# WHO'S WHO 2020

AN ANNUAL
BIOGRAPHICAL DICTIONARY

ONE HUNDRED AND SEVENTY-SECOND
YEAR OF ISSUE

A & C BLACK
LONDON · OXFORD · NEW YORK · NEW DELHI · SYDNEY

BLOOMSBURY YEARBOOKS
Bloomsbury Publishing Plc
50 Bedford Square, London, WC1B 3DP, UK

BLOOMSBURY, BLOOMSBURY YEARBOOKS, A&C BLACK and the 'WHO'S WHO PUBLISHED ANNUALLY SINCE 1849' belt logo are trademarks of Bloomsbury Publishing Plc

Published annually in Great Britain since 1849

172nd edition © Bloomsbury Publishing Plc, 2019

**Entries from *Who's Who* may not be reproduced, in any form whatsoever, without the written permission of the publishers.**

All rights reserved. No part of this publication may be reproduced ortransmitted in any form or by any means, electronic or mechanical, including photocopying, recording, or any information storage or retrieval system, without prior permission in writing from the publishers.

Bloomsbury Publishing Plc does not have any control over, or responsibility for, any third-party websites referred to or in this book. All internet addresses given in this book were correct at the time of going to press. The author and publisher regret any inconvenience caused if addresses have changed or sites have ceased to exist, but can accept no responsibility for any such changes.

The publishers make no representation, express or implied, with regard to the accuracy of the information contained in this book and cannot accept any legal responsibility for any errors or omissions that may take place.

A catalogue record for this book is available from the British Library.

ISBN: HB: 978-1-472-94759-8; Print and Online: 978-1-472-97909-4
www.ukwhoswho.com

2 4 6 8 10 9 7 5 3 1

Printed and bound in Italy by L.E.G.O. S.p.A.

To find out more about our authors and books visit www.bloomsbury.com and sign up for our newsletters.

## CONTENTS

| | |
|---|---|
| HISTORICAL NOTE | *4* |
| PREFACE | *5* |
| OBITUARY | *6* |
| ABBREVIATIONS USED IN THIS BOOK | *11* |
| THE ROYAL FAMILY | *46* |
| EDITORS' NOTE | *48* |
| BIOGRAPHIES | *1* |

# HISTORICAL NOTE

The first edition of *Who's Who* was published in 1849. It consisted of an almanac followed by thirty-nine lists of ranks and appointments and the names of those holding them. As might be expected, there were lists of peers, members of the House of Commons, judges, archbishops and bishops. Additionally, however, there were the names of the Governor and board of directors of the Bank of England, of British envoys abroad, of the directors of the East India Company and of the officers (including the actuaries) of the life and fire assurance companies in London.

The range of lists was expanded over the next half century to more than two hundred and fifty, to include, amongst others, the Police Commissioners, the officers of the principal railways, the members of the London School Board and the Crown Agents – together with the editors of significant newspapers and magazines whose names, the editor noted, were "given here, not for contributors, but that the public may know who lead public opinion".

In 1897 substantial changes were made to the nature and content of the book. The major change was the addition of a section of biographies in which details were given of the lives of some five and a half thousand leading figures of the day.

Now, as then, the book aims to list people who, through their careers, affect the political, economic, scientific and artistic life of the country. *Who's Who* places its emphasis on careers whilst giving opportunity for the inclusion of family and other individual details, such as the recreations which have become a distinctive feature of the book.

An invitation to appear in *Who's Who* has, on occasion, been thought of as conferring distinction; that is the last thing it can do. It recognises distinction and influence. The attitude of the present editorial board remains that of the editor of the 1897 edition, who stated in his preface that the book seeks to recognise people whose "prominence is inherited, or depending upon office, or the result of ability which singles them out from their fellows in occupations open to every educated man or woman".

# PREFACE

*Who's Who* is the recognised source book of information on people of influence and interest in all fields.

This, the 2020 edition, contains more than 33,000 biographies, approximately one thousand of these making their first appearance in *Who's Who*. They are of all kinds of people from all parts of the world and from all walks of life: the arts, business and finance, the church, the civil service, education, entertainment and sport, government, the law, local government, the media, medicine, professional institutions, science and the trade unions.

Each entry is in a standard form, full name and present post being followed by date of birth and family details, education, career in date order, publications, recreations and address.

The entries are carefully updated both from information supplied by biographees on their annual proofs and from many independent sources of reference. As a result, tens of thousands of amendments are made, more than half the entries requiring change. The book includes an obituary and a comprehensive list of abbreviations used in the entries.

# OBITUARY

Deaths notified from mid-September 2018 to mid-September 2019

**Abram,** Henry Charles, VRD, 7 Aug. 2019.
**Abrams,** Dr Michael Ellis, CB, 2019.
**Adams,** Terence David, CMG, 20 April 2019.
**Adamson,** (Samuel) Ian (Gamble), OBE, 9 Jan. 2019.
**Ainsworth,** Prof. Roger William, 23 Feb. 2019.
**Alexander,** Maj.-Gen. Paul Donald, CB, MBE, 11 Nov. 2018.
**Alferov,** Prof. Zhores Ivanovich, 1 March 2019.
**Allan,** James Nicholas, CMG, CBE, 18 Sept. 2018.
**Allen,** Paul Gardner, 15 Oct. 2018.
**Alvey,** John, CB, 19 Jan. 2019.
**Amano,** Yukiya, 18 July 2019.
**Anderson,** (Clarence) Eugene, 28 June 2019.
**Anderson,** Sir John Anthony, KBE, 13 Nov. 2018.
**Anderson,** Ray Thomas, OAM, 3 Feb. 2015.
**Andrews,** Peter John, QC, 29 Dec. 2017.
**Andriessen,** Prof. Frans, (Franciscus H. J. J.), 22 March 2019.
**Anthony,** Evelyn Bridget Patricia, (Mrs Michael Ward-Thomas), 25 Sept. 2018.
**Appleby,** Dom Raphael, OSB, 24 June 2018.
**Ashdown of Norton-sub-Hamdon,** Baron (Life Peer); Jeremy John Durham Ashdown, (Paddy), GCMG, CH, KBE, PC, 22 Dec. 2018.
**Asher,** Bernard Harry, 15 April 2019.
**Atherton,** Brig. Maurice Alan, CBE, 15 July 2019.
**Atiyah,** Sir Michael Francis, OM, FRS, 11 Jan. 2019.
**Atkin,** Prof. Wendy Sheila, OBE, 2 Oct. 2018.
**Atkinson,** Harry Hindmarsh, 30 Dec. 2018.
**Austin,** David Charles Henshaw, OBE, 18 Dec. 2018.
**Austin,** Ven. George Bernard, 30 Jan. 2019.
**Axworthy,** Michael George Andrew, 16 March 2019.
**Ayong,** Most Rev. James Simon, 5 April 2018.

**Bader,** Alfred, Hon. CBE, 23 Dec. 2018.
**Baker,** Richard Douglas James, OBE, RD, 17 Nov. 2018.
**Baldwin,** Brian Paul, 1 June 2018.
**Ball,** Rt Rev. Peter John, 21 June 2019.
**Banks,** Frank David, 21 Nov. 2018.
**Barker,** Paul, 21 July 2019.
**Barnes,** Rev. Mgr Edwin Ronald, 6 Feb. 2019.
**Barrett,** David, OC, OBC, 2 Feb. 2018.
**Basset,** Gerard Francis Claude, OBE, 16 Jan. 2019.
**Batley-Jackson,** Dame Temuranga, (Dame June), DNZM, QSM, 26 July 2019.
**Bayliss,** Hon. Mary Selina, CVO, 30 March 2019.
**Beach,** Gen. Sir (William Gerald) Hugh, GBE, KCB, MC, 4 Sept. 2019.
**Beardsworth,** Maj.-Gen. Simon John, CB, 8 July 2019.
**Beaurepaire,** Dame Beryl Edith, AC, DBE, 24 Oct. 2018.
**Beckett,** Maj.-Gen. Edwin Horace Alexander, CB, MBE, 15 Nov. 2018.
**Bedbrook,** Jack Harry, 10 July 2019.
**Beddow,** Prof. Michael, 2 Sept. 2019.
**Beér,** Prof. János Miklós, 8 Dec. 2018.
**Bell,** Baron (Life Peer); Timothy John Leigh Bell, 25 Aug. 2019.
**Benjamin,** Ralph, CB, 7 May 2019.
**Benner,** Patrick, CB, 14 July 2018.
**Bennett,** Robin, 18 March 2019.
**Bentham,** Prof. Richard Walker, 21 Feb. 2019.
**Berasategui,** Vicente Ernesto, 25 Sept. 2018.
**Berlins,** Marcel Joseph, 31 July 2019.
**Berry,** Cicely Frances, (Mrs H. D. Moore), CBE, 15 Oct. 2018.
**Berry,** (Roger) Simon, QC, 15 Dec. 2018.
**Bevan,** Rear-Adm. Timothy Michael, CB, 6 June 2019.
**Bewes,** Rev. Preb. Richard Thomas, OBE, 10 May 2019.
**Bhattacharyya,** Baron (Life Peer); Sushantha Kumar Bhattacharyya, CBE, FRS, 1 March 2019.
**Bicester,** 4th Baron; Hugh Charles Vivian, (Hugo) Smith, 11 Aug. 2016.
**Billington,** James Hadley, 20 Nov. 2018.
**Birkin,** Sir (John) Derek, TD, 25 Aug. 2019.
**Black,** John Newman, 6 March 2019.
**Black,** John Nicholson, 6 Oct. 2018.
**Blacker,** Norman, 4 April 2019.
**Blamey,** Marjorie Netta, MBE, 8 Sept. 2019.
**Blom-Cooper,** Sir Louis Jacques, QC, 19 Sept. 2018.
**Blythe,** Rex Arnold, 29 Jan. 2019.
**Boizot,** Peter James, MBE, 5 Dec. 2018.
**Booker,** Christopher John Penrice, 3 July 2019.
**Boord,** Sir Nicolas John Charles, 4th Bt, 7 Jan. 2019.
**Booth,** Richard George William Pitt, MBE, 20 Aug. 2019.
**Botha,** Roelof Frederik, (Pik), DMS, 12 Oct. 2018.
**Bott,** Prof. Martin Harold Phillips, FRS, 20 Oct. 2018.
**Bowen,** John Griffith, 18 April 2019.
**Boyd,** Sir Alexander Walter, 3rd Bt, 4 Dec. 2018.

**Bradley,** Stanley Walter, 5 June 2019.
**Breen,** His Honour Geoffrey Brian, 25 Jan. 2019.
**Brenner,** Sydney, CH, FRS, 5 April 2019.
**Brett,** Kieran James, Dec. 2018.
**Brodie,** Robert, CB, 4 Nov. 2018.
**Brogan,** Prof. (Denis) Hugh (Vercingetorix), 26 July 2019.
**Brooker,** Mervyn Edward William, 23 Jan. 2019.
**Broomfield,** Sir Nigel Hugh Robert Allen, KCMG, 29 Oct. 2018.
**Brothwood,** Rev. John, 8 Jan. 2018.
**Brown,** Harold, 4 Jan. 2019.
**Brown,** Robert Glencairn, 30 Dec. 2015.
**Brown,** Rt Rev. Ronald, 13 June 2019.
**Brown,** Prof. William Arthur, CBE, 1 Aug. 2019.
**Brownrigg,** Sir Nicholas Gawen, 5th Bt, 28 Sept. 2018.
**Browse,** Sir Norman Leslie, 12 Sept. 2019.
**Bull,** Sir Simeon George, 4th Bt, 7 April 2019.
**Buller,** Prof. Arthur John, ERD, 9 May 2019.
**Burgess,** Ven. John Edward, 9 March 2019.
**Burgoyne,** Rear-Adm. (Robert) Michael, CB, 1 July 2019.
**Burke,** Prof. Derek Clissold, CBE, 15 March 2019.
**Burke,** His Honour John Kenneth, QC, 23 March 2018.
**Burke,** Prof. Philip George, CBE, FRS, 4 June 2019.
**Burningham,** John Mackintosh, 4 Jan. 2019.
**Busch,** Constantinus Albertus Maria, 1 July 2018.
**Bush,** George Herbert Walker, Hon. GCB, 30 Nov. 2018.
**Buttrey,** Prof. Theodore Vern, 9 Jan. 2018.
**Buxton,** Adrian Clarence, CMG, 29 March 2019.
**Buzan,** Anthony Peter, 13 April 2019.
**Byrne,** Rev. Father Paul Laurence, OBE, 4 Dec. 2018.

**Caballé,** Montserrat, 6 Oct. 2018.
**Cagiati,** Andrea, Hon. GCVO, 17 Nov. 2018.
**Cairns,** Hugh John Forster, FRS, 12 Nov. 2018.
**Campbell,** Prof. Michael, OBE, 29 Sept. 2017.
**Carlisle,** John Russell, 18 Feb. 2019.
**Carr,** Alan Michael, 6 Sept. 2015.
**Carr,** Hon. Sir Henry James; Hon. Mr Justice Henry Carr, 18 July 2019.
**Casely-Hayford,** Joseph Ephraim, OBE, 3 Jan. 2019.
**Casida,** Prof. John Edward, 30 June 2018.
**Cassels,** Adm. Sir Simon Alastair Cassillis, KCB, CBE, 6 March 2019.
**Castle,** John Christopher, 7 Jan. 2019.
**Cazalet,** Sir Peter Grenville, 3 May 2019.
**Chadwick,** Peter, FRS, 12 Aug. 2018.
**Chamberlain,** Rt Rev. Neville, 8 Oct. 2018.
**Chambers,** Prof. Richard Dickinson, FRS, 18 April 2019.
**Chapman,** Ven. Michael Robin, 15 March 2019.
**Cherryman,** John Richard, QC, 23 June 2019.
**Chiswick,** Prof. Malcolm Leon, 8 Feb. 2019.
**Christofias,** Demetris, 21 June 2019.
**Christopher,** John Anthony, CB, 18 Aug. 2019.
**Chung,** Sir Sze-yuen, GBE, 14 Nov. 2018.
**Clare,** John Robert, 11 Sept. 2019.
**Clark,** Prof. Robin Jon Hawes, CNZM, FRS, 6 Dec. 2018.
**Clark,** Prof. Ronald George, 7 Nov. 2018.
**Clayton,** Prof. Robert Norman, FRS, 30 Dec. 2017.
**Cohen,** Ven. Clive Ronald Franklin, 8 April 2019.
**Cohen,** Lt-Col Mordaunt, MBE, TD, 16 March 2019.
**Cole,** Sir (Robert) William, 8 Jan. 2019.
**Coles,** His Honour (Norman) Bruce (Cameron), QC, 2 May 2018.
**Collins,** Sir David John, CBE, 14 Feb. 2019.
**Conville,** David Henry, OBE, 24 Nov. 2018.
**Cooper,** Philip John, CB, 17 Jan. 2019.
**Coppen,** Dr Alec James, 15 March 2019.
**Coulter,** Rev. Robert James, MBE, 5 Sept. 2018.
**Couper,** Prof. Alastair Dougal, 12 Sept. 2018.
**Coutts,** T(homas) Gordon, QC (Scot.), 16 Aug. 2019.
**Cox,** Peter Arthur, 17 Nov. 2018.
**Craft,** Prof. Ian Logan, 3 June 2019.
**Crampton,** Prof. Julian Moray, CBE, 26 June 2019.
**Crawford,** Prof. Robert James, (Roy), CNZM, 23 June 2016.
**Creese,** Nigel Arthur Holloway, AM, 29 Aug. 2018.
**Cresswell,** Rev. Amos Samuel, 10 Sept. 2018.
**Cretney,** Stephen Michael, FBA, 30 Aug. 2019.
**Crichton,** Nicholas, CBE, 17 Dec. 2018.
**Croft,** Frederick Lister, 21 Aug. 2018.
**Crofton,** Sir Julian Malby, 7th Bt, 14 July 2018.
**Cunningham,** Lt-Gen. Sir Hugh Patrick, KBE, 12 Sept. 2019.
**Custis,** Patrick James, CBE, 10 June 2019.

**Dalrymple,** Sir Hew Fleetwood Hamilton-, 10th Bt, GCVO, 26 Dec. 2018.
**d'Ancona,** John Edward William, CB, 24 June 2019.
**Davey,** Jon Colin, 12 June 2018.
**Davidson,** James Patton, CBE, 19 Oct. 2018.
**Davies of Coity,** Baron (Life Peer); David Garfield Davies, CBE, 4 March 2019.
**Davies,** Rt Hon. (David John) Denzil, PC, 10 Oct. 2018.
**Davies,** Her Honour Jacqueline, (Mrs P. N. R. Clark), 18 April 2019.
**Davis,** William, 2 Feb. 2019.
**Dawbarn,** Sir Simon Yelverton, KCVO, CMG, 29 June 2019.
**Dawson,** (Edward) John, 22 Nov. 2018.
**Day,** Prof. Alan Charles Lynn, 2 Dec. 2018.
**Deacon,** Keith Vivian, 16 Sept. 2018.
**Dean,** (Cecil) Roy, 25 Dec. 2018.
**de Clifford,** 27th Baron; John Edward Southwell Russell, 2 Nov. 2018.
**de Hamel,** Mette Tang, 6 June 2019.
**de La Barre de Nanteuil,** Luc, 14 Aug. 2018.
**Delacour,** Jean-Paul, 18 June 2019.
**de la Rúa,** Fernando, 9 July 2019.
**Denham,** Ernest William, 27 Aug. 2019.
**Denman,** Sylvia Elaine, CBE, 1 May 2019.
**Dennis,** Simon Richard, 2018.
**Denny,** Ronald Maurice, 26 June 2019.
**Devereux,** Alan Robert, CBE, 1 Feb. 2019.
**Devine,** Rt Rev. Joseph, 24 May 2019.
**Dewe,** Roderick Gorrie, 18 March 2019.
**Dick,** Dennis John Nicoll, MBE, 3 Feb. 2019.
**Dicks,** Prof. Anthony Richard, QC (Hong Kong), 8 Nov. 2018.
**Dobson,** Sir Christopher Martin, FRS, 8 Sept. 2019.
**Dobson,** Roger Swinburne, OBE, 7 Sept. 2019.
**Doerr,** Michael Frank, 23 March 2018.
**Donovan,** Mgr Paul Anthony, 8 Feb. 2017.
**Dore,** Prof. Ronald Philip, CBE, FBA, 13 Nov. 2018.
**Dorin,** Bernard Jean Robert, Hon. GCVO, 20 Feb. 2019.
**Downes,** Prof. Kerry John, OBE, 11 Aug. 2019.
**Drinkwater,** Sir John Muir, QC, 13 Aug. 2019.
**Drumm,** Rev. Mgr Walter Gregory, 17 Aug. 2015.
**Dunbar,** John Greenwell, OBE, 6 May 2018.
**Dyer,** James Archibald Thomson, OBE, 24 Jan. 2019.
**Dyson,** John Michael, 28 March 2019.

**Edwardes,** Sir Michael Owen, 15 Sept. 2019.
**Egginton,** Anthony Joseph, CBE, 4 Jan. 2019.
**Eichelbaum,** Rt Hon. Sir (Johann) Thomas, GBE, PC, 31 Oct. 2018.
**Eigen,** Manfred, 6 Feb. 2019.
**Elliott,** Sir Clive Christopher Hugh, 4th Bt, 18 April 2018.
**Elliott,** Michael Alwyn, 2 July 2019.
**Ellis,** Sir Herbert Douglas, (Sir Doug), OBE, 11 Oct. 2018.
**Eltis,** Walter Alfred, 5 April 2019.
**Elton,** Sir Arnold, CBE, 3 Oct. 2018.
**Elton,** Prof. Lewis Richard Benjamin, 29 Sept. 2018.
**English,** Gerald, 6 Feb. 2019.
**English,** Michael, 13 July 2019.
**Ephraums,** Maj.-Gen. Roderick Jarvis, CB, OBE, 6 Jan. 2019.
**Ershad,** Lt-Gen. Hussain Muhammad, 14 July 2019.
**Evans,** Dr (Noel) John (Bebbington), CB, 20 Oct. 2018.
**Evans,** Prof. Timothy William, 9 Nov. 2018.
**Eyre,** Sir Reginald Edwin, 26 Jan. 2019.

**Fairbairn,** David Ritchie, OBE, 19 Feb. 2019.
**Falkender,** Baroness (Life Peer); Marcia Matilda Falkender, CBE, 6 Feb. 2019.
**Fallows,** Geoffrey Michael, 11 June 2019.
**Farley,** Prof. Francis James Macdonald, FRS, 16 July 2018.
**Farquharson,** Jonathan, CBE, 9 Aug. 2018.
**Fauset,** Ian David, CB, 8 Dec. 2018.
**Feldstein,** Prof. Martin Stuart, 11 June 2019.
**Ferguson,** Air Vice-Marshal Gordon MacArthur, CB, CBE, 8 July 2019.
**Ferris,** Paul Frederick, 16 Nov. 2018.
**Field,** Maj.-Gen. Geoffrey William, CB, CVO, OBE, 1 Feb. 2019.
**Fieldhouse,** Prof. David Kenneth, FBA, 28 Oct. 2018.
**Finney,** Albert, 7 Feb. 2019.
**Finney,** Prof. David John, CBE, FRS, 12 Nov. 2018.
**Fischer,** Hon. Timothy Andrew, AC, 22 Aug. 2019.
**Flynn,** Paul Phillip, MP, 17 Feb. 2019.
**Forbes Adam,** Rev. Sir (Stephen) Timothy (Beilby), 4th Bt, 22 March 2019.
**Forrest,** John Richard, CBE, 11 March 2019.
**Forwood,** Sir Peter Noel, 4th Bt, 12 Sept. 2019 (*ext*).
**Foster of Bishop Auckland,** Baron (Life Peer); Derek Foster, PC, 6 Jan. 2019.
**Foster,** Joan Mary, 9 Feb. 2019.
**Foubister,** Stuart Russell, 19 April 2018.
**Fowler,** Robert Asa, 12 Jan. 2018.
**Fraenkel,** Prof. Ludwig Edward, FRS, 27 April 2019.
**Frame,** Rt Rev. John Timothy, 4 Aug. 2017.
**Franklin,** Sir Michael David Milroy, KCB, CMG, 7 July 2019.
**Fraser,** Sir Iain Michael Duncan, 3rd Bt, 3 April 2019.

**Fraser,** James Owen Arthur, 5 Sept. 2017.
**Fricker,** Rt Rev. Joachim Carl, 28 Oct. 2018.
**Friel,** (Michael) John, 28 Oct. 2014.
**Furlonger,** Robert William, CB, 19 Jan. 2019.

**Galton,** Raymond Percy, OBE, 5 Oct. 2018.
**Gardiner,** Peter Dod Robin, 5 Feb. 2019.
**Gardner,** Prof. John, FBA, 11 July 2019.
**Gates,** Emeritus Prof. Ronald Cecil, AO, 26 April 2018.
**Gell-Mann,** Murray, 24 May 2019.
**George,** Rt Rev. Ian Gordon Combe, AO, 28 Jan. 2019.
**Giacconi,** Prof. Riccardo, 9 Dec. 2018.
**Gibbons,** Prof. Ian Read, FRS, 30 Jan. 2018.
**Gibbs,** Air Vice-Marshal Charles Melvin, CB, CBE, DFC, 3 Oct. 2018.
**Gibbs,** Sir Roger Geoffrey, 3 Oct. 2018.
**Gill,** Sir Anthony Keith, 6 Aug. 2018.
**Gilliland,** David Jervois Thetford, 4 Feb. 2019.
**Gittus,** John Henry, 22 Jan. 2019.
**Glass,** Anthony Trevor, QC, 11 July 2019.
**Glauber,** Prof. Roy Jay, 26 Dec. 2018.
**Gledhill,** Keith Ainsworth, MBE, 7 Oct. 2018.
**Glover,** William James, QC, 10 March 2019.
**Goddard,** Harold Keith, QC, 15 Aug. 2019.
**Godfrey,** Peter, 27 April 2019.
**Godman,** Patricia, (Trish), 21 July 2019.
**Goldberg,** Rabbi David Julian, OBE, 30 April 2019.
**Goodyear,** Roger Maxwell, MBE, 30 May 2019.
**Gore,** Prof. Martin Eric, CBE, 10 Jan. 2019.
**Gourlay,** Sir Simon Alexander, 31 July 2019.
**Gowenlock,** Prof. Brian Glover, CBE, 17 March 2019.
**Graham,** Antony Richard Malise, 7 Feb. 2019.
**Grant,** Rt Rev. James Alexander, AM, 10 July 2019.
**Grattan,** Donald Henry, CBE, 22 Aug. 2019.
**Gray,** Anthony James, 1 Aug. 2019.
**Gray,** Prof. Douglas, FBA, 7 Dec. 2017.
**Gray,** George Gowans, CBE, 11 Oct. 2018.
**Green,** Rev. Canon (Edward) Michael (Bankes), 6 Feb. 2019.
**Greengard,** Prof. Paul, 13 April 2019.
**Guinness,** Sir Howard Christian Sheldon, VRD, 23 June 2019.

**Habgood,** Baron (Life Peer); Rt Rev. and Rt Hon. John Stapylton Habgood, PC, 6 March 2019.
**Hale,** Norman Morgan, CB, 5 Oct. 2018.
**Haley,** Prof. Keith Brian, 25 Dec. 2016.
**Halliday,** Prof. Timothy Richard, 10 April 2019.
**Hamblin,** Jeffrey John, OBE, 26 Dec. 2018.
**Hammond,** Hon. Sir (Robert) Grant, KNZM, 31 May 2019.
**Harbison,** Air Vice-Marshal William, CB, CBE, AFC, 25 Dec. 2018.
**Harper,** Heather Mary, (Mrs E. J. Benarroch), CBE, 22 April 2019.
**Harris,** Air Marshal Sir John Hulme, (Win), KCB, CBE, 2 July 2019.
**Harrison,** Sir Michael James Harwood, 2nd Bt, 13 Aug. 2019.
**Harrison,** Sir Terence, 21 June 2019.
**Hart,** Hon. Sir Anthony Ronald, 9 July 2019.
**Harvey,** Prof. Leonard Patrick, 7 Aug. 2018.
**Hawke,** Hon. Robert James Lee, AC, 16 May 2019.
**Hawkins-Leth,** Air Vice-Marshal David Richard, CB, LVO, MBE, 31 Jan. 2019.
**Haworth,** Sir Philip, 3rd Bt, 3 Sept. 2019.
**Haynes,** John Harold, OBE, 8 Feb. 2019.
**Hazell,** Ven. Frederick Roy, 16 July 2019.
**Healy,** Prof. Thomas Edward John, 3 Nov. 2018.
**Heath,** Samantha Louise, 29 March 2019.
**Hedges,** Anthony John, 19 June 2019.
**Held,** Prof. David Jonathan Andrew, 2 March 2019.
**Henderson,** (Patrick) David, CMG, 30 Sept. 2018.
**Herbert,** (Elizabeth) Jane, 18 March 2019.
**Herbert,** Adm. Sir Peter Geoffrey Marshall, KCB, OBE, 3 May 2019.
**Heron,** Sir Conrad Frederick, KCB, OBE, 22 July 2019.
**Herzberg,** Charles Francis, 13 June 2019.
**Hewett,** Major Richard William, 23 March 2019.
**Hewitt,** Prof. Geoffrey Frederick, FRS, 18 Jan. 2019.
**Heywood of Whitehall,** Baron (Life Peer); Jeremy John Heywood, GCB, CVO, 4 Nov. 2018.
**Hill,** Air Cdre Dame Felicity Barbara, DBE, 30 Jan. 2019.
**Hochhauser,** Victor, CBE, 22 March 2019.
**Hodgkins,** David John, CB, 19 April 2019.
**Hodgkinson,** Terence, CBE, 12 July 2019.
**Holland,** Rt Rev. Alfred Charles, 8 Oct. 2018.
**Hollingworth,** John Harold, 4 March 2018.
**Hollis of Heigham,** Baroness (Life Peer); Patricia Lesley Hollis, PC, 13 Oct. 2018.
**Honoré,** Prof. Antony Maurice, QC, FBA, 26 Feb. 2019.
**Hooley,** Prof. Christopher, FRS, 13 Dec. 2018.
**Hopkinson,** David Hugh, 29 Sept. 2018.
**Horden,** Richard, 5 Oct. 2018.

**Horsey,** Gordon, 8 June 2019.
**Hoult,** Frederick Wilson, 6 May 2019.
**Hourston,** Sir Gordon Minto, 18 Sept. 2018.
**Howard,** Rear-Adm. Christopher John, (Jack), 18 Jan. 2019.
**Howarth,** His Honour Nigel John Graham, 18 March 2019.
**Howden,** Timothy Simon, 19 Feb. 2019.
**Huffinley,** Beryl, 30 Sept. 2018.
**Hugh-Jones,** Sir Wynn Normington, (Sir Hugh Jones), LVO, 5 July 2019.
**Hughes,** David Glyn, 16 Oct. 2018.
**Hume,** James Bell, 8 July 2017.
**Huntington-Whiteley,** Lt Comdr Sir (John) Miles, 4th Bt, 19 Feb. 2019.
**Hurford,** Peter John, OBE, 3 March 2019.
**Hutchison,** Sir Peter Craft, 2nd Bt, CBE, 20 Jan. 2019.
**Huxtable,** Gen. Sir Charles Richard, KCB, CBE, 26 Nov. 2018.

**Imison,** Dame Tamsyn, DBE, 18 Sept. 2017.
**Inwood,** Rt Rev. Richard Neil, 14 April 2019.
**Iredale,** Peter, 10 July 2019.
**Irvine,** Sir Donald Hamilton, CBE, 19 Nov. 2018.
**Irwin,** Ian Sutherland, CBE, 7 June 2017.
**Isaacson,** Laurence Ivor, CBE, 23 Oct. 2018.
**Isaaman,** Gerald Michael, OBE, 29 April 2019.
**Israelachvili,** Prof. Jacob Nissim, FRS, 20 Sept. 2018.

**Jackson,** Alan Robert, AO, 4 Aug. 2018.
**Jackson,** (Michael) Rodney, 31 March 2018.
**Jaitley,** Arun, 24 Aug. 2019.
**James,** Prof. Vivian Hector Thomas, 6 Oct. 2018.
**Jawara,** Alhaji Sir Dawda Kairaba, Hon. GCMG, 27 Aug. 2019.
**Jefferson Smith,** Peter, CB, 22 Dec. 2018.
**Jeffrey,** Robin Campbell, 4 Nov. 2018.
**Jeffries,** Hon. Sir John Francis, 25 Jan. 2019.
**Jeffs,** Kenneth Peter, CMG, 25 April 2019.
**Jessel,** Toby Francis Henry, 3 Dec. 2018.
**Jessell,** Prof. Thomas Michael, FRS, 28 April 2019.
**Johnson,** Sir John Rodney, KCMG, 15 Oct. 2018.
**Jones,** Prof. James Eirug Thomas, 3 Dec. 2018.
**Jones,** His Honour Nicholas Graham, 5 June 2019.
**Jones,** Philip Graham, 17 Oct. 2018.
**Judge,** Harry George, 2 April 2019.

**Kao,** Sir Charles Kuen, KBE, FRS, 23 Sept. 2018.
**Kelleher,** Dame Joan, (Joanna), DBE, 23 Sept. 2018.
**Kennett,** Ronald John, 4 Feb. 2019.
**Kensington,** 8th Baron; Hugh Ivor Edwardes, 12 Sept. 2018.
**Kenyon,** 6th Baron; Lloyd Tyrell-Kenyon, 17 Aug. 2019.
**Kerr,** (Anne) Judith, OBE, 22 May 2019.
**Kettle,** Captain Alan Stafford Howard, CB, RN, 15 March 2019.
**Khoo,** Francis Kah Siang, 20 Nov. 2011.
**Kingshott,** Air Vice-Marshal Kenneth, CBE, DFC, 8 Nov. 2018.
**Kirby,** Maj.-Gen. Norman George, OBE, 25 July 2019.
**Kitching,** Peter Marshall, 21 May 2019.
**Kitson,** Sir Timothy Peter Geoffrey, 18 May 2019.
**Klug,** Sir Aaron, OM, FRS, 20 Nov. 2018.
**Knowles,** George Peter, 27 April 2018.
**Knox,** Prof. John Henderson, FRS, 15 Oct. 2018.
**Kok,** William, (Wim), 20 Oct. 2018.
**Koltai,** Ralph, CBE, RDI, 15 Dec. 2018.

**Lacey,** Prof. Richard Westgarth, 3 Feb. 2019.
**Lackey,** Mary Josephine, CB, OBE, 11 March 2019.
**Landau,** Sir Dennis Marcus, 27 Oct. 2018.
**Landry,** Prof. (Jean-) Bernard, GOQ, 6 Nov. 2018.
**Laqueur,** Walter, 30 Sept. 2018.
**Lavery,** (Charles) Michael, QC (NI), 25 April 2019.
**Law,** George Llewellyn, 25 Dec. 2018.
**Layton,** 3rd Baron; Geoffrey Michael Layton, 4 Aug. 2018.
**Leadbetter,** Alan James, CBE, 11 March 2019.
**Lederman,** Leon Max, 3 Oct. 2018.
**Leeming,** John Coates, 23 March 2019.
**Le Grice,** (Andrew) Valentine, QC, 23 Dec. 2018.
**Leighton,** Leonard Horace, 26 July 2019.
**Lemon,** Jane Katherine, QC, 24 April 2019.
**Levy,** Andrea Doreen, 14 Feb. 2019.
**Lewis,** Very Rev. John Thomas, 18 Feb. 2019.
**Lewis,** Steffan, 11 Jan. 2019.
**Lochore,** Sir Brian James, ONZ, KNZM, OBE, 3 Aug. 2019.
**Lockwood,** Baroness (Life Peer); Betty Lockwood, 29 April 2019.
**Long,** Athelstan Charles Ethelwulf, CMG, CBE, 31 July 2019.
**Lowther,** Col Sir Charles Douglas, 6th Bt, 2 Oct. 2018.
**Loy,** Francis David Lindley, CBE, 10 July 2019.
**Luff,** Geoffrey Shadrack, 8 April 2016.

**McAdam,** James, CBE, 31 Oct. 2017.
**McAleese,** Kevin Stanley, CBE, 13 March 2019.
**MacArthur,** Brian Roger, 24 March 2019.
**McCabe,** Bernice Alda, OBE, 18 Feb. 2019.
**McCoy,** Hugh O'Neill, 6 April 2019.
**McCullough,** Sir (Iain) Charles (Robert), 9 Oct. 2018.
**Macdonald,** Hon. Donald Stovel, PC (Can.), CC, 14 Oct. 2018.
**McDonald,** Elaine Maria, OBE, 8 Dec. 2018.
**Mace,** (Alan) Christopher (Hugh), CBE, 18 Sept. 2018.
**Macfarlane,** Maj.-Gen. William Thomson, CB, 14 April 2019.
**MacFarquhar,** Prof. Roderick Lemonde, 10 Feb. 2019.
**McGregor,** Prof. Gordon Peter, 2019.
**McGuire,** Michael Thomas Francis, 16 Aug. 2018.
**McIntosh,** Sir Ronald Robert Duncan, KCB, 1 April 2019.
**McIvor,** (Frances) Jill, CBE, 8 Jan. 2019.
**McKee,** (Charles Dean) Grant, 7 April 2019.
**McKee,** William Stewart, CBE, 12 Dec. 2018.
**McKeown,** John, 26 Nov. 2018.
**Mackie,** Clive David Andrew, 24 June 2019.
**McLaggan,** Murray Adams, 12 Feb. 2019.
**McLean,** Philip Alexander, CMG, 5 June 2019.
**McMahon,** Sir Brian Patrick, 8th Bt, 30 Jan. 2019.
**Macmillan,** Iain Alexander, CBE, 8 May 2019.
**McNee,** Sir David Blackstock, QPM, 26 April 2019.
**McPartlin,** Noel, 23 June 2019.
**MacQueen,** Prof. John, 15 Sept. 2019.
**MacTaggart,** Air Vice-Marshal William Keith, CBE, 12 Jan. 2019.
**Maddison,** Hon. Sir David George, 29 June 2019.
**Maddox,** Brenda Power, (Lady Maddox), 16 June 2019.
**Maddox,** Ronald, 14 Nov. 2018.
**Magee,** Bryan, 26 July 2019.
**Malcolm,** Wilfred Gordon, CBE, 6 Oct. 2018.
**Male,** David Ronald, CBE, 4 Oct. 2018.
**Malpas,** Prof. James Spencer, 29 April 2019.
**Maltby,** Antony John, 18 May 2019.
**Mander,** His Honour Michael Harold, 2 May 2018.
**Manning,** Prof. Aubrey William George, OBE, 20 Oct. 2018.
**Marshall,** Sir Michael John, CBE, 27 July 2019.
**Martin,** Rev. Prof. David Alfred, FBA, 8 March 2019.
**Martin,** Evelyn Fairfax, OBE, 18 Feb. 2019.
**Martin,** John William Prior, 2 June 2019.
**Martin,** Robert Logan, (Roy), QC (Scot.), QC, 26 Aug. 2019.
**Mason,** Rt Rev. Kenneth Bruce, AM, 20 Dec. 2018.
**Matev,** Lachezar Nikolov, 28 Sept. 2017.
**Matlhabaphiri,** Gaotlhaetse Utlwang Sankoloba, PH, 27 June 2018.
**Maunder,** Prof. Leonard, OBE, 20 April 2019.
**Maystadt,** Philippe, 7 Dec. 2017.
**Melinsky,** Rev. Canon (Michael Arthur) Hugh, 22 Oct. 2018.
**Mepham,** David John, OBE, 21 Oct. 2018.
**Mercer,** Roger James, OBE, 3 Dec. 2018.
**Merritt,** Prof. Neil, 25 Feb. 2019.
**Metcalf,** Prof. David Michael, 25 Oct. 2018.
**Michaels,** Prof. Leslie, 28 Dec. 2018.
**Middleton,** Bernard Chester, MBE, 28 Jan. 2019.
**Middleton,** Dame Elaine Madoline, DCMG, MBE, 21 April 2019.
**Middleton,** Sir John Maxwell, OBE, 1 Dec. 2018.
**Millar,** Sir Fergus Graham Burtholme, FBA, 15 July 2019.
**Millar,** John Stanley, CBE, 20 March 2019.
**Milroy,** Very Rev. Dominic Liston, OSB, 1 Jan. 2019.
**Mitchell,** John Matthew, CBE, 9 April 2019.
**Mitchell,** Terence Croft, 21 April 2019.
**Moate,** Sir Roger Denis, 15 April 2019.
**Mockford,** Caroline Frances, 5 March 2019.
**Montagnon,** Peter James, 25 June 2019.
**Moore of Lower Marsh,** Baron (Life Peer); John Edward Michael Moore, PC, 20 May 2019.
**Moore,** Prof. Stuart Alfred, 21 Feb. 2019.
**Moore,** Sir William Roger Clotworthy, 3rd Bt, TD, 19 May 2019.
**Morland,** Charles Francis Harold, 8 Nov. 2018.
**Morris,** Air Marshal Sir Alec, KBE, CB, 7 Nov. 2018.
**Morris,** Sir Allan Lindsay, 11th Bt, 16 Oct. 2016.
**Morrison,** Chloe Anthony, (Toni), 5 Aug. 2019.
**Morton,** Rev. Andrew Queen, 31 Dec. 2018.
**Moss,** Gabriel Stephen, QC, 15 March 2019.
**Moss,** John Ringer, CB, 31 July 2018.
**Mosselmans,** Carel Maurits, TD, 1 March 2019.
**Mott,** Gregory George Sidney, CBE, 28 May 2019.
**Mouatt,** (Richard) Brian, CBE, 29 Oct. 2018.
**Moxon,** Very Rev. Michael Anthony, LVO, 28 July 2019.
**Mugabe,** Robert Gabriel, 6 Sept. 2019.
**Mullis,** Kary Banks, 7 Aug. 2019.
**Mulryne,** Prof. (James) Ronald, 28 Jan. 2019.
**Murray,** Leo Joseph, CB, QC (Aust.), 21 June 2018.
**Murray,** Leslie Allan, (Les), AO, 29 April 2019.
**Mustow,** Stuart Norman, CBE, 3 June 2019.

**Myers,** Sir Rupert Horace, KBE, AO, 21 Feb. 2019.
**Myles,** David Fairlie, CBE, 16 Dec. 2018.

**Naish,** Sir (Charles) David, 28 March 2019.
**Neild,** Prof. Robert Ralph, 18 Dec. 2018.
**Neill,** Alistair, 8 Dec. 2018.
**Nevill,** Prof. Bernard Richard, 30 Jan. 2019.
**Newing,** Rt Rev. Dom Kenneth Albert, OSB, 15 May 2019.
**Newman,** Hon. Sir George Michael, 9 June 2019.
**Newman,** Dr Lotte Therese, (Mrs N. E. Aronsohn), CBE, 26 April 2019.
**Newport,** Ronald William, 26 May 2019.
**Newton,** Clive Trevor, CB, 16 Sept. 2018.
**Nicholas,** (Angela) Jane (Udale), OBE, 3 April 2019.
**Nicholas,** Sir John William, KCVO, CMG, 15 Feb. 2019.
**Nicholls,** Michael William Newbery, 17 Feb. 2018.
**Nichols,** Peter Richard, CBE, 7 Sept. 2018.
**Norden,** Denis, CBE, 19 Sept. 2018.
**Normanton,** 6th Earl of; Shaun James Christian Welbore Ellis Agar, 13 Feb. 2019.
**Norris,** Gilbert Frank, 16 Aug. 2018.
**Norris,** Sydney George, CB, 27 Nov. 2018.
**North,** John Joseph, 21 Feb. 2019.
**Northbourne,** 5th Baron; Christopher George Walter James, 8 Sept. 2019.
**Norton,** Hugh Edward, 11 Aug. 2019.
**Nuttall,** Peter Francis, 13 May 2019.
**Nye,** Prof. John Frederick, FRS, 8 Jan. 2019.

**O'Brien,** Prof. Paul, CBE, FRS, 16 Oct. 2018.
**O'Donnell,** Dr Michael, 6 April 2019.
**Oglesby,** Peter Rogerson, CB, 15 March 2018.
**Olszewski,** Jan, 7 Feb. 2019.
**O'Neill,** Prof. Michael Stephen Charles, 21 Dec. 2018.
**Orme,** Howard Peter, CB, 17 May 2018.
**Ormerod,** Prof. (Lawrence) Peter, 29 Jan. 2019.
**Orrego-Vicuña,** Prof. Francisco, 2 Oct. 2018.
**Ost,** Michael Stuart, 30 Aug. 2018.
**Owen,** Trevor Bryan, CBE, 23 April 2019.
**Oz,** Amos, 28 Dec. 2018.

**Palmer,** David Vereker, 4 Sept. 2019.
**Palmer,** Sir John Edward Somerset, 8th Bt, 7 June 2019.
**Parbo,** Sir Arvi Hillar, AC, 1 May 2019.
**Parker-Jervis,** Roger, 25 May 2019.
**Parry,** Anthony Joseph, QFSM, 1 July 2018.
**Patel of Blackburn,** Baron (Life Peer); Adam Hafejee Patel, 29 May 2019.
**Payne,** Christopher Frederick, CBE, QPM, 27 Feb. 2019.
**Peach,** Prof. (Guthlac) Ceri (Klaus), 2 Oct. 2018.
**Peart,** Prof. Sir (William) Stanley, FRS, 14 March 2019.
**Pei,** Ieoh Ming, 16 May 2019.
**Pepper,** Simon Richard, OBE, 18 Sept. 2018.
**Perrow,** (Joseph) Howard, 6 Sept. 2018.
**Peters,** Prof. Wallace, 26 Dec. 2018.
**Petersen,** Niels Helveg, 3 June 2017.
**Pettigrew,** Prof. John Douglas, FRS, 7 May 2019.
**Pheloung,** Barrington Somers James, 31 July 2019.
**Phipps,** Air Vice-Marshal Jeremy Leslie William, CB, AFC, 3 March 2019.
**Piëch,** Ferdinand Karl, 25 Aug. 2019.
**Piercy,** Prof. Nigel Francis, 13 Oct. 2017.
**Pilcher,** Rosamunde, OBE, 6 Feb. 2019.
**Plastow,** Sir David Arnold Stuart, 5 June 2019.
**Plume,** John Trevor, 10 Dec. 2018.
**Porteous,** Christopher Selwyn, CBE, 23 Dec. 2018.
**Porter,** Arthur Thomas, 26 March 2019.
**Powell,** Geoffrey Colin, CBE, 13 May 2019.
**Powell,** Sir Nicholas Folliott Douglas, 4th Bt, 7 March 2019.
**Prendergast,** His Honour Robert James Christie, 17 May 2019.
**Preston,** Walter James, 30 July 2018.
**Previn,** André George, Hon. KBE, 28 Feb. 2019.
**Price,** (Alan) Anthony, 30 May 2019.
**Price,** Air Vice-Marshal John Walter, CBE, 26 April 2019.
**Price,** Air Vice-Marshal Robert George, CB, 3 Oct. 2018.
**Priest,** Prof. Robert George, 2 Oct. 2018.
**Prince,** Harold, 31 July 2019.
**Pugh,** Alastair Tarrant, CBE, 6 March 2019.

**Quinn,** (James) Aiden O'Brien, QC (Seychelles), 28 Dec. 2018.

**Ramsden,** (John) Michael, 28 July 2019.
**Ramshaw,** Wendy Anne Jopling, (Mrs D. J. Watkins), CBE, RDI, 9 Dec. 2018.
**Ranfurly,** 7th Earl of; Gerald François Needham Knox, 4 Dec. 2018.
**Rausing,** Hans A., Hon. KBE, 30 Aug. 2019.
**Reese,** Prof. Jason Meredith, 8 March 2019.

**Reich,** Peter Gordon, 1 July 2018.
**Reid,** Sir Alexander James, 3rd Bt, 8 April 2019.
**Reid,** Derek Donald, 8 Feb. 2019.
**René,** (France) Albert, 27 Feb. 2019.
**Revell,** Surg. Vice-Adm. Anthony Leslie, CB, 30 Dec. 2018.
**Ribbins,** Maureen Margaret, 20 Oct. 2018.
**Richards,** Sir Rex Edward, FRS, 15 July 2019.
**Richards,** Roderick, 13 July 2019.
**Richardson,** George Barclay, CBE, 2 July 2019.
**Richardson,** Sir John Patrick, KBE, 12 March 2019.
**Robbins,** Prof. Keith Gilbert, 12 Sept. 2019.
**Robertson,** Andrew James, QC, 23 Oct. 2018.
**Robinson,** Rt Rev. Donald William Bradley, AO, 7 Sept. 2018.
**Robinson,** Lee Fisher, 12 April 2019.
**Robinson,** Air Vice-Marshal Michael Maurice Jeffries, CB, 5 June 2019.
**Roeg,** Nicolas Jack, CBE, 23 Nov. 2018.
**Rogers,** Peter Richard, 16 Jan. 2019.
**Rose,** Brian, 18 Nov. 2018.
**Rose,** Major Charles Frederick, CBE, 11 April 2019.
**Rose,** Sir Clive Martin, GCMG, 17 April 2019.
**Roseveare,** Robert William, CBE, 8 July 2019.
**Rosier,** Rt Rev. Stanley Bruce, AM, 28 Feb. 2019.
**Rowe,** Prof. Adrian Harold Redfern, 22 May 2019.
**Rowe,** Dorothy, 25 March 2019.
**Rowland,** Sir (John) David, 18 Feb. 2019.
**Roxburghe,** 10th Duke of; Guy David Innes-Ker, 29 Aug. 2019.
**Ruhfus,** Jürgen, 25 Feb. 2018.
**Rumble,** Peter William, CB, 21 Sept. 2018.
**Russell,** Alan Keith, OBE, 6 Feb. 2019.

**Sadeque,** Shahwar, 6 Jan. 2019.
**Sampson,** Sir Colin, CBE, QPM, 15 Oct. 2018.
**Sanders,** Sir Robert Tait, KBE, CMG, 8 May 2019.
**Sargent,** Prof. Roger William Herbert, 11 Sept. 2018.
**Schofield,** Roger Snowden, FBA, 8 April 2019.
**Scholes,** Hon. Gordon Glen Denton, AO, 9 Dec. 2018.
**Schrieffer,** Prof. John Robert, 27 July 2019.
**Scott,** Sir Anthony Percy, 3rd Bt, 27 Feb. 2019.
**Scott,** Dame Margaret, (Dame Catherine Margaret Mary Denton), AC, DBE, 24 Feb. 2019.
**Scott,** Paul Henderson, CMG, 16 March 2019.
**Seaga,** Most Hon. Edward Philip George, PC, ON, 28 May 2019.
**Seaward,** Colin Hugh, CBE, 14 April 2019.
**Seely,** Sir Nigel Edward, 5th Bt, 25 April 2019.
**Sellar,** W(illiam) David H(amilton), MVO, 26 Jan. 2019.
**Semple,** Prof. Stephen John Greenhill, 2 Dec. 2018.
**Shagari,** Alhaji Shehu Usman Aliyu, GCFR, 28 Dec. 2018.
**Shaw,** Prof. Charles Timothy, 21 April 2017.
**Shaw,** David, 4 Aug. 2018.
**Shaw,** Prof. William V., 30 July 2018.
**Sheehy,** Sir Patrick, 23 July 2019.
**Shelvey,** (Elsie) Miriam, 12 July 2017.
**Shiffner,** Sir Henry David, 8th Bt, 22 Aug. 2018.
**Shimomura,** Osamu, 19 Oct. 2018.
**Shirley,** Malcolm Christopher, 24 Aug. 2019.
**Short,** Peter, 25 July 2019.
**Shotter,** Very Rev. Edward Frank, 3 July 2019.
**Shuffrey,** Ralph Frederick Dendy, CB, CVO, 4 Jan. 2019.
**Sieff,** Hon. Sir David Daniel, 27 May 2019.
**Silk,** Dennis Raoul Whitehall, CBE, 19 June 2019.
**Silver,** Clinton Vita, CBE, 15 Feb. 2019.
**Simmonds,** John Andrew, 11 Feb. 2019.
**Simpson,** Edward Hugh, CB, 5 Feb. 2019.
**Simpson,** Very Rev. John Arthur, OBE, 24 April 2019.
**Sims,** Monica Louie, OBE, 20 Nov. 2018.
**Sinclair,** Andrew Annandale, 30 May 2019.
**Sinclair,** Murray Alexander, 27 Sept. 2018.
**Singer,** Sir (Jan) Peter, 22 Dec. 2018.
**Skelmersdale,** 7th Baron; Roger Bootle-Wilbraham, 31 Oct. 2018.
**Skingsley,** Air Chief Marshal Sir Anthony Gerald, GBE, KCB, 15 Jan. 2019.
**Slabas,** Prof. Antoni Ryszard, 2019.
**Slack,** Sir William Willatt, KCVO, 28 April 2019.
**Slater,** Kenneth Frederick, 24 June 2018.
**Slater,** William John, CBE, 18 Dec. 2018.
**Slim,** 2nd Viscount; John Douglas Slim, OBE, 12 Jan. 2019.
**Smart,** John Dalziel Beveridge, CVO, 12 Aug. 2019.
**Smith,** Arnold Terence, MBE, 18 Aug. 2016.
**Smith,** Prof. Barry Edward, 27 Sept. 2018.
**Smith,** Brian Stanley, 3 Nov. 2018.
**Smith,** (Charles) Philip, MBE, 27 Dec. 2018.
**Smith,** Rev. Christopher Hughes, 28 Jan. 2019.
**Smith,** Prof. Colin John, CBE, 15 Dec. 2018.
**Smith,** James Cadzow, CBE, 10 July 2018.
**Smith,** Walter Purvis, CB, OBE, 11 Dec. 2018.

**Smithies,** Frederick Albert, 24 Sept. 2018.
**Sondheimer,** Prof. Ernst Helmut, 9 June 2019.
**Soutar,** (Samuel) Ian, 29 April 2019.
**Sowden,** Terence Cubitt, QC, 9 April 2019.
**Sowrey,** Air Marshal Sir Frederick Beresford, KCB, CBE, AFC, 24 July 2019.
**Spicer,** Baron (Life Peer); William Michael Hardy Spicer, PC, 29 May 2019.
**Spooner,** Sir James Douglas, 8 Aug. 2019.
**Stavordale,** Lord; Simon James Fox-Strangways, 9 Feb. 2018.
**Steele-Bodger,** Michael Roland, CBE, 8 May 2019.
**Steitz,** Prof. Thomas Arthur, 9 Oct. 2018.
**Stephens,** Rt Rev. Prof. (William) Peter, 1 April 2019.
**Stevens,** Hon. John Paul, 16 July 2019.
**Stirling,** Prof. (William) James, CBE, FRS, 9 Nov. 2018.
**Stoddart,** Prof. John Little, CBE, 13 July 2016.
**Stoker,** Dr Dennis James, 24 Sept. 2017.
**Stone,** Prof. Norman, 18 June 2019.
**Stones,** (Elsie) Margaret, AM, MBE, 26 Dec. 2018.
**Streator,** Edward James, 16 April 2019.
**Streeten,** Paul Patrick, 6 Jan. 2019.
**Stringer,** Sir Donald Edgar, CBE, 16 Dec. 2018.
**Stuart,** Ven. Canon Herbert James, CB, 24 Feb. 2019.
**Sutherland,** Prof. Rosamund Jane, 26 Jan. 2019.
**Swan,** Sir Conrad Marshall John Fisher, KCVO, 10 Jan. 2019.
**Swanston,** Roderick Brian, 12 April 2018.
**Swift,** Clive Walter, 1 Feb. 2019.
**Swinnerton-Dyer,** Sir (Henry) Peter (Francis), 16th Bt, KBE, FRS, 26 Dec. 2018.
**Swinton,** Maj.-Gen Sir John, KCVO, OBE, 4 Oct. 2018.

**Taylor,** Prof. Ronald Wentworth, 27 Feb. 2016.
**Taylorson,** John Brown, OBE, 12 Dec. 2018.
**Thomas,** Gwyn Edward Ward, CBE, DFC, 4 Feb. 2019.
**Thorne,** Benjamin, CMG, MBE, 12 July 2019.
**Thouless,** Prof. David James, FRS, 6 April 2019.
**Thuysbaert,** Jonkheer Prosper, 27 May 2018.
**Thynne,** John Corelli James, CB, 23 Oct. 2018.
**Tilling,** George Henry Garfield, 23 Jan. 2019.
**Timms,** Prof. Edward Francis, OBE, FBA, 21 Nov. 2018.
**Tiwari,** Narayan Datt, 18 Oct. 2018.
**Tordoff,** Baron (Life Peer); Geoffrey Johnson Tordoff, 22 June 2019.
**ToRobert,** Sir Henry Thomas, KBE, 18 Oct. 2018.
**Townend,** James Barrie Stanley, QC, 17 Dec. 2018.
**Treitel,** Sir Guenter Heinz, QC, FBA, 14 June 2019.
**Triffitt,** Jayne, 3 July 2018.
**Trumpington,** Baroness (Life Peer); Jean Alys Barker, DCVO, PC, 26 Nov. 2018.
**Tryon,** 3rd Baron; Anthony George Merrik Tryon, OBE, 22 Dec. 2018.
**Turner,** Sir Michael John, 7 Oct. 2018.
**Tyrrell,** Prof. John, 4 Oct. 2018.

**Ungerer,** Jean Thomas, (Tomi), 8 Feb. 2019.
**Utley,** Prof. James Henry Paul, 30 Jan. 2019.

**Venturi,** Robert, 18 Sept. 2018.
**Venugopal,** Dr Sriramashetty, OBE, 2 March 2018.

**Wagerman,** Josephine Miriam, OBE, 16 Oct. 2018.
**Walden,** (Alastair) Brian, 9 May 2019.
**Walden,** Ian Mennie, MBE, 9 Sept. 2019.
**Waldron-Ramsey,** Waldo Emerson, QC (Barbados), 23 July 2018.
**Walker,** Surgeon Vice Adm. Alasdair James, CB, OBE, 1 June 2019.
**Walker,** His Honour Michael, 31 Oct. 2018.
**Walsh,** Arthur Stephen, CBE, 8 Feb. 2019.
**Ward,** Prof. Ian Macmillan, FRS, 6 Nov. 2018.
**Wardington,** 3rd Baron; William Simon Pease, 19 March 2019 (*ext*).
**Warnock,** Baroness (Life Peer); (Helen) Mary Warnock, CH, DBE, 20 March 2019.
**Warren,** Sir Kenneth Robin, 29 June 2019.
**Warren,** Ven. Norman Leonard, 19 June 2019.
**Watling,** His Honour Rev. (David) Brian, QC, 30 Nov. 2018.
**Watson,** James Kenneth, 11 Dec. 2018.
**Watson,** Prof. William Alexander Jardine, (Alan), 7 Nov. 2018.
**Weatherall,** Sir David John, GBE, FRS, 8 Dec. 2018.
**Webber,** Roy Seymour, 7 April 2019.
**Weldon,** Duncan Clark, 30 Jan. 2019.
**Westwood,** 3rd Baron; William Gavin Westwood, 28 July 2019.
**Wheatley,** Derek Peter Francis, QC, 23 Sept. 2018.
**Whitfield,** Dame June Rosemary (Mrs T. J. Aitchison), DBE, 29 Dec. 2018.
**Whitfield,** Sir William, CBE, 16 March 2019.
**Whiting,** Rev. Peter Graham, CBE, 31 March 2019.
**Whybrew,** Edward Graham, (Ted), CBE, 20 Jan. 2019.
**Wilding,** Richard William Longworth, CB, 29 Dec. 2018.
**Wilkinson,** John Francis, 15 Oct. 2016.
**Wilks,** (David) Michael (Worsley), 12 Jan. 2019.
**Williams,** (Albert) Trevor, 22 Aug. 2019.
**Williams,** Francis Julian, CBE, 5 Jan. 2019.
**Williams,** Nigel Christopher Ransome, CMG, 27 Aug. 2019.
**Wintersgill,** Dr William, 5 Dec. 2017.
**Winterton,** Nicholas Hugh, OBE, 29 Sept. 2018.
**Witteveen,** (Hendrikus) Johannes, 23 April 2019.
**Wolfson,** (Geoffrey) Mark, OBE, 14 Nov. 2018.
**Wolzfeld,** Jean-Louis, 14 Oct. 2018.
**Wood,** Tan Sri Alan John, CBE, 7 June 2018.
**Wouk,** Herman, 17 May 2019.
**Wroath,** His Honour John Herbert, 23 April 2019.
**Wyn,** Eurig, 25 June 2019.
**Wyngaarden,** James Barnes, 14 June 2019.

**Yarrow,** Sir Eric Grant, 3rd Bt, MBE, 22 Sept. 2018.
**Yorke,** Very Rev. Michael Leslie, 19 April 2019.
**Young,** Sir Leslie Clarence, CBE, 20 Oct. 2018.
**Younger,** Sir Julian William Richard, 4th Bt, 18 Feb. 2019.

**Zakharov,** Prof. Vasilii, (Basil), 29 Sept. 2018.
**Zamboni,** Richard Frederick Charles, 15 Sept. 2019.
**Zealley,** Christopher Bennett, 24 Sept. 2018.
**Zeffirelli,** Gian Franco Corsi, Hon. KBE, 15 June 2019.
**Zunz,** Sir Gerhard Jacob, (Sir Jack), 11 Dec. 2018.

# ABBREVIATIONS USED IN THIS BOOK

Some of the designatory letters in this list are used merely for economy of space and do not necessarily imply any professional or other qualification.

## A

| | |
|---|---|
| AA | Anti-aircraft; Automobile Association; Architectural Association; Augustinians of the Assumption; Associate in Arts |
| AAA | Amateur Athletic Association; American Accounting Association; Abdominal Aortic Aneurysm |
| AAAL | American Academy of Arts and Letters |
| AA&QMG | Assistant Adjutant and Quartermaster-General |
| AAArb | Member, Association of Arbitrators (South Africa) |
| AAAS | American Association for the Advancement of Science |
| AABC | (Register of) Architects Accredited in Building Conservation |
| AAC | Army Air Corps; Amateur Athletic Club |
| AADB | Accountancy and Actuarial Discipline Board |
| AAF | Auxiliary Air Force (*now see* RAuxAF) |
| AAFCE | Allied Air Forces in Central Europe |
| AAG | Assistant Adjutant-General |
| AAI | Associate, Chartered Auctioneers' and Estate Agents' Institute (later, after amalgamation, ARICS) |
| AAIL | American Academy and Institute of Arts and Letters (*now see* AAAL) |
| AAMC | Australian Army Medical Corps (*now see* RAAMC) |
| A&AEE | Aeroplane and Armament Experimental Establishment |
| A&E | Accident and Emergency |
| A&R | Artists and Repertoire |
| A and SH | Argyll and Sutherland Highlanders |
| AAPS | Aquatic and Atmospheric Physical Sciences |
| AAS | American Astronomical Society |
| AASA | Associate, Australian Society of Accountants (*now see* FCPA) |
| AASC | Australian Army Service Corps |
| AATSE | Australian Academy of Technological Sciences and Engineering |
| AAUQ | Associate in Accountancy, University of Queensland |
| AB | Bachelor of Arts (US); able-bodied seaman; airborne; Alberta (postal) |
| ABA | Amateur Boxing Association; Antiquarian Booksellers' Association; American Bar Association |
| ABAE | Amateur Boxing Association of England |
| ABBSI | Associate Member, British Boot and Shoe Institute |
| ABC | Australian Broadcasting Commission; American Broadcasting Companies; Amateur Boxing Club; Associate, Birmingham Conservatoire; Accredited Business Communicator |
| ABCC | Association of British Chambers of Commerce |
| ABF | Army Benevolent Fund |
| ABI | Association of British Insurers |
| ABIPP | Associate, British Institute of Professional Photography |
| ABM | Advisory Board of Ministry |
| ABNM | American Board of Nuclear Medicine |
| ABP | Associated British Ports |
| Abp | Archbishop |
| ABPI | Association of British Pharmaceutical Industry |
| ABPsS | Associate, British Psychological Society (*now see* AFBPsS) |
| ABRC | Advisory Board for the Research Councils |
| ABSA | Association for Business Sponsorship of the Arts |
| ABSM | Associate, Birmingham and Midland Institute School of Music |
| ABTA | Association of British Travel Agents |
| AC | Companion, Order of Australia; *Ante Christum* (before Christ) |
| ACA | Associate, Institute of Chartered Accountants |
| Acad. | Academy |
| ACARD | Advisory Council for Applied Research and Development |
| ACAS | Advisory, Conciliation and Arbitration Service; Assistant Chief of the Air Staff |
| ACC | Association of County Councils; Anglican Consultative Council |
| ACCA | Associate, Association of Chartered Certified Accountants (*formerly* Chartered Association of Certified Accountants) |
| ACCE | Association of County Chief Executives |
| ACCEL | American College of Cardiology Extended Learning |
| ACCM | Advisory Council for the Church's Ministry (*now see* ABM) |
| AcDip | Academic Diploma in the History of Art |
| AcDipEd | Academic Diploma in Education |
| ACDP | Australian Committee of Directors and Principals |
| ACDS | Assistant Chief of Defence Staff |
| ACE | Association of Consulting Engineers; Member, Association of Conference Executives; Allied Command Europe |
| ACENVO | Association of Chief Executives of National Voluntary Organisations (*now see* ACEVO) |
| ACEO | Association of Chief Education Officers |
| ACEVO | Association of Chief Executives of Voluntary Organisations |
| ACF | Army Cadet Force |
| ACFA | Army Cadet Force Association |
| ACFAS | Association Canadienne-Française pour l'avancement des sciences |
| ACFHE | Association of Colleges for Further and Higher Education |
| ACG | Assistant Chaplain-General |
| ACGI | Associate, City and Guilds of London Institute |
| ACGS | Assistant Chief of the General Staff |
| ACI | Airports Council International (Europe) |
| ACIArb | Associate, Chartered Institute of Arbitrators |
| ACIB | Associate, Chartered Institute of Bankers |
| ACIBS | Associate, Chartered Institute of Bankers in Scotland |
| ACIEA | Associate, Chartered Institute of Educational Assessors |
| ACIHort | Associate, Chartered Institute of Horticulture |
| ACII | Associate, Chartered Insurance Institute |
| ACIM | Associate, Chartered Institute of Marketing |
| ACIS | Associate, Institute of Chartered Secretaries and Administrators (*formerly* Chartered Institute of Secretaries) |
| ACLS | American Council of Learned Societies |
| ACM | Association of Computing Machinery |
| ACMA | Associate, Chartered Institute of Management Accountants (*formerly* Institute of Cost and Management Accountants) |
| ACMI | Associate, Chartered Management Institute |
| ACNS | Assistant Chief of Naval Staff |
| ACommA | Associate, Society of Commercial Accountants (*now see* ASCA) |
| ACORD | Advisory Committee on Research and Development |
| ACOS | Assistant Chief of Staff |
| ACOST | Advisory Council on Science and Technology |
| ACP | Association of Clinical Pathologists; Associate, College of Preceptors; African/Caribbean/Pacific |
| ACPO | Association of Chief Police Officers |
| ACR | Accredited Conservator-Restorer |
| ACRE | Action with Rural Communities in England |
| ACS | American Chemical Society; Additional Curates Society |
| acsc | passed Advanced Command and Staff Course |
| ACSM | Associate, Camborne School of Mines |
| AcSS | Member, Academy of Learned Societies for the Social Sciences (*now see* FAcSS) |
| ACT | Australian Capital Territory; Australian College of Theology; Associate, College of Technology; Association of Corporate Treasurers |
| ACTT | Association of Cinematograph, Television and Allied Technicians |
| ACTU | Australian Council of Trade Unions |
| ACU | Association of Commonwealth Universities |
| ACWA | Associate, Institute of Cost and Works Accountants (*now see* ACMA) |
| AD | Dame of the Order of Australia; *Anno Domini* (in the year of the Lord); Air Defence |
| ADAS | Agricultural Development and Advisory Service |
| ADASS | Association of Directors of Adult Social Services |
| ADB | Asian Development Bank; Associate of the Drama Board (Education) |
| ADC | Aide-de-camp; Association of District Councils |
| ADCM | Archbishop of Canterbury's Diploma in Church Music |
| AD Corps | Army Dental Corps (*now* RADC) |
| ADC(P) | Personal Aide-de-camp to HM The Queen |
| ADEME | Assistant Director Electrical and Mechanical Engineering |
| Ad eund | *Ad eundem gradum* ; and *see under* aeg |
| ADGMS | Assistant Director-General of Medical Services |
| ADipC | Advanced Postgraduate Diploma in Management Consulting |
| Adjt | Adjutant |
| ADJAG | Assistant Deputy Judge Advocate General |
| ADM | Advanced Diploma in Midwifery |
| Adm. | Admiral |
| ADMS | Assistant Director of Medical Services |
| ADOS | Assistant Director of Ordnance Services |
| ADP | Automatic Data Processing |
| ADPA | Associate Diploma of Public Administration |
| ADS&T | Assistant Director of Supplies and Transport |
| ADSS | Association of Directors of Social Services |
| ADSW | Association of Directors of Social Work |
| Adv. | Advisory; Advocate |
| AdvDip | Advanced Diploma |
| ADVS | Assistant Director of Veterinary Services |
| ADWE&M | Assistant Director of Works, Electrical and Mechanical |
| AE | Air Efficiency Award |

| | | | |
|---|---|---|---|
| AEA | Atomic Energy Authority; Air Efficiency Award (*now see* AE); American Economic Association | AIE | Associate, Institute of Education |
| AEAF | Allied Expeditionary Air Force | AIEE | Associate, Institution of Electrical Engineers |
| AEC | Agriculture Executive Council; Army Educational Corps (*now see* RAEC); Atomic Energy Commission | AIF | Australian Imperial Forces |
| | | AIFireE | Associate, Institution of Fire Engineers |
| AEE | Atomic Energy Establishment | AIG | Adjutant-Inspector-General |
| AEEU | Amalgamated Engineering and Electrical Union | AIH | Associate, Institute of Housing |
| AEF | Amalgamated Union of Engineering and Foundry Workers (later AEU, then AEEU); American Expeditionary Forces; Air Experience Flight | AIHort | Associate, Institute of Horticulture (*now see* ACIHort) |
| | | AIIA | Associate, Insurance Institute of America; Associate, Indian Institute of Architects |
| aeg | *ad eundem gradum* (to the same degree-of the admission of a graduate of one university to the same degree at another without examination) | AIIMR | Associate, Institute of Investment Management and Research (later ASIP; *now see* CFA) |
| | | AIIRA | Associate, International Industrial Relations Association |
| AEI | Associated Electrical Industries | AIL | Associate, Institute of Linguists |
| AELTC | All England Lawn Tennis Club | AILA | Associate, Institute of Landscape Architects (later ALI) |
| AEM | Air Efficiency Medal | AIM | Associate, Institution of Metallurgists (later MIM); Australian Institute of Management; Alternative Investment Market; Advanced Institute of Management Research |
| AER | Army Emergency Reserve | | |
| AERE | Atomic Energy Research Establishment (Harwell) | | |
| Æt. or Ætat. | *Ætatis* (aged) | AIMarE | Associate, Institute of Marine Engineers |
| AEU | Amalgamated Engineering Union (later AEEU) | AIMBE | American Institute for Medical and Biological Engineering |
| AEWVH | Association for the Education and Welfare of the Visually Handicapped | AIMC | Associate, Institute of Management Consultants |
| | | AIME | American Institute of Mechanical Engineers |
| AF | Admiral of the Fleet | AIMgt | Associate, Institute of Management (*now see* ACMI) |
| AFB | Air Force Base | AIMMM | Associate, Institute of Materials, Minerals and Mining |
| AFBPsS | Associate Fellow, British Psychological Society | AIMSW | Associate, Institute of Medical Social Work |
| AFC | Air Force Cross; Association Football Club | AInstP | Associate, Institute of Physics |
| AFCEA | Armed Forces Communications and Electronics Association | AIP | Association of Independent Producers; American Institute of Physics |
| AFCENT | Allied Forces in Central Europe | AIPR | Associate, Institute of Public Relations |
| AFD | Doctor of Fine Arts (US) | AIQS | Associate Member, Institute of Quantity Surveyors |
| AFDS | Air Fighting Development Squadron | AIRCENT | Allied Air Forces Central Europe |
| AFGE | Associate Fellow, Guild of Glass Engravers | AIRTO | Association of Independent Research and Technology Organizations |
| AFHQ | Allied Force Headquarters | | |
| AFI | American Film Institute | AIS | Associate, Institute of Statisticians (later MIS) |
| AFIAP | Artiste, Fédération Internationale de l'Art Photographique | AIStructE | Associate, Institution of Structural Engineers |
| AFIAS | Associate Fellow, Institute of Aeronautical Sciences (US) (*now see* AFAIAA) | AITP | Associate, Institute of Town Planners, India |
| | | AJAG | Assistant Judge Advocate General |
| AFIMA | Associate Fellow, Institute of Mathematics and its Applications | AJEX | Association of Jewish Ex-Service Men and Women |
| AFM | Air Force Medal | AK | Knight, Order of Australia; Alaska (postal) |
| AFNORTH | Allied Forces in Northern Europe | AKC | Associate, King's College London |
| AFOM | Associate, Faculty of Occupational Medicine | AL | Alabama (postal) |
| AFRAeS | Associate Fellow, Royal Aeronautical Society (*now see* MRAeS) | ALA | Associate, Library Association (*now see* MCLIP); Association of London Authorities |
| AFRC | Agricultural and Food Research Council (*now see* BBSRC) | Ala | Alabama |
| AFSOUTH | Allied Forces in Southern Europe | ALAA | Associate, Library Association of Australia |
| AFV | Armoured Fighting Vehicles | ALAI | Associate, Library Association of Ireland |
| AG | Attorney-General | ALAM | Associate, London Academy of Music and Dramatic Art |
| AGARD | Advisory Group for Aerospace Research and Development | ALCD | Associate, London College of Divinity |
| AGAvA | Associate, Guild of Aviation Artists | ALCM | Associate, London College of Music |
| AGC | Adjutant General's Corps | ALCM (TD) | Associate, London College of Music (Teaching Diploma) |
| AGI | Alliance Graphique Internationale; Associate, Institute of Certificated Grocers | ALCS | Authors Lending and Copyright Society |
| | | ALI | Argyll Light Infantry; Associate, Landscape Institute (*now see* MLI) |
| AGR | Advanced Gas-cooled Reactor | | |
| AGRA | Army Group Royal Artillery; Association of Genealogists and Record Agents | ALICE | Autistic and Language Impaired Children's Education |
| | | ALLC | Association for Literary and Linguistic Computing |
| AGRI | Animal Genetic Resources Information | ALP | Australian Labor Party |
| AGSM | Associate, Guildhall School of Music and Drama; Australian Graduate School of Management | ALPSP | Association of Learned and Professional Society Publishers |
| | | ALS | Associate, Linnean Society; Amyotrophic Lateral Sclerosis |
| AHA | Area Health Authority; American Hospitals Association; Associate, Institute of Health Service Administrators (later AHSM) | Alta | Alberta |
| | | ALVA | Association of Leading Visitor Attractions |
| | | AM | Albert Medal; Member, Order of Australia; Master of Arts (US); Alpes Maritimes |
| AHA(T) | Area Health Authority (Teaching) | | |
| AHI | Association of Heritage Interpretation | AMA | Association of Metropolitan Authorities; Assistant Masters Association (later AMMA, *now see* ATL); Associate, Museums Association; Australian Medical Association |
| AHQ | Army Headquarters | | |
| AHRB | Arts and Humanities Research Board (*now see* AHRC) | | |
| AHRC | Arts and Humanities Research Council | AMARC | Associated Marine and Related Charities |
| AHSM | Associate, Institute of Health Services Management | Amb. | Ambulance; Ambassador |
| ai | *ad interim* | AMBIM | Associate Member, British Institute of Management (later AIMgt) |
| AIA | Associate, Institute of Actuaries; American Institute of Architects; Association of International Artists | | |
| | | AMC | Association of Municipal Corporations |
| AIAA | American Institute of Aeronautics and Astronautics | AMCST | Associate, Manchester College of Science and Technology |
| AIACE | Association Internationale des Anciens des Communautés Européennes | AMCT | Associate, Manchester College of Technology |
| | | AMDEA | Association of Manufacturers of Domestic Electrical Appliances |
| AIAgrE | Associate, Institution of Agricultural Engineers | AMF | Australian Military Forces |
| AIAS | Associate Surveyor Member, Incorporated Association of Architects and Surveyors | AMFL | Allied Command Europe Mobile Force Land |
| | | AMICE | Associate Member, Institution of Civil Engineers (*now see* MICE) |
| AIB | Associate, Institute of Bankers (*now see* ACIB) | | |
| AIBD | Associate, Institute of British Decorators | AMIChemE | Associate Member, Institution of Chemical Engineers |
| AIC | Agricultural Improvement Council; Associate of the Institute of Chemistry (later ARIC, MRIC; *now see* MRSC) | AMIEE | Associate Member, Institution of Electrical Engineers (later MIEE) |
| aic | armour infantry course | AMIERE | Associate Member, Institution of Electronic and Radio Engineers |
| AICA | Associate Member, Commonwealth Institute of Accountants; Association Internationale des Critiques d'Art | AMIMechE | Associate Member, Institution of Mechanical Engineers (*now see* MIMechE) |
| AICE | Associate, Institution of Civil Engineers | | |
| AIChE | American Institute of Chemical Engineers | AMInstCE | Associate Member, Institution of Civil Engineers (*now see* MICE) |
| AICPA | American Institute of Certified Public Accountants | | |
| AICS | Associate, Institute of Chartered Shipbrokers | AmInstEE | American Institute of Electrical Engineers |
| AID | Artificial Insemination by Donor | AMMA | Assistant Masters & Mistresses Association (*now see* ATL) |
| AIDB | Accountancy Investigation and Discipline Board (*now see* AADB) | AMN | Ahli Mangku Negara (Malaysia) |
| AIDS | Acquired Immunity Deficiency Syndrome | AMP | Advanced Management Program; Air Member for Personnel |

| | | | |
|---|---|---|---|
| AMRAeS | Associate Member, Royal Aeronautical Society | ARP | Air Raid Precautions |
| AMRC | Association of Medical Research Charities | ARPS | Associate, Royal Photographic Society |
| AMREF | African Medical and Research Foundation | ARR | Association of Radiation Research |
| AMRI | Associate Member, Royal Institution | ARRC | Associate, Royal Red Cross; Allied (formerly Allied Command Europe) Rapid Reaction Corps |
| AMRS | Associate, Market Research Society | | |
| AMRSH | Associate Member, Royal Society of Health | ARSA | Associate, Royal Scottish Academy |
| AMS | Assistant Military Secretary; Army Medical Services | ARSC | Association for Recorded Sound Collections |
| AMSI | Associate Member, Securities Institute | ARSCM | Associate, Royal School of Church Music |
| AMSO | Air Member for Supply and Organisation | ARSM | Associate, Royal School of Mines |
| AMTRI | Advanced Manufacturing Technology Research Institute | ARTC | Associate, Royal Technical College (Glasgow) (*now see* ARCST) |
| AMusA | Associate Musician of Australia | ARVO | Association for Research in Vision and Ophthalmology |
| Anat. | Anatomy; Anatomical | | |
| ANC | African National Congress | ARWA | Associate, Royal West of England Academy |
| Anon. | Anonymously | ARWS | Associate, Royal Society of Painters in Water-Colours |
| ANU | Australian National University | AS | Anglo-Saxon |
| ANZAAS | Australian and New Zealand Association for the Advancement of Science | ASA | Associate Member, Society of Actuaries; Associate of Society of Actuaries (US); Australian Society of Accountants; Army Sailing Association; Advertising Standards Authority; Alment Aksjeselskap |
| Anzac | Australian and New Zealand Army Corps | | |
| AO | Officer, Order of Australia; Air Officer | | |
| AOA | Air Officer in charge of Administration | ASAA | Associate, Society of Incorporated Accountants and Auditors |
| AOC | Air Officer Commanding | ASAI | Associate, Society of Architectural Illustrators |
| AOC-in-C | Air Officer Commanding-in-Chief | ASAQS | Association of South African Quantity Surveyors |
| AOD | Army Ordnance Department | ASBAH | Association for Spina Bifida and Hydrocephalus |
| AOE | Alberta Order of Excellence | ASC | Administrative Staff College, Henley |
| AOER | Army Officers Emergency Reserve | ASCAP | American Society of Composers, Authors and Publishers |
| APA | American Psychiatric Association | ASCE | American Society of Civil Engineers |
| APACS | Association of Payment and Clearing Systems | ASCHB | Association for Study of Conservation of Historic Buildings |
| APD | Army Pay Department | ASCL | Association of School and College Leaders |
| APEX | Association of Professional, Executive, Clerical and Computer Staff | AScW | Association of Scientific Workers (later ASTMS) |
| | | ASD | Armament Supply Department |
| APHA | American Public Health Association | ASE | Amalgamated Society of Engineers (later AUEW, then AEU, subsequently AEEU); Association for Science Education |
| APIS | Army Photographic Intelligence Service | | |
| APM | Assistant Provost Marshal | ASEAN | Association of South East Asian Nations |
| APMI | Associate, Pensions Management Institute | ASEEES | Association for Slavic, East European and Eurasian Studies |
| APNI | Alliance Party of Northern Ireland | ASH | Action on Smoking and Health |
| APR | Accredited Public Relations Practitioner | ASIAD | Associate, Society of Industrial Artists and Designers |
| APS | Aborigines Protection Society; American Physical Society; American Philosophical Society | ASIP | Associate, UK Society of Investment Professionals (*now see* CFA) |
| APSW | Association of Psychiatric Social Workers | ASLE | American Society of Lubrication Engineers |
| APT&C | Administrative, Professional, Technical and Clerical | ASLEF | Associated Society of Locomotive Engineers and Firemen |
| APTC | Army Physical Training Corps | ASLIB or Aslib | Association for Information Management (*formerly* Association of Special Libraries and Information Bureaux) |
| AQ | Administration and Quartering | | |
| AQMG | Assistant Quartermaster-General | ASM | Association of Senior Members; Australian Service Medal |
| AR | Associated Rediffusion (Television); Arkansas (postal) | ASME | American Society of Mechanical Engineers; Association for the Study of Medical Education |
| ARA | Associate, Royal Academy; Armada de la República Argentina | | |
| ARACI | Associate, Royal Australian Chemical Institute | ASO | Air Staff Officer |
| ARAD | Associate, Royal Academy of Dancing | ASSET | Association of Supervisory Staffs, Executives and Technicians (later ASTMS) |
| ARAeS | Associate, Royal Aeronautical Society | | |
| ARAgS | Associate, Royal Agricultural Societies (*ie* of England, Scotland and Wales) | Asst | Assistant |
| | | ASTA | Association of Short Circuit Testing Authorities |
| ARAIA | Associate, Royal Australian Institute of Architects | ASTC | Administrative Service Training Course |
| ARAM | Associate, Royal Academy of Music | ASTMS | Association of Scientific, Technical and Managerial Staffs (subsequently part of MSF) |
| ARAS | Associate, Royal Astronomical Society | | |
| ARB | Architects' Registration Board | ASTS | Army School of Training Support |
| ARBA | Associate, Royal Society of British Artists | ASVU | Army Security Vetting Unit |
| ARBS | Associate, Royal Society of British Sculptors | ASWE | Admiralty Surface Weapons Establishment |
| ARC | Architects' Registration Council (*now see* ARB); Agricultural Research Council (later AFRC); Aeronautical Research Council; Arthritis and Rheumatism Council | ATA | Air Transport Auxiliary |
| | | ATAE | Association of Tutors in Adult Education |
| | | ATAF | Allied Tactical Air Force |
| | | ATC | Air Training Corps; Art Teacher's Certificate |
| ARCA | Associate, Royal College of Art; Associate, Royal Canadian Academy | ATCDE | Association of Teachers in Colleges and Departments of Education (*now see* NATFHE) |
| ARCamA | Associate, Royal Cambrian Academy of Art | ATCL | Associate, Trinity College of Music, London |
| ARCIC | Anglican-Roman Catholic International Commission | ATD | Art Teacher's Diploma |
| ARCM | Associate, Royal College of Music | ATI | Associate, Textile Institute |
| ARCO | Associate, Royal College of Organists | ATII | Associate Member, Chartered Institute (*formerly* Incorporated Institute, then Institute) of Taxation |
| ARCO(CHM) | Associate, Royal College of Organists with Diploma in Choir Training | | |
| | | ATL | Association of Teachers and Lecturers |
| ARCP | Affiliate, Royal College of Physicians | ato | Ammunition Technical Officer |
| ARCS | Associate, Royal College of Science; Accreditation Review and Consulting Service (*now see* ISI) | ATP | Association of Tennis Professionals |
| | | ATPL (A) or (H) | Airline Transport Pilot's Licence (Aeroplanes), or (Helicopters) |
| ARCST | Associate, Royal College of Science and Technology (Glasgow) | | |
| ARCUK | Architects' Registration Council of the United Kingdom (*now see* ARB) | ATR (BC) | Art Therapist Registered (Board Certified) |
| | | ATS | Auxiliary Territorial Service (later WRAC) |
| ARCVS | Associate, Royal College of Veterinary Surgeons | ATTI | Association of Teachers in Technical Institutions (*now see* NATFHE) |
| ARE | Associate, Royal Society of Painter-Printmakers (*formerly* of Painter-Etchers and Engravers); Arab Republic of Egypt; Admiralty Research Establishment | | |
| | | ATV | Associated Television (*formerly* Association TeleVision) |
| | | AUA | American Urological Association; Association of University Administrators |
| AREINZ | Associate, Real Estate Institute, New Zealand | | |
| ARHistS | Associate, Royal Historical Society | AUEW | Amalgamated Union of Engineering Workers (later AEU, then AEEU) |
| ARIAS | Associate, Royal Incorporation of Architects in Scotland | | |
| ARIBA | Associate, Royal Institute of British Architects (*now see* RIBA) | AUS | Army of the United States |
| ARIC | Associate, Royal Institute of Chemistry (later MRIC; *now see* MRSC) | AUT | Association of University Teachers |
| | | AVCC | Australian Vice-Chancellors' Committee |
| ARICS | Professional Associate, Royal Institution of Chartered Surveyors (*now see* MRICS) | AVD | Army Veterinary Department |
| | | AVMA | Association for Victims of Medical Accidents |
| ARINA | Associate, Royal Institution of Naval Architects | AVR | Army Volunteer Reserve |
| ARLIS | Art Libraries Association | AWA | Anglian Water Authority |
| ARMS | Associate, Royal Society of Miniature Painters | | |

| | |
|---|---|
| AWHCT | Associate, West Ham College of Technology |
| AWO | Association of Water Officers (*now see* IWO) |
| AWRE | Atomic Weapons Research Establishment |
| aws | Graduate of Air Warfare Course |
| AZ | Arizona (postal) |

# B

| | |
|---|---|
| b | born; brother |
| BA | Bachelor of Arts |
| BAA | British Airports Authority; British Accounting Association |
| BAAB | British Amateur Athletic Board |
| BAAL | British Association for Applied Linguistics |
| BAAS | British Association for the Advancement of Science |
| BAC | British Aircraft Corporation |
| BAcc | Bachelor of Accountancy |
| BaccPhil | Baccalaureate in Philosophy |
| BACS | British Academy of Composers & Songwriters (*now see* BASCA) |
| BACSA | British Association for Cemeteries in South Asia |
| BACUP | British Association of Cancer United Patients |
| BADA | British American Drama Academy |
| BAe | British Aerospace |
| BAED | Bachelor of Arts in Environmental Design |
| BAFTA | British Academy of Film and Television Arts |
| BAgricAdmin | Bachelor of Agricultural Administration |
| BAgrSc | Bachelor of Agricultural Science |
| BAI | *Baccalarius in Arte Ingeniaria* (Bachelor of Engineering) |
| BAIE | British Association of Industrial Editors |
| BALPA | British Air Line Pilots' Association |
| BAME | Black, Asian and minority ethnic |
| BAO | Bachelor of Art of Obstetrics |
| BAOMS | British Association of Oral and Maxillo-Facial Surgeons |
| BAOR | British Army of the Rhine (*formerly* on the Rhine) |
| BAOS | British Association of Oral Surgeons (*now see* BAOMS) |
| BAppSc(MT) | Bachelor of Applied Science (Medical Technology) |
| BAPS | British Association of Plastic Surgeons |
| BARB | Broadcasters' Audience Research Board |
| BARC | British Automobile Racing Club |
| BArch | Bachelor of Architecture |
| Bart | Baronet |
| BAS | Bachelor in Agricultural Science |
| BASc | Bachelor of Applied Science |
| BASCA | British Academy of Songwriters, Composers and Authors |
| BASE | British Association for Service to the Elderly |
| BASEEFA | British Approvals Service for Electrical Equipment in Flammable Atmospheres |
| BASES | British Association of Sport and Exercise Sciences |
| BASHH | British Association for Sexual Health and HIV |
| BASIC | British American Security Information Council |
| BASW | British Association of Social Workers |
| Batt. | Battery |
| BBA | British Bankers' Association; Bachelor of Business Administration |
| BBB of C | British Boxing Board of Control |
| BBC | British Broadcasting Corporation |
| BBFC | British Board of Film Classification |
| BBS | Bachelor of Business Studies |
| BBSRC | Biotechnology and Biological Sciences Research Council |
| BC | Before Christ; British Columbia; Borough Council |
| BCA | Bachelor of Commerce and Administration |
| BCC | British Council of Churches (later CCBI) |
| BCE | Bachelor of Civil Engineering; Before the Christian Era |
| BCh or BChir | Bachelor of Surgery |
| BChD | Bachelor of Dental Surgery |
| BCL | Bachelor of Civil Law |
| BCMF | British Ceramic Manufacturers' Federation |
| BCom or BComm | Bachelor of Commerce |
| BCompt | Bachelor of Accounting |
| BComSc | Bachelor of Commercial Science |
| BCPC | British Crop Protection Council |
| BCS | Bengal Civil Service; British Computer Society; Bachelor of Combined Studies |
| BCSA | British Constructional Steelwork Association |
| BCSC | British Council of Shopping Centres |
| BCTS | Bristol Certificate in Theological Studies |
| BCURA | British Coal Utilization Research Association |
| BD | Bachelor of Divinity |
| Bd | Board |
| BDA | British Dental Association; British Deaf Association; British Dyslexia Association |
| Bde | Brigade |
| BDQ | Bachelor of Divinity Qualifying |
| BDS | Bachelor of Dental Surgery |
| BDSc | Bachelor of Dental Science |
| BE | Bachelor of Engineering; British Element |
| BEA | British East Africa; British European Airways; British Epilepsy Association |
| BEAMA | Federation of British Electrotechnical and Allied Manufacturers' Associations (*formerly* British Electrical and Allied Manufacturers' Association) |
| BE&A | Bachelor of Engineering and Architecture (Malta) |
| BEARR | British Emergency Aid for Russia and the Republics |
| BEC | Business Education Council (*now see* BTEC) |
| BEc | Bachelor of Economics |
| BECTU | Broadcasting, Entertainment, Cinematograph and Theatre Union |
| BEd | Bachelor of Education |
| Beds | Bedfordshire |
| BEE | Bachelor of Electrical Engineering |
| BEF | British Expeditionary Force; British Equestrian Federation |
| BEIS | Department for Business, Energy and Industrial Strategy |
| BEM | British Empire Medal |
| BEMAS | British Educational Management and Administration Society |
| BEME | Brigade Electrical and Mechanical Engineer |
| BEng | Bachelor of Engineering |
| BEO | Base Engineer Officer |
| Berks | Berkshire |
| BERR | Department for Business, Enterprise and Regulatory Reform |
| BES | Bachelor of Environmental Studies |
| BESO | British Executive Service Overseas |
| BEVA | British Equine Veterinary Association |
| BFA | Bachelor of Fine Arts |
| BFI | British Film Institute |
| BFMIRA | British Food Manufacturing Industries Research Association |
| BFPO | British Forces Post Office |
| BFSS | British Field Sports Society |
| BFUW | British Federation of University Women (*now see* BFWG) |
| BGCStJ | Bailiff Grand Cross, Most Venerable Order of the Hospital of St John of Jerusalem |
| BGS | Brigadier General Staff |
| BHA | British Hospitality Association |
| BHB | Bachelor of Human Biology |
| Bhd | Berhad |
| BHF | British Heart Foundation |
| BHL | Bachelor of Hebrew Letters |
| BHRA | British Hydromechanics Research Association |
| BHRCA | British Hotels, Restaurants and Caterers' Association (*now see* BHA) |
| BHS | British Horse Society |
| BHSc | Bachelor of Home Science |
| BI | British Invisibles |
| BIBA | British Insurance Brokers' Association |
| BIBRA | British Industrial Biological Research Association |
| BICC | British Insulated Callender's Cables |
| BICERA | British Internal Combustion Engine Research Association (*now see* BICERI) |
| BICERI | British Internal Combustion Engine Research Institute |
| BICSc | British Institute of Cleaning Science |
| BIDA | British Interior Design Association |
| BIEC | British Invisible Exports Council (*now see* BI) |
| BIEE | British Institute of Energy Economics |
| BIFA | British Independent Film Awards |
| BIFU | Banking Insurance and Finance Union |
| BII | British Institute of Innkeeping |
| BIIBA | British Insurance & Investment Brokers' Association (*now see* BIBA) |
| BIM | British Institute of Management |
| BIR | British Institute of Radiology |
| BIS | Bank for International Settlements; British Interplanetary Society; Department for Business, Innovation and Skills |
| BISPA | British Independent Steel Producers Association |
| BISRA | British Iron and Steel Research Association |
| BITC | Business in the Community |
| BJ | Bachelor of Journalism |
| BJOG | British Journal of Obstetrics and Gynaecology |
| BJP | Bharatiya Janata Party |
| BJSM | British Joint Services Mission |
| BJur | Bachelor of Law |
| BKSTS | British Kinematograph, Sound and Television Society |
| BL | Bachelor of Law; British Library |
| BLE | Bachelor of Land Economy |
| BLegS | Bachelor of Legal Studies |
| BLESMA | British Limbless Ex-Servicemen's Association |
| BLitt | Bachelor of Letters |
| BM | British Museum; Bachelor of Medicine; Brigade Major; British Monomark |
| BMA | British Medical Association |
| BMedSci | Bachelor of Medical Science |
| BMet | Bachelor of Metallurgy |
| BMEWS | Ballistic Missile Early Warning System |
| BMG | British Military Government |
| BMH | British Military Hospital |
| BMilSc | Bachelor of Military Science |
| BMJ | British Medical Journal |

| | |
|---|---|
| BMR | Bureau of Mineral Resources |
| BMRA | Brigade Major Royal Artillery |
| BMS | Bachelor of Management Studies |
| BMus | Bachelor of Music |
| Bn | Battalion |
| BN | Bachelor of Nursing |
| BNA | British Nursing Association |
| BNC | Brasenose College |
| BNF | British National Formulary |
| BNFL | British Nuclear Fuels Ltd |
| BNOC | British National Oil Corporation; British National Opera Company |
| BNP | Banque Nationale de Paris; British National Party |
| BNSC | British National Space Centre |
| BNSc | Bachelor of Nursing Science |
| BOAC | British Overseas Airways Corporation |
| BOst | Bachelor of Osteopathy |
| BoT | Board of Trade |
| Bot. | Botany; Botanical |
| BOTB | British Overseas Trade Board |
| BOU | British Ornithologists' Union |
| Bp | Bishop |
| BPA | British Paediatric Association (later CPCH; *now see* RCPCH); Bachelor of Performing Arts |
| BPG | Broadcasting Press Guild |
| BPharm | Bachelor of Pharmacy |
| BPhty | Bachelor of Physiotherapy |
| BPIF | British Printing Industries Federation |
| BPMF | British Postgraduate Medical Federation |
| BProc | Bachelor of Procurationis |
| BPsS | British Psychological Society |
| BR | British Rail |
| Br. | Branch |
| BRA | Brigadier Royal Artillery; British Rheumatism & Arthritis Association |
| BRB | British Railways Board |
| BRCS | British Red Cross Society |
| BRE | Building Research Establishment |
| Brig. | Brigadier |
| BRIT | British Recording Industry Trust |
| BritIRE | British Institution of Radio Engineers (*now see* IERE) |
| BRNC | Britannia Royal Naval College |
| BRS | British Road Services |
| BRTP | Bachelor of Regional and Town Planning |
| BRurSc | Bachelor of Rural Science |
| BS | Bachelor of Surgery; Bachelor of Science; British Standard |
| BSA | Bachelor of Scientific Agriculture; Birmingham Small Arms; Building Societies' Association |
| BSAP | British South Africa Police |
| BSBI | Botanical Society of the British Isles |
| BSC | British Steel Corporation; Bengal Staff Corps |
| BSc | Bachelor of Science |
| BScA or BScAgr | Bachelor of Science in Agriculture |
| BSc(Dent) | Bachelor of Science in Dentistry |
| BScEcon | Bachelor of Science in Economics |
| BScEng | Bachelor of Science in Engineering |
| BSc (Est. Man.) | Bachelor of Science in Estate Management |
| BScN | Bachelor of Science in Nursing |
| BScSoc | Bachelor of Social Sciences |
| BSE | Bachelor of Science in Engineering (US); Bovine Spongiform Encephalopathy |
| BSEE | Bachelor of Science in Electrical Engineering |
| BSES | British Schools Exploring Society |
| BSF | British Salonica Force |
| BSFA | British Science Fiction Association |
| BSFS | Bachelor of Science in Foreign Service |
| BSI | British Standards Institution |
| BSIA | British Security Industry Association |
| BSJA | British Show Jumping Association |
| BSME | Bachelor of Science in Mechanical Engineering; British Society of Magazine Editors |
| BSN | Bachelor of Science in Nursing |
| BSNS | Bachelor of Naval Science |
| BSocSc | Bachelor of Social Science |
| BSocStud | Bachelor of Social Studies |
| BSRA | British Ship Research Association |
| BSRIA | Building Services Research and Information Association |
| BSS | Bachelor of Science (Social Science) |
| BSSc | Bachelor of Social Science |
| BST | Bachelor of Sacred Theology |
| BSurv | Bachelor of Surveying |
| BSW | Bachelor of Social Work |
| BT | Bachelor of Teaching; British Telecommunications |
| Bt | Baronet; Brevet |
| BTA | British Tourist Authority (*formerly* British Travel Association) |
| BTCV | British Trust for Conservation Volunteers |
| BTDB | British Transport Docks Board (*now see* ABP) |
| BTEC | Business and Technology (*formerly* Technician) Education Council |
| BTech | Bachelor of Technology |
| BTh | Bachelor of Theology |
| BTP | Bachelor of Town Planning |
| BTS | Bachelor of Theological Studies |
| Btss | Baroneteess |
| BUAS | British Universities Association of Slavists |
| Bucks | Buckinghamshire |
| BUGB | Baptist Union of Great Britain |
| BUNAC | British Universities North America Club |
| BUniv | Bachelor of the University |
| BUPA | British United Provident Association |
| BURA | British Urban Regeneration Association |
| BV | Besloten Vennootschap |
| BVA | British Veterinary Association; British Video Association |
| BVC | Bar Vocational Course |
| BVCA | British Private Equity and Venture Capital Association |
| BVetMed | Bachelor of Veterinary Medicine |
| BVI | British Virgin Islands |
| BVM | Blessed Virgin Mary |
| BVMS | Bachelor of Veterinary Medicine and Surgery |
| BVPA | British Veterinary Poultry Association |
| BVSc | Bachelor of Veterinary Science |
| BWI | British West Indies |
| BWM | British War Medal |

# C

| | |
|---|---|
| C | Conservative; 100 |
| c | child; cousin; *circa* (about) |
| CA | Central America; County Alderman; Chartered Accountant (Scotland and Canada); California (postal) |
| CAA | Civil Aviation Authority |
| CAABU | Council for the Advancement of Arab and British Understanding |
| CAAV | (Member of) Central Association of Agricultural Valuers |
| CAB | Citizens' Advice Bureau; Centre for Agricultural and Biosciences (*formerly* Commonwealth Agricultural Bureau) |
| CABE | Commission for Architecture and the Built Environment |
| CACTM | Central Advisory Council of Training for the Ministry (later ACCM; *now see* ABM) |
| CAER | Conservative Action for Electoral Reform |
| CAF | Charities Aid Foundation |
| CAFCASS | Child and Family Court Advisory and Support Service |
| CAFOD | Catholic Agency for Overseas Development |
| CAJ | Committee on the Administration of Justice |
| Calif | California |
| CAM | Communications, Advertising and Marketing |
| Cambs | Cambridgeshire |
| CAMC | Canadian Army Medical Corps |
| CAMRA | Campaign for Real Ale |
| CAMS | Certificate of Advanced Musical Study |
| C&G | City and Guilds of London Institute |
| Cantab | *Cantabrigiensis* (of Cambridge) |
| Cantuar | *Cantuariensis* (of Canterbury) |
| CAP | Common Agricultural Policy |
| Capt. | Captain |
| CARD | Campaign against Racial Discrimination |
| CARDS | Community Assistance for Reconstruction, Development and Stabilisation |
| CARE | Cottage and Rural Enterprises |
| CARICOM | Caribbean Community |
| CARIFTA | Caribbean Free Trade Area (*now see* CARICOM) |
| Carms | Carmarthenshire |
| CAS | Chief of the Air Staff |
| CASE | Council for the Advancement and Suppport of Education |
| CAT | College of Advanced Technology; Countryside Around Towns |
| CATE | Council for the Accreditation of Teacher Education |
| Cav. | Cavalry |
| CAWU | Clerical and Administrative Workers' Union (later APEX) |
| CB | Companion, Order of the Bath; County Borough |
| CBC | County Borough Council |
| CBE | Commander, Order of the British Empire |
| CBI | Confederation of British Industry |
| CBII | Companion, British Institute of Innkeeping |
| CBIM | Companion, British Institute of Management (later CIMgt) |
| CBiol | Chartered Biologist |
| CBNS | Commander British Navy Staff |
| CBS | Columbia Broadcasting System |
| CBSI | Chartered Building Societies Institute (*now see* CIB) |
| CBSO | City of Birmingham Symphony Orchestra |
| CC | Companion, Order of Canada; City Council; County Council; Cricket Club; Cycling Club; County Court |
| CCAB | Consultative Committee of Accountancy Bodies |
| CCAHC | Central Council for Agricultural and Horticultural Co-operation |

| | | | |
|---|---|---|---|
| CCBE | Commission Consultative des Barreaux de la Communauté Européenne | CETSW | Council for Education and Training in Social Work |
| CCBI | Council of Churches for Britain and Ireland (*now see* CTBI) | CF | Chaplain to the Forces; Companion, Order of Fiji; Corporate Finance; Corporate Financier |
| CCC | Corpus Christi College; Central Criminal Court; County Cricket Club | CFA | Canadian Field Artillery; Chartered Financial Analyst |
| CCE | Chartered Civil Engineer | CFE | Central Fighter Establishment |
| CCETSW | Central Council for Education and Training in Social Work | CFM | Cadet Forces Medal |
| CCF | Combined Cadet Force | CFPS | Certificate of Further Professional Studies |
| CCFM | Combined Cadet Forces Medal | CFR | Commander, Order of the Federal Republic of Nigeria |
| CCG | Control Commission Germany; Clinical Commissioning Group | CFS | Central Flying School; Chronic Fatigue Syndrome |
| CCH | Cacique's Crown of Honour, Order of Service of Guyana | CGA | Community of the Glorious Ascension; Country Gentlemen's Association |
| CChem | Chartered Chemist | CGeog | Chartered Geographer |
| CCIPD | Companion, Chartered Institute of Personnel and Development | CGeol | Chartered Geologist |
| CCIS | Command Control Information System | CGIA | Insignia Award of City and Guilds of London Institute (*now see* FCGI) |
| CCJ | Council of Christians and Jews | CGLI | City and Guilds of London Institute (*now see* C&G) |
| CCLRC | Council for the Central Laboratory of the Research Councils | CGM | Conspicuous Gallantry Medal |
| CCMI | Companion, Chartered Management Institute | CGMA | Chartered Global Management Accountant |
| CCMS | Committee on the Challenges of Modern Society | CGRM | Commandant-General Royal Marines |
| CCPR | Central Council of Physical Recreation | CGS | Chief of the General Staff |
| CCQI | Companion, Chartered Quality Institute | CH | Companion of Honour |
| CCRA | Commander Corps of Royal Artillery | Chap. | Chaplain |
| CCRE | Commander Corps of Royal Engineers | ChapStJ | Chaplain, Order of St John of Jerusalem (*now see* ChStJ) |
| CCREME | Commander Corps of Royal Electrical and Mechanical Engineers | CHAR | Campaign for the Homeless and Rootless |
| CCRSigs | Commander Corps of Royal Signals | CHB | Companion of Honour of Barbados |
| CCS | Casualty Clearing Station; Ceylon Civil Service; Countryside Commission for Scotland | ChB | Bachelor of Surgery |
| | | CHC | Community Health Council |
| CCSU | Council of Civil Service Unions | CHIU | Committee for Heads of Irish Universities |
| CCTA | Commission de Coöpération Technique pour l'Afrique; Central Computer and Telecommunications Authority | ChLJ | Chaplain, Order of St Lazarus of Jerusalem |
| | | (CHM) | *see under* ARCO(CHM), FRCO(CHM) |
| CCTS | Combat Crew Training Squadron | ChM | Master of Surgery |
| CD | Canadian Forces Decoration; Commander, Order of Distinction (Jamaica); Civil Defence; Compact Disc | Chm. | Chairman or Chairwoman |
| | | CHN | Community of the Holy Name |
| CDA | Co-operative Development Agency; Christian Democratic Alliance | CHort | Chartered Horticulturalist |
| | | ChStJ | Chaplain, Most Venerable Order of the Hospital of St John of Jerusalem |
| CDC | Centers for Disease Control and Prevention | | |
| CDEE | Chemical Defence Experimental Establishment | CI | Imperial Order of the Crown of India; Channel Islands |
| CDipAF | Certified Diploma in Accounting and Finance | CIA | Chemical Industries Association; Central Intelligence Agency |
| CDir | Chartered Director | CIAgrE | Companion, Institution of Agricultural Engineers |
| CDISS | Centre for Defence and International Security Studies | CIArb | Chartered Institute of Arbitrators |
| Cdo | Commando | CIB | Chartered Institute of Bankers |
| Cdre | Commodore | CIBS | Chartered Institution of Building Services (*now see* CIBSE) |
| CDS | Chief of the Defence Staff | CIBSE | Chartered Institution of Building Services Engineers |
| CDU | Christlich-Demokratische Union | CIC | Chemical Institute of Canada; Community Interest Company |
| CE | Civil Engineer | CICAP | Criminal Injuries Compensation Appeal Panel |
| CEA | Central Electricity Authority | CICB | Criminal Injuries Compensation Board |
| CEC | Commission of the European Communities | CICHE | Committee for International Co-operation in Higher Education |
| CECAM | Centre Européen de Calcul Atomique et Moléculaire | CICI | Confederation of Information Communication Industries |
| CECD | Confédération Européenne du Commerce de Détail | CID | Criminal Investigation Department |
| CEDA | Committee for Economic Development of Australia | CIE | Companion, Order of the Indian Empire; Confédération Internationale des Etudiants |
| CEDEP | Centre Européen d'Education Permanente | | |
| CEDR | Centre for Effective Dispute Resolution | CIES | Companion, Institution of Engineers and Shipbuilders in Scotland |
| CEE | Communauté Economique Européenne | | |
| CEED | Centre for Economic and Environmental Development | CIEx | Companion, Institute of Export |
| CEF | Canadian Expeditionary Force | CIFE | Council (*formerly* Conference) for Independent Further Education |
| CeFA | Certificate for Financial Advisers | | |
| CEFAS | Centre for Environment, Fisheries and Aquaculture Science | CIGasE | Companion, Institution of Gas Engineers (*now see* CIGEM) |
| CEFIC | Conseil Européen des Fédérations de l'Industrie Chimique | CIGEM | Companion, Institution of Gas Engineers and Managers |
| CEGB | Central Electricity Generating Board | CIGRE | Conférence Internationale des Grands Réseaux Electriques |
| CEH | Centre for Ecology & Hydrology | CIGS | Chief of the Imperial General Staff (*now see* CGS) |
| CEI | Council of Engineering Institutions | CIHM | Companion, Institute of Healthcare Management |
| CEIR | Corporation for Economic and Industrial Research | CIHR | Canadian Institutes of Health Research |
| CEM | Council of European Municipalities (*now see* CEMR); College of Emergency Medicine | CIIA | Canadian Institute of International Affairs |
| | | CIL | *Corpus inscriptionum latinarum* |
| CeMAP | Certificate in Mortgage Advice and Practice | CILIP | Chartered Institute of Library and Information Professionals |
| CEMR | Council of European Municipalities and Regions | CILT | Chartered Institute of Logistics and Transport |
| CEMS | Church of England Men's Society | CIM | China Inland Mission; Chartered Institute of Marketing |
| CEN | Comité Européen de Normalisation | CIMA | Chartered Institute of Management Accountants |
| CENELEC | European Committee for Electrotechnical Standardization | CIMarE | Companion, Institute of Marine Engineers |
| CEng | Chartered Engineer | CIMEMME | Companion, Institution of Mining Electrical and Mining Mechanical Engineers |
| Cento | Central Treaty Organisation | | |
| CEnv | Chartered Environmentalist | CIMgt | Companion, Institute of Management (*now see* CCMI) |
| CEO | Chief Executive Officer | CIMGTechE | Companion, Institution of Mechanical and General Technician Engineers |
| CEPS | Center for Economic Policy Studies | | |
| CERA | Chartered Enterprise Risk Analyst | CIMO | Commission for Instruments and Methods of Observation |
| CeRGI | Certificate of Regulated General Insurance | CIMR | Cambridge Institute for Medical Research |
| CERL | Central Electricity Research Laboratories | C-in-C | Commander-in-Chief |
| CERN | Organisation (*formerly* Centre) Européenne pour la Recherche Nucléaire | CINCHAN | Allied Commander-in-Chief Channel |
| | | CInstLM | Companion, Institute of Leadership and Management |
| CERT | Charities Effectiveness Review Trust | CINOA | Confédération Internationale des Négotiants en Œuvres d'Art |
| CertCPE | Certificate in Clinical Pastoral Education | CIOB | Chartered Institute of Building |
| CertDS | Certificate in Dramatic Studies | CIPA | Chartered Institute of Patent Agents |
| Cert Ed | Certificate of Education | CIPD | Companion, Institute of Personnel and Development (*now see* CCIPD); Chartered Institute of Personnel and Development |
| CertHE | Certificate in Higher Education | | |
| CertITP | Certificate of International Teachers' Program (Harvard) | CIPFA | Chartered Institute of Public Finance and Accountancy |
| CertTP | Certificate in Town Planning | CIPM | Companion, Institute of Personnel Management (later CIPD) |
| CEST | Centre for Exploitation of Science and Technology | CIPR | Chartered Institute of Public Relations |
| CET | Council for Educational Technology | CIQA | Companion, Institute of Quality Assurance (*now see* CCQI) |

| | | | |
|---|---|---|---|
| CIR | Commission on Industrial Relations | Col.-Sergt | Colour-Sergeant |
| CIRES | Co-operative Institute for Research in Environmental Sciences | Com | Communist |
| CIRIA | Construction Industry Research and Information Association | Comd | Command |
| CIRP | Collège Internationale pour Recherche et Production | Comdg | Commanding |
| CIS | Institute of Chartered Secretaries and Administrators (*formerly* Chartered Institute of Secretaries); Command Control Communications and Information Systems; Commonwealth of Independent States | Comdr | Commander |
| | | Comdt | Commandant |
| | | COMEC | Council of the Military Education Committees of the Universities of the UK |
| CISAC | Confédération Internationale des Sociétés d'Auteurs et Compositeurs; Centre for International Security and Arms Control | Commn | Commission |
| | | Commnd | Commissioned |
| | | CompICE | Companion, Institution of Civil Engineers |
| CISI | Chartered Institute for Securities & Investment | CompIEE | Companion, Institution of Electrical Engineers (later FIEE) |
| CIT | Chartered Institute of Transport; California Institute of Technology | CompIERE | Companion, Institution of Electronic and Radio Engineers |
| | | CompIGasE | Companion, Institution of Gas Engineers |
| CITB | Construction Industry Training Board | CompILE | Companion, Institution of Lighting Engineers |
| CITD | Certificate of Institute of Training and Development | CompIMechE | Companion, Institution of Mechanical Engineers |
| CITP | Chartered Information Technology Professional | CompInstE | Companion, Institute of Energy |
| CIV | City Imperial Volunteers | CompInstMC | Companion, Institute of Measurement and Control |
| CIWEM | Chartered Institution of Water and Environmental Management | CompOR | Companion, Operational Research Society |
| CJM | Congregation of Jesus and Mary (Eudist Fathers) | CompTI | Companion of the Textile Institute |
| CL | Commander, Order of Leopold | Comr | Commissioner |
| cl | *cum laude* | Comy.-Gen. | Commissary-General |
| Cl. | Class | CON | Commander, Order of the Niger |
| CLA | Country Land & Business Association (*formerly* Country Landowners' Association) | ConfEd | Confederation of Education Service Managers |
| | | Conn | Connecticut |
| CLIC | Cancer and Leukemia in Childhood | Const. | Constitutional |
| CLit | Companion of Literature (Royal Society of Literature Award) | CONUL | Council of National and University Librarians |
| CLJ | Commander, Order of St Lazarus of Jerusalem | Co-op. | Co-operative |
| CLP | Constituency Labour Party | COPA | Comité des Organisations Professionels Agricoles de la CEE |
| CLRAE | Congress (*formerly* Conference) of Local and Regional Authorities of Europe | COPEC | Conference of Politics, Economics and Christianity |
| | | COPUS | Committee on the Public Understanding of Science |
| CLY | City of London Yeomanry | Corp. | Corporation; Corporal |
| CM | Member, Order of Canada; Congregation of the Mission (Vincentians); Master in Surgery; Certificated Master; Canadian Militia | Corresp. Mem. | Corresponding Member |
| | | COS | Chief of Staff; Charity Organization Society |
| | | CoSIRA | Council for Small Industries in Rural Areas |
| CMA | Canadian Medical Association; Cost and Management Accountant (NZ); Competition and Markets Authority | COSLA | Convention of Scottish Local Authorities |
| | | COSPAR | Committee on Space Research |
| CMarEng | Chartered Marine Engineer | COSSAC | Chief of Staff to Supreme Allied Commander |
| CMarSci | Chartered Marine Scientist | COTC | Canadian Officers' Training Corps |
| CMath | Chartered Mathematician | CP | Central Provinces; Cape Province; Congregation of the Passion |
| CMB | Central Midwives' Board | CPA | Commonwealth Parliamentary Association; Chartered Patent Agent; Certified Public Accountant (USA) |
| CMC | Certified Management Consultant; Civil Mediation Council | | |
| CME | Continuing Ministerial Education | CPAG | Child Poverty Action Group |
| CMet | Chartered Meteorologist | CPAGB | Credit, Photographic Alliance of Great Britain |
| CMF | Commonwealth Military Forces; Central Mediterranean Force | CPAS | Church Pastoral Aid Society |
| CMG | Companion, Order of St Michael and St George | CPC | Conservative Political Centre |
| CMgr | Chartered Manager | CPCH | College of Paediatrics and Child Health (*now see* RCPCH) |
| CMILT | Chartered Member, Chartered Institute of Logistics and Transport | CPD | Continuing Professional Development |
| | | CPE | Common Professional Examination; Clinical Pastoral Education |
| CMIWSc | Certified Member, Institute of Wood Science | CPEng | Chartered Professional Engineer (of Institution of Engineers of Australia) |
| CMJ | Commander, Supreme Military Order of the Temple of Jerusalem | | |
| | | CPFA | Member or Associate, Chartered Institute of Public Finance and Accountancy |
| CMktr | Chartered Marketer | | |
| CMLI | Chartered Member, Landscape Institute | CPHVA | Community Practitioners & Health Visitors' Association |
| CMLJ | Commander of Merit, Order of St Lazarus of Jerusalem | CPhys | Chartered Physicist |
| CMM | Commander, Order of Military Merit (Canada) | CPL | Chief Personnel and Logistics |
| CMO | Chief Medical Officer | CPLS | Certificate of Professional Legal Studies |
| CMP | Corps of Military Police (*now see* CRMP) | CPM | Colonial Police Medal |
| CMS | Church Mission (*formerly* Church Missionary) Society; Certificate in Management Studies | CPR | Canadian Pacific Railway |
| | | CPRE | Campaign to Protect Rural England (*formerly* Council for the Protection of Rural England) |
| CMT | Chaconia Medal of Trinidad | | |
| CNAA | Council for National Academic Awards | CPRW | Campaign for the Protection of Rural Wales |
| CND | Campaign for Nuclear Disarmament | CPS | Crown Prosecution Service; Certificate in Pastoral Studies |
| CNI | Companion, Nautical Institute | CPSA | Civil and Public Services Association (*now see* PCS); Church of the Province of South Africa |
| CNO | Chief of Naval Operations | | |
| CNOCS | Captain Naval Operational Command Systems | CPSU | Communist Party of the Soviet Union |
| CNR | Canadian National Railways | CPsychol | Chartered Psychologist |
| CNRS | Centre National de la Recherche Scientifique | CPU | Commonwealth Press Union |
| CNS | Clinical Nurse Specialist | CQ | Chevalier, National Order of Quebec |
| CNZM | Companion, New Zealand Order of Merit | CQI | Chartered Quality Institute |
| CO | Commanding Officer; Commonwealth Office (after Aug. 1966) (*now see* FCO); Colonial Office (before Aug. 1966); Conscientious Objector; Colorado (postal); Congregation of the Oratory | CQP | Chartered Quality Professional |
| | | CQSW | Certificate of Qualification in Social Work |
| | | CR | Community of the Resurrection |
| | | cr | created or creation |
| Co. | County; Company | CRA | Commander, Royal Artillery |
| Coal.L or Co.L | Coalition Liberal | CRAC | Careers Research and Advisory Centre |
| Coal.U or Co.U | Coalition Unionist | CRadP | Chartered Radiation Protection Professional |
| COBSEO | Confederation of British Service and Ex-Service Organisations | CRAeS | Companion, Royal Aeronautical Society |
| CODEST | Committee for the Development of European Science and Technology | CRASC | Commander, Royal Army Service Corps |
| | | CRC | Cancer Research Campaign (*now see* CRUK); Community Relations Council |
| C of E | Church of England | | |
| C of I | Church of Ireland | CRE | Commander, Royal Engineers; Commission for Racial Equality; Commercial Relations and Exports; Conference of Rectors of European Universities (*formerly* Association of European Universities) |
| C of S | Chief of Staff; Church of Scotland | | |
| COHSE | Confederation of Health Service Employees | | |
| COI | Central Office of Information | | |
| CoID | Council of Industrial Design (*now* Design Council) | | |
| Col | Colonel | Cres. | Crescent |
| Coll. | College; Collegiate | CRMP | Corps of Royal Military Police |
| Colo | Colorado | CRNCM | Companion, Royal Northern College of Music |

| | |
|---|---|
| CRO | Commonwealth Relations Office (*now see* FCO) |
| CRSNZ | Companion, Royal Society of New Zealand |
| CRUK | Cancer Research United Kingdom |
| CS | Civil Service; Clerk to the Signet; Companion, Order of Samoa |
| CSA | Confederate States of America; Child Support Agency |
| CSAB | Civil Service Appeal Board |
| CSB | Bachelor of Christian Science |
| CSC | Conspicuous Service Cross; Congregation of the Holy Cross |
| CSCA | Civil Service Clerical Association (later CPSA) |
| CSCE | Conference on Security and Co-operation in Europe |
| CSci | Chartered Scientist |
| CSD | Civil Service Department; Co-operative Secretaries Diploma; Chartered Society of Designers |
| CSDE | Central Servicing Development Establishment |
| CSEU | Confederation of Shipbuilding and Engineering Unions |
| CSG | Companion, Order of the Star of Ghana; Company of the Servants of God |
| CSI | Companion, Order of the Star of India; Cross, Order of Solomon Islands |
| CSIR | Commonwealth Council for Scientific and Industrial Research (*now see* CSIRO); Council of Scientific and Industrial Research, India |
| CSIRO | Commonwealth Scientific and Industrial Research Organization (Australia) |
| CSM | Civil Service Medal (Fiji); Companion, Star of Merit (Federation of Saint Kitts and Nevis); Companion, Star of Melanesia (Papua New Guinea) |
| CSO | Chief Scientific Officer; Chief Signal Officer; Chief Staff Officer; Central Statistical Office (*now see* ONS) |
| CSP | Chartered Society of Physiotherapists; Civil Service of Pakistan |
| CSPQ | Certificat de Spécialiste de la Province de Québec |
| CSS | Companion, Star of Sarawak; Council for Science and Society; Certificate in Social Studies |
| CSSB | Civil Service Selection Board |
| CSSD | Czech Social Democratic Party |
| CSSp | Holy Ghost Father |
| CSSR | Congregation of the Most Holy Redeemer (Redemptorist Order) |
| CStat | Chartered Statistician |
| CSTI | Council of Science and Technology Institutes |
| CStJ | Commander, Most Venerable Order of the Hospital of St John of Jerusalem |
| CSU | Christlich-Soziale Union in Bayern |
| CSV | Community Service Volunteers |
| CSW | Certificate in Social Work |
| CT | Connecticut (postal) |
| CTA | Chaplain Territorial Army; Chartered Tax Adviser |
| CTBI | Churches Together in Britain and Ireland |
| CTC | Cyclists' Touring Club; Commando Training Centre; City Technology College |
| CText | Chartered Textile Technologist |
| CTh | Certificate in Theology |
| CTL | Companion, Trinity Laban |
| CTM | Certificate of Theology for Ministry |
| CTS | Certificate in Terrorism Studies |
| CU | Cambridge University |
| CUAC | Cambridge University Athletic Club; Colleges and Universities of the Anglican Communion |
| CUAFC | Cambridge University Association Football Club |
| CUCC | Cambridge University Cricket Club |
| CUF | Common University Fund |
| CUNY | City University of New York |
| CUP | Cambridge University Press |
| CUPGRA | Cambridge University Postgraduate Research Association |
| CURUFC | Cambridge University Rugby Union Football Club |
| CV | Cross of Valour (Canada) |
| CVCP | Committee of Vice-Chancellors and Principals of the Universities of the United Kingdom (*now see* UUK) |
| CVO | Commander, Royal Victorian Order |
| CVS | Council for Voluntary Service |
| CWA | Crime Writers Association |
| CWEM | Chartered Water and Environmental Manager |
| CWGC | Commonwealth War Graves Commission |
| CWS | Co-operative Wholesale Society |
| CWU | Communication Workers Union |

# D

| | |
|---|---|
| D | Duke |
| d | died; daughter |
| DA | Dame of St Andrew, Order of Barbados; Diploma in Anaesthesia; Diploma in Art; Doctor of Arts |
| DAA | Diploma in Archive Administration |
| DAA&QMG | Deputy Assistant Adjutant and Quartermaster-General |
| DAAD | Designers and Art Directors Association |
| DAAG | Deputy Assistant Adjutant-General |
| DA&QMG | Deputy Adjutant and Quartermaster-General |
| DAC | Development Assistance Committee; Diocesan Advisory Committee |
| DAcad | Doctor of the Academy |
| DACG | Deputy Assistant Chaplain-General |
| DACLAM | Diplomate, American College of Laboratory Animal Medicine |
| DACOS | Deputy Assistant Chief of Staff |
| DAD | Deputy Assistant Director |
| DAdmin | Doctor of Administration |
| DADMS | Deputy Assistant Director of Medical Services |
| DADOS | Deputy Assistant Director of Ordnance Services |
| DADQ | Deputy Assistant Director of Quartering |
| DADST | Deputy Assistant Director of Supplies and Transport |
| DAEd | Diploma in Art Education |
| DAG | Deputy Adjutant-General |
| DAgr | Doctor of Agriculture |
| DAgrFor | Doctor of Agriculture and Forestry |
| DAgrSc | Doctor of Agricultural Science |
| DAMS | Deputy Assistant Military Secretary |
| D&AD | Design and Art Direction (*formerly* Designers and Art Directors Association) |
| DAppSc | Doctor of Applied Science |
| DAQMG | Deputy Assistant Quartermaster-General |
| DArch | Doctor of Architecture |
| DArt | Doctor of Art |
| DArts | Doctor of Arts |
| DASc | Doctor in Agricultural Sciences |
| DASS | Diploma in Applied Social Studies |
| DATA | Draughtsmen's and Allied Technicians' Association (later AUEW(TASS)) |
| DATEC | Art and Design Committee, Technician Education Council |
| DAvMed | Diploma in Aviation Medicine, Royal College of Physicians |
| DBA | Doctor of Business Administration |
| DBE | Dame Commander, Order of the British Empire |
| DBTS | Diploma in Biblical and Theological Studies |
| DBus | Doctor of Business |
| DC | District Council; District of Columbia |
| DCA | Doctor of Creative Arts; Department for Constitutional Affairs |
| DCAS | Deputy Chief of the Air Staff |
| DCB | Dame Commander, Order of the Bath |
| DCC | Diploma of Chelsea College |
| DCCH | Diploma in Community Child Health |
| DCDS | Deputy Chief of Defence Staff |
| DCE | Diploma of a College of Education |
| DCG | Deputy Chaplain-General |
| DCGS | Deputy Chief of the General Staff |
| DCh | Doctor of Surgery |
| DCH | Diploma in Child Health |
| DChA | Diploma in Charity Accounting |
| DCHS | Dame Commander, Order of the Holy Sepulchre |
| DCL | Doctor of Civil Law; Doctor of Canon Law |
| DCLG | Department for Communities and Local Government |
| DCLI | Duke of Cornwall's Light Infantry |
| DCLJ | Dame Commander, Order of St Lazarus of Jerusalem |
| DCM | Distinguished Conduct Medal |
| DCMG | Dame Commander, Order of St Michael and St George |
| DCMS | Department for Digital, Culture, Media and Sport (*formerly* Department for Culture, Media and Sport) |
| DCnL | Doctor of Canon Law |
| DCNZM | Distinguished Companion, New Zealand Order of Merit |
| DCO | Duke of Cambridge's Own |
| DCom *or* DComm | Doctor of Commerce |
| DCP | Diploma in Clinical Pathology; Diploma in Conservation of Paintings |
| DCS | Deputy Chief of Staff; Doctor of Commercial Sciences |
| DCSF | Department for Children, Schools and Families |
| DCSG | Dame Commander, Order of St Gregory the Great |
| DCSO | Deputy Chief Scientific Officer |
| DCT | Doctor of Christian Theology |
| DCVO | Dame Commander, Royal Victorian Order |
| DD | Doctor of Divinity |
| DDAM | Diploma in Disability Assessment Medicine |
| DDes | Doctor of Design |
| DDGAMS | Deputy Director General, Army Medical Services |
| DDH | Diploma in Dental Health |
| DDL | Deputy Director of Labour |
| DDME | Deputy Director of Mechanical Engineering |
| DDMI | Deputy Director of Military Intelligence |
| DDMO | Deputy Director of Military Operations |
| DDMS | Deputy Director of Medical Services |
| DDMT | Deputy Director of Military Training |
| DDNI | Deputy Director of Naval Intelligence |
| DDO | Diploma in Dental Orthopaedics |
| DDPH | Diploma in Dental Public Health |
| DDPR | Deputy Director of Public Relations |
| DDPS | Deputy Director of Personal Services |
| DDR | Deutsche Demokratische Republik |
| DDRA | Deputy Director Royal Artillery |

| | | | |
|---|---|---|---|
| DDra | Doctor of Drama | DIH | Diploma in Industrial Health |
| DDS | Doctor of Dental Surgery; Director of Dental Services | DIMP | Darjah Indera Mahkota Pahang (Malaysia) |
| DDSc | Doctor of Dental Science | DIntLaw | Diploma in International Law |
| DDSD | Deputy Director Staff Duties | Dio. | Diocese |
| DDSM | Defense Distinguished Service Medal | DipA | Diploma of Arts in Theology |
| DDST | Deputy Director of Supplies and Transport | DipAA | Diploma in Applied Art |
| DDWE&M | Deputy Director of Works, Electrical and Mechanical | DipABRSM | Diploma, Associated Board of Royal Schools of Music |
| DE | Doctor of Engineering; Delaware (postal) | DipAD | Diploma in Art and Design |
| DEA | Department of Economic Affairs; Diplôme d'Etudes Approfondies | DipAE | Diploma in Adult Education |
| | | DipAe | Diploma in Aeronautics |
| DEc | Doctor of Economics | DipAgr | Diploma in Agriculture |
| DECC | Department of Energy and Climate Change | DipArch | Diploma in Architecture |
| decd | deceased | DipASE | Diploma in Advanced Study of Education, College of Preceptors |
| DEcon | Doctor of Economics | DipASS | Diploma in Applied Social Studies |
| DEconSc | Doctor of Economic Science | DipBA | Diploma in Business Administration |
| DEd | Doctor of Education | DipBS | Diploma in Fine Art, Byam Shaw School |
| DEFRA | Department for Environment, Food and Rural Affairs | DipCAM | Diploma in Communications, Advertising and Marketing of CAM Foundation |
| Deleg. | Delegate | | |
| DEME | Directorate of Electrical and Mechanical Engineering | DipCAT | Diploma in Cognitive Analytic Therapy |
| DEMS | Defensively Equipped Merchant Ships | DipCD | Diploma in Civic Design |
| (DemU) | Democratic Unionist | DipCE | Diploma in Civil Engineering; Diploma of a College of Education (Scotland) |
| DenD | Docteur en Droit | | |
| DEng | Doctor of Engineering | DipChA | Diploma in Chartered Accounting |
| DenM | Docteur en Médicine | DipCII | Diploma in Insurance, Chartered Insurance Institute |
| DEOVR | Duke of Edinburgh's Own Volunteer Rifles | DipCons | Diploma in Conservation |
| DEP | Department of Employment and Productivity; European Progressive Democrats | DipCS | Diploma in Classical Studies |
| | | DipECLAM | Diplomate, European College of Laboratory Animal Medicine |
| Dep. | Deputy | DipEcon | Diploma in Economics |
| DERA | Defence Evaluation and Research Agency | DipECVO | Diploma in Veterinary Ophthalmology, European College of Veterinary Ophthalmologists |
| DES | Department of Education and Science (later DFE); Dr in Environmental Studies | | |
| | | DipEd | Diploma in Education |
| DèsL | Docteur ès lettres | DipEE | Diploma in Electrical Engineering |
| DèsS or DèsSc | Docteur ès sciences | DipEl | Diploma in Electronics |
| DesRCA | Designer of the Royal College of Art | DipESL | Diploma in English as a Second Language |
| DESS | Diplôme d'Etudes Supérieures Specialisées | DipEth | Diploma in Ethnology |
| DESU | Diplôme d'Etudes Supérieures d'Université | DipEurHum | Diploma in European Humanities |
| DETR | Department of the Environment, Transport and the Regions | DipEVPC | Diplomate, European Veterinary Parasitology College |
| DExEU | Department for Exiting the European Union | DipFBOM | Diploma in Farm Business Organisation and Management |
| DFA | Doctor of Fine Arts | DipFD | Diploma in Funeral Directing |
| DFAS | Decorative and Fine Art Society | DipFE | Diploma in Further Education |
| DFC | Distinguished Flying Cross | DipFM | Diploma in Forensic Medicine; Diploma in Financial Management |
| DFE | Department for Education | | |
| DFEE or DfEE | Department for Education and Employment (later DFES) | DipFMS | Diploma in Forensic Medicine and Science |
| DFES or DfES | Department for Education and Skills | DipFS | Diploma in Financial Services |
| DFFP | Diploma in Fertility and Family Planning | DipGSM | Diploma in Music, Guildhall School of Music and Drama |
| DFH | Diploma of Faraday House | DipHA | Diploma in Hospital Administration |
| DFID | Department for International Development | DipHE | Diploma in Higher Education |
| DFil | Doctor en Filosofia | DipHSM | Diploma in Health Services Management |
| DFM | Distinguished Flying Medal; Diploma of Forensic Medicine | DipHIC | Diploma in Hospital Infection Control |
| | | DipHum | Diploma in Humanities |
| DFPHM | Diplomate Member, Faculty of Public Health Medicine | DipHV | Diploma in Health Visiting |
| DfT | Department for Transport | DipICArb | Diploma in International Commercial Arbitration |
| DG | Director General; Directorate General; Dragoon Guards | DipIT | Diploma in Information Technology |
| DGAA | Distressed Gentlefolks Aid Association | DipLA | Diploma in Landscape Architecture |
| DGAMS | Director-General Army Medical Services | DipLaw | Diploma in Law |
| DGCHS | Dame Grand Cross, Order of the Holy Sepulchre | DipLib | Diploma of Librarianship |
| DGDP | Diploma in General Dental Practice, Royal College of Physicians | DipLLP | Diploma in Law and Legal Practice |
| DGEME | Director General Electrical and Mechanical Engineering | DipLP | Diploma in Legal Practice |
| DGLP(A) | Director General Logistic Policy (Army) | DipLS | Diploma of Legal Studies |
| DGMS | Director-General of Medical Services | DipM | Diploma in Marketing |
| DGMT | Director-General of Military Training | DipMed | Diploma in Medicine |
| DGMW | Director-General of Military Works | DipMin | Diploma in Ministry |
| DGNPS | Director-General of Naval Personal Services | DipN | Diploma in Nursing |
| DGP | Director-General of Personnel | DipNEC | Diploma of Northampton Engineering College (now City University) |
| DGPS | Director-General of Personal Services | | |
| DGS | Diploma in Graduate Studies | DIPP | Diploma of Interventional Pain Practice |
| DGStJ | Dame of Grace, Order of St John of Jerusalem (now see DStJ) | DipPA | Diploma of Practitioners in Advertising (now see DipCAM) |
| DGU | Doctor of Griffith University | DipPE | Diploma in Physical Education |
| DH | Doctor of Humanities; Doctor of Health | DipPFS | Diploma in Financial Planning, Chartered Insurance Institute |
| DHA | District Health Authority | DipPSA | Diploma in Public Service Administration |
| Dhc or DHC | Doctor honoris causa | DipPSW | Diploma in Psychiatric Social Work |
| DHE | Defence Housing Executive | DipPsych | Diploma in Psychology |
| DHEW | Department of Health Education and Welfare (US) | DipRE | Diploma in Religious Education |
| DHL | Doctor of Humane Letters; Doctor of Hebrew Literature | DipREM | Diploma in Rural Estate Management |
| DHLitt | Doctor of Humane Letters | DipRS | Diploma in Religious Studies |
| DHM | Dean Hole Medal | DipSMS | Diploma in School Management Studies |
| DHMSA | Diploma in the History of Medicine (Society of Apothecaries) | DipSoc | Diploma in Sociology |
| DHQ | District Headquarters | DipSocSc | Diploma in Social Science |
| DHS | Dame, Order of the Holy Sepulchre | DipSRAA | Diploma in the Study of Records and Administration of Archives |
| DHSC | Department of Health and Social Care | DipStat | Diploma in Statistics |
| DHSS | Department of Health and Social Security | DipSW | Diploma in Social Work |
| DHum | Doctor of Humanities | DipTA | Diploma in Tropical Agriculture |
| DHumLit | Doctor of Humane Letters | DipT&CP | Diploma in Town and Country Planning |
| DIA | Diploma in Industrial Administration | DipTh | Diploma in Theology |
| DIB | Doctor of International Business | DipTMHA | Diploma in Training and Further Education of Mentally Handicapped Adults |
| DIC | Diploma of the Imperial College | | |
| DIFC | Dubai International Financial Centre | DipTP | Diploma in Town Planning |
| DIG | Deputy Inspector-General | | |

| | | | |
|---|---|---|---|
| DipTPT | Diploma in Theory and Practice of Teaching | DPhilMed | Diploma in Philosophy of Medicine |
| DipTRP | Diploma in Town and Regional Planning | DPhysMed | Diploma in Physical Medicine |
| DipURP | Diploma in Urban and Regional Planning | DPLG | Diplômé par le Gouvernement |
| DipYCS | Diploma in Youth and Community Studies | DPM | Diploma in Psychological Medicine; Diploma in Personnel Management |
| DIS | Diploma in Industrial Studies | DPMS | Dato Paduka Mahkota Selangor (Malaysia) |
| DistTP | Distinction in Town Planning | DPMSA | Diploma in Philosophy and Ethics of Medicine, Society of Apothecaries |
| DIT | Department for International Trade | | |
| DIur | Doctor of Law | DPP | Director of Public Prosecutions |
| DIUS | Department for Innovation, Universities and Skills | DPR | Director of Public Relations |
| Div. | Division; Divorced | DProf | Doctor of Professional Studies |
| DJAG | Deputy Judge Advocate General | DPS | Director of Postal Services; Director of Personal Services; Doctor of Public Service; Diploma in Pastoral Studies |
| DJPD | Dato Jasa Purba Di-Raja Negeri Sembilan (Malaysia) | | |
| DJStJ | Dame of Justice, Order of St John of Jerusalem (*now see* DStJ) | DPSA | Diploma in Public and Social Administration |
| | | DPSE | Diploma in Professional Studies in Education |
| DJur | *Doctor Juris* (Doctor of Law) | DPSM | Diploma in Public Sector Management |
| DK | Most Esteemed Family Order (Brunei) | DPSN | Diploma in Professional Studies in Nursing |
| DL | Deputy Lieutenant; Democratie Libérale | DPsych | Doctor of Psychology |
| DLAS | Diploma in Laboratory Animal Science, Royal College of Veterinary Surgeons | DQMG | Deputy Quartermaster-General |
| | | Dr | Doctor |
| DLaws | Doctor of Laws | DRA | Defence Research Agency (later DERA) |
| DLC | Diploma of Loughborough College | DRAC | Director Royal Armoured Corps |
| DLES | Doctor of Letters in Economic Studies | DRC | Diploma of Royal College of Science and Technology, Glasgow |
| DLI | Durham Light Infantry | DRCOG | Diploma of Royal College of Obstetricians and Gynaecologists |
| DLIS | Diploma in Library and Information Studies | DRD | Diploma in Restorative Dentistry |
| DLit or DLitt | Doctor of Literature; Doctor of Letters | Dr hab. | Doctor of Habilitation |
| DLittS | Doctor of Sacred Letters | Dr ing | Doctor of Engineering |
| DLJ | Dame of Grace, Order of St Lazarus of Jerusalem | Dr jur | Doctor of Laws |
| DLO | Diploma in Laryngology and Otology | DrŒcPol | *Doctor Œconomiæ Politicæ* (Doctor of Political Economy) |
| DLP | Diploma in Legal Practice; Democratic Labour Party | Dr phil | Doctor of Philosophy |
| DLR | Docklands Light Railway | Dr rer. nat. | Doctor of Natural Science |
| DM | Doctor of Medicine | Dr rer. pol. | Doctor of Political Science |
| DMA | Diploma in Municipal Administration | Dr rer. soc. oec. | Doctor of Social and Economic Sciences |
| DMan | Doctor of Management | DRS | Diploma in Religious Studies |
| DMCC | Diploma in the Medical Care of Catastrophe, Society of Apothecaries | Drs | Doctorandus |
| | | DRSAMD | Diploma of the Royal Scottish Academy of Music and Drama |
| DMD | Doctor of Medical Dentistry (Australia) | DS | Directing Staff; Doctor of Science |
| DME | Director of Mechanical Engineering | DSA | Diploma in Social Administration |
| DMed | Doctor of Medicine | DSAC | Defence Scientific Advisory Council |
| DMedSci | Doctor of Medical Science | DSAO | Diplomatic Service Administration Office |
| DMet | Doctor of Metallurgy | DSC | Distinguished Service Cross |
| DMI | Director of Military Intelligence | DSc | Doctor of Science |
| DMin | Doctor of Ministry | DScA | Docteur en sciences agricoles |
| DMiss | Doctor of Missiology | DSc(Eng) | Doctor of Engineering Science |
| DMJ | Diploma in Medical Jurisprudence | DSCHE | Diploma of the Scottish Council for Health Education |
| DMJ(Path) | Diploma in Medical Jurisprudence (Pathology) | DSCM | Diploma of the Sydney Conservatorium of Music |
| DMLJ | Dame of Merit, Order of St Lazarus of Jerusalem | DScMil | Doctor of Military Science |
| DMO | Director of Military Operations | DSc (SocSci) | Doctor of Science in Social Science |
| DMR | Diploma in Medical Radiology | DSD | Director Staff Duties; Diploma in Speech and Drama |
| DMRD | Diploma in Medical Radiological Diagnosis | DSF | Director Special Forces |
| DMRE | Diploma in Medical Radiology and Electrology | DSG | Dame, Order of St Gregory the Great |
| DMRT | Diploma in Medical Radio-Therapy | DSIR | Department of Scientific and Industrial Research (later SRC; then SERC) |
| DMS | Director of Medical Services; Decoration for Meritorious Service (South Africa); Diploma in Management Studies | DSL | Doctor of Sacred Letters |
| | | DSLJ | Dato Seri Laila Jasa (Brunei) |
| DMSc | Doctor of Medical Science | DSM | Distinguished Service Medal |
| DMT | Director of Military Training | DSMOM | Dame, Sovereign Military Order of Malta |
| DMus | Doctor of Music | DSNB | Dato Setia Negara Brunei |
| DN | Diploma in Nursing | DSNS | Dato Setia Negeri Sembilan (Malaysia) |
| DNB | Dictionary of National Biography | DSO | Companion of the Distinguished Service Order |
| DNE | Director of Naval Equipment | DSocSc | Doctor of Social Science |
| DNH | Department of National Heritage | DSP | Director of Selection of Personnel; Docteur en sciences politiques (Montreal) |
| DNI | Director of Naval Intelligence | | |
| DNursing | Professional Doctorate in Nursing | dsp | *decessit sine prole* (died without issue) |
| DNZM | Dame Companion, New Zealand Order of Merit | DSport | Doctor of Sport |
| DO | Diploma in Ophthalmology | DSS | Department of Social Security; Doctor of Sacred Scripture |
| DOAE | Defence Operational Analysis Establishment | Dss | Deaconess |
| DObstRCOG | Diploma of Royal College of Obstetricians and Gynaecologists (*now see* DRCOG) | DSSc | Doctor of Social Science |
| | | DST | Director of Supplies and Transport |
| DOC | District Officer Commanding | DStJ | Dame of Grace, Most Venerable Order of the Hospital of St John of Jerusalem; Dame of Justice, Most Venerable Order of the Hospital of St John of Jerusalem |
| DocArts | Doctor of Arts | | |
| DocEng | Doctor of Engineering | | |
| DoE | Department of the Environment | | |
| DoH | Department of Health | DSTL | Defence Science and Technology Laboratory |
| DoI | Department of Industry | DTA | Diploma in Tropical Agriculture |
| DOL | Doctor of Oriental Learning | DTech | Doctor of Technology |
| Dom. | *Dominus* (Lord) | DTH | Diploma in Tropical Hygiene |
| DOMS | Diploma in Ophthalmic Medicine and Surgery | DTh or DTheol | Doctor of Theology |
| DOR | Director of Operational Requirements | DThMin | Doctor of Theology and Ministry |
| DOrthRCS | Diploma in Orthodontics, Royal College of Surgeons | DThPT | Diploma in Theory and Practice of Teaching |
| DOS | Director of Ordnance Services; Doctor of Ocular Science | DTI | Department of Trade and Industry |
| DP | Data Processing | DTLR | Department for Transport, Local Government and the Regions |
| DPA | Diploma in Public Administration; Discharged Prisoners' Aid; Doctor of Public Administration | DTM&H | Diploma in Tropical Medicine and Hygiene |
| | | DU or DUniv | Honorary Doctor of the University |
| DPD | Diploma in Public Dentistry | Dunelm | *Dunelmensis* (of Durham) |
| DPEc | Doctor of Political Economy | DUP | Democratic Unionist Party; Docteur de l'Université de Paris |
| DPed | Doctor of Pedagogy | | |
| DPH | Diploma in Public Health | DVA | Diploma of Veterinary Anaesthesia |
| DPh or DPhil | Doctor of Philosophy | DVH | Diploma in Veterinary Hygiene |
| DPharm | Doctor of Pharmacy | | |

| | |
|---|---|
| DVLA | Driver and Vehicle Licensing Agency |
| DVLC | Driver and Vehicle Licensing Centre |
| DVM or DVetMed | Doctor of Veterinary Medicine |
| DVMS or DVM&S | Doctor of Veterinary Medicine and Surgery |
| DVO | Driver, Vehicle and Operator |
| DVOphthal | Diploma in Veterinary Ophthalmology |
| DVR | Diploma in Veterinary Radiology |
| DVSc | Doctor of Veterinary Science |
| DVSM | Diploma in Veterinary State Medicine |
| DWP | Department for Work and Pensions |

# E

| | |
|---|---|
| E | East; Earl; England; E-mail |
| e | eldest |
| EA | Environment Agency |
| EAA | Edinburgh Architectural Association |
| EACR | European Association for Cancer Research |
| EADS | European Aeronautics Defence and Space Company |
| EAF | East African Forces |
| EAGA | Energy Action Grants Agency |
| EAHY | European Architectural Heritage Year |
| EASD | European Association of Securities Dealers; European Association for the Study of Diabetes |
| EBC | English Benedictine Congregation |
| Ebor | *Eboracensis* (of York) |
| EBRD | European Bank for Reconstruction and Development |
| EBU | European Broadcasting Union |
| EC | Etoile du Courage (Canada); European Community; European Commission; Emergency Commission |
| ECA | Economic Co-operation Administration; Economic Commission for Africa |
| ECAFE | Economic Commission for Asia and the Far East (*now see* ESCAP) |
| ECB | England and Wales Cricket Board |
| ECCTIS | Education Courses and Credit Transfer Information Systems |
| ECE | Economic Commission for Europe |
| ECGD | Export Credits Guarantee Department |
| ECHR | European Court of Human Rights |
| ECLAC | United Nations Economic Commission for Latin America and the Caribbean |
| ECOSOC | Economic and Social Committee of the United Nations |
| ECR | European Conservatives and Reformists Group |
| ECSC | European Coal and Steel Community |
| ED | Efficiency Decoration; Doctor of Engineering (US); European Democrat |
| ed | edited |
| EdB | Bachelor of Education |
| EDC | Economic Development Committee |
| EdD | Doctor of Education |
| EDF | European Development Fund |
| EDG | European Democratic Group; Employment Department Group |
| Edin. | Edinburgh |
| Edn | Edition |
| EDP | Executive Development Programme |
| EdS | Specialist in Education |
| EDSAC | Electronic Delay Storage Automatic Calculator |
| Educ | Educated |
| Educn | Education |
| EEA | European Environment Agency |
| EEC | European Economic Community (*now see* EC); Commission of the European Communities |
| EEF | Engineering Employers' Federation; Egyptian Expeditionary Force |
| EETPU | Electrical Electronic Telecommunication & Plumbing Union (later AEEU) |
| EETS | Early English Text Society |
| EFCE | European Federation of Chemical Engineering |
| EFIAP | Excellence, Fédération Internationale de l'Art Photographique |
| EFQM | European Foundation Quality Management |
| EFTA | European Free Trade Association |
| EGCLJ | Ecclesiastical Grand Cross Chaplain, Order of St Lazarus of Jerusalem |
| eh | ehrenhalber (honorary) |
| EI | East Indian; East Indies |
| EIA | Engineering Industries Association |
| EIB | European Investment Bank |
| EIEMA | Electrical Installation Equipment Manufacturers' Association |
| E-in-C | Engineer-in-Chief |
| EIS | Educational Institute of Scotland |
| EISCAT | European Incoherent Scatter Association |
| EIU | Economist Intelligence Unit |
| ELBS | English Language Book Society |
| ELDR | European Liberal, Democrat and Reform Party |
| ELT | English Language Teaching |
| EM | Edward Medal; Earl Marshal |

| | |
|---|---|
| EMBL | European Molecular Biology Laboratory |
| EMBO | European Molecular Biology Organisation |
| EMEA | European Medicines Agency (*formerly* European Agency for the Evaluation of Medical Products); Europe, Middle East and Africa |
| EMI | European Monetary Institute |
| EMP | Electro Magnetic Pulse; Executive Management Program Diploma |
| EMS | Emergency Medical Service |
| EMU | European Monetary Union |
| Eng. | England |
| EngD | Doctor of Engineering |
| Engr | Engineer |
| ENO | English National Opera |
| ENT | Ear Nose and Throat |
| ENTO | Employment National Training Organisation |
| EO | Executive Officer |
| EOC | Equal Opportunities Commission |
| EOPH | Examined Officer of Public Health |
| EORTC | European Organisation for Research on Treatment of Cancer |
| EP | European Parliament |
| EPOS | Electronic Point of Sale |
| EPP | European People's Party |
| EPSA | Excellence, Photographic Society of America |
| EPSRC | Engineering and Physical Sciences Research Council |
| EPsS | Experimental Psychology Society |
| er | elder |
| ER | Eastern Region (BR); East Riding |
| ERA | Electrical Research Association |
| ERC | Electronics Research Council |
| ERD | Emergency Reserve Decoration (Army) |
| ESA | European Space Agency |
| ESC | European Society of Cardiology |
| ESCAP | Economic and Social Commission for Asia and the Pacific |
| ESCP-EAP | Ecole Supérieure de Commerce de Paris-Ecole des Affaires de Paris |
| ESF | European Science Foundation |
| ESL | English as a Second Language |
| ESOL | English for Speakers of Other Languages |
| ESP | English for Special Purposes |
| ESPID | European Society for Paediatric Infectious Diseases |
| EsqStJ | Esquire, Most Venerable Order of the Hospital of St John of Jerusalem |
| ESRC | Economic and Social Research Council; Electricity Supply Research Council |
| ESRO | European Space Research Organization (*now see* ESA) |
| ESSKA | European Society for Surgery of the Knee and Arthroscopy |
| ESTA | European Science and Technology Assembly |
| ESU | English-Speaking Union |
| ETA | Engineering Training Authority |
| ETH | Eidgenössische Technische Hochschule |
| ETS | Educational and Training Services |
| ETS(A) | Educational and Training Services (Army) |
| ETU | Electrical Trades Union |
| ETUC | European Trade Union Confederation |
| ETUCE | European Trade Union Committee for Education |
| EU | European Union |
| Euratom | European Atomic Energy Community |
| EurBiol | European Biologist (*now see* EurProBiol) |
| EurChem | European Chemist |
| EurGeol | European Geologist |
| Eur Ing | European Engineer |
| EUROM | European Federation for Optics and Precision Mechanics |
| EurProBiol | European Professional Biologist |
| EUW | European Union of Women |
| eV | eingetragener Verein |
| EVPC | European Veterinary Parasitology College |
| Ext | Extinct; external |

# F

| | |
|---|---|
| FA | Football Association |
| FAA | Fellow, Australian Academy of Science; Fleet Air Arm |
| FAAAI | Fellow, Association for the Advancement of Artificial Intelligence (formerly American Association for Artificial Intelligence) |
| FAAAS | Fellow, American Association for the Advancement of Science |
| FAACR | Fellow, American Association for Cancer Research |
| FAAHMS | Fellow, Australian Academy of Health and Sciences |
| FAAN | Fellow, American Academy of Neurology; Fellow, American Academy of Nursing |
| FAAO | Fellow, American Academy of Optometry |
| FAAP | Fellow, American Academy of Pediatrics |
| FAARM | Fellow, American Academy of Reproductive Medicine |
| FAAV | Fellow, Central Association of Agricultural Valuers |

| | |
|---|---|
| FAAVCT | Fellow, American Academy of Veterinary and Comparative Toxicology |
| FABE | Fellow, Association of Building Engineers |
| FAcadMed | Fellow, Academy of Medical Educators |
| FACB | Fellow, National Academy of Clinical Biochemistry, USA |
| FACC | Fellow, American College of Cardiology |
| FACCA | Fellow, Association of Certified and Corporate Accountants (*now see* FCCA) |
| FACCP | Fellow, American College of Chest Physicians |
| FACD | Fellow, American College of Dentistry |
| FACDS | Fellow, Australian College of Dental Surgeons (*now see* FRACDS) |
| FACE | Fellow, Australian College of Educators (*formerly* of Education) |
| FACerS | Fellow, American Ceramic Society |
| FAChAM | Fellow, Australasian Chapter of Addiction Medicine, Royal Australian College of Physicians |
| FAChPM | Fellow, Australasian Chapter of Palliative Medicine, Royal Australian College of Physicians |
| FACHSE | Fellow, Australian College of Health Service Executives |
| FACI | Fellow, Australian Chemical Institute (*now see* FRACI) |
| FACM | Fellow, Associaton of Computing Machinery |
| FACMA | Fellow, Australian College of Medical Administrators (*now see* FRACMA) |
| FACMG | Fellow, American College of Medicinal Genetics |
| FACOG | Fellow, American College of Obstetricians and Gynæcologists |
| FACOM | Fellow, Australian College of Occupational Medicine |
| FACP | Fellow, American College of Physicians |
| FACPM | Fellow, American College of Preventive Medicine |
| FACR | Fellow, American College of Radiology |
| FACRM | Fellow, Australian College of Rehabilitation Medicine |
| FACS | Fellow, American College of Surgeons |
| FAcSS | Fellow, Academy of Social Sciences |
| FACVSc | Fellow, Australian College of Veterinary Scientists |
| FACVT | Fellow, American College of Veterinary Toxicology (*now see* FAAVCT) |
| FADM | Fellow, Academy of Dental Materials |
| FADO | Fellow, Association of Dispensing Opticians |
| FAEM | Faculty of Accident and Emergency Medicine (*now see* CEM) |
| FAeSI | Fellow, Aeronautical Society of India |
| FAFMS | Fellow, Academy of Forensic Medical Sciences |
| FAfN | Fellow, Association for Nutrition |
| FAFPHM | Fellow, Australian Faculty of Public Health Medicine |
| FAGS | Fellow, American Geographical Society |
| FAHA | Fellow, Australian Academy of the Humanities; Fellow, American Heart Association |
| FAHMS | Fellow, Australian Academy of Health and Medical Sciences |
| FAI | Fellow, Chartered Auctioneers' and Estate Agents' Institute (*now* (after amalgamation) *see* FRICS); Fédération Aéronautique Internationale |
| FAIA | Fellow, American Institute of Architects; Fellow, Association of International Accountants |
| FAIAA | Fellow, American Institute of Aeronautics and Astronautics |
| FAIAS | Fellow, Australian Institute of Agricultural Science (*now see* FAIAST) |
| FAIAST | Fellow, Australian Institute of Agricultural Science and Technology |
| FAIB | Fellow, Australian Institute of Bankers |
| FAIBF | Fellow, Australasian Institute of Bankers + Finance |
| FAIBiol | Fellow, Australian Institute of Biology |
| FAICD | Fellow, Australian Institute of Company Directors |
| FAIE | Fellow, Australian Institute of Energy |
| FAIEx | Fellow, Australian Institute of Export |
| FAIFST | Fellow, Australian Institute of Food Science and Technology |
| FAII | Fellow, Australian Insurance Institute |
| FAIIA | Fellow, Australian Information Industry Association |
| FAIM | Fellow, Australian Institute of Management |
| FAIMBE | Fellow, American Institute for Medical and Biological Engineering |
| FAIP | Fellow, Australian Institute of Physics |
| FAISB | Fellow, Society for the Study of Artificial Intelligence and the Simulation of Behaviour |
| FAM | Fellow, Academy of Marketing |
| FAMA | Fellow, Australian Medical Association |
| FAMI | Fellow, Australian Marketing Institute |
| FAMINZ(Arb) | Fellow, Arbitrators and Mediators Institute of New Zealand |
| FAMM | Fellow, Academy of Medicine, Malaysia |
| FAmNucSoc | Fellow, American Nuclear Society |
| FAMS | Fellow, Ancient Monuments Society; Fellow, Academy of Medicine, Singapore; Fellow, American Mathematical Society |
| FANA | Fellow, American Neurological Association |
| F and GP | Finance and General Purposes |
| FANY | First Aid Nursing Yeomanry |
| FANZCA | Fellow, Australian and New Zealand College of Anaesthetists |
| FANZCP | Fellow, Australian and New Zealand College of Psychiatrists (*now see* FRANZCP) |
| FAO | Food and Agriculture Organization of the United Nations |
| FAOrthA | Fellow, Australian Orthopaedic Association |
| FAPA | Fellow, American Psychiatric Association |
| FAPHA | Fellow, American Public Health Association |
| FAPI | Fellow, Association of Physicians of India |
| FAPM | Fellow, Association for Project Management (*formerly* of Project Managers) |
| FAPS | Fellow, American Phytopathological Society |
| FAPT | Fellow, Association for Preservation Technology (US) |
| FArborA | Fellow, Arboricultural Association |
| FARE | Federation of Alcoholic Rehabilitation Establishments |
| FARELF | Far East Land Forces |
| FAS | Fellow, Antiquarian Society; Fellow, Nigerian Academy of Science; Funding Agency for Schools; Fellow, Anatomical Society |
| FASA | Fellow, Australian Society of Accountants (*now see* FCPA) |
| FASc | Fellow, Indian Academy of Sciences |
| fasc. | fascicule |
| FASCE | Fellow, American Society of Civil Engineers |
| FASI | Fellow, Architects' and Surveyors' Institute |
| FASME | Fellow, American Society of Mechanical Engineers |
| FASPOG | Fellow, Australian Society for Psychosomatic Obstetrics and Gynaecology |
| FASSA | Fellow, Academy of the Social Sciences in Australia |
| FAusIMM | Fellow, Australasian Institute of Mining and Metallurgy |
| FAustCOG | Fellow, Australian College of Obstetricians and Gynæcologists (later FRACOG; *now see* FRANZCOG) |
| FBA | Fellow, British Academy; Federation of British Artists |
| FBAHA | Fellow, British Association of Hotel Accountants |
| FBAM | Fellow, British Academy of Management |
| FBC | Fellow, Birmingham Conservatoire (*now see* FRBC) |
| FBCartS | Fellow, British Cartographic Society |
| FBCO | Fellow, British College of Optometrists (*formerly* of Ophthalmic Opticians (Optometrists)) (*now see* FCOptom) |
| FBCS | Fellow, British Computer Society |
| FBCS CITP | Fellow, British Computer Society, with Chartered Professional Status |
| FBEng | Fellow, Association of Building Engineers |
| FBES | Fellow, Biological Engineering Society (*now see* FIPEM) |
| FBHA | Fellow, British Hospitality Association |
| FBHI | Fellow, British Horological Institute |
| FBHS | Fellow, British Horse Society; Fellow, British Hypertension Society |
| FBI | Federation of British Industries (*now see* CBI); Federal Bureau of Investigation |
| FBIAT | Fellow, British Institute of Architectural Technicians |
| FBIBA | Fellow, British Insurance Brokers' Association (*now see* FBIIBA) |
| FBID | Fellow, British Institute of Interior Design |
| FBIDA | Fellow, British Interior Design Association |
| FBIDST | Fellow, British Institute of Dental and Surgical Technologists |
| FBII | Fellow, British Institute of Innkeeping |
| FBIIBA | Fellow, British Insurance and Investment Brokers' Association |
| FBIM | Fellow, British Institute of Management (later FIMgt) |
| FBINZ | Fellow, Bankers' Institute of New Zealand |
| FBIPM | Fellow, British Institute of Payroll Management (*now see* FIPPM) |
| FBIPP | Fellow, British Institute of Professional Photography |
| FBIR | Fellow, British Institute of Radiology |
| FBIRA | Fellow, British Institute of Regulatory Affairs |
| FBIS | Fellow, British Interplanetary Society |
| FBKS | Fellow, British Kinematograph Society (*now see* FBKSTS) |
| FBKSTS | Fellow, British Kinematograph, Sound and Television Society |
| FBNA | Fellow, British Naturalists' Association |
| FBOA | Fellow, British Optical Association |
| FBOU | Fellow, British Ornithologists' Union |
| FBPharmacolS | Fellow, British Pharmacological Society (*now see* FBPhS) |
| FBPhS | Fellow, British Pharmacological Society |
| FBPICS | Fellow, British Production and Inventory Control Society |
| FBPsS | Fellow, British Psychological Society |
| FBritIRE | Fellow, British Institution of Radio Engineers (later FIERE) |
| FBS | Fellow, Building Societies Institute (later FCBSI; *now see* FCIB) |
| FBSE | Fellow, Biomaterials Science and Engineering |
| FBSG | Fellow, British Society for Geomorphology |
| FBSI | Fellow, Boot and Shoe Institution (*now see* FCFI) |
| FBSM | Fellow, Birmingham School of Music (*now see* FBC) |
| FBTS | Fellow, British Toxicology Society |
| FC | Football Club |
| FCA | Fellow, Institute of Chartered Accountants; Fellow, Institute of Chartered Accountants in Australia; Fellow, New Zealand Society of Accountants; Federation of Canadian Artists |
| FCAE | Fellow, Canadian Academy of Engineering |
| FCAHS | Fellow, Canadian Academy of Health Sciences |
| FCAI | Fellow, New Zealand Institute of Cost Accountants; Fellow, Canadian Aeronautical Institute (*now see* FCASI); Fellow, College of Anaesthetists of Ireland |
| FCAM | Fellow, CAM Foundation |
| FCAnaes | Fellow, College of Anaesthetists (*now see* FRCA) |
| FCARCSI | Fellow, College of Anaesthetists, Royal College of Surgeons of Ireland |
| FCA(SA) | Fellow, College of Anaesthetists (South Africa) |

| | | | |
|---|---|---|---|
| FCASI | Fellow, Canadian Aeronautics and Space Institute | FCP(SoAf) | Fellow, College of Physicians, South Africa |
| FCBSI | Fellow, Chartered Building Societies Institute (merged with Chartered Institute of Bankers; *now see* FCIB) | FCPSO(SoAf) | Fellow, College of Physicians and Surgeons and Obstetricians, South Africa |
| FCCA | Fellow, Chartered Association of Certified Accountants | FCPS (Pak) | Fellow, College of Physicians and Surgeons of Pakistan |
| FCCEA | Fellow, Commonwealth Council for Educational Administration | FCQI | Fellow, Chartered Quality Institute |
| FCCP | Fellow, American College of Chest Physicians | FCRA | Fellow, College of Radiologists of Australia (*now see* FRACR) |
| FCCS | Fellow, Corporation of Secretaries (*formerly* of Certified Secretaries) | FCS | Federation of Conservative Students |
| FCCT | Fellow, Canadian College of Teachers; Fellow, Chartered College of Teaching | FCS or FChemSoc | Fellow, Chemical Society (now absorbed into Royal Society of Chemistry) |
| FCDSHK | Fellow, College of Dental Surgeons of Hong Kong | FCSD | Fellow, Chartered Society of Designers |
| FCEC | Federation of Civil Engineering Contractors | FCSFS | Fellow, Chartered Society of Forensic Sciences |
| FCEM | Fellow, College of Emergency Medicine (*now see* FRCEM) | FCSHK | Fellow, College of Surgeons of Hong Kong |
| FCFI | Fellow, Clothing and Footwear Institute | FCSI | Fellow, Chartered Institute for Securities & Investment |
| FCGA | Fellow, Certified General Accountants of Canada | FCSLT | Fellow, College of Speech and Language Therapists (*now see* FRCSLT) |
| FCGC | Fellow, Council of Geriatric Cardiology | FCSM | Fellow, Cambridge School of Music |
| FCGI | Fellow, City and Guilds of London Institute | FCSP | Fellow, Chartered Society of Physiotherapy |
| FCGP | Fellow, College of General Practitioners (*now see* FRCGP) | FCSSA or FCS(SoAf) | Fellow, College of Surgeons, South Africa |
| FChS | Fellow, Society of Chiropodists | FCSSL | Fellow, College of Surgeons of Sri Lanka |
| FCI | Fellow, Institute of Commerce | FCST | Fellow, College of Speech Therapists (later FCSLT; *now see* FRCSLT) |
| FCIA | Fellow, Corporation of Insurance Agents | | |
| FCIArb | Fellow, Chartered Institute of Arbitrators | FCT | Federal Capital Territory (*now see* ACT); Fellow, Association of Corporate Treasurers; Fellow, College of Teachers |
| FCIB | Fellow, Corporation of Insurance Brokers; Fellow, Chartered Institute of Bankers | | |
| FCIBS | Fellow, Chartered Institution of Building Services (*now see* FCIBSE); Fellow, Chartered Institute of Bankers in Scotland | FCTB | Fellow, College of Teachers of the Blind |
| | | FCU | Fighter Control Unit |
| FCIBSE | Fellow, Chartered Institution of Building Services Engineers | FCWA | Fellow, Institute of Costs and Works Accountants (*now see* FCMA) |
| FCIC | Fellow, Chemical Institute of Canada (*formerly* Canadian Institute of Chemistry) | FD | Doctor of Philosophy |
| | | FDA | Association of First Division Civil Servants |
| FCICM | Fellow, Chartered Institute of Credit Management | FdA | Foundation Degree of Arts |
| FCIEEM | Fellow, Chartered Institute of Ecology and Environmental Management | FDF | Food and Drink Federation |
| | | FDI | Fédération Dentaire Internationale |
| FCIEH | Fellow, Chartered Institute of Environmental Health | FDP | Freie Demokratische Partei |
| FCIFE | Fellow, Chartered Institution for Further Education | FDS | Fellow in Dental Surgery |
| FCIH | Fellow, Chartered Institute of Housing | FdSc | Foundation Degree in Science |
| FCIHort | Fellow, Chartered Institute of Horticulture | FDSRCPSGlas | Fellow in Dental Surgery, Royal College of Physicians and Surgeons of Glasgow |
| FCIHT | Fellow, Chartered Institution of Highways & Transportation | | |
| FCII | Fellow, Chartered Insurance Institute | FDSRCS or FDS RCS | Fellow in Dental Surgery, Royal College of Surgeons of England |
| FCIJ | Fellow, Chartered Institute of Journalists | | |
| FCIL | Fellow, Chartered Institute of Linguists | FDSRCSE | Fellow in Dental Surgery, Royal College of Surgeons of Edinburgh |
| FCILA | Fellow, Chartered Institute of Loss Adjusters | | |
| FCILT | Chartered Fellow, Chartered Institute of Logistics and Transport | FE | Far East; Further Education |
| FCIM | Fellow, Chartered Institute of Marketing; Fellow, Institute of Corporate Managers (Australia) | FEA | Fellow, English Association |
| | | FEAF | Far East Air Force |
| FCInstCES | Fellow, Chartered Institution of Civil Engineering Surveyors | FEAN | Fellow, European Academy of Neurology |
| FCIOB | Fellow, Chartered Institute of Building | FEANI | Fédération Européenne d'Associations Nationales d'Ingénieurs |
| FCIPA | Fellow, Chartered Institute of Patent Agents (*now see* CPA) | FEBS | Federation of European Biochemical Societies; Fellow, European Board of Surgery |
| FCIPD | Fellow, Chartered Institute of Personnel and Development | | |
| FCIPHE | Fellow, Chartered Institute of Plumbing and Heating Engineering | FECI | Fellow, Institute of Employment Consultants |
| | | FECTS | Fellow, European Association for Cardiothoracic Surgery |
| FCIPR | Fellow, Chartered Institute of Public Relations | FEE | Fédération des Expertes Comptables Européens |
| FCIPS | Fellow, Chartered Institute of Procurement (formerly Purchasing) and Supply | FEF | Far East Fleet |
| | | FEFC or FEFCE | Further Education Funding Council for England |
| FCIS | Fellow, Institute of Chartered Secretaries and Administrators (*formerly* Chartered Institute of Secretaries) | FEFCW | Further Education Funding Council for Wales |
| | | FEI | Fédération Equestre Internationale; Fellow, Energy Institute |
| FCISA | Fellow, Chartered Institute of Secretaries and Administrators (Australia) | FEIC | Fellow, Engineering Institute of Canada |
| | | FEIDCT | Fellow, Educational Institute of Design Craft and Technology |
| FCIT | Fellow, Chartered Institute of Transport (*now see* FCILT) | FEIS | Fellow, Educational Institute of Scotland |
| FCIWEM | Fellow, Chartered Institution of Water and Environmental Management | FEMAC | Fellow, European Marketing Academy |
| | | FEng | Fellow, Royal Academy (*formerly* Fellowship) of Engineering (*now see* FREng) |
| FCIWM | Fellow, Chartered Institution of Wastes Management | | |
| FCJEI | Fellow, Commonwealth Judicial Education Institute | FEPS | Federation of European Physiological Societies |
| FCLIP | Fellow, Chartered Institute of Library and Information Professionals | FERS | Fellow, European Respiratory Society |
| | | FES | Fellow, Entomological Society; Fellow, Ethnological Society |
| FCM | Faculty of Community Medicine | FESC | Fellow, European Society of Cardiology |
| FCMA | Fellow, Chartered Institute of Management Accountants (*formerly* Institute of Cost and Management Accountants); Fellow, Communications Management Association | FETCS | Fellow, European Board of Thoracic and Cardiovascular Surgeons |
| | | FF | Fianna Fáil; Field Force |
| FCMC | Fellow grade, Certified Management Consultant | FFA | Fellow, Faculty of Actuaries (in Scotland); Fellow, Institute of Financial Accountants |
| FCMI | Fellow, Chartered Management Institute | | |
| FCMSA | Fellow, College of Medicine of South Africa | FFAEM | Fellow, Faculty of Accident and Emergency Medicine (later FCEM) |
| FCNA | Fellow, College of Nursing, Australia | | |
| FCO | Foreign and Commonwealth Office | FFARACS | Fellow, Faculty of Anaesthetists, Royal Australasian College of Surgeons (*now see* FANZCA) |
| FCOG(SA) | Fellow, South African College of Obstetricians and Gynæcology | | |
| FCollH | Fellow, College of Handicraft | FFARCS | Fellow, Faculty of Anaesthetists, Royal College of Surgeons of England (*now see* FRCA) |
| FCollP | Fellow, College of Preceptors | | |
| FCollT | Fellow, College of Teachers | FFARCSI | Fellow, Faculty of Anaesthetists, Royal College of Surgeons in Ireland (*now see* FCAI) |
| FCommA | Fellow, Society of Commercial Accountants (*now see* FSCA) | | |
| FCOphth | Fellow, College of Ophthalmologists (*now see* FRCOphth) | FFAS | Fellow, Faculty of Architects and Surveyors, London (*now see* FASI) |
| FCOptom | Fellow, College of Optometrists | | |
| FCOT | Fellow, College of Teachers | FFA(SA) | Fellow, Faculty of Anaesthetists (South Africa) (*now see* FCA(SA)) |
| FCP | Fellow, College of Preceptors | | |
| FCPA | Fellow, Australian Society of Certified Practising Accountants | FFB | Fellow, Faculty of Building |
| FCPath | Fellow, College of Pathologists (*now see* FRCPath) | FFCM | Fellow, Faculty of Community Medicine (*now see* FFPH); Fellow, Faculty of Church Music |
| FCPCH | Fellow, College of Paediatrics and Child Health (*now see* FRCPCH) | | |
| | | FFCMI | Fellow, Faculty of Community Medicine of Ireland |
| FCPFA | Fellow Chartered Public Finance Accountant | FFCS | Founding Fellow, Contemporary Scotland |
| FCPodMed | Fellow, College of Podiatric Medicine | FFDRCSI | Fellow, Faculty of Dentistry, Royal College of Surgeons in Ireland |
| FCPS | Fellow, College of Physicians and Surgeons | | |

| | | | |
|---|---|---|---|
| FFFLM | Fellow, Faculty of Forensic and Legal Medicine, Royal College of Physicians | FIAP | Fellow, Institution of Analysts and Programmers; Fellow, Indian Academy of Paediatrics |
| FFFP | Fellow, Faculty of Family Planning & Reproductive Health Care of the Royal College of Obstetricians and Gynaecologists (*now see* FFSRH) | FIArb | Fellow, Institute of Arbitrators (*now see* FCIArb) |
| | | FIArbA | Fellow, Institute of Arbitrators of Australia |
| FFGDP(UK) | Fellow, Faculty of General Dental Practitioners of the Royal College of Surgeons | FIAS | Fellow, Institute of Aeronautical Sciences (US) (*now see* FAIAA) |
| FFHom | Fellow, Faculty of Homeopathy | FIASc | Fellow, Indian Academy of Sciences |
| FFI | Finance for Industry; Fauna & Flora International | FIASSID | Fellow, International Association for the Scientific Study of Intellectual Disability |
| FFICM | Fellow, Faculty of Intensive Care Medicine | FIB | Fellow, Institute of Bankers (*now see* FCIB) |
| FFOM | Fellow, Faculty of Occupational Medicine | FIBA | Fellow, Institute of Business Administration, Australia (*now see* FCIM) |
| FFOMI | Fellow, Faculty of Occupational Medicine of Ireland | | |
| FFOP (RCPA) | Fellow, Faculty of Oral Pathology, Royal College of Pathologists of Australasia | FIBC | Fellow, Institute of Business Consulting (*now see* FIC) |
| | | FIBI | Fellow, Institute of Bankers of Ireland |
| FFPath, RCPI | Fellow, Faculty of Pathologists of the Royal College of Physicians of Ireland | FIBiol | Fellow, Institute of Biology (later FSB, *now see* FRSB) |
| | | FIBiotech | Fellow, Institute for Biotechnical Studies |
| FFPH | Fellow, Faculty of Public Health | FIBMS | Fellow, Institute of Biomedical Sciences |
| FFPHM | Fellow, Faculty of Public Health Medicine (*now see* FFPH) | FIBScot | Fellow, Institute of Bankers in Scotland (*now see* FCIBS) |
| FFPHMI | Fellow, Faculty of Public Health Medicine of Ireland | FIC | Fellow, Institute of Chemistry (then FRIC; *now see* FRSC); Fellow, Imperial College, London; Fellow, Institute of Consulting |
| FFPM | Fellow, Faculty of Pharmaceutical Medicine | | |
| FFPMRCA | Fellow, Faculty of Pain Medicine, Royal College of Anaesthetists | FICA | Fellow, Commonwealth Institute of Accountants; Fellow, Institute of Chartered Accountants in England and Wales (*now see* FCA) |
| FFPRHC | Faculty of Family Planning & Reproductive Health Care, Royal College of Obstetricians and Gynaecologists (*now see* FSRH) | | |
| | | FICAI | Fellow, Institute of Chartered Accountants in Ireland |
| FFPS | Fauna and Flora Preservation Society (*now see* FFI) | FICB | Fellow, Institute of Canadian Bankers |
| FFR | Fellow, Faculty of Radiologists (*now see* FRCR) | FICD | Fellow, Institute of Civil Defence; Fellow, Indian College of Dentists; Fellow, International College of Dentists |
| FFRRCSI | Fellow, Faculty of Radiologists of the Royal College of Surgeons in Ireland | | |
| | | FICE | Fellow, Institution of Civil Engineers |
| FFSEM | Fellow, Faculty of Sports and Exercise Medicine, Royal College of Physicians of Ireland and Royal College of Surgeons in Ireland | FICeram | Fellow, Institute of Ceramics (later FIM) |
| | | FICES | Fellow, Institution of Chartered Engineering Surveyors |
| | | FICFM | Fellow, Institute of Charity Fundraising Managers (*now see* FInstF) |
| FFSRH | Fellow, Faculty of Sexual and Reproductive Healthcare of the Royal College of Obstetricians and Gynaecologists | FICFor | Fellow, Institute of Chartered Foresters |
| | | FIChemE | Fellow, Institution of Chemical Engineers |
| FFSSoc | Fellow, Forensic Science Society (*now see* FCSFS) | FICM | Fellow, Institute of Credit Management (*now see* FCICM) |
| FFSTEd | Fellow, Faculty of Surgical Trainers, Royal College of Surgeons of Edinburgh | FICMA | Fellow, Institute of Cost and Management Accountants |
| | | FICOG | Fellow, Indian College of Obstetricians and Gynaecologists |
| FFTM(Glas) | Fellow, Faculty of Travel Medicine, Royal College of Physicians and Surgeons of Glasgow | FICorr | Fellow, Institute of Corrosion |
| | | FICorrST | Fellow, Institution of Corrosion Science and Technology (*now see* FICorr) |
| FG | Fine Gael | | |
| FGA | Fellow, Gemmological Association | FICPD | Fellow, Institute of Continuing Professional Development |
| FGCL | Fellow, Goldsmiths' College, London | FICPEM | Fellow, Institute of Civil Protection and Emergency Management |
| FGCM | Fellow, Guild of Church Musicians | | |
| FGDP(UK) | Fellow, Faculty of General Dental Practice of the Royal College of Surgeons of England | FICS | Fellow, Institute of Chartered Shipbrokers; Fellow, International College of Surgeons |
| FGDS | Fédération de la Gauche Démocratique et Socialiste | FICT | Fellow, Institute of Concrete Technology |
| FGE | Fellow, Guild of Glass Engravers | FIDA | Fellow, Institute of Directors, Australia (*now see* FAICD) |
| FGGE | Fellow, Guild of Glass Engravers (*now see* FGE) | FIDDA | Fellow, Interior Decorators and Designers Association (*now see* FBIDA) |
| FGI | Fellow, Institute of Certificated Grocers | | |
| FGMS | Fellow, Guild of Musicians and Singers | FIDE | Fédération Internationale des Echecs; Fellow, Institute of Design Engineers; Fédération Internationale pour le Droit Européen |
| FGS | Fellow, Geological Society; Fellow, Guildhall School of Music and Drama | | |
| | | FIDEM | Fédération Internationale de la Médaille d'Art |
| FGSM | Fellow, Guildhall School of Music and Drama (*now see* FGS) | FIDM | Fellow, Institute of Direct Marketing |
| FGSM(MT) | Fellow, Guildhall School of Music and Drama (Music Therapy) | FIDPM | Fellow, Institute of Data Processing Management |
| FHA | Fellow, Institute of Health Service Administrators (*formerly* Hospital Administrators) (later FHSM); Fellow, Historical Association | FIEAust | Fellow, Institution of Engineers, Australia |
| | | FIED | Fellow, Institution of Engineering Designers |
| | | FIEE | Fellow, Institution of Electrical Engineers (*now see* FIET) |
| FHAS | Fellow, Highland and Agricultural Society of Scotland | FIEEE | Fellow, Institute of Electrical and Electronics Engineers (NY) |
| FHCIMA | Fellow, Hotel Catering and International (formerly Institutional) Management Association (*now see* FIH) | FIEEIE | Fellow, Institution of Electronics and Electrical Incorporated Engineers (later FIIE) |
| FHEA | Fellow, Higher Education Academy | FIEEM | Fellow, Institute of Ecology and Environmental Management (*now see* FCIEEM) |
| FHKAES | Fellow, Hong Kong Academy of Engineering Sciences | | |
| FHKAM | Fellow, Hong Kong Academy of Medicine | FIEHK | Fellow, Institution of Engineering, Hong Kong |
| FHKCCM | Fellow, Hong Kong College of Community Medicine | FIEI | Fellow, Institution of Engineering Inspection (later FIQA); Fellow, Institution of Engineers of Ireland |
| FHKCP | Fellow, Hong Kong College of Physicians | | |
| FHKCPath | Fellow, Hong Kong College of Pathologists | FIEIE | Fellow, Institution of Electronic Incorporated Engineers (later FIEEIE) |
| FHKCS | Fellow, Hong Kong College of Surgeons | | |
| FHKIE | Fellow, Hong Kong Institution of Engineers | FIEJ | Fédération Internationale des Editeurs de Journaux et Publications |
| FHMAAAS | Foreign Honorary Member, American Academy of Arts and Sciences | | |
| | | FIEMA | Fellow, Institute of Environmental Management and Assessment |
| FHRS | Fellow, Heart Rhythm Society | FIEnvSc | Fellow, Institute of Environmental Sciences |
| FHS | Fellow, Heraldry Society; Forces Help Society and Lord Roberts Workshops (*now see* SSAFA) | FIERE | Fellow, Institution of Electronic and Radio Engineers (later FIEE) |
| FHSA | Family Health Services Authority | FIES | Fellow, Illuminating Engineering Society (later FIllumES; *now see* FCIBSE); Fellow, Institution of Engineers and Shipbuilders, Scotland |
| FHSM | Fellow, Institute of Health Services Management (later FIHM) | | |
| FIA | Fellow, Institute and Faculty of Actuaries (formerly Institute of Actuaries) | | |
| | | FIET | Fédération Internationale des Employés, Techniciens et Cadres; Fellow, Institution of Engineering and Technology |
| FIAA | Fellow, Institute of Actuaries of Australia | | |
| FIAAS | Fellow, Institute of Australian Agricultural Science | FIEx | Fellow, Institute of Export |
| FIAA&S | Fellow, Incorporated Association of Architects and Surveyors | FIExpE | Fellow, Institute of Explosives Engineers |
| FIACM | Fellow, International Association of Computational Mechanics | FIFA | Fédération Internationale de Football Association |
| FIAE | Fellow, Irish Academy of Engineering | FIFEM | Fellow, International Federation of Emergency Medicine |
| FIAFoST | Fellow, International Academy of Food Science and Technology | FIFF | Fellow, Institute of Freight Forwarders (*now see* FIFP) |
| FIAgrE | Fellow, Institution of Agricultural Engineers | FIFireE | Fellow, Institution of Fire Engineers |
| FIAgrM | Fellow, Institute of Agricultural Management | FIFM | Fellow, Institute of Fisheries Management |
| FIALD | Fellow, International Association of Lighting Designers | FIFor | Fellow, Institute of Foresters (*now see* FICFor) |
| FIAM | Fellow, International Academy of Management | FIFP | Fellow, Institute of Freight Professionals |
| FIAMBE | Fellow, International Academy for Medical and Biological Engineering | FIFST | Fellow, Institute of Food Science and Technology |

| | | | |
|---|---|---|---|
| FIGasE | Fellow, Institution of Gas Engineers (*now see* FIGEM) | FInstKT | Fellow, Institute of Knowledge Transfer |
| FIGCM | Fellow, Incorporated Guild of Church Musicians | FInstLEx | Fellow, Institute of Legal Executives |
| FIGD | Fellow, Institute of Grocery Distribution | FInstLM | Fellow, Institute of Leadership and Management |
| FIGEM | Fellow, Institution of Gas Engineers and Managers | FInstM | Fellow, Institute of Meat; Fellow, Institute of Marketing (*now see* FCIM) |
| FIGO | International Federation of Gynaecology and Obstetrics | | |
| FIH | Fellow, Institute of Housing (*now see* FCIH); Fellow, Institute of the Horse; Fellow, Institute of Hospitality | FInstMC | Fellow, Institute of Measurement and Control |
| | | FInstMSM | Fellow, Institute of Marketing and Sales Management (later FInstM; *now see* FCIM) |
| FIHE | Fellow, Institute of Health Education | | |
| FIHEEM | Fellow, Institute of Healthcare Engineering and Estate Management | FInstMet | Fellow, Institute of Metals (later part of Metals Society; then FIM) |
| FIHM | Fellow, Institute of Housing Managers (later FIH; *now see* FCIH); Fellow, Institute of Healthcare Management | FInstNDT | Fellow, Institute of Non-Destructive Testing |
| | | FInstP | Fellow, Institute of Physics |
| FIHort | Fellow, Institute of Horticulture (*now see* FCIHort) | FInstPet | Fellow, Institute of Petroleum (*now see* FEI) |
| FIHospE | Fellow, Institute of Hospital Engineering | FInstPkg | Fellow, Institute of Packaging |
| FIHT | Fellow, Institution of Highways & Transportation (*now see* FCIHT) | FInstPS | Fellow, Institute of Purchasing and Supply (*now see* FCIPS) |
| | | FInstRE | Fellow, Institution of Royal Engineers |
| FIHVE | Fellow, Institution of Heating & Ventilating Engineers (later FCIBS and MCIBS) | FInstSM | Fellow, Institute of Sales Management (*now see* FInstSMM) |
| | | FInstSMM | Fellow, Institute of Sales and Marketing Management |
| FIIA | Fellow, Institute of Industrial Administration (later CBIM and FBIM); Fellow, Institute of Internal Auditors | FInstTT | Fellow, Institute of Travel & Tourism |
| | | FInstW | Fellow, Institute of Welding (*now see* FWeldI) |
| FIIB | Fellow, International Institute of Biotechnology | FINucE | Fellow, Institution of Nuclear Engineers (*now see* FNucI) |
| FIIC | Fellow, International Institute for Conservation of Historic and Artistic Works | FIOA | Fellow, Institute of Acoustics |
| | | FIOB | Fellow, Institute of Building (*now see* FCIOB) |
| FIIDA | Fellow, International Interior Design Association | FIOH | Fellow, Institute of Occupational Hygiene |
| FIIE | Fellow, Institution of Incorporated Engineers in Electronic, Electrical and Mechanical Engineering (*now see* FIET) | FIOM | Fellow, Institute of Office Management (*now see* FIAM) |
| | | FIOP | Fellow, Institute of Printing (*now see* FIP3) |
| FIIM | Fellow, Institution of Industrial Managers | FIOSH | Fellow, Institution of Occupational Safety and Health |
| FIInfSc | Fellow, Institute of Information Scientists (*now see* FCLIP) | FIP | Fellow, Australian Institute of Petroleum |
| FIIP | Fellow, Institute of Incorporated Photographers (*now see* FBIPP) | FIPA | Fellow, Institute of Practitioners in Advertising; Fellow, Insolvency Practitioners Association |
| FIIT | Fellow, Institute of Indirect Taxation | | |
| FIL | Fellow, Institute of Linguists (*now see* FCIL) | FIPAA | Fellow, Institute of Public Administration Australia |
| FILA | Fellow, Institute of Landscape Architects (*now see* FLI) | FIPD | Fellow, Institute of Personnel and Development (*now see* FCIPD) |
| FILAM | Fellow, Institute of Leisure and Amenity Management | | |
| FILDM | Fellow, Institute of Logistics and Distribution Management (later FILog) | FIPDM | Fellow, Institute of Physical Distribution Management (later FILDM) |
| FilDr | Doctor of Philosophy | FIPEM | Fellow, Institute of Physics and Engineering in Medicine |
| Fil.Hed. | Filosofie Hedersdoktor | FIPENZ | Fellow, Institution of Professional Engineers, New Zealand |
| FIllumES | Fellow, Illuminating Engineering Society (*now see* FCIBSE) | FIPG | Fellow, Institute of Professional Goldsmiths |
| FILog | Fellow, Institute of Logistics (later FILT) | FIPharmM | Fellow, Institute of Pharmacy Management |
| FILT | Fellow, Institute of Logistics and Transport (*now see* FCILT) | FIPHE | Fellow, Institution of Public Health Engineers (later FIWEM) |
| FIM | Fellow, Institute of Materials (*formerly* Institution of Metallurgists, then Institute of Metals) (*now see* FIMMM) | FIPlantE | Fellow, Institution of Plant Engineers |
| | | FIPM | Fellow, Institute of Personnel Management (later FIPD) |
| FIMA | Fellow, Institute of Mathematics and its Applications | FIPPM | Fellow, Institute of Payroll and Pensions Management |
| FIMarE | Fellow, Institute of Marine Engineers (*now see* FIMarEST) | FIPR | Fellow, Institute of Public Relations (*now see* FCIPR) |
| FIMarEST | Fellow, Institute of Marine Engineering, Science and Technology | FIProdE | Fellow, Institution of Production Engineers (later FIMfgE) |
| | | FIPSM | Fellow, Institute of Physical Sciences in Medicine (*now see* FIPEM) |
| FIMatM | Fellow, Institute of Materials Management (later FILog) | | |
| FIMBRA | Financial Intermediaries, Managers and Brokers Regulatory Association | FIP3 | Fellow, Institute of Paper, Printing and Publishing |
| | | FIQ | Fellow, Institute of Quarrying |
| FIMC | Fellow, Institute of Management Consultants (*now see* FCMC) | FIQA | Fellow, Institute of Quality Assurance (*now see* FCQI) |
| FIMCB | Fellow, International Management Centre from Buckingham | FIRI | Fellow, Institution of the Rubber Industry (later FPRI) |
| FIMCRCSE | Fellow in Immediate Medical Care, Royal College of Surgeons of Edinburgh | FIRM | Fellow, Institute of Risk Management |
| | | FIRO | Fellow, Institution of Railway Operators |
| FIMechE | Fellow, Institution of Mechanical Engineers | FIRRV | Fellow, Institute of Revenues Rating and Valuation |
| FIMF | Fellow, Institute of Materials Finishing | FIRSE | Fellow, Institute of Railway Signalling Engineers |
| FIMfgE | Fellow, Institution of Manufacturing Engineers (later FIEE) | FIRTE | Fellow, Institute of Road Transport Engineers |
| FIMgt | Fellow, Institute of Management (*now see* FCMI) | FIS | Fellow, Institute of Statisticians |
| FIMH | Fellow, Institute of Materials Handling (later FIMatM); Fellow, Institute of Military History | FISA | Fellow, Incorporated Secretaries' Association; Fédération Internationale des Sociétés d'Aviron |
| FIMI | Fellow, Institute of the Motor Industry | FISE | Fellow, Institution of Sales Engineers; Fellow, Institution of Sanitary Engineers |
| FIMinE | Fellow, Institution of Mining Engineers (later FIMM) | | |
| FIMIT | Fellow, Institute of Musical Instrument Technology | FISITA | Fédération Internationale des Sociétés d'Ingénieurs des Techniques de l'Automobile |
| FIMLS | Fellow, Institute of Medical Laboratory Sciences (*now see* FIBMS) | | |
| | | FISM | Fellow, Institute of Supervisory Managers (*now see* FInstLM); Fellow, Institute of Sports Medicine |
| FIMLT | Fellow, Institute of Medical Laboratory Technology (later FIMLS) | | |
| | | FISOB | Fellow, Incorporated Society of Organ Builders |
| FIMM | Fellow, Institution of Mining and Metallurgy (*now see* FIMMM) | FISPAL | Fellow, Institute for Sport, Parks and Leisure |
| FIMMA | Fellow, Institute of Metals and Materials Australasia | FISTC | Fellow, Institute of Scientific and Technical Communicators |
| FIMMM | Fellow, Institute of Materials, Minerals and Mining | FISTD | Fellow, Imperial Society of Teachers of Dancing |
| FIMS | Fellow, Institute of Mathematical Statistics | FIStructE | Fellow, Institution of Structural Engineers |
| FIMT | Fellow, Institute of the Motor Trade (*now see* FIMI) | FITD | Fellow, Institute of Training and Development (later FIPD) |
| FIMTA | Fellow, Institute of Municipal Treasurers and Accountants (*now see* IPFA) | FITE | Fellow, Institution of Electrical and Electronics Technician Engineers |
| FIMunE | Fellow, Institution of Municipal Engineers (now amalgamated with Institution of Civil Engineers) | FITSA | Fellow, Institute of Trading Standards Administration |
| | | FIW | Fellow, Welding Institute (*now see* FWeldI) |
| FIN | Fellow, Institute of Navigation (*now see* FRIN) | FIWE | Fellow, Institution of Water Engineers (later FIWES) |
| FINRA | Financial Industry Regulatory Authority | FIWEM | Fellow, Institution of Water and Environmental Management (*now see* FCIWEM) |
| FInstAM | Fellow, Institute of Administrative Management | | |
| FInstArb(NZ) | Fellow, Institute of Arbitrators of New Zealand | FIWES | Fellow, Institution of Water Engineers and Scientists (later FIWEM) |
| FInstBiol | Fellow, Institute of Biology (later FIBiol) | | |
| FInstCES | Fellow, Institution of Civil Engineering Surveyors (*now see* FCInstCES) | FIWM | Fellow, Institution of Works Managers (*now see* FIIM); Fellow, Institute of Wastes Management (*now see* FCIWM) |
| FInstD | Fellow, Institute of Directors | FIWO | Fellow, Institute of Water Officers |
| FInstE | Fellow, Institute of Energy (*now see* FEI) | FIWPC | Fellow, Institute of Water Pollution Control (later FIWEM) |
| FInstF | Fellow, Institute of Fuel (later FInstE); Fellow, Institute of Fundraising | FIWSc | Fellow, Institute of Wood Science |
| | | FIWSP | Fellow, Institute of Work Study Practitioners (*now see* FMS) |
| FInstFF | Fellow, Institute of Freight Forwarders Ltd (later FIFF) | FJI | Fellow, Institute of Journalists (*now see* FCIJ) |
| FInstHE | Fellow, Institution of Highways Engineers (later FIHT, *now see* FCIHT) | FJIE | Fellow, Junior Institution of Engineers (*now see* CIMGTechE) |

| | | | |
|---|---|---|---|
| FKC | Fellow, King's College London | FRAgS | Fellow, Royal Agricultural Societies (*ie* of England, Scotland and Wales) |
| FKCHMS | Fellow, King's College Hospital Medical School | FRAHS | Fellow, Royal Australian Historical Society |
| FL | Florida (postal) | FRAI | Fellow, Royal Anthropological Institute of Great Britain & Ireland |
| FLA | Fellow, Library Association (*now see* FCLIP) | | |
| Fla | Florida | FRAIA | Fellow, Royal Australian Institute of Architects |
| FLAS | Fellow, Chartered Land Agents' Society (*now* (after amalgamation) *see* FRICS) | FRAIB | Fellow, Royal Australian Institute of Building |
| | | FRAIC | Fellow, Royal Architectural Institute of Canada |
| FLCM | Fellow, London College of Music | FRAIPA | Fellow, Royal Australian Institute of Public Administration |
| FLI | Fellow, Landscape Institute | FRAM | Fellow, Royal Academy of Music |
| FLIA | Fellow, Life Insurance Association | FRAME | Fund for the Replacement of Animals in Medical Experiments |
| FLLA | Fellow, Association of Lawyers and Legal Advisers | FRANZCOG | Fellow, Royal Australian and New Zealand College of Obstetricians and Gynaecologists |
| FLS | Fellow, Linnean Society | | |
| FLSW | Fellow, Learned Society of Wales | FRANZCP | Fellow, Royal Australian and New Zealand College of Psychiatrists |
| Flt | Flight | | |
| FM | Field-Marshal | FRANZCR | Fellow, Royal Australian and New Zealand College of Radiologists |
| FMA | Fellow, Museums Association | | |
| FMAAT | Fellow Member, Association of Accounting Technicians | FRAPI | Fellow, Royal Australian Planning Institute (*now see* FPIA) |
| FMBA | Fellow, Marine Biological Association | FRAS | Fellow, Royal Astronomical Society; Fellow, Royal Asiatic Society |
| FMedSci | Fellow, Academy of Medical Sciences | | |
| FMES | Fellow, Minerals Engineering Society | FRASE | Fellow, Royal Agricultural Society of England |
| FMI | Foundation for Manufacturing and Industry | FRBC | Fellow, Royal Birmingham Conservatoire |
| FMinSoc | Fellow, Mineralogical Society of Great Britain and Ireland | FRBS | Fellow, Royal Society of British Sculptors (*now see* FRSS); Fellow, Royal Botanic Society |
| FMLM | Faculty of Medical Leadership and Management | | |
| FMS | Federated Malay States; Fellow, Medical Society; Fellow, Institute of Management Services | FRCA | Fellow, Royal College of Art; Fellow, Royal College of Anaesthetists |
| | | FRCCO | Fellow, Royal Canadian College of Organists |
| FMSA | Fellow, Mineralogical Society of America | FRCD(Can.) | Fellow, Royal College of Dentists of Canada |
| FNA | Fellow, Indian National Science Academy | FRCEM | Fellow, Royal College of Emergency Medicine |
| FNAEA | Fellow, National Association of Estate Agents | FRCGP | Fellow, Royal College of General Practitioners |
| FNCO | Fleet Naval Constructor Officer | FRCM | Fellow, Royal College of Music |
| FNECInst | Fellow, North East Coast Institution of Engineers and Shipbuilders | FRCN | Fellow, Royal College of Nursing |
| | | FRCO | Fellow, Royal College of Organists |
| FNI | Fellow, Nautical Institute; Fellow, National Institute of Sciences in India (*now see* FNA) | FRCO(CHM) | Fellow, Royal College of Organists with Diploma in Choir Training |
| FNIA | Fellow, Nigerian Institute of Architects | FRCOG | Fellow, Royal College of Obstetricians and Gynaecologists |
| FNM | Free National Movement | FRCOphth | Fellow, Royal College of Ophthalmologists |
| FNMCP | Fellow, Nigerian Medical College of Physicians | FRCP | Fellow, Royal College of Physicians, London |
| FNMSM | Fellow, North and Midlands School of Music | FRCPA | Fellow, Royal College of Pathologists of Australasia |
| FNucI | Fellow, Nuclear Institute | FRCP&S (Canada) | Fellow, Royal College of Physicians and Surgeons of Canada |
| FNZIA | Fellow, New Zealand Institute of Architects | | |
| FNZIAS | Fellow, New Zealand Institute of Agricultural Science | FRCPath | Fellow, Royal College of Pathologists |
| FNZIC | Fellow, New Zealand Institute of Chemistry | FRCPC | Fellow, Royal College of Physicians of Canada |
| FNZIE | Fellow, New Zealand Institution of Engineers (*now see* FIPENZ) | FRCPCH | Fellow, Royal College of Paediatrics and Child Health |
| FNZIM | Fellow, New Zealand Institute of Management | FRCPE or FRCPEd | Fellow, Royal College of Physicians, Edinburgh |
| FNZPsS | Fellow, New Zealand Psychological Society | FRCPGlas | Fellow, Royal College of Physicians and Surgeons of Glasgow |
| FO | Foreign Office (*now see* FCO); Field Officer; Flag Officer; Flying Officer | FRCPI | Fellow, Royal College of Physicians of Ireland |
| | | FRCPSGlas | Hon. Fellow, Royal College of Physicians and Surgeons of Glasgow |
| FODC | Franciscan Order of the Divine Compassion | | |
| FOIC | Flag Officer in charge | FRCPsych | Fellow, Royal College of Psychiatrists |
| FOMA | Flag Officer, Maritime Aviation | FRCR | Fellow, Royal College of Radiologists |
| FOMI | Faculty of Occupational Medicine of Ireland | FRCS | Fellow, Royal College of Surgeons of England; Fellow, Royal Conservatoire of Scotland |
| FONA | Flag Officer, Naval Aviation | | |
| FONAC | Flag Officer, Naval Air Command | FRCSCan | Fellow, Royal College of Surgeons of Canada |
| For. | Foreign | FRCSE or FRCSEd | Fellow, Royal College of Surgeons of Edinburgh |
| FOSA | Fellow, Optical Society of America | FRCSGlas | Fellow, Royal College of Physicians and Surgeons of Glasgow |
| FOST | Flag Officer Sea Training | FRCSI | Fellow, Royal College of Surgeons in Ireland |
| FPA | Family Planning Association | FRCSLT | Fellow, Royal College of Speech and Language Therapists |
| FPC | Family Practitioner Committee (later FHSA); Financial Planning Certificate | FRCSoc | Fellow, Royal Commonwealth Society |
| | | FRCS (OMFS) | Fellow, Royal College of Surgeons of England (Oral and Maxillofacial Surgery) |
| FPH | Faculty of Public Health | | |
| FPHM | Faculty of Public Health Medicine (*see now* FPH) | FRCST | Fellow, Royal College of Surgeons of Thailand |
| FPhS | Fellow, Philosophical Society of England | FRCUS | Fellow, Royal College of University Surgeons (Denmark) |
| FPhysiol | Fellow, Physiological Society of London | FRCVS | Fellow, Royal College of Veterinary Surgeons |
| FPhysS | Fellow, Physical Society | FREconS | Fellow, Royal Economic Society |
| FPI | Fellow, Plastics Institute (later FPRI) | FREng | Fellow, Royal Academy of Engineering |
| FPIA | Fellow, Plastics Institute of Australia; Fellow, Planning Institute of Australia | FRES | Fellow, Royal Entomological Society of London |
| | | FRFPSG | Fellow, Royal Faculty of Physicians and Surgeons, Glasgow (*now see* FRCPGlas) |
| FPM | Faculty of Pharmaceutical Medicine | | |
| FPMI | Fellow, Pensions Management Institute | FRG | Federal Republic of Germany |
| FPRI | Fellow, Plastics and Rubber Institute (later FIM) | FRGS | Fellow, Royal Geographical Society |
| FPS | Fellow, Pharmaceutical Society (*now also* FRPharmS); Fauna Preservation Society (later FFPS) | FRGSA | Fellow, Royal Geographical Society of Australasia |
| | | FRHistS | Fellow, Royal Historical Society |
| FPWI | Fellow, Permanent Way Institution | FRHS | Fellow, Royal Horticultural Society (*now see* MRHS) |
| FQNI | Fellow, Queen's Nursing Institute | FRI | Fellow, Royal Institution |
| FRA | Fellow, Royal Academy | FRIAI | Fellow, Royal Institute of the Architects of Ireland |
| FRAC | Fellow, Royal Agricultural College | FRIAS | Fellow, Royal Incorporation of Architects of Scotland; Royal Institute for the Advancement of Science |
| FRACDS | Fellow, Royal Australian College of Dental Surgeons | | |
| FRACGP | Fellow, Royal Australian College of General Practitioners | FRIBA | Fellow, Royal Institute of British Architects (*and see* RIBA) |
| FRACI | Fellow, Royal Australian Chemical Institute | FRIC | Fellow, Royal Institute of Chemistry (*now see* FRSC) |
| FRACMA | Fellow, Royal Australian College of Medical Administrators | FRICS | Fellow, Royal Institution of Chartered Surveyors |
| FRACO | Fellow, Royal Australian College of Ophthalmologists | FRIH | Fellow, Royal Institute of Horticulture (NZ) |
| FRACOG | Fellow, Royal Australian College of Obstetricians and Gynaecologists (*now see* FRANZCOG) | FRIN | Fellow, Royal Institute of Navigation |
| | | FRINA | Fellow, Royal Institution of Naval Architects |
| FRACP | Fellow, Royal Australasian College of Physicians | FRIPA | Fellow, Royal Institute of Public Administration (the Institute no longer has Fellows) |
| FRACR | Fellow, Royal Australasian College of Radiologists | | |
| FRACS | Fellow, Royal Australasian College of Surgeons | FRIPH | Fellow, Royal Institute of Public Health (*now see* FRSPH) |
| FRAD | Fellow, Royal Academy of Dancing | | |
| FRAeS | Fellow, Royal Aeronautical Society | | |

| | |
|---|---|
| FRIPHH | Fellow, Royal Institute of Public Health and Hygiene (later FRIPH; *now see* FRSPH) |
| FRMCM | Fellow, Royal Manchester College of Music |
| FRMedSoc | Fellow, Royal Medical Society |
| FRMetS | Fellow, Royal Meteorological Society |
| FRMIA | Fellow, Retail Management Institute of Australia |
| FRMS | Fellow, Royal Microscopical Society |
| FRNCM | Fellow, Royal Northern College of Music |
| FRNS | Fellow, Royal Numismatic Society |
| FRPharmS | Fellow, Royal Pharmaceutical Society |
| FRPS | Fellow, Royal Photographic Society |
| FRPSL | Fellow, Royal Philatelic Society, London |
| FRS | Fellow, Royal Society |
| FRSA | Fellow, Royal Society of Arts |
| FRSAI | Fellow, Royal Society of Antiquaries of Ireland |
| FRSAMD | Fellow, Royal Scottish Academy of Music and Drama |
| FRSB | Fellow, Royal Society of Biology |
| FRSC | Fellow, Royal Society of Canada; Fellow, Royal Society of Chemistry |
| FRS(Can) | Fellow, Royal Society of Canada (used when a person is also a Fellow of the Royal Society of Chemistry) |
| FRSCM | Hon. Fellow, Royal School of Church Music |
| FRSC(UK) | Fellow, Royal Society of Chemistry (used when a person is also a Fellow of the Royal Society of Canada) |
| FRSE | Fellow, Royal Society of Edinburgh |
| FRSGS | Fellow, Royal Scottish Geographical Society |
| FRSH | Fellow, Royal Society for the Promotion of Health (*now see* FRSPH) |
| FRSL | Fellow, Royal Society of Literature |
| FRSM | Fellow, Royal Schools of Music |
| FRSN | Fellow, Royal Society of New South Wales |
| FRSocMed | Fellow, Royal Society of Medicine |
| FRSNZ | Fellow, Royal Society of New Zealand |
| FRSPH | Fellow, Royal Society for Public Health |
| FRSPS | Fellow, Remote Sensing and Photogrammetry Society |
| FRSS | Fellow, Royal Society of Sculptors |
| FRSSA | Fellow, Royal Scottish Society for the Arts |
| FRSSAf | Fellow, Royal Society of South Africa |
| FRSTM&H | Fellow, Royal Society of Tropical Medicine and Hygiene |
| FRSV | Fellow, Royal Society of Victoria |
| FRTPI | Fellow, Royal Town Planning Institute |
| FRTS | Fellow, Royal Television Society |
| FRUSI | Fellow, Royal United Services Institute |
| FRVA | Fellow, Rating and Valuation Association (*now see* IRRV) |
| FRVC | Fellow, Royal Veterinary College |
| FRWCMD | Fellow, Royal Welsh College of Music and Drama |
| FRZSScot | Fellow, Royal Zoological Society of Scotland |
| FS | Field Security |
| fs | Graduate, Royal Air Force Staff College |
| FSA | Fellow, Society of Antiquaries; Financial Services Authority |
| FSACOG | Fellow, South African College of Obstetricians and Gynaecologists |
| FSAE | Fellow, Society of Automotive Engineers; Fellow, Society of Art Education |
| FSAI | Fellow, Society of Architectural Illustrators |
| FSArc | Fellow, Society of Architects (merged with the RIBA 1952) |
| FSaRS | Fellow, Safety and Reliability Society |
| FSAScot | Fellow, Society of Antiquaries of Scotland |
| FSB | Fellow, Society of Biology (*now see* FRSB) |
| FSBE | Fellow, Society of Business Economists |
| fsc | Foreign Staff College |
| FSCA | Fellow, Society of Company and Commercial Accountants |
| FScotvec | Fellow, Scottish Vocational Education Council |
| FSCRE | Fellow, Scottish Council for Research in Education |
| FSDC | Fellow, Society of Dyers and Colourists |
| FSE | Fellow, Society of Engineers; Fellow, Society for the Environment |
| FSEDA | Fellow, Staff and Higher Educational Development Association |
| FSES | Fellow, Society for Educational Studies |
| FSG | Fellow, Society of Genealogists |
| FSGD | Fellow, Society of Garden Designers |
| FSGT | Fellow, Society of Glass Technology |
| FSI | Fellow, Chartered Surveyors' Institution (*now see* FRICS); Fellow, Securities Institute (later Securities & Investment Institute, *now see* FCSI) |
| FSIA | Fellow, Securities Institute of Australia; Fellow, Society of Industrial Artists (later FSIAD) |
| FSIAD | Fellow, Society of Industrial Artists and Designers (*now see* FCSD) |
| FSIP | Fellow, Society of Investment Professionals |
| FSLCOG | Fellow, Sri Lankan College of Obstetrics and Gynaecology |
| FSLCPaed | Fellow, Sri Lanka College of Paediatricians |
| FSLTC | Fellow, Society of Leather Technologists and Chemists |
| FSMA | Fellow, Incorporated Sales Managers' Association (later FInstMSM, then FInstM) |
| FSMC | Freeman of the Spectacle-Makers' Company |
| FSME | Fellow, Society of Manufacturing Engineers |
| FSMPTE | Fellow, Society of Motion Picture and Television Engineers (US) |
| FSMS | Fellow, Strategic Management Society |
| FSNAD | Fellow, Society of Numismatic Artists and Designers |
| FSNAME | Fellow, American Society of Naval Architects and Marine Engineers |
| FSOE | Fellow, Society of Operations Engineers |
| FSOGC | Fellow, Society of Obstetricians and Gynaecologists of Canada |
| FSPE | Fellow, Society of Professional Economists |
| FSPI | Fellow, Society of Practitioners of Insolvency |
| FSQA | Fellow, Scottish Qualifications Authority |
| FSRH | Faculty of Sexual and Reproduction Healthcare, Royal College of Obstetricians and Gynaecologists |
| FSRHE | Fellow, Society for Research into Higher Education |
| FSRP | Fellow, Society for Radiological Protection |
| FSS | Fellow, Royal Statistical Society |
| FSSI | Fellow, Society of Scribes and Illuminators |
| FSTD | Fellow, Society of Typographic Designers |
| FSVA | Fellow, Incorporated Society of Valuers and Auctioneers (*now see* RICS) |
| FT | Financial Times |
| FTC | Flying Training Command; Full Technological Certificate, City and Guilds of London Institute |
| FTCD | Fellow, Trinity College, Dublin |
| FTCL | Fellow, Trinity College of Music, London |
| FTI | Fellow, Textile Institute |
| FTII | Fellow, Chartered Institute (*formerly* Incorporated Institute, then Institute) of Taxation |
| FTMA | Fellow, Telecommunications Managers Association (*now see* FCMA) |
| FTS | Fellow, Australian Academy of Technological Sciences and Engineering (*now see* FTSE); Flying Training School; Fellow, Tourism Society |
| FTSE | Fellow, Australian Academy of Technological Sciences and Engineering |
| FUCEB | Fellow, University of Central England in Birmingham |
| FUCUA | Federation of University Conservative and Unionist Associations (*now see* FCS) |
| FUMIST | Fellow, University of Manchester Institute of Science and Technology |
| FVCM | Fellow, Victoria College of Music |
| FVRDE | Fighting Vehicles Research and Development Establishment |
| FWAAS | Fellow, World Academy of Arts and Sciences |
| FWACP | Fellow, West African College of Physicians |
| FWAG | Farming and Wildlife Advisory Group |
| FWCB | Fellow, Worshipful Company of Blacksmiths |
| FWCMD | Fellow, Welsh College of Music and Drama (*now see* FRWCMD) |
| FWeldI | Fellow, Welding Institute |
| FWES | Fellow, Women's Engineering Society |
| FWSOM | Fellow, Institute of Practitioners in Work Study, Organisation and Method (*now see* FMS) |
| FZS | Fellow, Zoological Society |
| FZSScot | Fellow, Zoological Society of Scotland (*now see* FRZSScot) |

# G

| | |
|---|---|
| GA | Geologists' Association; Gaelic Athletic (Club); Georgia (postal) |
| Ga | Georgia |
| GAI | Guild of Architectural Ironmongers |
| GAICD | Graduate Member, Australian Institute of Company Directors |
| GAP | Gap Activity Projects |
| GAPAN | Guild of Air Pilots and Air Navigators |
| GATT | General Agreement on Tariffs and Trade (*now* World Trade Organisation) |
| GB | Great Britain |
| GBA | Governing Bodies Association |
| GBE | Knight or Dame Grand Cross, Order of the British Empire |
| GBGSA | Governing Bodies of Girls' Schools Association (*formerly* Association of Governing Bodies of Girls' Public Schools) |
| GBM | Grand Bauhinia Medal (Hong Kong) |
| GBS | Gold Bauhinia Star (Hong Kong) |
| GC | George Cross |
| GCB | Knight or Dame Grand Cross, Order of the Bath |
| GCBS | General Council of British Shipping |
| GCC | General Chiropractic Council |
| GCCC | Gonville and Caius College, Cambridge |
| GCCF | Grand Commander, Companion Order of Freedom (Zambia) |
| GCFR | Grand Commander, Order of the Federal Republic of Nigeria |
| GCH | Knight Grand Cross, Hanoverian Order |
| GCHQ | Government Communications Headquarters |
| GCIE | Knight Grand Commander, Order of the Indian Empire |
| GCL | Grand Chief, Order of Logohu (Papua New Guinea) |
| GCLJ | Grand Cross, Order of St Lazarus of Jerusalem |
| GCM | Gold Crown of Merit (Barbados) |
| GCMA | Global Certified Management Accountant |
| GCMG | Knight or Dame Grand Cross, Order of St Michael and St George |

| | |
|---|---|
| GCMJ | Knight or Dame Grand Cross, Supreme Military Order of the Temple of Jerusalem |
| GCNG | Knight Grand Cross, Order of the Nation (Grenada) |
| GCON | Grand Cross, Order of the Niger |
| GCSE | General Certificate of Secondary Education |
| GCSG | Knight Grand Cross, Order of St Gregory the Great |
| GCSI | Knight Grand Commander, Order of the Star of India |
| GCSJ | Knight Grand Cross of Justice, Sovereign Order of St John of Jerusalem (Knights Hospitaller) |
| GCSK | Grand Commander, Order of the Star and Key of the Indian Ocean (Mauritius) |
| GCSL | Grand Cross, Order of St Lucia |
| GCStG | Knight Grand Cross, Order of St George |
| GCStJ | Bailiff or Dame Grand Cross, Most Venerable Order of the Hospital of St John of Jerusalem |
| GCVO | Knight or Dame Grand Cross, Royal Victorian Order |
| gd | grand-daughter |
| GDBA | Guide Dogs for the Blind Association |
| GDC | General Dental Council |
| GDL | Graduate Diploma in Law |
| Gdns | Gardens |
| GDR | German Democratic Republic |
| GDST | Girls' Day School Trust |
| Gen. | General |
| Ges. | Gesellschaft |
| GFD | Geophysical Fluid Dynamics |
| GFS | Girls' Friendly Society |
| ggd | great-grand-daughter |
| ggs | great-grandson |
| GGSM | Graduate in Music, Guildhall School of Music and Drama |
| GHQ | General Headquarters |
| Gib. | Gibraltar |
| GIMechE | Graduate, Institution of Mechanical Engineers |
| GIS | Geographic Information Systems |
| GKT | Guy's, King's and St Thomas' (Medical and Dental School of King's College London) |
| GL | Grand Lodge |
| GLA | Greater London Authority |
| GLAA | Greater London Arts Association (*now see* GLAB) |
| GLC | Greater London Council |
| Glos | Gloucestershire |
| GM | George Medal; Grand Medal (Ghana); genetically modified |
| GMB | (Union for) General, Municipal, Boilermakers |
| GMBATU | General, Municipal, Boilermakers and Allied Trades Union (*now see* GMB) |
| GmbH | Gesellschaft mit beschränkter Haftung |
| GMBPS | Graduate Member, British Psychological Society |
| GMC | General Medical Council; Guild of Memorial Craftsmen; General Management Course (Henley) |
| GMH | Gibraltar Medallion of Honour |
| GMWU | General and Municipal Workers' Union (later GMBATU; *now see* GMB) |
| GNC | General Nursing Council |
| GNVQ | General National Vocational Qualification |
| GNZM | Knight or Dame Grand Companion, New Zealand Order of Merit |
| GOC | General Officer Commanding |
| GOC-in-C | General Officer Commanding-in-Chief |
| GOE | General Ordination Examination |
| GOMLJ | Grand Officer of Merit, Order of St Lazarus of Jerusalem |
| GOQ | Grand Officer, National Order of Quebec |
| GOSK | Grand Officer, Order of the Star and Key of the Indian Ocean (Mauritius) |
| Gov. | Governor |
| Govt | Government |
| GP | General Practitioner; Grand Prix |
| Gp | Group |
| GPDST | Girls' Public Day School Trust (*now see* GDST) |
| GPMU | Graphical, Paper and Media Union |
| GPO | General Post Office |
| GR | General Reconnaissance |
| Gr. | Greek |
| GRNCM | Graduate of the Royal Northern College of Music |
| GRSM | Graduate of the Royal Schools of Music |
| GS | General Staff; Grammar School |
| g s | grandson |
| GSA | Girls' Schools Association |
| GSD | Gibraltar Social Democrats |
| GSM | General Service Medal; (Member of) Guildhall School of Music and Drama |
| GSMD | Guildhall School of Music and Drama |
| GSO | General Staff Officer |
| GTCL | Graduate, Trinity College of Music |
| GTS | General Theological Seminary (New York) |
| GWR | Great Western Railway |

# H

| | |
|---|---|
| HA | Historical Association; Health Authority |
| HAA | Heavy Anti-Aircraft |
| HAC | Honourable Artillery Company |
| HACAS | Housing Association Consultancy and Advisory Service |
| Hants | Hampshire |
| HAT | Housing Action Trust |
| HBM | His (or Her) Britannic Majesty (Majesty's); Humming Bird Gold Medal (Trinidad) |
| hc | *honoris causa* (honorary) |
| HCA | Hospital Corporation of America |
| HCF | Honorary Chaplain to the Forces |
| HCIMA | Hotel, Catering and International (*formerly* Institutional) Management Association |
| HCO | Higher Clerical Officer |
| HCPC | Health and Care Professions Council |
| HCSC | Higher Command and Staff Course |
| HDA | Hawkesbury Diploma in Agriculture (Australia); Health Development Agency |
| HDD | Higher Dental Diploma |
| HDE | Higher Diploma in Education |
| HDFA | Higher Diploma in Fine Art |
| HDipEd | Higher Diploma in Education |
| HDR | Habilitation à diriger des recherches |
| HE | His (or Her) Excellency; His Eminence; Higher Education |
| HEA | Health Education Authority (later HDA) |
| HEC | Ecole des Hautes Etudes Commerciales; Higher Education Corporation |
| HEFCE | Higher Education Funding Council for England |
| HEFCW | Higher Education Funding Council for Wales |
| HEH | His (or Her) Exalted Highness |
| Heir-pres. | Heir-presumptive |
| HEO | Higher Executive Officer |
| HEQC | Higher Education Quality Council (*now see* QAA) |
| HERDA-SW | Higher Education Regional Development Association - South West |
| HERO | Higher Education Research Opportunities |
| Herts | Hertfordshire |
| HFEA | Human Fertilisation and Embryology Authority |
| HGTAC | Home Grown Timber Advisory Committee |
| HH | His (or Her) Highness; His Holiness; Member, Hesketh Hubbard Art Society |
| HHA | Historic Houses Association |
| HHD | Doctor of Humanities (US) |
| HI | Hawaii (postal) |
| HIH | His (or Her) Imperial Highness |
| HIllH | His (or Her) Illustrious Highness |
| HIM | His (or Her) Imperial Majesty |
| HIV | Human Immunodeficiency Virus |
| HJ | Hilal-e-Jurat (Pakistan) |
| HKIA | Hong Kong Institute of Architects |
| HKSAR | Hong Kong Special Administrative Region |
| HLD | Doctor of Humane Letters |
| HLF | Heritage Lottery Fund |
| HLI | Highland Light Infantry |
| HM | His (or Her) Majesty, or Majesty's |
| HMA | Head Masters' Association |
| HMAS | His (or Her) Majesty's Australian Ship |
| HMC | Headmasters' and Headmistresses' (*formerly* Headmasters') Conference; Hospital Management Committee |
| HMCIC | His (or Her) Majesty's Chief Inspector of Constabulary |
| HMCS | His (or Her) Majesty's Canadian Ship |
| HMHS | His (or Her) Majesty's Hospital Ship |
| HMI | His (or Her) Majesty's Inspector |
| HMMTB | His (or Her) Majesty's Motor Torpedo Boat |
| HMNZS | His (or Her) Majesty's New Zealand Ship |
| HMOCS | His (or Her) Majesty's Overseas Civil Service |
| HMP | His (or Her) Majesty's Prison |
| HMRC | His (or Her) Majesty's Revenue and Customs |
| HMS | His (or Her) Majesty's Ship |
| HMSO | His (or Her) Majesty's Stationery Office |
| HNC | Higher National Certificate |
| HND | Higher National Diploma |
| H of C | House of Commons |
| H of L | House of Lords |
| Hon. | Honourable; Honorary |
| HPA | Health Protection Agency |
| HPk | Hilal-e-Pakistan |
| HPV | Human Papilloma Virus |
| HQ | Headquarters |
| HQA | Hilali-Quaid-i-Azam (Pakistan) |
| HR | Human Resources |
| HRA | Horseracing Regulatory Authority |
| HRGI | Honorary Member, The Royal Glasgow Institute of the Fine Arts |
| HRH | His (or Her) Royal Highness |
| HRHA | Honorary Member, Royal Hibernian Academy |

| | |
|---|---|
| HRI | Honorary Member, Royal Institute of Painters in Water Colours |
| HROI | Honorary Member, Royal Institute of Oil Painters |
| HRSA | Honorary Member, Royal Scottish Academy |
| HRSW | Honorary Member, Royal Scottish Water Colour Society |
| HRUA | Hon. Member, Royal Ulster Academy |
| HSC | Health and Safety Commission; Higher School Certificate |
| HSE | Health and Safety Executive |
| HSH | His (or Her) Serene Highness |
| HSO | Higher Scientific Officer |
| HSS | Health and Social Services |
| Hum. | Humanity; Humanities (Classics) |
| Hunts | Huntingdonshire |
| HVCert | Health Visitor's Certificate |

# I

| | |
|---|---|
| I | Island; Ireland |
| IA | Indian Army; Iowa (postal) |
| IAA | International Academy of Architecture |
| IAAF | International Association of Athletics Federations (formerly International Amateur Athletic Federation) |
| IABSE | International Association of Bridge and Structural Engineers |
| IAC | Indian Armoured Corps; Institute of Amateur Cinematographers |
| IACP | International Association of Chiefs of Police |
| IACR | Institute of Arable Crops Research |
| IADB | Inter American Development Bank |
| IADR | International Association for Dental Research |
| IAEA | International Atomic Energy Agency |
| IAF | Indian Air Force; Indian Auxiliary Force |
| IAHS | International Association of Hydrological Sciences |
| IALD | Member, International Association of Lighting Designers |
| IAM | Institute of Advanced Motorists; Institute of Aviation Medicine |
| IAMAS | International Association of Meteorology and Atmospheric Sciences |
| IAMC | Indian Army Medical Corps |
| IAO | Incorporated Association of Organists |
| IAOC | Indian Army Ordnance Corps |
| IAPS | Independent Association of Prep Schools (*formerly* Incorporated Association of Preparatory Schools) |
| IAPSO | International Association for the Physical Sciences of the Oceans |
| IARO | Indian Army Reserve of Officers |
| IAS | Indian Administrative Service; Institute for Advanced Studies; International Academy of Science |
| IASC | International Arctic Science Committee |
| IASE | Institute of Advanced Studies in Education |
| IASPEI | International Association of Seismology and Physics of the Earth's Interior |
| IATA | International Air Transport Association |
| IATUL | International Association of Technological University Libraries |
| IAU | International Astronomical Union |
| IAVCEI | International Assembly of Volcanology and Chemistry of the Earth's Interior |
| IAWPRC | International Association on Water Pollution Research and Control |
| ib. or ibid. | *ibidem* (in the same place) |
| IB | International Baccalaureate |
| IBA | Independent Broadcasting Authority; International Bar Association |
| IBBY | International Board for Books for Young People |
| IBCA | International Braille Chess Association |
| IBG | Institute of British Geographers (now part of RGS) |
| IBRD | International Bank for Reconstruction and Development (World Bank) |
| IBRO | International Bank Research Organisation; International Brain Research Organisation |
| IBTE | Institution of British Telecommunications Engineers |
| IBVM | Institute of the Blessed Virgin Mary |
| i/c | in charge; in command |
| ICA | Institute of Contemporary Arts; Institute of Chartered Accountants in England and Wales (*now see* ICAEW) |
| ICAC | Independent Commission Against Corruption, Hong Kong |
| ICAEW | Institute of Chartered Accountants in England and Wales |
| ICAI | Institute of Chartered Accountants in Ireland |
| ICAO | International Civil Aviation Organization |
| ICAS | Institute of Chartered Accountants of Scotland |
| ICBP | International Council for Bird Preservation |
| ICC | International Chamber of Commerce; International Cricket Council (*formerly* International Cricket Conference) |
| ICCA | International Council for Commercial Arbitration |
| ICCROM | International Centre for Conservation at Rome |
| ICD | *Iuris Canonici Doctor* (Doctor of Canon Law); Independence Commemorative Decoration (Rhodesia) |
| ICD.D | Institute of Corporate Directors Director (Canada) |
| ICE | Institution of Civil Engineers |
| ICED | International Council for Educational Development |
| ICEF | International Federation of Chemical, Energy and General Workers' Unions |
| ICES | International Council for the Exploration of the Sea |
| ICF | International Federation of Chemical and General Workers' Unions (*now see* ICEF) |
| ICFC | Industrial and Commercial Finance Corporation (later part of Investors in Industry) |
| ICFR | International Centre for Financial Regulation |
| ICFTU | International Confederation of Free Trade Unions |
| ICH | International Conference on Harmonisation |
| ICHCA | International Cargo Handling Co-ordination Association |
| IChemE | Institution of Chemical Engineers |
| ICI | Imperial Chemical Industries |
| ICJ | International Commission of Jurists |
| ICL | International Computers Ltd |
| ICM | International Confederation of Midwives |
| ICMA | Institute of Cost and Management Accountants (*now see* CIMA) |
| ICNL | International Center for Not for Profit Law |
| ICOM | International Council of Museums |
| ICOMOS | International Council on Monuments and Sites |
| ICorrST | Institution of Corrosion Science and Technology (*now see* ICorr) |
| ICPO | International Criminal Police Organization (Interpol) |
| ICRC | International Committee of the Red Cross |
| ICREA | Institució Catalana de Recerca i Estudis Avançats |
| ICRF | Imperial Cancer Research Fund (*now see* CRUK) |
| ICS | Indian Civil Service |
| ICSA | Institute of Chartered Secretaries and Administrators |
| ICSD | International Council for Scientific Development |
| ICSID | International Council of Societies of Industrial Design; International Centre for Settlement of Investment Disputes |
| ICSM | Imperial College School of Medicine |
| ICSTIS | Independent Committee for Supervision of Telephone Information Services |
| ICSTM | Imperial College of Science, Technology and Medicine, London |
| ICSU | International Council for Science (*formerly* International Council of Scientific Unions) |
| ICT | International Computers and Tabulators Ltd (later ICL); Information and Communications Technology |
| ID | Independence Decoration (Rhodesia); Idaho (postal) |
| IDA | International Development Association |
| IDB | Internal Drainage Board; Industrial Development Board |
| IDC | Imperial Defence College (*now see* RCDS); Inter-Diocesan Certificate |
| idc | completed a course at, or served for a year on the Staff of, the Imperial Defence College (*now see* rcds) |
| IDDA | Interior Decorators and Designers Association (*now see* BIDA) |
| IDeA | Improvement and Development Agency for Local Government |
| IDRC | International Development Research Centre |
| IDS | Institute of Development Studies; Industry Department for Scotland |
| IEA | Institute of Economic Affairs |
| IEC | International Electrotechnical Commission |
| IED | Institution of Engineering Designers; improvised explosive device |
| IEE | Institution of Electrical Engineers (*now see* IET) |
| IEEE | Institute of Electrical and Electronics Engineers (NY) |
| IEEIE | Institution of Electrical and Electronics Incorporated Engineers (later IIE) |
| IEETE | Institution of Electrical and Electronics Technician Engineers (later IIE) |
| IEI | Institution of Engineers of Ireland |
| IEIE | Institution of Electronics and Electrical Incorporated Engineers (later IIE) |
| IEMA | Institute of Environmental Management Assessment |
| IEME | Inspectorate of Electrical and Mechanical Engineering |
| IEng | Incorporated Engineer |
| IERE | Institution of Electronic and Radio Engineers |
| IES | Indian Educational Service; Institution of Engineers and Shipbuilders in Scotland; International Electron Paramagnetic Resonance Society |
| IET | Institution of Engineering and Technology |
| IExpE | Institute of Explosives Engineers |
| IFAC | International Federation of Automatic Control; International Federation of Accountants |
| IFAD | International Fund for Agricultural Development (UNO) |
| IFAW | International Fund for Animal Welfare |
| IFBWW | International Federation of Building Woodworkers |
| IFC | International Finance Corporation |
| IFIAS | International Federation of Institutes of Advanced Study |
| IFIP | International Federation for Information Processing |
| IFLA | International Federation of Library Associations; Institute of Family Law Arbitrators |
| IFMGA | (Member of) International Federation of Mountain Guides Associations |
| IFOR | Implementation Force |
| IFORS | International Federation of Operational Research Societies |
| IFPI | International Federation of the Phonographic Industry |
| IFS | Irish Free State; Indian Forest Service; Institute for Fiscal Studies |
| IG | Instructor in Gunnery |
| IGasE | Institution of Gas Engineers |
| IGCSE | International General Certificate of Secondary Education |

| | | | |
|---|---|---|---|
| IGPP | Institute of Geophysics and Planetary Physics | IPE | International Petroleum Exchange |
| IGS | Independent Grammar School | IPFA | Member or Associate, Chartered Institute of Public Finance and Accountancy (*now see* CPFA) |
| IGU | International Geographical Union; International Gas Union | | |
| IHA | Institute of Health Service Administrators (later IHSM) | IPHE | Institution of Public Health Engineers (later IWEM) |
| IHBC | (Member of) Institute of Historic Building Conservation | IPI | International Press Institute; Institute of Patentees and Inventors |
| IHM | Institute of Healthcare Management | IPM | Institute of Personnel Management (later CIPD) |
| IHSM | Institute of Health Services Management (*now see* IHM) | IPPA | Independent Programme Producers' Association |
| IHVE | Institution of Heating and Ventilating Engineers (later CIBS) | IPPF | International Planned Parenthood Federation |
| IIE | Institution of Incorporated Engineers (*now see* IET) | IPPR | Institute for Public Policy Research |
| IIEB | Institut International d'Etudes Bancaires | IPPS | Institute of Physics and The Physical Society |
| IIExE | Institution of Incorporated Executive Engineers | IPR | Institute of Public Relations (*now see* CIPR) |
| IIM | Institution of Industrial Managers | IPRA | International Public Relations Association |
| IIRSM | International Institute of Risk and Safety Management | IProdE | Institution of Production Engineers (later Institution of Manufacturing Engineering) |
| IIS | International Institute of Sociology | | |
| IISI | International Iron and Steel Institute | IPS | Indian Police Service; Indian Political Service; Institute of Procurement (formerly Purchasing) and Supply |
| IISS | International Institute of Strategic Studies | | |
| IIT | Indian Institute of Technology | IPSM | Institute of Public Sector Managers |
| IL | Illinois (postal) | IPSO | Independent Press Standards Organisation |
| ILA | International Law Association | IPU | Inter-Parliamentary Union |
| ILAC | International Laboratory Accreditation Co-operation | IRA | Irish Republican Army |
| ILEA | Inner London Education Authority | IRAD | Institute for Research on Animal Diseases |
| Ill | Illinois | IRC | Industrial Reorganization Corporation; Interdisciplinary Research Centre |
| ILM | Institute of Leadership and Management | | |
| ILO | International Labour Office; International Labour Organisation | IRCAM | Institute for Research and Co-ordination in Acoustics and Music |
| ILP | Independent Labour Party | IRCert | Industrial Relations Certificate |
| ILR | Independent Local Radio; International Labour Review | IRI | Institution of the Rubber Industry (*now see* PRI) |
| ILTM | Member, Institute for Learning and Teaching in Higher Education (*now see* FHEA) | IRPA | International Radiation Protection Association |
| | | IRRV | (Member of) Institute of Revenues, Rating and Valuation |
| IM | Individual Merit | IRTE | Institute of Road Transport Engineers |
| IMA | International Music Association; Institute of Mathematics and its Applications | IS | International Society of Sculptors, Painters and Gravers; Information Systems |
| IMC | Instrument Meteorological Conditions | Is | Island(s) |
| IMCB | International Management Centre from Buckingham | ISAA | International Spill Response Accreditation Association |
| IMCO | Inter-Governmental Maritime Consultative Organization (*now see* IMO) | ISAF | International Sailing Federation; International Security Assistance Force |
| IME | Institute of Medical Ethics | ISAKOS | International Society for Arthroscopy and Knee Surgery |
| IMechE | Institution of Mechanical Engineers | ISBA | Incorporated Society of British Advertisers |
| IMechIE | Institution of Mechanical Incorporated Engineers (later IIE) | ISC | Imperial Service College, Haileybury; Indian Staff Corps; Independent Schools Council |
| IMEDE | Institut pour l'Etude des Méthodes de Direction de l'Entreprise | | |
| IMF | International Monetary Fund | ISCis | Independent Schools Council Information Service |
| IMGTechE | Institution of Mechanical and General Technician Engineers | ISCM | International Society for Contemporary Music |
| IMinE | Institution of Mining Engineers | ISCO | Independent Schools Careers Organisation |
| IMM | Institution of Mining and Metallurgy (*now see* IMMM) | ISI | International Statistical Institute; Independent Schools Inspectorate |
| IMMM | Institute of Materials, Minerals and Mining | | |
| IMO | International Maritime Organization | ISIL | Islamic State in Iraq and the Levant |
| Imp. | Imperial | ISIS | Independent Schools Information Service (*see now* ISCis) |
| IMRO | Investment Management Regulatory Organisation | ISJC | Independent Schools Joint Council (*now see* ISC) |
| IMS | Indian Medical Service; Institute of Management Services; International Military Staff | ISM | Incorporated Society of Musicians |
| | | ISMAR | International Society of Magnetic Resonance |
| IMTA | Institute of Municipal Treasurers and Accountants (*now see* CIPFA) | ISME | International Society for Musical Education |
| | | ISMP | International Senior Management Program |
| IMU | International Mathematical Union | ISO | Imperial Service Order; International Organization for Standardization |
| IMunE | Institution of Municipal Engineers (now amalgamated with Institution of Civil Engineers) | | |
| | | ISPRS | International Society for Photogrammetry and Remote Sensing |
| IN | Indian Navy; Indiana (postal) | ISSA | International Social Security Association |
| INASFMH | International Sports Association for People with Mental Handicap | ISTAR | Intelligence, Surveillance, Target Acquisition and Reconnaissance |
| Inc. | Incorporated | | |
| INCA | International Newspaper Colour Association | ISTC | Iron and Steel Trades Confederation; Institute of Scientific and Technical Communicators |
| Incog. | Incognito | | |
| Ind. | Independent | ISTD | Imperial Society of Teachers of Dancing; Institute for the Study and Treatment of Delinquency |
| Inf. | Infantry | | |
| INFORM | Information Network Focus on New Religious Movements | IStructE | Institution of Structural Engineers |
| INFORMS | Institute for Operations Research and the Management Sciences | ISVA | Incorporated Society of Valuers and Auctioneers |
| | | IT | Information Technology; Indian Territory (US) |
| INSA | Indian National Science Academy | It. or Ital. | Italian |
| INSEAD or Insead | Institut Européen d'Administration des Affaires | ITA | Independent Television Authority (later IBA) |
| | | ITAB | Information Technology Advisory Board |
| Insp. | Inspector | ITB | Industry Training Board |
| Inst. | Institute | ITC | International Trade Centre; Independent Television Commission |
| Instn | Institution | | |
| InstSMM | Institute of Sales and Marketing Management | ITCA | Independent Television Association (*formerly* Independent Television Companies Association Ltd) |
| INTELSAT | International Telecommunications Satellite Organisation | | |
| IOC | International Olympic Committee; Intergovernmental Oceanographic Commission | ITDG | Intermediate Technology Development Group |
| | | ITF | International Transport Workers' Federation; International Tennis Federation |
| IOCD | International Organisation for Chemical Science in Development | | |
| IoD | Institute of Directors | ITN | Independent Television News |
| I of M | Isle of Man | ITSA | Information Technology Services Agency |
| IOM | Isle of Man; Indian Order of Merit | ITU | International Telecommunication Union |
| IOP | Institute of Painters in Oil Colours | ITUC | International Trade Union Confederation |
| IOSCO | International Organisation of Securities Commissions | ITV | Independent Television |
| IOSH | Institution of Occupational Safety and Health | ITVA | International Television Association |
| IOTA | (Fellow of) Institute of Transport Administration | IUA | International Union of Architects |
| IoW | Isle of Wight | IUB | International Union of Biochemistry (*now see* IUBMB) |
| IP | Intellectual Property | IUBMB | International Union of Biochemistry and Molecular Biology |
| IPA | International Publishers' Association | IUC | Inter-University Council for Higher Education Overseas (*now see* IUPC) |
| IPC | International Property Corporation | | |
| IPCC | Intergovernmental Panel on Climate Change | IUCN | International Union for Conservation of Nature (*formerly* International Union for the Conservation of Nature and Natural Resources, then World Conservation Union) |
| IPCIS | International Institute for Practitioners in Credit Insurance and Surety | | |

| | |
|---|---|
| IUF | International Union of Food, Agricultural, Hotel, Restaurant, Catering, Tobacco and Allied Workers' Associations |
| IUGG | International Union of Geodesy & Geophysics |
| IUGS | International Union of Geological Sciences |
| IUHPS | International Union of the History and Philosophy of Science |
| IULA | International Union of Local Authorities |
| IUPAB | International Union of Pure and Applied Biophysics |
| IUPAC | International Union of Pure and Applied Chemistry |
| IUPAP | International Union of Pure and Applied Physics |
| IUPC | Inter-University and Polytechnic Council for Higher Education Overseas |
| IUPS | International Union of Physiological Sciences |
| IUSSP | International Union for the Scientific Study of Population |
| IUTAM | International Union of Theoretical and Applied Mechanics |
| IVF | In-vitro Fertilisation |
| IVS | International Voluntary Service |
| IWA | Inland Waterways Association |
| IWEM | Institution of Water and Environmental Management (*now see* CIWEM) |
| IWES | Institution of Water Engineers and Scientists (later IWEM) |
| IWGC | Imperial War Graves Commission (*now see* CWGC) |
| IWM | Institution of Works Managers (*now see* IIM) |
| IWO | Institution of Water Officers |
| IWPC | Institute of Water Pollution Control (later IWEM) |
| IWSA | International Water Supply Association |
| IWSOM | Institute of Practitioners in Work Study Organisation and Methods (*now see* IMS) |
| IWSP | Institute of Work Study Practitioners (*now see* IMS) |
| IYRU | International Yacht Racing Union (*now see* ISAF) |
| IZ | I Zingari |

# J

| | |
|---|---|
| JA | Judge Advocate |
| JACT | Joint Association of Classical Teachers |
| JAG | Judge Advocate General |
| Jas | James |
| JCB | *Juris Canonici* (or *Civilis*) *Baccalaureus* (Bachelor of Canon (or Civil) Law) |
| JCR | Junior Common Room |
| JCS | Journal of the Chemical Society |
| JCD | *Juris Canonici* (or *Civilis*) *Doctor* (Doctor of Canon (or Civil) Law) |
| JCHMT | Joint Committee on Higher Medical Training, Royal Medical Colleges (*now see* JRCPTB) |
| JCI | Junior Chamber International |
| JCL | *Juris Canonici* (or *Civilis*) *Licentiatus* (Licentiate in Canon (or Civil) Law) |
| JCO | Joint Consultative Organisation (of AFRC, MAFF, and Department of Agriculture and Fisheries for Scotland) |
| JCPTGP | Joint Committee on Postgraduate Training for General Practice |
| JD | Doctor of Jurisprudence |
| jd | *jure dignitatis* (by virtue of status) |
| JDipMA | Joint Diploma in Management Accounting Services |
| JG | Junior Grade |
| JILA | Joint Institute for Laboratory Astrophysics |
| JInstE | Junior Institution of Engineers (*now see* IMGTechE) |
| JISC or Jisc | Joint Information Systems Committee, Higher Education Funding Council |
| jl(s) | journal(s) |
| JMB | Joint Matriculation Board |
| JMN | Johan Mangku Negara (Malaysia) |
| JMOTS | Joint Maritime Operational Training Staff |
| JNCC | Joint Nature Conservation Committee |
| Jno. or Joh. | John |
| JP | Justice of the Peace |
| Jr | Junior |
| JRCPTB | Joint Royal Colleges of Physicians Training Board |
| jsc | qualified at a Junior Staff Course, or the equivalent, 1942-46 |
| JSCSC | Joint Services Command and Staff College |
| jscsc | completed a course at Joint Services Command and Staff College |
| JSD | Doctor of Juristic Science |
| JSDC | Joint Service Defence College |
| jsdc | completed a course at Joint Service Defence College |
| JSLO | Joint Service Liaison Officer |
| JSLS | Joint Services Liaison Staff |
| JSM | Johan Setia Mahkota (Malaysia); Master of the Science of Jurisprudence |
| JSPS | Japan Society for the Promotion of Science |
| JSSC | Joint Services Staff College |
| jssc | completed a course at Joint Services Staff College |
| JSU | Joint Support Unit |
| jt, jtly | joint, jointly |
| JUD | *Juris Utriusque Doctor* (Doctor of Both Laws (Canon and Civil)) |
| Jun. | Junior |
| Jun.Opt. | Junior Optime |
| JWS or jws | Joint Warfare Staff |

# K

| | |
|---|---|
| KA | Knight of St Andrew, Order of Barbados |
| Kans | Kansas |
| KAR | King's African Rifles |
| KBE | Knight Commander, Order of the British Empire |
| KC | King's Counsel |
| KCB | Knight Commander, Order of the Bath |
| KCC | Commander, Order of the Crown, Belgium and Congo Free State |
| KCGSJ | Knight Commander of Magisterial Grace, Order of St John of Jerusalem (Knights Hospitaller) |
| KCH | King's College Hospital; Knight Commander, Hanoverian Order |
| KCHS | Knight Commander, Order of the Holy Sepulchre |
| KCIE | Knight Commander, Order of the Indian Empire |
| KCJSJ | Knight Commander of Justice, Sovereign Order of St John of Jerusalem (Knights Hospitaller) |
| KCL | King's College London |
| KCLJ | Knight Commander, Order of St Lazarus of Jerusalem |
| KCMG | Knight Commander, Order of St Michael and St George |
| KCN | Knight Commander, Most Distinguished Order of the Nation (Antigua and Barbuda) |
| KCSA | Knight Commander, Military Order of the Collar of St Agatha of Paternò |
| KCSG | Knight Commander, Order of St Gregory the Great |
| KCSHS or KC*HS | Knight Commander with Star, Order of the Holy Sepulchre |
| KCSI | Knight Commander, Order of the Star of India |
| KCSJ | Knight Commander, Sovereign Order of St John of Jerusalem (Knights Hospitaller) |
| KCSS | Knight Commander, Order of St Silvester |
| KCVO | Knight Commander, Royal Victorian Order |
| KEO | King Edward's Own |
| KFOR | Kosovo Force |
| KG | Knight, Order of the Garter |
| KGB | Komitet Gosudarstvennoi Bezopanosti (Committee of State Security, USSR) |
| KGCHS | Knight Grand Cross, Order of the Holy Sepulchre |
| KGCN | Knight Grand Cross, Most Distinguished Order of the Nation (Antigua and Barbuda) |
| KGCSS | Knight Grand Cross, Order of St Silvester |
| KGN | Knight Grand Collar, Most Distinguished Order of the Nation (Antigua and Barbuda) |
| KGSJ | Knight of Grace, Sovereign Order of St John of Jerusalem (Knights Hospitaller) |
| KGStJ | Knight of Grace, Order of St John of Jerusalem (*now see* KStJ) |
| KHC | Hon. Chaplain to the King |
| KHDS | Hon. Dental Surgeon to the King |
| KHP | Hon. Physician to the King |
| KHS | Hon. Surgeon to the King; Knight, Order of the Holy Sepulchre |
| K-i-H | Kaisar-i-Hind |
| KJSJ | Knight of Justice, Sovereign Order of St John of Jerusalem (Knights Hospitaller) |
| KJStJ | Knight of Justice, Order of St John of Jerusalem (*now see* KStJ) |
| KLJ | Knight, Order of St Lazarus of Jerusalem |
| KM | Knight of Malta |
| KMJ | Knight, Supreme Military Order of the Temple of Jerusalem |
| KMLJ | Knight of Merit, Order of St Lazarus of Jerusalem |
| KNH | Knight Companion, Most Exalted Order of National Hero (Antigua and Barbuda) |
| KNZM | Knight Companion, New Zealand Order of Merit |
| KOM | Companion, National Order of Merit (Malta) |
| KORR | King's Own Royal Regiment |
| KOSB | King's Own Scottish Borderers |
| KOYLI | King's Own Yorkshire Light Infantry |
| KP | Knight, Order of St Patrick |
| KPM | King's Police Medal |
| KrF | Kristelig Folkeparti |
| KRRC | King's Royal Rifle Corps |
| KS | King's Scholar; Kansas (postal) |
| KSC | Knight of St Columba |
| KSG | Knight, Order of St Gregory the Great |
| KSJ | Knight, Sovereign Order of St John of Jerusalem (Knights Hospitaller) |
| KSLI | King's Shropshire Light Infantry |
| KSMOM | Knight Grand Cross with Star, Sovereign Military Order of Malta |
| KSS | Knight, Order of St Sylvester |
| KStJ | Knight, Most Venerable Order of the Hospital of St John of Jerusalem |
| KStJ(A) | Associate Knight of Justice, Most Venerable Order of the Hospital of St John of Jerusalem |
| KT | Knight, Order of the Thistle |
| Kt | Knight |
| KUOM | Companion of Honour, National Order of Merit (Malta) |
| KY | Kentucky (postal) |
| Ky | Kentucky |

# L

| | |
|---|---|
| L | Liberal |
| LA | Los Angeles; Library Association; Liverpool Academy; Louisiana (postal) |
| La | Louisiana |
| LAA | Light Anti-Aircraft |
| Lab | Labour |
| LAC | London Athletic Club; Los Angeles County |
| LACSAB | Local Authorities Conditions of Service Advisory Board |
| LAMDA | London Academy of Music and Dramatic Art |
| LAMTPI | Legal Associate Member, Town Planning Institute (*now see* LMRTPI) |
| Lance-Corp. | Lance-Corporal |
| Lancs | Lancashire |
| LAPADA | London & Provincial Antique Dealers' Association |
| LARSP | Language Assessment, Remediation and Screening Procedure |
| LARTPI | Legal Associate, Royal Town Planning Institute |
| Lautro | Life Assurance and Unit Trust Regulatory Organisation |
| LBC | London Broadcasting Company; London Borough Council |
| LBHI | Licentiate, British Horological Institute |
| LBIPP | Licentiate, British Institute of Professional Photography |
| LC | Cross of Leo |
| LCA | Licensed Companies Auditor |
| LCAD | London Certificate in Art and Design (University of London) |
| LCC | London County Council (later GLC) |
| LCCI | London Chamber of Commerce and Industry |
| LCD | Lord Chancellor's Department |
| LCh | Licentiate in Surgery |
| LCL | Licentiate of Canon Law |
| LCM | (Member of) London College of Music and Media |
| LCP | Licentiate, College of Preceptors |
| LCST | Licentiate, College of Speech Therapists |
| LD | Liberal and Democratic; Licentiate in Divinity |
| LDDC | London Docklands Development Corporation |
| LDiv | Licentiate in Divinity |
| LDP | Liberal Democratic Party (Japan) |
| Ldr | Leader |
| LDS | Licentiate in Dental Surgery |
| LDV | Local Defence Volunteers |
| LEA | Local Education Authority |
| LEAD | Leadership in Environment and Development |
| LEADR | Lawyers Engaged in Alternative Dispute Resolution |
| LEDU | Local Enterprise Development Unit |
| LEP | Local Ecumenical Project; Local Enterprise Partnership |
| LEPRA | British Leprosy Relief Association |
| LèsL | Licencié ès lettres |
| LèsSc | Licencié ès Sciences |
| LG | Lady Companion, Order of the Garter |
| LGA | Local Government Association |
| LGBT | Lesbian, gay, bisexual and transgender |
| LGBTI | Lesbian, gay, bisexual, transgender and intersex |
| LGBTQ | Lesbian, gay, bisexual, transgender and queer or questioning |
| LGSM | Licentiate, Guildhall School of Music and Drama |
| LGTB | Local Government Training Board |
| LH | Light Horse |
| LHD | *Literarum Humaniorum Doctor* (Doctor of Literature) |
| LHSM | Licentiate, Institute of Health Services Management |
| LI | Light Infantry; Long Island |
| LIBA | Lloyd's Insurance Brokers' Association |
| Lib Dem | Liberal Democrat |
| LIBER | Ligue des Bibliothèques Européennes de Recherche |
| LicMed | Licentiate in Medicine |
| Lieut | Lieutenant |
| LIFFE | London International Financial Futures and Options Exchange |
| LIFT | Local Improvement Finance Trust |
| LIMA | Licentiate, Institute of Mathematics and its Applications; International Licensing Industry Merchandisers' Association |
| Lincs | Lincolnshire |
| LIOB | Licentiate, Institute of Building |
| LISTD | Licentiate, Imperial Society of Teachers of Dancing |
| Lit. | Literature; Literary |
| LitD | Doctor of Literature; Doctor of Letters |
| Lit.Hum. | *Literae Humaniores* (Classics) |
| LittD | Doctor of Literature; Doctor of Letters |
| LJ | Lord Justice |
| LLAM | Licentiate, London Academy of Music and Dramatic Art |
| LLB | Bachelor of Laws |
| LLC | Limited Liability Company |
| LLCM | Licentiate, London College of Music |
| LLD | Doctor of Laws |
| LLL | Licentiate in Laws |
| LLM | Master of Laws |
| LLP | Limited Liability Partnership |
| LLSC | Local Learning and Skills Council |
| LM | Licentiate in Midwifery |
| LMBC | Lady Margaret Boat Club |
| LMC | Local Medical Committee |
| LMCC | Licentiate, Medical Council of Canada |
| LMed | Licentiate in Medicine |
| LMH | Lady Margaret Hall, Oxford |
| LMR | London Midland Region (BR) |
| LMS | London, Midland and Scottish Railway; London Missionary Society; London Mathematical Society |
| LMSSA | Licentiate in Medicine and Surgery, Society of Apothecaries |
| LMRTPI | Legal Member, Royal Town Planning Institute |
| LNat | Liberal National |
| LNER | London and North Eastern Railway |
| LOCOG | London Organising Committee of the Olympic and Paralympic Games |
| L of C | Library of Congress; Lines of Communication |
| LP | Limited Partnership |
| LPh | Licentiate in Philosophy |
| LPO | London Philharmonic Orchestra |
| LPTB | London Passenger Transport Board (later LTE) |
| LRAD | Licentiate, Royal Academy of Dancing |
| LRAM | Licentiate, Royal Academy of Music |
| LRCP | Licentiate, Royal College of Physicians, London |
| LRCPE | Licentiate, Royal College of Physicians, Edinburgh |
| LRCPI | Licentiate, Royal College of Physicians of Ireland |
| LRCPSGlas | Licentiate, Royal College of Physicians and Surgeons of Glasgow |
| LRCS | Licentiate, Royal College of Surgeons of England |
| LRCSE | Licentiate, Royal College of Surgeons, Edinburgh |
| LRCSI | Licentiate, Royal College of Surgeons in Ireland |
| LRelSc | Licentiate in Religious Sciences |
| LRFPS(G) | Licentiate, Royal Faculty of Physicians and Surgeons, Glasgow (*now see* LRCPSGlas) |
| LRIBA | Licentiate, Royal Institute of British Architects (*now see* RIBA) |
| LRPS | Licentiate, Royal Photographic Society |
| LRSM | Licentiate, Royal Schools of Music |
| LRT | London Regional Transport |
| LSA | Licentiate, Society of Apothecaries; Licence in Agricultural Sciences |
| LSC | Learning and Skills Council |
| LSE | London School of Economics and Political Science |
| LSHTM | London School of Hygiene and Tropical Medicine |
| LSO | London Symphony Orchestra |
| LSS | Licentiate in Sacred Scripture |
| Lt | Lieutenant; Light |
| LT | Lady, Order of the Thistle; London Transport (later LRT); Licentiate in Teaching |
| LTA | Lawn Tennis Association |
| LTB | London Transport Board (later LTE) |
| LTCL | Licentiate of Trinity College of Music, London |
| Lt Col | Lieutenant Colonel |
| LTE | London Transport Executive (later LRT) |
| Lt Gen. | Lieutenant General |
| LTh | Licentiate in Theology |
| LTS | London Topographical Society |
| LU | Liberal Unionist |
| LUOTC | London University Officers' Training Corps |
| LVO | Lieutenant, Royal Victorian Order (*formerly* MVO (Fourth Class)) |
| LWT | London Weekend Television |
| LXX | Septuagint |

# M

| | |
|---|---|
| M | Marquess; Member; Monsieur |
| m | married |
| MA | Master of Arts; Military Assistant; Massachusetts (postal) |
| MAAT | Member, Association of Accounting Technicians |
| MACE | Member, Australian College of Education; Member, Association of Conference Executives |
| MACM | Member, Association of Computing Machines |
| MACS | Member, American Chemical Society |
| MADO | Member, Association of Dispensing Opticians |
| MAE | Member, Academia Europaea |
| MAF | Ministry of Agriculture and Fisheries |
| MAFF | Ministry of Agriculture, Fisheries and Food |
| MAHL | Master of Arts in Hebrew Letters |
| MAI | *Magister in Arte Ingeniaria* (Master of Engineering) |
| MAIAA | Member, American Institute of Aeronautics and Astronautics |
| MAIBC | Member, Architectural Institute of British Columbia |
| MAICD | Member, Australian Institute of Company Directors |
| Maj. Gen. | Major General |
| MALD | Master of Arts in Law and Diplomacy |
| Man | Manitoba |
| M&A | Mergers and Acquisitions |
| MAO | Master of Obstetric Art |
| MAOT | Member, Association of Occupational Therapists |
| MAOU | Member, American Ornithologists' Union |

| | |
|---|---|
| MAP | Ministry of Aircraft Production |
| MAPM | Member, Association for Project Management |
| MAppSc | Master of Applied Science |
| MAPsS | Member, Australian Psychological Society |
| MARAC | Member, Australian Register of Agricultural Consultants |
| MArch | Master of Architecture |
| MARIS | Multi-State Aquatic Resources Information System |
| Marq. | Marquess |
| MAS | Minimal Access Surgery |
| MASc | Master of Applied Science |
| MASCE | Member, American Society of Civil Engineers |
| MASME | Member, American Society of Mechanical Engineers |
| Mass | Massachusetts |
| MAT | Master of Arts and Teaching (US) |
| MATh | Master of Arts in Theology |
| Math. | Mathematics; Mathematical |
| MAusIMM | Member, Australasian Institute of Mining and Metallurgy |
| MB | Medal of Bravery (Canada); Bachelor of Medicine; Manitoba (postal) |
| MBA | Master of Business Administration |
| MBASW | Member, British Association of Social Workers |
| MBC | Metropolitan/Municipal Borough Council |
| MBCS | Member, British Computer Society |
| MBE | Member, Order of the British Empire |
| MBES | Member, Biological Engineering Society |
| MBFR | Mutual and Balanced Force Reductions (negotiations) |
| MBHI | Member, British Horological Institute |
| MBIFD | Member, British Institute of Funeral Directors |
| MBII | Member, British Institute of Innkeeping |
| MBIID | Member, British Institute of Interior Design |
| MBIM | Member, British Institute of Management (later MIMgt) |
| MBKS | Member, British Kinematograph Society (*now see* MBKSTS) |
| MBKSTS | Member, British Kinematograph, Sound and Television Society |
| MBL | Master of Business Leadership |
| MBOU | Member, British Ornithologists' Union |
| MBPsS | Graduate Member, British Psychological Society |
| MBritIRE | Member, British Institution of Radio Engineers (later MIERE) |
| MBS | Member, Building Societies Institute (*now see* MCBSI) |
| MBSc | Master of Business Science |
| MC | Military Cross; Missionaries of Charity |
| MCB | Master in Clinical Biochemistry; Muslim Council of Britain |
| MCBSI | Member, Chartered Building Societies Institute |
| MCC | Marylebone Cricket Club; Metropolitan County Council |
| MCCDRCS | Member in Clinical Community Dentistry, Royal College of Surgeons |
| MCD | Master of Civic Design |
| MCE | Master of Civil Engineering |
| MCFP | Member, College of Family Physicians (Canada) |
| MCGI | Member, City and Guilds of London Institute |
| MCh or MChir | Master in Surgery |
| MChD | Master of Dental Surgery |
| MChE | Master of Chemical Engineering |
| MChemA | Master in Chemical Analysis |
| MChOrth | Master of Orthopaedic Surgery |
| MCIArb | Member, Chartered Institute of Arbitrators |
| MCIBS | Member, Chartered Institution of Building Services (*now see* MCIBSE); Member, Chartered Institute of Bankers in Scotland |
| MCIBSE | Member, Chartered Institution of Building Services Engineers |
| MCICM | Member, Chartered Institute of Credit Management |
| MCIEEM | Member, Chartered Institute of Ecology and Environmental Management |
| MCIfA | Member, Chartered Institute for Archaeologists |
| MCIH | Member, Chartered Institute of Housing |
| MCIHort | Member, Chartered Institute of Horticulture |
| MCIHT | Member, Chartered Institution of Highways & Transportation |
| MCIJ | Member, Chartered Institute of Journalists |
| MCIL | Member, Chartered Institute of Linguists |
| MCIM | Member, Chartered Institute of Marketing |
| MCIMarE | Member, Canadian Institute of Marine Engineers |
| MCIOB | Member, Chartered Institute of Building |
| MCIPD | Member, Charted Institute of Personnel and Development |
| MCIPR | Member, Charted Institute of Public Relations |
| MCIPS | Member, Chartered Institute of Procurement (formerly Purchasing) and Supply |
| MCIS | Member, Institute of Chartered Secretaries and Administrators |
| MCIT | Member, Chartered Institute of Transport (*now see* CMILT) |
| MCIWEM | Member, Chartered Institution of Water and Environmental Management |
| MCIWM | Member, Chartered Institution of Wastes Management |
| MCL | Master in Civil Law |
| MCLIP | Member, Chartered Institute of Library and Information Professionals |
| MCMI | Member, Chartered Management Institute |
| MCollP | Member, College of Preceptors |
| MCom | Master of Commerce |
| MCommH | Master of Community Health |
| MConsE | Member, Association of Consulting Engineers |
| MConsEI | Member, Association of Consulting Engineers of Ireland |
| MCOphth | Member, College of Ophthalmologists (*now see* MRCOphth) |
| MCP | Member of Colonial Parliament; Master of City Planning (US) |
| MCPA | Member, College of Pathologists of Australia (*now see* MRCPA) |
| MCPP | Member, College of Pharmacy Practice |
| MCPS | Member, College of Physicians and Surgeons |
| MCS | Malayan Civil Service |
| MCSD | Member, Chartered Society of Designers |
| MCSEE | Member, Canadian Society of Electrical Engineers |
| MCSI | Member, Chartered Institute for Securities & Investment |
| MCSP | Member, Chartered Society of Physiotherapy |
| MCST | Member, College of Speech Therapists |
| MCT | Member, Association of Corporate Treasurers |
| MD | Doctor of Medicine; Military District; Maryland (postal) |
| Md | Maryland |
| MDA | Masters in Defence Administration |
| MDC | Metropolitan District Council |
| MDes | Master of Design |
| MDiv | Master of Divinity |
| MDS | Master of Dental Surgery |
| MDSc | Master of Dental Science |
| ME | Mining Engineer; Middle East; Master of Engineering; Maine (postal); Myalgic Encephalomyelitis |
| MEAF | Middle East Air Force |
| MEC | Member of Executive Council; Middle East Command |
| MEc | Master of Economics |
| MECAS | Middle East Centre for Arab Studies |
| Mech. | Mechanics; Mechanical |
| MECI | Member, Institute of Employment Consultants |
| Med. | Medical |
| MEd | Master of Education |
| MED | Master of Environmental Design |
| MEdSt | Master of Educational Studies |
| MEF | Middle East Force |
| MEI | Member, Energy Institute |
| MEIC | Member, Engineering Institute of Canada |
| MELF | Middle East Land Forces |
| Mencap | Royal Society for Mentally Handicapped Children and Adults |
| MEng | Master of Engineering |
| MEnvS | Master of Environmental Studies |
| MEO | Marine Engineering Officer |
| MEP | Member of the European Parliament |
| MES | Master of Environmental Studies |
| MESc | Master of Engineering Science |
| MetSoc | Metals Society (formed by amalgamation of Institute of Metals and Iron and Steel Institute; now merged with Institution of Metallurgists to form Institute of Metals) |
| MF | Master of Forestry |
| MFA | Master of Fine Arts |
| MFC | Mastership in Food Control |
| MFCM | Member, Faculty of Community Medicine (later MFPHM) |
| MFFLM | Member, Faculty of Forensic and Legal Medicine, Royal College of Physicians |
| MFFP | Member, Faculty of Family Planning, Royal College of Obstetricians and Gynaecologists |
| MFGB | Miners' Federation of Great Britain (*now see* NUM) |
| MFGDP | Member, Faculty of General Dental Practitioners, Royal College of Surgeons |
| MFH | Master of Foxhounds |
| MFHom | Member, Faculty of Homoeopathy |
| MFOM | Member, Faculty of Occupational Medicine |
| MFPaed | Member, Faculty of Paediatrics, Royal College of Physicians of Ireland |
| MFPH | Member, Faculty of Public Health |
| MFPHM | Member, Faculty of Public Health Medicine (*now see* MFPH) |
| MFPHMI | Member, Faculty of Public Health Medicine of Ireland |
| MFPM | Member, Faculty of Pharmaceutical Medicine |
| MGDSRCS | Member in General Dental Surgery, Royal College of Surgeons |
| MGI | Member, Institute of Certificated Grocers |
| MGO | Master General of the Ordnance; Master of Gynaecology and Obstetrics |
| Mgr | Monsignor |
| MHA | Member of House of Assembly; Master of Health Administration |
| MHCIMA | Member, Hotel Catering and International (*formerly* Institutional) Management Association (*now see* MIH) |
| MHCLG | Ministry of Housing, Communities and Local Government |
| MHK | Member of the House of Keys |
| MHM | Master of Health Management |
| MHort (RHS) | Master of Horticulture, Royal Horticultural Society |
| MHR | Member of the House of Representatives |
| MHRA | Modern Humanities Research Association |
| MHSM | Member, Institute of Health Services Management (*now see* MIHM) |
| MI | Military Intelligence; Michigan (postal) |
| MIAeE | Member, Institute of Aeronautical Engineers |
| MIAgrE | Member, Institution of Agricultural Engineers |
| MIAM | Member, Institute of Administrative Management |

| | | | |
|---|---|---|---|
| MIAS | Member, Institute of Aeronautical Science (US) (*now see* MAIAA); Member, Institute of Architects and Surveyors | MInstBE | Member, Institution of British Engineers |
| MIBC | Member, Institute of Business Counsellors; Member, Institute of Building Control | MInstCE | Member, Institution of Civil Engineers (*now see* FICE) |
| | | MInstD | Member, Institute of Directors |
| MIBiol | Member, Institute of Biology (later MSB, *now see* MRSB) | MInstE | Member, Institute of Energy (*now see* MEI) |
| MICE | Member, Institution of Civil Engineers | MInstF | Member, Institute of Fuel (later MInstE) |
| MICEI | Member, Institution of Civil Engineers of Ireland | MInstHE | Member, Institution of Highway Engineers (later MIHT, *now see* MCIHT) |
| MICeram | Member, Institute of Ceramics (later MIM) | | |
| MICFor | Member, Institute of Chartered Foresters | MInstKT | Member, Institute of Knowledge Transfer |
| Mich | Michigan | MInstLM | Member, Institute of Leadership and Management |
| MIChemE | Member, Institution of Chemical Engineers | MInstM | Member, Institute of Marketing (*now see* MCIM) |
| MICM | Member, Institute of Credit Management (*now see* MCICM) | MInstMC | Member, Institute of Measurement and Control |
| MICorr | Member, Institute of Corrosion | MInstME | Member, Institution of Mining Engineers |
| MICorrST | Member, Institution of Corrosion Science and Technology (*now see* MICorr) | MInstMet | Member, Institute of Metals (later part of Metals Society; then MIM) |
| MICS | Member, Institute of Chartered Shipbrokers | MInstP | Member, Institute of Physics |
| MIE(Aust) | Member, Institution of Engineers, Australia | MInstPet | Member, Institute of Petroleum (*now see* MEI) |
| MIED | Member, Institution of Engineering Designers | MInstPkg | Member, Institute of Packaging |
| MIEE | Member, Institution of Electrical Engineers (*now see* MIET) | MInstPS | Member, Institute of Purchasing and Supply |
| | | MInstRA | Member, Institute of Registered Architects |
| MIEEE | Member, Institute of Electrical and Electronics Engineers (NY) | MInstRE | Member, Institution of Royal Engineers |
| | | MInstT | Member, Institute of Transport (later MCIT) |
| MIEEM | Member, Institute of Ecology and Environmental Management (*now see* MCIEEM) | MInstTA | Member, Institute of Transport Administration |
| | | MInstW | Member, Institute of Welding (*now see* MWeldI) |
| MIEI | Member, Institution of Engineering Inspection | MInstWM | Member, Institute of Wastes Management (*now see* MCIWM) |
| MIEMA | Member, Institute of Environmental Management and Assessment | MINucE | Member, Institution of Nuclear Engineers (*now see* MNucI) |
| | | MIOA | Member, Institute of Acoustics |
| MIEMgt | Member, Institute of Environmental Management (*now see* MIEMA) | MIOB | Member, Institute of Building (*now see* MCIOB) |
| | | MIOM | Member, Institute of Office Management (*now see* MIAM) |
| MIEnvSc | Member, Institution of Environmental Sciences | MIOSH | Member, Institution of Occupational Safety and Health |
| MIERE | Member, Institution of Electronic and Radio Engineers (later MIEE) | MIPA | Member, Institute of Practitioners in Advertising |
| | | MIPD | Member, Institute of Personnel and Development (*now see* MCIPD) |
| MIES | Member, Institution of Engineers and Shipbuilders, Scotland | | |
| MIET | Member, Institute of Engineering and Technology (*formerly* Member, Institute of Engineers and Technicians) | MIPEM | Member, Institute of Physics and Engineering in Medicine |
| | | MIPlantE | Member, Institution of Plant Engineers |
| MIEx | Member, Institute of Export | MIPM | Member, Institute of Personnel Management (later MIPD) |
| MIExpE | Member, Institute of Explosives Engineers | MIPR | Member, Institute of Public Relations (*now see* MCIPR) |
| MIfA | Member, Institute for Archaeologists (*now see* MCIfA) | MIProdE | Member, Institution of Production Engineers (later MIEE) |
| MIFA | Member, Institute of Field Archaeologists (later MIfA) | MIQ | Member, Institute of Quarrying |
| MIFF | Member, Institute of Freight Forwarders (*now see* MIFP) | MIQA | Member, Institute of Quality Assurance |
| MIFireE | Member, Institution of Fire Engineers | MIRE | Member, Institution of Radio Engineers (later MIERE) |
| MIFM | Member, Institute of Fisheries Management | MIREE(Aust) | Member, Institution of Radio and Electronics Engineers (Australia) |
| MIFor | Member, Institute of Foresters (*now see* MICFor) | | |
| MIFP | Member, Institute of Freight Professionals | MIRM | Member, Institute of Risk Management |
| MIGasE | Member, Institution of Gas Engineers (*now see* MIGEM) | MIRO | Mineral Industry Research Organisation; Member, Institution of Railway Operators |
| MIGEM | Member, Institution of Gas Engineers and Managers | | |
| MIGeol | Member, Institution of Geologists | MIRPM | Member, Institute of Residential Property Management |
| MIH | Member, Institute of Housing (*now see* MCIH); Member, Institute of Hospitality | MIRT | Member, Institute of Reprographic Technicians |
| | | MIRTE | Member, Institute of Road Transport Engineers |
| MIHM | Member, Institute of Housing Managers (later MIH); Member, Institute of Healthcare Management | MIS | Member, Institute of Statisticians |
| | | MISI | Member, Iron and Steel Institute (later part of Metals Society) |
| MIHort | Member, Institute of Horticulture (*now see* MCIHort) | Miss | Mississippi |
| MIHT | Member, Institution of Highways and Transportation (*now see* MCIHT) | MIStructE | Member, Institution of Structural Engineers |
| | | MIT | Massachusetts Institute of Technology |
| MIHVE | Member, Institution of Heating and Ventilating Engineers (later MCIBS) | MITA | Member, Industrial Transport Association |
| | | MITD | Member, Institute of Training and Development (later MIPD) |
| MIIA | Member, Institute of Industrial Administration (later FBIM) | MITE | Member, Institution of Electrical and Electronics Technician Engineers |
| MIIE | Member, Institute of Incorporated Engineers in Electronic, Electrical and Mechanical Engineering (*now see* MIET) | | |
| | | MITI | Member, Institute of Translation & Interpreting |
| MIIM | Member, Institution of Industrial Managers | MITSA | Member, Institute of Trading Standards Administration |
| MIInfSc | Member, Institute of Information Sciences (*now see* MCLIP) | MITT | Member, Institute of Travel and Tourism |
| MIL | Member, Institute of Linguists (*now see* MCIL) | MIWE | Member, Institution of Water Engineers (later MIWES) |
| Mil. | Military | MIWEM | Member, Institution of Water and Environmental Management (*now see* MCIWEM) |
| MILGA | Member, Institute of Local Government Administrators | | |
| MILocoE | Member, Institution of Locomotive Engineers | MIWES | Member, Institution of Water Engineers and Scientists (later MIWEM) |
| MILog | Member, Institute of Logistics (*now see* MILT) | | |
| MILT | Member, Chartered Institute of Logistics and Transport | MIWM | Member, Institution of Works Managers (*now see* MIIM) |
| MIM | Member, Institute of Materials (*formerly* Institution of Metallurgists, then Institute of Metals) (*now see* MIMMM) | MIWPC | Member, Institute of Water Pollution Control (later MIWEM) |
| | | MIWSP | Member, Institute of Work Study Practitioners (*now see* MMS) |
| MIMA | Member, Institute of Mathematics and its Applications | MJA | Medical Journalists Association |
| MIMarE | Member, Institute of Marine Engineers (*now see* MIMarEST) | MJI | Member, Institute of Journalists (*now see* MCIJ) |
| MIMarEST | Member, Institute of Marine Engineering, Science and Technology | MJIE | Member, Junior Institution of Engineers (*now see* MIGTechE) |
| | | MJur | *Magister Juris* (Master of Law) |
| MIMC | Member, Institute of Management Consultants | ML | Licentiate in Medicine; Master of Laws |
| MIMechE | Member, Institution of Mechanical Engineers | MLA | Member of Legislative Assembly; Modern Language Association; Master in Landscape Architecture; Museums, Libraries and Archives Council |
| MIMEMME | Member, Institution of Mining Electrical & Mining Mechanical Engineers (later MIMinE) | | |
| MIMgt | Member, Institute of Management (*see now* MCMI) | MLC | Member of Legislative Council; Meat and Livestock Commission |
| MIMGTechE | Member, Institution of Mechanical and General Technician Engineers | | |
| | | MLCOM | Member, London College of Osteopathic Medicine |
| MIMI | Member, Institute of the Motor Industry | MLI | Member, Landscape Institute |
| MIMinE | Member, Institution of Mining Engineers (later MIMM) | MLib | Master of Librarianship |
| MIMM | Member, Institution of Mining and Metallurgy (*now see* MIMMM) | MLitt | Master of Letters |
| | | Mlle | Mademoiselle |
| MIMMM | Member, Institute of Materials, Minerals and Mining | MLO | Military Liaison Officer |
| MIMunE | Member, Institution of Municipal Engineers (now amalgamated with Institution of Civil Engineers) | MLR | Modern Language Review |
| | | MLS | Master of Library Science |
| MIN | Member, Institute of Navigation (*now see* MRIN) | MM | Military Medal; Merchant Marine |
| Min. | Ministry | MMA | Metropolitan Museum of Art |
| Minn | Minnesota | | |
| MInstAM | Member, Institute of Administrative Management | | |

| | | | |
|---|---|---|---|
| MMan | Master of Management | MRCPsych | Member, Royal College of Psychiatrists |
| MMath | Master of Mathematics | MRCS | Member, Royal College of Surgeons of England |
| MMB | Milk Marketing Board | MRCSE | Member, Royal College of Surgeons of Edinburgh |
| MMD | Movement for Multi-Party Democracy | MRCSI | Member, Royal College of Surgeons in Ireland |
| MME | Master of Mining Engineering | MRCVS | Member, Royal College of Veterinary Surgeons |
| Mme | Madame | MRD RCS | Member in Restorative Dentistry, Royal College of Surgeons |
| MMechE | Master of Mechanical Engineering | MRE | Master of Religious Education |
| MMEd | Master in Medical Education | MRes | Master of Research |
| MMedSci | Master in Medical Science | MRHS | Member, Royal Horticultural Society |
| MMet | Master of Metallurgy | MRI | Magnetic Resonance Imaging; Member, Royal Institution |
| MMGI | Member, Mining, Geological and Metallurgical Institute of India | MRIA | Member, Royal Irish Academy |
| MMin | Master of Ministry | MRIAI | Member, Royal Institute of the Architects of Ireland |
| MML | Masters in Medical Law | MRIC | Member, Royal Institute of Chemistry (*now see* MRSC) |
| MMLJ | Member of Merit, Order of St Lazarus of Jerusalem | MRICS | Member, Royal Institution of Chartered Surveyors |
| MMM | Member, Order of Military Merit (Canada) | MRIN | Member, Royal Institute of Navigation |
| MMRS | Member, Market Research Society | MRINA | Member, Royal Institution of Naval Architects |
| MMS | Member, Institute of Management Services | MRNZCGP | Member, Royal New Zealand College of General Practitioners |
| MMus | Master of Music | MRPharmS | Member, Royal Pharmaceutical Society |
| MN | Merchant Navy; Minnesota (postal) | MRSB | Member, Royal Society of Biology |
| MNAM | Member, National Academy of Medicine (US) | MRSC | Member, Royal Society of Chemistry |
| MNAS | Member, National Academy of Sciences (US) | MRSH | Member, Royal Society for the Promotion of Health (*now see* MRSPH) |
| MND | Motor Neurone Disease | | |
| MNECInst | Member, North East Coast Institution of Engineers and Shipbuilders | MRSL | Member, Order of the Republic of Sierra Leone |
| | | MRSocMed | Member, Royal Society of Medicine |
| MNI | Member, Nautical Institute | MRSPH | Member, Royal Society for Public Health |
| MNIMH | Member, National Institute of Medical Herbalists | MRTPI | Member, Royal Town Planning Institute |
| MNucI | Member, Nuclear Institute | MRurSc | Master of Rural Science |
| MNZIS | Member, New Zealand Institute of Surveyors | MRUSI | Member, Royal United Service Institution |
| MNZM | Member, New Zealand Order of Merit | MRVA | Member, Rating and Valuation Association |
| MNZPI | Member, New Zealand Planning Institute | MS | Master of Surgery; Master of Science (US); Mississippi (postal); Multiple Sclerosis; Motor Ship |
| MO | Medical Officer; Military Operations; Missouri (postal) | | |
| Mo | Missouri | MS, MSS | Manuscript, Manuscripts |
| MoD | Ministry of Defence | MSA | Master of Science, Agriculture (US); Mineralogical Society of America; Motor Sports Association |
| Mods | Moderations (Oxford) | | |
| MOH | Medical Officer(s) of Health | MSAAIE | Member, Southern African Association of Industrial Editors |
| MoJ | Ministry of Justice | MSAE | Member, Society of Automotive Engineeers (US) |
| MOM | Member, Order of Merit (Malta) | MSAICE | Member, South African Institution of Civil Engineers |
| MOMA | Museum of Modern Art | MSAInstMM | Member, South African Institute of Mining and Metallurgy |
| MOMI | Museum of the Moving Image | MSB | Member, Society of Biology (*now see* MRSB) |
| Mon | Monmouthshire | MSC | Manpower Services Commission; Missionaries of the Sacred Heart |
| Mont | Montgomeryshire | | |
| MOP | Ministry of Power | MSc | Master of Science |
| MOrthRCS | Member in Orthodontics, Royal College of Surgeons | MScD | Master of Dental Science |
| Most Rev. | Most Reverend | MScE | Master of Science in Engineering |
| MoT | Ministry of Transport | MSci | Master of Natural Sciences |
| MOV | Member, Order of Volta (Ghana) | MScSoc | Master of Social Sciences |
| MP | Member of Parliament | MScSocMed | Master of Science in Social Medicine |
| MPA | Master of Public Administration; Member, Parliamentary Assembly, Northern Ireland | MSD | Meritorious Service Decoration (Fiji) |
| | | MSE | Master of Science in Engineering (US) |
| MPAGB | Member, Photographic Alliance of Great Britain | MSF | (Union for) Manufacturing, Science, Finance |
| MPBW | Ministry of Public Building and Works | MSFA | Member, Society of Financial Advisers |
| MPH | Master of Public Health | MSHyg | Master of Science in Hygiene |
| MPhil | Master of Philosophy | MSI | Member, Securities Institute (later Securities & Investment Institute, *now see* MCSI) |
| MPhys | Master of Physics | | |
| MPIA | Master of Public and International Affairs | MSIA | Member, Society of Industrial Artists |
| MPLA | Major Projects Leadership Academy | MSIAD | Member, Society of Industrial Artists and Designers (*now see* MCSD) |
| MPMI | Member, Property Management Institute | | |
| MPO | Management and Personnel Office | MSIT | Member, Society of Instrument Technology (*now see* MInstMC) |
| MPodA | Member, Podiatry Association | MSL | Master of Studies in Law |
| MPP | Member, Provincial Parliament; Master in Public Policy (Harvard) | MSLS | Master of Science in Library Science |
| | | MSM | Meritorious Service Medal; Madras Sappers and Miners; Master in Science Management |
| MPRISA | Member, Public Relations Institute of South Africa | | |
| MProf | Masters in Professional Studies | MSN | Master of Science in Nursing |
| MPS | Member, Pharmaceutical Society (*now see* MRPharmS) | MSocAdmin | Master of Social Administration |
| MPTS | Medical Practitioners Tribunal Service | MSocIS | Member, Société des Ingénieurs et Scientistes de France |
| MR | Master of the Rolls; Municipal Reform | MSocSc | Master of Social Sciences |
| MRAC | Member, Royal Agricultural College | MSocWork | Master of Social Work |
| MRACP | Member, Royal Australasian College of Physicians | MSoFHT | Member, Society of Food Hygiene Technology |
| MRACS | Member, Royal Australasian College of Surgeons | MSP | Member, Scottish Parliament; Managing Successful Programmes |
| MRad | Master of Radiology | | |
| MRAeS | Member, Royal Aeronautical Society | MSR | Member, Society of Radiographers |
| MRAIC | Member, Royal Architectural Institute of Canada | MSRP | Member, Society for Radiological Protection |
| MRAS | Member, Royal Asiatic Society | MSSc | Master of Social Sciences |
| MRC | Medical Research Council | MSSC | Marine Society & Sea Cadets |
| MRCA | Multi-Role Combat Aircraft | MSt | Master of Studies |
| MRCGP | Member, Royal College of General Practitioners | MSTD | Member, Society of Typographic Designers |
| MRC-LMB | Medical Research Council Laboratory of Molecular Biology | MStJ | Member, Most Venerable Order of the Hospital of St John of Jerusalem |
| MRCOG | Member, Royal College of Obstetricians and Gynaecologists | | |
| MRCOphth | Member, Royal College of Ophthalmologists | MSW | Master of Social Work |
| MRCP | Member, Royal College of Physicians, London; Member, Royal College of Physicians, United Kingdom | MSzP | Magyar Szocialista Párt |
| | | MT | Mechanical Transport; Montana (postal) |
| MRCPA | Member, Royal College of Pathologists of Australia | Mt | Mount; Mountain |
| MRCPath | Member, Royal College of Pathologists | MTA | Music Trades Association |
| MRCPCH | Member, Royal College of Paediatrics and Child Health | MTB | Motor Torpedo Boat |
| MRCPE | Member, Royal College of Physicians, Edinburgh | MTCA | Ministry of Transport and Civil Aviation |
| MRCPGlas | Member, Royal College of Physicians and Surgeons of Glasgow | MTD | Midwife Teachers' Diploma |
| MRCPI | Member, Royal College of Physicians of Ireland | MTech | Master of Technology |

| | |
|---|---|
| MTEFL | Master in the Teaching of English as a Foreign or Second Language |
| MTh | Master of Theology |
| MTIA | Metal Trades Industry Association |
| MTIRA | Machine Tool Industry Research Association (*now see* AMTRI) |
| MTPI | Member, Town Planning Institute (*now see* MRTPI) |
| MTS | Master of Theological Studies; Ministerial Training Scheme |
| MUniv | Honorary Master of the University |
| MusB | Bachelor of Music |
| MusD | Doctor of Music |
| MusM | Master of Music |
| MV | Merchant Vessel, Motor Vessel (naval) |
| MVB | Bachelor of Veterinary Medicine |
| MVEE | Military Vehicles and Engineering Establishment |
| MVO | Member, Royal Victorian Order |
| MVSc | Master of Veterinary Science |
| MW | Master of Wine |
| MWA | Mystery Writers of America |
| MWeldI | Member, Welding Institute |
| MWSOM | Member, Institute of Practitioners in Work Study Organisation and Methods (*now see* MMS) |

# N

| | |
|---|---|
| N | Nationalist; Navigating Duties; North |
| n | nephew |
| NA | National Academician (America) |
| NAACP | National Association for the Advancement of Colored People |
| NAAFI | Navy, Army and Air Force Institutes |
| NAAS | National Agricultural Advisory Service |
| NAB | National Advisory Body for Public Sector Higher Education |
| NABC | National Association of Boys' Clubs (later NABC-CYP) |
| NABC-CYP | National Association of Boys' Clubs - Clubs for Young People |
| NAC | National Agriculture Centre |
| NACAB | National Association of Citizens' Advice Bureaux |
| NACCB | National Accreditation Council for Certification Bodies |
| NACETT | National Advisory Council for Education and Training Targets |
| NACF | National Art-Collections Fund |
| NACRO | National Association for the Care and Resettlement of Offenders |
| NADFAS | National Association of Decorative and Fine Arts Societies |
| NAE | National Academy of Engineering |
| NAEW | Nato Airborn Early Warning |
| NAHA | National Association of Health Authorities (*now see* NAHAT) |
| NAHAT | National Association of Health Authorities and Trusts |
| NAHT | National Association of Head Teachers |
| NALGO or Nalgo | National and Local Government Officers' Association |
| NAMAS | National Measurement and Accreditation Service |
| NAMCW | National Association for Maternal and Child Welfare |
| NAMH | MIND (National Association for Mental Health) |
| NAMMA | NATO MRCA Management Agency |
| NAPAG | National Academies Policy Advisory Group |
| NARM | National Association of Recording Merchandisers (US) |
| NAS | National Academy of Sciences |
| NASA | National Aeronautics and Space Administration (US) |
| NASD | National Association of Securities Dealers |
| NASDAQ | National Association of Securities Dealers Automated Quotation System |
| NASDIM | National Association of Securities Dealers and Investment Managers (later FIMBRA) |
| NAS/UWT | National Association of Schoolmasters/Union of Women Teachers |
| NATCS | National Air Traffic Control Services (*now see* NATS) |
| NATFHE | National Association of Teachers in Further and Higher Education (combining ATCDE and ATTI) |
| NATLAS | National Testing Laboratory Accreditation Scheme |
| NATO | North Atlantic Treaty Organisation |
| NATS | National Air Traffic Services |
| Nat. Sci. | Natural Sciences |
| NATSOPA | National Society of Operative Printers, Graphical and Media Personnel (*formerly* of Operative Printers and Assistants) |
| NAYC | Youth Clubs UK (*formerly* National Association of Youth Clubs) |
| NB | New Brunswick; Nebraska (postal) |
| NBA | North British Academy |
| NBC | National Book Council (later NBL); National Broadcasting Company (US) |
| NBL | National Book League |
| NBPI | National Board for Prices and Incomes |
| NC | National Certificate; North Carolina |
| NCA | National Certificate of Agriculture |
| NCARB | National Council of Architectural Registration Boards |
| NCAS | Natural Environment Research Council Centres for Atmospheric Science |
| NCB | National Coal Board |
| NCC | National Computing Centre; Nature Conservancy Council (later NCCE); National Consumer Council |
| NCCE | Nature Conservancy Council for England (English Nature) |
| NCCL | National Council for Civil Liberties |
| NCD | National Capital District, Papua New Guinea |
| NCDAD | National Council for Diplomas in Art and Design |
| NCEA | National Council for Educational Awards |
| NCET | National Council for Educational Technology |
| NCH | National Children's Homes |
| NCLC | National Council of Labour Colleges |
| NCOP | National Council of Provinces (South Africa) |
| NCOPF | National Council for One Parent Families |
| NCRI | National Cancer Research Institute |
| NCSS | National Council of Social Service |
| NCTJ | National Council for the Training of Journalists |
| NCVCCO | National Council of Voluntary Child Care Organisations |
| NCVO | National Council for Voluntary Organisations |
| NCVQ | National Council for Vocational Qualifications |
| NCYPE | National Centre for Young People with Epilepsy |
| ND | North Dakota |
| NDA | National Diploma in Agriculture |
| NDC | National Defence College; NATO Defence College |
| NDD | National Diploma in Dairying; National Diploma in Design |
| NDEA | National Defense Education Act |
| NDH | National Diploma in Horticulture |
| NDIC | National Defence Industries Council |
| NDP | New Democratic Party |
| NDRI | National Disease Research Interchange |
| NDTA | National Defense Transportation Association (US) |
| NE | North-east |
| NEAB | Northern Examinations and Assessment Board |
| NEAC | New English Art Club |
| NEAF | Near East Air Force |
| NEARELF | Near East Land Forces |
| NEB | National Enterprise Board |
| NEC | National Executive Committee |
| NECInst | North East Coast Institution of Engineers and Shipbuilders |
| NEDC | National Economic Development Council; North East Development Council |
| NEDO | National Economic Development Office |
| NEH | National Endowment for the Humanities |
| NEL | National Engineering Laboratory |
| NERC | Natural Environment Research Council |
| NESTA | National Endowment for Science, Technology and the Arts |
| NF | Newfoundland and Labrador (postal) |
| NFC | National Freight Consortium (*formerly* Corporation, then Company) |
| NFCG | National Federation of Consumer Groups |
| NFER | National Foundation for Educational Research |
| NFHA | National Federation of Housing Associations |
| NFMS | National Federation of Music Societies |
| NFSH | National Federation of Spiritual Healers |
| NFT | National Film Theatre |
| NFU | National Farmers' Union |
| NFWI | National Federation of Women's Institutes |
| NGO | Non-Governmental Organisation(s) |
| NGTE | National Gas Turbine Establishment |
| NH | New Hampshire |
| NH&MRC | National Health and Medical Research Council (Australia) |
| NHBC | National House-Building Council |
| NHMF | National Heritage Memorial Fund |
| NHS | National Health Service |
| NHSU | National Health Service University |
| NI | Northern Ireland; Native Infantry |
| NIAB | National Institute of Agricultural Botany |
| NIACE | National Institute of Adult Continuing Education |
| NIACRO | Northern Ireland Association for the Care and Resettlement of Offenders |
| NIAE | National Institute of Agricultural Engineering |
| NIAID | National Institute of Allergy and Infectious Diseases |
| NICE | National Institute for Health and Care Excellence (formerly National Institute of Clinical Excellence, then National Institute for Health and Clinical Excellence) |
| NICEC | National Institute for Careers Education and Counselling |
| NICEIC | National Inspection Council for Electrical Installation Contracting |
| NICG | Nationalised Industries Chairmen's Group |
| NICRO | National Institute for Crime Prevention and Re-integration of Offenders |
| NICS | Northern Ireland Civil Service |
| NID | Naval Intelligence Division; National Institute for the Deaf; Northern Ireland District; National Institute of Design (India) |
| NIESR | National Institute of Economic and Social Research |
| NIH | National Institutes of Health (US) |
| NIHEC | Northern Ireland Higher Education Council |
| NIHR | National Institute of Health Research |
| NII | Nuclear Installations Inspectorate |
| NILP | Northern Ireland Labour Party |
| NIMR | National Institute for Medical Research |
| NISTRO | Northern Ireland Science and Technology Regional Organisation |

| | |
|---|---|
| NISW | National Institute of Social Work |
| NIU | Northern Ireland Unionist |
| NJ | New Jersey |
| NL | National Liberal; No Liability; Newfoundland and Labrador |
| NLCS | North London Collegiate School |
| NLHF | National Lottery Heritage Fund |
| NLYL | National League of Young Liberals |
| NM | New Mexico (postal) |
| NMC | Nursing and Midwifery Council |
| NMR | Nuclear Magnetic Resonance |
| NMRS | National Monuments Record of Scotland |
| NMSI | National Museum of Science and Industry |
| NNMA | Nigerian National Merit Award |
| NNOM | Nigerian National Order of Merit |
| NO | Navigating Officer |
| NODA | National Operatic and Dramatic Association |
| Northants | Northamptonshire |
| Notts | Nottinghamshire |
| NP | Notary Public |
| NPA | Newspaper Publishers' Association |
| NPFA | National Playing Fields Association |
| NPG | National Portrait Gallery |
| NPk | Nishan-e-Pakistan |
| NPL | National Physical Laboratory |
| NPQH | National Professional Qualification for Headship |
| NRA | National Rifle Association; National Recovery Administration (US); National Rivers Authority |
| NRAO | National Radio Astronomy Observatory |
| NRCC | National Research Council of Canada |
| NRD | National Registered Designer |
| NRDC | National Research Development Corporation |
| NRMA | National Roads and Motorists' Association |
| NRPB | National Radiological Protection Board |
| NRR | Northern Rhodesia Regiment |
| NRSA | National Research Service Award (US) |
| NS | Nova Scotia; New Style in the Calendar (in Great Britain since 1752); National Society; National Service |
| ns | Graduate of Royal Naval Staff College, Greenwich |
| NSA | National Skating Association (*now see* NISA) |
| NSAIV | Distinguished Order of Shaheed Ali (Maldives) |
| NSERC | Natural Sciences and Engineering Research Council, Canada |
| NSF | National Science Foundation (US) |
| NSM | Non-Stipendiary Minister |
| NSMHC | National Society for Mentally Handicapped Children (*now see* Mencap) |
| NSPCC | National Society for Prevention of Cruelty to Children |
| NSRA | National Small-bore Rifle Association |
| N/SSF | Novice, Society of St Francis |
| NSW | New South Wales |
| NT | New Testament; Northern Territory (Australia); Northwest Territories (Canada); National Theatre; National Trust |
| NT&SA | National Trust & Savings Association |
| NTO | National Training Organisation |
| NTUC | National Trades Union Congress |
| NUAAW | National Union of Agricultural and Allied Workers |
| NUBE | National Union of Bank Employees (later BIFU) |
| NUFLAT | National Union of Footwear Leather and Allied Trades (*now see* NUKFAT) |
| NUGMW | National Union of General and Municipal Workers (later GMBATU) |
| NUHKW | National Union of Hosiery and Knitwear Workers (*now see* NUKFAT) |
| NUI | National University of Ireland |
| NUJ | National Union of Journalists |
| NUJMB | Northern Universities Joint Matriculation Board |
| NUM | National Union of Mineworkers |
| NUMAST | National Union of Marine, Aviation and Shipping Transport Officers |
| NUPE | National Union of Public Employees |
| NUR | National Union of Railwaymen (*now see* RMT) |
| NUS | National Union of Students; National University of Singapore |
| NUT | National Union of Teachers |
| NUU | New University of Ulster |
| NV | Nevada (postal) |
| NVQ | National Vocational Qualification |
| NW | North-west |
| NWC | National Water Council |
| NWFP | North-West Frontier Province |
| NWP | North-Western Province |
| NWT | North-Western Territories |
| NY | New York |
| NYC | New York City |
| NYO | National Youth Orchestra |
| NYT | National Youth Theatre |
| NZ | New Zealand |
| NZEF | New Zealand Expeditionary Force |
| NZIA | New Zealand Institute of Architects |
| NZTF | New Zealand Territorial Force |

# O

| | |
|---|---|
| o | only |
| OAM | Medal of the Order of Australia |
| O&M | organisation and method |
| OAP | Old Age Pensioner |
| OAS | Organisation of American States; On Active Service |
| OASC | Officer Aircrew Selection Centre |
| OAU | Organisation for African Unity |
| OB | Order of Barbados; Order of Belize |
| OBC | Order of British Columbia |
| OBE | Officer, Order of the British Empire |
| OC | Officer, Order of Canada (equivalent to former award SM) |
| OC or o/c | Officer Commanding |
| oc | only child |
| OCC | Order of the Caribbean Community |
| OCDS or ocds Can | Overseas College of Defence Studies (Canada) |
| OCF | Officiating Chaplain to the Forces |
| OCHA | Office for the Coordination of Humanitarian Affairs |
| OCPA | Office of the Commissioner for Public Appointments |
| OCS | Officer Candidates School; Officer Cadet School |
| OCSS | Oxford and Cambridge Shakespeare Society |
| OCTU | Officer Cadet Training Unit |
| OCU | Operational Conversion Unit |
| OD | Officer, Order of Distinction (Jamaica); Order of Distinction (Antigua) |
| ODA | Overseas Development Administration |
| ODI | Overseas Development Institute |
| ODM | Ministry of Overseas Development |
| ODPM | Office of the Deputy Prime Minister |
| ODSM | Order of Diplomatic Service Merit (Lesotho) |
| OE | Order of Excellence (Guyana) |
| OECD | Organization for Economic Co-operation and Development |
| OED | Oxford English Dictionary |
| OEEC | Organization for European Economic Co-operation (*now see* OECD) |
| OF | Order of the Founder, Salvation Army |
| OFCOM or Ofcom | Office of Communications |
| OFEMA | Office Française d'Exportation de Matériel Aéronautique |
| OFFER | Office of Electricity Regulation |
| Ofgem | Office of Gas and Electricity Markets |
| OFM | Order of Friars Minor (Franciscans) |
| OFMCap | Order of Friars Minor Capuchin (Franciscans) |
| OFMConv | Order of Friars Minor Conventual (Franciscans) |
| Ofqual | Office of Qualifications and Examinations Regulation |
| OFR | Order of the Federal Republic of Nigeria |
| OFS | Orange Free State |
| OFSTED | Office for Standards in Education |
| OFT | Office of Fair Trading |
| Oftel | Office of Telecommunications |
| Ofwat | Office of Water Services |
| OGC | Office of Government Commerce |
| OGS | Oratory of the Good Shepherd |
| OH | Ohio (postal) |
| OHMS | On His (or Her) Majesty's Service |
| O i/c | Officer in charge |
| OJ | Order of Jamaica |
| OK | Oklahoma (postal) |
| OL | Officer, Order of Leopold; Order of the Leopard (Lesotho) |
| OLJ | Officer, Order of St Lazarus of Jerusalem |
| OLM | Officer, Legion of Merit (Rhodesia); Ordained Local Minister |
| OM | Order of Merit; Order of Manitoba |
| OMCS | Office of the Minister for the Civil Service |
| OMFIF | Official Monetary and Financial Institutions Forum |
| OMI | Oblate of Mary Immaculate |
| OMLJ | Officer, Order of Merit, Order of St Lazarus of Jerusalem |
| OMM | Officer, Order of Military Merit (Canada) |
| ON | Order of the Nation (Jamaica); Ontario (postal) |
| ONC | Ordinary National Certificate |
| OND | Ordinary National Diploma |
| ONDA | Ordinary National Diploma in Agriculture |
| ONS | Office for National Statistics; Order of Nova Scotia |
| Ont | Ontario |
| ONZ | Order of New Zealand |
| ONZM | Officer, New Zealand Order of Merit |
| OON | Officer, Order of the Niger |
| OOnt | Order of Ontario |
| OOV | Officer, Order of the Volta (Ghana) |
| OP | *Ordinis Praedicatorum* (of the Order of Preachers (Dominican)); Observation Post |
| OPCON | Operational Control |

| | | | |
|---|---|---|---|
| OPCS | Office of Population Censuses and Surveys (*now see* ONS) | PdD | Doctor of Pedagogy (US) |
| OPCW | Organisation for the Prohibition of Chemical Weapons | PDG | Président Directeur Général |
| OPEC | Organisation of Petroleum Exporting Countries | PDipHEd | Postgraduate Diploma in Health Education |
| OPEI | Order of Prince Edward Island | PDR | People's Democratic Republic |
| OPM | Owner President Management program | PDRA | post doctoral research assistant |
| OPRA | Occupational Pensions Regulatory Authority | PDSA | People's Dispensary for Sick Animals |
| OPS | Office of Public Service | PDTC | Professional Dancer's Training Course Diploma |
| OPSS | Office of Public Service and Science (later OPS) | PDTDip | Professional Dancer's Teaching Diploma |
| OQ | Officer, National Order of Quebec | PE | Procurement Executive; Prince Edward Island (postal) |
| OR | Order of Rorima (Guyana); Operational Research; Oregon (postal) | PEI | Prince Edward Island |
| | | PEN | Poets, Playwrights, Editors, Essayists, Novelists (Club) |
| ORGALIME | Organisme de Liaison des Industries Métalliques Européennes | PEng | Registered Professional Engineer (Canada); Member, Society of Professional Engineers |
| ORHA/CPA | Office of Reconstruction and Humanitarian Assistance/Coalition Provisional Authority | Penn | Pennsylvania |
| | | PEP | Political and Economic Planning (*now see* PSI) |
| ORL | Otorhinolaryngology | PER | Professional and Executive Recruitment |
| ORS | Operational Research Society | PES | Party of European Socialists |
| ORSA | Operations Research Society of America (*now see* INFORMS) | PEST | Pressure for Economic and Social Toryism |
| ORSL | Order of the Republic of Sierra Leone | PF | Procurator-Fiscal |
| ORT | Organization for Rehabilitation through Training | PFA | Professional Footballers' Association |
| ORTF | Office de la Radiodiffusion et Télévision Française | pfc | Graduate of RAF Flying College |
| ORTT | Order of the Republic of Trinidad and Tobago | PFHEA | Principal Fellow, Higher Education Academy |
| o s | only son | PFI | Private Finance Initiative |
| OSA | Order of St Augustine (Augustinian); Ontario Society of Artists | PGA | Professional Golfers' Association |
| OSB | Order of St Benedict (Benedictine) | PGCA | Post Graduate Certificate of Adjudication |
| OSC | Order of Simon of Cyrene | PGCE | Post Graduate Certificate of Education |
| osc | Graduate of Overseas Staff College | PGCFHE | Post Graduate Certificate in Further and Higher Education |
| OSCE | Organisation for Security and Co-operation in Europe | PGCHE | Post Graduate Certificate in Higher Education |
| OSCHR | Office for Strategic Co-ordination of Health Research | PGCTh | Postgraduate Certificate in Theology |
| OSFC | Franciscan (Capuchin) Order | PGDCCI | Postgraduate Diploma in Computing for Commerce and Industry |
| O/Sig | Ordinary Signalman | PGDipMin | Postgraduate Diploma in Ministry |
| OSMTH | Ordo Supremus Militaris Templi Hierosolymitani (Supreme Military Order of the Temple of Jerusalem) | PGDPT | Postgraduate Diploma in Pastoral Theology |
| | | PGTC | Postgraduate Teaching Certificate |
| osp | *obiit sine prole* (died without issue) | PGTCSE | Postgraduate Teaching Certificate in Secondary Education |
| OSS | Office of Strategic Services | PH | Presidential Order of Honour (Botswana) |
| OST | Office of Science and Technology | PHAB | Physically Handicapped & Able-bodied |
| OStJ | Officer, Most Venerable Order of the Hospital of St John of Jerusalem | PhB | Bachelor of Philosophy |
| | | PhC | Pharmaceutical Chemist |
| OSUK | Ophthalmological Society of the United Kingdom | PhD | Doctor of Philosophy |
| OT | Old Testament | PHE | Public Health England |
| OTC | Officers' Training Corps | Phil. | Philology; Philological; Philosophy; Philosophical |
| OTL | Officer, Order of Toussaint L'Ouverture (Haiti) | PhL | Licentiate in Philosophy |
| OTS | Office of the Third Sector | PHLS | Public Health Laboratory Service |
| OTU | Operational Training Unit | PhM | Master of Philosophy (USA) |
| OTWSA | Ou-Testamentiese Werkgemeenskap in Suider-Afrika | PhmB | Bachelor of Pharmacy |
| OU | Oxford University; Open University | Phys. | Physical |
| OUAC | Oxford University Athletic Club | PIA | Personal Investment Authority |
| OUAFC | Oxford University Association Football Club | PIARC | Permanent International Association of Road Congresses |
| OUBC | Oxford University Boat Club | PIB | Prices and Incomes Board (later NBPI) |
| OUCC | Oxford University Cricket Club | PICAO | Provisional International Civil Aviation Organization (*now* ICAO) |
| OUDS | Oxford University Dramatic Society | | |
| OUP | Oxford University Press; Official Unionist Party | PICTFOR | Parliamentary Internet Communications and Technology Forum |
| OURC | Oxford University Rifle Club | pinx. | *pinxit* (he painted it) |
| OURFC | Oxford University Rugby Football Club | PITCOM | Parliamentary Information Technology Committee (*now see* PICTFOR) |
| OURT | Order of the United Republic of Tanzania | | |
| Oxon | Oxfordshire; *Oxoniensis* (of Oxford) | PJG | Pingat Jasa Gemilang (Singapore) |
| | | PJHQ | Permanent Joint Headquarters |
| | | PJK | Pingkat Jasa Kebaktian (Malaysia) |

# P

| | | | |
|---|---|---|---|
| | | Pl. | Place; Plural |
| PA | Pakistan Army; Personal Assistant; Pennsylvania (postal) | PLA | Port of London Authority |
| PAA | President, Australian Academy of Science | PLAB | Professional and Linguistic Assessments Board |
| pac | passed the final examination of the Advanced Class, The Military College of Science | PLC or plc | public limited company |
| | | Plen. | Plenipotentiary |
| PACE | Protestant and Catholic Encounter; Property Advisers to the Civil Estate | PLI | President, Landscape Institute |
| | | PLP | Parliamentary Labour Party; Progressive Liberal Party (Bahamas) |
| PACTA | Professional Associate, Clinical Theology Association | | |
| PALS | Partnership for Active Leisure Scheme for Disabled Children | PLR | Public Lending Right |
| P&O | Peninsular and Oriental Steamship Co. | PMA | Personal Military Assistant |
| P&OSNCo. | Peninsular and Oriental Steam Navigation Co. | PMC | Personnel Management Centre |
| PAO | Prince Albert's Own | PMD | Program for Management Development |
| PASOK | Panhellenic Socialist Movement | PMedSci | President, Academy of Medical Sciences |
| PBFA | Provincial Booksellers Fairs Association | PMETB | Postgraduate Medical Education and Training Board |
| PBS | Public Broadcasting Service | PMG | Postmaster-General |
| PC | Privy Counsellor; Police Constable; Perpetual Curate; Peace Commissioner (Ireland); Progressive Conservative (Canada) | PMN | Panglima Mangku Negara (Malaysia) |
| | | PMO | Principal Medical Officer; Princess Mary's Own |
| pc | *per centum* (in the hundred) | PMRAFNS | Princess Mary's Royal Air Force Nursing Service |
| PCC | Parochial Church Council; Protected Cell Company (Guernsey); Private Cell Company | PMS | Presidential Order of Meritorious Service (Botswana); President, Miniature Society |
| PCE | Postgraduate Certificate of Education | PNBS | Panglima Negara Bintang Sarawak |
| pce | passed command examinations | PNEU | Parents' National Educational Union |
| PCFC | Polytechnics and Colleges Funding Council | PNG | Papua New Guinea |
| PCG | Primary Care Group | PNP | People's National Party |
| PCL | Polytechnic of Central London | PO | Post Office |
| PCMO | Principal Colonial Medical Officer | POB | Presidential Order of Botswana |
| PCNZM | Principal Companion, New Zealand Order of Merit | Pop. | Population |
| PCS | Parti Chrétien-Social; Public and Commercial Services Union | POST | Parliamentary Office of Science and Technology |
| PCT | Primary Care Trust | POUNC | Post Office Users' National Council |

| | |
|---|---|
| POW | Prisoner of War; Prince of Wales's |
| PP | Parish Priest; Past President |
| pp | pages |
| PPA | Periodical Publishers Association |
| PPARC | Particle Physics and Astronomy Research Council |
| PPCLI | Princess Patricia's Canadian Light Infantry |
| PPCSD | Past President, Chartered Society of Designers |
| PPDF | Parti Populaire pour la Démocratie Française |
| PPE | Philosophy, Politics and Economics |
| PPInstHE | Past President, Institution of Highway Engineers |
| PPIStructE | Past President, Institution of Structural Engineers |
| PPITB | Printing and Publishing Industry Training Board |
| PPP | Private Patients Plan; Psychology, Philosophy and Physiology |
| PPRA | Past President, Royal Academy |
| PPRBA | Past President, Royal Society of British Artists |
| PPRBS | Past President, Royal Society of British Sculptors |
| PPRE | Past President, Royal Society of Painter-Printmakers (*formerly* of Painter-Etchers and Engravers) |
| PPRIBA | Past President, Royal Institute of British Architects |
| PPRNCM | Diploma in Professional Performance, Royal Northern College of Music |
| PPROI | Past President, Royal Institute of Oil Painters |
| PPRP | Past President, Royal Society of Portrait Painters |
| PPRSA | Past President, Royal Scottish Academy |
| PPRSW | Past President, Royal Scottish Society of Painters in Water Colours |
| PPRTPI | Past President, Royal Town Planning Institute |
| PPRWA | Past President, Royal Watercolour Association |
| PPRWS | Past President, Royal Society of Painters in Water Colours |
| PPS | Parliamentary Private Secretary |
| PPSA | Proficiency, Photographic Society of America |
| PPSIAD | Past President, Society of Industrial Artists and Designers |
| PQ | Province of Quebec |
| PQCCC | Post Qualification Certificate in Child Care |
| PQE | Professional Qualifying Examination |
| PR | Public Relations; Parti républicain |
| PRA | President, Royal Academy |
| PRASEG | Associate Parliamentary Renewable and Sustainable Energy Group |
| PRBS | President, Royal Society of British Sculptors |
| PRCA | Public Relations Consultants Association |
| PRCS | President, Royal College of Surgeons |
| PrD | Doctor of Professional Practice |
| PRE | President, Royal Society of Painter-Printmakers (*formerly* of Painter-Etchers and Engravers) |
| Preb. | Prebendary |
| Prep. | Preparatory |
| Pres. | President |
| PRHA | President, Royal Hibernian Academy |
| PRI | President, Royal Institute of Painters in Water Colours; Plastics and Rubber Institute |
| PRIA | President, Royal Irish Academy |
| PRIAS | President, Royal Incorporation of Architects in Scotland |
| Prin. | Principal |
| PRISA | Public Relations Institute of South Africa |
| PRL | Liberal Reform Party (Belgium) |
| PRO | Public Relations Officer; Public Records Office |
| Proc. | Proctor; Proceedings |
| Prof. | Professor; Professional |
| PROI | President, Royal Institute of Oil Painters |
| PRO NED | Promotion of Non-Executive Directors |
| Pro tem. | *Pro tempore* (for the time being) |
| ProtU | Protestant Unionist Party |
| Prov. | Provost; Provincial |
| Prox. | *Proximo* (next) |
| Prox.acc. | *Proxime accessit* (next in order of merit to the winner) |
| PRS | President, Royal Society; Performing Right Society Ltd |
| PRSA | President, Royal Scottish Academy |
| PRSE | President, Royal Society of Edinburgh |
| PRSH | President, Royal Society for the Promotion of Health |
| PRSW | President, Royal Scottish Water Colour Society |
| PRUAA | President, Royal Ulster Academy of Arts |
| PRWA | President, Royal West of England Academy |
| PRWS | President, Royal Society of Painters in Water Colours |
| PS | Pastel Society; Paddle Steamer |
| ps | passed School of Instruction (of Officers) |
| PSA | Property Services Agency; Petty Sessions Area |
| psa | Graduate of RAF Staff College |
| psc | Graduate of Staff College († indicates Graduate of Senior Wing Staff College); Personal Services Company |
| PSD | Petty Sessional Division; Social Democratic Party (Portugal); Panglima Setia Diraja |
| PSE | Party of European Socialists |
| PSGB | Pharmaceutical Society of Great Britain (*now see* RPSGB) |
| PSI | Policy Studies Institute |
| PSIAD | President, Society of Industrial Artists and Designers |
| PSM | Panglima Setia Mahkota (Malaysia) |
| psm | Certificate of Royal Military School of Music |
| PSMA | President, Society of Marine Artists |
| PSO | Principal Scientific Officer; Personal Staff Officer |
| PSOE | Partido Socialista Obrero Español |
| PSS | Society of Priests of St Sulpice |
| PsyD | Doctor of Psychology |
| PTA | Passenger Transport Authority; Parent-Teacher Association |
| PTC | Personnel and Training Command |
| PTE | Passenger Transport Executive |
| Pte | Private |
| PThD | Doctor of Pastoral Theology |
| ptsc | passed Technical Staff College |
| Pty | Proprietary |
| PUP | People's United Party; Progressive Unionist Party |
| PVSM | Param Vishishc Seva Medal (India) |
| PWO | Prince of Wales's Own |
| PWO(CEW) | Principal Warfare Officer (Communications and Electronic Warfare) |
| PWO(U) | Principal Warfare Officer (Underwater Warfare) |
| PWR | Pressurized Water Reactor |
| PYBT | Prince's Youth Business Trust |

# Q

| | |
|---|---|
| Q | Queen |
| QAA | Quality Assurance Agency for Higher Education |
| QAIMNS | Queen Alexandra's Imperial Military Nursing Service |
| QARANC | Queen Alexandra's Royal Army Nursing Corps |
| QARNNS | Queen Alexandra's Royal Naval Nursing Service |
| QBD | Queen's Bench Division |
| QC | Queen's Counsel; Quebec (postal) |
| QCA | Qualifications and Curriculum Authority |
| QCB | Queen's Commendation for Bravery |
| QCDA | Qualifications and Curriculum Development Agency |
| QCVS | Queen's Commendation for Valuable Service |
| QCVSA | Queen's Commendation for Valuable Service in the Air |
| QDR | Qualified in Dispute Resolution |
| QEH | Queen Elizabeth Hall |
| QEO | Queen Elizabeth's Own |
| QFSM | Queen's Fire Service Medal for Distinguished Service |
| QGM | Queen's Gallantry Medal |
| QHC | Honorary Chaplain to the Queen |
| QHDS | Honorary Dental Surgeon to the Queen |
| QHNS | Honorary Nursing Sister to the Queen |
| QHP | Honorary Physician to the Queen |
| QHS | Honorary Surgeon to the Queen |
| Qld | Queensland |
| Qly | Quarterly |
| QMAAC | Queen Mary's Army Auxiliary Corps |
| QMC | Queen Mary College, London |
| QMG | Quartermaster-General |
| QMIPRI | Queen Mary Intellectual Property Research Institute |
| QMO | Queen Mary's Own |
| QMUL | Queen Mary, University of London |
| QMW | Queen Mary and Westfield College, London (*now see* QMUL) |
| QO | Qualified Officer |
| QOOH | Queen's Own Oxfordshire Hussars |
| Q(ops) | Quartering (operations) |
| QOY | Queen's Own Yeomanry |
| QPM | Queen's Police Medal |
| QPSM | Queen's Public Service Medal (New Zealand) |
| Qr | Quarter |
| QRIH | Queen's Royal Irish Hussars |
| QS | Quarter Sessions; Quantity Surveying |
| qs | RAF graduates of the Military or Naval Staff College |
| QSM | Queen's Service Medal (NZ) |
| QSO | Queen's Service Order (NZ) |
| QTS | Qualified Teacher Status |
| QUB | Queen's University, Belfast |
| qv | *quod vide* (which see) |
| QVRM | Queen's Volunteer Reserve Medal |
| qwi | Qualified Weapons Instructor |

# R

| | |
|---|---|
| (R) | Reserve |
| RA | Royal Academician; Royal Academy; Royal (Regiment of) Artillery |
| RAA | Regional Arts Association; Royal Australian Artillery |
| RAAF | Royal Australian Air Force |
| RAAMC | Royal Australian Army Medical Corps |
| RABI | Royal Agricultural Benevolent Institution |
| RAC | Royal Automobile Club; Royal Agricultural College; Royal Armoured Corps |

| | | | |
|---|---|---|---|
| RACDS | Royal Australian College of Dental Surgeons | RCT | Royal Corps of Transport |
| RACGP | Royal Australian College of General Practitioners | RCVS | Royal College of Veterinary Surgeons |
| RAChD | Royal Army Chaplains' Department | RD | Rural Dean; Royal Naval and Royal Marine Forces Reserve Decoration |
| RACI | Royal Australian Chemical Institute | | |
| RACO | Royal Australian College of Ophthalmologists | Rd | Road |
| RACOG | Royal Australian College of Obstetricians and Gynaecologists | RDA | Diploma of Roseworthy Agricultural College, South Australia; Regional Development Agency |
| RACP | Royal Australasian College of Physicians | | |
| RACS | Royal Australasian College of Surgeons; Royal Arsenal Co-operative Society | RDC | Rural District Council |
| | | RDF | Royal Dublin Fusiliers |
| RAD | Royal Academy of Dance | RDI | Royal Designer for Industry (Royal Society of Arts) |
| RADA | Royal Academy of Dramatic Art | RE | Royal Engineers; Fellow, Royal Society of Painter-Printmakers (*formerly* of Painter-Etchers and Engravers); Religious Education |
| RADAR | Royal Association for Disability Rights (*formerly* Royal Association for Disability and Rehabilitation) | | |
| RADC | Royal Army Dental Corps | REACH | Retired Executives Action Clearing House |
| RAE | Royal Australian Engineers; Royal Aerospace Establishment (*formerly* Royal Aircraft Establishment); Research Assessment Exercise | Rear Adm. | Rear Admiral |
| | | REconS | Royal Economic Society |
| | | REF | Research Excellence Framework |
| RAEC | Royal Army Educational Corps | Regt | Regiment |
| RAEng | Royal Academy of Engineering | REIT | Real Estate Investment Trust |
| RAeS | Royal Aeronautical Society | REME | Royal Electrical and Mechanical Engineers |
| RAF | Royal Air Force | REngDes | Registered Engineering Designer |
| RAFA | Royal Air Forces Association | RERO | Royal Engineers Reserve of Officers |
| RAFO | Reserve of Air Force Officers (*now see* RAFRO) | Res. | Resigned; Reserve; Resident; Research |
| RAFR | Royal Air Force Reserve | Rev. | Reverend; Review |
| RAFRO | Royal Air Force Reserve of Officers | RFA | Royal Field Artillery |
| RAFVR | Royal Air Force Volunteer Reserve | RFC | Royal Flying Corps (*now* RAF); Rugby Football Club |
| RAI | Royal Anthropological Institute of Great Britain & Ireland; Radio Audizioni Italiane | RFCA | Reserve Forces and Cadets Association |
| | | RFD | Reserve Force Decoration |
| RAIA | Royal Australian Institute of Architects | RFH | Royal Festival Hall |
| RAIC | Royal Architectural Institute of Canada | RFP | Registered Forensic Practitioner |
| RAM | (Member of) Royal Academy of Music | RFPS(G) | Royal Faculty of Physicians and Surgeons, Glasgow (*now see* RCPSG) |
| RAMC | Royal Army Medical Corps | | |
| RAN | Royal Australian Navy | RFR | Rassemblement des Français pour la République |
| R&D | Research and Development | RFU | Rugby Football Union |
| RANR | Royal Australian Naval Reserve | RGA | Royal Garrison Artillery |
| RANVR | Royal Australian Naval Volunteer Reserve | RGI | Royal Glasgow Institute of the Fine Arts |
| RAOC | Royal Army Ordnance Corps | RGJ | Royal Green Jackets |
| RAPC | Royal Army Pay Corps | RGN | Registered General Nurse |
| RARDE | Royal Armament Research and Development Establishment | RGS | Royal Geographical Society |
| RARO | Regular Army Reserve of Officers | RGSA | Royal Geographical Society of Australasia |
| RAS | Royal Astronomical Society; Royal Asiatic Society; Recruitment and Assessment Services | RHA | Royal Hibernian Academy; Royal Horse Artillery; Regional Health Authority |
| RASC | Royal Army Service Corps (*now see* RCT) | RHASS | Royal Highland and Agricultural Society of Scotland |
| RASE | Royal Agricultural Society of England | RHB | Regional Hospital Board |
| RAU | Royal Agricultural University | RHBNC | Royal Holloway and Bedford New College, London |
| RAuxAF | Royal Auxiliary Air Force | RHC | Royal Holloway College, London (later RHBNC) |
| RAVC | Royal Army Veterinary Corps | RHF | Royal Highland Fusiliers |
| RB | Rifle Brigade | RHG | Royal Horse Guards |
| RBA | Member, Royal Society of British Artists | RHistS | Royal Historical Society |
| RBK&C | Royal Borough of Kensington and Chelsea | RHQ | Regional Headquarters |
| RBL | Royal British Legion | RHR | Royal Highland Regiment |
| RBS | Royal Society of British Sculptors (*now see* RSS) | RHS | Royal Horticultural Society; Royal Humane Society |
| RBSA | (Member of) Royal Birmingham Society of Artists | RHUL | Royal Holloway, University of London |
| RBY | Royal Bucks Yeomanry | RHV | Royal Health Visitor; Registered Health Visitor |
| RC | Roman Catholic | RI | (Member of) Royal Institute of Painters in Water Colours; Rhode Island |
| RCA | Member, Royal Canadian Academy of Arts; Royal College of Art; (Member of) Royal Cambrian Academy | | |
| | | RIA | Royal Irish Academy |
| RCAC | Royal Canadian Armoured Corps | RIAI | Royal Institute of the Architects of Ireland |
| RCAF | Royal Canadian Air Force | RIAS | Royal Incorporation of Architects in Scotland |
| RCamA | Member, Royal Cambrian Academy | RIASC | Royal Indian Army Service Corps |
| RCAnaes | Royal College of Anaesthetists | RIBA | (Member of) Royal Institute of British Architects |
| RCAS | Royal Central Asian Society (*now see* RSAA) | RIBI | Rotary International in Great Britain and Ireland |
| RCDS | Royal College of Defence Studies | RIC | Royal Irish Constabulary; Royal Institute of Chemistry (*now see* RSC) |
| rcds | completed a course at, or served for a year on the Staff of, the Royal College of Defence Studies | | |
| | | RICS | (Member of) Royal Institution of Chartered Surveyors |
| RCGP | Royal College of General Practitioners | RIF | Royal Inniskilling Fusiliers |
| RCHA | Royal Canadian Horse Artillery | RIIA | Royal Institute of International Affairs |
| RCHME | Royal Commission on Historical Monuments of England | RILEM | Réunion internationale des laboratoires d'essais et de recherches sur les matériaux et les constructions |
| RCM | (Member of) Royal College of Music | | |
| RCN | Royal Canadian Navy; Royal College of Nursing | RIN | Royal Indian Navy |
| RCNC | Royal Corps of Naval Constructors | RINA | Royal Institution of Naval Architects |
| RCNR | Royal Canadian Naval Reserve | RIPA | Royal Institute of Public Administration |
| RCNVR | Royal Canadian Naval Volunteer Reserve | RIPH | Royal Institute of Public Health (*now see* RSPH) |
| RCO | Royal College of Organists | RIPH&H | Royal Institute of Public Health and Hygiene (later RIPH; *now see* RSPH) |
| RCOG | Royal College of Obstetricians and Gynaecologists | | |
| RCP | Royal College of Physicians, London | RIrF | Royal Irish Fusiliers |
| RCPA | Royal College of Pathologists of Australia | RLC | Royal Logistic Corps |
| RCPath | Royal College of Pathologists | RLFC | Rugby League Football Club |
| RCPCH | Royal College of Paediatrics and Child Health | RLSS | Royal Life Saving Society |
| RCPE or RCPEd | Royal College of Physicians, Edinburgh | RM | Royal Marines; Resident Magistrate; Registered Midwife |
| RCPI | Royal College of Physicians of Ireland | RMA | Royal Marine Artillery; Royal Military Academy Sandhurst (*now incorporating* Royal Military Academy, Woolwich) |
| RCPSG | Royal College of Physicians and Surgeons of Glasgow | | |
| RCPsych | Royal College of Psychiatrists | RMC | Royal Military College Sandhurst (*now see* RMA) |
| RCR | Royal College of Radiologists | RMCM | (Member of) Royal Manchester College of Music |
| RCS | Royal College of Surgeons of England; Royal Corps of Signals; Royal College of Science | RMCS | Royal Military College of Science |
| | | RMedSoc | Royal Medical Society, Edinburgh |
| RCSE or RCSEd | Royal College of Surgeons of Edinburgh | RMetS | Royal Meteorological Society |
| RCSI | Royal College of Surgeons in Ireland | RMFVR | Royal Marine Forces Volunteer Reserve |

| | |
|---|---|
| RMIT | Royal Melbourne Institute of Technology |
| RMLI | Royal Marine Light Infantry |
| RMN | Registered Mental Nurse |
| RMO | Resident Medical Officer(s) |
| RMP | Royal Military Police |
| RMPA | Royal Medico-Psychological Association |
| RMS | Royal Microscopical Society; Royal Mail Steamer; Royal Society of Miniature Painters; Royal Mail Ship |
| RMT | National Union of Rail, Maritime and Transport Workers; Registered Massage Therapist |
| RN | Royal Navy; Royal Naval; Registered Nurse |
| RNAS | Royal Naval Air Service |
| RNAY | Royal Naval Aircraft Yard |
| RNC | Royal Naval College |
| RNCM | (Member of) Royal Northern College of Music |
| RNEC | Royal Naval Engineering College |
| RNIB | Royal National Institute of Blind People (*formerly* Royal National Institute for the Blind, then Royal National Institute of the Blind) |
| RNID | Royal National Institute for Deaf People (*formerly* Royal National Institute for the Deaf) |
| RNLI | Royal National Life-boat Institution |
| RNLO | Royal Naval Liaison Officer |
| RNLTA | Royal Naval Lawn Tennis Association |
| RNR | Royal Naval Reserve |
| RNRU | Royal Navy Rugby Union |
| RNS | Royal Numismatic Society |
| RNSA | Royal Naval Sailing Association |
| RNSC | Royal Naval Staff College |
| RNT | Registered Nurse Tutor; Royal National Theatre |
| RNTNEH | Royal National Throat, Nose and Ear Hospital |
| RNutr | Registered Nutritionist |
| RNVR | Royal Naval Volunteer Reserve |
| RNVSR | Royal Naval Volunteer Supplementary Reserve |
| RNXS | Royal Naval Auxiliary Service |
| RNZA | Royal New Zealand Artillery |
| RNZAC | Royal New Zealand Armoured Corps |
| RNZAF | Royal New Zealand Air Force |
| RNZIR | Royal New Zealand Infantry Regiment |
| RNZN | Royal New Zealand Navy |
| RNZNVR | Royal New Zealand Naval Volunteer Reserve |
| ROC | Royal Observer Corps |
| ROF | Royal Ordnance Factories |
| R of O | Reserve of Officers |
| ROH | Royal Opera House |
| ROI | Member, Royal Institute of Oil Painters |
| RoSPA | Royal Society for the Prevention of Accidents |
| RP | (Member of) Royal Society of Portrait Painters |
| RPC | Royal Pioneer Corps |
| RPE | Rocket Propulsion Establishment |
| RPF | Rassemblement pour la France |
| RPMS | Royal Postgraduate Medical School |
| RPO | Royal Philharmonic Orchestra |
| RPP | Registered Project Professional |
| RPR | Rassemblement pour la République |
| RPS | Royal Photographic Society |
| RPSGB | Royal Pharmaceutical Society of Great Britain |
| RRC | Royal Red Cross; Rapid Reaction Corps |
| RRE | Royal Radar Establishment (later RSRE) |
| RRF | Royal Regiment of Fusiliers |
| RRS | Royal Research Ship |
| RSA | Royal Scottish Academician; Royal Society of Arts; Republic of South Africa |
| RSAA | Royal Society for Asian Affairs |
| RSAF | Royal Small Arms Factory |
| RSAI | Royal Society of Antiquaries of Ireland |
| RSAMD | Royal Scottish Academy of Music and Drama |
| RSanI | Royal Sanitary Institute (later RSH; *now see* RSPH) |
| RSAS | Royal Surgical Aid Society |
| RSC | Royal Society of Canada; Royal Society of Chemistry; Royal Shakespeare Company |
| RSCM | (Member of) Royal School of Church Music |
| RSCN | Registered Sick Children's Nurse |
| RSE | Royal Society of Edinburgh |
| RSF | Royal Scots Fusiliers |
| RSFSR | Russian Soviet Federated Socialist Republic |
| RSGS | Royal Scottish Geographical Society |
| RSH | Royal Society for the Promotion of Health (*now see* RSPH) |
| RSL | Royal Society of Literature; Returned Services League of Australia |
| RSM | Royal School of Mines |
| RSM or RSocMed | Royal Society of Medicine |
| RSMA | (Member of) Royal Society of Marine Artists |
| RSME | Royal School of Military Engineering |
| RSMHCA | Royal Society for Mentally Handicapped Children and Adults (*see* Mencap) |
| RSNC | Royal Society for Nature Conservation |
| RSO | Rural Sub-Office; Railway Sub-Office; Resident Surgical Officer |
| RSPB | Royal Society for Protection of Birds |
| RSPCA | Royal Society for Prevention of Cruelty to Animals |
| RSPH | Royal Society for Public Health |
| RSRE | Royal Signals and Radar Establishment |
| RSS | Royal Society of Sculptors |
| RSSAf | Royal Society of South Africa |
| RSSAILA | Returned Sailors, Soldiers and Airmen's Imperial League of Australia (*now see* RSL) |
| RSSPCC | Royal Scottish Society for Prevention of Cruelty to Children |
| RSTM&H | Royal Society of Tropical Medicine and Hygiene |
| RSUA | Royal Society of Ulster Architects |
| RSV | Revised Standard Version; Respiratory Syncytial Virus |
| RSW | Member, Royal Scottish Society of Painters in Water Colours |
| RTE | Radio Telefis Eireann |
| Rt Hon. | Right Honourable |
| RTL | Radio-Télévision Luxembourg |
| RTPI | Royal Town Planning Institute |
| RTR | Royal Tank Regiment |
| Rt Rev. | Right Reverend |
| RTS | Religious Tract Society; Royal Toxophilite Society; Royal Television Society |
| RTYC | Royal Thames Yacht Club |
| RU | Rugby Union |
| RUA | Royal Ulster Academy |
| RUC | Royal Ulster Constabulary |
| RUKBA | Royal United Kingdom Beneficent Association |
| RUR | Royal Ulster Regiment |
| RURAL | Society for the Responsible Use of Resources in Agriculture & on the Land |
| RUSI | Royal United Services Institute for Defence and Security Studies (*formerly* Royal United Service Institution) |
| RVC | Royal Veterinary College |
| RVS | Royal Voluntary Service |
| RWA | (Member of) Royal West of England Academy |
| RWAFF | Royal West African Frontier Force |
| RWCMD | Royal Welsh College of Music and Drama |
| RWF | Royal Welch Fusiliers |
| RWS | (Member of) Royal Society of Painters in Water Colours |
| RYA | Royal Yachting Association |
| RYS | Royal Yacht Squadron |
| RZSScot | Royal Zoological Society of Scotland |

# S

| | |
|---|---|
| (S) | (in Navy) Paymaster; Scotland |
| S | Succeeded; South; Saint |
| s | son |
| SA | South Australia; South Africa; Société Anonyme; Society of the Atonement |
| SAAF | South African Air Force |
| SABC | South African Broadcasting Corporation |
| SAC | Scientific Advisory Committee |
| sac | qualified at small arms technical long course |
| SACC | South African Council of Churches |
| SACEUR | Supreme Allied Commander Europe |
| SACIF | sociedad anónima commercial industrial financiera |
| SACLANT | Supreme Allied Commander Atlantic |
| SACRO | Scottish Association for the Care and Resettlement of Offenders |
| SA de CV | sociedad anónima de capital variable |
| SADG | Société des Architectes Diplômés par le Gouvernement |
| SAE | Society of Automobile Engineers (US) |
| SAHFOS | Sir Alister Hardy Foundation for Ocean Science |
| SAN | Senior Advocate of Nigeria |
| SARL | Société à Responsabilité Limitée |
| Sarum | Salisbury |
| SAS | Special Air Service |
| Sask | Saskatchewan |
| SASO | Senior Air Staff Officer |
| SAT | Senior Member, Association of Accounting Technicians |
| SATB | Soprano, Alto, Tenor, Bass |
| SATRO | Science and Technology Regional Organisation |
| SB | Bachelor of Science (US) |
| SBAA | Sovereign Base Areas Administration |
| SBAC | Society of British Aerospace Companies (*formerly* Society of British Aircraft Constructors) |
| SBS | Special Boat Service; Silver Bauhinia Star (Hong Kong) |
| SBStJ | Serving Brother, Most Venerable Order of the Hospital of St John of Jerusalem |
| SC | Star of Courage (Canada); Senior Counsel; South Carolina |
| sc | student at the Staff College |
| SCA | Society of Catholic Apostolate (Pallottine Fathers); Société en Commandité par Actions |
| SCAA | School Curriculum and Assessment Authority |
| SCAO | Senior Civil Affairs Officer |

| | |
|---|---|
| SCAR | Scientific Committee for Antarctic Research |
| ScD | Doctor of Science |
| SCDI | Scottish Council for Development and Industry |
| SCF | Senior Chaplain to the Forces; Save the Children Fund |
| Sch. | School |
| SChStJ | Senior Chaplain, Order of St John of Jerusalem |
| SCI | Society of Chemical Industry |
| SCIE | Social Care Institute of Excellence |
| SCIO | Scottish Charitable Incorporated Organisation |
| SCIS | Scottish Council of Independent Schools |
| SCL | Student in Civil Law |
| SCLC | Short Service Limited Commission |
| SCLI | Somerset and Cornwall Light Infantry |
| SCM | State Certified Midwife; Student Christian Movement |
| SCOB | Supreme Counsellor of Baobab (South Africa) |
| SCONUL | Standing Conference of National and University Libraries |
| Scot. | Scotland |
| ScotBIC | Scottish Business in the Community |
| SCOTVEC | Scottish Vocational Education Council |
| SCRL | Sociedade Cooperativa de Responsabilidade Limitada |
| SCVO | Scottish Council for Voluntary Organisations |
| SD | Staff Duties; South Dakota (postal) |
| SDA | Social Democratic Alliance; Scottish Diploma in Agriculture; Scottish Development Agency |
| SDF | Sudan Defence Force; Social Democratic Federation |
| SDI | Strategic Defence Initiative |
| SDLP | Social Democratic and Labour Party |
| SDP | Social Democratic Party |
| SE | South-east |
| SEAC | South-East Asia Command |
| SEATO | South-East Asia Treaty Organization |
| SEC | Security Exchange Commission |
| Sec. | Secretary |
| SED | Scottish Education Department |
| SEE | Society of Environmental Engineers |
| SEEDA | South East England Development Agency |
| SEFI | European Society for Engineering Education |
| SEN | State Enrolled Nurse; Special Educational Needs |
| SEP | Stanford Executive Program |
| SEPA | Scottish Environmental Protection Agency |
| SERC | Science and Engineering Research Council |
| SERT | Society of Electronic and Radio Technicians (later IEIE) |
| SESO | Senior Equipment Staff Officer |
| SF | Sinn Féin |
| SFA | Securities and Futures Authority |
| SFC | Scottish Further and Higher Education Funding Council |
| SFFMLM | Senior Fellow, Faculty of Medical Leadership and Management |
| SFHEA | Senior Fellow, Higher Education Academy |
| SFOR | Stabilisation Force |
| SFSEDA | Senior Fellow, Staff and Higher Educational Development Association |
| SFTA | Society of Film and Television Arts (*now see* BAFTA) |
| SG | Solicitor-General |
| SGA | Member, Society of Graphic Art |
| Sgt | Sergeant |
| SHA | Secondary Heads Association (*now see* ASCL); Special Health Authority |
| SHAC | London Housing Aid Centre |
| SHAEF | Supreme Headquarters, Allied Expeditionary Force |
| SHAPE | Supreme Headquarters, Allied Powers, Europe |
| SHEFC | Scottish Higher Education Funding Council (*now see* SFC) |
| SHHD | Scottish Home and Health Department |
| SHND | Scottish Higher National Diploma |
| SHO | Senior House Officer |
| SIA | Security Industry Authority |
| SIAD | Society of Industrial Artists and Designers (*now see* CSD) |
| SIAM | Society of Industrial and Applied Mathematics (US) |
| SIB | Shipbuilding Industry Board; Securities and Investments Board (*now see* FSA) |
| SICA-FICA | Foundation for International Commercial Arbitration |
| SICAV | Société d'Investissement à Capital Variable |
| SICOT | Société Internationale de Chirurgie Orthopédique et de Traumatologie |
| SID | Society for International Development |
| SIME | Security Intelligence Middle East |
| SIMG | *Societas Internationalis Medicinae Generalis* |
| SIROT | Société Internationale pour Recherche en Orthopédie et Traumatologie |
| SIS | Secret Intelligence Service |
| SITA | Société Internationale de Télécommunications Aéronautiques |
| SITPRO | Simpler Trade Procedures Board (*formerly* Simplification of International Trade Procedures) |
| SJ | Society of Jesus (Jesuits) |
| SJAB | St John Ambulance Brigade |
| SJD | Doctor of Juristic Science |
| SK | Saskatchewan (postal) |
| SL | Serjeant-at-Law; Sociedad Limitada |
| SLAC | Stanford Linear Accelerator Centre |
| SLC | St Lucia Cross |
| SLD | Social and Liberal Democrats |
| SLJ | Seri Laila Jasa (Brunei) |
| SLP | Scottish Labour Party |
| SLS | Society of Legal Scholars |
| SM | Medal of Service (Canada) (*now see* OC); Master of Science; Officer qualified for Submarine Duties |
| SMA | Society of Marine Artists (*now see* RSMA) |
| SMB | Setia Mahkota Brunei |
| SMCC | Submarine Commanding Officers' Command Course |
| SME | School of Military Engineering (*now see* RSME) |
| SMEO | Squadron Marine Engineer Officer |
| SMHO | Sovereign Military Hospitaller Order (Malta) |
| SMIEE | Senior Member, Institute of Electrical and Electronics Engineers (New York) |
| SMMT | Society of Motor Manufacturers and Traders Ltd |
| SMN | Seri Maharaja Mangku Negara (Malaysia) |
| SMO | Senior Medical Officer; Sovereign Military Order |
| SMP | Senior Managers' Program |
| SMPTE | Society of Motion Picture and Television Engineers (US) |
| SMS | Short Message Service |
| SNAME | Society of Naval Architects and Marine Engineers (US) |
| SNCF | Société Nationale des Chemins de Fer Français |
| SND | Sisters of Notre Dame |
| SNH | Scottish Natural Heritage |
| SNP | Scottish National Party |
| SNTS | Society for New Testament Studies |
| SO | Staff Officer; Scientific Officer; Symphony Orchestra |
| SOAF | Sultan of Oman's Air Force |
| SOAS | School of Oriental and African Studies |
| Soc. | Society; Socialist (France, Belgium) |
| SOCA | Serious and Organised Crime Agency |
| Soc & Lib Dem | Social and Liberal Democrats (*now see* Lib Dem) |
| Soc Dem | Social Democrats |
| SOE | Special Operations Executive; Society of Operations Engineers |
| SOGAT | Society of Graphical and Allied Trades (*now see* GPMU) |
| SOLACE or Solace | Society of Local Authority Chief Executives |
| SOLT | Society of London Theatre |
| SOM | Society of Occupational Medicine; Saskatchewan Order of Merit (Canada) |
| SOSc | Society of Ordained Scientists |
| SOTS | Society for Old Testament Study |
| sowc | Senior Officers' War Course |
| SP | Self-Propelled (Anti-Tank Regiment) |
| sp | *sine prole* (without issue) |
| SpA | Società per Azioni |
| SPAB | Society for the Protection of Ancient Buildings |
| SPARKS | Sport Aiding Medical Research for Children |
| SPCA | Society for the Prevention of Cruelty to Animals |
| SPCK | Society for Promoting Christian Knowledge |
| SPCM | Darjah Seri Paduka Cura Si Manja Kini (Malaysia) |
| SPD | Salisbury Plain District; Sozialdemokratische Partei Deutschlands |
| SPDK | Seri Panglima Darjal Kinabalu |
| SPG | Society for the Propagation of the Gospel (*now see* USPG) |
| SPk | Sitara-e-Pakistan |
| SPMB | Seri Paduka Makhota Brunei |
| SPMK | Darjah Kebasaran Seri Paduka Mahkota Kelantan (Malaysia) |
| SPMO | Senior Principal Medical Officer |
| SPNC | Society for the Promotion of Nature Conservation (*now see* RSNC) |
| SPNM | Society for the Promotion of New Music |
| SPR | Society for Psychical Research |
| sprl | société de personnes à responsabilité limitée |
| SPSO | Senior Principal Scientific Officer |
| SPTL | Society of Public Teachers of Law (*now see* SLS) |
| SPUC | Society for the Protection of Unborn Children (*formerly* the Unborn Child) |
| Sq. | Square |
| sq | staff qualified |
| SQA | Sitara-i-Quaid-i-Azam (Pakistan) |
| Sqdn or Sqn | Squadron |
| SR | Special Reserve; Southern Railway; Southern Region (BR) |
| SRA | Solicitors Regulation Authority |
| SRC | Science Research Council (later SERC); Students' Representative Council |
| SRCh | State Registered Chiropodist |
| SRHE | Society for Research into Higher Education |
| SRIS | Science Reference Information Service |
| SRN | State Registered Nurse |
| SRO | Supplementary Reserve of Officers; Self-Regulatory Organisation |
| SRP | State Registered Physiotherapist |
| SS | Saints; Straits Settlements; Steamship |
| SSA | Society of Scottish Artists; Side Saddle Association |
| SSAC | Social Security Advisory Committee |

| | |
|---|---|
| SSAFA | Soldiers, Sailors, Airmen and Families Association (*formerly* Soldiers', Sailors', and Airmen's Families Association, then Soldiers, Sailors, Airmen and Families Association Forces Help) |
| SSBN | Nuclear Submarine, Ballistic |
| SSC | Solicitor before Supreme Court (Scotland); Sculptors Society of Canada; *Societas Sanctae Crucis* (Society of the Holy Cross); Short Service Commission |
| SSEB | South of Scotland Electricity Board |
| SSEES | School of Slavonic and East European Studies |
| SSF | Society of St Francis |
| SSJE | Society of St John the Evangelist |
| SSLC | Short Service Limited Commission |
| SSM | Society of the Sacred Mission; Seri Setia Mahkota (Malaysia) |
| SSO | Senior Supply Officer; Senior Scientific Officer |
| SSR | Soviet Socialist Republic |
| SSRC | Social Science Research Council (*now see* ESRC) |
| SSSI | Sites of Special Scientific Interest |
| SSSR | Society for the Scientific Study of Religion |
| SSStJ | Serving Sister, Most Venerable Order of the Hospital of St John of Jerusalem |
| St | Street; Saint |
| STA | Sail Training Association |
| STB | *Sacrae Theologiae Baccalaureus* (Bachelor of Sacred Theology) |
| STC | Senior Training Corps |
| STD | *Sacrae Theologiae Doctor* (Doctor of Sacred Theology) |
| STEP | Skills To Empower Programme |
| STETS | Southern Theological Education and Training Scheme |
| STFC | Science and Technology Facilities Council |
| STh | Scholar in Theology |
| Stip. | Stipend; Stipendiary |
| STL | *Sacrae Theologiae Lector* (Reader or a Professor of Sacred Theology) |
| STM | *Sacrae Theologiae Magister* (Master of Sacred Theology) |
| STP | *Sacrae Theologiae Professor* (Professor of Divinity, old form of DD) |
| STSO | Senior Technical Staff Officer |
| STV | Scottish Television |
| SUNY | State University of New York |
| Supp. Res. | Supplementary Reserve (of Officers) |
| Supt | Superintendent |
| Surg. | Surgeon |
| Surv. | Surviving |
| SW | South-west |
| SWET | Society of West End Theatre (*now see* SOLT) |
| SWO | Staff Warfare Officer |
| SWRB | Sadler's Wells Royal Ballet |

# T

| | |
|---|---|
| T | Telephone; Territorial |
| TA | Telegraphic Address; Territorial Army |
| TAF | Tactical Air Force |
| T&AVR | Territorial and Army Volunteer Reserve |
| TARO | Territorial Army Reserve of Officers |
| TAS | Torpedo and Anti Submarine Course |
| TASS | Technical, Administrative and Supervisory Section of AUEW (now part of MSF) |
| TAVRA or TA&VRA | Territorial Auxiliary and Volunteer Reserve Association (*now see* RFCA) |
| TC | Order of the Trinity Cross (Trinidad and Tobago) |
| TCCB | Test and County Cricket Board (*now see* ECB) |
| TCD | Trinity College, Dublin (University of Dublin, Trinity College) |
| TCF | Temporary Chaplain to the Forces |
| TCPA | Town and Country Planning Association |
| TD | Territorial Efficiency Decoration; Efficiency Decoration (T&AVR) (since April 1967); Teachta Dala (Member of the Dáil, Eire) |
| TDA | Training and Development Agency for Schools |
| TDD | Tubercular Diseases Diploma |
| TE | Technical Engineer |
| TEC | Technician Education Council (later BTEC); Training and Enterprise Council |
| Tech(CEI) | Technician |
| TechRICS | Technical Member, Royal Institution of Chartered Surveyors |
| TEF | Teaching Excellence Framework |
| TEFL | Teaching English as a Foreign Language |
| TEFLA | Teaching English as a Foreign Language to Adults |
| TEM | Territorial Efficiency Medal |
| TEMA | Telecommunication Engineering and Manufacturing Association |
| Temp. | Temperature; Temporary |
| TEng(CEI) | Technician Engineer (*now see* IEng) |
| Tenn | Tennessee |
| TEO | Teaching English Overseas |
| TES | Times Educational Supplement |
| TESL | Teaching English as a Second Language |
| TESOL | Teaching English to Speakers of other Languages |
| Tex | Texas |
| TF | Territorial Force |
| TfL | Transport for London |
| TFR | Territorial Force Reserve |
| TFTS | Tactical Fighter Training Squadron |
| TGEW | Timber Growers England and Wales Ltd |
| TGO | Timber Growers' Organisation (*now see* TGEW) |
| TGWU | Transport and General Workers' Union |
| ThD | Doctor of Theology |
| THES | Times Higher Education Supplement |
| ThL | Theological Licentiate |
| ThM | Master of Theology |
| ThSchol | Scholar in Theology |
| TIMS | The Institute of Management Sciences (*now see* INFORMS) |
| TISCA | The Independent Schools Christian Alliance |
| TLS | Times Literary Supplement |
| TMA | Theatrical Management Association |
| TN | Tennessee (postal) |
| TNC | Theatres National Committee |
| TOPSS | Training Organisation for the Personal Social Services |
| TPI | Town Planning Institute (*now see* RTPI) |
| TPP | Transport Planning Professional |
| TPsych | Trainer in Psychiatry |
| TQ | Teaching Qualification |
| TRA | Tenants' and Residents' Association |
| Trans. | Translation; Translated |
| Transf. | Transferred |
| TrATB | Treble, Alto, Tenor, Bass |
| TRC | Thames Rowing Club |
| TRE | Telecommunications Research Establishment (later RRE) |
| TRH | Their Royal Highnesses |
| TRIC | Television and Radio Industries Club |
| Trin. | Trinity |
| TRL | Transport Research Laboratory |
| TRRL | Transport and Road Research Laboratory (*now see* TRL) |
| TS | Training Ship; Turbine Steamer |
| TSB | Trustee Savings Bank |
| tsc | passed a Territorial Army Course in Staff Duties |
| TSE | Transmissible Spongiform Encephalopathies |
| TSSA | Transport Salaried Staffs' Association |
| TSSF | Tertiary, Society of St Francis |
| TSWA | Television South West Arts |
| TTA | Teacher Training Agency (*now see* TDA) |
| TUC | Trades Union Congress |
| TUS | Trade Union Side |
| TUSC | Trade Unionist and Socialist Coalition |
| TUV | Traditional Unionist Voice |
| TV | Television |
| TVEI | Technical and Vocational Education Initiative |
| TWA | Thames Water Authority |
| TX | Texas (postal) |

# U

| | |
|---|---|
| U | Unionist |
| u | uncle |
| UA | Unitary Authority |
| UACE | Universities Association for Continuing Education |
| UAE | United Arab Emirates |
| UAL | University of the Arts London |
| UAU | Universities Athletic Union |
| UBC | University of British Columbia |
| UC | University College |
| UCAS | Universities and Colleges Admissions Service |
| UCCA | Universities Central Council on Admissions |
| UCCF | Universities and Colleges Christian Fellowship of Evangelical Unions |
| UCD | University College Dublin |
| UCE | University of Central England |
| UCEA | Universities and Colleges Employers Association |
| UCET | Universities Council for Education of Teachers |
| UCH | University College Hospital (London) |
| UCI | Union Cycliste Internationale |
| UCL | University College London |
| UCLA | University of California at Los Angeles |
| UCLES | University of Cambridge Local Examinations Syndicate |
| UCLH | University College London Hospital |
| UCMSM | University College and Middlesex School of Medicine |
| UCNW | University College of North Wales |
| UCS | University College School |
| UCSB | University of California at Santa Barbara |
| UCSD | University of California at San Diego |
| UCSF | University of California at San Francisco |
| UCUNF | Ulster Conservatives and Unionists - New Force |

| | |
|---|---|
| **UCW** | University College of Wales; Union of Communication Workers (*now see* CWU) |
| **UDC** | Urban District Council; Urban Development Corporation |
| **UDF** | Union Defence Force; Union pour la démocratie française |
| **UDM** | United Democratic Movement (South Africa) |
| **UDR** | Ulster Defence Regiment; Union des Démocrates pour la V<sup>ème</sup> République (later RPR) |
| **UDSR** | Union Démocratique et Socialiste de la Résistance |
| **UEA** | University of East Anglia |
| **UEFA** | Union of European Football Associations |
| **UEL** | University of East London |
| **UEMS** | Union Européenne des Médecins Spécialistes |
| **UF** | United Free Church |
| **UFAW** | Universities Federation for Animal Welfare |
| **UFC** | Universities' Funding Council |
| **UGC** | University Grants Committee (later UFC) |
| **UHI** | University of the Highlands and Islands (*formerly* University of the Highlands and Islands Millennium Institute) |
| **UIAA** | Union Internationale des Associations d'Alpinisme |
| **UICC** | Union Internationale contre le Cancer |
| **UIE** | Union Internationale des Etudiants |
| **UISPP** | Union Internationale des Sciences Préhistoriques et Protohistoriques |
| **UITP** | International Union of Public Transport |
| **UJD** | *Utriusque Juris Doctor* (Doctor of both Laws, Doctor of Canon and Civil Law) |
| **UK** | United Kingdom |
| **UKAEA** | United Kingdom Atomic Energy Authority |
| **UKCC** | United Kingdom Central Council for Nursing, Midwifery and Health Visiting |
| **UKCCCR** | United Kingdom Co-ordinating Committee on Cancer Research |
| **UKCICC** | United Kingdom Commanders-in-Chief Committees |
| **UKCISA** | United Kingdom Council for International Student Affairs |
| **UKCOSA** | United Kingdom Council for Overseas Student Affairs (*now see* UKCISA) |
| **UKCP** | United Kingdom Council for Psychotherapy |
| **UKERNA** | United Kingdom Education and Research Networking Association |
| **UKIAS** | United Kingdom Immigrants' Advisory Service |
| **UKIC** | United Kingdom Institute for Conservation |
| **UKIP** | United Kingdom Independence Party |
| **UKLF** | United Kingdom Land Forces |
| **UKMEA** | United Kingdom, Middle East and Africa |
| **UKMF(L)** | United Kingdom Military Forces (Land) |
| **UKMILREP** | United Kingdom Military Representative |
| **UKMIS** | United Kingdom Mission |
| **UKOLN** | United Kingdom Office of Library Networking |
| **UKOOA** | United Kingdom Offshore Operators Association |
| **UKPIA** | United Kingdom Petroleum Industry Association Ltd |
| **UKRI** | UK Research and Innovation |
| **UKSC** | United Kingdom Support Command |
| **UKSLS** | United Kingdom Services Liaison Staff |
| **UKTI** | UK Trade & Investment |
| **UKU** | United Kingdom Unionist |
| **ULPS** | Union of Liberal and Progressive Synagogues |
| **UMDS** | United Medical and Dental Schools |
| **UMIST** | University of Manchester Institute of Science and Technology |
| **UMP** | Union pour un Mouvement Populaire (*formerly* Union pour la Majorité Présidentielle) |
| **UN** | United Nations |
| **UNA** | United Nations Association |
| **UNCAST** | United Nations Conference on the Applications of Science and Technology |
| **UNCIO** | United Nations Conference on International Organisation |
| **UNCITRAL** | United Nations Commission on International Trade Law |
| **UNCSTD** | United Nations Conference on Science and Technology for Development |
| **UNCTAD** or **Unctad** | United Nations Commission for Trade and Development |
| **UNDP** | United Nations Development Programme |
| **UNDRO** | United Nations Disaster Relief Organisation |
| **UNECA** | United Nations Economic Commission for Asia |
| **UNECE** | United Nations Economic Commission for Europe |
| **UNED** | United Nations Environment and Development |
| **UNEP** | United Nations Environment Programme |
| **UNESCO** or **Unesco** | United Nations Educational, Scientific and Cultural Organisation |
| **UNFAO** | United Nations Food and Agriculture Organisation |
| **UNFICYP** | United Nations Force in Cyprus |
| **UNHCR** | United Nations High Commissioner for Refugees |
| **UNICE** | Union des Industries de la Communauté Européenne |
| **UNICEF** or **Unicef** | United Nations Children's Fund (*formerly* United Nations International Children's Emergency Fund) |
| **UNIDO** | United Nations Industrial Development Organisation |
| **UNIDROIT** | Institut International pour l'Unification du Droit Privé |
| **UNIFEM** | United Nations Development Fund for Women |
| **UNIFIL** | United Nations Interim Force in Lebanon |
| **UNIPEDE** | Union Internationale des Producteurs et Distributeurs d'Energie Electrique |
| **UNISIST** | Universal System for Information in Science and Technology |
| **UNITAR** | United Nations Institute of Training and Research |
| **Univ.** | University |
| **UNO** | United Nations Organization |
| **UNODC** | United Nations Office on Drugs and Crime |
| **UNRRA** | United Nations Relief and Rehabilitation Administration |
| **UNRWA** | United Nations Relief and Works Agency |
| **UNSCOB** | United Nations Special Commission on the Balkans |
| **UP** | United Provinces; Uttar Pradesh; United Presbyterian |
| **UPGC** | University and Polytechnic Grants Committee |
| **UPNI** | Unionist Party of Northern Ireland |
| **UPU** | Universal Postal Union |
| **UPUP** | Ulster Popular Unionist Party |
| **URC** | United Reformed Church; Urban Regeneration Company |
| **URSI** | Union Radio-Scientifique Internationale |
| **US** | United States |
| **USA** | United States of America |
| **USAAF** | United States Army Air Force |
| **USAF** | United States Air Force |
| **USAID** | United States Agency for International Development |
| **USAR** | United States Army Reserve |
| **USC** | University of Southern California |
| **USDAW** | Union of Shop Distributive and Allied Workers |
| **USM** | Unlisted Securities Market |
| **USMA** | United States Military Academy |
| **USMC** | United States Marine Corps |
| **USN** | United States Navy |
| **USNR** | United States Naval Reserve |
| **USPG** | United Society Partners in the Gospel (*formerly* United Society for the Propagation of the Gospel) |
| **USPHS** | United States Public Health Service |
| **USPS** | United States Postal Service |
| **USS** | United States Ship |
| **USSR** | Union of Soviet Socialist Republics |
| **USVI** | United States Virgin Islands |
| **UT** | Utah (postal) |
| **UTC** | University Training Corps |
| **U3A** | University of the Third Age |
| **UTS** | University of Technology, Sydney |
| **UU** | Ulster Unionist |
| **UUK** | Universities UK |
| **UUP** | Ulster Unionist Party |
| **UUUC** | United Ulster Unionist Coalition |
| **UUUP** | United Ulster Unionist Party |
| **UWCC** | University of Wales College of Cardiff |
| **UWCM** | University of Wales College of Medicine |
| **UWE** | University of the West of England |
| **UWIC** | University of Wales Institute, Cardiff |
| **UWIST** | University of Wales Institute of Science and Technology |
| **UWP** | United Workers' Party (Dominica) |
| **UWS** | University of the West of Scotland |
| **UWT** | Union of Women Teachers |
| **UWTSD** | University of Wales Trinity Saint David |

# V

| | |
|---|---|
| **V** | Five (Roman numerals); Version; Vicar; Viscount; Vice |
| **v** | *versus* (against) |
| **v** or **vid.** | *vide* (see) |
| **VA** | Virginia (postal) |
| **Va** | Virginia |
| **VAD** | Voluntary Aid Detachment |
| **V&A** | Victoria and Albert |
| **VAT** | Value Added Tax |
| **VC** | Victoria Cross; Voluntary Controlled |
| **VCAS** | Vice Chief of the Air Staff |
| **VCDS** | Vice Chief of the Defence Staff |
| **VCGS** | Vice Chief of the General Staff |
| **VCM** | Member, Victoria College of Music |
| **VCNS** | Vice Chief of the Naval Staff |
| **VCT** | Venture Capital Trust |
| **VD** | Royal Naval Volunteer Reserve Officers' Decoration (*now* VRD); Volunteer Officers' Decoration; Victorian Decoration |
| **VDC** | Volunteer Defence Corps |
| **VDI** | (Member) Verein Deutscher Ingenieure |
| **Ven.** | Venerable |
| **Vet.** | Veterinary |
| **VetMB** | Bachelor of Veterinary Medicine |
| **VG** | Vicar-General |
| **Vic** | Victoria |
| **Vice Adm.** | Vice Admiral |
| **VIP** | Very Important Person |
| **Visc.** | Viscount |
| **VLSI** | Very Large Scale Integration |
| **VLV** | Voice of the Listener and Viewer |

| | | | |
|---|---|---|---|
| **VM** | Victory Medal | **YT** | Yukon Territory (postal) |
| **VMA** | Fixed Wing Marine Attack | **YTS** | Youth Training Scheme |
| **VMGO** | Vice Master General of the Ordnance | **YVFF** | Young Volunteer Force Foundation |
| **VMH** | Victoria Medal of Honour (Royal Horticultural Society) | **YWCA** | Young Women's Christian Association |
| **VMSM** | Voluntary Medical Services Medal | **ZANU PF** | Zimbabwe African National Union Patriotic Front |
| **Vol.** | Volume; Voluntary; Volunteers | **ZAPU** | Zimbabwe African People's Union |
| **VP** | Vice-President | **ZIPRA** | Zimbabwe People's Revolutionary Army |
| **VPP** | Volunteer Political Party | | |
| **VPRP** | Vice-President, Royal Society of Portrait Painters | | |
| **VQMG** | Vice-Quartermaster-General | | |
| **VR** | *Victoria Regina* (Queen Victoria); Volunteer Reserve | | |
| **VRD** | Royal Naval Volunteer Reserve Officers' Decoration | | |
| **VRSM** | Volunteer Reserves Service Medal | | |
| **VSO** | Voluntary Service Overseas | | |
| **VT** | Vermont (postal) | | |
| **Vt** | Vermont | | |
| **VUP** | Vanguard Unionist Party | | |
| **VVD** | Volkspartij voor Vrijheiden Democratie | | |

# W

| | |
|---|---|
| **W** | West; Website |
| **WA** | Western Australia; Washington (postal) |
| **WAAF** | Women's Auxiliary Air Force (later WRAF) |
| **WACL** | Women in Advertising and Communications, London |
| **WAOS** | Welsh Agricultural Organisations Society |
| **Wash** | Washington State |
| **WCC** | World Council of Churches |
| **W/Cdr** | Wing Commander |
| **WCMD** | Welsh College of Music and Drama (*now see* RWCMD) |
| **WDA** | Welsh Development Agency |
| **WEA** | Workers' Educational Association; Royal West of England Academy |
| **WEF** | World Economic Forum |
| **WEU** | Western European Union |
| **WFEO** | World Federation of Engineering Organisations |
| **WFSW** | World Federation of Scientific Workers |
| **WFTU** | World Federation of Trade Unions |
| **WhF** | Whitworth Fellow |
| **WHO** | World Health Organization |
| **WhSch** | Whitworth Scholar |
| **WI** | West Indies; Women's Institute; Wisconsin (postal) |
| **Wilts** | Wiltshire |
| **WIPO** | World Intellectual Property Organization |
| **Wis** | Wisconsin |
| **Wits** | Witwatersrand |
| **WJEC** | Welsh Joint Education Committee |
| **WLD** | Women Liberal Democrats |
| **Wm** | William |
| **WMA** | World Medical Association |
| **WMO** | World Meteorological Organization |
| **WNO** | Welsh National Opera |
| **WO** | War Office; Warrant Officer |
| **Worcs** | Worcestershire |
| **WR** | West Riding; Western Region (BR) |
| **WRAC** | Women's Royal Army Corps |
| **WRAF** | Women's Royal Air Force |
| **WRNS** | Women's Royal Naval Service |
| **WRVS** | Women's Royal Voluntary Service (*now see* RVS) |
| **WS** | Writer to the Signet |
| **WSAVA** | World Small Animal Veterinary Association |
| **WSET** | Wine and Spirits Educational Trust |
| **WSPA** | World Society for the Protection of Animals |
| **WTO** | World Trade Organisation |
| **WV** | West Virginia (postal) |
| **WVS** | Women's Voluntary Services (later WRVS) |
| **WWF** | World Wide Fund for Nature (*formerly* World Wildlife Fund) |
| **WY** | Wyoming (postal) |

# XYZ

| | |
|---|---|
| **X** | Ten (Roman numerals) |
| **XO** | Executive Officer |
| **y** | youngest |
| **YC** | Young Conservative |
| **YCNAC** | Young Conservatives National Advisory Committee |
| **Yeo.** | Yeomanry |
| **YHA** | Youth Hostels Association |
| **YMCA** | Young Men's Christian Association |
| **YOI** | Young Offenders Institute |
| **Yorks** | Yorkshire |
| **YPTES** | Young People's Trust for Endangered Species |
| **yr** | younger |
| **yrs** | years |

# THE ROYAL FAMILY

*Born*

## THE SOVEREIGN

**Her Majesty Queen Elizabeth II, (Elizabeth Alexandra Mary).** . . . . . . 21 April 1926
Succeeded her father, King George VI, 6 February 1952
Married 20 Nov. 1947, HRH The Duke of Edinburgh, *now* HRH The Prince Philip, Duke of Edinburgh, KG, KT, OM, GCVO, GBE, ONZ, QSO, AK, GCL, CC, CMM (*b* 10 June 1921, *s* of HRH Prince Andrew of Greece (*d* 1944) and of HRH Princess Andrew of Greece (*d* 1969), *gg-d* of Queen Victoria; *cr* 1947, Baron Greenwich, Earl of Merioneth and Duke of Edinburgh)
*Residences:* Buckingham Palace, SW1A 1AA; Windsor Castle, Berkshire SL4 1NJ; Sandringham House, Norfolk PE35 6EN; Balmoral Castle, Aberdeenshire AB35 5TB.

## SONS AND DAUGHTER OF HER MAJESTY

**HRH The Prince of Wales, (Prince Charles Philip Arthur George),** . . . . . 14 Nov. 1948
KG, KT, GCB, OM, AK, QSO, CC, ADC; *cr* 1958, Prince of Wales and Earl of Chester; Duke of Cornwall; Duke of Rothesay, Earl of Carrick and Baron of Renfrew; Lord of the Isles and Great Steward of Scotland
Married 1st, 29 July 1981, Lady Diana Frances Spencer (*b* 1 July 1961, *y d* of 8th Earl Spencer, LVO, she *d* 31 Aug. 1997), (marriage dissolved, 1996), and has issue –
HRH THE DUKE OF CAMBRIDGE, (PRINCE WILLIAM ARTHUR PHILIP LOUIS), KG, KT, ADC;
*cr* 2011, Baron Carrickfergus, Earl of Strathearn and Duke of Cambridge . . . 21 June 1982
Married 29 April 2011, Catherine Elizabeth Middleton, GCVO, *d* of Michael and Carole Middleton, and has issue –
HRH PRINCE GEORGE OF CAMBRIDGE, (PRINCE GEORGE ALEXANDER LOUIS) . . 22 July 2013
HRH PRINCESS CHARLOTTE OF CAMBRIDGE, (PRINCESS CHARLOTTE ELIZABETH DIANA) 2 May 2015
HRH PRINCE LOUIS OF CAMBRIDGE, (PRINCE LOUIS ARTHUR CHARLES). . . 23 April 2018
HRH THE DUKE OF SUSSEX, (PRINCE HENRY CHARLES ALBERT DAVID), KCVO, ADC; .
*cr* 2018, Baron Kilkeel, Earl of Dumbarton and Duke of Sussex . . . 15 Sept. 1984
Married 19 May 2018, (Rachel) Meghan Markle, *d* of Thomas Markle and Doria Ragland, and has issue –
ARCHIE HARRISON MOUNTBATTEN-WINDSOR . . . . . . 6 May 2019
Married 2nd, 9 April 2005, Mrs Camilla Rosemary Parker Bowles (*now* HRH The Duchess of Cornwall, GCVO), *d* of late Major Bruce Shand, MC
*Office:* Clarence House, SW1A 1BA; *residences:* Highgrove, Doughton, Tetbury, Gloucestershire GL8 8TN; Birkhall, Ballater, Aberdeenshire.

**HRH The Duke of York, (Prince Andrew Albert Christian Edward),** KG, GCVO, ADC; . 19 Feb. 1960
*cr* 1986, Baron Killyleagh, Earl of Inverness and Duke of York
Married 23 July 1986, Sarah Margaret Ferguson, *now* Sarah, Duchess of York (*b* 15 Oct. 1959, 2nd *d* of late Major Ronald Ivor Ferguson, Life Guards), (marriage dissolved, 1996), and has issue –
HRH PRINCESS BEATRICE OF YORK, (PRINCESS BEATRICE ELIZABETH MARY) . . . 8 Aug. 1988
HRH PRINCESS EUGENIE OF YORK, (PRINCESS EUGENIE VICTORIA HELENA), (MRS J. C. S. BROOKSBANK) 23 March 1990
Married 12 Oct. 2018, Jack Christopher Stamp Brooksbank
*Office:* Buckingham Palace, SW1A 1AA; *residence:* Royal Lodge, Windsor Great Park, Windsor, Berkshire SL4 2HW.

**HRH The Earl of Wessex, (Prince Edward Antony Richard Louis),** KG, GCVO, ADC; . . 10 March 1964
*cr* 1999, Viscount Severn and Earl of Wessex; Earl of Forfar
Married 19 June 1999, Sophie Helen Rhys-Jones, GCVO (*b* 20 Jan. 1965, *d* of Christopher and late Mary Rhys-Jones), and has issue –
JAMES ALEXANDER PHILIP THEO MOUNTBATTEN-WINDSOR, (VISCOUNT SEVERN, *qv*). . 17 Dec. 2007
LOUISE ALICE ELIZABETH MARY MOUNTBATTEN-WINDSOR, (LADY LOUISE WINDSOR) . 8 Nov. 2003
*Office:* Buckingham Palace, SW1A 1AA; *residence:* Bagshot Park, Bagshot, Surrey GU19 5PL.

**HRH The Princess Royal, (Princess Anne Elizabeth Alice Louise),** KG, KT, GCVO, QSO . . 15 Aug. 1950
Married 1st, 14 Nov. 1973, Captain Mark Anthony Peter Phillips, *qv* (marriage dissolved, 1992), and has issue –
PETER MARK ANDREW PHILLIPS . . . . . . . . . . 15 Nov. 1977
Married 17 May 2008, Autumn Patricia, *d* of Brian Kelly, and has issue –
SAVANNAH ANNE KATHLEEN PHILLIPS . . . . . . . . 29 Dec. 2010
ISLA ELIZABETH PHILLIPS . . . . . . . . . . 29 March 2012
ZARA ANNE ELIZABETH PHILLIPS, MBE, (MRS M. J. TINDALL) . . . . 15 May 1981
Married 30 July 2011, Michael James Tindall, MBE, *s* of Philip and Linda Tindall, and has issue –
MIA GRACE TINDALL . . . . . . . . . . . 17 Jan. 2014
LENA ELIZABETH TINDALL. . . . . . . . . . . 18 June 2018
Married 2nd, 12 Dec. 1992, Vice Admiral Sir Timothy James Hamilton Laurence, *qv*
*Office:* Buckingham Palace, SW1A 1AA; *residence:* Gatcombe Park, Minchinhampton, Stroud, Gloucestershire GL6 9AT.

## NEPHEW AND NIECE OF HER MAJESTY

Children of HRH The Princess Margaret (Rose), (Countess of Snowdon, CI, GCVO, *b* 21 Aug. 1930, *d* 9 Feb. 2002) and 1st Earl of Snowdon, GCVO, RDI (*b* 7 March 1930, *d* 13 Jan. 2017)

**2nd Earl of Snowdon, (David Albert Charles Armstrong-Jones),** *qv*. . . . . 3 Nov. 1961
Married 8 Oct. 1993, Hon. Serena Alleyne Stanhope, *o d* of Earl of Harrington, *qv* and has issue –
HON. CHARLES PATRICK INIGO ARMSTRONG-JONES, (VISCOUNT LINLEY, *qv*) . . 1 July 1999
HON. MARGARITA ELIZABETH ALLEYNE ARMSTRONG-JONES . . . . . 14 May 2002

**Lady Sarah Chatto, (Sarah Frances Elizabeth Chatto)** . . . . . . 1 May 1964
Married 14 July 1994, Daniel Chatto, *s* of late Thomas Chatto and Rosalind Chatto, and has issue –
SAMUEL DAVID BENEDICT CHATTO . . . . . . . . . 28 July 1996
ARTHUR ROBERT NATHANIEL CHATTO . . . . . . . . 5 Feb. 1999

## COUSINS OF HER MAJESTY

Child of HRH The Duke of Gloucester (Prince Henry William Frederick Albert, *b* 31 March 1900, *d* 10 June 1974) and HRH Princess Alice Christabel, Duchess of Gloucester, GCB, CI, GCVO, GBE (*b* 25 Dec. 1901, *d* 29 Oct. 2004), 3rd *d* of 7th Duke of Buccleuch

**HRH The Duke of Gloucester, (Prince Richard Alexander Walter George),** KG, GCVO . . 26 Aug. 1944
   Married 8 July 1972, Birgitte Eva van Deurs, GCVO (*b* 20 June 1946, *d* of Asger Preben Wissing Henriksen), and has issue –
     ALEXANDER PATRICK GREGERS RICHARD, (EARL OF ULSTER, *qv*) . . . . 24 Oct. 1974
       Married 22 June 2002, Dr Claire Alexandra, *d* of Mr and Mrs Robert Booth, and has issue –
         XAN RICHARD ANDERS, (LORD CULLODEN, *qv*) . . . . . . 12 March 2007
         COSIMA ROSE ALEXANDRA, (LADY COSIMA WINDSOR) . . . . 20 May 2010
     DAVINA ELIZABETH ALICE BENEDIKTE . . . . . . . . 19 Nov. 1977
       Married 31 July 2004, Gary Christie Lewis (marriage dissolved, 2018), and has issue –
         TĀNE MAHUTA LEWIS . . . . . . . . . . 25 May 2012
         SENNA KOWHAI LEWIS . . . . . . . . . . 22 June 2010
     ROSE VICTORIA BIRGITTE LOUISE, (LADY ROSE GILMAN) . . . . . 1 March 1980
       Married 19 July 2008, George Edward Gilman, and has issue –
         LYLA BEATRIX CHRISTABEL GILMAN . . . . . . . . 30 May 2010
         RUFUS FREDERICK MONTAGU GILMAN . . . . . . . . 2 Nov. 2012
   *Residence:* Kensington Palace, W8 4PU.

Children of HRH The Duke of Kent (Prince George Edward Alexander Edmund, *b* 20 Dec. 1902, *d* 25 Aug. 1942) and HRH Princess Marina, Duchess of Kent (*b* 13 Dec. 1906, *d* 27 Aug. 1968), *y d* of late Prince Nicholas of Greece

**HRH The Duke of Kent, (Prince Edward George Nicholas Paul Patrick),** KG, GCMG, GCVO . 9 Oct. 1935
   Married 8 June 1961, Katharine Lucy Mary Worsley, GCVO (*b* 22 Feb. 1933, *o d* of Sir William Worsley, 4th Bt), and has issue –
     GEORGE PHILIP NICHOLAS, (EARL OF ST ANDREWS, *qv*) . . . . . 26 June 1962
       Married 9 Jan. 1988, Sylvana Tomaselli, and has issue –
         EDWARD EDMUND MAXIMILIAN GEORGE, (BARON DOWNPATRICK, *qv*) . 2 Dec. 1988
         MARINA-CHARLOTTE ALEXANDRA KATHARINE HELEN, (LADY MARINA-CHARLOTTE WINDSOR) 30 Sept. 1992
         AMELIA SOPHIA THEODORA MARY MARGARET, (LADY AMELIA WINDSOR) . . 24 Aug. 1995
     NICHOLAS CHARLES EDWARD JONATHAN, (LORD NICHOLAS WINDSOR) . . . 25 July 1970
       Married 19 Oct. 2006, Princess Paola Doimi de Lupis Frankopan Šubic Zrinski, and has issue –
         ALBERT LOUIS PHILIP EDWARD WINDSOR . . . . . . . 22 Sept. 2007
         LEOPOLD ERNEST AUGUSTUS GUELPH WINDSOR . . . . . . 8 Sept. 2009
         LOUIS ARTHUR NICHOLAS FELIX WINDSOR . . . . . . . 27 May 2014
     HELEN MARINA LUCY, (LADY HELEN TAYLOR) . . . . . . . 28 April 1964
       Married 18 July 1992, Timothy Verner Taylor, *e s* of Commander Michael Taylor, RN and Mrs Colin Walkinshaw, and has issue –
         COLUMBUS GEORGE DONALD TAYLOR . . . . . . . . 6 Aug. 1994
         CASSIUS EDWARD TAYLOR . . . . . . . . . . 26 Dec. 1996
         ELOISE OLIVIA KATHARINE TAYLOR . . . . . . . . 2 March 2003
         ESTELLA OLGA ELIZABETH TAYLOR . . . . . . . . 21 Dec. 2004
   *Office:* St James's Palace, SW1A 1BQ; *residence:* Wren House, Palace Green, W8 4PY.

**HRH Prince Michael of Kent, (Prince Michael George Charles Franklin),** GCVO . . . 4 July 1942
   Married 30 June 1978, Baroness Marie-Christine Agnes Hedwig Ida von Reibnitz (*b* 15 Jan. 1945, *d* of Baron Günther Hubertus von Reibnitz), and has issue –
     FREDERICK MICHAEL GEORGE DAVID LOUIS, (LORD FREDERICK WINDSOR) . . . 6 April 1979
       Married 12 Sept. 2009, Sophie Lara, *d* of Barry and Cynthia Winkleman, and has issue –
         MAUD ELIZABETH DAPHNE MARINA WINDSOR . . . . . . . 15 Aug. 2013
         ISABELLA ALEXANDRA MAY WINDSOR . . . . . . . . 16 Jan. 2016
     GABRIELLA MARINA ALEXANDRA OPHELIA, (LADY GABRIELLA KINGSTON) . . . 23 April 1981
       Married 18 May 2019, Thomas Kingston
   *Residence:* Kensington Palace, W8 4PU.

**HRH Princess Alexandra (Helen Elizabeth Olga Christabel), The Hon. Lady Ogilvy,** . . 25 Dec. 1936
KG, GCVO
   Married 24 April 1963, Rt Hon. Sir Angus (James Bruce) Ogilvy, KCVO, PC (*b* 14 Sept. 1928, *d* 26 Dec. 2004, *s* of 12th Earl of Airlie, KT, GCVO, MC), and has issue –
     JAMES ROBERT BRUCE OGILVY . . . . . . . . . . 29 Feb. 1964
       Married 30 July 1988, Julia, *d* of Charles Frederick Melville Rawlinson, *qv*, and has issue –
         ALEXANDER CHARLES OGILVY . . . . . . . . . 12 Nov. 1996
         FLORA ALEXANDRA OGILVY . . . . . . . . . . 15 Dec. 1994
     MARINA VICTORIA ALEXANDRA OGILVY . . . . . . . . 31 July 1966
       Married 2 Feb. 1990, Paul Julian Mowatt (marriage dissolved, 1997), and has issue –
         CHRISTIAN ALEXANDER MOWATT . . . . . . . . . 4 June 1993
         ZENOUSKA MAY MOWATT . . . . . . . . . . 26 May 1990
   *Office:* Buckingham Palace, SW1A 1AA; *residence:* Thatched House Lodge, Richmond, Surrey TW10 5HP.

# EDITORS' NOTE

A proof of each entry is sent to its subject every year for personal revision. Any editorial queries concerning content and accuracy are raised with the biographee at this stage, for amendment in the next edition.

Addresses printed in *Who's Who* are those which the subjects of the entries have submitted for publication. Addresses in London, and the names of London clubs, are unaccompanied by the word 'London'.

Entries are listed alphabetically by surname; forenames follow, those which are not customarily used by the subject being placed within brackets. Where a diminutive or alternative name is preferred, this is shown in brackets after all the given names.

Inclusion in *Who's Who* has never, at any time, been a matter for payment or of obligation to purchase.

# A

**AARONBERG, David Jeffrey;** QC 2010; **His Honour Judge Aaronberg;** a Circuit Judge, since 2018; *b* Edgware, Middx, 16 June 1958; *s* of Sidney and Yvonne Aaronberg; *m* 1990, Linda Aaronson; two *d*. *Educ:* Merchant Taylors' Sch.; Poly. of Central London (BA Law). Called to the Bar, Inner Temple, 1981, Bencher, 2017; a Recorder, 2007–18. *Recreations:* theatre, cinema, travel, ski-ing. *Address:* Wood Green Crown Court, Woodall House, Lordship Lane, N22 5LF.

**AARONOVITCH, David Morris;** columnist, The Times, since 2005; *b* 8 July 1954; *s* of Dr Sam Aaronovitch and late Lavender Aaronovitch; *m* 2005, Sarah Powell; three *d*. *Educ:* William Ellis Sch., Highgate; Manchester Univ. (BA Hons Hist.). Pres., NUS, 1980–82. Researcher and producer, Weekend World, LWT, 1982–87; BBC: Ed., On the Record, 1988–90; Hd, Political News, 1990–93; Managing Ed., Current Affairs, 1993–94; Chief Leader Writer, Independent, 1995–97; columnist: Independent, 1997–2003; Guardian and Observer, 2003–05. *Publications:* Paddling to Jerusalem, 2000; Voodoo Histories: the role of the conspiracy theory in shaping modern history, 2009; Party Animals: my family and other communists, 2016. *Recreations:* running, theatre, film, watching football. *Address:* The Times, 1 London Bridge Street, SE1 9GF. *E:* David.Aaronovitch@btinternet.com.

**AARONSON, Graham Raphael;** QC 1982; *b* 31 Dec. 1944; *s* of late John and Dora Aaronson; *m*; two *s* one *d*; *m* 1993, Pearl Isobel Buchler; two step *s* one step *d*. *Educ:* City of London Sch.; Trinity Hall, Cambridge (Thomas Waraker Law Schol.; MA). Called to the Bar, Middle Temple, 1966, Bencher 1991; practised Revenue law, 1968–73 and 1978–; Founding Mem. and Partner, Joseph Hage Aaronson LLP, 2013–. Chairman: Tax Law Review Cttee, 1994–97; Revenue Bar Assoc., 1995–98; Gen. Anti-Avoidance Rule Study Gp, HM Treasury, 2010–11; Interim Gen. Anti-Abuse Rule Adv. Panel, 2012–13. Advr on tax reform to Treasury, Israel, 1986–90. Chm., Dietary Res. Foundn, 1989–93. Founder, Standford Grange residential rehabilitation centre for ex-offenders, 1974; Man. Dir, Worldwide Plastics Development, 1973–77; Dir, Bridgend Group PLC, 1973–92. *Address:* Joseph Hage Aaronson LLP, 280 High Holborn, WC1V 7EE.

**AARONSON, Sir Michael (John),** Kt 2006; CBE 2000; independent management consultant and leadership coach, since 2007; Chair, Strategic Advisory Group, Global Challenges Research Fund, since 2016; *b* 8 Sept. 1947; *s* of late Edward John Aaronson and Marian Aaronson (*née* Davies); *m* 1988, Andrene Margaret Sutherland; two *s* one *d*. *Educ:* Merchant Taylors' Sch.; St John's Coll., Oxford (Sir Thomas White Scholar, Trevelyan Scholar; MA). Field Co-ordinator, SCF, Nigeria, 1969–71; HM Diplomatic Service, 1972–88, served Paris, Lagos, Rangoon; Save the Children Fund: Overseas Dir, 1988–95; Dir-Gen., 1995–2005. Chm., Frimley Health (Frimley Park Hosp.) NHS Foundn Trust, 2006–16. Non-exec. Dir, Oxford Policy Mgt Ltd, 2006–18. Professorial Res. Fellow and Exec. Dir, cii - The Centre for Internat. Intervention, 2011–15, Hon. Vis. Prof., 2008–11 and 2015–, Univ. of Surrey. A Civil Service Comr, 2007–12. Chm. Bd, Centre for Humanitarian Dialogue (Geneva), 2001–08; Gov., Westminster Foundn for Democracy, 2001–07 (Vice-Chm., 2005–07); non-exec. Dir, Nat. Sch. of Govt Internat., 2012–15. Mem. Council, RSA, 2004–09. Vis. Fellow, Nuffield Coll., Oxford, 2004–12 (Hon. Fellow, 2012–). Freeman: City of London, 1989; Merchant Taylors' Co., 1989. DUniv Surrey, 2011. *Recreations:* sports, the performing arts. *T:* 07785 571416. *Club:* MCC.

**AARTS, Prof. Sebastiaan Henri Lucas Marie, (Bas),** PhD; Professor of English Linguistics, since 2003, and Vice-Dean, Enterprise, since 2016, University College London; *b* Nijmegen, The Netherlands; *s* of Florent Gérard Antoin Marie Aarts and Marie Josephine Victoria Servatia Postmes; *m* 2002, Dr Gergana Popova; two *d*. *Educ:* Elshof Coll., Nijmegen; Univ. of Utrecht (Drs); University Coll. London (MA; PhD 1990). University College London: Lectr, 1989–96; Sen. Lectr, 1996–99; Reader, 1999–2003. Jt Founding Editor, English Lang. and Linguistics, 1997–2004. *Publications:* Small Clauses in English: the nonverbal types, 1992; (ed with C. F. Meyer) The Verb in Contemporary English, 1995; English Syntax and Argumentation, 1997, 5th edn 2018; (jtly) Investigating Natural Language: working with the British component of the international corpus of English, 2002; (ed jtly) Fuzzy Grammar: a reader, 2004; (ed with A. McMahon) The Handbook of English Linguistics, 2006; Syntactic Gradience: the nature of grammatical indeterminacy, 2007; Oxford Modern English Grammar, 2011; (ed jtly) The Verb Phrase in English: investigating recent language change with corpora, 2013; (jtly) Oxford Dictionary of English Grammar, 2nd edn, 2014; (jtly) How to Teach Grammar, 2019; articles in jls and books. *Address:* Department of English, University College London, Gower Street, WC1E 6BT. *T:* (020) 7679 3130. *E:* b.aarts@ucl.ac.uk.

**ABAS, Madeleine Nasim;** Senior Partner, Osborn Abas Hunt, since 2004; *b* Bangor, Gwynedd, 26 Aug. 1970; *d* of Dr Jan Abas and Rosemary Ann Abas. *Educ:* David Hughes Sch., Anglesey; Nottingham Trent Univ. (LLB Hons Law); Nottingham Law Sch. (Postgrad. DipLP). Trainee, Asst Solicitor and Associate, Irwin Mitchell Solicitors, 1988–2000; Associate, DLA Piper, 2000–02; Partner, Cooper Kenyon Burrows, 2002–04. Mem., Inst. of Industrial Accident Investigators. Founder, and Chair, 2005–12, Health and Safety Lawyers Assoc. Mem., Editl Panel, Construction Industry Pubns Health and Safety Manual, 2011–. *Recreation:* Formula 1. *Address:* OAH Law Ltd, Elizabeth House, 8A Princess Street, Knutsford, Cheshire WA16 6DD. *T:* (01565) 655837. *E:* madeleine.abas@oahlaw.com.

**ABBERLEY, Robert;** self-employed consultant, since 2013; Assistant General Secretary, UNISON, 2002–13; *b* 29 Oct. 1952; *s* of late Fred Abberley and of Lillian Abberley. *Educ:* Kingsland Co. Primary Sch., Hereford; Wigmore Co. Secondary Sch., Hereford. C&G Operating Dept Practitioner. Labourer, 1969; apprentice toolmaker, Halls Engrg, Shrewsbury, 1969–70; driver, builders merchants, 1971–72; operating dept asst, Hereford Hosps, 1972–79. Trade Union officer, COHSE, 1979–93; Hd of Health, UNISON, 1993–2002. Member: Adv. Bd, TUC Partnership Inst.; TUC Gen. Council, 2005; Bd, TUC Stakeholder Pension, 2009–; Trustee: UNISON Pension Fund, 2012–; COHSE Pension Scheme, 2014–. Non-exec. Dir, UIA, 2013– (Chm., Nominations and Remunerations Cttee). Member: NHS Task Force on Staff Involvement in decision making, 1998–99; NHS Modernisation Bd, 1999–; NHS shifting the balance of power task force, 2001; Community Cohesion Rev. Team, 2001–02; Ministerial Adv. Panel on Social Cohesion, 2002; NHSUniv. SHA, 2003–05; NHS Nat. Leadership Network, 2005–; NHS Ministerial Sounding Bd, 2006; Chair, NHS widening participation in learning steering gp, 2005–. Board Member: Care Connect Learning, until 2009; Coll. of Operating Dept Practitioners, 2007; Managers in Partnership, 2007–13; Workforce Develt Trust (formerly Skills for Health), 2009– (Mem., Shadow Bd, Nat. Skills Acad., 2011–13); Nat. Cohesion Forum, Inst. of Community Cohesion, 2009–; Involvement and Participation Assoc., 2010–14; TUC Unionlearn, 2010–; Movement for Change, 2013–17 (Vice Chair, 2014). Pres., Health and Social Services Cttee, Eur. Fedn of Trade Unions, 1983–2002. Member: IAM (Middx); TR Register. *Recreations:* classic car restoration, motorcycling, music, going to the gym, Manchester United, watching movies, reading biographies, watching Hereford FC. *E:* bobabberley1@gmail.com.

**ABBOTT, Anthony John,** CMG 2001; OBE 1997 (MBE 1986); HM Diplomatic Service, retired; Head, Pitcairn Logistics Team, New Zealand, 2001–04; *b* Ashton-under-Lyne, 9 Sept. 1941; *s* of Walter Abbott and Mary Abbott (*née* Delaney); *m* 1962, Margaret Stuart Green; three *s* one *d*. *Educ:* All Souls' Sch., Salford; De La Salle Coll., Pendleton. Joined HM Diplomatic Service, 1959: Vice-Consul, Khorramshahr, 1963–65; Helsinki, 1965–68; Press Officer, FCO, 1969–72; Passport Officer, Lusaka, 1972–75; Consul, Santiago, 1976–80; UK Presidency Secretariat to EC, 1981; on secondment to BOTB, 1981–82; Consul, Lisbon, 1983–87; First Sec., Calcutta, 1987–91; EC Monitor, Croatia and Bosnia Herzogovina, 1991; Dep. Head, Trng Dept, FCO, 1992–93; Consul-Gen., Perth, 1993–97; Governor, Montserrat, 1997–2001. Mem., Como Conf., St Vincent de Paul Soc., WA, 2005– (Pres., 2009–17). EC Monitoring Medal, 1994. Officer, Order of Enfante Dom Henrique (Portugal), 1985. *Recreations:* travel, driving, golf, spectator (all sports). *Address:* 6 James Street, Shenton Park, WA 6008, Australia. *Club:* Royal Over-Seas League (Chm., WA Br., 2011–16).

**ABBOTT, Hon. Anthony John;** MP (L) Warringah, New South Wales, since 1994; Prime Minister of Australia, 2013–15; Leader of the Liberal Party, Australia, 2009–15; *b* 4 Nov. 1957; *s* of Richard Abbott and Fay Abbott; *m* 1988, Margaret Aitken; three *d*. *Educ:* St Ignatius' Coll., Riverview; Univ. of Sydney (BEc; LLB); Queen's Coll., Oxford (Rhodes Schol. 1981; MA PPE). Journalist and feature writer, The Bulletin and The Australian; Press Sec. and Political Advr to Leader of Opposition, 1990–93; Exec. Dir, Australians for Constitutional Monarchy, 1993–94; Parly Sec. to Minister for Employment, Educn, Trng and Youth Affairs, 1996–98; Minister for Employment Services, 1998–2001, for Employment, Workplace Relns and Small Business, 2001, for Employment and Workplace Relns, 2001–03, asstg Prime Minister for Public Service, 2001–03; Leader, House of Reps, 2001–07; Minister for Health and Ageing, 2003–07; Shadow Minister for Families, Community Services, Indigenous Affairs and Voluntary Sector, then for Families, Housing, Community Services and Indigenous Affairs, 2008–09; Leader of the Opposition, 2009–13. Centenary Medal (Australia), 2003. *Publications:* The Minimal Monarch, 1995; How to Win the Constitutional War, 1997; Battlelines, 2009. *Address:* Parliament House, Canberra, ACT 2600, Australia.

**ABBOTT, Rt Hon. Diane (Julie);** PC 2016; MP (Lab) Hackney North and Stoke Newington, since 1987; *b* 27 Sept. 1953; *d* of late Reginald and Julia Abbott; *m* 1991, David Thompson (marr. diss. 1993); one *s*. *Educ:* Harrow County Girls' Grammar Sch.; Newnham Coll., Cambridge. Formerly: Admin. Trainee, Home Office; Race Relations Officer, NCCL; Researcher, Thames Television; Reporter, TV-am; Equality Officer, ACTT; Press and PR Officer, GLC; Principal Press Officer, Lambeth Borough Council. Joined Labour Party, 1971; Mem., NEC, 1994–97. Mem., Westminster City Council, 1982–86. Mem. resp. for equality and women's issues, Mayor of London's Cabinet, 2000–08. Shadow Minister of Public Health, 2010–13; Shadow Sec. of State for Internat. Develt, 2015–16; Shadow Sec. of State for Health, 2016; Shadow Home Sec., 2016–. *Address:* House of Commons, SW1A 0AA.

**ABBOTT, John Martin,** CBE 2000; QPM 1996; Director General, National Criminal Intelligence Service, 1997–2003; Vice President, Interpol, 1999–2002; *b* 22 March 1949; *s* of late Geoffrey Lowick Abbott and Gladys Lilian Abbott; *m* 1972, Christine Sowter; two *d*. *Educ:* Univ. of Sussex (BA Hons History 1982). Joined Sussex Police, 1968: served in various ranks throughout Sussex, 1968–86; Supt, seconded to Royal Hong Kong Police, 1986–88; Chief Supt, seconded to Police Staff Coll., Bramshill, 1989–91; Asst Chief Constable, 1991–94; Asst Insp. of Constabulary, 1994–96. Pres., Sussex CCC, 2017–. *Recreations:* reading, history, golf, cricket.

**ABBOTT, Paul;** film and television writer; *b* 22 Feb. 1960; *s* of late Alan Abbott and Doreen Abbott; *m* 1993, Saskia (marr. diss.); one *s* one *d*. *Educ:* Barden High Sch., Burnley. Writer: television series: Coronation Street, 1985–89; Cracker (episodes), 1993 (Best Drama Series, BAFTA award, 1995); Reckless, 1997; Touching Evil, 1997; Butterfly Collectors, 1999; Secret Life of Michael Fry, 2000; Clocking Off, 2000–03 (Best Drama Series, BAFTA award, 2001); Linda Green, 2001; State of Play, 2003; Shameless, 2004–13 (Best Drama Series, BAFTA award, 2005); Hit and Miss, 2012; No Offence, 2015, 2017, 2018; TV film, Reckless: The Movie, 1999. Exec. Prod., State of Play (film), 2009. *Recreations:* film, theatre, novels, rumours. *Address:* c/o The Agency, 24 Pottery Lane, Holland Park, W11 4LZ. *Clubs:* Ivy; Writers' Guild of Great Britain.

**ABBOTT, Roderick Evelyn;** senior adviser, international trade; *b* 16 April 1938; *e s* of late Stuart Abbott, OBE; *m* 1963, Elizabeth Isobel McLean; three *d*. *Educ:* Rugby Sch.; Merton Coll., Oxford. Board of Trade, 1962–68 (Private Sec. to Pres. of BoT, 1965–66; seconded to DEA, 1966–68); UK Mission to UN, Geneva, 1968–71; Foreign Office, London, 1971–73; EEC, Brussels, 1973–75; EEC Delegation, Geneva, 1975–79; EEC, Brussels, 1979–82; Dir, D-G of External Relns, then External Econ. Relns, EC, Brussels, 1982–96; Ambassador and Perm. Rep. of EC to UN and WTO, Geneva, 1996–2000; Dep. Dir Gen., Trade, EC, Brussels, 2000–02; Dep. Dir-Gen., WTO, 2002–05. Sen. Trade Advr, Eur. Centre for Internat. Pol Economy, 2006–. *Recreation:* travel. *Address:* Avenue Grandchamp 98A, 1150 Brussels, Belgium.

**ABBOTT-WATT, Thorhilda Mary Vivia, (Thorda),** OBE 2017; HM Diplomatic Service; Ambassador to Turkmenistan, 2016–19; *b* 11 Feb. 1955; *d* of Samuel Abbott-Watt and Elva Mary Abbott-Watt (*née* Clare Gibson); partner, Reef Talbot Hogg. *Educ:* Stonar

Sch., Atworth, Wilts. Joined HM Diplomatic Service, 1974; Third Sec., FCO, 1974–79; temp. duty tours in Latin America, Middle and Far East, 1979–80; Vice Consul, Paris, 1981–84; Third Sec. (Chancery), UK Repn to EU, 1984–86; Second Secretary: FCO, 1986–88; Bonn, 1988–91; First Sec., EU Dept and Western Eur. Dept, FCO, 1991–95; Hd, Commercial Section, Kiev, 1995–98; First Sec. (Political), Belgrade, 1998–99; Hd, Visa Policy Section, Jt Entry Clearance Unit, FCO, 1999–2001; Chargé d'Affaires, Tajikistan, 2001–02; Ambassador to Armenia, 2003–06; Conflict Issues Gp, FCO, 2006; Hd, Political/Military Gp, Kabul, 2006; Afghanistan Gp, FCO, 2006–07; Migration Directorate, FCO, 2007–08; Hd of Strategy and Performance, UKTI, 2008; Ambassador to Mongolia, 2008–09 and 2011–12; Finance Directorate, FCO, 2009–10; Internat. Liaison Section, MoD, 2010; Dep. Hd, 2012, Acting Hd, 2012–15, Project Task Force, FCO. Life Mem., NACF. *Recreations:* riding, theatre, the arts, sitting in a comfortable chair with a good book. *Address:* c/o Foreign and Commonwealth Office, King Charles Street, SW1A 2AH. *E:* Thorda.Abbott-Watt@fco.gov.uk.

**ABDALLA, Hossam Ibrahim, (Sam),** FRCOG; Clinical Director, Lister Fertility Clinic, London, since 1988; *b* Illinois, 23 May 1952; *s* of Ibrahim Abdalla and Alia Abdalla; *m* 1975, Mediha Elsawi; one *s* one *d*. *Educ:* Orman High Sch., Cairo; University of Baghdad (MB ChB 1977). MRCOG 1983, FRCOG 2001, Infertility and IVF Specialist, Cromwell Hosp., London, 1986–87. Mem. Bd, HFEA, 2004–14. *Publications:* Fast Facts: endometriosis, 1998, 2nd edn 2003; articles in learned jls. *Address:* Lister Hospital, Lister Fertility Clinic, Chelsea Bridge Road, SW1W 8RH. *T:* (020) 7881 4035. *E:* pa@lfclinic.com.

**ABDEL-HAQ, Prof. Mohammed Kayed,** PhD; Founder and Chief Executive Officer, Oakstone Merchant Bank, since 2012; Chairman: Centre for Opposition Studies, since 2010; Centre for Islamic Finance, University of Bolton, since 2012; *b* Jordan, 22 April 1964; *s* of Dr Kayed Abdel-Haq and Fatima Abdel-Haq; *m* 1993, Lynn Rhymes; four *d*. *Educ:* Islamic Scientific Coll., Amman; Yarmouk Univ., Jordan (BSc; MA); Oxford Brookes Univ. and Centre for Islamic Studies, St Cross Coll., Univ. of Oxford (PhD 1993). With Aitken Hume Bank, then Arbuthnot Latham & Co., 1994–95; UK Bank of Kuwait, London, 1995–96; Vice-Pres., Private Bank, ME Reg., ABN Amro Bank, London, 1997–99; Dir and Sen. Private Banker, Saudi Arabia and Levant, Citigroup Private Bank, London, 1999–2003; Dir and Hd, ME and N Africa Div., Deutsche Bank AG, London, 2003–04; Man. Dir and Global Hd, HSBC Amanah Private Banking, 2004–07; CEO, Barwa Capital (UK) Ltd, 2007–11; Chm., Complyport Ltd (UK), 2008–12; CEO and Founder Mem., Rosette Merchant Bank LLP, 2011–12. Chm., Ministerial Adv. Gp on Extremism in Univs and Further Educn Colls, 2011. Member: Adv. Bd, Centre for Social Justice, 2011–; Council, Chatham Hse, 2011–14; Adv. Bd, Centre for Contemp. Arab Music, Brunel Univ., 2012–. Pres., Disability Partnership, 2009–14. Chm., Amman Arab Univ., 2008–12. Chm., Adv. Bd, Cons. ME Council, 2010–. Contested (C) Swansea W, 2005. Chm., Oxford E Cons. Assoc., 2004. Freeman, City of Oxford, 2010. MInstD 2009. *Publications:* (jtly) Islamic Banking: theory, practice and challenges, 1996. *Recreations:* swimming, squash, chess. *Address:* University of Bolton, Deane Road, Bolton BL3 5AB. *T:* 07881 506785. *E:* m.abdelhaq@btinternet.com; Oakstone Merchant Bank, 53 Davies Street, W1K 5JH. *Clubs:* Lansdowne; Royal Automobile (Amman).

**ABDELA, Lesley Julia,** MBE 1990; journalist and broadcaster, since 1986; Chief Executive: Project Parity, 1996; Project Parity Partnerships for Peace, since 2005; Senior Partner: Eyecatcher Associates, since 1986; Shevolution, since 1998; specialist in post-conflict reconstruction, since 1999; *b* London, 17 Nov. 1945; *d* of late Frederick Abdela and Henrietta (*née* Hardy); *m* 1972 (marr. diss.); one *s*; partner, Tim Symonds. *Educ:* Queen Anne's Sch., Caversham; Châtelard Sch., Les Avants, Switzerland; Queen's Coll., Harley Street; Hammersmith Coll. of Art and Building; London Coll. of Printing. Advertising Exec., Royds of London, 1968–72; Derek Forsyth Design Partnership, 1972–73; researcher for Liberal Party, H of C, 1977–79; Founder, 1980, Chair, 1980–85, Trustee, 1980–95, 300 Group (for women in politics). UK Consultant, Project Liberty, Kennedy Sch. of Govt, Harvard Univ., 1992–98. OSCE Dep. Dir for Democracy, UN Interim Admin in Kosovo, 1999; Sen. Civil Soc. Expert in governance, democratisation, gender and human rights, Kosovo, Sierra Leone, Iraq, Afghanistan and Aceh (Indonesia); Sen. Gender Advr to UN OCHA Chief Coordinator Kathmandu, 2007–08. Political Editor: Cosmopolitan, 1993–96 (first Pol Ed. of a women's mag.); Radio Viva!, 1995; regular contributor to Exec. Woman mag., Mail on Sunday, Sunday Times, Guardian, Times, Independent, Glasgow Herald, etc; writer, researcher and presenter of radio and TV documentaries, incl. Women with X Appeal, 1993, Breaking Glass, 1994. Board Member: Internat. Inst. for Envmt and Develt, 1992–96; British Council, 1995–2000; Mem. Exec. Bd, Women in Mgt, 1985–88. Vice Pres., Electoral Reform Soc., 1995–. Contested (L) E Herts, 1979. Gov., Nottingham Trent Univ., 1997–2000. FRGS; FRSA; MCIJ. Hon. DLitt Nottingham Trent, 1996. Political Journalist of the Year, Women in Public Life Awards, 2009. *Publications:* Women with X Appeal, 1989; Breaking Through the Glass Ceilings, 1991; What Women Want, 1994; Do It! - Walk the Talk, 1995. *Recreations:* painting, ski-ing, scuba, reading, looking forward to true equality between women and men in politics and society. *Address:* Park Farm Oast, Bateman's Lane, Burwash, Etchingham, East Sussex TN19 7DR. *E:* lesley.abdela@shevolution.com.

**ABDIN, Dr Hasan;** Ambassador of Sudan to the Court of St James's, 2000–06; *b* 1 Jan. 1939; *m* 1966, Manahil A. Abu Kashwa; two *s* three *d*. *Educ:* Univ. of Khartoum (BA 1965); Univ. of Wisconsin (MA 1967; PhD 1970). Lectr in African Hist., Univ. of Khartoum, 1970–77; State Minister, Sudan, 1977–78; Mem., Nat. Assembly, 1978–80; Asst Prof. of Hist., Univ. of King Saud, Riyyadh, Saudi Arabia, 1983–88; Inst. of Asian and African Studies, Univ. of Khartoum, 1988–90; Ambassador to: Algeria, 1990–92; Iraq, 1993–97; Under Sec., Min. of Foreign Affairs, Khartoum, 1998–2000. *Publications:* Introduction to African History (in Arabic), 1974; Early Sudanese Nationalism, 1986. *Recreations:* reading, walking. *Address:* c/o Embassy of the Republic of the Sudan, 3 Cleveland Row, St James's, SW1A 1DD.

**ABDULAH, Frank Owen;** Deputy Secretary-General, Caribbean Community Secretariat, Guyana, 1989–93; Member, Public Service Commission of Trinidad and Tobago, since 2012; *b* 8 Nov. 1928; *m*; four *d*. *Educ:* Queen's Royal Coll., Trinidad; Oxford (MA, DipEd Oxon). Held several govt posts, 1953–62, before entering Diplomatic Service at Trinidad and Tobago's Independence, 1962; Dep. Perm. Rep. (Minister Counsellor), 1970–73, Perm. Rep. (Ambassador), 1975–83, Trinidad and Tobago Perm. Mission to UN, NY; Perm. Sec. (Acting), Ministry of External Affairs, Port of Spain, 1973–75; High Comr for Trinidad and Tobago in London with concurrent accreditations as Ambassador to Denmark, Finland, France, FRG, Norway and Sweden, 1983–85; Permanent Sec., Min. of External Affairs and Internat. Trade, Trinidad and Tobago, 1985–88. Caribbean Community Special Advr to Pres. of UN Gen. Assembly, 1993–94. Pres., UNA Trinidad and Tobago, 1987–88, 1997–2001. *Recreations:* music, sports. *Address:* 8 Nock Road, Maraval, Trinidad and Tobago.

**ABDY, Sir Robert Etienne Eric,** 7th Bt *cr* 1850, of Albyns, Essex; *b* 22 Feb. 1978; *o s* of Sir Valentine Robert Duff Abdy, 6th Bt and of Mathilde (*née* Coche de la Ferté); *S* father, 2012, but his name does not appear on the Official Roll of the Baronetage. *Heir:* none.

**ABED, Sir Fazle Hasan,** KCMG 2010; social entrepreneur and development professional; Founder, 1972, and Chairman, since 2001, BRAC (formerly Bangladesh Rural Advancement Committee) (Executive Director, 1972); *b* Bengal, 27 April 1936; *m* Syeda Sarwat; one *s* one *d*. *Educ:* Dhaka Univ.; Glasgow Univ. Chartered Mgt Accountant, 1962; Sen. Exec., Shell Oil, Pakistan, 1968–71. Founder Mem., Ashoka Global Acad. for Social Entrepreneurship; Mem., Eminent Persons Gp for Least Developed Countries, UN, 2010–. Hon. LLD: Queen's, Kingston, 1994; Columbia, 2008; Bath, 2010; Manchester, 2012; Princeton, 2014; Hon. DEd: Manchester, 2003; Bradford, 2016; Hon. DHL: Yale, 2007; Rikkyo, 2009; Hon. DLitt Oxon, 2009; Hon. DCL Univ. of the South, 2014. Ramon Magsaysay Award for Community Leadership, 1980; Olof Palme Award, 2001; Social Entrepreneurship Award, Schwab Foundn, 2003; Internat. Activist Award, Gleitsman Foundn, 2003; Mahbub ul Haq Award for Outstanding Contribn in Human Develt, UNDP, 2004; Gates Award for Global Health, Bill and Melinda Gates Foundn, 2004; Lifetime Achievement Award, Palli Karma Shahayak Foundn, 2007; Inaugural Clinton Global Citizen Award, 2007; Henry R. Kravis Leadership Prize, 2007; David Rockefeller Bridging Leadership Award, 2008; Inaugural World Innovation Summit for Educn Prize, Qatar, 2011; Open Soc. Prize, Central European Univ., 2013; Leo Tolstoy Internat. Gold Medal, 2014; Trust Women Hero Award, 2014; World Food Prize, 2015; Thomas Francis, Jr Medal in Global Public Health, Univ. of Michigan, 2016; LEGO Prize, 2018. Order of Civil Merit (Spain), 2014. *Address:* BRAC, BRAC Centre, 75 Mohakhali, Dhaka 1212, Bangladesh.

**ABED, Ringo F.;** Head of Mission of Namibia to China, 2013–16, and also Ambassador of Namibia (non-resident) to Vietnam and to Pakistan, 2014–16; *b* 6 June 1956; *s* of late Benjamin Abed and Albertina Matheus; *m* 1979, Johanna; three *d* (two *s* decd). *Educ:* UN Inst. for Namibia (Dip. Mgt and Develt Studies 1981); Makerere Univ., Kampala (BA Hons Pol Sci. and Public Admin 1986). Mem., SW African People's Orgn; in exile in Zambia, then Angola, 1974–89; Dep. Dir, reception and food distribn centres for returning veterans, 1989–92; Mem., OAU Observer Mission to SA, 1992–94; Ministry of Foreign Affairs, Namibia: First Sec. (Pol) and Dep. Hd of Mission, Botswana, 1995; First Sec. (Pol), SA, 1996; Hd, Privileges and Immunities, 1999, Functions and Ceremonies, 2000, Protocol Dept, Min. of Foreign Affairs; Counsellor and Dep. Hd of Mission, Congo, 2000–03; Dir, Protocol, Office of the Prime Minister, 2003–04; Actg Chief of Protocol, Min. of Foreign Affairs, 2004–05; High Comr to the Court of St James's, 2005–06; Ambassador to Democratic Republic of the Congo and (non-resident) to Republic of Congo, 2006–13. *Recreations:* reading, music, travelling.

**ABEL, Sir Christopher Charles,** Kt 2018; OBE 2007; Chairman, Masurina Ltd, since 1990; *b* New Zealand, 18 May 1941; *s* of Russell Abel and Sheila Abel; *m* 1968, Barbara Kauvu; three *s* one *d*. *Educ:* Geelong Grammar Sch., Vic; Dookie Agricl Coll., Vic. Agricl Extension Officer, colonial admin of Papua and New Guinea, subseq. PNG, then Officer, Milne Bay Province, PNG Development Bank, 1963–75; Dir and Co. Sec., Masurina Ltd, Milne Bay Province, PNG, 1975–90. *Publications:* A Dictionary of the Suau Language of Milne Bay, 2016. *Recreations:* playing tennis, watching sports live and on TV. *Address:* PO Box 390, Alotau, Papua New Guinea. *T:* 6411393, 79233305. *Club:* Cameron (Alotau).

**ABEL, Prof. Edward William,** CBE 1997; PhD, DSc; FRSC; Professor of Inorganic Chemistry, University of Exeter, 1972–97, now Emeritus (Head of Department of Chemistry, 1977–88; Deputy Vice-Chancellor, 1991–94); *b* 3 Dec. 1931; *s* of Sydney and Donna Abel; *m* 1960, Margaret R. Edwards (*d* 2018); one *s* one *d*. *Educ:* Bridgend Grammar Sch.; University Coll., Cardiff (BSc 1952); Northern Polytechnic, London (PhD 1957). Served Army, 1953–55. Research Fellow, Imperial Coll., 1957–59; Lectr, later Reader, Univ. of Bristol, 1957–71. Vis. Professor: Univ. of British Columbia, 1970; Japanese Soc. for Promotion of Science, 1971; Tech. Univ. of Braunschweig, 1973; ANU, Canberra, 1990; Robert E. Welch Lectures, Texas, 1994. Royal Society of Chemistry: Mem. Council, 1977–82, 1983–87 and 1989–2002; Pres., 1996–98; Chairman: Local Affairs Bd, 1983–87; Divl Affairs Bd, 1989–92; Scientific Affairs Bd, 1992–95; Parly Cttee, 1995–2003; Laboratory of the Govt Chemist Adv. Cttee, 1998–2003; Mem., Dalton Div. Council, 1977–83, 1987–91 (Sec./Treasurer, 1977–82; Vice-Pres., 1983, 1989–91; Pres., 1987–89); Main Group Chem. Medal, 1976; Tilden Medal and Lectr, 1981; Service Medal, 2007. Perm. Sec., Internat. Confs on Organometallic Chem., 1972–89; Mem., UGC, 1986–89 (Chm., Phys. Scis Sub-Cttee, 1986–89); Nat. Advr for Chem., UFC, 1989–92; CNAA: Mem., 1991–93; Chm., Phys. Scis Cttee, 1987–91; Mem., Cttee for Academic Affairs, 1989–91. DUniv North London, 1998; Hon. DSc: Exeter, 2000; Glamorgan, 2004. *Publications:* (ed jtly) Organometallic Chemistry, vols 1–25, 1970–95; (exec. editor) Comprehensive Organometallic Chemistry, 9 vols, 1984; (exec. editor) Comprehensive Organometallic Chemistry II, 14 vols, 1995; papers to learned jls. *Address:* 1A Rosebarn Avenue, Exeter EX4 6DY. *T:* (01392) 270272. *E:* Rosebarn9@icloud.com.

**ABEL, Keith Russell;** Founding Director, Abel & Cole, organic food business, 1988–2015; Chairman, Freddie's Flowers Ltd; *b* London, 13 Nov. 1963; *s* of Keith Paterson Abel and Sally Anne Neame; *m* 1992, Catherine Ciapparelli; one *s* one *d*. *Educ:* Rugby Sch.; Leeds Univ. (BA Hons); City Univ. (CPE Law); Inns of Court Sch. of Law. Called to the Bar, 1992. Queen's Award for Industry (Sustainable Develt), 2005. *Publications:* Cooking Outside the Box, 2005. *Recreations:* ski-ing, tennis, shooting, sleeping on Sunday afternoons!

**ABEL, Roger Lee;** Director, Cygnus Oil and Gas Corporation (formerly Touchstone Resources USA Inc.), 2005–07 (Chairman and Chief Executive Officer, 2005–06); *b* Nebraska, 12 Aug. 1943. *Educ:* Colorado Sch. of Mines (BSc Petroleum Engrg 1965); MIT (MSc 1979). FInstPet. Served US Army, 1966–68 (Capt.). Joined Conoco Inc., 1968: prodn engr, 1968–72; Supervising Reservoir Engr, Lake Charles, Louisiana, 1972–73; Staff Engr, N America, 1973–74; Co-ordinator for W Hemisphere Planning Dept, 1974–75; Manager, Planning and Budgets, 1975–77; Exec. Asst to Conoco's Dep. Chm., 1977–78; Sloan Fellow, MIT, 1978–79; Asst Div. Manager, Offshore Div., 1979–80; Vice Pres. and Gen. Manager of Ops for Dubai Petroleum Co., 1980–82; Manager: of Ops, UK and Europe, 1982–84; of Planning, Admin and Engrg, N American Prodn, 1984–86; General Manager: Offshore and Frontier, N American Prodn, 1986–88; Prodn Engrg and Res. Dept, 1988–90; Vice-Pres. and Gen. Manager, Prodn Engrg and Res., 1990–91; Vice Pres., Exploration Prodn-Russia, 1991–93; Chm., Conoco Exploration Prodn Europe Ltd, 1993–97; Pres. and Chief Operating Officer, Occidental Oil & Gas Corp., 1997–99; Exec. Vice Pres., Occidental Petroleum Corp., 1999–2000; Pres., Austex Production Co. LLC, 2002–05. Chm. Bd, Offshore Technol. Conf., 1994–2002; Co-Vice Chm., Mgt Cttee, E&P Forum, 1995–97; Chm., Energy Sub-Cttee, Gore-Chernomyrdin Commn, 1997–98. Dist. Mem., Soc. of Petroleum Engrs (Pres., 1992). Former Mem., Adv. Cttee, Petroleum Engrg Dept, and Trustee Develt Council, Colorado Sch. of Mines. Dist. Achievement Medal, Colorado Sch. of Mines, 1998; Bronze Star Medal, 1967 (USA). *Address:* 8045 Chalk Knoll Drive, Austin, TX 78735–1706, USA.

**ABELL, Prof. Christopher,** PhD; FRS 2016; FMedSci; Professor of Biological Chemistry, since 2002, and Pro-Vice-Chancellor for Research, since 2016, University of Cambridge; Fellow, since 1986, and Todd-Hamied Fellow, since 1997, Christ's College, Cambridge; *b* Fulford, 11 Nov. 1957; *s* of Norman and Barbara Abell; *m* 1981, Dr Katherine Tang; one *s*. *Educ:* St John's Coll., Cambridge (BA 1st Cl. Chem. 1979; PhD Chem. 1982). SERC

NATO Postdoctoral Fellow, Brown Univ., RI, 1982–83; Res. Fellow, King's Coll., Cambridge, 1983–86; University of Cambridge: demonstrator, 1984–88, Lectr, 1988–89, Reader, 1999–2002, Dept of Chemistry; Dir of Postdoctoral Affairs, 2013–15. Co-Founder and Mem., Scientific Adv. Bd, Astex Therapeutics, then Astex Pharmaceuticals, 1999–; Co-Founder: Akubio, 2002; Sphere Fluidics, 2010; Aqdot, 2013. Iberdrola Vis. Prof., Univ. of Santiago de Compostela, Spain, 1999–2000; David P. Craig Vis. Prof., ANU, 2003; Vis. Prof., Univ. Paul Sabatier, Toulouse, 2008–09; Erskine Fellow, 2000, BIC Internat. Fellow, 2011, Univ. of Canterbury, Christchurch, NZ. FMedSci 2012. *Publications:* over 310 articles in scientific jls. *Recreation:* running. *Address:* Department of Chemistry, University of Cambridge, Lensfield Road, Cambridge CB2 1EW.

**ABELL, (John) David;** Chairman, Jourdan (formerly Thomas Jourdan) plc, since 1997; Director, Leicester Football Club plc, since 1999; *b* 15 Dec. 1942; *s* of Leonard Abell and Irene (*née* Anderson); *m* 1st, 1967, Anne Janette Priestley (marr. diss. 1977); three *s*; 2nd, 1981, Sandra Dawn Atkinson (marr. diss. 1986); one *s* one *d*; 3rd, 1988, Juliana, *d* of late Prof. J. L. I. Fennell, PhD, FRSL and of Marina Lopukhin. *Educ:* Univ. of Leeds (BAEcon); London School of Economics (Dip. Business Admin). Assistant to Cash and Investment Manager, Ford Motor Co., 1962–65; Asst, Treasurer's Office, AEI, 1965–67; British Leyland: Central Staffs, 1968–69; Manager, Investments and Banking, 1969–70; Chm. and Chief Exec., Prestcold Div., 1970–72; Corporate Treasurer, 1972; First Nat. Finance Corp., Nov. 1972–Aug. 1973; re-joined British Leyland as Man. Dir, Leyland Australia, 1974–75; Group Man. Dir, Leyland Special Products, 1975; Man. Dir, BL Commercial Vehicles, Chm. and Chief Exec., Leyland Vehicles Ltd, 1978–81; Chm. and Chief Exec., Suter Electrical, subseq. Suter plc, 1981–96. *Recreations:* horse racing and breeding, wine, tennis, music, Rugby, soccer. *Address:* Jourdan plc, Elm House, Elmer Street North, Grantham, Lincs NG31 6RE.

**ABELL, Stephen Paul, (Stig);** Editor/Publisher, Times Literary Supplement, since 2016; *b* Nottingham, 10 April 1980; *s* of Steve Abell and Vera Abell; *m* 2008, Nadine Sanders; one *s* two *d*. *Educ:* Loughborough Grammar Sch.; Emmanuel Coll., Cambridge (BA 2001). Press Complaints Commission: Complaints Officer, 2001–04; Asst Dir, 2004–08; Dep. Dir, 2008–10; Dir, 2010–12; Partner, Pagefield Communications, 2012–13. Fiction Reviewer: TLS, 2001–12; Spectator, 2003–12; Telegraph, 2005–13; Man. Ed., The Sun, 2013–16. Contributor, Sky News, 2012–. Presenter: Sunday Morning Breakfast, 2014–16, Sunday Afternoon Drivetime, 2016–18, LBC; Front Row, BBC Radio 4, 2018–. *Publications:* How Britain Really Works: understanding the ideas and institutions of a nation, 2018. *Recreations:* reading, writing, pogonotrophy. *E:* stigabell@gmail.com.

**ABELSON, Michael Andrew;** a District Judge (Magistrates' Courts), Merseyside, 2001–17; a Recorder, 2000–17; *b* 22 March 1952; *s* of Harvey Abelson and Eva Abelson (*née* Newman); *m* 1994, Angela Bernadette Therese Walsh, BEd, DipEFL, *d* of Joseph Walsh and Frances Walsh (*née* Begley); one *s*. *Educ:* Leyton County High Sch.; University Coll., London (LLB Hons 1975). Called to the Bar, Middle Temple, 1976; in practice at the Bar, Northern, and Wales and Chester Circuits, 1977–98; Asst Recorder, 1997–2000; acting Stipendiary Magistrate: S Yorks, 1993–98; Gtr Manchester, 1995–98; Stipendiary Magistrate, later a Dist Judge (Magistrates' Courts), Gtr Manchester, 1998–2001. *Recreations:* travel, ski-ing, tennis, badminton.

**ABENSUR, Eric;** Executive Coach, Abensur Consulting, since 2015; Founder and President, Spot.coach, since 2016; *b* 7 Jan. 1964. *Educ:* Univ. Paris IX Dauphine (DESS Finance d'Entreprise). Sen. Manager, Ernst & Young, Paris and Los Angeles, 1989–98; Finance Dir, Pay-TV Div., France Telecom, 1998–2001; Chief Finance Officer, 2001–02, CEO, 2002–06, Freeserve, then Wanadoo UK, plc; Vice Pres., Orange Home UK plc, 2006–07; Dep. Man. Dir, 2007–08, Gp CEO, 2008–15, Venda Ltd. *Recreations:* cinema, history of 20th century, golf, squash.

**ABERCONWAY, 4th Baron** *cr* 1911, of Bodnant; **Henry Charles McLaren;** Bt 1902; *b* 26 May 1948; *s* of 3rd Baron Aberconway and his 1st wife, Deirdre Knewstub; *S* father, 2003; *m* 1st, 1981, Sally (marr. diss. 1993), *yr d* of Captain C. N. Lentaigne, RN; one *s* one *d*; 2nd, 2005, Brigitte E. Hasler (*d* 2007). *Educ:* Eton; Sussex Univ. (BA). *Heir:* *s* Hon. Charles Stephen McLaren, *b* 27 Dec. 1984. *Address:* 10 Rose Farm Cottages, Shotley, Ipswich, Suffolk IP9 1PH.

**ABERCORN, 5th Duke of,** *cr* 1868; **James Hamilton,** KG 1999; Lord of Paisley, 1587; Lord of Abercorn, 1603; Earl of Abercorn and Lord of Hamilton, Mountcastle and Kilpatrick, 1606; Baron of Strabane, 1617; Viscount of Strabane, 1701; Viscount Hamilton, 1786; Marquess of Abercorn, 1790; Marquess of Hamilton, 1868; Bt 1660; Chancellor, Order of the Garter, since 2012; Lord Lieutenant of Co. Tyrone, 1987–2009; Lord Steward of HM Household, 2001–09; company director; *b* 4 July 1934; *er s* of 4th Duke of Abercorn, and Lady Mary Kathleen Crichton (Dowager Duchess of Abercorn, GCVO) (*d* 1990); *S* father, 1979; *m* 1966, Anastasia Alexandra (OBE 2008) (*d* 2018), *e d* of late Lt-Col Harold Phillips, Checkendon Court, Reading; two *s* one *d*. *Educ:* Eton Coll.; Royal Agricultural Coll., Cirencester, Glos. Joined HM Army, Oct. 1952; Lieut, Grenadier Guards. MP (UU) Fermanagh and South Tyrone, 1964–70. Dir, Northern Bank Ltd, 1970–97. Chm., Laganside Develt Corp., 1989–96 (Laganside Ltd, 1986–89); Dir, NI Industrial Develt Bd, 1982–87. Member: Council of Europe, 1968–70; European Economic and Social Cttee, 1973–78. President: Royal UK Beneficent Assoc., 1979–2013; Building Socs Assoc., 1986–92; Patron, Royal Ulster Agricl Soc., 1990–96. Trustee, Winston Churchill Meml Trust, 1991–2001. Col, Irish Guards, 2000–08. High Sheriff of Co. Tyrone, 1970. Hon. Mem., RICS, 1995. Hon. LLB QUB, 1997. *Recreations:* shooting, ski-ing. *Heir:* *s* Marquess of Hamilton, *qv*. *Address:* Barons Court, Omagh, Northern Ireland BT78 4EZ. *T:* (028) 8166 1470. *E:* duke.baronscourt@btinternet.com. *Club:* Brooks's.

**ABERCROMBIE, Ian Ralph;** QC (Scot.) 1994; Sheriff Principal of South Strathclyde, Dumfries and Galloway, since 2015; Vice President, Sheriff Appeal Court, since 2016; *b* 7 July 1955; *s* of late Ralph Abercrombie and Jean Abercrombie (*née* Lithgow). *Educ:* Edinburgh Univ. (LLB Hons 1978). Called to the Bar: Scotland, 1981; Lincoln's Inn, 1992. Sheriff of Grampian, Highland and Islands at Inverness, 2009–13, of Tayside Central and Fife at Dunfermline, 2013–15. *Address:* Sheriff Principal's Chambers, Sheriff Court House, Graham Street, Airdrie ML6 6EE. *T:* (01236) 439170.

**ABERDARE, 5th Baron** *cr* 1873, of Duffryn, co. Glamorgan; **Alastair John Lyndhurst Bruce;** DL; *b* 2 May 1947; *s* of 4th Baron Aberdare, KBE, PC and Lady Aberdare (*née* (Maud Helen) Sarah Dashwood); *S* father, 2005; *m* 1971, Elizabeth Mary Culbert Foulkes; one *s* one *d*. *Educ:* Eton; Christ Church, Oxford (MA Hons Lit.Hum.). IBM, 1969–91; Partner, Bruce Naughton Wade, 1991–99; Dir, ProbusBNW Ltd (corporate reputation consultants), 1999–2009; Dir, WALTZ Programmes Ltd, 2009–13. Trustee: Nat. Botanic Gdn of Wales, 1994–2006; St John Cymru Wales, 2008–; Berlioz Soc., 2008– (Chm., 2014–); Nat. Liby of Wales, 2012–; Berlioz 2019, 2017– (Chm., 2017–). Vice President: Fountain Soc., 2016–11; Public Monuments and Sculpture Assoc., 2011–. Elected Mem., H of L, July 2009. FRGS 1997; FRSA. Hon. Fellow, Cardiff Univ., 2008. DL Dyfed, 2009. KStJ 2015. *Publications:* (trans. and ed.) Hector Berlioz: the musical madhouse, 2003; (contrib.) Berlioz: scenes from the life and work, 2008; (contrib.) The Cambridge Berlioz Encyclopedia, 2018. *Recreations:* music (esp. Berlioz), Wales, family, crosswords. *Heir:* *s* Hon. Hector Morys Napier Bruce, *b* 25 July 1974. *Address:* 16 Beverley Road, SW13 0LX. *Club:* MCC.

**ABERDEEN, Bishop of, (RC),** since 2011; **Rt Rev. Hugh Gilbert,** OSB; *b* Emsworth, Hants, 15 March 1952; *s* of Robert Gilbert and Philippa Gilbert (*née* Fordyce Jones). *Educ:* St Paul's Sch., London; King's Coll. London (BA Hons History). Entered Benedictine community of Pluscarden, 1974; ordained deacon, 1981, priest, 1982; Abbot, Pluscarden Abbey, Moray, 1992–2011. *Publications:* Unfolding the Mystery: monastic conferences on the liturgical year, 2007; Living the Mystery: monastic markers on the Christian way, 2008. *Recreations:* arts, walking. *Address:* St Mary's House, 14 Chanonry, Aberdeen AB24 1RP. *T:* (01224) 319154, *Fax:* (01224) 325570.

**ABERDEEN, (St Andrew's Cathedral), Provost of;** *see* Poobalan, Very Rev. Dr I. M.

**ABERDEEN AND ORKNEY, Bishop of,** since 2018; **Rt Rev. Anne Catherine Dyer;** *b* 1957. *Educ:* St Anne's Coll., Oxford (MA Chem. 1980); King's Coll. London (MTh 1989); Wycliffe Hall, Oxford. Business Systems Analyst, Unilever; ordained deacon, 1987, priest, 1994; non-stipendiary Minister: St John the Baptist, Eden Park, 1987–88; St George, Beckenham, 1988–89; Hon. Parish Deacon, Christ Church, Luton, Chatham, 1989–94; Chaplain for Evangelism, Dio. of Rochester, 1993–98; non-stipendiary Minister, St Barnabas, Istead Rise, Gravesend, 1994–98; Ministry Develt Officer, Dio. of Rochester, 1998–2004; Warden, Cranmer Hall, Durham, 2005–11; Rector, Holy Trinity, Haddington, Edinburgh, 2011–18. Honorary Canon: Rochester Cathedral, 2000–04; Durham Cathedral, 2008–11. *Address:* Ashley House, Ashley Gardens, Aberdeen AB10 6RQ.

**ABERDEEN AND ORKNEY, Dean of;** *no new appointment at time of going to press.*

**ABERDEEN AND TEMAIR, 7th Marquess of,** *cr* 1915; **Alexander George Gordon;** DL; landowner and property developer; Bt (NS) 1642; Earl of Aberdeen, Viscount Formartine, Lord Haddo, Methlic, Tarves, and Kellie, 1682 (Scot.); Viscount Gordon 1814, Earl of Haddo 1915 (UK); *b* 31 March 1955; *s* of 6th Marquess of Aberdeen and Temair and Anne, *d* of Lt-Col Gerald Barry, MC; *S* father, 2002; *m* 1981, Joanna Clodagh Houldsworth; three *s* one *d*. *Educ:* Cothill House, Abingdon; Harrow School; Polytechnic of Central London (DipBE). ARICS 1979–95. With Gardiner and Theobald, Chartered Quantity Surveyors, 1976–82; Speyhawk plc, Property Developers, 1982–86; London & Edinburgh Trust plc, Property Developers, 1986–94; Managing Director: Letinvest, 1989–94; Kellie Estates Ltd, 1995–2008; Gordon Land Ltd, 2000–; Braiklay Estates Ltd, 2007–; non-executive Director: Mobile Cardiovascular Science plc, 1992–99; Gordon Enterprise Trust, 1998–2002. DL Aberdeenshire, 1998. *Recreations:* golf, music, theatre. *Heir:* *s* Earl of Haddo, *qv*. *Address:* House of Formartine, Methlick, Ellon, Aberdeenshire AB41 7EQ. *T:* (01651) 851664. *Clubs:* MCC; New (Edinburgh); Royal Aberdeen Golf; Meldrum House Golf.

**ABERDOUR, Lord; John David Sholto Douglas;** Partner, Dalmahoy Farms, Kirknewton; *b* 28 May 1986; *s* and *heir* of Earl of Morton, *qv*; *m* 2017, Sarah Rosemary, *e d* of Salvatore Rizzo; one *s*. *Educ:* Merchiston Castle Sch., Edinburgh; RAC, Cirencester (BSc Hons Agric. (Land Mgt) 2008).

**ABERGAVENNY, 6th Marquess of,** *cr* 1876; **Christopher George Charles Nevill;** Baron Abergavenny 1450; Earl of Abergavenny and Viscount Nevill 1784; Earl of Lewes 1876; DL; landowner; *b* 23 April 1955; *yr s* of Lord Rupert Charles Montacute Nevill, CVO, *yr s* of 4th Marquess of Abergavenny and of Lady Anne Camilla Eveline Wallop, *d* of 9th Earl of Portsmouth; *S* uncle, 2000; *m* 1985, Venetia Jane, *er d* of late Frederick Gerard Maynard; one *d* (one *s* decd). *Educ:* Harrow. Dir, Nevill Estate Co. Ltd, 1985–. Mem. (C), Wealden DC, 1999. Chairman: St John Ambulance, Kent, 2004–10; Cons. Rural Forum (formerly Cons. Rural Affairs Gp), 2016– (Vice Chm., 2014–16). President: Royal Tunbridge Wells Civic Soc., 2008–; Friends of Tunbridge Wells Mus. and Art Gall., 2008–; S of England Agricl Soc., 2009–10. Patron: Sussex Housing Care, 2007–; Rotherfield St Martin, 2007–; Spa Valley Rly, 2008–; Pepenbury Residential Care Home, 2008–13; Searchlight, 2009–12. Trustee, Royal British Legion Industries, 2010–16. DL E Sussex, 2011. *Heir:* (to Earldom and Barony of Abergavenny and Viscountcy of Nevill only) *kinsman* David Michael Ralph Nevill [*b* 20 June 1941; *m* 1972, Katherine Mary, *d* of Rossmore Derrick Westenra; one *s* two *d*]. *Address:* Eridge Park, Eridge Green, Tunbridge Wells, Kent TN3 9JT. *T:* (01892) 752808. *Club:* White's.

**ABERNETHY, Rt Hon. Lord; John Alastair Cameron;** PC 2005; a Senator of the College of Justice in Scotland, 1992–2007; *b* 1 Feb. 1938; *s* of William Philip Legerwood Cameron and Kathleen Milthorpe (*née* Parker); *m* 1968, Elspeth Mary Dunlop Miller; three *s*. *Educ:* Clergy House Sch., Khartoum; St Mary's Sch., Melrose; Trinity Coll., Glenalmond; Pembroke Coll., Oxford (MA 1961; Hon. Fellow, 1993). Nat. Service, 1956–58 (2nd Lieut, RASC). Called to the Bar, Inner Temple, 1963; admitted Mem., Faculty of Advocates, 1966, Vice-Dean, 1983–92; QC (Scotland) 1979. Advocate-Depute, 1972–75; Standing Jun. Counsel; to Dept of Energy, 1976–79; to Scottish Develt Dept, 1978–79. Legal Chm., Pensions Appeal Tribunals for Scotland, 1979–92 (Pres., 1985–92). Dir, Faculty Services Ltd, 1979–89 (Chm., 1983–89). International Bar Association: Chm., Judges' Forum, 1994–98 (Vice-Chm., 1993–94); Mem. Council, Section on Legal Practice, 1998–2002; Mem. Council, Human Rights Inst., 1998–2000, 2002–05. Mem., Internat. Legal Assistance Consortium, 2002–. Comr, NI (Remission of Sentences) Act 1995, 2008–. Justice of Appeal, Botswana, 2009–18; Judge of Interim Ind. Constitutional Dispute Resolution Ct, Kenya, 2010. Pres., Scottish Medico-Legal Soc., 1996–2000. Mem. Exec. Cttee, Soc. for Welfare and Teaching of the Blind (Edinburgh and SE Scotland), 1979–92. Trustee: Arthur Smith Meml Trust, 1975–2001 (Chm., 1990–2001); Faculty of Advocates 1985 Charitable Trust, 1985–; Southern Africa Litigation Centre, 2008–15. Gov., St Mary's Sch. (Melrose) Ltd, 1998–2012 (Dep. Chm., 2004–12). *Publications:* Medical Negligence: an introduction, 1983; (contrib.) Reproductive Medicine and the Law, 1990. *Recreations:* travel, nature conservation, Africana. *Address:* 4 Garscube Terrace, Edinburgh EH12 6BQ. *T:* (0131) 337 3460, *Fax:* (0131) 240 6711. *Club:* New (Edinburgh).

**ABERNETHY, Rt Rev. Alan Francis;** *see* Connor, Bishop of.

**ABIMBOLA, Olufunke Akindolie, (Funke),** MBE 2017; Director of Operations for Dispute Resolution, Mishcon de Reya LLP, since 2019; *b* Lagos, Nigeria, 16 June 1973; *d* of Dr Frank Olufemi Akindolie and Dr Sarah Omodele Akindolie; one *s*. *Educ:* Burgess Hill Girls' Sch., W Sussex; Newcastle Univ. Law Sch. (LLB Hons); Nigerian Law Sch. (Nigerian Bar qualif.); BPP Law Sch. (Qualified Lawyers Transfer Test). Assistant Solicitor: Charles Russell Speechlys, 2001–05; Pictons Solicitors, 2006–07; Sen. Solicitor, IBB Solicitors, 2007–11; Roche UK: Man. Counsel, 2012–15; Gen. Counsel and Co. Sec., 2015–17; Gen. Counsel and Hd of Financial Compliance, 2017–18. Professional Ambassador, 2013–, Mem., Sen. Adv. Bd, 2016–, Aspiring Solicitors; Champion, 2014–, Mem., Adv. Bd, 2016–, Women in Law London Network. Patron: Power Up, 2016–; Precious Awards, 2016–; InterLaw Diversity Forum BAME and Allies Network, 2016–; Univ. Leadership and Mgt Soc., UCL, 2017–. Founder, Women Leaders in Life Scis Law, 2015. *Recreations:* travel (hot countries only), cinema, meals out, quality time with my son. *Address:* Mishcon de Reya LLP, Africa House, 70 Kingsway, WC2B 6AH.

**ABINERI, Claudia;** *see* Rosencrantz, C. E.

**ABINGDON, Earl of;** *see* Lindsey and Abingdon, Earl of.

**ABINGER, 9th Baron** *cr* 1835; **James Harry Scarlett;** music publisher; Managing Director, Editions Abinger SPRL, since 2017; *b* 28 May 1959; *er s* of 8th Baron Abinger and Isla Carolyn, *o d* of Vice-Adm. J. W. Rivett-Carnac, CB, CBE, DSC; *S* father, 2002; *m* 1995, Tracy Lee, *d* of N. Cloutier, Ottawa; one *s* one *d* (adopted twins). *Educ:* Eton; Univ. of Aberdeen (BSc 1982); Magdalene Coll., Cambridge (MPhil 1994). FRGS, FLS. Dir Gen., A-Music, 2005–17. *Recreations:* diving for treasure, playing the cello, sailing, music, Gainsborough, Keats and Shelley. *Heir: b* Hon. Peter Richard Scarlett [*b* 21 March 1961; *m* 1992, Sharon Elizabeth Turl; one *s* one *d*].

**ABLE, Graham George;** Deputy Chairman, Alpha Plus Group, since 2014 (Chief Executive Officer, 2009–14); Master, Dulwich College, 1997–2009; *b* 28 July 1947; *s* of George Jasper Able and Irene Helen Able (*née* Gaff); *m* 1969, Mary Susan Munro; one *s* one *d*. *Educ:* Worksop Coll.; Trinity Coll., Cambridge (MA Nat. Scis 1968, PGCE 1969); MA Social Scis Dunelm 1983. Teacher, Sutton Valence Sch., 1969–83 (Boarding Housemaster, 1976–83); Second Master, Barnard Castle Sch., 1983–88; Headmaster, Hampton Sch., 1988–96. Co-Chm., HMC and GSA Educn and Academic Policy Cttee, 1998–2001; Chairman: HMC, 2003; Exporting Educn (UK), 2012–. Member: Council and Court, ICSTM, 1999–2006; Council, Roedean Sch., 2000–09. Pres., Internat. Boys' Schs' Coalition, 2006–09; Sen. Vice-Pres. (Acad.), Dulwich Coll. Mgt Internat., 2009–. Governor: Beeston Hall Sch., 2012–; Gresham's Sch., 2013–. Fellow, Dulwich Coll., 2009. Mem., Bd of Trustees, Cricket Foundn, 2009–14. FRSA 1994. MInstD 1995. *Publications:* (jtly) Head to Head, 1992; (jtly) Head to HoD, 1998; (jtly) Education: A Great British Export?, 2012. *Recreations:* cricket, golf, sailing, contract bridge. *Address:* The Old Smithy, High Street, Wighton, Norfolk NR23 1AL. *Clubs:* MCC, East India (Hon. Mem.).

**ABNEY-HASTINGS,** family name of **Earl of Loudoun**.

**ABOUSEIF, Doris B.;** *see* Behrens-Abouseif.

**ABOYNE, Earl of; Alistair Granville Gordon;** *b* 26 July 1973; *s* and *heir* of Marquess of Huntly, *qv*; *m* 2004, Sophia, *d* of Michael Cunningham; one *s* three *d*. *Educ:* Harrow. *Heir: s* Lord Strathavon, *qv*. *Address:* c/o Aboyne Castle, Aberdeenshire AB34 5JP.

**ABRAHAM, Ann;** UK Parliamentary Ombudsman and Health Service Ombudsman for England, 2002–12; *b* 25 Aug. 1952; *d* of John Kenneth and Kathleen Mary Marsden; *m* 2011, Geoffrey Leonard Mitchell. *Educ:* Bedford Coll., Univ. of London (BA Hons German); Postgrad. DMS. MCIH. Housing Manager, Local Govt, 1975–80; Ops Manager, Regional Dir and Ops Dir, Housing Corp., 1980–90; Chief Exec., NACAB, 1991–97; Legal Services Ombudsman for England and Wales, 1997–2002; Health Service Comr for Wales, 2002–03; Welsh Admin Ombudsman, 2002–04. Non-executive Director: Benefits Agency, 1997–2001; Health Educn England, 2012–14. Mem., Cttee on Standards in Public Life, 2000–02; ex officio Member: Commn for Local Admin in England, 2002–11; Administrative Justice and Tribunals Council (formerly Council on Tribunals), 2002–11 (Mem., Scottish Cttee, 2002–11, Welsh Cttee, 2008–11). Mem. Validation Cttee, Ombudsman Assoc. (formerly British and Irish Ombudsman Assoc.), 2006–11, 2012–15 (Mem. 2001–06, Chair, 2004–06, Exec. Cttee). Trustee, Picker Inst. Europe, 2013–19. Chair, Dorset HealthCare Univ. NHS Foundn Trust, 2014–17 (non-exec. Dir, 2013–14); Trustee, Dorset Mental Health Forum, 2018–. Comr, Jersey Care Commn, 2017–. Pro-Chancellor, Bournemouth Univ., 2019–. Hon LLD Winchester, 2012; Hon. DBA Bournemouth, 2018. *Recreations:* family, friends, walking, gardening. *E:* ann.abraham@btinternet.com.

**ABRAHAM, David;** Co-Founder and Chief Executive Officer, Wonderhood Studios, since 2018; *b* Lincs, 7 Aug. 1963; *s* of Esmond and Jeanette Abraham; one *s* one *d*; partner, Tiina Le-Seong Lee, *qv*. *Educ:* Ingatestone Sch.; Magdalen Coll., Oxford (BA Modern Hist. 1984). Account Manager, Benton & Bowles, 1984–87; Account Manager, 1987–88, Account Dir, 1989–90, CDP; Account Dir, 1990–93, Dep. Man. Dir, 1993–95, Chiat Day; Founder and Chief Operating Officer, St Luke's, 1995–2000; Gen. Manager, Discovery Networks UK, 2001–04; Pres., TLC, USA, 2005–07; Chief Executive: UKTV, 2007–10; Channel Four, 2010–17. Mem. Bd, Creative Skillset (formerly Skillset), 2008–17. Mem., BAFTA; Patron, RTS.

**ABRAHAM, Eric Antony;** film, theatre and television producer; *b* Cape Town, S Africa, 3 March 1954; *s* of George Abraham; *m* 1st, 1978, Katarina Krausova (marr. diss. 2002); one *s* one *d*; 2nd, 2003, Sigrid Maria Elisabet Rausing, *qv*. *Educ:* Univ. of Cape Town (BA Comparative African Govt and Law 1976). Organiser, Amnesty Internat. first global campaign against torture and Conf. for Abolition of Torture, Paris, 1973–74; human rights worker and foreign corresp., S Africa, 1974–76; banned and house-arrested by apartheid govt, 1976; adopted as Amnesty Prisoner of Conscience; escaped and granted political asylum in UK, 1977. Producer, Panorama, BBC TV, 1977–82; Exec. Producer, Primetime TV, 1983–86; Founder, Portobello Pictures, 1987; productions include: *films:* Danny, the Champion of the World, 1989; A Murder of Quality, 1991; Kolya, 1996; IDA, 2013; *television:* Dalziel & Pascoe, 1997–99; Mojo, 1997; *theatre:* Embers, Duke of York's, 2006; South African version of Mozart's Magic Flute, Young Vic, transf. Duke of York's, 2008; Exec. Producer and Founder, Fugard Th., Cape Town, 2010–. Member: BAFTA, 1990–; Acad. of Motion Picture Arts and Scis, 1997–; Czech Film Acad., 1997–; Eur. Film Acad., 1998–. *Recreations:* cinema, theatre, ski-ing, walking. *Address:* Portobello Pictures, 12 Penzance Place, W11 4PA. *Clubs:* Athenæum, Chelsea Arts, Soho House, Groucho.

**ABRAHAM, Maj. Gen. Kevin David,** CB 2014; Director, AWCTS Ltd, since 2015; *b* Magherafelt, 11 Feb. 1960; *s* of David Abraham and Mary Patricia Abraham (*née* Nesbitt); *m* 1996, Julia Caroline Williams; two step *s*. *Educ:* Dr Challoner's Grammar Sch.; Univ. of St Andrews (MA 1983); King's Coll. London (MA 2000). Jun. officer posts in Germany and UK, 1983–2000; psc 1992; psc JSCSC 1999; CO, 1st Regt RHA, 2000–02; ACOS Plans, HQ ARRC, 2002–04; hcsc 2003; Comdr, 1st UK Armd Div., RA, 2004–05; rcds 2006; ACOS J7, PJHQ, 2006–08; Director: Jt Capability, MoD, 2008–10; Force Develt, Army HQ, 2010–12; Dir Gen. Army Reform, Army HQ, 2012–14. Dir, Strategic Engagement, Army Reserve, 2015–. Mem., Regtl Council, HAC, 2013–19. Hon. Col, Tayforth Univ. OTC, 2013–18. Dir, Shared Outcomes Prog., Inst. of Statecraft, 2015–19. Hon. Fellow, Strategy and Security Inst., Exeter Univ., 2015–. Pres., Army Ornithological Soc., 2017–. *Recreations:* ski-ing, sailing, Rugby, birding. *Club:* Naval and Military.

**ABRAHAM, Neville Victor,** CBE 2001; Chairman: Liberty Wines Ltd, since 2003; Metabolic Services Ltd, since 2013; Groupe Chez Gérard plc, 1994–2003 (Joint Founder, 1986; Chief Executive, 1994–99); *b* 22 Jan. 1937; *s* of late Solomon Abraham and of Sarah (*née* Raphael); *m* 2005, Nicola Leach. *Educ:* Brighton Coll.; London Sch. of Econs (BSc Hons). Marketing Asst, Young & Rubicam, 1961–63; Sen. Principal, DTI, 1963–71; Corporate Policy Advr, Harold Whitehead & Partners, 1971–74; Founder, Les Amis du Vin, 1974 (Man. Dir, 1974–86); Chm., Amis du Vin Gp, 1980–84; Dir, Kennedy Brookes plc, 1984–86. Non-exec. Dir, Draft House Hldgs Ltd, 2009–16. Vis. Lectr, several business schools, 1972–81. Chairman: Exec. Cttee, Covent Garden Fest., 1993–99; London String Quartet Foundn, 2000–06. Gov., Brighton Coll., 2006– (Vice Chm., 2017–). *Publications:* Big Business and Government: the new disorder, 1974. *Recreations:* music, opera, walking, good food and wine, cricket. *Clubs:* Royal Automobile, Home House, MCC.

**ABRAHAM, Ronny Jacob;** Judge, International Court of Justice, since 2005 (President, 2015–18); *b* Egypt, 5 Sept. 1951; *s* of Joseph Abraham and Greta Abraham (*née* Saldinger). *Educ:* Institut d'études politiques, Paris (Dip. 1973); Univ. of Paris I (Dip. Advanced Studies Public Law 1974); Ecole nationale d'administration (graduate). Judge sitting in administrative court of Versailles, 1978–88; Asst Dir, Office of Legal Affairs, Min. of Foreign Affairs, France, 1986–87; Maître des requêtes, Conseil d'Etat, 1988–98; Dir of Legal Affairs, Min. of Foreign Affairs, France, 1998–2005. Hon. Mem., Amer. Acad. of Arts and Scis, 2016. Chevalier, Ordre Nat. du Mérite (France), 1991. *Publications:* Droit international, droit communautaire et droit français, 1989. *Recreation:* cinema. *Address:* International Court of Justice, Carnegieplein 2, 2517 KJ, The Hague, The Netherlands. *T:* (70) 3022462. *E:* r.abraham@icj-cij.org.

**ABRAHAM, Sigrid Maria Elisabeth;** *see* Rausing, S. M. E.

**ABRAHAMS, David;** *see* Abrahams, I. D.

**ABRAHAMS, Deborah Angela Elspeth;** MP (Lab) Oldham East and Saddleworth, since Jan. 2011; *b* Sheffield, 1960; *m* John Abrahams; two *d*. *Educ:* Univ. of Salford; Univ. of Liverpool. FFPH 2012. Hd, Healthy Cities for Knowsley, 1992–2000; Sen. Res. Fellow, Univ. of Liverpool, full time, 2000–02, pt time, 2002–06; Chm., Rochdale PCT, 2002–06; Dir, Internat. Health Impact Assessment Consortium, Univ. of Liverpool, 2006–10. Mem. Bd, Bury and Rochdale HA, 1998–2002. Contested (Lab) Colne Valley, 2010. Mem., Work and Pensions Select Cttee, 2011–15; Shadow Minister of State for Disabled People, 2015–16; Shadow Sec. of State for Work and Pensions, 2016–18. *Address:* House of Commons, SW1A 0AA.

**ABRAHAMS, Prof. (Ian) David,** PhD; FRSE; N. M. Rothschild and Sons Professor of Mathematical Sciences and Director, Isaac Newton Institute for Mathematical Sciences, University of Cambridge, since 2016; Fellow, Corpus Christi College, Cambridge, since 2016; *b* Manchester, 15 Jan. 1958; *s* of late Harry Abrahams and of Leila Abrahams; *m* 2004, Penelope Lawrence Warwick; one *d* and two step *s*. *Educ:* Imperial Coll. London (BSc Eng. Hons 1979; PhD Applied Maths 1982; DIC 1982). Temp. Lectr, Dept of Maths, Univ. of Manchester, 1982–83; Lectr, Sch. of Maths, Univ. of Newcastle upon Tyne, 1983–90; Reader, 1990–93, Prof., 1994–98, Dept of Maths, Keele Univ.; Beyer Prof. of Applied Maths, 1998–2016, Hd, Applied Maths, Sch. of Maths, 1998–2007, Univ. of Manchester; Scientific Dir, Internat. Centre for Math. Scis, Edinburgh, 2014–16. Nuffield Foundn Sci. Res. Fellow, 1990–91; Royal Soc. Leverhulme Trust Sen. Res. Fellow, 2002–03; Royal Soc. Wolfson Res. Merit Award, 2013–16. Member: Council: IMA, 1998–2015 (Pres., 2008–09); Eur. Mechanics Soc., 2000–06; LMS, 2002–06; Bd, Internat. Council for Industrial and Applied Maths, 2003–. FRSE 2019. *Publications:* contrib. scientific papers on propagation, refraction and diffraction of waves in solids, fluids and electromagnetics. *Recreations:* distance running, motorcycling, fiddling with ALL things mechanical and electrical, watching (almost) all sports. *Address:* Isaac Newton Institute for Mathematical Sciences, 20 Clarkson Road, Cambridge CB3 0EH.

**ABRAHAMS, James;** QC 2016; *b* Port Elizabeth, S Africa, 7 March 1974; *s* of Kenneth Abrahams and Niall Geraldine D'Altera Abrahams; *m* 2002, Joanne Welsh; one *s* one *d*. *Educ:* Bournemouth Sch.; St Anne's Coll., Oxford (BA 1995; BCL 1996). Called to the Bar, Gray's Inn, 1997; in practice as a barrister specialising in patents and other intellectual property rights, 1999–. *Publications:* (contrib.) Halsbury's Laws of England, Vol. 48, 4th edn reissue 2000; (contrib.) Bullen & Leake & Jacob's Precedents of Pleadings, 14th edn 2001, 15th edn 2004. *Recreations:* football, cricket, long walks that finish in a pub. *Address:* 8 New Square, Lincoln's Inn, WC2A 3QP. *Clubs:* St Anne's Allstars Cricket (Founder Mem.); Tottenham Hotspur Football.

**ABRAHAMS, Michael David,** CBE 1994 (MBE 1988); DL; Chairman, Ferrexpo plc, 2007–17; *b* 23 Nov. 1937; *s* of Alexander Abrahams and Anne Abrahams (*née* Sokoloff); *m* 1968, Amanda Atha; one *s* two *d*. *Educ:* Shrewsbury; Worcester Coll., Oxford. Nat. Service, RM (commnd). Man. Dir, AW (Securities) Ltd, 1968–73; Chairman: Champion Associated Weavers Ltd, 1974–80; Associated Weavers Europe NV, 1974–83; Weavercraft Carpets Ltd, 1980–85; Dep. Chm., John Crowther PLC, 1985–88; Director: Prudential Corp. plc, 1984–2000 (Dep. Chm., 1991–2000); John Waddington plc, 1984–2000; Cavaghan & Gray plc, 1987–98 (Chm., 1992–98); Drummond Gp plc, 1989–2001. Chairman: Prudential Staff Pension Scheme, 1991–; Mgt Cttee, Hunt Staff Benefit Soc., 1993–; Minorplanet Systems plc, 1997–2004; Kingston Communications plc, 1999–2009; imJack plc (formerly Amteus plc), 2006–11. Chm., The London Clinic, 1996–2012. Pres., British Carpet Mfrs Assoc., 1979–80. Dep. Chm. Council, Prince of Wales's Inst. of Architecture, 1991–96; Dir, Rank Foundn, 1992–2007; Regl Chm., NT for Yorks, 1996–2003; Chm., Ripon City Partnership, 2005–09. Jt Chm., Yorks Children's Hosp. Fund (Co-founder), 1989–2011; Trustee, Hackfall Trust, 1987–. Pres., Yorks Agricl Soc., 2007–08. Master, Woolmen's Co., 1996–97. High Sheriff, 1993–94, DL, 1994, N Yorks. Hon. Freeman, City of Ripon, 2002. *Recreations:* art, architecture. *Address:* Newfield, Mickley, Ripon, N Yorks HG4 3JH. *T:* (01765) 635426. *Club:* Garrick.

**ABRAHAMSEN, Egil;** Comdr, Order of St Olav, 1987 (Kt Comdr 1979); Chairman, Norwegian Telecommunications, 1980–95; *b* 7 Feb. 1923; *s* of Anker Christian Abrahamsen and Aagot (*née* Kjølberg); *m* 1950, Randi Wiborg; one *s* two *d*. *Educ:* Technical Univ. of Norway (Naval Architect, 1949); Durham Univ., King's Coll., Newcastle upon Tyne (post-grad. studies and res.); Univ. of Calif, Berkeley (post-grad. studies). Sales Engr, Maschinen-Fabrik Augsburg-Nürnberg, and Karlstads Mekaniska Verkstad AB, Sweden, 1949–50; projects and planning, A/S Rosenberg Mekaniske Verksted, Stavanger, 1951–52; Det Norske Veritas, 1952–85: Surveyor, 1952; Sen. Surveyor, 1954 (resp. for building up Res. Dept); Principal Surveyor, 1957; Dep. Pres., 1966; Vice Pres., 1966; Pres., 1967. Chairman: Norsk Hydro, 1985–92; OPAK, 1985–99; Royal Caribbean Cruise-Line, 1987–88; Kosmos, 1988–99; IKO Group, 1988–; Eikland, 1990–99; IM Skaugen ASA, 1990–99. Editor, European Shipbuilding, 1952–60. Fellow, Nat. Acad. of Engrg, USA, 1978; Member: Norwegian Acad. of Technical Scis, 1968 (Hon. Mem., 2008); Royal Swedish Acad. of Engrg Scis, 1979; Hon. Mem., Soc. of Naval Architects and Marine Engrs, USA, 1987. DTech *hc* Royal Inst. of Technol., Sweden, 1977. Owes Hon. Prize, for contribn to res. and educn, 1971. Grand Officer, Order of Infante Dom Henrique (Portugal), 1977; Comdr, Order of the Lion (Finland), 1982; Kt, Nat. Order of Merit (France), 1982. *Address:* Borgenveien 50, 0373 Oslo, Norway.

**ABRAM, Rev. Paul Robert Carrington,** MVO 2007; a Deputy Priest in Ordinary to the Queen, 1996–2007; Chaplain of the Chapel Royal of St Peter ad Vincula, Tower of London, 1996–2007; *b* 21 July 1936; *s* of Norman and Madge Alice Abram; *m* 1961, Joanna Rose (*née* Headley); four *d*. *Educ:* The English Sch., Cairo; King Alfred Sch., Plon; Hymers

Coll., Hull; Keble Coll., Oxford (BA 1962; MA 1965); Chichester Theol Coll. Ordained deacon, 1962, priest, 1963; Asst Curate, Redcar, 1962–65; Chaplain to the Forces, 1965–89; Vicar of Salcombe and Chaplain, Missions to Seamen, 1989–96; Chaplain for the Pool of London, Mission to Seafarers (formerly Missions to Seamen), 1996–2007. Chaplain: HMS President, 1996–2007; Solicitors' Co., 1996–2007; Builders' Merchants' Co., 1996–2007 (Life Liveryman, 2007); Aldermanic Sheriff, 1999–2000; Security Professionals, 2001–07; NEAC, 2001–07; Lord Mayor of London, 2003–04. FRGS 1960. Medal, Order of St Melitus, 2007. *Recreations:* sailing, pre-nineteenth century maps, travel, people. *Address:* Paddock End, Kimpton, Andover, Hants SP11 8PG. *Club:* Special Forces.

**ABRAMS, Prof. (William) Dominic (Joshua),** PhD; FBA 2013; FAcSS; Professor of Social Psychology, since 1993 and Director, Centre for the Study of Group Processes, since 1995, University of Kent; *b* Cambridge, 11 April 1958; *s* of late Prof. Philip Abrams and of Prof. Sonia Jackson (*née* Edelman); *m* 1989, Prof. Diane Margaret Houston; one *s* two *d*. *Educ:* Impington Village Coll.; Brooksbank Comp. Sch.; Greenhead Coll.; Univ. of Manchester (BA Hons Psychol.); London Sch. of Econs and Pol Sci. (MSc Social Psychol.); Univ. of Kent (PhD Social Psychol. 1984). CPsychol 1989. Lectr in Social Psychol., Univ. of Bristol, 1983–85; Lectr in Social Cognition, Dundee Univ., 1985–89; Lectr, 1989–91, Sen. Lectr, 1991–92, Reader, 1992–93, in Social Psychol., Univ. of Kent. Member: res. bds, ESRC, 2008–13; HEFCE Res. Evaluation Framework Panel 4, 2013–14. British Psychological Society: Sec./Treas., Social Psychol. Section, 1985–89; Chm., Res. Bd and Mem., Bd of Trustees, 2003–06; Fellow, 2011. Mem. Council and Chm., Learned Socs, Acad. of Social Scis, 2000–06, 2009–14; Sec., Eur. Assoc. of Social Psychol., 2002–05; Pres., Soc. for Psychol Study of Social Issues, 2012–14 (Fellow, 1999); Founder Chair, Soc. for Psychol Study of Social Issues-UK, 2014–16; Vice Pres. (Social Scis), British Acad., 2016–July 2020. Trustee, Anne Frank Trust, 2013–15. Editor, Group Processes and Intergroup Relations, 1997–. Fellow: Soc. of Experimental Social Psychol., 2006; Soc. for Personality and Social Psychol., 2009. FAcSS (AcSS 2004). *Publications:* with M. A. Hogg: Social Identifications: a social psychology of intergroup relations and group processes, 1988 (Chinese edn 1995); (ed) Social Identity Theory: constructive and critical advances, 1990; (ed) Group Motivation: social psychological perspectives, 1993; (ed) Social Identity and Social Cognition, 1999; Intergroup Relations, 2001; (ed jtly) The Social Psychology of Exclusion and Inclusion, 2005; (ed jtly) Multidisciplinary Handbook of Social Exclusion Research, 2007; over 200 papers on prejudice, social cohesion and social gps in jls. *Recreation:* folk, blues and jazz guitar and violin. *Address:* Centre for the Study of Group Processes, University of Kent, Canterbury CT2 7NP. *E:* D.Abrams@kent.ac.uk.

**ABRAMSKY, Dame Jennifer (Gita),** DBE 2009 (CBE 2001); Chair: Royal Academy of Music, since 2014; National Life Stories, since 2015; *b* 7 Oct. 1946; *d* of late Prof. Chimen Abramsky and Miriam (*née* Nirenstein); *m* 1976, Alasdair Donald MacDuff Liddell, CBE (*d* 2012); one *s* one *d*. *Educ:* Holland Park Sch.; Univ. of East Anglia (BA Hons English) (Dep. Chm., New Univs Fest., 1968). BBC: joined as Prog. Operations Asst, 1969; Producer, World at One, 1973; Jt Producer and Compiler of Special Prog. on 'Nixon', 1974; Editor: PM Prog., 1978–81; Radio Four Budget Prog., 1979–86; World at One, 1981–86; Today, 1986–87; News and Current Affairs, BBC Radio, 1987–93; set up Radio 4 News FM for duration of Gulf War, 1991; Controller, BBC Radio Five Live, 1993–96; Dir, Continuous News Services, BBC, incl. Radio 5 Live, BBC World, 24 Hour UK TV News, Ceefax and Multimedia News, 1996–98; Dir, BBC Radio, 1999–2000; Dir, BBC Radio and Music, subseq. Audio and Music, 2000–08. Member: ESRC, 1992–96; Editl Bd, British Journalism Rev., 1993–98. Chair, NHMF and HLF, 2008–14. Director: Hampstead Th., 2003– (Chm., 2006–12); Birmingham Royal Ballet, 2011–. A Governor, BFI, 2000–06; Vice Chm., Digital Radio Develt Bureau, 2002–08. News Internat. Vis. Prof. of Broadcast Media, Oxford Univ., 2001–02. Gov., Royal Ballet, 2008– (Chair, Bd of Govs, 2013–); Chair, Bd of Trustees, Univ. of London, 2008–14; Trustee: Central Sch. of Ballet, 2007–13; Shakespeare Schs Foundn, 2008–17; English Touring Th., 2015–; Canal and River Trust, 2016– (Dep. Chm., 2017–). Chair, Trustees, You Make It (formerly Ladies Who L-EARN), 2014–17. Fellow, Radio Acad., 1998. Hon. Fellow, Central Sch. of Speech and Drama, 2009. Hon. RAM 2002. Hon. MA Salford, 1997; Hon. LittD UAE, 2003; Hon. DLitt: Westminster, 2005; Kent, 2012. Woman of Distinction, Jewish Care, 1990; Sony Radio Acad. Award, 1995. *Recreations:* theatre, music, dance.

**ABRAMSKY, Prof. Samson,** PhD; FRS 2004; FRSE; Christopher Strachey Professor of Computing, University of Oxford, since 2000; Fellow, Wolfson College, Oxford, since 2000; *b* 12 March 1953; *s* of Moshe and Chaya-Sarah Abramsky; *m* 1976, Rosalind Susan Herman; two *s*. *Educ:* King's Coll., Cambridge (BA 1975; MA Philosophy 1979; Dip. Computer Sci.); Queen Mary Coll., London (PhD Computer Sci. 1988). FRSE 2000. Programmer, GEC Computers Ltd, 1976–78; Lectr, Dept of Computer Sci. and Stats, QMC, 1980–83; Lectr, 1983–88, Reader, 1988–90, Prof., 1990–95, Dept of Computing, Imperial Coll., London; Prof. of Theoretical Computer Sci., Univ. of Edinburgh, 1996–2000. MAE 1993. *Publications:* (ed jtly) Handbook of Logic in Computer Science, 5 vols, 1992–2000; contrib. numerous articles to computer sci. jls and confs. *Recreations:* reading, music, walking. *Address:* Department of Computer Science, University of Oxford, Wolfson Building, Parks Road, Oxford OX1 3QD. *T:* (01865) 283558; Wolfson College, Linton Road, Oxford OX2 6UD.

**ABSALOM, Emily Helen;** *see* Wilson, E. H.

**ABTS, Tomma;** artist; Professor of Painting, Kunstakademie, Düsseldorf, since 2010; *b* Kiel, 26 Dec. 1967; *d* of Hermann Abts and Imke Tammena. *Educ:* Hochschule der Künste, Berlin (Dip. 1993, MA 1995). Trustee, Tate, 2011–15. *Solo exhibitions* include: greengrassi, London, 1999, 2002, 2005, 2011, 2016; Galerie Giti Nourbakhsch, Berlin, 2001, 2004, 2009; Wrong Gall., NY, 2003; Galerie Daniel Buchholz, subseq. Galerie Buchholz, Cologne, 2003, 2006, Berlin, 2013, 2017; Douglas Hyde Gall., Dublin, Kunsthalle Basel, 2005; Kunsthalle Kiel, 2006; David Zwirner, NY, New Mus. of Contemporary Art, NY, travelling to Hammer Mus., LA, 2008; Kunsthalle Düsseldorf, 2011; David Zwirner, NY, 2014; Aspen Art Mus., 2014; Serpentine Gall., London, 2018; Art Inst. of Chicago, 2018; *group exhibitions* include: Egofugal, 7th Internat. Istanbul Biennial, 2001; deutschemalereizweitausenddrei, Frankfurter Kunstverein, 2003; 54th Carnegie Internat., Carnegie Mus. of Art, Pittsburgh, 2004; British Art Show 6, Gateshead, Manchester, Nottingham and Bristol, 2005; Of Mice and Men, 4th Berlin Biennale, Shanghai Biennale - Hyper Design, 2006; Art Sheffield 08, 2008; 4th Tirana Biennale, 2009; Painting Now: Five Contemporary Artists, Tate Britain, 2013; Drawing Now, Albertina Mus., Vienna, 2015; Abstraction: Aspects of Contemporary Art, Nat. Mus. of Art, Osaka. Stipendium for London, DAAD, 1995; Paul Hamlyn Foundn Award, 2004; Turner Prize, 2006. *Publications:* exhibition catalogues.

**ABULAFIA, Prof. Anna Brechta Sapir,** DTh, LittD; FRHistS; Professor of the Study of the Abrahamic Religions, University of Oxford, since 2015; Fellow, Lady Margaret Hall, since 2015; *b* New York, 8 May 1952; *d* of Boris and Berti Sapir; *m* 1979, David Samuel Harvard Abulafia, *qv*; two *d*. *Educ:* St Hilda's and St Hugh's, NY; Bronx High Sch. of Sci.; Goois Lyceum, Netherlands; Univ. of Amsterdam (Candidaats 1974; Doctoraal Hist. 1978; DTh 1984); Lucy Cavendish Coll., Cambridge (MA 1985; LittD 2014); Univ. of Oxford (DLitt 2015). FRHistS 1998. Lectr in Medieval Hist., Univ. of Amsterdam, 1979; Res. Fellow, Clare Hall, Cambridge, 1981–86; Lucy Cavendish Coll., Cambridge: Laura Ashley Res. Fellow, 1987–90; Fellow, Coll. Lectr and Dir of Studies in Hist., 1990–2015; Tutor for grad. students, 1992–96; Sen. Tutor, 1996–2002; Vice Pres., 2002–10; Affiliated Coll. Lectr and Dir of Studies in Hist., Newnham Coll., Cambridge, 2013–15. *Publications:* (ed jtly) The Works of Gilbert Crispin, Abbot of Westminster, 1986; Christians and Jews in the Twelfth-century Renaissance, 1995; Christians and Jews in Dispute, 1998; (ed) Religious Violence between Christians and Jews: medieval roots, modern perspectives, 2002; Christian-Jewish Relations, 1000–1300: Jews in the service of medieval Christendom, 2011; contrib. articles to learned jls, conf. proceedings and vols of collected essays. *Recreations:* knitting, gardening. *Address:* Lady Margaret Hall, Norham Gardens, Oxford OX2 6QA. *T:* (01865) 284268. *E:* anna.sapirabulafia@theology.ox.ac.uk.

**ABULAFIA, Prof. David Samuel Harvard,** PhD, LittD; FBA 2010; FRHistS, FSA; Professor of Mediterranean History, History Faculty, University of Cambridge, 2000–17, now Emeritus; Fellow, since 1974, and Papathomas Professorial Fellow, since 2014, Gonville and Caius College, Cambridge; *b* Twickenham, 12 Dec. 1949; *s* of Leon and Rachel Abulafia; *m* 1979, Anna Brechta Sapir (*see* A. B. S. Abulafia); two *d*. *Educ:* St Paul's Sch.; King's Coll., Cambridge (BA 1971; MA); PhD 1975, LittD 1994, Cantab. FRHistS 1981. FSA 2010. Rome Schol., British Sch. at Rome, 1972–74; Cambridge University: Asst Lectr, 1978–83; Lectr, 1983–91; Reader, 1991–2000; Chm., History Faculty, 2003–05; Tutor for Grad. Students, Gonville and Caius Coll., 1984–91. Dorfler Meml Lectr, Leo Baeck Coll., 1992; Guest Lectr, project on Objective Cultural Resources, Tokyo Univ., 2000; Crayenborgh Lectr, Leiden Univ., 2002. Vis. Beacon Prof., Univ. of Gibraltar, 2017–; Vis. Prof., Coll. of Europe, Natolin, 2018–; Res. Fellow, John Carter Brown Liby, Brown Univ., 2017; Fellow, Erasmus Forum, 2018–. Project co-ordinator, EU Culture 2000, 2000–03. Mem., Rev. Cttee, Ben Gurion Univ. of the Negev, 1999–2000. Member, Council: Mediterranean Studies Assoc., 1998–2003; Cambridge Univ., 2008–12; British Acad., 2015–; Mem., Academic Bd, Univ. of Gibraltar, 2015–. Chm., Historians for Britain, 2015–16. Gov., Perse Sch., 2002–10. Mem., Jury, Galasso Prize, 2019. Gen. Ed., Jl of Medieval Hist., 1989–95. MAE 2002. Fellow, Legatum Inst., 2015–17. British Acad. Medal, 2013. Commendatore dell'Ordine della Stella della Solidarietà Italiana (Italy), 2003; Mediterranean Award (Malta), 2014. *Publications:* The Two Italies, 1977 (trans. Italian 1991); Italy, Sicily and the Mediterranean, 1987; Frederick II, 1988, 3rd edn 2002 (trans. Italian 1990, German 1991); Spain and 1492, 1992; (ed jtly) Church and City, 1992; Commerce and Conquest in the Mediterranean, 1993; A Mediterranean Emporium, 1994 (trans. Spanish 1996); (ed) The French Descent into Renaissance Italy, 1995 (trans. Italian 2005); The Western Mediterranean Kingdoms, 1997 (trans. Italian 1999); (ed jtly) En las costas del Mediterráneo occidental, 1997; (ed) New Cambridge Medieval History, vol. 5, 1999; Mediterranean Encounters, 2000; (ed jtly) Medieval Frontiers, 2002; (ed) The Mediterranean in History, 2003 (trans. Spanish and German, 2003, French and Greek, 2004, Turkish, 2005); (ed) Italy in the Central Middle Ages, 2004; The Discovery of Mankind, 2008 (trans. Spanish 2009, Italian 2010); (with M. Naro) Il Duomo di Monreale, 2009 (trans. French 2013); The Great Sea (Mountbatten Maritime Award for Literary Excellence, Maritime Foundn), 2011 (trans. Dutch, 2011, Greek, Turkish, 2012, Spanish, German, Italian, Korean, 2013, Romanian, Portuguese (Brazil), 2014, Chinese (Taiwan), 2017, Chinese, 2018); The Boundless Sea: a human history of the oceans, 2019. *Recreation:* travel in reality and in imagination. *Address:* Gonville and Caius College, Cambridge CB2 1TA. *T:* (01223) 332473. *Club:* Athenæum.

**ABUSSEITOV, Kairat;** Ambassador of the Republic of Kazakhstan to Norway, since 2014; *b* Almaty, 20 Oct. 1955; *s* of Khuat Abusseitov and Maira Abusseitova; *m* Rosa Aidarova; one *s*. *Educ:* Kazakh State Univ. (degree 1979); Moscow State Univ. (PhD 1984). Sen. Lectr, Dep. of Dean, Kazakh State Univ., Almaty, 1985–89; Sen. Lectr, World Pols and Internat. Relns, Almaty High Party Sch., 1989–91; Hd, Foreign Policy and Nat. Security Prog. of Presidential Center for Strategic Studies, 1991–93; Ministry of Foreign Affairs: Hd, Internat. Security and Arms Control Section, 1993–94; Hd, Internat. Security and Arms Control Dept, 1994–96; Counsellor, Embassy of Kazakhstan to USA, 1996–98; Dir, Multilateral Cooperation Dept, and Ambassador-at-Large, Min. of Foreign Affairs, 1998–99; Dep. Minister of Foreign Affairs, 1999–2002; First Dep. Minister of Foreign Affairs, 2002–04; Ambassador: to Switzerland, 2004–08; to UK, 2008–14. Kurmet Order, 2002. *Publications:* more than 40 scientific articles on internat. security, arms control and disarmament issues. *Recreations:* jazz music, tennis. *Address:* c/o Embassy of the Republic of Kazakhstan, Nedre Vollgate 3, 2nd Floor, 0158 Oslo, Norway.

**ACHARYA, Prof. Diwakar Nath,** PhD; Spalding Professor of Eastern Religions and Ethics, University of Oxford, since 2016; Fellow of All Souls College, Oxford, since 2016; *b* Kathmandu, 6 Nov. 1969; *s* of Loknath Acharya and Durga Devi Acharya; *m* 1997, Shobha; one *s* one *d*. *Educ:* Faculty of Sanskrit Studies, Tribhuvan Univ.; Mahendra Sanskrit Univ., Nepal (BA 1988); Sampurnananda Sanskrit Univ., Benares (MA 1992); Hamburg Univ. (PhD 2004). Asst Prof., Mahendra Sanskrit Univ., Nepal, 1993–2003; Res. Associate, Hamburg Univ., 2003–06; Vis. Lectr, 2006–11, Associate Prof., 2011–16, Kyoto Univ. Local Dir, Nepal Res. Centre and Nepal-German Manuscript Cataloguing Proj., 2003–04. Vis. Prof., Groningen Univ., 2012; Numata Prof. of Buddhism, 2015. *Publications:* Vācaspatimiśra's Tattvasamīkṣā: the earliest commentary on Maṇḍanamiśra's Brahmasiddhi, 2006; (trans.) The Little Clay Cart, 2009; (ed) Early Tantric Vaiṣṇavism: three newly discovered works of the Pañcarātra, 2015. *Recreations:* walking, reading, family. *Address:* All Souls College, Oxford OX1 4AL. *T:* (01865) 281413. *E:* acharyadiwakar@gmail.com.

**ACHER, Sir Gerald,** Kt 2012; CBE 1999; LVO 2002; Deputy Chairman, Camelot UK Lotteries Ltd (formerly Camelot Group plc), 2002–15 (non-executive Director, 2002–15; Interim Chairman, 2004); *b* 30 April 1945; *s* of late David Acher and Andrée Diana Acher (*née* Laredo); *m* 1970, Joyce Kathleen White; two *s*. *Educ:* King's Coll. Sch., Wimbledon. Articled clerk, Bird Potter & Co., 1961–66; Peat, Marwick, Mitchell & Co., subseq. KPMG: Asst Manager, 1967–73; Manager, 1973–75; Sen. Manager, 1975–80; Partner, 1980–2001; Mem., UK Bd, 1987–2001; Hd, Corporate Finance, 1990–93; UK Hd of Audit and Accounting, 1993–98; Sen. Partner, London Office, 1998–2001; Chairman: Worldwide Audit and Accounting Cttee, 1995–98; UK Client Service Bd, 1998–2001; Sen. Advr, 2002–10. Non-executive Director: BPB Industries plc, 2002–05; Imperial Coll. Healthcare NHS Trust, 2012– (Dep. Chm., 2015–). Member: Adv. Cttee on Business and the Envmt, 1999–2004; DTI Foresight Panel on Crime and Business, 2001–02. Dep. Chm., London First, 2000–05; Dir, London First Centre, 1998–2001; Chm., London Mayoral Commn investigating feasibility of an internat. convention centre in London, 2004–06. Institute of Chartered Accountants in England and Wales: Mem., 1967–; Mem. Council, 1995–2001; Chm., Audit and Assce Faculty, 1995–2001. Trustee, KPMG Foundn, 2005–. MCSI (MSI 1992). Hon. Treas., Queen's Golden Jubilee Weekend Trust, 2001–02. Chairman: Heart of the City, 2005–12; London Climate Change Partnership, 2005–12; Cobham Conservation and Heritage Trust, 2005–; Cobham Community Bus CIC, 2014–; Chm. and Trustee, Brooklands Mus. Trust, 2015–. Pres., Young Epilepsy, 2011–; Gov., 1990–, and Vice Chm., 1995–, Motability; Trustee, Motability Tenth Anniversary Trust, 1991–. Trustee, Aston Martin Heritage Trust, 2001–07; Chm., Awards for Young Musicians, 1998–2004. Royal Society of Arts: Fellow, 1998; Treas., 1999; Trustee, 2000–09; Chm., 2006–09; Mem. Council, 2000–04. Liveryman, Chartered Accountants'

Co. (Mem., Ct of Assistants; Master, 2003–04). Chm. Govs, Milbourne Lodge Jun. Sch., 1986–2007. Outstanding Achievement Award, ICAEW, 2017. *Recreations:* classic and vintage car rallying, restoring old houses, mountain walking, opera, classical music, travel, gardening. *Club:* Travellers.

**ACHESON,** family name of **Earl of Gosford**.

**ACHESON, Peter Newton,** MBE 2019; DL; Vice Lord-Lieutenant of County Tyrone, 2009–13; Solicitor and Senior Partner, Ronald Rosser & Co., 1974–98; *b* Belfast, 21 April 1938; *s* of David A. Acheson and Kathleen F. Acheson (*née* Newton); *m* 1962, Hilary J. McMaster (*d* 2010); one *s* three *d*. *Educ:* Elm Park Sch., Armagh; Merchiston Castle Sch., Edinburgh; Brasenose Coll., Oxford (BA Modern Hist. 1960). Dir, David Acheson Ltd, linen manufacturers, 1960–70. Admitted solicitor, 1973. Pres., Solicitors Disciplinary Tribunal (NI), 1996–98. Chm. Govs, Charles Sheils Charity, 1975–2019. DL Co. Tyrone, 1997. *Recreations:* boating, lawnmowing and weeding. *Address:* Castlecaulfield House, Castlecaulfield, Dungannon, Co. Tyrone, Northern Ireland BT70 3NY. *T:* (028) 8776 1223. *E:* pnacheson@yahoo.com. *Clubs:* Armagh; Kildare St and University (Dublin).
*See also Sir D. R. J. B. Finlay, Bt.*

**ACHTMAN, Prof. Mark,** PhD, Dr hab.; FRS 2015; Professor of Bacterial Population Genetics, University of Warwick, since 2013; *b* 30 Sept. 1943; *s* of Joseph Achtman and Helen Achtman (*née* Berland); two *c*. *Educ:* McGill Univ., Montreal (BSc Bacteriol. and Immunol. 1963); Univ. of Manitoba (MSc Microbiol. 1965); Univ. of Calif, Berkeley (PhD 1969); Dr hab. 1975. Res. gp leader, 1972–85, res. gp leader with tenure, 1985–2008, Max-Planck-Inst. für molekulare Genetik, Berlin; Prof. of Microbiol. and Sci. Foundn of Ireland Fellow, Envmtl Res. Inst., UC Cork, 2007–12. Foreign Mem., Norwegian Acad. Scis and Letters, 2014. Main Prize, Deutsche Gesellschaft für Hygiene und Mikrobiologie, 2004. *Publications:* contribs to learned scientific jls. *Address:* Department of Microbiology and Infection, Warwick Medical School, University of Warwick, Coventry CV4 7AL.

**ACKERLEY, Ian;** Chief Executive Officer, National Savings and Investments, since 2017; *b* Manchester, 12 April 1963; *s* of John Ackerley and Maureen Ackerley; *m* 1996, Kate Teasdale; one *s* one *d*. *Educ:* William Hulme's Grammar Sch., Manchester; Univ. of St Andrews (BSc Hons Psychol. 1985); London Business Sch. (MBA 1992). Business Consultant, 1985–88, Motorsport Manager, 1988–89, Shell Internat.; Territory Manager, Shell UK, 1989–90; Consultant, McKinsey & Co., 1992–96; Hd, Corp. Develt, Axa Sun Life, 1996–98; Man. Dir, Sun Life Internat., 1998–2001; Strategy Dir, 2001–02, Dir, Direct Distribution, 2002–03, AMP UK Financial Services; Man. Dir, APLC Ltd, 2004–14; Dir, Insurance and Investments, Impact Plus, 2005–06; Man. Dir, Investments and Pensions, Virgin Money, 2009–11; Barclays plc: Director: Investments, 2011–13; Barclays Financial Planning, 2013–17. *Recreations:* photography, cars, family, art, ski-ing. *Address:* National Savings and Investments, 1 Drummond Gate, SW1V 2QX. *T:* (020) 7932 6600. *E:* ian.ackerley@nsandi.com.

**ACKLAND, Joss, (Sidney Edmond Jocelyn),** CBE 2001; actor; *b* 29 Feb. 1928; *s* of Norman Ackland and Ruth Izod; *m* 1951, Rosemary Jean Kirkcaldy (*d* 2002); one *s* five *d* (and one *s* decd). *Educ:* Dame Alice Owen's Sch.; Central Sch. of Speech Training and Dramatic Art. Has worked in theatre, 1945–; repertory includes Stratford–upon–Avon, Arts Th., Buxton, Croydon, Embassy, Coventry, Oxford, Chesterfield, Windsor, Pitlochry; tea planter, Central Africa, 1954–55; disc jockey, Cape Town, 1955–57; Mem., Old Vic Theatre Co., 1958–61: parts include Toby Belch, in Twelfth Night, Caliban, in The Tempest, Pistol, in Henry IV, Lord Froth, in The Double Dealer, Aegisthus, in The Oresteia, Falstaff, in Henry IV Pt I and the Merry Wives of Windsor; Associate Dir, Mermaid Theatre, 1961–63: dir, The Plough and the Stars; parts include title rôle, Galileo, Bluntschli, in Arms and the Man, Scrofulovsky, in The Bedbug, Kirilov, in The Possessed. *West End theatre* rôles include: title rôle, The Professor, 1966; Gus, in Hotel in Amsterdam, 1968–69; Come As You Are, 1969–70; Brassbound, in Captain Brassbound's Conversion, 1971; Sam, in The Collaborators, 1973; Mitch, in A Streetcar Named Desire, 1974; Stewart, in A Pack of Lies, 1984; Clarence Darrow, in Never the Sinner, 1990; Weller Martin, in The Gin Game, 1999; King George V, in The King's Speech, 2002; *West End musicals:* Justice Squeezum, in Lock up your Daughters, 1962; title rôle, Jorrocks, 1967; Frederik, in a Little Night Music, 1975–76; Juan Perón, in Evita, 1978; Captain Hook and Mr Darling, in Peter Pan—the musical, 1985–86; *other musical rôles:* Honoré Lachailles, in Gigi; The King, in The King and I; *National Theatre:* Eustace Perry State, in The Madras House, 1977; Romain Gary, in Jean Seberg (musical), 1983; *Barbican Theatre:* Falstaff, in Henry IV pts I and II (opening prodn), 1982; Captain Hook and Mr Darling, in Peter Pan, 1982; *Chichester Theatre:* Gaev, in The Cherry Orchard, 1981; Ill, in The Visit, 1995; John Tarleton in Misalliance, 1997; Captain Shotover, in Heartbreak House, 2000; *tours:* Petruchio, in The Taming of the Shrew, 1977; Sir, in The Dresser, 1981; title rôle, King Lear, gala play reading, Old Vic and St James Theatres, 2013. *Films* include: Seven Days to Noon, 1949; Crescendo, 1969; The House that Dripped Blood, Villain, 1970; The Happiness Cage, England Made Me, 1971; The Little Prince, The Black Windmill, S-P-Y-S, The Three Musketeers, 1973; Great Expectations, One of our Dinosaurs is Missing, 1974; Operation Daybreak, Royal Flash, 1975; The Silver Bears, 1976; The End of Civilisation as we know it, The Greek Tycoon, Who is Killing the Great Chefs of Europe, 1977; Saint Jack, The Apple, Rough Cut, 1978; Lady Jane, 1984; A Zed and Two Noughts, 1985; Don Masino, in The Sicilian, 1987; Sir Jock Broughton, in White Mischief, The Colonel, in To Kill a Priest, 1988; Lethal Weapon II, The Hunt for Red October, The Palermo Connection, 1989; The Object of Beauty, The Sheltering Desert, 1991; The Bridge, Nowhere to Run, Pin for the Butterfly, The Mighty Ducks, 1992; Occhio Pinocchio (Italy), 1993; Miracle on 34th Street, Mad Dogs and Englishmen, A Kid in King Arthur's Court, Citizen X, 1994; Daisies in December, 'Til the End of Time, Mighty Ducks 3, Surviving Picasso, Deadly Voyage, Giorgino (France), 1995; Firelight, Swept from the Sea, 1996; Son of Sandokan, Game of Mirrors, Milk, 1999; Mumbo Jumbo, 2000; K-19: The Widowmaker, No Good Deed, I'll Be There, 2002; A Different Loyalty, Asylum, 2003; These Foolish Things, 2004; Tolstoy, in Moscow Zero, 2005; Flawless, How About You, 2007. Numerous TV plays and serials, incl. title rôle in Kipling, Alan Holly in First and Last, C. S. Lewis in Shadowlands, Barrett in The Barretts of Wimpole Street, Archie in Voices in the Garden, Terence Fielding in A Murder of Quality, Isaac in The Bible, Onassis in A Woman Named Jackie, Goering in The Man who lived at the Ritz, Heat of the Sun, Henry VII in Henry VIII, title rôle in Icon, 2004; Sir Winston Churchill in Above and Beyond, 2005; John Narbutowiz in Kingdom, Ridcully in The Hogfather, 2006; Pinocchio, 2008. *Radio* includes: title rôle in Macbeth; Falstaff in Henry IV, parts 1 and 2; Victor Hugo in Les Misérables; The Dog in Investigations of a Dog; God in The Little World of Don Camillo; 1966 And All That; Flashman in Flashman at the Charge; Big Daddy in Cat on a Hot Tin Roof; Socrates in The Life and Death of Socrates. Ambassador, MND Assoc.; Member: Drug Helpline; Amnesty Internat. *Publications:* I Must Be in There Somewhere (autobiog.), 1989; (with Rosemary Ackland) My Better Half and Me, 2009. *Recreations:* writing, painting, thirty-four grandchildren, nineteen great-grandchildren.

**ACKNER, Her Honour the Hon. Claudia Madeleine, (Hon. Mrs Hughes);** a Circuit Judge, 2007–17; *b* 13 Dec. 1954; *d* of Baron Ackner, PC and Joan May Evans; *m* 1978, Iain Hughes, *qv*; one *s* one *d* (and one *s* decd). *Educ:* Roedean Sch.; Girton Coll., Cambridge (BA 1976; MA). Called to the Bar, Middle Temple, 1977, Bencher, 2009; District Judge, 2000–07; Recorder, 2002–07. *Recreations:* theatre, opera, other people's dogs.

**ACKROYD, Keith,** CBE 1994; FRPharmS; Chairman, Silentnight Holdings plc, 1995–2002 (Director, 1993–2002); *b* 6 July 1934; *s* of Edward Ackroyd and Ethel (*née* Bates); *m* 1958, Ellen Gwenda Thomas; one *s* one *d* (and one *s* decd). *Educ:* Heath Grammar Sch.; Bradford Sch. of Pharmacy; London Business Sch. FRPharmS 1981. Boots The Chemists Ltd: Apprentice Pharmacist, 1952; Dir, 1975–94; Midlands Area Dir, 1976–77; Man. Dir, 1983–89; Pres., Boots Drug Stores (Canada) Ltd, 1977–79; Boots Company plc: Dir, 1979–94; Man. Dir, Retail Div., 1984–94; Chairman: Halfords Ltd, 1989–94; A. G. Stanley, 1989–94; Do It All Ltd, 1992–94; Director: Carefirst (formerly Takare) plc, 1994–98 (Dep. Chm., 1996–98); Navara (formerly Nottingham Gp) plc, 1994–2001; Cowie plc, 1994–96; Victoria plc, 1998–2008. Chairman: Company Chemists Assoc., 1983–89; British Retailers Assoc., 1988–92; British Retail Consortium, 1992–94; Regl Chm., Trent RHA, later NHS Exec., Trent, 1994–97; Mem., NHS Policy Bd, 1994–97. Member: Passport Agency Bd, 1991–2000; Nat. Bd for Crime Prevention, 1993–95. CCMI (CIMgt 1981); FInstD 1979. Liveryman, Soc. of Apothecaries, 1990–. *Recreations:* drinking wine, country sport. *Address:* Millfield, Bradmore, Nottingham NG11 6PF. *T:* (0115) 921 6052.

**ACKROYD, Norman,** CBE 2007; RA 1991 (ARA 1988); RE 1985; artist (painter and etcher); *b* 26 March 1938; *s* of late Albert Ackroyd, master butcher, and Clara Briggs, weaver; *m* 1st, 1963, Sylvia Buckland (marr. diss. 1975); two *d*; 2nd, 1978, Penelope Hughes-Stanton; one *s* one *d*. *Educ:* Cockburn High Sch., Leeds; Leeds Coll. of Art; Royal Coll. of Art (ARCA 1964; Sen. FRCA 2000). Teaches occasionally at RA, Slade, RCA and in N America; Tutor in Etching, Central Sch. of Arts, London, 1965–93; Prof. of Etching, London Inst., 1992. Over 50 one-man exhibns, 1970–, mainly in UK and USA; work in public collections includes: Tate Gall.; BM; V&A; Arts Council; British Council; Mus. of Modern Art, NY; Nat. Galls of Scotland, Norway, Canada, S Africa; Albertina, Vienna; Rijksmus. and Stedelijk, Amsterdam; Musée d'Art Histoire, Geneva; Nat. Gall. of Art, Washington. Mural commissions include: Albany, Glasgow, 1975; Haringey Cultural Centre, 1985; Lloyds Bank Technol. Centre, London, 1990; British Airways, 1991; Freshfields, London, 1992; Tetrapak, London, 1993; British Embassy, Moscow, 2000; Lazards Bank, London, 2003; Sainsbury Lab. for the Study of Plant Devel., Univ. of Cambridge, 2010. TV work includes: Artists in Print (etching), 1981; A Prospect of Rivers, 1988; Painting with Acid, 2000. Awards: Bradford Internat. Biennale, 1972, 1982; Royal Soc. of Etchers and Engravers, 1984, 1985; Bronze Medal, Frechen, Germany, 1986. *Publications:* A Cumberland Journey, 1981; Travels with Copper and Zinc, 1983; (with Douglas Dunn) The Pictish Coast, 1988; St Kilda: the furthest land, 1989; Windrush, 1990; A Song for Ireland, 1999; Aran Islands, 2001; Skellig to Skibbereen, 2002; High Islands, 2003; Brancaster Roads, 2004; The Furthest Lands, 2005; From Cuillin to Kintyre, 2006; Shannon, 2007; Malin, 2008; Random Journeys, 2009; St Kilda Revisited, 2010; Beyond Cape Wrath, 2011; Shetland, 2012; Donegal Bay, 2013; numerous collections of etchings from travels in the British Isles, occasionally with poets. *Recreations:* cricket, archæology. *Address:* Royal Academy of Arts, Piccadilly, W1J 0BD. *T:* (020) 7378 6001. *Clubs:* Chelsea Arts, Arts.

**ACKROYD, Peter,** CBE 2003; writer; Chief Book Reviewer, The Times, 1986–2010; *b* 5 Oct. 1949; *s* of Graham Ackroyd and Audrey Whiteside. *Educ:* St Benedict's Sch., Ealing; Clare Coll., Cambridge (MA; Hon. Fellow, 2006); Yale Univ. (Mellon Fellow). Literary Editor, 1973–77, Jt Managing Editor, 1978–82, The Spectator. Writer and presenter, TV series: Dickens, 2003; Peter Ackroyd's London, 2004; The Romantics, 2006; Peter Ackroyd's Thames, 2008; Peter Ackroyd's Venice, 2009. Freeman, City of London, 2006. FRSL 1984. Hon. Fellow, Amer. Acad. of Arts and Scis, 2006; Hon. FRIBA 2009. Hon. DLitt: Exeter, 1992; London Guildhall, 1999; City, 2000; London, 2001; Brunel, 2006. *Publications:* poetry: London Lickpenny, 1973; Country Life, 1978; The Diversions of Purley, 1987; *novels:* The Great Fire of London, 1982; The Last Testament of Oscar Wilde, 1983 (Somerset Maugham Award, 1984); Hawksmoor, 1985 (Whitbread Award; Guardian Fiction Prize); Chatterton, 1987; First Light, 1989; English Music, 1992; The House of Doctor Dee, 1993; Dan Leno and the Limehouse Golem, 1994 (filmed, 2017); Milton in America, 1996; The Plato Papers, 1999; The Clerkenwell Tales, 2003; The Lambs of London, 2004; The Fall of Troy, 2006; The Casebook of Victor Frankenstein, 2008; Three Brothers, 2013; *non-fiction:* Notes for a New Culture, 1976; Dressing Up, 1979; Ezra Pound and his World, 1980; T. S. Eliot, 1984 (Whitbread Award; Heinemann Award); Dickens, 1990; Introduction to Dickens, 1991; Blake, 1995; The Life of Thomas More, 1998; London: the biography, 2000; The Collection, 2001; Albion, 2002; Dickens: public life and private passion, 2002; Chaucer, 2004; Turner, 2005; Shakespeare: the biography, 2005; Newton, 2006; Thames: sacred river, 2007; Poe: a life cut short, 2008; Venice: pure city, 2009; The English Ghost: spectres through time, 2010; London Under, 2011; The History of England, vol. 1, Foundation, 2011, vol. 2, Tudors, 2012, vol. 3, Civil War, 2014, vol. 4, Revolution, 2016, vol. 5, Dominion, 2018; Wilkie Collins, 2012; Charles Chaplin, 2014; Hitchcock, 2015; Queer City, 2017; *translation:* The Canterbury Tales, 2009; The Death of King Arthur, 2010. *Address:* c/o Anthony Sheil Associates Ltd, 43 Doughty Street, WC1N 2LF. *T:* (020) 7405 9351.

**ACKROYD, Sir Timothy Robert Whyte,** 3rd Bt *cr* 1956; *of* Dewsbury, West Riding of Yorkshire; actor; *b* 7 Oct. 1958; *er s* of Sir John Robert Whyte Ackroyd, 2nd Bt and Jennifer Eileen McLeod (*d* 1997), *d* of H. G. S. Bishop; *S* father, 1995. *Educ:* Bradfield; LAMDA. *Theatre* includes: Agamemnon, 1976; On Approval, 1979; Much Ado About Nothing, 1980; Macbeth, Old Vic Co., 1980; Man and Superman, 1982; A Sleep of Prisoners, 1983; Pygmalion, 1984; Another Country, 1986; No Sex Please - We're British, 1987; Black Coffee, 1988; Jeffrey Bernard is Unwell, 1989, 1999 (televised); Journey's End, 1993; Bad Soldier Smith, 1995; Saki, 1997; The Rivals, Iphigenia at Aulis, 2000; A Step Out of Time, 2000; A Village Wooing, 2002; Red Lanterns, 2002; Falstaff, in Henry IV, Part I, 2003; Les Parents Terribles, 2004; Hogarth: the compassionate satirist, 2005–07; narrator, Gogol with Jurowski, 2009; narrator, An Oxford Elegy, 2010; The Fuse, 2011; *television:* Jack Be Nimble, 1979; Luther, 1983; Man and Superman, 1985; Pied Piper, 1989; A Royal Scandal, 1996; The New Professionals, 1998; *films:* Creator, 1984; Bullseye, 1990; Tembo Kali, 1992; *radio* includes: Fugitive Pieces, 1999; Life Story, 2004; Beau Geste, 2009. Director: Martingale Productions, 1985–86; Archview Films, 1991–95; Ackroyd Pullan, 1995–98; Zuma Productions, 2000–; Messiah Pictures, 2001; Ackroyd & Company, 2004–. Hon. Mem., Theatre of Comedy, 1984. Chm., Ackroyd Trust; Hon. Vice-Pres., Tusk Trust; Trustee, Marjorie and Dorothy Whyte Meml Fund; Patron, London & Internat. Sch. of Acting. Freeman and Liveryman, Carpenters' Co., 1982. *Publications:* Ackroyd's Ark, 2004, vol. II, 2010; Tripe (poetry), 2009. *Recreations:* Rugby, cricket, literature, Sumo wrestling. *Heir: b* Andrew John Armitage Ackroyd, *b* 17 Sept. 1961. *Clubs:* Garrick, MCC, Lazarusians.

**ACLAND,** family name of **Baroness Valentine**.

**ACLAND, Sir Antony (Arthur)**, KG 2001; GCMG 1986 (KCMG 1982; CMG 1976); GCVO 1991 (KCVO 1976); HM Diplomatic Service, retired; Provost of Eton, 1991–2000; *b* 12 March 1930; *s* of late Brig. P. B. E. Acland, OBE, MC, TD and Bridget Susan (*née* Barnett); *m* 1956, Clare Anne Verdon (*d* 1984); two *s* one *d*; *m* 1987, Jennifer McGougan (*née* Dyke). *Educ:* Eton; Christ Church, Oxford (MA 1956). Joined Diplomatic Service, 1953; ME Centre for Arab Studies, 1954; Dubai, 1955; Kuwait, 1956; FO, 1958–62; Asst Private Sec. to Sec. of State, 1959–62; UK Mission to UN, 1962–66; Head of Chancery, UK Mission, Geneva, 1966–68; FCO, 1968, Hd of Arabian Dept, 1970–72; Principal Private Sec. to Foreign and Commonwealth Sec., 1972–75; Ambassador to Luxembourg, 1975–77, to Spain, 1977–79; Deputy Under-Sec. of State, FCO, 1980–82, Perm. Under-Sec. of State, FCO, and Head of Diplomatic Service, 1982–86; Ambassador to Washington, 1986–91. Director: Shell Transport and Trading, 1991–2000; Booker plc, 1992–99. Chairman: Council, Ditchley Foundn, 1991–96; Tidy Britain Gp, 1992–96 (Pres., 1996–2002). Trustee: Nat. Portrait Gall., 1991–98; Esmée Fairbairn Foundn, 1991–2005. Chancellor, Order of St Michael and St George, 1994–2005. Pres., Exmoor Soc., 2007–. Hon. DCL: Exeter, 1988; William and Mary Coll., USA, 1990; Reading, 1992. *Address:* Staddon Farm, near Winsford, Minehead, Som TA24 7HY. *T:* (01643) 831489. *Club:* Brooks's.

**ACLAND, Lt-Col Sir (Christopher) Guy (Dyke)**, 6th Bt *cr* 1890; LVO 1999 (MVO 1990); an Extra Equerry to the Queen, since 1999; Vice Lord-Lieutenant, Isle of Wight, since 2006; *b* 24 March 1946; *s* of Major Sir Antony Guy Acland, 5th Bt, and Margaret Joan, *e d* of late Major Nelson Rooke; *S* father, 1983; *m* 1971, Christine Mary Carden, *y d* of late Dr John Waring, Totland Bay, Isle of Wight; two *s*. *Educ:* Allhallows School; RMA Sandhurst. Commissioned RA, 1966; served BAOR (26 Field Regt), 1967–70; UK and Hong Kong (3 RHA), 1970–73; BAOR and UK (22 AD Regt), 1974–77; Staff Coll. Camberley, 1978 (psc); served on Staff of HQ Eastern District, 1979–80; commanded Q (Sanna's Post) Bty in BAOR (5 Regt), 1981–83; SO2, Army Staff Duties Directorate, MoD, 1983–85; 2 i/c 1 RHA BAOR, 1986–88; Equerry to HRH The Duke of Edinburgh, 1988–90; SO1, Management Services Orgn 3, MoD, 1990–92; CO, Southampton Univ. OTC, 1992–94; retired 1994. Dep. Master of the Household and Equerry to the Queen, 1994–99. Administrator, HSA Charitable Trust, 2000–06. DL Isle of Wight, 2002. *Recreations:* sailing, gardening. *Heir: s* Alexander John Dyke Acland [*b* 29 May 1973; *m* 2007, Susannah Katharine Janet, *d* of Charles James Bell; two *d*]. *Clubs:* Royal Solent Yacht, Royal Artillery Yacht.

**ACLAND, Sir Dominic (Dyke)**, 17th Bt *cr* 1644, of Columb John, Devon; Managing Director, Embercombe, 2014–15; *b* 19 Nov. 1962; *er s* of Sir John Dyke Acland, 16th Bt and of Virginia, *yr d* of Roland Forge; *S* father, 2009, but his name does not appear on the Official Roll of the Baronetage; *m* 1990, Sarah Anne (marr. diss. 2011), 3rd *d* of Ven. Kenneth Unwin, *qv*; two *s* two *d* (of whom one *s* one *d* are twins). *Educ:* Edinburgh Univ. (MA). Dir, Torbay Coast and Countryside Trust, 1999–2013. *Heir: s* Patrick Acland, *b* 18 Nov. 1993.
 See also P. D. Acland.

**ACLAND, Lt-Col Sir Guy;** *see* Acland, Lt-Col Sir C. G. D.

**ACLAND, Piers Dyke;** QC 2010; barrister; *b* Nairobi, 2 Feb. 1965; *yr s* of Sir John Dyke Acland, 16th Bt and Virginia Acland; *m* 1993, Lucinda Raiman; one *s* two *d*. *Educ:* University Coll. London (BSc Biochem. 1987); Imperial Cancer Research Fund, Univ. of London (PhD 1991). Called to the Bar, Lincoln's Inn, 1993; in practice as barrister, specialising in intellectual property, 1993–. *Address:* 11 South Square, Gray's Inn, WC1R 5EY. *E:* pacland@11southsquare.com.
 See also Sir D. D. Acland, Bt.

**ACLAND-HOOD, Susan Elizabeth;** Chief Executive, HM Courts and Tribunal Service, since 2016; *b* London, 6 June 1977; *d* of Frank Blackaby and Mary Acland-Hood; *m* 2006, John Kenneth Frederick Andrews; two *d*. *Educ:* St Paul's Girls' Sch.; Trinity Coll., Cambridge (BA 1st Cl. Hons Hist. 1998; MPhil Intellectual Hist. and Hist. of Political Thought). Private Sec. to Prime Minister on Home Affairs, Justice and Counter-terrorism, 2007–08; Hd, Strategy, Partnerships and Performance, London Bor. of Tower Hamlets, 2009–10; Sen. Advr to Prime Minister and Dep. Prime Minister, Policy Unit, No 10 Downing St, 2011–12; Director: Educn Funding, DFE, 2013–15; Enterprise and Growth, HM Treasury, 2015–16. Mem., Adv. Bd, Centre for Business Res., Univ. of Cambridge. Gov., Bow Sch., Tower Hamlets. *Recreations:* singing, reading, cooking and eating, film and theatre, enjoying my children.

**ACLAND-HOOD-GASS, Dame Elizabeth Periam;** *see* Gass, Dame E. P. A. H.

**ACOSTA QUESADA, Carlos Yunior, (Carlos Acosta)**, CBE 2014; ballet dancer; President, Carlos Acosta International Dance Foundation, since 2012; founder, Acosta Danza, 2016; Director, Birmingham Royal Ballet, from Jan. 2020; *b* Havana, Cuba, 1973; partner, Charlotte Holland; three *d*. Trained with Nat. Ballet Sch. of Cuba; guest performer with cos incl. Compagnia Teatro Nuovo, Turin, 1989–91; Principal, English Nat. Ballet, 1991–92; with Nat. Ballet of Cuba, 1992–93 and 1994; Principal, Houston Ballet, 1993–98; with Royal Ballet, 1998–2015 (Principal Guest Artist, 2003–15); Guest Principal Artist with ballet companies including: American Ballet Th., 2002 (and Principal Dancer, 2003); Paris Opera, 2008; Australian Ballet, 2008. Performances include: English National Ballet: Polovtsian Dances from Prince Igor, 1991; The Nutcracker, Cinderella, 1992; National Ballet of Cuba: Giselle, Don Quixote, Swan Lake, 1994; Houston Ballet: The Nutcracker, Swan Lake, La Bayadère, Don Quixote, 1993; Royal Ballet: In the middle somewhat elevated, 1998; Raymonda, Swan Lake, My Brother, My Sisters, Rhapsody, Le Corsaire, The Nutcracker, Coppelia, Shadowplay, 2000; Don Quixote, 2001; Apollo, 2002; Manon, 2003; Mayerling, Giselle, 2004; La Fille mal gardée, 2005; Romeo and Juliet, 2006; Spartacus with Bolshoi Ballet, 2007; Elizabeth, 2013; writer and choreographer, Tocororo, 2003; choreographer: Premieres, 2010; Don Quixote, 2013; Guys and Dolls, 2014; Carmen, 2015. Hon. DLitt London Metropolitan, 2006. Gold Medal, Prix de Lausanne, 1990; Grand Prix, Concours Internat. de Danse de Paris, 1990; Vignale Danza Prize, Italy, 1990; Frédéric Chopin Prize, Polish Artistic Corp., 1990; Best Male Dancer, Nat. Dance Awards, 2004; Outstanding Achievement in Dance, Laurence Olivier Awards, 2007; Queen Elizabeth II Coronation Award, RAD, 2018. *Publications:* No Way Home: a Cuban dancer's story (autobiog.), 2007 (filmed as Yuli, 2019); Pig's Foot (novel), 2013. *Address:* c/o Carlos Acosta Management, Aberdeen House, South Road, Haywards Heath, W Sussex RH16 4NG.

**ACRES, Paul,** QPM 1997; Chief Constable of Hertfordshire, 2000–04; Chairman, Sefton NHS Primary Care Trust, 2006; *b* 15 April 1948; *s* of Albert George Acres and Kathleen Acres (*née* Jones); *m* 1971, Jean Parsons; three *s*. *Educ:* City of Bath Boys' Sch. Liverpool and Bootle Constabulary, 1968–74; joined Merseyside Police, 1974: Asst Chief Constable, 1992–94; rcds, 1994; Dep. Chief Constable, 1995–2000. Police Long Service and Good Conduct Medal, 1991. *Recreations:* walking, motor cycling, golf, cycling. *Club:* West Lancashire Golf.

**ACTON, 5th Baron** *cr* 1869, of Aldenham, Salop; **John Charles Ferdinand Harold Lyon-Dalberg-Acton;** Bt 1644; *b* 19 Aug. 1966; *o s* of 4th Baron Acton and Hilary Juliet Sarah (*née* Cookson); *S* father, 2010; *m* 1998, Lucinda, *d* of Brig. James Percival, OBE. *Educ:* Winchester; Balliol Coll., Oxford. *Heir: uncle* Hon. Robert Peter Acton [*b* 1946; *m* 1974, Michele Laigle; three *s*].

**ACTON, Prof. Edward David Joseph Lyon-Dalberg-,** PhD; Vice-Chancellor, University of East Anglia, 2009–14; *b* Harare; *s* of 3rd Baron Acton, CMG, MBE, TD and Hon. Daphne, *o d* of 4th Baron Rayleigh, FRS; *m* 1972, Stella, *d* of Henry Conroy; two *d*. *Educ:* St George's Coll., Harare; Univ. of York (BA Hons Hist.); St Edmund's Coll., Cambridge (PhD Hist. 1976). Bank of England, 1975–76; Lectr, Univ. of Liverpool, 1976–88; Sen Lectr, Univ. of Manchester, 1988–91; University of East Anglia: Prof. of Modern Eur. Hist., 1991–2014, now Emeritus; Pro-Vice-Chancellor, 2003–09. *Publications:* Alexander Herzen and the role of the intellectual revolutionary, 1979; Russia: the present and the past, 1986; Rethinking the Russian Revolution, 1990; Russia: the Tsarist and Soviet legacy, 1995; (ed jtly) Critical Companion to the Russian Revolution, 1914–1921, 1997; Nazism and Stalinism: a suitable case for comparison?, 1998; (ed jtly) La transición a la política de masas, 2001; The Soviet Union: a documentary history, vol. I, 1917–1940, 2005, vol. II, 1939–1991, 2007. *Recreations:* bridge, racing. *Address:* 365 Unthank Road, Norwich NR4 7QG.
 See also Baron Acton.

**ACTON DAVIS, Jonathan James;** QC 1996; a Recorder, since 2000; a Deputy High Court Judge, since 2008; *b* 15 Jan. 1953; *s* of Michael James and Elizabeth Acton Davis; *m* 1987; one *s*. *Educ:* Harrow Sch.; Poly. of Central London (LLB London). Called to the Bar, Inner Temple, 1977 (Bencher, 1995, Master of the House, 1999–2005); an Asst Recorder, 1997–2000. General Council of the Bar: Mem., 1993–98; Chm., Professional Conduct and Complaints Cttee, 2001–02 (Vice-Chm., 1999–2000); Mem., Legal Services Consultative Panel, 2004–09. *Recreations:* cricket, walking. *Address:* 1 Atkin Building, Gray's Inn, WC1R 5AT. *T:* (020) 7404 0102. *E:* clerks@atkinchambers.com. *Clubs:* Garrick, Beefsteak, MCC, Chelsea Arts.

**ACTON DAVIS, Lindsay Alice;** *see* Boswell, L. A.

**ACTON SMITH, Michael,** OBE 2014; Founder, 2004, and Chairman and Creative Director, Mind Candy (Chief Executive Officer, 2004–15); Co-founder and Co-Chief Executive Officer, Calm, since 2012; *b* London, 3 Sept. 1974; *s* of Charles and Colette Smith. *Educ:* Danesfield Primary Sch.; Sir William Borlase Grammar Sch.; Birmingham Univ. (BSc Geog.). Co-founder and CEO, Firebox.com, 1998–2004; Co-founder, Second Chance Tuesday, 2006. Inventor, Shot Glass Chess Set, 1998; creator of games: Perplex City, 2005; Moshi Monsters, 2008. *Publications:* Calm, 2015. *Recreations:* games, memes, monsters, poker, puzzles, parties and prime numbers. *Address:* Mind Candy, Floor 4, 15 Bonhill Street, EC2A 4DN. *T:* (020) 7501 1901. *E:* michael@mindcandy.com. *Clubs:* Soho House, Adam Street, Paramount.

**ACWORTH, Ven. Richard Foote;** Archdeacon of Wells, 1993–2003; *b* 19 Oct. 1936; *s* of late Rev. Oswald Roney Acworth and Jean Margaret Acworth; *m* 1966, Margaret Caroline Marie Jennings; two *s* one *d*. *Educ:* St John's Sch., Leatherhead; Sidney Sussex Coll., Cambridge (BA Hist. and Theol. 1962; MA 1965); Cuddesdon Theol Coll. Nat. service, RNVR, 1956–58. Ordained deacon, 1963, priest, 1964; Assistant Curate: St Etheldreda's, Fulham, 1963; All Saints and Martyrs, Langley, Mancs, 1964–66; St Mary's, Bridgwater, 1966–69; Vicar, Yatton, 1969–81; Priest-in-charge, St John's and St Mary's, Taunton, 1981–85; Vicar of St Mary Magdalene, Taunton, 1985–93. Trustee, Rethink Mental Illness, 2014–16 (Chm., SW Regl Cttee, 2008–14). *Recreations:* walking, gardening, DIY, ornithology. *Address:* Corvedale Cottage, Croscombe, Wells, Som BA5 3QJ. *T:* (01749) 342242.
 See also Brig. R. W. Acworth.

**ACWORTH, Brig. Robert William,** CBE 1986; Registrar of St Paul's Cathedral, 1991–2001; *b* 11 Dec. 1938; *s* of late Rev. Oswald Roney Acworth and Jean Margaret (*née* Coupland); *m* 1967, Elizabeth Mary, *e d* of late J. N. S. Ridgers; two *s* one *d*. *Educ:* St John's Sch., Leatherhead; RMA, Sandhurst. Commnd, Queen's Royal Regt, 1958; served in Germany, Holland, Norway, Gibraltar, Aden, Oman, Hong Kong, UK and NI; *sc* 1970; staff and regtl duty, 1971–81; Comdr, 10 UDR, 1981–83 (despatches 1983); Asst COS, HQ NI, 1983–85; Coll. Comdr, RMA, Sandhurst, 1985–87; Asst COS (Intelligence), HQ AFCENT, 1987–90; Dep. Comdr and COS, SE Dist, 1990–91, retd. Deputy Colonel: Queen's Regt, 1986–92; Princess of Wales's Royal Regt, 1992–94. Pres., Queen's Royal Surrey Regt Assoc., 1995–2005. *Recreations:* gardening, fishing, golf. *Address:* The Close, Netton, Salisbury, Wilts SP4 6AP. *T:* (01722) 782539. *Club:* Army and Navy.
 See also Ven. R. F. Acworth.

**ADAIR, Brian Campbell,** TD 1979; NP 1975; Senior Partner, 1973–2005, Consultant, 2005–08, Adairs, Solicitors, Dumbarton; President, Law Society of Scotland, 1992–93; *b* 28 Aug. 1945; *s* of Alan William Adair and Helen Mary Scott or Adair; *m* 1969, Elaine Jean Morrison; one *s* two *d*. *Educ:* Milngavie Primary Sch.; High Sch., Glasgow; Glasgow Univ. (LLB 1967). Commnd TA 1965, 1st Bn Glasgow Highlanders; served Glasgow & Strathclyde Univs OTC, 1967–73, 2nd Bn Lowland Volunteers, 1973–79; retired rank Major. Apprentice Solicitor, McGrigor Donald, Glasgow, 1967–70; Solicitor, Dumbarton CC, 1970–73; constituted own firm, 1973. Temp. Sheriff, 1995–99; part-time Sheriff, 2000–15. Mem., Scottish Legal Aid Bd, 1998–2002. Mem. Council, Law Soc. of Scotland, 1980–94 (Vice Pres., 1991–92). Elder, St Paul's Church, Milngavie. Chm. of Govs, High Sch. of Glasgow, 2006–18 (Gov., 1992–2018). *Recreations:* holidaying in Arran, entertaining, golf. *Address:* 21 James Watt Road, Milngavie, Glasgow G62 7JX. *T:* (0141) 956 3070. *Clubs:* Milngavie Golf (Captain, Centenary Year, 1995), Whiting Bay Golf.

**ADAIR, John Eric,** PhD; author and teacher of leadership; *b* Luton, 18 May 1934; *s* of Robin and Dorothy Adair; *m* 1977, Thea Talbot; two *s* one *d*. *Educ:* St Paul's Sch.; Hull Nautical Coll. (qualified Arctic trawler deckhand 1955); Trinity Hall, Cambridge (BA 1959); Univ. of London (PhD 1966); Jesus Coll., Oxford (BLitt 1971). FRHistS 1966. National Service: 2nd Lt Scots Guards and Adjutant 9 Regt Arab Legion, 1953–55. Arctic trawler deckhand, 1955. Sen. Lectr, RMA Sandhurst, 1961–67; Hon. Dir of Studies, St George's House, Windsor Castle, 1968; Asst Dir and Hd, Leadership Dept, 1969–71, Associate Dir, 1972–75, Industrial Soc.; Prof. of Leadership Studies, Univ. of Surrey, 1979–84. Vis. Prof., Univ. of Exeter, 1990–2000; Hon. Prof. of Leadership, China Exec. Leadership Acad., Pudong, 2006–; Chair, Strategic Leadership Studies, UN System Staff Coll., 2009–. Pres., John Hampden Soc., 1992–. Fellow, Windsor Leadership Trust, 2001–. *Publications:* Hastings to Culloden: battles of Britain (with Peter Young), 1964, 4th edn 2009; Training for Leadership, 1968; Training for Decisions, 1969; Roundhead General: the life of Sir William Waller, 1969, 2nd edn 1997; Cheriton 1644: the campaign and the battle, 1973; Training for Communication, 1973; Action Centred Leadership, 1973; Management and Morality: the problems and opportunities of social capitalism, 1974; A Life of John Hampden The Patriot 1594–1643, 1976; The Becoming Church, 1976; The Pilgrims' Way: shrines and saints in Britain and Ireland, 1978; The Royal Palaces of Britain, 1981; Founding Fathers: the Puritans in England and America, 1982, 2nd edn 1998; By the

Sword Divided: eyewitness accounts of the English Civil War, 1983, 2nd edn 1998; Effective Leadership, 1983, 2nd edn 2009; Effective Decision-Making, 1985, 2nd edn 2009; Effective Teambuilding, 1986, 2nd edn 2009; How to Manage Your Time, 1987, 3rd edn as Effective Time Management, 2009; No Bosses But Leaders, 1987, 3rd edn 2003; Developing Leaders, 1988; Great Leaders, 1989, 2nd edn as Inspiring Leadership, 2002; Understanding Motivation, 1990, 2nd edn as Leadership and Motivation, 2006; The Challenge of Innovation, 1990, 2nd edn as Leadership for Innovation, 1990; The Art of Creative Thinking, 1990, 2nd edn 2007; Effective Innovation, 1994, 2nd edn 2009; Effective Motivation, 1996, 2nd edn 2009; Leadership Skills, 1996, 2nd edn as Develop Your Leadership Skills, 2007; Effective Communication, 1997, 2nd edn 2009; Decision Making and Problem Solving, 1997, 2nd edn as Decision Making and Problem Solving Strategies; How to Find Your Vocation, 2000; The Leadership of Jesus, 2001; Effective Strategic Leadership, 2002, 2nd edn 2010; The Inspirational Leader, 2003; How to Grow Leaders, 2005; Effective Leadership Development, 2006; The Leadership of Muhammad, 2010; Lexicon of Leadership, 2011; John Adair's 100 Greatest Ideas (series), 2011; Confucius on Leadership, 2013. *Recreations:* English countryside, sketching, reading. *Address:* Westbury Manor, Compton, Guildford GU3 1EE. *T:* (01483) 810241. *E:* ja@johnadair.co.uk.

**ADAIR, Robert Gribben,** CBE 2015; Chief Executive Officer, Sonas CS, since 2018; Chief Executive, Belfast Harbour Commissioners, 2005–18; *b* Belfast, 21 Dec. 1956; *s* of late James Adair and Jane Adair; *m* 1978, Evelyn Joan McAllister; one *s* two *d*. *Educ:* Belfast Boys Model Sch.; Queen's Univ., Belfast (BSc Hons 1st Cl. Mech. Engrg 1980); Ulster Univ. (MBA 1991). Prodn Engr, Rothmans International, 1976–86; Dir and Gen. Manager, Flexibox Ltd, 1986–90; Chief Exec., NI Quality Centre, 1990–94; Man. Dir, SMTEK Europe Ltd, 1994–99; Man. Dir and Owner, Irlandus Circuits Ltd, 1999–2005. Non-executive Director: Market Growth Internat., 1996–2000; Laganside Corp., 2006–07; Ardmore Advertising, 2018–; Dir, Invest NI, 2008–14; Dep. Chm., UK Major Ports Gp Ltd, 2005–18; Pres. Emeritus, Gen. Stevedoring Council, 2005–; Chm., Northern Irish Connections, 2011–18. Mem. Bd, Business in the Community NI, 1994–2013; NI Chm., Business in the Community, 2013– (Nat. Trustee, 2013–). Prince of Wales' Ambassador for Corporate Social Responsibility, NI, 2007–08; Mem., Prince's Trust Council - NI, 2009–. Mem. Bd, Econ. Policy Centre, Ulster Univ., 2013–18. Dir, Belfast Boys Model Bursary Fund, 2015–. Nat. Judge, Nat. Trng Awards, 2009–11. Woodvale RFC Rep., Irish Rugby Football Union, 1977–95. Hon. DSc Econ QUB, 2018. *Recreations:* family, golf, travel, theatre, cooking, technology.

**ADAM, Prof. Andreas Ntinou,** CBE 2012; FRCR, FRCP, FRCS, FMedSci; Professor of Interventional Radiology, Guy's, King's and St Thomas' School of Medicine (formerly United Medical and Dental Schools of Guy's and St Thomas' Hospital and King's College Medical School), since 1992; President, Royal College of Radiologists, 2007–10; *b* 4 May 1951; *s* of Constantinos Adam and Hera Adam (*née* Spanou); *m* 1977, Dr Jane Williams; two *d*. *Educ:* Middlesex Hosp. Med. Sch. (MB BS Hons 1977). MRCP 1979, FRCP 1994; FRCR 1985; FRCS 1998. Hse physician, Middx Hosp., 1977–78; hse surgeon, Kettering Gen. Hosp., 1978; Senior House Officer: Hammersmith Hosp., 1978–79; Middx Hosp., 1979; National Hosp., 1979–80; Registrar: Whittington Hosp., 1980–81; UCH, 1981; Hammersmith Hosp., 1981–83; Senior Registrar: Hammersmith and Hillingdon Hosps, 1983–84; Hammersmith Hosp., 1984–86; Sen. Lectr, 1987–91, Reader, 1991–92, RPMS; Hon. Consultant Radiologist, Guy's and St Thomas' NHS Foundn Trust, 1992–. Dean, Med. Sch., Univ. of Cyprus, 2012–15. Jt Ed.-in-Chief, Jl Interventional Radiol., 1992–95; Ed.-in-Chief, Cardiovascular and Interventional Radiol., 1995–2003; Asst Ed., Jl Hepato-Pancreato-Biliary Assoc., 1998–2001; mem., editl bds of numerous jls. Advr to EU on digital imaging, 1991–92; Consultant in Radiol. to WHO, 1999; Specialist Advr on Interventional Radiol., NICE, 2000–; Mem., Adv. Gp on Ionising Radiation, Subgp on High Dose Radiation Effects and Tissue Injury, HPA, 2005–. Rep. of Eur. Assoc. of Radiol., Eur. Agency for Evaluation of Medicinal Products, 2000–04. Lectures include: Alan Goldin Oration, Royal Australasian Coll. of Radiologists, 1993; John Wickham, Internat. Soc. Minimally Invasive Therapy, 1998; Hounsfield, BIR, 2006; Haughton, RCSI, 2007; Holmes, New England Roentgen Ray Soc., 2008. President: Soc. for Minimal Invasive Therapy, 1996–97; British Soc. Interventional Radiologists, 1997–99; BIR, 1998–99; Internat. Soc. Hepatobiliary Radiol., 1998–99; Cardiovascular and Interventional Radiol Soc. of Europe, 2005–07; Eur. Congress of Radiol., 2006; Soc. of Gastrointestinal Intervention, 2007–09; Eur. Soc. Radiol., 2007–08. Fellow: Soc. of Cardiovascular and Interventional Radiol., USA, 1993; Eur. Soc. Gastrointestinal and Abdominal Radiol., 1998; FBIR 2007; FMedSci 2009; Academician, Russian Acad. Med. Scis, 2005. Hon. FRANZCR 2007; Hon. Fellow: Faculty of Radiologists, RCSI, 2007; Greek Soc. Interventional Radiol., 2007; Hong Kong Coll. of Radiologists, 2010; American Coll. of Radiol., 2011. Hon. PhD: Crete, 2012; Cyprus, 2016. Medal, Russian Acad. Med. Scis, 2004; Gold Medal, British Soc. Interventional Radiologists, 2005; President's Medal, RCR, 2006; Gold Medal, Cardiovascular and Interventional Radiol Soc. Europe, 2007; Gold Medal, Soc. of Interventional Radiol., USA, 2009; Gold Medal, Eur. Soc. of Radiol., 2010. *Publications: Clinical Gastroenterology: interventional radiology of the abdomen,* 1993; *Practical Interventional Radiology of the Hepatobiliary System and Gastrointestinal Tract,* 1994; *Interventional Radiology: a practical guide,* 1995; *A Textbook of Metallic Stents,* 1996; *Interventional Radiology: a multimedia virtual textbook,* 1997; *Practical Management of Oesophageal Disease,* 2000; *Diagnostic Radiology,* 4th edn 2001, 5th edn 2008; *Interventional Radiology in Cancer,* 2003; *Interventional Radiological Treatment of Liver Tumours,* 2008; *Interventional Oncology,* 2012; contrib. numerous scientific papers on aspects of interventional radiol., esp. focusing on use of metallic stents in various organs, and on aspects of thermal ablation of renal tumours. *Recreation:* reading history. *Address:* Department of Radiology, 1st Floor Lambeth Wing, St Thomas' Hospital, SE1 7EH. *T:* (020) 7188 5550, *Fax:* (020) 7188 5454. *E:* andy.adam@kcl.ac.uk. *Club:* Athenæum.

**ADAM, George;** Lord Provost and Lord-Lieutenant of Aberdeen, 2012–17; *b* Montrose, 26 Jan. 1957; *s* of late George Smith Adam and of Helen Adam (*née* Aitken). *Educ:* Brechin High Sch.; Duncan of Jordanstone Coll. of Art, Dundee. Graphic Designer, 1979–83, Event Producer and Co-Dir, 1983–90, Format Communications, Aberdeen; Owner, The Presentation Business, Aberdeen, 1990–2012. Mem. (Lab), Aberdeen CC, 1999–2017. Hon. LLD Aberdeen, 2017. *Recreations:* gardening, visual arts, music, cinema and theatre.

**ADAM, Gordon Johnston,** PhD; Member (Lab) North East Region, England, European Parliament, Feb. 2000–2004; *b* 28 March 1934; *s* of John Craig Adam and Deborah Armstrong Johnston; *m* 1973, Sarah Jane Seely; one *s*. *Educ:* Leeds Univ. (BSc Hons PhD). CEng, MIMMM; FEI. NCB, 1959–79. Mem., Whitley Bay Bor. Council, 1971–74; Mem. 1973–80, and Dep. Leader 1975–80, North Tyneside Metrop. Bor. Council (Chm., 1973–74; Mayor, 1974–75). Mem., Whitley Bay Playhouse Theatre Trust, 1975–2007 (Chm., 1975–80). MEP (Lab) Northumbria, 1979–99; contested (Lab) NE Region, 1999; Vice-Chm., Energy, Res. and Technol. Ctree, EP, 1984–99; Chm., Jt Parly Cttee, EU-Lithuania, 2000–04. Chairman: Northumbria Energy Advice Centre, 1994–; Northern Energy Initiative, 1996–2000; NE Reg. Energy Forum, 2004–06; Member: Northern Econ. Planning Council, 1974–79; Northern Arts Gen. Council, 1975–78; Northern Sinfonia Management Cttee, 1978–80; Bd, Northern Stage Co., 1989–2001; Bd, S Tyneside & Newcastle Groundwork Trust, 2004–10; NE Energy Leadership Council, 2011–. Sen. Advr, Energy Policy Consulting, 2006–08. Contested (Lab): Tynemouth, 1966; Berwick-upon-Tweed, Nov. 1973 (by-election), Feb. 1974 and 1992. *Recreation:* gardening. *Address:* The Old Farm House, East House Farm, Killingworth Village, Newcastle upon Tyne NE12 6BQ. *T:* (0191) 216 0154.

**ADAM, Ian Clark;** Chairman, Britannia Building Society, 2004–08 (Director, 1998–2008); *b* 2 Sept. 1943; *s* of George Adam and Natalie Jane Gibson Adam; *m* 1967, Betty Anne Crosbie; one *s* one *d*. *Educ:* Harris Acad., Dundee. CA 1967. Partner, 1976, Sen. Partner, Scotland, 1985–95, Price Waterhouse; Finance Dir, Christian Salvesen plc, 1995–98. Mem., SHEFC, 2003–05, SFC, 2005–11. Chm.: St Columba's Hospice, 2011–16 (Gov., 2010–11); Trustee, Worldwide Cancer Res., 2017–. Gov., St Leonards Sch., St Andrews, 2010–16. *Recreations:* gardening, golf, reading. *Address:* Gowanfield, 2 Cammo Road, Edinburgh EH4 8EB. *T:* (0131) 339 6401. *E:* iancadam@talktalk.net. *Clubs:* Royal and Ancient Golf (St Andrews); Royal Burgess Golfing Society (Edinburgh); Kilspindie Golf.

**ADAM, Robert,** RIBA; Director, ADAM Architecture (formerly Robert Adam Architect), since 1995; *b* 10 April 1948; *s* of Dr Robert Wilson Adam and Margaret Adam; *m* 1970, Sarah Jane Chalcraft; one *s* one *d*. *Educ:* Canford Sch., Dorset; Regent Street Poly. (DipArch 1973). RIBA 1977. Partner, 1977–, Dir, 1987–, Evans Roberts & Partners, subseq. Winchester Design (Architects) Ltd, later Robert Adam Architects, then ADAM Architecture. Principal buildings include: Sackler Liby, Oxford; Solar House, Wakeham; Dogmersfield Park, Odiham; Millennium Pavilion, Preston Candover, Hants; 198–202 Piccadilly; The Nadler Soho, London; new country houses in Hants, Dorset and Wilts; New district, Leith masterplans; William Wake House, Northampton. Trustee, 1989–98, Chm., Faculty of Fine Arts, 1993–97, British Sch. at Rome; Chm., Popular Housing Gp 1995–2003; Mem. Council, RIBA, 1999, 2002 (Hon. Sec., 2000–03); Design Advr, CABE, 1999–2003; Founder and Chair, Coll. of Chapters, Internat. Network for Traditional Building, Architecture and Urbanism, 2000–12 (Chair, UK Chapter, 2009–); Academician, Acad. of Urbanism, 2006–; Mem., Design Review Panel, London CABE, 2012–. Hon. FRIAS 2014. *Publications:* Classical Architecture: a complete handbook, 1990; (contrib.) Building Classical, 1993; (contrib.) Companion to Contemporary Architectural Thought, 1993; Buildings by Design, 1994; (ed jtly and contrib.) Tradition Today, 2008; The 7 Sins of Architects, 2010; (contrib.) Urban Identity, Learning from Place 2, 2011; The Globalisation of Modern Architecture, 2012; (contrib.) Architecture and Globalisation in the Persian Gulf Region, 2013; (contrib.) The Architectural Capriccio, 2014; Classic Columns: 40 years of writing on architecture, 2017; *relevant publications:* Robert Adam: the search for a modern classicism, by Richard John, 2010; The Country House Ideal: recent work by ADAM Architecture, by Jeremy Musson, 2015; papers in Architectl Review, Architects Jl, RIBA Jl, Architectl Design, Context 79, City Jl (USA), Archis (Holland). *Recreations:* ceramics, politics, economics. *Address:* Old Hyde House, 75 Hyde Street, Winchester, Hants SO23 7DW. *T:* (01962) 843843. *Clubs:* Athenæum, Home House.

**ADAM, Sheila Anne,** MD; FRCP, FFPH, FRCGP; Interim Director of Public Health, NHS London (Strategic Health Authority for London), 2006–07; *b* 24 Nov. 1949. *Educ:* Nottingham High Sch. for Girls; Edinburgh Univ. (MB ChB 1972; MD 1983). DCH 1974. MRCP 1976, FRCP 1993; MFPHM 1981, FFPHM 1986; FRCGP 2002. Public Health Registrar, 1975–77, Sen. Registrar and MRC Trng Fellow in Public Health, 1977–81, Oxford RHA; Public Health Consultant, Brent HA, 1981–83; Public Health Consultant, 1983–89, Dir of Public Health, 1989–95, NW Thames RHA; NHS Executive, Department of Health: Hd of Mental Health and NHS Community Care, 1995–97; Dep. Dir of Health Services, 1997–99; Dir of Health Services, 1999–2001; Dep. CMO, 1999–2002, and Dir of Policy, 2001–02, DoH; Dir of Public Health, NE London Strategic HA, 2002–06. QHP 1996–99.

**ADAM, Thomas Noble;** QC 2008; *b* London, 6 Jan. 1965; *s* of Bruce and Sheila Adam; *m* 1991, Helen Gooch; three *s*. *Educ:* Norwich Sch.; Trinity Coll., Cambridge (BA 1987; MA; boxing blue 1987). Solicitor, Macfarlanes, 1988–91; called to the Bar, Inner Temple, 1991; in practice as a barrister, specialising in commercial law, 1991–. *Publications:* (with C. Hollander) Documentary Evidence, 7th edn, 2000; (contrib.) Professional Negligence and Liability Encyclopedia. *Recreations:* family, fishing, shooting, hill-walking, light verse, wine and whisky. *Address:* c/o Brick Court Chambers, 7–8 Essex Street, WC2R 3LD. *Clubs:* 67 Pall Mall; Hawks.

**ADAMI, Edward F.;** see Fenech-Adami.

**ADAMISHIN, Dr Anatoly;** Consultant, Sistema Joint-Stock Financial Corporation, Russia, since 2003 (Vice President, International Affairs, 1998–2003); President, Association for Euro-Atlantic Co-operation; *b* 11 Oct. 1934; *s* of Leonid Adamishin and Vera Gusovskaya; *m* 2000, Svetlana Kharlamova; one *d* by previous marriage. *Educ:* Lomonosov Moscow State Univ.; Diplomatic Acad. of USSR (Dr in Historic Sci. 1979). Joined USSR Diplomatic Service, 1957; First European Dept, Min. of Foreign Affairs, 1957–59; served embassy in Italy, 1959–65; First European Dept, 1965–71; Foreign Policy Planning Dept, 1971–73; Head, Gen. Internat. Issues Dept, 1973–78; Head, First European Dept and Mem., Min. of Foreign Affairs Collegium, 1978–86; Dep. Minister for Foreign Affairs, 1986–90; also Head, USSR Commn for UNESCO Affairs, 1987–90; Ambassador to Italy, 1990–92; First Dep. Minister for Foreign Affairs of Russia, 1992–94; Ambassador to UK, 1994–97; Minister for relations with CIS, Min. of Foreign Affairs, 1997–98. Sen. Fellow, US Inst. of Peace, Washington, 2005–06. *Publications:* Tramonto e rinascita di una grande potenza, 1995; The White Sun of Angola, 2001; (with R. Schifter) Human Rights, Perestroika, and the End of the Cold War, 2009; Vraznye gody: vneshnepoliticheskie ocherki, 2016. *Recreation:* lawn tennis. *Address:* (office) 13 Mokhovaya Street, 125009 Moscow, Russia.

**ADAMKUS, Valdas;** President, Republic of Lithuania, 1998–2003 and 2004–09; *b* Kaunas, 3 Nov. 1926; *s* of Ignas Adamkavičius and Genovaite Bacevičiūte; *m* 1951, Alma Adamkiene. *Educ:* Munich Univ.; Illinois Inst. of Technology, Chicago. Qualified civil engr, 1960; Chicago Car Plant, 1949–50; Draftsman, Meissner Consulting Engrs, 1950–59; owner and operator, summer resort, Sodus, Michigan, 1960–69; Dir, Envmt Res. Centre, US Envmt Protection Agency, 1969–71; Dep. Adminr, 1971–81, Adminr, 1981–97, Reg. 5 (Great Lakes), US Envmt Protection Agency. Mem., US Delegn in Co-operation with USSR under bilateral envmtl agreement, 1972–91; Chm., US Delegn, Internat. Jt Commn for Great Lakes (US-Canada), 1980–97. Vice Chm., 1958–65, Chm., 1967–97, Santara-Sviesa Cultural-political Fedn; Vice-Chm., Exec. Cttee, American-Lithuanian Community; Mem., American-Lithuanian Council. Hon. Dr: Vilnius, 1989; Indiana St Joseph Coll., 1991; Northwestern, 1994; Kaunas Technology Univ., 1998. *Publications:* Lithuania: the name of my destiny, 1997. *Recreations:* sport activities (golf, swimming), classical music.

**ADAMS,** family name of **Baroness Adams of Craigielea.**

**ADAMS OF CRAIGIELEA,** Baroness *cr* 2005 (Life Peer), of Craigielea in Renfrewshire; **(Katherine Patricia) Irene Adams;** JP; *b* 27 Dec. 1947; *m* 1968, Allen S. Adams (*d* 1990), MP Paisley North; one *s* two *d*. *Educ:* Stanley Green High Sch., Paisley. Councillor, Paisley Town, 1970; Member: Renfrew DC, 1974–78; Strathclyde Regl Council, 1979–84. MP (Lab) Paisley North, Nov. 1990–2005. *Address:* House of Lords, SW1A 0PW.

**ADAMS, Dr Aileen Kirkpatrick,** CBE 1988; FRCS; FRCA; Emerita Consultant Anaesthetist, Addenbrooke's Hospital, Cambridge, since 1983; *b* 5 Sept. 1923; *d* of F. Joseph Adams and M. Agnes Adams (*née* Munro). *Educ:* Farringtons School, Chislehurst; Sheffield Univ. (MB ChB Sheffield, 1945); MA Cantab 1977. FFARCS 1954; FFA(SA) 1987; FRCS 1988; FRCA 1989; FDSRCS 1989. Fellow in anaesthesia, Harvard Univ. and Mass. Gen. Hosp., Boston, 1955–57; Consultant Anaesthetist, Addenbrooke's Hosp., Cambridge, 1960–83; Associate Lectr, Univ. of Cambridge, 1977–85; Dean, Faculty of Anaesthetists, RCS, 1985–88. Sen. Lectr, Lagos Univ. Med. Sch., Nigeria, 1963–64. Mem., Cambridge Health Authy, 1978–82. Royal College of Surgeons of England: Mem. Council, 1982–88; Hunterian Prof., 1993; Trustee, Hunterian Collection, 1996–2012; Royal Society of Medicine: Hon. Treas., 1995–99; Hon. Mem., Anaesthesia Section, 1998– (Pres., 1985–86); Pres., History of Medicine Section, 1994–95; Vice-Pres., Comparative Medicine Section, 2003–04. Hon. Mem., History of Anaesthesia Soc., 1994– (Pres., 1990–92); Pres., British Soc. for the History of Medicine, 2003–05. Hon. Archivist, Royal Coll. of Anaesthetists, 1989–98. Former Examr, Cambridge Univ. and FFARCS. Hon. Mem., Assoc. of Anaesthetists, GB and Ire. Lectures: Monckton Copeman, Soc. of Apothecaries, 2002; Arthur Thompson, Univ. of Birmingham, 2004. Mem., Editl Bd, Anaesthesia, 1972–85. Hon. MD Sheffield, 2016. *Publications:* book chapters and papers in med. jls on anaesthetic and related topics, and on history of medicine. *Recreations:* history of medicine, music, walking. *Address:* 12 Redwood Lodge, Grange Road, Cambridge CB3 9AR. *T:* (01223) 356460.

**ADAMS, Alan Edgar;** Deputy Chief Executive and Executive Director for Children's, Housing and Adult Services, London Borough of Hounslow, since 2014; *b* 1 June 1954; *s* of Anthony Adams and Olive Adams; one *d*. *Educ:* Nottingham Univ. (BA (Sociol.) 1976; MA (Social Work), Cert. Social Work 1978); Paddington Coll. of Further Educn, London (Further Educn Teachers' Cert.); Hendon Business Sch., Middlesex Poly. (MBA 1991). Dir, Housing and Social Services, Wokingham UA, 1997–2002; Exec. Dir for Adults and Community Care, Surrey CC, 2002–06; Interim Director: Havering LBC, 2007; Newham LBC, 2008–09; Dep. Chief Exec. for Families, Waltham Forest LBC, 2009–13. Dir, A. A. Leadership Ltd, 2007–16. *Recreations:* family, watching sport, flying light aircraft, drums, writing, optimism. *Address:* 9 Edgcumbe Park Drive, Crowthorne, Berks RG45 6HB. *T:* (01344) 773955. *E:* alan32b@hotmail.co.uk.

**ADAMS, Alastair Christian,** RP; portrait painter, since 1995; President, Royal Society of Portrait Painters, 2008–14; *b* Kingston upon Thames, 24 Dec. 1969; *s* of Gordon and Carolyn Adams; *m* 1997, Amy Wilkinson; one *s* one *d*. *Educ:* Formby High Sch.; Hugh Baird Coll., Bootle (Foundn Course 1989); Leicester Poly. (BA Hons Illustration 1992). RP 2002. Commissions include: Rear-Adm. Nicholas Wilkinson, Sir Ian Blair, Tony Blair, Dame Sandra Burslem, Sir Colin Campbell, Sir William Dale, Rt Hon. Lord Hope of Craighead, Sir John Jennings, Sir Rob Margetts, Rt Hon. Lord Nolan, Capt. John Powell, Rt Hon. Lord Scarman, Rt Hon. Lord Woolf, David Swensen, Rt Hon. Lord Skidelsky, Clare Marx, Kamalesh Sharma, Sir David Greenaway, Dr Marvin Chun. Prog. Coordinator, Sch. of the Arts, Loughborough Univ., 2006–13. Treas., RP, 2006–08. Trustee, Fedn of British Artists, 2008–14. *Publications:* contribs to Internat. Jl Humanities, Internat. Jl Arts in Society. *Recreations:* family, painting, travel, music, charity work. *T:* 07808 585366. *E:* alastair.adams@virgin.net.

**ADAMS, Prof. Alfred Rodney,** FRS 1996; Professor of Physics, 1987–2003, Distinguished Professor of Physics, 2003–08, University of Surrey, now Emeritus; *b* 11 Nov. 1939; *s* of Alfred Walter Adams and Lucy Elizabeth Adams; *m* 1966, Helga Fehringer; two *d*. *Educ:* Rayleigh Technical Sch.; Westcliff High Sch.; Univ. of Leicester (BSc, PhD, DSc). FInstP 1982; FIET 1997, Hon. FIET 2012; FIEEE 2001, Life FIEEE 2011. Research Fellow: Univ. of Leicester, 1964; Univ. of Karlsruhe, 1965; Lectr, 1967, Reader, 1984, Univ. of Surrey. Royal Soc./Japanese Soc. for Promotion of Science Fellow, 1980, Hitachi Prof., 1992, Tokyo Inst. Tech; CNRS Vis. Researcher, Univ. of Montpellier, 1993. Duddell Medal and Prize, Inst. of Physics, 1995; Rank Prize for Optoelectronics, 2014; Guildford Roll of Honour, 2017. *Publications:* (ed with Y. Suematsu) Semiconductor Lasers and Photonic Integrated Circuits, 1994; numerous papers in jls on physics and on quantum electronics. *Recreations:* walking, travel, sailing. *Address:* Advanced Technology Institute, Faculty of Engineering and Physical Sciences, University of Surrey, Guildford, Surrey GU2 7XH. *T:* (01483) 689310.

**ADAMS, Prof. Anthony Peter,** FRCA, FANZCA; Professor of Anaesthetics in the University of London, 1979–2001, now Emeritus, and Joint Vice-Chairman, Division of Surgery and Anaesthesia, 1998–2001, at Guy's, King's and St Thomas' Medical and Dental School of King's College, London; *b* 17 Oct. 1936; *s* of late H. W. J. Adams and W. L. Adams; *m* 1973, Veronica Rosemary Kohn; three *s* one *d*. *Educ:* Epsom College; London Univ. MB BS 1960, PhD 1970; DA 1962; MRCS 1960, LRCP 1960, FRCA (FFARCS 1964); FANZCA (FFARACS 1987). Wellcome Res. Fellow, RPMS, 1964–66; Consultant Anaesthetist and Clinical Lectr, Nuffield Dept of Anaesthetics, Univ. of Oxford, 1968–79; Guy's Hosp. Med. Sch., subseq. UMDS of Guy's and St Thomas' Hospitals, 1979–98: Chm., Div. of Anaesthetics, 1984–89, 1996–97; Vice-Chm., Div. of Surgery and Anaesthesia, 1997–98; Mem., Council of Govs, 1997–98. Civilian Consultant in Anaesthesia to Army, 1988–2001, Consultant Emeritus, 2001–. Member: Standing Cttee, Bd of Studies in Surgery, London Univ., 1979–92; Academic Bd of Medicine, London Univ., 1980–83; Jt Cttee for Higher Trng of Anaesthetists, 1985–90; Specialist Adv. Cttee on Accident and Emergency Medicine, Jt Cttee for Higher Trng in Medicine, 1986–90; Exec. Cttee, Fedn of Assocs of Clin. Profs, 1979–87; Exec. Cttee, Anaesthetic Res. Soc., 1983–94 (Chm., 1991–94; Hon. Mem., 2002–); Council, Royal Coll. of Anaesthetists, 1989–97; Chm., Assoc. of Profs of Anaesthesia, 1984–88; Senator, Eur. Acad. of Anaesthesiology, 1985–95, 2000–03 (Mem. Exec. Cttee, 1997–2003). Regional Educnl Adviser (SE Thames RHA) to Faculty of Anaesthetists of RCS, 1980–87; Examiner: FFARCS, 1974–86; DVA, 1986–93; DA and DM, Univ. of WI, 1986–88, 1995, 1997, 1998; MSc, Univ. of Wales Coll. of Medicine, 1988–93; PhD: Univ. of London, 1989, 1997, 1999, 2001, 2004; Univ. of Manchester, 1993; Univ. of Liverpool, 1995; NUI, Galway, 2000; MB ChB Chinese Univ. of Hong Kong, 1990; Professional and Linguistic Assessment Bd Pt 2, GMC, UK, 2001–06; Mem. of Faculty, Key Skills in Surgery Courses, RCSE, 2006–10. Mem., Bd of Govs, Sutton High Sch. for Girls, 1988–95 (Chm., 1991–95). President: Sutton & Dist Med. Soc., 2006–08; Cheam Br., Arthritis Research UK (formerly Arthritis and Rheumatism Council), 2011–14. Hon. Life Mem., Assoc. Dental Anaesthetists, 2006. Asst Editor, Anaesthesia, 1976–82; Associate Editor: Survey of Anesthesiology, 1984–2001; European Jl of Anaesthesiology, 1987–94; Jl of Anesthesia (Japan), 1995–2002; Mem. Editl Bd, British Jl of Anaesthesia, 1984–97; Chm. Editl Bd, 1997–2000, Editor-in-Chief, 2000–03, European Jl of Anaesthesiology. *Publications:* Principles and Practice of Blood-Gas Analysis, 1979, 2nd edn 1982; Intensive Care, 1984 (trans. Spanish 1987, Greek 1990); (ed jtly) Recent Advances in Anaesthesia and Analgesia, vol. 15, 1985, vol. 16, 1989, vol. 17, 1992, vol. 18, 1994, vol. 19, 1995, vol. 20, 1998, vol. 21, 2000, vol. 22, 2003; (ed jtly) Emergency Anaesthesia, 1986 and 1988, Japanese edn 1998; (ed jtly) Anaesthesia, Analgesia and Intensive Care, 1991; contribs to medical jls. *Recreations:* badger watching, English castles, history, tennis, croquet, cinema, theatre, ballet. *Clubs:* Royal Automobile, Royal Society of Medicine; Halifax House (Oxford).

**ADAMS, Dr Cheryll Mary,** CBE 2016; Executive Director, Institute of Health Visiting, since 2012; *b* Ipswich, 20 March 1953; *d* of John Gwilym Howells and Ola Margaret Howells; *m* 1978, John Graham Adams; one *s* one *d*. *Educ:* Ipswich High Sch. for Girls; Univ. of Surrey (BSc); Univ. of Southampton (MSc); Univ. of Portsmouth (DNursing 2007). RN 1978; RHV 1982. Health Visitor, 1982–2001; Res. and Develt Coordinator, 1996–98, Manager, 1998, Portsmouth Health Res. and Develt Consortium; Professional Officer, Res. and Practice, 2001–07, Lead Professional Officer, 2007–09, CPHVA; Sen. Safeguarding Advr, DoH, 2010; ind. advr in health visiting and children's public health evidence and policy, 2010–12. *Publications:* Clinical Effectiveness: a practical guide for the community nurse, 2000, 2nd edn 2003; (with N. Brocklehurst) Corporate Working in Health Visiting and Public Health Nursing Teams, 2004. *Recreations:* theatre, sailing, walking, travel, reading, swimming. *E:* Cheryll.Adams@ihv.org.uk. *Clubs:* Emsworth Sailing, Emsworth Slipper Sailing.

**ADAMS, Rev. David;** see Adams, Rev. J. D. A.

**ADAMS, Prof. David,** PhD; Ian Mactaggart Professor of Property and Urban Studies, University of Glasgow, since 2004; *b* Menston, 10 Sept. 1954; *s* of Richard Adams and Sylvia Adams; *m* 1989, Judith Banks; one *s* one *d*. *Educ:* Emmanuel Coll., Cambridge (BA Hons Land Economy 1976; MA 1980; PhD 1997); Univ. of Liverpool (MCD 1978). MRTPI 1981, FRTPI 2001; MRICS 1999, FRICS 2012. Planning Asst, Leeds CC, 1978–83; Res. Asst, Univ. of Reading, 1983–84; Lectr in Urban Planning and Develt, Univ. of Manchester, 1984–93; University of Aberdeen: Sen. Lectr, 1993–95, Reader, 1995–97, in Land Economy; Prof. of Land Economy, 1997–2004. Dep. Chair, Architecture, Planning and Built Envmt Sub-Panel, REF 2014, 2011–14. Mem., Scottish Land Commn, 2016–. FRSA 1998; FAcSS (AcSS 2013). *Publications:* Urban Planning and the Development Process, 1994; (jtly) Land for Industrial Development, 1994; (with C. Watkins) Greenfields, Brownfields and Housing Development, 2002; (ed jtly) Planning, Public Policy and Property Markets, 2005; (ed jtly) Urban Design in the Real Estate Development Process, 2011; (with S. Tiesdell) Shaping Places: urban planning, design and development, 2013. *Recreations:* walking, reading, classical music. *Address:* Urban Studies, School of Social and Political Sciences, University of Glasgow, 25 Bute Gardens, Glasgow G12 8RS. *T:* (0141) 330 6280, *Fax:* (0141) 330 6032. *E:* david.adams@glasgow.ac.uk.

**ADAMS, Sir David H.;** see Hempleman-Adams.

**ADAMS, Prof. David Harvey,** MD; FRCP, FMedSci; Professor of Hepatology, since 1997, Dean of Medicine, since 2013 and Pro-Vice Chancellor and Head, College of Medical and Dental Sciences, since 2015, University of Birmingham; Consultant Physician, Queen Elizabeth Hospital, Birmingham, since 1993; *b* Nottingham, 26 Feb. 1958; *s* of late Stewart Adams and Mary Adams (*née* Harvey); *m* 1984, Rosalind Hicks; two *s* one *d*. *Educ:* Univ. of Birmingham (MB ChB 1981; MD 1990). MRCP 1984, FRCP 1996. University of Birmingham: Lectr, Dept of Medicine, 1985–87; MRC Res. Fellow, 1987–90; MRC Travelling Fellow and Vis. Associate, Fogarty Exchange Prog., Experimental Immunol. Br., Nat. Cancer Inst., NIH, Bethesda, Md, 1991–93; Dir, Birmingham NIHR Biomed. Unit for Liver Disease, 2008–; Dir, Translational Res. MRC Centre for Immune Regulation, 2009–14, Hd, Sch. of Immunity and Infection, 2011–13, Univ. of Birmingham. Mem., Clin. Trng and Career Develt Panel, MRC, 2009–13. Chm., Wkg Gp on Mentoring, 2009–, Mem. Council, 2011–, Acad. of Med. Scis; Chm., Academic Cttee, British Soc. of Gastroenterol., 2011–14. Mem. Council, Eur. Soc. for Organ Transplantation, 2004–08; Mem., Scientific Cttee and Gov. Bd, 2004–07, Founder Mem., Ethics Cttee, 2011–14, Eur. Assoc. for Study of the Liver. Associate Editor: Liver, 1997–2002; Gut, 1998–2004; Clinical Sci., 1998–2010; Transplant Internat., 2006–10; Liver Transplantation, 2009–14; Amer. Jl of Physiol., 2009–15; Jl of Hepatol., 2009–. *Publications:* over 200 articles in scientific jls on immunol. and liver disease. *Recreations:* walking, fishing, reading, music. *Address:* College of Medical and Dental Sciences, University of Birmingham Medical School, Birmingham B15 2TT. *T:* (0121) 415 8700. *E:* d.h.adams@bham.ac.uk.

**ADAMS, Prof. David Robert Hutchinson, (Robin);** Librarian and College Archivist, Trinity College Dublin, 2002–12; *b* 9 June 1951; *s* of Cecil David and Ann Gilmore Adams; *m* 1st, 1984, Linda Jean Carter (*d* 2011); one *s* one *d*; 2nd, 2017, Amanda Jocelyn Piesse. *Educ:* Royal Belfast Academical Instn; Univ. of Ulster (BA); Queen's Univ. of Belfast (Dip. Liby Studies); Univ. of Dublin (MA). Asst Librarian, QUB, 1975–78; Asst Under-Librarian, Cambridge Univ., 1978–86; Principal Asst Librarian, Glasgow Univ., 1986–90; Dep. Librarian, TCD, 1991–2002. Member: Bd, Nat. Preservation Office, 2002–09; An Chomhairle Leabharlanna (Liby Council), 2002–12; Consortium of Nat. and Univ. Libraries, 2002–12; Legal Deposit Adv. Panel, 2005–09; Bd, NI Publications Resource, 2006– (Chm., 2013–); Council, Liby Assoc. of Ireland, 2012–13; BL Adv. Council, 2013–. Dir, Res. Libraries UK (formerly Consortium of Univ. Res. Libraries), 2002–12; Chm., Newsplan Ireland, 2008–12. Dir, Iris Document Delivery Services Ltd, 2002–12. Trustee, Worth Liby, 2002–12. *Publications:* contrib. articles to professional jls. *Recreations:* fishing, theatre, walking, permaculture and organic gardening, choral singing, distance running. *Address:* 40 Springvale Road, Ballywalter, Co. Down BT22 2RS. *E:* radams@tcd.ie.

**ADAMS, Dr Derek Westwood,** FRPharmS; Director, Pharmaceutical Compliance Europe, Merck Sharpe and Dohme, 1996–99; *b* Leeds, 13 April 1941; *s* of Ernest Wilfred Adams and Hilda Adams (*née* Wightman); *m* 1972, Kathryn Robinson. *Educ:* Archbp Holgate's Grammar Sch., York; Roundhay Sch., Leeds; Univ. of Manchester (BSc Pharmacy); Wolfson Coll., Cambridge (MA Hist.); Univ. of Hertfordshire (PhD 2010). Qualified Person status under provisions of Directive EEC 75/319, 1982. FRPharmS 1989. Merck Sharpe and Dohme: formulation pharmacist, Pharmaceutical R&D Dept, 1966–78; Manufg Manager, 1978–79; Prodn Manager, 1979–84; Distribn Services Manager, 1984–87; Gp Quality Control Manager, 1987–92; Director: Quality Ops, GB and Ireland, 1992–94; Ext. Quality Ops, 1994–96. Assessor of applicants for Qualified Persons under provisions of Directive EEC 75/319, RPharmS, 1980–99. RPharmS Nominee, Pharmacy Practices Cttee, FPC, 1983–88; Mem., Antibiotics Sub-Cttee, British Pharmacopoeia Commn, 1988–99. Master, Soc. of Apothecaries, 2016–17. Diocesan Gov., Tewin Cowper C of E Primary Sch., 2011–16. Mem., Rotary Club of Amwell (Pres., 1995–96); Gov., Rotary Internat. Dist 1260 (Beds, Bucks and Herts), 2000–01. *Recreations:* cycling, walking, music, reading. *Club:* Oxford and Cambridge.

**ADAMS, Most Rev. Edward Joseph;** Apostolic Nuncio to the Court of St James's, since 2017; *b* Philadelphia, Penn, 24 Aug. 1944; *s* of Albert Aloysius Adams, Sr and Mary Ella Youell Adams. *Educ:* St Charles Borromeo Seminary, Philadelphia (AB 1966; MDiv 1970); Villanova Univ. (MA 1968); Univ. of St Thomas, Rome (JCD 1975); Pontifical Ecclesiastical Acad., Rome. Ordained priest, 1970; entered Diplomatic Service of the Holy See, 1976; served in Rwanda, Kenya, Honduras, Ireland, Denmark, Czech Rep. and

Vatican Secretariat of State; apptd Titular Archbishop of Scala, 1996; Apostolic Nuncio to: Bangladesh, 1996–2002; Zimbabwe, 2002–07; Philippines, 2007–11; Greece, 2011–17. Comdr, Order of the Dannebrog (Denmark), 1993; Grand Cross, Order of the Phoenix (Greece), 2017. *Address:* Apostolic Nunciature, Great Britain, 54 Parkside, SW19 5NE. *T:* (020) 8944 7189, *Fax:* (020) 8947 2494. *E:* nuntius@globalnet.co.uk.

**ADAMS, Sir Geoffrey (Doyne)**, KCMG 2008 (CMG 2003); HM Diplomatic Service; Ambassador to Egypt, since 2018; *b* 11 June 1957; *s* of late Sir Philip George Doyne Adams, KCMG, and Hon. (Mary) Elizabeth, *e d* of Baron Trevethin and Oaksey (3rd and 1st Baron respectively); *m* 1999, Mary Emma Baxter; two *s* one *d*. *Educ:* Eton; Magdalen Coll., Oxford (BA). Joined HM Diplomatic Service, 1979; Third, later Second, Sec., Jedda, 1982–85; Ecole Nat. d'Admin, Paris, 1985–87; Private Sec. to Perm. Under-Sec. of State, FCO, 1987–91; First Sec., Pretoria and Cape Town, 1991–94; European Secretariat, Cabinet Office, 1995–98; Counsellor and Dep. Hd of Mission, Cairo, 1998–2001; Consul-Gen., Jerusalem, 2001–03; Principal Private Sec. to Sec. of State for Foreign and Commonwealth Affairs, 2003–05; Ambassador to Iran, 2006–09; Dir Gen. (Political), FCO, 2009–12; Ambassador to the Netherlands, 2013–17. *Address:* c/o Foreign and Commonwealth Office, King Charles Street, SW1A 2AH.

**ADAMS, Gerard, (Gerry);** Member of the Dáil (TD) (SF) Louth, since 2011; President, Sinn Féin, 1983–2018 (Vice-President, 1978–83); *b* 6 Oct. 1948; *s* of late Gerard Adams and Annie (*née* Hannaway); *m* 1971, Colette McArdle; one *s*. *Educ:* St Mary's Christian Brothers' Sch., Belfast. Interned without trial, 1971, 1973; subseq. imprisoned; released, 1976. Mem., NI Assembly, 1982; MP (SF) Belfast W, 1983–92; contested (SF) same seat, 1992; MP (SF) Belfast W, 1997–Jan. 2011; Mem. (SF) Belfast W, NI Assembly, 1998–Dec. 2010. Thorr Award, Switzerland, 1995. Blog, www.leargas.blogspot.com. *Publications:* Falls Memories (autobiog.), 1982; Politics of Irish Freedom, 1986; Pathway to Peace, 1988; Cage Eleven (autobiog.), 1990; The Street and Other Stories, 1992; Selected Writings, 1994; Before the Dawn (autobiog.), 1996; An Irish Voice: the quest for peace, 1997; An Irish Journal, 2001; Hope and History (memoirs), 2003; The New Ireland: a vision for the future, 2005; An Irish Eye, 2007. *Address:* Dáil Éireann, Leinster House, Kildare Street, Dublin 2, Ireland.

**ADAMS, Guy Luke V.;** *see* Vassall-Adams. G. L.

**ADAMS, Sir James;** *see* Adams, Sir W. J.

**ADAMS, James Noel,** CBE 2015; DPhil; FBA 1992; FAHA; Senior Research Fellow, All Souls College, Oxford, 1998–2010, now Emeritus Fellow; *b* 24 Sept. 1943. *Educ:* North Sydney Boys' High Sch.; Univ. of Sydney (BA); Brasenose Coll., Oxford (MA; DPhil; Hon. Fellow, 2012); MA Cantab. Teaching Fellow, Dept of Latin, Univ. of Sydney, 1965–66; Commonwealth Schol., Brasenose Coll., Oxford, 1967–70; Rouse Res. Fellow in Classics, Christ's Coll., Cambridge, 1970–72; University of Manchester: Lectr and Sen. Lectr in Greek and Latin, 1972–82; Reader in Latin, 1982–93; Prof. of Latin, 1993–95; Prof. of Latin, Univ. of Reading, 1995–97. Vis. Sen. Res. Fellow, St John's Coll., Oxford, 1994–95; Professorial Res. Fellow, Univ. of Manchester, 2013–14. FAHA 2002. Kenyon Medal, British Acad., 2009. *Publications:* The Text and Language of a Vulgar Latin Chronicle (Anonymus Valesianus), 1976; The Vulgar Latin of the Letters of Claudius Terentianus, 1977; The Latin Sexual Vocabulary, 1982; Wackernagel's Law and the Placement of the Copula Esse in Classical Latin, 1994; Pelagonius and Latin Veterinary Terminology in the Roman Empire, 1995; Bilingualism and the Latin Language, 2003; The Regional Diversification of Latin 200 BC–AD 600, 2007; Social Variation and the Latin Language, 2013; (ed) An Anthology of Informal Latin 200 BC–AD 900, 2016; articles in learned jls. *Recreation:* cricket. *Address:* All Souls College, Oxford OX1 4AL.

**ADAMS, Jennifer,** LVO 1993; OBE 2008; Director of Open Spaces, City of London Corporation (formerly Corporation of London), 2001–08; *b* 1 Feb. 1948; *d* of Arthur Roy Thomas Crisp and Joyce Muriel Crisp (*née* Davey); *m* 1968, Terence William Adams (*d* 2011). *Educ:* City of London School for Girls. Final Diploma, Inst. of Leisure and Amenity (FILAM DipPRA); FCIHort. Various positions in Parks Dept, London Borough of Wandsworth, 1971–83; Manager, Inner Parks, 1983–90; Acting Bailiff, Royal Parks, 1990–92; Hd of Inner Parks and Commerce, Royal Parks, 1992–2001. Pres., Inst. of Horticulture, 1996–98. Vice Chm., 2006–15, Treas., 2006–, Royal Parks Guild. Liveryman, Gardeners' Co., 1985. Associate of Honour, RHS, 1999. *Recreations:* walking, gardening, nature conservation.

**ADAMS, John;** composer; *b* 15 Feb. 1947. *Educ:* Harvard Univ. (scholar). Teacher, San Francisco Conservatory of Music, 1972–82; Music Advr, 1978–82, Composer-in-Residence, 1982–85, San Francisco Symphony; Creative Chair, LA Philharmonic, 2006–; Composer-in-Residence, Berlin Philharmonic, 2016–17. *Compositions include: opera:* Nixon in China, 1987; The Death of Klinghoffer, 1990; I Was Looking at the Ceiling and Then I Saw the Sky, 1995; El Niño, 2000; Doctor Atomic, 2005; A Flowering Tree, 2007; The Gospel According to the Other Mary, 2013; Girls of the Golden West, 2017; *orchestral works:* Shaker Loops, 1978; Common Tones in Simple Time, 1979; Harmonium, 1980–81; Grand Pianola Music, 1981–82; Harmonielehre, 1984–85; The Chairman Dances, 1985; Short Ride in a Fast Machine, 1986; Tromba Lontana, 1986; Fearful Symmetries, 1988; The Wound-Dresser, 1988–89; Eros Piano, 1989; El Dorado, 1991; Violin Concerto, 1993 (Grawemeyer Award for Music Composition, 1995); Gnarly Buttons, 1996; Century Rolls, piano concerto, 1998; Guide to Strange Places, 2002; My Father Knew Charles Ives, 2003; The Dharma at Big Sur, 2004; City Noir, 2010; Absolute Jest, string quartet and orch., 2012; Saxophone Concerto, 2013; Scheherezade.2, 2015; Must the Devil Have All the Good Tunes?, concerto for piano and orch., 2018; *chorus and orchestra:* On the Transmigration of Souls, 2002 (Pulitzer Prize, 2003); In the Name of the Earth, 2019; *chamber and ensemble works:* Christian Zeal and Activity, 1973; Chamber Symphony, 1992; John's Book of Alleged Dances, 1994; Road Movies, 1995; Son of Chamber Symphony, 2007; String Quartet, 2008; String Quartet No 2, 2016; *piano:* China Gates, 1977; Phrygian Gates, 1977; (for 2 pianos) Hallelujah Junction, 2001; *dance:* Available Light, 2017; numerous recordings. *Publications:* Hallelujah Junction: composing an American life (memoir), 2008. *Address:* c/o Boosey & Hawkes Music Publishers Ltd, Aldwych House, 71–91 Aldwych, WC2B 4HN.

**ADAMS, Rev. (John) David (Andrew);** Headmaster, Weydon School, Farnham, 1982–98; Chaplain to the Queen, 1994–2007; Secondary School consultant, 1998–2010; *b* 27 Nov. 1937; *s* of John McCullough McConnell Adams and Sylvia Pansy (*née* Pinner); *m* 1970, Maria Carmen de Azpiazu-Cruz; one *s* one *d*. *Educ:* Trinity Coll., Dublin (BA 1960; Div. Test. 1961; MA 1964; BD 1965); Univ. of Reading (MEd 1974). Curate, St Stephen's, Belfast, 1962–65; part-time teaching and vol. chaplaincy in Europe, 1965–67; Hd, Religious Educn, Tower Ramparts, Ipswich, 1967–70; Counsellor, later Sen. Teacher, Robert Haining Sch., Surrey, 1970–74; Headmaster, St Paul's, Addlestone, 1974–82. Non-stipendiary Curate, 1976–2007, Retired Priest (formerly Hon. Priest), 2007–, St Thomas-on-the-Bourne, Farnham. Bishop's Assessor, Dio. of Guildford, 2005–18. *Recreations:* gardening, household chores, birding; the life of George Morley, Bishop of Winchester, 1597–1684. *Address:* Brookside Farm, Oast House Crescent, Farnham, Surrey GU9 0NP. *T:* (01252) 726888.

**ADAMS, His Honour John Douglas Richard;** a Circuit Judge, 1998–2002; *b* 19 March 1940; *o s* of late Gordon Arthur Richard Adams and Marjorie Ethel Adams (*née* Ongley); *m* 1966, Anne Easton Todd, *o d* of late Robert Easton Todd and Mary Ann Margaret Todd; two *d*. *Educ:* Watford Grammar School; Durham Univ. (LLB 1963). Called to Bar, Lincoln's Inn, 1967; Bencher, Inner Temple, 1997. Lecturer: Newcastle Univ., 1963–71; University College London, 1971–78; also practised at Revenue Bar until 1978; Special Comr of Income Tax, 1978–82; Registrar of Civil Appeals, 1982–98; a Recorder, 1992–98. Hon. Lecturer, St Edmund Hall, Oxford, 1978–2008; Vis. Lectr, Oxford Univ., 1995–2008. Mem. Bd of Trustees, Hospice of St Francis, Berkhamsted, 2004–11. *Publications:* (with J. Whalley) The International Taxation of Multinational Enterprises, 1977; (contrib.) Atkin's Court Forms, 1984, 1992; (ed jtly) Supreme Court Practice, 1985, 1991, 1993, 1995, 1997, 1999; (ed jtly) Chitty and Jacob's Queen's Bench Forms, 21st edn, 1986; (ed jtly) Sweet & Maxwell's County Court Litigation, 1993; (ed jtly) Emergency Remedies in the Family Courts, 3rd edn, 1997; (ed jtly) Jordan's Civil Court Service, 2002; (ed jtly) Halsbury's Laws of England, 4th edn, vol. 10. *Recreations:* music, walking, dining. *E:* johndradams@btinternet.com.

**ADAMS, (John) Giles Selby C.;** *see* Coode-Adams.

**ADAMS, His Honour (John) Roderick (Seton);** a Circuit Judge, 1990–2003; *b* 29 Feb. 1936; *s* of George Adams and Winifred (*née* Wilson); *m* 1965, Pamela Bridget, *e d* of Rev. D. E. Rice, MC; three *s*. *Educ:* Whitgift Sch.; Trinity Coll., Cambridge. BA, 1959, MA 1963. Commnd, Seaforth Highlanders, 1955–56; Parachute Regt, TA, 1959–66. Legal Adviser in industry, 1960–66. Called to the Bar, Inner Temple, 1962; began practice at the Bar, 1967; Dep. Circuit Judge, 1978–80; a Recorder, 1980–90. *Recreations:* hill-walking, fishing, growing old roses, microlight flying. *Address:* 8 Melville Road, Eskbank, Midlothian EH22 3BY. *T:* (0131) 654 9274; Melness House, Sutherland IV27 4YR. *T:* (01847) 601255.
*See also* R. G. S. *Adams*.

**ADAMS, Justin Peter Renwick;** Chief Executive Officer, Global Chair Components Ltd, since 2018; *b* Cheltenham, 30 Sept. 1965; *s* of James Frederick Renwick Adams and Dawn Adams (*née* Cozens); *m* 1989, Philippa Bailey; two *s* two *d*. *Educ:* Cheltenham Coll.; Univ. of St Andrews (MA Hons Mgt with Internat. Relns); Cranfield Sch. of Mgt (MBA). Asst Area Manager (Asia Pacific), 1989–90, Product Manager, 1990–92, ICI C&P Ltd; Consultant, Arthur D. Little Ltd, 1992–94; Investment Manager, Doughty Hanson, 1995–96; Business Develt Manager, Guinness Worldwide Ltd, 1996–98; Man. Dir, Guinness Germany, 1998–2001; Man. Dir, UK and Ireland, Maxxium Worldwide, 2001–05; Greene King plc: Man. Dir, Greene King Brewing Co., 2005–11; Dir, Main Bd, 2005–11; CEO, SealSkinz Ltd, 2012–14; Man. Dir, Connect Books and Exec. Dir, Connect Gp plc, 2014–18. *Recreations:* coach and play hockey, watch Rugby, enjoy all racquet and water sports, family, food, reading, travel. *Address:* The Old Rectory, The Street, Horringer, Suffolk IP29 5SA. *T:* (01284) 735960. *E:* justinadams111@aol.com.

**ADAMS, Lewis Drummond,** OBE 1999; General Secretary, Associated Society of Locomotive Engineers and Firemen, 1994–99; *b* London, 16 Aug. 1939; *s* of Lewis John Adams and Margaret (*née* Drummond); *m* 1958, Jean Marion Bass; one *s* one *d*. *Educ:* Impington Coll., Cambridge; NCLC; Tavistock Inst., London. British Railways: engine cleaner, 1954–55; engine fireman and driver asst, 1955–67; engine driver, 1967–80. Associated Society of Locomotive Engineers and Firemen: Sec., London Dist Council No 1, 1970–80; Executive Committee: Mem., 1981–90; Vice-Pres., 1985–90; Asst Gen. Sec., 1990–93. British Railways: Mem., later Chm., Pension Fund, 1982–93; Member: Wages Grade Pension Fund, 1982–93; Superannuation Fund, 1982–93. Dir, Millennium Drivers Ltd, 1998–2015. Bd Mem., SRA, 1999–2004. Member: TUC Pension Cttee, 1987–90; Railway Industries Adv. Cttee, 1985–90; British Transport Police Authy, 2004–15 (Mem. Mgt Cttee, Superannuation Pension Fund, 2006–15). *Recreations:* travel, gardening.

**ADAMS, Air Vice-Marshal Michael Keith,** CB 1986; AFC 1970; FRAeS; *b* 23 Jan. 1934; *s* of late William Frederick Adams and Jean Mary Adams; *m* 1966, Susan (*née* Trudgian); two *s* one *d*. *Educ:* Bedford Sch.; City of London Sch. FRAeS 1978. Joined RAF, 1952; qualified Pilot, 1954; Flying Instr, 1960; Test Pilot, 1963 (QCVSA 1967); Staff Coll., Toronto, 1969; CO Empire Test Pilots' Sch., 1975; Dir of Operational Requirements, 1978–81; RCDS, 1982; AOC Training Units, 1983; ACAS (Op. Requirements), MoD, 1984; ACDS (Op. Requirements) Air, MoD, 1985–86; Sen. Directing Staff (Air), RCDS, 1987–88; retd. Dir, Thomson-CSF (UK) Ltd, 1988–94; Dir, International Aerospace, 1989–96 (Chm., 1996). Vice-Pres., RAeS, 1992–95. Chm. Govs, Duke of Kent Sch., Cranleigh, Surrey, 1997–2003. *Recreation:* silversmithing.

**ADAMS, Nigel;** MP (C) Selby and Ainsty, since 2010; Minister of State, Department for Digital, Culture, Media and Sport, since 2019; *b* Goole, E Yorks, 30 Nov. 1966; *s* of Derek Adams and late Isabella Adams; *m* 1992, Claire Robson; one *s* three *d*. *Educ:* Selby Grammar Sch.; Selby High Sch. Sales and mktg roles in advertising and telecommunications industry, 1985–93; Founder and Man. Dir, Advanced Digital Telecom Ltd, 1993–99; Dir, JWE Telecom plc, 1999–2000; non-exec. Chm., Pareto Law plc, 2001–02; Director: Ebor Events Ltd, 2003–05; Yorks Tourist Bd, 2005–06; NGC Networks Ltd, 2006–; NGC Network Services Ltd, 2007–. An Asst Govt Whip, 2017–18; a Lord Comr of HM Treasury (Govt Whip), 2018; Parly Under-Sec. of State, MHCLG, 2018, Wales Office, 2018–19; an Asst Govt Whip, 2018–19. Hon. Sec., All Party Parly Cricket Gp, 2010–17. *Recreations:* cricket, playing and watching (Member: Yorks CCC; Carlton Club CC; Hovingham CC; Sec., Lords and Commons CC), darts. *Address:* House of Commons, SW1A 0AA. *E:* nigel.adams.mp@parliament.uk; 17 High Street, Tadcaster, N Yorks LS24 9AP. *Club:* Carlton.

**ADAMS, Paul Nicholas;** JP; Chief Executive, British American Tobacco plc, 2004–11; *b* 12 March 1953; *s* of Peter Adams and Joan Adams (*née* Smith); *m* 1978, Gail Edwina McCann; one *s* two *d*. *Educ:* Culford Sch.; Ealing Coll., London (BA Hons 1977). Mktg Dir, Beecham Products Internat., 1983–86; Vice Pres. Mktg Europe, Pepsi-Cola Internat., 1986–91; British American Tobacco plc: Regl Dir, Asia Pacific, 1991–98, Europe, 1999–2001; Dep. Man. Dir, 2001; Man. Dir, 2002–03. Non-exec. Dir, Allied Domecq plc, 2003–05. JP Central London, 2014. *Recreations:* reading, country pursuits, theatre. *Address:* c/o British American Tobacco plc, Globe House, 4 Temple Place, WC2R 2PG.

**ADAMS, Piers Dermot Meredith;** musician; professional virtuoso recorder player, since 1985; *b* 21 Dec. 1963; *s* of late John Adams and of Susan Adams; one *d*. *Educ:* Reading Blue Coat Sch.; Univ. of Bristol (BSc Physics 1984); Guildhall Sch. of Music & Drama (Cert. Perf. in Early Music 1985). Winner (jtly), Moeck Recorder Competition, 1985; début recital, Wigmore Hall, London, 1985; performed, 1986–, in all Eur. countries, most US states, Canada, Mexico, Cuba, Russia, China, Japan, Singapore, Thailand and Australia; soloist: in all South Bank concert halls, London; with many orchs incl. BBC Symphony Philharmonia, Acad. of Ancient Music and Singapore Symphony; commnd over 25 works by mod. composers, 1986–; Founder and Dir, Red Priest (cult baroque ensemble), 1997–; Co-Founder, Red Priest Recordings, 2009–; performed private concerts for the Prince of Wales and the Duke of Edinburgh, 2001, 2002; frequent radio broadcasts; many TV appearances. Twelve CD recordings (début CD, 1988). *Address:* c/o Maureen Phillips, Upbeat Classical Management, 170 Thirlmere Gardens, Northwood HA6 2RU. *T:* (01923) 836220. *E:* admin@upbeatclassical.co.uk.

**ADAMS, Richard Clive;** Chairman, Crosswater Solutions Ltd, 2000–14; *b* 22 June 1945; *s* of William Henry Adams and Alberta Sarah Adams (*née* Steed); *m* 1971, Elizabeth Anne Coleman; two *s. Educ:* Cotham Grammar Sch., Bristol; Exeter Univ. (BA). Post Office: Asst Postal Controller, 1966–78; Dir of Studies, PO Mgt Coll., 1978–82; Head Postmaster, Northampton, 1982–85; Asst Dir, Corporate Planning, 1985–92; Gp Planning Dir, 1992–97; Sec., 1997–99. Chm., Postal and Logistics Consulting Worldwide Ltd, 2003–06. Mem. Council, CBI, 1998–99. Sec., Postal Heritage Trust, 2004–15. *Recreations:* applied arts, railways, wine. *Address:* 48 Overton Drive, Wanstead, E11 2NJ. *T:* (020) 8989 0021.

**ADAMS, Robert George Seton; His Honour Judge Adams;** a Circuit Judge, since 2014; *b* London, 5 Jan. 1966; *s* of His Honour (John) Roderick (Seton) Adams, *qv*, *m* 1994, Theresa Campbell; two *s* one *d. Educ:* Dulwich Coll.; Trinity Coll., Cambridge (BA 1987; MA 1991). Commnd Queen's Own Highlanders, 1987–92. Called to the Bar, Inner Temple, 1993; a Recorder, 2008–14. *Recreations:* running, swimming, walking, fly-fishing. *Address:* Newcastle upon Tyne Crown Court, Quayside, Newcastle upon Tyne NE1 2LA. *T:* (0191) 201 2000. *E:* HHJ.Robert.Adams@eJudiciary.net. *Club:* Old Alleynian.

**ADAMS, Prof. Robert Merrihew,** PhD; FBA 2006; Clark Professor of Philosophy, Yale University, 1995–2003, Emeritus, 2004; *b* 8 Sept. 1937; *s* of Rev. Arthur Merrihew Adams and Margaret Baker Adams; *m* 1966, Marilyn McCord, (Rev. Prof. Marilyn McCord Adams) (*d* 2017). *Educ:* Princeton Univ. (AB 1959); Mansfield Coll., Oxford (BA 1961, MA 1965); Princeton Theological Seminary (BD 1962); Cornell Univ. (MA 1967; PhD 1969). Pastor, Montauk Community Ch (Presbyterian), Montauk, NY, 1962–65; Lectr, 1968, Asst Prof., 1969–72, Univ. of Michigan, Ann Arbor; University of California, Los Angeles: Assoc. Prof., 1972–76; Prof., 1976–93; Chm., Philos. Dept, 1975–79; Yale University: Prof., 1993–2003; Chm., Philos. Dept, 1993–2001. Vis. Prof. of Philos., Univ. of Oxford, 2004–09; Sen. Res. Fellow, Mansfield Coll., Oxford, 2004–11; Dist. Res. Prof. of Philos., Univ. of N Carolina at Chapel Hill, 2009–13; Vis. Prof. of Philos., Rutgers Univ., 2013–16. Wilde Lectr in Natural Religion, Univ. of Oxford, 1989; Gifford Lectr, Univ. of St Andrews, 1999. Fellow, Amer. Acad. of Arts and Scis, 1991. *Publications:* The Virtue of Faith and Other Essays in Philosophical Theology, 1987; (ed with Marilyn McCord Adams) The Problem of Evil, 1990; Leibniz: determinist, theist, idealist, 1994; Finite and Infinite Goods: a framework for ethics, 1999; A Theory of Virtue, 2006; jl articles on topics in ethics, metaphysics, philos. of religion and hist. of mod. philos. *Recreations:* travel, museum visits, birdwatching.

**ADAMS, Robin;** *see* Adams, D. R. H.

**ADAMS, Roderick;** *see* Adams, His Honour J. R. S.

**ADAMS, Sheenagh;** Keeper of the Registers of Scotland, 2009–18; *b* Dundee, 31 Aug. 1957; *d* of James McIntosh Adams and Isabella Bruce Adams (*née* Ross); *m* 1997, Peter William Craig; two *d. Educ:* Harris Acad., Dundee; St Andrews Univ. (MA Hons Medieval Hist.); Glasgow Univ. (Dip. Housing Studies). Welfare Rights Officer, Strathclyde Regl Council, 1979–82; Tenant Participation Officer, Clydebank DC, 1982–83; Develt Manager, Tenant Participation Adv. Service, 1983–85; Principal Mgt Officer, Falkirk DC, 1985–90; various hd of branch posts, Scottish Office, 1990–99; Hd, Voluntary Issues Unit, Scottish Govt, 1999–2002; Dir of Policy, Historic Scotland, 2002–06; Man. Dir, Registers of Scotland, 2006–09. *Recreations:* reading, theatre, Spain.

**ADAMS, Suzanne;** *see* Cory, S.

**ADAMS, Tony Alexander,** MBE 1999; Founder and President, Sporting Chance Charity Clinic, since 2000; *b* Romford, Essex, 10 Oct. 1966; *s* of Alexander Adams and Caroline Adams (*née* Banks); *m* 1st, 1992, Jane Shea (marr. diss. 1996); one *s* one *d*; 2nd, 2004, Poppy Teacher; two *s* one *d. Educ:* Eastbrook Comp. Sch. Footballer: Arsenal FC, 1983–2002 (signed forms, 1979; Captain, 1987–2002; approx. 669 appearances, 10 major titles); England team, 1987–2000 (Captain, 1995–97; 66 caps); Manager: Wycombe Wanderers FC, 2003–04; Portsmouth FC, 2008–09; Manager, 2010–12, Football Dir, 2012–16, Gabala, Azerbaijan; Technical Dir, 2016–17, Caretaker Manager, 2017, Granada, Spain; Vice-Pres. and Gp Sports Dir, DDMC FC Mgt Co., 2016–17. Hon. Pres., Rugby Football League, 2019–. Patron: Forward Trust (formerly Rehabilitation for Addicted Prisoners Trust), 1999–; Nat. Assoc. for Children of Alcoholics, 2001–; School-Home Support, 2016–. *Publications:* Addicted, 1998; Sober, 2017. *Recreations:* AA, therapy, avoiding people and parties, theatre, singing, ski-ing, bodysurfing, talking about myself, family. *Address:* Sporting Chance Charity Clinic, Crouch House, Forest Mere, Liphook, Hants GU30 7JQ. *E:* office@tonyadams.uk.com. *Club:* House of St Barnabas.

**ADAMS, William David B.;** *see* Butler-Adams.

**ADAMS, Sir (William) James,** KCMG 1991 (CMG 1976); HM Diplomatic Service, retired; *b* 30 April 1932; *s* of late William Adams and late Norah (*née* Walker); *m* 1961, Donatella, *d* of late Andrea Pais-Tarsilia; two *s* one *d. Educ:* Wolverhampton Grammar Sch.; Shrewsbury Sch.; Queen's Coll., Oxford. 2nd Lieut RA, MELF, 1950–51. Foreign Office, 1954; MECAS, 1955; 3rd Sec., Bahrain, 1956; Asst Political Agent, Trucial States, 1957; FO, 1958; 2nd Sec., 1959; Manila, 1960; 1st Sec. and Private Sec. to Minister of State, FO, 1963; 1st Sec. (Information), Paris, 1965–69; FCO, 1969; Counsellor, 1971; Head of European Integration Dept (2), FCO, 1971–72; seconded to Economic Commn for Africa, Addis Ababa, 1972–73; Counsellor (Developing Countries), UK Permanent Representation to EEC, 1973–77; Head of Chancery and Counsellor (Economic), Rome, 1977–80; Asst Under-Sec. of State (Public Depts, then Energy), FCO, 1980–84; Ambassador and Consul-Gen. to Tunisia, 1984–87; Ambassador to Egypt, 1987–92. Consultant, Control Risks Group, 1992–2001. Chm., Egyptian-British Chamber of Commerce, 1992–99. Mem., RC Cttee for Other Faiths, 1995–2002. Chairman: Egyptian Growth Investment Co. Ltd, 1997–2012; Coral Growth Investments Ltd Funds, 2011–18. Order of the Star of Honour (Hon.), Ethiopia, 1965; Order of the Two Niles (Hon.), Sudan, 1965. *Address:* 20 Park Close, Ilchester Place, W14 8ND.

**ADAMS, Prof. William Mark,** PhD; Moran Professor of Conservation and Development, University of Cambridge, since 2006; Fellow, Downing College, Cambridge, since 1984; *b* 4 July 1955; *s* of Jimmie and Margaret Adams; *m* 1983, Dr Francine Hughes; one *s* one *d. Educ:* Downing Coll., Cambridge (BA 1976; PhD 1984); University Coll. London (MSc). Asst Lectr, 1984–89, Lectr, 1989–99, Reader, 1999–2004, and Prof. of Conservation and Develt, 2005–06, Dept of Geog., Univ. of Cambridge. *Publications:* Nature's Place, 1986; Green Development, 1990, 3rd edn 2009; Wasting the Rain, 1992; Future Nature, 1995; (with M. Mortimore) Working the Sahel, 1999; (with M. Mulligan) Decolonising Nature, 2003; Against Extinction, 2004. *Recreations:* poetry, mountains, cycling. *Address:* Downing College, Cambridge CB2 1DQ.

**ADAMS-CAIRNS, (Andrew) Ruaraidh;** Head of Litigation Support, Savills, since 1995; *b* 12 Oct. 1953; *s* of late Alastair Adams-Cairns and Fiona Lauder (*née* Paton of Grandhome); *m* 1983, Susan Ann Foll; two *s. Educ:* Gordonstoun Sch.; Reading Univ. (BSc Est. Man.); RMA Sandhurst. FRICS; MCIArb. Commissioned Queen's Own Highlanders, 1971; Platoon Comdr, Germany, UK, Belize, Gibraltar; Royal Guard, Balmoral (Capt.); Intell. Officer, NI, 1978–79. Joined Savills, 1980; Partner in charge, Salisbury office, 1985–87; Dir, Mixed Develt, 1987–91; Man. Dir, Savills Propriedades, Portugal, 1989–96; Dir, Savills (UK) Ltd (formerly Land and Property), 1987–; Dir and Hd, Residential Valuations, 1998–2004; Hd of Training and Talent Devlt, 2004–11. FRGS. *Publications:* The Somme Battlefield: a pocket guide to places and people with maps, 2014; The Somme Battlefield: the top 20 places to visit, 2015; occasional contribs to Estates Gazette, Family Law and Liability Today. *Recreations:* field sports, carpentry, tennis, Somme Battlefield. *Address:* Savills, 33 Margaret Street, W1G 0JD. *T:* (020) 7499 8644. *Club:* Army and Navy.

**ADAMSON, Clare Anne;** Member (SNP) Motherwell and Wishaw, Scottish Parliament, since 2016 (Scotland Central, 2011–16); *b* Motherwell, 1 Aug. 1967; *d* of George Pickering and Eileen Pickering; *m* 2002, John Adamson; one *s*, and three step *c. Educ:* Glasgow Caledonian Univ. (BSc Computer Information Systems). MBCS. Mem. (SNP), N Lanarkshire Council, 2007–. Parly Liaison Officer to Cabinet Sec. for Culture and External Affairs, Scottish Govt, 2011–16. Vice Chm., Home Safety Cttee, Scottish Accident Prevention Council; Mem., Organising Cttee, Lanarkshire 2011 Internat. Children's Games. *Address:* Scottish Parliament, Edinburgh EH99 1SP. *T:* (0131) 348 6377.

**ADAMSON, Clive Peter;** Director, Supervision, and Executive Director of Board, Financial Conduct Authority, 2013–15; *b* Bath, 17 March 1956; *s* of David Adamson and Cynthia Adamson; *m* 1988, Barbara Elizabeth; two *s* one *d. Educ:* Trinity Hall, Cambridge (BA 1977). Asst Manager, Citibank, London, 1977–81; Sen. Vice Pres., and Hd, UK and N Europe Reg., Bank of America, London, 1981–97; Sen. Advr, 1997–2008, Dir, Supervision (formerly Major Retail Gps) Div., 2008–13, FSA. Non-executive Director: Prudential UK, 2015–; JP Morgan Internat. Bank Ltd, 2015– (Chm., 2016–); Ashmore Gp plc, 2015–; CYBG plc, 2016–. Gov., St Paul's Cathedral Sch., 2005–. *Recreations:* sailing, ski-ing, reading.

**ADAMSON, Hamish Christopher,** OBE 1996; Director (International), The Law Society, 1987–95; *b* 17 Sept. 1935; *s* of John Adamson, Perth, Scotland, and Denise Adamson (*née* Colman-Sadd). *Educ:* Stonyhurst Coll.; Lincoln Coll., Oxford (Schol.; MA Hons Jurisprudence). Solicitor (Hons). Law Society: Asst Sec., then Sen. Asst Sec. (Law Reform), 1966–81; Sec., Law Reform and Internat. Relations, 1981–87. Sec., UK Delegn, Council of the Bars and Law Socs of EC, 1981–95; Exec. Sec., Commonwealth Lawyers' Assoc., 1983–95. Chm., Trustee Cttee, Commonwealth Human Rights Initiative, 1993–95; Mem. Bd Trustees, Acad. of European Law, 1995–2003. Dir, Franco-British Lawyers' Soc., 1991–2009. *Publications:* The Solicitors Act 1974, 1975; Free Movement of Lawyers, 1992, 2nd edn 1998. *Recreations:* plants, books, travel. *Address:* 133 Hartington Road, SW8 2EY.

**ADAMSON, Joanne,** OBE 2014; HM Diplomatic Service; Deputy Special Representative for the United Nations Multidimensional Integrated Stabilization Mission in Mali, since 2018; civil partnership, Elizabeth Eastwood. *Educ:* Girton Coll., Cambridge (BA Modern Langs 1989); Saïd Business Sch., Univ. of Oxford; Harvard Kennedy Sch. of Govt (MPA 2014). Entered FCO, 1989; Asst Desk officer (Nuclear Issues), Security Policy Dept, FCO, 1989–90; Arabic lang. trng, 1990–92; Third, later Second Sec., Jerusalem, 1992–95; Cttee Support Officer, UKMIS to UN, NY, 1995; Desk Officer, ME Dept, FCO, 1996–97; Team Leader, Mgt Consultancy and Inspection Dept, FCO, 1997–99; special unpaid leave working for UN in Gaza, Kosovo and NY, 1999–2002, incl. Pol Affairs Officer to COS, UN Mission, Kosovo, 2001–02; First Sec. (ME), Washington, 2002–07; Dep. Hd, Counter Proliferation Dept, FCO, 2007–09; Dep. Perm. Rep. to Conf. on Disarmament, Geneva, 2009–11; Ambassador for Multilateral Arms Control and Disarmament and UK Perm. Rep. to Conf. on Disarmament, Geneva, 2011–13; Ambassador to Mali and (non-resident) to Niger, 2014–15; Dep. Hd, EU Delegn to UN, 2016–18. *Address:* c/o Foreign and Commonwealth Office, King Charles Street, SW1A 2AH.

**ADAMSON, Martin Gardiner,** CA; Chairman, Associated British Foods, 2002–09 (non-executive Director, 1999–2009); *b* Shanghai, 14 Sept. 1939; *s* of Alan S. Adamson and Janet J. Adamson (*née* Gardiner); *m* 1964, Kathleen Jane Darby; two *s* one *d. Educ:* St Mary's Sch., Melrose; Sedbergh Sch. CA (with Dist.) 1962. Trained with Graham, Smart & Annan, Edinburgh, 1957–62; joined Thomson McLintock & Co., London, 1963: Partner, 1967; Staff Partner, i/c audit practice, 1970–83; Man. Partner, London Office, 1983–86, until merger with Peat Marwick Mitchell to form KPMG, mgt roles with KPMG, 1986–96, including: Partner i/c risk mgt; Mem. Bd. *Recreations:* gardening, golf, reading, theatre. *Clubs:* Caledonian, MCC; Wildernesse Golf (Sevenoaks); Tantallon Golf (N Berwick).

**ADAMSON, Nicolas Clark,** CVO 2008 (LVO 2002); OBE 1982; Private Secretary to the Duke and Duchess of Kent, 1993–2011; an Extra Equerry to the Duke of Kent, since 2011; *s* of Joseph Clark Adamson and Prudence Mary (*née* Paine); *m* 1971, Hilary Jane Edwards; two *d. Educ:* St Edward's Sch., Oxford; RAF Coll., Cranwell. Commnd, 1959, served 1959–69, RAF; transferred to FCO, 1969; served: Brussels (EC), 1972–75; Islamabad, 1979–82; Paris, 1985–90; Counsellor, FCO, 1990–92; retd from FCO, 1993. *Club:* Athenæum.

**ADCOCK, Christopher John,** LVO 2016; Chief Financial Officer, since 2003, and Member of Council, since 2007, Duchy of Lancaster; *b* Berlin, 7 Aug. 1962; *s* of late Col Alfred John Adcock, OBE and Eileen Joan Adcock (*née* Linton); *m* 1990, Joanna Sarah Mackinder; one *s* one *d. Educ:* Wellington Coll., Berks; Exeter Coll., Oxford (BA 1984; MA). ACA 1988, FCA 2015. With Ernst & Whinney, 1984–89. *Recreations:* golf, running, tennis, ski-ing. *Address:* Duchy of Lancaster Office, 1 Lancaster Place, WC2E 7ED. *T:* (020) 7269 1700. *Club:* East Berkshire Golf.

**ADCOCK, Fleur,** CNZM 2008; OBE 1996; FRSL; poet; *b* 10 Feb. 1934; *d* of Cyril John Adcock and Irene Adcock (*née* Robinson); *m* 1952, Alistair Teariki Campbell (marr. diss. 1958); two *s. Educ:* numerous schs in England and NZ; Victoria Univ., Wellington, NZ (MA 1st cl. Hons (Classics) 1956). Worked in libraries, NZ, 1959–62; settled in England, 1963; asst librarian, FCO, 1963–79. Arts Council Writing Fellow, Charlotte Mason Coll. of Educn, Ambleside, 1977–78; Northern Arts Fellow in Lit., Univs of Newcastle upon Tyne and Durham, 1979–81; Eastern Arts Fellow, UEA, 1984. FRSL 1984. Awards include: Cholmondeley, Soc. of Authors, 1976; NZ Nat. Book Award, 1984; Queen's Gold Medal for Poetry, 2006. *Publications:* The Eye of the Hurricane, 1964; Tigers, 1967; High Tide in the Garden, 1971; The Scenic Route, 1974; The Inner Harbour, 1979; (ed) The Oxford Book of Contemporary NZ Poetry, 1982; Selected Poems, 1983; (trans.) The Virgin and the Nightingale: medieval Latin poems, 1983; The Incident Book, 1986; (ed) The Faber Book of 20th Century Women's Poetry, 1987; (trans.) Orient Express: poems by Grete Tartler, 1989; Time Zones, 1991; (trans.) Letters from Darkness: poems by Daniela Crasnaru, 1991; (ed and trans.) Hugh Primas and the Archpoet, 1994; (ed jtly) The Oxford Book of Creatures, 1995; Looking Back, 1997; Poems 1960–2000, 2000; Dragon Talk, 2010; Glass Wings, 2013; The Land Ballot, 2015; Hoard, 2017. *Recreation:* genealogy. *Address:* 14 Lincoln Road, N2 9DL. *T:* (020) 8444 7881.

**ADDERLEY,** family name of **Baron Norton**.

**ADDERLEY, Mark David;** Director, Adderley Ltd, since 2018; President, Scottish Squash (formerly Scottish Squash and Racketball) Ltd, since 2018 (Director, since 2013); *b* 15 Jan. 1965; *s* of David Adderley and Gill Adderley (now Boden); *m* 1989, Miranda Jones; four *d*. *Educ:* King Edward's Sch., Birmingham; Emmanuel Coll., Cambridge (BA 1987; MEng 1988); London Business Sch. (MBA 1999). Analyst, then Sen. Analyst, Associate, then Sen. Associate, Gemini Consulting, 1988–94; Head of Ops, then Sen. Manager Group Integration, Royal Bank of Scotland, 1994–2002; Dir, Scottish Water, 2002–07; Chief Exec., Nat. Trust for Scotland, 2007–08; Dir, Adderley Associates Ltd, 2008–11; Exec. Dir, People and Orgnl Develt, NHS Ayrshire and Arran, 2009–11; Dir, Human Resource Devlt, Heriot-Watt Univ., 2011–18. Director: Quality Scotland, 2003–07; Scottish Bible Soc., 2012–18; Social Investment Scotland, 2013–19. FCIPD 2011; CDir 2011; FInstD 2012. *Recreations:* family, outdoor activity, sport, keeping track of five girls. *Address:* 18 Murrayfield Gardens, Edinburgh EH12 6DF.

**ADDINGTON,** family name of **Viscount Sidmouth.**

**ADDINGTON, 6th Baron** *cr* 1887; **Dominic Bryce Hubbard;** *b* 24 Aug. 1963; *s* of 5th Baron Addington and of Alexandra Patricia, *yr d* of late Norman Ford Millar; *S* father, 1982; *m* 1999, (Elizabeth) Ann Morris; one *d*. *Educ:* Aberdeen Univ. (MA Hons). Lib Dem spokesman on disability and on sport, H of L; elected Mem., H of L, 1999. Pres., British Dyslexia Assoc.; Vice President: Adult Dyslexia Orgn; UK Sport Assoc. for People with Learning Disability; Lonsdale Sporting Club; Lakenham Hewett RFC. *Recreation:* Rugby football. *Heir: b* Hon. Michael Walter Leslie Hubbard [*b* 6 July 1965; *m* 1999, Emmanuella Ononye]. *Address:* House of Lords, SW1A 0PW.

**ADDIS, Richard James;** Founder, Chairman and Editor-in-Chief, The Day, since 2010; *b* 23 Aug. 1956; *s* of late Richard Thomas Addis and Jane Addis; *m* 1983, Eunice Minogue (marr. diss. 2000); one *s* two *d*; partner, Helen Slater; two *s*. *Educ:* West Downs Prep. Sch.; Rugby; Downing Coll., Cambridge (MA). Evening Standard, 1985–89; Dep. Editor, Sunday Telegraph, 1989–91; Exec. Editor, Daily Mail, 1991–95; Editor, The Express, 1995–98; Consultant Editor, Mail on Sunday, 1998–99; Editor, The Globe and Mail, Toronto, 1999–2002; Asst Editor, Financial Times, 2002–06; Founder and Man. Partner, Shakeup Media, 2006–10; Ed.-in-Chief, Newsweek (Europe), 2014–15. *Recreations:* tennis, climbing, herb-surfing, dendron-leaping, portacenare. *Clubs:* Boodle's, Garrick, Academy, 5 Hertford Street.

**ADDISON,** family name of **Viscount Addison.**

**ADDISON, 4th Viscount** *cr* 1945, of Stallingborough; **William Matthew Wand Addison;** Baron Addison 1937; consultant, environmental impact assessment, 2002–10; *b* 13 June 1945; *s* of 3rd Viscount Addison and Kathleen Amy, *d* of Rt Rev. and Rt Hon. J. W. C. Wand, PC, KCVO; *S* father, 1992; *m* 1st, 1970, Joanna Mary (marr. diss. 1990), *e d* of late J. I. C. Dickinson; one *s* two *d*; 2nd, 1991, Lesley Ann, *d* of George Colin Mawer. *Educ:* Westminster; King's Sch., Bruton; Essex Inst. of Agriculture. Chm., DCL Telecommunications, 1997–99; Dir, Commensus, 1999–2002. Mem., Cttee on Jt Statutory Instruments, 1993–99. Vice President: Council for Nat. Parks, 1994–; British Trust for Conservation Volunteers, 1996–2006. Pres., Motor Activities Trng Council, 1996–2009. *Heir: s* Hon. Paul Wand Addison, *b* 18 March 1973.

**ADDISON, Lynda Helen,** OBE 2007; freelance consultant, 2011–18; Director, Malcolm Baker Consulting Ltd, since 2014; Managing Director, Addison & Associates, 1996–2011; *b* Manchester, 2 Dec. 1945; *d* of Cyril Shepley and Kathleen Shepley; *m* 1st, 1973, Alan Addison (marr. diss. 1999); one *s* one *d*; 2nd, 2014, Malcolm Baker. *Educ:* Gainsborough High Sch. for Girls; Portsmouth Poly. (BSc Geog. 1967); Central London Poly. (DipTP 1972). Asst Bor. Planner, Southwark LBC, 1978–83; Controller, Planning, Harrow LBC, 1983–87; Dir, Planning, 1987–91, Dir, Planning and Transport, 1991–95, Hounslow LBC. Historic England (formerly English Heritage): Comr, 2008–16; Chm., London Adv. Cttee, 2011–16. Director: Paddington Business Improvement District, 2005–13; Garden Cities Develt CIC, 2014–. Mem., Planning Cttee, London Legacy Develt Corp., 2012–16. Trustee: TCPA, 2004–13; Living Streets, 2009–15; Chair, Trustees, Raheli Trust, 2008–; Mem. Council, Nat. Infrastructure Planning Assoc., 2011–15; Chm., Sustainable Transport Panel, Chartered Instn of Highways and Transportation, 2012–; Mem., Transport Planning Soc., 2017– (Chair, 2017–19). Built Envmt Expert, Design Council Cabe, 2016–. Vis. Prof., Univ. of Westminster, 2008–16. Academician, Acad. of Urbanism, 2009–16. FRSA 1992; FCIHT 2012. *Publications:* (contrib.) The Routledge Handbook of Planning for Health and Well-Being, 2015; best practice guidance and research reports for DfT and DCLG; various articles in professional jls. *Recreations:* family, theatre, opera, walking, skiing, sailing, three grandchildren - two boys and one girl. *E:* lynda@lynda-addison.co.uk. *T:* 07956 173267.

**ADDISON, Mark Eric,** CB 2005; Director General, Department for Environment, Food and Rural Affairs, 2001–06; *b* 22 Jan. 1951; *s* of Sydney Robert James Addison and Prudence Margaret Addison (*née* Russell); *m* 1987, Lucinda Clare Booth. *Educ:* Marlborough Coll.; St John's Coll., Cambridge (BA, MA); City Univ. (MBA); Imperial Coll. (DIC, PhD). Department of Employment, 1978–95: Private Sec. to Parly Under-Sec. of State, 1982; Private Sec. to Prime Minister (Home Affairs, then Parly Affairs), 1985–88; Regl Dir for London, Training Agency, 1988–91; Dir, Finance and Resource Management, 1991–94; DoE, 1995–97: Dir, Safety Policy, HSE, 1994–97; Dir, Better Regulation Unit, OPS, 1997–98; Chief Exec., Crown Prosecution Service, 1998–2001. A Civil Service Comr, 2007–12; Public Appts Assessor, 2012–17. Member: Adv. Cttee on Business Appts, 2012–17; State Honours Cttee, 2017– (Chair, 2017–). Chairman: Nursing and Midwifery Council, 2012–14; Dorset Co. Hosp. NHS Foundn Trust, 2016–. Non-executive Director: Salix Finance Ltd, 2006–11; National Archives, 2007–12. Mem., Council, Which?, 2010–16. Vice Chair, Charity for Civil Servants, 2016–. *Recreations:* classic motorbikes, the Dorset garden and the meadow. *E:* mark@addisonbooth.com.

**ADDISON, His Honour Michael Francis;** a Circuit Judge, 1987–2014; *b* 14 Sept. 1942; *s* of late Joseph Addison and Wendy Blyth Addison; *m* 1979, Rosemary Hardy (*d* 1994); one *s*; *m* 1998, Lucy Carter; one *s* one *d*. *Educ:* Eton; Trinity College, Cambridge (BA). Called to the Bar, Inner Temple, 1965. *Recreation:* gardening.

**ADDYMAN, Peter Vincent,** CBE 2000; FSA; Director, York Archaeological Trust, 1972–2002; *b* 12 July 1939; *y s* of Erik Thomas Waterhouse Addyman and Evelyn Mary (*née* Fisher); *m* 1965, Shelton (*née* Oliver), Atlanta, Ga (*d* 2016); one *s* one *d*. *Educ:* Sedbergh Sch.; Peterhouse, Cambridge (MA). MCIfA (MIFA 1982); FSA 1967. Asst Lectr in Archaeology, 1962–64, Lectr, 1964–67, QUB; Lectr in Archaeol., Univ. of Southampton, 1967–72. Hon. Fellow, Univ. of York, 1972; Hon. Reader, Univ. of Bradford, 1974–81. Directed excavations: Maxey, 1960; Lydford, 1964–67; Ludgershall Castle, 1964–72; Chalton, 1970–72. Vice-President: Council for British Archaeol., 1981–85 (Pres., 1992–95); Royal Archaeol. Inst., 1979–83; Chairman: Standing Conf. of Archaeol Unit Managers, 1975–78; Inst. of Field Archaeologists, 1983–85; Standing Conf. on Portable Antiquities, 1995–2005; Standing Conf. on London Archaeology, 2005–07; Yorks Dales Landscape Res. Trust, 2006–16; Malton Museum Foundn, 2012–; York Civic Trust, 2012–15 (Pres., 2015–); Member: RCHME, 1997–99; Ancient Monuments Adv. Cttee, 1998–2001, Places of Worship Panel, 2001–04, English Heritage. Chm., Cultural Resource Management Ltd, 1989–95 (Dir, 1979–95); Academic Director, Heritage Projects Ltd, 1984–2007; Dir, Continuum Gp Ltd, 2007–; Jt Instigator, Jorvik Viking Centre, York. President: Yorks Archaeol Soc., 1999–2005; Yorks Philosophical Soc., 1999–2013; York Consortium for Conservation and Craftsmanship, 2002–16 (Medal, 2016). Trustee, Nat. Coal Mining Mus., 1995–2002. Gov., Co. of Merchant Adventurers of York, 2006–07. Hon. Freeman, City of York, 2008. Honorary Professor: Univ. of Bradford, 1998; Univ. of York, 1998. Hon. DSc Bradford, 1984; DUniv York, 1985. President's Medal, British Acad., 2015. Comdr, Royal Norwegian Order of Merit, 2004. *Publications:* (gen. editor) The Archaeology of York, vols 1–20, 1976–2002; (ed with V. E. Black) Archaeological Papers from York, 1984; (ed) British Historic Towns Atlas, vol. V, York, 2015; papers in archaeol jls. *Recreations:* gardening, watercolours, travel. *Address:* 15 St Mary's, York YO30 7DD. *T:* (01904) 624311. *Club:* Athenæum.

**ADEAGBO, Dr Ade;** Chief Operations Officer, Halogen Security, since 2017; *b* Nigeria, 9 Nov. 1960; *s* of Joseph and Christiana Adeagbo; *m* 1992, Ibironke Bawala; one *s* three *d*. *Educ:* Ogun State Univ., Nigeria (BA Philosophy); Thames Valley Univ. (MBA 1998); Bournemouth Univ. (DBA 2008). Admin Manager, London Bor. of Southwark, 1992–96; Retail Manager, Shell UK, 1996–2001; Res., Systems and Admin Manager, Help the Aged, 2001–03; Chief Exec., Age Concern Bexley, 2003–07; Ops Dir, Mission Care, 2007–08; Dir, Organisational Develt, and Interim CEO, National Voices, 2008–09; Interim CEO, African Health Policy Network, 2009–11; Interim Dir, African Diaspora Youth Network in Europe, 2011–12. Chm., Non-exec. Dirs Network, 2009–, Treas., 2010–, NHS Alliance; Chair, Community Alliance, 2009–11. Non-exec. Dir and Chm., Audit Cttee, NHS Greenwich, 2001–11. Dir, Nest Exchange, 2010–. Chm., EU Community Health Orgns, Netherlands, 2010–. Fellow and Mem., Coll. of Medicine, 2010–. *Address:* 28 Birkdale Road, Abbey Wood, SE2 9HX. *T:* (020) 8311 2207. *E:* dr.adeagbo@gmail.com.

**ADEBAYO, Oludiran Oludele Abimbola, (Diran),** FRSL; writer, novelist, academic; *b* London, 30 Aug. 1968; *s* of Dr Solomon Layi Adebayo and Phebean Olufunke Adebayo (*née* Agbe). *Educ:* Malvern Coll., Worcs (Major Schol.); Wadham Coll., Oxford (BA Hons Law 1989; MA). Reporter, then Chief News Reporter, The Voice, 1989–91; Reporter/Researcher, BBC TV, 1991–93; Sen. Researcher, LWT, 1994–95; Lectr (pt-time) in English and Creative Writing, Lancaster Univ., 2009–12; Lectr, Kingston Univ., London, 2015–. Fellow, Santa Maddalena Foundn, 2002; Internat. Writing Fellow, Southampton Univ., 2006–07; Royal Literary Fund Fellow, London Coll. of Fashion, 2012–14. Dir, Book Trust, 2000–04; Trustee, Nat. Council, Arts Council of England, 2004–10. FRSL 2006. *Publications:* Some Kind of Black, 1996; My Once Upon A Time, 2000; (ed jtly) New Writing, 2003. *Recreations:* music, sports, cricket history, general knowledge.

**ADEBOWALE, Baron** *cr* 2001 (Life Peer), of Thornes in the County of West Yorkshire; **Victor Olufemi Adebowale,** CBE 2000; Chief Executive Officer, Turning Point, since 2001; Chairman, Social Enterprise UK, since 2017; *b* 21 July 1962; *s* of Ezekiel Adebowale and Grace Adebowale. *Educ:* Thornes House Sch., Wakefield; Poly. of E London; City Univ. (MA Adv. Organisational Consulting 2008); Tavistock Inst., London (Dip. Adv. Organisational Consulting 2008). London Borough of Newham: Private Sector Repairs Administrator and Estate Officer, 1983–84; Sen. Estate Manager, 1984–86; Perm. Property Manager, Patchwork Community Housing Assoc., 1986–88; Regl Dir, Ujima Housing Assoc., 1988–90; Dir, Alcohol Recovery Project, 1990–95; Chief Exec., Centrepoint, 1995–2001. Dir, Leadership in Mind Ltd, 2006–; non-executive Director: Three Sixty Action Ltd, 2011–; NHS England, 2012–18. Mem. Bd, THP Innovate, 2012–. Member: Nat. Council, NFHA, 1991; Adv. Gp, New Deal Task Force, 1997–; Nat. Employment Panel, 2000–; Mental Health Task Force; UK Commn for Employment and Skills, 2009–; Adv. Council on Misuse of Drugs; Locality; NHS Commng Bd. Mem. Council, Inst. for Fiscal Studies. Chair, Collaborate CIC, London South Bank Univ., 2012–; Member, Board: English Touring Theatre; Urban Development. Director: Leadership in Mind, 2005–; 360; THP. Fellow, Sunningdale Inst. Mem. Bd Trustees, New Economics Foundn, 2006–07. Patron, British Nursing Council on Alcohol. Chancellor, Lincoln Univ., 2008– (Hon. Vis. Prof., 2007–). DUniv UCE, 2001; Hon. Dr: UEL; Birmingham. *Recreations:* poetry writing, kite flying, music, playing the saxophone. *Address:* Turning Point, Standon House, 21 Mansell Street, E1 8AA. *T:* (020) 7481 7600.
*See also M. Adebowale-Schwarte.*

**ADEBOWALE-SCHWARTE, Maria;** Executive Director, Foundation for Future London, since 2019; Founding Director, Living Space Project, since 2013; *d* of Ezekiel Adebowale and Grace Olurin Adebowale; *m* 2002, Christoph Schwarte; one *s* one *d*. *Educ:* Lancaster Univ. (BA Hons Orgn Studies and Business Law); Huddersfield Poly. (Postgrad. Dip. Law); SOAS, London Univ. (LLM Public Internat. Law); Univ. of East London (Postgrad. Dip. Architecture, Design and Sustainability). Prog. Asst, Climate Change and Trade, Foundn for Internat. Envmtl Law and Develt, 1994–98; Public Law Tutor, SOAS, 1996–97; Director: Envmtl Law Foundn, 1998–2001; Capacity Global, 2001–13. Cities and urban placemaking strategist, 2009–. Non-exec. Dir, Shared Assets, 2012–16. Mem., UK Sustainable Develt Commn, 2000–03 (Chair, World Summit for Sustainable Develt Wkg Gp, 2002); Comr, English Heritage, 2003–11; London Leader, 2011–, Mem., 2008–, London Sustainable Develt Commn; Mem. Bd, Envmt Agency, 2016–. Chair, SE Cttee, 2016–18, Mem. Bd, 2018–, Heritage Lottery Fund. Mem., Adv. Gp, Artist Project Earth, 2011–. Chair, Waterwise, 2005–09. Trustee: Allavida, 2006–09; Conservation Volunteers, 2013–; Matron, Women's Envmtl Network, 2006–; Patron, UK Envmtl Law Assoc., 2011–. Clore Social Leadership Fellow (Envmt), 2013–16. FRSA 2001. *Publications:* The Place Making Factor, 2017; contribs to acad. and non-acad. pubns on urban place making and green spaces, collaborative and inclusive urban renewal. *Recreations:* arguing about politics with my husband, collecting and reading knackered old Penguin paperback books, spending time with my son and daughter. *Address:* Living Space Project, 60 Farringdon Road, Free Word Centre, EC1R 3GA. *E:* hello@livingspaceproject.com.
*See also Baron Adebowale.*

**ADEKUNLE, Ven. Elizabeth;** Archdeacon of Hackney, since 2016; a Chaplain to the Queen, since 2017; Priest-in-charge, St Leonard's, Shoreditch, since 2019; *b* N London. *Educ:* Birmingham Univ. (BTh); Sch. of Oriental and African Studies, Univ. of London (MA African Christianity and Develt); Ridley Hall, Cambridge (MA Pastoral Care and Counselling). Curate, later Priest-in-charge, St Luke's Church, Homerton, 2007–11; Chaplain, St John's Coll., Cambridge, until 2016. Chaplain: St Mellitus Theol Coll. London; Homerton Hosp., Hackney. Mem., Archbishops' Task Gp on Evangelism.

**ADER, Peter Charles; His Honour Judge Ader;** a Circuit Judge, since 1999; *b* 14 May 1950; *s* of late Max Ader and Inge Ader (*née* Nord); *m* 1979, Margaret Taylor (marr. diss 2005); one *s* two *d*. *Educ:* Highgate Sch.; Southampton Univ. (LLB). Called to the Bar, Middle Temple, 1973; a Recorder, 1995–99. *Recreations:* squash, tennis, golf, ski-ing, travel *Address:* 3 Temple Gardens, Temple, EC4Y 9AU. *T:* (020) 7353 3102.

**ADERIN-POCOCK, Dr Margaret Ebunoluwa,** MBE 2009; Managing Director Science Innovation Ltd, since 2004; *b* London, 9 March 1968; *d* of Justus Adebayo Aderin and Caroline Philips; *m* 2002, Dr Martin Pocock; one *d*. *Educ:* La Sainte Union Conven Sch.; Imperial Coll. London (BSc Phys; PhD Mech. Engrg 1994). System Scientist

1996–97, Project Manager, 1997–99, DERA; Project and Engrg Manager, UCL, 1999–2004; Sen. Project Manager, Surrey Satellite Technol. Ltd, 2004–06; Sen. Res. Fellow, UCL, 2006–; Optical Instrumentation Manager UK, Astrium Ltd, 2006–10. Television and radio presenter, incl. BBC TV: Do We Really Need the Moon?, 2011; In Orbit: How Satellites Rule Our Lives, 2012; CBeebies Stargazing, 2014; The Sky at Night (series), 2014–. Trustee, IPPR, 2015–18. FInstP; FRAS. Fellow, Assoc. of Project Managers. Hon. Fellow, BAAS, 2010. Hon. DSc: Staffordshire, 2009; Bath, 2014; Open, 2015; Brunel, 2017; Leicester, 2018; London, 2018. *Publications:* The Knowledge: stargazing, 2015; The Sky at Night Book of the Moon: a guide to our nearest neighbour, 2018. *Recreations:* star gazing, travel, cinema, cooking, art, photography. *E:* m.aderin@science-innovation.com.

**ADÈS, Prof. (Josephine) Dawn,** CBE 2013 (OBE 2002); FBA 1996; Professor of Art History and Theory, University of Essex, 1989–2014, now Emeritus; *b* 6 May 1943; *d* of A. E. Tylden-Pattenson, CSI; *m* 1966, Timothy Raymond Adès; three *s*. *Educ:* St Hilda's Coll., Oxford (BA 1965); MA London 1968. Essex University: Lectr, 1971–85; Sen. Lectr, 1985–88; Reader, 1988–89; Head of Dept of Art History and Theory, 1989–92. Prof. of History of Art, Royal Acad., 2009–; Slade Prof. of the History of Art, Oxford Univ., 2010. Trustee: Tate Gall., 1995–2005; Nat. Gall., 1998–2005; Elephant Trust, 2000–; Henry Moore Foundn, 2003–13. *Publications:* Dada and Surrealism Reviewed, 1978; Salvador Dali, 1982, 2nd edn 1995; (jtly) The Twentieth Century Poster: design of the avant garde, 1984; (jtly) Francis Bacon, 1985; Photomontage, 1986; Art in Latin America: the modern era 1820–1980, 1989; Andre Masson, 1994; Figures and Likenesses: the paintings of Siron Franco, 1995; Surrealist Art: the Bergman Collection in the Art Institute of Chicago, 1997; (jtly) Marcel Duchamp, 1999; Salvador Dali's Optical Illusions, 2000; Dali: centenary retrospective, 2004; (jtly) Undercover Surrealism: Georges Bataille and Documents, 2006; (jtly) Close-Up, 2008; The Colour of My Dreams: the Surrealist revolution in art, 2011; Selected Writings, 2015. *Address:* School of Philosophy and Art History, University of Essex, Wivenhoe Park, Colchester, Essex CO4 3SQ.

See also T. J. E. Adès.

**ADÈS, Thomas Joseph Edmund,** CBE 2018; composer, pianist and conductor; *b* 1 March 1971; *s* of Timothy Adès and Prof. Dawn Adès, *qv*. *Educ:* University Coll. Sch.; Guildhall Sch. of Music and Drama; King's Coll., Cambridge (MA); St John's Coll., Cambridge (MPhil; Hon. Fellow, 2013). Composer in Association, Hallé Orch., 1993–95; Lectr, Univ. of Manchester, 1993–94; Fellow Commoner in Creative Arts, Trinity Coll., Cambridge, 1995–97; Benjamin Britten Prof. of Music, RAM, 1997–2000; Musical Dir, Birmingham Contemporary Music Gp, 1998–2000; Artistic Dir, Aldeburgh Fest., 1999–2008; Artistic Partner, Boston SO, 2016–. *Principal compositions:* Five Eliot Landscapes, 1990; Chamber Symphony, 1990; Catch, 1991; Darknesse Visible, 1992; Still Sorrowing, 1993; Life Story, 1993; Living Toys, 1993; … but all shall be well, 1993; Sonata da Caccia, 1993; Arcadiana (for string quartet), 1994; Powder Her Face (Chamber opera), 1995; Traced Overhead, 1996; These Premises are Alarmed, 1996; Asyla, 1997 (Grawemeyer Award for Music Composition, 2000); Concerto Conciso, 1997–98; America (A Prophecy), 1999; Piano Quintet, 2000; Brahms, 2001; The Tempest (opera), 2003; Violin Concerto, 2005; Tevót, 2007; Dances from Powder Her Face, 2007; In Seven Days, 2008; Concert Paraphrase on Powder Her Face, 2009; Lieux retrouvés, 2009; Three Mazurkas, 2010; Polaris, 2010; The Four Quarters, 2010; Totentanz, 2013; The Exterminating Angel, 2016; Concerto for Piano and Orchestra, 2019. Works performed at numerous festivals incl. Musica Nova, Helsinki, 1999; Salzburg Easter Fest., 2004; Présences, Radio France, 2007; Traced Overhead, Barbican, 2007; New Horizons Fest., St Petersburg, 2007; Tonsattarfestival, Stockholm, 2009; Composer in Focus, Melbourne, 2010; Aspects of Adès, LA, 2011; Portrait at Gulbenkian, Lisbon, 2012; See the Music, Hear the Dance, Sadler's Wells Ballet, 2014; Léonie Sonning Music Prizegiving, Copenhagen, 2015. Leoš Janáček Foundn award, 2018. *Address:* c/o Faber Music, Bloomsbury House, 74–77 Great Russell Street, WC1B 3DA. *T:* (020) 7908 5310, *Fax:* (020) 7908 5339. *Club:* Black's.

**ADEY, John Fuller;** company director; Chief Executive, National Blood Authority, 1993–98; *b* 12 May 1941; *s* of Frank Douglas Adey and Doreen Adey (*née* Fuller); *m* 1965, Marianne Alyce Banning; two *s* two *d*. *Educ:* Glyn GS, Epsom; St Edmund Hall, Oxford (MA); Harvard Univ. (MBA). CEng 1970; MIMechE 1970; MIEE 1976. Graduate Trainee, AEI Ltd, 1963–65; Design Engineer: Montreal Engrg, 1965–67; Nat. Steel & Shipbuilding, San Diego, 1967–70; various positions, Raychem Ltd, 1972–83; Chief Exec., Chemicals and Plastics, Courtaulds, 1983–86; Man. Dir, Baxter Healthcare, 1986–93. Director: API, 1987–97; Seton Healthcare Gp, 1996–98; non-executive Chairman: Adams Healthcare, 1999–2000; Medical Engineering Investments, 2003–05; non-executive Director: Swindon and Marlborough NHS Trust, 2002–06; New Horizons Ltd, 2005–08. Chm., Aldbourne Nursing Home, 2000–. A Gen. Comr of Income Tax, 1985–2009. Trustee, Royal Merchant Navy Sch. Foundn, 1999–2019 (Chm., 2002); Gov., John O'Gaunt Sch., Hungerford, 2000 (Chm. Govs, 2001–12). Treas., St Michael's Ch, Aldbourne, 2006–14. *Recreations:* tennis, tinkering with old cars, village life. *Address:* The Old Malt House, Aldbourne, Marlborough, Wilts SN8 2DW.

**ADHANOM GHEBREYESUS, Dr Tedros;** Director-General, World Health Organisation, since 2017; *b* Asmara, Eritrea, 1965; *s* of Adhanom Ghebreyesus and Letenkiel Weldegiorgis; *m* 1991, Kidist Meresa Kebede; five *c*. *Educ:* Asmara Univ., Ethiopia (BSc Biol. 1986); Univ. of London (MSc Immunol. of Infectious Diseases 1992); Univ. of Nottingham (PhD Community Health 2000). Minister of Health, 2005–12, of Foreign Affairs, 2012–16, Ethiopia. Hon. Fellow, LSHTM, 2012. Order of Serbian Flag (Serbia), 2016. *Publications:* (jtly) Innovative Health Partnerships: the diplomacy of diversity, 2011; (jtly) The Labor Market for Health Workers in Africa: a new look at the crisis, 2013; contribs to learned scientific jls incl. BMJ, Acta Tropica, Lancet, Jl Global Health, Nature, Prehospital and Disaster Medicine. *Recreations:* reading, travelling. *Address:* World Health Organisation, 20 Avenue Appia, 1211 Geneva 27, Switzerland.

**ADIE, Kathryn, (Kate),** CBE 2018 (OBE 1993); DL; author and freelance broadcaster; Presenter, From Our Own Correspondent, BBC Radio 4, since 1998; *b* 19 Sept. 1945; *d* of late Babe Dunnet (*née* Issitt), and adopted *d* of late John Wilfrid Adie and Maud Adie (*née* Fambely). *Educ:* Sunderland Church High Sch.; Newcastle Univ. (BA Hons Scandinavian Studies). FJI 1990. Technician and Producer, BBC Radio Bristol, 1969–76; Reporter, BBC TV South, 1977–78; Reporter, TV News, 1979–81, Correspondent, 1982; Chief News Correspondent, BBC TV, 1989–2003. Trustee: Imperial War Mus., 1998–2007; Services Sound and Vision Corp., 2004–11. Mem., First World War Centenary Adv. Gp, 2014–. Hon. Prof., Broadcasting and Journalism, Univ. of Sunderland, 1995. Chancellor, Bournemouth Univ., 2019–. Freeman, City of London, 1995; Liveryman, Glaziers' Co., 1996. DL Dorset, 2013. Hon. Freeman, Borough of Sunderland, 1989. Hon. Fellow: Royal Holloway, London Univ., 1996; Univ. of Central Lancs 2002; Cardiff Univ., 2004; York St John UC, 2006. Hon. MA: Bath, 1987; Newcastle upon Tyne, 1990; MUniv Open, 1996; Hon. DLitt: City, 1989; Loughborough, 1991; Sunderland, 1993; Robert Gordon, 1996; Nottingham, 1998; Nottingham Trent, 1998; Plymouth, 2013; Queen Margaret, 2014; DUniv: Anglia Polytechnic Univ., 1999; Oxford Brookes, 2002; Hon. DLaws: St Andrews, 2010; Bristol, 2012. RTS News Award, 1981 and 1987, Judges' Award, 1989; Monte Carlo Internat. TV News Award, 1981 and 1990; BAFTA Richard Dimbleby Award, 1989; BAFTA Fellowship, 2018. *Publications:* The Kindness of Strangers (memoirs), 2002; Corsets to Camouflage: women and war, 2003; Nobody's Child: the lives of abandoned children, 2005; Into Danger, 2008; Fighting on the Home Front: the legacy of women in World War One, 2013. *Address:* c/o Louise Greenberg Books Ltd, End House, Church Crescent, N3 1BG. *E:* louisegreenberg@btinternet.com. *W:* www.kateadie.co.uk.

**ADIE, Rt Rev. Michael Edgar,** CBE 1994; Bishop of Guildford, 1983–94; *b* 22 Nov. 1929; *s* of Walter Granville Adie and Kate Emily Adie (*née* Parrish); *m* 1957, Anne Devonald Roynon; one *s* three *d*. *Educ:* Westminster School; St John's Coll., Oxford (MA). Assistant Curate, St Luke, Pallion, Sunderland, 1954–57; Resident Chaplain to the Archbishop of Canterbury, 1957–60; Vicar of St Mark, Sheffield, 1960–69; Rural Dean of Hallam, 1966–69; Rector of Louth, 1969–76; Vicar of Morton with Hacconby, 1976–83; Archdeacon of Lincoln, 1977–83. Chm., Gen. Synod Bd of Education and of National Soc., 1989–94. DUniv Surrey, 1995. *Publications:* Held Together: an exploration of coherence, 1997. *Recreations:* gardening, walking. *Address:* 4 Lochnager Way, Ballater, Aberdeenshire AB35 5PB.

**ADIE, Susan Myraid;** see Sinclair, S. M.

**ADJAYE, Sir David (Frank),** Kt 2017; OBE 2007; RA 2017; Founder and Principal Architect, Adjaye Associates, since 2000; *b* 22 Sept. 1966; *s* of Affram Adjaye and Cecilia Affram-Adjaye. *Educ:* South Bank Univ. (BA Hons Arch. 1990; RIBA Pt 1); Royal Coll. of Art, London (MA Arch. 1993; Sen. Fellow 2007). RIBA 1998. *Building projects* include: Nobel Peace Center, Oslo, 2005; Idea Store Whitechapel, London, 2005 (Inclusive Design Award, RIBA, 2006); Bernie Grant Centre, Stephen Lawrence Centre and Rivington Place, London, 2007 (London Award, RIBA, 2008); Mus. of Contemporary Art, Denver, 2007 (Internat. Award, RIBA, 2008); Moscow Sch. of Mgt, Skolkovo, 2010; Nat. Mus. of African American History and Culture, Washington DC, 2016 (Beazley Design of the Year, 2018). Advr, Thames Gateway Design Panel, 2004. Mem. Bd, Greenwich Dance Agency, 2004–; Trustee: Architectl Educn Trust; South London Gall., 2003–; V&A Mus., 2008–10. Hon. Dr Arts UEL, 2007. W. E. B. Du Bois Medal, Harvard Univ., 2014. *Publications:* (ed Peter Allison) David Adjaye Houses: recycling, reconfiguring, rebuilding, 2005; (ed Peter Allison) David Adjaye: making public buildings, 2006; contribs to jls incl. Frame, Domus, RIBA Jl, Architects Jl, Archithese, Architectural Record, A+U, El Croquis. *Address:* Adjaye Associates, The Edison, 223–231 Old Marylebone Road, NW1 5QT. *E:* info@adjaye.com. *Club:* Shoreditch House.

**ADKIN, Jonathan William;** QC 2013; *b* Leicester, 2 March 1973; *s* of David and Prudence Adkin; *m* 2010, Ruth. *Educ:* Loughborough Grammar Sch.; Balliol Coll., Oxford (MA). Called to the Bar, Gray's Inn, 1997; in practice as barrister, 1997–. *Recreations:* riding, walking. *Address:* Serle Court, 6 New Square, Lincoln's Inn, WC2A 3QS. *T:* (020) 7242 6105.

**ADKIN, Tana Marie Therese, (Mrs Barry Danielson);** QC 2017; *b* Beckenham, Kent, 9 Dec. 1968; *d* of John and Pauline Adkin; *m* 1993, Barry Danielson; three *s* two *d*. *Educ:* Coloma Convent Girls' Sch., Shirley; Leicester Univ. (BA Hons Hist. 1990); City Univ. (DipLaw 1991); Inns of Court Sch. of Law. Dip. Forensic Med. Scis 2014. Called to the Bar, Inner Temple, 1992; in practice as barrister, specialising in criminal law, 1992–. Mem., Retention Panel, Bar Council, 2015–. Mem., Exec. Cttee, Criminal Bar Assoc., 2018–. Gov., Coloma Convent Girls' Sch., 2009–. *Recreations:* scouting (Asst Dist Comr, Croydon Beaver Scouts), music, sport. *Address:* Charter Chambers, 33 John Street, WC1N 2AT. *T:* (020) 7618 4400. *E:* tana.adkin@charterchambers.com. *Clubs:* Warlingham Rugby Football; Croydon Amphibians Swimming and Water Polo.

**ADLER, Prof. Jeremy David,** PhD; Professor of German, 1994–2003, Visiting Professor, 2003–05, Emeritus Professor and Senior Research Fellow, Department of German, since 2005, King's College London; *b* 1 Oct. 1947; *s* of H. G. and Bettina Adler; *m* 1983, Eva Mikulašová. *Educ:* St Marylebone GS; Queen Mary Coll., Univ. of London (BA 1st cl. Hons 1969); Westfield Coll., Univ. of London (PhD 1977). Lectr in German, Westfield Coll., 1970–89; Queen Mary and Westfield College, London: Reader, 1989–91; Prof. of German, 1991–94; Founding Chm., Centre for Modern European Studies, 1990–94. Mem., Council, 1997–99, Senate, 2000–01, London Univ. Mem. Council, Poetry Soc., 1973–77; Jt Hon. Sec., English Goethe Soc., 1987–2004; Member: Bielefeld Colloquium für Neue Poesie, 1979–2002; Council, Goethe Ges., Weimar, 1995–2003; Res. Cttee, Freies Deutsches Hochstift, 2003–; Editl Bd, Central Europe, 2003–; Res. Gp on Prague and Dublin Lit., Osaka, 2006–. Chm., M. L. v. Motesiczky Trust, 1997–2006. Schol., Herzog August Bibliothek, Wolfenbüttel, 1979; Fellow, Inst. of Advanced Study, Berlin, 1985–86, 2012. Corresp. Mem., German Acad. of Lang. and Lit., 2005. Goethe Prize, English Goethe Soc., 1977. *Publications:* (ed with J. J. White) August Stramm: Kritische Essays und unveröffentlichtes Quellenmaterial aus dem Nachlass des Dichters, 1979; (ed) Allegorie und Eros: Texte von und über Albert Paris Gütersloh, 1986; Eine fast magische Anziehungskraft: Goethes Wahlverwandtschaften und die Chemie seiner Zeit, 1987; (with Ulrich Ernst) Text als Figur: Visuelle Poesie von der Antike bis zur Moderne, 1987, 3rd edn 1990; (ed) August Stramm: Die Dichtungen, Sämtliche Gedichte, Dramen, Prosa, 1990; (ed) August Stramm: Alles ist Gedicht: Briefe, Gedichte, Bilder, Dokumente, 1990; (ed) Friedrich Hölderlin: Poems and Fragments, 1998; (ed) H. G. Adler: Der Wahrheit verpflichtet, 1998; (ed) E. T. A. Hoffmann: The Life and Opinions of the Tomcat Murr, 1999; (ed) H. G. Adler: Eine Reise, 1999; (ed jtly) F. B. Steiner: Selected Writings, 2 vols, 1999; (ed jtly) Goethe at 250, 2000; (ed) F. B. Steiner: Am Stürzenden Pfad, Gesammelte Gedichte, 2000; Franz Kafka, 2001; (ed jtly) Models of Wholeness, 2002; (ed jtly) From Prague poet to Oxford anthropologist: Franz Buermann Steiner celebrated, 2003; (ed) H. G. Adler: Die Dichtung der Prager Schule, 2003; (ed) H. G. Adler: Theresienstadt 1941–1945, 2005; (ed) E. Canetti: Aufzeichnungen für Marie-Louise, 2005; (ed jtly) Marie-Louise von Motesiczky 1906–1996: the paintings, 2006; (ed jtly) H. G. Adler: über Franz Baermann Steiner, 2006; (ed jtly) F. B. Steiner: Zivilization und Gefahr, 2008; (ed jtly) Friedrich Hölderlin: essays and letters, 2009; (ed with Peter Filkins) H. G. Adler: Nach der Befreiung, 2013; (ed with Peter Filkins) H. G. Adler: Orthodoxie des Herzens, 2014; (ed with Gesa Dane) Literatur und Anthropologie: H. G. Adler, Elias Canetti und Franz Baermann Steiner in London, 2014; Das bittere Brot: H. G. Adler, Elias Canetti und Franz Baermann Steiner im Londoner Exil, 2015; Das absolute Boese: Zur Neuedition von 'Mein Kampf', 2017; The Great Transformation: the contribution of German-Jewish exiles to British culture, 2019; Goethe: a critical life, 2019; *poetry:* Alphabox, 1973; Alphabet Music, 1974; Fragments Towards the City, 1977; Even in April, Ferrara and Liberty, 1978; A Short History of London, 1979; The Wedding and Other Marriages, 1980; Triplets, 1980; Homage to Theocritus, 1985; Notes from the Correspondence, 1983; The Electric Alphabet, 1986, 3rd edn 2001; To Cythera!, 1993; At the Edge of the World, 1994; Big Skies and Little Stones, 1997; *novels:* The Magus of Portobello Road, 2015; A Night at the Troubadour, 2017; Coriander Bowman's Party, 2019; pamphlets; articles in learned jls, daily press, New York Times, TLS, London Rev. of Books. *Recreations:* mountaineering, painting and drawing, music. *Address:* Department of German, King's College London, WC2R 2LS. *T:* (020) 7848 2124.

**ADLER, Prof. Michael William,** CBE 1999; MD; FRCP, FFPH; Professor of Genito Urinary Medicine and Consultant Physician, University College London (formerly Middlesex Hospital) Medical School, 1979–2004, now Emeritus Professor; *b* 12 June 1939; *s* of late Gerhard and of Hella Adler; *m* 1st, 1966, Susan Jean (marr. diss. 1978); 2nd, 1979, Karen Hope Dunnell (*see* Dame K. H. Dunnell) (marr. diss. 1994); two *d*; 3rd, 1994, Margaret Jay (*see* Baroness Jay of Paddington). *Educ:* Bryanston Sch.; Middlesex Hosp. Med. Sch. MB BS 1965, MD 1977; MRCP 1970, FRCP 1984; FFPH (MFCM 1977, FFCM 1983). House Officer and Registrar in Medicine, Middlesex, Central Middlesex and Whittington Hosps, 1965–69; Lectr, St Thomas' Hosp. Med. Sch., 1970–75; Sen. Lectr, Middlesex Hosp. Med. Sch., 1975–79. Consultant Physician: Middlesex Hosp., 1979–; Camden and Islington Community Health Services NHS Trust, 1992– (non-exec. Dir, 1992–94); non-exec. Dir, Health Develt Agency, 1999–2003. Advr in Venereology, WHO, 1983–2010; Department of Health (formerly DHSS): Mem., Expert Adv. Gp on AIDS, 1984–92; Mem., Sub-Gps on Monitoring and Surveillance, 1987–88 and Health Care Workers, 1987–92; Mem., AIDS Action Gp, 1991–92; Mem., Stocktake Gp, 1997–99; Chief Scientist's Advr, Res. Liaison Gp (Child Health), 1985–90; Mem., and Chm. Steering Gp, Develt of Sexual Health and HIV Strategy, 1999–2001; Mem., Ind. Adv. Gp on Sexual Health, 2000–. Medical Research Council: Member: Res. Adv. Gp on Epidemiol Studies of Sexually Transmitted Diseases, 1975–80; Working Party to co-ordinate Lab. Studies on the Gonococcus, 1979–83; Working Party on AIDS, 1981–87; Sub-Cttee on Therapeutic Studies, 1985–87; Cttee on Epidemiol Studies on AIDS, 1985–94; Cttee on Clinical Studies of Prototype Vaccines against AIDS, 1987–89; RCS Cttee on HIV infection/AIDS, 1991–96. Member: Med. Adv. Cttee, Brook Adv. Centres, 1984–94; Working Gp on AIDS, European Commn, 1985–; AIDS Working Party, BMA, 1986–92; Exec. Cttee, Internat. Union Against Sexually Transmitted Infections (formerly Against the Venereal Diseases and Treponematoses), 1986–; DFID (formerly ODA) Health and Population Adv. Cttee on R&D, 1995–99; Steering Cttee, Assoc. of NHS Providers of AIDS Care and Treatment, 1996–2003; Exec. Cttee, Assoc. of Genito Urinary Medicine, 1997–99. Mem., Specialist Adv. Cttee on Genito Urinary Medicine, Jt Cttee of Higher Med. Trng, 1981–86 (Sec., 1981–82; Chm., 1983–86). Royal College of Physicians: Member: Cttee on Genito Urinary Medicine, 1984–91 (Sec., 1984–87; Chm., 1987–91); Working Gp on AIDS, FCM (now FPH), 1985–; Lumleian Lectr, 1996; Member Council: Med. Soc. for the Study of Venereal Diseases, 1999–2002 (Pres., 1997–99); RIPH&H, 1993–94; RCP, 1999–2002. Dir, Terrence Higgins Trust, 1982–88; Mem. Governing Council, Internat. AIDS Soc., 1993–98; Trustee, 1987–2000, Chm., 1991–2000, Nat. AIDS Trust (Chm., Grants and Gen. Purposes Cttee, 1988–91); Member, Board: Care UK, 2007–; LEPRA, 2007–; Adviser: AIDS Crisis Trust, 1986–98; Parly All Party Cttee on AIDS, 1987–. Mem. Bd, Rose Th., Kingston, 2009–11. Patron, Albany Soc., 1987–91. Evian Health Award, 1990. Member, Editorial Panel: Sexually Transmitted Infections; Current Opinion on Infectious Diseases; Enfermedades de Transmission Sexual; Venereology; also Ed., AIDS, 1986–94; Consultant Editor, AIDS Letter, RSM, 1987–89. *Publications:* ABC of Sexually Transmitted Diseases, 1984, 5th edn 2004; (ed) ABC of AIDS, 1987, 6th edn 2012; (ed) Diseases in the Homosexual Male, 1988; (jtly) Sexual Health and Care Guidelines for Prevention and Treatment, 1998; articles on sexually transmitted diseases and AIDS in med. jls. *Recreations:* walking, theatre.

**ADLER, Rachel Vivienne;** *see* Karp, R. V.

**ADNAMS, Jonathan Patrick Adair,** OBE 2009; Chairman, Adnams plc, since 2006; *b* Halesworth, 25 Nov. 1956; *s* of John Adnams and Patricia Adnams. *Educ:* Framlingham Coll. Adnams: Brewery Engr, 1973–88; Pubs and Property Dir, 1988–97; Man. Dir, 1997–2006. Helmsman, Southwold RNLI, 1973–2001. *Recreations:* sailing, bluegrass banjo, Lithuanian language. *Address:* Adnams, Sole Bay Brewery, East Green, Southwold, Suffolk IP18 6JW. *T:* (01802) 727200, *Fax:* (01802) 727201. *E:* jonathan.adnams@adnams.co.uk.

**ADONIS,** family name of **Baron Adonis**.

**ADONIS,** Baron *cr* 2005 (Life Peer), of Camden Town in the London Borough of Camden; **Andrew Adonis;** PC 2009; Chairman, National Infrastructure Commission, 2015–17; *b* 22 Feb. 1963; one *s* one *d*. *Educ:* Kingham Hill Sch., Oxon; Keble Coll., Oxford; Christ Church, Oxford (DPhil 1988). Mem., HQ Secretariat, British Gas Corp., 1984–85; Nuffield College, University of Oxford: Res. student, 1985–86; Fellow in Politics, 1988–91; Financial Times: Public Policy corresp., 1991–93; Industry corresp., 1993–94; Public Policy Editor, 1994–96; political columnist and contributing editor, The Observer, 1996–98; Mem., Prime Minister's Policy Unit, 1998–2001; Head of Policy, 2001–03; Sen. Advr on Educn and Public Services, 2003–05, Prime Minister's Office. Parly Under-Sec. of State, DFES, later DCSF, 2005–08; Minister of State, DfT, 2008–09; Sec. of State for Transport, 2009–10. Dir, Inst. for Government, 2010–12. Non-exec. Dir, HS2 Ltd, 2015–17. Mem., Oxford City Council, 1987–91. Chm., Commn on East Thames Crossings, 2014. Chm. Trustees, IPPR, 2012–16. *Publications:* Parliament Today, 1990; Making Aristocracy Work: the peerage and the political system in Britain 1884–1914, 1993; (with T. Hames) A Conservative Revolution?: the Thatcher-Reagan decade in perspective, 1994; (with D. Butler and T. Travers) Failure in British Government: the politics of the poll tax, 1994 (with S. Pollard) A Class Act: the myth of Britain's classless society, 1997; (ed with Keith Thomas) Roy Jenkins: a retrospective, 2004; Five Days in May, 2013; (with Will Hutton) Saving Britain: how we must change to prosper in Europe, 2018; Half In Half Out: prime ministers on Europe, 2018. *Address:* House of Lords, SW1A 0PW. *T:* (020) 7219 5904.

**ADSETTS, Sir (William) Norman,** Kt 1999; OBE 1988; President, Sheffield Theatres Trust, since 2006 (Chairman, 1996–2006); *b* 6 April 1931; *s* of Ernest Norman Adsetts and Hilda Rachel Adsetts (*née* Wheeler); *m* 1956, Eve Stefanuti; one *s* one *d*. *Educ:* King Edward VII Sch., Sheffield; Queen's Coll., Oxford (BA 1955; MA). Commissioned RAF, 1950–52; Marketing Manager, Fibreglass Ltd, 1955–66; Sheffield Insulating Co.: Dir, 1966–89; Man. Dir, 1970–85; Chm., 1985–89; Chm., 1989–96, Pres., 1996–, Sheffield Insulations Gp, subseq. SIG plc. Dir, 1988–91, Dep. Chm., 1991–97, Sheffield Develt Corp.; Chairman: Kelham Riverside Develt Agency, 1998–2002; Sheffield Supertram Trust, 1993–98; Sheffield Partnerships, 1988–93; Sheffield First for Investment, 1999–2002. Chairman: Assoc. for Conservation of Energy, 1985–90, 1993–95; Yorkshire Humberside CBI, 1989–91; Pres., Sheffield Chamber of Commerce, 1988–89. Mem., Arts Council England, 2002–05 (Chm., Yorks Arts Regl Council, 2002–05). Chairman: Kelham Island Mus., subseq. Sheffield Industrial Mus Trust, 1994–98 (Pres., 2016–); Autism Plus, 2007–12; Adsetts Partnership, 2009–; Trustee, Research Autism, 2006–14. Chairman of Governors: Sheffield Hallam Univ., 1993–99; Mount St Mary's Coll., 1999–2009 (Pres., 2010–). Patron of local charities. *Publications:* A Man of Sheffield: the Adsetts story, 2017. *Recreations:* writing family history, two autistic grandchildren, reading. *Address:* Danes Balk, 8 Rotherham Road, Eckington, Sheffield S21 4FH. *T:* (01246) 431008.

**ADSHEAD, Fiona Jane,** FRCP, FFPH; Chief Wellbeing and Public Health Officer, Bupa, 2012–17; *b* 31 July 1962; *d* of late Lt Comdr and Mrs J. R. Adshead. *Educ:* University Coll. London (BSc 1983; MB BS 1986; MSc 1994). MRCP 1989, FRCP 2005; MFPHM 1999, FFPH 2003. Sen. hse officer posts, Nat. Hosp. for Nervous Diseases, Royal Marsden Hosp., Brompton Hosp. and RPMS, 1987–89; Med. Registrar, St George's Hosp., 1989–90; Clinical Res. Fellow, Inst. of Cancer Res. and Royal Marsden Hosp., 1990–92; Registrar, then Sen. Registrar, Croydon HA, 1993–96; Clinical Lectr, St George's Hosp. Med. Sch., 1996–2000; Consultant in Public Health Medicine, Camden and Islington HA, 2000–02; Dir of Public Health, Camden PCT, 2002–04; Dep. Chief Med. Officer, DoH, 2004–08; Dir, Chronic Diseases and Health Promotion, WHO, 2008–10; Sen. Sustainability and Health Advr, PricewaterhouseCoopers, 2010–12. *Publications:* contrib. numerous articles to scientific jls. *Recreations:* art, travel, gardening, film, theatre.

**ADYE, Sir John (Anthony),** KCMG 1993; Director, Government Communications Headquarters, 1989–96; *b* 24 Oct. 1939; *s* of Arthur Francis Capel Adye and Hilda Marjorie Adye (*née* Elkes); *m* 1961, Anne Barbara, *d* of Dr John Aeschlimann, Montclair, NJ; two *s* one *d*. *Educ:* Leighton Park Sch.; Lincoln Coll., Oxford (MA; Hon. Fellow, 2018). Joined GCHQ, 1962; Principal, 1968; British Embassy, Washington, 1973–75; Nat. Defence Coll., Latimer, 1975–76; Asst Sec., 1977–83; Under Sec., 1983–89; Dep. Sec., 1989–92; 2nd Perm. Sec., 1992–96. Chairman: Country Houses Assoc., 1999–2002; CPRE Glos, 2005–11; Identity Assurance Systems Ltd, 2010–. Director: Nat. Biometric Security Project, Washington, 2003–10; Northwick Park Ltd, 2014–. Gov., Dean Close Sch., Cheltenham, until 2014. *Address:* c/o Campaign to Protect Rural England, Community House, Gloucester GL1 2LZ. *Club:* Naval and Military.

**AEPPLI, Prof. Gabriel,** PhD; FRS 2010; Head, Photon Science Division (formerly Department of Synchroton Radiation and Nanotechnology), Paul Scherrer Institute, Switzerland, since 2014; Professor of Physics, ETH Zurich and École Polytechnique Fédérale de Lausanne, since 2014; *b* Zurich, 25 Nov. 1956; *s* of late Alfred Aeppli and Dorothea Aeppli; *m* 2005, Yeong-Ah Soh; one *d*. *Educ:* Massachusetts Inst. of Technol. (BSc Electrical Engrg and Maths 1978; MSc Electrical Engrg; PhD Electrical Engrg 1983). Res. asst, MIT, 1978–82; Mem., Tech. Staff, 1982–93, Dist. Mem., Tech. Staff, 1993–96, AT&T Bell Labs, Murray Hill, NJ; Sen. Res. Scientist, Nippon Electric Co. Res. Inst. Inc., Princeton, NJ, 1996–2002; University College London: Quain Prof. of Physics and Hon. Prof. of Medicine, 2002–15; Dir, London Centre for Nanotechnol., 2002–14. Co-founder and Mem. Bd, Bio Nano Consulting, 2007–. Resident, Bellagio Study and Conf. Center, Rockefeller Foundn, 2007. Lectures: Mildner, Dept of Electronic and Electrical Engrg, UCL, 2002; Liddiard Meml, Inst. Materials, Minerals and Mining, London, 2006; James A. Morrison, McMaster Univ., Ontario, 2008; J. C. Bose Meml, Saha Inst. of Nuclear Physics, Kolkata, 2009. Fellow: Japan Soc. for Promotion of Sci., 1996; Amer. Physical Soc., 1997; Riso Nat. Lab., Denmark, 2002. Member: Amer. Acad. of Arts and Scis, 2002; US NAS, 2015. Mem., Physical Soc. Club, London, 2003. Wolfson Res. Merit Award, Royal Soc., 2002; (jtly) Neel Medal/Magnetism Prize, IUPAP, 2003; Majumdar Meml Award, Indian Assoc. for Cultivation of Sci., 2005; (jtly) Oliver Buckley Prize, APS, 2005; Mott Medal, Inst. of Physics, 2008. *Publications:* contribs to jls incl. Nature, Science, Proceedings of NAS, Physics Rev. Letters, Nature Materials, Nanomedicine and Jl Applied Physics. *Address:* Paul Scherrer Institut, WSLA/117, 5232 Villigen PSI, Switzerland.

**AFFLECK, Prof. Ian Keith,** PhD; FRS 2010; FRSC; Killam University Professor, University of British Columbia, since 2003; *b* Vancouver, BC, 2 July 1952; *s* of William Burchill Affleck and Evelyn Mary Colenso Affleck (*née* Carter); *m* 1977, Glenda Ruth Harman; one *s* one *d*. *Educ:* Trent Univ., Ont (BSc 1975); Harvard Univ. (AM Physics 1976; PhD Physics 1979). Jun. Fellow, Harvard Soc. of Fellows, 1979–81; Asst Prof., Princeton Univ., 1981–87; Prof., Univ. of BC, 1987–; on leave as Prof., Boston Univ., 2001–03. Fellow: Canadian Inst. for Advanced Res., 1987–2001 and 2008–; Inst. for Theoretical Physics, UCSB, 1999–2000. FRSC 1991; Fellow: APS, 2003; Japanese Soc. for Promotion of Sci., 2004; Foreign Associate, French Acad. of Scis, 2016. Hon. LLD Trent, 1998. Steacie Prize, NRCC, 1988; Herzberg Medal, Canadian Assoc. Physicists, 1990; Rutherford Medal in Physics, RSC, 1991; Lars Onsager Prize, APS, 2012. *Publications:* contribs to scientific jls, incl. Nuclear Physics, Physics Letters, Physics Rev. Letters, Physics Rev. D and B, Jl of Physics A, Jl of Statistical Mechanics, Nature. *Recreations:* bicycling, swimming, hiking, wind-surfing, ski-ing. *Address:* Department of Physics and Astronomy, University of British Columbia, Vancouver, BC V6T 1Z1, Canada. *T:* (604) 8222137, *Fax:* (604) 8225324. *E:* iaffleck@phas.ubc.ca.

**AFOLAMI, Abimbola, (Bim);** MP (C) Hitchin and Harpenden, since 2017; *b* 11 Feb. 1986; *s* of Dr Samuel Afolami and Bassey Afolami; *m* 2013, Henrietta Jackson-Stops; three *s*. *Educ:* Eton Coll.; University Coll., Oxford (BA Mod. Hist. 2007). Vice Pres., Oxford Union, 2006. Associate: Freshfields Bruckhaus Deringer, 2009–12; Simpson, Thacher & Bartlett, 2012–15; Sen. Exec., HSBC plc, 2015–17. Mem., Public Accounts Cttee, 2017–. *Recreations:* history, the Archers, The Years of Lyndon Johnson, dinners and dancing. *Address:* House of Commons, SW1A 0AA. *E:* bim.afolami.mp@parliament.uk. *Club:* Carlton.

**AFRIYIE, Adam;** MP (C) Windsor, since 2005; *b* 4 Aug. 1965. *Educ:* Addey and Stanhope Sch., New Cross; Imperial Coll., London (BSc 1987). Man. Dir, then non-exec. Chm., Connect Services, 1993–2017; Exec. Chm., DeHavilland Inf. Services, 1998–2005; non-exec. Chm., Axonn Media Ltd (formerly Adfero), 2005–. Shadow Minister for Sci. and Innovation, 2007–10; Prime Minister's Trade Envoy, 2016–. Chairman: Parly Space Cttee, 2010–15 (Patron, 2015–); Parly Office of Sci. and Technol., 2010–; Members' Expenses Cttee, 2011–15; Parly Financial Technol. Cttee, 2015–. Mem. Bd, Policy Exchange, 2003–05. Gov., Mus. of London, 1999–2005. *Address:* House of Commons, SW1A 0AA.

**AFSHAR,** Baroness *cr* 2007 (Life Peer), of Heslington in the County of North Yorkshire; **Haleh Afshar,** OBE 2005; PhD; FAcSS; Professor of Politics and Women's Studies, University of York, 1999–2011, now Emeritus; *b* 1944; *d* of Hassan Afshar and Pouran Afshar (*née* Khabir); *m* 1974, Maurice Dodson; one *s* one *d*. *Educ:* Ecole Jean d'Arc, Tehran; St Martin's Sch., Solihull; Davis's Coll., Brighton; Univ. of York (BA Hons Soc. Scis 1967); Univ. of Strasbourg (Diplôme de Droit Comparé Communauté Européen 1972); PhD Land Economy Cantab 1974. Sen. Res. Officer, Ministry of Co-operatives and Rural Develt, Rural Res. Centre, Tehran; Econ. and Envmt Corresp. and Feature Writer, Kayhan International, English lang. daily newspaper, Tehran, 1971–74; Lectr in Develt, Univ. of Bradford, 1976–85; University of York: Dep. Dir and Lectr in Health Econs, Inst. for Res. in Social Scis, 1985–87; Dept of Politics and Centre for Women's Studies, 1987–. Founder and Co-Chm., 2002–09, Pres., 2009–, Muslim Women's Network; Chm. and Facilitator, Listening to Women exercise, conducted by Muslim Women's Network and Women's Nat. Commn, 2005–06. Advr to various pts of Govt on public policy on Muslim women and Islamic law; speaker on various media on Muslim community. Member: Wkg Gp on Ethics and Pharmacogenetics, Nuffield Council on Bioethics, 2002–04; UK Drug Policy Commn, 2006–; Educn Honours Cttee, 2007–; Women's Nat. Commn, 2008–10. FAcSS (AcSS 2009). Launched Democracy Series, Hansard Soc., with Democracy and Islam (pamphlet), 2006. Mem. editl bds of 10 learned jls. *Publications:* Islam and the Post-revolutionary State in Iran (as Homa Omid), 1994; Islam and Feminisms, 1998; edited: Iran a revolution in turmoil, 1985; Women, Work and Ideology in the Third World, 1985; Women, State and Ideology, 1987; (jtly) Women, Poverty and Ideology, 1989; Women Development and Survival in the Third World, 1991; (jtly) Women and Adjustment Policies in the Third World, 1992; Women in the Middle East, 1993; (jtly) The Dynamic of Race and Gender, 1994; Women and Politics in the Third World, 1996; (jtly)

Empowering Women for Development, 1997; Women and Empowerment: illustrations from the Third World, 1998; (jtly) Women and Globalization and Fragmentation in the Developing World, 1999; (jtly) Development, Women, and War, 2004; (jtly) Women in Later Life, 2008; Women and Fluid Identities, 2012. *Recreations:* music, opera, ballet, movies, books, cooking, entertaining, Paris, the Pennines. *Address:* House of Lords, SW1A 0PW; Department of Politics, University of York, York YO10 5DD.

**AFZAL RAUF, Mariya;** Director, Canada, British Council, since 2015; *b* Lahore, 1 Oct. 1977; *d* of Nargis Afzal and Afzal Rahman; *m* 2007, Abdul Rauf; two *s. Educ:* Kinnaird Coll. for Women Univ., Lahore (BA Internat. Relns, Political Sci., Psychol.); McGill Univ. (Exec. Develt Course 2017). British Council: Arts and Progs Officer, 2000–02, Arts and Governance Manager, 2002–04, Dep. Dir, 2005–08, Lahore; Hd, Progs, Pakistan, 2008–10; Regl Dir, London Sch. of Business and Finance, Pakistan, 2010; Hd, Develt, The Power Plant Contemp. Art Gall., Toronto, 2013–15. *E:* mariya.afzal@britishcouncil.org, mariya.afzal@hotmail.com.

**AGA KHAN (IV), His Highness Prince Karim,** granted title His Highness by the Queen, 1957, granted title His Royal Highness by the Shah of Iran, 1959; KBE 2004; *b* Genthod, Geneva, 13 Dec. 1936; *s* of late Prince Aly Salomon Khan and Princess Joan Aly Khan, later Viscountess Camrose (*née* Joan Barbara Yarde-Buller, *e d* of 3rd Baron Churston, MVO, OBE); became Aga Khan, spiritual leader and hereditary Imam of Ismaili Muslims all over the world on the death of his grandfather, Sir Sultan Mahomed Shah, Aga Khan III, GCSI, GCIE, GCVO, 11 July 1957; *m* 1969, Sarah Frances Croker-Poole (marr. diss. 1995); two *s* one *d*; *m* 1998, Princess Gabriele zu Leiningen (Begum Inaara Aga Khan) (marr. diss. 2014); one *s*, and one step *d. Educ:* Le Rosey, Switzerland; Harvard University (BA Hons 1959). Founder and Chairman: Aga Khan Foundn, Geneva, 1967 (also branches/ affiliates in Afghanistan, Bangladesh, Canada, India, Kenya, Kyrgyzstan, Mozambique, Pakistan, Portugal, Syria, Tajikistan, Tanzania, Uganda, UK and US); Aga Khan Award for Architecture, 1977–; Inst. of Ismaili Studies, 1977–; Aga Khan Fund for Econ. Develt, Geneva, 1984–; Aga Khan Trust for Culture, Geneva, 1988; Aga Khan Agency for Microfinance, 2005. Founder and Chancellor: Aga Khan Univ., Pakistan, 1983; Univ. of Central Asia, 2001. Leading owner and breeder of race horses in France, Ireland and UK; won: Derby, 1981 (Shergar), 1986 (Shahrastani), 1988 (Kahyasi), 2000 (Sinndar); Irish Derby, 1981 (Shergar), 1986 (Shahrastani), 1988 (Kahyasi), 2000 (Sinndar), 2003 (Alamshar); King George VI and Queen Elizabeth Diamond Stakes, 2003 (Alamshar), 2005 (Azamour); St James's Palace Stakes, 2004 (Azamour); Prix de L'Arc de Triomphe, 1982 (Akiyda), 2000 (Sinndar), 2003 (Dalakhani), 2008 (Zarkava); Prix du Jockey Club, 1960 (Charlottesville), 1979 (Top Ville), 1984 (Darshaan), 1985 (Mouktar), 1987 (Natroun), 2003 (Dalakhani); Prix de Diane, 1993 (Shemaka), 1997 (Vereva), 1998 (Zainta), 1999 (Daryaba), 2008 (Zarkava). Hon. Citizen of Canada, 2010. Hon. FRIBA 1991; Hon. Mem., AIA, 1992. Associate Foreign Mem., Académie des Beaux Arts, France, 2008. Doctor of Laws (*hc*): McGill, 1983; McMaster, 1987; Wales, 1993; Brown, 1996; Toronto, 2004; Ireland, 2006; Hon. DLitt London, 1989; DHLitt (*hc*) Amer. Univ. Beirut, 2005; Hon. Dr: Evora, 2005; Ottawa, 2012; Hon. DHumLit Amer. Univ., Cairo, 2006; Hon. DD Cambridge, 2008. Thomas Jefferson Meml Foundn Medal in Architecture, 1984; Amer. Inst. of Architects' Inst. Honor, 1984; Médaille d'argent, Académie d'Architecture, Paris 1991; Vincent Scully Prize, USA, 2005; Die Quadriga, Germany, 2005; Carnegie Medal of Philanthropy, Scotland, 2005; Grand Patron and Grand Donor of Culture, France, 2009; Medal, UCSF, 2011; J. C. Nichols Prize for Visionaries in Urban Develt, Urban Land Inst., 2011. Grand Croix: Order of Prince Henry the Navigator, Portugal, 1960; Ordem Militar de Cristo, Portugal, 2005; Order of Merit, Portugal, 1998; Cavaliere, Gran Croce, Ordine al Merito della Repubblica Italiana, 1977; Grand Cordon, Ouissam-al Arch, Morocco, 1986; Cavaliere del Lavoro, Italy, 1988; Commandeur, Légion d'Honneur, France, 1990; Gran Cruz, Orden del Mérito Civil, Spain, 1991; Order of Bahrain (1st cl.), 2003; Hon. CC, 2004; Comdr, Order of Arts and Letters (France), 2010. *Address:* Aiglemont, 60270 Gouvieux, France. *Clubs:* Royal Yacht Squadron; Yacht Club Costa Smeralda (Founder Pres.) (Sardinia).

**AGAR,** family name of **Earl of Normanton.**

**AGARWAL, Prof. Girish Saran,** PhD; FRS 2008; Professor of Biological and Agricultural Engineering, Physics and Astronomy, Texas A and M University, since 2016; *b* Bareilly, Uttar Pradesh, 7 July 1946; *s* of late Keladevi and Bhagwat Saran; *m* 1970, Sneh (*d* 2006); two *d. Educ:* Banaras Hindu Univ., India (MSc 1966); Univ. of Rochester, USA (PhD 1969). Res. Associate, 1969–71, and Asst Prof., 1970–71, Dept of Physics and Astronomy, Univ. of Rochester, NY; Asst Prof., Inst. für Theoretische Physik, Univ. of Stuttgart, 1971–73; Prof. and Hd, Dept of Physics, Inst. of Sci., Bombay, 1975–77; University of Hyderabad: Prof., Sch. of Physics, 1977–95, Dean, Sch. of Physics, 1977–80; Dir and Dist. Scientist, Physical Res. Lab., Ahmedabad, 1995–2006. Albert Einstein Centenary Res. Prof., Indian Nat. Sci. Acad., 2001–05; Noble Foundn Chair and Regents' Prof., Dept of Physics, Oklahoma State Univ., 2004–17. Hon. Prof., Jawaharlal Nehru Centre for Advanced Scientific Res., Jakkur, Bangalore, 1995–2000; Visiting Professor: Univ. of Ulm, Germany; Univ. of Essen, Germany; Max-Planck-Inst. für Quantenoptik, Garching; Technische Univ., Vienna; Vis. Fellow, 1973–75, J. R. D. Tata Vis. Prof., 2011–13, Tata Inst. of Fundamental Res., Mumbai; Vis. Fellow, Jt Inst. for Lab. Astrophysics, Univ. of Colo, Boulder, 1981–82; SERC Sen. Vis. Fellow, UMIST, 1985–86. Dr *hc* Liege, 2007; Hon. Dr Hyderabad, 2011. Fellow: Amer. Physical Soc., 1981; Indian Acad. of Scis, 1981; Indian Nat. Sci. Acad., 1985; Optical Soc. of America, 1988; Third World Acad. of Scis, 1997. Eastman Kodak Prize, Univ. of Rochester, 1969; Shanti Swaroop Bhatnagar Award in Physical Scis, Govt of India, 1982; Max-Born Award, Optical Soc. of America, 1988; Einstein Medal, Optical and Quantum Electronics Soc., USA, 1994; G. D. Birla Prize for Scientific Res., K. K. Birla Foundn, 1994; Third World Acad. of Scis Prize in Physics, 1994; R. D. Birla Prize, Indian Physics Assoc., 1997; Humboldt Res. Award, Germany, 1997; Eminent Faculty Award, Oklahoma State Univ., 2012. *Publications:* Quantum Optics, 2013; monographs; papers on stochastic processes and quantum optics; contrib. res. articles to jls of Amer. Physical Soc., Inst. of Physics, Optical Soc. of America. *Recreations:* reading magazines and newspapers, watching comedy and movies with message. *Address:* Institute for Quantum Science and Engineering and Department of Biological and Agricultural Engineering, Texas A and M University, College Station, TX 77843, USA. *T:* (979) 4587939. *E:* girish.agarwal@tamu.edu.

**AGASSI, André;** tennis player; *b* Las Vegas, 29 April 1970; *s* of Emmanuel (Mike) and Betty Agassi; *m* 1997, Brooke Shields (marr. diss.); *m* 2001, Stefanie Graf, *qv*; one *s* one *d*. Trained at Nick Bollettieri Tennis Acad., Fla. Professional tennis player, 1986–2006; winner: (inaugural) ATP World Championship, Frankfurt, 1991; Wimbledon, 1992; US Open, 1994, 1999; Australian Open, 1995, 2000, 2001, 2003; French Open, 1999 (one of only five players ever to win all four men's grand-slam titles); Gold Medallist, Olympic Games, 1996. Founder, André Agassi Charitable Foundn, 1996. *Publications:* Open: an autobiography, 2009.

**AGG, Stephen James,** FCILT; Chief Executive, Chartered Institute of Logistics and Transport, 2006–15; *b* 25 Sept. 1952; *s* of Douglas and Ivy Agg; *m* 2007, Maggie; one *s* one *d* by a previous marriage. Lowfield Distribn, 1981–86; Jacob's Bakery, 1986–96; Distribn Dir, Danone UK, 1996–99; Logistics Dir, Danone Waters UK, 1999–2002; Man. Dir, Business Services, Freight Transport Assoc., 2002–06. Director: PTRC Educn and Res. Services, 2008–15; Eur. Logistics Assoc., 2011–15; Mem., Adv. Bd, Cranfield Centre for Logistics and Supply Mgt. FCILT 2006. *Recreations:* classic cars, walking, rural life, English Setters.

**AGGARWAL, Prof. Varinder Kumar,** PhD; FRS 2012; Professor of Synthetic Chemistry, University of Bristol, since 2000; *b* Kalianpur, N India, 1961. *Educ:* Pembroke Coll., Cambridge (BA 1st Cl. Hons Natural Scis 1983; PhD 1987). Harkness Fellow, 1986–88; Postdoctoral Res. Fellow, Columbia Univ., NY, 1986–88; Lectr in Chem., Bath Univ., 1988–91; Lectr in Chem., 1991–95, Reader, 1995–97, Prof. of Chem., 1997–2000, Sheffield Univ. Hickinbottom Fellow, RSC, 1997; Nuffield Foundn Fellow, 1997–98. Pfizer Academic Award, 1996, 1998; Glaxo Wellcome Academic Award, 1996; Zeneca Academic Award, 1996; Corday Morgan Prize and Medal, 1999, Green Chem. Award, 2003, RSC. *Address:* School of Chemistry, University of Bristol, Cantock's Close, Bristol BS8 1TS.

**AGGLETON, Prof. John Patrick,** DPhil; FRS 2012; Professor of Cognitive Neuroscience, Cardiff University, since 1994; *b* Cardiff, 14 June 1955; *s* of Patrick and Judy Aggleton; *m* 1978, Jane; two *s. Educ:* Trinity Sch., Croydon; Clare Coll., Cambridge (BA Natural Scis 1976); Jesus Coll., Oxford (DPhil 1980). Lectr, Durham Univ., 1983–94. FMedSci 2002; FLSW 2011. *Recreations:* bird watching, fell running (selected to run for Wales, Masters over 60, 2015; over 60 Welsh Open Fell Running champion, 2016), cycling. *Address:* c/o School of Psychology, Cardiff University, Tower Building, 70 Park Place, Cardiff CF10 3AT. *T:* (029) 2087 4563, *Fax:* (029) 2087 4858. *E:* aggleton@cf.ac.uk. *Club:* Mynyddwyr de Cymru.

**AGGLETON, Prof. Peter Jeremy,** PhD; CPsychol, FBPsS; FAcSS; FASSA; Professor of Education and Health, Centre for Social Research in Health (formerly National Centre in HIV Social Research), 2012–17, and Scientia Professor, 2015–17, University of New South Wales, Emeritus Professor, 2018; *b* 16 Oct. 1952; *s* of David Charles and Pauline Betty Aggleton; partner, Preecha Anurakpongpee. *Educ:* Worcester Coll., Oxford (BA 1974); Aberdeen Univ. (MEd 1977); PhD London 1984. CPsychol 1989; FBPsS 1996; FRSPH (FRIPHH 2001); FAcSS (AcSS 2004); FASSA 2016. Lecturer: Psychol. and Sociol., Worthing Coll. of Technol., 1975–76; Teacher Educn, City of Bath Tech. Coll., 1977–84; Sen. Lectr, Sociol., Bath Coll. of Higher Educn, 1984–85; Sen. Lectr, 1985–89, Hd, 1989–90, Educn Policy Studies, Bristol Poly.; Dir, Health and Educn Res. Unit, Goldsmiths' Coll., Univ. of London, 1990–92; Chief, Social and Behavioural Studies and Support Unit, Global Prog. on AIDS, WHO, Geneva, 1992–94; Prof., 1994–2009, and Dir, 1996–2006, Thomas Coram Res. Unit, Inst. of Educn, Univ. of London; Prof. of Educn, Health and Social Care, and Hd, Sch. of Educn and Social Work, Univ. of Sussex, 2009–11. Visiting Professor: Univ. of NSW, 2003–12; Univ. of Oslo, 2006–; Inst. of Educn, Univ. of London, 2012–. Hon. Dist. Prof., Coll. of Arts and Soc. Scis, ANU, 2017–; Hon. Prof., Inst. for Global Health, UCL, 2018–. FRSN. Editor: Culture, Health and Sexuality, 1999–; Sex Education, 2011–; Health Educn Jl, 2013–. *Publications:* (with H. A. Chalmers) Nursing Models and the Nursing Process, 1986; Deviance, 1987; Health, 1990; Health Promotion and Young People, 1996; (with H. A. Chalmers) Nursing Models and Nursing Practice, 2000; (ed jtly) Young People and Mental Health, 2000; (ed jtly) Sex, Drugs and Young People, 2006; contribs to learned jls incl. Science, Lancet, AIDS Care, AIDS Educn and Prevention, Health Educn Res. *Recreations:* walking, writing, travel, learning languages. *Address:* Centre for Social Research in Health, UNSW Sydney, Sydney, NSW 2052, Australia. *T:* (2) 93856776, *Fax:* (2) 93856455. *E:* csrh@unsw.edu.au.

**AGIUS, Prof. Dionisius A.,** PhD; FBA 2011; FRGS; Al Qasimi Professor of Arabic Studies (formerly Arabic) and Islamic Material Culture, University of Exeter, 2009, Professor Emeritus, 2011; *b* Mosta, Malta, 21 Dec. 1945; *s* of Pietro Agius and Giovanna Agius (*née* Griscti Soler); *m* 1987, Anne Phillips; one *d*, and one step *s* one step *d. Educ:* Univ. St Joseph, Beirut (Diplôme d'Études Arabes 1967); Pontificio Istituto di Studi Arabi, Rome (Diploma di Studi Arabi *cum laude* 1974); Univ. of Toronto (MA 1977; PhD 1984). Teacher Assistant, in Classical and Modern Arabic, 1977–84, in Field Methods, 1979–81, Univ. of Toronto; Teacher, Arabic as Second Lang., Kuwait Univ., 1984–85; Burnham Lectr in Arabic, Defence Sch. of Langs, 1986–87; University of Leeds: Teaching Fellow, 1987–89, Lectr, 1989–94, Sen. Lectr, 1994–98, in Arabic; Reader in Arabic and Medieval Mediterranean, 1998–2003; Prof. of Arabic and Islamic Material Culture, 2003–07. Co-Founding Ed., Scripta Mediterranea: Bull. Soc. Mediterranean Studies, 1980; Founding Ed., Al-Masāq: Jl Medieval Mediterranean, 1988. FRSA 2013; FRGS 2015. *Publications:* Arabic Literary Works as a Source of Documentation for Technical Terms of the Material Culture, 1984; Siculo Arabic, 1996; In the Wake of the Dhow: the Arabian Gulf and Oman, 2002, 2nd edn 2009; Seafaring in the Arabian Gulf and Oman: people of the dhow, 2005 (Abdullah Al-Mubarak Al-Sabah Foundn and British-Kuwait Friendship Soc. Book Prize); Classic Ships of Islam: from Mesopotamia to the Indian Ocean, 2008; (ed) Georgio Scala and the Moorish Slaves: the Inquisition Malta 1598, 2013; (ed jtly) Ships, Saints and Sealore: maritime ethnography of the Mediterranean and the Red Sea, 2014; (ed jtly) Human Interaction with the Environment in the Red Sea, 2017; The Life of the Red Sea Dhow: a cultural history of seaborne exploration of the Islamic world, 2019. *Recreations:* walking, reading, travel, gardening. *Address:* Institute of Arab and Islamic Studies, University of Exeter, Exeter EX4 4ND. *T:* (01395) 445538. *E:* d.a.agius@exeter.ac.uk.

**AGIUS, Kate Juliette de R.;** *see* Rothschild Agius.

**AGIUS, Marcus Ambrose Paul;** Deputy Chairman, PA Consulting Group, since 2018 (Chairman, 2014–18); *b* 22 July 1946; *s* of late Lt-Col Alfred Victor Louis Benedict Agius, MC, TD and Ena Eleanora Alberta Agius (*née* Hueffer); *m* 1971, Kate Juliette de Rothschild (*see* K. J. de Rothschild Agius); two *d. Educ:* Trinity Hall, Cambridge (MA); Harvard Business Sch. (MBA). With Vickers plc, 1968–70; joined Lazard Brothers & Co. Ltd, subseq. Lazard London, 1972; Chm., 2001–06; a Dep. Chm., Lazard LLC, 2002–06; Chm., Barclays PLC, 2007–12. Non-executive Director: Exbury Gardens Ltd, 1977–; BAA plc, 1995–2006 (Dep. Chm., 1998–2002; Chm., 2002–06); Sen. Ind. Dir, BBC, 2006–12. Chm., BBA, 2010–12. British Business Ambassador, 2010–12. Member: Adv. Council, TheCityUK, 2010–12; Exec. Cttee, IIEB, 2010–12; Takeover Panel, 2010–12. Chm., Bd of Trustees, Royal Botanic Gdns, Kew, 2009–19 (Chm., Foundn and Friends, 2004–; Trustee, 2006–09). *Recreations:* gardening, shooting, ski-ing, fine art, sailing. *Address:* PA Consulting Group, 10 Bressenden Place, SW1E 5DH. *Clubs:* White's; Swinley Forest Golf; Beaulieu River Sailing.

**AGLIETTI, Prof. Guglielmo Saverio,** PhD; FREng; Director, and Royal Academy of Engineering/SSTL Research Professor in Space Engineering, Surrey Space Centre, University of Surrey, since 2013; *b* La Spezia, Italy, 14 July 1965; *s* of Brunero Aglietti and Carlotta Aglietti; *m* 2002, Anita Whitlock; one *s* two *d. Educ:* Politecnico di Milano (Dottore Ingegria Aeronautica 1991); Univ. of Southampton (PhD 1999). CEng 1998. Structural Engr, Alenia Spazio, Italy, 1991–92; Engrg Duty Corps Officer, Italian Navy, 1992–93; Structural Engr, Young Graduate Trainee, ESA, 1993–94; University of Southampton: Lectr, 1998–2003; Sen. Lectr, 2003–08; Reader in Aerospace Structural Dynamics, 2008–11; Hd, Astronautics Res. Gp, 2009–12; Prof. of Aerospace Structures,

2011. Principal Investigator for Space Missions: De-Orbit Sail, 2015; Alsat Nano, 2016; RemoveDEBRIS, 2018. FREng 2018. *Publications:* (contrib.) Spacecraft System Engineering, 3rd edn 2003, 4th edn 2011; (contrib.) ECSS-E-Handbook-32-26A, 2013; articles in academic jls incl. AIAA Jl, JASA, JSV, Acta Astronautica, IEEE Trans. *Address:* Surrey Space Centre, University of Surrey, BA Building, Guildford, Surrey GU2 7XH. *T:* (01483) 683417, *Fax:* (01483) 689503. *E:* g.aglietti@surrey.ac.uk.

**AGLIONBY, Dr Julia Catherine Weir;** Executive Director, Foundation for Common Land, since 2012; *b* London, 4 Oct. 1969; *d* of late Francis John Aglionby and of Susan Victoria Mary Aglionby; *m* 2000, Charles Alexander Forbes Weir; one *s* one *d. Educ:* St Paul's Girls' Sch.; Somerville Coll., Oxford (MA); University Coll. London (MSc); Newcastle Univ. (PhD 2014). FRGS 1989; MRICS 2000; FAAV 2000. Envmtl economist, ODA, 1993–95; Land Agent, H&H Bowe Ltd, 1997–2013. Director: Nat. Centre for the Uplands, 2013; Susan's Farm, CIC, 2015–. Mem. Bd, Natural England, 2014–19. FRSA. *Publications:* contribs on common land and natural park mgt. *Recreations:* wild swimming, cycling expeditions. *Address:* Wallacefield, Armathwaite, Carlisle CA4 9SR. *T:* 07702 100111. *E:* julia.aglionby@wallacefield.org.

**AGNELLO, Raquel, (Mrs Michel Hanns);** QC 2009; *b* London, 29 July 1963; *d* of Jose Agnello de Vaz Carreiro and Maria Eduarda Tavares Botelho Machado de Vaz Carreiro; *m* 2000, Michel Hanns; one *s* one *d. Educ:* Norra Reals Gymnasium, Stockholm; Univ. of Sussex (BA Hons Law with French); Univ. of Strasbourg (Dip. d'Etudes Juridiques Françaises). MCIArb 1989. Called to the Bar, Inner Temple, 1986, Bencher, 2011; Dep. Insolvency and Companies Court Judge (formerly Dep. Registrar in Bankruptcy), 2001–. *Recreations:* ski-ing, listening to music (opera and classical). *Address:* Erskine Chambers, 33 Chancery Lane, WC2A 1EN. *T:* (020) 7242 5532, *Fax:* (020) 7831 0125. *E:* ragnello@erskinechambers.com.

**AGNEW,** family name of **Baron Agnew of Oulton**.

**AGNEW OF OULTON,** Baron *cr* 2017 (Life Peer), of Oulton in the County of Norfolk; **Theodore Thomas More Agnew,** Kt 2015; DL; philanthropist; Parliamentary Under-Secretary of State, Department for Education, since 2017; *b* UK, 17 Jan. 1961; *s* of Stephen and Elizabeth Agnew; *m* 1993, Clare; one *s* one *d. Educ:* Rugby Sch. Non-executive Board Member: DfE, 2010–15 (Chm., Acads Bd, 2013–15); MoJ, 2015–17. Founder and Chm., Inspiration Trust, 2012–17; Trustee: New Schs Network, 2009–12; Educn Policy Inst. (formerly CentreForum), 2015–. DL Norfolk, 2012. *Recreation:* European military history. *Clubs:* Boodle's, Cavalry and Guards.

**AGNEW, Christine;** QC 2015; a Recorder, since 2016; *b* Northern Ireland; *d* of Robert and Amy Agnew; *m* 1997, Caspar Hilary Gordon Glyn, *qv*; two *s* one *d. Educ:* Methodist Coll., Belfast; Univ. of W of England (LLB). Called to the Bar, Inner Temple, 1992. *Recreations:* theatre, eating out, ski-ing, home, friends and family, Chelsea Football and Ireland Rugby supporter, touchline Mum. *Address:* 2 Bedford Row, WC1R 4BU. *T:* (020) 7440 8888. *E:* cagnew@2bedfordrow.co.uk.

**AGNEW of Lochnaw, Sir Crispin Hamlyn,** 11th Bt *cr* 1629; QC (Scot.) 1995; Rothesay Herald of Arms, since 1986; Chief of the Name and Arms of Agnew; *b* 13 May 1944; *s* of (Sir) Fulque Melville Gerald Noel Agnew of Lochnaw, 10th Bt and Swanzie, *d* of late Major Esmé Nourse Erskine, CMG, MC; *S* father, 1975; *m* 1980, Susan Rachel (careers adviser, formerly journalist, broadcaster, Advertising Exec.), *yr d* of late J. W. Strang Steel, Logie, Kirriemuir, Angus; one *s* three *d. Educ:* Uppingham; RMA, Sandhurst. Major (retd 1981), late RHF. Admitted to Faculty of Advocates, 1982. A Dep. Upper Tribunal Judge (formerly Dep. Social Security and Child Support Comr), 2000–19; Part-time Chm., Pension Appeal Tribunal, 2002–12; Convenor, Mental Health Tribunal for Scotland, 2016–19. Slains Pursuivant of Arms to Lord High Constable of Scotland, 1978–81; Unicorn Pursuivant of Arms, 1981–86. Trustee, John Muir Trust, 1989–2005. Mem. Council, 2008–10, Mem. Bd, 2010–12, Scottish Youth Hostels Assoc. Patron, UK Envmtl Law Assoc., 2010–18 (Convenor, Scottish Cttee, 2010–12). Leader: Army Expedn to E Greenland, 1968; Jt Services Expedn to Chilean Patagonia, 1972–73; Army Expedn to Api, NW Nepal, 1980; Member: RN Expedn to E Greenland, 1966; Jt Services to Elephant Island (Antarctica), 1970–71; Army Nuptse Expedn, 1975; Jt British and Royal Nepalese Army Everest Expedn, 1976 (reached the South Col). FRGS 1969. *Publications:* (jtly) Allan and Chapman, Licensing (Scotland) Act 1976, 2nd edn 1989, 5th edn 2002; (jtly) Connell on the Agricultural Holdings Acts, 7th edn 1996; Agricultural Law in Scotland, 1996; Land Obligations, 1999; Crofting Law, 2000; (contrib.) The Law of Trees, Forests and Hedgerows, 2nd edn, 2011; articles in newspapers and magazines, and in legal and heraldic jls. *Recreations:* mountaineering, sailing (Yacht Pippa's Song), heraldry, mountain biking. *Heir: s* Mark Douglas Noel Agnew of Lochnaw, yr, *b* 24 April 1991. *Address:* 6 Palmerston Road, Edinburgh EH9 1TN.

**AGNEW, Fraser;** *see* Agnew, W. A. F.

**AGNEW, Sir George (Anthony),** 7th Bt *cr* 1895, of Great Stanhope Street, London; joint owner, Rougham Estate, Suffolk, since 1994; *b* Rougham, 18 Aug. 1953; *yr s* of Major Sir (George) Keith Agnew, 5th Bt, TD and Anne Merete Louise Schaffalitzky de Muckadell; *S* brother, 2011; civil partnership 2007, Adrian Paul White. *Educ:* Gresham's Sch., Holt; Univ. of East Anglia (BA Hons). Director: Blackthorpe Barn Arts, 1993–; Summer Music at Blackthorpe Barn, 1993–2011. Chm. Trustees, Rougham Estate Trust, 2014–. *Recreations:* gardening, classical music, cooking, travel. *Heir: cousin* John Stuart Agnew [*b* 30 Aug. 1949; *m* 1982, Diana Margaret Zoë Baker; three *s*]. *Address:* Estate Office, Rougham, Bury St Edmunds, Suffolk IP30 9LZ. *T:* (01359) 270238, *Fax:* (01359) 271555. *E:* george@roughamestate.com.

**AGNEW, (John) Stuart;** Member (UK Ind) Eastern, European Parliament, 2009–19; *b* Oulton, Norwich, 30 Aug. 1949; *s* of Stephen William Agnew and Elizabeth Agnew (*née* Close); *m* 1982, Diana Margaret Zoe Baker; three *s. Educ:* Gordonstoun Sch.; Royal Agricultural Coll. (NDA 1971; McClennan Silver Medal 1971). MRAC 1971. Teacher, Church Mission Sch., Srinaga, Kashmir, 1968; farm pupil, Maj. C. Maude, 1968–69; Farm Manager, Narford Farm, 1971–74; Soil and Water Conservation Officer, Min. of Agric., Rhodesia, 1975–76; Rhodesian Army, 1976; Farm Manager, C. W. Cave, 1976–77 and 1978–81, Rogate Farms Ltd, 1977–83; farmer, free-range eggs, sheep and arable crops, 1983–. Chm., Norfolk Co., NFU, 1997; Norfolk Deleg., NFU Council, 2000–09; Local Dir, NFU Mutual Insce Soc., 2001–09. Contested (UK Ind) Eastern, EP, 2019. *Recreations:* country sports, cricket, snooker. *Address:* Paxfield Farm, Helhoughton, Fakenham, Norfolk NR21 7HJ. *T:* (01485) 528917, 07850 269424. *Club:* Farmers.

**AGNEW, Jonathan Geoffrey William;** Chairman, Fleet Mortgages Ltd, since 2014; *b* 30 July 1941; *er s* of Sir Geoffrey Agnew and Hon. Doreen Maud, *y d* of 1st Baron Jessel, CB, CMG; *m* 1st, 1966, Hon. Joanna Campbell (marr. diss. 1985); one *s* two *d*; 2nd, 1990, Marie-Claire Dreesmann; one *s* one *d. Educ:* Eton College; Trinity College, Cambridge (MA). The Economist, 1964–65; World Bank, 1965–67; Hill Samuel & Co., 1967–73. Dir, 1971–73; Morgan Stanley & Co., 1973–82, Man. Dir, 1977–82; J. G. W. Agnew & Co., 1983–86; Kleinwort Benson Gp, 1987–93, Gp Chief Exec., 1989–93; Chairman: Limit, 1993–2000; Gerrard Gp, 1998–2000; Nationwide Bldg Soc., 2002–07 (Dep. Chm.,

1999–2002; non-exec. Dir, 1997–2007); Beazley (formerly Beazley Gp), 2003–12 (non-exec. Dir, 2002–12); LMS Capital (formerly Leo Capital), 2006–10; The Cayenne Trust, 2006–15; Ashmore Global Opportunities, 2007–13; non-executive Director: Thos Agnew & Sons Ltd, 1969–2007; Thos Agnew and Sons Hldgs Ltd, 2007–13; Sen. Ind. Dir, Rightmove plc, 2007–15. Mem. Council, Lloyd's, 1995–99. *Address:* Flat E, 51 Eaton Square, SW1W 9BE. *Clubs:* White's; Automobile (Paris).

**AGNEW, Jonathan Philip,** MBE 2017; DL; cricket correspondent, BBC, since 1991; *b* 4 April 1960; *s* of Philip Agnew and Margaret Agnew; *m* 1996, Emma Norris; two *d* by former marriage. *Educ:* Uppingham Sch. Professional cricketer: début, Leics CCC, 1978; played for England, 1984–85; retd from first class cricket, 1990; cricket corresp., Today, 1990–91. DL Leics, 2015. Sports Reporter of Year, Sony, 1992. *Publications:* 8 Days a Week, 1988; (ed) Cricket Year (annually), 1989–2010; Over to You, Aggers (autobiog.), 1997; (with Peter Baxter) Inside the Box, 2009; (with Bill Frindall) Ask Bearders, 2009; Thanks, Johnners, 2010; Aggers' Ashes, 2011; Cricket: a modern anthology, 2013. *Address:* c/o Jane Morgan Management, Argentum, 2 Queen Caroline Street, W6 9DX. *T:* (020) 3178 8071.

**AGNEW, Rosemary;** Scottish Public Services Ombudsman, since 2017. *Educ:* Manchester Business Sch. (MBA (dist.)). CEO, Scottish Legal Complaints Commn, 2009–12; Scottish Information Comr, 2012–17. *Address:* Scottish Public Services Ombudsman, 99 McDonald Road, Edinburgh EH7 4NS. *T:* 0800 377 7330. *E:* ask@spso.org.uk.

**AGNEW, Sir Rudolph (Ion Joseph),** Kt 2002; Chairman, Stena International BV, 1990–2007; Director, 2004–09, Consultant, 2009–11, Petropavlovsk (formerly Peter Hambro Mining) PLC; *b* 12 March 1934; *s* of Rudolph John Agnew and Pamela Geraldine (*née* Campbell); *m* 1980, Whitney Warren (*d* 2018); one *s* one *d* by previous marriage. *Educ:* Downside School. Commissioned officer, 8th King's Royal Irish Hussars, 1953–57. Joined Consolidated Gold Fields, 1957; Dep. Chm., 1978–82; Gp Chief Exec., 1978–89; Chm., 1983–89; Mem., Cttee of Man. Dirs, 1986–89. Chairman: TVS Entertainment, 1990–93; Federated Aggregates PLC, 1991–95; Global Stone Corp. (Canada), 1993–94; Bona Shipholding Ltd, Bermuda, 1993–98; LASMO PLC, 1994–2000; Redland plc, 1995–97; Star Mining Corp., 1995–98; Wentworth Wooden Jigsaw Co., 2011–17; non-executive Director: Internat. Tool and Supply (formerly New London) PLC, 1985–96; Standard Chartered PLC, 1988–97; Newmont Mining Corp., USA, 1989–98; Newmont Gold Co., USA, 1989–99; Stena (UK) Ltd, 1990–99; Director: Gold Fields of South Africa Ltd, 1978–89; Renison Goldfields Consolidated, 1978–90; Anglo American Corp. of South Africa, 1980–88; Hanson PLC, 1989–91. Vice President: Nat. Assoc. of Boys' Clubs; Game Conservancy (Fellow); Hawk Trust; Chm., World Conservation Monitoring Centre, 1989–2006 (Hon. Pres., 2013); Fellow, WWF (UK), 2006 (Trustee, 1983–89). CCMI (FBIM 1980); FRSA. *Recreations:* shooting, racing. *Clubs:* White's, Cavalry and Guards.

**AGNEW, Steven;** Member (Green) North Down, Northern Ireland Assembly, since 2011; *b* Dundonald, Belfast, 12 Oct. 1979; *s* of H. Bell and step *s* of R. Bell; one *s* one *d. Educ:* Brooklands Primary Sch., Dundonald, Belfast; Grosvenor Grammar Sch., Belfast; Queen's Univ., Belfast (BA Hons Philosophy). Porter, HSE NI, 2002; Homeless Support Worker: First Housing Aid and Support Services, 2003–04; Simon Community, 2004–07; Res. Officer to Brian Wilson, MLA, 2007–11. Contested (Green) N Down, 2015, 2017. *Recreations:* music, film, football, acting (appeared in I Wanted to Talk to You Last Night and Endless Life, directed by Michael MacBroom). *Address:* Northern Ireland Assembly, Parliament Buildings, Stormont, Belfast BT4 3XX. *T:* (028) 9052 1790. *E:* steven.agnew@mla.niassembly.gov.uk; (office) 76 Abbey Street, Bangor BT20 4JB. *T:* (028) 9145 9110.

**AGNEW, Stuart;** *see* Agnew, J. S.

**AGNEW, (William Alexander) Fraser,** MBE 2015; Cultural Co-ordinator, Farset Youth and Community Group, 1981–85; *b* 16 Aug. 1942; *s* of late James Agnew and Maureen Barbara Agnew (*née* Fraser); *m* 1972, Lila McCausland; one *s. Educ:* Ballyclare High Sch.; Univ. of Ulster at Jordanstown; Belfast Tech. Coll.; Coll. of Business Studies. MCIOB (MIOB 1968). Irish League footballer, 1960–68. Architectural draughtsman and company dir, until 1990; part-time sports journalist; presenter, history programmes on community radio; lecturer. Mem., NI Assembly, 1982–86; Mem. (UU) Belfast North, NI Assembly, 1998–2003. Mem. (UU, 1980–90 and 2011–, Ind., 1990–2011) Newtownabbey BC (Chairman: Corporate Services Cttee, 1993–94, 1995–96; Culture and Tourism Cttee, 1995–96); Mayor, Newtownabbey, 1990–91, 2013–14. Director: Woodvale and Shankill Housing Assoc., 2005–; Farset Internat., 2010–. Gov., Mossley Primary Sch., 2000–. Formerly Chm., Ulster Tourist Develt Assoc. Chm., Ulster Young Unionist Council, 1970. Associate Mem., Inst. of Engrg Technol., 1969. Freeman, Newtownabbey, 2007. *Publications:* numerous pamphlets on aspects of Ireland's history. *Recreations:* soccer coaching for children (qualified coach), 5-a-side football, golf. *Address:* 1 Knockview Crescent, Newtownabbey BT36 6UD. *T:* (028) 9050 6147; (office) Mossley Mill, Newtownabbey, Co. Antrim BT36 5QA.

**AGNEW-SOMERVILLE, Sir (James) Lockett (Charles),** 3rd Bt *cr* 1957, of Clendry, Co. Wigtown; plumbing and heating engineer; *b* Dublin, 26 May 1970; *o s* of Sir Quentin Agnew-Somerville, 2nd Bt and of Hon. April Drummond, *y d* of 15th Baron Strange; *S* father, 2010. *Educ:* Headfort, Co. Meath; Milton Abbey. NVQ Level 3 Plumbing and Heating; Gas Safe. *Publications:* (as Lockett Somerville) The London Eye (poetry). *Recreations:* tents, dogs, music. *Heir:* none. *Address:* 6 Albion Terrace, Ramsey, Isle of Man IM8 2LW.

**AGRAN, Linda Valerie,** Executive Producer, Sky Arts Theatre Live!, 2009; *b* 9 May 1947; *d* of Albert and Gertrude Agran; *m* 1991, Alexander Gordon Scott. *Educ:* Queen Elizabeth's Girls' Grammar Sch., Barnet. William Morris Agency, Columbia Pictures, Paramount Pictures, Warner Bros, 1973–76; Head of Development, 1976, Director, 1982, Euston Films; Writer in Residence, Aust. Film & TV Sch.; Dep. Controller of Drama and Arts, LWT, 1986; Chief Exec., Paravision (UK) Ltd, 1989; completed management buyout to form Agran Barton TV, 1993, Jt Chief Exec., 1993–2000; Founder, Linda Agran Clothes Storage, 2004. Consultant to Hartswood Films. FRSA. *Television* (as producer or executive producer): series include: Minder; Widows; Paradise Postponed; London's Burning; Hercule Poirot; Moving Story. *Recreations:* cooking good food, drinking fine wines, horse racing, reading, all in the company of close friends.

**AGRAWAL, Rajesh;** Deputy Mayor of London for Business, since 2016; *b* Indore, India, 9 June 1977; *s* of Sobhagmal Agrawal and Krishnakanta Agrawal; *m* 2008, Charu Jain; two *d. Educ:* Prestige Inst. of Mgt and Res. (BBA, MBA). Chairman and Chief Executive Officer: RationalFX, 2005–16; Xendpay, 2012–16. Chm., London & Partners, 2016–. FRSA 2008. *Recreations:* reading, travelling, socialising. *Address:* City Hall, Queen's Walk, SE1 2AA. *Club:* Royal Automobile.

**AGRE, Prof. Peter Courtland,** MD; Director, Malaria Research Institute, since 2008, and Bloomberg Distinguished Professor, since 2014, Johns Hopkins Bloomberg School of Public Health; *b* 30 Jan. 1949; *s* of late Courtland Leverne Agre and of Ellen Violet Agre (*née* Swedberg); *m* 1975, Mary Macgill; one *s* three *d* (and one *d* decd). *Educ:* Theodore Roosevelt High Sch., Minneapolis; Augsburg Coll., Minneapolis (BA 1970); Johns

Hopkins Univ. (MD 1974). Fellow, 1978–80, Asst Prof. of Medicine, 1980–81, Univ. of N Carolina; Sen. Clin. Res. Scientist, Wellcome Labs, Research Triangle Park, NC, 1980–81; Johns Hopkins University: Res. Associate, 1981–83, Asst Prof., 1984–88, Associate Prof., 1988–93, Sch. of Medicine; Prof. of Biol Chemistry and of Medicine, 1993–2005; Vice-Chancellor for Sci. and Technol., Duke Univ. Med. Center, 2005–07. (Jtly) Nobel Prize for Chemistry, 2003. *Publications:* articles in learned jls. *Address:* Malaria Research Institute, Johns Hopkins Bloomberg School of Public Health, Room E5146, 615 North Wolfe Street, Baltimore, MD 21205, USA.

**AGUIRRE, Marcelino O.;** *see* Oreja Aguirre.

**ÁGÚSTSSON, Helgi,** Hon. GCVO 1990; Icelandic Grand Order of the Falcon, 1990 (Order of the Falcon, 1979); Headmaster, Diplomatic School, Ministry of Foreign Affairs, Iceland, 2010–11; *b* 16 Oct. 1941; *s* of Ágúst Pétursson and Helga Jóhannesdóttir; *m* 1963, Hervör Jónasdóttir (*d* 2016); three *s* one *d. Educ:* Univ. of Iceland (Law degree 1970); Icelandic Sch. of Travel and Tourism (dip. tour guide, 2010). Joined Foreign Ministry, 1970; served London, 1973–77; Counsellor, 1977; Dir, Defence Div., Foreign Min., 1979 and Chm., US-Icelandic Defence Council; Minister-Counsellor, 1980; served Washington, 1983–87; Dep. Perm. Under-Sec., Foreign Min., 1987, in rank of Ambassador; Ambassador to UK, 1989–94, and to Ireland, Holland and Nigeria, 1990–94; Perm. Under-Sec., Min. for Foreign Affairs, Iceland, 1995–99; Ambassador: to Denmark, also accredited to Lithuania, Turkey, Israel and Romania, 1999–2002; to USA, also accredited to Argentina, Brazil, Chile, El Salvador, Guatemala, Mexico and Uruguay, 2002–06; Special Assignments, Min. of Foreign Affairs, 2007–08; Chief of Protocol, Min. of Foreign Affairs, Iceland, 2008; Advr, 2008–09. Chm. Bd, Save the Children, Iceland, 2009–12. Former Pres., Icelandic Basketball Fedn. Decorations from Finland, Denmark, Sweden, Norway, Italy, Spain, Netherlands. *Recreations:* theatre, music, reading, salmon fishing, playing pool.

**AGUTTER, Jennifer Ann,** OBE 2012; actress; *b* 20 Dec. 1952; *d* of late Derek and of Catherine Agutter; *m* 1990, Johan Tham; one *s. Educ:* Elmhurst Ballet School, Camberley. *Films:* East of Sudan, 1964; Ballerina, 1964; Gates of Paradise, 1967; Star, 1968; Walkabout, I Start Counting, The Railway Children, 1969 (Royal Variety Club Most Promising Artist, 1971); Logan's Run, 1975; The Eagle Has Landed, Equus (BAFTA Best Supporting Actress, 1977), The Man In The Iron Mask, 1976; Dominique, Clayton and Catherine, 1977; The Riddle of the Sands, Sweet William, 1978; The Survivor, 1980; An American Werewolf in London, 1981; Secret Places, 1983; Dark Tower, 1987; King of the Wind, 1989; Child's Play 2, 1991; Freddie as Fro7, 1992; Blue Juice, 1995; The Parole Officer, 2001; Number One, Longing, Number Two, Regret, 2004; Heroes and Villains, 2006; Irina Palm, 2008; Glorious 39, 2009; Outside Bet, 2012; Avengers Assemble, 2012; Captain America: The Winter Soldier, 2014; Sometimes Always Never, 2019; *stage:* School for Scandal, 1972; Rooted, Arms and the Man, The Ride Across Lake Constance, 1973; National Theatre: The Tempest, Spring Awakening, 1974; Hedda, Betrayal, 1980; Peter Pan, 1997; Royal Shakespeare Co.: Arden of Faversham, Lear, King Lear, The Body, 1982–83; Breaking the Silence, 1985; Shrew, The Unified Field, LA, 1987; Breaking the Code, NY, 1987; Love's Labour's Lost, Barbican, 1995; Mothers and Daughters, Chichester, 1996; Equus, Gielgud, 2007; *television includes:* Long After Summer, 1967; The Wild Duck, The Cherry Orchard, The Snow Goose (Emmy Best Supporting Actress), 1971; A War of Children, 1972; School Play, 1979; Amy, 1980; Love's Labour's Lost, This Office Life, 1984; Silas Marner, 1985; Murder She Wrote, 1986; The Equaliser, Magnum, 1988; Dear John, 1989; Not a Penny More, Not a Penny Less, Tecx, 1990; The Good Guys, Puss in Boots, 1991; The Buccaneers, 1995; And the Beat Goes On, 1996; Bramwell, A Respectable Trade, 1998; The Railway Children, 2000; Spooks, 2002, 2003; The Alan Clark Diaries, 2004; The Invisibles, 2008; Monday Monday, 2009; Call the Midwife, 2012–. Hon. DLitt Bradford, 2004. *Publications:* Snap, 1983. *Address:* c/o The Artists Partnership, 21–22 Warwick Street, W1B 5NE. *T:* (020) 7439 1456.

**AGUTTER, Richard Devenish;** corporate finance adviser, since 1976; Senior Adviser, KPMG, 1998–2005; *b* 17 Sept. 1941; *s* of late Anthony Tom Devenish Agutter and Joan Hildegare Sabina (*née* Machen); *m* 1968, Lesley Anne Ballard; three *s. Educ:* Marlborough Coll. CA 1964. With W. T. Walton, 1960–64; joined Peat Marwick Mitchell, subsequently KPMG, 1964: Partner, 1977–98; Chm., KPMG Internat. Corporate Finance, 1990–96. City of London: Alderman, Ward of Castle Baynard, 1995–2005; Sheriff, 2000–01. Liveryman: Goldsmiths' Co., 1979– (Mem., Ct of Assts, 1999–; Prime Warden, 2013–14); Co. of Marketors, 1999–2016; Hon. Liveryman, Co. of Tax Advisers, 2005 (Mem., Ct of Assts, 2005–; Master, 2008–09); Master, Guild of Freemen, 2004. Hon. Fellow, Birkbeck, Univ. of London, 2011. *Recreations:* wine, gardening, sailing. *Address:* Leabridge Farmhouse, West Burton, near Pulborough, West Sussex RH20 1HD. *T:* (01798) 839169.

**AHEARNE, Stephen James,** FCA; Chief Financial Officer, 1990–96, and Managing Director, 1992–96, British Petroleum Company PLC; *b* 7 Sept. 1939; *s* of James Joseph Ahearne and Phyllis Eva (*née* Grigsby); *m* 1965, Janet Elizabeth Edwards; two *s*. Qualified as Chartered Accountant, 1962; joined British Petroleum, 1964: Man. Dir, BP Denmark, 1978–81; Exec. Dir, BP Chems, 1981–86; Gp Controller, 1986–88; Gp Planner, 1988–90. Mem., Restrictive Practices Court, 1993–99. Gov., Felsted Sch., 1996–2015. *Recreations:* tennis, gardening, walking, reading, learning languages.

**AHERN, Bertie;** Member of the Dáil (TD) (FF), 1977–2011; Taoiseach (Prime Minister of Ireland), 1997–2008; President, Fianna Fáil, 1994–2008; *b* 12 Sept. 1951; *s* of Cornelius and Julia Ahern; *m* 1975 (separated); two *d. Educ:* Rathmines Coll. of Commerce; University Coll., Dublin. Accountant. Asst Chief Whip, 1980–81; spokesman on youth affairs, 1981; Govt Chief Whip and Minister of State at Depts of Taoiseach and Defence, 1982; Minister for Labour, 1987–91; Minister for Finance, 1991–94; Leader of the Opposition, 1994–97. Lord Mayor of Dublin, 1986–87. Member, Board of Governors, 1991–94: IMF; World Bank; EIB (Chm., 1991–92). Involved in conflict resolution in several countries, 2008–19. Co-Chm. Council, InterAction; Chm., Bougainville Referendum Commn, PNG. Grand Cross, Order of Merit with Star and Sash (Germany), 1991. *Recreations:* sports, reading. *Address:* Drumcondra Business Centre, 120 Upper Drumcondra Road, Drumcondra, Dublin 9, Ireland.

**AHERN, Dermot;** Member of the Dáil (TD) (FF) for Louth, 1987–2011; Minister for Justice, Equality and Law Reform, Republic of Ireland, 2008–11; solicitor, mediator; *b* 2 Feb. 1955; *s* of Jerry Ahern; *m* 1980, Maeve Coleman; two *d. Educ:* St Mary's Coll. Secondary Sch., Dundalk; University Coll., Dublin (BCL); Law Soc. of Ireland. Mem. (FF) Louth CC, 1979–91. Asst Govt Whip, 1988–91; Minister of State, Dept of Defence and Dept of Taoiseach, and Govt Chief Whip, 1991–92; Minister: for Social, Community and Family Affairs, 1997–2002; for Communications, Marine and Natural Resources, 2002–04; for Foreign Affairs, 2004–08. Mem., British-Irish Parly Body, 1991–97 (Co-Chm., 1993–95). *Recreations:* windsurfing, ski-ing, golf. *Address:* Blackrock, Dundalk, Co. Louth, Ireland.

**AHERNE, Gerald Paul;** Managing Partner, Javelin Capital Partners LLP, since 2003; *b* London, 15 Jan. 1946; *s* of John Aherne and Eileen Aherne (*née* Peters); *m* 1st, 1971, Mary Wright (marr. diss. 1987); one *s* one *d*; 2nd, 1995, Robina Handley (marr. diss. 2006); two *d*; *m* 2018, Saralynn Gallafent. *Educ:* St Joseph's Acad., Blackheath; Univ. of Surrey (BSc Maths). AIA 1980. Actuarial and investment mgt rôles in UK and Europe, Equity & Law, 1968–86; Investment Dir, Schroder Investment Mgt, 1986–2002; Founding Dir, PRI Gp plc, 2002–03; Founding Partner and Chief Exec., Javelin Capital LLP, 2009–11; Chairman: Cenkos Securities plc, 2012–18; Electric & General Investment Fund (formerly Trust plc), 2012– (non-exec. Dir, 2003–11); non-executive Director: Henderson Global Investors Ltd, 2004–12; Majedie Investments plc, 2006–09, 2011–12; Hadleigh plc, 2007–11; Mecom Gp plc, 2009–12; TSM Agencies Ltd, 2010–12; Omnis Investments Ltd, 2012–15; Iveagh Ltd, 2012–14; Linear Investments, 2013–14. *Recreations:* film, fishing, travel, politics, gardening, France. *Club:* City of London.

**AHMAD,** family name of **Baron Ahmad of Wimbledon**.

**AHMAD OF WIMBLEDON,** Baron *cr* 2011 (Life Peer), of Wimbledon in the London Borough of Merton; **Tariq Mahmood Ahmad;** Minister of State, Foreign and Commonwealth Office, since 2017; Prime Minister's Special Representative on Preventing Sexual Violence in Conflict, since 2017; *b* London, 3 April 1968; *s* of Chaudhry Mansoor Ahmad, BT and Amtul Matin Ahmad (*née* Mir); *m* 2011, Siddiquea Masud; two *s* one *d. Educ:* Rutlish Sch.; London South Bank Univ. (BA Hons Business 1990); City Univ. (ACIB 1996). Mgt roles in corporate banking and Hd Office, NatWest Gp, 1991–2000; Vice Pres., and Dir, Marketing, Alliance Berstein, 2000–03; Dir, Strategy and Marketing, Sucden Financial Ltd, 2004–12. Mem. (C) Merton LBC, 2002–12 (Mem. Cabinet for Envmt, 2006–08, for Community Safety and Policing, 2008–09). A Lord in Waiting (Govt Whip), 2012–14; Parly Under-Sec. of State, DCLG, 2014–15, Home Office and DfT, 2015–16, DfT, 2016–17; Prime Minister's Special Envoy on Freedom of Religion or Belief, 2018–19. Contested (C) Croydon N, 2005. Vice Pres., Conservative Party, 2008–10. MInstD. *Recreations:* charity work, various sports, charity runs. *Address:* House of Lords, SW1A 0PW. *E:* ahmadt@parliament.uk.

**AHMAD, Asif Anwar,** CMG 2017; HM Diplomatic Service; High Commissioner to Jamaica, since 2017; *b* London, 21 Jan. 1956; *s* of late Salahuddin Ahmad and of Bandana Ahmad; two *s. Educ:* Community High Sch., Tehran; Carlisle Tech. Coll.; Durham Univ. (BA Hons Econs 1977); INSEAD (Internat. Exec. Prog. 1991). Nat. Westminster Bank, later NatWest, 1977–96, incl. Coutts, Sen. Manager, internat., domestic and private banking; business advr, Business Link London, 1996–99; joined FCO, 1999; Dep. Hd, Resource Budgeting Dept, 1999–2000; Hd, Commonwealth Co-ordination Dept, 2001–04; Hd, Communication and Inf. Centre, Prime Minister's Office, 2003–04; Dir, Asia, UK Trade and Investment, 2004–08; Hd, SE Asia and Pacific Dept, FCO, 2008–10; Ambassador: to Thailand, 2010–12; to the Philippines, 2013–17; High Comr to the Bahamas, 2017–19. *Recreations:* passionate Liverpool FC fan, cricket, theatre, music, travel. *Address:* c/o Foreign and Commonwealth Office, King Charles Street, SW1A 2AH. *E:* asif.ahmad@fco.gov.uk.

**AHMAD, Khurshid;** Chairman: Institute of Policy Studies, Islamabad, Pakistan, since 1979; Board of Trustees, Islamic Foundation, Leicester, 1978–2015; Member, Senate of Pakistan, 1985–97, and 2003–12; *b* 23 March 1932; three *s* three *d. Educ:* Karachi Univ. (LLB; MA Economics; MA Islamic Studies). Dir-Gen., Islamic Foundn, Leicester, 1973–78; Federal Minister for Planning and Develt and Dep. Chm., Planning Commn, Govt of Pakistan, 1978–79. Chm., Internat. Inst. of Islamic Econs, Islamic Univ., Islamabad, 1983–87. Hon. PhD: Educn, Nat. Univ. of Malaya; Internat. Islamic Univ., Kuala Lumpur; Hon. DLitt Loughborough, 2003. Islamic Develt Bank Laureate for dist. contribn to Islamic econs, 1988; King Faisal, Internat. Prize for service to Islam, 1990. *Publications:* Essays on Pakistan Economy (Karachi), 1958; An Analysis of Munir Report (Lahore), 1958; (ed) Studies in the Family Law of Islam (Karachi), 1960; (ed) The Quran: an Introduction (Karachi), 1966; The Prophet of Islam (Karachi), 1967; Principles of Islamic Education (Lahore), 1970; Fanaticism, Intolerance and Islam (Lahore), 1970; Islam and the West (Lahore), 1972; The Religion of Islam (Lahore), 1973; (ed) Islam: its meaning and message (London, Islamic Council of Europe), 1976; Development Strategy for the Sixth Plan (Islamabad), 1983; Islamic Approach to Development: some policy implications (Islamabad), 1994; Islamic Resurgence: challenges, directions and future perspectives, ed I. M. Abu-Rabi, 1995; The Crisis of the Political System in Pakistan and the Jamaat-e-Islami, 1996; *for Islamic Foundation, Leicester:* Islam: Basic Principles and Characteristics, 1974; Family Life in Islam, 1974; Islamic Perspectives: Studies in honour of Maulana Mawdudi, 1979; The Quran: Basic Teachings, 1979; Studies in Islamic Economics, 1980; contrib. The Third World's Dilemma of Development, Non-Aligned Third World Annual, (USA) 1970. *Recreations:* travelling, reading. *Address:* Islamic Foundation, Markfield Conference Centre, Ratby Lane, Markfield, Leics LE67 9SY. *T:* (01530) 244944; Institute of Policy Studies, House 1, Islamabad 44000, Pakistan. *T:* (51) 8438391. *E:* khurshid@ips.net.pk.

**AHMAD, Mushtaq,** OBE 2007; JP; Lord-Lieutenant of Lanarkshire, 2010–17; *b* Chhinah, India, 12 Nov. 1942; *s* of Choudary Inayat Ali Ahmadi and Khurshaid Begum; three *s* two *d* by Ann-Marie Razia Anne. *Educ:* Punjab Univ. (BA 1962); Univ. of Glasgow (MA 1969; Dip. Adult Educn 1993); Jordanhill Coll. of Educn, Glasgow (PGCE 1971). Migrated to Pakistan, 1947, moved to UK, 1963; worked in British industry, 1963–66; teacher: of modern studies, Earnock High Sch., Hamilton, 1972–74; of English, Daneford High Sch., London, 1974–77; Specialist Organiser of Adult Basic Educn, Lanarks, 1977–97. Chm.- Consultant (pt-time), Lifeskills Central, 2007–; Chm., Hamilton Dist, CAB, 2008–. Mem., Hamilton DC, then South Lanarks Council, 1988–2007, Provost, South Lanarks Council, 2003–07. Founder Pres., 2003–08, Vice Pres., 2008–, Scottish Provost's Assoc. JP Hamilton, 1988 (Chm., Justice's Cttee, 1988–2003). Mem., Amnesty Internat. *Recreations:* charity work to help alleviate the difficulties experienced by the disadvantaged, reading, current affairs. *Address:* 79 Rosevale Crescent, Hamilton, Lanarks ML3 8NX. *T:* and *Fax:* (01698) 429993, *T:* 07768 093979. *E:* mushtaq.ahmad@blueyonder.co.uk.

**AHMADI, Hon. Aziz Mushabber;** Chief Justice of India, 1994–97; *b* 25 March 1932; *s* of M. I. Ahmadi and Shirin I. Ahmadi; *m* 1960, Amena A. Muchhala; one *s* one *d. Educ:* Ahmedabad and Surat (LLB). Called to the Bar, Ahmedabad, 1954; Judge, City Civil and Sessions Court, Ahmedabad, 1964–74; Sec., Legal Dept, Govt of Gujarat, 1974–76; Judge, High Court of Gujarat, 1976–88; Judge, Supreme Court of India, 1988–94. Pres., Supreme Court Legal Aid Cttee, 1989; Exec. Chm., Cttee for Implementing Legal Aid Schemes in India, 1994. Chairman: Adv. Bd, Conservation of Foreign Exchange and Prevention of Smuggling Activities Act, 1974; Adv. Bd, Prevention of Black Marketing, Maintenance of Supplies of Essential Commodities Act, 1982–83; Gujarat Third Pay Commn, 1982–85. Member: UN Commn of Inquiry, East Timor, 1999; Internat. Bar Assoc. Mission to Zimbabwe, 2001. Chancellor, Aligarh Muslim Univ., 2003–06. Hon. Bencher, Middle Temple, 1996. Hon. LLD: Kurukshetra, 1994; Maharishi Dayanand, 1995; Kanpur, 1995; Sardar Patel, 1996; Cochin, 1997; Leicester, 1998. *Recreations:* reading, music. *E:* amahmadi@bol.net.in. *Clubs:* Delhi Gymkhana, India International Centre (New Delhi).

**AHMED,** Baron *cr* 1998 (Life Peer), of Rotherham in the co. of South Yorkshire; **Nazir Ahmed;** business development manager; *b* 24 April 1957; *s* of Haji Sain Mohammed and Rashim Bibi; *m* 1974, Sakina Bibi; two *s* one *d. Educ:* Thomas Rotherham Coll.; Sheffield Hallam Univ. Business development manager: mini-markets, 1979–82; fish and chip shops, 1979–2003; petrol station, 1982–84; marble mining, Azad, Kashmir, 1985–87; business park and property develt, 1990–. Advisor to Nestlé, 2003–06. Mem. (Lab) Rotherham MBC,

1990–2000. Founder, British Muslim Councillors Forum; founder Chm., Muslims for Labour. Chm., S Yorks Lab. Party, 1993–98. Chairman: All-Pty Parly Libya Gp, 1999–2001; All-Pty Parly Interfaith Inter-religious Gp; All-Pty Parly Financial Exploitation Gp; founder and Chm., All-Pty Parly Entrepreneurship Gp, 2009–13 (Vice-Chm., 2013–); founder, All-Pty Parly Enterprise Gp, 2009–13; Pres., All-Pty Parly Gp on Kashmir (Chm., 2010). Founder and Co-Chm., Govt's Forced Marriage Wkg Gp, 1999–; Chm., Preventing Extremism Together Working Gp on Imams trng and role of mosques, 2005. Mem., Channel 4 Hate Commn (on hate crime), 1999–. Mem. Council, BHF, 2007–. Pres., S Yorks Victim Support. Led first Hajj delegn on behalf of British govt, 2000; leader, British Muslim Peace and Reconciliation Initiative, 2009–. Advr to many internat. orgns on dialogue, tolerance and co-operation. Chancellor, British Inst. of Technol. and E-commerce, 2009–13. JP Rotherham, 1992. *Recreation:* volleyball. *Address:* 152 East Bawtry Road, Rotherham S60 4LG. *T:* (01709) 730140; House of Lords, SW1A 0PW.

**AHMED, Aaqil;** Head of Religion and Ethics, BBC, 2009–16; *b* Wigan, 5 June 1969; *s* of Maqbool Ahmed and Farhat Ahmed; *m* 1996, Saima Javed; one *s* two *d*. *Educ:* Univ. of Westminster (BA Hons Photography, Film and Video); London Business Sch. (Accelerated Develt Prog. 2010). BBC: Researcher, 1992–94, Asst Producer, 1994–95, Producer, 1995–96, Network TV; Producer, Network News and Current Affairs, 1997–2000; Exec. Producer, Religion and Ethics, 2000–03; Hd, Religion and Multicultural Progs, Channel 4, 2003–09. Chair: Mosaic Media Network, 2008–11; Cultural Diversity Network North, 2009–13; Mem. Bd, Mosaic, 2009–; Pres., BBC Black and Asian Workers Forum, 2014–. Trustee: Runnymede Trust, 2008–11; Rugby League Foundn, 2014–; Patron, Curriculum for Cohesion, 2013–. Professor: of Media, Middlesex Univ., 2013–15 (Vis. Prof. of Media, 2011–13); Univ. of Bolton, 2016–. Hon. Dr: Lancaster, 2012; Bolton, 2012. *Publications:* (contrib.) The Future of Public Service Broadcasting, 2008. *Recreations:* keen cyclist and regular five-a-side football player, coach and manager of under 15s football team, supporter of Bolton Wanderers, keen gardener and cook, learning the Arabic language in between reliving my youth on my Vespa scooter. *W:* www.twitter.com/aaqil1969.

**AHMED, Prof. Haroon,** ScD; FREng; Professor of Microelectronics, University of Cambridge, 1992–2003, now Emeritus; Fellow, 1967–2007, now Honorary Fellow, Master, 2000–06, Corpus Christi College, Cambridge (Warden of Leckhampton, 1993–98); *b* 2 March 1936; *s* of Mohammad Nizam Ahmed and Bilquis Jehan Ahmed; *m* 1969, Evelyn Anne Travers Goodrich; one *s* two *d*. *Educ:* St Patrick's Sch., Karachi; Imperial College London; King's College, Cambridge (PhD 1963); ScD Cantab 1996. GEC and Hirst Research Centre, 1958–59; Turner and Newall Res. Fellow, 1962–63; University of Cambridge: Univ. Demonstrator, Engineering Dept, 1963–66; Lectr, Engineering Dept, 1966–84; Reader in Microelectronics, 1984–92. Vis. Prof., Computer Lab., 2010–14, Engrg Dept, 2014–, Univ. of Cambridge. Non-exec. Dir, Addenbrooke's NHS Trust, 2001–04. Pres., Cambridge Philosophical Soc., 2004–06. Syndic, CUP, 1996–2002. Higher Educn Advr, Govt of Pakistan, 2006–08. Trustee: Noon Educnl Foundn, 2001–; Edith Evelyn Wali Mohammad Trust, 2009–. Mem., Develt Bd, Imperial Coll. London, 2006–10. FREng (FEng 1990). *Publications:* (with A. H. W. Beck) Introduction to Physical Electronics, 1968; (with P. J. Spreadbury) Electronics for Engineers, 1973, 2nd edn 1984; Cambridge Computing, 2013; (with P. N. Denbigh) Cambridge Depicted, 2013; Cambridge Engineering, 2017. *Recreations:* golf, table tennis, bridge. *Address:* Corpus Christi College, Cambridge CB2 1RH.

**AHMED, Kamal;** Editorial Director, BBC News, since 2018; *b* London, 8 Nov. 1967; *s* of late Abubaker Ismail Ahmed and of Elaine Ahmed (*née* Sturman); *m* (marr. diss.); one *s* one *d*. *Educ:* Drayton Manor High Sch.; Univ. of Leeds (BA Hons Politics); City University (Dip. Newspaper Journalism). Reporter, Lennox Herald, 1990–92; Chief Reporter, Scotland on Sunday, 1992–95; Royal Corresp., 1995–97, Media Editor, 1997–2000, The Guardian; Political Editor, 2000–04, Hd, News, 2004–07, The Observer; Dir, Communications, Equality and Human Rights Commn, 2007–09; Business Editor, Sunday Telegraph, 2009–14; Business Editor, 2014–16, Economics Editor, 2016–18, BBC. *Publications:* The Life and Times of a Very British Man, 2018. *Recreation:* gardening (badly). *Address:* BBC News, Broadcasting House, Portland Place, W1A 1AA.

**AHMED, Masood;** President, Center for Global Development, since 2017; *b* 13 Jan. 1953; *s* of late Aziz Ahmed and Phool Aziz Ahmed; *m* 1979, Priscilla Macleod; one *d*. *Educ:* St Joseph's Sch., Dhaka; Karachi Grammar Sch., Karachi; LSE (BSc Econ. 1974, MSc Econ. with dist. 1975). Res. Asst, then Lectr, LSE, 1975–78; joined World Bank, 1979: Economist, then Dep. Div. Chief, Energy Dept, 1980–86; Div. Chief, N Africa Country Dept, 1987–91; Div. Chief, Internat. Debt and Finance, 1991–93; Dir, Internat. Econs Dept, 1993–97; Vice Pres., Poverty Reduction and Econ. Mgt, 1997–2000; Dep. Dir, Policy Develt and Review, IMF, 2000–03; Dir Gen., Policy and Internat., DFID, 2003–06; Dir, External Relns, 2006–08, Dir, Middle East and Central Asia, 2008–16, IMF. Member, Board: Nutrition Internat.; Astana Financial Services Authy. *Recreations:* Urdu poetry, biographies, walking. *Address:* Center for Global Development, Washington, DC 20036, USA. *E:* mahmed@cgdev.org. *Club:* Reform.

**AHMED, Muddassar;** Founder and Managing Partner, Unitas Communications Ltd, since 2008; *b* London, 16 March 1983. Worked in television and production. Founder and President: Concordia Forum, 2008–; John Adams Soc., 2010–. Ind. Advr to UK Govt, 2015–16. Dir, Eur. Network of Amer. Alumni, 2012–; Member: Bd, British Pakistan Foundn, 2013–16; Inst. of Islamic Thought and Civilisation, Internat. Islamic Univ. of Malaysia, 2018–; Inst. for Rural Mgt, Pakistan, 2018–. Vis. Fellow, German Marshall Fund, USA, 2018–. Mem. Adv. Council, US Atlantic Council, 2017–; Patron, Faith's Forum for London, 2015–. *Recreations:* reading, travelling, antique collecting, cricket. *Address:* Unitas Communications Ltd, 1 St Mark Street, E1 8DA. *T:* (020) 7060 3955. *E:* ma@unitascommunications.com.

**AHMED, Samira;** freelance journalist, broadcaster and documentary maker, radio and television, since 2011; *b* 15 June 1968; *d* of Athar Ahmad and Lalita Ahmed (*née* Chatterjee); *m* 1996, Brian Michael Millar; one *s* one *d*. *Educ:* Wimbledon High Sch.; St Edmund Hall, Oxford (BA Hons English 1989); City Univ., London (Postgrad. Dip. Newspaper Journalism 1990). BBC: news trainee, 1990–92; network radio news reporter, 1992; Presenter, World Service TV, 1993; Reporter, Newsnight, 1993–94; News Corresp., 1994–97; LA Corresp., 1996–97; Presenter: Deutsche Welle TV, Berlin, 1998; BBC News 24/BBC World, 1998–99; (and writer) Islam Unveiled, documentary series, Channel 4, 2004; Presenter/Corresp., Channel 4 News, 2000–11; Presenter: Newswatch, BBC News Channel, 2012–; Front Row, BBC Radio 4, 2014–. Vis. Prof. of Journalism, Kingston Univ., 2011–. Hon. Dr City, London, 2019. Broadcaster of the Year, Stonewall, 2009. *Recreations:* reading, cinema, theatre, Berlin, collecting Amar Chitra Katha comics, swimming. *Address:* c/o Knight Ayton Management, 29 Gloucester Place, W1U 8HX. *W:* www.samiraahmed.co.uk.

**AHMED-SHEIKH, Tasmina,** OBE 2014; politician; producer and television presenter; columnist; *b* Chelsea; *m* Zulfikar Sheikh; one *s* three *d*. *Educ:* Univ. of Edinburgh (MA 1991); Strathclyde Univ. (LLB 1995; Postgrad. DipLaw 1996). NP; WS 2009. Mem., Faculty of Procurators, 1996; admitted as solicitor, 1997; Partner, 2006–10, Equity Partner, 2010–15, Hamilton Burns, WS. Columnist, The National. Mem., Adv. Bd, Yes Scotland Campaign, Yes Scotland Ltd, 2012–14. MP (SNP) Ochil and S Perthshire, 2015–17; contested (SNP) same seat, 2017. SNP spokesperson on internat. trade and investment, 2015–17. Scottish National Party: Mem. Bd, Finance and Audit Cttee, 2012–17; Nat. Women's and Equalities Convenor, 2012–17. Mem. Bd, Scottish Women in Sport. Advr, The Parliament Project.

**AHO, Esko Tapani;** Executive Chairman of Board, East Office of Finnish Industries, since 2013; Prime Minister of Finland, 1991–95; *b* Veteli, 20 May 1954; *s* of Kauko Kaleva Aho and Laura Kyllikki Aho (*née* Harjupatana); *m* 1980, Kirsti Hannele Söderkultalahti; three *s* one *d*. *Educ:* Univ. of Helsinki (Master of Pol Scis). Political Sec. to Minister for Foreign Affairs, Finland, 1979–80; MP (Centre Party), Helsinki, 1983–2003; Chm., Finnish Parlt, April 1991; Member: Traffic Commn, 1983–86; Finances Commn, 1987–90. Member: CSCE Cttee, 1984–90; Finnish Delegn, Nordic Council, 1983–89; Finnish Delegn, Council of Europe, 1989–91. Chairman: League, Centre Party Youth, 1974–80; Finnish Centre Party, 1990–2002. Vice-Chm., Liberal Internat., 1994–2002; Chm., Finnish Ski Assoc., 1996–2000; Vice-Chm., Finnish Olympic Cttee, 1997–2000. Elector, Presidential Elections, 1978, 1982 and 1998. Member, Advisory Board: Outokumpu Oy (Metal Ind.), 1985–91; OKO (Bank), 1991; SOK (Diversified Co-op.), 1990–91. Lectr, Harvard Univ., 2001–02; Chm., Verbatum Oy, corporate consulting co., 2002–; Pres., Finnish Innovation Fund (Sitra) (formerly Finnish Nat. Fund for Res. and Develt), 2004–08; Exec. Vice Pres., Corporate Relns and Responsibility, Nokia Corp., 2008–12 (Mem., Nokia Leadership Team, 2009–12; Consultative Partner, 2012–); Sen. Fellow, Mossavar-Rahmani Center for Business and Govt, Harvard Univ., 2012–14; Member: Bd, Fortum Corp., 2006–12; Bd of Dirs, Russian Venture Co., 2007–10; Bd of Dirs, Terveystalo Gp, 2012–13. Vice-Chm. Bd, Technol. Industries of Finland, 2009–; Mem., Bd of Dirs, Technol. Acad. of Finland, 2009–; Mem., Sci. and Technol. in Soc. Forum. Member: Club of Madrid; InterAction Council. Mem., World Council, and Vice Chm., Finland, ICC, 2009–. Exec. in Residence, Aalto Univ., 2016–. Grand Cross, Order of White Rose (Finland), 1992; Cavaliere di Gran Croce, Order of Merit (Italy), 1993. *Recreations:* literature, golf.

**AHRENDS, Peter;** Founding Partner, 1961, Director, 1961–2009, and Consultant, 2009–12, Ahrends, Burton & Koralek, Architects; *b* 30 April 1933; *s* of Steffen Bruno Ahrends and Margarete Marie Sophie Visino; *m* 1954, Elizabeth Robertson (*d* 2007); two *d*. *Educ:* King Edward VII Sch., Johannesburg; Architectural Assoc. Sch. of Architecture (Dipl., Hons). RIBA 1959. Steffen Ahrends & Partners, Johannesburg, 1957–58; Denys Lasdun & Partners, 1959–60; Julian Keable & Partners; major projects, 1961–, include: *public buildings:* Hampton Site, Nat. Gall. Extn, 1982–85 (comp. winning entry); St Mary's Hosp., Newport, IoW (nucleus low energy hosp.), 1990; White Cliffs Heritage Centre, Dover, 1991; Techniquest Science Centre, 1995 (RIBA Arch. Award); Dublin Dental Hosp., 1994–; Sculpture Court, Whitworth Art Gall., Manchester, 1995 (RIBA Arch. Award); Waterford Visitor Centre, 1998; N Tipperary Council civic offices, Nenagh, 2000–; Offaly Council offices, Tullamore, 2002 (RIBA Award, 2003); Galway Council office extension, library and HQ, 2002; *educational buildings:* New Liby, TCD, 1961 (internat. comp.); Templeton Coll., Oxford, phased completion over 25 years from 1969; residential bldg, Keble Coll., Oxford, 1976 (RIBA Arch. Award, 1978); Arts Faculty Bldg, TCD, 1979; Loughborough Univ. Business Sch., 1997; IT bldg and catering bldg, Inst. of Technology, Tralee, 1998; tourism and leisure bldg, Waterford Inst. of Technology, 1999; first phase bldgs, Inst. of Technology, Blanchardstown, 1999; *residential buildings:* Nebenzahl House, Jerusalem, 1972; Whitmore Court Housing, 1975 (RIBA Good Design in Housing Award, 1977); housing, Newcastle West, Limerick, 2004; *commercial/industrial buildings:* warehouse, showroom and offices, Habitat, 1974 (Structural Steel Design Award, FT Industrial Arch. Award, 1976); factory, Cummins Engines (Struct. Steel Design Award, 1980); Sainsbury supermarket, Canterbury, 1984 (Struct. Steel Design Award, 1985); W. H. Smith offices, Swindon, 1985; British Embassy, Moscow, 1988–99; John Lewis dept store, Kingston-upon-Thames, 1990; office develt for Stanhope Trafalgar, 1990–; office building, Tel Aviv, 1998; *sports buildings:* Carrickmines Croquet and Lawn Tennis Club, Dublin, 1998; *transport:* Docklands Light Railway Beckton Extension stations, 1987–93; *development plans:* MBA Sch., Templeton Coll., Univ. of Oxford, 1992; Falmer Develt Plan, Univ. of Brighton, 1992; Cardiff Inner Harbour, 1993; Inst. of Technology, Tralee, 1998; Waterford Inst. of Technology, 1998; City Block, Dublin, 2000; Dublin Corp. NEIC Civic Centre, Dublin, 2000; TCD Dublin Docklands Innovation Centre, 2001; Inst. of Technol., Blanchardstown, 2002; Arts Faculty Extension Bldg, TCD, 2002; Bexhill Town Centre Develt Plan, 2004; *competition wins:* Campus Develt Plan, Univ. of Grenoble, 1990–93; Designs on Democracy, Stockport, 2003. Chair: UK Architects Against Apartheid, 1988–93; Newham Design Review Panel, 2007–13 (Design Advr, Newham Strategic Develt Cttee, 2010–13); Member: Design Council, 1988–93; Council, AA, 1965–67. Vis. Prof. of Architecture, Kingston Poly., 1983–84; Bartlett Prof. of Arch., Bartlett Sch. of Arch. and Planning, UCL, 1986–89; part-time teaching posts and workshops at AA Sch. of Arch., Canterbury Sch. of Art, Edinburgh Univ., Winter Sch. Edinburgh, Plymouth Poly., Kingston Poly., and Plymouth Sch. of Art; vis. critic and/or ext. examr at Kumasi Univ., AA Sch. of Arch., Nova Scotia Tech. Univ., Strathclyde Univ. Exhibitions of drawings and works: RIBA Heinz Gall., 1980; RIAI, 1981; Douglas Hyde Gall., Dublin, 1981; Braunschweig Tech. Univ., Tech. Univ. of Hanover, Museum of Finnish Arch., 1982; Univ. of Oulu, Alvar Aalto Museum, Finland, 1982; AA HQ, Oslo, 1983. *Publications:* (contrib.) Ahrends Burton & Koralek, Architects (monograph), 1991; A3: threads and connections, 2015; Stream of Sketches, 2017; *relevant publications:* Collaborations: the work of ABK, ed by Kenneth Powell, 2002; Ahrends, Burton and Koralek, 2012, by Kenneth Powell; papers and articles in RIBA Jl and other prof. jls. *Recreation:* architecture. *Address:* 16 Rochester Road, NW1 9JH. *E:* pahrends@gmail.com.

**AHTISAARI, Martti Oiva Kalevi;** President, Republic of Finland, 1994–2000; Founder and Chairman of Board, Crisis Management Initiative, since 2000; *b* 23 June 1937; *s* of Oiva and Tyyne Ahtisaari; *m* 1968, Eeva Irmeli Hyvärinen; one *s*. Finnish diplomat; joined Ministry for Foreign Affairs, 1965; Ambassador to Tanzania, 1973–76; Under-Sec. of State, Internat. Develt Co-operation, 1984–86; Under-Sec. Gen., Admin and Mgt, 1987–91; Sec. of State for Foreign Affairs, 1991–94; UN envoy; UN Comr for Namibia, 1977–81; head, operation monitoring Namibia's transition to independence, 1989–90; senior envoy in Yugoslavia, 1992–93; EU Special envoy in Kosovo, 1999; Mem., observer gp on Austrian govt human rights record, 2000; co-inspector, IRA arms dumps, 2000; Chm., panel on security and safety of UN personnel in Iraq, 2003; special envoy of UN Secretary-General: for the Horn of Africa, 2003–06; for future status process for Kosovo, 2005–08. Chairman: Balkan Children and Youth Foundn, 2000–; Governing Council, Interpeace, 2000–09, now Chm. Emeritus and Special Advr; Ind. Commn on Turkey, 2004–. Co-Chair, Eur. Council on Foreign Relns, 2007–. Dir-at-Large, ImagineNations Gp, 2008–. Member: Internat. Sen. Adv. Bd, W Asia N Africa Regl Forum, 2008–; The Elders, 2009–; Bd of Trustees, Silatech. Mem., Prize Cttee, Mo Ibrahim Foundn, 2017–. Chm. Supervisory Bd, Finnish Nat. Opera, 2004–. Holds numerous honorary doctorates. Hon. AO 2002. Nobel Peace Prize, 2008. *Address:* (office) Eteläranta 12, 2nd Floor, 00130 Helsinki, Finland.

**AIKEN, Alexander Stuart;** Executive Director, Government Communications, Cabinet Office, since 2013; *b* London, 22 Sept. 1966; *s* of James and Stella Aiken; *m* 2000, Nicola Jane Durbin (*see* N. J. Aiken); one *s* one *d*. *Educ:* Dame Alice Owen's Sch., Potters Bar;

London Sch. of Econs and Pol Sci. (BSc Econ Hons 1988). Parly researcher, 1988–89; Nat. Chm., Cons. Students, 1989–90; Dir, Radical Soc., 1990–92; Conservative Party: Press Officer, 1992–95; Chief Press Officer, 1995–97; Hd of News, 1997–99; Dep. Dir, 1999–2000; Dir, Communications and Strategy, Westminster CC, 2000–12. *Recreation:* football (Chm., Westminster Wanderers FC). *Address:* Cabinet Office, 70 Whitehall, SW1A 2AS. *T:* (020) 7276 6009. *E:* alex.aiken@cabinetoffice.gov.uk. *Club:* Civil Service.

**AIKEN, Nicola Jane;** Member (C) and Leader, since 2017, Westminster City Council; *b* London, 4 Feb. 1969; *d* of John Durbin and Pamela Durbin; *m* 2000, Alexander Stuart Aiken, *qv*; one *s* one *d*. *Educ:* Radyr Comp. Sch., Cardiff; Univ. of Exeter (BA Hons Sociol. 1991). Hd, Public Relns, Bradford & Bingley plc, 2001–09. Mem. Bd, CAFCASS, 2015–18; Trustee, Bd, Royal Parks, 2017–. *Recreation:* walking. *Address:* Westminster City Council, City Hall, 64 Victoria Street, SW1E 6QP. *T:* (020) 7641 3255. *E:* naiken@westminster.gov.uk.

**AIKEN, Philip Stanley,** AM 2013; Chairman: Aveva Group plc, since 2012; Balfour Beatty, since 2015; *b* Sydney, Australia, 9 Jan. 1949; *s* of Stanley Ernest Aiken and Aileen Winifred Aiken; *m* 1976, Frances Barbara McCluskey; three *s*. *Educ:* Univ. of Sydney (BE Chem. Engrg 1970); Harvard Business Sch. (AMP 1989). BOC: Prodn Engr, 1970–72; Gas Supply Manager, 1972–78; Deptl Manager, 1978–82; Gen. Manager, W Australia, 1983–85, Medishield, 1985–87; Chief Exec., Gases, 1987–89; Man. Dir, CIG and Regl Dir, S Pacific, 1989–93; Man. Dir, Gases Europe, 1993–95; Man. Dir, BTR Nylex, 1995–97 and Exec. Dir, BTR, 1996–97; Pres. and CEO, 1997–2004, Gp Pres., Energy, 2004–06, BHP Petroleum Billiton Pty Ltd. Senior Independent Director: Kazakhmys, 2006–13; Essar Energy plc, 2010–14; non-executive Director: National Grid plc, 2008–15; Newcrest Mining Ltd, 2013–. *Recreations:* golf, ski-ing, Rugby, football, cricket. *Address:* 12/36 Sloane Court West, SW3 4TB. *T:* (020) 7730 4167. *E:* philipaiken1@gmail.com. *Clubs:* Wentworth; Melbourne; Royal Sydney Yacht Squadron.

**AIKEN, Stephen Ronald,** OBE 2004; Member (UU) South Antrim, Northern Ireland Assembly, since 2016. *Educ:* Britannia Royal Naval Coll., Dartmouth; King's Coll. London (MA); Univ. of Cambridge (MPhil). Served RN, 1978–2011. Chief Executive Officer: British-Irish Chamber of Commerce, 2011–14; Dublin City Univ. Educnl Trust, 2014–15. Opposition Spokesman on the Economy, NI Assembly, 2016–. Mem. Bd, British-Irish Assoc. MInstD. *Recreations:* hill walking, history. *Address:* Northern Ireland Assembly, Parliament Buildings, Stormont, Belfast BT4 3XX.

**AIKENS, Rt Hon. Sir Richard (John Pearson),** Kt 1999; PC 2008; arbitrator, since 2015; a Lord Justice of Appeal, 2008–15; *b* 28 Aug. 1948; *s* of late Basil Aikens and Jean Eleanor Aikens; *m* 1979, Penelope Anne Hartley Rockley (*née* Baker); two *s* two step *d*. *Educ:* Norwich Sch.; St John's Coll., Cambridge (BA 1970, MA 1973; Hon. Fellow, 2005). Called to Bar, Middle Temple, 1973 (Harmsworth scholar, 1971; Bencher, 1994); in practice, 1974–99; a Junior Counsel to the Crown, Common Law, 1981–86; QC 1986; a Recorder, 1993–99; a Judge of the High Court of Justice, QBD, 1999–2008; Presiding Judge, SE Circuit, 2001–04; Judge in charge of Commercial Ct, 2005–06. Mem., Supreme Court Rules Cttee, 1984–88. Dir, Bar Mutual Indemnity Fund Ltd, 1988–2000 (Chm., 1998–99). Visiting Professor: QMUL, 2016–; KCL, 2016–. Mem., Bd of Dirs, Franco-British Lawyers Soc., 2016–. Dir, ENO, 1995–2004. Chm., 2002–17, Pres., 2017–, Temple Music Foundn; Chm., Music and Theatre for All, 2017–; Trustee, Razumovsky Foundn, 2017–. Governor, Sedbergh Sch., 1988–97. *Publications:* (contributing editor) Bullen and Leake and Jacob, Precedents of Pleading, 13th edn 1990; (jtly) Bills of Lading, 2006, 2nd edn 2016; (contrib.) Reforming Marine and Commercial Insurance Law, 2008; (contrib.) Tom Bingham and the Transformation of the Law: a liber amicorum, 2009; (ed jtly) Law and Society: who shall be master?, 2011; (contributing editor) Dicey, Morris and Collins, The Conflict of Laws, 15th edn, 3rd Cumulative Supplement, 2016 to 5th Cumulative Supplement, 2017. *Recreations:* music, cycling, wine, le pays basque. *Address:* Brick Court Chambers, 7–8 Essex Street, WC2R 3LD, (020) 7379 3550. *Clubs:* Groucho; Leander.

**AIKIN, Olga Lindholm, (Mrs J. M. Driver),** CBE 1997; Partner, Aikin Driver Partnership, 1988; Visiting Lecturer, London Business School, 1985; Council Member, Advisory Conciliation and Arbitration Service, 1982–95; *b* 10 Sept. 1934; *d* of Sidney Richard Daly and Lilian May Daly (*née* Lindholm); *m* 1st, 1959, Ronald Sidney Aikin (marr. diss. 1979); one *d*; 2nd, 1982, John Michael Driver; one step *d*. *Educ:* London School of Economics (LLB); King's Coll., London. Called to Bar, Gray's Inn, 1956. Assistant Lecturer, King's Coll., London, 1956–59; Lecturer, London School of Economics, 1959–70; London Business School: Sloan Fellowship Programme, 1970–71; Vis. Lectr, 1971–79; Lectr in Law, 1979–85. Dir, Gen. Law Div., Lion Internat. (Keiser Enterprises Inc.), 1985–90; Chm. Bd of Mgt, Nat. Conciliation Service of Qualitas Furnishing Standards Ltd, 1992–94. *Publications:* (with Judith Reid) Employment, Welfare and Safety at Work, 1971; (with Sonia Pearson) Legal Problems of Employment Contracts, 1990; (ed) IPM Law and Employment series (Discipline; Industrial Tribunals; Redundancy), 1992; articles in Personnel Management. *Recreation:* collecting cookery books and pressed glass. *Address:* 22 St Luke's Road, W11 1DP. *T:* (office) (020) 7727 9791.
See also Hon. F. L. Daly.

**AILESBURY, 8th Marquess of,** *cr* 1821; **Michael Sydney Cedric Brudenell-Bruce;** Bt 1611; Baron Brudenell 1628; Earl of Cardigan 1661; Baron Bruce 1746; Earl of Ailesbury 1776; Earl Bruce 1821; Viscount Savernake 1821; 30th Hereditary Warden of Savernake Forest; *b* 31 March 1926; *e s* of 7th Marquess of Ailesbury and Joan (*d* 1937), *d* of Stephen Salter, Ryde, Isle of Wight; *S* father, 1974; *m* 1st, 1952, Edwina Sylvia de Winton (from whom he obtained a divorce, 1961), *yr d* of Lt-Col Sir (Ernest) Edward de Winton Wills, 4th Bt; one *s* two *d*; 2nd, 1963, Juliet Adrienne (marr. diss. 1974), *d* of late Hilary Lethbridge Kingsford and Mrs Latham Hobrow, Marlborough; two *d*; 3rd, 1974, Mrs Caroline Elizabeth Romilly (marr. diss. 1990), *d* of late Commander O. F. M. Wethered, RN, DL, JP. *Educ:* Eton. Lt RHG, 1946. *Heir: s* Earl of Cardigan, *qv*. *Address:* 4 Abdale Road, W12 7ET.

**AILION, Philipa Ann, (Pippa),** MBE 2018; Director, Pippa Ailion Casting, since 1997; *b* London, 20 Sept. 1947; *d* of Philip and Pamela Mary Ailion; one *s* by Roger Sell; *m* 2008, Paul Hale. *Educ:* Hove Co. Grammar Sch. for Girls; Bulmershe Coll. of Educn, Reading (Teachers' Cert. and Dip. 1968). Hd of Drama, Dick Sheppard Sch., London, 1968–71; actor, Greenwich Th. and Northcott Th., Exeter, 1971–73; asst to Neil Simon, playwright, NYC, 1974; Asst to Hd of Wardrobe (pt-time), Th. Dept, Dartington Coll. of Arts, Devon, 1975–81; Asst Dir and Co. Manager, Children of a Lesser God, Mermaid, then Albery, Dublin, Australia, SA, 1981–84; Resident Dir and Co. Manager, West End, incl. West Side Story, Her Majesty's Th. and Opera House Manchester, When We Are Married, Whitehall Th., Italian Straw Hat, Shaftesbury Th., A Month of Sundays, Duchess Th., 1984–87; Resident Associate Dir and Casting Dir, Old Vic Th., 1987–91; freelance casting dir, 1991–94; Hd, BA Acting, Central Sch. of Speech and Drama, 1994–97; casting dir, West End, incl. Dreamgirls, Motown, Wicked, The Book of Mormon, The Lion King, Gypsy, Sweeney Todd, Billy Elliot, Charlie and the Chocolate Factory, Funny Girl, We Will Rock You, Come From Away. Mem., Bd of Trustees, Regent's Park Open Air Th., 2012–17; Gov., Italia Conti Acad. of Th. Arts, 2017–; Patron, Urdang Acad., 2018–. Member:

BAFTA, 2001; Casting Dirs' Guild, 2008–. Hon. Companion, Liverpool Inst. Performing Arts, 2009. *Recreations:* theatre, gardening, travel, swimming, film. *Address:* Pippa Ailion Casting, Unit 65a Eurolink Business Centre, SW2 1BZ. *T:* (020) 7738 7556. *E:* pippa@pippaailioncasting.co.uk.

**AILSA, 9th Marquess of,** *cr* 1831; **David Thomas Kennedy;** Baron Kennedy 1452; Earl of Cassillis 1509; Baron Ailsa (UK) 1806; *b* Ayrshire, 3 July 1958; *yr s* of 7th Marquess of Ailsa, OBE and Mary Kennedy (*née* Burn); *S* brother, 2015; *m* 1991, Anne Kelly; one *s* one *d*. *Educ:* Strathallan Sch.; Berks Coll. of Agriculture. *Heir: s* Lord Archibald David Kennedy, *b* 7 Sept. 1995. *Address:* Morriston, Culzean, Maybole, Ayrshire KA19 8LB. *Clubs:* Farmers; New (Edinburgh); Glasgow Art.

**AINA, Benjamin Adejuwon Olufemi;** QC 2009; barrister; *b* London, 14 Feb. 1964; *s* of Johnson Olusola Aina and Elizabeth Taiwo Awolesi; *m* 2002, Mwanida Elizabeth Sakala; three *s* four *d* (and one *s* decd). *Educ:* Woolverstone Hall, Ipswich; Chelmer Inst. of Higher Educn (LLB Hons 1985); University Coll. London (LLM 1986). Called to the Bar, Lincoln's Inn, 1987. Admitted Attorney at Law, Cayman Is, 2010. Standing Counsel to Revenue and Customs Prosecution Office, 2008–; QC List, Serious Fraud Office, 2009–. *Publications:* Holborn Law Tutors Company Law Manual, rev. edn 1989. *Recreations:* running, travelling. *Address:* Church Court Chambers, Second Floor, Goldsmith Building Temple, EC4Y 7BL.

**AINGER, Nicholas Richard, (Nick);** *b* Sheffield, 24 Oct. 1949; *m* 1976, Sally Robinson; one *d*. *Educ:* Netherthorpe Grammar Sch., Staveley. Rigger, Marine and Port Services Ltd, Pembroke Dock, 1977–92. Mem. (Lab) Dyfed CC, 1981–93. Branch Sec., TGWU, 1978–92. MP (Lab) Pembroke, 1992–97, Carmarthen W and Pembrokeshire S, 1997–2010; contested (Lab) same seat, 2010. PPS to Sec. of State for Wales, 1997–2001; a Lord Comr, HM Treasury (Govt Whip), 2001–05; Parly Under-Sec. of State, Wales Office, 2005–07. Chair: Pembrokeshire Coastal Forum CIC, 2013–; Danny Fellows Training Trust, 2016–. *E:* nick.ainger@live.co.uk.

**AINGER, Stephen David;** Chief Executive, Partnerships For Renewables, 2007–16; *b* 27 Nov. 1951; *s* of Peter Jackson Ainger and Aileen (*née* Simpson); *m* 1992, Nicola Jane Corbett; one *s* one *d*. *Educ:* Towcester Grammar Sch.; Bath Univ. (BSc 1st cl. Hons (Physics) 1974). Exploration and Prodn posts with British Petroleum Co. Plc, London, Colombia, Brazil, Spain, Venezuela and Kuwait, 1974–99; Strategy and Business Develt Dir, Transco Plc, BG Gp, 1999–2000; Dir, Business Develt, Lattice Gp Plc, 2000–02; Chief Exec., Charities Aid Foundn, 2002–06. Trustee: Artsadmin, 2003–14; ATL Trust Fund, 2017–. Non-exec. Dir, Royal Free London Foundn Trust (formerly Royal Free Hampstead NHS Trust), 2011–18. *Recreations:* classic cars, architectural heritage, theatre angel. *Address:* 8 Downshire Hill, NW3 1NR. *E:* stephen.ainger@outlook.com. *Club:* Reform.

**AINLEY, Prof. Janet Mary,** PhD; Professor of Education, University of Leicester, since 2006 (Director, School of Education, 2007–14); *b* London, 13 March 1952; *d* of (James) Henry and Joyce Ainley; *m* 2001, Ronnie Goldstein; one *d* and two step *s* one step *d*. *Educ:* Sydenham High Sch.; Univ. of York (BA Hons Phil.); St Luke's Coll., Exeter (PGCE); Univ. of Warwick (MEd; PhD 1996). Primary sch. teacher, Solihull LEA, 1974–81; University of Warwick: Res. Asst, 1981–83; Lectr, 1983–98; Sen. Lectr, 1998–2002; Reader, 2002–06; Dep. Dir, 1999–2004, Dir of Teacher Educn, 2004–06, Warwick Inst. of Educn. Vice-Pres., Internat. Gp for Psychol. of Maths Educn, 1999–2000; Treas., Eur. Soc. for Res. in Maths Educn, 2007–13; Chair, British Soc. for Res. in Learning of Maths, 2008–11. *Publications:* (with R. Goldstein) Making Logo Work, 1988; Enriching Primary Mathematics with IT, 1996; contrib. For the Learning of Maths, Educnl Studies in Maths, Internat. Jl Computers for Math. Learning, British Educnl Res. Jl. *Recreations:* gardening, cooking, reading, family history. *Address:* School of Education, University of Leicester, 21 University Road, Leicester LE1 7RF. *T:* (0116) 252 3690, *Fax:* (0116) 252 3653. *E:* janet.ainley@le.ac.uk.

**AINLEY, Nicholas John; His Honour Judge Ainley;** a Circuit Judge, since 2003; Vice President, Immigration Appeal Tribunal, 2003–05; *b* 18 March 1952; *s* of late Edgar Ainley and Jean Olga Ainley (*née* Simister); *m* 1980, Susan Elizabeth Waugh; two *s* one *d*. *Educ:* Sevenoaks Sch. Called to the Bar, Lincoln's Inn, 1973; Supplementary Panel Counsel to the Crown (Common Law), 1995–2001; Asst Recorder, 1996–2000; a Recorder, 2000–03. *Publications:* (jtly) Disclosure and Confidentiality, 1996. *Recreations:* family, travel, books. *Address:* c/o The Law Courts, Altyre Road, Croydon CR9 5AB. *Clubs:* Sussex Yacht (Shoreham); Royal de Panne Sand Yacht (Belgium); Hove Deep Sea Anglers.

**AINLEY, Vivien Lesley;** Headmistress, South Hampstead High School, 2001–04; *b* 29 March 1950; *d* of late Herbert John Matthews and Win Matthews; *m* 1975, Eric Michael Ainley (marr. diss. 2015); two *d*. *Educ:* Univ. of Durham (BA Econs 1971); Hughes Hall, Cambridge (PGCE with distinction 1979); Univ. of Maryland (MA Secondary Educn (Maths) 1982); Royal Holloway, Univ. of London (Postgrad. Dip. Psychol. with distinction 2008); MSc Human Neurosci. with distinction 2010; PhD 2015). CSIR, Pretoria, South Africa, 1972–73; Bank of England, 1973–77; UCNW, Bangor, 1976–77; CEGB, 1977–78; Teacher of Econs and Stats, 1985–91, Hd of Sixth Form, 1991–94, Haberdashers' Aske's Sch. for Girls; Sen. Mistress, Oundle Sch., 1994–96; Surmistress, St Paul's Girls' Sch., 1996–2001. Hon. Res. Associate, Dept of Psychol., RHUL, 2015–. *Recreations:* theatre, travel, gardening, voluntary work in mental health. *Address:* 75 Bolingbroke Road, W14 0AA.

**AINSCOUGH, Jill Patricia;** Chief Operating Officer, 2007–14 and Board Member, 2010–14, Ofcom; *b* Leicester, 28 Dec. 1957; *d* of Philip and Jean Needham; three *d*. *Educ:* Univ. of Sheffield (BA Hons); Univ. of Warwick (MBA). ACIS 1988, FCIS 2012. Sen. Financial Analyst, Granada Gp, 1990–92; Business Planner, Cambridge Cable Gp, 1994–95; Financial Planning and Analysis Manager, Barclaycard, 1995–97; Head, Marketing Develt, NTL; Man. Dir, Easynet, 2001–06. Non-executive Director: BMJ, 2014–; Lakehouse plc, 2015–16; bpha, 2016–. Mem. Bd, Sport England, 2007–13. Gov., Univ. of Northampton, 2014–15.

**AINSCOUGH, Martin,** CBE 2016; DL; Chairman, Ainscough Group of Companies, since 2007; *b* Wigan, 6 June 1952; *s* of Gerald Ainscough and Evelyn Ainscough; *m* 1986, Judith Gibson; three *s* two *d*. *Educ:* St Peter's Secondary Modern Sch., Wigan. Co-Founder, 1976, Chm., 1985–2007, Ainscough Crane Hire Ltd. Co-Founder and Chm., Wigan Youth Zone, 2013–. DL Gtr Manchester, 2014. *Recreation:* driven game shooting. *Address:* Wrennalls Hall, Worthington, Wigan WN1 2XH. *T:* 07836 794990.

**AINSCOW, Prof. Melvyn, (Mel),** CBE 2012; PhD; Professor of Education, University of Manchester, 1995–2016, now Emeritus; *b* Manchester, 25 May 1943; *s* of Richard and Sarah Ainscow; one *s* one *d*. *Educ:* Ducie High Sch., Manchester; Univ. of Birmingham (MEd); Univ. of E Anglia (PhD 1995). Teacher, 1964–74; Headteacher, Castle Sch., Walsall, 1974–79; School Inspector, 1979–85; Lectr, Univ. of Cambridge, 1985–95. Chief Adviser, Greater Manchester Challenge, 2007–11. FRSA 2012. *Publications:* Understanding the Development of Inclusive Schools, 1999; Improving Schools, Developing Inclusion, 2006; Developing Equitable Education Systems, 2012; Towards Self-improving School

Systems: lessons from a city challenge, 2015; Struggles for Equity in Education: the selected works of Mel Ainscow, 2015. *Recreations:* music, reading, sport. *Address:* 31 Appleby Lodge, Manchester M14 6HQ. *T:* (0161) 275 3503. *E:* Mel_Ainscow@yahoo.co.uk.

**AINSCOW, Robert Morrison,** CB 1989; Deputy Secretary, Overseas Development Administration, Foreign and Commonwealth Office, 1986–96; *b* 3 June 1936; *s* of Robert M. Ainscow and Hilda Ainscow (*née* Cleminson); *m* 1965, Faye Bider; one *s* one *d*. *Educ:* Salford Grammar School; Liverpool Univ. (BA Econ Hons). Statistician: Govt of Rhodesia and Nyasaland, 1957–61; UN Secretariat, New York, 1961–65 and 1966–68; Dept of Economic Affairs, London, 1965–66. Ministry of Overseas Development: Economic Adviser, 1968–70; Senior Economic Adviser, 1971–76; Head, South Asia Dept, 1976–79; Under Secretary and Principal Finance Officer, FCO (ODA), 1979–86. Chm., OECD (DAC) Working Party on Financial Aspects of Develt Assistance, 1982–86; Member: World Bank/IMF Develt Cttee Task Force on Concessional Flows, 1983–85, on Multilateral Develt Banks, 1994–96; Asian Develt Bank Inspection Panel, 1996–2002. Consultant to UN, World Bank, OECD, DFID, Ireland Aid, and Overseas Develt Council, Washington, 1996. Mem. Bd Trustees, BRCS, 2000–06.

**AINSLEY, John Mark;** tenor; *b* 9 July 1963; *s* of John Alwyn Ainsley and Dorothy Sylvia (*née* Anderson). *Educ:* Royal Grammar Sch., Worcester; Magdalen Coll., Oxford. Début in Stravinsky's Mass, RFH, 1984; subsequent débuts: USA, in NY and Boston, 1990; with Berlin Philharmonic Orch., 1992; Glyndebourne Fest., in Così fan Tutte, 1992; Aix-en-Provence, in Don Giovanni, 1993; San Francisco, in Don Giovanni, 1995; appears regularly with ENO, Royal Opera, and leading orchestras incl. LPO, LSO, Scottish Chamber Orch. and Orchestre de Paris. Has made numerous recordings. Grammy Award for best opera recording, 1995. *Recreation:* chocolate. *Address:* Askonas Holt Ltd, 15 Fetter Lane, EC4A 1BW. *T:* (020) 7400 1700.

**AINSLIE, Sir Charles Benedict, (Sir Ben),** Kt 2013; CBE 2009 (OBE 2005; MBE 2001); professional yachtsman; Principal, Ben Ainslie Racing, since 2014; *b* 5 Feb. 1977; *s* of late Michael Roderick and of Susan Linda Ainslie; *m* 2014, Georgie Thompson; one *d*. *Educ:* Truro Sch.; Peter Symonds Coll., Winchester. Laser Cl. World Champion, 1998 and 1999; Silver Medal, Laser Cl. Sailing, Atlanta Olympics, 1998; Gold Medal, Laser Cl. Sailing, Sydney Olympics, 2000; Finn Cl. World Champion, 2002, 2003, 2004, 2005, 2008 and 2012; Gold Medal, Finn Cl. Sailing, Athens Olympics, 2004, Beijing Olympics, 2008, London Olympics, 2012; ISAF World Match Racing Champion, 2010. Crew, Oracle Team USA, America's Cup winners, San Francisco, 2013. ISAF World Sailor of the Year, 1998, 2002, 2008 and 2012. Hon. MSc UC Chichester, 2001; Hon. LLD Exeter, 2005; Hon. DSport Southampton Solent, 2007. *Publications:* The Laser Campaign Manual, 2002; Close to the Wind, 2009. *Recreations:* motor racing, cycling, flying. *Address:* Carne Vean, Manaccan, Helston, Cornwall TR12 6HD. *Clubs:* Royal Thames Yacht (Hon. Mem.), Royal Cornwall Yacht (Hon. Mem.), Stokes Bay Sailing (Gosport) (Hon. Mem.), Restronguet Sailing (Falmouth) (Hon. Mem.), Royal Lymington Yacht (Hon. Mem.), Royal Southern Yacht (Hon. Mem.), Royal Corinthian Yacht (Hon. Mem.), Royal Yacht Squadron (Hon. Mem.), Royal Ocean Racing (Hon. Mem.).

**AINSWORTH, Sir Anthony (Thomas Hugh),** 5th Bt *cr* 1916, of Ardanaiseig, co. Argyll; Director, Richard Glynn Consultants, since 2000; *b* 30 March 1962; *er s* of Sir David Ainsworth, 4th Bt and Sarah Mary, *d* of Lt-Col H. C. Walford; *S* father, 1999; *m* 2003, Anong Pradith; one *d*. *Educ:* Harrow. Lt, Royal Hussars (PWO), 1982–85. *Heir: b* Charles David Ainsworth, *b* 24 Aug. 1966. *Address:* Bangkok, Thailand. *E:* anthony@rglynn.th.com.

**AINSWORTH, James Bernard;** restaurant consultant; Editor, Good Food Guide, 1994–2002 (Consultant Editor, 2003); *b* 1 Feb. 1944; *s* of Henry Bernard Ainsworth and Margaret Ainsworth (*née* Fletcher); *m* 2002, Valerie (*née* McCully); two step *d*. *Educ:* Duke St Primary Sch.; Chorley Grammar Sch.; Liverpool Univ. (BA Psychol.). Lectr in Psychol. and Educn, Chorley Coll. of Educn, 1970–78; Proprietor, Vineyard Restaurant, Northampton, 1979–84; drinks columnist, Punch, 1984–92; freelance wine writer and restaurant reviewer, 1984–. *Publications:* Mitchell Beazley Red Wine Guide, 1990; Mitchell Beazley White Wine Guide, 1990. *Recreation:* no time for recreation now I'm retired. *Address:* Bicton Pool House, Bicton, Kingsland, Leominster, Herefordshire HR6 9PR.

**AINSWORTH, Rev. Janina Helen Margaret;** Chief Education Officer, Church of England, 2007–14; General Secretary, National Society, 2007–14; House for Duty Team Vicar, Turton Moorland Team Ministry, Manchester, since 2014; *b* 23 Dec. 1950; *d* of Paul and Isobel Brych; *m* 1974, Michael Ronald Ainsworth; two *s* two *d*. *Educ:* Nottingham High Sch. for Girls; Homerton Coll., Cambridge (Cert Ed 1972); Newnham Coll., Cambridge (BEd 1973); Lancaster Univ. (MA Religious Studies 1974); Ripon Coll. Cuddesdon. RE Teacher: Manor Sch., Arbury, 1974–75; Greaves Sch., Lancaster, 1975–78; pt-time Lectr and Warden, St Martin's Coll., Lancaster, 1978–82; Manchester Diocesan Board of Education: Children's Work Advr, 1986–91; RE and Schs Advr, 1991–98; Diocesan Dir of Educn, 1998–2007. Ordained deacon, 2005, priest, 2006; non-stipendiary Curate, E Farnworth and Kearsley, 2005–07; Asst Priest, St George-in-the-East with St Paul, London, 2012–14. FRSA. *Publications:* (with Alan Brown) Moral Education, 1994; Clergy and Church Schools, 1995. *Recreations:* singing church music, cinema, crime novels.

**AINSWORTH, (Mervyn) John,** OBE 2008; FCIS; Chief Executive and Secretary, Institute of Chartered Secretaries and Administrators, 1990–2007; *b* 28 Jan. 1947; *s* of late Gordon John Ainsworth and Eileen Ainsworth; *m* 1973, Marta Christina Marmolak; two *s* one *d*. *Educ:* Stanfields Technical High Sch., Stoke-on-Trent; Goldsmiths' Coll., Univ. of London (CertEd; DipEd). Asst Clerk to Govs and Bursar, Dulwich Coll., 1969–74; Principal Assistant, Sec. and Solicitors' Dept, CEGB, 1974–77; Secretarial Asst, BTDB, 1977–78; Sec., 1978–83, Sec. and Dir of Finance, 1983–84, BPIF; Sec. General, Inst. of Administrative Management, 1984–90. Director: ICSA Publishing, 1990–2007; ICSA Consultants, 1992–2007; ICSA Software, 1993–2007; Inst. of Business Administration, 1992–2007. Special Advr, Assets Reunited (UK) LLP, 2008–10. Member: Bd, Nat. Examining Bd for Supervisory Management, 1984–99; Academic Bd, Greenwich Coll., 1984–97; Open and Distance Learning Quality Council (formerly Council for Certification of Correspondence Colls), 1984–2015 (Chm., 1998–2015); Court, Cranfield Univ. (formerly Inst. of Technology), 1990–2010; Council for Admin (formerly Admin Lead Body), 1991–2007; City & Guilds Quality Standards Cttee, 1999–2005; Commonwealth Assoc. for Corporate Governance, 2000–07. Gov., Rokeby Sch., 2010– (Vice-Chair, 2014–16; Chair, 2016–); Chair, Newham Community Schs Trust, 2016–. Sec., Shepway Econ. Regeneration Partnership, 2010–14. Liveryman, Worshipful Co. of Chartered Secs and Administrators, 1992– (Mem. Ct of Assts, 2006–12); Mem., Livery Cos Financial Service Gp, 2008–14. Hon. Fellow, Canadian Inst. of Certified Administrative Managers, 1987; Hon. MCGI 2006. Hon. DBA Bournemouth, 1997; DUniv Anglia Ruskin, 2006. *Recreations:* golf, motoring, travel. *Address:* 2 Aspen House, West Terrace, Folkestone, Kent CT20 1TH.

**AINSWORTH, Peter Michael;** *b* 16 Nov. 1956; *s* of late Lt-Comdr Michael Lionel Yeoward Ainsworth, RN and Patricia Mary Ainsworth (*née* Bedford, later Beeny); *m* 1981, Claire Alison Burnett; one *s* two *d*. *Educ:* Ludgrove, Wokingham; Bradfield Coll.; Lincoln Coll., Oxford (MA Eng. Lit. and Lang.). Res. Asst to Sir J. Stewart-Clark, MEP, 1979–81; Investment Analyst, Laing & Cruickshank, 1981–85; Sen. Investment Analyst, S. G. Warburg Securities, 1985–87; Asst Dir, 1987–89, Dir, 1989–92, S. G. Warburg Securities Corporate Finance. Mem., Wandsworth Borough Council, 1986–94 (Chm., Cons. Group, 1990–92). MP (C) E Surrey, 1992–2010. PPS to Chief Sec. to HM Treasury, 1994–95, to Sec. of State for Nat. Heritage, 1996; an Asst Govt Whip, 1996–97; Opposition Dep. Chief Whip, 1997–98; Shadow Secretary of State: for Culture, Media and Sport, 1998–2001; for Envmt, Food and Rural Affairs, 2001–02, 2005–09. Member, Select Committee: on Envmt, 1993–94; on Public Affairs, 1996; on Envmtl Audit, 2003–05 (Chm., 2003–05); on Culture, Media and Sport. Sec., All-Party Conservation Gp, 1994–97; Chm., All-Party Parly Gp for the Envmt; Chm., All-Party Parly Gp for Sustainable Aviation; Treas., All-Party Parly Climate Change Gp. Mem., Speaker's Adv. Cttee on Works of Art. Mem. Council, Bow Group, 1984–86. Chairman: Cons. Arts and Creative Industries Network, 2009–10; Cons. Environment Network, 2010–12. Mem., London Sustainable Develt Commn, 2014–16. Chairman: Big Lottery Fund, then Nat. Lottery Community Fund, 2011–19; Churches Conservation Trust, 2016–; Heritage Alliance, 2019–; Mem. Bd, Envmt Agency, 2012–18. Founder Partner, Robertsbridge Gp, 2010–. Member: Bd, Plantlife, 2003– (Chm., 2010–15); CPRE; Friends of the Earth; Surrey Wildlife Trust. Chm., Elgar Foundn, 2005–13 (Trustee, 2013–16); Vice-Pres., Arthur Bliss Soc. Trustee, Surrey CPRE, 2010–11. Hon. Fellow: CIWM, 2010; Soc. for the Envmt, 2013. Presenter, Discord, Music and Dissent, radio, 2000. *Recreations:* music, versifying. *Clubs:* MCC, Garrick.

**AINSWORTH, Rt Hon. Robert (William);** PC 2005; *b* 19 June 1952; *s* of late Stanley Ewart Ainsworth and Monica Pearl Ainsworth (later Mrs D. J. Scullion); *m* 1974, Gloria Jean Sandall; two *d*. *Educ:* Foxford Comprehensive School. Sheet metal worker and fitter, Jaguar, 1971–91 (Shop Steward, MSF, 1974–91; Sec., Joint Stewards, 1980–91). City Councillor, Coventry, 1984–93 (Dep. Leader, 1988–91; Chm., Finance, 1989–92). MP (Lab) Coventry NE, 1992–2015. An Opposition Whip, 1995–97; a Lord Comr of HM Treasury (Govt Whip), 1997–2001; Parly Under-Sec. of State, DETR, 2001, Home Office, 2001–03; Treasurer of HM Household (Dep. Chief Whip), 2003–07; Minister of State, MoD, 2007–09; Sec. of State for Defence, 2009–10; Shadow Secretary of State for Defence, 2010. Member: Select Cttee on environmental affairs, 1993–95; Foreign Affairs Select Cttee, 2010–15. Vice-Chm., W Midlands Gp of Labour MPs, 1995–97. *Recreations:* walking, reading, chess, golf, photography, orchid growing, bird watching. *E:* bobainsworth14@gmail.com. *Club:* Copeswood Grange Golf.

**AIRD, Fiona Violet, (Lady Aird),** CVO 2001 (LVO 1980); Extra Lady-in-Waiting to HRH Princess Margaret, Countess of Snowdon, 1963–2002; *b* 24 Sept. 1934; *d* of late Lt Col Ririd Myddelton, LVO, and of Lady Margaret Myddelton; *m* 1963, Capt. Sir Alastair Sturgis Aird, GCVO (*d* 2009); two *d*. *Educ:* Westonbirt Sch.; in France. Lady-in-Waiting to HRH Princess Margaret, 1960–63. Mem. Council, UCL, 1987–97 (Hon. Fellow, 2003). Chm., Middx Hosp. League of Friends, 1987–2002; Vice-Pres., England, Attend (formerly Nat. Assoc. of Hosp. and Community Friends), 2000–; Chm., Florence Nightingale Aid in Sickness Trust, 1994–. *Recreations:* reading, fishing. *Address:* The Paddock, Lovells Court, Marnhull, Sturminster Newton, Dorset DT10 1JJ.

**AIRD, Sir (George) John,** 4th Bt *cr* 1901; Chairman, Matcon plc, 1980–2013; Chairman and Managing Director, Sir John Aird & Co. Ltd, 1969–96; *b* 30 Jan. 1940; *e s* of Sir John Renton Aird, 3rd Bt, MVO, MC, and Lady Priscilla Aird, *yr d* of 2nd Earl of Ancaster; *S* father, 1973; *m* 1st, 1968, Margaret (*d* 2010), *yr d* of Sir John Muir, 3rd Bt; one *s* two *d*; 2nd, 2011, Xiao Fen, *d* of Jin Fen Wang, Beijing. *Educ:* Eton; Oxford Univ.; Harvard Business Sch. MICE. Trainee, Sir Alexander Gibb & Partners, 1961–65; Manager, John Laing & Son Ltd, 1967–69. Dir, Healthcare Development Services Ltd, 1994–2006. *Recreations:* tennis, ski-ing, classic cars. *Heir: s* James John Aird [*b* 12 June 1978; *m* 2007, Dr Tara Clare Harrop, *d* of Dr Brian Harrop, Nairobi]. *Address:* Two Leys, Evenlode, Moreton-in-Marsh, Glos GL56 0NT. *T:* (01608) 650607. *E:* johnaird@aol.com.
See also Baroness Willoughby de Eresby.

**AIREY, Dawn Elizabeth;** Chief Executive, Getty Images Inc., 2015–18 (non-executive Director, since 2019); *b* Preston, Lancs, 15 Nov. 1960; *m* 2015, Jacqueline Lawrence; two *d*. *Educ:* Kelly College; Girton College, Cambridge (MA Hons). Central TV: management trainee, 1985–86; Channel 4 Liaison Officer, 1987; Associate Producer, 1988; Controller, later Dir, Programme Planning, Central Broadcasting, 1988–93; Controller of Network Children's and Daytime Progs, ITV Network Centre, 1993–94; Controller of Arts and Entertainment, Channel 4, 1994–96; Dir of Progs, 1996–2000, Chief Exec., 2000–02, Channel 5; Man. Dir, Sky Networks, 2003–07, Man. Dir, Channels and Services, 2006–07, BSkyB; Man. Dir, Global Content, ITV, 2007–08; Chm. and Chief Exec., Five, 2008–10; Man. Dir, 2010–11, Pres., 2011–13, CLT-UFA UK Television, RTL Gp; Sen. Vice-Pres. for EMEA, Yahoo!, 2013–15. Chair, Digital Theatre+, 2019–; non-executive Director: easyJet, 2004–08; Thomas Cook, 2010–19 (Sen. Ind. Dir, 2017–19); Grosvenor Britain and Ire., 2019–. Member: Film Council, 1999–2002; Bd, Internat. Acad. of Television Arts and Scis, 2003–08; British Liby Bd, 2007–13. Patron, Birmingham Film and TV Festival, 1996–; Gov., Banff Fest., 1999–2008; Chm., Edinburgh Internat. Television Fest., 2000; Exec. Chm., Guardian Edin. Internat. Television Fest., 2002–06. Chairman: Grierson Trust, 2010–13; NYT, 2011–. Patron, Skillset, 2002–08. Trustee, Media Trust, 2004–11. FRSA 1996; FRTS 1999 (Vice-Pres., 2002–). *Recreations:* tennis, fine wines, cinema, TV, theatre, collecting antique maps. *Address:* The Moat House, 25 Church Lane, Hampton Poyle, Kidlington, OX5 2QF.

**AIREY, Janet Claire;** *see* Bazley, J. C.

**AIRLIE, 13th Earl of,** *cr* 1639 (*de facto* 11th Earl, 13th but for the Attainder); **David George Coke Patrick Ogilvy,** KT 1985; GCVO 1984; PC 1984; Royal Victorian Chain, 1997; JP; Baron Ogilvy of Airlie, 1491; Baron Ogilvy of Alith and Lintrathen, 1639; Captain late Scots Guards; Lord Chamberlain of HM Household, 1984–97; Lord-Lieutenant of Angus, 1989–2001; a Permanent Lord-in-Waiting to the Queen, since 1997; Chancellor, Order of the Thistle, since 2007; *b* 17 May 1926; *e s* of 12th Earl of Airlie, KT, GCVO, MC, and Lady Alexandra Marie Bridget Coke (*d* 1984), *d* of 3rd Earl of Leicester, GCVO; *S* father, 1968; *m* 1952, Virginia Fortune Ryan (*see* Countess of Airlie); three *s* three *d*. *Educ:* Eton. Lieutenant Scots Guards, 1944; serving 3rd Battalion Germany, 1945; Captain, ADC to High Comr and C-in-C Austria, 1947–48; Malaya, 1948–49; resigned commission, 1950. Ensign, 1975–85, Lieutenant, 1985–2000, Pres., 2000, Captain-Gen. and Gold Stick, 2004–12, Queen's Body Guard for Scotland, Royal Company of Archers. Chancellor, Royal Victorian Order, 1984–97. Chairman: Schroders plc, 1977–84; Gen. Accident Fire & Life Assurance Corp., 1987–97 (Dir, 1962–97; Dep. Chm., 1975–87); Director: J. Henry Schroder Wagg & Co. Ltd, 1961–84 (Chm., 1973–84); Scottish & Newcastle Breweries plc, 1969–83; The Royal Bank of Scotland Gp, 1983–93; Baring Stratton Investment Trust (formerly Stratton Investment Trust), 1986–97. Chm., Historic Royal Palaces Trust, 1998–2002; Dep. Chm., Royal Collection Trust, 1992–97; Pres., NT for Scotland

1997–2002; Trustee, Prince's Foundn for Built Envmt, 2003–06. Treasurer, Scout Assoc., 1962–86; Hon. Pres., Scottish Council of Scout Assoc., 1988–2001. Gov., Nuffield Nursing Homes Trust, 1985–89; Chancellor, Univ. of Abertay Dundee, 1994–2009. DL Angus, 1964; JP Angus, 1990. Hon. LLD Dundee, 1990. *Heir: s* Lord Ogilvy, *qv*. *Address:* Airlie House, Cortachy, Kirriemuir, Angus DD8 4QJ; 36 Sloane Court West, SW3 4TB. *T:* (020) 7823 6246.
*See also Hon. J. D. D. Ogilvy.*

**AIRLIE, Countess of; Virginia Fortune Ogilvy,** DCVO 1995 (CVO 1983); Lady of the Bedchamber to the Queen, since 1973; *b* 9 Feb. 1933; *d* of John Barry Ryan, Newport, RI, USA; *m* 1952, Lord Ogilvy (now Earl of Airlie, *qv*); three *s* three *d*. *Educ:* Brearley School, New York City. Founder Governor, Cobham School, Kent, 1958. Mem., Industrial Design Panel, British Rail, 1974–94; Comr, Royal Fine Arts Commn, 1975–88. Trustee: Tate Gallery, 1983–95 (Chm. Friends of Tate Gallery, 1978–83); Amer. Mus. in Britain, 1985–89 (Chm., 2001); Nat. Gallery, 1989–95; Nat. Galls of Scotland, 1995 (Chm., 1997–2000). Pres., Angus Br., BRCS, 1988. *Address:* Airlie House, Cortachy, Kirriemuir, Angus DD8 4QJ; 36 Sloane Court West, SW3 4TB.

**AIRS, Prof. Malcolm Russell,** OBE 2019; DPhil; FSA, FRHistS; Fellow, Kellogg College (formerly Rewley House), Oxford, 1991–2008, now Emeritus (Director, Centre for the Historic Environment, 2008–12); Professor of Conservation and the Historic Environment, University of Oxford, 2002–06; *b* 7 March 1941; *s* of George William Laurence Airs and Gwendoline Elizabeth Airs (*née* Little); partner, 1971, Megan Parry; one *s*. *Educ:* Bushey Grammar Sch.; Oriel Coll., Oxford (BA Hons Modern Hist. 1963, MA, DPhil 1970). FSA 1980; IHBC 1998; FRHistS 2003. Historian, Historic Bldgs Div., GLC, 1966–73; Architectural Ed., Survey of London, 1973–74; Conservation Officer, S Oxfordshire DC, 1974–91; Lectr, 1991–96, Reader, 1996–2002, in Conservation and Historic Envmt, Univ. of Oxford; Vice-Pres., Kellogg Coll., Oxford, 2006–08. Member: Historic Bldgs and Areas Adv. Cttee, 1988–2003, Adv. Cttee, 2012–15, English Heritage; Historic Buildings and Land Panel, Heritage Lottery Fund, 2004–05; Architectural Panel, 2004–15, Council, 2012–14, NT; Adv. Cttee, Historic England, 2015–18. Comr, RCHM, 1993–99. Chm., 1998–2001, Pres., 2001–03, Inst. of Historic Building Conservation; Pres., Soc. of Architectl Historians of GB, 2008–13. Trustee: Oxford Preservation Trust, 1993–2016 (Vice-Pres., 2016–); Standing Conf. on Trng of Architects in Conservation, 1996–2004; Landmark Trust, 2007–16; Herbert Lane Trust, 2016–; Oxfordshire Historic Churches Trust, 2018–. Pres., Oxford Architectl and Histl Soc., 2001–05; Vice-Pres., Assoc. of Small Historic Towns and Villages, 2006–17, Mem. Bd, Historic Towns and Villages Forum, 2017–. *Publications:* The Making of the English Country House 1500–1640, 1975; The Buildings of Britain: Tudor and Jacobean, 1982; The Tudor and Jacobean Country House, 1995; numerous articles on architectural hist. and historic conservation. *Recreations:* visiting buildings, cultivating my allotment, following the lost cause of Oxford United. *Address:* 39 High Street, Dorchester on Thames, Wallingford OX10 7HN. *Club:* Oxford United Supporters.

**AIRY, Maj.-Gen. Sir Christopher (John),** KCVO 1989; CBE 1984; General Officer Commanding London District and Major General Commanding Household Division, 1986; an Extra Equerry to the Prince of Wales, since 1991; *b* 8 March 1934; *m* 1959, Judith Stephenson; one *s* two *d*. *Educ:* Marlborough Coll.; RMA Sandhurst. 2nd Lieut, Grenadier Guards, 1954; Scots Guards, 1974. PMA to Sec. of State for War, 1960; sc 1966; DAAG, Regtl Adjt, 1967; Bde Major, 4th Guards Armoured Bde, 1971; ndc 1973; CO, 1st Bn Scots Guards, 1974; Mil. Asst (GSO1) to Master Gen. of the Ordnance, 1976; Comdr 5th Field Force, 1979; rcds 1981; ACOS, HQ UKLF, 1982–83; Sen. Army Mem., RCDS, 1984–85; retd 1989. Private Sec. and Treas. to TRH The Prince and Princess of Wales, 1990–91. Chm., C. N. Unwin Ltd, 2006–09 (non-exec. Dir, 2003–06). Chairman: Not Forgotten Assoc., 1992–2001; Nat. Assoc. of Air Ambulance Services, 1999–2002; Comr, Royal Hosp., Chelsea, 1990–96; Mem., Prince of Wales's Council, 1990–91. Vice-Pres., Brainwave, 2000–. Trustee: Hedley Foundn, 1994–2002; The Voices Foundn, 2003–13. Patron, Soc. of Mary and Martha, 1998–. *Recreations:* gardening, smallholding, music, art, churches. *Address:* c/o Headquarters Scots Guards, Wellington Barracks, Birdcage Walk, SW1E 6HQ.

**AITCHISON, Prof. Cara Carmichael,** PhD; FHEA; FAcSS; FRGS; President and Vice-Chancellor, and Professor of Geography and Cultural Economy, Cardiff Metropolitan University, since 2016; *b* Falkirk, 5 Feb. 1965; *d* of James Aitchison and Norma Nicol. *Educ:* High Sch. of Stirling; Univ. of Edinburgh (MA Hons Geog. 1987); Moray House Coll. of Educn (Postgrad. Dip. Recreation and Leisure Practice 1988); Thames Poly. (CertEd Further and Higher Educn 1990); Middlesex Univ. (MA Gender and Society 1993); Univ. of Bristol (PhD Soc. Sci. 1999). Lectr, Croydon Coll., 1988–89; Polytechnic, then University of North London: Lectr, 1989–90; Sen. Lectr, 1990–93; Prin. Lectr, 1993–97; Cheltenham and Gloucester College of Higher Educn, then University of Gloucestershire: Sen. Res. Fellow, 1997–99; Reader, 1999–2003; Hd, Leisure and Sport Res. Unit, 2001–03; Prof. in Human Geog., UWE Bristol (formerly UWE), 2003–08; University of Bedfordshire: Dean, Faculty of Educn and Sport, 2008–10; Prof. in Leisure and Tourism Studies, 2008–10; University of Edinburgh: Hd, Moray House Sch. of Educn, 2010–13; Prof. in Social and Envmtl Justice, 2010–13; Vice-Chancellor and Chief Exec., Univ. of St Mark and St John, Plymouth, 2013–16. Hon. Prof., Univ. of Bath, 2015–. Sen. Fellow, World Leisure Acad., 2011–. Member: AHRC Peer Review Coll., 2004–07; ESRC Peer Review Coll., 2010–; Scottish Commn on Rural Educn, 2011–13; Student Opportunity and Achievement Cttee, HEFCW, 2016–; Longer Term Policy Gp, Univs UK, 2016–; Council, CBI Wales, 2016–. Chair: World Leisure Commn on Women and Gender, 2002–08; REF Panel for Sport and Exercise Scis, Leisure and Tourism, 2010–14. Board Member: Plymouth Area Business Council, 2013–16; Plymouth Culture, 2014–16; Equality Challenge Unit, 2015–. Mem. Council, Acad. of Social Scis, 2015–. Chair, Leisure Studies Assoc., 2001–04. Member, Board: Askel Veur Acads Umbrella Co., 2015–16; Arab Eur. Leadership Educn Network, 2016–. FHEA 2001; FAcSS (AcSS 2003); FRGS 2016. *Publications:* (jtly) Leisure and Tourism Landscapes: social and cultural geographies, 2000; Gender and Leisure: social and cultural perspectives, 2003; (ed jtly) Geographies of Muslim Identities: diaspora, gender and belonging, 2007; (ed) Sport and Gender Identities: masculinities, femininities and sexualities, 2007; articles in jls on educn, geog., sociol., gender, disability, leisure, sport, tourism and rural studies. *Recreations:* travel, camping, active outdoor recreation including swimming and kayaking, contemporary landscape art, music. *Address:* Vice-Chancellor's Office, Cardiff Metropolitan University, Western Avenue, Cardiff CF5 2YB. *T:* (029) 2041 6070. *E:* caitchison@cardiffmet.ac.uk.

**AITCHISON, Sir Charles (Walter de Lancey),** 4th Bt *cr* 1938; *b* 27 May 1951; *er s* of Sir Stephen Charles de Lancey Aitchison, 3rd Bt, and (Elizabeth) Anne (Milburn), *er d* of late Lt-Col Edward Reed, Ghyllheugh, Longhorsley, Northumberland; *S* father, 1958; *m* 1984, Susan (marr. diss 2009), *yr d* of late Edward Ellis; one *s* one *d*. Lieut, 15/19th The King's Royal Hussars, 1974; RARO, 1974–78. *Recreation:* fishing. *Heir: s* Rory Edward de Lancey Aitchison, *b* 7 March 1986.

**AITCHISON, Prof. Jean Margaret;** Rupert Murdoch Professor of Language and Communication, University of Oxford, 1993–2003; Fellow, Worcester College, Oxford, 1993–2003, now Emeritus; *b* 3 July 1938; *d* of late John Frederick and Joan Eileen Aitchison; *m* 2000, John Robert Ayto. *Educ:* Wimbledon High Sch.; Girton Coll., Cambridge (BA 1st Cl. Hons Classics 1960; MA 1964); Radcliffe Coll., Harvard (AM Linguistics 1961). University of London: Asst Lectr in Ancient Greek, Bedford Coll., 1960–65; Lectr, 1965–82, Sen. Lectr, 1982–92, Reader, 1992, in Linguistics, LSE. Reith Lectr, BBC, 1996. *Publications:* Linguistics, 1972, 7th edn (as Aitchison's Linguistics) 2010; The Articulate Mammal: an introduction to psycholinguistics, 1976, 5th edn 2008; Language Change: progress or decay?, 1981, 4th edn 2013; Words in the Mind: an introduction to the mental lexicon, 1987, 5th edn 2012; The Seeds of Speech: language origin and evolution, 1996, extended edn 2000; The Language Web: the power and problem of words (Reith lectures), 1997; A Glossary of Language and Mind, 2003; (ed with Diana Lewis) New Media Language, 2003; The Word Weavers: newshounds and wordsmiths, 2007; Linguistics Made Easy, 2012. *Recreations:* gardening, reading. *Address:* 45 Malvern Road, E8 3LP. *T:* (020) 7249 3734. *E:* jean.aitchison@worc.ox.ac.uk.

**AITCHISON, Thomas Nisbet,** CBE 2005; Chief Executive, City of Edinburgh Council, 1995–2010; *b* 24 Feb. 1951; *s* of Thomas Aitchison and Mary (*née* Millar); *m* 1973, Kathleen Sadler; one *s* two *d*. *Educ:* Univ. of Glasgow (MA 1st Class Hons); Heriot-Watt Univ. (MSc). Lothian Regional Council: various posts, 1975–91; Depute Chief Exec., 1991–94; Chief Exec., 1994–95. Regl Returning Officer for Scotland Region, European elecns, 1999, 2004 and 2009. Chm., SOLACE Scotland, 2001–03. Mem. Court, Napier Univ., 1997–2002. Sec., Edinburgh Internat. Fest. Soc., 1996–2010. *Recreations:* hill-walking, football, music, fine wines and malt whiskies.

**AITHRIE, Viscount; Charles Adrian Bristow William Hope;** *b* 25 July 2001; *s* and *heir* of Earl of Hopetoun, *qv*. A Page of Honour to the Queen, 2013–15.

**AITKEN,** family name of **Baron Beaverbrook**.

**AITKEN, Anne Elizabeth, (Mrs Charles Collinson);** District Judge, Central Family Court (formerly Principal Registry, Family Division), 2008–18; *b* Dewsbury, W Yorks, 14 Oct. 1952; *d* of late William Allen Crowther and of Mary Eileen Crowther; *m* 1st, 1979, Robert Aitken (marr. diss.); 2nd, 1990, Charles Collinson; one *d*. *Educ:* St Margaret Clitherow Grammar Sch., Bradford; Univ. of Warwick (BA Hons 1974); College of Law. Admitted solicitor, 1982; solicitor in private practice, 1982–92; Partner, Aitken Associates, Islington, 1992–2008; Dep. District Judge, 2000–08.

**AITKEN, Gill,** CB 2019; Registrar, University of Oxford, since 2018; *b* 23 March 1960; *d* of Bill and Pamela Parker; *m* 1998, Robert Aitken; one *s*, and two step *s*. *Educ:* St Hugh's Coll., Oxford (BA Hons Philosophy and Theol. 1982). Admitted solicitor, 1988; solicitor in private practice, 1988–93; lawyer in Govt Legal Service, 1993–; Department for Environment, Food and Rural Affairs: Dir, Legal Services, 2004–07; Director General: Law and Human Resources (formerly Legal Gp), 2007–09; Law and Corporate Services, 2009–10; Gen. Counsel and solicitor, HMRC, 2014–18. *Recreations:* family, cycling, art history, theatre, conversation and ideas.

**AITKEN, Rev. Jonathan William Patrick;** Assistant Prison Chaplain, HM Prison Pentonville, since 2018; Assistant Curate, St Matthew's, Westminster, since 2018; *b* 30 Aug. 1942; *s* of Sir William Traven Aitken, KBE and Hon. Penelope Loader Maffey, MBE, JP; *m* 1st, 1979, Lolicia Olivera (marr. diss. 1998), *d* of Mr and Mrs O. Azucki, Zürich; one *s* twin *d*; one *d* by Soraya Khashoggi; 2nd, 2003, Hon. Elizabeth Harris, *d* of 1st Baron Ogmore, TD, PC. *Educ:* Eton Coll.; Christ Church, Oxford (MA Hons Law); HMPs Belmarsh and Standford Hill; Wycliffe Hall, Oxford (CTh Dist.). Private Sec. to Selwyn Lloyd, 1964–66; Foreign Corresp., London Evening Standard, 1966–71; Man. Dir, Slater Walker (Middle East) Ltd, 1973–75; Dep. Chm., Aitken Hume Internat. PLC, 1990–92 (Co-founder, 1981; Chm., 1981–90); Dir, TV-am PLC, 1981–88. Contested (C) Meriden, 1966; MP (C) Thanet East, Feb. 1974–83, Thanet South, 1983–97; contested (C) Thanet South, 1997. Minister of State for Defence Procurement, MoD, 1992–94; PC, 1994–97; Chief Sec. to HM Treasury, 1994–95. Mem., Select Cttee on Employment, 1979–82. Dir, Prison Fellowship Internat., 2003–; Exec. Dir, Trinity Forum Europe, 2006–; Chm., Prison Reform Gp, Centre for Social Justice, 2007– (Fellow, 2014); Advr to World Bank on offender rehabilitation projects, 2010–. Ordained deacon, 2018, priest, 2019. Trustee: Caring for Ex-Offenders, 2003–; Saïd Foundn, 2007–; NACRO, 2011–18. President: Christian Solidarity Worldwide, 2006–; Tempus Novo, 2017–; Vice Pres., New Bridge Soc., 2007–. *Publications:* A Short Walk on the Campus, 1966; The Young Meteors, 1967; Land of Fortune: A Study of Australia, 1969; Officially Secret, 1970; Richard Nixon: a life, 1993; Pride and Perjury, 2000; Psalms for People under Pressure, 2004; Prayers for People under Pressure, 2004; Porridge and Passion, 2005; Charles W. Colson: a life redeemed, 2005; Heroes and Contemporaries, 2006; John Newton: from disgrace to amazing grace, 2007; Nazarbayev and the Making of Kazakhstan, 2009; Margaret Thatcher: power and personality, 2013; Meaningful Mentoring, 2014; (with J. E. A. Samuels) What Happened to the Rehabilitation Revolution?, 2017; The St Mellitus Story, 2018; articles in Spectator, Sunday Telegraph, Sunday Times, Guardian, American Spectator, Sydney Morning Herald, Washington Post, Independent, Daily Mail, Mail on Sunday, etc. *Address:* 83 Barkston Gardens, SW5 0EU. *T:* (office) (020) 7373 5800. *E:* jonathanaitken@jwpaitken.co.uk.
*See also M. P. K. Aitken.*

**AITKEN, Maria Penelope Katharine;** actress; Director, Dramatis Personae Co.; *b* 12 Sept. 1945; *d* of Sir William Traven Aitken, KBE and Hon. Penelope Loader Maffey, MBE, JP; *m* 1st, 1968, Mark Durden-Smith (marr. diss.); 2nd, 1972, (Arthur) Nigel Davenport (marr. diss.; he *d* 2013); one *s*; 3rd, 1991, Patrick McGrath, *qv*. *Educ:* Riddlesworth Hall, Norfolk; Sherborne Girls' Sch.; St Anne's Coll., Oxford. Associate Prof., Yale Sch. of Drama, 1990; Faculty Member: Juilliard Sch., NY, 1991–97; Drama Dept, NY Univ., 1995–96. *Stage includes:* first professional appearance, Belgrade Th., Coventry, 1967; rep., Th. Royal, Northampton, 1970–71; Travesties, RSC, 1974; A Little Night Music, Adelphi, 1975; Blithe Spirit, NT, 1976; Bedroom Farce, NT, 1977; Private Lives, Duchess, 1980; Design for Living, Queen's, 1982; Sister Mary Ignatius (also dir.), Ambassadors, 1983; Happy Family (dir.), Duke of York's, 1983; Private Lives (also dir.), 1984; After the Ball (dir.), Old Vic, 1985; The Rivals (dir.), Court, Chicago, 1985; Waste, RSC, 1985; The Women, Old Vic, 1986; The Vortex, Garrick, 1989; Other People's Money, Lyric, 1990; The Mystery of Irma Vep (dir.), Ambassadors, 1990; As You Like It (dir.), Regent's Park Open Air Th., 1992; Hay Fever, Albery, 1992; The Picture of Dorian Gray, Lyric, Hammersmith, 1994; Sylvia, Lyric, 1997; Easy Virtue (dir.), Chichester, 1999; Humble Boy, Gielgud, 2002; Man and Boy (dir.), Duchess, 2005; The 39 Steps (dir.), Criterion, 2006; Sherlock's Last Case (dir.), Watermill Th., Newbury, 2013; *films:* A Fish Called Wanda, 1988; Fierce Creatures, 1997; Jinnah, 1998; Asylum, 2005; producer, director and actor for TV and radio. *Publications:* A Girdle Round the Earth, 1986; Style: acting in high comedy, 1996.
*See also J. W. P. Aitken, J. A. Davenport.*

**AITKEN, Oonagh Melrose**; Chief Executive, Volunteering Matters (formerly Community Service Volunteers), 2014–19 (Director, Social Action, Volunteering, Fundraising and Policy, 2012–14); *b* 11 March 1956. *Educ:* Paisley Grammar Sch.; Glasgow University (MA Hons, MEd); Open Univ. (MA Art Hist. 2008). Teacher of modern languages, Linwood High Sch., Braidfield High Sch., and Garrion Acad., Wishaw (also Asst Head Teacher), 1982–90; Strathclyde Regional Council: Educn Officer, 1990–93; Brussels Officer, 1993–95; Actg Asst Chief Exec., 1995–96; Hd, Social Policy, Glasgow CC, 1996; Corporate Manager (Social Strategy), Fife Council, 1996–99; Chief Exec., COSLA, 1999–2001; Improvement and Development Agency: Regl Associate Dir, 2001–02, Regl Associate, 2002–03, South East; Acting Dir, Strategy, Inf. and Develt, 2003–04; Consultant, 2004–05; sessional lectr, project manager and researcher, McGill Sch. of Social Work, Montreal, 2006–09; Nat. Advr, Children, Young People and Families, Improvement and Develt Agency, subseq. Local Govt Improvement and Develt, 2009–12. *Recreations:* literature, cinema, current affairs.

**AITKEN, Brig. Robert Hanbury Tenison**, CBE 2009; Director, Music in Hospitals and Care (formerly Music in Hospitals), Cymru/Wales, since 2013; Lord-Lieutenant for Gwent, since 2016; *b* Kingston, Jamaica, 18 May 1956; *s* of Harry Aitken, MC, and Anne Aitken (*née* Tenison); *m* 1987, Joanna Napier; two *s*. *Educ:* Eton; Queen's Coll., Oxford; RMA, Sandhurst. Commnd Royal Regt of Wales, 1977; CO, 1995–97; Col of Regt, 2004–06; retd, 2011. Ops Manager, RWCMD, 2011–13. DL Gwent, 2012. Churchwarden, Llandegvedd Ch, 2011–. CStJ 2016 (OStJ 2003). *Recreations:* singing, fishing. *Address:* Walnut Tree Farm, Croesyceiliog, Cwmbran, Gwent NP44 2DE. *T:* (01633) 450706. *E:* robertaitken895@btinternet.com.

**AITKEN, William Mackie**; JP; DL; Member (C) Glasgow, Scottish Parliament, 1999–2011; *b* 15 April 1947; *s* of William Aitken and Nell Aitken. *Educ:* Allan Glen's Sch., Glasgow; Glasgow Coll. of Technol. ACII 1971. Underwriter and sales exec., insurance industry, 1965–98. Glasgow City Council: Mem. (C), 1976–99; Convenor, Licensing Cttee, 1977–80; Leader of Opposition, 1980–84 and 1992–96; Bailie of City, 1980–84, 1988–92 and 1996–99. Scottish Parliament: Dep. Opposition spokesman on justice, 2001–03; Vice Convenor, Justice 2 Cttee, 2000–03; Cons. Chief Whip and Parly Business Mgr, 2003–07; Shadow Sec. for Justice, 2007–11; Convener, Justice Cttee, 2007–11. JP 1985, DL 1992, Glasgow. *Publications:* contrib. articles to newspapers. *Recreations:* reading, walking, foreign travel, wining and dining with friends.

**AITKENHEAD, Gary John**, CEng; Chief Executive, Defence Science and Technology Laboratory, since 2017; *b* Glasgow, 26 Sept. 1968; *s* of Bill Aitkenhead and Karen Watson (*née* McGregor); *m* 2004, Sys Hansen; three *d*. *Educ:* Univ. of Strathclyde (BEng 1st Cl. Hons Electrical and Electronic Engrg). MIET 1989; CEng 1995. R&D Engr, Racal Res. Ltd, 1989–91; Motorola Solutions: R&D Engr, 1991–97; R&D Dept Manager, 1997–2003; Director: Project Mgt, 2003–04; Global Products, 2004–06; EMEA Pre-Sales, 2006–07; EMEA Public Safety, Services Business, 2007–09; Vice President: EMEA Enterprise Service, 2009–11; EMEA Services and Global Support, 2011–14; Global Managed Services Business, 2014–15; Vice Pres., Devices, Sepura plc, 2016–17. *Recreations:* mountain and road biking, entertaining, cooking. *Address:* Defence Science and Technology Laboratory, Porton Down, Salisbury, Wilts SP4 0JQ. *T:* (01980) 951161. *E:* gaitkenhead@dstl.gov.uk.

**AITKIN, Prof. Donald Alexander**, AO 1998; PhD; Chairman: Cultural Facilities Corporation, 2002–11; National Capital Authority, 2008–11; Chief Executive Officer, Agrecon Pty Ltd, 2002–03 (Chairman, 1992–2002); *b* 4 Aug. 1937; *e s* of late Alexander George Aitkin and Edna Irene (*née* Taylor); *m* 1st, 1958, Janice Wood (marr. diss. 1977); one *s* three *d*; 2nd, 1977, Susan Elderton (marr. diss. 1991); one *s*; 3rd, 1991, Beverley Benger. *Educ:* Univ. of New England (MA 1961); ANU (PhD 1964). Postdoctoral Travelling Fellow, Nuffield Coll., Oxford, 1964–65; Australian National University: Res. Fellow in Pol Sci., 1965–68; Sen. Res. Fellow, 1968–71; Prof. of Politics (Foundn Prof.), Macquarie Univ., 1971–80; Institute of Advanced Studies, Australian National University: Prof. of Pol Sci., 1980–88; Chm. Bd, 1986–88; Vice-Chancellor, 1991–2002, Pres., 1997–2002, Prof. Emeritus, 2003–, Univ. of Canberra. Chairman: Aust. Res. Grants Cttee, 1986–87; Aust. Res. Council, 1988–90; ACT Schs Legislation Review, 1999–2000; Dep. Chm., ACT Sci. and Technol. Council, 1999–; Member: Aust. Sci. and Technol. Council, 1986–92; Tourism Ministerial Adv. Council, 2006–08. Vice-Pres., Australian Vice-Chancellors' Cttee, 1994–95. Chairman: Aust. Maths Trust, 1995–2004; Nat. Olympiad Council, 1996–2004; NRMA/ACT Road Safety Trust, 2001–. Mem. Bd, Canberra Theatre Trust, 1993–97; Pres., Pro Musica Inc., 2002–09; Chm., Canberra Internat. Music Fest., 2009–12; Dir, Artsound FM, 2004–06. Patron and Ambassador, Alzheimer's Australia ACT, 2016–. FASSA 1975; FACE 1995; Hon. Fellow, Royal Aust. Planning Inst., 2001. DUniv Canberra, 2002; Hon. DLitt New England, 2004. *Publications:* The Colonel, 1969; The Country Party in New South Wales, 1972; Stability and Change in Australian Politics, 1977, 2nd edn 1982; The Second Chair (novel), 1977; (with B. Jinks) Australian Political Institutions, 1980 (trans. Japanese, 1985), 10th edn 2012; (ed) The Life of Politics, 1984; (ed) Surveys of Australian Political Science, 1985; What Was It All For? The Reshaping of Australia, 2005; Edna and Alec: a memoir, 2006; Turning Point (novel), 2015; The Canonbury Tales (novel), 2015; Nobody's Hero (novel), 2016; Moving On (novel), 2017; Critical Mass: how the Commonwealth got into funding research in universities, 2017; The Innings Biography (novel), 2018; Harry's Choice (novel), 2019. *Recreations:* walking, music, cooking. *Address:* 80 Banks Street, Yarralumla, ACT 2600, Australia.

**AITMAN, David Charles**; Partner, Freshfields Bruckhaus Deringer LLP, since 2001 (Global Managing Partner, 2014–16). *Educ:* Clifton Coll.; Univ. of Sheffield (BA). Admitted as solicitor, 1982; Partner, Denton Wilde Sapte, 1988–2001; Freshfields Bruckhaus Deringer LLP: Deptl Man. Partner, 2003–06; Global Practice Leader, 2006–10. *Publications:* contributor: Butterworth's Encyclopaedia of Competition Law, 1991; Practical Intellectual Property; Yearbook of Media Law; Bellamy & Child's European Community Law of Competition. *Recreations:* tennis, windsurfing, music (performing and concert going). *Address:* Freshfields Bruckhaus Deringer LLP, 65 Fleet Street, EC4Y 1HS. *T:* (020) 7832 7240. *E:* david.aitman@freshfields.com.

**AITMAN, Prof. Timothy John**, DPhil; FRCP; FRSB; FMedSci; FRSE; Professor of Molecular Pathology and Genetics, and Director, Centre for Genomic and Experimental Medicine, University of Edinburgh, since 2014; *b* Northwood, 9 June 1958; *s* of Gabriel and Irene Aitman; *m* 1989, Megan Rowley; one *s* one *d*. *Educ:* Birmingham Med. Sch. (BSc Physiol. 1979; MB ChB 1982); King's Coll. London (MSc Gen. Biochem. 1988); Wolfson Coll., Oxford (DPhil 1992). MRCP 1985, FRCP 2000; FRSB (FSB 2012). Clinical Res. Fellow and Hon. Sen. Registrar, Nuffield Dept of Surgery and Radcliffe Infirmary, Univ. of Oxford, 1989–92; Sen. Registrar, St Bartholomew's Hosp., 1993; Gp Hd and Section Chair, Physiol Genomics and Medicine Gp, MRC Clin. Scis Centre, Hammersmith Hosp., 1993–2014; Hon. Consultant Physician, Hammersmith Hosps NHS Trust, 1994–2014; Prof. of Clin. and Molecular Genetics, Faculty of Medicine, Imperial Coll. London, 2001–14. Specialist Advr for H of L Genomic Medicine Report, 2009. FMedSci 2001; FRSE 2017. *Address:* Centre for Genomic and Experimental Medicine, MRC Institute of Genetics and Molecular Medicine, University of Edinburgh, Western General Hospital, Crewe Road South, Edinburgh EH4 2XU. *T:* (0131) 651 2081. *E:* tim.aitman@ed.ac.uk.

**AITTCHISEN, Sir Lance Walter**; *see* Aitchison, Sir C. W. de L.

**AJEGBO, Sir Keith Onyema**, Kt 2007; OBE 1994; education consultant; Headteacher, Deptford Green School, 1986–2006; *b* 31 Oct. 1946; *s* of late Michael Ajegbo and Dorothy Ajegbo; *m* 1991, Deborah Caroline Fry; one *s* one *d*. *Educ:* Greenacres Primary Sch., Eltham; Eltham Coll.; Downing Coll., Cambridge (BA Eng. Lit. 1969); Univ. of Nottingham (PGCE 1970); Birkbeck, Univ. of London (MA Culture, Diaspora, Ethnicity 2014, MA Contemp. Lit. and Culture 2017). Dep. Hd, Elliott Sch., Putney, 1981–86. Education consultant for: DFES, subseq. DCSF, later DFE, 2006–10, researched and wrote report for Sec. of State for Educn (Curriculum Review: Diversity and Citizenship, 2007); London Bor. of Newham, 2004–10; UBS Investment Bank, 2006–07; Leadership Develt Advr, Future Leaders, 2006–15; Chm., 14–19 Diploma in Humanities Steering Gp, DFE (formerly DCSF), 2008–10; Mem., Speaker's Adv. Cttee on Public Engagement, 2010–. Governor: Nat. Coll. of Sch. Leadership, 2001–03; Goldsmiths, London, 2003–07; Bridge Acad., Hackney, 2007–15. Trustee: Citizenship Foundn, 2007–11; Stephen Lawrence Trust, 2007– (Vice Chair, 2011–13; Chair, 2013–); A Partner in Educn, Rwanda, 2014–; Wimbledon Foundn, 2015–. Hon. Fellow, Goldsmiths, London, 1997. Hon. DEd De Montfort, 2002; Hon. DLit(Ed) London, 2011. *Publications:* Black Lives, White Worlds, 1982; numerous articles for educn jls. *Recreations:* playing tennis (Capt., Cambridge Univ. 1969, Prentice Cup tour, 1968; Kent county team, 1966–82, county colours), reading novels, extensive library of pop music. *Clubs:* Hurlingham; All England Lawn Tennis (Wimbledon).

**AJIBOLA, Prince Bola Adesumbo**, Hon. KBE 1989; CFR; SAN 1986; High Commissioner for Nigeria in the United Kingdom, 1999–2002; Leader of Nigerian Delegation, Cameroon-Nigeria Mixed Commission, 2002; Founder, Bola Ajibola & Co., 1963; *b* 22 March 1934; *s* of Oba A. S. Ajibola and Adikatu Ashakun Ajibola; *m* 1961, Ona Olugbemi (*d* 2016); three *s* two *d*. *Educ:* Owu Baptist Day Sch., Abeokuta, Nigeria; Baptist Boys' High Sch., Abeokuta. Called to the Bar, Lincoln's Inn, London, 1962. Principal Partner, Bola Ajobola & Co., Nigeria, 1967–85 (specialising in commercial law and internat. arbitration); Hon. Attorney-Gen. and Minister of Justice, Nigeria, 1985–91; Judge: Internat. Court of Justice, The Hague, 1991–94; World Bank Admin. Tribunal, 1994; Constitutional Court, Fedn of Bosnia and Herzegovina, 1995; delegate to numerous internat. confs. President: Nigerian Bar Assoc., 1984–85 (Chm., Human Rights Cttee, 1980–84); Pan African Council, London Court of Internat. Arbitration, 1994; Pres. and Founder, African Concern, 1995–; Chairman: Gen. Council of the Bar, Nigeria, 1985–91; Body of Sen. Advocates of Nigeria, 1985–91; Adv. Cttee of Prerogative of Mercy, Nigeria, 1989–91; Task Force for Revision of Laws, Nigeria, 1990; Member: Privileges Cttee, Nigerian Bar, 1985–91; Nigerian Police Council, 1989–91; Internat. Bar Assoc.; Internat. Chamber of Commerce; World Arbitration Inst.; Perm. Court of Arbitration, The Hague (also Mem., Bd of Trustees); Governing Bd, Internat. Maritime Law Inst., IMO; Internat. Law Commn, UN, 1986–91; Internat. Court of Arbitration, ICC (Vice Chm., Commn; arbitrator, numerous internat. cases); Internat. Maritime Arbitration Commn; Governing Body, African Soc. of Internat. and Comparative Law. Fellow, Nigerian Inst. of Advanced Legal Studies; FCIArb. Editor: All Nigeria Law Reports, 1961–90; Nigeria's Treaties in Force, 1970–90; Ed.-in-Chief, Justice; Gen. Editor, Federal Min. of Justice Law Review Series. *Publications:* Law Development and Administration in Nigeria, 1987; Towards a Better Administration of Justice System in Nigeria, 1988; Narcotics, Law and Policy in Nigeria, 1989; Compensation and Remedies for Victims of Crime, 1989; Banking Frauds and Other Financial Malpractices in Nigeria, 1989; Unification and Reform of Criminal Laws and Procedure Codes of Nigeria, 1990; Women and Children under Nigerian Law, 1990; Customary Law in Nigeria, 1991; Democracy and the Law; Dispute Resolution by International Court of Justice; papers and articles in learned jls. *Address:* Bola Ajibola & Co., PO Box 6624, Marina, Lagos, Nigeria. *Clubs:* Abeokuta (Abeokuta); Metropolitan (Lagos); Yoruba Tennis.

**AJITSARIA, Shruti**; Head, since 2017, and Partner, since 2019, Fuse, Allen & Overy; *b* London, 19 Dec. 1978; *d* of Nand Kishore Ajitsaria and Aruna Ajitsaria; *m* 2005, Nilesh Jethwa; one *s* two *d*. *Educ:* Haberdashers' Aske's Sch. for Girls, Elstree; Downing Coll., Cambridge (BA Law 2000); Nottingham Law Sch. (LPC 2001). Admitted solicitor, 2004; Allen & Overy: trainee, 2002–04; Associate, 2004–14; Counsel, 2014–19. *Recreations:* ferrying my kids around, travel, restaurants, friends and family. *Address:* Allen & Overy, One Bishops Square, E1 6AD. *T:* (020) 3088 1831. *E:* shruti.ajitsaria@allenovery.com.

**AKAM, Prof. Michael Edwin**, DPhil; FRS 2000; FRES, FLS; Professor of Zoology (1866), University of Cambridge, 2010–19, now Emeritus (Head of Department, 2010–16); Fellow, Darwin College, Cambridge, since 2006; *b* 19 June 1952; *s* of William Edwin Akam and Evelyn Warriner Akam (*née* Thorne); *m* 1979, Margaret Madeleine Bray; two *s*. *Educ:* King's Coll., Cambridge (BA Nat. Scis 1974); Magdalen Coll., Oxford (DPhil Genetics 1978). FRES 1985; FLS 1999. Australian Sci. Schol., Royal Instn, 1970. Coll. Lectr in Zoology, Magdalen Coll., Oxford, 1978; Res. Fellow, King's Coll., Cambridge, 1978–86; MRC Fellow, Lab. of Molecular Biology, Cambridge, 1978–79; Fellow, Dept of Biochemistry, Stanford Univ., 1979–81 (Damon-Runyon/Walter Winchell Fellow, 1979); Cambridge University: MRC Sen. Fellow, Dept of Genetics, 1982–90; Wellcome Principal Fellow, and Founding Mem., Wellcome/CRC Inst., 1990–97; Prof. of Zoology, 1997–2010; Dir, Univ. Mus. of Zoology, 1997–2010. Chm., British Soc. for Developmental Biology, 1989–94 (Waddington Medal, 2005). Mem., EMBO, 1987. FAAAS 2006. Kowalevsky Medal, St Petersburg Soc. of Naturalists, 2007; Linnean Medal for Zool., Linnean Soc., 2009; Frink Medal, ZSL, 2013. *Publications:* (ed jtly) The Evolution of Developmental Mechanisms, 1994; res. papers and reviews in jls, Proc. Royal Soc., etc. *Recreation:* the living world. *Address:* Department of Zoology, University of Cambridge, Downing Street, Cambridge CB2 3EJ. *T:* (01223) 330114.

**AKENHEAD, Hon. Sir Robert**, Kt 2008; a Judge of the High Court of Justice, Queen's Bench Division, 2007–15; Judge in charge, Technology and Construction Court, 2010–13; *b* 15 Sept. 1949; *s* of late Edmund and Angela Akenhead; *m* 1972, Elizabeth Anne Jackson; one *s* three *d*. *Educ:* Rugby School; Exeter Univ. (LLB). Called to the Bar, Inner Temple, 1972, Bencher, 1997; in practice as barrister, 1973–2007; QC 1989; Head of Chambers, 2001–06; Asst Recorder, 1991–94; Recorder, 1994–2007. Arbitrator, mediator and adjudicator, 2015–. Examiner, Dio. of Canterbury, 1991–2007. Ed., Building Law Reports, 1999–. *Publications:* Site Investigation and the Law, 1984; Technology and Construction Court Practice and Procedure, 2006. *Recreations:* theatre, cricket, ski-ing, golf.

**AKER, Tim Mark**; Member for Eastern Region, European Parliament, 2014–19 (UK Ind, 2014–18; Ind, 2018–19); *b* Orsett, Essex, 23 May 1985. *Educ:* Havering Sixth Form Coll.; Univ. of Nottingham. Public affairs, TaxPayers' Alliance and Get Britain Out; Hd, Policy Unit, UKIP, 2013–15. Mem., Thurrock Council, 2014–19 (UK Ind, 2014–18; Ind, 2018–19). Contested (UK Ind) Thurrock, 2015, 2017.

**AKERLOF, Prof. George Arthur,** PhD; Professor of Economics, University of California at Berkeley, 1980, now Daniel E. Koshland, Sr Distinguished Professor Emeritus of Economics; Cassel Professor of Economics, London School of Economics and Political Science, 1978–81; *b* 17 June 1940; *s* of Gosta C. Akerlof and Rosalie C. Akerlof; *m* 1978, Janet Yellen; one *s*. *Educ*: Yale Univ. (BA 1962); MIT (PhD 1966). Fellowships: Woodrow Wilson, 1962–63; National Science Co-op., 1963–66; Fulbright, 1967–68; Guggenheim, 1973–74. Univ. of Calif, Berkeley: Asst Prof. of Econs, 1966–70; Associate Prof., 1970–77; Prof., 1977–78. Vis. Prof., Indian Statistical Inst., New Delhi, 1967–68. Sen. Economist, Council of Econ. Advisors, USA, 1973–74; Vis. Economist, Bd of Governors of Fed. Reserve System, USA, 1977–78. (Jtly) Nobel Prize for Economics, 2001. *Publications*: (with R. J. Shiller) Phishing for Phools: the economics of manipulation and deception, 2015; contrib. American Econ. Rev., Econ. Jl, Qly Jl Econs, Jl Polit. Econ., Rev. of Econ. Studies, Internat. Econ. Rev., Jl Econ. Theory, Indian Econ. Rev., and Rev. of Econs and Stats. *Address*: Department of Economics, University of California, Berkeley, CA 94720–3880, USA. *Club*: Piggy (Center Harbor, NH, USA).

**AKERS-DOUGLAS,** family name of **Viscount Chilston**.

**AKERS-JONES, Sir David,** KBE 1985; CMG 1978; GBM 2002; Chief Secretary, Hong Kong, 1985–86; Acting Governor, Hong Kong, Dec. 1986–April 1987; *b* 14 April 1927; *s* of Walter George and Dorothy Jones; *m* 1951, Jane Spickernell (MBE 1988) (*d* 2002); one *d* (one *s* decd). *Educ*: Worthing High Sch.; Brasenose Coll., Oxford (MA; Hon. Fellow, 2005). British India Steam Navigation Co., 1945–49. Malayan Civil Service (studied Hokkien and Malay), 1954–57; Hong Kong Civil Service, 1957–86; Government Secretary: for New Territories, 1973–81; for City and New Territories, 1981–83; for Dist Admin, 1983–85; Advr to Gov., April–Sept. 1987. Chm., Hong Kong Housing Authy, 1988–93; Advr to China on Hong Kong Affairs. Chm., Operation Smile China Medical Mission, 1992–. Pres., Business and Professionals Fedn, 2005–. Hon. Pres., Outward Bound Trust, Hong Kong, 1996– (Pres., 1986–95); Vice-Patron, Hong Kong Football Assoc. Hon. Member: RICS, 1991; HKIA, 2006. Hon. DCL Kent, 1987; Hon. LLD Chinese Univ. of Hong Kong, 1988; Hon. DSSc City Univ. of Hong Kong, 1993. *Publications*: Feeling the Stones: reminiscences, 2004. *Recreations*: painting, music. *Address*: Flat C, 33rd Floor, Tower 1, Sorrento, 1 Austin Road West, West Kowloon, Hong Kong. *Clubs*: Royal Over-Seas League; Hong Kong, Dynasty, China, Gold Coast and Country (Hong Kong).

**AKHTAR, Prof. Muhammad,** FRS 1980; Professor of Biochemistry, University of Southampton, 1973–98, now Emeritus; Distinguished National Professor, School of Biological Sciences, University of the Punjab, Lahore, since 2004; *b* 23 Feb. 1933; *m* 1963, Monika E. Schurmann; two *s*. *Educ*: Punjab Univ., Pakistan (MSc 1st class 1954); Imperial College, London (PhD, DIC 1959). Research Scientist, Inst. for Medicine and Chemistry, Cambridge, Mass, USA, 1959–63; University of Southampton: Lecturer in Biochemistry, 1963–66; Senior Lectr, 1966–68; Reader, 1968–73; Hd of Dept of Biochemistry, 1978–93; Chm., Sch. of Biochem. and Physiol. Scis, 1983–87; Dir, SERC Centre for Molecular Recognition, 1990–94. Chm., Inst. of Biomolecular Scis, 1989–90. Member: Chemical Soc. of GB; American Chemical Soc.; Biochemical Soc. of GB; Council, Royal Soc., 1983–85; Founding Fellow, Third World Acad. of Sciences, 1983 (Mem. Council and Treas., 1993–98; Vice-Pres., 1998–2004; Medal, 1996). Fellow, UCL, 2010. Hon. DSc Karachi, 2002. Flintoff Medal, RSC, 1993. Sitara-I-Imtiaz (Pakistan), 1981. *Publications*: numerous works on: enzyme mechanisms; synthesis and biosynthesis of steroids and porphyrins; biochemistry of vision; synthesis of anti-microbial compounds. *Address*: Biological Sciences, University of Southampton, Southampton SO17 1BJ. *T*: (home) (023) 8076 7718.

**AKIHITO, Emperor of Japan,** 1989–2019; Collar, Supreme Order of Chrysanthemum, 1989; KG 1998; *b* Tokyo, 23 Dec. 1933; *e s* of Emperor Hirohito (Showa) and Empress Nagako (Kojun); *m* 1959, Michiko Shoda; two *s* one *d*. *Educ*: Gakushuin Primary, Jun. and Sen. High Schs; Dept of Politics, Faculty of Politics and Econs, Gakushuin Univ. Official Investiture as Crown Prince of Japan, 1952; abdicated, 2019. Res. Associate, Australian Mus.; Mem., Ichthyological Soc. of Japan; For. Member: Linnean Soc. of London; Zool Soc. of London, 1992. King Charles II Medal, Royal Soc., 1998. *Publications*: (contrib. jtly) Fishes of the Japanese Archipelago, 1984; (jtly) The Fresh Water Fishes of Japan, 1987; 30 papers on gobies. *Recreation*: tennis. Heir: *er s* Naruhito, Emperor of Japan, since 2019 [*b* Tokyo, 23 Feb. 1960; *m* 1993, Masako Owada; one *d*]. *Address*: Imperial Palace, 1–1 Chiyoda, Chiyoda-ku, Tokyo 100–8111, Japan. *T*: (3) 32131111.

**AKINKUGBE, Prof. Oladipo Olujimi,** NNOM 1997; CON 1979; CFR 2004; Officier de l'Ordre National de la République de Côte d'Ivoire, 1981; MD, DPhil; FRCP, FRCPE, FWACP, FAS; Professor of Medicine, University of Ibadan, Nigeria, 1968–95, now Emeritus; *b* 17 July 1933; *s* of late Chief David Akinbobola and Chief (Mrs) Grace Akinkugbe; *m* 1965, Dr Folasade Modupeore Dina, *d* of late Chief I. O. Dina, CFR, OBE; two *s*. *Educ*: Univs of Ibadan (Fellow, 1998), London (MD), Liverpool (DTM&H) and Oxford (DPhil). FRCPE 1968; FWACP 1975; FAS 1980; FRCP 2012. House Surg., London Hosp., 1958; House Phys., King's Coll. Hosp., London, 1959; Commonwealth Res. Fellow, Balliol Coll. and Regius Dept of Medicine, Oxford, 1962–64; Head of Dept of Medicine, 1972, Dean of Medicine, 1970–74, and Chm., Cttee of Deans, 1972–74, Univ. of Ibadan; Vice-Chancellor: Univ. of Ilorin, 1977–78 (Principal, 1975–77); Ahmadu Bello Univ., Zaria, 1978–79. Rockefeller Vis. Fellow, US Renal Centres, 1966; Vis. Fellow in Medicine, Univs of Manchester, Cambridge and London, 1969; Visiting Professor of Medicine: Harvard Univ., 1974–75; Univ. of Oxford (and Vis. Fellow, Balliol Coll.), 1981–82; Univ. of Cape Town, 1996. Adviser on Postgrad. Med. Educn to Fed. Govt of Nigeria, 1972–75; Chairman: Nat. Implementation Commn on Rev. of Higher Educn in Nigeria, 1992; Presidential Project on Revamping Teaching Hosps, 2003–07; Member: Univ. Grants Commn, Uganda Govt; OAU Scientific Panels on Health Manpower Develt; Council, Internat. Soc. of Hypertension, 1982–90; Bd of Trustees, African Assoc. of Nephrology, 1986–94; Bd of Trustees, Nigerian Educare Trust, 1997–; internat. socs of hypertension, cardiology, and nephrology; Med. Res. Soc. of GB; Scientific Adv. Panel, Ciba Foundn, 1970–98; WHO Expert Adv. Panels on Cardiovascular Diseases, 1973–78, on Health Manpower, 1979–, on Health Sci. and Technol., 2003–; WHO Adv. Council on Health Res., 1990–95; Sec. to WHO 1984 Technical Discussions. Pro-Chancellor, and Chairman of Council: Univ. of Port-Harcourt, Nigeria, 1986–90; Univ. of Med. Scis, Ondo, Nigeria, 2015–; Chairman: Bd of Mgt, UCH, Ibadan, 2000–; Bd of Trustees, Ajayi Crowther Univ., Oyo, 2004–; Bd of Trustees, Bells Univ. of Technol., Ota, 2011–; Member: Governing Council and Bd of Trustees, Obafemi Awolowo Foundn, 1992; Governing Council, Nigeria Heart (formerly Heartcare) Foundn, 1994– (Chm., Bd of Trustees, 2000–); Exec. Council, World Innovation Foundn, 1998–; Bd of Trustees, Heritage Resources Conservation, 1999–; Bd, World Heart Fedn, 2004–; Chairman: Governing Council, Ajumogobia Science Foundn, 1997–; Bd of Trustees and Governing Council, Nigeria Soc. for Inf., Arts and Culture, 2002. President: Nigerian Assoc. of Nephrology, 1987–90; Nigerian Hypertension Soc., 1994; African Heart Network, 2001. Member, Editorial Bd: Jl of Hypertension, 1984–90; Jl of Human Hypertension, 1988–; Kidney International, 1990–98; Blood Pressure, 1991–; News in Physiological Scis, 1992–98. Hon. Fellow, Balliol Coll., Oxford, 2009. Hon. DSc: Ilorin, 1982; Fed. Univ. of Technol., Akure, 1992; Port Harcourt, 1997; Ogun State, 1998; Ibadan, 2006; Obafemi Awolowo, Ile-Ife, 2009; Bells Univ. of Technol., Ota, 2010. Searle Dist. Res. Award, 1989; Boehringer Ingelheim Award, Internat. Soc. of Hypertension, 2004; Hallmarks of Labour Award, 2004; Life Achievement Award: Nigerian Acad. of Sci., 2004; Nat. Univs Commn, 2006; Pioneer Award for Africa, Internat. Soc. of Nephrology, 2019. Traditional title, Atobase of Ife, 1991; Babalofin of Ijebu-Igbo, 1994; Adengbua of Ondo, 1995; Ikolaba Balogun Basegun of Ibadan, 1997; Aare Basegun of Ibadan, 2008. *Publications*: High Blood Pressure in the African, 1972; (ed) Priorities in National Health Planning, 1974; (ed) Cardiovascular Disease in Africa, 1976; (ed) Nigeria and Education: the challenges ahead, 1994; (ed jtly) Nigeria's Health in the 90s, 1996; (ed) Non-Communicable Diseases in Nigeria: final report of a national survey, 1997; (ed jtly) A Compendium of Clinical Medicine, 1999; (ed jtly) Clinical Medicine in the Tropics Series, 1987–; Footprints and Footnotes: an autobiography, 2010; papers on hypertension and renal disease in African, Eur. and Amer. med. jls, and papers on med. and higher educn. *Recreations*: music, gardening, clocks, birdwatching, golf. *Address*: c/o Department of Medicine, University of Ibadan, Ibadan, Nigeria; The Little Summit, Olubadan Aleshinloye Way, Iyaganku, Ibadan, Nigeria. *T*: 8036063327. *E*: akin3317@yahoo.com. *Clubs*: Dining (Ibadan); Oxford and Cambridge (Nigeria).

**AKINOLA, Most Rev. Peter Jasper,** CON 2003; Metropolitan, Archbishop and Primate of Nigeria, 2000–10; *b* 27 Jan. 1944; *m* 1969, Susan A. Akinola; three *s* three *d*. *Educ*: Diocesan Trng Centre, Wusasa; Theol Coll. of Northern Nigeria (Higher Dip. in Theol.); Virginia Theol Seminary, USA (MTS 1981). Catechist, Nguru, Nigeria, 1972; ordained deacon, 1978, priest, 1979; Vicar, St James, Suleija, Abuja, 1978–83; Canon (Missioner), Abuja, 1983–88; Bishop of Abuja, 1989–2010; Archbishop, Province Three, Nigeria, 1998–2000. Chairman: Global South, 2002; Conf. of Anglican Provinces in Africa, 2003–; Global Anglicans Future Conf. Primates' Council.

**AKKER, John Richard,** MBE 2012; Research Fellow, Human Rights Centre, University of Essex, since 2016 (Visiting Professor, 2012–16); Executive Secretary, Council for Assisting Refugee Academics, 1999–2012; *b* 6 May 1943; *s* of Alec Louis Morris Akker and Ruby (*née* Bryant); *m* 1st, 1967, Jean-Anne Roxburgh (marr. diss. 1990); two *d*; 2nd, 2007, Elaine Hill. *Educ*: SW Essex Tech. Coll.; Ruskin Coll., Oxford (L. C. White Schol.; Dip. Econ./Pol.); Univ. of York (BA Hons 1969); Cranfield Inst. of Technol. Mgt Sch. Clerical Officer, Ministry of Works, 1959–64; Asst Nat. Officer, 1969–71, Dep. Nat. Local Govt Officer, 1972–73, NALGO; Association of University Teachers: Asst Gen. Sec., 1973–77; Dep. Gen. Sec., 1978–94; Gen. Sec., NATFHE, 1994–97. Advr to EC, 1985–88. Exec. Dir, Network for Educn and Academic Rights, 2001–12. Visiting Lecturer: CIT, 1970–74; Univ. of Wisconsin, 1977–78; Vis. Prof., London South Bank Univ., 2005–12. Winston Churchill Fellowship, USA, 1976. Trustee: Refugee Council, 2000–09; Immigration Adv. Service, 2002–09; Student Action for Refugees, 2012– (Chm., 2012–16). Mem., Employment Tribunal Service, 1986–2013; Arbitrator, ACAS, 2012–16. Mem. (Ind), West Mersea Town Council, 2019–. Freeman, Guild of Educators, 2009–. *Recreations*: motor sport, sailing, football. *Address*: Human Rights Centre, University of Essex, Wivenhoe Park, Colchester CO4 3SQ. *E*: jakker@essex.ac.uk. *Clubs*: National Liberal; Colchester United FC Supporters.

**ALABASTER, Rear Adm. Martin Brian,** CBE 2011; CEng, FIET; Managing Director, Martin Alabaster Associates Ltd, since 2012; *b* 10 Aug. 1958; *s* of late Instructor Comdr Alan James Alabaster, RN and of Eileen Muriel (*née* Willshee); *m* 1981, Moira Bain; one *s* one *d*. *Educ*: Dulwich Coll.; Queens' Coll., Cambridge (BA Engrg Tripos 1980); Southampton Univ. (MSc Electronics 1985). CEng 2007; FIET 2007. HMS Bristol, 1982–84; Seawolf Project, MoD, 1985–89; RN Staff Course, Greenwich, 1989; BRNC Dartmouth, 1990–91; HMS London, 1992–93; Fleet Support, MoD, 1993–96; Project Horizon, 1996–98; Operational Requirements, MoD, 1998–2000; rcds 2001; Hd, Project Mgt, MoD, 2002–05; Sen. Engr, Fleet HQ, 2005–07. Cdre, BRNC Dartmouth, 2007–08; FO Scotland, Northern England and NI and FO Reserves, 2008–11. FInstLM 2007. Hon. DTech Plymouth, 2008. *Recreations*: running, sailing, bird-watching (Chm., RN Birdwatching Soc., 2006–), photography, cycling, opera (Dir, Iford Arts, 2018–).

**ALAGIAH, George Maxwell,** OBE 2008; presenter, BBC TV News at Six (formerly BBC TV 6 o'clock News), since 2003; *b* 22 Nov. 1955; *s* of Donald and Therese Alagiah; *m* 1984, Frances Robathan; two *s*. *Educ*: St John's Coll., Southsea; Van Mildert Coll., Durham Univ. South Magazine, 1982–89; BBC Foreign Affairs Correspondent, 1989–99, Africa Correspondent, 1994–99; News Presenter and journalist, BBC, 1999–2002; presenter, GMT with George Alagiah, 2010. Monte Carlo TV Fest. Award; BAFTA commendation; awards as Journalist of the Year from: Amnesty Internat., 1994; BPG, 1994; James Cameron Meml Trust, 1995; Bayeux Award for War Reporting, 1996. *Publications*: A Passage to Africa, 2001; (jtly) The Day That Shook the World, 2001; A Home from Home, 2006; The Burning Land (novel), 2019. *Recreations*: sport, tennis, music, hiking. *Address*: BBC News Centre, Broadcasting House, Portland Place, W1A 1AA.

**ALAGNA, Roberto;** French tenor; *b* 7 June 1963; *m* 1st, Florence Lancien (*d* 1994); one *d*; 2nd, 1996, Angela Gheorghiu, *qv* (marr. diss. 2013); *m* 2015, Aleksandra Kurzak; one *d*. Worked as accountant, electrician and cabaret singer; studied under Rafael Ruiz; Pavarotti Internat. Voice Competition Prize, 1988. Débuts: Alfredo in La Traviata, Glyndebourne Touring Opera, 1988; Royal Opera, Covent Garden, 1992; La Scala, Milan, 1992; Gran Teatre del Liceu, Barcelona, 1992; Chicago Opera, 1994; Vienna Staatsoper, 1995; Théâtre du Châtelet, Paris, 1996; Metropolitan Opera, NY, 1996; Palermo Opera, 2002; Copenhagen Opera, 2002; Bayerische Staatsoper, 2005; Teatro Real, Madrid, 2007; Deutsche Oper, Berlin, 2010. Rôles include: Roméo in Roméo et Juliette (Laurence Olivier Award, Covent Garden, 1995); title rôle in Don Carlos; Rodolpho in La Bohème; Nemorino in L'elisir d'amore; Edgard in Lucia di Lammermoor; Cavaradossi in Tosca; Radamès in Aida; title rôle in Gounod's Faust; Calaf in Turandot; title rôle in Otello; title rôle in Vasco da Gama; title rôle in Werther; Chevalier des Grieux in Manon Lescaut; Samson in Samson et Dalila; Don José in Carmen. Films: Tosca, 2002; Celles qui aimaient Wagner, 2011. Co-writer (with Frédérico Alagna), libretto, Le Dernier jour d'un condamné (composer, David Alagna). Numerous recordings. Officier des Arts et des Lettres (France), 2002 (Chevalier, 1996); Victoires de la Musique, 2002, 2004; Ordre Nat. du Mérite (France), 2003; Chevalier de la Légion d'Honneur (France), 2008. *Publications*: Je ne suis pas le fruit du hasard (autobiog.), 2007; Mon Dictionnaire intime, 2019.

**ALAMBRITIS, Stephen;** Leader of the Council, Merton London Borough Council, since 2010 (Member (Lab), since 2003; Leader, Labour Group, since 2007); *b* Larnaca, Cyprus, 22 Feb. 1957; *s* of late Andreas Alambritis, Cyprus and Christina Alambritis (*née* Skardashi); *m* 1987, Athanasia Georgiou; one *s* one *d*. *Educ*: Elliott Sch., Putney; Birmingham Poly. (BA Hons Govt); London Sch. of Econs (MSc); City Poly. (MA Business Law). Researcher, Assoc. of Ind. Businesses, 1984–88; Hd of Public Affairs, Fedn of Small Businesses, 1988–2010 (Mem., 2011–). Owner of small unincorporated property business, 2009–. Member: Better Regulation Task Force, Cabinet Office, 1998–2001; Rural Affairs Task Force, DEFRA, 2001–02; Consumer Adv. Panel, DCA, then MoJ, 2005–10. Member: Disability Rights Commn, 2004–07; Equality and Human Rights Commn, 2009–12. Trustee, Enterprise Insight UK, later Enterprise UK, 2009–10. Member, Board: London Pensions Fund Authy, 2010–18; South London Business Ltd, 2010–12; Sutton, Croydon and Merton Credit Union Ltd, 2011–12; Smart Energy Gp (formerly Smart Meter Central Delivery Body), 2013–16; London CIV Ltd, 2018–. Chair, South London Partnership, 2012–. Consultant, Adam Smith Internat., 2012–. Member: Labour Party Small Business Task Force, 2011–15; Labour Party Skills Task Force, 2012–15; EU Cttee of the Regions, 2015–. Member: NUJ, 1985–2010; Unite (formerly Amicus), 1999–2010; GMB, 2009–; CWU, 2009–10; London Councils, 2010–. FCIPR 2008 (MIPR 1990). Recreation: FA referee grade 1. Address: 10 Woodland Way, Morden, Surrey SM4 4DS. T: (020) 8543 6003, 07958 139498. E: stephen.alambritis@btinternet.com. W: www.twitter.com/cllr_alambritis; The Leader's Office, Merton London Borough Council, Civic Centre, London Road, Morden, Surrey SM4 5DX. T: (020) 8545 3424. E: stephen.alambritis@merton.gov.uk.

**ALAZREG, Abdullahi Hamad Ali;** Ambassador of Sudan to Ireland, since 2016; b El Gadaref, Sudan, 1 Jan. 1955; s of Hamad Ali Alazreg and Nafeesa Albashir Ahmad; m 2010, Sumaya Omer Hussain Abdelrahman; one s three d. Educ: Omdurman Univ., Sudan (BA Econs); Lincoln Univ., USA (MA Sociol.); NY Poly. (Dip. Energy Resources and Technol.). Min. of Energy and Mining, Sudan, 1980–88; Islamic African Relief Agency, Sudan, 1989–90; diplomat serving in Saudi Arabia, Kenya, USA, UN Office, Geneva, China, 1990–2004; Ambassador to Bulgaria, 2004–08; Dir, Res. and Studies Dept, Arab Affairs Dept and Dir Gen., Bilateral Relns Directorate, Min. of Foreign Affairs, 2008–10; Ambassador to UK, 2010–14; Under-Sec., Min. of Foreign Affairs, 2014–16. Publications: contrib. magazines in Sudan and Bulgaria. Recreations: reading, writing poetry. Address: Embassy of Republic of Sudan, 16 Herbert Street, Dublin 2, D02 FY01, Ireland. E: abalazreg@yahoo.com.

**ALBANESE, Thomas;** Chairman, Vedanta Resources Holdings Ltd, 2013–14; Chief Executive, Vedanta Resources plc, 2014–17; b 9 Sept. 1957; s of Paul Albanese and Rosemarie Albanese (née Helm); m 1979, Mary Delane; two d (and one d decd). Educ: Univ. of Alaska (BS Mining Econs (cum laude) 1979; MS Mining Engrg 1981). Chief Operating Officer, Nerco Minerals Co., 1982–93; Rio Tinto plc, 1993–2013: Gen. Manager, Greeks Creek Mine, Alaska, 1993–95; Gp Exploration Exec., London, 1995–97; Vice Pres. Engrg and Gen. Manager Smelting and Refining, Kennecott Utah Copper, Salt Lake City, 1997–2000; Man. Dir, North Ltd, Australia, 2000–01; Chief Executive: Industrial Minerals Div., 2001–04; Copper, and Hd of Exploration, 2004–06; Dir, Gp Resources, 2006–07; CEO, Rio Tinto plc, 2007–13. Director: Franco-Nevada Corp., 2013–; Nevada Copper Corp., 2018–. Recreations: walking, swimming, canal boats.

**ALBARN, Damon,** OBE 2016; musician, singer and songwriter; b 23 March 1968; partner, Suzi Winstanley; one d. Educ: Stanway Sch., Colchester. Lead singer, Blur, 1989–; co-creator, Gorillaz, 1998–; albums: with Blur: Leisure, 1991; Modern Life is Rubbish, 1993; Parklife, 1994 (BRIT Award, 1995); The Great Escape, 1995; Blur, 1997; 13, 1999; Think Tank, 2003; The Magic Whip, 2015; with Gorillaz: Gorillaz, 2001; Demon Days, 2005; Plastic Beach, 2010; The Fall, 2011; Humanz, 2017; The Now Now, 2018; other projects: Mali Music, 2002; The Good, The Bad & The Queen, 2007; Monkey: Journey to the West, 2008; Kinshasa One Two, 2011; Rocket Juice & The Moon, 2012; Dr Dee, 2012; solo: Everyday Robots, 2014. Composer of musical, wonder.land, 2015. BRIT Award for best group (jtly), 1995, for outstanding contribution to music (jtly), 2012; Ivor Novello Lifetime Achievement Award, 2016.

**ALBEMARLE,** 10th Earl of, cr 1696; **Rufus Arnold Alexis Keppel;** Baron Ashford, 1696; Viscount Bury, 1696; b 16 July 1965; s of Derek William Charles Keppel, Viscount Bury (d 1968), and Marina, yr d of late Count Serge Orloff-Davidoff; S grandfather, 1979; m 2001, Sally Claire Tadayon (marr. diss. 2016); one s. Educ: Central Sch. of Art (BA (Hons) Industrial Design, 1990). Heir: s Viscount Bury, qv. Address: Hurst Barns Farm, East Chiltington, Lewes, Sussex BN7 3QU.

**ALBERTI, Sir (Kurt) George (Matthew Mayer),** Kt 2000; DPhil; FRCP, FRCPE, FRCPath; Senior Research Investigator, Imperial College, London, since 2002; Professor of Medicine, University of Newcastle upon Tyne, 1985–2002 (Dean of Medicine, 1995–97); President, Royal College of Physicians, 1997–2002; b 27 Sept. 1937; s of late William Peter Matthew Alberti and Edith Elizabeth Alberti; m 1st, 1964; three s; m 2nd, 1998, Prof. Stephanie Anne Amiel, qv. Educ: Balliol Coll., Oxford (MA; DPhil 1964; BM, BCh 1965; Hon. Fellow 1999). FRCP 1978; FRCPath 1985; FRCPE 1988. Res. Fellow, Harvard Univ., Boston, USA, 1966–69; Res. Officer, Dept of Medicine, Oxford Univ., 1969–73; Prof. of Chemical Pathology and Human Metabolism, Univ. of Southampton, 1973–78; Prof. of Clinical Biochemistry and Metabolic Medicine, Univ. of Newcastle, 1978–85; Prof. of Medicine, ICSTM, 2000–02. Vis. Prof. of Diabetes and Metabolism, KCL, 2012–. Mem., WHO Expert Adv. Panel on Diabetes, 1979–. Nat. Clin. Dir for Emergency Access, DoH, 2002–09; Clin. Advr, NHS London, 2009–10. Pres., Internat. Diabetes Fedn, 2000–03 (Vice-Pres., 1988–94); Vice-Chm., British Diabetic Assoc., 1996–99; Chm., Diabetes UK, 2009–12 (Vice Pres., 2000–09). Chm., King's College Hosp. NHS Foundn Trust, 2011–15 (non-exec. Dir, 2010–11). Founder FMedSci 1998 (Mem. Council, 1998–2002). Hon. FRCPGlas 1999; Hon. FRCPI 1999. Hon. Member: Hungarian Diabetes Assoc., 1986; Argentinian Diabetes Assoc., 1991. Hon. MD: Aarhus, 1998; Athens, 2002; Hon. DM Southampton, 1999; Hon. DSc: Warwick, Cranfield, 2005. Publications: edited more than 30 medical books, including: Diabetes Annual, Vols 1–6; Internat. Textbook of Diabetes Mellitus, 1992, 2nd edn 1997; author of more than 1100 pubns in learned jls. Recreations: hill walking, jogging, crime fiction, opera.
See also S. J. M. M. Alberti.

**ALBERTI, Samuel John Matthew Mayer,** PhD; Keeper, Science and Technology, National Museums Scotland, since 2016; b Southampton, 7 June 1974; s of Sir (Kurt) George (Matthew Mayer) Alberti, qv and Johanna Mary Mayer Alberti; m 2005, Fay Bound; one s one d. Educ: Durham Univ. (BSc 1995); Imperial Coll. London (MSc 1997); Univ. of Sheffield (PhD 2001). Lectr and Res. Fellow, Univ. of Manchester, 2001–10; Dir, Mus and Archives, RCS, 2010–16. James M. Graham Vis. Prof., Univ. of Edinburgh 2014–15; Hon. Prof., Univ. of Stirling, 2016–. Publications: Nature and Culture: objects, disciplines and the Manchester Museum, 2009; Morbid Curiosities: medical museums in nineteenth-century Britain, 2011; (ed) The Afterlives of Animals: a museum menagerie, 2011; (ed) Medical Museums: past, present, future, 2013; (ed) War, Art and Surgery, 2014; 50 articles and chapters. Recreation: jogging. Address: National Museums Scotland, Chambers Street, Edinburgh EH1 1JF. E: s.alberti@nms.ac.uk.

**ALBERTI, Stephanie Anne, (Lady Alberti);** see Amiel, S. A.

**ALBERY, Ian Bronson;** theatre producer, manager and consultant, West End, London; Theatre Design Consultant, Nimax Theatres Ltd, since 2007; b 21 Sept. 1936; s of Sir Donald Albery and Rubina Albery (née McGilchrist); m Barbara Yu Ling Lee (d 1997); two s; one d by Jenny Beavan, qv; m 2003, Judy Monahan. Educ: Stowe; Lycée de Briançon, France. Trained in West End theatres as box office asst, stagehand, flyman, electrician and stage manager, 1955–57; Dep. Chief Electrician, New Th., Oxford, 1957; Dep. Stage Manager for H. M. Tennent, Irma La Douce and West Side Story, 1958; Stage Manager for Associated Rediffusion and Associated TV, 1958; Th. Manager, Ambassador's Th., 1959; Prodn Manager, The World of Suzie Wong, Prince of Wales Th., 1959; Stage Manager, Marlene Dietrich, Paris, 1959; Chief Electrician for European tours: musical, Free and Easy, 1960; US State Dept Cultural Exchange tour by American Ballet Th., Lisbon to Moscow, 1960; Prodn Manager for Donmar Prodns, incl. Oliver! UK tour and USA tour, incl. NY, and Tokyo, 1960–64; Manager, Donmar Rehearsal Th., subseq Donmar Warehouse Th., 1961–87; Tech. Dir, London Fest. Ballet, 1964–68; Producer or Co-Producer for over 50 West End prodns, 1978–; Managing Director: Wyndham Theatres, Piccadilly Theatre, Donmar Productions, Omega Stage (Producer) (Donmar Warehouse Th.), 1978–87; Theatre of Comedy, 1987–90; Dep. Chm., English Nat. Ballet, 1984–90; Dir, Ticketmaster (UK) Ltd, 1985–92; Chief Exec. and Producer, Sadler's Wells, Peacock and Lilian Baylis Theatres, 1994–2002; Theatre Consultant for rebuilding of Sadler's Wells Th., 1995–99; Chief Exec., Guildford Sch. of Acting Conservatoire, 2002–04. Consultant, Japan Satellite Broadcasting, 1991–92. Member: Bd of Mgt, British Th. Assoc., 1968–79; Drama Panel, Arts Council of GB, 1974–76; Drama and Dance Adv. Panel, British Council, 1978–88. Vice-Chm., Assoc. of British Th. Technicians, 1974–78 (Hon. Mem., 2007; Fellow, 2013). Trustee, Theatres Trust, 1977–96. Pres., 1977–79, Vice-Pres., 1979–80, Soc. of West End Th., later Soc. of London Th. (Hon. Mem., 2003–); Hon. Treas., Soc. of Th. Consultants, 1990–96 (Founder Mem., 1964–); Hon. Vice Pres., Sadler's Wells Foundn, 2009–. Address: 1090 Chemin de la Rochette, 26450 Roynac, France. T: (4) 75901221. E: ian.albery@gmail.com.

**ALBERY, Tim;** theatre and opera director; b 20 May 1952. Theatre productions include: War Crimes, ICA, 1981; Secret Gardens, Amsterdam and ICA, 1983; Venice Preserv'd, Almeida, 1983; Hedda Gabler, Almeida, 1984; The Princess of Cleves, ICA, 1985; Mary Stuart, Greenwich, 1988; As You Like It, Old Vic, 1989; Berenice, NT, 1990; Wallenstein, RSC, 1993; Macbeth, RSC, 1996; Attempts on her Life, Royal Court, 1997; Nathan the Wise, Toronto, 2005; opera productions include: for English National Opera: Billy Budd, 1988; Beatrice and Benedict, 1990; Peter Grimes, 1991; Lohengrin, 1993; From the House of the Dead, 1997; La Bohème, 2000; War and Peace, 2001; Boris Godunov, 2008; for Opera North: The Midsummer Marriage, 1985; The Trojans, 1986; La finta giardiniera, 1989; Don Giovanni, 1991; Don Carlos, 1992; Luisa Miller, 1995; Così fan Tutte, 1997, 2004; Katya Kabanova, 1999, rev. 2019; Idomeneo, 2003; King Croesus, Madama Butterfly, 2007; Macbeth, 2008; Giulio Cesare, 2012; Otello, 2013; Poppea, 2014; Pleasure, 2016; Ballo in Maschera, 2018; Silent Night, 2018; for Royal Opera: Chérubin, 1994; Der Fliegende Hollander, 2009; Tannhäuser, 2010; for Welsh National Opera: The Trojans, 1987; La finta giardiniera, 1994; Nabucco, 1995; for Scottish Opera: The Midsummer Marriage, 1988; The Trojans, 1990; Fidelio, 1994, 2005; The Ring Cycle, 2000–03; Don Giovanni, 2006; for Garsington Opera: Idomeneo, 2016; Capriccio, 2018; Mitridate, 2020; for Australian Opera, The Marriage of Figaro, 1992; for Netherlands Opera: Benvenuto Cellini, 1991; La Wally, 1993; Beatrice and Benedict, 2001; for Santa Fé Opera: Beatrice and Benedict, 1998; The Magic Flute, 2006; Arabella, 2012; La Finta Giordiniera, 2015; Capriccio, 2016; Ariadne, 2018; for Batignano Fest., Italy, The Turn of the Screw, 1983; for Bregenz Fest., Austria, La Wally, 1990; for Bayerische Staatsoper, Munich: Peter Grimes, 1991; Simon Boccanegra, 1995; Ariadne auf Naxos, 1996; for Metropolitan Opera, NY: A Midsummer Night's Dream, 1996; The Merry Widow, 2000; for Canadian Opera: Rodelinda, 2005; Götterdämmerung, 2006; War and Peace, 2008; Aida, 2010; Arabella, 2017; for Glimmerglass Fest., Così fan Tutte, 2005; for Boston Lyric Opera: The Lighthouse, 2012; Katya Kabanova, 2015; for Luminato Festival, Toronto: The Children's Crusade, 2009; Prima Donna, 2010; Hell's Fury, 2019; Maada'ookii Songlines, 2019; for Aldeburgh Fest., Peter Grimes, 2013; for Dallas Opera, The Aspern Papers, 2013; for Soundstreams, Toronto, Airline Icarus, 2014; for Tapestry, Toronto, M'dea Undone, 2015; for Philadelphia Opera, Don Carlo, 2015; for Chicago Lyric Opera: Tannhauser, 2015; Les Troyens, 2016; for Opera Theatre of St Louis, Coronation of Poppea, 2019; for Royal Danish Opera, Così fan Tutte; 2019; musicals include: Passion, Minnesota Opera, 2004; One Touch of Venus, Opera North, 2004.

**ALBON, Sarah;** Chief Executive Officer and Inspector General, Insolvency Service, since 2015. Principal Private Sec. to Lord Chancellor, 2001–03; Dep. Dir, Finance, DCA, 2004; Dep. Dir, Criminal Legal Aid Strategy, 2005–09, Dir, Civil Family and Legal Aid Policy, 2009–11, MoJ; Dir, Strategy and Change, HM Courts and Tribunal Service, 2011–15. Address: Insolvency Service, 4 Abbey Orchard Street, SW1P 2HT. T: (020) 7291 6713. E: sarah.albon@insolvency.gsi.gov.uk. W: www.twitter.com/insolvencyCEO.

**ALBRIGHT, Madeleine Korbel,** PhD; Secretary of State, United States of America, 1997–2001; Chairman, Albright Stonebridge Group, since 2009 (Founder and Principal, Albright Group LLC, 2001–09); b 15 May 1937; m Joseph Albright (marr. diss.); three d. Educ: Wellesley Coll. (BA Hons Pol Sci. 1959); Sch. of Advanced Internat. Studies, Johns Hopkins Univ.; Columbia Univ. (BA 1968; PhD 1976). Chief Legislative Asst to Senator Edmund Muskie, 1976–78; Staff Mem., Nat. Security Council and Mem., White House Staff, 1978–81; Sen. Fellow in Soviet and E European Affairs, Center for Strategic and Internat. Studies; Fellow, Woodrow Wilson Internat. Center for Scholars, 1981–82; Res. Prof. of Internat. Affairs and Dir, Women in Foreign Service Program, Georgetown Univ. Sch. of Foreign Service, 1982–92; Pres., Center for Nat. Policy, 1989–92 (Mem., Bd of Dirs); US Perm. Rep. to UN, 1993–96; Mem., Nat. Security Council, USA, 1993–2001. Member: Bd of Dirs, Atlantic Council of US; US Nat. Commn, UNESCO. Chm., Nat. Democratic Inst. for Internat. Affairs, 2001–. Presidential Medal of Freedom (USA), 2012. Publications: Poland: the role of the press in political change, 1983; Madam Secretary (autobiog.), 2003; The Mighty and the Almighty: reflections on America, God, and world affairs, 2006; Memo to the President: how we can restore America's reputation and leadership, 2008; Read My Pins: stories from a diplomat's jewel box, 2009; Fascism: a warning, 2018; articles in professional jls and chapters in books.

**ALBROW, Dame Susan Jane;** see Owen, Dame S. J.

**ALBU, Sir George,** 3rd Bt cr (UK) 1912, of Grosvenor Place, City of Westminster, and Johannesburg, Province of Transvaal, South Africa; farmer; b 5 June 1944; o s of Major Sir George Werner Albu, 2nd Bt, and Kathleen Betty (d 1956), d of Edward Charles Dicey, Parktown, Johannesburg; S father, 1963; m 1969, Joan Valerie Millar (d 2015), London; two d. Recreation: horse racing. Heir: none. Address: Glen Hamish Farm, PO Box 62, Richmond, Natal, 3780, South Africa. T: 824436045. Clubs: Victoria Country (Pietermaritzburg); Durban Country.

**ALBURY, Simon Albert,** MBE 2019; Chair, Campaign for Broadcasting Equality CIO, since 2014; b 9 Feb. 1944; s of Cyril Lyon Albury and Eileen Palmer Albury (née Lloyd-Jones); m 1989, Phillida Bartels-Ellis; one s. Educ: Univ. of Nottingham (BA Sociol. 1966); Wien Scholar and Special Student, Brandeis Univ.; Univ. of Sussex (MA Sociol. of Deviant Behaviour 1968). Information Officer, Govt Social Survey, 1967; Res. Associate, Amer. Psychol. Assoc. project on Scientific Information Exchange in Psychol., 1968; reporter, World In Action, Granada TV, 1969; prod. and dir, BBC Current Affairs Gp, 1969–73; BBC Open Univ., 1973–74; Sen. Producer, Granada TV (progs incl. World in Action, What the Papers Say, End of Empire, The Outrageous Millie Jackson), 1974–89; Dir, Campaign for Quality TV, 1989–90; Dir of Strategy, 1991, Dir of Public Affairs, 1991–99, Meridian Broadcasting Ltd; Director of Public Affairs: MAI Broadcasting, 1994–95; MAI Media, 1995–96; United Broadcasting and Entertainment, 1996–99; Chief Exec., RTS,

2000–12 (Fellow, 2012). Presenter (as Sam Scott), gospel music show, Hallelujah, Capital Radio, 1973–75. Chm., Cttee for Ethnic Minority Employment in Film, British Screen Adv. Council, 2000–07; Mem. Bd, Internat. Broadcasting Convention, 2001–12. Chm., Centre for Investigative Journalism, 2005–08; Special Advr, Nafsiyat Intercultural Therapy Centre, 2001–08 (non-exec. Dir, 2000–01). Trustee, Meridian Broadcasting Charitable Trust, 1993–99; Mem., Adv. Bd, Elizabeth R Fund, 2002–03. Mem., BAFTA, 2000. *Recreations:* travel, music, ballet. *Address:* Campaign for Broadcasting Equality CIO, 12 Blenheim Gardens, NW2 4NS. *E:* cequalitybroadcasting@gmail.com.

**ALCOCK, Michael Reginald;** Chair, Johnson & Alcock Ltd, Literary Agent, since 2003; *b* Hammersmith, London, 11 Feb. 1948; *s* of Dr Rex Alcock and Venetia Alcock (*née* Brealey); *m* 1st, 1972, Caroline Clary Prentice (marr. diss. 1991); 2nd, 1993, Nadia Manuelli; one *s* one *d. Educ:* Rugby Sch.; Univ. of Bristol (BA Classics 1970). N Eur. Rep., OUP, 1970–72; Editor, Tom Stacey Ltd, 1972–73; Editl Dir, Macmillan London, 1974–86; Publishing Dir, Aurum Press, 1986–90; Book Publisher, Newspaper Publishing plc, 1991; Publishing Dir, Boxtree, 1991–97; Literary Agent, Michael Alcock Mgt, 1997–2003. *Recreations:* music (especially opera), reading, classical antiquity. *Address:* 27 Manchester Street, W1U 4DJ. *E:* michael@johnsonandalcock.co.uk. *Club:* Garrick.

**ALCOCK, Air Chief Marshal Sir (Robert James) Michael,** GCB 1996 (CB 1989); KBE 1992; FREng; Royal Air Force, retired; aerospace consultant, since 1997; Director, Cygnae Ltd, 1997–2013; Chairman, AMSS Ltd, 2003–13; *b* 11 July 1936; *s* of late William George and Doris Alcock; *m* 1965, Pauline Mary Oades; two *d. Educ:* Victoria College, Jersey; Royal Aircraft Establishment. FIMechE; FRAeS. Commissioned, Engineer Branch, RAF, 1959; RAF Tech. Coll., Henlow, 1961; Goose Bay, Labrador, 1964; Units in Bomber Comd, 1959–69; RAF Staff Coll., Bracknell, 1970; PSO to DG Eng (RAF), 1971–73; OC Eng. Wing, RAF Coningsby, 1973–75; OC No 23 Maintenance Unit, RAF Aldergrove, 1975–77; Group Captain (Plans), HQ RAF Support Command, 1977–79; MoD, 1979–81; Dep. Comdt, RAF Staff Coll., Bracknell, 1981–84; RCDS, 1984; Dir Gen. of Communications, Inf. Systems and Orgn (RAF), 1985–88; AO Engrg, HQ Strike Comd, 1988–91; Chief Engr (RAF), 1991–96; Chief of Logistic Support, RAF, 1991–93; Air Mem. for Supply and Orgn, MoD, 1993–94; Air Member for Logistics and AOC-in-C, Logistics Comd, 1994–96. Trustee, RAF Benevolent Fund, 1996–2002. Chm., Bd of Mgt, Princess Marina Hse, 1996–2002. Pres., British Model Flyers' Assoc., 2000–; Mem., RAF Sailing Assoc. Governor, Victoria Coll., Jersey, 1995–2004. FREng (FEng 1995). Hon. DSc Cranfield, 1994. *Recreations:* golf, model aircraft, sailing. *Address:* c/o NatWest Farnborough North, Lawrie Road, Victoria Road, Farnborough, Hants GU14 7NR. *Clubs:* Royal Air Force; Berkshire Golf, St Enodoc Golf.

**ALDENHAM,** 6th Baron *cr* 1896, of Aldenham, Co. Hertford, **AND HUNSDON OF HUNSDON,** 4th Baron *cr* 1923, of Briggens, Co. Hertford; **Vicary Tyser Gibbs;** *b* 9 June 1948; *s* of 5th Baron Aldenham and of Mary Elizabeth, *o d* of late Walter Parkyns Tyser; *S* father, 1986; *m* 1980, Josephine Nicola, *er d* of John Richmond Fell, Lower Bourne, Farnham, Surrey; three *s* one *d. Educ:* Eton; Oriel College, Oxford; RAC, Cirencester. Capel-Cure Myers Ltd, 1975–79; Dir, 1986–, Chm., 2012–, Montclare Shipping Co.; Man. Partner, Aldenham Aviation, 2004–. Chairman: Herts CLA, 1995–98; Watling Chase Community Forest, 1997–99. Freeman, City of London, 1979; Liveryman, Merchant Taylors' Co., 1979. *Heir: s* Hon. Humphrey William Fell Gibbs, *b* 31 Jan. 1989. *Address:* c/o Aldenham Estate Office, Elstree Aerodrome, Hogg Lane, Elstree, Herts WD6 3AR.

**ALDER, Debbie, (Mrs M. A. T. Johnstone),** CB 2019; Human Resources Director General, Department for Work and Pensions, since 2014; *b* Bexley, Kent, 1 March 1966; *m* Mark Alexander Talbot Johnstone; two step *d. Educ:* Haberdashers' Aske's Hatcham Girls' Sch.; Univ. of Bristol (BSc Hons Psychol. and Zool. 1988). FCIPD. Hd, HR, W London, Marks and Spencer plc, 1988–2000; Hd, Internal HR Consultancy, Ford Motor Co. (Europe), 2000–04; Associate Consultant, Aspiren; Dir, Change 2 Perform; Human Resources Director: DWP, 2009–10; DEFRA, 2011–13; MoJ, 2013–14. *Recreations:* solo and choral singing, travel, movies, dog walking. *Address:* Department for Work and Pensions, Level 7, Caxton House, 6–12 Tothill Street, SW1H 9NA. *T:* (020) 7340 4193. *E:* debbie.alder@dwp.gov.uk.

**ALDER, Lucette, (Mrs Alan Alder);** *see* Aldous, L.

**ALDER, Michael;** Controller, English Regional Television, British Broadcasting Corporation, 1977–86, retired; *b* 3 Nov. 1928; *s* of late Thomas Alder and Winifred Miller; *m* 1955, Freda, *d* of late John and Doris Hall; two *d. Educ:* Ranelagh Sch., Bracknell, Berks; Rutherford Coll., Newcastle-upon-Tyne. Newcastle Evening Chronicle, 1947–59; BBC North-East: Chief News Asst, Newcastle; Area News Editor, Newcastle; Representative, NE England, 1959–69; Head of Regional Television Development, BBC, 1969–77. Mem., Exec. Cttee, Relate (formerly Nat. Marriage Guidance Council), 1987–94 (Chm., S Warwicks, 1987–89; Chm., Appeals Cttee, 1988–94). Chm., Tanworth Educnl Foundn, 2004–08 (Vice Chm., 1994–2004). Mem., Incorporated Co. of Butchers, 1948. Freeman, City of Newcastle upon Tyne. *Recreations:* gardening, walking, country pursuits. *Address:* 1 Lune Close, Kirkby Lonsdale, Carnforth, Lancs LA6 2DA.

**ALDER, Prof. Roger William,** DPhil, DSc; FRS 2006; FRSC; Professor of Organic Chemistry, University of Bristol, 1996–2002, now Professor Emeritus and Senior Research Fellow; *b* 26 April 1937; *s* of William John Alder and Mona Amelia Alder (*née* Nevitt); *m* 1961, Judy Anne Sweet; one *s* two *d. Educ:* Rendcomb Coll., Cirencester; Pembroke Coll., Oxford (MA, DPhil); DSc Bristol. FRSC 1980. Lectr in Organic Chem., 1966–81, Reader, 1981–96, Univ. of Bristol. *Publications:* (jtly) Mechanism in Organic Chemistry, 1971; contrib. numerous papers on aspects of organic chem. *Address:* School of Chemistry, University of Bristol, Cantock's Close, Bristol BS8 1TS. *E:* rog.alder@bristol.ac.uk.

**ALDERDICE,** family name of **Baron Alderdice.**

**ALDERDICE,** Baron *cr* 1996 (Life Peer), of Knock, in the City of Belfast; **John Thomas Alderdice,** FRCPsych; consultant psychiatrist in psychotherapy, Belfast Health and Social Services Trust (formerly Eastern Health and Social Services Board, then South and East Belfast Health and Social Services Trust), 1988–2010; Convenor, Liberal Democrat Parliamentary Party, House of Lords, 2010–14; *b* 28 March 1955; *s* of late Rev. David Alderdice and Helena Alderdice (*née* Shields); *m* 1977, Dr Joan Margaret Alderdice (*née* Hill), former consultant pathologist; two *s* one *d. Educ:* Ballymena Acad.; Queen's Univ., Belfast (MB, BCh, BAO 1978). MRCPsych 1983; FRCPsych 1991; Jun. House Officer, Lagan Valley Hosp., 1978–79; Sen. House Officer, Belfast City Hosp., 1979–80; Registrar: Holywell and Whiteabbey Hosps, 1980–81; Shaftesbury Square Hosp., 1981–82; Lissue and Belfast City Hosps, 1982–83; Sen. Tutor and Sen. Registrar, Belfast City Hosp. and Queen's Univ., Belfast, 1983–87. Exec. Med. Dir, S and E Belfast HSS Trust, 1993–97. Hon. Lectr/Sen. Lectr, QUB, 1991–99; Hon. Prof., Univ. of San Marcos, Peru, 1999; Vis. Prof., Dept of Psychiatry and Neurobehavioral Scis, Univ. of Virginia, USA, 2006–10; Sen. Res. Fellow, 2012–, Dir, Centre for Resolution of Intractable Conflict, 2013–, Harris Manchester Coll., Oxford; Res. Associate, Centre for Internat. Studies, Oxford, 2014–; Clinical Prof., Sch. of Medicine, Univ. of Maryland, 2016–; Dist. Vis. Prof., Nanyang Technol Univ., Singapore, 2017; Sen. Res. Fellow, St Benet's Hall, Oxford, 2019–. Chm., Centre for Democracy and Peace Bldg, Belfast, 2014–. Dir, NI Inst. of Human Relns, 1991–94. Contested (Alliance): Belfast E, 1987, 1992; NI, European Parly Election, 1989. Alliance Party of Northern Ireland: Mem., Exec. Cttee, 1984–98; Chm., Policy Cttee, 1985–87; Vice-Chm., March–Oct. 1987; Leader, 1987–98; Leader: delegn at Inter-Party and Inter-Governmental Talks on the future of NI, 1991–98; delegn at Forum for Peace and Reconciliation, Dublin Castle, 1994–96; Mem., NI Forum, 1996–98; Speaker, NI Assembly, 1998–2004 (Mem. for Belfast East). European Liberal, Democrat and Reform Party (formerly Fedn of European Liberal, Democratic and Reform Parties): Mem., Exec. Cttee, 1987–2003; Treas., 1995–99; Vice-Pres., 1999–2003; Pres., Liberal International, 2005–09 (Mem. Bureau, 1996–2014; Vice Pres., 1992–99; Dep. Pres., 2000–05; Hon. Pres., 2015–). Member: Ind. Monitoring Commn, 2004–11; Commonwealth Commn on Respect and Understanding, 2006–07; Cttee on Standards in Public Life, 2010–16; Panel on Disbanding of Paramilitary Gps, 2015–16. Mem. (Vic. Area), Belfast City Council, 1989–97. Pres., ARTIS (Europe) Ltd, 2009–. Vice Pres., Internat. Dialogue Initiative, 2007–. Trustee, Ulster Museum, 1993–97. Hon. FRCPI 1997; Hon. FRCPsych 2001; Hon Mem., Peruvian Psychiatric Assoc., 2000; Hon. Affiliate, British Psychoanalytical Soc., 2001. Hon. DLitt UEL, 2008; Hon. LLD: Robert Gordon, Aberdeen, 2009; Queen's, Kingston, Ont, 2017; DUniv: Open, 2014; Uskudar Univ., Istanbul, 2019; Hon. DHum American Univ., Bogota, 2018. Silver Medal, Congress of Peru, 1999; Medal of Honour, Coll. of Medicine, Peru, 1999; Erice Prize, World Fedn of Scientists, 2005; Extraordinarily Meritorious Service to Psychoanalysis Award, Internat. Psychoanalytical Assoc., 2005; Prize for Freedom, Liberal Internat., 2015; Award for Excellence in Promoting Peace and Collaboration, Global Thinkers Forum, 2016. Kt Comdr, Royal Order of Francis I, 2002. *Publications:* professional articles on psychology of fundamentalism, radicalisation, terrorism, violent political conflict and its resolution and rule of law; political articles. *Recreations:* reading, music, gastronomy, travel. *Address:* House of Lords, SW1A 0PW. *T:* (020) 7219 5050. *E:* john.alderdice@hmc.ox.ac.uk, alderdicej@parliament.uk. *Club:* National Liberal (Trustee, 2010–; Chm. Trustees, 2011–14).

*See also* D. K. *Alderdice.*

**ALDERDICE, David King,** OBE 1999; Consultant Dermatologist, Ulster Hospital, since 2010; Lord Mayor of Belfast, 1998–99; *b* 2 June 1966; *s* of Rev. David and Helena Alderdice; *m* 1989, Fiona Alison Johnston; one *s* two *d. Educ:* Queen's Univ., Belfast (MB BCh BAO 1989); Manchester Coll., Oxford (BA PPE 1994; MA 1998). MRCPI 1996, FRCPI 2008. Jun., subseq. Sen., House Officer, Royal Victoria Hosp., Belfast, 1989–92; Specialist Registrar in Dermatology, Royal Victoria Hosp., Belfast and Belfast City Hosp., 1997–2002; Clin. Res. Fellow, Ulster Hosp., Dundonald, 1997–98; Consultant Dermatologist, Causeway Hosp., Coleraine, 2002–10. Regl Lead, NI psychodermatology service, 2019–. Contested (Alliance), N Antrim, Forum, 1996, parly elecns, 1997. Member (Alliance): Belfast CC, 1997–2005; N Down BC, 2005–10. Chair, Youth Lyric, 2002–12. *Publications:* articles in dermatology, genitourinary and psychol learned jls. *Recreations:* squash racquets, hill walking. *Address:* c/o Ulster Hospital, Upper Newtownards Road, Dundonald, Belfast BT16 1RH.

*See also* Baron *Alderdice.*

**ALDERMAN, Richard John;** Director, Serious Fraud Office, 2008–12; *s* of John Edward Alderman and late Patricia Eileen Alderman; *m* 1981, Joyce Sheelagh, *d* of late Herrick Edwin and Joyce Hilda Wickens; one *d. Educ:* Woking Grammar Sch.; University College London (LLB). Called to the Bar, Gray's Inn, 1974; joined Solicitor's Office, Inland Revenue, 1975; seconded to Legal Secretariat to the Law Officers, 1991–93; Principal Asst Solicitor, 1996–2003, Dir, Special Compliance Office, 2003–05, Bd of Inland Revenue; Dir, Special Civil Investigations, HMRC, 2005–08. Member: Adv. Council, Sch. of Ethics and Law, UCL, 2011–16; Anti-Corruption Council, WEF, 2011–13. *Recreations:* family life, country walking.

**ALDERSLADE, Prof. Richard,** FRCP, FFPH; Adjunct Associate Professor of Public Health Administration, Robert F. Wagner Graduate School of Public Service, New York University, since 2008; *b* 11 Aug. 1947; *s* of Herbert Raymond Alderslade and Edna F. Alderslade; *m* 1st, 1974, Elizabeth Rose (marr. diss. 1999); two *s* one *d* (and one *d* decd); 2nd, 1999, Angela Hendriksen (marr. diss. 2010); one step *d. Educ:* Chichester High Sch. for Boys; Christ Church, Oxford (BM BCh; MA); St George's Hosp. FFPH (FFPHM 1987); FRCP 1993. GP, 1974–76; Registrar in Community Medicine, 1976–78, Lectr, 1978–79; MO and SMO, DHSS, 1979–85; Specialist in Community Medicine, 1985–88 and Community Unit Gen. Manager, 1986–88, Hull HA; Regl Dir of Public Health and Regl MO, Trent RHA, 1988–94; Prof. of Community Care, Univ. of Sheffield, 1994–95; Regl Advr, Humanitarian Assistance, WHO Regl Office for Europe, Copenhagen, 1995–2001; Chief Officer, High Level Gp for Romanian Children and Advr to Prime Minister of Romania, 2001–02; Sen. External Relns Officer, WHO Office, UN, NY, 2002–06; Chief Exec., Children's High Level Gp, 2006–10; Sen. Health Policy Advr, WHO Regl Office for Europe, 2010–12. Teaching Fellow in Public Health, St George's Hosp. Med. Sch., 2013–. *Publications:* articles on public health, BMJ and other jls. *Recreations:* walking, railways, photography. *Address:* 112A Osborne Street, Hull HU1 2PN.

**ALDERSON, Brian Wouldhave;** freelance editor and writer; Children's Books Editor, The Times, 1967–95; *b* 19 Sept. 1930; *s* of John William Alderson and Helen Marjory Alderson; *m* 1953, Valerie Christine (*née* Wells) (*d* 2005); three *s* (and two *s* decd). *Educ:* Ackworth Sch.; University College of the South-West, Exeter (BA Hons). Work in the book trade, 1952–63; Tutor-librarian, East Herts Coll. of Further Educn, 1963–65; Sen. Lectr, (on Children's Literature and on the Book Trade), Polytechnic of N London, 1965–83. Visiting Professor: Univ. of Southern Mississippi, 1985; UCLA, 1986. Lectr, London Rare Books Sch., 2008–. Founder and first Chm., Children's Books Hist. Soc., 1969–78 and 1995–2001. Pres., Beatrix Potter Soc., 1995–. Exhibition organiser: (with descriptive notes): Early English Children's Books, BM, 1968; Looking at Picture Books, NBL, 1973; Grimm Tales in England, British Library, 1985–86; Randolph Caldecott and the Art of the English Picture Book, British Library, 1986–87; Be Merry and Wise: the early development of English children's books, Pierpont Morgan Library, NY, 1990–91; Childhood Re-Collected, Christ Church, Oxford, 1994; This Book Belongs to Me, Nat. Liby of Scotland, Edinburgh, 2002. DUniv Surrey, 2002; Hon. DLit Newcastle, 2016. Eleanor Farjeon Award, 1968. *Publications:* Sing a Song for Sixpence, 1986; (with Iona and Robert Opie) Treasures of Childhood, 1989; The Arabian Nights, 1992; Ezra Jack Keats: artist and picture book maker, vol. 1, 1994, vol. 2, 2002; Edward Ardizzone: a bibliographic commentary, 2003; (with Felix de Marez Oyens) Be Merry and Wise: origins of children's book publishing in England 1650–1800, 2006; (with Andrea Immel) Tommy Thumb's Pretty Song-Book: a commentary, 2013; (with Lorraine Johnson) The Ladybird Story, 2014; 100 Best Books for Children, 2019; *translations:* Hürlimann: Three Centuries of Children's Books in Europe, 1967; Picture-book World, 1968; Grimm, Popular Folk Tales, 1978; Andersen, The Swan's Stories, 1997; Andersen, Fairy Tales, 2013; *edited:* The Juvenile Library, 1966–74; The Colour Fairy Books, by Andrew Lang, 1975–82; Lear, A Book of Bosh, 1975; Children's Books in England, by F. J. Harvey Darton, 1982; Hans

Christian Andersen and his Eventyr in England, 1982. *Recreations:* book collecting, uncorking bottles. *Address:* Jail-house View, Victoria Road, Richmond, North Yorks DL10 4AS. *T:* (01748) 823648.

**ALDERSON, Daphne Elizabeth, (Mrs J. K. A. Alderson);** *see* Wickham, D. E.

**ALDERSON, (George) Lawrence (Hastings),** CBE 2004; FRAgS; Chairman: Countrywide Livestock Ltd, since 1974; International Caspian Society, since 2017; Trustee and Founder Chairman, Rare Breeds International, since 1991 (President, 2011–14); *b* 24 June 1939; *s* of late John Henry Alderson and Mary Hilda Alderson (*née* Hastings), Teesdale; *m* 2nd, 1971, Jacqueline Mary (marr. diss. 1983), *y d* of John Pasfield, OBE; one *s* one *d*; 4th, 1994, Marie Bridgette (marr. diss. 2014), *e d* of John Lynch. *Educ:* Barnard Castle Sch.; Selwyn Coll., Cambridge (BA 1962, MA; boxing blue). Farmer, 1968–92: created new breed, British Milksheep; Chm., Westwater Farm Partners, 1974–81. Consultant: on internat. genetic resources, 1974–; EEC studies of endangered breeds, 1992–93. Dir, Traditional Breeds Meat Mktg Co., 1998–2000. Chm., Preserving Cttee, DEFRA Nat. Steering Cttee, 2003–06. Consultant: Internat. Evaluation Cttee, Danish Farm Animal Genetic Resources, 2001–02; Indian Horse Breeds, 2013–. Rare Breeds Survival Trust: Founder and Tech. Consultant, 1973–90; Dir, 1990–2000; Chm., 2003–07; Internat. Ambassador, 2010–13; Chm., Traditional Livestock Foundn, 1994–2003; Dir, Kelmscott Rare Breeds Foundn, USA, 1995–2003. Member: Council, Grazing Advice Partnership, 1997–2009; Council, Eur. Livestock Assoc. (formerly Eur. Livestock Alliance), 2001–17; Mgt Bd, PigBioDiv (Eur.), 2002–12 (Chm., 2008–12); Mgt Bd, Semen Archive, 2003–08; Co-Chm., Mgt Bd, Ovine Semen Archive, 2010–13. President: White Park Cattle Soc., 1988–; Red Poll Cattle Soc., 2001–02 (Mem. Council, 2001–04). Chm., Combined Flock Book, 1974–81, 2007–08; Mem., Editl Adv. Bd, AGRI (FAO), 2003–16. FRAgS 2012. Hon. Fellow, Rare Breeds Internat., 2011. *Publications:* The Chance to Survive, 1978, 3rd edn 1994; Rare Breeds, 1984, 4th edn 2001; Genetic Conservation of Domestic Livestock, Vol. I 1990, Vol. II 1992; Saving the Breeds, 1994; Coloured Sheep, 1994; A Breed of Distinction, 1997; The Adaptation of Rare Breeds of British Livestock to Different Environments, 1998; Conservation Genetics of Endangered Horse Breeds, 2005; A Pennine Dynasty (novel), 2009; Encyclopaedia of Livestock Breeds and Breeding, 2016; White Park Cattle, 2018. *Recreations:* sport, writing, genealogy, travel, breeding White Park cattle. *E:* ecnewal@gmail.com. *Club:* Farmers.

**ALDERSON, Joanne Hazel;** District Judge (Magistrates' Courts) (formerly Stipendiary Magistrate), Derbyshire, 1997–2014; *b* 18 March 1954; *d* of Colin and Joan Fleetwood; *m* 1983, Richard Alderson; two *s*. *Educ:* Wolverhampton Girls' High Sch.; Liverpool Univ. (LLB Hons); College of Law. Called to the Bar, Middle Temple, 1978. Legal Advr, W Midlands Prosecuting Solicitors' Dept, 1977–78; Court Clerk/Principal Asst, Wolverhampton Magistrates' Court, 1978–85; Deputy Clerk: to Warley Justices, 1985–86; to Wolverhampton Justices, 1986–97; Dep. Chief Exec., Wolverhampton Magistrates' Courts Cttee, 1995–97. *Recreations:* travel, bridge, swimming, reading.

**ALDERSON, Lawrence;** *see* Alderson, G. L. H.

**ALDERSON, Margaret Hanne, (Maggie);** journalist and novelist; *b* 31 July 1959; *d* of Douglas Arthur Alderson and Margaret Dura Alderson (*née* Mackay); *m* 1st, 1991, Geoffrey Francis Laurence (marr. diss. 1996); 2nd, 2002, Radenko Popovic; one *d*. *Educ:* Alleyne's Sch., Stone, Staffs; Univ. of St Andrews (MA Hons History of Art). Features Editor: Look Now, 1983; Honey, 1984; Commng Editor, You, 1985; Metropolitan Features Editor, Evening Standard, 1986; Editor: ES Magazine, 1988; Elle, 1989–92; Dep. Editor, Cleo magazine, 1993–94; Editor, Mode, 1994–95; sen. writer, Sydney Morning Herald, 1996–2001. Editor of the Year, Colour Supplements, British Soc. of Magazine Eds, 1989. *Publications:* Shoe Money, 1998; Pants On Fire, 2000; Handbag Heaven, 2001; (ed jtly) Big Night Out, 2002; Mad About the Boy, 2002; Handbags and Gladrags, 2004; (ed jtly) Ladies Night, 2005; Cents and Sensibility, 2006; How to Break Your Own Heart, 2008; (ed jtly) In Bed With, 2009; Shall We Dance?, 2010; Style Notes, 2011; Evangeline, the Wish Keeper's Helper, 2011; Everything Changes But You, 2012; Secret Keeping For Beginners, 2015; The Scent of You, 2017. *Address:* c/o Curtis Brown, 28–29 Haymarket, SW1Y 4SP. *W:* www.maggiealderson.com. *Club:* Groucho.

**ALDERSON, Martha, (Matti);** international advisor on regulatory policy and strategy; Managing Director, FireHorses Ltd, since 2000; *b* 20 Dec. 1951; *d* of Edward Connelly and Helen Connelly (*née* Peacock); *m* 1970, Alan Alderson. *Educ:* Bearsden Acad., Dunbartonshire; Open Univ. (BA Hons 1994). Legal Exec., Scotland, 1970–72; Advertising Agency Poster Bureau, 1972–74; Advertising Standards Authority: Executive, 1975–80; Manager, 1980–89; Dep. Dir Gen., 1989–90; Dir Gen., 1990–2000. Vice Chm., European Advertising Standards Alliance, Brussels, 1991–2000. Sec., Cttee of Advertising Practice, 1990–99. Member: Food Adv. Cttee, MAFF, 1997–2002; Better Regulation Task Force, 1998–2004; Doctors' and Dentists' Remuneration Review Body, 1998–2001; Press Complaints Commn, 2002–10; Bd, PhonepayPlus, 2008–14; IMCB, 2008–14; Cttee, BSI, 2008–11; Chm., Direct Mkting Commn (formerly Authy), 2007–10; Removals Ombudsman, 2008–11. Vice Pres., SRDA – Centre for Responsibility in the Digital Age, Brussels, 2017–. Mem., IAM, 2008 (Sec., High Wycombe Gp, 2015–). FCAM 1993; FRSA 1993; CCMI 2010. *Publications:* Report on Children, Advertising and Regulation in Europe, 2001; Alcohol Regulation in the Asia Pacific Region, 2006; columnist and contrib. numerous advertising and mktg textbooks, and jls in UK and EU. *Recreations:* design, cars, reading, studying. *Address:* Raglan House, Windsor Road, Gerrards Cross, Bucks SL9 7ND. *Club:* Royal Over-Seas League.

**ALDERTON, Clive,** CVO 2019 (LVO 2013); HM Diplomatic Service; Principal Private Secretary to the Prince of Wales and the Duchess of Cornwall, since 2015; *b* 9 May 1967; *m* 1990, Catriona Canning; one *s* one *d*. Joined FCO, 1986; Vice-Consul, Poland, 1988–90; Third Sec., UK Repn to EU, Brussels, 1990–93; Desk Officer, Far Eastern Dept, FCO, 1993–96; Hd, Indo-China Section, SE Asia Dept, FCO, 1996–98; Hd of Chancery and Dep. Hd of Mission, Singapore, 1998–2003; Consul-Gen., Lille, 2004–06; Dep. Private Sec., 2006–08, Private Sec. 2009–12, to the Prince of Wales and the Duchess of Cornwall; Ambassador to Morocco and concurrently (non-resident) Ambassador to Mauritania, 2012–15. *Address:* Clarence House, SW1A 1BA.

**ALDERTON, John;** actor (stage, films, television); *b* Gainsborough, Lincs, 27 Nov. 1940; *s* of Gordon John Alderton and Ivy Handley; *m* 1st, 1964, Jill Browne (marr. diss. 1970; she *d* 1991); 2nd, Pauline Collins, *qv*; two *s* one *d*. *Educ:* Kingston High Sch., Hull. *Stage:* 1st appearance (Rep.) Theatre Royal, York, in Badger's Green, 1961; cont. Rep.; 1st London appearance, Spring and Port Wine, Mermaid (later Apollo), 1965; Dutch Uncle, RSC, Aldwych, 1969; The Night I Chased the Women with an Eel, Comedy, 1969; Punch and Judy Stories, Howff, 1973; Judies, Comedy, 1974; The Birthday Party, Shaw, 1975; Confusions (4 parts), Apollo, 1976; Rattle of a Simple Man, Savoy, 1980; Special Occasions, Ambassadors, 1983; The Maintenance Man, Comedy, 1986; Waiting for Godot, NT, 1987; What the Butler Saw, RNT, 1995; Honeymoon Suite, Royal Court, 2004; *films:* (1962–): incl. Duffy, Hannibal Brooks, Zardoz, It Shouldn't Happen to a Vet, Please Sir, Calendar Girls; *television:* series: Please Sir, No Honestly, My Wife Next Door, P. G. Wodehouse, Thomas and Sarah, Father's Day, Forever Green, Little Dorrit and various plays. *Address:* c/o Curtis Brown, Haymarket House, 28–29 Haymarket, SW1Y 4SP.

**ALDHOUSE-GREEN, Prof. Miranda Jane,** PhD; FSA, FLSW; Professor of Archaeology, Cardiff University, 2006–13, now Emeritus; *b* 24 July 1947; *d* of Eric Aldhouse and Eunice Henriques; *m* 1970, Stephen Green (later Aldhouse-Green; he *d* 2016); one *d*. *Educ:* Cardiff Univ. (BA Hons Archaeol. 1969); Lady Margaret Hall, Oxford (MLitt 1974); Open Univ. (PhD 1981). FSA 1979. Pt-time Classical Studies Tutor, OU in Wales, 1982–94; Lectr, Cardiff Univ., 1990–94; University of Wales College, Newport, subseq. University of Wales, Newport: Sen. Lectr, 1994–97; Reader, 1997–98; Head, SCARAB Res. Centre, 1996–2006; Prof. of Archaeology, 1998–2006. Prof. John Mulvaney Lecture, ANU, 2011. Mem., Ancient Monuments Bd for Wales, 2001–10. Academic and Tech. Advr for drama series, Britannia, Sky Atlantic TV, 2014–. Pres., Prehistoric Soc., 2005 (Vice-Pres., 2002). FLSW 2011. Hon. Fellow, Centre for Advanced Welsh and Celtic Studies, Univ. of Wales, Aberystwyth, 1990–2001. *Publications:* The Gods of the Celts, 1986; Symbol and Image in Celtic Religious Art, 1989; The Sun Gods of Ancient Europe, 1991; Animals in Celtic Life and Myth, 1992; Dictionary of Celtic Myth and Legend, 1992; Celtic Goddesses, 1995; (ed) The Celtic World, 1995; Celtic Art, 1996; The World of the Druids, 1997; Dying for the Gods, 2001; An Archaeology of Images, 2004; (with S. Aldhouse-Green) The Quest for the Shaman in European Antiquity, 2005; Boudica Britannia, 2006; Caesar's Druids: archaeology of an ancient priesthood, 2010; The Celtic Myths; a guide to the ancient gods and legends, 2015; Bog Bodies Uncovered: solving Europe's ancient mystery, 2015 (Popular Book Award, Soc. for Amer. Archaeol., 2016; Felicia A. Holton Book Award, Archaeol Inst. of America, 2017); Sacred Britannia, 2018; about 80 articles in learned archaeol. jls. *Recreations:* choral singing, wine, travel, early and baroque music, swimming, Burmese cats, walking. *Address:* Department of Archaeology, School of History, Archaeology and Religion, Cardiff University, John Percival Building, Colum Drive, Cardiff CF10 3EU. *T:* (029) 2087 5651. *E:* Aldhouse-GreenMJ@cardiff.ac.uk.

**ALDINGTON,** 2nd Baron *cr* 1962; **Charles Harold Stuart Low;** Chairman, 2002–09, Senior Adviser, 2009–12, Deutsche Bank London; Chairman: Intramuros Ltd, since 2009; MACHEMC2 Ltd, since 2017; *b* 22 June 1948; *s* of 1st Baron Aldington, KCMG, CBE, DSO, TD, PC and Araminta Bowman, *d* of Sir Harold MacMichael, GCMG, DSO; *S* father, 2000; *m* 1989, Dr Regine, *d* of Erwin von Csongrady-Schopf and Liselotte (*née* Horstmann); one *s* twin *d*. *Educ:* Winchester Coll.; New Coll., Oxford (BA Hons); INSEAD; Baden-Badener Unternehmergespräche. Citibank NA (NY), Hong Kong and Dusseldorf, 1971–77; Head of Ship Finance, then Head of UK Corporate Lending, then Dir, Continental Europe, Grindlays Bank, 1978–86; Deutsche Bank AG: Dir, Duisburg Br., 1986–87; Man. Dir, London, 1988–96; Man. Dir, Investment Banking, 1996–2002. Chm., Stramongate Ltd, 2007–11. Chairman: Eur. Vocational Coll., 1991–96; CENTEC, subseq. FOCUS Central London, Central London TEC, 1995–99; Member: Council, British-German Chamber of Commerce and Industry, 1995–2008; Chairman's Cttee, LIBA, 2003–09; Chairman's Cttee, BBA, 2003–09. Member: Oxford Univ. Ct of Benefactors, 1990–2012; Business Adv. Council, Saïd Business Sch., 2001–11; Chm., New Coll. 2019 Cttee, New Coll., Oxford, 2009–. Dep. Chm., Royal Acad. Trust, 2003–12 (Trustee Emeritus, 2012); Trustee: English Internat., 1979–86; Whitechapel Art Gall. Foundn, 1991–96; Inst. for Philanthropy, 2008–14. Vice Pres., Nat. Churches Trust, 2008–17. Gov., Ditchley Foundn, 2006–. (Chm., Finance and Gen. Purposes Cttee, 2013–). *Heir: s* Hon. Philip Toby Augustus Low, *b* 1 Sept. 1990. *Clubs:* Brooks's; Hong Kong.
*See also* Hon. P. J. S. Roberts.

**ALDOUS, Charles;** QC 1985; *b* 3 June 1943; *s* of Guy Travers Aldous, QC and Elizabeth Angela Aldous (*née* Paul); *m* 1969, Hermione Sara de Courcy-Ireland; one *s* two *d* (and one *d* decd). *Educ:* Harrow; University College London (LLB). Called to the Bar, Inner Temple, 1967 (Bencher, 1994), Lincoln's Inn *ad eund*, 1967 (Bencher, 1993). *Address:* Ravensfield Farm, Bures Hamlet, Suffolk CO8 5DP.

**ALDOUS, Prof. David John,** PhD; FRS 1994; Professor of Statistics, University of California, Berkeley, since 1986; *b* 13 July 1952; *s* of Kenneth George Aldous and Joyce Minnie Aldous (*née* Finch); *m* 1986, Katy Edwards; one *s*. *Educ:* St John's Coll., Cambridge (BA 1973; PhD 1977). Res. Fellow, St John's Coll., Cambridge, 1977–79; Asst Prof., 1979–82, Associate Prof., 1982–86, Univ. of Calif, Berkeley. *Publications:* Probability Approximations via the Poisson Clumping Heuristic, 1989. *Recreations:* volley-ball, science fiction, geopolitical forecasting. *Address:* Department of Statistics, University of California, 367 Evans Hall #3860, Berkeley, CA 94720–3860, USA. *T:* (510) 6422781.

**ALDOUS, Grahame Linley;** QC 2008; a Recorder, since 2000; *b* London, 8 June 1956; *s* of Howard Aldous and Jocelyn Murray Aldous; partner, Vanessa Knapp, OBE; three *s*. *Educ:* Univ. of Exeter (LLB Hons 1978). Called to the Bar, Inner Temple, 1979, Bencher, 2009; in practice at the Bar, specialising in clinical and professional negligence and personal injury; Hd of Chambers, 9 Gough Square, 2008–13. Fellow, Assoc. of Personal Injury Lawyers, 2007. Contributing Ed., Kemp & Kemp Personal Injury Law Practice and Procedure, 2000–. *Publications:* Housing Law for the Elderly, 1982; Applications for Judicial Review, 1985, 2nd edn 1993; Work Accidents at Sea, 2008; Clinical Negligence Claims, 2008, 2nd edn 2011; APIL Guide to Catastrophic Injury Claims, 2010. *Recreations:* ocean racing, naval history. *Address:* 9 Gough Square, EC4A 3DG. *T:* (020) 7832 0500, *Fax:* (020) 7353 1344. *E:* galdous@9goughsquare.co.uk. *Club:* Royal Ocean Racing.

**ALDOUS, Hugh (Graham Cazalet),** FCA; Partner, Grant Thornton UK LLP (formerly Robson Rhodes, then RSM Robson Rhodes LLP), 1976–2008; Member, Competition Commission (formerly Monopolies and Mergers Commission), 1998–2001; *b* 1 June 1944; *s* of Maj. Hugh Francis Travers Aldous and Emily Aldous; *m* 1967, Christabel Marshall. *Educ:* Leeds Univ. (BCom). ACA 1970, FCA 1976. Robson Rhodes, later RSM Robson Rhodes, then Grant Thornton, 1967–2008: on secondment to Depts of Transport and the Envmt, 1976–79; Man. Partner, 1987–97; DTI Inspector: House of Fraser Hldgs plc 1987–88; TransTec plc, 2000–03. Chairman: RSM Internat., 1997–2000; Eastern European (formerly First Russian Frontiers) Trust plc, 2000–09 (Dir, 1995–2011); Protoco Associates NV, 2000–02; Craegmoor Ltd, 2001–05; Smart Educn Ltd, 2005–14; Capit Sinclair Henderson Ltd, 2007–15; Melorio plc, 2009–10 (Dir, 2007–10); SPL Guernse ICC Ltd, 2010–; Downing Strategic Micro-Cap Investment Trust plc, 2017–; Director Freightliner Ltd, 1979–84; Sealink UK Ltd, 1981–84; British Waterways Bd, 1983–86 CILNTEC Ltd, 1991–96; FOCUS Ltd, 1996–98; Draper Esprit VCT plc (formerly Gartmore Venture Capital Trust plc, then Millennium Venture Capital Trust, subseq Elderstreet VCT plc, then Elderstreet Draper Esprit VCT plc), 1996–; Asian Total Return Investment Co. plc (formerly Henderson TR Pacific Investment Trust plc, then Henderson Asian Growth Trust plc), 2003–14; Innospec Inc. (formerly Octel Inc.), 2005–; Pola Capital Holdings plc, 2007–18. *Publications:* Guide to Government Incentives to Industry 1979; Study of Businesses Financed under the Small Business Loan Guarantee Scheme 1984; (with H. Brooke) Report into the affairs of House of Fraser Holdings plc, 1988

Review of the UK Financial and Professional Services Industry, 1992; (with R. Kaye) Report into the affairs of TransTec plc, 2003; Performance Fees: a question of purpose, 2008. *Recreations:* classical music, walking. *Club:* Royal Automobile.

**ALDOUS, Lucette,** AC 2018; Senior Lecturer in Classical Ballet, Edith Cowan University, since 1994; Head of Classical Dance, Dance Department, Western Australian Academy of Performing Arts, 1984–99, now Senior Lecturer; Senior Adjudicator, National Eisteddfods, since 1979; *b* 26 Sept. 1938; *d* of Charles Fellows Aldous and Marie (*née* Rutherford); *m* 1972, Alan Alder; one *d*. *Educ:* Toronto Public Sch., NSW; Brisbane Public Sch., Qld; Randwick Girls' High Sch., NSW. Awarded Frances Scully Meml Schol. (Aust.) to study at Royal Ballet Sch., London, 1955; joined Ballet Rambert, 1957, Ballerina, 1958–63; Ballerina with: London Fest. Ballet, 1963–66; Royal Ballet, 1966–71; Prima Ballerina, The Australian Ballet, 1971; Master Teacher, Australian Ballet Sch., 1979; Guest Teacher: Australian Ballet, 1988–; Royal NZ Ballet Co., 1988–; West Australian Ballet Co., 1988–. Rep. Australia, 1st Internat. Ballet Competition, Jackson, Miss, USA, 1979; Guest, Kirov Ballet and Ballet School, Leningrad, 1975–76. Guest appearances: Giselle, with John Gilpin, NY, 1968; Lisbon, 1969; with Rudolf Nureyev, in Don Quixote: Aust., 1970, NY, Hamburg and Marseilles, 1971; Carmen, Johannesburg, 1970; The Sleeping Beauty: E Berlin, 1970, Teheran, 1970, 1975; partnered Edward Villela at Expo '74, Spokane, USA. *Television:* title rôle, La Sylphide, with Fleming Flindt, BBC, 1960. *Films:* as Kitri, in Don Quixote, with Rudolf Nureyev and Robert Helpmann, Aust., 1972; The Turning Point, 1977. Mem., Australia Council for the Arts, 1996–98. Patron, Australian Cecchetti Soc., 1991–. Hon. DLitt Edith Cowan, 1999. DStJ 2008. *Recreations:* music, reading, gardening, breeding Burmese cats. *Address:* c/o Dance Department, Western Australian Academy of Performing Arts, 2 Bradford Street, Mount Lawley, Perth, WA 6050, Australia.

**ALDOUS, Peter;** MP (C) Waveney, since 2010; *b* Ipswich, 26 Aug. 1961. *Educ:* Harrow Sch.; Reading Univ. (BSc Land Mgt 1982). Chartered Surveyor, in private practice, Norwich and Ipswich, 1983–2010. Member (C): Waveney DC, 1999–2002; Suffolk CC, 2001–05. *Recreations:* cricket, squash, football, horse racing. *Address:* House of Commons, SW1A 0AA. *E:* peter.aldous.mp@parliament.uk.

**ALDRED, Brian Gordon;** Chief Executive, Lancashire Police Authority, 2003–07; *b* 27 April 1951; *s* of late James Bernard Aldred and of Jean Margaret Layton Aldred; *m* 1973, Miriam Constance Shaw; one *s* one *d*. *Educ:* Queen Elizabeth's Grammar Sch., Blackburn; Jesus Coll., Oxford (BA Modern Hist.; MA); Liverpool Poly. CIPFA. Cheshire CC, 1972–82; Dep. Dir of Finance, Bolton MBC, 1982–85; Lancashire County Council: Dep. County Treas., 1985–92; County Treas., 1992–2000; Dir of Resources, 2000–02. *Recreations:* cycling, fell-walking, archaeology.

**ALDRED, (Patricia) Margaret,** CB 2009; CBE 1991; Secretary, Iraq Inquiry (on secondment from Cabinet Office), 2009–16. *Educ:* Univ. of Bristol (BSc Geog. 1975). Joined Civil Service as grad. trainee, 1975; posts at MoD incl. Principal Private Sec., 1994–97; Asst Under-Sec. of State, Service Personnel, 1997–98, and Dir Gen., Mgt and Orgn, 1998–2000; Dir, Public Services, HM Treasury, 2001; Dir Gen., Resources and Performance, Home Office, 2001–04; Dep. Hd, Defence and Overseas Secretariat, Cabinet Office, 2004–09.

**ALDRIDGE, Dr John Frederick Lewis,** OBE 1990, FRCP, FRCPEd, FFOM; consultant in occupational medicine, 1987–97; Civil Consultant in Occupational Medicine to the Royal Navy, 1983–92, Emeritus Consultant, since 1992; *b* 28 Dec. 1926; *s* of Dr Frederick James Aldridge and Kathleen Marietta Micaela (*née* White); *m* 1955, Barbara Sheila Bolland (*d* 2014); three *s* one *d*. *Educ:* Gresham's Sch.; St Thomas's Hosp. Med. Sch. (MB, BS 1951). DIH 1963; FRCPEd 1980; FFOM 1981; FRCP 1984. Served RAMC, 1953–60 (retd, Major). Indust. MO, Reed Paper Gp, 1960–63; CMO, IBM United Kingdom Ltd, 1963–87; part-time Hon. Clin. Asst, Dept of Psychol Medicine, UCH, 1970–76. Faculty of Occupational Medicine, Royal Coll. of Physicians: Vice-Dean, 1984–86; Dean, 1986–88; Chm., Ethics Cttee, 1991–96; Royal Soc. of Medicine: Fellow, 1964–2002; Hon. Sec., 1970–72 and Vice-Pres., 1974–77, Occupl Medicine Section; Soc. of Occupational Medicine: Mem., 1960–; Hon. Meetings Sec., 1969–71. Member: Specialist Adv. Cttee on Occupl Medicine, Jt Cttee of Higher Med. Trng, 1970–74; Nat. Occupl Health and Safety Cttee, RoSPA, 1979–81; Standing Med. Adv. Cttee, DHSS, 1986–88; Defence Med. Emergency Steering Cttee, 1986–88; Indust. Soc. Med. Adv. Cttee, 1986–89 (Chm., 1987–89); CEGB Med. Adv. Cttee, 1988–89. Mem., Council and Cttee of Management, Shipwrecked Mariners' Royal Benevolent Soc., 1987–96; Dir, Shipwrecked Mariners' Trading Ltd, 1999–2001. Chm., W Sussex Assoc. for the Disabled, 1995–97 (Mem. Council and Mgt Cttee, 1991–2006; Vice-Pres., 1997–2012); Vice Chm., Chichester DFAS, 2000–04 (Librarian, 1999–2003); Trustee, Southampton and Wessex Med. Sch. Trust, 1978–82. Liveryman, Worshipful Soc. of Apothecaries, 1984–. *Publications:* papers on occupnl med. topics and occupnl mental health. *Recreations:* art in general, geriatric golf, my family. *Address:* 2 Summersdale Road, Chichester, W Sussex PO19 6PL. *T:* (01243) 784705. *Clubs:* Vintage Sports Car; Goodwood Golf.

**ALDRIDGE, Sir Rodney (Malcolm),** Kt 2012; OBE 1994; Founder and Chairman, Capita Group, 1984–2006; Chair, Aldridge Foundation, since 2006. Qualif. accountant, CIPFA 1970. With CIPFA, 1974, latterly as Tech. Dir; work in local govt, E Sussex CC, Brighton BC, Crawley DC and W Sussex CC. Non-exec. Dir, Xafinity. Chair, Dance Champions Gp, DoH, 2009. Member Board: NESTA Lab.; Equiniti; Centre for Public Sector Partnerships, Univ. of Birmingham. Chm., Public Services Strategy Bd, CBI, 2003–06. Chairman: V, 2006; Acorn Care and Educn; The Lowry, Salford, 2007–. Mem., Prince of Wales Charities Council; Patron, Prince's Trust. Freeman, City of London, 1996; Mem. Court, Information Technologists' Co. *Address:* Aldridge Foundation, 3rd Floor, 30 Millbank, SW1P 4DU.

**ALDRIDGE, Stephen Charles,** CB 2007; Director, Analysis and Data (formerly Analysis and Innovation), Ministry of Housing, Communities and Local Government (formerly Department for Communities and Local Government), since 2009; *b* 30 April 1957; *s* of Dennis and Pamela Aldridge; *m* 1995, Katie Iakovleva; one *d*. *Educ:* City Univ., London (BSc Econ 1978); University Coll. London (MSc Econ 1982). Public Services Econs Div., HM Treasury, 1991–93; Housing and Urban Econs, DoE, subseq. DETR, 1993–98; Cabinet Office: Chief Economist, Perf. and Innovation Unit, 1998–2002; Dep. Dir, 2002–04, Dir, 2004–09, Strategy Unit. *Address:* Ministry of Housing, Communities and Local Government, 2 Marsham Street, SW1P 4DF. *T:* 0303 444 3339.

**ALDRIN, Dr Buzz;** President, Starcraft Enterprises International (research and development of space technology, manned flight to Mars), since 1988; *b* Montclair, NJ, USA, 20 Jan. 1930; *s* of late Col Edwin E. Aldrin, USAF retd, Brielle, NJ, and Marion Aldrin (*née* Moon); named Edwin Eugene, changed legally to Buzz, 1979; *m* 1988, Lois Driggs-Cannon; two *s* one *d* of former marriage. *Educ:* Montclair High Sch., Montclair, NJ (grad.); US Mil. Academy, West Point, NY (BSc); Mass Inst. of Technology (DSc in Astronautics). Received wings (USAF), 1952. Served in Korea (66 combat missions) with 51st Fighter Interceptor Wing. Aerial Gunnery Instr, Nellis Air Force Base, Nevada; attended Sqdn Officers Sch., Air Univ., Maxwell Air Force Base, Alabama; Aide to Dean of Faculty, USAF Academy; Flt Comdr with 36th Tactical Fighter Wing, Bitburg, Germany. Subseq. assigned to Gemini Target Office of Air Force Space Systems Div., Los Angeles, Calif; later transf. to USAF Field Office, Manned Spacecraft Center. One of 3rd group of astronauts named by NASA, Oct. 1963; served as back up pilot, Gemini 9 Mission and prime pilot, Gemini 12 Mission (launched into space, with James Lovell, 11 Nov. 1966), 4 day 59 revolution flight which brought Gemini Program to successful close; he established a new record for extravehicular activity and obtained first pictures taken from space of an eclipse of the sun; also made a rendezvous with the previously launched Agena; later assigned to 2nd manned Apollo flight, as back-up command module pilot; Lunar Module Pilot, Apollo 11 rocket flight to the Moon; first lunar landing with Neil Armstrong, July 1969; left NASA to return to USAF as Commandant, Aerospace Res. Pilots Sch., Edwards Air Force Base, Calif, 1971; retired USAF 1972. Mem., Soc. of Experimental Test Pilots; FAIAA; Tau Beta Pi, Sigma Xi. Further honours include Presidential Medal of Freedom, 1969; Air Force DSM with Oak Leaf Cluster; Legion of Merit; Air Force DFC with Oak Leaf Cluster; Air Medal with 2 Oak Leaf Clusters; and NASA DSM, Exceptional Service Medal, and Group Achievement Award. Various hon. memberships and hon. doctorates. *Publications:* Return to Earth (autobiography), 1973; Men From Earth: the Apollo Project, 1989; (jtly) Encounter with Tiber (science fiction), 1996; The Return (science fiction), 2000; Reaching for the Moon (for children), 2005; (with K. Abraham) Magnificent Desolation: the long journey home from the Moon, 2009; Look to the Stars (for children), 2009. *Recreations:* athletics, scuba diving, ski-ing, golf, etc.

**ALEKSANDER, Prof. Igor,** PhD; FREng; Professor of Neural Systems Engineering, and Head of Department of Electrical Engineering, Imperial College of Science, Technology and Medicine, University of London, 1988–2002, now Emeritus, and Senior Research Investigator, since 2002; *b* 26 Jan. 1937. *Educ:* Marist Brothers' Coll., S Africa; Univ. of the Witwatersrand (BSc Eng); Univ. of London (PhD). Section Head of STC, Footscray, 1958–61; Lectr, Queen Mary Coll., Univ. of London, 1961–65; Reader in Electronics, Univ. of Kent, 1965–74; Prof. of Electronics and Head of Electrical Engrg Dept, Brunel Univ., 1974–84; Prof. of Information Technology Management, Computing Dept, Imperial Coll., 1984–88. FREng (FEng 1989); FCGI 1994. *Publications:* An Introduction to Logic Circuit Theory, 1971; Automata Theory: an engineering approach, 1976; The Human Machine, 1978; Reinventing Man, 1983 (USA 1984); Designing Intelligent Systems, 1984; Thinking Machines, 1987; An Introduction to Neural Computing, 1990; Neurons and Symbols: the stuff that mind is made of, 1993; Impossible Minds: my neurons, my consciousness, 1996, 2nd edn 2015; How to Build a Mind, 2000; The World in My Mind, 2005; Aristotle's Laptop, 2012; *c* 120 papers on computing and human modelling. *Recreations:* tennis, ski-ing, music, architecture. *Address:* Imperial College of Science, Technology and Medicine, Exhibition Road, SW7 2AZ. *T:* (020) 7594 6176.

**ALEKSIC, Jocelyn;** see Pook, J.

**ALESSI, Charles, (Charles Sammut Alessi);** Chief Clinical Officer, Health Information and Management Systems Society, since 2018; Senior Advisor, Public Health England, since 2012; *b* Mgarr, Malta, 1 May 1954; *s* of William and Mary Sammut Alessi; *m* 2008, Dr Anu Jain. *Educ:* St Aloysius Coll., Malta; St George's Hosp. Med. Sch., Univ. of London (LRCP 1980). MRCS 1980. Kingston Hospital: Hse Officer, 1980–81; Anaesthetic SHO, 1981–82; Registrar, 1983–84; in practice as GP, SW London, 1984–2013; Dir, Medicine and Clin. Governance, SSAFA/Guy's and St Thomas's Care LLP, British Armed Forces, Germany, 2008–11; Med. Dir, Kingston PCT, subseq. CCG, 2009–11; Chm., 2012–14, Co-Chm., 2014–15, Nat. Assoc. of Primary Care; Chm., 2012–14, Sen. Advr, 2014–15, NHS Clin. Comrs. Vice Chm., Kingston and Richmond HA, 2002–. Adjunct Res. Prof. of Health Innovation, Richard Ivey Sch. of Business, 2012–15, Adjunct Res. Prof. of Clin. Neurosics, Schulich Sch. of Medicine, 2013–, Univ. of Western Ont; Vis. Prof., Psychol. and Lang. Scis, Clinical Educnl and Health Psychol., UCL, 2014–; Vis. Schol., World Health Innovation Network, Odette Business Sch., Univ. of Windsor, Ont, 2015–. Mem., RSA. *Recreation:* opera. *Address:* Public Health England, Wellington House, 133–155 Waterloo Road, SE1 8UG. *T:* (020) 7654 8090. *E:* charles.alessi@phe.gov.uk; Health Information and Management Systems Society, 33 West Monroe Street, Suite 1700, Chicago, IL 60603, USA. *E:* calessi@himss.org. *Clubs:* Athenæum, Royal Society of Medicine.

**ALESSI, Prof. Dario Renato,** PhD; FMedSci; FRS 2008; FRSE; Principal Investigator, since 1997, and Director, since 2012, MRC Protein Phosphorylation and Ubiquitylation Unit, University of Dundee (Deputy Director, 2006–12); *b* Dec. 1967. *Educ:* Univ. of Birmingham (BSc 1st Cl. Hons Biochem. with Biotech. 1988; PhD 1991). Postdoctoral res., MRC Protein Phosphorylation Unit, Univ. of Dundee, 1991–96. Hon. Reader, 2001, Hon. Prof. of Signal Transduction, 2003, Univ. of Dundee. R. D. Lawrence Lectr, Diabetes UK, 2004; Francis Crick Prize Lectr, Royal Soc., 2006. Mem., EMBO, 2005. FRSE 2002; FMedSci 2012. Colworth Medal, British Biochem. Soc., 1999; Eppendorf Young Eur. Investigator, 2000; Morgagni Young Investigator Prize, Servier Labs, 2002; Pfizer Acad. Award for Europe, 2002; Makdougall Brisbane Prize, RSE, 2002; Philip Leverhulme Prize, Leverhulme Trust, 2002; FEBS Anniv. Prize, 2003; Jun. Chamber Internat. Young Persons of Year Award, 2005; Gold Medal, EMBO, 2005. *Address:* MRC Protein Phosphorylation and Ubiquitylation Unit, Sir James Black Centre, University of Dundee, Dundee DD1 5EH. *T:* (01382) 385602, *Fax:* (01382) 223778. *E:* d.r.alessi@dundee.ac.uk.

**ALEX;** see Peattie, C. W. D. and Taylor, R. P.

**ALEXANDER,** family name of **Earl Alexander of Tunis** and **Earl of Caledon.**

**ALEXANDER, Viscount; Frederick James Alexander;** *b* 15 Oct. 1990; *s* and *heir* of Earl of Caledon, *qv*. *Educ:* Stowe.

**ALEXANDER OF TUNIS,** 2nd Earl *cr* 1952; **Shane William Desmond Alexander;** Viscount, 1946; Baron Rideau, 1952; Lieutenant Irish Guards, retired, 1958; Director: International Hospitals Group and associated companies, 1981–2016; Pathfinder Financial Corporation, Toronto, 1980–2015; *b* 30 June 1935; *er s* of 1st Earl Alexander of Tunis, KG, PC, GCB, OM, GCMG, CSI, DSO, MC, and Lady Margaret Diana Bingham (Countess Alexander of Tunis), GBE, DStJ, DL (*d* 1977); *yr d* of 5th Earl of Lucan, PC, GCVO, KBE, CB; *S* father, 1969; *m* 1981, Hon. Davina Woodhouse (LVO 1991; Lady-in-Waiting to Princess Margaret, 1975–2002), *y d* of 4th Baron Terrington; two *d*. *Educ:* Ashbury Coll., Ottawa, Canada; Harrow. A Lord in Waiting (Govt Whip), 1974. Dir, Marketform Ltd, 1996–2009. Trustee, 1987–, and Chm., 1989–, Canada Meml Foundn; Pres., British-American-Canadian Associates, 1989–94. Patron, British-Tunisian Soc., 1979–99. Freeman, City of London, 1964; Liveryman, Mercers Company. Freedom, City of New Orleans, 1993. Order of Republic of Tunisia, 1995. *Heir: b* Hon. Brian James Alexander, *qv*. *Address:* 28 Clonmel Road, SW6 5BJ. *T:* (020) 7736 2604. *Clubs:* MCC; Quis Separabit; Stoke Park Golf and Country.

*See also* Earl of Normanton.

**ALEXANDER, Prof. Alan,** OBE 2010; FRSE; FAcSS; General Secretary, Royal Society of Edinburgh, 2013–18; Professor of Local and Public Management, University of Strathclyde, 1993–2000, now Emeritus (Professor of Management in Local Government, 1987–93); *b* 13 Dec. 1943; *s* of Alexander Alexander and Rose (*née* Rein); *m* 1964, Morag

MacInnes (see M. Alexander); one s one d. *Educ*: Possil Secondary Sch., Glasgow; Albert Secondary Sch., Glasgow; Univ. of Glasgow (MA 1965). Lectr/Asst Prof. of Political Sci., Lakehead Univ., Ontario, 1966–71; Lectr in Politics, Univ. of Reading, 1971–87; Dir, Scottish Local Authorities Management Centre, 1987–93, and Hd, Dept of Human Resource Mgt, 1993–96, Univ. of Strathclyde. Scholar-in-Residence, Rockefeller Foundn, Villa Serbelloni, Bellagio, Italy, Feb.–March 1984; Fulbright Vis. Prof. of Politics, Randolph-Macon Woman's Coll., Virginia, 1986; Vis. Prof., Univ. of Edinburgh Mgt Sch., 2006–18. Member: Board, Housing Corp., 1977–80; Council, Quarriers', 1995–2000; Ind. Commn on Relations between Local Govt and the Scottish Parlt, 1998–99; Accounts Commn for Scotland, 2002–08; ESRC, 2003–09; Ind. non-exec. Mem. Bd, Audit Scotland, 2018–. Chairman: Glasgow Regeneration Fund, 1998–2001; W of Scotland Water Authy, 1999–2002; Scottish Water, 2002–06; Distance Lab Ltd, 2006–10; Postwatch Scotland, 2007–08; Waterwise, 2010–15. Chairman: Res. Councils UK/Univs UK Rev. of Full Economic Costing of Univ. Res., 2008–09; Data Access Cttee and Mem., Scientific Adv. Cttee, Understanding Soc., ESRC, 2010–15. Pres., Instn of Water Officers, 2005–06; Mem. Exec. Cttee, Advanced Inst. of Mgt Res., 2003–08. Member: Reading BC, 1972–74; Berks CC, 1973–77. Chair, Adv. Council, Sch. of Mgt, Univ. of St Andrews, 2016–; Member: Standing Res. Cttee on Local and Central Govt Relns, Joseph Rowntree Foundn, 1988–92; Adv. Bd, Edinburgh Univ. Mgt Sch., 2004–07. Conducted independent inquiry into relations between Western Isles Islands Council and Bank of Credit and Commerce Internat., 1991. Contested (Lab) Henley, Feb. 1974. Pres., Raglan Housing Assoc., 1987–2014 (Chm., 1975–87); Trustee: WaterAid, 2001–06; David Hume Inst., 2012–18; Mem., Scottish Council, Outward Bound, 2011–14 (Chm., 2012–14). Mem. Council, RSE, 2012–18 (Vice Chm., Digital Scotland Spreading the Benefits (formerly Digital Scotland: Reaping the Social Benefits) Inquiry, 2012–14). FRSE 2003; FAcSS 2015. *Publications*: Local Government in Britain since Reorganisation, 1982 (Italian edn, revised, 1984); The Politics of Local Government in the United Kingdom, 1982; Borough Government and Politics: Reading 1835–1985, 1985; Managing the Fragmented Authority, 1994; *fiction*: By All Means, 2014; Bloody Royals, 2015; Twin Track to Death, 2015; Flightpath, 2017; articles in Local Govt Studies, Public Admin, Brit. Jl Pol Sci. and others. *Recreations*: walking, theatre, opera, cinema, avoiding gardening. *Address*: 68 Comiston Drive, Edinburgh EH10 5QS.

**ALEXANDER, Anthony George Laurence**; Deputy Chairman, Imperial Tobacco Group, 1996–2008; *b* 4 April 1938; *s* of George and Margaret Alexander; *m* 1962, Frances, *d* of Cyril Burdett; one *s* two *d*. *Educ*: St Edward's School, Oxford. FCA. Hanson plc: Dir, 1976–96; UK Chief Operating Officer, 1986–96. *Recreations*: tennis, golf. *Address*: Crafnant, Gregories Farm Lane, Beaconsfield, Bucks HP9 1HJ. *T*: (01494) 672882.

**ALEXANDER, Bill, (William Alexander Paterson)**; Artistic Director, Birmingham Repertory Theatre, 1993–2000; Hon. Associate Director, Royal Shakespeare Company, since 1991 (Associate Director, 1984–91); *b* 23 Feb. 1948; *s* of Bill and Rosemary Paterson; *m* 1977, Juliet Harmer; two *d*. *Educ*: St Lawrence Coll., Ramsgate; Keele Univ. (BA Hons English/Politics). Seasons with The Other Company, Bristol Old Vic, Royal Court, 1972–78; Asst Dir, 1978–80, Resident Dir, 1980–84, RSC. Laurence Olivier award, Best Director, 1986. *Productions directed*: *Bristol Old Vic*: The Ride Across Lake Constance; Twelfth Night; Old Times; Butley; How the Other Half Loves; *Royal Court*: Sex and Kinship in a Savage Society, 1976; Amy and the Price of Cotton, 1977; Class Enemy, 1978; Sugar and Spice, 1979; *Royal Shakespeare Company*: Factory Birds, 1977; Shout Across the River, The Hang of the Gaol, Captain Swing, 1978; Men's Beano, 1979; Bastard Angel, Henry IV tour, 1980; Accrington Pals, 1981; Money, Clay, Molière, 1982; Tartuffe, Volpone, 1983; Richard III, Today, The Merry Wives of Windsor, 1984; Crimes in Hot Countries, Downchild (co-dir), 1985; Country Dancing, A Midsummer Night's Dream, 1986; Cymbeline, Twelfth Night, The Merchant of Venice, 1987; The Duchess of Malfi, Cymbeline, 1989; Much Ado About Nothing, The Taming of the Shrew (dir, regional tour), 1990; The Bright and Bold Design, 1991; The Taming of the Shrew, The School of Night, 1992; Titus Andronicus, 2003; King Lear, 2004, transf. Albery, 2005; *Birmingham*: Othello, Volpone, Old Times, 1993; The Snowman, 1993, 1997, transf. Peacock Th., London, annually, 1997–; Awake and Sing, The Tempest, 1994; The Servant, Macbeth, The Way of the World, 1995; Divine Right, The Alchemist, 1996; The Merchant of Venice, 1997; Frozen, Hamlet, 1998; The Four Alice Bakers, Jumpers, Nativity, 1999; Quarantine, Twelfth Night, 2000; *National Theatre*: Mappa Mundi, Frozen, 2002; *other productions* include: Entertaining Mr Sloane, Nottingham Playhouse, 1977; The Gingerbread Lady, Ipswich, 1977; The Last of the Knuckle Men, Edin. Fest. Fringe, 1977; Julius Caesar, Newcastle upon Tyne, 1979; One White Day, Soho Poly, 1976; Mates, Leicester Square, 1980; Betrayal, 1980; Anna Christie, 1981, Cameri Th., Tel Aviv; Talk of the Devil, Watford Palace, 1986; Romeo and Juliet, Victory Theatre, NY, 1990; Troilus and Cressida, 1992, Henry IV, 2004, Shakespeare Theatre, Washington; The Importance of Being Earnest, Th. Royal, Northampton, 2002; Enemy of the People, Th. Clwyd, 2002; The School of Night, Mark Taper Forum, LA, 2008; Glamour, Nottingham Playhouse, 2009; Bette and Joan, Arts Th., 2011; Twelfth Night, 2012, Summerfolk, Measure for Measure, 2013, Merchant of Venice, 2015, As You Like It, 2017, LAMDA; Othello, Northwest Classical Th. Co., Portland, Oregon, 2012; Merchant of Venice, 2015, The Two Gentlemen of Verona, 2017, The Taming of the Shrew, 2018, Bristol Old Vic Th. Sch.; The Sea, adaption for Radio 4, 2015. *Recreation*: tennis. *Address*: Rose Cottage, Tunley, Glos GL7 6LP.

**ALEXANDER, Hon. Brian (James)**, CMG 2000; Managing Director, Mustique Company, 1980–2008, now Chairman Emeritus; *b* 31 July 1939; *s* of 1st Earl Alexander of Tunis, KG, GCB, OM, GCMG, CSI, DSO, MC, PC, and Lady Margaret Diana Bingham, GBE, DStJ, DL (*d* 1977), *yr d* of 5th Earl of Lucan, GCVO, KBE, CB, PC; *heir-presumptive* to brother, Earl Alexander of Tunis, *qv*; *m* 1999, Johanna Williamson Miller. *Educ*: Ashbury Coll., Ottawa; Harrow Sch.; Grenoble Univ. Served Irish Guards, 1958–61. Mgt trainee, Bowater Corp., 1961–62; Advertising Films Div., then Central Marketing Dept, subseq. Marketing Exec., Hotels Div., Rank Orgn, 1962–68; Manager, Previews Internat., 1968–71; self-employed, 1971–80. Resort Consultant, 2008–16. *Recreations*: windsurfing, tennis, golf, reading. *Address*: Sapphire House, Mustique, St Vincent, W Indies. *E*: brian@mustique.vc; PO Box 349, Kingstown, St Vincent, W Indies. *Clubs*: White's, Queen's, MCC.

**ALEXANDER of Ballochmyle, Sir Claud Hagart-**, 4th Bt *cr* 1886, of Ballochmyle; *b* 5 Nov. 1963; *s* of Sir Claud Hagart-Alexander of Ballochmyle, 3rd Bt and Hilda Etain Acheson; *S* father, 2006; *m* 1994, Elaine Susan, *d* of Vincent Park, Winnipeg; one *s*. *Educ*: Trinity Coll., Glenalmond; Glasgow Univ. (BSc). *Heir*: *s* Claud Miles Hagart-Alexander, *b* 28 Sept. 1998.

**ALEXANDER, Clodagh Maria**; *see* Bradley, C. M.

**ALEXANDER, Rt Hon. Sir Daniel (Grian)**, Kt 2015; PC 2010; Vice-President and Corporate Secretary, Asian Infrastructure Investment Bank, since 2016; *b* 15 May 1972; *s* of Dion Ralph Alexander and Jane Alexander; *m* 2005, Rebecca Louise Hoar; two *d*. *Educ*: St Anne's Coll., Oxford (BA Hons PPE). Researcher, Campaign for Freedom of Information, 1991; Press Officer, Scottish Lib Dems, 1993–96; Press Officer, 1996–97, Hd of Communications, 1997–2003, European Movt, subseq. Britain in Europe; Hd of Communications, Cairngorms Nat. Park, 2004–05. MP (Lib Dem) Inverness, Nairn, Badenoch and Strathspey, 2005–15; contested (Lib Dem) same seat, 2015. Lib Dem spokesman on disability, 2005–07; Lib Dem Shadow Sec. of State for Work and Pensions, 2007–08; COS to Rt Hon. Nicholas Clegg, 2007–10; Sec. of State for Scotland, 2010; Chief Sec. to the Treasury, 2010–15. Chairman: All Party Gp on Media Literacy, 2006–08; Manifesto Gp, 2007–10; Vice-Chm., All Party Gp on Citizens Advice, 2006–10. Trustee, Joseph Rowntree Reform Trust, 2007–10. *Publications*: Why Vote Liberal Democrat?, 2010. *Recreations*: hill-walking, fishing, cricket.

**ALEXANDER, Sir Douglas**, 3rd Bt *cr* 1921; with Cowen & Co.; *b* 9 Sept. 1936; *s* of Lt-Comdr Archibald Gillespie Alexander (*d* 1978) (2nd *s* of 1st Bt), and of Margery Isabel, *d* of Arthur Brown Griffith; *S* uncle, 1981; *m* 1st 1958, Marylon, *d* of Leonidas Collins Scatterday; two *s*; 2nd, Deborah J. Marcus. *Educ*: Rice Univ., Houston, Texas (MA 1961); PhD 1967 (Univ. of N Carolina). Formerly Assoc. Prof. and Chairman, French, State Univ. of New York at Albany. *Heir*: *s* Douglas Gillespie Alexander [*b* 24 July 1962; *m* 1993, Marsha Sue, *d* of Robert Fink].

**ALEXANDER, Rt Hon. Douglas (Garven)**; PC 2005; *b* 26 Oct. 1967; *s* of Rev. Douglas N. Alexander and Dr Joyce O. Alexander; *m* 2000, Jacqueline Christian; one *s* one *d*. *Educ*: Univ. of Edinburgh (MA 1st cl. Hons 1990; LLB (Dist.) 1993; DipLP 1994); Univ. of Pennsylvania. Admitted Solicitor, 1995; Brodies WS, 1994–96; Digby Brown, 1996–97. MP (Lab) Paisley S, Nov., 1997–2005, Paisley S and Renfrewshire S, 2005–15; contested (Lab) same seat, 2015. Minister of State: (Minister for E-Commerce and Competitiveness), DTI, 2001–02; Cabinet Office, 2002–03: Minister for the Cabinet Office and Chancellor of the Duchy of Lancaster, 2003–04; Minister of State: FCO and DTI, 2004–05; for Europe, 2005–06; Sec. of State for Transport, and for Scotland, 2006–07, for Internat. Develt, 2007–10; Shadow Sec. of State for Internat. Develt, 2010, for Work and Pensions, 2010–11, for Foreign and Commonwealth Affairs, 2011–15. Fisher Family Fellow, 2015, Sen. Fellow, 2016–, Harvard Univ. Chair, Trustees, Unicef UK, 2018–; Trustee, RUSI, 2017–. *Recreation*: fishing on the Isle of Mull.
*See also* W. C. Alexander.

**ALEXANDER, Fiona Jane, (Mrs Stanko Ilic)**; Director of Communications, University Hospital Birmingham NHS Foundation Trust, since 2006; *b* 18 July 1967; *d* of David Charles Alexander and Susan Margaret Heywood (*née* Lewis); *m* 2004, Stanko Ilic; one *d*. *Educ*: S Glamorgan Inst. of Higher Educn, Cardiff (NCTJ); DipM; ACIM. Asst Ed., MATCH mag., 1989–96; Editor: Leics Herald Post, 1996–97; Sunday Mercury, 1997–2000; Editor-in-Chief, Midland Independent Mags, 2000–02; Business Develt Dir, Trinity Mirror Midlands, 2002–03; Ed., Birmingham Post, 2003–06. *Recreations*: football clubs Arsenal and Birmingham City, fine food and wine. *Address*: University Hospital Birmingham NHS Foundation Trust, Queen Elizabeth Medical Centre, Edgbaston, Birmingham B15 2TH. *T*: (0121) 371 4325. *E*: fiona.alexander@uhb.nhs.uk.

**ALEXANDER, Heidi**; Deputy Mayor for Transport, Greater London Authority, since 2018; *b* Swindon, 17 April 1975; *d* of Malcolm and Elaine Alexander; *m* 2011, Martin Ballantyne. *Educ*: Churchfields Secondary Sch., Swindon; Durham Univ. (BA Geog. 1996; MA Eur. Urban and Regl Change 1999). Researcher to Joan Ruddock, MP, 1999–2005; Campaign Manager, Clothes Aid, 2006. Dir and Chair, Gtr London Enterprise, 2007–09; Dir, Lewisham Schs for the Future Local Educn Partnership, 2007–09. Mem. (Lab) Lewisham LBC, 2004–10 (Dep. Mayor, 2006–10; Cabinet Mem. for Regeneration, 2006–10). MP (Lab) Lewisham E, 2010–May 2018. Shadow Health Sec., 2015–16. *Address*: Greater London Authority, City Hall, Queen's Walk, SE1 2AA.

**ALEXANDER, His Honour Ian Douglas Gavin**; QC 1989; a Circuit Judge, 2002–11; *b* 10 April 1941; *s* of late Dr A. D. P. Alexander, MB ChB, and of Mrs D. Alexander; *m* 1969, Rosemary Kirkbride Richards; one *s* one *d*. *Educ*: Tonbridge; University College London (LLB). Called to Bar, Lincoln's Inn, 1964, Bencher, 1998; a Recorder, Midland and Oxford Circuit, 1982–2002. A Pres., Mental Health Review Tribunal, 2000–11. Freemason; Grand Registrar of Craft and Chapter, United Grand Lodge of England, 2001–07. *Recreations*: horses, gardening, Freemasonry, Church of England. *Address*: The Folly, Fifield, Chipping Norton, Oxon OX7 6HW. *Club*: Naval and Military.

**ALEXANDER, Jonathan James Graham**, DPhil; FBA 1985; FSA 1981; Sherman Fairchild Professor of Fine Arts, Institute of Fine Arts, New York, 2002–11, now Emeritus (Professor of Fine Arts, 1988–2011); *b* 20 Aug. 1935; *s* of Arthur Ronald Brown and Frederica Emma Graham (who *m* 2nd, Boyd Alexander); *m* 1st, 1974, Mary Davey (marr. diss. 1995); one *s*; 2nd, 1996, Serita Winthrop (marr. diss. 2001). *Educ*: Magdalen Coll., Oxford (BA, MA, DPhil). Assistant, Dept of Western MSS, Bodleian Library, Oxford, 1963–71; Lecturer, 1971–73, Reader, 1973–87, History of Art Dept, Manchester Univ. Lyell Reader in Bibliography, Univ. of Oxford, 1982–83; Sen. Kress Fellow, Center for Adv. Study in Visual Arts, Nat. Gall. of Art, Washington DC, 1984–85; Sandars Reader in Bibliography, Cambridge Univ., 1984–85. Vis. Prof., UCL, 1991–93; John Simon Guggenheim Meml Fellow, 1995–96; Rio Tinto Distinguished Vis. Fellow, La Trobe Univ., Melbourne, 1997; Vis. Fellow, All Souls Coll., Oxford, 1998; J. Clawson Mills Art Hist. Fellowship, Met. Mus. of Art, NY, 2002; Samuel H. Kress Prof., Center for Advanced Study in the Visual Arts, Nat. Gall. of Art, Washington DC, 2004–05; J. Paul Getty Mus Guest Scholar, 2006. Panizzi Lectures, BL, 2007–08. Fellow, Medieval Acad. of America 1999. Hon. Fellow, Pierpont Morgan Liby, NY, 1995. *Publications*: (with Otto Pächt Illuminated Manuscripts in the Bodleian Library, Oxford, 3 vols, 1966, 1970, 1973; (with A. C. de la Mare) Italian Illuminated Manuscripts in the Library of Major J. R. Abbey, 1969 Norman Illumination at Mont St Michel c 966–1100, 1970; The Master of Mary o Burgundy, A Book of Hours, 1970; Italian Renaissance Illuminations, 1977; Insula Manuscripts 6th–9th Century, 1978; The Decorated Letter, 1978; (with E. Temple Illuminated Manuscripts in Oxford College Libraries, 1986; (ed with Paul Binski) Age o Chivalry: Art in Plantagenet England 1200–1400, 1987; Medieval Illuminators and Their Methods of Work, 1993; (ed) The Painted Page: Italian Renaissance book illuminatio 1450–1550, 1994; The Towneley Lectionary illuminated for Cardinal Alessandro Farnes by Giulio Clovio, 1997; Studies in Italian Manuscript Illumination, 2002; articles i Burlington Magazine, Art Bull., Arte Veneta, Pantheon, etc. *Recreation*: music. *Address* Institute of Fine Arts, 1 East 78th Street, New York, NY 10075-0178, USA.

**ALEXANDER, Lesley-Anne**, CBE 2012; Chief Executive, Royal National Institute o Blind People (formerly Royal National Institute of the Blind), 2004–16; *b* 20 Sept. 1959; of N. J. Davies and D. E. Davies; *m*; one *s*, *m* 1995, Colin James Reith. *Educ*: Thames Valle Univ. (MSc Ops Mgt). Housing Department: Ealing LBC, 1980–92; Enfield LBC 1992–98; Dir of Ops, Peabody Trust, 1998–2003. Chairman: British Judo Assoc 1997–2001; ACEVO, 2009–15; Red Door Ventures, 2016–; non-executive Directo Royal Brompton and Harefield NHS Foundn Trust, 2013–; Metropolitan Thames Valle (formerly Metropolitan), 2016–; Big Society Capital, 2018–; Trustee, MicroLoan Found 2016–. *Address*: 20 Grimsdyke Road, Pinner, Middx HA5 4PH.

**ALEXANDER, Michael Richard**, CEng, FIET; FIGEM; FIChemE; Chief Executive, British Energy plc, 2003–05; Senior Independent Director, Seplat Petroleum Development Company plc, since 2013; *b* 17 Nov. 1947; *s* of Humphrey and Pauline Alexander; *m* (marr. diss. 2011); two *s*. *Educ*: King George Grammar Sch., Southport; Univ. of Manchester Inst. of Sci. and Technol. (BSc 1st Cl. Hons Chem. Engrg; MSc Control Engrg). CEng 1975; MIChemE 1975, FIChemE 2004; FIGEM (FIGasE 1995); FIET (FIEE 2001); CSci 2004–15. Dir, CIS, Eastern Europe, British Gas Exploration and Production Ltd, 1991–93; Managing Director: Public Gas Supply, British Gas plc, 1993–96; British Gas Trading Ltd, 1996–2001; Exec. Dir, 1996–2003, Chief Operating Officer, 2002–03, Centrica plc. Chairman: Goldfish Bank Ltd, 2002–03; TGE Marine AG, 2008–10; Dep. Chm. and Sen. Ind. Dir, Russian Platinum, 2011–13; non-executive Director: Associated British Foods plc, 2002–07; Costain plc, 2007–13; Board Adviser: Marwyn Investment Mgt LLP, 2006–09; Landis+Gyr Gp, 2007–16; EGS Energy Ltd, 2010–16. Ind. Dir, UK Payments Council, 2007–14. Chm., Assoc. of Train Operating Cos, 2008–09. *Recreations*: Rugby, walking, family. *Address*: c/o Seplat Petroleum Development Company plc, 4th Floor, 50 Pall Mall, SW1Y 5JH.

**ALEXANDER, Michael Stuart**; Lead News Feature Writer, The Courier, Dundee, since 2015; *b* St Andrews, 17 Jan. 1973; *s* of Robert and Lorraine Alexander; *m* 2006, Lindsey Quinn; one *s* one *d*. *Educ*: Madras Coll., St Andrews; Univ. of Dundee (MA Hons Geog. 1995). Cinema projectionist (pt-time), St Andrews, 1990–95; The Courier, Dundee: reporter, 1995–2005; features writer, 2005–06; News Ed., 2007–12; Chief Reporter, The Courier, Fife, 2012–15. *Recreations*: mountain biking, hill walking, cinema, family, community events. *Address*: The Courier, 2 Albert Square, Dundee DD1 1DD. *E*: malexander@thecourier.co.uk. *Club*: St Andrews Golf.

**ALEXANDER, Morag**, OBE 2001; Member and Scotland Commissioner, Equality and Human Rights Commission, 2007–10; Convener, Scottish Social Services Council, 2001–07; *b* 10 Oct. 1943; *d* of Coll MacInnes and Sarah MacInnes (*née* Carberry); *m* 1964, Prof. Alan Alexander, *qv*; one *s* one *d*. *Educ*: Our Lady of Lourdes Sch., Glasgow; Glasgow Univ.; Lakehead Univ., Ont. (BA Hons). Res. Asst, ASTMS, 1971–73; editor and researcher, RIPA, 1973–82; freelance journalist and consultant, 1982–90; Founding Dir, TRAINING 2000 (Scotland) Ltd, Scottish Alliance for Women's Trng, 1990–92; Dir, EOC, Scotland, 1992–2001. Board Member: Children in Scotland, 1995–2000 (Chm., Early Years Adv. Gp, 1995–2002); Scottish Commn for Regulation of Care, 2001–07; Chairman: Fair Play Scotland, 2001–06; TOPSS UK Alliance, 2002–05; Co-Chm., Scottish Commn on Older Women, 2015–; Mem., E Lothian Poverty Commn, 2016–. Member: Bd, Partnership for a Parliament, 1997; Scottish Senate, the Windsor Meetings, 1997–2000; Women's Adv. Gp to Scottish Exec. (formerly Scottish Office), 1997–2000; Expert Panel on Procedures and Standing Orders, Scottish Parlt, 1997–98; Bd, Turning Point Scotland, 1998–2006; Bd, Skills for Health, 2003–05; Skills for Care and Develt, 2005–07; Bd and Trustee, ELCAP, 2010– (Vice Chm., 2012–14; Chair, 2014–). Mem., Gen. Optical Council, 2009–15. Mem., Cttee of Inquiry into Student Finance, 1999–2000. Member: Governing Body, Queen Margaret UC, 2001–07; Court, Queen Margaret Univ., Edinburgh, 2007–08. Founding Ed., Women in Europe, 1985–89; UK corresp., Women of Europe, 1987–92. *Recreations*: reading, walking, theatre, opera, spending time with family.

**ALEXANDER, Pamela Elizabeth**, OBE 2012; Chair, Commonplace Digital Ltd, since 2018; *b* 17 April 1954; *d* of late Reginald William Purchase Alexander and Marion Elizabeth Alexander (*née* Ross); *m* 1994, Dr Roger Booker; three step *s* one step *d*. *Educ*: Lady Eleanor Holles Sch.; Newnham Coll., Cambridge (BA Hons Geog.; MA). CGeog 2004. Department of the Environment, 1975–94: Asst Private Sec. to Minister for Housing, 1978–81; seconded to UK Rep., EC, Brussels, 1981–82; Hd, Publicity, 1987–90; Hd, Finance, Deptl Services, 1990–92; Hd, Housing Assocs Div., 1992–94; Dep. Chief Exec. (Ops), Housing Corp., 1995–97; Chief Exec., Historic Buildings and Monuments Commn (English Heritage), 1997–2001; Leader, Agency Policy Rev., Cabinet Office, 2001–02; Chief Exec., SEEDA, 2004–11. Non-executive Director: Housing Finance Corp., 2002–11; Quintain E&D plc, 2003; Crest Nicholson Hldgs plc (formerly Ltd), 2011–15; Future Cities Catapult, 2015–19, Connected Cities Catapult, 2019–; Crossrail Ltd, 2015–18. Chair: Thanet Regeneration Bd, 2011–14; Design Council Cabe, 2014–18 (non-exec. Dir, 2011–14; Built Envmt Expert, 2012–); Covent Garden Mkt Authy, 2013–19; non-executive Director: Acad. of Urbanism, 2010–15; London Legacy Develt Corp., 2018–. Ambassador, London Mayor's Cultural Leadership Bd, 2017–. Member: London Mayor's Design Adv. Gp, 2012–16; Watts Gall. Limnerslease Appeal Cttee, 2012–14. Governor, Peabody Trust, 2000–09 (Chm., 2004–09); Trustee: Brighton Dome and Festival Ltd, 2006–16; Design Council, 2011–18. Advr, Joseph Rowntree Foundn Res. Cttee, 1997–2004; Diversity Advr, Grimshaw LLP, 2018–. Pres., Roll Cttee, Newnham Coll., Cambridge, 2015–18. Associate, New Economics Foundn, 2002–06. FRSA 1998; FRGS 1999. Academician, Acad. of Urbanism, 2006. *Recreations*: choral singing, walking, talking, theatre. *E*: pamalexander@bookeralexander.com.

**ALEXANDER, Lt-Col Sir Patrick Desmond William C.;** *see* Cable-Alexander.

**ALEXANDER, Prof. Paul**, PhD; Professor of Radio Astronomy, University of Cambridge, since 2010; *b* Brighton, 20 Dec. 1960; *s* of Reginald and Iris Alexander; partner, Prof. Lynn Patt Gladden, *qv*. *Educ*: Brighton, Hove and Sussex Grammar Sch. and Sixth Form Coll.; Trinity Coll., Cambridge (BA 1982; PhD 1986). Res. Fellow, Sidney Sussex Coll., Cambridge, 1985–89; Lectr, 1989–2008, Reader, 2008–10, Univ. of Cambridge; Fellow, Jesus Coll., Cambridge, 1989–2015. UK Sci. Dir, Square Kilometre Array Orgn, 2011–17. Dir, Stratospheric Platforms Ltd, 2015–. *Publications*: contribs on astrophysics and data analysis. *Recreations*: gardening, cooking, wine. *Address*: Cavendish Laboratory, JJ Thomson Avenue, Cambridge CB3 0HE. *T*: (01223) 337477. *E*: p.alexander@mrao.cam.ac.uk.

**ALEXANDER, Prof. Philip Stephen**, DPhil; FBA 2005; Professor of Post-Biblical Jewish Literature, Manchester University, 1995–2011, now Emeritus; Co-Director, Manchester University Centre for Jewish Studies, 1995–2011; *b* 10 March 1947; *s* of Robert and Priscilla Alexander; *m* 1973, Loveday Constance Anne Earl (Rev. Canon Prof. L. Alexander); one *s* one *d*. *Educ*: Pembroke Coll., Oxford (Hon. Mods Greek and Latin Lit. 1967; BA Oriental Studies 1969; DPhil Oriental Studies 1974; MA 1992). University of Manchester: Nathan Laski Lectr in Post-Biblical Jewish Studies, Dept of Near Eastern Studies, 1972–86; Sen. Lectr in Jewish Studies, 1986–91; Prof. of Post-Biblical Jewish Lit., Dept of Middle Eastern Studies, 1991–92; University of Oxford: Speaker's Lectr (pt-time), 1985–88; Pres., Oxford Centre for Hebrew and Jewish Studies, 1992–95; Hebrew Centre Lectr, Oriental Faculty, 1992–95; Fellow, St Cross Coll., 1992–95. *Publications*: Textual Sources for the Study of Judaism, 1984; (with G. Vermes) Serekh ha-Yahad and Two Related Texts, 1998; The Targum of Canticles: translated with a critical introduction, apparatus and notes, 2003; Companions to the Dead Sea Scrolls: the Mystical Texts, 2005; contrib. to major ref. works in field of Jewish studies; contribs to Jl Jewish Studies, Jl Semitic Studies. *Recreations*: hill-walking, swimming, Rembrandt, Bach, Shakespeare. *Address*: c/o Centre for Jewish Studies, Religions and Theology, School of Arts, Languages and Cultures, University of Manchester, Manchester M13 9PL. *T*: (0161) 275 3977, *Fax*: (0161) 275 3151. *E*: philip.alexander@manchester.ac.uk.

**ALEXANDER, Sir Richard**, 3rd Bt *cr* 1945, of Sundridge Park, co. Kent; *b* London, 1 Sept. 1947; *o s* of Sir Charles Gundry Alexander, 2nd Bt, and of Mary Neale, *oc* of Stanley Richardson; *S* father, 2009; *m* 1971, Lesley Jane Jordan (marr. diss. 2002); two *s*. *Educ*: Bishop's Stortford Coll. MCIPR (MIPR 1980). Manager, Burntisland Shipbuilding, 1966–68; Shipbroker, Cory Mann George, 1968–70; Ship Manager, Houlder Brothers, 1970–79; PR Officer, Furness Gp, 1979–90; PR consultant, 1990–2012. Dir, Bentley Drivers Club Ltd, 1997–2014, 2017–; Editor, The BDC Review, 1997–2014; SE Reg. BDC Cttee, 2015–. Chm., Detling Village Hall, 1999–. Freeman, City of London; Liveryman, Merchant Taylors' Co. *Recreations*: vintage motoring, clay pigeon shooting, barebow archery. *Heir*: *s* Edward Samuel Alexander [*b* 1 Oct. 1974; *m* 2005, Michelle, *d* of Nicholas Goodhew, Sittingbourne; two *d*]. *Address*: 1 Northdowns View, Harrietsham, Maidstone, Kent ME17 1AQ. *T*: 07976 413091.

**ALEXANDER, Prof. Robin John**, PhD, LittD; FBA 2011; Fellow of Wolfson College, Cambridge, since 2004; Professor of Education, University of Warwick, 1995–2001, now Emeritus; *b* 10 Nov. 1941; *s* of Donald Alexander and Isabel Alexander (*née* Manton); *m* 1st, 1964, Elizabeth Walbank (marr. diss. 1986); one *s* one *d*; 2nd, 2001, Karen Lennox Mills. *Educ*: Downing Coll., Cambridge (BA 1964; MA 1968; PhD 1985; LittD 2006); Durham Univ. (PGCE 1966); Trinity Coll. of Music (ATCL 1966); London Univ. (AcDipEd 1970); Univ. of Manchester (MEd 1975). Teacher, schs and colls, 1964–77; University of Leeds: Lectr, Sen. Lectr, then Reader in Educn, 1977–90; Prof. of Educn, 1990–95; Leverhulme Res. Fellow, 1994–95; Dir, Centre for Res. in Elementary and Primary Educn, Univ. of Warwick, 1995–2001; Leverhulme Emeritus Fellow, 2002–04. Vis. Fellow, Hughes Hall, Cambridge, 2001–02; Sir Edward Youde Vis. Prof., Hong Kong Inst. of Educn, 2005–06; Professorial Dir of Res., Faculty of Educn, Univ. of Cambridge, 2006–12, Dir, Cambridge Primary Rev., 2006–12; Chm., Cambridge Primary Rev. Trust, 2012–17; C. K. Koh Prof., Nat. Inst. of Educn, Singapore, 2010; Miegunyah Dist. Vis. Fellow, Univ. of Melbourne, 2010; Vis. Prof., Univ. Gabriela Mistral, Santiago, 2012; Hon. Prof. of Educn, Univ. of York, 2013–17. Internat. educational consultant to DFID, EC, Ofsted, UGC of HK Govt, Knowledge and Human Devlt Authy, Dubai. Member: Cttees, CNAA, 1975–84; Council, CATE, 1989–94; DES Inquiry into Curriculum Orgn and Classroom Practice in Primary Schs, 1991–92; BFI/TES Commn on Teaching of English, 1992–93; Bd and Cttees, QCA, 1997–2002; Teach First Global Strategy Adv. Gp, 2011; Internat. Steering Cttee, Van Leer Jerusalem Inst., 2012–13; Strategic Bd, Expert Subject Adv. Gp, DFE, 2013–17; Court, Bishop Grosseteste Univ., 2013–; Chm., Assoc. for Study of Primary Educn, 1987–89; Pres., British Assoc. for Internat. and Comparative Educn, 2008–09; Vice-Pres., Early Educn, 2014–15. Director: Dialogos UK Ltd, 2004–; Isart Press Ltd, 2016–. Advr, Artis Educn, 2013–18. Trustee and Bd Mem., Children and the Arts (formerly Prince's Foundn for Children and the Arts), 2015–; Mem., Bd of Trustees, Creativity, Culture and Educn, 2017–18. Gov., Bath Spa Univ., 2013–17. Patron, Nat. Assoc. for Primary Educn, 2018–. FRSA 2006; FAcSS (AcSS 2011). Hon. FCollT 2009. Hon. DEd Manchester Metropolitan, 2010; DUniv: Bishop Grosseteste, 2010; Open, 2018. Award for Services to Educn, Assoc. of Managers in Educn, 2010; Fred and Anne Jarvis Award, NUT, 2011; Public Impact Award, British Educnl Res. Assoc./SAGE Publishing, 2015. *Publications*: (jtly) The Self-Evaluating Institution, 1982; Primary Teaching, 1984; (jtly) Change in Teacher Education, 1984; (jtly) Changing Primary Practice, 1989; Policy and Practice in Primary Education, 1992, 2nd edn 1997; Versions of Primary Education, 1995; (jtly) Learning from Comparing, vol 1, Classrooms, Contexts and Outcomes, 1999, vol. 2, Policy, Professionals and Development, 2000; Culture and Pedagogy, 2001 (Outstanding Book Award, Amer. Educnl Res. Assoc., 2002; First Prize, Soc. for Educn Studies Book Awards, 2002); Towards Dialogic Teaching, 2004, 5th edn 2017; Education as Dialogue, 2006; Essays on Pedagogy, 2008; Education for All: the quality imperative and the problem of pedagogy, 2008; (jtly) Children, their World, their Education: final report of the Cambridge Primary Review, 2010 (1st Prize, Soc. for Educn Studies Book Awards, 2011); (jtly) The Cambridge Primary Review Research Surveys, 2010; Primary Colours, 2015; A Dialogic Teaching Companion, 2019. *Recreations*: the arts, travel. *Address*: Wolfson College, Cambridge CB3 9BB. *E*: rja40@cam.ac.uk.

**ALEXANDER, Roger Michael**; non-executive Group Chairman, Walker Books Ltd, since 2010 (non-executive Director, 1999–2009); *b* Edinburgh, 29 June 1942; *s* of Hyman and Anna Alexander; *m* 1966, Monica Anne Freedman; two *d*. *Educ*: Dulwich Coll.; Coll. of Law. Admitted as solicitor, 1965; Lewis Silkin LLP: articled to Hon. John E. Silkin, 1960–65; Partner, 1965–2010; Head: Corporate Dept, 1986–89; Mktg Services Law Gp, 1986–99; Lead Partner, 1989–99; Sen. Partner, 1999–2005; Chm., 2005–10. Non-executive Director: EDS Financial Services Div., 1995–96; The Communications Agency Ltd, 2010–13; Advr to Bd, Strategy & Investment Partners LLP, 2010–. Non-exec. Dir, London String Quartet Foundn, 2001–07; non-exec. Dir, 2005–14, Mem., Capital Develt Gp, 2016–18, Royal Central Sch. of Speech and Drama (formerly Central Sch. of Speech and Drama); Mem., Strategy Develt Cttee, Dulwich Coll., 2013–16. Non-exec. Dir, and Hon. Solicitor, London Marriage Guidance Council, 1983–89. *Recreations*: literature, theatre, photography, cricket, gardening, bridge, family, travel, opera. *Address*: 24 Lyndhurst Road, NW3 5NX. *E*: roger.m.alexander@btinternet.com.

**ALEXANDER, Rosemary Anne, (Mrs G. L. S. Dobry)**; Founder and Principal, English Gardening School, since 1983; *b* 15 Dec. 1937; *d* of late Charles Sleigh and Violet Allison (*née* Petrie); *m* 1st, 1956, Walter Ronald Alexander, CBE (marr. diss. 1975; he *d* 2006); two *s* two *d*; 2nd, 1982, His Honour George Leon Severyn Dobry, CBE, QC (*d* 2018). *Educ*: Beacon Sch., Bridge of Allan, Stirlingshire. ACIHort (AIHort 1994). Trained as landscape architect; with Brian Clouston & Partners, Glasgow and London, 1973–79, then in private practice as garden designer. Expert witness, historic gardens, 2011–12. Internat. lectr, Kiev, 2012, NZ and Australia, 2013. Show Gardens Judge, RHS, 2011–17; Judge: Imperial Russian Flower and Garden Show, St Petersburg, 2014; Moscow Garden Fest., 2016. FSGD 1981. Veitch Meml Medal, RHS, 2011. *Publications*: (with Tony Aldous) Landscape By Design, 1979; The English Gardening School, 1987; A Handbook for Garden Designers, 1994; Terraced, Town and Village Gardens, 1999; Garden Design, 2000; Caring for Your Garden, 2001; The Essential Garden Design Workbook, 2004, 3rd edn 2017; The Garden Maker's Manual, 2005; The Essential Garden Maintenance Workbook, 2006; Dear Christo, 2010. *Recreations*: opera, travel to remote places, horse racing. *Address*: Sandhill Farm House, Rogate, Petersfield, Hants GU31 5HU. *T*: (01730) 818373, 07551 777873; English Gardening School, Chelsea Physic Garden, 66 Royal Hospital Road, SW3 4HS. *T*: (020) 7352 4347; 65 Burton Court, Franklins Row, SW3 4SY.

**ALEXANDER, Sian**; Chief Executive, Lyric Hammersmith, since 2015; *b* Changi, Singapore; *d* of Roger and Ceridwen Jenkins; *m* 1997, Robert Alexander; two *d*. *Educ*: St Felix Sch., Southwold; Balliol Coll., Oxford (MA Modern Hist.). Exec. Dir, Siobhan Davies Dance Co., 1996–2000; Hd of Theatre (London), Arts Council England, 2000–10; Associate Dir, Julie's Bicycle, 2010–13; Exec. Dir, Bush Th., 2012–14; arts mgt consultant, 2010–15. Clore Fellow, 2006–08. Dir, London Th. Consortium, 2016– (Vice Chair, 2016–). Trustee, Gate Th., 2015–; Vice Chair of Trustees, Julie's Bicycle, 2013–; Chair of

Trustees, Frantic Assembly, 2010–. *Recreations:* theatre, museums and galleries, family. *Address:* Lyric Hammersmith, Lyric Square, King Street, W6 0QL. *E:* sian.alexander@lyric.co.uk.

**ALEXANDER, Steven;** Chief Executive, Pre-School Learning Alliance, 2004–10; *b* 23 Oct. 1954; *s* of late Louisa and James Alexander; two *s*. *Educ:* Blue Coat C of E Sch.; Coventry Univ. (CQSW; CSS; DMS; MBA); Putteridge Bury Business Sch. (PhD 1994). Operational Services Manager, Coventry Social Services, 1976–92; Asst Gen. Manager, S Birmingham Community NHS Trust, 1992–95; Dir of Ops, Sense, 1995–2001; CEO, British Dyslexia Assoc., 2001–04. Associate Consultant, Nat. Develt Team, 1992–94. Dir, Children's Workforce Develt Council, 2005. Mem., Disability Employment Adv. Cttee, DWP, 2003. Treas., Eur. Dyslexia Assoc. FRSA. *Recreations:* classic cars, antiques, supporting Coventry FC, music, horses. *Address:* Potfords Dam Farm, Coventry Road, Cawston, Rugby CV23 9JP. *T:* (020) 7697 2519.

**ALEXANDER, Wendy Cowan;** Vice Principal, University of Dundee, since 2015; *b* 27 June 1963; *d* of Rev. Douglas N. Alexander and Dr Joyce O. Alexander; *m* 2003, Prof. Brian Ashcroft; one *s* one *d* (twins). *Educ:* Park Mains Sch., Erskine; Pearson Coll., Canada; Glasgow Univ. (MA Hons), Warwick Univ. (MA Econ); INSEAD, France (MBA). Research Officer, Lab. Party, 1988–92; with Booz & Co., 1994–97; Advr to Sec. of State for Scotland, 1997–98. Mem. (Lab) Paisley N, Scottish Parlt, 1999–2011. Scottish Executive, subseq. Scottish Government: Minister for Communities, 1999–2000; Minister for Enterprise and Lifelong Learning, 2000–02, and for Transport, 2001–02; Convenor: Finance Cttee, 2006–07; Scotland Bill Cttee, 2010–11; Lab Shadow Cabinet Sec. for Finance and Sustainable Growth, 2007. Leader, Scottish Labour Party, 2007–08. Associate Dean, London Business Sch., 2012–15. Vis. Prof., Univ. of Strathclyde Business Sch., 2003–12. FRSA 2011. DUniv Strathclyde, 2007; DUniv UWS, 2012.
*See also* Rt Hon. D. G. Alexander.

**ALEXANDER, William John,** CBE 2005; FREng, FIMechE; Chairman: Invesco Perpetual Income and Growth Investment Trust, since 2006; Beyond Analysis Ltd, 2008; *b* 15 Feb. 1947; *s* of late John Fryer Alexander and of Kathleen Mary (*née* Berry); *m* 1968, Dorothy Full; one *s* one *d*. FIMechE 1987; FREng (FEng 1996). British Coal: trng scheme, 1970; Chief Engr, Scottish Reg., 1982–86; Chief Mechanical Engr, 1986–87; Hd of Engrg, 1987–89; Thames Water Utilities: Engrg Dir, 1989–91; Technical Dir, 1991–92; Man. Dir, 1992–96; Dir, 1994–2005, Gp Man. Dir, 1996–97, Chief Executive, 1997–2005, Thames Water plc, later RWE Thames Water plc. Non-exec. Dir, RMC, 2001–05; Chairman: Henley Festival Ltd, 2003–11; Xansa plc, 2004–07; Clearview Traffic Ltd, 2006–09. Mem. Bd, CBI, 2005–09. Freeman, City of London, 1994; Liveryman, Engineers' Co., 1997–. Hon. FIMMM (Hon. FIMinE 1990); Hon. FCIWEM 2002. Hon. DSc: Cranfield, 2003; Reading, 2003. *Recreations:* classic cars, travel, golf. *Address:* Invesco Perpetual Income and Growth plc, 30 Finsbury Square, EC2A 1AG. *Club:* Phyllis Court (Henley).

**ALEXANDER-SINCLAIR of Freswick, James Boyd;** garden designer, writer, lecturer and broadcaster; *b* Münster, Germany, 30 July 1959; *s* of Maj.-Gen. David Boyd Alexander-Sinclair of Freswick, CB; *m* 1987, Celestria Fenwick; two *s* one *d*. *Educ:* Eton Coll. Estabd Terra Firma Landscapes, 1984–; gardens designed and built throughout UK and parts of Europe; freelance garden journalist, 2000–; columnist, Gardeners' World mag., 2007–. Contributor, BBC gardening progs. Gardens Judge, 2008–, Mem. Council, 2011–, Chm., Gardens Cttee, 2015–, RHS. Chm. Judges, Moscow Flower Show, 2012–. Blog of Year, Garden Media Guild, 2008, 2009, 2013. *Recreations:* gardening, cinema, drainage. *Address:* Green Rise, Ledwell, Oxon OX7 7AN. *E:* james@jamesalexandersinclair.com.

**AL FAYED, Mohamed;** Chairman: Harrods Holdings Ltd, 1994–2010; Harrods Ltd, 1985–2010; Fulham Football Club, 1997–2013; Chairman and Owner, Ritz Hotel, Paris, since 1979; *b* Egypt, Jan. 1933; *m*; two *s* two *d* (and one *s* decd). *Educ:* Alexandria Univ. Hon. Mem., Emmanuel Coll., Cambridge, 1995. Officier, Légion d'Honneur, 1993 (Chevalier, 1985); La Grande Médaille de la Ville de Paris, 1985; Plaque de Paris, 1989; Commendatore, Order of Merit (Italy), 1990.

**ALFÖLDY, Tádé;** Chairman, 1997, and Chief Executive Officer, 2005, ATI Depo Zrt; Chairman: Preventiv Security Rt, since 2000; ATI Sziget Industrial Park Kft, since 2005; Supervisory Board, Gundel Kft, since 2014 (Managing Director, 2010–14); *b* 6 Aug. 1946; *s* of László Alföldy and Erzsébet (*née* Ujvári); *m* 1968, Orsolya Baraczka; two *d*. *Educ:* Karl Marx Univ. of Economics, Budapest. Hungarian Shipping Agency, 1968–70; Hungarian Youth Union, 1970–74; Sec.-Gen., Internat. Cttee, Children's and Adolescents' Movements, 1974–79; joined Ministry of Foreign Affairs, Hungary, 1979; Arab Desk Officer, 1979–80; 2nd, later 1st, Sec., Kuwait, 1980–85; British Desk Officer, 1985–89; Dir, N Atlantic Dept, 1989–90; Dep. State Sec., 1990–91; Ambassador: to Greece, 1991–94; to the UK, 1994–97. Jt Chm., Investor Holding Rt, 1997–2005; Sen. Exec. Officer, Investor/Interag Gp, 1997–. Vice Pres., 1997–2002, Mem. Bd of Auditors, 2002–, Hungarian Atlantic Council, Budapest. Mem., Foreign Policy Assoc., Budapest, 1991–. *Recreations:* family, tennis, gardening. *Address:* Interag Zrt, Budapest 1051, Szent István tér 11, Hungary.

**ALFORD, Prof. Neil McNeill,** MBE 2013; PhD; FREng, FInstP, FRSC, FIET; Professor of Physical Electronics and Thin Film Materials, Department of Materials, since 2006, and Associate Provost (Academic Planning), since 2016, Imperial College London; *b* Newport, Mon, 9 Nov. 1949; *s* of David and Jean Alford; *m* 1988, Lesley Frances Cohen; three *s* one *d*. *Educ:* Harrow Sch.; Univ. of St Andrews (BSc; PhD 1979). FInstP 2003; CEng 2003; FIMMM 2003; FIET 2004; FREng 2007; FRSC 2011. Div. Res. Associate, ICI, 1981–94; Prof. and Pro-Dean of Faculty, London South Bank Univ., 1994–2006; Hd, Dept of Materials, Imperial Coll. London, 2010–15. Fellow, Amer. Ceramic Soc., 2011; FCGI 2011; FRSA. *Publications:* contribs to jls; 22 patents. *Recreations:* walking, playing the guitar, reading. *Address:* Imperial College London, Exhibition Road, SW7 2AZ. *T:* (020) 7594 6724, *Fax:* (020) 7594 6736. *E:* n.alford@imperial.ac.uk.

**ALFORD, Richard Harding,** CMG 2003; OBE 1988; Secretary, Charles Wallace India Trust, 2004–18; British Council Director, Italy, 1996–2003; *b* 28 Dec. 1943; *s* of Jack Harding Alford and Sylvia Alford; *m* 1968, Penelope Jane Wort; one *s* two *d*. *Educ:* Dulwich Coll.; Keble Coll., Oxford (MA; Diploma in History and Philosophy of Science). Asst Cultural Attaché, British Embassy, Prague, 1969–72; posts in ME Dept, Policy Res. Dept, and Educnl Contracts Dept, British Council, 1972–77; Project Planning Centre, Bradford Univ., 1977; Inst. of Educn, London Univ., 1978; British Council: Asst Rep., New Delhi, 1978–81; Dir, E Europe and N Asia Dept, 1982–85; Rep., Poland, 1985–89; Dir of Personnel, 1989–93; Regl Dir, Central Europe, 1993–96. Chm., Adv. Panel, British Centre for Literary Translation, 2009–11. Governor: Centre for Internat. Briefing, Farnham Castle, 1992–96; British Inst., Florence, 1996–2003; Atlantic Coll., 2005–14 (Mem., Adv. Council, 2014–). *Recreation:* theatre.

**ALFORD, Stuart Robert;** QC 2014; Partner, Latham & Watkins LLP, since 2016 (Co-Chair, London Litigation and Trial Department, 2017–18); *b* Westminster, 20 May 1967; *s* of Philip Alford and Heather Alford (*née* Porter); *m* 1995, Sylvia Philippa Theresa de Bertodano, *qv* (separated 2017); two *s* two *d*; one *s*. *Educ:* Kenilworth Sch.; Univ. of Reading (BSc Hons Geog. 1989); Univ. of Westminster (DipLaw 1991); Inns of Court Sch. of Law. Called to the Bar, Middle Temple, 1992; in practice as barrister, 1992–2001 and 2003–12; UN Prosecutor (E Timor), 2001–03; Legal Advr, Iraq High Tribunal, 2005–06; Special Advocate of Attorney Gen., 2009–17; Case Controller, 2012–13, Hd of Div. (Fraud), 2013–16, Serious Fraud Office. Chm., War Crimes Cttee, Internat. Bar Assoc., 2008–13. Chm. Govs, St Mary's Catholic Primary Sch., Aston-le-Walls, Northants, 2010–15. *Publications:* (contrib.) Oxford Companion to International Criminal Justice, 2009; contribs to Internat. Criminal Law Rev. *Recreations:* flying (Private Pilot's Licence Australia and Europe), scuba diving, opera (Mem., Glyndebourne Fest. Soc.), collecting fossilised wood. *Address:* Latham & Watkins LLP, 99 Bishopsgate, EC2M 3XF. *T:* (020) 7710 4502. *E:* stuart.alford.qc@lw.com.

**ALFORD, Sylvia Philippa Theresa;** *see* de Bertodano, S. P. T.

**ALHAJI, Alhaji Abubakar,** Hon. KBE 1989; Economic Adviser to Nigerian States of Sokoto, Kebbi and Zamfara, since 1999; High Commissioner for Nigeria in the United Kingdom, 1992–97; *b* 22 Nov. 1938; *m* Hajiya Amina Abubakar; three *s* three *d*. *Educ:* Univ. of Reading (BA Hons Political Economy); IMF Inst. course in public finance, 1974; Hague Inst. for Social Scis (course on industrialisation, 1970). Permanent Secretary, Ministries of: Trade, 1975–78; Industries, 1978–79; Finance, 1979–84; Nat. Planning, 1984–88; Hon. Minister, Ministries of: Budget and Planning, 1988–90; Finance and Economic Develt, 1990–92. Chm., Group 24 Cttee, 1991–92. Vice-Pres., Commonwealth Soc. for the Deaf. Sardauna of Sokoto, 1991. Hon. DSc Sokoto Univ., 1991. *Recreations:* horse riding, walking, reading. *Address:* c/o Government House, Sokoto State, Nigeria.

**AL HINAI, Shaikh Abdulaziz Abdullah Zahir;** Ambassador of Oman to the Court of St James's, since 2009; *b* Bahla Al Ghafat, 20 Jan. 1961. *Educ:* Univ. of Jordan (Bachelor Pol Sci. 1983). Joined Min. of Foreign Affairs, Oman, 1983; Second Sec., 1983–88; Chargé d'Affaires *ad interim*, London, 1988–90; Ambassador: to Netherlands, 1990–94; to Russian Fedn, 1994–2000; to Egypt, and Perm. Rep. to Arab League, 2000–09. *Address:* Embassy of Oman, 167 Queen's Gate, SW7 5HE. *T:* (020) 7589 3233, *Fax:* (020) 7589 2505. *E:* London2@mofa.gov.om.

**ALI, Ebrahim Mahomed;** Solicitor, Reynolds Porter Chamberlain LLP, 2013–14; *b* 9 April 1951; *s* of Mahomed and Katija Ali; *m* 1981, Susan Linda Kirkby; two *s* one *d*. *Educ:* Morgan High Sch., Harare; Univ. of Zimbabwe (LLB); UCL (LLM); Columbia Univ., NY (LLM). Called to the Bar, Middle Temple, 1978; admitted as legal practitioner, Zimbabwe, 1982; Attorney Gen.'s Chambers, Zimbabwe, 1982–83; Kantor & Immerman, Zimbabwe, 1983–84; admitted solicitor, England and Wales, 1989; Solicitor, Inland Revenue: Principal Legal Officer, 1989–94; on secondment to Competition Br., Legal Dept, OFT, 1994–97; Asst Solicitor (special appeals, internat., EC, oil), 1997–2002; on secondment to Legal Dept, Ofgem, 2002–03; Principal Assistant Solicitor (Taxes), Bd of Inland Revenue, subseq. HMRC, 2003–06; Consultant, Freshfields Bruckhaus Deringer, 2006–08; with PricewaterhouseCoopers Legal, 2008–09. *Recreations:* relaxing, sport.

**ALI, Rt Rev. Dr Michael N.;** *see* Nazir-Ali.

**ALI, Monica;** writer; *b* Dhaka, 20 Oct. 1967; *m* 2002, Simon Torrance; one *s* one *d*. *Educ:* Bolton Sch.; Wadham Coll., Oxford (BA Hons PPE). Mktg Manager, Verso, 1992–94; Account Dir, Newell & Sorrell (Interbrand), 1995–97; Gp Account Dir, Lambie-Nairn, 1997–98; freelance copy-writer, 1999–2001. Vis. Prof., MFA Course, Columbia Univ., 2010; Dist. Writer in Residence, Surrey Univ., 2016–18. Chm. Judges, Asian Man Booker Prize, 2011. *Publications:* Brick Lane, 2003; Alentejo Blue, 2006; In the Kitchen, 2009; Untold Story, 2011. *Recreations:* eating, cooking, yoga, riding, having baths. *Address:* c/o Curtis Brown, Haymarket House, 28–29 Haymarket, SW1Y 4SP.

**ALI, Rushanara;** MP (Lab) Bethnal Green and Bow, since 2010; *b* Bangladesh, 14 March 1975. *Educ:* Mulberry Sch. for Girls; Tower Hamlets Coll.; St John's Coll., Oxford (BA PPE). Res. asst to Lord Young of Dartington on estabt of Tower Hamlets Summer Univ., 1995; helped to develop Language Line; Parly Asst to Oona King, MP, 1997–99; FCO, 2000–01; Communities Directorate, Home Office, 2002–05; Associate Dir, Young Foundn, 2005–10. Res. Fellow, IPPR, 1999–2002. Shadow Minister: for Internat. Develt, 2010–14; for Educn, 2013–14. Member: Treasury Select Cttee, 2014–15, 2017–; Energy and Climate Change Select Cttee, 2015–16; DCLG Select Cttee, 2016–17. Chair, UpRising Leadership Prog.; Chair and Co-Founder, One Million Mentors. *Address:* House of Commons, SW1A 0AA.

**ALI, Tariq;** *b* 21 Oct. 1943; *s* of Tahira Hyat and Mazhar Ali Khan; partner, Susan Watkins; one *s* two *d*. *Educ:* Government Coll., Lahore (BA Hons); Exeter Coll., Oxford (PPE). Editor: The Black Dwarf, 1968–70; The Red Mole, 1970–73; Mem., Editorial Bd, New Left Review, 1982– (Chm., 1999–); Series Producer, Channel Four TV: Bandung File, 1984–89; Rear Window, 1990–94; Editorial Dir, 2001–05, Chm., 2005–, Verso Books; Series Editor, The World Today With Tariq Ali, 2014–. *Publications: non-fiction:* Pakistan: military rule or people's power, 1970; 1968 and After: inside the Revolution, 1978; Can Pakistan Survive?, 1982; Who's Afraid of Margaret Thatcher?, 1984; The Nehrus and the Gandhis: an Indian dynasty, 1985, 4th edn 2005; Streetfighting Years: an autobiography of the sixties, 1987, 2nd edn 2005; Revolution from Above: where is the Soviet Union going?, 1988; The Clash of Fundamentalisms, 2002; Bush in Babylon, 2003; Speaking of Empire and Resistance (interviews with David Barsamian), 2005; Rough Music: Blair/bombs/Baghdad/London/terror, 2005; Pirates of the Caribbean: axis of hope, 2006; The Duel: Pakistan on the flight path of American power, 2008; The Idea of Communism, 2009; The Protocols of the Elders of Sodom and other essays, 2009; The Obama Syndrome, 2010; On History: Tariq Ali and Oliver Stone in conversation, 2011; The Extreme Centre, 2015; The Dilemmas of Lenin, 2017; *fiction:* Redemption, 1990; Shadows of the Pomegranate Tree, 1992; The Book of Saladin, 1998; Fear of Mirrors, 1998; The Stone Woman, 2000; A Sultan in Palermo, 2005; Night of the Golden Butterfly, 2010; *plays:* Spinoza, 1993; Necklaces, 1994; The Illustrious Corpse, 2003; Zahra, 2007; (with Thorvald Steen) Desert Storms, 2010; The New Adventures of Don Quixote, 2013; with Howard Brenton: Iranian Nights, 1989; Moscow Gold, 1990; Ugly Rumours, 1998. *Recreations:* swimming, cinema, cricket, theatre, re-reading the classics. *Address:* 6 Meard Street, W1F 0EG. *T:* (020) 7437 3546, *Fax:* (020) 7734 0059. *E:* tariq.ali3@btinternet.com *W:* www.tariqali.org.

**ALI, Sayyid Zafar Gilani;** QC 2012; *b* London, 22 Feb. 1965; *s* of Mohsin and Jamila Ali; *m* 2004, Melissa Tollman; two *d*. *Educ:* Sutton Valence Sch., Kent; Pakistan Mil. Acad. Warwick Univ. (BA Hons 1990); City Univ. (DipLaw 1992); Inns of Court Sch. of Law. Called to the Bar, Middle Temple, 1994; in practice as barrister, specialising in criminal defence, 1994–. *Recreations:* boxing, family, study of Shia Islam. *Address:* 25 Frenchay Road, Oxford OX2 6TG; 5 Sheffield Terrace, W8 7NG. *Club:* Cavalry and Guards.

**ALIBHAI-BROWN, Yasmin;** journalist, broadcaster, author; Professor (part-time) Middlesex University, since 2013; columnist, i newspaper, since 2016; *b* 10 Dec. 1949; *d* of Kassim Damji and Jena Ramji; *m* (marr. diss.); one *s*; *m* 1990, Colin Brown; one *d*. *Educ:* Makerere Univ., Uganda (BA Hons 1972); MPhil Oxon 1975. Arrived in UK from Uganda, 1972; journalist; contributions to: Guardian; Observer; NY Times; Time mag.; Newsweek; Daily Mail; radio and TV broadcaster. Res. Fellow, IPPR, 1996–2001. Adv to instns on race matters; Founder and Co-Chair, British Muslims for Secular Democracy, 2006–. Pres., Inst. Family Therapy. One-woman show, commnd and dir by RSC, 2005–06, UK and Indian tour, 2007. Visiting Professor in Journalism: Cardiff Univ., 2008; Univ. of Lincoln, 2008; UWE, 2008. Winston Churchill Meml Trust Fellow, 2011. DUniv: Open, 1999; Oxford Brookes, 2004; Hon. Dr Liverpool John Moores, 2003; DLitt York St John, 2008. Asia Award for achievement in writing, BBC, 1999; Special Award for outstanding contrib. to journalism, CRE, 2000; Media Personality of Year Award, 2000, Award for Journalism, 2004, Ethnic Minority Media Award; Windrush Outstanding Merit Award, 2000; GG2 Leadership and Diversity Award for Media Personality of Year, 2001; George Orwell Prize for political journalism, 2002; Columnist of the Year: Asian Voice Political and Public Life Awards, 2011; Nat. Press Awards, 2017; Outstanding Contribution to Journalism, Asian Media Awards, 2017. *Publications:* No Place Like Home, 1995; After Multiculturalism, 2000; Who Do We Think We Are?, 2001; Mixed Feelings, 2001; Some of My Best Friends Are, 2004; The Settler's Story: a memoir of love, migration and food, 2009; Exotic England, 2013; In Defence of Political Correctness, 2018. *Recreations:* theatre, reading, volunteering to assist children in need, cooking. *Address:* i newspaper, Northcliffe House, Derry Street, W8 5HF. *E:* y.alibhai-brown@ntlworld.com.

**AL JABER, Mohamed Bin Issa;** Founder and Chairman, MBI Group; *b* Jeddah, 17 Jan. 1959; *m*; one *s* two *d*. Founder and Chairman: Jadawel Internat. Construction and Develt, 1982–; JJW Hotels and Resorts, 1989–; AJWA Gp for Agro and Food Industries, 1992–. UNESCO Special Envoy, 2004–; UN spokesperson for global forums on reinventing govt, 2007–. Founder, MBI Trust at SOAS, 2000; Founder and Chairman: MBI Foundn, 2002–; MBI Al Jaber Foundn; Vice-Chm., Internat. Adv. Bd, 2002–, Mem., Adv. Bd, London Middle East Inst., 2002–, SOAS, Univ. of London; Mem., Adv. Bd, Middle East Centre, LSE, 2016–. Hon. Fellow: SOAS, Univ. of London, 2002; Corpus Christi Coll., Oxford, 2009; UCL, 2012. Senator, Modul Univ., 2013–. Hon. DLitt Westminster, 2004; Hon. DSc City, 2004. Gold Medal: Arab League Educnl, Cultural and Scientific Orgn, 2007; UNESCO, 2007; City of Vienna, 2009; Islamic Educnl, Cultural and Scientific Orgn, 2012. Medaille d'Or du Tourisme (France), 2005. *Publications:* Yes, the Arabs Can Too, Arabic edn 2009, English edn 2013, French edn 2014, German edn 2015. *Recreations:* poetry, history, reading. *Address:* MBI Group, 78 Wigmore Street, W1U 2SJ. *T:* (020) 7935 5859, *Fax:* (020) 7535 1569.

**ALKER, (Frederick) Douglas;** Chair, since 1980, and Managing Director, since 2001, East Lancashire Deaf Society; Chief Executive, Royal National Institute for Deaf People, 1995–97; *b* 23 Nov. 1940. *Educ:* London Univ. (BSc 1967); Birmingham Univ. (MBA 1993). Analytical Chemist, Pilkington Bros, 1959–64; Exptl Officer, ICI, 1964–85; Researcher, BBC, 1985–87; Royal National Institute for Deaf People: Principal Regl Officer, 1987; Dir, Community Services, 1987–90; Dir, Quality and Res., 1990–94. Member: Nat. Disability Council, 1995–2000; Exec. Cttee, RADAR, 1997–2000; Chair: Fedn of Deaf People, 1997–2001 (Pres., 2001–); BDA, 2002–06. Chair, Kings Court (Blackburn) Ltd, 2000–. Ind. Assessor for DETR, 1999–2002. Hon. Fellow, Univ. of Central Lancashire, 1995. *Address:* Playing Field Cottage, Darwen, Lancs BB3 3PN.

**ALKER, Rt Rev. Mgr (John) Stephen,** MBE 1997; Pastor and Parish Priest, St Leonhard's International English-speaking Roman Catholic Parish, Frankfurt am Main and St Mary's, Lieberbach, Germany, 2010–16; *b* 1 July 1953; *s* of John Alker and Alice Alker (*née* Ashurst). *Educ:* St Joseph's Coll., Upholland, Wigan; St Cuthbert's Coll., Ushaw, Durham; Pontifical N American Coll., Rome (Inst. of Continuing Theol Educn Course, 2009). Ordained priest, Liverpool Archdio., 1978; Assistant Priest: St Joseph's, Leigh, 1978–80; Metropolitan Cath., Liverpool, 1980–83; Chaplain, TA, 1981, Regular Army, 1983–2009, served Germany, NI, Australia, Cyprus, Bosnia, UK; first RC Asst Chaplain Gen., RAChD, 2003–09; Principal RC Chaplain and Vicar Gen. to the Army, 2006–09; Asst Chaplain Gen., HQ Land Comd, later HQ Land Forces, 2006–09. QHC, 2007–09. Prelate of Honour, 2006. Mem., NW RFCA, 2017–. KCHS 2010 (KHS 2002). *Recreations:* ornithology, country walks, classical music, ecclesiastical heraldry. *E:* jstephen.a@gmail.com. *Clubs:* Athenæum, Artists (Liverpool).

**AL KHALIFA, Shaikh Abdul Aziz bin Mubarak;** International Media Advisor, Information Affairs Authority, Bahrain; *b* 10 Oct. 1962; *m* 1988, Shaikha Lamees Daij Al Khalifa. *Educ:* Wellington Sch., Som; Newbury Coll. (HND); Amer. Univ. Sch. of Internat. Service, Washington (BA); Inst. for Social and Economic Policy in Middle East, Harvard. Prime Minister's Court, Bahrain: Researcher on Political and Economic Affairs, 1987–90; Asst Dir of Information, 1990–94; acting Dir of Admin and Public Relations, 1994–96; Ambassador for Bahrain to UK, Denmark, Ireland, Holland, Norway and Sweden, 1996–2001; Asst Under Sec. for Policy Co-ordination, 2001, Asst Under Sec. for Co-ordination and Follow-up, 2002, Ministry of Foreign Affairs, Bahrain. *Address:* Information Affairs Authority, PO Box 253, Isa Town, Bahrain.

**AL KHALIFA, Shaikh Fawaz bin Mohamed;** Ambassador of Bahrain to the Court of St James's, since 2015, and accredited to The Netherlands, Ireland, Spain and Sweden, since 2016, and to Norway, since 2017; *b* Manama, Bahrain, 16 Sept. 1965; *s* of Shaikh Mohamed Bin Khalifa Al-Khalifa; *m* 2005, Shaikha Buthaina Bint Mohamed Alotaibi; two *s* one *d*. *Educ:* Bahrain Internat. Sch.; American Univ., Washington, DC (BA Law and Society); Univ. of S Calif (MA Public Admin); RMA, Sandhurst (Commns Course). Dir of Investments, Pension Fund Commn, Bahrain, 1992–2000; President, with ministerial rank: Gen. Orgn of Youth and Sport, 2000–10; Information Affairs Authy, 2010–12; Minister of State for Communication, 2012–14. Isa Bin Salman Award (Bahrain), 2000; Medal of First Degree (Bahrain), 2004. *Recreations:* sport, football, motor-racing sport. *Address:* Embassy of the Kingdom of Bahrain, 30 Belgrave Square, SW1X 8QB. *T:* (020) 7201 9183. *E:* information@bahrainembassy.co.uk. *Club:* Travellers.

**AL KHALIFA, Shaikh Khalifa bin Abdullah;** Secretary General, Supreme Defence Council, Bahrain, and National Security Adviser to the King of Bahrain, 2011; *b* 4 March 1965; *m* 1989, Shaikha Mayar bint Khalifa Al Khalifa; three *s* one *d*. *Educ:* West Rifaa Sch. for Boys; Huston Tillotson Univ., Texas (BBA); South West Texas State Univ. (MBA). Ministry of Information, Bahrain: Tourism Sector, 1989–96; set up and expanded Foreign Media Affairs, 1996–2002; Asst Under Sec. for Foreign Media Affairs, 2002–06; Chief Exec., Bahrain Radio and TV Corp., 2006–07; Ambassador of Bahrain to the Court of St James's, 2007–08; Hd, Nat. Security Agency, Bahrain, 2008–11. Chm. of regl, nat. and internat. seminars and confs in media field. Shaikh Isa bin Salman Al Khalifa Medal 4th class. *Recreation:* reading about politics and social affairs.

**AL KHALIFA, Shaikh Khalifa bin Ali bin Rashid;** Ambassador of Bahrain to the Court of St James's, 2008–11; *b* 1957; *m*; one *s* three *d*. *Educ:* Royal Mil. Coll. of Sci., Shrivenham (BSc Hons Aeronautical Engrg 1979); Southampton Univ. (MSc Aeronautical Engrg 1981); RAF Cranwell (Initial Officers Trng Course with dist. 1982). Joined Bahrain Defence Force, 1976; operational and staff posts, then Dep. Comdr, Bahraini Amiri Air Force, 1982–94 (Air Comd and Staff Course, Maxwell AFB, Ala); Defence Attaché, Washington, 1994–2001; Brig. 2001; Ambassador to USA and Canada, 2001–04; Hd, Nat. Security Agency, Bahrain, 2005–08. Trustee, Bahrain Center for Strategic, Internat. and Energy Studies, 2011–15. *Address:* c/o Embassy of Bahrain, 30 Belgrave Square, SW1X 8QB. *T:* (020) 7201 9170, *Fax:* (020) 7201 9183. *Clubs:* Mark's, Mosimann's, Harry's Bar.

**AL-KHALILI, Prof. Jameel S., (Jim),** OBE 2008; PhD; FRS 2018; FInstP; scientist, author and broadcaster; Professor of Physics and Professor of Public Engagement in Science, University of Surrey, since 2005; *b* Baghdad, 20 Sept. 1962; *s* of Sadik and Jean Al-Khalili; *m* 1986, Julie Frampton; one *s* one *d*. *Educ:* Univ. of Surrey (BSc Hons Physics 1986; PhD 1989). FInstP 2000. Res. Fellow, UCL, 1989–91; University of Surrey: Res. Fellow, 1991–92; Lectr in Physics, 1992–94; Advanced Res. Fellow, 1994–99; Sen. Lectr, 2000–05. Adjunct Prof., Michigan State Univ., 1999–2000. Sen. Advr on Sci. and Technol. to British Council, 2007–. British Association for Advancement of Science, later British Science Association: Trustee, 2006–; Vice Pres., 2008–18; Pres., 2018–19; Hon. Fellow, 2007; Pres., British Humanist Assoc., 2013–16. Presenter: *television* documentaries: The Riddle of Einstein's Brain, 2004; Atom, 2007; Lost Horizons: The Big Bang, 2008; Science and Islam, 2009; The Secret Life of Chaos, 2010; Chemistry: A Volatile History, 2010; Everything and Nothing, 2011; Shock and Awe: The Story of Electricity, 2011; Horizon: Is Nuclear Power Safe, 2012; Horizon: The Search for the Higgs, 2012; Order and Disorder, 2012; Light and Dark, 2013; The Secrets of Quantum Physics, 2014; Inside Sellafield: Britain's Nuclear Secrets, 2015; The Beginning and End of the Universe, 2016; Gravity and Me: the force that shapes our lives, 2017; Revolutions: Ideas that Changed the World, 2019; *radio:* The Secret Scientists, 2009; The Life Scientific, 2011–; Too Old to be a Genius, 2015; The Beauty of Equations, 2016. Hon. DSc: Royal Holloway, 2013; Bradford, 2014; Portsmouth, 2015; Open, 2015; York, 2017. Michael Faraday Medal for Sci. Communication, Royal Soc., 2007; Kelvin Medal for Public Awareness of Physics, Inst. of Physics, 2011; Stephen Hawking Medal for Sci. Communication, 2016. *Publications:* Black Holes, Wormholes and Time Machines, 1999; Nucleus: a trip into the heart of matter, 2001; Quantum: a guide for the perplexed, 2004; (ed) Lecture Notes in Physics: Nuclear Physics with Exotic Beams, vol. I 2004, vol. II 2006, vol. III 2008; Pathfinders: the golden age of Arabic science, 2010; Paradox: the nine greatest enigmas in science, 2012; (with J. McFadden) Life on the Edge: the coming of the age of quantum biology, 2014; Aliens, 2016; Quantum Mechanics (Ladybird Expert Book), 2017; Sunfall, 2019; contrib. res. papers in jls, newspaper and mag. articles. *Recreations:* reading non-fiction (particularly history and philosophy), hiking, running, cycling, oil painting, playing guitar, following Leeds United FC. *Address:* Department of Physics, University of Surrey, Guildford, Surrey GU2 7XH. *T:* (01483) 686808, *Fax:* (01483) 686781. *E:* j.al-khalili@surrey.ac.uk.

**ALKIN, Lawrence Michael;** Chairman, Metro Inns Ltd; *b* 16 June 1939; *s* of Henry and Phyllis Alkin. *Educ:* Mill Hill Sch.; University Coll. London (LLM). Sen. Partner, Alkin Colombotti and Partners, 1965–72; Managing Director: Filross Securities, 1972–; Holmes Place Ltd, 1979–96; Jt CEO, Holmes Place PLC, 1997–2000. Non-exec. Dir, M Winkworth plc, 2009–. *Recreations:* fishing (badly), cooking (moderately), dining out (well). *Address:* Flat 101, Block E, Montevetro Building, 100 Battersea Church Road, SW11 3YL.

**ALLABY, (John) Michael;** author, since 1973; *b* 18 Sept. 1933; *s* of Albert Theodore Allaby and Jessica May Allaby (*née* King); *m* 1957, Ailsa Marthe McGregor; one *s* one *d*. *Educ:* George Dixon Grammar Sch., Birmingham; Birmingham Sch. of Speech Training and Dramatic Art. Left sch. at 15, 1948; clerk, 1949; police cadet, Birmingham City Police, 1950–51; pilot, RAF, 1952–64; actor, 1955–64; Editorial Asst, Soil Assoc., 1964–72; Managing Editor, The Ecologist, 1972–73. *Publications:* The Eco-Activists, 1971; Who Will Eat?, 1972; (with Floyd Allen) Robots Behind the Plow, 1974; Ecology, 1975; (jtly) The Survival Handbook, 1975; Inventing Tomorrow, 1976; World Food Resources: actual and potential, 1977; (with Colin Tudge) Home Farm, 1977; (ed) A Dictionary of the Environment, 1977, 4th edn 1994; Making and Managing a Smallholding, 1979, 2nd edn 1986; Animals that Hunt, 1979; Wildlife of North America, 1979; (with Peter Bunyard) The Politics of Self-Sufficiency, 1980; A Year in the Life of a Field, 1981; (with Peter Crawford) The Curious Cat, 1982; Animal Artisans, 1982; (with James Lovelock) The Great Extinction, 1983; The Food Chain, 1984; (with James Lovelock) The Greening of Mars, 1984; (ed) The Oxford Dictionary of Natural History, 1985; Your Child and the Computer, 1985; (with Jane Burton) Nine Lives, 1985; 2040: our world in the future, 1985; (with Jane Burton) A Dog's Life, 1986; The Woodland Trust Book of British Woodlands, 1986; Ecology Facts, 1986, 2nd edn as Green Facts, 1989; The Ordnance Survey Outdoor Handbook, 1987; (with Jane Burton) A Pony's Tale, 1987; Conservation at Home, 1988; (ed) Thinking Green: an anthology of essential ecological writing, 1989; Guide to Gaia, 1989; Into Harmony with the Planet, 1990; Living in the Greenhouse, 1990; (ed with Ailsa Allaby) The Concise Oxford Dictionary of Earth Sciences, 1991, (ed) 4th edn as Oxford Dictionary of Geology and Earth Sciences, 2013; (ed) The Concise Oxford Dictionary of Zoology, 1991, 3rd edn as Oxford Dictionary of Zoology, 2009; (ed) The Concise Oxford Dictionary of Botany, 1992, 3rd edn as Oxford Dictionary of Plant Sciences, 2012; Elements: water, 1992; Elements: air, 1992; Elements: earth, 1993; Elements: fire, 1993; (with Neil Curtis) Planet Earth: a visual factfinder, 1993; (ed) The Concise Oxford Dictionary of Ecology, 1994, 5th edn as Oxford Dictionary of Ecology, 2015; How the Weather Works, 1995; Facing the Future, 1995; Basics of Environmental Science, 1996, 2nd edn 2000; (with Michael Kent) Collins Pocket Reference Biology, 1996; How it Works: the environment, 1996; Ecosystem: temperate forests, 1999, 2nd edn 2007; Biomes of the World, 9 vols, 1999; DK Guide to Weather, 2000; Plants and Plant Life, 5 vols of 10-vol. series: Plant Ecology, Plants Used By People, Conifers, Flowering Plants - The Monocotyledons, Flowering Plants - The Dicotyledons, 2001; Ecosystem: deserts, 2001, 2nd edn 2007; Megabites: tornadoes and other dramatic weather systems, 2001; (with Derek Gjertsen) Makers of Science, 5 vols, 2001; Encyclopedia of Weather and Climate, 2 vols, 2002, 2nd edn 2007; How it Works: the world's weather, 2002; The Facts on File Weather and Climate Handbook, 2002; (ed with Chris Park) Oxford Dictionary of Environment and Conservation, 2nd edn 2013; Dictionary of Science for Gardeners, 2015; Gardener's Guide to Weather and Climate, 2015; Plant Love, 2016; *series:* Dangerous Weather: Hurricanes, 1997, 2nd edn 2003, Tornadoes, 1997, 2nd edn 2003, Blizzards, 1997, 2nd edn 2003, Droughts, 1998, 2nd edn 2003, A Chronology of Weather, 1998, 2nd edn 2003, Floods, 1998, 2nd edn 2003, A Change in the Weather, 2003, Fog, Smog, and Poisoned Rain, 2003; Biomes of the Earth: Deserts, 2005, Grasslands, 2005, Temperate Forests, 2005, Tropical Forests, 2005; Countries of the World: India, 2005; Discovering the Earth: Earth Sciences, 2009, Atmosphere, 2009, Oceans, 2009, Ecology 2009, Animals, 2010, Plants, 2010, Exploration, 2010. *Recreations:* gardening, reading, watching movies. *Address:* Braehead Cottage, Tighnabruaich, Argyll PA21 2ED. *T:* and *Fax:* (01700) 811332. *E:* m.allaby@btinternet.com; c/o Rupert Crew Ltd, 6 Windsor Road, N3 3SS. *T:* (020) 8346 3000. *W:* www.michaelallaby.com.

**ALLAIN, Prof. Jean-Pierre Charles,** MD, PhD; FRCPath, FMedSci; Professor of Transfusion Medicine, University of Cambridge, 1991–2011, now Emeritus; *b* 26 Jan. 1942; *s* of Jacques Louis Allain and Marthe Charlotte (*née* Petitjean); *m* 1st, 1962, DucDung Nguyen (marr. diss.); two *s* two *d*; 2nd, 1978, Helen Lee. *Educ:* Univ. of Paris (MD 1967; PhD 1986; MSc 1995). FRCPath 1992. Asst Prof. of Haematol., Univ. of Paris, 1967–70; Dir, French Red Cross Haemophilia Centre, 1970–77; Head, Coagulation Res. Lab., Nat. Blood Transfusion Centre, Paris, 1977–81; Head, Dept of R&D Plasma Protein Derivatives, Nat. Blood Transfusion Centre, Paris, 1981–86; Dir of Med. Res., Diagnostic Div., Abbott Labs, Chicago, 1986–91; Dir, E Anglian Blood Transfusion Centre, 1991–94.

FMedSci 2000. *Publications:* over 300 articles in Nature, N Engl. Jl Med., Lancet, Jl of Clin. Invest., BMJ, Blood, PLoS Medicine, Hepatology, Jl Hepatol., Jl of Infectious Diseases, Transfusion. *Recreations:* tennis, ceramics, painting.

**ALLAIN CHAPMAN, Ven. Dr Justine Penelope Heathcote;** Archdeacon of Boston, since 2013; *b* Durham, 30 June 1967; *d* of Albert and Eileen Chapman; *m* 1990, Thomas Allain; one *s* three *d*. *Educ:* King's Coll. London (BA Hons 1988; AKC 1988; PGCE 1989; DThMin 2012); Lincoln Theol Coll. (MDiv Nottingham Univ. 1993). Hd of Religious Studies, S Hampstead High Sch., 1989–91; ordained deacon, 1993, priest, 1994; Curate, Christ Church and St Paul, Forest Hill, 1993–96; Vicar, St Paul, Clapham, 1996–2004; Dir of Mission and Pastoral Studies, 2004–13, Vice-Principal, 2007–13, SE Inst. for Theol Educn. *Publications:* Resilient Pastors: the role of adversity in healing and growth, 2012; The Resilient Disciple: a Lenten journey from adversity to maturity, 2018. *Recreations:* family, Norfolk, detective fiction, yoga, music. *Address:* Archdeacon's House, Castle Hill, Welbourn, Lincoln LN5 0NF. *T:* (01400) 273335. *E:* archdeacon.boston@lincoln.anglican.org.

**ALLAM, Christopher James,** FREng; Executive Group Director Engineering, MBDA, since 2018; *b* Lytham St Annes, 1 April 1967; *s* of Roy James Allam and Hilda Allam; one *s* one *d*. *Educ:* Hatfield Poly. (BEng Hons Aeronautical Engrg 1989). FRAeS 2010; FREng 2015. British Aerospace, then BAE Systems: Aerodynamicist, 1988–2000; Proj. Manager, 2000–06; Proj. Dir, Taranis, 2006–08; Managing Director: Future Capability, 2008–11; F-35, 2011–14; Engrg Dir, 2014–17. *Recreations:* golf, football. *Address:* MBDA UK Ltd, Six Hills Way, Stevenage SG1 2DA. *E:* chris.allam@mbda.co.uk.

**ALLAM, Peter John;** Architect Principal in private practice of Peter Allam, Chartered Architect, Dollar and Edinburgh, 1964–68, 1971–78 and 1987–2008; *b* 17 June 1927; *er s* of late Leslie Francis Allam and Annette Farquharson (*née* Lawson); *m* 1961, Pamela Mackie Haynes; two *d*. *Educ:* Royal High Sch., Edinburgh; Glasgow Sch. of Architecture. War service, 1944–48, Far East; commnd in Seaforth Highlanders, 1946. Architectural trng, 1948–53. Bahrain Petroleum Co., Engrg Div., 1954–55; Asst in private architectural practices, 1956–64; Partner in private practice of Haswell-Smith & Partners, Edinburgh, 1978–79; Director, Saltire Soc., 1968–70; Dir of Sales, Smith & Wellstood Ltd, Manufg ironfounders, 1979–81. ARIBA 1964; FRIAS 1985 (Associate, 1964). VMSM 1999. *Recreations:* trying to keep up with all my grandchildren and their modern technology, also some drawing and painting. *Address:* 15 St Thomas' Place, Stirling FK7 9LX. *T:* 07803 205620.

**ALLAM, Roger William;** actor; *b* 26 Oct. 1953; *s* of Rev. William Sydney Allam and Kathleen Allam (*née* Service); partner, Rebecca Saire; two *s*. *Educ:* Christ's Hosp.; Univ. of Manchester (BA). With Royal Shakespeare Co., 1981–, Associate Artist, 1990–: rôles include: Mercutio in Romeo and Juliet, Oberon in Midsummer Night's Dream, 1984; Javert in Les Misérables, transf. Palace Th., 1985; Brutus in Julius Caesar, Duke Vincentio in Measure for Measure, Toby Belch in Twelfth Night, 1987; Benedick in Much Ado About Nothing, 1990; title rôle in Macbeth, 1996; National Theatre, 1999–: rôles include: Graves in Money (Olivier Award for Best Supporting Actor, 2000), Ulysses in Troilus and Cressida (Clarence Derwent Award), Bassov in Summerfolk, 1999; Hitler in Albert Speer, Lophakin in The Cherry Orchard, 2000; Willy Brandt in Democracy, 2003, transf. Wyndham's, 2004; Reinhardt in Afterlife, 2008; Rutherford in Rutherford and Son, 2019; West End includes: City of Angels, Prince of Wales, 1993; Arcadia, Haymarket, 1994; Importance of Being Earnest, Old Vic, 1995; Art, Wyndham's, 1997; Privates on Parade, Donmar, 2001 (Olivier Award for Best Actor, 2002); Aladdin, Old Vic, 2004, 2005; Boeing-Boeing, Comedy, 2007; La Cage aux Folles, Playhouse, 2009; Henry IV Parts I and II, Shakespeare's Globe, 2010 (Olivier Award for Best Actor, 2011); The Tempest, Shakespeare's Globe, 2013; Limehouse, Donmar, 2017; The Moderate Soprano, Duke of York's, 2018; other performances include: Blackbird, Edinburgh Fest., 2005, transf. Albery, 2006; Pravda, Chichester Festival Th., 2006; God of Carnage, Th. Royal Bath, 2009; Uncle Vanya, Chichester Festival Th., 2012; Seminar, Hampstead Th., 2014; The Moderate Soprano, Hampstead Th., 2015; *films* include: A Cock & Bull Story, 2005; V for Vendetta, The Wind That Shakes the Barley, The Queen, 2006; Speed Racer, 2008; Tamara Drewe, 2010 (Peter Sellers Award for Comedy, Evening Standard British Film Awards, 2011); The Iron Lady, The Angel's Share, 2011; The Book Thief, 2014; Mr Holmes, A Royal Night Out, 2015; The Lady in the Van, 2015; The Truth Commissioner, 2016; The Hippopotamus, 2017; *television* includes: The Thick of It (series), 2007–12; Endeavour, 2012, 2013, 2014, 2016, 2017, 2018, 2019; Parades End (series), 2012; The Missing 2 (series), 2016. *Publications:* contrib. chapters to Players of Shakespeare, vol. II and vol. III. *Address:* c/o Claire Maroussas, Independent Talent Group Ltd, 40 Whitfield Street, W1T 2RH. *T:* (020) 7636 6565, *Fax:* (020) 7323 9867.

**ALLAN;** see Havelock-Allan.

**ALLAN,** family name of **Baron Allan of Hallam**.

**ALLAN OF HALLAM,** Baron *cr* 2010 (Life Peer), of Ecclesall in the County of South Yorkshire; **Richard Beecroft Allan;** Vice President, Public Policy, Europe, Middle East and Africa, Facebook, since 2014 (Director of European Public Policy, 2009–14); *b* 11 Feb. 1966; *s* of John and Elizabeth Allan; *m* 1991, Louise Maria Netley (marr. diss. 2001); one *d*. *Educ:* Pembroke Coll., Cambridge (BA Hons Archaeology and Anthropology); Bristol Poly. (MSc IT). Archaeologist, 1988–90; NHS Computer Manager, 1991–97. MP (Lib Dem) Sheffield, Hallam, 1997–2005. Hd of Govt Relns, UK and Ireland, Cisco Systems, 2005–09. Chm., Power of Inf. Task Force, 2008–. *Recreation:* visiting sites of historical interest and natural beauty.

**ALLAN, Dr Alasdair James;** Member (SNP) Na h-Eileanan an Iar, Scottish Parliament, since 2011 (Western Isles, 2007–11); *b* Edinburgh, 6 May 1971; *s* of late John H. Allan and of Christine M. Allan. *Educ:* Selkirk High Sch.; Glasgow Univ. (MA Scottish Lang. and Lit.); Aberdeen Univ. (PhD Scots Lang. 1998). Sen. Vice Pres., Students' Rep. Council, Glasgow Univ., 1991–92. Teaching asst, English Dept, Aberdeen Univ., 1995–97; researcher, SNP HQ, 1998–99; Parliamentary Assistant: to Michael Russell, MSP, 1999–2002; to Alex Salmond, MP, 2002–04; Policy and Parly Affairs Manager, Carers Scotland, 2004–05; Sen. Media Relns Officer, Ch of Scotland, 2005–06; Parly Asst to Angus MacNeil, MP, 2006–07. Minister for Learning and Skills, then Learning, Sci. and Scotland's Languages, 2011–16, for Internat. Develt and Europe, 2016–18, Scottish Parlt. Nat. Sec., SNP, 2003–06. Member, Cross-Party Group: Epilepsy; Malawi; Internat. Develt; Crofting; Convener, Cross-Party Gp on Gaelic. Vice-Pres., Scots Lang. Soc., 1996–99. *Publications:* Talking Independence, 2001. *Recreations:* campaigning for independence, cutting peat, singing in local Gaelic choir (Mem., Back Gaelic Choir, Isle of Lewis), learning Norwegian, hillwalking. *Address:* (office) 20 Kenneth Street, Stornoway, Isle of Lewis HS1 2DR. *T:* (01851) 700357. *E:* Alasdair.allan.msp@parliament.scot. *W:* www.alasdairallan.scot.

**ALLAN, Sir Alexander (Claud Stuart), (Sir Alex),** KCB 2012; Independent Adviser to Prime Minister on Ministers' Interests, since 2011; *b* 9 Feb. 1951; *s* of Lord Allan of Kilmahew, DSO, OBE and of Maureen (*née* Stuart Clark); *m* 1st, 1978, Katie Christine Clemson (*d* 2007); 2nd, 2012, Sarah Stacey. *Educ:* Harrow Sch.; Clare College, Cambridge; University College London (MSc). HM Customs and Excise, 1973–76; HM Treasury, 1976–92; secondments in Australia, 1983–84; Principal Private Sec. to Chancellor of the Exchequer, 1986–89; Under Sec. (Internat. Finance), 1989–90; Under Sec. (Gen. Expenditure Policy), 1990–92; Principal Private Sec. to PM, 1992–97; High Comr, Australia, 1997–99; UK Govt e-envoy, 1999–2000; Perm. Sec., DCA, subseq. MoJ, 2004–07; Chm., Jt Intelligence Cttee and Hd of Intelligence Assessment, Cabinet Office, 2007–11. Member: QC Selection Panel, 2013–; Adv. Council on Business Appts, 2015–. Mem., Premier's Science Council, WA, 2001–04. Mem., Senate, Univ. of WA, 2002–04. Mem., Royal S Beach Cycling Assoc., WA, 1983–. Trustee, Treloar Trust, 2010–. *Recreations:* Grateful Dead music, sailing, computers. *E:* alex@whitegum.com. *Club:* Royal Ocean Racing.

**ALLAN, (Christopher) David;** QC 1995; a Recorder, since 1993; a Deputy High Court Judge, since 2007; *b* 5 April 1952; *s* of Herbert Roy Allan and Joan (*née* Womersly); *m* 1977, Lynne Margaret Hosking; one *s* three *d*. *Educ:* Teignmouth Grammar Sch.; Manchester Univ. (LLB). Called to the Bar, Gray's Inn, 1974; Mem., Northern Circuit, 1975–. *Recreations:* tennis, theatre, walking.

**ALLAN, Christopher John;** HM Diplomatic Service; Ambassador to Uzbekistan, 2015–19; *b* Edinburgh, 18 Dec. 1975; *s* of John Richard Allan and Margaret Anne Allan; *m* 2004, Alice Mary Edith Hackett; two *d*. *Educ:* George Watson's Coll., Edinburgh; Pembroke Coll., Cambridge (BA Natural Scis and Social and Pol Scis 1996); London Sch. of Econs and Pol Sci. (MSc Envmt and Develt). Joined FCO, 2000; First Sec., Energy and Envmt, Tokyo, 2003–06; Hd, Nuclear and Missile Defence Team, FCO, 2007–08; Dep. Hd, 2009, Hd, 2009–10, S Asia Gp, FCO; Dep. Hd of Mission, Addis Ababa, 2011–14. *Recreations:* mountain walking, cycling, bridge, music. *Address:* c/o Foreign and Commonwealth Office, King Charles Street, SW1A 2AH.

**ALLAN, Prof. Cliff Charles;** Vice-Chancellor, Birmingham City University, 2012–17; *b* Tynemouth, 20 Feb. 1959; *s* of James and Irene Allan; *m* 1988, Alison Francis; one *s* one *d*. *Educ:* Allerton Grange High Sch., Leeds; Coventry Poly. (BA Hons Modern Studies 1981); Univ. of Birmingham (MA W African Studies 1982); Univ. of Bristol (MA Res. and Professional Studies in Educn 2007). Hd, Regl Activities (S), ActionAid, 1985–89; Sen. Prog. Officer, PCFC, 1989–93; Mgt Consultant, JM Consulting, 1993; Principal Policy Officer, 1993–96, Hd, Teaching and Learning, 1996–2000, HEFCE; Dir, Learning and Teaching Support Network, 2000–04; Dep. CEO, Higher Educn Acad., 2004–07; Deputy Vice-Chancellor: Teesside Univ., 2007–09; Sheffield Hallam Univ., 2010–12. FRSA. *Recreations:* swimming, cycling, walking, cinema, Leeds United. *E:* cliffcallan@gmail.com.

**ALLAN, David;** *see* Allan, C. D.

**ALLAN, Diana Rosemary, (Mrs R. B. Allan);** *see* Cotton, D. R.

**ALLAN, Douglas;** *see* Allan, J. D.

**ALLAN, Douglas George;** freelance wildlife and documentary cameraman, since 1984; Director, Tartan Dragon Ltd, since 2002; public speaker on marine conservation and climate change, since 2012; *b* Dunfermline, 17 July 1951; *s* of Morris and Betty Allan; *m* 1st, 1985, Elisabeth Smith (marr. diss. 2000); one *s*; 2nd, 2000, Sue Flood (marr. diss. 2011). *Educ:* Dunfermline High Sch.; Univ. of Stirling (BSc Hons Biol. 1973). Pearl diver, 1974; res. diver, 1974; dive instructor, 1975; diver, scientist, 1976–84, Base Comdr, 1983, British Antarctic Survey. Professional speaking engagements and theatre tours incl. Life Behind the Lens, In the Company of Giants, Wild Images Wild Life, 2012–. Fellow, NY Explorer's Club, 2007; Hon. FRPS 2012; Hon. FRSGS 2015; Hon. Fellow, Falmouth Univ., 2014. DUniv Stirling, 2007; Hon. DA Edinburgh Napier, 2009; Hon. DSc St Andrews, 2010. Cherry Kearton Photographic Award, RGS, 1993; BAFTA Awards for Cinematography: Life in the Freezer, 1993; Wildlife Special, 1997; The Blue Planet, 2002; Human Planet, 2011; Emmy Awards for Cinematography, 1994, 1995, 2002, 2007, 2010, 2012, 2014. Fuchs Medal, British Antarctic Survey, 1982; Polar Medal, 1983, and Bar, 2012; Scottish BAFTA for Outstanding Contribn to Craft (cinematography), 2017; Mungo Park Medal, RSGS, 2018. *Publications:* Freeze Frame: a wildlife cameraman's adventures on ice, 2012; articles in travel and adventure/expedition magazines. *Recreations:* travelling slowly, diving, cycling, occasional caving, reading, ocean conservation, meeting and talking with unknown people. *Address:* 13 Rockleaze Court, Rockleaze Avenue, Bristol BS9 1NN. *T:* 07876 032608; c/o Jo Sarsby Management, 154 Cheltenham Road, Bristol BS6 5RL. *T:* (0117) 927 9423. *E:* jo@josarsby.com. *W:* www.dougallan.com, www.twitter.com/dougallancamera.

**ALLAN, Fiona Jean Sutcliffe;** Artistic Director and Chief Executive, Birmingham Hippodrome, since 2015; *b* Sydney, 1967; *d* of Dr Graeme Allan and Roslyn Allan, AO. *Educ:* Abbotsleigh, Wahroongah; Univ. of Sydney (BMus Hons); Univ. of Technol., Sydney (MBA). Sen. Producer, Sydney Opera House, 1997–2001; Chief Exec., Sydney Film Fest., 2002–04; Artistic Dir, Wales Millennium Centre, 2004–11; Chief Exec., Curve Theatre, 2011–15. Chair, The Space, Birmingham, 2015–. Pres., UK Theatre, 2016–. *Recreations:* travel, equestrian sports. *Address:* Birmingham Hippodrome, Hurst Street, Birmingham B5 4TB. *T:* (0121) 689 3042. *E:* fionaallan@birminghamhippodrome.com. *Club:* Ivy.

**ALLAN, Gary James Graham;** QC (Scot.) 2007; *b* Aberdeen, 21 Jan. 1958; *s* of Stanley Gibson Allan and Margaret Harrison Allan (*née* Graham); *m* 1986, Margaret Muriel Glass; one *s* one *d*. *Educ:* Aberdeen Grammar Sch.; Univ. of Aberdeen (LLB Hons). Apprentice solicitor, McGrigor Donald and Co., Glasgow, 1980–82; Hughes Dowdall, Glasgow Solicitor, 1982–86; Partner, 1986–93; admitted Faculty of Advocates, 1994; in practice a Scottish Bar; Senior Advocate Depute (Crown Counsel), 2007–11. Appeal Chm., Judicial Panel, Scottish FA, 2011–18. *Recreations:* enjoying the outdoors, watching sport, music, theatre, cinema, reading, food and drink with friends, the pursuit of opportunities to do absolutely nothing. *Address:* Advocates Library, Parliament House, Edinburgh EH1 1RF. *T:* (0131) 226 5071. *E:* gary.allan@advocates.org.uk.

**ALLAN, George Alexander,** MA; Headmaster, Robert Gordon's College, Aberdeen, 1978–96; *b* 3 Feb. 1936; *s* of William Allan and Janet Peters (*née* Watt); *m* 1962, Anne Violet Veevers; two *s*. *Educ:* Daniel Stewart's Coll., Edinburgh; Edinburgh Univ. (MA 1st Cl. Hons Classics; Bruce of Grangehill Scholar, 1957). Classics Master, Glasgow Acad., 1958–60; Daniel Stewart's College: Classics Master, 1960–63; Head of Classics, 1963–73; Housemaster, 1966–73; Schoolmaster Fellow, Corpus Christi Coll., Cambridge, 1972; Dep. Headmaster, Robert Gordon's Coll., 1973–77. Headmasters' Conference: Sec., 1980–86, Chm., 1988, 1989, Scottish Div.; Mem. Cttee, 1982, 1983; Mem., ISIS Scotland Cttee, 1984–93; Council Mem., Scottish Council of Ind. Schs, 1988–96, 1997–2002. Dir, Edinburgh Acad., 1996–2003; Governor: Welbeck Coll., 1980–89; Longridge Towers Sch., 2004–08. Mem., Scottish Adv. Cttee, ICRF, 1996–97. *Recreations:* gardening, music. *Address:* Maxwiel, 5 Abbey View, Kelso TD5 8HX. *T:* (01573) 225128.

*See also* T. E. D. Allan.

**ALLAN, Prof. James Wilson,** DPhil; Professor of Eastern Art, University of Oxford, 1996–2012, now Emeritus; Fellow of St Cross College, Oxford, 1990–2005, now Emeritus; *b* 5 May 1945; *s* of John Bellerby Allan and Evelyn Mary Allan; *m* 1970, Jennifer Robin Hawksworth; two *s* two *d*. *Educ:* Marlborough Coll.; St Edmund Hall, Oxford (MA 1966; DPhil 1976). Ashmolean Museum: Asst Keeper, 1966–88, Sen. Asst Keeper, 1988–91, Keeper, 1991–2005, Eastern Art Dept; Dir, Ashmolean Inter-Faith Exhibitions Service, 2005–06. *Publications:* Medieval Middle Eastern Pottery, 1971; Persian Metal Technology 700–1300 AD, 1978; Islamic Metalwork: the Nuhad Es-Said Collection, 1982; Nishapur: metalwork of the early Islamic period, 1982; Metalwork of the Islamic World: the Aron Collection, 1986; (ed) Creswell: A Short Account of Early Muslim Architecture, 1989; (with B. Gilmour) Persian Steel: the Tanavoli Collection, 2000; The Art and Architecture of Twelver Shi'ism: Iraq, Iran and the Indian Sub-Continent, 2012. *Recreations:* music, ornithology, walking, travel.

**ALLAN, (John) Douglas,** OBE 2006; Sheriff of Lothian and Borders at Edinburgh, 2000–08; *b* 2 Oct. 1941; *s* of late Robert Taylor Allan and Christina Helen Blythe Reid or Allan; *m* 1966, Helen Elizabeth Jean Aiton or Allan; one *s* one *d*. *Educ:* George Watson's Coll.; Edinburgh Univ. (BL); Napier Coll., Edinburgh (DMS). Solicitor and Notary Public. Solicitor, 1963–67; Depute Procurator Fiscal, 1967–71; Sen. Legal Asst, Crown Office, 1971–76; Asst Procurator Fiscal, Glasgow, 1976–77; Sen. Asst Procurator Fiscal, Glasgow, 1978–79; Asst Solicitor, Crown Office, 1979–83; Regl Procurator Fiscal for Lothian and Borders and Procurator Fiscal for Edinburgh, 1983–88; Sheriff of South Strathclyde, Dumfries and Galloway at Lanark, 1988–2000. Bd Mem., Scottish Children's Reporter Admin, 1995–2003 (Dep. Chm., 2002–03); Mem., Judicial Appts Bd for Scotland, 2002–08. Chm., Judicial Commn, Gen. Assembly of C of S, 1998–2003 (Mem., 2009–). Pres., Sheriffs' Assoc., 2000–02 (Vice Pres., 1997–2000; Sec., 1991–97); Regl Vice-Pres., Commonwealth Magistrates' and Judges' Assoc., 2003–09 (Mem., Council, 2000–03, 2009–). Chm., Exec. Cttee, Scottish Council, 2009–13, Vice-Pres., SE Scotland Reg., 2014–, Scout Assoc. *Recreations:* youth work, church work, walking. *Address:* Minard, 80 Greenbank Crescent, Edinburgh EH10 5SW. *T:* (0131) 447 2593. *E:* jdouglasallan@lumison.co.uk.

**ALLAN, John Murray,** CBE 2005; Chairman: Barratt Developments, since 2014; Tesco plc, since 2015; *b* 20 Aug. 1948; *s* of Archibald John and Anna Allan; *m* 1st, 1970, Ewa Gaczol (marr. diss. 1998); two *d*; 2nd, 1999, Carole Thomas. *Educ:* Edinburgh Univ. (BSc Hons Mathematical Sci.). Brand Manager, Lever Bros, 1970–73; Mkting Manager, Bristol Myers, 1973–77; Fine Fare: Mkting Dir, 1977–83; Dir, 1980; Mkting and Buying Dir, 1983–84; Dir and Gen. Manager, 1984–85; BET: Divl Chm., 1985–87; Dir, 1987–94; Chief Exec., Ocean Gp, later Exel plc, 1994–2005; Chief Exec., DHL Logistics, 2006–07; Chief Financial Officer, Deutsche Post World Net, 2007–09 (Mem., Mgt Bd, 2006–09). Pres., CBI, 2018–July 2020 (Chm., Transport Policy Cttee, 1998–2001; Mem., President's Cttee, 2001–; Vice-Pres., 2017–18). Chm., Dixons Retail (formerly DSG internat.) plc, 2009–14; Co-Dep. Chm. and Sen. Ind. Dir, Dixons Carphone plc, 2014–15; Chairman: Care UK, 2010–13; Worldpay, 2011–15; London First, 2015–18; Council, Imperial Coll. London, 2019–; non-executive Director: Wolseley plc, 1999–2004; PHS plc, 2001–05; 3i, 2009–11; Royal Mail Gp, 2013–15. Chm., Freight Forwarders Europe, 2006–07 (Vice Chm., 2002–06). Chm., Mkting Soc. of GB, 1983–84. Mem., Internat. Adv. Cttee, Singapore Economic Develt Bd, 2002–07. Trustee, Univ. of Edinburgh Develt Trusts, 1991–2000; Mem., Univ. of Edinburgh Campaign Bd, 2000–. FInstD 1986 (Mem. Council, 1991–99); CCMI (CIMgt 1995). FRSA 1995. *Recreations:* reading, conversation, history. *Address:* Tesco plc, Tesco House, Shire Park, Kestrel Way, Welwyn Garden City AL7 1GA.

**ALLAN, Keith Rennie;** HM Diplomatic Service; High Commissioner, Mauritius, and Head, British Indian Ocean Network, since 2017; *b* 25 Aug. 1968; *m* 1996, Marja Harriette Medendorp; one *s* two *d*. *Educ:* Bannerman High Sch., Glasgow. MoD 1986–88; entered FCO, 1988; Botswana, 1990–93; worldwide floater duties, 1993–95; Counter Terrorism Policy Dept, FCO, 1996–97; Dep. Hd of Mission, Uzbekistan, 1997–2000; Hd, Central NW Eur. Dept, FCO, 2000–02; Consul, Kabul, 2002; Dep. Dir, Africa and ME, UK Trade and Investment, 2002–03; Dep. High Comr, Trinidad and Tobago, 2003–06; Consul Gen., Miami, 2006–09; Ambassador to Turkmenistan, 2010–13; Consul Gen., St Petersburg, 2013–17. *Address:* c/o Foreign and Commonwealth Office, King Charles Street, SW1A 2AH.

**ALLAN, Lucy;** MP (C) Telford, since 2015. *Educ:* Durham Univ. (BA Hons Anthropol. 1986); Kingston Univ. (LLM Employment Law 2006). CA 1992; Chartered Sec. Insolvency Manager, Price Waterhouse, 1987–94; Mercury Asset Mgt plc, 1994–95; De La Rue plc, 1995–97; Hd, Investment Trusts, Gartmore Investment, 1997–2001; Dir, Investment Trust Team, UBS Warburg, 2001–02; Hd, Investment Trusts, First State Investment, 2002–04; freelance employment law advr, Workplacelaw Ltd, 2004–. Non-exec. Dir, NHS Wandsworth, 2009–11. Mem. (C) Wandsworth LBC, 2006–12. Trustee, Wandsworth Women's Aid, 2007–09. *Address:* House of Commons, SW1A 0AA.

**ALLAN, Timothy Edward Douglas;** DL; President, Scottish Chambers of Commerce, since 2017 (Board Member, since 2016); *b* Edinburgh, 5 June 1966; *s* of George Alexander Allan, *qv*; *m* 1994, Kim Cowan; two *d*. *Educ:* Robert Gordon's Coll., Aberdeen; Univ. of St Andrews (MA Hist. 1988); Royal Mil. Acad. Sandhurst. RTR, British Army, 1988–98; Equerry to the Duke of York, 1996–98; Vice Pres., Citigroup Private Bank, 1998–2003; Dir, UBS Wealth Mgt, 2003–06; Owner, Unicorn Property Gp, 2006–. Non-exec. Dir, Motor Fuel Gp, 2011–. Pres., Dundee and Angus Chamber of Commerce, 2014–16. Dir, 2003–09, Chm., 2006–09, Young Enterprise Scotland; Member: Cttee, Big Lottery Fund, Scotland, 2007–14; Vice Chm., V&A Mus. of Design Campaign, 2011–18; Dir, V&A Mus. Dundee, 2018–. Mem. Ct, Univ. of St. Andrews, 2015–. Mem., Queen's Body Guard for Scotland, Royal Co. of Archers, 2015–. FRSA 2010. DL Clackmannanshire, 2017. Queen's Award for Enterprise Promotion, 2010. *Recreations:* field sports, theatre, wine, our farm. *Address:* Drumburn Farm, Muckhart, Clackmannanshire FK14 7JW. *E:* tallan@unicornpropertygroup.com. *Club:* Cavalry and Guards.

**ALLAN, Timothy Neil;** Managing Director, Portland, since 2001. *Educ:* Royal Grammar Sch., Guildford; Godalming Sixth Form Coll.; Pembroke Coll., Cambridge (BA 1992); INSEAD (MBA). Researcher to Tony Blair, MP, 1992–94; producer, A Week in Politics, 1994; Press Officer to Rt Hon. Tony Blair, MP, Leader of the Opposition, 1994–97; Dep. Press Sec., 10 Downing St, 1997–98; Dir, Corporate Communications, BSkyB plc, 1998–2000. *Recreations:* golf, ski-ing. *Address:* Portland, 85 Strand, WC2R 0DW. *T:* (020) 7554 1601. *E:* Tim.Allan@portland-communications.com. *Clubs:* Oxford & Cambridge, Soho House, 67 Pall Mall.

**ALLAN, Prof. Trevor Robert Seaward,** LLD; FBA 2016; Professor of Jurisprudence and Public Law, University of Cambridge, since 2003; Fellow, Pembroke College, Cambridge, since 1985; *b* Luton, 9 May 1955; *s* of Robert William Allan and Pamela Dorothy Allan. *Educ:* St Albans Sch.; Worcester Coll., Oxford (BA, BCL); LLD Cantab. Called to the Bar, Middle Temple, 1979. Lectr in Law, Univ. of Nottingham, 1980–85; University of Cambridge: Lectr, 1989–95; Reader in Legal and Constitl Theory, 1995–2003; British Acad./Leverhulme Trust Sen. Res. Fellow, 1991–92; Leverhulme Trust Maj. Res. Fellow, 2010–12. *Publications:* Law, Liberty and Justice: the legal foundations of British constitutionalism, 1993; Constitutional Justice: a liberal theory of the rule of law, 2001; The Sovereignty of Law: freedom, constitution and common law, 2013. *Recreations:* music (pianist), badminton, walking, cycling. *Address:* Pembroke College, Cambridge CB2 1RF. *E:* trsa2@cam.ac.uk.

**ALLAN, William Roderick Buchanan;** formerly Arts Consultant to United Technologies Corporation, working with Tate Gallery, National Portrait Gallery and National Maritime Museum; *b* 11 Sept. 1945; *s* of James Buchanan Allan and Mildred Pattenden; *m* 1973, Gillian Gail Colgan (*d* 2004); two *s*. *Educ:* Trinity Coll., Cambridge (MA Hons History, 1970). Joined staff of The Connoisseur, 1972, Editor 1976–80; Editorial Consultant to Omnific, 1980–83. Author of seven radio plays with nineteenth century historical themes. *Publications:* contrib. to several books dealing with British history; contrib. to History Today, The Connoisseur, and Antique Collector. *Recreations:* military history, cooking. *Address:* 52 Jamieson House, Edgar Road, Hounslow, Middlesex TW4 5QH.

**ALLARD, Christian;** Member (SNP), Aberdeen City Council, since 2017; Member (SNP) Scotland, European Parliament, since 2019; *b* Dijon, France, 31 March 1964; *s* of Maurice and Solange Allard; *m* Jacquelene Kerrigan (*d* 2000); three *d*. *Educ:* Lycée Montchapet, Dijon. With STEF-TFE (seafood haulage), 1982–93, Scottish Develt Manager, 1987–93; Seafood Export Manager, Charles & Caie (seafood export), 1994–2013. Mem. (SNP) Scotland NE, Scottish Parlt, May 2013–2016. *Recreations:* campaigning for an independent Scotland, family, swimming.

**ALLARDYCE, Samuel;** Manager, Everton Football Club, 2017–18; *b* Dudley, 19 Oct. 1954; *s* of late Robert Allardyce and Mary Agnes Maxwell Allardyce; *m* 1974, Lynne Ward; one *s* one *d*. *Educ:* Wren's Nest Comp. Sch., Dudley; St Helen's Coll. UEFA Pro Licence 2005. Football player for: Bolton Wanderers, 1969–80; Sunderland, 1980–81; Millwall, 1981–83; Tampa Bay Rowdies, 1983; Coventry City, 1983–84; Huddersfield Town, 1984–85; Bolton Wanderers, 1985–86; Preston North End, 1986–89; West Bromwich Albion, 1989–91; player and Manager, Limerick, 1991–92; Coach and Asst Manager, then Manager, Preston North End, 1992; Manager: Blackpool, 1994–96; Notts County, 1997–99; Bolton Wanderers, 1999–2007; Newcastle United, 2007–08; Blackburn Rovers, 2008–10; West Ham United, 2011–15; Sunderland FC, 2016; England Football Team, 2016; Crystal Palace FC, 2016–17. Mem. Cttee, League Managers Assoc., 1997–. Patron, Prince's Trust, 2004–. Hon. Dr Bolton, 2010. *Publications:* Big Sam: my autobiography, 2015. *Recreations:* golf, tennis, food and wine.

**ALLAS, Tera Pauliina,** CBE 2019; Senior Fellow, McKinsey Center for Government, since 2017 (Visiting Fellow, McKinsey Global Institute, 2015–17); *b* Finland, 1968; *m* 1992, Petri Allas; one *s* one *d*. *Educ:* Helsinki Univ. of Technol. (MSc Technol./Industrial Econs); INSEAD (MBA). Consultant, McKinsey & Co., Inc., 1992–2004; Chief Energy Economist, DTI, then BERR, later DECC, 2004–09; Dir, Transport Analysis and Econs, and Chief Economist, DfT, 2009–10; Dir Gen., Strategy, Analysis and Better Regulation (formerly Economics, Strategy and Better Regulation), and Dep. Hd, Govt Economic Service, 2011–13, Dir Gen., Strategic Advice, 2013–14, BIS. Mem., States of Jersey Fiscal Policy Panel, 2014–18. Member: Sci., Technol. and Innovation Adv. Bd, OECD, 2014–16; Evidence Cttee, ScaleUp Inst., 2016–; Comr, LSE Growth Commn, 2016–. Future Directors Participant, non-exec. Bd, Green Investment Bank, 2015–16; Mem., Governing Bd, Innovate UK, 2015–17. Gov., 2014–15, Trustee, 2015–, NIESR; Trustee, Productivity Gp/Be the Business, 2017–.

**ALLASON, Rupert William Simon;** European Editor, World Intelligence Review (formerly Intelligence Quarterly), since 1985; *b* 8 Nov. 1951; *s* of Lt-Col James Harry Allason, OBE and Nuala Elveen Allason; *m* 1st, 1979, Nicole Jane (marr. diss. 1996), *y d* of late M. L. Van Moppes; one *s* one *d*; 2nd, 2012, Nicola Loud. *Educ:* Grenoble Univ.; London Univ. (external). Special Constable, 1975–82. BBC TV, 1978–82. Contested (C): Kettering, 1979; Battersea, 1983. MP (C) Torbay, 1987–97; contested (C) same seat, 1997. *Publications:* The Branch: A History of the Metropolitan Police Special Branch 1883–1983, 1983; *as Nigel West:* non-fiction: Spy! (with Richard Deacon), 1980; MI5: British Security Service Operations 1909–45, 1981; A Matter of Trust: MI5 1945–72, 1982; MI6: British Secret Intelligence Service Operations 1909–45, 1983; Unreliable Witnesses: espionage myths of World War II, 1984; Garbo (with Juan Pujol), 1985; GCHQ: The Secret Wireless War, 1986; Molehunt; 1987; The Friends: Britain's post-war secret intelligence operations, 1988; Games of Intelligence, 1989; Seven Spies Who Changed the World, 1991; Secret War, 1992; The Illegals, 1993; (ed) Faber Book of Espionage, 1993; (ed) Faber Book of Treachery, 1995; The Secret War for the Falklands, 1997; Counterfeit Spies, 1998; (with Oleg Tsarev) The Crown Jewels: the British secrets at the heart of the KGB archives, 1998; (ed) British Security Co-ordination: the secret history of British Intelligence in the Americas 1940–1945, 1998; Venona: the greatest secret of the Cold War, 1999; The Third Secret, 2000; Mortal Crimes, 2004; (ed) The Guy Liddell Diaries, 2005; Mask, 2005; Historical Dictionary of British Intelligence, 2005; At Her Majesty's Secret Service, 2006; Historical Dictionary of International Intelligence, 2006; Historical Dictionary of Cold War Counterintelligence, 2007; Historical Dictionary of World War II Intelligence, 2008; (with Oleg Tsarev) TRIPLEX, 2009; Historical Dictionary of Naval Intelligence, 2010; (with Madoc Roberts) Snow: the double life of a WW II spy, 2011; Historical Dictionary of Signals Intelligence, 2012; (with I. C. Smith) Historical Dictionary of Chinese Intelligence, 2012; Historical Dictionary of World War I Intelligence, 2014; MI5 and the Great War, 2014; Double Cross in Cairo, 2015; Cold War Counterfeit Spies, 2016; Spycraft Secrets, 2016; Cold War Spymaster, 2018; Churchill's Spy Files, 2018; Codeword Overlord, 2019; fiction: The Blue List, 1989; Cuban Bluff, 1990; Murder in the Commons, 1992; Murder in the Lords, 1994. *Recreations:* sailing, ski-ing. *Clubs:* White's, Special Forces.

**ALLCOCK, Anthony,** OBE 2019 (MBE 1998); Chief Executive, Bowls England, since 2008; *b* Thurmaston, Leics, 11 June 1955; *s* of Ernest Stacey Allcock and Joan Winifred Allcock. *Educ:* Norwich City Coll. Teacher, Millfield Day Centre, Hinckley; Head Teacher; company and managing director. Bowls player: world outdoor champion, 1980, 1984, 1988; world outdoor singles champion, 1992, 1996; world indoor singles champion, 1986, 1987, 2002; world indoor pairs champion, 1986, 1987, 2002, 2003; England Bowls Captain, 1998–2002. Performance Dir, Bowls England, 1998–2002; Chief Exec., English Bowling Assoc., 2003–08. Hon. Fellow, Univ. of Gloucestershire, 2002. Hon. LLD Leicester, 2016. *Publications:* Improve Your Bowls, 1987; Step by Step Guide to Bowls, 1988; End to End, 1989; Bowl to Win, 1994. *Recreation:* dog show exhibitor and international judge. *Address:* Bowls England, Riverside House, Milverton Hill, Royal Leamington Spa, Warwickshire CV32 5HZ. *E:* tony@bowlsengland.com. *Clubs:* Kennel (Dir, 2015–); Cheltenham Bowling, Falcon (Painswick) Bowling.

**ALLCOCK, Stephen James;** QC 1993; *b* 29 Jan. 1952; *s* of James Allcock and Pamela Eve Allcock. *Educ:* Bristol Grammar Sch.; Jesus Coll., Cambridge (BA). Called to the Bar, Gray's Inn, 1975; private practice, 1977–99; with PricewaterhouseCoopers, 2001–04. *Recreations:* motor cars, business, stock market, piano.

**ALLDEN, Alison,** OBE 2016; Higher Education consultant and coach, since 2015; Chief Executive, Higher Education Statistics Agency, 2009–15; *b* 3 April 1954; *d* of late Michael Allden and Jean Allden (*née* Reynolds); *m* 1989, David McCutcheon (*d* 2004); one *s* one *d*; *m* 2018, Kevin Charles Gordon White, *qv. Educ:* Sch. of St Helen and St Katharine, Abingdon; Univ. of Bristol (BA Hons 1976); London Sch. of Econs (MSc Dist. 1988). MCIfA (MIFA 1985); MBCS 1988, FBCS 2007; MCLIP 1992. Archaeologist, DoE, 1977–82; Co. Archaeologist, Glos CC, 1982–85; Researcher: BM, 1985–89; Nat. Maritime Mus., 1989–91; Hd, IT, CCETSW, 1991–94; Computer Services Manager, Goldsmiths' Coll., Univ. of London, 1994–98; Dir, IT Services, Univ. of Warwick, 1998–2003; Dep. Registrar, Librarian and Dir of Inf. Services, Univ. of Bristol, 2003–09. Member: Res. Resources Bd, ESRC, 2002–05; JISC Bd, HEFC, 2005–12 (Mem., 1998–2011, Chm., 2005–11, JISC sub-cttees); Educn and Trng Forum, BCS, 2007–10; Bar Standards Bd, 2017–. Mem., Bd of Govs, Northumbria Univ., 2011–. Mem., Glos Co. History Trust, 2012–. Trustee and Governor: Sch. of St Helen and St Katharine, Abingdon, 2002–16; Badminton Sch., Bristol, 2009–17; Mem., Bd of Govs, Regent's Univ. London, 2015–. FRSA 2010. *Publications:* contrib. articles on archaeol., computing and mus. mgt to books and jls. *Recreations:* family, archaeology and culture, life-long learning.

**ALLEN OF KENSINGTON, Baron** *cr* 2013 (Life Peer), of Kensington in the Royal Borough of Kensington and Chelsea; **Charles Lamb Allen,** Kt 2012; CBE 2003; FCMA; Chairman: Global Media & Entertainment (formerly Global Radio Group), since 2007; 2 Sisters Food Group, since 2011; ISS A/S, since 2013; Advisory Chair, Moelis & Company, since 2015; *b* 4 Jan. 1957. *Educ:* Bell Coll., Hamilton. FCMA 1989. Accountant, British Steel, 1974–79; Dep. Audit Manager, Gallaghers plc, 1979–82; Dir, Management Services, Grandmet Internat. Services Ltd, 1982–85; Gp Man. Dir, Compass Vending, Grandmet Innovations Ltd, 1986–87; Man. Dir, Compass Gp Ltd, 1988–91; Chief Exec., Leisure Div., Granada Gp, 1991–92; Chief Exec., 1992–96, Chm., 1996–2006, Granada TV; Chief Exec., 1994–96, Chm., 1996–2006, LWT; Chief Exec., Granada Gp, 1996–2000; Exec. Chm., Granada Media, subseq. Granada plc, 2000–04; Chief Exec., ITV plc, 2004–06; Chief Advr to Home Office, 2006–08; Sen. Advr, Goldman Sachs Equity Partners, 2008–15. Chairman: Granada Leisure and Services, 1993–2000; Boxclever, 1994–2000; Tyne Tees TV, 1997–2006; Yorkshire TV, 1997–2006; Anglia TV, 2000–06; Meridian TV, 2000–06; ITV Digital, 2001–02; non-exec. Chm., 2009–10, Exec. Chm., 2010, Advr, 2010–, EMI Music; Dep. Chm., 1994–96, Chm., 1996–2000, GMTV; non-executive Director: Tesco plc, 2009–2010; Endemol, 2008–14; Virgin Media, 2008–13; Get AS, 2009–14. Dep. Chm., BITC, 1997–2007. Vice-Pres., RTS, 1996–2010. Chairman: British Commonwealth Games, 2000–02; Manchester 2002 Ltd, 2000–02; Vice-Chm., London 2012 Olympic Bid, 2004–05; Dir, London Organising Cttee of the Olympic Games, 2005–13. Chm., Creative Industries Adv. Gp, 1999–2002; Mem., Talent and Enterprise Taskforce Adv. Gp, 2006–. Chairman: Join In Trust Ltd, 2012–16; British Red Cross, 2013–14. Mem., Internat. Acad. of Television Arts and Scis, 1996. FRSA. Hon. DBA Manchester Metropolitan, 1999; Hon. DLitt Salford, 2002; Hon. DEcon Southampton Solent, 2006. *Recreations:* visual and performing arts, international travel, boating.

**ALLEN, Dame Anita Mildred,** DBE 2016; President, Court of Appeal of the Bahamas, 2010–17; *b* New Providence, Bahamas, 21 Dec. 1947; *d* of late Gerald E. Bethell and Gertrude Emily Bethell; *m* 1974, Hon. Alernon S. P. B. Allen; two *s* three *d. Educ:* Govt High Sch.; Univ. of W Indies; Coll. of Law. Called to the Bar, Gray's Inn, 1973; Asst Counsel, Counsel, Legal Draftsman, and Principal Legal Draftsman, Dept of Legal Affairs and Attorney Gen.'s Chambers, 1973–86; Associate Counsel, Paton, Toothe, Co. and Toothe Unwala & Co., 1986–89; Managing Partner, Allen, Allen & Co., 1989–96; Justice of Supreme Court, 1996–2005; Sen. Justice of Supreme Court, 2005–10. Pres., Bahamas Public Services Bd of Appeal, 2005–10; Mem., Judicial and Legal Services Commn, 2005–10. Ed., West Indian Law Reports, 2006–. *Recreations:* reading, cooking, gardening, music. *Address:* PO Box N 10250, Nassau, Bahamas. *T:* 3579481. *E:* aallen46@hotmail.com. *Club:* Zonta (Bahamas) (Founding Mem.).

**ALLEN, Anthony John,** CBE 1994; Chief Executive, and Clerk to Lieutenancy, Royal County of Berkshire, 1986–93; public sector consultant, 1996–2010; *b* 7 Oct. 1939; *s* of late Raymond Houghton Allen and Elsie Zillah Allen; *m* 1st, 1964, Suzanne Myfanwy Davies; two *s*; 2nd, 1987, Helen Leah Graney; two *s. Educ:* Battersea Grammar Sch.; Univ. of Exeter (LLB 1961). Admitted Solicitor, 1964. Asst Solicitor: Hendon Bor. Council, 1964–65; Barnet Bor. Council, 1965; Watford Bor. Council, 1966–68; Asst Town Clerk, Coventry CBC, 1968–71; Asst Chief Exec., Lewisham Bor. Council, 1971–72; Solicitor to the Council and Dep. Town Clerk, Southwark Bor. Council, 1972–76; Chief Exec., Hammersmith and Fulham Bor. Council, 1976–86; Chief Exec., NHBC, 1994–96. Lay Inspector of Constabulary, 1997–2001. Non-exec. Dir, BSI, 1992–95. Vice Pres. and Founder Dir, London Youth Games Ltd, 1979–2013 (Vice Chm., 2006–13). Chm., Working Party on Social and Psychol Aspects of Major Disasters (report published, 1990). CCMI (CIMgt 1992). Trustee, W Berks CAB, 2003–09 (Chm., 2005–09). Gov., Newbury Coll., 1997–2015 (Chm., 2003–11); Mem., Govs' Council, Assoc. of Colleges, 2008–13 (non-exec. Dir, 2006–08); non-exec. Dir, AoC Create (formerly Mgt Services), 2008–18. *Recreations:* golf, travel. *Address:* Woolton Hill, Hants RG20 9XE. *T:* 07971 924144.

**ALLEN, Benedict Colin;** author, adventurer, explorer and broadcaster; *b* 1 March 1960; *s* of late Colin Allen and Virginia Stafford; *m* 2007, Lenka Flidrova; one *s* two *d. Educ:* Bradfield Coll.; Univ. of E Anglia (BSc Hons). Television programmes: Raiders of the Lost Lake, 1995; Great Railway Journeys: Mombasa to the Mts of the Moon, 1996; The Skeleton Coast, 1997; Edge of Blue Heaven, 1998; The Bones of Col Fawcett, 1998; Last of the Medicine Men, 2000; Icedogs, 2002; Adventure for Boys: the Lost Worlds of Rider Haggard, 2006; Traveller's Century, 2008; Unbreakable, 2008; Expedition Africa, 2009; Birds of Paradise: the Ultimate Quest, 2017; radio: (with Hugh Thomson) Two Men and a Mule, 2015. Mem. Council and Trustee, RGS, 2010–13. Patron: Save the Rhino Trust, 2001–; Envmtl Justice Foundn, 2003–; Tony Trust, 2012–. *Publications:* Mad White Giant, 1985; Into the Crocodile Nest, 1987; Hunting the Gugu, 1989; The Proving Grounds, 1991; Through Jaguar Eyes, 1994; (jtly) More Great Railway Journeys, 1996; The Skeleton Coast, 1997; Edge of Blue Heaven, 1998; Last of the Medicine Men, 2000; Faber Book of Exploration, 2002; Into the Abyss, 2006. *Recreations:* writing diary, reading biographies at home, taking family into the wilds. *E:* info@benedictallen.com.

**ALLEN, Brian,** PhD; Chairman, Hazlitt Group, since 2012; *b* 3 Oct. 1952; *s* of Herbert and Mary Allen; *m* 1978, Katina Michael; two *s. Educ:* Univ. of East Anglia (BA 1974); Courtauld Inst. of Art, Univ. of London (MA 1975; PhD 1984). Research Asst, Witt Library, Courtauld Inst. of Art, 1975–76; Paul Mellon Centre for Studies in British Art: Asst Dir and Librarian, 1977–85, Dep. Dir of Studies, 1985–92; Dir of Studies, 1993–2012. Adjunct Prof. of History of Art, Yale Univ., 1993–2012; Vis. Prof. of History of Art, Birkbeck Coll., Univ. of London, 1999–2004. Hon. Sec. and Editor, 1977–85, Chm., 1996–2003, Walpole Soc.; Pres., Johnson Club, 1993–97. Member: Paintings and Sculpture Cttee, Victorian Soc., 1981–84; Bd of Studies in History of Art, Univ. of London, 1986–93; Adv. Cttee, Yale Center for British Art, 1993–2012; Bd, Assoc. of Research Insts in Art History, 1993–2003; Council, Attingham Trust for Study of Country Houses and Collections, 1995–2005; Adv. Council, Sotheby's Inst. of Art, 2002–; Adv. Cttee, Getty Res. Inst. Provenance Index, 2002–04; Council, Tate Britain, 2003–08; Internat. Adv. Bd, Ben Uri Gall., London Jewish Mus. of Art, 2003–; Adv. Council, NACF, 2004–12 (Mem. Exec. Cttee, 1998–2004; Chm., 2003–04); Appeal Cttee, Holburne Mus. of Art, Bath, 2005–12 (Trustee, 2000–03; Vice-Chm., Trustees, 2011–); Adv. Cttee, Chantrey Proj., Ashmolean Mus., Oxford, 2006–09; Kettle's Yard Appeal Gp, Univ. of Cambridge, 2009–12; Scientific Cttee, Hogarth, Reynolds, Turner: Pittura inglese verso la modernità, Fondazione Roma, Rome, 2011–14; Steering Cttee, Walpole Collection and Houghton Hall exhibn, 2011–13; Nat. Steering Gp, Wright of Derby Campaign, 2011–12; Appeals Cttee, Limnerslease Proj., Watts Gall., 2011–14; Acceptance in Lieu Panel, Arts Council England, 2012–; Adv. Panel, Nat. Heritage Meml Fund, 2012–; Exhibns and Prog. Cttee, Nat. Horse Racing Mus., Newmarket Heritage Centre, 2014–; Vetting Cttee, Eur. Fine Art Fair Maastricht, 2014–18; Res. Adv. Council, 2014–, Ethics Cttee, 2018–, NPG; Cttee, Masterpiece Awards, 2015. Lectures: Opening, Newport Symposium, Newport Histl Soc., USA, 1998; Meml, Christie's/Nat. Art Collections Fund, 2003; Spring, Scottish Nat. Art Collections Fund, 2004; 1st Paul Mellon, World Monuments Fund, 2004; 1st Lunar Soc., 2004. Trustee and Gov., Dr Johnson's House Trust, 1998–2012; Trustee: Foundling Mus., 1998–2007 (Vice Pres., 2010–); The Buildings Book Trust, 2002–11; Strawberry Hill Collection Trust, 2011–18; Hermitage Foundn UK, 2011– (Chm., 2013–); NPG, 2012–; British Sporting Art Trust, 2012–; Compton Verney Collections Settlement Trust, 2016–; Gov., Gainsborough's House Trust, 2000–05; Member Committee: Friends of Strawberry Hill, 2000–03; American Friends of the Strawberry Hill Trust, 2007–; Co. Sec., UK Friends, Yale Charitable Corp., 2003–12; Mem. Council, Academia Rossica, 2004–12. Chm., Judging Panel, Sunday Times/Singer and Friedlander Watercolour Competition, subseq. RWS and Sunday Times Watercolour Competition, 1997–2009; Judge, Garrick/Milne Prize, 2000. Chm., Works of Art Cttee, Garrick Club, 2005–13. Chm., Modern Art Press, 2007–12 (Mem., Adv. Cttee, 2017–). Mem., Editorial Adv. Panel, Apollo, 1990–2010; Associate Editor, Oxford DNB, 1997–2004; Member: Panel of Specialist Advrs, Architectural Heritage, 1998–2012; Internat. Adv. Bd, British Art Jl, 1999–2012; Adv. Bd, Visual Culture in Britain, 2000–10; Internat. Adv. Bd, Courtauld Inst. of Art Res. Forum, 2004–10; Editl Bd, English Heritage Histl Rev., 2006–; Advr to Editl Bd, Art and Architecture of Ireland, 2010–12. Hon. DLitt: Southampton Inst. (Nottingham Trent Univ.), 1999; Birmingham, 2006. *Publications:* Francis Hayman, 1987; (ed.) Towards a Modern Art World, 1995; (ed with L. Dukelskaya) British Art Treasures from Russian Imperial Collections in The Hermitage, 1996; The Paul Mellon Centre for Studies in British Art: a history 1970–2010, 2011; numerous articles in Apollo, Burlington Mag., Jl RSA, etc. *Recreations:* watching association football, opera. *Address:* Hazlitt Ltd, 38 Bury Street, SW1Y 6BB. *Club:* Garrick.

**ALLEN, David Charles Keith,** AO 1990; Chairman, Florey Neuroscience Institutes, 2007–12; *b* 3 April 1936; *s* of G. Keith Allen and Dorothy M. Allen; *m* 1st, 1964, Angela Mary Evatt (*d* 2001); two *s* one *d*; 2nd, 2002, Jocelyn Claire Searby. *Educ:* Oundle Sch.; Corpus Christi Coll., Cambridge (MA); Imperial Coll., London (MSc, DIC). Nat. Service, RE, Malaya, 1954–56. Joined Shell International, 1961: geophysicist, in Holland, NZ, Turkey and Nigeria, 1961–71; Chief Geophysicist, Shell Expro, London, 1971–74; Area Geologist, Shell Internat. Petroleum, The Hague, 1974–75; Western Division, Shell BP, Nigeria: Ops Manager, 1975–77; Divl Manager, 1977–79; Chm., Australian NW Shelf Liquid Natural Gas Project, 1980–95; Woodside Petroleum Ltd: Exec. Dir, 1980–82; Man. Dir, 1982–96; Chm., CSIRO, 1996–2001. Chm., National Australia Bank Ltd, 2001–04 (Dir, 1992–2004); Director: Metals Manufacturers Ltd, 1990–92; Amcor Ltd, 1996–2005; AGL, 1996–2008; Air Liquide (Aust.), 1997–2008 (Chm., 2005–08). Pres., Aust. Mines and Metals Assoc., 1989–91; Chm., Cambridge Australia Trust, 1996–2002; Director: Aust. Confedn of Commerce and Industry, 1989–91; Earthwatch Australia, 1994–2005. Hon. LLD: Monash, 1994; Melbourne, 2013. Reg Spriggs Gold Medal, 1996, Lewis G. Weeks Gold Medal, 2001, Australian Petroleum Prodn and Exploration Assoc. Centenary Medal (Australia), 2003. *Recreations:* golf, travel, fishing, music. *Clubs:* MCC; Grannies Cricket (UK); Australian, Melbourne, Metropolitan Golf (Melbourne).

**ALLEN, David James,** OBE 2012; Chair, Higher Education Funding Council for Wales, since 2014 (Board Member, since 2008); *b* Cardiff, 11 Feb. 1952; *s* of Aubrey and Joyce Allen; *m* 2008, Elaine Cotter; three *s* two *d. Educ:* Barry Comprehensive Sch.; University Coll. of Swansea (BA English 1973); University Coll., Cardiff (MEd 1986). Travel, casual and temp. work, 1973–74; Housing Asst, Vale of Glamorgan BC, 1974–76; Admin. Asst, Univ. of Wales Registry, 1976–80; Asst Registrar, Univ. of Wales Coll. of Medicine, 1980–86; Dep. Dir, Admin. Services, Univ. of Southampton, 1986–91; Sec., Jt Planning and Resources Cttee, Univ. of Wales, 1991–94; Registrar, Univ. of Nottingham, 1994–98; Registrar and Sec., Univ. of Birmingham, 1998–2003; Registrar and Dep. Chief Exec., Univ. of Exeter, 2003–13; Principal Consultant, Perrett Laver Exec. Recruitment, 2013–14. Chair: Assoc. of Univ. Administrators, 1998–2000; Assoc. of Heads of Univ. Admin, 2003–06; Member, Board: Leadership Foundn for Higher Educn, 2005–11; Heart of SW LEP, 2011–13. Non-exec. Dir, S Devon Healthcare, later Torbay and S Devon NHS Foundn Trust, 2011–17 (Vice Chair, 2014–17); Chair, Torbay Pharmaceuticals, 2017; Consulting Fellow and Sen. Advr, Halpin Partnership, 2017–. Gov., Exeter Coll., 2014– (Chair, 2017–). Hon. LLD Exeter, 2013. *Recreations:* supporting Exeter Chiefs Rugby team, boating, gardening, walking. *Address:* Higher Education Funding Council for Wales, Tŷ Afon, Bedwas Road, Bedwas, Caerphilly CF83 8WT. *T:* (029) 2068 2280. *E:* david.allen@hefcw.ac.uk. *Club:* Lansdowne.

**ALLEN, David Kenneth;** a Judge of the Upper Tribunal (Immigration and Asylum Chamber) (formerly a Vice-President, Immigration Appeal Tribunal, later a Senior Immigration Judge, Asylum and Immigration Tribunal), since 2000; Legal Member, Special Immigration Appeals Commission, since 2002; a Deputy High Court Judge, since 2016; *b* 23 Feb. 1950; *yr s* of late Philip Hernaman Allen and of Dorothy Allen (*née* Modral); *m* 1974, Joan Rosalind, *d* of late Rev. E. N. O. Gray and V. Gray; two *s* one *d. Educ:* Loughborough Grammar Sch.; Merton Coll., Oxford (BA Hons Juris; MA); McGill Univ., Montreal (LLM). Called to the Bar, Middle Temple, 1975; Lectr in Law, Inns of Court Sch. of Law, 1974–76; Department of Law, University of Leicester: Lectr, 1976–88; Sen. Lectr, 1988–99; Hd of Dept, 1993–96; Hon. Vis. Fellow, 1999–2005; in practice, Midland and Oxford Circuit, 1990–99. Immigration Adjudicator, 1989–2000 (pt-time, 1989–99). Vis. Prof., Dalhousie Univ., Halifax, NS, 1982–83. *Publications:* (jtly) Accident Compensation after Pearson, 1979; (jtly) Civil Liability for Defective Premises, 1982; (jtly) Fire, Safety and the Law, 1983, 2nd edn 1990; Misrepresentation, 1988; (jtly) Damages in Tort, 2000; essays; contrib. articles and notes in various jls. *Recreations:* golf, music. *Address:* Upper Tribunal (Immigration and Asylum Chamber), Field House, 15–25 Bream's Buildings, EC4A 1DZ.
*See also* P. R. H. Allen.

**ALLEN, David Paul;** Partner, PricewaterhouseCoopers LLP, since 2018 (Director 2016–18); *b* Bracknell, 1 Jan. 1979; *s* of John Allen and Linda Allen; *m* 2007, Nadia Mortali two *s. Educ:* Trinity Catholic High Sch. CIMA 2004. Joined NHS, 1999; Deputy Director of Finance: DWP, 2007–08; DFE, 2008–10; Dir, Finance and Shared Services, then Finance, BIS, 2010–14; Dir, Public Spending, HM Treasury, 2014–16. *Recreation:* hill walking. *Address:* PricewaterhouseCoopers LLP, 7 More London Riverside, SE1 2RT.

**ALLEN, Elizabeth Martin, (Mrs T. Bennett)**, CBE 2014; MA; Director of Secondary Education, Bright Futures Educational Trust, 2014–17; *b* 5 March 1946; *d* of Alfred (David) Trory and Alvena Trory (*née* Fisk); *m* 1st, 1967, Trevor Winston Allen (marr. diss. 1985); two *d*; 2nd, 1999, Terence Bennett; three step *s*. *Educ:* Whitelands Coll. of Educn (Cert Ed Divinity); Birkbeck Coll., Univ. of London (BA Hons English); Inst. of Educn, Univ. of London (MA Curriculum Studies). Hd of Religious Studies, Wallington High Sch. for Girls, 1969–73; 2nd i/c English Dept, St Bede's Ecumenical Sch., Redhill, 1981–84; Hd of English, Court Lodge Sch., Horley, 1984–88; Dep. Headteacher, Carshalton High Sch. for Girls, 1988–93; Headteacher: Altwood C of E Sch., Maidenhead, 1993–2001; Newstead Wood Sch. for Girls, 2001–13. FRSA 2000. *Recreations:* literature, the theatre, the garden, adding to the porcelain collection, the children and grandchildren.

**ALLEN, Franklin;** *see* Allen, H. F.

**ALLEN, Prof. Sir Geoffrey**, Kt 1979; PhD; FRS 1976; FREng; FRSC; FInstP; Executive Adviser, Kobe Steel Ltd, 1990–2000; Head of Research, Unilever PLC, 1981–90 (Director, Unilever PLC and NV, 1982–90); *b* 29 Oct. 1928; *s* of John James and Marjorie Allen; *m* 1973, Valerie Frances Duckworth; one *d*. *Educ:* Clay Cross Tupton Hall Grammar Sch.; Univ. of Leeds (BSc, PhD). FInstP 1972; FPRI 1974; FRSC 1984; Hon. FIMMM 2002 (FIM 1991); FREng (FEng 1993). Postdoctoral Fellow, Nat. Res. Council, Canada, 1952–54; Lectr, Univ. of Manchester, 1955–65, Prof. of Chemical Physics, 1965–75; Prof. of Polymer Science, 1975–76, Prof. of Chemical Technology, 1976–81, Imperial Coll. of Science and Technology (Fellow, 1986); Vis. Fellow, Robinson Coll., Cambridge, 1980–. Non-exec. Dir, Courtaulds, 1987–93. Member: Science Research Council, 1976, Chm., 1977–81; Royal Commn on Envmtl Pollution, 1991–99; Nat. Consumer Council, 1993–96; Council, Foundn for Sci. and Technol., 1995–2000; President: SCI, 1989–91; PRI, 1990–92; Inst. of Materials, 1994–95. A Vice-Pres., Royal Soc., 1991–93. Chancellor, UEA, 1994–2003. Fellow, St Catherine's Coll., Oxford, 1992. Hon. FUMIST 1993. Hon. FIChemE 1988; Hon. FCGI 1990; Hon. FIM 2002. Hon. MSc Manchester; DUniv Open, 1981; Hon. DSc: Durham, East Anglia, 1984; Bath, Bradford, Loughborough, 1985; Essex, Keele, Leeds, 1986; Cranfield, 1988; Surrey, 1989; Sheffield, 1993; London Metropolitan, 1998. Monbu Daijin Sho, Min. of Sci. and Educn, Japan, 2000. *Publications:* papers on chemical physics of polymers in Trans Faraday Soc., Polymer. *Recreations:* opera, walking, talking. *Address:* Flat 21, Battersea Place, 73 Albert Bridge Road, SW11 4DS.

**ALLEN, Graham James;** Director, Adults' Health and Care, Hampshire County Council, since 2016; *b* Truro, Cornwall, 5 Oct. 1966; *s* of Marcus James, (Jim), Allen and Marie Sarah Allen (*née* Hynes); *m* 1991, Gabrielle Cooper; one *s* one *d*. *Educ:* Richard Lander Sch., Truro; Truro Sixth Form; South Glamorgan Inst. of HE; Univ. of Bristol (DipSW 1994). Probation Officer, 1994–98, Probation Manager, 1998–2001, Cornwall Probation Service; Probation Manager, Devon and Cornwall Probation Service, 2001–03; Sen. Manager, 2003–07, Asst Dir, 2007–09, Hd of Ops, Adult Services, 2009–14, Cornwall CC, later Cornwall Council; Integrated Services Dir, Hampshire CC, 2015–16. *Recreations:* travel, family and friends, arts. *Address:* Hampshire County Council, Elizabeth II Court, Winchester, Hants SO23 8UQ. *T:* (01962) 847200. *E:* Graham.Allen@hants.gov.uk.

**ALLEN, Graham Leslie;** consultant to local authorities on arts, museum and cultural services; *b* 27 May 1949; *s* of William Leslie Allen and Doris Allen (*née* Fraser). *Educ:* Ladywood Comprehensive Sch., Birmingham. Joined Birmingham City Council, 1973; Assistant Director: Museums Services, 1994–99; Mgt Services, 1994–95; acting Head of Museums Services, 1995; Asst Dir (Museums and Arts), 1995–2001; Sen. Asst Dir (Museums and Heritage Projects), 2001–04. Associate: 4ps Consultancy; Invigour Consultancy. Trustee and Director: Thinktank, Birmingham Mus. of Sci. and Industry, 2004–12; Birmingham Mus Trust, 2011–; Trustee: Birmingham Mus Develt Bd, 2010–12; Millennium Point Birmingham, 2014–. Chm., Selly Park Residents' Assoc., 2007–10. *Recreations:* the arts, museums, hill walking, gardening, environmental issues. *Address:* 61 Sir Johns Road, Selly Park, Birmingham B29 7EP. *T:* (0121) 472 7953.

**ALLEN, Graham William;** *b* 11 Jan. 1953; *s* of William and Edna Allen. *Educ:* Robert Shaw Primary Sch.; Forest Fields Grammar Sch.; City of London Polytechnic; Leeds Univ. Warehouseman, Nottingham, 1971–72; Labour Party Res. Officer, 1978–83; Local Govt Officer, GLC, 1983–84; Trades Union National Co-ordinator, Political Fund Ballots Campaign, 1984–86; Regional Res. and Educn Officer, GMBATU, 1986–87. MP (Lab) Nottingham N, 1987–2017. Opposition front bench spokesman on social security, 1991–92, on democracy and the constitution, 1992–94, on the media, 1994, on transport, 1995, on environment, 1996–97; a Lord Comr of HM Treasury (Govt Whip), 1997–98; Vice Chamberlain of HM Household, 1998–2001. Member: Public Accounts Cttee, 1988–91; Procedure Cttee, 1989–91; 1990 Financial Bill Cttee. Chm., PLP Treasury Cttee, 1990–91. Chm., One Nottingham, 2005–10. *Publications:* Reinventing Democracy, 1995; The Last Prime Minister: being honest about the UK Presidency, 2002; (jtly) Early Intervention: good parents, great kids, better citizens, 2009. *Recreations:* cricket, golf, painting, cooking. *Clubs:* Strelley Social, Beechdale Community Centre, Bulwell Community Centre, Basford Hall Miners Welfare (Nottingham).

**ALLEN, Prof. (Harry) Franklin**, DPhil; FBA 2017; Professor of Finance and Economics, and Director (formerly Executive Director), Brevan Howard Centre, Imperial College London, since 2014; *b* Amersham, Bucks, 6 March 1956; *s* of Harry Cranbrook Allen and Mary Kathleen Allen; *m* 1st, Sally Riley (marr. diss. 2016); two *s*; 2nd, 2017, Agnieszka Wysokinska. *Educ:* Merchant Taylors' Sch.; Norwich City Coll.; Univ. of East Anglia (BA 1st Cl. Econs and Computing Studies 1977); Nuffield Coll., Oxford (MPhil 1979; DPhil 1980). Wharton School, University of Pennsylvania: Asst Prof. of Finance, 1980–86; Associate Prof. (with Tenure) of Finance and Econs, 1987–90; Prof. of Finance and Econs, 1990–94; Prof. of Econs and Nippon Life Prof. of Finance, 1994–2016, now Nippon Life Prof. Emeritus. *Publications:* with Douglas Gale: Financial Innovation and Risk Sharing, 1994; Comparing Financial Systems, 2000; Understanding Financial Crises, 2007. *Recreation:* travel. *Address:* Imperial College Business School, Tanaka Building, South Kensington Campus, SW7 2AZ. *T:* (020) 7594 9195, *Fax:* (020) 7596 9184. *E:* f.allen@imperial.ac.uk.

**ALLEN, Heidi Suzanne;** MP for South Cambridgeshire, since 2015 (C, 2015–19; Ind, since 2019); *b* Notton, Yorks; *m* Phil Allen. *Educ:* University Coll. London (BSc Hons Astrophysics 1996); London Business Sch. (Exxon Develt prog.); BPP London (DipLaw 2007). *Address:* House of Commons, SW1A 0AA.

**ALLEN, Dame Ingrid (Victoria), (Dame Ingrid Barnes Thompson)**, DBE 2001 (CBE 1993); DL; MD, FRCPath, FMedSci; MRIA; Director of Research and Development, Health and Personal Social Services, Northern Ireland, 1997–2001; Professor of Neuropathology, Queen's University of Belfast, 1979–97, now Emerita; *b* 30 July 1932; *d* of Rev. Robert Allen, MA, PhD, DD and Doris V. Allen (*née* Shaw); *m* 1st, 1972, Alan Watson Barnes, MA, ARIBA, Past Pres., RSUA (*d* 1987); 2nd, 1996, Prof. John Thompson (*d* 2010). *Educ:* Ashleigh House, Cheltenham Ladies' College; QUB. House Officer, Royal Victoria Hosp., Belfast, 1957–58; Musgrave Res. Fellow, Tutor in Path., Calvert Res. Fellow, QUB, 1958–64; Sen. Registrar, RVH, 1964–65; Sen. Lectr and Consultant in Neuropathol., QUB/RVH, 1966–78; Reader and Consultant, 1978–79; Head, NI Regional Neuropathol. Service, RVH, Belfast, 1979–97. Vis. Prof., Univ. of Ulster, 1988. Mem., MRC, 1989–92 (Chm., Neuroscis Bd, 1989–92); President: British Neuropathological Soc., 1993–95; Irish Neurological Assoc., 1993–; Vice-President: Internat. Soc. of Neuropathol., 1988–92; RCPath, 1993–96 (Mem. Council and Coll. Cttees, 1990–97). MRIA 1993 (Fellow, 1993). Founder FMedSci 1998. DL Belfast 1989. Mem. editl bds of various scientific jls. *Publications:* (contrib.) Greenfield's Neuropathology, 1984; (contrib.) McAlpine's Multiple Sclerosis, 1990; contribs to jls on neuropathology, demyelinating diseases, neurovirology and neuro-oncology. *Recreations:* doing research on molecular virology and demyelinating diseases, church activities, reading, playing the piano (badly), idling on an island in Donegal. *Address:* 95 Malone Road, Belfast BT9 6SP. *T:* (028) 9066 6662.

**ALLEN, Irene Mary Carmel;** *see* Tracey, I. M. C.

**ALLEN, Janet Rosemary;** Headmistress of Benenden School, Kent, 1976–85; *b* 11 April 1936; *d* of John Algernon Allen and Edna Mary Allen (*née* Orton). *Educ:* Cheltenham Ladies' Coll.; University Coll., Leicester; Hughes Hall, Cambridge. BA London 1958; CertEd Cambridge 1959. Asst Mistress, Howell's Sch., Denbigh, North Wales, 1959: Head of History Dept, 1961; in charge of First Year Sixth Form, 1968; Housemistress, 1968 and 1973–75. Acting Headmistress: Sch. of St Mary and St Anne, Abbots Bromley, Sept.–Dec. 1988; Selwyn Sch., Gloucester, 1989–90. Member: E-SU Scholarship Selection Panel, 1977–85; South East ISIS Cttee, 1978–84; Boarding Schs Assoc. Cttee, 1980–83; GSA Educnl sub-cttee, 1983–85; Gloucester Diocesan Bd of Educn, 1992–97; Mem., Winchcombe Ministry Leadership Team, 1997–2010. Vice-Pres., Women's Career Foundn (formerly Girls of the Realm Guild), 1981–90. Governor: St Catherine's Sch., Bramley, 1986–91; The King's Sch., Worcester, 1996–2008. *Recreations:* music, theatre, pottery, helping to preserve national heritage. *Address:* Bourne Rise, Queen's Square, Winchcombe, Cheltenham, Glos GL54 5LR.

**ALLEN, Prof. John Anthony**, PhD, DSc; FRSB; FRSE; Professor of Marine Biology, University of London, and Director, University Marine Biological Station, Millport, Isle of Cumbrae, 1976–91, now Professor Emeritus; Hon. Research Fellow, University Marine Biological Station, 1991–2013; *b* 27 May 1926; *s* of George Leonard John Allen and Dorothy Mary Allen; *m* 1st, 1952, Marion Ferguson Crow (marr. diss. 1983); one *s* one *d*; 2nd, 1983, Margaret Porteous Aitken; one adopted step *s*. *Educ:* High Pavement Sch., Nottingham; London Univ. (PhD, DSc). FRSB (FIBiol 1969); FRSE 1968 (Mem. Council, 1970–73). Served in Sherwood Foresters, 1945–46, and RAMC, 1946–48. Asst Lectr, Univ. of Glasgow, 1951–54; John Murray Student, Royal Soc., 1952–54; Lectr/Sen. Lectr in Zool., then Reader in Marine Biol., Univ. of Newcastle upon Tyne, 1954–76. Post Doctoral Fellow and Guest Investigator, Woods Hole Oceanographic Instn, USA, 1965–2005; Vis. Prof., Univ. of Washington, 1968, 1970, 1971; Royal Soc. Vis. Prof., Univ. of West Indies, 1976. Member: NERC, 1977–83 (Chm., Univ. Affairs Cttee, 1978–83); Council, Scottish Marine Biol Assoc., 1977–83; Council, Marine Biol Assoc. UK, 1981–83, 1990–93; Life Sciences Bd, CNAA, 1981–84; Nature Conservancy Council, 1982–90 (Chm., Adv. Cttee Sci., 1984–90); British Nat. Cttee for Oceanic Res., 1988–90. Pres., Malacological Soc. of London, 1982–84. *Publications:* many papers on decapod crustacea and molluscs, and deep sea benthos, in learned jls. *Recreations:* travel, appreciation of gardens, pub-lunching. *Address:* Drialstone, Millport, Isle of Cumbrae, Scotland KA28 0EP. *T:* (01475) 530479.

**ALLEN, Prof. John Robert Lawrence**, DSc; FRS 1979; Research Professor, Postgraduate Research Institute for Sedimentology, University of Reading, 1993–2001 (Director, 1988–93), Professor Emeritus and Visiting Professor, Department of Archaeology, since 2001; *b* 25 Oct. 1932; *s* of George Eustace Allen and Alice Josephine (*née* Formby); *m* 1959, Jean Mary (*née* Wood); four *s* one *d*. *Educ:* St Philip's Grammar Sch., Birmingham; Univ. of Sheffield (BSc; DSc 1972). Academic career in University of Reading, 1959–, Prof. of Geology, then of Sedimentology, 1972. Mem., NERC, 1992–94. FGS 1905; FSA 1991. Assoc. Mem., Royal Belgian Acad. of Scis, 1991. Hon. LLD Sheffield, 1994; Hon. DSc Reading, 2010. Lyell Medal, Geol Soc., 1980; David Linton Award, British Geomorphological Research Group, 1983; Twenhofel Medal, Soc. of Economic Paleontologists and Mineralogists, 1987; G. K. Warren Prize, Nat. Acad. of Scis, USA, 1990; Sorby Medal, Internat. Assoc. of Sedimentologists, 1994; Penrose Medal, Geol Soc. of Amer., 1996. *Publications:* Current Ripples, 1968; Physical Processes of Sedimentation, 1970; Sedimentary Structures, 1982; Principles of Physical Sedimentology, 1985; Geology for Archaeologists, 2017; numerous contribs to professional jls; several archaeol books on bldgs, monuments and bldg materials. *Recreations:* cooking, music, opera, pottery. *Address:* 17c Whiteknights Road, Reading RG6 7BY. *T:* (0118) 926 4621.

**ALLEN, Jonathan Guy;** HM Diplomatic Service; Ambassador and Deputy Permanent Representative to the United Nations in New York, since 2017; *b* Nottingham, 5 March 1974; *s* of late Jeremy Allen and of Maggie Allen; *m* 2010, Elizabeth Sleeman; one *s* one *d*. *Educ:* Nottingham High Sch.; St Catharine's Coll., Cambridge (BA 1996; MPhil 1997). Joined FCO, 1997; Second Sec. (Press/Pol), Cyprus, 1999–2002; Hd, Cyprus Section, FCO, 2002–03; Spokesman, UK Perm. Repn to the EU, Brussels, 2003–06; Asst Dir, Internat. Directorate, Home Office, 2006–07; Hd, Res., Inf. and Communications Unit, Office for Security and Counter-Terrorism, 2007–09; Hd, Africa Dept (E Africa, Great Lakes and Strategy), FCO, 2009–11; Ambassador to Bulgaria, 2012–15; Nat. Security Dir, FCO, 2015–17. *Recreations:* reading, theatre, walking, flying, travelling, Nottingham Forest, Strollers Cricket Club, Yacht Fund, eating and drinking well. *Address:* c/o Foreign and Commonwealth Office, King Charles Street, SW1A 2AH.

**ALLEN, Jonathan Guy H.;** *see* Holl-Allen, J. G.

**ALLEN, Joyce;** *see* Moseley, J.

**ALLEN, Katherine, (Kate);** Director, Amnesty International UK, since 2000; *b* 25 Jan. 1955; *d* of William and Patricia Allen (*née* Middleton). *Educ:* Brasenose Coll., Oxford (BA Hons PPE; Hon. Fellow, 2006). Policy Officer, GLC, 1977–79; Scientific Officer, SSRC, 1979–80; Policy Officer, Haringey LBC, 1980–81; Sen. Policy Officer (Social Services), ACC, 1981–87; Dep. Chief Exec., Refugee Council, 1987–99.

**ALLEN, Kay**, OBE 2011; consultant on diversity and inclusion; coach; Director, Diverse Advice Ltd consultancy, since 2003; Founding Director: Trading for Good, since 2011; Really Useful Stuff, since 2012; *b* 31 Jan. 1964; *d* of Frank Garside Allen and Gladys Allen. *Educ:* Oldham Coll.; Huddersfield Univ. (BA Hons Business Studies 1989). CIPD 1991, MCIPD 1994, FCIPD. Personnel Manager, Shorrock Security, 1986–90; Dir of Human Resources, Royal Philharmonic Orch., 1990–95; Head of Diversity, B&Q, 1995–2000; Consultant, Grass Roots Gp, 2000–02; Head of Diversity, BSkyB, 2002–07; Gp Hd of Social Policy and Inclusion, 2007–10, Special Advr on Social Action, 2010–11, Royal Mail Gp. Commissioner: Disability Rights Commn, 2000–03; Commn for Equality and Human Rights, 2007–09. Mem., Prime Minister's Council on Social Action, 2007–09; non-exec. Dir, Pension, Disability and Carers Bd, DWP, 2010–11. Dir, Every Business Commits, Prime Minister's Office, 2011–13. Member: Bd of Advrs, Helen Hamlyn Centre, 2004–; Ofcom Customer Communication Panel. Mem., Editl Bd, Equal Opportunities Rev.,

2003–. Chm., Tollard Royal Parish Council, 2014–. FRSA 2011. Lord Dahrendorf Award for Responsible Capitalism, First Mag., 2014. *Publications*: (jtly) Equality and Diversity, 2001; Corporates are from Mars, Charities are from Venus, 2012. *Recreations*: passionate about Arabian horses (owner of two Arabian stallions), country pursuits. *Address*: Salisbury, Wilts. *T*: (01725) 553099. *E*: kay.allen@diverseadvice.com. *Club*: Royal Over-Seas League.

**ALLEN, Kenton Paul Benbow;** Chief Executive, Big Talk Productions, since 2008; *b* Birmingham, 16 June 1965; *s* of Benbow Robert Sydney Allen and Pauline Allen; *m* 1999, Imogen Edwards-Jones; two *s* one *d*. *Educ*: Grange Comprehensive Sch., Stourbridge; King Edward's Sixth Form, Stourbridge. Producer: BBC Radio 4, 1990–94; BBC Radio 1, 1994–98; The Royle Family, 1998–2000; Creative Dir, Shine, 2000–02; Hd of Comedy, BBC, 2002–08. Producer, Six Shooter, 2005 (Academy Award for Best Short Film, 2006). *Recreations*: sailing, looking at boats, sitting on a hill in Ibiza, gazing into space, child taming. *Address*: Big Talk Productions, 26 Nassau Street, W1W 7AQ; Finca 15, St Joan, Ibiza. *E*: kenton@bigtalkproductions.com. *Clubs*: Royal Automobile, Groucho, Soho House, Bath & Racquets.

**ALLEN, Sir Mark (John Spurgeon),** Kt 2005; CMG 2002; HM Diplomatic Service, retired; Special Adviser to BP Group, since 2004; *b* 3 July 1950; *s* of Peter Muir Spurgeon Allen and Heather Anne Allen (*née* Roney); *m* 1976, Margaret Mary Watson; one *s* one *d*. *Educ*: Dragon Sch.; Downside; Exeter Coll., Oxford (MA). Entered FCO, 1973; MECAS, 1974; Third Secretary: Abu Dhabi, 1975–77; FCO, 1977–78; Second, later First, Sec., Cairo, 1978–81; First Secretary: Belgrade, 1982–86; FCO, 1986–90; Counsellor: Amman, 1990–94; FCO, 1994–2004. Senior Adviser: Monitor Gp, 2006–11; Palantir Technologies, Palo Alto, 2006–; Mem., Adv. Bd, Millennium Finance Corp., Private Equity Energy Fund, 2008–10. Sen. Associate Mem., St Antony's Coll., Oxford, 2004–10 (Hon. Fellow, 2010). Member: Adv. Council, London ME Inst., 2005–09; IDEAS Centre, LSE, 2008–14. Trustee, St John and St Elizabeth Hosp., 2008– (Chm., 2019–). KCSG 2009. Hon. Medal, Pres. of Republic of Bulgaria, 2011. *Publications*: Falconry in Arabia, 1980; (with Ruth Burrows) Letters on Prayer, 1999; First Holy Communion, 2002; Arabs, 2006; (ed) Sacred Script: Muhaqqaq in Islamic calligraphy, 2014. *Recreations*: falconry, Islamic calligraphy (traditional qualification (ijaza) in Arabic calligraphy (Muhaqqaq) from Nassar Mansour and Hasan Çelebi, 2010; exhibited Nat. Calligraphy Mus., Sharjah, 2018). *E*: Muhaqqaq@gmail.com. *Clubs*: Travellers, Beefsteak, Grillions; Leander.

**ALLEN, Mary Fitzgerald;** executive coach and mentor; *d* of Dr Fergus Hamilton Allen, CB and of Joan Allen; *m* 1st, 1980, Robin George Woodhead, *qv* (marr. diss. 1990); 2nd, 1991, Nigel Pantling (marr. diss. 2004). *Educ*: School of St Helen and St Katharine; New Hall, Cambridge; UEA (MA Creative Writing 2002). Actress, West End and repertory, 1973–76; Agent, London Management, 1977–78; Arts, Sponsorship Manager, Mobil Oil Co., 1978–81; Assoc. for Business Sponsorship of the Arts, 1982–83; arts management consultant, 1983–90; Director: Cheek by Jowl Theatre Co., 1989–93; Watermans Arts Centre, 1990–92; Dep. Sec.-Gen., Arts Council of GB, 1992–94; Sec.-Gen., Arts Council of England, 1994–97; Chief Exec., Royal Opera House, Covent Garden, 1997–98. Mem., Brighton and Hove Arts and Creative Industries Commn, 2013–. Chairman: High Tide Fest., 2008–12; Wonderful Beast, 2009–11; New Writing South, 2013–; Director: City of London Fest., 2003–06; Zap Art, 2013–; Brighton Fringe, 2014–; Phoenix Gall., 2015–. Public Art Develt Trust: Trustee, 1983–92; Chm., 1987–92. Chm., Breast Cancer Campaign, 2002–06. *Publications*: Sponsoring the Arts: new business strategies for the 1990s, 1990; A House Divided, 1998. *Recreations*: opera, theatre, collecting contemporary art, gardening, playing the spoons, astronomy, poetry.

**ALLEN, Michael David Prior,** FRICS; FCIArb; QC 2008; a Recorder, since 2005; *b* Liverpool, 24 March 1963; *s* of late Terence Roy Allen and of Margaret Prior Allen; *m* 1995, Lorraine Brown; one *s* one *d*. *Educ*: BSc Building Econs; LLB; King's Coll. London (LLM; MA). ARICS 1987, FRICS 1992; FCIArb 2006. Called to the Bar, Gray's Inn, 1990; in practice at the Bar, 1990–. *Publications*: Company Law and the Human Rights Act, 2000. *Recreations*: playing and teaching squash, ski-ing, cheering the children on in their sports. *Address*: 7 King's Bench Walk, Temple, EC4Y 7DS. *T*: (020) 7583 0404, *Fax*: (020) 7583 0950. *E*: dallen@7kbw.co.uk.

**ALLEN, Prof. Myles Robert,** DPhil; FInstP; Professor of Geosystem Science, School of Geography and the Environment and Head, Climate Dynamics Group, Department of Physics, University of Oxford, since 2011; Fellow, Linacre College, Oxford; *b* Farnham, 11 Aug. 1965; *s* of Hubert Allen and Phoebe Allen; *m* 1994, Prof. Irene Mary Carmel Tracey, *qv*; two *s* one *d*. *Educ*: British Sch. in the Netherlands; St John's Coll., Oxford (MA Phys and Philos. 1987; DPhil 1992). Tech. Manager, Bellerive Foundn, 1987–89; Consultant, UN Envmt Prog., 1989; Research Fellow, Rutherford Appleton Lab., 1993–94 and 1996–2001; Nat. Oceanic and Atmospheric Admin Postdoctoral Res. Fellow, MIT, 1994–95; Univ. Lectr, Dept of Phys, Univ. of Oxford, 2001–11. FInstP 2010. Appleton Medal, Inst. of Phys, 2010. *Publications*: contrib. and review ed. of chapters in Intergovtl Panel on Climate Change reports. *Recreations*: being a father, husband, son. *Address*: School of Geography and the Environment, University of Oxford, South Parks Road, Oxford OX1 3QY. *T*: (01865) 275848. *E*: myles.allen@ouce.ox.ac.uk.

**ALLEN, Nicholas Paul Thomas;** QC 2018; a Recorder, since 2015; *b* Leeds, 14 Sept. 1972; *s* of Edmund Allen and late Stephanie Allen; *m* 2013, Alexander Thomas. *Educ*: Leeds Grammar Sch.; Emmanuel Coll., Cambridge (BA 1993; LLM 1994). Called to the Bar, Middle Temple, 1995; admitted NY Bar, 1998; in practice as a barrister, specialising in matrimonial finance, 29 Bedford Row, 1997–. Arbitrator, Inst. of Family Law Arbitrators, 2016. Vis. Scholar, Harvard Law Sch., 1995–96. Chm., Emmanuel Coll., Cambridge Alumni Soc., 2013–. *Recreations*: theatre, cricket, gym. *Address*: 29 Bedford Row Chambers, WC1R 4HE. *T*: (020) 7404 1044. *E*: nallen@29br.co.uk. *Club*: Ivy.

**ALLEN, Sir Patrick (Linton),** ON 2009; GCMG 2009; CD 2006; Governor-General of Jamaica, since 2009; *b* Fruitful Vale, Portland, Jamaica, 7 Feb. 1951; *s* of Ferdinand Linton Allen and Christiana Eugenia Allen; *m* 1975, Patricia Denise; two *s* one *d*. *Educ*: Moneague Coll. (DipEd); Andrews Univ. (BA Hist. and Religion 1985; MA Systematic Theol. 1986; PhD Educnl Admin and Supervision 1998). Teacher, Water Valley All-age Sch., 1972–76; Principal: Robin's Bay All-age Sch., 1976–79; Hillside Primary Sch., 1979–81; Port Maria High Sch., 1981–83; Dir, Educn and Communication, Central Jamaica Conf. (Reg.), 1986–89 (Pres., 1998–2000); Dir, Educn and Family Life, WI Union Conf. of Seventh Day Adventists, 1990–93 (Pres., 2000–09); Asst Registrar, Andrews Univ., 1996–98. Chairman: Northern Caribbean Univ., 2000–09; Andrews Meml Hosp., 2000–09; Adventist Develt and Relief Agency, 2000–09; Book and Nutrition Centre, 2004–08. Vice-Chm., Bible Soc. of WI, 2006–09. Hon. Dr Public Service N Caribbean Univ., 2009; Hon. DLaws Andrews, 2010; Hon. Dr Oakwood, 2010. KStJ 2013. *Recreations*: avid sports fan, enjoys badminton, track and field, basketball and cricket. *Address*: Office of the Governor-General, King's House, Kingston 6, Jamaica, West Indies. *T*: 9276424, ext. 2030, *Fax*: 9786025. *E*: kingshouse@kingshouse.gov.jm. *Clubs*: Kiwanis (Kingston, Jamaica), Rotary, Lions.

**ALLEN, Hon. Sir Peter (Austin Philip Jermyn),** Kt 1987; High Court Judge, Lesotho, 1987–89; *b* 20 Oct. 1929; *yr s* of late Donovan Jermyn Allen and Edith Jane Bates. *Educ*: Headlands School, Swindon; LLB London. Army service, 1947–55, Lieut RA, 1952–55. HM Overseas Police Service, Asst Supt Uganda Police, 1955–62; ADC to Governor of Uganda, 1957; called to the Bar, Gray's Inn, 1964; Lectr, 1962–64, Principal, 1964–70, Uganda Law School; Judicial Adviser, Buganda Kingdom, 1964; Advocate, High Court of Uganda, 1965; Chief Magistrate, Uganda, 1970–73; Judge, Uganda High Court, 1973–85; Chief Justice (Head of Uganda Judiciary, Chm., Judicial Service Commn), 1985–86. Member: Uganda Law Reform Commn, 1964–68; Foundn Cttee, Uganda YMCA, 1959; Dir, Mbarara Branch, YMCA, 1970–73; Chairman: Presidential Commn of Inquiry into Kampala City Council, 1971; Judicial Review of Caribbean Dependent Territories (Allen Report for FCO), 1990; Commn of Inquiry into Grand Cayman New Hospital Contracts, 1993; Mem., Cayman Islands Anti-Corruption Commn, 2010–15. Mem., Uganda Law Soc., 1964–70. Uganda Independence Medal, 1962. *Publications*: An Introduction to the Law of Uganda (co-author), 1968; Days of Judgment, 1987; Interesting Times—Uganda Diaries 1955–1986, 2000; Inspector Beadle's Progress (fiction), 2007. *Address*: PO Box 38, Savannah, Grand Cayman KY1–1501, Cayman Islands, British West Indies.

**ALLEN, Peter William,** FCA; Managing Partner, 1984–90, Deputy Chairman, 1990–94, Coopers & Lybrand; *b* 22 July 1938; *s* of late Alfred William Allen, Sittingbourne, Kent, and Myra Nora (*née* Rogers); *m* 1965, Patricia Mary, *d* of late Joseph Frederick Dunk, FCA, Sheffield; three *d*. *Educ*: Borden Grammar Sch.; Cambridge Univ. (MA). Served RAF, 1957–59. Joined Coopers & Lybrand, 1963; qualified CA, 1966; Partner, 1973; Chm., Internat. Personnel Cttee, 1975–78; Partner in Charge, London Office, 1983; Member: UK Bd, 1984–94; Internat. Exec. Cttee, 1988–90, 1992–94. Non-executive Director: Charter, 1994–2001; Schroder Ventures, 1994–2015; Bd Mem., Post Office, 1995–98. Mem. and Hon. Treas., Governing Bd, Lister Inst. of Preventive Medicine, 1998–2005; Bd Mem., BRCS, 1999–2000. CCMI (CIMgt 1993). Freeman, City of London, 1988; Liveryman, Co. of Glaziers and Painters of Glass, 1989–2003. *Recreations*: golf, painting. *Address*: Fordham House, Abbotsbrook, Bourne End, Bucks SL8 5QS. *Club*: Reform.

**ALLEN, (Philip) Richard (Hernaman),** CB 2006; independent management and change consultant, since 2005; author and composer; *b* 26 Jan. 1949; *s* of late Philip Hernaman Allen and Dorothy Allen (*née* Modral); *m* 1970, Vanessa (*née* Lampard); two *d*. *Educ*: Loughborough Grammar Sch.; Merton Coll., Oxford (BA (Hons) Mod. History). Asst Principal, HM Customs and Excise, 1970; Assistant Private Secretary: to Paymaster Gen., 1973; to Chancellor of the Duchy of Lancaster, 1974; HM Customs and Excise: Principal, 1975; Asst Sec., 1984; Comr of Customs and Excise, 1990; Director: Internal Taxes, 1990; Orgn, 1991; Dir, Policy, DSS, 1994; HM Customs and Excise: Comr, 1997–2001; Director: Ops (Compliance), 1997–98; Personnel and Finance, 1998–2000; Human Resources, 2000–01; Prin. Estabs Officer and Dir Reorgn Project, 2001; Dir, Corporate Services, DEFRA, 2001–05. FRSA. *Publications*: The Waterguard, 2012; The Summer of Love, 2013; Through Fire, 2014; Bankers' Draught, 2014; A Well-respected Man, 2015; Nothing was Delivered, 2015; Something in the Air, 2015; Along the Watchtower, 2015; Murder at the Baltic Coast Hotel, 2015; By Water, 2016; Heard it on the Grapevine, 2016; Brussels Sprout, 2016; Our Friends in the South, 2016; Out of Sight, 2017; Fools' Copper, 2017; Kisses Sweeter Than Wine, 2017; Copper Kettle, 2017; Magic Clarinet, 2017; On a Carousel, 2018; The Ballad of a Thin Man, 2018; The Corridors of Secrecy, 2018; Old Ghosts, 2018; Medicine Man, 2018; Eight Miles High, 2018. *Recreations*: music, badminton, running, writing. *W*: www.richardhernamanallen.com.

See also D. K. Allen.

**ALLEN, Richard Ian Gordon,** Visiting Scholar, International Monetary Fund, since 2014 (Deputy Division Chief, Fiscal Affairs Department, 2005–09; consultant on public finance issues, 2010–14); Senior Research Associate, Overseas Development Institute, since 2011; *b* 13 Dec. 1944; *s* of Reginald Arthur Hill Allen and Edith Alice Allen (*née* Manger). *Educ*: Edinburgh Academy; Edinburgh Univ. (MA); York Univ. (BPhil). Consultant, UN Economic Commn for Europe, Geneva, 1970; Research Officer, NIESR, 1971–75; Economic Adviser: Dept of Energy, 1975–78; HM Treasury, 1978–81; Senior Economic Adviser, later Asst Sec., HM Treasury, 1981–85; Counsellor (Economic), Washington, 1985–87; Press Sec. to Chancellor of the Exchequer, 1987–88; Under Sec., HM Treasury, 1988–95; Financial Advr, Govt of Bahrain, 1995–96; Sen. Counsellor, SIGMA prog., OECD, Paris, 1996–2001; Sen. Advr on Governance, Asian Develt Bank, 2001; World Bank: Dir, Public Expenditure and Financial Accountability Prog., 2001–03; Lead Economist for Public Sector Issues, ME and N Africa Reg., 2003–05. Mem., Bd of Dirs, European Investment Bank, 1988–90. *Publications*: (with Daniel Tommasi) Managing Public Expenditure: a reference book for transition countries, 2001; (with Salvatore Schiavo-Campo and Thomas Columkill Garrity) Assessing and Reforming Public Financial Management, 2004; (with Richard Hemming and Barry Potter) International Handbook of Public Financial Management, 2013. *Recreations*: collecting art, music, golf. *Club*: Royal Wimbledon Golf.

**ALLEN, Prof. Robert Carson,** PhD; FRSCan; FBA 2003; Global Distinguished Professor of Economic History, New York University, Abu Dhabi, since 2014; *b* 10 Jan. 1947; *s* of Richard Carson Allen and Barbara Tudbury Allen; *m* 1990, Dianne Frank; one *s*. *Educ*: Carleton Coll. (BA 1969); Harvard Univ. (MA 1972; PhD 1975). FRSCan 1994. Asst Prof., Hamilton Coll., 1973–75; University of British Columbia: Asst Prof., 1975–80; Associate Prof., 1980–85; Prof., 1985–2000; Reader in Recent Social and Econ. Hist., Oxford Univ., 2001–02; Prof. of Econ. History, Univ. of Oxford, 2002–13; Fellow, 2011–13, Emeritus Fellow, 2014, Nuffield Coll., Oxford, now Sen. Res. Fellow. Vis. Prof., Harvard Univ., 1993–94, 1999–2000. *Publications*: (with G. Rosenbluth) Restraining the Economy: social credit economic policies for BC in the Eighties, 1986; (with G. Rosenbluth) False Promises: the failure of conservative economics, 1992; Enclosure and the Yeoman: agrarian change and English economic development 1450–1850, 1992; Farm to Factory: a reinterpretation of the Soviet industrial revolution, 2003; The British Industrial Revolution in Global Perspective, 2009; Global Economic History: a very short introduction, 2011; The Industrial Revolution: a very short introduction, 2017. *Recreations*: mountaineering, carpentry, running, weight lifting. *Address*: New York University, Abu Dhabi, PO Box 129188, Abu Dhabi, United Arab Emirates.

**ALLEN, Robert Geoffrey Bruère, (Robin);** QC 1995; a Recorder, since 2000; *b* 13 Feb. 1951; *s* of Rev. Canon R. E. T. Allen and Isabel (*née* Otter-Barry); *m* 1977, Elizabeth Gay Moon; two *s*. *Educ*: Rugby; University Coll., Oxford (BA PPE 1972). Called to the Bar, Middle Temple, 1974 (Bencher, 2004), NI, 2009; in practice, specialising in discrimination, employment and public law, and human rights, 1976–; an Asst Recorder, 1997–2000; Hd of Chambers, 2002–18 (Jt Head, 2002–05, 2016–18). Co-organiser and first Treas., Free Representation Unit, 1973. Employment Law Advr to Legal Action Gp, 1978–80; Legal Advr to Local Govt Gp, Inst. Public Relns, 1988–90; expert advr to EC on law affecting most disadvantaged, 1993. Founder Mem. Cttee, Employment Law Bar Assoc., 1994–99 (Chm., 1997–99); Chairman: Bar in the Community, 2000–02; Bar Pro Bono Unit, 2000–02; Mem., Bar Council, 1999–2001 and 2013– (Chm., Equality and Diversity Cttee 2013–, Social Mobility Cttee, 2015–); Chm., Bar Conf. Organising Bd, 2002. Mem., Home Office Human Rights Task Force, 1999–2001. Special Advr to Disability Rights

Commn, 2002–07; Consultant: Age Concern and Age Europe, 2004–09; Age UK, 2012–14. Hamlyn Lectr, QUB, Fac. of Advocates, Edinburgh, and Middle Temple, 2018. Trustee: London Bombing Relief Charitable Fund, 2005–08; Equal Rights Trust, 2018; Dir, London Emergencies Trust, 2016–. Patron, Andrea Adams Trust, 2008–09. Mem., Eur. Social Platform Virtual Network of Legal Experts, 2009–19. Sec., Lambeth Central CLP, 1977. Chm., London Youth Adv. Centre, 1984–90. Chairman: Bd of Govs, Eleanor Palmer Primary Sch., 1988–91; Brandon Centre for Psychotherapy, 1991–93. Chambers and Partners Employment Law Silk Award, 2008, 2012. *Publications:* How to Prepare a Case for an Industrial Tribunal, 1987; (ed and contrib.) Home Office/Bar Council Study Guide to the Human Rights Act, 2000, rev. edn for Dept of Constitutional Affairs/Bar Council, 2004; Employment Law and Human Rights, 2002, 3rd edn 2018; Family Rights at Work, 2012; contributed to: The Legal Framework and Social Consequences of Free Movement of Persons in the European Union, 1998; Women, Work and Inequality: the challenge of equal pay in a de-regulated labour market, 1999; Anti-Discrimination: the way forward, 1999; Race Discrimination: developing and using a new legal framework, 2000; Bullen and Leake and Jacob's Precedents of Pleadings, 2000; The Legal Regulation of the Employment Relationship, 2001; Equality Law in an Enlarged Europe, 2007; Blackstone's Guide to the Equality Act, 2010, 2nd edn 2012; Why Does Equality Seem So Difficult? Three Problems in Comparison, 2019. *Recreations:* family life, fireworks, fishing, growing chrysanthemums, singing. *Address:* Cloisters, 1 Pump Court, Temple, EC4Y 7AA. *T:* (020) 7827 4000, *Fax:* (020) 7827 4100. *Club:* Vincent's (Oxford).

**ALLEN, Shane;** Controller, Comedy Commissioning, BBC, since 2013; *b* Carrickfergus, 24 Nov. 1972; *s* of Joe Allen and Carole Allen; partner, Catherine Lovesey; two *s*. *Educ:* Belfast Royal Acad.; Univ. of Edinburgh (MA Hons Social Hist. 1996). Producer and writer, 11 O'Clock Show and Brass Eye, Talkback TV, 1998–2001; writer, Shooting Stars, BBC, 2002; Dir, Ali G in da USAiii, Talkback TV, 2003; Commng Editor, Comedy, Channel 4, 2004–09; Hd of Comedy, Channel 4, 2009–12. Mem., BAFTA, 2005–. *Recreations:* snooker, table tennis, American literature, print collecting, snail genocide. *Address:* 3 West Drive, Brighton BN2 0GD.

**ALLEN, Sir Thomas,** Kt 1999; CBE 1989; singer; *b* 10 Sept. 1944; *s* of Thomas Boaz Allen and Florence Allen; *m* 1st, 1968, Margaret Holley (marr. diss. 1986); one *s*; 2nd, 1988, Jeannie Gordon Lascelles. *Educ:* Robert Richardson Grammar Sch., Ryhope; Royal College of Music. ARCM; FRCM 1988. Welsh Nat. Opera, 1969–72; Principal Baritone, Royal Opera, Covent Garden, 1972–78; appearances include: Glyndebourne Fest. Opera; English Opera Group; Paris Opera; Florence; Teatro Colon, Buenos Aires; Met. Opera, NY; Hamburg; La Scala, Milan; BBC TV (The Gondoliers, The Marriage of Figaro); all major orchestras and various concert engagements abroad. Major rôles include: Figaro in Barber of Seville; Figaro and the Count in Marriage of Figaro; Papageno in The Magic Flute; Billy Budd; Marcello in La Bohème; Belcore in l'Elisir d'Amore; Sid in Albert Herring; Tarquinius in Rape of Lucretia; Guglielmo, and Don Alfonso, in Così fan Tutte; Demetrius in A Midsummer Night's Dream; Valentin in Faust; Dr Falke, and Eisenstein, in Die Fledermaus; King Arthur; The Count in Voice of Ariadne; Silvio in Pagliacci; Pelléas in Pelléas and Mélisande; Germont in La Traviata; Don Giovanni; Mandryka in Arabella; Malatesta in Don Pasquale; title rôle in Il ritorno d'Ulisse; Beckmesser in Die Meistersinger; Prosdocimo in The Turk in Italy; Music Master in Ariadne auf Naxos; title rôle in Sweeney Todd, and many others. Director: Albert Herring, RCM, 2002; Il Barbiere di Siviglia, Th. Royal, Glasgow, 2007; Don Giovanni, Sage, Gateshead, 2007; Marriage of Figaro, Scottish Opera, 2010; The Magic Flute, Th. Royal, Glasgow, 2012; prod., Così fan Tutte, Sage, Gateshead. Hambro Vis. Prof. of Opera, Oxford Univ., 2000–01. Kammersänger, Bayerische Staatsoper, 2003. Chancellor, Durham Univ., 2012–. Patron, Samling Foundn. Hon. RAM 1988. Hon. MA Newcastle, 1984; Hon. DMus Durham, 1988. Queen's Medal for Music, 2013. *Publications:* Foreign Parts: a singer's journal, 1993. *Recreations:* gardening, golf, sailing, painting, ornithology. *Address:* c/o Askonas Holt Ltd, 15 Fetter Lane, EC4A 1BW.

**ALLEN, Thomas Michael Chard;** QC 2015; *b* Beaconsfield, Bucks, 21 Feb. 1968; *s* of Michael and Susan Allen; *m* 1998, Natalie Baylis; two *s* one *d*. *Educ:* King's Sch., Bruton, Som; Durham Univ.; Inns of Court Sch. of Law. Called to the Bar, Middle Temple, 1994. *Address:* Cloth Fair Chambers, Cloth Fair, EC1A 7NT.

**ALLEN, Twink;** see Allen, W. R.

**ALLEN, William Anthony;** economic consultant, since 2004; Visitor, National Institute of Economic and Social Research, since 2017; *b* 13 May 1949; *s* of Derek William Allen and Margaret Winifred Allen (*née* Jones); *m* 1972, Rosemary Margaret Eminson; one *s* two *d*. *Educ:* King's College Sch., Wimbledon; Balliol College, Oxford (BA); LSE (MScEcon). Joined Bank of England, 1972; Economic Intell. Dept, 1972–77; Gold and Foreign Exchange Office, 1977–78; seconded to Bank for Internat. Settlements, Basle, 1978–80; Bank of England: Asst Adviser, Economics Div. (working on monetary policy), 1980–82; Manager, Gilt-Edged Div., 1982–86; Hd of Money Market Operations Div., 1986–90; Hd of Foreign Exchange Div., 1990–94; Dep. Dir, 1994–2003; Dir for Europe, 2002–04; Econ. Advr, Brevan Howard Asset Mgt LLP, 2004–07; Chief Economist, Denholm Hall Gp, 2007–10. Specialist Adviser: Treasury Cttee, H of C, 2010–17; Parly Commn on Banking Standards, 2012–13. Pt-time Advr, Nat. Bank of Poland, 1990–2001. Vis. Sen. Fellow, Faculty of Finance, Cass Business Sch., 2004–16. *Publications:* International Liquidity and the Financial Crisis, 2013; Monetary Policy and Financial Repression in Britain, 1951–59, 2014; The Bank of England and the National Debt: operations in the gilt-edged market 1928–72, 2019; articles in economics jls. *Recreations:* grandchildren, monetary history. *E:* bill@allen-economics.com.

**ALLEN, Hon. Sir William (Clifford),** KCMG 2000; accountant; Minister of Finance and Planning, Bahamas, 1995–2002; *b* 15 March 1937; *m* 1960, Aloma Munnings; three *s* one *d*. *Educ:* St Augustine's Coll., Nassau; Rhodes Sch., NYC; NY Univ. (BSc Accounting); CUNY (MBA). Internal auditor, Stone and Webster Securities Corp., NY, 1965–68; budget supervisor, J. C. Penny Co., NY, 1968–70; Res. Manager, Bahamas Monetary Authy, 1970–74; Dep. Gov., 1974–80, Gov., 1980–87, Central Bank of Bahamas; Pres., Matrix Investment Ltd, 1987–92. Mem., Bahamas Senate, 1992–94; MP (Free Nat. Movt) Montagu, Bahamas, Nov. 1994–2002; Minister of State, Ministry of Finance and Planning, 1992–93; Minister of Planning and Public Service, 1993–95. JP. *Address:* Old Fort Bay, POB CB10993, Nassau, Bahamas.

**ALLEN, Sir William (Guilford),** Kt 1981; Chairman, family group of companies; *b* 22 April 1932; *s* of Sir William Guilford Allen, CBE, and Mona Maree Allen; *m* 1959, Elaine Therese Doyle; two *s* one *d*. *Educ:* Downlands Coll., Toowoomba, Qld. In grazing industry, Merino sheep; Principal, Historic Malvern Hills Registered Merino Stud; stud Santa Gertrudis cattle breeder. Commercial broadcasting industry. Chm., Qld Transport and Technology Centre, 1984; Director: Qantas, 1981; Suncorp Insurance and Building Soc., 1985–89; Power Brewing Co., 1989. Former Mem. Bd, Care Australia. Mem., Longreach Base Hosp. Bd, 1960–83. Treas., 1981, Trustee, 1989–, Nat. Party, Qld. Councillor, Longreach Shire, 1958. Fellow, Hon. Co. of Air Pilots (formerly GAPAN). *Recreation:* aviation. *Clubs:* Brisbane, Tattersalls, Australian, Longreach, Queensland Turf, Brisbane Amateur Turf (Brisbane); Australian, Royal Sydney Golf (Sydney).

**ALLEN, Maj.-Gen. William Maurice,** CB 1983; FCIT, FIMI, FILDM; MInstPet; Senior Military Consultant to Mondial Defence Systems (formerly Mondial & Co.), 1985–95; Regional Vice President and Senior Defence Adviser, Fortis Aviation Group, 1995–99; *b* 29 May 1931; *s* of William James Allen and Elizabeth Jane Henrietta Allen; *m* 1st, 1955, Patricia Mary (*née* Fletcher) (*d* 1998); one *d* decd; 2nd, 1998, Elizabeth (*née* Irving). *Educ:* Dunstable Sch. FCIT 1972; FIMI 1982; FILDM (FIPDM 1982), FCMI (FBIM 1983); MInstPet 1982. Commnd RASC, 1950; RCT, 1965; regtl and staff appts, Korea, Cyprus, Germany and UK; Student, Staff Coll., Camberley, 1961; Instructor, Staff Coll., Camberley and RMCS Shrivenham, 1968–70; Student, RCDS, 1976; Asst Comdt, RMA Sandhurst, 1979–81; Dir Gen. of Transport and Movements (Army), 1981–83. Dir of Educn and Trng, Burroughs Machines Ltd, 1983–85. Jt Man. Dir, Marina Moraira Yacht Brokers, 1989–92; Man. Dir, Fortis Internat. Ltd, 1991–92; Director: Govt Projects, Unisys Corp. (formerly Systems Develt Corp.), Heidelberg, 1985–86; Fortis Aviation Gp, Spain, 1988–89; European Management Information, 1989–92. Member, Council: IAM, 1982–85; NDTA, 1983–90. Chm., Milton Keynes Information Technol. Trng Centre, 1983–85. Associate, St George's House. Freeman, City of London, 1981; Hon. Liveryman, Worshipful Co. of Carmen, 1981. *Recreations:* economics, trout fishing, gardening, vigneron et oleiculteur de Languedoc. *Address:* c/o Royal Bank of Scotland, Holts Farnborough Branch, Lawrie House, 31–37 Victoria Road, Farnborough, Hants GU14 7NR.

**ALLEN, Prof. William Richard, (Twink),** CBE 2002; PhD, ScD; FRCVS; Jim Joel Professor of Equine Reproduction, Department of Veterinary Medicine (formerly Clinical Veterinary Medicine), University of Cambridge, 1995–2007, now Professor Emeritus; Fellow, Robinson College, Cambridge, 1995–2007, now Emeritus; Director, Thoroughbred Breeders' Association Equine Fertility Unit, Newmarket, 1989–2007; Scientific Director, Paul Mellon Laboratory of Equine Reproduction, since 2008; *b* 29 Aug. 1940; *s* of Francis Cecil Allen and Rose St Ledger Allen (*née* Sinclair); *m* 1965, Diana Margaret Emms; one *s* two *d*. *Educ:* Auckland Grammar Sch.; Univ. of Auckland; Univ. of Sydney (BVSc 1965); Univ. of Cambridge (PhD in Equine Reproductive Physiology 1970); Royal Coll. of Veterinary Surgeons (Dip. Equine Stud Medicine 1986). FIBiol 2002–09; FRCVS 2004. In vet. practice, Kaitaia, NZ, 1965; res. student, Dept of Clinical Vet. Medicine, Univ. of Cambridge, 1966–70; Post Doctoral Scientist, AFRC Unit of Reproductive Physiol. and Biochem., Cambridge, 1970–72; Prin. Vet. Res. Officer, Thoroughbred Breeders' Assoc. Equine Fertility Unit, Animal Res. Stn, Cambridge, 1972–89. *Publications:* (ed) Equine Reproduction, vols I–V, 1975–91; contrib. Proc. Internat. Symposia on Equine Reproduction; numerous papers in scientific jls and reference books. *Recreations:* fox hunting, horse racing, wildlife conservation. *Address:* Paul Mellon Laboratory of Equine Reproduction, Brunswick, 18 Woodditton Road, Newmarket, Suffolk CB8 9BJ. *T:* (01638) 428233. *E:* twinkallen100@gmail.com.
See also L. Dettori.

**ALLEN, Woody, (Allen Stewart Konigsberg);** writer, actor, director; *b* Brooklyn, 1 Dec. 1935; *s* of late Martin and of Nettie Konigsberg; *m* 1966, Louise Lasser (marr. diss.), one *s* by Mia Farrow, *qv*; *m* 1997, Soon-Yi Previn. TV script writer, 1953–64, and appeared as a comedian in nightclubs and on TV shows. Sylvania Award, 1957. *Plays:* (writer) Don't Drink the Water, 1966; (writer and actor) Play It Again Sam, 1969 (filmed 1972); The Floating Light Bulb, 1990; (writer and dir) A Second Hand Memory, 2005. *Films:* (writer and actor) What's New Pussycat?, 1965; (actor): Casino Royale, 1967; Scenes from a Mall, 1991; Fading Gigolo, 2014; (writer, actor and director): What's Up Tiger Lily?, 1966; Take the Money and Run, 1969; Bananas, 1971; Everything You Always Wanted to Know About Sex But Were Afraid to Ask, 1972; Sleeper, 1973; Love and Death, 1975; The Front, 1976; Annie Hall (Academy Award), 1977; Manhattan, 1979; Stardust Memories, 1980; A Midsummer Night's Sex Comedy, 1982; Zelig, 1983; Broadway Danny Rose, 1984; Hannah and her Sisters (Academy Award), 1986; New York Stories, 1989; Shadows and Fog, 1992; Husbands and Wives, 1992; Manhattan Murder Mystery, 1994; Mighty Aphrodite, 1995; Everyone Says I Love You, 1996; Deconstructing Harry, 1997; Small Time Crooks, 2000; The Curse of the Jade Scorpion, 2002; Hollywood Ending, 2002; Anything Else, 2003; Whatever Works, 2010; To Rome with Love, 2012; (writer and director): Interiors, 1978; The Purple Rose of Cairo, 1985; Radio Days, 1987; September, 1988; Another Woman, 1989; Crimes and Misdemeanours, 1989; Alice, 1990; Bullets over Broadway, 1995 (writer, stage version, 2014); Celebrity, 1998; Sweet and Lowdown, 1999; Melinda and Melinda, 2005; Match Point, 2007; Cassandra's Dream, 2008; Vicky Cristina Barcelona, 2009; You Will Meet a Tall Dark Stranger, 2011; Midnight in Paris, 2011 (Academy Award for Best Original Screenplay, 2012); Blue Jasmine, 2013; Magic in the Moonlight, 2014; Irrational Man, 2015; Café Society, 2016; (writer and director) Wonder Wheel, 2018. *Television series:* (writer and actor) Crisis in Six Scenes, 2016. *Publications:* Getting Even, 1971; Without Feathers, 1975; Side Effects, 1981; Three One-Act Plays, 2004; Mere Anarchy (short stories), 2007; The Insanity Defense, 2007; contribs to New Yorker, etc.

**ALLEN-JONES, Charles Martin;** Senior Partner, Linklaters (formerly Linklaters & Paines), 1996–2001; Joint Chairman, Linklaters & Alliance, 1998–2001; *b* 7 Aug. 1939; *s* of late Air Vice-Marshal John Ernest Allen-Jones, CBE, and Margaret Allen-Jones (*née* Rix); *m* 1st, 1966, Caroline Beale (*d* 2016); one *s* two *d*; 2nd, 2018, Pepita Allsopp. *Educ:* Clifton Coll., Bristol. Admitted Solicitor, 1963. Articled Clerk: to the Clerk to the Justices, Uxbridge Magistrates Court, 1958–60; Vizard Oldham Crowder & Cash, London, 1960–63; Solicitor, Supreme Court, London, 1963; Linklaters & Paines, subseq. Linklaters: Solicitor, 1966; Partner, 1968–2001; Head, Hong Kong office, 1976–81; Head, Corporate Dept, 1985–91. Director: Caledonia Investments plc, 2001–15; Hongkong Land Holdings Ltd, 2001–; Jardine Strategic Hldgs Ltd, 2008–. Mem., Financial Reporting Council, 2001–07 (Member: Corporate Governance Cttee, 2004–07; Financial Reporting Review Panel, 2006–11). Trustee: BM, 2000–04; Asia House, 2001–09 (Chm., 2005–06). Member: Barbican Adv. Council, 1997–2005; Council, RCA, 2004–16 (Vice Chm., 2007–16); Internat. Adv. Council, SOAS, 2007–10. Mem., Cttee, Hong Kong Assoc., 2002–. Consultant Ed., CUP Law Practitioner Series, 2003–09. *Recreations:* keeping in touch, Asia, travel, tennis, reading. *Address:* 11 Campden Street, W8 7EP. *Clubs:* Brooks's; Hong Kong (Hong Kong).

**ALLENBY,** family name of **Viscount Allenby.**

**ALLENBY,** 4th Viscount *cr* 1919; **Henry Jaffray Hynman Allenby;** *b* 29 July 1968; *o s* of 3rd Viscount Allenby and of Sara Margaret Allenby (*née* Wiggin); *S* father, 2014; *m* 1996, Louise Victoria, *yr d* of Michael Green; two *s*.

**ALLENBY, Katherine Fiona,** MBE 2007; athlete; sports teacher, Monkton Coombe Preparatory School, Bath, since 2016; Fencing Manager of Modern Pentathlon, London 2012 Olympic Games, 2011–12; *b* London, 16 March 1974; *d* of William James and Gillian Mary Allenby; *m* 2005, Ian David Pocock; two *d*. *Educ:* St Joseph's Sch., Launceston; Kelly Coll., Tavistock; Brighton Univ. (BSc Hons Sport Sci.); QTS 2005. Modern Pentathlon athlete, 1993–2004: Individual bronze medal, 1994, silver medal, 1995, World Jun. Modern Pentathlon Championships; Eur. Champion, 1997; Eur. Team Champion, 1999, 2000, 2001, 2002, 2003; World Cup Champion, 1998, 2004; World Team Champion, 2000, 2001, 2003, 2004; Bronze Medal, Sydney Olympics, 2000; Individual bronze medal, 2003, silver medal, 2004, World Modern Pentathlon Championships; National Fencing Champion, 2005. Trainee teacher of Physical Educn, Wellington Sch., Som, 2004–05; PE teacher and Hd of Modern Pentathlon, Whitgift Sch., Croydon, 2005–09; Games Teacher, Paragon Sch., Bath, 2009–15. Dir of Fencing in Modern Pentathlon for 2011 Eur. Modern Pentathlon Championships and 2011 World Cup trial and Olympic Test event, 2010–11. Motivational/public speaker, 2000–. Chm., British Athletes' Commn, 2003–07; Member: Athletes' Cttee, British Olympic Assoc., 1997–2003, 2010–12; Nat. Olympic Cttee, 2000–09; Athlete Steering Gp advising Exec. Bd of London 2012 Olympics, 2003–05. Member: Athletes' Cttee, Union Internat. de Pentathlon Moderne, 2004–08; Tetrathlon Nat. Cttee, Pony Club, 2009–13. Founder Mem. and Vice Chm., Modern Pentathlon Club, Bath, 2009–11. Jim Fox Award for Excellence in Modern Pentathlon, Pentathlon GB, 2004. *Recreations:* foreign languages, cooking, especially with chocolate, reading paperback bestsellers, global exploration, baking celebration cakes. *Address:* c/o British Olympic Association, 101 Cavendish Street, W1W 6XH. *E:* ktlnb@hotmail.com.

**ALLENDALE**, 4th Viscount *cr* 1911; **Wentworth Peter Ismay Beaumont;** Baron 1906; *b* 13 Nov. 1948; *e s* of 3rd Viscount Allendale and of Hon. Sarah, 2nd *d* of 1st Baron Ismay, KG, GCB, CH, DSO, PC; *S* father, 2002; *m* 1975, Theresa Mary Magdalene (*née* More O'Ferrall); one *s* three *d*. *Educ:* Harrow. Landowner. *Recreations:* shooting, ski-ing, horseracing. *Heir: s* Hon. Wentworth Ambrose Ismay Beaumont [*b* 11 June 1979; *m* 2011, Vanessa, *d* of Peter Webb; two *s* one *d*]. *Address:* Allendale Estates, Unit 2, Bearl Farm, Stocksfield, Northumberland NE43 7AL. *T:* (01661) 843296. *Clubs:* Jockey, White's.

**ALLENDE, Isabel;** writer; *b* 2 Aug. 1942; *d* of Tomás Allende Pesce and Francisca Llona Barros; *m* 1st, 1962, Miguel Frías (marr. diss. 1987); one *s* (one *d* deced); 2nd, 1988, William C. Gordon. *Educ:* Ursulinas (German nuns), Chile; Dunalastaid Amer. Sch., La Paz; British Lebanese Trng Coll., Lebanon; La Maisonette, Chile. Journalist: Chile, 1964–74 (Paula (women's mag.), Mampato (children's mag.), TV programmes, film documentaries); El Nacional, Venezuela, 1975–84; Lecturer in Literature: Montclair Coll., USA; Univ. of Calif at Berkeley, 1988; Univ. of Virginia, 1988. Member: Academía de la Lengua, Chile, 1989; Academía de Artes y Ciencias, Puerto Rico, 1995. Hon. Prof. of Literature, Univ. of Chile, 1991. Lecture tours, N America and Europe. Work has been translated into more than 27 languages and has received numerous literary awards. Hon. DLitt: SUNY, 1991; Bates Coll., USA, 1994; Dominican Coll., USA, 1994; Columbia Coll., USA, 1996; Hon. DHL Florida Atlantic, 1996. Condecoración Gabriela Mistral (Chile), 1994; Chevalier, Ordre des Arts et des Lettres (France), 1994. *Plays:* El Embajador, 1971; La Balada del Medio Pelo, 1973; Los Siete Espejos, 1974. *Publications: novels:* La Casa de los Espíritus (The House of Spirits), 1982 (filmed; adapted for stage); De Amor y de Sombra (Of Love and Shadows), 1984 (filmed); Eva Luna, 1985 (adapted for stage); El Plan Infinito (The Infinite Plan), 1991; Paula, 1994 (adapted for stage); Hija de la Fortuna (Daughter of Fortune), 1999; Retrato en Sepia (Portrait in Sepia), 2000; La Ciudad de las Bestias (City of the Beasts), 2002; El reino del Dragón de Oro (Kingdom of the Golden Dragon), 2003; El Bosque de los Pigmeos (Forest of the Pygmies), 2005; Zorro, 2005; Inés del Alma Mía (Inés of My Soul), 2006; La Isla Bajo el Mar (The Island Beneath the Sea), 2010; El Cuaderno de Maya (Maya's Notebook), 2011; Ripper, 2014; The Japanese Lover, 2015; In The Midst of Winter, 2017; *short stories:* La Gorda de Porcelana, 1983; Cuentos de Eva Luna (Stories of Eva Luna), 1989 (adapted for theatre, opera, and ballet); Afrodita (Aphrodite), 1997; *memoirs:* Mi país inventado (My Invented Country), 2003; The Sum of Our Days, 2008; articles in jls in N America and Europe. *Address:* 116 Caledonia Street, Sausalito, CA 94965, USA.

**ALLERA, Marc;** Chief Executive Officer, Consumer, BT plc, since 2017 (Chief Executive Officer, EE, 2016–17); *b* 5 April 1972; *m* Lisa; three *s*. *Educ:* London Business Sch.; Sheffield Business Sch., Sheffield Hallam Univ. Gen. Manager, Saga UK, 1997–2001; Sales and Mktg Dir, Three, 2004–11; Chief Commercial Officer, EE, 2011–15. Mem., Mktg Gp of GB. *Recreation:* tennis. *Address:* BT Centre, 81 Newgate Street, EC1A 7AJ.

**ALLEYNE, Sir George (Allanmore Ogarren),** Kt 1990; OCC 2001; MD, FRCP; Director, Pan American Health Organization, 1995–2003 (Assistant Director, 1990–95), now Director Emeritus; Special Envoy of the UN Secretary-General for HIV/AIDS in the Caribbean, 2003–10; *b* 7 Oct. 1932; *s* of Clinton O. Alleyne and Eileen A. Alleyne (*née* Gaskin); *m* 1958, Sylvan Ionie (*née* Chen); two *s* one *d*. *Educ:* Harrison College, Barbados; University College of the West Indies (MB BS London 1977, MD). Completed training as physician in Barbados and UCH, London, 1958–62; Sen. Med. Registrar, UCH, Jamaica, 1962–63; Res. Fellow, Sen. Res. Fellow, MRC Tropical Metabolism Res. Unit, 1963–72; Prof. of Medicine, Univ. of W Indies, 1972–81 (Chm., Dept of Medicine, 1976–81); Pan American Health Organization: Head of Res. Unit, 1981–83; Dir of Health Programs Devolt, 1983–90. Mem., Lancet Commn on Investing in Health; Chm., Bd of Dirs, Center for Disease Dynamics, Econs and Policy, Washington. Chancellor, Univ. of W Indies, 2003–17. Sir Arthur Sims Travelling Prof., 1977. Hon. FACP. Hon. DSc Univ. of W Indies, 1989. Jamaica Assoc. of Scientists Award, 1979. Jamaica Centenary Medal, 1980. *Publications:* The Grooming of a Chancellor, 2018; contribs to learned jls on medicine, renal physiology and biochemistry, health and develt issues. *Recreations:* reading, gardening.

**ALLEYNE, Rev. Sir John (Olpherts Campbell),** 5th Bt *cr* 1769; Rector of Weeke, Diocese of Winchester, 1975–93; *b* 18 Jan. 1928; *s* of Captain Sir John Meynell Alleyne, 4th Bt, DSO, DSC, RN, and Alice Violet (*d* 1985), *d* of late James Campbell; *S* father, 1983; *m* 1968, Honor, *d* of late William Albert Irwin, Belfast; one *s* one *d*. *Educ:* Eton; Jesus Coll., Cambridge (BA 1950, MA 1955). Deacon 1955, priest 1956; Curate, Southampton, 1955–58; Chaplain: Coventry Cathedral, 1958–62; Clare Coll., Cambridge, 1962–66; to Bishop of Bristol, 1966–68; Toc H Area Sec., SW England, 1968–71; Vicar of Speke, 1971–73, Rector, 1973–75. *Heir: s* Richard Meynell Alleyne, *b* 23 June 1972. *Address:* 18 Ashbarn Crescent, Winchester, Hants SO22 4LW.

**ALLEYNE, Selwyn Eugene,** CBE 1986; Hong Kong Commissioner in London, 1987–89, retired; *b* 4 Dec. 1930; *s* of Gilbert Sydney Alleyne and Dorothy Alleyne; *m* 1956, Ellie Lynn Wong, MBE. *Educ:* Queen's Royal Coll., Trinidad; Jesus Coll., Oxford (MA). Joined Hong Kong Govt, 1956; Dep. Dir of Urban Services, 1974; Dep. Sec. for Civil Service, 1979; Dir of Social Welfare, and MLC, 1980; Dep. Financial Sec., 1983–87. *Recreations:* tennis, chess, collecting Chinese ceramics. *Clubs:* Civil Service; Hong Kong Jockey.

**ALLI,** Baron *cr* 1998 (Life Peer), of Norbury in the London Borough of Croydon; **Waheed Alli;** Chief Executive, Silvergate Media (Director, since 2011); *b* 16 Nov. 1964. *Educ:* Norbury Manor Sch. Formed televised production co., 24 Hour Productions, later Planet 24 Productions Ltd, with partner Charlie Parsons, Jt Man. Dir, 1992–99; Man. Dir, Carlton Productions, 1998–2000; Dir, Carlton Television, 1998–2000. Director: Shine Entertainment Ltd, 2000; Castaway Television; Chairman: ASOS, 2001–12; Chorion Ltd, 2003–11. Chancellor, De Montfort Univ., 2006–15. Pres., NYT. Trustee, Elton John Aids Foundn. *Address:* House of Lords, SW1A 0PW.

**ALLIANCE,** Baron *cr* 2004 (Life Peer), of Manchester in the County of Greater Manchester; **David Alliance,** Kt 1989; CBE 1984; Chairman, N. Brown Group plc, 1968–2012 (non-executive Director, since 2012); *b* 15 June 1932; *s* of Eliahoo and Sarahi Alliance. *Educ:* Iran. First acquisition, Thomas Hoghton (Oswaldtwistle), 1956; acquired Spirella, 1968, then Vantona Ltd, 1975, to form Vantona Group, 1975; acquired Carrington Viyella to form Vantona Viyella, 1983, Nottingham Manufacturing, 1985, Coats Patons to form Coats Viyella, 1986; Gp Chief Exec., 1975–90, Chm., 1989–99; Chm., Tootal Gp, 1991–99. Gov., Tel Aviv Univ., 1989–. CCMI (CBIM 1985); CompTI 1984. FRSA 1988. Hon. Fellow: UMIST 1988; Shenkar Coll. of Textile Tech. and Fashion, Israel, 1990. Hon. FCGI 1991. Hon. LLD: Victoria Univ. of Manchester, 1989; Liverpool, 1996; Hon. DSc Heriot-Watt, 1991; Hon. DPhil Tel Aviv, 2009. *Publications:* A Bazaar Life (autobiog.), 2015. *Address:* House of Lords, SW1A 0PW.

**ALLIES, Edgar Robin, (Bob),** OBE 2016; RIBA; Partner, Allies and Morrison, architects, since 1983; *b* Singapore, 5 Sept. 1953; *s* of Edgar Martyn Allies, MBE, DFC and Lily Maud Allies; *m* 1991, Jill Anne Franklin; one *s* one *d*. *Educ:* Reading Sch.; Univ. of Edinburgh (MA Hons 1976; DipArch 1977). RIBA 1980. Rome Schol. in Architecture, 1981–82; Lectr, Univ. of Cambridge, 1984–88; George Simpson Vis. Prof., Univ. of Edinburgh, 1995; Vis. Prof., Univ. of Bath, 1996–99; Kea Dist. Visiting Professor: Univ. of Maryland, 1999; Univ. of Reading, 2016–. Mem., Faculty of Fine Arts, Brit. Sch. at Rome, 1997–2002. Mem. Council, AA, 2004–07. Member: CABE Nat. Design Rev. Panel, 2006–17; RIBA Awards Gp, 2009–11; Mayor's Design Adv. Gp, 2012–16; RIAS; Chair: Brick Awards, 2009–12; Shape East Panel, 2011–14; Design South East Review Panel, 2014–. With G. Morrison, founded Allies and Morrison, 1983; *completed projects* include: Rosalind Franklin Bldg, Newnham Coll., Cambridge, 1995 (RIBA Award 1996); British Embassy, Dublin, 1995 (RIBA Award 1997); Abbey Mills Pumping Station, Stratford (RIBA Award), 1997; Centenary Bldg, Horniman Mus., 2002 (RIBA Award 2004); 85 Southwark Street, 2003 (RIBA London Bldg of the Year, 2004); BBC Media Village, White City, 2004 (RIBA Award 2005); Fitzwilliam Coll. Gatehouse and Auditorium, 2004 (RIBA Award 2005); Girton Coll. Library, Cambridge, 2005 (RIBA Award 2006); Royal Festival Hall restoration, 2007 (RIBA Design for London Space Award, 2007; RIBA Award 2008); Planetarium, Royal Observatory, Greenwich, 2007 (RIBA Award 2008); Paradise Street, Liverpool One, 2009 (RIBA Award 2009); Highbury Square, London, 2009 (RIBA Award 2010); Bankside 123, London, 2009 (RIBA Award 2010); Masterplan London 2012 Stratford (RIBA Nat. Award 2013); Rambert London, 2014 (RIBA Award 2014); Ash Court, Girton Coll., 2014 (RIBA Award 2014); St Thomas the Apostle, London (RIBA Award 2015). FRSA. Edinburgh Architectural Assoc. Medal for Architecture, 1977; Building Design Architect of the Year Award, 2007. *Publications:* Model Futures, 1983; Allies and Morrison, 1996; Cultivating the City: London before and after 2012, 2009; Allies and Morrison vol. 1, 2011, vol. 2, 2019; The Fabric of Place, 2013. *Recreation:* contemporary music. *Address:* Allies and Morrison, 85 Southwark Street, SE1 0HX. *T:* (020) 7921 0100. *E:* boballies@alliesandmorrison.com; 12 Well Road, NW3 1LH.

**ALLIN-KHAN, Dr Rosena;** MP (Lab) Tooting, since June 2016; *b* Tooting; *m* Robert T. Allin; two *d*. *Educ:* Brunel Univ. (BSc Med. Biochem.); Univ. of Cambridge. Scholarships for cancer res. in USA and for study of peace-keeping and conflict resolution in Switzerland. NHS doctor, 2005–; posts at Royal London and Homerton Hosps; jun. A&E doctor, St George's Univ. Hosps NHS Foundn Trust, Tooting. Mem. (Lab) Wandsworth LBC, 2014–. *Address:* House of Commons, SW1A 0AA.

**ALLINSON, Sir (Walter) Leonard,** KCVO 1979 (MVO 1961); CMG 1976; HM Diplomatic Service, retired; *b* 1 May 1926; *o s* of Walter Allinson and Alice Frances Cassidy; *m* 1951, Margaret Patricia Watts (*d* 2017); three *d* (of whom two are twins). *Educ:* Friern Barnet Grammar Sch.; Merton Coll., Oxford (First class in History, 1947; MA). Asst Principal, Ministry of Fuel and Power (Petroleum Div.), 1947–48; Asst Principal, later Principal, Min. of Education, 1948–58 (Asst Private Sec. to Minister, 1953–54); transf. CRO, 1958; First Sec. in Lahore and Karachi, 1960–62, Madras and New Delhi, 1963–66; Counsellor and Head of Political Affairs Dept, March 1968; Dep. Head, later Head, of Permanent Under Secretary's Dept, FCO, 1968–70; Counsellor and Head of Chancery, subsequently Deputy High Comr, Nairobi, 1970–73; RCDS, 1974; Diplomatic Service Inspectorate, 1975; Dep. High Comr and Minister, New Delhi, 1975–77; High Comr, Lusaka, 1978–80; Asst Under-Sec. of State (Africa), 1980–82; High Comr in Kenya and Ambassador to UN Environment Programme, 1982–86. Vice Pres., Royal African Soc., 1982–99; Mem. Council, East Africa Inst., 1986–92; Hon. Vice Chm., Kenya Soc., 1989–; Chm., Finance Cttee, Cornwall Red Cross, 1996–98. Gov., Wendron Voluntary Primary Sch., 1990–2003. *Address:* 29 Thames Avenue, Pangbourne, Berks RG8 7BY.

*See also* N. Syfret.

**ALLIOT-MARIE, Dr Michèle Yvette Marie-Thérèse;** Minister of Foreign and European Affairs, France, 2010–11; *b* 10 Sept. 1946; *d* of Bernard Marie and Renée Leyko. *Educ:* Lycée Folie St-James, Neuilly-sur-Seine; Paris Sorbonne Univ. (BA Private Law, Pol Scis and Hist. of Law; Cert. Law and Econs in African Countries; MA Ethnol.; PhD Law and Politics). Sen. Lectr, Paris Sorbonne Univ., 1984–. Jun. Minister i/c teaching affairs, 1986–88; Mem. (RPR) EP, 1989–94, 2014–19; Minister: of Youth and Sports, 1993–95; of Defence, 2002–07; of the Interior, 2007–09; of Justice, 2009–10. Deputy for Pyrénées-Atlantiques: (RPR), 1986, 1988, 1993, 1995, 1997 (UMP), 2002, 2007. Member: Municipal Council: Ciboure, 1983–88; Biarritz, 1989–91; and First Vice-Pres., Gen. Council, Pyrénées-Atlantiques, 1994–2001. Mayor, St-Jean-de-Luz, 1995–2002. Rassemblement pour la République: various posts including: Mem., Central Cttee, 1984–2002, Exec. Cttee, 1985–2002; Dep. Gen. Sec. i/c foreign affairs, 1990–93; Mem., Party Exec., 1991–2002; National Secretary: i/c social affairs, 1998–99; i/c elections, 1999; Party Chm., 1999–2002. Chair, EP Delegn for relations with Arab Peninsula. Decorations include: Commandeur: Mérite de l'Educn Nat. and Croix de Comdr, Ordre Nat. (Ivory Coast); Ordre de la République (Egypt); Palmes magistrales 1st Cl. (Peru); Ordre de Stara Planina (Bulgaria); Grand Officier, Ordre Nat. du Lion (Senegal). *Publications:* La Décision Politique: attention! une République peut en cacher une autre, 1983; La Grande Peur des Classes Moyennes, 1996; Les Boursiers Étrangers en France: errements et potentialités, 1997; La République des Irresponsables, 1999; Le Chêne qu'on relève, 2005; La tentation totalitaire de la Gauche, 2014.

**ALLISON, Brian George;** Senior non-executive Director, Goodwood Estate Company Ltd, 2014–19 (non-executive Director 2007–19); *b* 4 April 1933; *s* of late Donald Brian Allison and Edith Maud Allison (*née* Humphries); *m* 1st, 1958, Glennis Mary Taylor (*d* 1993); one *s* one *d*. *m* 2nd, 1996, Joanne Valerie Norman (*d* 2010); 3rd, 2012, Alisa Ann Topham. *Educ:* Hele's Sch., Exeter; University Coll. London (BSc Econ). FCIM 1981. Flying Officer, RAF, 1955–58. Economist Statistician, Shell-Mex & BP, 1958; Marketing Res. Manager, Spicers, 1958–64; Business Intelligence Services, subseq. The BIS Group: Dir, 1964–91; Gen. Manager, 1964–69; Man. Dir and Dep. Chm., 1969–74; Chm. and Man. Dir, 1974–81; Chm. and Chief Exec., 1981–85; Exec. Chm., 1985–87. Director: NYNEX Inf. Solutions Gp, 1987–90; NYNEX Network Systems Co. (Brussels) SA, 1991–93; non-executive Director: English China Clays plc, subseq. ECC Gp, 1984–92; Brammer plc, 1988–97; Electra Corporate Ventures Ltd, 1989–96; Microgen Holdings plc, 1992–98; Unitech plc, 1993–96; Flexible Management Systems Ltd, 1998–2001; Mem., London Bd, Halifax Building Soc., 1991–95; Chm., Holt Lloyd Gp, 1995–97; Chm. and non-exec. Dir, Amtico Holdings Ltd, 1996–2006; Chm. and non-exec. Dir, Smith Gp Holdings, later Detica Gp plc, 1997–2001; Operating Partner, Electra Partners Europe Ltd, later Cogneta LLP, 2001–09. Mem., ESRC, 1986–90. University of Surrey: Vis. Prof., 1976–92, 1994–2009, 2010–; Chm., Industrial Adv. Panel, Sch. of Mechanical and

Materials Engrg, 1998–2001; Mem., Adv. Bd, Surrey Business Sch., 2016– (Chm., 2016–18). Distinguished Scholar, QUB, 1989. DUniv Surrey 2018. *Recreations:* tennis, travel, motoring, restoring historic properties. *Clubs:* Reform; Goodwood Road Racing, Bentley Drivers, Rolls-Royce Enthusiasts.

**ALLISON, David William;** QC 2014; *b* England, 25 June 1975; *s* of Graham and Susan Allison; *m* Fiona Crookall; one *s* one *d*. *Educ:* Norwich Sch.; Downing Coll., Cambridge (BA 1st Cl. 1997). Called to the Bar, Middle Temple, 1998. *Publications:* contribs to legal textbooks. *Recreations:* tennis, ski-ing, riding, wine. *Address:* South Square Chambers, 3–4 South Square, Gray's Inn, WC1R 5HP. *T:* (020) 7696 9900. *E:* davidallison@southsquare.com.

**ALLISON, Air Vice-Marshal Dennis,** CB 1987; Chief Executive, North Western Regional Health Authority, 1990–94 (General Manager, 1986–90); *b* 15 Oct. 1932; *m* 1964, Rachel Anne, *d* of Air Vice-Marshal J. G. Franks, CB, CBE; one *s* four *d*. *Educ:* RAF Halton; RAF Coll., Cranwell; Manchester Univ. (MA 1994). Commnd, 1954; No 87 Sqdn, 1955–58; cfs 1958; Flying Instructor and Coll. Adjt, RAF Coll., 1958–61; CO, RAF Sharjah, 1961–62; Indian Jt Services Staff Coll., 1965; HQ 224 Gp, 1965–68; MoD Central Staffs, 1968–70; ndc, 1973; MoD Central Staffs, 1973–74; CO, RAF Coningsby, 1974–76; Canadian Nat. Defence Coll., 1977; MoD Central Staffs, 1978–79; Comdt, Central Flying Sch., 1979–83; Dir of Training (Flying), MoD, 1983–84; Dir of Management and Support of Intelligence, MoD, 1985–86; retired 1987. Member: NHS Trng Authority, 1988–91; Standing Cttee on Postgrad. Medical Educn, 1988–93; Steering Cttee on Pharmacist Postgrad. Educn, 1991–94; Adv. Bd, NHS Estates, 1991–95; Family Health Service Computer Unit, 1992–94; Nat. Blood Authority, 1993–2001 (Vice Chm., 1994–2001). Gov., Salford Coll. of Technology, 1987–89. QCVSA 1959. *Address:* 5 Castlegate, Castle Bytham, Grantham, Lincs NG33 4RU. *T:* (01780) 410372. *Club:* Royal Air Force (Hon. Life Mem., 2004).

**ALLISON, Gillian Margaret Clarkson;** a District Judge (Magistrates' Courts), since 2005; *b* 23 Dec. 1960; *d* of Murray Penman Clarkson and Margaret Gladys Clarkson; *m* 1985, Glen Stuart Allison; two *s*. *Educ:* Merchant Taylors' Sch. for Girls; Surrey Univ.; Central London Poly. (Dip. Law, ext.); Inns of Court Sch. of Law. Called to the Bar, Gray's Inn, 1990; Bench Legal Manager, HM Courts Service, and Dep. Dist Judge, 2003–05. *Recreations:* family, friends, sport, theatre. *Address:* Highbury Corner Magistrates' Court, 51 Holloway Road, N7 8JA.

**ALLISON, John,** PhD; Editor, Opera, since 2000; Music Critic, Sunday Telegraph, since 2005; *b* 20 May 1965; *s* of David Allison and Adele Myrtle Allison (née Kirby); *m* 1991, Nicole Galgut; one *s*. *Educ:* Rondebosch Boys' High Sch., Cape Town; Univ. of Cape Town (BMus 1986, PhD 1989). ARCO. Asst Organist, St George's Cathedral, Cape Town, 1985–89; Music Master, Culford Sch., 1990–91; Asst Ed., 1991–97, Co-ed., 1998–99, Opera mag.; Music Critic, The Times, 1995–2005. Ed., Glyndebourne Fest. prog., 1999–. *Publications:* Edward Elgar: sacred music, 1994; The Pocket Companion to Opera, 1994; (contrib.) New Grove Dictionary of Music and Musicians, 2nd edn 2001; (contrib.) Words on Music: essays in honour of Andrew Porter on the occasion of his 75th birthday, 2004. *Recreations:* travel, art. *Address:* Opera Magazine, 36 Black Lion Lane, W6 9BE. *T:* (020) 8563 8893. *E:* john@opera.co.uk.

**ALLISON, Air Chief Marshal Sir John (Shakespeare),** KCB 1995; CBE 1986 (MBE 1971); non-executive Director, Oxford Health NHS Foundation Trust, since 2015; *b* 24 March 1943; *o s* of Walter Allison and Mollie Emmie Allison (née Poole); *m* 1966, Gillian Patricia Middleton; two *s* three *d*. *Educ:* Royal Grammar Sch., Guildford; RAF College, Cranwell; psc, rcds. Commissioned 1964; flying and staff appts include: 5 Sqn; 226 OCU; 310 TFTS (USAF), Arizona; OC 228 OCU; Station Comdr, RAF Wildenrath; Sec., Chiefs of Staff Cttee; Dir, Air Force Plans and Programmes, 1987–89; ACDS Operational Requirements (Air), MoD, 1989–91; AOC No 11 Gp, 1991–94; COS and Dep. C-in-C, Strike Command, 1994–96; Air Member for Logistics and AOC-in-C, Logistics Comd, 1996–97; AOC-in-C, Strike Comd, 1997–99; Air ADC to Queen, 1997–99. Gentleman Usher to Sword of State, 2005–13. Dir of Strategy, 2001–02, Ops Dir, 2002–04, Jaguar Racing Ltd; Project Director: Filton Site Develt, Rolls-Royce plc, 2005–07; Griffon Hoverwork Ltd, 2009–10. Mem., Criminal Injuries Compensation Tribunal (formerly Appeals Panel), 2000–13. Dir and Trustee, Shuttleworth Trust, 1999–2013. President: Europe Air Sports, 2004–09; Light Aircraft Assoc. (formerly Popular Flying Assoc.), 2006–15. FRAeS 1995–2013. *Recreation:* private flying. *Address:* c/o National Westminster Bank, 24 Broadgate, Coventry CV1 1ZZ. *Club:* Royal Air Force.

**ALLISON, Julia,** PhD; General Secretary, 1994–97, Vice President, since 1997, Royal College of Midwives; *b* 26 Sept. 1939; *d* of Alfred Arthur Richley and Amelia (née Douglas); *m* 1960, Barrie Allison; one *s* one *d*. *Educ:* Lilley and Stone Foundn for Girls, Newark, Notts; Univ. of Nottingham (MA); Wolverhampton Poly. (CertEd (Dist.)); Univ. of Manchester (PhD English and American Studies 2013). RM; ADM; MTD. Clerical officer, Civil Service, 1956–62; libv officer, Nottingham City Libraries, 1963–66; resident in Australia, 1966–68; libv officer, Nottingham City Libraries, 1968–79; direct entry pupil midwife, 1970–72; dist midwife, Nottingham Local Authy, 1972–76; midwifery sister, night duty, Nottingham AHA, 1976–77; registered foster mother, Nottingham Social Services, 1977–79; community midwife, Nottingham HA, 1979–86; midwife teacher, Kingsmill Hosp., 1986–89; Associate Researcher and Sen. Midwife Advr, Univ. of Nottingham, 1989–91; Head of Midwifery Educn, Norfolk Coll. of Nursing and Midwifery, 1991–94. Hon. Associate Prof., Univ. of Nottingham, 2014–. Norwich Diocesan Pres.; Mother's Union, 2001–06; Lay Canon, Norwich Cathedral, 2002–08, now Lay Canon Emeritus. Hon. DSc Nottingham, 2013. *Publications:* Delivered at Home, 1996; The Organisation of Midwifery Care, 1998; (ed) First World War Diary of Robert Douglas, 2002; A Lifetime of Happiness, 2007; The Oldest Oriental Carpet Emporium, 2007; Maternal Mortality in Six East Anglian Parishes, 1539–1619, 2015; Midwives of Sixteenth-Century East Anglia, 2016. *Recreations:* painting, writing. *Address:* Victory Cottage, 6 Jermyns Road, Reydon, Southwold, Suffolk IP18 6QB.

**ALLISON, Prof. Robert John,** PhD; Vice-Chancellor and President, Loughborough University, since 2012; *b* Bristol, 4 Feb. 1961; *s* of Gordon Allison and Elizabeth Ann Allison (née Oman). *Educ:* Northallerton Grammar Sch.; Hull Univ. (BA Geog.); King's Coll. London (PhD Geog. 1986). CGeog RGS (with IBG) 2002. Addison Wheeler Res. Fellow, Durham Univ., 1986–89; Lectr in Engrg Sedimentology, UCL, 1989–93; Durham University: Lectr in Geog., 1993–95; Reader in Geog., 1995–99; Prof. of Geog., 1999–2006; Chm., Bd of Studies in Geog. (Head of Dept), 2000–03; Dean, Faculty of Social Scis and Health, 2003–06; Sussex University: Prof. of Geog. and Pro-Vice-Chancellor for Res., 2006–12; Dep. Vice-Chancellor, 2010–11. Tutor, EPSRC Graduate Schs Trng Prog., 1996–2005; Prog. Dir, ESRC/NERC Graduate Sch., 1999; Scientist: Oman Wahiba Sands Res. Proj., RGS (with IBG), 1988; Kimberly Res. Proj., RGS (with IBG), 1988; Geomorphology Prog. Dir, 1992–94, Mem. Steering Cttee, 1998–2001, Jordan Badia Res. and Develt Prog., RGS (with IBG). Chm., British Geomorphol Res. Gp, 2006–07 (Jun. Vice-Chm., 2004–05; Vice-Chm., 2005–06). Gen. Sec., Internat. Assoc. of Geomorphologists, 1993–97; Hon. Sec., RGS (with IBG), 1998–2001. Director and Chairman: Sussex Innovation Centre Ltd, 2006–12; Sussex IP Ltd, 2006–12; Chm., West Sussex Envmt and Climate Change Bd, 2010–12. Mem. Bd, Leicester and Leics Enterprise Partnership, 2015–. Canon Prof., Leicester Cathedral, 2015–. Pres., Charnwood Athletics, 2016–; Vice-Pres., Leics Scouts, 2016–. Convener, keynote speaker and plenary lectr at internat. confs and symposia. Jan De Ploey Prize, Katholieke Universiteit Leuven, 1993; Charles Lyell Award, BAAS, 1995; Cuthbert Peek Award, RGS (with IBG), 1997. *Publications:* (ed) Landslides of the Dorset Coast, 1990; (ed) The Coastal Landforms of West Dorset, 1992; (ed jtly) Landscape Sensitivity, 1993; Australia: country fact file, 1999; (ed jtly) Applied Geomorphology: theory and practice, 2002; (ed jtly) Sediment Cascades: an integrated approach, 2010; over 100 articles in jls and other pubns. *Recreations:* mountain biking when not falling off, reading a good book preferably on the beach, exploring remote places. *Address:* Vice-Chancellor's Office, Loughborough University, Leics LE11 3TU. *T:* (01509) 222001. *E:* r.j.allison@lboro.ac.uk.

**ALLISON, Roderick Stuart,** CB 1996; Joint Chairman and Head of UK Delegation, Channel Tunnel Safety Authority, 1997–2003; Member, Inter-Governmental Commission, 1997–2003; *b* 28 Nov. 1936; *s* of Stuart Frew Allison and Poppy (née Hodges); *m* 1968, Anne Sergeant; one *s* one *d*. *Educ:* Manchester Grammar Sch.; Balliol Coll., Oxford. Entered Ministry of Labour, 1959; Private Sec. to Perm. Sec., 1963–64; Principal, 1964; Civil Service Dept, 1969–71; Asst Sec., 1971, Under Sec., 1977, Dept of Employment; Health and Safety Executive, 1989–96: Dir, Safety Policy Div., 1992–94; Chief Exec., Offshore Safety Div., 1994–96; Mem., 1995–96. *Recreations:* reading, swimming, music, grandchildren. *E:* rod23allison@gmail.com.

**ALLISON, Ronald William Paul,** CVO 1978; journalist, author, broadcaster; television consultant; *b* 26 Jan. 1932; *s* of Percy Allison and Dorothy (née Doyle); *m* 1st, 1956, Maureen Angela Macdonald (*d* 1992); two *d*; 2nd, 1993, Jennifer Loy Weider; one *s*. *Educ:* Weymouth Grammar Sch.; Taunton's Sch., Southampton. Reporter, Hampshire Chronicle, 1952–57; Reporter, BBC, 1957–67; freelance broadcaster, 1968–69; special correspondent, BBC, 1969–73; Press Sec. to Queen, 1973–78; regular presenter and commentator, Thames TV, 1978–90; Controller of Sport and Outside Broadcasts, 1980–85, Dir of Corporate Affairs, 1986–89, Thames TV; Chm. and Man. Dir, Grand Slam Sports, 1992–96; Dir, Corporate Affairs, BAFTA, 1993–98. Dir, Corporate Affairs, API Gp, 1996–98. Consultant on Royal Family to ITN, 1991–. Editor, BAFTA News, 1993–99. *Publications:* Look Back in Wonder, 1968; The Queen, 1973; Charles, Prince of our Time, 1978; The Country Life Book of Britain in the Seventies, 1980; (ed with Sarah Riddell) The Royal Encyclopedia, 1991; The Queen: 50 years—a celebration, 2001. *Recreations:* photography, watching football. *Clubs:* Lord's Taverners; Old Tauntonians (Southampton).

**ALLISS, Peter;** golfer; television commentator; golf course architect; writer; *b* 28 Feb. 1931; *s* of Percy Alliss and Dorothy Alliss (née Rust); *m* 1st, 1953, Joan; one *s* one *d*; 2nd, 1969, Jacqueline Anne; two *s* one *d* (and one *d* decd). *Educ:* Queen Elizabeth's Grammar Sch., Wimborne; Crosby House, Bournemouth. Nat. Service, RAF Regt, 1949–51. Professional golfer, 1946; played in 8 Ryder Cup matches and 10 Canada Cup (now World Cup) matches; winner of 21 major events; open championships of Spain, Portugal, Italy, Brazil. Past Pres., Ladies' PGA and British Green Keepers' Assoc.; twice Captain, British PGA. Hon. Member, Golf Clubs: Royal & Ancient, 2004; Royal Cinque Ports; Professional Golfers' Assoc.; Combe Hill; Moor Allerton; Beaconsfield; Trevose; Parkstone; Ferndown; Stoke Poges; W Cornwall; Peel; Muirfield Village; Wentworth; Guildford; Rosses Point; Lahinch; Broadstone; Chestfield; Auchterarder; Hindhead; Royal Porthcawl; Kemper Lakes; Helsby; Loch Lomond; Churston; President: Old Thorns; Remedy Oak. Hon. LLD St Andrews, 2005; Hon. DLitt: Humberside, 1993; Bournemouth, 2002. *Publications:* Easier Golf (with Paul Trevillion), 1969; Bedside Golf, 1980; Shell Book of Golf, 1981; The Duke, 1983; Play Golf with Peter Alliss, 1983; The Who's Who of Golf, 1983; (with Michael Hobbs) The Open, 1984; Golfer's Logbook, 1984; Lasting the Course, 1984; More Bedside Golf, 1984; Peter Alliss' Most Memorable Golf, 1986; Peter Alliss' Supreme Champions of Golf, 1986; (ed) Winning Golf, 1986; Yet More Bedside Golf, 1986; Play Better Golf with Peter Alliss, 1989; (with Michael Hobbs) Peter Alliss' Best 100 Golfers, 1989; (with Bob Ferrier) The Best of Golf, 1989; The Lazy Golfers' Guide, 1995; Peter Alliss' Golf Heroes, 2002; Alliss' 19th Hole, 2005; Golf: the cure for a grumpy old man, 2008; *autobiography:* Alliss through the Looking Glass, 1964; Peter Alliss: an autobiography, 1981; My Life, 2004. *Recreation:* talking and taking wine with chums. *Address:* Bucklands, Hindhead, Surrey GU26 6HY. *Clubs:* Lansdowne, Crockfords, Ritz Casino.

**ALLISTER, Rt Rev. Donald Spargo;** *see* Peterborough, Bishop of.

**ALLISTER, James Hugh;** QC (NI) 2001; Member (TUV) North Antrim, Northern Ireland Assembly, since 2011; Leader, Traditional Unionist Voice, since 2007; *b* 2 April 1953; *s* of Robert Allister and Mary Jane Allister (née McCrory); *m* 1978, Ruth McCullagh; two *s* one *d*. *Educ:* Regent House Grammar Sch., Newtownards; Queen's Univ., Belfast. Called to the NI Bar, 1976. Mem. (DemU) N Antrim, NI Assembly, 1982–86. Mem. for NI, European Parlt, 2004–09 (DemU, 2004–07, Traditional Unionist, 2007–09). Contested (TUV) North Antrim, 2010. *Address:* Northern Ireland Assembly, Parliament Buildings, Stormont, Belfast BT4 3XX.

**ALLMENDINGER, Prof. Philip Michael,** PhD; Professor of Land Economy, since 2008, Head, School of Humanities and Social Sciences, since 2015, University of Cambridge; Fellow of Clare College, Cambridge; *b* North Ferriby, 20 Jan. 1968; *s* of Michael Antoon Allmendinger and Janet Mary Allmendinger; *m* 2002, Claudia Wilma Alföldi; three *d*. *Educ:* BSc Hons, MA, PhD, Dip. Law. MRTPI; MRICS. Reader in Land Economy, Univ. of Aberdeen, 1998–2004; Prof. of Planning, Univ. of Reading, 2004–08; Hd, Dept of Land Econ. and Dep. Hd, Sch. of Humanities and Social Scis, Univ. of Cambridge, 2012–15. *Publications:* Planning and Thatcherism, 1997; Planning in Postmodern Times, 2001; Planning Theory, 2002, 2nd edn 2009; New Labour New Planning, 2011; Neoliberal Spatial Governance, 2016. *Recreations:* ski-ing, reading. *Address:* Department of Land Economy, 19 Silver Street, Cambridge CB3 9EP. *E:* pma32@cam.ac.uk.

**ALLNUTT, Denis Edwin;** former Director of Analytical Services, Department for Education and Employment; *b* 17 May 1946; *m* 1968, Patricia Livermore; one *s* one *d*. *Educ:* Hampton Sch., Middlesex; Univ. of Birmingham (BSc 1967). Statistician, Min. of Housing and Local Govt, DoE and Dept of Transport, 1967–82; Chief Statistician: Dept of Employment, 1982–88; DoE, 1988–90; Hd, subseq. Dir, Analytical Services, DES, then DFE, later DFEE, 1990–2000.

**ALLOTT, Nicholas David,** OBE 2014; Managing Director, Cameron Mackintosh Ltd, since 2000; *b* 25 March 1954; *s* of late Brig. David Allott and Shirley Allott; *m* 1989, Anneka Rice (separated 1993); two *s*; partner, Christa D'Souza; two *s*. *Educ:* Geelong Grammar Sch., Australia; Copthorne Sch., Sussex; Charterhouse, Surrey; Exeter Univ. Exec. Dir, Royal Th., Northampton, 1977–81; Cameron Mackintosh Ltd: Prodn Adminr, 1981–86; Exec. Producer, 1986–2000. UK Trade Ambassador, 2014–19. Chm., Soho Th., 2005–19. Member: London Cultural Strategy Gp, 2013–18; Selection Cttee for UK City of Culture, 2013–17. Trustee: Foundn for Sport and the Arts, 1996–2014; Oxford Sch. of Drama, 2000–19; Roundhouse Trust, 2005–; Member: Bd, Cultural Olympiad, 2010–13; Theatres Trust, 2011–17. Patron, Shakespeare Schs Fest., 2016–. *Recreations:* shooting, sailing, keeping the peace. *Address:* 101 Gunterstone Road, W14 9BT. *T:* (020) 7602 0412, *Fax:* (020) 7610 4346. *E:* nick@camack.co.uk. *Clubs:* Garrick, Soho House, Ivy, Academicians' Room.

**ALLOTT, Prof. Philip James,** LLD; FBA 2004; Professor of International Public Law, University of Cambridge, 2000–04; now Professor Emeritus; Fellow, Trinity College, Cambridge, since 1973; *b* Sheffield, 29 May 1937; *s* of Reginald William Allott and Dorothy Allott (*née* Dobson). *Educ:* Downside Sch.; Trinity Coll., Cambridge (MA, LLM; LLD 1998). Called to the Bar, Gray's Inn, 1960; HM Diplomatic Service, 1960–73: Asst Legal Advr, then Legal Counsellor, 1965, FCO; First Sec. and Legal Advr, BMG, Berlin, 1965–68; Legal Counsellor, UK Perm. Repn to EC, Brussels, 1972–73; Law Faculty, University of Cambridge: Mem., 1976–; Lectr, 1980–97; Reader, 1997–2000. Bertha Wilson Dist. Vis. Prof., Dalhousie Univ. Law Sch., 1992; Ganshof van der Meersch Chair, Univ. Libre de Bruxelles, 1996; Faculty Mem., Hauser Global Law Sch. Prog., NY Univ. Law Sch., 1995–. Alternate Rep., UK Delegn to UN Law of the Sea Conf., 1976–80. Internat. Envmtl Law Award, Center for Internat. Envmtl Law, 2014. *Publications:* Eunomia: new order for a new world, 1990, 2nd edn 2001; The Health of Nations: society and law beyond the state, 2002; Towards the International Rule of Law, 2005; Invisible Power: a philosophical adventure story, 2005; Invisible Power 2: a metaphysical adventure story, 2008; Trinity Minds 1317–1945: an intellectual account of Trinity College, Cambridge, 2015; Eutopia: new philosophy and new law for a troubled world, 2016, 2nd edn 2017; Invisible Power 3: a political adventure story, 2017. *Recreations:* high culture, the fine arts, conversation, gardening. *Address:* Trinity College, Cambridge CB2 1TQ. *E:* pja1001@cam.ac.uk. *Club:* Oxford and Cambridge.

**ALLPRESS, Dr Stephen Alan,** FREng; FIET; Co-Founder and Chief Technology Officer, Five AI (formerly Bluprint Technologies), 2015–17, now Advisor; *b* Billericay, Essex, 24 July 1968; *s* of Alan and Valerie Kathleen Allpress; *m* 2005, Sarah Bryn; two *d*. *Educ:* Univ. of Bristol (BEng Hons 1990; PhD 1994). FIET 2000; FREng 2013. Mem., tech. staff, 1994–98, Tech. Manager, 1998–2000, Bell Labs, USA; Principal Scientist, Broadcom, NJ, 2000–01; Chief Res. Fellow, Toshiba Res. Labs, Bristol, 2001–02; Co-Founder, Mem. Bd, Chief Tech. Officer and Vice Pres., Icera Inc., 2002–11; Nvidia: Chief Technol. Officer for Modern Software Develt, 2011–15; Vice. Pres., 2011–14; Sen. Vice Pres., 2014–15. *Recreations:* family, running, cycling, squash.

**ALLSHIRE, Prof. Robin Campbell,** PhD; FRS 2011; Professor of Chromosome Biology, and Wellcome Trust Principal Research Fellow, Wellcome (formerly Wellcome Trust) Centre for Cell Biology, University of Edinburgh. *Educ:* Trinity College, Dublin (BA); Univ. of Edinburgh (Royal Commn for Exhibn of 1851 Scholar; PhD). Postdoctoral researcher, MRC Human Genetics Unit; Vis. Scientist, Cold Spring Harbor Labs; established own res. gp, MRC Human Genetics Unit, 1990, subseq. moved to Wellcome Trust Centre for Cell Biol., 2002, Univ. of Edinburgh. Mem. EMBO, 1988. FRSE 2005. Genetics Soc. Medal, 2013. *Publications:* articles in jls. *Address:* Wellcome Centre for Cell Biology, University of Edinburgh, Michael Swann Building, Max Born Crescent, Edinburgh EH9 3BF.

**ALLSOP, Malcolm Vincent;** Director, Town House Films Ltd, since 2009; *b* 9 Sept. 1950; *s* of Bernard and Irene Allsop; *m* 1975, Elaine Jessica Cox; one *s*. *Educ:* Highbury Grammar Sch., London. Reporter: Ormskirk Advertiser, Lancs, 1967–68; W Lancs Press Agency, 1968–70; and Producer, BBC Radio Merseyside, 1970–71; BBC TV Manchester, 1971–72; Anglia TV, Norwich, 1973; BBC TV East, Norwich, 1974–77; Anglia Television: Political Ed., 1978–84; Sen. Producer, Current Affairs, 1984–89; Controller, Current Affairs and Religion, 1990–94; Dep. Dir of Progs, 1994–96; Controller of Progs and Prodn, 1996–97; Dir of Progs and Prodn, 1998–2000; Controller of Factual Entertainment, Formats and Daytime, LWT/United Prodns, 2001–02; Dir, Anglia TV, until 2002; Controller, Format Sales and Acquisitions, Granada Media, 2002–03; Creative Dir, TéVé Media Gp, 2004; CEO, TéVé Partners, 2004; Man. Dir, Town House TV Prodns Ltd, 2004–09. Mem., Cringleford Parish Council, 2014–15; Vice Chm., Wroxham Parish Council, 2017–. Co-founder, Broadland Ukulele Gp, 2017–. *Publications:* (jtly) Painting Light in Oil, 2011. *Recreations:* painting, bird-watching, Victorian criminology, astronomy, playing the ukulele. *Address:* Wroxham, Norfolk NR12 8TH.

**ALLSOP, Prof. Richard Edward,** OBE 1997; PhD, DSc; FREng, FICE; Professor of Transport Studies, University College London, 1976–2005, now Professor Emeritus; *b* 2 May 1940; *s* of Edward James Allsop and Grace Ada Allsop (*née* Tacey); *m* 1990, Frances Elizabeth Killick. *Educ:* Bemrose Sch., Derby; Queens' Coll., Cambridge (MA Maths); University Coll. London (PhD Maths, DSc Engrg). CEng, FICE, 1990; FREng 1996; FCILT (FCIT 1981); FCIHT (FIHT 1983); TPP 2009. Scientific Officer, Road Res. Lab., 1964–66; Res. Fellow, 1967–69, Lectr in Transport Studies, 1970–72, UCL; Dir, Transport Ops Res. Gp, Univ. of Newcastle upon Tyne, 1973–76; Dean of Engrg, UCL, 1983–85. Visiting Professor: Univ. of Karlsruhe, 1977; Univ. of Natural Resources and Applied Life Scis, Vienna, 2002; Newcastle Univ., 2006–; Adjunct Prof., Qld Univ. of Technol., 2006–09; Hon. Professor: Tech. Univ. of Cracow, 2000–; Moscow Automobile and Roads Inst. (State Tech. Univ.), 2001–; Vis. Fellow, Univ. of Osaka, 1981; Vis. Erskine Fellow, Univ. of Canterbury Christchurch, 1997; Vis. Choi Kin Chung Fellow, Univ. of Hong Kong, 2012. Ext. Res. Advr, Dept for Transport, 1993–2010; Dir, Parly Adv. Council for Transport Safety, 1995–2015. Mem., Road Traffic Law Rev., 1985–88. Visitor to Traffic Gp, Transport & Road Res. Lab., 1987–92. Bd Mem., Eur. Transport Safety Council, 2005–. Member: Northumberland and Newcastle Soc., 1973–; Chiltern Soc., 1977–. Highways and Transportation Award, Instn of Highways and Transportation, 1997; Prince Michael Internat. Road Safety Award, 2011; TRL Academy Award, 2015; Kometani-Sasaki Award, Japan, 2018. *Publications:* (with M. Tracz) Skrzyzowania z Sygnalizacja Swietlna, 1990; (with D. Zumkeller) Kleines Fachwörterbuch Verkehrswesen, 2003; (ed jtly) Transportation and Traffic Theory 2007, 2007; numerous papers in learned jls, edited proceedings. *Recreations:* photography, theatre, walking. *Address:* Centre for Transport Studies, University College London, Gower Street, WC1E 6BT. *E:* r.e.allsop@ucl.ac.uk.

**ALLSOPP,** family name of **Baron Hindlip**.

**ALLSOPP, Ven. Christine;** Archdeacon of Northampton, 2005–13, now Archdeacon Emeritus; *b* 19 Jan. 1947; *d* of John Rupert Goddard and Phyllis May Goddard; *m* 1970, Dr Dennis Allsopp; two *s* one *d*. *Educ:* St Albans Grammar Sch. for Girls; Univ. of Aston (BSc (Chem.) 1968); Salisbury and Wells Theol Coll. Res. Chemist, 1968–70, Inf. Officer, 1970–72, Albright and Wilson; freelance scientific ed. and abstractor, 1977–86. Ordained deacon, 1989, priest, 1994; Asst Curate, Caversham and Mapledurham, 1989–94; Team Vicar, Bracknell, 1994–98; Team Rector, Bourne Valley, 1998–2005. RD, Alderbury, 1999–2005; Canon and Preb., Salisbury Cathedral, 2002–05; Hon. Canon, Peterborough Cathedral, 2005–13. Dep. to Archdeacon of Berks for church building matters, 2014–. Mem., Gen. Synod of C of E, 2005–13. Member: Oxford DAC, 2014–; Exec. Cttee, Anglican-Lutheran Soc., 2015–. Trustee, Clergy Support Trust (formerly Sons & Friends of the Clergy), 2012–. *Recreations:* walking, swimming, Asian cooking, choral singing. *Address:* Mellor Cottage, Sunnybank, 2 Walker's Lane, Lambourn, Berks RG17 8YE. *T:* 07801 096345. *E:* venchrisallsopp@gmail.com.

**ALLSOPP, Christopher John,** CBE 2004; Director, Oxford Institute for Energy Studies, 2006–13; Fellow of New College, 1967–2008, now Emeritus, and Senior Research Fellow, Department of Economics, 2006, now Emeritus, Oxford University; *b* 6 April 1941; twin *s* of late (Harold) Bruce Allsopp, FSA; *m* 1967, Marian Elizabeth Pearce. *Educ:* Balliol Coll., Oxford (MA 1967); Nuffield Coll., Oxford (BPhil Econs 1967). Econ. Asst, HM Treasury, 1966–67; Oxford University: Tutor in Econs, New Coll., 1967–2008; Lectr in Econs, 1968–97 (on leave to OECD, Paris, 1973–74); Reader in Econ. Policy, 1997–2006. Bank of England: Advr, 1980–83; Mem., Ct of Dirs, 1997–2000; Mem., Monetary Policy Cttee, 2000–03. Leader, ind. Review of Statistics for Economic Policymaking, 2003. Ed., Oxford Review of Econ. Policy, 1985–.

**ALLTHORPE-GUYTON, Marjorie;** Secretary General, Association Internationale des Critiques d'Art, 2015–18 (President, UK section, 2009–18; Chair, Congress Commission, 2012–15); *b* 29 July 1948; *d* of Maurice Jack Allthorpe-Guyton and Edith Florence (*née* Clark); *m* 1st, 1970, Brian Collison (marr. diss. 1977); 2nd, 1989, John Mullis (marr. diss. 2000); one *s* one *d*; 3rd, 2000, Paul Dale. *Educ:* Univ. of East Anglia (BA Hons Fine Art); Courtauld Inst. AMA 1974. Asst Keeper, Norwich Castle Mus., 1969–79; Researcher, Norwich Sch. of Art, 1980–82; Selector, British Art Show, Arts Council, 1982–84; Associate Ed., 1988–91, Ed., 1990–92, Artscribe; Dir of Visual Arts, Arts Council of England, later Arts Council England, 1993–2006. External Assessor, Fine Art degrees, 1988–95, Mem. Council, 1997–2005, Goldsmiths' Coll., London Univ.; External Assessor: Fine Art, Oxford Brookes Univ., 1998–2000; Art Theory, City Univ., 2003–07; Ext. Examr, Painting, Slade Sch. of Art, UCL, 2010–14; Panel Mem., Art and Design RAE, HEFC, 2008. Trustee: Kenneth Armitage Foundn, 2011–; City and Guilds of London Art Sch., 2011–. FRSA 1994; FRCA 1999; RIBA 2003. Hon. Dr Anglia Ruskin Univ., 2005. Previews writer, Royal Acad. Mag. *Publications:* A Happy Eye: history of Norwich Sch. of Art 1845–1982, 1982; (jtly) Ian McKeever (monograph), 2009; catalogues: Henry Bright, 1973; John Sell Cotman, 1975; John Thirtle, 1977; Norwich Castle Museum, 1979; many essays and articles on contemporary art. *Recreations:* film, cooking, sailing, growing pomegranates. *Address:* 1 Thornhill Road, N1 1HX. *Club:* Chelsea Arts.

**ALLUM, Sarah Elizabeth Royle, (Mrs R. G. Allum);** *see* Walker, S. E. R.

**ALLWEIS, Martin Peter; His Honour Judge Allweis;** a Circuit Judge, since 1994; Designated Family Judge for Greater Manchester, 1996–2005; *b* 22 Dec. 1947; *s* of late Jack Allweis and Iris Allweis (*née* Mosco); *m* 1984, Tracy Ruth, *d* of late Hyam Barr and of Bernice Barr; one *s* one *d*. *Educ:* Manchester Grammar Sch.; Sidney Sussex Coll., Cambridge (BA Hons 1969). Called to the Bar, Inner Temple, 1970; in practice on Northern Circuit, 1971–94; a Recorder, 1990–94. *Recreations:* family interests, football (Manchester City FC), squash. *Address:* c/o Manchester County Court, Manchester Civil Justice Centre, 1 Bridge Street, Manchester M60 9DJ.

**ALLWOOD;** *see* Muirhead-Allwood.

**ALLWOOD, Prof. Julian Mark,** PhD; CEng, FREng; Professor of Engineering and the Environment, and Director, Use Less Group, Department of Engineering, University of Cambridge, since 2014; *b* Loughborough, 23 July 1965; *s* of Dr Roger James Allwood and Kathleen Margaret Mary Allwood (*née* Ford); *m* 1996, Dr Mary Drummond Moffat; one *s* two *d*. *Educ:* Loughborough Grammar Sch.; Corpus Christi Coll., Cambridge (BA 1987); Imperial Coll. London (PhD 1993; MBA 1997). CEng 2015; FREng 2017. Lectr in Mech. Engrg, Imperial Coll. London, 1996–2000; Lectr, 2000–04, Sen. Lectr, 2004–11, Reader, 2011–14, Dept of Engrg, Univ. of Cambridge. Sec., 2007–10, Vice Chm., 2010–13, Chm., 2013–16, Scientific Tech. Cttee on Metal Forming, Internat. Acad. of Production Engrg (Fellow, 2014). Hon. FIMMM 2015. Jt Editor-in-Chief, Jl of Materials Processing Technol., 2007–17. *Publications:* Sustainable Materials: with both eyes open (with J. M. Cullen), 2012; approx. 125 papers in acad. jls on metal forming technol., envmtl systems analysis and climate mitigation through reducing demand for energy and materials. *Recreations:* family, hillwalking, piano, woodwork, tennis. *Address:* Department of Engineering, University of Cambridge, Trumpington Street, Cambridge CB2 1PZ. *E:* Allwood-Office@eng.cam.ac.uk.

**ALMOND, David John,** FRSL; novelist, short story writer and playwright for children and adults; Professor of Creative Writing, Bath Spa University, since 2012; *b* 15 May 1951; *s* of James Arthur Almond and Catherine Almond (*née* Barber); one *d*. *Educ:* St John's, Felling; St Aidan's, Sunderland; St Joseph's Hebburn; Univ. of E Anglia (BA Hons Eng. and American Lit.); Univ. of Newcastle upon Tyne (PGCE). Postman; teacher (primary, adults and special needs), Tyneside, 1976–98. Vis. Prof. of Creative Writing, Nottingham Trent Univ., 2007–12; Dist. Writing Fellow, Newcastle Univ., 2013–. Commune mem., 1982–83. Ed., Panurge (fiction mag.), 1987–93. Artistic Dir, Bath Fest. of Children's Lit., 2013, 2014. Freeman, City of Gateshead, 2011. Hon. DLitt: Sunderland, 2001; Leicester, 2005; Newcastle, 2011; UEA, 2015. Hans Christian Andersen Award, 2010; Eleanor Farjeon Award, 2013. *Plays:* Wild Girl, Wild Boy, nat. tours, 2001, 2002; My Dad's a Birdman, Young Vic, 2003, 2010; *libretto:* Skellig, 2008, UK tour, 2009–10, Broadway, 2011; Angelo: an opera for Sunderland, 2015. *Publications:* Sleepless Nights, 1985; A Kind of Heaven, 1997; Counting Stars (short stories), 2000; Noah and the Fludd (play), 2010; Nesting (short stories), 2013; Half a Creature from the Sea (illus. Eleanor Taylor; short stories), 2014; Harry Miller's Run, 2015; *for children:* Skellig, 1998 (Library Assoc. Carnegie Medal, Whitbread Children's Book of the Year; Silver Pencil (Holland), 2000) (adapted for radio, and staged, Young Vic, 2003; adapted as opera, The Sage, Gateshead, 2008, and as film, 2009); Kit's Wilderness, 1999 (Smarties Silver Award, 1999; Silver Kiss (Holland), Michael L. Printz Award (USA), 2001; adapted for TV); Heaven Eyes, 2000 (adapted for radio, and staged, 2004); Secret Heart, 2001 (adapted for stage); Wild Girl, Wild Boy (play), 2002; The Fire-Eaters, 2003 (Smarties Gold Award, Whitbread Children's Book of the Year, 2003; Boston Globe-Horn Book Award (USA), 2004); Kate, the Cat and the Moon (illus. Stephen Lambert), 2004; Clay, 2005 (adapted for TV, 2008); My Dad's a Birdman, 2007; The Savage, 2008 (Le Prix Sorcières, 2011); Jackdaw Summer, 2008; Slog's Dad, 2010; The Boy who Climbed into the Moon, 2010; My Name is Mina, 2010; The Boy who Swam with Piranhas, 2012; Mouse Bird Snake Wolf, 2013; A Song for Ella Grey, 2014 (staged, 2017); Klaus Vogel and the Bad Lads, 2014; Island, 2017; The Colour of the Sun, 2018; The Dam, 2018; War is Over (illus. David Litchfield), 2018; Joe Quinn's Poltergeist (illus. Dave McKean), 2019; The New Kid, 2020; *for children and adults:* The True Tale of the Monster Billy Dean, 2011; The Tightrope Walkers, 2014; books trans. into more than 40 langs. *Recreations:* cycling, theatre, cinema.

**ALMOND, George Haylock,** CBE 2001 (MBE 1993); DL; international fire consultant since 2002; Commander, St John Ambulance for Greater Manchester, 2002–07; *b* 19 Jan 1944; *s* of late Arthur Ernest Almond and of Mrs Constance Violet Almond; *m* 1968, Elizabeth Allcock; one *s* one *d*. *Educ:* Portsmouth Tech. High Sch.; Eastleigh Tech. Coll. Fireman, then Leading Fireman, and Sub-Officer, Hants Fire Service, 1962–70; Cheshire Fire Brigade: Station Officer, 1970–72; Asst Divl Officer, 1972–75; Divl Officer, Grade III 1975–77; Divl Officer, Grade I, 1977–82; Divl Comdr, 1978–82; Greater Manchester County Fire Service: Asst County Fire Officer, 1982–90; Dep. County Fire Officer 1990–95; County Fire Officer and Chief Exec., 1995–2002. Chm., Fire Services Nat Benevolent Fund, 2000; Vice Chm., Emmaus Bolton, 1998–; Vice Chm., 1998–2012

Chm., 2012–, Emmaus North West Partnership. Life Patron, Fire Fighters Charity, 2010. Vice Chm., Broughton Hse for ex-service men and women, 2013–. Mem., Rotary Club, Manchester, 1996–2014 (Pres., 2002–03). FIFireE 1988, Life FIFireE 2016 (Internat. Pres., 1996–97); FRSPH (FRSH 1989–2013); FCIPD (FIPD 1991). Mem., Inst. of Advanced Motorists, 2017. Freeman, City of London, 1999. DL 1999, High Sheriff 2012–13, Greater Manchester. Hon. Fellow, Bolton Inst., 2000. Hon. MSc Salford, 2004; Hon. DEng Bolton, 2010. OStJ 2004 (SBStJ 2001). Fire Bde Long Service and Good Conduct Medal, 1982; Queen's Jubilee Medal, 2002. *Publications:* Accidents, Injuries and Illnesses to Firemen in Great Britain, 1972; (contrib.) Fire Service Drill Book, 1985; IFE Preliminary Certificate Students Handbook, 1994, 3rd edn as Elementary Fire Engineering Handbook, 2004, 4th edn 2017; contrib. papers to technical jls. *Recreations:* voluntary work, music, reading, walking. *Address:* 4 Stonehouse, Chapeltown Road, Bromley Cross, Bolton, Lancs BL7 9NB.

**ALMOND, Prof. Jeffrey William,** PhD; FMedSci; Vice President, Discovery Research (formerly Global Research) and External Research and Development, Sanofi Pasteur, 1999–2014; *b* 28 June 1951; *s* of Stanley Peter Almond and Joyce Mary Almond (*née* Fountain); *m* 1976, Karen Elizabeth Batley, BSc, PhD; two *s* one *d*. *Educ:* Univ. of Leeds (BSc); Downing Coll., Cambridge (PhD 1978). Lectr in Virology, Univ. of Leicester, 1979–85; Fellow, Lister Inst. of Preventive Medicine, 1985; University of Reading: Prof. of Microbiol., 1985–99; Hd, Sch. of Animal and Microbial Scis, 1991–95; Vis. Prof., 1999–. Vis. Prof., Sir William Dunn Sch. of Pathology, Univ. of Oxford, 2014–. Mem., Spongiform Encephalopathies Adv. Cttee, UK Govt, 1995–99. Chm., Virology Div., Internat. Union of Microbiol Socs, 1996–99; Chair, Scientific Adv. Bd, Pirbright Inst., 2016–. Mem. Council, MRC, 2008–14; Dir, Greenbank Bio Ltd, 2014–; former Chm., Virion Health Ltd; Member, Board: Virion Biotherapeutics; Eveliqure; Dgen. Unilever-Colworth Prize Lect., Microbiol. Soc., 2013. Fellow, Amer. Acad. of Microbiol., 1996; FMedSci 2006 (Mem. Council, 2008–11). Ivanosky Medal for Virology, Russian Acad. Med. Scis, 1999. *Publications:* over 160 scientific papers, book chapters and rev. articles in jls. *Recreations:* Alpine sports, golf, fitness, jogging. *Address:* Greenbank, Chalkhouse Green, Oxon RG4 9AH.

**ALMOND, Thomas Clive,** OBE 1989; HM Diplomatic Service, retired; Consul-General, Bordeaux, 1992–98; *b* 30 Nov. 1939; *s* of late Thomas and Eveline Almond; *m* 1965, Auriol Gala Elizabeth Annette Hendry (*d* 2014). *Educ:* Bristol Grammar Sch.; London Univ. Entered HM Diplomatic Service, 1967; Accra, 1968; Paris, 1971; FCO, 1975; Brussels, 1978; Jakarta, 1980; Brazzaville, 1983; Ambassador to People's Republic of the Congo, 1987–88; Asst Marshal of the Diplomatic Corps and Asst Head of Protocol Dept, 1988–92. *Recreations:* travelling, golf.

**AL-MULLA, Shwan Mohammad,** CBE 2011; President, Iraqi Consultants and Construction Bureau, since 2003; *b* Baghdad, 20 Oct. 1960; *s* of Mohammad and Neimat Al-Mulla; *m* 1981, Suzan; three *s* two *d*. *Educ:* Richmond Coll., London (BA(Econ)). Pres. and CEO, Sheermans Ltd, 1993–2004; Co-Founder and Pres., Empire Hldgs, 2006–09. Mem., Adv. Bd, Amar Internat. Charitable Foundn, 2012–. *Recreations:* art, car racing, boating. *Address:* Iraqi Consultants and Construction Bureau Centre, Queen Rania Al Abdullah Street, opposite Arena Hotel, Amman, Jordan. *E:* info@iccb.com.

**ALMUNIA AMANN, Joaquín;** Member, 2004–14, and a Vice-President, 2010–14, European Commission; *b* 17 June 1948; *m*; two *c*. *Educ:* Univ. of Deusto, Bilbao. Economist, Council Bureau, Spanish Chambers of Commerce, Brussels, 1972–75; Chief Economist, Unión Gen. de Trabajo, 1976–79. MP (PSOE), Spain, 1979–2004; Minister: of Employment and Social Security, 1982–86; of Public Admin, 1986–91. Parly Leader, 1994–97, Sec. Gen., 1997–2000, PSOE. *Publications:* Memorias Políticas, 2001.

**ALMUTAIWEE, Abdulrahman Ghanem,** Hon. CVO 2013; Ambassador of the United Arab Emirates to the Court of St James's, 2009–16; *b* Dubai, 1 July 1953; *m*; six *s* two *d*. *Educ:* Cairo Univ. (BSc Econs 1979). Dip. Banking and Financial Studies, Bankers Trust Co., NY, 1983. Nat. Bank of Abu Dhabi, Dubai, 1980–83; Dir-Gen., Dubai Chamber of Commerce and Industry, 1983–2006. Chm., Al Fordous PSCo., 2008–; Vice-Chm., Emirates Glass Co., 2007–; Mem. Bd, Emirates Petroleum Corp., 1990–2006. Board Member: Trade Agencies Cttee, Min. of Econ. and Trade, Dubai, 1990–2003; Higher Cttee, Econ. and Trade Exec. Office, Dubai, 2005–06; Government of Dubai: Board Member: Higher Cttee, Dubai Shopping Fest., 1997–2006; Higher Cttee, Dubai Quality Award, 1998–2006; Vice-Chm., Exec. Council, Central Grievance Cttee, 2008–. Member: Bd, Jebel Ali Free Zone, 1985–2000; Dubai Commerce and Tourism Promotion Bd, 1989–95. Mem. Bd, UAE Nat. Cttee for Internat. Chamber of Commerce, 2003–06. Chm., Mohammed bin Rashid Al Maktoum Business Award Cttee, 2004–06. Member, Board of Governors: Dubai UC, 1983–2006; Dubai Ethics Resource Centre, 2003–06. Mem. Bd, UAE Red Crescent, 2007–. Officer, Order of Civil Merit (Spain), 1999. *Recreations:* reading, swimming, jogging.

**ALPASS, John;** Head of Fraud Strategy, Department for Work and Pensions (formerly Head of Fraud Intelligence, Department of Social Security), 2000–05. Security Service, 1973–95; Intelligence Co-ordinator, Cabinet Office, 1996–99. Mem., Security Vetting Appeals Panel, 2009–15. Chm., Fees Adv. Commn, Gen. Synod, 2012–; Member: Guildford Diocesan Adv. Cttee, 2003– (Chm., 2011–); Bishop's Council, Dio. of Guildford, 2007–.

**ALPE, Pauline;** *see* Wallace, P.

**ALPERS, Prof. Michael Philip,** AO 2005; CSM 2008; FRS 2008; FAA; John Curtin Distinguished Professor of International Health, Curtin University, 2005–16, Emeritus Professor, 2017. *Educ:* Gonville and Caius Coll., Cambridge (BA 1957); Univ. of Adelaide (BSc, MB BS). FAA 2012. Kuru Res. Officer, Dept of Public Health, PNG, 1961–63; Vis. Scientist, NIH, 1964–67; Res. Fellow, Dept of Microbiol., Univ. of Western Australia, 1968–76; Dir, Inst. of Med. Res., PNG, 1977–2000; Adjunct Prof., Centre for Internat. Health, Curtin Univ. of Technol., 2001–04. Mem., Aust. TSE Adv. Cttee, 2001–12. Fellow: Australasian Coll. of Tropical Medicine, 1992; Qld Inst. of Med. Res., 1992; Faculty of Public Health Medicine, RACP, 2001; PNG Inst. of Med. Res., 2005. Fellow, World Acad. of Scis (Associate Fellow, Third World Acad. of Scis, 1991). Hon. Internat. Fellow (formerly Hon. Mem.), Amer. Soc. of Tropical Medicine and Hygiene, 1993; Hon. Life Mem., Australasian Soc. for Infectious Diseases, 1999; Life Member: Nat. Soc. of PNG, 2002; Australasian Epidemiol Assoc., 2011. DUniv Adelaide, 2012. Medal, Collège de France, 1984; Macdonald Medal, RSTM&H, 1990; Lifetime Achievement Award, Monash Univ., 2008. *Address:* Room 437, Building 400, Curtin University, GPO Box U1987, Perth, WA 6845, Australia; 3 Watkins Street, Fremantle, WA 6160, Australia.

**ALPHANDÉRY, Edmond Gérard;** Director, ENGIE (formerly Suez, then GDF Suez), since 2008; Senior Adviser: Nomura France, since 2012; Quadrille Capital, since 2013; Chairman, Euro (50) Group, since 1999; *b* 2 Sept. 1943; *m* 1972, Laurence Rivain; one *s*. *Educ:* Frédéric Mistral Lycée, Avignon; Inst. of Political Studies, Paris; Univs of Chicago and California at Berkeley. Asst Lectr, Univ. of Paris, IX, 1968–69; Lectr, Univ. of Aix-en-Provence, 1970–71; Sen. Lectr, and Dean, Faculty of Econ. Sci., Univ. of Nantes, 1971–74; Prof., Univ. of Angers, 1973; Associate Prof., Univ. of Pittsburgh, 1975; Prof. of Political Economy, Univ. of Paris II, 1974–92. Deputy (UDF-CDS) for Maine-et-Loire, French Nat. Assembly, 1978–93 (Mem., Finance Cttee, 1979–93); Minister of the Economy, France, 1993–95; Mem., Maine-et-Loire General Council, 1976–2008 (Vice-Pres., 1991–94, Pres., 1994–95); Mayor of Longué-Jumelles, 1977–2008. Vice-Pres., Centre des Démocrates Sociaux; numerous positions with economic and monetary bodies, incl. Chm., Adv. Cttee, Omnès Capital, 2013–19; Mem., Governance Cttee, Caisse des Dépôts et Consignations, 2003– (Mem., Supervisory Bd, 1988–93); Member: Consultative Cttee, Banque de France, 1998–; Adv. Cttee, A. T. Kearney, France, 2013–17. Chairman: Bd of Dirs, CNP Insurance SA, 1992–93; Electricité de France, 1995–98; Caisse Nationale de Prévoyance, subseq. CNP Assurances, 1998–2012; non-voting Dir, Crédit Agricole Corporate and Investment Bank (formerly Calyon), 2002–15; Dir, Icade, 2004–12. Pres., Centre for European Policy Studies, Brussels, 2013–16 (Pres., High Level Gp on Energy Infrastructure in Europe, 2015–16); Chm., Centre des Professions financières, 2003–14; Vice-Pres., Internat. Finance Forum, 2018–. Mem., Trilateral Commn, 1996–2014 (Hon. Mem., 2014). *Publications:* Les Politiques de stabilisation (with G. Delsupehe), 1974; Cours d'analyse macroéconomique, 1976; Analyse monétaire approfondie, 1978; 1986: le piège, 1985; La Rupture: le liberalisme à l'épreuve des faits (with A. Fourçans), 1987; La Réforme obligée: sous le soleil de l'euro, 2000.

**ALPS, Tess;** Chair, Thinkbox, since 2013 (Founding Chief Executive Officer, 2006–13); *b* Retford, Notts, 1953; *m* 1976, Tim Alps; one *s*. *Educ:* Durham Univ. (BA Hons Eng. Lang. and Lit.); Mountview Theatre Sch. (Postgrad. Dip. Drama). Sales, ITV, incl. ATV, TSW and YTV, 1977–92; Dir, PHD, 1993–2003; Chm., PHD Gp UK, 2003–06. Member, Advisory Panel: ASA; BBC Magazines. Trustee, Nat. Advertising Benevolent Soc. Former Pres., WACL. Member: Mktg Gp of GB; BAFTA. FRTS; Fellow, Marketing Soc. Outstanding Achievement Award, Women in Film and TV, 2007; Media Leader of Decade, 2013; Mackintosh Medal, Advertising Assoc., 2018. *Recreations:* classical music, theatre, literature, gardening, lots of TV of course. *Address:* Thinkbox, Manning House, 22 Carlisle Place, SW1P 1JA. *T:* (020) 7630 2320. *E:* tess.alps@thinkbox.tv.

**ALPTUNA, Akin,** PhD; Ambassador of Turkey to the Court of St James's, 2003–07; *b* 23 May 1942; *s* of Huseyin Kamil Alptuna and Cahide Alptuna; *m* 1967, Esin Arman; two *s*. *Educ:* Ankara Univ. (BA; PhD in Internat. Relns). Joined Min. of Foreign Affairs, Turkey, 1967; Second, then First Sec., Copenhagen, 1972–75; First Sec., Nicosia, 1975–77; Hd of Section, Internat. Econ. Agreements Dept and Mem. of Cabinet for Minister of Foreign Affairs, 1977–79; Counsellor, Perm. Delegn of Turkey to EC, Brussels, 1979–81; Consul, Düsseldorf, 1981–83; Hd, Dept for Internat. Econ. Orgns, 1983–85; Dep. Hd of Mission, Turkish Perm. Delegn to UN, 1985–89; Dep. Dir Gen., Multilateral Political Affairs, 1989–93; Dir Gen., EU Dept, 1993–95; Ambassador: Helsinki, 1995–97; Perm. Repn of Turkey to OECD, 1997–2000; Dep. Under-Sec. for EU and W Europe, 1999–2003. Lectr, TOBB Univ. of Econs and Technol. *Clubs:* Athenæum, Travellers, Cavalry and Guards.

**AL SAUD, HRH Prince Khalid bin Bandar bin Sultan bin Abdul Aziz;** Ambassador of the Kingdom of Saudi Arabia to the Court of St James's, since 2019; *b* Paris, 14 Aug. 1977; *s* of HRH Prince Bandar bin Sultan Al Saud and HRH Princess Haifa Al Faisal; *m* 2011, Lucy Caroline Cuthbert; two *d*. *Educ:* Green Hedges; Islamic Saudi Acad.; Eton Coll.; Univ. of Oxford; Fletcher Sch., Tufts Univ. Ambassador to Germany, 2017–18. *Recreations:* tobogganing, shooting. *Address:* Royal Embassy of Saudi Arabia, 30–32 Charles Street, Mayfair, W1J 5DZ. *Clubs:* 5 Hertford Street, Mark's, Harry's, George; St Moritz Tobogganning.

**AL SAUD, HRH Prince Mohammed Nawaf;** Ambassador of the Kingdom of Saudi Arabia to the Court of St James's and to Ireland, 2005–18; Adviser to the King of Saudi Arabia, since 2018; *b* 22 May 1953; *s* of HRH Prince Nawaf bin Abdulaziz and HH Princess Sharifa; *m* 1979, HH Princess Fadwa Khalid Abdullah; two *s* three *d*. *Educ:* Capital Institute High Sch., Riyadh; Sch. of Foreign Service, Georgetown Univ., Washington; John F. Kennedy Sch. of Govt, Harvard Univ. Diplomat; joined Royal Commn for Jubail and Yanbu, Saudi Arabia, 1981; joined Min. of Foreign Affairs, 1984, Minister's Cabinet; promoted to Inspector Gen.; Ambassador of Saudi Arabia to Italy and Malta, 1995; promoted to rank of Minister, 2005. Formerly: Dean, Arab Ambassadors in Italy; Chm., Islamic and Cultural Centre, Rome. Pres., Harvard Alumni Assoc., Saudi Arabia. *Recreations:* football, tennis. *Clubs:* Brooks's, Travellers.

**AL-SHAIKH-ALI, Dr Anas,** CBE 2009; Academic Advisor, International Institute of Islamic Thought, since 1991; *b* Mosul, 29 Sept. 1942; *s* of Saddiq and Khadija Al-Shaikh-Ali; *m* 1972, Dr Maryam Mahmood; one *s* one *d*. *Educ:* Al-Hikma Univ., Baghdad (BA English Lit. 1969); American Univ. of Beirut (MA English Lit. 1972); Univ. of Manchester (PhD American Studies 1983). Lectr, and Cultural and PR Dir, Univ. of Mosul, Iraq, 1973–79; Res. Fellow, Manchester Univ., 1983–85; Res. Fellow, St David's UC, Wales, 1985–86; personal res. work, 1986–91. Chair, Assoc. of Muslim Social Scientists, UK, 1999–. Mem., Mgt Bd, Islamic Centre, Cambridge Univ., 2008–14. Vice-Pres., Inst. of Epistemological Res., 2010–. *Publications:* (contrib.) Citizenship, Security and Democracy: Muslim engagement with the West, 2009; (contrib.) Islamophobia: the challenge of pluralism in the 21st century, 2011; (contrib.) Genocidal Nightmares: narratives of insecurity and the logic of mass atrocities, 2014. *Recreations:* reading, gardening, walking. *E:* iiit@iiituk.com.

**ALSOP, Marin;** conductor; Music Director: Baltimore Symphony Orchestra, since 2007; São Paulo Symphony Orchestra, 2013–19, Conductor of Honour, since 2019 (Chief Conductor, 2012–13); Artist in Residence, Southbank Centre, since 2011; Chief Conductor, Vienna Radio Symphony Orchestra, since 2019 (Chief Conductor Designate, 2018–19); *b* 16 Oct. 1956; *d* of K. LaMar Alsop and Ruth (*née* Condell). *Educ:* Juilliard Sch. (BM 1977, MM 1978). Music Director: Long Island Philharmonic Orch., 1989–96; Eugene SO, Oregon, 1989–96; Cabrillo Fest., 1992–; Colorado SO, 1993–2003 (Music Dir Laureate, 2003–); Principal Conductor, Bournemouth SO, 2002–08 (Conductor Emeritus, 2008–); Principal Guest Conductor: City of London Sinfonia, 2000–03; Royal Scottish Nat. Orch., 2000–03. Regular guest conductor: Philadelphia Orch.; Cleveland Orch., Los Angeles Philharmonic; NY Philharmonic; LSO; LPO. Conductor, Last Night of the Proms, 2013, 2015. MacArthur Foundn Fellow, 2005. Fellow, Amer. Acad. of Arts and Scis, 2008. Hon. RAM, 2011; Hon. Mem., Royal Philharmonic Soc., 2014. Grammy Award, 2010. *Recreations:* running, swimming, antique collecting, reading. *Address:* c/o Intermusica Artists' Management Ltd, 9 Kingsway, WC2B 6XF. *T:* (020) 7608 9900.

**ALSTON, David Ian;** Arts Director, Arts Council of Wales, 2005–19; *b* 26 June 1952; *s* of Cyril Alston and Dorothy Alston; *m* 1975, Christine Bodin (marr. diss. 1987); two *d*; partner, Lesley Webster; one *s* one *d*. *Educ:* Corpus Christi Coll., Oxford (Open Exhibn, MA); Postgrad. Dip. in History of Art (Dist.)). Asst Curator of Pictures, Christ Church, Oxford, 1978–82; Asst Keeper of Art (Ruskin Collection), Sheffield, 1982; Dep. Dir of Arts, Sheffield MDC, 1982–93; Sen. Principal Keeper, Sheffield Arts and Museums, 1993–94; Keeper of Art, Nat. Museums and Galls of Wales, 1994–98; Galls Dir, 1998–2002, Acting Chief Exec., 2001–02, The Lowry. Vice Chair, Anthem (Music Fund Wales), 2019–. Trustee, Evelyn Williams Trust. Co-Founder Ed., Oxford Art Jl, 1978. *Publications:* Under the Cover of Darkness: Night Prints, 1986; Piranesi's Prisons: a perspective, 1987;

Graham Sutherland: nature into art, 2004; Into Painting: Brendan Stuart Burns, 2007; Silent Explosion: Ivor Davies and destruction in art, 2014; sundry exhibn texts and articles. *Recreations:* listening, looking, cooking, talking, drinking, walking, cycling, loving, musing and other 'ings. *Address:* 168 Dobbin Hill, Sheffield S11 7JG. *E:* davidialston@hotmail.com.

**ALSTON, Nicholas Kenneth,** CBE 1997; DL; Chair, Policing Institute for the Eastern Region, Anglia Ruskin University, since 2016; *b* Harwich, 2 Sept. 1952; *s* of Kenneth Alston, QPM and Florence Alston; *m* 1974, Philippa Hilary Rust; one *s* one *d. Educ:* King Edward VI Grammar Sch., Chelmsford; Queens' Coll., Cambridge (BA Natural Scis 1974; MA 1978). Officer, RN, 1974–77; MoD, 1977–2006; Global Hd of Security, Goldman Sachs, 2006–11. Police and Crime Comr for Essex, 2012–16. Non-exec. Dir, Nat. Crime Agency, 2016–. Chair, Essex Community Foundn, 2018–. DL Essex, 2017. *Recreations:* sailing, choral singing. *Address:* c/o Essex Community Foundation, 121 New London Road, Chelmsford, Essex CM2 0QT. *E:* nkalston@aol.com.

**ALSTON, Sir Richard (John William),** Kt 2019; CBE 2001; choreographer; Artistic Director, The Place, 1994–2018, and Richard Alston Dance Company, 1994–March 2020; *b* 30 Oct. 1948; *s* of late Gordon Walter Alston and Margot Alston (*née* Whitworth). *Educ:* Eton; Croydon Coll. of Art. Choreographed for London Contemporary Dance Theatre, 1970–72; founded Strider, 1972; worked in USA, 1975–77; Resident Choreographer, 1980–86, Artistic Dir, 1986–92, Ballet Rambert, subseq. Rambert Dance Co. Principal Ballets: Nowhere Slowly; Tiger Balm; Blue Schubert Fragments; Soft Verges; Rainbow Bandit; Doublework; Soda Lake; for Ballet Rambert: Rainbow Ripples, 1980; The Rite of Spring, 1981; Apollo Distraught, 1982; Dangerous Liaisons, 1985; Zansa, 1986; Dutiful Ducks, 1986; Pulcinella, 1987; Strong Language, 1987; Hymnos, 1988; Roughcut, 1990; Cat's Eye, 1992. Created: The Kingdom of Pagodas, for Royal Danish Ballet, 1982; Midsummer, for Royal Ballet, 1983; Le Marteau Sans Maitre, for Compagnie Chopinot, 1992; Delicious Arbour, for Shobana Jeyasingh Dance Co., 1993; Movements from Petrushka, Lachrymae, Rumours Visions, for Aldeburgh Festival, 1994; Sheer Bravado, for Ballet Theatre Munich, 2006; Walk Through A Storm, for Ballet Black, 2008; Carmen, for Scottish Ballet, 2009, for Miami City Ballet, 2015; All Alight for Phoenix Dance Th., 2013; for Richard Alston Dance Co.: Shadow Realm, Something in the City, 1994; Stardust, 1995; Orpheus Singing and Dreaming, Beyond Measure, Okho, 1996; Brisk Singing, Light Flooding into Darkened Rooms, 1997; Red Run, Waltzes in Disorder, Sophisticated Curiosities, 1998; Slow Airs Almost All, A Sudden Exit, 1999; The Signal of a Shake, Tremor, 2000; Fever, Strange Company, Water Music, 2001; Touch and Go, Stampede, 2002; Overdrive, 2003; Shimmer, Gypsy Mixture, 2004; Such Longing, 2005; Volumina, 2005; The Devil in the Detail, Proverb, 2006; Fingerprint, Nigredo, 2007; Shuffle it Right, Blow Over, The Men in My Life, 2008; Alert, Serene Beneath, 2009; Out of the Strong, 2010; Unfinished Business, 2011; A Ceremony of Carols, Isthmus, Darkness Visible, 2012; Buzzing Round the Hunisuccle, Phaedra, Hölderlin Fragments, 2013; Rejoice in the Lamb, 2014; Nomadic, 2015; An Italian in Madrid, 2016; Chacony, 2017; Carnaval, 2017; Brahms Hungarian, 2018; Arrived, 2019. Chm., Youth Dance England, 2009–16. DUniv: Surrey, 1993; Kent, 2015; Kingston, 2016. Hon. Fellow, Trinity Laban, 2017. Chevalier, Ordre des Arts et des Lettres (France), 1995; Ninette de Valois Award for Outstanding Achievement, Nat. Dance Critics Circle, 2009. *Recreations:* music, reading. *Address:* The Place, 17 Duke's Road, WC1H 9PY.

**ALSTON, Hon. Richard Kenneth Robert,** AO 2015; Federal President, Liberal Party of Australia, 2014–17; High Commissioner for Australia in the United Kingdom, 2005–08; *b* 19 Dec. 1941; *s* of late Robert Bruce Alston and of Sheila Gertrude Alston; *m* 1973, Margaret Mary, (Megs), Kennedy; one *s* one *d. Educ:* Xavier Coll., Melbourne; Univ. of Melbourne (BA, LLB; BCom); Monash Univ. (LLM; MBA). Government of Australia: Senator (Lib) for Victoria, 1986–2004; Shadow Minister: for Communications, 1989–90 and 1993–96; for Social Security, Child Care and Retirement Incomes, 1990–92; for Superannuation and Child Care, 1992–93; for the Arts, 1994–96; Dep. Leader of the Opposition in Senate, 1993–96; Dep. Leader of Govt in Senate, 1996–2003; Minister for Communications, IT and the Arts, 1996–2003. Chm., Senate Select Cttees, 1991–96; Mem., Senate Standing Cttees on Finance and Public Admin, 1987–90, and Legal and Const. Affairs, 1989–90. Chm., Broadcasting Services Australia Ltd, 2004–05; Dir, Hansen Technologies Ltd, 2004–05. Chairman: TFS Ltd, 2011–12; Amex Resources Ltd, 2014–17; non-exec. Dir, Chime plc, 2008–13; Member: Internat. Adv. Bd, CQS Hedge Fund LLP, 2008–15; Nat. Bd, CPA Australia, 2015–17. Adjunct Prof. of Information Technol., Bond Univ., 2004–. Centenary Medal (Australia), 2003. *Recreations:* Aboriginal art, modern literature, oriental rugs, walking, pumping iron.

**ALSTON, Robert John,** CMG 1987; QSO 2004; HM Diplomatic Service, retired; High Commissioner to New Zealand, Governor (non-resident) of Pitcairn, Henderson, Ducie and Oeno Islands, and High Commissioner (non-resident) to Western Samoa, 1994–98; *b* 10 Feb. 1938; *s* of late Arthur William Alston and of Rita Alston; *m* 1969, Patricia Claire Essex; one *s* one *d. Educ:* Ardingly Coll.; New Coll., Oxford (MA Mod. Hist.). Third Sec., Kabul, 1963; Eastern Dept, FO, 1966; Head of Computer Study Team, FCO, 1969; First Sec. (Econ.), Paris, 1971; First Sec. and Head of Chancery, Tehran, 1974; Asst Head, Energy Science and Space Dept, FCO, 1977; Head, Joint Nuclear Unit, FCO, 1978; Political Counsellor, UK Delegn to NATO, 1981; Head, Defence Dept, FCO, 1984; Ambassador to Oman, 1986–90; seconded to NI Office, 1990–92; Asst Under-Sec. of State (Public Depts), FCO, 1992–94. Chm., Link Foundn for UK-NZ Relations, 1999–2004; Advr, Internat. Trade & Investment Missions Ltd, 1999–2002; Trustees Rep., Commonwealth Inst., 2002–17. Chm., Anglo-Omani Soc., 2014–. Dir, Romney Resource Centre, 1999–2006. Consultant on Anglican Communion affairs to Archbishop of Canterbury, 1999–2002. Trustee: Antarctic Heritage Trust, 1998–2008; Commonwealth Educn Trust, 2016–18; Dir, Antarctic Heritage Ltd, 2008–12; Member: Cttee, Romney Marsh Historic Churches Trust, 2003–10; Cttee, The Pilgrims, 2010–17 (Chm., Membership Cttee, 2010–17); Dir, Romney Tweed, 2014–. Chairman of Governors: Ardingly Coll., 2005–10; Marsh Acad., New Romney, 2007–13. Mem. Ct, World Traders' Co., 2003–13 (Master, 2007–08). DL Kent, 2004. *Publications:* (with Stuart Laing) Unshook Till the End of Time: a history of relations between Britain and Oman, 2012. *Recreations:* gardening, travel, music. *Address:* 97 Coast Drive, Lydd on Sea, Romney Marsh, Kent TN29 9NW. *T:* (01797) 321686.

**ALSTON-ROBERTS-WEST, Lt-Col George Arthur;** see West, Lt-Col G. A. A.-R.-.

**ALT, Deborah;** see Gribbon, D.

**AL TAJIR, Sayed Mohamed Mahdi;** Patron, Al Tajir World of Islam Trust, since 1977; *m*; five *s* one *d. Educ:* Bahrain Govt Sch.; Preston Grammar Sch. Director: Port and Customs, Dubai, 1955–63; HH the Ruler's Affairs and Petroleum Affairs Dept, Dubai, 1963–72; Ambassador of UAE: to UK, 1972–91; to France, 1972–91. Vice Chm., World of Islam Fest. Trust, 1974–77. *Address:* c/o Al Tajir World of Islam Trust, 11 Elvaston Place, SW7 5QG.

**ALTANGEREL, Bulgaa;** Ambassador of Mongolia to United States of America, and (non-resident) to Israel, since 2013, and Mexico, since 2014; *b* Khovd Province, Mongolia, 25 Oct. 1955; *s* of Puntsag Bulgaa and Dansran Nansalmaa; *m* 1980, Erdenee Chuluuntsetseg; three *d. Educ:* Secondary Sch., Khovd Province, Mongolia; Moscow Inst. of Internat. Relns (Master in Internat. Law 1979); Moscow Inst. Political Scis (Master in Pol Scis 1990); Columbia Univ., USA (Special Trng for Internat. Law and Internat. Public Affairs 1992); Kiev Nat. Taras Shevchenko Univ., Ukraine (PhD Internat. Law 2003); Harvard Kennedy Sch. (Sen. Exec. Prog. 2013); Asia-Pacific Center for Security Studies, Hawaii (Sen. Exec. course, 2014). Attaché, Min. of Foreign Affairs, Mongolia, 1979–81; Attaché, later Third Sec., Embassy of Mongolia in Afghanistan, 1981–85; Third, later Second Sec., Min. of Foreign Affairs, 1985–88; State Great Hural-SGH (Parliament of Mongolia): Advr on Foreign Policy, 1991; Dir, Foreign Relns Dept, SGH Secretariat, 1991–97; Ambassador to Turkey and Ambassador (non-resident) to Bulgaria, Lebanon, Romania and Uzbekistan, 1997–2003; Dir Gen. for Legal and Consular Affairs, Min. of Foreign Affairs, 2003–08; Ambassador to UK and Ambassador (non-resident) to RSA, Ireland and Iceland, 2008–13. Mem., Inter-Govtl Commn on inspection of state boundaries between Mongolia and USSR, 1985–88. Responsible Sec., Mongolian Inter-Parly Gp, 1990–97. Chair, Internat. Law Dept, Mongolian Nat. Univ., 1993–97; Professor: Law and Security Acad., Russian Fedn, 2006; Mongolian Nat. Inst., 2008. Hon. Prof., Law Sch., Nat. Univ. of Mongolia, 2011. Mem., Bd of Dirs, Trust Fund for Victims, Internat. Criminal Court, 2007–12. *Address:* Embassy of Mongolia, 2833 M Street NW, Washington, DC 20007, USA. *T:* (202) 3337117, ext. 119, (202) 4316344, *Fax:* (202) 2989227. *E:* ambassador@mongolianembassy.us.

**ALTARAS, Jonathan;** Chairman and Managing Director, Jonathan Altaras Associates, 1990–2006; *b* 5 Aug. 1948; *s* of Leonard and Joy Altaras. *Educ:* Cheadle Hulme Sch.; Manchester Univ. (MA). Trustee, V&A Mus., 2003–06. Chm., Mus. of Performance, 2003; Mem. Bd, Drama Centre, 1990. *Recreation:* eating. *Club:* Garrick.

**ALTHAM, John Robert Carr; His Honour Judge Altham;** a Circuit Judge, since 2011; *b* Morecambe, 30 March 1966; *s* of John Altham and Linda Altham; *m* 1992, Fiona Aubrey; one *s* two *d. Educ:* Lancaster Royal Grammar Sch.; University Coll. London (BA Hons Classics); Univ. of Birmingham (Common Professional Exam.). Called to the Bar, Gray's Inn, 1993; Junior, Northern Circuit, 1996–97; Recorder, 2008–11. *Recreations:* family, hiking, running, piano. *Address:* Preston Crown Court, Openshaw Place, Ringway, Preston, Lancs PR1 2LL.

**ALTHORP, Viscount; Louis Frederick John Spencer;** *b* 14 March 1994; *o s* and *heir of* Earl Spencer, *qv. Educ:* Western Province Prep. Sch., Cape Town; Reddam House Sch., Cape Town; Bishops Dio. Coll., Cape Town; Edinburgh Univ. *Address:* Althorp, Northampton NN7 4HG.

**ALTMAN, Brian;** QC 2008; a Recorder, since 2003; *b* 16 Aug. 1957; *s* of late Stanley Altman and of Pauline Altman; *m* 1996, Charlotte Parkin; one *s* one *d* and one *s* one *d* from previous *m. Educ:* Chingford Sen. High Sch.; King's Coll. London (LLB); Univ. of Amsterdam (Dip. Eur. Int.). Called to the Bar, Middle Temple, 1981, Bencher, 2010; Central Criminal Court: Jun. Treasury Counsel, 1997–2002; Sen. Treasury Counsel, 2002–10; First Sen. Treasury Counsel, and Chm., Bar Mess, 2010–13. *Recreations:* weight and fitness training, music, scuba diving. *Address:* (chambers) 2 Bedford Row, WC1R 4BU. *T:* (020) 7440 8888, *Fax:* (020) 7242 1738. *E:* baltman@2bedfordrow.co.uk.

**ALTMAN, His Honour John;** a Circuit Judge, 1995–2015; Senior Circuit Judge and Designated Family Judge for London, 2007–15; *b* 21 June 1944; *s* of Lionel and Vita Altman; *m* 1968, Elizabeth Brown; two *d. Educ:* Bootham Sch., York; Univ. of Bristol (LLB); Council of Legal Education. Called to the Bar, Middle Temple, 1967; part-time Chm., Industrial Tribunals, 1983; Asst Recorder, 1985; Chm., Industrial Tribunals, 1986; a Recorder, 1989; Designated Family Judge: for Milton Keynes, 2003–07; for Oxford, 2005–07. Chm., W Yorks Family Mediation Service, 1997–2002. *Publications:* contribs to Law Guardian and Family Law. *Recreations:* reading, photography, music, theatre. *E:* john_altman@me.com.

**ALTMANN,** Baroness *cr* 2015 (Life Peer), of Tottenham in the London Borough of Haringey; **Rosalind Miriam Altmann,** CBE 2014; PhD; *b* 8 April 1956; *d* of Leo and Renate Altmann; *m* 1982, Paul Richer; one *s* two *d. Educ:* University Coll. London (BSc Econ 1st Cl. Hons); Harvard Univ. (Kennedy Schol.); London Sch. of Econs (PhD 1981). Investment Mgt Cert. Fund Manager, Prudential Assce, London, 1981–84; Hd, Internat. Equities, Chase Manhattan Bank, 1984–89; Director: Rothschild Asset Mgt, 1989–91; Natwest Investment Mgt, 1991–93; ind. policy advr on pensions, investment, savings and retirement, 1993–2015; Dir-Gen., Saga Gp, 2010–13. Consultant to HM Treasury on Pension Fund Investment, 2000; Mem., Lord Chancellor's Strategic Investment Bd, 2004–15; Policy Advr to Number 10 Policy Unit on pensions, investments and savings, 2000–05; UK Govt Business Champion for Older Workers, 2014–15. Minister of State, DWP, 2015–16. Non-exec. Mem., Court Funds Office, 2004–15; Mem. Bd, IPSO, 2014–15. Gov., 1989–2017, and non-exec. Dir, 2004–17, LSE. Life Gov., Nightingale House for the Elderly, 1985. MCSI (MSI 1992); MInstD 2000. Hon. DLitt Westminster, 2010; Hon. DCL Newcastle, 2015. *Publications:* articles in newspapers, jls and industry magazines, incl. Financial Times, The Times, Pensions Week, Financial Advr, Money Mktg, Pensions World, Wall St Jl, Professional Investor, Global Finance, Instnl Investor. *Recreations:* charity fund-raising, swimming, walking, table tennis. *E:* altmannr@parliament.uk.

**ALTON,** family name of **Baron Alton of Liverpool.**

**ALTON OF LIVERPOOL,** Baron *cr* 1997 (Life Peer), of Mossley Hill, in the Co. of Merseyside; **David Patrick Paul Alton;** Chairman, Banner Ethical Investment Fund, 1999–2011; Chairman and Director, Merseyside Special Investment Fund, 2001–06; Professor of Citizenship, 1997–2016, and Director, 1997–2016, Roscoe Foundation for Citizenship (formerly Foundation for Citizenship), Liverpool John Moores University (Hon. Fellow, 2016); *b* 15 March 1951; *s* of Frederick and Bridget Alton; *m* 1988, Dilys Elizabeth, *yr d* of Rev. Philip Bell; three *s* one *d. Educ:* Edmund Campion Sch., Hornchurch; Christ's College of Education, Liverpool; St Andrews Univ. Elected to Liverpool City Council as Britain's youngest City Councillor, 1972; CC, 1972–80; Deputy Leader of the Council and Housing Chairman, 1978; Vice-Pres., AMA, later LGA, 1979– ; MP Liverpool, Edge Hill (by-election), March 1979–83, Liverpool, Mossley Hill, 1983–97 (L, 1979–88, Lib Dem, 1988–97). Liberal Party spokesman on: the environment and race relations, 1979–81; home affairs, 1981–82; NI, 1987–88 (Alliance spokesman on NI, 1987); Chief Whip, Liberal Party, 1985–87; Member: Select Cttee on the Environment, 1981–85; H of C Privileges Cttee, 1994–97; cross-bencher, 1997. All-Party Groups: Treasurer: Pro-Life, 1993–2004; Landmines, 1996–2000; Friends of CAFOD; Chairman: Street Children 1992–97; British-N Korea, 2003–; Vice Chairman: Tibet Gp, 2005–; Blood Cord and Adult Stem Cells, 2009–14; Foreign Affairs, 2010–16; Freedom of Religion and Belief 2014–16; Burma, 2017–; Egypt, 2017–; Uganda, 2017–; Eritrea, 2018–; Co-Chair, Pakistan Minorities, 2019–; Sec., Sudan Gp, 2005–. Chm., Liberal Candidates Cttee, 1985. Nat Pres., Nat. League of Young Liberals, 1979. Co-founder, Movement for Christian Democracy in Britain, 1990. Vis. Fellow, St Andrews Univ., 1996; Vis. Prof., Liverpool Hope Univ., 2017–. Former Chm., Council for Educn in Commonwealth. Nat. Vice Pres., Life; Pres., Liverpool Br., NSPCC, 1980–97; Vice-President: Liverpool YMCA

Crisis; Past Chairman: Forget-me-not Appeal (Royal Liverpool Hosp.); Merseyside CVS. Vice-Pres., Assoc. of Councillors. Patron: Jubilee Campaign for the release of prisoners of conscience, 1986–; Nat. Assoc. Child Contact Centres, 1997–2017; Karen Aid, 1999–2018; Merseyside Kidney Res.; Jospice; Liverpool Sch. of Tropical Medicine; G. K. Chesterton Inst.; Motec Life; Asylum Link Merseyside; Internat. Young Leaders Network. Mem., Catholic Writers' Guild; Trustee: Catholic Central Liby, 1998–2004; Partners In Hope, 1999–2006; Metta Educn Trust, 2002–06; Christian Heritage Centre, 2012– (Chm., 2012–); Arise Foundn, 2016–. Columnist, The Universe, 1989–2013. Hon. Prof., Yanbian Univ. of Sci. and Technol., 2012–. Michael Bell Meml Award, Knights of St Columba, 1987; Good Samaritan Advocates Internat. Award, Advocates Internat., 2001; Korean Mystery of Life Award, Archdio. of Seoul, 2009; Coptic Award, 2014; St Thomas More Award, 2016. Kt Comdr, Constantinian Order of St George, 2003; KCSG 2008; Commander's Cross, Order of Merit (Hungary), 2017. *Publications:* What Kind of Country?, 1987; Whose Choice Anyway?, 1988; Faith in Britain, 1991; Signs of Contradiction, 1996; Life After Death, 1997; Citizen Virtues, 1999; Citizen 21, 2001; Pilgrim Ways, 2001; Passion and Pain, 2003; Euthanasia: getting to the heart of the matter, 2005; Abortion: getting to the heart of the matter, 2005; Building Bridges: is there hope for North Korea?, 2013. *Recreations:* gardening, reading, walking, grandchildren. *Address:* House of Lords, SW1A 0PW. *E:* altond@parliament.uk. *W:* www.davidalton.net.

**ALTON, Roger;** freelance journalist; Executive Editor, The Times, 2010–15; *b* 20 Dec. 1947; *s* of late Reginald Ernest Alton, MC and Jeannine Beatrice Alton (*née* Gentis); divorced; one *d. Educ:* Clifton Coll.; Exeter Coll., Oxford. Liverpool Post, 1969–74; The Guardian, 1974–98; Editor: The Observer, 1998–2007; The Independent, 2008–10. Sports Columnist, The Spectator, 2008–; Contributing Editor, Daily Mail, 2015–. Editor of the Year: What the Papers Say Awards, 2000; GQ Men of the Year Awards, 2005. *Recreations:* sports, films, ski-ing, climbing. *Address:* 62 St Julian's Farm Road, SE27 0RS. *Clubs:* Climbers', Soho House, Groucho; Ski Club of GB.

**ALTRINCHAM,** 3rd Baron *cr* 1945, of Tormarton, co. Gloucester; **Anthony Ulick David Dundas Grigg;** *b* 12 Jan. 1934; *yr s* of 1st Baron Altrincham, KCMG, KCVO, DSO, MC, PC and Hon. Joan Dickson-Poynder; *S* brother, 2001; *m* 1965, Eliane, *d* of Marquis de Miramon; two *s* one *d. Educ:* Eton; New Coll., Oxford. *Heir: s* Hon. (Edward) Sebastian Grigg [*b* 18 Dec. 1965; *m* 1993, Rachel Sophia Kelly; three *s* two *d* (of whom one *s* one *d* are twins)]. *Address:* La Musclera, Tamariu 17212, Palafrugell, Girona, Spain.

**ALTY, John Henry Myers,** CB 2010; Director General, Trade Policy, Department for International Trade, since 2016; *b* Liverpool, 2 Dec. 1956; *s* of late Henry and Heather Alty; *m* 1981, Jane Cocks; three *s* one *d. Educ:* Liverpool Coll.; Worcester Coll., Oxford (BA Classics). Department of Industry, subseq. Department of Trade and Industry, later Department for Business, Enterprise and Regulatory Reform, then Department for Business, Innovation and Skills: various trng posts, 1978–81; Private Sec. to Minister of State, 1981–83; Grade 7, 1984–91, incl. period in Eur. Secretariat, Cabinet Office and as Prin. Private Sec. to Chancellor of Duchy of Lancaster; Competition Policy, 1992–94; Insurance Regulation, 1994–95; Prin. Private Sec. to Sec. of State for Trade and Industry, 1995–98; Director: Europe, 1998–2002; Business Relations, 2002–05; Dir Gen., Fair Mkts Gp, 2005–10; Acting Dir Gen., Knowledge and Innovation, BIS, 2012–13; Chief Exec., Intellectual Property Office, 2010–16. *Publications:* contrib. Jl Hellenic Studies. *Recreation:* Liverpool Football Club. *Address:* Department for International Trade, 3 Whitehall Place, SW1A 2AW. *E:* John.alty@trade.gov.uk.

**ALVAREZ, Al(fred);** poet and author; *b* London, 1929; *s* of late Bertie Alvarez and Katie Alvarez (*née* Levy); *m* 1st, 1956, Ursula Barr (marr. diss. 1961); one *s*; 2nd, 1966, Anne Adams; one *s* one *d. Educ:* Oundle Sch.; Corpus Christi Coll., Oxford (BA 1952, MA 1956; Hon. Fellow, 2001). Research Schol., CCC, Oxon, and Research Schol. of Goldsmiths' Company, 1952–53, 1954–55. Procter Visiting Fellowship, Princeton, 1953–54; Vis. Fellow of Rockefeller Foundn, USA, 1955–56, 1958; gave Christian Gauss Seminars in Criticism, Princeton, and was Lectr in Creative Writing, 1957–58; D. H. Lawrence Fellowship, New Mexico Univ., 1958; Poetry Critic and Editor, The Observer, 1956–66. Visiting Professor: Brandeis Univ., 1960; New York State Univ., Buffalo, 1966. Adv. Ed., Penguin Modern European Poets in Translation, 1966–78. Hon. DLitt East London, 1998. Vachel Lindsay Prize for Poetry (from Poetry, Chicago), 1961; Benson Medal for Literature, RSL, 2010, 2012. *Publications:* The Shaping Spirit (US title, Stewards of Excellence), 1958; The School of Donne, 1961; The New Poetry (ed and introd), 1962; Under Pressure, 1965; Beyond All This Fiddle, 1968; Lost (poems), 1968; Penguin Modern Poets, No 18, 1970; Apparition (poems, with paintings by Charles Blackman), 1971; The Savage God, 1971; Beckett, 1973; Hers (novel), 1974; Hunt (novel), 1978; Autumn to Autumn and Selected Poems 1953–76, 1978; Life After Marriage, 1982; The Biggest Game in Town, 1983; Offshore, 1986; Feeding the Rat, 1988; Rain Forest (with paintings by Charles Blackman), 1988; Day of Atonement (novel), 1991; The Faber Book of Modern European Poetry (ed and introd.), 1992; Night, 1995; Where Did It All Go Right? (autobiog.), 1999; Poker: bets, bluffs and bad beats, 2001; New and Selected Poems, 2002; The Writer's Voice, 2005; Risky Business, 2007; Pondlife: a swimmer's journal, 2013. *Recreations:* music, poker, cold water swimming. *Address:* c/o Aitken Alexander Associates, 291 Gray's Inn Road, WC1X 8EB. *Clubs:* Climbers', Alpine; Highgate Lifebuoys.

**ALVINGHAM,** 2nd Baron *cr* 1929, of Woodfold; **Maj.-Gen. Robert Guy Eardley Yerburgh,** CBE 1978 (OBE 1972); DL; *b* 16 Dec. 1926; *s* of 1st Baron and Dorothea Gertrude (*d* 1927), *d* of late J. Eardley Yerburgh; *S* father, 1955; *m* 1952, Beryl Elliott, *d* of late W. D. Williams; one *s* one *d. Educ:* Eton. Commissioned 1946, Coldstream Guards; served UK, Palestine, Tripolitania, BAOR, Farelf, British Guiana; Head of Staff, CDS, 1972–75; Dep. Dir, Army Staff Duties, 1975–78; Dir of Army Quartering, 1978–81, retired. Patron, Royal British Legion, Oxfordshire, 1994–2009; Co-Patron (with Lady Alvingham), Henley and District Agricultural Assoc., 2008–14. DL Oxfordshire, 1996. *Heir: s* Captain Hon. Robert Richard Guy Yerburgh, 17th/21st Lancers, retired [*b* 10 Dec. 1956; *m* 1st, 1981, Vanessa, *yr d* of Captain Duncan Kirk (marr. diss. 1993); two *s*; 2nd, 1994, Karen, *er d* of Antony Baldwin; one *s* one *d*].

**ALWARD, Peter Andrew Ulrich;** Intendant and Managing Director, Salzburg Easter Festival, 2010–15; President, EMI Classics, 2002–05; *b* 20 Nov. 1950; *s* of late Herbert Andrew Alward and Marion Evelyne (*née* Schreiber). *Educ:* Mowden Prep. Sch., Hove; Bryanston; Guildhall Sch. of Music and Drama. Simrock Music Publishers, London, 1968–70; with EMI, 1970–2005: EMI Records UK, London, 1970–74; Eur. Co-ordinator, EMI Classical Div., Munich, 1975–83; Exec. Producer, with Herbert von Karajan, for all EMI recordings, 1976–89; Artists and Repertoire, UK: Manager, 1983–84; Internat. Dir, 1985–88; Vice-Pres., 1989–97; Sen. Vice-Pres., 1998–2001. Trustee: Royal Opera House Enterprises Ltd, 2007–16; Bd, Opera Rara, 2007–11. Artistic Consultant, 2006–09, Mem., Eur. Adv. Bd, 2009–10, Cleveland Orch.; Hon. Artistic Consultant, West-Eastern Divan Orch., 2007–09; Consultant, BR Klassik, 2008–. Member: Adv. Bd, Royal Opera House, Covent Garden, 1998–99; Artistic Cttee, Herbert von Karajan Stiftung, 2003–10; Kuratorium, Internationale Stiftung Mozarteum, Salzburg, 2008–13; Jury Mem., Salzburg Fest. and Nestlé Young Conductor's Award, 2010–18; Chm., ARD Piano Competition, 2011; Vice-Chm., Santander Internat. Piano Competition, 2012. Mem., Bd of Trustees, Young Concert Artists Trust, 1999–2004; Trustee, Masterclass Media Foundn, 2006–14. Mem., Editl Adv. Bd, BBC Music, 2006–16. Special Achievement Award, Gramophone Mag., 2004. City of Salzburg Golden Ring, 2015. *Recreations:* all classical music sectors, exhibitions of painting and sculpture, theatre, books, collecting stage designs and costume designs, cooking, travelling. *Address:* 24 Midway, Walton-on-Thames, Surrey KT12 3HZ. *T:* (01932) 226741; Reiteralpestrasse 19, 83395 Freilassing, Germany. *T:* (8654) 3558.

**AMAKYE, Grace Augustina; Her Honour Judge Amakye;** a Circuit Judge, since 2015; *b* Takoradi, Ghana, 12 Aug. 1959; *d* of John Emmanuel Amakye and Augustina Amakye (*née* Jantuah); *m* Robert James Saunders; two *d. Educ:* Handmaids of Sacred Heart of Jesus, Beckenham, Kent; Univ. of London (LLB Hons ext.). Called to the Bar, Gray's Inn, 1983; in practice as a barrister, specialising in crime, 1983–2015; Asst Recorder, 1999–2000; Recorder, 2000–15. *Recreations:* theatre, ballet, reading, fine dining, travel. *Address:* Snaresbrook Crown Court, 75 Hollybush Hill, E11 1QW.

**AMAN, Dato' Sri Anifah;** MP Malaysia, since 1999; Minister of Foreign Affairs, Malaysia, 2009–18; *b* Keningau, Sabah, Malaysia, 16 Nov. 1953; *m* Siti Rubiah Abdul Samad; three *s. Educ:* Sabah Coll., Kota Kinabalu, Sabah, Malaysia; Univ. of Buckingham (BA Philosophy, Econs and Law 1979). Deputy Minister: of Primary Industries, 1999–2004; of Plantation Industries and Commodities, 2004–08. JP 1996. Ahli Setia Darjah Kinabalu, 1994; Panglima Gemilang Darjah Kinabalu, 1998; Darjah Indera Mahkota Pahang, 2004; Darjah Sri Sultan Ahmad Shah Pahang, 2009. *Recreations:* football, golf. *Address:* Parliament of Malaysia, Parliament Building, 50680 Kuala Lumpur.

**AMANN, Prof. Ronald,** PhD; Professor of Comparative Politics (formerly of Soviet Politics), University of Birmingham, 1986–2003, now Emeritus; *b* 21 Aug. 1943; *s* of George James Amann and Elizabeth Clementson Amann (*née* Towell); *m* 1965, Susan Frances Peters; two *s* one *d. Educ:* Heaton Grammar Sch., Newcastle upon Tyne; Univ. of Birmingham (MSocSc, PhD). Consultant, OECD, and Res. Associate, 1965–68; University of Birmingham: Asst Lectr, then Lectr and Sen. Lectr, 1968–83; Dir, Centre for Russian and E European Studies, 1983–89; Dean, Faculty of Commerce and Soc. Sci., 1989–91; Pro-Vice-Chancellor, 1991–94; Chief Exec. and Dep. Chm., ESRC, 1994–99; Dir-Gen., Centre for Mgt and Policy Studies, Cabinet Office, 1999–2002. Vis. Fellow, Osteuropa Inst., Munich, 1975. Special Advr, H of C Select Cttee on Sci. and Technol., 1976. Member: Technology Foresight Steering Cttee, 1995–2000; COPUS, 1996–99; Adv. Bd, Centre for Analysis of Risk and Regulation, LSE, 2000–; Chm. Adv. Bd, Centre for Res. on Innovation and Competitiveness, Univ. of Manchester, 2001–. Ind. Mem., W Midlands Police Authy, 2007–12. Mem. Council, SSEES, London Univ., 1986–89. Founding AcSS, 1999. FRSA. *Publications:* jointly: Science Policy in the USSR, 1969; The Technological Level of Soviet Industry, 1977; Industrial Innovation in the Soviet Union, 1982; Technical Progress and Soviet Economic Development, 1986. *Recreations:* modern jazz, walking. *Address:* 3 Niall Close, Edgbaston, Birmingham B15 3LU.

**AMARATUNGA, Prof. Gehan Anil Joseph,** PhD; CEng, FREng, FIET; 1966 Professor of Engineering (Electrical), University of Cambridge, since 1998; Fellow, Churchill College, Cambridge, 1987–95 and since 1998; *b* 6 April 1956; *s* of Carl Hermen Joseph Amaratunga and Mallika Swarna; *m* 1981, Praveen Dharshini Hitchcock (marr. diss. 2016); one *s* two *d. Educ:* Royal Coll., Colombo; Pelham Meml High Sch., NY; University Coll. Cardiff (BSc Hons); Wolfson Coll., Cambridge (PhD 1983). CEng, FREng 2004; FIET (FIEE 2004). University of Southampton: Res. Fellow in Microelectronics, 1983; Lectr in Electronics, 1984–86; Vis. Prof., Dept of Electronics and Computer Sci., 1998–; Lectr in Electrical Engrg, Univ. of Cambridge, 1987–95; Prof. of Electrical Engrg, Univ. of Liverpool, 1995–98. Nanyang Prof., 2010–12, Tan Chin Tuan Centennial Prof., 2012–14, Nangyang Vis. Prof., 2014–18, Nanyang Technol Univ., Singapore; Hon. Prof., Yunnan Univ., China, 2015–; Hon. Vis. Prof., Peking Univ., Shenzen, China, 2016–. Founder, Chief Scientific and Technol. Officer, Cambridge Semiconductor Ltd, 2000–15; Chm. and Dir, Wind Technologies Ltd, 2006–17; Founder and Director: Enecsys Ltd, 2004–11; Nanoinstruments Ltd, 2005–07; Chief of Res. and Innovation, Sri Lanka Inst. of Nanotechnol., 2011–; Founder and CSO, Camutronics, 2012–; Founder and Chm., Zinergy UK Ltd, 2016–. Royal Acad. Engrg Vis. Researcher, Stanford Univ., Calif, 1989. FRSA 2009. Silver Medal, Royal Acad. of Engrg, 2007. *Publications:* contrib. IEEE Trans, Physical Rev., Nature. *Recreations:* jazz, opera, cricket, classic cars, avant garde cinema. *Address:* Electrical Engineering Division, Engineering Department, Cambridge University, Cambridge CB3 0FA. *T:* (01223) 748320. *E:* gaja1@cam.ac.uk.

**AMAYO, Lazarus Ombai;** High Commissioner of Kenya to the Court of St James's, 2014–18; *b* Homa Bay Co., Kenya, 23 March 1955; *s* of Pastor Luke Amayo and Esther Akoth; *m* Nelly Abonyo; one *s* two *d. Educ:* Spicer Meml Coll., India (Bachelor of Liberal Arts); Univ. of Delhi (MA Political Sci.). HR Manager, Kenya Posts and Telecommunications Corp. and teacher, 1979–89; MP for Karachuonyo, Kenyan Nat. Assembly, and Asst Minister for Educn, 1989–92; CEO/Man. Dir, Catering Levy Trustees (State Corp.), 1993–97; entered Kenyan diplomatic service, 1999; High Comr to India, 1999–2004; Actg Perm. Sec., Dir of Admin and Hd, Internat. Orgns and Confs Div., Min. of Foreign Affairs, 2004–06; High Comr to Zambia and Malawi and Perm. Rep. to Common Mkt for Eastern and Southern Africa, 2006–10; Dir, Europe and Commonwealth Div., Min. of Foreign Affairs and Internat. Trade, 2010–14. Moran of Burning Spear (Kenya), 2011; CAV 2013. *E:* loamayo@gmail.com.

**AMBACHE, Jeremy Noel;** Member (Lab), Wandsworth London Borough Council, since 2014 (Opposition spokesperson for Education and Children's Services, since 2016); *b* 16 Dec. 1946; *s* of late Nachman and Stella Ambache; *m* 1973, Ann Campbell; two *d. Educ:* Bedales Sch.; Sussex Univ. (BA); York Univ. (MPhil); Kingston Univ. (MA). Social worker, Birmingham Social Services, 1971–73; Team Manager, Hammersmith Social Services, 1974–80; Co-ordinator for Community Homes, Brent Social Services, 1981–84; Area Manager, Croydon Social Services, 1984–90; Divl Dir, Berks Social Services, 1990–91; Asst Dir, Bedfordshire Social Services, 1991–93; Dir of Social Services, Knowsley, 1993–2000; Dir of Social Services and Housing, Bromley, 2000–02; mgt consultant in health and social care, 2002–05. Member, Board: Wandsworth PCT, 2011–12; Wandsworth CCG, 2012–14. Pol advr and campaigner, Liberal Democrats, 2004–10. Contested (Lib Dem) Putney, 2005. Sec., and Vice Chair (Campaigns), Putney Constituency, Lab. Party, 2011–14. Trustee: Wandsworth Age Concern, subseq. Age UK (Wandsworth), 2008–17; Wandsworth LINK, 2009–12 (Chm., 2009). *Recreations:* tennis, yoga, travel, walking. *Address:* 17 Hazlewell Road, Putney, SW15 6LT. *T:* (020) 8785 9650. *Club:* Putney Lawn Tennis.

**AMBLER, John Doss;** Vice-President, 1980–86, Vice-President, Human Resources, 1989–96, Texaco Inc.; *b* 24 July 1934; *m*; one *s* one *d. Educ:* Virginia Tech. (BS Business Admin 1956). Texaco Inc., USA: various assignments, Marketing Dept, Alexandra, Va, 1956–65; Dist Sales Manager, Harrisburg, Pa, 1965–67; Asst Divl Manager, Norfolk, Va, 1967–68; Staff Asst to Gen. Manager Marketing US, New York, 1968; various assignments, Chicago and New York, 1969–72; Gen. Manager, Texaco Olie Maatschappij BV, Rotterdam, 1972–75; Man. Dir, Texaco Oil AB, Stockholm, 1975–77; Asst to Pres., 1977,

Asst to Chm. of the Bd, 1980, Texaco Inc.; Pres., Texaco Europe, New York, 1981–82; Chm. and Chief Exec. Officer, Texaco Ltd, London, 1982–89. *Recreations:* hunting, fishing, tennis, photography.

**AMBROSE, Euan James; His Honour Judge Ambrose;** a Circuit Judge, since 2009; *b* 23 Nov. 1967. *Educ:* Magdalene Coll., Cambridge (BA 1989). Called to the Bar, Middle Temple, 1992; Treasury Counsel, 2000–09; Recorder, 2005–09. *Address:* Bristol Crown Court, Small Street, Bristol BS1 1DA.

**AMED, Imran,** MBE 2017; Founder and Chief Executive Officer, The Business of Fashion, since 2007; *b* Calgary, Canada, 20 April 1975; *s* of Miles Ahmed and Hamida Ahmed. *Educ:* McGill Univ. (BCom 1997); Harvard Business Sch. (MBA 2002). Associate, Braxton Associates, 1997–2000; Engagement Manager, McKinsey & Co., 2002–06. Contrib. Editor, GQ, 2014–. *Publications:* (jtly) Pattern: 100 fashion designers, 10 curators, 2013. *Address:* The Business of Fashion, Moray House, 6th Floor, 23–31 Great Titchfield Street, W1W 7PA. *E:* editor@businessoffashion.com.

**AMENT, Sharon Ann;** Director, Museum of London, since 2012; *b* London, 29 Sept. 1962; *d* of Horace Cecil Ament and Pauline Ament (*née* Anderson); *m* 2006, Nicholas Lane. *Educ:* Sterrix Lane Comprehensive Sch., Litherland, Liverpool; Univ. of Leeds (BA Hons Hist. of Art). PR Manager, Merseyside Council for Voluntary Service, 1985–86; Hd of Mktg, Martin Mere Wildfowl Centre, 1986–89; Nat. Mktg Manager, Wildfowl and Wetlands Trust, 1989–92; Hd of Mktg, Zool Soc. London, 1992–2000; Dir, Public Engagement, Natural Hist. Mus., 2000–12. Vice Pres., Eur. Network for Sci. Centres and Mus, 2009–12. Chair, Exhibn Rd Culture Gp, 2008–12. Mem., Internat. Bd, ArtSci. Mus., Singapore, 2012–. Fellow: Salzburg Seminar, 2011; Noyce Leadership Inst., 2011. *Recreations:* cycling (keen), wine, walking, culture, birdwatching, wild places, knitting. *Address:* Museum of London, 150 London Wall, EC2Y 5HN. *T:* (020) 7814 5700. *E:* Director@museumoflondon.org.uk.

**AMESBURY, Mike;** MP (Lab) Weaver Vale, since 2017; *b* Manchester; *s* of Bernard Amesbury and Maureen Amesbury; *m* 2006, Amanda; one *s*. *Educ:* Castleford High Sch.; Univ. of Bradford (BA Hons Community Studies); Univ. of Central England (DipCG). Careers Advr, then Connexions Manager, 2002–08. Sen. Parly Advr to Angela Rayner, MP, 2015–17; Advr to Rt Hon. Andrew Burnham, MP, 2016–17. Mem., Manchester CC, 2006–17. Mem., Communities and Local Govt Select Cttee, 2017–. Member: Unison; GMB. *Recreation:* keen interest in football and indie music. *Address:* House of Commons, SW1A 0AA. *E:* mike.amesbury.mp@parliament.uk.

**AMESS, Sir David (Anthony Andrew),** Kt 2015; MP (C) Southend West, since 1997 (Basildon, 1983–97); *b* Plaistow, 26 March 1952; *s* of late James Henry Valentine Amess and Maud Ethel Martin; *m* 1983, Julia Monica Margaret Arnold; one *s* four *d*. *Educ:* St Bonaventure's Grammar Sch.; Bournemouth Coll. of Technol. (BScEcon Hons 2.2, special subject Govt). Teacher, St John the Baptist Jun. Mixed Sch., Bethnal Green, 1970–71; Jun. Underwriter, Leslie & Godwin Agencies, 1974–76; Sen. Manager, Accountancy Personnel, 1976–79; Senior Consultant: Executemps Co. Agency, 1979–81; AA Recruitment Co., 1981–87; Chairman and Chief Executive: Accountancy Solutions, 1987–90; Accountancy Gp, 1990–96. Mem., Redbridge Council, 1982–86 (Vice Chm., Housing Cttee, 1982–85). Contested (C) Newham NW, 1979. Parliamentary Private Secretary: to Parly Under-Secs of State (Health), DHSS, 1987–88; to Minister of State and Parly Under-Sec of State, Dept of Transport, 1988–90; to Minister of State, DoE, 1990–92; to Chief Sec. to the Treasury, 1992–94; to Sec. of State for Employment, 1994–95; to Sec. of State for Defence, 1995–97. Member: Broadcasting Select Cttee, 1994–97; Health Select Cttee, 1998–2007; Chairman's Panel, 2001–. All-Party Groups: Chairman: Solvent Abuse, 2000; Fire Safety and Rescue, 2001–; Rheumatoid Arthritis, 2002; Liver Health (formerly Hepatology), 2004–; Holy See, 2006; FRAME, 2006; Maldives, 2009–; Democracy in Bahrain, 2013; Maternity, 2013–; Britain-Bermuda; Philippines; Photography; Bermuda; Endometriosis, 2018–; Co-Chm., Fairs and Showgrounds; Vice-Chairman: Guides, 2000; Hungary, 2003–; Obesity, 2003; Deep Vein Thrombosis Awareness, 2003–; Asthma, 2003; Funerals and Bereavement, 2005–; Thrombosis, 2006–; Mauritius, 2010–; Zoos and Aquariums; Treasurer: N Korea, 2004–; Cardiac Risk in the Young, 2011–. Chm., Cons. Back Bench Health Cttee, 1999–; Member: Backbench Business Cttee, 2012–15; Admin Cttee, 2015–. Mem. Exec., 1922 Cttee, 2004–12. Vice Pres., Nat. Lotteries Council, 1998. Chm. Trustees, Industry and Parlt Trust, 2015–17. Dir, Parly Broadcasting Unit Ltd, 1997–99. Chm., 1912 Club, 1996–; Vice Chm., Assoc. of Cons. Clubs, 1997–. Hon. Sec., Cons. Friends of Israel, 1998–. Fellow, Industry and Parliament Trust, 1994 (Chm., Fellowship Cttee, 2017–18). *Publications:* The Road to Basildon, 1993; Basildon Experience: Conservatives fight back, 1994; Against All Odds, 2012; Party of Opportunity, 2014, 2nd edn 2015; contrib. magazines and pamphlets. *Recreations:* gardening, music, sport, animals, theatre, travel. *Address:* c/o House of Commons, SW1A 0AA.

**AMET, Hon. Sir Arnold (Karibone),** Kt 1993; CBE 1987; MP (Nat. Alliance) Madang, Papua New Guinea, 2007–12; Attorney General, Papua New Guinea, 2010–11; *b* 30 Oct. 1952; *m* 1972, Miaru (*d* 2009); three *s* two *d*. *Educ:* Univ. of PNG (LLB 1975); Legal Trng Inst., PNG. Joined Public Solicitor's Office, PNG, 1976; qualified as barrister and solicitor, 1977; Legal Officer and Sec., Nat. Airline Commn, 1979–80; Dep. Public Solicitor, 1980–81; Public Solicitor, 1981–83; Judge of National Trial Court and Supreme Court of Appeal, 1983–93; Chief Justice, Papua New Guinea, 1993–2003; Governor, Madang, 2007. Hon. LLD PNG, 1993. *Recreations:* Christian Ministry, watching Rugby and cricket.

**AMEY, Julian Nigel Robert;** Chief Executive, Institute of Healthcare Engineering and Estate Management, 2012–18; *b* 19 June 1949; *s* of Robert Amey and Diana Amey (*née* Coles); *m* 1972, Ann Victoria Brenchley; three *d*. *Educ:* Wellingborough Sch.; Magdalene Coll., Cambridge (BA 1971, MA 1973). Longman Group: Exec. Trainee, 1971; Manager: Spain, 1972–76; Brazil, 1977–79; Latin America, 1979–83; Regional Manager, Asia Pacific Region, 1983–85; Dir, Internat. Sales and Mktg, 1985–89; Exec. Dir, BBC English, World Service, 1989–94; apptd to DTI, to assist in internat. promotion of British educn and media interest, 1994–96; Dir Gen., Canning House, 1996–2001; Chief Executive: CIBSE, 2001–06; Trinity Coll. London, 2006–09 (Gov., 2003–06); ISTD, 2009–11. Chm., Anglo-Chilean Soc., 2002–06. Gov., Bath Spa Univ. (formerly Univ. Coll.), 1996–2013. Chm., Ambassadors Circle, Bath Spa Univ., 2013–. Mem., Samuel Pepys Club, 2010– (Mem. Cttee, 2011; Chm., 2013–). FRSA 2009. *Publications:* Spanish Business Dictionary, 1979; Portuguese Business Dictionary, 1981. *Recreations:* cricket, tennis, ornithology, travel. *Clubs:* English-Speaking Union, Rumford; Hawks (Cambridge).

**AMHERST OF HACKNEY,** 5th Baron *cr* 1892; **Hugh William Amherst Cecil;** maritime lawyer; *b* 17 July 1968; *s* of 4th Baron Amherst of Hackney and of Elisabeth, *d* of Hugh Humphrey Merriman, DSO, MC, TD; *S* father, 2009; *m* 1996, Nicola Jane, *d* of Major Timothy Michels; one *s* two *d*. *Educ:* Eton; Bristol Univ. (BSc Hons Psychology). Admitted solicitor, 1994. *Recreation:* sailing. *Heir: s* Hon. Jack William Amherst Cecil, *b* 13 July 2001. *Club:* Royal Yacht Squadron.

**AMIEL, Prof. Stephanie Anne, (Lady Alberti),** MD; FRCP; R. D. Lawrence Professor of Diabetic Medicine, King's College London, since 1995; *b* Farnborough, Kent, 17 Oct. 1954; *d* of Gerald Joseph Amiel and Trudie Amiel; *m* 1998, Sir (Kurt) George (Matthew Mayer) Alberti, *qv*; three step *s*. *Educ:* Baston Sch. for Girls, Kent; Guy's Hosp. Sch. of Medicine, Univ. of London (BSc 1975; MB BS 1978; MD 1988). FRCP 1993. Res. Fellow, Yale Univ., 1983–86; Res. Fellow and Hon. Sen. Registrar, St Bartholomew's Hosp., London, 1986–89; Sen. Lectr and Hon. Consultant, Guy's Hosp., London, 1989–95. *Publications:* contrib. papers on diabetes, hypoglycaemia in diabetes and central control of metabolism. *Recreations:* fell-walking, painting, opera. *Address:* Diabetes Research Offices, King's College London School of Medicine, Denmark Hill Campus, Weston Education Centre, 10 Cutcombe Road, SE5 9RJ. *T:* (020) 7878 5639. *E:* stephanie.amiel@kcl.ac.uk. *Club:* Royal Society of Medicine.

**AMIN, Prof. Ash,** CBE 2014; PhD; FBA 2007; Professor of Geography, University of Cambridge, since 2011; *b* 31 Oct. 1955; *s* of late Harish and Vilas Amin; *m* 1989, Lynne Marie Brown; one *s* two *d*. *Educ:* Reading Univ. (BA Hons Italian Studies 1979; PhD Geog. 1986). Newcastle University: Res. Associate, Centre for Urban and Regl Develt Studies, 1982–89; Lectr, then Sen. Lectr, Geog., 1989–94; Prof. of Geog., 1994–95; University of Durham: Prof. of Geography, 1995–2011; Exec. Dir, Inst. of Advanced Study, 2005–11. Visiting Professor: Naples, 1989; Rotterdam, 1995; Copenhagen, 1995; International Fellow: Naples, 1987; Uppsala, 1999 and 2011. Foreign Sec. and Vice-Pres., British Acad., 2015–19. FAcSS (AcSS 2000). Corresp. Life Mem., Società Geografica Italiana, 1999. Edward Heath Award, RGS/IBG, 1998. *Publications:* (ed jtly) Technological Change, Industrial Restructuring and Regional Development, 1986; (ed jtly) Towards a New Europe?, 1991; (ed) Post-Fordism: a reader, 1994; (ed with N. Thrift) Globalisation, Institutions and Regional Development, 1994; (ed jtly) Behind the Myth of European Union, 1995; (ed with J. Hausner) Beyond Market and Hierarchy, 1997; (with D. Massey and N. Thrift) Cities for the Many not the Few, 2002 (trans. Italian); (with N. Thrift) Cities: reimagining the urban, 2002; (with A. Cameron and R. Hudson) Placing the Social Economy, 2002; (with D. Massey and N. Thrift) Decentering the Nation: a radical approach to regional inequality, 2003; (jtly) Organisational Learning: the role of communities, 2003; (ed jtly) The Blackwell Cultural Economy Reader, 2004; (with P. Cohendet) Architectures of Knowledge: firms, capabilities and communities, 2004; (ed jtly) Community, Economic Creativity and Organisation, 2008; (ed jtly) Thinking About Almost Everything, 2009; (ed) The Social Economy: international perspectives, 2009; Land of Strangers, 2012; (with N. Thrift) Arts of the Political: new openings for the Left, 2013; (with N. Thrift) Seeing Like a City, 2017; (ed with P. Howell) Releasing the Commons, 2016. *Recreations:* music, walking, tennis. *Address:* Department of Geography, University of Cambridge, Downing Place, Cambridge CB2 3EN. *T:* (01223) 768418.

**AMIN, Yogi;** Partner, since 2009, and National Head of Public Law and Human Rights, since 2013, Irwin Mitchell, UK; *b* Mombasa, Kenya, 8 Jan. 1973; *s* of Hasmukh and Kusum Amin; *m* 1998, Rachel Brown; two *s*. *Educ:* Liverpool John Moores Univ. (LLB 1994); Coll. of Law (DipLaw 1996); Univ. of Leeds (LLM Human Rights Law 2005). Admitted solicitor, 1999; Amphlett Lissimore Solicitors, 1997–2001; Irwin Mitchell, solicitors: 2001–; Associate, 2005–09. Trustee: Independent Living Fund, 2007–15; Royal Mencap Soc., 2018–. Gov., Hunter's Bar Jun. Sch., 2010–17 (Chm., Govs, 2013–18). *Recreations:* theatre, film, walking, family. *Address:* Irwin Mitchell, 2 Millsands, Sheffield S3 8DT; Irwin Mitchell, 40 Holborn Viaduct, EC1N 2PZ. *T:* 0370 150 0100. *E:* yogi.amin@irwinmitchell.com.

**AMIS, Prof. Andrew Arthur,** PhD, DSc(Eng); FREng; CEng, FIMechE; Professor of Orthopaedic Biomechanics, Imperial College London, since 2000; *b* London, 10 Oct. 1951; *s* of Peter Amis and Hilda Amis; *m* 1974, Teresa; one *s* one *d*. *Educ:* Univ. of Leeds (BSc Mech. Engrg 1973; PhD Biomechanics 1978); Univ. of London (DSc(Eng) 1999). FIMechE 1988; CEng 1988; FREng 2014. Imperial College London: Lectr, 1979–89, Sen. Lectr, 1989–94, in Mech. Engrg; Reader in Orthopaedic Biomechanics, 1994–2000. FRSA 1995. *Publications:* approx. 400 articles in orthopaedic surgery res. *Recreations:* sailing, travel, theatre, wine, underwater photography. *Address:* Mechanical Engineering Department, Imperial College London, SW7 2AZ. *T:* (020) 7594 7062. *E:* a.amis@imperial.ac.uk.

**AMIS, Martin Louis;** author; Professor of Creative Writing, Manchester University, 2007–11; special writer for The Observer, since 1980; *b* 25 Aug. 1949; *s* of Sir Kingsley Amis, CBE, and Hilary Bardwell; *m* 1984, Antonia Phillips (marr. diss. 1996); two *s*; *m* 1998, Isabel Fonseca; two *d*. *Educ:* various schools; Exeter Coll., Oxford (BA Hons 1st cl. in English). Fiction and Poetry Editor, TLS, 1974; Literary Editor, New Statesman, 1977–79. *Publications:* The Rachel Papers, 1973 (Somerset Maugham Award, 1974); Dead Babies, 1975; Success, 1978; Other People: a mystery story, 1981; Invasion of the Space Invaders, 1982; Money, 1984; The Moronic Inferno and Other Visits to America, 1986; Einstein's Monsters (short stories), 1987; London Fields, 1989; Time's Arrow, 1991; Visiting Mrs Nabokov and Other Excursions, 1993; The Information, 1995; Night Train, 1997; Heavy Water and Other Stories, 1998; Experience (memoir), 2000 (James Tait Black Meml Prize); The War Against Cliché: essays and reviews 1971–2000, 2001; Koba the Dread, 2002; Yellow Dog, 2003; House of Meetings, 2006; The Second Plane: September 11, 2001–2007, 2008; The Pregnant Widow, 2010; Lionel Asbo: state of England, 2012; The Zone of Interest, 2014; The Rub of Time: Bellow, Nabokov, Hitchens, Travolta, Trump: essays and reportage, 1986–2016, 2017. *Recreations:* tennis, chess, snooker. *Address:* c/o Wylie Agency (UK), 17 Bedford Square, WC1B 3JA. *E:* mail@wylieagency.co.uk. *Club:* Oxford and Cambridge.

**AMLOT, Roy Douglas;** QC 1989; barrister; *b* 22 Sept. 1942; *s* of Douglas Lloyd Amlot and Ruby Luise Amlot; *m* 1969, Susan Margaret (*née* McDowell); two *s*. *Educ:* Dulwich Coll. Called to the Bar, Lincoln's Inn, 1963 (Bencher, 1986; Treas., 2007). Second Prosecuting Counsel to the Inland Revenue, Central Criminal Court and London Crown Courts, 1974; First Prosecuting Counsel to the Crown, Inner London Crown Court, 1975 Jun. Prosecuting Counsel to the Crown, Central Criminal Court, 1977, Sen. Prosecuting Counsel, 1981; First Sen. Prosecuting Counsel, 1987–89. Chairman: Criminal Bar Assoc. 1997; Bar Council, 2001; Mem., QC Appts Cttee, 2006–09. *Publications:* (ed) 11th edn Phipson on Evidence. *Recreations:* ski-ing, cycling, windsurfing, music. *Address:* Treasury Office, Lincoln's Inn, WC2A 3TL.

**AMMON, Dr (Niels) Peter (Georg),** Cross, Order of Merit (Federal Republic o Germany), 1999; Ambassador of Germany to the Court of St James's, 2014–18; *b* Frankfurt am Main, Germany, 23 Feb. 1952; *s* of Georg Ammon and Rita Ammon (*née* Nielsen); *m* 1979, Marliese Heimann; two *d*. *Educ:* Augustinergymnasium, Friedberg; Clausthal Univ. of Technol. (Dip. Maths); Freie Univ. Berlin (PhD Econs 1978); German Govt Diplomatic Sch., Bonn. Entered German Federal Foreign Office, 1978; Second Sec. and COS to Ambassador, London, 1980–82; First Sec. (Press, Cultural and Develt), Dakar, 1982–85 Econ. Dept, Bonn, 1985–89; Press Attaché, New Delhi, 1989–91; Policy Planning Office Bonn, 1991–96; Hd, Policy Planning Staff of German Federal President, 1996–99; Ministe (Econs), Washington, 1999–2001; Dir-Gen. for Econ. Affairs, Berlin, 2001–0 Ambassador to France, 2007–08; State Sec., Berlin, 2008–11; Ambassador to USA 2011–14.

**AMORIM, Celso;** Minister of Defence, Brazil, 2011–15; *b* 3 June 1942; *s* of Vicente Matheus Amorim and Beatriz Nunes Amorim; *m* 1966, Ana Maria Carvalho; three *s* one *d*. *Educ*: Brazilian Diplomatic Acad., Rio Branco Inst.; Diplomatic Acad. of Vienna (Postgrad. Dip. Internat. Relns 1967). Postgrad. work in Pol Sci./Internat. Relns, LSE, 1968–71. Chm., Brazilian Film Corp., 1979–82; Dep. Hd of Mission, Brazilian Embassy, Netherlands, 1982–85; Asst Sec., Min. of Sci. and Technol., 1985–88; Dir for Cultural Affairs, 1989, Dir for Econ. Affairs, 1990–91, Min. of Foreign Relns; Perm. Rep. to UN, GATT and Conf. on Disarmament, Geneva, 1991–93; Minister of Foreign Affairs, 1993–94; Perm. Rep. to UN, NY, 1995–99; Perm. Rep. to UN and WTO, Geneva, 1999–2000; Ambassador to UK, 2001–02; Minister of Foreign Affairs, 2003–10. Chairman: UN Security Council, 1999; Conf. on Disarmament, 2000; Gov. Body, ILO, 2000–01; Convention on Tobacco Control, 2000–01; WTO Council for Trade in Services, 2001; Exec. Bd, UNITAID, 2016–. US Foreign Policy Assoc. Medal, 1999. Nat. and foreign decorations, incl. many Grand Crosses. *Publications*: Conversas com jovens diplomatas, 2011; Breves narrativas diplomáticas, 2013; Teerã, Ramalá e Doha, 2015; articles in Brazilian and foreign pubns in fields of political theory, internat. relations, cultural policy, sci. and technological development. *Recreations*: reading, travelling, art, film.

**AMORY;** *see* Heathcoat Amory and Heathcoat-Amory.

**AMOS,** Baroness *cr* 1997 (Life Peer), of Brondesbury in the London Borough of Brent; **Valerie Ann Amos,** CH 2016; PC 2003; Director, School of Oriental and African Studies, University of London, 2015–July 2020; Master, University College, Oxford, from Aug. 2020; *b* 13 March 1954; *d* of E. Michael Amos and Eunice Amos. *Educ*: Univ. of Warwick (BA Sociol.); Univ. of Birmingham (MA Cultural Studies); Univ. of E Anglia (doctoral research). With London Boroughs: Lambeth, 1981–82; Camden, 1983–85; Hackney, 1985–89 (Head of Trng; Head of Management Services); Management Consultant, 1984–89; Chief Exec., Equal Opportunities Commn, 1989–94; Dir, Amos Fraser Bernard, 1995–98. A Baroness in Waiting (Govt Whip), 1998–2001; Parly Under-Sec. of State, FCO, 2001–03; Sec. of State for Internat. Develt, 2003; Leader of H of L, 2003–07. High Comr to Australia, 2009–10; Under Sec. Gen. for Humanitarian Affairs and Emergency Relief Coordinator, UN, 2010–15. Mem., Fulbright Commn, 2009–. Chairman: Bd of Govs, RCN Inst., 1994–98; Afiya Trust (formerly Black Heath Foundn), 1995–98; Royal African Soc., 2008–10. Member: Adv. Cttee, Centre for Educnl Develt Appraisal and Res., Univ. of Warwick, 1991–98; Gen. Council, King's Fund, 1992–98; Council, Inst. of Employment Studies, 1993–98; Adv. Bd, Global Health Gp, UCSF, 2008–10; Trustee, IPPR, 1994–98. External Examiner: (MA Equal Opportunities), Univ. of Northumbria, at Newcastle (formerly Newcastle Poly.), 1989–93; Liverpool Univ., 1992–97. Fellow, Centre for Corporate Reputation, Saïd Business Sch., Oxford Univ., 2008–. Dir, UCL Hosps NHS Trust, 1995–98; Fellow, UCL Hosps, 2000–. Dir, Hampstead Theatre, 1992–98; Dep. Chm., Runnymede Trust, 1990–98; Trustee: VSO, 1997–98; Project Hope, 1997–98; NPG, 2003–07. Hon. LLD: Warwick, 2000; Staffordshire, 2000; Manchester, 2001; Bradford, 2006; Leicester, 2007; Birmingham, 2008; E Anglia, 2009; Stirling, 2010; Nottingham, 2012; Durham, 2013. *Publications*: various articles on race and gender issues. *Address*: (until July 2020) School of Oriental and African Studies, Thornaugh Street, WC1H 0XG. *T*: (020) 7898 4014; (from Aug. 2020) University College, Oxford OX1 4BH.

**AMOS, Alan Thomas;** investigator with Local Government Ombudsman, since 1993; Complaints Manager, Camden and Islington Health Authority, 2002–05; *b* 10 Nov. 1952; *s* of William Edmond Amos and Cynthia Florence Kathleen Amos. *Educ*: St Albans Sch.; St John's Coll., Oxford (MA(PPE) Hons); London Univ. Inst. of Educn (PGCE 1976). Pres., Oxford Univ. Cons. Assoc., 1974–75. Dir of Studies, Hd of Sixth Form, Hd of Econs and Politics Dept, Dame Alice Owen's Sch., Potters Bar, 1976–84; Hd of Agric. and Environment Sect., Cons. Res. Dept, 1984–86; Asst Prin., College of Further Educn, 1986–87. PA to Sec. of State for the Envmt, 1993. Councillor, 1978–90, Dep. Leader, and Chm. Educn Cttee, 1983–87, Enfield Bor. Council; Chm., London Boroughs Assoc. Educn Cttee, 1986–87; Member (Lab): Tower Hamlets LBC, 1998–2006 (Chm., Overview and Scrutiny Cttee, 2002–06); Worcester CC, 2008– (Cabinet Mem. for Econ. Prosperity and Tourism, 2016; Chairman: Planning Cttee, 2015–16; Audit and Governance Cttee, 2016–); Worcestershire CC, 2009– (Dep. Leader, Lab Gp, 2009–; Dep. Leader of Opposition, 2013–; Mayor, City of Worcester, 2014–15; Chm., Health Overview and Scrutiny Cttee, 2016–17; Cabinet Mem. for Highways, 2017–); Vice Chm., Audit and Standards Cttee, Hereford and Worcester Fire Authy, 2017–. Contested (C): Tottenham, GLC, 1981; Walthamstow, 1983; MP (C) Hexham, 1987–97; contested (Lab) Hitchin and Harpenden, 2001. Mem., Agriculture Select Cttee, 1989–92; Chairman: Cons. backbench Forestry Cttee, 1987–92; Parly ASH Gp, 1991–92; Secretary: Cons. backbench Transport Cttee, 1988–92 (Vice Chm., 1991–92); Cons. backbench Educn Cttee, 1989–92; British-Bulgarian All Party Gp, 1991–92; Chm., Northern Gp of Cons. MPs, 1991–92. Joined Labour party, 1994; Mem. Exec. Cttee, Poplar and Canning Town Lab Party, 1996– (Treas., 1997–); Chm., Millwall Lab Party, 2000–; Vice Chm., Worcestershire Co. Lab Party, 2009–. Sec., Nat. Agricl and Countryside Forum, 1984–86. Lay Chm., NHS Ind. Review Panel, 1998–; Mem., Candidates Panel for appt to NHS Authorities, 1999–. A Vice-Pres., Gtr London YCs, 1981. Member: ESU, 1982–; ASH, 1987– (Mem. Council, 1991–); SPUC, 1987–. Hon. US Citizen, 1991. *Recreations*: travel, badminton, USA politics, bibliophilia.

**AMOS, Brad;** *see* Amos, W. B.

**AMOS, Timothy Robert, (Tim);** QC 2008; a Recorder, since 2009; *b* 13 Jan. 1964; *s* of Edward and Jean Miriam Amos; *m* 1995, Elke Mund, Cologne. *Educ*: King's Sch., Canterbury; Oriel Coll., Oxford (BA Hist. 1985); Poly. of Central London. Called to the Bar, Lincoln's Inn, 1987; in practice at the Bar, specialising in family law, esp. big money family finance cases, those with a foreign or internat. element and particularly Anglo-German cases. Standing Counsel to Queen's Proctor, 2001–08. *Recreations*: music and wine (separately and together). *Address*: Queen Elizabeth Building, Temple, EC4Y 9BS.

**AMOS, William Bradshaw, (Brad),** PhD; FRS 2007; biologist and optical designer; Research Staff Member, since 1981, and Emeritus Group Leader, since 2010, MRC Laboratory of Molecular Biology, Cambridge; Visiting Research Scientist, since 2010, and Visiting Professor, since 2012, Strathclyde Institute of Pharmacology and Biomedical Sciences; *b* 21 Nov. 1945; *s* of James and Edna Amos; *m* 1969, Linda Ann Richardson; two *s*. *Educ*: King Edward VII Sch., Sheffield; Queen Elizabeth's Hosp., Bristol; Queen's Coll., Oxford (MA Natural Scis 1966); Pembroke Coll., Cambridge (PhD 1970). University of Cambridge: Res. Fellow, King's Coll., 1970–74; Univ. Demonstrator and Balfour Student, Dept of Zoology, 1978–81. Chief Design Consultant, Bio-Rad Microsciences Ltd, 1986–2002; Co-Founder and Dir, Mesolens Ltd, 2009–. Principal Organiser, MRC Course in Advanced Optical Microscopy (annual), Plymouth, 2003–. Leeuwenhoek Lect., Royal Soc., 2012. FMBA 2016. Hon. FRPS 2002; Hon. FRMS 2010. Mullard Award, Royal Soc., 1994; Rank Prize for Optoelectronics, 1995; Ernst Abbe Award, NY Microscopical Soc., 2005. *Publications*: Molecules of the Cytoskeleton (with L. A. Amos), 1991; numerous articles in learned sci. jls; five patents in field of laser scanning microscopy. *Recreations*: aquatic microscopy, gemstone faceting, amateur dramatics, metalwork. *Address*: MRC Laboratory of Molecular Biology, Francis Crick Avenue, Cambridge CB2 0QH. *T*: (01223) 246101, *Fax*: (01223) 213556. *E*: amos.brad@gmail.com.

**AMPLEFORTH, Abbot of;** *see* Madden, Rt Rev. C.

**AMPTHILL,** 5th Baron *cr* 1881; **David Whitney Erskine Russell;** *b* London, 27 May 1947; *s* of 4th Baron Ampthill, CBE, PC and Susan Mary Sheila (*d* 2001), *d* of Hon. Charles John Frederic Winn; *S* father, 2011; *m* 1st, 1980, April McKenzie Arbon (marr. diss. 1998); two *d*; 2nd, 2002, Christia, *d* of Harold Noregaard Ipsen and *widow* of Prince Rostislav Romanoff. *Educ*: Stowe Sch. Member (C): Mid Sussex DC, 1999–2003; Rother DC, 2007–19 (Chm., 2011–12). *Heir*: *b* Hon. Anthony John Mark Russell [*b* 10 May 1952; *m* 1st, 1985, Christine O'Dell; one *s*; 2nd, 1999, Mrs Catherine Agnès Lefebvre (*née* Veinstein)]. *Address*: Mountsfield, Rye Hill, E Sussex TN31 7NH. *Club*: White's.

**AMRAN, Mohammed;** Member (Lab), Bradford Council, since 2015; *b* 20 Nov. 1975; *s* of Mohammed Ramzan and Rakhmat Jan; *m* 1999, Saima Tabassum; two *s* one *d*. *Educ*: Huddersfield Tech. Coll. (BTEC Nat. Public Services 1995); Bradford and Ilkley Community Coll. (DipHE 1998). Youth work, Grange Interlink Community Centre, Bradford, 1994–96; Play Scheme Leader, Manningham Sport Centre, 1994–97, and Girlington Action Gp, 1996, Bradford; Co-ordinator, Youth for Understanding UK, 1996–97; Recruitment Officer, Prince's Trust Volunteers, 1997–98; remand worker, Youth Offending Team, 1998–99; Outreach Manager, Prince's Trust, 1999–2002; Fundraiser, Yorks Air Ambulance Service Charity, 2002–04; Lay Advisor: Developing Policy Excellence, Central Police Trng Develt Authy, 2005–07; Nat. Police Improvement Agency, 2007–09; Community Cohesion Manager, Greenhead High Sch., 2004–06. Mem., CRE, 1998–2002. Chm., Courts Bd, DCA, subseq. MoJ, 2004–; Member: Home Office Adv. Panel on Futurebuilders, 2005–08; England Cttee, Big Lottery Fund, 2007–. Mem. Panel, EC Cities Anti-Racism Project, 1996–97. Volunteer Trainer, Nat. Police Trng Sch., 1996–97. Member: Policy Action Team, DCMS, 1999; IPPR (Criminal Justice Reform), 2000–02; Advr, Steering Gp, Holocaust Meml Day, Home Office, 2000–01; Home Sec.'s Rep., Selection Panel, Police Authy, 2008–. Mem., Duke of York's Community Initiative, Bradford, 2001–03; Mem., Police Liaison Cttee, Bradford and Dist Minority Ethnic Communities, 1998–; Dir, Bradford Youth Develt Partnership, 2000–. Eur. Rep., Prince's Trust Action, 1996–99. Mem. Court, Univ. of Leeds, 2002–. FRSA 2002. DUniv Bradford, 2002. Awards include: Imran Foundn Special Award in Recognition of Promotion of Asian Community, 2001; Gold Standard Winner, Arts and Community, Windrush Achievement Awards, 2001; Community and Campaigning Volunteer of Year, Whitbread Volunteers Action Awards, 2001; Beacon Prize (Community Builder), 2004. *Address*: 8 Highfield Drive, Heaton, Bradford, Yorks BD9 6HN.

**AMWELL,** 3rd Baron *cr* 1947, of Islington; **Keith Norman Montague;** former consulting civil engineer, engineering geologist and company director; *b* 1 April 1943; *o s* of 2nd Baron Amwell and of Kathleen Elizabeth Montague (*née* Fountain); *S* father, 1990; *m* 1970, Mary, *d* of Frank Palfreyman; two *s*. *Educ*: Ealing Grammar Sch. for Boys; Nottingham Univ. (BSc Civil Engrg 1964); CEng 1972; FICE 1992; CGeol 1992; FGS 1971. Consulting civil engineer, 1965–96. Dir, Construction Industry Res. and Inf. Assoc., 1996–2005; independent consultant, 2005–10. *Publications*: papers to international construction confs. *Recreations*: gardening, walking, photography, badminton. *Heir*: *s* Hon. Ian Keith Montague [*b* 20 Sept. 1973; *m* 2001, Amanda, *d* of George Sweetland; one *s* one *d*].

**AMY, Ronald John,** OBE 1998; FFA; Chairman, Review Body on Doctors' and Dentists' Remuneration, 2007–13; *b* 17 June 1950; *s* of Ernest and Grace Amy; *m* 1st, 1975, Evelyn Morrison (marr. diss.); two *d*; 2nd, 1997, Patricia Groves. *Educ*: Glasgow Univ. (BSc Hons Pure Maths). FFA 1977. London Actuary, Scottish Mutual Assce Soc., 1978–80; UK Pensions Manager, Philips Electronics, 1980–84; Gp Pensions Dir, Metal Box Plc, 1984–86; Dir, New Business Develt, BZW Investment Mgt, 1986–87; Gp Pensions Dir, 1987–88, Gp Compensation and Benefits Dir, 1988–96, Grand Metropolitan PLC; Chm. and Chief Exec., Alexander Clay, 1996–97; Chief Exec., 1998–2005, Chm., 1998–2007, Aon Consulting. Non-exec. Dir, Aon Ltd, 2007–11. Chairman: Jersey Public Employees Contributory Retirement Scheme, 1990–2014; DHL Master Trust, 2000–April 2020; Jersey Teachers' Superannuation Fund, 2007–14; Chairman of Trustees: Allied Domecq Pension Fund, 2004–13; Santander UK Retirement Plan, 2008–18; Alliance & Leicester Pension Scheme, 2009–12; Scottish Mutual Assurance plc Staff Pension Scheme, 2011–12; Scottish Provident Instn Staff Pension Fund, 2011–12. Member: Occupational Pensions Bd, 1989–97; Bd, OPRA, 1996–2003. Chm., Nat. Assoc. of Pension Funds, 1993–95. *Recreation*: golf. *Clubs*: Royal Automobile, Caledonian; Cruden Bay Golf (Captain, 2015–17), Royal Aberdeen Golf, Trump Internat. Golf Links, Newburgh-on-Ythan Golf.

**AMYOT, Léopold Henri,** CVO 1990; Secretary to Governor General of Canada and Secretary General of Order of Canada and of Order of Military Merit, 1985–90; Herald Chancellor of Canada, 1988–90; *b* 25 Aug. 1930; *s* of S. Eugène Amyot and Juliette Gagnon; *m* 1958, (Marie Jeanne) Andrée Jobin; one *s* two *d*. *Educ*: Laval Univ., Québec (BLSc, BScSoc); Ottawa Univ. (BA); Geneva Univ. (course on Internat. Instns). Joined External Affairs, 1957; Second Secretary: Canberra, 1960; New Delhi, 1961; Counsellor, Paris, 1968; Amb. to Lebanon (with accredn to Syria, Jordan, Iraq), 1974; Dep. Sec. Gen., Agence de Co-opération culturelle et technique, Paris, 1976; Chief of Protocol, Ext. Affairs, Ottawa, 1980; Exec. Dir, Task Force, on Pope's Visit to Canada, 1983; Amb. to Morocco, 1983. Chm., Official Residences Collections (formerly Official Residences Art) Adv. Cttee, 1985–. Member: Professional Assoc. of For. Service Officers, Ottawa, 1957–; Inst. canadien des Affaires internat., Québec, 1985–90. Prix d'honneur (Sect. de Québec), Inst. canadien des Affaires internat., 1985. *Recreations*: tennis, golf, swimming, contemporary art collector.

**ANAND, Anjum, (Mrs Adarsh Sethia);** author, television presenter; Founder and Creative Director, The Spice Tailor, since 2010; *b* London, 25 Aug. 1971; *d* of Prem and Santosh Anand; *m* 2003, Adarsh Sethia; one *s* one *d*. *Educ*: Queen's Coll., London; European Business Sch., London (BA Eur. Business Admin). Cookery writer, 2003–; presenter of TV series: Indian Food Made Easy, 2007, 2008; Anjum's Spice Stories, 2016. *Publications*: Indian Every Day, 2003; Indian Food Made Easy, 2007; Anjum's New Indian, 2008; Eat Right for your Body Type, 2010; I Love Curry, 2010; Anjum's Indian Vegetarian Feast, 2012; Quick and Easy Indian, 2014; I Love India, 2017. *Recreations*: travelling, contemporary Indian art, theatre, ski-ing, yoga, friends and family. *Address*: The Spice Tailor, 37 Warren Street, W1T 6AD. *T*: (0151) 245 0178, *Fax*: (0151) 244 5401. *E*: anjum.anand@thespicetailor.com.

**ANANDALINGAM, Prof. Gnanalingam, (Anand),** PhD; Ralph J. Tyser Professor of Management Science, University of Maryland, since 2016; *b* Cambridge, UK, 27 Oct. 1953; *s* of Dr S. Gnanalingam and Pushpa Gnanalingam; *m* 1987, Dr Deepa Ollapally; one *s* one *d*. *Educ*: Trinity Coll., Cambridge (BA 1975); Harvard Univ. (PhD 1981). Prof., Wharton Sch. and Systems Engrg, Univ. of Pennsylvania, 1987–2001; Chair and Prof., Dept of Decision and Inf. Technol., 2001–07, Dean, 2007–13, Robert H. Smith Sch. of Business, Univ. of Maryland; Dean, Imperial Business Sch., Imperial Coll. London, 2013–16. MInstD. *Publications*: Beware the Winner's Curse, 2004; Telecommunications

Planning, 2006. *Recreations:* tennis, jazz, cinema, walking, biking. *Address:* Robert H. Smith School of Business, University of Maryland, College Park, MD 20742, USA. E: ganand@rhsmith.umd.edu. *Club:* Bangalore (Bangalore).

**ANANIA, Giorgio,** PhD; Co-Founder and Vice President, Executive Board, Phototonics 21, since 2006; Co-Founder, Chief Executive Officer and Chairman, Aledia (formerly HelioDel), since 2012; Chairman, Sicoya, since 2015; *b* 18 Oct. 1958; *s* of Spartaco and Fanny Anania; *m* 1979, Regine Boucher (*d* 2012); two *d*. *Educ:* Princeton Univ. (MA, PhD); Magdalen Coll., Oxford (BA). Sen. Associate, Booz-Allen & Hamilton, New York, 1982–87; Strategic Marketing Manager, and Gen. Manager Miniplex Product, Raychem Corp., California, 1987–91; Principal, OCC Strategy Consultants, Paris, 1991–93; Vice Pres., Sales, Mktg and Business Develt, Flamel Technologies, Lyon, 1993–98; Sen. Vice Pres., Sales and Mktg, 1998–2000, Pres., 2000–07, CEO, 2001–07, Bookham Technology plc; Chm., Cube Optics AG, 2008–14. Advr on Acquisitions, Trilantic Capital Partners, 2009–11. *Recreations:* flying private planes, guitar, most water sports, reading (non-fiction). T: (France) 626694007. E: giorgio.anania@gmail.com.

**ANASTASIADES, Nicos;** President of Cyprus, since 2013; *b* Limassol, Cyprus, 1945; *m* Andri Moustakoudi; two *d*. *Educ:* Univ. of Athens (Law); Univ. of London (postgrad. studies in Maritime Law). In practice as lawyer, 1972–. MHR (Democratic Rally), 1981–2013 (Vice-Pres., House of Reps, 1996–2001); Chairman: Cttee of Foreign Affairs; Cttee on Educnl Affairs; Inter-Parly Cttee on Foreign Affairs, until 2006. Mem., Nat. Council, 1995–2013. Hd, Cyprus delegn to IPU. Pres., Democratic Rally Party, 1997–2012 (Hon. Pres., 2013). *Address:* Presidential Palace, 1400 Nicosia, Cyprus.

**ANAWOMAH, Margo Ciara Essi B.;** *see* Boye-Anawomah.

**ANCONA, Ronni;** *see* Ancona, V. J.

**ANCONA, Rear Adm. Simon James,** CBE 2016; Chief Executive Officer, Whitehall and Industry Group, since 2019; *b* Emsworth, Hants, 7 Jan. 1963; *s* of Derek Thomas and Jane Ancona; *m* 1996, Lisa Maree Daniel; one *s* one *d*. *Educ:* Daniel Stewart's and Melville Coll., Edinburgh; King's Coll. London (MA Strategic Studies and Internat. Affairs). Flying and sea appts, 1982–96; CO, HM Ships Birmingham, Newcastle and Starling (Hong Kong), 1996–2000; MA to Minister of State for Armed Forces, 2001–03; CO, HMS Cumberland, 2005–06; Hd, Iraq Commitment and Global Maritime Commitments, MoD, 2006–09; Comdr, UK Carrier Strike Gp and Dep. Comdr, UK Maritime Force, 2009–11; Comdr, ME, UK Maritime Component, 2011–13; ACDS (Mil. Strategy, later Defence Engagement), 2013–17. Chief Operating Officer, Network Rail Anglia, 2017–19. Mem. Council, RUSI, 2005–. QCVS 2014.

*See also* V. J. Ancona.

**ANCONA, Veronica Jane, (Ronni);** actress, comedienne and author; *b* 4 July 1968; *d* of Derek Thomas Ancona and Jane Ancona; *m* 2004, Dr Gerard Hall; two *d* (one *s* decd). *Educ:* Marr Coll., Troon; St Martin's and Cental Sch. of Art and Design (BA Hons); Inst. of Educn, Univ. of London (PGCE). Art, Design and Technol. Teacher, Holloway Boys Sch., Islington, 1993–95; worked extensively in radio, theatre, TV and film, 1995–; *theatre* includes: Miss Conceptions, Edinburgh Fest., 1996; Singin' in the Rain, Sadler's Wells, 2004; The Hypochondriac, 2005, Little Revolution, 2014, Almeida; *television* includes: The Big Impression (with Alistair McGowan), 1999–2005 (Variety Club Comedy Award (jtly), 2002); Gideon's Daughter, 2005; Ronni Ancona & Co, 2007; Hope Springs, 2009; Skins, 2009–10; Last Tango in Halifax, 2012, 2013; The Week That Wasn't, 2018; various appearances in Bremner, Bird and Fortune; regular panellist on QI, 2006–; *films* include: The Calcium Kid, 2004; Stella Street—The Movie, 2004; A Cock and Bull Story, 2006; Penelope, 2006; Surviving Christmas with the Relatives, 2018. Ambassador for: Prince's Foundn for Children and the Arts, 2008–; Prince's Trust, 2010–; Sightsavers, 2011–. Mem., BAFTA. Best Actress, British Comedy Awards, 2003. *Publications:* A Matter of Life and Death, 2009. *Recreations:* cinema, walking, family, painting, running. *Address:* c/o BWH, 35 Soho Square, W1D 3QX. *Clubs:* Soho House; Groucho.

*See also* Rear Adm. S. J. Ancona.

**ANCRAM, Rt Hon. Michael;** *see* Lothian, Marquess of.

**ANDERSEN, Inger la Cour;** Under Secretary General and Executive Director, United Nations Environment Programme, since 2019; *b* Jerup, Denmark, 23 May 1958; *d* of Erik Andersen and Aagot la Cour Andersen. *Educ:* Midtfyns Gymnasium; Poly. of North London (BA Mod. Studies 1981); Sch. of Oriental and African Studies, Univ. of London (MA Area Studies 1982). High sch. teacher, Omdurman and Khartoum, Sudan, 1982–85; Dep. Relief Coordinator, Sudan, CAFOD, seconded to SudanAid, Sudan Catholic Bishops Conf., 1985–87; Prog. Officer, 1987–89, Prog. Manager, 1989–92, UN Sudano-Sahelian Office, NY; Regl Coordinator, Global Envmt Facility, Regl Bureau for Arab States, UNDP, NY, 1992–99; World Bank: Partnership Coordinator, Internat. Waters, 1999–2001; Sector Manager, Water and Urban Develt, W and Central Africa, 2001–04; Sector Dir, Sustainable Develt, Middle East and N Africa Reg., 2004–08; Sector Dir, Sustainable Develt, Africa Reg., 2008–10; Vice Pres., Sustainable Develt and Chair, Fund Council, Consultative Gp for Internat. Agricl Res., 2010–11; Vice Pres., Middle East and N Africa Reg., 2011–14; Dir Gen., IUCN, 2015–19. *Publications:* (contrib.) The Niger River Basin: a vision for sustainable management, 2005. *Recreations:* opera, nature, gardening, biking, running. *Address:* United Nations Environment Programme, United Nations Avenue, Gigiri, PO Box 30552, Nairobi, Kenya. T: (20) 7621234.

**ANDERSEN, Thomas Thune;** Chairman, Lloyd's Register Group Ltd, since 2010; *b* Gentofte, Denmark, 4 March 1955; *s* of William Thune Andersen and Mette Munck; *m* 1981, Eva Lillan Hansen; one *s* one *d*. *Educ:* Rungsted Gymnasium; Copenhagen Business Sch. (Higher Dip. Foreign Trade 1979); Columbia Univ. (Sen. Mgt Course 1988); Harvard Univ. (Sen. Mgt Prog. 1992). Served Danish Navy, 1972–73. A. P. Møller Maersk: Personal Asst to Chm. and CEO, 1979–81; various roles, Hong Kong and China, 1981–88; Country Manager, Maersk Line Jakarta, Indonesia, 1989–91; Man. Dir, Maersk Taiwan Gp of Cos, Taiwan, 1992–94; CEO and Man. Dir, Maersk Co., UK, 1994–2000; Pres. and CEO, Maersk Contractors, Denmark, 2000–04; Pres. and CEO, Maersk Inc., USA, 2001–04; CEO, Maersk Oil Denmark, 2004–09. Director: Scottish and Southern Energy, 2008–14; Petrofac Ltd, 2009–17 (Sen. Ind. Dir, 2014–17); Chairman: DeepOcean Gp Hldg BV, 2011–16; Ørsted (formerly Dong Energy) A/S, 2014–; Vice Chm., VKR Hldg, 2010–; Mem. Bd, Blue Water Energy LLP, 2011–15; non-executive Director: BW Offshore Ltd, 2016–; IMI plc, 2018–. Vice Chm., British Chamber of Commerce, 2014– (Chm., 2009–14). Fellow, Churchill Coll., Cambridge, 2001. Freeman, City of London, 2000; Liveryman, Shipwrights' Co., 2001. Knight's Cross (Denmark), 2018. *Recreations:* golf, hunting. *Address:* Lloyd's Register Group Ltd, 71 Fenchurch Street, EC3M 4BS. T: (020) 7423 2228. E: tta@thuneandersen.com. *Clubs:* Travellers, Special Forces.

**ANDERSON,** family name of **Viscount Waverley** and **Barons Anderson of Ipswich** and **Anderson of Swansea**.

**ANDERSON OF IPSWICH,** Baron *cr* 2018 (Life Peer), of Ipswich in the County of Suffolk; **David William Kinloch Anderson,** KBE 2018; QC 1999; Judge of Courts of Appeal of Guernsey and Jersey, since 2015; *b* 5 July 1961; *s* of Sir (William) Eric (Kinloch) Anderson, *qv* and Poppy (née Mason); *m* 1989, Margaret Beeton; two *d*. *Educ:* Eton Coll. (King's Schol.); New Coll., Oxford (Open Schol.; MA Ancient and Modern Hist. 1982); Downing Coll., Cambridge (BA Law 1984); Inns of Court Sch. of Law. Called to the Bar, Middle Temple, 1985, Bencher, 2007; Lawyer from Abroad, Covington & Burling, Washington, 1985–86; Stagiaire, Cabinet of Lord Cockfield, European Commn, 1987–88; in practice as barrister, Brick Court Chambers, 1988–; a Recorder, 2004–13. Vis. Lectr in European Law, 1989–95, Vis. Res. Fellow, 1995–99, Vis. Prof., 1999–, KCL. Ind. Expert monitoring freedom of expression and inf., Council of Europe, 2000–03; Ind. Reviewer of Terrorism Legislation, 2011–17; led: Investigatory Powers Rev., 2014–15; Bulk Powers Rev., 2016; intelligence-handling reviews, 2017–19. Mem. Exec. Cttee, Lord Slynn of Hadley European Law Foundn, 2002–09. Member: Governing Body, British Assoc. for Central and Eastern Europe, 2002–08; Adv. Bd, SSEES, 2007–10; Adv. Bd, UCL European Inst., 2018–; Chm., Inter Mediate, 2019–. Trustee, British Inst. of Internat. and Comparative Law, 2005–09. Mem., RIIA, 2012–. *Publications:* References to the European Court, 1995, 2nd edn 2002; A Question of Trust, 2015; various reports on counter-terrorism law and nat. security articles in legal jls. *Recreations:* sea kayaking, history, science. *Address:* Brick Court Chambers, 7–8 Essex Street, WC2R 3LD. T: (020) 7379 3550. *Clubs:* Alpine, Athenæum.

**ANDERSON OF SWANSEA,** Baron *cr* 2005 (Life Peer), of Swansea in the county of West Glamorgan; **Donald Anderson;** PC 2001; DL; barrister-at-law; *b* 17 June 1939; *s* of David Robert Anderson and Eva (née Mathias); *m* 1963, Dr Dorothy Trotman, BSc, PhD; three *s*. *Educ:* Swansea Grammar Sch.; University Coll. of Swansea (Hon. Fellow, 1985). 1st cl. hons Modern History and Politics, Swansea, 1960. Barrister; called to Bar, Inner Temple, 1969; Mem. of Chambers, Lamb Bldg, Temple. Member of HM Foreign Service, 1960–64: Foreign Office, 1960–63; 3rd Sec., British Embassy, Budapest, 1963–64; lectured in Dept of Political Theory and Govt, University Coll., Swansea, 1964–66. Councillor, Kensington and Chelsea, 1971–75. MP (Lab): Monmouth, 1966–70; Swansea E, Oct. 1974–2005. Mem. Estimates Cttee, 1966–69; Vice-Chm., Welsh Labour Group, 1969–70, Chm., 1977–78; PPS to Minister of Defence (Administration), 1969–70; PPS to Attorney General, 1974–79; opposition front-bench spokesman on foreign affairs, 1983–92, on defence, 1993–94; Shadow Solicitor General, 1994–95. Member: Select Cttee on Welsh Affairs, 1980–83 (Chm., 1981–83); Select Cttee on Home Affairs, 1992–93; Speaker's Panel of Chairmen, 1995–99; Chm., Foreign Affairs Cttee, 1997–2005. Chairman: Parly Lab. Party Environment Gp, 1974–79; Welsh Lab. Gp, 1977–78. Former: Chm., British-French, -German, -S African and -Norwegian Parly Gps; Co-Chm., Czech and Slovak Parly Gp; Vice Chm., British-Spanish, -Netherlands and -Hungarian Parly Gps; Mem. Exec., British Gp, IPU, 1983–2001, 2005–17 (Vice-Chm. Exec., 1985–88; Treas., 1988–90, 1992; Vice-Chm., 2015–); Chm., UK Br., CPA, 1997–2001 (Vice-Chm., 1986–97, 2010–11; Treas., 1990–93). Sen. Vice-Pres., Assoc. of European Parliamentarians for Africa (Southern), 1984–97; Member: North Atlantic Assembly, subseq. NATO Parly Assembly, 1992–2005 (Ldr, UK Delegn, 1997–2003; Chm., Socialist Gp, 1997–2001); UK Delegn to OSCE, 1997–2001 (Leader, 1997–98); UK Delegn, Parly Assembly Council of Europe, 2008– (Vice-Chm., 2012–14, Chm., 2014–16, Middle East Cttee; Mem., Legal Affairs and Human Rights Cttee, 2015–; Vice Pres., Cttee for Selection of Judges to ECHR, 2015–). Mem., H of L Sub-Cttee C, 2006–10, EU Cttee, 2006–10, Sub-Cttee E, 2011–13. Pres., Gower Soc., 1976–78. Chairman: Parly Christian Fellowship, 1990–93; Nat. Prayer Breakfast, 1989; President: Boys' Brigade of Wales, 1992–94; Swansea Male Choir; Mem. Bd, Mercy Ships, 2005–12; Hon. Mem., Morriston Rotary Club, 2000–; Hon. Vice Pres., Swansea Business Club, 2006. Vis. Parly Fellow, St Antony's Coll., Oxford, 1999–2000. DL W Glam, 2006–14. Freeman: City of London, 2005; City and County of Swansea, 2000. Hon. Fellow, Swansea Inst. of Higher Educn, 2005. Commander's Cross, Order of Merit (FRG), 1986; Foreign Minister's Medal (Republic of Slovakia), 2004; Chevalier, Légion d'Honneur (France), 2005; Officer's Cross, Order of Merit (Hungary), 2007. *Recreations:* church work, walking and talking. *Address:* House of Lords, SW1A 0PW.

**ANDERSON, Alexander Beveridge,** CBE 2015 (OBE 2010); DL; FREng, FIChemE; Chairman, Tees Valley Local Enterprise Partnership, 2010–15; *b* Methil, Fife, 16 April 1944; *s* of John Weir Anderson and Elizabeth Warrender Anderson; *m* 1970, May Wemyss (*d* 2001); three *s*. *Educ:* Buckhaven High Sch.; Heriot-Watt Univ. (BSc). FIChemE 1982. ICI: Gen. Manager, Teesside Ops, 1989–94; Dir, Engrg, 1994–96; Ops Dir, Tioxide Gp, 1994–97; Dir, ICI Pakistan, 1997–2000; Sen. Vice Pres., Technol., 1997–2000. Chm., Ensus UK, 2006–11; Dir, Eutech Engrg Solutions, 1997–2001. Chairman: Teesside Trng Enterprise, 1989–94; Teesside Tomorrow Ltd, 1990–94; Director: Teesside Develt Corp., 1989–2005; Teesside Trng and Enterprise Council, 1989–2004; Centre for Process Innovation, 2004–. Chm., S Durham NHS Health Trust, 2002–04. Chm., Univ. of Teesside, 2004–14. Gov., Durham Sch., 2002–12. FREng 1997. DL Durham, 1991. Hon. DLaws Teesside, 2014. *Recreations:* jazz, golf, gardening, travel. *Address:* Carperby Lodge, 39 Abbey Road, Darlington, Co. Durham DL3 8LR. E: sandy_anderson.t21@btinternet.com.

**ANDERSON, Maj.-Gen. Alistair Andrew Gibson,** CB 1980; *b* 26 Feb. 1927; *s* of Lt-Col John Gibson Anderson and Margaret Alice (née Scott); *m* 1953, Dr Margaret Grace Smith (*d* 2013); one *s* two *d*. *Educ:* George Watson's Boys' Coll., Edinburgh; University Coll. of SW of England, Exeter (Short Univ. Course, 1944); Staff Coll., Camberley; Jt Services Staff Coll., Latimer. Enlisted 1944; commnd Royal Corps of Signals, 1946; comd 18 Signal Regt, 1967–69; Defence Ops Centre, 1969–72; staff of Signal Officer-in-Chief, 1972–74; Comdt, Sch. of Signals, 1974–76; Signal Officer-in-Chief (Army), 1977–80, retired; Dir, Communications and Electronics Security Gp, GCHQ, 1980–85. Col Comdt, Royal Corps of Signals, 1980–86; Chm., Royal Signals Assoc., 1982–87. *Recreations:* walking, gardening as far as limited ability will allow.

**ANDERSON, Dr Alun Mark;** writer and publisher; Editor 1992–99, Editor-in-Chief and Publishing Director, 1999–2005, New Scientist (Senior Consultant, 2005–15, now Editor Emeritus); *b* 27 May 1948; *s* of Peter Marchmont Anderson and Jane Watkin Anderson (née James). *Educ:* Univ. of Sussex (BSc 1968); Univ. of Edinburgh (PhD 1972). IBM Res. Fellow, 1972–74, Jun. Res. Fellow, Wolfson Coll., 1972–76, Oxford; Royal Soc. Res. Fellow, Kyoto Univ., 1977–79; Nature: News and Views Ed., 1980–83; Tokyo Bureau Chief, 1984–86; Washington Ed., 1986–90; Internat. Ed., Science, 1991–92. Dir, IPC Magazines Ltd, 1997–98; Dir and Co-owner, Xconomy, 2007–16. Member: Royal Soc. COPUS, 1997–2000; Royal Soc. Faraday Prize Cttee, 1999–2004; British Council Sci. Engrg and Envmt Adv. Cttee, 2001–07. Member Council: Univ. of Sussex, 1998–2001; Royal Instn, 2005–10; Soc. for Experimental Biol., 2007–15. Trustee, St Andrews Prize, 1999–2016. Mem., Editl Adv. Bd, Oxford Today, 2010–15. Editor of the Year (Special Interest Magazines), BSME, 1993, 1995, 1997; Editors' Editor of the Year, BSME, 1997. *Publications:* Science and Technology in Japan, 1984, 2nd edn 1991; After the Ice: life, death and politics in the New Arctic, 2009; (contrib.) The Fast-Changing Arctic: rethinking

Arctic security for a warmer world, 2013. *Recreations:* mountain walking, travel. *Address:* New Scientist, 25 Bedford Street, WC2E 9ES. *T:* (020) 7611 1202. *E:* alun.anderson@gmail.com.

**ANDERSON, Prof. Anne Harper**, OBE 2002; PhD; FRSE; Vice Principal, and Head, College of Social Sciences, University of Glasgow, since 2010; *b* Glasgow, 19 Feb. 1954; *d* of James and Jean Thomson; *m* 1975, Ian Anderson; one *s* one *d. Educ:* Hutchesons' Girls' Grammar Sch., Glasgow; Univ. of Glasgow (MA Hons Psychol. 1976; PhD 1982). Res. Fellow, Univ. of Edinburgh, 1979–86; University of Glasgow: Lectr, 1986–97; Prof. of Psychol., 1997–2006; Dep. Dean, Faculty of Law, Business and Social Sci., 2005–06; Vice Principal, and Hd, Coll. of Art, Sci. and Engrg, Univ. of Dundee, 2006–10. Director: ESRC Cognitive Engrg Prog., 1995–2000; ESRC/EPSRC/DTI People at the Centre of Communication and Inf. Technols Prog., 2000–06; Mem., EPSRC, 2008–15. Dep. Chair, Commonwealth Scholarship Commn. Mem. Bd, VisitScotland; UK UNESCO Comr. FRSE 2015. *Publications:* (jtly) Teaching Talk, 1983; (with Tony Lynch) Listening, 1988; papers in learned jls incl. Jl of Memory and Lang., Lang. and Cognitive Processes, Computers in Human Behavior. *Recreations:* travel to nice places, good food, good fiction, relaxing with the family. *Address:* College of Social Sciences, University of Glasgow, Florentine House, Glasgow G12 8QF. *T:* (0141) 330 6076, *Fax:* (0141) 330 7491. *E:* anne.anderson@glasgow.ac.uk.

**ANDERSON, Anthony John**; QC 1982; a Recorder, 1995–99; *b* 12 Sept. 1938; *s* of late A. Fraser Anderson and Margaret Anderson; *m* 1970, Fenja Ragnhild Gunn. *Educ:* Harrow; Magdalen Coll., Oxford. MA. 2nd Lieut, The Gordon Highlanders, 1957–59. Called to the Bar, Inner Temple, 1964, Bencher, 1992; retired from practice, 2001. Chm. of Tribunals, SFA (formerly The Securities Assoc.), 1988–2001. *Recreations:* golf, fishing, gardening, choral singing. *Address:* Hedges, Mead Lane, Upper Basildon, Berkshire RG8 8NA. *Clubs:* Garrick, MCC.

**ANDERSON, Mrs Beverly Jean**; educator; former journalist and broadcaster; *b* 9 Dec. 1940; *d* of Arthur Benjamin Phillpotts and Sylvia Phillpotts; *m* 1st, 1968, Angus Walker, *qv* (marr. diss. 1976); 2nd, 1976, Andrew Anderson (marr. diss. 1986); one *s. Educ:* Wellesley Coll., Mass (BA History, and Politics 1962); London Univ. (PGCE 1967). Jamaican Foreign Service, Kingston and Washington, 1963–66; primary sch. teacher, London, 1968–71, Oxfordshire primary schs, 1971–81; Headteacher, Berwood First Sch., Oxford, 1981–83; Sen. Lectr in Educn, Oxford Poly., 1985–89; Lectr in Educn, Warwick Univ., and educn consultant, 1989–93; Chief Exec., Book Trust, 1993–94; Head, Village Sch., Pacific Palisades, Calif, 1995–99; Middle School Principal: Trinity Sch., NY, 1999–2004; Rye Country Day Sch., Rye, NY, 2004–06. Dir, Railtrack, 1993–94. Chairman: Equal Opportunities Wkg Gp, NAB, 1987–88; CNAA Steering Cttee on Access Courses to HE Framework, 1988–89; Member: Nat. Curriculum Council, 1989–91; Council, ABSA, 1989–95; Arts Council, 1990–94; Governor: BFI, 1985–93; Oxford Stage Co. Bd, 1986–96; S Bank Bd, 1989–94. Mem., Nuffield Council on Bioethics, 1991–94; Chm. Council, Charter '88, 1989–93. Columnist, TES, 1989–93. Television includes: Presenter: Black on Black, 1982–83; Nothing but the Best; Sixty Minutes; After Dark, 1989–90; Behind the Headlines, 1990–91. FRSA 1991. Hon. Fellow, Leeds Metropolitan Univ., 1991. Hon. LLM Teesside, 1993. *Publications:* Learning with Logo: a teacher's guide, 1985; numerous articles on education, social issues and media education. *Recreations:* plays, paintings, poems, movies, dancing.

**ANDERSON, Brian David Outram**, AC 2016 (AO 1993); PhD; FRS 1989; Distinguished Professor: Hangzhou Dianzi University, since 2016; Australian National University, 2002–16, now Emeritus Professor (Professor of Systems Engineering, 1981–2002); Distinguished Researcher, data61-CSIRO (formerly National ICT Australia), since 2006 (Chief Executive Officer and President, 2002–03; Chief Scientist, 2003–06); *b* 15 Jan. 1941; *s* of late David Outram Anderson and Nancy Anderson; *m* 1968, Dianne, *d* of M. Allen; three *d. Educ:* Sydney Univ.; Stanford Univ. (PhD 1966); California Univ. Res. Asst, Stanford Electronics Labs, 1964; Lectr in Electrical Engrg, Stanford Univ., 1965; Asst Prof. and Staff Consultant, Vidar Corp., Mount View, Calif., 1966; Hd of Dept, 1967–75, Prof., 1967–81, Dept of Electrical Engrg, Univ. of Newcastle; Dir, Res. Sch. of Information Scis and Engrg, ANU, 1994–2002. Mem., Scientific Adv. Bd, Rio Tinto (formerly CRA) Ltd, 1982–98; Director: Telectronics Hldgs Ltd, 1986–88; Nucleus Ltd, 1988–95; Cochlear Ltd, 1995–2005; Crasys Ltd, 1996–98; Anutech Pty Ltd, 1997–2000. Member: Aust. Res. Grants Cttee, 1972–77; Aust. Science and Technology Council, 1977–82; UNESCO Nat. Commn, 1982–83; Aust. Industrial Res. and Develt Incentives Bd, 1984–86; Prime Minister's Sci. and Engrg Council, 1989–93; Prime Minister's Sci., Engrg and Innovation Council, 1998–2002; Aust. Res. Council, 2000–01; Aust. Res. Council Bd, 2001–03; Nat. Res. Priorities Standing Cttee, 2005–07; DEST e-Res. Co-ordinating Cttee, 2005–06. Member, Advisory Board: Inst. for Telecoms Res., 2004–07; Centre for Complex Dynamic Systems and Control, Univ. of Newcastle, NSW, 2004–; Centre for Applied Philos. and Public Ethics, 2005–. Pres., Australian Acad. of Sci., 1998–2002. FAA; FTS; FIEEE; Hon. FIE(Aust). For. Assoc., US NAE, 2002. Dr *hc* Louvain, 1991; Swiss Federal Inst. of Technol., 1993; Hon. DEng: Sydney, 1995; Melbourne, 1997; Newcastle, NSW, 2005; Hon. DSc NSW, 2001; Hon. DEng UTS, 2012. Order of the Rising Sun, Gold Rays with Neck Ribbon (Japan), 2007. *Publications* include: Linear Optimal Control, 1971; Network Analysis and Synthesis, 1975; Optimal Filtering, 1980; Optimal Control, 1990. *Address:* Research School of Engineering, Australian National University, 115 North Road, Acton, ACT 2601, Australia.

**ANDERSON, Campbell McCheyne**; Managing Director, North Ltd, 1994–98; *b* 17 Sept. 1941; *s* of Allen Taylor Anderson and Ethel Catherine Rundle; *m* 1965, Sandra Maclean Harper; two *s* one *d. Educ:* The Armidale Sch., NSW, Aust.; Univ. of Sydney (BEcon). AASA. Trainee and General Administration, Boral Ltd, Australia, 1962–69; Gen. Manager/Man. Dir, Reef Oil NL, Australia, 1969–71; Asst Chief Representative, Burmah Oil Australia Ltd, 1972; Corporate Development, Burmah Oil Incorporated, New York, 1973; Corporate Development, 1974; Finance Director and Group Planning, Burmah Oil Trading Ltd, UK, 1975; Special Projects Dir, 1976, Shipping Dir, 1978, Industrial Dir, 1979, Man. Dir, 1982–84, Burmah Oil Co.; Man. Dir, 1985–93, Chief Exec. Officer, 1986–93, Renison Goldfields Consolidated. Director: Consolidated Gold Fields, 1985–89; Ampolex Ltd, 1991–97 (Chm., 1991–96); Macquarie Direct Investments Ltd, 1999–2006; Aviva Australia Hldgs (formerly CGNU Australia), 1999–2009; IBJ Australia Bank, 2000–02; Reconciliation Australia Ltd, 2001–07; Clough Ltd, 2003–08; ThoroughVisioN Ltd, 2004–11. Dir, Aust. Mines and Metals Assoc., 1985–93 (Pres., 1988–89); Councillor: Aust. Mining Industry Council, 1985–98 (Pres., 1991–93); Business Council of Aust., 1986–2000 (Pres., 1999–2000); Sentient Gp, 2001–; Chairman: Energy Resources Aust. Ltd, 1994–98; Southern Pacific Petroleum NL, 2001–08; Landcare Aust. Ltd, 2012–16. Pres., Australia-Japan Soc., Victoria, 1995–98. *Recreations:* golf, swimming, horse-racing. *Address:* 77 Drumalbyn Road, Bellevue Hill, NSW 2023, Australia. *Clubs:* Australian (Sydney); Royal Sydney Golf; Australian Turf (formerly Jockey); Elanora Country (NSW).

**ANDERSON, Clive Stuart**; barrister; television and radio presenter and writer; *b* 10 Dec. 1952; *s* of late Gordon Menzies Randall Anderson and Doris Elizabeth Anderson; *m* 1981, Jane Hughes (*see* Prof. Jane Anderson); one *s* two *d. Educ:* Harrow County Sch. for Boys; Selwyn Coll., Cambridge (MA). Called to the Bar, Middle Temple, 1976, Bencher 2017. *Radio:* Host, Cabaret Upstairs, 1986–88; Chm., Whose Line is it Anyway?, 1988; Presenter: Devil's Advocate, 1991–92; Unreliable Evidence, 1998–; The Real…, 2002–; Clive Anderson's Chat Room, 2004–05; Loose Ends, 2007–; *television:* Whose Line is it Anyway?, 1988–98; Clive Anderson Talks Back, 1989–95; Notes & Queries, 1993; Our Man In, 1995, 1996; Clive Anderson All Talk, 1996–99; If I Ruled the World, 1998–99; Clive Anderson Now, 2001–; various other progs. Pres., Woodland Trust, 2003–. Patron: Afghan Connection; Save the Rhino International; Phoenix Cinema, Oban. Ambassador, Prince's Trust. *Publications:* (jtly) Great Railway Journeys, 1994; (with Ian Brown) Patent Nonsense, 1994; Our Man In, 1995; Our Man in Heaven & Hell, 1996. *Recreations:* history, comedy, football, planting trees. *Address:* Curtis Brown, Haymarket House, 28–29 Haymarket, SW1Y 4SP. *T:* (020) 7393 4400; 6 KBW, College Hill, 21 College Hill, EC4R 2RP. *T:* (020) 7583 0410.

**ANDERSON, David**; *b* 2 Dec. 1953; *s* of Cyril and Janet Anderson; *m* 1973, Elizabeth Eva Jago. *Educ:* Doncaster and Durham Tech. Colls; Durham Univ. (DipSocSc); Moscow Higher Trade Union Sch. Colliery mechanic, 1969–89; care worker, 1989–2005. MP (Lab) Blaydon, 2005–17. PPS to Minister of State, DIUS, 2007–08, FCO, 2008–09, MoD, 2009–10; an Opposition Whip, 2010–11, 2016; Shadow Sec. of State for NI, 2016–17, for Scotland, 2016–17. Chm., All-Party Parly Gp on Third World Solidarity, on Muscular Dystrophy, on Coalfield Communities, on Industrial Heritage; Sec., All-Party Parly Gp on Kurdistan. Trade Union Lay Official: NUM, 1978–89; UNISON, 1989–2005; Pres., UNISON, 2003–04; Mem., TUC Gen. Council, 2000–05. *Recreations:* walking, travel, music, caravanning.

**ANDERSON, David Heywood**, CMG 1982; Judge of the International Tribunal for the Law of the Sea, 1996–2005 (Judge *ad hoc* in Arctic Sunrise case, 2013); *b* 14 Sept. 1937; *s* of late Harry Anderson; *m* 1961, Jennifer Ratcliffe; one *s* one *d. Educ:* King James' Grammar Sch., Almondbury; LLB (Leeds); LLM (London). Called to Bar, Gray's Inn, 1963. HM Diplomatic Service, 1960–96: Asst Legal Adviser, FCO 1960–69; Legal Adviser, British Embassy, Bonn, 1969–72; Legal Counsellor, FCO, 1972–79; Legal Adviser, UK Mission to UN, NY, 1979–82; Legal Counsellor, 1982–87, Dep. Legal Advr, 1987–89, Second Legal Advr, 1989–96, FCO. Mem., Greenwich Forum, 1996–2014. *Publications:* Modern Law of the Sea - Selected Essays, 2008; (contrib.) International Maritime Boundaries, 1993–; contribs to British Yearbook of Internat. Law and learned jls. *Recreation:* gardening.

**ANDERSON, David James Charles**, OBE 1999; Director General, Amgueddfa Cymru-National Museum Wales, since 2010; *b* Belfast, 22 Aug. 1952; *s* of Trevor and Sylvia Anderson; *m* 1977, Josephine Harrison; one *s* two *d. Educ:* Lawrence Sheriff Sch., Rugby; Lewes Comprehensive Sch.; Edinburgh Univ. (MA Hist. 1976); Univ. of Sussex (PGCE 1977). History teacher, Oathall Comprehensive Sch., Haywards Heath, 1977–79; Educn Officer, Royal Pavilion, Art Gall. and Museums, Brighton, 1979–85; Hd of Educn, Nat. Maritime Mus., 1985–89; Hd of Educn, 1990–2001, Dir of Learning and Interpretation, 2001–10, V&A Mus. Pres., Museums Assoc., 2013–15. *Publications:* The Spanish Armada, 1988; (jtly) The Mutiny on the Bounty, 1989; A Common Wealth: museums and learning in the United Kingdom, 1997, 2nd edn as A Common Wealth: museums in the learning age, 1999. *Recreations:* family, Celtic literature and music, opera, visual arts, Irish Rugby, film. *Address:* 52 Grange Road, Lewes, E Sussex BN7 1TU. *T:* 07920 027071. *E:* david@midsummernight.net.

**ANDERSON, Prof. David McBeath**, PhD; Professor of African History and Politics, University of Warwick, since 2013; *b* Wick, 12 May 1957; *s* of William Anderson and Isobel Anderson; *m* 1983, Angela Parrott; two *s* two *d. Educ:* Kingswood Sch., Northants; Sussex Univ. (BA 1st Cl. Hons); Trinity Coll., Cambridge (PhD Hist. 1982). Res. Associate, Hist. Dept, Univ. of Nairobi, 1980–81; Sen. Rouse-Ball Scholar (Postdoctoral), Trinity Coll., Cambridge, 1982–83; Res. Fellow in Hist., New Hall, Cambridge, 1983–84; Lectr in Imperial and Commonwealth Hist., Birkbeck Coll., Univ. of London, 1984–91; Leverhulme Trust Res. Fellow, 1990–91; Sen. Lectr in Hist., SOAS, 1991–2002, Dir, Centre of African Studies, 1998–2002, Univ. of London; University of Oxford: Res. Fellow, St Antony's Coll., Oxford, 2002–05; Lectr in African Politics, 2005–06; Prof. of African Politics, 2006–12; Dir, African Studies Centre, 2006–09; Fellow, St Cross Coll., Oxford, 2005–12. Actg Dir, British Inst. in Eastern Africa, Nairobi, 2009–10. Evans-Pritchard Vis. Lectr, All Souls Coll., Oxford, 2002; Vis. Prof., Internat. Faculty, Univ. of Cologne, 2016–; Vis. Res. Fellow, Stellenbosch Univ., 2017–. *Publications:* (ed) Conservation in Africa: people, policies and practice, 1987; (ed) The Ecology of Survival: case studies from Northeast African history, 1988; (ed) Policing the Empire: government, authority and control, 1830–1940, 1991; (ed) Policing and Decolonisation: nationalism, politics and the police, 1917–1965, 1992; (ed) Revealing Prophets: prophecy and history in Eastern Africa, 1998; Maasai: people of cattle, 1998; (ed) Africa's Urban Past, 1999; Eroding the Commons: politics of ecology in Baringo, Kenya, 1890–1963, 2002; Supporting Ownership: Swedish development cooperation with Kenya, Tanzania and Uganda, 2 vols, 2002; (ed) The Poor Are Not Us: poverty and pastoralism in Eastern Africa, 2002; Histories of the Hanged: Britain's dirty war in Kenya and the end of empire, 2005; The Khat Controversy - Stimulating the Debate on Drugs, 2007; (ed) Routledge Handbook of African Politics, 2013; (ed) Politics and Violence in Eastern Africa: struggles of emerging states, 2015; (ed) Resilience and Collapse in African Savannahs: causes and consequences of environmental change in Eastern Africa, 2017; (ed) Allies at the End of Empire: nationalists, loyalists and the Cold War 1945–76, 2017. *Recreations:* football, ski-ing, reading good history. *Address:* Department of History, University of Warwick, Humanities Building, University Road, Coventry CV4 7AL. *T:* (024) 7615 0991. *E:* d.m.anderson@warwick.ac.uk.

**ANDERSON, David Munro**; Chairman, Anderson Quantrend (formerly Allingham Anderson Roll Ross) Ltd, since 1990; *b* 15 Dec. 1937; *s* of Alexander Anderson and Jessica Anderson (*née* Vincent-Innes); *m* 1st, 1965, Veronica Jane (*née* Stevens) (marr. diss.); two *s* one *d*; 2nd, 1989, Ruth Lewis-Bowen. *Educ:* Morrison's Academy, Perthshire; Strathallan, Perthshire. Commissioned Black Watch; served W Africa; tea production with James Finlay & Co., India, 1959–62; London Chamber of Commerce and Industry, 1962–63; joined E. D. & F. Man Ltd, 1963; formed Anderson Man Ltd, 1981; formed E. D. & F. Man International Ltd, 1985, Chm. 1986–90; Man. Dir, Commodity Analysis Ltd, 1968; numerous directorships. Chairman, formation cttees: Internat. Petroleum Exchange; Baltic Internat. Freight Futures Exchange (jtly); former Vice-Chm., London Commodity Exchange; Dir, SIB, 1986–87. MCSI (MSI 1992). *Recreations:* ski-ing, shooting. *Address:* The Old Gardens, Kersey, Suffolk IP7 6ED. *Club:* Caledonian.

**ANDERSON, Dr Digby Carter**; Director, Social Affairs Unit, 1980–2004; *b* 25 May 1944; *s* of late Donald Anderson and Elizabeth Nance Ethel Anderson; *m* 1965, Judith Harris. *Educ:* St Lawrence Coll.; Univ. of Reading (BA Hons); Brunel Univ. (MPhil, PhD). Lectr, then Sen. Lectr, Luton Coll. of Higher Educn, 1965–77; Tutor, Brunel Univ. Youth Work Trng Unit, 1974–78; Res. Fellow, Univ. of Nottingham, 1977–80; Associate Lectr, Brunel Univ., 1977–78. Mem., ESRC, 1989–93. Mem., Health Studies Cttee, CNAA, 1987–92. Columnist: The Times, 1984–88; Sunday Telegraph, 1988–89; Sunday Times, 1989–90; Spectator, 1984–2000; National Review, 1991–2000. Ordained deacon 1985, priest 1986; asst priest, St Saviour's, Luton, 1986–. Mem., Mont Pelerin Soc. *Publications:* (ed) Health Education in Practice, 1979; Evaluation by Classroom Experience, 1979; Evaluating Curriculum Proposals, 1980; (ed) The Ignorance of Social Intervention, 1980; Breaking the Spell of the Welfare State, 1981; (ed) The Kindness that Kills, 1984; (ed) A Diet of Reason, 1986; The Spectator Book of Imperative Cooking, 1987; (ed) Full Circle, 1988; (ed) Health, Lifestyle and Environment, 1992; (ed) The Loss of Virtue: moral confusion and social disorder in Britain and America, 1993; (ed) This Will Hurt: the restoration of civic order in America and Britain, 1995; (ed) Gentility Recalled: mere manners and the making of social order, 1996; (ed jtly) Faking It: the sentimentalisation of modern society, 1998; (compiler) The Dictionary of Dangerous Wars, 2000; Losing Friends, 2001; All Oiks Now, 2004; The English at Table, 2006; contrib. Sociology, Jl Curriculum Studies, Econ. Affairs, Social Policy Rev. *Recreations:* non-Germanic music, the seaside, dinner. *Address:* 17 Hardwick Place, Woburn Sands, Bucks MK17 8QQ. *T:* (01908) 584526.

**ANDERSON, Prof. Donald Thomas,** AO 1986; PhD, DSc; FRS 1977; Challis Professor of Biology, University of Sydney, 1984–91, Professor Emeritus, since 1992 (Professor of Biology, 1972–84); *b* 29 Dec. 1931; *s* of Thomas and Flora Anderson; *m* 1960, Joanne Trevathan (*née* Claridge). *Educ:* King's Coll., London Univ. DSc London, 1966; DSc Sydney, 1983. Lectr in Zoology, Sydney Univ., 1958–61; Sen. Lectr, 1962–66; Reader in Biology, 1967–71. Clarke Medal, Royal Soc. of NSW, 1979; Alexander Kowalevsky Medal, St Petersburg Soc. Naturalists, 2001. *Publications:* Embryology and Phylogeny of Annelids and Arthropods, 1973; Barnacles: structure, function, development and evolution, 1993; Atlas of Invertebrate Anatomy, 1996; Invertebrate Zoology, 1998, 2nd edn 2001; papers in zool. jls. *Recreations:* gardening, photography. *Address:* 5 Angophora Close, Wamberal, NSW 2260, Australia. *T:* (2) 43116598.

**ANDERSON, Edmund John Seward;** Chairman, National Savings and Investments, since 2017 (non-executive Director, since 2016); Lord-Lieutenant of West Yorkshire, since 2018; *b* Singapore, 22 Dec. 1950; *s* of late Dick Anderson and of Irene Anderson (*née* Seward); *m* 1982, Heather Medcalf (*see* H. Anderson); two *s* two *d*. *Educ:* Beaumont Coll.; Stonyhurst Coll.; Leeds Poly. (BSc Econs). CPFA 1977. Various local govt appts, 1973–87; Dep. Man. Dir, E Midlands Airport, 1987–90; Exec. Dir, Leeds CC, 1990–97; Man. Dir, Leeds Bradford Internat. Airport, 1997–2007. Chm. Airport Operators Assoc., 2018–19. Non-executive Director: Kelda Gp plc, 2005–08; Marketing Leeds Ltd, 2005–09. Chm., Yorks Bldg Soc., 2007–15 (Dir, 2003–15). Leeds, York and North Yorkshire (formerly Leeds) Chamber of Commerce: non-exec. Dir, 1998–2010; Pres., 2000–02; Chm., 2005–10. Chm, Mid Yorks Hosps NHS Trust, 2009–12. Non-executive Director: Opera North, 2014–; Tablet Publishing Co., 2015– (Vice Chm., 2016–). Leeds Trinity University (formerly Leeds Trinity and All Saints College, then Leeds Trinity University College): Mem., Bd of Govs, 2001–13; Chm., 2007–13; Pro-Chancellor, 2014–; Mem. Council, Univ. of Leeds, 2007–. Trustee: St Gemma's Hospice, 1999–2011; Leeds Internat. Pianoforte Competition, 2004–14, 2015–; Ryedale Fest., 2018–. High Sheriff, 2015–16, DL, 2016, W Yorks. KSG 2011. *Recreations:* watching sport, music, walking in the Yorkshire Dales. *Clubs:* Royal Over-Seas League, MCC; Collingham and Linton Cricket; Yorkshire CC.

**ANDERSON, Sir Eric;** *see* Anderson, Sir W. E. K.

**ANDERSON, Fiona Kate;** *see* Scolding, F. K.

**ANDERSON, Gillian Leigh,** Hon. OBE 2016; actress; *b* Chicago, 9 Aug. 1968; *d* of Edward Homer Anderson, III, and Rosemary Alyce Anderson; two *s* one *d*. *Educ:* Goodman Theater Sch., De Paul Univ. (BA). *Theatre* includes: A Streetcar Named Desire, Young Vic, 2014 (Best Actress, Evening Standard Theatre Awards, 2014); All About Eve, Noël Coward Th., 2019; *television* includes: The X Files, 1993–2002, 2016, 2018 (Screen Actors Guild Award, 1996, 1997; Emmy Award, Golden Globe Award for Best Actress in a Drama Series, 1997); Bleak House, 2005; Any Human Heart, 2010; Great Expectations, 2011; The Fall, 2013, 2014, 2016; Hannibal, 2013, 2014; Moby Dick, 2015; War and Peace, 2016; American Gods, 2017; Agatha Christie's Crooked House, 2017; Sex Education, 2019; *films* include: The X Files, 1998; House of Mirth, 2000 (Best Actress, BIFA Awards); The Last King of Scotland, 2006; The X Files: I Want to Believe, 2008; How to Lose Friends and Alienate People, 2008; Johnny English Reborn, 2011; Shadow Dancer, 2012; Mr Morgan's Last Love, 2014; Robot Overlords, 2014; Viceroy's House, 2017; The Spy Who Dumped Me, 2018. *Publications:* (jtly) A Vision of Fire, 2014; (jtly) We: a manifesto for women everywhere, 2017. *Address:* c/o Jane Epstein, Independent Talent Group Ltd, 40 Whitfield Street, W1T 2RH. *T:* (020) 7636 6565.

**ANDERSON, Rt Rev. Gregory David;** *see* Northern Territory (Australia), Bishop of the.

**ANDERSON, Prof. Harry Laurence,** PhD; FRS 2013; FRSC; Professor of Chemistry, University of Oxford, since 2004; *b* Kingston upon Thames, 12 Jan. 1964; *s* of late Douglas Alexander Anderson and of Elinor Anderson; *m* 1992, Sally Nicholson; two *d*. *Educ:* Haslemere Prep. Sch.; Brecon High Sch.; Hereford Cathedral Sch.; Rugby Sch.; Christ Ch, Oxford (BA 1st Cl. Chem. 1987); Trinity Hall, Cambridge (PhD Chem. 1991). FRSC 2003. Res. Fellow, Magdalene Coll., Cambridge, 1990–93; Postdoctoral Res. Fellow, ETH, Zurich, 1993–94; Lectr in Organic Chem., Univ. of Oxford, 1994–2004. *Publications:* contribs to scientific jls. *Recreation:* playing with fire. *Address:* Department of Chemistry, University of Oxford, Chemistry Research Laboratory, Mansfield Road, Oxford OX1 3TA. *T:* (01865) 275704. *E:* harry.anderson@chem.ox.ac.uk.

**ANDERSON, Heather; Her Honour Judge Heather Anderson;** a Circuit Judge, since 2013; a Deputy High Court Judge, since 2011; *b* Withernsea, 20 Nov. 1954; *d* of Edward Harry Medcalf and late Marjorie Medcalf; *m* 1982, Edmund John Seward Anderson, *qv*; two *s* two *d*. *Educ:* Withernsea High Sch.; Univ. of Warwick (BA Hons). Admitted as solicitor, 1978; in practice as solicitor, 1978–2000; called to the Bar, Inner Temple, 2000; in practice as barrister, 2000–01; a Dep. Dist Judge, 1998–2001; a Dist Judge, 2001–13; a Recorder, 2005–13. Chm., Child Support Appeal Tribunal, 1993–99. *Recreations:* walking, music, eating with family and friends, Rugby League, travel. *Address:* Leeds Combined Court Centre, The Courthouse, 1 Oxford Row, Leeds, W Yorks LS1 3BG. *T:* (0113) 306 2800. *Clubs:* Royal Over-Seas League; Collingham and Linton Cricket.

**ANDERSON, Sir Iain;** *see* Anderson, Sir J. I. W.

**ANDERSON, James Frazer Gillan,** CBE 1979; JP; DL; Member, Scottish Development Agency, 1986–89; *b* 25 March 1929; *m* 1956, May Harley; one *s* one *d*. *Educ:* Maddiston Primary Sch.; Graeme High Sch., Falkirk. Member: Stirling CC, 1958–75 (Convener, 1971–75); Central Regional Council, Scotland, 1974–96 (Convener, 1974–86). Mem., Health and Safety Commission, 1974–80. DUniv Stirling, 1987. *Recreations:* gardening, walking.

**ANDERSON, Sir (James) Iain (Walker),** Kt 2008; CBE 2000; PhD; Director, Unilever PLC and NV, 1988–98; *b* Glasgow, 30 June 1938; *s* of John and Alice Anderson; *m* 1963, Katie McCrone; two *s*. *Educ:* King's Park Sch., Glasgow; Univ. of Glasgow (BSc Hons, PhD 1962). Res. Manager, Unilever, 1965–76; Chairman: Marine Harvest Ltd, 1976–79; Food Industries Ltd, 1979–80; PPF Ltd, 1980–82; Ops Dir, Unilever Chemicals Div., 1982–85; Chm., Batchelors Foods Ltd, 1985–88. Director: British Telecom plc, 1995–2001; BT Scotland, 1997–2004 (Chm., 1999–2004); Scottish and Newcastle plc, 1998–2006. Chairman: Intense Photonics Ltd, 2000–06; Schs Enterprise Scotland Ltd, 2000–06. Special Advr to Prime Minister on Millennium Compliance (Y2K), 1998–2000; conducted ind. inquiry into Lessons to be Learned from 2001 outbreak of foot and mouth disease in UK, 2001–02; conducted ind. rev. of Govt's handling of foot and mouth outbreak in England in 2007, 2007–08. Gov., NIESR, 1992–98. Trustee: British Occupational Health Res. Foundn, 1996–98; Scottish Sci. Trust, 1997–2002; Leverhulme Trust, 1999–2017. FRSE 2010. Hon. DEng Glasgow, 2012. *Recreations:* food and wine, horticulture, photography, reading, thinking about things. *Address:* Burnbank, Acharn, by Aberfeldy, Perthshire PH15 2HU. *Club:* New (Edinburgh).

**ANDERSON, Prof. Jane,** CBE 2015; PhD; FRCP; Consultant Physician in HIV Medicine, and Director, Centre for Study of Sexual Health and HIV, Homerton University Hospital NHS Foundation Trust, since 2004; *b* Swindon, Wilts, 23 Dec. 1952; *d* of Brig. Francis Edmund Charles Hughes and Irene Mary Winifred Hughes; *m* 1981, Clive Stuart Anderson, *qv*; one *s* two *d*. *Educ:* Cirencester Grammar Sch., subseq. Cirencester Comprehensive Sch.; Queen Elizabeth Coll., Univ. of London (BSc 1975; PhD 1979); St Mary's Hosp. Med. Sch., Univ. of London (MB BS 1984). MRCP 1987, FRCP 1994. Hse Office, St Mary's Hosp. and St Charles Hosp., 1984–85; SHO, Northwick Park Hosp., 1985–87; Registrar, St Mary's Hosp., 1987–88; Sen. Registrar, Middx Hosp., 1988–90; Sen. Lectr and Hon. Consultant, St Bartholomew's Hosp. Med. Coll., subseq. Barts and the London Sch. of Medicine and Dentistry, 1990–2004; Hon. Consultant Physician, St Luke's Healthcare for the Clergy, 1996–. Lead for HIV and Sexual Health, Wellbeing Directorate, Public Health England, 2013–16. Visiting Fellow: Centre for Study of Migration, Dept of Politics, QMUL, 2005– (Hon. Prof., 2008–); King's Fund, 2016–; Hon. Prof., UCL, 2010–. Chair: British HIV Assoc., 2011–13; Nat. AIDS Trust, 2016–. Ct Asst, Soc. of Apothecaries, 2011– (Jun. Warden, 2018–19). *Publications:* contributor: HIV Infection in Women, 1994; Textbook of Genitourinary Surgery, 2nd edn 1998; Gender and Insecurity: migrant women in Europe, 2003; Mobility, Sexuality and AIDS, 2009; Education and HIV/AIDS (Education as a Humanitarian Response), 2011; Clinical Medicine, 2nd edn 1994 to 8th edn 2012; London the Promised Land Revisited: the changing face of the London migrant landscape in the early 21st century, 2015; contribs to jls in field of medicine and HIV. *Recreations:* taking photographs, attempting to catch fish, reading, being with my family and friends. *Address:* Centre for the Study of Sexual Health and HIV, Homerton University University Hospital NHS Foundation Trust, Homerton Row, E9 6SR. *T:* (020) 8510 7983. *E:* janderson@nhs.net. *Club:* Shoreditch House.

**ANDERSON, Janet;** Director, Pearson-Anderson Communications Ltd, since 2015; *b* Newcastle upon Tyne, 6 Dec. 1949; *d* of late Thomas Anderson and Ethel Pearson; *m* 1st (marr. diss.); two *s* one *d*; 2nd, 2016, James Patrick Dowd, *qv*. *Educ:* Trowbridge Girls' High Sch.; Kingswood Grammar Sch.; Kingsfield Comprehensive Sch.; Polytechnic of Central London; Univ. of Nantes (Dip. Bi-lingual Business Studies in French and German). Asst to Rt Hon. Barbara Castle, 1974–81, to Jack Straw, MP, 1981–87; Campaign Officer, PLP, 1988–89; Regl Organiser, Shopping Hours Reform Council, 1991–92. Contested (Lab) Rossendale and Darwen, 1987. MP (Lab) Rossendale and Darwen, 1992–2010; contested (Lab) same seat, 2010. PPS to Dep. Leader of Labour Party, 1992–93; an Opposition Whip, 1995–97; Vice Chamberlain of HM Household, 1997–98; Parly Under-Sec. of State, DCMS, 1998–2001. Mem., H of C Commn, 1993–94; Member, Select Committee: on Home Affairs, 1994–95 (Home Affairs Campaigns Co-ordinator, 1994–95); on Culture, Media and Sport, 2002–10. Secretary: All-Party Footwear Gp, 1992–97; All-Party Tourism Gp, 2002–10; Chairman: All-Party Intellectual Property Gp, 2005–10; All-Party Writers Gp, 2008–10; All-Party Performers Alliance Gp, 2008–10; Mem., Chairmen's Panel, 2004–10. Sec., Tribune Gp of Lab MPs, 1993–97. Vis. Fellow, St Antony's Coll., Oxford, 1993–94. Mem. and Consultant, Authors' Licensing and Collecting Soc., 2010–. *Recreations:* gardening, reading, cooking, playing with my grandchildren, playing the piano, badly.

**ANDERSON, Jennifer Elizabeth;** HM Diplomatic Service; Minister Counsellor and Deputy Head of Mission, Ankara, since 2017; *m* 1997, Stephen Ashworth; one *s* one *d*. *Educ:* Australian Nat. Univ. (BA Hons, LLB Hons). ME and Africa analyst, Australian Office of Nat. Assessments, Canberra, 1993–95; Advr, Internat. Div., Australian Dept of Prime Minister and Cabinet, 1995; Harkness Fellow, Inst. of War and Peace Studies, Columbia Univ., NY, 1995–96; Res. Associate, IISS, 1996–97; entered FCO, 1997; Head: Visegrad Sect., Central Eur. Dept, FCO, 1997–99; Bosnia and Croatia Sect., Eastern Adriatic Dept, FCO, 1999–2000; Resident Clerk, FCO, 2000–01; First Sec. (Pol/Mil.), UK Perm. Representation to EU, Brussels, 2001–03; Dep. Hd, Security Policy Gp, FCO, 2003–05; Business Change Manager and Hd, Business Engagement Gp, Inf. and Technol. Directorate, FCO, 2006–09; High Comr to Botswana, 2010–13; Dep. Hd of Mission, Jakarta, 2013; Hd, Counter-Terrorism Dept, FCO, 2014–16. *Address:* c/o Foreign and Commonwealth Office, King Charles Street, SW1A 2AH.

**ANDERSON, Jeremy David Bruce,** CBE 2005; Chairman, Global Financial Services, KPMG LLP, 2010–17; *b* Penang, 8 June 1958; *s* of Bruce Anderson and Sheila Anderson; *m* 1985, Rachel Priscilla Naish; two *s* one *d*. *Educ:* Mill Sch., Potterne; Dauntsey's Sch.; University Coll. London (BSc (Econ) 1980). IT develt, Triad Computing Systems, 1980–85; Mgt Consulting - Financial Services, KPMG, 1985–98; Dep. CEO, 1998–2001, CEO, 2001–02, KPMG Consulting UK; Mem. Bd, KPMG UK LLP, 1998–2002; Mem. Mgt Bd, Atos Origin SA, 2002–04; KPMG: UK Financial Services Leader, 2004–06; Eur. Financial Services Leader, 2006–08; Eur. Hd of Mkts, 2008–10; Mem. Bd, KPMG Europe LLP, 2008–11. Non-exec. Dir, UBS Gp AG, 2018–. Member: Nat. Employment Panel, 2002–08 (Chm., 2006–08); Ethnic Minority Employment Task Force, 2006–08; UK Commn for Employment and Skills, 2008–17. Mem., Bretton Woods Cttee, 2014–. Trustee: Kingham Hill Trust, 2014–; Be The Business, 2017–. Chm. Council, Oakhill Theol Coll., 2015–. Churchwarden, St Helen's, Bishopsgate. *Recreations:* walking, ski-ing, travel, wine, family. *Club:* National.

**ANDERSON, His Honour John Adrian;** a Circuit Judge, 2009–17; *b* Manchester, 11 Jan 1950; *s* of Robert and Stella Anderson; *m* 1995, Helen Gordon. *Educ:* Trent Coll., Long Eaton, Notts. Commercial apprenticeship, Rolls Royce Aero Engine Div., 1967–71; commnd RN as pilot, Fleet Air Arm, 1972–88 (South Atlantic Medal, Falklands War 1982); Commercial and Airline Transport Pilot's Licences (Fixed and Rotary Wing), 1988 Called to the Bar, Middle Temple, 1989; in practice at the Bar, specialising in crime and serious fraud, 1990–2009. Standing Counsel to Revenue and Customs Prosecutions Office 2005–09. *Recreations:* boating, walking, DIY, Cornwall, getting beaten at Wii tennis by nieces. *Club:* Torpoint Mosquito Sailing.

**ANDERSON, Hon. John (Duncan),** AO 2011; Chairman, Eastern Star Gas, 2007–11 Chair, Crawford Fund, since 2017 (Board Member, since 2010); *b* 14 Nov. 1956; *s* o Duncan Anderson and Beryl Anderson (*née* Mann); *m* 1987, Julia Gillian Robertson; one three *d*. *Educ:* Univ. of Sydney (MA). Farmer and grazier. MP (Nat.) Gwydir, NSW

1989–2007; Minister for: Primary Industries and Energy, 1996–98; Transport and Regl Services, 1998–2005; Dep. Prime Minister, 1999–2005. Dep. Leader, 1993–99, Leader, 1999–2005, Nat. Party of Australia. *Club:* Australian (Sydney).

**ANDERSON, John Ferguson;** Chief Executive, Glasgow City Council, 1995–98; *b* 13 Dec. 1947; *s* of Charles and Isabella Anderson; *m* 1970, Sandra McFarlane; one *s* one *d*. *Educ:* Edinburgh Univ. (LLB Hons 1969). Legal Assistant, then Solicitor, later Asst Chief Solicitor, Glasgow Corp., 1969–75; Strathclyde Regional Council: Prin. Solicitor, 1975–78; Asst Dir of Admin, 1978–80; Sen. Exec. Officer, 1980–86; Prin. Exec. Officer, 1986–90; Dep. Chief Exec., 1990–95. *Recreations:* golf, watching football, transportation issues, church, bowls. *Address:* Balwearie, 41 Scott Brae, Kippen FK8 3DL.

**ANDERSON, John Graeme,** CBE 1989; CEng, FInstE; Deputy Chairman, Northern Engineering Industries plc, 1986–89; Director, Team General Partner, 1993–2002; *b* 3 June 1927; *s* of John Anderson and Ella (*née* Pusey); *m* 1953, Nancy Clarice Taylor Johnson; one *s* twin *d*. *Educ:* Merchant Taylors' Sch., Sandy Lodge; London Univ. (BScEng Hons). MIMechE. Served RN, Fleet Air Arm, 1945–48. International Combustion Ltd: graduate apprentice, 1952; Dir, 1968; Dep. Chief Exec., 1969; Man. Dir, 1974; Northern Engineering Industries: Man. Dir, NEI-Internat. Combustion Ltd, 1977; Managing Director: Mechanical Gp, 1980; Power Gp, 1982; Internat. and Projects Gp, 1984; Chm., NEI Pacific, 1984–88. Chm., Internat. Combustion-HUD Hong Kong, 1978–82; Dir, British Nuclear Associates, 1985–88; Alternate Dir, Nat. Nuclear Corp., 1986–88; Director: Rolls Royce, 1980–88, 1989–91; Tyne and Wear Develt Corp., 1987–93; The Newcastle Initiative, 1988–90. Mem., Duke of Kent's BOTB mission to Turkey, 1984. Chairman: Solid Waste Assoc., 1972–74; Watertube Boilermakers' Assoc., 1976–80; Member: Process Plant Assoc., 1968–87; Process Plant, EDC, 1972–76; Heavy Electrical, EDC, 1976–80. Gov., Derby Coll. of Technology, 1969–74. Chm., Upstage, 1977–79. *Recreations:* shooting, painting, music, fell walking. *Address:* Trinity Barns, Corbridge, Northumberland NE45 5HP. *T:* (01434) 633228.

**ANDERSON, John Huxley Fordyce,** OBE 2010; FCIOB; property and development consultant, since 2009; Group Managing Director, Byrne Group PLC, 2016–18; *b* 13 Jan. 1945; *s* of Alexander Robert Fordyce Anderson and Agnes Joan (*née* Huxley); *m* 1973, Tucker Lee Etherington; one *s* one *d*. *Educ:* Fan Court Sch.; Milton Abbey Sch.; Brixton Sch. of Building; Harvard Business Sch. (post-grad. PMD 1983). FCIOB 1988. Joined Higgs & Hill as indentured student, 1962; Project Planner on projects such as BBC TV Centre, RMA Sandhurst, 1966–69; Contract Manager, Sales and Marketing Manager then Dep. Man. Dir, Costains, Vale do Lobo, Portugal, 1969–74; with Town & City Properties in Holland, 1975–76; Develt Project Manager, Town & City Develts in London, 1976–83; Man. Dir, Town & City, then P&O, Develts, 1984–92; Director: Chelsea Harbour, 1984–92; P&O Property Hldgs, 1985–99; Managing Director: Bovis Construction Ltd, 1993–2000; Bovis Europe, 1996–2000; Jt Man. Dir, Bovis Construction Gp, 1997–2000 (Dir, 1988–2000). Man. Dir, PSA Building Mgt (on secondment to Govt), 1991–93. Non-exec. Dir, Maxxiom, 1997–2000. Director: British Council for Offices, 1996–2003; Land Securities Properties, 2000–03; Chelsfield plc, 2003–05; of Develt, Parkview (Battersea Power Station), 2006–07; Buckingham Develts Ltd, 2007–08; of Projects and Develts, Tellesma LLP, 2008–09; Construction Adviser: Sammy Ofer Wing Develt, Nat. Maritime Mus., 2009–12; Cutty Sark Conservation Project, 2009–13; Chief Advr of Major Projects and Infrastructures, Olympic Park Legacy Co., 2010–11. Chairman: Export Gp for Construction Industries, 1999–2001; Special Purpose Vehicle St Martin in the Fields Develts Ltd, 2006–11. Consultant: Deerbrook Gp, 2011–15; Cleveland Clinic, London, 2018–19. Hon. Property Consultant, Queen Elizabeth Foundn for the Disabled, 2001–. Chm., Lighthouse Club, 2005–08. Mem., Hambledon Parish Council, 1984– (Chm., 2004–). Dir, Hambledon Village Shop, 2007–18. *Recreations:* parish council, golf, ski-ing, gardening, Rugby, opera, theatre, ballet, eating and drinking with friends.

**ANDERSON, John M.,** PhD; FBA 1991; Professor of English Language, University of Edinburgh, 1988–2001, now Emeritus. *Educ:* Edinburgh Univ. (MA, PhD). Lectr until 1975, Reader, 1975–88, Edinburgh Univ. *Publications:* The Grammar of Case: towards a localistic theory, 1971; An Essay Concerning Aspect, 1973; (ed with C. Jones) Historical Linguistics, 2 vols, 1974; (with R. Lass) Old English Phonology, 1975; On Case Grammar, 1977; (with C. Jones) Phonological Structure and the History of English, 1977; (with C. J. Ewen) Principles of Dependency Phonology, 1987; Linguistic Representation: structural analogy and stratification, 1992; Notional Theory of Syntactic Categories, 1997; Modern Grammars of Case, 2006; The Grammar of Names, 2007; The Substance of Language (3 vols), 2011. *Address:* PO Box 348, Methoni Messinias 24006, Greece. *E:* frohn@otenet.gr.

**ANDERSON, Dame Josephine;** *see* Barstow, Dame J. C.

**ANDERSON, Julian Anthony;** Director General, Country Landowners' Association, 1990–2000; *b* 12 June 1938; *s* of Sir Kenneth Anderson, KBE, CB. *Educ:* King Alfred Sch.; Wadham Coll., Oxford (MA). Entered MAFF as Asst Principal, 1961; Asst Private Sec. to Minister of Agriculture, 1964–66; Principal, 1966; seconded to FCO, 1970–73; Asst Sec., 1973, Under Sec., 1982–90, MAFF; seconded as Minister (Food and Agriculture), UK Perm. Rep. to EEC, 1982–85. *Recreations:* music, sport, travel, photography, gardening, DIY. *Clubs:* Oxford and Cambridge, Civil Service.

**ANDERSON, Julian David;** composer; *b* 6 April 1967. *Educ:* Royal Coll. of Music (BMus London 1st cl.); Gonville and Caius Coll., Cambridge, 1990–91; King's Coll., Cambridge, 1992–94 (MPhil Composition). Prof. of Music, Harvard Univ., 2004–07; Prof. of Composition and Composer-in-Residence, Guildhall Sch., 2007–. Composer-in-Association, CBSO, 2001–05; Daniel R. Lewis Young Composer Fellow, Cleveland Orch., 2005–07; Composer-in-Residence: London Philharmonic Orch., 2010–; Wigmore Hall, 2013–. Works performed by numerous ensembles and orchestras in Europe, Japan, E Asia and USA, incl. Cleveland Orch., Boston SO, Deutsche SO, Orch. de Paris, NY Philharmonic Orch., Tokyo Metropolitan SO, Malaysian Philharmonic Orch., Seoul Philharmonic Orch., London Sinfonietta, Tokyo Sinfonietta, Schoenberg, Nash and Asko Ensembles. Broadcast talks on music on BBC Radio, French, German, Swiss, Finnish and American radios. *Compositions* include: Symphony, 2003; Book of Hours, 2004; The Comedy of Change, 2009; Fantasias, 2009; The Discovery of Heaven, 2012; Violin Concerto, 2015; Van Gogh Blue, 2015; commissions from: London Sinfonietta, 1994 (Khorovod) and 2000 (Alhambra Fantasy); BBC Proms, 1998 (The Stations of the Sun), 2006 (Heaven is Shy of Earth) and 2013 (Harmony); Cheltenham Festival, 1997 (The Crazed Moon); ENO, 2014 (Thebans). Young Composer Prize, 1990, Award, 2006, Royal Philharmonic Soc.; South Bank Show Award, 2002; BASCA Award, 2004, 2007, 2011 (two awards); South Bank Sky Arts Award, 2013. *Publications:* articles on music in Musical Times, Tempo, The Independent, Guardian, The Times, FT. *Recreations:* films, reading, poetry, swimming.

**ANDERSON, Kenneth Walter;** Senior Advisor, Greenhill and Co. International LLP, since 2014; Managing Partner, Woodhaven Partners, since 2017; *b* 22 Feb. 1960; *s* of late Walter Anderson and of Barbara Anderson; *m* 1983, Pamela Davison; three *s*. *Educ:* American Community Sch., London; Texas A&M Univ. Director: of Strategic Investment, MG Technologies AG, Germany, 2000–01; of Healthcare, Amey plc, 2001–02; Department of Health: Dir, Contract Procurement Prog., 2002–03; Commercial Dir Gen., 2003–06; Man. Dir, 2006–11, a Vice Chm., 2011–14, UBS Investment Bank. Advr to Texas A&M Genetics Res. Prog., 2012–; Sen. Advr, Min. of Health, Saudi Arabia. Dir, West One Restaurants Ltd, 2013–. Non-exec. Dir, Real Asset Energy Fund, 2012–. Adjunct Prof. of Finance, Imperial Business Coll. (formerly Tanaka Business Sch., Imperial Coll. London), 2005–. *Recreations:* ski-ing, reading, fishing, cycling, triathlon, sailing. *Address:* Kingdom Tower, Riyadh, Saudi Arabia. *T:* 0503881314. *E:* kanderson@moh.gov.uk.

**ANDERSON, Lesley Jane, (Mrs C. Crawford);** QC 2006; a Recorder, since 2006; a Deputy High Court Judge, Chancery Division, since 2008; *b* 6 April 1963; *d* of Ian Anderson and late Rosemary Campbell Anderson; *m* 1996, Colin Crawford; one step *s* one step *d*. *Educ:* King Edward VI Camp Hill Sch. for Girls, Birmingham; Univ. of Manchester (LLB Hons 1984). CEDR Accredited Mediator, 2000. Lectr in Law, Univ. of Manchester, 1984–89; called to the Bar, Middle Temple, 1989; Trng Manager, Norton Rose M5 Gp of Legal Practices, 1989–91; barrister, 40 King St Chambers, subseq. Kings Chambers, Manchester, 1991–, and Hardwicke Chambers, 2011–. *Publications:* articles in legal and professional jls. *Recreations:* food, wine, theatre, cinema, modern jazz. *Address:* Kings Chambers, 36 Young Street, Manchester M3 3FT. *T:* (0161) 819 8261, *Fax:* (0161) 835 2139. *E:* landersonqc@kingschambers.com.

**ANDERSON, Lucy;** Member (Lab) London Region, European Parliament, 2014–19. Policy and legal expert, TUC, 1997–2006; Business Manager, GLA; Sen. Manager, NUT. Mem. (Lab) Camden LBC, 2002–06.

**ANDERSON, Prof. Malcolm Grove;** Professor of Physical Geography, University of Bristol, 1989–2012, now Emeritus (Pro-Vice-Chancellor, 2005–09); *b* 27 June 1949; *s* of Wilfred Roy Anderson and Frances Betty Anderson; *m* 1972, Elizabeth Ann Roger; one *d*. *Educ:* Univ. of Nottingham (BSc); Univ. of Cambridge (PhD); Univ. of Bristol (DSc). FICE 1996. Research Fellow, Sidney Sussex Coll., Cambridge, 1972; University of Bristol: Lectr, 1973; Reader, 1985; Head, Dept of Geography, 1990–96, 2002–05; Dir, Inst. for Advanced Studies, 1997–2000 (Vice-Provost, 2000–02). Res. Hydrologist, US Corps of Engrs, 1981–82; Sen. Res. Geotechnical Engr, Hong Kong Govt, 1982–83; Nuffield Foundn, Sen. Science Fellowship, 1988–89; Quater Centenary Vis. Fellowship, Emmanuel Coll., Cambridge, 1989. Vis. Prof. of Hydrology, Univ. of Oxford, 2010–13. Technical Advr, Poverty Reduction Fund, 2004–09, Chm., Management of Slope Stability in Communities (MoSSaiC) Cttee, 2004–11, Govt of St Lucia, WI; Sen. Landslide Risk Specialist, Latin America and Caribbean, World Bank, 2008–16. Natural Environment Research Council: Mem., AAPS Cttee, 1990–93; Chm., Land-Ocean Interaction Study Steering Cttee, 1998–2001; Member: Council, 2002–07; Audit Cttee, 2003–07; Mem., Science Grants Panel, Nuffield Foundn, 1992–2007; Mem., Technology Opportunities Panel, EPSRC, 2009–11; Scholarship Assessor, ACU, 1993–97. Mem., Bristol Cathedral Council, 2002–09. Editor-in-Chief, Hydrological Processes, 1986–2014. Life Fellow, Indian Assoc. of Hydrologists, 1995. Gill Meml Award, RGS, 1986; Trevithick Premium Award, ICE, 1996, 2007. *Publications:* edited jointly: Hydrological Forecasting, 1985; Slope Stability: geotechnical engineering and geomorphology, 1987; Modelling Geomorphological Systems, 1988; Process Studies in Hillslope Hydrology, 1990; Floodplain Processes, 1996; Advances in Hillslope Processes, 1996; Model Validation: perspectives in hydrological science, 2001; Encyclopaedia of Hydrological Sciences, 2005; Landslides: hazard and risk, 2005; (authored jtly) Community-based Landslide Risk Reduction: managing disasters in small steps, 2013; numerous res. pubns in hydrological scis and geotechnics. *Recreation:* Carrick Roads. *Address:* Department of Civil Engineering, University of Bristol, Bristol BS8 1TR.

**ANDERSON, Marie;** Police Ombudsman for Northern Ireland, since 2019; *b* Belfast, 7 Dec. 1960; *d* of Michael and Ellen Maguire; *m* 1988, Thomas Anderson; three *s*. *Educ:* St Dominic's High Sch., Belfast; Queen's Univ. Belfast (LLB; CPLS); Brunel Univ. (MBA). Pupil Solicitor, Meehan Murphy Solicitors, 1984–85; Solicitor (Litigation), Michael M. Collins, Solicitor, 1985–86, Kieran Trainor, Solicitor, 1986–87; Northern Ireland Housing Executive: Legal Asst (Housing Law), 1987–88; Sen. Legal Asst (Litigation and Public Law), 1988–96; Acting Legal Advr, 1996–97; Asst Information Comr for NI, 2003–08; Dep. NI Ombudsman, 2009–16; NI Public Services Ombudsman, 2016–19. *Publications:* (jtly) Mapping the Administrative Justice Landscape in Northern Ireland, 2014. *Recreations:* reading, walking, crossword puzzles. *Address:* Police Ombudsman Office, New Cathedral Buildings, Writers' Square, 11 Church Street, Belfast BT1 1PG.

**ANDERSON, Mark Roger;** QC 2010; a Recorder, since 2003; a Deputy High Court Judge, Chancery Division, since 2013; *b* Birmingham, 1960; *s* of Roger John Anderson and Ethel Ann Anderson (*née* Beale); *m* 1986, Katharine Elizabeth Anne Dillon; one *s* one *d*. *Educ:* King Edward's Sch., Birmingham; Exeter Coll., Oxford (MA). Called to the Bar, Middle Temple, 1983; in practice as barrister, specialising in commercial dispute resolution and professional negligence; Hd, No 5 Chambers, 2016–. Chm., Midland Chancery and Commercial Bar Assoc., 2010–16. *E:* man@no5.com.

**ANDERSON, Martina;** Member (SF) Northern Ireland, European Parliament, since June 2012; *b* Derry, NI, 16 April 1962. *Educ:* St Cecilia's Coll. BA 1st Cl. Hons Social Scis 1996. Spent 13 years in prisons in England and Ireland; released under terms of Good Friday Agreement, 1998. Political researcher, 1999–2002; All Ireland Coordinator, 2002–06, Dir, Unionist Engagement, 2006–07, SF. Mem. (SF) Foyle, NI Assembly, 2007–June 2012; Jun. Minister, Office of First Minister and Dep. First Ministers, 2011–12. Mem., NI Policing Bd, 2007–11. Mem., All Party Gp on Internat. Develt, 2007–09, on Disability, 2008–11, NI Assembly. Mem., Cttee on Envmt, Public Health and Food Safety, 2012, Cttee on Regl Develt, 2012, Eur. Parlt. *Address:* European Parliament, Rue Wiertz, 1047 Brussels, Belgium.

**ANDERSON, Prof. Michael,** OBE 1999; FRSE; FBA 1989; Professor of Economic History, University of Edinburgh, 1979–2007, now Emeritus; *b* 21 Feb. 1942; *s* of Douglas Henry and Rose Lillian Anderson; *m* 1st, 1966, Rosemary Elizabeth Kitching (marr. diss.); one *s* one *d*; 2nd, 2007, Elspeth Catriona MacArthur. *Educ:* Kingston Grammar Sch.; Queens' Coll., Cambridge (BA 1964; MA 1968; PhD 1969). FRSE 1990. University of Edinburgh: Department of Sociology: Asst Lectr, 1967; Lectr, 1969; Reader, 1975; Department of Economic and Social History, 1979; Dean, Faculty of Social Scis, 1985–89; Vice-Principal, 1989–93, 1997–2000; Acting Principal, April–Aug. 1994; Sen. Vice-Principal, 2000–07. Member: Economic and Social History Cttee, SSRC, 1974–78; Computing Cttee, SSRC, 1980–82; Scot. Records Adv. Council, 1984–93; ESRC, 1990–94 (Member: Res. Resources and Methods Cttee, 1982–84; Society and Politics Res. Develt Gp, 1989–92); Chm., Res. Resources Bd, 1992–94); History of Medicine Cttee, Wellcome Trust, 1988–92; BL Bd, 1994–2003 (Dep. Chm., 2000–03); Council, British Acad., 1995–98; Res. Information Network Adv. Bd, 2005–11; HEFCE Res. and Innovation Cttee, 2006–09; Adv. Cttee, Nat. Statistics Centre for Demography, 2006–12; Scottish Census Steering Cttee, 2009–11; Population Theme Adv. Bd, ONS, 2012–. Chm., Res. Support Libraries Programme, 1998–2003. Curator, RSE, 1997–99. Chm., Bd of Trustees, Nat. Library of Scotland, 2000–12 (Trustee, 1998–2012). Hon. FFA 2007. Dr *hc* Edinburgh, 2007; Hon. LittD Leicester, 2014. *Publications:* Family Structure in Nineteenth

Century Lancashire, 1971; (ed) Sociology of the Family, 1972; Approaches to the History of the Western Family 1500–1914, 1981; The 1851 Census: a national sample of the enumerators returns, 1987; Population Change in Northwestern Europe 1750–1850, 1988; (ed) Social and Political Economy of the Household, 1995; (ed) British Population History, 1996; Scotland's Populations from the 1850s to Today, 2018; numerous papers on family sociology, population and family history. *Recreations:* natural history, gardening, the rise and fall of urban civilizations.

**ANDERSON, Michael James;** Senior Vice President, External Affairs, Government Relations and Security, Kosmos Energy, since 2015; *b* 3 April 1961; *s* of James and Beryl Anderson; *m* 1987, Julie Dickens; two *s* one *d*. *Educ:* Newcastle Royal Grammar Sch.; Hymers Coll., Hull; Trinity Coll., Cambridge (BA Hons Law 1983). Law Lectr, Univ. of Ill, Urbana-Champaign, 1983–84; Foreign and Commonwealth Office, 1984–2003: Moscow, 1988–89; UK Delegn to Conf. on Disarmament, Geneva, 1992–97; Private Secretary: to Sir David Spedding, 1997–99; to Sir Richard Dearlove, 1999–2000; UK Mission to UN, NY, 2000–03; Prin. Private Sec. to the Lord Chancellor and Sec. of State for Constitutional Affairs, 2003–06; Dir of Strategy and Communication, DCA, 2006–07; Dir Gen., Climate Change Gp, DEFRA, later DECC, 2007–09; on secondment to Nat. Grid, 2009; Dir Gen., Strategy, Finance, Perf. and Evidence Gp, later Green Economy and Corp. Services, DEFRA, 2009–11; Dir Gen., Internat. and Immigration Policy Gp (formerly Strategy, Immigration and Internat. Gp), Home Office, 2011–15. *Recreations:* doing, thinking, family, sports.

**ANDERSON, Michael Roy,** CB 2014; Chief Executive Officer, Children's Investment Fund Foundation, 2013–16; *b* Bellingham, WA, USA, 9 April 1962; *s* of Jerry McCush Anderson and Maria Schmitt Anderson; *m* 2002, Sian Harris; one *s*. *Educ:* Univ. of Washington (Marshall Schol.); BA Pol Sci. *summa cum laude*; President's Medal); St John's Coll., Oxford (Rhodes Schol.; MLitt Social Anthropol. 1988); Sch. of Oriental and African Studies, Univ. of London (LLM 1988). Consultant in internat. law and litigation, 1988–2002; Lectr in Law, SOAS, Univ. of London, 1988–96; Dir of Studies, British Inst. of Internat. and Comparative Law, 1996–2001; Co-founder and Chief Operating Officer, Bazian Ltd, 2000–02; Department for International Development: Team Leader for Justice, 2002–03, for Fragile States, 2003–05; Head, ME, 2005–08, India, 2008–10; Dir Gen., Policy and Global Issues, then Policy and Global Progs, 2010–13; Prime Minister's Special Envoy for UN Develt Goals, 2012–13. Vis. Fellow in Law, LSE, 1996–; Vis. Fellow, Center for Global Develt. *Publications:* books include: Human Rights Approaches to Environmental Protection, 1996; The International Law Commission and the Future of International Law, 1998; International Environmental Law in National Courts, 2001; Constitutional Human Rights in the Commonwealth, 2002; Seafarers' Rights, 2005. *Recreations:* hiking, theatre.

**ANDERSON, Paul James;** journalist and author; Lecturer in Journalism, University of Essex, since 2014; *b* 3 Oct. 1959; *s* of James George Anderson and Marjorie Rosemary Anderson (*née* Thorpe). *Educ:* Ipswich Sch.; Balliol Coll., Oxford (BA Hons PPE 1981); London College of Printing. Dep. Ed., European Nuclear Disarmament Jl, 1984–87; Reviews Ed., 1986–91, Editor, 1991–93, Tribune; Dep. Ed., New Statesman, 1993–96; News Ed., Red Pepper, 1997–99; Dep. Ed., New Times, 1999–2000; Lecturer in Journalism: City Univ., 2000–12; Brunel Univ., 2012–14; Univ. Campus Suffolk, 2012–14. Dir, People's Europe 98, 1998. *Publications:* (ed jtly) Mad Dogs: The US Raid on Libya, 1986; (with Nyta Mann) Safety First: the making of New Labour, 1997; (ed) Orwell in Tribune: 'As I Please' and other writings, 2006; (with K. Davey) Moscow Gold?: the Soviet Union and the British Left, 2014; Paint the West Red!: the strange story of British Maoism, 2018. *Address:* 119 Woodbridge Road, Ipswich IP4 2NJ.

**ANDERSON, Prof. Philip Warren;** Joseph Henry Professor of Physics, Princeton University, New Jersey, 1975–96, now Emeritus; *b* 13 Dec. 1923; *s* of Prof. H. W. Anderson and Mrs Elsie O. Anderson; *m* 1947, Joyce Gothwaite; one *d*. *Educ:* Harvard Univ. BS 1943; MA 1947; PhD 1949, Harvard. Naval Res. Lab., Washington, DC, 1943–45 (Chief Petty Officer, USN). Mem., Technical Staff, 1949–76, Dir, 1976–84, Bell Telephone Labs. Fulbright Lectr, Tokyo Univ., 1953–54; Overseas Fellow, Churchill Coll., Cambridge, 1961–62; Vis. Prof. of Theoretical Physics, Univ. of Cambridge, 1967–75, and Fellow of Jesus College, Cambridge, 1969–75, Hon. Fellow, 1978–; Cherwell-Simon Meml Lectureship, 1979–80, George Eastman Prof., 1993–94, Oxford Univ. Member: Amer. Acad. of Arts and Sciences, 1966; Nat. Acad. of Sciences, US, 1967; Amer. Philosophical Soc., 1991; Foreign Member: Royal Society, London, 1980; Japan Acad., 1988; Indian Nat. Acad. of Scis, 1990; Russian Nat. Acad. of Sci., 1994; Foreign Associate: Accademia Lincei, Rome, 1985; Indian Acad. of Sci., 1996. Hon. FInstP, 1986. Hon. DSc: Illinois, 1978; Rutgers, 1991; Ecole Normale Supérieure, Paris, 1995; Gustavus Adolphus Coll., Minn, 1995; Sheffield, 1996; Tsinghua, Beijing, 2008; Hon. PhD Tokyo, 2002. O. E. Buckley Prize, Amer. Phys. Soc., 1964; Dannie Heinemann Prize, Akad. Wiss. Göttingen, 1975; (jtly) Nobel Prize for Physics, 1977; Guthrie Medal, Inst. of Physics, 1978; Centennial Medal, Harvard, 1996; John Bardeen Prize, 1997; Prange Prize and Lectr, Univ. of Maryland, 2009. Nat. Medal of Science, US, 1984. *Publications:* Concepts in Solids, 1963; Basic Notions of Condensed Matter Physics, 1984; A Career in Theoretical Physics, 1994, 2nd edn 2004; The Theory of Superconductivity in the High Tc Cuprates, 1996; More and Different, 2011; numerous articles in scholarly jls. *Recreations:* go (Japanese game), rank shodan, rank 3-Dan (honorary). *Address:* 2439 Windrows Drive, Princeton, NJ 08540, USA.

**ANDERSON, Robert Edward;** QC 2006; barrister; *b* 12 Nov. 1963; *s* of late Edward and of Ivy Anderson (*née* Garland); one *s*; *m* 2017, Synnøve Naesheim; one step *s* one step *d*. *Educ:* Oundle Sch.; Pembroke Coll., Cambridge (BA Hons Law 1985). Called to the Bar, Gray's Inn and Middle Temple, 1986; in practice, specialising in commercial (particularly internat. fraud), sports and media law, 1986–. *Recreations:* late baroque music, jazz, cricket, the Turf, walking. *Address:* Blackstone Chambers, Temple, EC4Y 9BW. *T:* (020) 7583 1770, *Fax:* (020) 7822 7350. *E:* robertanderson@blackstonechambers.com. *Club:* Home House.

**ANDERSON, Robert Geoffrey William;** President and Chief Executive Officer, Science History Institute (formerly Chemical Heritage Foundation), Philadelphia, since 2016; Fellow, Clare Hall, Cambridge, 2006–14, now Emeritus (Vice-President, 2009–13); *b* 2 May 1944; *er s* of late Herbert Patrick Anderson and Kathleen Diana Anderson (*née* Burns); *m* 1st, 1973, Margaret Elizabeth Callis Lea (marr. diss. 2003); two *s*; 2nd, 2005, Jane Virginia Portal *qv* (marr. diss. 2017). *Educ:* Woodhouse Sch., London; St John's Coll., Oxford (Casberd exhibitioner; BSc, MA, DPhil; Hon. Fellow, 2000). FSA 1986; FRSE 1990. Assistant Keeper: Royal Scottish Museum, 1970–75; Science Museum, 1975–78; Dep. Keeper, Wellcome Museum of History of Medicine, and Sec., Adv. Council, Science Museum, 1978–80; Keeper, Dept of Chemistry, Science Mus., 1980–84; Director: Royal Scottish Mus., 1984–85; Nat. Museums of Scotland, 1985–92; British Mus., 1992–2002; Fellow, IAS, Princeton, 2002–03; By Fellow, Churchill Coll., Cambridge, 2003–04; Vis. Fellow, CCC, Cambridge, 2004–05. Sec., Royal Scottish Soc. of Arts, 1973–75; Member Council: Soc. for History of Alchemy and Chemistry, 1978– (Chm., 2007–); Gp for Scientific, Technological and Medical Collections, 1979–83; British Soc. History of Science, 1981–84 (Pres., 1988–90); Scottish Museums, 1984–91; Museums Assoc., 1988–92; Mem., British Nat. Cttee for Hist. of Science, 1985–89; Pres., Scientific Instrument Commn, IUHPS, 1982–97; Visitor, Mus. of the Hist. of Sci., Oxford, 2002–14; Mem., Bd of Dirs, Chemical Heritage Foundn, Philadelphia, 2006– (Vice-Chm., 2012–). Mem., Internat. Acad. of Hist. of Sci., 2002. Member Editorial Board: Annals of Science, 1981–; Annali di Storia della Scienza, 1986–. Trustee, Boerhaave Mus., Leiden, 1994–99. Hon. FSAScot 1991. Hon. DSc: Edinburgh, 1995; Durham, 1998. Dexter Prize, Amer. Chemical Soc., 1986; Paul Bunge Prize, Gesellschaft Deutscher Chemiker, 2016. Comdr, Ordre des Arts et des Lettres (France), 2002. *Publications:* The Mariner's Astrolabe, 1972; Edinburgh and Medicine, 1976; (ed) The Early Years of the Edinburgh Medical School, 1976; The Playfair Collection and the Teaching of Chemistry at the University of Edinburgh, 1978; (contrib.) The History of Technology, Vol. VI, ed T. I. Williams, 1978; Science in India, 1982; (ed) Science, Medicine and Dissent: Joseph Priestley (1733–1804), 1987; Scientific Instrument Makers Trade Catalogues, 1990; (ed) A New Museum for Scotland, 1990; (with G. Fyffe) Joseph Black: a Bibliography, 1992; (ed) Making Instruments Count, 1993; The Great Court at the British Museum, 2000; (ed) Chymica Acta, 2007; The Correspondence of Joseph Black, 2012; (ed) Cradle of Chemistry, 2015. *Recreation:* books. *Address:* 15 King Street, King's Lynn, Norfolk PE30 1ET. *T:* (01533) 691567. *Clubs:* Athenæum, Philadelphia.

**ANDERSON, Prof. Robert Henry;** Joseph Levy Professor of Paediatric Cardiac Morphology, Institute of Child Health, University College London, 1999–2007 (at National Heart and Lung Institute, Imperial College School of Medicine, 1979–99), University of London, now Emeritus Professorial Fellow (Professorial Fellow, 2007–08); Professor of Pediatrics, Medical University of South Carolina, 2007–13; *b* 4 April 1942; *s* of Henry Anderson and Doris Amy Anderson (*née* Callear); *m* 1966, Christine (*née* Ibbotson); one *s* one *d*. *Educ:* Wellington Grammar Sch., Shropshire; Manchester Univ. BSc (Hons); MD; FRCPath. House Officer, Professorial Surgical Unit, 1966, Medical Unit, 1967, Manchester Royal Infirmary; Asst Lectr in Anatomy, 1967–69, Lectr, 1969–73, Manchester Univ.; MRC Travelling Fellow, Dept of Cardiology, Univ. of Amsterdam, 1973–74; Cardiothoracic Institute, now National Heart and Lung Institute, University of London: British Heart Foundn Sen. Res. Fellow and Sen. Lectr in Paediatrics, 1974–77; Joseph Levy Reader, 1977–79, Joseph Levy Prof., 1979–2007, Paediatric Cardiac Morphology. Hon. Consultant: Royal Brompton & Harefield NHS Trust, 1974–99; Gt Ormond St Hosp., 1999–2007. Hon. Prof. of Surgery, Univ. of N Carolina, USA, 1984–; Visiting Professor: Univ. of Pittsburgh, Pa, 1985–; Liverpool Univ., 1989–; St George's Hosp. Med. Sch., 2000–; Paediatrics, Baylor Coll. of Med., Houston, Texas, 2012–; Vis. Professorial Fellow, Inst. of Med. Genetics, Univ. of Newcastle, 2008–; Emeritus Vis. Prof., Univ. of Manchester, 2009–. Excerpta Medica Travel Award, 1977; British Heart Foundn Prize for Cardiovascular Research, 1984. Associate Editor, Internat. Jl of Cardiology, 1985–91; Ed.-in-Chief, Cardiology in the Young, 1997–2007 (Exec. Ed., 1992–97). Hon. FRCSE 2017. Hon. PhD New Univ. of Lisbon, 2018. *Publications:* (ed jtly) Paediatric Cardiology, 1977, vol. 3, 1981, vol. 5, 1983, vol. 6, 1986; (with A. E. Becker) Cardiac Anatomy, 1980; (with E. A. Shinebourne) Current Paediatric Cardiology, 1980; (with A. E. Becker) Pathology of Congenital Heart Disease, 1981; (with M. J. Davies and A. E. Becker) Pathology of the Conduction Tissues, 1983; (jtly) Morphology of Congenital Heart Disease, 1983; (with A. E. Becker) Cardiac Pathology, 1984; (with G. A. H. Miller and M. L. Rigby) The Diagnosis of Congenital Heart Disease, 1985; (with B. R. Wilcox) Surgical Anatomy of the Heart, 1985, 3rd edn 2004; (jtly) Paediatric Cardiology, 2 vols, 1987, 2nd edn 2002; (with P. J. Oldershaw and J. R. Dawson) Clinician's Illustrated Dictionary of Cardiology, 1988; (jtly) Atlas of the Heart, 1988; (jtly) Transoesophageal Echocardiography in Clinical Practice, 1991; (with A. E. Becker) The Heart Structure in Health and Disease, 1992; over 250 invited chapters in published books and over 900 papers in jls. *Recreations:* golf, music, wine. *Address:* 60 Earlsfield Road, SW18 3DN. *T:* (020) 8870 4368. *Clubs:* Saintsbury, Roehampton; Walton Heath Golf.

**ANDERSON, Rodney Brian;** Director of Marine and Fisheries, Department for Environment, Food and Rural Affairs, 2006–08; *b* 12 July 1948; *s* of Guy and Phyllis Anderson; *m* 1974, Mavis Barker; two *d*. ACIS 1972. Local Govt career, 1964–89; various posts, DoE, subseq. DETR, then DEFRA, 1989–2008; Hd, Water Supply and Regulation, 2000–04; Director: Water, 2004; Fisheries, 2004–06. Man. Dir, R.B. Anderson and Associates, 2008–. Member, Board: Greenwich Forum, 2007–18; Marine Mgt Orgn, 2010–13; Adviser: North Sea Marine Cluster, 2008–18; (internat.), Marine Planning Consultants, 2012–18. Advr, Agric., Fisheries, Envmt and Energy Sub-Cttee, EU Cttee, H of L, 2014–15. Dir, IRIS Consulting Ltd, 2008–18. Trustee, Travel Foundn, 2009–. *Recreations:* spending time with my grandchildren and family, reading, walking, travelling, angling. *E:* rb.anderson@btinternet.com.

**ANDERSON, Rolande Jane Rita;** Director General, Office for Civil Society, Cabinet Office, 2009–10; Lay Member, Bar Standards Board, 2012–16 (Chairman, Equalities and Diversity Committee, since 2012); *d* of late Arthur Ingham Anderson and of Rolande Marie Anderson. *Educ:* Lycée Français de Londres; Newnham Coll., Cambridge (BA Hons Mod. and Mediaeval Langs, MA Mod. Langs). Fast Stream Admin Trainee, Depts of Industry and of Prices and Consumer Protection, 1976–79; HEO, Dept of Trade, 1979–83; Principal and Hd of Section, DTI, 1983–89; Grade 7, Eur. Secretariat, Cabinet Office, 1989–91; Hd (Asst Sec.), Policy and Planning, Insolvency Service Exec. Agency, 1991–92; Dir, Aerospace and Defence Industries Policy, 1994–96, Regl Fuel Funds, 1996–99, Competition Policy, 1999–2002, DTI; Chief Exec., Radiocommunications Agency, 2002–03; Dep. Dir Gen., Innovation Gp, DTI, 2003–05; Regl Dir, Govt Office for the SE, 2006–08; Dir-Gen. for Transformation and Corporate Services, 2008, for Corporate Ops, 2008–09, ONS. Mem., panel of assessors for Fast Stream recruitment, CSSB, 1988–91; DTI Member, Steering Board: Patent Office, 2004–05; Nat. Weights and Measures Lab., 2004–05. Non-exec. Dir, Genesis Housing Assoc., 2005–14 (Chm., Remuneration and Diversity Cttees, 2007–14; Sen. Ind. Dir, 2012–14). Selector and Mentor, Minority Ethnic Talent Assoc., 2010–11. Newnham College, Cambridge: Associate Fellow, 2004–07; Pres. of Associates, 2009–11, now Hon. Associate; Mem., Campaign Bd, 2012–15. Trustee and Mem. Council, Volunteering Matters (formerly Community Service Volunteers), 2012–16 (Chm., HR, Remuneration and Pensions Cttee, 2014–; Mem., Audit Cttee, 2015–); Trustee: Brightside Trust, 2011– (Mem., Finance and Governance Cttee, 2017–); St Mungo's, 2015– (Member: Finance Cttee, 2016–; People, Governance and Remuneration Cttee, 2016– (Chair, 2017–)); Citizens' Advice, 2016–. Gov., London Metropolitan Univ., 2015– (Chair: Finance and Resources Cttee, 2016–18; Remuneration Cttee, 2018–). Associate, Coll. of Policing (Sen. Assessor), 2016–. Life FRSA. *Club:* Athenæum.

**ANDERSON, Prof. Ross John,** FRS 2009; FREng; Professor of Security Engineering, University of Cambridge, since 2003; computer security consultant, since 1984; *b* 1956; *s* of William and Anne Anderson; *m* Shireen; one *d*. *Educ:* High Sch. of Glasgow; Trinity Coll., Cambridge (BA 1978; MA 1982; PhD 1995). FIMA 1993; FIET (FIEE 2000); FREng 2009; FInstP 2009. University of Cambridge: Lectr, 1995–2000, Reader, 2000–03; Mem. Council, 2003–10 and 2015–18. Ed., Computer and Communications Security Reviews, 1992–99. Chm., Foundn for Information Policy Research, 1998–. Lovelace Medal, BCS Acad. of Computing, 2015. *Publications:* Fast Software Encryption, 1993; Security in Clinical Information Systems, 1996; Information Hiding, 1996; Personal Medical Information: security, engineering and ethics, 1997; Security Engineering: a guide to building dependable distributed systems, 2001, 2nd edn 2008. *Recreation:* music. *Address:* Computer Laboratory, University of Cambridge, J. J. Thomson Avenue, Cambridge CB3 0FD. *T:* (01223) 334733. *E:* info@ross-anderson.com.

ANDERSON, Prof. Sir Roy (Malcolm), Kt 2006; FRS 1986; FMedSci; Professor of Infectious Disease Epidemiology, Imperial College London, since 2000 (Head of Department, 2000–04; Rector, 2008–09); Chief Scientific Adviser, Ministry of Defence, 2004–08; *b* 12 April 1947; *s* of James Anderson and Betty Watson-Weatherburn; *m* 1st, 1975, Dr Mary Joan Anderson (marr. diss. 1989); 2nd, 1990, Dr Claire Baron (marr. diss. 2013); 3rd, 2014, Janet Louise Meyrick. *Educ:* Duncombe Sch., Bengeo; Richard Hale Sch., Hertford; Imperial College, London (BSc, ARCS, PhD, DIC). CBiol, FRSB. IBM Research Fellow, Univ. of Oxford, 1971–73; Lectr, King's Coll., London, 1973–77; Lectr, 1977–80, Reader, 1980–82, Prof., 1982–93, Head of Dept of Biology, 1984–93, Imperial Coll., London Univ.; University of Oxford: Linacre Prof. of Zoology, 1993–2000, and Hd, Zoology Dept, 1993–98; Dir, Wellcome Trust Centre for Epidemiology of Infectious Diseases, 1994–2000; Fellow, Merton Coll., Oxford, 1993–2000. Vis. Prof., McGill Univ., 1982–; Alexander Langmuir Vis. Prof., Harvard, 1990–; Genentech Vis. Prof., Univ. of Washington, 1998; James McLaughlin Vis. Prof., Univ. of Texas, 1999. Nuffield Medal Lect., RSocMed, 2002. Member: NERC, 1988–91 (Chm., Services and Facilities Cttee, 1989–90); ACOST, 1989–93 (Chm., Standing Cttee on Envmt, 1990–93); Spongiform Encephalopathy Adv. Cttee, 1998–2003; EPSRC, 2004–08; Chm., Sci. Adv. Council, DEFRA, 2004–07; Mem., Govt's China Task Force, 2009–12. Chm., Oxford Biologica Ltd (formerly IBHSC Ltd), 1999–2001; non-executive Director: GlaxoSmithKline, 2007–18; Imperial Coll. Healthcare NHS Trust, 2008–09; Mem. Internat. Adv. Bd, Hakluyt and Co. Ltd, 2007–19; Chm., Baccalaureate Adv. Panel, Pearson plc, 2012–. Member, Scientific Advisory Board: IMS, 1997–99; deCode, 1998–2002; Bill & Melinda Gates Foundn Initiative on Grand Challenges in Global Health, 2003–11; Singapore Nat. Res. Foundn, 2009–13; Member: Bio-Internat. Adv. Panel, Malaysia, 2009–18; Adv. Bd, Partnership for Child Develt, 2012–18; Chairman: Adv. Bd, Schistosomiasis Control Initiative, 2000–18; Sci. Adv. Bd, Neglected Tropical Diseases prog., WHO, 2008–12; Dir, London Centre for Neglected Tropical Disease Res., 2012–; Oriole Global Health Ltd, 2018–. Member, Council: Zoological Soc., 1988–90; Royal Soc., 1989–91; RSTM&H, 1989–92; RPMS, 1994–97; Mem. Ct, LSHTM, 1993–2003. Governor: Wellcome Trust Ltd, 1992–2000 (Trustee, Wellcome Trust, 1991–92); Chairman: Infection and Immunity Grant Panel, 1990–92; Population Studies Panel); Inst. for Government, 2008–13. Trustee: Natural Hist. Mus., 2008–16; London Inst. of Math. Scis, 2018–. Mem. Internat. Adv. Cttee, Nat. Sci. and Technol. Develt Agency, Thailand, 2009–17; Chm., Internat. Adv. Panel Sci., PTT Public Co. Ltd, Thailand, 2013–18. Foreign Associate Member: Inst. of Medicine, NAS, USA, 2000; French Acad. of Scis, 2010. Founder FMedSci 1998. Hon. FIA 2000; Hon. FRCPath 2000; Hon. FSS 2002; Hon. FRAgS 2002. Hon. Fellow, Linacre Coll., Oxford, 1993. Hon. DSc: East Anglia, 1997; Stirling, 1998; Aberdeen, 2008. Zoological Soc. Scientific Medal, 1982; Huxley Meml Medal, Imperial Coll., London, 1983; Wright Meml Medal, British Soc. of Parasitology, 1986; David Starr Jordan Medal, Univs of Stanford, Cornell and Indiana, 1986; Chalmers Medal, RSTM&H, 1988; Weldon Medal, Oxford Univ., 1989; John Hill Grundy Medal, Royal Army Med. Coll., 1990; Frink Medal, Zoological Soc. of London, 1993; Joseph Smadel Medal, Infectious Diseases Soc. of Amer., 1994; Distinguished Statistical Ecologist Award, 1998; Dist. Parasitologists Award, Amer. Soc. of Parasitology, 1999. *Publications:* (ed) Population Dynamics of Infectious Disease Agents: theory and applications, 1982; (ed jtly) Population Biology of Infectious Diseases, 1982; (with R. M. May) Infectious Diseases of Humans: dynamics and control, 1991. *Recreations:* wildlife photography, croquet, natural history. *Address:* Department of Infectious Disease Epidemiology, Faculty of Medicine, Imperial College London, St Mary's Campus, Norfolk Place, Paddington, W2 1PG. *Club:* Athenæum.

ANDERSON, Roy William; District Judge (Magistrates' Courts) (formerly Stipendiary Magistrate), West Yorkshire, 1999–2015; *b* 10 Feb. 1950; *s* of William Patterson Bruce Anderson and Thirza Elizabeth Anderson (*née* Wakeham); *m* 1974, Pauline Mary Rylands; two *s*. *Educ:* King Edward VI Sch., Stratford-upon-Avon; University Coll. London (LLB). Articled clerk, City of Swansea, 1972–74; Prosecuting Solicitor, W Midlands CC, 1974–80; Solicitor, Jacobs Bird & Co., Birmingham, 1980–84; Sole Principal, Roy Anderson Solicitor, Birmingham, 1984–99. *Recreations:* reading, theatre, painting, gardening, U3A. *Clubs:* Silsden Golf; Ilkley Wharfedale Rotary.

ANDERSON, Sarah Lilian, CBE 2000; Chief Executive, The Listening Place, since 2016; *b* London, 19 June 1956; *d* of Derek and Joan Anderson; *m* 1989, Terrence Ivor Collis; one *s* one *d*. *Educ:* Queen's Coll., London; Westminster Coll. (HND Hotel and Catering Admin). Personnel and Trng Manager, Compass Gp, 1977–86; owner and Chief Exec., Mayday Gp, 1986–2006; Chair, Teddies Nurseries Ltd, 1991–95. Dir, Simple Solutions Ltd, 1994–; non-executive Director: Job Centre Plus, 2003–11; Albatross Gp Hldgs Ltd, 2009–; Action for Employment, 2014–15; Chair, Call Britannia, 2009–12. Member: Women and Work Commn, 2004–09; Commn for Employment and Skills, 2007–09; Leader, Ind. Rev. on Regulatory Guidance (Anderson Rev.), 2008–09. Member: Better Regulation Task Force, 1997–2002; Small Business Council, 2000–04; Council, ACAS, 2004–11; Equality and Human Rights Commn, 2011–14; Public Appts Assessor, 2012–16. Chair, Small and Medium-sized Enterprises Council, CBI, 2000–04. Dir, Central London Samaritans, 2005–08. *Recreations:* eating out, cinema. *Address:* 45 Sussex Street, SW1V 4RJ. *T:* (020) 7821 5530, 07836 274968. *E:* sarah@anderson2.demon.co.uk.

ANDERSON, Air Marshal Sir Timothy (Michael), KCB 2013 (CB 2009); DSO 1999; independent consultant, since 2013; Chief Operating Officer, Flybe, since 2018 (non-executive Director, since 2014); *b* 2 Feb. 1957; *s* of George Anderson and Beatrice Anderson; *m* 1979, Ursula Henderson; two *d*. *Educ:* Belfast Royal Acad.; King's Coll. London (MA 1994). Ops Flight Comdr No 1 Sqn, RAAF, 1988–90; Mil. Asst to DCDS (Systems), 1996–98; OC No 14 Sqdn, RAF, 1999–2000; CO RAF Bruggen, 2000–01; Dir, Equipment Capability (Deep Target Attack), MoD, 2003–05; Comdt, RAF Air Warfare Centre, 2005–07; ACAS, 2007–10; Dir Gen., Mil. Aviation Authy, 2010–13. President: NI Wing Air Training Corps, 2008–; No 14 Sqdn Assoc., 2009–; RAF Rugby Union, 2009–13. Hon. Air Cdre, No 622 Sqdn, RAuxAF, 2013–. Vice Patron, Royal Internat. Air Tattoo, 2013–. FRAeS 2002. *Recreations:* cycling, military history, golf, Asian cooking, motor sport. *Club:* Royal Air Force.

ANDERSON, Victor Frederick; Visiting Professor, Global Sustainability Institute, Anglia Ruskin University, since 2013; *b* 7 Feb. 1952; *s* of Tom and Iris Anderson; *m* 1987, Joan Rawlinson; one *s*. *Educ:* Whitgift Sch.; Brasenose Coll., Oxford (BA). Lectr, 1980–88, at Paddington Coll. of FE, 1982–88; Researcher: New Econs Foundn, 1987–92; Plaid Cymru Gp of MPs, 1992–2000 and 2004–05; Higher Economic Analyst, Sustainable Develt Commn, 2006–09; One Planet Economy Leader, 2009–12, economist, 2011–13, WWF-UK. Mem. (Green), London Assembly, GLA, 2000–03. Mem. Bd, London Develt Agency, 2000–04. Envmt Advr to Mayor of London, 2001–04; Mem., London Sustainable Develt Commn, 2002–04. Develt Manager, Green Econs Inst., 2005. Dir, Planetary Boundaries Initiative, 2014–. Mem., Mgt Cttee, Compass, 2011–14. Mem., Core Gp, Green House think-tank, 2010–. Res. Fellow, Centre for Understanding of Sustainable Prosperity,

2016–18. *Publications:* Alternative Economic Indicators, 1991, reissued 2013; Energy Efficiency Policies, 1993; Greens and the New Politics, 2001. *Recreations:* dancing, visiting museums. *Address:* 12 Glynwood Court, Dartmouth Road, Forest Hill, SE23 3HU.

ANDERSON, Sir (William) Eric (Kinloch), KT 2002; MA, MLitt, DLitt, FRSE; Provost of Eton College, 2000–09; *b* 27 May 1936; *er s* of late W. J. Kinloch Anderson and Margaret (*née* Harper), Edinburgh; *m* 1960, Poppy, *d* of late W. M. Mason, Skipton; one *s* one *d*. *Educ:* George Watson's Coll.; Univ. of St Andrews (MA); Balliol Coll., Oxford (MLitt; Hon. Fellow, 1989). Asst Master: Fettes Coll., 1960–64; Gordonstoun, 1964–66; Asst Master, Fettes Coll., and Housemaster, Arniston House, 1967–70; Headmaster: Abingdon Sch., 1970–75; Shrewsbury Sch., 1975–80; Eton Coll., 1980–94; Rector, Lincoln Coll., Oxford, 1994–2000 (Hon. Fellow, 2000). Chairman: King George VI and Queen Elizabeth Foundn of St Catharine's, Cumberland Lodge, 1997–2009; Nat. Heritage Meml Fund, 1998–2001 (Trustee, 1996–2001). President: Edinburgh Sir Walter Scott Club, 1981; Johnson Soc., 1992; Mem., DCMS Adv. Panel for Public Appointments, 1997–2004. Trustee: Said (formerly Karim Rida Said) Foundn, 1994–98, 2004–09; Wordsworth Trust, 1996–97; Royal Collection, 2000–06; Shakespeare Birthplace Trust, 2001–; Farmington Trust, 2005–17; Manifold Trust, 2008–17; Abbotsford Trust, 2012–16. Mem. Visiting Cttee, Harvard Meml Church, 2001–07. Council Mem., Royal Holloway, London Univ. (formerly RHBNC), 1990–95; Gov., Shrewsbury Sch., 1994–2000; Visitor, Harris Manchester Coll., Oxford Univ., 2001–18. Chm. of Judges, Whitbread Book Awards, 2000. FRSE 1985. Hon. DLitt: St Andrews, 1981; Hull, 1994; Siena, 1999; Birmingham, 2010; Aberdeen, 2013; Buckingham, 2019. *Publications:* The Written Word, 1964; (ed) The Journal of Sir Walter Scott, 1972, rev. edn 1998; (ed) The Percy Letters, vol. IX, 1988; The Sayings of Sir Walter Scott, 1995; (with Adam Nicolson) About Eton, 2010; Sir Walter's Wit and Wisdom, 2013; Sir Walter's Verse, 2013; Sir Walter's Tales, 2015; articles and reviews. *Recreations:* theatre, golf. *Address:* The Homestead, Kingham, Oxon OX7 6YA.
*See also* Baron Anderson of Ipswich.

ANDERSON-COLE, Ailsa Jane, LVO 2009; Director of Communications to the Archbishop of Canterbury, Lambeth Palace, since 2013; *b* Pembury, Kent, 20 April 1969; *d* of Roderick and Patricia McIntyre; *m* 2000, Rear Adm. Mark Anderson, CB (marr. diss. 2015); one *s* one *d*; *m* 2017, Thomas Henry Simon Cole. *Educ:* John Warner Sch., Herts; Univ. of Essex (BA English Lit.). Journalist, London and Essex Guardian Newspapers, 1989–92; Sen. Press Officer and Press Sec. to Minister of State to Armed Forces, 1993–99; Chief Press Officer, Cabinet Office, 1999–2001; Royal Household: Asst Press Sec., 2001–06; Dep. Press Sec. to the Queen and Hd of News, 2007–10; Communications and Press Sec. to the Queen, 2010–13. MIPR 2007. *Recreations:* riding, cinema and theatre, walking my black labrador. *Address:* Lambeth Palace, SE1 7JU. *T:* (020) 7898 1224, 07990 574916. *E:* ailsa.anderson-cole@lambethpalace.org.uk.

ANDERSSON, Hilary Harper; correspondent, Panorama, BBC, since 2006; *b* 23 Sept. 1967; *d* of Alfred McRae Andersson and Zosha Mary Andersson; two *s*. *Educ:* Cheltenham Ladies' Coll.; Univ. of Edinburgh (MA Hons Politics). Joined BBC, 1991: producer, World Service, 1992–94; sen. broadcast journalist, 1994–96; Lagos Corresp., 1996–99; Jerusalem Corresp., 1999–2001; Africa Corresp., 2001–05; special reports for Panorama: Secrets of the Camps, 2005; The New Killing Fields, 2005 (Peabody Award, 2004; RTS Award, 2005); Climate of Fear, 2006; Is America Ready for a Black President?, 2008; What Next Mr President?, 2009; Licence to Torture, 2009; Zimbabwe's Blood Diamonds, 2011; Poor America, 2012; The Brothers who Bombed Boston, 2013; America's Gun Addiction, 2013; Bedlam Behind Bars, 2014; Fighting Terror with Torture, 2015; Trump's Angry America, 2016; Trump's New America, 2016; Bagram Airbase, BBC Radio 4, 2010 (Radio Prize, Amnesty Internat. Media Awards); Fortress America, 2017; Smartphones: The Dark Side, 2018; Trump: What's Next?, 2018. Poynter Fellow, Yale Univ., 2017. RTS Specialist Journalist of the Year, 2003. *Publications:* Mozambique: a war against the people, 1992. *Recreations:* ski-ing, windsurfing, writing. *Address:* c/o BBC News Centre, Broadcasting House, Portland Place, W1A 1AA. *E:* Hilary.Andersson.01@bbc.co.uk.

ANDERTON, Prof. Brian Henry, PhD; FMedSci; Director, MRC Centre for Neurodegeneration Research, 2005–08, and Professor of Neuroscience, Institute of Psychiatry, 1989–2008, at King's College London; *b* 25 Dec. 1945; *s* of Henry Anderton and Mary Anderton (*née* Ashcroft); *m* 1969, Thérèse L. F. Loviny; one *s*. *Educ:* Alsop High Sch. for Boys, Liverpool; University College London (BSc 1967; PhD 1970). MRC Biophysics Unit, KCL, 1970–72; Lectr in Biochem., Poly. of Central London, 1972–77; Lectr in Biochem. and Immunology, Chelsea Coll., Univ. of London, 1977–79; St George's Hospital Medical School, University of London: Lectr in Immunology, 1979–81; Sen. Lectr in Immunology, 1981–86; Reader in Molecular Pathology, 1986–88. FMedSci 2007. *Publications:* contribs to sci. jls on nervous system and molecular pathology of Alzheimer's disease and other neurodegenerative diseases. *Recreations:* hill walking, cycling, general reading, theatre, cinema, listening to music, drawing, painting. *Address:* 19 Speldhurst Road, W4 1BX.

ANDERTON, Sir (Cyril) James, Kt 1991; CBE 1982; QPM 1977; DL; Chief Constable, Greater Manchester Police Force, 1976–91 (Deputy Chief Constable, 1975); *b* 24 May 1932; *o s* of late James Anderton and Lucy Anderton (*née* Occleshaw); *m* 1955, Joan Baron; one *d*. *Educ:* St Matthew's Church Sch., Highfield; Wigan Grammar Sch. Certif. Criminology, Manchester Univ., 1960; Sen. Comd Course, Police Coll., 1967. Corps of Royal Mil. Police, 1950–53; Constable to Chief Inspector, Manchester City Police, 1953–67; Chief Supt, Cheshire Constab., 1967–68; Asst Chief Constable, Leicester and Rutland Constab., 1968–72; Asst to HM Chief Inspector of Constab. for England and Wales, Home Office, London, 1972–75; Dep. Chief Constable, Leics Constabulary, 1975. Mem., ACPO, 1968–91 (Pres., 1986–87). FCO lect. tour, FE and SE Asia, 1973. UK Govt deleg., UN Congress on Prevention of Crime, Budapest, 1974. British Institute of Management: Pres., Manchester Br., 1984–93; Chm., 1986–90, Mem., 1983–90, NW Regl Bd; Cert. of Merit, 1990. President: Manchester NSPCC Jun. League, 1979–93; Christian Police Assoc., 1979–81; Manchester and Dist RSPCA, 1984–2000 (Vice-Pres., 1981–84); Wigan and Dist RSPCA, 1999–2000 (Patron, 1986–99); Wythenshawe Hosp. League of Friends, 1991–2004; Altrincham Town Centre Partnership, 1994–2003; Disabled Living, Manchester, 1995–2005 (Patron, 1991–; Hon. Life Mem., 2006); Bolton Outward Bound Assoc., 1995–2002 (Vice-Pres., 1991–95); NW Reg., YMCA, 1996–2002; Manchester YMCA, 2000–02 (Vice-Pres., 1976–2000); Greater Manchester Fedn of Clubs for Young People (formerly Boys' Clubs), 2001–05 (Vice-Pres., 1984–2001; Patron, 2005–). Member: Manchester Adv. Bd, Salvation Army, 1977–2001 (Chm., 1993–2001; Hon. Life Mem., Salvation Army Adv. Bd, 2000); Salvation Army Territorial Adv. Bd, 1996–2001; Exec. Cttee, Manchester NSPCC, 1979–93; Bd, Henshaws Soc. for the Blind, 1991–95; Royal Soc. of St George, 1992–; CCJ, 1992–; Friends of Israel Assoc., 1992–; Broughton Catholic Charitable Soc., 1996–; Nat. Adv. Gp, YMCA, 1997–2002 (Chm., Prisons Steering Gp, 1994–2002). Comdr, St John Amb., Greater Manchester, 1989–96 (County Dir, 1976–89); Vice-President: Manchester and District RLSS, 1976–2000; Adelphi Lads' Club, Salford, 1979–2006; Sharp Street Ragged Sch., Manchester, 1982–2002; Manchester Schools Football Assoc., 1976–91; Greater Manchester East Scout Council, 1977–91; Wigan Hospice, 1990–; Greater Manchester West Scout Council, 1992–; Manchester and Dist

NSPCC, 1994–. Boys' Brigade: Pres., Leics Bn, 1972–76; Hon. Nat. Vice-Pres., 1983–. Patron: NW Counties Schs ABA, 1988–91; NW Campaign for Kidney Donors, 1983–91; NW Eye Res. Trust, 1982–91; Internat. Spinal Res. Trust (Greater Manchester Cttee), 1983–91; Stockport Lourdes Gp HCPT (formerly ACROSS), 1993–2009; Trafford Multiple Sclerosis Soc., 1994–2004; Mottram and Hattersley ABC, 1994–2003; Rhodes Foundn Scholarship Trust, 1996–; Lancashire and Cheshire (formerly Gtr Manchester) Lupus Gp, 1996–2005; Gtr Manchester Youth Field Gun Assoc., 1996–2003 (Pres., 1992–96); Police Boxing Assoc. of England, 1997–2003; Manchester Stedfast Assoc., 1999–. British College of Accordionists: Chm., Governing Council, 1972–77; Vice-Pres., 1977–84; Pres., 1984–91; Patron, 1991–2002. Trustee, Manchester Olympic Bid Cttee, 1985–93; Chm. of Trustees, S Manchester Accident Rescue Team, 1996–2001; Chm., Manchester Concerts Cttee, Sargent Cancer Care for Children, 1992–2003. Hon. FBCA 1976; Hon. RNCM 1984. Member: Catholic Union of GB; NT; Wigan Little Theatre; Royal Exchange Th., Manchester; Corps of Royal Mil. Police Assoc. Mancunian of The Year, 1980. DL Greater Manchester, 1989. Freeman, City of London, 1990. KStJ 1989 (OStJ 1978; CStJ 1982; Mem., Chapter-Gen., 1993–99). KMLJ 1998; KHS 1999. Cross Pro Ecclesia et Pontifice, 1982. Chevalier de la Confrérie des Chevaliers du Tastevin, 1985. *Recreations:* opera, theatre, walking; Rugby League supporter. *Address:* 9 The Avenue, Sale, Cheshire M33 4PB.

**ANDERTON, Hon. James Patrick, (Jim),** CNZM 2017; MP Wigram, New Zealand, 1996–2011 (MP Sydenham, 1984–96) (Lab 1984–89, NewLab, then Alliance, 1989–2002, Progressive, 2002–11); *b* 21 Jan. 1938; *m* 1st, Joan Caulfield (marr. diss.); three *s* two *d*; 2nd, Carole Dianne. *Educ:* Seddon Meml Technical Coll.; Auckland Teachers' Trng Coll. Formerly: teacher; Child Welfare Officer, Educn Dept, Wanganui; Export Manager, UEB Textiles, 1969–70; Man. Dir, Anderton Hldgs, 1971–84. Member: Manukau CC, 1965–68; Auckland CC, 1974–80; Auckland Regl Authy, 1977–80. Dep. Prime Minister of NZ, 1999–2002; Minister: for Econ. Develt, and for Industry and Regl Develt, 1999–2005; of Forests, 2004–08; of Agriculture, of Fisheries and for Biosecurity, 2005–08. Labour Party, 1963–89: Pres., 1979–84; Mem., Policy Council, 1979–89; Leader, NewLabour Party, 1989–2002; Jt Founder, 1991, Leader, 1992–2001, Alliance; Leader, Progressive Party, 2002–11. Co-Chm., Gtr Christchurch Bldgs Trust, 2012–; Chm., AMI Stadium, Christchurch, 2012–. Dir of Habitat, Humanity Bd, Christchurch, 2012–. Organiser, Catholic Youth Movt, 1960–65; Sec., Catholic Diocesan Office, Auckland, 1967–69.

**ANDERTON, Stephen Hugh Garth;** garden journalist and author; *b* Skipton, 3 Feb. 1955; *s* of William and Winifred Anderton; *m* 1976, Judith Symonds; three *d*. *Educ:* Ermysted's Grammar Sch., Skipton; Univ. of Birmingham (BA Drama and Classics 1976). Gardener and Hd Gardener for private estates incl. Cadogan Estate, Abbots Ripton Hall, Great Comp, Belsay Hall and Brodsworth Hall, 1976–85; English Heritage: Horticultural Officer, 1985–95; Nat. Gardens Manager, 1995–96; garden writer, The Times, 1993–; contrib. consumer mags, garden tour leader, lectr and horticultural consultant; TV presenter, Britain's Best Back Gardens, 2004, 2005. Cttee work for Garden Media Guild, Plant Heritage, RHS, Professional Gardener's Guild, Garden Hist. Soc. Founder, Thinkingardens Gp, 2005. Patron, Professional Gardener's Guild, 2008. Garden Media Guild Awards, 1995, 1996, 2000, 2003. *Publications:* Stephen Anderton's Garden Answers, 1998; Rejuvenating a Garden, 1998; Urban Sanctuaries: creating peaceful havens for the city gardener, 2006; Discovering Welsh Gardens, 2009; Christopher Lloyd: his life at Great Dixter, 2010; The Lives of the Great Gardeners, 2016. *Recreations:* gardening, writing music and lyrics, opera. *Address:* c/o Greene and Heaton, 37 Goldhawk Road, W12 8QQ. *E:* stephenanderton95@btinternet.com; Abergavenny, Mon.

**ANDO, Tadao,** Hon. RA 2002; architect; Director, Tadao Ando Architect and Associates, since 1969; *b* 13 Sept. 1941; *s* of Mitsugu Kitayama and Asako Kitayama; adopted by grandparents Hikoichi Ando and Kikue Ando; *m* 1970, Yumiko Kato. *Educ:* self-educated in architecture. Visiting Professor: Yale Univ., 1987; Columbia Univ., 1988; Harvard, 1990. *Works include:* Row House, Sumiyoshi (Azuma House), 1975; Rokko Housing I and II, 1978–89; Kidosaki House, 1982; Church of The Light, Osaka, 1987; Japanese Pavilion, Expo '92, Seville, 1989; Suntory Mus., Osaka, 1994; Mus. of Literature, Himeji, 1996; Pulitzer Foundn for the Arts, St Louis, 2001; Hyōgu Prefectural Mus. of Art, 2002; Shibuya Station, Tokyo, 2008; Naniwabashi Station, Osaka, 2008; Punta della Dogana art gall. restoration, Venice, 2009; 152 Elizabeth St, NY, 2018. *Exhibitions include:* Mus. of Modern Art, NY, 1991; Centre Georges Pompidou, Paris, 1993, 2018; Basilica Palladiana, Vicenza, 1994; RA, 1998; Tadao Ando: Endeavors, Nat. Art Center, Tokyo, 2017; Armani/Silos, Milan, 2019. Hon. FAIA 1991; Hon. FRIBA 1993. Chevalier, Ordre des Arts et des Lettres (France), 1995. Alvar Aalto Medal, Finnish Assoc. Architects, 1986; Gold Medal of Architecture, French Acad. Architecture, 1989; Arnold W. Brunner Meml Prize, AAIL, 1991; Carlsberg Architectural Prize, 1992; Pritzker Architecture Prize, 1995; Royal Gold Medal, RIBA, 1997; Gold Medal, AIA, 2002. *Publications:* Tadao Ando Monographies, 1982; Tadao Ando: buildings, projects, writings, 1984; Tadao Ando Complete Works, 1995; (with Richard Pare) The Colours of Light, 1996. *Address:* 5–23 Toyosaki 2–chome, Kita-ku, Osaka 531–0072, Japan. *T:* (6) 63751148.

**ANDOR, László;** Member, European Commission, 2010–14; Associate Professor, since 2000, and Head of Department of Economic Policy, Corvinus University of Budapest; *b* Zalaegerszeg, Hungary, 3 June 1966; *m* Varsányi; two *s* one *d*. *Educ:* High Sch., Zalaegerszeg; Univ. of Budapest; Univ. of Manchester (MA Develtl Econs 1993). Res. Fellow, Econ. and Social Res. Inst. of Trade Unions, Hungary, 1989–91; Hd, Coll. for Advanced Studies in Social Theory, Budapest Univ. of Econ. Scis and Public Admin, 1993–97; Vis. Prof., Rutgers Univ., 1997–98; Advisor: Budgetary and Finance Cttee, Hungarian Nat. Assembly, 1998–99; World Bank on Structural Adjustment Participatory Rev. Initiative, 1999–2001; Sen. Researcher, Inst. for Political Scis, Hungary, 2002–05; Sen. Advr to Prime Minister's Office, Hungary, 2003–05; Mem., Bd of Dirs, EBRD, 2005–10. Associate Prof., Econs Dept, King Sigismund Coll., 2000–10; Sen. Fellow, Hertie Sch. of Governance, Berlin, 2015–. *Publications:* Amerikai politika a XX században, 1998; Pénz beszél, 1998; (jtly) Market Failure: a guide to the East European economic miracle, 1998; (jtly) Roosevelt - Churchill, 1999; Hungary on the Road to the European Union: transition in Blue Westport, 2000; (jtly) Tiz év után…, 2000; Amerika évszázada, 2002; Nemzetek és pénzügyek, 2003; (jtly) Paneltöl az óceánig, 2003; Irak: háborúra ítélve, 2004; (ed) Közgazdaság, 2005; (ed) Világgazdaság, 2006; (ed) Magyar gazdaság, 2006; Összehasonlító gazdaságtan, 2008; (ed) Az adóparadicsomtól a zöldmozgalomig, 2008. *Recreations:* listening to music, playing soccer. *Address:* Corvinus University of Budapest, Fővám tér 8, 1093 Budapest, Hungary.

**ANDOVER, Viscount; Alexander Charles Michael Winston Robsahm Howard;** Managing Director, guntrader.uk Ltd, since 1997; *b* 17 Sept. 1974; *s* and *heir* of 21st Earl of Suffolk and Berkshire, *qv*; *m* 2011, Victoria, *d* of James Hamilton (marr. diss. 2019); one *s* one *d*. *Educ:* Eton Coll.; Bristol Univ. *Heir: s* Hon. Arthur Charles Alexander Howard, *b* 17 July 2014. *E:* andover@charltonpark.com.

**ANDRE, Carl;** sculptor; *b* 16 Sept. 1935; *s* of George Hans Andre and Margaret Andre (née Johnson). First exhibn, 1964; represented in collections in: Tate Gall.; Mus. of Modern Art, NYC; Guggenheim Mus., NYC; La Jolla Mus. Contemporary Art; Mönchengladbach Mus., Germany; Kunstmuseum Basel, Switzerland; Stedelijk Mus., Amsterdam; Musée Nationale d'Art Moderne, Paris; Nat. Gall. of Canada, Ottawa; Seattle Art Mus.; Musèo de Arte Moderno, Bogotá; *solo exhibitions:* Tibor de Nagy Gall., NY, 1965; Konrad Fischer Gall., Düsseldorf, 1967, 2006; Guggenheim Mus., 1970; Univ. Art Mus., Berkeley, Calif, 1979; Paula Cooper Gall., NY, 1983; (retrospective) Whitechapel Art Gall., 2000; Sadie Coles HQ, London, 2001; Ace Gall., LA, 2002; Galerie Tschudi, Switzerland, 2003; Galerie Arnaud Lefebvre, Paris, 2004; Kunsthalle Basel, Switzerland, 2005; Andrea Rosen Gall., NY, 2007; Yvon Lambert, Paris, 2008; Turner Contemporary, Margate, 2013. *Address:* c/o Konrad Fischer Galerie, Platanenstrasse 7, 40233 Düsseldorf, Germany; c/o Paula Cooper, 534 W 21 St, New York, NY 10011, USA.

**ANDREAE, Sophie Clodagh Mary, (Mrs D. E. Blain),** FSA; *b* 10 Nov. 1954; *d* of Herman Kleinwort (Sonny) Andreae and Clodagh Mary (née Alleyn); *m* 1984, Douglas Ellis Blain; three *s* one *d*. *Educ:* St Mary's, Ascot; Newnham Coll., Cambridge. FSA 2012. SAVE Britain's Heritage: Sec., 1976–84; Chm., 1984–88; Head, London Div., English Heritage (Historic Bldgs and Monuments Commn for England), 1988–93. Member: Royal Fine Art Commn, 1996–99; CABE, 1999–2004 (Chm., CABE Educn Foundn, 2002–06); English Heritage/CABE Urban Panel, 2004–07; Places of Worship Forum, Historic England (formerly English Heritage), 2005–; Council, Nat. Trust, 2006–15. Trustee: Heritage of London Trust, 1985–2003; Greenwich Foundn, 2007–15. Member: London DAC, 1988–2001; St Paul's Cathedral Fabric Adv. Cttee, 1991–2011; Exec. Cttee, 1993–2011, Council, 2011–, Georgian Gp; Council, London Historic Parks and Gardens Trust, 1993–2002. Vice Chm., Patrimony Cttee, RC Bishops' Conf., 2002–. Dir, Action for Mkt Towns, 1998–2003. High Sheriff, Powys, 2002–03. Chairman: Friends of St Andrew's Church, Presteigne, Powys, 1998–; HLF Project Bd, Auckland Castle Trust, 2014–16; Trustee: Judge's Lodging Mus., Presteigne, Powys, 2007–17; Historic Royal Palaces, 2009–14. DSG 2011. *Publications:* (contrib.) Preserving the Past: the rise of heritage in modern Britain, 1996; ed and contrib. to numerous SAVE Britain's Heritage reports. *Address:* 23 Brompton Square, SW3 2AD.

**ANDREAE-JONES, William Pearce;** QC 1984; a Recorder of the Crown Court, since 1982; *b* 21 July 1942. *Educ:* Canford Sch.; Corpus Christi Coll., Cambridge (MA Hons). Called to the Bar, Inner Temple, 1965. Pres., Mental Health Review Tribunal (Legal Mem., 2002–12). *Address:* Citadel Chambers, 190 Corporation Street, Birmingham B4 6QD; King's Bench Chambers, Wellington House, 175 Holdenhurst Road, Bournemouth, Dorset BH8 8DQ.

**ANDREASEN, Marta;** Member for South East Region, European Parliament, 2009–14 (UK Ind, 2009–13, C, 2013–14); *b* 26 Nov. 1954; *d* of Svend Andreasen and Maria Elena Salaverri; *m* 1979, Octavio Otaño; one *s* one *d*. *Educ:* Catholic Univ., Argentina (CPA); Babson Coll., Boston (Postgrad. Exec. Educn). Economist, Educn Ministry, Spain; Auditor, Price Waterhouse, 1977–82; Regl Finance Dir, cos incl. Lotus Develt, Rockwell Automation, 1983–98; Hd of Accounting, OECD, 1998; Chief Accounting Officer, European Commn, 2002. Contested (C) SE Reg., EP, 2014. *Publications:* Brussels Laid Bare, 2009. *Recreations:* sailing, trekking, swimming, water ski-ing, reading.

**ANDREEV, Rt Rev. Gennady, (Rt Rev. Matthew);** see Sourozh, Archbishop of, (Russian Orthodox).

**ANDRES, Dame Clare;** see Tickell, Dame O. C.

**ANDRESEN GUIMARÃES, Fernando;** Ambassador of Portugal to the Court of St James's, 2003–06; *b* 13 Nov. 1941; *s* of Fernando João Andresen Guimarães and Maria Carlota da Rocha Vasconcelos Meireles de Lacerda Andresen Guimarães; *m* 1984, Graça Trocado; two *s* from a previous marriage. *Educ:* Univ. of Lisbon (Econs degree). Joined Portuguese Diplomatic Service, 1969; Sec., Malawi, 1970–73; First Sec., London, 1973–76; Min. of Foreign Affairs, 1976–77; NATO Defence Coll., Rome, 1977–78; Counsellor, UN, NY, 1978–82; Consul Gen., Angola, 1982–86; Ambassador to: Iraq, 1986–88; Algeria, 1988–91; Dir Gen., Aid to Develt, 1991–92; Pres., Interministerial Commn on Macau and Portuguese-Chinese Jt Liaison Gp, 1992–95; Ambassador to USA, 1995–99; Perm. Rep. to NATO, 1999–2003. Decorations include: Grand Cross, Order of Christ (Portugal); Grand Cross, Order Infante D. Henrique (Portugal); Naval Cross, 1st cl. (Portugal). *Recreations:* reading, golf, opera (as spectator).

**ANDREW, Prof. Christopher Maurice,** PhD; FRHistS; Professor of Modern and Contemporary History, 1993–2008, Director of Research, Department of History, 2008–11, University of Cambridge; Fellow, Corpus Christi College, Cambridge, since 1967; *b* 23 July 1941; *s* of Maurice Viccars Andrew and Freda Mary (née Sandall); *m* 1962, Jennifer Ann Alicia Garratt; one *s* two *d*. *Educ:* Norwich Sch.; Corpus Christi Coll., Cambridge (MA, PhD). FRHistS 1976. Res. Fellow, Gonville and Caius Coll., Cambridge, 1965–67; Dir of Studies in History, 1967–81 and 1988, Sen. Tutor, 1981–87, Corpus Christi Coll., Cambridge; Univ. Lectr in History, 1972–89, Reader in Mod. and Contemp. Hist., 1989–93, Univ. of Cambridge. Ext. Examr in History, NUI, 1977–84. Specialist Adviser, H of C Select Cttee on Educn, Science and the Arts, 1982–83. Chm., British Intelligence Study Gp, 1999–. Official historian, MI5, 2002–. Visiting Professor: Univ. of Toronto, 1991; Harvard Univ., 1992. Visiting Fellow: ANU, 1987; Wilson Center, Washington, 1987. TV Presenter: The Fatal Attraction of Adolf Hitler, 1989; Hess: an edge of conspiracy, 1990; The Cambridge Moles, 1990; All the King's Jews, 1990; A Cold War, 1991; BBC Radio Presenter (series): Tampering with the Past, 1990; What if?, 1990–94; Hindsight, 1993–95. Editor: The Historical Journal, 1976–85; Intelligence and National Security, 1986–. *Publications:* Théophile Delcasse and the making of the Entente Cordiale, 1968; The First World War: causes and consequences, 1970 (vol. 19 of Hamlyn History of the World); (with A. S. Kanya-Forstner) France Overseas: the First World War and the climax of French imperial expansion, 1981; (ed with Prof. D. Dilks) The Missing Dimension: governments and intelligence communities in the Twentieth Century, 1984; Secret Service: the making of the British Intelligence Community, 1985; Codebreaking and Signals Intelligence, 1986; (ed with Jeremy Noakes) Intelligence and International Relations 1900–1945, 1987; (with Oleg Gordievsky) KGB: the inside story of its foreign operations from Lenin to Gorbachev, 1990; (with Oleg Gordievsky) Instructions from The Centre: top secret files on KGB foreign operations, 1991; (with Oleg Gordievsky) More Instructions from The Centre, 1992; For The President's Eyes Only: secret intelligence and the American presidency from Washington to Bush, 1995; (with Vasili Mitrokhin) The Mitrokhin Archive: the KGB in Europe and the West, 1999, vol. II: the KGB and the world, 2005; The Defence of the Realm: the authorized history of MI5, 2009; The Secret World: a history of intelligence, 2018; broadcasts and articles on mod. history, Association football, secret intelligence, current internat. relations. *Address:* 67 Grantchester Meadows, Cambridge CB3 9JL. *T:* (01223) 353773.

**ANDREW, Christopher Robert, (Rob),** MBE 1995; Chief Executive, Sussex Cricket, since 2017; *b* 18 Feb. 1963; *m* 1989, Sara (marr. diss. 2014); three *d*. *Educ:* Barnard Castle; St John's Coll., Cambridge (BA 1985; M-A 1989; Rugby blue, cricket blue). MRICS (ARICS 1988). Chartered surveyor with Debenham, Tewson & Chinnocks, until 1995; Develt Dir, Newcastle RFC, then Dir of Rugby, Newcastle Falcons, 1995–2006; Elite Rugby Dir, 2006–11, Operations Dir, 2011, Professional Rugby Dir, 2011–16, RFU.

Played for: Nottingham RFC, 1984–87; Wasps FC, 1987–91, 1992–96; Toulouse RFC, 1991–92; Barbarians RFC, and Newcastle RFC, 1996–99; England, 1985–97 (71 caps); World Cup team 1987, 1991, 1995; Grand Slam side, 1991, 1992, 1995; British Lions tour, Australia, 1989, NZ 1993. *Publications:* A Game and a Half, 1994; Rugby, The Game of My Life: battling for England in the professional era, 2017. *Address:* Sussex Cricket Ltd, 1st Central County Ground, Eaton Road, Hove BN3 3AN.

**ANDREW, Prof. Colin;** Professor of Manufacturing Engineering, 1986–94, and Chairman of Council, School of Technology, 1993–94, Cambridge University; Fellow, Christ's College, Cambridge, 1986–94; *b* 22 May 1934; *s* of Arnold Roy and Kathleen Andrew; *m* 1952, Ruth E. Probert; two *s* two *d*. *Educ:* Bristol Grammar Sch.; Christ's Coll., Cambridge Univ. MA; PhD. Res. Engr, Rolls-Royce, 1955–58; research, Cambridge, 1958–60; Develt Engr, James Archdale & Co., 1960–61; Bristol University: Lectr, 1961–68; Reader, 1968–71; Prof. of Applied Mechanics, 1971–82; Hon. Prof., 1982–86. Managing Director: Flamgard Ltd, 1982–85; Bristol Technical Develts Ltd, 1985–94. Chairman: Engrg Processes Cttee, SERC, 1981–83; Production Cttee, SERC, 1983–84; Main Engrg Panel, and Mech., Aeronautical and Manufacturing Panel, UFC Res. Assessment Exercise, 1992; Mech., Aeronautical and Manufacturing Panel, HEFCE Res. Assessment Exercise, 1996; Member: Technology Sub-Cttee, UGC, 1986–89; Engrg Council, 1990–94 (Chm., Bd of Engrs Registration, 1992–94). *Publications:* (jtly) Creep Feed Grinding, 1985; papers in scientific jls. *Address:* Hybank, Itton, Chepstow NP16 6BZ.

**ANDREW, Hon. (John) Neil,** AO 2008; arbitrator and mediator, since 2006; Speaker, House of Representatives, Australia, 1998–2004; *b* 7 June 1944; *s* of Jack Clover Andrew and Elsie Mavis Andrew; *m* 1971, Carolyn Ann Ayles; two *s* one *d*. *Educ:* Waikerie High Sch.; Urrbrae Agricl Coll.; Australian Nuffield Schol. in Agric., UK, 1975; Univ. of Adelaide. Horticulture (fruit and vineyards), 1964–83. MP (L) Wakefield, SA, 1983–2004; Dep. Opposition Whip, 1985–89, 1990–93; Chief Govt Whip, House of Reps, 1997–98. Chm., Murray Darling Basin Authy, 2015–. Chairman: AATSE, 2005–11, now Hon. Mem.; Crawford Fund, Australia, 2006–12. *Recreations:* horticulture, camping, reading, aviation. *Address:* c/o Box 495, Walkerville, SA 5081, Australia.

**ANDREW, Ven. Philip John;** Archdeacon of Cheltenham, since 2017; *b* Eldoret, Kenya, 4 Dec. 1962; *s* of Brian Andrew and of Eileen Andrew; *m* 1987, Dr Susan; three *s*. *Educ:* King Edward's Sch., Witley; Univ. of Nottingham (BSc Hons 1984); St John's Coll., Nottingham (MTh 2002). Chartered Engineer and Project Manager, 1984–2000; ordained deacon, 2002, priest, 2003; Curate, Greyfriars Church, Reading, 2002–06; Vicar, St Mary's Church, Reigate, 2006–17; Hon. Canon, Southwark Cathedral, 2016–17. *Address:* 2 College Green, Gloucester GL1 2LR. *T:* (01452) 835594. *E:* archdchelt@glosdioc.org.uk.

**ANDREW, Rob;** *see* Andrew, C. R.

**ANDREW, Sir Robert (John),** KCB 1986 (CB 1979); civil servant, retired; *b* 25 Oct. 1928; *s* of late Robert Young Andrew and Elsie (*née* Heritage); *m* 1963, Elizabeth Bayley (OBE 2000) (*d* 2018); two *s*. *Educ:* King's College Sch., Wimbledon; Merton Coll., Oxford (MA; Hon. Fellow 2005). Intelligence Corps, 1947–49. Joined Civil Service, 1952: Asst Principal, War Office, Principal, 1957; Min. of Defence, 1963; Asst Sec., 1965; Defence Counsellor, UK Delegn to NATO, 1967–70; Private Sec. to Sec. of State for Defence, 1971–73; Under-Sec., CSD, 1973–75; Asst Under-Sec. of State, MoD, 1975–76; Dep. Under-Sec. of State, Home Office, 1976–83; Perm. Under-Sec. of State, NI Office, 1984–88; Cabinet Office, Review of Govt Legal Services, 1988. Dir, Esmée Fairbairn Charitable Trust, 1989–94. Conservator of Wimbledon and Putney Commons, 1973–2009. Governor, King's College Sch., 1975–2000 (Chm., 1990–2000; Hon. Fellow 2003). Mem. Council, Royal Holloway, Univ. of London (formerly RHBNC), 1989–99 (Chm., 1992–99; Hon. Fellow, 2000). Trustee, BBC Children in Need Appeal, 1993–99. FRSA 1992–2013. *Recreations:* reading, current affairs, grandchildren. *Address:* 8 High Cedar Drive, Wimbledon, SW20 0NU. *Club:* Oxford and Cambridge.

**ANDREW, Her Honour Sandra Christine;** a Circuit Judge, 1999–2004; Designated Family Judge, Canterbury Combined Court, 2000–04; a Deputy Circuit Judge, 2004–11; *b* 5 Nov. 1941; *d* of Albert Hugh Dudley Tyas and Anne Florence (*née* Preston); *m* 1963, John Andrew (*d* 2001); two *s*. *Educ:* various prep. schools; E Grinstead Co. Grammar Sch. Admitted Solicitor, 1964; in private practice, 1964–83; Registrar, SE Circuit, Bromley Co. Court, 1983, transf. to Maidstone, 1990; Trng Registrar, then Dist Judge, 1986–99; Care Dist Judge, 1991–99. Member: President's Ancillary Relief Adv. Gp (formerly Lord Chancellor's Adv. Cttee on Ancillary Relief), 1993–2004; Family Proceedings Rules Cttee, 1993–97; Litigant Inf. Sub-Cttee, Civil Justice Council, 1998–2001; Tutor team for Dep. Dist Judges, Judicial Studies Bd, 1998–2001. Chm., SE Circuit Assoc. Dist Judges, 1992–95; SE Circuit (S) Rep., Nat. Cttee, Assoc. Dist Judges, 1996–99 (Co-opted Mem., Family Sub-Cttee, 1993–96). *Recreations:* music, bridge, travel, reading. *Address:* c/o The Law Courts, Chaucer Road, Canterbury, Kent CT1 1ZA.

**ANDREW, Stuart James;** MP (C) Pudsey, since 2010; Vice Chamberlain of HM Household (Government Whip), since 2019; *b* Bangor, N Wales, 25 Nov. 1971; *s* of James Edward and Maureen Catherine Andrew; partner, 2001, Robin Rogers. *Educ:* Ysgol David Hughes, Menai Bridge. Fundraiser: BHF, 1994–98; Hope House Children's Hospice, 1998–2000; Hd of Fundraising, E Lancs Hospice, 2000–03. Mem. (C) Leeds CC, 2003–. PPS to Minister for Cabinet Office and Paymaster Gen., 2012–17, to Sec. of State for Transport, 2015–17, to Chm., Cons. Party; an Asst Govt Whip, 2017–18; Parly Under-Sec. of State, Wales Office, 2018, MoD, 2018–19. Treas., All Party Parly Gp on Hospice and Palliative Care, 2010–; Chair, All Party Parly Gp on Islamophobia, 2015–, on Heart Disease, 2015–. Vice Chm., Cons. Party. *Recreations:* walking Yorkshire Dales, attending gym, socialising. *Address:* House of Commons, SW1A 0AA. *T:* (020) 7219 7130. *E:* stuart.andrew.mp@parliament.uk.

**ANDREWS,** Baroness *cr* 2000 (Life Peer), of Southover in the co. of East Sussex; **Elizabeth Kay Andrews,** OBE 1998; DPhil; FSA; Chair, English Heritage, 2009–13; *b* 16 May 1943; *d* of Clifford and Louisa Andrews; *m* 1970, Prof. Roy MacLeod (marr. diss. 1992); one *s*. *Educ:* Univ. of Wales (BA 1964); Univ. of Sussex (MA 1970; DPhil 1975). FSA 2015. Res. Fellow, Science Policy Res. Unit, Univ. of Sussex, 1968–70; Res. Clerk, then Sen. Res. Clerk, H of C, 1970–85; Special Advr, Rt Hon. Neil Kinnock, MP, Leader of the Opposition, 1985–92; Dir, Education Extra (nat. charity for out-of-sch. learning), 1992–2002. A Baroness in Waiting (Govt Whip), 2002–05; Parly Under-Sec. of State, ODPM, later DCLG, 2005–09. Dep. Chair and Trustee for Wales, NHMF and NLHF (formerly HLF), 2016–. Gov., Charterhouse, 2015–. Hon. DLaws Sussex, 2012. *Publications:* (with J. B. Poole) The Government of Science, 1972; (with John Jacobs) Punishing the Poor, 1990; Good Practice & Policy for After School, 1997; Extra Learning, 2001; articles in history, science policy and social policy jls. *Recreations:* music, museums, walking, friends. *Address:* House of Lords, SW1A 0PW.

**ANDREWS, Ann;** *see* Beynon, A.

**ANDREWS, Anthony Peter Hamilton;** Chairman: Countryside Learning Scotland (formerly Scottish Country Alliance Educational Trust), since 2003; South Esk Catchment Management Partnership, since 2004; *b* 23 Dec. 1946; *s* of late Col Peter Edward Clinton Andrews and Jean Margaret Hamilton (*née* Cooke); *m* 1973, Alison Margaret Dudley Morgan; two *d* (one *s* decd). *Educ:* King's Sch., Worcester; Univ. of St Andrews (MA); UCNW, Bangor (Dip. TEFL). Served RM, 1964–71. Land agent, 1975–76; with British Council, 1976–2002: Kano, Nigeria, 1976–78; Belgrade, 1979–81; Muscat, Oman, 1981–85; Recife, Brazil, 1985–89; Director: Scotland, 1989–95; Russia and Central Asia, 1996–2000; Germany, 2000–02; Chief Exec., Scottish Countryside Alliance, 2002–08; Exec. Dir, then Chief Exec., Atlantic Salmon Trust, 2008–16. *Recreations:* angling, river management, sailing, the arts. *Address:* Milton of Finavon House, by Forfar, Angus DD8 3PY. *T:* (01307) 850275.

**ANDREWS, Rev. Canon Christopher Paul;** Rector of Grantham, 1996–2013; Chaplain to the Queen, 2009–17; *b* Leicester, 29 April 1947; *s* of Stephen James Andrews and Patricia Margaret Andrews (*née* Eyre); *m* 1975, Christine Helen Hawkins; one *s* one *d*. *Educ:* Brighton Grammar Sch., Melbourne; Bishop Wordsworth's Sch., Salisbury; Fitzwilliam Coll., Cambridge (BA 1970; MA 1973); Westcott House, Cambridge. Ordained deacon, 1972, priest, 1973; Assistant Curate: St John the Baptist, Croydon, 1972–75; All Saints', Gosforth, Newcastle upon Tyne, 1975–78; Team Vicar, Kingston Park, Newcastle upon Tyne, 1978–87; Rural Dean, Newcastle Central, 1982–87; Vicar of Alnwick, 1987–96. Canon and Preb., Lincoln Cathedral, 2004–13. Mem. Cttee, Egypt Diocesan Assoc., 2014–. Volunteer, Embrace the Middle East, 2010–. *Recreations:* walking, gardening, reading, music, architecture, sketching and watercolours, travelling, exploring Islam and relations with Christianity. *Address:* 74 Daisy Avenue, Bury St Edmunds, Suffolk IP32 7PH. *T:* (01284) 723785.

**ANDREWS, David;** Member of the Dáil (TD) (FF) for Dún Laoghaire, 1965–2002; Minister for Foreign Affairs, Republic of Ireland, 1997–2000; *b* 15 March 1935; *s* of Christopher Andrews and Mary Coyle; *m* Annette Cusack; two *s* three *d*. *Educ:* Coláiste Mhuire, Christian Brothers' Sch.; Cistercian College, Roscrea; University College Dublin (BCL). Called to the Bar, King's Inns, 1962; Senior Counsel. Parly Sec. to Taoiseach, and Govt Chief Whip, 1970–73; opposition frontbench spokesman on justice and social welfare, 1973–77; Minister of State: Dept of Foreign Affairs, 1977–79; Dept of Justice, 1978–79; Minister: for Foreign Affairs, 1992–93; for Defence and the Marine, 1993–94; opposition spokesman on tourism and trade, 1995–97; Minister for Defence, 1997. Member: Cttee on the Constitution, 1967; New Ireland Forum, 1983–84. Mem., British-Irish Interparly Body, 1990–92. Hon. FRCPI 2010. Chevalier, Légion d'Honneur, 2006. *Recreations:* fly fishing, walking, theatre.

**ANDREWS, Prof. David John,** PhD; FREng, FIMechE; FRINA; Professor of Engineering Design, Department of Mechanical Engineering, University College London, since 2000; *b* 9 Aug. 1947; *m* 1970, Philippa Vanette Whitehurst; one *s* (and one *d* decd). *Educ:* Stationers' Co. Sch.; University Coll. London (BSc Eng 1970; MSc 1971; PhD 1984). FRINA 1987; FREng 2000; FIMechE 2002. RCNC Cadetship, 1965; Constructor Lieut, RCNC, 1971; Ministry of Defence: professional design on in-service and new build submarines, Submarine Design Section, Ship Dept, Bath, 1972–75; Constructor Grade, working on Invincible carrier design and subseq. Forward Design Gp, 1975–80; Lectr in Naval Architecture, UCL, 1980–84; Ministry of Defence: Hd, Trident Submarine Hull Design Section, Bath, 1984–86; Hd, Amphibious Gp (Chief Constructor), Replacement Amphibious Shipping Prog., 1986–90; Hd, Concept Design Div., Future Projects (Naval), Whitehall, 1990–93; Prof. of Naval Architecture, UCL, 1993–98; Dir, Frigates and Mine Countermeasures, Defence Procurement Agency, then Integrated Project Team Leader, Future Surface Combatant, MoD, Bristol, 1998–2000. Royal Institution of Naval Architects: Chm.; Membership Cttee, 1993–2000; Chm., Future Directions Cttee, 2000–; Vice Pres., 2005–; Mem. Council, 2005–; Mem., Exec. Cttee and Bd of Trustees, 2005–17; Vice Chm., Council, 2010–12. Mem., Panel 28, 2008 RAE. Chm., Internat. Marine Design Confs, 2015–. FRSA 1996. Dep. Ed., Internat. Jl of Maritime Engrg, 2008–. *Publications:* Synthesis in Ship Design (thesis), 1984; (contrib.) Finite Element Methods Applied to Thin Walled Structures, 1987; (contrib.) Technology and Naval Combat in the Twentieth Century and Beyond, 2001; (contrib.) Ship Design and Construction, 2004; (contrib) The Royal Institution of Naval Architects, 1860–2010, 2010; (contrib.) Dreadnought to Daring, 2013; (contrib.) Improving Ship Operational Design, 2015; contrib. numerous papers on ship design published by RINA, Royal Soc., etc, and in conf. proc. *Recreations:* painting and sketching, reading, cinema and theatre going, re-exploring London with my wife. *Address:* Department of Mechanical Engineering, University College London, Torrington Place, WC1E 7JE. *T:* (020) 7679 3874. *E:* d.andrews@ucl.ac.uk.

**ANDREWS, David Roger Griffith,** CBE 1981; *b* 27 March 1933; *s* of C. H. R. Andrews and G. M. Andrews; *m* 1963, Dorothy Ann Campbell; two *s* one *d*. *Educ:* Abingdon Sch.; Pembroke Coll., Oxford (MA). FCMA. Pirelli-General, 1956–59; Ford Motor Company, 1960–69: Controller: Product Engrg, 1965–66; Transmission and Chassis Div., 1967; European Sales Ops, 1967–69; Asst Controller, Ford of Europe, 1969; BLMC: Controller, 1970; Finance Dir, Austin Morris, 1971–72; Man. Dir, Power and Transmission Div., 1973–75; British Leyland Ltd: Man. Dir, Leyland International, 1975–77; Exec. Vice Chm., BL Ltd, 1977–82; Chm., Leyland Gp and Land Rover Gp, 1981–82; Chm. and Chief Exec., Land Rover-Leyland, 1982–86; Chm., Gwion Ltd, 1986–95. Director: Clarges Pharmaceutical Trustees Ltd, 1983–91; Glaxo Trustees Ltd, 1983–91; Ex-Cell-O Ltd, 1987–88; Foundn for Sci. and Technology, 1990–95 (Mem. Council, 1990–95, and Hon. Treas., 1990–95; Foundn Medal, 1996). Member: CBI Council, 1981–86; Exec. Cttee, SMMT, 1981–86; Open Univ. Visiting Cttee, 1982–85. FRSA. *Recreation:* reading.

**ANDREWS, Elizabeth Mary Nesbit,** PhD; MBE 2006; Vice Lord-Lieutenant of Gwynedd, 2014–17; *b* Birmingham, 13 June 1942; *d* of Dermot Knox Lloyd Nesbit Evans and Mary Elizabeth Evans (*née* Ellison); *m* 1st, 1972, Major Rodney Thomas Elliott (marr. diss. 1977); 2nd, 1978, Peter John Andrews (marr. diss. 1998). *Educ:* Abbey Sch., Malvern; Girton Coll., Cambridge (BA 1971; PhD 1977). Researcher, Elsa Wildlife Trust, Kenya, 1967–68; Co-ordinator, Otter Haven Proj., Vincent Wildlife Trust, 1978–88; ICM (Plastic Moulding) Ltd: Exec. Chm., 1988–95; non-exec. Chm., 1995–2005. Non-exec. Dir, Tufnol Industries Ltd, 1978–99. Dir, Wales Eur. Centre, Brussels, 1999–2006. Member: Cttee, Brecon Beacons Nat. Park, 1984–96; Countryside Council for Wales, 1997–2005; Jt Nature Conservation Cttee, 2005; Pres., Brecknock Wildlife Trust, 1996–; Vice Pres., RSPB, 2003–. DL 2001, High Sheriff 2015–16, Gwynedd. *Publications:* scientific papers in East African Wildlife Jl, Paleobiology, Regulated Rivers. *Recreations:* walking, standing and staring, military history. *Address:* Aberdovey, Gwynedd.

**ANDREWS, Hon. Dame Finola Mary Lucy;** *see* O'Farrell, Hon. Dame F. M. L.

**ANDREWS, Hon. Dame Geraldine (Mary),** DBE 2013; **Hon. Mrs Justice Andrews;** a Judge of the High Court of Justice, Queen's Bench Division, since 2013; *b* 19 April 1959; *d* of Walter and Mary Andrews. *Educ:* King's Coll. London (LLB 1st Cl. Hons 1980, LLM 1982; AKC; Dip.). Called to the Bar, Gray's Inn, 1981, Bencher, 2004; barrister, 1983–2013, specialising in commercial law, esp. banking; called to Irish Bar, 1993; QC 2001; a Recorder, 2001–13; a Dep. High Ct Judge, 2005–13. FKC 2018. *Publications:* (with S. Gee) Mareva Injunctions, 1988; (with R. Millett) The Law of Guarantees, 1992, 7th edn

2015; (contrib.) Singapore International Arbitration Law and Practice, 2015, 2nd edn 2018. *Recreations:* keen violinist, theatre, music, sport, reading, learning modern languages. *Address:* Royal Courts of Justice, Strand, WC2A 2LL. *T:* (020) 7947 7303.

**ANDREWS, Gillian Margaret,** FSA; President, Society of Antiquaries of London, 2014–18; *b* Manchester, 19 April 1953; *d* of Harold Victor Walker and Margaret Esther Walker; *m* 1978, Richard Duncan Andrews; two *d*. *Educ:* Kendal High Sch. for Girls; Univ. of Bristol (BA Archaeol., Ancient Hist. and Latin); Hughes Hall, Cambridge (PGCE). MCIfA (MIfA 1982); FSA 2002. Finds Officer, Central Excavation Unit, DoE, 1976–84; Archaeol and cultural heritage consultant, 1984–2019. *Recreations:* Lake District mountains, South Coast beach hut. *Address:* 4 Beechworth Road, Havant, Hants PO9 1AX. *E:* gill.andrews@virgin.net.

**ANDREWS, Sir Ian (Charles Franklin),** Kt 2007; CBE 1992; TD 1989; senior consultant to organisations in public and third sectors and academia, since 2009; Chairman, UK Serious Organised Crime Agency, 2009–13; *b* 26 Nov. 1953; *s* of Peter Harry Andrews and Nancy Gwladys Andrews (*née* Franklin); *m* 1985, Moira Fraser McEwan; two *s* one *d*. *Educ:* Solihull Sch.; Univ. of Bristol (BSc Social Sci.). Joined Ministry of Defence, 1975: Private Sec. to 2nd Perm. Under Sec. of State, 1979–81; short service volunteer commn, RRF, 1981–82; Principal, 1982; NATO Defence Coll., 1984–85; Asst Private Sec. to Sec. of State for Defence, 1986–88; Head: Defence Lands, 1988–90; Resources and Prog. (Army), 1990–93; Civil Sec., British Forces Germany/BAOR, 1993–95; Man. Dir (Facilities), DERA, 1995–97; Chief Exec., Defence Estates Agency, 1998–2002; Second Perm. Under-Sec. of State, MoD, 2002–08. Non-exec. Dir, 2013–15, Sen. Ind. Dir, 2015–18, NHS Digital (formerly Health and Social Care Inf. Centre). Conservator, Wimbledon and Putney Commons, 2009–17; Trustee, Chatham Historic Dockyard, 2010–. Served TA in rank of Major, 1972–93. FRGS 1996. *Recreations:* travel, ski-ing.

**ANDREWS, Prof. John Albert,** CBE 2000; Pro Chancellor, University of South Wales (formerly University of Glamorgan), since 2005 (Member, Board of Governors, 2002–15; Vice Chairman, 2005–08; Chairman, 2008–13); *b* 29 Jan. 1935; *s* of late Arthur George Andrews and Hilda May Andrews (*née* Banwell); *m* 1960, Elizabeth Ann Mary Wilkes; two *d*. *Educ:* Newport High Sch.; Wadham Coll., Oxford (MA, BCL). Called to the Bar, Gray's Inn, 1960, Bencher, 1991. Asst Lectr, Univ. of Manchester, 1957–58; Lectr in English Law, Univ. of Birmingham, 1958–67; University College of Wales, Aberystwyth: Prof. of Law, 1967–92; Hon. Prof., 1992–2000; Emeritus Prof., 2000–; Head of Dept of Law, 1970–92; Vice-Principal, 1985–88. Chief Exec., FEFCW and HEFCW, 1992–2000; Chm., Gen. Teaching Council for Wales, 2000–04. Visiting Professor: Thessaloniki, 1974, 1990; Cracow, 1978; Maryland, 1983. Former chm. or mem., numerous educnl, police and adv. bodies; Member: Police Trng Council, 1987–2002 (Academic Advr, 1997–2002); Lord Chancellor's Adv. Cttee on Legal Educn, 1987–90; Welsh Econ. Council, 1994–96; Criminal Injuries Compensation Appeals Panel, 2000–06; Police Skills and Standards Orgn, 2001–04; Police Accreditation and Licensing Bd, 2002–06; Justice Sector Skills Council, Policing Cttee, 2004–06; Actuarial Profession Disciplinary Panel, 2004–13; Practice Assce Cttee, CIPFA, 2007–14; Chairman: Council of Validating Universities, 1987–90 (Vice Chm., 1982–87); Police Promotions Exams Bd, 1987–2002; Agricl Wages Bd, 1999–2003. Member Council: Cardiff Univ., 2000–08; Univ. of Wales Coll. of Medicine, 2000–04; Member, Court of Governors: Univ. of Wales, 1969–92, 2001–04; Nat. Liby of Wales, 1979–92; Member, Board of Governors: Penglais Sch., 1974–80; Llanishen High Sch., 2005–17 (Chm., 2010–14); Mem., Bd of Dirs, Royal Welsh Coll. of Music and Drama, 2006–14. Hon. Fellow: Univ. of Wales Coll., Newport, 2000; Cardiff Univ., 2008. Trustee: SLS (formerly SPTL), 1990–2004 (Pres., SPTL, 1988–89); Hamlyn Trust, 1969–2000; AHRB, 2001–05. Mem., Welsh Cttee, Action for Children (formerly NCH), 2004–10. FRSA 1992; FLSW 2014. Hon. LLD S Wales, 2016. JP N Ceredigion, 1975–91. Editor, Legal Studies, 1981–93. *Publications:* (ed) Welsh Studies in Public Law, 1970; (ed) Human Rights in Criminal Procedure, 1982; (with L. G. Henshaw) The Welsh Language in the Courts, 1984; (with W. D. Hines) Keyguide to the International Protection of Human Rights, 1987; (with D. M. Hirst) Criminal Evidence, 1987, 3rd edn 1997; Criminal Evidence: statutes and materials, 1990; numerous contribs to legal and educnl books and jls. *Recreations:* walking, theatre, food, opera. *Address:* The Croft, 110 Mill Road, Lisvane, Cardiff CF14 0UG. *T:* (029) 2075 3980; c/o Office of the Vice-Chancellor, University of South Wales, Pontypridd CF37 1DL. *T:* (01443) 482001. *Clubs:* Brynamlwg (Aberystwyth); Cardiff and County.

**ANDREWS, Dame Julie (Elizabeth),** DBE 2000; actress; *b* 1 Oct. 1935; *m* 1st, Anthony J. Walton (marr. diss. 1968); one *d*; 2nd, 1969, Blake Edwards (*d* 2010); one step *s* one step *d*, and two adopted *d*. *Educ:* Woodbrook Girls' Sch., Beckenham and private governess. Appeared in The Boy Friend, NY, 1954; My Fair Lady: New York, 1956, London, 1958; Camelot, New York, 1960; Victor/Victoria, New York, 1995; directorial début, The Boy Friend, Bay Street Th., NY, 2003; The Gift of Music, O$_2$ Arena, 2010. *Films:* (Walt Disney) Mary Poppins, 1963 (Academy Award, 1964); Americanisation of Emily, 1964; Sound of Music, 1964; Hawaii, 1965; Torn Curtain, 1966; Thoroughly Modern Millie, 1966; Star, 1967; Darling Lili, 1970; The Tamarind Seed, 1973; "10", 1980; Little Miss Marker, 1980; S.O.B., 1981; Victor/Victoria, 1982; The Man Who Loved Women, 1983; Duet for One, 1987; That's Life, 1987; Relative Values, 2000; The Princess Diaries, 2001; The Princess Diaries II, 2004; Shrek II, 2004; Shrek III, 2007; Enchanted, 2007; The Tooth Fairy, 2010; Aquaman, 2018; *television:* Cinderella, 1957; Julie & Carol at Carnegie Hall, 1961; An Evening with Julie Andrews and Harry Belafonte, 1969; Julie & Carol at Lincoln Center, 1971; The Julie Andrews Hour, 1972–73 (7 Emmy Awards); Julie & Dick at Covent Garden, 1973–74; Julie & Jackie—How Sweet it is, 1973–74; Julie & Perry & The Muppets, 1973–74; My Favourite Things, 1975; The Puzzle Children, 1976; ABC's Silver Anniversary Celebration, 1978; Julie Andrews… One Step into Spring, 1978; The Sound of Christmas (Emmy Award), 1987; Julie & Carol Together Again, 1989; Great Performances Live in Concert, 1990; Our Sons, 1991; The Julie Show, 1992; One Special Night, 1999; On Golden Pond, 2001; Eloise at the Plaza, 2003; Eloise at Christmastime, 2003. Golden Lion Lifetime Achievement Award, Venice Film Fest., 2019. *Publications:* (as Julie Andrews Edwards) Mandy, 1972; Last of the Really Great Whangdoodles, 1973; Little Bo, 1999; Little Bo in France, 2002; (with Emma Walton Hamilton) Dumpy the Dump Truck, 2000; Dumpy at School, 2000; Dumpy Saves Christmas, 2001; Dumpy and His Pals; Dumpy's Friends on the Farm; Dumpy and the Big Storm, 2002; Dumpy and the Firefighters, 2003; Dumpy's Apple Shop, 2004; Dumpy's Happy Holiday, 2005; Dumpy's Valentine, 2008; Dumpy's Extra-Busy Day, 2008; Simeon's Gift, 2003; Dragon, 2004; The Great American Musical, 2006; Thanks to You: wisdom from mother and child, 2007; Julie Andrews' Collection of Poems, Songs and Lullabies, 2010; The Very Fairy Princess, 2010; (as Julie Andrews) Home: a memoir of my early years, 2008; (with Emma Walton Hamilton) Home Work: a memoir of my Hollywood years, 2019. *Recreations:* gardening, boating, writing.

**ANDREWS, Hon. Kevin James;** MHR (L) Menzies, Victoria, since 1991; *b* Sale, Vic, Australia, 9 Nov. 1955; *s* of Roy Gebhardt Andrews and Sheila Andrews; *m* 1979, Margaret; three *s* two *d*. *Educ:* Rosedale Primary Sch.; St Patrick's Coll., Sale; Univ. of Melbourne (BA, LLB); Monash Univ. (LLM). Res. solicitor, 1980–81, Co-ordinator, Contg Legal Educn, 1981–83, Law Inst. of Vic; Associate to Hon. Sir James Gobbo, Supreme Court of Vic, 1983–85; in practice as barrister, 1985–91. Minister: of Ageing, 2001–03; for Employment and Workplace Relns, 2003–07; for Immigration and Citizenship, 2007; for Social Services, 2013–14; for Defence, 2014–15. *Publications:* Maybe 'I do': modern marriage and the pursuit of happiness, 2012. *Recreations:* cycling, horse racing. *Address:* Parliament House, Canberra, ACT 2600, Australia. *T:* (02) 62777800.

**ANDREWS, Prof. Leighton Russell;** Professor of Practice in Public Service Leadership and Innovation, Cardiff Business School, since 2016; *b* 11 Aug. 1957; *s* of Len and Peggy Andrews; *m* 1996, Ann Beynon, *qv*; one step *s* one step *d*. *Educ:* University Coll. of N Wales, Bangor (BA Hons English and Hist.); Univ. of Sussex (MA Hist.). Vice-Pres., NUS, 1980–81; Parly Officer, Age Concern, 1982–84; Campaign Dir, Internat. Year of Shelter, 1984–87; Dir, then Man. Dir, Sallingbury Casey, subseq. Rowland Sallingbury Casey, 1988–93; Hd, Public Affairs, BBC, 1993–96; Chm., Political Context, 1996–99; Dir, then Man. Dir, Westminster Strategy, 1999–2001; Man. Dir, Smart Co., 2001–02; Lectr, Sch. of Journalism, Cardiff Univ., 2002–03. Vis. Prof., Univ. of Westminster, 1997–2002; Hon. Prof., Cardiff Univ., 2004–16. Mem. (Lab) Rhondda, Nat. Assembly for Wales, 2003–16; contested (Lab) same seat, 2016. Welsh Government: Dep. Minister for Social Justice and Public Service Delivery, 2007, for Regeneration, 2007–09; Minister for Children, Educn and Lifelong Learning, then for Educn and Skills, 2009–13; Minister for Public Services, 2014–16. Chair, Cardiff City FC Community Foundn. *Publications:* Wales Says Yes, 1999; Ministering to Education, 2014; contrib. various articles and chapters. *Recreations:* watching Cardiff City FC, music, cinema, theatre, reading literature, history and political biography. *E:* AndrewsL7@Cardiff.ac.uk.

**ANDREWS, Mark Björnsen;** Partner (formerly Deputy Chairman), SNR Denton UK LLP (formerly Denton Wilde Sapte), solicitors, 2000–11; Consultant, Dentons UKMEA LLP (formerly SNR Denton UK), 2011–13; *b* 12 July 1952; *s* of Harry Field Andrews and Ruth Margaret Andrews (*née* Legge). *Educ:* Reading Grammar Sch.; Hertford Coll., Oxford (BA Jurisp. 1973); Coll. of Law, Guildford. Articled Clerk, Clarks, solicitors, Reading, 1974–76; Wilde Sapte, subseq. Denton Wilde Sapte: Asst Solicitor, 1976–79; Partner, 1979–2000; Head of Insolvency Gp, 1989–2000; Sen. Partner, 1996–2000; Head, Restructuring and Insolvency Gp, 2000–10. Non-executive Director: Healthcare Locums plc, 2011–13; Al Scheme Ltd, 2014–18; Sen. Ind. Dir, Zolfo Cooper LLP, 2013–15; Consultant, AlixPartners UK, 2015–. Chairman of Trustees: Pimlico Opera, 1991–2015; Grange Park Opera Endowment Fund, 2005–14; The Crescent Support Gp, 2013–; Central YMCA, 2017–; Trustee: Dulwich Picture Gall., 2012–; London Gypsy Traveller Unit, 2015–17. *Recreations:* music, art, history, ornithology, walking, watercolour painting. *E:* m.bjornsen@hotmail.com.

**ANDREWS, Nigel John;** Film Critic, Financial Times, since 1973; *b* 3 April 1947; *s* of Francis Yardley Andrews and Marguerite Joan Andrews. *Educ:* Lancing Coll., Sussex; Jesus Coll., Cambridge (MA English). Contributor and reviewer, Sight and Sound and Monthly Film Bulletin, 1969–73; Asst Ed., Cinema One books and Sight and Sound mag., 1972–73; regular broadcaster, BBC Radio; writer and presenter, Kaleidoscope, Radio 4, and other arts programmes, 1975–. Mem., BFI, 1971–. Critic of Year, British Press Awards, 1985, 2002. FRSA 2002. *Publications:* (contrib.) The Book of the Cinema, 1979; Horror Films, 1985; True Myths: the life and times of Arnold Schwarzenegger, 1995; Travolta: the life, 1998; Jaws, 1999. *Address:* c/o Curtis Brown, Haymarket House, 28–29 Haymarket, SW1Y 4SP.

**ANDREWS, Robert Graham M.;** *see* Marshall-Andrews.

**ANDREWS, Rt Rev. Rodney Osborne;** Bishop of Saskatoon, 2004–10; *b* 11 Nov. 1940; *s* of George William Andrews and Mary Isabel (*née* Smith); *m* 1990, Jacqueline Plante; one *s* one *d*. *Educ:* Univ. of Saskatchewan (BA 1963); Coll. of Emmanuel and St Chad, Saskatoon (BTh 1965; MDiv 1981). Ordained deacon, 1964, priest, 1965; parish work and native ministry, Dio. Calgary, 1965–84; parish work and military chaplaincy, Dio. Montreal, 1984–87; parish work, Dio. Ottawa, 1988–91; Exec. Archdeacon, Dio. Algoma, 1991–2000; Rector of St Alban's, Richmond, and Univ. Chaplain: UBC, Dio. New Westminster, BC, 2000–03; Royal Canadian Mounted Police, 2011–. Columnist, Country Guide, Canada's nat. farm mag., 1994–. Holds airline transport pilot's licence, Canada. Hon. DD Coll. of Emmanuel and St Chad, Saskatoon, 2009. Medal commemorating 100th anniv. of treaty betw. southern Alberta native tribes and Queen Victoria, 1977; Saskatchewan Centennial Medal, 2006. *Recreations:* flying, curling, camping. *Address:* 310 Kutz Court, Saskatoon, SK S7N 4S4, Canada.

**ANDREWS, Maj. Gen. Stephen Michael,** CBE 2001 (MBE 1992); CEng, FIET, CMgr, CCMI; Strategy Advisor, Ministry of Public Health, Qatar, since 2016; *b* Plymouth, 8 Jan. 1957; *s* of Gordon James Andrews and Monica Marion Andrews (*née* Mansfield); *m* 1988, Kim Victoria White; two *s* one *d*. *Educ:* Ravensbourne Sch.; Welbeck Coll.; RMA, Sandhurst; Pembroke Coll., Cambridge (MA 1981). CEng 1993; MIET (MIEE 1993); FIET 2009; CMgr, CCMI 2018 (FCMI 2016). Joined Army, 1975; commnd REME, 1976; served UK and BAOR, 1976–88; Staff Coll., Camberley, 1989; DCOS 22 Armd Bde, 1990–91; OC 3 Field Workshop, 1992–94; jsdc 1994; Mem. Directing Staff, RMCS, 1995–96; CO, 3 Bn REME, 1996–98; Col Army Discipline Policy, 1999–2001; rcds 2002; Director: Personal Services (Army), 2003–06; Personnel Strategy, MoD, 2006–09; Dir, Strategy and Change, Defence Medical Services, 2009–12; Exec. Dir, Hamad Medical Corp. (public hosp. service), Qatar, 2012–16. Col Comdt, REME, 2010–18; Chm. Trustees, REME Charity, 2014–. Trustee, ABF, 2007–12. Patron, Defence Medical Welfare Service, 2012–18. FRSA. *Recreations:* Wessex landscapes, running for pleasure, radio drama, crime fiction, Jane Austen. *Address:* c/o Corps Secretary, Regimental Headquarters Royal Electrical and Mechanical Engineers, MoD Lyneham, Lyneham, Chippenham SN15 4XX. *E:* stephenmandrews@btinternet.com.

**ANDREWS, Stuart Morrison;** Head Master of Clifton College, 1975–90; *b* 23 June 1932; *s* of William Hannaford Andrews and Eileen Elizabeth Andrews; *m* 1962, Marie Elizabeth van Wyk; two *s*. *Educ:* Newton Abbot Grammar Sch.; St Dunstan's Coll.; Sidney Sussex Coll., Cambridge (MA). Nat. service with Parachute Bde, 1952–53. Sen. History Master and Librarian, St Dunstan's Coll., 1956–60; Chief History Master and Librarian, Repton Sch., 1961–67; Head Master, Norwich Sch., 1967–75. Chm., Direct-grant Sub-cttee, HMC, 1974–75; Dep. Chm., Assisted Places Cttee, 1982–91; Nat. Rep., HMC, 1987–89; HMC Lead Inspector of Schs, 1994–96. Pres., Grateful Soc., Bristol, 1988. Trustee, Glastonbury Abbey Develt Trust, 1992–96; Chm. Trustees and Managers, Wells & Mendip Mus., 1999–2004 (Hon. Librarian, 2004–). Chm., Emmott Foundn, 1999–2006. Editor, Conference, 1972–82. *Publications:* Eighteenth-century Europe, 1965; Enlightened Despotism, 1967; Methodism and Society, 1970; Rediscovery of America, 1998; British Periodical Press and the French Revolution, 2000; Unitarian Radicalism: political rhetoric 1770–1814, 2003; Irish Rebellion: Protestant polemic 1798–1900, 2006; Robert Southey: history, politics, religion, 2011; articles in various historical and literary jls. *Recreations:* walking, writing. *Address:* 34 St Thomas Street, Wells, Somerset BA5 2UX.

**ANDREWS, Susan Elizabeth;** *see* Acland-Hood, S. E.

**ANDREWS, William Denys Cathcart,** CBE 1980; WS; Partner, Shepherd & Wedderburn, WS, Edinburgh, 1962–91; *b* 3 June 1931; *s* of Eugene Andrews and Agnes Armstrong; *m* 1955, May O'Beirne; two *s* two *d*. *Educ:* Girvan High Sch.; Worksop Coll.; Edinburgh Univ. (BL). Served RASC, 1950–52. Law Society of Scotland: Mem. Council, 1972–81; Vice Pres., 1977–78; Pres., 1978–79. Examr in Conveyancing, Edinburgh Univ., 1974–77. Pt-time Mem., Lands Tribunal for Scotland, 1980–91. Fiscal to Soc. of Writers to HM Signet, 1987–91. *Recreation:* gardening. *Address:* Auchairne, Ballantrae, South Ayrshire KA26 0NX. *T:* (01465) 831344.

**ANDRIUKAITIS, Vytenis Povilas;** Member, European Commission, 2014–19; *b* Kyusyur, Soviet Union, 9 Aug. 1951; *s* of Alfonsas Andriukaitis and Liuda Andriukaitiene; *m* 1980, Irena Meižytė; two *s* one *d*. *Educ:* Kaunas 24th High Sch.; Kaunas Med. Inst. (MD (Surgery Speciality) 1975); Univ. of Vilnius (Dip. *summa cum laude* Hist. and Political Sci. 1984; Master's Degree). Surgeon: Kaunas 3rd Hosp., 1975–76; Ignalina Central Hosp., 1976–84; Cardiac Surgeon, Republican Clin. Hosp., Vilnius, 1985–93. Lectr in Hist. and Pol Sci., Univ. of Vilnius. Supreme Soviet Dep. for Lithuanian Republic, 1990–92; Parliament of Lithuania: MP, 1992–2004 and 2008–14; Opposition Leader, 2000–01; Chm., 2001–04; Dep. Chm., 2009–12; Mem., Republic Cttee on Eur. Affairs, 2008–12, Republic Cttee on Foreign Affairs, 2001–02, 2003–04, 2008–12; Minister of Health, 2012–14. Mem., Vilnius CC, 2000–04. Social Democratic Party of Lithuania: Dep. Chm., 1989–99; Chm., 1999–2001; Vice-Chm., 2008–12. Co-signatory, Act of Re-establishment of State of Lithuania, 1990; jt author, Constitution of Republic of Lithuania, adopted 1992. Comdr, Order of Grand Duke Gediminas (Lithuania), 2004; Grand Cross, Order of Merit (Portugal), 2003; Officier, Légion d'Honneur (France), 2015. *Publications:* The Status of Freedom Fighter.

**ANELAY OF ST JOHNS,** Baroness *cr* 1996 (Life Peer), of St Johns in the county of Surrey; **Joyce Anne Anelay,** DBE 1995 (OBE 1990); PC 2009; *b* 17 July 1947; *d* of late Stanley Charles Clarke and of Annette Marjorie Clarke; *m* 1970, Richard Alfred Anelay, *qv*. *Educ:* Merryhills Primary Sch., Enfield; Enfield Co. Sch.; Bristol Univ. (BA Hons Hist.); London Univ. Inst. of Educn (Cert Ed); Brunel Univ. (MA Public and Social Admin). Teacher, St David's Sch., Ashford, Middx, 1969–74; Voluntary Advr, Woking CAB, 1976–85 (Chm., 1988–93; Pres., 1996–). Member: Social Security Appeal Tribunal, 1983–96; Social Security Adv. Cttee for GB and NI, 1989–96. Opposition spokesman on agriculture, 1997–98, on culture, media and sport, 1998–2002, on Home Affairs, 2002–07; an Opposition Whip, 1997–98, Opposition Chief Whip, 2007–10, H of L; Captain of the Honourable Corps of Gentlemen at Arms (Govt Chief Whip in H of L), 2010–14; Minister of State, DFID, 2016; Minister of State, FCO, 2014–17; Prime Minister's Special Rep. on Preventing Sexual Violence in Conflict, 2015–17; Minister of State, DExEU, 2017. Mem., Procedure Cttee, 1997–2000, 2007–. Conservative Women's Committee: Chm., SE Area, 1987–90; Vice-Chm., SE Area Exec. Cttee, 1990–93; Chm., Nat. Cttee, 1993–96; Member: Nat. Union of Cons. Party, 1987–97 (Vice-Pres., 1996–97); Women's Nat. Commission, 1990–93. Trustee: UNICEF UK, 2004–07; Just a Drop, 2004–06. JP NW Surrey, 1985–97. Chm. Govs, Hermitage First and Middle Schs, 1981–88. FRSA 1991. Hon. DSocSc Brunel, 1997. *Recreations:* golf, reading. *Address:* House of Lords, SW1A 0PW. *Club:* Woking Golf.

**ANELAY, Richard Alfred;** QC 1993; a Recorder, 1992–2019; a Deputy High Court Judge, Family Division, 1995–2016; *b* 26 March 1946; *s* of late Maurice Alfred Anelay and Bertha Anelay; *m* 1970, Joyce Anne Clarke (*see* Baroness Anelay of St Johns). *Educ:* Dodmire Primary Sch., Darlington; Queen Elizabeth Grammar Sch., Darlington; Bristol Univ. (BA Classics and Philosophy); Council of Legal Educn. Called to the Bar, Middle Temple, 1970, Bencher, 2003; Asst Recorder, 1987. Hd of Chambers, 2006–13. Acting Deemster, 2007–09, Deemster, 2009–16, I of M. Dir, Bar Mutual Indemnity Fund, 2005–13. Consulting Ed., Encyclopedia of Financial Provision in Family Matters, 1998–2014. Fellow, Internat. Acad. of Matrimonial Lawyers, 2008–. *Recreation:* golf. *Address:* 1 King's Bench Walk, Temple, EC4Y 7DB. *T:* (020) 7936 1500. *Club:* Woking Golf.

**ANFOM, Emmanuel E.;** *see* Evans-Anfom.

**ANGEL, Anthony Lionel;** Chairman, 4C Biomed Inc., since 2016; *b* 3 Dec. 1952; *s* of William and Frances Angel; *m* 1975, Ruth Hartog; two *s*. *Educ:* Haberdashers' Aske's Sch., Elstree; Queens' Coll., Cambridge (MA). Admitted Solicitor, 1978. Linklaters: Articled Clerk, 1976; Partner, 1984–2008; Hd of Tax, 1994–98; Man. Partner, 1998–2007; Exec. Man. Dir and Hd of Europe, Middle East and Africa, Standard & Poor's, 2008–10; Chief Exec., Vantage Diagnostics Ltd, 2010–11 (Dir, 2010–); Sen. Partner, DLA Piper Internat., 2011–15; Global Chm., DLA Piper, 2011–14; Chm., Jnetics, 2016–. Vis. Prof., Cass Business Sch., 2015–. Hon. DSc City, 2009. *Recreations:* golf, sailing, ski-ing, theatre.

**ANGEL, Gerald Bernard Nathaniel Aylmer;** Senior District Judge, Family Division of the High Court, 1991–2004 (Registrar, 1980–90; District Judge, 1991); *b* 4 Nov. 1937; *s* of late Bernard Francis and Ethel Angel; *m* 1968, Lesley Susan Kemp; three *s* one *d* (and one *s* decd). *Educ:* St Mary's Sch., Nairobi; Inns of Court Sch. of Law. Served Kenya Regt, 1956–57. Called to Bar, Inner Temple, 1959, Bencher 1992; Advocate, Kenya, 1960–62; practice at Bar, 1962–80. Member: Judicial Studies Bd, 1989–90 (Mem., Civil and Family Cttee, 1985–90); Supreme Ct Procedure Cttee, 1990–95; Matrimonial Causes Rule Cttee, 1991; Family Proceedings Rule Cttee, 1991–2003. *Publications:* (ed) Industrial Tribunals Reports, 1966–78; (contrib.) Atkin's Court Forms (Adv. Editor), 1988–2003. *Recreations:* reading, walking. *Address:* Garden House, 12 Aylsham Road, North Walsham, Norfolk NR28 0BH. *T:* (01692) 402401.

**ANGEL, Heather,** FRPS, FBIPP; professional wildlife photographer, author and lecturer; *b* 21 July 1941; *d* of Stanley Paul Le Rougetel and Hazel Marie Le Rougetel (*née* Sherwood); *m* 1964, Martin Vivian Angel; one *s*. *Educ:* 14 schools in England and NZ; Bristol Univ. (BSc Hons (Zoology) 1962; MSc 1965). FRPS 1972; FBIPP 1974. Solo exhibitions: The Natural History of Britain and Ireland, Sci. Mus., 1981; Nature in Focus, Natural Hist. Mus., 1987; The Art of Wildlife Photography, Gloucester, 1989; Natural Visions, UK tour, 2000–04, Cairo, 2002, Kuala Lumpur, 2002, Beijing, 2003; Wild Kew, Royal Botanic Gdns, Kew, 2010; Haslemere Mus., 2012. Television: demonstrating photographic techniques, Me and My Camera I, 1981; Me and My Camera II, 1983; Gardener's World, 1983; Nature, 1984; Nocon on Photography, 1988. Led British Photographic Delegn to China, 1985. Photos used worldwide in books, magazines, on TV, advertising, etc, 1972–. Vis. Prof., Sch. of Life Sci., Nottingham Univ., 1994–. Hon. FRPS 1986 (Pres., 1984–86). Hon. DSc Bath, 1986. Hood Medal, RPS, 1975; Médaille de Salverte, Soc. Française de Photographie, 1984; Louis Schmidt Award, Biocommunications Assoc., 1998. *Publications:* Nature Photography: its art and techniques, 1972; All Colour Book of Ocean Life, 1975; Photographing Nature: Trees, 1975, Insects, 1975, Seashore, 1975, Flowers, 1975, Fungi, 1975; Seashore Life on Rocky Shores, 1975; Seashore Life on Sandy Beaches, 1975; Seashells of the Seashore, 1976; Wild Animals in the Garden, 1976; Life in the Oceans, 1977; Life in our Estuaries, 1977; Life in our Rivers, 1977; British Wild Orchids, 1977; The Countryside of the New Forest, 1977; The Countryside of South Wales, 1977; Seaweeds of the Seashore, 1977; Seashells of the Seashore, Book 1, 1978, Book 2, 1978; The Countryside of Devon, 1980; The Guinness Book of Seashore Life, 1981; The Natural History of Britain and Ireland, 1981; The Family Water Naturalist, 1982; The Book of Nature Photography, 1982; The Book of Close-up Photography, 1983; Heather Angel's Countryside, 1983; A Camera in the Garden, 1984; Close-up Photography, 1986; Kodak Calendar, The Thames, 1987; A View from a Window, 1988; Nature in Focus, 1988; Landscape Photography, 1989; Animal Photography, 1991; Kew: a world of plants, 1993; Photographing the Natural World, 1994; Outdoor Photography: 101 tips and hints, 1997; How to Photograph Flowers, 1998; Pandas, 1998; How to Photograph Water, 1999; Natural Visions, 2000; Giant Pandas, 2006; Puffins, 2007; Green China, 2008; Snow Monkeys, 2009; Living Dinosaurs, 2009; Heather Angel's Wild Kew, 2009; Exploring Natural China, 2010; Digital Outdoor Photography: 101 top tips, 2012; Pollination Power, 2016; *for children:* Your Book of Fishes, 1972; The World of an Estuary, 1975; Fact Finder—Seashore, 1976; The World of a Stream, 1976; Fungi, 1979; Lichens, 1980; Mosses and Ferns, 1980. *Recreations:* exploring wilderness areas and photographing unusual aspects of animal behaviour, reading and writing haiku at airports and in planes. *W:* heatherangelphotography.co.uk.

**ANGEL, Prof. (James) Roger (Prior),** FRS 1990; Regents' Professor of Astronomy, since 1990, Regents' Professor of Optical Sciences, and Director, Steward Observatory Richard F. Caris Mirror Laboratory, since 1985, University of Arizona; *b* 7 Feb. 1941; *s* of James Lee Angel and Joan Angel; *m* 1965, Ellinor M. Goonan; one *s* one *d*. *Educ:* St Peter's Coll., Oxford (Hon. Schol.; BA 1963; Hon. Fellow, 1993); Calif Inst of Technology (MS 1966); DPhil Oxon 1967. Post Doctoral Assistant, then Asst Prof., later Associate Prof. of Physics, Columbia Univ., 1967–72; Alfred P. Sloan Res. Fellow, 1970–74; Associate Prof. and Prof. of Astronomy, Arizona Univ., 1973–90. Dir, Center for Astronomical Adaptative Optics, 1996–2011. Vice-Pres., Amer. Astronomical Soc., 1987–90 (Pierce Prize, 1976); Fellow, Amer. Acad. of Arts and Scis, 1990. MacArthur Fellow, John D. and Catherine T. MacArthur Foundn, 1996–2001. MNAS 2000. Kavli Prize in Astrophysics, 2010. *Publications:* numerous papers on white dwarf stars, quasars, the search for extra-solar planetary systems, astronomical mirrors, telescopes and their instruments, adaptive optics, geoengrg and current research in photovoltaic solar energy. *Recreation:* grandchildren. *Address:* Steward Observatory, University of Arizona, Tucson, AZ 85721–0065, USA. *T:* (520) 6216541.

**ANGEL, Timothy Morris,** CBE 2019 (OBE 1997); Chairman, Morris Angel & Son Ltd, since 1986; *b* London, 1 Aug. 1949; *s* of Daniel and Maureen Angel; *m* 1973, Eleanor Marx; two *s* one *d*. *Educ:* John Lyon Sch., Harrow on the Hill. With Angel Costumes, 1967– (Dir, 1980–); has provided costumes for 37 award-winning films; Award for Outstanding British Contribution to Cinema, BAFTA, 2016. Mem., BAFTA, 1993– (Chm., 1997–2000). Gov., BFI, 2002–08. Trustee and Treasurer: Hammerson House, 1980–2016; Nightingale Hammerson, 2012–16. *Publications:* Behind the Seams, 2015. *Recreations:* family, theatre, film, life-long 'Gooner', walking my dogs. *Address:* Angels Costumes, 1 Garrick Road, NW9 6AA. *T:* (020) 8202 2244, *Fax:* (020) 8202 1820. *Clubs:* Ivy, Soho House.

**ANGELINI, Prof. Gianni Davide,** MD; FRCSGlas, FMedSci; British Heart Foundation Professor of Cardiac Surgery, since 1992, and Director, since 1995, Bristol Heart Institute, University of Bristol; Professor of Cardiothoracic Surgery, Imperial College London, 2010–16; *b* Murlo, Siena, 29 Jan. 1953; *s* of Marzio and Erina Angelini; *m* 1985, Rosalind Gwendolin John; three *s*. *Educ:* Istituto T Sarrochi, Siena (Dip. Mech. Engrg 1972); Univ. of Siena (MD 1979; Fellow in Thoracic Surgery 1984); Univ. of Wales Coll. of Medicine, Cardiff (MCh 1986). FRCSGlas 1986. Senior House Officer: Cardiothoracic Surgery, Llandough Hosp., Cardiff, 1981; Gen. Surgery, University Hosp. of Wales, Cardiff, 1981–82; Casualty/Accident, Royal Gwent Hosp., Newport, 1982–83; Registrar in Cardiothoracic Surgery, 1983–86, Sen. Registrar, 1986–88, University Hosp. of Wales, Cardiff; Sen. Registrar, Cardiothoracic Surgery, Thoraxcenter, Erasmus Univ., Rotterdam, 1988–89; Lectr and BHF Intermediate Res. Fellow in Cardiothoracic Surgery, University Hosp. of Wales, April–Oct. 1989; Sen. Lectr and Consultant in Cardiothoracic Surgery, Univ. of Sheffield, 1989–92. Sen. Investigator, NIHR, 2009–. FETCS 1998; FMedSci 2011. Cavaliere, Order of Merit (Italy) 2003. *Publications:* (jtly) Arterial Conduits in Myocardial Revascularisation, 1995; contribs to jls incl. Lancet, Nature, Circulation, BMJ, Jl of Thoracic and Cardiovascular Surgery, Jl of the American Coll. of Cardiol. *Recreations:* running, tennis. *Address:* Bristol Heart Institute, Bristol Royal Infirmary, Bristol BS2 8HW. *T:* (0117) 342 3145. *E:* g.d.angelini@imperial.ac.uk.

**ANGEST, Sir Henry,** Kt 2015; Chairman and Chief Executive Officer, and Principal Shareholder, Arbuthnot Banking Group plc, since 1985; Chairman: Secure Trust Bank plc, 1982–2016; Arbuthnot Latham & Co. Ltd, since 1994; *b* Winterthur, Switzerland, 6 July 1940; *m* Dorothy Block; one *s* one *d*. *Educ:* Univ. of Basel, Switzerland (LLL). Nat. Service, Switzerland (1st Lieut (Intelligence and Mil. Court)) (pt-time), 1959–79. International Executive: Dow Chem. Co. and Dow Banking Corp., Zurich, Miami, Sao Paulo, Hong Kong, London, 1967–85. Chm., Banking Cttee, London Investment Banking Assoc., 1997–2009. Mem., Council and Bd, IoD, 1999–2004. Nat. Treas. and Banker, Cons. Party, 2000–. Patron: Royal Botanic Gdn, Edinburgh, 2001–; Royal Botanic Gdns, Kew, 2011–. Founder Fellow, RHS 2011–. Mem., then Liveryman, Lombard Assoc., later Overseas Bankers Club, then Guild of Internat. Bankers, subseq. Internat. Bankers' Co., 1979– (Master, 2008–09). Mem., Internat. Dendrology Soc., 2008–. *Recreations:* dendrology, farming, science, cosmology, politics. *Address:* Arbuthnot Banking Group plc, Arbuthnot House, 7 Wilson Street, EC2M 2SN. *T:* (020) 7012 2420. *E:* sirhenryangest@arbuthnot.co.uk. *Clubs:* White's, 5 Hertford St, Mosimann's, Carlton.

**ANGIOLINI, Rt Hon. Dame Elish (Frances),** DBE 2011; PC 2006; QC (Scot.) 2001; Principal, St Hugh's College, Oxford, since 2012; *b* 24 June 1960; *d* of James McPhilomy and Mary McPhilomy (*née* Magill); *m* 1985, Domenico Angiolini; two *s*. *Educ:* Notre Dame Sch., Glasgow; Univ. of Strathclyde (LLB Hons; DipLP). Admitted solicitor, 1985; admitted Mem., Faculty of Advocates, 2008; Depute Procurator Fiscal, Airdrie; Mgt Services Gp, Crown Office; Sen. Depute Procurator Fiscal, Asst Procurator Fiscal 1995–97, Glasgow; with Crown Office, 1997–2000; Regl Procurator Fiscal, Grampian, Highlands and Is, 2000–01; Solicitor Gen. for Scotland, 2001–06; Lord Advocate, Scottish Exec., later Scottish Govt, 2006–11. Non-practising Mem., Terra Firma Chambers, 2011–. Vis. Prof., Univ. of Strathclyde, 2011–; Hon. Prof., Univ. of Aberdeen, 2011–. Chancellor, Univ. of the West of Scotland, 2013–. FRSE 2017. *Recreations:* travel, walking, picking wild mushrooms, cinema, eating out. *Address:* St Hugh's College, St Margaret's Road, Oxford OX2 6LE; Terra Firma Chambers, Parliament House, Edinburgh EH1 1RF.

**ANGLE, Martin David,** FCA; Chairman, National Exhibition Centre Group, 2006–15; *b* London, 8 April 1950; *s* of Robert William Angle and Mary Angle; *m* 1977, Lindsey Blake (separated); two *s* one *d*. *Educ:* St Dunstan's Coll., London; Univ. of Warwick (BSc Hons). FCA 1975; MCSI 1992. Articled Clerk, Peat, Marwick, Mitchell & Co., London, 1972–76; Asst to Chief Exec., UAE Currency Bd, 1976–77; Dir, S G Warburg & Co. Ltd, 1978–88; Man. Dir, Morgan Stanley, 1988–92; Gp Dir, Kleinwort Benson, 1992–96; Gp Finance Dir, TI Gp plc, 1997–2000; Operational Man. Dir, Terra Firma Capital Partners, 2001–06. Non-executive Director: Savills plc, 2007–16; OAO Severstal, 2007–15; Pennon plc, 2008–18; Shuaa Capital psc, 2009–16; Bd Advr, Commercial Bank of Dubai, 2016–18; Sen. Ind. Dir, Gulf Keystone Petroleum Ltd, 2018–; Chm., Cybersec Innovation Partners Ltd,

2019–; Dep. Chm., Spire Healthcare Gp plc, 2019–. Vice Chm., Trustee and Treas., FIA Foundn, 2010–. Member: Governing Council, Univ. of Warwick, 2001–07; Adv. Bd, Warwick Business Sch., 2001–11. FRSA. *Recreations:* music and opera, mountain walking, historic motor racing, modern history. *Address:* Broomscroft Place, Canon Lane, Wateringbury, Kent ME18 5PQ. *E:* martindangle@aol.co.uk. *Club:* Royal Automobile.

**ANGLESEY,** 8th Marquess of, *cr* 1815; **Charles Alexander Vaughan Paget;** Baron Paget of Beaudesert 1549; Earl of Uxbridge 1784; Bt 1730; *b* 13 Nov. 1950; *s* of 7th Marquess of Anglesey and of (Elizabeth) Shirley Vaughan Paget, Dowager Marchioness of Anglesey; *S* father, 2013; *m* 1st, 1986, Georganne Elizabeth Elliott (marr. diss. 2011), *d* of Col John Alfred Downes, MBE, MC; one *s* one *d*; 2nd, 2015, Susan Blanche Louise De Paolis. *Educ:* Dragon School, Oxford; Eton; Exeter Coll., Oxford; Sussex Univ. (MA, DPhil). *Heir:* s Earl of Uxbridge, *qv*. *Address:* Plâs-Newydd, Llanfairpwll, Gwynedd LL61 6DZ.

**ANGLIN, Prof. Douglas (George);** Professor of Political Science, Carleton University, Ottawa, Canada, 1958–89, Adjunct Research Professor, 1989–93, Professor Emeritus, since 1993; *b* Toronto, Canada, 16 Dec. 1923; *s* of George Chambers Anglin, MD, and Ruth Cecilia Cale, MD; *m* 1948, Mary Elizabeth Watson; two *d*. *Educ:* Toronto Univ.; Corpus Christi and Nuffield Colls, Oxford Univ. BA Toronto; MA, DPhil Oxon. Lieut, RCNVR, 1943–45. Asst (later Associate) Prof. of Political Sci. and Internat. Relations, Univ. of Manitoba, Winnipeg, 1951–58; Associate Prof. (later Prof.), Carleton Univ., 1958–89. Vice-Chancellor, Univ. of Zambia, Lusaka, Zambia, 1965–69; Associate Research Fellow, Nigerian Inst. of Social and Economic Research, Univ. of Ibadan, Ibadan, Nigeria, 1962–63; Research Associate, Center of Internat. Studies, Princeton Univ., 1969–70. Canadian Association of African Studies: Pres., 1973–74; Distinguished Africanist Schol., 1989. Consultant, Educn for Democracy Prog., South African Council of Churches, Johannesburg, 1992–94. Hon. DLitt Zambia, 2011. *Publications:* The St Pierre and Miquelon Affaire of 1941: a study in diplomacy in the North Atlantic quadrangle, 1966, repr. 1999; Zambia's Foreign Policy: studies in diplomacy and dependence, 1979; Zambian Crisis Behaviour: confronting Rhodesia's unilateral declaration of independence 1965–1966, 1994; Confronting Rwandan Genocide: the military options, 2002; edited jointly: Africa: Problems and Prospects 1961; Conflict and Change in Southern Africa, 1978; Canada, Scandinavia and Southern Africa, 1978; articles on Internat. and African affairs in a variety of learned jls.

**ANGLO, Margaret Mary, (Mrs Sydney Anglo),** *see* McGowan, M. M.

**ANGLO, Prof. Sydney,** PhD; FBA 2005; Professor of the History of Ideas, 1981–86, Research Professor, 1986–99, now Professor Emeritus, University of Wales Swansea (formerly University College of Swansea); *b* 1 March 1934; *s* of Harry Anglo and Ray (*née* Pelter); *m* 1964, Margaret Mary McGowan, *qv*. *Educ:* Pinner Co. Grammar Sch.; London Sch. of Economics (BA 1955; PhD 1959). Sen. Res. Fellow, Univ. of Reading, 1958–61; Lectr in the Hist. of Ideas, 1961–69, Sen. Lectr, 1969–75, Reader, 1975–81, UC of Swansea. Sen. Fellow, Warburg Inst., 1970–71. Mem., Adv. Cttee, Ref. Div., BL, 1975–84. Sec., 1967–70, Chm., 1986–89, Soc. for Renaissance Studies. FSA 1965. Founding FLSW 2010. Lectr, Conférences Léopold Delisle, Bibliothèque nationale de France, 2010. Numerous contribs to BBC Radio; features include: The Leonardo Cylinders, 1989; The Big Fight Fiasco of 1467, 1992; Piping the Blues, 1992; The Great Snooker Final, 1994; Great Spy, Lousy Tapdancer, 1996; Cheese, 1997. Arms and Armour Soc. Medal, 2002. *Publications:* The Great Tournament Roll of Westminster, 1968; Spectacle, Pageantry and Early Tudor Policy, 1969, 2nd edn 1997; Machiavelli, a Dissection, 1969; La tryumphante Entrée de Charles Prince des Espargnes, 1974; (ed) The Damned Art: essays in the literature of witchcraft, 1977; (ed) Chivalry in the Renaissance, 1990; Images of Tudor Kingship, 1992; The Martial Arts of Renaissance Europe, 2000; Machiavelli - the First Century: studies in enthusiasm, hostility and irrelevance, 2005; L'escrime, la danse et l'art de la guerre: le livre et la représentation du mouvement, 2011; numerous contribs to learned jls, periodicals and collaborative vols. *Recreations:* telephone conversation with friends, listening to and reading about pianists past and present. *Address:* 59 Green Ridge, Brighton BN1 5LU. *Clubs:* East India, Royal Society of Medicine.

**ANGUS, Robert James Campbell;** Social Security and Child Support Commissioner, 1995–2007; *b* 7 Feb. 1935; *s* of James Angus and Jessie Macrae Angus; *m* 1968, Jean Anne, *d* of Andrew and Jessie Martin. *Educ:* Shawlands Acad.; Univ. of Glasgow (BL 1957). Nat. service, RA, 1958–60. Admitted solicitor, Scotland, 1960; in private practice, 1960–71; Legal Asst, Office of Solicitor to Sec. of State for Scotland, 1972–74, Sen. Legal Asst, 1974; on secondment as Administrator, SHHD, 1974–78; Solicitor's Office, 1978–82; Inquiry Reporter, Scottish Office, 1982–84; Chairman: Social Security, Medical and Vaccine Damage Appeal Tribunals, 1984–95; Child Support Appeal Tribunals, 1992–95. *Recreations:* history, music, history and mechanics of pianos, rough gardening. *Address:* Hunter Gap, Keenley, Allendale, Northumberland NE47 9NT. *Club:* Royal Scots (Edinburgh).

**ANGUS, Tracey Anne;** QC 2012; *b* Amersham, 10 Jan. 1967; *d* of Athol James Angus and Roberta Anne Angus (*née* Scott); *m* 1997, John Simon Jones; one *s* one *d*. *Educ:* St George's Sch., Edinburgh; Rugby Sch.; Edinburgh Univ. (MA Hons English Lit.); City Univ. (DipLaw). Called to the Bar, Inner Temple, 1991. *Publications:* (jtly) A Practical Guide to Inheritance Act Claims, 2007; (ed) Heywood & Massey Court of Protection Practice. *Address:* 5 Stone Buildings, Lincoln's Inn, WC2A 3XT. *T:* (020) 7242 6201.

**ANHOLT, Trudy Frances Charlene;** *see* Mackay, T. F. C.

**ANIM, Cecilia Akrisie,** CBE 2017; President, Royal College of Nursing, 2015–18; *b* Sekondi, Ghana, 20 Dec. 1947; *d* of late J. K. N. Mills and of Elizabeth Amoa; *m* 1977, B. O. Anim; one *s* four *d*. *Educ:* St Ann's Sch., Ghana; Hull Sch. of Nursing; London South Bank Univ. (Dip. Professional Studies in Nursing 2000). RGN 1977; CNS: Nursing and midwifery trng, Ghana, 1964–68. Staff nurse: Hull Royal Inf., 1977; Harley Street Clinic, 1979–80; Margaret Pyke Centre, 1979–83; Princess Grace Hosp., 1980–85; Clin. Nurse Specialist, sexual and reproductive health, 1983–. Dep. Pres., RCN, 2010–14 (Chair, Inner N Central Br., 2010–). Hon. DH Bradford, 2016; Hon. DLaw Nottingham, 2017; Hon. DSc Portsmouth, 2018. Merit Award, 2000, Long Service Award, 2011, RCN; Bevan Prize for Health and Wellbeing, 2013; UN African Women of Excellence Award, 2015; Chair's Award, Windrush Generation, 2018; GUBA Award for Outstanding Leadership, 2018; BJN Award for Lifetime Achievement, 2019. *Publications:* contrib. RCN Family Planning Nurses Forum Jl. *Recreations:* music, travelling, flower arranging.

**ANIONWU, Dame Elizabeth (Nneka),** DBE 2017 (CBE 2001); PhD; FRCN; Professor of Nursing, University of West London, 1997–2007, now Emeritus; *b* Birmingham, 2 July 1947; *d* of late Mary Furlong (later Hart) and Lawrence Odiatu Victor Anionwu; one *d*. *Educ:* Paddington Gen. Hosp. (SRN 1968); Chiswick Poly. (HVCert 1971); Univ. of Manchester (Dip. Advanced Nursing 1978); Inst. of Educn, Univ. of London (PhD 1988). FRCN 2004. Staff Nurse, Paddington Gen. Hosp., 1968–69; nurse and English teacher, Paris, 1969–70; Health Visitor, Brent, 1971–74; Community Nurse Tutor, Brent Health Dist, 1975–77, Hd, Brent Sickle Cell and Thalassaemia Centre, 1979–90; Sen. Lectr, Inst. of Child Health, Univ. of London, 1990–97. *Publications:* The Politics of Sickle Cell and Thalassaemia (with K. Atkin), 2001; A Short History of Mary Seacole, 2005; Mixed Blessings from a Cambridge Union (memoirs), 2016. *Recreations:* reading, music, walking, family, swimming. *W:* www.elizabethanionwu.co.uk, www.twitter.com/EAnionwu.

**ANKERSON, Dr Dudley Charles,** CMG 2013; HM Diplomatic Service, retired; Managing Director, Latin Insight Consulting, since 2006; *b* Hereford, 4 Sept. 1948; *s* of Richard and Norah Ankerson; *m* 1973, Silvia Galicia Morales; one *s* one *d*. *Educ:* Hereford Cathedral Sch.; Sidney Sussex Coll., Cambridge (BA 1971; MA 1975; PhD 1982). Entered FCO, 1976; Second Sec., Buenos Aires, 1978–81; Falkland Is Dept, FCO, 1982–85; First Sec., Mexico City, 1985–88; Soviet and Eastern Europe Dept, FCO, 1988–93; Counsellor: Madrid, 1993–97; Budapest, 1998–2001; Permanent Under-Sec.'s Dept, FCO, 2001–06. Vis. Lectr, Univ. of St Luis Potosí, Mexico, 2008; Vis. Fellow, Latin American Centre, Cambridge Univ., 2009. Consultant: BP, Latin America, 2006–; British cos in Latin America, incl. Anglo-American, HSBC, 2006–; Special Adviser: on Latin America to FCO, 2006–; to Mexican Govt, 2008–; to Govt of Colombia, 2011–; Advr, Inter Mediate Foundn, 2011–. Participant in N American Tri-Lateral Commn, 2013. Mil. Medal, 1st Cl. (Hungary), 2000; OM Col Guillermo Fergusson (Columbia), 2016; Aguila Azteca (Mexico), 2018. *Publications:* Agrarian Warlord: Saturnino Cedillo and the Mexican Revolution in San Luis Potosí, 1984; La Memoria Viva del General Saturnino Cedillo, 2010; Caudillos Agrarista, 2011. *Recreations:* history (especially of Latin America), classical studies, family, travel, cinema, theatre, sport. *Address:* c/o Latin Insight Consulting, 11 Quernmore Road, Bromley, Kent BR1 4EH. *T:* (020) 8290 0386. *E:* Ankergal@aol.com. *Clubs:* Athenæum, MCC; Penguins Internat. Rugby Football.

**ANNALY,** 6th Baron *cr* 1863; **Luke Richard White;** a Lord in Waiting (Government Whip), 1994; *b* 29 June 1954; *o s* of 5th Baron Annaly and Lady Marye Isabel Pepys (*d* 1958), *d* of 7th Earl of Cottenham; *S* father, 1990; *m* 1983, Caroline Nina (marr. diss.), *yr d* of Col Robert Garnett, MBE; one *s* three *d*. *Educ:* Eton; RMA Sandhurst. Commnd Royal Hussars, 1974–78, RARO, 1978–86. Freeman, Haberdashers' Co., 1997. *Heir: s* Hon. Luke Henry White, *b* 20 Sept. 1990.

**ANNANDALE AND HARTFELL,** 11th Earl of, *cr* 1662 (S) with precedence to 1643; **Patrick Andrew Wentworth Hope Johnstone of Annandale and of that Ilk;** Earl of the territorial earldom of Annandale and Hartfell, and of the Lordship of Johnstone; Hereditary Steward of the Stewartry of Annandale; Hereditary Keeper of the Castle of Lochmaben; Chief of the Name and Arms of Johnstone; landowner; Vice-Lord Lieutenant, Dumfries and Galloway Region, districts of Nithsdale, Annandale and Eskdale, 1992–2016; *b* 19 April 1941; *s* of Major Percy Wentworth Hope Johnstone of Annandale and of that Ilk, TD (*d* 1983) (*de jure* 10th Earl) and Margaret Jane (*d* 1998), *d* of Herbert William Francis Hunter-Arundell; claim to earldom admitted by Committee for Privileges, House of Lords, 1985; *m* 1969, Susan Josephine, *d* of late Col Walter John Macdonald Ross, CB, OBE, MC, TD, Netherhall, Castle Douglas; one *s* one *d*. *Educ:* Stowe School; RAC, Cirencester. Member: Dumfries CC, 1970–75; Dumfries and Galloway Regional Council, 1974–86; Scottish Valuation Advisory Council, 1983–85. Director: Bowring Members Agency, 1985–88; Murray Lawrence Members Agency, 1988–92; Solway River Purification Bd, 1970–86; Raehills Farms Ltd, 1997–; Skairfield Ltd, 1998–; Maclay Gp plc, 2001–15; Dir and Trustee, River Annan Trust, 2010–17; Chm., River Annan District Fishery Bd, 1988–2012. Chm., Royal Jubilee and Prince's Trusts for Dumfries and Galloway, 1984–88. Underwriting Member of Lloyds, 1976–2004. DL Nithsdale and Annandale and Eskdale, 1987. *Recreations:* golf, shooting. *Heir: s* Lord Johnstone, *qv*. *Address:* Annandale Estates Office, St Ann's, Lockerbie, Dumfriesshire DG11 1HQ. *Clubs:* Puffin's, New (Edinburgh).

**ANNAS, Rt Rev. Geoffrey Peter;** Area Bishop of Stafford, 2010–19; *b* London, 29 Nov. 1953; *s* of Derek and Betty Annas; *m* 1987, Ann Clover; one *s* one *d*. *Educ:* Therfield County Secondary Sch., Leatherhead; Univ. of Leicester (BA Hons Sociol. 1975; DipSW, CQSW 1977); Salisbury and Wells Theol Coll. (BTh Hons Southampton 1983). Sen. Social Worker, Surrey CC, 1975–80; ordained deacon, 1983, priest, 1984; Curate, Holy Trinity with St Matthew, Elephant and Castle, Dio. of Southwark, 1983–87; Team Vicar, St Christopher's, Walworth, and Coll. Missioner, Pembroke Coll., Cambridge, 1987–94; Vicar, St Christopher's, Thornhill, Southampton, 1994–2010; Theatre Chaplaincy UK (formerly Actors' Church Union): Chaplain, Mayflower Th., Southampton, 1996–2010; Regent Th., Stoke on Trent, 2011–; Mem. Council, 2009–. Asst Area Dean, Southampton, 2007–10; Canon, Winchester Cathedral, 2007–10. *Recreations:* theatre (Theatre Chaplaincy UK Chaplain of Regent Theatre, Stoke on Trent), holidays in Greece.

**ANNESLEY,** family name of **Earl Annesley** and **Viscount Valentia.**

**ANNESLEY,** 12th Earl *cr* 1789 (Ire.), of Castelwellan, co. Down; **Michael Robert Annesley;** Baron Annesley 1758; Viscount Glerawly 1766; *b* Egham, Surrey, 4 Dec. 1933; 3rd *s* of 9th Earl Annesley and Nora, *y d* of Walter Harrison; *S* brother, 2011; *m* 1956, Audrey Mary Goodwright (*d* 2013); two *s* one *d*. *Educ:* Sir Henry Strode's Sch., Egham; No 1 Sch. of Tech. Training, RAF Halton. RAF, 1949–73: aircraft engineer and aircrew, then Warrant Officer, retd. Flight simulator engineer and sen. installation mgr, 1976–91. *Recreation:* classic motorcycle racing. *Heir: er s* Viscount Glerawly, *qv*.

**ANNESLEY, (Arthur) Noël (Grove);** Hon. Chairman, Christie's UK (formerly Christie's International UK Ltd), since 2004; *b* 28 Dec. 1941; *s* of late E. P. Grove Annesley, OBE and Ruth, *d* of A. Norman Rushforth; *m* 1968, Caroline Lumley; two *s*. *Educ:* Harrow Sch. (entrance schol.); Worcester Coll., Oxford (Open Schol. in classics; MA). Joined Christie Manson & Woods Ltd, fine art auctioneers, 1964; founded Dept of Prints, Drawings and Watercolours; auctioneer, 1967–; holds world records for Michelangelo and Leonardo da Vinci drawings and for British watercolours (J. M. W. Turner); authority on Old Master Drawings; discoveries incl. drawings by Michelangelo, Sebastiano del Piombo, Raphael and Rubens; Dep. Chm., 1985–91; Dir, Christie's Internat. plc, 1989–98 (Dep. Chm., 1992–98); Dep. Chm., Christie's Fine Art Ltd, 1998–2000; Chairman: Christie's Fine Art Specialist Gp, 2000–03; Christie's Educn, 2000–11. Mem. Adv. Panel, Nat. Heritage Meml Fund, 2006–12. Mem. Council, American Mus. in Britain, 1988–; Trustee: Villiers David Foundn, 1996–2009; Dulwich Picture Gall., 1999–2010 (Vice Chm., 2006–10); Yehudi Menuhin Sch., 2000–16 (Chm., Appeal Cttee to raise funds for concert hall, 2000–05); Michael Marks Charitable Trust, 2007–. *Publications:* contribs to specialist books and jls. *Recreations:* music (especially chamber), exploring classical sites, gardening. *Address:* c/o Christie's, 8 King Street, St James's, SW1Y 6QT. *T:* (020) 7389 2241. *Clubs:* Brooks's, Garrick, MCC.

**ANNESLEY, Sir Hugh (Norman),** Kt 1992; QPM 1986; Chief Constable, Royal Ulster Constabulary, 1989–96; *b* 22 June 1939; *s* of late William Henry Annesley and of Agnes May (*née* Redmond); *m* 1970, Elizabeth Ann (*née* MacPherson) (*d* 2016); one *s* one *d*. *Educ:* St Andrew's Prep. Sch., Dublin; Avoca Sch. for Boys, Blackrock. Joined Metropolitan Police, 1958; Chief Supt, 1974; Police Staff College: Special Course, 1963; Intermed. Comd Course, 1971; Sen. Comd Course, 1975; Asst Chief Constable, Personnel and Ops, Sussex Police, 1976; RCDS 1980; Metropolitan Police, Deputy Assistant Commissioner: Central and NW London, 1981; Personnel, 1983; Dir, Force Re-organisation Team, 1984; Assistant Commissioner: Personnel and Training, 1985; Specialist Ops, 1987. Graduate:

Nat. Exec. Inst., FBI, 1986; Mem. Exec. Cttee, Interpol (British Rep.), 1987–90, and 1993–94. Bd of Govs, Burgess Hill Sch. for Girls, 1997 (Chm. Govs, 2000–05). *Recreations:* hockey, sailing. *Address:* Brooklyn, 65 Knock Road, Belfast BT5 6LE.

**ANNESLEY, Noël;** *see* Annesley, A. N. G.

**ANNETTS, Deborah Claire;** Chief Executive, Incorporated Society of Musicians, since 2008; *b* 7 Oct. 1960; *d* of Robert John Annetts and Patricia Margaret Annetts; *m* 2008, Simon Thomsett. *Educ:* St Albans Girls' Grammar Sch.; St Hilda's Coll., Oxford (BA PPE 1983). Admitted solicitor, 1989; Hd, Employment Law, 1994–99, Partner, 1998–99, Stephens Innocent, solicitors; Partner and Hd, Employment Law, Tarlo Lyons, Solicitors, 1999–2000; Asst Dir, Public Concern at Work, 2000–01; Chief Executive: Voluntary Euthanasia Soc., subseq. Dignity in Dying, 2001–07; YWCA, 2007. Board Member: London Museums Agency, 2001–03; Medic Alert, 2003–07 (Vice Chair, 2005–07); Law Soc. Charity, 2003–09; Fair Trials International, 2008– (Chair, 2014–); Nat. Music Council, 2009–12; Music Educn Council, 2009– (Chm., 2010–13); NYO, 2011–13; Educnl Resource Agency, 2011– (Interim Chair, 2012–13; Chair, 2013–). *Recreations:* music, theatre, film, social history, tennis, yoga. *Address:* Incorporated Society of Musicians, 4/5 Inverness Mews, W2 3JQ.

**ANNING, Raymon Harry,** CBE 1982; QPM 1975; Commissioner of Police, The Royal Hong Kong Police Force, 1985–90; *b* 22 July 1930; *s* of Frederick Charles Anning and Doris Mabel Anning (*née* Wakefield); *m* 1949, Beryl Joan Boxall; one *s* (and one *d* decd). *Educ:* Richmond and East Sheen Grammar School. Army (East Surrey Regt and Royal Military Police), 1948–50. Metropolitan Police, 1952–79: Constable to Chief Supt, Divisions and Headquarters, 1952–69; Officer i/c Anguilla Police Unit, W Indies, 1969; Chief Supt i/c Discipline Office, New Scotland Yard, 1970–72; Commander i/c A 10 (Complaints Investigation) Branch, NSY, 1972–75; seconded to Hong Kong Govt, 1974; Dep. Asst Commissioner C (CID) Dept, 1975–78; Inspector of Metropolitan Police (Dep. Asst Comr), 1979; HM Inspector of Constabulary for England and Wales, 1979–83; Dep. Comr of Police, Hong Kong, 1983–85. Graduate of Nat. Exec. Inst., FBI Academy, Quantico, Virginia, USA, 1979. *Recreation:* walking. *Clubs:* Royal Automobile; Hong Kong Golf.

**ANNIS, Francesca;** actress; *b* 1945. *Theatre:* Royal Shakespeare Company: Romeo and Juliet, 1976; Troilus and Cressida, 1976; Luciana in Comedy of Errors, 1976; Natalya in A Month in the Country, NT, 1981; Masha in Three Sisters, Albery, 1987; Melitta in Mrs Klein, NT, 1988; Rosmersholm, Young Vic, 1992; Lady Windermere's Fan, Albery, 1994; Hamlet, Hackney Empire, 1995; Ghosts, Comedy, 2001; The Vortex, Donmar Warehouse, 2002; Blood, Royal Court, 2003; Henry IV, Donmar Warehouse, 2004; The Shoreditch Madonna, Soho Th.; Epitaph for George Dillon, Comedy, 2005; Time and the Conways, NT, 2009; Company, Sheffield Crucible, 2011; Versailles, Donmar Warehouse, 2014; The Children, Royal Court, 2016, transf. NY, 2017. *Films* include: Penny Gold, 1972; Macbeth, 1973; Krull, 1983; Dune, 1984; The Golden River; Under the Cherry Moon; The Debt Collector, 1999; The Libertine, 2004; Revolver, 2005; Shifty, 2009. *Television:* A Pin to see the Peepshow, 1973; Madame Bovary, 1975; Stronger than the Sun, 1977; The Ragazza, 1978; Lillie (series), 1978; Partners in Crime (series), 1983; Inside Story (series), 1986; Parnell and the Englishwoman, Absolute Hell, 1991; The Gravy Train Goes East (series), 1991; Between the Lines (series), 1993; Reckless (series), 1997; Deadly Summer, 1997; Wives and Daughters, Milk, 1999; Deceit, 2000; Jericho, 2005; Cranford, 2007, 2009; The Little House, 2010; Loving Miss Hatto, 2012; Home Fires (series), 2015. *Address:* c/o Independent Talent Group Ltd, 40 Whitfield Street, W1T 2RH.

**ANSBRO, David Anthony;** Chairman, SFL Ltd, 2006–10; *b* 3 April 1945; *s* of late David T. Ansbro and Kathleen Mary Ansbro (*née* Mallett); *m* 1967, Veronica Mary (*née* Auton); two *d. Educ:* Xaverian Coll., Manchester; Leeds Univ. (LLB Hons). Articled to Town Clerk, Leeds, 1966–69; admitted Solicitor, 1969; Solicitor, Leeds City Council, 1969–73; Asst Dir of Admin, 1973–77, Dep. Dir of Admin, 1977–81, W Yorks County Council; Town Clerk and Chief Exec., York City Council, 1981–85; Chief Exec., Kirklees Council, 1985–87; Rees & Co., Solicitors, Huddersfield, 1987–88; Chief Exec., Leeds City Council, 1988–91; Partner, Hepworth & Chadwick, then Eversheds, 1991–2003, Managing Partner, 2000–03; Managing Partner, Eversheds, Leeds and Manchester, 1995–2000. Consultant, Grant Thornton, 2003–08. Mem., Local Govt Commn for England, 1992–95. Dir, Leeds TEC, 1990–99; Chm., Leeds Renaissance Partnership, 2005–10. Pro-Chancellor, Leeds Univ., 2000–07. Chm., Airton Parish Meeting, 2011–. Trustee: Henry Moore Foundn, 2003–10; Nat. Centre for Early Music, 2003–09. Hon. LLD Leeds, 2007. Papal Medal Pro Ecclesia et Pontifice, 1982; KSG 2008. *Recreations:* family, friends, golf, watching Manchester City, visiting Thorpeness and Singapore. *Address:* The Green, Airton, Skipton, N Yorks BD23 4AH. *T:* (01729) 830451. *Clubs:* Honley Cricket; Skipton Golf; Thorpeness Golf; Wharfedale Rugby Union Football.

**ANSELL, His Honour Anthony Ronald Louis;** a Circuit Judge, 1995–2016, a Deputy Circuit Judge, since 2016; a Deputy High Court Judge, Family Division, 2009–16; *b* 9 Sept. 1946; *s* of Samuel Ansell and Joan Ansell; *m* 1970, Karen Kaye; one *s* one *d. Educ:* Dulwich Coll.; University Coll. London (LLB). Called to the Bar, Gray's Inn, 1968; in practice at the Bar, 1968–80; admitted Solicitor, 1980; in practice as solicitor, 1980–95; Asst Recorder, 1987–91; Recorder, 1991–95; a Judge of Employment Appeal Tribunal, 2002–10. Member: Sentencing Adv. Panel, 2005–10; Parole Bd, 2016–. Vice-Pres., United Synagogue, 1997–. *Publications:* (jtly) A Time for Change: the Kalms review of United Synagogue, 1992. *Recreations:* walking, opera, Chelsea Football Club.

**ANSELL, Caroline Julie Porte;** *b* 1971; *m* 1997, Nicholas Ansell; three *s. Educ:* Royal Holloway Coll., Univ. of London (BA French); MEd 2001. NPQH. Teacher; Schs Inspector. Mem. (C) Eastbourne BC, 2012–15. MP (C) Eastbourne, 2015–17; contested (C) same seat, 2017.

**ANSELL, Maj.-Gen. Nicholas George Picton,** CB 1992; OBE 1980; JP, DL; Clerk of the Course, Exeter Racecourse, 1995–2002; Director, Devon and Exeter Steeplechases Ltd, 2003–07; *b* 17 Aug. 1937; *s* of Col Sir Michael Ansell, CBE, DSO and Victoria Jacintha Fleetwood Fuller; *m* 1961, Vivien, *e d* of Col Anthony Taylor, DSO, MC; two *s* one *d. Educ:* Wellington Coll.; Magdalene Coll., Cambridge (MA). Commnd into 5th Royal Inniskilling Dragoon Guards, 1956; served BAOR, Libya, Cyprus; sc Camberley, 1970; Bde Major RAC HQ 1 (BR) Corps, 1971–72; Instructor Staff Coll., 1976–77; CO 5th Royal Inniskilling Dragoon Guards, 1977–80; Col GS Staff Coll., 1980–81; comd 20 Armd Bde, 1982–83; RCDS, 1984; Dep. Chief of Staff HQ BAOR, 1985–86; Dir, RAC, 1987–89; Sen. DS, Army, RCDS, 1990–92. Chm., Army Ornithol Soc., 1989–95. JP N Devon, 1994; DL Devon, 1996; High Sheriff, Devon, 2002–03. *Recreations:* fishing, bird watching, horse racing. *Address:* The Potting Shed, Pillhead, Bideford, Devon EX39 4NF.

**ANSELL, Rachel Louise;** QC 2014; *b* Amersham, Bucks, 14 June 1973; *d* of Michael and Laraine Ansell. *Educ:* St Clement Danes Sch., Chorleywood; Downing Coll., Cambridge (BA 1st Cl. Law 1994). Called to the Bar, Middle Temple, 1995. *Recreations:* avid Rugby fan supporting Wales and Saracens (season ticket holder) and cricket enthusiast supporting England cricket team and Middlesex County Cricket Club; working out at the gym, going to the ballet and opera. *Address:* 4 Pump Court, Temple, EC4Y 7AN. *T:* (020) 7842 5555, *Fax:* (020) 7583 2036. *E:* ransell@4pumpcourt.com.

**ANSIP, Andrus;** Member (Eesti Reformierakond), European Parliament, since 2019; Prime Minister of Estonia, 2005–14; *b* Tartu, Estonia, 1 Oct. 1956; *m*; three *d. Educ:* Tartu Univ. (Dip. Chem. 1979); York Univ., Toronto (Business Mgt 1992). Hd, Tartu Regl Office, Jt Venture Estkompexim, 1989–93; Mem., Bd of Dirs, Rahvapank (People's Bank), 1993–95; Chairman, Management Board: Radio Tartu Ltd, 1994–98; Fondijuhtide AS (Fundmanager Ltd), 1995–96; Livonia Privatization IF, 1995–96; Bankruptcy Trustee, Tartu Commercial Bank, 1995–98; Mayor of Jartu, 1998–2004; Minister of Econ. Affairs and Communications, Estonia, 2004–05; Mem. and a Vice-Pres., EC, 2014–19. Mem., Estonia Reform Party. Order of White Star, 3rd Cl. (Estonia), 2005; Officer, Nat. Order of Merit (Malta), 2001. *Address:* European Parliament, 60 rue Wiertz, 1047 Brussels, Belgium.

**ANSON,** family name of **Earl of Lichfield**.

**ANSON, Viscount; (Thomas) Ossian (Patrick Wolfe) Anson;** *b* 20 May 2011; *s* and heir of Earl of Lichfield, *qv*.

**ANSON, Andrew Edward;** Chief Executive Officer, British Olympic Association, since 2019 (non-executive Director, 2011–19); *b* Oldham, Lancs, 28 Oct. 1964; *s* of Kenneth Anson and Sheila Anson; *m* 1996, Lisa May Whewell (*see* L. M. W. Anson); two *s* one *d. Educ:* Oulder Hill Sch., Rochdale; Exeter Coll., Oxford (BA Maths 1986); INSEAD Business Sch. (MBA (distinction) 1993). Andersen Consulting, 1988–93; Kalchas Gp, 1994–96; Walt Disney Co., 1996–99; Channel Four Television Ltd, 1999–2001; OC&C Strategy Consultants, 2001–04; Commercial Dir, Manchester United plc, 2004–07; Chief Executive Officer: ATP Europe, 2007–09; England 2018, 2009–10; Kitbag Ltd, 2011–17; Goals Soccer plc, 2018–19. Non-executive Director: UTV Media plc, 2012–16; Racecourse Media Gp, 2017–. *Recreations:* cycling, golf, football, guitar. *Address:* British Olympic Association, 101 New Cavendish Street, W1W 6XH. *T:* (020) 7842 5700. *E:* andy.anson@teamgb.com. *Club:* Royal Automobile.

**ANSON, Charles Vernon,** CVO 1996 (LVO 1983); DL; Vice Chairman, Cubitt Consulting PR, 2002–17 (non-executive Director, 2001–18); *b* 11 March 1944; *s* of Philip Vernon Anson and Stella Anson; *m* 1st, 1976, Clarissa Rosamund Denton (marr. diss. 2005); one *s* one *d*; 2nd, 2009, Juliet Nicolson, *qv*. *Educ:* Lancing College; Jesus College, Cambridge (BA History). Joined Diplomatic Service, 1966; Third, later Second Sec. (Commercial), Washington, 1968–71; FCO, 1971–74; Asst Private Sec. to Minister of State, 1974–76; Second Sec. (Commercial), Tehran, 1976–79; seconded to Press Office, 10 Downing St, 1979–81; First Sec. (Inf.), Washington, 1981–85; FCO, 1985–87; Dir of Public Relations, Kleinwort Benson, 1987–90; Press Sec. to the Queen, 1990–97; Gp Corporate Relns Dir, Grand Metropolitan, later Diageo plc, 1997–98; Hd of Communications, EBU, 1998–2000; Dir of Corporate Commns, Hilton Gp, 2000–01; Communications Advr, The Queen's Golden Jubilee Weekend Trust, 2001–02. Mem., Press Complaints Commn, 2012–14. Mem., Regl Adv. Bd for London and SE, Nat. Trust, 2013–. Non-exec. Dir, Siren Communications, 2003–. Trustee: Elizabeth Finn Trust, 2002–08; Brogdale Horticultural Trust, 2008–18; Sussex Heritage Trust, 2015–; Cumberland Lodge, 2017–. Chm., S Downs Jt Cttee, 2009–11. DL E Sussex, 2011. *Address:* Winton House, Winton Street, Alfriston, E Sussex BN26 5UH. *T:* (01323) 871769. *Club:* Hurlingham.

**ANSON, Dame Elizabeth (Audrey), (Lady Anson),** DBE 1995; JP, DL; Chairman, Independent Appeals Authority for School Examinations, 1990–99; Independent Monitor to Parliament on Entry Clearance Refusals, 1994–2000; *b* 9 Jan. 1931; *d* of late Rear-Adm. Sir Philip Clarke, KBE, CB, DSO, and Audrey (*née* White); *m* 1955, Rear-Adm. Sir Peter Anson, 7th Bt (*d* 2018); two *s* two *d. Educ:* Weirfield Sch., Taunton; Royal Naval Sch., Haslemere; King's Coll., London (LLB). Called to Bar, Inner Temple, 1953; joined Western Circuit, 1953; practice at Bar, 1952–56; part-time Adjudicator, 1979–87, an Adjudicator, 1987–91, Immigration Appeals. Councillor, Waverley Bor. Council, 1974–95, Mayor, 1987–89. Association of District Councils of England and Wales: Mem., 1983–95; Vice-Chm., 1989–91; Chm., 1991–93; Dep. Chm., and Chm. Exec. Cttee, 1993–95; Chm., Housing and Environmental Health Cttee, 1987–89. Dep. Chm., Local Govt Management Bd, 1991–93; Member: Local Govt Audit Commn, 1987–90; Cons. Nat. Local Govt Adv. Cttee, 1991–95; Nat. Union Exec. Cttee, 1992–95; Local and Central Govt Relations Res. Cttee, Joseph Rowntree Meml Trust, 1992–96; EU Cttee of the Regions, 1993–98; Packaging Standards Council, 1992–96. Chm., Eagle Radio (formerly Surrey and NE Hampshire Radio Ltd, then County Sound Radio Network Ltd), 1994–2006. Chm., Nat. Mobility Scheme, 1987–88. Mem. Council and Chm. W Surrey Br., IoD, 2002–05; Chair of Judges, Surrey Business Awards, 2005–07. Vice President: Inst. of Envmtl Health Officers, 1989–2001; Assoc. of Drainage Authorities, 1995–2010. Vice Pres., SW Surrey Conservative Assoc., 2006–15 (Pres. 2003–06). Mem. Schs Forum, Hants CC, 2005–10. Gov., Rowledge C of E Primary Sch., 1981–2013 (Chm., 1995–2003). President: Farnham Venison Dinner, 2012–18 (Chm., 2005–10); Farnham and Alton Talking Newspapers, 2012–. FRSA 1992. JP 1977, DL 1984, Surrey. *Recreations:* travel, needlecraft, swimming. *Address:* Rosefield, Rowledge, Farnham, Surrey GU10 4AT. *T:* (01252) 792724.

See also Sir P. R. Anson, Bt.

**ANSON, Sir John,** KCB 1990 (CB 1981); Second Permanent Secretary (Public Expenditure), HM Treasury, 1987–90; *b* 3 Aug. 1930; *yr s* of Sir Edward Anson, 6th Bt, and Alison (*née* Pollock) (*d* 1997); *m* 1957, Myrica Fergie-Woods; one *s* two *d* (and one *s* decd). *Educ:* Winchester; Magdalene Coll., Cambridge (MA; Smith's Prize). Served in HM Treasury, 1954–68; Financial Counsellor, British Embassy, Paris, 1968–71; Asst Sec., 1971–72, Under-Sec., 1972–74, Cabinet Office; Under-Sec., 1974–77, Dep. Sec., 1977–87, HM Treasury; Economic Minister, British Embassy, Washington, and UK Exec. Dir, IMF and World Bank, 1980–83. Chairman: Public Finance Foundn, 1991–94; Retirement Income Inquiry, 1994–96. Hon. Treas., Council of Churches for Britain and Ireland, 1990–92; Chair, House of Laity, Southwark Diocesan Synod, 1996–97.

**ANSON, Lisa Mary Whewell;** Chief Executive Officer, Redx Pharmaceuticals, since 2018; President, Association of British Pharmaceutical Industry, since 2017; *b* Amersham, 26 April 1968; *d* of Roger and Elaine Whewell; *m* 1996, Andrew Edward Anson, *qv*; two *s* one *d. Educ:* Cheltenham Ladies' Coll.; St John's Coll., Cambridge (BA 1st Cl. Natural Scis); INSEAD, Fontainebleau (MBA (Dist.) 1993). Consultant, KPMG, London, 1990–96; Vice Pres., Strategy and Business Develt, Salick Health Care, Calif, 1996–2000; Dir roles, AstraZeneca UK/US, 2000–05; Vice Pres. roles, incl. Vice Pres., Oncol., AstraZeneca plc, 2005–12; Pres., AstraZeneca UK, 2012–18. Gov., Wilmslow Prep. Sch. *Recreations:* walking, Scotland, eventing. *Address:* Redx Pharmaceuticals, 33 Mereside, Alderley Park, Cheshire SK10 4TG. *T:* (01625) 521165. *E:* lmwanson@outlook.com.

**ANSON, Sir Philip (Roland),** 8th Bt *cr* 1831; pharmacist, Alliance-Boots UK Ltd, since 2008; *b* 4 Oct. 1957; *s* of Rear-Adm. Sir Peter Anson, 7th Bt and of Dame Elizabeth (Audrey) Anson, *qv*; S father, 2018. *Educ:* Charterhouse; Chelsea Coll., London (BPharm

Hons 1979). MRPharmS 1980. Pharmacist: Boots, 1979–84; Waremoss Ltd, 1984–96; Moss Chemists, 1996–2008. Chm., SE Reg., Royal Pharmaceutical Soc., 1996–98. *Heir: brother* Hugo William Anson [*b* 30 April 1962; *m* 1986, Sharon, *d* of L. J. Gardner; one *s* two *d*]. *Address:* 34 Martello Road, Eastbourne, E Sussex BN22 7SS. *T*: (01323) 411906, *Fax:* 0872 115 0963. *E*: Ansonpr@aol.com.

**ANSTEE, Eric Edward,** FCA; *b* 1 Jan. 1951; *s* of Reginald Thomas Anstee and Margaret Doris Anstee (*née* Hampshire); *m* 1982, Suzanne Joy Piller; one *s* three *d*. *Educ:* St Albans Sch. FCA 1974. Ernst and Young: London and Singapore, 1974–83; on secondment as Commercial Accountancy Advr to HM Treasury, 1983–86; Partner, London, 1986–93; Gp Finance Dir, Eastern Electricity plc, 1993–95; Advr to Lord Hanson, Hanson plc, 1995–96; Group Finance Director: Energy Gp plc, 1996–98; Old Mutual plc, 1998–2000; Chief Executive: Old Mutual Financial Services plc, 2000–01; Old Mutual Asset Management Inc., 2000–01; non-exec. Chm., Mansell plc, 2001–03; Chief Exec., ICAEW, 2003–06; Chief Exec., City of London Gp, 2009–13. Non-executive Director: Severn Trent plc, 1999–2003; Insight Investment Funds Mgt Ltd, 2006–; Insight Investment Mgt (Global) Ltd, 2006–; Financial Reporting Council, 2007–11; Paypoint plc, 2008–15; Sun Life Financial of Canada (UK) Ltd, 2011–19; Vocalink Hldgs Ltd, 2015–17; One Savings Bank plc, 2015–; Chm., CPP Gp plc, 2015. Chm., Eastern Reg. Industrial Develt Bd, DTI, 1993–99. Mem., Takeover Panel Appeals Bd, 2006–. FFA 2007–15. *Recreations:* tennis, golf, gardening. *E*: e.anstee@btinternet.com.

**ANSTEE, Nicholas John,** FCA; Senior Director, King & Wood Mallesons LLP (formerly S J Berwin LLP), since 2007; Lord Mayor of London, 2009–10; *b* 27 May 1958; *s* of Wing Comdr Peter John Anstee and Ann Tudor Anstee (*née* Price); *m* 1983, Claire Mary Carson Cooper; three *d*. *Educ:* Stamford Sch. ICAEW 1982; FCA 1987. Dearden Farrow, 1984–86; Binder Hamlyn, 1987–94; Partner, Andersen, 1994. Director: London Marathon, 2004–; Barts and The London Charity, 2008–. Common Councilman, City of London, 1987–96; Alderman, Aldersgate Ward, 1996–; Sheriff, City of London, 2003–04; Liveryman: Butchers' Co., 1996– (Master, 2014–15); Plaisterers' Co., 2005–. Mem., Adv. Council, LSO, 2010–. Trustee, Cricket Foundn, 2010–. Governor: City of London Sch. for Girls, 1993–2003; Christ's Hosp., 1996–; King Edward Sch., 1996–. KStJ 2010. *Recreations:* marathon running, cricket, tennis. *Address:* 8 Wallside, Monkwell Square, Barbican, EC2Y 8BH. *T*: (020) 7588 6851. *E*: nick.anstee@btinternet.com. *Clubs:* Aldersgate Ward, MCC.

**ANSTRUTHER, Sir Sebastian Paten Campbell,** 9th Bt *cr* 1694 (NS), of Balcaskie, and 14th Bt *cr* 1700 (NS) of Anstruther; *b* 13 Sept. 1962; *s* of Sir Ian Fife Campbell Anstruther of that Ilk, 8th, 13th and 10th Bt and Susan Margaret Walker (*née* Paten); *S* to father's NS Baronetcies, 2007; *m* 1992, Pornpan Pinitwong, Thailand; one *s* one *d*. *Heir: s* Maximilian Sengtawan Pinitwong Anstruther, *b* 27 Jan. 1995. *Address:* The Barlavington Estate Office, Dye House Lane, Duncton Mill, Petworth, W Sussex GU28 0LF.

**ANSTRUTHER-GOUGH-CALTHORPE, Sir Euan (Hamilton),** 3rd Bt *cr* 1929; Director, Calthorpe Holdings Ltd, since 2000; *b* 22 June 1966; *s* of Niall Hamilton Anstruther-Gough-Calthorpe (*d* 1970) and of Martha Rodman (who *m* 2nd, 1975, Sir Charles C. Nicholson, Bt, *qv*), *d* of Stuart Warren Don; *S* grandfather, 1985; *m* 1st, 2002, Anna Joan Wright (marr. diss. 2015); two *s* two *d*; 2nd, 2017, Susannah Ellen Muffley Prins. *Educ:* Hawtreys, Savernake Forest; Harrow School; Royal Agricultural Coll., Cirencester (Dip. in Estate Mgt). Pres., Birmingham Botanical Gdns, 1985–99. Director: STG Hldgs plc, 1999–2004; Estate Insce Gp, 1999–2003; Enterprise Heritage Capital Ltd, 2000–06; HTTP Technol. Inc., 2000–03; Richmond & Hampshire Ltd, 2001–; Beck & Call Delivery Ltd, 2001–04; Quantum Land Ltd, 2005–11; Capstone Foster Care Ltd, 2007–. DUniv Birmingham, 2008. *Heir: s* Barnaby Charles Anstruther-Gough-Calthorpe, *b* 28 Oct. 2005. *Clubs:* Brooks's; Edgbaston Priory (Pres., 1985–).

**ANTELME, Alexander John;** QC 2014; *b* London, 2 Oct. 1968; *s* of late Leopold Antelme and of Patricia Antelme (*née* Kane); *m* 1992, Rachel Alexa McMullen; one *s* two *d*. *Educ:* St Bede's, Bishton Hall, Staffs; Douai Sch.; Berks; Exeter Coll., Oxford (Open Schol.; MA Hons); City Univ., London (DipLaw). Called to the Bar, Gray's Inn, 1993; in practice as barrister, 1994–. *Address:* Crown Office Chambers, 2 Crown Office Row, Temple, EC4Y 7HJ. *T*: (020) 7797 8100.

**ANTHONY, Rear Adm. Derek James,** MBE 1983; Clerk to the Shipwrights' Company, 2003–08; *b* 2 Nov. 1947; *s* of late James Kenwood Anthony and Nora Evelyn Anthony (*née* Honnor); *m* 1970, Denyse Irene Hopper Wright; two *d*. *Educ:* New Beacon Prep. Sch., Sevenoaks; Eastbourne Coll.; BRNC, Dartmouth. Joined Royal Navy, 1966: sea-going appts, HM Ships Opossum, Revenge, Andrew, Oxley, Oberon, Sovereign, 1970–80; CO, HMS Onslaught, 1981–82; Exchange Service, USN, 1982–84; jsdc, 1985; CO, HMS Warspite, 1986–88; CO, Submarine Comd Course, 1988–90; Head, RN Seaman Officers Policy, MoD, 1990–91; CO, HMS Cumberland, 1991–93; Dir, Naval Service Conditions, 1993–96; hcsc, Camberley, 1996; Dep. Flag Officer Submarines, 1996–97; Naval Attaché, Asst Defence Attaché, Washington, and UK Nat. Liaison Rep. to SACLANT, 1997–2000; FO Scotland, Northern England and NI, 2000–03. Chairman: Assoc. of RN Officers, 2004–13; RN Officers' Charity, 2004–13. Trustee and Dir, Medway Kingfisher Trust, 2010–. Liveryman, Shipwrights' Co., 2009–. Mem., Incorp. of Wrights of Glasgow, 2002–. *Recreations:* golf, music, clarinet, history, family, fly fishing. *Address:* Bocton House, Faversham Road, Boughton Lees, Ashford, Kent TN25 4HS. *Clubs:* Royal Navy of 1765 and 1785, Victory Services.

**ANTHONY, Rt Hon. Douglas;** *see* Anthony, Rt Hon. J. D.

**ANTHONY, His Honour Guy;** *see* Anthony, His Honour M. G.

**ANTHONY, Rt Hon. (John) Douglas,** AC 2003; CH 1982; PC 1971; company director and farmer; *b* 31 Dec. 1929; *s* of late H. L. Anthony; *m* 1957, Margot Macdonald Budd; two *s* one *d*. *Educ:* Murwillumbah Primary and High Schs, The King's Sch., Parramatta; Queensland Agricultural Coll. (QDA). MP, Country Party, later National Party, Richmond, NSW, 1957–84, (Mem., Exec. Council, 1963–72, 1975–83). Minister for Interior, 1964–67; Minister for Primary Industry, 1967–71; Dep. Prime Minister and Minister for Trade and Industry, 1971–72; Minister for Overseas Trade, Minerals and Energy, Nov.–Dec. 1975; Dep. Prime Minister and Minister for Trade and Resources, 1975–83. Dep. Leader, Aust. Country Party, 1966–71; Leader, Nat. Country Party, later Nat. Party, 1971–84. Chairman: Pan Australian Mining Ltd, then Mt Leyshon Gold Mines, 1986–92; Resource Finance Corp., 1986–2003; Commonwealth Regl Telecommunications Infrastructure Fund, then Networking Nation, 1997–2002; Director: John Swires & Sons Pty Ltd (Australia), 1987–2007; Clyde Agriculture Ltd, 1988–2008; Normandy Mining Ltd, 1992–2000. Chm. Governing Council, Old Parlt House, 1998–2008. Hon. Fellow, AATSE, 1990. Hon. LLD Victoria Univ. of Wellington, NZ, 1983; DUniv: Sydney, 1997; Southern Cross, 2014. Council Gold Medal, Qld Agricl Coll., 1985. Canberra Medal, 1989; NZ Commemorative Medal, 1990. *Recreations:* golf, fishing, swimming. *Address:* PO Box 71, Murwillumbah, NSW 2484, Australia. *Clubs:* Australian, Royal Sydney Golf (Sydney); Queensland (Brisbane).

**ANTHONY, Louise Frances;** *see* Chunn, L. F.

**ANTHONY, His Honour (Michael) Guy;** a Circuit Judge, 1998–2018; *b* 5 March 1950; *s* of Kenneth Anthony and June Anthony (*née* Gallifent); *m* 1974, Jane Farrer; one *s*. *Educ:* St Paul's Sch.; Magdalen Coll., Oxford (BA 1971; MA). Called to the Bar, Middle Temple, 1972; in practice at the Bar, 1972–98; an Asst Recorder, 1989–93; a Recorder, 1993–98; SE Circuit. Mem., Mental Health Review Tribunal, 2002–14. *Recreations:* travel, reading, spending time with family, Rugby and other sports, opera. *Address:* Dene Edge, 12 Deepdene Wood, Dorking, Surrey RH5 4BG. *T*: (01306) 742622. *Club:* Army and Navy.

**ANTHONY, Robert Brown;** QC (Scot.) 2002; Sheriff of Glasgow and Strathkelvin, 2007–10; *b* Bathgate, 1 June 1962; *s* of Michael Anthony and Elizabeth Campbell Anthony (*née* Brown); *m* 1987, Shona Catherine Struthers; one *s* two *d*. *Educ:* Univ. of Aberdeen (LLB 1983; DipLP 1984). Admitted solicitor, 1984; admitted to Faculty of Advocates, 1988; Advocate Depute, 2001–02; Sen. Advocate Depute, 2002–04; pt-time Sheriff, 2005–07; in practice at Scottish Bar, 2010–13. Part-time Chairman: Judicial Panel, Scottish FA, 2011–16; Anti-Discriminatory Disciplinary Panel, FA, 2013–. Mem., Scottish Criminal Cases Review Commn, 2007. Dir, Scottish Youth FA, Hampden, Glasgow, 2014–. Registered Humanist Celebrant authorised to conduct funerals and legal weddings, Scotland, 2014–.

**ANTHONY, Vivian Stanley;** educational consultant; Reporting Inspector of Independent Schools, 1994–2010; Secretary, Headmasters' and Headmistresses' (formerly Headmasters') Conference, 1990–2000; *b* 5 May 1938; *s* of Captain and Mrs A. S. Anthony; *m* 1969, Rosamund Anne MacDermot Byrn; one *s* one *d*. *Educ:* Cardiff High Sch.; LSE (1st Div. 2nd Cl. Hons BSc Econ); Fitzwilliam Coll., Cambridge (DipEd); Merton Coll., Oxford (schoolmaster student). Asst Master, Leeds Grammar Sch., 1960–64; Asst Master and Housemaster, Tonbridge Sch., 1964–69; Lectr in Educn, Univ. of Leeds, 1969–71; Dep. Headmaster, The King's Sch., Macclesfield, 1971–76; Headmaster, Colfe's Sch., London, 1976–90. Asst Examr, Econ. Hist., London Univ., 1964–71; Asst Examr, Econs, Oxford and Cambridge Bd, 1970–76, Chief Examr (Awarder), Econs, 1976–92; Ext. Examr, Educn, Univs of Manchester, 1972–75, Birmingham, 1975–78, and Lancaster, 1977–79. Mem., DFEE Wkg Gp on Sch. Security, 1996–2000. Chm., Econs Assoc., 1974–77; Member: Schools Council Social Science Cttee, 1976–83; London Univ. Schs Examinations Cttee, 1981–85; Secondary Examinations Council Economics Panel, 1984–89; CBI/Schools Panel, 1984–88. Sabbatical tour, US indep. schools, 1983. Chm., London Area, 1988–89, Mem. Council, 1989–2000, SHA; Headmasters' Conference: elected, 1980; Chm., Academic Policy Cttee, 1988–90 (Mem., 1983–2000); Mem., Professional Develt Cttee, 1985–2004, Teacher Shortage Wkg Party, 1987–88, Assisted Places Cttee, 1987–89; Chm., Records of Achievement Wkg Party, 1987–90; Trng Coordinator, 2000–04; Hon. Associate, 2000. Member: Exec. Cttee, Nat. Professional Qualification for Headship (E Midlands), 1996–99; Exec., Boarding Schs Assoc., 2000–04. Mem., Admiralty Interview Bd, 1980–2004. Comr, Inland Revenue, 1989–90. Mem. Court, Univ. of Kent, 1985–90; Governor: Stamford Sch., 1992–2009 Chm. of Educn, 1996–2009); King's Sch., Macclesfield, 1993–96; Bromsgrove Sch., 1995–2010 (Chm. of Educn, 2001–10); Pres., 2010–18; Vice-Pres., 2018–; Mem., Hd Selection team, 2013); Uppingham Sch., 1996–2006; British Sch. in Colombo, 1999–2007; Hosp. of St John and St Anne Oakham, 2007–16 (Chm. 2010–16); Bromsgrove Internat. Sch. in Thailand, 2009–13. Mem., Uppingham PCC, 2009–12; Chairman: Allexton Parish Meeting, 2005–14; Three Villages Conservation Trust, 2005–15. Member: Uppingham Local Hist. Study Gp, 2005– (Chm., 2014–19; Pres., 2019–); Rutland Arts Soc. (formerly Rutland Decorative and Fine Arts Soc.), 2005–. Volunteer, Churches Conservation Trust, 2003– (Allexton, 2003–16). Founder Chm., 2006–09, Pres., 2009–, Uppingham White Hart Dining Club. Hon. Freeman, Leathersellers' Co., 1990. Hon. FCP 1991. Hon. DEd De Montfort, 1999. *Publications:* Monopoly, 1968, 3rd edn 1976; Overseas Trade, 1969, 4th edn 1981; Banks and Markets, 1970, 3rd edn 1979; Objective Tests in A Level Economics, 1971, 2nd edn 1974; Objective Tests in Introductory Economics, 1975, 3rd edn 1983; History of Rugby Football at Colfe's, 1980; US Independent Schools, 1984; 150 Years of Cricket at Colfe's, 1986; (ed) Head to Head, 1993; (ed) Manual of Guidance, 1995; (ed) Head to HoD, 1998; (ed) Head to House, 2000; Allexton Church Guide, 2007; The Survival of a Village: the history of Allexton, 2009; Good Wit and Capacity: the history of Colfe's School 1972–2002, 2012; The History of Uppingham: principal town of Rutland in 1800, 2015; *contributor:* The Teaching of Economics in Secondary Schools, 1970; Curriculum Development in Secondary Schools, 1973; Control of the Economy, 1974; Comparative Economics in Teaching Economics, 1984; The Search for Standards, 1992; Access and Affordability, 1994; Uppingham in Peacetime, 2007; The History of Uppingham to 1800, 2015; articles in Economics, Leicestershire & Rutland Life. *Recreations:* choral singing (Uppingham Parish Ch Choir, 1990–; Chm., 1998–2004, Pres., 2007–, Leics Chorale; Chm., Youth Find A Voice, 2005–), Rugby football, local and family history, travelling. *Address:* 24 Ayston Road, Uppingham, Rutland LE15 9RL. *T*: (01572) 821674. *Clubs:* East India, Devonshire, Sports and Public Schools, Old Colfeians' Association; Uppingham Probus (Mem., 2000–; Sec., 2008–09; Pres., 2011–12; Speaker Sec., 2012–16; Vice-Pres., 2017–).

**ANTONIADES, Reno Michael;** Managing Partner, Lee & Thompson LLP, since 2012; *b* London, 27 July 1966; *s* of Michael and Joy Antoniades; *m* 1997, Julieanne Cunningham; one *s* one *d*. *Educ:* Alleyn's Sch., Dulwich; Leicester Univ. (LLB Hons 1987). Trainee solicitor, then Solicitor, Herbert Smith, 1989–93; Solicitor: Olswang, 1993–94; Lee & Thompson LLP, 1994–. Mem., Edward Alleyn Club. *Recreations:* cinema, football, family. *Address:* 19 Riggindale Road, SW16 1QL. *T*: 07872 118422. *E*: renoantoniades@leeandthompson.com. *Club:* Soho House.

**ANTONIAZZI, Antonia Louise, (Tonia);** MP (Lab) Gower, since 2017; one *s*. *Educ:* Gorseinon Coll. Former Wales Women's Rugby player. Language teacher; Hd, Mod. Foreign Langs, Ysgol Bryngwyn Sch., until 2017. Member: Welsh Affairs Cttee, 2017–; Women and Equalities Cttee, 2017–. *Address:* House of Commons, SW1A 0AA.

**ANTONIAZZI, Manon Bonner,** LVO 2012 (MVO 1998); PhD; Chief Executive and Clerk, National Assembly for Wales, since 2017; *b* Cardiff, 15 April 1965; *d* of (John) Emyr Jenkins, *qv*; *m* 1991, Jeremy Huw Williams (marr. diss. 2009); one *d*; *m* 2014, John Lawrence Antoniazzi. *Educ:* Llanhari Welsh Comp. Sch.; St John's Coll., Cambridge (BA 1986; PhD 1990). Hd, Press and Public Relns, S4C, 1991–93; Asst Private Sec. to the Prince of Wales, 1994–98; Dir, Communications Services, Nat. Assembly for Wales, 1999–2000; Sec. and Hd of Public Affairs, BBC Wales, 2000–03; Hd, Public Policy, BBC Nations and Regions, 2003–04; Private Sec. for Wales to the Prince of Wales and the Duchess of Cornwall, 2004–12; CEO, Tourism and Mktg, 2012–14, Dir, Tourism Heritage and Sport, then Culture, Sport and Tourism, 2014–17, Welsh Govt. Associate CMi, 2011–12. Mem., Tourism Panel, Welsh Govt, 2011–12. Trustee, Wales: Prince's Trust, 2001–04; Nat. Heritage Meml Fund and Heritage Lottery Fund, 2012–15. Gov. RSC, 2001–04; Non-executive Director: London Philharmonic Orch., 2012–16 RWCMD, 2018–. *Recreations:* music (as a harpist), walking, heritage. *Address:* Nationa Assembly for Wales, Cardiff Bay, Cardiff CF99 1NA. *E*: manon@manonbonner.com *Club:* Royal Automobile.

*See also* F. L. Hague.

**ANTONIAZZI, Tonia;** *see* Antoniazzi, A. L.

**ANTONIW, Michael;** Member (Lab) Pontypridd, National Assembly for Wales, since 2011; *b* 2 Sept. 1954; *s* of Mychajlo Antoniw and Agnes Rigmor Antoniw (*née* Sørensen); *m* 1983, Elaine Baynton; one adopted *s* two adopted *d*. *Educ:* Presentation Coll., Reading; University Coll., Cardiff (LLB Hons). Thompsons Solicitors, 1980–2011, Partner, 1987–2011. Counsel Gen. for Wales, 2016–17. Fellow, Assoc. of Personal Injury Lawyers, 2006–. Vis. Fellow, Univ. of S Wales. *Recreations:* football, playing the mandolin. *Address:* National Assembly for Wales, Cardiff Bay, Cardiff CF99 1NA. *Club:* Llantrisant Working Men's.

**ANTRIM,** 14th Earl of, *cr* 1620; **Alexander Randal Mark McDonnell;** Viscount Dunluce; Keeper of Conservation, 1975–95, and Director (formerly Head) of Collection Services, 1990–95, Tate Gallery; *b* 3 Feb. 1935; *er s* of 13th Earl of Antrim, KBE, and Angela Christina (*d* 1984), *d* of Sir Mark Sykes, 6th Bt; *S* father, 1977 (but continued to be known as Viscount Dunluce until 1995); *m* 1963, Sarah Elizabeth Anne (marr. diss. 1974), 2nd *d* of St John Harmsworth; one *s* two *d*; *m* 1977, Elizabeth, *d* of late Michael Moses Sacher; one *d*. *Educ:* Downside; Christ Church, Oxford; Ruskin Sch. of Art. Restorer: the Ulster Museum, 1969–71; Tate Gall., 1965–75. Dir, Ulster Television, 1982–2000; Chm., Northern Salmon Co. Ltd, 2000–08 (Dir, 2000–14). Mem., Exec. Cttee, City and Guilds Art School, 1983–2009. FRSA 1984. Prime Warden, Fishmongers' Co., 1995–96. *Recreations:* painting, vintage cars. *Heir: s* Viscount Dunluce, *qv. Address:* Deerpark Cottage, Castle Lane, Glenarm, Ballymena, Co. Antrim BT44 0BQ. *Club:* Beefsteak.

**ANTROBUS, Sir Edward (Philip),** 8th Bt *cr* 1815, of Antrobus, Cheshire; *b* 28 Sept. 1938; *er s* of Sir Philip Coutts Antrobus, 7th Bt and his 1st wife, Dorothy Margaret Mary (*d* 1973), *d* of Rev. W. G. Davis; *S* father, 1995; *m* 1st, 1966, Janet Sarah Elizabeth (*d* 1990), *d* of Philip Sceales, Johannesburg; one *s* one *d* (and one *d* decd); 2nd, 1996, Rozanne Penelope, *d* of Neville Simpson. *Educ:* Witwatersrand Univ. (BSc Mining Engrg); Magdalene Coll., Cambridge (MA). *Heir: s* Francis Edward Sceales Antrobus, BSc Eng Cape Town, *b* 24 Oct. 1972. *Address:* 54A 3rd Avenue, Parktown North, 2193 Johannesburg, South Africa.

**ANTROBUS, Simon James;** QC 2018; *b* Croydon, 10 Sept. 1973; *s* of Roger Antrobus and Jean Antrobus; *m* 2005, Nicola Bannon; two *s*. *Educ:* Warden Park Comp. Sch.; Univ. of Sheffield (LLB 1st Cl. Law). Called to the Bar, Inner Temple, 1995; in practice as barrister, specialising in criminal regulatory law, 1995–. *Recreations:* fighting a mid-life crisis with exercise, travelling the world with my family, supporting Chelsea FC.

**ANWYL, Her Honour Shirley Anne;** QC 1979; a Circuit Judge, 1995–2008; Resident Judge, Woolwich Crown Court, 1999–2007; *b* 10 Dec. 1940; *d* of James Ritchie and Helen Sutherland Ritchie; *m* 1969, Robin Hamilton Corson Anwyl (*d* 2016); two *s*. *Educ:* St Mary's Diocesan Sch. for Girls, Pretoria; Rhodes Univ., S Africa (BA, LLB). Called to the South African Bar, 1963; called to the Bar, Inner Temple, 1966, Bencher, 1985. A Recorder, 1981–95; a Dep. High Court Judge, Family Div., 1981–99. Member: Senate of Inns of Court and Bar, 1978–81; Gen. Council of the Bar, 1987; Criminal Injuries Compensation Bd, 1980–95; Mental Health Review Tribunal, 1983–99. Chm., Barristers' Benevolent Assoc., 1989–95. FRSA 1989. Freeman, City of London, 1994; Liveryman, Fruiterers' Co., 1996. *Recreations:* theatre, music, reading. *Address:* 30/31 The Cedars, St George's Park, Ditchling Common, Burgess Hill, E Sussex RH15 0GR. *Club:* Guild of Freemen of City of London.

**ANYAOKU, Eleazar Chukwuemeka, (Emeka),** CFR 2003; CON 1982; Hon. GCVO 2000; Ndichie Chief Adazie of Obosi; Ugwumba of Idemili; Secretary-General of the Commonwealth, 1990–2000; *b* 18 Jan. 1933; *e s* of late Emmanuel Chukwuemeka Anyaoku, Ononukpo of Okpuno Ire, Obosi, Nigeria, and Cecilia Adiba (*née* Ogbogu); *m* 1962, Ebunola Olubunmi, *yr d* of late barrister Olusola Akanbi Solanke, of Abeokuta, Nigeria; three *s* one *d*. *Educ:* Merchants of Light Sch., Oba; Univ. of Ibadan (Schol.), Nigeria; courses in England and France. Exec. Asst, Commonwealth Develt Corp., in London and Lagos, 1959–62. Joined Nigerian Diplomatic Service, 1962; Mem. Nigerian Permanent Mission to the UN, New York, 1963–66; seconded to Commonwealth Secretariat as Asst Dir, 1966–71, and Dir, 1971–75, Internat. Affairs Div.; Asst Sec.-Gen., 1975–77, Dep. Sec.-Gen (Political), 1977–83 and 1984–90, of the Commonwealth. Minister of External Affairs, Nigeria, Nov.–Dec. 1983. Chm., Presidential Adv. Council on Internat. Relns, Nigeria, 2001–. Served as Secretary: Review Cttee on Commonwealth inter-governmental organisations, June–Aug., 1966; Commonwealth Observer Team for Gibraltar Referendum, Aug.–Sept., 1967; Anguilla Commn, WI, Jan.–Sept. 1970; Leader, Commonwealth Mission for Mozambique, 1975; Commonwealth Observer, Zimbabwe Talks, Geneva, 1976; accompanied Commonwealth Eminent Persons Gp, SA, 1986. Pres., Royal Commonwealth Society, London, 2000–08 (Vice-Pres., 1975–2000); Mem. Council, Overseas Develt Inst., 1979–90. Trustee, BM, 2005–13. Mem., Governing Council: SCF, 1984–90; IISS, London, 1987; Mem., Governing Bd, South Centre, Geneva, 2002–10; Hon. Mem., Club of Rome, 1992–. Internat. Pres., WWF, 2001–09. FRSA 1984. Hon. Fellow, Inst. of Educn, Univ. of London, 1994. Hon. DLitt: Ibadan, 1990; Buckingham, 1994; Bradford, 1995; Rhodes, 2002; Lagos, 2010; Internat. Univ. of Geneva, 2010; Paul, Awka, Nigeria, 2014; Hon. DPhil Ahmadu Bello, 1991; Hon. LLD: Nigeria, 1991; Aberdeen, Reading, 1992; Bristol, Oxford Brookes, 1993; Leeds, South Bank, 1994; New Brunswick, North London, 1995; Liverpool, London, 1997; Nottingham. Livingstone Medal, RSGS, 1996. Freeman, City of London, 1998. Trinity Cross, Trinidad and Tobago, 1999; Grand Officer, Nat. Order of Valour, Cameroon, 1999; Comdr, Most Courteous Order of Lesotho, 1999; Order of Welwitchia (1st Class), Namibia, 2000; highest nat. civilian honour, Madagascar, 2005; Supreme Companion of O. R. Tambo (Gold), S Africa, 2008. *Publications:* The Missing Headlines, 1997; The Inside Story of the Modern Commonwealth, 2004; essays in various pubns. *Recreations:* tennis, swimming, reading. *Address:* 36 Lugard Avenue, PO Box 56236, Ikoyi, Lagos, Nigeria. *Clubs:* Travellers; Metropolitan (Lagos).

**AOTEAROA, NEW ZEALAND AND POLYNESIA, Co-Archbishop of;** *see* Polynesia, Bishop of.

**AOUN, Michel;** President, Republic of Lebanon, since 2016; *b* Haret Hreik, 30 Sept. 1933; *s* of Naim and Marie Aoun; *m* 1968, Nadia El-Chami; three *d*. *Educ:* Sch. of Sacré-Coeur, Gemmayzé, Beirut; Military Acad. Army Artillery Comdr, 1976–78; Special Rep. to US Govt for re-equipment of Lebanese Army, 1978; Commander: Defence Bde, 1980–83; Eighth Bde, 1983–84; Comdr in Chief, Armed Forces, 1984–88. Nominated as Prime Minister of Lebanon, Minister of Defence and Minister of Information by Pres., Republic of Lebanon, 1988–90; MP, 2005; Leader, Free Patriotic Movement party, 2005–15; Hd, Change and Reform Parly Bloc, 2005. Commemorative Medal, 1961; Extraordinary Grade, Order of Merit (Lebanon) (Third Grade, 1971; Second Grade, 1983; First Grade, 1986; Grand Cordon); Grand Collar, Nat. Order of the Cedar (Lebanon) (Knight, 1983; Officer, 1988; Grand Cordon, 1988); 4 War Medals; Medal for battle wounds, 1983; Comdr, Légion d'honneur (France) 1986. *Publications:* My Vision of Lebanon, 2007; Ce que je crois, 2017. *Address:* Presidency of the Republic of Lebanon, Baabda, Lebanon. *T:* (5) 900031, *Fax:* (5) 900001. *E:* president_office@presidency.gov.lb. *W:* www.presidency.gov.lb.

**APLIN, Paul Stephen,** OBE 2009; Tax Partner, A C Mole & Sons, since 1992; President, Institute of Chartered Accountants of England and Wales, 2018–19; *b* Taunton, 11 June 1957; *s* of James Aplin and Marjorie Aplin (*née* Townsley); *m* 1991, Sharon Binns. *Educ:* Cambridge Coll. of Arts and Technol. (BSc Jt Hons Biol. and Chem. 1985). ACA 1985, FCA 1996; CTA 1989, CTA (Fellow) 2010. A C Mole & Sons, 1980–. Institute of Chartered Accountants in England and Wales: Mem. Council, 2007– (Chm. Tax Faculty, 2007–09 (Chm., Tech. Cttee, 2010–16); Mem., Tech. Strategy Bd, 2007–09); Mem. Bd, 2015–; Vice Pres., 2016–17; Dep. Pres., 2017–18. Mem., Tech. Cttee, 2010–16, Mem., Council, 2017–, Chartered Inst. of Taxation. Mem., Admin. Burdens Adv. Bd, 2008–, Powers Oversight Forum, 2009–13, HMRC. Mem., Editl Bd, Tax Jl, 2012–. Lectr and broadcaster on tax issues. Freeman, Tax Advisers' Co., 2009 (Liveryman, 2016); Liveryman, Chartered Accountants' Co., 2018. Tax Personality of Year, Taxation Awards, 2007; External Engagement Award, HMRC, 2012; Outstanding Industry Contribution Award, British Accountancy Awards, 2013. *Publications:* contrib. Tax Jl, Taxation, TAXLine, Economia and other tax and accountancy jls. *Recreations:* photography (LRPS 1999), hillwalking and mountaineering, ballroom dancing, reading, theatre, early music, endeavouring (generally unsuccessfully) to stay one intellectual step ahead of my border collie. *Address:* A C Mole & Sons, Stafford House, Blackbrock Park Avenue, Taunton, Somerset TA1 2PX. *T:* (01823) 624450. *E:* paulaplin@acmole.co.uk.

**APPIGNANESI, Dr Lisa,** OBE 2013; FRSL; writer, since 1990; Chair, Royal Society of Literature, since 2016; *b* Poland, 4 Jan. 1946; *d* of Aron Borenstein and Hena Borenstein; *m* 2013, Prof. John Forrester; one *d*; one *s* by a previous marriage. *Educ:* McGill Univ., Montreal (BA 1966; MA 1967); Univ. of Sussex (PhD 1970). Lecturer: Univ. of Essex, 1971–73; New England Coll., 1974–81; Institute of Contemporary Arts: Dir, Talks, 1981–86; Dep. Dir, 1986–90; Mem. Bd, 2001–05. Dep. Pres., 2003–07, Pres., 2008–11, English PEN. Chm., Freud Mus., 2006–14. Vis. Prof., KCL, 2012–. Chair, Man Booker Internat. Prize, 2017–18. FRSL 2015. Chevalier, Ordre des Arts et des Lettres (France), 1987. *Publications: non-fiction:* Dialogue of the Generations, 1974; Femininity and the Creative Imagination: James, Proust and Musil, 1974; The Cabaret: the first hundred years, 1976, 2nd edn 1986 (trans. several langs), 3rd edn 2004; (ed with Steven Rose), Science and Beyond, 1986; Simone de Beauvoir, 1988, 2nd edn 2005 (trans. several langs); (ed) Postmodernism, 1989; (ed) Ideas from France, 1989; (ed with Hilary Lawson) Dismantling Truth, 1989; (ed with Sara Maitland) The Rushdie File, 1989; (with John Forrester) Freud's Women, 1992, 3rd edn 2004 (trans. German, Spanish and other langs); Losing the Dead, 1999, 2nd edn 2014; (ed) Free Expression is No Offence, 2005; Mad, Bad and Sad: a history of women and the mind doctors since 1800, 2008 (BMA Award for Public Understanding of Sci., 2009); All About Love: anatomy of an unruly emotion, 2011; (ed jtly) Fifty Shades of Feminism, 2013; Trials of Passion: crimes in the name of love and madness, 2014; Everyday Madness: on grief, anger, loss and love, 2018; *fiction:* Memory and Desire, 1991; Dreams of Innocence, 1994; A Good Woman, 1996; The Things We Do for Love, 1997; The Dead of Winter, 1999; Sanctuary, 2000; Paris Requiem, 2002, 2nd edn 2014; The Memory Man, 2004 (Holocaust Literature Award, 2005); Sacred Ends, 2014; *translations* include: (with John Berger) Bielski, Oranges for the Son of Alexander Levy, 2000; Latifa, My Forbidden Face: a memoir of an Afghan girl, 2002; (with John Berger) Bielski, The Year is 42, 2003 (Scott Moncrieff Prize for French Trans., 2005); articles in NY Rev. of Books, Guardian, Observer, Independent, Telegraph. *Recreation:* friends. *Address:* c/o Tracy Bohan, Wiley Agency, 17 Bedford Square, WC1B 3JA.

**APPLEBY, His Honour Brian John;** QC 1971; a Circuit Judge, 1988–2003, a Deputy Circuit Judge, since 2003; *b* 25 Feb. 1930; *s* of Ernest Joel and Gertrude Appleby; *m* 1st, 1958, Rosa Helena (*née* Flitterman) (*d* 1996); one *s* one *d*; 2nd, 1998, Lynda Jane Eaton (*d* 2014). *Educ:* Uppingham; St John's Coll., Cambridge (BA). Called to Bar, Middle Temple, 1953; Bencher, 1980. Dep. Chm., Notts QS, 1970–71; a Recorder, 1972–88. Mem., Nottingham City Council, 1955–58 and 1960–63. District Referee, Nottinghamshire Wages Conciliation Board, NCB, 1980–88. President, Court of Appeal: St Helena, 1998–2007; Falkland Is, 2002–07; Indian Ocean Territory, 2002–07. *Recreations:* watching good football (preferably Nottingham Forest). Mem. Club Cttee, 1965–82, Life Mem., 1982; Vice-Chm., 1972–75, Chm., 1975–78); swimming, reading and enjoying, when possible, company of children. *Address:* The Briars, Old Melton Road, Normanton on the Wolds, Nottingham NG12 5NN.

**APPLEBY, Douglas Edward Surtees;** retired Managing Director, The Boots Co. Ltd; *b* 17 May 1929; *s* of Robert Edward Appleby, MSc and Muriel (*née* Surtees); one *s* one *d*; *m* Judith Anne de la Cour. *Educ:* Durham Johnston Sch.; Univ. of London (BSc); Univ. of Nottingham (BSc). Chartered Accountant, 1957. Commissioned, RAF, Cranwell, 1950–54. Moore, Stephens & Co., Chartered Accountants, London, 1954–57; Distillers Co. Ltd, 1957–58; Corn Products Co., New York, 1959–63; Finance Dir, 1964–66, Internat. Man. Dir, 1966–68, Wilkinson Sword Ltd; The Boots Co. Ltd, 1968–81 (Finance Dir, 1968–72, Man. Dir, 1973–81). Regional Dir, Nat. Westminster Bank, 1978–88; Chairman: John H. Mason Ltd, 1982–96; Meadow Farm Produce plc, 1984–86; Sims Food Gp plc, 1987–89. Member Council: Inst. Chartered Accountants, 1971–75; Loughborough Univ., 1973–75; CBI, 1977–81. *Address:* c/o Bank of Scotland, The Mound, Edinburgh EH1 1YZ.

**APPLEBY, Elizabeth;** *see* Appleby, L. E.

**APPLEBY, Dame Hazel Gillian;** *see* Genn, Dame H. G.

**APPLEBY, Prof. (James) Louis (John),** CBE 2006; MD; FRCPE, FRCPsych, FRCP; Professor of Psychiatry, University of Manchester, since 1996; *b* 27 Feb. 1955; *s* of late James Appleby and Doris May Appleby; *m* 1992, Juliet Haselden; two *s* two *d*. *Educ:* Bathgate Acad.; Univ. of Edinburgh (BSc Hons; MB ChB; MD 1995). MRCP 1983, FRCPE 1995; MRCPsych 1986, FRCPsych 1997; FRCP 2008. Sen. Lectr, Univ. of Manchester, 1991–96. Nat. Dir for Mental Health, DoH, 2000–10; Nat. Clinical Dir for Health and Criminal Justice, DoH, 2010–14. Dir, Nat. Confidential Inquiry into suicide and homicide by people with mental illness, 1996–; Chm., Nat. Suicide Prevention Strategy Adv. Gp, 2002–; Ind. Advr, GMC, 2015–16. Non-exec. Dir, Care Quality Commn, 2013–19. Hon. FRCPsych 2011. *Publications:* A Medical Tour Through the Whole Island of Great Britain, 1994, 2nd edn 1995; contrib. numerous res. pubns on suicide, homicide and parental mental illness. *Recreations:* trying to impress my kids, cleaning my clarinet, keeping lists. *Address:* Centre for Mental Health and Safety, University Place, University of Manchester, Oxford Road, Manchester M13 9PL.

**APPLEBY, John Laurence;** Director of Research and Chief Economist, Nuffield Trust, since 2016; *b* 26 April 1958; *s* of Will Appleby and Margaret Sheila Appleby; partner, Claire Helen Melamed; three *s* one *d*. *Educ:* Univ. of Essex (BA Hons Econs 1979); Univ. of York (MSc Health Econs 1981). Economist in NHS, Birmingham and London, 1981–88; Manager of Res., NAHAT, 1988–93; Senior Lecturer in Health Economics: Univ. of Birmingham, 1993–95; Univ. of East Anglia, 1995–98; Chief Economist, King's Fund,

1998–2016. Hon. Vis. Prof., Dept of Econs, City Univ., London, 2002–. *Publications:* Financing Health Care in the 1990s, 1992; (jtly) The Reorganised NHS, 5th edn 1995, 6th edn 1998; numerous book chapters and peer-reviewed papers. *Recreations:* when not painting, reading, iPodding or DIYing, slumped in front of TV with a bottle of wine. *Address:* Nuffield Trust, 59 New Cavendish Street, W1G 7LP.

**APPLEBY, His Honour John Montague;** a Circuit Judge, Northern Circuit, 2003–15; *b* 8 Nov. 1945; *s* of Montague Eric Appleby and Carmen Irene Appleby; *m* 1970, Barbara Joan Plumb; (one *s* decd). *Educ:* Dauntsey's; Univ. of Nottingham (LLB Hons). Admitted solicitor, 1970; Asst Solicitor, Leicester, 1970–72; joined Truman & Appleby, later Truman Close Kendall & Appleby, 1972; Partner, 1974–88; Man. Partner, 1988–98; merged to form Nelsons, 1999; Mem., Mgt Bd, 1999–2000; Partner, 1999–2003; Asst Recorder, 1993–99; Recorder, 1999–2003. Mem. Council, Law Soc., 1984–99; Pres., Notts Law Soc., 1997. Pres., Notts Hockey Assoc., 1994–96. *Publications:* (contrib.) Professional Management of a Solicitor's Practice, 1980. *Recreations:* golf, travel, wine, theatre. *Clubs:* Nottingham Hockey (Vice-Pres.); Nottingham Cricket (Vice-Pres.); Hale Golf.

**APPLEBY, (Lesley) Elizabeth, (Mrs Michael Kenneth Collins);** QC 1979; barrister-at-law; a Deputy High Court Judge, 1985–2006; a Recorder, 1989–2001; *b* 12 Aug. 1942; *o d* of late Arthur Leslie Appleby and Dorothy Evelyn Appleby (*née* Edwards); *m* 1978, Michael Kenneth Collins, OBE, BSc, MICE (*d* 2008); one *s* one *d*. *Educ:* Dominican Convent, Brewood, Staffs; Wolverhampton Girls' High Sch.; Manchester Univ. (LLB Hons). Called to Bar, Gray's Inn, 1965 (Richardson Schol.); ad eundem Lincoln's Inn, 1975, Bencher, 1986, Treas., 2009–10; in practice at Chancery Bar, 1966–2013; inspector of five cos, Dept of Trade, 1983; Chm., Inquiry into Lambeth BC, 1993. Mem., Senate of Inns of Court and Bar, 1977–80, 1981–82. Chm., Ethics and Integrity Cttee, Cons. Party, 1998–2000. *Recreations:* walking, gardening. *Address:* 4/5 Gray's Inn Square, Gray's Inn, WC1R 5AH. *T:* (020) 7404 5252.

**APPLEBY, Lindsay C.;** *see* Croisdale-Appleby, L.

**APPLEBY, Louis;** *see* Appleby, J. L. J.

**APPLEBY, Malcolm Arthur,** MBE 2014; engraver designer, mentor and teacher; *b* 6 Jan. 1946; *s* of James William and Marjory Appleby; *m* 2000, Philippa Swann; one *d*. *Educ:* Hawes Down County Secondary Modern School for Boys; Beckenham Sch. of Art; Ravensbourne Coll. of Art and Design; Central Sch. of Arts and Crafts; Sir John Cass Sch. of Art; Royal Coll. of Art. Set up shop, 1968; bought Crathes station, 1970; moved workshop to Perthshire, 1996; developed fresh approaches to engraving on silver, forging after engraving; created first pure gold and pure silver pieces to bear Scottish hallmark, 1999; works designed and executed include: engraving on Prince of Wales coronet; model of moon (subseq. gift to first moon astronauts); steel and gold cylinder box for Goldsmiths' Co.; steel, gold, ivory and silver chess set, 1977; 500th anniv. silver for London Assay Office; King George VI Diamond Stakes trophy, 1978; seal for the Board of Trustees, V & A; silver condiment set for 10 Downing Street, commnd by Silver Trust; major silver commn for Royal Mus. of Scotland; silver table centre for new Scottish Parlt; gold Royal Medal for RSE, 2000; sporting guns (product designer, Holland & Holland, gunmakers, 1991–97); 'Loving Cups' for 35th anniv. of George Heriot's Sch., Edinburgh, silver bowls, jewels, prints; Banchory Bangle award for Children First charity, annually, 1976–; Diamond Jubilee Jewel; Prime Ministers' catch phrases silver beaker series, 2011–; medal for FIDEM XXXII Art Medal Congress, 2012; Candlesticks for St Giles' Cath., Edinburgh, 2013. Goldsmiths' Craftsmanship and Design Awards: Gold Awards, Trafalgar Medal, 2007, Peacock Bangle, 2008; Silver Award, Raven Beaker, 2009; Gold, Silver and Special Awards for engraving, 2011; Gold and Special Council Award, 2012. Work in collections: Aberdeen Art Gallery; Royal Scottish Museum; Scottish Craft Collection; East Midlands Arts; Fitzwilliam Mus., Cambridge; BM; Goldsmiths' Co.; V&A; Crafts Council; Contemporary Arts Soc.; Tower of London Royal Armouries; Nat. Mus. of Finland; Åland Maritime Mus.; S Australia Maritime Mus.; Perth Art Gall. and Mus.; Ashmolean Mus.; Alice & Louis Koch Collection, Swiss Nat. Mus., Zurich. Exhibitions: one-man retrospective, Aberdeen Art Gall., 1998; (contrib.) Creation, Goldsmiths' Hall, 2004; (jt retrospective) Precious Statements, Goldsmiths' Hall, 2006; The Cutting Edge, Royal Mus. of Scotland, Mus. of Modern Art Glasgow, Aberdeen Art Gall. and Mus., 2007; Raising the Bar, Dovecot, Edinburgh, Ruthin Craft Centre, Wales, Middlesbrough Inst. of Modern Art, 2008; Contemporary Silver for Bishopsland, V&A, 2009, Dovecot, Edinburgh, 2010; Maker, Scottish Gall., Edinburgh, 2012; Silver, the Aberdeen Story, Aberdeen Art Gall., 2012; Passing it On, Scottish Gall., 2014; (contrib.) The Silversmith's Art, Nat. Mus. of Scotland, Edinburgh, 2015; Malcolm Appleby at 70, Scottish Gall., 2016; Silver, Light and Shade, Holbourne Mus., Bath, 2016; 175th Anniv. Exhibn, Scottish Gall., 2017; Malcolm Appleby: 50 golden years in Scotland, Scottish Gall., 2019. Glenmorangie Lect., Nat. Mus. of Scotland, 2015. Fellow, Bishopsland Educnl Trust. Founder, British Art Postage Stamp Soc., 1986; Mem., British Art Medal Soc., 1987–; Founding Mem., British Hand Engravers Assoc.; estab. Malcolm Appleby Hand Engraving Award, British Silver Week, 2010. Chm., Crathes Drumoak Community Council, 1981. Life Member: NT for Scotland, 1971; SPAB, 1989; British Dragon Fly Soc., 2001; Orkney Boat Mus.; Cluny Gardens; Highland Perthshire Community Land Trust; McLaren Soc.; NE Mountain Trust. Member: Silver Soc.; Butterfly Conservation Soc.; John Muir Trust; Bumble Bee Conservation Trust. Sponsor, Friends of Birks Cinema, Aberfeldy restoration project. Hon. Mem., Grandtully and Strathtay Br., Women's Rural Inst., 1997. Liveryman, Goldsmiths' Co. Hon. DLitt Heriot-Watt, 2000. Lifetime Achievement Award, Hand Engravers Assoc., 2015. *Recreations:* work, walking, garden design, drinking herbal tea with friends, acting in pantomime, conservation matters, tree planting with Philippa Swann, playing pom pom ping pong with daughter May, inventor of celebrity frisbee quoits. *Address:* Aultbeag, Grandtully, by Aberfeldy, Perthshire PH15 2QU. *T:* (01887) 840484.

**APPLEBY, Rt Rev. Richard Franklin;** Bishop of the Northern Region and an Assistant Bishop, Diocese of Brisbane, 1999–2006; *b* 17 Nov. 1940; *s* of Julian Paul Leonard Appleby and Lilian Margaret Appleby (*née* Pragnell); *m* 1966, Elizabeth Clark; two *d*. *Educ:* Eltham High Sch.; Univ. of Melbourne (BSc); St John's Coll., Morpeth (ThL (Hons)). Curate of Glenroy, 1967–68; Curate of N Balwyn and Chaplain to Apprentices and Probation Hostels, 1969–70; Chaplain to Christchurch Grammar Sch., 1970–71; Warden of Wollaston Coll. and Chaplain to the Archbishop of Perth, 1972–75; Rector of Belmont, 1975–80; Dean of Bathurst and Examining Chaplain to the Bishop of Bathurst, 1980–83; Auxiliary Bishop of Newcastle, 1983–92; Bishop of the Northern Territory (Australia), 1992–99. President: NSW Ecumenical Council, 1987–89; Qld Churches Together, 2004–05; Nat. Council of Churches in Australia, 2006–09. Visitor, CSC Aust., 1991–2001; Protector SSF Aust./NZ, 1992–2002; Protector Gen. SSF, 1996–2002, SSA, 2000–06. ChStJ 2002. *Recreations:* gardening, walking, listening to music. *Address:* 13/212 David Road, Nuffield Village, Castle Hill, NSW 2154, Australia. *T:* (2) 96801681. *E:* rfappleby@gmail.com.

**APPLEGARTH, Adam John;** Senior Advisor to Private Equity, since 2009; *b* 3 Aug. 1962; *s* of late John Speed Applegarth and Mary Applegarth; *m* 1984, Patricia Catherine Killeen; two *s*. *Educ:* Sedbergh Sch.; Grey Coll., Durham Univ. (BA). Gen. Manager, 1993–96, Exec. Dir, 1996–97, Northern Rock Building Soc.; Exec. Dir, 1997–2007, Chief Exec., 2001–07, Northern Rock plc; Dir, Northern Rock (Guernsey) Ltd, 1996–2001; Chief Exec., Legal & General Bank, 2002–03; non-exec. Dir, Persimmon, 2006–07. Senior Advisor: Apollo Mgt, 2009–13; HCL Europe, 2013–17. Trustee, Internat. Centre for Life Trust, 1997–2001. Gov., RGS, Newcastle, 2002–17. *Recreations:* cricket, Rugby, Newcastle United FC. *Club:* Ashbrooke Sporting.

**APPLEGATE, Ven. John,** PhD; Principal, All Saints Centre for Mission and Ministry (formerly Course Principal, Southern North-West Training Partnership), since 2008; Archdeacon of Bolton, 2002–08, now Emeritus; *b* 1956. *Educ:* Bristol Univ. (BSc 1975); Trinity Coll., Bristol (DipHE; PhD). Ordained deacon, 1984, priest, 1985; Curate: Collyhurst, Dio. of Manchester, 1984–87; St John, Broughton and St James, Higher Broughton, and St Clement with St Matthias, Lower Broughton, 1987–92; St John, Broughton and St James with St Clement, and St Matthias, Broughton, 1992–94; Rector, St John, Broughton, 1994–96; Team Rector, Broughton, 1996–2002. Area Dean, Salford, 1996–2002. Pt-time Lectr and Hon. Res. Fellow, Univ. of Manchester, 2001–.

**APPLEGATE, Lt Gen. Richard Arthur David,** CB 2010; OBE 1996; Managing Director, Eagle Strategic Consulting Ltd, since 2010; Head of Strategy and New Business (formerly Chairman), Elbit Systems (UK), since 2011; *b* 20 March 1955; *s* of late Arthur Applegate and Elsie Applegate; *m* 1979, Rachael Bridgeman; two *d*. *Educ:* Chislehurst and Sidcup Grammar Sch.; Manchester Univ. (BA Hons Politics and Mod. Hist.); Staff Coll., Camberley (psc† 1987); Joint Staff Coll., Bracknell (hcsc(j) 1998); Boeing Exec. Leadership Prog. 2009; IoD 2009. Service in Bosnia, Kosovo, NI, Belize, Hong Kong, Kenya, Germany, Belgium and UK; Mil. Asst/Speechwriter to SACEUR, 1992–94; Comdr UN and European Rapid Reaction Bde Artillery Gps, Mount Igman/Sarajevo, 1995; CO 19th Regt RA (Highland Gunners), 1994–96; Col Force Devel, 1996–98; CRA 3rd (UK) Div., 1998–2000; Director: Indirect Battlefield Engagement; Deep Target Attack, 2000–03; Capability Manager (Battlespace Manoeuvre), MoD, 2003–06, and Master Gen. of the Ordnance, 2006; Chief of Materiel (Land), Defence Equipment and Support Orgn, 2007–09; Quartermaster Gen., 2007–09; Defence Career Partner, 2009–10. Col Comdt, RA, 2006–11 (Chm., RA Fundraising, 2009–). Director: Design Blue, 2011–16; UAV Tactical Systems Ltd, 2011–; Ferranti Technologies Ltd, 2012–16; Remitia Ltd, 2014–16. Patron, Heropreneurs, 2012–. Chair, Salisbury Plain Heritage Centre Fundraising Council, 2015–. Corporate Friends Ambassador, SSAFA, 2017–. CCMI 2010; FCGI 2011. City and Guilds Inst. Award, 1986; Légionnaire 1st cl. d'Honneur, Légion Étrangère, 1996; Officer, Legion of Merit (USA), 2007. *Publications:* numerous articles in RUSI Jl, Defense Analysis and in-house jls; winner, Thales essay competition, 2002. *Recreations:* walking, coarse gardening, military history.

**APPLETON, His Honour John Fortnam;** a Circuit Judge, 1992–2011; Designated Civil Judge, Lancashire and Cumbria (formerly Preston) Group of Courts, 1998–2011; *b* 8 April 1946; *s* of late George Fortnam Appleton, OBE, TD, JP, DL and Patricia Margaret Appleton; *m* 1983, Maureen Sellers; one *s*. *Educ:* Harrow; Bristol Univ. (LLB Hons). Called to the Bar, Middle Temple, 1969; Asst Recorder, 1981–85; a Recorder of the Crown Court, 1985–92. *Recreations:* family, country pursuits. *Address:* Park Cottage, Deer Park Lane, Hornby, Lancaster LA2 8LF. *E:* jfappleton@btinternet.com.

**APPLETON, Margaret Mary,** MBE 2012; Chief Executive, Royal Air Force Museum, since 2015; *b* Lytham, Lancs, 1965; *d* of Thomas Appleton and Veronica Ball; partner, 1986, *m* 2005, Anthony Nicolson; two *s*. *Educ:* Lark Hill House Sch., Preston; Cardinal Newman Coll., Preston; Univ. of Liverpool (BA Hons Med. and Mod. Hist. 1988); Univ. of Birmingham (MSocSc Heritage Mgt 1991). AMA. Asst Registrar, Royal Armouries, 1990; Asst Curator, then Curator/Cultural Services Manager, Stevenage BC, 1991–2002; Dir, Museums, Luton BC, 2003–08; Chief Exec., Luton Culture, 2008–15. Mem., E of England Cttee, HLF, 2010–16. Pres., Mus Assoc., 2018–; Co-Chair, Women Leaders in Mus Network, 2015–18. *Recreations:* book group, cycling, museums, theatre. *Address:* Royal Air Force Museum, Grahame Park Way, NW9 5LL. *T:* (020) 8358 4823. *E:* maggie.appleton@rafmuseum.org.

**APPLEYARD, James;** *see* Appleyard, W. J.

**APPLEYARD, Joan Ena, (Lady Appleyard);** DL; Headmistress, St Swithun's School, Winchester, 1986–94; *b* 15 Aug. 1946; *d* of William Jefferson and Ruth Ena Leake; *m* 1994, Sir Leonard Appleyard, *qv*. *Educ:* Univ. of Newcastle (BA Hons History); Westminster Coll., Oxford (Dip Ed). Asst Mistress, 1968–70, Head of History, 1970–73, Scarborough Girls' High Sch.; Head of Humanities, Graham Sch., Scarborough, 1973–75; Dep. Head, 1975–79, Headmistress, 1979–86, Hunmanby Hall Sch., Filey. President: GSA, 1992–93; Futures for Women (formerly Soc. for Promoting the Training of Women), 2007–. Dep. Chm., ESU, 1999–2005. Chm., Hants Historic Churches Trust, 2008–. DL Hants, 2010. *Recreations:* drama, opera, reading, cooking.

**APPLEYARD, Sir Leonard (Vincent),** KCMG 1994 (CMG 1986); Pro Chancellor, Bournemouth University, 2004–12; Senior Fellow and Visiting Professor, Southampton University, 2009–11; *b* 2 Sept. 1938; *s* of Thomas William Appleyard; *m* 1st, 1964, Elizabeth Margaret West (marr. diss. 1994); two *d*; 2nd, 1994, Joan Ena Jefferson (*see* J. E. Appleyard). *Educ:* Read School, Drax, W Yorks; Queens' Coll., Cambridge (MA). Foreign Office, 1962; Third Secretary, Hong Kong, 1964; Second Secretary, Peking, 1966; Second, later First, Secretary, Foreign Office, 1969; First Secretary, Delhi, 1970; Moscow, 1975; HM Treasury, 1978; Financial Counsellor, Paris, 1979–82; Head of Economic Relations Dept, FCO, 1982–84; Principal Private Sec. to Sec. of State for Foreign and Commonwealth Affairs, 1984–86; Ambassador to Hungary, 1986–89; Dep. Sec., Cabinet Office, 1989–91 (on secondment); Political Dir and Dep. Under-Sec. of State, FCO, 1991–94; Ambassador to People's Republic of China, 1994–97. Vice-Chm., Barclays Capital, 1998–2003. Chairman: Farnham Castle Conf. Centre, 2003–07; Hants Archives Trust, 2011–12. Chm., Council, Winchester Cathedral, 2007–12. *Recreations:* music, shooting.

**APPLEYARD, Dr (William) James,** FRCP, FRCPCH; Dean of Clinical Sciences, Kigesi International School of Medicine, Uganda, 2000–04; Consultant Paediatrician, 1971–98, Hon. Consultant Paediatrician, 1998–99, and Clinical Director, Paediatric Directorate, 1992–98, Kent and Canterbury Hospitals NHS Trust (formerly Canterbury and Thanet Health District); *b* 25 Oct. 1935; *s* of late E. R. Appleyard and Maud Oliver Collingwood (*née* Marshall); *m* 1964, Elizabeth Anne Ward; one *s* two *d*. *Educ:* Canford Sch.; Exeter College, Oxford (BM BCh, MA); Guy's Hosp. Med. Sch., Univ. of London DObstRCOG; FRCP 1978; FRCPCH 1998. Junior paediat. posts, Guy's and Gt Ormond St; Resident in Pediat., Univ. of Louisville, 1964–65; Dyers' Co. Res. Registrar, St Thomas' Hosp., 1968–69. British Medical Association: Treas., 1996–2002; Member: Jt Consultants Cttee, 1976–95; Consultants Cttee, 1971–2002 (Dep. Chm., 1979–83); Dep Chm., 1989–91, Chm., 1992–95, Rep. Body. Treasurer, BPA, 1988; Mem., GMC 1984–2003 (Mem., Educn Cttee, 1993–96); Member Council: RCP, 1988–91 (Member Standing Cttee, 1970–72; Res. Cttee, 1971–74; Paed. Cttee, 1987–91; Examng Bd 1992–98); World Med. Assoc., 1995–2005 (Chm., Med. Ethics Cttee, 1996–99; Pres. 2003–04; immed. Past Pres., 2005); Chm. Ethics Cttee and a Site Visitor, 2006–, Vice Pres. 2012–15, Pres., 2015–, Internat. Assoc. of Med. Colls (Hon. Sec. to Bd of Trustees 2007–12); Pres., Internat. Coll. of Person Centered Medicine, 2013–17. Member: Health

Service Inf. Steering Gp, Korner Cttee, 1985; DoH Inf. Adv. Gp, 1986–90; Nat. Specialist Commissioning Adv. Gp, DoH, 1995–96; London Univ. Nominee, Kent AHA, 1974–78. Mem. Bd, Urbani Internat., Geneva, 2004–. Hon. Tutor in Paed., Guy's Hosp.; Hon. Lectr in Paed., St Thomas' Hosp.; Dean of Clin. Studies, (UK), St George's Univ. Sch. of Medicine, Grenada, 1995–97 (Associate Prof., 1985–90; Prof. of Paediatrics, 1991–95; Chm., Senate, 1991–93). Hon. Treas., Kent Postgrad. Med. Centre, Canterbury, 1998–2000. Patron, Dyspraxia Trust, 1988–. Trustee, St John's Hosp., Canterbury, 2007–June 2020 (Chm., 2012–17). Liveryman, Apothecaries' Soc., 1983. Hon. FRCPCH 2002. Hon. MD Kent at Canterbury, 1999; Hon. DHL St George's, Grenada, 2000. Alumnus Award for Paed. Res., Univ. of Louisville, 1965. Member, Editorial Board: Jl Chinese Med. Assoc., 2003–13; Internat. Jl of Person Centered Medicine, 2011–. *Publications:* contribs to med. jls and textbooks. *Recreations:* croquet, photography, erstwhile allotment digger. *Address:* Thimble Hall, Blean Common, Blean, Kent CT2 9JJ. *T:* (01227) 781771. *Club:* Athenæum.

**ApSIMON, Prof. Helen Mary,** CBE 2013; PhD; Professor of Air Pollution Studies, Imperial College London, since 2001; *b* Ashby-de-la-Zouch, 28 April 1942; *d* of Dr Geoffrey and Margery Hollingsworth; *m* 1967, Dr Hugh Ellis Gardiner ApSimon (*d* 1998). *Educ:* Northampton High Sch.; Somerville Coll., Oxford (MA Maths 1963); St Andrews Univ. (PhD Astrophysics 1967). Res., W S Atkins, 1972–74; Imperial College London: pt-time PDRA, 1974–86; Res. Fellow, 1986–91; Reader in Air Pollution Studies, 1991–2000; Churchill Travelling Fellowship on air pollution in Eastern Europe, 1988; work for UK govt on air pollution, 1991–. Mem., task forces under UNECE Convention on Long-Range Transboundary Air Pollution, 1991–. Founder Mem. and Pres., Eur. Assoc. for Sci. of Air Pollution, 1994–2000; Founder Mem. and Chair, Air Pollution Res. in London res. network, 2000–10. Member: expert gps, incl. Air Quality Expert Gp, 2003–12, Air Quality Modelling Steering Gp, 2013–15, DEFRA; Expert Panel, Airports Commn, 2013–15; Chm., Air Quality Expert Rev. Gp on Heathrow expansion, 2016–. *Recreations:* keeping a horse, dressage judging, walking, gardening, reading, volunteer in A&E at Frimley Park Hospital. *Address:* Centre for Environmental Policy, Imperial College London, Exhibition Road, SW7 2AZ. *T:* (020) 7594 9292. *E:* h.apsimon@imperial.ac.uk.

**APSLEY, Lord; Benjamin George Henry Bathurst;** Director, TruU (formerly Doctor's Link), since 2018; *b* 6 March 1990; *s* and *heir* of Earl Bathurst, *qv*. Captain, 40 Commando RM, 2013–17.

**APSLEY, Dr Norman,** OBE 2012; FREng; FInstP; FIAE; Chief Executive, Catalyst Inc. (formerly Northern Ireland Science Park Foundation Ltd), 2000–18; *b* Larne, Co. Antrim, 9 Dec. 1950; *s* of Robert and Edith Muriel Apsley; *m* 2009, Jacqui McCarroll; one *s* one *d*. *Educ:* Larne Grammar Sch.; Ulster Univ. (BSc Physics 1st Cl.); Peterhouse, Cambridge (MA 1976); Jesus Coll., Cambridge (PhD 1977). FInstP 1996; FREng 2011. Res. Fellow, Jesus Coll., Cambridge, 1976–79; Sen. Res. Scientist, 1979–83, Principal Res. Scientist, 1983–90, Royal Signals & Radar Estabt Malvern; Superintendent, Optical and Display Sci., 1990–92, Business Develt Manager, 1992–96, DRA; Dir, Electronics Sector, DERA, 1996–2000. Vis. Prof., Ulster Univ., 2000–. Vice Pres. (Business and Innovation), Inst. of Physics, 2008–12. FIAE 2011. Hon. DSc QUB, 2019. Lifetime Achievement Award, Belfast Telegraph Business Awards, 2018. *Publications:* contribs to learned jls. *Recreations:* photography, walking, camping, music.

**APTED, Michael David,** CMG 2008; director and producer of television and films; *b* 10 Feb. 1941; *m* (marr. diss.); one *s* (and one *s* decd); *m*; one *s*. *Educ:* Downing Coll., Cambridge (BA 1963). With Granada TV, 1963–70: researcher, 1963; dir, episodes of Coronation Street; investigative reporter, World in Action, incl. research, 1964, on 7 Up, which became first of series (director: Seven Plus Seven, 1970; 21 Up, 1977; 28 Up, 1985; 35 Up, 1991; 42 Up, 1998; 49 Up, 2005; 56 Up, 2012; 21 Up New Generation, 2014; 63 Up, 2019). Director: *television*: series: Big Breadwinner Hog, 1969; The Lovers, 1970; Folly Foot (for children), 1972; My Life and Times, 1991; plays and films: Slattery's Mounted Foot, 1970; The Mosedale Horseshoe, 1971; The Reporters, 1972; Kisses at Fifty, 1972; Another Sunday and Sweet FA, 1972; The Collection, 1975; Stronger than the Sun, 1977; P'tang Yang Kipperbang, 1982; The Long Way Home, 1989; Always Outnumbered, 1998; Nathan Dixon, 1999; *films include*: Triple Echo, 1973; Stardust, 1975; The Squeeze, 1977; Agatha, 1979; Coal Miner's Daughter, 1980; Continental Divide, 1981; Gorky Park, 1983; Firstborn, 1984; Bring on the Night, 1985; Critical Condition, 1987; Gorillas in the Mist, 1988; Class Action, 1991; Incident at Oglala, 1992; Thunderheart, 1992; Blink, 1994; Moving the Mountain, 1994; Nell, 1995; Extreme Measures, 1997; (also prod) Inspirations (documentary), 1997; The World is Not Enough, 1999; Me and Isaac Newton, 1999; Enigma, 2001; Enough, 2002; Amazing Grace, 2007; The Chronicles of Narnia: the Voyage of the Dawn Treader, 2010; Unlocked, 2017; *executive producer*: The River Rat, 1984; Dracula, 1992. Prod., TV series, Rome, 2006. *Publications:* 7 Up, 1999. *Address:* c/o United Agents, 12–26 Lexington Street, W1F 0LE.

**APTHORP, John Dorrington,** CBE 2014 (OBE 1999); Chairman, Majestic Wine Warehouses (formerly Wizard Wine), 1989–2005; *b* 25 April 1935; *s* of late Eric and Mildred Apthorp; *m* 1959, Jane Frances Arnold (*d* 2018); three *s* one *d*. *Educ:* Aldenham School. Sub-Lieut RNVR, 1953–55. Family business, Appypak, 1956–68; started Bejam Group, 1968, Exec. Chm., 1968–87, non-exec. Chm., 1987–88. Mem., Tay River Bd, 2002–09. Councillor, London Bor. of Barnet, 1968–74. Liveryman: Butchers' Co., 1974–; Vintners' Co., 1999–. Gov., London Acad., 2004–. FCMI (FBIM 1977); FInstD 1978; FIGD 1981. Hon. DArts Herts, 2014. Guardian Young Business Man of Year, 1974. Commandeur d'Honneur pour Commanderie du Bontemps de Médoc et des Graves, 1977. Freedom: Bor. of Barnet, 2009; Parish of Aldenham. *Recreations:* shooting, wine. *Address:* The Field House Farm, 29 Newlands Avenue, Radlett, Herts WD7 8EJ. *T:* (01923) 855201. *Club:* Radlett Tennis and Squash.

**ARAD, Prof. Ron,** RDI 2002; RA 2013; architect and designer; Professor of Product Design, Royal College of Art, 1998–2009; *b* 24 April 1951; *s* of Grisha and Itai Arad; *m* 1975, Dr Alma Erlich; two *d*. *Educ:* Jerusalem Acad. of Art; Architectural Assoc. (dip. 1979). Professor of Product Design, Hochschule für Angewandte Kunst, Vienna, 1994–97; of Furniture Design, RCA, 1997. Retrospective exhibn, Restless, Barbican, 2010; solo exhibn, Ben Brown Gall., 2016; sculpture, Spyre, RA Summer Exhibn, 2016; installation, Curtain Call, Roundhouse, 2016. Guest Ed., Internat. Design Yearbook, 1994. Designer of Year, Salon du Meuble, Paris, 1994; Barcelona Primavera Internat. Award for Design, 2001; Gio Ponti Internat. Design Award, Denver, 2001; Oribe Art and Design Award, Japan, 2001; Architektur und Wohnen Designer of the Year Award, 2004; FX Mag. Designer of the Year Award, 2005; Visionary Award, Mus. of Arts & Design, NY, 2006; Laureate, Contemporary Art Prize, French Friends of Tel Aviv Mus. of Art, 2007; London Design Medal, 2011. *Recreations:* tennis, ping-pong. *Address:* 62 Chalk Farm Road, NW1 8AN. *T:* (020) 7284 4963. *W:* www.ronarad.com.

**ARAGONA, Giancarlo,** Hon. KCVO 2005; Ambassador of Italy to the Court of St James's, 2004–09; Chairman: Mediterranean Institute of Hematology, 2010; Sogin SpA, 2010–13; *b* 14 Nov. 1942; *s* of late Giovanni Aragona and of Bianca Maria Aragona (*née* Vinci); *m* 1968, Sandra Pauline Jackson; two *d*. *Educ:* Messina Univ., Italy (degree in Internat. Law). Entered Italian Diplomatic Service, 1969: served in Vienna, Freiburg im Breisgau and Lagos, 1969–80; Foreign Ministry, Rome, 1980–84; First Counsellor (Political), London, 1984–87; First Counsellor, then Minister-Counsellor and Dep. Perm. Rep., Delegn to NATO, 1987–92; Diplomatic Advr to Defence Minister, Rome, 1992–95; Dir of Cabinet of Foreign Minister, 1995–96; Sec. Gen., OSCE, 1996–99; Ambassador to Russian Fedn, 1999–2001; Dir Gen., Political Affairs and Human Rights, Min. of Foreign Affairs, 2001–04. Pres., Italian Inst. for Internat. Political Studies, 2012–16. Cavaliere di Gran Croce dell'Ordine al Merito della Repubblica Italiana, 2007. *Address:* Largo dell'Olgiata 15, 00123 Roma, Italy.

**ARAM, Zeev,** OBE 2014; FCSD; Chairman, Aram Designs Ltd and Aram Store, since 2002; *b* 5 Oct. 1931; *s* of Aaron and Palma Ungar; *m* 1958, Elizabeth Bunzl; one *s* three *d*. *Educ:* Central Sch. of Arts and Design (NDD). Worked in architects practices of Ernő Goldfinger, RIBA, Sir Basil Spence & Partners and Andrew Renton Associates, 1960–63; estabd own design practice, Zeev Aram and Associates, 1963; founded Aram Designs, 1964; opened furniture and design showroom in Chelsea, 1964, 2nd showroom in Hampstead, 1991; design and furniture showrooms, Aram Store, Drury Lane, opened 2002. Estabd Grad. Show of Young Designers, 1987. FCSD 1973; FRSA 1982. Hon. FRIBA 2006; Hon. FRCA 1992; Hon. Fellow, Univ. of the Arts, London, 2004. Arts Bicentenary Medal, RSA, 1996. *Recreations:* walking, music, sailing. *Address:* c/o Aram Designs Ltd, 110 Drury Lane, Covent Garden, WC2B 5SG. *T:* (020) 7240 3933, *Fax:* (020) 240 3697. *E:* zeev@aram.co.uk. *Club:* Chelsea Arts.

**ARBER, Prof. Sara Lynne,** PhD; FBA 2008; FAcSS; Professor of Sociology, 1994–2017, now Emeritus, and Co-Director, Centre for Research on Ageing and Gender, since 2000, University of Surrey; *b* Essex, 19 March 1949; *d* of late George Arber and Katie Arber; *m* 1979, Geoff Herrington (*d* 2005); one *s* one *d*. *Educ:* London Sch. of Econs (BSc 1st Cl. Sociol. 1972); Bedford Coll., Univ. of London (MSc Med. Sociol. 1973); Univ. of Surrey (PhD 1991). University of Surrey: Lectr, 1974–86; Sen. Lectr, 1986–94; Head: Dept of Sociol., 1996–2002; Sch. of Human Scis, 2001–04. Member: SW Surrey Community Health Council, 1976–81; SW Surrey District HA, 1981–89; Social Affairs Bd, 1984–87, Res. Grants Bd, 2008–10, Grants Assessment Panel, 2010–12, ESRC; Statistics Users Council, 1999–2006. British Sociological Association: Treas., 1988–90; Pres., 1999–2001; Vice Pres., 2002–; Vice Pres., Eur. Sociol Assoc., 2005–07; Pres., Res. Cttee 11 on Ageing, Internat. Sociol. Assoc., 2006–10. FAcSS (AcSS 2000). Fellow, Gerontol Soc. of America, 2012; FRSA 2012. Chm., Editl Bd, Sociology, 1992–95. Outstanding Achievement Award, British Soc. of Gerontology, 2011; Dist. Service to Sociol. Award, British Sociol Assoc., 2017. *Publications:* Gender and Later Life, 1991; (ed) Women and Working Lives, 1991; (ed) Ageing, Independence and the Life Course, 1993; (ed) Connecting Gender and Ageing, 1995; (ed) The Myth of Generational Conflict, 2000; (ed) Gender and Ageing, 2003; (ed) Contemporary Grandparenting, 2012; over 300 articles on health inequalities, gender, ageing and sociology of sleep. *Recreations:* travel, walking, swimming, ruins in exotic places. *Address:* Department of Sociology, University of Surrey, Guildford, Surrey GU2 7XH. *T:* (01483) 686989, *Fax:* (01483) 689551. *E:* S.Arber@surrey.ac.uk.

**ARBER, Prof. Werner;** Professor of Molecular Microbiology, Basle University, 1971–96; President, Pontifical Academy of Sciences, 2011–17. President, International Council of Scientific Unions, 1996–99. Discovered restriction enzymes at Geneva in 1960s; Nobel Prize in Physiology or Medicine (jointly), 1978. *Address:* Department of Microbiology, Biozentrum der Universität Basel, 50–70 Klingelbergstrasse, 4056 Basel, Switzerland.

**ARBIB, Sir Martyn,** Kt 2003; DL; Founder and Chairman, Perpetual plc, 1973–2000; *b* 27 June 1939; *s* of late Richard Arbib and Denise Arbib; *m* 1969, Anne Hermione Parton; two *s* two *d*. *Educ:* Felsted Sch. FCA 1962. Trained with Spicer & Pegler, 1956–62; qualified Chartered Accountant, 1962; Kelsey Industries PLC, 1966–72 (non-exec. Dir, 1975–2000). Dir, Perpetual Income & Growth Investment Trust, 1996–2015. Trustee: Annabel Arbib Foundn (formerly Arbib Foundn), 1987–; Langley Acad. Trust, 2006–16; Dir, 1991–, Dep. Chm., 1994–2001, Chm., 2001–12, River and Rowing Mus. Foundn, Henley on Thames; Dir, 1992, Jt Chm., 1994–2003, Henley Fest. of Music and the Arts. DL Oxon, 2001. *Recreations:* golf, dry fly fishing, flat racehorse owner and breeder. *Address:* 61 Grosvenor Street, W1K 3JE. *Clubs:* Alfred's; Huntercombe Golf, Queenwood Golf, Royal Westmorland Golf.

**ARBOUR, Anthony Francis;** JP; Member (C) South West, since 2000, and Chairman, since 2016, London Assembly, Greater London Authority; *b* 30 Aug. 1945; *s* of late Charles and Magdalen Arbour; *m* 1970, Caroline Anne Cooper; three *s* one *d*. *Educ:* St Andrew's Sch., Ham Common; Surbiton Co. Grammar Sch.; Kingston Coll. of Technol. (BSc Econ); City Univ. Business Sch. (MBA). Admitted to the Bar, Gray's Inn, 1967. Sen. Lectr, Kingston Univ. Business Sch., 1967–2000 (Vis. Hon. Fellow, 2000–08). Mem., Employment Tribunals, London Central (formerly Industrial Tribunals, London North), 1993–2012. Member (C): Richmond upon Thames BC, 1968–2018 (Chm., Planning Cttee, 1974–80; Leader, Cons. Gp, 1996–2002; Leader of Council, 2002–06); Surbiton, GLC, 1983–86. London Assembly, GLA: Chm., Planning Cttee, 2000–02; Cons. spokesman on planning and standards, 2004–; Chm., Planning and Spatial Develt Cttee, 2005–08; Dep. Chm., 2015–16. Vice-Chm., Kingston and Richmond FHSA, 1990–96; Member: Metropolitan Police Authy, 2000–08, 2010–12; London Fire and Emergency Planning Authy, 2008–18. JP Richmond upon Thames, 1974. Chm., Hampton Wick United Charity, 1972–. Governor: Kingston Poly., 1988–90; Tiffin Sch., 1988–92; St Mary's Univ. Coll., 2010–16. *Recreations:* book collecting, watching TV soap operas, car booting, eBaying. *Address:* 3 Holmesdale Road, Teddington, Middx TW11 9LJ; Greater London Authority, City Hall, Queen's Walk, SE1 2AA.

**ARBUCKLE, Andrew,** FRAgS; Rural Affairs Editor, The Scotsman; *b* 12 April 1944; *s* of John and Lydia Arbuckle; *m* Margaret Elizabeth Arbuckle (marr. diss. 1985); two *d*. *Educ:* Bell Baxter High Sch., Cupar; Elmwood Coll., Cupar (NDA). Farmer, E Fife; Agricl Ed., Dundee Courier & Advertiser, 1986–2005. MSP (Lib Dem) Scotland Mid and Fife, Jan. 2005–2007; Lib Dem spokesman on finance, Scottish Parlt, 2005–07. Member (Lib Dem): Fife Regl Council, 1986–95; Fife Council, 1995–2012. Mem., Tay Bridge Bd, 1996–2012. Pres., Fife NFU, 1989–91. Mem. Ct, St Andrews Univ., 1990–95. Chm., Fife Athletic Club, 1980–81. FRAgS 2000. *Recreations:* sport, reading, music. *Address:* Lower Cottage West, Fliskmillan, Newburgh, Cupar, Fife KY14 6HN.

**ARBUTHNOT,** family name of **Baron Arbuthnot of Edrom**.

**ARBUTHNOT OF EDROM,** Baron *cr* 2015 (Life Peer), of Edrom in the County of Berwick; **James Norwich Arbuthnot;** PC 1998; *b* 4 Aug. 1952; 2nd *s* of Sir John Arbuthnot, 1st Bt, MBE, TD and of Margaret Jean, *yr d* of late Alexander G. Duff; *m* 1984, Emma Louise Broadbent (*see* E. L. Arbuthnot); one *s* three *d*. *Educ:* Wellesley House, Broadstairs; Eton Coll. (Captain of School); Trinity Coll., Cambridge (MA). Called to the Bar, 1975; practising barrister, 1977–92 and 2002–03. Councillor, Royal Bor. of Kensington and Chelsea, 1978–87. Contested (C) Cynon Valley, 1983, May 1984. MP (C) Wanstead and Woodford, 1987–97, NE Hampshire, 1997–2015. An Asst Govt Whip, 1992–94; Parly Under-Sec. of State, DSS, 1994–95; Minister of State for Defence Procurement, MoD, 1995–97; Opposition Chief Whip, 1997–2001; Shadow Sec. of State for Trade, 2003–05. Chm., Defence Select Cttee, 2005–14. Chm., Neuro-Bio Ltd, 2016–;

non-executive Director: Gusbourne Estates plc, 2015–; SC Strategy Ltd, 2016–17 (Sen. Consultant, 2018–). Mem., Adv. Bd, Thales UK, 2015–. (Chm., 2016–). President: Cynon Valley Cons. Assoc., 1983–92; NE Hants Cons. Assoc., 2015–. *Recreations:* playing guitar, ski-ing, cooking. *Address:* House of Lords, SW1A 0PW.
*See also Sir W. R. Arbuthnot, Bt.*

**ARBUTHNOT, Emma Louise, (Lady Arbuthnot of Edrom);** Chief Magistrate of England and Wales, and Senior District Judge (Magistrates' Courts), since 2016; a District Judge (Magistrates' Courts), since 2005; a Recorder, since 2002; *b* 9 Jan. 1959; *d* of (John) Michael Broadbent, *qv*; *m* 1984, Rt Hon. James Norwich Arbuthnot (*see* Baron Arbuthnot of Edrom); one *s* three *d*. *Educ*: Lycée Français de Londres; Queen Mary Coll., Univ. of London (BA); City Univ. (Dip. Law); Coll. of Legal Educn. Called to the Bar, Inner Temple, 1986, Bencher, 2007; Tenant, 6 King's Bench Walk, 1988–2005; a Dep. Dist Judge, 2000–05; Dep. Chief Magistrate of England and Wales and Dep. Sen. Dist Judge (Magistrates' Cts), 2012–16. Member: Cttee, Criminal Bar Assoc., 1996–2002; Bar Council, 1998–2005 (Mem., Professional Conduct and Complaints Cttee, 1998–2005; Vice-Chm., Public Affairs Cttee, 2003–05). Chm., 1987–2008, Vice Chm., 2008–, Earls Court Youth Club; Dir, Feathers' Clubs Assoc., 1999–; Chm., Fourth Feathers' Youth Club, 2017–. Judge: Asian Women of Achievement Awards, 2004–13 (Chm., 2017–); Women of the Future Awards, 2006–08. *Recreations:* city cycling, su doku, weeding, reading. *Address:* c/o Westminster Magistrates' Court, 181 Marylebone Road, NW1 5BR.

**ARBUTHNOT, Sir Keith Robert Charles,** 8th Bt *cr* 1823, of Edinburgh; *b* 23 Sept. 1951; *s* of Sir Hugh Fitz-Gerald Arbuthnot, 7th Bt and Elizabeth Kathleen (*d* 1972), *d* of late Sqdn-Ldr G. G. A. Williams; *S* father, 1983; *m* 1st, 1982, Anne (marr. diss. 2001), *yr d* of late Brig. Peter Moore; two *s* one *d*; 2nd, 2003, Alison Jane, *d* of John Warner and Ann Casson. *Educ*: Wellington; Univ. of Edinburgh. BSc (Soc. Sci.). *Heir*: *s* Robert Hugh Peter Arbuthnot, *b* 2 March 1986. *Address*: Ivy House, High Street, Edgmond, Newport, Shropshire TF10 8JY.

**ARBUTHNOT, Sir William (Reierson),** 2nd Bt *cr* 1964, of Kittybrewster, Aberdeen; *b* 2 Sept. 1950; *s* of Sir John Sinclair-Wemyss Arbuthnot, 1st Bt, MBE, TD, sometime MP (C) Dover Div. of Kent, and of (Margaret) Jean, *yr d* of late (Alexander) Gordon Duff; *S* father, 1992; one *d*; *m* 2010, Louise Alexandra Mary Barry; two *s* (twins). *Educ*: Eton; Coll. of Law, London. Arbuthnot Latham Holdings, 1970–76; Joynson-Hicks & Co., solicitors, 1978–81. Dir, Assoc. of Lloyd's Members, 1997–2005. Dep. Chm., High Premium Gp, 1994–2010. Liveryman, Grocers' Co., 1981. *Recreations:* genealogy; webmaster, Arbuthnot Family Assoc. and Kittybrewster.com. *Heir*: *s* Henry William Arbuthnot, *b* 21 March 2011. *Address*: 37 Cathcart Road, SW10 9JG. *T*: (020) 7795 0707. *E*: wra@kittybrewster.com.
*See also Baron Arbuthnot of Edrom.*

**ARBUTHNOTT,** family name of **Viscount of Arbuthnott.**

**ARBUTHNOTT, 17th Viscount of,** *cr* 1641; **John Keith Oxley Arbuthnott,** DL; *b* 18 July 1950; *o s* of 16th Viscount of Arbuthnott, KT, CBE, DSC and Mary Elizabeth Darley Oxley (*d* 2010); *S* father, 2012; *m* 1974, Jillian Mary, *er d* of late Captain Colin Farquharson of Whitehouse; one *s* two *d*. *Educ*: Fettes College; Aberdeen Univ. Mem., Grampian Health Bd, 1993–97; Vice-Convenor, Scottish Landowners' Fedn, 2003–05; Chm., Scottish Rural Property and Business Assoc., 2005–08. DL Kincardineshire, 2000. *Heir*: *s* Master of Arbuthnott, *qv*. *Address*: Kilternan, Arbuthnott, Laurencekirk, Kincardineshire AB30 1NA. *T*: (01561) 320417.

**ARBUTHNOTT, Master of; Hon. Christopher Keith Arbuthnott;** *b* 20 July 1977; *o s* and heir of 17th Viscount of Arbuthnott, *qv*; *m* 2003, Emily Jane Agg-Manning; one *s* two *d*.

**ARBUTHNOTT, Hugh James,** CMG 1984; HM Diplomatic Service, retired; *b* 27 Dec. 1936; *m*; two *s* (and one *s* decd). *Educ*: Ampleforth Coll., Yorks; New Coll., Oxford. Nat. Service, Black Watch, 1955–57. Joined Foreign (subseq. Diplomatic) Service, 1960; 3rd Sec., Tehran, 1962–64; 2nd, later 1st Sec., FO, 1964–66; Private Sec., Minister of State for Foreign Affairs, 1966–68; Lagos, 1968–71; 1st Sec. (Head of Chancery), Tehran, 1971–74; Asst, later Head of European Integration Dept (External), FCO, 1974–77; Counsellor (Agric. and Econ.), Paris, 1978–80; Head of Chancery, Paris, 1980–83; Under Sec., Internat. Div., ODA, 1983–85; Ambassador to Romania, 1986–89, to Portugal, 1989–93, to Denmark, 1993–96. Chm., Martin Currie Eur. Investment Trust, 1997–2004. Chm., Charities Evaluation Services, 1997–2003. Chm., Iran Soc., 2006–08. Trustee, Children at Risk Foundn (UK), 1997–2007. *Publications:* Common Man's Guide to the Common Market (ed with G. Edwards), 1979, 2nd edn (co-author with G. Edwards), 1989; (jtly) British Missions around the Gulf 1575–2005, 2008.

**ARBUTHNOTT, Sir John (Peebles),** Kt 1998; PhD, ScD; FRCPath, FMedSci; FRSE; FRSB; President, Royal Society of Edinburgh, 2011–14; Chairman, Greater Glasgow and Clyde (formerly Greater Glasgow) NHS Board, 2002–07; *b* 8 April 1939; *s* of James Anderson Arbuthnott and Jean (*née* Kelly); *m* 1962, Elinor Rutherford Smillie; one *s* two *d*. *Educ*: Univ. of Glasgow (BSc 1960; PhD 1966); Trinity Coll., Dublin (ScD 1984; Hon. FTCD 1992). FRSB (FIBiol 1988); FRSE 1993; FIIB 1993; FRCPath 1995. University of Glasgow: Lectr, Dept of Bacteriology, 1963–67; Alan Johnston, Lawrence and Moseley Res. Fellow of Royal Soc., 1968–72; Sen. Lectr, Dept of Microbiol., 1972–73; Sen. Lectr, Dept of Bacteriol., 1973–75; Professor of Microbiology: TCD, 1976–88 (Bursar, 1983–86); Univ. of Nottingham, 1988–91; Prin. and Vice Chancellor, Strathclyde Univ., 1991–2000. Vis. Lectr, Dept of Microbiol., New York Univ. Med. Centre, 1966–67. Sec. and Treas., Carnegie Trust for Univs of Scotland, 2000–04. Chair, External Adv. Bd, Wolfson Inst. for Health & Wellbeing, Univ. of Durham, 2000–08 (Mem., Internat. Adv. Bd, 2012–). Chair, Med. and Scientific Bd, Lamellar Biomedical Ltd, 2011–. Bd Mem., Food Standards Agency and Chm., Scottish Food Adv. Cttee, 2000–02; Member: Bd, PHLS, 1991–97; Bd, Glasgow Development Agency, 1995–2000; Bd, British Council Educn Counselling Service, 1995–96; Cttee, DTI Multimedia Industry Adv. Gp, 1995–97; Nat. Cttee of Inquiry into Higher Educn, 1996–97; Chm., Commn on Boundary Changes and Voting Systems, 2004–05 (report, 2006). Chm., Jt Inf. Systems Cttee, HEFC, 1994–98; Convenor, Cttee of Scottish Higher Educn Principals, 1994–96. Pres., Scottish Assoc. of Marine Sci., 2004–10. Treas., Soc. for Gen. Microbiol., 1987–92. Chairman: Nat. Review of allocation of health resources in Scotland, 1998–2000 (report, 2000); Standing Cttee on resource allocation to health services in Scotland, 2001–03; Clyde Valley Review, 2008; Chair: Expert Gp on Integrated and Social Care in Scotland, 2010–11; Adv. Bd, Fiscal Affairs Scotland, 2014–. Foundn Trustee, Africa Oxford Cancer Foundn, 2007–13; Trustee, Lloyds TSB Foundn for Scotland, 2009–. Hon. Sec., UK Bioscis Fedn, 2002–06. Founder FMedSci 1998. Hon. FRCPSGlas 1997. MRIA 1985. Hon. Fellow, Internat. Med. Univ., Kuala Lumpur; Hon. Principal Fellow, Dept of Clinical Pharmacol., Univ. of Oxford, 2008. Hon. DSc: Łódź, 1995; Univ. Teknologi, Malaysia, 1997; Glasgow, 1999; Durham, 2007; Edinburgh Napier, 2013; Open, 2014; Hon. LLD: QUB, 1996; Aberdeen, 1998; Hon. DEd Queen Margaret's UC, 2000. *Publications:* Breaking the Mould (autobiog.), 2015; edited: (jtly) Isoelectric Focusing, 1975; (jtly) The Determinants of Bacterial and Viral Pathogenicity, 1983; (jtly) Foodborne Illness: a Lancet review, 1991; more than 100 in prestigious scientific learned jls and books. *Recreations:* golf, birdwatching. *Address:* 9 Curlinghall, Broomfield Crescent, Largs KA30 8LB. *Club:* New (Edinburgh) (Hon. Mem.).

**ARBUTHNOTT, Robert,** CBE 1991; Minister (Cultural Affairs), India, British Council, 1988–93; *b* 28 Sept. 1936; *s* of late Archibald Arbuthnott, MBE, ED, and Barbara Joan (*née* Worters); *m* 1962, Sophie Robina (*née* Axford); one *s* two *d*. *Educ*: Sedbergh Sch. (scholar); Emmanuel Coll., Cambridge (exhibnr; BA Mod Langs, MA). Nat. service, 1955–57 (2nd Lieut The Black Watch RHR). British Council, 1960–94: Karachi, 1960–62; Lahore, 1962–64; London, 1964–67; Representative, Nepal, 1967–72; London Inst. of Education, 1972–73; Representative, Malaysia, 1973–76; Director, Educational Contracts Dept, 1976–77; Controller, Personnel and Staff Recruitment Div., 1978–81; Representative, Germany, 1981–85; RCDS, 1986; Controller, America, Pacific and S Asia Div., 1987. Member: Adv. Panel, Nehru Centre, 1998–2002; Council, Royal Soc. for Asian Affairs, 2006–09. Member: Mgt Cttee, St Anthony's Cheshire Home, Wolverhampton, 1995–2000; English Haydn Fest. Cttee, Bridgnorth, 1995–2000; Internat. Cttee, Leonard Cheshire Foundn, 1997–2003. FRAS 1995 (Mem. Council, 1996–2000). *Recreations:* music-making, the arts, historic buildings. *Club:* Oxford and Cambridge.

**ARCAYA, Ignacio;** international and political consultant; Ambassador of Venezuela to the United States of America, 2001–02; *b* Caracas, 3 June 1939; *s* of Ignacio Luis Arcaya and Antonieta (*née* Smith); *m* 1966, Lydia Vincenti; one *s* one *d*. *Educ*: Central Univ. of Venezuela (Internat. Affairs, 1964; Law, 1968). Third Sec., Perm. Mission of Venezuela to UN, Geneva, 1966–68; Second Sec., Min. for Foreign Affairs, 1968–69; First Sec., Mission to OAS, Washington, 1969–72; Counsellor, Inst. of Foreign Trade, Min. for Foreign Affairs, 1972–75; Minister Counsellor of Econ. Affairs, Paris, 1975–78; Ambassador to Australia and non-resident Ambassador to NZ, Fiji and Philippines, 1978–84; Sec. Gen., Assoc. of Iron Ore Exporting Countries, Geneva, 1984–88; Ambassador-at-large, Min. for Foreign Affairs, 1988; Ambassador: to Chile, 1988–92; to UK, 1992–95 and (non-resident) to Ireland, 1994–95; to Argentina, 1995–98; Perm. Rep. to UN, 1998–99 and 2000–01; Minister of Govt and Justice, 1999–2000; acting Pres. of Venezuela, Oct. 1999. Venezuelan orders: Order of Liberator, 1992; Orden Francisco de Miranda, 1995; Orden Andrés Bello, 1995; Orden al Merito en el Trabajo, 1998; Orden J. C. Falcón, 1999; numerous foreign orders. *Recreation:* golf. *E:* ia@arcaya.com. *Clubs:* Caracas Country; Royal Berkshire Polo; Royal & Ancient Golf (St Andrews); Chantilly Polo (Paris).

**ARCHARD, Prof. David William,** PhD; Professor of Philosophy, Queen's University Belfast, 2012–18, now Emeritus; *b* Reading, 19 Jan. 1951; *s* of John Frederick Archard and Peggy Muriel Archard (*née* Pratt); *m* 2015, Marie Bernarde Lynn. *Educ*: Wyggeston Boys' Sch., Leicester; Corpus Christi Coll., Oxford (Open Scholar; BA PPE 1972); London Sch. of Econs and Political Sci. (PhD 1976). Lectr, then Sen. Lectr, Ulster Poly., subseq. Univ. of Ulster, Jordanstown, 1976–85; Reader in Moral Philos., Univ. of St Andrews, 1985–2003; Prof. of Philosophy and Public Policy, Univ. of Lancaster, 2003–12. Mem., HFEA, 2004–16. Chm., Nuffield Council on Bioethics, 2017–. Hon. Vice-Pres., Soc. for Applied Philosophy, 2015–. *Publications:* Marxism and Existentialism: the political philosophy of Jean-Paul Sartre and Maurice Merleau-Ponty, 1980; Consciousness and the Unconscious, 1984; (ed) Philosophy and Pluralism, 1996; Sexual Consent, 1998; (jtly) The Moral and Political Status of Children, 2002; Children, Family and the State, 2003; Children: rights and childhood, 2004, 3rd edn 2015; The Family: a liberal defence, 2010; (ed jtly) Procreation and Parenthood: the ethics of bearing and rearing children, 2010; (ed jtly) Reading Onora O'Neill, 2013. *Recreations:* walking, travel by campervan and otherwise, food and drink, growing spuds. *Address:* School of History, Anthropology, Philosophy and Politics, Queen's University Belfast, University Road, Belfast BT7 1NN. *T:* (028) 9097 3681. *E:* d.archard@qub.ac.uk.

**ARCHDALE, Sir Nicholas (Edward),** 4th Bt *cr* 1928, of Riversdale, co. Fermanagh; *b* 2 Dec. 1965; *o s* of Sir Edward Folmer Archdale, 3rd Bt and Elizabeth Ann Stewart Archdale (*née* Lukis); *S* father, 2009 but his name does not appear on the Official Roll of the Baronetage. *Heir*: *cousin* Mervyn Talbot Archdale [*b* 30 Oct. 1924; *m* 1951, Aureole Helen Whelan (*d* 1998); one *s* one *d*].

**ARCHER,** family name of **Baron Archer of Weston-super-Mare.**

**ARCHER OF WESTON-SUPER-MARE,** Baron *cr* 1992 (Life Peer), of Mark in the County of Somerset; **Jeffrey Howard Archer;** author; *b* 15 April 1940; *s* of late William Archer and Lola Archer (*née* Cook); *m* 1966, Mary Weeden (*see* Dame M. D. Archer); two *s*. *Educ*: by my wife since leaving Wellington Sch., Somerset; Brasenose Coll., Oxford. Athletics Blues, 1963–65, Gymnastics Blue, 1963, Pres. OUAC 1965; ran for Great Britain (never fast enough); Oxford 100 yards record (9.6 sec.), 1966. Mem. GLC for Havering, 1966–70; MP (C) Louth, Dec. 1969–Sept. 1974. Dep. Chm., Cons. Party, 1985–86. Former Pres., Somerset AAA; Pres., World Snooker Assoc. (formerly World Professional Billiards & Snooker Assoc.), 1997–99. Co-ordinator, Simple Truth Campaign, 1991. *Plays:* Beyond Reasonable Doubt, Queen's, 1987; Exclusive, Strand, 1990; The Accused (and acted), Haymarket Theatre Royal, 2000. *Publications:* Not a Penny More, Not a Penny Less, 1975 (televised, 1990); Shall We Tell the President?, 1977; Kane and Abel, 1979, rev. 30th anniv. edn 2009 (televised, 1986); A Quiver Full of Arrows (short stories), 1980; The Prodigal Daughter, 1982; First Among Equals, 1984 (televised, 1986); A Matter of Honour, 1986; A Twist in the Tale (short stories), 1988; As the Crow Flies, 1991; Honour Among Thieves, 1993; Twelve Red Herrings (short stories), 1994; The Fourth Estate, 1996; The Collected Short Stories, 1997; The Eleventh Commandment, 1998; To Cut a Long Story Short (short stories), 2000; A Prison Diary, vol. I, Hell, 2002, vol. II, Purgatory, 2003, vol. III, Heaven, 2004; Sons of Fortune, 2003; False Impression (also screenplay), 2006; Cat O'Nine Tales (short stories), 2006; (with Francis J. Moloney) The Gospel according to Judas, 2007; A Prisoner of Birth, 2008; Paths of Glory (also screenplay), 2009; And Thereby Hangs a Tale (short stories), 2010; Only Time Will Tell, 2011; The Sins of the Father, 2012; Best Kept Secret, 2013; Be Careful What You Wish For, 2014; Mightier Than The Sword, 2015; Cometh the Hour, 2016; This was a Man, 2016; Tell Tale (short stories), 2017; Heads You Win, 2018; Nothing Ventured, 2019. *Recreations:* charity auctioneer, theatre, watching Somerset try to win the County Championship. *Address:* 93 Albert Embankment, SE1 7TY. *W:* www.jeffreyarcher.com.

**ARCHER OF WESTON-SUPER-MARE, Lady;** *see* Archer, Dame M. D.

**ARCHER, Anthony William;** Partner, JWA Governance Services LLP, since 2012; Managing Partner, Bridgewater Leadership Advisory (formerly Bridgewater Associates) since 2010; *b* 17 Jan. 1953; *s* of late George William Frederic Archer and Mary Archer (*née* Deeming); *m* 1979, Louise Marion Rhodes; one *s* two *d*. *Educ*: St Edward's Sch., Oxford Univ. of Birmingham (LLB Hons 1975); Anglia Ruskin Univ. (Cert. Higher Educn Christian Theology 2013). ACA 1979. Asst Manager, Tax, Price Waterhouse & Co. 1975–80; Asst Manager, Corporate Finance, S. G. Warburg & Co. Ltd, 1980–83; various posts in London and NY, County NatWest Ltd, 1983–88 (Dir, 1988); Man. Dir MacLennan & Partners, 1988–92; Principal, TASA Ltd, 1992–95; Partner, Ray & Berndtson, later Odgers Berndtson, 1995–2010. Sen. Advr, Steele Solutions Ltd, 2016–18 Mem., Crown Nominations Commn, 2005–07, 2017–. Chm., Council for Discipleship and Ministry, Dio. of St Albans, 2014–17. Member: Gen. Synod of C of E, 1993–2010, 2015–; Dioceses Commn, 2016–18. Gov., Royal Brompton & Harefield NHS Foundn Trust, 2016–19. Member, Council: Oak Hill Coll., 1995–2000; Wycliffe Hall, Oxford, 2000–11. Freeman, City of London, 2001; Liveryman, Wheelwrights' Co., 2001–. *Recreations:* gardening, narrow boating, grandparenting. *Address:* Barn Cottage, Little Gaddesden, Berkhamsted, Herts HP4 1PH. *T:* (01442) 842397. *E:* anthony.archer@jwagovernance.com.

**ARCHER, Gilbert Baird;** Vice Lord-Lieutenant for Tweeddale, 2018–17; Director, Tods of Orkney Ltd (oatcake and biscuit manufacturers), since 1970 (Chairman, 1970–2017); *b* Edinburgh, 24 Aug. 1942; *s* of late John Mark Archer, CBE and Marjorie Carmichael (*née* Baird); *m* 1967, Irené, *er d* of late Rev. Dr John C. M. Conn and Jess (*née* Stewart); two *d*. *Educ:* Melville Coll. Chairman: John Dickson & Son Ltd, 1985–97; Borders 1996 Ltd, 1996–98; Dir, EPS Moulders Ltd, 1985–88. Dir, Scottish Council Develt and Industry, 1993–96. Chm., Leith Chamber of Commerce, 1986–88; Pres., Edinburgh Chamber of Commerce, 1990–92; Chm., Assoc. of Scottish Chambers of Commerce, 1993–96; Dep. Pres., British Chambers of Commerce, 1995–96. Chm., Edinburgh Common Purpose, 1991–94. Dir, Scottish Council of Ind. Schs, 1988–91; Mem. Council, Governing Bodies Assoc. of Ind. Schs, 1988–91. Chm., St Columba's Hospice, 1998–2004 (now Vice Pres.). Vice Convener, George Watson's Coll., 1978–80; Governor: Fettes Coll., 1986–90; Napier Univ., 1991–97. Master: Co. of Merchants of the City of Edinburgh, 1997–99; Gunmakers' Co., 2006–07. Moderator, High Constables of Port of Leith, 1990–91. DL Tweeddale, 1994. *Recreations:* previously flying, now country pursuits. *Address:* 10 Broughton Place Lane, Edinburgh EH1 3RS. *T:* (0131) 556 4518. *Clubs:* Army and Navy; New (Edinburgh).

**ARCHER, Graham Robertson,** CMG 1997; HM Diplomatic Service, retired; High Commissioner to Malta, 1995–99; *b* 4 July 1939; *s* of late Henry Robertson Archer and Winifred Archer; *m* 1963, Pauline Cowan; two *d*. *Educ:* Judd School, Tonbridge. Joined Commonwealth Relations Office, 1962; British High Commission, New Delhi, 1964; Vice Consul, Kuwait, 1966; CRO (later FCO), 1967; Second Secretary (Commercial), Washington, 1970; First Secretary: FCO, 1972; Wellington, NZ, 1975; FCO, 1979; Counsellor: Pretoria, 1982; The Hague, 1986; FCO, 1990. Chm., Commonwealth Soc. for the Deaf, 2001–03; Dep. Chm., Adv. Bd, London and SE Reg. (formerly Cttee, SE and London Reg.), NT, 1999–2012. KStJ 1999. *Club:* Royal Over-Seas League (Mem., Council and Exec. Cttee, 2001–18).

**ARCHER, Malcolm David,** FRCO; Director of Chapel Music, Winchester College, 2007–18; *b* 29 April 1952; *s* of Gordon Austin Archer and Joan Eddleston Archer; *m* 1994, Alison Jane Robinson; one *s* one *d*. *Educ:* King Edward VII Sch., Lytham; Royal Coll. of Music (ARCM 1971); Jesus Coll., Cambridge (Organ Schol.; MA, CertEd). FRCO 1974. Asst Dir of Music, Magdalen Coll. Sch., Oxford, 1976–78; Asst Organist, Norwich Cathedral, 1978–83; Organist and Master of the Choristers, Bristol Cathedral, 1983–90; freelance organist, conductor and composer, 1990–96; music staff, 1990–96, Head of Chapel Music, 1994–96, Clifton Coll.; Organist and Master of the Choristers, Wells Cathedral, 1996–2004; Organist and Dir of Music, St Paul's Cathedral, 2004–07. Founder and Musical Dir, City of Bristol Choir, 1991–2000; Conductor, Wells Cathedral Oratorio Soc., 1996–2004. Hon. FNMSM, 2002; Hon. FGCM, 2005; Hon. FRSCM 2009. *Publications:* A Year of Praise, 1991; (ed jtly) Carols Old and New, 1991; After the Last Verse, 1995; (ed jtly) Advent for Choirs, 1999; (ed jtly) Epiphany to All Saints for Choirs, 2004; over 200 compositions; major works include: Love Unknown, 1992; Requiem, 1993; The Coming of the Kingdom, 1999; Three Psalms of David, 2000; Veni Creator Spiritus, 2004; The Garden of Love, 2004; Nowell! Nowell!, 2010; George and the Dragon, 2014; Vespers, 2016. *Recreations:* watercolour painting, cooking, classic cars, antique clocks. *Address:* St Paul's Church House, Staverton BA14 6PE.

**ARCHER, Dame Mary (Doreen),** DBE 2012; PhD; Chair: Science Museum Group, since 2015 (Trustee, National Museum of Science and Industry, 1990–2000); External Advisory Board, Centre for Personalised Medicine, St Anne's College, Oxford, since 2013; *b* 22 Dec. 1944; *d* of late Harold Norman Weeden and Doreen Weeden (*née* Cox); *m* 1966, Jeffrey Howard Archer (*see* Baron Archer of Weston-super-Mare); two *s*. *Educ:* Cheltenham Ladies' College; St Anne's Coll., Oxford (Nuffield Schol.; MA 1972; Hon. Fellow, 2013); Imperial Coll., London Univ. (PhD 1968); MA Cantab 1976. CChem, FRSC 1987; CSci 2006. Junior Res. Fellow, St Hilda's Coll., Oxford, 1968–71; temp. Lectr in Chemistry, Somerville Coll., Oxford, 1971–72; Res. Fellow, Royal Instn of GB, 1972–76 (Dewar Fellow, 1975–76); Lector in Chemistry, Trinity Coll., Cambridge, 1976–86; Fellow and Coll. Lectr in Chem., Newnham Coll., Cambridge, 1976–86 (Bye-Fellow, 1987–2002). Sen. Academic Fellow, De Montfort Univ. (formerly Leicester Polytechnic), 1990–; Vis. Prof., Dept of Biochem., 1991–99, Centre for Energy Policy and Technol., 2000–03, Imperial Coll., London; Visitor, Univ. of Hertfordshire, 1993–2005. Chm., Cambridge Univ. Hosps NHS Foundn Trust (formerly Addenbrooke's NHS Trust), 2002–12 (Dir, 1992–2012; Vice-Chm., 1999–2002). Chair, Imperial Coll. Health Partners Adv. Council (formerly Expert Adv. Bd, then Expert Adv. Council), 2013–17. Member: Renewable Energy Adv. Gp, Dept of Energy/DTI, 1991–92; Energy Adv. Panel, DTI, 1992–98; COPUS, 1995–2000; Energy Policy Adv. Gp, Royal Soc., 1998–2004. Chm., E of England Stem Cell Network Steering Gp, 2004–08. Convenor (formerly Chm.), UK Univ. Hosps Chairs' Gp, 2008–12. Trustee: UK Stem Cell Foundn, 2005–15; CRAC, 2007–12; icould, 2012–19; Global eHealth Foundn, 2015–18. Mem. Council, Cheltenham Ladies' Coll., 1991–2000. Mem. Bd of Dirs, Internat. Solar Energy Soc., 1975–81 (Sec., UK Section, 1973–76); Manager, 1982–84, Mem. Council, 1984–85 and 1997–2002, Royal Instn; Chm., Nat. Energy Foundn, 1990–2000 (Pres., 2000–17); Pres., Solar Energy Soc., 2001–. Director: Anglia Television Gp, 1987–95; Mid Anglia Radio, 1988–94; Q103 (formerly Cambridge & Newmarket FM Radio), 1988–97; Hydrodec, 2014–. Mem. Council of Lloyd's, 1989–92. Pres., Guild of Church Musicians, 1989–; non-exec. Dir, Britten Sinfonia, 1998–; Chm., Cambridge Early Music, 2015–. Hon. Liveryman: Fuellers' Co., 2016; Salters' Co., 2018. Hon. DSc: Hertfordshire, 1994; Imperial Coll. London, 2018. Melchett Medal, Inst. of Energy, 2002; Eva Philbin Award, Inst. of Chem. of Ireland, 2007. *Publications:* Rupert Brooke and the Old Vicarage, Grantchester, 1989; (ed jtly) Clean Electricity from Photovoltaics, 2001, 2nd edn 2014; (ed jtly) Molecular to Global Photosynthesis, 2004; (ed jtly) Transformation and Change: the 1702 Chair of Chemistry at Cambridge, 2004; (ed jtly) Solar Photon Conversion in Nanostructured and Photoelectrochemical Systems, 2008; The Story of The Old Vicarage, Grantchester, 2012; contribs to chem. jls. *Recreations:* reading, writing, singing. *Address:* The Old Vicarage, Grantchester, Cambridge CB3 9ND. *T:* (01223) 840213.

**ARCHER, Nicholas Stewart,** MVO 2001; HM Diplomatic Service; Ambassador to Czech Republic, since 2018; *b* 24 Dec. 1960; *s* of Thomas Stewart Archer and Marjorie Anne Archer (*née* Mackenzie); *m* 1999, Erica Margaret Power; two *s*. *Educ:* Denstone Coll.; Univ. of Durham (BA 1982). With Sotheby's, 1983; entered FCO, 1983: Third, later Second Sec., Amman, 1986–89; FCO, 1989–92; Private Sec. to Minister of State, FCO, 1992–94; First Sec., Oslo, 1995–97; Asst Private Sec. to the Prince of Wales, 1997–2000; Head: NE Asia and Pacific Dept, FCO, 2001–02; Near East and N Africa Dept, FCO, 2002–05; High Comr, Malta, 2006–08; Ambassador to Denmark, 2008–12; Dir, Strategic Trade, 2012–14, Man. Dir, Policy and Network Develt, 2014–16, UK Trade and Investment. *Address:* c/o Foreign and Commonwealth Office, King Charles Street, SW1A 2AH.

**ARCHER, Stephen Frederick Julian;** Director, Infrastructure Services, Aberdeenshire Council, since 2011; *b* Montrose, 20 July 1960; *s* of Edward Archer and Eileen Archer; *m* 1991, Dawn; one *s* one *d*. *Educ:* Jordanhill College Sch., Glasgow; Univ. of Liverpool; Liverpool Poly.; Univ. of West of England. Envmtl Health Officer, Ipswich BC, 1985–88; Cotswold DC, 1988–98; Hd of Service, Bracknell Forest BC, 1998–2002; North Kesteven DC, 2002–05; Waveney DC, 2005–11. *Recreations:* Rugby (used to play), photography, bird watching, music, RSPM Member. *Address:* Aberdeenshire Council, Woodhill House, Westburn Road, Aberdeen AB16 5EB.

**ARCHER, Thomas;** Controller, Factual Production, BBC, 2008–12; *b* Tunbridge Wells, 7 Jan. 1953; *s* of Michael and Carol Carr-Archer; two *d*. *Educ:* Tonbridge Sch.; Univ. of Bristol (BA; PhD African Hist. 1982). Freelance investigative journalist, 1982–95; Head: of Factual Progs, HTV, 1995–96; of Factual Progs, United News and Media, 1997–2000; of Factual, Granada West, 2000–02; of Progs, BBC TV, Bristol, 2002–04; Comr, Features and Documentaries, BBC, 2004–08. Vis. Prof., UWE, 2013–.

**ARCHER, Timothy John;** Consultant, Reed Smith LLP (formerly Richards Butler, then Reed Smith Richards Butler), since 2001 (Partner, 1973–2001; Senior Partner, 1991–2000); *b* 9 Feb. 1943; *s* of Jack Valentine Archer and Phyllis Emma Archer (*née* Cotton); *m* 1972, Gillian Karen Davies; one *s* one *d*. *Educ:* Sutton Valence Sch.; Merton Coll., Oxford (MA); Coll. of Law. Alfred Syrett Prize, Law Soc., 1966; admitted Solicitor, 1969. Richards Butler, Solicitors, subseq. Reed Smith Richards Butler, later Reed Smith LLP, 1965–. Associate, Byrne Dean Associates Ltd, 2003–. Part-time Chm., Employment Tribunals, 2002–06. Director: Royal Philharmonic Orch., 1993–95; Philharmonia Orch. Trust, 1997–2010; Harefield Res. Foundn, 2002–03; NSO Trust Ltd, 2010–17. Mem., Management Cttee, Univ. of Exeter Centre for Legal Practice, 1993–96. *Publications:* (contrib.) International Handbook on Contracts of Employment, 1988, 2nd edn 1991; with Prof. G. S. Morris: Trade Unions, Employers and the Law, 1991; Collective Labour Law, 2000. *Recreations:* sport, travel, music, art. *Club:* City of London.

**ARCHER, William Ernest;** Chairman, Focus DIY Ltd (formerly Focus DIY, later Focus Do It All, then Focus Wickes Group), 1992–2007 (Chief Executive Officer, 1992–2002); *b* 6 May 1944; *s* of Joseph and Elizabeth Archer; *m* 1963, Shirley Patricia Clarke; one *s* two *d*. *Educ:* Wellington Sch. for Boys. Sales Manager Nat. Accounts, Crown Dec. Prod., Reed Internat. Ltd, 1968–83; Man. Dir, Signpost/Ashfield Paints, 1983–87; (with business partner) acquired retailer Choice DIY Ltd, 1987; Man. Dir, Choice DIY Ltd, subseq. Focus DIY, 1987–92. MInstD; MCIM. *Recreations:* golf, swimming, walking, reading, football, tennis. *Address:* Withington Hall Offices, Holmes Chapel Road, Lower Withington, Cheshire SK11 9DS. *E:* vicki@bandscharters.com. *Clubs:* Pleasington Golf; La Manga.

**ARCULUS, Sir (Thomas) David (Guy),** Kt 2005; Chairman: O$_2$ plc (formerly mmO$_2$), 2004–06; Aldermore Bank plc, 2010–13; *b* 2 June 1946; *s* of Thomas Guy Arculus and Mary (*née* Barton); *m* 1973, Anne Murdoch Sleeman; two *s* one *d*. *Educ:* Bromsgrove Sch.; Oriel Coll., Oxford (MA 1968); London Graduate Sch. of Business Studies (MSc 1972). VSO, 1964–65. BBC Producer, 1968–70; EMAP plc: Publisher, 1972–84; Dep. Man. Dir, 1984–89; Gp Man. Dir, 1989–97; Chief Operating Officer, United News and Media plc, 1997–98; Chairman: ipc Gp, 1998–2001; Severn Trent plc, 1998–2004; Earls Court and Olympia Ltd, 2002–04; Shortlist Media, 2007–14; Boat Internat., 2007–10; LIEC, 2008–12 (non-exec. Dir, LIEC Hldgs, 2008–12); Numis Corp., 2009–14. Non-executive Director: Norcros, 1993–96; Barclays plc, 1997–2006; Guiton Gp, 2000–02; Telefónica (formerly Telefónica O$_2$) Europe plc, 2006–12; Telefónica SA, 2006–12; Pearson plc, 2006–15; Chm., Energy UK, 2015–17. Chm., Better Regulation Task Force, Cabinet Office, 2002–05. Mem., President's Cttee, 2003–, Dep. Pres., 2005–06, CBI. Chairman: PPA, 1988–90; NCC, 1993–96. Deleg., Finance Cttee, OUP, 2000–06; Chm., Investment Cttee, Oriel Coll., Oxford, 2000–04. A Comr, Public Works Loan Bd, 2001–02. Trustee, Industry and Parliament Trust, 2006–11 (Fellow, 1994). Freeman, City of London, 1989. High Sheriff, Cambs, 2016–17. DUniv Central England, 2003. Marcus Morris Award, PPA, 1993. *Recreations:* cricket, hill walking, reading. *E:* david.arculus@integral2.com. *Clubs:* Oxford and Cambridge, Groucho, Thirty, MCC.

**ARDAGH, Philip;** *see* Roxbee Cox, P. A.

**ARDAGH AND CLONMACNOISE, Bishop of, (RC),** since 2013; **Most Rev. Francis Duffy;** *b* Templeport, Co. Cavan, 21 April 1958; *s* of late Frank Duffy and of Mary Catherine Duffy (*née* Dolan). *Educ:* Munlough Nat. Sch., Bawnboy; St Patrick's Coll., Co. Cavan; St Patrick's Coll., Maynooth. Ordained priest, 1982; Teacher of history, religion and Irish, St Patrick's Coll., Co. Cavan; Principal, Fatima and Felim's Secondary Sch., Ballinamore, Co. Leitrim, 1996–2008; Diocesan Sec. and Chancellor, Dio. of Kilmore, 2009; Resident Priest, Parish of Laragh, Co. Cavan, 2009–13. *Address:* Diocesan Office, Ballinalee Road, Longford, Co. Longford, Ireland.

**ARDEE, Lord; Anthony Jacques Brabazon;** *b* 30 Jan. 1977; *o s* of Earl of Meath, *qv*; *m* 2004, Fionnuala, *d* of Joseph Aston; one *s* one *d*. *Educ:* Harrow Sch. *Heir: s* Hon. Aldus Jack Brabazon, *b* 21 April 2010.

**ARDEN OF HESWALL, Rt Hon. Lady; Mary Howarth Arden,** DBE 1993; PC 2000; a Justice of the Supreme Court of the United Kingdom, since 2018; *d* of late Lt-Col E. C. Arden, LLB, TD and M. M. Arden (*née* Smith); *m* 1973, Jonathan Hugh Mance (*see* Baron Mance); one *s* two *d*. *Educ:* Huyton College; Girton College, Cambridge (MA, LLM; Hon. Fellow, 1995); Harvard Law School (LLM). Called to the Bar, Gray's Inn, 1971 (Arden and Birkenhead Scholarships, 1971); admitted *ad eundem* to Lincoln's Inn, 1973 (Bencher, 1993); QC 1986; Attorney Gen., Duchy of Lancaster, 1991–93; a Judge of the High Ct of Justice, Chancery Div., 1993–2000; UK *ad hoc* Judge, Eur. Ct of Human Rights, 2000; a Lady Justice of Appeal, 2000–18; Hd, Internat. Judicial Relns for England and Wales, 2005–18. Chm., Law Commn, 1996–99. Bar Mem., Law Society's Standing Cttee on Company Law, 1976–2007; Member: Financial Law Panel, 1993–2000; Steering Gp, Company Law Review Project, 1998–2001; Chairman: Wking Party of Judges' Council on Constitutional Reform, 2004–06; Papers Cttee, Commonwealth Law Conf., 2005. DTI Inspector, Rotaprint PLC, 1988–91. Mem. Council, Statute Law Soc., 2001–07. Member: Exec. Cttee, 2004–05, Advr to Bd of Trustees, 2005–, British Inst. of Internat. and Comparative Law; Ext. Adv. Bd, Faculty of Modern History, Univ. of Oxford, 2000–06; Amer. Law Inst., 2003–; Adv. Bd, Centre of European Law, KCL, 2008–; Permanent Ct of Arbitration, 2011–; Adv. Bd, Centre of Eur. Law Studies, Univ. of Cambridge, 2018–; Adv. Council, Bonavero Inst. Human Rights, Univ. of Oxford; Visitor, Royal Holloway, Univ. of London, 2008–; Dist. Judicial Visitor, UCL, 2008–; Chair, Septemviri, Univ. of Cambridge, 2017–. Acad. Trustee, Kennedy Meml Trust, 1995–2005. Pres., Assoc. of Women Barristers, 1994–98. Chair, CAB, Royal Cts of Justice, 1994–97; Patron, Free Repn Unit, 2007–. Hon. Fellow: Liverpool John Moores Univ., 2006 (Pres. of Moots, 2016); Amer. Coll. of Trial Lawyers, 2016. DUniv Essex, 1997; Hon. LLD: Liverpool, 1998; Warwick, 1999; RHBNC, 1999; Nottingham, 2002; UCL, 2011. Editor, Chancery

Guide, 1995, 1999. *Publications:* Negligence and the Public Accountant (contrib.), 1972; Legal Editor, Current Accounting Law and Practice, by Robert Willott, 1976; (with George Eccles) Tolley's Companies Act 1980, 1980; Legal Consultant Editor: Tolley's Companies Act 1981, 1981; Tolley's Accounting Problems of the Companies Acts, 1984; Accounting Provisions of the Companies Act 1985, 1985; Coopers & Lybrand Deloitte Manual of Accounting, vols 1 and 2, 1990, 1995; Jt Gen. Editor and Contributor, Buckley on the Companies Acts, 14th edn: Special Bulletin, 1990, 15th edn 2000 (updated biannually); (contrib.) Accounting and the Law, 1992; (contrib.) Perspectives on Company Law, 1995; (contrib.) Law, Society and Economy, 1997; Human Rights and European Law: building new legal orders, 2015; Common Law and Modern Society: keeping pace with change, 2015; articles in legal jls. *Recreations:* travel, reading, theatre. *Address:* Supreme Court of the United Kingdom, Parliament Square, SW1P 3BD.

**ARDEN, Andrew Paul Russel;** QC 1991; *b* 20 April 1948; *m* 1991, Joanne Leahy; one *d*. *Educ:* Stowe; University College Sch.; University Coll. London (LLB). MCIH 2002–14. Called to the Bar, Gray's Inn, 1974; Dir, Small Heath Community Law Centre, Birmingham, 1976–78. Local government inquiries/reviews: for GLC, 1982–83; for Bristol CC, 1985; for Hackney LBC, 1985–87, 1993–94; for Camden LBC, 1992. Founder and Head, Arden Chambers, 1993–2003. Vis. Prof. of Law, Faculty of Develt and Soc., Sheffield Hallam Univ., 2001–07. General Editor: Encyclopaedia of Housing Law, 1978–; Housing Law Reports, 1981–; Jl of Housing Law, 1997–; Consultant Ed., Local Government Law Reports, 2000–01 (Gen. Ed., 1999–2000). *Publications:* Manual of Housing Law, 1978, 10th edn (with Andrew Dymond), 2017; Housing Act 1980 (annotations), 1980; (with Prof. M. Partington) Quiet Enjoyment, 1980, 8th edn (with R. Brown and S. Madge-Wyld), 2017; (with Prof. M. Partington) Housing Law, 1983, 2nd edn (also with C. Hunter), 1994; (with Prof. J. T. Farrand) Rent Acts & Regulations, amended and annotated, 1981; (with C. Cross) Housing & Building Control Act 1984 (annotations), 1984; Private Tenants Handbook, 1985, 2nd edn 1989; Public Tenants Handbook, 1985, 2nd edn 1989; (with S. McGrath) Landlord & Tenant Act 1985 (annotations), 1986; Housing Act 1985 (annotations), 1986; (with J. Ramage) Housing Associations Act 1985 (annotations), 1986; Homeless Persons Handbook, 1986, 2nd edn 1988; (with C. Hunter) Housing Act 1988 (annotations), 1989; (with Sir Robert Megarry) Assured Tenancies, Vol. 3, The Rent Acts, 11th edn 1989; (with C. Hunter) Local Government & Housing Act 1989 (annotations), 1990; (with C. Hunter) Local Government Finance Law, 1994; (with C. Hunter) Housing Act 1996 (annotations), 1996; (with C. Hunter) Housing Grants, Construction and Renewal Act 1996 (annotations), 1996; Homeless Persons Act, 1982, 11th edn as Homelessness and Allocations (with J. Bates and T. Vanhegan), 2018; (jtly) Local Government Constitutional and Administrative Law, 1999, 2nd edn 2008; *fiction:* The Motive Not The Deed, 1974; No Certain Roof, 1985; The Object Man, 1986; The Programme, 2001; thrillers under pseudonym Bernard Bannerman: The Last Wednesday, 1990; Controlling Interest, 1990; The Judge's Song, 1991; Orbach's Judgement, 1991; Disappearance, 2018; Carson's Confession, 2018; From Wednesday to Judgement, 2018. *Recreations:* Southern Comfort, Hill Street Blues, Camel cigarettes. *Address:* Nexus Chambers, 7 New Square, WC2A 3QS. *T:* (020) 7404 1147. *E:* andrew.arden@nexuschambers.com.

**ARDEN, Annabel Kate, (Mrs Stephen Jeffreys);** freelance theatre and opera director; Co-Founder, Complicité (formerly Théâtre de Complicité), since 1983; *b* London, 11 Nov. 1959; *d* of Prof. Geoffrey Bernard Arden and Sheila Barbara Arden (*née* Gordon); *m* 1999, Stephen Jeffreys (*d* 2018); two *s*. *Educ:* St Paul's Girls' Sch.; Newnham Coll., Cambridge (BA Hons English Lit. 1981). For Complicité: *as performer.* Put It on Your Head, 1983; Foodstuff, 1986; Anything for a Quiet Life, 1987 (adapted for TV, 1989); The Street of Crocodiles, world tour, 1992–93 and revival, 1998–99; *as director.* productions include: Please, Please, Please, 1986; The Lamentations of Thel, 1989; (with S. McBurney) The Visit, 1989, revival, 1991; (with A. Castledine) The Winter's Tale, 1992; (with A. Castledine) India Song, 1993; Lionboy, 2013; semi-staging of Das Rheingold and The Miserly Knight, RFH, 2015; Il Barbiere di Siviglia, Glyndebourne, 2016, revival, 2019; for Opera North: The Magic Flute, 1993, 1997; The Return of Ulysses, 1995–97; La Traviata, 2001, 2002, 2003, 2004; The Cunning Little Vixen, 2001; Andrea Chénier, 2016; Turandot, L'enfant et les sortilèges, Osud, 2017; Aida, 2019; La Traviata, Sadler's Wells, 1999; Picasso's Women, RNT, 1999; The Rake's Progress, ENO, 2001; Gianni Schicchi, The Miserly Knight, Glyndebourne, 2004; L'Elisir d'Amore, Glyndebourne on Tour, 2007, Houston, 2009, revival at Glyndebourne, 2011, 2019; Little Red Riding Hood, Almeida, 2005; The Art of War, Sydney Th. Co., 2007; Heldenplatz, Arcola, 2010; concert. perf., The Soldier's Tale, Chicago SO, 2012; La Bohème, WNO, 2012; The Commission/Café Kafka, Linbury Studio Th., 2014; Carmen, Grange Fest., 2017; has created many concert stagings incl. (with Sir John Eliot Gardiner) Leonore, 1996 and (with V. Jurowski) Faust, 2012–14. Has conducted internat. workshops. Union of Eur. Women of Achievement Award, 2003. *Publications:* (contrib.) Actor Training, 2010. *Recreations:* family, gardening, singing. *E:* annabelarden@me.com.

**ARDEN, Peter Leonard;** QC 2006; *b* 5 April 1960; *s* of Surgeon Captain Leonard Arden and Ann Arden; *m* 1999, Zia Kurban Bhaloo, *qv*; one *d*. *Educ:* University Coll. London (LLB); Queens' Coll., Cambridge (LLB 1982). Called to the Bar, Gray's Inn, 1983.

**ARDEN, Sian S.;** *see* Sutherland-Arden.

**ARFIELD, John Alan;** University Librarian, University of Western Australia, 1996–2010; *b* 15 March 1949; *s* of Donald Sidney Arfield and Barbara Winifred Arfield (*née* Alderton); *m* 1st, 1970, Paula May Perrin (marr. diss. 1998); one *s* two *d*; 2nd, 2004, Susan June Henshall. *Educ:* Kingston Grammar Sch.; Jesus Coll., Cambridge (BA 1971; MA 1975); Univ. of Sheffield (MA 1973). Cambridge University Library: Asst Liby Officer, 1973–78; Asst Under-Librarian, 1978–79; Under-Librarian, 1979–81; Sub-Librarian (Tech. Services), UC, Cardiff, 1981–88; Dep. Librarian, Reading Univ., 1988–92; University Librarian, Loughborough Univ., 1992–96. *Publications:* articles in librarianship. *Recreations:* cricket, theatre, music, gardening.

**ARFON-JONES, Elisabeth, (Mrs B. Watkins);** DL; Senior Tribunals Liaison Judge (Wales), since 2011; a Vice President, Upper Tribunal (Immigration and Asylum Chamber) (formerly Deputy President, Asylum and Immigration Tribunal), 2005–14; a Public Appointments Assessor, 2012–16; *b* 2 July 1950; *d* of late Arfon Arfon-Jones and Margaret Arfon-Jones (*née* Price); *m* 1982, Brian Watkins, *qv*; one *d*. *Educ:* University Coll. London (LLB 1971). Called to the Bar, Gray's Inn, 1972 (William Shaw Schol.; Fellow, 2008; Bencher, 2010; Mem., Mgt Cttee); in practice at the Bar, 1973–77; Sen. Prosecuting Solicitor, Cheshire, 1977–80; Crown Counsel, Bermuda, 1980–81; Registrar, Supreme Court, Bermuda, 1981–83; an Immigration Adjudicator, 1997–2005; Dep. Chief Immigration Adjudicator, 2001–04; Chief Immigration Adjudicator, 2004–05. A Civil Service Comr, 2005–12. A Lay Chm., NHS Complaints Rev. Panels in Wales, 1995–2006. US Liby of Congress Rep. (pt-time), Islamabad, 1984–86; Chm., Internat. Cttee, BC Red Cross, Vancouver, 1986–90; Founding Chm., Swaziland Hospice at Home, 1990–93. Mem. Bd, Community Fund (formerly National Lottery Charities Bd), 1998–2004 (Chm., Wales Cttee, 2000–02). Member: Ministerial Adv. Gp on Community Volunteering, 1999–2004; Multi-Centre Res. Ethics Cttee for Wales, 2001–03. Lay Mem., Lord Chancellor's Adv. Cttee for Appointment of JPs in Gwent, 2000–09. Hon. Sec., Assoc. of Women Barristers, 1999–2001. Tenant Dir, Dolphin Sq. 2005 Ltd, 2018–. Member, Council: Barnardo's, 2001–08 (Chm., Wales Cttee, 2007–08); Canada-Royal Commonwealth Ex-Services League, 2013–. Mem., Livery Co. of Wales (formerly Welsh Livery Guild), 2009–. Trustee, Lord Edmund-Davies Legal Educn Trust, 2013–. DL Gwent, 2006. *Recreations:* 'laughter and the love of friends' (worldwide), theatre, ski-ing. *Address:* c/o Drummonds, 49 Charing Cross, SW1A 2DX. *E:* libby.watkins@gmail.com. *Clubs:* Athenæum (Mem., Gen. Cttee, 2016–), Royal Over-Seas League.

**ARGAR, Edward John Comport;** MP (C) Charnwood, since 2015; Minister of State, Department of Health and Social Care, since 2019; *b* Ashford, Kent, 9 Dec. 1977; *s* of Edward Henry Argar and Patricia Joan Argar. *Educ:* Harvey Grammar Sch., Folkestone; Oriel Coll., Oxford (BA; MSt). Political Advr to Shadow Foreign Sec., 2001–05; Mgt Consultant, Hedra plc, then Mouchel, 2005–11; Hd, Public Affairs, UK and Europe, Serco Gp plc, 2011–14. Parly Under Sec. of State, MoJ, 2018–19. Non-exec. Mem. Bd, NHS Westminster PCT, 2008–10. Trustee, Groundwork London, 2010–15. Mem., Westminster CC, 2006–15. *Recreations:* reading, ski-ing, tennis, cricket, gardening. *Address:* House of Commons, SW1A 0AA. *T:* (020) 7219 8140. *E:* edward.argar.mp@parliament.uk. *Club:* Travellers.

**ARGENT, Malcolm,** CBE 1985; Deputy Chairman, Civil Aviation Authority, 1995–98; *b* 14 Aug. 1935; *s* of Leonard James and Winifred Hilda Argent; *m* 1st, 1961, Mary Patricia Addis Stimson (marr. diss. 1983); one *s* one *d*; 2nd, 1986, Thelma Hazel Eddleston. *Educ:* Palmer's Sch., Grays, Essex. General Post Office, London Telecommunications Region: Exec. Officer, 1953–62; Higher Exec. Officer, 1962–66; Principal, PO Headquarters, 1966–70; Private Sec., Man. Dir, Telecommunications, 1970–74; Personnel Controller, External Telecommun. Exec., 1974–75; Dir, Chairman's Office, PO Central Headquarters, 1975–77; Dir, Eastern Telecommun. Region, 1977; Secretary: of the Post Office, 1978–81; British Telecommunications Corp., 1981–94; British Telecommunications plc, 1984–94 (Dir, 1989–98); Chm., NATS, 1996–98. Trustee, British Telecommunications Staff Superannuation Fund, 1981–94. Director: McCaw Cellular Communications Inc., 1989–94; Westminster Health Care plc, 1992–99; Clerical, Medical & Gen. Assce Soc., 1994–2001; Clerical Medical Investment Gp, 1997–2001; Chm., Envision Licensing Ltd, 1999. Member: Council, CBI, 1994–95; Cttee, Essex Magistrates' Courts, 2000–04. Freeman, City of London, 1987. CCMI (CIMgt 1992; CBIM 1991; FBIM 1980). Hon. DSc Aston, 2004. *Recreation:* golf. *Address:* 64 Tor Bryan, Ingatestone, Essex CM4 9HN.

**ARGENTA, Nancy Maureen;** soprano; *b* Nelson, Canada, 17 Jan. 1957; *d* of Hugh and Agnes Herbison; adopted Argenta as professional name. *Educ:* Vancouver Community Coll.; Univ. of Western Ontario (Artist Dip. in Performance). Début, Hippolyte and Aricie, Fest. d'Aix en Provence, 1983; has performed in Australia, Europe, Japan, N America, S America, with major orchestras and companies, including Boston SO, Leipzig Gewandhaus Orch., Montreal SO, LPO and Philharmonia Orch.; also tours as a recitalist. Has made over 50 recordings. *Recreations:* walking, gardening, cycling, woodwork.

**ARGENTINA, Bishop of,** since 2002; **Most Rev. Gregory James Venables;** Presiding Bishop (Primate) of the Province of South America, since 2016; *b* 6 Dec. 1949; *s* of Rev. Dudley James Venables and May Norah Venables (*née* Saddington); *m* 1970, Sylvia Margaret Norton; one *s* two *d*. *Educ:* Chatham House; Kingston Univ.; Christchurch Coll., Canterbury. Computer Systems Officer, Sterling Winthrop, 1971–72; English master, Holy Cross Sch., Broadstairs, 1974–77; Headmaster, St Andrews Coll., Asunción, Paraguay, 1978–89; ordained deacon, March 1984, priest, Nov. 1984; Asst Curate, St Helen's and St Giles, Rainham with St Mary's, Wennington, dio. of Chelmsford, 1990–93; Asst Bishop, dio. of Peru and Bolivia, 1993–95; Bishop of Bolivia, and Vice-Primate, Province of the Southern Cone of America, 1995–2000; Coadjutor Bishop of Argentina, 2000–02; Presiding Bishop (Primate) of the Province of the Southern Cone of America, 2001–10. *Publications:* Look to the Scars, 1973. *Recreations:* reading, music, walking. *Address:* 25 de Mayo 282, 1001 Buenos Aires, Argentina. *T:* (11) 43424618, *Fax:* (11) 43310234. *E:* diocesisanglibue@fibertel.com.ar.

**ARGERICH, Martha;** pianist; *b* Buenos Aires, 5 June 1941; *m* 1st, 1963, Robert Chen (marr. diss.); one *d*; 2nd, 1969, Charles Dutoit, conductor (marr. diss.); one *d*. Studied with Vincenzo Scaramuzza, Madeleine Lipatti, Nikita Magaloff, Friedrich Gulda, Arturo Benedetti Michelangeli, Stefan Askenase. Début in Buenos Aires, 1949, in London, 1964; soloist with leading orchestras. Gen. Dir, Argerich's Meeting Point, Beppu, 1996–; Founder, Martha Argerich Project, 2002; Co-Founder, Alink-Argerich Foundn. Numerous recordings. First Prize: Ferruccio Busoni Internat. Competition, Bolzano, Italy, 1957; Internat. Music Competition, Geneva, 1957; Internat. Chopin Competition, Warsaw, 1965. Comdr, Ordre des Arts et des Lettres (France), 2004 (Officier, 1996); Gold Rays with Rosette, Order of Rising Sun (Japan), 2005; Kennedy Center Honor (USA), 2016. *Address:* c/o Jacques Thelen Agence Artistique, 15 avenue Montaigne, 75008 Paris, France.

**ARGUS, Donald Robert,** AC 2010 (AO 1998); Chairman, BHP Billiton (formerly BHP Ltd), 1999–2010 (Director, 1996–2010); *b* 1 Aug. 1938; *s* of Dudley Francis and Evelyn Argus; *m* 1961, Patricia Anne Hutson; three *d*. *Educ:* C of E GS, Brisbane; RMIT; Harvard Univ. FAIB; FCPA; FAICD. National Australia Bank: General Manager: Credit Bureau, 1984–87; Gp Strategic Develt, 1987–89; Chief Operating Officer, 1989–90; Man. Dir and Chief Exec., 1990–99. Chm. and Dir, Brambles Ltd (formerly Brambles Industries), 1999–2008; Director: Southcorp Ltd, 1999–2003; Australian Foundn Investment Co., 1999–2015; Member: Allianz Internat. Adv. Bd, 2000–09; Internat. Adv. Bd, NYSE, 2005–09; Chm., Australia Adv. Bd, Bank of America Merrill Lynch, 2010– (Mem., Global Adv. Council, 2013–19). Hon. LLD Monash; DUniv Griffith. *Recreations:* golf, reading, hockey. *Address:* PO Box 252, Caulfield East, Melbourne, Vic 3145, Australia. *T:* (3) 96592726, *Fax:* (3) 90171313. *Clubs:* Australian, Melbourne (Melbourne); Kingston Heath Golf; Queensland Cricketers (Brisbane).

**ARGYLL, 13th Duke of,** *cr* 1701 (Scotland), 1892 (UK); **Torquhil Ian Campbell;** Marquess of Lorne and Kintyre; Earl of Campbell and Cowal; Viscount Lochow and Glenyla; Baron Inveraray, Mull, Morvern and Tiry, 1701; Baron Campbell, 1445; Earl of Argyll, 1457; Baron Lorne, 1470; Baron Kintyre, 1633 (Scotland); Baron Sundridge, 1766; Baron Hamilton of Hameldon, 1776; Bt 1627; 37th Baron and 47th Knight of Lochow; Celtic title, Mac Cailein Mor, Chief of Clan Campbell; Hereditary Master of the Royal Household, Scotland; Hereditary High Sheriff of the County of Argyll; Admiral of the Western Coast and Isles; Keeper of the Great Seal of Scotland and of the Castles of Dunstaffnage, Dunoon, and Carrick and Tarbert; *b* 29 May 1968; *s* of 12th Duke of Argyll and Iona Mary, *d* of Capt. Sir Ivar Colquhoun, 8th Bt; *S* father, 2001; *m* 2002, Eleanor Mary, *d* of Peter H. G. Cadbury; two *s* one *d*. *Educ:* Craigflower; Cargilfield; Glenalmond Coll.; Royal Agricultural Coll., Cirencester. A Page of Honour to the Queen, 1981–83. Pres., Scottish Chapter, World Elephant Polo Assoc., 2006–. Patron, Keeper of the Quaich 2006–. Liveryman, Distillers' Co., 2006–. *Heir: s* Marquess of Lorne, *qv. Address:* Inveraray Castle, Inveraray, Argyll PA32 8XF.

**ARGYLL AND THE ISLES, Bishop of,** since 2011; **Rt Rev. Kevin Pearson;** *b* 27 Aug. 1954; *s* of Edward and Nancy Pearson; *m* 1992, Dr Elspeth Atkinson. *Educ:* Leeds Univ. (BA 1975); Edinburgh Univ. (BD 1979); Edinburgh Theol Coll. Ordained deacon, 1979, priest, 1980; Curate, St Mary, Horden, 1979–81; Chaplain, Leeds Univ., 1981–87; Rector, St Salvador, Edinburgh, 1987–93; Chaplain, Napier Poly., subseq. Napier Univ., 1988–94; Diocesan Dir of Ordinands, Dio. Edinburgh, 1990–95; Provincial Dir of Ordinands, Scottish Episcopal Church, 1991–2011; Associate Rector, Old St Paul, Edinburgh, 1993–94; Priest-in-charge, Linlithgow, 1994–95; Rector, St Michael and All Saints, Edinburgh, 1995–2011; Dean, Dio. of Edinburgh, 2004–10. Hon. Canon, St Mary's Cathedral, Edinburgh, 2003–04. *Recreations:* Italy, the Victorian novel, food and drink. *Address:* Bishop's House, Ganavan Sands, Oban PA34 5TB. *T:* (01631) 562617. *E:* bishop@argyll.anglican.org; St Moluag's Diocesan Centre, Croft Avenue, Oban PA34 5JJ. *T:* (01631) 570870.

**ARGYLL AND THE ISLES, Bishop of, (RC),** since 2016; **Rt Rev. Brian Thomas McGee;** *b* Greenock, 8 Oct. 1965; *s* of Seamus and Brighid McGee. *Educ:* St Vincent's Coll., Langbank; St Mary's Coll., Blairs; St Patrick's Coll., Thurles (Cert. Philosophy; DipTh); Sarum Coll., Salisbury (MA Christian Spirituality 2011). Ordained priest, 1989; Assistant Priest: St Charles Borromeo Parish, Paisley, 1989–95; Holy Family Parish, Port Glasgow, 1995–97; Parish Priest, St Joseph's Parish, Clarkston, 1997–2007; Spiritual Dir, Scotus Coll., Nat. Seminary, 2007–09; Parish Priest, Holy Family Parish, Port Glasgow, 2009–15; Vicar Episcopal for Marriage and Family, 2006–14, Vicar Gen., 2014–16, Dio. of Paisley. *Address:* Bishop's House, Esplanade, Oban, Argyll PA34 5AB. *T:* (01631) 567436.

**ARGYLL AND THE ISLES, Dean of;** *no new appointment at time of going to press.*

**ARGYLL AND THE ISLES, Provost in;** *see* Campbell, Very Rev. Canon M. R.

**ARGYRIS, Nicholas John Hadji-;** Director, Communications Services: policy and regulatory framework (formerly Telecommunications Trans European Networks and Services and Postal Services), European Commission, 1993–2001; *b* 22 March 1943; *s* of late Costas Argyris, (Costas Hadjiargyris), and Eileen Argyris (*née* Pollard); *m* 1st, 1966, Carol Bartlett (marr. diss. 1991); one *s* two *d*; 2nd, 1992, Danielle Canneel. *Educ:* St Paul's Sch.; Clare Coll., Cambridge (BA Hons Econs 1965; Cert. Ed. 1966). Schoolmaster, 1966–68; with Govt Econ. Service, in Depts of Econ. Affairs, Technol. and Trade and Ind., 1969–73; joined European Commission, 1973: worked in Directorate General for: Competition, 1973–84 (State Aids); Develt, 1985–86 (Trade and Private Investment Issues); Competition, 1987–91 (Head of Div., Transport and Tourist Industries); Dir for internal market, DG for Energy, 1991–93. Former Mem., England junior chess team (London junior champion, 1960). *Publications:* articles on air transport, energy and telecommunications policy. *Recreations:* reading, walking, music, gardening, chess problems, cinema.

**ARIAS SÁNCHEZ, Oscar,** PhD; President of Costa Rica, 1986–90 and 2006–10; President, Arias Foundation for Peace, 1990–2010; *b* 13 Sept. 1940; *m* Margarita; one *s* one *d*; *m* 2012, Suzanne Fischel. *Educ:* Univ. of Costa Rica; Univ. of Essex. Prof., Sch. of Political Sciences, Univ. of Costa Rica, 1969–72; Minister of Nat. Planning and Economic Policy, 1972–77; Gen. Sec., 1979–86, Liberación Nacional Party; Congressman, 1978–82. Formulated Central American Peace Agreement, 1986–87. Member: Stockholm Internat. Peace Res. Inst.; Carter Center; Inst. for Internat. Studies, Stanford Univ.; ILD Rockefeller Foundn; Internat. Centre for Human Rights and Democratic Develt; Inter Press Service; Bd of Dirs, WWF. Hon. PhD: Harvard, 1988; Essex, 1988; Dartmouth, 1992. Nobel Peace Prize, 1987; Martin Luther King Peace Prize, Martin Luther King Foundn, 1987; Prince of Asturias Prize, 1988; Nat. Audubon Soc. Prize, 1988; Liberty Medal, Univ. of Pennsylvania, 1991. *Publications:* Pressure Groups in Costa Rica, 1970; Who Governs in Costa Rica?, 1976; Latin American Democracy, Independence and Society, 1977; Roads for Costa Rica's Development, 1977; New Ways for Costa Rican Development, 1980. *Address:* c/o Arias Foundation/Center for Peace, PO Box 8–6410–1000, San José, Costa Rica. *T:* 2552955, *Fax:* 2552244.

**ARIE, Prof. Thomas Harry David,** CBE 1995; FRCPsych, FRCP, FFPH; Foundation Professor of Health Care of the Elderly, University of Nottingham, 1977–95, now Professor Emeritus, and Hon. Consultant Psychiatrist, Nottingham Health Authority, 1977–95; *b* 9 Aug. 1933; *s* of late Dr O. M. Arie and Hedy Arie; *m* 1963, Eleanor, FRCP, *yr d* of Sir Robert Aitken, FRCP, FRACP; two *d* one *s*. *Educ:* Reading Sch.; Balliol Coll., Oxford (Open Exhibnr in Classics; 1st cl. Hons, Classical Mods); MA, BM 1960; DPM. Training, Radcliffe Infirmary, Oxford, and Maudsley and London Hosps; Consultant Psychiatrist, Goodmayes Hosp., 1969–77; Sen. Lectr in Social Medicine, London Hosp. Med. Coll.; Hon. Sen. Lectr in Psychiatry, UCH Med. Sch. Royal College of Psychiatrists: Mem. Council, 1975–79, 1981–86, 1991–97; Vice-Pres., 1984–86; Chm., Specialist Section on Psychiatry of Old Age, 1981–86; Jt Cttee on Higher Psychiatric Training, 1978–84; Hon. FRCPsych 2001; Royal College of Physicians: Geriatrics Cttee, 1984–90; Examining Bd for Dip. in Geriatric Medicine, 1983–92. Member: Central Council for Educn and Trng in Social Work, 1975–81; Standing Med. Adv. Cttee, DHSS, 1980–84; Cttee on Review of Medicines, 1981–90; Res. Adv. Council, Nat. Inst. for Social Work, 1982–90; Med. Adv. Cttee to Registrar General, 1990–93; Council, AgeCare, Royal Surgical Aid Soc., 1995–2008 (Vice-Chm., 1998–2008). Fotheringham Lectr, Univ. of Toronto, 1979; Vis. Prof., NZ Geriatrics Soc., 1980; Dozor Vis. Prof., Univ. of the Negev, Israel, 1988; Fröhlich Vis. Prof., UCLA, 1991; Vis. Prof., Keele Univ., 1997. Chm., Geriatric Psych. Section, World Psych. Assoc., 1989–93. Governor, Centre for Policy on Ageing, 1992–98. Founders' Medal, British Geriatrics Soc., 2005; Lifetime Award, Internat. Psychogeriatric Assoc., 1999; Lifetime Award, Old Age Faculty, RCPsych, 2012. *Publications:* (ed) Health Care of the Elderly, 1981; (ed) Recent Advances in Psychogeriatrics, Vol. 1 1985, Vol. 2 1992; articles in med. jls and chapters in other people's books. *Address:* Cromwell House, West Church Street, Kenninghall, Norfolk NR16 2EN.

**ARIS, Aung San Suu Kyi, (Mrs M. V. Aris);** *see* Aung San Suu Kyi.

**ARKELL, John Hardy,** MA; Headmaster, Gresham's School, Holt, 1991–2002; *b* 10 July 1939; *s* of Hardy Arkell and Vivienne (*née* Le Sueur); *m* 1963, Jean Harding, JP; two *s* one *d*. *Educ:* Stowe Sch.; Selwyn Coll., Cambridge (BA Hons English Tripos; MA). National Service, HM Submarines, 1958–60 (Sub Lieut). Asst Master, Abingdon Sch., 1963–64; Head of VI form English, Framlingham Coll., 1964–70; Fettes College, 1970–83: Head of English Dept, 1971–73, 1976–78; Founder Headmaster, Fettes Jun. Sch., 1973–79; Housemaster, Glencorse House, 1979–83; Headmaster, Wrekin Coll., 1983–91. Chm., ISIS, Central England, 1989–91; Sec., HMC Midland Div., 1990–91; HMC Rep., ISC (formerly ISJC) Special Needs Cttee, 1991–2002. Governor: Oakham Sch., 2001–13; Beeston Hall Prep. Sch., 2003–11. Lay Reader, Benefice of Weybourne, 2006–. Mem., Fishmongers' Co., 2002–. *Recreations:* tennis, sailing, motor cars, drama. *Address:* Church Farm House, Lower Bodham, Holt, Norfolk NR25 6PS. *T:* (01263) 715582.

**ARKLESS, Richard Lambert Thomas;** lawyer and campaigner for Scottish independence; *b* Stranraer, 1975; *m* Anne; two *c*. *Educ:* Glasgow Caledonian Univ. (BA Hons Financial Services); Strathclyde Univ. (LLB); Glasgow Grad. Sch. of Law (DipLP). Solicitor trainee, Edinburgh incl. secondment to RBS; solicitor, specialising in consumer litigation, Cheshire, until 2013; set up small online business, 2013. MP (SNP) Dumfries and Galloway, 2015–17; contested (SNP) same seat, 2017. *E:* arkless.richard@gmail.com.

**ARKLEY, Alistair Grant,** CBE 2006; DL; Chairman, New Century Enterprises (formerly New Century Inns) Ltd, since 1999; *b* 13 May 1947; *s* of Alexander Arkley and Victoria Margaret Arkley (*née* Grant); *m* 1972, Kathleen Ann Raeburn; three *s*. *Educ:* Aberdeen Acad.; Aberdeen Univ. (BSc Engrg). Engrg Officer, R&D, ICI, 1971–72; various posts, selling and mktg, Procter & Gamble, 1972–79; Sales and Mktg Dir, Scottish Breweries, Scottish & Newcastle plc, 1979–85; Man. Dir, J. W. Cameron & Co. Ltd, 1985–91; Chief Exec., Century Inns plc, 1991–99. Chairman: Chameleon Pub. Co., 1999–; Steelite Internat. plc, 2006–; Hospitality Data Insights, 2012–; Dir, S. A. Brain & Co. Ltd, 2014–. Dir, UK (formerly British) Business Angels Assoc., 2008. Hon. ML, Teesside Univ., 2000. DL Co. Durham, 2007. *Recreations:* countryside, gardening, football (spectating). *Address:* New Century Enterprises Ltd, Belasis Business Centre, Coxwold Way, Billingham, Tees Valley TS23 4EA. *T:* (01642) 343415, *Fax:* (01642) 345729. *E:* a.arkley@new-century.co.uk. *Clubs:* Royal Automobile; Northern Counties (Newcastle upon Tyne).

**ARKUSH, Jonathan Harry Samuel;** President, Board of Deputies of British Jews, 2015–18; *b* London, 20 June 1954; *s* of David and Shirley Arkush; *m* 1983, Carol Haas; one *s* two *d*. *Educ:* University Coll. Sch.; Mansfield Coll., Oxford (MA Juris. 1976). Called to the Bar: Middle Temple, 1977, Bencher, 2017; Lincoln's Inn, 1978; in practice as barrister, 1978–; Accredited Mediator, ADR Gp, 2000; Dep. Chancery Master, Royal Courts of Justice, 2002–. Chm. Govs, Hertsmere Jewish Primary Sch., 1999–2005. Mem., Scotch Malt Whisky Soc.; Life Mem., Friends of Lake District. *Recreations:* fell walking, opera, travel, family. *Address:* Enterprise Chambers, 9 Old Square, Lincoln's Inn, WC2A 3SR.

**ARKWRIGHT, Paul Thomas,** CMG 2016; HM Diplomatic Service; High Commissioner to Nigeria, 2015–18; *b* Bolton, 2 March 1962; *s* of Thomas Arkwright and Muriel Arkwright (*née* Hague); *m* 1997, Patricia Holland; one *s* one *d*. *Educ:* Ampleforth Coll.; Trinity Coll., Cambridge (BA Hons English 1983). Entered FCO, 1987; Second Sec. (Political), BMG Berlin (later Berlin Office), 1988–91; Hd, Conventional Arms Section, Non-proliferation and Defence Dept, FCO, 1991–93; First Sec. (Political), UK Mission to UN, 1993–97; on secondment to Min. of Foreign Affairs, France, 1997–98; First Sec. (Political), Paris, 1998–2001; Political Counsellor, UK Delegn to NATO, 2001–05; Hd, Counter-proliferation Dept, FCO, 2006–09; Ambassador to the Netherlands, 2009–13; Dir, Multilateral Policy, FCO, 2013–15. *Recreations:* cycling, swimming, watching football. *Address:* c/o Foreign and Commonwealth Office, King Charles Street, SW1A 2AH. *Club:* London Supporters of Bolton Wanderers Football.

**ARLINGTON,** Baroness (11th in line), *cr* 1664; **Jennifer Jane Forwood;** *b* 7 May 1939; *er d* of Maj.-Gen. Sir John Nelson, KCVO, CB, DSO, OBE, MC, and Lady Jane Nelson; *S* in 1999 to Barony of uncle, 9th Duke of Grafton, which had fallen into abeyance in 1936; *m* 1964, Rodney Forwood (*d* 1999); two *s*. *Educ:* Downham. *Recreations:* horse racing, bridge, gardening. *Heir: s* Hon. Patrick John Dudley Forwood [*b* 23 April 1967; *m* 2001, Alexandra, *yr d* of late Anthony Psychopulos and of Mrs Neil Maconochie].

**ARLOW, Ruth Marian;** barrister; Chancellor: Diocese of Norwich, since 2012 (Deputy Chancellor, 2008–12); Diocese of Salisbury, since 2016; *b* Bristol, 31 Jan. 1975; *d* of James Terence Arlow and Lynne Margaret Arlow (*née* Martinson); *m* 1997, Jonathan Chambers; three *d*. *Educ:* St Edmund Hall, Oxford (BA 1996); Cardiff Univ. (LLM Canon Law 2003). Called to the Bar, Inner Temple, 1997; Mem., Pump Court Chambers, 1997–. Deputy Chancellor: Dio. of Chichester, 2006–16; Dio. of Oxford, 2014–16. Lectr and Dir of Teaching, Postgraduate Dip. in Legal Practise, Monash Univ., 2003–06; Sen. Lectr, Bristol Law Sch., 2007–. Gov., Berrow C of E Primary Sch., Som, 2009–17. Casenotes Ed., Ecclesiastical Law Jl, 2001–. *Recreations:* family, reading, walking. *Address:* Norwich Diocesan Registry, Kingfisher House, 1 Gilders Way, Norwich NR3 1UB. *T:* (01603) 756501, *Fax:* (01603) 766554.

**ARMAGH, Archbishop of, and Primate of All Ireland,** since 2012; **Most Rev. Richard Lionel Clarke,** PhD; *b* 25 June 1949; *s* of Dudley Hall Clarke and Norah Constance (*née* Quine); *m* 1975, Linda Margaret Thompson (*d* 2009); one *s* one *d*. *Educ:* Trinity Coll., Dublin (MA 1979; PhD 1990); King's Coll., London (BD 1975). Ordained deacon, 1975, priest, 1976; Assistant Curate: Holywood, Down, 1975–77; St Bartholomew with Christ Church, Leeson Park, Dublin, 1977–79; Dean of Residence, Trinity Coll., Dublin, 1979–84; Rector, Bandon Union of Parishes, Dio. of Cork, 1984–93; Dean of Cork and Incumbent of St Fin Barre's Union of Parishes, Cork, 1993–96; Bishop of Meath and Kildare, 1996–2012. *Publications:* And Is It True?, 2000; A Whisper of God, 2006; Shouldering the Lamb, 2017. *Recreation:* music. *Address:* Church House, 46 Abbey Street, Armagh BT61 7DZ. *T:* (028) 3752 7144.

**ARMAGH, Archbishop of, (RC), and Primate of All Ireland,** since 2014; **Most Rev. Eamon Martin;** *b* Derry, 30 Oct. 1961; *s* of John James Martin and Catherine Martin (*née* Crossan). *Educ:* St Columb's Coll., Derry; St Patrick's Coll., Maynooth (BSc Math. Scis; BD Theol.); Queen's Univ. Belfast; St Edmund's Coll., Cambridge (MPhil). Ordained priest, 1987; Asst Priest, St Eugene's Cathedral, Derry, 1987–89; Teacher, 1990–98, Pres., 1999–2008, St Columb's Coll., Derry; Dio. Sec. Gen., 2008–10, Pres. 2014–, Irish Episcopal Conf.; Vicar Gen., 2010–11, Diocesan Administrator, 2011–13, Diocese of Derry; Coadjutor Archbishop of Armagh, (RC), 2013–14. Chaplain to HH The Pope, 2010–13. *Address:* Archdiocese of Armagh, Ara Coeli, Cathedral Road, Armagh BT61 7QY. *T:* (028) 3752 2045, *Fax:* (028) 3752 6182. *E:* admin@aracoeli.com.

**ARMAGH, Dean of;** *see* Dunstan, Very Rev. G. J. O.

**ARMANI, Giorgio;** Italian fashion designer; *b* 11 July 1934; *s* of late Ugo Armani and of Maria Raimondi. *Educ:* Univ. of Milan. Mil. Service, 1957. La Rinascente, Milan, 1957–64; Designer and Product Developer, Nino Cerruti, 1964–70; freelance designer, 1970–; founded Giorgio Armani SpA, 1975 and created own-label ready-to-wear clothing; has since introduced other Armani lines, incl. accessories, fragrances and eyewear. Dr *hc* RCA, 1991. Numerous fashion awards. Gran Cavaliere dell'ordine al merito della Repubblica Italiana, 1987 (Commendatore, 1985; Grand'Ufficiale, 1986). *Publications:* Giorgio Armani (autobiog.), 2015. *Address:* Giorgio Armani SpA, Via Borgonuovo 11, 20121 Milan, Italy. *T:* (02) 723181; Giorgio Armani Corporation, 114 Fifth Avenue, New York, NY 10011, USA.

**ARME, Prof. Christopher,** PhD, DSc; CBiol, FRSB; Professor of Zoology, University of Keele, 1979–2007, now Emeritus, *b* 10 Aug. 1939; *s* of Cyril Boddington and Monica Henrietta Arme; *m* 1962; three *s*. *Educ:* Heanor Grammar Sch.; Univ. of Leeds (BSc 1961; PhD 1964); Univ. of Keele (DSc 1985). FRSB (FIBiol 1980); CBiol 1980. SRC/NATO Res. Fellow, Univ. of Leeds, 1964–66; Res. Associate, Rice Univ., Texas, 1966–68; Lectr, later Reader, QUB, 1968–76; Head of Biology Gp, N Staffs Polytechnic, 1976–79; Head, Dept of Biol Scis, 1981–88, Dean of Natural Scis, 1998–2001, Univ. of Keele; Dir of Terrestrial and Freshwater Scis, NERC, 1993–95 (on leave of absence from Keele Univ.). British Society for Parasitology: Hon. Gen. Sec., 1980–83; Silver Jubilee Lectr, 1987; Vice Pres., 1988–90; Pres., 1990–92; Hon. Mem., 1992. Chm., Heads of Zool. Depts of Univs

Gp, 1981–82; Institute of Biology: Hon. Treas. and Chm., Finance Cttee, 1986–93; Chm., Staffing Cttee, 1993–99; Treas., Eur. Fedn of Parasitologists, 1992–2000. Mem., Biol Scis Cttee, and Chm., Animal Scis and Psychol. Sub-Cttee, SERC, 1989–92; Chairman: Steering Cttee, NERC special topic prog. on wildlife diseases, 1992–93; Policy Adv. Cttee, Envmtl Res. Prog., DFID (formerly ODA), 1995–99; Molecular Genetics in Ecology Initiative, Aberdeen Univ./Inst. of Terrestrial Ecology, Banchory, 1995–99; Mem., Adv. Cttee, Centre for Ecology and Hydrology, NERC, 1998–2002. Mem. Bd of Govs, Harper Adams Agricl Coll., 1996–2002. Hon. Member: Czechoslovakian Parasitological Soc., 1989; All-Russia Soc. of Helminthologists, 1992; Bulgarian Soc. for Parasitology, 1995; World Assoc. for Advancement of Veterinary Parasitol., 2017. Jt Editor, Parasitology, 1987–2006; Ed.-in-Chief, Parasites and Vectors, 2008–16. Hon. DSc Slovak Acad. of Scis, 1995. K. I. Skryabin Medal, All-Russian Soc. of Helminthologists, 1994; Hovorka Medal, Slovak Acad. of Scis, 1995; Charter Award Medal, Inst. of Biology, 1995; Dist. Parasitologist Award, World Fedn of Parasitologists, 2018. *Publications:* (ed jtly) Biology of the Eucestoda, Vols I and II, 1983; (ed) Molecular Transfer across Parasite Membranes, 1988; (ed jtly) Toxic Reactions of the Liver, 1992; contribs to parasitological jls. *Address:* School of Life Sciences, University of Keele, Keele, Staffs ST5 5BG. *T:* (01782) 733028.

**ARMES, Rt Rev. John Andrew;** *see* Edinburgh, Bishop of.

**ARMES, Prof. Steven Peter,** PhD; FRS 2014; Professor of Polymer and Colloid Chemistry, University of Sheffield, since 2004; *m;* two *c. Educ:* Whitley Abbey Comprehensive Sch., Coventry; Univ. of Bristol (BSc 1st Cl. Hons Chem. 1983; PhD 1987). Postdoctoral Fellow, Los Alamos Nat. Lab., New Mexico, 1987–89; Lectr, Sen. Lectr and Reader, 1989–2000, Prof. of Polymer Chem., 2000–04, Univ. of Sussex. Thomas Graham Lect., RSC/SCI, 2014; Colloid and Polymer Sci. Lectr, German Colloid Soc., 2015. Macro Gp Medal for Polymer Sci., 2007 and 2017, Peter Day Award for Soft Matter Res., 2010, Interdisciplinary Prize, 2014, RSC; Tilden Medal, 2013; Materials Sci. Award, DSM, 2016; Eur. Colloid and Interface Sci. Award, Solvay Prize, 2017; Armourers and Brasiers' Co. Prize, Royal Soc., 2018. *Publications:* contrib. scientific papers to peer-reviewed jls. *Address:* Department of Chemistry, University of Sheffield, Sheffield S3 7HF.

**ARMFIELD, Diana Maxwell, (Mrs Bernard Dunstan),** RA 1991 (ARA 1989); RWS 1983 (ARWS 1977); RWA; RCA; painter, since 1965; *b* 11 June 1920; *d* of Joseph Harold Armfield and Gertrude Mary Uttley; *m* 1949, (Andrew Harold) Bernard Dunstan, RA (*d* 2017); two *s* (and one *s* decd). *Educ:* Bedales; Bournemouth Art Sch.; Slade Sch.; Central School of Arts and Crafts. MCSD. Textile/wallpaper designer, 1949–65; work in Fest. of Britain, 1951, and Permanent Collection, V& A Mus. One woman exhibitions: Browse & Darby (London), regularly, 1979–, 90th Birthday show, 2010; RCA Conwy, and Cardiff, 2001; other exhibitions include: regular contribs RA Summer Exhibn, 1966–; Friends' Room, RA, also Cardiff and Llanbedrog, 1995; Bala, 1996; Wassenaar, Holland, 1998; Nat. Mus. of Cardiff, 1998; Bedales Art & Design Centenary Exhibn, 1999; Kentucky, USA, 2005; Arts Club, London, 2006; Curwen & New Acad. Gall. 50th Anniv. Show, 2008; Director's Choice, Curwen & New Academy Gall., 2009; Pure Gold: 50 Years of the FBA, Mall Gall., 2011; Featured Artist: RWS Spring Exhibn, 2011; RA Now Exhibn, 2012; exhibn with Bernard Dunstan, Belle Shenkman Room, RA, 2015–16; Russell-Cotes exhibn for 250th Anniv., RA, 2018. Artist in Residence: Perth, WA, 1985; Jackson, Wyoming, 1989. Work in Permanent Collections: Govt picture collection, RWA; Yale Center for British Art; Nat. Trust; Contemporary Art Soc. for Wales; Lancaster City Mus.; Faringdon Trust; RWS Queen's birthday collection, 1996; Royal Acad. Queen's Diamond Jubilee Collection, 2012; Commissions: Reuters, Nat. Trust, 1989; Prince of Wales, 1989; Royal Acad. diploma collection. RWA 1975, now Hon. Retired RWA; RCA 1991, now Hon. Retired RCA; Hon. Mem., Pastel Soc., 1988; Hon. NEAC 2000. *Publications:* (jtly) Painting in Oils, 1982; (jtly) Drawing, 1982; *relevant publication:* The Art of Diana Armfield, by Julian Halsby, 1995. *Recreations:* music, gardening, travel. *Address:* 10 High Park Road, Kew, Richmond, Surrey TW9 4BH; Llwynhir, Parc, Bala, Gwynedd, North Wales LL23 7YU. *Club:* Arts.

**ARMIDALE, Bishop of,** since 2012; **Rt Rev. Richard Alexander Lewers;** *b* Sydney, 18 March 1958; *s* of Basil Richard Lewers and Lois Lewers; *m* 1981, Janene; three *c. Educ:* Sydney Missionary and Bible Coll. (Dip.); Moore Coll. (DipA; BTh). Curate, Liverpool, NSW, 1988–92; Asst Minister, later Rector, Wanniassa, ACT, 1992–2002; Evangelism Ministries, 2002–05; Engadine Anglican Church, 2005–12. Dep. Chair, Evangelical Fellowship Anglican Church; Mem., Gospel Coalition (Australia). *Recreations:* fishing, golf, family. *Address:* PO Box 198, Armidale Diocesan Office, NSW 2350, Australia. *T:* (2) 67724491. *E:* bishop@armidaleanglicandiocese.com. *Club:* Armidale Golf.

**ARMITAGE, His Honour (Ernest) Keith;** QC 1994; a Circuit Judge, 2001–15; *b* 15 May 1949; *s* of Selwyn and Marjorie Armitage; *m* 1972, Anita Sharples; one *s* one *d. Educ:* Trent Coll., Notts; Univ. of Liverpool (LLB Hons). Called to the Bar, Middle Temple, 1970; in practice, Northern Circuit, 1971–2001; a Recorder, 1989–2001. *Recreations:* travel, gliding (soaring).

**ARMITAGE, John Vernon,** PhD; Principal, 1975–97, and Hon. Senior Fellow in Mathematical Sciences, since 1997, College of St Hild and St Bede, Durham; *b* 21 May 1932; *s* of Horace Armitage and Evelyn (*née* Hauton); *m* 1963, Sarah Catherine Clay; two *s. Educ:* Rothwell Grammar Sch., Yorks; UCL (BSc, PhD); Cuddesdon Coll., Oxford. Asst Master: Pontefract High Sch., 1956–58; Shrewsbury Sch., 1958–59; Lectr in Maths, Univ. of Durham, 1959–67; Sen. Lectr in Maths, King's Coll., London, 1967–70; Prof. of Mathematical Educn, Univ. of Nottingham, 1970–75; Special Prof., Nottingham Univ., 1976–79. Chm., Math. Instruction Sub-Cttee, Brit. Nat. Cttee for Maths, Royal Soc., 1975–78. *Publications:* (with H. B. Griffiths) A Companion to Advanced Mathematics, 1969; (with W. F. Eberlein) Elliptic Functions, 2006; papers on theory of numbers in various jls. *Recreations:* railways, cricket and most games inexpertly. *Address:* 7 Potters Close, Potters Bank, Durham DH1 3UB.

**ARMITAGE, Prof. Judith Patricia,** PhD; FRS 2013; Professor of Biochemistry, University of Oxford, since 1996; Fellow, Merton College, Oxford, since 1996; *b* Shelley, Yorks, 21 Feb. 1951; *d* of George Arthur Armitage and Eleanor Armitage (*née* Emmott); *m* 1975, John Gordon R. Jefferys; two *d. Educ:* Selby Girls' High Sch.; University Coll. London (BSc Hons 1972; PhD 1976). Lister Inst. Res. Fellow, 1982–85; Lectr, Univ. of Oxford, 1985–96. Pres., Microbiol. Soc., 2019–. *Publications:* contrib. papers to scientific jls. *Recreations:* theatre, travel, art, good food and wine, reading history. *Address:* Department of Biochemistry, University of Oxford, South Parks Road, Oxford OX1 3QU. *T:* (01865) 613293. *E:* judith.armitage@bioch.ox.ac.uk.

**ARMITAGE, Keith;** *see* Armitage, E. K.

**ARMITAGE, Air Chief Marshal Sir Michael (John),** KCB 1983; CBE 1975; Commandant, Royal College of Defence Studies, 1988–89; *b* 25 Aug. 1930; *m* 1st, 1955 (marr. diss. 1969); three *s;* 2nd, 1970, Gretl Renate Steinig. *Educ:* Newport Secondary Grammar Sch., IW; Halton Apprentice; RAF Coll., Cranwell. psc 1965, jssc 1970, rcds 1975. Commnd 1953; flying and staff appts, incl. 28 Sqn, Hong Kong, and No 4 and No 1 Flying Trng Schools; Personal Staff Officer to Comdr 2ATAF, 1966; OC 17 Sqdn, 1967–70; Directing Staff, JSSC and NDC, 1971–72; Stn Comdr, RAF Luqa, Malta, 1972–74; Dir Forward Policy, Ministry of Defence (Air Force Dept), 1976–78; Dep. Comdr, RAF Germany, 1978–80; Senior RAF Mem., RCDS, 1980–81; Dir of Service Intelligence, 1982; Dep. Chief of Defence Staff (Intelligence), 1983–84; Chief of Defence Intelligence and Dep. Chm., Jt Intelligence Cttee, 1985–86; Air Mem. for Supply and Orgn, Air Force Dept, MoD, 1986–87. Mem. Council, RUSI, 1986. Trustee: RAF Mus., 1986–87; Headley Ct, 1986–87; Chm., Mus. of E Asian Art, Bath, 1996–2000. Freeman, City of London, 1996. *Publications:* (jtly) Air Power in the Nuclear Age, 1982; Unmanned Aircraft, 1988; The Royal Air Force: an illustrated history, 1993, 3rd edn 1999; (ed) Great Air Battles of the Royal Air Force, 1996; contrib. prof. jls. *Recreations:* military history, shooting, reading, writing. *Address:* c/o Lloyds, Cox & King's Branch, 7 Pall Mall, SW1Y 5NA. *Club:* Royal Air Force.

**ARMITAGE, Prof. Peter,** CBE 1984; Professor of Applied Statistics (formerly of Biomathematics), 1976–90, now Emeritus, and Fellow, St Peter's College, University of Oxford, 1976–90, now Emeritus Fellow; *b* 15 June 1924; *s* of Harry and Florence Armitage, Huddersfield; *m* 1st, 1947, Phyllis Enid Perry (*d* 2001), London; one *s* two *d;* 2nd, 2003, Cecil Dione Rowlatt (*d* 2018), Wallingford. *Educ:* Huddersfield Coll.; Trinity Coll., Cambridge (Wrangler, 1947; MA 1952); PhD London, 1951. Ministry of Supply, 1943–45; National Physical Laboratory, 1945–46; Mem. Statistical Research Unit of Med. Research Council, London Sch. of Hygiene and Trop. Med., 1947–61; Prof. of Medical Statistics, Univ. of London, 1961–76. President: Biometric Soc., 1972–73 (Hon. Life Mem., 1998); Royal Statistical Soc., 1982–84 (Hon. Sec., 1958–64); Internat. Soc. for Clinical Biostatistics, 1990–91; Mem., International Statistical Institute, 1961. Hon. FFPM 1991. Hon. DSc De Montfort, 1998. (Jtly) J. Allyn Taylor Prize, John P. Robarts Res. Inst., London, Ont, 1987; Guy Medals in bronze, silver and gold, Royal Statistical Soc., 1962, 1978, 1990. Editor, Biometrics, 1980–84. *Publications:* Sequential Medical Trials, 1960, 2nd edn 1975; Statistical Methods in Medical Research, 1971, 4th edn (jtly), 2001; (ed with H. A. David) Advances in Biometry, 1996; (ed with T. Colton) Encyclopedia of Biostatistics, 1998, 2nd edn 2005; papers in statistical and medical journals. *Recreations:* music, genealogy. *Address:* 2 Reading Road, Wallingford, Oxon OX10 9DP. *T:* (01491) 835840.

**ARMITAGE, Sarah Joanne;** *see* Lee, S. J.

**ARMITAGE, Simon Robert,** CBE 2010; FRSL; poet, novelist, playwright, song-lyricist, screen-writer and broadcaster; Poet Laureate, since 2019; Professor of Poetry, University of Leeds, since 2017; *b* 26 May 1963. Writer of song-lyrics for film, Feltham Sings, 2002 (BAFTA and Ivor Novello Awards, 2004). Professor of Poetry: Univ. of Sheffield, 2011–17; Univ. of Oxford, 2015–19. FRSL 2004. Queen's Gold Medal for Poetry, 2018. *Publications: poetry:* Zoom!, 1989; Xanadu, 1992; Kid, 1992; Book of Matches, 1993; (with G. Maxwell) Moon Country, 1995; The Dead Sea Poems, 1996; CloudCuckooLand, 1997; Killing Time, 1999; Selected Poems, 2001; The Universal Home Doctor, 2002; Travelling Songs, 2002; Tyrannosaurus Rex Versus the Corduroy Kid, 2006; The Not Dead, 2008; Seeing Stars, 2010; Black Roses: the killing of Sophie Lancaster, 2012; Still, 2016; The Unaccompanied, 2017; New Cemetery, 2017; Flit, 2018; Sandettie Light Vessel Automatic, 2019; *prose:* All Points North, 1998; Walking Home: travels with a troubadour on the Pennine Way, 2012; Walking Away: further travels with a troubadour on the South West Coast Path, 2015; *plays:* Mister Heracles, 2000; Jerusalem, 2005; Gig, 2008; *novels:* Little Green Man, 2001; The White Stuff, 2004; *dramatisation:* The Odyssey, 2005; The Odyssey: missing, presumed dead, 2015; *libretto:* The Assassin Tree, 2006; Hansel and Gretel, 2018; *translations:* Sir Gawain and the Green Knight, 2007; The Death of King Arthur, 2012; Pearl, 2016. *Address:* c/o DGA, 55 Monmouth Street, WC2H 9DG.

**ARMITSTEAD, Claire Louise, (Mrs J. C. Yandell);** Associate Editor, Culture, Guardian News and Media, since 2017; *b* 2 Dec. 1958; *d* of Charles Henry Wilfrid Armitstead and Gillian Louise Armitstead (*née* Bartley); *m* 1983, John Christopher Yandell; one *s* one *d. Educ:* Zaria Children's Sch., Nigeria; Bedales Sch.; St Hilda's Coll., Oxford (BA). Reporter, S Wales Argus, 1980–84; sub-ed. and Theatre Critic, Hampstead and Highgate Express, 1984–88; Theatre Critic, Financial Times, 1988–92; The Guardian: Theatre Critic, 1992–95; Arts Ed., 1995–99; Literary Ed., 1999–2011; Books Ed., 2011–17. Trustee, English PEN, 2013–. *Publications:* (ed) Tales of Two Londons: stories from a fractured city, 2018. *Recreations:* reading, writing, gardening, trying to play the piano. *Address:* The Guardian, Kings Place, 90 York Way, N1 9AG.

**ARMITSTEAD, Elizabeth Mary;** *see* Deignan, E. M.

**ARMITT, Sir John (Alexander),** Kt 2012; CBE 1996; FREng, FICE, FCGI; Chairman: City and Guilds, since 2012; National Express, since 2013 (non-executive Director, since 2013); *b* 2 Feb. 1946; *s* of Alexander Walter Armitt and Lily Irene (*née* Dunce); *m* 1969, Mavis Dorothy Sage (marr. diss.); one *s* one *d. Educ:* Portsmouth Northern Grammar Sch.; Portsmouth Coll. of Technology. FREng (FEng 1993); FICE 1989. John Laing Construction, 1966–93; Jt Man. Dir, 1988–93; Chairman: J. Laing Internat., 1988–93; Laing Civil Engrg, 1988–93; Chief Executive: Union Railways, 1993–97; Costain Gp, 1997–2001; Railtrack plc, 2001–02; Network Rail, 2002–07. Chairman: EPSRC, 2007–12; Olympic Delivery Authy, 2007–14. Non-exec. Dir, Berkeley Gp, 2007– (Dep. Chm., 2012–). Member, Advisory Board: Siemens UK, 2009–12; PricewaterhouseCoopers, 2010–12. Council Member: ICE, 1989–92 (Chm., Mgt Bd 1989–92; Pres., 2015–16); FCEC, 1986–93 (Chm., European Affairs Cttee, 1989–92). Pres., Export Gp for Constructional Inds, 1992–93; Member: Overseas Project Bd, DTI, 1992–93; Export Guarantees Adv. Council, 2001–04; Commn for Integrated Transport, 2004–07; Bd, TfL, 2012–; Nat. Infrastructure Commn, 2015– (Chm., 2018–). Mem. Bd, Major Projects Assoc., 1994–2004. FCGI 2010. Hon. Dr: Imperial Coll. London; Birmingham; Portsmouth; Warwickshire. *Recreations:* sailing, fishing, golf, theatre, music. *E:* john_armitt@hotmail.com.

**ARMOND, Ralph Peter;** Director General, Zoological Society of London, 2004–17; *b* 30 May 1957; *s* of John Walter Armond and Helene Maria Armond; *m* 1984, Jane Caroline Everitt; one *s* one *d. Educ:* King's Coll. Sch., Wimbledon; Emmanuel Coll., Cambridge (BA Geog. 1978). Retail Mktg, Boots Co. Plc, 1978–84; Mktg Manager, Dixons Stores Gp, 1984–88; Tussauds Group Ltd, 1988–2004: Mktg Manager, Chessington World of Adventures, 1988–91; Gen. Manager, Warwick Castle, 1991–95; Divl Dir, Alton Towers Resort, 1995–2004. Outstanding Personal Contribn to Tourism award, Heart of England Tourist Bd, 2003. *Recreations:* mountain biking, jogging, learning to play the guitar, overseas travel. *Address:* 7 Princess Mary Close, Guildford GU2 9UZ.

**ARMOUR, Prof. Sir James,** Kt 1995; CBE 1989; FRSE; FMedSci; Vice-Principal, 1990–95, and Professor of Veterinary Parasitology, 1976–95, now Emeritus, University of Glasgow; Chairman, Glasgow Dental Hospital and School NHS Trust, 1995–98; *b* 17 Sept. 1929; *s* of James Angus Armour and Margaret Brown Roy; *m* 1st, 1953, Irene Morris (*d* 1988); two *s* two *d;* 2nd, 1992, Christine Strickland. *Educ:* Marr Coll., Troon; Univ. of Glasgow (PhD 1967; BVMS 2010). MRCVS 1952 Hon. FRCVS 1995); FRSE 1991. Colonial Service, Nigeria: Vet. Officer, 1953–57; Vet. Parasitologist, 1957–60; Parasitologist, Cooper Technical Bureau, Berkhamsted, 1960–63; University of Glasgow: Research Fellow, 1963–67; Lectr, 1967–70; Sen. Lectr, 1970–73; Reader, 1973–76; Dean,

Vet. Faculty, 1986–91. Chairman: Vet. Products Cttee, Medicines Commn, 1987–96; Governing Body, Inst. of Animal Health, Compton, 1991–97; Member: Adv. Bd, Inst. of Aquaculture, Univ. of Stirling, 1997–2003; Bd, Hannah Res. Inst., Ayr, 1999–2011; RSE Inquiry into Foot and Mouth Disease in Scotland, 2001–03; Chm., HEFCE RAE Panels for Agriculture, Food Sci. and Vet. Sci., 1999–2001. Chairman: Moredun Foundn for Animal Health and Welfare, 2000–04; St Andrews Clinics for Children in Africa, 1996–2010; Vice Chm., Hannah Trust, 2012–; Trustee, Scottish Sci. Trust, 1999–2001. Vice-Pres., RSE, 1998–2000. Founder FMedSci 1998. Hon. FIBiol 2001. Dr *hc* Utrecht, 1981; DVM&S Edinburgh, 1995; DU: Glasgow, 2001; Stirling, 2005. John Henry Steel Medal, RCVS, 1979; Bledisloe Award, Royal Agricl Soc., 1990; Wooldridge Medal, BVA, 1990; World Assoc. for Advancement of Vet. Parasitol./Pfizer Award, 1993; Chiron Medal, BVA, 1997; Bicentenary Medal, RSE, 2002. *Publications:* (with Urquhart and Duncan) Veterinary Parasitology, 1988; numerous contribs to vet. and parasitology jls. *Recreations:* golf (British Boys Golf Champion, Hoylake, 1947), watching soccer and Rugby. *Address:* 4b Towans Court, Prestwick KA9 2AY. *Clubs:* Royal Troon Golf (Captain, 1990–92; Hon. Pres., 2007–10); Atlanta Athletic (USA).

**ARMOUR, Prof. John Hamish**, FBA 2017; Professor (formerly Lovells, then Hogan Lovells Professor) of Law and Finance, Oxford University, since 2007; Fellow, Oriel College, Oxford, since 2007; *b* Nottingham, 24 Dec. 1971; *s* of Edward and Suzanne Armour; *m* 2007, Rebecca Ann Williams; one *s* two *d*. *Educ:* Pembroke Coll., Oxford (BA 1994; BCL 1995); Yale Law Sch. (LLM 1996). University of Nottingham: Lectr in Law, 1996–2000; Norton Rose Lectr in Corporate and Financial Law, 2000–01; University of Cambridge: Res. Fellow, Centre for Business Res., 1999–2000; Sen. Res. Fellow, 2001–02; Lectr in Law, 2002–05; Sen. Lectr in Law, 2005–07. *Publications:* (ed) Vulnerable Transactions in Corporate Insolvency, 2003; (ed) After Enron: modernising corporate and securities law in Europe and the US, 2006; The Anatomy of Corporate Law, 2nd edn 2009, 3rd edn 2017; (ed) Rationality in Company Law, 2009; Principles of Financial Regulation, 2016; Negotiating Brexit, 2017; contrib. to academic jls. *Recreations:* cycling, hill-walking. *Address:* Faculty of Law, University of Oxford, St Cross Building, St Cross Road, Oxford OX1 3UL. *T:* (01865) 281616. *E:* john.armour@law.ox.ac.uk.

**ARMOUR, Nicholas Hilary Stuart**; HM Diplomatic Service, retired; business consultant, since 2013; *b* 12 June 1951; *s* of late Brig. William Stanley Gibson Armour and of Penelope Jean Armour; *m* 1982, Georgina Elizabeth Fortescue (*d* 2003); two *d*. *Educ:* Ampleforth Coll.; Exeter Univ. (BA). FCO, 1974; MECAS: Lebanon, Beaconsfield, Jordan, 1975; Beirut, 1977; FCO, 1980; Head of Chancery, Athens, 1984; Asst Head of Dept, FCO, 1989; Counsellor, Muscat, 1991; on loan to DTI, 1994–97; Consul-Gen., Dubai and the Northern Emirates, 1997–99; on loan to Royal Mail ViaCode, 2000; Head, North America Dept, FCO, 2000–03; Sen. DS (Civil), RCDS, 2003–05 (on secondment); Consul-Gen., Toronto, and Dir, UK Trade and Investment, Canada, 2005–09; Dir, Internat. Gp, UK Trade and Investment, 2009–12. Dir and Chief Exec., Internat. Chamber of Commerce UK, 2012–13. Mem., Canada UK Council, 2018–. Mem., Madrigal Soc., 1995– (Hon. Sec., 2017–). *Recreations:* music, singing, sailing, ski-ing.

**ARMSON, (Frederick) Simon (Arden)**; mental health professional, since 2004; *b* 11 Sept. 1948; *s* of late Frank Gerald Arden Armson and Margaret Fenella Armson (*née* Newton); *m* 1975, Marion Albinia (*née* Hamilton-Russell); one *s* two *d*. *Educ:* Denstone Coll.; MSc (Mental Health Studies) Guy's Hosp. Med. Sch., London, 1996; Dip. Clin. Psychotherapy, CAT, 2002; Dip. Neuro-linguistic programming, Internat. Neuro-linguistic Programming Trainers' Assoc., 2007; registered UKCP, 2005. Various administrative and managerial posts, NHS, 1970–84; Asst Gen. Sec. 1984–89, Gen. Sec. 1989, Chief Exec., 1990–2004, The Samaritans. Dir, The Samaritans Enterprises Ltd, 1996–2004. Clinical Psychotherapist, 2004–; Develt Coach, 2004–. Chair: BBC Radio Helpline Adv. Gp, 1995–98; Telephone Helplines Gp, 1992–96; Develt Adv. Cttee, Cancer Bacup Service, 1998–2001. UK Rep., 1996–2005, Chm., Nat. Delegs, 2001–03, Mem. Exec. Cttee, 2003–03, Internat. Assoc. for Suicide Prevention; Member: Suicide Prevention Sub-Gp, DoH Wider Health Wkg Gp, 1995–97; RCN Men's Health Forum, 1995–97; Steering Cttee for Structure Review of British Red Cross, 1995; Adv. Cttee, Inst. of Volunteer Research, 1996–2002; Wkg Gp, Rev. of BACUP Cancer Counselling Service, 1997; Cttee, ICSTIS, 2001–07; Ind. Adv. Panel to Ministerial Council on Deaths in Custody, 2009–14; Lay Mem., Mental Health Rev. Tribunal, later Specialist Mem., First-tier Tribunal (Mental Health), 2006–19 (Mentor, 2016–19). Mental Health Act Comr, 2002–08 and 2009–12 (Mem. Bd, 2004–09; Chm., Mental Health Act Commn, 2008–09); Ind. Mem., Mkt Res. Disciplinary Authy, 2009–; Mental Health Act Manager, W London NHS Trust (Broadmoor Hosp.), 2012–; Associate Hospital Manager: Apple Hill Ind. Hosp., 2016–; Cardinal Clinic, 2018–. Trustee: Yoxall Town Lands Charity, 1974–; Yoxall United Charities, 1982–; ChildLine, 1999–2006; Broadcasting Support Services, 2003–09; Mental Health Media Trust, 2004–09; National Nightline, 2005–06; Maytree Respite Centre, 2005–14 (Chm., 2009–14; Patron, 2015–); CLIC Sargent, 2006–09; Partnership for Children, 2009–16 (Vice Chm., 2012–15). Hon. Mem., Telephone Helplines Assoc., 1999. Chairman of Judges: Guardian Jerwood Award, 1995–99; Guardian Charity Award, 2000–03; Mem. Cttee, Ringel Award, 2001–03. CCMI (CIMgt 1995; Pres., Mid Thames Br., 2006–). FRSA 1993. *Publications:* (contrib.) International Handbook of Suicide and Attempted Suicide, 2000; (contrib.) Every Family in the Land, 2004; (contrib.) Prevention and Treatment of Suicidal Behaviour, 2005. *Recreations:* music, cycling (cross country), walking, sailing, mental health and emotional wellbeing; grand paternal activities. *Address:* Broad Oak, Old Honey Lane, Hurley, Maidenhead, Berkshire SL6 5LW. *T:* (01628) 824322, 07788 186339. *E:* armson@btinternet.com. *Club:* Reform.

**ARMSON, Rev. Canon John Moss**, PhD; Canon Residentiary, Rochester Cathedral, 1989–2001, now Canon Emeritus; *b* 21 Dec. 1939; *s* of Arthur Eric Armson and Edith Isobel Moss. *Educ:* Wyggeston Sch.; Selwyn Coll., Cambridge (MA); St Andrews Univ. (PhD); College of the Resurrection, Mirfield. Curate, St John, Notting Hill, 1966; Chaplain and Fellow, Downing Coll., Cambridge, 1969; Chaplain, 1973–77, Vice-Principal, 1977–82, Westcott House, Cambridge; Principal, Edinburgh Theol Coll., 1982–89. Mem., Hengrave Ecumenical Community, 2001–03. *Recreations:* music, theatre, gardening, landscaping. *Address:* Stuart Court, High Street, Kibworth, Leics LE8 0LR. *T:* (01162) 793341.

**ARMSON, Simon**; *see* Armson, F. S. A.

**ARMSTRONG**, family name of **Baron Armstrong of Ilminster**.

**ARMSTRONG OF HILL TOP**, Baroness *cr* 2010 (Life Peer), of Crook in the County of Durham; **Hilary Jane Armstrong**; PC 1999; DL; *b* 30 Nov. 1945; *d* of Rt Hon. Ernest Armstrong, PC and of Hannah P. Lamb; *m* 1992, Dr Paul Corrigan. *Educ:* Monkwearmouth Comp. Sch., Sunderland; West Ham Coll. of Technology (BSc Sociology); Univ. of Birmingham (Dip. in Social Work). VSO, Murray Girls' High Sch., Kenya, 1967–69; Social Worker, Newcastle City Social Services Dept, 1970–73; Community Worker, Southwick Neighbourhood Action Project, Sunderland, 1973–75; Lectr, Community and Youth Work, Sunderland Polytechnic, 1975–86. MP (Lab) NW Durham, 1987–2010. Frontbench spokesperson on education, 1988–92 (under-fives, primary, and special educn), on Treasury affairs, 1994–95; PPS to Leader of the Opposition, 1992–94; Minister of State, DETR,

1997–2001; Parly Sec. to HM Treasury (Govt Chief Whip), 2001–06; Chancellor of the Duchy of Lancaster and Minister for the Cabinet Office, 2006–07. DL Durham, 2010. *Recreations:* reading, theatre, football. *Address:* House of Lords, SW1A 0PW.

**ARMSTRONG OF ILMINSTER**, Baron *cr* 1988 (Life Peer), of Ashill in the county of Somerset; **Robert Temple Armstrong**, GCB 1983 (KCB 1978; CB 1974); CVO 1975; Secretary of the Cabinet, 1979–87, and Head of the Home Civil Service, 1983–87 (Joint Head, 1981–83), retired; director of companies; *b* 30 March 1927; *o s* of Sir Thomas (Henry Wait) Armstrong, DMus, FRCM; *m* 1st, 1953, Serena Mary Benedicta (marr. diss. 1985; she *d* 1994), *er d* of Sir Roger Chance, 3rd Bt, MC; two *d*; 2nd, 1985, (Mary) Patricia, *d* of late C. C. Carlow. *Educ:* Dragon Sch., Oxford; Eton; Christ Church, Oxford (Hon. Student 1985). Asst Principal, Treasury, 1950–55; Private Secretary to: Rt Hon. Reginald Maudling, MP (when Economic Sec. to Treasury), 1953–54; Rt Hon. R. A. Butler, CH, MP (when Chancellor of the Exchequer), 1954–55; Principal, Treasury, 1955–57; Sec., Radcliffe Cttee on Working of Monetary System, 1957–59; returned to Treasury as Principal, 1959–64; Sec., Armitage Cttee on Pay of Postmen, 1964; Asst Sec., Cabinet Office, 1964–66; Sec. of Kindersley Review Body on Doctors' and Dentists' Remuneration and of Franks Cttee on Pay of Higher Civil Service, 1964–66; Asst Sec., Treasury, 1967–68; Jt Prin. Private Sec. to Rt Hon. Roy Jenkins, MP (Chancellor of the Exchequer), 1968; Under Secretary (Home Finance), Treasury, 1968–70; Principal Private Sec. to Prime Minister, 1970–75; Dep. Sec., 1973; Dep. Under-Sec. of State, Home Office, 1975–77, Permt Under Sec. of State, 1977–79. Director: BAT Industries, 1988–97; Inchcape, 1988–95; Bristol and West plc (formerly Bristol and West Building Soc.), 1988–97 (Chm., 1993–97); N. M. Rothschild & Sons, 1988–97; RTZ Corporation, 1988–97; Shell Transport & Trading Co., 1988–97; Lucas Industries, 1989–92; Biotechnology Investments Ltd, subseq. 3i Bioscience Investment Trust, 1989–2002 (Chm., 1989–2001); Carlton Television, 1991–95; IAMGold Ltd, 1996–2003; Bank of Ireland, 1997–2001; Chm., Forensic Investigative Associates, 1997–2003; Mem., Supervisory Bd, Robeco Gp, 1988–97. Chancellor, Univ. of Hull, 1994–2006. Chairman: Bd of Trustees, V & A Museum, 1988–98; Hestercombe Gardens Trust, 1996–2005; Bd of Govs, RNCM, 2000–05; Sir Edward Heath Charitable Foundn, 2005–13; Trustee: Ralph Vaughan Williams Trust, 1956–; Leeds Castle Foundn, 1988–2007 (Chm., 2001–07); Derek Hill Foundn, 2000–; Wells Cathedral Sch. Foundn, 2007–12; Dir, RAM, 1975–98 (Hon. Fellow 1985); Member: Council of Management, Royal Philharmonic Soc., 1975–2002; Rhodes Trust, 1975–97; Bd of Dirs, Royal Opera House, Covent Garden, 1988–93 (Sec., 1968–88); Royal Acad. of Music Foundn, 1988–2000. Fellow of Eton Coll., 1979–94. Hon. Bencher, Inner Temple, 1986. *Recreation:* music. *Address:* House of Lords, SW1A 0PW. *Clubs:* Brooks's, Garrick.

**ARMSTRONG, Hon. Lord; Iain Gillies Armstrong;** a Senator of the College of Justice in Scotland, since 2013; *b* 26 May 1956; *s* of John Gillies Armstrong and June Bell Armstrong (*née* Black); *m* 1977, Deirdre Elizabeth Mary Mackenzie; one *s* one *d*. *Educ:* Inverness Royal Acad.; Glasgow Univ. Called to Scottish Bar, 1986; QC (Scot.) 2000; Clerk of Faculty of Advocates, 1995–99 (Vice Dean, 2008–13); Standing Jun. Counsel in Scotland, DSS, 1998–2000; Crown Counsel, 2000–03. Member: Jt Standing Cttee on Legal Educn in Scotland, 1995–99; Adv. Panel, Sch. of Law, Univ. of Glasgow, 2009–15; Judicial Appts Bd for Scotland, 2010–12. Gov., Fettes Coll., 2000–11. *Address:* Supreme Courts, Parliament House, Parliament Square, Edinburgh EH1 1RQ. *T:* (0131) 225 2595. *Club:* New (Edinburgh).

**ARMSTRONG, Alan Gordon;** Senior Lecturer in Economics, University of Bristol, 1977–97; *b* 11 Feb. 1937; *s* of late Joseph Gordon Armstrong and Evelyn Armstrong (*née* Aird); *m* 1963, Margaret Louise Harwood; one *s* one *d*. *Educ:* Bede Grammar Sch., Sunderland; Queens' Coll., Cambridge (MA). Economist, Reed Paper Gp, 1960–62; Res. Officer, Dept of Applied Econs, Univ. of Cambridge, 1962–69; Fellow, Selwyn Coll., Cambridge, 1967–69; Lectr in Econs, Univ. of Bristol, 1970–77. Part-time Mem., Monopolies and Mergers Commn, 1989–95; Consultant on Economic Statistics to: UN Statistical Office, OECD, EEC, ONS, DTI, NEDO, various times, 1970–2001; Member: EC Adv. Cttee on Econ. and Social Statistics, 1992–97; UK Central Statistical Office (formerly Central Statistical Office Users') Adv. Cttee, 1992–96. *Publications:* Input-Output Tables and Analysis, 1973; Structural Change in UK, 1974; Review of DTI Statistics, 1989; res. papers and jl articles on input-output, nat. accounts and the motor industry. *Recreations:* gardening (by necessity), family history, cricket, church affairs. *Address:* 70 Causeway View, Nailsea, Bristol BS48 2XL. *T:* (01275) 853197.

**ARMSTRONG, Alexander Henry Fenwick;** television presenter, comedian, singer and actor, since 1996; *b* Rothbury, Northumberland, 2 March 1970; *s* of Angus and Virginia Armstrong; *m* 2004, Hannah Snow; four *s*. *Educ:* Durham Sch.; Trinity Coll., Cambridge (Choral Schol.; BA 1992). *Television* includes: Beast, 2000–01; (with Ben Miller) The Armstrong and Miller Show, 2000–01 and 2007–10; Life Begins, 2004–06; The Trial of Tony Blair, 2007; Mutual Friends, 2008; Dr Who, 2008, 2011; Pointless, 2009–; SJA: Alien Files, 2010; Reggie Perrin, 2010; The Sarah Jane Adventures, 2011; Love Life, 2012; The Twelve Drinks of Christmas, 2013; Rome's Invisible City, 2015; Land of the Midnight Sun, 2015; The Sound of Music, 2015; film, Horrible Histories: the movie, 2019. Dir, Toff Media, 2006–. *Recordings:* A Year of Songs, 2015; Upon a Different Shore, 2016; Peter and the Wolf, 2017. Pres., Newcastle Literary and Philosophical Soc., 2011–. Mem. Cttee, St Paul's Knightsbridge Foundn, 2006–. *Publications:* (with R. Osman) The Very Pointless Quiz Book, 2014; Land of the Midnight Sun: my Arctic adventures, 2015. *Recreations:* wine, fishing, friends, singing. *Address:* c/o PBJ Management, 22 Rathbone Street, W1T 1LG. *Clubs:* Brooks's, Groucho, Aspinalls.

**ARMSTRONG, Very Rev. Christopher John;** Dean of Blackburn, 2001–16; Priest-in-charge, Welland Fosse Benefice, Peterborough, since 2016; *b* 18 Dec. 1947; *s* of John Armstrong and Susan Elizabeth Armstrong; *m* 1976, Geraldine Anne Clementsen; two *s* one *d*. *Educ:* Dunstable Grammar Sch.; Bede Coll., Univ. of Durham (Cert Ed 1969); Kelham Theol Coll.; Univ. of Nottingham (BTh 1975). Ordained deacon, 1975, priest, 1976; Asst Curate, All Saints, Mansfield, 1975–79; Chaplain, Coll. of St Hild and St Bede, Univ. of Durham, 1979–85; Domestic Chaplain to Archbp of York and Diocesan Dir of Ordinands, Dio. York, 1985–91; Vicar, St Martin, Scarborough, 1991–2001, Chm., Lancs Fairness Commn, 2014–15. *Recreations:* sport, mountaineering, gardening, theatre and cinema, travel. *Address:* The Rectory, 11 Church Lane, Barrowden, Oakham, Rutland LE15 8ED.

**ARMSTRONG, Lt-Col Sir Christopher (John Edmund Stuart)**, 7th Bt *cr* 1841, of Gallen Priory, King's County; MBE 1979; *b* 15 Jan. 1940; *s* of Sir Andrew Clarence Francis Armstrong, 6th Bt, CMG and Laurel May (*née* Stuart; *d* 1988); *S* father, 1997; *m* 1972, Georgina Elizabeth Carey, *d* of Lt-Col W. G. Lewis; three *s* one *d*. *Educ:* Ampleforth; RMA, Sandhurst. Lt-Col, RCT. *Heir: s* Charles Andrew Armstrong, *b* 21 Feb. 1973.

**ARMSTRONG, Prof. (Christopher) Mark**, DPhil; FBA 2007; Professor of Economics, University of Oxford, since 2011; Fellow, All Souls College, Oxford, since 2011; *b* 26 Dec. 1964; *s* of John Armstrong and Jane Armstrong; *m* 1999, Carli Coetzee; one *s* one *d*. *Educ:* Bedales Sch., Petersfield; Queens' Coll., Cambridge (BA Hons Math. 1987); St John's Coll., Oxford (DPhil Econs 1992). Lectr in Econs, Univ. of Cambridge, 1992–94; Eric Roll Prof. of Econ. Policy, Univ. of Southampton, 1994–97; Fellow in Econs, Nuffield Coll., Oxford,

1997–2003; Prof. of Econs, UCL, 2003–11. Editor: Rev. of Econ. Studies, 1999–2003; Rand Jl of Econs, 2005–. *Publications:* (with S. Cowan and J. Vickers) Regulatory Reform: economic analysis and UK experience, 1994; articles in academic jls on industrial economics, competition policy and consumer behaviour. *Recreations:* playing the piano, architecture old and new, keeping up with my children Harriet and Joseph. *Address:* Department of Economics, University of Oxford, Manor Road, Oxford OX1 3UL.

**ARMSTRONG, Colin Robert,** CMG 2012; OBE 1995; Founder, and Executive President, since 1976, Agripac SA (Manager, 1972–76); *b* Manchester, 9 Sept. 1915; *s* of Gerald Armstrong and Margaret Armstrong (*née* Wilson); *m* 1974, Cecilia Alexandra Luna; one *s* two *d*. *Educ:* Rossall Sch.; Harper Adams Agricl Coll. (NDA); Essex Inst. of Agric. (Dip. Mgt) ICI Plant Protection Div., Malaysia, Mexico and Ecuador, 1968–76. Hon. Consul, Guayaquil, 1982–2017. Designer, Forbidden Corner, Coverdale, N Yorks (visitor attraction, opened 1994). *Publications:* Behind the Forbidden Corner, 1999. *Recreations:* reading, opera, walking, riding and cattle ranching in Ecuador. *Address:* Agripac SA, PO Box 09 01 8598, Guayaquil, Ecuador. *E:* carmstrong@agripac.com.ec. *Club:* Union (Guayaquil).

**ARMSTRONG, Dean Paul;** QC 2014; *b* Halstead, Kent; *s* of Paul Armstrong and Merle Armstrong; one *s*. *Educ:* Sevenoaks Sch.; Fitzwilliam Coll., Cambridge (BA 1983; MA 1986). Called to the Bar, Gray's Inn, 1985; in practice as barrister, specialising in fraud, data security and cyber law. Regular commentator on Sky News and BBC TV and Radio. *Publications:* (jtly) Cyber Security: law and practice, 2017, 2nd edn 2019; (contrib.) Blockchain and Cryptocurrency: international legal and regulatory challenges, 2019. *Recreations:* follower of Chelsea Football Club and Kent County Cricket Club, music. *Address:* The 36 Group, 4 Field Court, Gray's Inn, WC1R 5EF.

**ARMSTRONG, Douglas;** see Armstrong, R. D.

**ARMSTRONG, Dr Ernest McAlpine,** CB 2005; FRCSE, FRCPE, FRCPGlas, FRCGP, FFPH; Chief Medical Officer, Scottish Executive Department of Health, 2000–05; Chairman, Alcohol Focus Scotland, 2011–16; *b* 3 June 1945; *s* of Ernest Armstrong and Mary Brownlie McLean Armstrong (*née* McAlpine); *m* 1970, Dr Katherine Mary Dickson Young; two *s*. *Educ:* Hamilton Acad.; Glasgow Univ. (BSc Hons 1968; MB ChB Hons 1970); Open Univ. (BA Hons 2016). MRCP 1975; FRCGP 1987; FRCPGlas 1988; FRCPE 1996; FFPH (FFPHM 2001); FRCSE 2001. Lectr in Pathology, Glasgow Univ., 1971–74; Trainee Assistant, Douglas, 1974–75; Principal in gen. practice, Argyll, 1975–93; Sec., BMA, 1993–2000. Chm., Oban Hospice Ltd, 2007–13. Hon. Col, 205 (S) Field Hosp. (V), 2005–12. Hon. LLD Aberdeen, 2008. *Publications:* articles on ultrastructure, clinical immunology and med. politics. *Recreations:* church music, opera, sailing, travelling. *Address:* The Captain's House, 4 The Square, Plymouth PL1 3JX.

**ARMSTRONG, Dr Fiona, (Lady MacGregor of MacGregor);** broadcaster and writer; Lord-Lieutenant of Dumfries, since 2016; *b* Preston, 28 Nov. 1956; *d* of Robert and Pauline Armstrong; *m* 1st, 1987, Rodney Potts (marr. diss. 2002); one *d*; 2nd, 2005, Sir Malcolm Gregor Charles MacGregor of MacGregor, *qv*. *Educ:* St Thomas More Comprehensive Sch., Preston; W. R. Tuson Coll., Preston; University Coll. London (BA Hons German); Univ. of Strathclyde (PhD Hist. 2017). Reporter, Radio 210, 1982–83; production journalist, BBC TV Manchester, 1983–85; news reporter, then newsreader, ITV Border, 1985–87; newsreader, ITN, 1987–92; presenter, GMTV, 1992–93; freelance work for ITV Border, Sky Sports, BBC World, Grampian TV, NBC; newsreader, BBC News Channel, 2010–14; presenter, Border Life, ITV Tyne Tees and Border, 2013–. Columnist: Scottish Field mag., 2009–; Scotbanner newspaper, USA, 2009–; The Courier, 2013–. Lay Advr, Scottish Cttee, Community Integrated Care, 2015–. Mem. Bd, Univ. of Central Lancs, 2013–. Founder, Border Reiver Trail, 2008. Chm., Clan Armstrong Trust, 2013–18; Trustee, Community Integrated Care, 2017–. Patron: Angling for Youth Develt, 2008–; Second Chance, 2008–. Hon. Fellow: Univ. of Central Lancs 2006; Univ. of Cumbria, 2018. *Publications:* 'F' is for Fly-Fishing, 1993; The Commuter's Cookbook, 1995; Let's Start Fly-Fishing, 1999; Big Food for Wee Macs, 2004. *Recreations:* fishing, cooking, swimming, clan research. *Address:* c/o Knight Ayton Management, 29 Gloucester Place, W1U 8HX. *T:* (020) 3795 1806. *E:* info@knightayton.co.uk. *Club:* New (Edinburgh).

**ARMSTRONG, Frank William,** FREng; FIMechE; FRAeS; independent technical consultant, since 1991; *b* 26 March 1931; *s* of Frank Armstrong and Millicent L. Armstrong; *m* 1957, Diane T. Varley; three *d*. *Educ:* Stretford Grammar Sch.; Royal Technical Coll., Salford; Queen Mary Coll., Univ. of London (BSc Eng; MSc Eng 1956). FIMechE 1981; FRAeS 1981; FREng (FEng 1991). Massey-Harris Ltd, 1947–51; De Havilland Engine Co., 1956–58; Admiralty Engineering Lab., 1958–59; NGTE, 1959–78; Engine Div., MoD (PE), 1978–81; Dep. Dir, R&D, NGTE, 1981–83; Royal Aircraft, later Royal Aerospace, Establishment: Head of Propulsion Dept, 1983–87; Dep. Dir (Aircraft), 1987–88; Dep. Dir (Aerospace Vehicles), 1988–90; Dir (Aerospace Vehicles), 1990–91. *Publications:* contribs on aeronautics research, gas turbines and aircraft propulsion to learned jls. *Recreations:* mountaineering (nowadays mainly of the armchair variety!), music, aviation history. *Address:* 6 Corringway, Church Crookham, Fleet, Hants GU52 6AN. *T:* (01252) 616526.

**ARMSTRONG, Prof. Fraser Andrew,** PhD; FRS 2008; Professor of Chemistry, University of Oxford; Fellow of St John's College, Oxford, since 1993. *Educ:* Univ. of Leeds (BSc; PhD 1978); Univ. of Oxford (MA). Royal Soc. Univ. Res. Fellow, Univ. of Oxford, 1983–89; Chemistry Faculty, Univ. of Calif, Irvine, 1989–93; Lectr, then Reader, Dept of Chem., Univ. of Oxford, 1993. European Medal for Biol Inorganic Chem., 1998; Award for Inorganic Biochem., 2000, Medal for Interdisciplinary Chem., 2006, RSC; Carbon Trust Innovation Award, 2003; Max Planck Award for Frontiers in Biol Chem., 2004. *Publications:* Bioinorganic Chemistry, 1990; (jtly) Inorganic Chemistry, 4th edn 2006, 5th edn as Shriver & Atkins' Inorganic Chemistry, 2009; (jtly) Energy… beyond oil, 2007; articles in learned jls. *Address:* Department of Chemistry, University of Oxford, South Parks Road, Oxford OX1 3QR.

**ARMSTRONG, Iain Gillies;** see Armstrong, Hon. Lord.

**ARMSTRONG, Prof. Isobel Mair,** PhD; FBA 2003; Professor of English, Birkbeck College, University of London, 1989–2002, now Professor Emeritus, and Hon. Fellow, 2002; *b* 25 March 1937; *d* of Richard Aneurin Jones and Marjorie Jackson; *m* 1961, John Michael Armstrong; two *s* one *d*. *Educ:* Friends' Sch., Saffron Walden; Univ. of Leicester (BA 1959; PhD 1963). Asst Lectr and Lectr in English, UCL, 1963–70; Lectr and Sen. Lectr in English, Univ. of Leicester, 1971–79; Prof. of English, Univ. of Southampton, 1979–89. Vis. Prof., Princeton Univ., 1983–84; Frank and Eleanor Griffiths Chair, Bread Loaf Sch. of English, 1990, Robert Frost Chair, 2002, Middlebury Coll.; Vis. Prof., Harvard Univ., 1995–96, 1999, 2004, 2008; Sen. Res. Fellow, Inst. of English Studies, 2002; John Hinkley Vis. Prof., Johns Hopkins Univ., 2005, 2013; Council of Humanities Fellow, Princeton Univ., 2016. Lectures: Warton, on English Poetry, British Acad., 2011; F. T. Prince, Univ. of Southampton, 2017; Jacques Berthoud, Univ. of York, 2017; Lisa Jardine, QMUL, 2018; Megan Morris, Univ. of Surrey; Lorna Sage, UEA. Internat. School. (formerly For. Mem.), Amer. Acad. of Arts and Scis, 2014. Hon. DLitt Leicester, 2005. Jt Editor, Women: a cultural review, 1990–2015; Gen. Editor, Writers and their Work, British Council, 1992–2006. *Publications:* Victorian Scrutinies: reviews of poetry 1830–70, 1972; Language as Living Form in Nineteenth Century Poetry, 1982; Jane Austen: Mansfield Park, 1988; Victorian Poetry, 1993, 2nd edn 2019; Jane Austen: Sense and Sensibility, 1994; Nineteenth Century Women Poets, 1996; (ed with Virginia Blain) Women's Poetry in the Enlightenment, 1999; (ed with Virginia Blain) Women's Poetry, Late Romantic to Late Victorian, 1999; The Radical Aesthetic, 2000; Victorian Glassworlds: glass culture and the imagination, 1830–1880, 2008 (John Russell Lowell Prize, MLA, 2009); Novel Politics: democratic imaginations in nineteenth-century fiction, 2016. *Recreation:* drawing in pen and ink. *Address:* Department of English and Humanities, Birkbeck College, Malet Street, WC1E 7HX. *T:* (020) 7631 6078.

**ARMSTRONG, Dr Jennifer Louise,** FFPH; Medical Director, NHS Greater Glasgow and Clyde, since 2012; *b* Glasgow, 19 Nov. 1965; *d* of James Armstrong and Irene Armstrong; *m* 1993, Prof. Martin McIntyre; two *s* one *d*. *Educ:* Laurel Bank Sch., Glasgow; Langside Coll., Glasgow; Univ. of Glasgow (MB ChB 1988; MPH 1995); Caledonian Univ. (Dip. Mgt 1999). MRCPGlas 1993; MFPH 1998, FFPH 2007. Trng in clin. posts, 1988–94; specialty trng in public health, West of Scotland, 1994–2000; Gen. Manager, N Glasgow Trust, 2000–04; Dir, Acute Services Rev., 2001–02; Consultant in Public Health Medicine, Nat. Services Div., NHS Nat. Services Scotland, 2004–07; SMO, Health Dept, Scottish Govt, 2007–12. *Recreations:* running 10K, script writing, cycling. *Address:* NHS Greater Glasgow and Clyde, J B Russell House, Gartnavel, 1055 Great Western Road, Glasgow G12 0XH. *T:* (0141) 201 4407. *E:* Jennifer.Armstrong2@ggc.scot.nhs.uk.

**ARMSTRONG, Karen Andersen,** OBE 2015; writer, since 1982; *b* 14 Nov. 1944; *d* of John Oliver Seymour Armstrong and Eileen Hastings Armstrong (*née* McHale). *Educ:* Convent of Holy Child Jesus, Edgbaston; St Anne's Coll., Oxford (MA; MLitt). Mem., Soc. of the Holy Child Jesus, 1962–69. Tutorial Res. Fellow, Bedford Coll., Univ. of London, 1973–76; Hd of English, James Allen's Girls' Sch., Dulwich, 1976–82. Trustee, British Mus., 2008–16. Hon. DLitt: Georgetown; Exeter; Aston; St Andrews; Free, Amsterdam, 2017; Hon. DD Kingston, Ont. TED Prize, 2008; Franklin D. Roosevelt Four Freedoms Medal, 2008; Leopold Lucas Meml Prize, Tubingen Univ., 2009; Internat. Hon. Knowledge Award (Sweden), 2011; Jack P. Blaney Award for Dialogue, Simon Fraser Univ., 2012; Al-Rodhan Prize, British Acad., 2013; Princess of Asturias Prize for Social Scis, Princess Asturias Foundn, 2017. *Publications:* Through the Narrow Gate, 1981; Beginning the World, 1983; The First Christian, 1984; Tongues of Fire, 1985; The Gospel According to Woman, 1986; Holy War: the Crusades and their impact on today's world, 1988; Muhammad: a biography of the Prophet, 1991; A History of God, 1993; In the Beginning, 1996; Jerusalem, One City, Three Faiths, 1996; The Battle for God: a history of Fundamentalism, 2000; Islam: a short history, 2000; Buddha, 2001; The Spiral Staircase: a memoir, 2004; A Short History of Myth, 2005; The Great Transformation: the world at the time of Buddha, Socrates, Confucius and Jeremiah, 2006; Muhammad: a prophet for our time, 2006; The Bible: a biography, 2007; The Case for God: what religion really means, 2009; Twelve Steps to a Compassionate Life, 2011; Fields of Blood: religion and the history of violence, 2014; St Paul, the Misunderstood Apostle, 2015; The Lost Art of Scripture: rescuing the sacred texts, 2019. *Recreations:* literature, music, theatre. *Address:* c/o Felicity Bryan, 2A North Parade, Banbury Road, Oxford OX2 6LX. *T:* (01865) 513816, *Fax:* (01865) 310055.

**ARMSTRONG, Kellie;** Member (Alliance) Strangford, Northern Ireland Assembly, since 2016; *b* Newtownards, 8 Sept. 1970; *d* of Eamonn and Geraldine McGrattan; *m* 1995, Barry L. Armstrong; one *d*. *Educ:* Assumption Grammar Sch.; Queen's Univ. Belfast (BA Hons). Manager: Peninsula Community Transport, 2002–06; NBLT, 2006–07; Dir for NI, Community Transport Assoc., 2007–16. Chm., Kinship Care NI, 2014–16. Vice Chm., Alliance Party, 2013–14. Mem. (Alliance) Ards BC, 2013. *Address:* 19A Upper Ballygelagh Road, Kircubbin, Co. Down BT22 1JH. *T:* 07739 371558. *E:* kellie.armstrong@mla.niassembly.gov.uk.

**ARMSTRONG, Lance;** professional cyclist, retired 2005, returned to racing, 2009–11; *b* Plano, Texas, 18 Sept. 1971; *s* of Linda Armstrong (*née* Walling); *m* 1998, Kristin Richard (marr. diss. 2003); one *s* twin *d*; one *s* one *d* by Anna Hansen. Nat. Amateur Champion, USA, 1991; Member: US Olympic Team, 1992, 1996, 2000 (Bronze Medal, subseq. disqualified); Motorola Team, 1993–96; Cofidis Team, 1996–97; US Postal Service, subseq. Discovery Channel, Pro Cycling Team, 1998–2005; Team Astana, 2009; RadioShack, 2009–11. Winner, numerous races, including: World Cycling Championships, Oslo, 1993; Tour DuPont, 1995, 1996; Tour de Luxembourg, 1998; Tour de France, 1999, 2000, 2001, 2002, 2003, 2004, 2005 (1st person to win 7 consecutive races, but subseq. stripped of titles); Grand Prix du Midi Libre, 2002. Founder and Chm., Lance Armstrong Foundn for Cancer, later Livestrong Foundn, 1996–2012. *Publications:* It's Not About the Bike: my journey back to life, 2000; (jtly) The Lance Armstrong Performance Program, 2001; (with S. Jenkins) Every Second Counts, 2003. *Address:* c/o Livestrong Foundation, 2201 E Sixth Street, Austin, TX 78702, USA.

**ARMSTRONG, Lisa, (Mrs P. Hadaway);** Fashion Director, The Daily Telegraph, since 2015 (Fashion Editor, 2011–15); Contributing Editor, Vogue, since 1999; *b* 12 Oct. 1961; *d* of Royston Myers and Rosalind Armstrong, and step *d* of Clement Armstrong; *m* 1988, Paul Hadaway; two *d*. *Educ:* Dorchester Grammar Sch. for Girls; Bristol Univ. (BA Hons English Lit.); City Univ. (Postgrad. Dip. Journalism). Asst Ed., Fitness Mag., 1985–86; Insight Ed., Elle, 1986–88; Dep. Features Ed., Vogue, 1988–91; Fashion Ed., The Independent and Independent on Sunday, 1991–93; Fashion Features Dir, Vogue, 1993–98; Fashion Ed., The Times, 1998–2011. Trustee, Style for Soldiers, 2012– (Patron). Fashion Writer of the Year, British Fashion Council, 2001. Hon. DArts London Univ. of Arts 2011. *Publications:* Front Row, 1998; Dead Stylish, 2001; Bad Manors, 2003; Deja View, 2004. *Recreations:* reading, riding, needlepoint, finding places to put finished needlepoint, increasingly travel - fashion is now a global beat. *Address:* Daily Telegraph, 111 Buckingham Palace Road, SW1W 0DT.

**ARMSTRONG, Lucy Victoria Winwood;** Chief Executive, The Alchemists Ltd, since 2003; *b* Manchester, 13 July 1968; *d* of late David Winwood Armstrong and of Jennifer Susan Armstrong. *Educ:* Aylesbury High Sch.; St Hilda's Coll., Oxford (BA Hons PPE 1989); Open Univ. (MBA 1999; MSc Forensic Psychol. and Criminol. 2010). Investment Controller, 3i plc, 1989–96; Business Develt Manager, Courtaulds Textiles plc, 1996–98; Consultant, Tyzack & Partners, 1998–2003. Non-exec. Chm., Capital for Enterprise Ltd, 2012–13. Actg Chair, Northumbria Univ., 2010–12. Non-exec. Chm., Small and Medium Enterprises Council, CBI, 2004–13. Chair: Professional Standards Council, Asset Based Finance Assoc., 2013–; Enterprise Res. Centre, 2014–; Tyneside Cinema, 2015–; Port of Tyne, 2017–. Chair, TDI, 2015–. FRSA. *Recreations:* church bell ringing, chain-sawing, diving. *Address:* The Alchemists Ltd, Fifth Avenue Business Park, Gateshead NE11 0XA. *T:* (0191) 491 2391. *E:* lucy.armstrong@the-alchemists.com. *Club:* Northern Counties (Newcastle upon Tyne).

**ARMSTRONG, Mark;** see Armstrong, C. M.

**ARMSTRONG, Prof. Peter;** Professor of Diagnostic Radiology, St Bartholomew's Hospital, 1989–2005; President, Royal College of Radiologists, 1998–2001; *b* 31 Aug. 1940; *s* of Alexander Armstrong and Ada Armstrong (*née* Lapidas); *m* 1967, Carole J. Gray (*d* 2017); one *s* one *d* (one *s* decd). *Educ:* Marylebone Grammar Sch.; Middlesex Hosp. Med. Sch. (MB BS 1963). Jun. hosp. posts, Middlesex Hosp. and Guy's Hosp., 1963–70; Consultant Radiologist, KCH, 1970–77; Prof. of Radiology and Dir, Diagnostic Radiology Dept, Univ. of Virginia, 1977–89. Ed., Clinical Radiology, 1990–94. Warden for Clinical Radiology, RCR, 1994–98. *Publications:* (with M. Wastie) Diagnostic Imaging, 1981, 6th edn 2009; (jtly) Imaging Diseases of the Chest, 1990, 4th edn 2005; contrib. numerous articles on radiological topics to med. jls and books. *Recreations:* reading, theatre, opera. *Address:* 8 Westrow, SW15 6RH. *Club:* Shadows Radiology.

**ARMSTRONG, Peter John Bowden; His Honour Judge Armstrong;** a Circuit Judge, since 2000; *b* 19 Dec. 1951; *s* of late William David Armstrong, MBE and Kathleen Mary Armstrong; *m* 1976, Joanna Cox; two *d*. *Educ:* Durham Johnston Grammar Technical Sch.; Trinity Coll., Cambridge (MA). Called to the Bar, Middle Temple, 1974; in practice at the Bar, Middlesbrough, 1976–2000; Asst Recorder, 1990–94; a Recorder, 1994–2000; North Eastern Circuit. *Recreations:* golf, cricket, Rugby, music. *Address:* c/o Teesside Court Centre, Russell Street, Middlesbrough TS1 2AE. *Clubs:* Eaglescliffe Golf (Stockton-on-Tees); Durham CC.

**ARMSTRONG, Sir Richard,** Kt 2004; CBE 1993; FRSE; conductor; Music Director, Scottish Opera, 1993–2005; *b* 7 Jan. 1943. *Educ:* Wyggeston School, Leicester; Corpus Christi College, Cambridge (Hon. Fellow, 1994). Music staff, Royal Opera House, Covent Garden, 1966–68; Welsh National Opera: head of music staff, 1968–73; Musical Director, 1973–86; Principal Guest Conductor, Frankfurt Opera, 1987–90. FRSE 2002. Hon. DMus: De Montfort, 1992; Glasgow, 2001; Aberdeen, 2002; St Andrews, 2004. Janáček Medal, 1978. *Recreations:* walking, food. *W:* www.sirrichardarmstrong.com.

**ARMSTRONG, (Robert) Douglas,** QC (Scot.) 2005; *m* Sally Grossart; two *d*. *Educ:* Melville Coll., later Daniel Stewart's and Melville Coll.; Aberdeen Univ. (LLB Hons 1986; DipLP 1987). Admitted Faculty of Advocates, 1990; called to the Bar, Inner Temple, 1999; in practice as barrister, 1999–, specialising in planning, envmt and admin. and constitutional law; Vice Chm., Terra Firma Chambers, 2008–12. *Address:* Terra Firma Chambers, Advocates' Library, Parliament House, Edinburgh EH1 1RF. *Clubs:* Lansdowne; New (Edinburgh); Hon. Company of Edinburgh Golfers (Muirfield).

**ARMSTRONG, Sheila Ann;** soprano; *b* 13 Aug. 1942; *m* 1980, Prof. David Edward Cooper, *qv* (marr. diss. 1998). *Educ:* Hirst Park Girls' Sch., Ashington, Northumberland; Royal Academy of Music, London. Debut Sadler's Wells, 1965, Glyndebourne, 1966, Covent Garden, 1973. Sang all over Europe, Far East, N and S America; has made many recordings. Pres., Kathleen Ferrier Soc., 1996–2012 (former Trustee, Kathleen Ferrier Awards). K. Ferrier and Mozart Prize, 1965; Hon. RAM 1970, FRAM 1973. Hon. MA Newcastle, 1979; Hon. DMus Durham, 1991. *Recreations:* interior design and decoration, collecting antique keys, gardening, flower arranging, sewing, bird watching.

**ARMSTRONG-JONES,** family name of **Earl of Snowdon**.

**ARMYTAGE, John McDonald G.;** *see* Green-Armytage.

**ARMYTAGE, Sir (John) Martin,** 9th Bt *cr* 1738, of Kirklees, Yorkshire; *b* 26 Feb. 1933; *s* of Sir John Lionel Armytage, 8th Bt, and of Evelyn Mary Jessamine, *d* of Edward Herbert Fox, Adbury Park, Newbury; *S* father, 1983. *Educ:* Eton; Worcester Coll., Oxford. *Heir:* cousin Hugh Anthony Armytage [*b* 6 Aug. 1955; *m* 1999, Rachel, *yr d* of Michael Wesson; one *s* one *d*]. *Address:* 5 St James's Place, Cheltenham, Glos GL50 2EG. *T:* (01242) 525869.

**ARNAULT, Bernard Jean Etienne,** Hon. KBE 2012; President, since 1984, and Chairman, Christian Dior; President, since 1989, and Chairman, since 1992, Louis Vuitton Moët Hennessy; *b* Roubaix, 5 March 1949; *s* of Jean Arnault and Marie-Jo (*née* Savinel); *m* 1991, Hélène Mercier; three *s*; one *s* one *d* by former marriage. *Educ:* Ecole Polytechnique, Paris. Qualified as engineer, 1971. President: Ferret Savinel, 1978–84; Financière Agache SA, 1984–89. Pres., Fondation Louis Vuitton 2014–. Man of the Year, NY, 1991. Officier, 2001, Commandeur, 2007, Légion d'Honneur; Commandeur, Ordre des Arts et des Lettres, 2002. *Recreations:* music, piano, tennis. *Address:* Louis Vuitton Moët Hennessy, 22 avenue Montaigne, 75008 Paris, France. *T:* (1) 44132222.

**ARNELL, Prof. Nigel William,** PhD; FRGS, FRMetS; Professor of Climate Systems Science, University of Reading, since 2007 (Director, Walker Institute for Climate System Research, 2007–15); *b* Newport, IoW, 10 Dec. 1959; *s* of Roy and Audrey Arnell; *m* 1993, Hilary Kathryn Stevens (*née* Burn); one *d*, and one step *s* one step *d*. *Educ:* W Kidlington Primary Sch.; Gosford Hill Secondary Sch.; Univ. of Southampton (BSc Hons Geog.; PhD Geog. 1985). FRGS 2003; FRMetS 2016. Hydrologist, Inst. of Hydrol., 1984–94; University of Southampton: Reader in Geog., 1995–99; Prof. of Geog., 1999–2007; Hd, Sch. of Geog., 2003–07. *Publications:* Global Warming, River Flows and Water Resources, 1996; Hydrology and Global Environmental Change, 2002; lead author, 2nd, 3rd, 4th and 5th Assessment Reports of InterGovtl Panel on Climate Change, 1995, 2001, 2007, 2013; Short Guide to Climate Change Risk, 2015; contrib. jls incl. Climatic Change, Jl Hydrol., Jl Geophysical Res., Nature Climate Change, Global Envmtl Change. *Recreations:* walking in the country, especially the remoter parts of the British Isles, gardening, badminton, old maps, 10k runs. *Address:* Department of Meteorology, University of Reading, Earley Gate, Reading RG6 6AR. *E:* n.w.arnell@reading.ac.uk.

**ARNEY, Claudia Isobel;** non-executive Director and Chair of Remuneration Committee, Halfords plc, since 2011; Independent non-executive Director, Aviva plc, since 2016; *b* 25 Jan. 1971; *d* of Hon. Martin Jay, *qv*; *m* 2000, John Arney; one *s* two *d*. *Educ:* Hertford Coll., Oxford (BA English Lit.); INSEAD (MBA). Business Analyst, McKinsey and Co., 1992–94; Strategy and Develt Exec., Pearson plc, 1994–97; Product Develt Manager, FT, 1997–99; Man. Dir, thestreet.co.uk, 1999–2000; Exec. Dir, Goldman Sachs, 2000–06; Dir, Enterprise and Growth Unit, HM Treasury, 2006–08; Gp Man. Dir, Digital, Emap, 2008–10. Sen. Ind. Dir and Dep. Chm., Telecity plc, 2013–16; non-executive Director: Partnerships UK, 2006–10; Transport for London, 2009–12; Which?, 2011–15; Huawei, 2011–14; Premier League, 2015–; Derwent London plc, 2015–; Kingfisher plc, 2018–. Mem., Adv. Bd, Shareholder Exec., 2008–. Chair, Public Data Gp, 2012–15.

**ARNISON, Maj.-Gen. Peter Maurice,** AC 2001 (AO 1992); CVO 2002; company director; Governor of Queensland, Australia, 1997–2003; Chancellor, Queensland University of Technology, 2004–12; *b* 21 Oct. 1940; *s* of Frank and Norma Arnison; *m* 1964, Barbara Ruth Smith; one *s* one *d*. *Educ:* Lismore High Sch.; Royal Mil. Coll., Duntroon; Army Staff Coll., Queenscliff; Univ. of Queensland (BEc 1976); Securities Inst. of Australia (Grad. Dip. in Applied Finance and Investment 1993). CO 5th 7th Bn Royal Aust. Regt, 1981–82; COS HQ 1st Div., Brisbane, 1983–84; Comdt Land Warfare Centre, Canungra, Qld, 1985–86; Comdr 3rd Bde, Townsville, Qld, 1987–88; jssc, Canberra; rcds 1989; Dir-Gen. Jt Ops and Plans, HQ Aust. Defence Force, Canberra, 1990; Comdr 1st Div., Brisbane, Qld, 1991–94; Land Comdr Australia, Sydney, 1994–96. Exec. Dir, Allied Rubber Products (Qld), 1996–97; Mem. Bd, Energex Ltd, 2004. Chairman: Centre for Military and Veterans' Health, 2004–10; Australian Bravery Decorations Council, 2009–10. DUniv: Griffith, 1998; Qld Univ. of Technology, 1999; Southern Cross, 2009. Hon. DLit Southern Qld, 2001; Hon. LLD Qld, 2002. KStJ 1997. *Publications:* Australia's Security Arrangements in the South West Pacific, 1989. *Recreations:* golf, watching Rugby and cricket, theatre, opera, ballet, reading, computing. *Address:* 86 Yabba Street, Ascot, Qld 4007, Australia. *Clubs:* Queensland, Brisbane, United Service (Brisbane); Royal Queensland Golf.

**ARNOLD, Anne Mary; Her Honour Judge Arnold;** a Circuit Judge, since 2019; *b* 16 March 1958; *d* of late Lt Comdr Stanley Hugh Childs Plant, RNR, RD, and of Enid Edith Plant (*née* Morgan); *m* 1987, Peter Roderick Arnold. *Educ:* Talbot Heath, Bournemouth; Dorset Inst. Higher Educn and Université de Caen (BA Hons); Univ. of Birmingham (MBA Public Service); Homerton Coll., Cambridge (AdvDip Professional Trng and Develt). Called to the Bar, Inner Temple, 1981; Dorset Magistrates' Courts, 1979–99: Legal Advr, 1980–82; Principal Legal Advr, 1982–92; Dep. Justices' Trng Officer, 1991–94; Bench Legal Advr, 1992–94; Dir of Legal Services, 1994–99; Jt Staff Trng Officer, 1995–99; Associate Inspector, HM Magistrates' Courts Inspectorate, 1998; Actg Provincial Stipendiary Magistrate, E and W Sussex Commn Areas, 1997–99; a Provincial Stipendiary Magistrate, then District Judge (Magistrates' Cts), E Sussex, 1999–2006; a Recorder, 2005–19; a District Judge (Magistrates' Cts), Hants, 2006–19. Adjudicator, Prison Rule 53(A)2 and Young Offender Instn Rule 58(A)2, 2002–19. Mem., Sentencing Council for England and Wales, 2010–14. *Publications:* (contrib.) Atkin's Court Forms, vol. 5, 2nd edn (2012 issue), 2012, vol. 25, 2002, vol. 5(i), 2nd edn, 2004, vol. 19(1A) and 19(1B), 2005, vol. 25(1), 2007. *Recreations:* travel, being by the water, in the water and on the water, and a little bit of water-colouring too. *Address:* The Law Courts, High Street, Lewes BN7 1YB. *Club:* Bar Yacht.

**ARNOLD, Dr Bruce,** OBE 2003; writer; *b* 6 Sept. 1936; *s* of George Croft Arnold and Margaret Shaw; *m* 1959, Ysabel Mavis Cleave (*d* 2017); one *s* one *d* (and one *s* decd). *Educ:* Kingham Hill Sch., Oxon; Trinity Coll., Dublin (MA); National Univ. of Ireland (DLitt 2000). Political commentator and arts journalist: Irish Times, 1961–67; Sunday Independent, 1967–70; Irish Independent, 1972–2014: Literary Ed., 1986–2001; Chief Critic, 1986–2014. *Publications:* A Concise History of Irish Art, 1969, rev. edn 1998; Coppinger quartet: A Singer at the Wedding, 1978; The Song of the Nightingale, 1980; The Muted Swan, 1981; Running to Paradise, 1983; Orpen: mirror to an age, 1981; What Kind of Country, 1984; Margaret Thatcher: a study in power, 1984; An Art Atlas of Britain and Ireland, 1991; The Scandal of Ulysses, 1991, rev. edn 2004; Mainie Jellett and the Modern Movement in Ireland, 1991 (Amer. Conf. for Irish Studies Prize); Haughey: his life and unlucky deeds, 1993, rev. edn 2007; Jack Yeats, 1998; Jonathan Swift: an illustrated life, 1999; Jack Lynch: hero in crisis, 2001; The Spire and other essays in Irish culture, 2003; He That Is Down Need Fear No Fall, 2008; The Fight for Democracy: the Libertas voice in Europe, 2009; The Irish Gulag: how the Irish state betrayed its innocent children, 2009; Derek Hill, 2010; (with Jason O'Toole) The End of the Party: how Fianna Fail lost its grip on power, 2011. *Recreations:* camellias, snowdrops, singing madrigals. *E:* arnoldbruce@mac.com. *Club:* Athenæum.

**ARNOLD, Catherine Elizabeth Jane,** OBE 2019; Master, St Edmund's College, Cambridge, since 2019; *b* Pusan, S Korea, 10 Nov. 1978; *d* of late Rev. Ernest Stephen Arnold and of Pamela Ann Arnold (*née* Murray). *Educ:* Overseas Sch., Colombo; Ryde Sch. with Upper Chine (Head Girl); Trinity Coll., Cambridge (BA Maths and Theol.; MPhil Philosophy of Religion); Nottingham Univ. (MA Religious Conflict). Consultant, Oliver Wyman and Co., 2001–03; journalist, 2003–06; entered FCO 2006; Desk Officer, Prevent (Counter Terrorism), FCO, 2006–07; Second Secretary: Political, Press and Public Affairs, Muscat, 2007–08; Baghdad, 2008; Political, Human Rights, Tehran, 2009–11; Hd of Communication and Spokesman, Kabul, 2011–13; Hd, Emerging Powers Initiative, FCO, 2013–14; Hd, Philanthropic Investment, FCO and UKTI, 2014; Ambassador to Mongolia, 2015–18; Hd, Illegal Wildlife Trade Unit, FCO, 2018–19; HCSC 2019. *Publications:* Bradt City Guide to Baghdad, 2004. *Recreations:* riding, trekking, music, poetry. *Address:* St Edmund's College, Cambridge CB3 0BN. *E:* master@st-edmunds.cam.ac.uk. *Club:* Frontline.

**ARNOLD, Prof. Dana Rebecca,** PhD; FSA; Professor of Art History, University of East Anglia, since 2016; *b* 22 June 1961; *d* of late Edward Cyril Arnold and of Josephine Arnold; *m* 1989, Dr Kenneth Haynes (marr. diss. 2007). *Educ:* Westfield Coll., London (BA 1983); Bartlett Sch. of Architecture, UCL (MSc 1984; PhD 1997). Sen. Lectr, Dept of Fine Art, Univ. of Leeds, 1994–99; Prof. of Architectural History, 1999–2012, Hd of Res., Sch. of Humanities, 2003–12, Univ. of Southampton; Prof. of Architectural Hist., Middx Univ., 2012–16. Research Fellow: Yale Univ., 1997 and 2005; Getty Res. Inst., Calif, 2002; Univ. of Cambridge, 2003, 2013. Hon. Prof., Faculty of Architecture, Middle East Tech. Univ., Ankara, 2010–15; Guest Prof., Internat. Res. Centre for Chinese Cultural Heritage Conservation, Tianjin Univ., 2011–. Member: AHRC (formerly AHRB), 2004–; Adv. Panel, AHRC/EPSRC Sci. and Heritage Res. Prog., 2008–14; sub-panel 32, REF 2021, UKRI, 2019–. FRSA 2000; FSA 2006; FRHistS 2007. Ed., Art History jl, 1997–2002; General Editor: New Interventions in Art History (book series), 2002–; Blackwell Companions to Art History, 2004–; Jt Ed., special issue of Synergies jl, London and Paris: capitals of the nineteenth century, 2009. *Publications:* (ed) Belov'd by Ev'ry Muse: Richard Boyle, 3rd Earl of Burlington and 4th Earl of Cork (1694–1753), 1994; (ed) Squandrous and Lavish Profusion: George IV, his image and patronage of the arts, 1995; (ed) The Georgian Villa, 1995, 2nd edn 1998; (ed) The Georgian Country House, 1998, 2nd edn 2003; (ed) The Metropolis and its Image, 1999; Re-presenting the Metropolis: architecture, urban experience and social life in London 1800–1840, 2000; Reading Architectural History, 2002; (ed jtly) Tracing Architecture, 2003; (ed jtly) Art and Thought, 2003; Art History: a very short introduction, 2004; (ed) Cultural Identities and the Aesthetics of Britishness, 2004; (ed jtly) Architecture as Experience, 2004; Rural Urbanism: London landscapes in the early nineteenth century, 2006; (ed jtly) Re-thinking Architectural Historiography, 2006; (ed jtly) Biographies and Space, 2007; (ed) Art History: contemporary perspectives on method, 2010; (ed jtly) A Companion to British Art 1600 to the Present, 2013; The Spaces of the Hospital: spatiality and urban change in London 1680–1820, 2013; (ed) Interdisciplinary Encounters: hidden and visible explorations of the work of Adrian Rifkin, 2014; A Short Book about Art, 2015; (ed jtly) Londres et Paris s'observent, 2015. *Address:* Department of Art History, University of East Anglia, Norwich NR4 7TJ. *E:* darnold@talk21.com.

**ARNOLD, David George;** film composer, songwriter and record producer; *b* 23 Jan. 1962; *s* of George and Rita Arnold; one *s* three *d* (incl. twin *d*). Composer: for *films* including: The Young Americans, 1993; Stargate, 1994; Last of the Dogmen, 1995; Independence Day (Grammy Award for Best Film Score), 1996; Tomorrow Never Dies, A Life Less Ordinary, 1997; Godzilla, 1998; The World is not Enough, 1999 (Ivor Novello Award for Best Film Score), 2000; Shaft, 2000; Zoolander, Baby Boy, 2001; Enough, Changing Lanes, Die Another Day, 2002; 2 Fast 2 Furious, 2003; Stepford Wives, 2004; Stoned, Four Brothers, 2005; Casino Royale, Venus, Amazing Grace, 2006; Hot Fuzz, 2007; How to Lose Friends and Alienate People, Quantum of Solace, 2008; Narnia: The Voyage of the Dawn Treader, 2010; Made in Dagenham, 2010; Paul, 2011; for *television* including: The

Visitor (series), 1997; Randall & Hopkirk Deceased (series), 2000; Little Britain (series), 2003 (RTS Award for Best Music, 2005); Sherlock, 2010 (Emmy Award, 2014); for *stage* including: Made In Dagenham - The Musical, Adelphi, 2014; Mood Music, Old Vic, 2018. Music Dir, London 2012 Olympics Closing and Paralympics Closing Ceremonies, 2012. Composer and producer of numerous recordings. Fellow, British Acad. of Composers & Songwriters, 2005. *Recreations:* watching cooking on TV, wandering round streets in a daze, Twitterer @davidgarnold. *Address:* Air Studios, Lyndhurst Road, NW3 5NG. *T:* (020) 7794 0660, *Fax:* (020) 7794 8518. *E:* davidgarnold@gmail.com.

**ARNOLD, Prof. David John**, DPhil; FBA 2004; Professor of Asian and Global History, University of Warwick, 2006–11, now Emeritus; *b* 1 Oct. 1946; *s* of Mansel John and May Arnold; *m* 1988, Juliet Elizabeth Miller. *Educ:* Univ. of Exeter (BA Hons (Hist.) 1968); Univ. of Sussex (DPhil 1973). Lectr in History, Univ. of Dar es Salaam, 1972–75; Res. Fellow, Flinders Univ., Australia, 1975–77; Res. Fellow, SOAS, 1977–78; Lectr in History, Univ. of Lancaster, 1979–88; Prof. of S Asian Hist., 1988–2006, Hd, Dept of Hist., 1992–96, Pro-Dir for Res., 1999–2002, SOAS. Dist. Vis. Prof., Dept of Hist., Univ. of Chicago, 2008; Vis. Prof., ETH, Zurich, 2013. *Publications:* The Age of Discovery 1400–1600, 1983, 2nd edn 2002; Famine: social crisis and historical change, 1988; Colonizing the Body: state medicine and epidemic disease in nineteenth-century India, 1993; The Problem of Nature: environment, culture and European expansion, 1996; Science, Technology and Medicine in Colonial India, 2000; Gandhi, 2001; The Tropics and the Travelling Gaze: India, landscape and science 1800–1856, 2005; Everyday Technology: machines and the making of India's modernity, 2013; Toxic Histories: poison and pollution in modern India, 2016. *Recreations:* travel, gardening. *Address:* 12 Eyot Green, Chiswick, W4 2PT. *E:* d.arnold@warwick.ac.uk.

**ARNOLD, Rev. Duane Wade-Hampton**, PhD; Principal, St Chad's College, and Cummings Fellow in Liturgy, University of Durham, 1994–97; *b* 5 Aug. 1953; *s* of Wade H. Arnold and Louise Elizabeth (*née* Hensley); *m* 1980, Janet Lee Drew. *Educ:* Univ. of State of New York (AA 1978); AA 1979); Concordia Theological Seminary (MA 1981); Cambridge Dip. Religious Studies (LES) 1984; STh (Lambeth Dip. Theol.) 1984; St Chad's Coll., Durham (PhD 1989). Minister, First Church, Detroit, Michigan, 1985–87; Precentor, St Paul's Cathedral, Detroit, 1987; Chaplain, Wayne State Univ., Detroit, 1988–91; Curate, St Thomas Church, Fifth Ave, NY, 1991–93. Tutor, St Chad's Coll., Durham, 1983–85; Adjunct Lecturer: in Religious Studies, Univ. of Detroit, 1985–88; in Church History, Ashland Seminary, Ohio, 1987–91; Sen. Res. Fellow, Centre for Reformation Studies, Sheffield Univ., 1987. Producer, CDs: Martyrs Prayers, 2012; Mystic Chapel, 2015. Fellow, Coll. of Preachers, Washington Nat. Cathedral, 1991. ChStJ 1990. Governor's Award, Michigan, 1988. *Publications:* A Lutheran Reader, 1982; The Way, the Truth and the Life, 1982; Francis, A Call to Conversion, 1990; Prayers of the Martyrs, 1991; The Early Episcopal Career of Athanasius of Alexandria, 1991; Praying with John Donne and George Herbert, 1992; *De Doctrina Christiana*, Classic of Western Civilization, 1995; Martyrs' Prayers: seeking God in the midst of suffering, 2018; with R. Hudson: Beyond Belief: what the Martyrs said to God, 2002; Más allá de la Fe, 2004; Fiés até o Fim, 2008; contribs to learned jls. *Recreations:* shooting, heraldry.

**ARNOLD, Glynis, (Mrs Elliott Arnold)**; *see* Johns, G.

**ARNOLD, Jacques Arnold**; DL; consultant on Latin America; *b* London, 27 Aug. 1947; *s* of late Samuel Arnold and Eugenie (*née* Patentini); *m* 1976, Patricia Anne, *er d* of late Dennis Maunder, Windsor; one *s* two *d*. *Educ:* schools in Brazil and by correspondence; London School of Economics (BSc (Econ) 1972). Asst Gp Rep., Midland Bank, São Paulo, 1976–78; Regl Dir, Thomas Cook Gp, 1978–84; Asst Trade Finance Dir, Midland Bank, 1984–85; Dir, American Express Europe Ltd, 1985–87; Adviser for Latin America: GEC plc, 1998–2000; BAE Systems, 2000–04; FIRST Mag., 2006–; has travelled to over 90 countries on business. County Councillor for Oundle, Northants, 1981–85. Contested (C) Coventry SE, 1983. MP (C) Gravesham, 1987–97; contested (C) same seat, 1997, 2001. PPS to Minister of State: for Envmt and Countryside, 1992–93; Home Office, 1993–95. Member: Educn, Arts and Sci. Select Cttee, 1989–92; Treasury and CS Select Cttee, 1997; Sec., Cons. Backbench Cttee on Foreign and Commonwealth Affairs, 1990–92, 1995–97; Vice-Chm., 1995–96, Chm., 1996–97, Cons. Backbench Cttee on Constitutional Affairs. Secretary: British-Latin-American Parly Gp, 1987–97; Scout Assoc. Parly Gp, 1987–97; Chairman: British Brazilian Parly Gp, 1992–97; British Portuguese Parly Gp, 1995–97. Chm., LSE Cons. Soc., 1971–72; Treasurer, Nat. Assoc. of Cons. Graduates, 1974–76; Chairman: Hyde Park Tories, 1975–76; Tonbridge and Malling Cons. Assoc., 2012–16 (Pres., 2018–); Vice-Chairman: Croydon NE Cons. Assoc., 1974–76; Corby Cons. Assoc., 1983–85. Chm., Kent County Scout Council, 1998–2000. Trustee: Environment Foundn, 1989–2003; Monarchist Movement Trust, 2010–. DL Kent, 2013. Grand Official, Order of Southern Cross (Brazil), 1993. *Publications:* Democracy for Europe, 1977; (ed) Royal Houses of Europe (series), 1998–; (ed) History of Britain's Parliamentary Constituencies (annually), 2009–; A Senate of Interests: a proposal for reform of the House of Lords, 2013. *Recreations:* family life, travel, genealogy. *Address:* Fairlawn, 243 London Road, West Malling, Kent ME19 5AD. *T:* and *Fax:* (01732) 848388. *Club:* Carlton.

**ARNOLD, Jennette**, OBE 2009; Member (Lab), London Assembly, Greater London Authority, since July 2000 (London, 2000–04, North East, since 2004) (Chairman, 2008–09 and 2011–13; Deputy Chairman, 2009–11 and 2014–15). Formerly: nurse; health visitor; Regl Dir, RCN. Mem. (Lab) Islington BC, 1994–2002 (Dep. Mayor, 1999–2000). Chair: Cultural Strategy Gp for London, 2000–04; London Health Commn, 2004; Vice-Chair, London Cultural Consortium, 2005. Member: Metropolitan Police Authy, 2000–12; Mayor of London's Adv. Cabinet, 2000; UK Delegn to EU Cttee of the Regions, 2002–. Mem. Bd, Arts Council England - London, 2002–06. *Address:* Greater London Authority, City Hall, Queen's Walk, SE1 2AA.

**ARNOLD, Prof. John André**, FCA; Director, Manchester Business School, and KPMG Professor of Accounting and Financial Management, University of Manchester, 1994–2006; *b* 30 April 1944; *s* of André Eugene Arnold and May Arnold (*née* Vickers); *m* 1997, Sylvia Bailey; two *d*. *Educ:* London Sch. of Econs (MSc 1969). FCA 1967. Teaching Fellow, LSE, 1967–69; Lectr in Accounting, Univ. of Kent, 1969–71; Lectr, 1971–75, Sen. Lectr, 1975–77, Prof. of Accounting, 1977–94, Univ. of Manchester. Vis. Prof., Grad. Sch. of Business, Univ. of Washington, 1981–82. Chm., pro.manchester, 2007–08; non-exec. Dir, PZ Cussons plc, 2007–16. Pres., Manchester Soc. of Chartered Accountants, 1991–92. CCMI 1995. Chm., Feelgood Theatre Prodns, 2008–. *Publications:* Pricing and Output Decisions, 1973; Accounting for Management Decisions, 1983, 3rd edn 1996; Financial Accounting, 1985, 2nd edn 1994; contrib. numerous articles to learned jls. *Recreations:* tennis, golf, watching Stockport County FC. *Address:* 3 Green Meadows, Marple, Stockport, Cheshire SK6 6QF. *T:* (0161) 449 9432. *E:* john.arnold@manchester.ac.uk. *Club:* Marple Golf.

**ARNOLD, Very Rev. John Robert**, OBE 2002; Dean of Durham, 1989–2002, now Emeritus; *b* 1 Nov. 1933; *s* of John Stanley and Ivy Arnold; *m* 1963, Livia Anneliese Franke; one *s* two *d*. *Educ:* Christ's Hospital; Sidney Sussex Coll., Cambridge (MA); Westcott House Theol College. Curate of Holy Trinity, Millhouses, Sheffield 1960–63; Sir Henry Stephenson Fellow, Univ. of Sheffield, 1962–63; Chaplain and Lectr, Univ. of Southampton, 1963–72; Secretary, Board for Mission and Unity, General Synod of the Church of England, 1972–78; Dean of Rochester, 1978–89. Pt-time Lectr, Univ. of Durham, 1992–2002. Hon. Canon of Winchester Cathedral, 1974–78; Mem., General Synod, 1980–2002. Mem., European Ecumenical Commn for Church and Society, 1986–98; Pres., Conference of European Churches, 1986–2001 (Vice-Chm., 1986–92; Chm., 1993–97). Pres., Anglican-Lutheran Soc., 1999–; Vice Pres., Faith in Europe, 2005–. Patron, ChildAid to Russia and the Republics, 1978–; Trustee, St Ethelburga's Centre for Peace and Reconciliation, 2003–13. Hon. Fellow, St Chad's Coll., Univ. of Durham, 2002. DD Lambeth, 1999; Hon. DD Dunelm, 2002. Order of Saint Vladimir (Russian Orthodox Church), 1977. Officers' Cross, Order of Merit (Germany), 1991. *Publications:* (trans.) Eucharistic Liturgy of Taizé, 1962; (contrib.) Hewitt, Strategist for the Spirit, 1985; Rochester Cathedral, 1987; (contrib.) Cathedrals Now, 1996; (contrib.) Preaching from Cathedrals, 1998; Life Conquers Death, 2007; contribs to Theology, Crucible, St Luke's Journal of Theology, Ecclesiology. *Recreations:* music, European languages and literature. *Address:* 26 Hawks Lane, Canterbury CT1 2NU.

**ARNOLD, Rt Rev. John Stanley Kenneth**; *see* Salford, Bishop of, (RC).

**ARNOLD, Rt Rev. Keith Appleby**; Hon. Assistant Bishop, Diocese of Oxford, since 1996; *b* 1 Oct. 1926; *s* of Dr Frederick Arnold, Hale, Cheshire, and Alice Mary Appleby Arnold (*née* Holt); *m* 1955, Deborah Noreen Glenwright; one *s* one *d*. *Educ:* Winchester; Trinity Coll., Cambridge (MA); Westcott House, Cambridge. Served as Lieut, Coldstream Guards, 1944–48. Curate: Haltwhistle, Northumberland, 1952–55; St John's, Princes St, Edinburgh, 1955–61; Chaplain, TA, 1956–61; Rector of St John's, Edinburgh, 1961–69; Vicar of Kirkby Lonsdale, Cumbria, 1969–73; Team Rector of Hemel Hempstead, 1973–80; Bishop Suffragan of Warwick, 1980–90; Hon. Assistant Bishop: dio. Newcastle, 1991–96; dio. Oxford, 1997–2009. Vice-Pres., Abbeyfield Soc., 1981–91; Chairman: Housing Assocs Charitable Trust, 1980–86; Rural Housing Trust, 1987–2008. Pres., S Warwicks Marriage Guidance Council, subseq. Relate, 1980–90. *Recreations:* 19th century history, gardening. *Address:* 9 Dingleerry, Olney, Bucks MK46 5ES. *T:* (01234) 713044.

**ARNOLD, Hon. Rev. Lynn Maurice Ferguson**, AO 2004; Priest Assistant, St Peter's Cathedral, Adelaide, since 2014; Chief Executive Officer, Anglicare SA, 2008–12; *b* 27 Jan. 1949; *s* of Maurice and Jean Arnold; *m* 1978, Elaine Palmer; two *s* three *d*. *Educ:* Adelaide Boys' High Sch.; Univ. of Adelaide (BA, BEd; PhD 2003). Dip. en la Alta Dirección de Empresas, ESADE, 1996. Teacher, Salisbury N High Sch., 1971–74; Adv. Teacher, Health Educn Project Team, 1975–76; Personal Assistant to MHR, 1977–79; MHA (ALP) Salisbury, 1979–87; MP (ALP) Ramsay, 1987–93, Taylor, 1993–94; Minister of: Education, 1982–85; Technology, 1982–87; Children's Services, 1985; Employment and Further Educn, and State Develt, 1985–89; Industry, Trade & Technol., also Agriculture, Fisheries, and Ethnic Affairs, 1989–92; Economic Develt, and Multicultural and Ethnic Affairs, 1992–93; Premier of S Australia, 1992–93; Leader of the Opposition and Shadow Minister of Econ. Develt and of Multicultural and Ethnic Affairs, 1993–94; Vis. Scholar, Univ. of Oviedo, Spain, 1994–95; student, Escuela Superior de Administración y Dirección de Empresas, Barcelona, 1995–96; CEO, World Vision Australia, 1997–2003; Regl Vice-Pres. (Asia/Pacific), World Vision Internat., 2003–08. Chair, Board: Ahava Holdings Pty Ltd, 2009–; Ahava Energy Pty Ltd, 2009–. Sec. and Pres., Campaign for Peace in Vietnam, 1970–73. Mem. Council, Univ. of Adelaide, 1979–82; Mem. Bd, ICFAI Australia, 2008–. Ordained deacon, 2013, priest, 2014. Mem. Council, Anglicare Australia, 2008; Pres., SA Br., CMS, 2009–; Mem., Gen. Synod, Anglican Ch of Australia, 2010–. Reconciliation Ambassador for SA, 2010–. Trustee, Cttee for the Economic Develt of Australia, 1997–2003, 2008–; Chair, Bd of Trustees, Don Dunstan Foundn, 2009–. Mem., Australian Inst. of Co. Dirs, 1997–. *Publications:* Nigeria-Biafra Conflict, 1968; (jtly) Hoa Binh Third Force in Vietnam, 1970; (jtly) You and Me, 1975; (jtly) All Together, 1976. *Recreations:* sociolinguistics, history. *Address:* St Peter's Cathedral, St Peter's Cathedral Close, 27 King William Road, North Adelaide, SA 5006, Australia.

**ARNOLD, Mark Graham**; QC 2013; *b* Colwyn Bay, 1965; *s* of Alan Arnold and Carole Arnold (*née* McCann); *m* 1991, Halldis Gribbin; two *s* one *d*. *Educ:* Rydal Sch.; Norwich Sch.; Downing Coll., Cambridge (BA 1987; MA 1990). Called to the Bar, Middle Temple, 1988; in practice as barrister, specialising in company, insolvency and restructuring, 1989–; Jt Hd of Chambers, South Sq. *Publications:* (contrib.) Company Directors: duties, liabilities and remedies, 2009, 3rd edn 2017; (contrib.) Cross Border Insolvency, 3rd edn 2012, 4th edn 2015. *Recreations:* music, wine, playing the piano. *Address:* South Square, 3–4 South Square, Gray's Inn, WC1R 5HP. *T:* (020) 7696 9900. *E:* markarnold@southsquare.com.

**ARNOLD, Prof. Polly Louise**, OBE 2017; DPhil; FRS 2018; FRSE; FRSC; Crum Brown Chair of Chemistry, University of Edinburgh, since 2013; *b* London, 24 July 1972; *d* of Eric Leslie Arnold and (Jennifer) Anne (Louise) Powell. *Educ:* Notting Hill and Ealing High Sch. GPDST; Westminster Sch.; Brasenose Coll., Oxford (BA Chem. 1994); Univ. of Sussex (DPhil Chem. 1997). Fulbright Scholar, MIT, 1997–99; Univ. of Nottingham, 1999–2007; Univ. of Edinburgh, 2007–. FRSE 2012; FRSC 2012. *Publications:* articles in jls. *T:* (0131) 650 5429. *E:* polly.arnold@ed.ac.uk.

**ARNOLD, Rt Hon. Sir Richard David**, Kt 2008; PC 2019; **Rt Hon. Lord Justice Arnold**; a Lord Justice of Appeal, since 2019; *b* 23 June 1961; *s* of late Francis Arnold and of Ann Arnold (*née* Churchill); *m* 1990, Mary Elford; two *d*. *Educ:* Highgate Sch.; Magdalen Coll., Oxford (BA Nat. Sci. 1983, MA 1986); Univ. of Westminster (Dip. Law 1984). Called to the Bar, Middle Temple, 1985, Bencher, 2008. QC 2000; Dep. High Court Judge, 2004–08; a Judge of the High Court of Justice, Chancery Div., 2008–19; Judge in charge, Patents Court, 2013–19. Chm. Cttee, Code of Practice for Promotion of Animal Medicines, Nat. Office of Animal Health, 2002–08. Apptd to hear Trade Mark appeals, 2003–08; Mem., Panel of Chairmen, Competition Appeal Tribunal, 2008–; Ext. Mem., Enlarged Bd of Appeal, Eur. Patent Office, 2016–. Ed., Entertainment and Media Law Reports, 1993–2004. Hon. LLD Westminster, 2017. *Publications:* Performers' Rights, 1990, 5th edn 2015; (jtly) Computer Software: legal protection in the UK, 2nd edn 1992; (ed) Halsbury's Laws—Trade Marks, 4th edn reissue 2007, 5th edn 2014. *Recreations:* music, cinema, theatre, opera, exhibitions, cooking, walking in Suffolk. *Address:* Royal Courts of Justice, Strand, WC2A 2LL. *Club:* MCC.

**ARNOLD, Sir Thomas (Richard)**, Kt 1990; theatre producer; publisher; *b* 25 Jan. 1947; *s* of late Thomas Charles Arnold, OBE and Helen Breen; *m* 1984, Elizabeth Jane (marr. diss. 1993), *widow* of Robin Smithers; one *d*. *Educ:* Bedales Sch.; Le Rosey, Geneva; Pembroke Coll., Oxford (MA). Contested (C): Manchester Cheetham, 1970; Hazel Grove, Feb. 1974. MP (C) Hazel Grove, Oct. 1974–1997. PPS to Sec. of State for NI, 1979–81, to Lord Privy Seal, FCO, 1981–82; Chm., Treasury and CS Select Cttee, 1994–97 (Mem., 1992–94). Vice-Chm., Conservative Party, 1983–92. *Address:* No 1 Manchester Square, W1U 3AB.

**ARNOLD, Wallace**; *see* Brown, C. E. M.

**ARNOLD, William**; Director, Corporate Services, Supreme Court of the United Kingdom, 2009–18; *b* 13 May 1953; *s* of Rev. William and Mrs Ruth Arnold; *m* 1992, Elizabeth Anne McLellan; twin *s*. *Educ:* Bury Grammar Sch.; King's Coll., Cambridge (MA Classics). Joined Lord Chancellor's Department, 1974: Asst Private Sec. to Lord Chancellor,

1977–79; Principal, 1979; Head of Legal Services Div., 1987; Hd of Remuneration and Competition Div., 1988; Hd, Courts and Legal Services Bill Div., 1989; Dir of Corporate Services and Principal Estabt and Finance Officer, PRO, 1991–92; on loan to Dept of PM and Cabinet, Canberra, Australia, 1993–94; Hd, Family Policy Div., LCD, 1994–99; Hd of Govt Offices and Regl Policy, then Regl Policy and Regeneration, Div. 1, DETR, 1999–2001; Dir, Regl Develt Agency Policy, Finance and Sponsorship, DTI, 2001–03; Hd, Criminal Justice System Confidence Unit, Home Office, 2003; Sec. to the Judicial Appointments Comrs, 2004–06; Interim Chief Exec., Family Justice Council, 2006; Hd, Court Broadcasting Unit, Min. of Justice, 2006–07; Chief Exec., Law Commn, 2008–09. Reader: St Margaret's Church, Putney, 1989–2008; Mortlake with East Sheen, 2008–. Manager (pro bono), Friends of Richmond Park, Richmond Park Visitor Centre, 2019–. FRSA 2000. *Recreations:* ski-ing, swimming, long-distance trekking, opera, ballet. *E:* wbmjarnold@gmail.com.

**ARNOT, Prof. Madeleine Mary, (Lady Young),** PhD; Professor of Sociology of Education, University of Cambridge, 2004–17, now Emeritus; Fellow, Jesus College, Cambridge, 1990–2017, now Emeritus; *b* 9 Jan. 1950; *d* of Eric Maxwell-Arnot and Marie Madeleine (née Rzewuska); *m* 1st, 1973, Neil MacDonald (marr. diss. 1980); 2nd, 1982, R. Allan Drummond (*d* 1994); one *s* one *d;* 3rd, 1998, Sir Robin Urquhart Young, *qv. Educ:* More House Convent, London; Univ. of Edinburgh (MA 1st Cl. Hons 1972); Univ. of London Inst. of Educn; PhD Open 1989; MA Cantab 1998. Lectr, Open Univ., 1975–88; Lectr, 1988–2000, Reader, 2000–04, Cambridge Univ.; Leverhulme Trust Res. Fellow, 1996–97; Dir of Studies in Educn, Jesus Coll., Cambridge, 1990–. Noted Schol., Univ. of BC, 1993; George A. Miller Vis. Prof., Univ. of Illinois, Champagne Urbana, 2000; Visiting Professor: Univ. of Porto, 2001–; Aristotle Univ. of Thessaloniki, 2003–; Univ. of Stockholm, 2005. Commonwealth Scholarship Comr, 2018. Member: Wkg Gp on Citizenship and Initial Teacher Educn, 2000, DfEE; Gender Policy Gp, QCA, 1998–99; Consultative Gp, EOC, 1999–2002; Steering Gp Global Monitoring Report, UNESCO, 2003; Gender expert for Council of Europe Jt Cttee on Human Rights and Educn, 1999. FRSA 1996; FAcSS (AcSS 2004). FilDr *hc* Uppsala, 2008. *Publications:* (jtly) Educational Reforms and Gender Equality in Schools, 1996; (jtly) Recent Research on Gender and Educational Performance, 1998; (jtly) Closing the Gender Gap: post-war education and social change, 1999; Reproducing Gender?: essays on educational theory and feminist politics, 2002; (jtly) Consultation in the Classroom, 2004; Educating the Gendered Citizen, 2009; (jtly) Education, Asylum and the 'Non-Citizen' Child, 2010; (jtly) School Approaches to the Education of EAL Students, 2014; (jtly) Girls' Education and Gender Equality 2014; *anthologies:* as M. M. MacDonald: (ed jtly) Schooling and Capitalism, 1977; Education and the State, Vol. 1: Schooling and the National Interest, 1981, Vol. 2: Politics, Patriarchy and Practice, 1981; as M. Arnot: (ed) Race and Gender: equal opportunities policies in education, 1985; (ed) The Sociology of Disability and Inclusive Education: a tribute to Len Barton, 2012; edited jointly: Gender and the Politics of Schooling, 1987; Gender Under Scrutiny: new inquiries in education, 1987; Voicing Concerns: sociological perspectives on contemporary education reforms, 1992; Feminism and Social Justice in Education, 1993; Challenging Democracy?: international perspectives on gender, education and citizenship, 2000; Gender Education and Equality in a Global Context, 2008; The RoutledgeFalmer Reader in Gender and Education, 2009; Knowledge, Power and Educational Reform: applying the sociology of Basil Bernstein, 2009; Youth Citizenship and the Politics of Belonging, 2013; Education, Mobilities and Migration: people, ideas and resources, 2016. *Address:* Jesus College, Cambridge CB5 8BL. *T:* (01223) 339339, *Fax:* (01223) 339313.

**ARNOTT;** *see* Walker-Arnott.

**ARNOTT, Sir Alexander John Maxwell,** 6th Bt *cr* 1896, of Woodlands, Shandon, Co. Cork; *b* 18 Sept. 1975; *s* of Sir John Robert Alexander Arnott, 5th Bt, and of Ann Margaret, *d* of late T. A. Farrelly, Kilcar, Co. Cavan; *S* father, 1981. *Heir: b* Andrew John Eric Arnott, *b* 20 June 1978.

**ARNOTT, Very Rev. (Andrew) David (Keltie);** Moderator of the General Assembly of the Church of Scotland, 2011–12; *b* Dunfermline, Fife, 22 July 1945; *s* of Robert Scott Gibb Arnott and Christian Keltie Arnott (née Taylor); *m* 1972, Rosemary Jane Batchelor; two *s* one *d. Educ:* George Watson's Coll., Edinburgh; Univ. of St Andrews (MA); Univ. of Edinburgh (BD). Ordained, 1971; Minister: Gorebridge, Midlothian, 1971–77; Netherlee, Glasgow, 1977–96; Hope Park, St Andrews linked with Strathkinness, 1996–2010. *Recreations:* golf, photography. *Address:* 53 Whitehaugh Park, Peebles EH45 9DB. *T:* (01721) 725979.

**ARNOTT, (Ann) Rosemary,** OBE 2001; Gender and Development Specialist, UNICEF Pakistan, since 2016; *b* Hull, 30 Jan. 1961; *d* of Prof. W(illiam) Geoffrey Arnott, FBA and Vera Arnott (née Hodson); *m* 1993, Abdu Mozayen (*d* 2013); twin *s. Educ:* Leeds Girls' High Sch.; Trinity Coll., Cambridge (BA Mod. Langs 1984); Univ. of Muenster; Inst. of Educn, Univ. of London (PGCE TESOL 1987); Univ. of Manchester (MA Econ Develt Studies (Dist.) 2000). Teacher of English: Hubei Teachers Coll., Wuhan, China, 1984–85; Lhasa Educn Office, Lhasa, Tibet, 1985–86; British Council, 1987–2014: Assistant Director: Romania, 1988–89; Ethiopia, 1989–93; Ghana, 1993–95; Consultant, gender and social develt, Manchester, 1996–98; Country Dir, Ethiopia, 1999–2003; Regl Dir, Southern Africa, 2003–08; Dir, Turkey and Black Sea, 2008–11; Dir, Bangladesh, 2011–14; Country Dir, Burma, VSO, 2014–15. *Recreations:* literature, travel, cultural relations. *Address:* 65 Little Normans, Longlevens, Gloucester GL2 0EH.

**ARNOTT, Deborah;** Chief Executive (formerly Director), Action on Smoking and Health, since 2003; *b* 23 June 1955; *d* of Michael MacMillan Arnott and Felicity Arnott (née Hugh-Jones); *m* 1996, Jon Davies; two *s. Educ:* Brunel Univ. (BSc Hons Govt, Politics and Mod. Hist. 1977); Cranfield (MBA 1981). Grad. trainee and Industrial Relns Officer, Triumph Cars, 1977–80; business consultant, planning, research and systems, 1981–82; journalist, Management Today, 1982–83; LWT Factual Programmes: researcher, 1984–86; producer director, 1986–93; series producer and prog. editor, 1993–98; Hd, Consumer Educn, Financial Services Authy, 1998–2002. Equality Officer and Shop Steward, ACTT, later BECTU, at LWT, 1983–93; Mem., Nat. Exec. and Standing Orders Cttees, ACTT, 1984–86. Chair, Mgt Cttee, and Special Advr to Bd, Personal Finance Educn Gp, 1998–2002; Mem., Govt Task Force on Tackling Over-indebtedness, 2000–02. Member: Eur. Bd, Framework Convention Alliance, 2003–12; Tobacco Adv. Gp, RCP, 2003–; Bd, IMPRESS, 2015–. Numerous policy submissions to govt depts, incl. HM Treasury and DoH, and to EC and WHO. Mem. Cttee, Kingsway workplace nursery, 1983–94; Governor: Walnut Tree Walk Primary Sch., 1995–2001; Pimlico Comprehensive, Westminster, 2002–06. Hon. Associate Prof., Univ. of Nottingham, 2011–. Hon. FRCP 2012. Alwyn Smith prize for most outstanding contrib. to public health, FPH, 2007. *Publications:* letters, articles and edlts in sci. jls incl. The Lancet and BMJ's Tobacco Control; articles in The Guardian and other newspapers and pubns. *Recreation:* the usual. *Address:* Action on Smoking and Health, New House, 67–68 Hatton Garden, EC1N 8JY. *T:* (020) 7404 0242. *E:* deborah.arnott@ash.org.uk.
*See also* J. J. Arnott.

**ARNOTT, John Jacob, (Jake);** novelist; *b* 11 March 1961; *s* of Michael MacMillan Arnott and Felicity Arnott (née Hugh-Jones); one *s. Educ:* Aylesbury Grammar Sch. Labourer, lab technician, theatrical agent's asst, artist's life model, actor, sign lang. interpreter, 1978–91; care worker, Leeds Social Services, 1991–98. *Publications:* The Long Firm, 1999; He Kills Coppers, 2001; truecrime, 2003; Johnny Come Home, 2006; The Devil's Paintbrush, 2009; The House of Rumour, 2012; The Fatal Tree, 2017. *Recreations:* t'ai chi chuan, swimming, wandering. *Address:* c/o Curtis Brown Group Ltd, Haymarket House, 28–29 Haymarket, SW1Y 4SP. *T:* (020) 7393 4409.
*See also* D. Arnott.

**ARNOTT, Jonathan;** Member for North East Region, European Parliament, 2014–19 (UK Ind, 2014–18; Ind, 2018–19); *b* Sheffield, 12 Jan. 1981; *m. Educ:* Sheffield Univ. (MMath Hons). Former teacher. Gen. Sec., UKIP, 2008–14.

**ARNOTT, Rosemary;** *see* Arnott, A. R.

**ARON, Michael Douglas;** HM Diplomatic Service; Ambassador to Yemen, since 2018; *b* 22 March 1959; *s* of late Maurice Aron and Sheila Aron (née Torrens); *m* 1986, Rachel Ann Golding Barker (*see* R. A. G. Aron) (marr. diss. 2016); two *s* two *d; m* 2018, Kate Joanne Orrick. *Educ:* Exeter Sch.; Leeds Univ. (BA Hons Arabic and French); Poly. of Central London. English lang. teacher, Sudan, 1981–83; joined FCO, 1984: Conf. Support Officer, UK Mission to UN, NY, 1985; on secondment to EC, 1986; Second, later First Sec., FCO, 1986–88; First Secretary: (Commercial and Econ.), Brasilia, 1988–91; FCO, 1991–93; UK Mission to UN, 1993–96; Dep. Hd, ME Dept, FCO, 1996–97; Head: Comprehensive Spending Review Unit, FCO, 1997–98; Mgt Consultancy Services, FCO, 1998–99; Counsellor and Dep. Hd of Mission, Amman, Jordan, 1999–2002; Political Counsellor, UK Repn to EU, Brussels, 2002–06; EU Dir and Hd, Scottish Govt (formerly Exec.) EU Office, Brussels (on secondment), 2006–08; Ambassador to Kuwait, 2008–09; Hd of Middle East Gp, FCO, 2010–11; Ambassador: to Iraq, 2011–12; to Libya, 2012–15; to Sudan, 2015–18. *Recreations:* football, Arsenal, tennis, walking, France. *Address:* c/o Foreign and Commonwealth Office, King Charles Street, SW1A 2AH.

**ARON, Rachel Ann Golding,** PhD; HM Diplomatic Service, retired; executive coach and consultant, since 2010; *b* 18 July 1951; *d* of Guy Barker and Ailsa Barker (née Gladdish); *m* 1986, Michael Douglas Aron, *qv* (marr. diss. 2016); two *s* two *d. Educ:* Ashford Sch. for Girls; Westfield Coll., Univ. of London (BA Hons Hist. 1973); Inst. of Educn, Univ. of London (PGCE 1974); Darwin Coll., Cambridge (PhD 1978). Res. Asst to Sir Frederick Catherwood, MEP, 1979–84; joined FCO, 1984; First Sec. and Cyprus Desk Officer, 1984–86; Privileges and Immunities Desk Officer, 1987–88; Hd of Chancery, Brasilia, 1988–91; Asst Hd, Eastern Dept, 1991–93; First Sec. (Pol), UK Mission to UN, NY, 1993–96; FCO Chair, CSSB, 1997–99; remote project work for HR Directorate in Amman and Brussels, 2000–03; Ambassador to Belgium, 2007–10. Chair, Parents' Assoc., 2003–05, Bd of Govs, 2005–07, Trustee, 2010–, British Sch. of Brussels. Chair, Stanmore Community Assoc., 2011–; Chair, Citizens Advice Winchester Dist (formerly Winchester Dist CAB), 2017– (Vice Chair, 2012–17); Trustee, Carroll Centre, Stanmore, Winchester, 2017–. *Publications:* Conscience, Government and War, 1978. *Recreations:* walking, gardening. *Address:* 64 Middle Brook Street, Winchester, Hants SO23 8DQ. *E:* rachel.aron12@gmail.com.

**ARONSON, Hazel Josephine;** *see* Cosgrove, Rt Hon. Lady.

**ARORA, Rev. Arun;** Vicar, St Nicholas', Durham, since 2017; *b* Birmingham, 10 Oct. 1971; *s* of Gucharan and Sudarshan Arora; *m* 2006, Joanne Logan; one *d. Educ:* King Edward VI Five Ways Sch., Birmingham; Univ. of Birmingham (LLB 1993); Univ. of Durham (BA 2006). Admitted solicitor, 1998; with Thompsons Solicitors, 1996–2000; Diocesan Communications Officer, Dio. of Birmingham, 2000–04; Dir of Communications for Archbishop of York, 2006–09; ordained deacon, 2007, priest, 2008; Curate, St Marks, Harrogate, 2007–10; Team Leader, Wolverhampton Pioneer Ministries, 2010–12; Dir of Communications, C of E, 2012–17. *Publications:* (with A. Francis) The Rule of Lawyers, 1998. *Address:* St Nicholas Church, Market Place, Durham DH1 3NJ. *Club:* Aston Villa Football.

**ARORA, Simon;** Chief Executive, B&M Retail Ltd, since 2005; *b* UK, 1969; *s* of Surjit and Rani Arora; *m* 1995, Shalni; two *d. Educ:* Manchester Grammar Sch.; Fitzwilliam Coll., Cambridge (BA 1991). McKinsey & Co., 1992–94; 3i plc, 1994–95; Barclays Bank plc, 1995–96; Orient Sourcing Services Ltd, 1996–2003. Mem., Young Presidents' Orgn, 2002–. *Recreations:* travel, art, fine dining. *Address:* B&M Retail Ltd, The Vault, Dakota Drive, Estuary Commerce Park, Speke, Liverpool L24 8RJ. *Clubs:* Arts, 5 Hertford Street, Annabel's, 67 Pall Mall.

**ARRAN, 9th Earl of,** *cr* 1762, of the Arran Islands, Co. Galway; **Arthur Desmond Colquhoun Gore;** Bt 1662; Viscount Sudley, Baron Saunders, 1758; Baron Sudley (UK), 1884; *b* 14 July 1938; *er s* of 8th Earl of Arran and Fiona Bryde, *er d* of Sir Iain Colquhoun of Luss, 7th Bt, KT, DSO; *S* father, 1983; *m* 1974, Eleanor, (MBE 2008), *er d* of Bernard van Cutsem and Lady Margaret Fortescue; two *d. Educ:* Eton; Balliol College, Oxford. 2nd Lieutenant, 1st Bn Grenadier Guards (National Service). Asst Manager, Daily Mail, 1972–73; Man. Dir, Clark Nelson, 1973–74; Asst Gen. Manager, Daily and Sunday Express, June–Nov. 1974. Dir, Waterstone & Co. Ltd, 1984–87. A Lord in Waiting (Govt Whip), 1987–89; Parliamentary Under-Secretary of State: for the Armed Forces, MoD, 1989–92; NI Office, 1992–94; Parly Under-Sec. of State, DoE, 1994; Captain of the Yeomen of the Guard (Dep. Govt Chief Whip), 1994–95; elected Mem., H of L, 1999. Director: HMV, 1995–98; Bonham's, 1997–2000; Weather World, 2005–. Chm., Waste Mgt Industry NTO, 2000–. Pres., Children's Country Holidays Fund, 2008–18. Trustee, Chelsea Physic Garden, 1994–2014. *Recreations:* tennis, shooting, gardening, croquet. *Address:* c/o House of Lords, SW1A 0PW. *Clubs:* White's, Pratt's, Turf, Beefsteak.

**ARRAN, His Honour Graham Kent;** a Circuit Judge, 2007–17; Resident Judge, Harrow Crown Court, 2013–17; a Deputy Circuit Judge, since 2018; *b* Manchester, 13 April 1947; *s* of Carl and Dorothy Arran; *m* 1st, 1973, Carol Quellmalz (*d* 1986); one *s* two *d;* 2nd, 1992, Susan Duncan. *Educ:* N Manchester Grammar Sch.; London Sch. of Econs and Pol Sci. (LLB). Called to the Bar, Lincoln's Inn, 1969; in practice at the Bar, London, specialising in criminal law, 1969–2007; Asst Recorder, 1990–94; Recorder, 1994–2007. Judicial Mem., Parole Bd, 2018–. Chm., Lord Chancellor's Adv. Cttee on JPs for London West, 2012–17. *Recreations:* being a grandfather, the occasional holiday.

**ARRAND, Ven. Geoffrey William;** Archdeacon of Suffolk, 1994–2009, now Archdeacon Emeritus; *b* 24 July 1944; *s* of Thomas Staniforth Arrand and Alice Ada Arrand; *m* 1st, 1968, Mary Marshall (marr. diss.); one *s* two *d;* 2nd, 2005, Margaret Elizabeth Frost. *Educ:* King's Coll., London (BD 1966, AKC). Ordained deacon, 1967, priest, 1968; Assistant Curate: Washington, dio. of Durham, 1967–70; S Ormsby Gp, 1970–73; Team Vicar, Great Grimsby, 1973–79; Team Rector, Halesworth, 1979–85; Dean of Bocking and Rector of Hadleigh with Layham and Shelley, 1985–94; RD of Hadleigh, 1986–94. Hon. Canon, St Edmundsbury Cathedral, 1991–2009. Mem., Gen. Synod, 2005–09. OStJ 1994 (County Chaplain, Suffolk, 1995–2009). *Recreation:* golf. *Address:* 86 Broadway, Lincoln LN2 1SR. *T:* (01522) 826967. *E:* garrand@virginmedia.com. *Club:* Lincoln Golf.

**ARROWSMITH, Amanda Jane Elizabeth**; Chair, Eastern Region Committee, Heritage Lottery Fund, 2001–04; *b* 28 Dec. 1947; *d* of late Michael St George Arrowsmith and Elizabeth Arrowsmith (*née* Bartlett). *Educ*: Lady Margaret Hall, Oxford (MA); MBA Open Univ. Archive trng, Bodleian Liby, Oxford, 1971–72; asst, sen. asst and dep. archivist posts, Northumberland and Suffolk CCs, 1972–79; Co. Archivist, Berks, 1979–82, Suffolk, 1982–87; Dep. Dir of Arts and Libraries, 1987–90, Dir of Libraries and Heritage, 1990–2001, Suffolk. Comr, RCHME, 1994–98; Mem., Hist. Bldgs and Monuments Commn (Eng. Heritage), 1998–2001. Member: Adv. Council on Public Records, 1995–2000; Eastern Reg. Cttee, SE Museums Service, 1999–2003; Exec. Cttee, Friends of Nat. Libraries, 1993–96 and 1999–2003; Reviewing Cttee on Export of Works of Art, 2002–06 (Chm., Manuscripts and Documents Wkg Gp, 2002–06); Pres., 1996–99, Vice-Pres., 2002–, Soc. of Archivists. Dir, Victim Support Suffolk, 2002–03 (Chm., Magistrates' Courts Witness Support Service Cttee, 2002–03). Mem. Bd, Living East, 1999–2002. Hon. Ed., Chapels Soc., 2004–07. *Publications*: contrib. articles to Archives, Jl Soc. Archivists, New Liby World. *Address*: 30 Underhill, Stowmarket, Suffolk IP14 1QY.

**ARROWSMITH, Pat**; peace activist and socialist; on staff of Amnesty International, 1971–94, retired; *b* 2 March 1930; *d* of late George Ernest Arrowsmith and late Margaret Vera (*née* Kingham); *m* Mr Gardner, 11 Aug. 1979, separated 11 Aug. 1979; lesbian partnership with Wendy Butlin, 1962–76. *Educ*: Farringtons; Stover Sch.; Cheltenham Ladies' Coll.; Newnham Coll., Cambridge (BA history); Univ. of Ohio; Liverpool Univ. (Cert. in Social Science). Has held many jobs, incl.: Community Organizer in Chicago, 1952–53; Cinema Usher, 1953–54; Social Caseworker, Liverpool Family Service Unit, 1954; Child Care Officer, 1955 and 1964; Nursing Asst, Deva Psychiatric Hosp., 1956–57; Reporter for Peace News, 1965; Gardener for Camden BC, 1966–68; Researcher for Soc. of Friends Race Relations Cttee, 1969–71; Case Worker for NCCL, 1971; and on farms, as waiter in cafes, in a factory, as a toy demonstrator, as a 'temp' in numerous offices, as asst in children's home, as newspaper deliverer and sales agent, as cleaner, as bartender, and in a holiday camp. Organizer for Direct Action Cttee against Nuclear War, Cttee of 100 and Campaign for Nuclear Disarmament, 1958–68; gaoled 11 times as political prisoner, 1958–85 (adopted twice as Prisoner of Conscience by Amnesty International); awarded: Holloway Prison Green Band, 1964; Girl Crusaders knighthood, 1940; Americans Removing Injustice, Suppression and Exploitation peace prize, 1991; Unsung Woman award, Haringey Council, 2001. Contested: Fulham, 1966 (Radical Alliance) and 1970 (Hammersmith Stop the SE Asia War Cttee), on peace issues; Cardiff South East (Independent Socialist), 1979. Member: War Resisters' Internat.; Campaign for Nuclear Disarmament (Vice-Pres., 2008–). *Publications*: Jericho (novel), 1965; Somewhere Like This (novel), 1970; To Asia in Peace, 1972; The Colour of Six Schools, 1972; Breakout (poems and drawings from prison), 1975; On the Brink (anti-war poems with pictures), 1981; The Prisoner (novel), 1982; Thin Ice (anti-nuclear poems), 1984; Nine Lives (poems and pictures), 1990; I Should Have Been a Hornby Train (fiction-cum-memoir), 1995; Many are Called (novel), 1998; Drawing to Extinction (poems and pictures), 2000; Going On (poems), 2005; Dark Light (poems and pictures), 2009. *Recreations*: water colour painting (has held and contrib. exhibns), swimming, writing poetry. *Address*: 132c Middle Lane, N8 7JP. *T*: (020) 8340 2661.

**ARROYO, Gloria M.**; *see* Macapagal-Arroyo.

**ARROYO, James José-Maria**, OBE 2003; Director, Ditchley Foundation, since 2016; *b* Leicester, 25 March 1967; *s* of José-Maria Arroyo and Susan Josephine Arroyo (*née* Joyce); *m* 1992, Kerry Ford; two *d*. *Educ*: Loughborough Grammar Sch.; Jesus Coll., Cambridge (BA Eng. Lit. 1989). Joined FCO, 1990; Second Sec., Amman, 1992–95; First Sec., Cairo, 1996–99; Vice Consul, Jerusalem, 1999–2002; Counsellor, Paris, 2008–12; Dir, Eur. and Econ. Affairs, FCO; Dir for Data, FCO. Advr to technol. start ups and cos; writer on technol. *Recreations*: literature, languages, researching technology, writing novels and other books. *Address*: Ditchley Foundation, Ditchley Park, Enstone, Chipping Norton, Oxon OX7 4ER. *T*: (01608) 667346. *E*: info@ditchley.com.

**ARRUDA, Cláudio Frederico de Matos, (Fred)**; Ambassador of Brazil to the Court of St James's, since 2018; *b* Fortaleza, 20 Sept. 1957; *s* of João Tarcisio Cartaxo Arruda and Silvia Maria Matos Arruda; *m* 1980, Lenice de Almeida Nóbrega; one *s* one *d*. *Educ*: Univ. of Brasília (BA Econs 1979). Joined Foreign Service of Brazil, 1980; Montevideo, 1985–88; OAS, Washington, 1988–91; Office of Minister of Justice, 1991–92; Dep. Sec. of Communications, Pres.'s Press Office, 1992; Geneva, 1993–95; Advr to Sec.-Gen. of Foreign Affairs, 1996–97; Federal Senate, 1997–2001; Counsellor, Ottawa, 2001–04; Minister, Consulate-Gen., NY, 2004–09; Chamber of Deputies, 2009–10; Chief Diplomatic Adviser to Vice-Pres.'s Office, 2011–14; to Pres., 2016–18. *Address*: Embassy of Brazil, 14–16 Cockspur Street, SW1Y 5BL.

**ARSCOTT, John Robert Dare**, FRAeS; Director, Airspace Policy, Civil Aviation Authority, 1999–2009; *b* 19 April 1947; *s* of Richard Arscott and Janet Arscott (*née* Knibbs); *m* 1971, Kyrle Margaret Bradley; one *d* and one *s* decd. *Educ*: Lindisfarne Coll. RAF, 1966; jsdc 1984; aws 1987; posts in NATS and Mil. Air Traffic Ops, 1990–95; AOC Mil. Air Traffic Ops, 1996–99; retired in rank of Air Vice-Marshal, 2001. Dep. Chm., 2007–09, Chm., 2009–11, Eurocontrol Performance Rev. Commn. FRAeS 2001. *Recreations*: aviation, railways, walking, DIY, grandfathering. *Address*: Lilac Cottage, Kemble Wick, Cirencester, Glos GL7 6EQ. *Club*: Royal Air Force.

**ARSHAD, Dr Rowena, (Mrs M. Q. Parnell)**, OBE 2001; Director, Centre for Education for Racial Equality in Scotland, since 1994, Senior Lecturer, since 1997, and Head, Moray House School of Education, since 2013, University of Edinburgh; *b* 27 April 1960; *d* of Zainal Arshad bin Zainal Abidin and Teoh Phaik Choo; *m* 1985, Malcolm Quarrie Parnell; one *s* one *d*. *Educ*: Methodist Girls' Sch., Penang, W Malaysia; St Francis' Coll., Letchworth; Bulmershe Coll. of Higher Educn (Cert. in Youth and Community Work 1985); Moray House, Heriot-Watt Univ. (MEd 1995); Univ. of Edinburgh (DEd 2008). Scottish Educn and Action for Develt, 1985–88; Multicultural Educn Centre, Edinburgh, 1988–91; Lectr, Moray House Inst. of Educn, Edinburgh, 1991–97; Hd, Inst. for Educn, Community and Soc., Univ. of Edinburgh, 2010–13. Member: SHEFC, then SFC, 1999–2008; Independent Inquiry into Student Finance, 1999; Working Party on Guidelines in Sex Educn in Scottish Schs, 2000; Equal Opportunities Commn, 2001–07; Scotland Cttee, Equality and Human Rights Commn; Convenor Educn Sub Gp, Race Equality Adv. Forum, Scottish Exec., 1999–2001. Board Member: Telford Coll., Edinburgh, 2001–03; Inspectorate of Educn, 2001–05; Member: Governance Adv. Team, British Council, 2002–08; Inst. of Contemporary Scotland, 2002–. *Recreations*: reading political literature on Scotland, equity, justice, travelling (particularly to favourite city Toronto), cooking for family and friends, playing with border collie Perry. *Address*: Old Moray House, Moray House School of Education and Sport, University of Edinburgh, Holyrood Road, Edinburgh EH8 8AQ. *T*: (0131) 651 6371, *Fax*: (0131) 651 6511. *E*: Rowena.Arshad@ed.ac.uk.

**ARTER, Anthony Lewis**; Pensions Ombudsman and Pension Protection Fund Ombudsman, since 2015; *b* Harrow, 9 Jan. 1947; *s* of Jack and Louise Arter; *m* Catherine; one *s* one *d*. *Educ*: Wandsworth Comprehensive Sch.; Jesus Coll., Cambridge (BA 1988); Coll. of Law. Detective Superintendent, Metropolitan Police, 1990–92; admitted as solicitor, 1995; Eversheds LLP: Partner, 2001–14; Hd, Pensions Gp, 2005–13; London Sen. Partner, 2009–14. London Ambassador for Employee Volunteering, 2009, Mem., London Adv. Bd, 2009–14, BITC. Mem. Exec. Cttee, 2016–, Vice Chm., 2018–, Ombudsman Assoc. Trustee Dir, Action for Children Pension Fund, 2019–. Police Long Service and Good Conduct Medal, 1991. *Recreations*: sailing, cycling, walking. *Address*: Pensions Ombudsman, 10 South Colonnade, Canary Wharf, E14 4PU. *T*: (020) 7630 2210. *E*: anthony.arter@pensions-ombudsman.org.uk. *Clubs*: Reform; Royal Fowey Yacht.

**ARTHANAYAKE, Nihal**; Presenter, Afternoon Edition, BBC Radio 5 Live, since 2016; *b* 1 June 1971; *s* of Tilak Arthanayake and Rohini Arthanayake; *m* 2005, Eesha; one *s* one *d*. *Educ*: St Mary's Coll., Strawberry Hill (BA Hons). Disc Jockey, BBC Radio 1, 2002–14; presenter, BBC Asian Network, 2007–16; television presenter: The Drop, 2001; Saturday Show Extra; Whitey Blighty (documentary), 2003; Desi DNA, 2004–07; Where's Your F\*\*\*ing Manners (documentary), 2004; God is a DJ for Heaven and Earth Show, 2007; jt programmer, with Radio 1, London Flavas stage, 2004; promoter and creator, Bombay Bronx clubnight. Member, Board: British Council, 2006–12; Metal Arts Think Tank, 2007–. Cultural Ambassador, London 2012 Olympics, 2004–12; Ambassador, Football Aid Charity, 2007. *Recreations*: walking my Staffordshire Bull Terrier, Luna, swimming, going to see the mighty Tottenham Hotspur, listening to music, DJing, looking at my My Space page, messageboards. *E*: dj.nihal@bbc.co.uk.

**ARTHUIS, Jean Raymond Francis Marcel**; Member, European Parliament, 2014–19; *b* 7 Oct. 1944; *m* 1971, Brigitte Lafont; one *s* one *d*. *Educ*: Ecole Supérieure de Commerce, Nantes; Institut d'Etudes Politiques, Paris. Sen. consultant in internat. auditing office; Founder of a soc. for accounting expertise and auditors. Senator, Mayenne, 1983–86, 1988–95 and 1997–2014 (President: Gpe de l'Union Centriste, 1998–2002; Finance Commn, 2002–14); Pres., Gen. Council of Mayenne, 1992–2014 (Rapporteur général of budget to Senate, 1992–95). Secretary of State: Ministry of Social Affairs and Employment, 1986–87; for competition and consumption, Ministry of Economy, Finance and Privatization, 1987–88; Minister of: Economic Development and Planning, May–Aug. 1995; the Economy, Finance and Planning, Aug.–Nov. 1995; the Economy and of Finance, 1995–97. Chm., Cttee on Budgets, Eur. Parlt. Mayor, Château-Gontier, Mayenne, 1971–2001. *Publications*: (with H. Haenel) Justice Sinistrée: démocratie en danger, 1991; Les Délocalisations et l'emploi, 1993; Dans les coulisses de Bercy, 1998; Mondialisation: la France à contre emploi, 2007; SOS Finances publiques: osons les vraies réformes, 2011; (with Michel Sapin) La France peut s'en sortir, 2012; L'Europe: dernière chance pour la France, 2014. *Recreation*: horse-riding. *Address*: 8 rue René Homo, 53200 Château-Gontier, France.

**ARTHUR**, family name of **Baron Glenarthur**.

**ARTHUR, Adrian**; Editor, The Courier, Dundee, 1993–2002; *b* 28 Sept. 1937; *s* of Alastair and Jean Arthur, Kirkcaldy; *m* 1962, Patricia Mill; one *s* two *d*. *Educ*: Harris Academy, Dundee; Univ. of St Andrews (BL). Sub-Editor, People's Journal, 1954–56; Nat. Service, RAF, 1956–58; editorial staff, The Courier, Dundee, 1958–2002 (Dep. Editor, 1978–93). Hon. Fellow, Univ. of Abertay, Dundee, 2003. *Recreations*: golf, reading, travel, Rotary. *Address*: 33 Seaforth Crescent, West Ferry, Dundee DD5 1QD. *T*: (01382) 776842. *Club*: Dalhousie Golf (Carnoustie).

**ARTHUR, Sir Benjamin Nathan**, 7th Bt *cr* 1841, of Upper Canada; *b* 27 March 1979; *o s* of Sir Stephen John Arthur, 6th Bt, and of Carolyn Margaret, *d* of Burney Lawrence Diamond, Cairns, Qld; *S* father, 2010, but his name does not yet appear on the Official Roll of the Baronetage.

**ARTHUR, Hugh Anthony Victor**, OBE 2010; Director, Barbados Tourism Marketing Inc., since 2014; *b* Bridgetown, Barbados, 1945; *s* of Beresford Arthur and Louise Arthur; *m* 1972, Rose Anne Burnham (marr. diss. 2000); one *s* one *d*. *Educ*: Modern High Sch., Bridgetown; Trent Univ., Ont (BA Hons Sociol. and Econs 1969); Univ. of Surrey (MSc Tourism 1977). Barbados Tourist Board: Travel Develt Officer, Toronto, 1971–74; Exec. Officer, Bridgetown, 1974–76; Lectr in Tourism, Univ. of West Indies, Nassau, 1979–80; Barbados Tourist Board, subseq. Barbados Board of Tourism, then Barbados Tourism Authority: Mktg Manager, 1980–85; Dep. Dir of Tourism, 1985–91; Dir, Mktg and Sales, N America, 1991–92; CEO, 1992–95; Tourism Develt Planner, Grenada Tourism Master Plan Proj., Govt of Grenada/Orgn of Amer. States, 1995–97; Lectr/Coordinator, Hospitality and Mgt Degree Prog., Univ. of West Indies, Cave Hill, 1998–2008; High Comr for Barbados in UK, 2008–13. *Recreations*: reading, walking, guitar. *Address*: 9 Roehampton Gate, Roehampton, SW15 5JR. *T*: (020) 7299 7150, *Fax*: (020) 7323 6872.

**ARTHUR, Prof. James Greig**, CC 2018; FRS 1992; FRSC 1981; University Professor, since 1987, and Professor of Mathematics, since 1979, University of Toronto; *b* 18 May 1944; *s* of John Greig Arthur and Katherine Mary Patricia Scott; *m* 1972, Dorothy Pendleton Helm; two *s*. *Educ*: Upper Canada Coll.; Univ. of Toronto (BSc, MSc); Yale Univ. (PhD). Instructor, Princeton Univ., 1970–72; Asst Prof., Yale Univ., 1972–76; Prof., Duke Univ., 1976–79. Sloan Fellowship, 1976; E. W. R. Steacie Meml Fellowship, 1982. Pres., American Math. Soc., 2005–07. FHMAAAS 2003; MNAS 2014. Synge Award, RSC, 1987; Wolf Prize in Maths, Wolf Foundn, 2015. *Publications*: Simple Algebras, Base Change and the Advanced Theory of the Trace Formula (with Laurent Clozel), 1989. *Recreations*: tennis, golf. *Address*: 23 Woodlawn Avenue W, Toronto, ON M4V 1G6, Canada. *T*: (416) 9640975.

**ARTHUR, Lt-Gen. Sir (John) Norman (Stewart)**, KCB 1985; CVO 2007; Lord-Lieutenant, Stewartry of Kirkcudbright (Dumfries and Galloway Region), 1996–2006; General Officer Commanding Scotland and Governor of Edinburgh Castle, 1985–88, retired; *b* 6 March 1931; *s* of Col Evelyn Stewart Arthur, DL, and Mrs E. S. Arthur (*née* Burnett-Stuart); *m* 1st, 1960, Theresa Mary Hopkinson (*d* 2011); one *s* one *d* (and one *s* decd); 2nd, 2012, Jillian Constance Andrews. *Educ*: Eton Coll.; RMA, Sandhurst. rcds, jssc, psc. Commnd Royal Scots Greys, 1951; commanded: Royal Scots Dragoon Guards, 1972–74 (despatches, 1974); 7th Armoured Bde, 1976–77; Brig., Gen. Staff, Intelligence, MoD, 1978–80; GOC 3rd Armoured Div., 1980–82; Dir of Personal Services (Army), MoD, 1983–85. Col Comdt, Military Provost Staff Corps, 1985–88; Col, The Royal Scots Dragoon Gds (Carabiniers and Greys), 1984–92; Hon. Col, 205 (Scottish) Gen. Hosp., RAMC(V), 1988–93, The Scottish Yeomanry, 1993–97. Chm., Cavalry Colonels, 1987–92. Officer, Royal Co. of Archers, Queen's Body Guard for Scotland. Chairman: Scotland, Army Benevolent Fund, 1988–2000; Leonard Cheshire Services, SW Scotland, 1994–2000; President: Combined Cavalry Old Comrades Assoc., 1995–2000; Lowland RFCA, 2001–06; Vice Pres., Edinburgh and Borders, Riding for the Disabled Assoc., 1988–94; Dir, Edinburgh Mil. Tattoo Co., 1988–91; Pres., Scottish Conservation Projects, 1989–94; Mem., Automobile Assoc. Cttee, 1990–98. Humanitarian aid work to Balkans, 1992–2013. Mem., British Olympic Team, Equestrian Three-Day Event, 1960. DL Stewartry, 1989; JP 1996. *Recreations*: field and country sports and pursuits, horsemanship, military history. *Address*: Newbarns, Dalbeattie, Kirkcudbrightshire DG5 4PY. *T*: (01556) 630227; The Garden House, Sparsholt, Winchester, Hants SO21 2NS. *T*: (01962) 776279. *E*: jilliancarthur@hotmail.com.

**ARTHUR, Sir Michael (Anthony)**, KCMG 2004 (CMG 1992); HM Diplomatic Service, retired; President: Boeing UK, 2014; Boeing Europe, and Managing Director, Boeing UK/Ireland, since 2016; Boeing International, and Member, Executive Council, since 2019; consultant, since 2010; *b* 28 Aug. 1950; *s* of late John Richard Arthur and of Mary Deirdre (*née* Chaundy); *m* 1974, Plaxy Gillian Beatrice (*née* Corke); two *s* two *d. Educ:* Watford GS; Rugby; Balliol Coll., Oxford. Entered HM Diplomatic Service, 1972; UK Mission to UN, NY, 1972; FCO, 1973; 3rd, later 2nd Sec., UK Perm. Representation to Eur. Communities, 1974–76; 2nd Sec., Kinshasa, 1976–78; FCO, 1978–83; Private Secretary: to Lord Privy Seal, 1981; to Minister of State, FCO, 1982; 1st Sec., Bonn, 1984–88; Hd, EC Dept (Internal), FCO, 1988–93; Sen. Associate Mem., St Antony's Coll., Oxford, 1993; Counsellor and Hd of Chancery, Paris, 1993–97; Dir (Resources) and Chief Inspector, FCO, 1997–99; Minister and Dep. Hd of Mission, Washington, 1999–2000; Econ. Dir, then Dir-Gen., EU and Econ., FCO, 2001–03; High Comr, India, 2003–07; Ambassador to Germany, 2007–10. UK Chm., Koenigswinter, 2010; Partner, Ambassador Partnership (formerly ADRg Ambassadors) LLP, 2011–14. Non-exec. Dir, Diligentia plc, 2012–. Member: FCO Locarno Gp, 2011–; Sen. European Experts Gp, European Movement, 2013–; Member, Advisory Board: Kings India Inst., 2011–; Global Economic Symposium, 2011–; Humboldt Univ. GB Centre, 2011–15. Associate Mem., BUPA, 2011–. Trustee: Orbis, 2011–; Nehru Trust, 2011–. Regular speaker on India, Germany and Europe. Freeman, City of Oxford, 1970. Hon. Bencher, Inner Temple, 2017. *Recreations:* music, travel, books.

**ARTHUR, Prof. Michael James Paul**, DM; FRCP, FMedSci; Provost and President, University College London, since 2013; *b* 3 Aug. 1954; *s* of Reginald Alfred John Arthur and Patricia Margaret Arthur; *m* 1979, Elizabeth Susan McCaughey; one *s* two *d. Educ:* Burnt Mill Comprehensive Sch., Harlow; Sch. of Medicine, Univ. of Southampton (BM 1977; DM 1986). FRCP 1993. Med. Registrar, Wessex Reg., 1980–82; University of Southampton: Lectr in Medicine, 1982–89; Sen. Lectr, 1989–92; Prof. of Medicine, 1992–2004; Hd, Sch. of Medicine, 1998–2001; Dir of Res., Sch. of Medicine, 2001–02; Dean, Faculty of Medicine, Health and Life Scis, 2003–04; Vice-Chancellor, Univ. of Leeds, 2004–13. Fogarty Internat. Travelling Fellow, Liver Center Lab., Univ. of Calif, San Francisco, 1986–88; Fulbright Dist. Scholar, Mount Sinai Sch. of Medicine, NY, 2002. Mem., Adv. Gp on Hepatitis, 1998–2004, Chm., Adv. Gp on Nat. Specialist Services, 2010–13, DoH. Member: Molecular and Cell Panel, Wellcome Trust, 1998–2002 and 2003–04 (Vice-Chm., 2000; Chm., 2003–04); Council, MRC, 2008–14. US/UK Fulbright Comr, 2008–14. Pres., British Assoc. for Study of the Liver, 2001–03. Chair, Nat. Student Survey Steering Gp, 2006–08; Mem. Bd, QCA, later QCDA, 2007–10. Board Member: Yorkshire Forward, 2007–11; Opera North, 2007–13; Nat. Sci. Learning Centre, 2006–13. Chair: Worldwide Univs Network, 2007–09; Russell Gp of Univs, 2009–12. FMedSci 1998; FRSA 2006; PFHEA 2016. Hon. Fellow, Assoc. of Physicians of GB and Ireland, 2006. Hon. DLitt Southampton, 2010; Hon. DLaws Leeds, 2014. Res. Prize, Amer. Liver Foundn, 1987; Linacre Medal, RCP, 1994. *Publications:* (ed jtly) Wright's Liver and Biliary Disease, 3rd edn 1992; numerous contribs to biomed. jls relating to liver disease and the pathogenesis of liver fibrosis. *Recreation:* sailing and yacht racing in the Solent. *Address:* Provost's Office, University College London, Gower Street, WC1E 6BT. *T:* (020) 7679 7234. *Clubs:* Royal Southern Yacht (Hamble), Royal Southampton Yacht.

**ARTHUR, Lt-Gen. Sir Norman;** *see* Arthur, Lt-Gen. Sir J. N. S.

**ARTHUR, Rt Hon. Owen Seymour;** PC 1995; MP (Lab) Barbados, 1984–2018; Leader of the Opposition, 2010–13; *b* 17 Oct. 1949; *m* 1st, 1978, Beverley Jeanne Batchelor (marr. diss.); 2nd, 2006, Julie Ann Price. *Educ:* Harrison Coll., Barbados; Univ. of West Indies at Cave Hill (BA) and at Mona (MSc). Research Asst, UWI, Jamaica, 1973; Asst Economic Planner, then Chief Econ. Planner, Nat. Planning Agency, Jamaica, 1974–79; Dir of Econs, Jamaica Bauxite Inst., 1979–81; Chief Project Analyst, Min. of Finance, Barbados, 1981–83; Lectr, Dept of Management, UWI, Cave Hill, 1986, Res. Fellow, 1993. Mem., Barbados Senate, 1983–84; Parly Sec., Min. of Finance, 1985–86; Chm., Barbados Labour Party, 1993–96, 1998–; Leader of Opposition, 1993–94; Prime Minister of Barbados, 1994–2008; Minister of Finance and Econ. Affairs, Defence and Security and Civil Service, 1994–2008. *Publications:* The Commercialisation of Technology in Jamaica, 1979; Energy and Mineral Resource Development in the Jamaica Bauxite Industry, 1981; The IMF and Economic Stabilisation Policies in Barbados, 1984. *Recreations:* cooking, gardening.

**ARTHUR, Richard Andrew;** Chairman, Camden and Islington NHS Foundation Trust, 2009–13; *b* 24 March 1944; *s* of late Cyril Stuart Arthur and Cicely Arthur; *m* 1st, 1968, Diana Thompson (marr. diss.); one *s* one *d.* 2nd, 1986, Akiko Shindo; one step *s. Educ:* King's Sch., Canterbury; Christ's Coll., Cambridge (MA Econs); London Business Sch. (MSc Business). Commonwealth Development Finance Co.: Regl Dir, SE Asia, 1976–80; Chief Exec., Australia, 1981–82; Hd of Ops, 1982–86; Exec. Dir, Scimitar Develt Capital, 1986–93. Mem., Audit Commn, 1995–2003; Bd Mem., Housing Corp., 2000–04 (Chm., Regulation and Supervisory Cttee, 2001–04); Chm., CSA, 2006–08. Chm., Public Private Partnerships Prog., 1998–2000; Vice-Chm., Central London Partnership, 1998–2000. Dir, Accord plc, 2000–07. Chm., Renaissance Bedford, 2005–11. London Borough of Camden: Mem. (Lab), 1971–76 and 1990–2002; Chm. of Staff, 1975–76; Chm., Social Services, 1991–93; Leader, 1993–2000. Vice-Chm., Assoc. of London Govt, 2000–02. Mem. Ct, Middlesex Univ., 1996–2000. Hon. Chief, Bresua, Ghana, 2016. *Recreations:* swimming, gardening, reading, travel, tai ji. *Address:* 11d Highgate West Hill, N6 6JR. *T:* (020) 8341 9148. *Club:* Singapore Cricket.

**ARTHUR, Sandra Joy;** Midwife Lecturer, School of Nursing and Midwifery Studies, Cardiff University, 1998; *b* 16 April 1957; *d* of William Chapman and Evelyn Joy Chapman; *m* 1981, Stephen Laurence Arthur; two *s. Educ:* Queen Elizabeth Hosp., Birmingham (SRN 1979); Good Hope Hosp., Sutton Coldfield (SCM 1980); Cardiff Univ. (PGCE; LLM Legal Aspects in Med. Practice). Midwife, S Glamorgan, Cardiff and Vale NHS Trust, 1980. Hon. Supervisor of Midwives, 1996. Mem. Council, Royal Coll. of Midwives, 1993–98; President: Assoc. of Supervisors of Midwives, 2002; NMC, 2006–17. *Recreations:* tennis, sailing, gardening. *Clubs:* Penarth Yacht, Penarth Lawn Tennis.

**ARTHUR, Thomas;** Member (SNP), Renfrewshire South, Scottish Parliament, since 2016; *b* Paisley, 1 Oct. 1985; *s* of Tom Arthur and Maureen Arthur. *Educ:* Barrhead High Sch.; Univ. of Glasgow (BMus 2010; MMus 2012). Freelance piano teacher, 2012–16; freelance musician, 2012–16; Dir, Velvet Music Ltd, 2013–15. *Recreations:* theatre, opera, ballet, art, reading, composing. *Address:* (office) 49 High Street, Johnstone PA5 8AS. *T:* (01505) 331990. *E:* tom.arthur.msp@parliament.scot.

**ARTHURS, Prof. Harry William**, OC 1989; OOnt 1995; FRSC 1982; University Professor, Osgoode Hall Law School, York University, Canada, 1995–2005, now Emeritus (Professor of Law, 1968–95); *b* 9 May 1935; *s* of Leon and Ellen Arthurs; *m* 1974, Penelope Geraldine Ann Milnes; two *s. Educ:* Univ. of Toronto (BA, LLB); Harvard Univ. (LLM). Barrister and Solicitor, 1961. York University: Asst Prof. 1961, Associate Prof. 1964, Associate Dean 1967, Dean 1972–77, Osgoode Hall Law Sch.; Pres., 1985–92, Pres. Emeritus, 1992–. Mem., Economic Council of Can., 1978–82; Bencher, Law Soc. of Upper Can., 1979–84; Chm., Consultative Gp on Res. and Educn in Law, 1981–84; Arbitrator, Mediator in Labour Disputes, 1962–84; Chair, Council of Ontario Univs, 1987–89; a Dir, Internat. Centre for Human Rights and Democratic Develt, 1999–2002; Commissioner: Rev. of Federal Labour Standards, 2004–06; Rev. of Ontario Pensions Legislation, 2006–08; Chm., Ind. Funding Review, Workplace Safety and Insurance Bd, 2010–12. Visiting Professor: Univ. of Toronto, 1965; McGill, 1967; Visiting Scholar: Clare Hall, Cambridge, 1971; Inst. for Socio-Legal Res., Oxford, 1977–78; Vis. Research Prof., UCL, 1984, 2003. Killam Laureate, 2002. Corresp. FBA 2003. Hon. LLD: Sherbrooke, 1986; Brock, 1986; Law Soc. of Upper Can., 1987; McGill, 1995; Montreal, 2002; Toronto, 2002; York, 2008; Simon Fraser, 2012; Hon. DLitt Lethbridge, 1991; Hon. DCL Windsor, 2004. (jtly with J. Stiglitz) Decent Work Res. Prize, ILO, 2008. *Publications:* Law and Learning, 1983; (jtly) Industrial Relations and Labour Law in Canada, 1979, 3rd edn 1988; Without the Law, 1985; (ed jtly) Rethinking Workplace Regulation: beyond the standard contract of employment, 2013. *Address:* Osgoode Hall Law School, York University, 4700 Keele Street, Toronto, Ontario M3J 1P3, Canada. *T:* (416) 9206184.

**ARTHURS, Kate Daisy;** Director, Arts, British Council, since 2018; *b* Bristol, 4 Dec. 1978; *d* of Alan John Arthurs and Caroline Joan Arthurs. *Educ:* Keble Coll., Oxford (BA PPE). British Council: Project Manager, Europe, Brussels, 2002–04; Hd, Arts, Mexico, 2004–07; Dep. Dir, Vietnam, 2007–08; freelance arts consultant, 2009–15; Dir Strategy, Arts, British Council, 2015–18. Dir, Wasafari mag., 2011–. *Recreations:* shipping containers, witchcraft, Venn diagrams.

**ARTHURSON, Hon. Lord; Paul Andrew Arthurson;** a Senator of the College of Justice in Scotland, since 2017; *b* 16 Dec. 1964; *s* of Dr Iain Hayden Arthurson and Margaret Arthurson; *m* 1997, Dr Sharon Elizabeth McAuslane; two *d. Educ:* Daniel Stewart's and Melville Coll., Edinburgh; Univ. of Edinburgh (LLB Hons 1986); Worcester Coll., Oxford (Dip Law 1990). Advocate, 1991–2005; Temp. Sheriff, 1999; Pt-time Sheriff, 2003–05; QC (Scot.) 2005; All Scotland Floating Sheriff, 2005–11; Sheriff of Lothian and Borders at Edinburgh, 2011–17; Temp. Judge, Ct of Session and High Ct of Justiciary, 2013–17; Appeal Sheriff, Sheriff Appeal Ct, 2015–17. Chm., Mental Health Tribunals (restricted patients), 2008–09; Legal Mem., Parole Bd for Scotland, 2008–11. *Recreations:* church, choral singing, cycling in rural France and on Scottish Islands. *Address:* Court of Sessions, Parliament House, Edinburgh EH1 1RQ.

**ARTON, His Honour Simon Nicholas B.;** *see* Bourne-Arton.

**ARULKUMARAN, Prof. Sabaratnam,** Kt 2009; PhD; FRCS, FRCOG; Professor and Head of Obstetrics and Gynaecology, St George's, University of London (formerly St George's Hospital Medical School), 2001–13, now Emeritus; President, British Medical Association, 2013–14; *b* Jaffna, Ceylon, 17 Jan. 1948; *s* of Kathiravelu Sabaratnam and Gnanambikai Sabaratnam; *m* 1975, Gayatri Muttuthamby; two *s* one *d. Educ:* Univ. of Ceylon (MB BS Hons 1972); Univ. of Singapore (PhD 1992). FRCS 1979; FRCOG 1993. Hon. Sen. Lectr, Inst. of Obstetrics and Gynaecol., Queen Charlotte's Hosp., London, 1988–89. National University of Singapore: Associate Prof., 1990–92, Prof., 1992–97, of Obstetrics and Gynaecol.; Dep. Hd, 1992–94, Hd, 1994–97, of Obstetrics and Gynaecol.; Prof. of Obstetrics and Gynaecol., Univ. of Nottingham, 1997–2001. Vice Pres., 2005–07, Pres., 2007–10, RCOG. Treas. and Sec. Gen., Internat. Fedn of Obstetrics and Gynaecol., 1997–2006. Ed.-in-Chief, Best Practice in Clin. Res. in Obstetrics and Gynaecol., 1998–. *Publications:* (ed jtly) Fetal Monitoring in Practice, 1992, 3rd edn 2008; (ed jtly) Management of Labour, 1996, 2nd edn 2005; Emergencies in Obstetrics and Gynaecology, 2006; (ed jtly) Munro Kerr's Operative Obstetrics, 11th edn 2007; (ed jtly) Oxford Handbook of Obstetrics and Gynaecology, 2nd edn 2008; Best Practice in Labour and Delivery, 2009; (ed jtly) Obstetrics and Gynaecology for Postgraduates, vols 1 and 2, 3rd edn 2009; contrib. chapters in books and peer-reviewed indexed articles. *Recreations:* reading, philosophy, walking, listening to classical music. *Address:* Division of Obstetrics and Gynaecology, St George's, University of London, Cranmer Terrace, SW17 0RE. *T:* (020) 8725 5956, *Fax:* (020) 8725 5958. *E:* sarulkum@sgul.ac.uk.

**ARUNDEL AND BRIGHTON, Bishop of, (RC),** since 2015; **Rt Rev. (Charles Phillip) Richard Moth;** *b* Chingola, Zambia, 8 July 1958; *s* of Charles Ernest Moth and Barbara Yvonne Moth (*née* Hambly). *Educ:* Judd Sch., Tonbridge; St John's Seminary, Wonersh; St Paul Univ., Ottawa (MA; JCL 1987). Ordained priest, 1982; Assistant Priest: Clapham Park, 1982–85; Lewisham, 1987–92; Private Sec. to Archbishop of Southwark, 1992–2001; Vocations Dir, 1992–2001; Vicar Gen. and Chancellor, RC Archdio. of Southwark, 2001–09; RC Bishop of the Forces, 2009–15. Hon. Canon: Guildford Cathedral, 2018; Chichester Cathedral, 2018. Liaison Bishop for Catholic Scouting, 2010–, for Prisons, 2013–. Pres., Southwark Metropolitan Appeal Tribunal, 1994–2002; Catholic Bishops' Conference. Mem., Dept of Christian Responsibility and Citizenship, 2009–; Chair, Mental Health Reference Gp, 2009–. Chair of Govs, St Mary's UC, later St Mary's Univ., Twickenham, 2011–. Mem., Canon Law Soc. of GB and Ireland, 1985. Freeman: City of London, 2013; Skinners' Co., 2013 (Liveryman, 2017). KC★HS 2009. *Recreations:* horse riding, walking, music. *Address:* High Oaks, Old Brighton Road North, Pease Pottage, W Sussex RH11 9AJ. *Club:* Naval and Military.

**ARUNDEL AND SURREY, Earl of; Henry Miles Fitzalan-Howard;** *b* 3 Dec. 1987; *s* and *heir* of Duke of Norfolk, *qv; m* 2016, Cecilia Mary Elizabeth; *d* of William Colacicchi; one *d. Educ:* Radley College; Bristol Univ. Formula BMW UK Rookie Champion, 2006.

**ARUNDELL,** family name of **Baron Talbot of Malahide**.

**ARVILL, Robert;** *see* Boote, R. E.

**ASANTE-MENSAH, Evelyn Justina,** OBE 2006; Chairman, Pennine Care NHS Foundation Trust, since 2017; *b* 11 Oct. 1965; *d* of late Kwaku Asante-Mensah and of Beatrice Gyamfi (*née* Amoo-Mensah); step *d* of Alfred Gyamfi; partner, Yoni Ejo; one *s* three *d. Educ:* Nicholls Ardwick High Sch., Manchester; Manchester Metropolitan Univ. (MA 2001). Joined Black Health Agency, 1992; Chief Exec., Black Health Agency, 1999–2005; Strategic Advr on Community Cohesion and Diversity, Govt Office for NW, 2006–07; Head of Equality and Econ. Inclusion, NW Develt Agency, 2007–10. Chairman: Central Manchester PCT, 2000–06; NHS Manchester (formerly Manchester PCT), 2006–13; Manchester Locality Assce, 2011–13. Non-executive Director: Manchester HA, 1998–2000; NHS Greater Manchester, 2010–. Dir, EAM Solutions Ltd, 2011–. Chairman: Race for Health, 2002–08; Appt Commn, Black and Minority Ethnic Adv. Gp, 2004–07; Brook, 2007–09; Member: Equal Opportunities Commn, 2005–07; Community, Voluntary and Local Services Hons Cttee, Cabinet Office, 2011–; Bd, Partners of Prisoners, 2011–; EHRC, 2013–17. Chm., Arawak Walton Housing Assoc., 2014–. Governor: St Mary's C of E Primary Sch., Moss Side, 2012–; Manchester Metropolitan Univ. Hon. DLitt Manchester Metropolitan, 2003. *Recreations:* reading, gardening, cooking, spending time with family. *E:* evelynasante-mensah@hotmail.co.uk.

**ASBIL, Rt Rev. Walter Gordon;** Bishop of Niagara, 1991–97; *b* 3 Oct. 1932; *m* 1957, Mavis Asbil; three *s* one *d. Educ:* Concordia Univ., Montreal (BA); McGill Univ. (BD, STM). Ordained deacon, 1957, priest, 1957; Rector: Aylwin River Desert, 1957–60; Montreal South Shore, 1960–65; St Stephen's, Montreal, 1965–67; St George, St Anne de Bellevue, 1967–70; St George, St Catharine's, 1970–86; Rector and Dean, Christ Church

Cathedral, Ottawa, 1986–90; Co-adjutor Bishop of Niagara, 1990–91. Hon. DD Montreal Dio. Theol Coll., 1991. *Address:* 1107, 3 Towering Heights Boulevard, St Catharines, ON L2T 4A4, Canada.

**ASBRIDGE, Sir Jonathan (Elliott),** Kt 2006; Chief Clinical Officer (formerly Clinical Director), Healthcare at Home, since 2016 (Director of Quality and Governance, 2013–16); *b* 16 Feb. 1959; *s* of late Roy Derek Asbridge and Doris Enid Asbridge; *m* 1986, Helen Catherine Lewis-Smith; two *s* two *d*. *Educ:* Nightingale Sch., St Thomas' Hosp., London (SRN 1980); UC Swansea (DipN 1987). Dir, Clinical Care Services, Addenbrooke's Hosp., 1989–92; Executive Nurse Director: Llandough Hosp., Cardiff, 1992–94; Oxford Radcliffe Hosp., 1994–97; Chief Nurse, Barts and the London NHS Trust, 1997–2003; Nat. Clinical Dir, Emergency Care, DoH, 2003–06; Dir of Nursing and Clinical Services, 2007–08, Ops Dir, 2008–12, Clinicenta Ltd; Prog. Dir, Reconfiguration of Health Services, NE Sector, Gtr Manchester, 2008–12. Pres., NMC, 2001–06. Mem., Council for Health Regulatory Excellence, 2002–06 (Vice Chm., 2004–05). Chm., Eur. Health Wkg Gp, Conseil Européen des Professions Libérales, 2004–07; Mem., Internat. Council of Nurses Observatory of Licensure and Regulation, 2004–07. Non-exec. Dir, Oxford Health NHS Foundn Trust, 2014–. Council Mem., Florence Nightingale Foundn, 2002–06; Life Vice Pres., Nightingale Fellowship, 2005–. Hon. DSc City, 2004; Hon. Dr Health Service Mgt Anglia Ruskin, 2016. *Recreations:* tennis, running, walking, biographies, aviation.

**ASCHERSON, (Charles) Neal;** journalist and author; *b* 5 Oct. 1932; *s* of late Stephen Romer Ascherson and Evelyn Mabel Ascherson; *m* 1st, 1958, Corinna Adam (marr. diss. 1982; she *d* 2012); two *d*; 2nd, 1984, Isabel Hilton; one *s* one *d*. *Educ:* Eton College; King's College, Cambridge (MA; Hon. Fellow, 1993). Served RM, 1950–52. Reporter and leader writer, Manchester Guardian, 1956–58; Commonwealth corresp., Scotsman, 1959–60; The Observer: reporter, 1960–63; Central Europe corresp., 1963–68; Eastern Europe corresp., 1968–75; foreign writer, 1979–85; columnist, 1985–90; Associate Editor, 1985–89; columnist, The Independent on Sunday, 1990–98. Scottish politics corresp., Scotsman, 1975–79. Asst Lectr, 1998–2009, Hon. Prof., 2008–, Inst. of Archaeology, UCL; Hon. Fellow: UCL, 2010; UHI, 2010. Hon. FSAScot 2011. Hon. DLitt: Strathclyde, 1988; Bradford, 2006; Aberdeen, 2010; Goldsmiths, Univ. of London, 2011; Hon. DSc (SocSci) Edinburgh, 1990; DUniv: Open, 1991; Paisley, 2003; Hon. LLD St Andrews, 1999. Reporter of the Year 1982, Journalist of the Year 1987, Granada Awards; James Cameron Award, 1989; David Watt Meml Prize, 1991; (jtly) George Orwell Award, Political Qly, 1993; Saltire Award for Literature, 1995. Golden Insignia, Order of Merit (Poland), 1992; Bene Merito Insignia (Poland), 2011. *Publications:* The King Incorporated, 1963; The Polish August, 1981; The Struggles for Poland, 1987; Games with Shadows, 1988; Black Sea, 1995; Stone Voices, 2002; The Death of the Fronsac, 2017. *Address:* 27 Corsica Street, N5 1JT. *Club:* Ognisko Polskie (Polish Hearth Club).

**ASFARI, Ayman,** FREng; Group Chief Executive, Petrofac plc, since 2002; *b* 8 July 1958; *s* of Dr Adeeb Asfari and Lamia Haroun; *m* 1983, Sawsan El-Himani; four *s*. *Educ:* Villanova Univ. (BSc Civil Engrg 1979); Univ. of Pennsylvania (MSc Civil and Urban Engrg 1980). Resident Engr, Conser Consulting Gp, 1980–81; Man. Dir, Desert Line Projects (DLP), Muscat, Oman, 1982–91; Man. Dir, Petrofac UK Ltd, Chm. and Chief Exec., Petrofac Internat. Ltd, and Dir in all other Petrofac cos, 1991–2002. FREng 2014. *Recreations:* tennis, golf, ski-ing, boating. *Address:* Petrofac plc, 4th Floor, 117 Jermyn Street, SW1Y 6HH. *T:* (020) 7811 4900. *Club:* Royal Automobile.

**ASGHAR, Mohammad;** Member (C) South Wales East, National Assembly for Wales, since 2009 (Plaid Cymru, 2007–09); *b* Peshawar, 30 Sept. 1945; *s* of M. Aslam Khan and Zubaida Aslam; *m* 1983, Firdaus; one *d*. *Educ:* Peshawar Univ. (BA 1968). Certified Public Accountant. Asst to Principal, R. J. Minty, chartered accountants, 1972–83; Principal, MA Associates, accountants, 1983–. National Assembly for Wales: Shadow Minister for Equalities and Sport, 2011, for Further Educn, Faith and Skills, 2018–; Member: Equalities, Local Govt and Community Cttee; Public Accounts Cttee. Chairman: Cons. Friends of India; Cons. Friends of Pakistan. Member: Assoc. of Accounting Technicians, 1975–; Inst. of Financial Accountants, 2001–. Mem., CPA. *Recreations:* holder of Private Pilot's Licence, keen sportsman, cricket, athletics, badminton. *Address:* National Assembly for Wales, Cardiff Bay, Cardiff CF99 1NA. *T:* 0300 200 7239. *E:* mohammad.asghar@assembly.wales.

**ASH, Brian Maxwell,** QC 1990; *b* 31 Jan. 1941; *s* of late Carl Ash and of Irene Ash (*née* Atkinson); *m* 1971, Barbara Anne Maxwell, creator and founding editor of BBC TV Question Time; two *s* one *d*. *Educ:* Mercers' Sch.; City of London Sch.; New Coll., Oxford (Open Exhibnr; BA). BBC TV Current Affairs Producer, Reporter and Programme Presenter, 1967–73; called to the Bar, Gray's Inn, 1975. Chm. of Panel, Examination in Public of First Alteration to Devon Structure Plan, 1986; Sec., Local Govt, Planning and Envmtl Bar Assoc., 1990–92. *Recreations:* golf, sailing, ski-ing, music. *Address:* Thirty Nine Essex Chambers, 81 Chancery Lane, WC2A 1DD. *T:* (020) 7832 1111. *Clubs:* Royal Mid-Surrey Golf; Royal Norwich Golf.

**ASH, Daniel Victor,** FRCP, FRCR; Consultant in Clinical Oncology, Cookridge Hospital, Leeds, 1979–2007; President, Royal College of Radiologists, 2001–04 (Dean, Faculty of Clinical Oncology, 1998–2000); *b* 18 Oct. 1943; *s* of Vivien and Isidore Ash; *m* 1969, Deirdre Meikle; one *s* one *d*. *Educ:* Royal London Hosp. Medical Coll. (MB BS). FRCR 1976; FRCP 1992. Lectr in Medicine, Makerere Univ., Kampala, 1971–72; Registrar in Radiotherapy, Churchill Hosp., Oxford, 1973–76; Lectr in Radiotherapy, Royal Marsden Hosp., London, 1976–79. President: British Oncology Assoc., 1994–97; European Brachytherapy Gp, 1995–98. *Publications:* (jtly) Practical Radiotherapy Planning, 1985, 3rd edn 2000; (jtly) Effective Treatment of Prostate Cancer, 2002; clinical res. papers on radiation sensitisers, photodynamic therapy and brachytherapy. *Recreations:* music (classical and jazz), walking, ceramics. *Address:* 10 Oakwood Park, Leeds LS8 2PJ.

**ASH, Prof. Sir Eric (Albert),** Kt 1990; CBE 1983; FRS 1977; FREng; Emeritus Professor of Electrical Engineering, University College London, since 1993; *b* 31 Jan. 1928; *s* of Walter and Dorothea Ash; *m* 1954, Clare (*née* Babb); five *d*. *Educ:* University College Sch.; Imperial Coll. of Science and Technology. BSc(Eng), PhD, DSc, FCGI, DIC. FREng (FEng 1978); FIET; FIEEE; FInstP. Research Fellow: Stanford Univ., Calif, 1952–54; QMC, 1954–55; Res. Engr, Standard Telecommunication Laboratories Ltd, 1955–63; Sen. Lectr, 1963–65, Reader, 1965–67, Prof., 1967–85, Pender Prof. and Head of Dept, 1980–85, Dept of Electronic and Electrical Engrg, UCL (Hon. Fellow, 1985); Rector, Imperial Coll., London Univ., 1985–93 (Hon. Fellow, 1995). Dir (non-exec.), BT (formerly British Telecom), 1987–93; Chairman: Hydroventuri Ltd, 2001–03; Ocean Power Technologies, Inc., 2003–08. Pres., IEE, 1987–88 (Vice-Pres., 1980–83; Dep. Pres., 1984–86); Treas. and Vice-Pres., Royal Soc., 1997–2002; Mem., Exec. Bd, Fellowship of Engrg, 1981–84. Chm., BBC Science Advisory Cttee, 1987–90. Trustee: Science Mus., 1987–91; Wolfson Foundn, 1988–. Sec., Royal Instn, 1984–88 (Vice Pres., 1980–82; Manager, 1980–84; Vice Pres. and Chm. of Council, 1995–99). Foreign Member: NAE, US, 2001; Russian Acad. of Sci., 2003. Marconi International Fellowship, 1984. Dr *hc* Aston, 1987; Leicester, 1987; Institut National Polytechnique de Grenoble, 1987; Edinburgh, 1988; Polytechnic Univ., NY, 1988; Westminster, 1992; Sussex, 1993; Glasgow, 1994; Chinese Univ. of Hong Kong, 1994; City Univ. of Hong Kong, 1998; Surrey, 2001; Nanyang Technol Univ., Singapore, 2002. Faraday Medal, IEE, 1980; Royal Medal, Royal Soc., 1986. National Order of Merit (France), 1990. *Publications:* patents; papers on topics in physical electronics in various engrg and physics jls. *Recreations:* music, swimming, cycling. *Address:* 11 Ripplevale Grove, N1 1HS.

**ASH, Dame Margaret;** *see* Barbour, Dame M.

**ASH, Timothy John G.;** *see* Garton Ash.

**ASHBERG, Judith;** *see* Piatkus, J.

**ASHBOURNE, 4th Baron** *cr* 1885; **Edward Barry Greynville Gibson;** Lieutenant-Commander RN, retired; *b* 28 Jan. 1933; *s* of 3rd Baron Ashbourne, CB, DSO, and Reta Frances Manning (*d* 1996), *e d* of E. M. Hazeland, Hong Kong; *S* father, 1983; *m* 1967, Yvonne Georgina, *d* of Mrs Flora Ham (*née* Harvey), of Malin, County Donegal; three *s*. *Educ:* Rugby. RN, 1951–72; Kitcat and Aitken, stockbrokers, 1972–73, 1976–79; Vickers, da Costa & Co. Ltd, stockbrokers, 1973–76; Save & Prosper Gp, 1979–81; GT Management, 1981–88; MoD, 1989–93. Pres., Christian Broadcasting Council, 1998–. Pres., Hampshire Autistic Soc. *Heir:* *s* Hon. Edward Charles d'Olier Gibson [*b* 31 Dec. 1967; *m* 2001, Tanya Louise (marr. diss. 2013), *d* of Bryan Beckett, OBE; two *s* one *d*]. *Address:* Colebrook Barn, East Harting Farm, Petersfield, Hants GU31 5LU.

**ASHBOURNE, (Kenneth) John (Turner);** artist (primarily sculpture and photography); public and private sector chief executive and company chairman, now retired; *b* 16 July 1938; *s* of Ernest John Ashbourne and Phyllis Turner Ashbourne; *m* 1959, Valerie Anne Sado, artist; one *s* one *d*. *Educ:* St Dunstan's Coll.; London Sch. of Econs (BSc Econs 1959). Teacher, then lectr, 1959–68; Mgt Develt Officer, BAC, 1968–71; Hd, Corporate Planning, London Borough of Lewisham, 1971–74; Asst Chief Exec., Suffolk CC, 1974–77; Chief Exec., Royal Borough of Kingston-upon-Thames, 1977–80; Dep. Man. Dir, Express Newspaper Gp 1980–83; Sen. Consultant, Hay-MSL, 1983–85; Chief Executive: Cambridge HA, 1985–91; Addenbrooke's Hosp., then Addenbrooke's NHS Trust, 1991–98; E Anglian Ambulance NHS Trust, 1999. Chairman: Chapter Ltd, 1999–2012; Enterprise Cradle Ltd, 2001–12. Sen. Mem., Hughes Hall, 1992–2000, and Affiliate Lectr, Clinical Sch., 1994–2000, Univ. of Cambridge. Chm., UK Univ. Hosps Forum, 1998–2000. Founder and Hon. Dir, Shelby Transplant Trust, 1994–2000. Gov., Anglia Poly. Univ., 1996–2000. Mem. Nat. Council, British Falconers' Club, 1977–88; Mem., 1980–86, Vice-Chm., 1983–86, Hawk Bd, DoE. Mem., Ontario Soc. of Artists, 2014. Annual Award, Ontario Soc. of Artists, 2016. *Recreations:* music, reading, working. *Address:* 248400 5th Side Road, Mono, ON L9W 6L2, Canada. *W:* www.johnashbourne.com.

**ASHBROOK, 11th Viscount** *cr* 1751 (Ire.); **Michael Llowarch Warburton Flower;** JP; DL; Baron Castle Durrow 1733; landowner; Vice Lord-Lieutenant, Cheshire, 1990–2010; *b* 9 Dec. 1935; *s* of 10th Viscount Ashbrook and Elizabeth, *er d* of Capt. John Egerton-Warburton and Hon. Mrs Waters; *S* father, 1995; *m* 1971, Zoë Mary Engleheart; two *s* one *d*. *Educ:* Eton; Worcester Coll., Oxford (MA Mod. Hist.). 2nd Lieut, Grenadier Guards, 1955. Solicitor, 1963; Partner, Farrer & Co., Solicitors, 1966–76; Partner, then Consultant, Pannone & Partners (formerly March Pearson & Skelton), 1985–96. Chm., Taxation Sub-Cttee, 1984–86, Pres., Cheshire Branch, 1990–99, CLA. Hon. DBA Chester, 2012. DL 1982, JP 1983, Cheshire. *Recreations:* gardening, the countryside, shooting. *Heir:* *s* Hon. Rowland Francis Warburton Flower [*b* 16 Jan. 1975; *m* 2004, Annika Jane, *d* of Julian Beavan; one *s* two *d*]. *Address:* Woodlands, Arley, Northwich, Cheshire CW9 6LZ. *T:* (01565) 777277. *Club:* Brooks's.
*See also* Sir C. J. Hoare, Bt.

**ASHBROOK, Kate Jessie;** General Secretary, Open Spaces Society, since 1984; *b* 1 Feb. 1955; *d* of John Ashbrook and Margaret Balfour; lives with Christopher Myles Hall, *qv*. *Educ:* Benenden Sch., Kent; Exeter Univ. (BSc). Mem., Exec. Cttee, Open Spaces Soc., 1978–84; Campaign for National Parks (formerly Council for National Parks): Mem., Exec. Cttee, later Trustee, 1983–; Vice-Chm., 1998–2003 and 2016–; Chm., 2003–09; Ramblers' Association: Trustee, 1982–2012, 2016–; Vice-Chm., 1993–95, 2017–18; Chm., Exec. Cttee, later Bd of Trustees, 1995–98, 2006–09 and 2018–; Pres., 2012–16; Vice-Pres., 2016–; Chm., Access Cttee, 1997–2009; Footpath Sec., Bucks and W Middx, 1986–; Member: Common Land Forum, 1984–86; Countryside Agency, 1999–2006; Nat. Parks Review Adv. Panel, DEFRA, 2002; Common Land Stakeholder Wkg Gp, DEFRA, 2002–03; Natural England Rights of Way Stakeholder Gp, 2008–; Adv. Mem., Thames Basin Heaths Special Protection Area Jt Strategic Partnership Bd, 2007–. Chm., Central Rights of Way Cttee, 1991–98; Sec., Countryside Link, 1989–92; Pres., Dartmoor Preservation Assoc., 1995–2011 (Hon. Sec., 1981–84; Trustee, 2011–); Vice-Pres., Peak and Northern Footpaths Soc., 2018–. Mem., Inst. of Public Rights of Way and Access Mgt (formerly Inst. of Public Rights of Way Officers), 1999–. Patron, Walkers are Welcome Towns Network, 2008–. Chm., Turville Sch. Trust, 1994–95. Editor, Open Space, 1984–. Outdoor Personality of the Year, Great Outdoors Mag., 2015. *Publications:* (contrib.) The Walks of South-East England, 1975; (contrib.) Severnside: a guide to family walks, 1976; Saving Open Spaces, 2015; pamphlets; contribs to Oxford DNB, The Countryman and various jls. *Recreations:* pedantry, finding illegally blocked footpaths, learning British birdsong. *Address:* Telfer's Cottage, Turville, Henley-on-Thames RG9 6QL. *T:* (01491) 638396, (office) (01491) 573535.

**ASHBURNER, Prof. Michael,** PhD, ScD; FRS 1990; Professor of Biology, University of Cambridge, 1991–2009, Professor Emeritus, 2010 (Director of Research, 2009–11) Fellow, Churchill College, Cambridge, 1980, now Fellow Emeritus; *b* 23 May 1942; *s* of Geoffrey Staton Ashburner and Diane Ashburner (*née* Leff); *m* 1963, Francesca Ryan, *d* of Desmond Francis Ryan and Isabel Ryan; one *s* two *d*. *Educ:* Royal Grammar Sch., High Wycombe; Churchill Coll., Cambridge (BA 1964, PhD 1968, ScD 1978). FRES 1975 University of Cambridge: Asst in Research, 1966–68; Univ. Demonstrator, 1968–73; Univ Lectr, 1973–80; Reader in Developmental Genetics, 1980–91. Gordon Ross Res. Fellow Calif Inst. of Technology, 1968–69; Visiting Professor: Univ. of California Sch. of Medicine, San Francisco, 1977–78; Univ. of Crete, 1985; Univ. of Pavia, Italy, 1990–96 Miller Vis. Prof., Univ. of California at Berkeley, 1986. Lectures: Goldschmidt, Hebrew Univ., Jerusalem, 1985; Osborne, Edinburgh Univ., 1991; Dacre, Peterhouse, Cambridge 1992. Res. Co-ordinator, EMBL, 1994–98; Jt Hd, EMBL-European Bioinformatics Inst 1998–2001. Member: EMBO, 1977, Council, 1988–91; Governing Council, Internat Centre for Insect Physiology and Ecology, Nairobi, 1991–96; Council, Royal Soc. 2001–03. Pres., Genetical Soc., 1997–2000. Mem., Academia Europaea, 1989; Fellow Japan Soc. for Promotion of Sci., 1992. Hon. Foreign Mem., Amer. Acad. of Arts and Scis 1993; Hon. FRES 2012. Hon. Dr Biol Crete, 2002; Hon. DSc Edinburgh, 2003 *Publications:* (ed) The Genetics and Biology of Drosophila, 1976–86, 12 vols; (ed) Insec Cytogenetics, 1980; (ed) Heat Shock: from bacteria to man, 1982; Drosophila: a laborator handbook, 1989, (jtly) 2nd edn 2005; Won for All: how the Drosophila genome wa sequenced, 2006; contribs to scientific jls. *Recreations:* walking, watching birds. *Address:* 2 Commercial End, Swaffham Bulbeck, Cambs CB25 0NE. *T:* (01223) 812451.

**ASHBURNHAM, Sir James Fleetwood,** 13th Bt *cr* 1661, of Broomham, Sussex; *b* 17 Dec. 1979; *s* of John Anchitel Fleetwood Ashburnham (*d* 1981) and of Corinne Ashburnham (*née* O'Brien, now Merricks); *S* grandfather, 1999; *m* 2011, Yasmin, *e d* of Jurgen Effertz; one *s* one *d*. *Educ:* Sherborne; King's Coll., London. *Heir: s* Levent John Ashburnham, *b* 12 April 2013.

**ASHBURTON,** 7th Baron *cr* 1835; **John Francis Harcourt Baring,** KG 1994; KCVO 1990 (CVO 1980); Kt 1983; DL; Chairman: Barings plc, 1985–89 (non-executive Director, 1989–94); Baring Brothers & Co. Ltd, 1974–89 (a Managing Director, 1955–74); BP Co. plc, 1992–95 (Director, 1982–95); *b* 2 Nov. 1928; *er s* of 6th Baron Ashburton, KG, KCVO, DL and Hon. Doris Mary Thérèse Harcourt (*d* 1981), *e d* of 1st Viscount Harcourt; *S* father, 1991; *m* 1st, 1955, Susan Mary Renwick (marr. diss. 1984), *e d* of 1st Baron Renwick, KBE, and Mrs John Ormiston; two *s* two *d*; 2nd, 1987, Mrs Sarah Crewe, *q d* late J. G. Spencer Churchill. *Educ:* Eton Coll. (Fellow, 1982–97); Trinity Coll., Oxford (MA; Hon. Fellow 1989). Dep. Chm., Royal Insurance Co. Ltd, 1975–82 (Dir, 1964–82); Chairman: Outwich Investment Trust Ltd, 1968–86; Baring Stratton Investment Trust, 1986–97; Director: Trafford Park Estates Ltd, 1964–77; Dunlop Holdings Ltd, 1981–84; Jaguar, 1989–91; Mem. Court, Bank of England, 1983–91. Duchy of Cornwall: Receiver-Gen., 1974–90; Lord Warden of the Stannaries, 1990–94. Vice-Pres., British Bankers' Assoc., 1977–81; Pres., Overseas Bankers' Club, 1977–78. Chm., Accepting Houses Cttee, 1977–81; Chm., Cttee on Finance for Industry, NEDC, 1980–86. Member: British Transport Docks Bd, 1966–71; President's Cttee, CBI, 1976–79; Trustee and Hon. Treas., Police Foundn, 1989–2001; Member: Council, Baring Foundn, 1971–99 (Chm., 1987–98); Exec. Cttee, NACF, 1989–99. Trustee: Rhodes Trust, 1970–99 (Chm., 1987–99); Southampton Univ. Develt Trust, 1986–96 (Chm., 1989–96); Nat. Gall., 1981–87; Winchester Cathedral Trust, 1989– (Chm., 1993–2006). High Steward, Winchester Cathedral, 1991–2013. DL Hants, 1994. Hon. Fellow, Hertford Coll., Oxford, 1976. DUniv Southampton, 2007. *Heir: s* Hon. Mark Francis Robert Baring [*b* 17 Aug. 1958; *m* 1st, 1983, Miranda Caroline (marr. diss. 2014), *d* of Captain Charles St John Graham Moncrieff; two *s* two *d*; 2nd, 2016, Sophie Grenville]. *Address:* Lake House, Northington, Alresford, Hants SO24 9TG; 52 Carthew Road, W6 0DX. *Clubs:* Pratt's, Flyfishers', Beefsteak, Grillions.

**ASHBY, David Glynn;** *b* 14 May 1940; *s* of Robert M. Ashby and Isobel A. Davidson; *m* 1965, Silvana Morena (marr. diss. 1998); one *d*. *Educ:* Royal Grammar Sch., High Wycombe; Bristol Univ. (LLB Hons). Called to the Bar, Gray's Inn, 1963; formerly in practice on SE Circuit. Member: Hammersmith Bor. Council, 1968–71; for W Woolwich, GLC, 1977–81; ILEA, 1977–81. MP (C) NW Leics, 1983–97. *Recreations:* gardening, sailing (Transatlantic 2003–04, Mediterranean 2005–06), music.

**ASHBY, Prof. Deborah,** OBE 2009; PhD; FMedSci; Professor of Medical Statistics and Clinical Trials, since 2008, and Director, School of Public Health, since 2018, Imperial College London; NIHR Senior Investigator, 2010–18, now Emeritus; *b* London, 21 Aug. 1959; *d* of George Herbert Davis and Jean Davis (*née* Martin); *m* 1982, Michael Owen Ashby (marr. diss. 2014); one *s* one *d*. *Educ:* Southend High Sch. for Girls; Univ. of Exeter (BSc Maths 1980); London Sch. of Hygiene and Tropical Medicine (MSc Med. Stats 1981); Royal Free Hosp. Sch. of Medicine (PhD 1984). CStat 1994. Res. Fellow, Royal Free Hosp. Sch. of Medicine, 1983–86; Lectr, 1987–92, Sen. Lectr, 1992–95, Reader, 1995–97, in Medical Statistics, Univ. of Liverpool; Prof. of Med. Stats, QMUL, 1997–2008. Member: Cttee on Safety of Medicines, 1999–2005; Commn on Human Medicines, 2005–14. Royal Statistical Society: Mem. Council, 1992–97; Vice Pres., 1993–95; Hon. Sec., 1998–2004; Pres., 2019–Dec. 2020. FMedSci 2012. *Publications:* (with S. Eldridge) Statistical Concepts, 2000. *Recreations:* seeing family and friends, walking and cycling in cities and countryside, genealogy, visiting art galleries. *Address:* School of Public Health, Imperial College London, St Mary's Campus, Norfolk Place, W2 1PG. *T:* (020) 7594 8704. *E:* deborah.ashby@imperial.ac.uk.

**ASHBY, Rt Rev. Godfrey William Ernest Candler;** an Honorary Assistant Bishop, Diocese of Exeter, since 2012; *b* 6 Nov. 1930; *s* of late William Candler Ashby and Vera Fane Ashby (*née* Hickey); *m* 1957, Sally Hawtree (*d* 2015); four *s* two *d*. *Educ:* King's School, Chester; King's Coll., London (BD, AKC, PhD). Deacon 1955, priest 1956; Assistant Curate: St Peter, St Helier, Morden, 1955–57; Clydesdale Mission, 1958; Priest-in-charge, St Mark's Mission, 1958–60; Subwarden, St Paul's Coll., Grahamstown, 1960–65; Priest-in-charge, St Philip's, Grahamstown, 1962–63; Rector of Alice and Lectr, Federal Theological Seminary, 1966–68; Sen. Lecturer, Old Testament and Hebrew, Rhodes Univ., Grahamstown, 1969–75; Assoc. Professor, 1974–75; Overseas Visiting Scholar, St John's Coll., Cambridge, 1975; Dean and Archdeacon, Cathedral of St Michael and St George, Grahamstown, 1976–80; Bishop of St John's (Transkei and S Africa), 1980–84; Prof. of Divinity, Univ. of Witwatersrand, Johannesburg, 1985–88; Asst Bp of Leicester, 1988–95; Priest-in-Charge, Newtown Linford, 1992–95; Hon. Assistant Bishop: George, S Africa, 1995–2008; Portsmouth, 2008–12. Hon. Canon, Leicester Cathedral, 1994. *Publications:* Theodoret of Cyrrhus as Exegete of the Old Testament, 1970; Sacrifice, 1988; Exodus (commentary), 1998; (trans.) Alphonse de Lamartine, The Stonemason of Saint Point, 2015; articles in theological jls. *Recreations:* ornithology, French literature.

**ASHBY, Prof. Michael Farries,** CBE 1997; FRS 1979; FREng; Royal Society Research Professor, Department of Engineering, University of Cambridge, since 1989 (Professor of Engineering Materials, 1973–89); *b* 20 Nov. 1935; *s* of Baron Ashby, FRS; *m* 1962, Maureen Stewart; two *s* one *d*. *Educ:* Campbell Coll., Belfast; Queens' Coll., Cambridge (BA, MA, PhD). Post-doctoral work, Cambridge, 1960–62; Asst, Univ. of Göttingen, 1962–65; Asst Prof., Harvard Univ., 1965–69; Prof. of Metallurgy, Harvard Univ., 1969–73. Mem., Akad. der Wissenschaften zu Göttingen, 1980–. FREng (FEng 1993). Hon. MA Harvard, 1969. Editor: Acta Metallurgica, 1974–96; Progress in Materials Science, 1995–. *Publications:* Deformation Mechanism Maps, 1982; Engineering Materials, pt 1 1986, pt 2 1996; Materials Selection in Design, 1992, 3rd edn 2004; Cellular Solids, 1997; Materials and Design, 2002; Materials: engineering, properties, science, design, 2007; Materials and the Environment, 2009; Materials: engineering, science, processing and design, 2014, 4th edn 2019; Materials and Sustainable Development, 2015. *Recreations:* music, design. *Address:* 51 Maids Causeway, Cambridge CB5 8DE. *T:* (01223) 301333.

**ASHCOMBE,** 5th Baron *cr* 1892; **Mark Edward Cubitt;** *b* 29 Feb. 1964; *s* of Mark Robin Cubitt and Juliet Perpetua Cubitt (*née* Woodall); *S* cousin, 2013; *m* 1992, Melissa Mary, *o d* of Maj. Charles Hay; two *s*. *Heir: s* Hon. Richard Robin Alexander Cubitt, *b* 14 June 1995.

**ASHCROFT,** Baron *cr* 2000 (Life Peer), of Chichester in the County of West Sussex; **Michael Anthony Ashcroft,** KCMG 2000; PC 2012; international businessman, philanthropist, author and pollster; *b* 4 March 1946; *s* of Frederic Parker Ashcroft and Mary Lavinia Long; *m* 1st, 1972, Wendy Mahoney (marr. diss. 1984); two *s* one *d*; 2nd, 1986, Susi Anstey. *Educ:* King Edward VI Grammar Sch., Norwich; Royal Grammar Sch., High Wycombe; Mid-Essex Tech. Coll., Chelmsford. Varied business interests in public and private cos in UK, USA and Caribbean. Chairman: Hawley Group, later ADT Ltd, 1977–97; BB Hldgs, later BCB Hldgs, then Caribbean Investment Hldgs, 1987–2010; Dir, Tyco Internat., 1984–2002. Ambassador from Belize to the UN, 1998–2000. Party Treas., Conservative Party, 1998–2001; a Dep. Chm., Conservative and Unionist Party, 2005–10; Treas., Internat. Democratic Union, 2007–. Mem., H of L, 2000–15. Sen. Ind. Advr on Sovereign Base Areas, Cyprus, 2011; Govt Special Rep. for Veterans' Transition, 2012– (report, Veterans' Transition Review, 2014). Founder and Chm, Crimestoppers Trust, 1988–. Chm., Ashcroft Technology Acad. (formerly ADT Coll.), 1991–; Chancellor, Anglia Ruskin Univ., 2001–. Pres. and Trustee, W India Cttee, 2011–; Trustee: Cleveland Clinic, 2004–; Imperial War Mus. and Foundn, 2010–18. Vice Patron, Intelligence Corps Mus., 2009–. Fellow, Royal Canadian Geographical Soc., 2016. Hon. Dr Anglia Poly., 1999. Kt Grand Cross, Imperial Order of Holy Trinity (Ethiopia), 2016. *Publications:* Smell the Coffee: a wake up call to the Conservative Party, 2005; Dirty Politics, Dirty Times, 2005; Victoria Cross Heroes, 2006, Vol II, 2016; Special Forces Heroes, 2008; George Cross Heroes, 2010; Minority Verdict: the Conservative Party, the voters and the 2010 election, 2010; Heroes of the Skies, 2012; Special Ops Heroes, 2014; Call Me Dave, 2015; Well You Did Ask: why the UK voted to leave the EU, 2016; Hopes and Fears: Trump, Clinton, the voters and the future, 2017; The Lost Majority, 2017; White Flag: an examination of Britain's modern day defence capability, 2018; Half-Time: American public opinion midway through Trump's (first?) term - and the race to 2020, 2019; Jacob's Ladder: the unauthorised biography of Jacob Rees-Mogg, 2019. *Recreations:* researching the Victoria Cross, entertaining friends, trying something new, messing about in boats. *W:* www.lordashcroft.com.

**ASHCROFT, Andrew Richard;** HM Diplomatic Service, retired; Joint Executive Director, Koolkompany Ltd/Koolskools Ethical School Clothing (formerly Astro Inc./Koolskools Ethical School Clothing), since 2015 (Joint Director, 2009–15); *b* 28 May 1961; *s* of Ivor John Ashcroft and Amy Joan Ashcroft; *m* 1st, 2001, Dr Amanda Sives (marr. diss. 2006); 2nd, 2012, Anna Zofia Danielewicz. *Educ:* Worle Sch., Weston-super-Mare; Millfield Sch. Entered FCO, 1980; Finance Dept, then S Asian Dept, FCO, 1980–82; 3rd Sec. (Commercial), Muscat, 1982–86; 3rd, later 2nd Sec. (Chancery), Tel Aviv, 1987–91; Asst Private Sec. to Minister of State (ME, Near East, N Africa and Former Soviet Union and Central Eastern Europe), FCO, 1991–95; 1st Sec. (Commercial), Harare, 1996–99; Hd, Caribbean Section, FCO, 1999–2001; Ambassador, Dominican Republic and Haiti, 2002–06; FCO, London, 2006–07. Chief Exec., Ambassador Communications, 2008–11; Jt Dir, FAIR4DR, 2011–14. Mem. Bd, New Forest Business Partnership, 2010–15. *Recreations:* music (solo euphonium and Chair, Downton Brass Band, piano and singing), cricket, golf, tennis. *Address:* 103 The Meadows, Lyndhurst, Hants SO43 7EJ. *T:* (023) 8028 3223, 07757 978898. *Club:* Royal Harare Golf.

**ASHCROFT, Emma Georgina Annalies;** *see* Fielding, E. G. A.

**ASHCROFT, Dame Frances (Mary),** DBE 2015; PhD; ScD; FRS 1999; Professor of Physiology, University of Oxford, 1996–2001 and since 2011 (Royal Society GlaxoSmithKline Research Professor, 2001–11); Fellow, Trinity College, Oxford, since 1992; *b* 15 Feb. 1952; *d* of John and Kathleen Ashcroft. *Educ:* Talbot Heath Sch., Bournemouth; Girton Coll., Cambridge (BA 1974; MA 1978; PhD 1979; ScD 1996; Hon. Fellow, 2015). MRC Trng Fellow, Physiol., Leicester Univ., 1978–82; Oxford University: Demonstrator in Physiol., 1982–85; EPA Cephalosporin Jun. Res. Fellow, Linacre Coll., 1983–85; Royal Soc. 1983 Univ. Res. Fellow, Physiol., 1985–90; Lecturer in Physiology: Christ Church, 1986–87; Trinity Coll., 1988–89; Univ. Lectr in Physiol., 1990–96; Tutorial Fellow in Medicine, St Hilda's Coll., 1990–91. Grass Foundn Fellow, 1978; Muscular Dystrophy Assoc. Fellow, Physiol., UCLA, 1981–82. G. L. Brown Prize Lectr, 1997; Peter Curran Lectr, Yale Univ., 1999; Charitable Infirmary Lectr, RCSI, 2003; Linacre Lect., Cambridge Univ., 2006; Kroc Lect., Uppsala Univ., 2008; Rodney Porter Lect., Oxford Univ., 2008; Mendel Lect., Brno, 2009; Croonian Lect., Royal Soc., 2013; Winston Scott Meml Lect., Barbados, 2014; Royal Soc. of NZ Dist. Speaker, 2015; Forbes Lect., Marine Biol Lab., Woods Hole, Mass, 2017. Mem., EMBO, 2000. FMedSci 1999. DUniv Open, 2003; Hon. DSc: Leicester, 2007; Radboud, 2013; Aberdeen, 2014; Lund, 2017; E Anglia, 2019; Cambridge, 2019. Frank Smart Prize, Cambridge Univ., 1974; Andrew Cudworth Meml Prize, 1990; G. B. Morgagni Young Investigator Award, 1991; Charter Award, Inst. of Biology, 2004; Walter Cannon Award, Amer. Physiol. Soc., 2007; Albert Renold Prize, Eur. Assoc. for the Study of Diabetes, 2007; Feldberg Foundn Prize, 2010; Eur. Laureate, L'Oréal/UNESCO Women in Sci. Award, 2012; Lewis Thomas Prize for Writing about Science, Rockefeller Univ., 2013; Jacobaeus Prize, Novo Nordisk Foundn, 2014; Jacob Henlé Medal, Georg-August Univ., Göttingen, 2019. *Publications:* (with S. J. H. Ashcroft) Insulin-Molecular Biology to Pathology, 1992; Ion Channels and Disease, 1999; Life at the Extremes: the science of survival, 2000; The Spark of Life, 2012; res. papers in Nature, Jl Physiology, etc. *Recreations:* reading, writing, walking, sailing, pottery. *Address:* Department of Physiology, Anatomy and Genetics, Parks Road, Oxford OX1 3PT.

**ASHCROFT, Jane Rachel,** CBE 2014; Chief Executive, Anchor Hanover (formerly Anchor Trust), since 2010; *b* Liverpool, 17 June 1966; *d* of Alan Geoffrey and June Rachel Williams; *m* 1990, Andrew Jonathan Ashcroft. *Educ:* Univ. of Stirling (BA Hons Modern Hist. 1988). Grad. trainee, 1988–89, Co. Secretarial Asst, 1989–91, Personnel Officer, 1991–93, Midlands Electricity plc; HR Mgr, 1993–95, Co. Sec., 1995–97, Bromford Housing Gp; Personnel Dir (Care First), BUPA, 1997–99; Hd of HR, then Man. Dir, Care Services, Anchor Trust, 1999–2010. Non-executive Director: Stroud and Swindon Building Soc., 2007–10; Dignity plc, 2012–. Chm., Care England (formerly English Community Care Assoc.), 2009–15 (Mem. Bd, 2015–). Trustee, Silver Line, 2014–. MCIPD 1995. FCIS 2006. *Recreations:* reading, historical biography, running, theatre, ballet. *Address:* Anchor Hanover, The Heals Building, 22–24 Torrington Place, WC1E 7HJ. *T:* (020) 7759 7231. *E:* jane.ashcroft@anchorhanover.org.uk.

**ASHCROFT, Hon. John David,** JD; Attorney General of the United States of America, 2001–04; Founder and Chairman, Ashcroft Group, LLC, since 2005; *b* Chicago, 9 May 1942; *m* Janet Elise; two *s* one *d*. *Educ:* Yale Univ.; Univ. of Chicago (JD 1967). Admitted: Missouri State Bar; US Supreme Court Bar. In private practice, Springfield, Mo, 1967–73; Associate Prof., SW Missouri State Univ., Springfield, 1967–72; State Auditor, 1973–75, Asst Attorney Gen., 1975–77, Attorney Gen., 1977–84, Gov., 1985–93, Missouri; Attorney, Suelthaus and Kaplan, 1993–94; US Senator Missouri, 1995–2001. Dist. Prof., Schs of Law and Govt, Regent Univ., 2005–. *Publications:* (with Janet E. Ashcroft) College Law for Business; (with Janet E. Ashcroft) It's the Law, 1979; Lessons From a Father to his Son, 1998.

**ASHCROFT, John Kevin,** CBE 1990; Chief Executive, pro.manchester, 2009–18; Consultant, Equilibrium Asset Management LLP, since 2019; *b* 24 Dec. 1948; *s* of Cumania Manion and late John Ashcroft; *m* 1972, Jennifer Ann (*née* King) (marr. diss. 2015); two *s* one *d*; *m* 2015, Mary Louise (*née* Pye). *Educ:* Upholland Grammar School; LSE (BSc Econ Hons); PhD Manchester Metropolitan Univ., 1996. Marketing Trainee, Tube Investments, 1970; Brand Manager, Crown Wallcoverings Internat. Div., 1974; Marketing Dir, Crown Wallcoverings French Subsidiary, 1976; Man. Dir, Coloroll, 1978–82, Dep. Chm. and Chief Exec., 1982–86, Chm., 1986–90; Chief Exec., Crabtree Consultancy Gp Ltd, 1990–2007. Dir, Marketing Manchester, 2010–; Mem., Gtr Manchester Business

Leadership Council, 2010–. Vis. Prof., Business Sch., Manchester Metropolitan Univ., 2010–18; Executive in Residence, Manchester Business Sch., 2012. Young Business Man of the Year, The Guardian, 1987. *Recreations:* fine arts, opera, sports, wine.

**ASHCROFT, Prof. Margaret,** PhD; FRSB; Professor of Hypoxia Signalling and Cell Biology, University of Cambridge, since 2014; *b* Stirling, Scotland, 22 Jan. 1969; *d* of James Galbraith and Ann Armour Galbraith (*née* Miller); *m* 1991, Neville Richard Ashcroft; one *s*. *Educ:* Univ. of Bristol (BSc Hons Pharmacol. 1991; PhD Molecular/Cellular Biol. 1995). FRSB (FSB 2010). Postdoctoral Researcher, Nat. Cancer Inst., Frederick Cancer Res. and Develt Center, Frederick, Md, 1995–2000; Team Leader, Inst. of Cancer Res., 2000–08; University College London: Reader in Cancer Biol., 2008–12; Hd, Centre for Cell Signalling and Molecular Genetics, 2008–14; Prof. of Molecular Cell Biol., 2012–14 (Hon. Prof. of Molecular Cell Biol., 2014–). Res. Fellow, Human Frontier Scientific Prog., 1997–2000. Hon. Mem., RCR 2014. Young Investigator Award, EACR, 2005. *Publications:* (contrib.) Tumor Suppressor Genes in Human Cancer, 2000; articles in learned jls. *Recreation:* martial arts. *Address:* Department of Medicine, University of Cambridge, Clifford Allbutt Building, Cambridge Biomedical Campus, Hills Road, Cambridge CB2 0AH. *E:* m.ashcroft@medschl.cam.ac.uk.

**ASHCROFT, Rt Rev. Mark David;** *see* Bolton, Bishop Suffragan of.

**ASHCROFT, Noel Graham,** AM 2012; JP; company director, leadership training and change management consultant; Chairman, Dandaragan Camel Dairies Pty Ltd, since 2017; Agent General for Western Australia in London, 2005–08; *b* 2 May 1944; *s* of Arthur Joseph Ashcroft and late Eileen May Ashcroft; *m* 1st, 1968, Penelope Anthea Edwards (marr. diss. 2000); four *d*; 2nd, 2003, Susan Mary Feeney (*née* Zanco); two step *s*. *Educ:* St Francis Xavier Coll., Bunbury; St Ildephonsus Coll., New Norcia; Australian National Univ. (BSc Forestry 1967); Linacre Coll., Oxford (MSc 1974). Divl Forest Officer, 1968–80, Regl Forest Manager, 1980–83, Forests Dept, WA; Project Manager, Govt of WA Functional Review Cttee, 1983–86; Associate Dir, Barrack House Gp Pty, Ltd, 1986–89; Government of Western Australia: Dir, Dept of Resources Develt, 1989–2001; Exec. Dir, Office of Major Projects, 2001–03; Dep. Dir Gen., Dept of Industry and Resources, 2003–05; Co. Exec., Griffin Gp, Australia, 2008–11; Dep. Chm., Mid West Ports Authy, WA, 2012–18. Member, Board: Australian Coal Research Ltd, 2010–; Geraldton Port Authy, 2012–. Member: Oxford Soc. (WA), 2001–; Britain-Australia Soc., 2005–; Cook Soc., 2005–. JP WA, 2005–. Mem., Guild of Freemen of City of London, 2006–10. Mem. and volunteer, St Vincent de Paul Soc., 2016–. Mem., Catenian Assoc. of Australia. *Recreations:* building, furniture restoration, golf, fishing, sightseeing and touring, spiritual reading. *Address:* PO Box 955, Mount Lawley, WA 6929, Australia.

**ASHCROFT, Wendy Cowan, (Mrs B. Ashcroft);** *see* Alexander, W. C.

**ASHCROFT, Zoë Jane;** Co-Founder, Capital Partner and Head, Corporate and Finance Group, Winston & Strawn London LLP, since 2003; *b* 6 Oct. 1965; *d* of Peter Ashcroft and Christine Zillah (*née* Hawley); *m* 2014, Piers Alexander Adamson. *Educ:* Clifton Prep. Sch., York; York Coll. for Girls; St Peter's Sch., York; Univ. of Bristol (LLB 1986); Guildford Coll. of Law. Admitted solicitor, 1989. Lawyer, Turner Kenneth Brown, London and Hong Kong, 1987–94; Morgan, Lewis & Bockius: Associate, 1994–98; Partner, 1998–2003; Hd, UK Corporate/Business and Finance Gp, 2000–03; Member: Global Exec. Cttee, Winston & Strawn LLP, 2015–18; Winston Global Women's Leadership Initiative. Dir, Sponsors for Educnl Opportunity, 2003–; Trustee, Climate Gp, 2006–. *Recreations:* travel, art, comedy, horse racing. *Address:* Winston & Strawn London LLP, CityPoint, One Ropemaker Street, EC2Y 9AW. *E:* zashcroft@winston.com, zoeashcroft1@gmail.com. *Clubs:* Home House, Morton's, The Ned.

**ASHE, Ven. (Francis) John;** Archdeacon of Lynn, 2009–18; *b* London, 11 Feb. 1953; *s* of Francis Patrick Bellesme and Marion Islay Ashe; *m* 1979, Shelagh Lesley Prouse; three *d*. *Educ:* Christ's Hospital, Horsham; Univ. of Sheffield (BMet 1974); Ridley Hall, Cambridge (CTh 1979). Metallurgist, Hadfield's Steel, Sheffield, 1974–75; Dir, Witley Enterprises, 1976–77; ordained deacon, 1979, priest, 1980; Curate, Parish of St Giles and St George, Ashtead, 1979–82; Priest-in-charge, St Faith's, Plumstead, SA, 1982–87; Rector, Wisley with Pyrford, Guildford, 1987–93; Vicar, Godalming, 1993–2001; Rural Dean of Godalming, 1996–2002; Team Rector, Godalming, 2001–09; Warden of Readers, Dio. of Norwich, 2009–15. Hon. Canon, Guildford Cathedral, 2003–09. Chaplain (pt-time), Rowley Bristow Hosp., Pyrford, 1987–91; Hon. Chaplain, Dunkirk Veterans, Pyrford Br., 1987–93. Mem., Gen. Synod, 2004–09. *Recreations:* woodturning/carpentry, gardening, running, photography. *Address:* Kirkleigh Farmhouse, Virginstow, Beaworthy, Devon EX21 5DZ.

**ASHE, (Thomas) Michael;** QC 1994; QC (NI) 1998; SC (Ire.) 2000; *b* 10 March 1949; *s* of John Ashe and Nancy (*née* O'Connor); *m* 1977, Helen Morag Nicholson (marr. diss. 2007). *Educ:* Finchley Catholic Grammar Sch. Called to the Bar, Middle Temple, 1971, Bencher, 1998; called to Irish Bar, 1975, Northern Irish Bar, 1993. Estate Duty Office, CS, 1967–70; merchant banking, 1971–76; practice at the Bar, 1978–. Dep. Public Prosecutor, Min. of Finance, Singapore, 1988–90; an Asst Recorder, 1998–2000; a Recorder, 2000–19. Editor, Company Lawyer, 1983–2009. Hon. General Counsel to Brit. Inst. of Securities Laws, 1980–; Hon. Consultant to Commercial Crime Unit, Commonwealth Secretariat, 1980–84. Mem. Bd, Centre for Internat. Documentation on Organised and Economic Crime, Cambridge, 1990–; Guest Lectr, Fac. of Laws, Univ. of Cambridge, 1990–95. Diocese of Brentwood: Auditor and Notary, 1997–; Defender of the Bond, 2006–; Mem., Safeguarding Commn, Dio. of Westminster, 2012–. *Publications:* (jtly) Insider Trading, 1990, 2nd edn 1994; (jtly) Insider Dealing (Ireland), 1992; (jtly) Insider Crime, 1994; (jtly) Money Laundering, 2000, 2nd edn 2007; (jtly) Anti-Money Laundering Risks, Compliance and Governance, 2013; contrib. Money, 1980, and (jtly) Injunctions, 1991, in Halsbury's Laws of England, 4th edn; articles in legal periodicals. *Recreations:* walking, railways, Gregorian Chant, classical music, Irish traditional music. *Address:* 9 Stone Buildings, Lincoln's Inn, WC2A 3NN. *T:* (020) 7404 5055.

**ASHENDEN, Rt Rev. Dr Gavin Roy Pelham;** theologian, author, commentator; Missionary Bishop for UK and Europe, Christian Episcopal Church, since 2017; Chaplain to the Queen, 2008–17; *b* London, 3 June 1954; *s* of Michael Roy Edward Ashenden and Carol Ashenden (*née* Simpson, now Salmon); *m* 1996, Helen Mary Lowe; one *s* two *d*. *Educ:* Univ. of Bristol (LLB 1976); Oak Hill Theol Coll. (BA 1980); Heythrop Coll., Univ. of London (MTh 1989); Univ. of Sussex (PhD 1998). Ordained deacon, 1980, priest, 1981; Curate, St James, Bermondsey, 1980–82; Vicar, St Antony's, Hamsey Green, Sanderstead, 1982–89; University of Sussex: Univ. Chaplain, 1989–2012; Sen. Lectr, Dept of English, 1989–2012; Vicar, St Martin de Gouray, Jersey, 2012–16. Canon, later Bursalis Canon, Chichester Cathedral, 2005–16. Consecrated as Bishop, Christian Episcopal Ch (USA and Canada), 2017. Mem., Gen. Synod for Southern Univs, 1994–2012. Hon. Prof., St Mary's Univ., Twickenham, 2019–. Presenter: on faith and ethics, BBC Radio, BBC Sussex, BBC Surrey, 2008–11; Faith in England, BBC podcast, 2009–12; Anglican TV, 2017–; columnist, Jersey Evening Post, 2015–. Dir, Aid to Russian Christians, 1982–92; Patron, Child Aid to Russia, 2005–. Mem. Council, Keston Coll., 1982–92 (Vice Chm., 1990–92). *Publications:* Charles Williams: alchemy and integration, 2007; (contrib.) Charles Williams and His Contemporaries, 2009; (contrib.) Persona and Paradox: issues of identity in C. S. Lewis, 2012; contrib. to jls incl. Church Times, Anglo American Literary Jl, Seven, Third Way, Jersey Evening Post. *Recreations:* singing, walking, reading, talking, writing. *Address:* Shropshire and Normandy. *E:* Gavin@ashenden.org. *W:* https://ashenden.org. *Club:* United (St Helier).

**ASHER, Jane;** actress, writer and businesswoman; *b* 5 April 1946; *d* of late Richard A. J. Asher, MD, FRCP and Margaret Asher (*née* Eliot); *m* Gerald Scarfe, *qv*; two *s* one *d*. *Educ:* North Bridge House; Miss Lambert's PNEU. *Stage:* Will You Walk a Little Faster, Duke of York's, 1960; Wendy in Peter Pan, Scala, 1961; Bristol Old Vic, 1965; Romeo and Juliet and Measure for Measure, NY, 1967; Look Back in Anger, Royal Court, 1969; The Philanthropist, Mayfair and NY, 1970; Treats, Royal Court, 1975; National Theatre, 1976; Whose Life is it Anyway?, Mermaid and Savoy, 1978; Before the Party, Queen's, 1978; Blithe Spirit, Vaudeville, 1986; Henceforward, Vaudeville, 1988; The School for Scandal, NT, 1990; Making it Better, Criterion, 1992; The Shallow End, Royal Court, 1997; Things We Do For Love, Gielgud, 1998; House, and Garden, RNT, 2000; What the Butler Saw, tour, 2001; Festen, Almeida, transf. Lyric, 2004; The World's Biggest Diamond, Royal Court, 2005; Bedroom Farce, Rose Th., Kingston, 2009; Snow White and the Seven Dwarfs, Richmond Th., 2009; The Reluctant Debutante, tour, 2011; Farewell to the Theatre, The Importance of Being Earnest, Rose Th., Kingston, 2011; Charley's Aunt, Menier Chocolate Factory, 2012; Pride & Prejudice, Regent's Park, 2013; Moon Tiger, tour, 2014; The Gathered Leaves, Park Th., 2015; Great Expectations, W. Yorkshire Playhouse, 2016; An American in Paris, 2017; A Song at Twilight, tour, 2019; *films include:* Mandy, 1951; Greengage Summer, 1961; Alfie, 1966; Deep End, 1970; Henry VIII and his Six Wives, 1970; Runners, 1984; Dream Child, 1985; Paris by Night, 1988; The Maidens' Conspiracy, 2005; Death at a Funeral, 2007; I Give It a Year, 2013; Burn, Burn, Burn, 2015; The Visitor (short), 2018; *television includes:* Brideshead Revisited, 1981; The Mistress, 1986; Wish Me Luck, 1987–89; Eats for Treats, 1990; Tonight at 8.30, Murder Most Horrid, 1991; Closing Numbers, 1993; The Choir, 1995; Good Living, 1997, 1998; Crossroads, 2003; Miss Marple, 2004; New Tricks, 2005; A For Andromeda, 2006; Holby City, 2007, 2008, 2009, 2010; The Palace (series), 2008; Maestro, 2008; The Old Guys, 2009, 2010; Poirot, 2009; Dancing on the Edge, 2012; Eve, 2015–16; Stella, 2015; Brian Pern: a tribute, 2017; numerous plays for radio; Radio Actress of the Year Award, 1986. Member: BBC Gen. Adv. Council, 1991–96; BAFTA, 1985; Forum, 1993–. President: Nat. Autistic Soc., 1997– (Vice Pres., 1990–97); Arthritis Care, 2003–; Parkinson's UK (formerly Parkinson's Disease Soc.), 2007–; Vice-President: Nat. Deaf Children's Soc., 2003–08; Autistica, 2010–; Trustee: Child Accident Prevention Trust, 1992–96; Ford Martin Trust for Cancer in Children, 1993–95; WWF, 1994–98; Children in Need, 1995–99. Governor, Molecule Theatre. Ran business, Jane Asher Party Cakes, London, 1990–2016; designer and consultant for Sainsbury's cakes, 1992–99; Consultant, Debenhams, 1999–2004; own range of cake-decorating supplies and edibles: Poundland, 2014–18; Home Bargains, 2018–. Columnist: Today newspaper, 1994–95; The Express, 1998–2001. FRSA 1989. Hon. LLD Bristol, 2001. *Publications:* Jane Asher's Party Cakes, 1982; Jane Asher's Fancy Dress, 1983; Silent Nights for You and Your Baby, 1984; Jane Asher's Quick Party Cakes, 1986; Moppy is Happy, 1987; Moppy is Angry, 1987; Easy Entertaining, 1987; Keep Your Baby Safe, 1988; Children's Parties, 1988; Calendar of Cakes, 1989; Eats for Treats, 1990; Jane Asher's Book of Cake Decorating Ideas, 1993; Round the World Cookbook, 1994; Time to Play, 1995; The Longing, 1996; 101 Things I wish I'd known before…, 1996; The Best of Good Living, 1998; The Question, 1998; Good Living at Christmas, 1998; Tricks of the Trade, 1999; Losing It, 2002; Cakes For Fun, 2005; Moppy is Calm, 2005; Moppy is Sad, 2005; Beautiful Baking, 2007; journalism for newspapers and magazines. *Recreations:* reading, The Times crossword. *Address:* c/o United Agents, 12–26 Lexington Street, W1F 0LE. *T:* (020) 3214 0800.

**ASHFOLD, Prof. Michael Norman Royston,** PhD; FRS 2009; FRSC; FInstP; Professor of Physical Chemistry, University of Bristol, since 1992; *b* Bridgwater, Som, 19 June 1954; *s* of Kenneth Norman George and Gwendoline May Ashfold; *m* 1977, Julie Carolyn Favell; two *s*. *Educ:* Weston-super-Mare Grammar Sch. for Boys; Birmingham Univ. (BSc Hons Chem.; PhD Phys. Chem. 1978). Guy Newton Jun. Res. Fellow, Jesus Coll., Oxford, 1978–81; School of Chemistry, University of Bristol: Lectr in Chem. Physics, 1981–90; Reader in Chem. Physics, 1990–92. Vis. Fellow, Jt Inst. for Lab. Astrophysics, Univ. of Colo, 1990; EPSRC Sen. Res. Fellow, 1997–2002; Royal Soc. Leverhulme Trust Sen. Res. Fellow, 2011–12. Royal Society of Chemistry: Pres., Faraday Div., 2009–12; Chair, Sci., Educn and Industry Bd, 2012–; Mem. Council, 2012–. Marlow Award, 1987, Corday-Morgan Prize, 1989, Tilden Prize, 1996, Liversidge Award, 2014, RSC; Herbert P. Broida Prize, Amer. Physical Soc., 2015. *Publications:* contribs to physical chem./chem. physics jls describing res. in broad areas of gas-phase and gas-surface chemistry. *Recreations:* family, walking, half-marathons, watching many other sports. *Address:* School of Chemistry, University of Bristol, Bristol BS8 1TS. *T:* (0117) 928 8312, *Fax:* (0117) 925 0612. *E:* mike.ashfold@bris.ac.uk.

**ASHFORD, Archdeacon of;** *see* Miller, Ven. D. N.

**ASHKEN, Kenneth Richard,** CB 1996; Director (Policy), Crown Prosecution Service, 1990–95; *b* 13 June 1945; *s* of Karol and Dulcinea Ashken; *m* 1st, 1969, Linda Salemink (marr. diss.); two *s* one *d*; partner, 1986, *m* 2nd, 1996, Patricia Almond (*d* 1996); one *d* partner, Linda Demaris Wood. *Educ:* Whitgift Sch., Croydon; London Univ. (LLB Hons) Cambridge Inst. of Criminology (DipCrim). Admitted solicitor, 1972. Office of Director of Public Prosecutions, 1972; Asst Dir of Public Prosecutions, 1984; Hd of Policy and Inf Div., 1986, Dir, Policy and Communications Gp (Grade 3), 1990, Crown Prosecution Service. UK Govt consultant to S African Ministry of Justice, 1998–99. Lay Chm., ind review panels, NHS, 1998–2001; non-exec. Dir, Bromley Primary Care NHS Trust 2001–04. Member: Cttee, SE London Probation Service, 1997–2001; London Area Bd Nat. Probation Service, 2001–07. Mem., Funding Panel, Victim Support, 1997–2008 (Vice-Chair, 2006–08); Chair: S London Youth Panel, 2012; S London Trng and Devel Cttee, 2014. FRSA 1990. JP SE London, 2000–15. *Recreations:* travel, opera, wine and othe decadent retirement activities, working an allotment. *Club:* Royal Automobile.

**ASHKENAZY, Vladimir;** concert pianist; conductor; Music Director, European Unio Youth Orchestra, 2000–15; *b* Gorky, Russia, 6 July 1937; *m* 1961, Thorunn Johannsdotti *d* of Johann Tryggvason, Iceland; two *s* three *d*. *Educ:* Central Musical Sch., Moscow Conservatoire, Moscow. Studied under Sumbatyan; Lev Oborin class, 1955: grad 196( Internat. Chopin Comp., Warsaw, at age of 17 (gained 2nd prize); won Queen Elisabet Internat. Piano Comp., Brussels, at age of 18 (gold medal). Joint winner (with John Ogdon of Tchaikovsky Piano Comp., Moscow, 1962. London debut with London Symph. Orch under George Hurst, and subseq., solo recital, Festival Hall, 1963. Music Dir, RPC 1987–94; Chief Conductor, Berlin Radio SO, subseq. Deutsches Symphonie-Orcheste Berlin, 1989–99; Music Dir and Chief Conductor, Czech Philharmonic Orchestra 1998–2003; Music Dir, NHK SO, Tokyo, 2004–07; Principal Guest Conductor, Orch della Svizzera Italiana, Lugano, 2012–; Prin. Conductor and Artistic Advr, Sydney SC 2009–13. Has played in many countries. Makes recordings (Grammy Awards, 1973, 197

1981, 1985, 1987; 1999, 2009). Hon. RAM 1972. Hon. Dr Sibelius Acad., Helsinki. Icelandic Order of the Falcon, 1971. *Publications:* (with Jasper Parrott) Beyond Frontiers, 1985. *Address:* Pilatusstrasse 13, 6045 Meggen, Switzerland.

**ASHLEY, Cedric,** CBE 1984; PhD; CEng, FIMechE; automotive engineering and e-learning consultant; land developer; Chairman: Cedric Ashley and Associates, since 1989; Euromotor Autotrain LLP, since 2006; Kings Gate Management Company (Cambridge) Ltd, since 2008; Director, AlphaPillars Ltd, since 2012; *b* 11 Nov. 1936; *s* of Ronald Ashley and Gladys Fincher; *m* 1st, 1960, Pamela Jane Turner (decd); one *s*; 2nd, 1965, (Marjorie) Vivien Gooch (marr. diss. 1991); one *s* one *d*; 3rd, 1991, Auriol Mary Keogh. *Educ:* King Edward's Sch., Birmingham; Mech. Engrg Dept, Univ. of Birmingham (BSc 1958, PhD 1964). CEng 1972; FIMechE 1978. Rolls-Royce Ltd, Derby, 1955–60; Univ. of Birmingham, 1960–73: ICI Res. Fellow, 1963; Lectr, 1966; Internat. Technical Dir, Bostrom Div., Universal Oil Products Ltd, 1973–77; Dir, Motor Industry Res. Assoc., 1977–87; Man. Dir, Lotus Engineering, 1987; Chief Exec., BICERI, 1989–91. Dir, Euromotor, Univ. of Birmingham, 1992–2006. Chairman: SEE, 1970–72; RAC Tech. Cttee, 1980–87; Member: SMMT Technical Bds, 1977–87; Board, Assoc. Ind. Contract Res. Orgns, 1977–86 (Pres., 1982–84); Automobile Div., IMechE, 1978–93 (Chm., 1990–91); Court, Cranfield Inst. of Technol., 1977–87; Engine and Vehicles Cttee, DTI, 1980–88; Three-Dimensional Design Bd, CNAA, 1981–87. Trustee, Sir Henry Royce Meml Foundn, 2006–13, 2014–. Liveryman, Carmen's Co., 1987. FRSA 1983. Cementation Muffelite Award, SEE, 1968; Design Council Award, 1974. TA, 1959–68. *Publications:* (contrib.) Infrasound and Low Frequency Vibration, ed Tempest, 1976; over 40 papers on various automotive and ICT topics incl. engine technol., vehicle ride, effect of vibration and shock on man and buildings, and e-learning, in learned jls. *Recreations:* travel, reading, classic cars. *Address:* (office) Euromotor Autotrain LLP, 17 Buchanan's Wharf North, Ferry Street, Bristol BS1 6HN. *E:* c.ashley@autotrain.org.

**ASHLEY, Jacqueline;** President, Lucy Cavendish College, Cambridge, 2015–18; *b* 10 Sept. 1954; *d* of Baron Ashley of Stoke, CH, PC; *m* 1987, Andrew William Stevenson Marr, *qv*; one *s* two *d*. *Educ:* Rosebery Grammar Sch., Epsom; St Anne's Coll., Oxford (MA PPE). Producer and Newsreader, Newsnight, BBC TV, 1980–83; Producer and Reporter, TV-am, 1983–84; Politics Producer, Channel 4 News, 1984–87; Editor, Their Lordships' House, Channel 4, 1987–88; Presenter, The Parliament Programme, Channel 4, 1988–89; Political Corresp., ITN, 1989–98; Presenter, People and Politics, BBC World Service, 1998–2000; Political Editor, New Statesman, 2000–02; columnist, The Guardian, 2002–15. Presenter, The Week in Westminster, BBC Radio 4, 1999–2015. *Recreations:* reading, swimming.

**ASHLEY, Michael St John,** FCA; non-executive Director, since 2013, and Chairman, Audit Committee, since 2014, Barclays plc; *b* Redhill, Surrey, 19 Sept. 1954; *s* of John Gordon Ashley and Alice Ellen Ashley; *m* 1977, Janet Perry; four *s*. *Educ:* Dulwich Coll.; Trinity Coll., Cambridge (BA Maths 1976). ACA 1979, FCA 2002. Peat, Marwick, Mitchell & Co., later KPMG: Trainee Acct, 1976–78; Sen. Acct, 1978–79; Supervising Sen. Acct, 1979–81; Asst Manager, 1981–82; Consultant, 1982–84; Manager, 1984–85; Sen. Manager, 1985–89; Partner, 1989–95; Chief Financial Officer, NatWest Mkts, 1995–97; Partner, KPMG LLP, 1997–2013; Hd, Quality and Risk Mgt, KPMG Europe LLP, 2007–13. Chairman: Audit and Risk Cttee, Asset Protection Agency, 2009–12; Govt Internal Audit Agency, 2014–18; Member: Audit and Risk Cttee, HM Treasury, 2009–15; Charity Commn, 2014– (Chairman: Audit and Risk Cttee, 2014–18; Policy and Guidance Cttee, 2019–); non-exec. Dir, Cabinet Office, 2018– (Chm., Audit and Risk Cttee, 2018–). Member: Accounting Standards Bd, 2004–10; Ethics Standards Cttee, ICAEW, 2006–; Steering Gp, Financial Reporting Lab, 2011–18; Internat. Ethics Standards Bd for Accountants, 2016–. Mem., Tech. Expert Gp, Eur. Financial Reporting Adv. Gp, 2005–16 (Vice Chm., 2010–16). Trustee, Dulwich Prep. Schs Trust, 2013–; Gov., Dulwich Prep. Cranbrook, 2017–. *Recreations:* genealogy, dinghy sailing, fine wine. *Address:* Barclays plc, Level 31, One Churchill Place, E14 5HP. *Club:* Athenæum.

**ASHLEY, Neil;** Founder Chairman, Amey plc, 1989–2001; *b* 14 Nov. 1936; *s* of late Bernard Stephenson Ashley and of Nora Ashley (*née* Daxon); *m* 1st, 1961, Jane Evelyn Victoria (*d* 1995), *d* of late Granville Canty and of Vera Canty; two *s*; 2nd, 2002, Dr Shirley Anne, *d* of late Col George Frederick Preston Bradbrooke and Lillian (*née* Sibley). *Educ:* Barton-on-Humber Grammar Sch.; Battersea Poly. Inst.; Ashridge Mgt Coll. Man. Dir, ARC Construction Ltd, 1971–79; Dir, Balfour Beatty Construction Ltd, 1979–84; Man. Dir, Balfour Beatty Internat. Ltd, 1984–88; Jt Man. Dir, Balfour Beatty plc, 1985–89; Chairman: Balfour Beatty Projects Ltd, 1985–88; Balfour Beatty Canada Ltd, 1986–89; Balfour Beatty Malaysia SND BYD, 1986–88; Balfour Beatty Inc., 1987–89; Heery Internat. Inc. USA, 1987–89; Amey Construction Ltd, 1989–98; Amey Facilities Mgt Ltd, 1990–98; Amey Homes Ltd, 1991–98; Amey Building Ltd, 1992–98; Amey Railways Ltd, 1996–98. Chairman: Energy Power Resources, 1997–2003; Heritage Property Gp, 1997–2009; Courtenay Develts, 1998–2004; BPO Gp, 1999–2004; Oxford Radcliffe Hospitals NHS Trust, 2000–03; Vectra Gp, 2003–07; BPOSS Ltd, 2005–09. Non-executive Director: Volvere plc, 2002–11; Clarsen Goff Mgt Ltd, 2008–12. Mem., Nat. Council, 1994–2000, Chm., Southern Regl Council, 1995–97, CBI. Mem. Bd, British Road Fedn, 1993–98. Mem. Court, Oxford Brookes Univ., 2005–15 (Ind. Gov., 1997–2005; Chm., Audit Cttee, 1999–2005); Member: Med. Scis Bd, Oxford Univ., 2000–03; Inst. of Cancer Res., 2004 (Dep. Chm., Develt Bd, 2004–07). Vice Pres. and Mem. Council, Lighthouse Club (Construction Ind. Charity), 1991– (Chm., 1998–2001); Chairman: Oxford Radcliffe Charities and Radcliffe Med. Foundn, 2000–03; Oxford Cancer Campaign, 2008–10; Oxford Univ. Hosps Trust (formerly Oxford Radcliffe Hosps Charitable Funds) Cancer Benefactors' Bd, 2010–15. Chairman of Trustees: OCCTOPUS, 2004–17 (Patron, 2017–); Ashley (formerly Jane Ashley) Charitable Trust, 1995–; Patron: Dorchester Abbey Appeal, 1998–2006; Mulberry Bush Sch. (for care and educn of troubled children), 1998–; Vice-Patron, Purley Park Trust, 2003–07. FRSA 1993. Freeman, City of London, 1979; Liveryman, and Mem. Ct, Paviors' Co., 1979–. DUniv Oxford Brookes, 2006; Hon. Bachelor Surrey, 2011. *Publications:* contrib. numerous technical and commercial papers to jls and presentations on wide range of business topics. *Recreations:* boating, shooting, dogs, pyrotechnics. *Address:* Burcot Grange, Burcot, Abingdon, Oxon OX14 3DJ. *T:* (01865) 407106, *Fax:* (01865) 409969; 52 Upper Montagu Street, W1H 1SJ. *T:* and *Fax:* (020) 7569 8595. *E:* neil@bpgroup.com. *Clubs:* Royal Automobile; Leander (Henley); Middlesex CC; Clifton Hampton Cricket; Henley Rugby.

**ASHLEY-COOPER,** family name of **Earl of Shaftesbury**.

**ASHLEY-NORMAN, Jonathan Charles;** QC 2016; a Recorder, since 2010; *b* London, 18 Feb. 1967; *s* of Derek Charles and Lyn Ashley-Norman; *m* 1991, Fiona Seok Hooi; four *c*. *Educ:* Univ. of Exeter (LLB). Called to the Bar, Middle Temple, 1989; in practice as barrister, specialising in business crime and regulation, incl. health and safety. *Recreation:* allotmenteering. *Address:* 3 Raymond Buildings, Gray's Inn, WC1R 5BH. *T:* (020) 7400 6400, *Fax:* (020) 7400 6464. *E:* jonathan.ashley-norman@3rblaw.com.

**ASHLEY-SMITH, Jonathan,** PhD; FMA, FRSC, FIIC; consultant in collections risk; Secretary General, International Institute for Conservation, 2003–06; *b* 25 Aug. 1946; *s* of Ewart Trist and Marian Tanfield Ashley-Smith; *m* 1967, Diane Louise (*née* Wagland); one *s* one *d*. *Educ:* Sutton Valence Public Sch.; Bristol Univ. (BSc (Hons), PhD). FMA 1988. Post-doctoral research, Cambridge Univ., 1970–72; Victoria and Albert Museum, 1973–2004: Hd of Conservation, 1977–2002; Sen. Res. Fellow (Conservation Studies), 2002–04. Leverhulme Fellow, 1995; Sen. Mem., Wolfson Coll., Cambridge, 1995. Gp leader, EU Climate for Culture project on effects of climate change on cultural heritage, 2009–14. Member: UKIC, 1974– (Accredited Mem., 1999); Mem., Exec. Cttee, 1978–; Vice-Chm., 1980; Chm., 1983–84); Crafts Council, 1980–83 (Mem., Conservation Cttee, 1978–83); Council for Care of Churches Conservation Cttee, 1978–85; Board of Governors, London Coll. of Furniture, 1983–85. Vis. Prof., RCA, 1999–2010; Guest Schol., Getty Conservation Inst., 2019. Trustee, Leather Conservation Centre, 2009–13. FRSC 1987; FIIC 1985; Hon. FRCA 1992; FRSA 2000. Scientific Editor, Science for Conservators (Crafts Council series), 1983–84. Plowden Medal, Royal Patentholders Assoc., 2000. *Publications:* Risk Assessment for Object Conservation, 1999; articles in learned jls on organometallic chemistry, conservation risk, conservation skills and scientific examination of art objects. *Recreations:* loud music, strong cider. *E:* jashleysmith@btinternet.com.

**ASHMAN, Stephen John;** Chief Constable, Northumbria Police, 2015–17; *b* Jarrow, S Tyneside, 7 Aug. 1968; *s* of Jack and Alice Ashman; *m* 2000, Alison Stewart; two *s*. *Educ:* St Wilfred's Sch., S Shields; Royal Grammar Sch., Newcastle upon Tyne. Joined Metropolitan Police, 1987; rôles as uniformed and plain-clothes officer in Tottenham, Kings Cross, Wood Green, Hornsey, Holloway and Edmonton; Territorial Support Gp Inspector, NW London; Superintendent, 2002–07, Chief Superintendent, 2007–09, Cleveland Police, serving in Middlesbrough and Hartlepool; Asst Chief Constable, 2009–13, Dep. Chief Constable, 2013–15, Northumbria Police (Gold Comdr, Operation Bulwark, 2010; Regl Gold Comdr, Olympic Games Torch Relay, 2012).

**ASHMORE, Gillian Margaret;** Recording Clerk, Society of Friends (Quakers), 2007–10; *b* 14 Oct. 1949; *d* of John Oxenham and Joan Oxenham; *m* 1971, Frederick Scott Ashmore; three *s* one *d*. *Educ:* Walthamstow Hall, Sevenoaks; Winchester Co. High Sch. for Girls; Newnham Coll., Cambridge (BA Hons Hist.); Open Univ. (BSc Hons). Depts of the Envmt and Tspt, 1971–86; seconded to Housing Corp., 1974; Dep. Dir, Enterprise and Deregulation Unit, Dept of Employment, 1986–87, then DTI, 1987–89; Head, Central Finance Div., Dept of Transport, 1990–92; Dir, Privatisation Studies, BRB, 1992–94; Regl Dir, Govt Office for SE, 1994–98; Principal, Mulberry Consulting, 1999–2007. Chief Exec., EOC, 2001–02. Chair: Kingston Victim Support, 1998–2001; Refugee Housing Assoc., 1999–2006; Exec. Dir, Fostering Network, 2003; Trustee: Metropolitan Housing Trust, then Metropolitan Housing Partnership, 1999–2006; Victim Support London, 1999–2001; Quaker Social Action, 2011–17; Joseph Rowntree Foundn, 2011– (Chair: Audit Cttee, 2008–11; Resources Cttee, 2017–). Gov., Richmond Adult and Community Coll., 2000–06. Associate, Newnham Coll., Cambridge, 1998–2009. FRSA 1995. *Recreations:* novels, history, talking, learning about science, walking, Religious Society of Friends (Quakers). *Address:* 47 Lower Teddington Road, Hampton Wick, Kingston, Surrey KT1 4HQ.

**ASHMORE, Prof. Jonathan Felix,** PhD; FRS 1996; FMedSci; FRSB; Bernard Katz Professor of Biophysics, University College London, since 1996; *b* 16 April 1948; *s* of late Eric Peter Ashmore, theatre director, and Rosalie Sylvia Crutchley, actress; *m* 1974, Sonia Elizabeth Newby; one *s* one *d*. *Educ:* Westminster; Univ. of Sussex (BSc 1st cl. Mathematical Physics); Imperial Coll., London (PhD); University College London (MSc Physiology). FRSB 2016. Vis. Scientist, Internat. Centre for Theoretical Physics, Trieste, Italy, 1971–72; Nuffield Biological Scholar, 1972–74; Res. Asst, Dept of Biophysics, UCL, 1974–77; Fulbright Scholar, and Vis. Physiologist, Ophthalmology Dept, Univ. of California, San Francisco, 1977–80; Lectr, Univ. of Sussex, 1980–83; Lectr, 1983–88, Reader in Physiology, 1988–93, Prof. of Biophysics, 1993–96, Univ. of Bristol; Dir, UCL Ear Inst., 2004. Chaire Blaise Pascal, Institut Pasteur, Paris, 2007–09; Yusuf Hamied Vis. Prof., India, 2019. G. L. Brown Lectr, Physiol Soc., 1992; Croonian Lectr, Royal Soc., 2017. Chief Scientific Advr, Defeating Deafness, subseq. Deafness Res. UK, 2002–07. Dir, London Interdisciplinary Doctoral Prog., 2017–. Pres., Physiol Soc., 2012–14 (Vice Pres., 2010–12). Trustee, Sir John Soane Mus., 2017–. Acted in film, A Kid for Two Farthings, 1955. FMedSci 2001. Hon. DSc Sussex, 2016. Croonian Medal, Royal Soc., 2016. *Publications:* contribs to learned jls on cellular basis of hearing. *Recreation:* travel. *Address:* Department of Neuroscience, Physiology and Pharmacology, University College London, Gower Street, WC1E 6BT. *T:* (020) 7679 2141, *Fax:* (020) 7813 0530. *E:* j.ashmore@ucl.ac.uk.

**ASHRAWI, Hanan;** Media Director and spokesperson, Arab League, since 2001; Member, Palestinian Legislative Council, since 1996; *b* 1946; *m* Emile Ashrawi; two *d*. *Educ:* American Univ., Beirut; Univ. of Virginia. Prof. of English Literature, Chm. of English Dept, and Dean of Arts, Birzeit Univ., West Bank, 1973–90; Dir Gen., Human Rights Instn, Jerusalem. Joined Fatah, PLO; official spokesperson, Palestinian Delegn, 1991–93; Mem., and former Head, Palestinian Independent Commn for Palestinian Republic; Minister of Higher Educn, Palestinian Legislative Council, 1996–98; Mem. Exec. Cttee, Palestine Liberation Orgn, 2009–. *Publications:* A Passion for Peace, 1994; This Side of Peace, 1995. *Address:* c/o Palestinian Legislative Council, Jerusalem, West Bank, via Israel.

**ASHTIANY, Saphié, (Mrs P. L. Davies);** Principal, Ashtiany Associates, since 2010; Special Counsel, Nabarro LLP, 2010–14; *b* Teheran, 2 Aug. 1949; *d* of Ali Asghar Nouredin Ashtiany and Amir Banou Faily; *m* 1973, Prof. Paul Lyndon Davies, *qv*; two *d*. *Educ:* Huntington Hse Sch.; Univ. of Warwick (BA Hons Philosophy and Politics); Univ. of Birmingham (MSocSc Pt 1 Internat. Relns). Refugee counsellor, UNHCR/UKIAS, 1976–79; volunteer, CAB, 1980–84; admitted as solicitor, 1986; Partner and Hd, Employment Dept, Cole & Cole Solicitors, subseq. Morgan Cole, 1989–2000; Partner and Hd, Employment and Discrimination Gp, Nabarro Nathanson, subseq. Nabarro LLP, 2001–10. Vis. Professorial Fellow, QMUL, 2012–. Mem., EOC, 2000–07. Non-exec. Dir, 1993–2003, Vice-Chair, 1996–2001, Actg Chair, 2001–03, Oxon Ambulance NHS Trust. Non-exec. Dir, Channel 4 Corp., 2003–09. Vice Chair, CAF, 2012–18 (non-exec. Dir, 2009–). Mem., Planning and Resources Cttee, Royal Soc., 2016–. Chm., Nationwide Foundn, 2018–. Trustee: Oxford Philharmonic Orch. (formerly Philomusica), 2010– (Chair, Adv. Council); Equal Rights Trust (Chair, 2014–19); Joseph Rowntree Foundn and Joseph Rowntree Housing Trust, 2016–; Oxford Playhouse, 2011–19; Mem., Adv. Bd, WNO, 2013–. *Publications:* (contrib.) Tottles Encyclopaedia on Employment Law, 1996–; contribs to Solicitors' Jl. *Recreations:* music, theatre, walking, cricket. *Address:* 21 Warnborough Road, Oxford OX2 6JA. *T:* (01865) 310232, 07585 771373. *E:* saphieh@ashtianyassociates.com.

**ASHTON,** family name of **Baron Ashton of Hyde**.

**ASHTON OF HYDE,** 4th Baron *cr* 1911; **Thomas Henry Ashton;** Captain of the Honourable Corps of Gentlemen at Arms (Government Chief Whip in House of Lords), since 2019; *b* 18 July 1958; *s* of 3rd Baron Ashton of Hyde and Pauline Trewlove Ashton (*née* Brackenbury); *S* father, 2008; *m* 1987, Emma Louise, *d* of C. N. G. Allinson and Mrs J. R. W. Palmer; four *d*. *Educ:* Eton; Trinity Coll., Oxford (MA). Late Lt Royal Hussars (PWO), Royal Wessex Yeo. Vice Pres., Guy Carpenter & Co., Inc., 1990–92; Director:

C. T. Bowring Reinsurance Ltd, 1992–93; D. P. Mann Ltd, 1996–99; Chief Executive Officer: Faraday Underwriting Ltd, 2005–13 (Dir, 1999–2013); Faraday Reinsurance Co. Ltd, 2005–13 (Dir, 2002–13). Member: Council of Lloyd's, 2010–13; Adv. Council, Century Capital LLP, Boston, 2006–14. Elected Mem., H of L, 2011. A Lord in Waiting (Govt Whip), 2014–17; Parly Under-Sec. of State, DCMS, 2016–19. Mem., RCDS, 2013–14. Jt Master, Heythrop Hunt, 2007–09. *Heir: b* Hon. Jack Edward Ashton, *b* 30 Jan. 1966. *Address:* Broadwell Hill, Moreton-in-Marsh, Glos GL56 0UD. *Club:* Boodle's.

**ASHTON OF UPHOLLAND**, Baroness *cr* 1999 (Life Peer), of St Albans in the county of Hertfordshire; **Catherine Margaret Ashton**, GCMG 2015; PC 2006; High Representative of the European Union for Foreign Affairs and Security Policy, 2009–14, and a Vice-President, European Commission, 2010–14 (Member, 2008–14); King of Arms, Most Distinguished Order of St Michael and St George, since 2019; *b* 20 March 1956; *d* of late Harold and Clare Margaret Ashton; *m* 1988, Peter Jon Kellner, *qv*; one *s* one *d*. *Educ:* Upholland Grammar Sch.; Bedford Coll., Univ. of London (BSc 1977). Admin. Sec., CND, 1977–79; Business Manager, The Coverdale Orgn, 1979–81; Dir of Public Affairs, BITC, 1983–89; freelance policy advr, 1989–99; on secondment from London First to Home Office, 1998–2001. Chm., E and N Herts, subseq. Herts, HA, 1998–2001. Parliamentary Under-Secretary of State: DFES, 2001–04; DCA, subseq. MoJ, 2004–07; Leader of the H of L, 2007–08. Vice Pres., Nat. Council for One-Parent Families. Trustee: Verulamium Mus.; RUSI, 2017–. Chancellor, Univ. of Warwick, 2017–. Chm. Governors, Spencer Jun. Sch., 1995–2001. *Recreations:* theatre, family.

**ASHTON, Rt Rev. Cyril Guy**; Bishop Suffragan of Doncaster, 2000–11; an Honorary Assistant Bishop in the Diocese of Liverpool and in the Diocese of Blackburn, since 2011, and in the Diocese of Carlisle, since 2015; *b* 6 April 1942; *s* of William Joseph Ashton and Margaret Anne Ashton (*née* Todd); *m* 1965, Muriel Ramshaw; three *s* one *d*. *Educ:* Oak Hill Theol Coll.; Lancaster Univ. (MA 1986). Ordained deacon, 1967, priest, 1968; Curate, St Thomas', Blackpool, 1967–70; Vocations Sec., CPAS, 1970–74; Vicar, St Thomas', Lancaster, 1974–91; Dir of Training, Dio. Blackburn, 1991–2000. Hon. Canon, Blackburn Cathedral, 1991–2000. *Publications:* Church on the Threshold, 1988, 2nd edn 1991; Threshold God, 1992; (with Jack Nicholls) A Faith Worth Sharing?: a Church Worth Joining?, 1995. *Recreations:* poetry, writing, music, motor bikes and classic cars. *Address:* Charis, 17c Quernmore Road, Lancaster LA1 3EB.

**ASHTON, John**, CBE 2012; independent speaker and activist, since 2012; Co-founder, E3G, 2004 (Chief Executive, 2004–06; Director, 2004–14); *b* 7 Nov. 1956; *s* of Prof. John Ashton and Prof. Heather Ashton; *m* 1983, Kao Fengning, (Judy); one *s*. *Educ:* Royal Grammar Sch., Newcastle upon Tyne; St John's Coll., Cambridge (MA). Radio Astronomy Gp, New Cavendish Lab., Cambridge, 1977–78; FCO 1978; Science Officer, Peking, 1981–84; Head, China Section, FCO, 1984–86; Cabinet Office, 1986–88; Rome, 1988–93; Dep. Political Advr to Governor, Hong Kong, 1993–97; Vis. Fellow, Green Coll., Oxford, 1997–98; Hd of Envmt, Sci. and Energy, then Envmt Policy, Dept, FCO, 1998–2002; Dir for Strategic Partnerships, LEAD Internat., 2002–04. Foreign Sec.'s Special Rep. for Climate Change, FCO, 2006–12. Vis. Prof., 2006–13, Dist. Policy Fellow, Grantham Inst. for Climate Change, 2013–14, Imperial Coll. London; Vis. Prof., Grantham Res. Inst., LSE, 2013–. Trustee: Tipping Point, 2012–15; UK Youth Climate Coalition, 2012–16. Mem., Adv. Bd, Rethinking (formerly Post-Crash) Economics, 2015–. FRSA. *Recreations:* cricket, nature. *Address:* c/o E3G, 47 Great Guildford Street, SE1 0ES. *Clubs:* MCC; Kew Cricket; Kowloon Cricket.

**ASHTON, Prof. John Richard**, CBE 2000; Professor of Public Health Policy and Strategy, University of Liverpool, since 1993; Honorary Professor, Faculty of Public Health and Policy, London School of Hygiene and Tropical Medicine, since 2014; *b* Liverpool, 27 May 1947; *s* of Edward Ashton and Irene Ashton (*née* Pettit); *m* 1st, 1968, Pamela Scott (marr. diss. 2001); three *s*; 2nd, 2004, Catherine Benedicte, (Maggi), Montague; one *s*, and two step *s*. *Educ:* Quarry Bank High Sch., Liverpool; Univ. of Newcastle upon Tyne (MB BS 1970); London Sch. of Hygiene and Trop. Medicine (MSc Soc. Med. 1978). FFPHM 1986; FRCPsych 1993; FFSRH (MFFP 1993), now Hon. FFSRH; FRCPE 2003; FRCP 2004; FRSocMed 2004. House physician and surgeon, Newcastle Univ. Hosps, 1970–71; Registrar in Psychiatry and Family Practitioner, Newcastle, 1971–75; Lectr in Primary Care, Southampton Univ., 1975–76; Sen. Lectr in Preventive Medicine, LSHTM, 1980–82; Sen. Lectr in Public Health, Univ. of Liverpool, 1983–93); Regional Director of Public Health and Regional Medical Officer, Mersey, 1993–94; Govt Office for NW (formerly NW RHA, then NW Region, NHS Exec., DoH), 1994–2006; Dir of Public Health and County Medical Officer, NHS Cumbria (formerly Cumbria PCT) and Cumbria CC, 2007–13; Interim Dir of Public Health and Sen. Public Health Advr, RBK&C/Grenfell, 2018–19. Visiting Professor: Valencia Inst. Public Health, 1988; Liverpool John Moores Univ., 1998; Med. Sch., Univ. of Manchester, 2001–; Univ. of Central Lancs, 2004–; Univ. of Cumbria, 2008–; Professorial Fellow, Liverpool Sch. of Trop. Medicine, 1994; Fellow, Liverpool John Moores Univ., 2003. Advr on Urban Health, Health Policy, Public Health Educn and Violence, WHO, 2017–; WHO Advr to WHO Copenhagen, 1986–; Sen. Consultant to WHO Eur. Healthy Cities Network, 2017–; Neighbourhood Renewal Advr to UK govt, 2006–09; Consultant Advr on NHS New Care Models, 2015–17; Specialist Advr on Brexit to H of C Select Cttee on Health, 2016–. Mem. Bd, Baywind Energy Co-op., 2016–. Mem., Liverpool Health Instn, 1990–. President: FPH, RCP, 2013–16; Epidemiol. and Public Health Section, RSM, 2014–17. Hon. Pres., Liverpool Med. Students Soc., 2016–17; Member: John Snow Soc.; Duncan Soc., 1998– (Life Pres., 2011); Chm., Wootton Soc., 2001–03. Trustee and Chm., UK Public Health Assoc., 2009–11; Trustee: Carlisle Youth Zone, 2010–13; Mus and Galls Liverpool, 2011–15; Kendal Arts Internat., 2012–13. Freeman, City of London, 2017; Yeoman, Soc. of Apothecaries, 2016. FRSA 2012. Ed., Jl of Epidemiology and Community Health, 1997–2008. *Publications:* Everyday Psychiatry, 1980; The New Public Health, 1988; Esmedune 2000, 1988; Healthy Cities, 1992; (ed) The Epidemiological Imagination, 1994; The Pool of Life, 1997; contrib. articles on medical, public health and social issues. *Recreations:* Liverpool FC, fell walking, cycling, keeping chickens, outdoor education, trainee humanist wedding celebrant. *Address:* Ginny Hall, Dent, Cumbria LA10 5TD. *T:* (01539) 625281; 8 Church Road, Much Woolton, Liverpool L25 5JF. *Club:* Athenæum (Liverpool).

**ASHTON, Joseph William**, OBE 2007; journalist; *b* 9 Oct. 1933; *s* of Arthur and Nellie Ashton, Sheffield; *m* 1957, Margaret Patricia Lee; one *d*. *Educ:* High Storrs Grammar Sch.; Rotherham Technical Coll. Engineering Apprentice, 1949–54; RAF National Service, 1954–56; Cost Control Design Engineer, 1956–68; Sheffield City Councillor, 1962–69. MP (Lab) Bassetlaw Div. of Notts, Nov. 1968–2001. PPS to Sec. of State for Energy, formerly Sec. of State for Industry, 1975–76; an Asst Govt Whip, 1976–77; Opposition Spokesman on Energy, 1979–81. Member, Select Committee: on Trade and Industry, 1987–92; on Home Affairs, 1989–92; on Nat. Heritage, 1992–97; on Modernising the House, 1997–98; Chm., Parly All-Party Football Cttee, 1992–2001. Dir, Sheffield Wednesday, 1990–99. Founder and Chm., Assoc. of Former Members of Parliament, 2001–11. Columnist for: Sheffield Star, 1970–75, 1979–80, 1990–91; Labour Weekly, 1971–82; Daily Star, 1979–87; Sunday People, 1987–88; Plus magazine, 1988–89.

Columnist of the Year, What the Papers Say, Granada TV, 1984. *Publications:* Grass Roots, 1977; A Majority of One (stage play), 1981; Red Rose Blues (memoirs), 2000; Joe Blow, 2014. *Recreations:* football, reading, do-it-yourself, motoring, travel, films, theatre.

**ASHTON, Robin James**; Chairman, Leeds Building Society, since 2013 (non-executive Director, since 2011); Senior Independent Director, Shawbrook Group plc and Shawbrook Bank, since 2011; *b* 19 Jan. 1958; *s* of late Frederick James Ashton and of Florence Mary Ashton; *m* 1st, 1985, Elizabeth Miles (marr. diss. 2002); one *s* one *d*; 2nd, 2004, Jasna Mozetič; one *s*. *Educ:* Bradford Grammar Sch.; Durham Univ. (BA Hons Econs and Law). ACA. Coopers & Lybrand, 1979–83; Finance Dir, Provident Insurance plc, 1983–85; Finance Dir and Dep. Man. Dir, H. T. Greenwood Ltd, 1986–88; Man. Dir, Provident Investments Ltd, 1989; Provident Financial plc: Gp Treas., 1989–93; Finance Dir, 1993–99; Dep. Chief Exec., 1999–2001; Chief Exec., 2001–06; Chief Exec., London Scottish Bank plc, 2007–09; non-exec. Chm., Apple Holdco Ltd, 2010–11; non-executive Director: Albemarle & Bond Hldgs plc, 2012–13; Non-Standard Finance plc, 2014–16. *Address:* 105 Albion Street, Leeds LS1 5AS.

**ASHTON, Prof. Rosemary Doreen**, OBE 1999; FRSL; FBA 2000; Quain Professor of English Language and Literature, University College London, 2002–12, now Emeritus; *b* 11 April 1947; *d* of late David Thomson and Doreen Sidley Thomson (*née* Rose); *m* 1971, Gerard Ashton (*d* 1999); two *s* one *d*. *Educ:* Univ. of Aberdeen (MA Hons English and German 1969); Newnham Coll., Cambridge (PhD 1974). Temp. Lectr, English Dept, Univ. of Birmingham, 1973–74; Lectr, 1974–86, Reader, 1986–91, Prof., 1991–2002, English Dept, UCL. Sen. Res. Fellow, Sch. of Advanced Study, Univ. of London, 2012–. FRSL 1999; Founding Fellow, English Assoc., 1999. FRSA 2002. Hon. Fellow, UCL, 2013. *Publications:* The German Idea: four English writers and the reception of German thought 1800–1860, 1980; Little Germany: exile and asylum in Victorian England, 1986; The Mill on the Floss: a natural history, 1990; G. H. Lewes: a life, 1991; The Life of Samuel Taylor Coleridge: a critical biography, 1996; George Eliot: a life, 1996; Thomas and Jane Carlyle: portrait of a marriage, 2002; 142 Strand: a radical address in Victorian London, 2006; Victorian Bloomsbury, 2012; One Hot Summer: Dickens, Darwin, Disraeli and the Great Stink of 1858, 2017. *Recreations:* gardening, table tennis, listening to music.

**ASHTON, Ruth Mary, (Mrs E. F. Henschel)**, OBE 1991; RN, RM, MTD; non-executive Director and Vice-Chairman, Bromley Primary Care NHS Trust, 2001–07; *b* 27 March 1939; *d* of Leigh Perry Ashton and Marion Lucy Ashton (*née* Tryon); *m* 1984, E. Fred Henschel. *Educ:* Kenya High Sch. for Girls; Clarendon Sch. (lately Abergele); London Hosp. and Queen Mother's Hosp., Glasgow; High Coombe Midwife Teachers' Training College (RN 1964; RM 1967; MTD 1970). Staff Midwife and Midwifery Sister, Queen Mother's Hosp., Glasgow, 1967–69; Nursing Officer and Midwifery Tutor, King's College Hosp., 1971–75; Tutor, 1975–79, Professional Officer, 1979, Gen. Sec., 1980–94, Royal College of Midwives. Non-executive Director: Optimum Health Services NHS Trust, 1994–99; Community Health S London NHS Trust, 1999–2000. Chm., Workforce Develt Confedn, NHS SE London, 2002–06. Temp. Advr on Midwifery, WHO, 1995. Treas., Internat. Confedn of Midwives, 1997–2002. Temp. Prof. March of Dimes, Los Angeles, 1982. Lay Mem., London Deanery Sch. of Gen. Practice Bd, 2007–11. ACIArb 1995. OStJ 1988. *Publications:* midwifery related articles. *Recreations:* gardening, travel, photography. *Address:* c/o National Westminster Bank, PO Box 192, 116 Fenchurch Street, EC3M 5AN. *T:* (home) (020) 8851 7403. *E:* ruhens@tiscali.co.uk.

**ASHTON, William Michael Allingham**, OBE 2010 (MBE 1978); Founding Musical Director, National Youth Jazz Orchestra of Great Britain, 1968–2010, now Life President; *b* Blackpool, 6 Dec. 1936; *s* of Eric Sandiford Ashton and Zilla Dorothea (*née* Miles); *m* 1966, Kay Carol Watkins; two *s* one *d*. *Educ:* Rossall Sch., Fleetwood; St Peter's Coll., Oxford (MA Hons Mod. Langs; DipEd 1962). Nat. Service, RAF, 1955–57. Professional musician, 1962–63; teacher of French in London schs, 1963–73. Founded London Schs Jazz Orch., 1965; became Nat. Youth Jazz Orch., 1968. Editor, News from NYJO, 1988–. Appeared in Royal Variety Perf., 1978; visits to America, Russia, Australasia, France, Poland, Portugal, Germany, Bulgaria, Turkey, Malta, Spain, Italy, etc.; appearances at festivals, film premières, etc. Numerous recordings. Has written over 60 recorded songs, incl. Wait and See, Much Too Much, It's Over, Accident Prone, Thought I'd Ask, Let's Settle Down, Why Don't They Write Songs Like This Any More?, Don't Go to Her. Member: Arts Sub-cttee, Internat. Year of the Child, 1979; Cttee, Assoc. British Jazz Musicians, 1988–. Fellow, City of Leeds Coll. of Music, 1995. BP ABSA Award, 1991; Music Retailers Assoc. Annual Awards for Excellence, 1984, 1990; NYJO voted Best British Big Band, British Jazz Awards, 1993, 1995, 1998, 2002; BBC R2 Award for services to British jazz, 1995; Silver Medal for Jazz, Musicians' Co., 1996; Special Award, All Party Jazz Appreciation Gp, 2007. *Recreations:* song writing, snorkelling, reading. *Address:* 11 Victor Road, Harrow, Middx HA2 6PT. *T:* (020) 8863 2717. *E:* bill.ashton@virgin.net.

**ASHTOWN**, 8th Baron *cr* 1800 (Ire.); **Roderick Nigel Godolphin Trench**; *b* 17 Nov. 1944; *o s* of 7th Baron Ashtown, KCMG and Marcelle Clotterbooke Patijn; *S* father, 2010; *m* 1st, 1967, Janet (*d* 1971), *d* of Harold Hamilton-Faulkner; one *s*; 2nd, 1973, Susan Barbara Wright, *d* of Lewis Frank Day, FRCS, DLO; one *d*. *Educ:* Eton; Stanford Univ., USA. Mem. Cttee, Irish Peers Assoc., 2006–. *Recreations:* reading, family history. *Heir: s* Hon. Timothy Roderick Hamilton Trench [*b* 29 Feb. 1968; partner; one *d*]. *Address:* Plonk Barn, Lullington Road, Lullington, Polegate, E Sussex BN26 5QU. *E:* roderickashtown@gmail.com.

**ASHURST, Deborah Ann;** see Sherwin, D. A.

**ASHURST, (Kenneth William) Stewart**; DL; Chief Executive and Clerk, Essex County Council, 1995–2005; Partner, Odgers Ray & Berndtson, 2006–07; *b* 19 May 1945; *s* of Kenneth Latham Ashurst, OBE and Helen Ferguson Ashurst (*née* Rae); *m* 1984, Catherine Mary Sample; two *s* one *d*. *Educ:* Royal Grammar Sch., Newcastle upon Tyne; King Edward VI Grammar Sch., Lichfield; Exeter Coll., Oxford Univ. (MA); Guildford Coll. of Law; Birmingham Univ. (MSocSc). Trainee solicitor, Leicester and Newcastle upon Tyne CBCs, 1967–68; Assistant Solicitor: Newcastle upon Tyne, 1968–71; Cumberland CC, 1972–73; Asst Co. Clerk, Cumbria CC, 1973–79; Dep. Co. Sec., 1979–81, Co. Solicitor and Dep. Co. Clerk, 1981–85, Suffolk CC; Dep. Chief Exec. and Clerk, Essex CC 1985–94. Clerk to: Essex Police Authy, 1995–2002; Essex Fire Authy, 1998–2004; Essex Lieutenancy, 1995–2004; River Crouch Harbour Authy, 1995–2004; Secretary: Lord Chancellor's Adv. Cttee in Essex, 1995–2004; Stansted Airport Consultative Cttee 1995–2004 (Chm., 2007–); Mem., Essex TEC Bd, 1995–2001. Director: Disability Essex 2005–07; Children's Legal Centre, Essex Univ., 2006–07. Nat. Chm., ACCE, 2003–04 Law Society: Council Mem., 1989–97; Chm., Local Govt Gp, 1986–87. Mem. Council Industrial Soc., 1997–2001. Chairman: Trustees, Aldeburgh Mus., 2008–13; Alde and Ore Assoc., 2010–12. Dir, Year of Opera and Musical Theatre, 1996–97. DL Essex, 2004 FCMI (FIMgt 1982); FRSA 1998. *Recreations:* wine and dining, art, music, loafing. *Address* 3 The Cygnets, Saxmundham Road, Aldeburgh, Suffolk IP15 5PD.

**ASHURST, Stephen John; His Honour Judge Ashurst**; a Circuit Judge, since 2004; 19 April 1957; *s* of John Anthony Ashurst and Doris Ashurst; *m* 1981, Deborah An Sherwin, *qv*; one *s* one *d*. *Educ:* South Hunsley Sch., E Yorks; Univ. of Newcastle upon

Tyne (LLB). Called to the Bar, Inner Temple, 1979; in practice as barrister, Leeds and Middlesbrough, 1979–2004; an Asst Recorder, 1994–98, Recorder, 1998–2004; Resident Judge, York Crown Court, 2007–15. Judicial Mem., N Yorks Probation Bd, 2006–10. Hon. Pres., N Yorks Magistrates' Assoc., 2011–15. Mem. Council, 2010–, Mem., Ethics Cttee, 2011–, Univ. of York. Hon. Recorder, City of York, 2008–15. *Recreations:* music, cycling, walking. *Address:* Teesside Combined Court Centre, Russell Street, Middlesbrough TS1 2AE.

ASHWIN, Mary Christine; *see* Vitoria, M. C.

ASHWORTH, Prof. Alan, PhD; FRS 2008; President, Helen Diller Family Comprehensive Cancer Center, Professor of Medicine, Division of Hematology/Oncology, E. Dixon Heise Distinguished Professor in Oncology, and Senior Vice President for Cancer Services, University of California, San Francisco, since 2015; *b* 26 Aug. 1960; *s* of Arthur and Dorothy Ashworth; *m* 2011, Dr Amanda McGuigan. *Educ:* Thornleigh Salesian Coll., Bolton; Imperial Coll. London (BSc Hons 1981); UCL (PhD 1984). Institute of Cancer Research, University of London: Gp Leader, 1988–2014; Prof. of Molecular Biology, 1997–2014; Chm., Section of Gene Function, 1997–99; Dir, Breakthrough Breast Cancer Res. Centre, 1999–2011; Chief Exec., 2011–14. Mem., EMBO, 1999. FMedSci 2002. *Publications:* contribs to scientific jls. *Recreations:* cinema, theatre, reading, writing. *Address:* Helen Diller Family Comprehensive Cancer Center, University of California, San Francisco, 1450 3rd Street, San Francisco, CA 94158, USA.

ASHWORTH, Prof. Andrew John, CBE 2009; PhD, DCL; FBA 1993; Vinerian Professor of English Law, University of Oxford, 1997–2013, now Emeritus; Fellow of All Souls College, Oxford, 1997–2013, now Emeritus; *b* 11 Oct. 1947; *s* of late Clifford Ashworth and Amy Ashworth (*née* Ogden); *m* 1st, 1971, Gillian Frisby (marr. diss. 2002); two *d*; 2nd, 2006, Veronica Bagnall. *Educ:* London Sch. of Economics (LLB 1968); New Coll., Oxford (BCL 1970; DCL 1993); Manchester Univ. (PhD 1973). Lectr, then Sen. Lectr, in Law, Manchester Univ., 1970–78; Fellow and Tutor in Law, Worcester Coll., Oxford, 1978–88; Edmund-Davies Prof. of Criminal Law and Criminal Justice, KCL, 1988–97. Mem., Sentencing Adv. Panel, 1999–2010 (Chm., 2007–10). Editor, Criminal Law Rev., 1975–99. Hon. QC 1997. Hon. LLD: De Montfort, 1998; LSE, 2014; Hon. DJur Uppsala, 2003. *Publications:* Sentencing and Penal Policy, 1983; Principles of Criminal Law, 1991, 7th edn (with Jeremy Horder) 2013; Sentencing and Criminal Justice, 1992, 6th edn 2015; The Criminal Process, 1994, 4th edn (with Mike Redmayne) 2010; (with Ben Emmerson) Human Rights and Criminal Justice, 2001, 3rd edn 2012; Human Rights, Serious Crime and Criminal Procedure, 2002; Positive Obligations in Criminal Law, 2013; (with Lucia Zedner) Preventive Justice, 2014. *Recreations:* bridge, travel. *Address:* All Souls College, Oxford OX1 4AL.

ASHWORTH, Anne Mary Catherine; Assistant Editor (Property), The Times, since 2006; *b* 13 June 1954; *d* of Peter Ashworth and Joan Ashworth (*née* Kay); *m* 1985, Tom Maddocks; one *s*. *Educ:* Ursuline Convent High Sch., Wimbledon; King's Coll. London (BA Hons French and German). Reporter: Sunday Express, 1982–86; Today, 1986; Daily Mail, 1986–87; Personal Finance Editor: Mail on Sunday, 1987–94; The Times, 1994–2006. Property Columnist of the Year, Property Press Awards, 2014. *Recreations:* art, architecture, cinema. *Address:* The Times, News Building, 1 London Bridge Street, SE1 9GF. *T:* (020) 7782 5083. *E:* anne.ashworth@thetimes.co.uk.

ASHWORTH, Auriol, (Lady Ashworth); *see* Stevens, A.

ASHWORTH, Jennifer Elizabeth; *see* Anderson, J. E.

ASHWORTH, Sir John (Michael), Kt 2008; DSc; Chairman: Barts and the London NHS Trust, 2003–07; Wivenhoe Pub Co. Ltd, since 2016; *b* 27 Nov. 1938; *s* of late Jack Ashworth and late Constance Mary Ousman; *m* 1st, 1963, Ann Knight (*d* 1985); one *s* three *d*; 2nd, 1988, Auriol Stevens, *qv*. *Educ:* West Buckland Sch., N Devon; Exeter Coll. Oxford (MA, DSc; Hon. Fellow, 1983); Leicester Univ. (PhD). FRSB (FIBiol 1974). Dept of Biochemistry, Univ. of Leicester: Res. Demonstr, 1961–63; Lectr, 1963–71; Reader, 1971–73; Prof. of Biology, Univ. of Essex, 1974–79 (on secondment to Cabinet Office, 1976–79); Under-Sec., Cabinet Office, 1979–81 and Chief Scientist, Central Policy Review Staff, 1976–81; Vice-Chancellor, Univ. of Salford, 1981–90; Dir, LSE, 1990–96; Chm., British Liby Bd, 1996–2001. Harkness Fellow of Commonwealth Fund, NY, at Brandeis Univ. and Univ. of Calif, 1965–67. NEDO: Chm., Information Technology EDC, 1983–86; Mem., Electronics EDC, 1983–86. Chairman: Nat. Accreditation Council for Certification Bodies, BSI, 1984–88; NCC, 1983–92. Director: Granada TV, 1987–89; Granada Group, 1990–2002; J. Sainsbury, 1993–97; London First, 1993–98. Non-exec. Dir, Colchester Hosp. Univ. Foundn Trust, 2010–14. Fellow, Inst. of Cancer Res., 2007 (Mem. Council, 2000–07). Pres., Council for Assisting Refugee Academics, 2002–06. Colworth Medal, Biochem. Soc., 1972. *Publications:* Cell Differentiation, 1972; (with J. Dee) The Slime Moulds, 1976; over 100 pubns in prof. jls on biochem., genet., cell biol. and educnl topics. *Recreation:* sailing. *Address:* Garden House, Wivenhoe, Essex CO7 9BD. *Clubs:* Royal Overseas League; Wivenhoe Sailing.

ASHWORTH, Jonathan Michael Graham; MP (Lab Co-op) Leicester South, since May 2011; *b* Salford, 14 Oct. 1978; *m* 2010, Emilie Oldknow; two *d*. *Educ:* Philips High Sch.; Bury Coll.; Durham Univ. (BA Hons Politics and Philosophy). Pol Res. Officer, 2001, Econs and Welfare Policy Officer, 2002–03, Labour Party; Special Advr, HM Treasury, 2003–07; Dep. Political Sec. to Prime Minister, 2007–10; Political Sec. to Acting Leader, Labour Party, 2010; Hd, Labour Party Relns for Rt Hon. Edward Miliband, MP, 2010–11. Shadow Cabinet Office Minister, 2013–15; Shadow Minister without Portfolio, 2015–16; Shadow Sec. of State for Health, then Health and Social Care, 2016–. *Address:* House of Commons, SW1A 0AA.

ASHWORTH, Lance Dominic Piers; QC 2006; a Recorder of the Crown Court, since 2005, and of the County Court, since 2007; a Deputy High Court Judge, since 2016; *b* 13 June 1964; *s* of Piers Ashworth, QC and of Iolene Jennifer Scholes (*née* Foxley); *m* 1989, Sally Elizabeth Downs (marr. diss. 2015); two *s* one *d*. *Educ:* Oundle Sch.; Pembroke Coll., Cambridge (BA 1986, MA 1990). Called to the Bar, Middle Temple, 1987; specialises in commercial and insolvency law. Chm., Midlands Legal Support Trust, 2008–11. Founder Trustee, Medical Res. Foundn, Coventry and Warwicks, 2004–; Trustee, Access to Justice Foundn, 2014–. Lord's Taverners: Mem., W Midlands Cttee, 2010–12; Mem., Middlesex Cttee, 2012–16 (Chm., 2017–). *Publications:* (contrib.) Mithani: Directors' Disqualification, nos 8 to 27, 1995–2007. *Recreations:* tennis, golf, cricket. *Address:* Serle Court, 6 New Square, Lincoln's Inn, WC2A 3QS. *T:* (020) 7242 6105. *E:* lashworth@serlecourt.co.uk.

ASHWORTH, Patrick; HM Diplomatic Service, retired; High Commissioner to Belize, 2009–13 (Acting High Commissioner, 2008–09); *b* Maryport, Cumberland, 2 Nov. 1950; *s* of late Tom Ashworth and of Mary Josephine Ashworth (*née* Mulgrew); *m* 1973, Pauline Mary Harrison; one *s* one *d*. *Educ:* St Patrick's RC Sch., Maryport; Cockermouth Grammar Sch. Joined HM Diplomatic Service, 1968; Dar es Salaam, 1971–75; Castries, 1975–78; Attaché, Moscow, 1978–80; Security Dept, FCO, 1980–81; Diplomatic Service Trade Union Side Sec., FCO, 1981–83; Consular Officer, Valletta, 1983–87; Vice Consul Commercial, Sao Paulo, 1987–92; Second Sec., UN Conf. on Envmt and Develt Co-ordinator, Brasilia/Rio de Janeiro, 1992; Hd, Council of Europe Section, W Eur. Dept, FCO, 1992–95; Press Officer, The Hague, 1995–2000; Dep. Consul Gen., Sao Paulo and Dep. Dir of Trade for Brazil, 2000–05; Hd of Liaison, Whitehall Liaison Dept, FCO, 2005–08. *Recreations:* walking, running, sport, music, reading, photography. *Club:* Civil Service.

ASHWORTH, Peter Anthony Frank; Director, Leeds Permanent Building Society, 1971–92 (President, 1978); *b* 24 Aug. 1935; *s* of Peter Ormerod and Dorothy Catherine Ashworth; *m* 1964, Elisabeth Crompton; one *s* one *d*. *Educ:* Leeds Grammar School. Articled to Hollis & Webb, Chartered Surveyors, Leeds (later Weatherall, Green & Smith, now Sanderson Weatherall), 1953–56; Partner, 1961–80. *Recreations:* golf, gardening. *Address:* 4 Bridge Paddock, Collingham, Wetherby LS22 5BN. *T:* (01937) 572953. *Club:* Alwoodley Golf (Leeds).

ASHWORTH, Richard James; Member for South East Region, European Parliament, 2004–19 (C, 2004–17; Ind, 2017–19); *b* 17 Sept. 1947; *s* of late Maurice Ashworth and Eileen Ashworth; *m* 1972, Sally Poulton; three *d*. *Educ:* King's Sch., Canterbury; Seale-Hayne Coll., Devon (DipAgr; Dip. in Farm Mgt; NDA). Farmer, 1970–2001. Chairman: United Milk Plc, 1996–2002; NFU Corporate, 2000–02. Contested (C) Devon North, 1997. European Parliament: Member: Budget Cttee, 2005–19; Climate Change Cttee, 2005–09; Agriculture Cttee, 2009–19; Chief Whip, 2006–09; Dep. Leader, 2009–11, Leader, 2012, British Cons. MEPs. Contested (Change UK) SE, EP, 2019. *Recreations:* sport, music, theatre, country pursuits. *Address:* Woodside, Brickhouse Lane, Newchapel, Lingfield, Surrey RH7 6HY. *Club:* Farmers.

ASHWORTH, Thomas Leslie, MSc; Head Master, Ermysted's Grammar School, Skipton, 1998–2008; *b* 17 Sept. 1949; *s* of late William Leslie Ashworth and Katharine Elizabeth Ashworth; *m* 1979, Roslyn Williams; two *d*. *Educ:* Birkenhead Inst.; Queen Mary Coll. London (BSc Hons Maths 1971); Univ. of Liverpool (MSc Maths 1973). Maths teacher, Birkenhead Sch., 1973–83; Sen. Teacher and Hd of Maths, Ripon GS, 1983–88; Dep. Head Master, Reading Sch., 1988–98. Trustee, Skipton Mechanics Inst., 2005– (Vice Chm., 2012–15; Chm., 2015–18). *Recreations:* Rugby (RFU panel referee, 1988–2000); Member: Yorks Referees' Soc., 1983–88, 2008–15; London Soc. of Rugby Referees, 1989–99), golf, Rotary (Skipton Craven, 2009–, Treas., 2011–), philately, ICT, travel. *Address:* 22 Cross Bank, Skipton, N Yorks BD23 6AH. *E:* tla179@aol.com. *Clubs:* Birkenhead Park Football; Skipton Golf; Skipton Craven Rotary.

ASHWORTH, Tracy; *see* Borman, T.

ASIF, (Mohammed) Jalil (Akhter); QC 2010; a Recorder, 2004–16; *b* London, 25 March 1965; *s* of Mohammed Asif and Carola Mary Asif (*née* Paine); *m* 1994, (Katharine) Clare Harding Price; one *s* two *d*. *Educ:* Twyford High Sch., London; St Paul's Sch., London; Peterhouse, Cambridge (BA 1987). Called to the Bar, Lincoln's Inn, 1988, Bencher, 2011; in practice as a barrister, 1988–. Mem. Bd and Trustee, Royal and Derngate Theatres, Northampton, 2010–16. *Publications:* (ed jtly) Professional Negligence Liability Reports, 1996–; contributing editor: Jackson & Powell's Professional Liability Precedents, 2000; APIL Clinical Negligence, 2008, 2nd edn 2014; The Law and Regulation of Medicines, 2008. *Recreations:* scuba diving, ski-ing, cinema, music. *Address:* Kobre & Kim LLP, Tower 42, 25 Old Broad Street, EC2N 1HQ. *T:* (020) 3301 5700, *Fax:* (020) 3301 5720. *E:* jalil.asif@kobrekim.com.

ASIM, Dr Mohamed; Minister of Foreign Affairs, Maldives, since 2016; *b* 1960; *m* Mariyam Ali Manik; one *s* one *d*. *Educ:* American Univ. of Beirut (BA Public Admin); California State Univ., Sacramento (MA Internat. Relns); Australian National Univ. (PhD Pol Sci. and Internat. Relns 1999). Government of the Maldives: admin. officer, Min. of Educn, 1982–83; President's Office, 1983–96; Dir Gen., Employment Affairs, 1996–99; Dir Gen., Public Service Div., President's Office, 1999–2004; High Comr, Sri Lanka and concurrently to Bangladesh and Pakistan, 2004–07; High Comr, UK, 2007–08; Addnl Sec., Min. of Foreign Affairs, Maldives, 2009; Minister/Chargé d'affaires, Belgium and Maldives Mission to EU, 2013–14; High Comr to Bangladesh, 2015–16. *Publications:* contrib. articles on public admin and public sector reform in the Maldives to Labour and Mgt in Develt Jl and Public Admin and Develt Jl.

ASKARI, Hasan; Chairman, Aberdeen New India (formerly New India) Investment Trust plc, since 2014 (Director, since 2012); *s* of late Syed Mohammad and Kishwar Jahan Askari; *m* 1976, Nasreen Hassam Ismail; one *s* one *d*. *Educ:* University Coll., Oxford (MA 1975). S. G. Warburg & Co. Ltd, London, 1975–80; Chase Manhattan Bank: Dir, Hong Kong, 1981–85; Man. Dir, Tokyo, 1985–89; Man. Dir, Barclays de Zoete Wedd Ltd, Tokyo, 1989–92, London, 1992–99; Dir, 1999–2003, Chief Exec., 2003–07, Old Mutual Financial Services plc. Chm., Aqua Resources Fund Ltd, 2008–18; Sen. Advr, Kotak Mahindra Bank Gp, India, 2008–; non-exec. Dir, Sun Life of Canada (UK) Ltd, 2011–17. Dir, Lloyd George Indian Ocean Fund, Hong Kong, 2017–. Dir, Gt Ormond St Hosp. for Children NHS Trust, 1999–2007. Chm., Turquoise Mountain Foundn, 2007–08. Trustee, BM, 1999–2007. Mem., RSAA, 1979; FRAS 1979. *Publications:* The Flowering Desert: textiles from Sindh, 2019. *Recreations:* cricket, South Asian art, walking (preferably in solitude). *Address:* 22 Ovington Square, SW3 1LR. *E:* hasan.askari@btinternet.com. *Clubs:* Oriental, Walbrook; Vincent's (Oxford); American (Tokyo).

ASKE, Sir Robert John Bingham, 3rd Bt *cr* 1922; *b* 12 March 1941; *s* of late Robert Edward Aske (*yr s* of Sir Robert Aske, 1st Bt) and Joan, *o d* of late Capt. Eric Bingham Ackerley; *S* uncle, 2001. *Educ:* King's Sch., Canterbury. *Heir:* none. *Address:* 5 Bicton Place, Heavitree, Exeter EX1 2PF.

ASKEW, Sir Bryan, Kt 1989; Personnel Director, Samuel Smith Old Brewery (Tadcaster), 1982–95; Chairman, Yorkshire Regional Health Authority, 1983–94; *b* 18 Aug. 1930; *s* of John Pinkney Askew and Matilda Askew; *m* 1955, Millicent Rose Holder (*d* 2015); two *d*. *Educ:* Wellfield Grammar Sch., Wingate, Co. Durham; Fitzwilliam Coll., Cambridge (MA Hons History). ICI Ltd, 1952–59; Consett Iron Co. Ltd (later part of British Steel Corporation), 1959–71; own consultancy, 1971–74; Samuel Smith Old Brewery (Tadcaster), 1974–95. Chm., Advanced Digital Telecom Ltd, 1997–99. Member, Consett UDC, 1967–71; contested (C) General Elections: Penistone, 1964 and 1966; York, 1970. Mem., Duke of Edinburgh's Third Commonwealth Study Conf., Australia, 1968. Mem., Working Gp on Young People and Alcohol, Home Office Standing Conf. on Crime Prevention, 1987. Chm., British Polio Fellowship, 2004–08. Mem. Court, 1985–2006, Mem. Council, 1988–2000, Univ. of Leeds. Chm., Burgage Holders of Alnmouth Common, 2003–13. FRSA 1986 (Chm., Yorks Region, 1997–99); FRSocMed 1988. Hon. LLD Hull, 1992. *Recreations:* listening to music, reading, politics.

ASKEW, Christopher Richard Thompson; Chief Executive, Diabetes UK, since 2015; *b* Amersham, 1965; *s* of late Canon Richard George Askew and of Margaret Askew; *m* 2002, Liza Juliet; one *s* one *d*. *Educ:* Monkton Combe Sch., Bath; Brasenose Coll., Oxford (BA Hons Classics). Dir, GMT Shipping and Chartering Ltd, 1994–97; Asst Dir, External Affairs, NCH, 2001–03; Dir of Fundraising, Crisis, 2003–06; Dir of Fundraising, 2006–10, Chief Exec., 2010–15, Breakthrough Breast Cancer. *Recreations:* cycling, sailing, family. *Address:* Diabetes UK, Wells Lawrence House, 126 Back Church Lane, E1 1FH.

**ASKEW, Clinton Graham;** Founder and Director, Citywide Financial Partners Ltd, since 2004; *b* Cardiff, 31 May 1958; *s* of Douglas Askew and Muriel Askew; *m* 1991, Dr Leslie Becker; two *s* two *d*. *Educ:* Univ. of West of England (BA Hons Business Studies). Mem., Smaller Business Practitioner Panel, FCA (formerly FSA), 2009–17 (Chm., 2015–17). Mem., RYA. *Recreations:* Scout group leader, rock climbing, sailing, cycling. *Address:* Citywide Financial Partners Ltd, Riverbridge House, Guildford Road, Leatherhead, Surrey KT22 9AD. *T:* (01372) 365950. *E:* clinton.askew@citywidefinancial.co.uk.

**ASLET, Clive William;** Editor-at-Large, Country Life, 2006–15 (Deputy Editor, 1989–92; Editor, 1993–2006); Editor in Chief, Country Life Books, 1994–2006; Co-founder and Board Member, Remember WW1, since 2013; *b* 15 Feb. 1955; *s* of Kenneth and Monica Aslet; *m* 1980, Naomi Roth; three *s*. *Educ:* King's College Sch., Wimbledon; Peterhouse, Cambridge. Joined Country Life, 1977, Architectural Editor, 1984–88; Ed. in Chief, New Eden, 1999–2000. Dir, Country and Leisure Media Ltd, 1999–2006. Founding Hon. Sec., Thirties Soc., 1979–87. Trustee: Plantlife International, 2015–; Internat. Network for Traditional Building, Architecture and Urbanism, 2016–; Lutyens Trust, 2018–. Gov., St Peter's Eaton Sq. C of E Sch., 1999–2006. FRSA. *Publications:* The Last Country Houses, 1982; (with Alan Powers) The National Trust Book of the English House, 1985; Quinlan Terry, the Revival of Architecture, 1986; The American Country House, 1990; Countryblast, 1991; (introd.) The American Houses of Robert A. M. Stern, 1991; Anyone for England? a search for British identity, 1997; (with Derry Moore) The House of Lords, 1998; The Story of Greenwich, 1999; Greenwich Millennium, 2000; A Horse in the Country: a diary of a year in the heart of England, 2001; The Landmarks of Britain, 2005; The English House: the story of a nation at home, 2008; Villages of Britain, 2010; The Edwardian Country House, 2012; War Memorial: the story of one village's sacrifice from 1914 to 2003, 2012; Exuberant Catalogue of Dreams, 2013; The Birdcage, 2014; The Age of Empire, 2015. *Recreations:* pleasures of the table, wool gathering. *Address:* c/o Adrian Sington, Kruger Cowne Rights, Unit 7, 15 Lots Road, Canary Wharf, SW10 0QJ. *T:* (020) 7352 2277. *W:* www.cliveaslet.com. *Club:* Garrick.

**ASLETT, Anne;** Global Chief Executive Officer, Elton John Aids Foundation, since 2018; *b* Sydney, Australia, 5 Aug. 1964; *d* of Derek Anthony Ewen Maclaren and Pamela Anne Maclaren; *m* 1993, William David Aslett; one *s* one *d*. *Educ:* Francis Holland Girls Sch., London; OISE, Paris (Dip. Business French 1993). Edit asst, House & Garden, 1983–85; prodn asst, Strategy Prodns, 1985–86; Prodn Manager, Park Prodns Ltd, 1986–88; photographic assignment, Middle East, 1988; Publications Manager, Profile Systems Ltd, News Media Information, 1989–92; freelance journalist and documentary/film researcher (pt-time), BBC and Channel 4, 1994–97; Elton John Aids Foundation: Prog. Officer (pt-time), 1997–2001; Internat. Develt Dir, 2001–09; Exec. Dir, 2009–18. Chm., Eur. Funders Gp, 2010–. Mem., Internat. Grants Cttee, Comic Relief, 2004–. *Recreations:* reading, family, badminton, art, travel. *Address:* Elton John Aids Foundation, 1 Blythe Road, W14 0HG. *T:* (020) 7603 9996, *Fax:* (020) 7348 4848. *E:* anne.aslett@ejaf.com.

**ASPEL, Michael Terence,** OBE 1993; broadcaster and writer; *b* 12 Jan. 1933; *s* of late Edward and of Violet Aspel; *m* 1st, 1957, Dian; one *s* (and one *s* decd); 2nd, 1962, Ann; twin *s* and *d*; 3rd, 1977, Elizabeth; two *s*. *Educ:* Emanuel School. Tea boy, publishers, 1949–51. Nat. Service, KRRC and Para Regt, TA, 1951–53. Radio actor, 1954–57; television announcer, 1957–60, newsreader, 1960–68; freelance broadcaster, radio and TV, 1968–; presenter: Aspel and Company, 1984–93; This is Your Life, 1988–2003; Antiques Roadshow, 2000–08; A Hundred Years of Us, 2011; occasional stage appearances. Vice-Pres., BLISS (Baby Life Support Systems), 1981–; Patron: Plan International, 1986–; Evacuees Reunion Assoc., 2005–. Member: Equity, 1955–; Lord's Taverners; RYA. Hon. Fellow, Cardiff Univ., 2002. Mem., RTS Hall of Fame, 1996. Hon. Freeman, Elmbridge, 2008. *Publications:* Polly Wants a Zebra (autobiog.), 1974; Hang On! (for children), 1982; (with Richard Hearsey) Child's Play, 1985; regular contribs to magazines. *Recreations:* water sports, theatre, cinema, eating, travel. *Address:* c/o CSA, 3rd Floor, Joel House, 17–21 Garrick Street, WC2E 9EL.

**ASPINALL, Beverley Ann;** Managing Director, Bond Street Development Group, New West End Company, 2013–15; Interim Retail Director, Snape Maltings, 2015; *b* Dunstable, 4 Dec. 1958; *d* of late T. Domas and of Mrs R. J. Browning; *m* 2002, David Aspinall; one *s* one *d*. *Educ:* Redbourne Community Coll., Ampthill; Univ. of York (BA Hons). Managing Director: John Lewis, Peterborough, 1996–98; Peter Jones, 1998–2005; Fortnum & Mason plc, 2005–12. Dir, Aspinalls Gp, 2012–; non exec. Dir, W. & G. Foyle Ltd, 2014–. Dir, V&A Enterprises, 2007–. Dir, Develt Bd, Univ. of York, 2007–. Gov., King's Sch., Ely, 2008–11. *Recreations:* classical music, gardening.

**ASPINALL, John Michael,** CEng, FICE; Director of Major Projects, Ministry of Justice, 2012–13; Member, International Tennis Federation, playing on Seniors Tennis Tour, since 2013; *b* Leeds, 3 July 1959; *s* of Ronald and Margaret Aspinall; *m* 1983, Jill Hutton; one *s* two *d*. *Educ:* Allerton Grange High Sch., Leeds; Bradford Univ. (BEng Hons Civil and Structural Engrg). CEng 1986; MCIHT (MIHT 1991); FICE 2008. Grad. Civil Engr, S Yorks CC, 1982–86; Sen. Section Engr, W Yorks Highways Engrg and Tech. Services, 1986–91; Associate, Smithers Purslow, Cons. Engrs, 1991–93; Project Manager, Highways Agency, 1993–98; Policy Advr, World Bank, Washington, 1998–99 (on secondment); Gp Leader, Highways Agency, 1999–2002; Divl Manager, Rail Directorate, DfT, 2002–04; Regl Dir for SE, Highways Agency, 2004–08; Ministry of Justice: Dir of Estate Capacity, Nat. Offender Mgt Service, 2008–09; Strategic Estates Dir, 2009–11; Dir, Transforming Justice Portfolio and Estates, 2011–12. *Recreations:* cricket, reading, pottering about. *Address:* 92 Kennylands Road, Sonning Common, Oxon RG4 9JX. *T:* (0118) 9242567. *E:* aspinall562@btinternet.com.

**ASPINALL, Margaret Mary,** CBE 2015; Chairman, Hillsborough Family Support Group, since 1999; *b* Liverpool, 25 Sept. 1946; *d* of James and Margaret McCormick; *m* 1970, James Aspinall; two *s* two *d* (and one *s* decd). *Educ:* St Augustine's Secondary Modern RC High Sch. Voluntary work for Hillsborough Family Support Gp, 1989– (Mem. Cttee; Vice Chm.). Voluntary work for Liverpool Capital of Culture, 2008. *Address:* Hillsborough Family Support Group, Anfield Sports and Community Centre, Lower Breck Road, Anfield, Liverpool L6 0AG. *T:* (0151) 263 8138. *E:* info@HFSG.co.uk.

**ASPINALL, Most Rev. Phillip John;** *see* Brisbane, Archbishop of.

**ASPINALL, Wilfred;** European Union policy and strategy adviser; Director, Aspinall & Associates, since 1988; Hon. Chairman (formerly Director) and Strategy Adviser, Forum in the European Parliament for Construction and Energy Users (formerly European Parliament Forum for Construction, then Forum in the European Parliament for Construction, Energy, Finance and Sustainability, then Forum in the European Parliament for Construction and Sustainable Energy), since 2002; *b* 14 Sept. 1942; *s* of late Charles Aspinall and Elizabeth Aspinall; *m* 1973, Judith Mary (*d* 2005), *d* of late Leonard James Pimlott and Kathleen Mary Pimlott; one *d*. *Educ:* Poynton Secondary Modern; Stockport Coll. for Further Educn. Staff, National Provincial Bank Ltd, 1960–69; Asst Gen. Sec., National Westminster Staff Assoc., 1969–75; Dep. Sec. (part-time), Council of Bank Staff Assocs, 1969–75; Mem., Banking Staff Council, 1970–77; Gen. Sec., Confedn of Bank Staff Assocs, 1975–79; Exec. Dir, Fedn of Managerial, Professional and Gen. Assocs, 1978–94. Advr, Eversheds Financial Services Forum, 1998–2009. Dir, Doddingselles Manor Develt, 2014–. Mem., European Economic and Social Cttee, 1986–98. Dir, The Strategy Centre, Brussels, 2004–14. Vice-Pres., Confédération Internat. des Cadres, 1979–94. Member: N Herts DHA, 1981–86; NW Thames RHA, 1986–88; Hammersmith and Queen Charlotte's SHA, 1981–90; Professions Allied to Medicine, Whitley Management Negotiating Cttee, 1983–87. *Recreations:* motoring, travel - particularly to places of historical interest, social affairs and political history, pressing for reform of the planning process, submissions on Brexit to Ministers and Select Committees in both Houses of Parliament from 2016, available at www.eustrategy.wordpress.com. *Address:* Doddingselles Manor, Shillington Road, Pirton, Hitchin, Herts SG5 3QJ. *T:* 07872 953922. *E:* wa@wilfredaspinall.eu, wilfredaspinall@me.com. *W:* www.wilfredaspinallblog.wordpress.com.

**ASPLIN, Rt Hon. Dame Sarah (Jane), (Rt Hon. Dame Sarah Sherwin),** DBE 2012; PC 2017; **Rt Hon. Lady Justice Asplin;** a Lady Justice of Appeal, since 2017; *b* 16 Sept. 1959; *d* of Raymond Asplin and Florence Grace Asplin; *m* 1986, Nicholas Adrian Sherwin; two *d*. *Educ:* Southampton Coll. for Girls; Fitzwilliam Coll., Cambridge (MA; Hon. Fellow, 2013); St Edmund Hall, Oxford (BCL; Hon. Fellow). Called to the Bar, Gray's Inn, 1984, Bencher, 2006; in practice as barrister, specialising in Chancery and pensions law and life assurance, 1985–2012; QC 2002; Dep. High Court Judge, Chancery Div. Head of Chambers, 3 Stone Bldgs, 2009–12; a Judge of the High Court of Justice, Chancery Div., 2012–17. Member: Chancery Bar Assoc., 1985–2012; Assoc. Pension Lawyers, 1990–2012 (Mem., Litigation Sub-Cttee, 2000–09; Hon. Mem., 2014); Fees Collection Cttee and Implementation Cttee, Bar Council. Vice-Pres., UK Assoc. of Women Judges, 2017–. *Recreations:* playing the violin, cooking. *Address:* Royal Courts of Justice, Strand, WC2A 2LL.

**ASPRAY, Rodney George,** FCA; Managing Director, Worthbase Ltd, 1990–2000; *b* 1934. Secretary, Manchester and Salford Cooperative Society, 1965–69; Chief Exec. Officer, Norwest Co-op. Soc., 1969–91. Director: Co-operative Bank, 1980–89 (Chm. 1986–89); Co-operative Wholesale Soc. Ltd, 1980–89; Mersey Docks & Harbour Co., 1987–94; Piccadilly Radio Plc, 1989–90. Mem., Monopolies and Mergers Commn, 1975–81. FCA 1960.

**ASQUITH,** family name of **Earl of Oxford and Asquith**.

**ASQUITH, Viscount; Mark Julian Asquith;** *b* 13 May 1979; *o s* and heir of Earl of Oxford and Asquith, *qv*; *m* 2008, Helen, *d* of Christopher Norman Russell Prentice, *qv*; one *s*. *Educ:* Ampleforth; St Andrews Univ. (MA 2001). Investment manager, Somerset Capital Management LLP.

**ASQUITH, Hon. Sir Dominic (Anthony Gerard),** KCMG 2012 (CMG 2004); HM Diplomatic Service; High Commissioner to India, since 2016; *b* 7 Feb. 1957; *y s* of 2nd Earl of Oxford and Asquith, KCMG; *m* 1988, Louise Cotton; two *s* two *d*. Joined HM Diplomatic Service, 1983; FCO, 1983–86; Second Sec., Damascus, 1986–87; First Secretary: Muscat, 1987–89; FCO, 1989–92; Washington, 1992–96; Minister and Dep. Hd of Mission, Argentina, 1997–2001; Dep. Hd of Mission and Consul Gen., Saudi Arabia, 2001–04; Dep. Special Rep. and Dep. Head of Mission, Iraq, 2004; Dir, Iraq Directorate, FCO, 2004–06; Ambassador to: Iraq, 2006–07; Egypt, 2007–11; Libya, 2011–12. Sen. Advr, Dentons US LLP, 2013–16; Senior Director: Macro Advisory Partners, 2014–16; Strategic Advr, Gp DF Internat., 2014–16. Chm., Libyan British Business Council, 2014–16. *Address:* 22 Cyril Mansions, Prince of Wales Drive, SW11 4HP.

*See also Earl of Oxford and Asquith.*

**ASSAMBA, Aloun N.;** *see* Ndombet-Assamba, A.

**ASSHETON,** family name of **Baron Clitheroe**.

**ASSIM, Donna-Maria;** *see* Cullen, D.-M.

**ASSIRATI, Robert,** CBE 2012; Major Projects Director, Office of Government Commerce, HM Treasury, 2007–11 (Executive Director, 2001–07); Vice President, BCS - The Chartered Institute for IT, 2008–13; *b* 27 May 1947; *s* of late Frederick Louis Assirati and Mary Violet Assirati (*née* Dillon); *m* 1968, Lynne Elizabeth Yeend; one *s* one *d*. *Educ:* Stationers' Company's Sch., London; Hertford Coll., Oxford (MA PPE). MCIPS 1997; CITP 2007. Nat. Coal Bd, 1968; Data Processing Manager, Eli Lilly & Co., 1972; Management Services Manager, British Carpets, 1976; Company Dir, C Squared, 1984; Commercial Dir, Inland Revenue IT Office, 1986; Chief Exec., CCTA, 1996–2001. Freeman, City of London; Liveryman, Co. of Information Technologists, 2003. FBCS. Hon. FAPM 1997. *Recreations:* bridge, tennis, travel, theatre. *Address:* The Alders, Capel, Tonbridge, Kent TN12 6SU. *T:* (01892) 836609.

**ASTAIRE, Jarvis Joseph,** OBE 2004; Chairman: GRA (formerly Greyhound Racing Association), 1993–2005; First Artist Corporation plc, 2006–09; *b* 6 Oct. 1923; *s* of late Max and Esther Astaire; *m* 1st, 1948, Phyllis Oppenheim (*d* 1974); one *s* one *d*; 2nd, 1981, Nadine Hyman (*d* 1986). *Educ:* Kilburn Grammar Sch., London. Dir, Lewis & Burrows Ltd, 1957–60; Managing Director: Mappin & Webb Ltd, 1958–60; Hurst Park Syndicate, 1962–71; Dep. Chm., Wembley Stadium, 1984–99; Director: Perthpoint Investments Ltd, 1959–70; Associated Suburban Properties Ltd, 1963–81; Anglo-Continental Investment & Finance Co. Ltd, 1964–75; William Hill Org., 1971–82; First Artists Prodns Inc. (USA), 1976–79; Wembley PLC (formerly GRA Gp), 1987–99; Revlon Group Ltd, 1991–98. Mem. Bd, British Greyhound Racing, 1991–2004. Introduced into UK showing of sporting events on large screen in cinemas, 1964. Pres., Royal Free Hosp. and Med. Sch Appeal Trust, 1991–97 (Chm., 1974); Hon. Treas., 1976–, and Vice Pres., 1982–, Fedn of London Youth Clubs (formerly London Fedn of Boys' Clubs); Chm., Police Dependants Trust Appeal, 1999–; Trustee: Nightingale House Home for Aged Jews, 1984–; Bowles Outdoor Centre, 1985–; Royal Free Cancer Res. Trust, 2001–. Chm., Associated City Properties, 1981–2001. Chief Barker (Pres.), Variety Club of GB, 1983; Pres., Variety Clubs Internat. (Worldwide), 1991–93. Mem. Adv. Council, LSO, 1996–2004. Freeman City of London, 1983. *Recreations:* watching cricket and football. *Club:* MCC.

**ASTASIO, Sarah Jane;** *see* Stennett, S. J.

**ASTBURY, Nicholas John,** FRCS, FRCOphth, FRCP; Clinical Associate Professor (part-time), International Centre for Eye Health, London School of Hygiene and Tropical Medicine, since 2014 (Consultant Adviser, 2006–14); *b* 21 Feb. 1949; *s* of late Dr John Schonberg Astbury and Dr Noel Hope Astbury (*née* Gunn); *m* 1970, Susan Patricia Whall two *s* two *d*. *Educ:* Rugby Sch.; Guy's Hosp. Med. Sch. (MB BS 1972). LRCP 1972 MRCS 1972, FRCS 1977; DO 1974; FRCOphth 1989; FRCP 2005. Sen. Registrar, KCH and Moorfields Eye Hosp., 1981–83; Consultant Ophthalmic Surgeon (part-time), W Norwich Hosp., later Norfolk and Norwich Univ. Hosp. NHS Trust, 1983–2013. Vice Chm., Impact Foundn, 2004–; Chairman: Duke-Elder Foundn, 2004–; VISION 2020 UK 2008–14; Regional Co-Chm. for Europe, Internat. Agency for the Prevention of Blindness 2009–. Med. Advr, St John of Jerusalem Eye Hosp., 2009–15; Lead, Clinical Fellowship Prog., Queen Elizabeth Diamond Jubilee Trust, 2014–19. Pres., Royal Coll. of Ophthalmologists, 2003–06. Hon. FCOptom 2014. CStJ 2014. *Recreations:* walking cycling, sailing, horology, photography, drawing and painting, making automata, pottery. *Address:* Rectory Farmhouse, The Street, Shotesham, Norwich NR15 1YL. *T:* (01508) 550377. *E:* njastbury@gmail.com.

**ASTBURY, Nicholas Paul;** HM Diplomatic Service; Deputy High Commissioner, Jamaica and the Bahamas, since 2016; *b* 13 Aug. 1971; *s* of Nigel Astbury and Yvonne Susan Astbury (*née* Harburn). *Educ:* Hills Rd Sixth Form Coll., Cambridge; University Coll. London (BA Internat. Historical Studies; MA Legal and Political Theory); Open Univ. (MBA). Entered FCO, 1994; Second Secretary: Colombo, 1995–99; FCO, 1999–2001; Private Sec. to Parly Under-Sec. of State, 2001–02; Deputy Head: UKvisas, 2002–04; Drugs Team, Kabul, 2005; Ambassador to Eritrea, 2006–08; Hd of Sudan Unit, FCO, 2009–11; Dep. Consul Gen. and Dep. Hd of Mission, NY, 2012–16. FRSA 2014. Fellow, British American Project, 2015. *Recreations:* photography, diving, numismatics, beer. *Address:* c/o Foreign and Commonwealth Office, King Charles Street, SW1A 2AH. *Club:* Bentham Boat.

**ASTHANA, Anushka;** Joint Political Editor, since 2016, and presenter, Today in Focus podcast, since 2018, The Guardian; *b* Scunthorpe, 31 March 1980; *d* of Jagdish Asthana and Aruna Asthana; *m* 2009, Toby Jones; two *s*. *Educ:* Manchester High Sch. for Girls; Christ's Coll., Cambridge (BA Econs); City Univ. (Post Grad. Journalism). Gen. reporter, Educn Corresp., Dep. News Ed., Policy Ed., The Observer, 2003–10; Chief Political Corresp. and columnist, The Times, 2010–12; Sen. Political Corresp., Sky News, 2012–15. Laurence Stern Fellow, Washington Post, 2006. *Address:* The Guardian, Kings Place, 90 York Way, N1 9GU.

**ASTILL, Prof. Grenville George,** PhD; FSA; Professor of Archaeology, University of Reading, 1999, now Emeritus; *b* Coventry, 15 June 1950; *s* of George and Hazel Astill. *Educ:* Warwick Sch., Warwick; Univ. of Birmingham (BA Hons Hist.; PhD 1978). FSA 1987. Tutorial Fellow, Sch. of Hist., Univ. of Birmingham, 1974–75; Dir, Berks Archaeol Unit, 1975–78; University of Reading: Lectr in Eur. Medieval Archaeol., 1978–95; British Acad. Reader, 1990–92; Reader in Archaeol., 1995–99. *Publications:* Historic Towns in Berkshire, 1978; (ed with A. Grant) The Countryside of Medieval England, 1988; A Medieval Industrial Complex and its Landscape: the metalworking watermills and workshops of Bordesley Abbey, 1993; (with W. Davies) The East Brittany Survey: fieldwork and field data, 1994; (with W. Davies) A Breton Landscape, 1997; (ed with J. Langdon) Medieval Farming and Technology: the impact of agricultural change in Northwest Europe, 1997; (with W. Davies) Un Paysage Breton, 2001; over 70 chapters and articles on Eur. and British urbanisation, rural soc., medieval industry and technol change, medieval religion, particularly monasticism. *Recreations:* early and contemporary music, vegetable gardening, cooking, walking to find monuments. *Address:* c/o Department of Archaeology, University of Reading, Whiteknights, PO Box 218, Reading RG6 6AA. *T:* (0118) 378 7363. *E:* g.g.astill@reading.ac.uk.

**ASTILL, Hon. Sir Michael (John),** Kt 1996; a Judge of the High Court of Justice, Queen's Bench Division, 1996–2004; *b* 31 Jan. 1938; *s* of Cyril Norman Astill and Winifred Astill; *m* 1968, Jean Elizabeth, *d* of Dr J. C. H. Mackenzie; three *s* one *d*. *Educ:* Blackfriars School, Laxton, Northants. Admitted solicitor, 1962; called to the Bar, Middle Temple, 1972, Bencher, 1996; a Recorder, 1980–84; a Circuit Judge, 1984–96; a Pres., Mental Health Tribunals, 1986–96; Presiding Judge, Midland and Oxford Circuit, 1999–2002. Mem., Judicial Studies Bd, 1995–99 (Chm.), Magisterial Cttee, 1995–99). *Recreations:* music, reading, sport. *Address:* c/o Royal Courts of Justice, Strand, WC2A 2LL.

**ASTIN, Ven. Moira Anne Elizabeth;** Archdeacon of Reigate, since 2016; *b* Egham, 18 Feb. 1965; *d* of Roy Williams and Winifred Williams; *m* 1986, Timothy Astin; one *s*. *Educ:* Clare Coll., Cambridge (BA Natural Scis 1986; MA 1990); Wycliffe Hall, Oxford. Ordained deacon, 1995, priest, 1996; Asst Curate, St Nicolas, Newbury, 1995–99; Team Vicar, Thatcham, 1999–2005; Vicar, St James, Woodley, 2005–11; Vicar, Frodingham and New Brumby, and Area Dean, N Lincolnshire, 2011–16. *Recreations:* watching puffins, painting in acrylics, researching England 400–600 AD. *Address:* The Vicarage, 1 The Avenue, Tadworth, Surrey KT20 5AS. *E:* moira.astin@southwark.anglican.org.

**ASTLEY,** family name of **Baron Hastings**.

**ASTLEY, Neil Philip;** Editor and Managing Director, Bloodaxe Books Ltd, since 1978; *b* 12 May 1953; *s* of Philip Thomas Astley and late Margaret Ivy Astley (*née* Solman). *Educ:* Price's Sch., Fareham; Alliance Française, Paris; Univ. of Newcastle upon Tyne (BA 1st Cl. Hons). Journalist, England and Australia, 1972–74. Hon. FRSL 2018. Hon. DLitt Newcastle upon Tyne, 1996. Eric Gregory Award, Soc. of Authors, 1982. *Publications:* (ed) Ten North-East Poets, 1980; The Speechless Act, 1984; (ed) Bossy Parrot, 1987; Darwin Survivor (Recommendation, Poetry Book Soc.), 1988; (ed) Poetry with an Edge, 1988, 2nd edn 1993; (ed) Tony Harrison (critical anthology), 1991; Biting My Tongue, 1995; (ed) New Blood, 1999; The End of My Tether (novel), 2002; (ed) Staying Alive: real poems for unreal times, 2002; (ed) Pleased to See Me, 2002; (ed) Do Not Go Gentle, 2003; (ed) Being Alive: the sequel to Staying Alive, 2004; The Sheep Who Changed the World (novel), 2005; (ed) Passionfood: 100 love poems, 2005; (ed) Bloodaxe Poetry Introductions: vol. 1, 2006, vol. 2, 2006, vol. 3, 2007; (ed jtly) Soul Food: nourishing poems for starved minds, 2007; (ed) Earth Shattering: ecopoems, 2007; (ed jtly) In Person: 30 poets filmed by Pamela Robertson-Pearce, 2008; (ed) Being Human, 2011; (ed) Ten Poems About Sheep, 2012; (ed) Essential Poems from the Staying Alive Trilogy, 2012; (ed jtly) The World Record, 2012; (ed) The Hundred Years' War: modern war poems, 2014; (ed) Funny Ha-Ha, Funny Peculiar: a book of strange and comic poems, 2015; (ed jtly) In Person: world poets filmed by Neil Astley and Pamela Robertson-Pearce, 2017; (ed) Land of Three Rivers: the poetry of North-East England, 2017. *Recreations:* reading, film, enjoying countryside, folklore, sheep. *Address:* Bloodaxe Books Ltd, Eastburn, South Park, Hexham, Northumberland NE46 1BS. *T:* (01434) 611581.

**ASTLEY, Philip Sinton,** CVO 1999 (LVO 1979); HM Diplomatic Service, retired; Ambassador to Denmark, 1999–2003; *b* 18 Aug. 1943; *s* of Bernard Astley and Barbara Astley (*née* Sinton); *m* 1966, Susanne Poulsen; two *d*. *Educ:* St Albans Sch.; Magdalene Coll., Cambridge (BA 1965). Asst Representative, British Council, Madras, 1966–70; British Council, London, 1970–73; First Sec., FCO, 1973–76, Copenhagen, 1976–79; First Sec. and Head of Chancery, East Berlin, 1980–82; First Sec., FCO, 1982–84; Counsellor and Head of Management Review Staff, FCO, 1984–86; Econ. Counsellor and Consul Gen., Islamabad, 1986–90; Dep. Head of Mission, Copenhagen, 1990–94; Counsellor, and Hd of Human Rights Policy Dept, FCO, 1994–96; Asst Under-Sec. of State, FCO, and HM Vice-Marshal of the Diplomatic Corps, 1996–99. Freeman, City of London, 1999. Grand Cross, Order of Dannebrog (Denmark), 2000. *Recreations:* oriental ceramics and textiles, vernacular furniture, gardening, cooking. *Address:* Korsebøllevej 5, 5953 Tranekær, Denmark.

**ASTLEY, Rita Ann;** *see* Clifton, R. A.

**ASTLING, (Alistair) Vivian,** OBE 2005; DL; Chairman, National Forest Co., 1999–2005; *b* 6 Sept. 1943; *s* of late Alec William Astling, MBE and Barbara Grace Astling; *m* 1967, Hazel Ruth Clarke. *Educ:* Glyn Grammar Sch., Epsom; Sheffield Univ. (LLB 1965; LLM 1967); Birmingham Univ. (MSocSci 1973). West Bromwich County Borough Council: articled clerk, 1967; Asst Solicitor, 1971; Asst Town Clerk, 1973; Walsall Metropolitan Borough Council: Corporate Planner, 1974; Chief Exec. and Town Clerk, 1982–88; Chief Exec., Dudley MBC, 1988–99. Clerk to W Midlands Police Authy, 1988–99; Sec. to Shareholders' Forum, 1988–97, Chm., Consultative Cttee, 2002–12, Birmingham Internat. Airport. Member Board: Midlands Arts Centre, 1999–2013; Artsites, 2002–06; Dudley Coll. Corp., 2003–11 (Chm., 2004–11). Mem., Birmingham Art Circle, 2009–. RBSA 2012 (Hon. Sec., 2011–). Trustee, Heart of the Nat. Forest Foundn, 2005–10. DL W Midlands, 2008. Hon. Graduate Wolverhampton, 1999. *Recreations:* sculpture, theatre, music, planting trees. *Address:* 16 Knighton Drive, Sutton Coldfield, W Midlands B74 4QP.

**ASTON, Bishop Suffragan of,** since 2015; **Rt Rev. Anne Elizabeth Hollinghurst;** *b* 4 March 1964; *d* of William and Audrey Bailey; *m* 1984, Rev. Steve Hollinghurst. *Educ:* Trinity Coll., Bristol (BA 1996); Hughes Hall, Cambridge (MSt 2010). Youth worker, Sussex, then Nottingham; ordained deacon, 1996, priest, 1997; Curate, St Saviours in the Meadows, Nottingham, 1996–99; Chaplain, Derby Univ. and Derby Cathedral, 1999–2005; Bishop's Domestic Chaplain and Canon Res., Manchester Cathedral, 2005–10; Vicar, St Peter's, St Albans, 2010–15. *Address:* Diocesan Office, 1 Colmore Row, Birmingham B3 2BJ.

**ASTON, Archdeacon of;** *see* Heathfield, Ven. S. D.

**ASTON, Felicity Ann Dawn,** MBE 2015; polar explorer, author and speaker, since 2005; *b* Sevenoaks, 7 Oct. 1977; *d* of Richard Aston and Jacqueline Aston; *m* 2015, Gísli Jónsson. *Educ:* Tonbridge Grammar Sch. for Girls; University Coll. London (BSc Phys and Astronomy 1999); Univ. of Reading (MSc Applied Meteorol. 2000). Sen. Meteorologist, British Antarctic Survey, 2000–03; Expedition Officer, British Schs Exploring Soc., 2003–04; Team Mem., Pink Lady Polecats Polar Challenge, 2005; Expedition Leader: Yippee! Timberland Expedition, 2005; Arctic Foxes Greenland Quest, 2006; Kaspersky Lab Commonwealth Antarctic Expedition, 2009; Kaspersky One Trans-Antarctic Expedition, 2011; Pole of Cold Expedition, 2013; Women's Euro-Arabian North Pole Expedition, 2018; polar guide and instructor, Wettlauf Zum Südpol, 2010; expedition guide and lecturer: 50 Let Pobedy (icebreaker), 2015; Sea Spirit, 2016. Presenter: Operation Cloud Lab: Secrets of the Skies, BBC TV, 2013; Operation Gold Rush, BBC TV, 2016. FRGS 2014; Fellow, Wings World Quest, 2014. Hon Dr Canterbury Christ Church, 2015. Polar Medal, 2014. *Publications:* Call of the White: taking the world to the South Pole, 2011; Alone in Antarctica, 2013; Chasing Winter: a journey to the Pole of Cold, 2014. *Recreations:* scouring maps for any unexplored fringes, plotting new adventures. *Address:* c/o United Agents, 12–26 Lexington Street, W1F 0LE. *T:* 07809 626107. *E:* felicity@felicityaston.com. *Club:* Explorers (New York).

**ASTOR,** family name of **Viscount Astor** and **Baron Astor of Hever**.

**ASTOR,** 4th Viscount *cr* 1917, of Hever Castle; **William Waldorf Astor;** Baron 1916; *b* 27 Dec. 1951; *s* of 3rd Viscount Astor; *S* father, 1966; *m* 1976, Annabel Lucy Veronica Sheffield (*see* Viscountess Astor); two *s* one *d*. *Educ:* Eton Coll. A Lord in Waiting (Govt Whip), 1990–93. Parliamentary Under-Secretary of State: DSS, 1993–94; Dept of Nat. Heritage, 1994–95; an Opposition spokesman, H of L, 1996–2009; elected Mem., H of L, 1999; Dir, Silvergate Media Ltd, 2012– (Chm., 2013–). Trustee, Sir Stanley Spencer Gall., Cookham, 1975–. *Heir: s* Hon. William Waldorf Astor [*b* 18 Jan. 1979; *m* 2009 Lohralee Stutz; one *s* one *d*]. *Address:* Ginge Manor, Wantage, Oxon OX12 8QT. *Club:* White's.

**ASTOR, Viscountess; Annabel Lucy Veronica Astor;** Chairman, Oka Direct Ltd, since 2017 (Founder and Chief Executive Officer, 1999–2016; Director, since 1999); *b* London, 14 Aug. 1948; *d* of late Timothy Angus Jones and Pandora Jones (*née* Clifford); *m* 1st, 1969, Sir Reginald Adrian Berkeley Sheffield, Bt, *qv* (marr. diss. 1975); two *d*; 2nd, 1976, Viscount Astor, *qv*; two *s* one *d*. *Educ:* Hatherop Castle Sch.; Lycée Français de Londres. Owner, Annabel Jones Ltd, jewellery, 1969–99. *Address:* Ginge Manor, Wantage, Oxon OX12 8QT.

*See also* Rt Hon. D. W. D. Cameron.

**ASTOR OF HEVER,** 3rd Baron *cr* 1956, of Hever Castle; **John Jacob Astor;** PC 2015; DL; *b* 16 June 1946; *s* of 2nd Baron Astor of Hever and Lady Irene Haig, *d* of Field Marshal 1st Earl Haig, KT, GCB, OM, GCVO, KCIE; *S* father, 1984; *m* 1st, 1970, Fiona Diana Lennox Harvey (marr. diss. 1990), *d* of Captain Roger Harvey; three *d*; 2nd, 1990, Hon. Elizabeth, *d* of 2nd Viscount Mackintosh of Halifax, OBE, BEM; one *s* one *d*. *Educ:* Eton College. Lieut Life Guards, 1966–70, Malaysia, Hong Kong, Ulster. Director: Terres Blanches Services Sarl, 1975–77; Valberg Plaza Sarl, 1977–82; Managing Director: Honon et Cie, 1982–; Astor France Sarl, 1989–. An Opposition Whip, H of L, 1998–2010; elected Mem., H of L, 1999. Shadow Defence Minister, 2003–10; a Lord in Waiting (Govt Whip), 2010–11; Parly Under-Sec. of State, MoD, 2010–15. Vice-Chm., All Party Parly Gp for the Army; Secretary: Anglo-Swiss Parly Assoc., 1992–2010; All Party Motor Gp, 1998–2010; All Party Gp on Autism, 2000–10; All Party Gp on Shooting and Conservation, 2002–10; Jt Treas., British-S African Parly Assoc., 1994. Trustee: Astor Foundn; Astor of Hever Trust; Pres., RoSPA, 1996–99. Gov., Cobham Hall Sch., 1993–96. DL Kent, 1996. Chm., Council of St John, Kent, 1987–97; KStJ 1998. *Heir: s* Hon. Charles Gavin John Astor, *b* 10 Nov. 1990. *Address:* Frenchstreet House, Westerham, Kent TN16 1PW. *Club:* White's.

**ASTOR, David Waldorf,** CBE 1994; DL; farmer, since 1973; *b* 9 Aug. 1943; *s* of late Michael Langhorne Astor and Barbara Mary (*née* McNeill); *m* 1968, Clare Pamela St John; two *s* two *d*. *Educ:* Eton Coll. Short service commn in Royal Scots Greys, 1962–65. United Newspapers, 1970–72; Housing Corp., 1972–75; Head of Develt, National Th., 1978–79; Director: Jupiter Tarbutt Merlin, 1985–91; Priory Investments Ltd, 1990–2007. Chairman: CPRE, 1983–93; Southern Arts Bd, 1998–2002. Chairman: Action for Prisoners' Families, 2003–09; Turn2Us, 2007–09. Trustee: Glyndebourne Arts Trust, 1995–2005; Elizabeth Finn Care (formerly Elizabeth Finn Trust), 2004–11; Oxford Community Foundn, 2010–16. Patron: Mulberry Bush Sch., 1998–; Wychwood Project, 2010– (Chm., 2018–); Oxfordshire Family Mediation, 2010–16. Pres., Oxfordshire Playing Fields Assoc., 2018–. Contested (SDP/Alliance) Plymouth Drake, 1987. FRSA. DL Oxon, 2007. *Recreations:* reading, walking, cricket, wine. *Address:* Bruern Grange, Milton under Wychwood, Oxford OX7 6HA. *T:* (01993) 830413. *Clubs:* Brooks's, Beefsteak, Academy, MCC.

**ASTWOOD, Hon. Sir James (Rufus),** KBE 1994; Kt 1982; JP; President, Court of Appeal: Bermuda, 1994–2003; Turks and Caicos Islands, 1997–2002; *b* 4 Oct. 1923; *s* of late James Rufus Astwood, Sr, and Mabel Winifred Astwood; *m* 1952, Gloria Preston Norton; one *s* two *d*. *Educ:* Berkeley Inst., Bermuda; Univ. of Toronto, Canada. Called to the Bar, Gray's Inn, London, Feb. 1956, Hon. Bencher, 1985; admitted to practice at Jamaican Bar, Oct. 1956; joined Jamaican Legal Service, 1957; Dep. Clerk of Courts, 1957–58; Clerk of Courts, Jamaica, 1958–63; Stipendiary Magistrate and Judge of Grand Court, Cayman Islands (on secondment from Jamaica), 1958–59; Resident Magistrate, Jamaica, 1963–74; Puisne Judge, Jamaica, during 1971 and 1973; retd from Jamaican Legal Service, 1974; Sen. Magistrate, Bermuda, 1974–76; Solicitor General, 1976–77; Acting Attorney General, during 1976 and 1977; Acting Dep. Governor for a period in 1977; Chief

Justice, 1977–93, Justice of Appeal, 1993–94, Bermuda. Has served on several cttees, tribunals and bds of enquiry, in both Bermuda and Jamaica. *Recreations:* golf, cricket, photography, reading, bridge, travel. *Address:* The Pebble, 7 Astwood Walk, Warwick WK08, Bermuda; PO Box HM 1674, Hamilton HMGX, Bermuda. *Club:* Bermuda Senior Golfers Society (Bermuda).

**ATALLA, Ashraf Albert**; Managing Director, Roughcut Television Ltd, since 2007; *b* Cairo, 18 June 1972; *s* of Albert and Adele Atalla. *Educ:* Lord Mayor Treloar Coll.; Bath Univ. (BSc Business Admin 1994). Stockbroker, Panmure Gordon, 1995–97; Researcher, BBC, 1997–2001; Producer, The Office, BBC TV, 2001–04; Hd of Comedy, Talkback Thames, 2004–07. Exec. Producer, TV series incl. The IT Crowd, 2006–07, Clone, 2008, Trinity, 2009, Trollied, 2011–12, People Just Do Nothing, 2015–17, Hospital People, 2017. Columnist, Guardian, 2006–08. *Publications:* contribs to newspapers. *Recreations:* audio books, sitting in the sun, Indian food, watching any football that happens to be on. *Address:* PBJ Management, 22 Rathbone Street, W1T 1LG. *Clubs:* Groucho, Soho House, Ivy.

**ATHA, Bernard Peter**, CBE 2007 (OBE 1991); Principal Lecturer in Business Studies, Huddersfield Technical College, 1973–90; Lord Mayor, City of Leeds, 2000–01; *b* 27 Aug. 1928; *s* of Horace Michael Atha and Mary Quinlan; unmarried. *Educ:* Leeds Modern Sch.; Leeds Univ. (LLB Hons). Barrister-at-law, Gray's Inn. Commn, RAF, 1950–52. Variety artist on stage; Mem. Equity; films and TV plays. Elected Leeds City Council, 1957–2014 (Hon. Alderman, 2014); Chm., Leeds Leisure Services Cttee, 1988–99; former Chairman: Watch Cttee; Social Services Cttee; Educn Cttee. Vice-Chm., W Leeds HA, 1988–90. Contested (Lab) Penrith and the Border, 1959; Pudsey, 1964. Pres., Leeds Co-op. Soc., 1976–96; Chairman: Leeds Playhouse, 1974–2007; Northern Ballet Theatre, 1995–2010. Member: Arts Council, 1979–82; Ministerial Working Party on Sport and Recreation, 1974, on Sport for the Disabled, 1989; EU (formerly EC) Sport for Disabled Cttee, 1992–99 (Vice-Chm., 1997–99); Internat. Paralympic Cttee, 1993–98; Sports Lottery Bd, 1995–2003; Vice-Chm., Sports Council, 1976–80; Chairman: Yorks and Humberside Reg. Sports Council, 1966–76; Nat. Water Sports Centre, 1978–84; UK Sports Assoc. for People with Learning Disability (formerly UK Sports Assoc. for People with Mental Handicap), 1980– (Pres., INASFMH, 1993–2007); British Paralympics Assoc., 1989. Vice-Chm., St James' Univ. Hosp. NHS Trust, 1993–98 (Dir, 1990–98); Chm., United Leeds Teaching Hosps NHS Trust, subseq. United Leeds Hosps Charitable Foundn, 2009–14 (Mem., 2000–14; Vice Chm., 2001–09). Chairman: Disability Sports Develt Trust (formerly British Paralympic Trust), 1990–; English Fedn Disability Sport, 1999–2009. Chairman: Yorks Dance Centre Trust, 1987–2007; Red Ladder Theatre Co., 1987–2014; Craft Centre and Design Gall., Leeds, 1988–2015; Liz Dawn Cancer Appeal; Yorkshire Youth Ballet (formerly Yorkshire Youth Dance), 2006–08. Pres., British and Internat. Fedn of Festivals, 2002–14, now Emeritus. Mem., Lord Renton Foundn, 1991–2015; Trustee, London Marathon Charitable Foundn, 2007–11. Governor: Sports Aid Foundn; Opera North. FRSA. Hon. Fellow, Leeds Coll. of Music, 2002. British Gas/Arts Council Award, 1993. *Recreations:* sport, the arts, travel. *Address:* 25 Moseley Wood Croft, Leeds, West Yorks LS16 7JJ. *T:* (0113) 267 2485. *E:* bernard.atha@outlook.com.

**ATHA, Air Marshal Sir Stuart David**, KBE 2019; CB 2015; DSO 2003; Deputy Commander Operations, Headquarters Air Command, 2016–19; *b* Irvine, 30 April 1962; *s* of Wright Atha and Myra Atha; *m* 1989, Caroline Dick; one *s* four *d*. *Educ:* Kilmarnock Acad.; Univ. of Glasgow (BSc 1984); King's Coll. London (MA 2000). Joined RAF, 1984; Hawk flying instructor, 1986–90; Harrier pilot, 1 (Fighter) Sqdn, IV (Army Cooperation) Sqdn and Air Warfare Centre, 1990–2000; OC 3 (Fighter) Sqdn, 2000–03; PSO to CAS, 2003–05; Station Comdr, RAF Coningsby, 2006–08; AOC No 83 Expeditionary Air Gp, 2009–10; Hd, Jt Capability, MoD, 2010–11; AOC No 1 Gp, RAF, 2011–14; COS (Ops), Perm. Jt HQ, 2014–16. *Recreations:* high handicap piano player and golfer, children's taxi driver. *Club:* Royal Air Force.

**ATHANASOU, Prof. Nicholas Anthony**, PhD, MD; FRCPath; Professor of Musculoskeletal Pathology, University of Oxford, since 2002; Fellow of Wadham College, Oxford, since 2002; *b* Perth, Australia, 26 April 1953; *s* of Anthony Athanasou and Angella Athanasou (*née* Pappas); *m* 1985, Linda Hulls. *Educ:* Sydney High Sch.; Univ. of Sydney (MB BS 1978; MD 1998); St Bartholomew's Hosp. Medical Coll., Univ. of London (PhD 1985). MRCP 1981; FRCPath 1986. Arthritis Res. Campaign Fellow in Osteoarticular Pathology, Univ. of Oxford, 1988–91; Consultant Pathologist, Nuffield Orthopaedic Centre, Oxford, 1991–. Reader, Univ. of Oxford, 2002. Res. Line Leader, EuroBoNeT, 2006–11. Committee Member: Nat. Cancer Intelligence Network, 2008–; Nat. Cancer Res. Network (sarcoma), 2011–14; Nat. Cancer Peer Rev. (sarcoma), 2012–14. *Publications:* Hybrids: stories of Greek Australia, 1995; Atlas of Bone, Joint and Soft Tissue Pathology, 1999; Pathological Basis of Orthopaedic and Rheumatic Disease, 2001; *novels:* The Greek Liar, 2002; The Person of the Man, 2012; Palindrome, 2016. *Recreations:* walking, music, theatre, sports, travel. *Address:* Department of Pathology, Nuffield Orthopaedic Centre, Oxford OX3 7LD. *T:* (01865) 738136, *Fax:* (01865) 738140. *E:* nick.athanasou@ndorms.ox.ac.uk.

**ATHERTON, Alan Royle**, CB 1990; Director, The Argyll Consultancies PLC, 1991–99 (Deputy Chairman, 1992–94; Chairman, 1994–99); *b* 25 April 1931; *s* of Harold Atherton and Hilda (*née* Royle); *m* 1959, Valerie Kemp (marr. diss. 1996; she *d* 2017); three *s* one *d*. *Educ:* Cowley Sch., St Helens; Sheffield Univ. (BSc (Hons Chem.)). ICI Ltd, 1955–58; Department of Scientific and Industrial Research: SSO, 1959–64; Private Sec. to Permanent Sec., 1960–64; PSO, Road Res. Lab., 1964–65; Principal, Min. of Housing and Local Govt, 1965–70; Asst Sec., Ordnance Survey, 1970–74; Under-Sec., 1975–87, Dep. Sec., 1987–91, DoE. Chm., Local Govt Staff Commn (Eng.), 1993–98. Vice Chm., CS Med. Assoc., then CS Healthcare, 1987–98. Chm., Queen Elizabeth II Conf. Centre Bd, 1990–93; Dir, Internat. Centre for Facilities, Canada, 1993–2001; Member: Letchworth Garden City Corp., 1991–94; Historic Royal Palaces Agency Adv. Gp, 1991–98. *Recreations:* reading, bonsai, ballet. *Club:* Athenæum.

**ATHERTON, Prof. Andrew Michael**, PhD; Principal and Vice-Chancellor, University of Dundee, since 2019; *b* Liverpool, 27 June 1966; *s* of Dr Michael Atherton and Catherine Atherton; *m* 2008; two *s*. *Educ:* Sch. of Oriental and African Studies, Univ. of London (BA Chinese and Econs 1989); Yale Univ. (MA Internat. and Develt Econs 1992); Univ. of Lincoln (PhD 2012). Durham University: Dir, Policy Res. Unit, Small Business Centre, 1995–99; Hd, Enterprise and SME Develt Dept, 1999–2002; University of Lincoln: Prof., 2003–06; Pro-Vice Chancellor, 2006–10; Sen. Dep. Vice-Chancellor, 2010–12; Dep. Vice-Chancellor and Prof. of Enterprise, Lancaster Univ., 2013–18. *Publications:* (with A. Newman) Entrepreneurial China: the emergence of the private sector, 2018; contrib. articles and papers on enterprise, entrepreneurship and small business. *Recreations:* ski-ing, walking, mountain biking. *Address:* University of Dundee, Nethergate, Dundee DD1 4HN. *T:* (01382) 385561. *E:* a.m.atherton@dundee.ac.uk. *Club:* Caledonian.

**ATHERTON, David**, OBE 1999; Founder and Artistic Director, Mainly Mozart Festival, Southern California and Northern Mexico, 1988–2013; Conductor Laureate, Hong Kong Philharmonic Orchestra, 2000–09 (Music Director and Principal Conductor, 1989–2000); *b* 3 Jan. 1944; *s* of Robert and Lavinia Atherton; *m* 1970, Ann Gianetta Drake (marr. diss.

2012); one *s* two *d*; *m* 2012, Eleanor Ann Roth. *Educ:* Cambridge Univ. (MA). LRAM, LTCL. Music Dir, London Sinfonietta, 1967–73 and 1989–91 (Co-Founder, 1967); Repetiteur, Royal Opera House, Covent Garden, 1967–68; Resident Conductor, Royal Opera House, 1968–80; Principal Conductor and Artistic Advr, 1980–83, Principal Guest Conductor, 1983–86, Royal Liverpool Philharmonic Orch.; Music Dir and Principal Conductor, San Diego Symphony Orch., 1980–87; Artistic Director and Conductor: London Schubert/Webern Fest., 1978–79; Stravinsky Fest., 1979–82; Ravel/Varèse Fest., 1983–84; Principal Guest Conductor: BBC SO, 1985–89; BBC Nat. Orch. of Wales, 1994–97. Co-Founder, Pres. and Artistic Dir, Global Music Network, 1998–2002. Became youngest conductor in history of Henry Wood Promenade Concerts at Royal Albert Hall, and also at Royal Opera House, 1968; Royal Festival Hall debut, 1969; from 1968 performances in Europe, Middle East, Far East, Australasia, N and S America. Adapted and arranged Pandora by Roberto Gerhard for Royal Ballet, 1975. Conductor of the Year Award (Composers' Guild of GB), 1971; Edison Award, 1973; Grand Prix du Disque award, 1977; Koussevitzky Award, 1981; Internat. Record Critics Award, 1982; Prix Caecilia, 1982. *Publications:* (ed) The Complete Instrumental and Chamber Music of Arnold Schoenberg and Roberto Gerhard, 1973; (ed) Pandora and Don Quixote Suites by Roberto Gerhard, 1973; contrib., The Musical Companion, 1978, The New Grove Dictionary, 1981. *Recreations:* travel, computers, theatre.

**ATHERTON, James Bernard**; Secretary-General, British Bankers' Association, 1982–85; *b* 3 Dec. 1927; *s* of late James Atherton and Edith (*née* Atkinson); *m* 1953, Eileen Margaret Birch; two *s*. *Educ:* Alsop High Sch., Liverpool. Served RAF, 1946–48; Martins Bank, 1943–46 and 1948–69 (Asst Chief Accountant, 1966–69); Barclays Bank, 1969–82 (Chief Clearing Manager, 1969–73, Asst Gen. Manager, 1973–78, Divl Gen. Manager, 1978–82). *Recreations:* opera, gardening. *Address:* c/o Barclays Bank, 10 The Square, Petersfield, Hants GU32 3HW.

**ATHERTON, Jason**; chef; Chief Executive Officer, Jason Atherton Restaurants, since 2010; *b* Worksop, Notts, 6 Sept. 1971; *s* of Vic and Sandra Atherton; *m* 2004, Irha; two *d*. *Educ:* Earl of Scarborough High Sch.; Boston Coll. of Further Educn. Commis chef, La Tante Claire; chef de partie: Chez Nico; The Restaurant; L'Auberge de l'Ill, France; sous chef, Coast; hd chef, Mash and Air; chef de partie, El Bulli, Spain; hd chef, Frith St Restaurant; Exec. Chef, Maze Restaurants, 2001–10, incl. Verre, Dubai, 2001–05, Maze London, Maze Grill and Maze Prague; Chef: Pollen St Social Restaurant, 2011– (Michelin Star, 2012); Little Social, 2013; Social Eating House, 2013 (Michelin Star, 2013); Berners Tavern, 2013; City Social, 2014; Social Wine and Tapas, 2015; Sosharu, 2016; Nova, 2017; Hai Cenato, 2017; Pavlova's, 2019; Chef/owner, restaurants in China, Hong Kong, Singapore, Dubai, New York and Sydney. Presenter, TV series: My Kitchen Rules, 2014; The Chefs' Brigade, 2019. Chef of Year, Catey Awards, 2012. *Publications:* Maze: the cookbook, 2008; Gourmet Food for a Fiver, 2010; Pollen Street: the cookbook, 2018. *Recreations:* golf, keeping fit, running. *Address:* 7B Balham Grove, SW12 8AZ. *E:* jason@pollenstreetsocial.com.

**ATHERTON, Michael Andrew**, OBE 1997; journalist, sports commentator and broadcaster; *b* 23 March 1968; *s* of Alan and Wendy Atherton; one *s* one *d*. *Educ:* Manchester Grammar Sch.; Downing Coll., Cambridge (BA Hons History; MA). 1st class début, Cambridge *v* Essex, 1987; played for Lancashire CCC, 1987–2001; Captain: Young England, Sri Lanka 1987, Australia 1988; Cambridge Univ., 1988–89; Combined Universities, 1989; Mem., England Test team, 115 matches, 1989–2001; captained 54 Test matches, 1993–98 and 2001; scored 16 Test centuries. Mem., Editl Board, Wisden Cricket Monthly, 1993–2003; columnist: Sunday Telegraph, 2001–07; The Times, 2008–. Cricket commentator: Channel 4, 2001–05; Sky Sports (formerly BSkyB), 2006–. *Publications:* Opening Up: my autobiography, 2002; Gambling: a story of triumph and disaster, 2007. *Recreations:* golf, reading, writing. *Address:* The Farm House, The Green, Letchmore Heath, Herts WD25 8ES. *Club:* Groucho.

**ATHERTON, Air Vice-Marshal Paul Ashley**, OBE 2005; RAF Commander Croughton, since 2017; *b* W Hartlepool, 10 Feb. 1964; *s* of Wilfred and Melva Atherton; *m* 1987, Jane Mary Richards; two *d*. *Educ:* Peterlee Grammar Tech. Sch.; RAF Coll., Cranwell. VIP and trng pilot, Sqdn Exec., No 10 Sqdn, 1985–95; sc 1996; Directorate of Jt Warfare, MoD, 1997–99; OC No 216 Sqdn, 1999–2002; Future Strategic Tanker Aircraft Project Team, Defence Procurement Agency, 2002–04; Comdr, Basrah Air Stn, Iraq, 2004–05; OC, RAF Lyneham, 2006–07; rcds, 2008; ACOS Strategy, Policy and Plans, 2008–10, AO Ops, 2010–12, HQ Air Comd; Dir Military Aviation Authy, 2012–15; COS Ops, HQ Air Comd, 2016. Chm., Combined Services Cricket Assoc., 2012–14; President: RAF Cricket Assoc., 2008–16; 216 Sqdn Assoc., 2009–. Freeman, Fuellers' Co., 2002. *Recreations:* growing vegetables from seed, reading, the countryside, watching football, Rugby Union and cricket (sadly no longer playing!). *T:* 07557 053677. *Clubs:* Royal Air Force Innominate; Adastrian Cricket (Pres., 2007–16).

**ATHERTON, Rev. Mgr Richard**, OBE 1989; Chaplain to the Archbishop of Liverpool, 1996–2002; *b* 15 Feb. 1928; *s* of Richard Atherton and Winifred Mary Atherton (*née* Hurst). *Educ:* St Francis Xavier's Coll., Liverpool; Upholland Coll., Wigan; Dip. Criminology, London Univ., 1979; BA Hons Maryvale Inst., Birmingham, 1995; MA Durham. 1997. Ordained priest, 1954; Curate: St Cecilia's, Tuebrook, Liverpool, 1954–60; St Philip Neri's, Liverpool, 1960–65; Prison Chaplain: Walton, Liverpool, 1965–75; Appleton Thorne, Warrington, 1975–77; Principal RC Prison Chaplain, 1977–89; Parish Priest, St Joseph's, Leigh, Lancs, 1989–91; Pres., Ushaw Coll., 1991–96. *Publications:* Summons to Serve, 1987; New Light on the Psalms, 1993; Praying the Prayer of the Church, 1998; Praying the Sunday Psalms, Year A, 2001, Year B, 2003, Year C, 2004; Let's Meet the Prophets, 2008. *Recreations:* walking, reading. *Address:* 27 Seabank Road, Southport PR9 0EJ. *T:* (01704) 631071.

**ATHERTON, His Honour Robert Kenneth**; a Circuit Judge, 2000–15; *b* 22 June 1947; *s* of late John and Evelyn Atherton; civil partnership 2006, Michael Montgomery. *Educ:* Boteler Grammar Sch., Warrington; Univ. of Liverpool (LLB Hons). Called to the Bar, Gray's Inn, 1970; in practice at the Bar, 1971–2000; Asst Recorder, 1994–99; a Recorder, 1999–2000. Legal Mem., Mental Health Review Tribunal, 1989–2000 (Mem., Restricted Panel, 2001–). Asst Comr, Parly Boundary Commn, 1993–95. Mem., Council of HM Circuit Judges, 2006–14 (Chm., Criminal Sub-cttee, 2011–14). Mem., Lincoln's Inn, 2008, Bencher, 2012. *Recreations:* travel, music, gardening.

**ATHERTON, Stephen Nicholas**; QC 2006; barrister; *b* 6 May 1966; *s* of James Alan Atherton and late Ann Margaret Atherton; *m* 1992, Lucy-Jane Coppock; one *d*. *Educ:* West Park Sch.; Univ. of Lancaster (LLB Hons); Magdalene Coll., Cambridge (LLM 1988). Called to the Bar, Middle Temple, 1989, and Gray's Inn. Barrister specialising in domestic and internat. corporate insolvency and restructuring, and civil aspects of domestic and internat. commercial fraud. *Publications:* various legal texts and articles. *Recreations:* Rugby Union, Rugby League, cricket, films, food, family, collecting ancient Chinese ceramics and British watercolours and drawings. *Address:* 20 Essex Street, WC2R 3AL. *T:* (020) 7842 1200. *E:* satherton@20essexst.com; Old Isleworth, Middlesex; Hinton St George Somerset; Turtle's Nest, Jamaica. *Clubs:* Hinton St George Cricket; Treasure Beach Pirates Cricket.

**ATHOLL**, 12th Duke of, *cr* 1703; **Bruce George Ronald Murray**; Lord Murray of Tullibardine 1604; Earl of Tullibardine 1606; Earl of Atholl 1629; Marquess of Atholl, Viscount of Balquhidder, Lord Murray, Balvenie and Gask, 1676; Marquess of Tullibardine, Earl of Strathtay and Strathardle, Viscount Glenalmond and Glenlyon, 1703 - all in the peerage of Scotland; *b* 6 April 1960; *er s* of 11th Duke of Atholl and of Margaret Yvonne Murray (*née* Leach); *S* father, 2012; *m* 1st, 1984, Lynne Elizabeth (marr. diss. 2003), *e d* of Nicholas Andrew; two *s* one *d*; *m* 2nd, 2009, Charmaine Myrna (marr. diss. 2016), *d* of Dirk Du Toit. Lieut, Transvaal Scottish, 1983; Col, Atholl Highlanders, 2012. CStJ 2015. *Heir: s* Marquess of Tullibardine, *qv*. *Address:* PO Box 1522, Louis Trichardt, 0920, South Africa.

**ATKIN, Becky;** *see* Parker, B.

**ATKIN, Prof. Christopher John,** PhD; CEng, FRAeS, FREng; Professor of Aeronautical Engineering, since 2008, and Head of Engineering, since 2017, City, University of London (formerly City University, London); *b* Santiago, Chile, 16 Dec. 1964; *s* of late William Richard Bourchier Atkin and Ellen Mary Atkin (*née* Young); *m* 1998, Siobhan Lesley Dowling; two *d*. *Educ:* Stonyhurst Coll., Lancs; St John's Coll., Cambridge (BA 1986; MA 1990; PhD Transonic Aerodynamics 1991). FRAeS 1991; CEng 1997; FREng 2018. Sen. Res. Engr, British Aerospace Commercial Aircraft, 1991–94; Defence Research Agency, then Defence Evaluation and Research Agency, later QinetiQ plc: SSO, 1994–97; PSO, 1997–2007; Fellow in Aerodynamics and Flow Control, 2002–07; Tech. Manager, Aerodynamics Dept, 2006–07; Asst Dean, 2008–11, Dep. Dean, 2012, City Univ., London. Chm., Engrg Council, 2017–. Pres., RAeS, 2016–17. *Address:* City, University of London, 10 Northampton Square, EC1V 0HB. *T:* (020) 7040 4203.

**ATKIN, Gavin Mark;** journalist and editor, Wilmington Healthcare (formerly Wellards), since 2012; *b* 2 Jan. 1956; *s* of Alistair Brian and Sunya Mary Atkin; one *s* one *d*; *m* 2009, Julie Arnott. *Educ:* Univ. of Newcastle upon Tyne (BSc Gen. Scis). Man. Editor, 1994–2000, Ed., 2000–06, The Practitioner; Clin. Ed., Chemist & Druggist, 2006–10; Ed. and Publisher, intheboatshed.net, 2006–. *Publications:* Ultrasimple Boatbuilding, 2007. *Recreations:* enjoying, performing and teaching traditional music; playing Jeffries duet concertina; sailing, boat building and design; weblogging about boats at intheboatshed.net.

**ATKIN, Timothy John;** freelance wine writer and photographer; *b* Dartford, 26 Aug. 1961; *s* of Ronald George Atkin and late Brenda Irene Atkin; *m* 2009, Sue Wixley. *Educ:* Durham Univ. (BA Hons French); London Sch. of Econs (MSc Eur. Studies). With Haymarket Publishing, 1985–89; wine correspondent: Guardian, 1989–93; Observer, 1993–2010. Mem., Inst. of Masters of Wine, 2001–. Chevalier du Tastevin, 2000; Master of Wine, 2001; Caballero del Vino, 2007. *Publications:* Chardonnay, 1991; Vins de Pays d'Oc, 1992; (with A. Rose) Grapevine, annually, 1993–97. *Recreations:* golf, piano, reading, cinema, guitar, collecting black and white photography. *Address:* c/o PFD, 55 New Oxford Street, WC1A 1BS. *T:* (020) 7344 1000. *Clubs:* Groucho, 67 Pall Mall; Royal Wimbledon Golf.

**ATKINS, Andrew Windham;** Chief Executive, A Rocha UK, since 2016; *b* Eastleigh, Hants, 9 Oct. 1960; *s* of Rev. Roger Atkins and Diana Atkins (*née* Gilbard); *m* 1985, Sarah Witts; one *s* two *d*. *Educ:* University Coll. London (BA Hons Geog. 1982); Inst. of Latin American Studies, Univ. of London (MA Latin American Studies 1983). Nat. Coordinator, 1985, Gen. Sec., 1986–88, Chile Cttee for Human Rights; Partnership Scheme Coordinator, CAFOD, 1988–90; Latin America Desk Officer, Catholic Inst. for Internat. Relns, 1990–97; Tearfund: Public Policy Advr, 1997–98; Public Policy Team Leader, 1998–2000; Advocacy (Policy and Campaigns) Dir, 2000–08; Exec. Dir, Friends of the Earth (England, Wales and NI), 2008–15. Board Member: Make Poverty Hist. Campaign, 2004–06; Micah Challenge Campaign, 2004–08. FRSA. *Recreations:* landscape painting, cycling, world literature, theatre. *E:* andy2atkins@gmail.com.

**ATKINS, Charlotte;** *b* 24 Sept. 1950; *d* of Ronald and Jessie Atkins; *m* 1990, Gus Brain (*d* 2015); one *d*. *Educ:* Colchester County High Sch.; LSE (BSc(Econ)); MA London Univ. Asst Community Relations Officer, Luton CRC, 1974–76; Res. Officer, then Hd of Res., UCATT, 1976–80; Res. and Political Officer, AUEW (TASS), 1980–83; Press Officer, 1983–92, Parly Officer, 1992–97, COHSE, then UNISON. Contested (Lab) Eastbourne, Oct. 1990. MP (Lab) Staffordshire Moorlands, 1997–2010; contested (Lab) same seat, 2010. PPS to Minister of State for Trade, DTI and FCO, 2001–02; an Asst Govt Whip, 2002–05; Parly Under-Sec. of State, DfT, 2004–05. Member: Select Cttee on Educn and Employment, 1997–2001; Cttee of Selection, 1997–2000; Select Cttee on Health, 2005–10. Mem., PLP Parly Cttee, 1997–2000. Member (Lab): Staffordshire Moorlands DC, 2012–; Staffordshire CC, 2013– (Shadow Cabinet Mem. for Social Care, subseq. for Health and Social Care, 2013–; Dep. Leader, Labour Gp, 2016–). Chm., Central Shires Canal and River Trust Waterways Partnership, 2012–16; Mem., Staffs and Stoke on Trent Fire and Rescue Authy, 2013–14.

**ATKINS, Charlotte Elizabeth Mary;** *see* Voake, C. E. M.

**ATKINS, Dame Eileen,** DBE 2001 (CBE 1990); actress and writer; *b* 16 June 1934; *d* of Arthur Thomas Atkins and late Annie Ellen (*née* Elkins); *m* Bill Shepherd (*d* 2016). *Educ:* Latymer Grammar Sch., Edmonton; Guildhall Sch. of Music and Drama. *Stage appearances include:* Twelfth Night, Richard III, The Tempest, Old Vic, 1962; The Killing of Sister George (Best Actress, Standard Awards), Bristol Old Vic, transf. Duke of York's, 1965; The Cocktail Party, Wyndham's, transf. Haymarket, 1968; Vivat! Vivat Regina! (Variety Award), Piccadilly, 1970; Suzanne Andler, Aldwych, 1973; As You Like It, Stratford, 1973; St Joan, Old Vic, 1977; Passion Play, Aldwych, 1981; Medea, Young Vic, 1986; The Winter's Tale, and Cymbeline (Olivier Award), Mountain Language, NT, 1988; A Room of One's Own, Hampstead, 1989; Exclusive, Strand, 1989; Prin, NY, 1990; The Night of the Iguana, NT, 1992; Vita and Virginia, Ambassadors, 1993, NY, 1994; Indiscretions, NY, 1995; John Gabriel Borkman, NT, 1996; A Delicate Balance, Haymarket (Best Actress, Evening Standard Awards), 1997; The Unexpected Man, RSC, transf. Duchess (Best Actress, Olivier Awards), 1998; Honour, NT, 2003; The Retreat from Moscow, NY, 2003; The Birthday Party, Duchess, 2005; Doubt, NY, 2006; There Came a Gypsy Riding, Almeida, 2007; The Sea, Haymarket, 2008; The Female of the Species, Vaudeville, 2008; All That Fall, Jermyn Street Th., transf. Arts, 2012 (Best Actress, Offie Awards); (one-woman show) Ellen Terry with Eileen Atkins, Sam Wanamaker Playhouse, 2014; The Witch of Edmonton, Stratford, 2014; The Height of the Storm, Wyndham's, 2018, transf. NY, 2019; *films include:* Equus, 1974; The Dresser, 1984; Let Him Have It, 1990; Wolf, 1994; Women Talking Dirty, 2001; Gosford Park, 2002; What a Girl Wants, 2003; Vanity Fair, 2005; Evening, 2007; Wild Target, 2008; Last Chance Harvey, 2009; Robin Hood, 2009; Beautiful Creatures, 2013; Magic in the Moonlight, 2014; Suite Française, 2015; Nothing Like a Dame, 2018; *TV appearances include:* The Duchess of Malfi; Sons and Lovers; Smiley's People; Nelly's Version; The Burston Rebellion; Breaking Up; The Vision; Mrs Pankhurst in In My Defence (series), 1990; A Room of One's Own, 1990; The Lost Language of Cranes, 1993; The Maitlands, 1993; Cold Comfort Farm, 1995 (film, 1997); Talking Heads 2, 1998; Madame Bovary, 2000; Bertie and Elizabeth, 2002; Love Again, 2003; Waking the Dead, Cranford, 2007 (Best Actress, BAFTA, 2008; Best Supporting Actress, Emmy Awards, 2008); Upstairs Downstairs, 2010; Doc Martin, 2011, 2013, 2015, 2017; The Scapegoat, 2012; The Crown, 2016. Co-created television series: Upstairs Downstairs; The House of Eliott; *screenplay:* Mrs Dalloway (Best Screenplay, Evening Standard British Film Awards), 1998; (with Chanya Button) Vita and Virginia, 2019. Hon. DLitt Oxford, 2010. Gielgud Award, Shakespeare Guild, 2015. *Address:* c/o Paul Lyon Maris, Independent Talent Group Ltd, 40 Whitfield Street, W1T 2RH.

**ATKINS, John King,** AO 2019; Chairman, Anglicare Western Australia, since 2018; *b* Perth, WA, 24 Dec. 1954; *s* of Alfred and Margaret Atkins; *m* 1986, Kate Fischer; one *s* three *d*. *Educ:* Hale Sch.; Univ. of Western Australia (BJur; LLB); University Coll. London (LLM). Solicitor, 1978–86, Partner, 1986–97, Parker and Parker; Partner, Freehills (formerly Freehill Hollingdale & Page), 1997–2008; Chairman: Western Australia ANZ Bank, 2008–13; Lotterywest, 2011–15; Agent Gen. for WA, London, 2015–18. Former Director: Minotaur Resources Ltd; BWP Property Trust; Australian Finance Gp Ltd; Aurora Oil & Gas Ltd; Asialink; Foodbank Inc. Member, Board: Metropolitan Health Service Bd of WA; Fremantle Hosp. and Health Service; Princess Margaret Hosp. Inc.; Lions Eye Inst. Ltd. Director: Western Australian Healthcare Assoc.; Australian Healthcare Assoc. Member, Board: Australian Chamber of Commerce and Industry; Australian Chamber Alliance; Chamber of Commerce and Industry of WA. Pres. and Mem. Council, Mortgage Industry Assoc. of WA; Dir, Mortgage Industry Assoc. of Australia. Mem. Council, Law Soc. of WA. *Recreations:* golf, tennis, walking, boating. *Clubs:* Weld (Perth); Cottesloe Golf; Royal Freshwater Bay Yacht.

**ATKINS, Prof. Dame Madeleine (Julia),** DBE 2019 (CBE 2012); DL; PhD; President, Lucy Cavendish College, Cambridge, since 2018; *b* 2 July 1952; *d* of Harold and Juliana Dunkerley; *m* 1975, John Michael Atkins; two *s*. *Educ:* Girton Coll., Cambridge (BA Hons 1974); Lady Margaret Hall, Oxford (PGCE); Nottingham Univ. (PhD 1982). Teacher, Hinchingbrooke Comprehensive Sch., 1975–79; post-doctoral res., Nottingham Univ., 1982–83; University Newcastle upon Tyne: Lectr, 1984–88; Sen. Lectr, 1988–2004; Head, Dept of Educn, 1991–96; Dean, Faculty of Educn, 1996–98; Pro-Vice-Chancellor, 1998–2004; Vice-Chancellor, Coventry Univ., 2004–14; Chief Exec., HEFCE, 2014–18. Mem. Bd, HEFCE, 2009–14. Trustee, Nesta Operating Co., 2012–17. DL W Midlands, 2013–18. *Publications:* (with G. A. Brown) Effective Teaching in Higher Education, 1988; contrib. numerous articles on mgt in higher educn and on use of multimedia applications in learning to jls. *Recreations:* theatre, walking. *Address:* Lucy Cavendish College, Lady Margaret Road, Cambridge CB3 0BU.

**ATKINS, Rev. Dr Martyn David;** Superintendent Minister and Team Leader, Methodist Central Hall, Westminster, since 2015; *b* 16 June 1955; *s* of Raymond and Marion Atkins; *m* 1980, Helen Claire Robinson; three *s*. *Educ:* Victoria Univ. of Manchester (BA; PhD 1990). Ordained Methodist Minister, 1981; Leeds (S) Methodist circuit, 1981–86; Shipley and Bingley Methodist circuit, 1986–91; Chaplain, Edgehill Coll., Bideford, Devon, 1991–96; Postgrad. Tutor, 1996–2004, Principal, 2004–08, Cliff Coll., Sheffield; Gen. Sec., Methodist Ch of GB, and Sec., Methodist Conf., 2008–15. Chm. Bd, Fresh Expressions, 2014–18. Pres., Methodist Conference, 2007–08. Mem. Coll., Westminster Abbey, 2015–. Hon. Ecumenical Canon, Sheffield Cathedral, 2010–15. *Publications:* Preaching in a Cultural Context, 2001; Sermon on the Mount, 2002; Resourcing Renewal, 2007; Discipleship and the people called Methodists, 2010. *Recreations:* supporting Leeds United Football Club, book collecting, reading. *Address:* Methodist Central Hall, Storeys Gate, Westminster, SW1H 9NH. *T:* (020) 7654 3809.

**ATKINS, Rt Rev. Peter Geoffrey;** Bishop of Waiapu, 1983–90; Dean, Theological College of St John the Evangelist, Auckland, 1991–96; *b* 29 April 1936; *s* of late Lt-Col Owen Ivan Atkins and Mrs Mary Atkins; *m* 1968, Rosemary Elizabeth (*née* Allen); one *d*. *Educ:* Merchant Taylors' School, Crosby, Liverpool; Sidney Sussex Coll., Cambridge; St John's Coll., Auckland, NZ. MA (Cantab), BD (Otago), LTh (NZ). Ordained deacon, 1962, priest, 1963; Curate, Karori Parish, Wellington, 1962–66; Priest-Tutor, St Peter's Theological Coll., Siota, Solomon Is, 1966–67; Curate, Dannevirke Parish, dio. Waiapu, 1968–70; Vicar of Waipukurau Parish, 1970–73; Diocesan Sec. and Registrar, Diocese of Waiapu, 1973–79; Canon of St John's Cathedral, Napier, 1974–79; Vicar of Havelock North, 1979–83; Archdeacon of Hawkes Bay, 1979–83; Vicar-Gen., Diocese of Waiapu, 1980–83; Commissary to Archbishop of NZ, 1983; Lectr in Liturgy and Evangelism, Univ. of Auckland and Melbourne Coll. of Divinity, 1991–97. Permission to Officiate, Dio. of Auckland, 1997–2012, as bishop and priest, 2013–. Hon. Sen. Res. Fellow, Univ. of Birmingham, 1996. Contributor, Reviews in Religion and Theology, 1997–2006; Mem., Editl Bd, Rural Theology, 2006–13. *Publications:* Good News in Evangelism, 1992; (contrib.) Counselling Issues and South Pacific Communities, 1997; Worship 2000, 1999; Soul Time, 2000; (jtly) Personality Type and Scripture: exploring Luke's gospel, 2000, exploring Matthew's gospel, 2001, exploring Mark's gospel, 2002; Soul Care, 2001; Ascension Now, 2001; (jtly) Family Prayers, 2003; Memory and Liturgy, 2004; (jtly) Cool Prayers, 2004; (jtly) Prayer Kids, 2008; (contrib.) Journeying into Prayer: people and pathways, 2012. *Recreations:* writing, gardening, music, University of the Third Age. *Address:* 9A Paunui Street, St Helier's Bay, Auckland 1071, New Zealand. *T:* (9) 5754775. *E:* peter.rosemary@xtra.co.nz.

**ATKINS, Prof. Peter William,** PhD; FRSC; Professor of Chemistry, University of Oxford, 1998–2007; Fellow and Tutor, Lincoln College, Oxford, 1965–2007, now Supernumerary Fellow (Acting Rector, 2007); author; *b* 10 Aug. 1940; *s* of William Henry Atkins and Ellen Louise Atkins; *m* 1st, 1964, Judith Ann Kearton (marr. diss. 1983); one *d*; 2nd, 1991, Susan Adele Greenfield (*see* Baroness Greenfield) (marr. diss. 2005); 3rd, 2008, Patricia-Jean Nobes. *Educ:* Dr Challoner's Sch., Amersham; Univ. of Leicester (BSc 1961; PhD 1964); MA Oxon 1965. FRSC 2002. Harkness Fellow, UCLA, 1964–65; Lectr, Univ. of Oxford, 1965–2007. Vis. Prof. in China, Japan, France, NZ and Israel. Nyholm Lectr, 1999; Hon. Prof., Mendeleyev Univ., Moscow, 2006. Chairman: Davy-Faraday Lab. Cttee, 1999–2005; Educn Strategy Develt Cttee, 2000, Cttee on Chemistry Educn, 2002–05, IUPAC. Mem. Council, Royal Instn, 1999–2005; Mem. Ct, Leicester Univ., 2000–13. Foreign Mem., Acad. of Sci., Bologna, 2007. Hon. Associate: Rationalist Assoc., 1993; Nat. Secular Soc., 2000; Patron (formerly Dist. Supporter), Humanists UK (formerly British Humanist Assoc.), 2010. Hon. DSc: Utrecht, 1992; Leicester, 2002; Kazan State Technol Univ., 2009. Meldola Medal, RSC, 1969; Grady-Stack Award, ACS, 2016. *Publications:* The Structure of Inorganic Radicals, 1967; Tables for Group Theory, 1970; Molecular Quantum Mechanics, 1970, 5th edn 2011; Physical Chemistry, 1978, 11th edn 2018; Solutions Manual for Physical Chemistry, 1978, 8th edn 2006; Quanta: a handbook of concepts, 1974, 2nd edn 1991; Principles of Physical Chemistry, 1981; The Creation, 1981; Quantization, 1981; Solutions Manual for Molecular Quantum Mechanics, 1983, 2nd edn 1997; The Second Law, 1984; Molecules, 1987, 2nd edn as Atkins' Molecules, 2003; General Chemistry, 1987, 2nd edn 1992; Chemistry: principles and applications, 1988; Inorganic Chemistry, 1990, 5th edn 2010; Atoms, Electrons and Change, 1991; The Elements of Physical Chemistry, 1992, 7th edn 2017; Creation Revisited, 1992; The Periodic Kingdom, 1995; Concepts of Physical Chemistry, 1995; Chemistry: molecules, matter, and change, 1997, 4th edn 1999; Chemical Principles, 1999, 7th edn 2016; Galileo's Finger: the ten great ideas of science, 2003; Physical Chemistry for Life Sciences, 2006, 2nd edn 2011; Four Laws that Drive the Universe, 2007; Quanta, Matter and Change, 2009, 2nd edn as Physical Chemistry: quanta, matter and change, 2014; A Very Short Introduction to: The Laws of Thermodynamics, 2010; On Being, 2011; Reactions: the private life of atoms, 2011; What is Chemistry?, 2013; Physical Chemistry: a very short introduction, 2014; Conjuring the Universe: the origins of the laws of nature, 2018; Molecular Thermodynamics and Kinetics, 2019. *Recreation:* working. *Address:* Lincoln College, Oxford OX1 3DR. *Club:* Athenæum.

**ATKINS, Richard James,** CBE 2016; Further Education Commissioner, since 2016; *b* Bristol, 10 May 1953; *s* of Jim Atkins and Betty Atkins; *m* 1978, Vicky Rooney; two *d*. *Educ:* Bulmershe Coll. (BEd); Univ. of Surrey (MSc). Principal and Chief Executive: Yeovil Coll., 1994–2001; Exeter Coll., 2002–16. Pres., Assoc. of Colls, 2014–15. Chm., AoC Sport, 2012–16. Pro-Chancellor and Mem. Council, Univ. of Exeter, 2016–. Member: RA; Tate; Nat. Trust. FRSA. Hon. Freeman, City of Exeter, 2016. Hon. LLD Exeter, 2015. *Recreations:* spending time with family, supporter of Yeovil Town FC, Exeter City FC and Exeter Chiefs RFC, theatre, art, travel, exploring England's railway network. *Address:* Department for Education, Sanctuary Building, Great Smith Street, SW1P 3BT. *T:* 07887 528739. *Clubs:* Lansdowne; Somerset County Cricket.

**ATKINS, Richard Paul;** QC 2011; a Recorder, since 2005; *b* Coventry, 31 May 1966; *s* of late Michael Richard Atkins and of Margaret Atkins; *m* 1998, Nicola Mary Rutherford-Jones; one *s* one *d*. *Educ:* King Henry VIII Sch., Coventry; St Catherine's Coll., Oxford (BA Hons Juris. 1988; MA). Called to the Bar, Gray's Inn, 1989, Bencher, 2014; in practice as a barrister: 1 Fountain Court Chambers, Birmingham, 1991–2002; St Philips Chambers, Birmingham, 2002– (Head: Criminal Gp, 2011–14; Regulatory Gp, 2014–17); Leader, Midland Circuit, 2014–17; Fee-paid Judge, Restricted Patients Panel, First-tier Tribunal Health Educn and Social Care Chamber (Mental Health), 2014–. Tutor Judge, Judicial Coll., 2012–; a Chm., Disciplinary Tribunal, Financial Reporting Council, 2013–. Mem., Gen. Council of the Bar, 2003– (Chairman: Member Services Bd, 2010–16; Bar Conf. Organising Bd, 2014; Bar Representation Bd, 2016–; Mem., Gen. Mgt Cttee, 2011–; Vice-Chair, 2018; Chair, 2019). Mem. Council, Birmingham Law Soc., 2013–15. Gov., Coventry Sch. Foundn (King Henry VIII and Bablake Schs), 1999–2014 (Chm., 2011–14). *Recreations:* family, wine, humour, member of Coventry School of Music Old Boys' Band. *Address:* St Philips Chambers, 55 Temple Row, Birmingham B2 5LS. *T:* (0121) 246 7000, *Fax:* (0121) 246 7001. *E:* rpatkins@st-philips.com.

**ATKINS, Rt Hon. Sir Robert (James),** Kt 1997; PC 1995; Member (C) North West Region, England, European Parliament, 1999–2014; *b* 5 Feb. 1946; *s* of late Reginald Alfred and of Winifred Margaret Atkins; *m* 1969, Dulcie Mary (*née* Chaplin); one *s* one *d*. *Educ:* Highgate School. Councillor, London Borough of Haringey, 1968–71; Vice-Chm., Greater London Young Conservatives, 1969–70, 1971–72. Contested (C) Luton West, Feb. 1974 and Oct. 1974 general elections. MP (C) Preston North, 1979–83, South Ribble, 1983–97; contested (C) South Ribble, 1997. PPS to Minister of State, DoI, then DTI, 1982–84, to Minister without Portfolio, 1984–85, to Sec. of State for Employment, 1985–87; Parly Under Sec. of State, DTI, 1987–89, Dept of Transport, 1989–90, DoE (Minister for Sport), 1990, DES (Minister for Sport), 1990–92; Minister of State, NI Office, 1992–94; Minister of State for the Environment and the Countryside, DoE, 1994–95. Vice-Chm., Cons. Aviation Cttee, 1979–82; Jt Sec., Cons. Defence Cttee, 1979–82. Chm., NW Cons. MPs, 1996–97; Dep. Leader, British Cons. MEPs, 2004–07; Chief Whip (C), Eur. Parlt, 2008–10. President: Cons. Trade Unionists, 1984–87; Wyre & Preston N Cons. Assoc., 2007–; Preston Cons. Assoc., 2013–; Lancs Assoc. of Local Councils, 2014–; Chm., NW Conservatives, 2015–17. Member: Victorian Soc.; Sherlock Holmes Soc. of London; English Heritage; Historic Churches Preservation Trust; Nat. Trust. Chm., Lancs CCC Develt Assoc., 2002–12. Trustee, Inland Waterways Assoc., 2017– (Chm., NW Region, 2017–). Freeman, City of London, 1989. *Publications:* (contrib.) Changing Gear, 1981. *Recreations:* cricket, ecclesiology, wine, Holmesiana, Pepysiana. *Address:* Manor House, Lancaster Road, Garstang, Lancs PR3 1JA. *Clubs:* Carlton, MCC, Lord's Taverners; Middlesex County Cricket (Hon. Mem.), Lords and Commons Cricket, Lancashire County Cricket (Vice-Pres., 2005–), Garstang Cricket (Pres., 2007–), Preston Grasshoppers Rugby Football (Vice-Pres., 1990–), Garstang Rugby Union Football (Vice-Pres., 2007–).
See also V. M. Atkins.

**ATKINS, Ronald Henry;** *b* Barry, Glam, 13 June 1916; *s* of Frank and Elizabeth Atkins; *m* 1st (marr. diss. 1979); three *s* two *d*; 2nd, 2012, Elizabeth Alison Wildgoose. *Educ:* Barry County Sch.; London Univ. (BA Hons). Teacher, 1949–66 (latterly Head, Eng. Dept, Halstead Sec. Sch.); Lectr, Accrington Coll. of Further Educn, 1970–74. Member: Braintree RDC, 1952–61; (Lab) Preston Dist Council, 1974–76, 1980–2010. Contested (Lab) Lowestoft, 1964; MP (Lab) Preston North, 1966–70 and Feb. 1974–1979. *Recreations:* jazz, dancing, walking, local and national politics, connoisseur of good coffee. *Address:* 38 James Street, Preston, Lancs PR1 4JU. *T:* (01772) 251910.

**ATKINS, Rosemary Jean, (Rosie),** FLS; Curator, Chelsea Physic Garden, 2002–10; *b* 9 Oct. 1947; *m* 1973, Eric James Brown; one *s* one *d*. *Educ:* St Michael's Sch. for Girls, Limpsfield; Ravensbourne Sch. of Art. Sunday Times, 1968–82; freelance journalist and gardening writer, 1982–84; Jt Producer, In the Air, BBC Radio 4; gardening corresp., Today, 1985–92; launch Editor, Gardens Illustrated Mag., 1993–2002. Royal Horticultural Society: a Judge, 2004–; Mem., Nominations, Appts and Governance Cttee, 2006–13; Mem., Mgt Council, 2010–15; Chairman: Awards Adv. Cttee, 2010–15; Woody Plant Cttee, 2016–. Member: Garden Panel, English Heritage, 2011–; Exec. Cttee, Metropolitan Public Gardens Assoc., 2012–16 (Vice Pres., 2017–). Chm., London Gardens Network, 2009–12. Trustee: Thrive, 1998–2003; Gardening for Disabled Trust, 1998–2011; Gt Dixter Charitable Trust, 2008–; Professional Gardeners' Trust, 2015–; Vice Pres., Linnean Soc., 2017– (Trustee, 2015–17). Mem., London Liby. FLS 2004. Editor's Editor Award, BSME, 1996. *Publications:* (jtly) The Sunday Times Book of the Countryside, 1978; (contrib.) Making a Garden: the history of the National Garden Scheme, 2001; (ed) Gardens Illustrated Plant Profiles, 2003; Roses, 2004; (contrib.) Plant: exploring the botanical world, 2016. *Recreations:* gardening, lecturing, painting, travel. *E:* rosie19@ymail.com. *Club:* Chelsea Arts.

**ATKINS, Dr Susan Ruth Elizabeth,** CB 2014; Service Complaints Commissioner for the Armed Forces, 2007–15; *b* 4 March 1952; *d* of late Victor Charles Rodney Prickett and Marian Sarah Gertrude Prickett; *m* 1977, Stephen Thomas Atkins; one *s* one *d*. *Educ:* Manchester High Sch. for Girls; Univ. of Birmingham (LLB Hons); Univ. of Calif, Berkeley (Master of Criminol.); Univ. of Southampton (PhD 1986). Admitted solicitor, 1977. Articled clerk, GLC, 1974–77; Lectr in Law, Univ. of Southampton, 1977–89; Principal, Home Office, 1989–93; Dep. Chief Exec., EOC, 1993–95; Home Office: Head: of Extradition, 1995–96; of Personnel Policy, 1996–99; of Probation, 1999–2000; Dir, Women and Equality Unit, Cabinet Office, 2000–02; Chief Exec., Ind. Police Complaints Commn, 2003–06; Interim Chief Exec., Appts Commn, 2007. Vis. Fellow, 1989–95, Vis. Prof., 1995–2001, Univ. of Southampton. Non-exec. Bd Mem., HMP Manchester, 1994–95; Bd Mem., QAA, 2004–10; non-exec. Dir, Leadership Foundn for Higher Educn, 2007–13. Member, Advisory Board: Geneva Centre for Democratic Control of Armed Forces, 2015–18; Centre for Women, Peace and Security, LSE, 2015– (Interim Chair, 2016–17); Mem., Ind. Adv. Bd, RMA Sandhurst, 2015–. *Publications:* (with B. Hoggett) Women and the Law, 1984, 2018; contribs to books and legal jls on sex discrimination, European law, the Armed Forces and human rights. *Recreations:* reading, travel, tapestry.

**ATKINS, Victoria Mary;** MP (C) Louth and Horncastle, since 2015; Parliamentary Under-Secretary of State, Home Office, since 2017; Minister for Women, since 2018; *d* of Rt Hon. Sir Robert (James) Atkins, *qv*; *m* Paul; one *s*. *Educ:* Corpus Christi Coll., Cambridge (BA Law). Called to the Bar, Middle Temple, 1998; in practice as barrister, specialising in serious organised crime, 1998–2015. *Address:* House of Commons, SW1A 0AA.

**ATKINSON, Prof. Alan,** PhD; FInstP, FIMMM; Professor of Materials Chemistry, Imperial College London, since 1995 (part-time, since 2010); *b* Heckmondwike, W Yorks, 4 Oct. 1944; *s* of Norman Atkinson and Marion Atkinson; *m* 1979, Rita Jain; one *s* one *d*. *Educ:* Batley Grammar Sch.; Selwyn Coll., Cambridge (BA Natural Scis 1967); Univ. of Leeds (PhD Phys 1971). FInstP 1989; FIMMM 1994. Res. Fellow, Univ. of Leeds, 1970–75; Res. Scientist, AERE Harwell, 1975–90; Hd, Materials Chem., AERE Harwell, subseq. AEA Technol., 1990–95; Dean, Faculty of Engrg, Imperial Coll. London, 2007–10. Fellow, Amer. Ceramic Soc., 2010. *Publications:* over 300 contribs to learned jls and technical books. *Recreations:* tennis, golf, cycling, photography, music. *Address:* Department of Materials, Imperial College London, SW7 2AZ. *T:* (020) 7594 6780. *E:* alan.atkinson@imperial.ac.uk.

**ATKINSON, Prof. Bernard,** OBE 2001; FREng, FIChemE; Director-General, BRF International (formerly Director, Brewing Research Foundation), 1981–96; *b* 17 March 1936; *s* of late Thomas Atkinson and of Elizabeth Ann (*née* Wilcox); *m* 1957, Kathleen Mary Richardson; two *s*. *Educ:* Farnworth Grammar Sch.; Univ. of Birmingham (BSc); Univ. of Manchester Inst. of Science and Technology; PhD Univ. of Manchester. FREng (FEng 1980). Post-Doctoral Fellow and Asst Prof., Rice Univ., Houston, Texas, 1960–63; Lectr, Sen. Lectr in Chem. Engrg, and latterly Reader in Biochem. Engrg, University Coll. of Swansea, 1963–74 (Hon. Fellow, 1991); Prof. and Head of Dept of Chem. Engrg, UMIST, 1974–81; Visiting Professor: UMIST, 1981–86; Swansea, 1986–96; Heriot-Watt, 1991–96. European Brewery Convention: Mem., Management Cttee and Council, 1990–97; Vice Pres., 1991–97. Mem., BBSRC, 1996–2001. Gov., Queen Victoria Hosp. NHS Foundn Trust, 2004–11 (Vice-Chm., 2009–11; Gov. Rep., Bd of Dirs, 2007–10). Editor, Biochemical Engineering Journal, 1983–93. Senior Moulton Medal, IChemE, 1976; Gairn EEC Medal, Soc. of Engrs, 1985; Presidential Award, Master Brewers' Assoc. of the Americas, 1988; Donald Medal, IChemE, 1996. *Publications:* Biochemical Reactors, 1974, trans. Japanese, Russian, Spanish; (with P. F. Cooper) Biological Fluidised Bed Treatment of Water and Waste Water, 1981; (with F. Mavituna) Biochemical Engineering and Biotechnology Handbook, 1982, 2nd edn 1991; (ed) Research and Innovation in the 1990s: the chemical engineering challenge, 1986; (with C. Webb and G. M. Black) Process Engineering Aspects of Immobilised Cell Systems, 1986; numerous contribs to chemical engrg and biochemical engrg jls. *Recreations:* cycling, sailing, walking. *Address:* Little Mieders, Borers Arms Road, Copthorne, Crawley, West Sussex RH10 3LJ. *T:* (01342) 713181. *Club:* Square Rigger (Gosport) (Sec., 2007–12).

**ATKINSON, Prof. Bruce Wilson,** PhD; Professor of Geography, Queen Mary and Westfield College (formerly at Queen Mary College), University of London, 1983–2004, now Emeritus; *b* 28 Sept. 1941; *s* of J. and S. A. Atkinson. *Educ:* University Coll., London (BSc, PhD). CGeog 2002. Queen Mary, subseq. Queen Mary and Westfield College, University of London: Lectr, 1964–78; Reader, 1978–83; Hd, Dept of Geog., 1985–89; Dean of Social Scis, 1991–94; Mem., Senate and Acad. Council, Univ. of London, 1991–94. Natural Environment Research Council: Mem., 1982–85, Chm., 1988–91, Aquatic & Atmospheric Phys. Sci. Cttee; Member: Neutral Atmosphere Adv. Panel to British Antarctic Survey, 1984; Atmos. Sci., Marine Sci., Terrestrial and Freshwater Sci. and Higher Educn Affairs Cttees, 1988–91; British Antarctic Survey (Ice and Climate Div.) Peer and Merit Rev. Gp, 1989–96; Rev. Gp on Hydrogeology, 1990; Scientific Steering Gp, UK Global Atmosphere Modelling Prog., 1991–93. Mem., RAE (Envmtl Sci.) 2001. Member: Meteorol and Atmos. Phys. Sub-cttee, Nat. Cttee on Geodesy and Geophysics, 1988–90; Scientific Adv. Cttee, Meteorol Office, 1996–2004. Mem. Council and cttees, and Editor, Weather, RMetS, 1972–79; Chm., Pubns Cttee, 1992–98, Mem. Council, 1993–95, RGS-IBG (formerly RGS); Mem., Assoc. Brit. Climatologists, 1970– (Chm., 1976–78). Ed., Progress in Physical Geography, 1977–2008. Hugh Robert Mill Medal, RMetS, 1974; Back Award, RGS, 1981. *Publications:* Weather Business, 1968; (ed) Dynamical Meteorology, 1981; Meso-scale Atmospheric Circulations, 1981; Weather: Review of UK Statistical Sources, 1985; (ed jtly) Encyclopædic Dictionary of Physical Geography, 1986; (with A. Gadd) Weather: a modern guide to forecasting, 1986; articles in geographical, geophys. and meteorol jls. *Recreations:* walking, music. *Clubs:* Athenæum, Geographical.

**ATKINSON, Carol Lesley, (Mrs C. A. Kinch); Her Honour Judge Atkinson,** a Circuit Judge, since 2007; Designated Family Judge, East London, since 2014; *b* N Yorks, 29 Sept. 1962; *d* of George Atkinson and Maureen Atkinson (*née* Heslop); *m* 1994, Christopher Anthony Kinch, *qv*; one *s* two *d*. *Educ:* Cleveland Girls Grammar Sch.; Rye Hills Sch., Redcar; Sir William Turner's Sixth Form Coll.; Lancaster Univ. (LLB Hons); Inns of Court Sch. of Law. Called to the Bar, Gray's Inn, 1985 (Karmel Schol. 1986); Recorder, 2001–07. Mem., Bar Council, 1997–2007. Sec., Family Law Bar Assoc., 2004–07. *Recreations:* my children, running, swimming, music, Middlesbrough FC; Black Belt, 1st Dan, Karate, playing alto sax. *Address:* East London Family Court, 11 Westferry Circus, E14 4HD.

**ATKINSON, David Alastair;** Headmaster, Dr Challoner's Grammar School, Amersham, since 2016; *b* Reading, 2 June 1973; *s* of Keith Atkinson and Sandra Atkinson; *m* 1999, Clare Ireland; one *d*. *Educ:* Reading Blue Coat Sch.; Hertford Coll., Oxford (BA Hons Geog. 1994). PGCE 1996). Dr Challoner's Grammar School: Teacher of Geography, 1996–98; Hd of Geography, 1998–2003; Asst Dir, Sixth Form, 2003–08; Dir, Sixth Form, 2008–14; Dep. Headmaster, 2014–16. Chief Accounting Officer, Astra Sch. Centred Initial Teacher Trng provider and Teaching Sch. Alliance, 2016–. Chair, Bucks Schs Cricket Assoc., 2016– (Sec., 2002–16). Vice-Pres. and Trustee, RGS (with IBG), 2018–. *Publications:* Weathering, Slopes and Landforms, 2004. *Recreations:* cricket, music, travel, geocaching. *Address:* Dr Challoner's Grammar School, Chesham Road, Amersham HP5 6HA. *E:* headmaster@challoners.com. *Clubs:* MCC, Lansdowne.

**ATKINSON, Rt Rev. Dr David John;** Bishop Suffragan of Thetford, 2001–09; an Hon. Assistant Bishop, Diocese of Southwark, since 2009; *b* 5 Sept. 1943; *s* of Thomas John Collins and Adèle Mary Atkinson; *m* 1969, Suzan Elizabeth; one *s* one *d*. *Educ:* King's Coll., London (BSc, PhD, AKC); Bristol Univ. (MLitt); Oxford Univ. (MA); Tyndale Hall, Bristol. Teacher of Chemistry, Maidstone Tech. High Sch. for Boys, 1968–69. Ordained deacon, 1972, priest, 1973; Assistant Curate: St Peter Halliwell, Bolton, 1972–74; Harborne Heath, Birmingham, 1974–77; Librarian, Latimer House, Oxford, 1977–80; Chaplain, 1980–93, Fellow, 1984–93, Corpus Christi Coll., Oxford; Canon Chancellor and Missioner, Southwark Cathedral, 1993–96; Archdeacon of Lewisham, 1996–2001. Co-Founder, Oxford Christian Inst. for Counselling, 1985. Mem., SOSc, 1987. *Publications:* To Have and To Hold, 1979; The Bible Speaks Today (series): Ruth, 1983; Genesis 1–11, 1990; Job, 1991; Proverbs, 1996; Peace in Our Time?, 1985; Pastoral Ethics, 1989, 2nd edn 1994; (jtly) Counselling in Context, 1994, 2nd edn 1998; (ed jtly) New Dictionary of

Christian Ethics and Pastoral Theology, 1995; Jesus, Lamb of God, 1996; God So Loved the World, 1999; Renewing the Face of the Earth: a theological and pastoral response to climate change, 2008; The Church's Healing Ministry, 2011; Hope Rediscovered: biblical wisdom for an anxious world, 2018; articles and reviews in jls. *Recreations:* music, walking, photography, enjoying being with my eight grandchildren. *Address:* 6 Bynes Road, South Croydon CR2 0PR. *T:* (020) 8406 0895. *E:* davidatkinson43@virginmedia.com.

**ATKINSON, David Rowland;** Regional Chairman, British Gas East Midlands, 1987–92; *b* 18 June 1930; *s* of late Rowland Hodgson Atkinson and Nora Marian (*née* Coleman); *m* 1956, Marian Eileen Sales (*d* 2016); one *d*. *Educ:* Wrekin College. FCA, CCMI, CompIGasE. National Coal Board: NW Div., 1955; E Midlands Div., 1961; Chief Accountant, W Midlands Gas, 1969; Dir of Finance, E Midlands Gas, 1977; Dep. Chm., SE Gas, 1983; Dir of Finance, British Gas, 1985. *Recreations:* Rugby, gardening, ciné photography. *Address:* 28 Browning Court, Bourne, Lincs PE10 9FA.

**ATKINSON, Duncan;** *see* Atkinson, R. D.

**ATKINSON, Eileen Maria;** *see* Milner, E. M.

**ATKINSON, Prof. Helen Valerie,** CBE 2014; PhD; CEng, FREng, FIMMM, FIMechE; Pro-Vice-Chancellor, School of Aerospace, Transport and Manufacturing, Cranfield University, since 2017; *b* Portadown, NI, 29 April 1960; *d* of Arthur and Sheila Bavister; *m* 1984, Rt Rev. Richard William Bryant Atkinson, *qv*; one *s* two *d*. *Educ:* South Park High Sch., Lincoln; Girton Coll., Cambridge (BA 1981); Imperial Coll. of Sci. and Technol., Univ. of London (PhD 1986; DIC 1986). MIM 1985, FIMMM 1998; CEng 1986; FIMechE 2004; FREng 2007. SO, 1981–83, HSO, 1983–87, SSO, 1987, Materials Develt Div., UKAEA, Harwell; Sen. Lectr in Materials, Sheffield City Poly., 1987–89; Lectr, 1989–96, Sen. Lectr, 1996–2000, Reader, 2000–02, in Materials, Univ. of Sheffield; University of Leicester: Prof. of Materials Processing, 2002–17; Head: Mechanics of Materials Gp, 2004–14, Dept of Engrg, 2012–16; Interim Graduate Dean, 2016–17. Vis. Prof., Ecole d'Arts et Métiers, ParisTech, Centre Paris, 2010–. Member: UK Foresight Panel on Materials, 1994–99; Action Gp on Sensors, Office of Sci. and Technol., 1996–97; British Transport Police Cttee, 1998–2003; Chem. and Materials Task Force, UK Foresight Crime Prevention Panel, 1999–2001; Lord Chancellor's Adv. Cttee for Appt of Magistrates in Rotherham, 2000–02; Implementation Gp for Govt's Strategy on Women in Sci., Engrg and Technol., DTI, 2004–07; Advanced Materials Leadership Council, BEIS (formerly BIS)/EPSRC, 2015–16. Member: Bd of Dirs, Eur. Soc. of Material Forming, 2007–12; Educn and Trng Panel, EngineeringUK (formerly Engrg and Technol. Bd), 2008–12; Royal Academy of Engineering: Mem., Standing Cttee on Educn and Trng, 2008–11 (Chair, 2012–17); Trustee, 2011–16; Vice Pres., 2012–14; Chair, Engrg Talent Campaign Ref. Gp, 2017–. Jt Chm., Engrg Professors' Council/Engrg and Technol. Bd Cttee on costs of teaching engrg degrees, 2007–08. Member, Council: Inst. of Metals, 1989–91; Inst. of Materials, 1992–96. Mem. Cttee, Engrg Professors' Council, 2004–. Mem., Strategic Facilities Adv. Bd, Sir Henry Royce Inst., 2016–. Member: Oxford Diocesan Bd of Social Responsibility, 1986–87; Sheffield Diocesan Bd of Social Responsibility, 1990–91. Pres., Engrg Professors' Council, 2011–13. Member, Editorial Board: Jl Fatigue and Fracture of Engrg Materials and Structures, 1996–2002; Internat. Jl Microstructure and Material Properties, 2004–16. Dr hc Liège, 2010. Plowden Prize, British Nuclear Energy Soc., 1985; (jtly) Williams Prize, IMMM, 2002; Woman of Outstanding Achievement, UK Resource Centre for Women in Sci., Engrg and Technol., 2010. *Publications:* (with B. A. Rickinson) Hot Isostatic Processing, 1991; (ed) Modelling of Semi-Solid Processing, 2008; (ed) Thixoforming Steel, 2010; contrib. papers on metallurgy and materials sci. *Recreations:* gardening, singing, walking. *Address:* School of Aerospace, Transport and Manufacturing, Cranfield University, Cranfield MK43 0AL. *T:* (01234) 754769.

**ATKINSON, Prof. Janette,** PhD; FBA 2015; FMedSci; Professor of Psychology and Developmental Cognitive Neuroscience, University College London, 1993–2010, now Emeritus; *m* 1979, Prof. Oliver John Braddick, *qv*; two *s* two *d*. *Educ:* Univ. of Bristol (BSc Psychol. 1965); Univ. of Cambridge (George Henry Lewes Student; PhD Adult Vision 1970). Henry George Plimmer Fellow, Imperial Coll. London, 1968–70; Research Associate: Inst. of Behavioral Genetics, Colorado, 1971–72; Dept of Psychol., Johns Hopkins Univ., 1972; Sen. Res. Associate, 1972–83, MRC Ext. Scientific Staff, 1983–2009, Dept of Exptl Psychol., Univ. of Cambridge, then UCL, later Univ. of Oxford; estabd Visual Develt Unit, Univ. of Cambridge, 1976, UCL, 1993, Univ. of Oxford, 2003; University College London: Vice-Dean, Faculty of Life Sci., 1998–2002; Internat. Pro Provost, N America, 2005–08; Mem., Nat. Steering Cttee, Athena Scientific Women's Academic Network, 2005–14; Ambassador, Athena Scientific Women's Academic Network and Survey of Sci., Engrg and Technol., 2004–10; Sen. Advr, Gender Equality Scheme, 2007; Leverhulme Emeritus Fellow, 2012–14. Visiting Professor: UCSD, 1981–; Salk Inst., San Diego, 1987; Nankai Univ., Tianjin, China, 2008; Univ. of Oxford, 2003. MAE 2008. FMedSci 2002. Young Inventor's Award, MRC, 1989; Dist. Speaker's Medal, Sch. of Optometry, Ohio State Univ., 1992; Kurt Koffka Medal, Giessen Univ., 2009; Davida Teller Award, Vision Scis Soc., 2016. *Publications:* The Developing Visual Brain, 2000; over 200 chapters; contrib. scientific jls on vision and visual brain develt. *Address:* Division of Psychology and Language Sciences, Faculty of Brain Sciences, University College London, Gower Street, WC1E 6BT.

**ATKINSON, Janice Ann;** Member for South East Region, European Parliament, 2014–19 (UK Ind, 2014–15, Ind, 2015–19); *b* London, 31 Aug. 1962; *d* of George and Lillian Coombs; *m* 1st, Steve Small (marr. diss.); two *s*; 2nd, Simon Atkinson; one step *s* one step *d*. Owner, media and mktg agency; Global PR Dir, Byronwilde Ltd, 2012–. Jt Founder, WomenOn.org. Founder, Europe of Nations and Freedom Gp, EP, 2015–19 (Vice Pres., 2015–19); Sen. Mem., EU/US Delegn Cttee, EP. Contested (C) Batley and Spen, 2010. Writer, UK Sputnik; reporter, Rebel Media, Canada, 2019–.

**ATKINSON, Kent;** *see* Atkinson, M. K.

**ATKINSON, Dr Margaret Elizabeth;** Founder and Chief Executive Officer, Maggie Atkinson Consulting Ltd, since 2016; *b* Barnsley, S Yorks, 16 Sept. 1956; *d* of Colin Cragg and Kathleen Cragg; *m* 1999, Andrew Atkinson; one step *s* one step *d*. *Educ:* Pope Pius X RC Comp. Sch., Wath-on-Dearne; Mexborough VI Form Coll.; Newnham Coll., Cambridge (BA Hons Hist. 1978); Sheffield Univ. (PGCE 1979); Keele Univ. (EdD 2008). Teacher of English and Drama, Hungerhill Comp. Sch., Doncaster, 1979–87; Hd of English, Birkdale Comp. Sch., Dewsbury, 1987–89; W and N Yorks Co-ordinator, Lang. in the Nat. Curriculum Proj., 1989–91; Educn Adviser and Inspector: Birmingham, 1991–92; Kirklees, 1992–98; Asst Dir of Educn, Warrington, 1998–99, seconded as Dep. Dir of Educn to Liverpool CC, 1999; County Manager, Cheshire LEA, 1999–2003; Gp Dir Learning and Culture and Dir of Educn, later Gp Dir Learning and Children and Dir of Children's Services, Gateshead Council, 2003–10; Children's Comr for England, 2010–15. Member: Children and Young People's Health Outcomes Forum, 2011–14; DoH Children and Young People's Mental Health and Well-Being Taskforce, 2014–15. Chm., Bd of Dirs, A New Direction, 2015–; Chair: Wirral Safeguarding Children Bd, 2017–; Wigan Educn Partnership Bd, 2018–; Trustee, Michael Sieff Foundn, 2015–; Member: Think Tank, KidZania London, 2015–; Calouste Gulbenkian Foundn Inquiry into Arts Orgns and Civic Roles, 2017–; Adult Adv. Bd, Children's Comr, States of Jersey, 2018–; Advr on cultural strategies to incl. children and young people as rights holders in arts and culture settings, Rotherham Council. Hon. Prof., Keele Univ., 2013–. Pres., Assoc. of Dirs of Children's Services, 2008–09. Mem. Court, Bishop Grosseteste Univ., Lincoln, 2013–15. FRSA; FIAM; Fellow, ILM; Mem., Internat. Fedn of Professional Aromatherapists. Mem., Northumberland Pipers' Soc. Hon. DCL: Northumbria, 2010; Keele, 2015; Hon. EdD Nottingham Trent, 2017. Pres.'s Medal, RCPsych, 2014. *Publications:* (contrib.) Research in Practice, 2016; (contrib.) Justice for Children and Families: a developmental perspective, 2018; (contrib.) Including Children and Young People with Special Educational Needs and Disabilities in Learning and Life, 2019; articles in TES, Children and Young People Now Mag., BMJ Archives of Diseases in Childhood, Local Govt Chronicle. *Recreations:* playing Northumbrian small pipes, gardening, piano, singing, travel, arts (watching, making, celebrating), family, DIY, aromatherapy (qualified aromatherapist, 1997), church affairs, walking, good food, wine and company, birdwatching, range of hand crafts, cycling (road, beach and wild country settings), gym and cross-fit activities. *E:* maggieatkinsonconsulting@gmail.com.

**ATKINSON, (Michael) Kent;** Group Finance Director, Lloyds TSB Group plc, 1994–2002 (non-executive Director, 2002–03); *b* 19 May 1945; *s* of late Carl Kent Atkinson and Edith Atkinson (*née* Gilbert); *m* 1970, Eufemia Alexandra Alarcón; two *s*. *Educ:* Blundell's Sch. Entered Bank of London & South America Ltd, 1964: sen. appts, Bank of London/Lloyds Bank Internat. Ltd in Colombia, Ecuador, Panama, Bahrain, Dubai, Paraguay and Argentina, 1967–86; Gen. Manager, Argentina, Chile, Peru, Bolivia, Paraguay and Uruguay, 1987–89; Lloyds Bank plc: Regl Exec. Dir, 1989–94; Gen. Manager, Retail Ops, 1994. Non-executive Director: Coca-Cola HBC SA (formerly Coca-Cola Beverages), 1998–2013; telent plc (formerly Marconi Corp.), 2002–07; Cookson Gp plc, 2003–05; Standard Life plc (formerly Standard Life Assurance Co.), 2005–11; Gemalto (formerly Axalto) NV, 2005–13; Millicom Internat. SA, 2007–10; Northern Rock plc, 2008–09; Northern Rock (Asset Mgt) plc, 2010–16; Bradford & Bingley plc, 2010–16; UK Asset Resolution Ltd, 2010–16; BILT Paper plc, 2011; Bank of Ireland Gp plc, 2012–; Chairman: Standard Life Bank Ltd, 2007; Link Plus Corp., 2006–08. *Recreations:* tennis, golf, Rugby, soccer, cricket, theatre, opera, technology. *Clubs:* Effingham Golf, Horsley Sports.

**ATKINSON, Michael William,** CMG 1985; MBE 1970; HM Diplomatic Service, retired; *b* 11 April 1932; *m* 1963, Veronica Bobrovsky; two *s* one *d*. *Educ:* Purley County Grammar School; Queen's College, Oxford (BA Hons). Served FO, Vientiane, Buenos Aires, British Honduras, Madrid; FCO 1975; NATO Defence Coll., 1976; Counsellor, Budapest, 1977–80, Peking, 1980–82; Hd of Consular Dept, FCO, 1982–85; Ambassador: to Ecuador, 1985–89; to Romania, 1989–92; Personnel Assessor, FCO, 1992–98.

**ATKINSON, Nigel John Bewley;** Lord-Lieutenant of Hampshire, since 2014 (Vice Lord-Lieutenant, 2007–14); Chairman, Centurion Safety Products Ltd, since 2009; *b* London, 25 Dec. 1953; *s* of John Bewley Atkinson, MBE and Jean Margaret Atkinson; *m* 1987, Christine Pamela Oliver; one *d* and one step *s* one step *d*. *Educ:* Haileybury Coll.; RMA Sandhurst. Served RGJ, Captain and Adjt, 1973–79. Courage Ltd: District Manager, 1979–83; Retail Services Manager, 1983–85; Regl Gen. Manager, 1985–87; Sales Dir, 1987–90; Chief Exec., George Gale & Co. Ltd, 1990–2006. Non-executive Chairman: S E Hants Enterprise Agencies, 1992–2003; Ocean Radio Gp, 2001–07. Chm., Flowrite Services Ltd, 2012–15; non-executive Director: Fuller, Smith & Turner plc, 2006–12; Wadworth & Co. Ltd, 2012–; David Cover and Son Ltd, 2014–. Chm., St John Ambulance, Hants, 2001–09; Vice-Pres., Duke of Edinburgh Award, Hants, 1998–2014. Trustee, HMS Warrior 1860, 2001–17. Honorary Colonel: Hants & IoW ACF, 2009–; 4 Princess of Wales's Royal Regt, 2018–. Patron: King Edward VI Sch., Southampton, 2014–; Hants Constabulary Volunteer Police Cadets, 2014–. Liveryman, Brewers' Co., 1994 (Court Asst, 1999; Master, 2010–11). DL Hants, 1999. KStJ 2015 (CStJ 2007). *Recreations:* tennis, ski-ing. *Address:* c/o Hampshire Lieutenancy Office, Serle's House, Gar Street, Winchester, Hants SO23 8GQ. *Clubs:* Lansdowne, Royal Green Jackets; Royal Naval and Royal Albert Yacht (Southsea), Royal Southampton Yacht.

**ATKINSON, Very Rev. Peter Gordon;** Dean of Worcester, since 2007; *b* 26 Aug. 1952; *m* 1983, Lynne Wilcock; two *s* one *d*. *Educ:* St John's Coll., Oxford (BA 1974; MA 1978); Westcott House, Cambridge. Ordained: deacon, 1979; priest, 1980; Asst Curate, Clapham Old Town Ministry, 1979–83; Priest-in-charge, St Mary, Tatsfield, 1983–90; Rector, Holy Trinity, Bath, 1990–91; Principal, Chichester Theol Coll., 1991–94; Rector, Lavant, 1994–97; Bursalis Preb., 1991–97, Canon Residentiary and Chancellor, 1997–2007, Chichester Cathedral; Dio. Warden of Readers, Chichester, 2001–03. Mem., Gen. Synod of C of E, 2000–05. Vice-Chm., 2002–07, Chm., 2007–, Cathedral Libraries and Archives Assoc.; Mem., Cathedrals Fabric Commn for England, 2001–05, 2015–. Master, St Oswald's Hosp., Worcester, 2007–. FRSA 2006. Hon. DLitt Worcester, 2014. *Publications:* (contrib.) Stepping Stones: joint essays on Anglican Catholic and Evangelical Unity, ed C. Baxter, 1987; Friendship and the Body of Christ, 2005; The Lion Encyclopedia of the Bible, 2009; (contrib.) Holy Ground: cathedrals in the Twenty-First Century, ed S. Platten, 2017; (contrib.) Life After Tragedy: essays on faith and the First World War evoked by Geoffrey Studdert Kennedy, ed M. Brierley and G. Byrne, 2017. *Recreations:* English literature, European history, living in Normandy. *Address:* The Deanery, 10 College Green, Worcester WR1 2LH. *T:* (01905) 732909, 732939.

**ATKINSON, Peter Landreth;** *b* 19 Jan. 1943; *s* of Major Douglas Wilson Atkinson, RTR (*d* Burma, 1945) and of Amy Landreth; *m* 1976, Brione, *d* of late Comdr Arthur Darley, RN and Elspeth Darley; two *d*. *Educ:* Cheltenham Coll. Journalist, 1961–87 (formerly News Editor, Evening Standard); Dep. Dir, British Field Sports Soc., 1987–92. Councillor: London Borough of Wandsworth, 1978–82; Suffolk County Council, 1989–92. MP (C) Hexham, 1992–2010. PPS to Chm. of Cons. Pty, 1994–95, 1997–98, to Sec. of State for Transport, 1996–97; an Opposition Whip, 1999–2002, 2003–05. Member: Select Cttee on Scottish Affairs, 1992–2002; Speaker's Panel of Chairmen, 1997–99, 2005–10; Procedure Cttee, 2003–05. *Recreations:* shooting, racing, gardening. *Club:* Northern Counties (Newcastle).

**ATKINSON, (Richard) Duncan;** QC 2016; a Recorder, since 2012; Senior Treasury Counsel, Central Criminal Court, since 2015; *b* Maidstone, 9 June 1973; *s* of David and Elisabeth Atkinson; *m* 2014, Duncan Campbell. *Educ:* King's Sch., Rochester (Chorister, then Hd Chorister, Rochester Cathedral); Westhill Acad., Aberdeen; Bristol Univ. (Organ Schol.; LLB 1st Cl. Law); Inns of Court Sch. of Law. Called to the Bar, Gray's Inn, 1995; Jun. Prosecuting Counsel, Central Criminal Court, 2009–15. Dir of Music, St Margaret's, Lee, 2006–. *Publications:* (contrib.) Blackstone's Guide to Criminal Procedure Rules, 2005; (contrib.) Blackstone's Criminal Practice, 2017–; (ed) EU Law in Criminal Practice, 2013. *Recreations:* music (opera, organ playing), art, good food and good friends. *Address:* 6KBW College Hill, 21 College Hill, EC4R 2RP. *T:* (020) 3301 0910, *Fax:* (020) 3301 0911. *E:* duncan.atkinson@6kbw.com.

**ATKINSON, Rt Rev. Richard William Bryant;** *see* Bedford, Bishop Suffragan of.

**ATKINSON, Rowan Sebastian,** CBE 2013; actor and writer; *b* 6 Jan. 1955; *s* of late Eric Atkinson and Ella May Atkinson; one *s* two *d*. *Educ*: Durham Cathedral Choristers' Sch.; St Bees Sch.; Newcastle Univ.; Oxford Univ. (BSc, MSc). *Stage*: Beyond a Joke, Hampstead, 1978; The Secret Policeman's Ball, 1979; The Secret Policeman's Other Ball, 1981; Revue (with Richard Curtis), 1980–81; youngest person to have a one-man show in the West End of London, 1981; The Nerd, 1984; Rowan Atkinson at the Atkinson (with Angus Deayton), 1986; The Sneeze, 1988; Rowan Atkinson, UK tour, 1991; Oliver!, Th. Royal, 2009; Quartermaine's Terms, Wyndham's Th., 2013; *television*: Rowan Atkinson Presents… Canned Laughter, 1979; Not the Nine O'clock News, 1979–82; The Black Adder, 1983; Blackadder II, 1985; Comic Relief, 1986–2016; Blackadder the Third, 1987; Blackadder's Christmas Carol, 1988; Blackadder goes Forth, 1989; Mr Bean, 1990–94; Bernard and the Genie, 1991; Funny Business (documentary), 1992; Rowan Atkinson on Location in Boston, 1992; The Driven Man, 1993; Heroes and Villains: Full Throttle, 1995; The Thin Blue Line, 1995; A Royal Birthday Celebration, 1998; The Royal Variety Performance, 2000; The Jubilee Girl, 2002; Mr Bean (animated series), 2003–19; Horrible Histories, 2015; Maigret Sets a Trap, 2016; Maigret's Dead Man, 2016; Maigret's Night at the Crossroads, Maigret in Montmartre, 2017; *films*: Never Say Never Again, 1983; The Tall Guy, The Appointments of Dennis Jennings, 1989; The Witches, 1990; Hot Shots—Part Deux, 1993; Four Weddings and a Funeral, The Lion King, 1994; Bean—The Ultimate Disaster Movie, 1997; Maybe Baby, 2000; Rat Race, Scooby Doo, 2002; Johnny English, Love Actually, 2003; Keeping Mum, 2005; Mr Bean's Holiday, 2007; Johnny English Reborn, 2011; Johnny English Strikes Again, 2018. *Recreations*: motor cars, motor sport. *Address*: c/o PBJ Management Ltd, 22 Rathbone Street, W1T 1LG. *T*: (020) 7287 1112. *E*: general@pbjmanagement.co.uk.

**ATKINSON, Shirley Anne,** OBE 2019; Vice Chancellor and Chief Executive, University of Sunderland, 2015–18, now Emeritus Professor; *b* Morpeth, Northumberland, 6 April 1960; *d* of Samuel Franklin and Mary Theresa Franklin (*née* Lannon); *m* 1979, David Ross Atkinson; one *s* one *d*. *Educ*: Liverpool John Moores Univ.; Univ. of Northampton (MSc Finance); Harvard Business Sch. (Global Leadership Prog.). Principal Accountant, Newcastle CC, 1987–96; Sen. Advr, CIPFA, 1996–2002; Exec. Dir, Nexus, Tyne and Wear PTE, 2002–08; Dep. Vice Chancellor, 2008–14, Interim Vice Chancellor, 2014–15, Univ. of Sunderland. Dir, Sunderland BID, 2016–18; Mem., Sunderland Econ. Leadership Bd, 2014–18. Gov., City of Sunderland Coll., 2011–18. Trustee, SW Durham UTC, 2013–18. Fellow, CIPFA 2016 (CPFA 1989); FRSA. *Recreations*: walking, family, reading.

**ATKINSON, Dr Susan, (Sue),** CBE 2002; FFPH; Visiting Professor, Department of Epidemiology and Public Health, University College London, since 2002; Chairman, Public Health Action Support Team, since 2007; *b* 10 Aug. 1946; *d* of Fredrick Booth Atkinson and Jay Atkinson (*née* Carruthers); *m*; one *d*. *Educ*: Merchant Taylors' Sch. for Girls; UCNW (BSc Zoology); New Hall, Cambridge (MA 1976; MB BChir 1975); Middlesex Hosp. Med. Sch. DCH 1977; FFPH (FFPHM 1989). Res. Associate in animal behaviour/zool., Univ. of Cambridge, 1969–70; Registrar and SHO posts, Paediatrics, Bristol Children's Hosp. and Addenbrooke's Hosp., 1976–78; Registrar in Public Health Medicine, Avon Area HA, 1979–80; Res. Fellow, NH and MRC Perinatal Epidemiology Unit, Univ. of WA, 1980–81; GP, Bristol, 1981–82; Sen. Registrar in Public Health Medicine, Bristol and Weston HA, 1982–84; Public Health Consultant, Bristol HA, 1985–87; Dir, Public Health, and Chief Exec., SE London HA, 1987–93; Regional Director of Public Health: Wessex, then Wessex and SW RHA, 1993–94; S Thames RHA, then S Thames Regl Office, NHS Exec., 1994–99; Regl Dir of Public Health, 1999–2006, Med. Dir, 1999–2003, London, DoH; Health Advr to Mayor of London and GLA, 2000–06. Special Advr to Health Select Cttee, 1991–92. Interim Dir, Public Health Triborough, London, 2013–14. Chm., Greater London Alcohol and Drug Alliance, 2007–08; Mem. Bd, Food Standards Agency, 2008–13; Co-Chair, Climate and Health Council, 2009–. Non-executive Director: UCL Hosps NHS Foundn Trust, 2007–13; Dorset County Hosp. NHS Foundn Trust, 2016–. Member: Council, Public Health and Epidemiology Section, RSM, 2014–; Gen. Bd, FPH, 2016–. Joan H. Tisch Dist. Fellow in Public Health, Hunter Coll., NY, 2012. Mem., London Sports Bd, 2003–08. Mem. Bd and Ct, LSHTM, 2001–10. FRSA. *Publications*: articles and chapters on spastic diplegia, vision screening, public health in UK and internationally, health impact assessment, health inequality, food and health. *Recreations*: cinema, art, music, furniture restoration. *E*: sueatkinsonph@gmail.com. *T*: 07884 473280.

**ATKINSON, William Alexander;** Managing Director and Publisher, Atlantic Books Ltd, since 2014; *b* Singapore, 30 April 1962; *s* of Keith Atkinson and Diana Atkinson. *Educ*: Tonbridge Sch.; Univ. of Exeter (BA Hons English). Manager, Waterstone's Booksellers Ltd, 1988–94; Faber and Faber Ltd: Paperback Manager, 1994–96; Sales and Mktg Manager, 1996–98; UK Sales Dir, 1998–2004; Sales and Mktg Dir, 2004–14. Dir, Edinburgh Book Fest., 2000–05. Member: Bd, Independent Publishers Guild, 2003–13 (Chm., 2009–10); Publisher Assoc. Trade Council, 2018–. Mem., Publishing Course Adv. Bd, Univ. of Stirling, 2005–10. Sales Person of the Year, 2004, Book Industry Achievement Award, 2008, British Book Awards; Outstanding Contribn to Ind. Bookselling Award, Booksellers Assoc., 2009. *Recreation*: modern art. *Address*: Atlantic Books Ltd, Ormond House, 26–27 Boswell Street, WC1N 3JZ. *E*: willatkinson@atlantic-books.co.uk. *Club*: Rye Golf.

**ATKINSON, Sir William (Samuel),** Kt 2008; DL; Executive Headteacher, Phoenix Canberra Schools Federation, 2010–13 (Headteacher, Phoenix High School, Hammersmith and Fulham, 1995–2010); *b* St Ann, Jamaica, 9 April 1950; *s* of late William Benjamin Atkinson and Sara Jane Atkinson; *m* 1974, Jacqueline Ann Burley; three *s* one *d*. *Educ*: King's Coll. London (MA 1981). Teacher, Portsmouth Modern Boys' Sch., 1971–72; Asst Hd of Year, Islington Green Sch., 1973–74; Hd of Year, Holloway Boys' Sch., 1974–81; Deputy Head: Henry Thornton Sch., 1981–83; White Hart Lane Sch., Haringey, 1983–86; Headteacher: Copland Community Sch., Brent, 1986–87; Cranford Community Sch., 1987–95. Member: Special Measures Action Recovery Team, 1997, Standards Task Force, 1997–2001, DfEE; Justice Task Force, 1999, London Youth Crime Reduction Task Force, 2003–04, Home Office; London Black and Minority Ethnic Communities Cracking Crime Partnership Bd, until 2006; Adv. Panel on Children's Viewing, BBFC, until 2010; a Comr, Family Commn. Designated Nat. Leader, Nat. Coll. for Leadership of Schs and Children's Services, 2010. Nat. Judge, 2002–09, Dep. Chm., Nat. Judging Panel, 2006, Teaching Awards; Chm., London Teaching Awards Panel, 2003. Member: Fulham Sch. Commn, 2007; Haringey Educn Commn, 2012; Chm., Hammersmith and Fulham Youth Task Force, 2007. Dir, Lyric Th., Hammersmith, 2010–18. Mem. Bd, RSC, 2012– (Gov., 2011–12). Trustee: Inst. for Citizenship, 2001–06; Shaftesbury Homes and Arethusa, 2001–06; Research Autism. Mem. Council, Industrial Soc. FRSA (Mem., Council, 2004). Media roles and appearances incl. contribs to wide range of TV and radio progs; role of headteacher in The Unteachables (documentary series), 2005. Hon. Dr North London, 2002. DL Gtr London, 2016. *Recreations*: Rugby, theatre, family.

**ATTALI, Jacques;** Member, Conseil d'Etat, France, 1981–90 and since 1993; Président: Attali et Associés, since 1994; Positive Planet Foundation (formerly PlaNet Finance), since 1999; *b* 1 Nov. 1943. *Educ*: Ecole Polytechnique; Inst. d'Etudes Politiques, Paris; Ecole des Mines; Ecole Nat. d'Admin. Dr d'Etat en Sci. Econ. Conseil d'Etat: Auditeur, 1970; Maître des Requêtes, 1977; Conseiller, 1989; Special Advr to President of French Republic, 1981–91; Founding Pres., EBRD, 1991–93; Pres., Commn for Liberation of French Econ. Growth, 2007–08. *Publications*: Analyse économique de la vie politique, 1972; Modèles Politiques, 1973; (with Marc Guillaume) L'Anti-Economique, 1974; La Parole et l'outil, 1975; Bruits, 1976; La nouvelle Economie Française, 1977; L'Ordre Cannibale, 1979; Les Trois Mondes, 1981; Histoire du Temps, 1982; La figure de Fraser, 1984; Un homme d'influence, 1985; Au propre et au figuré, 1988; Lignes d'Horizon, 1990; 1492, 1991; Verbatim, 1993; Europe(s), 1994; L'Economie de l'Apocalypse, 1995; Verbatim II, 1995; Verbatim III, 1996; Chemins de Sagesse: traité du labyrinthe, 1996; Mémoire de Sabliers, 1997; Dictionnaire du XXI$^e$ siècle, 1998; Fraternités, 1999; Blaise Pascal, 2000; Economic History of the Jewish People, 2002; L'homme nomade, 2003; La Voie humaine, 2004; La confrérie des éveillés, 2004; Karl Marx ou l'esprit du monde, 2005; C'était François Mitterrand, 2005; Une brève histoire de l'avenir, 2006; Devenir soi, 2014; *fiction*: La vie éternelle, 1989; Le premier Jour après moi, 1990; Il viendra, 1994; Manuel, l'Enfant Rêve (for children), 1994; Au-delà de nulle part, 1997; La femme du menteur, 1999; *play*: Les portes du Ciel, 1999.

**ATTALIDES, Michalis A.;** Rector, 2007–16, now Rector Emeritus, and Jean Monnet Professor, since 2011, University of Nicosia (formerly Intercollege) (Dean, School of Humanities, Social Sciences and Law, 2003–06); *b* 15 Nov. 1941; *s* of Antonis Attalides and Katina Loizou; *m* 1991, Alexandra Alexandrou; one *s* one *d* from previous marriages. *Educ*: London Sch. of Econs (BSc Econ); Princeton Univ. (PhD 1975). Lectr in Sociology, Univ. of Leicester, 1966–68; sociologist, Cyprus Town and Country Planning Project, 1968–70; Counterpart of UNESCO Expert, Social Research Centre, Cyprus, 1971 and 1973–74; mil. service, 1972; Guest Lectr, Otto Suhr Inst., Free Univ. of Berlin, 1974–75; journalist, 1975–76; Internat. Relns Service, House of Representatives of Cyprus, 1977–89 (Dir, 1979–89); Dir, Pol Affairs Div. B (Cyprus Question) (with rank of Ambassador), Min. of Foreign Affairs, 1989–91; Ambassador to France, also accredited to Morocco, Portugal and Spain, 1991–95; Perm. Delegate to EU, also accredited to Belgium and Luxembourg, 1995–98; High Comr in London, 1998–2000; Perm. Sec., Min. of Foreign Affairs, Cyprus, 2000–01; Rep. of Govt of Cyprus, Eur. Convention, 2002–03. *Publications*: Social Change and Urbanization in Cyprus: a study of Nicosia, 1971; Cyprus: nationalism and international politics, 1980; Cyprus: State, Society and International Environment (in Greek), 2009. *Address*: 8 Sachtouris Street, 1080 Nicosia, Cyprus. *E*: attalides.m@cytanet.com.cy.

**ATTALLAH, Naim Ibrahim,** CBE 2017; Book Publisher and Proprietor: Quartet Books, since 1976; The Women's Press, since 1977; Robin Clark, since 1980; *b* 1 May 1931; *s* of Ibrahim and Genevieve Attallah; *m* 1957, Maria Attallah (*née* Nykolyn); one *s*. *Educ*: Battersea Polytechnic. Foreign Exchange Dealer, 1957; Financial Consultant, 1966; Dir of cos, 1969–; Financial Dir and Jt Man. Dir, Asprey of Bond Street, 1979–92; Gp Chief Exec., Asprey PLC, 1992–96; Managing Director: Mappin & Webb, 1990–95; Watches of Switzerland, 1990–95; Exec. Dir, Garrard, 1990–95; Magazine Proprietor: The Literary Review, 1981–2001; The Wire, 1984–2000; The Oldie, 1991–2001. Proprietor, Academy Club, 1989–96. Launched Parfums Namara, Avant l'Amour and Après l'Amour, 1985, Naïdor, 1987, l'Amour de Namara, 1990; launched Namara Fine Art, 1997. *Theatre*: co-presenter, Happy End, Lyric, 1975; presented and produced, The Beastly Beatitudes of Balthazar B, Duke of York's, 1981; co-prod, Trafford Tanzi, Mermaid, 1982; *films*: co-prod (with David Frost), The Slipper and the Rose, 1974–75; exec. producer, Brimstone and Treacle, 1982; also prod and presented TV docs. MUnic Surrey, 1993. *Publications*: Women, 1987; Singular Encounters, 1990; Of a Certain Age, 1992; More of a Certain Age, 1993; Speaking for the Oldie, 1995; A Timeless Passion (novel), 1995; Asking Questions, 1996; Tara & Claire (novel), 1996; A Woman a Week, 1998; In Conversation with Naim Attallah, 1998; Insights, 1999; Dialogues, 2000; The Old Ladies of Nazareth, 2004; The Boy in England, 2005; In Touch With His Roots, 2006; Fulfilment & Betrayal, 2007; (ed) A Scribbler in Soho, 2019; contrib. Literary Review, Oldie, and most nat. newspapers. *Recreations*: classical music, opera, theatre, cinema, photography. *Address*: 26 Shepherd Market, W1J 7PP. *T*: (020) 7499 2901, *Fax*: (020) 7499 2914. *E*: nattallah@aol.com. *W*: http://quartetbooks.wordpress.com.

**ATTANASIO, Prof. Orazio Pietro,** PhD; FBA 2004; Professor of Economics, since 1995, and Head, Department of Economics, since 2014, University College London; *b* 31 Oct. 1959. *Educ*: Univ. of Bologna; London Sch. of Econs and Pol Sci. (MSc 1984; PhD 1988). Asst Prof. of Econs, 1988–94, Fellow, Hoover Instn, 1993–94, Stanford Univ.; Associate Prof. of Econs, Univ. of Bologna, 1993–95; Res. Fellow, Inst. for Fiscal Studies, 1995–; Dir, Centre for the Evaluation of Develt Policies, UCL and Inst. for Fiscal Studies, 2002–. Man. Ed., Quantitative Economics, 2009–. *Publications*: contrib. learned jls. *Address*: Department of Economics, University College London, Gower Street, WC1E 6BT; Institute for Fiscal Studies, 7 Ridgmount Street, WC1E 7AE.

**ATTENBOROUGH, Sir David (Frederick),** OM 2005; CH 1996; Kt 1985; CVO 1991; CBE 1974; FRS 1983; FLS; FSA; broadcaster and naturalist; *b* 8 May 1926; *s* of late Frederick Levi Attenborough and Mary Attenborough (*née* Clegg); *m* 1950, Jane Elizabeth Ebsworth Oriel (*d* 1997); one *s* one *d*. *Educ*: Wyggeston Grammar Sch. for Boys, Leicester; Clare Coll., Cambridge (Hon. Fellow, 1980). Served in Royal Navy, 1947–49. Editorial Asst in an educational publishing house, 1949–52; joined BBC Television Service as trainee producer, 1952; undertook zoological and ethnographic filming expeditions to: Sierra Leone, 1954; British Guiana, 1955; Indonesia, 1956; New Guinea, 1957; Paraguay and Argentina, 1958; South West Pacific, 1959; Madagascar, 1960; Northern Territory of Australia, 1962; the Zambesi, 1964; Bali, 1969; Central New Guinea, 1971; Celebes, Borneo, Peru and Colombia, 1973; Mali, British Columbia, Iran, Solomon Islands, 1974; Nigeria, 1975; Controller, BBC2, BBC Television Service, 1965–68; Dir of Programmes, Television, and Mem., Bd of Management, BBC, 1969–72. Writer and presenter: TV series: Tribal Eye, 1976; Wildlife on One, 1977–2004; Life on Earth, 1979; The Living Planet, 1984; The First Eden, 1987; Lost Worlds, Vanished Lives, 1989; The Trials of Life, 1990; Life in the Freezer, 1993; The Private Life of Plants, 1995; The Life of Birds, 1998; State of the Planet, 2000; The Life of Mammals, 2002; Life in the Undergrowth, 2005; Life in Cold Blood, 2008; Darwin and the Tree of Life, 2009; First Life, 2010; Flying Monsters 3D, 2010; Frozen Planet, 2011; Kingdom of Plants 3D, 2011; Madagascar, 2011; 60 Years in the Wild, 2012; Galapagos 3D, 2012; Attenborough's Ark, 2012; Africa, 2013; Micromonsters 3D, 2013; Natural Curiosities, 2013–14; Rise of Animals: triumph of the vertebrates, 2013; Life Story, 2014; Natural History Museum Alive 3D, 2014; Conquest of the Skies 3D, 2015; The Hunt, 2015; The Great Barrier Reef, 2015; Attenborough and the Giant Dinosaur, 2016; Zoo Quest in Colour, 2016; Giraffes: Africa's gentle giants, 2016; Life that Glows, 2016; Planet Earth II, 2016; Dynasties, 2018; Our Planet, 2019; Seven Worlds, One Planet, 2019; BBC Radio 4: Life Stories, 2009; Tweet of the Day, 2013. Huw Wheldon Meml Lecture, RTS, 1987. President: BAAS, 1990–91; RSNC, 1991–96; Mem., Nature Conservancy Council, 1973–82. Trustee: WWF UK, 1965–69, 1972–82, 1984–90; WWF Internat., 1979–86; British Museum, 1980–2001; Science Museum, 1984–87; Royal Botanic Gardens, Kew, 1986–92 (Kew Award, 1996). Corresp. Mem., Amer. Mus. Nat. Hist., 1985. Fellow: BAFTA 1980; FRSE 2006; FLS 2007 (Hon. FLS 1998); FSA 2008. Hon. Fellow: Manchester Polytechnic, 1976; UMIST, 1980; Hon. FRCP 1991; Hon. FIBiol 2000. Special Award, SFTA, 1961; Silver Medal, Zool Soc. of London, 1966; Silver

Medal, RTS, 1966; Desmond Davis Award, SFTA, 1970; Cherry Kearton Medal, RGS, 1972; Kalinga Prize, UNESCO, 1981; Washburn Award, Boston Mus. of Sci., 1983; Hopper Day Medal, Acad. of Natural Scis, Philadelphia, 1983; Founder's Gold Medal, RGS, 1985; Internat. Emmy Award, 1985; Encyclopaedia Britannica Award, 1987; Livingstone Medal, RSGS, 1990; Franklin Medal, RSA, 1990; Gold Medal, RTS, 1991; Golden Kamera Award, Berlin, 1993; Edinburgh Medal, Edinburgh Sci. Fest., 1998; Internat. Cosmos Prize, Osaka, 2000; Michael Faraday Prize, Royal Soc., 2003; Raffles Medal, Zool Soc. of London, 2004; Caird Medal, Nat. Maritime Mus., 2004; Bicentennial Medal, Smithsonian Instn, 2004; Petersen Medal, Harvard, 2004; Descartes Prize, EC, 2004; Prince of Asturias Award, 2009; Crystal Award, World Economic Forum, 2019. Hon. DLitt: Leicester, 1970; City, 1972; London, 1980; Birmingham, 1982; Hon. DSc: Liverpool, 1974; Heriot-Watt, 1978; Sussex, 1979; Bath, 1981; Ulster, Durham, 1982; Keele, 1986; Oxford, 1988; Plymouth, 1992; Bradford, 1998; Nottingham, 1999; UWE, Iceland, Guelph, 2003; UEA, 2005; Uppsala, 2007; Nottingham Trent, Westminster, 2010; St Andrews, 2011; QUB, 2013; Hon. LLD: Bristol, 1977; Glasgow, 1980; DUniv: Open Univ., 1980; Essex, 1987; Antwerp, 1993; Hon. ScD Cambridge, 1984; Hon. DVetMed Edinburgh, 1994. Hon. Freeman, City of Leicester, 1990. Comdr of Golden Ark (Netherlands), 1983. *Publications:* Zoo Quest to Guiana, 1956; Zoo Quest for a Dragon, 1957; Zoo Quest in Paraguay, 1959; Quest in Paradise, 1960; Zoo Quest to Madagascar, 1961; Quest under Capricorn, 1963; (with Molly Cox) Fabulous Animals, 1975; The Tribal Eye, 1976; Life on Earth, 1979; The Living Planet, 1984; The First Eden, 1987; The Atlas of the Living World, 1989; The Trials of Life, 1990; The Private Life of Plants, 1994; The Life of Birds, 1998; Life on Air (memoirs), 2002, 2nd edn 2009; The Life of Mammals, 2002; Life in the Undergrowth, 2005; (jtly) Amazing Rare Things, 2007; Life in Cold Blood, 2008; Life Stories, 2009; New Life Stories, 2011; (with Errol Fuller) Drawn from Paradise, 2012; Adventures of a Young Naturalist: the zoo quest expeditions, 2017; Journeys to the Other Side of the World: further adventures of a young naturalist, 2018. *Recreations:* music, tribal art, natural history. *Address:* 5 Park Road, Richmond, Surrey TW10 6NS.

**ATTENBOROUGH, (Hon.) Michael John,** CBE 2013; freelance theatre director and teacher; *b* 13 Feb. 1950; *s* of Baron Attenborough, CBE; *m* 1st, 1971, Jane Seymour (*née* Joyce Frankenberg) (marr. diss. 1976); 2nd, 1984, Karen Lewis; two *s*. *Educ:* Westminster Sch.; Sussex Univ. (BA Hons English). Associate Director: Mercury Theatre, Colchester, 1972–74; Leeds Playhouse, 1974–79; Young Vic Theatre, 1979–80; Artistic Director: Palace Theatre, Watford, 1980–84; Hampstead Theatre, 1984–89; Turnstyle Gp, 1989–90; Exec. Producer and Resident Dir, 1990–95, Principal Associate Dir, 1995–2002, RSC; Artistic Dir, Almeida Theatre, 2002–13; freelance theatre dir incl. NT, Royal Court, Hampstead Th., Tricycle Th., Broadway, Abbey Th. Dublin, Queensland Th. Co., Washington Shakespeare Co. Dir Emeritus, RADA, 2016. Hon. Prof. of English, Univ. of Sussex, 2011–; Hon. Dist. Fellow, Univ. of Leicester, 2017. Patron: Attenborough Arts Centre, Leicester, 2014–; Attenborough Centre for the Creative Arts, Univ. of Sussex, 2016–. Hon. DLitt: Sussex, 2005; Leicester, 2009. Excellence in the Theatre Award, Internat. Theatre Inst., 2012. *Recreations:* music, football, reading, being with my family. *Address:* c/o Rose Cobbe, United Agents, 12–16 Lexington Street, W1F 0LE.

**ATTENBOROUGH, Peter John;** Director of Educational and Community Care Projects, 1994–2004, Administrator, Leadership and Fellowship Schemes, 2004–06, The Rank Foundation; Headmaster of Charterhouse, 1982–93; *b* 4 April 1938; *m* 1967, Alexandra Deidre Campbell Page; one *s* one *d*. *Educ:* Christ's Hospital; Peterhouse, Cambridge. BA Classics 1960, MA 1964. Asst Master, Uppingham Sch., 1960–75 (Housemaster, Senior Classics Master); Asst Master, Starehe Boys' Centre, Nairobi, 1966–67; Headmaster, Sedbergh Sch., 1975–81. Chairman: Common Entrance Cttee of Independent Schs, 1983–88; Schools Arabic Project, 1986–87; Mem., HMC Cttee, 1986–90. Almoner, Christ's Hosp., 1987–2001; Governor: Ashdown House, 1983–93; Haslemere Prep. Sch., 1986–93; St Edmund's Sch., 1986–94; Brambletye Sch., 1989–99; Caldicott Sch., 1990–93; Haberdashers' Monmouth Schs, 1996–2007; Trustee, Uppingham Sch., 1993–2002. Trustee: Inner City Young People's Project, 1989–98; Starehe Endowment Fund (UK), 1995–2008. Freeman, City of London, 1965; Liveryman, Skinners' Co., 1978. *Address:* Oaklea, Belle Orchard, Ledbury, Herefordshire HR8 1DD.

**ATTERBURY, Paul Rowley;** self-employed writer, lecturer, broadcaster, curator and antiques expert, since 1981; *b* London, 8 April 1945; *s* of Rowley Streatfeild Atterbury and Audrey Atterbury; *m* 1st, 1974, Avril Thompson (marr. diss. 1987); two *d*; 2nd, 2002, Chrissie Bursey; two step *d*. *Educ:* Westminster Sch.; London Sch. of Printing (Co. Cert. Typography 1967); Univ. of E Anglia (BA Hons 1972). Prodn Manager, Sotheby Pubns, 1973–76; historical advr, Royal Doulton, 1976–80; Ed., Connoisseur mag., 1980–81; exhibn curator, V&A Mus., 1976, 1979, 1994, 2001; lectr, UK and internationally, 1970–. Mem., team of experts, Antiques Roadshow, 1990–. Judge, Nat. Heritage Rlwy Awards, 2010–. Trustee, Dorset Co. Mus., 2014–; Co-Dir, Dorchester Literary Fest., 2015–. Hon. DLitt Keele, 2005. *Publications:* Nicholson's Guide to the Thames, 1969; (with A. Darwin) Nicholson's Guides to the Waterways, 5 vols, 1970–74; (with J. Moran) Henry George: printer and publisher in Westerham, Kent, 1830–1946, 1972; (ed) Antiques: an encyclopedia of the decorative arts, 1979; English Pottery and Porcelain: historical survey, 1980; History of Porcelain, 1982; English Rivers and Canals, 1984; A Golden Adventure: the first 50 years of Ultramar, 1985; Moorcroft Pottery: guide to the pottery of William and Walter Moorcroft, 1897–1986, 1987, 4th edn as Moorcroft: a guide to Moorcroft Pottery, 1897–1993, 2008; See Britain by Train, 1989; (ed) The Interior Design Year Book 1989; The Parian Phenomenon: survey of Victorian Parian porcelain statuary and busts, 1989; Art Deco Patterns, 1990; South East England by Train, 1991; (with J. Henson) Ruskin Pottery: pottery of Edward Richard Taylor and William Howson Taylor, 1993; The Great Antiques Treasure Hunt, 1993, 2nd edn 1997; (ed with Lars Tharp) The Little, Brown Illustrated Encyclopedia of Antiques, 1994, 2nd edn 1998; End of the Line: exploration of Britain's threatened rural railways, 1994; (with Lars Tharp) The Bullfinch Illustrated Encyclopedia of Antiques, 1994; Exploring Britain's Canals, 1995; (with L. Hayward) Poole Pottery: Carter and Co. and their successors, 1873–1995, 1995, rev. edn as Poole Pottery: Carter and Company and their successors, 1873–2011, 2011; A. W. N. Pugin: master of Gothic revival, 1996; (with I. Burgum) Country Railways, 1996; (with T. Forrest) The Bullfinch Anatomy of Antique Furniture, 1996; (with T. Forrest) Know Your Antiques, 1996; Walking Britain's Rivers and Canals, 1997, 2nd edn 1999; (with A. Haines) Thames: from source to the sea, 1998; (with M. Batkin) The Dictionary of Minton, 1999; (jtly) Twentieth-Century Ceramics, 2000, 2nd edn 2005; (with S. F. Cooper) Victorians at Home and Abroad, 2001; Miller's 20th Century Ceramics Antiques Checklist, 2003; Branch Line Britain, 2004; (with J. Benjamin) The Jewellery and Silver of H. G. Murphy: arts and crafts to art deco, 2005; (jtly) The Antiques Roadshow, 2005; Along Country Lines: exploring the rural railways of yesterday, 2005; Tickets Please!: a nostalgic journey through railway station life, 2006; (with H. Kay) The Wedding: 150 years of down-the-aisle style, 2006; Along Lost Lines, 2007; On Holiday: the way we were, 2008; All Change: visiting the byways of Britain's railway network, 2009; (with A. Hart-Davis) Discovering Britain's Lost Railways, 2009; Life Along the Line: a nostalgic celebration of railways and railway people, 2010; An A-Z of Railways: a nostalgic celebration of British railway heritage, 2010; Along Main Lines: the great trains, stations and routes of Britain's railways, 2011; Paul Atterbury's Lost Railway Journeys: rediscover Britain's forgotten railway routes, 2011; Paul Atterbury's Railway Collection, 2012; Paul Atterbury's Wonder Book of Trains, 2012; Mapping Lost Branch Lines: a nostalgic look at Britain's branch lines in old maps and photographs, 2013; Paul Atterbury's Favourite Railway Journeys, 2013; The First World War in 100 Family Treasures, 2014. *Recreations:* going to Australia, visiting antique fairs, walking the Somme, exploring lost railways. *Address:* 9 Kempston Road, Weymouth, Dorset DT4 8XB. *T:* (01305) 759769. *E:* paul@pcpress.co.uk.

**ATTEWELL, Brian;** HM Diplomatic Service, retired; *b* 29 May 1937; *s* of late William John Geldard Attewell and Marie Evelyn Attewell; *m* 1st, 1963, Mary Gillian Tandy (*d* 2000); two *s* one *d*; 2nd, 2002, Angelika Pathak. *Educ:* Dulwich Coll.; London School of Economics and Political Science (BScEcon 1961); Birkbeck Coll., London (Dip. Hist. of Art, 2006). BoT, 1956–58, 1961–66; Private Sec. to Parly Sec., 1964–66; transf. to Diplomatic Service, 1966: Washington, 1967–70; Buenos Aires, 1970–73; FCO, 1974–78; Canberra, 1978–80; FCO, 1980–83; Dubai, 1984–87; Brussels, 1988–92; High Comr, Bahamas, 1992–96. *Recreations:* golf, walking, listening to music (classical and jazz), watercolours, following fortunes of Charlton Athletic. *Club:* Wimbledon Park Golf.

**ATTFIELD, Prof. (John) Paul,** DPhil; FRS 2014; FRSC; FRSE; Professor of Materials Science at Extreme Conditions, University of Edinburgh, since 2003; *b* Birmingham, 27 July 1962; *s* of David George Attfield and Janet Attfield (*née* White); *m* 1987, Diane Louise Gallagher (marr. diss. 2014); two *s* one *d*. *Educ:* Durham Johnston Sch., Durham; Magdalen Coll., Oxford (BA Hons Chem. 1984; DPhil Chem. 1987). FRSC 2005. Jun. Res. Fellow, Christ Church, Oxford, 1987–91; Lectr in Chem., 1991–2000, Reader in Materials Chem., 2000–03, Univ. of Cambridge; Fellow, Jesus Coll., Cambridge, 1991–2003. FRSE 2006. *Recreations:* walking, travel, visiting galleries and museums. *Address:* Centre for Science at Extreme Conditions, King's Buildings, University of Edinburgh, Mayfield Road, Edinburgh EH9 3JZ; School of Chemistry, King's Buildings, University of Edinburgh, West Mains Road, Edinburgh EH9 3JJ. *T:* (0131) 651 7229, *Fax:* (0131) 651 7049. *E:* j.p.attfield@ed.ac.uk.

**ATTLEE,** family name of **Earl Attlee.**

**ATTLEE, 3rd Earl** *cr* 1955; **John Richard Attlee,** TD; Viscount Prestwood, 1955; *b* 3 Oct. 1956; *s* of 2nd Earl Attlee and Anne Barbara, *er d* of late James Henderson, CBE; *S* father, 1991; *m* 2008, Teresa Ahern. *Educ:* Stowe. Engrg and automotive industries until 1993; British Direct Aid: Bosnia, 1993–94; Rwanda, 1995. TA officer, Maj. REME (V), Op. Lodestar, 1997–98, OC 150 Recovery Company, 1998–2000; Op. TELIC, 2003–17. Opposition Whip, H of L, 1997–99; opposition spokesman, in H of L, for transport, 1997 and 1999–2001, for NI, 1997 and 1998–99, for energy, 1998, and for defence, 1998–2001, for transport and defence, 2002–03, for trade and industry, 2003–05; for maritime and shipping, 2007–10; govt spokesman in H of L, for Transport, Home Office, and NI, 2010–14, for Wales, 2012–14, and for Scotland, 2013–14; a Lord in Waiting (Govt Whip), 2010–13. Elected Mem., H of L, 1999. *Address:* House of Lords, SW1A 0PW. *T:* (020) 7219 6071. *E:* attleej@parliament.uk.

**ATTLEE, Air Vice-Marshal Donald Laurence,** CB 1978; LVO 1964; DL; fruit farmer, 1977–95, retired; *b* 2 Sept. 1922; *s* of Major Laurence Attlee; *m* 1952, Jane Hamilton Young; one *s* two *d*. *Educ:* Haileybury. Pilot trng in Canada, 1942–44; Flying Instructor, 1944–48; Staff, Trng Comd, 1949–52; 12 Sqdn, 1952–54; Air Ministry, Air Staff, 1954–55; RAF Staff Coll., 1956; 59 Sqdn, 1957–59; CO, The Queen's Flight (W/Cdr), 1960–63; HQ, RAF Germany, 1964–67; CO, RAF Brize Norton, 1968–69; IDC, 1970; MoD Policy Staff, 1971–72; Dir of RAF Recruiting, 1973–74; Air Cdre, Intell., 1974–75; AOA Trng Comd, 1975–77, retired. Chm., Mid-Devon Business Club, 1985–87; Mem. Bd, Mid-Devon Enterprise Agency, 1983–93. Mem., Mid-Devon DC, 1982–2003 (Vice-Chm., 1987–89; Chm., 1989–91; Leader, 2002–03; Hon. Alderman, 2003). DL Devon, 1991. *Recreations:* genealogy, gardening. *Address:* Wintergold, 31 Longmead, Hemyock, Devon EX15 3SG. *T:* (01823) 680317. *Club:* Royal Air Force.

**ATTRIDGE, Prof. Derek,** PhD; FBA 2007; Professor of English and Related Literature, University of York, 2003–16, now Emeritus (Head, Department of English and Related Literature, 2004–07); *b* 6 May 1945; *s* of Henry Lester Attridge and Marjorie Julia Attridge (*née* Lloyd); *m* 1st, 1969, Anna Mary Ridehalgh (marr. diss. 1976); 2nd, 1986, Suzanne Hall; two *d*. *Educ:* Scottsville Govt Sch., S Africa; Maritzburg Coll., S Africa; Univ. of Natal (BA Hons English 1966); Clare Coll., Cambridge (BA English 1968; PhD 1972). Res. Lectr, Christ Church, Oxford, 1971–73; Lectr, then Sen. Lectr in English, Univ. of Southampton, 1973–84; Prof. of English Studies, 1984–88, Hd of Dept, 1985–86, Univ. of Strathclyde; Prof. of English, 1988–98, Dir of Grad. Studies, 1994–98, Rutgers Univ.; Leverhulme Res. Prof., Univ. of York, 1998–2003. Visiting Professor: Univ. of Illinois, 1979; Univ. of Orléans, 1990; NYU Abu Dhabi, 2018; Vis. Prof., 1984, 1987, Dist. Vis. Prof., 1998–2006, Rutgers Univ.; Vis. Scholar, New Hall, Cambridge, 1993–97; S. W. Brooks Fellow, Univ. of Qld, 2007; Vis. Fellow, All Souls Coll., Oxford, 2012; Fellow: Stellenbosch Inst. for Advanced Studies, 2013, 2017; Bogliasco Foundn, 2014; Birkelund Sen. Fellow, Nat. Humanities Center, USA, 2015; Christensen Fellow, St Catherine's Coll., Oxford, 2016. Mem., Scottish Adv. Bd, British Council, 1985–88. Mem., Bd of Trustees, Internat. James Joyce Foundn, 1986–96, 2007–12. Member, Editorial Board: Derrida Today; Interventions; James Joyce Qly, Joyce Studies Annual; Jl of Narrative Theory; Language and Literature; Modern Fiction Studies, etc. *Publications:* Well-weighed Syllables: Elizabethan verse in classical metres, 1974; The Rhythms of English Poetry, 1982; (ed with D. Ferrer) Post-structuralist Joyce: essays from the French, 1984; (ed jtly) Post-structuralism and the Question of History, 1987; (ed jtly) The Linguistics of Writing: arguments between language and literature, 1987; Peculiar Language: literature as difference from the Renaissance to James Joyce, 1988, 2nd edn 2004; (ed) The Cambridge Companion to James Joyce, 1990, 2nd edn 2004; (ed) Jacques Derrida: acts of literature, 1992; Poetic Rhythm: an introduction, 1995; (ed with R. Jolly) Writing South Africa: literature, apartheid, and democracy 1970–1995, 1998; Joyce Effects: on language, theory, and history, 2000; (ed with M. Howes) Semicolonial Joyce, 2000; (with T. Carper) Meter and Meaning: an introduction to rhythm in poetry, 2003; The Singularity of Literature, 2004; J. M. Coetzee and the Ethics of Reading: literature in the event, 2004; (ed) James Joyce's Ulysses: a casebook, 2004; How to Read Joyce, 2007; Reading and Responsibility: deconstruction's traces, 2010; (ed with J. Elliott) Theory after 'Theory', 2011; (ed with D. Attwell) The Cambridge History of South African Literature, 2012; Moving Words: forms of English poetry, 2013; The Work of Literature, 2015; (with Henry Staten) The Craft of Poetry: dialogues on minimal interpretation, 2015; Derek Attridge in Conversation, 2015; (ed with K. Easton) Zoe Wicomb & the Translocal: Scotland & South Africa, 2017; The Experience of Poetry: from Homer's listeners to Shakespeare's readers, 2019; articles in Essays in Criticism, Jl of Postcolonial Writing, MLN, Modernism/Modernity, New Literary History, Novel, Paragraph, PMLA, Poetics Today, South Atlantic Quarterly, etc. *Address:* Department of English and Related Literature, University of York, Heslington, York YO10 5DD.

**ATTWELL, Prof. David Ian,** PhD; FMedSci; FRS 2001; Jodrell Professor of Physiology, University College London, since 1995; *b* 18 Feb. 1953; *s* of Arthur Attwell and Vera Eileen Attwell (*née* Slade); *m* 1988, Ulrike Schmidt; one *s*. *Educ:* Magdalen Coll., Oxford (BA 1st

Cl. Physics 1974; BA 2nd Cl. Physiological Scis 1975; PhD Physiol. 1979). Fellow, Magdalen Coll., Oxford, 1977–79 and 1980–81; University College London: Lectr in Physiol., 1981–88; Reader, 1988–91; Prof. of Physiol., 1991–95. SRC Postdoctoral Fellow, Berkeley, Calif, 1979–80; Henry Head Fellow, Royal Soc., 1984–89. FMedSci 2000. *Publications*: contribs to learned jls on neuroscience. *Recreation*: travel. *Address*: Department of Physiology, University College London, Gower Street, WC1E 6BT. *T*: (020) 7679 7342.

**ATTWOOD, Alex;** Member (SDLP) Belfast West, Northern Ireland Assembly, 1998–2017; *b* Belfast, 26 April 1959; *s* of Benjamin and Claire Attwood. *Educ*: St Malachy's Coll.; Queen's Univ. Belfast (LLB). Solicitor, Belfast. Mem. (SDLP), Belfast CC, 1985–2005 (Leader, SDLP Gp). Minister for Social Develt, 2010–11, of the Envmt, 2011–13, NI. Mem., NI Policing Bd, 2001–07, 2009–10. Contested (SDLP): Belfast W, 2015, 2017; Belfast W, NI Assembly, 2017.

**ATTWOOD, Brian Christopher;** Editorial Director, Synthesis Media, since 2016; *b* New Brighton, Cheshire, 29 Feb. 1960; *s* of Raymond Attwood and Eileen Attwood (*née* Power); *m* 2002, Lisa Frances Martland; one *s* one *d*. *Educ*: St Joseph's RC Primary Sch., South Oxhey; Watford Boys' Grammar Sch.; Univ. of Stirling (BA Hons Social Anthropol.); Centre for Journalism, Cardiff (Dip.). The Stage: Chief Reporter, 1989–92; Dep. Ed., 1992–94; Ed., The Stage Newspaper, 1994–2014; Editl Dir, The Stage Media Co. Ltd, 2011–14; LinkedIn Channel Manager, Open Univ., 2014–17. *Recreations*: history (especially Irish), fine art, autism issues. *Address*: Synthesis Media, Castle House, 89 High Street, Berkhamsted, Herts HP4 2DF.

**ATTWOOD, Jonathan F.;** *see* Freeman-Attwood.

**ATTWOOD, Philip;** Keeper of Coins and Medals, British Museum, since 2010; *b* Sheffield, 23 March 1954; *s* of Frank Eric Attwood and Doreen Hilda Attwood; partner, Anthony J. Daniels. *Educ*: Cambridgeshire High Sch. for Boys, Cambridge; Univ. of Birmingham (BA Hons). British Museum: mus. asst, 1978–87; Curator: of Medals, 1987–90; of Modern Coins, 1990–2002; of Medals, 2002–10. Ed., The Medal, 1990–. Hon. Curator of Medals, Cutlers' Co., 1996–. President: British Art Medal Soc., 2008–18 (Vice-Pres., 2018–); FIDEM, 2012–. *Publications*: Artistic Circles: the medal in Britain 1880–1918, 1992; British Art Medals 1982–2002, 2002; Italian Medals, *c*. 1530–1600, in British Public Collections, 2003; Badges, 2004; (with Felicity Powell) Medals of Dishonour, 2009; Hard at Work: the diary of Leonard Wyon 1853–1867, 2014. *Recreations*: architectural history, local history, transport, swimming. *Address*: Department of Coins and Medals, British Museum, WC1B 3DG. *E*: pattwood@thebritishmuseum.ac.uk.

**ATTWOOLL, Elspeth Mary-Ann Muncy;** Member (Lib Dem) Scotland, European Parliament, 1999–2009; *b* 1 Feb. 1943; *d* of Hugh Robert Rhind Attwooll and Joan Attwooll (*née* Fidler); *m* 1990, Donald Gordon Henry. *Educ*: Tiffin Girls' Sch., Kingston upon Thames; St Andrews Univ.; Queen's Coll., Dundee (LLB, MA Hons Politics and Philosophy). University of Glasgow: Asst Lectr, Lectr, Sen. Lectr in Jurisp., 1966–98; ILO, Geneva, 1968–69. *Publications*: The Tapestry of the Law, 1997; articles and essays on legal philosophy. *Recreation*: reading, particularly detective fiction.

**ATWELL, Very Rev. James Edgar;** Dean of Winchester, 2006–16, now Dean Emeritus; *b* 3 June 1946; *s* of Joseph Norman Edgar Atwell and Sybil Marion Atwell (*née* Burnett); *m* 1976, Lorna Goodwin; one *s* two *d*. *Educ*: Dauntsey's Sch.; Exeter Coll., Oxford (MA, BD); Harvard Univ. (ThM). Ordained deacon, 1970, priest, 1971; Assistant Curate: St John the Evangelist, E Dulwich, 1970–74; Great St Mary's, Cambridge, 1974–77; Chaplain, Jesus Coll., Cambridge, 1977–81; Vicar of Towcester, 1981–95; RD, Towcester, 1983–91; Provost, subseq. Dean, of St Edmundsbury, 1995–2006. Vis. Prof., Univ. of Winchester, 2011–. Member: Cathedral Fabric Commn for England, 2006–16; Cttee to Visit, Harvard Meml Ch, USA, 2006–12. Pres., New Forest and Hants County Show, 2015–16. Hon. DD Winchester, 2016. Order of St Edmund, Dio. St Edmund and Ipswich, 2011. *Publications*: Sources of the Old Testament, 2004; (contrib.) Dreaming Spires?, 2005; (contrib.) Speaking of Faith, 2016; contrib. to Jl Theol Studies. *Recreations*: countryside, driving a Land Rover, travel, fairground organs, theology. *Address*: 12 Ventress Farm Court, Cambridge CB1 8HD.

**ATWELL, Rt Rev. Robert Ronald;** *see* Exeter, Bishop of.

**ATWOOD, Barry Thomas;** public and European Community law consultant, 1995–2010; Principal Assistant Solicitor (Under Secretary), Ministry of Agriculture, Fisheries and Food, 1989–95; *b* 25 Feb. 1940; *s* of Percival Atwood and Vera Fanny Atwood (*née* Stoneham); *m* 1965, Jennifer Ann Burgess; two *s*. *Educ*: Bristol Grammar Sch.; Bristol Univ. (LLB); University College London. Solicitor. Articled John Robinson and Jarvis, Isle of Wight, 1961; Solicitor with Robert Smith & Co., Bristol, 1965; Legal Dept, Ministry of Agriculture, Fisheries and Food: conveyancing, 1966; food legislation, 1970; Common Agricultural Policy, 1977; i/c European Court litigation, 1982; Agricultural Commodities and Food Safety Bill, 1986; Legal Gp B (domestic and EC litigation and commercial work), 1989–92; Legal Gp A (legislation and adv. work), 1992–95. *Publications*: (contrib.) Law of the European Communities, 1999; Butterworth's Food Law, 2nd edn 2000, 3rd edn as Food Law (with K. Thompson and C. Willett) 2009. *Recreations*: family, music, walking, France, Italy.

**ATWOOD, Margaret Eleanor,** CH 2019; CC (Can.) 1981; FRSC 1987; writer; *b* Ottawa, 18 Nov. 1939; *m* Graeme Gibson (*d* 2019); one *d*. *Educ*: Univ. of Toronto (BA 1961); Radcliffe Coll., Cambridge, Mass (AM 1962); Harvard Univ., Cambridge, Mass. Lectr in English, Univ. of BC, Vancouver, 1964–65; Instructor in English: Sir George Williams Univ., Montreal, 1967–68; Univ. of Alberta, 1969–70; Asst Prof. of English, York Univ., Toronto, 1971–72; Writer-in-Residence: Univ. of Toronto, 1972–73; Macquarie Univ., Australia, 1987; Hon. Chair, Univ. of Alabama, Tuscaloosa, 1985; Berg Prof., New York Univ., 1986. Holds hon. degrees from univs and colls; recipient of awards, medals and prizes for writing. TV scripts: The Servant Girl, 1974; Snowbird, 1981; (with Peter Pearson) Heaven on Earth, 1986; radio script, The Trumpets of Summer, 1964. PEN Pinter Prize, English PEN, 2016. *Publications*: *poetry*: The Circle Game, 1966; The Animals in That Country, 1969; The Journals of Susanna Moodie, 1970 (illus. edn, 1997); Procedures for Underground, 1970; Power Politics, 1971; You Are Happy, 1974; Selected Poems, 1976; Two-Headed Poems, 1978; True Stories, 1981; Notes Towards a Poem that Can Never be Written, 1981; (ed) The New Oxford Book of Canadian Verse in English, 1982; Snake Poems, 1983; Interlunar, 1984; Selected Poems II: poems selected and new 1976–1986, 1986; Selected Poems 1966–1984, 1990; Margaret Atwood Poems 1965–1975, 1991; Poems 1976–1986, 1992; Morning in the Burned House, 1995; The Door, 2007; also poetry in art and small press edns; *fiction*: The Edible Woman, 1969; Surfacing, 1972; Lady Oracle, 1976; Dancing Girls (short stories), 1977; Up in the Tree (for children), 1978; Anna's Pet (for children), 1980; Life Before Man, 1979; Bodily Harm, 1981; Encounters with the Element Man, 1982; Murder in the Dark (short stories), 1983; Bluebeard's Egg (short stories), 1983; Unearthing Suite, 1983; The Handmaid's Tale, 1985 (Governor General's Award, 1986; filmed 1990; televised 2017); (ed with Robert Weaver) The Oxford Book of Canadian Short Stories in English, 1986, new edn as The New Oxford Book of Canadian Short Stories in English, 1995; Cat's Eye, 1989; (ed with Shannon Ravenel) The Best American Short Stories, 1989; For the Birds (for children), 1990; Wilderness Tips (short stories), 1991; Good Bones (short stories), 1992; The Robber Bride, 1993; Princess Prunella and the Purple Peanut (for children), 1995; Alias Grace (Giller Prize, Giller Foundn, Canada; Canadian Booksellers Assoc. Author of the Year; Nat. Arts Club Medal of Honor for Literature; televised 2017), 1996; The Blind Assassin (Booker Prize), 2000; Oryx and Crake, 2003; Rude Ramsay and the Roaring Radishes (for children), 2003; Bashful Bob and Doleful Dorinda (for children), 2004; The Penelopiad, 2005; The Tent (short stories), 2006; Moral Disorder (short stories), 2006; The Penelopiad: the play, 2007; The Year of the Flood, 2009; Wandering Wenda and the Widow Wallop (for children), 2011; MaddAddam, 2013; Stone Mattress (short stories), 2014; The Heart Goes Last, 2015; Hag-Seed, 2016; Angel Catbird (graphic novel), vol. I, 2016, vol. II, 2017, vol. III, 2017; War Bears (graphic novel), vol. 1–3, 2018; The Testaments, 2019; *opera*: Pauline, York Theatre, Vancouver, 2014; *non-fiction*: Survival: a thematic guide to Canadian literature, 1972; Days of the Rebels 1815–1840, 1977; Second Words: selected critical prose, 1982; Strange Things: the malevolent North in Canadian literature, 1995; Negotiating with the Dead: a writer on writing, 2002; Moving Targets: writing with intent 1982–2004, 2004; Curious Pursuits: occasional writing, 2005; Payback: debt and the shadow side of wealth, 2008; In Other Worlds: SF and the human imagination, 2011. *Address*: c/o Penguin Random House Canada, 320 Front Street West, Suite 1400, Toronto, ON M5V 3B6, Canada.

**AUBREY, David John;** QC 1996; a Recorder, since 1998; Head of Advocacy, Public Defender Service, since 2014; *b* 6 Jan. 1950; *s* of Raymond John Morgan Aubrey and Dorothy Mary (*née* Griffiths); *m* 1980, Julia Catherine Drew; one *d*. *Educ*: Cathays High Sch., Cardiff; University Coll., Cardiff (LLB Hons); Inns of Court Sch. of Law. Called to the Bar, Middle Temple, 1976, Bencher, 2002; Hd of Chambers, Temple Chambers, Cardiff and Newport, 2001–11; Hd of Temple Court Chambers, Cardiff, 2012–14. Treas., Wales and Chester Circuit, 2000–03. Legal Pres., Mental Health Review Tribunal, 1999–. Member: Criminal Bar Assoc., 1988–; Bar Council, 1998–2013. Pres., Boys' Brigade in Wales, 2004– (Vice Pres., 2002–04). *Recreations*: gardening, music, cricket, collecting Boys' Brigade memorabilia, genealogy. *E*: david.aubrey1@virgin.net.

**AUBREY-FLETCHER,** family name of **Baroness Braye.**

**AUBREY-FLETCHER, Sir Henry (Egerton),** 8th Bt *cr* 1782, of Clea Hall, Cumberland; KCVO 2019; farmer and company director; Lord-Lieutenant of Buckinghamshire, since 2006 (Vice Lord-Lieutenant, 1997–2006); *b* 27 Nov. 1945; *s* of Sir John Henry Lancelot Aubrey-Fletcher, 7th Bt and Diana Mary Fynvola (*d* 1996), *o c* of Lt-Col Arthur Egerton; *S* father, 1992; *m* 1976, Sara Roberta, *d* of late Major Robert Gilliam Buchanan and Mrs Margaret Ogden-White; three *s*. *Educ*: Eton. Chm., Chilton House Nursing Home, 1987–. Chm., Fox FM ILR, 2000 (Dir, 1989–2006). Dep. Chm., NT, 2003–06; Member: Landscape Adv. Cttee, Dept of Transport, 1990–94. Pres., CLA, 2007–09. Chairman: Berks, Bucks and Oxon Wildlife (formerly Naturalist) Trust, 1995–2001; Cothill Educnl Trust, 2010–16; Trustee, Chequers Trust, 1991–. High Sheriff, Bucks, 1995–96. KStJ 2014. *Recreations*: IT, media and rural affairs. *Heir*: *s* John Robert Aubrey-Fletcher, *b* 20 June 1977. *Address*: Estate Office, Chilton, Aylesbury, Bucks HP18 9LR. *T*: (01844) 265201.

**AUCKLAND,** 10th Baron *cr* 1789 (Ire.), 1793 (GB); **Robert Ian Burnard Eden;** *b* 25 July 1962; *s* of 9th Baron Auckland and Dorothy Margaret, *d* of H. J. Manser; *S* father, 1997; *m* 1986, Geraldine Caroll; one *d*. *Educ*: Blundell's Sch., Tiverton; Dublin City Univ. (BBS). *Heir*: *cousin* Henry Vane Eden [*b* 11 March 1958; *m* 1988, Alice Claire Needham; one *s* two *d* (and one *s* decd)].

**AUCKLAND (NZ), Bishop of,** since 2010; **Rt Rev. Ross Bay;** *b* Auckland, NZ, 22 Jan. 1965; *s* of Max and Valerie Bay; *m* 1987, Jacqueline Hedge. *Educ*: Australian Coll. of Theol. (BTh); Univ. of London (Postgrad. Dip. Pastoral Theol.). Ordained deacon, 1989, priest 1989; Vicar: of Ellerslie, Auckland, 1994–2001; of Remuera, Auckland, 2001–07; Archdeacon of Auckland, 2006–07; Dean of Auckland, 2007–10; Vicar-Gen., Dio. of Auckland, 2007–10. *Recreation*: squash. *Address*: PO Box 37242, Parnell, Auckland, New Zealand. *T*: (office) (9) 3027288. *E*: bishopoffice@aucklandanglican.org.nz.

**AUCKLAND (NZ), Bishop of, (RC),** since 1994; **Most Rev. Patrick James Dunn;** *b* London, 5 Feb. 1950; *s* of Hugh Patrick Dunn and June Mary (*née* Grevatt). *Educ*: Sacred Heart Coll., Auckland; Canterbury Univ. (BA); Otago Univ. (BTh); Melbourne Coll. of Divinity, Australia (MTheol 1989). Ordained priest, 1976; Catholic Maori Mission, Auckland, 1976–77; Assistant Priest: Mangere E, 1978–79; Takapuna, 1980–84; Co-Pastor, Pakuranga, 1985; Dir, First Year Formation House, Dio. of Auckland, 1986–87; Parish Priest, Northcote, 1990–92; Pastoral Asst to RC Bp of Auckland, and VG, 1993–94. *Publications*: Priesthood, 1990. *Address*: Catholic Diocese of Auckland, Private Bag 47904, Ponsonby, Auckland 1144, New Zealand. *T*: (9) 3603002.

**AUCKLAND Archdeacon of;** *see* Simpson, Ven. R. L.

**AUCKLAND, Mary Josephine,** OBE 2002; Librarian, School of Oriental and African Studies, University of London, 1992–98; *b* 22 Nov. 1950; *d* of Reginald George Auckland and Annie Auckland (*née* Sullivan); *m* 2003, Terence John Beck. *Educ*: Poly. of N London (LA Professional Exams 1971; University Coll. London (BSc Hons Anthropol. 1977); London Sch. of Econs (MSc Industrial Relns and Personnel Mgt 1986). MCLIP (ALA 1973). Res. Asst, Sch. of Librarianship and Inf. Studies, Poly. of N London, 1971–72; Res. Librarian, Liby and Learning Resources Service, City of London Poly., 1972–74; Asst Librarian, 1979–88, Sub-Librarian, 1988–89, British Liby of Pol and Econ. Sci., LSE; Dep. Librarian and Hd, User Services, Univ. of Southampton Liby, 1990–92; Dir of Liby and Learning Resources, London Inst., subseq. Univ. of the Arts London, 1998–2005. Conf. Dir, Computers in Libraries Internat., 1993–95. Member: Cttee for Inf. Envmt (formerly for Electronic Inf.), Jt Inf. Systems Cttee, 1996–2003 (Chair, Content Wkg Gp, 1999–2000); UK Office for Liby Networking Mgt Cttee, 1999–2001; UKOLN Strategic Adv. Gp, 2002–03; British Council Knowledge and Inf. Adv. Cttee, 2002–06; Artifact Exec. Bd, 2002–05; ARLIS Nat. Co-ordinating Cttee, 2004–05. Mem., Higher Educn/British Liby Task Force, 2000–01. Mem. Council, LA, 1991–99 (Chm. Council, 1997–99; Chm., Acad. and Res. Libraries Cttee, 1993–95). Acad. Gov., Ct of Govs, SOAS, 1996–98; Acad. Bd Gov., Ct of Govs, London Inst. (later Univ. of the Arts London), 1999–2005. Mem. Trustees, CILIP Benevolent Fund, 2004–14. Hon. FCLIP 2002. Cawthorne Prize, LA, 1970. *Publications*: contrib. various articles, chapters, etc, in professional pubns, reports, and conf. papers. *Recreations*: good company, travel.

**AUDLAND, Sir Christopher (John),** KCMG 1987 (CMG 1973); HM Diplomatic Service and Commission of the European Communities, retired; *b* 7 July 1926; *s* of late Brig. Edward Gordon Audland, CB, CBE, MC, and Violet Mary, *d* of late Herbert Shepherd-Cross, MP; *m* 1955, Maura Daphne Sullivan; two *s* one *d*. *Educ*: Twyford Sch.; Winchester Coll. RA, 1944–48 (Temp. Capt.). Entered Foreign (subseq. Diplomatic) Service, 1948; served in: Berlin and Bonn, 1949–52; British Representation to Council of Europe, Strasbourg, 1952–55; Washington, 1955–58; Foreign Office, 1958–61; UK Delegn to negotiations for British Membership of European Communities, Brussels, 1961–63; Co-ordinator and Ed.-in-Chief, FCO report on negotiations for UK entry into EC, 1963; Buenos Aires, 1963–67; Head of Science and Technology Dept, FCO, 1968–70; Counsellor (Head of Chancery), Bonn, 1970–73; seconded to Commn of Eur. Communities, 1973: Dep. Sec.-Gen., 1973–81; Dir-Gen. for Energy, 1981–86. British Negotiator, Allied/FRG Bonn Conventions, 1950–52; Head, UK Delegn to 1st UN Conf. on Seabed and Ocean Floor, 1968 and 1969; Dep. Head, UK Delegn to Four-Power Negotiations on Berlin, 1970–72. Hon. Fellow, Faculty of Law, and Vis. Lectr on European Instns, Edinburgh Univ., 1986–90. Vice President: Europa Nostra, 1988–91; Internat. Castles Inst., 1988–90 (Pres., 1990–91); Europa Nostra united with Internat. Castles Inst., 1991–96 (Exec. Pres., 1992; Hon. Pres., 1997–). Member: NW Regl Cttee, National Trust, 1987–95; European Strategy Bd, ICL, 1988–96; Lake District Nat. Park Authority, 1989–95; Pro-Chancellor, Lancaster Univ., 1990–97 (Mem., Council, 1988–97; Hon. Fellow, 2007). Trustee: Peter Kirk Meml Fund, 1989–96; Ruskin Foundn, 1994–2001; European Opera Centre, 1996–2002, 2014–16. DL Cumbria, 1996–2006. *Publications:* (contrib.) Berlin: von Brennpunkt der Teilung zur Brücke der Einheit, 1990; Right Place, Right Time (autobiog.), 2004; Jenny: the life and times of a Victorian Lady, 2008; contrib. Jl Soc. of Archivists. *Address:* The Old House, Ackenthwaite, Milnthorpe, Cumbria LA7 7DH. *T:* (015395) 62202. *E:* cja_ack@btinternet.com. *Club:* Oxford and Cambridge.

See also W. G. Audland.

**AUDLAND, William Grant;** QC 2015; *b* Buenos Aires, 27 Aug. 1966; *s of* Sir Christopher (John) Audland, *qv*; *m* 1994, Antonella Bonetti; one *s* one *d*. *Educ:* Winchester Coll.; Queen's Coll., Oxford (BA Hons Mod. Langs); City Univ., London (DipLaw). Called to the Bar, Gray's Inn, 1992 (Scarman Scholar); in practice as a barrister, 1993–; Accredited Mediator, 2011–. *Publications:* (contrib.) Personal Injury Schedules: calculating damages, 2001, 4th edn 2018. *Recreations:* ascent and descent of mountains on foot, ski(n)s or by bicycle; diving, foreign travel, the arts. *Address:* 12 King's Bench Walk, Temple, EC4Y 7EL. *T:* (020) 7583 0811. *E:* audland@12kbw.co.uk.

**AUDLEY,** Barony *cr* 1312–13; in abeyance. *Co-heiresses:* Hon. Patricia Ann Mackinnon [*b* 10 Aug. 1946; *m* 1969, Carey Leigh Mackinnon; one *s* one *d*]; Hon. Jennifer Michelle Carrington [*b* 23 May 1948; *m* 1978, Michael William Carrington; two *s* one *d*]; Hon. Amanda Elizabeth Souter [*b* 5 May 1958; one *d*].

**AUDLEY, Prof. Robert John,** PhD; FBPsS; Professor of Psychology, University College London, 1965–94, now Professor Emeritus; *b* 15 Dec. 1928; *s of* Walter Audley and Agnes Lilian (*née* Baker); *m* 1st, 1952, Patricia Mary Bannister (marr. diss. 1977); one *s* (and one *s* decd); 2nd, 1990, Vera Elyashiv Bickerdike. *Educ:* Battersea Grammar Sch.; University Coll. London (BSc 1st Cl. Hons Psychology, 1952; PhD 1955). Fulbright Scholar and Res. Asst, Washington State Univ., 1952; University College London: Res. Worker, MRC Gp for Exptl Investigation of Behaviour, 1955–57; Lectr in Psychology, 1957–64; Reader in Psychology, 1964; Head, Psychology Dept, 1979–93; Dean, Faculty of Science, 1985–88; Vice-Provost, 1988–94; Fellow, 1989. Vis. Prof., Columbia Univ., NY, 1962; Vis. Miller Prof., Univ. of Calif, Berkeley, 1971; Vis Fellow, Inst. for Advanced Study, Princeton, 1970. Member: UGC Social Studies Sub-Cttee, 1975–82; UGC Equipment Sub-Cttee, 1982–89; Computer Bd for Univs and Res. Councils, 1986–90; MRC/RN Personnel Res. Cttee, 1984 (Chm., Psychology Sub-Cttee, 1984–95); Chm., Jt Wkg Gp, ESRC/HEFC Jt Inf. Systems Cttee, 1990–99 (Mem., New Technology Sub-Cttee, Jt Inf. Systems Cttee, 1993–95). President: British Psychological Soc., 1969–70; Exptl Psychology Soc., 1975–76. Editor, British Jl of Math. and Stat. Psychology, 1965–70. *Publications:* papers on choice, judgement, medical mishaps. *Recreations:* crosswords, cooking, the arts. *Address:* 22 Keats Grove, NW3 2RS. *T:* (020) 7435 6655.

**AUDLEY-CHARLES, Prof. Michael Geoffrey,** PhD; Yates-Goldsmid Professor of Geology, 1982–93, now Emeritus Professor, and Head of the Department of Geological Sciences, 1982–92, University College London; *b* 10 Jan. 1935; *s of* Laurence Geoffrey Audley-Charles and Elsie Ada (*née* Ustonson); *m* 1965, Brenda Amy Cordeiro; one *s* one *d*. *Educ:* Royal Wanstead Sch.; Chelsea Polytechnic (BSc); Imperial Coll., London (PhD). Geologist with mining and petroleum cos, Canada and Australia, 1957–62; Imperial Coll. of Science and Technology, London: research in geology, 1962–67; Lectr in Geol., 1967–73; Reader in Geol., 1973–77; Prof. of Geol. and Head of Dept of Geol Sciences, Queen Mary Coll., London, 1977–82. Hon. Fellow, UCL, 1996. *Publications:* geological papers dealing with stratigraphy of British Triassic, regional geol. of Indonesia and Crete, evolution of Gondwanaland, and deep orogenic trough tectonic processes, in learned jls. *Recreation:* gardening.

**AUERBACH, Frank Helmuth;** painter; *b* 29 April 1931; *s of* Max Auerbach, lawyer, and Charlotte Norah Auerbach; *m* 1958, Julia Wolstenholme; one *s*. *Educ:* privately; St Martin's Sch. of Art; Royal Coll. of Art. *One-man exhibitions:* Beaux Arts Gallery, 1956, 1959, 1961, 1962, 1963; Marlborough Fine Art, 1965, 1967, 1971, 1974, 1983, 1987, 1990, 1997, 2004, 2009, 2012, 2015; Marlborough Gall., New York, 1969, 1982, 1994, 1998, 2006; Villiers, Sydney, Australia, 1972; Bergamini, Milan, 1973; Univ. of Essex, 1973; Mun. Gall. of Modern Art, Dublin, 1975; Marlborough, Zurich, 1976; Anthony D'Offay, London, 1978; Arts Council Retrospective, Hayward Gall., Fruit Market Gall., Edinburgh, 1978; Jacobson, NY, 1979; Anne Berthoud, London, 1983; Venice Biennale, British Pavilion, 1986 (Golden Lion Prize); Kunstverein, Hamburg; Museum Folkwang, Essen; Centro de Arte Reina Sofia, Madrid, 1986–87; Rijksmuseum Vincent van Gogh, Amsterdam, 1989; Yale Center for British Art, New Haven, 1991; Nat. Gall., 1995; Campbell-Thiebaud Gall., San Francisco, 1995; Rex Irwin, Woollahra, 1996, 2000; Charlottenborg, Copenhagen, 2000; RA 2001; Marlborough, Madrid, 2002; (with Lucian Freud) V&A Mus., 2006; Fitzwilliam Mus., Cambridge; Abbot Hall Art Gall., Kendal, 2007–08; Courtauld Gall., London, 2009; Offer Waterman, London, 2012; Kunstmus., Bonn, 2015; Tate Britain, London, 2015–16. *Mixed exhibitions:* Carnegie International, Pittsburgh, 1958, 1961; Dunn International, Fredericton, 1963; Gulbenkian International, Tate Gallery, 1964; Peter Stuyvesant Foundn Collection, London, 1967; The Human Clay, Hayward Gall., 1976; European Painting in the Seventies, Los Angeles County Mus. and tour, 1976; Annual Exhibn, part I, Hayward Gall., 1977; Westkunst, Cologne, 1981; New Spirit in Painting, RA, 1981; Internat. Survey, MoMA, NY, 1984; The Hard Won Image, Tate Gall., 1984; The British Show, Art Gall. of WA, Perth, and tour, 1985; British Art in the Twentieth Century, RA, 1987; Current Affairs, Mus. of Modern Art, Oxford, and tour, 1987; A School of London, Kunstnernes Hus, Oslo, and tour, 1987–88; Pursuit of the Real, Manchester City Art Gall., 1990; British Figurative Painting of the Twentieth Century, Israel Mus., Jerusalem, 1992–93; From London, Scottish Nat. Gall. of Modern Art, Edinburgh, and tour, 1995–96; School of London, Fondation Dina Vierny, Musée Maillol, Paris, and tour, 1998–99; La Mirada Fuerte: Pintura Figurativa de Londres, Museo de Arte Moderno and Museo de Monterrey, Mexico, 2000; Raw Truth: Auerbach-Rembrandt, Ordovas, London and Rijksmuseum, Amsterdam, 2013; Bare Life, LWL-Mus. für Kunst und Kultur, Münster, 2014–15. *Public collections:* Arts Council; Brit. Council; Brit. Museum; Tate Gallery, London; Courtauld Gall.; Metropolitan Museum, NY; Mus. of Modern Art, NY; National Gallery of Victoria, Melbourne; Nat. Galls of Australia, W Australia and NSW; County Museum of LA, Calif; Cleveland Mus., Ohio; Art Inst., Chicago; Univ. of Cincinnati; St Louis Art Mus.; Yale Center for British Art, New Haven; Tamayo Mus., Mexico; Aberdeen, Bedford, Belfast, Birmingham, Bolton, Bristol, Cambridge, Cardiff, Edinburgh, Glasgow Mus, Hartlepool, Huddersfield, Hull, Kendal, Leeds, Leicester, Manchester, Newcastle, Norwich, Nottingham, Oldham, Oxford, Rochdale, Sheffield, Southampton, Tyne and Wear Mus, Wakefield, Walsall Galls; Contemporary Art Soc., etc. *Address:* c/o Marlborough Fine Art, 6 Albemarle Street, W1S 4BY.

**AUERBACH, Simon Joseph,** DPhil; **His Honour Judge Auerbach;** a Circuit Judge, since 2018; a Senior Circuit Judge, Employment Appeal Tribunal, since 2018; *b* London, 12 July 1961; *s of* Cyril Auerbach and late Anita Auerbach (*née* Feingold); *m* 1991, Julie George; one *s* one *d*. *Educ:* Westminster Sch.; Balliol Coll., Oxford (BA Juris. 1st Cl. 1982; DPhil 1988); Coll. of Law (Solicitors' Finals 1st Cl. 1983). Admitted solicitor, 1985; in practice as a solicitor, 1988–2007; pt-time Chm., Employment Tribunals, 2004–07; an Employment Judge, 2007–18; a Recorder, 2011–18. Ind. Mem., Council, ACAS, 2001–08. *Publications:* Legislating for Conflict, 1990; *contributor:* The New Oxford Companion to Law, 2008; Harvey on Industrial Relations and Employment Law, 2015–; Civil Procedure (the White Book), 2016–; contrib. articles on employment law. *Recreations:* piano, guitar, cinema, theatre, live music, books. *Address:* Employment Appeal Tribunal, The Rolls Building, 7 Rolls Buildings, Fetter Lane, EC4A 1NL.

**AUGAR, Philip John;** author; *b* Northampton, 18 June 1951; *s of* John and Helen Augar; *m* 1978; one *s* one *d*. *Educ:* Cambridgeshire High Sch.; Clare Coll., Cambridge (BA 1973; PhD 1979; PGCE 1974). Investment analyst, Wood Mackenzie, 1978–87; Bursar and Fellow, St Catharine's Coll., Cambridge, 1987–89; Sen. Man. Dir, NatWest Mkts, 1989–95; Gp Man. Dir, Securities, Schroders plc, 1995–2000. Non-executive Director: Fuller Smith & Turner plc, 1999–2002; TSB, 2014–15. Chm., UK Border Agency, 2012–13; non-executive Director: DFE, 2004–10; Home Office, 2010–14. Chm., UK govt Post-18 educn review panel, 2018. Member: Public Interest Cttee, KPMG, 2013–16; Adv. Bd, New City Agenda, 2014–. Visiting Fellow: Cranfield Sch. of Mgt, 2001–09; Inst. of Historical Res., 2010–17; Leadership Fellow, Alliance Manchester Business Sch., 2017. *Publications:* The Death of Gentlemanly Capitalism, 2001; (with Joy Palmer) The Rise of the Player Manager, 2003; The Greed Merchants, 2005; (with Robin Cane) Skiing Better, 2006; Chasing Alpha, 2009, new edn as Reckless: the rise and fall of the City, 2010; The Bank that Lived a Little: Barclays in the age of the very free market, 2018. *Recreations:* Leeds United, tennis, ski-ing, rock music. *W:* www.philipaugar.com.

**AUGIER, Sir Fitzroy (Richard),** Kt 1996; OJ 2014; Professor of History, University of the West Indies, 1989–95, now Professor Emeritus; *b* 17 Dec. 1924; *s of* Frank John Augier and Lucie Lastique; *m* 1959, Leila Yvette Gibbs; two *s* one *d*. *Educ:* St Mary's Coll., Castries; Univ. of St Andrews (MA 1949; PhD 1954); London Univ. Inst. of Educn (DipEd 1950); Inst. Commonwealth Studies. Served RAF, 1942–46. Pres., West Indian Students' Union, 1952–54; University of the West Indies: Jun. Res. Fellow, 1954; Lectr, Dept of Hist., 1955–65; Sen. Lectr, 1965–89; Dean, Faculty of Arts and Gen. Studies, 1967–72; Pro Vice Chancellor, 1972–90. Rockefeller Fellow, Inst. of Historical Res., London Univ., 1962. Chairman: Drafting Cttee, UNESCO Gen. Hist. of Caribbean, 1981–2014; Caribbean Exams Council, 1986–96; Teachers' Service Commn, Jamaica, 2005–08. Mem., Univ. Council of Jamaica, 2012–15. Fellow, Inst. of Jamaica, 2003. Medal, Internat. Council on Archives, 1980; Musgrave Medal (Gold), Council, Inst. of Jamaica, 1996; Five Continents Medal, UNESCO, 2009. Chevalier, Ordre des Arts et des Lettres (France), 1989. *Publications:* (jtly) The Making of the West Indies, 1960; (jtly) Sources of West Indian History: documents with commentary, 1962; contrib. to Caribbean Qly, New World Qly, Jl Caribbean Hist. *Recreation:* gardening. *Address:* Department of History, University of the West Indies, Mona, Kingston 7, Jamaica, West Indies. *T:* 9271922. *E:* history@uwimona.edu.jm; 70 Donhead Close, Kingston 6, Jamaica, West Indies. *T:* 9275385.

**AUGUST, Dame Kathryn (Mary),** DBE 2014; education researcher, writer and consultant, since 2013; *b* Blackpool, 1 July 1952; *d of* James and Ann Daly; *m* 1977, Richard August; two *s*. *Educ:* Convent of Holy Child Jesus, Blackpool; Manchester Poly. (BA; PGCE; MA). North Manchester High School for Girls: Teacher of History, 1975–80; Project Leader, Alternative Curriculum, 1980–83; Dep. Headteacher, 1983–85; Headteacher, 1988–93; Headteacher, Priestall Sch., Stockport, 1993–97; Dir of Educn, Trafford MBC, 1997–99; Sen. Educn Advr, DFES, 1999–2002; Dir of Educn, Stockport MBC, 2002–03; Principal, Manchester Acad., 2003–10; Dep. Chief Exec., then Actg Chief Exec., United Learning Trust, 2010–12; Exec. Dir of Educn, The Educn Fellowship, 2012–13. Mem. Bd, Ofsted, 2018–. *Recreations:* reading, travel, theatre. *T:* 07803 525644. *E:* kathryn.august@gmail.com.

**AUKIN, David;** Director, David Aukin Productions Ltd, since 2003; Consultant, Daybreak Pictures Ltd, since 2016 (Chief Executive Officer, 2006–16); *b* 12 Feb. 1942; *s of* late Charles and Regina Aukin; *m* 1969, Nancy Meckler, theatre director; two *s*. *Educ:* St Paul's Sch., London; St Edmund Hall, Oxford (BA). Admitted Solicitor, 1965. Literary Advr, Traverse Theatre Club, 1970–73; Administrator, Oxford Playhouse Co., 1974–75; Administrator, 1975–79, Dir, 1979–84, Hampstead Theatre; Dir, Leicester Haymarket Theatre, 1984–86; Exec. Dir, NT, 1986–90; Hd of Drama, 1990–97, Hd of Film, 1997–98, Channel 4 Television; Jt Chief Exec., HAL Films, 1998–2000; Dir, Act Prodns Ltd, 2001–04; Hd of Drama, Mentorn, 2003–06. Chm., Artichoke Prodns Ltd, 2005–14. Chm., Soho Theatre and Writers' Centre, 1994–2005; Dir, Soho Theatre Ltd, 1995–. Gov., London Film Sch., 2008–16. *Recreation:* golf. *Address:* 20 Balmoral House, 45 Windsor Way, W14 0UE. *Club:* Century.

**AULD, Alasdair Alpin,** FMA; Director, Glasgow Museums and Art Galleries, 1979–88, retired; *b* 16 Nov. 1930; *s of* Herbert Bruce Auld and Janetta Isabel MacAlpine; *m* 1959, Mary Hendry Paul; one *s* one *d*. *Educ:* Shawlands Acad., Glasgow; Glasgow Sch. of Art (DA). FMA 1971. Glasgow Museums and Art Galleries: Asst Curator, 1956–72; Keeper of Fine Art, 1972–76; Depute Dir, 1976–79. Pres., Scottish Fedn of Museums and Art Galls, 1981–84. Hon. Curator, RCPSG, 1991–. Hon. FRCPSGlas 2001. *Publications:* catalogues; articles on museum subjects. *Recreations:* golf, travel, painting. *Address:* 3 Dalziel Drive, Pollokshields, Glasgow G41 4JA. *T:* (0141) 427 1720.

**AULD, Very Rev. Jeremy Rodger;** Provost, St Paul's Cathedral, Dundee, since 2010; *b* Perth, 5 Nov. 1966; *s of* late Derek William Auld and of Jennifer Anne Auld (*née* Rodger); *m* 2000, Christine Marie Arjun; two *s*. *Educ:* Perth Acad.; Univ. of Edinburgh (LLB 1987; DipLP; BD 2004); Theol Inst. of Scottish Episcopal Church (Cert. Theol. 2004). Admitted solicitor, Scotland, 1988; Solicitor, Tods Murray, Edinburgh, 1992–97; admitted to the Bar, Fiji, 1997; Principal Legal Officer, Govt of Fiji, 1997–99; Solicitor, MacRoberts, Edinburgh, 1999–2002; ordained deacon, 2004, priest, 2005; Asst Curate, St Peter's, Edinburgh, 2004–06; Rector, St James the Great, Dollar, 2006–10. Convenor, Provincial Cttee on Canons, 2008–13, Mem., Organisational Rev. Cttee, 2012–, Scottish Episcopal Church; Mem., Gen. Synod, 2011–; Trustee, Scottish Churches Architectural Heritage Trust, 2010–12. Chm., Bd of Dirs, Ark Nursery, Dundee, 2010–. *Publications:* contribs to Expository Times. *Recreations:* travel, music, architecture, theatre, amateur dramatics. *Address:* Castlehill House, 1 High Street, Dundee DD1 1TD. *E:* provost@saintpaulscathedral.net.

**AULD, Rt Hon. Sir Robin (Ernest),** Kt 1988; PC 1995; a Lord Justice of Appeal, 1995–2007; Vice-Chairman, Judicial Appointments Commission, 2006–07; *b* 19 July 1937; *s* of late Ernest Auld and Adelaide Mackie; *m* 1st, 1963, Mary Pritchard (marr. diss. 2005); one *s* one *d*; 2nd, 2014, Prof. Catherine Alison Geissler. *Educ:* Brooklands Coll.; King's Coll. London (LLB 1st cl. Hons 1958; PhD 1963; FKC 1987). Called to Bar, Gray's Inn, 1959 (first in order of merit, Bar finals; Macaskie Schol., Lord Justice Holker Sen. Schol.), Bencher, 1984; in practice at English Bar, 1960–87; admitted to Bar: State of NY, USA, 1984; NSW, Australia, 1986 and other overseas jurisdictions. QC 1975; a Recorder, 1977–87; a Judge of the High Court of Justice, QBD, 1987–95; Presiding Judge, Western Circuit, 1991–94; Sen. Presiding Judge for England and Wales, 1995–98. Sen. Res. Scholar, Yale Law Sch., 2001; Vis. Prof., KCL, 2007–10; Arthur Goodhart Prof. in Legal Sci., Cambridge Univ., 2009–10; Vis. Fellow, Selwyn and Wolfson Colls, Cambridge, 2009–10. Legal Assessor, GMC and GDC, 1982–87. Mem., Judicial Studies Bd, 1989–91. Mem., Commn of Inquiry into Casino Gambling in the Bahamas, 1967; Chm., William Tyndale Schools' Inquiry, 1975–76; Dept of Trade Inspector, Ashbourne Investments Ltd, 1975–79; Counsel to Inquiry into Brixton Disorders, 1981; Chm., Home Office Cttee of Inquiry into Sunday Trading, 1983–84; Counsel to UK, Australian Royal Commn of Inquiry into British nuclear tests in Australia, 1984–85; conducted Criminal Courts Review, 1999–2001; Chm., Inquiry into Governmental Corruption, Turks and Caicos Islands, 2008–09; a Justice, Court of Appeal, Bermuda, 2008–15; Pres., Court of Appeal, Solomon Islands, 2009–14; Mem., Tribunal of Inquiry into alleged misconduct in office of Prime Minister of PNG, 2011. Mem., Oxford Univ. Appeal Ct, 2009–. Trustee, Slynn Foundn, 2008–. Master, Woolmen's Co., 1984–85. Hon. LLD Hertfordshire, 2002. *Address:* Lamb Chambers, Temple, EC4Y 7AS. *T:* (020) 7797 8366. *Clubs:* Athenæum; Yale (New York).

**AUMANN, Prof. Robert John,** PhD; Professor of Mathematics, 1968–2000, now Emeritus, and Member, Federmann Center for the Study of Rationality (formerly Center for the Study of Rationality), since 1991, Hebrew University of Jerusalem; *b* Frankfurt am Main, 8 June 1930; *s* of Siegmund Aumann and Miriam Aumann (*née* Landau); *m* 1st, 1955, Esther Schlesinger (*d* 1998); four *c* (and one *s* decd); 2nd, 2005, Batya Cohn (*née* Schlesinger). *Educ:* Yeshiva High Sch., NY; City Coll. of New York (BS 1950); Mass Inst. of Technol. (SM 1952; PhD 1955). Mathematics Department, Hebrew University of Jerusalem: Instructor, 1956–58; Lectr, 1958–61; Sen. Lectr, 1961–64; Associate Prof. 1964–68. Foreign Hon. Mem., Amer. Acad. of Arts and Scis, 1974; Mem., Nat. Acad. of Scis, USA, 1985; Mem., Israel Acad. of Scis and Humanities, 1989; Corresp. FBA 1995; Corresp. Mem., Royal Acad. of Financial Sci. and Econs, Spain, 2011. Hon. dr: Bonn, 1988; Univ. Catholique de Louvain, 1989; Chicago, 1992; City Univ. of NY; Bar Ilan, 2006; Ben Gurion, 2015. Harvey Prize in Sci. and Technol., Technion-Israel Inst. of Technol., 1983; Israel Prize in Econs, 1994; Lanchester Prize in Operations Res., 1995, von Neumann Theory Prize in Operations Res., 2005, INFORMS; Erwin Plein Nemmers Prize in Econs, Northwestern Univ., USA, 1998; EMET Prize in Econs, Israel, 2002; (jtly) Nobel Prize in Econs, 2005. *Publications:* (with L. S. Shapley) Values of Non-Atomic Games, 1974; (with Y. Tauman and S. Zamir) Game Theory (2 vols), 1981; (ed jtly) Handbook of Game Theory with Economic Applications, vol. 1, 1992, vol. 2, 1994, vol. 3, 2002; (with M. Maschler) Repeated Games with Incomplete Information, 1995; Collected Papers (2 vols), 2000; articles in learned jls. *Address:* Federmann Center for the Study of Rationality, Hebrew University of Jerusalem, 91904 Jerusalem, Israel.

**AUNG SAN SUU KYI;** MP for Kawhmu, Burma, since 2012; Minister for Foreign Affairs, for Energy, for Education and of the President's Office, since 2016; Co-Founder and General Secretary, National League for Democracy, Burma, since 1988; Burmese prisoner of conscience, 1989–95; *b* Rangoon, 19 June 1945; *d* of U Aung San (assassinated, 19 July 1947) and late Daw Khin Kyi; *m* 1972, Michael Vaillancourt Aris (*d* 1999); two *s. Educ:* St Francis Convent, Rangoon; Methodist English High Sch., Rangoon; Lady Shri Ram Coll., Delhi Univ.; St Hugh's Coll., Oxford (BA PPE 1967; MA; Hon. Fellow, 1990). Asst Sec., Adv. Cttee on Admin. and Budgetary Questions, UN Secretariat, NY, 1969–71; Res. Officer, Min. of Foreign Affairs, Bhutan, 1972. Vis. Schol., Centre for SE Asian Studies, Kyoto Univ., Japan, 1985–86. Fellow, Indian Inst. of Advanced Studies, Simla, 1987. Hon. Mem., World Commn on Culture and Develt, Unesco, 1992–95; Mem., Acad. Universelle des Cultures, Paris, 1993. Hon. Pres., LSE Students' Union, 1992–2017; Hon. Life Mem., Univ. of London Union, 1992. Hon. doctorates: Thammasat Univ., Bangkok, 1992; Toronto Univ., 1993; Oxford Univ., 1993; Vrije Univ., Brussels, 1994; Queen's Univ., Kingston, 1995. Thorolf Rafto Award for Human Rights, Norway, 1990; Nobel Peace Prize, 1991; Sakharov Prize for Freedom of Thought, European Parlt, 1991; Annual Award, Internat. Human Rights Law Group, USA, 1992; Simón Bolívar Prize, Unesco, 1992; Prix Littéraire des Droits de l'Homme, Paris, 1992; Rose Prize, Internat. Forum of Danish Lab. Movement, 1993; Victor Jara Internat. Human Rights Award, Center for Human Rights and Constitutional Law, LA, 1993; Bremen Solidarity Prize, 1993; Liberal Internat. Prize for Freedom, 1995; Jawaharlal Nehru Award for Internat. Understanding, 1995; Freedom Award of Internat. Rescue Cttee, 1995; Congressional Gold Medal, USA, 2012. *Publications:* (ed with Michael Aris) Tibetan Studies in Honour of Hugh Richardson, 1980; Aung San, 1984, 2nd edn as Aung San of Burma: a biographical portrait by his daughter, 1990; (contrib.) Burma and Japan: basic studies on their cultural and social structure, 1987; Burma and India: some aspects of intellectual life under colonialism, 1990; Freedom from Fear and Other Writings, 1991, 2nd edn 1995; Towards a True Refuge (Joyce Pearce Meml Lect.), 1993; numerous speeches. *Address:* 54–6 University Avenue, Rangoon, Burma.

**AUPETIT, Most Rev. Michel Christian Alain;** see Paris, Archbishop of, (RC).

**AUSTEN, Patrick George;** Operating Partner, Nova Capital Management Ltd, 2003–13; *b* 22 Sept. 1943; *m* 1968, Margaret; three *s* one *d. Educ:* Bristol Coll. of Commerce; Leicester Sch. of Textiles; Leicester Poly.; Centre d'Etudes Industrielles, Geneva. ICI Fibres, 1961–83: commercial apprentice, British Nylon Spinners (later ICI Fibres), 1961–65; mgt trainee, 1965–67; Trade Sales Manager, 1967–70; Fibres Manager, Republic of Ireland, 1970–73; Business Area Manager, 1974–79; Commercial Manager, Textile Fibres, 1979–83; BTR, 1983–93; Managing Director: Pretty Polly, 1983–85; Pretty Polly and Dunlopillo, 1985–87; Chief Exec., Liberty plc, 1993–96. *Recreations:* golf, motor-racing.

**AUSTEN, Richard James,** MBE 1996; HM Diplomatic Service, retired; Africa Directorate, Foreign and Commonwealth Office, 2012–13; *b* 25 May 1955; *s* of late Capt. George Albert Austen, MN and Joyce Margaret Austen. *Educ:* Steyning Grammar Sch.; Univ. of Bristol (BA Hons (Theol.) 1977). Grad. trainee, Midland Bank, 1977–81; joined FCO, 1981; Desk Officer, Consular Dept, 1981–82, ME Dept, 1982–83, FCO; Attaché, Dar Es Salaam, 1983–87; 3rd Sec., Ottawa, 1987–90; Desk Officer, Protocol Dept, FCO, 1990–93; Dep. High Comr, Banjul, 1993–96; Desk Officer, Perm. Under-Sec.'s Dept, FCO, 1996–97; Dep. Hd, Conference Dept, FCO, 1997–98; Hd of Section, Latin America and Caribbean Dept, FCO, 1998–2001; Dep. High Comr, Port Louis, 2001–03; Ambassador: to Mongolia, 2004–06; to Panama, 2006–11; Hd, Pol Ext. Section, Moscow, 2011; Chargé d'Affaires, Mali, 2012. Chair: Anglo Latin Amer. Foundn, 2015–; Nikaean Club, Lambeth Palace, 2017–. Lay Reader, St Luke's and the Barn, Kew, 2015–. *Recreations:* walking, cycling, religion, travelling, family history. *Address:* 8 Tunstall Court, Hatherley Road, Richmond, Surrey TW9 3LJ.

**AUSTEN-SMITH, Air Marshal Sir Roy (David),** KBE 1979; CB 1975; CVO 1994; DFC 1953; retired; a Gentleman Usher to HM the Queen, 1982–94, an Extra Gentleman Usher, since 1994; *b* 28 June 1924; *m* 1951, Ann (*née* Alderson); two *s. Educ:* Hurstpierpoint College. Pilot trng, Canada, 1943–44; No 41 Sqn (2 TAF), 1945; No 33 Sqdn, Malaya, 1950–53; Sqn Comdr, RAF Coll., Cranwell, 1953–56; OC No 73 Sqdn, Cyprus, 1956–59; Air Min., 1960–63; OC No 57 Sqdn, 1964–66; HQ 2 ATAF, 1966–68; CO, RAF Wattisham, 1968–70; MoD, 1970–72; AOC and Comdt, RAF Coll., Cranwell, 1972–75; SASO Near East Air Force, 1975–76; Comdr British Forces, Cyprus, AOC Air HQ Cyprus and Administrator, Sovereign Base Areas, Cyprus, 1976–78; Hd of British Defence Staff, Washington, and Defence Attaché, 1978–81. *Recreation:* golf. *Address:* c/o National Westminster Bank, Swanley, Kent BR8 7WL. *Club:* Royal Air Force.

**AUSTIN, Brian Patrick;** HM Diplomatic Service, retired; *b* 18 March 1938; *s* of Edward William Austin and Winifred Alice Austin (*née* Villiger); *m* 1st, 1968, Gusti Lina (*d* 2002); one *s* one *d*; 2nd, 2007, Dr Mary Laurie-Pile. *Educ:* St Olave's Grammar Sch.; Clare Coll., Cambridge. National Service, 1956–58. Joined CRO, 1961; Central African Office, 1962; Lagos, 1963; The Hague, 1966; First Sec., FCO, 1969; Montreal, 1973; FCO, 1978; Dep. High Comr, Kaduna, 1981–84; Counsellor: FCO, 1984–88; Stockholm, 1989–93; Consul-Gen., Vancouver, 1993–98. *Recreation:* birdwatching. *Address:* Clinton, Nightingale Avenue, West Horsley, Surrey KT24 6PB.

**AUSTIN, Prof. Gareth Meredith,** PhD; Professor of Economic History, University of Cambridge, since 2016; Fellow, King's College, Cambridge, since 2016; *b* Ibadan, Nigeria, 20 May 1956; *s* of Frederick and Margaret Austin; *m* 1989, Felicity, (Pip), Slipper; three *d. Educ:* Sevenoaks Sch.; Clare Coll., Cambridge (BA Hist. 1978); Univ. of Birmingham (PhD Econ. Hist. 1984). Teacher, Kiamuya Secondary Sch., Othaya, Kenya, 1975; Lecturer: Univ. of Birmingham, 1981–82; Univ. of Ghana, 1982–85; ESSRC Postdoctoral Fellow, Inst. of Commonwealth Studies, Univ. of London, 1986–88; Lectr, 1988–2004, Sen. Lectr, 2004–07, Reader, 2007–10, LSE; Prof., Grad. Inst. of Internat. and Develt Studies, Geneva, 2010–16. Guest or Vis. Scholar: Univ. of Cape Town, 1990; Kyoto Univ., 2006; Jawaharlal Nehru Univ., 2008; Kansai Univ., 2009; Macquarie Univ., 2010; Ecole d'économie de Paris, 2014; Univ. of Ghana, Univ. de la República, Montevideo, Univ. of Witwatersrand, 2015. Ed., Jl African Hist., 2001–05. Pres., Eur. Network in Universal and Global Hist., 2008–12. *Publications:* (ed with Kaom Sugihara) Local Suppliers of Credit in the Third World, 1750–1960, 1993; Labour, Land and Capital in Ghana: from slavery to free labour in Asante, 1807–1956, 2005; Labour-Intensive Industrialization in Global History, 2013; (ed) Economic Development and Environmental History in the Anthropocene: perspectives on Asia and Africa, 2017; contrib. articles to jls on African hist., African studies, develt studies, business hist., econ. hist. and social hist. *Recreation:* running. *Address:* King's College, 5 King's Parade, Cambridge CB2 1ST. *E:* gma31@cam.ac.uk.

**AUSTIN, Gary Ronald;** non-executive Director, Intellectual Property Office, 2009–18 (Chair, Audit and Risk Committee, 2010–18); *b* 28 May 1956; *s* of late Ronald Austin and Doris Austin (*née* Pearce); *m* 1980, Susan Ann Horridge; one *s* one *d. Educ:* Univ. of Nottingham (BSc Hons (Geog.) 1978); City Univ. Business Sch. (MBA 1984). Bank clerk, Nat. Westminster Bank, 1974–75; Econ. Planning Asst, N. Lichfield & Partners, 1978–79; Manpower Planner, City Area, 1980–84, City Dist, 1984–86, British Telecom plc; Dep. Regl Personnel Dir, SW Regl HA, 1986–92; Chief Exec., Blood Services SW, 1992–94; Exec. Dir, Nat. Blood Service, 1994–99; Chief Exec., Driving Standards Agency, 2000–06; Man. Dir, a²om academy, 2006–08, Chief Exec., a²om International, 2008–09. Non-exec. Dir, E Midlands Ambulance Service NHS Trust, 2006–14 (Dep. Chm., 2009–14). Lay Mem., Employment Tribunals Service, 2010–. Trustee, Lincs and Notts Air Ambulance Charitable Trust, 2013–15. London Olympic Games Maker team leader, 2012. CCMI 2003. *Recreations:* Bath Rugby, family, walking, Tai Ji Quan classes. *Address:* No 2 The Furlongs, Main Street, Bleasby, Notts NG14 7GH.

**AUSTIN, Ian;** MP for Dudley North, since 2005 (Lab, 2005–19; Ind, since 2019); *b* 6 March 1965; *s* of Alfred and Margaret Austin; *m* 1993, Catherine Miles; two *s* one *d. Educ:* Dudley Sch.; Univ. of Essex (BA Hons Govt). Communications Manager, Focus Housing, 1989–94; Press Officer, Labour Party, 1995–98; Dep. Dir of Communications, Scottish Labour Party, 1998–99; political advr to Chancellor of Exchequer, 1999–2005. Mem. (Lab) Dudley MBC, 1991–95. PPS to Prime Minister, 2007–08; an Asst Govt Whip, 2008–09; Minister for the W Midlands, 2008–10; Parly Under-Sec. of State, DCLG, 2009–10. *Recreations:* reading, watching football, cycling. *Address:* House of Commons, SW1A 0AA. *T:* (020) 7219 8012, *Fax:* (020) 7219 4408; St James House, Trinity Road, Dudley DY1 1JB. *T:* (01384) 342503.

**AUSTIN, Hon. Jacob, (Jack),** CM 2014; OBC 2010; PC (Canada) 1981; QC (British Columbia) 1970; Member of the Senate, 1975–2007, and Minister and Leader of the Government in the Senate, 2003–06, Canadian Parliament; Senior Advisor, International, Stern Partners Inc., since 2007; *b* 2 March 1932; *s* of Morris Austin and Clara Edith (*née* Chetner); *m* (marr. diss.); three *d*; *m* 1978, Natalie Veiner Freeman. *Educ:* Univ. of British Columbia (BA, LLB); Harvard Univ. (LLM). Barrister and Solicitor, BC and Yukon Territory. Asst Prof. of Law, Univ. of Brit. Columbia, 1955–58; practising lawyer, Vancouver, BC, 1958–63; Exec. Asst to Minister of Northern Affairs and Nat. Resources, 1963–65; contested (Liberal) Vancouver-Kingsway, Can. Federal Election, 1965; practising lawyer, Vancouver, BC, 1966–70; Dep. Minister, Dept of Energy, Mines and Resources, Ottawa, 1970–74; Principal Sec. to Prime Minister, Ottawa, May 1974–Aug. 1975; Minister of State for Aboriginal and Northern Affairs, 1981–82; Minister of State for Social Develt, responsible for Canada Devlt Investment Corp., and Minister for Expo '86, 1982–84; Chm., Ministerial Sub-Cttee on Broadcasting and Cultural Affairs, 1982–84. Pres., Internat. Div., Bank of British Columbia, 1985–86; Associate Counsel: Swinton & Co., 1986–92; Boughton Peterson & Co., 1992–2002; Chm. Board and Dir, Elite Insurance Management Ltd, 1986–90. Pres., Canada China Business Council, 1993–2001. Hon. Prof. and Sen. Fellow, Inst. of Asian Res., Univ. of BC, 2007–. Hon. DSocSc Univ. East Asia, 1987; Hon. LLD: BC, 2011; Royal Roads, 2016; Simon Fraser, 2017. Queen's Diamond Jubilee Medal, 2012. *Publications:* articles on law and public affairs in Canadian Bar Rev., Amer. Soc. of Internat. Law and other publns. *Recreations:* sailing, golf, reading, theatre. *Address:* Stern Partners Inc., Suite 2900, 650 West Georgia Street, Vancouver, BC V6B 4N8, Canada. *Clubs:* Vancouver, Shaughnessy Golf and Country (Vancouver, BC).

**AUSTIN, John Eric;** *b* 21 Aug. 1944; *s* of late Stanley George Austin and Ellen Elizabeth (*née* Day); adopted surname Austin-Walker, 1965, reverted to Austin, 1997; *m* 1st, 1965 Linda Margaret Walker (marr. diss. 1998); two *s* one *d*; 2nd, 2014, Sylvia Kelcher. *Educ:* Glyn Grammar Sch., Epsom; Goldsmiths' Coll., Univ. of London (Cert. Community and Youth Work 1972); Sch. for Advanced Urban Studies, Univ. of Bristol (MSc Policy Studies 1990). Hosp. lab. technician, 1961–63; Labour Party organiser, 1963–70; social worker, community worker, Bexley, 1972–74; Race Equality Officer (Dir, Bexley Council for Racial Equality), 1974–92. London Borough of Greenwich Council: Mem., 1970–94; Vice-Chm., 1971–74, Chm., 1974–78, Social Services; Dep. Leader, 1981–82; Leader 1982–87; Mayor of Greenwich, 1987–88 and 1988–89. Vice-Chairman: ALA, 1983–87 (Envmt Spokesperson, 1989–92); London Strategic Policy Unit, 1986–88; Chairman London Ecology Unit, 1990–92; London Emergency Planning Inf. Centre, 1990–92

Chairman: British Youth Council, 1969–71; Assoc. CHCs for England and Wales, 1986–88. Contested (Lab) Woolwich, 1987. MP (Lab) Woolwich, 1992–97, Erith and Thamesmead, 1997–2010. Mem., Select Cttee on Health, 1994–2005. Jt Chm., All Party Osteoporosis Gp, 1996–2010; Treasurer: Parly Human Rights Gp, 1997–98; Parly Gibraltar Gp, 1997–98; Secretary: British/Czech and Slovak Parly Gp, 1997–2010; British/Hungary Parly Gp, 1997–2010; Chairman: British/Slovenia Parly Gp, 1997–2010; British/Albania Parly Gp, 1997–2010; All Party UK Overseas Territories Parly Gp, 1998–2010; All Party Trinidad and Tobago Gp, 2005–10; Vice-Chm., British Falkland Is Gp, 1997–2006; Member: British Irish Parly Assembly, 2006–10; Jt Cttee on Human Rights, 2008–09. Vice Chm., London Gp of Labour MPs, 1992–97; Chm., Socialist Campaign Gp of Labour MPs, 1992–98. Deleg., Parly Assembly, Council of Europe and WEU, 2004–10 (Vice-Chm., Sub-Cttee on Human Trafficking); Vice-Chm., UK &, CPA, 2004–05 (Mem., 1997–2010, Chm., 2009–10, Exec. Cttee); Mem., Internat. Exec., IPU, 2004–07 (Mem. Exec. Cttee, British Gp, 1997–2010 (Chm., 2002–05); Pres., 12+ (Geopolitical Gp), 2006–10). Association of Former MPs: Mem., Exec. Cttee, 2010–; Mem. Editl Bd, Order Order, 2010–; Trustee and Chm., Parly Outreach Trust, 2015– (Sec., 2014–15). Hon. Chm., British Caribbean Assoc., 1997–2009. Mem. Bd, CAABU, 2001– (Co-Chair, 2001–11). Chm., George Croydon Marks Soc. (formerly Baron Marks Commemoration Cttee), 2011–. Trustee: London Marathon Charitable Trust, 1997–; Greenwich Community Coll. Trust, 2006–14; Crossness Engines Trust, 2007–17 (Chm., 2013–17); Conway Sch. Trust, 2008–10; Friends of Brighton and Hove Hosps, 2017–; Patron: Palestine Solidarity Campaign, 2007–; Archway Project, Thamesmead, 2008–; Patron (formerly Dist. Supporter), Humanists UK (formerly British Humanist Assoc.). *Recreations:* cooking, gardening, allotment holder, reminiscing about past marathons run, travel. *E:* johnaustin1944@gmail.com, admin@parlyoutreach.org.uk. *W:* www.johnaust.in.

**AUSTIN, Mark;** Presenter, Sky News, since 2018; *b* 1 Nov. 1958; *m* 1991; one *s* two *d. Educ:* Bournemouth Sch.; Highbury Coll., Portsmouth. Reporter, Bournemouth Evening Echo, 1976–80; newsroom writer, 1980–82, news reporter, 1982–85, sports reporter, 1985–86, BBC; joined ITV News as sports correspondent, 1986; Asia correspondent, 1990–93, 1996–98; Africa correspondent, 1993–96; Sen. Correspondent, 1998–2002; Presenter, ITV Evening News, 2003–16 (ITV News at 10.30pm, 2006–08, ITV News at Ten, 2008–15); US Corresp., Sky News, 2017–18. Presenter, TV series, Survivor, 2001. Best TV News Presenter, RTS, 2014, 2015. *Publications:* And Thank You For Watching: a memoir, 2018.

**AUSTIN, Neil;** lighting designer; *b* London, 22 June 1972; *s* of Anthony Charles Austin and Patricia Anne Austin (*née* Daly). *Educ:* St Paul's Sch., London; Guildhall Sch. of Music and Drama (Fellow 2008). Lighting designer for plays, musicals, opera and dance. *Productions include:* West End: Japes, Haymarket, 2000; A Life in the Theatre, Apollo, 2005; Dealer's Choice, Trafalgar, 2007; No Man's Land, Duke of York, 2008; The Prisoner of 2nd Avenue, Vaudeville, 2010; The Children's Hour, Comedy, Death and the Maiden, Pinter, Betty Blue Eyes, Novello, 2011; South Downs, The Browning Version, Pinter, The Sunshine Boys, Savoy, 2012, transf. LA, 2013; The Hothouse, Trafalgar, Henry V, Noël Coward, 2013; Shakespeare in Love, Noël Coward, Assassins, Menier Chocolate Factory, 2014; Bend it Like Beckham, Phoenix, Photograph 51, Noël Coward, 2015; Harry Potter and the Cursed Child, Palace, 2016, transf. NY, 2018, transf. Melbourne, 2019 (Whatsonstage Award, 2017; Olivier Award for Best Lighting Design, 2017; Tony Award for Best Lighting Design for a Play, 2018; Drama Desk Award for Outstanding Lighting Design, 2018; Outer Critics Circle Award for Outstanding Lighting Design, 2018); The Goat, Haymarket, Labour of Love, Noël Coward, 2017; Ink, Duke of York, 2017, transf. NY, 2019; Travesties, Apollo, 2017, transf. NY, 2018; The Lieutenant of Inishmore, Noël Coward, Company, Gielgud, 2018; Rosmersholm, Duke of York, The Starry Messenger, Wyndham's, Bitter Wheat, Garrick, The Night of the Iguana, Noël Coward, 2019; National Theatre: A Prayer for Owen Meany, 2002; Henry IV Pts 1 and 2, 2005; The Man of Mode, Philistines, The Emperor Jones, The Seafarer, transf. NY, 2007; Her Naked Skin, Oedipus, 2008; England People Very Nice, The Observer, 2009; London Assurance, The White Guard (Olivier Award for Best Lighting Design, 2011), Women Beware Women, Welcome to Thebes, 2010; The Cherry Orchard, 2011; She Stoops to Conquer, The Doctor's Dilemma, 2012; Port, Liolà, 2013; The Silver Tassie, Great Britain, 2014; Dara, Rules for Living, Three Days in the Country, 2015; Translations, 2018; Donmar Warehouse: Caligula, After Miss Julie, 2003; The Wild Duck, 2005; Frost Nixon, 2006, transf. NY, 2007; Don Juan in Soho, 2006; John Gabriel Borkman, Parade (Knight of Illumination Award, 2008), 2007; Piaf, Twelfth Night, 2008; Madame de Sade, Hamlet, transf. NY, A Streetcar Named Desire, Life is a Dream, 2009; Red, 2009, transf. NY, 2010 (Tony Award for Best Lighting Design of a Play, Drama Desk Award for Outstanding Lighting Design, 2010); The Prince of Homborg, Passion, King Lear, 2010; The 25th Annual Putnam County Spelling Bee, 2011; Julius Caesar, 2012, transf. NY, 2013; The Weir, 2013, transf. West End, 2014; The Night Alive, 2013, transf. NY, 2013; Henry IV, 2014; Company, Crucible, 2011 (Knight of Illumination Award, 2012); Royal Ballet: The Soldier's Tale, 2004; Rhapsody, 2005; As One, 2010; 24 Preludes, 2013; English National Ballet: The Sleeping Beauty, 2012; Le Corsaire, 2013; New Adventures: Cinderella, 2010, 2017; New York: Evita, 2012; Cat on a Hot Tin Roof, 2013; Macbeth, 2014. *Address:* c/o Rose Cobbe, United Agents, 12–26 Lexington Street, W1F 0LE. *W:* www.neilaustin.com.

**AUSTIN, Sir Peter John,** 7th Bt *cr* 1894, of Red Hill, Castleford, West Riding; *b* 29 July 1958; *s* of Sir Anthony Leonard Austin, 6th Bt and Mary Annette Austin (*née* Kelly); *S* father, 2017; *m* 1988, Jane Clare Dracup (marr. diss. 2012). *Educ:* Belmont Abbey Coll. *Heir: b* Nicholas Michael James Austin [*b* 1960; *m* 1996, Susan Margaret Sarjeant; two *d*].

**AUSTIN, Sir Roger (Mark),** KCB 1992; AFC 1973; aviation and defence consultant, 1998–2009; *b* 9 March 1940; *s* of Mark and Sylvia Joan Austin. *Educ:* King Alfred's Grammar Sch., Wantage. Commissioned in RAF, 1957; flying appts as Qualified Flying Instructor and with Nos 20 and 54 Sqns, 1960–68; commanded No 54 Sqn, 1969; flying appt with No 4 Sqn, 1970–72; Staff Coll., Camberley, 1973; commanded 233 OCU, 1974–77; PSO to AOC-in-C Strike Command, 1977–80; commanded RAF Chivenor, 1980–82; ADC to the Queen, 1980–82; Staff of HQ Strike Command, 1982–84; Dir of Op. Requirements, 1984–85; RCDS, 1986; AO i/c Central Tactics and Trials Orgn, 1987; DG Aircraft 1, MoD (PE), 1987–89; AOC and Comdt, RAF Coll., Cranwell, 1989–92; DCDS (Systems), MoD, 1992–94; Controller Aircraft, MoD, 1994–96; Dep. Chief of Defence Procurement (Ops), MoD (PE), 1995–96; Air Marshal, retd 1997. FO RAFVR (T), 1997–2009. President: RBL, 1997–2000; Victory Services Assoc., 2002–09 (Chm., 1997–2001); SE and E Area, RAFA, 2014–18; Trustee, RAF Benevolent Fund, 2000–09. *Recreations:* military history, transport systems, photography. *Address:* 29 Fen Road, Watlington, Kings Lynn PE33 0JA. *Club:* Royal Air Force.

**AUSTIN-SMITH, Michael Gerard;** QC 1990; a Recorder, 1986–2014; *b* 4 Sept. 1944; *s* of late Cyril John Austin-Smith and Joyce Austin-Smith; *m* 1971, Stephanie Maddocks; one *s* one *d. Educ:* Hampton Grammar Sch.; Exeter Univ. (LLB Hons). Called to the Bar, Inner Temple, 1969, Bencher, 2002. DTI Inspector, 1988–89 and 1989–90. *Clubs:* Royal Ocean Racing; Island Sailing, Cowes Corinthian, Baat (Cowes).

**AUSTIN-WALKER, John Eric;** *see* Austin, J. E.

**AUSTINS, Lynne Teresa;** *see* Matthews, L. T.

**AUSTRALIA, Primate of;** *see* Melbourne, Archbishop of.

**AUSTWICK, Dawn Jacquelyn,** OBE 2000; Chief Executive, National Lottery Community Fund (formerly Big Lottery Fund), since 2013; *b* Sheffield, 11 Dec. 1960; *d* of Prof. Kenneth Austwick, *qv*; *m* 1990, Henry Stewart; one *s* two *d. Educ:* Bath High Sch.; Westfield Coll., London (BA Combined Hons English and Drama); London Business Sch. (MBA). Projects Coordinator, Assoc. for Business Sponsorship of the Arts, 1983–85; Business Develt Manager, Half Moon Th., 1985–86; Principal Consultant, KPMG Mgt Consulting, 1986–94; Proj. Dir, Tate Modern, 1995–2000; Dep. Dir, BM, 2002–05; Chief Exec., Esmée Fairbairn Foundn, 2005–13. Dep. Chm., Women's Liby, 2004–05. Dir, Big Society Capital, 2011–13. Mem., Audit Cttee, AHRC, 2007–10. Trustee: Woodland Trust, 2001–09; Historic Royal Palaces, 2006–16; London Marathon Charitable Trust, 2017–. CCMI; FRSA. Hon. DBA London Metropolitan, 2006. *Recreations:* theatre, gardening, Arsenal Football Club, yoga. *Address:* National Lottery Community Fund, 1 Plough Place, EC4A 1DE. *Club:* Bath.

**AUSTWICK, Prof. Kenneth;** JP; Professor of Education, Bath University, 1966–91, now Emeritus; *b* 26 May 1927; *s* of Harry and Beatrice Austwick; *m* 1956, Gillian Griffin; one *s* one *d. Educ:* Morecambe Grammar Sch.; Sheffield Univ. BSc Maths, DipEd, MSc, PhD Sheffield. Schoolmaster, Bromsgrove, Frome and Nottingham, 1950–59; Lectr/Sen. Lectr, Sheffield Univ., 1959–65; Dep. Dir, Inst. of Educn, Reading Univ., 1965–66; Pro-Vice-Chancellor, Bath Univ., 1972–75. Vis. Lecturer: Univ. of BC, 1963; Univ. of Michigan, 1963; Univ. of Wits., 1967. Consultant, OECD, 1965; Adviser, Home Office, 1967–81; Chm., Nat. Savings SW Regional Educn, 1975–78. JP Bath 1970. FRSA. *Publications:* Logarithms, 1962; Equations and Graphs, 1963; (ed) Teaching Machines and Programming, 1964; (ed) Aspects of Educational Technology, 1972; Maths at Work, 1985; Mathematics Connections, 1985; Level by Level Mathematics, 1991; (ed) Working Science, 1991; (ed) Working English, 1991; articles and contribs on maths teaching and educnl technology. *Recreations:* painting, gardening, bridge. *Address:* The Coach House, Combe Hay, Bath BA2 7EG. *T:* (01225) 282726.
*See also* D. J. Austwick.

**AUTON, Sylvia Jean,** OBE 2014; Chairman, 2009–13, and Chief Executive, 2003–08 and 2011–13, IPC Media Ltd (Director, 1998–2013); *b* 8 June 1949; *m* 1978, William Auton; two *s. Educ:* Southampton Univ. (BSc Jt Hons). Publishing Dir, New Scientist, 1990–98; Man. Dir, IPC Country & Leisure Media, 1998–2003; Exec. Vice Pres., Time Inc., 2007–10. Trustee, 1998–2013, Chm., 2000–13, IPC Media Pension Trustee Ltd; Dir, PPA Ltd, 2003–13. *Recreations:* walking, travel.

**AUTY, Michael Roy;** QC 2013; *b* Nottingham, 30 July 1963; *s* of late Roy Mercer Auty and Phyllis Mary Auty; *m* 2007, Helen Catherine Asher-Hibbett; four *s. Educ:* Nottingham Bluecoat C of E Grammar Sch.; Nottingham Trent Univ. (BA Hons Law 1984); Chester Coll. of Law. Admitted as solicitor, 1987; Asst Solicitor, 1987–88, Partner, 1988–90, Messrs Fidler and Pepper; called to the Bar, Inner Temple, 1990; barrister in ind. practice, specialising in criminal law (homicide, major drugs ops and serious sexual offences), 1990–. *Recreations:* rock music, playing the guitar, food (American, Asian and Indian), motorcycling, films, relaxing with friends and family. *Address:* No 1 High Pavement Chambers, 1 High Pavement, Nottingham NG1 1HF. *T:* (0115) 941 8218, *Fax:* (0115) 941 8240. *E:* MichaelAutyqc@1highpavement.co.uk.

**AVEBURY, 5th Baron** *cr* 1900, of Avebury Wilts; **Lyulph Ambrose Jonathan Lubbock;** Bt 1806; *b* 15 June 1954; *e s* of 4th Baron Avebury and of Kina Maria Lubbock (*see* Kina, Lady Avebury); *S* father, 2016; *m* 1977, Susan Carol MacDonald; one *s* one *d. Educ:* Birmingham Univ. (BSc Physics). Roles in food testing and civil engrg labs; Business Team Leader and Project Manager, Bromley LBC, 1981–90; Consultant, CFM, 1993–97; Consultant, ICL, 1997–2001; Man. Consultant, 2001–07, Principal Consultant, 2007–16, Fujitsu. Chm., Maurice Lubbock Meml Trust, 2016–. MInstP. FLS. *Heir: s* Hon. Alexander Lyulph Robert Lubbock, *b* 17 Jan. 1985.

**AVEBURY, Kina, Lady; Kina-Maria Lubbock;** consultant on health and social policy; *b* 2 Sept. 1934; *d* of late Count Joseph O'Kelly de Gallagh and Mrs M. Bruce; *m* 1953, Eric Reginald Lubbock (later 4th Baron Avebury) (marr. diss. 1983; he *d* 2016); two *s* one *d. Educ:* Convent of the Sacred Heart, Tunbridge Wells; Goldsmiths' College (BScSoc Hons) and LSE, Univ. of London. Lectr, Royal Coll. of Nursing, 1970–74; campaign organizer, European Movement, 1975; Asst Dir, Nat. Assoc. for Mental Health, 1976–82; Sociologist, Dept of Psychiatry, London Hosp. Med. Coll., 1983–85; Mental Health Planner, Tower Hamlets Social Services, 1986–94. Chairman: Nat. Marriage Guidance Council, 1975–82; Family Service Units, 1984–87; Avebury Working Party, 1982–84 (produced Code of Practice for Residential Care for DHSS); Working Party for A Better Home Life, 1996, Working Party on Nat. Required Standards for Long Term Care, 1998–99, Centre for Policy on Ageing; Mem., Central Council for Educn and Trng in Social Work, 1986–90. JP Kent, 1974–79. Trustee: Neighbours in Poplar; George Green Almshouse Trust. *Publications:* Volunteers in Mental Health, 1985; (with R. Williams) A Place in Mind, 1995; (jtly) The Substance of Young Needs, 1996; articles on mental health and related social policy. *Recreations:* painting, cooking, gardening, music.
*See also* Baron Avebury.

**AVERY, Brian Stuart,** FDSRCS; FRCSE; Consultant Oral and Maxillofacial Surgeon, James Cook University Hospital, Middlesbrough, 1983–2009; Dean, Faculty of Dental Surgery, Royal College of Surgeons of England, 2004–08; *b* 15 Feb. 1947; *s* of Stuart and Edna Avery; *m* 1972, Fiona Gibson; two *s* two *d. Educ:* Fox Primary Sch., Notting Hill Gate; Abingdon Sch.; Guy's Hosp. Med. Sch., Univ. of London (BDS Hons 1970; MB BS 1974). LDSRCS 1970, FDSRCS 1976; LRCP 1974; MRCS 1974, Hon. FRCS 2005; FRCSE 1985; FRACDS 2008; FDSRCPSGlas 2009. House officer posts, Guy's Hosp., 1974–75; Registrar in Oral and Maxillofacial Surgery: Eastman Dental Hosp., 1975; Queen Mary Hosp., Roehampton and Westminster Hosp., 1976–78; Sen. Registrar in Oral and Maxillofacial Surgery, Canniesburn Hosp., Glasgow, 1978–83. Hon. Prof. of Oral and Maxillofacial Surgery, Univ. of Teesside, 2002–09. Consultant to the Army, 1995–2009. Pres., BAOMS, 2005. Member: Council, RCS, 2003–09; Acad. of Med. Royal Colls, 2004–09. Hon. Fellow: Indian Assoc. Oral and Maxillofacial Surgery, 1992; Amer. Assoc. Oral and Maxillofacial Surgery, 2005. Surgery Prize, 1992, Downs Surgical Prize, 2008, BAOMS; Colyer Gold Medal, Faculty of Dental Surgery, RCS, 2009. *Publications:* with G. Dimitroulis: Maxillofacial Injuries: a synopsis of basic principles, diagnosis and management, 1994; Oral Cancer: a synopsis of pathology and management, 1998; contrib. book chapters and articles related to oral and maxillofacial surgery. *Recreations:* reading, dining, travelling, cursing inefficiency of the National Health Service. *Address:* Mordon House, Mordon, Sedgefield, Stockton-on-Tees TS21 2EY. *T:* (01740) 620634. *E:* averyb@live.co.uk.

**AVERY, Graham John Lloyd,** CMG 2012; Senior Member, St Antony's College, Oxford, since 2005; Senior Adviser, European Policy Centre, Brussels, since 2006; Hon. Director General, European Commission, since 2006; *b* 29 Oct. 1943; *s* of Rev. Edward Avery and Alice Avery; *m* 1st, 1967, Susan Steele (marr. diss.); two *s*; 2nd, 2002, Annalisa

Cecchi; one s. *Educ*: Kingswood Sch., Bath; Balliol Coll., Oxford (MA). Joined MAFF, 1965; Principal responsible for negotiations for British entry to European Communities, 1969–72; PPS to Ministers, Fred Peart, John Silkin, 1976; Commission of the European Communities, subseq. European Commission, Brussels: Member of Cabinets: of President, Roy Jenkins, 1977–80; of Vice-Pres. for External Relns, Christopher Soames, 1973–76; of Comrs for Agric., Finn Gundelach 1981, Poul Dalsager 1981, Frans Andriessen 1985–86; served: in Directorate Gen. for Agric. as Hd of Div. for Econ. Affairs and Gen. Problems, 1981–84, as Dir for Rural Develt, 1987–90; in Directorate Gen. for External Relations as Dir for relns with USA, Canada, Australia and NZ, 1990–92, as Dir for relns with Austria, Switzerland, Iceland, Norway, Sweden and Finland, 1992–93, in Task Force for Enlargement as Dir, 1993–94; in Directorate Gen. for External Political Relations, as Head of Policy Planning, 1995, as Chief Advr for Enlargement, 1996–98; Inspector Gen., 1998–2000; Chief Advr, Directorate Gen. for Enlargement, 2000–03; Chief Advr, subseq. Dir for Strategy, Co-ordination and Analysis, Directorate Gen. for External Relations, 2003–06. Sen. Gen., Trans European Policy Studies Assoc., 2006–08. Vis. Prof., Coll. of Europe, 2003–05. Convenor, Adam von Trott Meml Cttee, Oxford, 2014–18. Fellow: Center for Internat. Affairs, Harvard Univ., 1986–87; Eur. Univ. Inst., Florence, 2002, 2009, 2010, 2019; Canterbury Univ., NZ, 2006; Sen. Mem., Mansfield Coll., Oxford, 2015–18. *Publications*: (with Fraser Cameron): The Enlargement of the European Union, 1998; chapter on Enlargement Negotiations in The Future of Europe: enlargement and integration, 2004; chapter on EU Expansion and Wider Europe in The European Union: how does it work?, 2nd edn 2008 to 4th edn 2015; articles in Internat. Affairs, World Today, Prospect, Jl of Eur. Public Policy, Internat. Spectator, Studia Diplomatica, Hungarian Qly, Internat. Jl Study of Christian Ch, Jl of Agricl Econs, Jl of Jane Austen Soc., Jl of Bristol Naturalists' Soc., European Policy Centre, Clarence Bicknell Assoc., etc. *Address*: 65 Southmoor Road, Oxford OX2 6RE.

**AVERY, James Royle, (Roy)**; Headmaster, Bristol Grammar School, 1975–86; *b* 7 Dec. 1925; *s* of Charles James Avery and Dorothy May Avery; *m* 1954, Marjorie Louise (*née* Smith); one *s* one *d*. *Educ*: Queen Elizabeth's Hosp., Bristol; Magdalen Coll., Oxford; Bristol Univ. MA Oxon, CertifEd Bristol. Asst History Master, Bristol Grammar Sch., 1951–59; Sen. History Master, Haberdashers' Aske's Sch. at Hampstead, then Elstree, 1960–65; Head Master, Harrow County Boys' Sch., 1965–75. Mem. Council, Bristol Univ., 1982–95. Hon. MLitt Bristol, 1996. *Publications*: The Story of Aldenham House, 1961; The Elstree Murder, 1962; The History of Queen Elizabeth's Hospital 1590–1990, 1990; The Sky's the Limit: the story of Bristol philanthropist John James, 1906–1996, 2001; contrib. Dictionary of World History, 1973; articles, reviews in educnl jls. *Recreations*: reading, walking, sport, music, the ecumenical movement, international studies. *Address*: 6 Willow Pool, Cote Lane, Bristol BS9 3FD. *T*: (0117) 962 3423.

**AVERY, John Ernest**, CB 1997; Deputy Parliamentary Commissioner for Administration, 1990–2000; *b* 18 April 1940; *s* of Ernest Charles Avery and Pauline Margaret Avery; *m* 1966, Anna Meddings; two *d*. *Educ*: Plymouth Coll.; Leeds Univ. (BSc). Called to the Bar, Gray's Inn, 1972. Patent Examiner, Bd of Trade, 1964–72; Office of Fair Trading, 1972–76; Dept of Industry, later DTI, 1976–89; Dir of Investigations, Office of Parly Comr for Admin (Ombudsman), 1989–90. *Recreations*: squash, theatre.

**AVERY, Mark Ian**, PhD; freelance writer on environmental issues; *b* Bristol, 29 March 1958; *s* of Charles Avery and Megan Avery; *m* 1985, Rosemary Cockerill; one *s* one *d*. *Educ*: Downing Coll., Cambridge (BA 1979); Aberdeen Univ. (PhD 1983). NERC Res. Fellow, Univ. of Oxford, 1984–85; Res. Biologist, 1986–88, Sen. Res. Biologist, 1988–92, Hd of Conservation Sci., 1992–98, Dir, Conservation, 1998–2011, RSPB. *Publications*: Birds and Forestry (with R. Leslie), 1989; Blogging for Nature, 2011; Fighting for Birds, 2012; A Message from Martha, 2014; (with K. Betton) Behind the Binoculars, 2015; Inglorious, 2015; Remarkable Birds, 2016. *Recreations*: National Hunt racing, opera, nature. *Address*: 9 Lawson Street, Raunds, Wellingborough, Northants NN9 6NG. *Club*: Reform.

**AVERY, Roy**; see Avery, J. R.

**AVERY JONES, Dr John Francis**, CBE 1987; a Judge of the Upper Tribunal (Tax and Chancery Chamber) and of the Tax Chamber of the First-tier Tribunal, 2009–11 (a Special Commissioner of Income Tax, 2002–09 (Deputy, 1991–2001); Chairman, VAT and Duties Tribunals, 2002–09 (part-time, 1991–2001)); *b* 5 April 1940; *s* of Sir Francis Avery Jones, CBE, FRCP; *m* 1994, Catherine Susan Bobbett. *Educ*: Rugby Sch.; Trinity Coll., Cambridge (MA, LLM, PhD 1993). Solicitor, 1966; Partner in Bircham & Co., 1970; Sen. Partner, Speechly Bircham, 1985–2001. Member: Meade Cttee, 1975–77; Keith Cttee, 1980–84. Pres., Inst. of Taxation, 1980–82 (Hon. FTII 2002); Chm., Law Soc.'s Revenue Law Cttee, 1983–87; Member Council: Law Soc., 1986–90; Inst. for Fiscal Studies, 1988–2011; Exec. Cttee, Internat. Fiscal Assoc., 1988–94 (1st Vice-Pres., 1993–94; Chm., British Br., 1989–91); Mem., Bd of Trustees, Internat. Bureau of Fiscal Documentation, 1989–2011 (Chm., 1991–2002). Vis. Prof. of Taxation, LSE, 1988–2009; Atax Cliffbrook Vis. Schol., Univ. of NSW, 1995. David R. Tillinghast Lectr on Internat. Taxation, New York Univ., 1997. Mem., Steering Cttee, Tax Law Rewrite, 1996–; Mem., Tax Law Review Cttee, 1997–2011 (Chm., 1997–2005). Member, Board of Governors: Voluntary Hosp. of St Bartholomew, 1984–2011; LSE, 1995–2010 (Chm., Audit Cttee, 1996–2003); Chm., Addington Soc., 1985–87. Master: Co. of Barbers, 1985–86; City of London Solicitors' Co., 1997–98. Consulting Editor: Encyclopedia of VAT, 1989–93 (Gen. Ed., 1972–89); British Tax Review, 1997– (Jt Ed., 1974–97); Mem. Editl Bd, Simon's Taxes, 1977–2001. Frans Banninck Cocq Medal, City of Amsterdam, 2002; Chartered Inst. of Taxation Council Award, 2012; Lifetime Achievement, Taxation Awards, 2014; (jtly) Frans Vanistendael Award for Internat. Tax Law, Internat. Bureau of Fiscal Documentation, 2015. *Publications*: (ed) Tax Havens and Measures Against Tax Avoidance and Evasion in the EEC, 1974; numerous articles on tax. *Recreation*: music, particularly opera. *Address*: Camilla, Frogham, Fordingbridge, Hants SP6 2HN. *T*: (01425) 653721. *Club*: Athenæum.

**AVES, Jonathan James**; HM Diplomatic Service, retired; Senior Political Counsellor for Russia, Central Asia and Mongolia, European Bank for Reconstruction and Development, since 2017; *m* Katherine Jane Leach, *qv*; one *s* two *d*. *Educ*: Univ. of Oxford (BA); Univ. of London (PhD). Lecturer: LSE; Univ. of Sussex; joined FCO, 1996; Res. Analyst, S Caucasus and Central Asia, FCO, 1996–2000; First Sec. (Pol), Moscow, 2000–04; Hd, Pol and Human Rights Section, Iraq Policy Unit, FCO, 2004–05; Hd, Pol Section, Tokyo, 2006–11; Hd, UN Team, Human Rights and Democracy Dept, FCO, 2011; Jt Ambassador to Armenia, 2012–14; Caucasus Prog. Sen. Advr, Conciliation Resources, 2016.

**AVES, Katherine Jane**; see Leach, K. J.

**AVIS, Rev. Dr Paul David Loup**; Chaplain to the Queen, 2008–17; Canon Theologian of Exeter Cathedral, 2008–13; *b* 21 July 1947; *s* of late Peter George Hobden Avis and Diana Joan (*née* Loup); *m* 1970, Susan Janet Haywood; three *s*. *Educ*: London Bible Coll. (BD Hons London Univ. (ext.) 1970; PhD 1976); Westcott House, Cambridge. Deacon 1975, priest 1976; Curate, South Molton, dio. Exeter, 1975–80; Vicar, Stoke Canon, Poltimore with Huxham, Rewe with Netherexe, 1980–98; Preb., 1993–2008, Sub Dean, 1997–2008, Exeter Cathedral. Hon. Asst Priest, Axe Valley Mission Community, 2003–. Gen. Sec., C of E Council for Christian Unity, 1998–2011; Theol Consultant to Anglican Communion Office, 2011–12. Hon. Dir, Centre for Study of Christian Church, 1997–, Hon. Vis. Prof., 2009–17, Hon. Res. Fellow, 2017–, Univ. of Exeter; Hon. Prof., Univ. of Durham, 2017–. Jt Ed., Internat. Jl for Study of the Christian Church, 2001–03; Convening Ed., 2004–11, Ed.-in-Chief, 2011–, Ecclesiology. *Publications*: The Church in the Theology of the Reformers, 1982; Ecumenical Theology, 1986; The Methods of Modern Theology, 1986; Foundations of Modern Historical Thought, 1986; Gore: Construction and Conflict, 1988; (ed and contrib.) The Threshold of Theology, 1988; Eros and the Sacred, 1989; Anglicanism and the Christian Church, 1989, 2nd edn 2002; Authority, Leadership and Conflict in the Church, 1992; (ed and contrib.) The Resurrection of Jesus Christ, 1993; (ed and contrib.) Divine Revelation, 1997; Faith in the Fires of Criticism, 1997; God and the Creative Imagination, 1999; The Anglican Understanding of the Church, 2000, 2nd edn 2013; Church, State and Establishment, 2001; (ed and contrib.) The Christian Church: an introduction to the major traditions, 2002; A Church Drawing Near, 2003; (ed and contrib.) Public Faith?, 2003; (ed and contrib.) Seeking the Truth of Change in the Church, 2003; (ed and contrib.) Paths to Unity, 2004; A Ministry Shaped by Mission, 2005; Beyond the Reformation?: authority, primacy and unity in the conciliar tradition, 2006; The Identity of Anglicanism: essentials of Anglican ecclesiology, 2008; Reshaping Ecumenical Theology: the Church made whole?, 2010; (ed and contrib.) The Journey of Christian Initiation: theological and pastoral perspectives, 2011; In Search of Authority: Anglican theological method from the Reformation to the Enlightenment, 2014; Becoming a Bishop: theological handbook of episcopal ministry, 2015; The Vocation of Anglicanism, 2016; (ed and contrib.) The Lambeth Conference: theology, history, polity and purpose, 2017; (ed and contrib.) The Oxford Handbook of Ecclesiology, 2018; (ed and contrib.) Incarnating Authority: a critical account of authority in the Church, 2019. *Recreations*: walking, literature, writing theology, logging trees. *Address*: Lea Hill, Membury, Axminster, Devon EX13 7AQ. *T*: (01404) 881881. *E*: dr.paul.avis@gmail.com.

**AVISON, Dr Gerald**; Co-Founder, 1988, and non-executive Director, since 2015, TTP Group plc (Chief Executive, 1988–2007; Chairman, 2007–15); *b* 23 Nov. 1940; *s* of Fred and Edith Avison; *m* 1971, Jean Margaret Mizen; one *s* one *d*. *Educ*: Manchester Grammar Sch.; Univ. of Bristol (BSc; PhD 1967). Engr, Guided Weapons Div., 1968–71, Manager, Electron Beam Welding Dept, 1971–73, BAC; PA Technology: Sen. Engr, 1973–75; Consultant, 1975–78, Sen. Consultant, 1978–85; Man. Dir, Cambridge Lab., 1985–87; Chm., TTP Communications plc, 2000–06. Director: TTP Venture Managers Ltd, 1999–; Cambridge Network, 2002–08. Trustee, Hirsch Trust for Camlab Employees, 2001–. *Recreations*: travel, family, curiosity. *Address*: 59 Victoria Park, Cambridge CB4 3EJ. *T*: (01223) 354553, *Fax*: (01763) 261582. *E*: ga@ttpgroup.com.

**AVISS, Prof. Derek William**, OBE 2013; 'cellist; freelance consultant, since 2012; Executive Director, Trinity Laban Conservatoire of Music and Dance, 2010–12 (Joint Principal, 2006–10), Emeritus Professor of Higher Education, 2013; *b* 21 Aug. 1948; *s* of Arthur William Archibald and Joan Gladys Aviss; *m* 1994, Jennifer Jane Smith; one *s* from previous marriage. *Educ*: Trinity Coll. of Music (LTCL 1970; Hon. FTCL 1986). FLCM 1979. Free-lance professional 'cellist, performing with Ariosti Piano Trio, Cantilena Ensemble, 1970–83. Trinity College of Music: Prof. of 'Cello, Jun. Dept, 1976–90, Prof. of 'Cello and Chamber Music, Sen. Dept, 1979–; Sen. Lectr in 'Cello and Chamber Music, 1986–90; Head: String Dept, 1990–94; Performance Studies, 1992–94; Dep. Principal, 1994–2005; Principal, 2005–10. Hon. Vis. Prof., City Univ., 2010–. FRSA 2000. *Recreations*: granddaughters Rowan and Ilona, motor cars, cricket, literature, music, theatre, travel. *Address*: The Clock House, The Dower Court, Somerford Keynes, Glos GL7 6DN. *T*: (01285) 861974. *E*: derek.aviss@gmail.com.

**AX, Emanuel**; concert pianist, since 1974; *b* 8 June 1949; *m* Yoko Nazaki; one *s* one *d*. *Educ*: Juilliard Sch. (studied with Mieczylaw Munz); Columbia Univ. Regular solo appearances with symphony orchs, incl. NY Philharmonic, National Symphony, Philadelphia Orch., Boston SO, Chicago SO, Cleveland Orch., Berlin Philharmonic, LPO, etc.; recitals at Carnegie Hall, Concertgebouw, Amsterdam, Barbican Centre, Théâtre des Champs Elysées, etc.; has played duo recitals with cellist Yo-Yo Ma annually since 1976; performed world premières of piano concertos by: Joseph Schwantner, 1988; Ezra Laderman, 1992; John Adams, 1997; Christopher Rouse, 1999; Bright Sheng, 2000, 2003; Krzysztof Penderecki, 2002; Melinda Wagner, 2003. Numerous recordings; Grammy Awards, 1985–86, 1992–95. First Prize, Arthur Rubinstein Internat. Piano Competition, 1974; Michael's Award, Young Concert Artists, 1975; Avery Fisher Prize, 1979. *Address*: c/o Opus 3, 470 Park Avenue South, 9th Floor North, New York, NY 10016, USA. *T*: (212) 5847500.

**AXEL, Prof. Richard**, MD; Professor of Biochemistry and Molecular Biophysics, Columbia University, since 1999; *b* 2 July 1946; two *s*. *Educ*: Columbia Univ. (AB 1967); Johns Hopkins Univ. (MD 1970). Res. Associate, NIH, 1972–74; Columbia University: Asst Prof., Inst. of Cancer Res., 1974–78; Prof. of Pathol. and Biochem., 1978; Investigator, Howard Hughes Medical Inst., 1984–. Foreign Mem. Royal Soc., 2014. (Jtly) Nobel Prize in Physiology or Medicine, 2004. *Address*: Axel Laboratory, Howard Hughes Medical Institute, Columbia University, Room 1016, 701 West 168th Street, New York, NY 10032, USA.

**AXFORD, David Norman**, PhD; CMet, CEng, FIET; international consultant meteorologist; Adviser to Earthwatch Europe, Oxford, 1996–2000; *b* 14 June 1934; *s* of Norman Axford and Joy Alicia Axford (*née* Williams); *m* 1st, 1962, Elizabeth Anne (*née* Stiles) (marr. diss. 1980); one *s* two *d*; 2nd, 1980, Diana Rosemary Joan (*née* Bufton); three step *s* one step *d*. *Educ*: Merchant Taylors' School, Sandy Lodge; Plymouth Coll.; St John's Coll., Cambridge (Baylis Open Scholarship in Maths; BA 1956, MA 1960, PhD (Met.) 1972); MSc (Electronics) Southampton 1963; Advanced Dip., 2004, Dip., 2006 (English Local Hist.), Oxford Univ. FIET (FIEE, CEng 1982). Entered Met. Office, 1958; Flying Officer, RAF, 1958–60; Meteorological Office: Forecasting and Research, 1960–68; Met. Research Flight, and Radiosondes, 1968–76; Operational Instrumentation, 1976–80; Telecommunications, 1980–82; Dep. Dir, Observational Services, 1982–84; Dir of Services, 1984–89; Dep. Sec.-Gen., WMO, 1989–95; Special Exec. Advr to Sec.-Gen., WMO, 1995. Chm., Cttee on Operational World Weather Watch Systems Evaluation, N Atlantic (CONA), 1985–89. Pres., N Atlantic Observing Stations (NAOS) Bd, 1983–86; Vice Pres., RMetS, 1989–91 (Mem. Council and Hon. Gen. Sec., 1983–88; Mem. 1998–2004, Chm., 1999–2004, Accreditation Bd); European Meteorological Society Chm., Accreditation Cttee, 2001–06; Vice Pres. and Treas., 2002–05. British Association of Former UN Civil Service: Mem., Exec. Cttee, 1996–; Vice Chm., 1998–99; Chm. 1999–2004, 2009–10; Vice-Pres., 2004–. Clerk/Correspondent of Trustees, Stanford-in-the-Vale Public Purposes Charity, 2002–18 (Chm., 2000–02); Chm., Stanford-in-the-Vale Local and Dist History Soc., 2004–13 (Hon. Mem., 2013–); Mem. and Trustee, Stanford-in-the-Vale Village Hall Mgt Cttee, 2010–15. Trustee: Thames Valley Hospice, 1996–98 Friends of the Ridgeway, 2008–15; Trustee and Mem. Cttee, Berkshire Local Hist. Assoc. 2016–18. L. G. Groves 2nd Meml Prize for Met., 1970. *Publications*: (contrib.) History of the Meteorological Office, 2012; papers in learned jls on met. and aspects of met instrumentation in GB and USA; articles on local history. *Recreations*: home and garden music, travel, good food, family history research, local English history, twelve grandchildren, two great grandsons, creating a family web-site. *Address:* 3 Penstones Court, Marlborough Lane, Stanford-in-the-Vale, Faringdon, Oxon SN7 8SW. *T:* (01367) 718480.

**AXON, Prof. Anthony Thomas Roger,** MD; FRCP; Consultant Physician and Gastroenterologist, Leeds General Infirmary, 1975–2006, now Emeritus Consultant Gastroenterologist; Hon. Professor of Gastroenterology, University of Leeds, since 1995; *b* 21 Nov. 1941; *s* of Robert and Ruth Axon; *m* 1965, Jill Coleman; two *s* one *d*. *Educ:* Woodhouse Grove Sch., W Yorks; St Bartholomew's Hosp. Med. Coll., London (MB BS Hons, Dist. in Medicine, MD 1973). FRCP 1980. Hse Physician and Resident in Pathology, St Bartholomew's Hosp., 1965–68; Registrar, 1968–70, Sen. Registrar, 1971–75, St Thomas' Hosp., London. Mem. Council, RCP, 1992–94. Vice-Pres. Endoscopy, British Soc. Gastroenterol., 1989–91; President: N of England Gastroenterol. Soc., 1999–2000; British Soc. of Gastroenterol., 2000–01; Eur. Soc. of Gastrointestinal Endoscopy, 2000–02; World Orgn of Gastrointestinal Endoscopy, 2005–09; United European Gastroenterology Fedn, 2006–07; Mem., Educn Cttee, World Orgn of Gastroenterology, 1999–2004. Life Achievement Award, United European Gastroenterology, 2017. *Publications:* contrib. numerous original papers on wide variety of gastrointestinal subjects, specifically inflammatory bowel disease, intestinal permeability, endoscopic retrograde cholangio-pancreatography, safety in endoscopy, Helicobacter pylori, cancer surveillance, aetiology of gastric cancer, to peer review jls and other pubns. *Recreations:* travel, gardening. *Address:* Nidd Park House, Nidd, N Yorks HG3 3BN. *T:* (01423) 779099.

**AXWORTHY, Hon. Lloyd,** CC 2015 (OC 2003); OM 2001; PC (Can.) 1980; PhD; President and Vice-Chancellor, University of Winnipeg, 2004–14; Chancellor, St Paul's University College, University of Waterloo, 2014; Chairman, World Refugee Council, since 2017; *b* 21 Dec. 1939; *s* of Norman Joseph and Gwen Anne Axworthy; *m* 1984, Denise Ommanney; two *s* one *d*. *Educ:* Univ. of Winnipeg (BA 1961); Princeton Univ. (MA 1963; PhD 1972). Asst Prof. of Pol Sci., 1969–79, and Dir, Inst. of Urban Studies, 1970–79, Univ. of Winnipeg. MLA(L) Manitoba, 1973–79; MP (L): Winnipeg-Fort Garry, 1979–88; Winnipeg S Centre, 1988–2001; Minister of State for Status of Women, Canada, 1980–81; Minister of Employment and Immigration, 1980–83; Minister of Transportation, 1983–84; Opposition spokesman on internat. trade, 1984–88; Liberal spokesman on external affairs, 1988–93; Minister of Human Resources Develt, and of Western Econ. Diversification, 1993–96; Minister for Foreign Affairs, 1996–2001; Dir, Liu Inst. for Global Issues, Univ. of BC, 2001–04 (Sen. Associate, 2004–). Mem., Commn for the Legal Empowerment of the Poor, UN Develt Prog., 2006–08; Head, OAS Electoral Observation Mission to Peru, 2006; Comr, Dialogue and Commn on Arctic Climate Change, Aspen Inst., 2008–. Richard von Weizsäcker Fellow, Robert Bosch Acad., 2016–17. Hon. DLitt Waterloo, 2014. Hubert H. Humphrey Award, American Pol Sci. Assoc., 2017. *Publications:* Navigating a New World: Canada's global future, 2003. *Recreation:* golf.

**AYAZ, Sir Iftikhar (Ahmad),** KBE 2015 (OBE 1998); PhD; Hon. Consul of Tuvalu in the United Kingdom, since 1995; *b* 3 Jan. 1933; *m* 1959, Amatul Basit; five *d*. *Educ:* secondary educn in Tanzania; Univ. of Newcastle upon Tyne (BEd Hons); Univ. of London (Dip. TEFL, Dip. Comparative Educn; MA Applied Linguistics); Univ. of Western Pacific, Calif (PhD Educn and Trng for Human Develt, 1993). Teacher, Inspector of Schs, Educn Administrator, Teacher Educn Officer, Sen. Curriculum Officer, and Sen. Lectr in Applied Linguistics, Govt of Tanzania Educn Admin, 1955–76; Commonwealth Fellow, Commonwealth Inst., London, 1976–77; Sen. Lectr and Sen. Curriculum Advr, Univ. of Dar-es-Salaam, Tanzania, 1979–81; Admin Officer, Centre on Integrated Rural Develt for Africa, UNFAO, 1981–84; Field Expert in Educn, Commonwealth Fund for Tech. Co-operation, 1984–91; Consultant: on Educn for Human Develt, UNO, 1991–93; on Educn for All, 1993–95. Associate Dir, Universal Consultants, UK; Advr, Minority Gp Rights, UN Human Rights Council, Geneva. Sec., E Africa Commonwealth Soc. for Prevention of Disablement. Chairman: Grass Roots Diplomat; Internat. Human Rights Cttee; Sec., Royal Soc. for Prevention of Cruelty to Animals, Tanzania. Founder and Sec. Gen., Tanzania Commonwealth Soc. Vice President: Pacific Peace Forum; Non-resident Indians' Welfare Soc. of India. Member: Commonwealth Partnership for Tech. Mgt; World Council for Poverty Alleviation. Member: Pacific Is Assoc.; Commonwealth Assoc.; ABI Res. Assoc. Peace Ambassador, Universal Peace Fedn. Award for Internat. Consultation on Skill-based Educn, OAD, 1979. *Publications:* contrib. papers on educn in small states, climate change and sustainable envmts, educn theory, philosophy and sociol., linguistics, literature and curriculum develt, human develt, culture in educn, peace educn, and universal and fundamental human rights. *Address:* Tuvalu House, 230 Worple Road, SW20 8RH. *T:* and *Fax:* (020) 8879 0985. *E:* TuvaluConsulate@netscape.net.

**AYCKBOURN, Sir Alan,** Kt 1997; CBE 1987; playwright and director; Artistic Director, Stephen Joseph Theatre, Scarborough, 1972–2009, Director Emeritus, 2018; *b* 12 April 1939; *s* of Horace Ayckbourn and Irene Maude (*née* Worley); *m* 1st, 1959, Christine Helen (*née* Roland); two *s*; 2nd, 1997, Heather Stoney. *Educ:* Haileybury. Worked in repertory as Stage Manager/Actor at Edinburgh, Worthing, Leatherhead, Oxford, and with late Stephen Joseph's Theatre-in-the-Round Co., at Scarborough. Founder Mem., Victoria Theatre, Stoke-on-Trent, 1962. BBC Radio Drama Producer, Leeds, 1964–70; Co. Dir, NT, 1986–87. Vis. Prof. of Contemporary Theatre, and Fellow, St Catherine's Coll., Oxford, 1991–92. Has written numerous full-length plays almost all premiered in Scarborough. London productions: Mr Whatnot, Arts, 1964; Relatively Speaking, Duke of York's, 1967, Wyndham's, 2013 (televised, 1969, 1989); How the Other Half Loves, Lyric, 1970, Duke of York's, 1988, 2016; Time and Time Again, Comedy, 1972 (televised, 1976); Absurd Person Singular, Criterion, 1973, transf. Vaudeville, 1974, Whitehall, 1990, Garrick, 2007 (Evening Standard Drama Award, Best Comedy, 1973) (televised, 1985); The Norman Conquests (Trilogy), Globe, 1974, transf. Apollo, 1975, Old Vic, 2008 (Evening Standard Drama Award, Best Play; Variety Club of GB Award; Plays and Players Award) (televised, 1977); Jeeves (musical, with Andrew Lloyd Webber), Her Majesty's, 1975, reworked as By Jeeves, Duke of York's, transf. Lyric, 1996, NY, 2001 (filmed, 2001); Absent Friends, Garrick, 1975, Harold Pinter, 2012 (televised, 1985); Confusions, Apollo, 1976; Bedroom Farce (dir), Nat. Theatre, 1977, transf. Prince of Wales, 1978, NY, 1979, Aldwych, 2002, Duke of York's, 2010 (televised, 1980); Just Between Ourselves, Queen's, 1977 (Evening Standard Drama Award, Best Play) (televised, 1978); Ten Times Table (dir), Globe, 1978; Family Circles, Orange Tree, 1978; Joking Apart (dir), Globe, 1979 (Shared Plays and Players Award); Sisterly Feelings (dir), Nat. Theatre, 1980; Taking Steps, Lyric, 1980, Orange Tree, 2010; Suburban Strains (musical with Paul Todd) (dir), Round House, 1981; Season's Greetings (dir), Apollo, 1982, Nat. Theatre, 2010 (televised, 1986); Way Upstream (dir), Nat. Theatre, 1982 (televised, 1988); Making Tracks (musical with Paul Todd) (dir), Greenwich, 1983; Intimate Exchanges (dir), Ambassadors, 1983 (filmed, 1993); A Chorus of Disapproval (dir), Nat. Theatre, 1985, transf. Lyric, 1986, Harold Pinter, 2012 (Evening Standard Drama Award, Best Comedy; Olivier Award, Best Comedy; DRAMA Award, Best Comedy, 1985) (filmed, 1989); Woman in Mind (dir), Vaudeville, 1986, 2009; A Small Family Business (dir), Nat. Theatre, 1987, 2014 (Evening Standard Drama Award, Best Play); Henceforward… (dir), Vaudeville, 1988 (Evening Standard Drama Award, Best Comedy, 1989); Man of the Moment (dir), Globe, 1990 (Evening Standard Drama Award, Best Comedy, 1990); The Revengers' Comedies (dir), Strand, 1991 (filmed 1989); Time of My Life (dir), Vaudeville, 1993; Wildest Dreams (dir), RSC, 1993; Communicating Doors (dir), Gielgud, 1995, transf. Savoy, 1996, Menier Chocolate Factory, 2015 (Writers' Guild of GB Award, Best West End Play, 1996); Things We Do For Love (dir), Gielgud, 1998, transf. Duchess, 1998 (Lloyds Pvte Banking Playwright of the Year); adapt. Ostrovsky's The Forest, RNT, 1999; Comic Potential (dir), Lyric, 1999; House & Garden (dir), RNT, 2000; Damsels in Distress (trilogy: GamePlan; FlatSpin; RolePlay), (dir), Duchess, 2002; Haunting Julia, Riverside Studios, 2011; Snake in the Grass, Print Room, 2011; Drowning on Dry Land, Jermyn St Th., 2011; Private Fears in Public Places, Orange Tree, 2011 (filmed, 2007); Neighbourhood Watch, Tricycle, 2012; Scarborough: It Could Be Any One Of Us, 1983; Body Language, 1990; Dreams from a Summer House (play with music by John Pattison), 1992; A Word from our Sponsor (musical with John Pattison), 1995; Sugar Daddies, 2003; Improbable Fiction, 2005; If I Were You, 2006; Life and Beth, 2008; Awaking Beauty (musical with Denis King), 2008; My Wonderful Day, 2009; Life of Riley, 2010 (filmed, 2015); Dear Uncle (adapt. Chekhov's Uncle Vanya), 2011; Surprises, 2012; Arrivals & Departures, 2013; Roundelay, 2014; Hero's Welcome, 2015; Consuming Passions, 2016; A Brief History of Women, 2017; Better Off Dead, 2018; Birthdays Past, Birthdays Present, 2019; other plays directed: Tons of Money, Nat. Theatre, 1986; A View from the Bridge, Nat. Theatre, transf. Aldwych, 1987; 'Tis Pity she's a Whore, Nat. Theatre, 1988; Two Weeks with the Queen, Nat. Theatre, 1994; Conversations with my Father, Old Vic, 1995; The Safari Party, Scarborough, 2002, Hampstead, 2003. *Plays for children and young people include:* Callisto 5, 1990; This Is Where We Came In, 1990; My Very Own Story, 1991; Invisible Friends (dir), Nat. Theatre, 1991; Mr A's Amazing Maze Plays, Nat. Theatre, 1993; The Musical Jigsaw Play, 1994; The Champion of Paribanou, 1996; The Boy Who Fell Into A Book, 1998, Lyric, 2012 (jtly reworked as musical, 2014); Callisto #7, 1999; Whenever (musical with Denis King), 2000; The Jollies, 2002; Orvin—Champion of Champions (musical with Denis King), 2003; My Sister Sadie, 2003; Miss Yesterday, 2004; (lyrics) Where is Peter Rabbit?, Old Laundry Th., 2016. Hon. Fellow, Oxford Literary Fest., 2016. Hon. DLitt: Hull, 1981; Keele, 1987; Leeds, 1987; Bradford, 1994; Univ. of Wales Coll. of Cardiff, 1995; Manchester, 2003; York St John, 2011; DUniv: York, 1992; Open, 1998. Sunday Times Award for Literary Achievement, 2000; Special Olivier Award, 2009; Critics' Circle Award for Services to the Arts, 2010; Tony Lifetime Achievement Award, 2010. *Publications:* The Crafty Art of Playmaking, 2002; the majority of his plays have been published and are currently in print. *Recreations:* music, cricket, films. *Address:* c/o Casarotto Ramsay & Associates Ltd, Waverley House, 7–12 Noel Street, W1F 8GQ. *T:* (020) 7287 4450. *W:* www.alanayckbourn.net.

**AYERS, John Gilbert;** Keeper, Far Eastern Department, Victoria and Albert Museum, 1970–82; *b* 27 July 1922; *s* of H. W. Ayers, CB, CBE; *m* 1957, Bridget Elspeth Jacqualine Fanshawe; one *s* two *d*. *Educ:* St Paul's Sch.; St Edmund Hall, Oxford. Served in RAF, 1941–46 (Sgt). Asst Keeper, Dept of Ceramics, Victoria and Albert Museum, 1950, Dep. Keeper 1963. Pres., Oriental Ceramic Soc., 1984–87. *Publications:* The Seligman Collection of Oriental Art, II, 1964; The Baur Collection: Chinese Ceramics, I–IV, 1968–74, Japanese Ceramics, 1982; (with R. J. Charleston) The James A. de Rothschild Collection: Meissen and Oriental Porcelain, 1971; Oriental Ceramics, The World's Great Collections: Victoria and Albert Museum, 1975; (with J. Rawson) Chinese Jade throughout the Ages, exhibn catalogue, 1975; (with D. Howard) China for the West, 2 vols, 1978; (with D. Howard) Masterpieces of Chinese Export Porcelain, 1980; Oriental Art in the Victoria and Albert Museum, 1983; (ed) Chinese Ceramics in the Topkapi Saray Museum, Istanbul, 3 vols, 1986; (with O. Impey and J. V. G. Mallet) Porcelain for Palaces: the fashion for Japan in Europe 1650–1750, 1990; Chinese Ceramic Tea Vessels: the K. S. Lo Collection, Hong Kong, 1991; A Jade Menagerie: creatures real and imaginary from the Worrell Collection, 1993; Chinese Ceramics in the Baur Collection, Geneva, 2 vols, 1999; Blanc de Chine: divine images in porcelain, exhibn catalogue, China Inst., NY, 2002; The Chinese Porcelain Collection of Marie Vergottis, Lausanne, 2004; Chinese and Japanese Works of Art in the Collection of Her Majesty The Queen, 3 vols, 2016. *Address:* 3 Bedford Gardens, W8 7ED. *T:* (020) 7229 5168.

**AYERS, Prof. Michael Richard,** PhD; FBA 2001; Professor of Philosophy, University of Oxford, 1996–2002; Fellow of Wadham College, Oxford, 1965–2002, now Emeritus; *b* 27 June 1935; *s* of Dick Ayers and Sybil Kerr Ayers (*née* Rutherglen); *m* 1962, Delia Mary Bell; one *s* one *d*. *Educ:* Battersea Grammar Sch.; St John's Coll., Cambridge (BA 1959; MA, PhD 1965). Jun. Res. Fellow, St John's Coll., Cambridge, 1962–65; Tutor in Philosophy, Wadham Coll., Oxford, 1965; CUF Lectr in Philosophy, 1965–94, Reader in Philosophy, 1994–2002, Univ. of Oxford. Vis. Lectr, 1964–65, Vis. Prof., 1979, 2007, Univ. of Calif. Berkeley; Vis. Prof., Univ. of Oregon, 1970–71; Vis. Fellow, Res. Sch. of Social Scis, ANU, 1993; Ida Beam Dist. Vis. Prof., Univ. of Iowa, 1995. MAE 2006. *Publications:* The Refutation of Determinism, 1968; (with J. Ree and A. Westoby) Philosophy and its Past, 1978; Locke: vol. 1, Epistemology, vol. 2, Ontology, 1991; Locke: ideas and things, 1997; (ed with D. Garber) The Cambridge History of Seventeenth Century Philosophy, 2 vols, 1998; (ed) Rationalism, Platonism and God, 2007; Knowing and Seeing: groundwork for a new empiricism, 2019; contrib. to jls, collections and works of reference. *Recreations:* walking, gardening, natural history, philosophy. *Address:* Wadham College, Oxford OX1 3PN.

**AYERS, Ven. Paul Nicholas;** Archdeacon of Leeds, since 2017; *b* Bradford, 1961. *Educ:* St Peter's Coll., Oxford (MA); Trinity Coll., Bristol. Ordained deacon, 1985, priest, 1986; Curate: St John the Baptist, Clayton, 1985–88; St Andrew, Keighley, 1988–91; Vicar: St Cuthbert, Wrose, 1991–97; St Lawrence and St Paul, Pudsey, 1997–2017. Hon. Canon, Bradford Cathedral, 2016–. *Address:* c/o Leeds Diocesan Office, Church House, 17–19 York Place, Leeds LS1 2EX. *T:* (0113) 2000 540. *E:* paul.ayers@leeds.anglican.org.

**AYKROYD, Sir Henry (Robert George),** 5th Bt *cr* 1920, of Lightcliffe, Yorks; *b* Leeds, 4 April 1954; *o s* of Sir Michael David Aykroyd, 4th Bt and of Oenene Gillian Diana (*née* Cowling); *S* father, 2010; *m* 1975, Lucy Merlin Houghton Brown (marr. diss. 2007); two *s* three *d* (of whom two *d* are twins). *Educ:* Charterhouse; Edinburgh Univ. (MA). Farmer. *Heir: s* George Jack Aykroyd [*b* 8 Jan. 1977; *m* 1999, Jodie Askew (marr. diss. 2012); two *s* one *d*]. *Address:* Amisfield Tower, Amisfield, Dumfriesshire DG1 3PA. *T:* 07836 757845. *E:* henryaykroyd@msn.com.

**AYKROYD, Sir James (Alexander Frederic),** 3rd Bt *cr* 1929, of Birstwith Hall, Hampsthwaite, co. York; *b* 6 Sept. 1943; *s* of Bertram Aykroyd (*d* 1983), *y s* of Sir Frederic Alfred Aykroyd, 1st Bt, and his 1st wife, Margot (later Dame Margot Smith, DBE), *d* of Leonard Graham Brown; *S* uncle, 1993; *m* 1973, Jennifer Marshall; two *d*. *Educ:* Eton Coll.; Univ. of Aix en Provence; Univ. of Madrid. Sen. Export Dir, James Buchanan & Co. Ltd, 1965–83; Export Man. Dir, Martini & Rossi SpA, 1983–87; Chm., Speyside Distillers Co. Ltd, 2001–12. *Recreation:* active sports esp. tennis and golf. *Heir: half b* Toby Nigel Bertram Aykroyd [*b* 13 Nov. 1955; *m* 2005, Rona Louise Birnie; one *s*]. *Address:* Birstwith Hall, near Harrogate, Yorks HG3 2JW. *T:* (01423) 770250. *Club:* Alwoodley Golf.

**AYLARD, Richard John,** CVO 1994; External Affairs and Sustainability Director, Thames Water, since 2010; Extra Equerry to the Prince of Wales, since 1996; *b* 10 April 1952; *s* of John and Joy Aylard; *m* 1st, 1977, Sally Williams (marr. diss. 1984); 2nd, 1984, Suzanne

Walker (marr. diss. 1998); two d; 3rd, 1998, Jennifer Jones; one s one d. Educ: Queen Elizabeth's Grammar Sch., Barnet; Reading Univ. (BSc Hons Applied Zoology with Maths). Joined RN as university cadet, 1972; served HM Ships Shavington, Ark Royal, Fox, 1974–77; Staff of Flag Officer Submarines, 1977–79; Flag Lieut to Dep. SACLANT, Norfolk, USA, 1979–81; Capt.'s Sec., HMS Invincible, 1981–83; Supply Officer, HMS Brazen, 1984–85; Equerry to the Princess of Wales, 1985–88; Comdr RN, 1987; Asst Private Sec. and Comptroller to the Prince and Princess of Wales, 1988–91; RN retd, 1989; Private Sec. and Treas. to the Prince of Wales, 1991–96; consultant on envmtl issues and public affairs, 1996–2002; Thames Water: Corporate Social Responsibility Dir, 2002–04; Ext. Affairs and Envmt Dir, 2004–08; Dir, 2008–10. Recreations: sailing, fishing, gardening.

**AYLEN, Walter Stafford;** QC 1983; a Deputy High Court Judge, 1993–2005; b St Helena, 21 May 1937; s of late Rt Rev. Charles Arthur William Aylen and Elisabeth Margaret Anna (née Hills); m 1967, Peggy Elizabeth Lainé Woodford; three d. Educ: Summer Fields Sch.; Winchester Coll. (schol.); New Coll., Oxford (schol., sen. schol.; BCL; MA). Northants County Cricket Club 2nd XI, 1955. Commnd 2nd Lieut KRRC, 1956–57. Called to the Bar, Middle Temple, 1962 (Bencher 1991); Head of Chambers, Hardwicke Bldg, 1991–2000; Mem., ADR Chambers, 2000–08. Asst Recorder, 1982; Recorder, 1985–2003. Mem., Internat. Panel, Alternative Dispute Resolution Gp, 2001–08. Mem., Bar Council, 1994–96 (Chm., Bar Services and IT Cttee, 1994; Vice-Chm., Finance Cttee, 1995–96). MCIArb 1999–2009. FRSA 1989–2009. Recreations: reading novels (especially his wife's), theatre, music. Address: 24 Fairmount Road, SW2 2BL.

**AYLESFORD,** 12th Earl of, cr 1714; **Charles Heneage Finch-Knightley;** Baron Guernsey, 1703; Vice Lord-Lieutenant for West Midlands, 1990–2015; b 27 March 1947; s of 11th Earl of Aylesford and Margaret Rosemary Tyer; S father, 2008; m 1971, Penelope Anstice, y d of Kenneth A. G. Crawley; one s four d (incl. twin d). Educ: Oundle; Trinity Coll., Cambridge. DL West Midlands, 1986. Recreations: shooting, fishing, Real tennis, cricket. Heir: s Lord Guernsey, qv. Address: Hetherington House, Idlicote Road, Halford, Shipton on Stour, Warwicks CV36 5BP. T: (01789) 740465.

**AYLETT, Crispin David William;** QC 2008; b 13 Aug. 1961; s of late David Leonard Nankivell Aylett and Freda Emily Aylett (née Montague, then Whitehead); m 1989, Louise Sheppard; two s two d. Educ: Dulwich Coll.; Bristol Univ. (BA Hons 1983); City Univ., London (Dip Law 1984). Called to the Bar, Inner Temple, 1985 (Scarman Schol.), Bencher, 2014. Jun. Treasury Counsel, 2001–06, Sen. Treasury Counsel, 2006–13, Central Criminal Court. Tribunal Mem., disciplinary panel, Lloyd's of London, 2013–. Sec., Cakemaker's Dozen, 1985–2002. Recreations: theatre, satire, cricket. Address: QEB Hollis Whiteman, 1–2 Laurence Pountney Hill, EC4R 0EU. T: (020) 7933 8855.

**AYLING, John Vernon,** OBE 2007; Executive Chairman, John Ayling and Associates, since 2014 (Chairman and Managing Director, 1978–2014); b Fulmer, Bucks, 18 April 1944; s of Stanley Harradine Ayling and Phyllis Evelyn Ayling; m 1982, Marilyn, (Lyn), Whinray; one d. Educ: East Grinstead Grammar Sch.; Univ. of Exeter (BA Hons Geog.). Media Manager, Garland-Compton, 1968–71; Media Dir, Kirkwood Co., 1971–78. Recreations: cricket, golf, travel, music, watching all sports. Address: John Ayling and Associates, 27 Soho Square, W1D 3QR. T: (020) 7439 6070. E: jaa@jaa-media.co.uk. Clubs: Lord's Taverners (Chm., 2002–03, 2010–12), MCC, Solus (Pres., 2007); Oxted Hockey (Pres.); Tandridge Golf; SWIGS Golf.

**AYLING, Robert John,** CBE 2018; Chief Executive, British Airways, 1996–2000; b 3 Aug. 1946; m 1972, Julia Crallan; two s one d. Educ: King's Coll. Sch., Wimbledon. Admitted solicitor, 1968; joined Elborne, Mitchell & Co., Solicitors, 1969, Partner, 1971; Department of Trade, later of Trade and Industry: Legal Advr, 1974 (work on UK accession to EEC, 1974–77); Asst Solicitor and Head, Aviation Law Br., 1979 (legislation to privatise British Airways Bd); UK deleg., UN Common for Internat. Trade Law, 1979–83; Under Sec. (Legal), 1983; British Airways: Legal Dir, 1985; Company Sec., 1987; Human Resources Dir, 1988; Marketing and Ops Dir, 1991; Gp Man. Dir, 1993. Chairman: New Millennium Experience Co., 1997–2000; Holidaybreak plc, 2003–09; Sanctuary Group plc, 2006–07. Non-executive Director: Royal & Sun Alliance, 1994–2004; Dyson Ltd, 2001–12 (Vice-Chm., 2005–10; Chm., 2010–12); Glas Cymru (Welsh Water), 2008–16 (Chm., 2010–16). Ind. Chm., HM Courts and Tribunals Service, 2011–18. Gov., King's Coll. Sch., 1996–2006. Hon. LLD Brunel, 1996. Hon. FRIBA. Recreations: hillwalking, sailing. Clubs: Brooks's; Royal Thames Yacht.

**AYLING, Tracy Jane, (Mrs C. A. Hutton);** QC 2006; b 27 April 1960; d of Rex John Ayling and Doreen Ayling (née Matthews); m 2004, Charles Adrian Hutton. Educ: Horndean Comprehensive Sch.; Durham Univ. (BA Hons 1982). Called to the Bar, Inner Temple, 1983, Bencher, 2010. Recreations: cuisine, travel, shoes. Address: 2 Bedford Row, WC1R 4BU. T: (020) 7440 8888, Fax: (020) 7242 1738.

**AYLMER,** family name of **Baron Aylmer**.

**AYLMER,** 14th Baron cr 1718; **(Anthony) Julian Aylmer;** Bt 1662; Partner, Reynolds Porter Chamberlain LLP, 1982–2009; b 10 Dec. 1951; o s of 13th Baron Aylmer and Countess Maddalena Sofia, d of late Count Arbeno Attems; S father, 2006; m 1990, Belinda Rosemary, e d of Major Peter Henry Parker; one s one d. Educ: Westminster; Trinity Hall, Cambridge (MA). Admitted solicitor, 1976. Chm., Irish Peers Assoc., 2011–. Recreations: history, genealogy, architecture. Heir: s Hon. Michael Henry Aylmer, b 21 March 1991. Address: 16 Edgarley Terrace, SW6 6QF. Clubs: Brooks's, Pratt's.

**AYLMER, Sir Richard John,** 16th Bt cr 1622, of Donadea, Co. Kildare; writer; b 23 April 1937; s of Sir Fenton Gerald Aylmer, 15th Bt and Rosalind Boultbee (d 1991), d of J. Percival Bell; S father, 1987; m 1962, Lise, d of Paul Demers; one s one d. Educ: Lower Canada Coll., Montreal; Western Ontario, London, Canada; Harvard Univ., Cambridge, Mass, USA. Heir: s Fenton Paul Aylmer [b 31 Oct. 1965; m 1989, Pina Mastromonaco; two s]. E: dickaylmer@gmail.com.

**AYLWARD, Adrian John Francis;** educational consultant; Headmaster, Leweston School (formerly St Antony's Leweston School), 2006–15; b 12 Nov. 1957; s of John James and Cynthia Aylward; m 1990, Caroline Cramer; one s two d. Educ: Worth Sch., Sussex; Exeter Coll., Oxford (BA); King's Coll. London (PGCE). Formerly investment banker; Royal Sovereign Group (Chief Exec., 1986–91); Dir, EMESS plc, 1990–91; Housemaster and Head of Religious Studies, Downside Sch., 1992–96; Headmaster, Stonyhurst Coll., 1996–2006. Mem., Irish Assoc. Knight of Malta. Recreations: fishing, philosophy, sport, travel. Address: Little Westcott, Doccombe, Moretonhampstead, Devon TQ13 8SU. Club: Brooks's.

**AYLWARD, (George) William,** MD; FRCS, FRCOphth; Consultant Ophthalmic Surgeon, Moorfields Eye Hospital, 1994–2017 (Medical Director, 2002–10); Director, OpenEyes Project, 2010–14; b 23 Dec. 1957; s of James Ernest Aylward and Martha Harvey Aylward; m 1983, Catherine Joy Otty; one s one d. Educ: Malvern Coll.; Corpus Christi Coll., Cambridge (MB BChir); Addenbrooke's Hosp. (Cambridge Univ. Med. Sch. (MD 1990)). FRCS 1987; FRCOphth 1989. SHO, Western Eye Hosp., London, 1985–86; Lectr, Sydney Univ., 1987–89; Sen. Registrar, 1989–92, Fellow in Vitreoretinal Surgery, 1992–93, Moorfields Eye Hosp. Fellow in Med. Retina, Bascom Palmer Eye Inst., Miami, 1993–94. President: Eur. Soc. of Retina Specialists, 2009–11 (Vice Pres., 2007–09); British and Eire Vitreoretinal Soc., 2012–14. Mem., Eur. Acad. of Ophthalmology, 2008. Pres., Club Jules Gonin, Lausanne, 2016– (Vice Pres., 2011–16); Mem., Ophthalmic Club, 1999–. Publications: contrib. chapters to books, including: Ophthalmology, 1997; Clinical Retina, 2002; Ryan's Retina, 2005, 4th edn 2017; over 115 articles in peer-reviewed ophthalmic jls. Recreations: sailing (sailed across Atlantic Ocean, 2016), cooking. Address: Moorfields Eye Hospital, City Road, EC1V 2PD. E: bill.aylward@moorfields.nhs.uk.

**AYLWARD, Prof. Sir Mansel,** Kt 2010; CB 2002; FRCP, FFPM, FFOM, FLSW; Professor of Public Health Education, Centre for Psychosocial Research, Occupational and Physician Health, since 2012, and Special Adviser to Vice Chancellor on Engagement, Reputation and International Links, since 2013, Cardiff University; Professor of Prudent Health and Wellbeing, Swansea University, since 2017; Chair: Bevan Commission, since 2008; Life Sciences Hub Wales, since 2017; b 29 Nov. 1942; s of John Aylward and Cora Doreen Aylward (née Evans); m 1963, Angela Bridget Besley; one s one d. Educ: Cyfarthfa Castle Grammar Sch., Merthyr Tydfil; London Hosp. Med. Coll., Univ. of London (BSc 1964; MB BS Hons 1967); FFPM 1991; DDAM RCP 2001; FFOM 2003; FRCP 2003; FLSW 2016. MRC Clin. Res. Fellow in Exptl Surgery, London Hosp., 1968–70; Lectr in Surgery, London Hosp. Med. Coll., 1969; GP, Merthyr Tydfil, 1970–73; Clin. Assistant in Dermatol. and Minor Surgery, St Tydfil's Hosp., 1970–76; Res. Physician, Singleton Hosp., Swansea and Merthyr and Cynon Valleys, 1973–76; Chm. and Man. Dir, Simbec Research Ltd, 1974–84; Dir of Clin. Res., Berk Pharmaceuticals, 1974–76; Dir, Women's Health Concern, London, 1976–86; Pres., Simbec Research (USA) Inc., 1980–84; Dir of Clin. Res., Lyonnaise Industrielle Pharmaceutique, France, 1982–84; Regl MO, DHSS, Cardiff, 1985–88; SMO, DSS, London, 1988–90; Sec. to Attendance Allowance Bd, London, 1991; PMO and Dir of Med. Policy, R&D, Benefits Agency, London, 1991–95; CMO and Chief Scientist, DSS, subseq. DWP, 1995–2005; Prof. of Psychosocial and Disability Res. and Dir, Centre for Psychosocial and Disability Res., Cardiff Univ., 2004–17. Chair, Public Health Wales NHS Trust, 2009–17. Hon. Prof., Sch. of Psychol., Cardiff Univ. and UWCM, 2001–04. Chief Med. Advr, War Pensions, later Veterans, Agency, MoD, 2001–05; Civilian Med. Advr in Disability Medicine to Army, 2004–. Expert Agréé Medecine Interne, France, 1982. Visiting Professor: Harvard Univ., 2004–; Leuven Univ., 2006–; Karolinska Univ., 2008–; First Ko Awatea Stevenson Chair and Vis. Prof., Univ. of Auckland, 2012–. Lectures include: Thakrah, SOM, 2006; Edward Jones, Cardiff Univ., 2006; Tudor Hart, Cardiff Univ., 2007; Dynamics of Disability Keynote, FLA, USA, 2008; Easter, RSM, 2009; Brackenridge Meml, Assurance Med. Soc. UK, 2011; Eumass, Padua Univ., 2013; Australasian Mil. Medicine Assoc., 2014. Chm., Standards Cttee, Merthyr Tydfil CB, 2002–14; Chair: Wales Centre for Health, Welsh Assembly Govt, 2004–09; Health Commn Wales Rev., 2007–08; All Wales Public Mental Health Network, 2007–17; Academic Forum, Faculty of Occupational Medicine, 2007–; Royal Mail Attendance Acad., 2007–11; Wales Occupational Health Review, 2008–09; All Wales Occupational Health Review, 2009–; Expert Panel Rev. of Growing Up in NZ Longitudinal Study, 2012; Parly Rev. on Health and Social Care in Wales, 2016–17. Member: Health Honours Cttee UK, 2005–12; Industrial Injuries Adv. Cttee, 2005–14; Workplace Health Expert Cttee, HSE, 2017–. Director: Elision Gp Ltd UK, 2005–07; Arkaga Health & Technology Ltd, 2008–09. Author of Reviews: Child Protection and Safeguarding in NHS Wales, 2009; Supporting People Programme (Wales), 2010; Health Improvement Prog. (Wales), 2011. Vice Pres., Soc. of Occupational Therapists, 2012–. Pres., Dowlais Male Voice Choir, 2013–; Patron: Vocational Rehabilitation Assoc. (UK), 2005–; Wellbeing Wales Lles Cymru, 2011–14. FRSocMed 1981 (Academic Dean (Wales), 2001–; Hon. Treas. and Dir, 2005–07); Fellow, Soc. of Occupational Medicine, 2006–. Hon. FFPH 2008. Hon. Mem., Soc. of Occupational Medicine, Ireland, 2004. Hon. DSc S Wales, 2013. Freeman, Merthyr Tydfil CB, 2013. Publications: Management of the Menopause and Post-Menopausal Years, 1975; The Disability Handbook, 1991, 2nd edn 1998; Back Pain: an international review, 2002; (contrib.) Malingering and Illness Deception, 2003; Scientific Concepts and Basis of Incapacity Benefits, 2005; The Power of Belief, 2006; (contrib.) Fitness for Work, 2nd edn, 1997 to 4th edn, 2012; Models of Disability, 2010; contribs on public health, disability assessment, rehabilitation, and social security issues to learned jls. Recreations: military history, travel, theatre, reading, grandchildren, poetry, public speaking, philosophy of science, innovation in health and care. Address: Life Sciences Hub Wales, 3 Assembly Square, Cardiff Bay, Cardiff CF10 4PL; (home) Cefn Cottage, Cefn Coed-y-Cymer, Merthyr Tydfil CF48 2PH. Club: Athenæum.

**AYLWARD, William;** see Aylward, G. W.

**AYNSLEY-GREEN, Sir Albert,** Kt 2006; DPhil; FRCP, FRCPE, FRCPCH, FMedSci; Founder and Director, Aynsley-Green Consulting, since 2010; Children's Commissioner for England, 2005–10; Nuffield Professor of Child Health, Institute of Child Health, University College London, 1993–2005, now Emeritus; President, British Medical Association, 2015–16; b 30 May 1943; m 1967, Rosemary Anne Boucher; two d. Educ: Glyn Grammar Sch., Epsom; Guy's Hosp. Med. Sch., Univ. of London (MB BS); Oriel Coll., Oxford (MA, DPhil; Hon. Fellow, 2014). MRCS 1967; FRCP 1982; FRCPE 1987; FRCPCH 1997 (Hon. FRCPCH 2008). House Officer posts at Guy's Hosp., London, St Luke's Hosp., Guildford, Radcliffe Infirmary, Oxford and RPMS, Hammersmith Hosp., London, 1967–70; Radcliffe Infirmary, Oxford: Wellcome Res. Fellow, 1970–72; Clinical Lectr in Internal Medicine, 1972–73; Sen. House Officer and Registrar posts in Paediatrics, Radcliffe Infirmary and John Radcliffe Hosp., Oxford, 1973–74; European Sci. Exchange Fellow, Royal Soc. and Swiss Nat. Res. Council, Univ. Children's Hosp., Zurich, 1974–75; University of Oxford: Clinical Lectr in Paediatrics, 1975–78; Univ. Lectr, 1978–83; Fellow, Green Coll., 1980–83; Hon. Consultant Paediatrician, Oxford AHA, 1978–83; University of Newcastle upon Tyne: James Spence Prof. of Child Health and Hd of Dept, 1984–93; Hd, Sch. of Clinical Med. Scis, 1991–93; Hon. Consultant Paediatrician: Royal Victoria Infirmary, Newcastle upon Tyne, 1984–93; Gt Ormond St Hosp. and UCL, 1993–2005; Vice-Dean for Clin. Res., Inst. of Child Health, Univ. of London, at UCL, 1999–2003; Dir, Clinical R&D, Gt Ormond St Hosp. for Children, 1993–2003; NHS Nat. Clin. Dir for Children and Chm., NHS Nat. Children's Taskforce, DoH, 2001–05. Non-exec. Mem., Bd of Govs, Hosp. for Sick Children, Gt Ormond St, 1990–93; Exec. Mem., Trust Bd, Gt Ormond St Hosp. for Children NHS Trust, 1993–2003; non-exec. Dir, Salisbury Foundn NHS Trust, 2007–08. Chm., Adv. Gp on NHS Priorities for R&D in Mother and Child Health, DoH, 1994–95; Mem., Central R&D Cttee, DoH, 1999–2002. Hon. Mem. Council, NSPCC, 2006–; Pres., Contact a Family, 2007–; Patron: Childhood Bereavement Network, 2010–; Coram Life Educn, 2014–; Mosaic Bereavement Care, 2014–. Visiting Professor: Univ. of Ulm, FRG, 1986; Harvard Univ., 1987; Columbus Children's Hosp., Ohio State Univ., 1991; Vis. Paediatrician in Residence, Royal Children's Hosp., Univ. of Qld, 1989; Vis. Lectr, Children's Hosp., Camperdown, Sydney, 1992; Queen Elizabeth the Queen Mother Fellow, Nuffield Trust, 2004–05; Vis. Prof. of advocacy for children and childhood, Nottingham Trent Univ., 2016–. Numerous lectures in Europe, USA and Australia including: Lockyer, RCP, 1988; Assoc. of Paediatric Anaesthetists of GB and Ire. (and Medal), 1990; Niilo Hallman, Univs of Helsinki and Tampere, Finland (and Medal), 1991; Killam, Killam Trusts, Canada, 2009. External Examiner in Paediatrics: Univ. of Malaya, 1990; Chinese Univ. of Hong Kong, 1994–98

Univ. of Kuwait, 1996. European Society for Paediatric Endocrinology: Sec., 1982–87; Pres., 1994–95; Pres., Assoc. of Clin. Profs of Paediatrics, 1999–2002. Hon. Lay Canon, Salisbury Cathedral, 2009–14, now Lay Canon Emeritus; Chair, Diocesan Bd of Educn, 2010–13. Founder FMedSci, 1998; Millennium Fellow, Paediatric Soc. NZ, 2000; FRSA 2010; Hon. FFPH 2007; Hon. FRCPI 2016; Hon. Fellow: UNICEF UK, 2010. Hon. Member: Hungarian Paediatric Assoc., 1988 (Silver Medal, 2004); S African Paediatric Assoc., 1998; Finnish Paediatric Soc., 2006. Dr *hc* Pécs, 1998; Hon. DCL Northumbria, 2005; Hon. MD Liverpool, 2006; DUniv: Northampton, 2007; York, 2008; Huddersfield, 2016; Hon. DEd Nottingham Trent, 2011. Andrea Prader Prize and Medal, 1991, (jtly) Henning Andersen Prize, 1999, European Soc. for Paediatric Endocrinology; Juvenile Justice Award, Internat. Juvenile Justice Observatory, 2010; James Spence Medal, RCPCH, 2013. *Publications:* The British Betrayal of Childhood, 2019; papers and articles on children in society, child health and childhood, and scientifically on endocrinology and metabolism in infancy. *Recreations:* family, walking, music, photography. *E:* al@aynsley-green.com. *Club:* Athenæum.

**AYOADE, Richard Ellef**; comedian, actor, writer and director; *b* London, 23 May 1977; *s* of Layide and Dagny Ayoade; *m* Lydia; one *d*. *Educ:* St Joseph's Coll., Ipswich; St Catharine's Coll., Cambridge (BA Law 1998). Pres., Footlights, Cambridge Univ., 1997–98. Actor: TV series including: The Mighty Boosh, 2003–07; Garth Marenghi's Dark Place, 2004; The IT Crowd, 2006–11; film, The Souvenir, 2019; presenter, TV series: Gadget Man, 2013–14; Travel Man, 2015–19; Crystal Maze, 2017; director and writer of screenplay: Submarine, 2011; The Double, 2014; Dir, music videos for bands incl. Arctic Monkeys, Kasabian. *Publications:* (jtly) The Mighty Book of Boosh, 2008; Ayoade on Ayoade: a cinematic odyssey, 2014; Ayoade on Top, 2019. *Address:* c/o PBJ Management, 22 Rathbone Street, W1T 1LG. *T:* (020) 7287 1112.

**AYOUB, Fouad**; Ambassador of the Hashemite Kingdom of Jordan to Canada, 2002–05; *b* 15 Aug. 1944; *m* 1974, Marie Vernazza; two *s* one *d*. *Educ:* California State Univ., San Francisco (BA; MA philosophy 1974). Press Secretary to King Hussein, 1977–91; Mem., Jordanian Delegn to Madrid Peace Conf., 1991; Ambassador of Jordan to UK, 1991–99, and (non-resident) to Iceland and Ireland, 1992–99; Ambassador of Jordan to Switzerland, 1999–2001. Fellow, Centre for Internat. Affairs, Harvard, 1983–84. Order of El Istiqlal (Jordan), 1991; numerous foreign orders. *Recreation:* reading.

**AYRAULT, Jean-Marc Joseph Marcel**; Minister of Foreign Affairs and International Development, France, 2016–17; *b* Maulévrier, France, 25 Jan. 1950; *s* of Joseph Ayrault and Georgette Ayrault (*née* Uzenot); *m* 1971, Brigitte Terrien; two *d*. *Educ:* Nantes Univ. (German degree; Teaching Cert.). German lang. teacher, Rezé, 1973–76, Saint-Herblain, 1976–86. Mem., Gen. Council, Loire-Atlantique, 1976–82; Mayor: Saint-Herblain, 1977–89; Nantes, 1989–2012; Chm., Dist of City of Nantes, 1992–2001; Pres., Nantes Métropole Urban Community, 2001–12. National Assembly: Mem. (Soc.) Loire-Atlantique, 1986–88, 3rd Dist, Loire-Atlantique, 1988–2012; Leader, Socialist Gp, 1997–2012; Prime Minister of France, 2012–14. Mem., Steering Cttee, 1977–, Exec. Bd, 1979–, Socialist Party.

**AYRE, Andrew**; HM Diplomatic Service; Deputy High Commissioner, Chandigarh, India, since 2017; *b* Bishop Auckland, 1966; *s* of Brian Ayre and Barbara Ayre; *m* 1990, Bettina Moosberger; one *s*. *Educ:* Douglas Ewart High Sch., Newton Stewart; King James I Comp. Sch., Bishop Auckland. Joined FCO, 1986; Accountant, Warsaw, 1988–89; Asst Mgt Officer, Rio de Janeiro, 1990–91; Travel Policy Officer, FCO, 1991–94; Entry Clearance Officer and Vice Consul, Nicosia, 1994–97; Entry Clearance Manager, Geneva, 1997; Second Secretary: Political, Tel Aviv, 1998–2001; EU, Vienna, 2001–06; Head: Arabian Peninsula Team, FCO, 2006–08; EU Budget and European Councils Team, FCO, 2009–11; High Comr to Guyana, and non-resident Ambassador to Suriname, 2011–15. *Recreations:* motorcycling, travelling, mountaineering, photography. *Address:* c/o Foreign and Commonwealth Office, King Charles Street, SW1A 2AH. *E:* andrew.ayre@fco.gov.uk, andrewayre@hotmail.co.uk.

**AYRES, Andrew John William**; QC 2015; *b* Bradford on Avon, 18 March 1971; *s* of late Lt Col Brian William Ayres, MBE and Margaret Elizabeth Ayres (*née* Moore); *m* 2000, Claire Alison Kavanaugh; two *s* one *d*. *Educ:* Eton Coll. (Oppidan Schol.); University Coll., Oxford (MA 1995); City Univ. (Dip. Law). Called to the Bar, Gray's Inn, 1996; in practice as barrister, specialising in commercial and chancery law, 1996–. Mem., Bar Council, 1999–2001. Asst Treas., S Eastern Circuit Bar Mess, 2003–06. Sec., Bar Boat Club, 1998–2003. *Recreations:* theatre, music, film, country pursuits. *Address:* Maitland Chambers, 7 Stone Buildings, Lincoln's Inn, WC2A 3SZ. *T:* (020) 7406 1200. *E:* AAyres@maitlandchambers.com. *Club:* Ivy.

**AYRES, Ian Leslie**; Chief Officer, NHS West Kent Clinical Commissioning Group, since 2012; *b* 14 Nov. 1954; *s* of Dennis Albert Walter Ayres and Patience Ayres; *m* 1980, Catherine Tucker; two *s* one *d*. *Educ:* Univ. of Surrey (BSc Hons Psychol. and Philosophy); Univ. of Warwick (MBA). Pres., Univ. of Surrey Students' Union, 1976–77. BP Oil UK: Asst Manpower Planner, 1977–80; Business Controller, 1980–84; Sales Manager, 1984–88; Project Manager, Business Process Re-engrg, 1990–94; Project Manager, Queen Mary's Christian Care Foundn, 1994–95; National Health Service: Chief Executive Officer: SW London Total Purchasing Project, 1995–99; Nelson PCG, 1999–2000; Nelson and W Merton PCT, 2000–02; Sutton and Merton PCT, 2002–06; Hillingdon PCT, 2006; Mgt Consultant and Dir, Downsview Ltd, 2007; Associate Dir, BUPA Health Dialog, 2008–09; Dir, Strategy and Innovation, 2009–12, Dir, Commissioning Develt, 2012, NHS Norfolk. *Recreations:* church going, ski-ing, reading. *Address:* 3 Cornwall Road, Cheam, Surrey SM2 6DR. *T:* (020) 8296 8645. *E:* IanLAyres@aol.com.

**AYRES, Pamela, (Mrs D. Russell)**, MBE 2004; writer, broadcaster and entertainer; *b* 14 March 1947; *d* of Stanley William Ayres and Phyllis Evelyn Ayres; *m* 1982, Dudley Russell; two *s*. *Educ:* Stanford-in-the-Vale Village Primary Sch., Berks; Faringdon Secondary Modern Sch., Berks. Served WRAF, 1965–69. Writer and performer: *television:* début on Opportunity Knocks, 1975; The World of Pam Ayres (series), 1977; TV specials in UK, Hong Kong and Canada, 1978–79; Women at War - 100 Years of Women in the Armed Forces, BBC TV, 2017; Celebrity Mastermind, 2017; *radio:* Pam Ayres Radio Show (series), 1995; presenter: Pam Ayres on Sunday, 1996–99; Pam Ayres' Open Road, 2000–01; Ayres on the Air (series), 2004, 2006, 2009, 2012, 2014, 2018; appeared in Royal Variety Show, Palladium, 1977; annual UK concert tours; regular concert tours in Australia and NZ; also perf. in Canada, France, Ireland, Hong Kong and Kenya; many appearances at Literary Festivals incl. Cheltenham, Hay, Woodstock, Gibraltar, Ledbury Poetry Fest., Dubai. *Publications:* Some of Me Poetry, 1976; Some More of Me Poetry, 1976; Thoughts of a Late-Night Knitter, 1978; All Pam's Poems, 1978; The Ballad of Bill Spinks' Bedstead and Other Poems, 1981; Dear Mum, 1985; Pam Ayres: The Works, 1992, new edn as The Works: the classic collection, 2010; With These Hands, 1997; Surgically Enhanced, 2006; The Necessary Aptitude (autobiog.), 2011; You Made Me Late Again!, 2013; The Last Hedgehog, 2018; Up in the Attic, 2019; *for children:* Bertha and the Racing Pigeon, 1979; Guess Who?, 1987; Guess What?, 1987; When Dad Fills In The Garden Pond, 1988; When Dad Cuts Down The Chestnut Tree, 1988; Piggo and the Nosebag, 1990; Piggo has a Train Ride, 1990; Piggo and the Fork-lift Truck, 1991; The Bear Who Was Left Behind, 1991; Jack Crater, 1992; Guess Why?, 1994; Guess Where?, 1994; The Nubbler, 1997 (trans. Japanese 1999). *Recreations:* gardening, bee-keeping, drawing, wildlife. *Address:* PO Box 64, Cirencester, Glos GL7 5YD. *T:* (01285) 644622. *W:* www.pamayres.com.

**AYRIS, Dr Paul**; Pro-Vice-Provost, UCL Library Services, University College London, since 2017 (Director, 1997–2016); Chief Executive Officer, UCL Press, since 2015; *b* 27 April 1957; *s* of Walter Roy Ayris and Irene Ayris (*née* Ball). *Educ:* Selwyn Coll., Cambridge (BA, MA); Gonville and Caius Coll., Cambridge (PhD 1984); Univ. of Sheffield (MA). Sir Henry Stephenson Fellow, Univ. of Sheffield, 1982–84; Cambridge University Library: Asst Librarian, Scientific Periodicals Liby, 1985–89; Automation Div., 1989–96; Hd, IT Services, 1994–96; Dep. Librarian, UCL, Jan.–Sept. 1997. Exec. Ed., Reformation & Renaissance Rev., 1999–2006. *Publications:* (ed with D. Selwyn) Thomas Cranmer, Churchman and Scholar, 1993, 2nd edn 1999. *Recreations:* ecclesiastical architecture, visiting foreign cities, classical music. *Address:* UCL Library Services, UCL, Gower Street, WC1E 6BT. *T:* (020) 7679 7834. *E:* p.ayris@ucl.ac.uk.

**AZA, Alberto**; Head of the Royal Household, Spain, 2002–11; *b* 22 May 1937; *s* of Alberto Aza and Marcela Arias; *m* 1963, María Eulalia Custodio Martí; two *s* four *d*. *Educ:* Univ. de Oviedo; Law Faculty of Madrid (Law Degree); BA, BSc. Joined Diplomatic Service, 1965; served Libreville, Algiers, Rome, Madrid; Dir, Cabinet of the Spanish Prime Minister, 1977–83; Chief Dir, OAS, Latin-America Dept, Min. of Foreign Affairs, 1983; Minister Counsellor, Lisbon, 1983–85; Ambassador: to OAS, Washington, 1985–89; to Belize (resident in Washington), 1985–89; to Mexico, 1990–92; to UK, 1992–99; Dir, Office of Diplomatic Inf., 1999–2002; Sec. Gen., Royal Household, Spain, 2002. Permanent Dir, Consejo de Estado, 2012–. Hon. DLitt Portsmouth, 1997. Gran Cruz del Mérito Civil (Spain), 1979; Gran Cruz del Mérito Naval (Spain), 1996. *Recreations:* fishing, golf, walking. *Address:* Consejo de Estado, C/ Mayor 79, 28013 Madrid, Spain. *Clubs:* Puerta de Hierro, Nuevo (Madrid).

**AZAPAGIC, Prof. Adisa**, PhD; FREng, FIChemE, FRSC; Professor of Sustainable Chemical Engineering, University of Manchester, since 2006; *b* Tuzla, Bosnia and Herzegovina, 10 April 1961; *d* of Bahrija Azapagic and Iza Balic; *m* 1992, Dr Slobodan Perdan. *Educ:* Gymnasium, Tuzla; Univ. of Tuzla (Dip. Ing. 1984; MSc 1987); Univ. of Surrey (PhD 1997). CEng 2000; CSci 2000; FIChemE 2000; FRSC 2000; FREng 2013. Teaching and Res. Asst, Univ. of Tuzla, 1985–92; British Council Fellow, Univ. of Leeds, 1992–93; University of Surrey: Res. Asst, 1993–97; Lectr, 1996–2000; Reader, 2000–04; Prof., 2004–06; Dir of Res., Sch. of Chem. Engrg and Analytical Sci., Univ. of Manchester, 2006–09. Dir, Industrial Ecology Solutions Ltd, 2001–07. Deutscher Akademischer Austausch Dienst Sen. Scholar, 2001; Vis. Scientist, German Aerospace Agency, 2002; RAEng Industrial Secondment, WBB Minerals, 2002; RAEng School, 2002, Leverhulme Trust Vis. Schol., 2002, Univ. of Sydney; UNESCO/ICSU/Third World Acad. of Sci. Vis. Prof., ITAM, Mexico City, 2003; Erskine Fellow, Univ. of Canterbury, Christchurch, 2006; Vis. Prof., Technical Univ. of Dresden, 2013. Member: Strategic Adv. Cttee for Energy, UK Res. Councils, 2005–10; UK Commonwealth Scholarships Adv. Panel, 2009–17; UK REF panel for Aeronaut., Mech., Chem. and Manufg Engrg, 2011–14, 2018–; Manufg Commn, 2014–17. Member: Internat. Adv. Panel, Helmholtz Assoc., 2009–16; Nat. Scientific Qualification Cttee for Commodity Sci., Italy, 2012–15; Chm., Sustainability Section, Eur. Fedn of Chem. Engrg, 2013– (Mem., Exec. Bd, 2018–). Fellow, Japanese Soc. for Promotion of Sci., 2012. Editor-in-Chief, (Envmt), Process Safety and Envmtl Protection, 2013–; Sustainable Prodn and Consumption, 2014–. Hon. FSE 2012. FRSA. Hon. Dr Envmtl Engrg Technical Univ., Iaşi, 2014. *Publications:* Polymers, the Environment and Sustainable Development, 2003 (trans. Chinese, 2005); Sustainable Development in Practice: case studies for engineers and scientists, 2004, 2nd edn 2011; papers on life cycle assessment, industrial sustainability and policy. *Recreations:* hiking, cross-country ski-ing, writing, leading even when I don't know where I am going (and trying to find my way afterwards). *Address:* University of Manchester, The Mill, Sackville Street, Manchester M13 9PL. *T:* (0161) 306 4363. *E:* adisa.azapagic@manchester.ac.uk.

**AZIZ, Mohammed Abdul**; Director, Aziz Foundation, since 2015; *b* 28 Feb. 1971; *s* of Moinul Islam and Sundora Khatun; *m* 1998, Duaa Izzidien; two *s* one *d*. *Educ:* UCL (LLB Hons (Law), LLM (Jurisprudence and Human Rights Law)). Called to the Bar, Gray's Inn, 1997. London Borough of Tower Hamlets: Policy Officer, 1997–2000; Lawyer, 1998–99; Chief Executive Officer: Forum Against Islamophobia and Racism, 2000–02; British Muslim Res. Centre, 2002–04; Director: FaithWise Ltd, 2003–11; Centre for Policy and Public Educn, Woolf Inst., Cambridge, 2012–15. Mem., Treasury Counsel Rev. Team, 2005; Advr on Religion and Belief Equality, DTI, 2004–07; Sen. Advr on Race, Religion and Community Cohesion, DCLG, 2007–11. Vis. Fellow, Univ. of Cambridge, 2011–12; Res. Associate, Centre of Islamic Studies, Univ. of Cambridge, 2012; Associate Mem., St Edmund's Coll., Cambridge, 2013–15; Nohoudh Scholar, Sch. of Law, SOAS, 2012. Member: CRE, 2003–07; EOC, 2005–07; TUC Commn on Vulnerable Employment, 2006–08; Commission for Equality and Human Rights: Member: Govt Task Force, 2003–04; Govt Steering Gp, 2004–06; Equalities Reference Gp, 2005–07. Member: Mgt Cttee, UK Race & Europe Network, 2003–; Bd, European Network Against Racism, 2004–10 (Chm., 2007–10); Council, Liberty, 2004–08. Mem., Honours Cttees for State and Community, Voluntary and Local Service, 2005–10. Founder Mem., Equality and Diversity Forum, 2002– (Trustee, 2010–; Vice Chm., 2011–). Trustee: E London Mosque and London Muslim Centre, 1992–2013; Book Foundn, 2000–. *Recreations:* swimming, gardening, travelling. *T:* (01322) 408220.

**AZIZ, Shaukat**; Member for Attock, National Assembly, Pakistan, 2004–07; Prime Minister of Pakistan, 2004–07, and Minister of Finance, 1999–2007; *b* 6 March 1949; *m*; three *c*. *Educ:* Gordon Coll., Rawalpindi (BSc 1967); Univ. of Karachi (MBA 1969). With Citibank, 1969–99, posts included: Hd of Corporate and Investment Banking for Asia Pacific Reg., then for Central and Eastern Europe; ME and Africa Corporate Planning Officer, Citicorp; Man. Dir, Saudi American Bank; Global Hd, Private Banking, Citigroup; Vice-Pres., 1992. Senator, Pakistan, 2002. Ind. non-exec. Dir, Millennium & Copthorne Hotels plc, 2009– (Sen. Ind. Dir, 2017–); former Mem., Internat. Adv. Bd, Blackstone Gp.

**AZIZ, Suhail Ibne**; international management consultant, since 1981; Chairman and Managing Director, Brettonwood Partnership Ltd, since 1990; *b* Bangladesh (then India), 3 Oct. 1937; permanently resident in England, since 1966; *s* of Azizur Rahman and Lutfunnessa Khatoon; *m* 1960, Elizabeth Ann Pyne, Dartmouth, Devon (*d* 2014); two *d*. *Educ:* Govt High Sec. Sch., Sylhet; Murarichand Coll., Dacca Univ., Sylhet (Intermed. in Science, 1954); Jt Services Pre-Cadet Trng Sch., Quetta; Cadet Trng Sch., PNS Himalaya, Karachi; BRNC, Dartmouth (Actg Sub-Lieut 1958); (mature student) Kingston upon Thames Polytechnic and Trent Polytech., Nottingham (Dipl. in Mgt Studies, 1970); (ext. student) London Univ. (BScEcon Hons 1972); (internal student) Birkbeck Coll., London Univ. (MScEcon 1976); Michigan Business Sch., USA (mgt courses, 1992). FCMI (FIMgt 1981); FIMC 1991; CMC 1994. Sub-Lieut and Lieut, Pakistan Navy Destroyers/Mine Sweeper (Exec. Br.), 1954–61. Personnel and indust. relations: Unilever (Pakistan); Royal Air Force; Commn on Indust. Relations, London; Ford Motor Co. (GB); Mars Ltd, 1963–78; Dir of Gen. Services Div., CRE, 1978–81; Dep. Dir of Econ. Develt, London Borough of Lewisham, 1984–89; Management Consultant, Fullemploy Consultancy Ltd,

1989–90; Mem. Exec. Sub-Cttee, and Bd Mem., Tower Hamlets, Education Business Partnership, 1993–2009. Mem., London Electricity Consumer Cttee, 1991–95. Chairman: Lambeth Healthcare NHS Trust, 1998–99; S London Community Health NHS Trust, 1999–2000; London Probation Bd, Nat. Probation Service, 2001–07. Leading Mem., Bangladesh Movement in UK, 1971. Member: Exec., Standing Conf. of Asian Orgs in UK, 1972–90; N Metropol. Conciliation Cttee, Race Relations Bd, 1971–74; Exec., Post Conf. Constituent Cttee, Black People in Britain - the Way Forward, 1975–76; Adv. Cttee to Gulbenkian Foundn on Area Resource Centre and Community Support Forum, 1976–81; Exec., Nottingham and Dist Community Relations Council, 1975–78; Dept of Employment Race Relations Employment Adv. Gp, 1977–78; BBC Asian programme Adv. Cttee, 1977–81; Industrial Tribunals, 1977–95; Exec., Nat. Org. of African, Asian and Caribbean Peoples, 1976–77; Home Sec.'s Standing Adv. Council on Race Relations, 1976–78; Steering Cttee, Asian Support Forum, 1984–86; Steering Cttee, Develt Policy Forum, DFID, 1998–2000; Jt Consultative Cttee with Ethnic Minorities, Merton BC, 1985–87; Plunkett Foundn for Co-operative Studies, 1985–97; "One World", 1986–90; Adv. Gp, City of London Polytechnic Ethnic Minority Business Develt Unit, 1987–94; Res. Adv. Bd, QMW, London Univ., 1988–99; (co-opted), Exec. Cttee, Tower Hamlets Assoc. for Racial Equality, 1988–91 (Mem., Action Tower Hamlets, 1987); Bangladeshis in Britain - a Response Forum, 1987–89; Tower Hamlets Consortium, 1994–97; Mgt Cttee, Faiths Together in Lambeth, 2017–; Exec. Mem. and Trustee, Docklands Forum, 1991–99; Chairman: Jalalabad Overseas Orgn in UK, 1983–; London Boroughs Bangladesh Assoc., 1984–; Founder Chm., East London Bangladeshi Enterprise Agency, 1985–. CRE Bursary to study Minority Business Develt initiatives in USA, 1986. Mem., Labour Econ. Finance Taxation Assoc., 1973–80; Institute of Management Consultants: Chm., Third World Specialist Gp, 1984–92; Mem. Council, 1995–. Jt Trustee, United Action-Bangladesh Relief Fund, 1971–90; Trustee: Brixton Neighbourhood Assoc., 1979–82; Trust for Educn and Develt, 1992–2004; Community Develt Foundn, 1999–2008; pact (Prison Advice & Care Trust), 2007–13; Advr and Trustee, SE London Community Foundn, 1996–2010. Comr, Commonwealth Scholarship Commn, 1996–2002. Governor: London Guildhall Univ., 1995–2003; Lambeth Coll., 1999–2011. Deeply interested in community and race relations and believes profoundly that future health of Brit. society depends on achieving good race relations. *Recreations:* travelling, seeing places of historical interest, meeting people, reading (e.g. political economy). *Club:* Royal Air Force.

**AZNAR LÓPEZ, José María;** Prime Minister of Spain, 1996–2004; Distinguished Scholar in the Practice of Global Leadership, Georgetown University, USA, 2004–11; *b* Madrid, 1953; *m* 1977, Ana Botella; two *s* one *d*. *Educ:* Univ. Complutense, Madrid (LLB). Tax Inspector, 1976. Mem., Cortes, 1982–2004; Chief Exec., Castile-León Reg.; Premier, Castilla y León Autonomous Reg., 1987. Joined Alianza Popular, later Partido Popular, 1978: Dep. Sec. Gen., 1982; Pres., 1990–2004; Vice-Pres., European Popular Party, 1993. Dir, News Corp., 2006–. Pres. Fundación para el Análisis y los Estudios Sociales, Madrid. *Publications:* Libertad y solidaridad, 1991; España: la segunda transición, 1994; La España en que yo creo, 1995; Ocho años de Gobierno, 2004; Retratos y Perfiles: de Fraga a Bush, 2005. *Recreations:* reading, sports, music.

**AZOULAY, Audrey Vanessa;** Director-General, United Nations Educational, Scientific and Cultural Organization, since 2017; *b* La Celle-Saint-Cloud, Yvelines, 4 Aug. 1972; *d* of André Azoulay, journalist, banker and politician and Katia Brami, writer. *Educ:* Lancaster Univ. (MBA); Paris IX-Dauphine Univ. (Master Mgt Scis); Inst. d'études politiques, Paris; Ecole Nationale d'Admin. Dep. to Chief, Office of Administrative and Financial Affairs of the Public Sector of Audiovisual Communication, Legal and Tech. Service of Information and Communication, Prime Minister's Office, 2000; Hd, Public Audiovisual Sector Office, Audiovisual Communication Subdirectorate, Directorate of Media Develt, Prime Minister's Office, 2000–03; Rapporteur to Regl Chamber of Accounts of Ile-de-France, 2003–06; National Centre of Cinematography and the Moving Image: Dep. Dir for Audiovisual Affairs, 2006–07; Chief Financial and Legal Officer, 2007–11; Dep. Dir Gen., 2011–14; Culture and Communication Councillor, Office of Pres. of France, 2014–16; Minister of Culture and Communication, 2016–17. Comdr des Arts et des Lettres (France), 2016. *Address:* UNESCO, 7 place de Fontenoy, 75352 Paris 07 SP, France. *T:* (1) 45681310. *E:* dg.secretariat@unesco.org. *W:* www.twitter.com/AAzoulay.

**AZZOPARDI, Joseph;** Chief Justice of Malta, since 2018; *b* Senglea, Malta, 8 April 1955; *s* of late Michael Azzopardi and Mary Azzopardi (née Azzopardi); *m* 1981, Maria Attard; one *d*. *Educ:* Govt primary and secondary schs; Univ. of Malta (LLD 1979). Called to the Bar, Malta, 1980; in private practice as a lawyer, Law Courts, 1980–2003; Pres., Chamber of Advocates, 2000–03; a Judge of Superior Courts, Malta, 2003. Pres., Fedn of Youth Orgns, 1980–82. Director: Mid-Med Bank, 1981–87; Housing Authy, 1996–2003. *Recreations:* football, athletics. *Address:* Law Courts, Valletta, Malta. *T:* 21652967, 99492939. *E:* azzjo55@gmail.com. *Club:* Casino Maltese 1852 (Valletta).

# B

**BABINGTON, Paula R.**; see Gooder, P. R.

**BABINGTON, Roger Vincent,** FREng; FRINA; Director General Ships and Chief Executive, Ships Support Agency, Ministry of Defence, 1996–97; b 6 April 1943; s of late George Cyril Babington and Rita Mary Babington (née Simpkins); m 1967, Susan Wendy Eaton; two s two d. Educ: King Edward's Sch., Bath; Univ. of Birmingham (BSc); University Coll. London (MSc). RCNC. Asst Constructor, MoD, 1965–73; Constructor, MoD, Bath, 1973–76; Naval Constructor Overseer, MoD, Barrow-in-Furness, 1976–81; HM Dockyard, Rosyth: Constructor, 1981–82; Chief Constructor, 1982–86; Dir of Progs and Planning, 1986–87; Ministry of Defence, Bath: Dir, Surface Ships D, 1987–89; Dir, SSN20, 1989–91; Dir, Submarines, 1991–93; Dir-Gen., Ship Refitting, 1993; Dir-Gen., Fleet Support (Ships), 1993–95; Dir-Gen. Ships, 1995–96; Managing Director: BMT Marine Procurement Ltd, 1998–99; BMT Defence Services Ltd, 1999–2001. FREng (FEng 1995). Recreations: badminton, golf, house, garden and vehicle maintenance, watching sport, listening. Address: Shoscombe Lodge, Shoscombe, Bath BA2 8LU. T: and Fax: (01761) 432436.

**BABINGTON-BROWNE, Gillian Brenda, (Mrs K. J. Wilson);** a District Judge (Magistrates' Courts) (formerly Metropolitan Stipendiary Magistrate), 1991–2008; b 20 May 1949; d of Derek Keith Babington-Browne and Olive Maude (née Seymour); m 1983, Kenneth John Wilson. Educ: Rochester Girls' Grammar Sch.; Coll. of Law, London. Admitted Solicitor, 1973; Asst Solicitor with Arnold, Tuff & Grimwade, Rochester, 1973–74; Assistant with Ronald A. Prior, 1974, with Edward Lewis Possart, London, 1974–78; own practice, 1978–89; freelance advocate and consultant, 1989–91. Hon. Mem., London Criminal Courts Solicitors' Assoc. (Pres., 1990–91; Associate Mem., 1991–). Publications: contribs to legal jls. Recreations: studio pottery, gardening, reading, interior design, swimming, tap dancing.

**BABIŠ, Ing. Andrej;** Prime Minister of the Czech Republic, since 2017; b Bratislava, 2 Sept. 1954; s of Štefan Babiš and Adriana Babišová; m 2017, Monika; two s two d. Educ: Univ. of Bratislava (Ing.). Founder and owner, Agrofert, 1993–2017. Vice Premier of Czech Republic, 2014–17; Finance Minister, 2016–17. Founder and Leader, ANO 2011, 2012–. Publications: What I Dream When I Happen to Sleep: vision 2035 for the Czech Republic, for our children, 2017. Address: Office of the Government of the Czech Republic, nábřeží Edvarda Beneše 4, 11801 Prague 1, Czech Republic. T: 224002527. E: premier@vlada.cz.

**BACH,** family name of **Baron Bach**.

**BACH, Baron** cr 1998 (Life Peer), of Lutterworth in the co. of Leicestershire; **William Stephen Goulden Bach;** Police and Crime Commissioner for Leicester, Leicestershire and Rutland, since 2016; b 25 Dec. 1946; s of late Stephen Craine Goulden Bach, CBE and Joan Bach; m 1984, Caroline Jones, er d of Eric and Cynthia Smeaton; one d, and one s one d from former marriage. Educ: Westminster Sch.; New Coll., Oxford (BA). Called to the Bar, Middle Temple, 1972; Midland and Oxford Circuit; Hd of Chambers. Member (Lab): Leicester City Council, 1976–87; Harborough DC, 1995–99; Mayor, Lutterworth, 1993–94. Labour Party: Treas., Leics W Const., 1974–87; Chm., Harborough Dist, 1989–95; Chm., Northants and Blaby Euro. Const., 1992–99. Member: Lab Party Econ. Commn, 1998–99; Lab Party Nat. Policy Forum, 1998–99. Government spokesman: Home Office, DfEE, LCD, 1999–2000; FCO, BIS (formerly BERR), MoJ, 2007–10; a Lord in Waiting (Govt Whip), 1999–2000, 2007–09; Parly Sec., LCD, 2000–01; Parliamentary Under-Secretary of State: MoD, 2001–05; DEFRA, 2005–06; MoJ, 2008–10; an Opposition spokesman for Justice, 2010–12, for Foreign Affairs, 2013–16; Shadow Attorney Gen., 2014–16. Contested (Lab): Gainsborough, 1979; Sherwood, 1983 and 1987. Mem. Court, Leicester Univ., 1980–94. Chair, Bach Commn on Access to Justice, 2015–17. Trustee, LawWorks. Patron, Coventry Law Centre. Recreations: playing and watching football and cricket, Leicester City FC supporter, music, reading hard-boiled American crime fiction. Address: House of Lords, SW1A 0PW.

**BACHE, Andrew Philip Foley,** CMG 1992; HM Diplomatic Service, retired; Ambassador to Denmark, 1996–99; b 29 Dec. 1939; s of late Robert Philip Sidney Bache, OBE and Jessie Bache; m 1963, Shân Headley; two s one d. Educ: Shrewsbury Sch.; Emmanuel Coll., Cambridge (MA). Joined HM Diplomatic Service, 1963; 3rd Sec., Nicosia, 1964–66; Treasury Centre for Admin. Studies, 1966; 2nd Sec., Sofia, 1966–68; FCO, 1968–71; 1st Sec., Lagos, 1971–74; FCO, 1974–78; 1st Sec. (Commercial), Vienna, 1978–81; Counsellor and Head of Chancery, Tokyo, 1981–85; Counsellor and Dep. Hd of Mission, Ankara, 1985–87; Hd of Personnel Services Dept, FCO, 1988–90; on secondment as Diplomatic Service Chm. to CSSB, 1990–91; Ambassador, Romania, 1992–96. Chief Exec., Westminster Foundn for Democracy, 2001–02. Chm., Hospices of Hope (formerly Hospices of Hope Romania Trust), 2000–12. JP West London, 2001–09. Conseiller, Chief Pleas, Sark, 2010–14; Dep. Seigneur of Sark, 2017–. Dr hc: Technical Univ., Cluj, 1994; Sibiu Univ., 1995. Recreations: diverse, including travel, history, ornithology, fine arts, tennis, cricket, Real tennis. Clubs: Oxford and Cambridge, MCC.

**BACHE, Jonathan Beesley, (John),** JP; FRCS, FRCSE; National Chairman, Magistrates' Association, since 2017 (Deputy Chairman, 2013–17); b Widnes, Lancs, 11 Nov. 1950; s of Noel Edwin Alan Bache and Audrey Chadwick Bache (née Beesley); m 1st, 1981, Lorraine Anne Newman (marr. diss. 2000); two d; 2nd, 2004, Anne Catherine Troop; one step s one step d. Educ: Liverpool Coll.; Univ. of Liverpool (MB ChB 1975). FRCSE 1979; FRCS 1997. Consultant in Accident and Emergency Medicine, Leighton Hosp., Crewe, 1983–2009; Associate Postgrad. Dean of Medicine, Univ. of Liverpool, 1998–2005. Pres., Section of Accident and Emergency Medicine, RSocMed, 2002–04. Trustee, Magistrates' Assoc., 2009– (Chm., Youth Courts Cttee, 2010–13). Gov., S Cheshire Coll., 2008–13. JP 1989. Publications: (jtly) A Colour Atlas of Nursing Procedures in Accidents and Emergencies, 1985 (trans. French, German, Spanish, Italian, Turkish); (with R. H. Hardy) Accidents and Emergencies, 5th edn 1987, 6th edn 1994; (jtly) Handbook of Emergency Department Procedures, 1998, 2nd edn 2003; articles in jls on accident and emergency medicine and the magistracy. Recreations: walking my dogs (Izzy and Larry), bird watching, name dropping, seeing London by bus, learning to cook (starting tomorrow), history, politics. Address: Magistrates' Association, 10A Flagstaff House, St George Wharf, SW8 2LE. T: (020) 7387 2353. E: jbache@doctors.org.uk. Club: Royal Society of Medicine.

**BACHER, Dr Aron, (Ali);** Chairman, Right to Care, since 2008; b 24 May 1942; s of Rose and Koppel Bacher; m 1965, Shira Ruth Teeger; one s two d. Educ: Yeoville Boys' Primary Sch.; King Edward VII High Sch.; Witwatersrand Univ. (MB BCh). Junior appts, Baragwanath and Natalspruit Hosps, 1968–69; private practice, Rosebank, Johannesburg, 1970–79. Man. Dir, Delta Distributors, 1979–81; Chief Executive Officer: Transvaal Cricket Council, 1981–86; South African Cricket Union, 1986–91; United Cricket Bd of S Africa, 1991–2000; Executive Director: 2003 ICC Cricket World Cup, 2001–03; Wits Foundn, 2003–06. Chairman: Stella Vista, 2007–09; Seniors' Finance, 2007–10. International Cricket Council: Mem. Exec. Bd, 1997–2000; Chm., Internat. Develt Cttee, 1996–2000. Cricket début for Transvaal, 1959–60; captained S Africa, 1970; played 12 Test matches, made 120 1st cl. appearances, 7,894 runs, 18 centuries, 110 catches, one stumping; retired, 1974; Transvaal and Nat. Selectors' Panels, 1976–83; Dir, S African Cricket Develt Club, 1986. Chm., Alexander Forbes Community Trust, 2012–. Hon. Dr: Rhodes; Witwatersrand. Numerous awards include: Jack Cheetham Meml, 1990, for doing the most to normalise sport in S Africa; Laureate Award for Social Architecture, Da Vinci Inst., 2013; Presidential Sports Award, S Africa. Recreation: jogging. Address: PO Box 55041, Northlands 2116, South Africa. T: (home) (11) 7831263.

**BACK, Philippa Lucy F.**; see Foster Back.

**BACKHOUSE, Sir Alfred (James Stott),** 5th Bt cr 1901; b 7 April 2002; s of Sir Jonathan Roger Backhouse, 4th Bt and of Sarah Ann, o d of J. A. Stott; S father, 2007.

**BACKHOUSE, David,** FRSS, RWA; sculptor; b 5 May 1941; s of late Joseph and Jessie Backhouse; m 1975, Sarah Barber; one s two d. Educ: Lord Weymouth Sch.; W of England Coll. of Art. RWA 1978; FRSS (FRBS 1983). Numerous one-man exhibns, London and NY; public sculptures include: Meml to Merchant Seamen, Bristol, 2001; Animals in War Meml, London, 2004; sculptures in public and private collections internationally. Address: Silenus, 8 Bishop Ken Close, Wells, Som BA5 3ND. E: db@backhousesculptures.com.

**BACKHOUSE, David Miles;** Chairman: South Farm Products Ltd, since 1964; Leo Consult Ltd, since 1986; b 30 Jan. 1939; s of late Jonathan Backhouse and Alice Joan (née Woodroffe); m 1969, Sophia Ann (née Townsend); one s one d. Educ: Summer Fields, Oxford; Eton Coll. Commenced career in banking with Schroders PLC, 1966; Chief Exec. Officer, Dunbar Gp, 1973–84; Chm., Henderson Admin Gp, 1990–92; Chm., Johnson Fry Hldgs, 1995–2000. Non-executive Director: Hambro Life Assce, 1982–84; TSB Group, 1985–92; Witan Investment Company, 1985–92; Royal Agricl Coll., 1987–2005. Recreations: tennis, riding. Address: South Farm House, Hatherop, Glos GL7 3PN. T: (01285) 712225.

**BACKHOUSE, Roger Bainbridge;** QC 1984; b 8 March 1938; s of late Leslie Bainbridge Backhouse and of Jean Backhouse; m 1962, Elizabeth Constance, d of Comdr J. A. Lowe, DSO, DSC; two s one d. Educ: Liverpool Coll.; Trinity Hall, Cambridge (History Tripos parts I & II). Nat. Service, RAF, 1956–58 (Pilot Officer). Worked in family business, 1961–62; Schoolmaster, 1962–64; called to the Bar, Middle Temple, 1965. Recreations: opera, military history, travel. Address: 14 Parchment Street, Winchester, Hants SO23 8AZ. T: (01962) 863053. Clubs: Royal Air Force; Hockley Golf.

**BACKHOUSE, Prof. Roger Edward,** PhD; FBA 2014; Professor of the History and Philosophy of Economics, University of Birmingham, since 1996; b 19 Jan. 1951; s of Edward Backhouse and Mary Backhouse (née Pillow); m 1st, 1980, Merida Jane Lee (d 1989); one s one d; 2nd, 2004, Ann Elizabeth Barnfield. Educ: Friends' Sch., Saffron Walden; Univ. of Bristol (BSc Econs and Econ. Hist. 1972); Univ. of Birmingham (PhD Econs 1977). Temp. Lectr in Econs, UCL, 1975–77; University of Birmingham: Lectr in Econs, 1980–89; Sen. Lectr, 1989–92; Reader, 1992–96. British Acad. Res. Reader, 1998–2000; Ludwig Lachman Res. Fellow, LSE, 2006–07; Leverhulme Trust Maj. Res. Fellow, 2011–14; Vis. Lectr, UCL, 1977–79; Vis. Lectr, then Vis. Prof., Univ. of Buckingham, 1992–2006; Vis. Prof., Univ. of Oporto, 1999–; Prof. of Hist. and Philosophy of Econs (pt-time), Erasmus Univ., Rotterdam, 2009–. Publications: Macroeconomics and the British Economy, 1983; A History of Modern Economic Analysis, 1985 (Spanish edn, 1988; Italian edn, 1990); Economists and the Economy, 1988, 2nd edn 1994 (Japanese edn); Applied UK Macroeconomics, 1991; (ed jtly) Economics and Language, 1993; Interpreting Macroeconomics: explorations in the history of macroeconomic thought, 1995; Truth and Progress in Economic Knowledge, 1997; (ed jtly) Economics and Methodology: crossing boundaries, 1997; Explorations in Economic Methodology: from Lakatos to empirical philosophy of science, 1998; (ed) Keynes: contemporary responses to the general theory, 1999; (ed with J. Creedy) From Classical Economics to the Theory of the Firm: essays in honour of D. P. O'Brien, 1999; (ed with R. Middleton) Exemplary Economists, 2 vols, 2000; (ed with A. Salanti) Macroeconomics and the Real World, 2 vols, 2000; (ed with J. Biddle) Toward a History of Applied Economics, 2000; The Ordinary Business of Life: a history of economics from ancient times to the Twenty-First Century, 2002; The Penguin History of Economics, 2002; (ed with B. W. Bateman) The Cambridge Companion to Keynes, 2006; (ed with T. Nishizawa) No Wealth But Life: welfare economics and the welfare state in Britain, 1800–1945, 2010; (ed with P. Fontaine) The History of the Social Sciences since 1945, 2010; (ed with P. Fontaine) The Unsocial Social Science? Economics and Neighbouring Disciplines since 1945, 2010; (with B. W. Bateman) Keynes: capitalist revolutionary, 2011; (with M. Boianovsky) Transforming Modern Macroeconomics: the search for disequilibrium microfoundations, 1956–2003, 2013; (ed with P. Fontaine) A Historiography of Modern Social Science, 2014; Founder of Modern Economics: Paul A. Samuelson, vol. I, Becoming Samuelson, 1915–1948, 2017; (with K. Tribe) The History of Economics: a guide for students and teachers, 2018. Address: Department of Economics, University of Birmingham, Edgbaston, Birmingham B15 2TT. E: R.E.Backhouse@bham.ac.uk.

**BACKLER, Dr Gary George;** strategy and management consultant; owner, Backler Consulting Ltd, since 2011; *b* 19 July 1955; *s* of Robert and Barbara Backler; *m* 1990, Elizabeth Ann Edes; two *d*. *Educ:* Merton Coll., Oxford (MA Modern Hist.); Univ. of BC (MSc Commerce & Business Admin); Leeds Univ. (PhD Econ. Studies 1987). Traffic mgt trainee, British Rail, 1976–78; res. asst, Centre for Transportation Studies, Vancouver, 1978–81; Sen. Associate, Booz, Allen & Hamilton, 1985–90; Supervising Consultant, Price Waterhouse, 1990–94; Asst Dir, Office of Passenger Rail Franchising, 1994–98; Dir, Franchise Mgt, Shadow Strategic Rail Authy, 1998–2000; Exec. Dir, Regl Networks, 2000–02, Franchise Dir, N & W, 2002–05, Strategic Rail Authy; Dir, Rail Service Delivery, DfT, 2005–10. Trustee, 2011–, Planning Dir, 2013–, Friends of River Crane Envmt. *Publications:* contribs to logistics jls. *Recreations:* gym, Merton Society Secretary. E: ggbackler@hotmail.co.uk.

**BACKUS, Rear Adm. Alexander Kirkwood,** CB 2003; OBE 1989; Chief of Staff (Warfare) and Rear Admiral Surface Ships, 2002–03; *b* 1 April 1948; *s* of late Jake Kirkwood Backus and Jean Backus (*née* Stobie); *m* 1971, Margaret Joan Pocock; two *s* one *d*. *Educ:* Sevenoaks Sch., Kent; BRNC, Dartmouth. Joined RN, 1966; served HM Ships Fiskerton, Intrepid, Eastbourne, Cavalier, Bacchante, Blake, Arrow, Cleopatra, and Torquay, 1967–84; CO, Arethusa, 1984; JSDC Greenwich, 1986; Comdr Sea Training, 1988; Capt. 6th Frigate Sqn, HMS Hermione, 1990; Comdr British Forces Falkland Islands, 1995–96; ACOS (Policy) to C-in-C Fleet, 1996–99; Flag Officer Sea Trng, 1999–2001; Flag Officer Surface Flotilla, 2001–02. Hon. Pres., Devon Rural Skills Trust, 2014 (Chm., 2002–12). Silver Jubilee Medal, 1977; Golden Jubilee Medal, 2002. *Recreations:* ornithology, photography. *Clubs:* Royal Naval (Argyll); Western Isles Yacht.

**BACON, Gareth Andrew;** Member (C) Bexley and Bromley, London Assembly, Greater London Authority, since 2016 (London-wide, 2008–16); *b* Hong Kong, 7 April 1972; *s* of Robert and Helen Bacon; *m* 2004, Cheryl Cooley; one *d*. *Educ:* Univ. of Kent, Canterbury (BA Hons Pols and Govt 1996; MA Eur. Pols 1997). Mem. (C), Bexley LBC, 1998– (Dep. Mayor, 2001–02; Cabinet Mem. for Envmt, 2006–14, for Finance and Corp. Services, 2014–15). Contested (C) Greenwich and Lewisham, GLA, 2004. Greater London Authority: Cons. spokesman on envmt, 2008–10, on budget, 2010–; Leader, Conservatives, 2015–; Chm., Budget and Perf. Cttee, 2016–. Mem., London Fire and Emergency Planning Authy, 2010–18 (Chm., 2015–16). Hd, public sector div., Randstad Financial & Professional (formerly Martin Ward Anderson), 2004–12. *Recreations:* former Rugby player, current squash player, season ticket holder at Manchester United Football Club. *Address:* Greater London Authority, City Hall, The Queen's Walk, SE1 2AA. *T:* (020) 7983 5784. *E:* gareth.bacon@london.gov.uk.

**BACON, Jennifer Helen,** CB 1995; Director-General, Health and Safety Executive, 1995–2000; *b* 16 April 1945; *d* of Dr Lionel James Bacon and Joyce Bacon (*née* Chapman). *Educ:* Bedales Sch., Petersfield; New Hall, Cambridge (BA Hons 1st cl.; Hon. Fellow, 1997). Joined Civil Service as Asst Principal, Min. of Labour, 1967; Private Sec. to Minister of State for Employment, 1971–72; Principal, 1972–78, worked on health and safety and industrial relations legislation; Principal Private Sec. to Sec. of State for Employment, 1977–78; Asst Sec., Controller of Trng Services, MSC, 1978–80; sabbatical, travelling in Latin America, 1980–81; Asst Sec., Machinery of Govt Div., CSD, later MPO, 1981–82; Under Sec., Dir of Adult (formerly Occupational) Trng, MSC, 1982–86; Under Sec., School Curriculum and Exams, DES, 1986–89; Department of Employment: Prin. Finance Officer (Grade 3), 1989–91; Dir of Resources and Strategy (Grade 2), 1991–92; Dep. Dir-Gen. (Policy), HSE, 1992–95; Head, Animal, Health and Envmt Directorate, MAFF, then DEFRA, 2000–01. Mem., External Review Gp, Water UK, 2004–09. Mem., Adv. Cttee on Degree Awarding Powers, QAA, 1998–2004. Mem. Bd, Sheffield Develt Corp., 1992–95. Vis. Fellow, Nuffield Coll., Oxford, 1989–97. Gov., Bedales Sch., 2002–05. Hon. DSc Aston, 2000. *Recreations:* classical music especially opera, travelling, walking.

**BACON, John William,** CB 2006; FCCA; Chairman: Community Health Partnerships Ltd, since 2011; Barts Health NHS Trust, 2015–16; Company Chemists' Association, since 2018; *b* 1 Nov. 1950; *s* of late William Bacon and Joy Bacon; *m* 1975, Margaret Clapson; one *d*. *Educ:* Cambridgeshire High Sch.; Univ. of Kent (BA). FCCA 1975. UKAEA, 1972–83; Chief Finance Officer, Culham Lab., 1979–82; Head of Finance, Harwell Lab., 1983; NHS, 1983–94; Department of Health: Dir of Finance and Performance, London Reg., 1995–2000; Dir, Health and Social Care, London, 2000–03; Dir of Service Delivery, 2003–05. Healthcare Consultant, Health Works, 2006–09; Associate Consultant, Grant Thornton Internat., 2007–09; Associate, KPMG Global Health Practice, 2011–15; Dir, UCL Partners, 2015–16. Chm., Sussex Partnership NHS Founds Trust, 2008–15. Sec., London Old Tablers Soc., 2007–09. Trustee, Barts Charity, 2015–16. Hon. Fellow, Univ. of Sussex, 2015. *Address:* 3 Ventnor Villas, Hove BN3 3DD.

**BACON, Kelyn Meher;** *see* Bacon Darwin, K. M.

**BACON, Maureen Anne;** QC 2009; **Her Honour Judge Bacon;** a Circuit Judge, since 2015; *b* London, 8 Jan. 1954; *d* of Stanley Clarke Bacon and Violet Bacon. *Educ:* George Farmer Sch., Holbeach, Lincs; De Montfort Univ. (BA Hons Law 1983); Inns of Court Sch. of Law 1984. NHS Adminr, 1971–80; called to the Bar, Gray's Inn, 1984; a Recorder, 2001–15; a Judge, Mental Health Tribunal (Restricted Patients Panel), 2012–. *Recreations:* theatre, cinema, jazz, travel, the pursuit of all things stylish. *Address:* Norwich Crown Court, The Law Courts, Bishopsgate, Norwich NR3 1UR.

**BACON, Sir Nicholas (Hickman Ponsonby),** 14th Bt of Redgrave, *cr* 1611, and 15th Bt of Mildenhall, *cr* 1627; OBE 2010; Premier Baronet of England; DL; Lord Warden of the Stannaries and Keeper of the Privy Seal, Duchy of Cornwall, since 2006; *b* 17 May 1953; *s* of Sir Edmund Castell Bacon, 13th and 14th Bt, KG, KBE, TD and Priscilla Dora, *d* of Col Sir Charles Edward Ponsonby, 1st Bt, TD; *S* father, 1982; *m* 1981, Susan, *d* of Raymond Dinnis, Edenbridge, Kent; four *s*. *Educ:* Eton; Dundee Univ. (MA). Barrister-at-law, Gray's Inn. A Page of Honour to the Queen, 1966–69. Pres., RHS, 2013–. DL Norfolk, 1998. *Heir: s* Henry Hickman Bacon, *b* 23 April 1984. *Address:* Raveningham Hall, Norfolk NR14 6NS. *Club:* Pratt's.

**BACON, Dame Patricia (Anne),** DBE 2011; Principal and Chief Executive, St Helens College, 2002–11 (Deputy Principal, 1990–2002); *b* London, 16 Jan. 1951; *d* of Reginald and Florence Bacon; *m* 1989, Anthony Paul Davison. *Educ:* Leicester Univ. (BA Hons English 1973); Wolverhampton Poly. (Cert Ed 1982); Univ. of S Bank (MBA Educn 1995). Exec. Officer, DHSS, 1969–70; grad. manager, Lewis's Dept Store, 1973–76; Retail Manager, Josiah Wedgwood, 1976–78; Lectr, Stoke Coll., 1978–81; Lectr, then Sen. Lectr, Warwickshire Coll., 1981–87; Associate Vice Principal, Wellingborough Coll., 1987–90. Association of Colleges: Pres., 2009–10; Chm., Beacon Awards Steering Gp, 2012–18; Trustee, 2012–18. Chm. Govs, Sutton Acad., 2008–11; Chair, Cheshire Coll. South and West (formerly South Cheshire Coll.), 2015–; Dir, Crewe Multi Acad. Trust, 2015–; Interim Exec. Bd Mem., Oakfield Lodge Sch., 2014–17. Non-exec. Dir, Mid-Cheshire Hosps and Foundn Trust, 2012–18 (Dep. Chair, 2014). Pres., British Red Cross, Cheshire, 2018– (Vice Pres., 2016–18). Hon. DEd Edgehill, 2011; Hon. DLitt Chester, 2014. *Recreations:* travel, theatre, music.

**BACON, Peter James;** HM Diplomatic Service, retired; Consul-General, Houston, 1995–2001; *b* 17 Sept. 1941; *s* of Alfred J. Bacon and Mildred (*née* Randall); *m* 1963, Valerie Ann Colby; one *s* one *d*. *Educ:* Huish's Grammar Sch., Taunton. GPO, 1958–63; joined HM Diplomatic Service, 1963; CRO, 1963–64; Nicosia, 1964–66; Kota Kinabalu, 1967–70; Brussels, 1970–71; Beirut, 1971–75; Asst Private Sec. to Minister of State, FCO, 1975–78; Suva, 1978–80; First Sec. (Energy), Washington, 1980–84; Hd, Parly Relns Dept, FCO, 1984–88; Consul (Commercial), Johannesburg, 1988–92; Counsellor (Commercial and Develt), Jakarta, 1992–95. *Recreations:* golf, travel. *Address:* The Pines, Blagdon Hill, Taunton, Somerset TA3 7SL.

**BACON, Richard Michael;** MP (C) South Norfolk, since 2001; *b* 3 Dec. 1962; *s* of Michael Edward Bacon and Sheila Margaret Bacon (*née* Taylor, now Campbell); *m* 2006, Victoria Louise Panton; two *s*. *Educ:* King's Sch., Worcester; LSE (BSc 1st cl. Hons 1986); Goethe Inst., Berlin. Investment banker, Barclays de Zoete Wedd Ltd, 1986–89; financial journalist, principally with Euromoney Publications, 1993–94; Dep. Dir, Mgt Consultancies Assoc., 1994–96; Associate Partner, Brunswick Public Relations, 1996–99; Founder, English Word Factory, 1999–. Member: Public Accounts Cttee, H of C, 2001–17; European Scrutiny Cttee, 2003–07; Public Accounts Commn, 2005–. Chm., Hammersmith Cons. Assoc., 1995–96. Co-founder, Cons. Party Geneva project, 2000. Contested (C) Vauxhall, 1997. *Publications:* (with Christopher Hope) Conundrum, 2013. *Recreation:* playing the bongos. *Address:* House of Commons, SW1A 0AA. *T:* (constituency office) (01379) 643728. *Club:* Ronnie Scott's.

**BACON, Susan Elizabeth;** *see* Sullivan, S. E.

**BACON DARWIN, Kelyn Meher, (Kelyn Bacon);** QC 2014; a Deputy High Court Judge, since 2017; *b* Bombay, 29 Oct. 1973; *d* of Martin and Barbara Bacon; *m* 2003, Peter Darwin; one *s* one *d*. *Educ:* Merton Coll., Oxford (MA Law with Law Studies in Europe 1996); Univ. of Konstanz, Germany; European Univ. Inst., Florence (LLB Eur. Law 1997); Inns of Court Sch. of Law. Called to the Bar, Inner Temple, 1998, Bencher, 2015; in practice as barrister, specialising in EU and competition law, 1998–. *Publications:* European Community Law of State Aid, 2009, 3rd edn as European Union Law of State Aid, 2017. *Recreations:* walking, cycling, singing, playing cello. *Address:* Brick Court Chambers, 7–8 Essex Street, WC2R 3LD. *T:* (020) 7379 3550.

**BACOW, Lawrence S.;** President, Harvard University, since 2018; *m* Adele Fleet; two *s*. *Educ:* Massachusetts Inst. of Technol. (SB Econs 1972); Harvard Univ. (JD 1976; MPP 1976; PhD Public Policy 1978). Massachusetts Institute of Technology: Lee and Geraldine Martin Prof. of Envmtl Studies; Chair, Faculty, 1995–97; Chancellor, 1998–2001; Co-Dir, Consortium on Global Envmtl Challenges; Tufts University: Pres., 2001–11; Harvard University: Pres.-in-Residence, Higher Educn Prog., Graduate Sch. of Educn, 2011–14; Hauser Leader-in-Residence, Center for Public Leadership, Harvard Kennedy Sch. of Govt, 2014–18; Mem., Harvard Corp., 2011–. Sen. Advr to Ithaka S+R. Member: White House Bd of Advrs on Historically Black Colls and Univs, 2010–15; Lincoln Proj., Amer. Acad. of Arts and Scis, 2014–16. Clark Kerr Lect., Univ. of Calif. Berkeley, 2017. Fellow, Amer. Acad. of Arts and Scis. *Recreations:* running, sailing, ski-ing. *Address:* Harvard University, Massachusetts Hall, Cambridge, MA 02138, USA.

**BADAWI, Zeinab;** broadcaster and journalist, BBC, since 1998; *d* of Mohammed-Khair Badawi and Asia Malik; *m*; two *s* two *d*. *Educ:* St Hilda's Coll., Oxford (BA Politics, Philosophy, Econs); Sch. of Oriental and African Studies, London Univ. (MA Middle East Hist.). Broadcast journalist: Yorkshire TV, 1982–86; BBC Manchester, 1986–87; News Reporter and Presenter, Channel 4 News, ITN, 1988–98. Dir, Kush Communications Ltd, 2010–. Chm., Article 19 (Internat. Centre Against Censorship), 1998–2002; Vice-Pres., UNA, 1998–; Council Member: ODI, 1990–; Bd, Inst. of Contemporary History, 2001–; Board Member: British Council, 2004–09; NPG, 2004–12. Chm., Africa Medical Partnership Fund, 2004–. Chm., Royal African Soc., 2014–. Trustee: Africa Centre, 2001–03; BBC World Service Trust, 2002–09; Historic Royal Palaces, 2016–; BBC Media Action, 2017–; Hampstead Theatre, 2018–. Hon DLitt SOAS, Univ. of London, 2011; Hon. Dr Univ. of the Arts, London, 2015. *Recreations:* family, cooking, ancient history, travel. *Address:* BBC New Broadcasting House, Portland Place, W1A 1AA.

**BADCOCK, Maj.-Gen. John Michael Watson,** MBE 1959; DL; Chairman, S. W. Mount & Sons, 1982–86; *b* 10 Nov. 1922; *s* of late R. D. Badcock, MC, JP and Mrs J. D. Badcock; *m* 1948, Gillian Pauline (*née* Attfield) (*d* 2007); one *s* two *d*. *Educ:* Sherborne Sch.; Worcester Coll., Oxford. Enlisted in ranks (Army), 1941; commnd Royal Corps of Signals, 1942; war service UK and BAOR; Ceylon, 1945–47; served in UK, Persian Gulf, BAOR and Cyprus; Comdr 2 Inf. Bde and Dep. Constable of Dover Castle, 1968–71; Dep. Mil. Sec., 1971–72; Dir of Manning (Army), 1972–74; Defence Advr and Head of British Defence Liaison Staff, Canberra, 1974–77; retired. psc, jssc, idc. Col Comdt, Royal Signals, 1974–80 and 1982–90; Master of Signals, 1982–90; Hon. Col, 31 (London) Signal Regt (Volunteers), 1978–83. Chm., SE TA&VRA, 1979–85. Chief Appeals Officer, CRC, 1978–82. Founder, 1981, now Pres., E Kent Br., Royal Signals Assoc., 2011–. DL Kent, 1980. *Recreations:* watching Rugby football, cricket, hockey, most field sports less horsemanship. *Address:* c/o RHQ Royal Signals, Blandford Camp, Blandford, Dorset DT11 8RH. *T:* (01258) 482082.

**BADDELEY, Prof. Alan David,** CBE 1999; PhD; FRS 1993; FBA 2008; Professor of Psychology, University of York, since 2003; *b* 23 March 1934; *s* of Donald and Nellie Baddeley; *m* 1964, Hilary Ann White; three *s*. *Educ:* University Coll., London (BA; Fellow, 1998); Princeton Univ. (MA); PhD Cantab, 1962. Walker Fellow, Princeton Univ., 1956–57; Scientist, MRC Applied Psychology Unit, Cambridge, 1958–67; Lectr then Reader, Sussex Univ., 1969–72; Prof. of Psychology, Stirling Univ., 1972–74; Dir, Applied Psychology Unit, MRC, Cambridge, 1974–95; Sen. Res. Fellow, Churchill Coll., Cambridge, 1988–95; Hon. Prof. of Cognitive Psychology, Cambridge Univ., 1991–95; Prof. of Psychology, Univ. of Bristol, 1995–2003. Vis. Fellow, Univ. of California, San Diego, 1970–71; Visiting Professor: Harvard Univ., 1984; Univ. of Queensland, 1990; Univ. of Texas, Austin, 1991; Fellow, Center for Advanced Study in Behavioral Scis, Stanford, 2001–02. President: Experimental Psychology Soc., 1984–86; European Soc. for Cognitive Psychology, 1986–90. Founder FMedSci 1998. Hon. FBPsS 1995. Mem., Academia Europaea, 1989; Hon. For. Mem., Amer. Acad. of Arts and Scis, 1996. Hon. DPhil Umeå, Sweden, 1991; DUniv: Stirling, 1996; Essex, 1999; Plymouth, 2000; Dr *hc* Edinburgh, 2005. Aristotle Prize, 2001; Dist. Scientific Contrib. Award, Amer. Psychol Assoc., 2001; Lifetime Achievement Award, BPsS, 2013; Award for Major Contrib. to Psychol Sci., IUPS, 2016. *Publications:* The Psychology of Memory, 1976; Your Memory: a user's guide, 1982; Working Memory, 1986; Human Memory: theory and practice, 1990; Essentials of Human Memory, 1999; Working Memory, Thought and Action, 2007; Memory, 2009, 2nd edn 2015; Working Memories: postmen, divers and the cognitive revolution, 2018. *Recreations:* walking, reading, travel. *Address:* Department of Psychology, University of York, Heslington, York YO10 5DD. *T:* (01904) 322882.

**BADDELEY, Sir John (Wolsey Beresford),** 4th Bt *cr* 1922; *b* 27 Jan. 1938; *s* of Sir John Beresford Baddeley, 3rd Bt, and Nancy Winifred (*d* 1994), *d* of late Thomas Wolsey; *S* father, 1979; *m* 1st, 1962, Sara Rosalind Crofts (marr. diss. 1992); three *d*; 2nd, 1998, Mrs

Carol Quinlan (*née* Greenham). *Educ:* Bradfield College, Berks. FCA. Qualified as Chartered Accountant, 1961. *Recreations:* inland waterways, gardening. *Heir:* kinsman Paul Allan Baddeley [*b* 15 Aug. 1948; *m* 1977, Lesley Springett; two *s*]. *Address:* Brooklands Farm, Swanwick Shore Road, Sarisbury Green, Southampton SO31 7EF. *T:* (01489) 880863.

**BADDELEY, Jonathan Andrew**; fine art auctioneer, broadcaster and author; Managing Director, Bonhams, since 2010; Director, Bonhams International, since 2016; *b* Woking, Surrey, 15 May 1952; *s* of Denis and Verney Baddeley; *m* 2007, Josephine Olley; two *s*. *Educ:* St Edmund's Sch., Canterbury; Univ. of Manchester; London Business Sch. Hd of Collectors' Dept, Sotheby's, 1972–75; Jeremy Cooper Ltd, 1975–81; Sotheby's, 1981–2001: Sen. Dir, 1990–2001; Gp Hd, Collectors' Div., 1990–2001; Hd of sothebys.com UK, Europe and Australasia, 2000–01; Man. Dir, Windsor Hse Antiques, 2001–03; Bonhams, 2003–. Guest Curator, Mariner's Mus., Newport News, USA, 1995. Expert, Antiques Roadshow, BBC TV, 1990–. *Publications:* The Birkenhead Della Robbia Pottery, 1893–1906, 1980; Nautical Antiques and Collectables, 1993, 3rd edn 2001. *Recreations:* London markets, performing arts, travel, family, scuba diving. *Address:* Bonhams, Montpelier Street, Knightsbridge, SW7 1HH. *T:* (020) 7393 3872, *Fax:* (020) 7393 3873.

**BADDELEY, Stephen John**; Director of Sport, University of Bath, since 2010; *b* 28 March 1961; *s* of William Baddeley and Barbara Isobel Baddeley (*née* Dufty); *m* 1984, Deirdre Ilene Sharman (marr. diss. 1997); one *s* one *d*; partner, Kirsten Irene Gwerder; one *s* one *d*. *Educ:* Chelsea Coll., Univ. of London (BSc 1982); Open Univ. (BA 1990). Professional badminton player, 1982–90; Dir of Coaching and Develt, Scottish Badminton Union, 1990–92; (pt-time) Manager, British Badminton Olympic Team, 1990–92; Head Coach, Nat. Badminton Centre, Lausanne, and Asst Nat. Coach for Switzerland, 1992–96; Dir of Elite Play, 1996–97, Performance Dir, 1997–99, Chief Exec., 1998–2004, Badminton Assoc. of England Ltd; Dir, Nat. Sport, Sport England, 2004–08 (Interim Chief Exec., 2006–07); Physical Activity Consultant, NHS Northants, 2008–10. Trustee: Bath Recreation Ground Trust, 2013–; SkillsActive, 2015–18. Member: Bd, Talented Athlete Scholarship Scheme, 2013–; Bd, Badminton GB Ltd, 2015– (Chair, 2016–); Council, LTA, 2016–. Mem., Gov. Bd, Royal High Sch., Bath, 2015–. *Publications:* Badminton in Action, 1988; Go and Play Badminton, 1992. *Recreations:* dog walking, swimming. *Address:* Department of Sports Development and Recreation, University of Bath, Claverton Down, Bath BA2 7AY.

**BADEN-POWELL**, family name of **Baron Baden-Powell**.

**BADEN-POWELL, 3rd Baron** *cr* 1929, of Gilwell; **Robert Crause Baden-Powell**; Bt 1922; Vice-President, Scout Association, since 1982; *b* 15 Oct. 1936; *s* of 2nd Baron and Carine Crause Baden-Powell (*née* Boardman) (*d* 1993); S father, 1962; *m* 1963, Patience Hélène Mary Batty (CBE 1986; *d* 2010). *Educ:* Bryanston (Blandford). Money broker, 1964–84; Director: City Share Trust, 1964–70; Bolton Bldg Soc., 1974–88; Managing Director: Fieldguard Ltd, 1984–; Highline Estates Ltd, 1986–95. Chief Scouts Comr, 1965–82; Pres., West Yorks Scout Council, 1972–88; Mem., 1965–, Mem. Cttee, 1972–78, Council, Scout Assoc. Mem. Council, British Quarter Horse Assoc., 1984–90 (Chm., 1990); Chm., Quarter Horse Racing UK, 1985–88. Vice Pres., Camping and Caravanning Club, 2002– (Pres., 1992–2002); Pres., Surrey Youth Focus, 2011–16. *Recreations:* horses, the arts. *Heir: b* Hon. David Michael Baden-Powell [*b* 11 Dec. 1940; *m* 1966, Joan Phillips, *d* of H. W. Berryman, Melbourne, Australia; three *s*]. *Address:* Weston Farmhouse, The Street, Albury, Surrey GU5 9AY. *T:* (01483) 205087.

**BADENOCH, David Fraser**, DM; FRCS; Hon. Consultant Urological Surgeon, St Bartholomew's and Royal London Hospitals, since 2000 (Consultant, 1988–2000); Urological Surgeon, King Edward VII Hospital for Officers, since 1996; *b* 7 Feb. 1949; 3rd *s* of late Alec Badenoch, MD, ChM, FRCS and Dr Jean Badenoch; *m* 1981, Michele Patricia Howard; two *s* two *d*. *Educ:* Marlborough Coll.; Lincoln Coll., Oxford (Rugby blue 1971; BA Animal Physiology 1970; BM BCh 1975; MA 1975; DM 1988; MCh 1988); Med. Coll., St Bartholomew's Hosp. FRCS 1979. House Surgeon, Registrar and Lectr in Surgery, St Bartholomew's Hosp., London, 1976–82; Sen. Registrar in Urology, London Hosp., 1982–87; Sen. Lectr in Urology, London Hosp. Med. Coll., London Univ., 1988–99. Surg. Lt Comdr, RNR, 1978–91. Hon. Surg., Royal Scottish Corp., 1993–2006. Vis. Prof. of Urology, Mayo Clinic, 2001. Member: British Assoc. of Urological Surgeons; Amer. Urological Assoc.; European Urological Assoc.; Société Internationale d'Urologie; British Fertility Soc.; RSocMed (Hon. Sec., 1997–99, Hon. Treas., 2000–05, Pres., 2008–09, Section of Urology); Pres., Chelsea Clin. Soc., 2011–12 (Hon. Sec., 2000–08; Trustee, 2015–19). Trustee: King Edward VII Hosp., 2009–18; London Consultants' Assoc., 2012–17. Fellow, Eur. Bd of Urology, 1995. Creevy Meml Lect., Minnesota Soc. of Urology, 2001. Trustee, Orchid Cancer Charity, 2006–. Surgitek Prize, British Assoc. of Urological Surgeons, 1987; Grand Prix, European Urological Assoc., 1988. *Publications:* Aids to Urology, 1987; contribs to textbooks and jls in urology and infertility. *Recreations:* reading, music, Rugby, opera, company of good friends. *Address:* 101 Harley Street, W1G 6AH. *T:* (020) 7935 3881. *Clubs:* Garrick, Lansdowne; Vincent's (Oxford).

**BADENOCH, (Ian) James (Forster)**; QC 1989; a Recorder, 1987–2012; a Deputy High Court Judge, 1994–2012; a President, Mental Health Review Tribunal, 2000–15; *b* 24 July 1945; *s* of Sir John Badenoch and of Anne, *d* of Prof. Lancelot Forster; *m* 1979, Marie-Thérèse Victoria Cabourn-Smith; two *s* one *d*. *Educ:* Dragon Sch., Oxford; Rugby Sch.; Magdalen Coll., Oxford (Open Scholar, Demyship; MA). Called to the Bar, Lincoln's Inn, 1968 (Hardwicke Scholar; Bencher, 2000); Mem., Inner Temple; admitted (*ad eundem*) Hong Kong Bar, 1999. Accredited Mediator, 2003–. Chm., Expert Witness Inst., 2004–13, now Chm. Emeritus. Vis. Lectr, 2016, Adjunct Prof., 2019–, Hong Kong Univ. Member: Medico-Legal Soc.; Harveian Soc. FRSocMed 2005. *Publications:* (contrib.) Medical Negligence, 1990, 4th edn 2008; Urology and the Law, 2007; articles in professional jls. *Recreations:* fossil hunting, travel, wildlife photography, the study of herons. *Address:* 1 Crown Office Row, Temple, EC4Y 7HH. *T:* (020) 7797 7500.

**BADENOCH, Kemi**; MP (C) Saffron Walden, since 2017; Parliamentary Under-Secretary of State, Department for Education, since 2019; *b* London, 1980; *d* of Dr Femi Adegoke and Prof. Feyi Adegoke; *m* 2012, Hamish Badenoch; one *s* two *d*. *Educ:* Univ. of Sussex (MEng Computer Systems Engrg 2003); Birkbeck Coll., Univ. of London (LLB 2009). Consultant Business Analyst, Logica CMG, 2003–06; Associate Dir, Coutts & Co., 2006–13; Digital Dir, Spectator Mag., 2015–16. Mem. (C), London Assembly, GLA, Sept. 2015–2017. Mem., Justice Cttee, H of C, 2017–. *Address:* House of Commons, SW1A 0AA.

**BADER, David John**; Director, Social Justice and Regeneration, Welsh Assembly Government, 2003–05; *b* 26 July 1945; *s* of Erling David Bader and Sybil Mary Bader (*née* Lewis); *m* 1969, Hilary Mary Organ; one *s* one *d*. *Educ:* Newport High Sch. for Boys. FCIH 1975. Dir, Housing and Architectural Services, Newport CBC, 1972–89; Dep. Chief Exec., Housing for Wales (Tai Cymru), 1989–98; Dir, Housing, Welsh Assembly Govt, 1998–2003. Mem., Ind. Remuneration Panel for Wales, 2008–. Director: Somer Housing Gp Ltd, 2005–10; Newport Housing Trust Ltd, 2008–; Arloes Ltd, 2011–. Trustee: Wales Community Fire Safety Trust, 2003–05; Somer Community Housing Trust, 2005–11 (Chm., 2005). *Recreations:* golf, classic car restoration, bidding on eBay, gardening, cinema, reading. *Address:* 20 Groves Road, Newport NP20 3SP. *Club:* Newport Golf.

**BADGE, Sir Peter (Gilmour Noto)**, Kt 1998; Chief Metropolitan Stipendiary Magistrate, 1992–97; a District Judge (Magistrates' Courts) (formerly Stipendiary Magistrate, Devon), 1997–2002; *b* 20 Nov. 1931; *s* of late Ernest Desmond Badge, LDS and Marie Benson Badge (*née* Clough); *m* 1956, Mary Rose Noble; four *d*. *Educ:* Univ. of Liverpool (LLB). National Service, 1956–58: RNVR, lower deck and commnd; UK, ME and FE; RNR, 1958–62. Solicitor, 1956; Mem., Solicitor's Dept, New Scotland Yard, 1958–61; Asst Solicitor and later Partner, 1961–75, Kidd, Rapinet, Badge & Co.; Notary Public; Metropolitan Stipendiary Magistrate, 1975–97; a Recorder, 1980–92, 1997–99; a Chm., Inner London Juvenile Panel, 1979–97; Pres., Mental Health Review Tribunals, 1997–2003. Member: Lord Chancellor's Adv. Cttee for Inner London, 1983–97; Magisterial Cttee, Judicial Studies Bd, 1985–90; Chm., Legal Cttee, Magistrates' Assoc., 1990–93. Mem., Basket Makers' Assoc., 1987–2002; Pres., Coracle Soc., 1997– (Chm., 1985–97); Chm., Binney Meml Awards Cttee, 1992–97. Mem. Bd of Green Cloth, Verge of the Palaces of St James's, Whitehall etc, 1992–2003. Liveryman, Co. of Basket Makers, 1995–2001. Contested (L) Windsor and Maidenhead, 1964. *Publications:* Coracles of the World, 2009; articles on coracles.

**BADGE, Robin Howard L.**; see Lovell-Badge.

**BADGER, Prof. Anthony John**, PhD; Master of Clare College, Cambridge, 2003–14; Paul Mellon Professor of American History, Cambridge University, 1992–2014; *b* 6 March 1947; *s* of Kenneth Badger and Iris G. (*née* Summerill); *m* 1979, Ruth Catherine Davis; two *s*. *Educ:* Cotham Grammar Sch.; Sidney Sussex Coll., Cambridge (BA, MA; Hon. Fellow, 2003); Hull Univ. (PhD). Department of History, Newcastle University: Lectr, 1971–81; Sen. Lectr, 1981–91; Prof., 1991; Fellow, Sidney Sussex Coll., Cambridge, 1992–2003. Ind. Reviewer for migration of FCO Colonial Admin files, 2011–. Chm., Kennedy Meml Trust, 2009–. Hon. Fellow, Brit. Assoc. for Amer. Studies, 2013; Jubilee Fellow, HA, 2015. Hon. DLitt Hull, 1999; Hon. DHumLit North Carolina State, 2013. *Publications:* Prosperity Road: the New Deal, North Carolina and tobacco, 1980; North Carolina and the New Deal, 1981; The New Deal: the Depression years, 1989; (ed jtly) The Making of Martin Luther King and the Civil Rights Movement, 1996; (ed jtly) Southern Landscapes, 1996; Race and War: Lyndon Johnson and William Fulbright, 2000; (ed jtly) Contesting Democracy: substance and structure in American political history 1775–2000, 2001; New Deal/New South, 2007; FDR: the first hundred days, 2008. *Recreations:* walking, supporting Bristol Rovers.

**BADHAM, Prof. Paul Brian Leslie**; Professor of Theology and Religious Studies, University of Wales, Lampeter, 1991–2010, now Emeritus Professor, University of Wales Trinity St David; *b* 26 Sept. 1942; *s* of Rev. Leslie Badham, QHC and Effie (*née* Garrett); *m* 1969, Dr Linda Frances Elson; one *s*. *Educ:* Reading Sch.; Jesus Coll., Oxford (BA 1965; MA 1969); Jesus Coll., Cambridge (BA 1968; MA 1972); Westcott House, Cambridge; Univ. of Birmingham (PhD 1973). Divinity Master, Churcher's Coll., Petersfield, 1965–66; ordained deacon, 1968, priest, 1969; Curate: Edgbaston, 1968–69; Rubery, 1969–73; St David's University College, Lampeter, then University of Wales, Lampeter: Lectr, 1973–83; Sen. Lectr, 1983–88; Reader, 1988–91; Chm. of Church History, 1982–86; Chm. of Religion and Ethics, 1987–91; Dean, Faculty of Theology, 1991–97; Hd, Dept of Theology and Religious Studies, 1991–99; Hd, Sch. of Anthropology, Classics, Philosophy, Theology and Religious Studies, 1999–2002. Chm., Subject Panel for Theology and Religious Studies, Univ. of Wales, 1998–2003; Sec., Assoc. of Univ. Depts of Theology and Religious Studies, 1990–94. Sen. Res. Fellow, Ian Ramsey Centre, Oxford, 2004–07. Member: Res. Panel for Philosophy, Law and Religious Studies, AHRB, 1999–2003; Benchmarking Panel for Theology and Religious Studies, QAA, 1999–2000 (Subject Reviewer, 2000–02). Dir, Alister Hardy Religious Experience Res. Centre, 2002–10 (Trustee, 1997–2002); Hon. Sec., Alister Hardy Trust, 2010–13. Vice-Pres., Modern Church (formerly Modern Churchpeople's Union), 2001– (Mem. Council, 1974–95). Patron, Dignity in Dying, 2006–. FRSocMed 2007. Ed., Modern Believing, 2006–11. *Publications:* Christian Beliefs about Life after Death, 1976; (with Linda Badham) Immortality or Extinction?, 1982; (ed jtly) Death and Immortality in the Religions of the World, 1987; (ed jtly) Perspectives on Death and Dying, 1987; (ed) Religion, State and Society in Modern Britain, 1989; (ed) A John Hick Reader, 1990; (ed) Ethics on the Frontiers of Human Existence, 1992; The Christian Understanding of God and Christ in Relation to True Pure-Land Buddhism, 1994; (ed jtly) Facing Death, 1996; The Contemporary Challenge of Modernist Theology, 1998; (with Xinzhong Yao) Religious Experience in Contemporary China, 2007; Is there a Christian Case for Assisted Dying?, 2009; A Christianity that Can be Believed, 2009; (ed) Verdict on Jesus, 2010; Making Sense of Death and Immortality, 2013; (ed) Assisted Dying: for and against, 2015; Thinking about Death and Immortality, 2015; contribs to jls. *Address:* 11 Petherton Mews, Llantrisant Road, Llandaff, Cardiff CF5 2SJ. *T:* 07968 626902. *E:* pblbadham@hotmail.com.

**BAGCHI, Andrew Kumar**; QC 2015; *b* Wakefield, W Yorks, 10 Dec. 1965; *s* of Dr Saral Bagchi and Angela Bagchi; *m* 2001, Carol Ann Teague; one *s*. *Educ:* Queen Elizabeth Grammar Sch., Wakefield; King's Coll. London (LLB Law). Called to the Bar, Middle Temple, 1989; in practice as a barrister, specialising in family law and court of protection. *Publications:* (contrib.) DIY Divorce and Separation: the expert guide to representing yourself, 2014. *Recreations:* cricket, golf, electronica, LUFC. *Address:* 1GC, 10 Lincoln's Inn Fields, WC2A 3BP. *E:* bagchi@1gc.com.

**BAGGE, Sir (John) Jeremy (Picton)**, 7th Bt *cr* 1867, of Stradsett Hall, Norfolk; DL; *b* 21 June 1945; *s* of Sir John Bagge, 6th Bt, ED, DL and Elizabeth Helena (*d* 1996), *d* of late Daniel James Davies, CBE; S father, 1990; *m* 1979, Sarah Margaret Phipps, *d* of late Maj. James Shelley Phipps Armstrong; two *s* one *d*. *Educ:* Eton. FCA 1968. Hon. Alderman, King's Lynn, 1995. DL Norfolk, 1996; High Sheriff, Norfolk, 2003–04. Pres., Royal Norfolk Show, 2010. *Heir: s* Alfred James John Bagge [*b* 1 July 1980; *m* 2009, Charlotte, *d* of Stanley Stride; two *s* one *d*]. *Address:* Marham House, Marham, King's Lynn, Norfolk PE33 9HS.

**BAGGINI, Dr Julian Guiseppe**; freelance writer, since 2000; Academic Director, Royal Institute of Philosophy, since 2019; *b* 1968. *Educ:* Harvey Grammar Sch.; Univ. of Reading (BA Hons Philosophy); University Coll. London (PhD Philosophy 1996). Co-Founder and Ed., The Philosophers' Mag., 1997–2010. *Publications:* Philosophy: key texts, 2002, 2nd edn (with G. Southwell), 2012; Philosophy: key themes, 2002, 2nd edn (with G. Southwell), 2012; (with P. S. Fosl) The Philosopher's Toolkit, 2002, 2nd edn 2010; Making Sense: philosophy behind the headlines, 2002; Atheism: a very short introduction, 2003; (ed with J. Stangroom) What Philosophers Think, 2003; (ed with J. Stangroom) Great Thinkers A-Z, 2004; What's It All About: philosophy and the meaning of life, 2004; The Pig That Wants to be Eaten, 2005; (with J. Stangroom) Do You Think What You Think You Think, 2006; Welcome to Everytown: a journey into the English mind, 2007; (with P. S. Fosl) The Ethics Toolkit, 2007; (ed with J. Stangroom) What More Philosophers Think, 2007; Complaint, 2008; The Duck That Won the Lottery, 2008 (pbk edn as Do They Think You're Stupid, 2010); Should You Judge This Book By Its Cover, 2009; (jtly) 30-

Second Philosophies, 2010; The Ego Trick, 2011; (with N. Choksi) Really Really Big Questions About Faith, 2011; (with A. Macaro) The Shrink and the Sage: a guide to modern dilemmas, 2012; The Big Questions: Ethics, 2012; Philosophy: all that matters, 2012; The Virtues of the Table: how to eat and think, 2014; Freedom Regained, 2015; The Edge of Reason: a rational skeptic in an irrational world, 2016; A Short History of Truth, 2017; How The World Thinks: a global history of philosophy, 2018. *Address:* c/o David Higham Associates, 7th Floor, Waverley House, 7–12 Noel Street, W1F 8GQ. *E:* julian@julianbaggini.com.

**BAGLIN, Richard John;** Chairman, Greenwich Healthcare NHS Trust, 1995–2000 (Director, 1993–2000); *b* 30 Oct. 1942; *s* of F. W. and C. C. Baglin; *m* 1964, Anne Christine; one d. *Educ:* Preston Manor County Grammar Sch.; St John's Coll., Cambridge (MA). Various posts with Abbey National BS, later Abbey National plc, 1964–93: Gen. Man., 1981–88; Dir, various subsidiaries, 1987–93; Man. Dir, New Businesses, 1988–92. Gov., Greenwich Univ., 2001–10. Chm., Greenwich Soc., 2010–16. DUniv Greenwich, 2011. *Recreations:* theatre, the arts. *Address:* 2 Feathers Place, Greenwich, SE10 9NE. *T:* (020) 8858 9895.

**BAGNALL, Air Chief Marshal Sir Anthony (John Crowther),** GBE 2003 (OBE 1982); KCB 1998 (CB 1994); Vice-Chief of Defence Staff, 2001–05; *b* 8 June 1945; *s* of Maurice Arthur Bagnall and Marjorie (*née* Crowther); *m* 1970, Pamela Diane Wilson; one *s* two *d*. *Educ:* Stretford Grammar Sch. RAF Coll., Cranwell, 1964; Flight Comdr, 5 Sqn, 1975; Advanced Staff College, 1978; Sqn Comdr, 43 Sqn, 1983, 23 Sqn, 1985; Dir, Air Staff Briefing and Co-ordination, 1985; Station Comdr, RAF Leuchars, 1987; RCDS 1990; Dir, Air Force Staff Duties, 1991; ACAS, 1992; AOC No 11 Gp, 1994; Dep. C-in-C, AFCENT, 1996–98; Air Mem. for Personnel, and AOC-in-C, Personnel and Trng Comd, 1998–2000; C-in-C Strike Comd, 2000–01; Air ADC to the Queen, 2000–01. Mem. Ct, St Andrews Univ., 2005–13. *Recreations:* golf, bridge, fell walking. *Club:* Royal Air Force.

**BAGNALL, Kenneth Reginald;** QC 1973; QC (Hong Kong) 1983; Chairman, The New Law Publishing Co. plc, 1993; Editor-in-Chief, New Property Cases, 1986; *b* 26 Nov. 1927; *s* of Reginald and Elizabeth Bagnall; *m* 1st, 1955, Margaret Edith Wall; one *s* one *d*; 2nd, 1963, Rosemary Hearn; one *s* one *d*. *Educ:* King Edward VI Sch., Birmingham; Univ. of Birmingham (LLB Hons). Yardley Scholar. Served Royal Air Force; Pilot Officer, 1947, Flt Lt, 1948. Called to the Bar, Gray's Inn, 1950; a Dep. Judge of Crown Court, 1975–83. Co-founder, 1980, Chm., 1980–82, and Life Gov., 1983, Anglo-American Real Property Inst. Mem., Crafts Council, 1982–85; Co-founder, Bagnall Gall., Crafts Council, 1982. Founder: The New Law Fax Reporting Service, 1992; Internat. Legal Index Online, 2006; Founder and Designer, New Law Online, 1995; Co-founder and Consultant, Law Alert Ltd, 1999. Mem., Inst. of Dirs. Freeman, City and Corp. of London, 1972; Freeman and Liveryman, Barber-Surgeons' Co., 1972. *Publications:* Guide to Business Tenancies, 1956; Atkins Court Forms and Precedents (Town Planning), 1973; (with K. Lewison) Development Land Tax, 1978; Judicial Review, 1985. *Recreations:* yachting, motoring, travel. *Address:* Flat 16, Eversley Court, St Anne's Road, Eastbourne BN21 2BS. *Clubs:* 1900, United and Cecil.

**BAGNALL, Peter Hill,** CBE 1999; DL; Chairman, Oxford Radcliffe Hospitals NHS Trust, 1993–2000; *b* 8 Oct. 1931; *s* of Reginald Stuart Bagnall and Mary Adelaide (*née* Hill); *m* 1st, 1955, Edith Ann Wood (marr. diss. 1979); one *s* one *d* (and one *s* decd); 2nd, 1979, Diana Elizabeth Rayner. *Educ:* Newcastle-under-Lyme Sch.; St Catharine's Coll., Cambridge (MA). Nat. Service and TA Commns, N Staffs Regt. Dir, W. H. Smith & Son Ltd, 1968–88; Dir and Man. Dir, W. H. Smith PLC, 1974–88, retd; Chm., Book Club Associates, 1972–88; Director: Book Tokens Ltd, 1975–2000; W. H. Smith Pension Trustees Ltd, 1979–2002; TSB/Trustcard, 1986–89; The Book Trust, 1986–93 (Chm., 1989–91); Longman/Ladybird Books, 1987–90; British Museum Co., 1988–2000; Blackwell Ltd, Oxford, 1989–96. Dir, Oxon HA, 1989–93. Trustee, Radcliffe Med. Foundn, 1993–2003; Chm., Oxford Radcliffe Hosps Charitable Funds, 2003–. Mem., Vis. Cttee, Open Univ., 1988–92; Chm. Govs and Pro-Chancellor, Oxford Brookes Univ., 1993–98 (Gov., 1988–98). Mem. Council, St Luke's Hospital, Oxford, 2003–14. DL Oxfordshire, 1995. Hon. LLD Oxford Brookes, 1998. *Recreations:* book collecting, theatre, travel. *Address:* Orchard House, Buckland, Faringdon, Oxon SN7 8QW. *Club:* Sloane.

**BAGOT,** family name of **Baron Bagot**.

**BAGOT,** 10th Baron *cr* 1780, of Bagot's Bromley, co. Stafford; **Charles Hugh Shaun Bagot;** Bt 1627; *b* 23 Feb. 1944; *s* of 9th Baron Bagot and of Muriel Patricia (*née* Moore-Boyle); *S* father, 2001; *m* 1986, Mrs Sally A. Stone, *d* of D. G. Blunden; one d. *Heir:* kinsman Julian William D'Arcy Bagot, *b* 24 Dec. 1943. *Address:* 16 Barclay Road, SW6 1EH.

**BAGOT, Charles Richard Milo;** QC 2018; a Recorder, since 2018; *b* Amersham, 27 May 1973; *s* of Christopher Bagot and Jennifer Bagot; *m* 2003, Nina Hills; one *s* one *d*. *Educ:* Dr Challoner's Grammar Sch.; Université Jean Moulin Lyon III (Dip. French Law 1995); Univ. of Leicester (LLB Law with French 1996). Called to the Bar, Inner Temple, 1997; barrister, Hardwicke, London, 1999–; a Dep. Dist Judge, 2010–18; a Dep. Queen's Bench Master, High Court, 2015–. Mem., Bar Disciplinary Tribunal Panel, 2012– (Chm., 2018). Member, Editorial Board: Kemp and Kemp: the Quantum of Damages, 2012–; Personal Injuries and Quantum Reports, 2015–. *Recreations:* open water swimming, British Swimming judge.

**BAGRI, Hon. Apurv;** President and Chief Executive Officer (formerly Managing Director), Metdist Group, since 1980; *b* 11 Nov. 1959; *s* of Baron Bagri, CBE; *m* 1982, Alka Rakyan; two d. *Educ:* University Coll. Sch., London; Cass Business Sch., London (BSc Business Admin 1980); Wharton Univ. (AMP 1993). Dir, Bagri Foundn, 1990–. Mem., Crown Estate Paving Commn, 1996–; non-exec. Dir and Mem. Bd, Royal Parks, 2003–17 (non-exec. Chm., 2008–17). Member, Board: Dubai FSA, 2004– (Dep. Chm., 2017–); Hong Kong Exchanges and Clearing Ltd, 2016–. Mem. Bd, Internat. Wrought Copper Council, 2000– (Chm., 2002–04). Mem. Bd, HEFCE, 2014–18. Vis. Prof., Cass Business Sch., London, 2004–. Member: Governing Council, City Univ., 2002–12 (Dep. Pro-Chancellor and Acting Chm. of Council, 2009; Pro-Chancellor and Chm. of Council, 2009–12; Hon. Rector, 2012–); Bd of Govs, London Business Sch., 2003– (Dep. Chm., 2006–14; Chm., 2014–); Corp., University Coll. Sch., 2000–. Trustee: Asia House, 2000–; Royal Parks Foundn, 2003–12. Mem., Adv. Bd, UK India Business Council (formerly Indo-British Partnership), 2009–11 (Mem. Bd, 2004–09). Hon. Fellow, London Business Sch., 2013. Hon. DSc City, 2006. *Recreations:* watching cricket, travel, reading. *Address:* Metdist Enterprises Ltd, 80 Cannon Street, EC4N 6EJ. *T:* (020) 7280 0000, *Fax:* (020) 7606 6650. *Club:* MCC.

**BAGSHAW, Prof. Michael,** FFOM; FRAeS; FRSB; Professor of Aviation Medicine, King's College London, 2005–08, now Emeritus; Associate Director, Jarvis Bagshaw Ltd, since 2012; *b* 9 July 1946; *s* of Robert and Alice Bagshaw; *m* 1970, Penelope Isaac; two d. *Educ:* Welsh Nat. Sch. of Medicine, Cardiff (MB BCh 1973); MRCS, LRCP 1973; DAvMed 1980; MFOM 1982, FFOM 2003; DFFP 1995; FRAeS 1995; FRSB 2015. Airline Transport Pilot's Licence; CAA Flying Examr. Clerical Asst, Architect's Dept, Swansea BC, 1966; Technical Photographer, Univ. of Swansea, 1967; medical student, Cardiff, 1967–70; RAF, 1970–86: Med. Br., 1970–75; Fast Jet Pilot (Hunter, Jaguar), 1975–78; Flying Instr, RAF Coll., Cranwell, 1978–80; Sen. Med. Officer Pilot, RAF Inst. of Aviation Medicine, 1980–86; Locum Consultant in Neuro-Otology, St George's Hosp., London, 1987; Principal, General Practice, Crowthorne, 1987–90; Establt MO, DERA, Farnborough, 1990–92; Sen. Aviation Physician, 1992–97, Hd of Med. Services, 1997–2004, British Airways. Hon. civilian consultant advr in aviation medicine to the Army, 2003–; Aeromedical Advr, Airbus, 2005–18. Vis. Prof., Cranfield Univ., 2005–. Pres., Aerospace Med. Assoc., 2005–06; Chm., UK Gen. Aviation Safety Council, 2018–. Lectures: Guest Technology, Royal Society, 1996; Armstrong, Aerospace Med. Assoc., 2014. Liveryman, Hon. Co. of Air Pilots (formerly GAPAN), 1992– (Award of Merit, 1997). Clarkson Trophy, RAF, 1978; Buchanan Barbour Award, RAeS, 1984; Louis H. Bauer Founders Award, Aerospace Med. Assoc., 2008; Allard Medal, Internat. Acad. of Aviation and Space Medicine, 2009; Boothby-Edwards Award, Aerospace Med. Assoc., 2011; Guthrie Meml Medal, RAMC, 2016. *Publications:* Human Performance and Limitations in Aviation, 1991; (contrib.) Principles and Practice of Travel Medicine, 2001; (contrib.) Oxford Textbook of Medicine, 2002; (contrib.) Ernsting's Aviation Medicine, 2007; (contrib.) Fundamentals of Aerospace Medicine, 2008; (contrib.) Occupational and Environmental Lung Diseases, 2010; papers and articles on aviation medicine. *Recreations:* violinist; bass singer, Royal Meml Chapel, Sandhurst; general aviation (flying instructor and examiner). *Address:* 3 Bramley Grove, Crowthorne, Berks RG45 6EB. *T:* (01344) 775647. *Club:* Royal Air Force.

**BAGSHAWE, Prof. Kenneth Dawson,** CBE 1990; MD; FRCP, FRCOG; FRCR; FRS 1989; Professor of Medical Oncology in the University of London at Imperial College School of Medicine (formerly Charing Cross Hospital Medical School, later Charing Cross and Westminster Medical School), 1974–90, now Emeritus; Hon. Consultant Physician, Charing Cross Hospital, since 1990 (Consultant Physician, 1961–90); *b* 17 Aug. 1925; *s* of Harry Bagshawe and Gladys (*née* Dawson); *m* 1st, 1946, Ann Kelly (marr. diss. 1976); she *d* 2000); one *s* one *d*; 2nd, 1977, Sylvia Dorothy Lawler (*née* Corben) (*d* 1996); 3rd, 1998, Surinder Kanta Sharma. *Educ:* Harrow County Sch.; London Sch. of Econs and Pol Science; St Mary's Hosp. Med. Sch. (MB, BS 1952; MD 1964). FRCP 1969; FRCR 1983; FRCOG *ad eundem* 1978. Served RN, 1942–46. Fellow, Johns Hopkins Univ., Baltimore, USA, 1955–56; Sen. Registrar, St Mary's Hosp., 1956–60. Visiting Professor: Down State Univ., NY, 1977; Univ. of Hong Kong, 1982, 1994. Chm., DHSS Wkg Gp on Acute Cancer Services, 1980–84. Cancer Research Campaign: Chm., Scientific Cttee, 1983–88; Chm., Exec. Cttee, 1988–90; Vice Chm. Bd, 1988–2002. Chm., Aepact Ltd, 1996–2000. Hon. FRSocMed 1993. Hon. DSc Bradford, 1990. Galen Medal, London Soc. of Apothecaries, 1993. *Publications:* Choriocarcinoma, 1969; Medical Oncology, 1975; 300 papers on cancer chemotherapy, tumour markers, drug targeting and antibody-directed enzyme prodrug therapy, etc. *Recreations:* (passive) music, art; (active) walking, travel, conservation. *Address:* 115 George Street, W1H 7HF. *T:* (020) 7262 8479. *Club:* Athenæum.

**BAGSHAWE, Louise;** *see* Mensch, L.

**BAGULEY, Adrian Duncan;** Director, Air Support, Defence Equipment and Support, Ministry of Defence, since 2015; *b* Thurso, Caithness, 29 Sept. 1964; *s* of Geoffrey and Barbara Baguley; *m* 1998, Rachel Bould; one s. *Educ:* Culcheth High Sch.; Imperial Coll. London (BEng 1987). CEng 1991; MIMechE 1991. Ministry of Defence: Engrg Trainee, 1987–88; Project Manager, DERA, 1988–90; Operational Analyst, Defence Operational Analysis Gp, Rheindhalen, 1990–92; Middle East Desk Officer, Overseas Secretariat, 1992–94; Avionics Lead, Eurofighter Directorate, 1994–97; Section Leader, Avionics, NATO Eurofighter and Tornado Mgt Agency, Munich, 1997–99; Private Sec. to Chief Scientific Advr, MoD, 1999–2002; Counsellor, Defence Sci. and Technol., British Embassy, Washington, DC, 2002–05; Hd, Helicopters 2, 2005–11, Dir, Helicopters, 2011–15, Defence Equipment and Support, MoD. *Recreations:* golf, photography.

**BAGWELL, Air Marshal Gregory Jack,** CB 2012; CBE 2007; Executive Vice President, Business Development, Cobham, since 2018 (Strategic Adviser, 2017); *b* Dartford, Kent, 6 Oct. 1961; *s* of Jack Bagwell and Maureen Bagwell; *m* 1989, Scarlett van Gelder; three *s* one d. *Educ:* Tonbridge Sch.; Univ. of Madras (MSc Defence and Politics). Royal Air Force: pilot, 1982–2016; OC IX (B) Sqdn, 1999–2004; Station Comdr, RAF Marham, 2004–07; Plans Dir, Perm. Jt HQ Northwood, 2007–09; AOC No 1 Gp, 2009–11; COS Jt Warfare Develt, 2011–13; Dep. Comdr Ops, HQ Air Comd, 2013–16. Pres., Air Power Assoc., 2016–. *Recreations:* cricket, golf.

**BAHL, Kamlesh, (Mrs N. Lakhani),** CBE 1997; Chief Executive, Lotus Resolutions Ltd, since 2009; Vice-President, Law Society, 1999–2000; *b* 28 May 1956; *d* of Swinder Nath Bahl and Leela Wati Bahl; *m* 1986, Dr Nitin Lakhani. *Educ:* Univ. of Birmingham (LLB 1977). Admitted Solicitor, 1980. GLC, 1978–81; BSC, 1981–84; Texaco Ltd, 1984–87; Data Logic Ltd: Legal and Commercial Manager, 1987–89; Company Sec. and Manager, Legal Services, 1989–93. Chm., EOC, 1993–98. Mem., Barnet HA, 1989–90; non-exec. Dir, Parkside HA, 1990–93. Law Society: Chm., Commerce and Industry Gp, 1988–89; Mem. Council, 1990–2000 and 2003. Member: Justice Sub-Cttee on Judiciary, 1991–92; Ethnic Minorities Adv. Cttee and Tribunals Cttee (Cttees of Lord Chancellor's Judicial Studies Bd), 1991–94; Council and Standing Cttee on HAs, NAHAT, 1993–94; Council, Justice, 1993–94. Ind. Mem., Diplomatic Service Appeal Bd, FCO, 1993–99. Bd Mem., London Transport, 1999–2003. EC Rep., EC Consultative Commn on Racism and Xenophobia, 1994–97; Vice Pres., Eur. Adv. Cttee on Equal Opportunities, 1998. Mem. Council, Scout Assoc., 1996–99. Mem. Council, Open Univ., 1999; Gov., Univ. of Westminster, 1997–2003. Foundn Gov., Krishna-Avanti Primary Sch., 2008. FRSA. Hon. Fellow, Liverpool John Moores Univ., 1998. Hon. MA North London, 1997; Hon. LLD: De Montfort, 1998; Birmingham, 1999; Hon. DCL Northumbria, 1999. *Publications:* (ed) Managing Legal Practice in Business, 1989. *Recreations:* swimming, dancing, travelling, theatre.

**BAILES, Christopher Peter;** horticulturist; Curator, Chelsea Physic Garden, 2011–14; *b* London, 3 April 1951; *s* of Charles Robert and Irene Francis Bailes; *m* 2003, Sue Lee; three *s* one d. *Educ:* Brockley Co. Grammar Sch.; Merrist Wood Coll. (Nat. Cert. Hort. 1976); Royal Botanic Gdns, Kew (Dip. Hort. Hons 1979). Supervisor, Tropical Section, Royal Botanic Gdns, Kew, 1979–85; Manager, Eric Young Orchid Foundn, 1985–88; Curator: RHS Garden, Rosemoor, 1988–2010; RHS Regl Gardens, 1995–2001. Ed., Orchid Rev., 1985–89. Mem., Orchid Cttee, 2011–17, Bursaries Cttee, 2013–, Gardens Cttee, 2015–16, RHS. President: Plant Heritage Devon Gp, 2008–; Alpine Garden Soc., 2017–; Patron, Professional Gardeners' Trust, 2008–. FCIHort (FIHort 2000). Gold Veitch Meml Medal, RHS, 2011. *Publications:* Orchids… and how to grow them, 1987; (with P. J. Cribb) Hardy Orchids, 1989; (with P. J. Cribb) Orchids: a guide to cultivation, 1993; Hollies for Gardeners, 2007; contrib. articles and papers on orchids and gen. horticulture to jls incl. The Garden, Orchid Rev., Curtis' Botanical Mag. *Address:* 21 Highfield, Northam, Bideford, Devon EX39 1BB.

**BAILEY,** family name of **Baron Glanusk**.

**BAILEY, Adrian Edward;** MP (Lab Co-op) West Bromwich West, since Nov. 2000; b 11 Dec. 1945; s of Edward Arthur Bailey and Sylvia Alice Bailey; m 1989, Jill Patricia Millard (née Hunscott); one step s. Educ: Cheltenham Grammar Sch.; Univ. of Exeter (BA Hons Econ. Hist.); Loughborough Coll. of Librarianship (Post Grad. DipLib). Librarian, Cheshire CC, 1971–82; Pol Organiser, Co-op Party, 1982–2000. Mem. (Lab), Sandwell MBC, 1991–2000 (Dep. Leader, 1997–2000). Contested (Lab): S Worcs, 1970; Nantwich, Feb. and Oct. 1974; Wirral, March 1976; Cheshire W, EP, 1979. Recreations: supporting Cheltenham Town FC, cricket, dog walking. Address: House of Commons, SW1A 0AA; 181 Oakham Road, Tividale, Oldbury, W Midlands B69 1PZ.

**BAILEY, Sir Alan (Marshall),** KCB 1986 (CB 1982); Permanent Secretary, Department of Transport, 1986–91; b 26 June 1931; s of John Marshall Bailey and Muriel May Bailey; m 1st, 1959, Stella Mary Scott (marr. diss. 1981); three s; 2nd, 1981, Shirley Jane Barrett. Educ: Bedford Sch.; St John's and Merton Colls, Oxford (MA, BPhil; Hon. Fellow, St John's Coll., 1991). Harmsworth Senior Scholarship, 1954; Harkness Commonwealth Fellowship, USA, 1963–64. Principal Private Sec. to Chancellor of the Exchequer, 1971–73; Under-Sec., HM Treasury, 1973–78, Dep. Sec., 1978–83 (Central Policy Review Staff, Cabinet Office, 1981–82), 2nd Perm. Sec., 1983–85. Board Mem., London Transport, 1991–2000. Hon. Treas., Hist. of Parliament Trust, 1994–2011. Address: 56 Greenfell Mansions, Glaisher Street, SE8 3EU.

**BAILEY, Prof. Allen Jackson,** FRSC; Professor of Biochemistry, University of Bristol, 1980–96, now Emeritus; b 31 Jan. 1931; s of late Horace Jackson Bailey and Mabel Bailey (née Young); m 1956, Beryl Lee; twin s two d. Educ: Eccles Grammar Sch.; BSc London (Chem.) 1954; MSc (Physics) 1958, PhD (Chem.) 1960, Birmingham; MA 1967, ScD 1973, Cambridge. FIFST. Shell Chemicals, 1954–57; Low Temp. Res. Station, Univ. of Cambridge, 1960–67; Harkness Fellow, Commonwealth Fund, USA, 1963–65; joined AFRC Meat Res. Inst., Bristol, 1967: SPSO (Special Merit), 1972; Head of Biochem. Dept, 1977–79; Director (DCSO), 1979–85; Hd of Lab., AFRC Inst. of Food Res., Bristol, 1985–90; Hd of Collagen Res. Gp, Bristol Univ., 1991–2001. Visiting Professor: São Paulo Univ., 1991; UCL, 2004–10. Scott Robertson Meml Lectr, QUB, 1986; Proctor Meml Lectr, Leeds, 1991. Hon. Fellow, British Connective Tissue Soc.; Hon. FRCP 2003. Senior Medal Food Science, RSC, 1987; Internat. Lectureship Award, Amer. Meat Sci. Assoc., 1989. Mem. Edıtl Bds, sci. jls. Publications: Recent Advances in Meat Science, 1985; Collagen as a Food, 1987; Connective Tissue in Meat and Meat Products, 1989; Elastomeric Proteins, 2003; sci. papers in learned jls. Recreations: travel, photography, painting. Address: 14A Well Close, Winscombe, N Somerset BS25 1HG. T: (01934) 843447.

**BAILEY, Anthony John James,** OBE 2008; Chairman, Anthony Bailey Ltd, since 2015; Special Economic Envoy of Government of Antigua and Barbuda to European Union, since 2015; b London, 13 Jan. 1970; s of late Colin Bailey and Veronica Bailey (née Riggs); m 2007, Princess Marie-Therese von Hohenberg (marr. diss. 2018; annulled, 2019); one s. Educ: Douay Martyrs Sch., Ickenham; University Coll. London (BA Hons Contemp. East Eur. Studies 1991). MCIPR 1997. Sen. Account Dir, Burson-Marsteller, 1991–95; Prog. Manager, Mgt Communications EMEA, IBM, 1995–96; Sen. Counsellor, Manning, Selvage & Lee Ltd, 1995–96; Chm., Eligo Internat. Ltd, 1997–2016. Special Counsel to Prince Khalid Al-Faisal, Gov. of Makkah Reg., Saudi Arabia, 1999–2012; Delegate for GB and Ire., Caribbean and Inter-Religious Relns, Sacred Mil. Constantinian Order of St George, 2003–; Special Envoy of Pres. of Montenegro to Middle E and N Africa, 2010–18; Special Advr to Chm. and Bd, TIMWE, 2014–. Chm., Painting and Patronage, 1999–; Trustee and Bd Dir, United Learning Trust, 2004–14. Member: London Challenge Ministerial Adv. Gp, DfES, 2004–07; Ministerial Task Force for Gifted and Talented Educn, DCSF, 2007–10. Mem., Adv. Bd, Three Faiths Forum, 2004–14; Chief Policy Advr to Bd of Dirs, Foreign Policy Centre, 2006–10. Co-Pres., British Influence, 2015–. Member: Govt House Restoration Cttee, Antigua and Barbuda, 2014–17; Govt House Restoration Cttee, Grenada, 2015–17; Chm., Portuguese Centenary Appeal, 2016–. Director: British Saudi Soc., 2002–15; Bahrain Soc., 2010–13. Governor: Douay Martyrs Sch., Ickenham, 2005–; Sheffield Springs Acad., 2006–13; Sheffield Park Acad., 2006–13; St Mary's Univ., Twickenham, 2009–16; Foundn Gov., RC Archdio. of Westminster, 2005–; Dir, Schola Foundn, London Oratory Sch., 2012–14. Dir, Waterford Mus. of Treasures, 2009–; UK Bd Mem., Co-operation Ireland, 2012–15. Mem. Council, Catholic Union of GB, 2009–15; Vice Pres., Assoc. of Papal Orders in Ireland, 2009–15; Patron, Faith Forum for London, 2014–. Sec. Gen., Royal Order of Francis I, 2014–. Member: Internat. Public Relns Assoc., 1996; Public Relns Inst. of Ireland, 2017. Freeman, City of London, 2004; Mem. Court, Guild of Freemen, 2010–17; Liveryman: Loriners' Co., 2004; Stationers' and Newspaper Makers' Co., 2015. Freedom, City of Glasgow, 2012. FRSA 2004; FRSocMed 2007. Hon. FCollT 2014. Commander: Nat. Order of Cedar (Lebanon), 2004; Royal Order of Al-Alaoui (Morocco), 2004; Knight Grand Cross: Nat. Order of Juan Mora Fernandez (Costa Rica), 2004; Pontifical Order of Pope St Sylvester (Vatican), 2008; Kt Comdr with Star, Nat. Order of Infante Dom Henrique (Portugal), 2005; First Class Grade: Order of Madara Horsemen (Bulgaria), 2007; Nat. Order of Montenegrin Flag (Montenegro), 2010; Sternberg Interfaith Gold Medallion, 2012; Grand Cordon, Order of Independence (Jordan), 2013; Grand Officer, Order of San Carlos (Colombia), 2013; Mother Teresa Humanitarian Presidential Award (Kosovo), 2014; President's Medal (Slovak Republic) 2016; KGCHS 2017. Publications: (contrib.) Travellers Tales: by members of the Travellers' Club, 1999; Painting and Patronage, 2000. Recreations: Irish history, heraldry, sleeping, global travel, Weimaraner dogs, Portugal, promoting European unity. Address: Anthony Bailey Ltd, 12 Queen's Gate Gardens, SW7 5LY. T: (020) 7591 0619. E: office@anthonybailey.org. Clubs: Travellers; Turf (Lisbon).

**BAILEY, Christopher,** CBE 2019 (MBE 2009); Chief Creative Officer, 2009–18, and President, 2017–18, Burberry Ltd (Creative Director, 2001–09; Chief Executive, 2014–17); b Yorks, 1971. Educ: Univ. of Westminster (BA 1990); Royal Coll. of Art (MA 1994; Hon. Fellow 2003). Womenswear Designer, Donna Karan, 1994–96; Sen. Designer, Womenswear, Gucci, Milan, 1996–2001. Co-Founder, Burberry Foundn, 2008–18. Hon. DLitt Westminster, 2006; Hon. DSc Huddersfield, 2007. Designer of the Year, 2005 and 2009, Menswear Designer of the Year, 2007, 2008 and 2013, British Fashion Awards; Internat. Award, Council of Fashion Designers of America, 2010.

**BAILEY, Colette Mary;** Artistic Director and Chief Executive, Metal Culture Ltd, since 2002; b Hartlepool, 13 April 1971; d of (William) John (Joseph) Bailey, qv; m 2019, Andrew Delaney; one d. Educ: English Martyrs RC Comprehensive Sch.; Cleveland Coll. of Art (Art Foundn 1990); Univ. of Newcastle-upon-Tyne (BA Hons Combined Studies 1993). Asst Ed., 1994–96, Ed., 1996, Sculpture IOB mag.; Project and Pubns Manager, The Sculpture Co., 1997–99; Man. Dir, RBS, 1999–2002. Member, Board: Southend Business Partnership Exec., 2005–; Opportunity South Essex, 2017–; SE LEP, 2017–. Mem. Bd, Wow Foundn, 2018–. Recreations: swimming, pilates, reading. Address: Metal, Chalkwell Hall, Chalkwell Avenue, Southend-on-Sea SS0 8NB. T: (01702) 470700. E: chalkwell@metalculture.com.

**BAILEY, Colin Frederick,** QPM 1993; Chief Constable, Nottinghamshire Constabulary, 1995–2000; b 17 Oct. 1943; s of late Fred Bailey and Mary (née Sivill); m 1st, 1966, Christine Lound (d 2009); one s one d; 2nd, 2012, Glenys Hayers. Educ: Queen Elizabeth's GS, Horncastle, Lincs; Univ. of Sheffield (LLB Hons). Lincolnshire Constab., 1960–86; Asst Chief Constable (Crime Ops), W Yorks Police, 1986–90; Dep. Chief Constable, Nottinghamshire Constab., 1990–95. Chairman: ACPO Race and Community Relns Sub Cttee, 1995–2000; ACPO Crime Prevention Sub Cttee, 1997–2000. Pres., Nottingham Br., RLSS, 1995–2000. Chm., E Midlands RLSS, 1998–2000. Chm., Police History Soc., 1998–2001. Pres., Carlton Male Voice Choir, 2005–. Vice Pres., Notts Br., Royal Soc. of St George, 2014–. Recreations: antique porcelain, wildlife, gardening, wine, foreign travel, Nottingham Forest FC. Address: Firs Barn, Top Street, Elston, Newark-on-Trent, Notts NG23 5NP. T: (01636) 526090.

**BAILEY, Prof. Colin Gareth,** PhD; CEng, FREng, FICE, FIStructE; President and Principal, Queen Mary University of London, since 2017; b Hillingdon, 1967; s of Norman and Iris Bailey; m 1999, Fiona Maclagan; two s one d. Educ: Abbotsfields Comprehensive Sch.; Slough Coll. (ONC); Richmond upon Thames Coll. (HNC); Univ. of Sheffield (BEng 1992; PhD 1995). CEng 2003; MIFireE 2004; FICE 2006; FIStructE 2011; FREng 2012. Trainee, technician/draughtsman, Design Dept, Lovell Construction Services Ltd, 1984–86; technician/draughtsman, Cameron Taylor Partners, Consulting Civil and Structural Engrs, 1986–88; Design Engr, Clarke Nicholls and Marcel, Consulting Civil and Structural Engrs, 1988–89; res. asst, Univ. of Sheffield, 1994–96; Sen. Engr, Steel Construction Inst., 1996–98; Principal Engr, BRE, 1998–2002; University of Manchester: Prof. of Structural Engrg, 2002–07; Hd, Sch. of Mech., Aerospace and Civil Engrg, 2007–09; Vice-Pres., and Dean, Faculty of Engrg and Physical Scis, 2009–14; Dep. Pres. and Dep. Vice Chancellor, 2014–17. Non-executive Director: Northern Consortium, 2010–17; Univ. of Manchester 13 Ltd, 2011–16; Univ. of Manchester Innovation Centre Ltd, 2011–16; Central Manchester Univ. Hosps NHS Trust, 2016–17. Member: Standing Cttee on Structural Safety, 2009–14; Expert Panel to advise on immediate safety action following Grenfell Tower fire, 2018–. Chm., Governing Bd, Knowledge Centre for Materials Chemistry, 2014–17; Mem., Adv. Bd, Manchester Mus. of Sci. and Industry, 2012–17. Trustee: Find a Better Way charity, 2011–17; RAEng, 2016–19. Associate Ed., Fire Safety Jl, 2010–14; Member, Editorial Board: Jl Steel Construction Res., 2008–11; Jl Structural Fire Engrg, 2010–. Publications: Design of Steel Framed Buildings without Applied Fire Protection, 1999; Fire Safe Design: a new approach to multi-storey-steel-framed buildings, 2000, 2nd edn 2006; New Fire Design Method for Steel Frames with Composite Floor Slabs, 2003; Guide to Evaluating Design Wind Loads to BS6399-2, 2003; Designers' Guide to EN1991-1-2, EN1992-1-2, EN1993-1-2 and EN1994-1-2, 2007; contribs to BRE Digest and Steel BRE Digest. Recreations: football, walking, family, DIY.

**BAILEY, David,** CBE 2001; FCSD; photographer, film maker; b 2 Jan. 1938; s of William Bailey and Agnes (née Green); m 1st, 1960, Rosemary Bramble; 2nd, 1967, Catherine Deneuve, qv (marr. diss.); 3rd, 1975, Marie Helvin (marr. diss. 1985); 4th, 1986, Catherine Dyer; two s one d. Educ: self taught. FRPS 1972 (Hon. FRPS 1999); FSIAD 1975. Photographer for Vogue, 1959–; dir of television commercials, 1966–, of documentaries, 1968–; director and producer: Who Dealt? (TV film), 1992; Models Close-Up (TV documentary), 1998; dir, The Intruder (film), 1999. Exhibitions: Nat. Portrait Gall., 1971; one-man retrospective, V&A, 1983; Internat. Centre of Photograph, NY, 1984; Photographs from the Sudan, ICA and tour, 1985; Bailey Now!, Nat. Centre of Photography, Bath, 1989; Hamilton's Gall., annually, 1995–; Camerawork, Berlin, 1997; Carla Sozzani Gall., Milan, 1997; Galerie Claire Fontaine, Luxembourg, 1997; A Gallery for Fine Photography, New Orleans; painting exhibn, Well Hung Gall., 1997; Barbican, 1999; Nat. Mus. of Photography, Film & TV, 1999; Modern a Museet, Stockholm, 2000; Helsinki City Art Mus., 2000; Bonham's, 2010; David Bailey: New Sculpture and Photography, Pangolin, 2010; David Bailey's East End, Compressor House, 2012; Bailey's Stardust, NPG, 2014; The Sixties, Davies Street, London, 2019. FRSA. Hon. FCGI. Hon. DLitt Bradford, 1999. D&AD President's Award, for outstanding contrib. to creativity, 1998; awards for commercials including Clios, D&AD Gold Award, Cannes Golden Lion and Emmy. RPS Centenary Medal, 2005. Publications: Box of Pinups, 1964; Goodbye Baby and Amen, 1969; Warhol, 1974; Beady Minces, 1974; Papua New Guinea, 1975; Mixed Moments, 1976; Trouble and Strife, 1980; David Bailey's London NW1, 1982; Black and White Memories, 1983; Nudes 1981–84, 1984; Imagine, 1985; If We Shadows, 1992; The Lady is a Tramp, 1995 (TV film, 1995); Rock & Roll Heroes, 1997; Models Close-Up, 1998; Archive One, 1957–69, 1999; Chasing Rainbows, 2001; (with Kate Kray) The Art of Violence, 2003; Archive Two: locations, 2003; Bailey's Democracy, 2005; Havana, 2006; NY JS DB 62, 2007; Pictures That Mark Can Do, 2007; Is that so Kid, 2008; 8 Minutes: Hirst and Bailey, 2009; Eye, 2009; Flowers, Skulls, Contacts, 2010; Sculpture +, 2010; Bailey Exposed, 2013; Bailey's Stardust, 2014; Bailey's East End, 2014; Tears and Tears, 2015; NW1, 2017; King's Cross, 2017; Bailey's Naga Hills, 2017; David Bailey, 2018; relevant publication: (with Jackie Higgins) David Bailey: Look, 2010. Recreations: aviculture, photography, travelling, painting.

**BAILEY, Ven. David Charles;** Archdeacon of Bolton, 2008–18, now Archdeacon Emeritus; b Shipley, W Yorks, 5 Dec. 1952; s of (George) Eric Bailey and Florence Violet, (Billie), Bailey; m 1978, Kathryn Ann Middleton; two s one d. Educ: Bradford Grammar Sch.; Lincoln Coll., Oxford (MSc 1977; MA 1978); St John's Coll., Nottingham (BA 1979). Ordained deacon, 1980, priest, 1981; Assistant Curate: St John's, Worksop, 1980–83; Edgware, 1983–87; Incumbent, S Cave and Ellerker with Broomfleet, York, 1987–97; Rural Dean, Howden, 1991–97; Incumbent, Beverley Minster, and Priest-in-charge, Routh, 1997–2008. Canon and Preb., York Minster, 1998–2008. Recreations: watching cricket, football (Leeds Utd), photography, music esp. jazz.

**BAILEY, David John;** QC 2006; b 6 March 1965; s of John Hardy Bailey and Joyce Marion de Havilland; m 1993, Catherine Crick; two s and one step s. Educ: Oundle Sch.; Mansfield Coll., Oxford (Eldon Schol.; BA 1st Cl. Hons); Univ. of Calif, Los Angeles (LLM). Called to the Bar, Gray's Inn, 1989; specialising in commercial law. Chm. and Dir, English Sinfonia, 2003–17. Trustee, Menat Trust, 2003–15. Mem., Old Oundelian Club. Publications: (contrib.) Insurance Disputes, 1999, 4th edn 2017. Recreations: shooting, skiing, music, theatre. Address: 7 King's Bench Walk, Temple, EC4Y 7DS. T: (020) 7583 0404, Fax: (020) 7583 0950. E: dbailey@7kbw.co.uk. Clubs: Royal Automobile, MCC.

**BAILEY, His Honour Edward Henry;** a Circuit Judge, Central London County Court, 2000–19; b 24 May 1949; s of Geoffrey Henry Bailey and Ninette Bailey; m 1983, Claire Dorothy Ann From; two d. Educ: King's Sch., Canterbury; Gonville and Caius Coll., Cambridge (MA, LLB). Called to the Bar, Middle Temple, 1970, Bencher, 2014; Lectr, Inns of Court Sch. of Law, 1970–72; in practice as barrister, 1972–2000. Mem., Judicial Wing, Insol-Europe, 2008–. Hon. Member: Pyramus and Thisbe Club, 2018; Faculty of Party Wall Surveyors, 2018. Publications: Personal Insolvency: law and practice, 1981, 4th edn 2008; Corporate Insolvency: law and practice, 1992, 5th edn 2017; Law of Voluntary Arrangements, 2003, 2nd edn 2007; (contrib.) Halsbury's Laws of England, 4th edn 1989. Recreations: music, gardening, lambing, pottering.

**BAILEY, Dame Glenda (Adrianne)**, DBE 2019 (OBE 2008); Editor-in-Chief, Harper's Bazaar, since 2001; *b* 16 Nov. 1958; *d* of late John Ernest Bailey and Constance Groome. *Educ:* Noel Baker Sch., Derby; Kingston Poly. (BA Fashion Design; Hon. MA). Editor: Honey Magazine, 1986; Folio Magazine, 1987; Marie Claire (UK edn), 1988–96; Editor-in-Chief, Marie Claire (US edn), 1996–2001. Women's Magazine Editor of the Year, 1989, 1992, Editor's Editor of the Year, 1992, BSME; Amnesty Internat. Award, 1997; Mediaweek Editor of the Year Award. Hon. PrD Derby, 2001. Chevalier, Ordre des Arts et Lettres (France), 2012. *Address:* (office) 300 West 57th Street, New York, NY 10019, USA.

**BAILEY, James Thomas;** QC 2019; *b* London, 1 Feb. 1975; *s* of Geoffrey Noel Bailey and Marion Isabel Bailey; *m* 2006, Blazenka Sumera; one *s* one *d. Educ:* Winchester Coll.; Brasenose Coll., Oxford (MA, BCL). Called to the Bar, Gray's Inn, 1999; in practice as a barrister, specialising in commercial chancery, insolvency and company law. *Publications:* (contrib.) Tolley's Insolvency Law, 2018–. *Recreations:* rowing, cycling, jazz piano. *Address:* c/o Wilberforce Chambers, 8 New Square, Lincoln's Inn, WC2A 3QP. *T:* (020) 7306 0102. *E:* jbailey@wilberforce.co.uk.

**BAILEY, Dame Jessica Lois;** *see* Corner, Dame J. L.

**BAILEY, John;** *see* Bailey, W. J. J.

**BAILEY, Sir John Bilsland,** KCB 1987 (CB 1982); Chief Adjudicator, 1989–2000, and Director, 1998–2002, Independent Committee for Supervision of Standards of Telephone Information Services; Chairman, Disciplinary Tribunal of Personal Investment Authority, 1994–2001; *b* 5 Nov. 1928; *o s* of late Walter Bailey and Ethel Edith Bailey, FRAM (who *m* 2nd, Sir Thomas George Spencer); *m* 1952, Marion Rosemary (née Carroll); two *s* one *d. Educ:* Eltham Coll.; University Coll., London (LLB). Solicitor of Supreme Court. Under-Sec. (Legal), Dept of HM Procurator General and Treasury Solicitor, 1973–77; Legal Dir, Office of Fair Trading, 1977–79; Dep. Treasury Solicitor, 1979–84; HM Procurator Gen. and Treasury Solicitor, 1984–88. Pres., Disciplinary Cttee, 1994, Public Interest Dir, 1993–94, LAUTRO; Dir, PIA, 1994–97. Gov., Anglo-European Coll. of Chiropractic, 1990–94. Chm., Westminster Soc., 1994–2000. *Recreation:* historical perambulations.

**BAILEY, Sir John Richard,** 4th Bt *cr* 1919, of Cradock, Province of Cape of Good Hope, Union of South Africa; *b* 11 June 1947; *s* of Sir Derrick Thomas Louis Bailey, 3rd Bt, DFC and Katharine Nancy Stormonth Darling; *S* father, 2009; *m* 1977, Philippa Jane, *o d* of John Sherwin Mervyn Pearson Gregory; two *s* one *d. Educ:* Winchester; Christ's Coll., Cambridge (BA 1969). *Heir: s* James Edward Bailey, *b* 7 Sept. 1983.

**BAILEY, Maj. Gen. Jonathan Bernard Appleton,** CB 2005; MBE 1980; PhD; Director, Boeing Defence UK, 2007–13; *b* 12 April 1951; *m* 1976, Deborah Smith; two *s* one *d. Educ:* Charterhouse; Univ. of Sussex (BA 1972); Univ. of Cranfield (PhD 2004). Commnd RA 1972; served NI; comd Assembly Place "ROMEO" (ZIPRA guerillas), Rhodesia, 1979–80; OC troops, MV Baltic Ferry, sailing to S Atlantic, then Ops Officer, 4th Field Regt RA, Falklands War, 1982; psc 1983; HCSC 1994; Chief Fire Co-ordination, ARRC, 1997–99; Chief Jt Implementation Commn, HQ Kosovo Force, and Chief Liaison Officer, Yugoslav Gen. Staff and Kosovo Liberation Army, 1999; Dir, RA, 2000–01; Dir Gen. Develt and Doctrine, MoD, 2002–05. Dir, Centre for Defence and Internat. Security Studies, 2005–06; defence analyst and consultant, 2005–07. Consultant, Leverhulme prog. on Changing Character of War, Oxford Univ., 2005–. Col Comdt, RA, 2003–08. QCVS 1999. *Publications:* Field Artillery and Firepower, 1989; Great Power Strategy in Asia 1905–2005, 2007; contributor: British Fighting Methods in the Great War, 1996; The Emerging Strategic Environment, 1999; The Dynamics of Military Revolution 1300–2050, 2001; The Past as Prologue, 2006; Contemporary Operations: reflections on and of Empire, 2007; (ed jtly) British Generals in Blair's Wars, 2013; contrib. professional jls.

**BAILEY, Mark David,** PhD; High Master, St Paul's School, 2011–Sept. 2020; Professor of Late Medieval History, University of East Anglia, 2010–11 and from Sept. 2020 (Visiting Professor, 2011–20); *b* 21 Nov. 1960; *s* of Ronald Bailey and Maureen Bailey (née Oates); *m* 1989, Julie Margaret Noy; one *s* one *d. Educ:* Univ. of Durham (BA Econ. Hist. 1982); Corpus Christi Coll., Cambridge (PhD History 1986; Rugby blue, 1982–85). Fellow, Gonville and Caius Coll., Cambridge, 1986–96; Lectr in Local History, Bd of Continuing Educn, Univ. of Cambridge, 1991–96; Fellow, Corpus Christi Coll., Cambridge, 1996–99; Headmaster, Leeds Grammar Sch., later The Grammar Sch. at Leeds, 1999–2010. Vis. Fellow, All Souls Coll., Oxford, 2010, 2018; James Ford Lectr in British History, Univ. of Oxford, 2019. Mem. Council, RFU, 1994–98. Played Rugby Union for England, 1984–90 (7 caps); Captain, Suffolk CCC, 1988–90. Mem. Council, Sir Winston Churchill Meml Trust, 2007–15. FRHistS 1999. T. S. Ashton Award, British Econ. Hist. Soc., 1988, 1994. *Publications:* A Marginal Economy?: East Anglian Breckland in the later Middle Ages, 1989; (ed) The Bailiffs' Minute Book of Dunwich 1404–1430, 1992; (with J. Hatcher) Modelling the Middle Ages: the history and theory of England's Economic Development, 2001; The English Manor *c* 1200–*c* 1500, 2002; Medieval Suffolk: an economic and social history 1200–1500, 2007; (with S. H. Rigby) Town and Countryside in Medieval England, 2012; The Decline of Serfdom in Late Medieval England, 2014; various articles in learned jls and contribs to collections of essays on medieval England. *Recreations:* local history, walking, sport, food, music. *Address:* (until Sept. 2020) St Paul's School, Lonsdale Road, Barnes, SW13 9JT; (from Sept. 2020) School of History, University of East Anglia, Norwich NR4 7TJ. *Clubs:* East India (Hon. Mem.); Hawks (Cambridge).

**BAILEY, Michael John;** Co-Founder and Chairman, Elior North America (formerly TrustHouse Services Group), since 2008 (Chief Executive, 2008–15); *b* 14 Oct. 1948; *s* of Sidney William Bailey and Joyce Mary Bailey; *m* 1st (marr. diss.); two *d*; 2nd, 2007, Michelle. *Educ:* Westminster Coll., London. Gardner Merchant: various posts, from Food Service Manager to Exec. Dir, UK South, 1964–85; Pres., US subsidiary, 1985–91; Man. Dir, UK contract feeding business, 1991–92; Exec. Vice Pres., Nutrition Mgt Food Services Co., 1992; Compass Group plc: Gp Develt Dir, 1993–94; Chief Exec., N America Div., 1994–99; Gp Chief Exec., 1999–2006. Non-exec. Dir, Allmanhall Ltd, 2007–. FHCIMA 1995. *Recreations:* music, watching sports, cooking. *Address:* Elior North America, 300 South Tryon Street, Charlotte, NC 28202, USA.

**BAILEY, Norman Stanley,** CBE 1977; operatic and concert baritone; *b* Birmingham, 23 March 1933; *s* of late Stanley and Agnes Bailey; *m* 1st, 1957, Doreen Simpson (marr. diss. 1983); two *s* one *d*; 2nd, 1985, Kristine Ciesinski (*d* 2018). *Educ:* Rhodes Univ., S Africa; Vienna State Academy. BMus; Performer's and Teacher's Licentiate in Singing; Diplomas, opera, lieder, oratorio. Principal baritone, Sadler's Wells Opera, 1967–71; regular engagements at world's major opera houses and festivals, including: La Scala, Milan (first British Wanderer in Siegfried, 1976); Royal Opera House, Covent Garden; Bayreuth Wagner Fest. (first British Hans Sachs in Meistersinger, 1969); Vienna State Opera; Metropolitan Opera, NY; Chicago Opera; Paris Opera; Edinburgh Fest.; Hamburg State Opera; Munich State Opera; Opera North; Glyndebourne Fest. BBC Television performances in Falstaff, La Traviata, The Flying Dutchman, Macbeth. Recordings include The Ring (Goodall); Meistersinger and Der Fliegende Holländer (Solti); Walküre (Klemperer), among others. Hon. RAM 1981; Hon. DMus Rhodes, 1986. *Recreations:*

Mem., Baha'i world community; chess, notaphily, golf, microcomputing, indoor rowing (Mem. 16 million meter club; Winner, N American Rowing Challenge, 2004). *Address:* PO Box 655, Victor, ID 83455, USA.

**BAILEY, Paul,** (christened **Peter Harry**); freelance writer, since 1967; radio broadcaster; *b* 16 Feb. 1937; *s* of Arthur Oswald Bailey and Helen Maud Burgess; civil partnership 2016, Jeremy Trevathan. *Educ:* Sir Walter St John's Sch., London; Central School of Speech and Drama. Actor, 1956–64: appeared in first productions of Ann Jellicoe's The Sport of My Mad Mother, 1958, and John Osborne's and Anthony Creighton's Epitaph for George Dillon, 1958. Literary Fellow at Univ. of Newcastle and Univ. of Durham, 1972–74; Bicentennial Fellowship, 1976; Visiting Lectr in English Literature, North Dakota State Univ., 1977–79; Sen. Res. Fellow, Kingston Univ., 2010–. Theatre critic, The Oldie, 2010–. Frequent radio broadcaster, mainly on Radio 3; has written and presented programmes on Karen Blixen, Henry Green, I. B. Singer and Primo Levi, among others. FRSL, 1982–84 and 1990. E. M. Forster Award, 1974; George Orwell Meml Prize, 1978, for broadcast essay The Limitations of Despair. *Publications:* At the Jerusalem, 1967 (Somerset Maugham Award, 1968; Arts Council Prize, 1968); Trespasses, 1970; A Distant Likeness, 1973; Peter Smart's Confessions, 1977; Old Soldiers, 1980; An English Madam, 1982; Gabriel's Lament, 1986; An Immaculate Mistake: scenes from childhood and beyond (autobiog.), 1990; Sugar Cane, 1993; (ed) The Oxford Book of London, 1995; (ed) First Love, 1997; Kitty and Virgil, 1998; (ed) The Stately Homo: a celebration of the life of Quentin Crisp, 2000; Three Queer Lives (Fred Barnes, Naomi Jacob and Arthur Marshall), 2001; Uncle Rudolf (novel), 2002; A Dog's Life (memoir), 2003; Chapman's Odyssey, 2011; The Prince's Boy, 2014; contribs to Independent, TLS, Daily Telegraph, Guardian. *Recreations:* wandering in Eastern Europe, visiting churches, chamber music, watching tennis. *Address:* 79 Davisville Road, W12 9SH. *T:* (020) 8749 2279, 07854 414917.

**BAILEY, Reginald William,** CBE 2013; Chief Executive, Mothers' Union, 1999–2015; *b* London, 9 July 1950; *s* of Reginald Arthur Bailey and Katherine Eleanor Bailey (née Perryment); *m* 1973, Alison Ferguson; one *s* one *d* (and one *d* decd). *Educ:* Stationers' Co. Sch.; Poly. of South Bank. MIBiol 1973. Graduate trainee, J Sainsbury, 1970–73; Marketing Manager, Spillers Foods, 1973–78; Managing Director: Swift & Co., 1978–82; Carnation Petfoods plc, 1982–84; Prestige Gp plc, 1984–86; Scientific Investment Corp., 1986–89; Del Monte Foods Internat. plc, 1989–94; Chief Exec., Danish Bacon Co. plc, 1994–99. Advr to Govt on Families and Children, 2010–; Ind. Reviewer for Govt on Sexualisation and Commercialisation of Children, 2011–17. Member: Consultative Council/Adv. Panel on Children's Viewing, BBFC, 2012–; Council, Advertising Standards Authy, 2016–. Chair, Trustees, Traidcraft Foundn, 2003–12; Chair: Still Birth and Neo-Natal Death Support Charity, 2016–18; YMCA Eng. and Wales, 2018–; non-exec. Dir, Children's Media Foundn, 2015–17. Reader, C of E, 1991–; Hon. Canon, St Albans Abbey and Cathedral Ch, 2014. *Publications:* Letting Children be Children: a review of the commercialisation and sexualisation of children, 2011. *E:* regbailey@aol.com.

**BAILEY, Sarah Joanne;** *see* Storey, Dame S. J.

**BAILEY, Dame Susan (Mary),** DBE 2014 (OBE 2002); FRCPsych; Chair, Children and Young People's Mental Health Coalition, since 2014; Senior National Lead for Mental Health, Health Education England; President, Royal College of Psychiatrists, 2011–14; *b* Manchester, 29 Aug. 1950; *d* of Frank and Edith Mary Bailey; two *d. Educ:* Hulme Grammar Sch. for Girls; Watford Grammar Sch. for Girls; Univ. of Manchester (MB ChB 1973). MRCPsych 1976, FRCPsych 1996. Consultant Child and Adolescent Psychiatrist, Bolton, Salford and Trafford Mental Health Trust, subseq. Gtr Manchester W Mental Health NHS Foundn Trust, 1983–; Hon. Prof. of Child Mental Health, Univ. of Central Lancs, 2004–. Non-exec. Dir, DoH, then DHSC, 2017–. Chair, Acad. of Med. Royal Colls, 2015–17 (Vice Chair, 2012–14). Section Chair, Eur. Assoc. of Child and Adolescent Psychiatry, 2005–14. Trustee: Centre for Mental Health; MAC-UK. Hon. Fellow, Coll. of Psychiatrists (SA). *Recreations:* with children and grandchildren, walking, visual arts, music. *Address:* FACts Team, Adult & Youth Specialised Services Directorate, Adolescent Forensic Service, Greater Manchester West Mental Health NHS Foundation Trust, Bury New Road, Prestwich, Manchester M25 3BL. *T:* (0161) 772 3601. *E:* Sue.Bailey@gmw.nhs.uk.

**BAILEY, Sylvia, (Sly);** Chief Executive, Trinity Mirror plc, 2003–12; *b* 24 Jan. 1962; *d* of Thomas Lewis Grice and Sylvia Grice (née Bantick); *m* 1998, Peter Bailey. *Educ:* St Saviour's and St Olave's Grammar Sch. for Girls. IPC Magazines, 1989–2000: Ad Sales Dir, 1990–97; Bd Dir, 1994–2002; Man. Dir, TX, 1997–99; Chief Exec., IPC Media, 1999–2002; non-executive Director: Littlewoods plc, 2002; EMI, 2004–07 (Sen. Ind. Dir, and Chm., Remuneration Cttee, 2007); Ladbrokes Coral Gp (formerly Ladbrokes plc), 2009–16 (Mem., Remuneration Cttee, 2009–16); Greencore Gp, 2013– (Mem. Audit, Nominations, 2013–); London Real Estate Exchange Ltd, 2015–. Mem., Press Assoc. Bd, 2003–12 (Chm., Remuneration Cttee, 2009–12). Pres., NewstrAid, 2003–12. Gov., English Nat. Ballet Sch. Ltd, 2009–13. Hon. MA East London, 2004. Marcus Morris Award, PPA, 2002. *Recreations:* family, dogs, fitness.

**BAILEY, (William) John (Joseph);** journalist; *b* 11 June 1940; *s* of Ernest Robert Bailey and Josephine Smith; *m* 1963, Maureen Anne, *d* of James Gibbs Neenan and Marjorie Dorema Wrigglesworth; five *s* three *d. Educ:* St Joseph's, Stanford-le-Hope, Essex; Campion Hall, Jamaica; St George's Coll., Kingston, Jamaica; St Chad's Coll., Wolverhampton. Reporter: Southend Standard, Essex, and Essex and Thurrock Gazette, 1960–63; Northern Daily Mail, 1963–64; Chief Reporter, Billingham and Stockton Express, 1964–72; Sub-Editor, Mail, Hartlepool, 1972–75; Features Editor, Echo, Sunderland, 1975–97; Editor, Northern Cross, 1981–2008 (corresp. and columnist, 2008–); Media Officer, Sunderland City Council, 1998–2005. Mem., Press Council, 1974–80 (Member: Complaints Cttee, 1974–76; Cttee for Evidence to Royal Commission on Press, 1975–76; Gen. Purposes Cttee, 1976–77; Secretariat Cttee, 1976–80). National Union of Journalists: Mem., Nat. Exec. Council, 1966–82; Pres., 1973–74; Gen. Treasurer, 1975–82; Mem. of Honour, 1999. Sec., Hartlepool People Ltd, 1983–2002. Member: NE Br., Catholic Writers' Guild of St Francis de Sales, 2003–; Tyneside Circle, Newman Assoc., 2008–. Life Mem., Friends of Nat. Glass Centre, Sunderland. Mem., Hartlepool Local Exchange Trading System. Minute-taker, Hartlepool Churches Together, 2015–; Adminr, Hartlepool Town Pastors (Street Angels), 2015–. Trustee, Journalists' Copyright Trust, 1996–2015. Provincial Journalist of the Year (jtly with Carol Roberton), British Press Awards, 1977 (commended, 1979); Special award Northern Cross, 1984–85, 1989, 1992, 1996, 1997, personal award, 2000, Tom Cordner North East Press Awards. *Address:* 225 Park Road, Hartlepool TS26 9NG. *Clubs:* Tyneside Irish Centre (Newcastle upon Tyne); Island Social (Seaham); Lindisfarne Social (Wallsend); Hartlepool Catholic Men's Social (Hartlepool).
*See also* C. M. Bailey.

**BAILHACHE, Sir Philip (Martin),** Kt 1996; a Judge of the Court of Appeal, Jersey, 1994–2011, and Guernsey, 1996–2011; Senator, States of Jersey, 2011–18; Minister for External Relations, 2013–18; *b* 28 Feb. 1946; *s* of late Jurat Lester Vivian Bailhache (Lieut-Bailiff of Jersey, 1980–82) and Nanette Ross (née Ferguson); *m* 1st, 1967 (marr. diss. 1982); two *s* two *d*; 2nd, 1984, Linda (née Le Vavasseur dit Durell); one *s* one *d. Educ:*

Charterhouse; Pembroke Coll., Oxford (Hon. Fellow, 1995). Called to the Bar, Middle Temple, 1968, Hon. Bencher, 2003; called to the Jersey Bar, 1969; QC (Jersey) 1989. In private practice as Advocate, Jersey, 1969–74; States of Jersey Dep. for Grouville, 1972–74; Solicitor-Gen., Jersey, 1975–85; Attorney Gen. for Jersey, 1986–93; Dep. Bailiff of Jersey, 1994–95, Bailiff, 1995–2009; Comr, Royal Court of Jersey, 2009–11. Asst Chief Minister, Govt of Jersey, 2011–13. Chm., Governing Body, Inst. of Law, Jersey, 2008–17. Chm., Jersey Arts Council, 1987–89. Exec. Vice-Pres., Commonwealth Magistrates' and Judges' Assoc., 2009–11. Editor, Jersey and Guernsey Law Review (formerly Jersey Law Review), 1997–. *Publications*: (ed) A Celebration of Autonomy, 2005; (ed) Dependency or Sovereignty, 2012. *Recreations*: books, wine, gardening, the arts. *Address*: L'Anquetinerie, Grouville, Jersey, Channel Islands JE3 9UX. *T*: (01534) 852533. *Clubs*: Reform; United (Jersey).

See also Sir W. J. Bailhache, V. M. Bird.

**BAILHACHE, Sir William (James),** Kt 2017; QC 2000; Bailiff of Jersey, 2015–19 (Deputy Bailiff, 2009–15); *b* 24 June 1953; *s* of late Jurat Lester Vivian Bailhache, sometime Lieut Bailiff of Jersey, and Nanette Ross Bailhache (*née* Ferguson); *m* 1975, Jennifer Laura Nudds; one *s* one *d*. *Educ*: Charterhouse; Merton Coll., Oxford (MA). Called to the Bar, Middle Temple, 1975, Bencher, 2015; Advocate, Royal Court of Jersey, 1976; Partner, Bailhache & Bailhache, 1977–94, Bailhache Labesse, 1994–99; HM Attorney Gen. for Jersey, 2000–09. Chm., Barclays Bank Finance Co. (Jersey) Ltd, 1996–99 (Dir, 1982–99); Dir, Jersey Gas Co. Ltd, 1992–94. *Recreations*: golf, cricket, reading, opera. *Address*: Seymour House, La Rocque, Jersey JE3 9BB. *T*: (01534) 854708. *Clubs*: Vincent's (Oxford); Royal Jersey Golf (Captain, 1995–96).

See also Sir P. M. Bailhache, V. M. Bird.

**BAILIE, Robert Ernest, (Roy),** OBE 1995; Chairman, W. & G. Baird (Holdings) Ltd, since 1982; *b* 2 June 1943; *s* of Robert and Rosetta Bailie; *m* 1971, Paddy Clark; two *s* one *d*. *Educ*: Belfast High Sch.; Queen's Univ., Belfast; Harvard Sch. of Business (grad. 1985). MSO Ltd, 1958–65; joined W. & G. Baird, 1965, Man. Dir, 1972, led mgt buy-out, 1977; Director: W. & G. Baird Ltd, 1977–; Graphic Plates Ltd, 1977–; MSO Ltd, 1984–2013; Blackstaff Press Ltd, 1995–; Corporate Document Services Ltd, 2000–. Non-executive Director: UTV, 1997–2013; Bank of England, 1998–2003; Bank of Ireland, 1999–2006 (Mem., NI Adv. Bd, 1994–98); Bank of Ireland UK Financial Services PLC, 2006–08. Pres., BPIF, 1999–2001 (Mem., Exec. Bd of Mgt, 1978–80, Chm., 1980–84, NW Reg.; Vice-Pres., 1997–99). Member: NI Council for Higher Educn, 1985–90; IDB for NI, 1990–95; Adv. Council on Alcohol and Drug Educn, 1990–99; Chairman: CBI (NI), 1992–94; NI Tourist Bd, 1996–2002; Opera Company NI, 2009–; Nat. Trust NI, 2010–17; Mem., Queen's Senate, 2018–. *Recreations*: sailing, golf, walking. *Address*: The Look Out, 49 Main Street, Castlerock, Coleraine, Co. Derry, Northern Ireland BT51 4RA. *T*: (028) 9334 0383.

**BAILIE, Rt Hon. Robin John;** PC (NI) 1971; Solicitor of the Supreme Court of Judicature, Northern Ireland, since 1961; *b* 6 March 1937; *m* 1961, Margaret F. (*née* Boggs); one *s* three *d*. *Educ*: Rainey Endowed Sch., Magherafelt, Co. Londonderry; Queen's Univ., Belfast (LLB). Founding Partner, Mills, Selig and Bailie, Solicitors, Belfast, 1961. MP (NI) for Newtonabbey, 1969–72; Minister of Commerce, Govt of NI, 1971–72. Estab. NI Finance Corpn; initiated cross border dialogue and develt. Chairman: Fine Wine Wholesalers, London, 1986–93; Innovative Integrations, 2018–; former Chm., Century Newspapers; Director: Walker Steel, 1974–77; Lumus Mackie (Engrg), 1991–94; former Dir, Goodyear Tyre and Rubber Co. *Recreations*: fine wine collection (Chevalier de Tastevin, Clos Vougouet, 1991); formerly tennis, golf, squash and ski-ing. *Address*: 7 Yattendon Court, Yattendon, Thatcham RG18 0UT. *T*: (01635) 200368; Calle Gamo 7, Los Monteros, Marbella 29603, Spain. *T*: (95) 2775568. *Club*: Sloane.

**BAILIE, Roy;** see Bailie, R. E.

**BAILIN, Alexander;** QC 2010; barrister; a Recorder, since 2012; a Deputy High Court Judge, since 2013; *b* Brighton, 23 Jan. 1969; *s* of late Prof. David Bailin and of Dr Anjali Bailin; *m* 2001, Emma Saunders; one *s* one *d*. *Educ*: Dorothy Stringer High Sch., Brighton; Brighton, Hove and Sussex Sixth Form Coll.; Emmanuel Coll., Cambridge (BA Hons 1991; MA); Univ. of Sussex (CPE 1994). Derivatives trader, 1991–93; called to the Bar, Lincoln's Inn, 1995; in practice as barrister, specialising in criminal, public and human rights law; Matrix Chambers, 2003–. *Publications*: contributions to: Criminal Justice and Human Rights, 2007; Fraud: criminal law and procedure, 2012; Blackstone's Criminal Practice, 2012; articles in nat. press and legal jls. *Recreations*: scuba diving, West African music, theatre, ski-ing, tennis. *Address*: Matrix Chambers, Griffin Building, Gray's Inn, WC1R 5LN. *T*: (020) 7404 3447. *E*: alexbailin@matrixlaw.co.uk.

**BAILLIE,** family name of **Baron Burton**.

**BAILLIE, Sir Adrian (Louis),** 8th Bt *cr* 1823, of Polkemmet, Linlithgowshire; *b* 26 March 1973; *o s* of Sir Gawaine George Hope Baillie, 7th Bt and of (Lucile) Margot Baillie; *S* father, 2003; *m* 2006, Amber Rose Laine; one *s* one *d*. *Educ*: Eton Coll.; Manchester Univ. (BA); City Univ. (Dip. Law); Inns of Court Sch. of Law; London Business Sch. (MBA). Called to the Bar, Middle Temple, 1999. Company Director. *Heir*: *s* Sebastian Gawaine Baillie, *b* 18 April 2011. *Address*: Freechase, Warninglid, Haywards Heath, West Sussex RH17 5SZ.

**BAILLIE, Alexander;** 'cellist; *b* 1956; *m* Christel; one *s* two *d*. *Educ*: Royal Coll. of Music; Hochschule für Musik, Vienna; studied with Jacqueline du Pré. Soloist with LSO, BBC SO, CBSO and orchestras worldwide; premières of works include Colin Matthew's Cello Concerto, 1984, Penderecki's 2nd Cello Concerto, and concerti by H. K. Gruber and Andrew MacDonald; recitals include Bach's Cello Suites (unaccompanied), Wigmore Hall, 1997; also appears with chamber music ensembles; Member: Villiers Piano Quartet; Heveningham Hall Piano Trio; Alia Musica, Berlin; formerly Mem., The Fires of London. Vis. Prof., Royal Coll. of Music; Prof. of Cello, Bremen Hochschule; Prof. of Cello and Chamber Music, GSMD, 2009–.

**BAILLIE, Andrew Bruce;** QC 2001; a Recorder, since 1989; *b* 17 May 1948; *s* of Edward Oswald Baillie and Molly Eva (Renée) Baillie (*née* Andrews); *m* 1976, Mary Lou Meech Palmer (*d* 1988); one *s* two *d*. *Educ*: King's Coll. Sch., Wimbledon; Univ. de Besançon; Univ. of Kent at Canterbury (BA Social Scis 1969). Called to the Bar, Inner Temple, 1970. *Recreations*: played Rugby for Univ. of Kent, E Kent and London Scottish; now bridge, cooking and visiting Spain. *Address*: 9 Gough Square, EC4A 3DE. *T*: (020) 7832 0500. *E*: abaillie@9goughsquare.co.uk.

**BAILLIE, Jacqueline, (Jackie);** Member (Lab) Dumbarton, Scottish Parliament, since 1999; *b* Hong Kong, 15 Jan. 1964; *d* of Frank and Sophie Barnes; one *d*. *Educ*: Glasgow Univ. (MSc). Resource Centre Manager, Strathkelvin DC, 1990–96; Community Economic Develt Manager, E Dumbartonshire Council, 1996–99. Scottish Parliament: Dep. Minister for Communities, 1999–2000; Minister for Social Justice, 2000–01; Shadow Cabinet Secretary for Health and Wellbeing, 2008–13, for Social Justice, Equalities and Welfare, 2013–14, for Finance and Economy, 2014–15, for Public Service and Wealth Creation, 2015–16, for Economy, Jobs and Fair Work, 2016–. Chair, Scottish Labour Party, 1997–98 (Mem., Exec. Cttee, 1990–99). *Address*: Scottish Parliament, Edinburgh EH99 1SP.

**BAILLIE, Prof. John,** CA; Chairman, Accounts Commission for Scotland, 2007–13 (Member, 2003–13); Honorary Professor of Accountancy, University of Edinburgh, since 2016 (Visiting Professor of Accountancy, 2013–15); *m* 1972, Annette; one *s* one *d*. *Educ*: Whitehill Sch. CA 1967 (Gold Medal and Distinction in final exams). Partner: Thomson McLintock & Co., later Peat Marwick McLintock, then KPMG, 1978–93; Scott-Moncrieff, 1993–2001. Johnstone-Smith Prof. of Accountancy, Univ. of Glasgow, 1983–88. Visiting Professor of Accountancy: Heriot-Watt Univ., 1989–2004; Univ. of Glasgow, 1996–2013. Member: Reporting Panel, Competition Commn, 2002–11; Ind. Local Govt Finance Review Cttee, 2004–07; Audit Scotland, 2004–13 (Chm., 2007–10); Gambling Commn, 2016–. Convenor, Res. Cttee, 1995–99, and Mem. various technical and professional affairs cttees, Inst. of Chartered Accountants of Scotland; Mem., CIPFA, 2008. Trustee, ICAS Foundn, 2008–17. FRSA 1996. Hon. MA Glasgow, 1983. *Publications*: Systems of Profit Measurement, 1985; Consolidated Accounts and the Seventh Directive, 1985; technical and professional papers; contribs to Accountants' Magazine and other professional jls. *Recreations*: keeping fit, reading, music, golf. *Club*: Kilmacolm Golf (Captain, 2002; Chm., 2018, 2019).

**BAILLIE-HAMILTON,** family name of **Earl of Haddington**.

**BAILLIEU,** family name of **Baron Baillieu**.

**BAILLIEU, 3rd Baron** *cr* 1953, of Sefton, Australia and Parkwood, Surrey; **James William Latham Baillieu;** Director, Anthony Baillieu and Associates (Hong Kong) Ltd, since 1992; Managing Director, Bank NIKoil, 2000; *b* 16 Nov. 1950; *s* of 2nd Baron Baillieu and Anne Bayliss, *d* of Leslie William Page, Southport, Queensland; *S* father, 1973; *m* 1st, 1974, Cornelia Masters Ladd (marr. diss. 1985), *d* of William Ladd; one *s*; 2nd, 1986, Clare Stephenson (marr. diss. 1995), *d* of Peter Stephenson; 3rd, 2004, Olga Vladimirovna; one *s*. *Educ*: Radley College; Monash Univ. (BEc 1977). Short Service Commission, Coldstream Guards, 1970–73. Banque Nationale de Paris, 1978–80; Asst Dir, Rothschild Australia Ltd, 1980–88; Dir, Manufacturers Hanover Australia Ltd, 1988–90; Dir, Standard Chartered Asia Ltd, 1990–92; Asst Dir, Credit Lyonnais Asia Ltd, 1992–94; Asst Dir, Nomura International (Hong Kong) Ltd, 1995; Gen. Dir, Regent European Securities, 1995–96; Dir, CentreInvest Gp, Moscow, 1996–99. *Heir*: *s* Hon. Robert Latham Baillieu, *b* 2 Feb. 1979. *Clubs*: Boodle's; Hong Kong (Hong Kong); Australian (Melbourne).

**BAILLIEU, Christopher Latham,** MBE 1977; Chairman, Sports Aid, 2012–18; *b* 12 Dec. 1949; *s* of late Hon. Edward Baillieu and Betty Anne Baillieu (*née* Taylor); *m* 1984, Jane Elizabeth Bowie; two *s* one *d*. *Educ*: Jesus Coll., Cambridge (BA 1972). Called to the Bar, Lincoln's Inn, 1976. Rowed in winning crew, Oxford v Cambridge Boat Race, 1970–73. Represented Great Britain in rowing, 1973–83; winner: Silver Medal, double sculls, Olympic Games, 1976; Gold Medal, World Championships, 1977; competed Olympic Games, 1980. Chairman: British Swimming, 2001–08; The Olympians, 2004–12; Wandsworth Active, 2009–15; sports coach UK, 2010–16; Trustee, Enable Leisure and Culture, 2015–. Steward, Henley Royal Regatta, 1985– (Trustee, Henley Stewards' Trust, 1992–). *Recreations*: exploring old buildings, hills, valleys and waterways. *Address*: 11 Woodthorpe Road, Putney, SW15 6UQ. *Clubs*: Hurlingham; Hawks (Cambridge); Leander.

**BAILLIEU, Colin Clive;** Director, Renata Baillieu Art Tours; Member, Monopolies and Mergers Commission, 1984–93; *b* 2 July 1930; *s* of Ian Baillieu and Joanna Baillieu (*née* Brinton); *m* 1st, 1955, Diana Robinson (marr. diss. 1968); two *d*; 2nd, 1968, Renata Richter; two *s*. *Educ*: Dragon Sch.; Eton. Commissioned Coldstream Guards, 1949. Local newspaper, Evening Standard, 1951–52; British Metal Corp., 1952–58; British Aluminium, 1958–60; Monsanto Fibres, 1960–66; Arthur Sanderson, 1966–68; Ultrasonic Machines, 1968–76. Chm., Gresham Underwriting Agencies, 1990–92. Mem., Council of Lloyd's, 1983–88. Lecturer: European Business Sch., London, 1995–2008; London Coll. of Printing, 1998–2005. Contested (C) Rossendale, Lancs 1964 and 1966. Dir, Orchestra of St John's, Smith Square, 1999–2000. Dist Comr, Cowdray Pony Club, 1998–2001. *Publications*: The Lion and the Lamb, 1996. *Recreations*: ski-ing, 17th Century history, trees. *Address*: 17 North Pallant, Chichester, W Sussex PO19 1TQ. *T*: (01243) 778675. *Clubs*: Travellers, Beefsteak, Shikar, MCC.

**BAILLIEU, Hon. Edward Norman, (Hon. Ted);** MLA (L) Hawthorn, Victoria, Australia, 1999–2014; Premier of Victoria, and Minister of the Arts, 2010–13; Leader, Parliamentary Liberal Party (Victorian Division), 2006–13; *b* Melbourne, 31 July 1953; *s* of Darren Baillieu and Diana Margaret Baillieu (*née* Knox); *m* Robyn Mary Jubb; one *s* two *d*. *Educ*: Melbourne Grammar Sch.; Univ. of Melbourne (BArch); Royal Melbourne Inst. of Technol. (Cert. Business Studies). FRAIA. Formerly Partner, Mayne & Baillieu, Architects, Melbourne. Formerly Dir, Knight Frank Hldgs. Shadow Minister: for Tertiary Educn and Trng, 1999–2001; for Gaming, 2000–02; for Planning, 2001–06; for the Arts, 2006–10; Leader of the Opposition, 2006–10. Chm., Vic Govt Anzac Centenary Cttee, 2013–; Chair, Wye River Reconstruction Fund, 2016–. Member: Bd, Tourism Vic, 1998–99; Melbourne Convention and Exhibn Trust, 1998–99; Australian India Business Council, 2014–. Dir, Australian Children's TV Foundn, 1997–99. Member: Vic Bd of Mgt, Assoc. of Consulting Architects, 1985–99; Australian Inst. Architects Foundn, 2017–. Member: Patron's Council, Epilepsy Foundn Vic; Bd, Nat. Breast Cancer Foundn, 2014–; Patron: Hawthorn Community Chest, Melbourne; Mental Health Foundn; Multicultural Arts Vic; Sovereign Hill Mus.; Friends of Auburn Uniting Church. 2015–; Sir Rupert Hamer Mgt Award, Public Records Office Victoria, 2016–; Queenscliffe Histl Mus., 2017–; Hawthorn Relay of Life; Patron-Chieftain, Vic Highland Pipe Bands Assoc., 2012–. Hon. Enterprise Prof., Univ. of Melbourne, 2016–; Adjunct Prof., Swinburne Univ., 2018–. Ashoka Award, Aust.-India Business Council, 2013; Special Public Service Award, ASEAN Leadership Network of Aust., 2014. *Recreations*: golf, swimming. *Address*: Level 1, Old Treasury Building, 20 Spring Street, Melbourne, Vic 3002, Australia. *E*: formerpremier46@gmail.com.

**BAIN, Andrew David,** OBE 1997; FRSE 1980; Visiting Professor of Political Economy, University of Glasgow, 1991–98; *b* 21 March 1936; *s* of Hugh Bain and Kathleen (*née* Eadie); *m* 1st, 1960, Anneliese Minna Frieda Kroggel (marr. diss. 1988); three *s*; 2nd, 1989, Eleanor Riches. *Educ*: Glasgow Academy; Christ's Coll., Cambridge; PhD Cantab 1963. Junior Res. Officer, Dept of Applied Econs, Cambridge Univ., 1958–60; Res. Fellow, Christ's Coll., Cambridge, 1960; Instructor, Cowles Foundn, Yale Univ., 1960–61; Lectr, Cambridge, 1961–66; Fellow, Corpus Christi Coll., Cambridge, 1962; on secondment to Bank of England, 1965–67; Prof. of Econs, 1967–70, Esmee Fairbairn Prof. of Econs of Finance and Investment, 1970–77, Univ. of Stirling; Walton Prof. of Monetary and Financial Econs, Univ. of Strathclyde, 1977–84; Gp Econ. Advr, Midland Bank, 1984–90. Member: Cttee to Review the Functioning of Financial Institutions, 1977–80; (part-time) Monopolies and Mergers Commn, 1981–82; TEC Nat. Council, 1994–97; (part-time) Appeal Panel, Competition Commn 2000–03; Competition Appeal Tribunal, 2003–11. Bd Mem., Scottish Enterprise, 1991–98. *Publications*: The Growth of Television Ownership

in the United Kingdom (monograph), 1964; The Control of the Money Supply, 1970; Company Financing in the UK, 1975; The Economics of the Financial System, 1981, 2nd edn 1992; articles on demand analysis, monetary policy and other subjects.
*See also* Colin D. Bain.

**BAIN, Christopher Derek,** CMG 2019; Director, Catholic Agency for Overseas Development, 2003–18; *b* 27 Nov. 1953; *s* of Derek Bain and Mary Bain (*née* Hill); *m* 2012, Philomena Cullen; one *d*. *Educ:* Leicester Univ. (BA); Middlesex Univ. (MBA); Open Univ. (MSc Develt Mgt). VSO develt worker, Fiji, 1975–77; VSO Field Officer, S Pacific, 1977–79; Dir, Churches' Housing Trust, Fiji, 1979–82; Regl Coordinator, Christian Aid, 1982–89; Oxfam: Sen. Campaigns Advr, 1989–93; Hd of Campaigns, 1993–96; Hd of Progs, VSO, 1996–2003. Hon. Dir, Disasters Emergency Cttee, 2003–; Chm., British Overseas Aid Gp, 2005–08; Member: Exec. Cttee, Caritas Europa, 2010–18; Internat. Governing Council, Caritas, 2015–18. Pres., Co-opération Internat. pour le Développement et la Solidarité (CIDSE), 2011–14. *Recreations:* long distance pilgrimages, ale and malt whiskey appreciation, friends.

**BAIN, Prof. Colin David,** PhD; Professor of Chemistry, since 2005, and Vice-Provost (Research), since 2019, Durham University; *b* 2 Jan. 1963; *s* of Andrew David Bain, *qv*; *m* 1992, Emma Victoria Claudia Kauffmann (marr. diss. 2012); one *s* two *d*. *Educ:* Dollar Acad.; Corpus Christi Coll., Cambridge (BA 1983); Harvard Univ. (PhD 1989). Mr & Mrs John Jaffe Res. Fellow, Univ. of Cambridge, and Fellow, Christ's Coll., Cambridge, 1988–91; Univ. Lectr, Univ. of Oxford, 1991–2005; Fellow, Magdalen Coll., Oxford, 1991–2005, Emeritus, 2005–; Durham University: Dir, Inst. of Advanced Study, 2008–12; Dean and Dep. Pro-Vice Chancellor (Res.), 2015–17; Dir, Centre for Doctoral Trng in Soft Matter and Functional Interfaces, 2018–. Director: Magdalen Develt Co. Ltd, 1998–2005; GTE for Oxfordshire Ltd, 1999–2004; Member, Scientific Advisory Board: Oxford Capital Partners, 2005–; Max Planck Inst. for Colloid and Interface Res., 2007–14; Res. Complex, Harwell, 2011–15. Mem., Faraday Council, RSC, 2006–08; Trustee, RSC Pension Fund, 2009–19 (Chm., 2015–19). *Publications:* approx. 160 book chapters and articles in learned jls. *Recreations:* hill-walking, cycling, sailing. *Address:* Department of Chemistry, Durham University, Stockton Road, Durham DH1 3LE. *T:* (0191) 334 2138, *Fax:* (0191) 334 2051. *E:* c.d.bain@durham.ac.uk.

**BAIN, Douglas John;** Industrial Adviser to the Secretary of State for Scotland, 1983–85; *b* 9 July 1924; *s* of Alexander Gillan Bain and Fanny Heaford; *m* 1946, Jean Wallace Fairbairn (*d* 2012); three *d*. *Educ:* Mosspark Elementary Sch.; Pollokshields Secondary School; Royal Technical Coll., Glasgow (DRTC). ATI. Royal Tech. Coll., 1941–43 and 1948–51. Trained and flew as pilot, RAF, 1943–48. J. & P. Coats Ltd, 1951–83: graduate trainee, 1951–55; overseas management, 1955–60; Hd, Office Management, 1960–68; Director, 1968–83; seconded to Scottish Office (Scottish Econ. Planning Dept) as Under Sec., 1979–82. *Recreations:* walking, cycling, reading, TV, spending time with my three daughters and new friends - Vanessa and Val. *Address:* Unit 4 Viewbank Gardens, 26–46 Rutherford Road, Viewbank, Melbourne, Vic 3084, Australia.

**BAIN, Prof. Sir George (Sayers),** Kt 2001; DPhil; President and Vice-Chancellor, Queen's University Belfast, 1998–2004, now Professor Emeritus; *b* 24 Feb. 1939; *s* of George Alexander Bain and Margaret Ioleen Bamford; *m* 1st, 1962, Carol Lynn Ogden White (marr. diss. 1987); one *s* one *d*; 2nd, 1988, Frances Gwynneth Rigby (*née* Vickers). *Educ:* Univ. of Manitoba (BA Hons 1961, MA 1964); Oxford Univ. (DPhil 1968). Lieut, Royal Canadian Naval Reserve, 1957–63. Exec. Cttee, 1961–63, Pres., 1962–63, Manitoba NDP. Lectr in Econs, Univ. of Manitoba, 1962–63; Res. Fellow, Nuffield Coll., Oxford, 1966–69; Frank Thomas Prof. of Indust. Relations, UMIST, 1969–70; University of Warwick: Dep. Dir, 1970–74, Dir, 1974–81, SSRC Industrial Relations Res. Unit; Pressed Steel Fisher Prof. of Industrial Relations, 1979–89; Chm., Sch. of Industrial and Business Studies, 1983–89; Principal, London Business Sch., 1989–97. Sec., British Univs Indust. Relations Assoc., 1971–74. Member: Mech. Engrg Econ. Develt Cttee, NEDO, 1974–76; Cttee of Inquiry on Indust. Democracy, Dept of Trade (Chm., Lord Bullock), 1975–76; Council: ESRC, 1986–91; Nat. Forum for Management Educn and Develt, 1987–90; Chm. Council, Univ. Management Schs, 1987–90. Member: Bd of Trustees, 1990–96, and Exec. Vice-Pres., 1991–95, European Foundn for Management Develt; Internat. Affairs Cttee, 1990–92, Bd of Dirs, 1992–94, Amer. Assembly of Collegiate Schs of Business; Council, Foundn for Mgt Educn, 1991–95; Council, IMgt (formerly BIM), 1991–93; Senior Salaries Review Body, 1993–96; Internat. Council, Amer. Mgt Assoc., 1993–95; Foundn for Canadian Studies in UK, 1993–2001, 2004–06; Exec. Cttee, Co-operation Ireland GB, 1994–97 (Dep. Chm., 1996–97); Bd of Dirs, Grad. Mgt Admission Council, 1996–97; Bd of Co-operation Ireland, 1998–2004; Educn Honours Cttee, 2005–10; Trustee: Navan at Armagh, 1999–2003; Scotch-Irish Trust, 1999–2007; Council for Advancement and Support of Educn (CASE), 2004–08; CASE Europe, 2004–07; McClay Foundn, 2008–. Chairman: Food Sector Wkg Gp, NEDO, 1991–92; Commn on Public Policy and British Business, 1995–97; Low Pay Commn, 1997–2002, 2008–09; NI Meml Fund, 1998–2002; Conf. of Univ. Rectors in Ireland, 2000–01; Work and Parents Task Force, DTI, 2001; Pensions Policy Inst., 2002–04; Ind. Review of Fire Service, ODPM, 2002; ACU, 2002–03; NI Legal Services Review Gp, 2005–06; Advr on Royal Mail to Sec. of State for Trade and Industry, 2005–06; NI Ind. Strategic Review of Educn, 2006; NI Rev. of Policy on Location of Public Sector Jobs, 2007–08; Commn on Future of Nat. Minimum Wage and Low Pay Commn, Resolution Foundn, 2013–14. Pres., Involvement and Participation Assoc., 2002–06. Director: Blackwell Publishers Ltd (formerly Basil Blackwell Ltd), 1990–97; The Economist Gp, 1992–2001; Canada Life Gp (UK) Ltd, 1994–2014; Canada Life Assce Co., 1996–2003; Electra Private Equity (formerly Electra Investment Trust PLC), 1998–2008; Bombardier Aerospace Shorts Brothers Plc, 1998–2007; NI Sci. Park Foundn, 1999–2004; NI Adv. Bd, Bank of Ireland, 2000–02; Canada Life Capital Corp., 2003–14; Iain More Associates, 2004–07; Entertainment One, 2007–10; Great-West Lifeco Inc., 2009–14. Consultant: Royal Commn on Trade Unions and Employers' Assocs (Donovan Commn), 1966–67; NBPI, 1967–69; Canadian Task Force on Labour Relns, 1968; Dept of Employment; Manitoba and Canada Depts of Labour; arbitrator and mediator in indust. disputes. Vice-Chm., Bd and Chm., Develt Trust, Lyric Theatre, Belfast, 2006–11; Chairman: Bd, Ulster Orch. Soc., 2011–16; Keeper's Council, Armagh Public Liby, 2014–16; Mem. Bd of Trustees, Ulster Histl Foundn, 2017–. Patron, Somme Assoc., 2004–13. FRSA 1987; CCMI (CIMgt 1991); Companion, Assoc. Business Schs, 2007; Fellow: British Acad. of Mgt, 1994; London Business Sch., 1999. FAcSS (AcSS 2000). Hon. Fellow, Nuffield Coll., Oxford, 2002. Hon. DBA De Montfort, 1994; Hon. LLD: NUI, 1998; Guelph, UC of Cape Breton, 1999; Manitoba, Warwick, 2003; Queen's, Canada, 2004; QUB, 2005; Winnipeg, 2016; Hon. DLitt: Ulster, 2002; New Brunswick, 2003; Hon. DSc Cranfield, 2005. Chief Exec. Leadership Award, CASE, 2003; Canadian High Comr's Award, 2003; Lifetime Achievement Award, British Acad. of Mgt, 2014. *Publications:* Trade Union Growth and Recognition, 1967; The Growth of White-Collar Unionism, 1970; (jtly) The Reform of Collective Bargaining at Plant and Company Level, 1971; (jtly) Social Stratification and Trade Unionism, 1973; (jtly) Union Growth and the Business Cycle, 1976; (jtly) A Bibliography of British Industrial Relations, 1979; (jtly) Profiles of Union Growth, 1980; (ed) Industrial Relations in Britain, 1983; (jtly) A Bibliography of British Industrial Relations 1971–1979, 1985; contrib. prof. and learned jls. *Recreations:* reading, genealogy, piano playing, Western riding, ice skating. *Address:* Vice-Chancellor's Office, Queen's University Belfast, University Road, Belfast BT7 1NN. *Club:* Ulster Reform (Belfast).

**BAIN, Iain Andrew;** Editor, Nairnshire Telegraph, since 1987; *b* 25 Feb. 1949; *s* of late Alastair I. R. Bain and Jean R. Forrest; *m* 1974, Maureen Beattie; three *d*. *Educ:* Nairn Acad.; Univ. of Aberdeen (MA). Research, Univ. of Durham, 1971–74; Sub-editor, 1974, Asst Editor, 1980, Editor, 1981–87, The Geographical Magazine. Chm. Trustees, Nairn Mus. Ltd, 1998–; Pres., Nairn Lit. Inst., 2002–05. *Publications:* Mountains and People, 1982; Water on the Land, 1983; Mountains and Earth Movements, 1984; various articles. *Recreations:* reading, walking, photography. *Address:* Rosebank, Leopold Street, Nairn IV12 4BE. *Club:* Nairn Golf.

**BAIN, Janet;** *see* Rossant, J.

**BAIN, John;** *see* Bain, K. J.

**BAIN, Ven. (John) Stuart;** Canon Provost, Sunderland Minster, since 2018; *b* 12 Oct. 1955; *s* of John and Doris Bain; *m* 1978, Angela Forster; two *s* one *d*. *Educ:* Van Mildert Coll., Univ. of Durham (BA Theol. 1977); Westcott House, Cambridge. Ordained deacon, 1980, priest, 1981; Assistant Curate: Holy Trinity, Washington, 1980–84; St Nicholas, Dunston, 1984–86; Vicar, Shiney Row and Herrington, 1986–92; Priest-in-charge: Whitworth and Spennymoor, 1992–97; Merrington, 1994–97; Area Dean, Auckland, 1996–2002; Vicar, Spennymoor, Whitworth and Merrington, 1997–2002; Asst Priest, 2002–03, Priest-in-charge, 2003–13, Parish of Hedworth; Archdeacon of Sunderland, 2002–18; Priest-in-charge, St George's, E Boldon, 2008–13, St Nicholas, Boldon, 2010–13; Curate, The Boldons, 2013–18. Hon. Canon, 1998–2002, (supernumerary) Non-Residentiary Canon, 2002–, Durham Cathedral. Chairman: DFW Adoption (formerly Durham Family Welfare), 1999–; Lord Crewe's Charity, 2006–. *Recreations:* music (very eclectic tastes), landscape photography, cooking, enjoying good wines, surfing the net, enjoying mountains. *Address:* Sunderland Minster, High Street, West Sunderland SR1 3ET.

**BAIN, (Kenneth) John,** OBE 2000; MA; Headmaster, The Purcell School, 1983–99; *b* 8 July 1939; *s* of Allan John and Hetty Bain; *m* 1962, Cynthia Mary Spain; one *s* one *d*. *Educ:* Bancroft's School; St Peter's College, Oxford (MA). Assistant Master, Stanbridge Earls School, 1962–70; Assistant Master and Housemaster, Cranleigh School, 1970–83. Gov., Arts Educnl Sch., Tring, 1999–2002. Dir, Endymion Ensemble, 1999–2003. Churchwarden, St Candida and Holy Cross, Whitechurch Canonicorum, 2008–11; Trustee, Friends of St Candida, 2014–. Hon. RCM 1999. *Publications:* occasional articles in educational jls. *Recreations:* Spanish language and culture, music, golf, walking, rough gardening. *Address:* Candida House, Whitechurch Canonicorum, Bridport, Dorset DT6 6RQ. *T:* (01297) 489629.

**BAIN, Ven. Stuart;** *see* Bain, Ven. J. S.

**BAIN, Tacey Marguerite;** *see* Cronin, T. M.

**BAIN, William Thomas;** Policy Advisor, Brexit and International Trade, British Retail Consortium, since 2017; *b* Glasgow, 29 Nov. 1972; *s* of Bill and Catherine Bain. *Educ:* St Roch's Secondary Sch., Glasgow; Univ. of Strathclyde (LLB Hons, DipLP, LLM). Sessional Lectr and Tutor, Univ. of Strathclyde Law Sch., 1996–2004; Sen. Lectr in Public Law, London South Bank Univ., 2004–09. MP (Lab) Glasgow NE, Nov. 2009–2015; contested (Lab) same seat, 2015. PPS to Minister of State, DfT, 2010; Shadow Minister for Transport, 2010, for Envmt, Food and Rural Affairs, 2010–11, for Scotland, 2011–13. Mem., Business, Innovation and Skills Select Cttee, 2013–15. Chair, All Party Gp on Sudan and S Sudan, 2012–15. Hd of Fintech, Financial Services and Brexit Adv. Unit, Inline Policy, 2016–17. *Publications:* (contrib.) Devolution to Scotland: the legal aspects, 1997; (contrib.) What Next for Labour?: ideas for a new generation, 2011; The New Social Contract: the future for Europe's centre-left, 2018. *Recreations:* films, modern music, walking, reading. *E:* williambain15@gmail.com. *W:* www.twitter.com/William_Bain.

**BAINBRIDGE, Cyril,** FCIJ; author and journalist; *b* 15 Nov. 1928; *o s* of late Arthur Herman and Edith Bainbridge; *m* 1953, Barbara Hannah (*née* Crook); one *s* two *d*. *Educ:* privately (Negus Coll., Bradford). Served Army, staff of CGS, WO, 1947–49. Entered journalism as Reporter, Bingley Guardian, 1944–45; Telegraph and Argus, and Yorkshire Observer, Bradford, 1945–54; Press Assoc., 1954–63; joined The Times, 1963: Asst News Editor, 1967; Dep. News Editor, 1967–69; Regional News Editor, 1969–77; Managing News Editor, 1977–82; Asst Managing Editor, 1982–86; Editorial Data Manager, Times Newspapers, 1986–88. Vice-Pres., 1977–78, Pres., 1978–79, Fellow, 1986, Chartered Inst. of Journalists; Member: Press Council, 1980–90; Nat. Council for Trng of Journalists, 1983–86. *Publications:* Taught With Care: a century of Church schooling, 1974; The Brontës and their Country, 1978, 3rd edn 1993; Brass Triumphant, 1980; North Yorkshire and North Humberside, 1984, 2nd edn 1989; (ed) One Hundred Years of Journalism, 1984; Pavilions on the Sea, 1986; (jtly) The News of the World Story, 1993; contrib. to various magazines. *Recreations:* reading, brass bands, water colour painting. *Address:* 6 Lea Road, Hemingford Grey, Huntingdon, Cambs PE28 9ED.

**BAINBRIDGE, Dr David Robert James;** Clinical Veterinary Anatomist, University of Cambridge, since 2003; Director of Studies, Tutor and Admissions Tutor, St Catharine's College, Cambridge, since 2003; Director of Studies, Trinity Hall, Cambridge, since 2007; *b* Chelmsford, 30 Oct. 1968; *s* of Robert and Peta Bainbridge; *m* 1997, Michelle; one *s* two *d*. *Educ:* Emmanuel Coll., Cambridge (BA 1989; VetMB 1992); Univ. of London (PhD 1997). MRCVS 1992. Postdoctoral researcher, Univ. of Oxford, 1996–99; Lectr, RVC, 1999–2003. Consultant, selfesteemteam.org, 2015–. *Publications:* A Visitor Within, 2000; The X in Sex, 2003; Beyond the Zonules of Zinn, 2008; Teenagers: a natural history, 2009; Middle Age: a natural history, 2012; Curvology, 2015. *Recreations:* travel, 70s music, astronomy, veterinary practice. *Address:* Department of Physiology, Development and Neuroscience, University of Cambridge, Downing Street, Cambridge CB2 3DY. *T:* (01223) 333799. *E:* db125@cam.ac.uk.

**BAINBRIDGE, Prof. Janet Mary,** OBE 2000; PhD; Senior Specialist Advisor, Bio-economy, Department for International Trade (formerly UK Trade and Investment) (Chief Executive, 2016); *b* 14 April 1947; *d* of Henry George Munn and Vera Doreen Munn; *m* 1st, 1970, Geoffrey Stathers Tuffnell (marr. diss. 1985); 2nd, 1987, Dr George Bainbridge (marr. diss. 2011); one *s* one *d*. *Educ:* Gravesend Girls' Grammar Sch.; Univ. of Newcastle upon Tyne (BSc Hons); Univ. of Leeds (PGCE); Univ. of Durham (PhD 1986). Microbiol. Res., Head Office, J. Sainsbury Ltd, 1968–70; NHS, 1970–71; secondary teaching, 1971–72; lectr, further educn, 1972–80; Teesside Polytechnic, then University: Lectr, then Sen. Lectr, 1980–85; Prin. Lectr, 1985–92; Divl Leader, 1992–98; Prof., 1996–2007, now Emeritus; Dir, Sch. of Sci. and Technol., 1998–2002; Tutor Counsellor, Sci. Foundn Degree, 1989–99, and Tutor, genetics, 1990–92, Open Univ. Chief Exec., European Process Industries Competitiveness Centre, 2001–04. Sen. Specialist Advr (Govt and Europe), One Northeast, 2004–07. UK Trade and Investment: Global Res. and Develt Specialist, 2007–13; Chief Exec., Agricultural Technol. Orgn, 2013–16. Mem., EPSRC, 2000–; Dep. Chm., Gen. Adv. Cttee on Sci., Food Standards Agency, 2010–; Chair: Govt

Adv. Cttee on novel foods and processes, 1997–2003; Ext. Adv. Panel, N8 AgriFood, 2002–16; Scientific Adv. Cttee on Genetic Manipulation (Contained Use), 2004–; Mem. Council, British Potato Council, 2003–07 (Chair, R&D Cttee, 2003–07); mem., other expert cttees and foresight panels. Non-exec. Dir, Virtual Vet. Trustee, Sense About Science, 2002–16. MSOFHT 1994; MILT 2000; FRSA 1998. *Publications:* numerous contribs to learned jls; expert papers for parly cttees, enquiries, etc. *Recreations:* family, gardening, travel.

**BAINBRIDGE, Prof. Simon;** freelance composer, conductor and lecturer; Professor, University of London, since 2001, and Senior Professor of Composition, since 2007, Royal Academy of Music (Senior Lecturer, 1999–2001; Head of Composition, 2001–07); *b* 30 Aug. 1952; *s* of John Bainbridge and Nan Knowles; *m* 1997, Lynda Richardson; one *d. Educ:* Central Tutorial Sch. for Young Musicians; Highgate Sch.; Royal Coll. of Music. Freelance composer, 1973–; Margaret Lee Crofts Fellowship (studying with Gunther Schuller), Berkshire Music Center, Tanglewood, USA, 1973; Leonard Bernstein Fellowship, 1974; Forman Fellow in Composition, Edinburgh Univ., 1976–78; US-UK Bicentennial Fellowship, 1978–79; Music Dir, Royal Nat. Theatre, 1980–82; Composer in residence, Southern Arts, 1982–86; Professor of Composition: RCM, 1989–99; GSMD, 1991–99; Composer in residence, Univ. of Wales Coll. of Cardiff, 1993–94. Hon. RAM 2002. Gemini Prize in Composition, Musicians' Co., 1988. *Compositions include:* Viola Concerto, 1978; Fantasia for Double Orchestra, 1984; Ad ora Incerta: four orchestral songs from Primo Levi, 1994 (Grawemeyer Award for Music Composition, Univ. of Louisville, 1997); Landscape and Memory, 1995; Four Primo Levi settings, 1996; (for chorus and ensemble) Chant, 1999; (for orchestra) Diptych, 2007; Music Space Reflection, 2007; (for chamber orchestra) Concerti Grossi, 2010; Counterpoints, 2015. *Recreations:* films, reading, cooking, swimming, walking. *Address:* c/o Novello & Co. (Music Sales Ltd), 14–15 Berners Street, W1T 3LJ.

**BAINES, (John) Christopher;** independent environmental consultant; Director, Chris Baines Associates Ltd, since 2011; *b* Sheffield, S Yorks, 4 May 1947; *s* of Stuart and Winifred Baines; partner, 1988, Nerys Jones. *Educ:* Ecclesfield Grammar Sch.; Wye Coll., Univ. of London (BSc Hons Horticulture); City of Birmingham Poly. (Postgrad. Dip. Landscape Architecture). FRSB (FIBiol 2009). Landscape architect, Blakedown Landscapes Ltd, 1969–74; Sen. Lectr in Landscape Design and Mgt, City of Birmingham Poly., 1974–88; Partner, Landscape Design Gp, 1974–79; Dir, Baines Environmental Ltd, 1979–2011. Presenter, TV progs incl. The Wild Side of Town, The ARK, Pebble Mill at One, Countryfile, Saturday Starship, The Big E, That's Gardening, throughout 1980s. Hon. Prof., UCE, 1986. Member: Rural Affairs Adv. Bd, BBC, 1998–2001; Adv. Gp, CABE Space, 2004–10; Urban Regeneration Panel, City of Bath, 2004–15; Expert Panel, Heritage Lottery Fund, 2005–11; Ind. Envmtl Rev. Panel, Stratford City and 2012 Olympic Village, 2007–12; CABE Design Rev. Panel for Ecotowns, 2009–11; Chm., Stakeholder Adv. Gp, Nat. Grid Visual Impact Provision, 2014–; independent adviser to: Alliance for Religions and Conservation, 2012–15; Royal Palaces, 2013; Thames Water plc, 2013; Lendlease, 2013–15. Nat. Vice Pres., Royal Soc. of Wildlife Trusts (formerly of Nature Conservation), 1987– (Chm., Strategic Develt Fund, 2011–16). Chm., Wyre Forest Landscape Partnership, 2013–. Hon. President: Assoc. for Envmt-Conscious Bldg, 1994–; Wildside Centre, Wolverhampton, 1997–; Urban Wildlife Partnership, 2000–12; Thames Estuary Partnership, 2001–; Essex Wildlife Trust, 2004–; Hon. Vice Pres., Wildlife Trust for Birmingham and the Black Country, 1990–. Trustee, Nat. Heritage Meml Fund, 1998–2004. Patron: Bankside Open Spaces Trust, 1999–; Landscape Design Trust, 2001–10; Countrywide Mgt Assoc., 2016–. Hon. FCIWEM 2000. Hon. Dr Envmtl Mgt Sheffield Hallam, 1998. Medal of Honour, RSPB, 2004; Peter Scott Meml Award, British Naturalists' Assoc., 2013. *Publications:* How to Make a Wildlife Garden, 1985, 2nd edn 2000; The Wild Side of Town, 1987 (Nat. Conservation Book Prize, Royal Soc. of Wildlife Trusts, 1987); A Guide to Habitat Creation, 1988, 2nd edn 1992; RHS Companion to Wildlife Gardening, 2016; *for children:* The Old Boot, The Nest, The Flower, The Picnic, 1996, 2nd edn 2002. *Recreations:* cooking, gardening, walking, nature conservation, watercolour painting, ski-ing. *Address:* 28 Parkdale West, Wolverhampton WV1 4TE. *T:* (01902) 424820. *E:* chris.baines@blueyonder.co.uk.

**BAINES, Prof. John Robert,** FBA 2011; Professor of Egyptology, University of Oxford, 1976–2013, Research Associate, 2013–14; Fellow of Queen's College, Oxford, 1976–2013, now Emeritus; *b* 17 March 1946; *o s* of late Edward Russell Baines and Dora Margaret Jean (*née* O'Brien); *m* 1971, Jennifer Christine Ann, *e d* of S. T. Smith; one *s* one *d. Educ:* Winchester Coll.; New Coll., Linacre Coll., Worcester Coll., Oxford (BA 1967, MA, DPhil 1976). Lectr in Egyptology, Univ. of Durham, 1970–75; Laycock Student, Worcester Coll., Oxford, 1973–75. Visiting Professor: Univ. of Arizona, 1982, 1988; Univ. of Michigan, 1989; Ecole Pratique des Hautes Etudes, Paris, 1994, 2003, 2012; Harvard Univ., 1995–96, 1999–2000; Univ. of Basel, 2003, 2011; Peking Univ., 2015; Dist. Vis. Prof., Amer. Univ., Cairo, 1999; Freehling Prof., Univ. of Michigan, 2002–03; Mem., Inst. for Advanced Study, Princeton, NJ, 2009–10; Old Dominion Fellow, Princeton Univ., 2014; MZAW-Gastprofessor, Ludwig-Maximilians-Universität, Munich, 2019–20. Fellow, Humboldt-Stiftung, 1982, 1989, 1996, 2016. Vice Pres., British Acad., 2014–18. Corresp. Mem., German Archaeol Inst., 1999; Mem., Amer. Philosophical Soc., 2011. *Publications:* (trans. and ed) H. Schäfer, Principles of Egyptian Art, 1974, rev. edn 1986; (with J. Malek) Atlas of Ancient Egypt, 1980 (trans. 11 langs), 2nd edn as Cultural Atlas of Ancient Egypt, 2000; (trans. and ed) E. Hornung, Conceptions of God in Ancient Egypt, 1982; Fecundity Figures, 1985; (ed jtly) Pyramid Studies and Other Essays presented to I. E. S. Edwards, 1988; (jtly) Religion in Ancient Egypt (ed B. E. Shafer), 1991; (ed) Stone Vessels, Pottery and Sealings from the Tomb of Tut'ankhamūn, 1993; (ed jtly) Civilizations of the Ancient Near East, 4 vols, 1995; (contrib.) Ancient Egyptian Kingship, 1995; Die Bedeutung des Reisens im alten Ägypten, 2004; Visual and Written Culture in Ancient Egypt, 2007; (ed jtly) The Disappearance of Writing Systems, 2008; High Culture and Experience in Ancient Egypt, 2013; (ed jtly) Historical Consciousness and the Use of the Past in the Ancient World, 2019; articles in collections and in Acta Orientalia, American Anthropologist, Art History, Encyclopaedia Britannica, Jl Egypt. Archaeol., Man, Orientalia, Studien altägypt. Kultur, etc. *Address:* Oriental Institute, Pusey Lane, Oxford OX1 2LE.

*See also P. J. Baines.*

**BAINES, Rt Rev. Nicholas;** *see* Leeds, Bishop of.

**BAINES, Priscilla Jean,** CB 2004; Librarian, House of Commons, 2000–04; *b* 5 Oct. 1942; *d* of late Edward Russell Baines and (Dora Margaret) Jean Baines (*née* O'Brien). *Educ:* Tonbridge Girls' Grammar Sch.; Somerville Coll., Oxford (BA Agric. 1963; MA 1967); Linacre Coll., Oxford (BLitt 1969). Adminr, Chelsea Coll., Univ. of London, 1965–68; House of Commons: Library Clerk, 1968–77; Head: Economic Affairs Section, 1977–88; Science and Envmt Section, 1988–91; Parly Div., 1991–93; Dep. Librarian and Dir of Human Resources, 1993–99. Associate, Hist. of Parlt, 2005–. *Publications:* (contrib.) New Select Committees, 1985, (contrib.) Westminster and Europe, 1996, 2004, and other pubns of Study of Parlt Gp; Colonel Josiah Wedgwood's Questionnaire: Members of Parliament, 1885–1918, 2012. *Recreations:* food, travel, opera. *Address:* 11 Ravensdon Street, SE11 4AQ.

*See also J. R. Baines.*

**BAINS, Rupinder;** solicitor; Founder and Managing Director, Pinder Reaux & Associates Ltd, since 2012; *b* Hillingdon, 20 Dec. 1974; *d* of Narinderjit Singh Hehar and Khushwant Kaur Hehar; *m* 1998, Justin Bains; one *s* one *d. Educ:* Greenford High Sch.; Nottingham Trent Univ. (LLB Hons Law 1996); Nottingham Law Sch. (LPC 1997); Univ. of Cambridge (Postgrad. Dip. Notarial Practice 2009). Admitted solicitor, 1999; partner in law firm, 2001; Founder, Bains Cohen LLP, 2003–12. Dir, Lily Foundn, 2013–. Non-exec. Dir, FA, 2017–. *Recreations:* avid football fan, enjoy watching football and spending time with my family. *Address:* Pinder Reaux & Associates Ltd, 502 Larkshall Road, E4 9HH. *T:* (020) 8252 7373. *E:* rbains@pinderreaux.com.

**BAINSFAIR, Paul Jeffrey,** FIPA; Director General, Institute of Practitioners in Advertising, since 2011; *b* London, 5 Jan. 1953; *s* of Leslie John and Doris May Bainsfair; *m* 1989, Sophie Giulietta Ray; two *s* one *d. Educ:* Watford Coll. Advertising (DipCAM). Account Exec., 1977–87, Man. Dir and Jt CEO, 1987–91, Saatchi & Saatchi; Co-Founder and Co-Chm., Bainsfair Sharkey Trott, 1991–99; Chm., 1999–2004, Pres., Europe, 2004–09, TBWA; Chm., IRIS Worldwide, 2009–11. Mem., Mktg Gp of GB. *Recreations:* golf, shooting, art, Queens Park Rangers. *Address:* Institute of Practitioners in Advertising, 44 Belgrave Square, SW1X 8QS. *T:* (020) 7235 7020. *E:* Paul@ipa.co.uk. *Clubs:* Groucho, Soho House; High Post Golf.

**BAIRD, Sir Andrew;** *see* Baird, Sir J. A. G.

**BAIRD, Sir Charles William Stuart,** 6th Bt *cr* 1809, of Newbyth, Haddingtonshire; *b* 8 June 1939; *s* of Robert William Stuart Baird and Maxine Christine, *oc* of Rupert Darrell, NY; *S* uncle, 2000; *m* 1965, Joanna Jane, *e d* of late Brig. A. Darley Bridge; three *d. Educ:* Switzerland. *Heir:* kinsman Andrew James Baird [*b* 23 Oct. 1970; *m* 2005, Katherine Louise Graham-Campbell; one *s* one *d*]. *Address:* 12 Falstaff Street, Sunnybank Hills, Brisbane, Qld 4109, Australia.

**BAIRD, Prof. David Tennent,** CBE 2000; FRCP, FRCOG, FMedSci; FRSE; Medical Research Council Clinical Research Professor of Reproductive Endocrinology, 1985–2000, now Emeritus, and Senior Professorial Research Fellow, MRC Centre for Reproductive Health and Obstetrics and Gynaecology, since 2000, University of Edinburgh; *b* 13 March 1935; *s* of Sir Dugald Baird, MD, FRCOG and Lady (May) Baird (*née* Tennent), CBE; *m* 1st, 1965, Frances Diana Lichtveld (marr. diss. 1995); two *s*; 2nd, 2000, Anna Frances Glasier. *Educ:* Aberdeen Grammar Sch.; Aberdeen Univ.; Trinity Coll., Cambridge (BA 1st cl.); Edinburgh Univ. (MB ChB; DSc). Junior med. posts, Royal Infirmary, Edinburgh, 1959–65; MRC Travelling Research Fellow, Worcester Foundn of Experimental Biology, USA, 1965–68; Lectr, later Sen. Lectr, Dept of Obstetrics, Univ. of Edinburgh, 1968–72; Dep. Dir, MRC Unit of Reproductive Biology, Edinburgh, 1972–77; Prof. of Obst. and Gyn., Univ. of Edinburgh, 1977–85. Consultant Gynaecologist, Royal Infirmary, Edinburgh, 1970–2000. Dir, Contraceptive Develt Network, 1995–2007. Mem., WHO Task Force on Infertility, 1976–82; Mem. and Chm., WHO Task Force on Postovulatory Methods, 1989–95. Leading developer of methods of med. abortion, contraception, ovulation induction. FRSE 1990. Founder FMedSci 1998. Hon. FRANZCOG 1997; Hon. FFPRHC 2008; Hon. FCMSA 2009. Hon. MD Nottingham, 2002. *Publications:* Contraceptives of the Future (with R. V. Short), 1976; Mechanism of Menstrual Bleeding, 1985; (jtly) Modern Methods of Inducing Abortion, 1995; contrib. 100 chapters in books and over 400 papers in med. and sci. jls on reproductive endocrinology, abortion and contraception. *Recreations:* ski mountaineering, golf. *Address:* 24 Moray Place, Edinburgh EH3 6DA. *T:* (0131) 281 4257.

**BAIRD, Gareth Thomas Gilroy;** DL; FRAgS; farmer, since 1979; Member, Board, Crown Estate, since 2010 (Scottish Commissioner, 2010–17); *b* Kelso, 11 May 1957; *s* of Roger and Margaret Baird; *m* 1985, Kirsty Stobbs; one *s* two *d. Educ:* St Mary's Prep. Sch.; Merchiston Castle Sch.; Edinburgh Sch. of Agric. (HND). Chm., Scottish Enterprise, S of Scotland Regl Adv. Bd, 2008–15. Chairman: Scott Country Potato Growers, 1995–; Pentlands Sci. Park, 2014–; Vice Chm., Grainco Ltd, 2005–; Director: Scotland Food and Drink, 2007–; Scottish Borders Produce, 2009–18. Dir, RHASS, 1995–2011. Chairman: Border Union Agricl Soc., 2000–01; Scottish Agricl Orgn Soc., 2000–03 and 2006–09. Chairman: St Mary's Sch., Melrose, 2005–; Merchiston Castle Sch., 2015– (Dep. Chm., 2014–15); Mem. Council, St George's Sch. for Girls, 2003–15. FRAgS 2005. Mem., Hon. Co. of Edinburgh Golfers. DL Roxburghshire, Ettrick and Lauderdale, 2008. *Recreations:* playing rugby, watching Rugby, spoofing. *Address:* Manorhill, Kelso, Roxburghshire TD5 7PA. *T:* (01573) 460237. *E:* gareth@baird.gbtbroadband.co.uk.

**BAIRD, Guy Martin,** FCA; Senior Adviser, European Investment Bank, Brussels, 2001–06; *b* 3 Jan. 1948; *s* of late Thomas Herbert Mertens Baird and Kathleen Florence Baird (*née* Mapley, later Ballard); *m* 1969, Juliet Hope Mears (marr. diss. 1984); two *d. Educ:* Wellington College. ACA 1970, FCA 1975. Bland Fielden & Co., 1966–69; Cooper Brothers & Co., subseq. Coopers & Lybrand, 1970–72; Manager, Fidital, Coopers & Lybrand SpA, Rome, 1972–74; Vice Pres. Finance, Italicor Inc., Atlanta and Milan, 1975–77; Manager, Andrew Moore & Co., 1978–79; European Investment Bank: Sen. Loan Officer, Luxembourg, 1980–83; Head of London Office, 1983–2001. *Recreations:* sailing, Wagner. *Club:* East India.

**BAIRD, Sir (James) Andrew (Gardiner),** 11th Bt *cr* 1695 (NS), of Saughton Hall, Edinburgh; *b* 2 May 1946; *s* of Sir James Baird, 10th Bt, MC and Mabel Ann, (Gay), *d* of A. Gill; *S* father, 1997, but his name does not appear on the Official Roll of the Baronetage; *m* 1984, Jean Margaret (marr. diss. 1988), *yr d* of Brig. Sir Ian Jardine, 4th Bt, OBE, MC; one *s. Educ:* Eton. *Heir:* *s* Alexander William Gardiner Baird, *b* 28 May 1986.

**BAIRD, James Hewson;** Chief Executive and Company Secretary, British Veterinary Association, 1997–2002; *b* 28 March 1944; *s* of James Baird, MBE, MRCVS and Ann Sarah Baird (*née* Hewson); *m* 1969, Clare Rosalind (*née* Langstaff); three *d. Educ:* Austin Friars; Creighton, Carlisle; Newcastle upon Tyne Univ. (BSc Hons Agric). Hydrologist, Essex River Authy, 1968–75; Policy Officer, Nat. Water Council, 1975–80. Institution of Civil Engineers: Asst Dir, 1980–81; Dir of Admin, 1981–86; Mem., Infrastructure Planning Gp, 1982–86; Dir, Assoc. of Municipal Engineers, 1984–86; Dir, External Affairs, Fedn of Civil Engineering Contractors, 1986–87. *Recreations:* Rugby, gardening, farming, countryside. *Address:* Hollyhock Cottage, Fen Street, Nayland, Suffolk CO6 4HT.

**BAIRD, Air Marshal Sir John (Alexander),** KBE 1999; DL; Surgeon General to the Armed Forces, 1997–2000; *b* 25 July 1937; *s* of late Dr David Alexander Baird, CBE and Isobel T. Baird; *m* 1963, Mary Clews. *Educ:* Merchiston Castle Sch.; Edinburgh Univ. (MB ChB). FFOM; FRCPE 1998; FRCSE 1999; DAvMed; FRAeS. Western Gen. Hosp., Edinburgh, 1961–62; MO Sarawak, 1962–63; commnd RAF, 1963; RAF Stations, UK and Singapore, 1963–80; exchange post, USA, 1970–73; HQ Strike Comd, 1980–83; MoD, 1983–86; OC Princess of Wales RAF Hosp., Ely, 1987–88; PMO, RAF Germany, 1988–91; PMO, HQ RAF Strike Comd, 1991–94; Dir Gen., RAF Med. Services, 1994–97. QHP 1991–2000. Mem., Internat. Acad. of Aviation and Space Medicine, 1993. FRSocMed 1983; Fellow: Aerospace Med. Assoc., 1992; Assoc. of Med. Secs, 2001. DL

Cambs, 1998. CStJ 1997. *Publications:* contribs to med. jls on aviation medicine subjects. *Recreations:* ornithology, wild-life conservation, cricket, music. *Address:* Braeburn, Barway, Ely, Cambs CB7 5UB. *Club:* Royal Air Force.

**BAIRD, Kenneth William;** Project Director/Chief Executive, European Opera Centre, since 1994; *b* 14 July 1950; *s* of William and Christine Baird. *Educ:* Uppingham School (Music Schol.); St Andrews Univ. (MA); Royal College of Music; Royal Sch. of Church Music. LRAM, ARCM. English National Opera, 1974–82; Gen. Manager, Aldeburgh Foundn, 1982–88; Music Dir, Arts Council, 1988–94. Sec., New Opera Co., 1981–82. Member: NW Arts Bd, 1998–2002; Arts Council NW, 2002–04; Bd, Huddersfield Contemporary Music Fest., 1997–2004; Bd, Birmingham Contemp. Music Gp, 2000–; Bd, Liverpool Hope Carter Preston Foundn (formerly Carter Preston Trust), 2015– (Chm., 2018–); Ina Boyle Develt Cttee, 2016–. Adv. Dir, Sonic Arts Network (Chm., 2003–08); Dir, Bittern Press, 2011–. Chairman: Snape Historical Trust, 1986–2001; British Arts Fests Assoc., 1988. Trustee, R. A. Vestey Meml Trust, 1991–2004. Mem., Nat. Adv. Council, Milap Fest. Trust, 2014– (Mem. Bd, 2016–). *Address:* c/o European Opera Centre, 1 Haigh Street, Liverpool L3 8QB. *Club:* Chelsea Arts.

**BAIRD, Nicholas Graham Faraday,** CMG 2010; CVO 2008; HM Diplomatic Service, retired; Group Corporate Affairs Director, Centrica plc, since 2014; *b* 15 May 1962; *s* of Colin and Elizabeth Baird; *m* 1985, Caroline Jane Ivett; one *s* two *d*. *Educ:* Dulwich Coll.; Emmanuel Coll., Cambridge (MA English Lit.). Joined FCO, 1983; Third Sec., Kuwait, 1986–89; First Sec., UK Repn to EU, Brussels, 1989–93; Private Sec. to Parly Under-Sec. of State, FCO, 1993–95; Hd, Amsterdam Intergovtl Conf. Unit, FCO, 1995–97; Counsellor and Dep. Hd of Mission, Muscat, 1997–98; Counsellor, UK Repn to EU, Brussels, 1998–2002; Hd, EU Dept (Internal), FCO, 2002–03; Sen. Dir, Internat. Immigration and Nationality Directorate, 2003–04; Policy, Immigration and Nationality Directorate, 2004–06; Home Office (on secondment); Ambassador to Turkey, 2006–09; Dir-Gen., Europe and Globalisation, 2009–11; Chief Exec., UK Trade and Investment, 2011–13. Ind. Dir, Nord Anglia Inc., 2015–17. Member: Cole Commn advising Labour Party on exports, 2014–15; President's Cttee, Inst. of Exports, 2017–. Member: Adv. Council, Sheffield Univ. Sch. of Mgt, 2014–; Develt Cttee, Prince's Teaching Inst., 2016–. Mem., Bd of Trustees, Royal Botanical Gardens, Kew, 2015–. *Recreations:* reading, theatre, running, travel. *Address:* Centrica plc, Millstream, Maidenhead Road, Windsor, Berks SL4 5GD.

**BAIRD, Vice-Adm. Sir Thomas (Henry Eustace),** KCB 1980; DL; *b* Canterbury, Kent, 17 May 1924; *s* of Geoffrey Henry and Helen Jane Baird; *m* 1953, Angela Florence Ann Paul (*d* 2009), Symington, Ayrshire; one *s* one *d*. *Educ:* RNC, Dartmouth. Served HM Ships: Trinidad, in support of convoys to Russia, 1941, Midshipman; Bermuda, Russian convoys and landings in N Africa, and Orwell, Russian convoys and Atlantic escort force, 1942; Howe, E Indies, 1943, Sub-Lt; Rapid, E Indies, 1944 until VJ Day, Lieut; St James, Home Fleet, 1946; Ganges, Ratings' New Entry Trng, 1948; Plucky, Exec. Officer, mine clearance in Mediterranean, 1950; Lt Comdr 1952; Veryan Bay, Exec. Officer, W Indies and Falkland Is., 1953; O-in-C, Petty Officers' Leadership Sch., Malta, 1954; Exec. Officer, HMS Whirlwind, Home Fleet and Med., for Suez Op., 1956; Comd, HMS Acute, Dartmouth Trng Sqdn, 1958; Comdr 1959; Comd, HMS Ulysses, Home Fleet, 1960; Staff, C-in-C, Home Fleet, Northwood, 1961; Exec. Officer, Jt Anti-Sub. Sch., Londonderry, 1963; EO, HMS Bulwark, Far East, 1965; Ch. Staff Officer to Cdre, Naval Drafting, 1966; Captain 1967; Dep. Dir, Naval Equipment, Adm., Bath, 1967; Captain: Mine Countermeasures; Fishery Protection and HMS Lochinvar (comd), 1969; Comd, HMS Glamorgan, Far East, W Indies, S Amer., Med., and UK Waters, 1971; Captain of the Fleet, 1973; Rear Adm. 1976; Chief of Staff to C-in-C Naval Home Comd, 1976–77; Dir Gen., Naval Personal Services, 1978–79; Vice-Adm. 1979; Flag Officer Scotland and NI, 1979–82. Chm. Exec. Cttee, Erskine Hosp., 1986–95. DL Ayrshire and Arran, 1982. *Recreations:* cricket, golf, shooting, fishing. *Address:* Craigrethill, Symington, Ayrshire KA1 5QN. *Club:* Prestwick Golf (Prestwick).

**BAIRD, Dame Vera,** DBE 2017; QC 2000; Victims' Commissioner, since 2019; *d* of Jack Thomas and Alice (*née* Marsland); *m* 1st, 1972, David John Taylor-Gooby (marr. diss. 1978); 2nd, 1978, Robert Brian Baird (*d* 1979); two step *s*. *Educ:* Newcastle Polytechnic (LLB Hons 1972); Open Univ. (BA 1982); London Guildhall Univ. (MA 2000). Called to the Bar, Gray's Inn, 1975, Bencher, 2004. MP (Lab) Redcar, 2001–10; contested (Lab) same seat, 2010. Parly Under-Sec. of State, DCA, then MoJ, 2006–07; Solicitor Gen., 2007–10. Police and Crime Comr (Lab) for Northumbria, 2012–19. Vis. Law Fellow, St Hilda's Coll., Oxford, 1999 (Hon. Fellow); Vis. Prof. of Legal Practice, Newcastle Univ., 2014–; Hon. Vis. Law Prof., London South Bank Univ.; Vis. Law Lectr, Teesside Univ. (Hon. Fellow). Chair, Bd of Dirs and Trustee, Centre for Criminal Appeals. Hon. Mem., Durham Miners' Assoc., 2000–. Hon. Fellow, Durham Univ. Law Sch. Hon. DCL Northumbria, 2014. *Publications:* Rape in Court, 1998; Defending Battered Women Who Kill, 2000; Seeing is Believing, 2017.

**BAIRD, William;** Under Secretary, Scottish Home and Health Department, 1978–87; *b* 13 Oct. 1927; *s* of Peter and Christina Baird, Airdrie; *m* 1954, Anne Templeton Macfarlane (*d* 2009); two *d*. *Educ:* Airdrie Academy; Glasgow Univ. Entered Scottish Home Dept, 1952; Private Sec. to Perm. Under-Sec. of State, Scottish Office, 1957; Principal, Scottish Educn Dept, 1958–63; Private Sec. to Minister of State and successive Secs of State for Scotland, 1963–65; Asst Sec., Scottish Educn Dept, 1965–66; Dept of Agriculture and Fisheries for Scotland, 1966–71; Scottish Office Finance Div., 1971–73; Registrar General for Scotland, 1973–78. *Address:* 8 Strathearn Road, North Berwick EH39 5BZ. *T:* (01620) 893190.

**BAIRSTO, Air Vice-Marshal Nigel Alexander,** CB 2007; MBE 1991; CEng, FIMechE, FRAeS; FCMI; Director, Bair Solutions Ltd, since 2013; *b* 27 Aug. 1953; *s* of Air Marshal Sir Peter Edward Bairsto, KBE, CB, AFC; *m* 1976, Alison Margaret Philippe; one *s* one *d*. *Educ:* King's Sch., Ely; Portsmouth Poly. (BSc 1975); RAF Coll., Cranwell; Cranfield Inst. of Technol. (MSc 1986); Cranfield Univ. (MDA 1999). CEng 1989; FIMechE 1997; FRAeS 2000. Commnd RAF Eng. Officer, 1971; RAF Leuchars, 1978–80; RAF Cottesmore, 1980–82; MoD, London, 1982–87; Sen. Engr Officer 14 Sqn, RAF Bruggen, 1987–91; RAF Staff Coll., Bracknell, 1991; Wing Comdr, Tornado, Strike Command, 1992–93; OC Eng & Supply, RAF Leeming, 1993–95; Gp Capt., Logistics, Strike Command, 1996–98; Station Comdr, Sealand, and Electronics Dir, DARA, 1998–2000; rcds 2000; ACOS Ops (Force Protection), Strike Command, and Comdt Gen., RAF Regt, 2001–03; Defence Logistics Organisation, Ministry of Defence: Tornado Integrated Project Team Leader, 2003–05; 1 Gp Cluster Leader, 2005; Dir Gen. Defence Logistics Transformation, 2005–07. Associate Partner, IBM Global Business Services, 2007–09; Vice Pres., 2009–11, Sen. Vice Pres., 2011–13, Selex Galileo; Transformation Dir, Wholesale, United Utilities plc, 2013–15. Chm., Central Council, RAFA, 2010–16, now Life Vice Pres. (Northern Area Pres., 2007–10, 2018–). Trustee, Air League, 2015– (Vice Chm., 2018–). Hon. Air Cdre, 2624 (Co. of Oxford) Regt Sqdn, RAuxAF, 2018–. FCMI 1997. *Recreations:* golf, shooting, ski-ing, private flying, gardening, sailing, hill walking. *Address:* Swayfield, Lincs. *T:* (01476) 550097. *E:* bears178@aol.com. *Clubs:* Royal Air Force; Royal Air Squadron; Royal and Ancient Golf; Luffenham Heath Golf; West Rheine Golf.

**BAIRSTOW, John;** Founder, 1968, Chairman, 1972–93, Queens Moat Houses PLC (formerly Queens Modern Hotels Ltd); *b* 25 Aug. 1930; *m*; four *d*. *Educ:* City of London Sch. FSVA. Founded Bairstow, Eves and Son, Valuers and Estate Agents, 1953. *Relevant publication:* Corporate Hijack? The John Bairstow Story, by Brian Lynch, 2005. *Recreation:* salmon fishing.

**BAISTER, Stephen,** PhD; Chief Bankruptcy Registrar of the High Court, Royal Courts of Justice, 2004–17 (Bankruptcy Registrar, 1996–2004); *b* 15 Feb. 1952; *s* of John Norman Baister and Bridget Baister. *Educ:* Merton Coll., Oxford (BA Mod. Langs 1974); Birkbeck Coll., London (MA German 1978); University Coll. London (PhD Law 1992). Admitted solicitor, 1981; solicitor in private practice, 1981–96. Non-exec. Dir, Manolete Partners plc, 2018–; Consultant, Moon Beevor Solicitors. Mediator, Three Stone Bldgs. Trustee, Condor Trust for Educn, 2005–. Hon. Mem., Insolvency Lawyers' Assoc., 1997–. Hon. FCICM (Hon. FICM 2011) (Pres., 2011–). *Publications:* with Chris Patrick: guide to East Germany, 1990; Latvia: the Bradt travel guide, 1999, 5th edn 2007; Riga: the Bradt city guide, 2005; William Le Queux: master of mystery, 2007; *contributions to:* Atkin's Court Forms; Butterworth's Encyclopaedia of Forms and Precedents; Civil Procedure; Muir Hunter on Personal Insolvency.

**BAJWA, Ali Naseem;** QC 2011; a Recorder, since 2018; *b* Lancs, 25 Aug. 1970; *s* of Naseem Bajwa and Yasmeen Bajwa; *m* 2000, Shine Khan; one *s* one *d*. *Educ:* Langley Grammar Sch.; London Sch. of Econs and Pol Sci. (LLB Hons); Inns of Court Sch. of Law (BVC). Called to the Bar, Gray's Inn, 1993, Bencher, 2015; in practice as a barrister specialising in criminal law, 1993–, 25 Bedford Row, 2000–11, Garden Court Chambers, 2011–. Pegasus Scholar, Crown Law Office, NZ, 1996. *Recreations:* cricket, tennis, ski-ing, international film. *Address:* Garden Court Chambers, 57–60 Lincoln's Inn Fields, WC2A 3LJ. *T:* (020) 7993 7600, *Fax:* (020) 7993 7700. *E:* alib@gclaw.co.uk.

**BAKAYA, Mohit;** Controller, BBC Radio 4 and BBC Radio 4 Extra, since 2019; *b* London, 12 Nov. 1964; *s* of Madan Bakaya and Uma Bakaya; *m* 2013, Victoria Shepherd; one *s*; one *s* one *d* by a previous marriage. *Educ:* Pimlico Sch.; Keble Coll., Oxford (BA Hons PPE). Trainee Producer, BBC Radio, 1993–95; Producer, Kaleidoscope, 1995–98, Sen. Producer, Front Row, 1998–2001, Commissioning Ed., Factual (current affairs, politics, history, sci. and religion), 2007–19, BBC Radio 4; Ed., Night Waves, BBC Radio 3, 2001–07. *Recreations:* music (PJ Harvey, Bruce Springsteen, Joni Mitchell, Bob Dylan), philosophy, wine, trying to cook the perfect consommé. *E:* mohit.bakaya@bbc.co.uk.

**BAKER,** family name of **Baron Baker of Dorking**.

**BAKER OF DORKING,** Baron *cr* 1997 (Life Peer), of Iford in the Co. of East Sussex; **Kenneth Wilfred Baker,** CH 1992; PC 1984; Chairman, Graphite Resources plc, 2007–12; *b* 3 Nov. 1934; *s* of late W. M. Baker, OBE and of Mrs Baker (*née* Harries); *m* 1963, Mary Elizabeth Gray-Muir; one *s* two *d*. *Educ:* Holy Trinity Primary, Southport; King George V Grammar Sch., Southport; Hampton Grammar Sch., Middx; St Paul's Sch.; Magdalen Coll., Oxford. Nat. Service, 1953–55: Lieut in Gunners, N Africa; Artillery Instructor to Libyan Army. Oxford, 1955–58 (Sec. of Union). Served Twickenham Borough Council, 1960–62. Contested (C): Poplar, 1964; Acton, 1966. MP (C): Acton, March 1968–1970; St Marylebone, Oct. 1970–1983; Mole Valley, 1983–97; Parly Sec., CSD, 1972–74; PPS to Leader of Opposition, 1974–75; Minister of State and Minister for Information Technology, DTI, 1981–84; Minister for Local Govt, DoE, 1984–85; Sec. of State for the Environment, 1985–86; Sec. of State for Educn and Sci., 1986–89; Chancellor of the Duchy of Lancaster, 1989–90; Chm., Conservative Party, 1989–90; Sec. of State for Home Dept, 1990–92. Mem., Public Accounts Cttee, 1969–70; Chm., H of L Inf. Cttee, 2002–06; Mem., House Cttee, H of L, 2007–12. Mem. Exec., 1922 Cttee, 1975–81. Chm., Teather & Greenwood plc, 2004–07. Chm., Hansard Soc., 1978–81. Sec. Gen., UN Conf. of Parliamentarians on World Population and Development, 1978. Pres., Royal London Soc. for the Blind, 1999–2010; Vice Chm., Cartoon Art Trust, 2003–; Trustee, Booker Prize Foundn, 2005–18; Chm. of Trustees, Baker Dearing Educnl Trust, 2008–; Chm., Edge Foundn, 2010–. Hon. Dr: Aston; Warwick; Plymouth; Chester; Wolverhampton; Brunel. *Publications:* (ed) I Have No Gun But I Can Spit, 1980; (ed) London Lines, 1982; (ed) The Faber Book of English History in Verse, 1988; (ed) Unauthorized Versions: poems and their parodies, 1990; (ed) The Faber Book of Conservatism, 1993; The Turbulent Years: my life in politics, 1993; The Prime Ministers: an irreverent political history in cartoons, 1995; (ed) The Faber Book of War Poetry, 1996; The Kings and Queens: an irreverent cartoon history of the British monarchy, 1996; (ed) A Children's English History in Verse, 2000; (ed) The Faber Book of Landscape Poetry, 2000; George IV: a life in caricature, 2005; George III: a life in caricature, 2007; (ed) Poems by G. K. Chesterton, 2007; George Washington's War in caricature and print, 2009; (jtly) 14–18 A New Vision for Secondary Education, 2013; On the Burning of the Books, 2018; On the Seven Deadly Sins, 2018. *Recreation:* collecting books and political caricatures. *Address:* House of Lords, Westminster, SW1A 0PW. *Clubs:* Athenæum, Garrick, Old Pauline (Pres., 2007–09).

**BAKER, Dr Alan Reginald Harold,** FBA 2010; Fellow, Emmanuel College, Cambridge, since 1970; *b* Canterbury, 20 Oct. 1938; *s* of Reginald Andrew Baker and Edith Georgina Baker (*née* Hackman); *m* 1960, Sandra Walker Teale; two *s*. *Educ:* Kent Coll., Canterbury; University Coll. London (BA 1960; PhD 1963); DLit London 1999. Asst Lectr in Geog., 1963–64, Lectr in Geog., 1964–66, UCL; University of Cambridge: Lectr in Geog., 1966–99, pt-time, 1999–2001; Hd, Dept of Geog., 1989–94; Tutor, 1973–76, Sen. Tutor, 1976–86, Vice-Master, 1990–94, Emmanuel Coll., Cambridge. Editor: Jl Histl Geog., 1987–96; Cambridge Studies in Histl Geog., 1980–2005. Mem. (Lib Dem) Cambridge CC, 2002–10 (Chair, Planning Cttee, 2003–10). Hon. Mem., Soc. de Géographie de Paris, 2003. Gill Meml Medal, 1974, Founder's Medal, 2009, RGS. Chevalier, Ordre des Palmes Académiques (France), 1997. *Publications:* (ed jtly) Geographical Interpretations of Historical Sources, 1970; (ed) Progress in Historical Geography, 1972; (ed jtly) Studies of Field Systems in the British Isles, 1973; (ed jtly) Period and Place: research methods in historical geography, 1982; (ed jtly) Explorations in Historical Geography, 1984; (ed jtly) Ideology and Landscape in Historical Perspective, 1992; Fraternity Among the French Peasantry: sociability and voluntary associations in the Loire Valley, 1815–1914, 1999; Geography and History: bridging the divide, 2003; (ed jtly) Geographies of England: the North-South divide, imagined and material, 2004; Amateur Musical Societies and Sports Clubs in Provincial France, 1848–1914, 2017; contrib. articles to learned jls. *Recreations:* walking, appreciating the landscapes, wines and foods of France, reading political biographies and autobiographies, theatre going, visiting art galleries, trying to follow my wife's instructions in our garden. *Address:* Emmanuel College, Cambridge CB2 3AP. *T:* (01223) 334200. *E:* arb1000@cam.ac.uk.

**BAKER, Alistair James;** Founder and Chief Executive Officer, Cogent Healthcare Systems (formerly Cogent Business Group), 2008–14; *b* 26 July 1962; one *s* three *d*. *Educ:* BSc Hons Computing and Informatics; Postgrad. DipM. Joined IBM, 1984; various rôles, IBM, Hewlett Packard, Morse Computers, 1984–96; joined Microsoft, 1996; Country Manager Scotland, 1996–98; Gp Dir, Microsoft Services Orgn, 1998–2002; Gen. Manager, Small and Mid-Mkt Solutions and Partners, 2002–04; Man. Dir, Microsoft Ltd, 2004–06; Vice Pres., Microsoft EMEA, 2004–06. FCIM. *Recreations:* cycling, snow-boarding, guitar.

BAKER, Andrew John, MA; freelance lecturer in contemporary history, since 2012; b Bolton, 13 Nov. 1946; s of late John and Lilian Baker; m 1971, Lynda Ann Revell; one s. Educ: Farnworth Grammar Sch.; Univ. of Sheffield (BA 1969; MA 1973). Teacher of Hist., Boteler Grammar Sch., Warrington, 1969–74; Hulme Grammar School, Oldham: Sen. Hist. Master, 1974–81; Dir, Sixth Form Studies, 1981–87; Dep. Headmaster, 1987–90; Headmaster, Westcliff High Sch. for Boys, 1990–2012. Lectr to educationalists and businessmen on contemp. educnl issues, 1987–2014. Chm., Essex Secondary Heads' Assoc., 1995–98, 2001–05, 2009–12. Sch. Improvement Partner, 2007–10. Governor: Immanuel Coll., Bushey, 2012–15; Hearts Acad. Trust Bd, Wickford, 2016–. *Publications:* Examining British Politics, 1979; Education, Society and the Pursuit of Values: a headmaster's reflections, 2015. *Recreations:* reading, contemporary affairs, conversation, music, theatre, cricket, walking. *Address:* 48 Burges Road, Thorpe Bay, Essex SS1 3AX. *E:* ajbaker48@hotmail.co.uk. *W:* www.ajbeducation.co.uk.

BAKER, Hon. Sir Andrew (William), Kt 2016; Hon. Mr Justice Andrew Baker; a Judge of the High Court of Justice, Queen's Bench Division, since 2016; b 21 Dec. 1965; s of Gordon Baker and Ann Baker (now Williamson); m 1986, Philippa Jane Ghaut; four s. Educ: Lenzie Acad., Strathclyde; Merton Coll., Oxford (BA Maths 1986; MA 1990); City Univ. (PGDipLaw 1987). Called to the Bar, Lincoln's Inn, 1988 (Hardwicke, Wolfson and Kennedy Scholar); Tutor, law of internat. trade, 1988–89; in practice at the Bar, 1989–2016; QC 2006; a Recorder, 2012–16; a Dep. High Court Judge, 2016. CEDR Accredited Mediator, 2008; Reg. Practitioner, Dubai Internat. Financial Centre Courts, 2011–16. Mem., Admiralty and Commercial Court Users' Cttee, 2009–16. Supporting Mem., London Maritime Arbitrators Assoc., 2004–16. Member: Panel of Arbitrators, Singapore Internat. Arbitration Centre, 2010–12; Singapore Maritime Arbitrators Assoc., 2010–16; Kuala Lumpur Regl Centre for Arbitration, 2010–16. Gov., Busbridge C of E (Aided) Jun. Sch., 2005–13 (Chm., 2011–13). Series Editor, Lloyd's Shipping Law Library, 2009–16. *Publications:* (jtly) Time Charters, 6th edn 2008, 7th edn 2014. *Recreations:* time with Philippa and the Fabulous Baker Boys, golf, tennis, football (playing and coaching), Lotus and McLaren cars, playing trumpet, music, films. *Address:* Royal Courts of Justice, Strand, WC2A 2LL.

BAKER, Ann Maureen, (Mrs D. R. Baker); see Jenner, A. M.

BAKER, Anthony Thomas; independent reviewer, Airports Slot Allocation Regulations, since 2005; Director, International Aviation Negotiations, Department for Transport, retired 2004; b 1944; s of Charles Arthur Baker and Ivy Louvain Baker; m 1969, Alicia Veronica Roberts; two s one d. Educ: Chatham House Grammar Sch., Ramsgate; Lincoln Coll., Oxford (BA Hons Modern History). Ministry of Transport: Asst Principal, 1965–70; Principal, 1970–75; Principal, HM Treasury, 1975–78; Asst Sec., 1978–88, and 1991–96, MOT; Dir, Internat. Aviation Negotiations, DoE, then DETR, subseq. DTLR, later DfT, 1996–2004. Dir, County NatWest Ltd, 1988–91. Co-Chair, 2008–14, Chair, 2014–18, Harington Scheme. Freeman, City of London. *Recreations:* theatre, opera, history, literature. *Address:* 68 Talbot Road, N6 4RA.

BAKER, Antonia; see Boström, A.

BAKER, Catherine Judith; see Cowton, C. J.

BAKER, Christopher John; Director, European and Scottish Art and Portraiture, National Galleries of Scotland, since 2018; b Bromley, Kent, 3 March 1967; s of D. W. W. Baker and J. Baker (née Askham); m 2001, Alison Brooks; one d. Educ: Univ. of York; Univ. of Manchester. Researcher, National Gall., 1989–95; Lectr (pt-time), Birkbeck Coll., Univ. of London, 1996–97; Asst Curator, Christ Church Picture Gall., Oxford, 1997–2003; Dep. Dir and Chief Curator, Nat. Gall. of Scotland, 2003–12; Dir, Scottish Nat. Portrait Gall., 2012–18. Vis. Fellow, Yale Univ. Expert Advr, Scottish Nat. Fund for Acquisitions, Nat. Mus, Edinburgh. Member: Steering Cttee, UK Nat. Inventory Res. Project/Subject Specialist Network: Eur. Paintings Pre-1900; UK Govt Spoliation Panel. Mem., Adv. Bd, Mus, Galls and Collections Inst., Univ. of St Andrews. *Publications:* Canaletto, 1994; (with T. Henry) The National Gallery Complete Illustrated Catalogue, 1995; Guide to Christ Church Picture Gallery, 2002; (ed jtly) Collecting Prints and Drawings in Europe, c. 1500–1800, 2003; J. M. W. Turner: The Vaughan Bequest, 2006; Turner and Italy, 2009; The Discovery of Spain, British Artists and Collectors, 2009; Catalogue of English Drawings and Watercolours, 1600–1900, 2011; Companion Guide to the Scottish National Portrait Gallery, 2014; John Ruskin, Artist and Observer, 2014; Jean-Etienne Liotard, 2015; Turner and the Poetics of Landscape, 2017; The Monarch of the Glen by Landseer, 2017; contribs to jls incl. Burlington Mag., Apollo, Jl Hist. of Collections, British Art Jl. *Recreations:* travel, cooking. *E:* cbaker@nationalgalleries.org.

BAKER, Air Vice-Marshal Christopher Paul, CB 1991; Chairman, Taylor Curnow Ltd, 1994–2013; b 14 June 1938; er s of late Paul Hocking Baker, FCA and Kathleen Minnie Florence Baker; m 1st, 1961, Heather Ann Laity (decd), d of late Cecil Henry Laity and Eleanor Hocking Laity; three s; 2nd, 1981, Francesca R. Aghabi, er d of late George Khalil Aghabi and Elizabeth Maria Regina Aghabi; two s. Educ: Bickley Hall, Kent; Tonbridge School. Commnd RAF, 1958; served 1958–61: RAF Khormaksar (Air Movements), Aden; Supply Sqdn, RAF Coll., Cranwell; RAF Labuan, N Borneo; No 389 Maintenance Unit, RAF Seletar, Singapore; MoD Harrogate; student, RAF Staff Coll., Bracknell; OC Supply Sqdn, RAF Linton-on-Ouse; SHAPE, Two ATAF; ndc; Directing Staff, RAF Staff Coll., Bracknell; HQ RAF Support Comd; Dep. Dir, RAF Supply Systems, MoD; Comd Supply Movements Officer, HQ Strike Comd, RAF High Wycombe, 1982–84; RCDS, 1985; Dir, Supply Systems, MoD, 1986–87; Dir, Supply Policy and Logistics Plans, MoD, 1988–89; Dir Gen. of Support Management, RAF, 1989–93. Gen. Manager, Defence Sector Business Gp, TNT Express (UK) Ltd, 1993–94. Freeman, City of London; Liveryman, Bakers' Co. *Publications:* papers on the crisis of authority, oil potential of the Arctic Basin, and German reunification. *Recreations:* Rugby, rowing, ski-ing, modern history.

BAKER, Claire Josephine, PhD; Member (Lab) Scotland Mid and Fife, Scottish Parliament, since 2007; b Dunfermline, 4 March 1971; d of James Brennan and Margaret Brennan (née Edgar); m 2004, Richard James Baker, qv; one d. Educ: Edinburgh Univ. (MA Hons English Lang. and Lit.); Glasgow Univ. (PhD English Lit. 1997). Labour researcher, Scottish Parlt, 1999–2002; Amicus researcher, 2002–04; Res. and Information Manager, RCN Scotland, 2004–05; Policy Manager, SCVO, 2005–07. *Publications:* Critical Guide to the Poetry of Sylvia Plath, 1998. *Address:* Ore Valley Business Centre, 93 Main Street, Lochgelly, Fife KY5 9AF. *T:* (01592) 786726, *Fax:* (01592) 566401. *E:* claire.baker.msp@parliament.scot.

BAKER, David Brian, OBE 2001; FSA; consultant, historic environment conservation, since 1997; b 20 Jan. 1941; s of Henry and Maie Baker; m 1963, Evelyn Amos; one s. Educ: Hertford Coll., Oxford (BA Hons Mod. Hist. 1963); Inst. of Educn, London (PGCE 1964). FSA 1972; MCIfA (MIFA 1982); IHBC 1998. Asst Hist. Master, Bedford Sch., 1964–68; Lectr in Hist., Portsmouth Poly., 1968–71; Conservation and Archaeol. Officer, Beds County Planning Dept, 1972–97. Member: various adv. cttees, English Heritage, 1990–2011; Council, NT, 1998–2006; Vice-Pres., 1999–2008, Chm., Historic Bldgs Panel, 2012–, Council for British Archaeol. Chm., Adv. Bd for Redundant Churches, C of E, 2005–08 (Mem., 2001–08); Member: St Albans DAC, 1973–; Rochester Fabric Adv. Cttee, 2007–; Cathedrals Fabric Commn for England, 2012–. Chm., Cowdray Heritage Trust, 2009–13 (Trustee, 1998–2013). *Publications:* Living with the Past, 1983; numerous papers in conservation and archaeol jls. *Recreations:* photography, music, gardening. *Address:* 3 Oldway, Bletsoe, Bedford MK44 1QG. *T:* (01234) 781179. *E:* dbb@suttons.org.uk.

BAKER, Derek Alexander; Permanent Secretary, Department of Education, Northern Ireland, since 2017; b 3 Nov. 1957; s of Alexander James Baker and Sarah Beatrice Baker; m 1989, Barbara Anne Haggan; one s two d. Educ: Queen's Univ., Belfast (BA Hons French and German). Joined NICS, 1980; Dept for Econ. Develt, 1980–84, and 1987–93; Harland & Wolff Shipbuilders (on secondment), 1985–87; Asst Sec., Dept of Health and Social Services, 1993–2002; Dep. Sec., Dept for Social Develt, 2002–06; Dir, Corporate HR (formerly Central Personnel Gp), Dept of Finance and Personnel, 2006–12; Dep. Sec., Dept of Educn, 2013; Perm. Sec., Dept for Employment and Learning, 2013–16.

BAKER, Dick; see Baker, F. E.

BAKER, Prof. Edward James, MD; FRCP, FRCPCH; Chief Inspector of Hospitals England, Care Quality Commission, since 2017 (Deputy Chief Inspector of Hospitals England, 2014–17); b 2 May 1956; s of late Christopher Baker and Dr Hazel Baker; m 1982, Patricia Hudswell; two d. Educ: Trinity Coll., Cambridge (MB BChir 1979; MA; MD 1987); St Thomas's Hosp. Med. Sch. FRCP 1994; FRCPCH 1997. Hon. Consultant Paediatric Cardiologist, Guy's Hosp., 1987–2010; Sen. Lectr, 1987–2010, Prof. of Paediatric Cardiol., 2010, KCL; Medical Director: Guy's and St Thomas' Hosp. NHS Trust, subseq. Guy's and St Thomas' NHS Foundn Trust, 2003–10; Oxford Radcliffe NHS Trust, subseq. Oxford Univ. Hosps NHS Trust, 2010–14. Editor-in-Chief, Cardiology in the Young, 2007–13. *Publications:* (ed jtly) Paediatric Cardiology, 1986, 3rd edn 2010. *Address:* Care Quality Commission, 151 Buckingham Palace Road, SW1W 9SZ. *T:* (020) 7448 9084.

BAKER, Elizabeth Margaret; Headmistress, Wimbledon High School, 1992–95, retired; b 13 Sept. 1945; d of Walter and Betty Gale; m; one d. Educ: University College of Wales, Swansea (BA, DipEd). Lectr, Derby Coll. of Further Educn, 1968–71; Classics Teacher: West Monmouth Sch., 1971–74; Cheltenham Bournside, 1974–81; Cheltenham Ladies' Coll., 1981–88; Headmistress, Ellerslie, Malvern, 1988–92. *Recreations:* wine, letter-writing, keeping the classics alive.

BAKER, Francis Eustace, (Dick), CBE 1984 (OBE 1979); business interests in property and the automotive industry; Partner, Crossroads Motors, since 1988; b 19 April 1933; s of Stephen and Jessica Wilhelmina Baker; m 1957, Constance Anne Shilling; two s two d. Educ: Borden Grammar Sch.; New Coll., Oxford (MA). Nat. Service, RNVR, 1955–57 (Sub Lieut; minesweeper navigating officer). Admin. Officer, HMOCS, 1957; Solomon Islands: Dist. Officer, W Solomons, 1958; Co-operatives Develt Officer, 1960; Secretariat Officer and Clerk to Legislative Council, 1961–63; farming in UK, 1963–67; Admin. Officer, British Service Condominium of New Hebrides, 1967–79 (Chief Co-operatives Officer, 1968–73; District Agent, Northern District, 1973–78; Political and Lands Sec., British Residency Secretariat, 1978–79); Chief Sec. to Falkland Is Govt and Deputy to Gov. and High Comr, British Antarctic Territory, 1979–84; Gov. and C-in-C, St Helena and Dependencies of Ascension and Tristan Da Cunha, 1984–88. Queen's Silver Jubilee Medal, 1977. *Recreations:* swimming, reading, travelling, interesting motor cars. *Address:* Fairway, Bannister Hill, Borden, Sittingbourne, Kent ME9 8HT. *T:* (01795) 423301.

BAKER, Francis Raymond, CMG 2018; OBE 1997; Ambassador to Libya, 2018–19; b 27 Jan. 1961; s of late Raymond Albert Baker and Pamela Annis Baker; m 1983, Maria Pilar Fernandez; one s one d. Educ: Dartford Grammar Sch. Entered FCO, 1981: Third Sec., Panama City, 1983–86; Third, later Second Sec., Buenos Aires, 1986–91; Second Sec., FCO, 1991–93; First Secretary: Ankara, 1993–96; on secondment to US State Dept, Washington, 1996–98; FCO, 1998; Private Sec. to Minister of State, FCO, 1998–2000; Head, Africa Dept (Equatorial), FCO, 2000–03; Counsellor (Pol/Mil.), 2003–04, Counsellor (Foreign and Security Policy), 2004–07, Washington; Dir (Iraq), FCO, 2007–10; Ambassador: to Kuwait, 2010–14; to Iraq, 2014–17. *Recreations:* cricket, watching football (Ebbsfleet Utd FC), American football, golf, rock music, sailing, road biking, travelling.

BAKER, Gerard Thomas; Editor at Large, Wall Street Journal, since 2018 (Editor-in-Chief, 2013–18); columnist, The Times; b Barnehurst, Kent, 24 Jan. 1962; s of Frederick Samuel Baker and Della Maria Baker (née O'Flynn); m 1993, Sally Hinton; five d. Educ: St Mary's Grammar Sch., Sidcup; Corpus Christi Coll., Oxford (MA 1st Cl. Hons PPE 1983; Hon. Fellow). Analyst, Bank of England, 1984–86; economist, Lloyds Bank, 1986; researcher, Weekend World, LWT, 1987–88; British Broadcasting Corporation: producer, News and Current Affairs, 1988–89; New York producer, 1989–90; producer, Panorama, 1990–93; economics corresp., 1993–94; Financial Times: Tokyo corresp., 1994–96; Washington corresp., 1996–98; Washington Bureau Chief, 1998–2002; Associate Ed. and Chief US Commentator, 2002–04; US Ed., The Times, 2004–09; Dep. Ed.-in-Chief, Dow Jones and Wall St Jl, 2009–13. *Recreations:* travel, running, reading. *Address:* Wall Street Journal, 1211 Avenue of the Americas, New York, NY 10036, USA. *T:* (212) 4163070. *E:* gerard.baker@wsj.com. *Club:* Soho House.

BAKER, Gordon Meldrum; HM Diplomatic Service, retired; Temporary Senior Clerk, Committee Office, House of Lords, 2002–06; Clerk, Sub-Committee G (Social Policy and Consumer Affairs), European Union Select Cttee, 2004–06; b 4 July 1941; o s of Walter John Ralph Gordon Baker and Kathleen Margaret Henrietta Dawe Baker (née Meldrum); m 1978, Sheila Mary Megson (d 2011). Educ: St Andrew's Sch., Bawdrip, near Bridgwater; Univ. of Bradford (MSc 1976). Lord Chancellor's Dept, 1959–66; transf. to HM Diplomatic Service, 1966; Commonwealth Office, 1966–68; FO (later FCO), 1968–69; Lagos, 1969–72; First Sec., FCO, 1973–75 (Resident Clerk, 1974–75); sabbatical at Postgrad. Sch. of Studies in Industrial Technol., Univ. of Bradford, 1975–76; FCO, 1976–78 (Res. Clerk, 1976–78); First Sec. (Chancery/Information), subseq. First Sec., Head of Chancery and Consul, Brasilia, 1978–81; Asst Head, Mexico and Central America Dept, FCO, 1982–84; Counsellor, 1984; on secondment to British Aerospace, 1984–86; Counsellor, Head of Chancery then Dep. Hd of Mission, and Consul-General, Santiago, 1986–89, Chargé d'Affaires, 1986, 1987 and 1989; RCDS, 1990–91; Head of W Indian and Atlantic Dept, FCO, 1991–94; High Commissioner: Belize, 1995–98; Barbados and Eastern Caribbean States, 1998–2001; Inquiry Sec., Competition Commn, 2002. Associate Fellow and Chm., Caribbean Study Gp, RIIA, 2001–07; Mem. Adv. Panel, Centre for Positive Ageing, Univ. of Greenwich, 2013–15. Mem., Local Socs Consultative Gp on Greenwich Park Olympics, 2010–12. Mem., Exec. Cttee, Anglo-Chilean Soc., 2002–06. Trustee: Friends of Georgian Soc. of Jamaica, 2003–05, 2008–16 (Chm., 2012–15); Blackheath Historic Bldgs Trust, 2009–13. Patron, Age Activity Centre, Wandsworth, 2001–09. Mem., Exec. Cttee, Westcombe Soc. (local community assoc.), 2002–13 (Chm., 2007–12); Trustee: Ramphal Centre, 2007–11; Carers Support (Bexley and Greenwich), 2011–12. Chairman: Stewardship Cttee, St Alfege's Ch, Greenwich, 2015–; Parish Meeting, Holwell, Oxon, 2017–. *Publications:* (ed) No Island is an Island: the impact of globalization on the

Commonwealth Caribbean, 2007. *Recreations:* walking, watching birds, browsing, enjoying the arts and the company of women and small animals, collecting clocks. *Address:* 78 Foyle Road, Blackheath, SE3 7RH.

**BAKER, Ian Michael;** a District Judge (Magistrates' Courts) (formerly Metropolitan Stipendiary Magistrate), 1990–2012; a Recorder, 2002–17; *b* 8 May 1947; *s* of late David Ernest Baker and Phyllis Hinds; *m* 1st, 1976, Sue Joel (marr. diss. 1985); one *s*; 2nd, 1991, Jill Sack (*d* 2001); 3rd, 2005, Jane Hinde. *Educ:* Cynffig Grammar Sch., Mid Glam; St Catharine's Coll., Cambridge (MA). Travelled, New England, Latin America and Asia, 1969–71. Articled, then Asst Solicitor to John Clitheroe, Kingsley Napley, 1972–76; Partner, Heninghem, Ambler & Gildener, York, 1976–79; Assistant Solicitor: Claude, Hornby & Cox, 1979; Seifert Sedley, 1980–83; Clinton Davis, 1984–87; Partner, T. V. Edwards, 1987–90. Mem., Equal Treatment Adv. Cttee, Judicial Studies Bd, 2002–08. Trustee, Nat. Council for Welfare of Prisoners Abroad, 1986–99 (Chm., 1993–99). *Recreations:* travel, especially visiting grandchildren in New Zealand, saxophone, theatre, music, art, gardening, bird watching, golf.

**BAKER, Dame Janet (Abbott),** CH 1994; DBE 1976 (CBE 1970); professional singer; *b* 21 Aug. 1933; *d* of Robert Abbott Baker and May (*née* Pollard); *m* 1957, James Keith Shelley. *Educ:* The College for Girls, York; Wintringham, Grimsby. Chancellor, Univ. of York, 1991–2004. Trustee, Foundn for Sport and the Arts, 1991–2012. Daily Mail Kathleen Ferrier Award, 1956; Queen's Prize, Royal College of Music, 1959; Shakespeare Prize, Hamburg, 1971; Copenhagen Sonning Prize, 1979; Lifetime Achievement Award, Gramophone, 2011. Hon. DMus: Birmingham, 1968; Leicester, 1974; London, 1974; Hull, 1975; Oxon, 1975; Leeds, 1980; Lancaster, 1983; York, 1984; Hon. MusD Cantab, 1984; Hon. LLD Aberdeen, 1980; Hon. DLitt Bradford, 1983. Hon. Fellow: St Anne's Coll., Oxford, 1975; Downing Coll., Cambridge, 1985. FRSA 1979. Gold Medal, Royal Philharmonic Soc., 1990. Comdr, Order of Arts and Letters (France), 1995. *Publications:* Full Circle (autobiog.), 1982. *Recreations:* reading, walking.

**BAKER, Hon. Sir Jeremy (Russell);** Kt 2013; **Hon. Mr Justice Jeremy Baker;** a Judge of the High Court of Justice, Queen's Bench Division, since 2013; a Presiding Judge, Midland Circuit, since 2017; *b* 9 Feb. 1958. Called to the Bar, Middle Temple, 1979, Bencher, 2013; QC 1999; Recorder, 2000–10; a Circuit Judge, 2010–13. *Address:* Royal Courts of Justice, Strand, WC2A 2LL.

**BAKER, Prof. Sir John Hamilton,** Kt 2003; LLD; FBA 1984; Downing Professor of the Laws of England, Cambridge University, 1998–2011, now Emeritus; Fellow, St Catharine's College, Cambridge, 1971–2011, Emeritus, 2011–12, now Honorary Fellow (President, 2004–07); *b* 10 April 1944; *s* of Kenneth Lee Vincent Baker, QPM and Marjorie (*née* Bagshaw); *m* 1st, 1968, Veronica Margaret (marr. diss. 1997), *d* of Rev. W. S. Lloyd; two *d*; 2nd, 2002, Fiona Rosalind Holdsworth (*née* Cantlay) (*d* 2005); 3rd, 2010, Prof. Elisabeth Maria Cornelia van Houts, *widow* of Thomas Erle Faber. *Educ:* King Edward VI Grammar School, Chelmsford; UCL (LLB 1965 (Andrews Medal), PhD 1968; Fellow 1990); MA Cantab 1971, LLD 1984, Yorke Prize, 1975. FRHistS 1980. Called to the Bar, Inner Temple, 1966 (Hon. Bencher 1988), *aeg* Gray's Inn, 1978 (Hon. Bencher 2013). Asst Lectr, Faculty of Laws, UCL, 1965–67, Lectr, 1967–71; Cambridge University: Librarian, Squire Law Library, 1971–73; Univ. Lectr in Law, 1973–83; Reader in English Legal History, 1983–88; Prof. of English Legal Hist., 1988–98; Junior Proctor, 1980–81; Chm., Faculty of Law, 1990–92. Visiting Professor: European Univ. Inst., Florence, 1979; Yale Law Sch., 1987; NY Univ. Sch. of Law, 1988–2010; Vis. Lectr, Harvard Law Sch., 1982; Mellon Senior Res. Fellow, H. E. Huntington Liby, San Marino, Calif., 1983; Ford Special Lectr, Oxford Univ., 1984; Vis. Fellow, All Souls Coll., Oxford, 1995. Corresp. Fellow, Amer. Soc. Legal History, 1993; Hon. Fellow, Soc. for Advanced Legal Studies, 1997; Hon. Foreign Mem., Amer. Acad. of Arts and Scis, 2001. Literary Dir, Selden Soc., 1981–2011 (Jt Dir, 1981–90). Hon. QC 1996. Hon. LLD Chicago, 1992. Ames Prize, Harvard, 1985; Gold Medal, Irish Soc. for Legal Hist., 2008. *Publications:* An Introduction to English Legal History, 1971, 4th edn 2002; English Legal Manuscripts, vol. I, 1975, vol. II, 1978; The Reports of Sir John Spelman, 1977–78; (ed) Legal Records and the Historian, 1978; Manual of Law French, 1979, 2nd edn 1990; The Order of Serjeants at Law, 1984; English Legal Manuscripts in the USA, vol. I 1985, vol. II 1991; The Legal Profession and the Common Law, 1986; (with S. F. C. Milsom) Sources of English Legal History, 1986, 2nd edn 2010; The Notebook of Sir John Port, 1986; (ed) Judicial Records, Law Reports and the Growth of Case Law, 1989; Readings and Moots in the Inns of Court, vol. II, 1990; Cases from the lost notebooks of Sir James Dyer, 1994; Catalogue of English Legal MSS in Cambridge University Library, 1996; Spelman's Reading on Quo Warranto, 1997; Monuments of Endlesse Labours, 1998; The Reports of John Caryll, 1999; The Common Law Tradition, 2000; The Law's Two Bodies, 2001; Readers and Readings at the Inns of Court, 2001; Oxford History of the Laws of England, vol. 6, 2003; An Inner Temple Miscellany, 2004; (with A. Taussig) Catalogue of the Legal Manuscripts of Anthony Taussig, 2007; The Reports of William Dalison, 2008; The English Legal Manuscripts of Sir Thomas Phillipps, 2009; The Men of Court, 2011; Collected Papers on English Legal History, 2013; The Reinvention of Magna Carta 1216–1616, 2017; The Inns of Chancery 1340–1640, 2017; articles in legal and hist. jls. *Address:* St Catharine's College, Cambridge CB2 1RL.

**BAKER, Sir John (William),** Kt 2007; CBE 2000; Chairman, Bladon Jets Holdings Ltd, since 2014; *b* 5 Dec. 1937; *s* of Reginald and Wilhelmina Baker; *m* 1st, 1962, Pauline (*née* Moore); one *s*; 2nd, 1976, Gillian (*née* Bullen). *Educ:* Harrow Weald County Grammar Sch.; Oriel Coll., Oxford. Served Army, 1961–70; MoT, 1961–70; DoE, 1970–74; Dep. Chief Exec., Housing Corp., 1974–78; Sec., 1979–80, Bd Mem., 1980–89, Corporate Man. Dir, 1986–89, CEGB; Chief Exec., 1990–95, Chm., 1995–97, National Power; Dir, 1995–2003, Dep. Chm., 2002–03, Royal and Sun Alliance Insurance Gp; Chm., Medeva PLC, 1996–2000; Dep. Chm., Celltech Gp, 2000–03. Chairman: Globeleq, 2003–07; The Maersk Co., 2003–10; Renewable Energy Hldgs plc, 2005–13; Momenta Hldgs, 2006–07; Mem. Business Adv. Council, A. P. Moller Gp, 1996–2008. Chm., Sen. Salaries Rev. Body, 2002–08. Vice Chm., Chelsea and Westminster Hosp. NHS Foundn Trust, 2011–15. Chairman: ENO, 1996–2001; Associated Bd, Royal Schs of Music, 2000–06. Chairman: Exec. Assembly, World Energy Council, 1995–98; Groundwork Foundn, 1996–2001. Chairman: Governing Body, Holland Park Sch., 2003–13; Friends of Yehudi Menuhin Sch., 2013–. *Recreations:* tennis, golf, bridge, music, theatre. *Club:* Athenæum.
See also Rt Rev. J. M. R. Baker.

**BAKER, Rt Hon. Sir Jonathan Leslie,** Kt 2009; PC 2018; **Rt Hon. Lord Justice Baker;** a Lord Justice of Appeal, since 2018; *b* 6 Aug. 1955; *s* of late Leslie Baker and Isobel Baker; *m* 1980, Helen Sharrock, DL; one *s* one *d*. *Educ:* St Albans Sch.; St John's Coll., Cambridge (MA). Called to the Bar, Middle Temple, 1978, Bencher, 2009; barrister, specialising in Family Law, 1979–2009; Recorder, 2000–09; QC 2001; Dep. High Ct Judge, 2003–09; Hd, Harcourt Chambers, 2004–09; a Judge of the High Ct, Family Div., 2009–18; Family Division Liaison Judge, Western Circuit, 2011–18; Judge in Charge of Appeals, Family Division, 2016–18; Sen. Family Liaison Judge, 2017–18. Mem. Cttee, Family Law Bar Assoc., 2005–09. Chm., Relate, Oxon, 1999–2008. Gov., Magdalen College Sch., Oxford, 2005–14. Ed.-in-Chief, Court of Protection Law Reports, 2011–;

Gen. Ed., Court of Protection Practice, 2018–. *Publications:* (jtly) Contact: the new deal, 2006; (jtly) The Public Law Outline: the court companion, 2008. *Recreations:* music, history, family life. *Address:* Royal Courts of Justice, Strand, WC2A 2LL.

**BAKER, Rt Rev. Jonathan Mark Richard;** see Fulham, Bishop Suffragan of.

**BAKER, Mark Alexander Wyndham,** CBE 1998; Chairman, Magnox Electric plc, 1996–98; *b* 19 June 1940; *s* of late Lt-Comdr Alexander Arthur Wyndham Baker, RN and Renée Gavrelle Stenson (*née* Macnaghten); *m* 1964, Meriel, *yr d* of late Capt. Hugh Chetwynd-Talbot, MBE and Cynthia Chetwynd-Talbot; one *s* one *d*. *Educ:* Prince Edward Sch., Salisbury, S Rhodesia; University Coll. of Rhodesia and Nyasaland (Beit Schol.; BA London); Christ Church, Oxford (Rhodes Schol.; MA). United Kingdom Atomic Energy Authority, 1964–89: Sec., 1976–78, Gen. Sec., 1978–81, AERE, Harwell; Dir of Personnel and Admin, Northern Div., 1981–84; Authority Personnel Officer, 1984–86; Authority Sec., 1986–89; Exec. Dir, Corporate Affairs and Personnel, Nuclear Electric plc, 1989–96. Chm., Electricity Pensions Ltd, 1996–2006; non-exec. Dir, Pension Protection Fund, 2004–09. Deputy Chairman: Police Negotiating Bd, 2000–04; Police Adv. Bd, 2001–04. Mem., Sen. Salaries Review Body, 2004–09. Mem., Adv. Cttee, Envmtl Change Inst., Oxford Univ., 1999–2004. Mem. Bd of Trustees, Save the Children, 1998–2004. Pres., Inst. of Energy, 1998–99. *Recreations:* gardening, golf, walking, poetry, words. *Address:* The Old Schol, Fyfield, Abingdon OX13 5LR. *T:* (01865) 390724. *E:* MarkWBaker@ aol.com. *Club:* Antrobus Dining (Cheshire).

**BAKER, Martin John;** Master of Music, Westminster Cathedral, since 2000; recitalist; *b* 26 July 1967. *Educ:* Royal Northern Coll. of Music Jun. Sch.; Chetham's Sch. of Music; Downing Coll., Cambridge (Organ Scholar; BA 1988; Hon. Fellow 2016). Organ Scholar, Westminster Cathedral, 1988–90; Assistant Organist: St Paul's Cathedral, 1990–91; Westminster Abbey, 1992–2000. Recitals include improvisations. Hon. FGCM 2015; Hon. FRSCM 2015. *Address:* Westminster Cathedral, 42 Francis Street, SW1P 1QW.

**BAKER, Martyn Murray,** OBE 2009; Director of Economic Development (formerly of Economic Development and Education), City of London Corporation, 1999–2008; *b* 10 March 1944; *s* of late Norman and Constance Baker; *m* 1970, Rosemary Caroline Holdich. *Educ:* Dulwich Coll.; Pembroke Coll., Oxford (MA). Asst Principal, Min. of Aviation, 1965–67; Private Sec. to Ministers, Min. of Aviation Supply, and DTI, 1968–71; Principal, 1971; Principal Private Sec. to Sec. of State for Trade, 1977–78; Counsellor, Civil Aviation and Shipping, Washington, 1978–82; Department of Trade and Industry: Asst Sec., Air Div., 1982–85; Projects and Export Policy Div., 1985–86; Under Sec., 1986; Regl Dir, NW, 1986–88; Dir, Enterprise and Deregulation Unit, 1988–90; Head of Overseas Trade Div., 1990–93; Head of Exports to Asia, Africa and Australasia Div., 1993–96; Hd of Chemicals and Biotechnology Directorate, 1996–99, and Hd of Consumer Goods, Business and Postal Services Directorate, 1997–99. Member: Export Guarantees Advisory Council, 1985–86; Cttee for ME Trade, 1990–96; Council, China Britain Trade Gp, 1993–96; Asia Pacific Adv. Gp, 1993–96; BBSRC, 1996–99. Leader, Manchester-Salford City Action Team, 1986–88; Chm., City Fringe Partnership Exec. Team, 1999–2005. Mem. Council, Chelsea Soc., 2007–. FRSA 1988–2012.

**BAKER, Mary Geraldine,** MBE 1995; President: European Parkinson's Disease Association, 1992–2006; European Federation of Neurological Associations, 2002–11; European Brain Council, 2010–14 (Vice President, 2002–10); *b* 27 Oct. 1936; *d* of George and Emily Wheeler; *m* 1960, Robert William John Baker; three *s*. *Educ:* Bromley High Sch.; Leeds Univ. (BA); Inst. of Almoners. AIMSW. Almoner, St Thomas' Hosp., 1959–61; housewife and mother, 1961–75; Social Worker, 1975–82; Principal Med. Social Worker, Frimley Park Hosp., 1982–83; Parkinson's Disease Society of UK: National Welfare Dir, 1984–91, 1992; Acting Chief Exec., 1991–92; Dir of Welfare Develt, 1994; Nat. and Internat. Develt Consultant, 1995–99; Chief Exec., 1999–2001. Mem., Adv. Gp on Rehabilitation, DoH, 1992–94; Chm., WHO Cttee of NGOs concerned with neurol disorders, 1998–2002. World Federation of Neurology: Mem., Med. Educn Res. Gp, 1998–; Mem., PR and WHO Liaison Cttee, 2002–; Mem., Code of Practice, 2001–; Council, 2007–, ABPI; Dir at Large, World Stroke Assoc., 2004–; Patient Representative Mem., Mgt Bd, EMEA, 2005–; Mem., Scientific Cttee, Innovative Medicines Initiative Jt Undertaking, 2008–. British Medical Journal: Patient Ed., 2004– (Mem., Editl Bd, 2000–); Chm., Patient Adv. Gp, 2005–. Hon. FCSLT 1991. Paul Harris Fellow, Rotary Foundn, 1997. DUniv Surrey, 2003; Hon. DSc Aston, 2013. Outstanding Contrib. to British Neurosci. and for Public Service, British Neurosci. Assoc., 2009. *Publications:* Speech Therapy in Practice, 1988; (with B. McCall) Care of the Elderly, 1990; (with P. Smith) The Role of the Social Worker in the Management of Parkinson's Disease, 1991; (jtly) The Wall between neurology and psychiatry, 2002; Practical Neurology: destigmatizing stigma in people with neurological problems, 2003; contribs to learned jls incl. BMJ. *Recreations:* music, theatre, reading, bridge, caravanning. *Address:* Kailua, Maybourne Rise, Mayford, Woking, Surrey GU22 0SH. *T:* (01483) 763626. *Club:* Soroptimists'.

**BAKER, Dr Maureen,** CBE 2004; FRCGP; Chair, Professional Record Standards Body, since 2017; *b* Motherwell, 20 Sept. 1958; *d* of William Murphy and Helen Murphy; *m* 1984, Peter Baker; two *d*. *Educ:* Holy Cross High Sch., Hamilton; Univ. of Dundee Med. Sch. (MB ChB 1981). DCH 1985; DRCOG 1985; DM 2003. FRCGP 1994. GP, Lincoln, 1985–2018. Dir, Primary Care, Nat. Patient Safety Agency, 2002–07; Clin. Dir for Patient Safety, NHS Digital (formerly Health and Social Care Information Centre), 2007–16. Hon. Sec., 1999–2009, Chair of Council, 2013–16, RCGP. *Publications:* contrib. jls and books. *Recreations:* cinema, reading fiction, theme parks.

**BAKER, Maureen Anne;** see Bacon, M. A.

**BAKER, His Honour Michael Findlay,** CBE 2016; QC 1990; DL; a Circuit Judge, 1995–2012; *b* 26 May 1943; *s* of Rt Hon. Sir George Baker, PC, OBE; *m* 1973, Sarah Hartley Overton; two *d*. *Educ:* Haileybury; Brasenose Coll., Oxford. Called to the Bar, Inner Temple, 1966; a Recorder, 1991–95; Resident Judge, St Albans Crown Court, 2000–10. Sec., Nat. Reference Tribunals for Coal-mining Industry, 1973–95. Chairman: Herts Criminal Justice Strategy (Liaison) Cttee, 1998–2003; Vale House Stabilisation Services, 2003–11; Mem., Herts Probation Bd (formerly Cttee), 1998–2010. Chm., Archer Trust, 1994–. Gov., Univ. of Hertfordshire, 2008–14. DL Herts, 2008. Hon. DLaws Herts, 2016. *Recreations:* mountain climbing and walking, gardening. *Address:* Oakford, Standon, Ware, Herts SG11 1LT. *Clubs:* Alpine, Climbers'; Thames Hare and Hounds.
See also Rt Hon. Sir T. S. G. Baker.

**BAKER, Prof. Michael John,** TD 1971; Professor of Marketing, Strathclyde University, 1971–99, now Emeritus; Chairman, Westburn Publishers Ltd, since 1984; *b* 5 Nov. 1935 *s* of John Overend Baker and Constance Dorothy (*née* Smith); *m* 1959, Sheila (*née* Bell); one *s* two *d*. *Educ:* Worksop Coll.; Gosforth and Harvey Grammar Schs; Durham Univ. (BA) London Univ. (BScEcon); Harvard Univ. (CertITP, DBA); DipM. FRSE 1995; FCIM 1971; FCAM 1983; FScotvec 1988; FSQA 1997. 2nd Lieut, RA, 1956–57. Salesman Richard Thomas & Baldwins (Sales) Ltd, 1958–64; Asst Lectr, Medway Coll. o Technology, 1964–66; Lectr, Hull Coll. of Technology, 1966–68; Foundn fo Management Educn Fellow, 1968–71, Res. Associate, 1969–71, Harvard Business Sch.

Dean, Strathclyde Bus. Sch., 1978–84; Dep. Principal, 1984–91, Sen. Advr to Principal, 1991–94, Strathclyde Univ. Mem., Vice Chm. and Chm., Scottish Bus. Educn Council, 1973–85; Pres., Acad. of Marketing (formerly Marketing Educn Gp), 1986–2005 (Chm., 1973–86); Member: Food and Drink, EDC, 1976–78; SSRC Management and Industrial Relns Cttee, 1976–80; Nat. Councillor, Inst. of Marketing, 1977, Vice Chm. 1984–86, Chm. 1987; Trustee, CIM, 2008–14. Member: Scottish Hosps Endowment Res. Trust, 1983–96; Chief Scientist's Cttee, SHHD, 1985–96; Bus. and Management Sub-Cttee, UGC, 1985–89. Chairman: Scottish Marketing Projects Ltd, 1986–2005; IBEX Ltd, 1991–2005; Director: Stoddard Sekers International (formerly Stoddard Hldgs) PLC, 1983–97; Scottish Transport Gp, 1986–90; ARIS plc, 1990–94; Reid Gp, 1989–91; SGBS Ltd, 1990–97; STAMP Ltd, 1992–96. Dir, Scottish Med. Res. Fund, 1992–96. Visiting Professor: Univ. of Surrey, 1995–; Nottingham Trent Univ., 1999–2001; Hon. Prof., Univ. of Wales, Aberystwyth, 1999–2011; Adjunct Prof., Monash Univ., 2000–08; Special Prof., Nottingham Univ., 2001–07. Governor, Lomond Sch., 1984–96. Dean, Senate, CIM, 1994–2002. Founding Editor: Jl of Marketing Management, 1985; Jl of Customer Behaviour, 2002; Social Business, 2011. FRSA 1986. Hon. FCIM 1989; Hon. FAM 1997; Hon. FEMAC 2004. Hon. LLD Portsmouth, 2000; DUniv Surrey, 2003. *Publications*: Marketing, 1971, 7th edn 2006; Marketing New Industrial Products, 1975; (with R. McTavish) Product Policy, 1976; (ed) Marketing in Adversity, 1976; (ed) Marketing Theory and Practice, 1976, 3rd edn 1995; (ed) Industrial Innovation, 1979; Market Development, 1983; (ed) Dictionary of Marketing, 1984, 3rd edn 1998; Marketing Strategy and Management, 1985, 5th edn 2014; (with S. T. Parkinson) Organisational Buying Behaviour, 1986; (ed) The Marketing Book, 1987, 7th edn (with S. Hart) 2016; (with D. Ughanwa) The Role of Design in International Competitiveness, 1989, re-issued as Industrial Economics, 2018; (with S. Hart) Marketing and Competitive Success, 1989; Research for Marketing, 1991; (ed) Perspectives on Marketing Management, vol. 1, 1991, vol. 2, 1992, vol. 3, 1993, vol. 4, 1994; Companion Encyclopedia of Marketing, 1995; The Marketing Manual, 1998; (with S. Hart) Product Strategy and Management, 1998, 2nd edn 2007; (ed) The Encyclopedia of Marketing, 1999; (ed) Marketing Theory, 2000, 3rd edn (with M. Saren) 2016; (ed) Marketing: critical perspectives, 5 vols, 2001; Business and Management Research, 2003, 3rd edn (with Anne Foy) 2010; The Leisure of the Theory Class, 2017. *Recreations*: foreign travel, building bridges and mending fences. *Address*: Westburn, Helensburgh G84 9NH. *T*: (01436) 674686.

**BAKER, His Honour Michael John David;** a Circuit Judge, 1988–99; *b* 17 April 1934; *s* of late Ernest Bowden Baker and Dulcie Baker; *m* 1958, Edna Harriet Lane; one *s* one *d*. *Educ*: Trinity Sch. of John Whitgift; Bristol Univ. (LLB Hons). Admitted solicitor, 1957. Flying Officer, RAF, 1957–60. Joined firm of Glanvilles, Solicitors, Portsmouth, 1960; Partner, 1963–88; a Recorder, 1980–88. Coroner, S Hampshire, 1973–88 (Asst Dep. Coroner, 1971; Dep. Coroner, 1972). Pres., Southern Coroners Soc., 1975–76; Mem. Council, Coroners Soc. of England and Wales, 1979–88 (Jun. Vice-Pres., 1987–88). Mem., Council of Mgt, Music at Boxgrove, 1997–2010; Chm., Friends of Boxgrove Priory, 2004–08; Hon. Patron, Chichester Festival Th., 2002–; Dir (formerly Mem. Cttee), Friends of Arundel Castle CC, 2003–; Mem., Chichester Singers, 2008–17. Churchwarden, St Margaret's Ch, Eartham, 2004–12. Trustee, Leonard Hawkins Trust, 2004–12. *Recreations*: watching cricket, the theatre, music (particularly choral singing), photography. *Address*: c/o Glanvilles, Solicitors, Langstone Gate, Solent Road, Havant, Hants PO9 1TR. *T*: (023) 9249 2300. *Clubs*: Law Society; Keats (Chichester); Emsworth Sailing.

**BAKER, Nicola Karina Christina;** *see* Horlick, N. K. C.

**BAKER, Nigel Marcus,** OBE 2010; MVO 2003; HM Diplomatic Service; Deputy Director, Americas, since 2016 and Head, Latin American Department, since 2018, Foreign and Commonwealth Office (Head, South America Department, 2016–18); *b* 9 Sept. 1966; *s* of late Clive Baker and Mary (*née* Appleyard, later Berg); *m* 1997, Alexandra Čechova; one *s*. *Educ*: Dulwich Coll.; Gonville and Caius Coll., Cambridge (BA Hons 1st cl. Hist. 1988; MA 1992). Researcher, Cons. Res. Dept, 1989; Third Sec., FCO, 1989; Third, later Second Sec., Prague, 1992–93; Dep. Hd of Mission, Bratislava, 1993–95; First Sec., FCO, 1998; Hd of Eur. Defence Section, Security Policy Dept, FCO, 1998–2000; Asst Private Sec. to Prince of Wales, 2000–03; Dep. Hd of Mission, Havana, 2003–06; Ambassador: to Bolivia, 2007–11; to Holy See, 2011–16. Writer and histl researcher, Verona, 1996–97. Trustee, St Catherine's Foundn, 2000–03; Mem. Cttee, Friends of Royal Opera House, 2000–03. *Publications*: (ed) Britain and the Holy See: a celebration of 1982 and the wider relationship, 2013; articles in British and Eur. pubns on Byron, Palmerston, Italian history, Britain and the Holy See. *Recreations*: history in all its forms, good food and drink, mountains, civilisation, escaping. *Address*: 4 Cadogan Gardens, Royal Tunbridge Wells, Kent TN1 2UL. *E*: baker.sn@gmail.com, nigel.baker@fco.gov.uk. *Clubs*: Travellers; Crystal Palace Football.

**BAKER, Nigel Robert James;** QC 1988; a Recorder, 1985–2015; a Deputy High Court Judge, Queen's Bench Division, 1994–2015; *b* 21 Dec. 1942; *s* of late Herbert James Baker and Amy Beatrice Baker; *m* 1973, Stephanie Joy Stephenson; one *s*. *Educ*: Norwich Sch.; Univ. of Southampton (BA Law 1st cl.); Queens' Coll., Cambridge (LLM). Lectr in Law, Univ. of Leicester, 1968–70; called to the Bar, Middle Temple, 1969, Bencher, 1997; practised in London and on Midland Circuit, 1970–2007. Mem., Bar Council, 1985. *Recreations*: football (supporting Barnet FC), fell walking, gardening. *Address*: 7 Bedford Row, WC1R 4BS. *T*: (020) 7242 3555.

**BAKER, Rt Hon. Norman (John);** PC 2014; *b* 26 July 1957. *Educ*: Royal Holloway Coll., London Univ. (BA Hons). Our Price Records, 1978–83; teacher, 1985–97. Member: Lewes DC, 1987–99 (Leader of Council, 1991–97); E Sussex CC, 1989–97. Contested (Lib Dem) Lewes, 1992. MP (Lib Dem) Lewes, 1997–2015; contested (Lib Dem) same seat, 2015. Parly Under-Sec. of State, DfT, 2010–13; Minister of State, Home Office, 2013–14. *Publications*: Against the Grain, 2015.

**BAKER, Prof. Philip Newton,** DM; FRCOG, FRCSCan, FMedSci; Pro-Vice-Chancellor and Head, College of Life Sciences (formerly College of Medicine, Biological Sciences and Psychology), and Dean, School of Medicine, University of Leicester, since 2015; *b* Leicester, 31 March 1962; *s* of John and Jennifer Baker; *m* 1987, Nicola MacGregor (marr. diss. 2011); one *s* two *d*. *Educ*: Oakham Sch., Rutland; Nottingham Univ. Med. Sch. (BMedSci; BM BS 1985; DM 1991). FRCOG 2003. Wellbeing/Amer. Coll. of Obstetricians and Gynaecologists Travelling Res. Fellow, Magee-Women's Res. Inst., Pittsburgh, 1994–95; Sen. Lectr and Hon. Consultant, Obstetrics and Gynaecol., 1996–98, Prof. of Obstetrics and Gynaecol., 1998–2001, Univ. of Nottingham; Prof. of Maternal and Fetal Health, Univ. of Manchester and Hon. Consultant Obstetrician, St Mary's Hosp., 2001–09; Dir, Manchester NIHR Biomedical Res. Centre, 2008–09; Hd of Res., Central Manchester Foundn NHS Trust, 2008–09; University of Alberta: Dean, Faculty of Medicine and Dentistry, 2009–11; Adjunct Prof., Dept of Physiol., Heritage Medical Res. Centre, 2011; Hon. Consultant Obstetrician, Royal Alexandra Hosp., Edmonton, Alberta, 2009–11; Prof. of Maternal and Fetal Health, Liggins Inst., and Dir, Gravida (Nat. Centre for Growth and Develt), Univ. of Auckland, 2012–15. Non-exec. Dir, NHS Direct Trust, 2007–09. Dist. Nat. Prof., Chongqing Medical Univ., 2013–. FMedSci 2008. *Publications*: (jtly) Obstetrics and Gynaecology: cases, questions and commentaries, 1997; (ed jtly) The Pathogenesis and Management of Intrauterine Growth Restriction, 2000; (ed) Best Practice of Labour Ward Management, 2000; A Problem-based Obstetrics and Gynaecology Textbook for Undergraduates, 2003; (ed) MRCOG: an evidence-based textbook, 2004, 2nd edn 2010; (ed) The Aetiology and Management of Pre-eclampsia, 2004; (ed) Obstetrics by Ten Teachers, 17th edn 2005, 18th edn 2010; (ed) The Placenta and Neurodisability, 2005; (ed) Midwifery by Ten Teachers, 2006; (ed) Multiple Pregnancy, 2006; (ed) Cardiac Disease and Pregnancy, 2006; (ed) Teenage Pregnancy, 2007; (ed) Obesity and Reproduction, 2007; (ed) Renal Disease and Pregnancy, 2008; contrib. articles and papers. *Recreations*: Leicester City FC, cricket (ECB coach), vintage cars, grandfather clocks. *T*: (0116) 252 2962. *E*: philip.baker@le.ac.uk.

**BAKER, Philip Woolf,** OBE 1997; QC 2002; *b* 14 July 1955; *s* of Lionel Baker and Frances Baker (*née* Roth); *m* 1992, Bing-Sum Lau; two *s* one *d*. *Educ*: Haberdashers' Aske's Sch., Elstree; Emmanuel Coll., Cambridge (MA); Balliol Coll., Oxford (BCL); University Coll., London (LLM); SOAS, London (PhD 1985); London Business Sch. (MBA). Called to the Bar, Gray's Inn, 1979, Bencher, 2009; Lectr in Law, SOAS, London Univ., 1979–87; in practice as barrister, 1987–. Vis. Prof., Queen Mary Coll., Univ. of London, 1997–2008; Vis. Fellow, 2005–08, Sen. Vis. Fellow, 2008–, Inst. of Advanced Legal Studies, Univ. of London; Vis. Prof. of Law, Univ. of Oxford, 2015–. *Publications*: Double Taxation Conventions and International Tax Law, 1991, 3rd edn 2001; contrib. articles on internat. tax law, Chinese law, Islamic law and human rights. *Recreations*: sinology, my family. *Address*: Field Court Tax Chambers, 3 Field Court, Gray's Inn, WC1R 5EP. *T*: (020) 3693 3700. *E*: pb@fieldtax.com. *Club*: Athenæum.

**BAKER, Piers Howard Burton,** PhD; HM Diplomatic Service, retired; Clerk, Tin Plate Workers' alias Wire Workers' Company, since 2012; *b* 23 July 1956; *s* of late Dr Donald Burton Baker and Marjorie Winifred Baker; *m* 1979, Maria Eugenia Vilaincour; three *s*. *Educ*: King's Sch., Canterbury; Corpus Christi Coll., Cambridge (MA 1981, PhD 1983). Joined HM Diplomatic Service, FCO, 1983; First Sec., Brussels, 1985–88; FCO, 1988–93; First Sec., UK Repn, Brussels, 1993–96; FCO, 1996–2001; Dep. Hd of Mission, Consul-Gen. and Dir, Trade Promotion, then Trade and Investment, Vienna, 2001–06. Dir, Internat. Office, Imperial Coll. London, 2007–09; Asst Dir, Engineering Professors' Council, 2009–12. *Publications*: Shahr-i Zohak and the History of the Bamiyan Valley, Afghanistan, 1991. *Recreations*: music, walking, historical research.

**BAKER, Prof. Raymond,** CBE 2002; PhD; FRS 1994; Chief Executive, Biotechnology and Biological Sciences Research Council, 1996–2001; *b* 1 Nov. 1936; *s* of Alfred Baker and May (*née* Golds); *m* 1960, Marian Slater; one *s* two *d*. *Educ*: Ilkeston Grammar Sch.; Leicester Univ. (BSc, PhD). Postdoctoral Fellow, UCLA, 1962–64; University of Southampton: Lectr in Organic Chem., 1964–72; Sen. Lectr, 1972–74; Reader, 1974–77; Prof., 1977–84; Dir, Wolfson Unit of Chemical Entomology, 1976–84; Dir 1984–89, Exec. Dir, 1989–96, of Medicinal Chem., Merck Sharp & Dohme Res. Labs. *Publications*: Mechanism in Organic Chemistry, 1971; contrib. numerous articles to Jl Chemical Soc., Jl Medicinal Chem., and other scientific jls. *Recreations*: golf, gardening. *Address*: 2 Thirlestaine Place, Cheltenham, Glos GL53 7ED. *T*: (01242) 243633.

**BAKER, Richard Andrew;** Operating Partner, Advent International, since 2009; *b* 6 Aug. 1962; *s* of John and Mary Baker; *m* Suzanne; two *d*. *Educ*: Bishop Vesey's Grammar Sch., Sutton Coldfield; Downing Coll., Cambridge (BA 1984). Nat. Account Manager, Brand Mktg and Hd of Sales, UK Multiples, Mars Confectionery, 1986–95; Gp Mktg Dir, then Chief Operating Officer, ASDA, 1995–2003; CEO, Alliance Boots (formerly Boots Gp) plc, 2003–07. Chairman: Virgin Active Ltd, 2008–14; DFS Furniture Co. Ltd, 2010–17; Global Adv. Council, Aimia Inc. (formerly Groupe Aeroplan), 2009–17; Whitbread plc, 2014–18 (non-exec. Dir, 2009–18). Chm., British Retail Consortium, 2016–18. Non-exec. Dir and Mem. Bd, LTA, 2010–18. *Recreations*: keen sportsman playing competitive hockey, tennis and golf. *Clubs*: Royal Automobile; Hawks (Cambridge).

**BAKER, Richard Hugh;** HM Diplomatic Service, retired; *b* 22 Oct. 1935; *s* of late Hugh Cuthbert Baker and (Muriel) Lovenda Baker (*née* Owens); *m* 1963, Patricia Marianne Haigh Thomas; one *s* three *d*. *Educ*: Marlborough Coll.; New Coll., Oxford. Army (2nd Lieut RA), 1954–56. Plebiscite Officer, UN Plebiscite, S Cameroons, 1960–61; joined Diplomatic Service, 1962; 3rd, later 2nd, then 1st Sec., Addis Ababa, 1963–66; Foreign Office, 1967; Private Sec. to Permanent Under-Sec. of State, Foreign Office (later FCO), 1967–70; 1st Sec. and Head of Chancery, Warsaw, 1970–72; FCO, 1973–76; RCDS 1977; Econ. and Financial Counsellor, and Dep. Head, UK Perm. Delegn to OECD, Paris, 1978–82; Dep. High Comr, Ottawa, 1982–86; Asst Under-Sec. of State, and Civilian Mem., Sen. Directing Staff, RCDS, 1986–89. *Recreations*: music, painting, literature, pottery, printmaking, writing, architecture, engineering. *Address*: 1 The Thatched Cottages, Water Lane, Radwinter, Saffron Walden CB10 2TX. *T*: (01799) 599355.

**BAKER, Richard James;** Policy Manager, Royal Blind and Scottish War Blinded, since 2017; *b* 29 May 1974; *s* of Rev. Canon James Baker, MBE and Rev. Anne Baker; *m* 2004, Claire Josephine Brennan (*see* C. J. Baker); one *d*. *Educ*: Aberdeen Univ. (MA English Lit.). Pres., NUS Scotland, 1998–2000; Scottish Press Officer, Help the Aged, 2000–02. MSP (Lab) Scotland NE, 2003–Jan. 2016. Contested (Lab Co-op) Aberdeen N, 2015. Policy and Communications Manager, Age Scotland, 2016–17. *Recreations*: choral singing, football, cinema, reading. *Address*: Royal Blind and Scottish War Blinded, 50 Gillespie Crescent, Edinburgh EH10 4JB.

**BAKER, Sir Robert George Humphrey S.;** *see* Sherston-Baker.

**BAKER, Prof. Robin William,** CMG 2005; PhD; Professor of Old Testament and Ancient Near Eastern Studies, University of Winchester, since 2016 (Visiting Professor, 2015–16); Visiting Scholar, Sarum College, since 2015; *b* 4 Oct. 1953; *s* of late William John David Baker and Brenda Olive Baker (*née* Hodges); *m* 1974, Miriam Joy Turpin (marr. diss. 1997); two *s*; *m* 2017, Rachel Victoria Elizabeth Forrester-Jones. *Educ*: Bishop Wordsworth's Sch., Salisbury; Sch. of Slavonic and East European Studies, Univ. of London (BA 1976); Univ. of East Anglia (PhD 1984). MoD, 1976–80; res. student, 1980–84; British Council: S Africa, 1984–89; Head of Recruitment, 1989; Hungary, 1990–93; Thessaloniki, Greece, 1994–96; Russia, 1996–99; Director: W and S Europe, 1999; Europe, 1999–2002; Dep. Dir-Gen., 2002–05; Pro-Vice-Chancellor, Univ. of Kent, 2005–07; Vice-Chancellor: Univ. of Chichester, 2007–10; Canterbury Christ Church Univ., 2010–12. Sen. Vis. Fellow, Inst. for Balkan Studies, Thessaloniki, 1995–; Vis. Fellow, SSEES, 1995–97, 1999. Member: Council for Assisting Refugee Academics, 2003–13; Council, Univ. of Kent, 2003–05; Internat. Policy Cttee, Royal Soc., 2003–05; Jamestown 2007 British Cttee, 2006–07. Member, Advisory Council: Inst. of Romance Studies, Univ. of London, 1999–2002; SSEES, 2000–09; W Sussex Econ. Skills and Enterprise Bd, 2008–10. Trustee and Director: Chichester Festival Th., 2007–10; Canterbury Fest., 2010–12; Creative Foundn, 2010–12; Trustee, Finnish Inst. UK and Ireland, 2009–15. Fellow, UCL, 2005. FRSA 1998. *Publications*: The Development of the Komi Case System: a dialectological investigation, 1985; Hollow Men, Strange Women: riddles, codes and otherness in the Book of Judges, 2016; papers on history and languages of E Europe, and Biblical and ancient Near Eastern theol texts. *Recreations*: opera, Budapest café life. *Club*: Travellers.

**BAKER, Roger,** QPM 2008; HM Inspector of Constabulary, 2009–14; b 15 Nov. 1958; s of William Ernest Baker and Norah Margaret Baker; m 1999, Patricia Anne O'Callaghan; two d (and one d decd). Educ: Shirebrook Comp. Sch., Mansfield; Univ. of Derby (MBA 1998); Univ. of Manchester (MA Organisational Mgt 2000). Derbyshire Constabulary, 1977–2001, Chief Supt, 1999; Asst Chief Constable, Staffs Police, 2001–03; Dep. Chief Constable, N Yorks Police, 2003–05; Chief Constable, Essex Police, 2005–09. Vis. Prof. of Criminol., Univ. of Derby, 2014–. Recreations: equestrian pursuits, golf, walking the dogs.

**BAKER, Samantha Jayne, (Sam);** novelist, editor, writer and brand consultant; b 7 July 1966; d of Cliff Baker and Di (née Riglar); m 1993, Jon Courtenay Grimwood; one step s. Educ: Winton Sch.; Cricklade Coll.; Birmingham Univ. (BSocSc Pol Sci.). Chat mag., 1988–92; writer, Take a Break, 1992–93; Features Ed., then Dep. Ed., New Woman, 1993–96; Editor: Just Seventeen, 1996–97; Minx, 1997–98; Company, 1998–2003; Cosmopolitan, 2004–06; Ed.-in-Chief, Red, 2006–13. Publications: Fashion Victim, 2005; This Year's Model, 2008; The Stepmothers Support Group, 2009; To My Best Friends, 2011; The Woman Who Ran, 2016. Clubs: Black's, Shoreditch House.

**BAKER, Rt Hon. Sir Scott;** see Baker, Rt Hon. Sir T. S. G.

**BAKER, Ven. Simon Nicholas Hartland;** Rector, United Benefice of St Michael and St Mary with St John at Wall, since 2013; Prebendary, Lichfield Cathedral, since 2019; b 1957; m Diana. Educ: King's Coll. London (BD 1978); Queen's Coll., Birmingham. Ordained deacon, 1981, priest, 1982; Asst Curate, St Paul, Tupsley, 1981–85; Vicar, Shinfield, 1985–98; Principal, Berks Christian Trng Scheme, 1993–98; Lay Trng Officer, 1998–2002; Dir of Discipleship and Ministry, and Warden of Readers, Dio. of Winchester, 2002–13; Archdeacon of Lichfield, 2013–19. Hon. Canon, Winchester Cath., 2008–13, now Canon Emeritus.

**BAKER, Steven John;** MP (C) Wycombe, since 2010; b St Austell, 6 June 1971; s of Michael Baker and Diane Vivienne Baker (née Brimble); m 1996, Julia Elizabeth Perks. Educ: Poltair Comp. Sch., St Austell; St Austell Sixth Form Coll.; Univ. of Southampton (BEng Aerospace Systems Engrg 1992); St Cross Coll., Oxford (MSc Computation (Computer Sci.) 2000). CEng 1999. Engr Officer (Aerosystems), RAF, 1989–99; Hd, Consulting and Product Manager, DecisionSoft Ltd, Oxford, 2000–01; Chief Technol. Officer, BASDA Ltd, Great Missenden, 2002–07; Dir, Product Develt, CoreFiling Ltd, Oxford, 2005–06; Chief Architect, Global Financing and Asset Servicing Platforms, Lehman Brothers, 2006–08. Principal, Ambriel Consulting Ltd, 2001–10. Associate Consultant, Centre for Social Justice, 2008–10; Corporate Affairs Dir, 2009–10, Trustee, 2010–17, Cobden Centre. Dir, Thermal Engineering Ltd, 2013. Trustee, GB Job Clubs, 2010–13. Parly Under-Sec. of State, DExEU, 2017–18. Mem., Treasury Select Cttee, H of C, 2014–17, 2018–; Chair, Eur. Res. Gp, 2016–18 (Dep. Chair, 2018–). Co-Chm., Conservatives for Britain, 2015–16. FRSA 2012. Recreations: skydiving, sailing, ski-ing, motorcycling, running. Address: (office) 150A West Wycombe Road, High Wycombe HP12 3AE. T: (01494) 448408. Club: Royal Air Force.

**BAKER, His Honour Stuart William;** a Circuit Judge, 1998–2017; b 1 June 1952; s of Henry Baker and Elizabeth Baker (née Hooker); m 1975, Christine Elizabeth Bennett; (one s decd). Educ: Univ. of Newcastle upon Tyne (LLB Hons 1973). Called to the Bar, Inner Temple, 1974; in practice at the Bar, 1975–98; Asst Recorder, 1991–94; a Recorder, 1994–98; Northern Circuit; Dep. Judge, High Court of Justice, 2001–17. Mem., Legal Aid Area Appeal Cttee, 1991–98; Legal Mem., Mental Health Review Tribunal, 1996–98. Recreations: fell walking, golf, woodturning, playing viola.

**BAKER, Rt Hon. Sir (Thomas) Scott (Gillespie),** Kt 1988; PC 2002; a Lord Justice of Appeal, 2002–10; President, Court of Appeal, Bermuda, 2015–18 (Member, 2011–18); Chair, Judicial and Legal Services Committee, Bermuda, 2015–18; b 10 Dec. 1937; s of the Rt Hon. Sir George Baker, PC, OBE and Jessie McCall Baker; m 1973, (Margaret) Joy Strange; two s one d. Educ: Haileybury; Brasenose Coll., Oxford (Hon. Fellow 2003). Called to the Bar, Middle Temple, 1961 (Astbury Schol.), Bencher 1985, Treasurer 2004; a Recorder, 1976–88; QC 1978; a Judge of the High Court, Family Div., 1988–92, QBD, 1993–2002; Family Div. Liaison Judge (Wales and Chester Circuit), 1990–92; Presiding Judge, Wales and Chester Circuit, 1991–95; Lead Judge, Administrative Ct, 2000–02. Member: Senate, Inns of Court, 1977–84; Bar Council, 1988. Chm., Panel apptd by Sec. of State for Home Office to review UK's extradition arrangements, 2010–11; Member: Govt Cttee of Inquiry into Human Fertilisation (Warnock Cttee), 1982–84; Parole Bd, 1999–2002 (Vice-Chm., 2000–02); Ind. Parly Standards Authy, 2010–13; a Surveillance Comr, 2010–16. Asst Dep. Coroner for Inquest into the deaths of Diana, Princess of Wales and Dodi Al Fayed, 2007–08. Mem., Chorleywood UDC, 1965–68. Dep. Chm., Cricket Council Appeals Cttee, 1986–88. Hon. Mem., Coroners' Soc., 2008–. Gov., Caldicott Sch., 1991–2005 (Chm., 1996–2003). Recreations: golf, fishing, shooting. Address: Highlands, Woodrow, Amersham, Bucks HP7 0QG. Clubs: MCC; Denham Golf (Captain, 1992, Chm., 1995–2001).
See also His Honour M. F. Baker.

**BAKER, Tristan Michael Douglas;** Producer, Runaway Entertainment, since 2012; Joint Founder and Chief Executive Officer: KX Tickets, since 2016; Troubadour Theatres, since 2017; b Birmingham, 5 Oct. 1978; s of Michael Baker and Pamela Baker. Educ: Rugby Sch.; Univ. of Birmingham (BA Hons 2001). Theatre producer, 2002–. Productions include: Calamity Jane, Shaftesbury, and tour, 2002–03; Kiss Me Kate, tour, 2004; Footloose, Novello and Playhouse, and tours, 2004–17; Love Shack, tour, 2005; Never Forget (co-producer), Savoy, and tours, 2007–08; The Railway Children at Waterloo Station, 2010–11; Guys and Dolls, Chichester, Savoy, Phoenix, and tours, 2014–16; The Railway Children at King's Cross, 2014–17; Lazarus, King's Cross, 2016–17; In the Heights, Southwark and King's Cross, 2014–17; Flashdance, tour, 2017–19; Girl from the North Country, Old Vic, 2017, transf. Noel Coward, 2018; The Public, NY, 2018. Recreations: theatre, cricket, golf, poker, dog walking, dining. Address: Suite 101, 72 Great Titchfield Street, W1W 7QW. T: (020) 7438 1562. E: info@runawayentertainment.com.

**BAKER, William John Clovis M.;** see Meath Baker.

**BAKER-BATES, Merrick Stuart,** CMG 1996; HM Diplomatic Service, retired; Historical Records Adviser, Foreign and Commonwealth Office, 2000–17; b 22 July 1939; s of late E. T. Baker-Bates, MD, FRCP, and of Norah Stuart (née Kirkham); m 1963, Chrystal Jacqueline Goodacre; one s one d. Educ: Shrewsbury Sch.; Hertford Coll., Oxford (MA); College of Europe, Bruges. Journalist, Brussels, 1962–63; entered HM Diplomatic Service, 1963; 3rd, later 2nd Sec., Tokyo, 1963–68; 1st Secretary: FCO, 1968–73; (Inf.), Washington, 1973–76; (Commercial), Tokyo, 1976–79; Counsellor (Commercial), Tokyo, 1979–82. Dir, Cornes & Co., Tokyo, 1982–85; Representative Dir, Gestetner Ltd (Japan), 1982–85; Dep. High Comr and Counsellor (Commercial/Econ.), Kuala Lumpur, 1986–89; Hd of S Atlantic and Antarctic Dept, FCO, and Comr, British Antarctic Territory, 1989–92; Consul-Gen., Los Angeles, 1992–97. Youth Offending Team mentor, Leicester Probation, 2002–07. Mem., Mgt Cttee, British-Malaysia Soc., 2004–08. Comdr, 1998–2005, Pres., 2005–12, St John Ambulance (Northants). Shakespeare's Globe Trust: Mem., Develt Council, 1998–2003; Chm., Internat. Cttee, 1999–2005; Bd Mem., 2001–05; Mem., Adv. Council, 2005–. Trustee, Oxford Univ. Soc., 2001–08. Street Pastor, Northampton, 2018. CStJ 2010 (OStJ 2000). Recreations: photography, golf, hill-walking, talking, restorative justice. E: merrick@bakerbates.com. Club: Tokyo (Tokyo).
See also R. P. Baker-Bates.

**BAKER-BATES, Rodney Pennington;** Chairman, Willis Ltd, since 2011; b 25 April 1944; s of Eric Tom Baker-Bates and Norah Stuart (née Kirkham); m 1972, Gail Elizabeth Roberts; one s. Educ: Shrewsbury Sch.; Hertford Coll., Oxford (MA History). FICA 1975; AIMC 1975; FCIB 1991. Glyn Mills & Co., 1966–68; Arthur Andersen & Co., 1968–77; Chase Manhattan Bank, 1977–84; Midland Bank, 1984–92; Dir of Finance and IT, BBC, 1993–98; Man. Dir, Corporate Pensions Business, Prudential Corp., 1998–99; Chief Exec., Gp Pensions, 1999–2000, Prudential Financial Services, 2000–01, Consultant, 2001–02, Prudential plc. Director: Dexia Municipal Bank, 1997–2000; Aspen Group, 1997–99; Lloyds Register of Shipping, 1998–2007; Prudential Assce Co. Ltd, 2000–01; Bedlam Asset Mgt plc, 2003–13; Chairman: Change Partnership Ltd, 1998–2001; Hydra Associates, 1999–2001; CoralEurobet plc, 1999–2002; Burns e-Commerce Solutions, 2002–04; Stobart Gp plc (formerly Westbury Property Fund), 2002–13; EG Consulting Ltd, 2003–13; First Assist Gp Ltd, 2003–09; The Music Solution Ltd, 2004–08; Cabot Financial Hldgs Gp, 2004–06; Helphire Gp plc, 2005–08; G's Gp Hldgs, 2006–16; Britannia Bldg Soc., 2008–09 (Mem. Bd, 2007–09); Assura Gp plc, 2008–10; Ridgeons Gp, 2012–16; Fram Farmers (formerly AtlasFram Gp Ltd), 2014– (non-exec. Dir, 2008–10; Vice-Chm., 2010–14); Push Energy Ltd, 2014–; G's Growers Ltd, 2018–; Deputy Chairman: Co-operative Bank, 2009–12; Co-operative Insurance Gp Ltd, 2009–12; Co-operative Life Fund, 2009–12; Co-operative Financial Services, 2009–12; non-exec. Dir, C. Hoare & Co., 2001–10 (Chm., Exec. Man. Partners, 2001–06); Dir, City of London Fest., 2001–04; Gov., RSC, 2003–08. Governor, Bedales Sch., 1993–2002. Trustee: Royal Nat. Pension Fund for Nurses, 1999–; Burdett Trust for Nursing, 2001–09; Dolphin Square Trust, 2001–13; Mem. Audit Cttee, Wellcome Trust, 2005–07; Chm., Outset Foundn, 2014–. Recreations: gardening, performing arts, classic cars. Address: c/o Mrs Julie Dyson, Willis Ltd, The Willis Building, 51 Lime Street, EC3M 7DQ. T: (020) 3124 6559. Club: Farmers.
See also M. S. Baker-Bates.

**BAKER WILBRAHAM, Sir Richard,** 8th Bt cr 1776; DL; Director, J. Henry Schroder Wagg & Co. Ltd, 1969–89; Chairman, Bibby Line Group, 1992–97 (Deputy Chairman, 1989–92); b 5 Feb. 1934; s of Sir Randle Baker Wilbraham, 7th Bt, and Betty Ann, CBE (d 1975), d of W. Matt Torrens; S father, 1980; m 1962, Anne Christine Peto, d of late Charles Peto Bennett, OBE; one s three d. Educ: Harrow. Welsh Guards, 1952–54. J. Henry Schroder Wagg & Co. Ltd, 1954–89. Director: Westpool Investment Trust, 1974–92; Brixton Estate, 1985–2001 (Dep. Chm., 1994–2001); The Really Useful Group plc, 1985–90; Charles Barker Group, 1986–89; Grosvenor Estates Hldgs, 1989–99 (Dep. Chm., 1989–99); Severn Trent, 1989–94; Majedie Investments, 1989–2001; Christie Hosp. NHS Trust, 1990–96. Mem., Gen. Council, King Edward's Hosp. Fund for London, 1986–98. Gov., Nuffield Hosps, 1990–2001. A Church Comr, 1994–2001. Trustee, Grosvenor Estate, 1981–99. Governor: Harrow Sch., 1982–92; The King's Sch., Macclesfield, 1986–2006; Manchester Metropolitan Univ., 1998–2001. Upper Bailiff, Weavers' Co., 1994–95. High Sheriff, Cheshire, 1991–92; DL Cheshire, 1992. Recreation: field sports. Heir: s Randle Baker Wilbraham [b 28 May 1963; m 1997, Amanda, e d of Robert Glossop; one s two d]. Address: Rode Home Farm, Scholar Green, Cheshire ST7 3QW. T: (01270) 877784. Club: Brooks's.

**BAKEWELL,** family name of Baroness Bakewell.

**BAKEWELL,** Baroness cr 2011 (Life Peer), of Stockport in the County of Greater Manchester; **Joan Dawson Bakewell,** DBE 2008 (CBE 1999); broadcaster and writer; b 16 April; d of John Rowlands and Rose Bland; m 1st, 1955, Michael Bakewell (marr. diss. 1972); one s one d; 2nd, 1975, Jack Emery (marr. diss. 2001). Educ: Stockport High Sch. for Girls; Newnham Coll., Cambridge (MA History and Econs). Associate, 1980–91, Associate Fellow, 1984–87, Newnham Coll., Cambridge. TV critic, The Times, 1978–81; columnist: Sunday Times, 1988–90; Guardian, 2003–05; Independent, 2006–08; The Times, 2008–09; Daily Telegraph, 2012–14. Gov., BFI, 1994–2003 (Dep. Chm., 1997–99; Chm., 1999–2003); Mem. Bd, RNT, 1996–2003. Chm., Nat. Campaign for the Arts, 2004–10. Chair, Shared Experience Theatre Co., 2007–12. Pres., Soc. of Arts Publicists, 1984–90. Mem. Council, Aldeburgh Foundn, 1985–99. Hon. Prof., Dept of Film and Media, Univ. of Stirling, 2006–. Pres., Birkbeck, Univ. of London, 2013–. Hon. FRCA 1994; Hon. Fellow, RHBNC, 1997; Hon. FBA 2018. Hon. DLitt: Queen Margaret UC, Edinburgh, 2005; Chester, 2007; Univ. of Arts, London, 2008; Staffordshire, 2009; Lancaster, 2010; Open, 2010; Essex, 2011; RHUL; Hon. DCL Newcastle, 2011; Hon. Dr Manchester, 2015. Television: BBC Television includes: Meeting Point, 1964; The Second Sex, 1964; Late Night Line Up, 1965–72; The Youthful Eye, 1968; Moviemakers at the National Film Theatre, 1971; Film 72, and Film 73, 1972–73; For the Sake of Appearance, Where is Your God?, Who Cares?, and The Affirmative Way (series), 1973; Holiday '74, '75, '76, '77 and '78 (series); What's it all About? (2 series) and Time Running Out (series), 1974; The Shakespeare Business, The Brontë Business, and Generation to Generation (series), 1976; My Day with the Children, 1977; Panorama, 2011–12 (Old Age Drinkers, 2016; Life at 100, 2017); Arts UK: OK?, 1980; Arts Correspondent, 1981–87; The Heart of the Matter, 1988–2000; Travels with Pevsner: Derbyshire, 1998; My Generation (series), 2000; Taboo (series), 2001; ITV includes: Sunday Break, 1962; Home at 4.30, 1964; (writer and producer) Thank You, Ron (documentary), 1974; Fairest Fortune and Edinburgh Festival Report, 1974; Reports Action (4 series), 1976–78; National Trust, 2017; Portrait Artist of the Year (series), 2013, 2014, 2015, 2016, 2017; Landscape Artist of the Year (series), 2016, 2017, Sky Arts. Radio: Away from it All, 1978–79; PM, 1979–81; Artist of the Week, 1998–2000; Midsummer Sins, 2004; Chm., The Brains Trust, 1998–2001; Belief, 2001–13; Inside the Ethics Cttee, 2010–16; Joan Bakewell's Lovers, 2013; We Need to Talk about Death, 2017, 2018, 2019; BBC Radio 4 plays: There and Back; Parish Magazine: 3 editions; Brought to Book, 2005; Keeping in Touch, 2017. Theatre: Brontës: The Private Faces, Edinburgh Fest., 1979. Publications: (with Nicholas Garnham) The New Priesthood: British television today, 1970; (with John Drummond) A Fine and Private Place, 1977; The Complete Traveller, 1977; The Heart of Heart of the Matter, 1996; The Centre of the Bed (autobiog.), 2003; Belief, 2005; The View from Here, 2006; All the Nice Girls (novel), 2009; She's Leaving Home (novel), 2011; Stop the Clocks, 2016. Recreations: theatre, travel, cinema. Address: Knight Ayton Management, 29 Gloucester Place, W1U 8HX. T: (020) 3795 1806.

**BAKEWELL OF HARDINGTON MANDEVILLE,** Baroness cr 2013 (Life Peer), of Hardington Mandeville in the County of Somerset; **Catherine Mary Bakewell,** MBE 1999. Member (Lib Dem): Somerset CC, 1993–2013 (Leader, 2001–07); South Somerset DC, 2009–. Address: House of Lords, SW1A 0PW.

**BAKHURST, Kevin Alexander;** Content Group Director, Ofcom, since 2016; b 10 Dec 1965; s of Christopher and Elizabeth Bakhurst; m 1990, Barbara King; two s one d. Educ: Haberdashers' Aske's Sch. for Boys, Elstree; St John's Coll., Cambridge (BA Modern Langs 1988). Audit Asst, Price Waterhouse, 1988–89; BBC: researcher and asst producer, Business Breakfast, 1989–90; Producer, Nine O'Clock News, 1990–94; Europe Producer, Brussels

1994–95; Asst Ed., News, 1996–2001; News Ed., BBC Millennium Eve prog., 2000; Evenings Ed., News 24, 2001–03; Ed., Ten O'Clock News, BBC TV, 2003–06 (BAFTA Award for News Coverage, 2004, 2005); Controller, BBC News Channel, BBC News at One O'Clock, 2006–12; Ed., Olympics Decision 2012 prog., 2005; Dep. Hd, BBC Newsroom, 2010–12; RTÉ: Man. Dir, News and Current Affairs, and Mem., Exec. Bd, 2012–16; Dep. Dir-Gen., 2014–16. JP St Albans, 2000–06. *Recreations:* travel, speaking French, film and cinema, watching Chelsea, reading and political autobiography, history. *Address:* Ofcom, Riverside House, 2a Southwark Bridge Road, SE1 9HA. *E:* kevin.bakhurst@ofcom.org.uk.

**BALASUBRAMANIAN, Sir Shankar,** Kt 2017; PhD; FRS 2012; FMedSci; Herchel Smith Professor of Medicinal Chemistry, University of Cambridge, since 2008; Fellow, Trinity College, Cambridge, since 1994; Senior Group Leader, CRUK Cambridge Research Institute, since 2010; *b* Madras, 30 Sept. 1966; *s* of Venkataraman Balasubramanian and Padma Balasubramanian; *m* 1999, Veena Krishnan; one *s* one *d. Educ:* Fitzwilliam Coll., Cambridge (BA Natural Sci 1988); PhD Cantab 1991. SERC/NATO Res. Fellow, Pennsylvania State Univ., 1991–93; University of Cambridge: Royal Soc. Res. Fellow, 1994–98; Lectr, 1998–2003; Reader in Chem. Biol., 2003–07; Prof. of Chem. Biol., 2007–08. Founder, 1998, and Dir, 1998–2004, Solexa Ltd UK; Founder, 2012, and Dir, 2012–, Cambridge Epigenetix Ltd. FMedSci 2011. *Recreations:* running, cycling, football, music, family. *Address:* Department of Chemistry, University of Cambridge, Lensfield Road, Cambridge CB2 1EW. *T:* (01223) 336347. *E:* sb10031@cam.ac.uk.

**BALÁZS, Prof. Péter;** Professor of International Relations and European Studies, and Director, Center for European Neighborhood Studies, Central European University, Budapest, since 2005; *b* 5 Dec. 1941; *s* of Sándor Balázs and Klára Pecz. *Educ:* Budapest Sch. of Econs (Dip. in Econs 1963; Dr habil 2000); Hungarian Acad. of Scis (Dr 2003). Economist, Elektroimpex Hungarian Foreign Trading Co., 1963–68; Desk Officer, then Dir, Min. of Foreign Trade, 1969–82; Counsellor i/c EC, Hungarian Embassy, Brussels, 1982–87; Prime Minister's Office, 1987–88; Dir Gen. for multilateral relns, Min. of Internat. Econ. Relns, 1988–92; Perm. State Sec., Min. of Industry and Trade, 1992–93; Ambassador of Hungary: to Denmark, 1994–96; to Germany, 1997–2000; Prof., Budapest Univ. of Econs and Public Admin, 2000–02; State Sec. for Integration and Ext. Econ. Relns, Min. of Foreign Affairs, 2002–03; Ambassador, Perm. Repn to EU, 2003–04; Mem., European Commn, 2004; Minister for Foreign Affairs, Hungary, 2009–10. *Publications:* Az Európai Unió külkapcsolatai és Magyarország, 1996; (contrib.) Enlarging the European Union, 1997; (contrib.) Őszinte Könyv az Európai Unióról, 1999; (contrib.) Az Európai Unió politikái, 2000; (contrib.) Európai Közjog és politika, 2000; (contrib.) Unser Europa-Gemeinsam stärker: die kooperation der Klein- und Mittelstaaten im EU-Konvent, 2004. *Recreations:* classical music, horse riding.

**BALBUS, Prof. Steven Andrew,** PhD; FRS 2016; Savilian Professor of Astronomy, since 2012 and Head of Astrophysics, since 2014, University of Oxford; Fellow, New College, Oxford, since 2012; *b* Philadelphia, 23 Nov. 1953; *s* of Theodore G. Balbus and Rita S. Balbus (*née* Frucht); *m* 2002, Caroline Terquem; three *s* one *d. Educ:* Massachusetts Inst. of Technol. (BSc Maths and Physics); Univ. of Calif, Berkeley (PhD Physics 1981). Research Associate: MIT, 1981–83; Princeton Univ., 1983–85; Asst Prof., 1985–91, Associate Prof., 1991–97, Prof., 1997–2004, of Astronomy, Univ. of Virginia; Prof. des Universités, Physics Dept, École Normale Supérieure de Paris, 2004–12. MNAS 2015. Chaire d'Excellence, 2004; Shaw Prize in Astronomy, 2013. *Publications:* contribs to Astrophysical Jl, Monthly Notices of RAS. *Recreations:* reading, music, cycling, cooking. *Address:* Physics Department, University of Oxford, Denys Wilkinson Building, Keble Road, Oxford OX1 3RH. *T:* (01865) 273639, *Fax:* (01865) 273390. *E:* Steven.Balbus@physics.ox.ac.uk.

**BALCHIN,** family name of **Baron Lingfield**.

**BALCOMBE, David Julian;** QC 2002; a Recorder, since 2000; *b* 4 Feb. 1958; *s* of Rt Hon. Sir (Alfred) John Balcombe and Jacqueline Rosemary, (Lady Balcombe); *m* 1992, Sally Jane Spence; two *s. Educ:* Winchester Coll.; Univ. of Kent at Canterbury (BA). Called to the Bar, Lincoln's Inn, 1980. *Address:* 1 Crown Office Row, Temple, EC4Y 7HH. *T:* (020) 7797 7500.

**BALDING, Clare Victoria,** OBE 2013; freelance sports presenter and author; *b* 29 Jan. 1971; *d* of Ian Balding, LVO, and Lady Emma Balding, *sister* of Earl of Huntingdon, *qv; m* 2006, Alice Arnold. *Educ:* Downe House; Newnham Coll., Cambridge (BA 2nd Cl. Hons English; Pres., Cambridge Union, 1992). Racing reporter, BBC Radio 5 Live, 1993–94; sports presenter, BBC Radio, 1994–; presenter: BBC horse-racing coverage, incl. Royal Ascot; Badminton, Derby and Grand National; BBC Grandstand and Sunday Grandstand, 2000–07; Sydney Olympics and Paralympics, 2000; Salt Lake City Winter Olympics, 2002; Athens Olympics and Paralympics, 2004; Crufts, 2005–; Commonwealth Games, Melbourne, 2006; Beijing Olympics and Paralympics, 2008; Vancouver Winter Olympics, 2010; Saturday Live and Woman's Hour, BBC Radio 4, 2008–09; Britain by Bike (BBC TV series), 2010; Countryfile, Britain's Hidden Heritage, 2011; London Olympics, BBC, 2012; London Paralympics, Channel 4, 2012; The Clare Balding Show, 2013–; horse-racing coverage, Channel 4, 2013–16; Britain's Brightest, 2013; Sochi Winter Olympics, 2014; Operation Wild, 2014; Sports Personality of the Year, 2014–; Wimbledon 2day, BBC, 2015; Rio Olympics and Paralympics, 2016; Seoul Winter Olympics, 2018; Commonwealth Games, Gold Coast, 2018. Sports columnist: Evening Standard, 1997–2003; Observer, 2004–07. Presenter, BBC Radio 4: Ramblings, 1998–; Sport and the British, 2012; Good Morning Sunday, BBC Radio 2, 2013. Sports Presenter of the Year, 2004, Presenter of the Year, 2013, RTS; BAFTA Special Award, 2013. *Publications:* My Animals and Other Family (Autobiog. of the Year, Nat. Book Awards), 2012; Walking Home: my family and other rambles, 2014; The Racehorse Who Wouldn't Gallop (for children), 2016. *Recreations:* riding, tennis, theatre, cinema, travel. *Address:* c/o YMU Group, 4th Floor, 180 Great Portland Street, W1W 5QZ.

**BALDOCK, Anne Elizabeth;** Partner, Allen & Overy LLP, 1990–2012; *b* Kent, 1959; *d* of Alec John Baldock and Violet Margery Baldock; *m* 1990, Graham David Vinter; two *s* one *d. Educ:* Wombwell Hall Sch. for Girls; London Sch. of Econs and Pol Sci. (LLB). Admitted as solicitor, 1982; Lawyer, Allen & Overy LLP, 1982–90. Consultant and lectr on project finance and infrastructure, 2012–. Non-executive Director: Hydrogen Gp plc, 2012–16; Thames Tideway Tunnel Ltd, 2014–; Low Carbon Contracts Co. Ltd, 2014–; Electricity Settlements Co. Ltd, 2014–; Submarine Develt Authy, 2018–; Electricity North West Ltd, 2018–; East West Railway Ltd, 2019–. Mem., Nuclear Liabilities Financial Assce Bd, 2009–15. Trustee, CRUK, 2011–15. MInstD. *Publications:* contrib. articles to jls incl. Project Finance Internat. *Recreations:* riding, running. *E:* abaldock@hotmail.co.uk. *Club:* Royal Automobile.

**BALDOCK, Brian Ford,** CBE 1997; Chairman, Mencap, 1998–2011; independent coach, since 2010; *b* 10 June 1934; *s* of Ernest A. and Florence F. Baldock; *m* 1st, 1956, Mary Lillian Bartolo (marr. diss. 1966); two *s*; 2nd, 1968, Carole Anthea Mason; one *s. Educ:* Clapham Coll., London. Army Officer, 1952–55. Procter & Gamble, 1956–61; Ted Bates Inc., 1961–63; Rank Orgn, 1963–66; Smith & Nephew, 1966–75; Revlon Inc., 1975–78; Imperial Group, 1978–86; Guinness PLC: Dir, 1986–96; Gp Man. Dir, 1989–96; Dep.

Chm., 1992–96. Chairman: Portman Group, 1989–96; Wellington Investments Ltd, 1997–2002; Dalgety, later Sygen Internat., 1998–2005 (Dir, 1992–2005); Marks & Spencer plc, 2000–01 (non-exec. Dir, 1996–2004); First Artist Corp., 2001–03; Dir, Cornhill Insurance, 1996–2002. Trustee, RTR Foundn, 2002–. Freeman, City of London, 1989. CInstM 1991 (FInstM 1976); Fellow, Marketing Soc., 1988. FRSA 1987. Hon. DA E London, 2008. *Recreations:* theatre (opera), cricket, travel. *E:* brianbaldock@outlook.com. *Clubs:* Garrick, MCC, Lord's Taverners (Mem. Council; Chm., 1992–95).

**BALDOCK, (Richard) Stephen;** High Master, St Paul's School, 1992–2004; *b* 19 Nov. 1944; *s* of John Allan Baldock and Marjorie Procter Baldock; *m* 1969, Dr Janet Elizabeth Cottrell; one *s* three *d. Educ:* St Paul's Sch.; King's Coll., Cambridge (John Stewart of Rannoch schol. in Greek and Latin 1964; BA 1967 Part I Classics, Part II Theology, MA 1970). St Paul's School: Asst Master, 1970–77; Housemaster, School House, 1977–84; Surmaster, 1984–92. Council Mem. and Educnl Advr, Overseas Missionary Fellowship, 1989–2010. Trustee, South Square Trust, 2007–19. Governor: Monkton Combe Sch., Bath, 2003–15; Gordonstoun Sch., 2006–16; Visitor, Collingham coll., SW London, 2004–. *Recreations:* family, computers, sport. *Address:* c/o Old Pauline Club, St Paul's School, Lonsdale Road, Barnes, SW13 9JT. *Club:* MCC.
*See also* S. R. Baldock.

**BALDOCK, Sarah Ruth,** FRCO; College Organist and Music Teacher, Cheltenham Ladies' College, since 2014; *b* Wembley, 5 April 1975; *d* of (Richard) Stephen Baldock, *qv. Educ:* St Paul's Girls' Sch., London; Pembroke Coll., Cambridge (BA 1996). FRCO 1997. Organist-in-Residence, Tonbridge Sch., 1996–98; Asst Organist and Dir of Girls' Choir, 1998–2002, Asst Dir of Music, 2002–08, Winchester Cathedral; Organist and Master of the Choristers, Chichester Cathedral, 2008–14. *Recreations:* cooking and eating, gardening. *Address:* Cheltenham Ladies' College, Bayshill Road, Cheltenham, Glos GL50 3EP.

**BALDOCK, Stephen;** *see* Baldock, R. S.

**BALDRY, Rt Hon. Sir Antony Brian, (Rt Hon. Sir Tony),** Kt 2012; PC 2013; DL; *b* 10 July 1950; *e s* of late Peter Edward Baldry and Oina (*née* Paterson); *m* 1st, 1979, Catherine Elizabeth (marr. diss. 1996), 2nd *d* of Captain James Weir, RN and Elizabeth Weir; one *s* one *d*; 2nd, 2001, Pippa Isbell, *e d* of Lt Col Penny Payne and Betty Payne. *Educ:* Leighton Park Sch., Reading; Univ. of Sussex (MA, LLB). Called to the Bar, Lincoln's Inn, 1975; barrister; Hd of Chambers, 1 Essex Court, 2007–. Director: New Opportunity Press, 1975–90; Newpoint Publishing Gp, 1983–90; Transense Technologies plc, 1998–2008; Gatenet plc, 2015–17; GNet plc, 2015–17; Chairman: Woburn Energy (formerly Black Rock Oil & Gas) plc, 2005–15; Westminster Oil Ltd, 2007–12; Mastermailer plc, 2008–10; Curve Capital Ltd, 2008–10; Partner Capital Ltd, 2008–10; Kazakhstan Kagazy plc, 2013–15; Mass Dragon Energy Ltd (formerly Blue Dragon Resources Ltd), 2015–; Anglo-Kazakh TransAsian Pipeline Corp. plc, 2015–18; Westminster Gp plc, 2018– (Dep. Chm., 2016–18). Contested (C) Thurrock, 1979. MP (C) Banbury, 1983–2015. PPS to Minister of State for Foreign and Commonwealth Affairs, 1986–87, to Lord Privy Seal and Leader of the House, 1987–89, to Sec. of State for Energy, 1989–90; Parliamentary Under-Secretary of State: Dept of Energy, 1990; DoE, 1990–94; FCO, 1994–95; Minister of State, MAFF, 1995–97. Mem., Parly Select Cttee on Employment, 1983–86; on Trade and Industry, 1997–2001; on Standards and Privileges, 2001; on Internat. Develt, 2001–05 (Chm., 2001–05). Second Church Estates Comr, 2010–15; Mem., Gen. Synod, 2010–. Chm., Church Bldgs Council, 2015–19; Chm. Trustees, St Ethelburga's Centre for Peace and Reconciliation, 2015–. Lay Canon, Christ Ch Cath., Oxford, 2015–. Joined Sussex Yeomanry, 1971; TA Officer, resigned 1990; Hon. Col, RLC (TA), 1997–2001. DL Oxon, 2016; High Steward of Banbury, 2016–. Robert Schuman Silver Medal, Stiftung FVS Hamburg, 1978. *Recreations:* walking in the country, reading historical biography, gardening, cricket. *Clubs:* Carlton, Garrick, Brass Monkey.

**BALDRY, Lorraine,** OBE 2012; Chairman: Inventa Partners, since 2002; Schroder Real Estate Investment Trust, since 2014; Sellafield Ltd, since 2018; *b* 22 May 1949; *m* 1973, Don Baldry. Prudential Corp. plc, 1990–98; Man. Dir, Regus plc, 1999–2000; Sen. Advr, Investment Banking Div., Morgan Stanley, 2000–02; Chief Exec., Chesterton plc, 2002–03; Chm., London Thames Gateway Develt Corp., 2004–08. Chairman: Central London Partnership, 1998–2008; Tri-Air Develts Ltd, 2009–17 (Dir, 2006–09); London & Continental Railways Ltd, 2011–19; non-executive Director: DTZ Gp plc, 2010–11; Thames Water Utilities Ltd, 2014–19; Sen. Ind. Dir, Circle Hldgs plc, 2011–17. Mem. Bd, Olympic Delivery Authy, 2006–14 (Chm., Planning, 2006–12). Gov., Univ. of Arts, London, 2008–18. *Address:* Inventa Partners Ltd, Central Court, 25 Southampton Buildings, WC2A 1AL. *E:* lorraine.baldry@inventapartners.com.

**BALDRY, Rupert Patrick Craig;** QC 2010; *b* Guildford, 30 March 1962; *s* of Brian and Patricia Baldry. *Educ:* Marlborough Coll.; Bedford Coll., Univ. of London (BA Hons); City Univ. (Dip. Law). Called to the Bar, Middle Temple, 1987; Jun. Counsel to the Crown, 1999–2005. *Recreations:* fly-fishing, Shakespeare, astronomy. *Address:* Pump Court Tax Chambers, 16 Bedford Row, WC1R 4EF. *T:* (020) 7414 8080, *Fax:* (020) 7414 8099. *E:* rbaldry@pumptax.com. *Club:* Travellers.

**BALDRY, Tony;** *see* Baldry, Rt Hon. Sir A. B.

**BALDWIN,** family name of **Earl Baldwin of Bewdley**.

**BALDWIN OF BEWDLEY,** 4th Earl *cr* 1937; **Edward Alfred Alexander Baldwin;** Viscount Corvedale, 1937; *b* 3 Jan. 1938; *o s* of 3rd Earl Baldwin of Bewdley and Joan Elspeth, *y d* of late C. Alexander Tomes, New York, USA; *S* father, 1976; *m* 1st, 1970, Sarah MacMurray (*d* 2001), *er d* of late Evan Maitland James; three *s*; 2nd, 2015, Lydia Segrave, widow of Dr I. M. D. Little. *Educ:* Eton; Trinity Coll., Cambridge (MA, PGCE). Chm., British Acupuncture Accreditation Bd, 1990–98. Joint Chairman: Parly Gp for Alternative and Complementary Medicine, 1992–2002; All Party Parly Gp Against Fluoridation, 2005–10; Sec., Associate Parly Food and Health Forum; elected Mem., H of L, 1999–2018; Mem., H of L Select Cttee inquiry into complementary and alternative medicine, 2000. *Publications:* (ed jtly) Baldwin Papers: a Conservative statesman 1908–47, 2004. *Heir: s* Viscount Corvedale, *qv. Address:* 2 Scholar Place, Cumnor Hill, Oxford OX2 9RD. *Club:* MCC.

**BALDWIN, Alan Charles;** a District Judge (Magistrates' Courts) (formerly Metropolitan Stipendiary Magistrate), 1990–2013; *b* 14 April 1948; *s* of Frederick Baldwin and Millicent Baldwin (*née* McCarthy); *m* 1974, Denise Maureen Jagger; two *s*. Admitted Solicitor, 1976.

**BALDWIN, (Anna) Lisbet (Kristina);** *see* Rausing, A. L. K.

**BALDWIN, David Arthur,** CBE 1990; CEng, FIET; Director Emeritus, Hewlett-Packard Ltd, since 1996 (Chairman, 1988–96); *b* 1 Sept. 1936; *s* of late Isaac Arthur Baldwin and Edith Mary Baldwin (*née* Collins); *m* 1961, (Jacqueline) Anne Westcott; one *s* one *d. Educ:* Twickenham Technical Coll.; Wimbledon Technical Coll. (qualified electronic engineer). CEng; FIET (FIEE 1989). R&D Engineer, EMI, 1954–63; Sales Engineer, Solartron, 1963–65; Hewlett-Packard: Sales Engineer and Sales Manager, 1965–73; European Marketing Manager, 1973–78; Man. Dir, Hewlett-Packard Ltd, 1978–88. Man. Dir, Hewlett-Packard Eur. Multi-Country Region, 1990; Pres., Hewlett-Packard Belgium,

1991; Chm., Hewlett-Packard Spain, 1991; Dir, Hewlett-Packard Finland, Sweden, Denmark, Netherlands and Austria, 1991–96. Mem., BOTB, 1994–98 (Chm., European Trade Cttee, 1994–98); Chm., Thames Action and Res. Gp for Educn and Trng Ltd, 1996–. Mem. Council, RSA, 1994–. Member, Court: Cranfield Univ. (formerly Inst. of Technol.), 1987–; Brunel Univ., 1988–. CCMI; FInstD; FInstM. Freeman City of London, 1988; Liveryman, Inf. Technologists' Co., 1994. DUniv Strathclyde, 1990. *Recreations*: golf, ski-ing, photography, painting, sailing. *Address*: c/o Hewlett-Packard Ltd, Cain Road, Bracknell, Berks RG12 1HN. *T*: (01344) 360000.

**BALDWIN, Gil Talbot,** MBE 1995; Chief Executive Officer, St Andrew's Healthcare, 2014–18; non-executive Chairman, Three Shires Hospital, since 2015; *b* Hong Kong, 27 Jan. 1960; *s* of Michael Baldwin and Jean Baldwin; *m* 2016, Fiona Oliver-Smith (*née* Tanner); four *c*. *Educ*: MBA 1999. Officer, British Army, 1981–2004 (despatches 1984); Army Command and Staff Coll., 1992. Dir, Post-Conflict Reconstruction Unit, Cabinet Office, 2004–06; CEO, Aviva Health, 2006–10; Gp CEO, Tunstall Healthcare Gp, 2010–14. Dir, UK Dementia Strategy, 2014. Ministerial Med. Technol. Strategy Gp; Vice Chm., 3Million Lives jt Govt and Industry Gp; Founder Mem., Eur. Stability Initiative. Visiting Lecturer: IISS; KCL. Windsor Leadership Trust. QCVS 2003. *Recreations*: renovations, tennis, cooking, opera.

**BALDWIN, Prof. Graham,** PhD; Vice-Chancellor, University of Central Lancashire, since 2019; *b* Carshalton, 28 July 1963; *s* of Brian Ernest Jones and Ruth Jones (*née* Pearson), and step *s* of Ralph Duncan Baldwin; *m* 1990, Sarah Moxon; two *s* one *d*. *Educ*: Madeley Sch. of Physical Educn (BA Hons Sport and Recreation Studies 1984); Univ. of Wales (PGCE 1985); Loughborough Univ. (MSc Sports Sci. 1991); Univ. of Wales, Bangor (PhD 2002); Ashridge Business Sch. (Sen. Exec. Prog. 2011). Teacher of Physical Educn, Coopers Sch., Chislehurst, 1985–87; Lectr, Stoke on Trent Coll., 1987–91; Liverpool Hope University College: Lectr, 1991–95; Dep. Hd, Sport Recreation and Physical Educn Dept, 1995–97; Hd, Dept of Sport and Health, 1997–2001; University of Central Lancashire: Hd, Dept of Tourism and Leisure Mgt, 2001–03; Dir for Cumbria, 2004–06; Dean, Academic Develt, 2006–07; Nat. Skills Res. Dir, Nuclear Decommng Authy (on secondment), 2007–08; University of Central Lancashire: Pro-Vice Chancellor, 2008–09; Dep. Vice Chancellor, 2010–13; Dep. Pres., 2013–14; Vice-Chancellor and Prof. of Employer Engagement, Solent (formerly Southampton Solent) Univ., 2014–19. Hon. Prof., Hebei Univ., 2014–; Vis. Prof., Nat. Acad. of Educn Admin, China, 2015–. Dir, Business South, 2015–; Mem. Bd, Solent LEP, 2018–. Mem. Bd, UCEA, 2016–. Outstanding Foreign Expert, Hebei Foreign Experts Bureau, China, 2014. *Recreations*: family, cycling, walking, watching sport, beer, wine, coffee. *Address*: University of Central Lancashire, Preston, Lancs PR1 2HE.

**BALDWIN, Harriett Mary Morison;** MP (C) West Worcestershire, since 2010; *b* Watford, 2 May 1960; *d* of Anthony Francis Eggleston, *qv*; *m* 2004, James Stanley Baldwin; two step *d*; one *s* by a previous marriage. *Educ*: Friends' Sch., Saffron Walden; Marlborough Coll.; Lady Margaret Hall, Oxford (BA French and Russian 1982); McGill Univ. (MBA 1985). J. P. Morgan, 1986–2008, Man. Dir, 1998–2008; Vice Chm., Social Investment Business, 2008–12. PPS to Minister for Employment, 2012–14; an Asst Govt Whip, 2014; a Lord Comr of HM Treasury (Govt Whip), 2014–15; Econ. Sec., HM Treasury, 2015–16; Parly Under-Sec. of State, MoD, 2016–18; Minister of State, DFID and FCO, 2018–19. Contested (C) Stockton N, 2005. *Recreations*: family, walking, swimming, travel. *Address*: House of Commons, SW1A 0AA. *T*: (020) 7219 7187. *E*: harriett.baldwin.mp@parliament.uk. *Club*: Carlton.

**BALDWIN, Sir Jack (Edward),** Kt 1997; PhD; FRS 1978; Waynflete Professor of Chemistry and Fellow of Magdalen College, University of Oxford, 1978–2006, now Professor Emeritus and Hon. Fellow; *b* 8 Aug. 1938; *s* of Frederick Charles Baldwin and Olive Frances Headland; *m* 1977, Christine Louise, *d* of William B. Franchi. *Educ*: Lewes County Grammar Sch.; Imperial Coll., London Univ. (BSc, DIC, PhD). ARCS. Asst Lectr in Chem., Imperial Coll., 1963, Lectr, 1966; Asst Prof. of Chem., Pa State Univ., 1967, Associate Prof., 1969; Alfred P. Sloan Fellow, 1969–70, Associate Prof. of Chem., 1970, Prof., 1972, MIT; Daniell Prof. of Chem., King's Coll., London, 1972; Prof. of Chem., MIT, 1972–78. Dir, Oxford Centre for Molecular Sciences, 1988–98. Mem., BBSRC, 1994–97. Lectures: Tilden, RSC, 1979; Simonsen, RSC, 1982. Corresp. Mem., Academia Scientiarum Gottingensis, Göttingen, 1988; For. Mem., Amer. Acad. of Arts and Scis, 1993. Hon. DSc: Warwick, 1988, Strathclyde, 1989. Corday Morgan Medal and Prize, Chem. Soc., 1975; Medal and Prize for Synthetic Organic Chemistry, RSC, 1980; Paul Karrer Medal and Prize, Zürich Univ., 1984; Medal and Prize for Natural Product Chemistry, RSC, 1984; Hugo Müller Medal, RSC, 1987; Max Tischler Award, Harvard Univ., 1987; Dr Paul Jansen Prize for Creativity in Organic Synthesis, Belgium, 1988; Davy Medal, 1994, Leverhulme Medal, 1999, Royal Soc.; Nakanishi Prize, Chem. Soc. of Japan, 2002; Paracelsus Prize, Swiss Chem. Soc., 2006. *Publications*: res. pubns in Jl of Amer. Chem. Soc., Jl of Chem. Soc., Tetrahedron. *Address*: Broom, Hinksey Hill, Oxford OX1 5BH.

**BALDWIN, John Paul;** QC 1991; barrister; a Recorder, 2004–17; a Deputy High Court Judge, 2008–17; *b* 15 Aug. 1947; *s* of late Frank Baldwin and Marjorie Baldwin (*née* Jay); *m* 1981, Julie Campbell; two *d*. *Educ*: Nelson Grammar Sch.; Univ. of Leeds (BSc 1st Cl. Hons 1968); St John's Coll., Oxford (DPhil 1972). Res. Fellow, Univ. of Oxford, 1972–75; called to the Bar, Gray's Inn, 1977, Bencher, 2000. Judge: Chancery Div., Patents Court, 2006–; Intellectual Property Enterprise Court (formerly Patents County Court), 2006–. *Publications*: numerous scientific pubns, 1969–75. *Recreations*: tennis, gardening. *Address*: 8 New Square, Lincoln's Inn, WC2A 3QP. *T*: (020) 7405 4321. *Clubs*: Queen's, Campden Hill.

**BALDWIN, Mark Phillip,** OBE 2015; founder and choreographer, Mark Baldwin Dance Co., since 1992; Artistic Director, Mark Baldwin Studios, since 2017; *b* 16 Jan. 1954; *s* of late Ronald William Baldwin and Rose Theresa Evans. *Educ*: St Kentigerns Coll., NZ; Pakuranga Coll., NZ; Suva Grammar Sch., Fiji; Elam Sch. of Fine Arts, Univ. of Auckland. Founder Dancer, Limbs Dance Co., NZ, New Zealand Ballet, Australian Dance Theatre, Rambert Dance Co., 1979–92; choreographer-in-residence, Sadler's Wells, 1993; resident artist, The Place, 1995–96; choreographer-in-residence, Scottish Ballet, 1996; Artistic Dir, Rambert Dance Company, 2002–18. Works choreographed for Rambert Dance Co. include: Island to Island, 1991; Gone, 1992; Spirit, 1994; Banter Banter, 1994; Constant Speed, 2005; Eternal Light, 2008; The Comedy of Change, 2009; Seven for a Secret, never to be told, 2011; What Wild Ecstasy, 2012; The Strange Charm of Mother Nature, 2014; Dark Arteries, 2015; The Creation, 2016; for Scottish Ballet: Haydn Pieces, 1995; Ae Fond Kiss, 1996; More Poulenc, 1996; for Staatsoper, Berlin: Labyrinth, 1997; The Demon, 1998; The Man with a Moustache (for City Ballet of London), 1998; Towards Poetry (for Royal Ballet), 1999; Pointe Blank (for TV), 1999; Ihi FrENZY (for Royal NZ Ballet), 2001; Frankenstein (for BBC4), 2003; The Wedding (for Royal NZ Ballet), 2006; M is for Man (for Dansgroep Amsterdam), 2009; The Rite of Spring (for Rambert Sch.), 2013; Not a Cloud in the Sky (for Staatstheater, Saarbrücken), 2014; Inala, Edinburgh Playhouse, then touring, 2014; G(Rave) (for B(old)), 2018. *Address*: Mark Baldwin Studios, 3a Southcombe Street, W14 0RA.

**BALDWIN, Nicholas Peter,** CBE 2017; CEng, CDir, FIMechE, FIET; Chair, Dimensions-UK, since 2018; *b* 17 Dec. 1952; *s* of Desmond Stanley Frederick Baldwin and Beatrix Marie Baldwin (*née* Walker); *m* 2002, Adrienne Ann Plunkett; one *s* one *d*. *Educ*: City Univ. (BSc Mechanical Engrg); Birkbeck Coll., Univ. of London (MSc Econs). CEng 1979; FIMechE 1996; FIET 2002; CDir 2007. Metropolitan Water Bd, 1971–74; Thames Water Authy, 1974–80; CEGB, 1980–89, Sen. Energy Analyst, 1986–89; PowerGen plc, 1989–2002: Econ. Studies Manager, 1989–90; Business Planning Manager, 1990–92; Head of Strategic Planning, 1992–94; Director: Strategy, 1994–95; Generation, 1995–96; Man. Dir, UK Electricity Prodn, 1996–98; Exec. Dir, UK Ops, 1998–2001; Chief Exec., 2001–02. Non-executive Director: Energy Gp Advisory Bd, DTI, 2002–06; Forensic Sci. Service, 2004–; Nuclear Decommng Authy, 2004–11 (Chm., 2007–08); Scottish and Southern Energy, 2006–11; Sanctuary Housing, 2008–09 (Chm., 2009–14). Chairman: Public Weather Service Customer Gp, 2007–13; Office for Nuclear Regulation, 2011–19. Mem., HSE, 2011–. Vice Chm., Worcs Local Area Partnership, 2014–. Chm., Ambitious About Autism (formerly TreeHouse Trust), 2008–14; Trustee, Land Trust, 2010–11. FRSA 1998; FInstD 2015; FEI 2015. *Publications*: articles in Energy Policy and Energy Economics. *Recreations*: long distance walking, photography, cinema, music, reading, family activities. *Club*: Worcester County Cricket.

**BALDWIN, Air Vice-Marshal Nigel Bruce,** CB 1996; CBE 1992; Chairman, RAF Historical Society, since 1997; *b* 20 Sept. 1941; *s* of Peter William Baldwin and Doris Baldwin; *m* 1963, Jennifer; one *d* (and one *d* decd). *Educ*: Peter Symonds' Sch., Winchester; RAF Coll., Cranwell. Pilot, Vulcans, 9/35 Sqns, 1963–68; ADC to AOC 11 Gp, 1968–70; Sqn Ldr, Vulcans, 35 Sqn, Cyprus, 1970–73; Staff Coll., Bracknell, 1974; HQ Strike Command, 1975–76; OC 50 Sqn, Vulcans, 1977–79; US Air War Coll. and Faculty, US Air Command and Staff Coll., 1979–82; Gp Captain and Station Comdr, Wyton, 1983–85; Internat. Fellow, Nat. Defense Univ., Washington, 1986; Asst Dir of Defence Policy, MoD, 1986–88; Air Cdre Plans, HQ Strike Command, 1989–92; ACDS (Overseas), 1993–96. Pres., RAF Vol. Band Assoc., 1996–; Vice Pres., Ex-Services Mental Welfare Soc., 2007– (Chm., 1997–2007). *Recreations*: Schubert, Nelson. *Club*: Royal Air Force.

**BALDWIN, Prof. Thomas Raymond,** PhD; Professor of Philosophy, University of York, since 1995; *b* 10 April 1947; *s* of Raymond Baldwin and Penelope Baldwin (*née* Barlow); *m* 1973, Anna Barber; two *d*. *Educ*: Trinity Coll., Cambridge (BA (Moral Scis) 1968; PhD (Philos.) 1971). Lectr in Philos., Makerere Univ., Kampala, 1971–72; Jun. Res. Fellow, Churchill Coll., Cambridge, 1973–74; Lecturer: Univ. of York, 1974–84; Philos. Faculty, Cambridge Univ., 1984–95; Fellow, Clare Coll., Cambridge, 1984–95. Ed., Mind, 2005–15. Member: Nuffield Council on Bioethics, 2000–06; HFEA, 2001–05 (Dep. Chm., 2002–05); Expert Adv. Cttee on Obesity, DoH, 2008–11; Human Genetics Commn, 2009–12. Trustee (non-alcoholic), Alcoholics Anonymous, 2019–. *Publications*: G. E. Moore, 1990; Contemporary Philosophy, 2001; Cambridge History of Philosophy, 2003. *Recreations*: walking, visiting gardens. *Address*: Department of Philosophy, University of York, York YO10 5DD. *T*: (01904) 323252. *E*: thomas.baldwin@york.ac.uk.

**BALFE,** family name of **Baron Balfe**.

**BALFE,** Baron *cr* 2013 (Life Peer), of Dulwich in the London Borough of Southwark; **Richard Andrew Balfe;** President, European Parliament Members Pension Fund, since 1994; adviser to pension funds on defined contribution pension rules; *b* 14 May 1944; *s* of Dr Richard J. Balfe and Mrs Dorothy L. Balfe (*née* de Cann); *m* 1986, Susan Jane Honeyford; one *s* one *d*, and one *s* by a previous marriage. *Educ*: Brook Secondary Sch., Sheffield; LSE (BSc Hons 1971). Fellow Royal Statistical Soc., 1972. HM Diplomatic Service, 1965–70; Res. Officer, Finer Cttee on One Parent Families, 1970–73; Political Sec., RACS, 1973–79; Dir, RACS and associated cos, 1978–85. European Parliament: Mem. (Lab 1979–2001, C 2002–04) London S Inner, 1979–99, London Reg., 1999–2004; Quaestor, 1994–2004; Member: Foreign Affairs Cttee, 1981–99; Security Cttee, 1989–99; Econ. and Monetary Cttee, 1999–2004; Petitions Cttee, 2001–04. Mem., Eur. Econ. and Social Cttee, 2012–13. Parly Candidate (Lab), Paddington South, 1970; contested (Lab) Southwark and Bermondsey, 1992. Mem., GLC for Southwark/Dulwich, 1973–77; Chairman: Thamesmead New Town Cttee, 1973–75; GLC Housing Cttee, 1975–77. Member: Exec. Cttee, Fabian Soc., 1981–82; London Labour Party Exec., 1973–95 (Chair, Policy Cttee, 1983–85); Chair, Political Cttee, Royal Arsenal Co-op (CWS), 1984–95. Cons. Party Envoy to Trades Union and Co-op movements, 2008–12. Dir, CERN Pension Fund, 2009–14 (Mem., Actuarial and Technical Cttee, 2011–17). Trustee, Pension Scheme, Royal Statistical Soc., 2012–13. Mem., Ct of Governors, LSE, 1973–91; Sen. Mem., Wolfson Coll., Cambridge, 2016–. Chm., Anglia Community Leisure, 2008–13. President: British Dietetic Assoc., 2016–; BALPA, 2018– (Vice Pres., 2017–18). *Recreations*: collecting books and pamphlets on political and social history topics, opera, Wagner, walking. *Address*: House of Lords, SW1A 0PW. *E*: richard.balfe@parliament.uk. *Club*: Reform (Chm., Finance Cttee, 2013–14; Member: Gen. Cttee, 2011–16; Library Cttee, 2015–).

**BALFOUR,** family name of **Earl of Balfour** and **Barons Kinross** and **Riverdale**.

**BALFOUR, 5th Earl of,** *cr* 1922; **Roderick Francis Arthur Balfour;** Viscount Traprain 1922; *b* 9 Dec. 1948; *s* of Eustace Arthur Goschen Balfour and Anne (*née* Yule); *S* cousin, 2003; *m* 1971, Lady Tessa Mary Isabel Fitzalan-Howard, *e d* of 17th Duke of Norfolk, KG, GCVO, CB, CBE, MC; four *d*. *Educ*: Eton; London Business Sch. Mem., London Stock Exchange, 1975–81; Dir, Union Discount Co. of London plc, 1983–90; Dir, Rothschild Trust Corp. Ltd, 1990–2005; Founder and Dir, Virtus Trust Gp, 2005–17; Dir, Business Develt, Equiom Gp, 2017–. Non-executive Director: Bateman Engrg NV, 2005–09; Nikanor plc, 2006–08; Dir, CTTC Archway (China), 2008–. Mem., Adv. Bd, Gateway Commodity Fund, Basel, 2009–. Member: City of London Cttee and Soc. of Trust and Estate Practitioners, 1996–; Internat. Tax Planning Assoc., 2010–. Liveryman, Clothworkers' Co., 1986. *Heir*: *b* Hon. Charles George Yule Balfour [*b* 23 April 1951; *m* 1st, 1978, Audrey Margaret Hoare; 2nd, 1987, Svea Maria Cecily Lucrezia von Goëss; one *s* one *d*]. *E*: EofBPrivate@aol.com. *Clubs*: White's, I Zingari, Eton Ramblers, Old Etonian Lawn Tennis and Racquets; Brook (New York).

**BALFOUR OF BURLEIGH, Lord** *cr* 1607 (*de facto* 8th Lord, 12th but for the Attainder); **Robert Bruce,** CEng, FIET; FRSE; Chancellor, Stirling University, 1988–98; Vice Lord-Lieutenant, Clackmannan, 1995–2001; *b* 6 Jan. 1927; *e s* of 11th Lord Balfour of Burleigh and Dorothy (*d* 1976), *d* of late R. H. Done; *S* father, 1967; *m* 1st, 1971, Mrs Jennifer Brittain-Catlin (marr. diss. 1993), *d* of late E. S. Manasseh; two *d*; 2nd, 1993, Janet Morgan (*see* Lady Balfour of Burleigh). *Educ*: Westminster Sch. Served Home Guard, 1944–45 as Private, 2nd Herefordshire Bn; RN, 1945–48, as Ldg Radio Electrician's Mate. Joined English Electric Co. Ltd, 1951; DFH; graduate apprentice, 1951–52; Asst Foreman, Heavy Electrical Plant Dept, Stafford Works, 1952–54; Asst Superintendent, Heavy Electrical Plant Dept, Netherton Works, Liverpool, 1954–57; Manager, English Electric Co. of India (Pvte) Ltd, Madras, 1957–60; Dir and Gen. Manager, English Electric Co. India Ltd, 1960–64 Dep. Gen. Manager, English Electric Co. Ltd, Netherton, Liverpool, 1964–65, Gen. Manager 1965–66; Dir and Gen. Manager, D. Napier & Son Ltd, 1966–68; Dep. Gov. Bank of Scotland, 1977–91 (Dir, 1968–91). Chairman: Viking Oil, 1971–80; NWS Bank (formerly North West Securities), 1978–91; Cappella Nova, 1988–2009; Canongate Press

1991–93; United Artists Communications (Scotland), 1993–96; Director: Scottish Investment Trust, 1971–97; Tarmac, 1981–90; William Lawson Distillers Ltd, 1984–97; Television Educnl Network, 1990–96; UAPT Infolink, 1991–94; Member: British Railways (Scottish) Board, 1982–93; Forestry Commn, 1971–74. Chm., Fedn of Scottish Bank Employers, 1977–86. Chairman: Scottish Arts Council, 1971–80; NBL Scotland, 1981–85; Turing Inst., 1983–91; Scottish Cttee, ABSA, 1990–94 (Mem. Council, 1976–94); Dir, Edinburgh Book Fest., 1981–97 (Chm., 1981–87). Pres., Friends of Vellore, 1973–. Vice-President: RNID, 1987–2004; Bletchley Park Trust, 2009– (Trustee, 2000–09); Treasurer: Royal Scottish Corp., 1967–2004; RSE, 1989–94; Trustee: Radcliffe Trust, 1975–2015; John Muir Trust, 1989–96; Dir, Eur. Brandenburg Ensemble, 2007–09. Hon. FRIAS, 1982. DUniv Stirling, 1988; Hon. DLitt Robert Gordon, 1995. Chevalier, Ordre Grand-Ducal de la Couronne de Chêne (Luxembourg), 2014. *Recreations:* music, climbing, woodwork, open air ice-skating. *Heir:* d Hon. Victoria Bruce-Winkler [b 7 May 1973; m 2002, Michail Winkler; two d]. *Address:* Brucefield, Clackmannanshire FK10 3QF. *Clubs:* Travellers, New (Edinburgh).

See also G. J. D. Bruce.

**BALFOUR OF BURLEIGH, Lady; Janet Bruce**, CBE 2008; writer and company director; b 5 Dec. 1945; e d of Frank Morgan and Shiela Sadler; m 1993, Lord Balfour of Burleigh, qv. *Educ:* Newbury Co. Girls Grammar Sch.; St Hugh's Coll., Oxford. MA, DPhil Oxon, MA Sussex. FSAScot 1992; FRSE 1999. Kennedy Meml Scholar, Harvard Univ., 1968–69; Student, Nuffield Coll., Oxford, 1969–71; Res. Fellow, Wolfson Coll., Oxford and Res. Officer, Univ. of Essex, 1971–72; Res. Fellow, Nuffield Coll., Oxford, 1972–74; Lectr in Politics, Exeter Coll., Oxford, 1974–76; Dir of Studies, St Hugh's Coll., Oxford, 1975–76 and Lectr in Politics, 1976–78; Mem., Central Policy Rev. Staff, Cabinet Office, 1978–81. Mem. Bd, British Council, 1989–99. Vis. Fellow, All Souls Coll., Oxford, 1983. Dir, Satellite Television PLC, 1981–83; Special Advr to Dir-Gen., BBC, 1983–86; Advr to Bd, Granada Gp, 1986–89; Mem., London Adv. Bd, Nat. and Provincial Bldg Soc., 1988–89; Chairman: Cable & Wireless Flexible Resource Ltd, 1993–97; Nuclear Liabilities Fund (formerly Nuclear Generation Decommissioning Co.), 2003–14 (Dir, 1996–2003); Nuclear Liabilities Financing Assurance Bd, 2008–15; Espirito Ltd, 2011–12; non-executive Director: Cable & Wireless, 1988–2004; W. H. Smith, 1989–95; Midlands Electricity, 1990–96; Pitney Bowes, 1991–93; Scottish American Investment Trust, 1991–2008; Scottish Med. Res. Fund, 1993–96; Scottish Life, 1995–2001; Scottish Oriental Smaller Cos Investment Trust, 1995–2017; NMT Gp, 1997–2004; BPB, 2000–05; Stagecoach Gp, 2001–10; Murray Internat. Investment Trust, 2003–16; Albion Enterprise (formerly Close Enterprise) VCT, 2006–; NDA Archives Ltd, 2014–. Vice-Pres., Videotext Industries Assoc., 1985–91; Dir, Hulton Deutsch Collection, 1988–90. Member: Lord Chancellor's Adv. Council on Public Records, 1982–86; Adv. Council, Inst. for Advanced Studies in the Humanities, Univ. of Edinburgh, 1988–96; Ancient Monuments Bd for Scotland, 1990–97; Book Trust (Scotland), 1992–99; Scottish Econ. Council, 1993–96; Chairman: Scotland's Book Campaign, 1994–96; Readiscovery Touring Ltd, 1996–99. Trustee: Amer. Sch. in London, 1985–88; Fairground Heritage Trust, 1987–90; Cyclotron Trust, 1988–90; Scottish Hosp. Endowments Res. Trust, 1992–96; Carnegie Trust for Univs of Scotland, 1994–2016; Nuclear Trust, 1996–2014; Scottish Science Trust, 1997–99; Nat. Library of Scotland, 2002–11; Trusthouse Charitable Foundn, 2006–17; Royal Anniversary Trust, 2010–; Chairman: Dorothy Burns Charitable Trust, 1992–2002; Scottish Cultural Resources Access Network Ltd, 1996–2004; Scottish Mus. of Year Awards, 1999–2004; Patron, Porthcurno Submarine Telegraph Mus., 2004–; Vice-Patron, Intelligence Corps Mus., 2014–. Mem., Editorial Bd, Political Quarterly, 1980–90. Mem., Amer. Philosophical Soc., 2012. Hon. LLD Strathclyde, 1999; Hon. DLitt Napier, 1999. Chevalier, Ordre Grand-Ducal de la Couronne de Chêne (Luxembourg), 2014. *Publications:* (as Janet Morgan): The House of Lords and the Labour Government 1964–70, 1975; Reinforcing Parliament, 1976; (ed) The Diaries of a Cabinet Minister 1964–70 by Richard Crossman, 3 vols 1975, 1976, 1977; (ed) Backbench Diaries 1951–63 by Richard Crossman, 1980; (ed with Richard Hoggart) The Future of Broadcasting, 1982; Agatha Christie: a biography, 1984; Edwina Mountbatten: a life of her own, 1991; The Secrets of rue St Roch, 2004. *Recreations:* music of Handel, sea-bathing, ice-skating out of doors, pruning. *Address:* Brucefield, Clackmannanshire FK10 3QF. *T:* (01259) 730228.

**BALFOUR, Alexander William;** Chief Executive Officer, Digital Brand Services (UK) Ltd, since 2017; b 26 Feb. 1971; s of late Peter Edward Gerald Balfour, CBE and of Diana Rosemary Balfour; m 2000, Samantha, (Sam), Walker; one s one d. *Educ:* St John's Coll., Cambridge (BA 1993). Reporter, Euromoney mag., 1994–95; freelance journalist, 1995–97; Editor, GE '97, 1997; Content Dir, UK Citizens Online Democracy, 1998; Producer, The Guardian, 1998–99; Dir, Business Develt, 2000–01, Chm., 2001–03, CricInfo Ltd; Dir of Strategy, Emerging Media, 2003–06; Hd of New Media, LOCOG, 2006–12; Chief Digital Officer, Engine Gp, 2013; Chief Digital Officer, Haymon Boxing Mgt, 2014–16. Non-executive Director: Pensions Adv. Service, 2010–14; DTracks Ltd, 2011–; Ardohr Ltd, 2012–. Sen. Consultant, Digital Strategy, TEAM Mktg AG, 2017–. Mem., HM Govt Digital Adv. Bd, 2012–16. Comr, Historic England (formerly English Heritage), 2014–; Trustee, English Heritage Trust, 2014–. *Recreations:* riding fixed gear bicycles, being bullied by my children, swimming in the sea, reading, watching cricket, DJing, surfing the Interweb. *Address:* c/o DBS, Camburgh House, 27 New Dover Road, Canterbury, Kent CT1 3DN. *Clubs:* Lansdowne, MCC; London Dynamo, Rye Wheelers.

**BALFOUR, (Elizabeth) Jean**, CBE 1981; FRSE 1980; FRSA; FICFor; JP; Chairman, Countryside Commission for Scotland, 1972–82; b 4 Nov. 1927; 2nd d of late Maj.-Gen. Sir James Syme Drew, KBE, CB, DSO, MC, and late Victoria Maxwell of Munches; m 1950, John Charles Balfour, OBE, MC (d 2009); three s. *Educ:* Edinburgh Univ. (BSc). Partner/Owner, Balbirnie Home Farms; Director: A. & J. Bowen & Co. Ltd; Loch Duart Ltd, 1999–2008 (Chm., 1999–2006); Mem. Bd, Scottish Quality Salmon, 2005–06. Pres., Royal Scottish Forestry Soc., 1969–71; Mem., Fife CC, 1958–70; Chm., Fife County and City and Royal Burgh of Dunfermline Joint Probation Cttee, 1967–69; Governor, East of Scotland Coll. of Agriculture, 1958–88, Vice Pres. 1982–88; Dir, Scottish Agricl Colls, 1987–88, Dir, Council, 1974–87; Member: Scottish Agric. Develt Council, 1972–77; Verney Working Party on Natural Resources, 1971–72; Nature Conservancy Council, 1973–80; Oil Develt Council, 1973–78; Scottish Economic Council, 1978–83; Forth River Purification Bd, 1992–96; Council, Scottish Landowners Fedn, 1996–99 (Chm., Forestry Cttee, 1997–99); Chairman: Regional Adv. Cttee, East (Scotland) Forestry Commn, 1976–85; Regional Adv. Cttee, Mid (Scotland) Forestry Commn, 1987–2000; Food and Farming Adv. Cttee, Scottish Cons. and Unionist Assoc., 1985–88; Crarae Gardens Charitable Trust, 1986–93; W Sutherland Fisheries Trust, 1996–99; Hon. Vice Pres., Scottish Wildlife Trust (Vice-Chm., 1968–72; Founder Council Mem.). Deputy Chairman: Seafish Industry Authority, 1987–90; Cttee on Women in Science, Engrg and Technol., OST, Cabinet Office, 1993–94. Member: Cttee of Enquiry on handling of geographical information, 1985–87; RSE Foot and Mouth Enquiry, 2001–02. Trustee: Buckland Foundn, 1989–94; Royal Botanic Gdns, Edinburgh, 1992–98. Mem. Council, RSE, 1983–86; Mem. Council and Chm., Policy and Legislation Cttee, Inst. of Chartered Foresters, 1986–88; Council Mem. and Chm., Mid Scotland Timber Growers' Assoc., 2000–02. Hon. Vice-Pres., Scottish YHA, 1983–. Mem. Court, St Andrews Univ.,

1983–87 (Chm. Ct Cttee, Estates and Buildings, 1983–87); Gov., Duncan of Jordanstone Coll. of Art, 1992–96. JP Fife, 1963. FRSA 1981; FRZSScot 1983; FRSB (FIBiol 1988); FRSGS 1997. Hon. DSc St Andrews, 1977; DUniv Stirling, 1991. Forestry Medal, Inst. of Chartered Foresters, 1996; Award for Dedicated Service to Forestry, Confedn of Forest Industries, 2015. Order of the Falcon (Iceland), 1994. Report to Government, A New Look at the Northern Ireland Countryside, 1984–85. *Recreations:* hill walking, fishing, painting, exploring arctic vegetation, shooting. *Address:* Kirkforthar House, Markinch, Fife KY7 6LS. *T:* (01592) 752233; Scourie, by Lairg, Sutherland IV27 4TH. *Clubs:* Farmers; New (Edinburgh).

See also R. W. Balfour.

**BALFOUR, Maj. Gen. James Melville John**, CBE 2001 (OBE 1992); DL; farmer; b 6 May 1951; s of late Comdr Colin James Balfour, RN; m 1981, Carolyn Laing; one s two d. *Educ:* Eton Coll.; Mons Officer Cadet Sch.; Army Staff Coll. Commnd into 3rd Bn RGJ, 1970; ADC to CGS, 1977; Defence Services Staff Coll., India, 1983; Major, Mil. Ops, MoD, 1984–85; Co. Comdr, 3rd Bn RGJ, 1986–88; JSDC, Greenwich, 1988; Directing Staff, Army Staff Coll., Camberley, 1988–90; CO, 3rd Bn, RGJ, 1990–92; MA to QMG, 1993; HCSC 1994; Col, Mil. Ops, MoD, 1994–95; Comdr, 3rd Inf. Bde, 1996–97; RCDS 1998; COS, HQ NI, 1999–2001; Comdr, British Forces, Bosnia, 2001; Dir, Infantry, MoD, 2002–04; Co-ordinator, Kosovo Protection Corps, 2005–06; Pres., Gen. Court Martial, 2006–07. Dir Gen., Winston Churchill Meml Trust, 2007–15. Chairman: Youth Clubs Hants and IoW, 2007–09; Winchester Downs Cluster Gp, 2017–; Hants County Chairman: Game and Wildlife Conservancy Trust, 2008–11; ABF, 2008–15 (Vice Pres., 2015–); Army Regular Reservist Chm., Service Complaint Appeal Bodies, 2015–; Pres., Hants CLA, 2014– (Mem. Cttee, 2006–11). Hon. Col, Eton College CCF, 2007–17. DL, 2009, High Sheriff, 2014–15, Hants. *Recreations:* field sports, rural conservation issues.

**BALFOUR, Jean;** see Balfour, E. J.

**BALFOUR, Jeremy Ross;** Member (C) Lothian, Scottish Parliament, since 2016; b Edinburgh, 11 March 1967; s of Ian and Joyce Balfour; m 2005, Jude Huddart; two d. *Educ:* Edinburgh Acad.; Edinburgh Univ. (DipLP 1992); London Sch. of Theol. (BA Theol. 1998). Trainee solicitor, Anderson Strathern, 1992–94; admitted solicitor, 1994; Parly Officer, Evangelical Alliance, 1999–2006; Church Property Mgr, Scottish Churches Housing Action, 2008–16. Mem. (C), Edinburgh CC, 2005–. Associate Minister, Morningside Baptist Ch, 2000–04. *Recreations:* sport, travelling, reading. *Address:* Scottish Parliament, Edinburgh EH99 1SP. *T:* (0131) 348 5960. *E:* jeremy.balfour.msp@parliament.scot.

**BALFOUR, Michael William,** OBE 2008; FCA; Founder and Chairman, The Hideaways Club Ltd, 2007–13; Chairman, Jatomi Fitness Ltd (formerly Pure Health and Fitness Sp. z o.o.), 2012–14; b 3 May 1949; s of Alexander and Winifred Balfour; m 1978, Margaret; one s one d. Gen. Manager, Lucas (Latina America) Inc., 1978–81; Man. Dir, Bytex Ltd, 1982–85; Dir, Mannai Investment Co., 1985–92; Fitness First Holdings Ltd: Founder, CEO, 1992–2004; Dep. Chm., 2005–06; Chm., 2006–09. Director: Fitness Industry Assoc., 2003–06; Skills Active, 2005–06. Non-exec. Dir, Tender Space Ltd, 2015–. Hon. DBA Bournemouth, 2004. *Recreations:* sailing, golf. *T:* (office) (01202) 331932.

**BALFOUR, Neil Roxburgh;** Chairman: Mermaid Holdings Ltd, 1991–2018; Mermaid Properties Sp. z o.o., since 2005; b 12 Aug. 1944; s of Archibald Roxburgh Balfour and Lilian Helen Cooper; m 1st, 1969, HRH Princess Elizabeth of Yugoslavia; one s; 2nd, 1978, Serena Mary Spencer-Churchill Russell; two s one d. *Educ:* Ampleforth Coll., Yorks; University Coll., Oxford Univ. (BA History). Called to the Bar, Middle Temple, 1969. Baring Brothers & Co., 1968–74; European Banking Co. Ltd, 1974–83 (Exec. Dir, 1980–83). Chm., York Trust Group plc, 1986–91; Pres., and CEO, Mostostal Warszawa SA, 2000–02. Mem. (C) N Yorks, European Parlt, 1979–84. *Publications:* Paul of Yugoslavia (biography), 1980. *Recreations:* bridge, golf, tennis, shooting, fishing. *Address:* Alma Grove, Combe, near Witney, Oxon OX29 8NA. *Clubs:* Turf, Pratt's, White's; Royal St George's (Sandwich), Sunningdale; Arcangues (Biarritz).

**BALFOUR, Robert William,** FRICS; Lord-Lieutenant of Fife, since 2014; Managing Partner, Balbirnie Home Farms, 1991–2018; b Edinburgh, 25 March 1952; s of late John Charles Balfour, OBE, MC and of (Elizabeth) Jean Balfour, qv; m 1975, Jessica McCrindle; three s (and one s decd). *Educ:* Eton Coll.; Univ. of Edinburgh (BSc Hons). FRICS 1990. Mgt trainee, Ocean Gp, 1974–78; Surveyor, Bell-Ingram, Perth, 1978–88; Bidwells, Chartered Surveyors, Perth, 1988–94 (Associate Partner, 1991–94). Chm., Kettle Growers Ltd, 2006–11. Dir, Paths for All Partnership, 2005–13. Mem., E Area Bd, Scottish Natural Heritage, 2003–07. Convener, Scottish Landowners Fedn, 1999–2002. Chm., RICS Rural Practice Div. (Scotland), 1990–91. Chm., Assoc. of Deer Mgt Gps, 2005–11. Dir, Fife Coast and Countryside Trust, 2003–15 (Chm., 2007–15). Vice Pres., RHASS, 2005–06. Gen. Trustee, Church of Scotland, 2012–. Mem., Bd of Mgt, Elmwood Coll., 2000–08. Mem., Royal Co. of Archers (Queen's Body Guard for Scotland), 1992–. DL Fife, 1994. Elder, Markinch Parish Ch, 1982–. *Recreations:* shooting, music, theatre, opera, restoring series 1 Land Rovers. *Address:* Little Kinloch, Ladybank, Fife KY15 7UT. *T:* (01337) 831400, 07774 833620. *E:* robertwbalfour@gmail.com. *Clubs:* Farmers; Royal and Ancient Golf.

**BALKWILL, Prof. Frances Rosemary,** OBE 2008; FMedSci; Professor of Cancer Biology and Centre Lead, Centre for Cancer and Inflammation (formerly Centre for Translational Oncology), Barts Cancer Institute (formerly Cancer Research UK Translational Oncology Laboratory, then Institute of Cancer), Barts and The London School of Medicine and Dentistry, Queen Mary University of London (formerly Barts and The London, Queen Mary's Medical School), since 2000; b 18 March 1952; d of late Elson Howard Lucas Leach and Rosemary Emily Leach; m 1973, Lewis Balkwill (marr. diss. 1987); one s one d. *Educ:* Surbiton High Sch.; Bristol Univ. (BSc); Univ. of London (PhD). Prin. Scientist and Lab. Hd, ICRF, 1979–2000; Dir, Centre of the Cell (sci. centre for children), Barts and The London Sch. of Medicine and Dentistry (formerly Barts and the London, Queen Mary's Med. Sch.), 2002–. Non-Parly Bd Mem., POST, 2000–19. Chairman: Public Engagement Strategy Cttee, Wellcome Trust, 2008–11; Understanding Animal Res., 2010–16; Mem., Scientific Adv. Cttee, Breakthrough Breast Cancer, 2012–15. Trustee, Bloodwise, 2018–. Judge, Wellcome Book Prize, 2016. Series Ed., Making Sense of Science, 1995–99. FMedSci 2006. Hon. Fellow, British Sci. Assoc., 2009. Hon. DSc Bristol, 2015. Award for Communication in the Life Scis, EMBO, 2004; Michael Faraday Prize, Royal Soc., 2005. *Publications:* Cytokines in Cancer Therapy, 1989; (ed) Cytokines: a practical approach, 1991, 3rd edn 2000; (ed jtly) Interleukin 2, 1992; (ed) Frontiers in Molecular Biology: the cytokine network, 2000; *books for children* (designed and illustrated by Mic Rolph): Cells are Us, 1990; Cell Wars, 1990; DNA is Here to Stay, 1992; Amazing Schemes within your Genes, 1993; The Egg and Sperm Race, 1994; Microbes, Bugs, and Wonder Drugs, 1995; Enjoy Your Cells (series), 2001–02; Staying Alive: fighting HIV/AIDS, 2002; SuperCells, 2003; You, Me and HIV, 2004; approx. 250 pubns in scientific jls. *Recreations:* writing, travel, bird watching, piano. *Address:* Centre for Cancer and Inflammation, Barts Cancer Institute, Queen Mary University of London, Charterhouse Square, EC1M 6BQ. *T:* (020) 7882 3587.

**BALL, Alison**; QC 1995; a Recorder, since 1998; *b* 12 Jan. 1948; *d* of Winifred Alice Ball and Hilary Noble Ball; *m* 1980, Richard; two *d*. *Educ:* Bedales Sch.; King's Coll., London (LLB Hons). Called to the Bar, Middle Temple, 1972, Bencher, 2002; founded Specialist Family Law Chambers, 1989, Joint Head, 1989–2010. *Recreation:* my family and other animals. *Address:* 1GC Family Law, 10 Lincoln's Inn Fields, WC2A 3BP. *T:* (020) 7797 7900.

**BALL, Anthony George, (Tony)**, MBE 1986; FCIM; FIMI; FCGI; Founder, 1983, and Chairman, 1983–2006, Tony Ball Associates (TBA) plc; *b* 14 Nov. 1934; *s* of Harry Ball and Mary Irene Ball, Bridgwater; *m* 1st, 1957, Ruth Parry Davies (marr. diss. 1997); two *s* one *d*; 2nd, 2000, Ms Jan Kennedy. *Educ:* Grammar Sch., Bridgwater. Indentured engineering apprentice, Austin Motor Co., 1951–55; responsible for launch of Mini, 1959; UK Car and Commercial Vehicle Sales Manager, 1961–66, Austin Motor Co.; Sales and Marketing Exec., British Motor Corp., 1966–67; Chm. and Man. Dir, Barlow Rand UK Motor Gp, 1967–78; Managing Director: Barlow Rand Ford, S Africa, 1971–73; Barlow Rand European Operations, 1973–78; returned to British Leyland as Man. Dir, Overseas Trading Operations, 1978; Dep. Man. Dir, Austin Morris Ltd, 1979; Chm. and Man. Dir, British Leyland Europe & Overseas, 1979–82; Director, 1979–82: BL Cars Ltd (World Sales Chief, 1979–82; responsible for launch of the Austin Metro in 1980); Austin Morris Ltd; Rover Triumph Ltd; Jaguar Rover Triumph Inc. (USA); Dir, Jaguar Cars Ltd, 1979–82; Chief Exec., Henlys plc, 1981–83. Dep. Chm., Lumley Insce Gp, 1983–95; Director: Jetmaster UK, 1989–97; Theatrical Agents Billy Marsh Associates Ltd, 1993–2016; Royal Carlton Hotel, Blackpool, 1998–2007. Dir, producer and stager of 'Industrial Theatre' Motivational confs, sponsorship, marketing, promotions, special events and new product launches, 1983–2014. Responsible for: staging new product launches for British Leyland, Austin, Rover, MG, Jaguar, General Motors, Vauxhall, Proton, Mercedes-Benz, Daihatsu, LDV, Land Rover, Bedford trucks, Optare buses, Pioneer-UK, Fiat and Gillette; production and staging of opening ceremony of Rugby World Cup, Twickenham, 1991; DoH European drug abuse prevention campaign, 1992. Apptd Marketing Adviser: to Minister of Agric. and 'Food from Britain', 1979–83; to Sec. of State for Energy, 1984–87; to Sec. of State for Wales, 1988–91; to SMMT for producing and promoting: British Internat. Motor Show, 1992–96; Scottish Motor Show, 1997–2001; to FA for producing opening and closing ceremonies of European Football Championships, Wembley, 1996, FA Cup Finals, 1996–2000 and promotional and presentation work for England World Cup Bid, 2006; to RFU for 125th Anniversary celebrations, 1996, for 5 Nations Championship activities, Twickenham, 1997–2006; to RFU Français for prodn of opening ceremony at Stade de France, Paris, 1998; to Welsh RU for producing opening and closing ceremonies, Rugby World Cup, Millennium Stadium, Cardiff Arms Park, 1999; to ECB for producing opening ceremony, Cricket World Cup, Lord's, 1999; responsible for: promoting London Zoo relaunch, 1993; creating and producing Lloyds Bank's Playwright of the Year Award, annually 1994–2003. President: Austin Ex-Apprentices Assoc., 2006–14; Fellowship of Motor Industry, 2011–14 (Chm., 2009–11). Lectr, public and after dinner speaker; guest after dinner speaker, P&O Cruises, 2008–16; TV and radio broadcasts on motivation, marketing, public speaking and industrial subjects; producer, The Birth of Rugby (TV); panellist, Any Questions (TV and radio). Mason Meml Lecture, Birmingham Univ., 1983. Governor, N Worcs Coll., 1984–91. Patron, Wordsworth Trust, 2004–16. Freeman of City of London, 1980; Liveryman: Worshipful Co. of Coach Makers and Coach Harness Makers, 1980; Worshipful Co. of Carmen, 1982. Fellowship of Inst. of Marketing awarded 1981, for services to Brit. Motor Industry; FCGI 1999; Hon. Mem. CGLI, 1982, for services to technical and vocational educn; Prince Philip Medal, CGLI, 1984, for Outstanding Lifetime Contribution to British marketing; Benedictine Award, Business After-Dinner Speaker of the Year, 1992, 1993; Outstanding Lifetime Individual Achievement Award for services to motor industry, Inst. of Motor Industry, 2016. *Publications:* (contrib.) Metro: the book of the car, 1981; (contrib.) Tales out of School: misdeeds of the famous, 1983; A Marketing Study of the Welsh Craft Industry (Welsh Office report, 1988); (contrib.) Making Better Business Presentations, 1988; (contrib.) Men and Motors of 'The Austin', 2000; (contrib.) Earls Court Motor Show, 2016; contribs to numerous industrial, management, marketing and public speaking books and jls. *Recreations:* theatre, British military history, sharing good humour. *Address:* Roe Lodge, Sowerby Row, North Lakes, Penrith, Cumbria CA4 0QH; 19 Grove End Gardens, St John's Wood, NW8 9LL. *Club:* Lord's Taverners.
See also M. A. Ball.

**BALL, Rev. Canon Anthony James**; Canon Steward, since 2016, and Almoner, since 2018, Westminster Abbey; *b* Harare, 18 Dec. 1968; *s* of David Romney Ball and Doreen Felicity-Anne Ball (*née* James); *m* 1995, Celia García-Marugán Miño; one *s*. *Educ:* King's Sch., Bruton; St Chad's Coll., Univ. of Durham (BA Hons Philosophy and Politics 1989); Heythrop Coll., Univ. of London (MA Christian Theology 2010). Joined FCO, 1990; Cairo, 1992; Kuwait, 1994–95; Madrid, 1999–2003; Damascus, 2003–05; ordained deacon, 2000, priest, 2001; Chaplain, All Saints' Church, Damascus, 2003–05; Archbp of Canterbury's Apokrisiarios, 2003–05; Archbp of Canterbury's Asst Sec. for Internat., Ecumenical and Anglican Communion Affairs, 2005–08; Archbp of Canterbury's Sec. for Internat. Inter Religious Relns, 2008–09; Archbp of Canterbury's Chaplain, 2009–11; Rector of Worth, Pound Hill and Maidenbower, 2011–16; Anglican Chaplain, Worth Sch., Sussex, 2012–16. Honorary Canon: All Saints' Cathedral, Cairo, 2007–; Cathedral of the Redeemer, Madrid, 2007–. Trustee: Embrace the Middle East, 2012– (Chair, 2016–); Jerusalem and Middle East Church Assoc., 2016– (Chair, 2018–); Sion Coll., 2017–; Christian Muslim Forum, 2018–. Governor: Holy Trinity Sch., Crawley, 2014–16; Westminster City Sch., 2016– (Chair, 2018–). *Recreations:* travel, food, reading. *Address:* The Chapter Office, 20 Dean's Yard, SW1P 3PA. *T:* (020) 7654 4805. *E:* anthony.ball@westminster-abbey.org. *Club:* Travellers.

**BALL, Sir Christopher (John Elinger)**, Kt 1988; MA; Chancellor, University of Derby, 1995–2003; *b* 22 April 1935; *er s* of late Laurence Elinger Ball, OBE, and Christine Florence Mary Ball (*née* Howe); *m* 1958, Wendy Ruth Colyer, *d* of late Cecil Frederick Colyer and Ruth Colyer (*née* Reddaway); three *s* three *d*. *Educ:* St George's School, Harpenden; Merton College, Oxford (Harmsworth Scholar 1959; Hon. Fellow, 1987); 1st Cl. English Language and Literature, 1959; Dipl. in Comparative Philology, 1962; MA Oxon, 1963. 2nd Lieut, Parachute Regt, 1955–56. Lectr in English Language, Merton Coll., Oxford, 1960–61; Lectr in Comparative Linguistics, Sch. of Oriental and African Studies (Univ. of London), 1961–64; Fellow and Tutor in English Language, Lincoln Coll., Oxford, 1964–79 (Bursar, 1972–79; Hon. Fellow, 1981); Warden, Keble College, Oxford, 1980–88 (Hon. Fellow, 1989). Founding Fellow, Kellogg Forum for Continuing Educn, Univ. of Oxford, 1988–89; Vis. Prof. in Higher Educn, Leeds Poly., 1989–91; Fellow in Continuing Educn, 1989–92, Dir of Learning, 1992–97, RSA. Sec., Linguistics Assoc. of GB, 1964–67; Pres., Oxford Assoc. of University Teachers, 1968–71; Publications Sec., Philological Soc., 1969–75; Chairman: Oxford Univ. English Bd, 1977–79; Bd of NAB, 1982–88; Higher Educn Inf. Services Trust, 1987–90; Member: General Bd of the Faculties, 1977–79; Hebdomadal Council, 1985–89; CNAA, 1982–88 (Chm., English Studies Bd, 1973–80, Linguistics Bd, 1977–82); BTEC, 1984–89 (Chm., Quality Assurance & Control Cttee, 1989–90); IT Skills Shortages Cttee (Butcher Cttee), 1984–85; CBI IT Skills Agency, 1985–88; CBI Task Force, 1988–89. Chairman: NICEC, 1989–93; Pegasus, 1989–92; Strategic Educn Fora for Kent, 1992–97, Oxfordshire, 1992–97, and Gtr Peterborough, 1992–95; Educn Policy Cttee, RSA Exams Bd, 1993–96; Patron: Campaign for Learning, RSA, 1998– (Chm., 1996–98); Research Autism, 2007–15; Vice-Pres., Autistica, 2009–. Vice-Chm., Jigsaw Gp, 1998–2004; founding Chm., The Talent Foundn, 1999–2004 (Patron, 2004–); Chairman: Global Univ. Alliance, 2000–04; WAVE Trust, 2004–07; Down Syndrome Educn Internat., 2010–15. Member: Council and Exec., Templeton Coll., Oxford, 1981–92; Centre for Medieval and Renaissance Studies, Oxford, 1987–90; Brathay Hall Trust, 1988–91 (Chm, 1990–91; Fellow, 2003–); Manchester Polytechnic, 1989–91 (Hon. Fellow, 1988). President: ACFHE, 1990–92; SEAL, 2000–05. Gov., St George's Sch., Harpenden, 1985–89; Trustee, Langley Hall Primary Acad., 2011–. Jt Founding Editor (with late Angus Cameron), Toronto Dictionary of Old English, 1970; Member Editorial Board: Oxford Rev. of Education, 1984–96; Science and Public Affairs, 1989–94. FRSA 1987. Hon. Fellow: Univ. of Westminster (formerly Poly. of Central London), 1991; Auckland Inst. of Technol., NZ, 1992; Glendower Univ. (formerly NE Wales Inst., Wrexham), 1996; Oxford Brookes Univ., 2007; Millennium Fellow, Auckland Univ. of Technol., NZ, 2000; Oxfordshire Charity and Volunteer Award, 2018. Hon. DLitt CNAA, 1989; DUniv: N London, 1993; Open, 2002; Derby, 2003; Hon. DEd Greenwich, 1994. *Publications:* Fitness for Purpose, 1985; Aim Higher, 1989; (ed jtly) Higher Education in the 1990s, 1989; More Means Different, 1990; Learning Pays, 1991; Sharks and Splashes, 1991; Profitable Learning, 1992; Start Right, 1994; (ed jtly) Early Childhood Education Redefined, 2018; *poetry* (as John Elinger): Still Life, 2008; Operatic Interludes, 2008; That Sweet City, 2013; That Mighty Heart, 2014; That Strange Necessity, 2015; Marriage: a sonnet sequence, 2018; pamphlets and various contributions to philological, linguistic, poetic and educational jls. *Address:* 45 Richmond Road, Oxford OX1 2JJ. *T:* (01865) 310800.

**BALL, Colin George;** Director, Commonwealth Foundation, 2000–04 (Deputy Director, 1998–99); *b* 22 July 1943; *s* of George Heyward Ball and Bessie Margaret Ball (*née* Henry); *m* 1st, 1968, Maureen Sheelagh Bryan (marr. diss. 1996); one *s* one *d*; 2nd, 1998, Susan Helen Armstrong. *Educ:* Sevenoaks Sch.; Univ. of Keele (BA (Hons)). Teaching, Malaysia, Ghana, Nigeria, UK, 1961–62, 1966–70; Dir Schs Adv. Service, CSV, 1970–72; Asst Principal, Birstall Community Coll., 1973–74; Principal, Home Office and MSC, 1975–79; Founder, Chm. and CEO, Centre for Employment Initiatives, 1980–88; freelance researcher, consultant and writer, 1988–97. Chm., Commonwealth Assoc. for Local Action and Econ. Develt, 1990–96. *Publications:* Education for a Change, 1973; Community Service and the Young Unemployed, 1977; Fit for Work?, 1979; Whose Business is Business, 1980; Locally Based Responses to Long-term Unemployment, 1988; Towards an Enterprising Culture, 1989; Non-governmental Organisations: guidelines for good policy and practice, 1995; Dupuytren's Contracture, 2010; It's the Community, Stupid!, 2011; Only Human Nature, 2017. *Recreations:* music, reading, writing, Italy. *Address:* 69 Franklings Road, Harcourt North, Vic 3453, Australia.

**BALL, David Christopher James;** Director, HR Insight and Research, Defence Equipment and Support, Ministry of Defence, since 2016 (Director: Human Resources, 2010–15; Learning and Talent, 2015–16); *b* Cardiff, 20 June 1959; *s* of late Peter Alec James Ball and Anne Stephen Ball; *m* 1998, Felicity Jane Unwin; two *s* one *d*. *Educ:* Winchester Coll.; Merton Coll., Oxford (BPhil Philos. 1983; MA Lit.Hum.). Chartered FCIPD 2012. Ministry of Defence, 1983–: Asst Private Sec. to Sec. of State, 1986–88; Legal Secretariat, 1988–90; on loan to Cabinet Office, 1990–92; Army Resources and Plans, 1992–95, Hd of Finance and Secretariat, Land Systems, 1995–98, Gp Leader, Central Finance and Planning Gp, 1998–2001, Defence Procurement Agency; Chief Exec., Pay and Personnel Agency, subseq. People, Pay and Pensions Agency, 2001–09. *Recreations:* family, singing in chamber choir, gardening. *Address:* Defence Equipment and Support, Ministry of Defence, Abbey Wood, Bristol BS34 8JH. *E:* david.ball248@mod.uk.

**BALL, Gillian,** OBE 2012; Director of Finance, University of Birmingham, 1995–2014; *b* Birmingham, 10 Nov. 1959; *d* of late John Henry Allcutt and Winifred Allcutt; *m* 1997, Michael Ball. *Educ:* Erdington Girls' Grammar Sch., Birmingham. ACCA 1983, FCCA 1988. Trainee Accountant, 1980–82, Internal Auditor, 1982–83, West Midlands CC; Accountant for Higher and Further Educn, Coventry CC, 1983–85; University of Birmingham: Systems Accountant, 1985–87; Principal Accountant, 1987–89; Dep. Dir, Finance, 1989–95; Actg Registrar and Sec., 2007–08. Mem. Bd, UM Assoc. Ltd and UM Services Ltd, 1999–2007 (Dep. Chm., 2003–07); Sec., British Univs Finance Dirs Gp, 2002–05. Mem. Council, 2001–10, Pres., 2007–08, ACCA. Mem., Financial Sustainability Strategy Gp, Office for Students (formerly HEFC), 1997–; Ind. Mem., Audit Cttee, ESRC, 2004–06; Mem., STFC, 2009–18 (Mem., 2009–14, Chm., 2015–18, Audit Cttee; Chm., 2010–15, Mem., 2015–18, Remuneration Cttee; Mem., Finance Cttee, 2015–18); Mem., Audit Cttee, Manufacturing Technol. Centre, 2012–14; Chm., Audit and Assurance Supervisory Bd, UK Res. Councils, 2015–18. Higher Educn Advr, Accelerus Educn Ltd, 2015–; Associate, Advance HE (formerly Leadership Foundn for Higher Educn), 2016–; Dir, Professional Higher Educn Services Ltd, 2016–. Governor: King Edward VI Foundn, Birmingham, 2003– (Chm., Audit Cttee, 2009–; Bailiff, 2014–15); King Edward VI Sch. for Girls, Handsworth, 2016– (Interim Chm., 2016). *Recreations:* racketball, golf, ski-ing, cooking.

**BALL, Graham Thalben, (Johnny);** writer, lecturer and television presenter; mathematical enthuser, since 1978; *b* Bristol, 23 May 1938; *s* of Daniel and Martha Anne Ball; *m* 1975, Dianne Cheryl Hicks; two *s* one *d*. *Educ:* Bolton Co. Grammar Sch. De Haviland Aircraft Corp., 1954–56; served RAF, 1957–59; Butlins Redcoat, 1960–62; comedian, 1964–76; BBC TV: presenter, Playschool, 1967–83; writer and presenter: Cabbages and Kings, 1972–74; Playaway, 1972–74; Think of a Number, 1978 (Rediffusion Star Award, 1979); Think Again, 1981 (Prix Jeunesse; Asia-Pacific Broadcast Union Singapore Prize); Johnny Ball Reveals All, ITV, 1989–94; corporate work, 1999–2003: Nat. Grid (incl. 3 videos); British Gas lectures; Engrg Council lecture tour; BAE Systems tour; writer and producer, science videos; co-writer: Cutting Edge Materials Technol., DTI; How is it Made? UK educnl package, Rover; writer and presenter, Torness Nuclear Power Stn launch video; speaker on carbon, putting the envmtl dangers into perspective, Toyota Lexus and Volvo Motors. Theatre: writer, presenter and actor: 5 educnl stage musicals, 1993–2003; Michael Faraday All Electric Roadshow; Energy Champions; Let the Force be with You; Tales of Maths and Legends, Tales of Blooming Science, DoE; With Your Mind and Tomorrow's Technology, Anything Possible, Mind Zone Live prodn, Millennium Dome and BAE Systems, 2000. Ambassador for British Engrg, 1995–. Presenter of Year, ITVA Craft Awards, 1986; Medal for Promotion of Engrg to Gen. Public, RAEng, 2007. *Publications:* Think of a Number, 1982; Think Box, 1982; Plays for Laughs, 1983; Second Thinks, 1987; Think of a Number, 2005 (US edn as Go Figure (Blue Ribbon, Chicago Depository of Great Books)); Mathmagicians, 2009 (US edn as Why Pi?); Ball of Confusion, 2011; Wonders Beyond Numbers: a brief history of all things mathematical, 2017. *Recreations:* drums, gazebo design, golf, humour. *Address:* Highfield, Beaconsfield Road, Farnham Common, S Bucks SL2 3JD. *T:* (01753) 643621. *E:* jballprods@aol.com. *W:* www.johnnyball.co.uk.

**BALL, Dr Harold William**; Keeper of Palæontology, British Museum (Natural History), 1966–86; *b* 11 July 1926; *s* of Harold Ball and Florence (*née* Harris); *m* 1955, Patricia Mary (*née* Silvester); two *s* two *d*. *Educ:* Yardley Gram. Sch.; Birmingham Univ. BSc 1947, PhD 1949, Birmingham. Geologist, Nyasaland Geological Survey, 1949–51; Asst Lectr in Geology, King's Coll., London, 1951–54; Dept of Palæontology, British Museum (Nat. Hist.), 1954–86: Dep. Keeper, 1965; Keeper, 1966. Adrian Vis. Fellow, Univ. of Leicester, 1972–77. Sec., 1968–72, Vice-Pres., 1972–73, 1984–86, Geological Soc. of London; Pres., 1981–84, Vice-Pres., 1984–86, Soc. for the History of Natural History. Wollaston Fund, Geological Soc. of London, 1965. *Publications:* papers on the stratigraphy of the Old Red Sandstone and on the palæontology of the Antarctic in several scientific jls. *Recreations:* music, gardening. *Address:* Wilderbrook, Dormans Park, East Grinstead, West Sussex RH19 2LT. *T:* (01342) 870426.

**BALL, Sir John (Macleod)**, Kt 2006; DPhil; FRS 1989; FRSE; FIMA; Sedleian Professor of Natural Philosophy, 1996–2018, now Emeritus, and Director, Oxford Centre for Nonlinear PDE, 2007–18, University of Oxford; Fellow, Queen's College, Oxford, 1996–2018, now Emeritus; Professor, Department of Mathematics, Heriot-Watt University, since 2018; *b* 19 May 1948; *s* of Ernest Frederick Ball and Dorothy Forbes Ball; *m* 1st, 1973, Mary Judith Hodges (marr. diss. 1977); 2nd, 1992, Sedhar Chozam; two *s* one *d*. *Educ:* Mill Hill Sch.; St John's Coll., Cambridge (BA Maths, 1969; Hon. Fellow, 2005); Univ. of Sussex (DPhil 1972). FRSE 1980; FIMA 2003. SRC Postdoctoral Res. Fellow, Dept of Maths, Heriot-Watt Univ., and Lefschetz Center for Dynamical Systems, Brown Univ., USA, 1972–74; Lectr in Maths, 1974–78, Reader in Maths, 1978–82, SERC Sen. Fellow, 1980–85, Prof. of Applied Analysis, 1982–96, Heriot-Watt Univ. Visiting Professor: Dept of Maths, Univ. of Calif, Berkeley, 1979–80; Laboratoire d'Analyse Numérique, Université Pierre et Marie Curie, Paris, 1987–88, 1994; Inst. for Advanced Study, Princeton, 1993–94, 2002–03; Univ. Montpellier II, 2003; Hon. Prof., Heriot-Watt Univ., 1998–2018. Member Council: EPSRC, 1994–99; Edinburgh Mathematical Soc., 1972 (Pres., 1989–90); London Math. Soc., 1982 (Pres., 1996–98 and 2009); Amer. Math. Soc., 1987–; Soc. for Nat. Phil., 1978–; Pres., IMU, 2003–06. Member: Programme Cttee, Internat. Centre for Mathematical Scis, Edinburgh, 1991– (Mem. Exec. Cttee, 1991–96, Chm., 1991–93); Bd of Govs, Weizmann Inst., 1998–; Exec. Bd, ICSU, 2011–16; Comité d'orientation stratégique, Sorbonne Univs, 2012–. Delegate, OUP, 1998–2008. Member, Conseil Scientifique: CNRS, 2010–14; EDF, 2010–14. John von Neumann Lect., Soc. for Industrial and Applied Maths, 2012. Associé Etranger, Acad. des Sciences, Paris, 2000; Foreign Member: Instituto Lombardo, 2005; Norwegian Acad. of Sci. and Letters, 2007; MAE, 2008; Hon. Mem., Edinburgh Math. Soc., 2008; Fellow, Amer. Math. Soc., 2012. Hon. DSc: Ecole Polytechnique Fédérale, Lausanne, 1992; Heriot-Watt, 1998; Sussex, 2000; Montpellier II, 2003; Edinburgh, 2004; Pierre et Marie Curie, Paris, 2010. Whittaker Prize, Edinburgh Math. Soc., 1981; Jun. Whitehead Prize, 1982, Naylor Prize, 1994, London Math. Soc.; Keith Prize, RSE, 1990; Theodore von Karman Prize, SIAM, 1999; David Crighton Medal, LMS/IMA, 2003; Royal Medal, RSE, 2006; Sylvester Medal, 2009, Wolfson Res. Merit Award, 2010, Royal Soc. Mem. Editorial Boards of various math. and scientific jls and book series. *Publications:* articles in math. and scientific jls. *Recreations:* travel, music, chess. *Address:* Department of Mathematics, Heriot-Watt University, Edinburgh Campus, Edinburgh EH14 4AS.

**BALL, Johnny;** see Ball, G. T.

**BALL, Prof. Keith Martin**, PhD; FRS 2013; FRSE; Professor, University of Warwick, since 2012; *b* New York, 26 Dec. 1960; *s* of Michael John and Margaret Ball; *m* 1995, Prof. Sachiko Kusukawa. *Educ:* Berkhamsted Sch.; Trinity Coll., Cambridge (BA 1982; PhD 1987). Prof., Texas A&M Univ., 1987–2006; University College London: Lectr, 1990–92; Reader, 1992–96; Prof., 1996–2007; Astor Prof. of Maths, 2007–11; Scientific Dir, Internat. Centre for Math. Scis, Edinburgh, 2010–14. Chair, Eur. Res. Centres on Maths, 2013–14; Mem. Council, Royal Soc., 2018–19. FRSE 2013. *Publications:* Strange Curves, Counting Rabbits and Other Mathematical Explorations, 2003; contrib. res. articles to math. jls. *Address:* Institute of Mathematics, University of Warwick, Coventry CV4 7AL. *T:* (024) 7652 3736. *E:* K.M.Ball@warwick.ac.uk.

**BALL, Matthew Eliot;** Principal Dancer, Royal Ballet, since 2018; *b* Liverpool, 14 Dec. 1993; *s* of Christopher Ball and Elizabeth Ball. *Educ:* Royal Ballet Sch. (Lynn Seymour Award 2011). Joined Royal Ballet, 2014; First Artist, 2015; Soloist, 2016; First Soloist, 2017; main rôles include: Romeo, in Romeo and Juliet; Prince Rudolf, in Mayerling; Albrecht, in Giselle; Siegfried, in Swan Lake; Basilio, in Don Quixote. Other performances include rôle as Swan/Stranger in Matthew Bourne's Swan Lake, 2018. Best Emerging Artist, Critics' Circle Nat. Dance Awards, 2016. *Recreations:* travel, photography, art, music, procrastination, bouts of hyperactivity. *Address:* Royal Ballet, Royal Opera House, Covent Garden, WC2E 9DD. *T:* (020) 7240 1200. *E:* matthew.eliot.ball@gmail.com.

**BALL, Michael Ashley**, OBE 2015; actor and singer; *b* 27 June 1962; *s* of Anthony George Ball, *qv*; partner, Cathy McGowan. *Educ:* Plymouth Coll.; Farnham Sixth Form Coll.; Guildford Sch. of Acting (Dip. Acting). *Theatre* includes: first professional rôle as Judas/John the Baptist, Godspell, 1984; first starring rôle, Frederick, The Pirates of Penzance, Manchester Opera House, 1985; West End début: created rôle of Marius, Les Misérables, Barbican and Palace, 1985; other major rôles include: Raoul, Phantom of the Opera, Her Majesty's, 1987; created rôle of Alex, Aspects of Love, Prince of Wales, 1989, NY 1990; Giorgio, Passion, Queen's, 1996; Alone Together, Divas Season, Donmar Warehouse, 2001; Caractacus Potts, Chitty Chitty Bang Bang, Palladium, 2002–03; Count Fosco, Woman in White, Palace, 2005; Kismet, ENO, 2007; Hairspray, Shaftesbury, 2007 (Laurence Olivier Award, 2008); Sweeney Todd, Chichester, 2011 (Olivier Award for Best Actor in a Musical, 2013), Adelphi, 2012; Mack & Mabel, Chichester Festival Th., 2015; Chess, Coliseum, 2018; *film:* England My England, 1996; *television* includes: GB rep., Eurovision Song Contest, 1992; two series of Michael Ball, 1993, 1994; That Day We Sang, 2014; Royal Variety Performances; numerous nat. and internat. concert tours; has made numerous recordings. Patron and Co-Founder, charity, Res. into Ovarian Cancer (ROC). Most Promising Artiste Award, 1989, Best Recording Artiste, 1998, Variety Club of GB; Most Popular Musical Actor, Theatregoers Club of GB, 1999. *Recreations:* collecting graphic novels and single malt whiskys, country walking, music, theatre. *Address:* c/o Live Nation (Music) UK Ltd, Regent Arcade House, 19–25 Argyll Street, W1F 7TS.

**BALL, Rt Rev. Michael Thomas;** Bishop of Truro, 1990–97; *b* 14 Feb. 1932; *s* of Thomas James Ball and Kathleen Obena Bradley Ball. *Educ:* Lancing Coll., Sussex; Queens' Coll., Cambridge (BA 1955; MA 1959). Schoolmastering, 1955–76; Co-Founder, Community of the Glorious Ascension, 1960; Prior at Stroud Priory, 1963–76; Curate, Whitehall, Stroud, Glos, 1971–76; Priest-in-charge of Stanmer with Falmer, and Senior Anglican Chaplain to Higher Education in Brighton, including Sussex Univ., 1976–80; Bishop Suffragan of Jarrow, 1980–90. Mem., H of L, 1996–97. Advr to Tyne Tees Television, 1983–89. Mem. Council, St Luke's Hosp. for the Clergy, 1994–2006. *Publications:* So There We Are, 1997; Foolish Risks of God, 2002. *Recreations:* music, housework. *Address:* The Coach House, The Manor, Aller, Langport, Somerset TA10 0RA.

**BALL, Rev. Canon Peter William;** Canon Emeritus, St Paul's Cathedral, since 1990 (Residentiary Canon, 1984–90); Public Preacher, diocese of Salisbury, since 1990; *b* 17 Jan. 1930; *s* of Leonard Wevell Ball and Dorothy Mary Ball; *m* 1956, Angela Jane Dunlop (*d* 2004); one *s* two *d*. *Educ:* Aldenham School; Worcester Coll., Oxford (MA); Cuddesdon Coll., Oxford. Asst Curate, All Saints, Poplar, 1955; Vicar, The Ascension, Wembley, 1961; Rector, St Nicholas, Shepperton, 1968; Area Dean of Spelthorne, 1972–83; Prebendary of St Paul's Cathedral, 1976. Dir, Post Ordination Trng and Continuing Ministerial Educn, Kensington Episcopal Area, 1984–87. Chaplain: Rediffusion Television, 1961–68; Thames Television, 1970–93. First Dir, Brent Samaritans, 1965–68; Dep. Dir, NW Surrey Samaritans, 1973–79. Mem., European Conf. on the Catechumenate, 1975– (Chm., 1983). Member: Spiritual Directors Internat., 1992–; Spiritual Directors Europe, 2000–. *Publications:* Journey into Faith, 1984; Adult Believing, 1988; Adult Way to Faith, 1992; Journey into Truth, 1996; Anglican Spiritual Direction, 1998; (with Ven. Malcolm Grundy) Faith on the Way, 2000; Introducing Spiritual Direction, 2003. *Recreations:* gardening, walking, music. *Address:* Whittonedge, Whittonditch Road, Ramsbury, Marlborough, Wilts SN8 2PX.

**BALL, Sir Richard Bentley**, 5th Bt *cr* 1911, of Merrion Square, Dublin and Killybegs, Donegal; *b* 29 Jan. 1953; *o s* of Sir Charles Ball, 4th Bt and Alison Mary (*née* Bentley); *S* father, 2002; *m* 1st, 1991, Beverley Ann, *d* of late Bertram Joffre Wright (marr. diss. 2015); one *d*; 2nd, 2016, Alexandra (*née* Watts). *Educ:* Sherborne; Leicester Univ. ACA. *Heir: cousin* Christopher Nigel Morton Ball [*b* 3 Nov. 1951; *m* 1974, Melanie Fenner; one *s* one *d*].

**BALL, Simon Coryndon L.;** *see* Luxmoore-Ball.

**BALL, Simon Peter**, FCA; Senior Adviser, Anchura Group Ltd, since 2017 (Chairman, 2014–17); *b* 2 May 1960; *s* of Peter Terence Ball and Maureen Eleanor Ball (*née* Bishop); *m* 1992, Sandra Marie Cameron; two *d*. *Educ:* Chislehurst and Sidcup Grammar Sch.; UCL (BSc (Econ)). ACA 1985; MCSI 2001; FCA 2009. Price Waterhouse & Co., 1981–85; Kleinwort Benson Group plc, 1985–98: Finance Dir, Kleinwort Benson Securities Ltd, 1990–93; Finance Dir, Kleinwort Benson Ltd, 1994–95; Chief Operating Officer, 1995–98; Robert Fleming Holdings Ltd, 1998–2000: Gp Finance Dir, 1998–2000; Chm., Robert Fleming Inc., 1999–2000; Exec. Dir, Intelligent Energy Ltd, 2001–02; Dir Gen., Finance, DCA, 2003–05; Gp Finance Dir, 3i Gp plc, 2005–08. Dep. Chm., Cable & Wireless Communications plc, 2010–15; non-executive Director: Leica Geosystems AG, Switzerland, 2001–05; Cable & Wireless Ltd, 2006–10; Tribal Gp plc, 2010–14; Allied Irish Bank Gp, 2011–19; AIB Mortgage Bank, 2017–; Morgan Stanley Internat., 2019–. Mem. Bd, Commonwealth Games England, 2013–; non-exec. Dir, Organising Cttee, 2022 Commonwealth Games, 2018–. FRSA 2003. *Recreations:* golf, cinema, theatre, running. *Clubs:* Royal Mid Surrey Golf; Roehampton.

**BALL, Prof. Stephen John**, DPhil; FBA 2006; Karl Mannheim Profes or of Sociology of Education, 2001–15, now Distinguished Service Professor of Sociology of Education, and Associate Director, Centre for Critical Education Policy Studies, 2005, Institute of Education, University College London (formerly Institute of Education, University of London); *b* 21 Jan. 1950; *s* of John and Betty Flora Joan Ball; *m* 1975, Trinidad Fructuoso-Gallego. *Educ:* Univ. of Essex (BA Hons Sociol. 1972); Univ. of Sussex (MA Sociol Studies 1975; DPhil Sociol. 1978). Lectr in Educn, Univ. of Sussex, 1975–85; King's College, London: Tutor in Urban Educn, 1985–89; Reader in Sociol. of Educn, 1990–91; Prof. of Educn, 1991–2001. FAcSS (AcSS 2000). Hon. Dr Turku, 2003; Hon. DLitt Leicester, 2014. *Publications:* Beachside Comprehensive, 1981; The Micropolitics of the School, 1987; Politics and Policy-making in Education, 1990; Education Reform, 1994; Class Strategies in the Education Market, 2003; Education Policy and Social Class: selected works, 2006; Education Plc, 2007; The Education Debate, 2008, 3rd edn 2017; Global Education Inc., 2012; Foucault, Power and Education, 2012; (jtly) Networks, New Governance and Education, 2012; (jtly) Edu.net: globalisation and education policy mobility, 2017. *Recreations:* film, novels, walking, horse-riding. *Address:* UCL Institute of Education, 20 Bedford Way, WC1H 0AL. *T:* (020) 7612 6973. *E:* s.ball@ioe.ac.uk.

**BALLADUR, Edouard;** Grand Officier, Légion d'Honneur; Grand Croix de l'Ordre National du Mérite; Member, Conseil d'Etat, France, since 1984; Prime Minister of France, 1993–95; *b* 2 May 1929; *s* of Pierre Balladur and Emilie Latour; *m* 1957, Marie-Josèphe Delacour; four *s*. *Educ:* Lycée Thiers, Marseille; Faculté de Droit, Aix-en-Provence; Inst. d'études Politiques; Ecole Nat. d'Admin. Jun. Auditeur, 1957, Maître des Requêtes, 1963, Conseil d'Etat; Adviser to Dir-Gen., ORTF, 1962–63 (Mem. Admin Council, 1967–68); Tech. Adviser, Office of Prime Minister Pompidou, 1963–68; Pres., French Co. for routier tunnel under Mont Blanc, 1968–80; Mem., Admin Council, Nat. Forestry Office, 1968–73; Asst Sec. Gen., later Sec. Gen., French President's Office, 1969–74; Chm. and Chief Exec., Générale de Service Informatique, 1977–86; Chm. and Chief Exec., Co. européenne d'accumulateurs, 1980–86; Deputy (RPR, later UMP) for Paris, French Nat. Assembly, 1986–2007 (re-elected 1988, 1993, 1995, 1997 and 2002); Minister for Economy, Finance and Privatization, 1986–88; Mem., Paris City Council, 1989–. President: Comité de réflexion et de proposition sur la modernisation et le rééquilibrage des instns de la V$^e$ République, 2007; Comité pour la réforme des collectivités locales, 2009. Numerous medals and awards, incl. Jacques Rueff Prize, NY, 1986; Euromoney Prize, IMF, 1987; Gold Medal for patronage, French Acad., 1988; Louise Michel Prize, 1993. *Publications:* L'Arbre de mai, 1979; Je crois en l'homme plus qu'en l'Etat, 1987; (jtly) Passion et longueur de temps, 1989; Douze lettres aux Français trop tranquilles, 1990; Des modes et des convictions, 1992; Le dictionnaire de la réforme, 1992; Deux ans à Matignon, 1995; Caractère de la France, 1997; Avenir de la différence, 1999; Renaissance de la droite, pour une alternance décomplexée, 2000; Les aventuriers de l'histoire, 2001; Jeanne d'Arc et la France, 2003; La fin de l'illusion jacobine, 2005; Machiavel en démocratie, 2006; L'Europe autrement, 2006; Laissons de Gaulle en paix!, 2006; Pour une Union occidentale entre l'Europe et les Etats-Unis, 2007; Une V$^e$ République plus démocratique, 2008; Il est temps de décider, 2009; Le pouvoir ne se partage pas, 2009 (Aujourd'hui Prize, François Guizot Prize, 2010); La liberté a-t-elle un avenir?, 2012; La tragédie du pouvoir, 2013; Grandeur, déclin et destin de la V$^e$ République, 2017.

**BALLANCE, Chris(topher);** playwright; Development Manager (formerly Development Officer), Moffat CAN, since 2009; *b* 7 July 1952; *s* of Howard and Gwyneth Ballance; *m* 2005, Alis Taylor; two *s*. *Educ:* Alderman Newton's Sch., Leicester; Reigate Grammar Sch.; St Andrews Univ. Work in anti-nuclear power and public transport campaigns; Co-founder, First of May Radical Bookshop, Edinburgh, 1977; self-employed writer for theatre and radio, 1990–; jt-owner, secondhand bookshop, Wigtown, 2000–. MSP (Green) Scotland S, 2003–07. Member: Scottish Soc. of Playwrights, 1992–; Writers Guild of GB, 1995–. Mem., Equity, 1994–. *Recreations:* film, theatre, hill-walking, swimming.

**BALLANTINE, (David) Grant**, FFA; Directing Actuary, Government Actuary's Department, 1991–2004; *b* 24 March 1941; *s* of James Williamson Ballantine and Robertha (*née* Fairley); *m* 1969, Marjorie Campbell Brown; one *s* one *d*. *Educ:* Daniel Stewart's Coll.; Edinburgh Univ. (BSc 1st Cl.). Scottish Widows' Fund, 1963–68; Asst Vice-Pres., Amer. Insce Gp (Far East), 1968–73; Government Actuary's Department, 1973–2004: Actuary, 1973–82; Chief Actuary, 1983–90. Mem. Council, Faculty of Actuaries, 1991–94. *Publications:* articles in trade and professional jls.

**BALLANTYNE, Fiona Catherine**, OBE 2014; Chair, Love Music Productions Ltd (formerly Music at the Brewhouse Ltd), 2009–18; *b* Bristol, 9 July 1950; *d* of James Douglas and Marjorie Mackay; *m* 1973, (Andrew) Neil Ballantyne. *Educ:* Univ. of Edinburgh (MA). FCIM 2004. Scottish Development Agency: Hd, Small Business Services, 1984–88; Dir, Tayside and Fife, 1988–90; Principal, Ballantyne Mackay Consultants, 1990–2012. Chm., Essentia Gp, 1997–2001; Director: 4-consulting Ltd, 2001–12; RIO Ltd, 2014–18; Mem. Bd, Edinburgh Print Studios Ltd, 2004–08. Vice Chm., BBC Broadcasting Council for Scotland, 1991–96; Member: Bd, Edinburgh Healthcare Trust, 1994–96; Consumer Panel, OFCOM, 2004–12; Bd, Office of the Scottish Charity Regulator, 2008–16; Water Customer Forum for Scotland, 2013–17; Chm., Museums Galls Scotland, 2007–12. Chm., Edinburgh Br., IoD, 2002–06. Vice Chairman: Duncan of Jordanstone Coll. of Art, 1988–94; Queen Margaret University, 1995–2005. Gov., Royal Conservatoire of Scotland, 2015–18. Trustee, Scottish Trust for Underwater Archaeology. *Recreations:* walking, gardening, reading, photography. *E:* fionaballantyne@me.com.

**BALLANTYNE, Sir Frederick (Nathaniel)**, GCMG 2002; Governor General, St Vincent and the Grenadines, since 2002; *b* 5 July 1936; *s* of Samuel and Olive Ballantyne; *m* 1996, Sally Ann; eight *c* (and one *c* decd). *Educ:* Syracuse Univ., NY (MD); Bd Certified Internal Medicine Cardiology. Med. Dir, Kingstown Gen. Hosp., 1970–83; CMO, St Vincent and Grenadines, 1983–88. *Recreations:* sailing, tennis, bridge. *Address:* Government House, Montrose, St Vincent and the Grenadines, West Indies. *T:* 4561401, *Fax:* 4579710. *E:* govthouse@vincysurf.com.

**BALLARAT, Bishop of**, since 2011; **Rt Rev. Garry John Weatherill**; *b* 3 Oct. 1956; *s* of Trevor Donald and Lorna Beryl Weatherill. *Educ:* Univ. of Adelaide (BA Hons 1978; DipEd 1979); St Barnabas' Theol Coll.; Flinders Univ. of SA (BTh 1991). Asst Master, Pulteney Grammar Sch., Adelaide, 1980–81; ordained deacon 1986, priest 1987; Asst Curate, St Jude's Ch, Brighton, 1986–88; Asst Priest, St Peter's Cathedral, Adelaide, 1988–90; Rector, Semaphore, 1990–97 and Area Dean, Western Suburbs of Adelaide, 1995–97; Ministry Develt Officer, 1997–2000, Archdeacon, 1999–2000, Willochra; Bishop of Willochra, 2001–11. Member: Standing Cttee, 2007–14, 2017–, Exec. Cttee of Standing Cttee, 2017–, Gen. Synod; Appellate Tribunal, Anglican Ch of Australia, 2016–; Chairman: Liturgy Commn of Anglican Church of Aust., 2013–; Adv. Council for Anglican Religious Life in Aust., 2013–; Anglican Bd of Mission, Australia, 2015–. Warden, Community of the Holy Name, 2013–; Episcopal Consultant, Oratory of Good Shepherd, 2015–. Chm., Australia Council of the Mission to Seafarers, 2006–12. Bp Protector, Third Order, Soc. of St Francis, 2014–. *Recreations:* contemporary fiction, poetry, drama, garden, godchildren. *Address:* The Diocesan Centre, PO Box 89, Ballarat, Vic 3353, Australia. *E:* bishop@ballaratanglican.org.au.

**BALLARD, Ven. Andrew Edgar**; Archdeacon of Manchester, 2005–09; *b* 14 Jan. 1944; *s* of Arthur Henry and Phyllis Marian Ballard; *m* 1970, Marian Caroline Conolly; one *s* two *d*. *Educ:* Rossall Sch.; St John's Coll., Durham Univ. (BA Hons Theol. 1966); Westcott House, Cambridge. Ordained deacon 1968, priest 1969; Asst Curate, St Mary, Bryanston Sq., and Asst Chaplain, Middlesex Hosp., London, 1968–72; Sen. Asst Curate, St Mary, Portsea, 1972–76; Vicar: St James, Haslingden with St Stephen, Haslingden Grane, 1976–82; St Paul, Walkden, 1982–93; Team Rector, St Paul, Walkden with St John the Baptist, Little Hulton, 1993–98; Area Dean, Farnworth, 1990–98; Priest in charge, 1998–2000, Team Rector, 2000, Rochdale Team Ministry; Archdeacon of Rochdale, 2000–05. Permission to officiate, dio. of Lincoln, 2010–. Hon. Canon, Manchester Cathedral, 1998–2000. *Recreations:* church music, playing the organ. *Address:* 30 Swift Drive, Scawby Brook, Brigg, N Lincs DN20 9FL.

**BALLARD, Jacqueline Margaret, (Jackie)**; Chief Executive, Alcohol Concern, 2014–16; *b* 4 Jan. 1953; *d* of late Alexander Mackenzie and Daisy Mackenzie (*née* Macdonald); *m* 1975, Derek Ballard (marr. diss. 1989); one *d*. *Educ:* Monmouth Sch. for Girls; London Sch. of Economics (BSc Social Psychology). Social Worker, Waltham Forest, 1974–76; Further Educn Lectr, Yeovil Coll., 1982–90. Member: (L then Lib Dem) S Somerset DC, 1987–91 (Leader, 1990–91); (Lib Dem) Somerset CC, 1993–97 (Dep. Leader, 1993–95); Council Support Officer, Assoc. of Lib Dem Councillors, 1993–97. MP (Lib Dem) Taunton, 1997–2001. Contested (Lib Dem) Taunton, 2001. Dir Gen., RSPCA, 2002–07; Chief Executive: RNID, later Action on Hearing Loss, 2007–12; Womankind Worldwide, 2012–13; Associate Dir, BB Gp, 2013–14. Member: Youth Justice Bd, 2003–05; Ind. Parly Standards Authy, 2009–13; Lambeth CCG, 2016–; Bd, London Travelwatch, 2017–. Mem. Bd, 2014–, Vice Chm., 2017–, Newlon Housing Trust.

**BALLARD, John Frederick**, CB 2001; non-executive Director, Lewisham and Greenwich NHS Trust, since 2013 (Deputy Chair, since 2015); *b* 8 Aug. 1943; *s* of Frederick and Margaret Ballard; *m* 1st, 1975, Ann Helm (marr. diss. 1999); one *s* two *d*; 2nd, 2000, Helena (*née* Rose). *Educ:* Roundhay Grammar Sch., Leeds; Ifield Grammar Sch., W Sussex; Southampton Univ. (BA); Exeter Univ. (CertEd). Academic Registrar's Dept, Univ. of Surrey, 1965–69; Asst Principal, MoT, 1969; Principal, DoE, 1972; Treasury, 1976; Asst Sec. 1978, Sec., Top Salaries Review Body and Police Negotiating Bd; DoE, 1979; Prin. Private Sec. to Sec. of State for the Environment, 1983–85; Under Sec., DoE and Dept of Transport, and Regl Dir, Yorks and Humberside Region, 1986; Dir, Housing Assocs and the Private Sector, DoE, 1990–92; Dir, Maxwell Pensions Unit, DSS, 1992–93 (on secondment); Dir, Town and Country Planning, DoE, 1993–97; Dir Finance, and Principal Finance Officer, DoE, subseq. DETR, 1997–2001; Dir, Water and Land, DETR, subseq. DEFRA, 2001–03. Dir, British Water, 2004–06; non-exec. Dir, NI Water, 2007–10. Mem. Steering Bd, Marine Fisheries Agency, 2005–10. Non-executive Director: Queen Elizabeth Hosp. NHS Trust, 2008–09; S London Healthcare NHS Trust, 2009–13 (Dep. Chm., 2010–11; Actg Chm., 2011–13). Trustee, Maxwell Pensioners Trust, 1993–97; Associate Special Trustee, 1992–99, Special Trustee, 1999–2010, Gt Ormond St Hosp. for Sick Children Charity (Chm., 2006–08). Gov., Brooklands Sch., Blackheath, 2005–09. *Recreations:* trekking, tennis, singing, reading. *Address:* 81 Humber Road, Blackheath, SE3 7LR.

**BALLARD, Mark**; Policy Manager, Children 1st, since 2019; *b* 27 June 1971; *s* of Roger and Cathy Ballard; *m* 2002, Heather Stacey; two *s*. *Educ:* Edinburgh Univ. (MA Hons (Econ. and Social Hist.) 1994). Various positions, European Youth Forest Action, Edinburgh and Amsterdam, 1994–98; Ed., Reforesting Scotland Jl, 1998–2001; estd and ran EMBE Environmental Communications, consultancy co., 2002–03. Scottish Green Party: spokesperson on internat. develt, 1999–2000; Convener, Nat. Council, 2000–02; Nat. Sec., 2002–03. Mem. (Green) Lothians, Scottish Parlt, 2003–07. Communications Manager, SCVO, 2008–09; Asst Dir, Barnardo's Scotland, 2009–16; Dir, Strategy and Communications, Chest Heart & Stroke Scotland, 2016–17; Hd of Scotland, Save the Children UK, 2017–18. Rector, Edinburgh Univ., 2006–09. *Recreations:* cycling, Indian cookery.

**BALLARD, Ven. Peter James**; Chief Executive, DBE Services, since 2010; Archdeacon of Lancaster, 2006–10; Vicar, Shireshead St James, Diocese of Blackburn, since 2017; *b* 10 March 1955; *m* 1978, Helen Lees; two *d*. *Educ:* Grammar Sch. for Boys, Chadderton; St Hild and St Bede's Coll., Durham (BEd 1978); DipTheol London (ext.) 1985; Sarum and Wells Theol Coll. Various posts with TEC, then BTEC, 1978–85; ordained deacon, 1987, priest, 1988; Asst Curate, Grantham, 1987–91; Vicar, Christ Ch, Lancaster, 1991–98; RD Lancaster, 1995–98; Canon Residentiary, Blackburn Cathedral, 1998–2006; Diocesan Dir of Educn, dio. of Blackburn, 1998–2010; permission to officiate, Dio. of Blackburn, 2016–17. Mem., Gen. Synod of C of E, 2000–10. Consulting Ed., Internat. Jl of Comparative Religious Educn and Values, 2001–10. Non-exec. Dir, Lancashire Care NHS Foundn Trust (formerly Lancashire NHS Trust), 2009–17 (Sen. Ind. Dir, 2012–15; Dep. Chm., 2013–17); Dir, Bay Learning Trust, 2018– (Vice Chm., 2019–). Hon. Treas., Nat. Soc., 2011–. Gov., St Martin's Coll. of Higher Educn, 1999–2007 (Actg Chm., 2005–07); Chm. and Pro Chancellor, Univ. of Cumbria, 2007–10 (Vice Chm., 2006–07). Trustee, Culham St Gabriel's, 2016– (Chm., Finance Cttee, 2017–). FRSA 2009. *Publications:* (with Brian Boughton) Construction Mathematics, vols I and II, 1983; (contrib.) Mission Shaped Youth, 2007. *Recreations:* bad golf, electronic gardening, watching most sports, spending time with the family. *Address:* Chapel House, Chapel Lane, Ellel, Lancaster LA2 0PW. *T:* (01524) 752466, 07970 923141. *E:* peter.j.ballard@btinternet.com.

**BALLARD, Dr Robert Duane**; oceanographer and marine explorer; Founder and President, Ocean Exploration Trust, since 2008; *b* 30 June 1942; *s* of Chester P. Ballard and Harriett N. Ballard; *m* 1991, Barbara Earle; two *s* one *d*. *Educ:* Univ. of California, Santa Barbara (BS 1965); Univ. of Hawaii; Univ. of Southern California; Univ. of Rhode Island (PhD 1974). 2nd Lieut, US Army Intelligence, 1965–67; USN, 1967–70, served Vietnam War; Comdr, USNR, 1987–2001. Woods Hole Oceanographic Institution: Res. Associate, 1969–74; Asst Scientist, 1974–76; Associate Scientist, 1976–83; Founder, Deep Submergence Lab., and Sen. Scientist, Dept of Applied Ocean Physics and Engrg, 1983–99; Dir, Center for Marine Exploration, 1989–95; Scientist Emeritus, 1997–. Founder, Jason Project (use of remotely operated vehicles for deep-sea exploration), 1989; Founder, 1989, and Chm. of Bd, 1990–95, Jason Foundn for Educn; Founder and Pres., Inst. for Exploration, then Ocean Exploration Center, 1995–2014. Expeditions include: exploration of Mid-ocean Ridge, 1974, of Galapagos Rift, 1977; discovery of polymetallic sulphides, 1979; Titanic, 1985; German battleship Bismarck, 1989; warships from lost fleet of Guadalcanal, 1992; Lusitania, 1994; Roman ships off coast of Tunisia, 1997; USS Yorktown, 1998; Black Sea, 2000. Presenter, Nat. Geographic Explorer TV prog., 1989–91; award-winning films for television incl. Secrets of the Titanic, 1985, and Last Voyage of the Lusitania, 1994. Many scientific, academic and multi-media awards and honours. *Publications:* Photographic Atlas of the Mid-Atlantic Ridge Rift Valley, 1977; (jtly) The Discovery of the Titanic, 1987 (trans. 10 langs); The Discovery of the Bismarck, 1990 (trans. 8 langs); Bright Shark (novel), 1992 (trans. 6 langs); The Lost Ships of Guadalcanal, 1993 (trans. 5 langs); (jtly) Exploring the Lusitania, 1995 (trans. 2 langs); Explorations (autobiog.), 1995 (trans. 2 langs); Lost Liners, 1997 (trans. 5 langs); History of Deep Submergence Science and Technology, 1998; At the Water's Edge: coastal images of America, 1998; Return to Midway, 1999; The Eternal Darkness: a personal history of deep-sea exploration, 2000; *for children:* Exploring the Titanic, 1988 (trans. 7 langs); The Lost Wreck of the Isis, 1990 (trans. 5 langs); Exploring the Bismarck, 1991 (trans. 2 langs); Explorer, 1992; Ghost Liners, 1998; contrib. many learned jls. *Address:* Ocean Exploration Trust, PO Box 42, Old Lyme, CT 06371, USA.

**BALLENTYNE, Donald Francis**, CMG 1985; HM Diplomatic Service, retired; Consul-General, Los Angeles, 1985–89; *b* 5 May 1929; *s* of late Henry Q. Ballentyne and Frances R. MacLaren; *m* 1950, Elizabeth Heywood, *d* of late Leslie A. Heywood; one *s* one *d*. *Educ:* Haberdashers' Aske's Hatcham Sch. FO, 1950–53; Berne and Ankara, 1953–56; Consul: Munich, 1957; Stanleyville, 1961; Cape Town, 1962; First Secretary: Luxembourg, 1965–69, Havana, 1969–72; FCO, 1972–74; Counsellor (Commercial), The Hague, 1974–78, Bonn, 1978–81; Counsellor, E Berlin, 1982–84. *Address:* Orford, Suffolk.

**BALLHEIMER, Andrew Mark**; Global Managing Partner, Allen & Overy LLP, since 2016; *b* London, 30 Nov. 1961; *s* of late Hans Reinhold Ballheimer and of Ellen Ballheimer; *m* 1996, Lisa Jane Mears; two *s* one *d*. *Educ:* Gonville and Caius Coll., Cambridge (BA Hons Law 1983). Admitted solicitor, 1987; Allen & Overy: has practised law in New York, Tokyo and UK; Associate, then Sen. Associate, 1987–94; Partner, 1994–; Global Co-Hd, Corporate, 2010–16. Trustee, Moorfields Eye Charity, 2011–. *Publications:* articles in Columbia Jl of Transnational Law and Univ. of Pennsylvania Jl of Internat. Business Law. *Recreations:* tennis, swimming, theatre, travel. *Address:* Allen & Overy LLP, One Bishops Square, E1 6AD. *T:* (020) 3088 0000, *Fax:* (020) 3088 0088. *E:* andrew.ballheimer@allenovery.com. *Clubs:* George; Chandos Lawn Tennis.

**BALLMER, Steve**; Owner, Los Angeles Clippers, since 2014; *b* March 1956; *m* Connie; three *c*. *Educ:* Harvard Univ. (BA); Stanford Univ. Graduate Sch. of Business. Asst Product Manager, Procter & Gamble Co.; joined Microsoft Corp., 1980; Vice-Pres., Marketing; Sen. Vice-Pres., Systems Software; Exec. Vice-Pres., Sales and Support, until 1998; Pres., 1998–2000; CEO, 2000–14. Dir, Accenture, 2001–06.

**BALLS, Alastair Gordon**, CB 1995; DL; Chairman, The International Centre for Life, since 2007 (Chief Executive, 1998–2007); *b* 18 March 1944; *s* of late Dr Ernest George Balls and Elspeth Russell Balls; *m* 1978, Beryl May Nichol (*d* 2017); one *s* one *d*. *Educ:* Hamilton Acad.; Univ. of St Andrews (MA); Univ. of Manchester (MA). Economist: Treasury, Govt of Tanzania, 1966–68; Min. of Transport, UK, 1969–74; Sec., Adv. Cttee on Channel Tunnel, 1974–75; Sen. Econ. Adviser, HM Treasury, 1976–79; Asst Sec., Dept of Environment, 1979–83; Regl Dir, Depts of Environment and Transport (Northern Region), 1984–87; Chief Exec., Tyne and Wear Develt Corp., 1987–98. Chairman: Newcastle Gateshead Initiative, 2004–07; Northern Rock Foundn, 2006–. Non-executive Director: Northumbrian Water Ltd, 2002–11; N Star Venture Capital, 2004–10. Mem. Bd, HEFCE, 2006–12. Mem., ITC, 1998–2003. Chm., Alzheimer's Soc., 2007–13. Vice-Chm., Council, Univ. of Newcastle upon Tyne, 1994–2000. DL Tyne and Wear, 2009. *Recreations:* sailing, fishing, maintaining rusty old cars. *Address:* The International Centre for Life Trust, Times Square, Newcastle upon Tyne NE1 4EP.

**BALLS, Rt Hon. Edward (Michael)**; PC 2007; Visiting Professor, Policy Institute, King's College London, since 2015; broadcaster, writer and speaker; *b* 25 Feb. 1967; *s* of Prof. Michael Balls and Carolyn Janet Balls; *m* 1998, Rt Hon. Yvette Cooper, *qv*; one *s* two *d*. *Educ:* Bawburgh Co. Primary Sch.; Crossdale Drive Primary Sch., Keyworth; Nottingham High Sch.; Keble Coll., Oxford (Keble Coll. Scholar; BA 1st Cl. Hons PPE; Hon. Fellow); John F. Kennedy Sch. of Govt, Harvard Univ. (Kennedy Scholar; MPA). Teaching Fellow, Dept of Econs, Harvard Univ., and Nat. Bureau of Econ. Res., 1989–90; econs leader writer and columnist, Financial Times, 1990–94; Econ. Advr to Shadow Chancellor, 1994–97; Sec., Labour Party Econ. Policy Commn, 1994–97; Econ. Advr to Chancellor of the Exchequer, HM Treasury, 1997–99; Chief Econ. Advr, HM Treasury, 1999–2004. G20 Deputy, 2000–04; Chm., Cttee of Deputies, IMF, 2002–04. Sen. Res. Fellow, Smith Inst., 2004–05. MP (Lab and Co-op) Normanton, 2005–10, Morley and Outwood, 2010–15; contested (Lab and Co-op) same seat, 2015. Econ. Sec. to HM Treasury, 2006–07; Sec. of State for Children, Schs and Families, 2007–10; Shadow Sec. of State for Educn, 2010, for Home Dept, 2010–11; Shadow Chancellor of the Exchequer, 2011–15. Chm., Fabian Soc., 2007. Co-Chair, Commn on Inclusive Prosperity, Center for Amer. Progress, 2013–15 (Report, 2015). Sen. Fellow, 2015–17, Res. Fellow, 2017–, Mossavar-Rahmani Center for Business and Govt, Harvard Kennedy Sch., Harvard Univ. Mem. Bd, UK Holocaust Meml

Foundn, 2015–. Chm., 2015–18, Vice Pres. and Club Ambassador, 2018–, Norwich City FC plc. Patron: British Stammering Assoc., 2011–; Whizz-Kidz, 2016–; Vice-Pres., Action for Stammering Children, 2016–. Contestant, Strictly Come Dancing, TV series, 2016; Presenter, Travels in Trumpland with Ed Balls, 2018. Hon. LLD: Nottingham, 2003; Trent, 2016. Spectator Parliamentarian of the Year Award, 2010; Opposition Politician of the Year, Political Studies Assoc., 2011. *Publications:* (Principal Ed.) World Bank Development Report, 1995; (ed with Gus O'Donnell) Reforming Britain's Economic and Financial Policy, 2002; (ed with Joe Grice and Gus O'Donnell) Microeconomic Reform in Britain, 2004; Speaking Out: lessons in life and politics, 2016; contribs to learned jls, incl. Scottish Jl Pol Economy, World Economics, and to reports published by Fabian Soc. and Social Justice Commn. *Recreations:* learning the piano, running marathons, cooking, dancing. *W:* www.edballs.co.uk.

**BALLS, Rt Hon. Yvette;** *see* Cooper, Rt Hon. Y.

**BALMAIN, Prof. Allan,** PhD; FRS 2015; FRSE; Barbara Bass Bakar Distinguished Professor of Cancer Genetics, University of California, San Francisco, since 2001; Co-Leader, Cancer Genetics Program, and Director, Genome Analysis Core Facility, UCSF Helen Diller Family Comprehensive Cancer Center; *b* Wick, Scotland. *Educ:* Univ. of Glasgow (BSc Chem. 1966; PhD 1969). Postdoctoral res., Univ. of Strasbourg, 1969–71; postdoctoral res., 1971–72, tenured mem. staff, 1972–76, German Cancer Res. Centre, Heidelberg; Beatson Institute for Cancer Research, Glasgow: Staff Scientist, 1976–82; Gp Leader, 1982–94; CRC Special Appt, 1987–94; Dir, Lab. Res., and Prof. of Molecular Oncol., Univ. of Glasgow, 1994–96; Jerry Turner Fellow, CRC, 1994–96; Vice-Pres., Res., Onyx Pharmaceutical, Richmond, Calif, 1996–98; Prof. of Cancer Genetics, UCSF, 1999–2001. FRSE 1995; FAAAS. *Publications:* contribs to learned scientific jls. *Address:* Helen Diller Family Comprehensive Cancer Center, University of California, San Francisco, 1450 3rd Street, San Francisco, CA 94158, USA.

**BALMER, Colin Victor,** CB 2001; Managing Director, Cabinet Office, 2003–06; *b* 22 Aug. 1946; *s* of Peter Lionel Balmer and Adelaide Currie Balmer; *m* 1978, Frances Mary Montrésor (marr. diss. 2006); two *s* one *d*; *m* 2006, Lesley Ann Pasricha. *Educ:* Liverpool Inst. High Sch. War Office, 1963, later Ministry of Defence: Asst Private Sec. to Minister of State, 1972; Private Sec. to Parly Under-Sec. of State (RAF), 1973; Civil Advr to GOC N Ireland, 1973; Cabinet Office, 1977; Private Sec. to Minister of State (Defence Procurement), 1980; UK Delegn to NATO, 1982; MoD 1984; Minister (Defence Materiel), Washington, 1990; Ministry of Defence: Asst Under-Sec. of State, 1992–96; Dep. Under-Sec. of State (Resources, Programmes and Finance), 1996–98; Finance Dir, 1998–2003. Technical Advr, IMF, 2006–08. Non-executive Director: QinetiQ Gp plc, 2006–14; Royal Mint, 2007–13. *Recreations:* Portesham Ukulele Band, golf, gardening, bridge, rock and roll music. *E:* colinvbalmer@btinternet.com.

**BALMER, Derek Rigby,** RWA 1970; painter and photographer; President, Royal West of England Academy, 2001–10; *b* 28 Dec. 1934; *s* of Geoffrey Johnstone Balmer and Barbara Winifred Balmer (*née* Rigby); *m* 1962, Elizabeth Mary Rose Hawkins; one *s* one *d*. *Educ:* Waterloo House Sch.; Sefton Park Sch.; West of England Coll. of Art. Photographer, Th. Royal, Bristol Old Vic, 1961–90. *One-man exhibitions* include: Fimbarrus Gall., Bath, 1960; Arnolfini Gall., Bristol, 1966, 1968; City Art Gall., Bristol, 1975; Sharples Gall., RWA, 1980; Anthony Hepworth Fine Art, Bath, 1992, 1994, 2005, London, 1994, 2000; Gisela van Beers, London, 1992; Montpelier Sandelson, London, 1995; Smelik and Stokking Galls, Holland, 1996, 1998, 2000, 2001; New Gall., RWA, 2003; Campden Gall., Chipping Campden, 2005, 2008, 2011; Catto Gall., London, 2010, 2012, 2014, 2016, 2018; Cube Gall., London, 2013; Bath Contemporary, Bath, 2015, 2017; RWA, 2015; *retrospective exhibition:* President's Eye: 1950–2007, RWA Galls, 2007; *group exhibitions* include: Arnolfini Gall., Bristol, 1963, 1964, 1983; Arts Council Touring Exhibn, 1967; Leicester Galls, London, 1968, 1969, 1970; Victoria Art Gall., Bath, 1970; New Art Centre, London, 1982; Louise Hallet Gall., London, 1985; London Contemp. Art Fair, annually 1990–; Campden Gall., Chipping Campden, 2004; RA Summer Show, 2005–10; Browse & Darby Gall., London, 2010; Hilton Fine Art, Bath, 2014; RWA, 2019. Chm., RWA, 1997–2000. Pro-Chancellor, UWE, 2003–10. Hon. DArts UWE, 2001. Hon. RA 2003. *Publications:* (monograph) Derek Balmer: a singular vision, 2012. *Recreations:* art history, reading, cricket, walking Newfoundland dogs and Leonberger dog. *Address:* Mulberry House, 12 Avon Grove, Sneyd Park, Bristol BS9 1PJ. *T:* (0117) 968 2953; c/o Catto Gallery, Heath Street, Hampstead, NW3 1DP. *T:* (020) 7435 6660. *Club:* Chelsea Arts.

**BALMFORD, Prof. Andrew Paul,** PhD; FRS 2011; Professor of Conservation Science, University of Cambridge, since 2007; Fellow, Clare College, Cambridge, since 2008; *b* Birmingham, 8 March 1963; *s* of John Edwin Balmford and Marie Diana Ruth Balmford; *m* 1989, Sarah Blakeman; two *s*. *Educ:* King Edward's Sch., Birmingham; Clare Coll., Cambridge (BA 1985; PhD 1990). Research Fellow: Girton Coll., Cambridge, 1991–92; Inst. of Zool., London, 1993–95; Lectr in Zool., Dept of Animal and Plant Scis, Univ. of Sheffield, 1995–98; University of Cambridge: Univ. Lectr, 1998–2001; Sen. Lectr, 2001–04; Reader in Conservation Sci., 2004–07. Pola Pasvolsky Prof. of Conservation Biol., Univ. of Cape Town, 2004–05. Marsh Award for Conservation Biol., Zool Soc. of London, 2000. *Publications:* Conservation in a Changing World (ed jtly), 1998; Wild Hope: on the frontlines of conservation success, 2012; contribs to learned jls. *Recreation:* enjoying wild nature, especially with my family. *Address:* Department of Zoology, Downing Street, Cambridge CB2 3EJ. *T:* (01223) 336600.

**BALMFORTH, Dr David John,** CEng, FICE, FCIWEM; Executive Technical Director, Stantec (formerly MWH), since 2007; President, Institution of Civil Engineers, 2014–15 (Vice President, 2009–14); *b* Grappenhall, Cheshire, 3 Feb. 1947; *s* of Philip and Ella Balmforth; *m* 1968, Gillian Waller; three *s* one *d*. *Educ:* Botelier Grammar Sch., Warrington; Hampton Grammar Sch., Middx; Bristol Univ. (BSc 1st Cl. Hons Civil Engrg 1968); Sheffield Univ. (PhD Civil Engrg 1976). CEng 1983; FCIWEM 1987; FICE 1999. Lectr, 1970–72, Sen. Lectr, 1972–87, Sheffield Poly.; Principal Lectr, 1988, Dean, Faculty of the Envmt, 1988–89, Sheffield City Poly.; Dir, Sch. of Construction, Sheffield Hallam Univ., 1989–99; Sen. Principal Engr, MWH, 1999–2007. Vis. Prof., Imperial Coll. London, 2003–. Ed., Jl Flood Risk Mgt, 2007–13. Pres., Engrg Section, British Sci. Acad., 1998–99. Non-exec. Dir, Construction Industry Res. and Information Assoc., 1999–2010. *Publications:* contribs to technical jls and conf. procs on flood risk mgt. *Recreation:* canal boating. *Address:* Institution of Civil Engineers, One Great George Street, SW1P 3AA. *T:* (020) 7665 2002, *Fax:* (020) 7222 0267.

**BALNIEL, Lord; Anthony Robert Lindsay;** DL; Partner, James Hambro and Partners, since 2010; *b* 24 Nov. 1958; *s* and *heir* of Earl of Crawford and Balcarres, *qv*; *m* 1989, Nicola A., *y d* of Antony Bicket; two *s* two *d*. *Educ:* Eton Coll.; Univ. of Edinburgh. Dir, 1987–2009, CEO, 2004–07, J. O. Hambro Investment Mgt. DL Fife, 2013. *Heir: s* Master of Lindsay, *qv. Address:* Balcarres, Colinsburgh, Leven, Fife KY9 1HN. *Clubs:* New (Edinburgh); XII.

**BALOGUN-LYNCH, Christopher Charles,** FRCSE, FRCOG; Consultant Obstetrician and Gynaecological Surgeon, Milton Keynes General Hospital, 1984–2010, now Emeritus; *b* 1 Oct. 1947; *s* of late Prof. Prince E. Balogun-Lynch and Jane A. Balogun-Lynch; *m* 1986, Julia Caroline Klinner; one *s* three *d*. *Educ:* Christ Church, Oxford (MA); St Bartholomew's Hosp., London (MB BS 1974). FRCSE 1979; FRCOG 1991; MCIArb 1999; QDR 1994. Surgeon in private practice, Harley St, 1984–. Royal Coll. Tutor and Trainer in Minimal Access Surgery, 1995–2010; Internat. Lectr and Simulation Trainer in post-partum haemorrhage, 2008–. Hon. Vis. Gynaecological Cancer Surgeon, Northampton Gen. Hosp., 2001. Introduced carbon dioxide laser, YAG laser and keyhole surgery techniques to Milton Keynes Hosp., 1985–2003; innovator of new technology and obstetric and gynaecological surgical techniques incl. the control of post-partum haemorrhage now in worldwide application. Vis. Prof., Cranfield Univ., 2006–; has lectured in Sydney, Cape Town, USA, Italy and various centres in UK, 1988–. Obstetrics and gynaecol. undergrad. Trainer and Examiner, Oxford Univ., 2007–. Publications Referee: British Jl Obstetrics and Gynaecol.; Eur. Jl Obstetrics and Gynaecol.; Internat. Jl Obstetrics and Gynaecol.; American Jl Obstetrics and Gynaecol. Mem., WHO Commn for Women's Health Improvement, 2010–; Hon. Comr, WHO Women's Health Prog., 2011–. Founder and Chair, Myrtle Peach Trust for Gynaecological Cancer Prevention and Res., 1985–. Liveryman, Soc. of Apothecaries, 1983–. MAE 1992; FLLA 1997. Fellow, Royal Soc. of St George, 2002. DUniv Open, 1997. Serono Labs (UK) Award for Assisted Conception, 1987. Grand Commanding Officer, Republic of Sierra Leone, 2007. *Publications:* (jtly) The Surgical Management of Post Partum Haemorrhage, 2005; (ed jtly) A Textbook of Postpartum Hemorrhage, 2006; (ed jtly) A Textbook of Preconceptional Medicine and Management, 2012; numerous contribs to medical, surgical, scientific, clinical, endoscopic surgery, medico-legal and educational papers in leading jls. *Recreations:* Rugby, cricket, occasional golf, family outings. *Address:* 3 Bessemer Lodge, 15 Ada Walk, Oakgrove Village, Milton Keynes MK10 9SW. *T:* and *Fax:* (01908) 397875. *Clubs:* Athenæum, Royal Automobile.

**BALSDON, Paula;** *see* Hodges, P.

**BALSHAW, Maria Jane,** CBE 2015; DPhil; Director, Tate Galleries, since 2017; *b* 24 Jan. 1970; *d* of Walter and Colette Balshaw; one *s* one *d*; *m* Nicholas Merriman. *Educ:* Univ. of Liverpool (BA Hons Eng. and Cultural Studies 1991); Univ. of Sussex (MA Critical Theory 1992; DPhil African American Visual Culture and Lit. 1997). Lectr in Cultural Studies, UC Northampton, 1993–97; Res. Fellow in American Urban Culture, Univ. of Birmingham, 1997–2002; Director: Creative Partnerships Birmingham, 2002–05; Dir, External Relns and Develt, Arts Council England, W Midlands, 2005–06; Whitworth Art Gall., Univ. of Manchester, 2006–17; Manchester City Galls, 2011–17. Mem. Bd, Arts Council England, 2014–18. Clore Leadership Fellow, 2004–05. *Publications:* Urban Space and Representation (ed with Liam Kennedy), 1999; Looking for Harlem: African American urban culture, 2000; (ed jtly) City Sites: multimedia essays on Chicago and New York, 2000. *Recreations:* dancing and watching dance, gardening, travelling anywhere, visiting art galleries, cooking, yoga.

**BALSOM, Alison Louise, (Mrs S. A. Mendes),** OBE 2016; classical trumpet soloist, since 2001; Professor of Trumpet, Guildhall School of Music and Drama, since 2006; Artistic Director, Cheltenham Music Festival, since 2018; music educator, campaigner, producer, arranger and presenter; *b* 7 Oct. 1978; *d* of William and Zena Balsom; *m* 2017, Samuel Alexander Mendes, *qv*; one *s*. *Educ:* Tannery Drift Primary Sch.; Greneway Middle Sch.; Meridian Sch., Royston; Hills Rd Sixth Form Coll., Cambridge; Guildhall Sch. of Music and Drama (BMus Hons 2001; FGS 2012); Paris Conservatoire. Has appeared as soloist with many of world's major orchestras incl. Last Night of the Proms, 2009. Young Concert Artists Trust Artist, 2001–04; BBC New Generation Artist, 2004–06. Commnd, produced and appeared in Gabriel, Shakespeare's Globe, 2013. Patron: Cherubim Music Trust, 2010–; Mayor's Fund for Young Musicians, 2011–; OHMI Trust, 2012–; Brass for Africa, 2013–. Pres., Deal Fest., 2014–. Hon. DA Anglia Ruskin, 2009; Hon. DMus Leicester, 2015. Brass Winner, BBC Young Musician of Year, 1998; Gramophone Award, Classic FM Listeners' Choice, 2006; Young British Classical Performer, 2006, Female Artist of the Year, 2009, 2011, Classical Brit Awards; Echo Klassik Award, Deutsche Phono-Akademie, 2007, 2010, 2012; Artist of the Year, Gramophone Awards, 2013; Silver Clef Award, Nordoff Robbins, 2013. *Recreations:* sailing, construction and design, furniture restoration. *Address:* c/o Askonas Holt, 15 Fetter Lane, EC4A 1BW.

**BALSTON, Michael Edward;** Senior Director, Balston Agius Ltd (formerly Balston & Company Ltd), since 1983; *b* London, 11 June 1944; *s* of Comdr Edward Francis Balston, DSO, RN and Diana Beatrice Louise Balston (*née* Ferrers); *m* 1978, Meriel Frances Stirling-Aird; two *s* one *d*. *Educ:* Downside Sch.; BRNC Dartmouth; Christ's Coll., Cambridge (BA 1968; DipArch 1972); Thames Poly. (DipLA). RIBA 1972; CMLI 1979. Landscape Architect and Planner, Robert Matthew Johnson-Marshall and Partners, 1972–77; Partner, Lennox-Boyd and Balston, 1978–83. Mem., Panel, Europa Nostra UK Awards, 1999–2003. Royal Horticultural Society: Gardens Judge, 1993–2012; Mem. Council, 2003–12; Vice Pres., 2013–. *Publications:* The Well-Furnished Garden, 1986; Ten Landscapes, 2001. *Recreations:* gardening, arts. *Address:* Balston Agius Ltd, Manor Farm Lane, Patney, Devizes, Wilts SN10 3RB. *T:* (01380) 848181, *Fax:* (01380) 848189. *E:* mb@balstonagius.co.uk.

**BALTIMORE, David,** PhD; Robert Andrews Millikan Professor of Biology, California Institute of Technology, since 2006 (President, 1997–2006, now Emeritus); *b* New York, 7 March 1938; *s* of Richard and Gertrude Baltimore; *m* 1968, Alice Huang; one *d*. *Educ:* Swarthmore Coll. (BA 1960); Rockefeller Univ. (PhD 1964). Postdoctoral Fellow, MIT, 1963–64; Albert Einstein Coll. of Med., NY, 1964–65; Research Associate, Salk Inst., La Jolla, Calif, 1965–68; Massachusetts Institute of Technology: Associate Prof., 1968–72; Amer. Cancer Soc. Prof. of Microbiol., 1973–83; Prof. of Biology, 1972–90; Dir, Whitehead Inst., 1982–90; Prof., 1990–94, Pres., 1990–91, Rockefeller Univ.; Ivan R. Cottrell Prof. of Molecular Biol. and Immunol., MIT, 1994–97. FAAAS 1980 (Pres., 2007–08; Chm., 2008–09). Chm., AIDS Vaccine Adv. Cttee, NIH, 1996–2002. Member: Nat. Acad. of Scis, 1974; Amer. Acad. of Arts and Scis, 1974; Pontifical Acad. of Scis, 1978; Foreign Mem., Royal Soc., 1987. Eli Lilly Award in Microbiology and Immunology, 1971; US Steel Foundn Award in Molecular Biology, 1974; (jtly) Nobel Prize for Physiology or Medicine, 1975; US Nat. Medal of Science, 1999; Warren Alpert Foundn Prize, 2000; AMA Scientific Achievement Award, 2002. *Address:* California Institute of Technology, 147–75, 1200 E California Boulevard, Pasadena, CA 91125, USA.

**BAMBERG, Harold Rolf,** CBE 1968; FRAeS; Chairman of Glos Air Ltd, 1985–2010; Via Nova Properties Ltd, 1985–2011; Bamberg Farms Ltd, 1996–2017; *b* 17 Nov. 1923; *m* 1957 (marr. diss. 1990); one *s* two *d*, and one *s* one *d* of a former marriage. *Educ:* Hampstead. Former Chm., British Independent Air Transport Assoc.; Life Vice Pres., British Business and Gen. Aviation (formerly GAMTA) (Chm., 1978–80); former Director: Cunard Steamship Co.; BOAC Cunard, etc; Founder: British Eagle International Airlines, 1948; Lunn Poly Ltd, 1956. Mem., NFU. FRAeS 1993. Kt, Order of Merit, Italian Republic, 1960. *Recreations:* horses, agriculture. *Address:* 18 Cheniston Court, Ridgemount Road, Ascot, Berks SL5 9SF. *T:* (01344) 625950, *Fax:* (01344) 872285. *E:* h.bamberg489@btinternet.com. *Club:* Guards' Polo (Life Mem.).

**BAMERT, Matthias;** conductor; Principal Guest Conductor, Daejeon Symphony Orchestra, Korea, since 2017; Chief Conductor, Sapporo Symphony Orchestra, Japan, since 2018; *b* Switzerland, 5 July 1942; *m* 1969, Susan Exline; one *s* one *d*. Asst conductor to Leopold Stokowski, 1970–71; Resident Conductor, Cleveland Orch., USA, 1971–78; Music Director: Swiss Radio Orch., Basel, 1977–83; London Mozart Players, 1993–2000; Chief Conductor, W Australian SO, 2004–06; Principal Conductor and Artistic Advr, Malaysian Philharmonic Orch., 2005–08. Principal Guest Conductor: Scottish Nat. Orch., 1985–90; NZ SO, 2000–02; Associate Guest Conductor, RPO, 2001–. Director: Musica Nova fest., Glasgow, 1985–90; Lucerne Fest., 1992–98. Has worked with orchestras incl. LPO, BBC Philharmonic, BBC SO, CBSO, Orchestre de Paris, Rotterdam Philharmonic, Cleveland Orchestra, Pittsburgh Symphony, Houston Symphony, Montreal Symphony, and appears regularly at Promenade concerts; tours each season in Europe, N America, Australia, NZ, Hong Kong and Japan, and has made over 60 recordings. *Address:* c/o Sarperi Artists Management, Breitingerstrasse 17, 8002 Zürich, Switzerland.

**BAMFORD,** family name of **Baron Bamford**.

**BAMFORD,** Baron *cr* 2013 (Life Peer), of Daylesford in the County of Gloucestershire and of Wootton in the County of Staffordshire; **Anthony Paul Bamford,** Kt 1990; DL; Chairman, J. C. Bamford Group, since 1975; *b* 23 Oct. 1945; *s* of late Joseph Cyril Bamford, CBE; *m* 1974, Carole Gray Whitt (OBE 2006); two *s* one *d*. *Educ:* Ampleforth Coll.; Grenoble Univ. FIAgrE 2003. Joined JCB, 1964. Dir, Tarmac, 1988–94. Member: Design Council, 1987–89; President's Cttee, CBI, 1986–88. Pres., Staffs Agricl Soc., 1987–88. Pres., Burton on Trent Cons. Assoc., 1987–90. High Sheriff, Staffs, 1985–86. DL Staffs, 1989. Hon. FCGI 1993; Hon. FCSD 1994; Hon. FIED 2008; Hon. FREng 2014; Hon. FIMechE 2015. Hon. MEng Birmingham, 1987; DUniv Keele, 1988; Hon. DSc: Cranfield, 1994; Harper Adams Univ. Coll., 2010; Hon. DTech: Staffordshire, 1998; Loughborough, 2002; Hon. DBA Robert Gordon, 1996. Young Exporter of the Year, 1972; Young Businessman of the Year, 1979; Top Exporter of the Year, 1995; Entrepreneurial Award, British Amer. Business Inc., 2003; Hall of Fame, Assoc. of Equipment Manufacturers, USA, 2008. Chevalier, l'Ordre National du Mérite (France), 1989; Commendatore al merito della Repubblica Italiana, 1995. *Recreations:* farming, gardening. *Address:* c/o J. C. Bamford Excavators Ltd, Rocester, Staffs ST14 5JP. *Clubs:* White's, British Racing Drivers'; Royal Yacht Squadron.

**BAMFORD, Louis Neville Jules;** Legal Executive with Margetts & Ritchie, Solicitors, Birmingham, since 1960; *b* 2 July 1932; *s* of Neville Barnes Bamford and Elise Marie Bamford; unmarried. *Educ:* local schools in Birmingham. Member (Lab): Birmingham CC, 1971–74; W Midlands CC, 1974–86 (Chm., 1981–82); Birmingham CC, 1986–2002 (Chm., Gen. Purposes Cttee; Chief Whip, Lab Gp; Hon. Alderman, 2002). *Recreations:* sport, music. *Address:* Apartment 25, Tudor Lodge, 331–335 Warwick Road, Solihull B92 7AA; (office) Coleridge Chambers, 177 Corporation Street, Birmingham B4 6RL.

**BAMPFYLDE,** family name of **Baron Poltimore**.

**BANATVALA, Prof. Jehangir Edalji, (Prof. Jangu Edal Banatvala),** CBE 1999; MD; FRCP, FRCPath, FMedSci; Professor of Clinical Virology, Guy's, King's College and St Thomas' Hospitals Medical and Dental School, 1975–99, now Emeritus; Hon. Consultant Virologist, Guy's and St Thomas' Hospital Trust, 1975–99; *b* 7 Jan. 1934; *s* of Dr Edal Banatvala and Ratti Banatvala (née Shroff); *m* 1959, Roshan (née Mugaseth); three *s* (one *d* decd). *Educ:* Forest Sch., London; Gonville and Caius Coll., Cambridge (MA 1958; MB BChir 1958; MD (Whitby Medal) 1964); London Hosp. Med. Coll. DPH London 1961 (Dist.); DCH 1961; MRCPath 1965, FRCPath 1977; MRCP 1986, FRCP 1995. Polio Fund Res. Fellow, Univ. of Cambridge, 1961–64; Fulbright Schol. and Amer. Thoracic Soc. Fellow, Yale Univ., 1964–65; Sen. Lectr, 1965–71, Reader, 1971–75, St Thomas' Hosp. Med. Sch., then UMDS of Guy's and St Thomas' Hosp.; Chm., St Thomas' Hosp. Mgt Team and Med. Adv. Cttee, 1983–84. Royal College of Pathologists: Registrar, 1985–87; Vice Pres., 1987–90; Mem. Council, 1993–96; Chm., sub-cttee on measles, mumps and rubella vaccines, 1985–95, Mem., Cttee on Develt of Vaccination and Immunisation Procedures, 1985–95, MRC; Member: Council, Med. Defence Union, 1987–2004; Jt Cttee on Vaccination and Immunisation, DoH, 1986–95; PHLS Bd, 1995–2001; Ind. Panel for Vaccine Reactions (Gulf Veterans Illnesses), MoD, 1998–2001; Chm., Adv. Gp on Hepatitis, DoH, 1990–98; Mem., European Soc. of Clin. Virology, 1997–; Pres., European Assoc. Against Virus Disease, 1981–83. Hon. Cons. Microbiologist to the Army, 1992–97. Dir, Clinical Pathology Accreditation (UK) Ltd, 1997–2002. Chm., Res. Cttee, CFS Foundn, 2008–; Trustee, Hepatitis B Foundn UK, 2008–. Vis. Prof., Univ. of Auckland Med. Sch., 1983. Examiner, Univs of London, Cambridge, Colombo, West Indies and Riyadh. Mem. Senate, London Univ., 1987–94; Governor: Forest Sch., E17, 1993–2014; Mill Hill Sch., 2001–14. Founder FMedSci 1998. Freeman, City of London, 1987; Liveryman, Co. of Apothecaries, 1986. *Publications:* (ed) Current Problems in Clinical Virology, 1971; (ed jtly) Principles and Practice of Clinical Virology, 1987, 6th edn 2009; (ed) Viral Infections of the Heart, 1993; papers in gen. and specialised med. jls on intrauterine and perinatal infections, blood-borne virus infections, viral vaccines, etc. *Recreations:* watching sports in which one no longer performs (rowing, cricket), playing tennis, music, good company in good restaurants. *Address:* Little Acre, Church End, Henham, Bishop's Stortford, Herts CM22 6AN. *T:* (01279) 850386. *Clubs:* Athenæum, MCC; Leander (Henley-on-Thames); Hawks (Hon. Mem.) (Cambridge).

**BANBURY,** family name of **Baron Banbury of Southam**.

**BANBURY OF SOUTHAM,** 3rd Baron *cr* 1924, of Southam; **Charles William Banbury;** Bt 1902; *b* 29 July 1953; *s* of 2nd Baron Banbury of Southam and of Hilda Ruth, *d* of late A. H. R. Carr; *S* father, 1981; *m* 1st, 1984, Lucinda Trehearne (marr. diss. 1986); 2nd, 1989, Inger Marianne Norton; three *d*. *Educ:* Eton College. *Heir:* none. *Address:* The Mill, Fossebridge, Glos GL54 3JN.

**BANCE, Prof. Manohar Lal;** Professor of Otology and Skull Base Surgery, University of Cambridge, since 2017; *b* India, 20 May 1961; *s* of Hazara Ram Bance and Chanan Kaur; *m* 1989, Diane Gorsky; one *s* one *d*. *Educ:* Challney High Sch. for Boys, Luton; Univ. of Manchester (BSc, MB ChB); Univ. of Toronto (MSc Neurophysiol.). FRCSCan 1995; Amer. Bd of Otolaryngol. Certification; Amer. Bd of Otolaryngol. Subspeciality Neurotol. Certification. Residency in Otolaryngol.-Hd and Neck Surgery, Univ. of Toronto and UCLA, 1990–95; Fellowship in Skull Base Surgery, Univ. of Manchester, 1995–96; Asst Prof., Dept of Otolaryngol.-Hd and Neck Surgery, Univ. of Toronto, 1996–2001; Associate Prof., 2001–07, Prof., 2007–17, Div. of Otolaryngol.-Hd and Neck Surgery, Dalhousie Univ. Four start-up cos. Member: Collegium Oto-Rhino-Laryngologicum Amicitae, 2009; Triological Soc., 2012; Amer. Otology Soc., 2013; Amer. Neurotol. Soc., 2016. *Publications:* (ed jtly) ENT Medicine and Surgery: illustrated clinical cases, 2017; nine book chapters; over 130 articles in scientific jls; nine patents. *Recreations:* current affairs, work!, science fiction, fitness, Shakespeare, what-if?, blue skying. *E:* mlb59@cam.ac.uk.

**BANCROFT, Anna Louise; Her Honour Judge Bancroft;** a Circuit Judge, since 2013; *b* Blackburn, 15 March 1961; *d* of Russell and Valerie Bancroft; *m* 1988, Stuart Henry MacDonald Denney, *qv*; one *s*. *Educ:* Casterton Sch., Cumbria; St Anne's Coll., Oxford (MA); Univ. of Westminster (Grad. DipLaw). Called to the Bar, Inner Temple, 1985; in practice as barrister, Deans Court Chambers, Manchester, 1985–2013; a Recorder 2002–13. Governor: Casterton Sch., 2007–13; Sedbergh Sch., 2013–. *Recreation:* choral singing. *Address:* Liverpool Civil and Family Court, 35 Vernon Street, Liverpool, Merseyside L2 2BX.

**BAND, Adm. Sir Jonathon,** GCB 2008 (KCB 2002); DL; non-executive Director, Carnival Corporation and Carnival plc, since 2010; Survitec Group, since 2015; *b* 2 Feb. 1950; *s* of Victor and Muriel Band; *m* 1979, Sarah Asbury; two *d*. *Educ:* Brambletye Sch. Haileybury Coll.; Exeter Univ. (BA 1972). Served: HMS Soberton, 1979–81; Fleet HQ 1981–83; HMS Phoebe, 1983–85; MoD, 1986–89; HMS Norfolk and Ninth Frigate Sqn 1989–91; MoD, 1991–95; HMS Illustrious, 1995–97; ACNS, MoD, 1997–99; Team Leader, Defence Trng and Educn Study, MoD, 2000–01; Dep. C-in-C Fleet, 2001–02; C-in-C Fleet, 2002–05; Comdr Allied Naval Forces N, 2002–04; Comdr Allied Maritime Component Comd Northwood, 2004–06; Chief of Naval Staff and First Sea Lord 2006–09; First and Principal Naval ADC to the Queen, 2006–09. Non-exec. Dir Lockheed Martin UK, 2010–16. Chairman: Nat. Mus. of RN, 2010–; White Ensign Assoc., 2013–15; Pres., RN and RM Charity, 2010–. Younger Brother, Trinity House 1998–. Liveryman, Shipwrights' Co., 2006–. DL Hants, 2009. *Recreations:* family, dominated, including boating, tennis. *Clubs:* Naval, Buck's; Royal Naval and Royal Alber Yacht (Portsmouth).

**BAND, Thomas Mollison,** FSAScot; Chairman, Perthshire Housing Association, 2003–09 (Director, since 1994); *b* 28 March 1934; *s* of late Robert Boyce Band and Elizabeth Band *m* 1959, Jean McKenzie Brien (*d* 2011); one *s* two *d*. *Educ:* Perth Academy. National Service, RAF, 1952–54. Joined Civil Service, 1954; Principal, BoT, 1969; Sen. Principal Dept of Industry, 1973; Scottish Econ. Planning Dept, 1975, Asst Sec., 1976; Scottish Development Dept, 1978; Scottish Office, Finance, 1981; Dir, Historic Bldgs and Monuments, Scottish Develt Dept, 1984–87; Chief Exec., Scottish Tourist Bd, 1987–94 Chairman: Made in Scotland Ltd, 1994–95; Anderson Enterprises Ltd, 1994–98; Edinburgh Europa Ltd, 1994–98; Perth Repertory Th. Ltd, 1995–2002. Dir, Edinburgh Telford Coll. 1989–98. Chm., Industrial Cttee, Napier Univ. (formerly Napier Poly. of Edinburgh) 1989–95. Gov., Queen Margaret UC, Edinburgh, 1995–2002. President: Perthshire Soc of Natural Sci., 2004–07; Scots Lang. Soc., 2004–08; Eur. Bureau of Lesser Used Langs (UK), 2005–08. FRSA 1993. *Recreations:* ski-ing, gardening. *Address:* Heathfield Pitcairngreen, Perthshire PH1 3LS. *T:* (01738) 583403.

**BANDA, Prof. Enric,** DSc; President, Euroscience, 2006–12; *b* 21 June 1948; *s* of Emilio and Maria Banda; *m* 1st, 1973 (marr. diss. 1982); 2nd, 1983, Gemma Lienas, writer. *Educ* Univ. of Barcelona (BSc Physics 1974; DSc Physics 1979). Researcher, ETH-Zürich 1980–83; Head, Geophysical Survey, Catalan Govt, 1983–87; Res. Prof., Consejo Superior de Investigaciones Científicas, 1987; Head, Inst. of Earth Sciences, Barcelona, 1988–91 Sec. Gen., Nat. Plan R&D, Spain, 1994; Sec. of State for Universities and Research, Spain 1995–96; Sec. Gen., ESF, 1998–2003. Dir, Catalan Res. and Innovation Foundn, 2004; Dir of Sci., Res. and Envmt, La Caixa Foundn, 2009–11. Mem., Royal Acad. of Scis and Arts Barcelona, 2014. Chevalier de la Légion d'Honneur (France), 1997. *Publications:* more than 150 scientific papers.

**BANDIERA, Prof. Oriana,** PhD; FBA 2015; Professor of Economics, since 2009, and Director, Suntory and Toyota International Centres for Economics and Related Disciplines since 2012, London School of Economics and Political Science; *b* Catania, Italy, 26 Aug. 1971; *d* of Antonio Bandiera and Nunzia Guzzardi; *m*; one *s* one *d*. *Educ:* Universita Bocconi, Milan (BSc Econs 1993; MSc Econs 1994); Boston Coll. (PhD Econs 2000) London School of Economics and Political Science: Lectr in Econs, 1999–2007; Reader in Econs, 2007–09. Visiting Assistant Professor: Univ. of Chicago, 2003; New York Univ. 2004; IIES, Stockholm, 2004, 2006; Università Bocconi, Milan, 2005; Yale Univ., 2005 Northwestern Univ., 2007. Co-Director: State Capabilities Prog., Internat. Growth Centre, 2008–; Develt Econs Prog., Centre for Econ. Policy Res., 2015– (Fellow); Fellow Bureau for Analysis of Econ. Develt. Member, Council: Eur. Econ. Assoc.; Royal Econ Soc. Co-Editor: Jl of Labor Economics, 2014–; Economica, 2016–. Carlo Alberto Medal Collegio Carlo Alberto, 2011. *Publications:* articles in economics jls. *Address:* Department o Economics, London School of Economics and Political Science, Houghton Street, WC2A 2AE. *T:* (020) 7955 7519. *E:* o.bandiera@lse.ac.uk.

**BANERJEE, Urmila, (Millie),** CBE 2002; Chair: College of Policing, since 2017 (non-executive Director, since 2012); NHS Blood and Transplant, since 2017; *b* Calcutta, 30 June 1946; *d* of late Shankar Ray-Chaudhuri and of Maya Ray-Chaudhuri; *m* 1st, 1970, Pradip Banerjee (marr. diss. 1985); 2nd, 1991, Christopher Anthony Seymour (*d* 2014). *Educ* University Coll. London (BSc Zool.); Poly. of N London (DMS); Massachusetts Inst. o Technol. (Sen. Exec. Prog.). Post Office Telecommunications: Operational Manager Internat. Telephones, 1970–76; Tutor, Telecoms Mgt Coll., 1976–79; Exec. Asst to MD Telecoms, 1979–84; British Telecommunications: Dep. Gen. Manager, London SW 1984–88; Dist Gen. Manager, London Networks, 1988–90; Director: Personnel Worldwide Networks, 1990–92; Integrated Systems, 1992–95; Pricing, 1995; Vice Pres. Prog. Mgt, 1995–97, Exec. Vice Pres., Ops, 1997–2000, ICO Global Communications Non-exec. Dir, Channel 4 TV, 2000–02. Mem. Bd, Ofcom, 2003–11; Chairman Postwatch, 2005–08; Postal Services Commn, 2011; British Transport Police Authy 2008–15; Working Links, 2011–16; non-executive Director: Prison Service Agency 1990–95; Focus Central London, 1997–2000; Cabinet Office Bd, 1999–2005; Sector Skills Develt Agency, 2001–04; Strategic Rail Authy, 2002–05; E London and City Primary Care Cluster (formerly Newham PCT), 2009–12; E London Foundn Trust, 2014–17; Member Nurses and Allied Professions Pay Rev. Bd, 1999–2002; Judicial Appts Commn, 2001–05 Bd, Barts Health, 2012–13. Gov., S Bank Univ., 1993–98; Mem. Adv. Bd, Tanaka Imperial Business Sch., 2003–07; External Examnr, UCL, 2014–17. Trustee, 2001–07, and Chm. 2005–07, Carnegie Trust UK; Gov., Peabody Trust, 2008–11; Chm., Nominet Trust 2011–14. High Sheriff, Greater London, 2012–13. *Recreations:* cooking, France. *Address:* 14 Marlborough Street, SW3 3PS. *T:* (020) 7581 1399. *E:* millie.banerjee@btinternet.com.

**BANFIELD, John Martin,** FEI; Diocesan Director of Finance, Diocese of Cyprus and the Gulf, Episcopal Church in Jerusalem and the Middle East, since 2011 (Member, Standing Committee, since 2007); *b* 15 Nov. 1947; *s* of late Jack Banfield and Peggy Winifred Banfield (née Parker); *m* 1978, Mary Gerrey Morton; one *s* one *d*. *Educ:* Haberdashers Aske's; St John's Coll., Cambridge (MA Geography). FEI (FInstPet 1996). Joined Mobil Oi Co., 1969; Man. Dir, Mobil Cyprus, 1986–87; Director: Mobil Benelux, 1988–89; Mobil Oil Co., 1990–91; Pres., Mobil Benelux, 1992; Dir, Mobil Germany, 1993; Chm., Mobil Oil Co., 1994–96; Dir, Mobil Europe, 1996–2001. Dep. Chm. and non-exec. Dir, Surrey and Borders NHS Trust, 2002–11. Vice-Pres., Inst. of Petroleum, 1996–99; Pres., Oi Industries Club, 1997–98. Hon. Lay Canon, St Christopher's Cathedral, Bahrain, 2011– Chm. of Govs, Box Hill Sch., 2009–19. *Recreations:* music, sailing, travel. *Address:* Garden Corner, Mickleham, Surrey. *Club:* MCC.

**BANGAY, Deborah Joanna Janet;** QC 2006; *b* 29 Nov. 1957; *d* of late Joe and of Jane Bangay; *m* (marr. diss. 2001); two *s* (twins). *Educ:* Cranwell Primary Sch.; Sleaford High Sch.; Wycombe High Sch.; Univ. of Exeter (LLB Hons 1979); Council of Legal Educn

Called to the Bar, Gray's Inn, 1981; in practice, specialising in family law. Mem., RADA Develt Bd. *Recreations:* theatre, ballet, football, keeping fit. *Address:* 1 Hare Court, Temple, EC4Y 7BE. *T:* (020) 7797 7070, *Fax:* (020) 7797 7435. *E:* bangay@1hc.com. *Club:* Soho House.

**BANGEMANN, Dr Martin;** a Member, European Commission (formerly Commission of the European Community), 1989–99 (a Vice-President, 1989–93); *b* 15 Nov. 1934; *s* of Martin Bangemann and Lotte Telge; *m* 1962, Renate Bauer; three *s* two *d*. *Educ:* Univ. of Tübingen; Univ. of Munich (DJur). Lawyer, 1964–79. Mem., Bundestag, 1972–80 and 1986–89; Mem., European Parliament, 1973–84 (Pres., Liberal Gp, 1979–84); Minister of Econs, FRG, 1984–88. Freie Demokratische Partei: Mem., 1963–; Chm., 1985–88. Fed. Cross of Merit with star (Germany); Bavarian Order of Merit.

**BANGHAM, Prof. Charles Richard Mark,** PhD, ScD; FRCPath, FMedSci; FRS 2019; Professor of Immunology, Imperial College London, since 1995 (Head, Division of Infectious Diseases, 2011–19); *b* London, 25 April 1955; *s* of Derek Bangham and Alison Bangham; *m* 1990, Jocelyne Marie Ragody Hughes; one *s* two *d*. *Educ:* Mill Hill Sch.; Downing Coll., Cambridge (BA 1976; ScD 2006); Lincoln Coll., Oxford (BM BCh 1980; PhD 1987). MRCP 1983; FRCPath 1999. House Physician, Nuffield Dept of Medicine, Oxford, 1980–81; House Surgeon, Royal United Hosp., Bath, 1981; SHO, University Hosp., Nottingham, 1981–83; MRC Trng Fellow, NIMR and Nuffield Dept of Medicine, Oxford, 1983–87; Wellcome Trust Sen. Res. Fellow, Univ. of Oxford, 1987–93; Consultant Virologist, John Radcliffe Hosp., Oxford, 1993–95; Dir, Public Health Lab., Oxford, 1995. Hon. Consultant, St Mary's Hosp., London, 1995–. FMedSci 2003. *Publications:* papers on lung function, genetics and fertility of Sherpas of Nepal, and on virol., immunol. and cell biol. of persistent viral infections, esp. human T cell leukaemia virus HTLV-1. *Recreations:* photography, music (violin), woodwork, travel. *Address:* River View, The Walk, Islip OX5 2SD. *T:* (01865) 373191. *E:* c.bangham@imperial.ac.uk.

**BANGOR, 8th Viscount** *cr* 1781 (Ire.); **William Maxwell David Ward;** Baron 1770 (Ire.); antiquarian bookseller; *b* 9 Aug. 1948; *s* of 7th Viscount Bangor and his 3rd wife, Leila Mary Heaton (*d* 1959); *S* father, 1993; *m* 1976, Sarah Mary Malet Bradford, *qv*. *Educ:* University Coll., London. *Recreations:* history, music, antiquity, Bolton Wanderers. *Heir: presumptive:* *b* Hon. (Edward) Nicholas Ward [*b* 16 Jan. 1953; *m* 1985, Rachel Mary, *d* of Hon. Hugh Waldorf Astor; two *d*]. *Address:* 31 Britannia Road, SW6 2HJ. *Club:* Chelsea Arts.

**BANGOR, Viscountess;** *see* Bradford, S. M. M. W.

**BANGOR, Bishop of,** since 2008; **Rt Rev. Andrew Thomas Griffith John;** *b* 1964; *m* Caroline; one *s* three *d*. *Educ:* Ysgol Penglais, Aberystwyth; Univ. of Wales (LLB 1986); Univ. of Nottingham (BA Theology 1988); St John's Coll., Nottingham (Dip. in Pastoral Studies 1989). Ordained deacon, 1989, priest, 1990; Asst Curate, St Mary's, Cardigan with Mwnt and Y Ferwg, 1989–91; Asst Curate, 1991–92, Team Vicar/Minister, 1992–99, St Michael's, Aberystwyth; Vicar: St David, Henfynyw with Aberaeron and Llanddewi Aberarth, 1999–2006; St Patrick, Pencarreg and Llanycrwys, 2006–08; Archdeacon of Cardigan, 2006–08. *Address:* Ty'r Esgob, Upper Garth Road, Bangor LL57 2SS. *T:* (01248) 362895. *E:* bishop.bangor@churchinwales.org.uk.

**BANGOR, Dean of;** *see* Jones, Very Rev. K. L.

**BANHAM, Sir John (Michael Middlecott),** Kt 1992; DL; Chairman: Future Homes Commission, 2011–13; Innoveas International Ltd, 2014–18; *b* 22 Aug. 1940; *s* of late Terence Middlecott Banham, FRCS and Belinda Joan Banham, CBE; *m* 1965, Frances Barbara Molyneux Favell; one *s* two *d*. *Educ:* Charterhouse; Queens' Coll., Cambridge (Foundn Schol.; BA 1st cl. in Natural Scis, 1962; Hon. Fellow, 1989). Asst Principal, HM Foreign Service, 1962–64; Dir of Marketing, Wallcoverings Div., Reed International, 1965–69; McKinsey & Co. Inc.: Associate, 1969–75; Principal, 1975–80; Dir, 1980–83. Controller, Audit Commn, 1983–87; Dir-Gen., CBI, 1987–92; Chm., Local Govt Commn for England, 1992–95. Chm., Retail and Consumer Affairs Foresight Panel, 1997–2001. Chairman: John Labatt (Europe), subseq. Labatt Breweries of Europe, 1992–95; Westcountry Television, 1992–95; Tarmac, 1994–2000 (Dir, 1992–2000); Kingfisher, 1996–2001; ECI Ventures, 1992–2005; Whitbread, 2000–05 (Dir, 1999–2005); Geest, 2002–05; Cyclacel Ltd, 2002–06; Spacelabs Healthcare Inc., 2005–08; Johnson Matthey plc, 2006–11; Director: National Westminster Bank, 1992–98; National Power, 1992–98; Merchants Trust, 1992–2005; Cyclacel Pharmaceuticals Inc. (formerly Cyclacel Therapeutics Inc.), 2006–; Sen. Ind. Dir, Invesco Inc. (formerly Amvescap plc), 1999–2014. Mem., BOTB, 1989–92; Dir and Mem. Bd, Business in the Community, 1989–92. Member Council: PSI, 1986–92; Forum for Management Educn and Develt, 1988–93; BESO, 1991–92. Member: Council of Management, PDSA, 1982–93; Governing Body, London Business Sch., 1987–92; Managing Trustee, Nuffield Foundn, 1988–97; Hon. Treas., Cancer Res. Campaign, 1991–2002. DL Cornwall, 1999. Hon. LLD Bath, 1987; Hon. DSc: Loughborough, 1989; Exeter, 1993; Strathclyde, 1995. *Publications:* Future of the British Car Industry, 1975; Realizing the Promise of a National Health Service, 1977; The Anatomy of Change: blueprint for a new era, 1994; numerous reports for Audit Commn on education, housing, social services and local government finance, 1984–87, and for CBI on UK economy, skills, transport, the infrastructure, urban regeneration and manufacturing. *Recreations:* walking, ground clearing, gardening. *Address:* Penberth, St Buryan, Penzance, Cornwall TR19 6HJ. *Fax:* (01736) 810722. *Club:* Travellers.

**BANISTER, Prof. David John,** PhD; Professor of Transport Studies, and Director, Transport Studies Unit, University of Oxford, 2006–15, now Emeritus Professor; Fellow of St Anne's College, Oxford, 2006–15, now Senior Research Fellow; *b* 10 July 1950; *s* of late Stephen Michael Alvin Banister and of Rachel Joan Banister; *m* 1985, Elizabeth Dawn Bucknell; three *d*. *Educ:* Royal Grammar Sch., Guildford; Nottingham Univ. (BA 1st Cl. Hons Geog.); Leeds Univ. (PhD Transport Studies 1976). CMILT (MCIT 1976; MILT 1999). Lectr in Geog., Univ. of Reading, 1975–78; University College London: Lectr in Transport Policy, 1979–88; Sen. Lectr, 1988–90; Reader in Transport Planning, 1990–95; Prof. of Transport Planning, 1995–2006; Acting Dir, Envmtl Change Inst., Oxford Univ., 2009–10. Vis. VSB Prof., Tinbergen Inst., Amsterdam, 1994–97; Vis. Prof., Univ. of Bodenkultur, Vienna, 2007. Non-exec. Dir, Taylor and Francis Gp PLC, 1990–2004. Dir, Res. Prog. on Transport and Envmt, ESRC, 1992–96; Chair, BIVEC-GIBET, 2012–13. Chair, Advanced Res. Grants SH3 Panel, European Res. Council, 2015–16; Member: Adv. Gps on Future Integrated Transport, Inland Surface Transport, Cities and Sustainability, EPSRC, 1994–2004; Team for Town and Country Planning, RAE 2001 and 2008, HEFCE. Chm., Econ. Commn for Europe's Task Force on Urban Transport Patterns and Land Use Planning, UN, 2000–02. FRSA 1988. Trustee: Ferguson Charitable Trust, 1979–; Civic Trust, 2005–09 (Chm., Policy Cttee, 2006–09). Jt Ed., Built Envmt, 1992–; Ed., Transport Reviews, 2001–; Ed., Spon series on Transport, Development and Sustainability, 1999–2006; Mem., editl bds of several jls. *Publications:* Transport Mobility and Deprivation in Inter-Urban Areas, 1980; (jtly) Transport and Public Policy Planning, 1981; Rural Transport and Planning, 1985; (jtly) Urban Transport and Planning, 1989; (jtly) Transport in a Free Market Economy, 1991; (jtly) Transport in Unified Europe: policies and challenges, 1993; (jtly) Transport, the Environment and Sustainable Development, 1993; Transport Planning, 1994, 2nd edn 2002; Transport and Urban Development, 1995; (jtly)

European Transport and Communications Networks: policy evolution and change, 1995; (jtly) Telematics and Transport Behaviour, 1996; Transport Policy and the Environment, 1998; (jtly) Environment, Land Use and Urban Policy, 1999; (jtly) European Transport Policy and Sustainable Mobility, 2000; (jtly) Encouraging Transport Alternatives: good practice in reducing travel, 2000; (jtly) Transport Investment and Economic Development, 2000; Unsustainable Transport, 2005; (jtly) Land Use and Transport: European perspectives on integrated policies, 2007; (jtly) Integrated Transport: from policy to practice, 2010; (jtly) The Transport System and Transport Policy, 2012; (jtly) Moving Towards Low Carbon Mobility, 2013; (jtly) Transport, Climate Change and the City, 2014; (jtly) Transport and Development, 2015; (jtly) The Imperatives of Sustainable Development: Needs, Justice, Limits, 2017; Inequality in Transport, 2018; (jtly) What Next for Sustainable Development?: our common future at thirty, 2019; contrib. books and internat. jls. *Recreations:* gardening, farming, walking, good company and conversation. *Address:* Transport Studies Unit, Oxford University Centre for the Environment, South Parks Road, Oxford OX1 3QY. *T:* (01865) 285066.

**BANKES-JONES, William Michael Roger;** Founder and Artistic Director, Tête à Tête, since 1998; *b* London, 23 Aug. 1963; *s* of Roger Myddleton Bankes-Jones and Patricia Mary Russell Bankes-Jones. *Educ:* Marlborough Coll., Wilts; Univ. of St Andrews (MA Hons Logic and Metaphysics and Moral Philosophy 1986). ITV Regl Th. Young Directors' Scheme, 1989–91; Associate Dir, Thorndike Th., Leatherhead, 1989; Associate Dir, Redgrave Th., Farnham, 1989–91; Staff Dir, ENO, 1991–97; productions for Tête à Tête include: Shorts, 1999–2001; Six-Pack, 2002; Push!, 2006; Odysseus Unwound, 2006; Salad Days, 2009–13; Britten's Canticles in Westminster Abbey for Tête à Tête and Streetwise Opera, 2002; A Nitro at the Opera for Royal Opera and BBC TV, 2003; directed and translated: Fledermaus, English Touring Opera, 2003; Hansel and Gretel, 2012, Pagliacci, 2018, Scottish Opera. Founder and Artistic Dir, Tête à Tête: the Opera Fest., 2007–. Chm., Opera and Music Th. Forum, 2002–. *Recreations:* surfing, cycling, campaigning, swimming against the tide. *Address:* c/o Performing Arts, A203 The Biscuit Factory, 100 Clements Road, SE16 4DG. *T:* (020) 7255 1362. *E:* info@performingarts.co.uk.

**BANKS, (Arthur) David;** journalist and broadcaster; Contributing Editor, Press Gazette, since 2006; Editor and Columnist, www.voiceofthenorth.net; *b* 13 Feb. 1948; *s* of Arthur Banks and Helen (*née* Renton); *m* 1975, Gemma Newton; one *s* one *d*. *Educ:* Boteler Grammar Sch., Warrington. Asst Man. Editor, NY Post, 1979–81; Night Editor, then Asst Editor, The Sun, 1981–86; Dep. Man. Editor, NY Daily News, 1986–87; Dep. Editor, The Australian, 1987–89; Editor: Daily Telegraph Mirror (Sydney), 1989–92; Daily Mirror, 1992–94; Editl Dir, Mirror Gp Newspapers, 1994–97; Consultant Ed., Sunday Mirror, 1997–98; Dir of Information, Mirror Gp, 1998–99. Presenter, Breakfast Show: LBC, 1997–99; Talk Radio, 1999–2000. *Recreations:* writing, enjoying my second-chance life. *Address:* Ross Cottage, 4 Crookham, Cornhill-on-Tweed, Northumberland TD12 4SY. *T:* 07931 501252. *E:* david_banks@hotmail.com.

**BANKS, Caroline;** Chairman, Home-Start Westminster, since 2016 (Trustee, since 2014); *b* 24 April 1950; *d* of Geoffrey Banks and Pamela Dane Banks. *Educ:* Kitwe Girls' High Sch., Zambia; Middlesex Poly. (BA Hons). Office of Fair Trading: various posts, 1975–82; Head, Consumer Credit Licensing Bureau, 1982–88; Principal Estabt and Finance Officer, 1988–97; Dir, Consumer Regulation Enforcement Div., OFT, 1998–2003; non-exec. Dir, Financial Ombudsman Service, 2004–08. Member: Billing and Direct Selling Codes Panel, Energy Retail Assoc., 2003–14; CSAB, 2004–12. *Recreations:* gardening, family history. *Address:* 40 Meadowcroft Road, Palmers Green, N13 4EA.

**BANKS, Charles Augustus,** III; Partner, Clayton, Dubilier & Rice Inc., 2006–10; *b* Greensboro, N Carolina, 20 Dec. 1940; *s* of late Charles Augustus Banks, Jr and Madge McMillan Banks; *m* 1962, Marie Ann Sullivan; two *s* one *d*. *Educ:* Brown Univ. (BA 1962); Young Exec. Inst. of Professional Mgt, Univ. of N Carolina; Wharton Sch., Univ. of Pennsylvania (AMP 1989). Ensign/Lt, USNR (Active), 1962–64. Plant manager, Minerals Recovery Corp., 1964–65; mortgage banker, Cameron-Brown Co., 1965–67; Ferguson Enterprises Inc.: Peebles Supply Div., 1967–69; Outside Sales, Lenz Supply Div., 1969–70; Vice-Pres. and Gen. Manager, Alexandria, Va, 1970–77; Pres. and Gen. Manager, Herndon, Va, 1977–81; Dir, 1977; Regl Manager, 1981–87; Sen. Exec. Vice-Pres., 1987–89; Pres. and Chief Ops Officer, 1989–93; Pres. and CEO, 1993–2001; Chm., 2001–06; Dir, Wolseley plc (parent co. of Ferguson Enterprises), 1992–2006, Chief Exec., 2001–06. Chm., US Foodservice Inc., 2007; non-exec. Dir, Bunzl PLC, 2002–11.

**BANKS, Christopher Nigel,** CBE 2003; Chairman: Quality Assurance Agency for Higher Education, since 2014; The Spice Tailor Ltd, since 2015; Cracker Drinks Co. Ltd, since 2016; Founder, Big Thoughts, since 2001; *b* 1 Sept. 1959; *s* of James Nigel Alexander and Pamela Ethel Banks; *m* 1982, Karen Jane Dauber; one *s* two *d*. *Educ:* Bristol Cathedral Sch.; Birmingham Univ. (BA Combined Hons Latin and French); Aston Univ. (MBA). Client Services, A. C. Nielsen, 1983–85; Marketing Manager, Mars Inc., 1985–89; Marketing Dir, H. P. Bulmer, 1989–92; Man. Dir, URM Agencies, part of Allied Domecq, 1992–95; CEO, Justerini & Brooks, part of Grand Metropolitan, 1996–97; Man. Dir, Coca-Cola GB, 1997–2001. Mem., Women and Work Commn, 2004–07. Chairman: London Employer Coalition, 1999–2004; Directgov, 2009–10; Public Chairs' Forum, 2009–16; Ind. Coll. Partnership, 2011–; Mem., Nat. Council, and Chm., Young People's Learning Cttee, 2000–04, Chm., 2004–10, LSC; Dep. Chm., Nat. Employment Panel, 2001–08. Dep. Pro Chancellor, Univ. of Birmingham, 2009–14. Pres., British Soft Drinks Assoc., 2003–05. Gov., University of Birmingham Sch., 2014– (Chm., 2015–). *Address:* Quality Assurance Agency for Higher Education, Southgate House, Southgate Street, Gloucester GL1 1UB.

**BANKS, David;** *see* Banks, A. D.

**BANKS, Elizabeth Christina,** CBE 2017; DL; President, Royal Horticultural Society, 2010–13, now Emeritus; *b* Rockingham Castle, 30 Sept. 1941; *d* of Leslie Swain Saunders and Elizabeth Saunders; *m* 1963, (William) Lawrence Banks; two *s*. *Educ:* Fritham House Sch.; New York Botanical Gardens; Greenwich Univ. (Dip. Landscape Architecture 1981). CMLI 1982. Associate, Land Use Consultants, 1981–86; Chm. and Man. Dir, Elizabeth Banks Associates, 1986–2006. Chairman: Gardens Cttee, Historic Houses Assoc., 1989–93; Queensway Coronation Fund, 1999–2010; Trustee: Gateway Gardens Trust, 2006–09; Member: Arboreta Adv. Cttee, Westonbirt Arboretum and Bedgebury Pinetum, 2004–; Council, RHS, 2007–13. Mem., Kington Town Council, 2001– (Mayor, 2006–10, 2015–17). Liveryman, Gardeners' Co., 2011. DL Herefordshire, 2008. FCIHort (FIHort 2011). Hon. DDes Greenwich, 2011; Hon. DSc Worcester, 2011. *Publications:* Creating Period Gardens, 1991; articles in Country Life and other mags. *Recreations:* gardening, fishing, travelling, walking. *Address:* Ridgebourne House, Ridgebourne Road, Kington, Herefordshire HR5 3EG. *T:* (01544) 230218. *E:* banks@hergest.co.uk. *Club:* Boodle's.

**BANKS, Mrs Gillian Theresa,** CB 1990; *b* 7 Feb. 1933; *d* of Percy and Enid Brimblecombe; *m* 1960, John Anthony Gorst Banks (marr. diss. 1993); one *s* two *d*. *Educ:* Walthamstow Hall Sch., Sevenoaks; Lady Margaret Hall, Oxford (BA). Asst Principal, Colonial Office, 1955; Principal, Treasury, 1966; Department of Health and Social Security: Asst Sec., 1972; Under Sec. 1981; Dir, Health Authy Finance, 1985; Dir, OPCS and Registrar Gen. for Eng. and Wales, 1986; Dir, Carnegie Inquiry into the Third Age,

1990; led Functions, Manpower and Sen. Management Review of Wider DoH, 1994; Dir, Retirement Income Inquiry, 1994; Mem., Camden and Islington HA, 1995; non-exec. Dir, Royal Free Hampstead NHS Trust, 1997–2004. Policy Consultant, Age Concern, England, 1996; Hon. Treas., Age Concern Camden, 1997–2002. Lay Mem., Council, RPSGB, 1996–2001. *Address:* Flat 3, Andrew Court, 2 Wedderburn Road, NW3 5QE. *T:* (020) 7435 4973.

BANKS, Gordon Raymond; Managing Director, Cartmore Building Supply Company Ltd, since 1986; *b* 14 June 1955; *s* of William Banks and Patricia Marion Banks (*née* Macknight); *m* 1981, Lynda Nicol; one *s* one *d*. *Educ:* Univ. of Stirling (BA Hons Hist. and Politics); Glasgow Coll. of Building and Printing (Construction Technician). Chief Buyer: Barratt (Edinburgh) Ltd, 1975–84; Barratt (Falkirk) Ltd, 1984–86. Parly Officer for Dr Richard Simpson, MSP, 1999–2003; researcher for Martin O'Neill, MP, 2003–05. Mem., Nat. Policy Forum, and Quality of Life Policy Forum, Lab. Party, 2002–05. MP (Lab) Ochil and S Perthshire, 2005–15; contested (Lab) same seat, 2015. PPS to Minister for Pension Reform, DWP, 2006–07, to Sec. of State for Culture, Media and Sport, 2007–08, to Sec. of State for Work and Pensions, 2008–10; Shadow Business Minister, 2010–11; Shadow Scotland Office Minister, 2012–15. Mem. Exec. Cttee, Assoc. of Former MPs, 2015– (Chm., Scottish Br., 2018–). *Recreations:* music (song-writing), motor sport, football.

BANKS, Jeremy, (Banx); pocket cartoonist, Financial Times, since 1989; Cartoon Editor, The Reaper, since 2015; *b* London, 10 May 1959; *s* of Peter William Banks and Sheila Lascelles Banks (*née* Fleming); *m* 1998, Elaine Pennicott; four *d*. *Educ:* Lycée français de Londres; Hounslow Bor. Coll.; Maidstone Coll. of Art. Freelance cartoonist, 1980–, for: Private Eye; Punch; London Evening Standard; Daily Express; Mail on Sunday; New Statesman; She; Men Only; Mayfair; Penthouse; Oink!; Toxic; Vice.com; Woodstock; Bladon News; Wall St Journal; Barron's; Weekly Humorist. Float designer, Nice Carnival, 2002–09. Pocket Cartoonist of Year, Cartoon Art Trust, 2008, 2012. *Publications:* Cubes, 1982; The Many Deaths of Norman Spittal, 1997; Big Fat Sleepy Cat, 2001; The Dewsburys, 2006; Frankenthing, 2014; Frankentruc, 2018. *Recreations:* family, art, reading, watching DVD box sets, swimming. *E:* banxcartoons@gmail.com.

BANKS, Lynne Reid; writer; *b* 1929; *d* of Dr James Reid-Banks and Muriel (Pat) (*née* Marsh); *m* 1965, Chaim Stephenson, sculptor; three *s*. *Educ:* schooling mainly in Canada; RADA. Actress, 1949–54; reporter for ITN, 1955–62; English teacher in kibbutz in Western Galilee, Israel, 1963–71; full-time writer, 1971–; writing includes plays for stage, television and radio. J. M. Barrie Award, Action for Children's Arts, 2013. *Publications: plays:* It Never Rains, 1954; All in a Row, 1956; The Killer Dies Twice, 1956; Already, It's Tomorrow, 1962; (for children) Travels of Yoshi and the Tea-Kettle, 1993; *fiction:* The L-Shaped Room, 1960 (trans. 10 langs; filmed 1962); An End to Running, 1962 (trans. 2 langs); Children at the Gate, 1968; The Backward Shadow, 1970; Two is Lonely, 1974; Defy the Wilderness, 1981; The Warning Bell, 1984; Casualties, 1986; Fair Exchange, 1998; *biographical fiction:* Dark Quartet: the story of the Brontes, 1976 (Yorks Arts Lit. Award, 1977); Path to the Silent Country: Charlotte Bronte's years of fame, 1977; *history:* Letters to my Israeli Sons, 1979; Torn Country, 1982; *for young adults:* One More River, 1973; Sarah and After, 1975; My Darling Villain, 1977 (trans. 3 langs); The Writing on the Wall, 1981; Melusine, 1988 (trans. 3 langs); Broken Bridge, 1994 (trans. 2 langs); *for children:* The Adventures of King Midas, 1976 (trans. 4 langs); The Farthest-Away Mountain, 1977; I, Houdini, 1978 (trans. 4 langs); The Indian in the Cupboard, 1980 (trans. 24 langs) (Pacific NW Choice Award, 1984; Calif. Young Readers Medal, 1985; Va Children's Choice, 1988; Mass. Children's Choice, 1988; Rebecca Caudill Award, Ill, 1989; Arizona Children's Choice, 1989; filmed, 1995); Maura's Angel, 1984 (trans. 2 langs); The Fairy Rebel, 1985 (trans. 3 langs); Return of the Indian, 1986 (trans. 5 langs); The Secret of the Indian, 1989 (trans. 4 langs); The Magic Hare, 1992; Mystery of the Cupboard, 1993 (trans. 3 langs); Harry the Poisonous Centipede, 1996; Angela and Diabola, 1997 (trans. 2 langs); The Key to the Indian, 1999; Moses in Egypt, 1998 (trans. 3 langs); Alice-by-Accident, 2000; Harry the Poisonous Centipede's Big Adventure, 2000; The Dungeon, 2002; Stealing Stacey, 2004; Tiger, Tiger, 2004; Harry the Poisonous Centipede Goes to Sea, 2005; Bad Cat, Good Cat, 2011; The Wrong-Coloured Dragon, 2012; Uprooted: a Canadian warstory, 2014; short stories; articles in The Times, The Guardian, Sunday Telegraph, Observer, TES, TLS, Independent on Sunday, Sunday Times, Spectator, Saga Magazine, and in overseas periodicals. *Recreations:* theatre, gardening, visiting schools overseas and at home. *Address:* c/o Watson, Little Ltd, Suite 315, Screenworks, 22 Highbury Grove, N5 2ER. *W:* www.lynnereidbanks.com.

BANKS, Matthew Richard William; *see* Gordon Banks, M. R. W.

BANKS, Rt Rev. Norman; *see* Richborough, Bishop Suffragan of.

BANKS, Richard Lee, CBE 2016; Chairman, Topaz Finance Ltd, since 2016; *b* 15 June 1951; *s* of Richard Cyril Banks and Mary Banks; *m* 1978, Elaine Helena Kret; two *s*. *Educ:* Stockport Secondary Technical High Sch.; Manchester Poly. (BA Hons Business Studies). Joined Midland Bank, 1974, various mgt posts, 1978–87; Girobank: Gen. Manager, 1987–91; Sen. Gen. Manager, 1991–94; Dir, Corporate Banking, 1994–96; Man. Dir, 1996–2000; Alliance & Leicester plc: Dir, 1998–2008; Distribution Ops Dir, 2000–02; Man. Dir, Wholesale Banking, 2002–08; Man. Dir, 2009–10, CEO, 2010–16, Bradford & Bingley plc; Chief Executive Officer: UK Asset Resolution Ltd, 2010–16; Northern Rock (Asset Mgt) plc, 2010–16; Computershare Mortgage Services Ltd, 2016. Non-exec. Chm., Shop Direct Finance, 2014–; non-exec. Dir, Ritz Club, 2017–. *Recreations:* reading, cottage renovation.

BANKS, Robert George; *b* 18 Jan. 1937; *s* of late George Walmsley Banks, MBE, and Olive Beryl Banks (*née* Tyler); *m* 1967, Diana Margaret Payne Crawford (marr. diss. 2004); four *s* one *d* (of whom one *s* one *d* are twins). *Educ:* Haileybury. Lt-Comdr RNR. Jt Founder Dir, Antocks Lairn Ltd, 1963–67. Mem., Alcohol Educn and Res. Council, 1982–88. Mem., Paddington BC, 1959–65. MP (C) Harrogate, Feb. 1974–97. PPS to Minister of State and to Under-Sec. of State, FCO, 1979–82. Member: Select Cttee on Foreign Affairs (and its Overseas Develt Sub-Cttee), 1982; Select Cttee on Trade and Industry, 1994–97; Jt Sec., Cons. Defence Cttee, 1976–79; Chairman: British-Sudan All Party Parly Gp, 1984–97; All-Party Tourism Gp, 1992–97 (Sec., 1973–79; Vice-Chm., 1979–92); Vice-Chm., Yorks Cons. Mems' Cttee, 1983–97. Member: Council of Europe, 1977–81; WEU, 1977–81; N Atlantic Assembly, 1981–95. Introd Licensing (Alcohol Educn and Res.) Act, 1981; sponsored Licensing (Restaurants Meals) Act, 1987. Reports: for Mil. Cttee of WEU, Report on Nuclear, Biol. and Chem. Protection, adopted by WEU Assembly April 1980; North Atlantic Assembly document, The Technology of Military Space Systems, 1982. *Publications:* (jtly) Britain's Home Defence Gamble (pamphlet), 1979; New Jobs from Pleasure, report on tourism, 1985; Tories for Tourism, 1995. *Recreations:* travel, architecture, contemporary art. *Address:* Brett House, 305 Munster Road, SW6 6BJ.

BANKS, Prof. William McKerrell, PhD; FREng, FIMechE; FRSE; Professor of Advanced Materials, University of Strathclyde, Glasgow, 1991–2008, now Emeritus; President, Institution of Mechanical Engineers, 2008–09; *b* Dreghorn, Ayrshire, 28 March 1943; *s* of William and Jeanie Banks; *m* 1966, Martha Ruthven (*née* Hair); three *s*. *Educ:* Univ. of Strathclyde (BSc 1st Cl. Hons Mech. Engrg 1965; MSc 1966; PhD 1977); FIMechE 1987; FIMMM 1993; FREng 2001. Sen. Res. Engr, G & J Weir Ltd, 1966–70; University of Strathclyde: Lectr, Sen. Lectr, then Reader, 1970–91; Dir, External Relns and Dir of Res., Dept of Mech. Engrg, 1990–2004. Director: Centre for Advanced Structural Materials, 1995–2008; Scottish Polymer Technol. Network, 1997–2006; Dir of Res. and Trng, Faraday Plastics Partnership, 2002–06; Pres., Engrg Professors' Council, 2001–03 (Mem. Cttee, 1999–2013); Assessor, DTI Technol. Prog., 2001–06; Member: DSAC, 1997–2002 (Mem., Wkg Party on Rev. of use of polymer composite materials in platforms, 1997–99); EPSRC Peer Rev. Coll., 2000–13; Exec. Cttee, Campaign for Sci. and Engrg, 2002–11; Fellowship Sectional Cttee for Engrg, RSE, 2003–07; Engrg Council, 2006–08; Engrg Technol. Bd, 2008–09; Educn and Skills Panel, Engrg UK, 2009–15; Qualifications Design Team for Technol Studies and Engrg, Scottish Qualifications Authy, 2010–14. Mem. and Lead Assessor for Mech. Engrg Res. and Secondments Cttee, 2007–11, Professorial Mentor, 2012–18, Steering Gp Mem., Res. Fellowships and Engrg for Develt Res. Fellowships, 2018–, Royal Acad. of Engrg. External Advr, Materials Prog., QinetiQ, 2002–06. Chm., Professional Engineering Publishing, 2004–06. Mem. Council, Inst. of Materials, 1997–2001; Chairman: Trustee Bd and Council, IMechE, 2008–09 (Chm., Awards Cttee, Trustee Bd, 2010–11); Resolution Panel, BCS, 2011–17 (Lay Mem., 2018–). Pres., Engrg and Technol. Assoc. (Scotland), 2010–11. FRSE 2003. Lectures internat. incl. China, Russia, Malaysia, Singapore, Australia. Ed. in Chief, IMechE Procs Jl of Materials: Design and Applications, 2000–14; served on several editl panels. James Clayton Res. Prize, 1977, Donald Julien Groen Prize, 1994, 2001, 150th Anniv. Gold Medal Award, 1998, James Clayton Prize, 2011, IMechE; James Alfred Ewing Medal, Royal Soc. and ICE, 2007. *Publications:* co-edited: Advances in Turbine Materials: design and manufacturing, 1997; Advanced Materials for 21st Century Turbines and Power Plant, 2000; Pressure Equipment Technology: theory and practice, 2003; Engineering Issues in Turbine Machinery, Power Plant and Renewables, 2003; What God hath Joined: an answer to contemporary issues in marriage, 2005; Power Generation in an Era of Climate Change, 2007; over 200 papers and chapters in books. *Recreations:* involved extensively in Bible teaching, enjoy gardening, reading, family and travelling. *Address:* 19 Dunure Drive, Hamilton ML3 9EY. *T:* (01698) 823730, *Fax:* (01698) 823730. *E:* bill.banks@strath.ac.uk.

BANN, Prof. Stephen, CBE 2004; PhD; FBA 1998; FSA; Professor of History of Art, 2000–08, now Emeritus, and Senior Research Fellow, since 2008, University of Bristol; *b* 1 Aug. 1942; *s* of Harry Bann, OBE and Edna Bann (*née* Pailin). *Educ:* Winchester Coll. (schol.); King's Coll., Cambridge (schol.; BA Hist. 1963; MA; PhD 1967). FSA 2009. State Res. Studentship, 1963–66, in Paris, 1964–65; University of Kent: Lectr, 1967–75, Sen. Lectr, 1975–80, in History; Reader in Modern Cultural Studies, 1980–88; Prof. of Modern Cultural Studies, 1988–2000; Sen. Fellow, 2003–08, Beatrix Farrand Distinguished Fellow, 2009, Dumbarton Oaks Res. Liby, Washington; Sen. Mellon Fellow, Canadian Centre for Architecture, Montreal, 2003; Leverhulme Emeritus Fellow, 2009–10. Visiting Professor: Rennes Univ., 1994; Johns Hopkins Univ., 1996–98; Bologna Univ., 1998; Warburg Foundn, Hamburg, 2002; Inst Nat. d'Histoire de l'Art, Paris, 2003; Edmond J. Safra Prof., Center for Advanced Studies in the Visual Arts, Washington, 2005; Pilkington Vis. Prof., Univ. of Manchester, 2010; Sen. Vis. Scholar, Yale Center for British Art, 2012–14; Hon. Prof., Univ. of Kent, 2011–14; Slade Prof. of Fine Art, Univ. of Cambridge, 2017–18. Getty Lectures, Univ. of Southern Calif, 2004. Member: Art Panel, Arts Council of GB, 1975–78; Humanities Res. Bd, British Acad., 1997–98; Chm. Res. Cttee, AHRB, 1998–2000; Res. Awards Adv. Cttee, Leverhulme Trust, 1998–2005. Pres., Comité Internat. d'Histoire de l'Art, 2000–04. Mem. Council, Friends of Canterbury Cathedral, 1990–2000. Trustee, Little Sparta Trust, 1994–2013. Dep. Ed., then Ed., 20th Century Studies, 1969–76; Adv. Ed., Reaktion Books, 1985–. MAE 2014. Hon. DLitt Kent, 2016. R. H. Gapper Prize for French Studies, Soc. for French Studies, 2002. *Publications:* (ed) Concrete Poetry: an international anthology, 1967; Experimental Painting, 1970; (ed) The Tradition of Constructivism, 1974; The Clothing of Clio, 1984; The True Vine: on visual representation and the Western tradition, 1989; The Inventions of History, 1990; Under the Sign: John Bargrave as collector, traveler and witness, 1994; The Sculpture of Stephen Cox, 1995; Romanticism and the Rise of History, 1995; Paul Delaroche: history painted, 1997; Parallel Lines: printmakers, painters and photographers in nineteenth-century France, 2001; Jannis Kounellis, 2003; (ed) The Reception of Walter Pater in Europe, 2004; Ways Around Modernism, 2007; (ed) The Coral Mind: Adrian Stokes' engagement with architecture, art history, criticism and psychoanalysis, 2007; (with L. Whiteley) Painting History: Delaroche and Lady Jane Grey, 2010; (ed) Art and the Early Photographic Album, 2011; (ed) Interlacing Words and Things: bridging the nature-culture opposition in gardens and landscape, 2012; Distinguished Images: prints in the visual economy of nineteenth-century France, 2013; (ed) Midway: letters from Ian Hamilton Finlay to Stephen Bann 1964–69, 2014; Bernard Lassus, the Landscape Approach, 2014; (ed) Stonypath Days: letters between Ian Hamilton Finlay and Stephen Bann 1970–72, 2016. *Recreations:* travel, collecting. *Address:* 2 New Street, St Dunstan's, Canterbury, Kent CT2 8AU. *T:* (01227) 761135; Department of History of Art, University of Bristol, Bristol BS8 1TB. *Club:* Savile.

BANNATYNE, Hon. Lord; Iain Alexander Scott Peebles; a Senator of the College of Justice in Scotland, since 2008. *Educ:* Strathclyde Univ. Admitted to Faculty of Advocates, 1979; Temp. Sheriff, 1991; Advocate Depute, 1992–95; QC (Scot.) 1993; Sheriff of Glasgow and Strathkelvin, 1995–99; Commercial Sheriff, 1999; Temp. Judge, Court of Session and High Court of Justiciary, 2003–08. *Address:* Court of Session, Parliament House, Edinburgh EH1 1RQ.

BANNATYNE, (Walker) Duncan, OBE 2004; Chairman, Bannatyne Group plc (Chairman: Bannatyne Fitness Ltd, 1996–2016; Bannatyne Hotels Ltd, 1996–97; Bannatyne Casinos Ltd, 2003–16; Bannatyne Housing Ltd, 2005–16); *b* 2 Feb. 1949; one *s* five *d*. RN, 1964–68. Started own business, Duncan's Super Ices; established: Quality Care Homes, 1986, sold 1996; Just Learning, 1996, sold 2002. Has appeared in BBC TV series, Dragons' Den, 2005–14. Funded Bannatyne Hospices for Children with HIV and Aids, Romania and Colombia; Founder, Bannatyne Charitable Trust, 2008. *Publications:* Anyone Can Do It: my story, 2006; Wake Up and Change Your Life, 2008; How to be Smart with Your Money, 2009; How to be Smart with Your Time, 2010; 43 Mistakes Businesses Make and How to Avoid Them, 2011; 37 Questions Everyone in Business Needs to Answer, 2012. *Address:* Bannatyne Group plc, Power House, Haughton Road, Darlington, Co. Durham DL1 1ST.

BANNENBERG, Jennifer Bridget; *see* Tanfield, J. B.

BANNER, Charles Edward Raymond; QC 2019; *b* Birmingham, 3 June 1980; *s* of Dr Edward Raymond Banner and Rachel Nimmo Banner (*née* Macfarlane); *m* 2013, Tetyana Nesterchuk; one *d*. *Educ:* King Edward's Sch., Birmingham; Lincoln Coll., Oxford (BA Hons Lit.Hum. 2002); City Univ., London (DipLaw 2003); King's Coll. London (Postgrad. Dip. Eur. Community Law 2004). Adv. Cert. Internat. Arbitration, MCIArb 2016. Res. Analyst, then Res. Fellow, Policy Exchange, 2002–04; intern (pt-time), AIRE Centre, 2003–04; called to the Bar, Lincoln's Inn, 2004; pupil barrister, 2004–05, barrister, 2006–, Landmark Chambers; on secondment: as Judicial Asst to Law Lords, H of L, 2005–06; as Pegasus Schol. to Mayer Brown JSM, Hong Kong, Hong Kong Court of Appeal and Court of Final Appeal, 2008. UK Mem., Mgt Bd, EU Fundamental Rights Agency, 2017–. Independent Member: JNCC, 2017–; UK and Ireland Regulatory Sub-Bd, RICS, 2018–. Associate Mem., Hong Kong Inst. of Arbitrators, 2016. Patron, Tate. *Publications:* (with

Alex Deane) Off With Their Wigs: judicial revolution in modern Britain, 2003; (ed) The Aarhus Convention: a guide for UK lawyers, 2015. *Recreations:* running, mountaineering, travel, collecting and viewing art, rock music, theatre. *Address:* Landmark Chambers, 180 Fleet Street, EC4A 2HG. *T:* (020) 7421 4234. *E:* cbanner@landmarkchambers.co.uk.

**BANNER, Gregory Stuart;** QC 2018; *b* Orpington, 24 Jan. 1966; *s* of late Francis John Banner and of Lillian May Banner; *m* 1996, Elisabeth Louise Heaton; two *d*. *Educ:* Dulwich Coll.; Trinity Hall, Cambridge (BA Hons Law 1988; MA). Called to the Bar, Gray's Inn, 1989; in practice as barrister, specialising in commercial chancery and company law, 1989–; Jun. Counsel to Crown, B Panel, 1997–2003. *Recreations:* cycling, triathlon, ski-ing. *Address:* Maitland Chambers, 7 Stone Buildings, Lincoln's Inn, WC2A 3SZ. *T:* (020) 7406 1200. *E:* gbanner@maitlandchambers.com.

**BANNER, Rev. Prof. Michael Charles,** DPhil; Dean of Chapel, Director of Studies, and Fellow, Trinity College, Cambridge, since 2006; *b* 19 April 1961; *s* of Maurice Banner and Maureen (*née* Ince); *m* 1st, 1983, Elizabeth Jane Wheare (marr. diss. 2001); two *d*; 2nd, 2007, Sally-Ann Gannon; two *d*. *Educ:* Bromsgrove Sch.; Balliol Coll., Oxford (BA Philos. and Theol. 1st cl. 1983; MA 1985; DPhil 1986); DD Cantab 2016. Ordained deacon 1986, priest 1987. Bampton Res. Fellow, St Peter's Coll., Oxford, 1985–88; Dean, Chaplain, Fellow and Dir of Studies in Philosophy and Theol., 1988–94, Tutor 1989–94, Peterhouse, Cambridge; F. D. Maurice Prof. of Moral and Social Theology, KCL, 1994–2004; Prof. of Public Policy and Ethics in the Life Scis, Univ. of Edinburgh, 2004–06; Dir, ESRC Genomics Policy and Res. Forum, 2004–06. Vis. Fellow, Merton Coll., Oxford, 1993; Peden Sen. Fellow, Rice Univ., 2012. Chairman: HM Govt Cttee of Enquiry on Ethics of Emerging Technologies in Breeding of Farm Animals, 1993–95; Home Office Animal Procedures Cttee, 1998–2006; CJD Incidents Panel, DoH, 2000–04; Shell Panel on Animal Testing, 2002–09. Member: Royal Commn on Envmtl Pollution, 1996–2002; Agric. and Envmt Biotech. Commn, 2000–03; Human Tissue Authy, 2005–14; Cttee of Reference, F&C Asset Mgt, 2007–14; Working Gp on animals containing human material, Acad. of Med. Scis, 2010–11; Scientific Adv. Cttee on Medical Implications of Less Lethal Weapons, MoD, 2012–; Adv. Stewardship Cttee, Friends Life, 2014–16; Nuffield Council on Bioethics, 2015–17. Asst Curate, Balsham, W Wratting, Weston Colville and W Wickham, 2000–04. Member: C of E Bd for Social Responsibility, 1995–2001; C of E Doctrine Commn, 1996–99. Trustee, Scott Holland Fund, 1996–99. Baron de Lancey Lectr, Cambridge Univ., 1998; Bampton Lectr, Oxford Univ., 2013. Consultant Editor, Studies in Christian Ethics, 1996–2007; Corresp. Editor, Jl of Ethical Theory and Moral Practice, 1997–2004; Mem. Editl Bd, Internat. Jl of Systematic Theology, 1998–2004. *Publications:* The Justification of Science and the Rationality of Religious Belief, 1990; The Practice of Abortion: a critique, 1999; Christian Ethics and Contemporary Moral Problems, 1999; The Doctrine of God and Theological Ethics, 2006; Christian Ethics: a brief history, 2009; Ethics of Everyday Life, 2014; various articles in learned jls. *Recreations:* galleries, mountain biking, cross country ski-ing, horse riding, rowing. *Address:* Trinity College, Cambridge CB2 1TQ. *Club:* National.

**BANNERMAN, Bernard;** *see* Arden, A. P. R.

**BANNERMAN, David C.;** *see* Campbell Bannerman.

**BANNERMAN, Sir David (Gordon),** 15th Bt *cr* 1682 (NS), of Elsick, Kincardineshire; OBE 1977; Ministry of Defence, 1963–97; *b* 18 Aug. 1935; *s* of Lt-Col Sir Donald Arthur Gordon Bannerman, 13th Bt and Barbara Charlotte, *d* of late Lt-Col Alexander Cameron, OBE, IMS; *S* brother, Sir Alexander Patrick Bannerman, 14th Bt, 1989; *m* 1960, Mary Prudence, *d* of Rev. Philip Frank Ardagh-Walter; four *d*. *Educ:* Gordonstoun; New Coll., Oxford (MA); University Coll. London (MSc 1999). 2nd Lieut Queen's Own Cameron Highlanders, 1954–56. HMOCS (Tanzania), 1960–63. Chm., Gordonstoun Assoc., 1997–2000. *Recreations:* painting, ornithology, architecture. *Address:* Old Hall Cottage, Woodley's Yard, Southwold, Suffolk IP18 6HP.
*See also* M. A. O'Neill.

**BANNISTER, Clive Christopher Roger;** Group Chief Executive, Phoenix Group plc, since 2011; *b* London, 28 Oct. 1958; *s* of Sir Roger Gilbert Bannister, CH, CBE and of Moyra Elver Bannister; *m* 1992, Marjorie Barfuss; three *s*. *Educ:* Exeter Coll., Oxford (BA PPE 2000; MA 2005). Banker, First Nat. Bank of Boston, 1981–85; Partner, Booz Allen and Hamilton, 1985–94; Gp Man. Dir, HSBC, 1994–2010. Dir, ABI, 2018–. Chm., Mus. of London, 2013–. *Recreations:* woodwork, military history, running, cycling. *Address:* Phoenix Group plc, Juxon House, 100 St Paul's Churchyard, EC4M 8BU. *T:* (020) 3735 0900, *Fax:* (020) 7489 4860. *E:* clive.bannister@thephoenixgroup.com. *Club:* Athenæum.

**BANNISTER, Edward Alexander,** CMG 2017; QC 1991; *b* Watford, 12 Aug. 1942; *s* of Edward Bannister and Antonina Bannister; *m* 1965, Pamela Fay Webber; two *s* one *d*. *Educ:* St John's Sch., Leatherhead; Keble Coll., Oxford (BA Lit.Hum.). Called to the Bar, Lincoln's Inn, 1974, Bencher, 1995; Commercial Court Judge, Eastern Caribbean Supreme Court, 2009–15.

**BANNISTER, (Richard) Matthew;** broadcaster and journalist; presenter: Last Word, Radio 4, since 2006; Folk on Foot podcast, since 2018; *b* 16 March 1957; *s* of late Richard Neville Bannister and Olga Margaret Bannister; *m* 1st, 1984, Amanda Gerrard Walker (*d* 1988); one *d*; 2nd, 1989, Shelagh Margaret Macleod (*d* 2005); one *s*; 3rd, 2007, Katherine Jane Hood (marr. diss. 2013); partner, 2013, Kate McGuire. *Educ:* King Edward VII Sch., Sheffield; Nottingham Univ. (LLB Hons). Presenter, BBC Radio Nottingham, 1978–81; Reporter/Presenter: Capital Radio, 1981–83; Newsbeat, Radio 1, 1983–85; Dep. Head, 1985–87, Head, 1987–88, News and Talks, Capital Radio; BBC, 1988–2000: Man. Ed., Gtr London Radio, 1988–91; Project Co-ordinator: Charter Renewal, 1991–93; Prog. Strategy Review, 1993; Controller, BBC Radio 1, 1993–98; Dir, BBC Radio, 1996–98; Chief Exec., BBC Prodn, 1999–2000; Dir of Mkting and Communications, BBC, 2000; presenter: BBC Radio 5 Live, 2002–06; Outlook, BBC World Service, 2008–18; Chairman: Trust the DJ, 2001–02; Wire Free Prodns Ltd, 2012–. Mem. Bd, Chichester Fest. Theatre, 1999–2003. Fellow, Radio Acad., 1998. Hon. DLitt Nottingham, 2011. *Recreations:* theatre, music, design, walking. *Address:* c/o Knight Ayton Management, 29 Gloucester Place, W1U 8HX. *T:* (020) 3795 1806. *E:* info@knightayton.co.uk.

**BANNON, Michael Joseph,** FRCPI, FRCPCH; Postgraduate Dean, Department of Postgraduate Medical and Dental Education, Oxford, since 2003; *b* 2 May 1954; *s* of Christopher Bannon and Ann (*née* Kelly); *m* 1988, Prof. Yvonne Helen Carter, CBE (*d* 2009); one *s*. *Educ:* Trinity Coll., Dublin (MB BCh, BAO 1978; MA 1992; DCH 1979); MA Oxon; Univ. of Keele (MSc). FRCPI 1993; FRCPCH 1993. Consultant Paediatrician: City Gen. Hosp., N Staffs, 1990–92; Warwick Hosp., 1992–96; Northwick Park Hosp., 1996–2003. Sen. Lectr, Warwick Univ., 1992–96. Hon. FFPH 2014. *Publications:* Protecting Children from Abuse and Neglect in Primary Care, 2003; contrib. papers on child protection and med. educn. *Recreation:* Irish folk music. *Address:* Health Education England, Chancellor Court, 4150, Oxford Business Park South, Oxford OX4 2GX. *T:* (01865) 785556.

**BANO, (Ernest) Andrew (Louis);** an Upper Tribunal Judge (formerly a Social Security and Child Support Commissioner), 2000–13; *b* 7 May 1944; *s* of late Imre Bano and Susanne Bano; *m* 1985, Elizabeth Anne Sheehy; three *s* one *d*. *Educ:* Cardinal Vaughan Meml Sch.; Inns of Court Sch. of Law. Trng Consultant, 1966–69; Trng Develt Officer, BEA, 1969–72; called to the Bar, Gray's Inn, 1973; in practice at Common Law Bar, 1973–88; Head of Chambers, 1986–88; Chm. (part-time), Industrial Tribunals, 1984–88; Chm., Employment Tribunals, 1988–2000; Dep. Social Security Comr, 1996–2000; Legal Chm. (part-time), Pensions Appeal Tribunals, 2001–05; Pres., War Pensions and Armed Forces Compensation Chamber, First-tier Tribunal, 2009–12. *Publications:* War Pensions and Armed Forces Compensation: law and practice, 2016; (ed jtly) Atkin's Court Forms Tribunals and Inquiries, 2016–; (ed jtly) Atkin's Court Forms Social Security, 2017. *Recreations:* opera, amateur radio, woodwork. *Club:* Athenæum.

**BANTING, Ven. (Kenneth) Mervyn (Lancelot Hadfield);** Archdeacon of the Isle of Wight, 1996–2003, now Archdeacon Emeritus; *b* 8 Sept. 1937; *s* of late Rev. Canon H. M. J. Banting and P. M. Banting; *m* 1970, Linda (*née* Gick); four *d*. *Educ:* Pembroke Coll., Cambridge (MA 1965); Cuddesdon Coll., Oxford; Univ. of Wales (MA 2007). Ordained deacon, 1965, priest, 1966; Chaplain, Winchester Coll., 1965–70; Asst Curate, St Francis, Leigh Park, Portsmouth, 1970–73; Team Vicar, Highfield, Hemel Hempstead, 1973–79; Vicar, Goldington, Bedford, 1979–88; Priest-in-charge, Renhold, 1980–82; RD, Bedford, 1984–87; Vicar, St Cuthbert's, Portsmouth, 1988–96; RD, Portsmouth, 1994–96. *Recreations:* sailing, horology. *Address:* Furzend, 38A Bosham Hoe, W Sussex PO18 8ET. *T:* (01243) 572340. *E:* furzend@merlinbanting.plus.com.

**BANVILLE, John;** writer; *b* Wexford, 8 Dec. 1945; *s* of Martin and Agnes Banville; two *s* with Janet Dunham Banville; two *d* with Patricia Quinn. *Educ:* Christian Brothers' Schs; St Peter's Coll., Wexford, Ireland. Journalist, 1970–99; Literary Ed., Irish Times, 1988–99. *Theatre:* The Broken Jug, Abbey Th., Dublin, 1994; God's Gift, Dublin Th. Fest. and tour, 2000; The Book of Evidence, Kilkenny Th. Fest., 2002 and Gate Th., Dublin, 2003; *television:* screenplay: Reflections, 1984; play: Seachange, 1994; *radio* includes: Stardust, series of monologues, 2004; plays: Kepler, 2004; Todtnauberg, 2005; Bowen and Betjeman, 2014; *film screenplays:* The Last September, 2000; (jtly) Albert Nobbs, 2012; The Sea, 2014. *Publications:* Long Lankin (short stories), 1970; *novels:* Nightspawn, 1971; Birchwood, 1974; Doctor Copernicus (James Tait Black Meml Prize), 1976; Kepler (Guardian Fiction Prize), 1980; The Newton Letter, 1982 (filmed for TV as Reflections, 1984); Mefisto, 1986; The Book of Evidence, 1989 (Guinness Peat Aviation Award, Premio Ennio Flaiano, Italy, 1991); Ghosts, 1993; Athena, 1995; The Untouchable, 1997; Eclipse, 2000; Shroud, 2002; The Sea (Man Booker Prize), 2005 (filmed 2014); The Infinities, 2009; Ancient Light, 2012; The Blue Guitar, 2015; Mrs Osmond, 2017; *non-fiction:* Prague Pictures: portraits of a city, 2003; Time Pieces: a Dublin memoir, 2016; *adaptations* of dramas by Heinrich von Kleist: The Broken Jug, 1994; God's Gift, 2000; Love in the Wars, 2005; as Benjamin Black: Christine Falls, 2006; The Silver Swan, 2007; The Lemur, 2008; Elegy for April, 2010; A Death in Summer, 2011; Vengeance, 2012; The Black-Eyed Blonde, 2014; Even the Dead, 2016; Prague Nights, 2017. *Recreation:* work. *Address:* c/o Jessica Kelly, 6 Priory Close, St Raphael's Manor, Celbridge, Co. Kildare, Ireland. *Clubs:* Kildare Street and University, St Stephen's Green (Dublin).

**BANX;** *see* Banks, Jeremy.

**BAPTISTA, João P. A.;** President, Eastern, Central and Southern Europe, 2015–16, and Member, Executive Committee, 2012–16, CGI (President, Nordics, Southern Europe and South America, 2012–15); *b* Lisbon, Portugal, 1958; *s* of Milton Baptista and Maria Baptista; *m* 1997, Elizabeth P. A. Allen; two *s* one *d*. *Educ:* Stanford Graduate Sch. of Business (MBA 1985); Swiss Federal Inst. of Technology, Lausanne (Dip. Mechanical Engrg and Energy). Man. Dir, Bd Mem., Hd of Technol., Information, Communication and Entertainment Worldwide, Mercer Management Consulting, 1985–2005; Global Leader of Technol., Information, Communication and Entertainment, Marsh & McLennan Cos, Inc., 2004–05; Lead Partner, UK Telecommunication Team, Booz Allen Hamilton, 2005–06; Chm. and CEO of Internat. Investments, Mem. of Exec. Cttee and Dir, Main Bd, Portugal Telecom SGPS, 2006–08; CEO, N and Central Europe, Iberia and Latam, Chm., Utilities and Telecommunications Practices and Special Businesses, and Mem., Exec. Cttee, Logica plc, 2008–12. Vice-Chm., Vivo, Brazil, 2006–08; CEO, Africatel Hldgs, 2006–08. Exec. Chm., iLOCL, 2017–18. Sen. Advr, Estin & Co., 2017–. Trustee, V&A Mus., 2011–15 (Chm., Audit Cttee, 2011–15; Mem., Finance Cttee, 2011–15). FRSA. *Publications:* (jtly) Grow to be Great, 1995, 2nd edn 2010. *Recreations:* painting, modern art, cinema, travelling, ski-ing, sailing.

**BAPTISTA DA SILVA, Dr Carlos Boaventura;** Secretary, Board of Trustees, Calouste Gulbenkian Foundation, 1974–2005; Executive Director, Grémio Literário Committee, Lisbon, since 2001; *b* 13 Feb. 1935; *s* of Fernando Baptista da Silva and Virginia Boaventura Baptista da Silva; *m* 1961, Emilia de Almeida Nadal; two *s* one *d*. *Educ:* Univ. of Lisbon (Lic. in Law). Lawyer, 1968–. Mem., Portuguese Mint Consulting Cttee, 1971–. Mem., Gen. Cttee, Oliveira Martins Foundn, Lisbon, 1980–. Pres., 2000–07, Counsellor, 2007–12, FIDEM (Hon. Mem., 2012); Vice-Pres., Gen. Assembly, Nat. Soc. of Fine Arts, Lisbon, until 2013. Comdr, Order of Public Instruction (Portugal), 1968. *Publications:* several texts on medal art. *Recreations:* collector of medals, coins and modern art, music, reading. *Address:* Rua dos Navegantes 53–5° DT°, 1200–730 Lisbon, Portugal. *T:* 213974242, 916000276, *Fax:* 213974242. *E:* cbsilva935@gmail.com.

**BAPTISTE, Alison Jill,** CBE 2018; Director, Operations, Infrastructure and Projects Authority, Cabinet Office, since 2018; *b* Shrewsbury, 9 Dec. 1965; *d* of Graham Garrett and Jill Garrett; *m* 1999, Anthony Baptiste; one *s* one *d*. *Educ:* Univ. of Nottingham (BEng Civil Engrg 1987); Univ. of Southampton (MSc Irrigation Engrg 1990). CEng 1993; MCIWEM 1997; FICE 2015. Design Engr, Design and Consulting Services, Nepal, 1987–88; Res. Engr, Sir M McDonald & Partners, Indonesia, 1989; Sen. Project Manager, Binnie, Black & Veatch, 1990–96; Environment Agency: Area Ops Manager, 1996–2001; SE Ops Manager, 2001–04; Envmtl Policy Advr, 2004–05; Making Space for Water Prog. Dir, 2005–07; Nat. Coastal Manager, 2008–11; Nat. Project/Prog. Manager, 2011–12; Prog. Exec. for Excellence Transformation Project, 2012–13; Exec. Flood and Coastal Risk Manager, 2012–14; Exec. Ops Manager SE, 2013; Nat. Recovery Manager, 2013–14; Dep. Dir, Strategy Develt, 2014–15; Dir, Strategy and Investment, 2015–18. Non-executive Director: Redcar Racecourse Ltd, 2006–; Assoc. of Drainage Authorities, 2015–17. Diamond Jubilee Medal, 2012. *Publications:* (ed) Coastal Management: changing coast, changing climate, changing minds, 2016. *Recreations:* hill walking, music, church, family. *Address:* Infrastructure and Projects Authority, Cabinet Office, 1 Horse Guards Road, SW1A 2HQ. *T:* 07591 382512. *E:* alison.baptiste@ipa.gov.uk. *Clubs:* Royal Air Force, Royal Automobile.

**BAR-HILLEL, Mira;** property and planning writer, commentator and broadcaster; Tenants' Champion, London Borough of Wandsworth, since 2019; *b* 30 Sept. 1946; *d* of late Prof. Yehoshua Bar-Hillel and Shulamit (*née* Aschkenazy); *m* 2017, Peter Fermoy. *Educ:* Hebrew Gymnasia, Jerusalem; Hebrew Univ., Jerusalem (BA Soviet Studies 1972). Military Service, Israel Defence Forces, 1963–65. News reporter: Voice of Israel, 1965–72; Building mag., 1973–82 (News Editor, 1978–82); freelance writer on property and also architecture and planning, 1982–; Property and Planning Corresp. (pt-time), Evening Standard, 1986–2017; commentator on Israel/Palestine, Independent Voices and other media, 2008–17. Internat. Bldg Press Award, 1979, 1980, 1983, 1988, 1994, 1995, 1996; RICS Award, 1985; Incorporated Soc. Valuers and Auctioneers Award, 1986, 1996; Laing Homes Award, 1989, 1991, 1993; Lifetime Achievement Award, LSL Property Press Awards, 2013. *Recreations:* cats, meeting interesting people, countering Zionist propaganda, promoting a proper Private Rented Sector (PRS) and cleaning up the rental industry. *T:* 07711 495158. *E:* mira.barhillel@gmail.com. *W:* www.twitter.com/mirabarhillel.

**BARAGWANATH, Hon. Sir (William) David**, KNZM 2011; QC (NZ) 1983; President, Special Tribunal for Lebanon, The Hague, 2011–15 (Judge, Appeals Chamber, since 2009); Chairman, Advisory Board, P.R.I.M.E. Finance Foundation, The Hague, since 2017; *b* Balclutha, NZ, 3 Aug. 1940; *s* of Very Rev. Owen Thomas Baragwanath and Eileen Georgia Baragwanath; *m*; four *c*. *Educ:* Auckland Grammar Sch.; Univ. of Auckland (LLB 1964); Balliol Coll., Oxford (Rhodes Scholar 1964; BCL 1966). Called to the Bar, NZ, 1964; Partner, Meredith Connell & Co., Auckland, 1966–77; Judge, High Court, 1995; Judge, Court of Appeal of NZ, 2008–10. Pres., NZ Law Commn, 1996–2001; Chm., Rules Cttee, Court of NZ, 2004–08. Presiding Judge, Court of Appeal, Samoa, 2006–12; NZ Mem., Perm. Court of Arbitration, The Hague, 2007–13. Sen. Academic Visitor, Wolfson Coll., Cambridge, 2010; Dist. Judicial Visitor, Univ. of Hong Kong, 2010; Dist. Vis. Fellow, QMUL, 2011; HUGO Fellow-in-Residence, Netherlands Inst. of Advanced Studies, 2011; Vis. Prof., Univ. of Northumbria. Hon. Prof., Univ. of Waikato. Overseas Bencher, Inner Temple, 2010; Hon. Door Tenant, 3 Hare Court, 2018–. Fulbright travel award to Univ. of Virginia, 1983. *Publications:* articles in legal jls. *Recreations:* ski-ing, walking, reading. *Address:* Special Tribunal for Lebanon, PO Box 115, 2260 Leidschendam, Netherlands. *Club:* Haagsche.

**BARAK, Jeff(rey);** Corporate Editor, Amdocs, since 2009; *b* 26 April 1961; *s* of Malcolm and Estelle Black; *m* 1989, Yemima Rabin; two *s* one *d*. *Educ:* Leeds Grammar Sch.; Univ. of Newcastle upon Tyne (BA Hons English Lit.). Formerly Middle East analyst for assorted media; Ed.-in-Chief, Jerusalem Post, 1996–2002; Dep. Ed., 2002–05, Man. Ed., 2005–06, Jewish Chronicle; Ed.-in-Chief, Ynetnews.com, 2007; Sen. Ed., Ha'aretz (English-language edn), 2007–08. *Recreations:* hiking, watching televised sport. *Address:* PO Box 85285, Mevasseret Zion 90805, Israel. *T:* 526453637.

**BARAŃSKI, Prof. Zygmunt Guido;** Serena Professor of Italian, University of Cambridge, 2002–11, now Emeritus; Fellow, Murray Edwards College (formerly New Hall), Cambridge, 2002–11; R. L. Canala Professor of Romance Languages and Literatures, University of Notre Dame, since 2019 (Notre Dame Chair of Dante and Italian Studies, 2011–19); *b* 13 April 1951; *s* of Henryk Barański and Sonia Mariotti; *m* 1979, Margaret Ellen Watt; one *s* one *d*. *Educ:* St Bede's Coll., Manchester; Hull Univ. (BA 1973). Lectr in Italian, Univ. of Aberdeen, 1976–79; University of Reading: Lectr, 1979–89, Sen. Lectr, 1989–92, in Italian Studies; Prof. of Italian Studies, 1992–2002. Visiting Professor: McGill Univ., 1988, 1997; Univ. of Virginia, Charlottesville, 1991; Univ. of Connecticut, 1993; Yale Univ., 1995; Univ. of Notre Dame, 1996, 1998, 2004, 2007, 2010; Univ. of Bari, 2001; Univ. of California, Berkeley, 2002; Univ. of Reading, 2002–; UCLA, 2008; Univ. of Leeds, 2011–14; Univ. of Basel, 2016; Hon. Faculty Res. Fellow, Univ. of Oxford, 2018–. Pres., Internat. Dante Seminar, 2003–08. Commendatore, Ordine della Stella della Solidarietà (Italy), 2005. *Publications:* (ed) *Libri poetarum in quattuor species dividuntur*. essays on Dante and genre, 1995; *Luce nuova, sole nuovo:* saggi sul rinnovamento culturale in Dante, 1996; Pasolini Old and New, 1999; Dante e i segni, 2000; *Chiosar con altro testo:* leggere Dante nel trecento, 2001; Petrarch and Dante: anti-Dantism, metaphysics, tradition, 2009; Dante in Context, 2015; (ed jtly) Cambridge Companion to Dante's Commedia, 2019; Dante, Petrarch, Boccaccio: literature, doctrine, reality, 2019; contribs to learned jls. *Recreations:* following Manchester United, cycling, music. *Address:* Department of Romance Languages and Literatures, University of Notre Dame, Notre Dame, IN 46556, USA. *T:* (574) 6316886, *Fax:* (574) 6313493. *E:* baranski.1@nd.edu, zgb20@cam.ac.uk.

**BARBER, Sir Brendan (Paul),** Kt 2013; General Secretary, Trades Union Congress, 2003–12; Chairman, Advisory Conciliation and Arbitration Service, 2014–19 (Council Member, 1995–2004); *b* 3 April 1951; *s* of John and Agnes Barber; *m* 1981, Mary Rose Gray; two *d*. *Educ:* St Mary's Coll., Crosby; City Univ., London (BSc Hons; Pres. Students Union, 1973–74). Volunteer teacher, VSO, Ghana, 1969–70; Researcher, ceramics, glass and mineral products, ITB, 1974–75; Trades Union Congress: Asst, Orgn Dept, 1975–79; Hd, Press and Information Dept, 1979–87; Hd, Orgn Dept, 1987–93; Dep. Gen. Sec., 1993–2003. Member: Council, Sport England, 1999–2002; Court, Bank of England, 2003–12; UK Commn on Employment and Skills, 2008–12; Bd, TfL, 2013–16; Banking Standards Bd, 2015–. Non-exec. Dir, Openreach, BT plc, 2017–. Visiting Fellow: Saïd Business Sch., Oxford, 2012–; Nuffield Coll., Oxford, 2013–. Member: Council, City Univ., 2013–18; Bd of Trustees, Mountview Acad. of the Theatre Arts, 2014–. *Recreations:* golf, football, theatre, cinema. *Club:* Muswell Hill Golf.

**BARBER, Chris;** see Barber, D. C.

**BARBER, Sir David;** see Barber, Sir T. D.

**BARBER, (Donald) Chris(topher),** OBE 1991; band leader, The Chris Barber Band; *b* 17 April 1930; *s* of Henrietta Mary Evelyn Barber, MA Cantab and Donald Barber, CBE, BA Cantab; *m*; one *s* one *d*; *m* Kate; one step *d*. *Educ:* King Alfred School; St Paul's School. Formed first amateur band, 1949; present band commenced on professional basis, 1954; plays trombone, baritone horn, double bass and trumpet. Hon. Citizen, New Orleans. Numerous recordings, including over 150 LPs and 100 CDs, with records in the hit parade of over 40 countries world wide. Hon. DMus Durham, 2006. *Recreations:* collecting jazz and blues records, snooker, motor racing. *Address:* c/o Belmont, Wycombe Road, Studley Green, High Wycombe, Bucks HP14 3XB. *T:* and *Fax:* (01494) 484488. *E:* sitedc@aol.com.

**BARBER, Edward Simon Dominic,** OBE 2013; RDI 2007; Founding Director and Co-owner: Barber & Osgerby, since 1996; Universal Design Studio, since 2001; Map Project Office Ltd, since 2011; *b* Shrewsbury, 6 April 1969; *s* of Simon Barber and Penelope Barber (*née* Baldock). *Educ:* Leeds Poly. (BA Hons Interior Design); Royal Coll. of Art (MA Arch. and Interior Design). Prof., University Coll. Falmouth. *Commissions* include: design for Torch for London 2012 Olympic Games, 2011; design for £2 coin to commemorate 150 years of London Underground. Co-Curator of exhibitions including: In the Making, Design Mus., London, 2014; Precision and Poetry in Motion, V&A Mus., 2014. FRSA 2005. Hon. Dr Middx, 2018. Jerwood Applied Arts Prize (jtly), Jerwood Foundn, 2004. *Publications:* (with Jay Osgerby) The Design Work of Edward Barber and Jay Osgerby, 2010; (with Jay Osgerby) One by One, 2015; (jtly) Barber Osgerby: projects, 2017. *Address:* Barber & Osgerby, 37–42 Charlotte Road, EC2A 3PG. *T:* (020) 7033 3884, *Fax:* (020) 7033 3882. *E:* mail@barberosgerby.com.

**BARBER, Frank;** Senior Partner, Morgan, Fentiman & Barber, 1993–97; Deputy Chairman of Lloyd's, 1983, 1984; *b* 5 July 1923; *s* of Sidney Barber and Florence (*née* Seath); *m* 1st, 1945, Gertrude Kathleen Carson (decd); one *s* one *d* (and one *s* decd); 2nd, 1994, Elizabeth Joan Charvet (*d* 2011). *Educ:* West Norwood Central School. RAFVR, 1942–46. Entered Lloyd's, 1939; Underwriter, Lloyd's syndicate, Frank Barber & others, 1962–81; Member: Cttee of Lloyd's, 1977–80, 1982–85 and 1987; Council of Lloyd's, 1983–85 and 1987; Chm., Finance Cttee, Lloyd's, 1984; Dep. Chm., Lloyd's Underwriters' Non-Marine Assoc., 1971, Chm., 1972; Dep. Chm., British Insurers' European Cttee, 1983. Partner: Morgan, Fentiman & Barber, 1968–97; G. S. Christensen & Partners, 1985–2000; Chairman: A. E. Grant (Underwriting Agencies) Ltd, 1991–96; Frank Barber Underwriting Ltd, 2000–13. *Recreations:* music, walking, sailing. *Address:* Lime Cottage, Horseshoe Lane, Ipthorpe, Hants SP11 0BY.

**BARBER, Prof. James,** PhD; FRS 2005; FRSC; Ernst Chain Professor of Biochemistry, since 1989, and Senior Research Investigator, since 2013, Imperial College London (formerly Imperial College of Science, Technology and Medicine) (Head of Department of Biochemistry, 1989–99); *b* 16 July 1940; *s* of Sophia Barber; *m* 1965, Marilyn Jane Emily Tyrrell; one *s* one *d*. *Educ:* Portsmouth Southern Grammar Sch.; Univ. of Wales (BSc Hons Chem.); Univ. of East Anglia (MSc, PhD Biophy.). FRSC 1983. Unilever Biochem. Soc. European Fellow, Univ. of Leiden, 1967–68; Imperial College: Lectr, Dept of Botany, 1968–74; Reader in Plant Physiology, 1974–79, Prof., 1979–89; Dean, Royal Coll. of Science, 1989–91. Miller Prof., Univ. of Calif at Berkeley, 1989–90, 2001; Burroughs Wellcome Fund Prof., Univ. of Calif, 2000. Lectures: Brookhaven Sci. Associates Dist., 2005; Drummond, Queen Mary, London, 2005; G8 Univ., Torino, 2009; Sir Ernst Chain Distinguished, Imperial Coll. London, 2011. Lee Kuan Yew Dist. Visitor, Singapore, 2008. Selby Fellow, Australian Acad. of Scis, 1996; Foreign Mem., Swedish Royal Acad. of Scis, 2003. Mem., Academia Europaea, 1989. Hon. Dr Univ. of Stockholm, 1992; Hon. DSc: UEA, 2010; Nanyang Technol Univ., Singapore, 2017. Flintoff Medal, RSC, 2002; Italgas Prize for Energy and Envmt, Academia Europaea, 2005; Novartis Medal and Prize, Biochem. Soc., 2006; Wheland Medal and Prize, Univ. of Chicago, 2007; Arnon Lect. and Prize, UC Berkeley, 2008; Interdisciplinary Medal and Prize, RSC, 2013; Porter Medal, Eur. Photochem. Assoc., Inter-American Photochemical Soc. and Asian and Oceanian Photochem. Assoc., 2016; Communications Award, Internat. Soc. for Photosynthesis Res., 2016. *Publications:* The Intact Chloroplast, 1976; Primary Processes in Photosynthesis, 1977; Photosynthesis in Relation to Model Systems, 1979; Electron Transport and Photophosphorylation, 1982; Chloroplast Biogenesis, 1984; Photosynthetic Mechanisms and the Environment, 1986; The Light Reactions, 1987; The Photosystems: structure, function and molecular biology, 1992; Molecular Processes of Photosynthesis, 1994; Molecular to Global Photosynthesis, 2004; Photosynthesis and Bioenergetics, 2017; articles and reviews. *Recreation:* gardening. *Address:* Sir Ernst Chain-Wolfson Building, Department of Life Sciences, Imperial College London, SW7 2AZ. *T:* (020) 7594 5266. *E:* j.barber@imperial.ac.uk.

**BARBER, Prof. Karin Judith,** CBE 2012; PhD; FBA 2003; Professor of African Cultural Anthropology, Department of African Studies and Anthropology, University of Birmingham, 1999–2017, now Emeritus; Centennial Professor of Anthropology, London School of Economics and Political Science, since 2018; *b* 2 July 1949; *d* of Charles and Barbara Barber; partner, Dr Paulo Fernando de Moraes Farias. *Educ:* Lawnswood High Sch., Leeds; Girton Coll., Cambridge (BA English 1st cl., MA); UCL (Dip. in Soc. Anthropol.); Univ. of Ife (PhD). Lectr, Dept of African Langs and Lits, Univ. of Ife, 1977–84; Centre of West African Studies, University of Birmingham: Lectr, 1985–93; Sen. Lectr, 1993–97; Reader, 1997–99; Dir, 1998–2001. Vis. Preceptor, Inst. for Adv. Study and Res. in African Humanities, 1993–94. Melville J. Herskovits Vis. Chair in African Studies, 1999, Northwestern Univ., Illinois. *Publications:* Yorùbá Dùn ún So: a beginners' course in Yorùbá, 1984, 2nd edn 1990; (ed with P. F. de Moraes Farias) Discourse and its Disguises: the interpretation of African oral texts, 1989; (ed with P. F. de Moraes Farias) Self-assertion and Brokerage: early cultural nationalism in West Africa, 1990; I Could Speak Until Tomorrow: Oríkì, women and the past in a Yorùbá town (Amaury Talbot Prize, RAI), 1991; (with Bayo Ogundijo) Yorùbá Popular Theatre: three plays by the Oyin Adejobi Company, 1994; (jtly) West African Popular Theatre, 1997; (ed) Readings in African Popular Culture, 1997; (with Akin Oyetade) Yorùbá Wuyi, 1999; The Generation of Plays: Yorùbá popular life in theater (Herskovits Award, African Studies Assoc., USA), 2000; (ed) Africa's Hidden Histories: everyday literacy and making the self, 2006; The Anthropology of Texts, Persons and Publics, 2007; Print Culture and the First Yoruba Novel (Paul Hair Prize, African Studies Assoc., USA), 2012; A History of African Popular Culture, 2018. *Recreations:* theatre, music. *Address:* Department of African Studies and Anthropology, University of Birmingham, Edgbaston, Birmingham B15 2TT. *T:* (0121) 414 5125, *Fax:* (0121) 414 3228. *E:* k.j.barber@bham.ac.uk.

**BARBER, Lionel;** Editor, Financial Times, since 2005; *b* 18 Jan. 1955; *s* of Frank Douglas Barber and Joan Elizabeth Barber (*née* Nolan); *m* 1986, Victoria Greenwood; one *s* one *d*. *Educ:* Dulwich Coll.; St Edmund Hall, Oxford (BA Jt Hons German and Modern Hist.). Reporter, Scotsman, 1978–81; business reporter, Sunday Times, 1981–85; Financial Times: UK company news reporter, 1985–86; Washington Corresp., 1986–92; Brussels Bureau Chief, 1992–98; News Ed., 1998–2000; European Ed., 2000–02; US Managing Ed., 2002–05. Trustee: Tate, 2011– (Chm., 2018–); Carnegie Corp., NY, 2014–. Chevalier, Légion d'Honneur (France), 2017. *Publications:* (jtly) The Delorean Tapes, 1984; (jtly) The Price of Truth: the story of Reuter's millions, 1985; (jtly) Not with Honour, 1986. *Recreations:* cycling, tennis, working out, reading American history, watching Rugby. *Address:* Financial Times, Bracken House, 1 Friday Street, EC4M 9BT. *T:* (020) 7873 4222.

**BARBER, Sir Michael (Bayldon),** Kt 2005; Founder and Chairman, Delivery Associates Ltd, since 2012; Chairman, Office for Students, since 2017; *b* 24 Nov. 1955; *s* of Christopher and Anne Barber; *m* 1982, Karen Alderman; three *d*. *Educ:* Bootham Sch., York; Queen's Coll., Oxford (BA Hons 1977); Georg-August Univ., Göttingen; Westminster Coll., Oxford (PGCE 1979); Inst. of Educn, London Univ. (MA 1991). History Teacher: Watford, 1979–83; Zimbabwe, 1983–85; Policy and Res. Officer 1985–89, Education Officer, 1989–93, NUT; Professor of Education: Keele Univ., 1993–95; Inst. of Educn, London Univ., 1995–97; Dir, Standards and Effectiveness Unit and Chief Advr to Sec. of State on Sch. Standards, DFEE, 1997–2001; Chief Advr to Prime Minister on Delivery, and Hd, Prime Minister's Delivery Unit, 2001–05; Expert Partner Global Public Sector Practice, later Head of Global Educn Practice, McKinsey & Co. 2005–11; Chief Educn Advr, Pearson plc, 2011–17. Non-exec. Dir, MoJ, 2015–17. Vis Fellow, Sch. of Public Health, Harvard Univ., 2014–15. Mem. (Lab), Hackney LBC 1986–90 (Chair, Educn Cttee, 1988–89). Contested (Lab) Henley-on-Thames, 1987. Hon DLaws Exeter, 2009; Hon. DLitt Wales, 2014; Hon. LLD Warwick, 2015. *Publications* Education and the Teacher Unions, 1992; The Making of 1944 Education Act, 1994; The National Curriculum: a study in policy, 1996; The Learning Game: arguments for an education revolution, 1996, revd edn 1997; Instruction to Deliver: Tony Blair, reform o public services and achievement of targets, 2007, 2nd edn as Instruction to Deliver: th battle to reform Britain's public services, 2008; (with Mona Moursbed) How the World' Best Performing Education Systems Come Out on Top, 2007; Deliverology 101: a fiel guide for education leaders, 2011; How to Run a Government so that Citizens Benefit an

Taxpayers don't go Crazy, 2015, 2nd edn 2016; (jtly) Deliverology in Practice, 2015. *Recreations:* Liverpool Football Club, cycling, reading history books. *Address:* N Devon. *T:* (020) 8244 1060.

**BARBER, Nicholas Charles Faithorn,** CBE 2004; Deputy Chairman, Bolero International Ltd, since 2016 (Chairman, 1998–2016); *b* 7 Sept. 1940; *s* of Bertram Harold and Nancy Lorraine Barber; *m* 1966, Sheena Macrae Graham; two *s* one *d*. *Educ:* Ludgrove Sch.; Shrewsbury Sch.; Wadham Coll., Oxford (MA; Hon. Fellow 2007); Columbia Univ., New York, 1969–71 (MBA). Lectr, Marlboro Coll., Vermont, USA, 1963–64; joined Ocean Steam Ship, subseq. Ocean Transport and Trading, later Ocean Group, 1964; Dir, 1980–94; Chief Exec., 1986–94. Divl Dir, NEB, 1977–79. Chairman: IEC Gp plc, 1996–99; Orion Publishing Gp, 1997–98; Kappa IT Ventures, 1998–2007; Director: Overseas Containers Ltd, 1984–86; Costain Gp, 1990–93; Royal Insurance Hldgs plc, 1991–96 (Dep. Chm., 1994–96); Royal & Sun Alliance Insurance Gp plc, 1996–2003; Barings plc, 1994–95; Bank of Ireland UK Financial Services plc (formerly Bristol & West Bldg Soc., then Bristol and West plc), 1994–2003 (Dep. Chm., 2001–03); Albright & Wilson plc, 1995–99; Fidelity Japanese Values PLC, 2000–12; The Maersk Co., 2004–08. Mem., NW Industrial Develt Bd, 1982–85; Gov., NIESR, 1991–2016 (Mem., Exec. Cttee, 2001–16). Mem. Bd, Liverpool Playhouse, 1982–87; Member: Adv. Cttee, Tate Gall., Liverpool, 1988–92; Council, Internat. Dendrological Soc., 2015–; Trustee: Nat. Museums and Galls on Merseyside, 1986–94; Shrewsbury Sch. Foundn, 1990–2006; British Mus., 1993–2003; Country Houses Foundn, 2004–; Chairman: British Mus. Friends (formerly British Mus. Soc.), 1992–2003; British Mus. Co. Ltd, 1996–2003; Ashmolean Mus., 2003–10. Governor: Shrewsbury Sch., 1983–2003 (Dep. Chm., 1997–2003); London Business Sch., 1993–2001; Vice-Pres., Liverpool Sch. of Tropical Medicine, 1988–2014, now Vice-Pres. Emeritus; Chm., Huron Univ. USA in London Ltd, 1998–2007; Member Council: Liverpool Univ., 1985–88; Industrial Soc., 1993–99; Mem., Adv. Council, Asia House, 1996–; Dir, Hult Internat. Business Sch., Boston, 2008–; Fellow, Ashridge Business Sch., 2015–. Pres., Classics for All, 2017– (Chm., 2013–16). FRSA 1994. Hon. DHL Marlboro Coll., Vermont, 2005. Distinguished Friend, Oxford Univ., 2010; Fellow, Ashmolean Mus., 2011. Pres., Salopian Club, 2018. *Recreations:* history, museums, dendrology, mountain walking, cricket. *Address:* 6 Lytton Court, 14 Barter Street, WC1A 2AH. *Clubs:* Brooks's, MCC; Denham Golf.

**BARBER, Pamela Gay, (Mrs Paul Barker);** DL; Headteacher, Lancaster Girls' Grammar School, 1987–2007; *b* 8 May 1947; *d* of Harold and Muriel Nunwick; *m* Paul Barker. *Educ:* N Western Poly., London (BA Hons Geog.); Leeds Univ. (PGCE). Class teacher, then Hd of Geog. and Hd of Sixth Form, Belle Vue Girls' Sch., Bradford, 1969–80; Deputy Head: Crossley and Porter Sch., Halifax, 1980–85; Crossley Heath Sch., Halifax, 1985–86. Boarding Headteacher, Admiralty Interview Bd, 1992–2005. Non-exec. Dir, Lancaster HA, 1990–93. Mem. Bd, Bay Radio, 1999–2003. Mem. Council, Lancaster Univ., 1989–95. Mem., Adv. Cttee, Arkwright Trust, 1998–2007; Trustee: Community Foundn for Lancs, 2008–15; Lancaster Charities, 2016–. Constable, Lancaster Castle, 2013–. DL Lancs, 2007. Hon. Fellow, Lancaster Univ., 2011. *Recreations:* foreign travel, horse riding, donkey keeping, gardening, fell-walking.

**BARBER, Rt Rev. Paul Everard;** Bishop Suffragan of Brixworth, 1989–2001; an Hon. Assistant Bishop, Diocese of Bath and Wells, since 2001; *b* 16 Sept. 1935; *s* of Cecil Arthur and Mollie Barber; *m* 1959, Patricia Jayne Walford; two *s* two *d* (and one *s* decd). *Educ:* Sherborne School; St John's Coll., Cambridge (BA 1958, MA 1966); Wells Theological College. Deacon 1960, priest 1961, dio. Guildford; Curate of St Francis, Westborough, 1960–66; Vicar: Camberley with Yorktown, 1966–73; St Thomas-on-the-Bourne, Farnham, 1973–80; Rural Dean of Farnham, 1974–79; Archdeacon of Surrey, 1980–89; Hon. Canon: of Guildford, 1980–89; of Peterborough, 1997–2001. General Synod, 1979–85; Member, Council of College of Preachers, 1969–98. Archbp of Canterbury's Advr to HMC, 1993–2001. Gov., Millfield Sch., 2002–08. *Recreations:* sport, theatre, cinema, walking. *Address:* Apartment 17, Parklands Manor, Parklands Drive, Chertsey, Surrey KT16 9FS. *T:* (01932) 876871.

**BARBER, Peter Ambrose,** Managing Director, Peter Barber Architects Ltd, since 1995; Reader in Architecture, University of Westminster, since 2008; *b* Guildford, Surrey, 30 Nov. 1960; *s* of Ambrose Cambridge Barber and Joan Barber; partner, Daisy Miller; two *s*. *Educ:* Reeds Sch., Cobham; Godalming 6th Form Coll.; Univ. of Sheffield (BA Arch.); Central London Poly. (DipArch). Architect: Richard Rogers Partnership, 2000–02; Will Alsop + Partners, 2002–03. Projects include Coldbath Town - Mount Pleasant Sorting Office site (RA Grand Prize for Arch., 2015). Lecturer: Kingston Univ., 1998; UCL, 1998–2005; Oxford Brookes Univ., 2005–10. Numerous RIBA awards. *Publications:* (contrib.) Project Interrupted, 2018; architectl projects featured in numerous publications internationally. *Recreations:* musician (piano, guitar, banjo, ukelele), sketching, painting, walking about. *Address:* Peter Barber Architects Ltd, 173 King's Cross Road, WC1X 9BZ. *E:* peter@peterbarberarchitects.com.

**BARBER, Stephen James;** social services consultant; Safeguarding Adviser (formerly Child Protection Adviser), Diocese of Oxford, 2003–16; Chief Children's Officer, and Director of Social Services, London Borough of Barnet, 1999–2000; *b* 15 Nov. 1946; *s* of John Barber and Jenny Barber (née Roshan Mirza); *m* 1972, Mary Margaret Hoffman; three *d*. *Educ:* Hall Sch., Hampstead; Uppingham Sch., Rutland; Trinity Coll., Cambridge (BA, MA); Brunel Univ. (MA, CQSW). Res. student, 1970–73; nursing asst, Cassell Hosp., 1973–74; social worker, 1974–79; Team Leader, 1979–85; Principal Officer, 1985–88, RBK&C; Asst Dir (Children and Families), London Borough of Ealing, 1988–93; Controller of Community Services, London Borough of Barnet, 1993–99. Chair, Local Safeguarding Children Bds, W Berks, Reading and Wokingham, 2009–14. Chm., Springboard Family Project, 2004–09. Trustee: British Assoc. (formerly Agencies) for Adoption and Fostering, 1999–2000; Parents and Children Together, 2004–09; Hampshire and Thames Valley Circles of Support and Accountability, 2008–09; Oxford Diocesan Schools Trust, 2018–. Treas., Charles Williams Soc., 2001–16. *Publications:* (ed) The Celian Moment and Other Essays, by Charles Williams, 2017; contrib. reviews and articles to Seven, Jl of Inklings Studies, Charles Williams Qly, TES, and various social work jls. *Recreations:* playing the piano, collecting books and CDs, visiting cathedral cities. *Address:* c/o Church House Oxford, Langford Locks, Kidlington, Oxford OX5 1GF.

**BARBER, Sir (Thomas) David,** 3rd Bt *cr* 1960, of Greasley, Nottingham; self-employed philatelist; *b* 18 Nov. 1937; *o s* of Col Sir William Francis Barber, 2nd Bt and his 1st wife, Diana Constance Barber (*née* Lloyd) (*d* 1984); *S* father, 1995; *m* 1st, 1971, Amanda Mary Healing (*née* Rabone) (marr. diss. 1976); one *s*; 2nd, 1978, Jeannine Mary Boyle (*née* Gurney); one *s* one *d*. *Educ:* Eton; Trinity Coll., Cambridge (MA). 2nd Lieut, RA, 1958–61. *Heir: s* Thomas Edward Barber [*b* 14 March 1973; *m* 2004, Davina Alice, *o d* of Anthony Duckworth-Chad, OBE; one *s* three *d* (of whom two *d* are twins)]. *Address:* Wicket House, Rivar Road, Shalbourne, Marlborough, Wilts SN8 3PU. *Club:* Free Foresters.

**BARBER, His Honour Trevor Wing;** a Circuit Judge, 1992–2014; *b* 10 June 1943; *s* of Robert and Margaret Barber; *m* 1967, Judith Penelope Downey; one *s* one *d*. *Educ:* Worksop Coll.; Newcastle Univ. (LLB). Called to the Bar, Inner Temple, 1967; practice in Sheffield, 1967–92. *Recreations:* gardening, golf, reading, bee keeping. *Address:* Juniper Lodge, Hillfoot Road, Totley, Sheffield S17 3AX.

**BARBIERI, Margaret Elizabeth, (Mrs M. E. Barbieri-Webb);** freelance ballet teacher and coach, since 1990; Assistant Director, Sarasota Ballet Company, Florida, since 2012; *b* 2 March 1947; *d* of Ettore Barbieri and Lea Barbieri; *m* 1982, Iain Webb, Artistic Dir, Sarasota Ballet Co.; one *s*. *Educ:* Convent High Sch., Durban, S Africa. Trained with Iris Manning and Brownie Sutton, S Africa; Royal Ballet Sen. Sch., 1963; joined Royal Ballet, 1965; Principal, 1970; Sen. Principal, SWRB, 1974–89. Dir, Classical Graduate Course, London Studio Centre, 1990–2012; Artistic Dir, Images of Dance, 1990–2012; guest teacher, Royal Ballet Sch., 1990–94. Roles: Gypsy Girl, Two Pigeons, 1966; 1st Giselle, Covent Garden, 1968; 1st Sleeping Beauty, Leeds, 1969; 1st Swan Lake, Frankfurt, 1977, Covent Garden, 1983; 1st Romeo and Juliet, Covent Garden, 1979; 1st Sleeping Beauty, Covent Garden, 1985. Other roles with Royal Ballet: La Fille mal Gardée, Two Pigeons, The Dream, Façade, Wedding Bouquet, Rendezvous (Ashton); Lady and the Fool, Card Game, Pineapple Poll (Cranko); The Invitation, Solitaire, (Summer) The Four Seasons (MacMillan); Checkmate, The Rake's Progress (de Valois); Grosse Fugue, Tilt (van Manen); Lilac Garden (Tudor); Fête Etrange (Howard); Grand Tour (Layton); Summer Garden (Hynd); Game Piano (Thorpe), 1978; Cinderella (Killar), 1978; Cinderella (Rodrigues), 1979; Papillon, The Taming of the Shrew, 1980; Coppélia, Les Sylphides, Raymonda Act III, Spectre de la Rose; La Vivandière, 1982; Petrushka, 1984. Roles created: Knight Errant (Tudor), 1968; From Waking Sleep (Drew), 1970; Ante-Room (Cauley), 1971; Oscar Wilde (Layton), 1972; Sacred Circles and The Sword (Drew), 1973; The Entertainers (Killar), 1974; Charlotte Brontë (Hynd), 1974; Summertide (Wright), 1977; Metamorphosis (Bintley), 1984; Flowers of the Forest (Bintley), 1985; The Wand of Youth (Corder), 1985. Recreated: Pavlova's Dragonfly Solo, 1977; The Dying Swan, produced by Dame Alicia Markova after Fokine, 1985. Guest artist, 1990–92, guest teacher, 1991–92, Birmingham Royal Ballet. Staged for Images of Dance: Les Sylphides, Façade, 1991; Rake's Progress, 1992; Pineapple Poll, La Bayadère, 1993; Raymonda, 1994; Swan Lake, 1995; Paquita, 1996; staged: Façade and Raymonda Act 3 for K Ballet Co., Japan, 2003; Façade for Oregon Ballet Th. Co., Portland, 2004; The Two Pigeons for K Ballet Co., Japan and State Ballet of Georgia, Tbilisi, 2006; staged for Sarasota Ballet, 2007–: Two Pigeons, Façade, Rendezvous, Les Patineurs, Birthday Offering, Valses Nobles et Sentimentales, La Fille mal Gardée, The Rake's Progress, Checkmate, The American and There Where She Loves (Wheeldon), Pineapple Poll, Grand Tour, Giselle, Les Sylphides, Boutique (Bourne), Scottish Dances (Bintley), Jazz Calendar (Ashton), Raymonda Act III (Nureyev), Summertide. Travelled with Royal Ballet to Australia, Canada, China, Egypt, Far East, France, Germany, Greece, Holland, Israel, Italy, Japan, New Zealand, Portugal, Spain, Switzerland, Yugoslavia, India and North and South America; guest appearances, USA, Germany, S Africa, France, Norway, Czechoslovakia. TV Appearances in: Spectre de la Rose; Grosse Fugue; Giselle; Coppelia; Checkmate; Metamorphosis; Markova master classes. Gov., Royal Ballet, 1994–2000. Ashton Associate, Frederick Ashton Foundn, 2013–. (Jtly) Luminaire Award, Fine Arts Soc. of Sarasota, 2014. *Recreations:* music (classical), theatre, gardening.

**BARBIZET, Patricia Marie Marguerite;** Commandeur: de l'ordre national du Mérite, 2010; de la Légion d'honneur, 2015; Chairman and Chief Executive Officer, Temaris & Associés, since 2018; *b* Paris, 17 April 1955; *d* of late Philippe Dussart and of Monique Dussart (*née* Cartier); *m* 1979, Jean Barbizet; one *d*. *Educ:* ESCP Europe (Master's degree 1976). Internat. Treas., Renault Véhicules Industriels, 1979–82; Chief Financial Officer, Renault Crédit Internat., 1982–89; Groupe Pinault: Chief Financial Officer, 1989; Dep. CEO, Pinault-CFAO, 1990–92; Chief Executive Officer: Artémis, 1992–2018; Financière Pinault, 1992–2018; Christie's International: Chm., 2002–16; CEO, 2014–16; Vice Chm., 2016–18; Vice-Chm., Kering (formerly PPR), 2005–. Member Board: Bouygues, 2000–13; Air France-KLM, 2003–13; Total, 2008–; AXA, 2018–; Pernod-Ricard, 2018–. *Recreations:* classical music, opera, theatre, literature. *Address:* Temaris & Associés, 40 rue Francois 1er, 75008 Paris, France. *T:* (1) 40750101. *E:* contact@temaris.fr.

**BARBOSA, Rubens Antonio,** Hon. GCVO 1997 (Hon. LVO 1969); President and Chief Executive Officer, Rubens Barbosa & Associates, since 2004; Senior Director, Albright Stonebridge Group, since 2005; Chief Executive Officer, Brazilian Wheat Industry Association, since 2017; board member of several industrial companies; *b* 13 June 1938; *s* of José Orlando Barbosa and Lice Farina Barbosa; *m* 1969, Maria Ignez Correa da Costa Barbosa; one *s* one *d*. *Educ:* Univ. of São Paulo, Brazil (BA Law); Foreign Service Acad., Brazil (BA Diplomacy); LSE (MA Latin Amer. Politics); other degrees in economics, finance and politics. Exec. Sec., Brazilian Trade Commn with socialist countries of Eastern Europe, 1976–84; Head of Staff, Min. of External Relations, 1985–86; Under-Sec. Gen., Multilateral and Special Pol Affairs, 1986; COS, Min. of Foreign Relations, 1986–87; Sec., Internat. Affairs, Min. of Economy, 1987–88; Ambassador and Perm. Rep. to Latin-Amer. Integration Assoc., 1988–91; Pres., Commn of Reps, 1991–92; Under-Sec. Gen., Trade, Regl Integration, Econ. Affairs and Foreign Trade, Min. of External Relations, and Co-ordinator for Mercosur, Brazil, 1991–93; Vice-Pres., Perm. Commn on Foreign Trade, 1992–93; Ambassador: to UK, 1994–99; to USA, 1999–2004. Pres., Assoc. of Coffee Producing Countries, 1993–99. Grand Cross, Order of Rio Branco (Brazil); French Legion of Honour; orders from Argentina and Mexico; honours from Germany, Belgium, Italy, Iran, Portugal. Publisher and Ed., Interesse Nacional, qly jl on pol, econ. and social issues, 2008–. *Publications:* America Latina em Perspectiva: a integração regional da retórica à realidade, 1991; The Mercosur Codes, 2000; Mercosur and Regional Integration, 2010; The Dissent in Washington, 2011 (Washington Dissensus, 2014); National Interest and Vision of the Future, 2012; The Place of Brazil in the World, 2018; A Diplomat at the Service of the State, 2018; articles in newspapers and learned jls. *Recreations:* tennis, classical music. *Address:* (office) Avenida Brigadeiro Faria Lima 2413, Sobreloja, Conjunto B, 01452-000 São Paulo, Brazil.

**BARBOUR, James Jack,** OBE 1992; FRCPE; Chief Executive, Lothian NHS Board, 2001–12; *b* 16 Jan. 1953; *s* of late Thomas Jack Barbour and Flora Jean Barbour (*née* Murray); one *s* two *d*; *m* Julie Barnes. *Educ:* Madras Coll., St Andrews; Univ. of Strathclyde (BA Jt Hons Politics, Sociol., Econs). MHSM 1983, CIHM 2010; FRCPE 2008. Grad. Mgt Trainee, NHS in Scotland, 1977–79; Administrator, Gtr Glasgow Health Bd, 1979–83; EEC Exchange scholarship in Germany, 1981; Unit Administration, Gt Ormond St Gp of Hosps, 1983–86; General Manager: Royal Manchester Children's Hosp., 1986–87; Aberdeen Royal Infirmary, 1987–92; Chief Executive: Aberdeen Royal Hosps NHS Trust, 1992–94; Central Manchester Healthcare NHS Trust, 1994–98; Sheffield HA, 1998–2001. Alumnus, London Business Sch. Develt Prog., 1989. Hon. Professor: Queen Margaret Univ. (formerly Queen Margaret UC), 2002–14; Univ. of Strathclyde, 2012–15. Burgess, City of Aberdeen, 1992. *Recreations:* travel, keeping fit, walking our labradoodle.

**BARBOUR, Dame Margaret,** DBE 2002 (CBE 1991); DL; Chairman, J. Barbour & Sons Ltd, since 1972 (Director, 1968–72); *b* 1 Feb. 1940; *d* of David and Mary Ann Davies; *m* 1st, 1964, John Malcolm Barbour (*d* 1968); one *d*; 2nd, 1991, David William Ash. *Educ:*

Middlesborough High Sch.; Battersea Poly. (DipEd). Teacher: Elliot Sch., Putney, 1961–64; Church High Sch., Newcastle upon Tyne, 1964–66. DL Tyne and Wear, 1992. Hon. DBA Sunderland, 1994; Hon. DCL Newcastle, 1998. *Recreations:* swimming, bridge, literature. *Address:* J. Barbour & Sons Ltd, Simonside, South Shields, Tyne and Wear NE34 9PD. *T:* (0191) 455 4444, *Fax:* (0191) 427 4259.

**BARBOUR, Muriel Janet;** *see* Gray, M. J.

**BARCA, Manuel David;** QC 2011; *b* Kensington, 1962; *o s* of Emilio and Sara Barca. *Educ:* Wimbledon Coll.; Churchill Coll., Cambridge (MA Law Tripos). Called to the Bar, Lincoln's Inn, 1986; in practice as a barrister, specialising in media and information law, One Brick Court, 1987–2019. *Recreations:* theatre, music, cinema, art history, Spain. *E:* mbarca@cantab.net.

**BARCLAY, Prof. (Alan) Neil,** DPhil; E. P. Abraham Professor of Chemical Pathology, 2011–15, and Titular Professor of Molecular Immunology, 1998–2015, now Professor Emeritus, University of Oxford; Fellow of Lincoln College, Oxford, since 2011; *b* 12 March 1950; *s* of late Frank Rodney Barclay and Betty Cowie Barclay (*née* Watson); *m* 1975, Ella Geraldine Quinn; two *s* one *d. Educ:* Hardye's Sch., Dorchester; Oriel Coll., Oxford (DPhil Biochem. 1976). Res. Fellow, Inst. of Neurobiology, Univ. of Göteborg, Sweden, 1976–78; Scientific Staff: MRC, Sir William Dunn Sch. of Pathol., Univ. of Oxford, 1978–2011; MRC Cellular Immunol. Unit, Oxford, 1978–99. Academic Advr, Oxford Univ. Bioinformatics Centre, 1990–2000. Chairman: Everest Biotech Ltd, 1999–; Absolute Antibody Ltd, 2012–. Chm., 2009–14, Treas., 2014–, CIU Trust; Chm., EPA Cephalosporin Trust Fund, 2000–. Hon. Mem., Scandinavian Soc. of Immunology, 1993. *Publications:* (jtly) The Leucocyte Antigen Factsbook, 1993, 2nd edn 1997; contribs to scientific jls. *Recreations:* literature, listening to music, writing stories (unpublished). *Address:* Sir William Dunn School of Pathology, Oxford University, South Parks Road, Oxford OX1 3RE. *T:* (01865) 275500.

**BARCLAY, Sir David (Rowat),** Kt 2000; Joint Proprietor: Littlewoods, since 2002; Woolworths and Ladybird Brands, since 2009; The Daily Telegraph, Sunday Telegraph, Spectator magazine and Apollo, since 2004. Joint Proprietor: Cadogan Hotel, 1968–78; Londonderry Hotel, 1970–80, 1985–87; Kensington Palace Hotel, 1973–77; Howard Hotel, 1975–2000; Mirabeau Hotel, Monte Carlo, 1979–2007; Ellerman Shipping, 1983–87; Tolly Cobold Brewery & JW Cameron Brewery, 1983–89; Howard Hotel, NY, 1984–87; Gotass Larsen Shipping, 1988–97; The European, 1992–98; Scotsman Publications, 1995–2006; Ritz Hotel, 1995–; Cavendish Hotel, London, 2006–12; Maybourne Hotel Gp, 2011–15. Jt Founder and Trustee, David and Frederick Barclay Foundn. Ambassador Extraordinaire at Large for Econ. Develt of Monaco, 2010. Hon. Dr Glasgow, 1998. KSG 2010. Officier, 2000, Commandeur, 2017, Ordre de Saint Charles (Monaco).

*See also* Sir F. H. Barclay.

**BARCLAY, Sir Frederick (Hugh),** Kt 2000; Joint Proprietor: Littlewoods, since 2002; Woolworths and Ladybird Brands, since 2009; The Daily Telegraph, Sunday Telegraph, Spectator magazine and Apollo, since 2004. Former estate agent. Joint Proprietor: Cadogan Hotel, 1968–78; Londonderry Hotel, 1970–80, 1985–87; Kensington Palace Hotel, 1973–77; Howard Hotel, 1975–2000; Mirabeau Hotel, Monte Carlo, 1979–2007; Ellerman Shipping, 1983–87; Tolly Cobold Brewery & JW Cameron Brewery, 1983–89; Howard Hotel, NY, 1984–87; Gotass Larsen Shipping, 1988–97; The European, 1992–98; Scotsman Publications, 1995–2006; Ritz Hotel, 1995–; Cavendish Hotel, London, 2006–12; Maybourne Hotel Gp, 2011–15. Jt Founder and Trustee, David and Frederick Barclay Foundn. Ambassador Extraordinaire at Large for Econ. Develt of Monaco. Hon. Dr Glasgow, 1998. KSG 2010. Officier, Ordre de Saint Charles (Monaco), 2000.

*See also* Sir D. R. Barclay.

**BARCLAY, James Christopher,** OBE 2006; Chairman and Managing Director, Cater Allen Holdings PLC, 1985–98; *b* 7 July 1945; *s* of late Theodore David Barclay and Anne Barclay; *m* 1974, Rolleen Anne, *d* of late Lt-Col Arthur Forbes and Joan Forbes; one *s* one *d. Educ:* Harrow. Served 15th/19th The King's Royal Hussars, 1964–67. Dep. Chm., Cater Allen Hldgs PLC, 1981–85; Chm., Cater Ryder & Co. Ltd, 1981. Chm., M & G Equity investment Trust PLC, 1998–2011 (Dir, 1996–2011); Director: Abbey National Treasury Services plc, 1997–98; Abbey National Offshore Hldgs Ltd, 1998–2000; Thos Agnew & Sons Ltd, 1998–2013; New Fulcrum Investment Trust plc, 1999–2006; Liontrust Knowledge Economy Trust PLC, 2001–03; Rathbone Brothers PLC, 2003–10. Dir, UK Debt Mgt Office, 2000–05. Chm., London Discount Market Assoc., 1988–90. *Recreation:* fresh air pursuits. *Address:* Rivers Hall, Waldringfield, Woodbridge, Suffolk IP12 4QX. *Clubs:* Boodle's, Pratt's.

**BARCLAY, John Alistair;** Executive Director, Royal Bank of Scotland Group plc, retired; *b* 5 Dec. 1933; *m* 1963, Mary Tierney (*née* Brown); three *d. Educ:* Banff Academy. FCIBS. Joined Royal Bank of Scotland, 1949; Chief City Manager, 1982–84; seconded to Williams & Glyn's Bank (Asst Gen. Manager), 1984–85; Exec. Vice-Pres., NY, 1985–88; Sen. Gen. Manager, UK Banking, 1988–89; Exec. Dir, International, 1989–90; Man. Dir, Corporate and Institutional Banking, 1990–92; Dep. Gp Chief Exec., 1992–94; non-exec. Dir, 1994–96. Chm., Direct Line Financial Services, 1994–2004. *Recreations:* travel, golf, reading, gardening, photography, good food and wine.

**BARCLAY, Prof. John Martyn Gurney,** PhD; Lightfoot Professor of Divinity, Durham University, since 2003; *b* 31 July 1958; *s* of late Oliver and Dorothy Barclay; *m* 1981, Diana Knox; two *s* one *d. Educ:* Queens' Coll., Cambridge (BA 1981; PhD 1986). University of Glasgow: Lectr, 1984–96; Sen. Lectr, 1996–2000; Prof., 2000–03. *Publications:* Obeying the Truth: Paul's ethics in Galatians, 1988; Jews in the Mediterranean Diaspora, 1996; Colossians and Philemon, 1997; Flavius Josephus: translation and commentary, Vol. 10, Against Apion, 2007; Pauline Churches and Diaspora Jews, 2011; Paul and the Gift, 2015; Paul: a very brief history, 2017. *Recreations:* cycling, walking. *Address:* Kimblesworth House, Kimblesworth, Chester-le-Street DH2 3QP. *T:* (0191) 371 0388. *E:* john.barclay@durham.ac.uk.

**BARCLAY, Neil;** *see* Barclay, A. N.

**BARCLAY, Patrick;** journalist, author, broadcaster; *b* 15 Aug. 1947; *s* of Guy Deghy and Patricia Wighton; one *s* one *d. Educ:* Dundee High Sch. Sub-editor, 1966–77, football writer, 1977–86, The Guardian; football columnist: Today, 1986; The Independent, 1986–91; The Observer, 1991–96; Sunday Telegraph, 1996–2009; Chief Football Commentator, The Times, 2009–12; columnist, Evening Standard, 2012–16. *Publications:* Mourinho: anatomy of a winner, 2005, rev. edn as Mourinho: further anatomy of a winner, 2011; Football - Bloody Hell!: the story of Alex Ferguson, 2010; The Life and Times of Herbert Chapman, 2014; Sir Matt Busby: the definitive biography, 2017. *Recreations:* reading, travel. *Address:* c/o 2 Brydges Place, WC2N 4HP.

**BARCLAY, His Honour Paul Robert;** a Circuit Judge, 1998–2013; *s* of late John Alexander Barclay and Mabel Elizabeth Barclay; *m* 1972, Sarah Louise Jones; two *s* two *d. Educ:* Nottingham High Sch.; St John's Coll., Cambridge (MA 1971). Called to the Bar, Middle Temple, 1972; in practice at the Bar, 1972–98; an Asst Recorder, 1992–96; a Recorder, 1996–98. *Recreation:* village cricket.

**BARCLAY, Sir Robert (Colraine),** 15th Bt *cr* 1668 (NS), of Pierston, Ayrshire; *b* 12 Feb. 1950; *e s* of Sir Colville Herbert Sanford Barclay, 14th Bt and Rosamond Grant Renton (*née* Elliott); *S* father, 2010; *m* 1980, Lucilia Saboia (marr. diss. 1986); one *s* one *d. Educ:* Eton; Univ. of East Anglia. Chartered accountant; stockbroker. *Publications:* Brazil: changing course, 1992. *Recreations:* Bach, bromeliads. *Heir: s* Henry William Saboia Barclay, *b* 16 Jan. 1982. *E:* robert.c.barclay@gmail.com. *Clubs:* Royal Over-Seas League; Naval (Rio de Janeiro).

**BARCLAY, Rt Hon. Stephen (Paul);** PC 2018; MP (C) North East Cambridgeshire, since 2010; Secretary of State for Exiting the European Union, since 2018; *b* Lytham, Lancs, 1972; *s* of Robert and Janice Barclay; *m* Karen; one *s* one *d. Educ:* King Edward VII Sch., Lancs; Peterhouse, Cambridge (BA Hist. 1994); Coll. of Law, Chester. 2nd Lieut, RRF, 1991. Trainee solicitor, Lawrence Graham, Solicitors, 1996–98; admitted as solicitor, 1998; Solicitor, Axa Insce, 1998–2001; FSA, 2002–06; Dir, Regulatory Affairs, then Hd, Antimoney Laundering and Sanction, Barclays UK Retail Bank, 2006–10. An Asst Govt Whip, 2015–16; a Lord Comr of HM Treasury (Govt Whip), 2016–17; Economic Sec., HM Treasury, 2017–18; Minister of State, DHSC, 2018. Contested (C): Manchester Blackley, 1997; Lancaster and Wyre, 2001. *Address:* House of Commons, SW1A 0AA.

**BARCLAY, Yvonne Fay, (Mrs William Barclay);** *see* Minton, Y. F.

**BARCLAY-SMITH, Ronald George;** Chair, British Transport Police Authority, since 2018; *b* 12 May 1954; *s* of John Hamilton Smith and Jean Lennox Smith (*née* Graeme); *m* 1st, 1978, Elaine Sheila Murdoch (*née* McClure) (marr. diss. 1988); two *s*; 2nd, 2004, Linsey Jane (*née* McDonald). *Educ:* George Heriot's Sch., Edinburgh; Edinburgh Univ. (MA Jt Hons Pol. and Mod. Hist., 1976); Queens' Coll., Cambridge (MPhil Internat. Relns, 1988); Kingston Poly. Business Sch. (MBA 1991). Commnd RAF, 1972; RAF Coll., Cranwell, 1976–77 (Queen's Medal); 51 Sqn RAF Regt, 1977–78; 63 Sqn RAF Regt, Gütersloh, 1978–81; HQ RAF Germany, Rheindahlen, 1981–82; RAF Lyneham, 1982–83; Dep. Sqn Ldr II Sqn (Para) RAF Regt, 1983–84; Sqn Ldr, 1984; Staff Officer, HQ 1 Gp, 1984; OC Short Range Air Defence, Belize, 1984–85; OC 1 (Light Armoured) Sqn RAF Regt, RAF Laarbruch, 1985–87; Wing Comdr, 1988; Desk Officer D Air Plans, 1988–92; retd RAF, 1992; Dep. Regl Dir, Corporate Planning, Trent RHA, 1992–93; Chief Executive: Lincs HA/FHSA, 1993–95; Defence Secondary Care Agency, MoD, 1995–98; mgt and consultancy rôles, 1998–2000; Chief Executive: Common Services Agency, NHS, Scotland, 2000–01; ESPC Gp of Cos (formerly ESPC (UK) Ltd), 2001–09; 9 Gough Square, 2010–11; South Square, 2011–17. Non-exec. Dir, Criminal Injuries Compensation Authy, 2017–. Mem., Conduct and Appeals Cttee, RICS, 2017–. Chm., Scottish Solicitors' Property Centres Cttee, 2002–04; Mem., Scottish Archæol Finds Allocation Panel (formerly Treasure Trove Adv. Panel for Scotland), 2004–10. Chm., Veterans Scotland, 2006–10. Hon. Pres., RAF Regt Assoc. in Scotland, 2006–. CDir 2004; FCMI 2005; FCIPD 2006; FInstD 2009. Mem., Merchant Co. of Edinburgh, 2002–10. *Publications:* articles in jls. *Recreations:* hillwalking, tennis, philately, model trains, fine wine, English landscape paintings. *Address:* c/o New Club, 86 Princes Street, Edinburgh EH2 2BB; British Transport Police Authority, Force Headquarters, 25 Camden Road, NW1 9LN. *Club:* New (Edinburgh).

**BARCROFT, Very Rev. Ian David;** Dean of the Diocese of Glasgow and Galloway, since 2010; Rector, St Mary's Episcopal Church, Hamilton, since 1997, and St Andrew's, Uddingston, since 2016; *b* Bury, Lancs, 29 Sept. 1960; *s* of Alan and Joyce Barcroft; *m* 1988, Heather Cowe; two *d. Educ:* Bury Grammar Sch.; Univ. of Manchester Inst. of Sci. and Technol. (BSc Hons 1983); Edinburgh Univ. (BD Jt Hons 1988); Glasgow Univ. (MTh (Res.) 2001). Ordained deacon 1988, priest 1989; Precentor, St Ninian's Cathedral, Perth, 1988–92; Priest, St Clement's, Aberdeen, 1992–97. *Recreations:* football, cricket, theatre, walking. *Address:* St Mary's Rectory, 4C Auchingramont Road, Hamilton ML3 6JT. *T:* (01698) 429895. *E:* ian.barcroft@btinternet.com.

**BARCROFT, Sam J. R.;** Founder and Chief Executive Officer, Barcroft Media Ltd, since 2003; *b* London, 4 June 1975; *s* of Roger Barcroft and Jan Etoile; *m* 2004, Faith Emmett; one *s* two *d. Educ:* Haverstock Sch. Library asst, Rex Features, 1994; Asst Picture Ed., Sunday People, 1995–98; freelance picture editor, 1998–2000; freelance photojournalist, 2000–03. *Recreations:* hip hop and jazz music, walking, ski-ing, football, world domination. *Address:* Barcroft Media Ltd, Studio 14, Shoreditch Stables, 138 Kingsland Road, E2 8DY. *Club:* Soho House.

**BARDA, Clive Blackmore,** OBE 2016; freelance photographer, since 1968; *b* 14 Jan. 1945; *s* of Gaston Barda and Marjorie (*née* Blackmore); *m* 1970, Rosalind Mary Whiteley; three *s. Educ:* Bryanston Sch.; Birkbeck Coll., London (BA Hons Modern Langs). Photographer, specialising in performing arts, esp. classical music, opera and theatre. *Exhibitions:* RFH, London, 1979; Science Museum, London, 1985; RNCM, Manchester, 1980; Perth, Australia, 1981; RPS, Bath, 1985; Nat. Mus. of Photography, Film and TV, Bradford, 1988; Nagaoka, Japan, 1996; Tokyo, 1998; Edinburgh, 2001; Paris, 2002; EXPOSURE! (retrospective), China and UK, 2012. FRSA 1996. Freeman, Musicians' Co., 2017. *Publications:* The Sculpture of David Wynne, 1975; The Complete Phantom of the Opera, 1988; The Complete Aspects of Love, 1990; Celebration!, 1996; Performance!, 2001; The Power of the Ring, 2007. *Recreations:* walking, singing in the church choir, classical music, opera, theatre, cinema, reading, watching cricket. *T:* (020) 8579 5202. *E:* clivebarda@pobox.com. *Clubs:* Garrick, MCC.

**BARDELL, Hannah Mary;** MP (SNP) Livingston, since 2015; *b* Craigshill, Livingston. *Educ:* Broxburn Acad.; Univ. of Stirling (BA Hons Film and Media, Politics and English 2005). Researcher, then Asst Producer, GMTV, 2005–07; Office Manager, Rt Hon. Alex Salmond, MSP, 2007–10; Protocol Exec. and Events Manager, American Consulate Edinburgh, 2010–12; Communications Manager, Subsea 7, 2012; Hd, Communications and Mktg (UK and Africa), Stork Tech. Services, 2013–15. SNP spokesperson for culture and media, 2018–. *Address:* House of Commons, SW1A 0AA.

**BARDER, Owen Matthew;** Senior Fellow and Europe Director, since 2011, and Vice President, since 2015, Center for Global Development; *b* 20 Feb. 1967; *s* of Sir Brian Leon Barder, KCMG and of Jane Maureen Barder; partner, Grethe Petersen. *Educ:* Sevenoaks Sch.; New Coll., Oxford (BA Hons PPE 1988); London Sch. of Econs (MSc Econs 1991). HM Treasury, 1988–96, Private Sec. to the Chancellor of the Exchequer, 1991–94; Dep of Finance, S Africa, 1997–99; Private Sec., Econ. Affairs, to the Prime Minister 1999–2000; Department for International Development: Hd, Africa Policy, 2000–02; Dir Inf., Communications, Knowledge, 2002–04; Center for Global Develt, Washington (on special leave), 2004–06; Dir, Global Develt Effectiveness, then Internat. Finance and Devel Effectiveness, DFID, 2006–08. Director: aidinfo, 2008–11; Publish What You Fund 2012–16. Vis. Scholar, Univ. of Calif, Berkeley, 2004–06; Vis. Fellow, Center for Globa

Develt, 2010–11; Vis. Prof. in Practice, LSE, 2015–. Non-exec. Dir, One World International, 2000–04. Producer and host, Development Drums podcast, 2008–. *Publications:* Making Markets for Vaccines (jtly), 2004; Running for Fitness, 2002; Get Fit Running, 2004; various articles. *Recreations:* running, information technology, triathlon. *T:* 07917 547979. *E:* owen@barder.com. *W:* www.owen.org, www.runningforfitness.org. *Clubs:* Lansdowne; Serpentine Running.

**BARDRICK, James David Kempster;** Chief Executive Officer, Citigroup Global Markets Ltd, and Country Officer - UK, Citigroup, since 2014; *b* Ilford, 22 Nov. 1962; *s* of Brian Bardrick and Enid Bardrick; *m* 2006, Sophie Lewington; one *s* three *d. Educ:* Bishop Luffa C of E Comp. Sch., Chichester; Bancroft's Sch., Woodford Green; Univ. of Birmingham (BSc and BCom Hons 1st Cl. Mech. Engrg and Econs). Engineer: GKN, 1981–84; F H Tomkins, 1984–86; Schroders, then Citigroup: banker, 1987–; Global Hd, Industrials Banking, 2006–09; EMEA Co-Hd, Corporate and Investment Banking, 2009–14. Director: BBA, 2014– (Chm., 2017–); Banking Standards Bd, 2015–; UK Finance, 2017–. Mem., Prudential Regulation Authy Practitioner Panel, Bank of England, 2014–. Trustee: Coggeshall Prentice Youth Work Trust, 2007– (Chm., 2015–); Career Ready, 2010– (Dep. Chm., 2015–). Mem., Chatham House (RIIA), 2010–. *Recreations:* sailing, ski-ing, tennis, cooking, reading, singing, family, charity. *Address:* Citigroup Centre, Canada Square, Canary Wharf, E14 5LB. *Clubs:* Reform; Tollesbury Sailing.

**BAREAU, Peter John,** CBE 2002; Chief Executive, National Savings and Investments (formerly National Savings), 1996–2002; *b* 1 June 1942; *s* of late Paul Bareau, OBE and Kitty Bareau (*née* Gibson); *m* 1st, 1967, Irene Nelson (marr. diss.); one *s* one *d*; 2nd, 1976, Karen Giesemann (*d* 2001); one *s* two *d*; 3rd, 2003, Ruth Holyoak (*née* Hardy); two step *s*. *Educ:* Eton Coll.; Queens' Coll., Cambridge (MA). With Bank of London & S America in UK, USA, Paraguay and Spain, 1966–72; with Lloyds Bank Internat. in UK and Brazil, 1973–84; Lloyds Bank PLC: General Manager: Strategic Planning, 1985–86; Europe, ME and Internat. Pvte Banking, 1987–91; Personnel, 1992–96. Sen. Advr, Corporate Value Associates, 2003–12. Chm., Surrey and Sussex SHA, 2003–06. Ind. Mem., Energy Gp Adv. Bd, DTI, 2004–06. Trustee, Breast Cancer Campaign, 2002–06. Hon. FCMC 2003. *Recreations:* writing biography of my father, playing chamber music, trying to defeat Brexit. *Address:* Red Rose Cottage, Ockham Road South, East Horsley, Surrey KT24 6RL. *T:* (01483) 286814.

**BAREHAM, Lindsey Margaret;** cookery writer, The Times, since 2006; *b* Chislehurst, 18 Sept. 1948; *s* of Frederick and Jean Bareham; *m* 1977, Ben John (*d* 2006); two *s. Educ:* St Philomena's Convent High Sch., Kent; Chislehurst and Sidcup Grammar Sch. Consumer and Eating-out Ed., Time Out, 1972–87; consumer columnist and restaurant critic, Sunday Telegraph, 1989–91; cookery columnist, Daily Telegraph, 1992–93; Evening Standard cook, 1996–2004; food writer, Saga mag., 2004–12. *Publications:* In Praise of the Potato, 1989; A Celebration of Soup, 1993; (with S. Hopkinson) Roast Chicken and Other Stories, 1994; Onions without Tears, 1995; Supper Won't Take Long, 1997; (with S. Hopkinson) The Prawn Cocktail Years, 1997; The Big Red Book of Tomatoes, 1999; A Wolf in the Kitchen, 2000, new edn as Hungry?, 2008; Just One Pot, 2004; The Fish Store, 2006; Dinner in a Dash, 2007; Pasties, 2008; The Trifle Bowl and Other Tales, 2013; One Pot Wonders, 2014; Dinner Tonight: 200 dishes you can cook in minutes, 2016. *Recreations:* Cornish coast walking, dancing, jazz, art, allotmenteering. *Clubs:* Chelsea Arts, Groucho, Union, Quo Vadis.

**BARENBOIM, Daniel,** Hon. KBE 2011; pianist and conductor; Music Director: Berlin State Opera, since 1992; La Scala, Milan, 2011–15 (Principal Guest Conductor, 2006–11); *b* Buenos Aires, 15 Nov. 1942; *s* of Enrique Barenboim and late Aida Barenboim (*née* Schuster); *m* 1st, 1967, Jacqueline du Pré (*d* 1987); 2nd, 1988, Elena Bashkirova; two *s. Educ:* Santa Cecilia Acad., Rome; studied with his father; coached by Edwin Fischer, Nadia Boulanger, and Igor Markevitch. Debut as pianist with: Israel Philharmonic Orchestra, 1953; Royal Philharmonic Orchestra, 1956; Berlin Philharmonic Orchestra, 1963; NY Philharmonic Orchestra, 1964; Music Director: Orchestre de Paris, 1975–88; Chicago SO, 1991–2006; tours include: Australia, North and South America, Far East; regular appearances at Bayreuth, Edinburgh, Lucerne, Prague and Salzburg Festivals; co-founded West-Eastern Divan Orchestra with Edward Saïd, 1998. Many recordings as conductor and pianist. BBC Reith Lectr, 2006. Beethoven Medal, 1958; Paderewski Medal, 1963; subsequently other awards. Grand Officier, Legion of Honour (France), 2011. *Publications:* A Life in Music, 1991; (with Edward Saïd) Parallels and Paradoxes, 2002; Everything is Connected, 2008; (with Patrice Chéreau) Dialoghi su musica e teatro: Tristano e Isotta, 2008. *Address:* c/o Konzert-Direktion Hans Adler OHG, Auguste-Victoria-Straße 64, 14199 Berlin, Germany.

**BARFIELD, Julia Barbara,** MBE 2000; Director, Marks Barfield Architects, since 1989; *b* 15 Nov. 1952; *d* of Arnold Robert Barfield and Iolanthe Mary Barfield; *m* 1981, David Joseph Marks, MBE (*d* 2017); one *s* two *d. Educ:* Godolphin and Latymer Sch.; AA Sch. of Architecture. Dir, Tetra Ltd, 1978–79; Architectural Asst, Richard Rogers Partnership, 1979–81; Project Architect, Foster Associates, 1981–88; Founding Director: London Eye Co., 1994–2006; Brighton i360, 2006–. Member: Council, AA, 2001–06; Design Review Panel, CABE, 2004–11; Chm., RIBA Nat. Awards Panel, 2016–18. Mem. Council, Guy's and St Thomas' Hosp., 2005–10; Gov., Godolphin and Latymer Sch., 2006–16. *Recreations:* family, travel, arts. *Address:* Marks Barfield Architects, 50 Bromell's Road, SW4 0BG. *T:* (020) 7501 0180. *E:* jbarfield@marksbarfield.com.

**BARFORD, Prof. David,** DPhil; FRS 2006; FMedSci; Team Leader, since 2013 and Co-Head, Division of Structural Studies, since 2015, MRC Laboratory of Molecular Biology, Cambridge; *b* 17 Aug. 1963; *s* of Jack and Mai Barford. *Educ:* Univ. of Bristol (BSc 1984); Univ. of Oxford (DPhil 1988). Research Fellow: Univ. of Oxford, 1988–90; Univ. of Dundee, 1990–91; Cold Spring Harbor Lab., NY, 1991–94; Lectr, Univ. of Oxford and Tutorial Fellow, Somerville Coll., Oxford, 1994–99; Prof. of Molecular Biol. and Co-Hd, Div. of Structural Biol., Inst. of Cancer Res., London, 1999–2013. Mem. Scientific Adv. Bd, Ceptyr Corp., Seattle, 1996–2004. Mem. EMBO, 2003. FMedSci 2003. Hon. DSc Bristol, 2017. *Publications:* contribs to scientific jls. *Recreations:* classical music, reading. *Address:* MRC Laboratory of Molecular Biology, Cambridge CB2 0QH. *T:* (01223) 267075. *E:* dbarford@mrc-lmb.cam.ac.uk.

**BARGERY, (Bruno Philip) Robert;** Director, Royal Fine Art Commission Trust, since 2015; *b* 4 April 1966; *s* of Geoffrey Maxwell Bargery and Barbara Ann Hill. *Educ:* Hinchley Wood Sch.; Kingston Coll.; Exeter Univ.; Exeter Coll., Oxford. DoE, 1991–95; Researcher, Royal Fine Art Commn, 1995–99; Head, Policy and Res., CABE, 1999–2001; Dir, The Georgian Gp, 2002–16. Dir, Georgian Enterprises and Trading Ltd, 2008–16. Mem., Adv. Council, Brighton and Hove Heritage Commn, 2015–; Heritage Advr, Hamish Ogston Foundn, 2018–. Trustee, Kelmarsh Trust, 2016–19. FRSA 2003. *Publications:* (ed) Good Design in Speculative Housing, 1998; The Amateur Artist, 2016; Decorating Parliament: Prince Albert and the first Royal Fine Art Commission 1841–1863, 2017; Design Champion: the twentieth century Royal Fine Art Commission 1924–1999, 2019. *Address:* 33 Merganser Court, Star Place, St Katharine Docks, E1W 1AQ. *E:* robertbargery@me.com.

**BARHAM, His Honour Geoffrey Simon;** a Circuit Judge, 1993–2010; *b* 23 Dec. 1945; *s* of late Denis Patrick Barham and Pleasance (*née* Brooke); *m* 1976, Sarah Seebold (*d* 2016); one *s* one *d. Educ:* Malvern Coll.; Christ's Coll., Cambridge (MA). Called to the Bar, Lincoln's Inn, 1968; Asst Recorder, 1983; Recorder, 1987. *Recreation:* golf. *Club:* Norfolk (Norwich).

**BARI, Dr Muhammad Abdul,** MBE 2003; DL; educationalist, parenting consultant, and writer and commentator on social and political issues; *b* 2 Oct. 1953; *s* of Muhammad Manikuddin and Karimunnesa; *m* Sayeda Akhter; three *s* one *d. Educ:* King's Coll., London (PhD; PGCE). Specialist Teacher, London Bor. of Tower Hamlets, 1997–2011. Chm., E London Mosque/London Muslim Centre, 2002–13; Sec. Gen., Muslim Council of GB, 2006–10. Trustee, Muslim Aid, 1996–2015. Non-exec. Dir, LOCOG, 2006–13. DL Gtr London, 2016. Hon. Fellow, Queen Mary, Univ. of London, 2008. Hon. DEd East London, 2012. FRSA 2005. *Publications:* The Greatest Gift: a guide to parenting from an Islamic perspective, 2002; Building Muslim Families: challenges and expectations, 2002; Race, Religion and Muslim Identity in Britain, 2005; Marriage and Family Building in Islam, 2007; A Guide to Parenting in Islam: addressing adolescence, 2011; British, Muslims, Citizens: introspection and renewal, 2012; A Guide to Parenting in Islam: cherishing childhood, 2015; The Rohingya Crisis: a people facing extinction, 2018; A Long Jihad: my quest for the middle way, 2018. *Recreations:* reading, travelling, writing, youth and community work. *E:* mabdulbari59@gmail.com.

**BARING,** family name of **Earl of Cromer** and **Barons Ashburton, Howick of Glendale, Northbrook,** and **Revelstoke.**

**BARING, Sir John (Francis),** 3rd Bt *cr* 1911, of Nubia House, Isle of Wight; Director, Camphill Village Copake Foundation, 2007–14; *b* 21 May 1947; *s* of Raymond Alexander Baring (*d* 1967) (2nd *s* of 1st Bt) and Margaret Fleetwood Baring (who *m* 1991, 6th Earl of Malmesbury, TD; she *d* 1994), *d* of late Col R. W. P. C. Campbell-Preston; *S* uncle, 1990; *m* 1st, 1971, Elizabeth Anne (marr. diss. 2004), *yr d* of Robert D. H. Pillitz; two *s* one *d*; 2nd, 2007, Penelope Ann Roberts, *e d* of Cdre John M. Doull, Canada Navy (retd). Citibank NA, 1971–72; Chemical Bank, 1972–84; Kidder, Peabody & Co. Inc., 1984–89; GPA Group Ltd, 1989; Hackman, Baring & Co., 1991–97; PricewaterhouseCoopers Securities LLC, 1997–99; Managing Partner and Mem., Mercator Capital LLC, 1999–2004. Director, Camphill Foundn, 2002–14; Camphill Village USA, 2005–14. Chm. Trustees, Rudolf Steiner Sch., 2002–08. *Recreations:* gardening, fishing. *Heir: s* Julian Alexander David Baring, *b* 10 Feb. 1975. *Address:* (residence) 126 Seacliff Drive, Aptos, CA 95003, USA; (mailing) 500 Cathedral Drive #2814, Aptos, CA 95001, USA.

*See also* A. H. Buchanan.

**BARING, Nicholas Hugo,** CBE 2003; Chairman, Baring Archive Trust, 2008–14; *b* 2 Jan. 1934; *er s* of Francis Anthony Baring (killed in action, 1940) and Lady Rose Baring, DCVO; *m* 1972, (Elizabeth) Diana, *d* of late Brig. Charles Crawfurd; three *s. Educ:* Eton (King's Schol.); Magdalene Coll., Cambridge (exhibnr, BA). Nat. service, 2nd Lieut Coldstream Guards, 1952–54. ADC to Governor of Kenya, 1957–58; joined Baring Brothers, 1958; Man. Dir, Baring Brothers & Co., 1963–86; Dir, Barings plc, 1985–94 (Dep. Chm., 1986–89); Mem., 1973–2004, Chm., 1998–2004, Council of Mgt, Baring Foundn. Dir, Commercial Union plc, 1968–98 (Chm., 1990–98). Mem., City Capital Markets Cttee, 1983–89 (Chm., 1983–87). Vice Pres., Liverpool Sch. of Tropical Medicine, 1982–89, 1996– (Pres., 1989–96); Chm., Bd of Trustees, Nat. Gall., 1992–98 (Trustee, 1989–96); Trustee, Fitzwilliam Museum Develt Trust (formerly Fitzwilliam Museum Trust), 1997–2011 (Chm., 2004–11). National Trust: Mem. Exec. Cttee, 1965–69 and 1979–2002; Mem. Council, 1978–2002; Chm., Finance Cttee, 1980–91. Mem. Council of Management, Architectl Heritage Fund, 1987–2010. Hon. LLD Liverpool, 1995; Hon. DCL: Kent, 1998; Northumbria, 2004. *Address:* The Old Rectory, Ham, Marlborough, Wilts SN8 3QR. *T:* (01488) 668805. *Clubs:* Brooks's, Beefsteak.

*See also* P. Baring.

**BARING, Peter;** *b* 28 Oct. 1935; *yr s* of Francis Anthony Baring (killed in action, 1940) and Lady Rose Baring, DCVO; *m* 1960, Teresa Anne Bridgeman (CBE 1998) (*d* 2019); three *s. Educ:* Magdalene College, Cambridge (MA English). Joined Baring Brothers & Co., 1959, Director, 1967; Chairman: Barings plc, 1989–95; Baring Asset Management, 1993–95. Dir, Inchcape, 1978–96. Dep. Chm., Provident Mutual Life Assurance Assoc., 1989–95. Chm., London Investment Banking Assoc., 1991–94. Gov., London Business Sch., 1991–95. Chm., Glyndebourne Arts Trust, 1994–96.

*See also* N. H. Baring.

**BARKE, Prof. Edmund James Stephen, (Prof. Edmund Sonuga-Barke),** PhD; FBA 2018; FMedSci; Professor of Developmental Psychology, Psychiatry and Neuroscience, King's College London, since 2017; *b* Derby, 20 May 1962; *s* of David Barke and Carmel Barke (*née* Hughes); *m* 1987, Funke Sonuga; one *s* one *d. Educ:* St Ralph Sherwin RC Comprehensive Sch., Derby; Wilmorton Tech. Coll., Derby; University Coll. of N Wales, Bangor (BSc Hons Psychol.); Univ. of Exeter (PhD Psychol. 1985). Researcher and Lectr, Inst. of Psychiatry, 1987–89; Lectr, 1989–95, Reader. 1995–97, Prof. of Develtl Psychopathol., 1997–2016, Univ. of Southampton. Visiting Professor: Univ. of Calif, Irvine, 2002–03; Ghent Univ., 2007–18; Aarhus Univ., 2013–; Univ. of Sussex, 2015–; Adjunct Prof., Child Study Center, NY Univ., 2004–10. Ed.-in-Chief, Jl Child Psychol. and Psychiatry, 2010–. FMedSci 2016. *Publications:* contribs to learned jls incl. Jl Child Psychol. and Psychiatry, Biological Psychiatry, Neurosci. Behaviour Res., Amer. Acad. Child and Adolescent Psychiatry, Amer. Jl Psychiatry, Lancet. *Recreations:* singing, dancing, joking, eating, praying. *E:* ejsbarke@gmail.com.

**BARKER,** family name of **Baron Barker of Battle.**

**BARKER,** Baroness *cr* 1999 (Life Peer), of Anagach in Highland; **Elizabeth Jean Barker;** Management Consultant, ThirdSectorBusiness, since 2008; Partner, Barker and Woodard Consulting, since 2007; *b* Outwood, W Yorks, 31 Jan. 1961. *Educ:* Dalziel High Sch., Motherwell; Broadway Sch., Oldham; Univ. of Southampton (BSc(SocSci) Hons Psychology). Pres., Union of Liberal Students, 1982–83. Age Concern England: Project Co-Ordinator, Opportunities for Volunteering Programme, 1983–88; Grants Officer, 1988–92; Field Officer, 1992–2008; Head of Business Develt, www.seethedifference.org, 2009–12. Chm., All Party Parly Gp on Sexual and Reproductive Health; Co-founder, All Party Parly Gp on Global LGBT Rights. Member: Liberal Party Nat. Exec., 1982–83; Liberal Assembly Cttee, 1984–88; Lib Dem Federal Conf. Cttee, 1988– (Chm., 1997–2004); Lib Dem Federal Policy Cttee, 1997–2003. Thought Leader, TheGivingLab, 2009–13. Trustee, Andy Lawson Meml Fund. Patron: Spare Tyre Theatre Co.; E London Out Project. Ambassador, Albert Kennedy Trust, 2013–. Volunteer, VSO, 2014–. *Address:* House of Lords, SW1A 0PW.

**BARKER OF BATTLE,** Baron *cr* 2015 (Life Peer), of Battle in the County of East Sussex; **Gregory Leonard George Barker;** PC 2012; Chairman, En+ Group plc, since 2017; *b* Sussex, 8 March 1966; *m* 1992, Celeste Harrison (marr. diss. 2008); two *s* one *d. Educ:* Steyning Grammar Sch.; Lancing Coll.; RHBNC (BA 1987). Researcher, Centre for Policy Studies, 1987–88 (Associate, 1988–); Equity Analyst, Gerrard Vivian Gray, 1988–90; Dir,

Internat. Pacific Securities, 1990–97; Associate Partner, Brunswick Gp Ltd, 1997–98; Hd, Investor Communications, Siberian Oil Co., 1998–2000. Dir, Daric plc, 1998–2001. MP (C) Bexhill and Battle, 2001–15. An Opposition Whip, 2003–05; Shadow Envmt Minister, 2005–08; Shadow Climate Change Minister, 2008–10; Minister of State, DECC, 2010–14. Mem., H of C Envmtl Audit Select Cttee, 2001–05. Contested (C) Eccles, 1997. Chm., Quercus, 2018–; non-executive Director: Dragon Harvest Gp, 2015–; Lightsource Renewable Energy Ltd, 2015–. Chm., London Sustainable Develt Commn, 2014–17. *Club:* Pratt's.

**BARKER, Alexandra Rose;** *see* Mahon, A. R.

**BARKER, Prof. Andrew Dennison,** PhD; FBA 2005; Professor of Classics, University of Birmingham, 1998–2008, now Emeritus; *b* 24 April 1943; *s* of Edwin Barker and Nancy Ethel Barker; *m* 1st, Susan Margaret Hough (marr. diss. 1976); two *s*; 2nd, 1978, Jill Davida Newman; two *s* one *d*. *Educ:* Christ's Hosp.; Queen's Coll., Oxford (BA); Australian Nat. Univ. (PhD). Lectr in Philosophy, 1970–87, Sen. Lectr, 1987–92, Univ. of Warwick; Asst Lectr in Classics, Univ. of Cambridge, 1976–78, and Fellow and Dir of Studies in Classics and Philosophy, Selwyn Coll., Cambridge, 1977–78 (on leave from Univ. of Warwick); Sen. Lectr in Classics, 1992–95, Prof., 1995, Univ. of Otago; Reader in Classics, Univ. of Birmingham, 1996–98. *Publications:* Greek Musical Writings, vol. 1, 1984, vol. 2, 1989; Scientific Method in Ptolemy's Harmonics, 2000; Euterpe: ricerche sulla musica Greca e Romana, 2002; Psicomusicologia Nella Grecia Antica, 2005; The Science of Harmonics in Classical Greece, 2007; Ancient Greek Writers on their Musical Past, 2014; Porphyry's Commentary on Ptolemy's Harmonics, 2015; articles on ancient Greek music and philosophy. *Recreations:* negotiations with dogs and family; DIY building and land-maintenance, natural history, listening to music, watercolour painting. *Address:* Department of Classics, Ancient History and Archaeology, University of Birmingham, Birmingham B15 2TT. *E:* andrewqbarker@hotmail.com.

**BARKER, Rt Hon. Dame Anne Judith;** *see* Rafferty, Rt Hon. Dame A. J.

**BARKER, Barry,** MBE 1960; FCIS; Secretary and Chief Executive, Institute of Chartered Secretaries and Administrators (formerly Chartered Institute of Secretaries), 1976–89; *b* 28 Dec. 1929; *s* of late Francis Walter Barker and Amy Barker; *m* 1954, Dr Vira Dubash; two *s*. *Educ:* Ipswich Sch.; Trinity Coll., Oxford (MA Class. Greats). Secretary: Bombay Chamber of Commerce and Industry, 1956–62; The Metal Box Co. of India Ltd, 1962–67. Dir, Shipbuilding Industry Bd, 1967–71; Consultant at Dept of Industry, 1972; Sec., Pye Holdings Ltd, 1972–76. Chairman: Consultative Council of Professional Management Orgns, 1981–90; Nat. Endorsement Bd, Management Charter Initiative, 1990–94. Member: BTEC, 1985–94; RSA Exams Bd, 1987–94; NCVQ, 1989–92; Bd of Management, Young Vic Co., 1984–90. *Recreation:* the theatre and the arts. *Address:* 82 Darwin Court, Gloucester Avenue, NW1 7BQ. *T:* (020) 7911 0570.

**BARKER, His Honour Brian John,** CBE 2015; QC 1990; a Senior Circuit Judge, 2000–15; Recorder of London, 2013–15; *b* 15 Jan. 1945; *s* of William Barker and Irene Barker (*née* Gillow); *m* 1977, Anne Judith Rafferty (*see* Rt Hon. Dame A. J. Rafferty); three *d* (and one *d* decd). *Educ:* Strode's School, Egham; Univ. of Birmingham (LLB); Univ. of Kansas (MA). Called to the Bar, Gray's Inn, 1969, Bencher, 1999. A Recorder, 1985–2000; Common Serjeant, City of London, 2005–13. Mem., Senate and Bar Council, 1976–79. A Pres., Mental Health Review Tribunals, 1993–2004. Asst Surveillance Comr, 2015–; Chair, NI Cttee on Protection, and Ind. Reviewer of Nat. Security Arrangements in NI, 2016–. Chm., Criminal Bar Assoc., 1998–2000. Course Dir, Criminal Continuation Seminars, Judicial Studies Bd, 2003–07. Chm., Judicial Panel, British Horseracing Authy, 2017–. Coroner, Deepcut Inquest, 2016. Judge, The Trial, Channel 4, 2017. Trustee, MAC-UK, 2012–. Governor: Strode's Coll., Egham, 1992–2003; Sir John Cass Foundn, Aldgate, 2003– (Treas., 2005–07); Mem., Coopers' Co. and Coborn Sch. Foundn Trust, 2018–. Patron, Kalisher Scholarship Trust, 2017–. Freeman, City of London; Liveryman: Coopers' Co., 1989– (Mem., Ct of Assts, 1995; Master, 2008–09); Cutlers' Co., 2006; Curriers' Co., 2013. Hon. Fellow, RHUL, 2016. Hon. LLD City, 2014. *Recreations:* sheep rearing, golf. *Address:* c/o Serjeants' Inn Chambers, 85 Fleet Street, EC4Y 1AE. *Clubs:* Bishopsgate Ward, Garrick; Rye Golf.
*See also* P. A. Darling.

**BARKER, Caroline;** *see* Norbury, C.

**BARKER, Prof. Eileen Vartan,** OBE 2000; PhD; FBA 1998; Professor of Sociology with Special Reference to the Study of Religion, London School of Economics, 1992–2003, now Emeritus; Leverhulme Emeritus Fellow, 2004–07; *b* 21 April 1938; *d* of Calman MacLennan and Mary Helen MacLennan (*née* Muir); *m* 1958, Peter Johnson Barker, MBE; two *d*. *Educ:* Cheltenham Ladies' Coll.; Webber Douglas Sch. of Singing and Dramatic Art; London Sch. of Econs (BSc 1st Cl. Hons Sociol. 1970; PhD 1984; Hon. Fellow, 2011). London School of Economics: Lectr, 1970–85; Sen. Lectr, 1985–90; Reader, 1990–92; Dean, Undergrad. Studies, 1982–86. Leonard Greenberg Distinguished Vis. Fellow, Trinity Coll., Hertford, USA, 2000; William James Guest Prof., Univ. of Bayreuth, 2012. Founder and Chm., INFORM, 1988– (Hon. Dir, 2001–13). President: Soc. for Scientific Study of Religion, 1991–93; Assoc. for Sociol. of Religion, 2001–02. Hon. Pres. for Life, Internat. Study of Religion in Eastern and Central Europe Assoc., 2006. FAcSS 2016. PhD *hc* Copenhagen, 2000. Martin E. Marty Award for Public Understanding of Religion, Amer. Acad. of Religion, 2000; Dist. Scholar Award, Communal Studies Assoc., 2010; George Leslie MacKay Award, Aletheia Univ., Taiwan, 2011; Lifetime Achievement Award, Internat. Cultic Studies Assoc., 2013. *Publications:* (ed) Of Gods and Men, 1982; (ed) New Religious Movements: a perspective for understanding society, 1982; The Making of a Moonie: brainwashing or choice?, 1984 (SSSR Dist. Book Award 1985); New Religious Movements: a practical introduction, 1989; (ed jtly) Secularization, Rationalism and Sectarianism, 1993; (ed jtly) Twenty Years On: changes in new religious movements, 1995; (ed) LSE on Freedom, 1995; (ed jtly) New Religions and New Religiosity, 1998; (ed) Freedom and Religion in Eastern Europe, 2003; (ed) The Centrality of Religion in Social Life, 2008; (ed) Revisionism and Diversification in New Religious Movements, 2013; numerous contribs to scholarly jls and books. *Address:* London School of Economics, Department of Sociology, Houghton Street, WC2A 2AE.

**BARKER, Prof. Graeme William Walter,** CBE 2015; FSA; FBA 1999; FRGS; Disney Professor of Archaeology, 2004–14, now Emeritus, and Senior Fellow, since 2014, McDonald Institute for Archaeological Research, University of Cambridge (Director, 2004–14); Fellow, St John's College, Cambridge, since 2004; *b* 23 Oct. 1946; *s* of Reginald Walter Barker and Kathleen (*née* Walton); *m* 1st, 1976, Sarah Miranda Buchanan (marr. diss. 1991); one *d* (and one *s* decd); 2nd, 2008, Annie Grant (marr. diss. 2016). *Educ:* Alleyn's Sch., Dulwich; St John's Coll., Cambridge (Henry Arthur Thomas Schol., 1965–67; MA; PhD 1973). FSA 1979; FRGS 2013. Rome Schol. in Classical Studies, British Sch. at Rome, 1969–71; Lectr, 1972–81, Sen. Lectr, 1981–88, in Prehist. and Archaeol., Sheffield Univ.; Dir, British Sch. at Rome, 1984–88; Leicester University: Prof. and Hd, Sch. of Archaeol Studies, 1988–2000; Graduate Dean, 2000–03; Pro-Vice-Chancellor, 2003–04. Member: Exec. Cttee, UK Council for Graduate Educn, 2001–03; AHRB, subseq. AHRC, 2003–09; Council, British Sch. at Rome, 2009–15; Chm., Archaeol. Sub-Panel, RAE, 2008. Pres., Prehistoric Soc., 2001–05; Hon. Vice Pres., Soc. for Libyan Studies, 2016–. Trustee: Antiquity, 2006–; Assoc. for Southeast Asianists UK, 2014–; Council for British Research in the Levant, 2017–; King Edward VII Sch. Foundn Charity, King's Lynn, 2018–. Gov., Bishop's Stortford Coll., 2019–. Hon. DLitt Sheffield, 2014. Dan David Prize, 2005; Field Discovery Award, Shanghai Archaeol Forum, 2017. *Publications:* Landscape and Society: Prehistoric Central Italy, 1981, Italian edn 1984; (with R. Hodges) Archaeology and Italian Society, 1981; Prehistoric Communities in Northern England, 1981; (jtly) La Casatico di Marcaria, 1991; (with C. S. Gamble) Beyond Domestication in Prehistoric Europe: Investigations in Subsistence Archaeology and Social Complexity, 1985; (with J. A. Lloyd) Roman Landscapes, 1991; (with R. Maggi and R. Nisbet) Archeologia della Pastorizia nell'Europa Meridionale, 1993; A Mediterranean Valley: landscape archaeology and *Annales* history in the Biferno Valley, 1995; The Biferno Valley Survey: the archaeological and geomorphological record, 1995; (jtly) Farming the Desert: the UNESCO Libyan valleys survey, 2 vols, 1996; (with T. Rasmussen) The Etruscans, 1998; (ed) The Companion Encyclopedia of Archaeology, 2 vols, 1999; (with D. Gilbertson) The Archaeology of Drylands: living at the margin, 2000; (ed jtly) The Human Use of Caves in Peninsular and Island Southeast Asia, 2005; The Agricultural Revolution in Prehistory: why did foragers become farmers?, 2006; (ed jtly) Archaeology and Desertification: the Wadi Faynan landscape survey, Southern Jordan, 2007; (ed jtly) Why Cultivate? anthropological and archaeological approaches to foraging-farming transitions in Southeast Asia, 2011; (ed) Foraging and Farming in Island Southeast Asia: the archaeology of the Niah Caves, 2013; (ed jtly) A World with Agriculture, 2015; (ed jtly) Archaeological Investigations in the Niah Caves, Sarawak, 2016; contribs to learned jls, esp. on landscape archaeol., ancient agric., dispersal of modern humans and Neanderthal demise. *Address:* McDonald Institute for Archaeological Research, Downing Street, Cambridge CB2 3ER. *T:* (01223) 339622.

**BARKER, Howard;** playwright and poet; *b* 28 June 1946. *Educ:* Univ. of Sussex (MA). Theatre productions, 1970–, include: *Royal Court:* No End of Blame, 1981; Victory, 1983; version of Thomas Middleton's Women Beware Women, 1986; The Last Supper, 1988; Golgo, 1990; Hated Nightfall, 1995; *RSC* at The Pit: The Castle, 1985; Downchild: a fantasy, 1985; The Bite of the Night, 1988; *Leicester:* The Last Supper, 1989; Seven Lears, 1990; Judith, 1995; (Uncle) Vanya, 1996; other productions: A Passion in Six Days, Crucible, Sheffield, 1983; The Power of the Dog, Hampstead, 1985; Possibilities, Almeida, 1988; The Forty, Aberystwyth, 2011; Scenes from an Execution, NT, 2012; Flesh and Blood, BBC SO, Coliseum, 2013. TV and radio plays include: Scenes from an Execution, Radio 3, 1984 (Best Drama Script, Sony Radio Awards, 1985; Prix Italia, 1985; perf. Almeida, 1990); Pity in History, BBC 2, 1985; A Hard Heart, Radio 3, 1992 (perf. Almeida, 1992); The Early Hours of a Reviled Man, Radio 3, 1992; A House of Correction, Albertina, Radio 3, 1999; Knowledge and a Girl, Radio 4, 2001; The Moving and The Still, Radio 3, 2003; The Road, The House, The Road, Radio 4, 2006; Let Me, Radio 3, 2006. Opera: (with Nigel Osborne) Terrible Mouth, ENO, Almeida, 1992; (with F. M. Einheit) Dead, Dead and Very Dead, 2007; In the Depths of Dead Love, Radio 3, 2013 (perf. Print Room at the Coronet, 2017). Formed The Wrestling School (company to perform own work), 1989: The Europeans, 1993; Wounds to the Face, 1997; Ursula, 1998; Und, 1999; The Ecstatic Bible, He Stumbled, 2000; A House of Correction, 2001; Gertrude - the Cry, 2002; 13 Objects, 2003; Dead Hands, 2004; The Fence in its Thousandth Year, 2005; The Seduction of Almighty God, 2006; I Saw Myself, The Dying of Today, 2008; Found in the Ground, 2009; Hurts Given and Received, Slowly, 2010. *Publications:* plays: Stripwell, and Claw, 1977; Fair Slaughter, 1978; Love of a Good Man, and All Bleeding, 1981; That Good Between Us, and Credentials of a Sympathiser, 1981; No End of Blame: scenes of overcoming, 1981; Two Plays for the Right: Birth on a Hard Shoulder, and The Loud Boy's Life, 1982; Hang of the Gaol, 1982; Victory: choices in reaction, 1983; The Castle, and Scenes from an Execution, 1984; Crimes in Hot Countries, and Fair Slaughter, 1984; Power of the Dog, 1985; A Passion in Six Days, and Downchild, 1985; The Last Supper: a New Testament, 1988; Lullabies for the Impatient, 1988; Possibilities, 1988; Pity in History, 1989; Seven Lears, and Golgo, 1990; Europeans, and Judith, 1990; Collected Plays, vol. I, 1990, vol. II, 1993, vol. III, 1996, vol. IV, 1997, vol. V, 1999; A Hard Heart, 1992; The Early Hours of a Reviled Man, 1992; Gertrude, and Knowledge and a Girl, 2002; The Ecstatic Bible, 2004; Dead Hands, 2004; The Fence in Its Thousandth Year, 2005; The Seduction of Almighty God, 2006; Collected Plays, vol. 1, 2006, vol. 2, 2006, vol. 3, 2008, vol. 4, 2008, vol. 5, 2009; The Dying of Today, 2008; Blok/Eko, 2011; *poetry:* Don't Exaggerate (Desire and Abuse), 1985; Breath of the Crowd, 1986; Gary the Thief/Gary Upright, 1987; The Ascent of Monte Grappa, 1991; The Tortmann Diaries, 1996; Sheer Detachment, 2009; *essays:* Arguments for a Theatre, 1989; Death, The One and the Art of Theatre, 2004; A Style and Its Origins, 2007; These Sad Places, Why Must You Enter Them?, 2014. *Address:* c/o Judy Daish Associates Ltd, 2 St Charles Place, W10 6EG.

**BARKER, Hon. Sir Ian;** *see* Barker, Hon. Sir R. I.

**BARKER, Jane Victoria,** CBE 2014; FCA; Chairman: Marsh Ltd, since 2013 (non-executive Director, since 2010); Mercer Ltd, since 2014 (non-executive Director, since 2011); *b* Stratford upon Avon, 11 Nov. 1949; *d* of Reginald Badger and Dorothy Badger; *m* 1976, Richard Barker (*d* 1995). *Educ:* Stratford upon Avon Grammar Sch. for Girls; Univ. of Reading (BSc Geol Geophysics 1971). FCA 1980 (ACA 1974). Articled clerk, Supervisor, then Manager, Coopers & Lybrand, 1971–76; various appts, then Chief Financial Officer, C. T. Bowring & Co. Ltd, 1976–90; Finance Dir, 1990–94, Chief Operating Officer, 1993–94, London Stock Exchange; Equitas Ltd: Finance Dir, 1995–2007; Chief Exec., 2007–14; non-exec. Dir, 2014–. Non-executive Director: Alliance & Leicester plc, 2004–11; Santander UK plc, 2008–11; Ind. Mem., Partnership Council, Clifford Chance, 2015–17. Member: Council, Open Univ., 1999–2005; Council, RCM, 2007– (Dep. Chm., 2008–; FRCM 2018). Mem., Chapter, Salisbury Cath., 2008–. DUniv Open, 2007. *Recreation:* enjoying life. *E:* jane.barker@marsh.com. *Club:* Athenæum.

**BARKER, Dame Katharine (Mary), (Dame Katharine Donovan),** DBE 2014 (CBE 2006); Chairman of Trustees, British Coal Staff Superannuation Scheme, since 2014; *b* 29 Nov. 1957; *d* of Wilfred Barker and Eileen May (*née* Pinhorn); *m* 1982, Peter Richard Donovan; two *s*. *Educ:* St Hilda's Coll., Oxford (BA Hons PPE). Investment analyst, PO Pension Fund, 1979–81; Res. Officer, NIESR, 1981–85; Chief Economist, Ford of Europe, 1985–94; Chief Econ. Advr, CBI, 1994–2001; Mem. Monetary Policy Cttee, Bank of England, 2001–10; non-exec. Mem., Office for Budget Responsibility, 2011–17 Mem., Panel of Independent Advrs, HM Treasury, 1996–97. Non-executive Director Yorkshire Bldg Soc., 1999–2001, 2010–16; Electra Private Equity, 2010–16; Taylor Wimpey, 2011–; Man Gp, 2017–. Sen. Advr, Credit Suisse, 2010–16. Member: Bd Housing Corp., 2005–08; Bd, Homes and Communities Agency, 2008–11; Nat Infrastructure Commn, 2017–; Industrial Strategy Council, 2018–. Chairman: Ind. Review of UK Housing Supply, 2003–04; Ind. Review of Land Use Planning, 2005–06; NI Econ Adv. Gp, 2010–15; Commn on the Future of Health and Social Care, King's Fund, 2014 Member: Football Regulatory Authy, 2006–12; Jersey Fiscal Policy Panel, 2014–. Ind

Comr, Geospatial Commn, 2019–. Mem., 1999–2007, Chm., 2007–10, Bd of Govs, Anglia Ruskin (formerly Anglia Poly.) Univ. *Publications:* Housing: where's the plan?, 2014; contribs to jls. *Recreation:* bell-ringing. *T:* 07866 546424.

**BARKER, Prof. Kenneth,** CBE 1994; Vice-Chancellor, Thames Valley University, 1999–2003; *b* 26 June 1934; *s* of Thomas William and Lillian Barker; *m* 1958, Jean Ivy Pearl; one *s* one *d. Educ:* Royal Coll. of Music (ARCM); King's Coll., London (BMus); Sussex Univ. (MA). GRSM, FTCL, FLCM. Schoolmaster, 1958–62; lectr and university teacher, 1962–75; Principal, Gipsy Hill Coll., 1975; Pro-Dir, Kingston Polytechnic, 1975–86; Dep. Dir/Dir Designate, 1986–87, Dir, 1987–92, Leicester Poly., then Chief Exec. and Vice-Chancellor, De Montfort Univ., 1992–99. Chm., Postgrad. Initial Teacher Trng Bd, 1975–80, Chm., Music Bd and Chm., Cttee for Creative Arts, 1980–90, CNAA. Board Member: London West LSC, 2001–03; London NHS Workforce Confedn, 2001–03. Trustee, Richmond Amer. Internat. Univ. in London, 1997–2004. FRSA; CCMI. Hon. DSc Moscow State Tech. Univ., 1995; DUniv: St Petersburg Univ. of Design and Technology, 1997; De Montfort, 1999; Thames Valley, 2004; Hon. DEd Kingston, 2003. *Publications:* contribs to jls. *Recreations:* music, theatre, watching Rugby. *Address:* Bramshott, Church Road, Surbiton, Surrey KT6 5HH. *T:* (020) 8398 4700. *Club:* Institute of Directors.

**BARKER, Neil Peter;** Managing Director, UK and Ireland, William Grant & Sons Ltd, since 2017; *b* Dorking, 27 July 1963; *s* of Peter Barker and Shirley Barker; *m* 2014, Nina Ferrier; one *s* one *d. Educ:* Univ. of Southampton (BSc Hons Physics and Chem. 1984). Esso Chemical Ltd, 1984–88; Mars Confectionery, 1988–93; Pepsico Inc., UK/Australia, 1993–2002; GM, Australia, Southcorp Wines, 2002–05; Country Manager, UK, Fosters Wines, Fosters Gp, 2006–10; Commercial Director: General Mills, 2011–14; Birds Eye Foods, 2014–17. *Recreations:* 400m runner to region/county level, travel. *Address:* c/o William Grant & Sons UK Ltd, Form 1, Bartley Wood Business Park, Hook RG27 9XA. *T:* 07787 884658. *E:* neil.barker@wgrant.com. *Clubs:* Home House; Lensbury (Teddington).

**BARKER, Nicholas; His Honour Judge Nicholas Barker;** a Circuit Judge, since 2018; *b* Thirsk, 19 Nov. 1968; *s* of Terence and Mary Barker; *m* 1997, Rachel Davinia; two *s* one *d. Educ:* Sedbergh Sch.; Newcastle Univ. (BA Hons). Called to the Bar, Gray's Inn, 1994; a Recorder, 2012–18. *Recreations:* fishing, Rugby, sailing, the Hebrides. *Address:* The Law Courts, Ring Way, Preston, Lancs PR1 2LL. *E:* hhj.nicholas.barker@ejudiciary.net. *Club:* Armstrong Rugby Football.

**BARKER, Ven. Nicholas John Willoughby;** Archdeacon of Auckland, 2007–17; Priest-in-Charge, Holy Trinity, Darlington, 2007–17; *b* 12 Dec. 1949; *s* of Rev. Arthur Barker and Peggy Barker; *m* 1980, Katherine Pritchard; three *s* one *d. Educ:* Sedbergh Sch.; Oriel Coll., Oxford (MA Metallurgy 1973; MA Theol. 1975). Ordained deacon, 1977, priest, 1978; Curate, St Mary's, Watford, 1977–80; Team Vicar, St James & Emmanuel, Didsbury, 1980–86; Team Rector, St George's, Kidderminster, 1986–2007; Rural Dean, Kidderminster, 2001–07. Hon. Canon, Worcester Cathedral, 2003–07; Hon. Supernumerary Canon, Durham Cathedral, 2007–17, now Canon Emeritus. *Recreations:* bee-keeping, hill-walking, sailing, gardening. *Address:* 4 Watson Park, Spennymoor DL16 6NB.

**BARKER, Nicolas John,** OBE 2002; FBA 1998; FSA; Editor, Book Collector, 1965–2015, now Consultant Editor; *b* 6 Dec. 1932; *s* of Sir Ernest Barker, FBA, and Olivia Stuart Horner; *m* 1962, Joanna Mary Sophia Nyda Cotton; two *s* three *d. Educ:* Westminster Sch.; New Coll., Oxford (MA; Hon. Fellow, 2011). With Baillière, Tindall & Cox, 1958 and Rupert Hart-Davis, 1959; Asst Keeper, National Portrait Gallery, 1964; with Macmillan & Co. Ltd, 1965; with OUP, 1971; Dep. Keeper, British Library, 1976–92. William Andrews Clark Vis. Prof., UCLA, 1986–87; Scholar, Getty Center for History of Art and the Humanities, 1996; Sandars Reader in Bibliography, Cambridge Univ., 1999–2000. Panizzi Lectr, BL, 2001; Rosenbach Lectr, Univ. of Pennsylvania, 2002. President: Amici Thomae Mori, 1978–89; Double Crown Club, 1980–81; Bibliographical Soc., 1981–85; Chm., London Liby, 1994–2004 (Mem. Cttee, 1971–2004; a Vice-Pres., 2005–); Member: Publication Bd of Dirs, RNIB, 1969–92; BBC and ITV Appeals Adv. Cttee, 1977–86; Nat. Trust Arts Panel, 1979–91 (Libraries Advr, 1991–99); Liby Cttee, RHS, 1996– (Chm., 1996–2004); Adv. Council, Science Mus., 2006–12. Gov., St Bride Foundn, 1976–; Trustee: The Pilgrim Trust, 1977–2007; York Glaziers Trust, 1990– (Chm., 2004–); Chm., Laurence Sterne Trust, 1984–2010; Chm. Trustees, Type Archive (formerly Type Mus.), 1995–. Feoffee, Chetham's Hosp., 2002–10. FSA 2012. DUniv York, 1994. *Publications:* The Publications of the Roxburghe Club, 1962; The Printer and the Poet, 1970; Stanley Morison, 1972; (ed) Essays and Papers of A. N. L. Munby, 1977; (ed) The Early Life of James McBey: an autobiography, 1883–1911, 1977; Bibliotheca Lindesiana, 1977; The Oxford University Press and the Spread of Learning 1478–1978, 1978; (with John Collins) A Sequel to an Enquiry, 1983; Aldus Manutius and the Development of Greek Script and Type, 1985; The Butterfly Books, 1987; Two East Anglian Picture Books, 1988; (ed) Treasures of the British Library, 1989; (ed) S. Morison, Early Italian Writing-Books, 1990; (with Sir Anthony Wagner and A. Payne) Medieval Pageant, 1993; Hortus Eystettensis: the Bishop's Garden and Besler's Magnificent Book, 1994; The Great Book of Thomas Trevilian, 2000; Form and Meaning in the History of the Book, 2002; The Devonshire Inheritance, 2003; The Library of Thomas Tresham and Thomas Brudenell, 2006; The Glory of the Art of Writing: the calligraphic work of Francesco Alunno, 2009; Lady Anne Barnard's Watercolours and Sketches: glimpses of the Cape of Good Hope, 2009; Horace Walpole's Description of the Villa at Strawberry-Hill, 2010; The Roxburghe Club: a bicentenary history, 2012; Esther Inglis's Les Proverbes de Salomon, 2012; Visible Voices, 2016. *Address:* 22 Clarendon Road, W11 3AB. *T:* (020) 7727 4340. *Clubs:* Garrick, Roxburghe; Roxburghe (San Francisco); Zamorano (Los Angeles).

**BARKER, Pamela Gay;** *see* Barber, P. G.

**BARKER, Patricia Margaret,** CBE 2000; novelist, since 1982; *b* 8 May 1943; *d* of Moyra Drake; *m* 1978, Prof. David Faubert Barker (*d* 2009); one *s* one *d. Educ:* Grangefield GS; London School of Economics (BScEcon; Hon. Fellow, 1998); Durham Univ. (DipEd). Teacher, until 1982. Hon. MLitt Teesside, 1994; Hon. DLitt: Napier, 1996; Durham, 1998; Hertfordshire, 1998; London, 2002; DUniv Open, 1997. Author of the Year Award, Booksellers' Assoc., 1996. *Publications:* Union Street (Fawcett Prize), 1982; Blow Your House Down, 1984; The Century's Daughter, 1986 (retitled Liza's England, 1996); The Man Who Wasn't There, 1989; The Regeneration Trilogy: Regeneration, 1991 (filmed 1997; adapted for stage 2014); The Eye in the Door, 1993 (Guardian Fiction Prize, Northern Electric Special Arts Award, 1994); The Ghost Road (Booker Prize), 1995; Another World, 1998; Border Crossing, 2001; Double Vision, 2003; Life Class, 2007; Toby's Room, 2012; Noonday, 2015; The Silence of the Girls, 2018. *Address:* c/o Aitken Alexander Associates, 291 Gray's Inn Road, WC1X 8EB. *T:* (020) 7373 8672.

**BARKER, Peter William,** CBE 1988; DL; Chairman, Fenner (formerly J. H. Fenner (Holdings)) PLC, 1982–93; *b* 24 Aug. 1928; *s* of William Henry George and Mabel Irene Barker; *m* 1961, Mary Rose Hainsworth, MBE, JP, DL; one *s* one *d. Educ:* Royal Liberty Sch., Romford; Dorking County High Sch.; South London Polytechnic. CCMI; FInstD; FCIM. J. H. Fenner & Co., 1953–67; Jt Managing Dir, Fenner International, 1967–71; Chief Exec., J. H. Fenner (Holdings), 1971–82. Dir, Neepsend plc, 1984–93. Member: Yorks and Humberside Regional Council, CBI, 1981–94 (Chm., 1991–93); National Council, CBI, 1985–95; Yorks and Humberside Regional Indust. Develt Bd, 1981–95 (Chm., 1992–95). Pro-Chancellor, Univ. of Hull, 1993–2002, now Emeritus. Hon. DSc (Econ) Hull, 1992. FRSA. DL E Yorks (formerly Humberside), 1990; High Sheriff, Humberside, 1993–94. *Recreations:* sailing, ski-ing, tennis, music. *Address:* Swanland Rise, West Ella, East Yorks HU10 7SF. *T:* (01482) 653050. *Clubs:* Royal Yorkshire Yacht, Royal Thames Yacht.

**BARKER, Hon. Sir (Richard) Ian,** Kt 1994; arbitrator and mediator; Senior Judge, High Court of New Zealand, 1991–97; Chairman, Banking Ombudsman Commission, New Zealand, 1997–2010; *b* 17 March 1934; *s* of Archibald Henry Barker and Kate Dorothy Barker (*née* Humphrys); *m* 1965, Mary Christine Allardyce; two *s* three *d. Educ:* Auckland Univ. (BA, LLB, 1958). FAMINZ(Arb/Med). Called to the Bar, NZ, 1958; Partner, Morpeth, Gould & Co., solicitors, Auckland, 1968–80; Barrister, 1968–76; QC (NZ) 1973; Judge, High Court of NZ, 1976–97; Member, Court of Appeal: Cook Is, 1990–; Fiji, 1997–2007; Samoa and Vanuatu, 1998–2001; Pitcairn, 2004–11; Kiribati, 2011–14. Door Tenant, Essex Ct Chambers, London, 1998–2014. Vis. Fellow, Wolfson Coll., Cambridge, 2006, 2009, 2011, 2017. Chancellor, Univ. of Auckland, 1991–99. Nominee of NZ Govt on ICSID Panel of Arbitrators, 1999–. President: Legal Res. Foundn of NZ, 1981–90; Arbitrators' and Mediators' Inst. of NZ, 2000–02. Chm., Sir George Elliot Trustees, Auckland, 2003–. Hon. LLD Auckland Univ., 1999. Ed.-in-Chief, New Zealand Forms and Precedents, 1990–2017. *Publications:* (Ed.-in-Chief) Law Stories: essays on the New Zealand legal profession, 2003; contrib. articles to NZ and Australian jls. *Recreations:* walking, reading, music, railways. *Address:* 10 Seaview Road, Auckland 1050, New Zealand. *Club:* Northern (Auckland).

**BARKER, Dr Richard William,** OBE 2012; Chairman: South London Academic Health Science Network, since 2012; South London Genomic Medicine Centre, since 2014; Founding Director: New Medicine Partners, since 2016; Lodgeadvice (formerly Metadvice), since 2019; *b* 18 Oct. 1948; *s* of late William Barker and Florence Barker; *m* 1st, 1969, Jennifer Ruth (marr. diss. 2000); two *s* one *d*; 2nd, 2008, Michaela. *Educ:* Alleyn's Sch.; Exeter Coll., Oxford (MA; DPhil 1973). Partner, Healthcare Practice Leader, McKinsey & Co., 1980–93; Gen. Manager, Healthcare Solutions, IBM, 1993–96; President: Chiron Diagnostics, 1996–2000; New Medicine Partners, 2001–03; Chm. and CEO, Molecular Staging, 2003–06; Dir-Gen., Assoc. of British Pharmaceutical Industry, 2004–11; Founding Dir, Centre for Accelerating Med. Innovation, Univ. of Oxford, then Oxford-UCL Centre for Advancement of Sustainable Med. Innovation, 2012–17. Chairman: Stem Cells for Safer Medicines, 2007–; Image Analysis, 2014–; Precision Medicine Catapult, 2015–17; Co-Chair, UK Therapeutic Capability Clusters, 2009–11; non-executive Director: Sunquest, 1997–2001; Exact Scis, 1999–2005; Adlyfe, 2004–09; Internat. Health Partners, 2005– (Chm., 2015–18); iCo Therapeutics, 2006–; Celgene Corp., 2012–. Member: Ministerial Industry Strategy Gp, 2005–11; NHS Stakeholder Forum, 2006–; NHS Nat. Leadership Network for Health and Social Care, 2006–10; UK Clin. Res. Consortium, 2006–11 (Vice-Chm., 2009–11); e-Health Record Res. Bd, OSCHR, 2007–10; Bd, Academy of Medical Scis Forum, 2009–11. Member: Bd, Eur. Fedn of Pharmaceutical Industry Assocs, 2004–11; Council, Internat. Fedn of Pharmaceutical Manufacturers and Assocs, 2004–11. Hon. Prof., UCL, 2013–; Associate Prof., 2014–16, Vis. Prof., 2016–, Univ. of Oxford. FRSocMed 2010. Hon. FBPhS. *Publications:* 2030: the future of medicine, 2010; Bioscience - Lost in Translation?, 2016. *Recreations:* hiking, kayaking, music (especially opera). *Address:* 14 Cottenham Park Road, SW20 0RZ. *T:* 07708 867655. *E:* richard.barker@newmedicine.io.

**BARKER, Prof. Roger Alistair,** PhD; FMedSci; Consultant Neurologist, Addenbrooke's Hospital, Cambridge, since 1999; Professor of Clinical Neuroscience, University of Cambridge, since 2011; *b* Coleford, Glos, 12 Sept. 1961; *s* of Gordon and Sylvia Barker; *m* 1986, Christine Sorenson; one *s* two *d* (and one *d* decd). *Educ:* Haberdashers' Aske's Sch., Elstree; Corpus Christi Coll., Oxford (BA 1983); St Thomas' Hosp. Med. Sch. (MB BS 1986); Univ. of Cambridge (PhD 1995). MRCP 1989. University of Cambridge: Health Trng Fellow, 1991–94; Lectr, 2000–05, Reader, 2006–11, in Clinical Neurosci.; Registrar in Neurology: Addenbrooke's Hosp., 1994–95; Nat. Hosp. for Neurol., 1995–96; Sen. Registrar in Neurol., Addenbrooke's Hosp. and Norfolk and Norwich Hosp., 1996–97; MRC Clinician Scientist, Cambridge Univ., 1997–2000. FMedSci 2015. *Publications:* Neuroscience at a Glance, 1999, 5th edn 2017; Neural Repair: transplantation and rehabilitation, 1999; A–Z of Neurological Practice, 2011. *Recreations:* art, walking, golf. *Address:* John van Geest Centre for Brain Repair, University of Cambridge, E. D. Adrian Building, Forvie Site, Robinson Way, Cambridge CB2 0PY. *T:* (01223) 331160, *Fax:* (01223) 331174. *E:* rab46@cam.ac.uk.

**BARKER, Sarah Anne, (Mrs D. M. Freeman);** Partner, and Head, Art and Fashion Groups, Lee & Thompson LLP, since 2017; *b* Manchester, May 1976; *d* of John Andrew Grahame Barker and Lorna Anne Barker; *m* 2011, Daniel Marc Freeman; one *s. Educ:* Wycombe Abbey Sch.; University Coll. London (LLB 1997); Coll. of Law; Sotheby's Inst. of Art (Art & Business 2006). Admitted as solicitor, 2001; with Herbert Smith, 1999–2006; SB Art consultancy, 2007–09; Man. Partner, Montgomery Barker, 2009–17. Member: Inst. of Art and Law, 2011; Assoc. of Women in the Art World, 2012; Professional Advrs to Internat. Art World, 2017. Liveryman, Mercers' Co., 2014– (Mem., Arts & Heritage Giving Cttee, 2003–12). Gov./Dir, St Paul's Sch. (Boys), 2015–. Chm., Patrons' Cttee, Royal Acad. Schs, 2016–18; Patron, Contemp. Art Soc., 2018–. *Recreations:* family, friends and food, art and design, spotting tomorrow's future leading contemporary artists, life drawing, tennis, politics. *Address:* Lee & Thompson LLP, 4 Gee's Court, St Christopher's Place, W1U 1JD. *T:* (020) 3073 7600. *E:* sarahbarker@leeandthompson.com. *Club:* Arts.

**BARKER, Simon George Harry,** FCA; QC 2008; **His Honour Judge Simon Barker;** a Specialist Chancery Circuit Judge, since 2010; *b* London, 1950; *s* of Edgar John Harry and Dorothy Joan Barker; *m* 1972, Eva-Marie; one *s* one *d. Educ:* Westminster Sch.; Ealing Tech. Coll. (BA Hons). ACA 1976, FCA 1981. Called to the Bar, Lincoln's Inn, 1979. Recorder, 1995–2010. *Recreations:* rowing, water sports, ski-ing, art, theatre, films, music, football. *Address:* Birmingham Civil Justice Centre, Bull Street, Birmingham B4 6DS. *Club:* London Rowing.

**BARKER, Timothy Gwynne;** Chairman, Highview Enterprises Ltd, 2010–17; *b* 8 April 1940; *s* of late Lt Col Frank Richard Peter Barker and Hon. Olwen Gwynne (*née* Philipps); *m* 1964, Philippa Rachel Mary Thursby-Pelham; one *s* one *d. Educ:* Eton Coll.; McGill Univ., Montreal; Jesus Coll., Cambridge (MA). Dir, 1973–2000 and Hd of Corporate Finance, 1986–90, Kleinwort Benson Ltd; Kleinwort Benson Group plc, subseq. Dresdner Kleinwort Benson: Dir, 1988–93; Dep. Chief Exec., 1990–93; Vice Chm., 1993–2000; Chm., Kleinwort Benson Private Bank Ltd, 1997–2004; Chm., Robert Walters plc, 2001–07. Director-General: City Panel on Take-overs and Mergers, 1984–85; Council for the Securities Industry, 1984–85. Sen. Ind. Dir, Drax Gp plc, 2004–13; Ind. Dir, 2000–07, Sen. Ind. Dir, 2007–09, Electrocomponents plc; Mem. Bd, Genesis Housing Gp Ltd,

2009–10; Sen. Ind. Dir, Jefferies Internat. Ltd, 2010–16. Member: Econ. Affairs Cttee, CBI, 1997–2003; Professional Oversight Bd, Financial Reporting Council, 2004–09. *E*: tgb@timothybarker.co.uk.

**BARKER, Very Rev. Timothy Reed;** Dean of Guernsey, and Rector, St André de la Pommeraye, since 2015; Priest-in-charge, Sark, since 2015; *b* 18 Aug. 1956; *s* of Norman and Marjorie Barker; *m* 1979, Judith Angela, *d* of Rev. Dr Elmore and Pamela Leske, Adelaide, SA; one *s* one *d*. *Educ*: Manchester Grammar Sch.; Queens' Coll., Cambridge (MA 1982); Westcott House, Cambridge. Ordained deacon, 1980, priest, 1981; Asst Curate, St Mary, Nantwich, 1980–83; Vicar: St Berteline and St Christopher, Norton, 1983–88; All Saints, Runcorn, 1988–94; Domestic Chaplain to Bishop of Chester, 1994–98; Vicar, St Mary and St Nicolas, Spalding, 1998–2009; Priest-in-charge, St Paul, Spalding, 2007–09; Rural Dean: Elloe W, 2000–09; Elloe E, 2008–09; Archdeacon of Lincoln, 2009–15. Diocese of Chester: Urban Ministry Officer, 1988–90; Commns Officer, 1991–98; Hon. Priest Asst, Chester Cathedral, 1994–98. Canon and Preb., Lincoln Cathedral, 2003–15 (Mem. Chapter, 2000–08); Canon, Winchester Cathedral, 2016–. Member: Gen. Synod, 2000–05 and 2008–; Church Bldgs Council, 2011–18; Chair, Nat. Archdeacons' Forum, 2015–. Ind. Mem., Cheshire Police Authy, 1994–98; Mem., Standards Cttee, Lincs CC, 2003–09 (Chair, 2006–07); Chair, Standards Cttee, S Holland DC, 2008–12. Vice Chair, Nat. Assoc. of Councils for Voluntary Service, 1990–94; Chair: Cheshire Relate, 1995–98; Lincs Community and Voluntary Service, 2010–15. Mem. of Council, Priaulx Library, Guernsey, 2015–. Chair of Dirs, Elizabeth Coll. Guernsey, 2015–; Gov. of primary and secondary schs. Trustee, Alcuin Club, 1986–. *Recreations*: walking, Dutch and Flemish art, travel, music (esp. early 20th century English music). *Address*: The Rectory, Route de St André, St Andrew, Guernsey GY6 8XN. *T*: (01481) 238568. *E*: deanofguernsey@gmail.com.

**BARKER, Trevor;** Chairman, Alpha Consolidated Holdings Ltd, 1988–2003; *b* 24 March 1935; *s* of Samuel Lawrence Barker and Lilian Barker (*née* Dawson); *m* 1957, Joan Elizabeth Cross; one *s* one *d*. *Educ*: Acklam Hall Grammar School. FCA. Price Waterhouse & Co., 1957–58; Cooper Brothers, 1958–62; sole practitioner, 1962–70; Chm. and Chief Exec., Gold Case Travel, 1964–77; Dir, Ellerman Wilson Lines, 1977–80; Chairman: John Crowther Gp, 1980–88; William Morris Fine Arts, 1981–88; Micklegate Gp, 1989–95; Drew Scientific Gp, 1993–95; Dep. Chm., Blanchards, 1988–94; Dir, Darlington Bldg Soc., 1994–2000. FRSA 1989. Liveryman, Co. of Woolmen, 1986. *Recreations*: grandchildren, breeding and racing thoroughbred horses, opera, music, literature, the arts.

**BARKING, Area Bishop of,** since 2014; **Rt Rev. Peter Hill;** *b* Swansea, 4 Feb. 1950; *s* of John and Megan Hill; *m* 1971, Ellen Purvis; one *s* one *d*. *Educ*: UMIST (BSc 1971); Manchester Univ. (PGCE 1973); Wycliffe Hall, Oxford (Cert. Theol 1983); Nottingham Univ. (MTh 1990). Teacher, Manchester and Cheshire, 1972–78; Dep. Head Teacher, The Beaches Primary Sch., Sale Moor, 1978–81; ordained deacon, 1983, priest, 1984; Asst Curate, St James, Porchester, 1983–86; Vicar, All Saints, Huthwaite, 1986–95; Priest-in-charge, St Wilfrid's, Calverton, 1995–2004; Area Dean, Southwell, 1997–2001; Chair, Dio. Bd of Educn, 2001–04, 2012–14; Chief Exec., Dio. of Southwell and Nottingham, 2004–07; Archdeacon of Nottingham, 2007–14. Hon. Canon. Southwell Minster, 2001–14. Mem., Gen. Synod of C of E, 1993–2004 and 2010–14; Vice Chair, Dioceses Commn, 2010–14. *Address*: Barking Lodge, 35A Verulam Avenue, Walthamstow, E17 8ES. *T*: (020) 8509 7377.

**BARKING, Archdeacon of;** *see* Burke, Ven. C. M.

**BARKLEM, Martyn Stephen; His Honour Judge Barklem;** a Circuit Judge, since 2012; a Judge of the Employment Appeal Tribunal, since 2017; *b* Ormskirk, 26 Dec. 1956; *s* of Thomas and Edna Barklem; *m* 2008, Naomi Lisa Ellenbogen, *qv*; two *s* by a former marriage. *Educ*: Dauntsey's Sch.; Univ. of London (LLB Hons ext. 1986). Served RN, 1976–78. Royal Hong Kong Police, 1979–88, Detective Chief Inspector, 1983–88. Called to the Bar, Middle Temple, 1989; in practice at the Bar, 1990–2012; a Recorder, 2002–12. *Recreations*: sailing, aviation, IT, cooking. *Address*: Kingston upon Thames Crown Court, 6–8 Penrhyn Road, Kingston upon Thames KT1 2BB. *T*: (020) 8240 2500. *E*: hhj.martyn.barklem@ejudiciary.net. *Clubs*: Bar Yacht, Royal Naval Volunteer Reserve Yacht; Hong Kong Cricket.

**BARKLEM, Naomi Lisa;** *see* Ellenbogen, N. L.

**BARKSHIRE, Robert Renny St John, (John),** CBE 1990; TD; JP; DL; banker; *b* 31 Aug. 1935; *s* of late Robert Hugh Barkshire, CBE; *m* 1st, 1960, Margaret Elizabeth Robinson (marr. diss. 1990; she *d* 2011); two *s* one *d*; 2nd, 1990, Audrey Mary Anne Witham. *Educ*: Bedford School. ACIB. Served Duke of Wellington's Regt, 2nd Lieut, 1953–55; HAC, 1955–74 (CO, 1970–72; Regtl Col, 1972–74). Joined Cater Ryder & Co., 1955, Jt Man. Dir, 1963–72; Chm., Mercantile House Holdings plc, 1972–87; Non-exec. Dir, Extel Gp PLC, 1979–87 (Dep. Chm., 1986–87); Chairman: CL-Alexanders Laing & Cruickshank Hldgs Ltd, 1984–88; Internat. Commodities Clearing House Ltd, 1986–90. Chm., Financial Futures Wkg Pty, 1980, later LIFFE Steering Cttee, 1981–82; Dir, LIFFE, 1982–91 (Chm., 1982–85); Member: Adv. Bd, Internat. Monetary Market Div., Chicago Mercantile Exchange, 1981–84; London Adv. Bd, Bank Julius Baer, 1988–91. Chairman: Uplink Ltd (EPN Satellite Service), 1988–90; Chaco Investments Ltd, 1994–2001; non-executive Director: Household Mortgage Corp., 1985–94 (Chm., 1993–94); Savills, 1988–95; Sun Life and Provincial Holdings plc, 1988–99; TR Property Investment Trust plc, 1993–2002. Chm., Eastbourne Hosps NHS Trust, 1993–99. Chm., Cttee on Market in Single Properties, 1985–2000. Gen. Comr for Income Tax, City of London, 1981–2009. Chairman: Reserve Forces Assoc., 1983–87; Sussex TA Cttee, 1983–85; SE TAVRA, 1985–91; Dep. Chm., TA Sport Bd, 1983–95 (Mem., 1979–95). Financial Advisor: Victory Services Assoc. (formerly Club), 1981–95; RE Central Mgt Investments Policy Cttee, 1988–2007; Army Central Fund, 1995–2007; Royal Signals Trustees Ltd, 1996–2005; Dir, Officers' Pensions Soc. Investment Co. Ltd, 1982–95; Member: Regular Forces Employment Assoc. Council, 1986–95; SSAFA Council (Trustee and Mem. Exec. and Finance Cttee), 1996–2008; Adv. Bd, Army Common Investment Fund, 2002–04; Chm., Nat. Meml Arboretum, 2003–11; Trustee: Regtl Assoc., Duke of Wellington's Regt, 1990–2011; Army Benevolent Fund, 1999–2010 (Pres., E Sussex Br., 1999–2011); RBL, 2005–10 (Co-opted Mem., Nat. Council, 1991–2005; Chm., Chiddingly and Dist, 1982–87; Pres., Burwash, 2012–15); Yorks Regt, 2006–11. Chairman: E Sussex Br., Magistrates' Assoc., 1986–91; E Sussex Magistrates' Courts Cttee, 1993–97 and 1999–2001; Sussex Magistrates' Courts Cttee, 2001–02. Mem., Chiddingly Parish Council, 1979–86; Treas., Burwash PCC, 1999–2016; Mem., Assets Cttee, Chichester Dio. Bd of Finance, 2015–. Treasurer and Trustee: Sussex Historic Churches Trust, 2003–; Friends of The Keep Archives (formerly E Sussex Record Office), 2008–18; Treas., Wealden, NADFAS, 2010–15. Dir, Brighton Philharmonic Orch., 2013–17. Governor: Harpur Trust, 1984–89 (Chm., Bedford Sch. Cttee, 1984–89); Eastbourne Coll., 1980–95 (Vice Chm., 1983–92); Roedean Sch., 1984–89; Burwash Primary C of E Sch., 1999–2007 (Chm., 1992–2007); Comr, Duke of York's Royal Military Sch., 1986–95. Freeman, City of London, 1973; Liveryman, Worshipful Co. of Farmers, 1981. JP Lewes, 1980; DL E Sussex, 1986.

*Recreations*: sailing, shooting. *Address*: 7 Maltravers Street, Arundel, W Sussex BN18 9AP. *T*: (01903) 889599. *Clubs*: City of London, Cavalry and Guards, MCC; Royal Fowey Yacht (Cornwall).

**BARLEY, Nicholas;** Director, Edinburgh International Book Festival, since 2009; *b* N Yorks, 22 June 1966; *s* of Anthony and Lesley Barley; *m* 1997, Fiona Bradley; one *s* one *d*. *Educ*: Univ. of Kent, Canterbury (BA Hons Social Psychol.). Publisher, Blueprint mag., 1994–98; Dir, August Publishing, 1998–2003; Ed., The List, 2003–07; Exec. Dir, The Lighthouse, Scotland's Centre for Architecture, Design and the City, 2007–09. Hon. FRSL 2018. *Publications*: Lost and Found: critical voices in new British design, 1999; Breathing Cities: the architecture of movement, 2000. *Address*: Edinburgh International Book Festival, 5 Charlotte Square, Edinburgh EH2 4DR.

**BARLING, Hon. Sir Gerald (Edward),** Kt 2007; a Judge of the High Court of Justice, Chancery Division, 2007–19; Vice-Chancellor, County Palatine of Lancaster, 2017–19; *b* 18 Sept. 1949; *s* of Banks Hubert Barling and Barbara Margarita (*née* Myerscough); *m* 1983, Myriam Frances (*née* Ponsford); three *d*. *Educ*: St Mary's Coll., Blackburn (Peel Foundn Scholar, 1968); New Coll., Oxford (Burnett Open Exhibnr in Classics, 1968; Hons Sch. of Jurisprudence (1st Cl.), 1971; MA). Called to the Bar, Middle Temple, 1972 (Harmsworth Entrance Exhibnr, 1971; Astbury Law Scholar, 1973; Bencher, 2001); called to the Bar, NI, 1992. Practised at Common Law Bar, Manchester, 1973–81; practising in fields of public and competition law, and in all aspects of EC and EU Law, Brick Court Chambers, London, 1981–2007; Asst Recorder, 1990–93; QC 1991; QC (NI) 1992; Recorder, 1993–2007; Dep. High Court Judge, 2007; Actg Deemster, I of M Court of Appeal, 2000–09. Pres., Competition Appeal Tribunal, 2007–13. Business and Property Courts Supervising Judge, North and North East Circuits, 2017–19. Lectr in Law, New Coll., Oxford, 1972–77. Chairman: Western European Sub-Cttee, Bar Council, 1991–92; Bar European Gp, 1994–96 (Vice-Chm., 1992–94). Pres., Thomas More Soc., 2014–18. Trustee, Develt Fund, New Coll., Oxford, 2003–14. *Publications*: (contrib.) Butterworth's European Court Practice, 1991; (co-ed) Practitioner's Handbook of EC Law, 1998; papers on different aspects of English and EU Law. *Recreation*: country pursuits. *Club*: Garrick.

**BARLOW, Celia Anne;** *b* 28 Sept. 1955; two *s* one *d*. *Educ*: King Edward High Sch. for Girls, Birmingham; New Hall, Cambridge (BA 1976); University Coll., Cardiff; Central St Martin's Coll. of Art and Design (MA); Sussex Univ. (PGDip). Reporter, Telegraph and Argus, Bradford, 1979–82; reporter and Asst Ed., Asia TV HK, 1982–83; journalist and Home News Ed., BBC TV News, 1983–95; freelance video producer, 1998–2000; Lectr in Video Prodn, Chichester Coll. of Arts, Sci. and Technol., 2000–05. Contested (Lab) Chichester, 2001. MP (Lab) Hove, 2005–10; contested (Lab) same seat, 2010. *Publications*: Spray of Pearls, 1993.

**BARLOW, Sir Christopher Hilaro,** 7th Bt *cr* 1803; architect; *b* 1 Dec. 1929; *s* of Sir Richard Barlow, 6th Bt, AFC, and Rosamund Sylvia, *d* of late F. S. Anderton (she *m* 2nd, 1950, Rev. Leonard Haslet Morrison, MA); *S* father, 1946; *m* 1st, 1952, J. C. de M. Audley (*d* 2002), *e d* of late J. E. Audley, Cheshire; one *s* two *d* (and one *s* decd); 2nd, 2003, Mrs Jeane Gage, *e d* of Douglas Stevens, Hamilton. *Educ*: Eton; McGill Univ., Montreal. BArch. MRAIC. Past Pres., Newfoundland Architects' Assoc. Lt Governor's Silver Medal, 1953. *Heir*: *s* Crispian John Edmund Audley Barlow, Tech. Advr, Protected Areas Enforcement, WWF, Laos [*b* 20 April 1958; *m* 1st, 1981, Anne Waiching Siu (marr. diss. 2005); one *d*; 2nd, 2006, Christi Lane, Philadelphia, Penn]. *Address*: 40 St James Place, Hamilton, ON L8P 2N4, Canada.

**BARLOW, Prof. David Hearnshaw,** MD; Executive Dean of Medicine, Faculty of Medicine, University of Glasgow, 2005–10, now Emeritus Professor; *b* 26 Dec. 1949; *s* of Archibald and Anne Barlow; *m* 1973, Norma Christie Woodrow; one *s* one *d*. *Educ*: Clydebank High Sch.; Univ. of Glasgow (BSc Hons Biochem. 1971; MB ChB 1975; MD 1982); MA Oxon 1985. FRCOG 1993; MRCP 2005. MRC Trng Fellowship, 1977–78; Hall Tutorial Fellow, Univ. of Glasgow, 1979–81; Sen. Registrar, Queen Mother's Hosp., Glasgow, 1981–84; Oxford University: Clinical Reader in Obstetrics and Gynaecology, 1984–90; Nuffield Professor of Obstetrics and Gynaecology, 1990–2004; Fellow: Green Coll., 1984–90; Oriel Coll., 1990–2004, Hon. Fellow, 2006; Hon. Consultant Obstetrician and Gynaecologist, The Women's Centre, Oxford Radcliffe Hosps NHS Trust (formerly John Radcliffe Hosp.), Oxford, 1984–2004. Chm., Dept of Obstetrics and Gynaecol., Women's Hosp., Qatar, 2012–17; Prof., Weill-Cornell Medical Coll., Qatar, 2014–17; Hamad Medical Corp., Qatar: Dir, Women's Services, 2012–17; Chm., Institutional Review Bd, 2015–17; Ext. Grant Reviewer, Medical Res. Centre, 2017–. Lectures: Blair Bell Meml, 1985, Simpson Oration, 2006, RCOG; Howard Jacobs, British Fertility Soc., 2005. Chairman: DoH Adv. Gp on Osteoporosis (report published, 1995); NICE Guideline Develt Gp on Fertility, 2002–04; NICE Guideline Develt Gp on Osteoporosis, 2003–08. Member: Bd, Acad. Medicine for Scotland, 2005–10; Oversight Bd, Scottish Academic Health Scis Collaboration, 2007–10; Univs of Scotland Health Cttee, 2007–10. Mem., HFEA, 1998–2006 (Mem., Scientific and Clinical Advances Adv. Cttee, 2006–10). Mem., FIGO Expert Panel on the Menopause, 1998–2005. Mem. Council, RCOG, 1996–2002. Chm., British Menopause Soc., 1999–2001; Trustee: Nat. Osteoporosis Soc., 1995–2006 (Chm., 2002–04); Mem., Clinical and Scientific Cttee, 2006–12; Clinical and Scientific Fellow, 2017–); Nat. Endometriosis Soc., 1997–2000. Pres., Eur. Menopause and Andropause Soc., 2007–09 (Vice-Pres., 2004–06). Chm., Oxford NHS R & D Consortium, 2001–04; NHS Greater Glasgow and Clyde Health Board: non-exec. Dir, 2005–10; Chm., Clinical Governance Cttee, 2005–10; Chm., Res. Ethics Governance Cttee, 2005–10; Chm., Glasgow Biomedicine; Mem., Scientific Adv. Bd, Preglem, Geneva, 2008–16. Member: Medical Scis Divisional Bd, Univ. of Oxford, 2000–04; RAE 2001 and RAE 2008 Panels, HEFCE; Sen. Investigator, Appts Panel, NIHR, 2008–; Fitness to Practise Panel, GMC, 2011–14. Ext. Assessor, Medical Council of Ireland, 2011–; Panel Mem., RAE 2014, Ext. Grant Reviewer, 2014–, Medical Res. Council of HK; Ext. review of maternity service, Matilda Internat. Hosp., HK, 2017. Internat. Trustee, Susan Mubarak Foundn for Women's Health, Egypt, 2006–11. Founder FMedSci 1998; FRSE 2008. Hon. FRCPGlas 2006. Mem., Editl Bd, Best Practice in Obstetrics and Gynaecology, 1995–2004; Ed., Menstrual Disorders & Subfertility Gp, Cochrane Collaboration, 1996–; Editor-in-Chief, Human Reproduction Jl, 2000–06. *Publications*: (ed) Clinical Guidelines on the Prevention and Treatment of Osteoporosis, 1999; over 330 pubns incl. 200 scientific papers in field of reproduction, reproductive medicine and women's health incl. infertility and assisted reproduction, endometriosis and pelvic pain, SPRM, menopause and osteoporosis. *Recreations*: wide-ranging interest in music, painting.

**BARLOW, David John;** broadcasting consultant; Adviser on International Relations, BBC, since 1993; *b* 20 Oct. 1937; *s* of Ralph and Joan Barlow; *m* 2001, Stella M. Waterman (*née* Hewer) (*d* 2015); one step *s* one step *d*, and five *s* one *d* of previous marriages. *Educ*: Leighton Park Sch.; The Queen's Coll., Oxford; Leeds Univ. MA, DipEd (Oxon); DipESI (Leeds). British Council, 1962–63; BBC, 1963–: Producer, African Service; Schools Broadcasting, 1965–67; Programme Organiser, Hindi, Tamil, Nepali and Bengali Services, 1967–70; Further Educn Radio, 1970–71; UNESCO, British Council Consultancies, 1970–73; Head of Liaison Internat. Relations, 1974–76; Chief Asst Regions, 1977–79; Gen. Sec., ITCA, 1980–81; BBC: Sec., 1981–84; Controller: Public Affairs and Internat.

Relations, 1984–86; Public Affairs, 1986–87; Regional Broadcasting, 1987–90; seconded to EBU as Co-ordinator for Audio Visual Eureka Project, 1990–91; Controller, Information Services and Regional Relns, 1991–92. Consultant, then Sec. Gen., Public Broadcasters Internat., 1999–2008. Non-exec. Dir, Bedford Hosp. NHS Trust, 2002–04. Mem., RTS, 1980–. Trustee, Children in Need, 1986–92. Chm., Govs, Sharnbrook Upper Sch., 2002–03 (Vice-Chm., 2001–02). *Recreations:* bird watching, mountains, books. *Address:* 6 Rue des Ecoles, 79120 Chenay, France. *T:* (5) 49293899. *E:* davidbarlow121@orange.fr.

**BARLOW, David Michael Rigby,** CB 1996; Under Secretary, Government Legal Service, 1989–96; *b* 8 June 1936; *s* of late Samuel Gordon Barlow and Eunice Hodson Barlow; *m* 1973, Valeree Elizabeth Rush-Smith; one *s*; one *d* by previous marr. *Educ:* Shrewsbury Sch.; Christ Church, Oxford (MA Law). National Service: Midshipman RNVR in Submarine Br. of RN, 1954–56; Sub-Lieut and Lieut in permanent RNR, 1956–61. Solicitor, England and Wales, 1965, NI, 1991. Appointments as a lawyer in the public service, 1965–73; Asst Sec. in Govt Legal Service, 1973–89. *Recreations:* Spanish language and culture, swimming, cinema.

**BARLOW, Francis;** *see* Barlow, R. F. D.

**BARLOW, Sir Frank,** Kt 1998; CBE 1993; Chairman, Logica, 1995–2002; *b* 25 March 1930; *s* of John and Isabella Barlow; *m* 1950, Constance Patricia Ginns (*d* 2000); one *s* two *d*. *Educ:* Barrow Grammar Sch., Cumbria. Nigerian Electricity Supply Corp., 1952–59; Daily Times, Nigeria, 1960–62; Managing Director: Ghana Graphic, 1962–63; Barbados Advocate, 1963; Trinidad Mirror Newspapers, 1963–64; Gen. Manager, Daily Mirror, 1964–67; Man. Dir, King & Hutchings, 1967–75; Dir and Gen. Manager, Westminster Press, 1975–83; Dir, Economist, 1983–99; Chief Executive: Financial Times Group, 1983–90 (Chm., 1993–96); Westminster Press Group, 1985–90; Man. Dir, Pearson plc, 1990–96; Chairman: BSkyB, 1991–95; Thames Television, 1995–97; Channel 5, 1997. Pres., Les Echos, Paris, 1988–90; Director: Elsevier (UK), 1991–94; Soc. Européene des Satellites SA, 2000–02; Chm., Lottery Products Ltd, 1997–99. Dir, Press Assoc., 1985–93. Chm., Printers' Charitable Corp., 1995–2000, Pres. Emeritus, 2006. Dir, Royal Philharmonic Orch., 1988–93. *Recreations:* golf, fell walking, angling. *Club:* Carlton.

**BARLOW, Gavin Galbraith;** Director, Capability, Cabinet Office, since 2018; *b* 5 May 1964; *s* of Peter John Barlow and Elizabeth Findlay Barlow; *m* 1991, Dr Alice Rebecca Chishick; three *s* two *d*. *Educ:* Univ. of Bristol (BSc Soc. Sci. 1986); Imperial Coll., London (MBA, DIC, 1997). Ministry of Defence, 1987–2015: Asst Private Sec. to Minister of State (Armed Forces), 1989–91; Administrative Sec., Sovereign Base Areas Admin, Cyprus, 1999–2002; Dir Policy Planning, 2002–06; Dir Gen. Mgt and Orgn, 2006–07; Dir Prison Population, MoJ (on secondment), 2007–08; Dir Service Personnel Policy, MoD, 2008–15; Dir of Strategy, Planning and International, Home Office, 2015–16; Dir, Economic Crime, Cabinet Office (on secondment), 2017. *Recreations:* cooking, cycling, books. *Address:* Cabinet Office, 70 Whitehall, SW1A 2AS.

**BARLOW, George Francis,** OBE 1998; FRICS; Chairman, London Development Agency, 2000–03; Chief Executive (formerly Director), Peabody Trust, 1987–99; *b* 26 May 1939; *s* of late George and Agnes Barlow; *m* 1969, Judith Alice Newton; one *s* two *d*. *Educ:* Wimbledon Coll.; Hammersmith Sch. of Art and Building; Polytechnic of Central London. Surveyor, Building Design Partnership, 1962–67; Develt Surveyor, GLC Housing Dept, 1967–70; The Housing Develt Officer, London Borough of Camden, 1970–76; Dir/Sec., Metropolitan Housing Trust, 1976–87. External Examiner, Polytechnic of Central London, 1989–90. Mem., Housing Cttee, 1986–91, Chm., Housing Policy Panel, 1996–99, RICS; Chm., London Housing Assocs Council, 1978–82; Dep. Chm., London Develt Partnership, 1998–2000; Member: Central YMCA Housing Assoc., 1982–85; Council, Nat. Fedn of Housing Assocs, 1985–89; Cttee, Community Self Build Agency, 1989–94; Cttee, Broomleigh Housing Assoc., 1989–95; Trustee: Kent Community Housing Trust, 1989–92; William Sutton Trust, 1999–2001; Mem. Bd, East London Partnership, 1991–99. Chm., Youth Homelessness Cttee, Prince's Trust/BITC, 1994–98. Gov., Univ. of E London, 1996–2000. Sen. Associate, King's Fund, 1999–2004. Hon. DLitt: Westminster, 2001; London South Bank, 2004. *Recreations:* theatre, horseracing.

**BARLOW, Dr Horace Basil,** FRS 1969; Royal Society Research Professor, Physiological Laboratory, Cambridge University, 1973–87; *b* 8 Dec. 1921; *s* of Sir (James) Alan (Noel) Barlow, 2nd Bt, GCB, KBE and Nora Barlow (*née* Darwin); *m* 1st, 1954, Ruthala (marr. diss., 1970), *d* of late Dr M. H. Salaman; four *d*; 2nd, 1980, Miranda, *d* of John Weston Smith; one *s* two *d*. *Educ:* Winchester; Trinity Coll., Cambridge. Research Fellow, Trinity Coll., 1950–54, Lectr, King's Coll., Cambridge, 1954–64. Demonstrator and Asst Dir of Research, Physiological Lab., Cambridge, 1954–64; Prof. of Physiological Optics and Physiology, Univ. of Calif, Berkeley, 1964–73. Australia Prize, 1993; Royal Medal, Royal Soc., 1993; Lashley Award, Amer. Philosophical Soc., 2003. *Publications:* several, on neurophysiology of vision in Jl of Physiology, and elsewhere. *Address:* Trinity College, Cambridge CB2 1TQ.

**BARLOW, Ian Edward;** Chairman, Racecourse Association, 2009–15; Chairman, Racing Foundation, since 2016; *b* Shipley, 30 Sept. 1951; *s* of Sir (George) William Barlow; *m* 1976, Judith Ann Jary; two *s*. *Educ:* Oundle Sch.; Clare Coll., Cambridge (BA Engrg Scis 1973). FCA 1976; CTA 2000, CTA (Fellow). KPMG, 1973–2010: Hd of Tax and Legal UK, 1994–2001; Sen. Partner, London, 2002–08; Sen. Advr, 2008–10. Chm., WSP Gp plc, 2011–12; non-executive Director: Candy & Candy Gp, 2008–11; PA Consulting Gp, 2008–12; Brunner Investment Trust plc, 2009–; Smith & Nephew plc, 2010–19 (Sen. Ind. Dir, 2017–19); Foxtons plc, 2013– (Sen. Ind. Dir); Goodwood Estate Co. Ltd, 2016–; Urban and Civic, 2016– (Sen. Ind. Dir); Lead non-exec. Dir, HMRC, 2012–16. Dir, China British Business Council, 2008–16. Chm., Think London, 2002–11; Dir, London First, 2005–11; Mem. Bd, London Develt Agency, 2008–12. Founder Chm., Safer London Foundn, 2005–08; Trustee: Historic Royal Palaces, 2010–13; Nat. Heritage Centre for Horseracing and Sporting Art, 2016–. *Recreations:* golf, horseracing. *E:* ian@ianebarlow.com. *Club:* Brooks's.

**BARLOW, Sir James (Alan),** 4th Bt *cr* 1902, of Wimpole Street, St Marylebone, co. London; Sales Executive, Preston Mobility, since 2014; *b* 10 July 1956; *s* of Sir Thomas Erasmus Barlow, 3rd Bt and of Isabel Barlow (*née* Body); *S* father, 2003; *m* 2004, Sylvia Lois Mann. *Educ:* Highgate Sch.; Manchester Univ. (BSc). US Steel Res. Center, Penn, USA, 1978; The Welding Inst., Cambridge, UK, 1979–82; Harland & Wolff, Shipbuilders, Belfast, 1982–84; Glassdrumman Lodge Hotel, Newcastle, Ire., 1985–92; Galgorm Manor Hotel, Ballymena, 1992–95; Covenant Life Coll., Fort St John, BC, 1996–98; IBM Canada, Vancouver, 1999–2002; Sales Exec. (formerly Communications Consultant), Bell Mobility, 2002–14. Dir, Destiny Encounters, 2010–12. Pres., Interjab Computer Support Services, Vancouver, 2002–12. Mem., Abbotsford Chamber of Commerce, BC, 2001– (Dir, 2007); Vice Pres., 2008; Pres., 2009; Chm., 2010); Dir, British Columbia Chamber of Commerce, 2010–13. Dir, Jimi Hendrix Family Foundn, 2013–15. Ambassador, Galapagos Conservation Trust, London, 2005–; Chm., Habitat for Humanity, Upper Fraser Valley, 2017–; Vice Chm., Bd of Trustees, Abbotsford Christ the King, 2006–16; Dir, Character Abbotsford, 2016–. *Recreations:* ornithology, the countryside, the Bible, technology, conservation. *Address:* #1–2475 Emerson Street, Abbotsford, BC V2T 4W5, Canada. *T:* (604) 5042412. *E:* jabathome@aol.com. *Clubs:* Savile, Royal Over-Seas League.

**BARLOW, Sir John (Kemp),** 3rd Bt *cr* 1907, of Bradwall Hall, Sandbach; merchant banker and farmer; Director, Majedie Investments plc, 1978–2000; Director of other companies; *b* 22 April 1934; *s* of Sir John Denman Barlow, 2nd Bt and Hon. Diana Helen (*d* 1986), *d* of 1st Baron Rochdale, CB and *sister* of 1st Viscount Rochdale, OBE, TD; *S* father, 1986; *m* 1st, 1962, Susan (marr. diss. 1998), *er d* of Col Sir Andrew Horsbrugh-Porter, 3rd Bt, DSO; four *s*; 2nd, 1998, Mrs Pauline Windsor. *Educ:* Winchester; Trinity Coll., Cambridge (MA 1958). Chm., Rubber Growers' Assoc., 1974. Steward of the Jockey Club, 1988–90. High Sheriff, Cheshire, 1979. *Recreations:* steeplechasing, hunting, shooting. *Heir: s* John William Marshall Barlow [*b* 12 March 1964; *m* 1991, Sarah Nobes; three *s*]. *Clubs:* Brooks's, City of London, Jockey.

**BARLOW, Prof. Martin Thomas,** ScD; FRS 2005; FRSC 1998; Professor of Mathematics, University of British Columbia, 1992–2018; *b* 16 June 1953; *s* of late Andrew Dalmahoy Barlow and Yvonne Rosalind Barlow; *m* 1994, Colleen Patricia McLaughlin. *Educ:* Sussex House Sch., London; St Paul's Sch., London; Trinity Coll., Cambridge (BA 1975; ScD 1993); University Coll. of Swansea (PhD). Fellow, Trinity Coll., Cambridge, 1979–92; Interim Dir, Pacific Inst. for Mathematical Scis, 2015–16. *Publications:* contrib. to learned jls. *Address:* Department of Mathematics, University of British Columbia, Vancouver, BC V6T 1Z2, Canada. *T:* (604) 8222666, *Fax:* (604) 8226074.

**BARLOW, Patrick;** actor, writer, director; *b* 18 March 1947; *s* of Edward Morgan and Sheila Maud Barlow; two *s* one *d*. *Educ:* Uppingham Sch.; Birmingham Univ. (BA 1968). Founder mem., Inter-Action Community Arts, 1968–72; Dir, Lancaster Young People's Theatre, 1972–74; Founder Dir, Solent People's Theatre, 1974–76; created Henrietta Sluggett and appeared nationwide in clubs, streets, theatres, incl. Crucible, Sheffield, Haymarket, Leicester and NT, 1976–79; created *National Theatre of Brent,* 1980, appeared in and wrote jointly: stage: Charge of the Light Brigade, 1980; Zulu!, 1981; Black Hole of Calcutta, 1982; Götterdämmerung, 1982; The Messiah, 1983; Complete Guide to Sex, 1984; Greatest Story Ever Told, 1987; Mysteries of Sex, 1997; Love Upon the Throne, 1998; The New Messiah, 2000; The Wonder of Sex, 2001; television: Messiah, 1983; Mighty Moments from World History, Lawrence of Arabia, Dawn of Man, Boadicea, Arthur and Guinevere, 1985; Revolution!!, 1989; created Royal Dingle Co. for Oh Dear Purcell!, 1995; Massive Landmarks of the Twentieth Century, Queen Victoria, Russian Revolution, Edward VIII and Mrs Simpson, Cuban Missile Crisis, First Man on the Moon, Clinton and Monica, 1999; *other stage appearances* incl.: Truscott, in Loot, Manchester Royal Exchange, 1987; Humphry, in Common Pursuit, Phoenix, 1988; Pseudolus, in A Funny Thing Happened on the Way to the Forum, Manchester Liby Th., 1988; Sidney, in Silly Cow, Haymarket, 1991; Toad, in Wind in the Willows, RNT, 1994; *television* incl.: Talk to Me, 1983; Victoria Wood: As Seen on TV, 1985; All Passion Spent, 1986; Thank You Miss Jones, 1987; Absolutely Fabulous, 1994, 2004; Aristophanes, 1995; Is It Legal?, 1995, 1996, 1998; Cows, 1996; Goodbye Mr Steadman, 1999; The Nearly Complete and Utter History of Everything, 2002; Hans Christian Anderson, 2002; Murder in Suburbia, 2004; Shakespeare's Happy Endings, 2005; Marple: By the Pricking of My Thumbs, 2006; Jam and Jerusalem, 2006, 2008, 2009; Sensitive Skin, 2007; Miranda, 2009; The Queen Mother's Visit, 2010; A Very English Scandal, 2018; regular appearances on French & Saunders; *films* incl.: Shakespeare in Love, 1999; Notting Hill, 1999; Girl from Rio, 2001; Bridget Jones's Diary, 2001; Nanny McPhee, 2005; Scoop, 2006; The Riot Club, 2014; *radio* incl. *National Theatre of Brent's:* All the World's a Globe, 1990 (Sony Radio award, 1990; Premier Ondas award, 1991); Desmond Dingle's Compleat Life and Works of William Shakespeare, 1995; Complete and Utter History of the Mona Lisa, 2004 (Sony Gold for Best Comedy, Gold award, NY Fests, 2005); Messiah, 2006; The Arts and How They Was Done, 6 episodes, 2007; Iconic Icons: episode 1, Bob Dylan and How He Done the Singing, 2009; episode 2, Tracey Emin and How She Done the Bed, 2010; Joan of Arc, and How She Finally Became a Saint, 2009 (also actor); The Dalai Lama and How He Done The Buddhism, 2011; Giant Ladies That Changed the World, 2011; Illustrated Guide to Sex and How it Was Done, 2011; *other radio* incl.: Midsummer Wedding, 1990; Noah, 1991; Rent, 1996, 1997, 1998; The Patrick and Maureen Maybe Music Experience, 1999; Just Plain Gardening, 2002, 2005; The Furniture Play, 2004; Volpone, 2004; Small Gods, 2006; The Skool Days of Nigel Molesworth, 2014; regular contrib., Looking Forward to the Past, Quote Unquote. Writer: for television: The Ghost of Faffner Hall (jtly), 1989; adaptation, The Growing Pains of Adrian Mole, 1986; screenplay, Van Gogh (Prix Futura, Berlin Film Fest.), 1990; Scarfe on Sex, 1991; The True Adventures of Christopher Columbus (also actor and dir), 1992; Queen of the East, 1994 (also actor); adaptation, The Young Visiters, 2003 (also actor); Marple: Why Didn't They Ask Evans?, 2009; for theatre: libretto, Judgement of Paris, Garden Venture, Royal Opera, 1991; How to Deal with Getting Dumped, GogMagog Theatre Co., 2002; The 39 Steps, W Yorks Playhouse, 2005, transf. Tricycle, then Criterion, 2006 (Best Comedy, Olivier Awards, 2007), transf. NY, 2008–11, UK tour, 2008, 2009–10, US tour, 2009–10, world tour, 2008–13, revived NY, 2015; Ben-Hur, Watermill Th., Newbury, 2012 (also co-dir); The Messiah, 2018 (also dir), Other Palace, Victoria, UK tour; adaptations: A Christmas Carol, US, 2012, 2013, Noel Coward Th., 2015; Comus, Sam Wanamaker Playhouse, 2016. *Publications:* All the World's a Globe, 1987 (adapted for radio); Shakespeare: The Truth, 1993; Love Upon the Throne, 1998; The Messiah, 2001, new edn 2018; The Wonder of Sex, 2001; Desmond Olivier Dingle's Complete History of the Whole World, 2002; The 39 Steps (play), 2010; A Christmas Carol (play), 2015. *Address:* (as writer/director) Casarotto Ramsay Associates, 7–12 Noel Street, W1F 8GQ; (as actor) Jonathan Altaras Associates Ltd, 60 St Martins Lane, WC2N 4JS. *Clubs:* Groucho, Two Brydges, Union, Academy.

**BARLOW, Phyllida,** CBE 2016; RA 2011; sculptor; *b* Newcastle upon Tyne, 4 April 1944; *d* of late Erasmus Darwin Barlow and Brigit Ursula Hope Barlow (*née* Black); *m* Fabian Peake; five *c*. *Educ:* Chelsea Coll. of Art, London; Slade Sch. of Fine Art, London. Former Prof. of Fine Art, and Dir, Undergrad. Studies, Slade Sch. of Fine Art, London. Solo exhibitions include: Mus. of Installation, London, 1991, 1995; Baltic Centre for Contemp. Art, Gateshead, 2004; Mead Gall., Warwick Arts Centre, 2008; Hauser & Wirth, London, 2011, NY, 2012; Tate Britain, 2014; Venice Biennale, 2017; RA, 2019; group exhibitions include Venice Biennale, 2013; work in public collections: Tate, London; Henry Moore Inst., Leeds. *Address:* c/o Hauser & Wirth, 23 Savile Row, W1S 2ET.

**BARLOW, (Richard) Francis (Dudley);** QC 2006; barrister; *b* 9 Oct. 1938; *y s* of late Dudley Barlow and Ruby Barlow (*née* Brews); *m* 1966, Helen Mary, *er d* of late Wilfrid Gawthorne and Maureen Gawthorne (*née* Nelson); three *s*. *Educ:* Dauntsey's Sch.; Christ Church, Oxford (BA 1962; MA 1966). Nat. Service, RN, 1957–59; Lt-Comdr RNR. Called to the Bar, Inner Temple, 1965; Bencher, Lincoln's Inn, 1994; in practice at Chancery Bar; Hd of Chambers, Ten Old Square, 2012–. *Address:* 10 Old Square, Lincoln's Inn, WC2A 3SU. *T:* (020) 7405 0758. *Club:* Garrick.

**BARLOW, Stephen William,** FGS, FRCO; conductor, composer and pianist; Artistic Director, Buxton Festival, 2012–18; *b* 30 June 1954; *s* of George William Barlow and Irene Catherine Barlow (*née* Moretti); *m* 1986, Joanna Lamond Lumley, qv. *Educ:* Canterbury

Cathedral Choir Sch.; King's Sch., Canterbury; Trinity Coll., Cambridge (BA 1975); Guildhall Sch. of Music and Drama. FRCO 1971; FGS (FGSM 1986). Associate Conductor, Glyndebourne Fest. Opera, 1980–81; Resident Conductor, ENO, 1980–83; Music Director: Opera 80, 1987–90 (co-founder, 1979); Queensland Philharmonic, 1996–99; Artistic Dir, Opera Northern Ireland, 1996–99. Début as conductor, Royal Opera House, Covent Garden, 1989, then San Francisco, Melbourne, Sydney, Detroit, Miami, Berlin, Auckland, Singapore, Vancouver, Amsterdam, Chicago, Copenhagen, Aarhus, Belgrade, Catania, Toronto, etc. Hon. DMus Chester, 2019. *Publications:* String Quartet, 2000; The Rainbow Bear (for children), 2000; Pas de Deux for Flute and Piano, 2002; King (opera for Canterbury Cathedral), 2004; Nocturne for Clarinet, Marimba and Strings, 2008. *Recreations:* wine, driving, cricket, composing and playing chamber music. *Address:* c/o Musichall, Oast House, Crouch's Farm, Hollow Lane, E Hoathly, E Sussex BN8 6QX. *E:* info@musichall.uk.com.

**BARNARD,** 12th Baron *cr* 1698, of Barnard Castle in the County Palatine of Durham; **Henry Francis Cecil Vane;** DL; *b* 11 March 1959; *o s* of 11th Baron Barnard and Lady Davina Vane (*née* Cecil), *e d* of 6th Marquess of Exeter, KCMG; *S* father, 2016; *m* 1998, Kate, *yr d* of Christopher Robson; one *s* two *d*. *Educ:* Eton; Univ. of Edinburgh (BSc). DL Durham 2011. *Heir: s* Hon. William Henry Cecil Vane, *b* 4 June 2005.

**BARNARD, Prof. Alan John,** PhD; FBA 2010; Professor of the Anthropology of Southern Africa, University of Edinburgh, 2001–15, now Emeritus Professor and Honorary Professorial Fellow; *b* Baton Rouge, Louisiana, 22 Feb. 1949; *s* of John H. Barnard and Doris P. Barnard; *m* 1990, Joy E. Maxwell. *Educ:* George Washington Univ. (BA 1971); McMaster Univ. (MA 1972); PhD London 1976. Jun. Lectr, Univ. of Cape Town, 1972–73; Lectr, UCL, 1976–78; Lectr, 1978–90, Sen. Lectr, 1990–94, Reader, 1994–2001, in Social Anthropol., Univ. of Edinburgh. Hon. Consul of Namibia in Scotland, 2007–. *Publications:* (with A. Good) Research Practices in the Study of Kinship, 1984; A Nharo Wordlist, with Notes on Grammar, 1985; Hunters and Herders of Southern Africa: a comparative ethnography of the Khoisan Peoples, 1992; Kalahari Bushmen, 1993; (ed with J. Spencer) Encyclopedia of Social and Cultural Anthropology, 1996, 2nd edn 2010; History and Theory in Anthropology, 2000; Social Anthropology: a concise introduction for students, 2000, 2nd edn as Social Anthropology: investigating human social life, 2006; Los pueblos cazadores recolectores: tres conferencias dictadas en Argentina (The Hunter-Gatherer Peoples: three lectures presented in Argentina), 2001; (ed) Hunter-Gatherers in History, Archaeology and Anthropology, 2004; Anthropology and the Bushman, 2007; Social Anthropology and Human Origins, 2011; Genesis of Symbolic Thought, 2012; Language in Prehistory, 2016; Bushmen: Kalahari hunter-gatherers and their descendants, 2019; contrib. articles to acad. jls and chapters in books. *Recreations:* black labradors, folk music, watercolour painting. *Address:* Social Anthropology, School of Social and Political Studies, University of Edinburgh, Chrystal Macmillan Building, 15a George Square, Edinburgh EH8 9LD. *E:* a.barnard@ed.ac.uk.

**BARNARD, David;** *see* Barnard, J. D. W.

**BARNARD, Surg. Rear Adm. Ernest Edward Peter,** DPhil; FFCM; Surgeon Rear Admiral, Operational Medical Services, 1982–84; retired 1984; *b* 22 Feb. 1927; *s* of Lionel Edward Barnard and Ernestine (*née* Lethbridge); *m* 1955, Dr Joan Barnard (*née* Gunn); one *s* one *d*. *Educ:* schools in England and Australia; Univ. of Adelaide; St Mary's Hosp., Univ. of London (MB, BS 1955); St John's Coll., Univ. of Oxford (student, 1966–68; DPhil 1969). MRCS, LRCP 1955; MFOM 1979; FFCM 1980. After house appts, joined RN, 1956; served, 1957–76: HMS Bulwark, Reclaim and Dolphin; RN Physiol Lab.; RN Med. Sch.; Inst. of Naval Medicine; Dept of Med. Dir Gen. (Naval); exchange service with US Navy at Naval Med. Res. Inst., Bethesda, Md, 1976–78; Inst. of Naval Medicine, 1978–80; QHP 1980–84; Dep. Med. Dir Gen. (Naval), 1980–82; Surgeon Rear-Adm., Inst. of Naval Medicine, and Dean of Naval Medicine, 1982. FRSocMed 1962. SBStJ 1984. *Publications:* papers on underwater medicine and physiology. *Recreations:* gardening, reading of history and archaeology, photography. *Address:* c/o Barclays Bank, PO Box 6, Portsmouth PO6 3DH.

**BARNARD, Dame Hermione;** *see* Lee, Dame H.

**BARNARD, (John) David (William),** CBE 2000; FRCS, FDSRCS; Consultant Oral and Maxillofacial Surgeon, Queen Alexandra Hospital, Portsmouth Hospitals NHS Trust, 1979–2005; *b* 5 March 1943; *s* of Dr George Edward Barnard and Gwenllian Mary Barnard (*née* Thomas); *m* 1980, Cheryl Barlow. *Educ:* St Marylebone Grammar Sch.; Guy's Hosp. Dental Sch. (BDS London 1966). FDSRCS 1974; FDSRCPSGlas 1974. Hse surgeon, Guy's Hosp., 1967; RN Dental Service, 1967–72; Asst Dental Surgeon, Queen Victoria Hosp., E Grinstead, 1973–75; Sen. Registrar, Oxford Hosps, 1975–79. Civil Consultant, Royal Navy, 1995 (formerly Royal Naval Hosp.), Haslar, 1983–2005; Consultant Advr in Oral and Maxillofacial Surgery, RN, 2002–05 Leverhulme Fellow in Oral Surgery, Univ. of California, 1978; Hunterian Prof., RCS, 1978. Clifford Ballard Meml Lecture, Consultant Orthodontists' Gp, British Orthodontic Soc., 2004. Member: Central Cttee, Hosp. Dental Services, 1988–99 (Chm., 1995–98); Jt Consultants Cttee, 1995–2001; Central Consultants and Specialists Cttee, BMA, 1995–2001; Standing Dental Adv. Cttee, 1998–2004. Mem., GDC, 1998–2004 (Chm., Postgrad. Sub Cttee, 2001–03; Chm., Educn Cttee, 2003–04); Hosps Gp Pres., 1985, Chm., Gp Cttee, 1988–99, Mem., Council and Rep. Bd, 1995–98, Fellow, 2004, BDA; Mem. Council, 1987–92, Hon. Treas., 1989–92, Pres., 2004, BAOMS; Odontological Section, Royal Society of Medicine: Mem. Council, 1990–99; Hon. Treas., 1993–96; Vice-Pres., 1996–99; Royal College of Surgeons of England: Bd Mem., 1995–2002, Dean, 1998–2001, Faculty of Dental Surgery; Mem. Council, 1998–2002; Trustee, Hunterian Collection, 2008–19 (Chm of Trustees, 2014–19). FDSRCSE (*ad hominem*) 1998; FRCS (by election) 2000; FFGDP(UK) 2008. Hon. Fellow, Amer. Assoc. of Oral and Maxillofacial Surgeons, 2004. Colyer Gold Medal, Faculty of Dental Surgery, RCS, 2004. *Publications:* contrib. chapters in books and articles to learned jls. *Recreations:* my border collies, historic motor sport, music. *Address:* Squirrels Leap, 59 Warblington Road, Emsworth, Hants PO10 7HG. *T:* (01243) 372987. *Clubs:* Army and Navy; Emsworth Sailing; Goodwood Road Racing.

**BARNARD, Prof. John Michael;** Professor of English Literature, School of English, University of Leeds, 1978–2001, now Emeritus; *b* Folkestone, 13 Feb. 1936; *s* of John Claude Southard Barnard and Dora Grace Barnard; *m* 1st, 1961, Katherine Duckham (marr. diss. 1975); one *s* two *d*; partner, 1975, *m* 2nd, 1991, Hermione Lee (*see* Dame H. Lee). *Educ:* Wadham Coll., Oxford (BA (Hons) Eng. Lang. and Lit.; BLitt; MA). Res. Asst, English Dept, Yale Univ., 1961–64; Vis. Lectr, English Dept, Univ. of California at Santa Barbara, 1964–65; Post-doctoral Fellow, William Andrews Clark Meml Liby, UCLA, 1965; Leeds University: Lectr and Sen. Lectr, Sch. of English, 1965–78; Dir, Inst. of Bibliography and Textual Criticism, Sch. of English, 1996–2001 (Actg Dir, 1982–96). Res. Fellow, William Andrews Clark Meml Liby, UCLA, and Huntington Liby, 1994. Mem., British Cttee, Eighteenth Century Short Title Catalogue, 1983–89; Pres., Bibliographical Soc., 2008–10 (Mem. Council, 1989–94, 2010–16; Vice-Pres., 1998–2008). Mem., English Panel, 1996 RAE, Chm., English Panel, 2001 RAE, HEFCE. Lectures: British Academy Warton, 1989; Friends of Bodleian Quatercentenary, 2002; D. F. McKenzie, Oxford Univ., 2005; Coffin Meml, London Univ., 2010. Internat. expert Verkenningscommissie Moderne Letteren, Netherlands, 1992–93. Sen. Res. Fellow, Inst. of English Studies, Univ. of London, 2007–. FEA 2000; Hon. Fellow, Wolfson Coll., Oxford, 2016. General Editor: Longman Annotated Poets, 1976–, with Paul Hammond, 2001–10; The Cambridge History of The Book, Vols 1–2 and 5–7, 2003–; Member, Editorial Board: English Poetry Full Text Database, 1991–93; English Verse Drama Full Text Database, 1993–95; English Prose Drama Full Text Database, 1994–96. *Publications:* (ed) William Congreve, The Way of the World, 1972; (ed) Pope: The Critical Heritage, 1973; (ed) John Keats: the complete poems, 1973, 3rd edn 1988; (ed) Etherege: The Man of Mode, 1979, rev. edn 2007; John Keats, 1987; (ed) John Keats: selected poems, 1988; (jtly) The Early Seventeenth-Century York Book Trade and John Foster's Inventory of 1616, 1994; (ed) The Folio Society John Keats, 2001; (ed jtly) The Cambridge History of the Book in Britain, Vol. 4 1557–1695, 2002; (ed) Selected Poems: John Keats, 2007; (ed) John Keats: selected letters, 2014; (ed) John Keats, 2017; chapters in books, articles in Brit. and Amer. learned jls, occasional reviews, etc. *Recreations:* travel, walking. *Address:* Lane End, Weeton Lane, Weeton, Leeds LS17 0AN.

**BARNARD, Toby Christopher,** DPhil; FBA 2007; Lecturer in History, University of Oxford, 1976–2012; Fellow and Tutor in History, 1976–2012, now Emeritus Fellow, and Archivist and Fellow Librarian, 2005–12, Hertford College, Oxford; *b* 17 April 1945; *s* of Robert John Barnard and Gina Barnard (*née* Motta). *Educ:* Torquay Boys' Grammar Sch.; Brighton, Hove and Sussex Grammar Sch.; Queen's Coll., Oxford (BA 1966; DPhil 1972). Bryce Sen. Scholar in Hist., Oxford Univ., 1968–69; Tutor in Hist., Univ. of Exeter, 1969–70; Lectr in Hist., Royal Holloway Coll., Univ. of London, 1970–76. Historical advr, Carroll Inst. of Irish Hist., 1991–94; British Acad. Res. Reader, 1997–99; Vis. Fellow, Archbishop Narcissus Marsh's Liby, Dublin, 2001–02; Leverhulme Sen. Res. Fellow, 2006–09. Dacre Lectr, Univ. of Oxford, 2013. Hon. MRIA 2001. FRHistS 1977. *Publications:* Cromwellian Ireland: English government and reform in Ireland 1649–1660, 1975, 2nd edn 2000; The English Republic 1649–1660, 1982, 2nd edn 1997; The Abduction of a Limerick Heiress: social and political relations in mid-eighteenth-century Ireland, 1998; A New Anatomy of Ireland: the Irish protestants 1641–1770, 2003; Making the Grand Figure: lives and possessions in Ireland 1641–1770, 2004; Irish Protestant Ascents and Descents 1641–1770, 2004; The Kingdom of Ireland 1641–1760, 2004; Guide to the Sources for the History of Material Culture in Ireland 1500–2000, 2005; Improving Ireland?: projectors, prophets and profiteers, 1641–1786, 2008; Brought to Book: print in Ireland, 1679–1784, 2016; *edited:* (with Jane Clark) Lord Burlington: architecture, art and life, 1995; (with D. Ó. Crónin and K. Simms) A Miracle of Learning: studies in manuscripts and Irish learning: essays in honour of William O'Sullivan, 1998; (with Jane Fenlon) The Dukes of Ormonde 1610–1745, 2000; (with W. G. Neely) The Clergy of the Church of Ireland 1000–2000: messengers, watchmen and stewards, 2006; (with B. McCormack) Archives of the Tholsel Court, Dublin, 2018; articles in historical jls and book reviews in TLS, Irish Times, English Historical Review, etc. *Recreations:* pugs (Member, Pug Dog Club), collecting, West Cork. *Address:* 44 High Street, Finstock, Oxon OX7 3DW. *E:* toby.barnard@hertford.ox.ac.uk. *Club:* Oxford and Cambridge.

**BARNBROOK, Richard John;** private fine art commissions and commercial international fine art and design projects; *b* Catford, London, 24 Feb. 1961; *s* of John and Janet Barnbrook. *Educ:* Immingham Comp. Sch.; Grimsby Sch. of Art (Foundn course); Royal Acad. of Arts (RA Dip; BA 1st Cl. Hons 1985); Limoges Coll. of Art and Design (Minor Schol. 1983); Silpakorn Univ., Bangkok (UNESCO Schol. 1986); Calif Inst. of Art (Interim MA); Greenwich Univ. (PGCE 1995). Practising artist and art lectr, England, Norway, Holland, Germany, France, Thailand and USA, 1985–2003; writer, director and actor, performance art and theatre, 1987–91, film (and film-maker), 1989–92; private commns of art works, 1989–2004; secondary sch. art teacher, 1996–2004. Nat. and internat. exhibns, 1971–2002. Mem. (BNP) Barking and Dagenham LBC, 2006–10 (Leader, 2006–08, Dep. Leader, 2008–10, BNP Gp); Mem., London Assembly, GLA, 2008–12 (BNP, 2008–10, Ind, 2010–12). Contested (BNP) Barking, 2005. Member: Labour Party, 1984–86; BNP, 1999–2010 (Br. Organiser, Lewisham and Bromley, 2000; London Regl Organiser, 2003–05; Mem., Adv. Council, 2004–06). *Recreations:* cycling, Rugby, swimming. *E:* richardbarnbrook2402@hotmail.com.

**BARNEBY, Col Michael Paul;** Clerk to the Salters' Company, 1990–2006; *b* 29 March 1939; *m* 1973, Bridget, *d* of Col A. G. Roberts, DSO, Crickhowell; three *d*. *Educ:* Radley Coll. Commissioned into 15th/19th King's Royal Hussars, 1958; served Germany, NI, Hong Kong; commanded Royal Hong Kong Regt (Volunteers), 1981–83; retired from Army, 1988; Dir of Planning and Admin, Clark Whitehill, 1988–89. *Recreations:* hunting, shooting, racing. *Address:* Woodseats House, Medstead, Hants GU34 5ND. *Club:* Cavalry and Guards.

**BARNES;** *see* Oppenheim-Barnes.

**BARNES,** family name of **Baron Gorell**.

**BARNES, Adrian Francis Patrick,** CVO 1996; DL; Remembrancer of the City of London, 1986–2003; *b* 25 Jan. 1943; *s* of late Francis Walter Ibbetson Barnes and of Heather Katherine (*née* Tamplin); *m* 1980, Sally Eve Whatley; one *s* one *d*. *Educ:* St Paul's School; Hague Acad. of Internat. Law; Council of Legal Educn; MA City of London Polytechnic 1981. Called to the Bar, Gray's Inn, 1973, Bencher, 2000 (Doyen, Seniors in Hall, 1992–2000); Solicitor's Dept, DTI, 1975; Dep. Remembrancer, Corp. of London, 1982. Chm., Wimbledon Guild of Social Welfare, 2004–08 (Mem., Exec. Cttee, 2003–08; Chairman: Counselling Mgt Cttee, 2004–08; Centenary Cttee, 2004–08). Chm., The Music Therapy Charity, 1997–2003 (Gov., 1995–2016; Chm., Res. Cttee, 2014–16). Pres., Merton Talking Newspaper Assoc., 2015–. Freeman: City of London, 1982; Arts Scholars' Co. (formerly Guild of Arts Scholars, Dealers and Collectors), 2007–; Liveryman, Merchant Taylors' Co., 1989–. DL Greater London, 2002. *Recreations:* music, cricket, rowing, chess, biography, City lore. *Clubs:* Garrick, Guildhall, MCC.

**BARNES, Anthony Hugh,** FSA; FCIPD; Director, Redundant Churches Fund, 1984–92; *b* 16 June 1931; *s* of Sir George Barnes and Anne Barnes; *m* 1st, 1956, Susan Dempsey; one *s* (and one *s* decd) one *d*; 2nd, 1984, Jennifer Carey. *Educ:* King's Coll., Cambridge (MA). Schweppes Ltd, 1954–66; Royal Opera House, 1966–70; ICI, 1970–82; self-employed, 1982–84. Trustee: Norfolk Churches Trust, 1995–2002 (Sec., 1992–95); Norwich Historic Churches Trust, 2001–08. Vice-Pres., Norwich Labour Party, 2000–01. FSA 2004. *Address:* 1 Dixon's Court, 52 Bethel Street, Norwich NR2 1NR. *T:* (01603) 666783.

**BARNES, Barbara Lucinda;** a District Judge (Magistrates' Courts), 2004–18; *b* 28 Nov. 1953; *d* of Arthur Frederick Barnes and Barbara Barnes (*née* Willisford). *Educ:* Blackheath High Sch.; St George's Sch., Harpenden; KCL (LLB 1975). Called to the Bar, Gray's Inn, 1976; Inner London Magistrates' Courts Service: Dep. Chief Clerk, 1979–88; Dep. Training Officer, 1988–91; Justices' Clerk, Greenwich, 1998–2003. Commng Ed., 2004–07, Ed.-in-Chief, 2007–18, Archbold: Magistrates' Courts Criminal Practice. *Recreations:* amateur dramatics, theatre, travel, reading.

**BARNES, Christopher John Andrew,** CB 1996; trainer, facilitator and coach; *b* 11 Oct. 1944; *s* of late Eric Vernon Barnes and Joan Mary Barnes; *m* 1st, 1978, Carolyn Elisabeth Douglass Johnston (*d* 1990); two *s*; 2nd, 1990, Susan Elizabeth Bird; two *s*. *Educ*: City of London Sch.; London School of Economics (BScEcon). Ministry of Agriculture, Fisheries and Food: Exec. Officer, 1962; Asst Principal, 1967; Private Sec. to Parly Sec., 1969–71; Principal, 1971; Sec. to Northfield Cttee on Agricultural Land Ownership and Occupancy, 1977–79; Asst Sec., 1980; Chief Reg. Officer, Nottingham and Reading, 1980–83; Hd of Personnel and R&D Requirements Divs, 1983–90; 'Barnes Review' of near market R&D, 1988; Under Sec. (Grade 3), 1990–96; Arable Crops and Hort., later Arable Crops and Alcoholic Drinks Gp, 1990–95; Dir of Estabs, 1995–96, retired. A Chm., CSSB, 1995–97. Ind. Accredited Assessor for DEFRA (formerly MAFF), 1996–2013. Sen. Consultant, Andersons, 1996–98; Associate Dir, Andersons Chamberlain Recruitment, 1996–98; Dir, Drew Associates Ltd, 1996–98; Associate, Nat. Sch. of Govt, 1996–2012; Senior Associate: McNeil Robertson Develt, 1996–2013; Miad UK Ltd, 2001–15; Res Consortium, 2003–14; Westminster Explained, 2004–14; Public Health Action Support Team, 2005–17; Facilitator, ISC Medical, 2012–; Exec. Search Consultant, Rundle Brownswood, 2002–12; Mem., Live Academy, 2005–10. Chairman: Assured Produce Ltd, 1999–2001; Chris Barnes Ltd (formerly Modernising Skills Ltd), 1999–2014; Assured Food Standards Ltd, 2000–03; Barnes Partnership, 2015–; Man. Dir, Currency Connect UK, 2004–05; Dir, Horticultural Business, Hartington Gp, 2003–05; non-exec. Dir, Booker Food Services, 1987–90. Chm., Governing Bd, CMi plc, 2005–12 (Mem., 2003–12). Mem. Management Cttee, CS Healthcare, 1992–99 (Vice-Chm., 1997–99); Chm., Bucks HA, 1999–2000 (non-exec. Dir, 1996–99). FRSA 1999; FCIHort (FIHort 2002). *Recreations*: competitive off-roading, France, study of First World War.

**BARNES, Sir David;** *see* Barnes, Sir J. D. F.

**BARNES, David John;** Head Master, Pate's Grammar School, Cheltenham, 1986–2000; *b* 6 Nov. 1939; *s* of David Alan Barnes and Norah Barnes (*née* Fleming); *m* 1961, Jan Crofts; one *s* one *d*. *Educ*: The Grammar Sch., Wolstanton, Staffs; Queen's Coll., Oxford (Open Schol.; MA); DipEd London; Post Grad. Cert. in Architectural Hist., Oxford, 2003. Assistant Master: Pocklington Sch., York, 1962–66; Nottingham High Sch., 1966–68; Vice-Principal, Newcastle-under-Lyme Sch., 1968–86. *Publications*: A Parent's Guide to GCSE, 1988; various check-lists and guides to students' reading, 1991. *Recreations*: fly-fishing, Homer, digging holes and other honest labour. *Address*: 32 Gretton Road, Gotherington, Cheltenham, Glos GL52 9QU.

**BARNES, (David) Michael (William);** QC 1981; a Recorder, since 1985; *b* 16 July 1943; *s* of David Charles Barnes and Florence Maud Barnes; *m* 1970, Susan Dorothy Turner; three *s*. *Educ*: Monmouth Sch.; Wadham Coll., Oxford. Called to Bar, Middle Temple, 1965, Bencher, 1989. Hon. Research Fellow, Lady Margaret Hall, Oxford, 1979; Vis. Fellow, Univ. of Auckland, NZ, 1995. Chm., Hinckley Point 'C' Public Inquiry, 1988. *Publications*: Leasehold Reform Act 1967, 1967; Hill and Redman's Law of Landlord and Tenant, 15th edn 1970 to 18th edn 1988; Hill and Redman's Guide to Rent Review, 2001; The Law of Compensation and Compulsory Purchase, 2014; The Law of Rights of Light, 2016. *Recreations*: walking, crime fiction. *Address*: Wilberforce Chambers, 8 New Square, WC2A 3QP. *Club*: Beefsteak.

**BARNES, Edward Campbell;** independent television producer/director and television consultant, 1986–2008; Head of Children's Programmes, BBC Television, 1978–86; *b* 8 Oct. 1928; *s* of Hubert Turnbull Barnes and Annie Mabel Barnes; *m* 1950, Dorothy Smith (*d* 1992); one *s* two *d*. *Educ*: Wigan Coll. British Forces Network, Vienna, 1946–49; stage management, provincial and West End theatre, 1949–55; BBC Television: studio management, 1955–62; Producer, Blue Peter, 1962–70; Dep. Head of Children's Progs, 1970–78, incl.: original Editor, John Craven's Newsround; Producer: Blue Peter Royal Safari with Princess Anne; 6 series of Blue Peter Special Assignments; Producer and Director: Treasure Houses, 1986; All Our Children, 1987–90; Boxpops, 1992; The Lowdown, 1992. Mem. Bd, Children's Film and Television Foundn Ltd, 1983–97; Dir, Christian Children's Fund, 1995–2002. Consultant, St Paul's Multi-media, 1995–96. Mem., RTS (Mem., Awards Cttee, 1989–91). Trustee, EveryChild, 2002–03. SFTA Award, 1969; RTS Silver Medal, 1986; Pye Television Award, 1986; Special Award as creator of Newsround to celebrate its 40th anniversary, BAFTA, 2012; (jtly) Harvey Lee Award in special recognition of Blue Peter, BPG, 2018. *Publications*: 25 Blue Peter Books and 8 Blue Peter Mini Books, 1964–; 6 Blue Peter Special Assignment Books, 1973–75; Blue Peter Royal Safari, 1971; Petra: a dog for everyone, 1977; Blue Peter: the inside story, 1989; numerous articles for nat. press. *Recreations*: cricket, music, birding, walking, Venice, Bali.

*See also* S. J. C. Barnes.

**BARNES, Eric Charles,** CBE 1992; GBS 2005; High Court Judge, Hong Kong, 1981–91; *b* 12 Sept. 1924; *m* 1st, Estelle Fay Barnes (*née* Darnell); four *s* one *d*; 2nd, 1978, Judianna Wai Ling Barnes (*née* Chang); one *s* one *d*. *Educ*: Univ. of Queensland (LLB). Chief Adjudicator, Immigration Tribunal, Hong Kong, 1993–2004; Chm., Appeal Bd on Public Meetings and Demonstrations, Hong Kong, 1995–99. Mem., Australian Assoc., Hong Kong, 1994–. *Recreations*: tennis, racing (horse), sports. *Address*: House 52, Manderly Garden, 48 Deep Water Bay Road, Hong Kong. *Clubs*: United Services Recreation, Kowloon Cricket, Hong Kong Jockey (Hong Kong); Tattersall's (Brisbane).

**BARNES, Harold, (Harry);** *b* 22 July 1936; *s* of late Joseph and Betsy Barnes; *m* 1963, Elizabeth Ann Stephenson; one *s* one *d*. *Educ*: Ruskin Coll., Oxford (Dip. Econs and Political Science); Hull Univ. (BA Philosophy and Political Studies). National Service, 1954–56. Railway clerk, 1952–54 and 1956–60; adult student, 1960–65; further educn lectr, 1965–66; Lectr, Sheffield Univ., 1966–87. MP (Lab) Derbys NE, 1987–2005. Jt Pres., New Dialogue (Britain), 1992–2005 (Chm., 1990–92); Vice-Pres., Labour Friends of Iraq, 2007–12 (Jt Pres., 2004–06). Mem., National Admin. Council, Ind. Labour Publications, 1977–80 and 1982–85. Writer, http://threescoreyearsandten.blogspot.com. *Publications*: pamphlets on local govt and on the public face of Militant; articles and reviews in Labour Leader, London Labour Briefing, Tribune, Morning Star, Local Socialism, New Socialist, Derbyshire Miner, Leeds Weekly Citizen, Sheffield Forward, Industrial Tutor, Political Studies, Dronfield Miscellany, Post-16 Educator, North East History, Labour Heritage. *Club*: Dronfield Contact.

**BARNES, Ian Colin,** PhD; FRCPath; independent pathology specialist advisor, since 2015; Specialist Advisor to Chief Scientific Officer, NHS England, 2014–15; *b* Jersey, CI, 16 Aug. 1950; *s* of Colin Barnes and Margaret Barnes; *m* 1969, Sarah Fraser-Thomson; two *s*. *Educ*: Hautlieu GS, Jersey; Univ. of Bath (BSc Applied Biochem.); Univ. of London (MSc Clin. Biochem.); Univ. of Bristol (PhD 1978). FRCPath 1996; CSci 2006. Leeds General Infirmary: Consultant Clinical Biochemist, 1987–92; Hd of Clin. Biochem., 1992–96; Dir of Pathol., 1996–98; Hd of Pathol., Leeds Teaching Hosps, 1998–2007. Nat. Pathol. Advr, 2002–09, Nat. Clinical Dir for Pathol., 2009–13, DoH; Chair, Pathol. Quality Assurance Rev. Bd, NHS England (formerly NHS Commng Bd), 2013–14. Chm., Assoc. of Clin. Biochemists, 1997–2000. *Recreations*: travel, golf, food and wine. *Address*: La Petite Rosaye, Rue des Landes, St John, Jersey, Channel Islands JE3 4AF. *E*: icsfbarnes@yahoo.co.uk.

**BARNES, Jack Henry;** Director of Administration, British Society for Allergy and Clinical Immunology, 2002–05; *b* 11 Dec. 1943; *s* of James Barnes and Joan Ivy (*née* Sears); *m* 1966, Nicola Pearse; two *d*. *Educ*: Hatfield Sch., Herts; Univ. of Sussex (BA); LSE (MSc). Dep. Chief Inspector, Social Services Inspectorate, DHSS, 1983–88; Department of Health: Dep. Chief Scientist and Dir, Res. Management, 1988–91; Under Sec., 1991–99; Head: Primary Care Div., NHS Exec., 1991–95; Internat. and Industry Div., 1995–99; Dir of Res. and Policy, Nat. Asthma Campaign, 2000–03. Trustee, Mental Health Foundn, 1997–2003. Non-exec. Dir, E Sussex Downs and Weald PCT, 2006–12; Ind. Mem., Governing Body, Eastbourne, Hailsham and Seaford CCG, 2012–. Gov. and Audit Chair, Goldsmiths, Univ. of London, 2005–10.

**BARNES, Sir (James) David (Francis),** Kt 1996; CBE 1987; Deputy Chairman, AstraZeneca PLC, 1999–2001; *b* 4 March 1936; *s* of Eric Cecil Barnes, CMG, and of Jean Margaret Barnes; *m* 1963, Wendy Fiona Mary (*née* Riddell); one *s* one *d*. *Educ*: Shrewsbury Sch.; Liverpool Univ. National Service, commnd 'N' Battery (Eagle Troop), 2nd Regt RA, 1958–60 (Malaya). ICI Pharmaceuticals Division: Overseas Dir 1971–77, Dep. Chm. 1977–83; Chm., ICI Paints Div., 1983–86; Exec. Dir, ICI, 1986–93; CEO, Zeneca Group PLC, 1993–99. Non-executive Director: Thorn EMI, 1987–94; Redland, 1994–98; Prudential, 1999–2003; non-exec. Chm., Imperial Cancer Res. Technol., 1999–2002; Dep. Chm., Syngenta AG, 2000–04. Chairman: Pharmaceuticals EDC, NEDO, 1983–92; Biotechnology Industries Working Party, NEDO, 1989–91. Vice-Pres., Thames Valley Hospice, 1986–. Mem. Council, VSO, 1996–99; a Dep. Chm., BITC, 1996–2000 (Chm., Economic Regeneration Leadership Team, 1996–2000). Mem. Bd of Governors, Ashridge (Bonar Law Meml) Trust, 1993–2006; Gov. and Bd Mem., Intellectual Property Inst., 1994–2000; Member: Governing Body, Shrewsbury Sch., 1997–2006; Bd of Trustees, BRCS, 1998–2004. FInstD; CCMI; FRSA 1988; Hon. Associate, 1995, Hon. Mem., 2006, BVA (Wooldridge Meml Medal, 1995). Hon. LLD Liverpool, 1996; Hon. DSc UMIST, 1998. Centenary Medal, SCI, 2000. *Recreations*: fishing, shooting, walking.

**BARNES, Janet,** CBE 2014; Chief Executive, York Museums Trust, 2002–15; *b* 23 April 1952; *d* of Frederick George Hagan and Margaret Hagan (*née* Wilson); *m* 1970, Philip Barnes. *Educ*: Sheffield Univ. (BA Hons English Lit.); Manchester Univ. (Postgrad. Dip. Mus and Art Gall. Studies). Keeper, Ruskin Gall. and Ruskin Craft Gall., 1985–94; Sen. Curator, Sheffield Galls and Museums, 1995–99; Dir, Crafts Council, 1999–2002. Chm., Yorks, Arts Council England, 2006–13; Mem., Adv. Panel, NHMF, 2014–. Trustee, Anthony Shaw Collection Trust, 2012–. Mem., ICOM UK, 2012–15. Mem., Challenge Panel, DCMS Museums Review, 2016–17. Pres., Arts Soc. York (formerly York Decorative and Fine Arts Soc.), 2016–19. Hon. Curator, Turner Mus. of Glass, Univ. of Sheffield, 1979–99. Dir, Guild of St George, 1994–2018. Hon. LLD Sheffield, 2000; DUniv Sheffield Hallam, 2001; DUniv York, 2013. *Publications*: Percy Horton: 1897–1970 Artist and Absolutist, 1982; Ruskin and Sheffield, 1985, 4th edn 2018; Catalogue of the Turner Museum of Glass, 1993. *Recreations*: swimming, pottery.

**BARNES, Dr Jennifer Chase, (Mrs R. P. Edgar-Wilson);** Partner, Saxton Bampfylde, since 2016; *b* Massachusetts, 30 July 1960; *d* of Prof. James John Barnes and Patience Plummer Barnes; *m* 1988, Richard Philip Edgar-Wilson; one *s* one *d*. *Educ*: Crawfordsville High Sch., Indiana; Smith Coll., Mass (BA Lit.); Britten Internat. Opera Sch., Royal Coll. of Music (MMus); Univ. of London (PhD 1997); MA Cantab 2008. Founder Mem., Mecklenburgh Opera, 1984–89; Associate Prof., RAM, 1989–91; Dir, Professional Integration Project, RCM, 1995–99; Dean and Asst Principal, Trinity Coll. of Music, 1999–2005; Dir, Global Educn, BP, 2005–08; Pres., New Hall, later Murray Edwards Coll., Cambridge, 2008–12; Pro-Vice-Chancellor, Internat. Strategy, 2010–15, Lady Margaret Preacher, 2013–14, Univ. of Cambridge. Member: Exec. Cttee, Centre for Sci. and Policy, Cambridge, 2010–15; Internat. Adv. Panel, Univ. of Oman 2015–; Supervisory Bd, Univ. of Maastricht, 2017–. Director: Univ. of Suffolk, 2016–; Cambridge India Research Foundn, 2016–17. Trustee, Charles and Julia Henry Fund, 2009–15. Mem., Soc. of Authors, 1989–. Hon. Fellow, Trinity Laban Conservatoire of Music and Dance, 2009. FRSA. *Publications*: Television Opera: the fall of opera commissioned for television, 2005; contributor: A Night in at the Opera, 1994; Girls, Girls, Girls, 1996; The New Grove Dictionary of Music and Musicians, 2nd edn 2001; Opera Quarterly. *Recreations*: family, dog walking, reading.

**BARNES, John;** a Senior Immigration Judge, Asylum and Immigration Tribunal (formerly a Vice-President, Immigration Appeal Tribunal), 2000–06; *b* 13 March 1938; *s* of Frederick Walter John Barnes, MBE, LLB and Phyllis Edna Barnes (*née* Brooks); *m* 1992, Frances (*née* Broadrick); three *s* by a previous marriage. *Educ*: Brentwood Sch., Essex; Univ. of London (LLB Hons ext.). Admitted solicitor, 1961; engaged in private practice, 1961–97. Part-time Chm., Industrial Tribunals, 1993–99; Immigration Adjudicator, part-time, 1995–97, full-time, 1997–2000. International Association of Refugee Law Judges: Mem., 2004–; Mem., Eur. Chapter, 2008–; Rep. to European Asylum Support Office, 2011–16. *Publications*: A Manual for Refugee Law Judges, 2007; (with A. R. Mackey) Judicial Criteria and Standards in Assessment of Credibility, 2013; (jtly) An Introduction to the CEAS for Courts and Tribunals, 2016; contrib. to Internat. Jl of Refugee Law. *Recreations*: learning to enjoy retirement, theatre, history, art. *Address*: Orchard Place, Triq ta' Sansuna, Xaghra XRA 1652, Gozo, Malta. *T*: 21561647.

**BARNES, John Nigel;** Chief Executive, Historic Royal Palaces, since 2017 (Conservation & Learning Director, 2001–17); *b* 24 June 1961; *s* of Geoffrey Philip Barnes and Shirley Anne (*née* Eaton); partner, Lauren Kathleen Agnew; two *d*. *Educ*: Judd Sch., Tonbridge; S Bank Poly. (BA Hons, Postgrad. DipArch). Registered Architect; ARB (ARC 1989). In private practice in architecture, 1984–94; English Heritage: Hd, Architecture and Survey, 1994–95; Director: Professional Services, 1995–98; Major Projects, 1998–2001. Trustee, Old RNC, Greenwich. Chm., DEMHIST, ICOM. *Recreations*: karate, life drawing. *Address*: Historic Royal Palaces, Hampton Court Palace, Surrey KT8 9AU. *T*: (020) 3166 6363, *Fax*: (020) 3166 6365. *E*: john.barnes@hrp.org.uk.

**BARNES, Prof. Jonathan,** FBA 1987; Professor of Ancient Philosophy, University of Paris-Sorbonne, 2002–06; *b* 26 Dec. 1942; *s* of late A. L. Barnes and K. M. Barnes; *m* 1965, Jennifer Postgate; two *d*. *Educ*: City of London Sch.; Balliol Coll., Oxford. Oxford University: Fellow, Oriel Coll., 1968–78; Fellow, 1978–94, Emeritus Fellow, 1994–, Balliol Coll.; Prof. of Ancient Philosophy, 1989–94; Prof. of Ancient Philosophy, Univ. of Geneva, 1994–2002. Visiting posts at: Inst. for Advanced Study, Princeton, 1972; Univ. of Texas, 1981; Wissenschaftskolleg zu Berlin, 1985; Univ. of Alberta, 1986; Univ. of Zurich, 1987; Istituto Italiano per gli studi filosofici, Naples, 1988, 1998; Ecole Normale Supérieure, Paris, 1996 (Condorcet Medal, 1996); Scuola Normale Superiore di Pisa, 2002. John Locke Lectr, Univ. of Oxford, 2004. Fellow, Amer. Acad. Arts and Scis, 1999. Hon. Fellow, Oriel Coll., Oxford, 2007. Hon. Dr: Geneva, 2010; Humboldt, Berlin, 2012. Hon. Citizen of Velia, 2010. *Publications*: The Ontological Argument, 1972; Aristotle's Posterior Analytics, 1975; The Presocratic Philosophers, 1979; Aristotle, 1982; Early Greek Philosophy, 1987; The Toils of Scepticism, 1991; The Cambridge Companion to Aristotle, 1995; Logic and the Imperial Stoa, 1997; Porphyry: introduction, 2003; Truth, etc, 2007; Coffee with Aristotle, 2008; Method and Metaphysics, 2011; Zenone e l'infinito, 2011;

Logical Matters, 2012; Proof, Knowledge and Scepticism, 2014; Mantissa, 2015. *Address:* Les Charmilles, 36200 Ceaulmont, France.
*See also* J. P. Barnes.

**BARNES, Joseph Harry George;** Chairman, Baxters of Speyside, 1994–98; Director, 1969–93, Joint Managing Director, 1988–90, J. Sainsbury plc; *b* 24 July 1930; *s* of William Henry Joseph Barnes and Dorothy Eleanor Barnes; *m* 1958, Rosemary Gander; two *s*. *Educ:* John Ruskin Grammar Sch., Croydon. FCA 1963. Articled clerk, Lever Honeyman & Co., 1946–52. National Service, 2nd Lieut RAPC, 1953–55. Joined J. Sainsbury plc, 1956. *Recreations:* tennis, fishing. *Address:* Tudor Court, 29 Grimwade Avenue, Croydon, Surrey CR0 5DJ. *T:* (020) 8654 5696.

**BARNES, Julian Patrick;** writer; *b* 19 Jan. 1946; *m* 1979, Pat Kavanagh (*d* 2008). *Educ:* City of London Sch.; Magdalen Coll., Oxford. Lexicographer, OED Supplement, 1969–72; freelance journalist; Contributing Ed., New Review, 1977; Asst Literary Ed., 1977–79, TV Critic, 1977–81, New Statesman; Dep. Literary Ed., Sunday Times, 1980–82; TV Critic, Observer, 1982–86; London correspondent, The New Yorker, 1990–95. E. M. Forster Award, US Acad. of Arts and Letters, 1986; Shakespeare Prize, Germany, 1993; Austrian State Prize for European Literature, 2004; David Cohen Prize for Literature, 2011. Commandeur de l'Ordre des Arts et des Lettres (France), 2004. *Publications:* Metroland, 1980 (Somerset Maugham Award, 1981); Before She Met Me, 1982; Flaubert's Parrot, 1984 (Geoffrey Faber Meml Prize, 1985; Prix Médicis, 1986; Grinzane Cavour Prize (Italy), 1988); Staring at the Sun, 1986; A History of the World in 10½ Chapters, 1989; Talking it Over, 1991 (Prix Femina, 1992); The Porcupine, 1992; Letters from London (essays), 1995; Cross Channel (short stories), 1996; England, England, 1998; Love, etc, 2000; Something to Declare (essays), 2002; trans. Daudet, In the Land of Pain, 2002; The Pedant in the Kitchen, 2003; The Lemon Table (short stories), 2004; Arthur & George, 2005; Nothing to be Frightened Of (non-fiction), 2008; Pulse (short stories), 2011; The Sense of an Ending, 2011 (Man Booker Prize, 2011; filmed 2017); Through the Window: seventeen essays (and one short story), 2012; Levels of Life, 2013; Keeping an Eye Open: essays on art, 2015; The Noise of Time, 2016; The Only Story, 2018; (as Dan Kavanagh): Duffy, 1980; Fiddle City, 1981; Putting the Boot In, 1985; Going to the Dogs, 1987. *Address:* c/o United Agents, 12–26 Lexington Street, W1F 0LE.
*See also* Jonathan Barnes.

**BARNES, Kristina Aileen;** *see* Montgomery, K. A.

**BARNES, Martin;** *see* Barnes, N. M. L.

**BARNES, Martin;** Senior Curator, Photographs, Victoria and Albert Museum, since 2007; *b* Southport, 31 July 1971; *s* of Brian Robinson Barnes and Josephine Barnes; two *d* by Imke Valentien; *m* 2015, Lydia Rebecca Goldblatt; one *d*. *Educ:* Univ. of Leicester (BA Combined Arts (Hist. of Art, Eng. Lit., Psychol.) 1994); Courtauld Inst. of Art, Univ. of London (MA Art Mus. Studies 1995). Cataloguer (pt-time), Walker Art Gall., Liverpool, 1994–95; Victoria and Albert Museum: Asst Curator, 1995–2001; Curator, Photographs, 2001–07. J. Dudley Johnston Medal, RPS, 2013. *Publications:* Benjamin Brecknell Turner: rural England through a Victorian lens, 2001; Illumine: photographs by Garry Fabian Miller, 2005; Shadow Catchers: camera-less photography, 2010, 2nd edn 2012; Horst: patterns from nature, 2014; Curtis Moffat: Silver Society: experimental photography and design, 1923–1935, 2016; Cameraless Photography, 2018. *Recreations:* guitar, music, writing, gardens, cycling. *Address:* Victoria and Albert Museum, Cromwell Road, South Kensington, SW7 2RL. *T:* (020) 7942 2534. *E:* m.barnes@vam.ac.uk.

**BARNES, Melvyn Peter Keith,** OBE 1990; MCLIP; Guildhall Librarian and Director of Libraries and Art Galleries, Corporation of London, 1984–2002; *b* 26 Sept. 1942; *s* of Harry and Doris Barnes; *m* 1965, Judith Anne Leicester; two *s*. *Educ:* Chatham House Sch., Ramsgate; North-Western Polytechnic, London. MCLIP (ALA 1965); DMA 1972; FCMI (FBIM 1980). Public library posts in Kent, Herts and Manchester, 1958–68; Dep. Bor. Librarian, Newcastle-under-Lyme, 1968–72; Chief Librarian, Ipswich, 1972–74; Bor. Librarian and Arts Officer, Kensington and Chelsea, 1974–80; City Librarian, Westminster, 1980–84. Hon. Librarian to Clockmakers' Co., and Gardeners' Co., 1984–2002. Member: LA Council, 1974–98 (Chm. Exec. Cttee, 1987–92; Vice-Pres., 1991–93; Pres., 1995); Liby and Inf. Services Council, 1984–89; Brit. Liby Adv. Council, 1986–91; Brit. Liby SRIS Adv. Cttee, 1986–91. Pres., Internat. Assoc. of Metropolitan City Libraries, 1989–92; Dep. Chm., Liby Services Trust and Liby Services Ltd, 1983–93. Hon. Treas., Victoria County History of Inner Middlesex, 1979–90. Gov., St Bride Inst., 1984–2002. Liveryman, Clockmakers' Co., 1990–2002; Hon. Freeman, Gardeners' Co., 1995. Editorial Cons., Journal of Librarianship, 1980–94; Editorial Advr, Librarianship & Information Work Worldwide, 1991–99. *Publications:* Youth Library Work, 1968, 2nd edn 1976; Best Detective Fiction, 1975; Murder in Print, 1986; Dick Francis, 1986; Root and Branch: a history of the Worshipful Company of Gardeners of London, 1994; Francis Durbridge: a centenary appreciation, 2015; (ed) Deerstalker series of classic crime fiction reprints, 1977–82; Francis Durbridge: the complete guide, 2018; contributor to numerous books and jls in fields of librarianship and crime fiction criticism. *Recreations:* reading and writing, going to the theatre, studying the history of the movies and stage musicals, performing amateur operatics.

**BARNES, Michael;** *see* Barnes, D. M. W.

**BARNES, Prof. Michael Patrick;** Professor of Scandinavian Studies, University College London, 1995–2005, now Professor Emeritus (Professor of Scandinavian Philology, 1983–94); *b* 28 June 1940; *s* of William Edward Clement Barnes and Gladys Constance Barnes (*née* Hooper); *m* 1970, Kirsten Heiberg (*née* Røer); one *s* three *d*. *Educ:* University College London (BA, MA); Univ. of Oslo. Asst Lectr, Lectr and Reader in Scandinavian Philology, UCL, 1964–83. Visiting Professor: Tórshavn, Faroe Islands, 1979 and 1990; Uppsala Univ., 1984; Hon. Prof., Centre for Study of the Viking Age, Univ. of Nottingham, 2012–; Hon. Res. Fellow, Univ. of Highlands and Islands, 2012–. Member: Gustav Adolfs Akademien, Uppsala, 1984 (Corresp. Mem., 1977); Det norske Videnskaps-Akademi, Oslo, 1997. Jt Ed., North-Western European Language Evolution, 1989– (Mem. Adv. Bd, 1981–88); Member, Editorial Board: Fróðskaparrit, 1995–; Maal og Minne, 1996–2009; Norsk lingvistisk tidsskrift, 1997–; Nordic Jl of Linguistics, 2000–; Beiträge zur nordischen Philologie, 2000–; Jt Hon. Sec., Viking Soc. for Northern Research, 1983–2006 (Mem. Editl Bd, 1970–76, Chief Editor, 1977–83, Saga Book of the Viking Soc.). Mem., Soc. of Antiquaries of Scotland, 2009. Hon. DPhil Uppsala, 2002. Knight: Order of the Falcon (Iceland), 1992; 1st Cl., Royal Norwegian Order of Merit, 2008. *Publications:* Draumkvæde: an edition and study, 1974; The Runic Inscriptions of Maeshowe, Orkney, 1994; (jtly) The Runic Inscriptions of Viking Age Dublin, 1997; The Norn Language of Orkney and Shetland, 1998; A New Introduction to Old Norse, vol. I: Grammar, 1999; Faroese Language Studies, 2001; (jtly) Introduction to Scandinavian Phonetics, 2005; (jtly) The Scandinavian Runic Inscriptions of Britain, 2006; Runes: a handbook, 2012; (jtly) The Runic Inscriptions of the Isle of Man, 2019; articles in learned jls. *Recreations:* badminton, being with family, walking disused railways. *Address:* 93 Longland Drive, N20 8HN. *T:* (020) 8445 4697.

**BARNES, Dr (Nicholas) Martin (Limer),** CBE 2009; FREng, FICE, FCInstCES; FAPM; project management consultant, since 1971; *b* Sutton Coldfield, 18 Jan. 1939; *s* of Geoffrey and Emily Barnes; *m* 1963, Diana Marion Campbell; one *s* one *d*. *Educ:* King Edward's Sch., Birmingham; Imperial Coll., London (BSc (Eng.) Hons 1960); Univ. of Manchester (PhD 1971). FCInstCES 1974; FICE 1977; FAPM 1984; FREng 1987. Partner: Martin Barnes & Partners, 1971–85; Deloitte, Haskins & Sells, subseq. Coopers & Lybrand Deloitte, then Coopers & Lybrand, 1985–96; Exec. Dir, Major Projects Assoc., 1997–2006. President: Chartered Instn of Civil Engrg Surveyors, 1978–86; Assoc. for Project Mgt, 2003–12. Churchill Fellow, 1973. *Publications:* Measurement in Contract Control, 1977; The CESMM3 Handbook, 1992. *Recreations:* choral singing, railway and canal history. *Address:* Cornbrash House, Kirtlington, Oxon OX5 3HF. *T:* (01869) 350828, *Fax:* (01869) 351314. *E:* cornbrash@aol.com.

**BARNES, Prof. Peter John,** DM, DSc; FRCP, FMedSci; FRS 2007; Margaret Turner-Warwick Professor of Thoracic Medicine (formerly Professor of Thoracic Medicine), Imperial College, London (National Heart and Lung Institute) and Hon. Consultant Physician, Royal Brompton Hospital, since 1987; Head of Respiratory Medicine, Imperial College, London, 1997–2017; *b* 29 Oct. 1946; *s* of late John Barnes and Eileen Gertrude Barnes (*née* Thurman); *m* 1976, Olivia Harvard-Watts; three *s*. *Educ:* Leamington Coll.; St Catharine's Coll., Cambridge (open schol., BA (1st class); MA; Hon. Fellow 2012); Worcester Coll., Oxford (DM, DSc). FRCP 1985. Jun. med. posts, then Registrar, Oxford and UCH, London; MRC fellowships, Univ. of Calif, San Francisco, and RPMS, London; Hammersmith Hospital, London: Sen. Registrar, 1979–82; Sen. Lectr and Consultant Physician, RPMS, 1982–85; Prof. of Clinical Pharmacol., Cardiothoracic Inst., London, 1985–87. NIHR Sen. Investigator, 2008–. Vis. Prof., RSocMed, 1993. Lectures: Linacre, RCP, 1994; Amberson, Amer. Thoracic Soc., 1996; Sadoul, Eur. Respiratory Soc., 1999; Croonian, RCP, 2009. Pres., Eur. Respiratory Soc., 2013–14. Master Fellow, Amer. Coll. Chest Physicians, 2012. MAE 2012. Founder FMedSci 1998. Mem., Assoc. of Amer. Physicians, 2014; Mem., Acad. of Athens, 2018. Hon. MD: Ferrara, Italy, 1997; Athens, 2001; Leuven, 2010; Maastricht, 2014. Dutch Med. Fedn Prize, 1995; Ariens Prize, Dutch Pharmacol. Soc., 2005; Quintiles Prize, British Pharmacol. Soc., 2005; Presidential Award, Eur. Respiratory Soc., 2007; Medal, British Thoracic Soc., 2007; Galen Medal, Soc. of Apothecaries, 2015. *Publications:* New Drugs for Asthma, 1982, 3rd edn 1998; Asthma: basic mechanisms and clinical management, 1989, 3rd edn 1998; (ed jtly) The Lung: scientific foundations, 1991, 3rd edn 1998; Recent Advances in Respiratory Medicine, 1993; (jtly) Conquering Asthma, 1994; (jtly) Molecular Biology of Lung Disease, 1994; Asthma (2 vols), 1997; (ed jtly) Autonomic Control of the Respiratory System, 1997; (jtly) Asthma Therapy, 1998; Managing Chronic Obstructive Pulmonary Disease, 1999; (jtly) Asthma and Chronic Obstructive Pulmonary Disease, 2002, 2nd edn 2009; over 1,000 pubns on lung pharmacol. and airway disease. *Recreations:* travel, ethnic art collecting, gardening, film and theatre going. *Address:* Airway Disease Section, National Heart and Lung Institute (Imperial College), Dovehouse Street, SW3 6LY. *T:* (020) 7351 8174.

**BARNES, Richard Michael;** Member (C) Ealing and Hillingdon, 2000–12, and Deputy Mayor of London, 2008–12, London Assembly, Greater London Authority; *b* 1 Dec. 1947; *s* of late John William Barnes and of Kate (Kitty) Barnes (*née* Harper). *Educ:* UWIST, Cardiff (BSc Hons Econs). Mem. (C) Hillingdon BC, 1982–2014 (Leader, Cons. Gp, 1992–2000; Leader, 1998–2000). Mem., Metropolitan Police Authority, 2000–12. London Assembly, Greater London Authority: Chm., Safer London Cttee, 2004–08; Chm., 7 July Rev. Cttee, 2005–12. Contested (C) Ealing and Hillingdon, London Assembly, GLA, 2012. Advr, Book Trust. *Recreations:* gardening, chelonia, opera, bibliophile. *Address:* 280 Northwood Road, Harefield, Middx UB9 6PU. *T:* (020) 7983 4387.

**BARNES, Prof. Robert Harrison,** DPhil; Professor of Social Anthropology, University of Oxford, 1996–2012; Fellow, St Antony's College, Oxford, 1987–2012, now Emeritus; *b* Jacksonville, Texas, 11 Oct. 1944; *s* of Robert Harrison Barnes and Edna Ruth Barnes (*née* Farrier); *m* 1968, Ruth Weinlich; one *s* one *d*. *Educ:* Bellaire High Sch., Texas; Reed Coll. (BA 1966, Phi Beta Kappa); St Catherine's Coll., Oxford (BLitt 1969; DPhil 1972). Lecturer in Social Anthropology: Univ. of Edinburgh, 1974–77; Univ. of Oxford, 1978–96; St Antony's College, Oxford: Dean, 1989–92; Dean of Degrees, 2001–02; Sub-Warden, 2005–06. Dir d'Etudes Associé, Ecole des Hautes Etudes en Scis Sociales, Paris, 1980; Vis. Fellow, Dept of Anthropol., Res. Sch. of Pacific Studies, ANU, 1986; Vis. Prof., Dept of Anthropol., Univ. of Michigan, 1986–87; Affiliated Fellow, Internat. Inst. for Asian Studies, Leiden, 2006 and 2007; Vis. Sen. Res. Fellow, Asia Res. Inst., NUS, 2008. FRAI 1969. *Publications:* Kédang: a study of the collective thought of an eastern Indonesian people, 1974; (trans. and ed with Ruth Barnes) Josef Kohler: On the Prehistory of Marriage, Totemism, Group Marriage, Mother Right, 1975; Two Crows Denies It: a history of controversy in Omaha sociology, 1984, 2nd edn 2005; (ed jtly) Contexts and Levels: anthropological essays on hierarchy, 1985; (ed jtly) Indigenous Peoples of Asia, 1995; Sea Hunters of Indonesia: fishers and weavers of Lamalera, 1996; (with U. B. Samely) A Dictionary of the Kedang Language: Kedang-Indonesian-English, 2013; Excursions into Eastern Indonesia: essays on history and social life, 2013; contrib. articles to scholarly jls. *Recreations:* bicycle riding, walking, gardening, mushroom hunting. *Address:* 156 East Rock Road, New Haven, CT 06511, USA. *T:* (203) 7529617; 105 6th Street, SE, Apt 103, Washington, DC 20003, USA. *T:* (202) 5432587.

**BARNES, Dr Robert Sandford;** Chairman, Robert S. Barnes Consultants Ltd, since 1978; Principal, Queen Elizabeth College, Kensington, London University, 1978–85; *b* 8 July 1924; *s* of William Edward and Ada Elsie Barnes (*née* Sutherst); *m* 1952, Julia Frances Marriott Grant; one *s* three *d*. *Educ:* Univ. of Manchester (BSc Hons 1948, MSc 1959, DSc 1962). FInstP 1961; FIMMM (FIM 1965); CEng 1977; CPhys 1985. Radar Research, Admiralty Signals Estab., Witley, Surrey, 1944–47; AERE, Harwell: Metallurgical Research on nuclear materials, 1948–62; Head of Irradiation Branch, 1962–65; Vis. Scientist, The Science Center, N Amer. Aviation Co., Calif, 1965; Head of Metallurgy Div., AERE, Harwell, 1966–68; Dep. Dir, BISRA, 1968–69; Dir, BISRA, 1969–70; Dir R&D, British Steel Corp., 1970–75; Chief Scientist, BSC, 1975–78. Technical Adviser: Bd of BOC Ltd, 1978–79; Bd of BOC International Ltd, 1979–81; Bd of New Ventures Secretariat, 1978–80. Chm., Ruthner Continuous Crop Systems Ltd, 1976–78. Member: CBI Res. and Technol. Cttee, 1968–75; Adv. Council on R&D for Iron and Steel, 1970–75; Materials Science and Technol. Cttee, SRC, 1975–79; European Industrial Res. Management Assoc., 1970 (Vice-Pres., 1974–78); Parly and Scientific Cttee, 1970–80, 1983–85; Foundn for Science and Technology, 1984– (Mem., Membership Cttee, 1987–98); Chm., Materials Technology Panel, Internat. Tin Res. Inst., 1988–94. Member: Council, Welding Inst., 1970–75; Council, Instn of Metallurgists, 1970–75 and 1979–85 (Vice Pres., 1979; Sen. Vice Pres., 1982; Pres., 1983–85); Council, Metals Soc., 1974–80, 1982–85 (Chm., Coordinating Cttee, 1976–78; Mem., Executive Cttee, 1976–80). Institute of Metals: Mem., Steering Gp, 1983–84; Mem. Council, 1985–92; Mem. Exec. Cttee, 1985–92; Past Pres., 1985–; Chm., Professional Bd, 1985–92; Institute of Materials Members Trust: Trustee, 1984–2003; Mem., 1986–2002; Chm., 1992–99. Chairman: Combined Operations Working Party, 1980–81; European Nuclear Steel-making Club, 1973–76; UK Mem., Conseil d'Association Européenne pour la Promotion de la Recherche Technique en Sidérurgie, 1972–78; Member: Adv. Council on Energy Conservation, Industry Group

1977–78; Council, Nat. Backpain Assoc., 1979–98. Hon. Mem. Council, Iron and Steel Inst., 1969–73. Governor, Sheffield Polytechnic, 1968–72; Member: Court of Univ. of Surrey, 1968–80; Collegiate Council, Univ. of London, 1978–85; Jt Finance and Gen. Purposes Cttee, Univ. of London, 1978–85; Senate, Univ. of London, 1980–85; Member Council: King's Coll. London, 1982–85; Chelsea Coll., 1983–85; Bd Mem., CSTI, 1984–88. Mem., Supporters of Nuclear Energy, 2003–. Numerous lectures at home and overseas including: Hatfield Meml, Iron and Steel Inst., 1973; John Player, IMechE, 1976. Freeman, City of London, 1984; Liveryman, Worshipful Co. of Engrs, 1985. Rosenhain Medallist, Inst. of Metals, 1964. FRSA 1976; FKC 1985; Life Member: RYA, 1976; Royal Instn, 1986; Nat. Trust, 1986. *Publications:* chapters in specialist books of science; scientific papers in various learned jls on the effects of atomic radiation on materials, on the rôle of energy in the production of engineering materials, etc. *Recreations:* cruising in the Mediterranean on sailing yacht Bombero, coupled with archaeology. *Address:* One The Mansion, Ashwood Place, Woking, Surrey GU22 7JR. *T:* (01483) 761529. *Clubs:* Athenæum, Cruising Association.

**BARNES, Roger Anthony;** Director, Hambros Bank Ltd, 1993–97; Assistant Director, Bank of England and Head of Banking Supervision Division, 1988–93; *b* 29 May 1937; *s* of Kenneth Ernest Barnes and Lilian Agnes (*née* King); *m* 1961, Tessa Margaret Soundy (*d* 2014); two *s* two *d. Educ:* Malvern College; St John's College, Oxford (BA). Bank of England, 1961–93. Mem. Council of Management, European Sch. of Management, 1994–2003. Trustee, CAF, 1999–2003. *Recreations:* golf, music. *Address:* 13 The Dell, St Albans, Herts AL1 4HE. *T:* (01727) 851987. *Club:* City of London.

**BARNES, Rosemary Susan, (Rosie),** OBE 2011; Chief Executive, Cystic Fibrosis Trust, 1996–2010; *b* 16 May 1946; *d* of Alan Allen and Kathleen (*née* Brown); *m* 1967, Graham Barnes; two *s* one *d. Educ:* Bilborough Grammar Sch.; Birmingham Univ. (BSocSci Hons). Management Trainee, Research Bureau Ltd, 1967–69; Product Manager, Yardley of London Ltd, 1969–72; primary teacher (briefly), 1972; freelance market researcher, 1973–87. MP Greenwich, Feb. 1987–1992 (SDP, 1987–90, Social Democrat, 1990–92); contested (Soc. Dem.) Greenwich, 1992. Dir, Birthright, subseq. WellBeing, 1992–96. *Recreations:* gardening, cooking, reading, travelling, walking, yoga, my dogs.

**BARNES, Scott,** FCA; Chairman, Global Board, Grant Thornton, since 2015; *b* Morley, Leeds, 3 Dec. 1955; *s* of Ronald and Sheila Barnes; *m* 1979, Irene Evans; one *s* one *d. Educ:* Batley Grammar Sch.; Keble Coll., Oxford (MA Hist.). ACA 1982, FCA 1992. Arthur Andersen, Leeds, 1978–84; Grant Thornton UK LLP: Manager, 1984–87; Partner, Leeds Office, 1987–91; Nat. Hd, Corporate Recovery, 1995–2001; UK Hd of Advisory, 2001–06; Global Hd of Advisory, 2006–08; CEO, 2008–15. Pres., Keble Assoc., 2014–. *Recreations:* cricket, watching football and Rugby, theatre, music. *Address:* Grant Thornton International, 20 Fenchurch Street, EC3M 3BY. *E:* scott.barnes@gti.gt.com. *Club:* Royal Automobile.

**BARNES, Shani Estelle; Her Honour Judge Barnes;** a Circuit Judge, since 2004; *b* 24 Sept. 1955; *d* of late Sidney Hurst and of Renée Hurst; *m* 1994, David Thomas Howker, QC (*d* 2016); two *s* three *d. Educ:* Central Foundn Grammar Sch. for Girls; Middlesex Univ. (BA 1st cl. Hons 1984). Called to the Bar, Middle Temple, 1986; Asst Recorder, 1999–2000; Recorder, 2000–04. Hon. Recorder, Brighton and Hove, 2013–. *Address:* c/o The Law Courts, High Street, Lewes, E Sussex BN7 1YB.

**BARNES, Simon John Campbell;** writer; chief sports writer, 2002–14, wildlife columnist, 2005–14, The Times (sports columnist, 1982–2002); *b* 22 July 1951; *s* of Edward Campbell Barnes, *qv* and late Dorothy Elsie Barnes (*née* Smith); *m* 1983, Cindy Lee Wright; two *s. Educ:* Emanuel Sch.; Bristol Univ. (BA Hons). Surrey and S London Newspapers, 1974–78; contributor to S China Morning Post, Asian Business and Asian Finance, based in Asia, 1978–82; wildlife writer, RSPB Birds magazine, 1994–, Sunday Times magazine; sports columnist, The Spectator, 1995–2002. Mem. Council, World Land Trust, 2008–. Patron: Spinal Research, 2000–08; Froglife, 2008–10; Save the Rhino, 2009–. Hon. DLitt Bristol, 2007. Sports Writer of Year: British Press Awards, 1987, What the Papers Say Awards, 2003; Sports Feature Writer of Year, Sports Council, 1988 and 1998; Sports Columnist of the Year: Sports Writers' Assoc., 2001, 2007; Sports Journalists' Assoc., 2007; Football Writer of Year, Football Supporters' Assoc., 1991; Sports Commentator of Year and Olympic Commentator of the Year, Comment Awards, 2012. *Publications:* Phil Edmonds: a singular man, 1986; Horsesweat and Tears, 1988; A Sportswriter's Year, 1989; A la Recherche du Cricket Perdu, 1989; Sportswriter's Eye, 1989; Flying in the Face of Nature, 1991; Tiger!, 1994; Planet Zoo, 2000; On Horseback, 2000; How to be a Bad Birdwatcher, 2004; A Bad Birdwatcher's Companion, 2005; The Meaning of Sport, 2006; How to be Wild, 2007; The Horsey Life, 2008; (with Rachel Barnes) The Horse: a celebration of horses in art, 2008; My Natural History, 2010; A Book of Heroes, 2010; Birdwatching With Your Eyes Closed, 2011; Ten Million Aliens: a journey through the entire animal kingdom, 2014; The Sacred Combe: a search for humanity's heartland, 2016; Losing It: a lifetime in pursuit of sporting excellence, 2016; Rewild Yourself, 2018; *novels:* Rogue Lion Safaris, 1997; Hong Kong Belongers, 1999; Miss Chance, 2000. *Recreations:* Africa, horses, birdsong, Bach. *Club:* Tewin Irregulars Cricket.

**BARNES, Stuart;** Rugby Union broadcaster, Sky Sports, since 1994; columnist, Sunday Times, since 2005; *b* Grays, Essex, 22 Nov. 1962; *s* of John and Joyce Barnes; *m* 1985, Lesley Patricia; one *s* one *d. Educ:* Bassaleg Comprehensive Sch., Newport, Gwent; St Edmund Hall, Oxford (BA Hons Modern Hist.). England Rugby player, 1984–93; Mem., British and Irish Lions team, 1993; Rugby writer and broadcaster, 1994–. Ambassador, Donald Woods Foundn, 2012–. Mem., RSC. *Publications:* Smelling of Roses: a Rugby autobiography, 1994; The Year of Living Dangerously, 1995; Rugby's New Age Travellers, 1997. *Recreations:* National Hunt horseracing (owner), red wine, literature. *Address:* Sky Sports, British Sky Broadcasting Ltd, Grant Way, Isleworth, Middx TW7 5QD.

**BARNES, Prof. Timothy David,** DPhil; FBA 2011; FRSC 1985; Hon. Professorial Fellow, School of Divinity and School of History, Classics and Archaeology, University of Edinburgh, since 2008; *b* Ossett, Yorks, 13 March 1942; *e s* of David Barnes and Margaret Barnes (*née* Baxter); *m* 1st, 1965, Anne Jenifer Dixon (marr. diss. 1996); four *s*; 2nd, 1998, Stella Sandahl (marr. diss. 2004); 3rd, 2005, Janet Fairchild Sidaway. *Educ:* Queen Elizabeth Grammar Sch., Wakefield; Balliol Coll., Oxford (Deakin Schol.; BA 1964; MA); Univ. of Oxford (DPhil 1970). Harmsworth Sen. Scholar, Merton Coll., Oxford and Craven Fellow, Univ. of Oxford, 1964–66; Jun. Res. Fellow, Queen's Coll., Oxford, 1966–70; University of Toronto: Asst Prof., 1970–72, Associate Prof., 1972–76, Prof., 1976–2007, of Classics; Associate Chm., 1979–83, 1995–96; Coordinator, Graduate Studies, 1979–83, 1986–89, 1995–96. Vis. Mem. and Herodotus Fellow, Inst. for Advanced Study, Princeton and Leave Fellow, Amer. Council of Learned Socs, 1976–77; Vis. Fellow, Wolfson Coll., Oxford and J. S. Guggenheim Meml Foundn Fellow, 1983–84; Vis. Scholar, ANU, Canberra, 1988; Townsend Lectr and Vis. Prof., Cornell Univ., 1994; Vis. Prof., Univ. di Roma 'La Sapienza' and Vis. Scholar, Amer. Acad. in Rome, 1997; Dist. Vis. Scholar, Princeton Univ., 2000. Connaught Sen. Fellow in Humanities, 1984–85, Fellow, Trinity Coll., 1991, Univ. of Toronto; Killam Sen. Res. Fellow, Humanities and Social Scis Res. Council of Canada, 2001–03. Hon. Res. Fellow, UCL, 2004–08. Ancient Hist. Prize, 1966, Conington Prize, 1974, Univ. of Oxford; Philip Schaff Meml Prize, Amer. Soc. of Ch Hist.,

1984; Charles J. Goodwin Award of Merit, Amer. Philol Assoc., 1984. *Publications:* Tertullian: a historical and literary study, 1971, 2nd edn 1985; The Sources of the Historia Augusta, 1978; Constantine and Eusebius, 1981; The New Empire of Diocletian and Constantine, 1982; Early Christianity and the Roman Empire, 1984; Athanasius and Constantius: theology and politics in the Constantinian Empire, 1993; From Eusebius to Augustine: selected papers 1982–1993, 1994; (ed) The Sciences in Greco-Roman Society, 1994; Ammianus Marcellinus and the Representation of Historical Reality, 1998; Early Christian Hagiography and Roman History, 2010, 2nd edn 2016; Constantine: dynasty, religion and power in the later Roman Empire, 2011, 2nd edn 2014; (with G. Bevan) The Funerary Speech for John Chrysostom, 2013; over 170 articles and essays; approx. 150 reviews. *Address:* 13 Marchhall Crescent, Edinburgh EH16 5HL. *T:* (0131) 662 0480, *Fax:* (0131) 650 7952.

**BARNES, Timothy Paul;** QC 1986; a Recorder, 1987–2014; *b* 23 April 1944; *s* of late Arthur Morley Barnes and Valerie Enid Mary Barnes; *m* 1969, Patricia Margaret Gale; one *s* three *d. Educ:* Bradfield Coll., Berkshire; Christ's Coll., Cambridge (MA). Called to Bar, Gray's Inn, 1968 (Hilbery Exhibn; Bencher, 2004); practises Midland and Oxford Circuit; Asst Recorder, 1983. Chm., Greenwich Soc., 2001. *Recreations:* gardening, theatre. *Address:* The White House, Crooms Hill, SE10 8HH. *T:* (020) 8858 1185, *Fax:* (020) 8858 0788. *Club:* MCC.

**BARNES JONES, Deborah Elizabeth Vavasseur;** HM Diplomatic Service, retired; Governor, Montserrat, 2004–07; *b* 6 Oct. 1956; *née* Barnes; *m* 1986, Frederick Richard Jones; twin *d. Educ:* Bristol Univ. (BA); Washburn Univ. (JD 2018). Joined FCO, 1980; Moscow, 1983–85; First Secretary: on loan to Cabinet Office, 1985–86; (Chancery), Israel, 1988–92; FCO, 1992–96; Dep. Hd of Mission, Uruguay, 1996–2001; Ambassador to Georgia, 2001–04. Mem., Vestry of Grace Cathedral, Topeka, 2014–17. *Recreation:* choral singing. *Club:* Athenæum.

**BARNES THOMPSON, Dame Ingrid Victoria;** *see* Allen, Dame I. V.

**BARNETT, Alexandra Louise;** *see* Marks, A. L.

**BARNETT, Andrew;** *see* Barnett, J. A.

**BARNETT, Andrew Charles Robert;** Director, Calouste Gulbenkian Foundation (UK), since 2007; *b* Nowra, NSW, Australia, 10 March 1968; *s* of Comdr Kenneth Malcolm Barnett, RAN, and Sheila Margaret Barnett. *Educ:* King's Sch., Bruton, Som; Univ. of St Andrews (MA). Public Affairs Advr, Foyer Fedn, 1992–94; Dep. Hd, Press and Public Affairs, Arts Council of England, 1994–97; Gp Corporate Affairs Manager, HSBC Hldgs plc, 1997–99; Hd, Public Affairs, Nat. Consumer Council, 1999–2001; Director: Communications, UK Sports Council, 2001–05; Policy and Communications, Joseph Rowntree Foundn, 2005–07. Non-exec. Dir, Yorks Metropolitan Housing Assoc., 2000–08. Advr to Jt Chair, All-Party Parly Gp on Homelessness, 1992–94. Mem. Council, Collaborate, 2012–; Mem., Church Council, 1996–2014, Church Warden, 2014–, St Dunstan-in-the-West. Chair of Trustees: SPACE Studios, 1998–2003 (Trustee/Dir, 1998–2003); People Can Gp, 2009–12; DV8 Physical Th., 2010–14; Trustee: St Christopher's Fellowship, 1995–98; Addaction, 2006–14; Forces in Mind Trust, 2015–18; Founder Trustee, Social Innovation Exchange, 2013–; Trustee, Assoc. of Charitable Foundns, 2016–; Chm. of Trustees, Church Urban Fund, 2018–. Mem. Cttee, Healthwatch England, 2014–. Gov., Clerkenwell Parochial Primary Sch., 1998–2000. Contested (C) Glasgow Springburn, 1992. FRSA 1995. *Recreations:* history, contemporary dance, aboriginal and modern art, swimming, food and wine, travelling, languages. *Address:* c/o Calouste Gulbenkian Foundation, 50 Hoxton Square, N1 6PB. *E:* acrbarnett@gmail.com.

**BARNETT, Andrew John; His Honour Judge Andrew Barnett;** a Circuit Judge, since 2004; Liaison Judge, North Hampshire Magistrates, since 2007; Honorary Recorder of Salisbury, since 2010; *b* 19 Sept. 1953; *s* of late Rev. Canon Norman Barnett and of Dorette Barnett; *m* 1978, Gillian Lindsey, *d* of late Patrick Leonard James; three *s* one *d. Educ:* Marlborough Coll.; KCL (BD). Called to the Bar, Gray's Inn, 1977; Asst Recorder, 1992–96; Recorder, 1996–2004. Mem. Cttee, Council of Circuit Judges, 2006– (Pres., 2018–); Pres., Wessex Magistrates' Assoc., 2009–. Patron, Sebastian's Action Trust, 2017–. *Recreations:* most outdoor activities, including golf. *Address:* Winchester Combined Court Centre, The Law Courts, Winchester, Hants SO23 9DL. *T:* (01962) 814100. *Clubs:* Lansdowne; High Post Golf.

**BARNETT, Benjamin Lawrence;** Chief Executive Officer, TFG Brands (London) Ltd, since 2015; *b* Reading, 23 Feb. 1979; *s* of Dr Christopher Andrew Barnett, *qv*; *m* 2004, Alina Marilena Grigoras; two *d. Educ:* St Catherine's Coll., Oxford (BA Econs and Mgt 2000); London Business Sch. (Masters in Finance 2003). Analyst, JP Morgan Chase, 2000–02; Associate, Kaupthing Bank, 2003–05; Investment Dir, Kaupthing Capital Partners, 2005–08; Finance Dir, 2009–13, CEO, 2014–19, Phase Eight (Fashion and Designs), Ltd; Chm., Whistles Ltd, 2016–. *Recreations:* family, travel, horse riding/racing, running, table tennis. *Address:* TFG Brands (London) Ltd, 55 Kimber Road, SW18 4NX. *T:* (020) 8877 4011. *E:* ben.barnett@tfg-brands.co.uk.

**BARNETT, Caroline Hannah;** Founder and Director, Arts Scape Ltd, since 2013; *b* London, 8 Nov. 1966; *d* of Brychan Powell and Noreen Avril Powell (*née* Berry); *m* 2004, Peter John Barnett. *Educ:* Lady Margaret Hall, Oxford (BA 1st Cl. Hons Ancient and Modern Hist.); Univ. of Westminster (Legal CPE (Commendation)); Coll. of Law (Dist.). Admitted as solicitor, 1995; Trainee, 1993–95, Solicitor, 1995–99, Slaughter and May; Intellectual Property Counsel, Reuters Gp, 1999–2003; Gen. Counsel, Royal Shakespeare Co., 2003–13. Non-exec. Dir, Belgrade Th. Trust (Coventry) Ltd, 2007–13. *Recreations:* hill walking, swimming, theatre, cinema, playing the cello, cooking.

**BARNETT, Charles Henry,** CVO 2015; Chief Executive, Ascot Racecourse, 2007–14; *b* 15 July 1948; *s* of late Major B. G. Barnett and D. Barnett; *m* 1978, Georgina Greig; one *s* two *d. Educ:* Eton Coll.; Christ Church, Oxford (BA 2nd Cl. Hons Jurisprudence; MA). Chief Executive: Haydock Park Racecourse, 1984–93; Chester Race Co. Ltd, 1996–2000; Man. Dir, Aintree Racecourse Co. Ltd, 1993–2007. *Recreation:* country pursuits.

**BARNETT, Dr Christopher Andrew,** MBE 2018; Headmaster, Whitgift School, Croydon, 1991–2017; *b* 1 Feb. 1953; *s* of Peter Alan Barnett and Joan Barnett (*née* Cullis); *m* 1976, Hon. Laura Miriam Elizabeth (marr. diss. 2015), *oc* of Baron Weidenfeld, GBE; three *s* one *d. Educ:* Cedars Sch., Leighton Buzzard; Oriel Coll., Oxford (Exhibnr; BA Hons History 1974; MA 1978; DPhil 1981). Lectr in Econs, Brunel Univ., 1975–77; Head of History Dept, Bradfield Coll., Berks, 1978–87; Second Master, Dauntsey's Sch., Wilts, 1987–91. Fellow Commoner, Downing Coll., Cambridge, 1987; Evelyn Wrench Scholar, ESU, 1990. Pres., Croydon Music Fest., 1992–2013. Match Dir, Surrey CCC Festival of Cricket, 2000–11. Exhibition Director: Hidden Treasures from the Mary Rose, 2009; Remembering 1916: life on the Western Front, 2016. Chevalier, Ordre des Palmes Académiques (France), 2012. *Publications:* John Whitgift, 2015; Remembering 1916, 2016. *Recreations:* opera, political Victoriana, hill-walking, travel, horse-racing. *Club:* Athenæum. *See also* B. L. Barnett.

**BARNETT, His Honour Christopher John Anthony;** QC 1983; a Circuit Judge, 1988–2003, a Deputy Circuit Judge, 2003–10; Designated Family Judge, Suffolk, 1991–2003; b 18 May 1936; s of Richard Adrian Barnett and Phyllis Barnett (née Cartwright); m 1959, Sylvia Marieliese (née Pritt); two s one d. Educ: Repton Sch., Derbyshire; College of Law, London. Called to the Bar, Gray's Inn, 1965. Volunteer, Kenya Regt, 1954–55; District Officer (Kikuyu Guard) and Kenya Government Service, 1955–60; a District Officer in HM Overseas Civil Service, serving in Kenya, 1960–62; in practice as barrister, 1965–88; a Recorder, 1982–88; Jt Hd of Chambers, 4 Paper Buildings, 1985–88; a Dep. High Court Judge, QBD, 1991–97. Led conf. promoting Unified Family Ct, Bermuda, 2010. A Pres., Mental Health Review Tribunal Restricted Patients Panel, 2002–11. Mem., Wine Cttee, SE Circuit, 1984–88; Chm., SE Circuit Area Liaison Cttee, 1985–88; Mem. Cttee, Council of Circuit Judges, 1992–2003; a Chm., Bar Disciplinary Tribunal, 2006–10. Chairman: Suffolk Community Alcohol Services, 1993–95; Ferriers Barn Ltd Centre for severely disabled adults, Bures, 2014–16; a Patron, Relate, W Suffolk, 1998–2019. Mem., Court of Essex Univ., 1983–2018. Foundn Gov., Colne Engaine C of E Voluntary Assisted Primary Sch., 2009–19. Pres., Old Reptonian Soc., 2002. Recreations: cricket, tennis, novice golfer, walking, travel, gardening under instruction. Address: c/o Judicial Secretariat, 2nd Floor, Rose Court, 2 Southwark Bridge, SE1 9HS. Clubs: MCC (Assoc. Mem.); Essex; Kenya Kongonis Cricket.

**BARNETT, Cindy;** see Barnett, L. J.

**BARNETT, Clive Durac,** MA; educational consultant, 2009–14; b 22 July 1949; s of Edgar Thomas Barnett and Betty Marian Barnett; m 1981, Patricia Michelle Morrissey. Educ: King's Coll. Sch., Wimbledon; Magdalen Coll., Oxford (BA Hons, MA, PGCE). Asst Teacher of History, 1971–79, Hd, Hist. Dept, 1975–79, Kingston GS; Head, History and Politics Depts, Watford Boys' GS, 1979–86; Dep. Headmaster, Portsmouth GS, 1986–92; Headmaster, Bishop Wordsworth's Sch., Salisbury, 1992–2002. HM Inspector of Schs, 2002–09. Consultant, Working Eye (non-exec. Dir, 2016). Member: Salisbury Diocesan Bd of Educn, 1998–2002; Salisbury Cathedral Chapter, 2009–12; Salisbury Cathedral Council, 2012; Lay Canon, Salisbury Cath., 2007–17, now Canon Emeritus. Trustee, Trade Aid, 1996–2006 (Chm., 1996–2002); Mem. Cttee, Bloxham Project, 1998–2005 (Vice-Chm., 1999–2002); Patron, EdUKaid, 2007– (Trustee, 2014–). Governor: Royal Grammar Sch., Guildford, 2009–; Salisbury Cathedral Sch., 2012–17; Trustee, Bishop Wordsworth's Sch., 2017–. Publications: (jtly) Smike (a musical), 1973 (televised 1974). Recreations: umpiring and watching cricket (Life Vice-Pres., Broadhalfpenny Brigands CC, 2016–), walking, going to the theatre, listening to most forms of music, travelling, spending time with my wife! Address: 111 Havant Road, Emsworth, Hants PO10 7LF. Club: MCC.

**BARNETT, Hon. Colin James;** MLA (L) Cottesloe, Western Australia, 1990–2018; Premier of Western Australia, 2008–17; b Nedlands, WA, 15 July 1950; s of James Henry Barnett and Coralle Cross Barnett; m 1989, Lynette Kathleen Ashby; one s, and three s from a previous marriage. Educ: Hollywood High Sch.; Univ. of Western Australia (BEc Hons, MEc). Cadet Res. Officer, then Sen. Res. Officer, Aust. Bureau of Statistics, 1973–75; Sen. Tutor, then Lectr in Econs, Western Australian Inst. of Technol., 1975–82; Confederation of Western Australian Industry, subseq. Chamber of Commerce and Industry of WA: on secondment, then Economist, and Editor, WA Economic Review, 1982–85; Exec. Dir, 1985–90. Western Australia: Shadow Minister for Housing, Works and Services, 1990, for Housing Fuel and Energy, Works and Services, 1991–92, for State Develt, 1992, for Resources, Fuel and Energy, 1992; Dep. Leader of the Opposition, 1992; Dep. Leader, Parly Liberal Party, 1992–2001; Leader, House of Legislative Assembly, 1993–2001; Minister: for Tourism, 1993; for Resources Develt, 1993–2001; for Energy, 1993–2001; for Educn, 1995–2001; Leader of the Opposition, 2001–05, 2008; Shadow Minister for the Arts, 2004–05, for Public Sector Mgt, 2004–05; Shadow Treasurer, 2004–05; Shadow Minister for State Develt, 2008; Treasurer, 2008; Minister for State Develt, 2008–16, for Sci., 2013–17, for Tourism, 2016–17. Centenary Medal (Australia), 2003. Recreations: tennis, walking, watching football. Clubs: Claremont Football, Cottesloe Tennis, Peppermint Grove Tennis.

**BARNETT, Correlli (Douglas),** CBE 1997; author; Fellow, Churchill College, Cambridge, since 1977; Keeper of the Churchill Archives Centre, 1977–95; b 28 June 1927; s of D. A. Barnett; m 1950, Ruth Murby; two d. Educ: Trinity Sch., Croydon; Exeter Coll., Oxford. Second class hons, Mod. Hist. with Mil. Hist. and the Theory of War as a special subject; MA 1954. Intell. Corps, 1945–48. North Thames Gas Bd, 1952–57; Public Relations, 1957–63. Vice-Pres., E Arts Assoc., 1978–91 (Chm. Literature Panel, and Mem. Exec. Cttee, 1972–78); Pres., East Anglian Writers, 1969–88; Member: Council, Royal Utd Services Inst. for Defence Studies, 1973–85; Cttee, London Library, 1977–79 and 1982–84. Leverhulme Res. Fellowship, 1976; apptd Lectr in Defence Studies, Univ. of Cambridge, 1980; resigned in order to devote more time to writing, 1983. Winston Churchill Meml Lectr, Switzerland, 1982. Hon. Pres., Western Front Assoc., 1998–2010. FRSL; FRHistS; FRSA. Hon. FCGI 2003. Hon. DSc Cranfield, 1993. Chesney Gold Medal, RUSI, 1991. Contrib., The Times, Daily Mail and The Spectator. Publications: The Hump Organisation, 1957; The Channel Tunnel (with Humphrey Slater), 1958; The Desert Generals, 1960, new enlarged edn, 1983; The Swordbearers, 1963; Britain and Her Army, 1970 (RSL award, 1971); The Collapse of British Power, 1972; Marlborough, 1974; Bonaparte, 1978; The Great War, 1979; The Audit of War, 1986 (US edn as The Pride and the Fall, 1987); Engage the Enemy More Closely: the Royal Navy in the Second World War, 1991 (Yorkshire Post Book of the Year Award, 1991); The Lost Victory: British dreams, British realities 1945–1950, 1995; The Verdict of Peace: Britain between her yesterday and the future, 2001; The Lords of War: supreme leadership from Lincoln to Churchill, 2012; (historical consultant and writer to) BBC Television series: The Great War, 1963–64; The Lost Peace, 1965–66; The Commanders, 1972–73; contrib. to: The Promise of Greatness (a symposium on the Great War), 1968; Governing Elites (a symposium), 1969; Decisive Battles of the Twentieth Century, 1976; The War Lords, 1976; The Economic System in the UK, 1985; Education for Capability, 1986; (ed) Hitler's Generals, 1989. Recreations: gardening, interior decorating, idling, eating, mole-hunting, travelling through France. Address: Catbridge House, East Carleton, Norwich NR14 8JX. T: (01508) 570410.

**BARNETT, Prof. David Braham,** CBE 2007; MD; FRCP; Professor of Clinical Pharmacology, University of Leicester Medical School, 1984–2009, now Emeritus (Head, Department of Medicine, 1999); b 17 July 1944. Educ: Sheffield Univ. Med. Sch. (MB ChB Hons 1967; MD 1979). FRCP 1981. Merck Internat. Travelling Fellow, 1975–76; Sen. Lectr, Univ. of Leicester, 1976–84; Hon. Consultant Physician, Leicester Royal Infirmary, 1976–. Non-exec. Dir, Leicester Royal Infirmary NHS Trust, 1993–2000. Chairman: Appraisals Cttee, NICE, 1999–2009. Publications: original research, rev. articles and book chapters in fields of molecular pharmacology and general cardiovascular clinical pharmacology, with specialist interest in ischaemic heart disease. Recreations: reading, theatre.

**BARNETT, Geoffrey Grant Fulton,** OBE 2001; Chair (formerly Chair of Council), Barnardo's, 2006–11 (Trustee, 2001–11; Hon. Treasurer, 2002–06); b 9 March 1943; s of Air Chief Marshal Sir Denis H. F. Barnett, GCB, CBE, DFC; m 1968, Fiona Katharine Milligan; two s two d. Educ: Winchester Coll.; Clare Coll., Cambridge (MA). Courtaulds Ltd, 1964–67; The Economist Intelligence Unit, 1967–70; British Printing Corp., 1970–71; Baring Brothers & Co. Ltd, 1971–95 (Dir, 1979–95); Man. Dir, Baring Brothers Asia, Hong Kong, 1979–83; seconded as Dir Gen., Panel on Takeovers and Mergers, 1989–92. Dir, Language Line Ltd, 1996–99; Trustee: Castelnau Centre Project, 2002–13 (Chm., 2002–13); StartHere, 2000–05; St Michael's Fellowship, 2002–06; Baring Foundn, 2005–13. Hon. Treas., VSO, 1984–2000; Mem., Governing Bd, London and Quadrant Housing Trust, 1985–2000. Lay Chm., Richmond and Barnes Deanery Synod, 2002–07; Lay Reader, C of E, 2003–. FRSA 1992. Recreations: Scotland, walking, music, bird watching. Address: 2 Mill Hill Road, SW13 0HR. T: (020) 8878 6975.

**BARNETT, Dame Jenifer W.;** see Wilson-Barnett.

**BARNETT, Jeremy John,** OBE 1982; independent tour consultant, 1994–2016; b 26 Jan. 1941; s of late Audrey Wickham Barnett and Lt-Comdr Charles Richard Barnett, RN; m 1968, Maureen Janet Cullum; one s one d. Educ: St Edward's Sch., Oxford; St Andrews Univ. (MA); Leeds Univ. (Dip TEFL); SOAS, London Univ. (MA 1994). Joined British Council, 1964; teaching, Victory Coll., Cairo, 1965–67; Lectr, Inst. of Educn, Istanbul, 1967–69; MECAS, Lebanon, 1969–70; Dir of Studies, Turco-British Assoc., Ankara, 1970–72; British Council Rep., Riyadh, 1972–75; Dir, ME Dept, 1975–78; Counsellor for British Council and Cultural Affairs, Ankara, 1978–82; British Council Rep., Warsaw, 1982–85; Dir, E Europe and N Asia Dept, 1985–88; Controller, S and W Asia Div., 1988–89; British Council Rep., later Dir, and Cultural Counsellor, British Embassy, Cairo, 1989–93. Dir, Westminster Classic Tours, 1994–2016 (Man. Dir, 1998–99). Recreation: long distance walking. Address: Oakdene, Station Road, Groombridge, Tunbridge Wells, Kent TN3 9NB. T: (01892) 864626.

**BARNETT, (John) Andrew;** Director, The Policy Practice Ltd, since 2004; b Repton, 1 Dec. 1946; s of William Gordon Barnett and Margaret Acton Barnett (née Wain); m 1977, Mary Jane Smith; two d. Educ: Repton Sch.; Univ. of Sussex (MA Develt Studies 1970). Economist, ODA, 1971–72; University of Sussex: Res. Officer, Inst. of Develt Studies, 1974–77; Prog. Officer, Internat. Develt Res. Centre, Canada, 1977–85; Fellow, 1985–96, Leader, Technol. and Develt Gp, 1987–93, Sci. Policy Res. Unit, subseq. Sci. and Technol. Policy Res. Unit (Hon. Fellow, 1996–); Dir of Res., Intermediate Technol. Develt Gp, 1994–98. Partner, Sussex Development Project Consultants Ltd, 1973–78; Dir, Sussex Research Associates Ltd, 1985–2018. Specialist Adviser: Select Cttee on Sci. and Technol., H of L, 1989; Select Cttee on Sci. and Technol., H of C, 2003–04; Mem., Tech. Adv. Gp, Energy Sector Mgt Assistance Prog., World Bank, 1996–2007. Member Board: Womankind Worldwide, London, 1999–2007 (Chm., 2006–07); ODI, 2000–11; Small Scale Sustainable Infrastructure Develt Fund, Cambridge, Mass, 2002–08; HEDON Household Energy Network, 2010–16. Publications: articles in learned jls, books and reports on energy policy, technol. policy and res. policy in developing countries. Recreations: walking, cooking, grandchildren. Address: c/o The Policy Practice Ltd, 33 Southdown Avenue, Brighton BN1 6EH. T: (01273) 330331.

**BARNETT, Joseph Anthony,** CBE 1983 (OBE 1975); Director (formerly Representative), British Council, Tokyo, 1983–91, retired; b 19 Dec. 1931; s of Joseph Edward Barnett and Helen Johnson; m 1960, Carolina Johnson Rice (d 1998); one s one d. Educ: St Albans Sch.; Pembroke Coll., Cambridge (BA (Hons) English and Psychology); Edinburgh Univ. (Diploma in Applied Linguistics). Served Army, 1950–51 (2nd Lieut). Teaching, Aylesford House, St Albans, 1954–55; Unilever Ltd, 1955–58; apptd British Council, 1958; Asst Educn Officer, Dacca, Pakistan, 1958; trng at Sch. of Applied Linguistics, Edinburgh Univ., 1960; Educn Officer, Dacca, 1961; seconded to Inst. of Educn, London Univ., 1963; Head, English Language Teaching Inst., London, 1964; Dir of Studies, Regional Inst. of English, Bangalore, India, 1968; Representative, Ethiopia, 1971; Controller, English Language Teaching Div., 1975; Representative, Brazil, 1978–82. Publications: (jtly) Getting on in English, 1960; Success with English (language laboratory materials), Books 1–3, 1966–69. Recreation: sport (tennis, armchair cricket, Rugby). Address: The Thatch, Stebbing Green, Dunmow, Essex CM6 3TE. T: (01371) 856014.

**BARNETT, Kenneth Thomas,** CB 1979; Deputy Secretary, Department of the Environment, 1976–80; b 12 Jan. 1921; yr s of late Frederick Charles Barnett and Ethel Barnett (née Powell); m 1943, Emily May Lovering (d 2016); one d. Educ: Howard Gardens High Sch., Cardiff. Entered Civil Service (Min. of Transport), 1937; Sea Transport Office, Port Said, 1951–54; Asst Sec., 1965; Under-Sec., Cabinet Office (on secondment), 1971–73; Under-Sec., DoE, 1970–76. Dir, Abbey Data Systems Ltd, 1984–2005.

**BARNETT, His Honour Kevin Edward;** a Circuit Judge, 1996–2014; b 2 Jan. 1948; s of Arthur and Winifred Barnett; m 1972, Patricia Margaret Smith; one d. Educ: Wellesbourne Sch.; Tudor Grange Grammar Sch.; London Univ. (LLB Hons ext.). Called to the Bar, Gray's Inn, 1971; Wales and Chester Circuit. Recreations: painting, photography, cooking. Club: Lansdowne.

**BARNETT, Lucinda Jane, (Cindy),** OBE 2009; JP; a Vice President, Magistrates' Association, since 2008 (Deputy Chairman, 2002–05; Chairman, 2005–08); b 21 March 1951; d of late Richard William Gilbert and Margaret Gwenllian Gilbert (née Edwards); m 1976, William Evans Barnett, qv; two s. Educ: Croydon High Sch. (GDST); King's Coll. London (Inglis studentship); BA 1st Cl. Hons 1972; MA 1973; PGCE 1974). ARCM 1971. Civil servant, DoE, 1974–77; teacher (pt-time), in schs, and private coaching, 1978–94. Member: Lord Chancellor's Adv. Cttee (SE London), 1993–2001; SE London Probation Cttee, 1998–2001; Magistrates' Courts' Sentencing Guidelines Wkg Party, 2002–03; Magisterial and Family Sub-cttee, 2005–07, Magisterial Cttee, 2007–08, Judicial Studies Bd; Judges' Council, 2005–08; Lay Mem., Council of Inns of Court Disciplinary Pool, 2013–18; Jt Chm., Nat. Sentencer/Probation Forum, 2005–08; Mem., Adv. Gp, Sentencing Adv. Panel on Definitive Magistrates' Ct Sentencing Guidelines, 2006–08; Lay Mem., Solicitors' Disciplinary Tribunal, 2009– (Lay Mem. Vice Pres., 2013–16); Ind. Mem., Parole Bd, 2010–11. Member, Board of Visitors: HMP Downview, 1994–2002 (Chm., 1997–2000); HMP Wandsworth, 2002. Member: Croydon Area Child Protection Cttee, 1994–2000 (Chm., Registration Appeals Panel); Croydon Magistrates' Courts' Cttee, 1999–2001; Chm., Croydon Family Panel, 2000–02. Panel Chm., Fitness to Practise Cttees, NMC, 2012–. Magistrates' Association: Mem. Council, 2001–13; Chm., Criminal Justice System, subseq. Judicial Policy and Practice, Cttee, 2002–05. JP Croydon, 1986 (Supplemental List, 2015). Gov., Croydon High Sch., 1993–2005 (Chm. Govs, 2000–05). Publications: contrib. Magistrate mag. Recreations: music, reading, computing. Address: c/o Magistrates' Association, 10A Flagstaff House, St George Wharf, SW8 2LE. T: (020) 7387 2353, Fax: (020) 7383 4020.

**BARNETT, Hon. Sir Michael (Lancelot Patrick),** Kt 2009; Chief Justice, The Bahamas, 2009–15; a Judge of the Court of Appeal, The Bahamas, since 2019; b Nassau, 21 Aug. 1954; s of Arthur Barnett and Beryl Barnett; m 1980, Camille Liverpool; two d. Educ: Georgetown Univ., Washington, DC (BA). Called to the Bar, Lincoln's Inn, 1978; Partner, 1983–2008, Of Counsel, 2015–19, Graham Thompson and Co., Nassau; Attorney Gen., Bahamas, 2008–09.

**BARNETT, Rt Rev. Paul William,** ThD; Bishop of North Sydney, and an Assistant Bishop, Diocese of Sydney, 1990–2001; *b* 23 Sept. 1935; *s* of William and Edna Barnett; *m* 1963, Anita Janet Simpson; two *s* two *d*. *Educ*: Univ. of London (BD Hons 1963, PhD 1978); Univ. of Sydney (MA Hons 1975). Deacon, 1963; priest, 1965; Lectr, Moore Theol Coll., 1964–67; Rector, St Barnabas, Broadway, 1967–73; Rector, Holy Trinity, Adelaide, 1973–79; Master, Robert Menzies Coll., Macquarie Univ., 1980–90. Lecturer, part time: Macquarie Univ., 1980–86; Univ. of Sydney, 1982–92. Vis. Prof., 1987, 1991, 1993, 1995, Res. Prof., 1996–, Regent Coll., Vancouver; Vis. Fellow in History, 1987–, Sen. Fellow in Ancient History Documentary Res., 2002–, Macquarie Univ.; Kingham Fellow, Oak Hill Theol Coll., 1996; Fellow, Inst. of Biblical Res., 2000. Hon. ThD Australian Coll. of Theology, 2009. Highly commended author, Christian Booksellers Conf., 1990; Christian Theol Writer's Award, Aust. Christian Lit. Soc., 2009. *Publications*: Is the New Testament History?, 1986; The Message of 2 Corinthians, 1988; Bethlehem to Patmos, 1989; Apocalypse Now and Then, 1990; The Two Faces of Jesus, 1990; The Servant King, 1991; The Truth About Jesus, 1994; Jesus and the Logic of History, 1997; Commentary on 2 Corinthians, 1997; Jesus and the Rise of Early Christianity, 1999; Commentary on 1 Corinthians, 2000; Commentary on Romans, 2003; Birth of Christianity, 2005; Shepherd King, 2005; First Peter, 2006; Paul, Missionary of Jesus, 2008; Messiah, 2009; Finding the Historical Christ, 2009; The Corinthian Question: why the Church opposed her founder, 2011; Paul the Pastor in Second Corinthians, 2012; Galatians: defending the truth, 2012; Following Jesus to Jerusalem, 2012; Gospel Truth: answering new atheist attacks on the Gospels, 2012; Paul in Syria: the background to Galatians, 2014; John the Pastor: encouragement to a struggling church, 2015; A Short Book about Jesus: the man from Heaven, 2015; The Importance of Peter in Early Christianity, 2016; Paul's Friends in Leadership, 2017. *Recreations*: tennis, swimming, fishing, fine music. *Address*: 59 Essex Street, Epping, NSW 2121, Australia.

**BARNETT, Richard;** historian, writer, broadcaster and poet; Faculty Member, Exeter Summer Programme, Exeter College, Oxford, since 2018; *b* Birmingham, 3 March 1980; *s* of Roy Barnett and Elizabeth Barnett (*née* Clayton); *m* 1st, 2006, Caroline Essex (marr. diss. 2013); 2nd, 2017, Lauren Summersgill. *Educ*: University Coll. London (BSc 1st Cl. Hons Hist. of Medicine and Basic Med. Scis 2001; MSc Hist. and Philosophy of Sci., Technol. and Medicine (Dist.) 2003; PhD Hist. of Medicine 2007). Lectr in Hist. of Medicine, Wellcome Trust Centre for Hist. of Medicine, UCL, 2007–08 and 2010–11; Teaching Associate in Hist. of Modern Medicine and Biol., Dept of Hist. and Philosophy of Sci., Univ. of Cambridge, 2008–10; Faculty Mem., Pembroke-King's Prog., Pembroke Coll., Cambridge, 2011–17. Hon. Res. Fellow, 2011–16, Teaching Fellow, 2017, Dept of Sci. and Technol. Studies, UCL. Wellcome Trust Engagement Fellow, 2011–14. Curatorial consultant, Teeth exhibition, Wellcome Collection, 2018. Chair of Judges, McCarthy Award for History of Medicine Research, RCPE, 2018. *Publications*: Medical London: city of diseases, city of cures, 2008; The Dedalus Book of Gin, 2011; (contrib.) Natural Death Handbook, 5th edn 2012; (contrib.) Pocket Horizon, 2013; The Sick Rose: disease and the art of medical illustration, 2014; Seahouses, 2015; contribs to Lancet, London Rev. of Books; Crucial Interventions: an illustrated treatise on the principles and practice of nineteenth-century surgery, 2015; The Smile Stealers: the fine and foul art of dentistry, 2017. *Recreations*: walking, cooking, reading, arguing. *E*: richard@richardbarnettwriter.com.

**BARNETT, Sir Richard (Robert),** Kt 2015; PhD; Vice Chancellor, 2006–15, and Professor of Public Finance and Management, 1990–2015, now Professor Emeritus, University of Ulster; *b* 17 Oct. 1952; *s* of late Sidney Barnett and Joyce Barnett (*née* Stocker). *Educ*: St Ivo Sch., St Ives; Abbey Sch., Ramsey; Univ. of Salford (BSc 1974; PhD 1983). Lecturer in Economics: Univ. of Salford, 1977–78; Univ. of York, 1978–90; University of Ulster: Dean, Faculty of Business and Mgt, 1994–2000; Pro Vice Chancellor, 2000–05; Actg Vice Chancellor, 2004–06. Vivienne Stewart Fellow, Univ. of Cambridge, and Vis. Scholar, Wolfson Coll., Cambridge, 1988; Vis. Prof. of Econs, Queen's Univ., Ontario, 1989–90. Non-exec. Dir, United Hosps HSS Trust, 1996–2004; Director: ILEX Urban Regeneration Co. Ltd, 2005–09; NI Sci. Park Foundn Ltd, 2006–15; non-exec. Dir, Bombadier-Shorts Aerospace (Belfast) Ltd, 2007–16. Member: NI Adv. Cttee, British Council, 2000–06; NIHEC, 2009–; NI Council, CBI, 2006–10; Chm., NI Ind. Review of Economic Policy, 2008–09. Chm., Nursing and Midwifery Task Gp, Dept of Health, NI, 2016–19. Trustee, Daphne Jackson Trust, 2008–11. CCMI 2007; Dist. Fellowship Award, Griffith Coll., Dublin, 2014. *Publications*: contrib. learned jls and chapters in books in area of econ. policy and public finance. *Recreations*: contemporary fiction, gardens. *Address*: Kidman Farm Cottage, Gravely Way, Hilton, Cambs PE28 9NN.

**BARNETT, Robert;** DL; Chairman, W & R Barnett Ltd, since 1981; *b* Belfast, 31 May 1944; *s* of William H. Barnett and Sarah C. Barnett; *m* 1975, Elizabeth Ann Bingham; one *s* three *d*. *Educ*: Malvern Coll., Brasenose Coll., Oxford (BA). Dir, W & R Barnett Ltd, 1976–. Mem., Belfast Harbour Comrs, 1981–98 (Chm., 1993–98); Dir, NI Electricity, 1991–96. DL Co. Down, 1998. *Recreations*: golf, tennis, horse breeding. *Address*: W & R Barnett Ltd, Clarendon House, 23 Clarendon Road, Belfast BT1 3BG. *Clubs*: Ulster Reform; Royal County Down Golf, Royal and Ancient Golf, Royal Belfast Golf.

**BARNETT, Robert William,** OBE 1993; HM Diplomatic Service, retired; Head of Science and Technology Unit, Foreign and Commonwealth Office, 2001–02; *b* 25 May 1954; *s* of late Harry Frederick Barnett, Wells-next-the-Sea, Norfolk and Dorothy Anne Barnett (*née* Williamson); *m* 1979, Caroline Sara Weale; two *s*. *Educ*: Wymondham Coll., Norfolk; St Catharine's Coll., Cambridge (BA Hons Mod. & Med. Langs 1977; MA 1979). Joined FCO, 1977: Japanese lang. trng, 1979; Third Sec., Tokyo, 1980–83; Policy Planning Staff, FCO, 1984; Asst Private Sec. to Minister of State, 1984–86; First Secretary: Western European Dept, FCO, 1986–88; Bonn, 1988–91; seconded to Saxony State Govt as Inward Investment Advr, 1992; Asst Hd, Eastern Adriatic Unit, FCO, 1993–94; Ambassador to Bosnia-Herzegovina, 1994–95; Counsellor (Sci., Technol. and Envmt), Bonn, 1995–99; Counsellor, Review of FCO Internat. Sci. and Technol. Work, 1999–2001. Mem. (Ind.), Cotswold DC, 2003. Trustee: Stow Fund, 2005–16; Kate's Home Nursing, 2011–15 (Chm., 2013–15). *Recreations*: walking, gardening.

**BARNETT, Robin Anthony,** CMG 2006; HM Diplomatic Service; Ambassador to Ireland, since 2016; *b* 8 March 1958; *s* of Bryan Anderson Barnett and Marion Barnett; *m* 1st, 1989, Debra Marianne Bunt (marr. diss. 1999); one *s*, and one step *s*; 2nd, 1999, Tesca Marie Osman; one step *s* one step *d*. *Educ*: Birmingham Univ. (LLB Hons 1979). Joined FCO, 1980: Second Secretary: Warsaw, 1982–85; FCO, 1985–90; First Secretary: UK Delegn to conventional forces in Europe negotiations, Vienna, 1990–91; UK Mission to UN, NY, 1991–95; FCO, 1996–98; Counsellor and Dep. Hd of Mission, Warsaw, 1998–2001; Hd, UKvisas, FCO, 2002–06; Ambassador to Romania, 2006–10; Dir, Business Gp, UK Trade & Investment, 2010–11; Ambassador to Poland, 2011–16. *Recreations*: travel, football (Manchester United), reading, film, cooking. *Address*: c/o Foreign and Commonwealth Office, King Charles Street, SW1A 2AH.

**BARNETT, Prof. Stephen Mark,** PhD; FRS 2006; CPhys; FRSE; Royal Society Research Professor, since 2016, Cargill Professor of Natural Philosophy, since 2014 and Professor of Quantum Theory, since 2013, University of Glasgow; *b* 20 Feb. 1961; *s* of Peter Symon Barnett and Rita Barnett; partner, Dr Claire Rosalie Gilson; one *s* one *d*. *Educ*: Imperial Coll., London (BSc, PhD 1985). Postdoctoral Res. Fellow, Imperial Coll., London, 1985–87; Harwell-Wolfson Res. Fellow, 1987–88; GEC and Fellowship of Engrg Fellow, Univ. of Oxford, 1988–90; Lectr in Physics, KCL, 1990–91; University of Strathclyde: RSE Res. Fellow, 1991–94; Reader, 1994–96; Prof. of Quantum Optics, 1996–2013. FRSE 1996; Fellow, Optical Soc. of America, 2009. Dirac Medal, Inst. of Physics, 2013. *Publications*: Methods in Theoretical Quantum Optics (with Dr P. M. Radmore), 1997; Quantum Information, 2009; (jtly) Phase Space Methods for Degenerate Quantum Cases, 2015. *Recreations*: croquet, playing the viola. *Address*: School of Physics and Astronomy, University of Glasgow, Kelvin Building, University Avenue, Glasgow G12 8QQ.

**BARNETT, His Honour William Evans;** QC 1984; a Circuit Judge, 1994–2009; a Deputy Circuit Judge, 2009–11; *b* 10 March 1937; *s* of late Alec Barnett and Esmé (*née* Leon); *m* 1976, Lucinda Jane Gilbert (*see* L. J. Barnett); two *s*. *Educ*: Repton; Keble Coll., Oxford (BA Jurisprudence, 1961; MA 1965). National Service, RCS, 1956–58. Called to the Bar, Inner Temple, 1962; Major Scholarship, Inner Temple, 1962. A Recorder, 1981–94. Mem., Personal Injuries Litigation Procedure Wkg Pty, 1976–78; Judicial Mem., Mental Health Rev. Tribunal, 1993–2004. Chm., Ind. Local Rev. Panel into rioting in Croydon in Aug. 2011, 2011–12. Mem., Whitgift Sch. Cttee, 1996–2002; Gov., Whitgift Foundn, 2004–17, now Emeritus. *Recreations*: photography, gardening. *Address*: c/o Judicial Secretariat for the London and South East Region, City of London Magistrates Court, 3rd Floor, 1 Queen Victoria Street, EC4N 4XY. *Club*: Royal Automobile.

**BARNEVIK, Percy;** Chairman of the Board: AstraZeneca PLC, 1999–2004; ABB (formerly ABB Asea Brown Boveri) Ltd, Zürich, Switzerland, 1996–2001 (President and Chief Executive Officer, 1988–96); Co-founder and Chairman, Hand in Hand International, 2004–14, now Honorary Chairman; *b* Simrishamn, Sweden, 1941. *Educ*: Sch. of Econs, Gothenburg, Sweden (MBA 1964). Stanford Univ. Johnson Group, 1966–69; Sandvik AB: Group Controller, 1969–75; Pres. of Sandvik, USA, 1975–79; Exec. Vice Pres., 1979–80, Chm., 1983–2002, Hon. Chm., 2002–, Sandvik AB Sweden; Pres. and Chief Exec. Officer, Asea, 1980–87. Chm. Bd, Investor AB, 1997–2002 (Bd Mem., Providentia, subseq. Investor, 1987–2002); Bd Mem., General Motors, 1996–2009. Hon. Fellow London Business Sch., 1996. Hon. FREng 1998. Hon. DTech Linköping, Sweden, 1989; Hon. DEcons Gothenburg, 1991; Hon. DLaws Babson Coll., Mass, USA, 1995; Hon. DSc Cranfield, 1997; Hon. Dr UMIST with Manchester, 1999. *Publications*: Jag Vill Förändra Världen (autobiog.), 2011; Ledarskap, 2013. *Address*: Caparo House, 101–103 Baker Street, W1U 6LN.

**BARNEWALL,** family name of **Baron Trimlestown**.

**BARNEWALL, Sir Peter (Joseph),** 14th Bt *cr* 1623; Managing Director, Langano Business Strategists, since 1995; *b* 26 Oct. 1963; *s* of Sir Reginald Robert Barnewall, 13th Bt and of Maureen Ellen Barnewall (*née* Daly); *S* father, 2018; *m* 1988, Kathryn Jane, *d* of Hugh Carroll; two *s* one *d*. *Educ*: St Joseph's Coll., Nudgee, NSW; Queensland Univ. (BAgrSc 1985; MBA 2001); Queensland Univ. of Technol. (Postgrad. Cert. Mgt 1995); Australian Inst. of Company Dirs (Dip. 2002). Lieut 2nd/14th Light Horse Regt, Qld Mounted Infantry, Royal Australian Armoured Corps, 1982. Economist, Qld Dept of Primary Industries, 1985–89; Agricl Economist, GRM Internat., 1989–93; Manager, Internat. Projects, UniQuest, 1996–99; Business Develt Manager, Brisbane City Enterprises, 1999–2001; Gen. Manager, Darling Downs Foods Ltd, 2002; CEO, Commerce Qld, 2002–06; CEO and Exec. Dir, Biolytix Gp, 2007–08; CEO and Sen. Associate, AshleyMunro Pty Ltd, 2009–10; Practice Manager, WG Gp, 2013–17. Director: Sunsuper Pty Ltd, 2003–06; Airline Acad. of Australia Ltd, 2008–12; Royal Queensland Aero Club Ltd, 2008–12. Mem., Adv. Bd, Asia Pacific Centre for Franchising Excellence, Griffith Univ., 2008–12. FAIM; FAICD. *Recreations*: cycling, bush walking, aviation. *Heir*: *s* Christopher Patrick Barnewall, *b* 3 June 1995. *E*: joe.barnewall@langano.com.au.

**BARNICOAT, Thomas Humphry;** Chairman, Somethin' Else, since 2008; *b* 21 Oct. 1952; *s* of John Barnicoat and Jane Barnicoat (*née* Selby, now Wright); *m* 1980, Katrina Noelle Chalmers; three *d*. *Educ*: Lycée Français de Londres; St John's Coll., Oxford (BA Hist. and French). Ed., Isis, 1976; joined BBC, 1977: grad. trainee, 1977–79; scriptwriter, TV News, 1979–81; producer and dir, TV Current Affairs, 1981–86; Producer, Crown TV, 1986; Dir, Public Affairs, Sotheby's, 1986–87; Producer, Business TV, 1987–89; Dir, Corporate Develt, 1990–93, Dep. Chief Exec., 1993–95, Broadcast Communications plc; Chief Exec., Broadcast Communications plc, subseq. Endemol UK, 1995–2004; Chief Operating Officer, Endemol Group, 2005–07. *Recreations*: swimming, walking, sleeping. *E*: tbarnicoat@mac.com. *Clubs*: Reform, Hurlingham.

**BARNIER, Michel Jean;** Officier de la Légion d'honneur; Conseiller d'Etat, since 2005; Chief Negotiator, European Commission Taskforce for Preparation and Conduct of Negotiations with the United Kingdom, since 2016; *b* 9 Jan. 1951; *m* 1982, Isabelle Altmayer; two *s* one *d*. *Educ*: Ecole Supérieure de Commerce de Paris (Dip. 1972). Govt service, 1973–78. Mem. (RPR) for Savoie, Nat. Assembly, 1978–93; Minister of the Environment, France, 1993–95; Minister of State for European Affairs, 1995–97; Minister of Foreign Affairs, 2004–05; Minister for Agriculture, 2007–09. Mem., EC, 1999–2004 and 2010–14; MEP, 2009–10; Special Advr, European Defence and Security Policy, EC, 2015–16. Corporate Vice Pres., Internat. Develt, Mérieux Alliance, 2006–07. Mem., 1973–99, Chm., 1982–99, Deptl Council of Savoie; Senator for Savoie, 1997–99; Pres., Senate Delegn for EU, 1998. Jt Pres., Organising Cttee, Olympic Games, Albertville and Savoie, 1987–92. *Publications*: Vive la politique, 1985; Chacun pour tous: le défi écologique, 1990; Atlas des risques majeurs, 1992; Vers une mer inconnue, 1994; Notre contrat pour l'alternance, 2001; Sortir l'Europe des idées reçues, 2005; Atlas for a Sustainable World, 2007; Who will Feed the World: a new agricultural revolution, 2008; Europe, Cards on the Table, 2008.

**BARNISH, Alan Joseph;** consultant, Cambridgeshire County Council, since 2003 (Chief Executive, 1997–2003); *b* 13 Oct. 1949; *s* of Sydney and Dora Barnish; *m* 1972, Elizabeth Sanders; one *s* one *d*. *Educ*: Leeds Univ. (BCom); IPFA. Mid Glam CC, 1975–90; Chief Exec. and Co. Treas., Powys CC, 1990–93; Chief Exec., Shropshire CC, 1993–97.

**BARNSLEY, John Corbitt;** company director; Chief Executive Officer, Business Process Outsourcing, PricewaterhouseCoopers, 1998–2001 (Managing Partner, UK, 1995–98); *b* 25 May 1948; *s* of William C. Barnsley, consultant thoracic surgeon, and Hilda C. Barnsley (*née* Robson); *m* (marr. diss.); one *s* one *d* (and one *d* decd); civil partnership 2006, James Ian Mackenzie. *Educ*: Heaton Grammar Sch., Newcastle upon Tyne; Newcastle upon Tyne Univ. (LLB 1st Cl. Hons 1969; Reynoldson Meml Prize). Joined Price Waterhouse, Newcastle, 1970: Sen. Tax Partner, UK, 1990–93; European Leader for Audit and Business Services, 1993–95; Joint Global Dir of Ops, 1996–98. Senior Independent non-executive Director: Northern Investors Co. PLC, 2005– (non-exec. Dir, 2002–); LMS Capital (formerly Leo Capital) plc, 2006–12; Grainger (formerly Grainger Trust) plc, 2011–15 (non-exec. Dir, 2003–11); non-executive Director: American Appraisal Associates, 2003–15; Hippodrome Casino, 2013–; Apperley Properties Ltd, 2013–16; Chairman:

American Appraisal Associates UK, 2005–15; Coverbox Ltd, 2014–; Customs Connect Ltd, 2016–. *Recreations:* Chinese porcelain, antique furniture. *Address:* Flat 21, Howard Building, Chelsea Bridge Wharf, SW8 4NN.

**BARNSLEY, Victoria, (Hon. Mrs Nicholas Howard),** OBE 2009; Executive Co-Chairman, Castle Howard Estate Ltd, since 2015; *b* 4 March 1954; *d* of late T. E. Barnsley, OBE and Margaret Gwyneth Barnsley (*née* Llewellin); *m* 1992, Hon. Nicholas Howard; one *d*, and one step *s*. *Educ:* University Coll. London (BA Hons English; Hon. Fellow, 2005); Univ. of York (MA French and English 19th Century Novel). Founder, and Chm. and Chief Exec., Fourth Estate Ltd, 1984–2000; CEO and Publisher, HarperCollins UK, 2000–13, HarperCollins Internat., 2008–13. Trustee: Tate Gall., 1998–2007; Tate Foundn, 2007–15; Dir, Tate Enterprises (formerly Tate Gall. Pubns) Ltd, 1998–2015. Trustee, Nat. Gall., 2004–07; Comr, English Heritage, 2014–15; Trustee, English Heritage Trust, 2015–. Mem. Council, Publishers' Assoc., 2001–13 (Pres., 2010–11).

**BARNSTAPLE, Archdeacon of;** *see* Butchers, Ven. Dr M. A.

**BARON, Hon. Francine,** Senator and Minister for Foreign and CARICOM Affairs, Dominica, since 2014; *b* Dominica; two *d*. *Educ:* Univ. of Wolverhampton (LLB). Called to the Bar: Middle Temple, 1995; Dominica, 1996; barrister in private practice, 1996–2007, 2010–12; Attorney Gen., Dominica, 2007–10; High Comr for Dominica in the UK, 2012–14. *Recreations:* hiking, reading. *Club:* Rotary (Dominica).

**BARON, Prof. Jean-Claude,** MD, ScD; FMedSci; Professor of Stroke Medicine, Department of Clinical Neurosciences (formerly Departments of Medicine and Neurology), University of Cambridge, 2000–10, now Emeritus; Director of Research, INSERM U894, and Deputy Director, Centre for Psychiatry and Neuroscience, Paris 5 University, 2010, now Emeritus; Honorary Consultant in Neurology, Sainte-Anne Hospital, Paris, since 2010; *b* 25 March 1949; *s* of Marcel and Yolaine Baron (*née* Bonan); *m* 1974, Annik Arnette de la Charlonny; one *s* two *d*. *Educ:* Univ. of Paris (MD); Univ. of Cambridge (ScD 2010). Clin. Lectr in Biophysics, 1979–82, then in Neurol., 1982–86, Univ. of Paris; Sen. Registrar in Nuclear Medicine, 1979–82, then in Neurol., 1982–86, Salpêtrière Hosp., Paris; Director: of Res., INSERM, France, 1986–2000; INSERM Res. Unit # 320, Caen, 1989–2000; Scientific Dir, CYCERON Neuroimaging Res. Centre, Univ. of Caen, 1987–2000; Hon. Consultant in Neurology, Addenbrooke's Hosp., Cambridge, 2000–10. FMedSci 2003. Johann Jacob Wepfer Award, Eur. Stroke Conf., 2005; Mérmain-Pelletier Biomed. Scis Prize, Acad. of Scis, France, 2014. *Publications:* (ed jtly) The Ischemic Penumbra, 2007; contrib. numerous peer-reviewed articles to learned jls, incl. Lancet, Brain, Annals of Neurol., Stroke; numerous book chapters and refereed abstracts. *Recreations:* music (playing the guitar), classic blues, J. S. Bach, Mozart. *Address:* Department of Neurology, Hôpital Sainte-Anne, INSERM U894, Paris 5 University, 1 rue Cabanis, 75014 Paris, France.

**BARON, John Charles;** MP (C) Basildon and Billericay, since 2010 (Billericay, 2001–10); *b* 21 June 1959; *s* of Raymond Arthur Ernest Baron and Kathleen Ruby Baron; *m* 1992, Thalia Anne Mayson Laird; two *d*. *Educ:* Jesus Coll., Cambridge (MA). Capt., RRF, 1984–88. Director: Henderson Private Investors, 1988–99; Rothschild Asset Mgt, 1999–2001. Contested (C) Basildon, 1997. Shadow Health Minister, 2002–03; an Opposition Whip, 2007–10. Founder and Dir, Equi Ltd. *Recreations:* financial journalism, walking. *Address:* c/o House of Commons, SW1A 0AA. *T:* (constituency office) (01268) 520765.

**BARON, Dr (Ora) Wendy,** OBE 1992; Director (formerly Curator), Government Art Collection, 1978–97; *b* 20 March 1937; *d* of late Dr S. B. Dimson and Gladys Felicia Dimson, CBE; *m* 1st, 1960, Jeremy Hugh Baron (marr. diss.; he *d* 2014); one *s* one *d*; 2nd, 1990, David Joseph Wyatt, *qv*. *Educ:* St Paul's Girls' Sch.; Courtauld Institute of Art (BA, PhD). Trustee: Public Art Commns Agency, 1990–99; Contemp. Art Soc., 1997–2001; Arts Res. Ltd, 1998–2004; NACF, 1998–2010. Has selected, researched and catalogued exhibitions, including: Sickert, Fine Art Soc., 1973; Camden Town Recalled, Fine Art Soc., 1976; The Camden Town Group, New Haven, USA, 1980; Late Sickert, Hayward Gall., 1981; Sickert, Royal Acad., 1992, Amsterdam, 1993. FRSA 1974; FSA 2007. *Publications:* Sickert, 1973; Miss Ethel Sands and her Circle, 1977; The Camden Town Group, 1979; Perfect Moderns, 2000; Sickert: paintings and drawings, 2006; articles and reviews in professional jls in the field of modern British art.

**BARON-COHEN, Prof. Simon,** PhD; FBA 2009; Professor of Developmental Psychopathology, since 2001, and Director, Autism Research Centre, since 1997, University of Cambridge; Fellow, Trinity College, Cambridge, since 1995; *b* 15 Aug. 1958; *m* 1987, Bridget Lindley (OBE 2014) (*d* 2016); two *s* one *d*. *Educ:* New Coll., Oxford (BA Human Scis); University Coll. London (PhD Psychol.); Inst. of Psychiatry, Univ. of London (MPhil Clin. Psychol.). Lectr, 1987–91, Sen. Lectr, 1991–94, Dept of Psychiatry, Univ. of London; Lectr, 1994–99, Reader, 1999–2001, Dept of Psychiatry, Univ. of Cambridge. FMedSci 2018. *Publications:* (with P. Bolton) Autism: the facts, 1993; (ed jtly) Understanding Other Minds: perspectives from autism, 1993, 3rd edn, 2013; Mindblindness: an essay on autism and the theory of mind, 1995; (ed jtly) Synaesthesia: classic and contemporary readings, 1996; (ed) Maladapted Mind: classic readings in evolutionary psychopathology, 1997; (with P. Howlin) Teaching Children with Autism to Mind-read, 1998; (with M. Robertson) Tourette Syndrome: the facts, 1998; The Essential Difference: men, women and the extreme male brain, 2003; (with S. Wheelwright) An Exact Mind: an artist with Asperger Syndrome, 2004; Prenatal Testosterone in Mind: amniotic fluid studies, 2004; Autism and Asperger's Syndrome: the facts, 2008; Zero Degrees of Empathy: a new theory of human cruelty, 2011; The Science of Evil: on empathy and the origins of cruelty, 2011; (ed jtly) Lego Therapy: how to build social competence for children with autism and related conditions, 2014; (ed jtly) Teaching Children with Autism to Mind-read: the workbook, 2015; contribs to jls incl. Eur. Jl Neurosci., Jl Child Psychol. and Psychiatry, Brain, Jl Amer. Acad. Child and Adolescent Psychiatry, Infant Behaviour and Develt, Jl Autism and Develtl Disorders. *Address:* Autism Research Centre, Section of Developmental Psychiatry, University of Cambridge, Douglas House, 18b Trumpington Road, Cambridge CB2 8AH.

**BARÓN CRESPO, Enrique Carlos;** lawyer; Member, European Parliament, 1986–2009 (President, 1989–92); *b* Madrid, 27 March 1944; *m*; one *s*. *Educ:* Univ. of Madrid (LLL); Inst. Católico de Dirección de Empresas (Lic. en Ciencias Empresariales); Ecole Supérieure des Scis Econ. et Commerciales, Paris (Dip.). Lectr in Agricl Econs, Inst. Nacional de Estudios Agrarios, Valladolid, and in Structural Econs, Univ. of Madrid, 1966–70; lawyer in private practice, 1970–77. Mem. (PSOE), Congress of Deputies, Spain, 1977–87; spokesman on econ. and budgetary affairs, 1977–82; Minister of Transport, Tourism and Communications, 1982–85. European Parliament: a Vice-Pres., 1986–89; Pres., Gp of Party of European Socialists, 1999–2004. President: Internat. European Movt, 1987–89; European Foundn for Information Soc. Mem. Adv. Bd, Gold Mercury Internat., 2006–. *Publications:* Población y Hambre en el Mundo; El Fin del Campesinado; La Civilización del Automóvil; Europa 92: el rapto del futuro; Europe at the Dawn of the Millennium, 1997; Más Europa, ¡unida! (memoirs), 2013 (Gaziel Prize, 2012); La Era Del Federalismo, 2014; contribs on economic and social questions to major Spanish periodicals.

**BARR, Clare Elizabeth;** *see* Pelham, C. E.

**BARR, Very Rev. Dr (George) Russell;** Minister, Cramond Kirk, Edinburgh, since 1993; Moderator of the General Assembly of the Church of Scotland, 2016–17; *b* Kilmarnock, 15 Oct. 1953; *s* of George and Isobel Barr; *m* 1978, Margaret Marion Wyllie; one *s* one *d*. *Educ:* Loanhead Primary; Kilmarnock Acad.; Langside Coll., Glasgow; Univ. of Edinburgh (BA 1975; BD Hons 1978; MTh 1993); Princeton Theol Seminary (DMin 2000). Minister: Garthamlock and Craigend E, Glasgow, 1979–88; St Luke's, Greenock, 1988–93. Chaplain to Lord High Comr, Gen. Assembly of the Church of Scotland, 2011–12; Moderator, Presbytery of Edinburgh, 2013. *Publications:* Just Sharing: a Christian approach to the distribution of wealth, income and benefits, 1988; The Realm of Reform, 1999; articles and reviews in Theology in Scotland; sermons, book reviews and prayers in Expository Times. *Recreations:* golf, Rugby, Scottish opera. *Address:* The Manse of Cramond, Edinburgh EH4 6NS. *T:* (0131) 336 2036. *E:* GBarr@churchofscotland.org.uk.

**BARR, Prof. Hugh,** MD; FRCS, FRCSE; Consultant General and Gastrointestinal Surgeon, Gloucestershire Hospitals NHS Trust, since 1992; *b* Penrith, 19 Sept. 1954; *s* of Hugh and Margaret Barr; *m* 1978, Judith Anne Hiscock; two *d*. *Educ:* Liverpool Univ. (MB ChB 1977; MD (Dist.) 1991; ChM 1996). FRCS 1982; FRCSE 1982. Wellcome Res. Fellow, UCL, 1982–88; Sen. Registrar Surgery, Oxford Hosps NHS Trust, 1988–92; Cranfield University: Clin. Prof., 1994–; Dir, Inst. Med. Scis, Glos Royal Hosp., Cranfield Postgrad. Med. Sch., 1998; Foundn Dean, Faculty of Medicine and Biosci., 1999; Clin. Dean, Cranfield Health, 2001. Hon. Prof., Univ. of Exeter, 2013–. FHEA 2007. *Publications:* contribs to scientific learned jls. *Recreations:* gardening, Church. *Address:* Edge Farm Cottage, Edge, Gloucester, Glos GL6 6NG.

**BARR, Maj.-Gen. John Alexander James Pooler,** CB 1993; CBE 1989; Engineer-in-Chief (Army), 1991–93; *b* 29 Jan. 1939. 2nd Lieut, RE, 1960; Lt-Col, 1978; GSO1 (DS) SC, 1978; Brig. 1983; Comdt, Royal Sch. of Mil. Engrg, Chatham, 1983–87; Dir of Army Staff Duties, MoD, 1987–89; DCS (Support), HQ Allied Forces Northern Europe, 1989–91; Maj.-Gen., 1991. Col Comdt, RE, 1993–2002. CompICE 1992.

**BARR, Kenneth Glen;** Sheriff of South Strathclyde, Dumfries and Galloway at Dumfries, 1976–2008; *b* 20 Jan. 1941; *o s* of late Rev. Gavin Barr and Catherine McLellan Barr (*née* McGhie); *m* 1970, Susanne Crichton Keir (*d* 1996). *Educ:* Ardrossan Acad.; Royal High Sch.; Edinburgh Univ. (MA, LLB). Admitted to Faculty of Advocates, 1964. *Address:* c/o Sheriff Court House, Dumfries DG1 2AN.

**BARR, Prof. Nicholas Adrian,** PhD; Professor of Public Economics, European Institute, London School of Economics and Political Science, since 2002; *b* London, 23 Nov. 1943; *s* of Herman and Edith Barr; *m* 1991, Gillian Lee (*née* Audigier); two step *s*. *Educ:* London Sch. of Econs and Political Sci. (BSc (Econ) 1965; MSc (Econ) 1967); Univ. of Calif, Berkeley (PhD 1971). Lectr in Econs, 1971–88, Sen. Lectr in Econs, 1988–2000, Reader, 2000–02, LSE. Vis. Schol., Fiscal Affairs Dept, IMF, 2000. World Bank: Consultant, Europe and Central Asia Reg., Central and Southern Eur. Depts, HR Ops Div., 1990–92; Principal Author, World Develt Report, 1995–96. Gov., LSE, 1999–95, 1999–2005. Trustee, HelpAge Internat., 2004–12. FRSA 1997. *Publications:* (jtly) Self-Assessment for Income Tax, 1977; (with A. Prest) Public Finance in Theory and Practice, 6th edn 1979, 7th edn 1985; The Economics of the Welfare State, 1987, 5th edn 2012 (trans. French, Greek, Hungarian, Korean and Polish); (with J. Barnes) Strategies for Higher Education: the alternative White Paper, 1988; Student Loans: the next steps, 1989; (ed with D. Whynes) Current Issues in the Economics of Welfare, 1993; (ed) Labor Markets and Social Policy in Central and Eastern Europe: the transition and beyond, 1994 (trans. Hungarian, Romanian and Russian); (contrib.) World Development Report 1996: from plan to market, 1996 (trans. Arabic, Chinese, French, German, Japanese, Russian and Spanish); The Welfare State as Piggy Bank: information, risk, uncertainty and the role of the State, 2001 (trans. Japanese); (ed) Economic Theory and the Welfare State, Vol. I: theory, Vol. II: income transfers, Vol. III: benefits in kind, 2001; (with I. Crawford) Financing Higher Education: answers from the UK, 2005; (ed) Labor Markets and Social Policy in Central and Eastern Europe: the accession and beyond, 2005; (with P. Diamond) Reforming Pensions: principles and policy choices, 2008; (with P. Diamond) Pension Reform: a short guide, 2010 (trans. Spanish, Chinese, Polish); (contrib.) Handbook of Contemporary Education Economics, 2017; contrib. jls incl. Jl Econ. Lit., Econ. Jl, Economica, Oxford Rev. of Econ. Policy, Educn Econs, Econs of Transition, Internat. Social Security Rev., British Tax Rev., Public Money and Mgt, Jl Public Policy, Jl Social Policy, Political Qly. *Recreations:* cricket, computers, grandchildren, photography. *Address:* Economics Department, London School of Economics, Houghton Street, WC2A 2AE. *T:* (020) 7955 7482. *E:* N.Barr@lse.ac.uk. *Club:* Middlesex County Cricket.

**BARR, Very Rev. Russell;** *see* Barr, Very Rev. Dr G. R.

**BARR, Stephen;** Managing Director, SAGE Publications Ltd, since 1996; President, SAGE International, since 2006; *b* Edinburgh, 7 Oct. 1956; *s* of James Barr and Jane Barr (*née* Hepburn); partner, Susan Worsey; four *s*. *Educ:* Queen's Coll., Oxford (BA 1st Cl. Hons Mod. Hist. 1978). Asst Editor, Europa Publications, 1978–79; Editor, Cambridge University Press, 1979–83; Sen. Commng Editor, Open University Press, 1983–86; SAGE: Sen. Commng Editor, 1986–87; Editl Dir, 1988–96; Exec. Vice Pres., SAGE Inc., 2001–; Director: SAGE India, 2006–; SAGE Asia Pacific, 2006–. Pres., Publishers Assoc., 2016–17 (Vice Pres., 2015–16). Dir, Phoenix Cinema Trust, 2007–16 (Chm., 2009–15). *Address:* SAGE Publications Ltd, 1 Oliver's Yard, 55 City Road, EC1Y 1SP.

**BARR YOUNG, His Honour Gavin Neil;** a Circuit Judge, 1988–2005; *b* 14 Aug. 1939; *s* of Dr James Barr Young and Elsie Barr Young (*née* Hodgkinson); *m* 1969, Barbara Elizabeth Breckon; two *d*. *Educ:* Loretto Sch., Musselburgh; Leeds Univ. (LLB). Called to the Bar, Gray's Inn, 1963; Member, North Eastern Circuit, 1964–88 (North Eastern Circuit Junior, 1968); a Recorder of the Crown Court, 1979–88. Part-time Legal Pres., Mental Health Rev. Tribunals (Restricted Patients Panel), 2001–10. *Recreations:* gardening, music. *Address:* Flaxbourne House, Great Ouseburn, York YO26 9RG.

**BARRACLOUGH, Richard Michael;** QC 2003; *b* 29 April 1953; *s* of Michael Alfred William Barraclough and Doreen Barraclough; *m* 1982, Lindsey Elsa Petronella Taylor; two *s* three *d*. *Educ:* St Michael's Coll., Leeds; St Catherine's Coll., Oxford (MA). Solicitor of the Supreme Court, 1978; called to the Bar, Inner Temple, 1980, Bencher, 2011. Legal Assessor: GMC, 1997–; GDC, 2000–. Chm., Disability Cttee, Bar Council, 2004–08. KHS. *Recreations:* motor-cycling, cellist, opera-singing, morganeering, sailing. *Address:* 6 Pump Court, Temple, EC4Y 7AR. *T:* (020) 7797 8400, *Fax:* (020) 7797 8401. *E:* facutvivas@hotmail.com; Stella Maris, Port Bannatyne, Island of Bute, Scotland. *Clubs:* Royal Automobile; Hog.

**BARRADELL, John Bernard,** OBE 2008; Town Clerk and Chief Executive, City of London Corporation, since 2012; *b* London, 20 Aug. 1960; *s* of Austin, (Jack), Barradell and Alice Mary Barradell (*née* O'Hara); Marian, (Maggie), Martin; one *d*, and two step *d*. *Educ:* Bishop Challoner Sch.; University Coll. London (BA Hons Geog. 1981). Various tech. and mktg mgt roles in IT and communications industries, 1981–2002; Westminster City Council: Hd of Crime and Disorder Reduction, 2002–03; Asst Dir, 2003–04; Dir,

2004–06, Dept of Community Protection; Dep. Chief Exec., 2006–09; Chief Exec., Brighton and Hove CC, 2009–12. Clerk to Lieutenancy of E Sussex, 2010–13. Special constabulary, Metropolitan Police, 1981–2007: Comdt, Central Area, 1997–99; Chief Comdt, 1999–2007. Member: Adv. Bd, Ind. Police Complaints Commn, 2003–07; London Resilience Partnership, 2012– (Dep. Chm., 2013–); Film London Taskforce, 2012–. Founding Dir, London Apprenticeship Co., 2008–09. Chairman: Caterham Barracks Community Trust, 2000–03; Sir Simon Milton Foundn, 2016–; Trustee, Epilepsy Soc., 2015–18. FRGS. *Recreations:* recreational cycling, philately, social history, National Public Radio. *Address:* City of London Corporation, Guildhall, EC2P 2EJ. *Clubs:* Athenæum, Guildhall.

**BARRAN**, family name of **Baroness Barran**.

**BARRAN**, Baroness *cr* 2018 (Life Peer), of Bathwick in the City of Bath; **Diana Francesca Caroline Barran**, MBE 2011; Parliamentary Under-Secretary of State, Department for Digital, Culture, Media and Sport, since 2019; *b* London, 10 Feb. 1959; *d* of Cosmo and Erica de Bosdari; *m* 1986, Julian Barran; three *s* one *d*. *Educ:* Benenden Sch.; King's Coll., Cambridge (BA Hons 1980; MA). Chief Exec., Barran and Partners, 1992–2000; Hd, Grant Develt, New Philanthropy Capital, 2001–04; Chief Exec., Co-ordinated Action Against Domestic Abuse, later SafeLives, 2004–17. A Baroness in Waiting (Govt Whip), 2018–19. Chair, Henry Smith Charity, 2002– (Chm.); Trustee: Comic Relief, 2010–; Royal Foundn, 2018–. *Address:* House of Lords, SW1A 0PW. *T:* (020) 7219 5353. *E:* barrand@parliament.uk.

**BARRAN, Sir John Ruthven,** 5th Bt *cr* 1895, of Chapel Allerton Hall, Chapel Allerton, West Riding co. York, and of Queen's Gate, St Mary Abbots, Kensington, co. London; *b* 10 Nov. 1971; *o s* of Sir John Napoleon Ruthven Barran, 4th Bt, and Jane Margaret, *d* of Sir Stanley George Hooker, CBE, FRS; *S* father, 2010, but his name does not appear on the Official Roll of the Baronetage; *m* 2005, Helen Elizabeth, *er d* of Robert Ward, Westbury-sub-Mendip, Som; two *s*. *Heir:* *s* John Robert Nicholson Barran, *b* 23 Dec. 2008.

**BARRASS, Gordon Stephen,** CMG 1992; HM Diplomatic Service, retired; *b* 5 Aug. 1940; *s* of James and Mary Barrass; *m* 1st, 1965, Alice Cecile Oberg (*d* 1984); 2nd, 1992, Dr Kristen Clarke Lippincott, *qv*. *Educ:* Hertford Grammar Sch.; LSE (BSc (Econs)); SOAS (postgrad.). FCO, 1965–67; Chinese Language student, Hong Kong Univ., 1967–69; in Office of HM Chargé d'Affaires, Peking, 1970–72; Cultural Exchange Dept, FCO, 1972–74; UKMIS Geneva, 1974–78; Planning Staff, FCO, 1979–82; RCDS, 1983; seconded to MoD, 1984, Cabinet Office, 1987; Under Sec., 1991–93. Advr, Internat. Affairs, Coopers & Lybrand, then PricewaterhouseCoopers, 1993–2002. Mem., Bd, 2008–, Vis. Prof., 2009–, LSE IDEAS. Guest Curator, Brushes with Surprise exhibn, BM, 2002. *Publications:* The Art of Calligraphy in Modern China, 2002; The Great Cold War, 2009. *Recreations:* Chinese and Western art, classical archaeology, opera, travel, books. *Address:* 3 Mount Vernon, NW3 6QS.

**BARRASS, Kristen Clarke;** *see* Lippincott, K. C.

**BARRATT, Francis Russell,** CB 1975; Deputy Secretary, HM Treasury, 1973–82; *b* 16 Nov. 1924; *s* of Frederick Russell Barratt; *m* 1st, 1949, Janet Mary Sherborne (marr. diss. 1978); three *s*; 2nd, 1979, Josephine Norah Harrison (*née* McCririck) (*d* 2005). *Educ:* Durban High Sch., SA; Clifton; University Coll., Oxford. War Service, 1943–46; Captain, Intelligence Corps, 1946. Asst Principal, HM Treasury, 1949; Principal, 1953; First Sec., UK High Commission, Karachi, 1956–58; Asst Sec., 1962, Under Sec., 1968, HM Treasury. Dir, Amdahl (UK), 1983–93; Trustee, Amdahl (UK) Pension Fund, 1984–95. Mem., Rev. Bd for Govt Contracts, 1984–93. *Address:* Little Paddocks, Smallthye Road, Tenterden, Kent TN30 7LY. *T:* (01580) 763734.

**BARRATT, Michael Fieldhouse;** communications consultant; broadcaster on radio and television; Chairman: Michael Barratt Ltd, 1977–97; Commercial Video Ltd, since 1981; *b* 3 Jan. 1928; *s* of late Wallace Milner Barratt and Doris Barratt; *m* 1st, 1952, Joan Francesca Warner (marr. diss.; she *d* 1995); three *s* three *d*; 2nd, 1977, Dilys Jane Morgan; two *s* one *d*. *Educ:* Rossall and Paisley Grammar Sch. Entered journalism, Kemsley Newspapers, 1944; Editor, Nigerian Citizen, 1956; *television:* Reporter, Panorama, 1963; Presenter: 24 Hours, 1965–69; Nationwide, 1969–77; Songs of Praise, 1977–82; Reporting London, 1983–88; *radio:* Question-Master, Gardeners' Question Time, 1973–79. Dir, Career Best Ltd, 1995–97. Chm. of Trustees, People to Places, 1996–2009; Trustee, Temple Holdings, 1992–96. Rector, Aberdeen Univ., 1973. Hon. LLD Aberdeen, 1975. *Publications:* Michael Barratt, 1973; Michael Barratt's Down-to-Earth Gardening Book, 1974; Michael Barratt's Complete Gardening Book, 1977; Golf with Tony Jacklin, 1978; Making the Most of the Media, 1996; Making the Most of Retirement, 1999; Mr Nationwide, 2012. *Recreations:* golf, cricket, listening. *Address:* 9 Andrews Reach, Bourne End, Bucks SL8 5GA. *T:* (01628) 530895. *E:* michael@mbarratt.co.uk.

**BARRATT, Michael John;** Principal, Priory School, Shrewsbury, since 2015; Executive Principal, Priory School Trust, since 2016; *b* Lancaster, 12 Oct. 1963; *s* of William Barratt and Muriel Barratt; *m* 1993, Susanna Busi; one *s* two *d*. *Educ:* Lancaster Royal Grammar Sch.; Liverpool Univ. (BA Mgt and Business Studies); Sheffield Poly. (PGCE); Univ. of Worcester (MSc Educn Mgt and Leadership); National Coll. of School Leadership (NPQH). Shrewsbury School: Teacher, 1988–2002; Hd of Business and Econs, 1991–2002; Housemaster, 1999–2003; Dep. Headmaster, 2003–08, Headmaster, 2008–14, Adams' Grammar Sch. Examr, UCLES, 1991–2005. *Publications:* Understanding Industry, 1996; A Level Business Studies, 2001. *Recreations:* cycling (lycra shorts), running (mud preferred), tennis (modest), golf (big handicap), watching my family enjoy life. *Address:* The Yews, Montford Bridge, Shrewsbury, Shropshire SY4 1EB.

**BARRATT, Nicholas David,** PhD; FRHistS; Director, Senate House Library, University of London, since 2018 (Associate Director, Collections and Engagement, 2015–17; Acting Director, 2017–18); *b* Chiswick, London, 16 May 1970; *s* of late David Frank Ernest Barratt and of Daphne June Barratt (*née* Miller). *Educ:* Newland House Prep. Sch.; Hampton Sch.; King's Coll. London (BA 1st cl. Hons Hist. 1991; PhD Medieval Hist. 1996). FRHistS 2013. Reader advr and Co-ordinator of Academic Inductions, PRO, 1996–2000; Specialist Researcher, BBC, 2000–02, incl. House Detectives, House Detectives at Large, Invasion, One Foot in the Past and Britain's Best Buildings; Founder and CEO, Sticks Research Agency, 2000–; Exec. Dir, FreeBMD, 2010–13; Associate, Ancestral Tourism Partnership, 2011–13; Hd, Medieval and Early Modern, Legal, Maps and Plans Teams, Nat. Archives, 2013–15. Co-Founder, 2005, CEO, 2007–12, Firebird Media. Ed. in Chief, Your Family Hist., 2010–13. Hon. Associate Prof. of Public History, Univ. of Nottingham, 2016–. Freelance broadcaster; television: on-screen document specialist, House Detectives, 1997–98; presenter: Small Piece of History, 2002; Family History Project, 2003; Secrets From the Attic, 2008; Brit Camp, 2008; specialist researcher: Wreck Detectives, 2003–04; Seven Wonders of the Industrial World, 2003; consultant and specialist researcher: Who Do You Think You Are?, BBC, 2004–07 (and co-presenter, 2004), SBS Australia, 2008–, RTÉ, 2008–09; Not Forgotten, 2007; co-presenter: History Mysteries, 2005; Hidden House History, 2006; So You Think You're Royal, 2007; Live The Dream as Seen on Screen, 2009; Missing Millions, 2011; Find My Past, 2011; radio: co-presenter, Tracing Your Roots, 2007–11. Columnist, Daily Telegraph, 2005–08. Co-creator, Nation's Memorybank personal heritage website, 2007; Principal Consultant and Co-founder, Who Do You Think You Are? Live, 2007–12. Co-ordinator, Action 4 Archives, 2009–10. Pres., Fedn of Family Hist. Socs, 2011– (Mem., Exec. Cttee, 2005–06); Member: Educn Cttee, British Assoc. for Local Hist., 2009–; Cttee for Public Hist., Historical Assoc., 2009–; Knowledge Transfer Adv. Gp, Fine Rolls Project, KCL, 2009–13; Televising History Adv. Bd, Univ. of Lincoln, 2009–10; Educn Cttee, Soc. of Genealogists, 2010–13; Council, Assoc. of Genealogists and Researchers in Archives, 2010–12; Cttee, Community Archives and Heritage Gp, 2011–13, 2016– (Treas., 2018–); Educn Sub-Cttee, Magna Carta Trust, 2013–15; Adv. Gp, Within the Walls, York, 2014–15. Ind. Advr and Chair, Partners Adv. Gp, Midlands 3 Cities Doctoral Trng Partnership, 2015–18. Trustee: Soc. of Genealogists, 2011–16 (Treas., 2013–16); Foundn for Medieval Genealogy, 2011–14; Vice Pres., AGRA, 2011–. Julian Bickersteth Meml Medal, Inst. of Heraldic and Genealogical Studies, 2008. *Publications:* Tracing the History of Your House, 2001, 2nd edn 2006; Receipt Rolls, 4, 5, 6, Henry III, 2003; Receipt Rolls, 7, 8, Henry III, 2007; (jtly) Who Do You Think You Are?, 2, 2005, 3, 2006; The Family Detective, 2006; (jtly) Genealogy Online for Dummies, 2006; The Who Do You Think You Are? Encyclopaedia of Family History, 2008; Lost Voices from the Titanic, 2009; Nick Barratt's Guide to Your Ancestors' Lives, 2010; Greater London: the story of the suburbs, 2012; The Forgotten Spy, 2015; The Restless Kings, 2018; *contributions to:* King John: new interpretations, 1999; Crises, Revolutions and Self-Sustained Growth, 1999; Family and Dynasty in Late Medieval England, 2003; English Government in the Thirteenth Century, 2004; Thirteenth Century England X, 2005; The Story of Where You Live, 2005; Henry II: new interpretations, 2007; Foundations of Medieval Scholarship, 2008; How to Trace Your Family History on the Internet, 2008; Thirteenth Century England XII, 2009; Researching Your Family History Online for Dummies, 2009; The Growth of Royal Government Under King Henry III, 2015; Baronial Reform and Revolution in England, 1258–1267, 2016; contrib. English Historical Rev., Internat. History Rev. *Recreations:* football (playing and managing), running (completed four London marathons), chess. *Address:* c/o HHB Agency Ltd, 6 Warwick Court, WC1R 5DJ. *E:* admin@sra-uk.com.

**BARRATT, Peter Frederick;** Speaker's Secretary, House of Commons, since 2011; *b* Forest Gate, London, 23 Nov. 1965; *s* of late Frederick Barratt and Mabel Jean Barratt (*née* John). *Educ:* Barking Abbey Comprehensive Sch., Barking. Registrar's Department, Bank of England: Grade 1 Clerk, Chief Registrar's Office, 1982–84, Dividend Office, 1984–86; Computer Officer, Computer Section, 1986–91; House of Commons: Department of Finance and Administration: Sen. Office Clerk, 1991–92; Computer Officer, 1992–93; Payroll Manager, 1993–96; Actg Financial Accountant, 1993–96; Financial Accountant, 1996–98; Members' Allowances Co-ordinator, 1998–2000; Speaker's Office: Asst Sec. to Speaker, 2000–04 and 2005–11; Actg Speaker's Sec., 2004–05. *Recreations:* reading, theatre, music, genealogy, socialising, regular lager and wine-tasting. *Address:* Speaker's Office, House of Commons, SW1A 0AA. *T:* (020) 7219 4111, *Fax:* (020) 7219 6901. *E:* barrattpf@parliament.uk.

**BARRATT, His Honour Robin Alexander;** QC 1989; a Circuit Judge, 1998–2011; *b* 24 April 1945; *s* of Harold and Phyllis Barratt; *m* 1st, 1972, Gillian Anne Ellis (marr. diss. 1999); one *s* three *d*; 2nd, 2009, Linda D. Shepley. *Educ:* Charterhouse; Worcester Coll., Oxford (Exhibnr; BA Hons, MA). Harmsworth Entrance Exhibnr, 1965, Schol. 1969; called to the Bar, Middle Temple, 1970. Lectr in Law, Kingston Polytechnic, 1968–71; Western Circuit, 1971; Asst Recorder, 1990; a Recorder, 1993–98. Councillor (C), London Bor. of Merton, 1978–86. Chm., Chichester Cathedral Community Cttee, 2014–17. *Recreations:* fell walking, music. *Address:* Court Barn, Salthill Park, Fishbourne, Chichester, W Sussex PO19 3PS.

**BARRÉ-SINOUSSI, Françoise Claire;** Commandeur, Légion d'Honneur, 2009; Director, Regulation of Retroviral Infections Unit (formerly Retrovirus Biology Unit), 1992–2015, and Professor, since 1996, Institut Pasteur, Paris; *b* Paris, 30 July 1947; *d* of Roger Sinoussi and Jeanine Sinoussi (*née* Fau); *m* 1978, Jean-Claude Barré. *Educ:* Lycée Bergson; Univ. de Paris (DèsSc 1975). Post-doctoral Fellow, NIH, Bethesda, 1975–76; Institut Pasteur, Paris: Res. Asst, 1975–80, Asst Prof., 1980–86, Res. Dir, 1986–, Institut nat. de la santé et de la recherche médicale; Hd, Retrovirus Biology Lab., 1986–91; Mem., Exec. Cttee, 2001–04; Dep. Dir, Scientific Affairs of Internat. Network, 2001–05. Co-discoverer of AIDS virus, 1983. (jtly) Nobel Prize in Physiology or Medicine, 2008. *Address:* Regulation of Retroviral Infections Unit, Virology Department, Institut Pasteur, 25 Rue du Docteur Roux, 75724 Paris Cedex 15, France.

**BARRELL, Dr Anthony Charles,** CB 1994; FREng; Chief Executive, North Sea Safety, Health and Safety Executive, 1991–94; *b* 4 June 1933; *s* of William Frederick Barrell and Ruth Eleanor Barrell (*née* Painter); *m* 1963, Jean, *d* of Francis Henry Hawkes and Clarice Jean (*née* Silke); one *s* one *d*. *Educ:* Friars Sch., Bangor; Kingston Grammar Sch.; Birmingham Univ.; Imperial Coll. BSc Hons chem. eng. CEng; FREng (FEng 1990); FIChemE 1984; Eur Ing 1988. Chemist, Ministry of Supply, later War Dept, 1959–64; Commissioning Engineer, African Explosives and Chemical Industries, 1964–65; Shift Manager, MoD, 1965–66; Chemical Inspector, then Supt Specialist Inspector, HM Factory Inspectorate, 1966–78; Head of Major Hazards Assessment Unit, HSE, 1978–85; Dir, Technology, HSE, 1985–90; Chief Exec., N Sea Safety, Dept of Energy, 1990–91. Non-executive Director: BAA, 1994–2001; Lloyd's Register (formerly Lloyd's Register of Shipping), 1998–2009; Partner, TBP, 1994–2009; Special Advr, NATS, 2000–09. Member, Council: IChemE, 1989–94 (Pres., 1993–94); Royal Acad. of Engrg, 1994–97. Hon. DEng Birmingham, 1995. *Publications:* papers on assessment and control of major hazards, on offshore safety and on fire and explosion risks. *Recreations:* walking, reading, boating, golf. *T:* (01803) 752266. *Clubs:* Royal Dart Yacht (Cdre, 2000–03; Pres., 2010–15); Churston Golf (Chm., 2004–06, 2009–11).
*See also* S. R. Barrell.

**BARRELL, Prof. John Charles,** PhD; FBA 2001; Professor of English, Queen Mary University of London, 2013–15, now Emeritus; *b* 3 Feb. 1943; *s* of John Ellis Barrell and Beatrice Mary Barrell; *m* 1st, 1965, Audrey Jones (marr. diss. 1975); two *s*; 2nd, 1975, Jania Miller (marr. diss. 1978); 3rd, 1992, Prof. Harriet Guest; one *d*. *Educ:* Trinity Coll., Cambridge (BA 1964; MA 1967); Univ. of Essex (PhD 1971). Lectr, Dept of Lit., Univ. of Essex, 1968–72; University of Cambridge: Lectr in English, and Fellow, King's Coll., 1972–85; Lectr, Newnham Coll., 1972–84; Professor of English: Univ. of Sussex, 1986–93; Univ. of York, 1993–2012. British Acad. Reader, 1991–93; Vis. Fellow, Inst. of Advanced Study, Indiana Univ., 2002; Schaffner Vis. Prof., Chicago Univ., 2002; Leverhulme Major Res. Fellow, 2002–04; Dist. Vis. Prof., Carleton Univ., Ottawa, 2009. FEA 2001. Hon. Fellow, King's Coll., Cambridge, 2013. Hon. DHL Chicago, 2008; Hon. DLitt Courtauld Inst. of Art, Univ. of London, 2010; Hon. Dip. Warsaw, 2011. *Publications:* The Idea of Landscape and the Sense of Place 1730–1840: an approach to the poetry of John Clare, 1972; The Dark Side of the Landscape: the rural poor in English painting 1730–1840, 1980; English Literature in History 1730–1780: an equal, wide survey, 1983; The Political Theory of Painting from Reynolds to Hazlitt, 1986; Poetry, Language and Politics, 1988; The Infection of Thomas De Quincey: a psychopathology of imperialism, 1991; The Birth of Pandora and the Division of Knowledge, 1992; Imagining the King's Death: figurative treason, fantasies of regicide 1793–1796, 2000; The Spirit of Despotism: invasions of privacy in the 1790s, 2006; *edited:* S. T. Coleridge, On the Constitution of the Church and State, 1972; (with John Bull) The Penguin Book of Pastoral Verse, 1972; Painting and the Politics of Culture: new essays on British Art 1700–1850, 1992; Exhibition Extraordinary!! Radical Broadsides of the Mid 1790s, 2001; (with Jon Mee) Trials for Treason and Sedition 1792–1794, 8 vols, 2006–07; (with Tim Whelan) The Complete Writings of William Fox, 2011; Edward Pugh of Ruthin, 1763–1813: 'a native artist', 2013. *Recreations:* gardening, print-collecting, watching television. *Address:* School of English and Drama, Queen Mary University of London, Mile End Road, E1 4NS.

**BARRELL, Dr Samantha Ruth,** CBE 2014; Chief Operating Officer, Francis Crick Institute, since 2017; *b* Taplow, Bucks, 22 Feb. 1968; *d* of Dr Anthony Charles Barrell, *qv*; *m* 1998, Justin Marney; three *d*. *Educ:* Cox Green Comp. Sch.; Charing Cross and Westminster Med. Sch. (MB BS, BSc). GP, 2001–15; Chief Clinical Officer, S Devon and Torbay CCG, 2012–15; Chief Exec., Taunton and Somerset NHS Foundn Trust, 2015–17. *Recreations:* open water swimming, cycling, triathlon, reading, sailing, ski-ing. *E:* sam.barrell@crick.ac.uk. *Club:* Royal Dart Yacht.

**BARRETT, Angela Jane;** illustrator; *b* 23 Aug. 1955; *d* of Donald and Dinah Patricia Barrett. *Educ:* Coborn Sch. for Girls, Bow; Maidstone Coll. of Art; Royal Coll. of Art. Mem., Art Workers' Guild. Illustrator, Jane Austen issue, Royal Mail stamps, 2013. *Publications:* illustrated: The King, the Cat and the Fiddle, by Yehudi Menuhin and Christopher Hope, 1983; Naomi Lewis, The Wild Swans, 1984; Susan Hill, Through the Kitchen Window, 1984; James Riordan, The Woman in the Moon, 1984; Christopher Hope, The Dragon Wore Pink, 1985; Susan Hill, Through the Garden Gate, 1986, Can it be true?, 1988 (Smarties Award); Naomi Lewis, The Snow Queen, 1988; Proud Knight, Fair Lady, trans. Naomi Lewis, 1989; Martin Waddell, The Hidden House, 1990 (W. H. Smith Award 1991); Susan Hill, The Walker Book of Ghost Stories, 1990; Snow White, re-told by Josephine Poole, 1991; Jenny Nimmo, The Witches and the Singing Mice, 1993; Susan Hill, Beware Beware, 1993; Geraldine McCaughrean, The Orchard Book of Stories from the Ballet, 1994; Angela McAllister, The Ice Palace, 1994; Candide, Voltaire, trans. Christopher Thacker, 1996; Naomi Lewis, The Emperor's New Clothes, 1997 (IBBY Award 2000); Josephine Poole, Joan of Arc, 1998; Rocking Horse Land and other classic tales of dolls and toys, compiled by Naomi Lewis, 2000; The Orchard Book of Shakespeare Stories, retold by Andrew Matthews, 2001; Sharon Darrow, Through the Tempests Dark and Wild, 2003; Josephine Poole, Anne Frank, 2005; Beauty and the Beast, re-told by Max Eilenberg, 2006; Paul Gallico, The Snow Goose, 2007; Leo Tolstoy, Anna Karenina, 2008; Tim Binding, Sylvie and the Songman, 2008; Laura Amy Schlitz, The Night Fairy, 2010; Robert Louis Stevenson, The Strange Case of Dr Jekyll and Mr Hyde, 2010 (Parrot Prize for Illustration, Fine Press Book Assoc., 2011); Clement C. Moore, The Night Before Christmas, 2012; Vivian French, The Most Wonderful Thing in the World, 2015; Charles Dickens, A Christmas Carol, 2015; Jessie Burton, The Restless Girls, 2018; Bram Stoker, Dracula, 2019. *Recreations:* reading, needlework, roaming about London. *Address:* c/o Caradoc King, A. P. Watt Ltd, 12–26 Lexington Street, W1F 0LE. *T:* (020) 3214 0800. *Club:* Double Crown.

**BARRETT, Prof. Ann,** OBE 2010; MD; FRCP, FRCR; FMedSci; Professor of Oncology, School of Medicine, University of East Anglia, 2002–08, now Emeritus; *b* 27 Feb. 1943; *d* of Robert Douglas and Elsie Mary Brown. *Educ:* St Bartholomew's Hosp. (MD). Junior posts, St Bartholomew's, UCH, Middlesex, Mount Vernon and Westminster Hosps, 1968–76; Chef de Clinique, Hôpital Tenon, Paris, 1976; Sen. Lectr and Consultant, Royal Marsden Hosp., 1977–86; Prof. of Radiation Oncology, Glasgow Univ., 1986–2002; Dir, Beatson Oncology Centre, Glasgow, 1987–91. Member: Cttee on Med. Aspects of Radiation in the Envmt, NRPB, 1988–93; Molecular and Cellular Med. Bd, MRC, 1991–94; Nat. Radiotherapy Adv. Gp, 2005–08; Psychosocial Gp, NCRI, 2005–08. Chm., Standing Scottish Cttee, 1992–95, Registrar, 2000–02, Dean, 2002–04, Faculty of Clin. Oncology, RCR; Pres., Scottish Radiological Soc., 1995–97; Pres., Eur. Soc. for Therapeutic Radiation Oncology, 1997–99. Trustee: The Big C Cancer Charity, 2008–11; Assoc. for Cultural Exchange, Cambridge, 2011–; Read Easy UK, 2014–18; Cobalt Health, 2016–18. Founder FMedSci 1998. *Publications:* Practical Radiotherapy Planning, 1985, 4th edn 2009; Cancer in Children, 1986, 5th edn 2005; (ed jtly) Oxford Desk Reference: Oncology, 2011, 2nd edn, 2019. *Recreations:* walking, travel, the Arts, gardening. *Address:* 110 Knightly Avenue, Cambridge CB2 0AL.

**BARRETT, Prof. Anthony Gerard Martin,** FMedSci; FRS 1999; Glaxo Professor of Organic Chemistry, and Director, Wolfson Centre for Organic Chemistry in Medical Science, since 1993, and Sir Derek Barton Professor of Synthetic Chemistry, since 1999, Imperial College London; *b* Exeter, Devon, 2 March 1952; *s* of Claude E. V. Barrett and Margaret Teresa Barrett (*née* Bannon); naturalised US citizen. *Educ:* Imperial Coll. of Science and Technology (BSc 1st Cl. Hons Chemistry 1973; PhD 1975; DIC 1975; SRC Student, 1973–75). Lectr, 1975–82, Sen. Lectr, 1982–83, Imperial Coll. of Science and Technology; Professor of Chemistry: Northwestern Univ., 1983–90; Colorado State Univ., 1990–93. Dir of Chemistry, 1998–2010, Dir of Sci. and Dir, 2000–10, Argenta Discovery (formerly ChemMedICa); Dir, iThemba Pharmaceuticals (S Africa), 2007–13. Fellow, Japan Soc. for Promotion of Science, 1989. Mem., Chemicals Panel, Technology Foresight Prog., Office of Sci. and Technology, 1994. FMedSci 2003. Lectureships: Tilden, RSC, 1994; Backer, Univ. of Groningen, 1996; Glaxo Wellcome, E Carolina Univ., 1998; Organic Divl Interim, Royal Aust. Chem. Inst., 1999; Eaborn-Cornforth, Sussex Univ., 1999; Allelix Dist., Queens Univ., Ont., 1999; Sir Robert Price, CSIRO, 1999; Novo Nordisk, Tech. Univ. of Denmark, 2000; Upper Rhine, 2001; AstraZeneca Pharmaceuticals, Ohio State Univ., 2002; Pattison, Univ. of Western Ont., 2002; Boehringer Ingelheim, Univ. of New Orleans, 2002; Weissberger-Williams, Kodak, NY, 2002; Novartis Chemistry, Basel, 2002; Troisième Cycle, Geneva, Fribourg, Bern and Lausanne, 2002; GlaxoSmithKline and Celltech, Univ. of Bristol, 2003; Pedler, RSC, 2004; Mich Chemistry, 2005; Simonsen, RSC, 2006. Dist. Schol., Hope Coll., Mich, 2003. Meldola Medal, 1980, Harrison Medal, 1982, Corday-Morgan Medal, 1986, Award in Natural Products Chemistry, 2001, RSC; Armstrong Medal, Imperial Coll., 1981; Glaxo Wellcome Award, 2000; Innovation Award, Specialised Organic Sector Assoc., 2000; iAc Award for Applied Catalysis, 2001; Royal Soc. Wolfson Res. Merit Award, 2002; Charles Rees Award, RSC, 2010; (jtly) President's Award for Excellence in Innovation and Entrepreneurship, Imperial Coll. London, 2017. *Address:* Department of Chemistry, Imperial College London, Molecular Sciences Research Hub, White City Campus, Wood Lane, W12 0BZ. *T:* (020) 7594 5766. *E:* agmb@ic.ac.uk.

**BARRETT, Prof. Hazel Rose,** PhD; Professor of Development Geography, since 2006 and Research Professor, Centre for Trust, Peace and Social Relations, since 2016, Coventry University; *b* London, 26 Aug. 1955; *d* of Leslie Peter Edgar Barrett and Hilda May Barrett; partner, Feike Pieter Twijnstra. *Educ:* Plume Comp. Sch., Maldon; Univ. of Sussex (BA Hons Geog. 1976); Univ. of Birmingham (MA W African Studies 1978; PhD Geog./W African Studies 1984); Inst. of Learning and Teaching (Learning and Teaching Cert. 2001). FRGS 1992; CGeog 2009. Lecturer: in Econ. Geog. (pt-time), Garrett's Green Tech. Coll., Birmingham, 1984–85; in Human Geog. (pt-time), Coventry Poly., 1984–85; in Human Geog., Derbyshire Coll. of Higher Educn 1985–92; in Develt Geog. (pt-time), Univ. of Sheffield, 1991–92; Coventry University: Sen. Lectr in Human Geog., 1992–98; Reader in Develt Geog., 1998–2005; Head: Geog. Subject Gp, 2001–04; Geog. and Envmtl Sci. Subject Gp, 2004–05; Geog., Envmtl Sci. and Disaster Mgt, 2005–10; Associate Dean for Applied Res., Faculty of Business, Envmt and Society, 2010–14; Exec. Dir, Centre for Communities and Social Justice, 2014–16. Global Woman Award, Educn, PEACE Foundn, 2018. Geographical Association: Mem., 1991–; Pres., 2013–14; Editor, Geography, 1995–2001. *Publications:* The Marketing of Foodstuffs in The Gambia, 1400–1980: a geographical analysis, 1988; Population Geography, 1992; over 40 papers in academic jls. *Recreations:* gardening, travelling, eating chocolate. *Address:* Centre for Trust, Peace and Social Relations, Coventry University, Priory Street, Coventry CV1 5FB. *T:* (024) 7688 7688. *E:* h.barrett@coventry.ac.uk.

**BARRETT, Dr Jane Margaret,** OBE 2014; FRCP, FRCR; Consultant Oncologist, Royal Berkshire Hospital, Reading, 1991–2013; President, Royal College of Radiologists, 2010–13; Chair, Thames Valley Clinical Senate, since 2014; *b* Pembury, 25 April 1953; *d* of Leonard Sidney Frank Walter and Lilian May Walter (*née* Filson); *m* 1977, Simon Anthony Barrett; two *s* one *d*. *Educ:* Newbury Co. Girls' Grammar Sch.; Bristol Univ. (BSc 1974; MB ChB 1977). FRCR 1988; FRCP 1996; FRCPE 2013. Hse Physician and Hse Surgeon, Bristol, 1977–78; Senior House Officer: Accident and Emergency, 1978–79; Pathol., Bristol, 1979–80; Registrar, Medicine, Royal Berks Hosp., 1980–82; Registrar, then Sen. Registrar (pt-time), Oncol., Oxford rotation, 1982–91; Med. Dir, Thames Valley Cancer Network, 2001–07. Registrar, 2006–08, Dean, 2008–10, Royal Coll. of Radiologists. Hon. FFRRCSI 2010; FAMS (Hon.) 2011; Hon. FRCPE 2013. *Recreations:* travel, ski-ing, walking, cycling, family history. *E:* janembarrett@me.com.

**BARRETT, John;** *b* 11 Feb. 1954; *s* of Andrew Barrett and Elizabeth Mary (*née* Benert); *m* 1975, Carol Pearson; one *d*. *Educ:* Forrester High Sch., Edinburgh; Napier Poly., Edinburgh. Director: ABC Productions, 1985–; Edinburgh Internat. Film Fest., 1995–2001; EDI Group, 1997–99; Edinburgh and Borders Screen Industries, 1997–2001; Edinburgh Film House, 1997–2001. Mem. (Lib Dem) Edinburgh CC, 1995–2001. MP (Lib Dem) Edinburgh W, 2001–10. Lib Dem spokesman on internat. develt, 2003–05. President: Scottish Liberal Club, 2010–15; Edinburgh W Lib Dems, 2013–15. Member: Adv. Council, Edinburgh Internat. Film Fest., 2001–; Microfinance Adv. Bd, RBS, 2009–12. *Recreations:* travel, film, theatre, music (playing and listening).

**BARRETT, Rev. John Charles Allanson;** Headmaster, The Leys School, Cambridge, 1990–2004; Principal, ACS (International), Singapore, 2004–09; Associate Minister, Wesley Methodist Church, Cambridge, 2011–15; *b* 8 June 1943; *s* of Leonard Wilfred Allanson Barrett and Marjorie Joyce Barrett; *m* 1967, Sally Elisabeth Hatley; one *s* one *d*. *Educ:* Culford Sch.; Univ. of Newcastle upon Tyne (BA Hons); Fitzwilliam Coll., Cambridge; Wesley House, Cambridge. MA Cantab. Ordained Methodist Minister. Chaplain and Lectr in Divinity, Westminster Coll., Oxford, 1968–69; Asst Tutor, Wesley Coll., Bristol, 1969–71; Circuit Minister, Hanley Trinity Circuit, Stoke on Trent, and actg Hd of Religious Studies, Birches High Sch., Hanley, 1971–73; Chaplain and Hd of Religious and Gen. Studies, Kingswood Sch., Bath, 1973–83; Headmaster, Kent Coll., Pembury, 1983–90. Mem., HMC Cttee, 1997–98 (Sec.), 1997, Chm., 1998, Eastern Div., HMC; Chm., HMC Working Party on Alcohol and Drug Abuse, 1996–99). World Methodist Council: Mem. Exec. Cttee, 1981–2016 (Vice Chm., 2001–06; Chm., 2006–11; Pres., 2011); Chairman: Educn Cttee, 1991–2001; Prog. Cttee, 1992–96; Brit. Cttee, 1999–2016 (Sec., 1986–97); Mem., Presidium, 1996–2016. Chm., Educn Commn, Methodist Ch, 2010–12; Trustee: Wesley House, Cambridge, 2011–; Methodist Ind. Schools Trust, 2015– (Chair, 2017–); Vice Chm., Trustees, Landmark Internat. Sch., Cambridge, 2019–. Vice-Pres., Internat. Assoc. of Methodist Schs, Colls and Univs, 1998–2006. Bloxham Project: Mem. Steering Cttee, 1986–92; Trustee, 2002–04. Governor: Queenswood Sch., 1997–2004; Kingswood Sch., 2010–17; ACS (Internat.) Singapore, 2010–; Ermine Street Church Acad., 2015–17. FRSA 1996. Hon. DD Florida Southern, 1992. *Publications:* What is a Christian School?, 1981; Family Worship in Theory and Practice, 1983; Methodist Education in Britain, 1990; Methodists and Education: from roots to fulfilment, 2000; (contrib.) Serving God with Heart and Mind, 2001; sections on Methodism in Encyc. Britannica Year Books, 1988–98. *Address:* Tudor Lodge, 151 High Street, Harston, Cambridge CB2 7QD. *T:* (01223) 872842. *E:* jcabarrett@aol.com.

**BARRETT, John Edward,** MBE 2007; tennis commentator and journalist; *b* 17 April 1931; *s* of Alfred Edward Barrett and Margaret Helen Barrett (*née* Walker); *m* 1967, (Florence) Angela (Margaret) Mortimer; one *s* one *d*. *Educ:* University College Sch., Hampstead; St John's Coll., Cambridge (MA History). National Schoolboy champion, 1948. Joined Slazengers as management trainee, 1957; Tournament Dir, 1975; Dir, 1978; Consultant, 1981–95 (latterly Dunlop Slazenger International). Tennis career: RAF champion, 1950, 1951; Captain of Cambridge, 1954; Nat. Indoor Doubles champion (with D. Black), 1953; Asian Doubles champion (with R. Becker), 1956; Davis Cup, 1956–57, non-playing Captain, 1959–62; Dir, LTA Trng Squad (Barrett Boys), 1965–68; qualified LTA coach, 1969; Founded: BP Internat. Tennis Fellowship, 1968–80 (and directed); BP Cup (21-and-under), 1973–80; Pepsi Junior Internat. Series, 1975–79. Financial Times: tennis corresp., 1963–2006; crossword contribs, 1986–. TV tennis commentator: BBC, 1971–2006; Australian networks, 1981–2007; USA, 1985–89. Annual Award, Lawn Tennis Writers' Assoc., 2004; Ron Bookman Media Excellence Award, ATP Tour, 2006. Inducted Internat. Tennis Hall of Fame, 2014. *Publications:* Tennis and Racket Games, 1975; Play Tennis with Rosewall, 1975; 100 Wimbledon Championships: a celebration, 1986; (with Dan Maskell) From Where I Sit, 1988; (with Dan Maskell) Oh, I Say, 1989; Wimbledon: the official history of The Championships, 2001, 4th edn as Wimbledon: the official history, 2014; (jt ed and contrib.) Centre Court: the jewel in Wimbledon's crown, 2009 (Best Illustrated Book, British Sports Book Awards, 2010); Wimbledon: the complete singles draws (1877–2012), 2013; (ed and contrib.) World of Tennis, annually, 1969–2001. *Recreations:* music, theatre, reading, bridge, croquet. *Address:* All England Lawn Tennis Club, Church Road, Wimbledon, SW19 5AE. *Clubs:* All England Lawn Tennis (Vice-Pres.), International Lawn Tennis (Vice-Pres.), Queen's (Hon. Mem.); Surbiton Croquet.

**BARRETT, Lorraine Jayne;** Member (Lab) Cardiff South and Penarth, National Assembly for Wales, 1999–2011; *b* 18 March 1950; *m* 1972, Paul Franklyn Barrett; one *s* one *d*. *Educ:* Porth County Sch. for Girls. Nursing, 1966–70; secretarial work, 1970–74; Personal and Political asst to Alun Michael, MP, 1987–99. Mem. (Lab), Vale of Glamorgan UA, 1995–99. Humanist celebrant. *Recreations:* reading horror and thriller books, walking, cinema.

**BARRETT, Matthew W.,** OC 1995; Chairman, Barclays PLC, 2004–06 (Group Chief Executive, 1999–2004); *b* Co. Kerry, 20 Sept. 1944. *Educ:* Christian Brothers Sch., Kells, Harvard Univ. (AMP 1981). Joined Bank of Montreal, 1962; Chief Operating Officer 1987–89; Chief Exec. Officer, 1989–99; Chm., 1990–99. Director: Harry Winston Diamond Corp., 2008–13; Samuel, Son & Co. Ltd, 2009–.

**BARRETT, Michael Paul,** OBE 1987; Chief Executive Officer, Great Britain Sasakawa Foundation, 2000–06; *b* 30 July 1941; *s* of William James Barrett and Irene (*née* Beynon); *m* 1966, Marie-Thérèse Françoise Juliette Lombard; two *s*. *Educ:* Westminster City Sch. Univ. of Durham (BA Hons Classics). Asst Tutor in English to Overseas Students, Univ. o

Birmingham, 1963–64; British Council: Asst Dir, Port Harcourt, 1964–65; Asst Rep., Addis Ababa, 1966–69; Educnl Television Officer, Tokyo, 1970–72; Dir, Films Dept, 1972–75; Educnl Technologist, Media Dept, 1975–77; Non-Formal Educn Specialist, Nairobi, 1977–80; Dep. Rep., Japan, 1980–84; Cultural Attaché, Washington, 1984–87; Dir, PR, 1987–88; Consultant, Goddard Kay Rogers & Associates Ltd, 1989; Man. Dir, GKR Japan Ltd, 1989–93; Dir, British Council, Japan, 1993–99. Vice-Pres., British Chamber of Commerce in Japan, 1992–99. Non-exec. Dir, S London & Maudsley NHS Trust, 2001–07. Mem. Council, Japan Soc., 2000–06; Mem. Culture Cttee, Asia House, 2001–09; Mem. Mgt Cttee, Sainsbury Inst. for Japanese Art & Culture, 2006–16. Trustee: British Sch. in Tokyo, 1992–99 (Chm., 1992–95); Mosaic Clubhouse Internat., 2013–. FRGS 1989; FRSA 2015. Order of the Rising Sun (Japan), 2006. *Recreations:* music (viola), fishing, sailing, languages. *Address:* 25 Offerton Road, SW4 0DJ; Rosalbert, Roullens 11290, France.
See also P. J. Barrett.

**BARRETT, Nicholas James;** Chief Executive, Outward Bound Trust, since 2006; *b* 3 Sept. 1960; *s* of Sir Stephen Jeremy Barrett, *qv*; *m* 2001, Fiona Lewis; one *s* four *d*. *Educ:* Christ Church, Oxford (BA Mod. Hist.; PGCE). Volunteer, VSO, Bhutan and Kenya, 1983–87; Regl Organiser, ActionAid, 1987–89; Voluntary Service Overseas: Prog. Dir, W Kenya, 1989–91; Head, New Services, 1991–95; Dir, Recruitment, 1995–2000; Chief Exec., Ramblers' Assoc., 2000–05. *Recreations:* climbing small mountains, family, reading. *Address:* Outward Bound Trust, Hackthorpe Hall, Hackthorpe, Penrith, Cumbria CA10 2HX. *Clubs:* Alpine; Ausable (NY).

**BARRETT, Oliver Grant,** MBE 2013; Director, Connector Unit, since 2016; *b* Beckenham, 31 Dec. 1977; *s* of Peter and Karen Barrett; *m* 2009, Verity Watts; one *d*. *Educ:* Bradfield Coll.; Edinburgh Univ.; Leeds Univ. Cast mem., Disney World, 1997; Redcoat, Butlins, 1998; Co-founder: Amazing You, 2000–03; Rainmakers, 2003; Tenner, 2008; Web Mission, 2008; StartUp Britain, 2011; Volunteer It Yourself, 2011; TOTS (Turn on the Subtitles), 2019. Dir, Cospa, 2011–16. *Recreations:* photography, running, travel, theatre, piano. *T:* 07812 835861. *E:* oli@olibarrett.com. *Clubs:* One Alfred Place, The Ivy, Home Grown.

**BARRETT, Paul Michael,** CMG 2001; OBE 1993; Director: Epipharma Ltd, since 2016; Basetrek Ltd, since 2016; non-executive Chairman, Noumed Life Sciences, since 2017; *b* 9 Nov. 1945; *s* of Thomas Barrett and Gladys Barrett (*née* Cook); *m* 1970, Mary Elizabeth Tuthill; one *s* one *d*. *Educ:* Sir Roger Manwood's Sch., Sandwich; Grey Coll., Univ. of Durham (BA Hons Modern Hist. 1967); Templeton Coll., Oxford (AMP 1985). VSO, Starene Boys' Centre, Nairobi, 1968–69; Beecham Gp Ltd, 1969–76: Gen. Manager, Nigeria, 1973–74; Regl Mktg Manager, Africa/Caribbean, 1974–76; Nat. Sales Manager, Servier Labs, 1976–78; Manager, Francophone Africa, Beecham Gp, 1978–89, Smithkline Beecham, 1989–93; Dir and Vice-Pres., Africa, Smithkline Beecham, 1993–2000. Chairman: Medreich plc, 1997–2013; Microsulis plc, 1999–2002; Medreich Ltd, Bangalore, India, 2005–13. Chm., Tropical Africa Adv. Gp, DTI, 1989–2000. Chm., British Francophone Business Gp, 1981–88. Vice-Chm., Harpsden Hall Trust, 2002–; Chm., John Hodges' Trust for Harpsden Hall, 2005–08; Mem. Cttee, 2001–02, Chm., 2002–, S Oxon Mencap; Mem., Major Gifts Cttee, African Med. and Res. Foundn, 2001–03; Chm., Chiltern Centre for Disabled Children Ltd, 2003–. Churchwarden, St Margaret's Ch, Harpsden, 2001–07. *Recreations:* reading, theatre, opera, walking, keep fit. *Address:* 1 Leicester Close, Henley-on-Thames, Oxon RG9 2LD. *T:* (01491) 578051. *E:* paulandmarybarrett@tiscali.co.uk.

**BARRETT, Dr Peter John,** CBE 2006; DL; Chair, Framework, 2016–17; *b* London, 12 Jan. 1947; *s* of William James and Irene Barrett; *m* 1970, Rosamund Briggs; two *s*. *Educ:* Westminster City Grammar Sch.; King's Coll. Hosp., London Univ. (MB BS 1970). MRCS, LRCP 1970. Principal in Gen. Practice, Nottingham, 1975–2006. Chairman: Nottingham Local Med. Cttee, 1990–98; Nottingham HA, 1998–99; Trent Reg. NHS Exec., 1999–2001; NHS Ind. Reconfiguration Panel, 2003–12; Nottingham Univ. Hosps NHS Trust, 2006–13. Chm., Regl Employer Engagement Gp (formerly Regl Employer Adv. Bd), E Midlands RFCA, 2012 (Mem., 2009). Chm., Midlands and E Reg., Eur. Inst. of Governance Awards, 2014–15. DL Notts, 2010. Hon. MD Nottingham, 2014. *Recreations:* playing the 'cello, listening to classical music. *E:* pete@barrett.uk.com.

**BARRETT, Richard Martin Donne,** CMG 2013; OBE 1992; counter-terrorism and violent extremism consultant; pundit; Director, Global Strategy Network, since 2016; Adjunct Professor of Law, Case Western Reserve University, Ohio, since 2014; *b* Taplow, 14 June 1949; *s* of Martin and Joan Barrett; *m* 1st, 1974, Irene Hogg (marr. diss. 2004); two *s* one *d* (and one *s* decd); 2nd, 2008, Lucy Sisman. *Educ:* Ampleforth Coll.; University Coll., Oxford (MA). Served British Govt, incl. in Canada, Turkey, USA and Jordan, 1975–2004; Co-ordinator, Al-Qaida and Taliban Monitoring Team, UN, NY, 2004–13; Sen. Vice-Pres., Special Projects, Soufan Gp, NY, 2014–16. Board Member: Internat. Centre for Counter Terrorism, The Hague, 2014–; Global Center on Cooperative Security, Washington, 2014–; Centre for Res. and Security Studies, Islamabad, 2014–; Inst. for Strategic Dialogue, London, 2017–; Women without Borders, Vienna, 2017–; Neem Foundn, Abuja, 2018–; Hiraal Inst., Mogadishu, 2018–. Mem., Ind. Review Panel, Global Community Engagement and Resilience Fund, Geneva, 2015–; Mem., Internat. Adv. Bd, Hedayah, Abu Dhabi, 2018–. Associate Fellow, RUSI, 2013–; Fellow, New America Foundn, Washington, 2013–. *Publications:* (contrib.) Using Human Rights to Counter Terrorism, 2018; book chapters, reports, papers and articles related to counter terrorism, counter radicalisation and reintegration. *E:* rmdbarrett@gmail.com.

**BARRETT, Prof. Spencer Charles Hilton,** PhD; FRS 2004; FRSC; Professor of Evolutionary Biology (formerly of Botany), 1977, and University Professor, 2008, University of Toronto (Canada Research Chair in Evolutionary Genetics, 2002–14), now Emeritus Professor; *b* 7 June 1948; *s* of Arthur Charles and Doris Barrett; *m* 1973, Suzanne Whittaker; two *s*. *Educ:* Univ. of Reading (BSc Hons (Horticultural Botany) 1971); Univ. of Calif, Berkeley (PhD (Botany) 1977). FRSC 1988. Member, Expert Panel: on Predicting Invasions, Nat. Res. Council, USA, 1999–2001; on Future of Food Biotechnol., RSC, 2000–01. Pres., Canadian Soc. for Ecol. and Evolution, 2010–12; Member: British Ecol Soc.; Soc. for Study of Evolution (Vice Pres. (N America), 2010–12); Botanical Soc. of America; European Evolutionary Biol. Soc. For. Hon. Mem., Amer. Acad. of Arts and Scis, 2009. Ed.-in-Chief, Procs of Royal Soc. Series B, 2015–. Sewall Wright Award, Amer. Soc. of Naturalists, 2008; Flavelle Medal, RSC, 2014. *Publications:* (ed) Evolution and Function of Heterostyly, 1992; (ed) Floral Biology: studies on floral evolution in animal-pollinated plants, 1996; (ed) Ecology and Evolution of Flowers, 2006; (ed) Major Evolutionary Transitions in Flowering Plant Reproduction, 2008; (ed) Invasion Genetics: the Baker and Stebbins legacy, 2017; numerous book chapters and articles in learned jls. *Recreations:* plant exploration, travel, gardening, photography, music of Brian Eno. *Address:* 182 Humbervale Boulevard, Toronto, ON M8Y 3P8, Canada. *T:* (416) 2341871; Department of Ecology and Evolutionary Biology, University of Toronto, 25 Willcocks Street, Toronto, ON M5S 3B2, Canada. *T:* (416) 9784151, *Fax:* (416) 9785878. *E:* spencer.barrett@utoronto.ca.

**BARRETT, Sir Stephen (Jeremy),** KCMG 1991 (CMG 1982); HM Diplomatic Service, retired; Ambassador to Poland, 1988–91; *b* 4 Dec. 1931; *s* of late W. P. Barrett and Dorothy Barrett; *m* 1958, Alison Mary Irvine; three *s*. *Educ:* Westminster Sch.; Christ Church, Oxford (MA). FO, 1955–57; 3rd, later 2nd Sec., Political Office with Middle East Forces, Cyprus, 1957–59; Berlin, 1959–62; 1st Sec., FO, 1962–65; Head of Chancery, Helsinki, 1965–68; 1st Sec., FCO, 1968–72; Counsellor and Head of Chancery, Prague, 1972–74; Head of SW European Dept, FCO, later Principal Private Sec. to Foreign and Commonwealth Sec., 1975; Head of Science and Technology Dept, FCO, 1976–77; Fellow, Center for Internat. Affairs, Harvard, 1977–78; Counsellor, Ankara, 1978–81; Head of British Interests Section, Tehran, 1981; Asst Under-Sec. of State, FCO, 1981–84; Ambassador to Czechoslovakia, 1985–88. *Recreations:* family, reading, moderate exercise. *Address:* 9 Redgrave Court, Patron's Way East, Denham Garden Village, Uxbridge UB9 5NT.
See also N. J. Barrett.

**BARRETT-BAXENDALE, Dr Denise,** MBE 2014; DL; Chief Executive Officer, since 2013, and Director, since 2016, Everton Football Club; Executive Chair, Everton in the Community, since 2016; *b* Merseyside. *Educ:* Manchester Metropolitan Univ. (BA Hons); Liverpool John Moores Univ. (MBA; EdD). Everton Football Club: Chief Exec., 2010; Chief Operating Officer, 2011–13. Mem. Bd, Sport England, 2016–. Dep. Chm., Adv. Bd, Liverpool Commonwealth Games, 2017–. Member: Liverpool Creativity Commn, 2014–; Adv. Bd, Children's Comr, 2016–; Adv. Team, Liverpool Hope Univ., 2016–. Regl Pres. for Girlguiding, 2017–. Mem., Panel of Expert Judges, Stadium Business Awards, Madrid, 2016. FRSA. Fellow: Liverpool Hope Univ. Business Sch., 2014; Angela Hall, Liverpool Hope Univ., 2015–. Hon. Fellow, Liverpool John Moores Univ., 2017. Patron, St Vincent's Sch. for Blind, 2013–. DL Merseyside, 2019. Woman of Year Award, and Special CEO Achievement Award, Downtown Liverpool, 2013; Outstanding Achievement Award, Stadium Business Awards, Barcelona, 2014; Lifetime Role Model Award, Football is More Conference, Switzerland, 2017.

**BARRETT-LENNARD, Sir Peter John,** 7th Bt *cr* 1801, of Belhus, Essex; *b* 26 Sept. 1942; *s* of Roy Barrett-Lennard and Joyce Christine Elizabeth (*née* Drinkwater); S cousin, 2007, but his name does not appear on the Official Roll of the Baronetage; *m* 1979, Sonja (separated), *d* of Vladimir Belačić, Zagreb; one *s*; partner, Phuong Xuan Ho; one *d*. *Heir:* s Simon James Barrett-Lennard, *b* 12 Aug. 1980.

**BARRICK, Jonathan;** Chief Executive Officer, Stroke Association, 2004–16 (Vice President, since 2016); President, Stroke Alliance for Europe, since 2015 (Trustee, 2006–12); *b* 14 Jan. 1954; *s* of Jack William Barrick and Audrey Joan Barrick (*née* Cook); *m* 1988, Susan Skinner; two *d*; partner, Olivia Belle. *Educ:* Davenant Foundn Grammar Sch.; Bath Univ. (BSc Sociol. 1978); Kent Univ.; Middlesex Univ. (PG Dip. Housing 1993); Henley Mgt Coll. (MBA 2002). FCMI. DHSS, 1979–81; Inspector Taxes, 1981–83; London Bor. of Haringey, 1983–89; RNIB, 1989–2004, Dir, Community Services, 1996–2004. Mem. Bd, World Stroke Orgn, 2009– (Chm., World Stroke Campaign, 2016–19). Trustee: Pocklington Trust, 1997–2004; Neurological Alliance, 2004–09, 2011–13; AMRC, 2006–10. Hon. Dr Policy Res. and Practice, Bath, 2017. *Publications:* (jtly) Building Sight, 1995; contribs to jls in vision impairment and inclusive access. *Recreations:* Tottenham Hotspur FC, travel, family interests, studying leadership and strategy issues. *Address:* Stroke Alliance for Europe, c/o Stroke Association House, 240 City Road, EC1V 2PR. *T:* (020) 7566 0300. *E:* Jon.Barrick@stroke.org.uk.

**BARRIE, (Charles) David (Ogilvy),** CBE 2010; campaigner and author; Chairman, Make Justice Work, 2010–13; *b* 9 Nov. 1953; *s* of late Alexander Ogilvy Barrie and Patricia Mary Tucker; *m* 1978, Mary Emily, *d* of Rt Hon. Sir Ralph Gibson, PC; two *d*. *Educ:* Bryanston Sch.; Brasenose Coll., Oxford (Exp. Psych. and Phil.). HM Diplomatic Service, 1975; served FCO 1975–76; Dublin, 1976–80; seconded to Cabinet Office, 1980–81; FCO, 1981–87; transf. Cabinet Office, 1988; seconded to Japan Festival 1991, as Exec. Dir, 1989–92; resigned from Cabinet Office, 1992. Dir, The Art Fund, 1992–2009. Advr, William Morris Gall. redevelt project, 2009–11; Project Advr, Two Temple Place, 2009–13. Bd Mem., MLA (formerly Resource: Council for Mus, Archives, and Libraries), 2000–06 (Mem., Acceptance-in-Lieu Panel, 2000–06). Hon. Res. Fellow, Univ. of Leicester, 2010–; Arthur Batchelor Lectr, UEA, 2010. Companion, Guild of St George, 1992 (Dir, 1992–2004). Trustee: Civitella Ranieri Foundn, 1995–99; Ruskin Foundn, 1996–; Baltic Centre for Contemporary Art, 2014–15; Founder and Chm., Ruskin To-Day, 1999–2016. Trustee: Butterfly Conservation, 2003–07; Pilgrim Trust, 2016–. Mem. Council, Royal Inst. of Navigation, 2015–18. FRIN 2015. Patron, J. M. Barrie Literary Soc., 2018–. *Publications:* (ed) John Ruskin's Modern Painters, 1987, 2nd edn 2000; Sextant: a voyage guided by the stars and the men who mapped the world, 2014; Incredible Journeys: exploring the wonders of animal navigation, 2019; numerous articles and reviews. *Recreations:* sailing (completed Observer Two-handed Round Britain Race, 1972), entomology, celestial navigation. *Address:* 13 Wingate Road, W6 0UR. *E:* cdobarrie@gmail.com. *Clubs:* Arts; Royal Cruising; Emsworth Sailing.

**BARRIE, Lesley;** General Manager and Member, Tayside Health Board, 1993–97, retired; *b* 20 Sept. 1944. *Educ:* Glasgow High Sch. for Girls; Univ. of Glasgow (DPA). MHSM; DipHSM. NHS admin. trainee, 1963–66; hosp. mgt, 1966–77; District General Manager: Inverclyde Dist, 1977–81; Glasgow SE, 1981–83; Dir, Admin Services, Glasgow Royal Infirmary, Royal Maternity Hosp. and Glasgow Dental Hosp., 1983–87; Unit Gen. Manager, Stirling Royal Infirmary, 1987–91; Gen. Manager and Mem., Forth Valley Health Bd, 1991–93. Chm., Social Security Appeal Tribunals, 1978–90; Mem., Industrial Tribunal, 1992–98. Hon. Sen. Lectr, Dept of Epidemiology and Public Health, Dundee Univ., 1994–97. MCMI. *Recreations:* table tennis (Scottish International, 1963–70), badminton, reading.

**BARRIE, Peter Anthony Stanfield; His Honour Judge Barrie;** a Circuit Judge, since 2010; Resident Judge, Shrewsbury Crown Court, since 2014; *b* Oxford, 12 March 1953; *m* 1980, Helen; three *s* one *d*. *Educ:* Kingswood Sch., Bath; New Coll., Oxford. Called to the Bar, Middle Temple, 1976; in practice as barrister, Guildhall Chambers, Bristol, 1976–2010; a Recorder, 1999–2010. *Publications:* Personal Injury Law, 1999, 2nd edn 2005. *Address:* Shrewsbury Crown Court, The Shirehall, Abbey Foregate, Shrewsbury SY2 6LU.

**BARRIE, (Thomas) Scott;** Member (Lab) Dunfermline West, Scottish Parliament, 1999–2007; *b* 10 March 1962; *s* of William Barrie and Helen McBain Barrie (*née* Scott). *Educ:* Auchmuty High Sch., Glenrothes; Edinburgh Univ. (MA Hons 1983); Stirling Univ. (CQSW 1986). Fife Regional Council: Social Worker, 1986–90; Sen. Social Worker, 1990–91; Team Manager, Social Work Dept, 1991–96; Team Leader, Social Work Service, Fife Council, 1996–99. Mem. (Lab), Dunfermline DC, 1988–92. *Recreations:* hill walking, supporter of Dunfermline Athletic.

**BARRINGTON, Sir Benjamin,** 8th Bt *cr* 1831, of Limerick; *b* 23 Jan. 1950; *s* of Major John William Barrington and his 1st wife, Annie, *d* of Florian Wetten; S cousin, 2003, but his name does not appear on the Official Roll of the Baronetage; *m* 1980, Carola Christel Mogck; one *s* one *d*. *Heir:* s Patrick Benjamin Barrington, *b* 5 May 1988. *Address:* 44 Cherovan Drive SW, Calgary, AB T2V 2P2, Canada.

**BARRINGTON, Edward John, (Ted);** Irish Ambassador to the Court of St James's, 1995–2001; *b* 26 July 1949; *s* of Edward Barrington and Sarah Barrington (*née* Byrne); *m* 1972, Clare O'Brien; one *s*. *Educ*: University College Dublin (BA). Entered Irish Diplomatic Service, 1971; 3rd Sec., 1971, 1st Sec., 1973; Perm. Rep. to EEC, 1975–80; 1st Sec., Press and Information, 1980; Counsellor, Political, 1980–85; Assistant Secretary: Admin, 1985–89; EC Div., 1989–91; Political Div. and Political Dir, 1991–95; Dep. Sec., 1995. Vis. Prof., Res. Inst. for Irish and Scottish Studies, Univ. of Aberdeen; Vis. Res. Fellow, Inst. for British-Irish Studies, UC Dublin. DUniv N London. *Recreations*: bird-watching, cinema, hiking, theatre, jazz, gardening. *Address*: Sun Villa, Mauritiustown, Rosslare Strand, Co. Wexford, Ireland. *T*: (53) 9132880.

**BARRINGTON, Jonah,** MBE; Consultant, England Squash (formerly Squash Rackets Association), since 1996; *b* 29 April 1941; *m* 1973, Madeline Ibbotson (*née* Wooller); two *s*. *Educ*: Cheltenham Coll.; Trinity Coll., Dublin. Professional squash rackets player, 1969–83; winner: British Open, 1967–68, 1970–73; Egyptian Open, 1968; Canadian Open, 1983. Coach, English Squash Rackets Team; Dir of Excellence, 1988–93, Pres., 1994, Squash Rackets Assoc. *Publications*: On Squash, 1973; (jtly) Tackle Squash, 1977; Murder in the Squash Court, 1982.

**BARRINGTON, Sir Nicholas (John),** KCMG 1990 (CMG 1982); CVO 1975; HM Diplomatic Service, retired; Ambassador, 1987–89, subsequently High Commissioner, 1989–94, to Pakistan; non-resident Ambassador to Afghanistan, 1994; *b* 23 July 1934; *s* of late Eric Alan Barrington and Mildred (*née* Bill). *Educ*: Repton (Pres., Old Reptonian Soc., 1995–96); Clare Coll., Cambridge (MA 1957; Hon. Fellow 1992). HM Forces, RA, 1952–54. Joined Diplomatic Service, 1957; Tehran (language student), 1958; Oriental Sec., Kabul, 1959; FO, 1961; 2nd Sec., UK Delegn to European Communities, Brussels, 1963; 1st Sec., Rawalpindi, 1965; FO, 1967; Private Sec. to Permanent Under Sec., Commonwealth Office, April 1968; Asst Private Sec. to Foreign and Commonwealth Sec., Oct. 1968; Head of Chancery, Tokyo, 1972–75 (promoted Counsellor and for a period apptd Chargé d'Affaires, Hanoi, 1973); Head of Guidance and Information Policy (subsequently Information Policy) Dept, FCO, 1976–78; Counsellor, Cairo, 1978–81; Minister and Head of British Interests Section, Tehran, 1981–83; Supernumerary Ambassador attached to UK Mission to UN, NY, for Gen. Assembly, autumn 1983; Co-ordinator for London Econ. Summit, 1984; Asst Under-Sec. of State (Public Depts), FCO, 1984–87. Chm., Management Cttee, Southwold Summer Theatre, 1995–2001; Co-Pres., Clare Coll. Develt Prog., 1995–2002; Member: Develt Cttee, Cambridge Univ. Divinity Faculty, 1994–97; Standing Cttee on Schs and Insts, British Acad., 1995–96; Special Projs Cttee, Sadler's Wells Th., 1996–2001; Friends of New River Walk, Islington, 1995–2002; Cttee to restore spire of St Stephen's Ch, Canonbury, 1998–2002. Member: Exec. Cttee, Asia Review, 1994–2000 (originator and Exhibn Comr, 50 Years of Painting and Sculpture in Pakistan, Brunei Gall., 2000); Pakistan Soc., 1995–2002 (acting Chm., 2001; Hon. Vice Pres., 2002–); Council: Royal Soc. for Asian Affairs, 1995–2000; British Inst. of Persian Studies, 1996–2001 (Mem., Adv. Council, 2002–09); British Assoc. for Cemeteries in S Asia, 1996–2014. Trustee: Ancient India and Iran Trust, 1993–; British Empire and Commonwealth Mus., Bristol, 1996–2013 (first Pres. of Friends, 1996–2002); Patron, Hindu Kush Conservation Assoc., 1995–2000. Principal Organiser, Symposium on history of Lahore and preservation of its historic buildings, Cambridge, 2017. Mem., Order of St Etheldreda, Ely Cathedral, 1996–. FRSA 1984. 3rd Cl., Order of the Sacred Treasure, Japan, 1975. *Publications*: (foreword and asst ed.) Old Roads, new Highways: 50 years of Pakistan, 1997; (jtly) A Passage to Nuristan, 2005; Envoy, 2013; Nicholas meets Barrington, 2013; Summary of life of Henry Fawcett, the blind Postmaster General, 2018. *Recreations*: theatre, drawing, prosopography, Persian poetry, pentominoes, pingminton. *Address*: 2 Banhams Close, Cambridge CB4 1HX. *T*: (01223) 360802. *Clubs*: Athenæum, Nikaean.

**BARRINGTON, Ted;** *see* Barrington, E. J.

**BARRINGTON BROWN, Amanda Margaret;** *see* Tincknell, A. M.

**BARRINGTON-WARD, Rt Rev. Simon,** KCMG 2001; Bishop of Coventry, 1985–97; Hon. Assistant Bishop, Diocese of Ely, since 1998; Prelate of the Most Distinguished Order of St Michael and St George, 1989–2005; *b* 27 May 1930; *s* of Robert McGowan Barrington-Ward and Margaret Adele Barrington-Ward; *m* 1963, Jean Caverhill Taylor; two *d*. *Educ*: Eton; Magdalene Coll., Cambridge (MA; Hon. Fellow, 1987). Lektor, Free Univ., Berlin, 1953–54; Westcott House, Cambridge, 1954–56; Chaplain, Magdalene Coll., Cambridge, 1956–60; Asst Lectr in Religious Studies, Univ. of Ibadan, 1960–63; Fellow and Dean of Chapel, Magdalene Coll., Cambridge, 1963–69; Principal, Crowther Hall, Selly Oak Colls, Birmingham, 1969–74; Gen. Sec., CMS, 1975–85; Hon. Canon of Derby Cathedral, 1975–85; a Chaplain to the Queen, 1984–85. Chairman: Partnership for World Mission, 1987–91; Internat. Affairs Cttee, Bd for Social Responsibility of Gen. Synod, 1986–96. Pres., St John's Coll., Nottingham, 1987–2000. FRAI. Hon. DD Wycliffe Coll., Toronto, 1984; Hon. DLitt Warwick, 1998. *Publications*: CMS Newsletter, 1975–85; Love Will Out (anthology of news letters), 1988; Why God?, 1993; The Jesus Prayer, 1996, rev. edn 2007; (jtly) Praying the Jesus Prayer Together, 2001; The Jesus Prayer and the Great Exchange, 2013; *contributor to*: Christianity in Independent Africa (ed Fasholé Luke and others), 1978; Today's Anglican Worship (ed C. Buchanan), 1980; Renewal—An Emerging Pattern, by Graham Pulkingham and others, 1980; A New Dictionary of Christian Theology (ed Alan Richardson and John Bowden), 1983; Christianity Today, 1988; The World's Religions, 1988; The Weight of Glory (ed D. W. Hardy and P. H. Sedgwick), 1991. *Address*: Magdalene College, Cambridge CB3 0AG.

**BARRON, Prof. Caroline Mary,** OBE 2019; PhD; FRHistS, FSA; Professor of the History of London, 2000–05 and Dean of the Graduate School, 1999–2003, Royal Holloway, University of London (Hon. Fellow, 2014); *b* 7 Dec. 1939; *d* of late William David Hogarth, OBE and Grace Allen Hogarth; *m* 1962, Prof. John Penrose Barron (*d* 2008); two *d*. *Educ*: North London Collegiate Sch.; Somerville Coll., Oxford (Exhibnr; MA Mod. Hist. 1966; Hon. Fellow, 2011); Westfield Coll., London (PhD 1970). Bedford College, subseq. Royal Holloway and Bedford New College, University of London: Asst Lectr, 1967, Lectr, 1968–83, Sen. Lectr, 1983–91, in Hist.; Dean, Faculty of Arts, 1983–85; Reader in Hist. of London, 1991–99. Reader, British Academy, 1988–90. Member: Cttee, Victoria County Hist., 1970–95; Council, London Record Soc., 1973–76, 1996– (Chm., 2005–); Royal Commn on Historical Manuscripts, 1999–2003; Adv. Council on Nat. Records and Archives, 2003–05. Mem. Council, GPDST, 1979–94 (Chm. Educn Cttee, 1992–94); Chm. Govs, Wimbledon High Sch., 1985–88; Gov., NLCS, 1985–91. Trustee, St Peter's Coll., Oxford, 2010–. President: Assoc. of Senior Mems, Somerville Coll., 1994–99; British Assoc. for Local History, 2016–; Chm. Friends, PRO, 1999–2002. Mem. Editorial Bd, Hist. of Parliament, 1988–2007. FRHistS (Mem. Council, 1989–94). Corresp. Fellow, Medieval Acad. of America, 2007. *Publications*: (ed and contrib.) The Reign of Richard II, 1971; The Medieval Guildhall of London, 1974; The Parish of St Andrew Holborn, 1979; Revolt in London 11th to 15th June 1381, 1981; (ed and contrib.) The Church in the Century before the Reformation, 1985; Hugh Alley's Caveat: markets of London in 1598, 1988; (ed and contrib.) Widows of Medieval London, 1994; (ed and contrib.) England and the Low Countries in the Late Middle Ages, 1995; (ed and contrib.) The Church and Learning in Later Medieval Society, 2001; London in the Later Middle Ages: government and people, 2004; *contributions to*: British Atlas of Historic Towns, 1990; New Cambridge Medieval History, 1999; Cambridge Urban History of England, 2000; St Paul's, the Cathedral Church of London, 2004; contrib. Oxford DNB. *Recreations*: travel, people. *Address*: Alhambra Cottage, 9 Boundary Road, NW8 0HE. *Club*: University Women's.

**BARRON, Derek Donald;** Chairman and Chief Executive, Ford Motor Co. Ltd, 1986–91; Chairman, Ford Motor Credit Co., 1986–91; *b* 7 June 1929; *s* of Donald Frederick James Barron and Hettie Barbara Barron; *m* 1963, Rosemary Ingrid Brian; two *s*. *Educ*: Beckenham Grammar School; University College London. Joined Ford Motor Co. Sales, 1951; Tractor Group, 1961; Tractor Manager, Ford Italiana 1963; Marketing Associate, Ford Motor Co. USA, 1970; Gen. Sales Manager, Overseas Markets, 1971; Man. Dir, Ford Italiana, 1973; Group Dir, Southern European Sales, Ford of Europe, 1977; Sales and Marketing Dir, Ford Brazil, 1979; Vice-Pres., Ford Motor de Venezuela, 1982; Dir-Vice-Pres., Operations, Ford Brazil, 1985. DUniv Essex, 1989.

**BARRON, Iann Marchant,** CBE 1994; Chairman, Division Group plc, 1990–99; *b* 16 June 1936; *s* of William Barron; *m* 1962, Jacqueline Almond (marr. diss. 1989); two *s* two *d*; one *s*. *Educ*: University College School; Christ's College, Cambridge (exhibitioner; MA). Elliott Automation, 1961–65; Managing Director: Computer Technology Ltd, 1965–72; Microcomputer Analysis Ltd, 1973–78; Exec. Dir, 1978–89, Chief Strategic Officer, 1984–89, INMOS International; Man. Dir, INMOS, 1981–88. Vis. Prof., Westfield Coll., London, 1976–78; Vis. Indust. Prof., Bristol Univ., 1985–; Vis. Fellow, QMC, 1976; Science Policy Res. Unit, 1977–78. Exec. Trustee, The Exploratory, 1992–98; Dir, Bristol 2000, 1995–2000. Mem. Council, UCS, 1983–2002. Distinguished FBCS, 1986. FIET (FIEE 1994). Hon. DSc: Bristol Polytechnic, 1988; Hull, 1989. R. W. Mitchell Medal, 1983; J. J. Thompson Medal, IEE, 1986; IEE Achievement Medal for computing and control, 1996. *Publications*: The Future with Microelectronics (with Ray Curnow), 1977; technical papers. *Address*: Barrow Court, Barrow Gurney, Somerset BS48 3RP.

**BARRON, Rt Hon. Sir Kevin (John);** Kt 2014; PC 2001; MP (Lab) Rother Valley, since 1983; *b* 26 Oct. 1946; *s* of Richard Barron; *m* 1969 (*d* 2008); one *s* two *d*. *Educ*: Maltby Hall Secondary Modern Sch.; Ruskin Coll., Oxford. NCB, 1962–83. PPS to Leader of the Opposition, 1985–87; Opposition spokesman on energy, 1988–92, on employment, 1993–95, on health, 1995–97. Member: Select Cttee on Energy, 1983–85; Select Cttee on Environmental Affairs, 1992–93; Parly Intelligence and Security Cttee, 1997–2005; Liaison Cttee, 2005–18; Chairman: Select Cttee on Health, 2005–10; Standards and Privileges Cttee, 2010–18 (Mem., 2005–10). Chm., Yorkshire Labour MPs, 1987–. Pres., Rotherham and Dist TUC, 1982–83. Trustee and Dir, Nat. Coal Mining Mus. for England. Vice Pres., RSPH (formerly RSH, then RIPH), 2007–. Hon. FRCP 2008. *Address*: House of Commons, SW1A 0AA.

**BARRON, Prof. Laurence David,** DPhil; FRS 2005; FRSE; FInstP, FRSC; Gardiner Professor of Chemistry, University of Glasgow, 1998–2008, now Emeritus; *b* 12 Feb. 1944; *s* of Edward Landon Barron and Stella Barron (*née* Gertz); *m* 1969, Sharon Aviva Wolf; one *s* one *d*. *Educ*: King Edward VI Grammar Sch., Southampton; Northern Poly. (BSc); Lincoln Coll., Oxford (DPhil 1969). FInstP 2005; FRSC 2005. Chemistry Department, University of Cambridge: SRC Fellow, 1969; Res. Asst, 1971; Ramsay Meml Fellow, 1974; University of Glasgow: Lectr in Physical Chem., 1975–80; Reader, 1980–84; Prof. of Physical Chem., 1984–98; EPSRC Sen. Fellow, 1995–2000. Vis. Miller Res. Prof., Univ. of Calif, Berkeley, 1995; Vis. Prof., Univ. Paul Sabatier, Toulouse, 2003; Tetelman Vis. Fellow, Jonathan Edwards Coll., Yale Univ., 2008. Lectures: Schmidt Meml, Weizmann Inst., Israel, 1984; Conover Meml, Vanderbilt Univ., USA, 1987; Schechter Meml, Bar Ilan Univ., Israel, 2012; Zhang Dayu Meml, Dalian Inst. of Chemical Physics, Chinese Acad. of Scis, 2012; Guest Review, Assoc. of Physicians of GB and Ireland, 1997; Chem. Soc. of Zürich, 1998. FRSE 1992. Corday-Morgan Medal and Prize, Chem. Soc., 1977; Sir Harold Thompson Award for Molecular Spectroscopy, 1992; Chirality Medal, Societa Chimica Italiana, 2011; Philip J. Stephens Award for Vibrational Optical Activity, 2016. *Publications*: Molecular Light Scattering and Optical Activity, 1982, 2nd edn 2004; contrib. res. papers to chemistry, physics and life sci. jls. *Recreations*: walking, listening to music (classical and jazz), water-colour painting, building and flying radio control model aircraft.

**BARRON, Prof. Nicholas Ian S.;** *see* Shepherd-Barron.

**BARRON, Peter Scott;** Vice President, Communications and Public Affairs, Europe, Middle East and Africa, Google, 2015–18; *b* Belfast, 16 Oct. 1962; *s* of Wilson and Greta Barron; *m* 1996, Julia Stroud; two *s* one *d*. *Educ*: Royal Belfast Academical Instn; Univ. of Manchester Inst. of Sci. and Technol. (BSc Hons Eur. Studies and Mod. Langs). Ed., Algarve News, 1987–88; news trainee, BBC News, 1988–90; Producer, BBC Newsnight, 1990–97; Deputy Editor: Channel 4 News, 1997–2002; Tonight with Trevor McDonald, 2002–03; Editor: If…, BBC Current Affairs, 2003–04; Newsnight, BBC, 2004–08; Google: Hd, Communications and Public Affairs, UK, Ireland and Benelux, 2008–09, N and Central Europe, 2009–11; Dir, Ext. Relns, EMEA, 2011–13; Dir, Communications and Public Affairs, EMEA, 2013–15. Adv. Chm., Edinburgh TV Fest., 2007. *Recreations*: playing the guitar, collecting records, spending time in Spain.

**BARRON, Maj.-Gen. Richard Edward,** CB 1993; *b* 22 Nov. 1940; *s* of John Barron and Lorna Frances Barron; *m* 1968, Margaret Ann Eggar; one *s* one *d*. *Educ*: Oundle; RMA. Commissioned Queen's Royal Irish Hussars, 1962; Staff College, 1973; DAA&QMG 7th Armoured Brigade, 1974–76; Instructor, Staff Coll., 1978–81; CO, QRIH, 1981–84; Comdr, 7th Armoured Brigade, 1984–86; RCDS 1987; QMG's Staff, 1988–89; Dir, RAC, 1989–92. Col, Queen's Royal Hussars, 1993–99. *Recreations*: reading, gardening, fishing. *Address*: Willow House, Whistley Road, Potterne, Wilts SN10 5TD. *Club*: Cavalry and Guards.

**BARRON, Roger Paul;** Partner, Paul Hastings (Europe) LLP, since 2018; *b* Rotherham, 29 March 1969; *s* of Michael Barron and Monica Barron; *m* 1995, Clare Osborough; two *s* one *d*. *Educ*: New Coll., Oxford (BA Juris. 1990; MA); Coll. of Law, Chester. Admitted solicitor, 1993; Linklaters LLP: articled clerk, 1991–93; Associate, 1993–2001; Partner, 2001–18. Mem., Develt Cttee, ROH, 2010–; Director and Trustee: Mayor's Music Fund, 2011–15; LPO, 2016–. *Recreations*: music, theatre, playing tennis and golf, watching football and Rugby. *Address*: Paul Hastings (Europe) LLP, 10 Bishops Square, E1 6EG. *T*: (020) 3023 5100. *Clubs*: Roehampton; Thurlestone Golf.

**BARRON, Tanya, (Mrs Gregory Knowles),** OBE 2016; Chief Executive Officer, Plan International UK, 2013–19; *b* London, 18 March 1954; *d* of Donald and Edna Barron; *m* 2000, Gregory Knowles; one *s* one *d*. *Educ*: Dartington Hall Sch.; Poly. of Central London (BA Hons 1985). Dairy worker, 1972–76; Zool Soc. of London, 1976–82; Lectr in Pol Philosophy, Open Univ., 1986–89; Prog. Manager, VSO, 1989–96; Hd of Progs, Eur Children's Trust, 1996–99; CEO, Home Start Internat., 1999–2004; Internat. Dir, Leonard Cheshire, 2004–13. Chair, UNICEF NGO Cttee for Central and E European States/CIS 1993–99. Non-exec. Dir, Herts Partnership NHS Foundn Trust. Chair, Affinity Trust

2019–. Hon Dr Health Scis York St John, 2009. *Publications:* Disability and Inclusive Development, 2007; Poverty and Disability, 2010. *Recreations:* wine-making, grandchildren. *Address:* 135 Whitehall Court, SW1A 2EP. *Club:* Farmers.

**BARRONS, John Lawson;** Director: Century Newspapers Ltd, Belfast, 1989–98 (Chief Executive, 1989–97); Praxis Care Ltd, Belfast, since 2011; *b* 10 Oct. 1932; *s* of late William Cowper Barrons, MBE and Amy Marie Barrons (*née* Lawson); *m* 1st, 1957, Caroline Anne (marr. diss. 1986), *d* of late George Edward Foster; three *s*; 2nd, 1987, Lauren Ruth, *d* of late Robert Z. Friedman. *Educ:* Caterham Sch. Nat. Service, 1st Bn Northamptonshire Regt, 1952–54. Journalist, UK and USA, 1950–57; Gen. Manager, Nuneaton Observer, 1957; Managing Editor, Northampton Chronicle & Echo, 1959; Gen. Manager, Edinburgh Evening News, 1961; Gen. Manager, 1965–76, Man. Dir, 1976–85, Westminster Press. Director: Pearson Longman, 1979–83; Stephen Austin Newspapers, 1986–91; Northern Press, 1986–91; Lincolnshire Standard Gp plc, 1987–88; President: Westminster (Florida) Inc., 1980–85; Westminster (Jacksonville) Inc., 1982–85. Dir, Evening Newspaper Advertising Bureau, 1978–81 (Chm. 1979–80); Dir, The Press Association Ltd, 1985–86; Chm., Printing Industry Res. Assoc., 1983–85 (Mem. Council, 1978, a Vice-Chm., 1979–83); Mem. Bd of Management, Internat. Electronic Publishing Res. Centre, 1981–85. Member, Council: Newspaper Soc., 1975–87 (Pres., 1981–82; Hon. Vice-Pres., 1983–); CPU, 1970–86. Director: BITC, NI, 1994–2006; City West Action Ltd, Belfast, 1995–2008. *Recreations:* walking, watching wolfhounds, reading. *Address:* 8 Harberton Avenue, Belfast BT9 6PH. *Clubs:* Flyfishers', MCC.

*See also Gen. Sir R. L. Barrons.*

**BARRONS, Gen. Sir Richard (Lawson),** KCB 2013; CBE 2003 (OBE 1999; MBE 1993); Managing Partner, Wychwood LLP, since 2017; Co-Chairman, Universal Defence and Security Solutions, since 2019; Commander Joint Forces Command, 2013–16; Aide-de-Camp General to the Queen, 2013–16; *b* Northampton, 17 May 1959; *s* of John Lawson Barrons, *qv*; *m* 1988, Cherry Louise Dedow; two *d*. *Educ:* Merchant Taylors' Sch., Northwood; Queen's Coll., Oxford (BA; Hon. Fellow 2013); Cranfield Inst. of Technol. (MDA). Psc 1991; COS, 11 Armd Bde, 1992–93; Battery Comdr, B Battery, RHA, 1994–96; MA to CGS, 1997–99; CO, 3rd Regt, RHA, 1999–2001; COS 3(UK) Div., 2002–03; HCSC(J) 2003; Comdr, 39 Infantry Bde, 2004–06; ACOS Commitments, HQ Land, 2006–07; Dep. Comdg Gen. Multinat. Corps (Iraq), 2008–09; COS, HQ ARRC, 2009; Dir, Force Reintegration, HQ ISAF - Afghanistan, 2009–10; Asst Chief of Gen. Staff, 2010–11; DCDS (Military Strategy and Ops), 2011–13. Hon. Col, 3rd Regt RHA, 2013–16; Pres. and Col Comdt, HAC, 2013–19. Dist. Fellow (formerly Sen. Associate Fellow), RUSI, 2016–; Sen. Vis. Fellow, LSE IDEAS, 2017–18. Chm., RA Mus. Ltd, 2009–13; Comr, Royal Hosp. Chelsea, 2010–11. Hon. DSc Cranfield, 2014. QCVS 2004 and 2006. Officer, Legion of Merit (USA), 2009. *Publications:* (with Deborah Tom) The Business General, 2006. *Recreations:* ski-ing, cycling, gardening, military history, finding world-beating cappuccino in glorious surroundings. *Address:* c/o Military Secretary, Army Personnel Centre, Kentigern House, 65 Brown Street, Glasgow G2 8EX. *E:* richardbarrons825@gmail.com. *Clubs:* Army and Navy; Victory Services.

**BARROS MELET, Cristián;** Permanent Representative of Chile to the United Nations, 2014–18; Ambassador (non-resident) of Chile to the Islamic Republic of Iran, 2014; *b* 19 Oct. 1952; *s* of Diego Barros and Tencha Melet; *m* 1976, Mary Florence Michell Nielsen; one *s*. *Educ:* St Gabriel's Sch.; Sagrados Corazones Padres Franceses; Sch. of Law, Univ. of Chile; Diplomatic Acad. Andrés Bello; Catholic Univ., Santiago. Entered Diplomatic Service, Consular Div., Chile, 1974; Legal Dept, 1975–78; Protocol Dept, 1978; Admin. Dept, 1978–79; Consul: Mendoza, Argentina, 1979; Bariloche, Argentina, 1980–83; Bilateral Policy Dept, America Div., 1983–85; Consul and Consul Gen., Chicago, 1985–88; First Sec., Canada, 1989–90; Hd of Cabinet for Dir Gen. of Foreign Policy, 1990; Dir of Personnel, 1990–91; Ambassador, Dir Gen., Admin. Dept, 1991–93; Ambassador to Denmark, 1993–96; Dir Gen., Admin. Dept, 1996–98; Dir Gen., Foreign Policy, 1998–99; Ambassador to UK, 2000–02; Vice Minister of Foreign Affairs, 2002–06; Ambassador: to Peru, 2006–08; to Italy, 2008–10; to India, 2010–14. Grand Cross: Order of Merit (Portugal), 1993; Order of Dannebrog (Denmark), 1996; Order of May (Argentina), 1998; Order of El Sol (Peru), 1999; Grand Order, Order of Merit (Brazil), 1999. *Address:* Ministry of Foreign Affairs, Teatinos 180, Santiago, Chile.

**BARROSO, José Manuel D.;** *see* Durão Barroso.

**BARROW, Sir Anthony (John Grenfell),** 7th Bt *cr* 1835, of Ulverston, Lancashire; Senior Risk Officer, International Labour Organization, since 2016; *b* London, 24 May 1962; *o s* of Captain Sir Richard John Uniacke Barrow, 6th Bt and Alison Kate (*née* Grenfell); *S* father, 2009; *m* 1st, 1990, Rebecca Mary Long (marr. diss. 1996); 2nd, 2001, Elisa Isabel Marzo Pérez; one *d*; and one *d*. *Educ:* Edinburgh Univ. (MA Classics 1985). CPFA 1993; Cert. Internat. Risk Mgt, Inst. of Risk Mgt, 2011. Nat. Insce Inspector, DHSS, 1986–88; National Audit Office: Asst Auditor, 1988–91; Auditor, 1991–93; Sen. Auditor, 1993–2000; seconded to Cour des Comptes as Rapporteur, 1998–99; Food and Agriculture Organisation of the UN: Internal Auditor, 2000–02; Regl Auditor, 2002–10; Sen. Auditor, 2010–11; Sen. Planning and Budget Officer, 2011–16. *Publications:* nine published reports to UK and French Parlts. *Heir: cousin* John Lendon Barrow [*b* 1934; *m* 1961, Maureen Ann, *d* of Alfred Stanley Gover; one *s* one *d*].

**BARROW, Colin,** CBE 2004; Chairman, Alpha Strategic plc, 2005–14; *b* 18 June 1952; *s* of Reginald Barrow and Margaret (*née* Jones); *m* 1994, Angelica Bortis (marr. diss. 2007); two *s*; *m* 2009, Ana Smaldon. *Educ:* Dulwich Coll.; Clare Coll., Cambridge (BA Moral Scis and Law 1974; MA). John Brown Gp, 1974–83; Man. Dir, Funds Mgt Div., ED&F Man, 1983–96; Chm., Sabre Fund Mgt, 1996–2005. Member (C): Suffolk CC, 1997–2002; Westminster CC, 2002–12 (Dep. Leader, 2005–08; Leader, 2008–12). Exec. Mem. for Health, London Councils, 2009–12; Member: Mayor of London's Commn on Health, 2013–14; Expert Adv. Bd, Imperial Coll. Health Partners, 2013–17. Chm., Central London Forward, 2009–10. Chm., Improvement and Develt Agency for Local Govt, 2000–04. DCI Fellow, Stanford Univ., 2018–19. Director: Rambert Dance Co., 1997–2003; Policy Exchange, 2002–05. Chm., Nat. Autistic Soc., 2005–11 (Treas., 2004). Vice Chm., Bd of Cllrs, Sol Price Sch. of Public Policy, USC, 2016– (Mem. Council, 2014–; Sen. Fellow, 2019–). CEDR Qualified Mediator, 2014–. *Recreations:* inexpert skier, scuba diver, bridge player. *T:* (020) 3286 7713. *E:* colin.barrow1@gmail.com.

**BARROW, Jill Helen;** Director, Big Blue Experience, since 2006; *b* 26 April 1951; *d* of Philip Eric Horwood and Mavis Mary (*née* Handscombe); *m* (marr. diss.); two *d*. *Educ:* Durham Univ. (Cert Ed 1972; MA Ed 1983); Open Univ. (BA 1980). Teaching in secondary, special and further educn, 1972–86; educn mgt and inspection, 1986–90; Dep. Dir of Educn, Essex CC, 1990–93; Dir of Educn, Surrey CC, 1993–95; Chief Exec., Lincs CC, 1995–98; Chief Exec., SW of England RDA, 1999–2001; Bd Mem. for England, New Ops Fund, 1999–2004; Dir, Consultancy and Develt, GatenbySanderson, 2004–06. *Recreations:* walking, outdoor activities, travelling, reading.

**BARROW, Dame Jocelyn (Anita),** DBE 1992 (OBE 1972); Development Director, Focus Consultancy Ltd, 1996–2002; Deputy Chairman, Broadcasting Standards Council, 1989–95; *b* 15 April 1929; *d* of Charles Newton Barrow and Olive Irene Barrow (*née* Pierre); *m* 1970, Henderson Downer. *Educ:* Univ. of London. Mem., Taylor Cttee on School Governors; Gen. Sec., later Vice-Chm., Campaign Against Racial Discrimination, 1964–69; Vice-Chm., Internat. Human Rights Year Cttee, 1968; Member: CRC, 1968–72; Parole Bd, 1983–87. A Governor, BBC, 1981–88. Chairman: Ind. Cttee of Mgt, Optical Consumer Complaints Service, 1992–; Independent Equal Opportunities Inquiry into Ethnicity and Trng and Assessment on Bar Vocational Course, 1993–94; Non-exec. Dir, Whittington Hosp. NHS Trust, 1993–99. Mem., Econ. and Social Cttee, EC, 1990–98. Nat. Vice-Pres., Nat. Towns-women's Guilds, 1978–80, 1987–; Pres. and Founder, Community Housing Assoc.; Governor: Farnham Castle, 1977–93; BFI, 1991–97. Patron: Blackliners, 1989–; Unifem UK, 1998. FRSA. Hon. DLitt E London, 1992. *Recreations:* theatre, music, cooking, reading. *Address:* c/o Focus Consultancy Ltd, 38 Grosvenor Gardens, SW1W 0EB. *Club:* Reform.

**BARROW, Prof. John David,** DPhil; FRS 2003; FRAS; CPhys, FInstP; Professor of Mathematical Sciences, Department of Applied Mathematics and Theoretical Physics, University of Cambridge, since 1999; Fellow, since 1999, and Dean, since 2017, Clare Hall, Cambridge (Vice President, 2004–07); Director, Millennium Mathematics Project, Cambridge, since 1999; *b* 29 Nov. 1952; *s* of Walter Henry Barrow and Lois Miriam Barrow (*née* Tucker); *m* 1975, Elizabeth Mary East; two *s* one *d*. *Educ:* Van Mildert Coll., Durham Univ. (BSc Hons 1974); Magdalen Coll., Oxford (DPhil Astrophysics 1977). FRAS 1981; CPhys 1998; FInstP 1998. Res. Lectr, Christ Church and Dept of Astrophysics, Oxford Univ., 1977–80; Lindemann Fellow, Dept of Astronomy, 1977–78, Miller Fellow, Dept of Physics, 1980–81, Univ. of Calif, Berkeley; Astronomy Centre, University of Sussex: Lectr, 1981–88; Sen. Lectr, 1988–89; Prof., 1989–99; Dir, 1989–90 and 1995–99. Gordon Godfrey Vis. Prof., Univ. of NSW, Sydney, 1998, 2000, 2003. Gresham College: Gresham Prof. of Astronomy, 2003–07, now Emeritus; Gresham Prof. of Geometry, 2008–12; Fellow, 2012–15; Hon. Fellow, 2018. Hon. Prof., Nanjing Univ., 2005. Lectures: Centenary Gifford, Glasgow, 1989; Scott, Leuven, 1989; Collingwood, Durham, 1990; George Darwin, London, 1992; Spinoza, Amsterdam, 1993; Spreadbury, London, 1994; Benedum, Va, 1997; Kelvin, Glasgow, 1999; Flamsteed, Derby, 2000; Tyndall, Bristol, 2001; Whitrow, London, 2002; Brasher, Kingston, 2002; Newton, Grantham, 2003; Gresham, London, 2003; Hubert James, Purdue, 2004; Carl Von Weizsäcker, Hamburg, 2004; McCrea Centenary, Sussex, 2004; Wood, Newcastle, 2005; Hamilton, Dublin, 2005; Boyle, St Mary-le-Bow, 2007; Roscoe, Liverpool, 2007; Borderlands, Durham, 2007; Källen, Lund, 2007; Si-Wei, Taiwan, 2008; Sciama, Oxford and Trieste, 2008; Phillips, Cardiff, 2008; Sir Henry Tizard, Westminster Sch., 2010; William Herschel, Bath, 2010; Van Mildert Trust, Van Mildert Coll., Durham, 2010; Anile Meml, Catania, 2011; Gregynog, Aberystwyth, 2011; Centenary, Real Sociedad Matemática Española, Paraninfo, Zaragoza, 2011; McCrea, RIA, Cork, 2013; Internat. Maths Olympiad, Cape Town, 2014; Enriques, Milan, 2014; British Soc. for the History of Maths, Gresham Coll., 2017; Jeremiah Horrocks, Lancs, 2019. Mem., Internat. Soc. for Sci. and Religion, 2002; Titular Mem., Acad. Internat. de Philosophie des Scis, 2009. Pres., Phys. and Astronomy Sect., BAAS, 2008–09; Pres., Maths Sect., BSA, 2011–12. MAE 2009. Forum Fellow, World Econ. Forum, 1999–2000. FRSA 1999. Hon. Fellow, Internat. Soc. for Sci. and Religion, 2017. Hon. DSc: Herts, 1999; Szczecin, 2007; Durham, 2008; Sussex, 2010; S Wales, 2014. Locker Prize, Birmingham Univ., 1989; Kelvin Medal, Royal Glasgow Philosophical Soc., 1999; Lacchini Medal, Union Astrofili Italiani, 2005; Templeton Prize, Templeton Foundn, 2006; Queen's Anniversary Prize, 2006; Faraday Prize, Royal Society, 2008; Kelvin Medal, Inst. of Physics, 2009; Gresham Prize, Gresham Coll., 2009; Colletti Sci. Prize, Colletti Foundn, 2010; Merck-Serono Prize for Sci. and Lit., Merck-Serono, Rome, 2011; Christopher Zeeman Medal, LMS and IMA, 2011; Dirac Gold Medal, Inst. of Physics, 2015; Gold Medal, RAS, 2016. *Publications:* The Left Hand of Creation, 1983, 2nd edn 1995; L'Homme et le Cosmos, 1984; The Anthropic Cosmological Principle, 1986, 2nd edn 1996; The World Within the World, 1988, 2nd edn 1995; Theories of Everything, 1991, 2nd edn 1994; Pi in the Sky, 1992, 2nd edn 1994; Perché il Mondo è Matematico?, 1992, 2nd edn 2001; The Origin of the Universe, 1993, 2nd edn 2001; The Artful Universe, 1995, 2nd edn 1997; Impossibility, 1998, 2nd edn 2000; Between Inner Space and Outer Space, 1999; The Universe that Discovered Itself, 2000; The Book of Nothing, 2000, 2nd edn 2002; The Constants of Nature, 2002; Science and Ultimate Reality, 2004; The Artful Universe Expanded, 2005; The Infinite Book, 2005; New Theories of Everything, 2007; Cosmic Imagery, 2008; 100 Essential Things You Didn't Know You Didn't Know, 2008; The Book of Universes, 2011 (Premio Antico Pignolo Literary Prize, Venice, 2012); 100 Essential Things You Didn't Know You Didn't Know About Sport, 2012; One Hundred Essential Things You Didn't Know about Maths and the Arts, 2014; *theatre script:* Infinities, 2002 (Premi Ubu Italian Theatre Award, 2002; Italgas Prize, 2003); contrib. to works of reference and 545 scientific articles to learned jls. *Recreations:* athletics, books, travelling, throwing things away. *Address:* Centre for Mathematical Sciences, Cambridge University, Wilberforce Road, Cambridge CB3 0WA. *Fax:* (01223) 765900. *E:* J.D.Barrow@damtp.cam.ac.uk.

**BARROW, Prof. Julia Steuart,** DPhil; FBA 2016; Professor of Medieval Studies, University of Leeds, since 2012; *b* London, 5 Dec. 1956; *d* of Geoffrey Wallis Steuart Barrow, FBA and Heather Elizabeth Agnes Barrow (*née* Lownie). *Educ:* Westfield Sch., Newcastle upon Tyne; Univ. of St Andrews (MA 1978); Corpus Christi Coll., Oxford (DPhil 1983). Research Fellow: Univ. of Sheffield, 1982–84; Alexander von Humboldt Foundn, 1984–86; British Acad. Postdoctoral Res. Fellow, Univ. of Birmingham, 1986–89; Asst Editor, Victoria County Hist. of Cheshire, 1989–90; University of Nottingham: Lectr, 1990–99; Sen. Lectr, 1999–2004; Reader, 2004–12. FRHistS 1990; FSA 1997. *Publications:* English Episcopal Acta, VII, Hereford 1079–1234, 1993, XXXV, Hereford 1234–1275, 2009; St Davids Episcopal Acta 1085–1280, 1998; (ed with Nicholas Brooks) St Wulfstan and his World, 2005; (ed with Andrew Wareham) Myth, Rulership, Church and Charters: essays in honour of Nicholas Brooks, 2008; The Clergy in the Medieval World: secular clerics, their families and careers in North-Western Europe c. 800–c. 1200, 2015; (ed jtly) Autour de Lanfranc: réforme et réformateurs dans l'Europe du nord-ouest (XIe-XIIe siècles), 2015; (ed jtly) The White Book (Liber Albus) of Southwell, 2 vols, 2018; (ed jtly) Italy and Early Medieval Europe: papers for Chris Wickham, 2018. *Recreations:* reading, music, walking. *Address:* School of History, University of Leeds, Leeds LS2 9JT. *T:* (0113) 343 4394. *E:* j.s.barrow@leeds.ac.uk.

**BARROW, Sir Timothy Earle, (Sir Tim),** KCMG 2015 (CMG 2006); LVO 1994; MBE 1994; HM Diplomatic Service; UK Permanent Representative to European Union (with rank of Ambassador), since 2017; *b* 15 Feb. 1964; *m* Alison; two *s* two *d*. Entered FCO, 1986; Second Sec. (Chancery), Moscow, 1989–93; First Sec., FCO, 1993–94; Pvte Sec. to Minister of State, FCO, 1994–96; First Sec., UK Rep. to EU, Brussels, 1996–98 ; Pvte Sec. to Sec. of State, FCO, 1998–2000; Hd, Common Foreign and Security Policy Dept, FCO, 2000–03; Asst Dir, EU (Ext.), FCO, 2003–06; Ambassador to Ukraine, 2006–08; UK Rep. to Political and Security Cttee, European Union, 2008–11; Ambassador to Russia, 2011–15; Political Dir, FCO, 2016–17. *Address:* c/o Foreign and Commonwealth Office, King Charles Street, SW1A 2AH.

**BARROW, Ursula Helen, (Viscountess Waverley),** PhD; Wisbech Schools Co-ordinator, Cambridgeshire Advisory Service, 2002; *b* 31 Oct. 1955; *d* of Raymond Hugh and Rita Helen Barrow; *m* 1994, Viscount Waverley, *qv*; one *s*. *Educ*: Newnham Coll., Cambridge (BA Hons 1977; MA 1981; PhD 1988; Fellow, 1999–2000); Jesus Coll., Cambridge (LLM 1992). Econ. Develt Planner, Planning and Govt of Belize, 1978; consultant for small business affairs, urban planning and marketing, Frazier & Assocs, 1979–85; Counsellor and Dep. High Comr, London, 1988–89; Perm. Rep. to UN, 1989–90; Asst Dir (Pol), Commonwealth Secretariat, 1991–93; High Comr for Belize in London, 1993–98, also Ambassador to EU, Belgium, France, Germany and Holy See. Dir, Belize Telecommunications Ltd, 2004–05.

**BARRY, Alison Ruth;** *see* Pople, A. R.

**BARRY, David;** *see* Barry, J. D.

**BARRY, Sir Edward;** *see* Barry, Sir L. E. A. T.

**BARRY, Hilary Alice S.;** *see* Samson-Barry.

**BARRY, Prof. (James) David,** PhD; Professor of Molecular Parasitology, 1996, now Honorary Senior Research Fellow, and Director, Wellcome Trust Centre for Molecular Parasitology, 1999–2012, University of Glasgow; *b* 13 Dec. 1949; *s* of James Barry and Helen Barry (*née* Cairns); *m* 1st, 1973, Mary Mowat (*d* 1992); one *s* two *d*; 2nd, 2001, Olwyn Byron; one *d*. *Educ*: Univ. of Glasgow (BSc Combined Biol.; PhD 1977). Res. Fellow, Univ. of Glasgow, 1977–86; Scientist, Internat. Lab. for Res. on Animal Diseases, Nairobi, 1978–80; Sen. Lectr, 1986–92, Reader, 1992–96, Univ. of Glasgow. Consultancy appts with scientific research funding bodies. *Publications*: 100 scientific contribs. *Recreations*: drawing and painting, swimming, reflection. *Address*: c/o Wellcome Centre for Molecular Parasitology, Sir Graeme Davies Building, 120 University Place, Glasgow G12 8TA. *E*: dave.barry@glasgow.ac.uk.

**BARRY, Sir (Lawrence) Edward (Anthony Tress),** 5th Bt *cr* 1899; Baron de Barry in Portugal *cr* 1876; *b* 1 Nov. 1939; *s* of Sir Rupert Rodney Francis Tress Barry, 4th Bt, MBE, and Diana Madeline (*d* 1948), *o d* of R. O'Brien Thompson; *S* father, 1977; *m* 1st, 1968, Fenella Hoult (marr. diss. 1991); one *s* one *d*; 2nd, 1992, (Elizabeth) Jill Dawe, *d* of G. Bradley, Fishtoft. *Educ*: Haileybury; Imperial Service Coll. Formerly Captain, Grenadier Guards. *Heir*: *s* William Rupert Philip Tress Barry [*b* 13 Dec. 1973; *m* 2004, Diana, d of Antoni Leidner, Germany; one *s* one *d*].

**BARRY, Sebastian;** writer, since 1977; Laureate for Irish Fiction, since 2018; *b* Dublin, 5 July 1955; *s* of Francis J. Barry, architect, and late Joan O'Hara, actress; *m* 1992, Alison Deegan; two *s* one *d*. *Educ*: Catholic University Sch., Dublin; Trinity Coll., Dublin (BA Hons). Writer in Association, Abbey Th., Dublin, 1990; Writer Fellow, TCD, 1995; Heimboldt Vis. Prof., Villanova Univ., Philadelphia, 2006. Mem., Aosdána, 1989–. FRSL 2009. Hon. DLitt: NUI, Galway, 2012; UEA, 2010; DUniv Open, 2014. Gold Medal of Hon. Patronage, Philosophical Soc., Trinity Coll., Dublin, 2019. *Publications*: poetry: The Water-Colourist, 1983; plays: Prayers of Sherkin/Boss Grady's Boys: two plays, 1990; The Steward of Christendom (Lloyds Private Banking Playwright of the Year Award, Ire./America Latest Prize, Christopher Ewart-Biggs Meml Prize), 1995; Our Lady of Sligo, 1998; The Pride of Parnell Street, 2007; On Blueberry Hill, 2017; novels: The Whereabouts of Eneas McNulty, 1998; A Long Long Way, 2005 (Kerry Gp Irish Novel of the Year, 2006); The Secret Scripture, 2008 (Costa Book of the Year, 2008; James Tait Black Meml Prize, 2009); On Canaan's Side, 2011 (Walter Scott Prize, 2012); The Temporary Gentleman, 2014; Days Without End, 2016 (Costa Book of the Year, 2017; Walter Scott Prize, 2017).

**BARSON, Jacqueline Anne,** MBE 1995; HM Diplomatic Service, retired; High Commissioner to Papua New Guinea, 2010–14; *b* Walsall, 26 May 1959; *d* of John and Brenda Barson. *Educ*: Arthur Terry Grammar Sch., Sutton Coldfield. Entered FCO, 1979; Desk Officer, Parly Unit, FCO, 1979–81; Archivist, Prague, then Belgrade, 1981–82; Archivist/Registrar: Abu Dhabi, 1982–85; Bandar Seri Begavan, 1985–86; Asst Admin Officer, UKMIS Geneva, 1986–89; Asst Visits Officer, FCO, 1989–91; Desk Officer, Security Coordination Dept, FCO, 1991–92; Presidency Liaison Officer, Copenhagen, Brussels and Athens, 1992–93; Second Sec. (Econ./Trade), Ottawa, 1994–99; Olympic Attaché to Team GB, Sydney, 1999–2000; on secondment to Manchester Organising Cttee, 2002 Commonwealth Games, 2001–02; Sen. Asst to Dir Gen. Corporate Affairs, FCO, 2002–04; Hd, Public Diplomacy Challenge Fund and Hd, London Press Service, FCO, 2004; on secondment to SOCA, 2005; Project Leader, UK/India Educn Initiative, S Asia Gp, FCO, 2005; Dep. Dir, Protocol and Asst Marshal of Diplomatic Corps, FCO, 2005–09; on loan to UK Trade and Investment for Prime Minister's Global Investment Conf., 2009–10. *Recreations*: sport, travel, reading, the arts.

**BARSTOW, Dame Josephine (Clare),** DBE 1995 (CBE 1985); opera singer, free-lance since 1971; *b* Sheffield, 27 Sept. 1940; *m* 1964, Terry Hands (marr. diss. 1967); *m* 1969, Ande Anderson (*d* 1996); no *c*. *Educ*: Birmingham Univ. (BA). Debut with Opera for All, 1964; studied at London Opera Centre, 1965–66; Opera for All, 1966; Glyndebourne Chorus, 1967; Sadler's Wells Contract Principal, 1967–68, sang Cherubino, Euridice, Violetta; *Welsh National Opera*: Contract Principal, 1968–70, sang Violetta, Countess, Fiordiligi, Mimi, Amelia, Simon Boccanegra; Don Carlos, 1974; Jenufa, 1975; Peter Grimes, 1978, 1983; Tatyana in Onegin, 1980; Tosca, 1985; Un Ballo in Maschera, 1986; The Makropoulos Case, 1994; *Covent Garden*: Denise, world première, Tippett's The Knot Garden, 1970 (recorded 1974); Falstaff, 1975; Salome, 1982; Santuzza, 1982; Peter Grimes, 1988 and 1995; Attila, 1990; Fidelio, 1993; Katya Kabanova, 2000; Queen of Spades, 2001; *Glyndebourne*: Lady Macbeth (for TV), 1972; Idomeneo, 1974; Fidelio, 1981; *English National Opera*: has sung all parts in Hoffman, Emilia Marty (Makropulos Case), Natasha (War and Peace) and Traviata; Der Rosenkavalier, 1975, 1984; Salome, 1975; Don Carlos, 1976, 1986; Tosca, 1976, 1987; Forza del Destino, 1978, 1992; Aida, 1979; Fidelio, Arabella, 1980; The Flying Dutchman, La Bohème, 1982; The Valkyrie, 1983; Don Giovanni, 1986; Lady Macbeth of Mtsensk, 1987, 1991; Street Scene, 1993; Jenufa, 1994; The Carmelites, 1999, 2005; *Opera North*: Gloriana, 1993, 1997, 2001; Jenufa, 1995; Medea, Wozzeck, 1996; Aida, 1997; Falstaff, 2000; Albert Herring, 2002, 2013; Queen of Spades, 2011; Jack the Ripper: the women of Whitechapel, 2019. Other appearances include: Alice in Falstaff, Aix-en-Provence Festival, 1971; Nitocris in Belshazzar, Geneva, 1972; Jeanne, British première, Penderecki's The Devils, 1973; Marguerite, world première, Crosse's The Story of Vasco, 1974; Fidelio, Jenufa, Scottish Opera, 1977; Gayle, world première, Tippett's The Ice Break, 1977; US début as Lady Macbeth, Miami, 1977; Musetta in La Bohème, NY Met., 1977; Salome, Staat Berlin, 1979 (Critics Prize); San Francisco, 1982; Abigaille in Nabucco, Miami, 1981; début in Chicago as Lady Macbeth, 1981; new prod. of Jenufa, Cologne, 1981; La Voix Humaine and Pagliacci, Chicago, 1982; The Makropulos Case (in Italian), Florence, 1983; Gutrune, Götterdämmerung, Bayreuth, 1983; Die Fledermaus, San Francisco, 1984; Peter Grimes, 1984, La Traviata, 1985, Salome, 1987, Der Rosenkavalier, 1990, Houston; Benigna, world première, Penderecki's Die Schwarze Maske, Salzburg, 1986, Vienna Staatsoper, 1986; Manon Lescaut, USA, 1986; Tosca, Bolshoi, Tbilisi, 1986; Tosca, and Macbeth, Riga, 1986; Macbeth, Zurich, 1986, Munich, 1987; Medea, Boston, 1988; Prokofiev's The Fiery Angel, Adelaide, 1988; Un Ballo in Maschera, Salzburg, 1989, 1990; Fanciulla del West, Toulouse, 1991; Chrysothemis, Houston, 1993; Fidelio, 1992, Salome, 1994, Amsterdam; Peter Grimes, Tokyo, 1998; first Jenufa in Czech, Antwerp, 1999; debut at Wigmore Hall, 2007; Mamma Lucia in Cavalleria Rusticana, Liceu, Barcelona, 2011; Heidi Schiller in Follies, RNT, 2017. Sings in other opera houses in USA, Canada and Europe. Recordings include: Un Ballo in Maschera; Verdi arias; scenes from Salome, Médée, Makropulos Case and Turandot; Kiss Me Kate; Kurt Weill's Street Scene, Gloriana; Albert Herring; Wozzeck; Jenufa; The Carmelites; Bernstein's Kaddish Symphony. Runs business of Arabian stud farm, Sussex. Fidelio medal, Assoc. of Internat. Opera Directors, 1985. *Recreations*: gardening, walking. *Address*: c/o Musichall Ltd, Oast House, Crouch's Farm, Hollow Lane, E Hoathly, E Sussex BN8 6QX.

**BARSTOW, Prof. Martin Adrian,** PhD; CPhys, FInstP; CSci; FRAS; Professor of Astrophysics and Space Science, since 2003, Pro Vice-Chancellor for Strategic Science Projects, since 2009, Director, Leicester Institute of Space and Earth Observation, since 2016, University of Leicester; *b* Scunthorpe, 18 May 1958; *s* of Brian Thomas Barstow and Marjorie Anona Barstow (*née* Willans); *m* 1981, Rachel Ann Howes; one *s* one *d*. *Educ*: Carlinghow Primary Sch.; Batley Boys' Grammar Sch.; Univ. of York (BA Physics 1979); Univ. of Leicester (PhD 1983). FRAS 1987; FInstP 1998; CSci 2004. Department of Physics and Astronomy, University of Leicester: Res. Associate, 1983–90; SERC/PPARC Advanced Fellow, 1991–98; Lectr, 1994–98; Reader, 1998–2003; Head of Dept, 2005–09; Head, Coll. of Science and Engrg, 2009–15. Member: Public Understanding of Sci. Judges Panel, PPARC, 1996–2000 (Chm., 1997–2000); Public Understanding of Sci. Adv. Panel, PPARC, 1997–2000; STFC, 2009–15. Consultant on Space Educn to BNSC, 2005. Chm., Educn Adv. Bd, Nat. Space Centre, 2001–; Member: Adv. Gp, Near Earth Object Inf. Centre, 2002–12; Mgt Bd, E Midlands Regl Sci. Learning Centre, 2003–12; Astronomy Working Gp, ESA, 2012–14; Sci. Prog. Adv. Cttee, UK Space Agency, 2012–; Adv. Bd, Nat. Space Acad., 2012–; Council, Space Telescope Inst., 2015– (Chair, 2016–); UK Space Conf. 2019 Organising Cttee, 2018–19 (Chair, Prog. Cttee, 2018–19). Mem., Time Allocation Cttee, 2001, 2003, 2006, 2012, Users' Cttee, 2004–08, Hubble Space Telescope. Member: Wakeham Panel, Res. Councils UK Rev. of Physics, 2008; Public Engagement with Res. Adv. Panel, Research Councils UK, 2009–15; Physics Panel, HEFCE REF impact pilot exercise, 2010; HEFCE Physics REF 2014 Panel, 2011–14; Bd, American Univs Res. Assoc., 2009–; Newton Agri-Tech Governance Bd, 2016–; Chm., Educn, Communication and Outreach Adv. Bd, STFC, 2010–12. UK Space Agency Observer, NASA LUVOIR Sci. and Technol. Develt Team, 2016–. Mem., Organizing Cttee, Physics Olympiad 2000, 1997–2000. Mem., 2005–08 and 2013–14, Sec., 2008–13, Pres., 2014–16, Council, RAS. Mem., Div. XI Cttee, IAU, 2009–13. Mem., Bd of Trustees, Univ. of Sharjah, 2015–. Member: Adv. Bd, Physics Rev., 1998–2009; Editl Bd, Springer-Praxis Astronomy and Astrophysics Liby, 2015–. *Publications*: (ed) White Dwarfs: advances in observation and theory, 1993; (with J. B. Holberg) Extreme Ultraviolet Astronomy, 2003; (ed jtly) UV Astronomy: stars from birth to death, 2007; contrib. astronomical and instrumentation jls. *Recreations*: choral singing with my family, Morris dancing, allotment and home gardening, church organ playing, folk music, theatre. *Address*: Department of Physics and Astronomy, University of Leicester, University Road, Leicester LE1 7RH. *T*: (0116) 252 3492, *Fax*: (0116) 252 3311. *E*: mab@le.ac.uk.

**BARTER, Nicholas Arthur Beamish;** theatre director and teacher; Principal, Royal Academy of Dramatic Art, 1993–2007; *b* 12 Sept. 1940; *s* of Paul André Valentine Spencer and Sylvia Theadora Essex Barter; *m* 1961, Brigid Alice Panet (marr. diss. 1981); one *s* one *d*; *m* 1998, Noriko Sasaki; one *d*. *Educ*: Cheltenham Coll.; Pembroke Coll., Cambridge (BA Hons, MA). ABC TV Trainee Directors Award, 1963; Asst Dir, Phoenix Th., Leicester, 1963–65; Dir of Prodns, Lincoln Theatre Royal, 1965–68; Dir. Artistic Dir, RSC Theatregoround, 1968; Dir, Ipswich Arts Th., 1968–71; Asst Drama Dir, Arts Council of GB, 1971–75; Artistic Dir, Unicorn Th., 1977–86 (Best Prodn for Young People Award, Drama mag., 1982, for Beowulf); Children's Th. Consultant, Los Angeles, 1986; Course Dir, and Dep. Principal, RADA, 1988–93. Guest Prof., Toho Gakuen Coll. of Drama and Music, Tokyo, 2007–; Guest Teacher, JOKO Acting Sch., Tokyo, 2007–; Guest Teacher, 2009, Vis. Prof., 2010–, Shanghai Th. Acad. Productions include: Julius Caesar, 2008, How the Other Half Loves, 2009, Gekidan Subaru, Tokyo; Major Barbara, 2008, Taming of the Shrew, 2011, Midsummer Night's Dream, 2012, Twelfth Night, 2013, The Winter's Tale, 2014, As You Like It, 2015, Two Gentlemen of Verona, 2016, Love's Labour's Lost, 2018, Shanghai Th. Acad.; Pericles, 2009, Merchant of Venice, 2010, Th. du Sygne, Tokyo; A Doll's House, Th. Green, Tokyo, 2012; Doubt, Yorozuya Shouten, Tokyo, 2013; As You Like It, Yunnan Arts Univ., 2014; Marlowe Soc. Agents Showcase, Cambridge Univ., 2015, 2016, 2017, 2018. Chm., Dharma Trust, 1990–97. *Publications*: Playing with Plays, 1979; contrib. Theatre Qly, Theatre Internat.

**BARTER, Sir Peter (Leslie Charles),** Kt 2001; OBE 1986; *b* Sydney, Australia, 26 March 1940; *s* of late John Frank Barter and of Wyn Emily Barter; *m* 1970 Janet Ellen Carter; one *s*. *Educ*: Newington Coll.; Wellington Coll., Sydney. MP (People's Progress) 1992–97, (Nat. Alliance), 2002–07, Madang, PNG. Gov., Madang Province, 1992–94; Minister for Health, PNG, 1994–96; Minister for Provincial Affairs and Bougainville, 1996–97; Provincial Minister, 1997–98; Minister for Intergovt Relns and Bougainville Affairs, 2002–06; Minister for Health and Bougainville Affairs, 2006–07. Work in aviation and tourism develt in Papua New Guinea: Chairman: Melanesian Foundn, 1980–2008; Mgt Gp, PNG Incentive Fund, 1997–2002; PNG Nat. Events Council, 2000–07; Nat. Aids Council, 2008–; Dep. Chm., PNG Tourist Authy, 1998–2000. Licensed commercial pilot of both fixed and rotary wing, 1967–. Hon. PhD Australian Catholic Univ., 2005. *Recreation*: sailing in motor yacht Kalibobo Spirit. *Address*: PO Box 707, Madang 511, Papua New Guinea. *T*: 4222766, *Fax*: 4223543.

**BARTFELD, Jason Maurice;** QC 2015; *b* St John's Wood, London, 7 Feb. 1972; *s* of Peter Bartfeld and Carol Bartfeld; *m* 2007, Annabel; three *c*. *Educ*: Westminster Sch.; Durham Univ. (BA Philos. and Politics). Called to the Bar, Middle Temple, 1995; in practice as a barrister, 1995–. *Recreations*: cooking, polo, family. *Address*: 187 Fleet Street, EC4A 2AT. *T*: (020) 7430 7430, *Fax*: (020) 7430 7431. *E*: jasonbartfeld@187fleetstreet.com. *Club*: Sussex Polo.

**BARTFIELD, Robert; His Honour Judge Bartfield;** a Circuit Judge, since 1996; *b* 30 Dec. 1949; *s* of Isaac and Emily Bartfield; *m* 1977, Susan Eleanor Griffin; one *s* one *d*. *Educ*: Leeds Grammar Sch.; Queen Mary Coll., London (LLB). Called to the Bar, Middle Temple, 1971; in practice as barrister, 1971–96; a Recorder, 1993–96. *Recreations*: tennis, football.

**BARTHOLOMEW, Prof. Stuart,** CBE 2014; DL; Principal and Vice Chancellor, Arts University Bournemouth (formerly Principal, Arts University College at Bournemouth), since 1997; *b* London, 20 Jan. 1953; *s* of William George and Ada Ellen Bartholomew; *m* 2002, Claire McIntyre; twin *s*. *Educ*: Christ Church Secondary Sch.; Christ Coll. Sch.; Univ. of Hull (BA Hons); Univ. of Nottingham (MEd); Univ. of Leicester (PGCE) McMaster Univ. (MA). Teaching Fellow, Univ. of Calgary, 1973–74; Lectr, Norwich Coll. of Art, 1974–75; Asst Dean, Univ. of Derby, 1975–90; Tutor, Open Univ. (pt-time),

1980–90; Dean of Media, 1990–95, Hd of Coll., 1995–96, Univ. of the Arts, London. Vis. Prof., Univ. of the Arts, London, 2001–04. Dir, Bournemouth SO, 2011–. Chm., UK Assoc. Specialist Colls of Art and Design, 2009–15. Chair, Trustees, Russell-Cotes Art Gall. and Mus., 2016–. FRSA 1999. DL Dorset, 2019. *Publications:* contrib. articles on specialist educn in arts and design and engagement in promotion of UK creative industries. *Recreations:* being alive, sports, generally using the seated position, the arts. *Address:* Arts University Bournemouth, Wallisdown, Poole BH12 5HH. *T:* (01202) 363203. *Club:* Royal Motor Yacht (Poole).

**BARTLAM, Edward Andrew Ashenhurst;** Founder and Director, Underbelly Ltd, since 2001; *b* London, 14 Nov. 1979; *s* of Thomas Hugh Bartlam and Gabriel Bartlam; *m* 2009, Lucinda Baring; one *s* one *d* (and one *s* decd). *Educ:* Eton Coll.; Univ. of Edinburgh (MA Eng. Lit.). *Recreations:* theatre, tennis, piano, museums, travel. *Address:* Underbelly Ltd, 36–38 Hatton Garden, EC1N 8EB. *T:* (020) 7307 8480, *Fax:* (020) 7307 8481. *E:* ed@underbelly.co.uk. *Club:* Soho House.

**BARTLE, Philip Martyn;** QC 2003; **His Honour Judge Bartle;** a Circuit Judge, since 2012; *b* 24 Dec. 1952; *s* of Leslie Bartle and Zena Bartle (*née* Unger). *Educ:* Manchester Grammar Sch.; Christ Church, Oxford (MA, BCL). Called to the Bar, Middle Temple, 1976, Bencher, 2006; in practice, 1976–2012, specialising in law of professional negligence and mediation. Recorder, 2004–12. *Publications:* (contrib.) ADR and Commercial Disputes, 2002; (consultant ed.) Halsbury's Laws of England, 5th edn, 2008; (contrib.) Security for Costs and Other Court Ordered Security, 2010. *Recreations:* theatre, classical music, travel, reading, Apostrophe Chambers. *Address:* Southwark Crown Court, 1 English Grounds, Southwark, SE1 2HU.

**BARTLE, Ronald David;** a Metropolitan Stipendiary Magistrate, 1972–99; Deputy to Chief Magistrate, 1992–99; *b* 14 April 1929; *s* of late Rev. George Clement Bartle and Winifred Marie Bartle; *m* 1st, 1963; one *s* one *d*; 2nd, 1981, Hisako (*née* Yagi) (*d* 2004); 3rd, 2006, Molly. *Educ:* St John's Sch., Leatherhead; Jesus Coll., Cambridge (MA). Nat. Service, 1947–49 (Army Athletic Colours). Called to Bar, Lincoln's Inn, 1954; practised at Criminal Bar, 1954–72; a Dep. Circuit Judge, 1975–79; a Chm., Inner London Juvenile Courts, 1975–79. Member: Home Office Council on Drug Abuse, 1987–; Home Office Cttee on Magistrates' Court Procedure, 1989–. Lectr on Advocacy, Council of Legal Educn, 1984–89. Contested (C) Islington N, 1958, 1959; Mem., Essex CC, 1963–66. Freeman, City of London, 1976; Liveryman, Basketmakers' Co., 1976– (Steward, 1990; Mem. Ct, 1997–; Prime Warden, 2005–06). Patron, Pathway to Recovery Trust. Governor: Clergy Support Trust (formerly Corp. of Sons of the Clergy), 1995–; RNLI, 1997–. Church Warden, St Mary the Boltons, Kensington, 1992–95; Church Warden and Trustee, St Margaret Pattens, 1999–; Member: City of London Deanery Synod, 2000–; Friends of City of London Churches, 2001–; Guild of Freemen, City of London; Royal Soc. of St George. *Publications:* Introduction to Shipping Law, 1958; The Police Officer in Court, 1984; Crime and the New Magistrate, 1985; The Law and the Lawless, 1987; Bow Street Beak, 1999; The Police Witness, 2002; The Telephone Murder: the mysterious death of Julia Wallace, 2012; Three Cases That Shook the Law, 2016; (contrib.) Atkin's Court Forms and Precedents; contrib. to legal jls. *Recreations:* music, reading. *Clubs:* Garrick, Hurlingham.

**BARTLETT, Sir Andrew (Alan),** 5th Bt *cr* 1913, of Hardington Mandeville, Somerset; *b* 26 May 1973; *er s* of Sir John Hardington David Bartlett, 4th Bt and of his 2nd wife, Elizabeth Joyce (*née* Raine); *S* father, 1998. *Heir: b* Stephen Mark Bartlett, *b* 5 July 1975.

**BARTLETT, Andrew Vincent Bramwell;** QC 1993; a Recorder, since 2004; chartered arbitrator; a Deputy High Court Judge, since 2010; *b* 1952; *s* of John Samuel Bartlett and Doris Jean Bartlett; *m* 1974, Elisabeth Jefferis. *Educ:* Jesus Coll., Oxford (BA). Called to the Bar, Middle Temple, 1974, Bencher, 2005. Chm., Technol. and Construction Bar Assoc., 2007–09. FCIArb. *Address:* Crown Office Chambers, 2 Crown Office Row, Temple, EC4Y 7HJ. *T:* (020) 7797 8100.

**BARTLETT, Dr Christopher Leslie Reginald,** FRCP, FFPH; Director, Public Health Laboratory Service Communicable Disease Surveillance Centre, 1988–2000; *b* 20 Dec. 1940; *s* of Reginald James Bartlett and Dorothea Amelia Bartlett; *m* 1979, Alicia Teresa Tower; one *s* two *d*. *Educ:* Milton Sch., Bulawayo, Southern Rhodesia; Lysses Sch., Hants; St Bartholomew's Hosp. Med. Coll. (MB, BS 1965); MSc LSHTM 1977. MRCS 1965; LRCP 1965, FRCP 1991; MFCM 1978, FFPH (FFPHM 1983). RAF SSC, 1967–72. Registrar, Wessex RHA, seconded to LSHTM, 1975–77; Public Health Laboratory Service: Sen. Registrar, 1977–79; Consultant Epidemiologist, 1979–88. Consultant Med. Epidemiologist, Caribbean Epidemiol. Centre, 1984–85. Hon. Lectr, Dept of Envmtl and Preventative Medicine, St Bartholomew's Hosp. Med. Coll., 1980; Hon. Sen. Lectr, Dept of Epidemiol. and Med. Stats, Royal London Hosp., 1990; Vis. Prof., LSHTM, 1997–. Chm., PHLS Cttee on Legionnaires' Disease, 1989; Member: DHSS Cttee on Aspects and Use of Biocides, 1986; Registrar-Gen's Med. Adv. Cttee, DoH, 1988–90; Expert Gp on Cryptosporidium in Water Supplies, DoE and DoH, 1989–90; Steering Gp on Microbiol Safety of Food, MAFF and DoH, 1991–95; CMO's Health of Nation Cttee, DoH, 1992–2000. Faculty of Public Health Medicine: Member: Bd, 1988–91; Educn Cttee, 1988–94; Pres., Sect. of Epidemiol. and Public Health, RSocMed. 1996 (Mem., Council, 1990–94); Mem. Council, RIPH&H, 1991–94. Member: Scientific Steering Cttee, Réseau Nat. de Santé Publique, France, 1992; Steering Gp, European Prog. for Intervention Epidemiol. Trng, 1994; PROMED Steering Cttee, Fedn of Amer. Scientists, 1995; Communicable Diseases Wkg Gp, G7 Nations Global Healthcare Applications Project, 1995; MRC CJD Epidemiol. Subcttee, 1996; EU/USA Task Force on Communicable Diseases, 1996 (Co-Chm., Surveillance and Response Wkg Gp, 1996); Project Leader, European Surveillance of Travel Associated Legionnaires' Disease, 1993; Jt Project Leader, SALMNET (EU Surveillance of Salmonella Infections), 1994; Chm., Charter Gp of Heads of Instns with responsibilities in nat. surveillance of disease in EU countries, 1994. Specialist Advr, Editl Bd, Jl Infection, 1991–. *Publications:* chapters, articles and papers in med. and scientific texts on aspects of epidemiology and prevention of infectious diseases. *Recreations:* family, walking, ski-ing, travelling. *Club:* Royal Society of Medicine.

**BARTLETT, Hon. David John;** Chairman: Fronde Systems Group Ltd, since 2017; Premier of Tasmania, Australia, 2008–11; *b* Hobart, 19 Jan. 1968; *s* of Neil Walker and Grace Lucinda Borella (*née* Bird); *m* 1st, 1994, Jacqui Swee Lan Lim (marr. diss. 1998); 2nd, 2004, Larissa Mary, *d* of Ben and Mary Marriss; one *s* one *d*. *Educ:* Hobart Matriculation Coll.; Univ. of Tasmania (BSc Computer Sci.; Grad. Dip. Business). Manager, SOE Business (Telecom), 1990–95; Dep. Dir, IT, Govt of Tasmania, 1995–97; Dir, IT, Dept of Educn, 1997–99; Manager, Innovation Sci. Technol., Dept of State Develt, 1999–2002; Sen. Private Sec., Office of the Treas., 2002–04; Sen. Advr, Office of the Premier of Tasmania, 2004. MHA (ALP) Denison, Tasmania, 2004–11. Dep. Premier of Tasmania, 2008; Minister for Education, 2006–11, for Planning, 2008, for Workplace Relns, 2008, for Skills, 2008–11. Chm., Asdeq Labs, 2011–17; Non-exec. Dir, Emprevo, 2018–. Chm., Wicking Dementia Res. and Educn Centre, 2017–.

**BARTLETT, George Robert;** QC 1986; President of the Lands Chamber of the Upper Tribunal (formerly Lands Tribunal), 1998–2012; a Deputy High Court Judge, 1994–2012; *b* 22 Oct. 1944; *s* of late Commander H. V. Bartlett, RN and Angela (*née* Webster); *m* 1972, Dr Clare Virginia, *y d* of G. C. Fortin; three *s*. *Educ:* Tonbridge Sch.; Trinity Coll., Oxford (MA). Called to the Bar, Middle Temple, 1966, Bencher, 1995. A Recorder, 1990–2000; an Asst Parly Boundary Comr, 1992–98. Hon. RICS 2000.

**BARTLETT, John Vernon,** CBE 1976; MA; FREng, FICE; consulting engineer, retired; *b* 18 June 1927; *s* of late Vernon F. Bartlett and Olga Bartlett (*née* Testrup); *m* 1951, Gillian, *d* of late Philip Hoffmann, Sturmer Hall, Essex; four *s*. *Educ:* Stowe; Trinity Coll., Cambridge. Served 9th Airborne Squadron, RE, 1946–48; Engineer and Railway Staff Corps, TA, 1978; Col 1986. Engineer with John Mowlem & Co. Ltd, 1951–57; joined staff of Mott, Hay & Anderson, 1957; Partner, 1966–88; Chm., 1973–88. Pres., ICE, 1982–83 (Vice-Pres., 1979–82; Mem. Council, 1974–77); Chm., British Tunnelling Soc., 1977–79. Gov., Imperial Coll., 1991–95. FRSA 1975. Hon. Sec., Overseas Affairs, RAEng, 1982–85; Mem. Council, Fellowship of Engrg, 1982–86. Master, Engineers' Co., 1992–93 (Mem., Court of Assts, 1986–2004). Telford Gold Medal, (jointly) 1971, 1973; S. G. Brown Medal, Royal Soc., 1973; Sir Frank Whittle Medal, RAEng, 2018. *Publications:* Tunnels: Planning Design and Construction (with T. M. Megaw), vol. 1, 1981, vol. 2, 1982; Ships of North Cornwall, 1996; contrib. various papers to ICE, ASCE, etc. *Recreations:* sailing, maritime history (Founder, Bartlett Library, Nat. Maritime Mus. Cornwall, 2002). *Address:* 6 Cottenham Park Road, SW20 0RZ. *T:* (020) 8946 9576. *Clubs:* Hawks (Cambridge); Harlequin Football; Royal Engineers Yacht.

**BARTLETT, Neil Vivian,** OBE 2000; writer, director; Artistic Director, Lyric Theatre, Hammersmith, 1994–2004; *b* 23 Aug. 1958; *s* of Trevor and Pam Bartlett; partner, James Gardiner. *Educ:* Magdalen Coll., Oxford (BA Hons Eng. Lit.). Works written, adapted and directed include: *theatre:* More Bigger Snacks Now, 1985; A Vision of Love Revealed in Sleep, 1987; Sarrasine, 1990; A Judgement in Stone, 1992; Night After Night, 1993; The Picture of Dorian Gray, 1994; Lady into Fox, 1996; The Seven Sacraments of Nicholas Poussin, 1997; Everybody Loves A Winner, 2009; Or You Could Kiss Me, 2010; For Alfonso, 2011; Stella, 2016; The Plague, 2017; *television:* That's What Friends are For, 1987; Where is Love?, 1988; Pedagogue, 1989; That's How Strong My Love Is, 1990; *film:* Now That It's Morning, 1992; *major productions directed:* Romeo and Juliet, 1994; The Letter, 1995; Mrs Warren's Profession, A Christmas Carol, 1996; Then Again, Treasure Island, 1997; Cause Célèbre, Seven Sonnets of Michelangelo, Cinderella, 1998; The Dispute, 1999; The Servant, 2001; The Prince of Homburg, The Island of Slaves, 2002; Pericles, 2003; Oliver Twist, Don Juan, 2004; Dido, Queen of Carthage, Amer. Rep. Co., Boston, 2005; The Rake's Progress, Aldeburgh Fest., 2006; The Maids, The Pianist, Twelfth Night, RSC, 2007; An Ideal Husband, Abbey, Dublin, 2008; Romeo and Juliet, RSC, 2008; The Turn of the Screw, Aldeburgh Fest., 2009; The Queen of Spades, Grand Th., Leeds, 2011; The Picture of Dorian Gray, Abbey, Dublin, 2012; Britten's Canticles, Aldeburgh and ROH, 2013; Great Expectations, Bristol Old Vic, 2013; Owen Wingrave, Aldeburgh and Edinburgh Fests, 2014; Stella, London Internat. Fest. of Theatre, and Holland Fest., 2016; The Plague, Arcola Th., De Profundis, Reading Jail, 2017; Medea, Brighton Fest., 2018; has performed at RNT, Royal Court, Blackpool Grand, Tate Britain and Vauxhall Tavern. Patron, Sussex Beacon, 2011–. Hon. DArts: Oxford Brookes, 2008; Brighton, 2013. *Publications:* Who Was That Man?, 1988; Ready to Catch Him Should He Fall, 1989; A Vision of Love Revealed in Sleep, 1990; (trans.) Berenice/The Misanthrope/School for Wives, 1991; (trans.) The Game of Love and Chance, 1992; Night After Night, 1993; Mr Clive and Mr Page, 1995; (trans.) Splendid's, 1995; (trans.) The Dispute, 1999; (trans.) The Threesome, 2000; In Extremis, 2000; (trans.) The Prince of Homburg, 2002; (trans.) The Island of Slaves, 2002; (trans.) Don Juan, 2005; Solo Voices, 2005; Skin Lane, 2007; Or You Could Kiss Me, 2010; Queer Voices, 2012; The Disappearance Boy, 2014; adaptations for stage: Camille, 2003; A Christmas Carol, 2003; Oliver Twist, 2004; Great Expectations, 2007; The Picture of Dorian Gray, 2012; Letter to an Unknown Soldier, 2014; Stella, 2016; The Plague, 2017. *Address:* c/o The Agency, 24 Pottery Lane, W11 4LZ. *T:* (020) 7727 1346. *E:* info@theagency.co.uk. *W:* www.neil-bartlett.com.

**BARTLETT, Nicholas Michael;** Partner, since 2004, and Head, Real Estate Investment, since 2012, Eversheds Sutherland (formerly Eversheds) LLP; *b* Chester, 16 May 1972; *s* of Pierre Nicholas and late Elizabeth Anne Bartlett; *m* 2000, Annabel Sophie Frearson; one *s* one *d*. *Educ:* Eton Coll.; Univ. of Warwick (LLB Hons Law 1993); Coll. of Law, London (Postgrad. DipLP with Commendation 1994). Admitted as solicitor, 1997; Linklaters: trainee solicitor, 1995–97; Associate, 1997–99; Man. Associate, 1999–2003. Dir, Colville Estate Ltd, 2016–. Member: Historic Houses Assoc.; Motorsports Assoc.; British Assoc. for Shooting and Conservation; Welsh Rifle Assoc.; Nat. Rifle Assoc. *Recreations:* Captain, Etonian Shooting Club (long range target shooting), motor-racing (owner driver), ski-ing, tennis, scuba diving. *Address:* Eversheds Sutherland LLP, One Wood Street, EC2V 7WS. *T:* (020) 7919 4570. *E:* nicholasbartlett@eversheds.com. *Clubs:* British Automobile Racing, Lancia Motor; N London Rifle.

**BARTLETT, Prof. Philip Nigel,** PhD; FRS 2012; Professor of Electrochemistry, University of Southampton, since 1993; *b* Sevenoaks, Kent, 27 July 1956; *s* of Stuart and Edith Bartlett; *m* 2000, Zoë Slattery; one *s* one *d*. *Educ:* University Coll., Oxford (BA 1978); Imperial Coll. London (PhD 1981). Royal Commn for Exhibn of 1851 Res. Fellow, 1981–83, Asst Dir, Wolfson Unit for Modified Electrodes, 1983–84, Imperial Coll. London; Lectr, Univ. of Warwick, 1984–91; Prof. of Physical Chem., Univ. of Bath, 1991–92. *Recreations:* anything with two wheels, modern literature. *Address:* Chemistry, University of Southampton, Highfield, Southampton SO17 1BJ. *T:* (023) 8059 2373. *E:* p.n.bartlett@soton.ac.uk.

**BARTLETT, Prof. Robert John,** CBE 2019; FBA 1997; FRSE, FSA, FR.HistS; Professor of Mediaeval History, University of St Andrews, 1992–2016, now Emeritus; *b* 27 Nov. 1950; *s* of Leonard Frederick Bartlett and Mabel Emily Adams; *m* 1979, Honora Elaine Hickey (*d* 2016); one *s* one *d*. *Educ:* Peterhouse, Cambridge (BA 1972; MA 1976); St John's Coll., Oxford (DPhil 1978). Lectr in History, Edinburgh Univ., 1980–86; Prof. of Medieval History, Univ. of Chicago, 1986–92; British Acad. Reader, 1995–97. Junior Fellow, Univ. of Michigan Soc. of Fellows, 1979–80; Fellow, Davis Center, 1983–84, Mem., Inst. for Advanced Study, 1983–84, 2014–15, Princeton; von Humboldt Fellow, Göttingen, 1988–89; Leverhulme Trust Major Res. Fellow, 2009–12. Presenter: Inside the Medieval Mind, BBC4, 2008; The Normans, BBC2, 2010; The Plantagenets, BBC2, 2014. Corresp. Fellow, Medieval Acad. of America, 2012. *Publications:* Gerald of Wales 1146–1223, 1982; Trial by Fire and Water, 1986; The Making of Europe, 1993; England under the Norman and Angevin Kings, 2000; (ed) Medieval Panorama, 2001; (ed) Geoffrey of Burton, Life and Miracles of St Modwenna, 2002; (ed) The Miracles of St Æbbe of Coldingham and St Margaret of Scotland, 2003; The Hanged Man, 2004; The Natural and the Supernatural in the Middle Ages, 2008; Why Can the Dead Do Such Great Things?: saints and worshippers from the martyrs to the Reformation, 2013; (ed) Gerald of Wales, Instruction for a Ruler, 2018; contribs to learned jls. *Address:* Department of Mediaeval History, University of St Andrews, St Andrews, Fife KY16 9AL. *T:* (01334) 463308.

**BARTLETT, Timothy Conn;** Director, Tourism and Hotel Advisory Services, since 2006; *b* 15 Dec. 1944; *s* of Gordon Thomas Bartlett and Margaret Decima Bartlett; *m* 1st, 1970, Deira Janis Vacher (marr. diss.); one *s* one *d*; 2nd, 1988, Xochitl Alicia Quintanilla; two *d*. *Educ:* Cranleigh Sch.; Pembroke Coll., Oxford (Hons French and Spanish). Morgan

Grampian Books, 1967–68; British Tourist Authority: London, 1968–70 and 1974–77; Sydney, 1970–74; Manager: Mexico, 1977–82; Western USA, based in LA, 1982–87; France, 1987–88; General Manager: S Europe, 1988–91; Asia Pacific, 1991–94; Europe, based in Brussels, 1994–95; Acting Chief Exec., 1995–96, Chief Exec., 1996–99, English Tourist Bd; Chief Exec., British Assoc. of Leisure Parks, Piers and Attractions, 1999–2001; Dir, Tourism Div., 1999–2001 and Dir, Spain, Portugal and Latin America, 2001–05, TRI Hospitality Consulting; Chief Exec., Newcastle-Gateshead Initiative, 2005. *Recreations:* tennis, reading, music, travel. *Address:* Madrid, Spain. *E:* timcbartlett@hotmail.com.

**BARTLEY, Jonathan Charles;** Co-Leader, Green Party, since 2016; Member (Green) and Leader, Green Group, Lambeth Council, since 2018; *b* London, 16 Oct. 1971; *s* of Christopher William Bartley and Madeleine Bartley; one *s* two *d. Educ:* London Sch. of Econs and Political Sci. (BSc Social Policy and Admin 1994). Founder, 2001, Dir, 2003–16, Ekklesia. Contested (Green Party) Streatham, 2015. *Publications:* Faith and Politics after Christendom, 2004. *Recreation:* drummer (in blues band The Mustangs). *Address:* 23 Tooting Bec Gardens, SW16 1QY. *E:* jonathan.bartley@greenparty.org.uk.

**BARTOLI, Cecilia;** mezzo soprano; Artistic Director, Salzburg Whitsun Festival, since 2012; *b* Rome, 4 June 1966; *d* of Pietro Angelo Bartoli and Silvana Bartoli (*née* Bazzoni). *Educ:* Acad. of Santa Cecilia, Rome. Début, Barber of Seville, Teatro dell'opera, Rome, 1986; has performed at La Scala, Milan, Opéra Bastille, Carnegie Hall, Maggio Musicale Fest., Florence, Salzburg Fest., Wigmore Hall, Aix-en-Provence Fest., NY Metropolitan Opera, Royal Opera House, Covent Garden, Zurich Opera, Theater an der Wien, Barbican, Edinburgh Fest.; also with major orchs, incl. Vienna Philharmonic and Berlin Philharmonic, and major period instrument ensembles. Numerous recordings. Hon. RAM; Hon. Mem., Royal Swedish Acad. of Music; Academician, Santa Cecilia, Rome. Hon. DMus University Coll. Dublin, 2010. Léonie Sonning Music Prize, Denmark, 2010; Handel Prize, Halle, Germany, 2010; Herbert von Karajan Music Prize, Germany, 2012; 5 Grammy Awards; Polar Music Prize, 2016. Knight: Order of Merit (Italy); Fine Arts (France); Officer, Order of Merit (France); Medalla de Oro al Mérito en las Bellas Artes (Spain), 2007; Médaille Grand Vermeil de la Ville de Paris, 2010.

**BARTON, Alan Burnell;** Head of Resource Management and Finance Division (formerly Under Secretary), Department of Health, 1993–98; *b* 2 May 1943; *s* of Charles Henry Barton and Rose Edith Barton; *m* 1969, Jirina Klapstova; one *s* one *d. Educ:* Glyn Grammar Sch., Ewell; Bristol Univ. (BSc Chem.). Operational Research Exec., NCB, 1966–73; Department of Health and Social Security: Principal, 1973–78; Asst Sec., 1979–90; Dir, Medical Devices Directorate, DoH, 1990–93. Advr, Rickmansworth CAB, 2000–; Social Policy Advr, Citizens Advice (formerly NACAB), 2000–12; Mem., Low Incomes Tax Reform Gp, 2005–. *Recreations:* jazz (Mem., Ronnie Scott's), theatre, country houses, walking, art galleries. *Address:* 67 Heronsgate Road, Chorleywood, Rickmansworth, Herts WD3 5PA.

**BARTON, Amanda Lucy;** *see* Foreman, A. L.

**BARTON, Ven. (Charles) John Greenwood;** Archdeacon of Aston, 1990–2003; Priest-in-charge, St Peter, Bickenhill, 2002–03; *b* 5 June 1936; *s* of Charles William Greenwood Barton and Doris Lilian Leach; *m* 1972 (marr. diss. 1981); one *s. Educ:* Battersea Grammar Sch.; London Coll. of Divinity (ALCD). Asst Curate, St Mary Bredin, Canterbury, 1963–66; Vicar, Whitfield with West Langdon, dio. Canterbury, 1966–75; Vicar, St Luke, South Kensington, 1975–83; Area Dean, Chelsea, 1980–83; Chief Broadcasting Officer, Church of England, 1983–90. Communications Advr, 2005–06, Acting Chief of Staff, 2007–08, Actg Chaplain/Researcher, 2008, to Archbishop of York. Mem., Gen. Synod of C of E, 2000–03. Chm., BBC W Midlands Regl Adv. Council, 1995–98; Mem., English Nat. Forum, 1995–98. Member, Council: Corp. of Church House, 1989–2009; St Luke's Hosp. for Clergy, 2000–03. Chm., 2000–02, Trustee, 2002–03, Midlands Ethnic Albanian Foundn. *Address:* 7 The Spires, Canterbury, Kent CT2 8SD. *T:* (01227) 379688. *E:* venjohnbarton@gmail.com. *Club:* Victory Services.

**BARTON, Fiona;** QC 2011; *b* Bromley, Kent, 11 April 1964; *d* of John Barton and Theresa Barton. *Educ:* Stratford House Sch., Bickley; London Univ. (LLB Hons Law ext. 1985). Called to the Bar, Middle Temple, 1986; in practice as a barrister, specialising in police law, 5 Essex Court, Temple, 1986–, Hd of Chambers, 2010–17. Mem., Disciplinary Panel, Bar Council, 2003–12. *Publications:* (contrib.) Civil Actions Against the Police, 3rd edn, 2004; regular contrib. to Police Law Reports. *Recreations:* horse riding, walking, travel. *Address:* 5 Essex Court, Temple, EC4Y 9AH. *T:* (020) 7410 2000, *Fax:* (020) 7410 2010. *E:* clerks@5essexcourt.co.uk.

**BARTON, Rev. Prof. John,** DPhil, DLitt; FBA 2007; Oriel and Laing Professor of the Interpretation of Holy Scripture, University of Oxford, 1991–2014, now Emeritus; Fellow of Oriel College, Oxford, 1991–2014, now Emeritus; Senior Research Fellow, Campion Hall, Oxford, since 2014; *b* 17 June 1948; *s* of Bernard Arthur Barton and Gwendolyn Harriet Barton; *m* 1973, Mary Burn; one *d. Educ:* Latymer Upper Sch., Hammersmith; Keble Coll., Oxford (MA; DPhil 1974; DLitt 1988). Deacon and priest, 1973. University of Oxford: Jun. Res. Fellow, Merton Coll., 1973–74; Official Fellow, St Cross Coll., 1974–91; University Lectr in Theology (OT), 1974–89; Reader in Biblical Studies, 1989–91; Chaplain, St Cross Coll., 1979–91. Canon Theologian, Winchester Cathedral, 1991–2003. Hon. Dr theol. Bonn, 1998. *Publications:* Amos's Oracles against the Nations, 1980; Reading the Old Testament: method in biblical study, 1984, 2nd edn 1996; Oracles of God: perceptions of ancient prophecy in Israel after the Exile, 1986; People of the Book?—the authority of the Bible in Christianity, 1988, 2nd edn 1993; Love Unknown: meditations on the Death and Resurrection of Jesus, 1990; What is the Bible?, 1991, 2nd edn 1997; Isaiah 1–39, 1995; The Spirit and the Letter: studies in the biblical canon, 1997; Making the Christian Bible, 1997; Ethics and the Old Testament, 1998; (ed) The Cambridge Companion to Biblical Interpretation, 1998; (ed jtly) The Oxford Bible Commentary, 2001; Joel and Obadiah, 2001; (ed) The Biblical World, 2002; Understanding Old Testament Ethics, 2003; (with J. L. V. Bowden) The Original Story: God, Israel and the World, 2004; Living Belief: being Christian, being human, 2005; The Nature of Biblical Criticism, 2007; The Old Testament: canon, literature, theology, 2007; The Bible: the basics, 2010; The Theology of the Book of Amos, 2012; Ethics in Ancient Israel, 2014; The Hebrew Bible: a critical companion, 2016; A History of the Bible: the book and its faiths, 2019. *Address:* Oriel College, Oxford OX1 4EW. *Club:* Athenæum.

**BARTON, John;** *see* Barton, R. J. O.

**BARTON, Ven. John Greenwood;** *see* Barton, Ven. C. J. G.

**BARTON, Prof. Leonard Francis;** Professor of Inclusive Education, Institute of Education, London University, 2001–05, now Emeritus; *b* 20 April 1941. *Educ:* Liverpool Univ. (BA Hons); Manchester Univ. (MEd). Prof. of Educn, Bristol Poly., 1986–90; Sheffield University: Head of Res. Degrees, and Dir of Inclusive Educn Res. Centre; Prof. of Educn, 1990–2001. Sir Allan Sewell Fellow, Griffiths Univ., Australia, 1995–96. Founder and Editor, Disability and Society, 1985, now Consulting Editor. *Publications:* (ed) Disability and Society: emerging issues and insights, 1996; (ed) Disability, Politics and the Struggle for Change, 2001. *Recreations:* swimming, walking, listening to music. *Address:* c/o UCL Institute of Education, 20 Bedford Way, WC1H 0AL.

**BARTON, Prof. Nicholas Hamilton,** PhD; FRS 1994; Professor, Institute of Science and Technology Austria, since 2008. *Educ:* Peterhouse, Cambridge (BA 1976; MA 1980); Univ. of E Anglia (PhD 1979). Cambridge University: Res. Fellow, Girton Coll., 1980; Demonstrator, Dept of Genetics, 1980–82; Lectr, then Reader, Dept of Genetics and Biometry, UCL, 1982–90; Darwin Trust Fellow, 1990, Prof., 1994, Inst. of Cell, Animal and Population Biol., later Inst. for Evolutionary Biol., Edinburgh Univ. FRSE 1995. Darwin Medal, Royal Soc., 2006; Darwin-Wallace Medal, Linnean Soc., 2009; Mendel Medal, German Nat. Acad. of Scis Leopoldina, 2013. *Publications:* (jtly) Evolution, 2007. *Address:* Institute of Science and Technology Austria, Am Campus 1, 3400 Klosterneuburg, Austria.

**BARTON, Philip Robert,** CMG 2007; OBE 1997; HM Diplomatic Service; Director General, Consular and Security, Foreign and Commonwealth Office, since 2017; *b* 18 Aug. 1963; *s* of late Geoffrey Howard Barton and Katharine Anne (*née* Stubbings); *m* 1999, Amanda Joy Bowen; one *s* one *d. Educ:* Warwick Univ. (BA Econs and Politics); London Sch. of Econs (MSc Econs). Joined FCO, 1986: Third, then Second, Sec., Caracas, 1987–91; Cabinet Office (on secondment), 1991–93; First Secretary: FCO, 1993–94; New Delhi, 1994–96; Private Sec. to Prime Minister (on secondment), 1997–2000; Dep. High Comr, Cyprus, 2000–04; Dep. Gov., Gibraltar, 2005–08; Dir, S Asia, FCO, 2008–09; Dir, Foreign Policy, and Afghanistan and Pakistan Co-ordinator, Cabinet Office, 2009–11; Dep. Hd of Mission, Washington, 2011–13; High Comr to Pakistan, 2014–16; Dir-Gen., Prime Minister's Anti-Corruption Summit, Cabinet Office, 2016; Consulting Sen. Fellow, IISS (on secondment), 2016; Acting Chm., Jt Intelligence Cttee, Cabinet Office, 2016–17. *Recreations:* football, tennis, hiking, travel, reading. *Address:* c/o Foreign and Commonwealth Office, King Charles Street, SW1A 2AH.

**BARTON, (Robert) John (Orr);** Chairman, easyJet plc, since 2013; *b* Lahore, Pakistan, 23 Aug. 1944; *s* of Kenneth Barton and Elizabeth Joan Boyd (*née* Orr); *m* 1972, Anne Marie Coffey; two *s* one *d. Educ:* Gordonstoun Sch., Elgin; Strathclyde Univ. (MBA); CA 1968. CEO, Jardine Insce Brokers Gp plc, 1984–97; Chm., Jardine Lloyd Thompson Gp plc, 1997–2001; Chairman: Wellington Underwriting plc, 2001–06; Next plc, 2006–17 (Dir, 2002–17; Dep. Chm., 2004–06); Brit Insce Hldgs plc, 2008–10; Cable & Wireless Worldwide plc, 2011–12 (Dep. Chm., 2010–11); Catlin Gp Ltd, 2012–15 (Dir, 2011–15). Non-executive Director: Hammerson plc, 1998–2007; W H Smith plc, 1999–2011; SSP Gp plc, 2014– (Chm., Remuneration Cttee, 2014–). *Recreations:* golf, travelling, ski-ing. *Clubs:* Boodle's, Hurlingham; Royal and Ancient Golf; New Zealand Golf.

**BARTON, Roger;** owned and ran Llama Trekking, Sheffield, 2007–10; *b* 6 Jan. 1945; *s* of late Joseph and Doreen Barton; *m* 1965, Joan; one *s* (and one *s* decd). *Educ:* Burngreave Secondary Modern Sch.; Granville Coll. (Engrg Technician's Cert.). Fitter, 1961–81; Sheffield TUC and Labour Party Sec., 1981–89. Mem., Sheffield CC, 1971–90. Mem. (Lab) Sheffield, Eur. Parlt, 1989–99; contested (Lab) Yorkshire and the Humber Region, 1999. Former Dir, Insight Dynamics. *Recreations:* walking, gentle cycling, water sports. *Address:* 50 Hartley Brook Avenue, Sheffield S5 0HN. *Clubs:* Trades and Labour, Wortley Hall Labour (Sheffield).

**BARTRAM, Christopher John,** FRICS; Founder and Chairman, Orchard Street Investment Management, 2004–15; *b* Cambridge, 8 April 1949; *s* of John and Irene Bartram; *m* 1974, Carolyn Bates; one *s* one *d. Educ:* Oundle Sch.; Downing Coll., Cambridge (BA 1972). FRICS 1989. In private practice, London, 1972–74; Asst Surveyor, Equitable Life Assce, 1974–78; Property Investment Manager, Scottish Amicable Life, 1978–85; Partner, Jones Lang Wootton, 1985–95, Man. Partner, 1991–94; CEO, Haslemere NV, 1995–2004. Non-exec. Dir, Land Securities Gp plc, 2009–. A Crown Estate Comr, 2007–14. Chm., Bank of England Property Forum, 2002–05. Pres., British Property Fedn, 2000–01. Wilkins Fellow, Downing Coll., Cambridge, 2009– (Associate Fellow, 2005–09). *Recreation:* golf. *Clubs:* Reform; Royal West Norfolk Golf, Royal Worlington Golf, Royal and Ancient Golf.

**BARTRAM, Prof. Clive Issell,** FRCS, FRCP, FRCR; Honorary Professor of Gastrointestinal Radiology, Imperial College School of Medicine, University of London, 1999–2004; *b* 30 June 1943; *s* of Henry George and Muriel Barbara Bartram; *m* 1966, Michele Juliette François; two *s. Educ:* Dragon Sch., Oxford; St Edward's Sch., Oxford; Westminster Hosp. Med. Sch. (MB BS 1966). FRCR 1972; FRCP 1985; FRCS 1999. Consultant Radiologist, St Bartholomew's Hosp., 1974–94; Consultant Radiologist, 1974–2004, Clinical Dir, 2001–04, St Mark's Hosp.; Dir, Radiology, Princess Grace Hosp., 1990–2012. Hon. Consultant Radiologist, Hammersmith Hosp., 1994–99. *Publications:* Radiology in Inflammatory Bowel Disease, 1983; Handbook of Anal Endosonography, 1997; Imaging of Pelvic Floor Disorders, 2003; contrib. articles on gastrointestinal radiology and pelvic floor disorders. *Recreations:* walking, photography, music, reading, some gardening. *E:* cibartram@gmail.com. *Club:* Royal Society of Medicine.

**BARTTELOT, Col Sir Brian Walter de Stopham,** 5th Bt *cr* 1875; OBE 1983; psc; DL; Vice Lord-Lieutenant for West Sussex, 1994–2009; Harbinger, HM Body Guard of the Honourable Corps of Gentlemen at Arms, 2010–11 (Member, 1993–2011); *b* 17 July 1941; *s* of Lt-Col Sir Walter de Stopham Barttelot, 4th Bt, DSO and Sara Patricia (who *m* 2nd, 1965, Comdr James Barttelot, RN retd; she *d* 1998), *d* of late Lieut-Col H. V. Ravenscroft; *S* father, 1944; *m* 1969, Hon. Mary Angela Fiona Weld Forester (MBE 2001; DL, GCStJ), *y d* of 7th Baron Forester, and of Marie Louise Priscilla, CStJ, *d* of Sir Herbert Perrott, 6th Bt, CH, CB; four *d. Educ:* Eton; RMA, Sandhurst. Commnd Coldstream Guards, 1961; Temp. Equerry to HM the Queen, 1970–71. Camberley Staff Coll., 1974; GSO2, Army Staff Duties Directorate, MoD, 1975–76; Second in comd, 2nd Bn, Coldstream Guards, 1977–78; Mil. Sec. to Maj.-Gen. comdg London Dist and Household Div., 1978–81; GSO1, MoD, 1981–82; CO 1st Bn Coldstream Gds, 1982–85; GSO1, HQ BAOR, 1985–86; Regtl Lt-Col Comdg Coldstream Guards, 1986–92. Col, Foot Guards, 1989–92; Hon. Col, Sussex ACF, 1996–2007. President: W Sussex Scout Council, 1993–2017; S of England Agricl Soc., 2001–02; Sussex Br., CLA, 2008–. Chm. Exec. Cttee, Standing Council of the Baronetage, 1996–2001; Chm., Baronets' Trust, 2002–. Liveryman, Gunmakers' Co., 1981. DL W Sussex, 1988, High Sheriff, W Sussex, 1997–98. *Heir: b* Robin Ravenscroft Barttelot [*b* 15 Dec. 1943; *m* 1987, Theresa, *er d* of late Kenneth Greenlees; one *s* one *d*]. *Address:* Stopham Park, Pulborough, W Sussex RH20 1DY. *Clubs:* Cavalry and Guards, Pratt's, Farmers, Boodle's.

**BARWELL, Charles;** *see* Barwell, J. C. F.

**BARWELL, Rt Hon. Gavin (Laurence);** PC 2017; Chief of Staff to the Prime Minister, 2017–19; *b* Cuckfield, W Sussex, 23 Jan. 1972; *s* of David and Jennifer Barwell; *m* 2001, Karen McKenzie; three *s. Educ:* Trinity Sch. of John Whitgift, Croydon; Trinity Coll. Cambridge (BA Natural Scis 1993). Envmt Desk Officer, Cons. Party Res. Dept, 1993–95; Special Advr to Sec. of State for Envmt, 1995–97; Press Officer, Cons. Party, 1997; Hd of Pol Sect., 1997–98, Hd of Local Govt Dept, 1998–2003, Cons. Campaign HQ; Chief

Operating Officer, Cons. Party, 2003–06; political consultant, 2006–10. MP (C) Croydon Central, 2010–17; contested (C) same seat, 2017. PPS to Minister of State, DCLG, 2012–13, to Sec. of State for Educn, 2013; an Asst Govt Whip. 2013–14; a Lord Comr of HM Treasury (Govt Whip), 2014–15; Comptroller of HM Household (Govt Whip), 2015–16; Minister of State (Minister for Housing and Planning and Minister for London), DCLG, 2016–17. Mem. (C) Croydon LBC, 1998–2010 (Cons. Chief Whip, 2006–07; Cabinet Mem. for Resources and Customer Services, 2007–08, for Community Safety and Cohesion, 2008–10). Mem., Sci. and Technol. Select Cttee, 2010–12. Mem. Exec., 1922 Cttee, 2010–12. Chm. Govs, Trinity Sch. Cons. Backbencher of the Year, Asian Voice, 2011. *Publications:* How to Win a Marginal Seat: my year fighting for my political life, 2016. *Recreations:* sport, particularly football and tennis, military history, travel.
*[Created a Baron (Life Peer), 2019 but title not gazetted at time of going to press.]*

**BARWELL, (John) Charles (Fiddian),** OBE 2013; Chairman, Facultas Associates, since 2017; *b* Birmingham, 3 Aug. 1968; *s* of late Bryan Fiddian Barwell and of Blanch Barwell; *m* 2010, Juliet Claire Allen; two *s. Educ:* Malvern Coll., Worcs; Loomis Chaffee Sch., Windsor, Conn, USA; Univ. of Manchester (BA Amer. Studies 1991); Univ. of Birmingham (DBA 1992). Investment Manager: Albert E Sharp, 1993–98; Capel Cure Sharp, 1998–2005; Associate Dir, Gerrard Investment Mgt Ltd, 2005–07; Vice-Pres., Wealth and Investment Mgt, Barclays, 2007–17. Vice Pres., 2007–10, Pres., 2010–11, Nat. Cons. Convention. Chm., 1999–2002, Pres., 2018–, Birmingham Edgbaston Cons. Assoc. Conf. Chm., British-American Project, 2005. Trustee: CBSO, 2005–15 (Dep. Chm., 2012–15; Chm., Finance Cttee, 2005–11); CBSO Develt Trust, 2013–; Cons. Agents Superannuation Fund, 2015–; Cons. Agents Benevolent Assoc., 2017–. Governor: ESU, 1999–2001; Malvern Coll., 2013–; Bilton Grange Sch., 2014– (Chm., 2016–); Assoc. of Governing Bodies of Ind. Schs, 2019–. Chartered FCSI (FSI 2000). *Recreations:* family, singing, the rare sight of a golf ball flying straight, gardens, sailing, ski-ing, classical music, cultural heritage, fresh air and sunshine. *Address:* 6 Carpenter Road, Edgbaston, Birmingham B15 2JT. *E:* mail@charlesbarwell.com. *Clubs:* Carlton; MCC, Edgbaston Golf, Edgbaston Priory Lawn Tennis, Royal Cinque Ports Golf.

**BARWICK, Brian Robert;** Director, Barwick Media & Sport, since 2009; Chairman, Rugby Football League, since 2013; *b* 21 June 1954; *s* of John Leonard Barwick and Jean Ellen Barwick; *m* 1982, Geraldine Lynch; two *s. Educ:* Rudston Rd Co. Primary Sch.; Quarry Bank Comprehensive Sch.; Liverpool Univ. (BA Hons Econs). Journalist/sub-editor, North Western Evening Mail, Barrow-in-Furness, 1976–79; BBC Television (Sport): Asst Producer, 1979–84; Producer, Football Focus, 1982–84; Asst Ed., Grandstand, 1984–88; Editor: Match of the Day, 1988–95; Sportsnight, 1990–94; World Cup coverage, 1990 and 1994; Olympics, 1992 and 1996; Sports Rev. of the Year, 1991–95; Hd, Sport (Prodn), 1995–97; Controller, ITV Sport, 1998–2004; Dir of Programming, ITV2, 1998–2001; Chief Exec., FA, 2005–08. Vis. Prof. of Strategic Mgt, Univ. of Liverpool, 2009–. *Publications:* The Great Derbies: Everton *v* Liverpool (with G. Sinstadt), 1988; Anfield Days and Wembley Ways, 2011; Are You Watching the Match Tonight?, 2013. *Recreations:* watching sport, football, Rugby League, boxing and cricket; British TV comedy, sports and comedy memorabilia collecting, contemporary music, holidaying with family.

**BARWISE, Stephanie Nicola, (Mrs N. P. O'Donohoe);** QC 2006; *b* 17 Feb. 1964; *d* of Frank Barwise and Dorothy Carlyle Barwise (*née* Armstrong); *m* 2003, Nicholas Peter O'Donohoe, *qv*; one *s* two *d*, and two step *d. Educ:* Downing Coll., Cambridge (BA Law 1986; LLM 1987). Called to the Bar, Middle Temple, 1988, Bencher, 2010; in practice as barrister, specialising in commercial and construction law, 1989–. Chm., Middle Temple Estates Cttee, 2015–18 (Vice Chm., 2014). *Recreations:* horse riding, scuba-diving, ski-ing, yoga. *Address:* 1 Atkin Building, Gray's Inn, WC1R 5AT. *Clubs:* Kit Kat; Leander (Henley-on-Thames); Ospreys (Cambridge).

**BARWISE, Prof. (Thomas) Patrick,** PhD; Professor of Management and Marketing, London Business School, 1990–2006, Emeritus Professor, 2007; *b* 26 June 1946; *s* of (Henry) Balfour and Lily Barwise (*née* Abeles); *m* 1st, 1973, Mary Campbell (separated 2002; marr. diss. 2012); one *s* one *d*; 2nd, 2012, Dr Catherine Horwood (*née* Galitzine). *Educ:* Lincoln Coll., Oxford (Old Members' Scholar; BA Engrg Sci. with Econs 1968; MA 1973); London Business Sch. (MSc with Dist. Business Studies 1973; PhD 1985). Systems Engr, IBM, 1968–71; Asst to Chief Exec., Austin-Hall Gp, 1973–74; Mktg Manager, Graphic Systems Internat., 1974–76; London Business School: Sen. Res. Officer, 1976–82; Lectr, then Sen. Lectr in Mktg, 1982–90. Vis. Fellow, Reuters Inst. for Study of Journalism, Univ. of Oxford, 2011–14; Vis. Sen. Fellow in Media and Communications, LSE, 2015–16. Mem. Council, Which? (Consumers' Assoc.), 1995–2000, 2006–15 (Dep. Chm., 1998–2000; Chm., 2010–15); led ind. review of BBC digital television services, DCMS, 2004; Specialist Advr to H of L Select Cttee on Communications inquiry into regulation of TV advertising, 2010–11; expert witness for internat. commercial, tax and competition cases. Mem., Hansard Soc. Commn on Parlt and the Public, 2004–05. Mem. Cttee of Mgt, Soc. of Authors, 2010–13. Fellow, Sunningdale Inst., 2005–11. Hon. Fellow, Marketing Soc., 2006–. Patron, Market Res. Soc., 2013–. *Publications:* Online Searching, 1979; (with A. Ehrenberg) Television and its Audience, 1988; Accounting for Brands, 1989; Strategic Decisions, 1997; Marketing Expenditure Trends, 2002, 2nd edn 2003; (with S. Meehan) Simply Better: winning and keeping customers by delivering what matters most, 2004 (Berry-AMA Prize, 2005); (with S. Meehan) Beyond the Familiar: long-term growth through customer focus and innovation, 2011; (with R. G. Picard) The Economics of Television in a Digital World, 2012; (with R. G. Picard) What if There Were No BBC Television?, 2014; (with T. Barta) The 12 Powers of a Marketing Leader: how to succeed by building customer and company value, 2016; (with P. York) The War Against the BBC, 2020; numerous publications on mgt, mktg and media. *Recreation:* talking. *Address:* London Business School, Regent's Park, NW1 4SA.

**BARYSHNIKOV, Mikhail;** dancer, actor, producer; Artistic Director, Baryshnikov Arts Center, since 2005; *b* 27 Jan. 1948; *s* of Nicolai Baryshnikov and Alexandra (*née* Kisselov). *Educ:* Ballet Sch. of Riga, Latvia; Kirov Ballet Sch., Leningrad. Soloist, Kirov Ballet Co., 1969–74; Principal Dancer, NY City Ballet, 1978–79; Artistic Dir, 1980–89, Principal Dancer, 1974–78 and 1980–89, American Ballet Theater; Co-Founder (with Mark Morris) and Dir, White Oak Dance Proj., 1990–2002. Guest Artist, 1974–, with: Royal Ballet; National Ballet of Canada; Hamburg Ballet; Ballet Victoria, Aust.; Stuttgart Ballet; Alvin Ailey Dance Co., and Eliot Feld Ballet, New York; Spoleto Festival. Repertoire includes: Shadowplay (Tudor); Le Jeune Homme et la Morte (Petit); Sacré du Printemps (Tetley); Prodigal Son, Apollo, Theme and Variations (Balanchine); Afternoon of a Faun (Robbins); Romeo and Juliet, Wild Boy (MacMillan); Configurations (Choo San Goh); Les Patineurs, A Month in the Country (Ashton); Spectre de la Rose, Le Pavillon d'Armide, Petrouchka (Fokine); Santa Fe Saga (Feld); La Sylphide, La Bayadère, Coppélia, La Fille mal gardée (Bournonville); Swan Lake (Sergeyev and Bruhn); The Nutcracker, Don Quixote (own choreography). Works created: Medea (Butler), 1975; Push Comes to Shove, and, Once More Frank (Tharp), Connotations on Hamlet (Neumeier), Pas de Duke (Ailey), Other Dances (Robbins), 1976; Variations on America (Feld), 1977; Rubies (Balanchine), Opus Nineteen (Robbins), 1979; Rhapsody (Ashton), 1980. Over 50 works commissioned by White Oak Dance Project including: Waiting for the Sunrise (Lubovitch); Three Preludes (Morris); Punch and Judy (Gordon); Pergolesi (Tharp); Unspoken Territory (Reitz); Journey of a Poet (Hawkins); Heartbeat:mb (Janney and Rudner); Blue Heron (Schlömer); The Good Army (O'Day); Piano Bar (Béjart); See Through Knot (Jasperse); Single Duet (Hay); Chacony (Childs); The Show/Achilles Heels (Move); Yazoo (Feld). Actor: *films:* The Turning Point, 1978; White Nights, 1986; Dancers, 1987; Company Business, 1991; The Cabinet of Dr Ramirez, 1991; *television:* Sex in the City, 2004; *theatre:* Forbidden Patient or The Doctor and the Patient, NY, 2004; Beckett Shorts, NY, 2007; In Paris, Helsinki, 2011; Man in a Case, CT, 2013; The Old Woman, 2013; Letter to a Man, Spoleto, 2015; Brodsky/Baryshnikov, 2015; *photography exhibition:* Dancing Away, Contini Art UK, 2014–15. Gold Medal: Varna Competition, Bulgaria, 1966; 1st Internat. Ballet Comp., Moscow, 1968 (also awarded Nijinsky Prize by Paris Acad. of Dance); Dance Magazine Award, NYC, 1978; Kennedy Center Honors, 2000; Nat. Medal of Arts, 2000; Nijinsky Award for choreographic work Past Forward, 2002; Chubb Fellowship Award, Yale Univ., 2003; Liberty Prize, 2004; Jerome Robbins Award, 2004; Nixon Center Award, 2004; Arison Award, 2005. Commandeur, Ordre des Arts et des Lettres (France), 2010; Officier, Légion d'Honneur (France), 2010; Praemium Imperiale (Japan), 2017. *Publications:* (with Charles Engell France, photographs by Martha Swope) Baryshnikov at Work, 1976; (with John Fraser, photographs by Eve Arnold) Private View: inside Baryshnikov's American Ballet Theatre, 1988; Baryshnikov in Black and White, 2002; Merce My Way, 2008. *Recreations:* fishing, golf, photography.

**BARZUN, Matthew Winthrop;** Ambassador of the United States of America to the Court of St James's, 2013–17; Publisher, Louisville Magazine, since 2018; *b* NYC, 23 Oct. 1970; *m* 1999, Brooke Lee Brown; two *s* one *d. Educ:* St Paul's Sch., New Hampshire; Harvard Univ. (AB Hist. and Lit. 1993). With CNET Networks, 1993–2004: Vice Pres., Software Services, 1995–98; Exec. Vice-Pres., 1998–2000; Chief Strategy Officer, 2000–04; Founder, Brickpath LLC, internet media consultancy, 2004; Mem., Barack Obama's Nat. Finance Cttee for Presidential campaign, 2008; Ambassador to Sweden, 2009–11; Chair, Barack Obama's Nat. Finance Cttee for Presidential re-election campaign, 2012.

**BASBAUM, Prof. Allan Irwin,** PhD; FRS 2006; Professor, since 1984, and Chairman, Department of Anatomy, since 1977, University of California, San Francisco. *Educ:* McGill Univ. (BS 1968); Univ. of Penn (PhD 1972). Postdoctoral research: in neurophysiol., UCL, 1972–74; in neuroanatomy, UCSF, 1974–76; Associate Prof., Depts of Anatomy and of Physiol., UCSF, 1980–84. Co-founder and Mem., Scientific Adv. Bd, BiPar Sciences Inc. Chm., French American Internat. Sch. (Mem. Bd, 1988, Pres., until 2004). FMedSci 2019. *Publications:* articles in jls. *Address:* Department of Anatomy, University of California, Box 2722, 1550 4th Street, Rock Hall, San Francisco, CA 94158, USA.

**BĂSESCU, Traian;** Member (Partidul Mişcarea Populară), European Parliament, since 2019; President of Romania, 2004–14; *b* 4 Nov. 1951; *s* of Dimitru and Elena Traian; *m* 1975, Maria; two *d. Educ:* Mircea cel Bătrân Naval Inst. (grad 1976); Norwegian Acad. (schol.; advanced courses Mgt in Shipping Ind. 1995). Naval Officer, NAVROM, 1976–81; Captain, Comdr, Arges, Crisana and Biruinta ships, 1981–87; Chief, NAVROM Agency, Belgium, 1987–89; Gen. Manager, State Inspectorate for Civil Navigation, 1989–90, Under-Sec. of State and Chief, Shipping Dept, 1990–91, Min. of Transportation; Minister of Transportation, 1991–92; Deputy (Democratic), Vaslui, 1992–96; Minister of Transportation, 1996–2000; Mayor of Bucharest, 2000–04. Mem. (Partidul Mişcarea Populară), Senate, Romania, 2016–19. Democratic Party (PD): Bucharest Orgn, 2000–01; Pres., 2001–04; Co-Pres., DA (Justice and Truth) Alliance, 2001–04; Pres., People's Movement Party, 2016, now Hon. Pres. Hon. Dr Pol Scis Hankuk, Seoul, 2005; Hon. Dr Diplomatic and Strategic Centre of Studies, Paris, 2005. Comdr, Nat. Order of Merit (Romania), 2000; Medal of Renaissance, 1st Cl. (Jordan), 2005. *Recreations:* spending time with my family, taking long walks in nature. *Address:* European Parliament, 60 rue Wiertz, 1047 Brussels, Belgium.

**BASHAM, Brian Arthur;** *b* 30 July 1943; *s* of late Arthur Edgar Basham and Gladys Florence Alice (*née* Turner); *m* 1st, 1968, Charlotte Blackman; two *d*; 2nd, 1988, Eileen Wise (marr. diss. 1996); 3rd, 1998, Lynne Goodson. *Educ:* Brownhill Road Primary Sch., Catford; Catford Secondary Sch. GEC Export Clerk, 1961; Daily Mail City Office: Stock Exchange prices collector, 1962; City Press reporter, 1963; Prodn Editor, Daily Mail City Page, 1964; Financial Journalist: Daily Telegraph, 1966; The Times, 1968; Fund Man., Regent Fund Managers, 1971; Dir, John Addey Associates, 1973; Founder, 1976, subseq. Dep. Chm., Broad Street Gp; Co-Founder and Dep. Chm., Primrose Care, 1993–98; Founder Chairman: Equity Development, 2006–; ArchOver, 2013–16; Chm., Skin and Tonic, 2017–; Jt Founder and Chm., Affordable Access to Justice, 2017–. Founder Trustee, Centre for Investigative Journalism, 2005–15. *Publications:* (with Craig Pickering) Tomorrow's Giants, 1998; Thorium: the eighth element, 2013. *Recreations:* politics, reading, constitutional reform, motorcycling, gardening, walking. *Address:* Nashes Farmhouse, Crowhurst, E Sussex TN33 9BU. *T:* 07771 828828. *Clubs:* Army and Navy, Establishment (Chm., 2012–16).

**BASHEER, Prof. (Paliakarakadu Assen) Muhammed,** PhD, DSc; FREng; Professor of Structural Engineering, since 2014 and Head, School of Civil Engineering, since 2015, University of Leeds; *b* Puramattom, India, 9 Feb. 1959; *s* of Peerukhan Assen and Marium Beevi; *m* 1985, Lulu Bahauddin; one *s* one *d. Educ:* Univ. of Kerala (BSc Engrg); Univ. of Calicut (MSc Engrg); Queen's Univ., Belfast (PhD 1991; DSc 2014). CEng 1998. Asst Engr, Kerala Public Health Engrg Dept, 1982; Lectr, Calicut Regl Engrg Coll., 1982–90; Queen's University, Belfast: Res. Asst, 1990–92; Lectr, 1993–96; Sen. Lectr, 1996–98; Reader, 1998–99; Prof., 1999–2014. FREng 2014. *Publications:* Resistance of Concrete to Chloride Ingress: testing and modelling, 2012; approx. 85 papers in learned jls. *Recreations:* classical music, driving through countryside, family. *Address:* School of Civil Engineering, University of Leeds, Leeds LS2 9JT. *T:* (0113) 343 2272, *Fax:* (0113) 343 2265. *E:* p.a.m.basheer@leeds.ac.uk.

**BASHFORD, Prof. Alison Caroline,** PhD; FBA 2017; FRHistS; Research Professor of History, University of New South Wales, since 2017; *b* Sydney, Australia, 7 Sept. 1963; *d* of Keith and Marjorie Bashford; one *s* one *d* (twins). *Educ:* Univ. of Sydney (BA Hons 1990; PhD 1996); MA Cantab 2015. FRHistS 2015. Lectr in History, 1996–2009, Prof. of Modern Hist., 2009–13, Univ. of Sydney; Whitlam & Fraser Chair of Australian Studies, Harvard Univ., 2009–10; Vere Harmsworth Prof. of Imperial and Naval Hist., Univ. of Cambridge, 2013–17; Fellow, Jesus Coll., Cambridge, 2013–17. FAHA 2008. Trustee, Royal Mus Greenwich, 2014–17. *Publications:* Purity and Pollution, 1998; Imperial Hygiene, 2004; Thomas Griffith Taylor, 2008; Global Population, 2014; (ed with D. Armitage) Pacific Histories, 2014; (with J. E. Chaplin) The New Worlds of Thomas Robert Malthus, 2016. *Recreation:* horse riding. *Address:* School of Humanities and Languages, University of New South Wales, Sydney, NSW 2052, Australia. *E:* a.bashford@unsw.edu.au.

**BASHIR, Amjad Mahmood;** Member for Yorkshire and the Humber Region, European Parliament, 2014–19 (UK Ind, 2014–15, C, 2015–19); *b* Jhelum, Pakistan, 17 Sept. 1952. *Educ:* Thornton Grammar Sch.; Univ. of Bradford (degree in Chem. Engrg). Worked with Kodak; owner, Zouk Tea Bar and Grill, Bradford, 2006, Manchester, 2008. Contested (C) Yorks and the Humber Reg., EP, 2019.

**BASHIR, Hon. Prof. Dame Marie (Roslyn),** AD 2014 (AC 2001; AO 1988); CVO 2005; FRANZCP; Governor of New South Wales, Australia, 2001–14; *d* of M. Bashir; *m* 1957, Sir Nicholas Michael Shehadie, AC, OBE (*d* 2018); one *s* two *d*. *Educ:* Sydney Girls' High Sch.; Univ. of Sydney (MB, BS 1956). Taught at Univs of Sydney and of NSW; Clinical Prof. of Psychiatry, Univ. of Sydney, 1993–2001; Area Dir, Mental Health Services, Central Sydney, 1994–2001; Sen. Consultant, Aboriginal Med. Services, Redfern and Kempsey, 1996–2001. Chancellor, Univ. of Sydney, 2007–12. Chevalier, Légion d'Honneur (France), 2009.

**BASHIR, Martin;** Religious Affairs Editor, BBC, since 2016; *b* London, 19 Jan. 1963; *m* 1986, Deborah Judith Knox; one *s* two *d*. *Educ:* Southampton Univ. (BA Hons); King's Coll. London. BBC: news corresp., 1987–92; Panorama, 1992–99; presenter, Sunday prog., Radio 4, 2004, 2017–; Anchor/corresp., ITV Current Affairs; Anchor, Nightline, ABC News, 2004–10; Anchor/corresp., NBC News, 2010–13; freelance TV journalist, 2013–15. BAFTA Award, 1996; Journalist of Year, 1996, Best Piece of TV Journalism Award, 2000, RTS. *Recreations:* music - playing bass and produced two albums, sports - Rugby, football, cricket, theatre. *Address:* BBC TV, New Broadcasting House, Portland Place, W1A 1AA. *Club:* Reform.

**BASHMET, Yuri Abramovich;** viola player; Principal Conductor, Symphony Orchestra of New Russia, since 2002; *b* 24 Jan. 1953; *m* Natalia Timofeevna; one *s* one *d*. *Educ:* Moscow State Conservatory. Winner, Munich International Viola Competition, 1976; Founder and Dir, Chamber Orchestra Moscow Soloists, 1989–; Artistic Dir, Sviatoslav Richter's December Nights Fest., Moscow. Has performed with the world's major orchestras including: Berlin Philharmonic; Boston Symphony; Concertgebouw; LSO; Los Angeles Philharmonic; Montreal Symphony; first performance of viola concerti by Alfred Schnittke, Aleksander Tchaikovsky, Poul Ruders, Sofia Gubaidulina, Mark-Anthony Turnage, Giya Kancheli and Alexander Raskatov. Founder, Yuri Bashmet Internat. Foundn, 1994. *Address:* Apartment 16, Nezhdanovoy str. 7, 103009, Moscow, Russia.

**BASING, 6th Baron** *cr* 1887; **Stuart Anthony Whitfield Sclater-Booth;** *b* 18 Dec. 1969; *s* of 5th Baron Basing and of Patricia Ann, *d* of late George Bryan Whitfield, New Haven, Conn; *S* father, 2007; *m* 1997, Kirsten Erica (marr. diss.), *d* of Eric Henry Oxboel; two *s* one *d*. *Educ:* Collegiate Sch.; Vassar Coll.; Boston Univ. (MA). *Heir:* *s* Hon. Luke Waters Sclater-Booth, *b* 1 Sept. 2000.

**BASINGSTOKE, Bishop Suffragan of,** since 2014; **Rt Rev. David Grant Williams;** *b* Reading, 16 April 1961; *s* of Malcolm Williams and Brenda Williams; *m* 1986, Helen Pacey; one *s* one *d*. *Educ:* Bristol Univ. (BSocSc 1983); Wycliffe Hall, Oxford. Dep. Hd Teacher, St Luke's Yatta, CMS, E Kenya, 1983–85; ordained deacon, 1989, priest, 1990; Asst Curate, All Saints, Ecclesall, 1989–92; Vicar, Christ Church, Dore, 1992–2002; Rural Dean, Ecclesall, 1997–2002; Vicar, Christ Church, Winchester, 2002–14; Hon. Canon, Winchester Cathedral, 2012–14. Elected Gen. Synod, C of E, 2010–14; Chair, House of Clergy, Winchester Diocesan Synod, 2012–14. *Recreations:* sailing, long distance motorcycle journeys, theatre and film. *Address:* Bishop's Lodge, Colden Lane, Old Alresford, Alresford SO24 9DY. *T:* (01962) 737330. *E:* bishop.david@winchester.anglican.org.

**BASS;** see Hastings Bass, family name of Earl of Huntingdon.

**BASS, Rear-Adm. Paul Eric,** CB 1981; CEng, FIMechE, MIMarEST; *b* 7 March 1925; *s* of C. H. P. Bass, Ipswich; *m* 1948, Audrey Bruce Tomlinson (*d* 2002); one *s*. *Educ:* Northgate School, Ipswich; Royal Naval Engineering Coll., Keyham. Served as Midshipman in HM Ships Cambrian, Mauritius, Premier and Rodney; Lieut in Belfast, Phoebe and Implacable; Lt Comdr in Ulysses; Comdr in Lion and Tiger; Naval Staff Course, 1962; Captain, Weapons Trials, 1969–72; NATO Defense Course, 1972–73; Asst Chief of Staff (Intelligence), SACLANT, 1973–75; Dir, Naval Manning and Training (Engineering), 1975–78; Flag Officer, Portsmouth and Port Admiral, Portsmouth, 1979–81, retired 1981. Naval Advr to Internat. Military Services Ltd, 1982–85. *Recreations:* sailing, painting. *Clubs:* Royal Naval Sailing Association; Royal Naval and Royal Albert Yacht (Portsmouth).

**BASSAM OF BRIGHTON, Baron** *cr* 1997 (Life Peer), of Brighton in the co. of East Sussex; **John Steven Bassam;** PC 2009; *b* 11 June 1953; *s* of late Sydney Stevens and Enid Bassam; partner, Jill Whittaker; one *s* two *d* (and one *s* decd). *Educ:* Univ. of Sussex (BA Hons History 1975; Hon. Fellow, 2001); Univ. of Kent (MA Social Work 1979). Social Worker, E Sussex CC, 1976–77; Legal Advr, N Lewisham Law Centre, 1979–83; Policy Adviser: LB Camden, 1983–84; GLC (Police Cttee), 1984–86; London Strategic Policy Unit (Policing), 1986–87; Asst Sec., Police, Fire, Envmtl Health and Consumer Affairs, AMA, 1988–97; Consultant Advr, KPMG, 1997–99. Parly Under-Sec. of State, Home Office, 1999–2001; a Lord in Waiting (Govt Whip), 2001–08; Captain of Hon. Corps of Gentlemen at Arms (Govt Chief Whip in H of L), 2008–10; Opposition Chief Whip, H of L, 2010–18. Member (Lab): Brighton BC, 1983–97 (Leader, 1987–97); Brighton & Hove Unitary Council, 1996–99 (Leader, 1996–99). Fellow, Brighton Coll., 2002–. *Publications:* articles for local govt pubns. *Recreations:* cricket (plays for Preston Village CC), walking, running, watching football, reading, history of churches. *Address:* Longstone, 25 Church Place, Brighton BN2 5JN. *T:* (01273) 609473.

**BASSETT, Claire Elisabeth Rachel;** Chief Executive, UK Trade Remedies Authority, since 2019; *b* Londonderry, 23 Jan. 1974; *d* of Col Keith Whiteman and Jenny Whiteman; *m* 2002, Jason Bassett. *Educ:* Sherborne Sch. for Girls; Univ. of Wales Coll., Cardiff (LLB Hons). Mgt Trainee, SIG plc, 1996–99; Account Manager, Legal Services Commn, 1999–2003; Chief Exec., Connexions Milton Keynes, Oxon and Bucks, 2003–06; Services Dir, NACRO, 2006–09; Chief Executive: Criminal Cases Rev. Commn, 2009–12; Parole Bd for England and Wales, 2012–15; Electoral Commn, 2015–18. Mem. Bd, Home Gp, 2013–. Mem. Bd, Assoc. of Chief Execs, 2010–17 (Vice-Chair, 2014–17). Trustee, Internet Watch Foundn, 2018–. *Recreations:* horse riding, walking, friends and family, pet dachshund. *Address:* North Gate House, 21–23 Valpy Street, Reading RG1 1AF.

**BASSETT, John Anthony Seward,** FRICS; Consultant, Jones Lang LaSalle (formerly Jones, Lang, Wootton), since 1997 (Senior Partner, 1991–97); *b* 8 Sept. 1936; *s* of Roger Seward and Marjorie Bassett; *m* 1st, 1960, Jean Margaret Cooper (marr. diss. 1993; remarried 2006); one *s* one *d*; 2nd, 1994, Jennifer David (marr. diss. 2003). *Educ:* Blundell's Sch.; Coll. of Estate Management, London Univ. FRICS 1972. Joined Folkard & Hayward, 1957; Donaldson & Sons, 1960–63; joined Jones, Lang, Wootton, 1963, Partner 1967–97. Chairman: MWB Leisure Funds, 1996–2003; X-Leisure (Gen. Partner) Ltd, 2004–. Hon. Treas., Westminster Property Owners' Assoc., 1989–98. Trustee, Chatham Historic Dockyard Trust, 1997–. *Recreations:* ocean racing, ski-ing, travel, fly fishing. *Address:* 6 Ranelagh Grove, SW1W 8PD. *Clubs:* Pilgrims; Royal Thames Yacht, Royal Ocean Racing.

**BASSETT CROSS, Alistair Robert Sinclair;** District Judge, 1991–2011, Deputy District Judge, 2013–15, Central Family Court (formerly Principal Registry, Family Division), High Court of Justice; *b* 25 Aug. 1944; *s* of late Edward Bassett Cross and Marguerite Sinclair Bassett Cross (*née* Mitchell); *m* 1977, Margaret Victoria Janes; one *s* one *d*. *Educ:* Bishop Challoner Sch., Shortlands; Coll. of Law, Lancaster Gate. FInstLEx 1971. Legal Exec. with Lawrence Graham, 1964–77; solicitor, 1980; Legal Exec. and Solicitor, Payne Hicks Beach, 1977–91 (Partner, 1988–91); Dep. County Court and Dist Registrar, 1990. Mem., Solicitors' Family Law Assoc., 1984; Mem., Family Mediators' Assoc., 1989; Accredited Family Mediator, 1990; Mem., Adv. Bd of Mediation Service, Inst. of Family Therapy, 1995–98; Trustee, Mediation for Families (London E and City), 1999–2001; Accredited Civil and Commercial Mediator, 2012; Mem., Civil Mediation Council, 2012–. HAC, 1965, commnd, 1969; Mem., Co. of Pikemen and Musketeers, Lord Mayor's Bodyguard, 1993 (Elder Serjeant, 2003–06; Captain, 2011–14). Freeman, City of London, 1993; Liveryman, Poulters' Co., 1996 (Ct Asst, 2009; Master, 2014–15). Mem., Lime Street Ward Club, 1996 (Master, 2009–10). *Publications:* (ed) Supreme Court Practice, 1994–99; Civil Procedure, 2000–06; (ed) The Family Court Practice, 2004–06. *Recreations:* family, anything and everything. *Club:* Victory Services.

**BASSEY, Dame Shirley (Veronica),** DBE 2000 (CBE 1994); singer; *b* Tiger Bay, Cardiff, 8 Jan. 1937; *d* of late Henry and Eliza Jane Bassey; one *d*; *m* 1st, 1961, Kenneth Hume (marr. diss. 1965; decd); 2nd, 1971, Sergio Novak (marr. diss. 1981); one adopted *s* (one *d* decd). Appeared in Such is Life, 1955; *recordings* include: *singles:* Burn My Candle; Banana Boat Song, 1957; As I Love You, 1959; Kiss Me Honey; Reach for the Stars/Climb Every Mountain, 1961; What Now My Love; I Am What I Am; I (Who Have Nothing); Goldfinger, 1964; Diamonds Are Forever, 1971; Something; For All We Know; Never Never Never; Moonraker, 1979; *albums:* Born to Sing the Blues, 1958; And I Love You So, 1972; Live at Carnegie Hall, 1973; Magic Is You, 1978; Sassy Bassey, 1985; La Mujer, 1989; New York, New York, 1991; Great Shirley Bassey, 1999; The Performance, 2009; Hello Like Before, 2014; numerous concerts and tours; series, BBC TV; appeared in film, La Passione, 1996. Artist for Peace, UNESCO, 2000; Internat. Ambassador, Variety Club, 2001. Britannia Award for Best Female Singer, 1977; Lifetime Achievement Award, Nat. Music Awards, 2003. Légion d'Honneur (France), 2003; Freedom of City of Cardiff, 2012. *Address:* c/o Victoria Settepassi, 31 Avenue Princess Grace, MC 98000, Monaco.

**BASSI, (Paramjit) Paul Singh,** CBE 2010; DL; Chief Executive, Real Estate Investors plc, since 2007; Founder Chairman, Bond Wolfe, since 1985; *b* Birmingham, 21 March 1962; *s* of Santokh Singh Bassi and Avtar Kaur (*née* Chaudry); *m* 2008, Priya Paula (*née* Narang); one *d*; one *s* one *d* by a previous marriage. *Educ:* Harlington Comp. Sch., Hayes; Sandwell Coll. Regl Chm., Coutts Bank, 2001–07 (Mem., Exec. Steering Bd, 2006); non-exec. Chm., Corporatewear UK, 2004; Vice Chm., 2006, Chm., 2006–15, CP Bigwood (formerly Bigwood) Chartered Surveyors; Chm., Midlands, Kaupthing Singer & Friedlander, 2007–09; Director: Birmingham Hippodrome, 2005–10; InvestBX, 2007–11; Dir, Ind. Financial Advrs, EFG, 2011. Pres., Birmingham Chamber of Commerce, 2009–10 (Vice Pres., 2008–09). DL 2008, High Sheriff 2009, W Midlands. DUniv Birmingham City, 2009; Hon. DSc Aston, 2011. Lifetime Achievement Award, Lloyds TSB, 2005. *Recreations:* sport, reading, travel, prestige cars. *Address:* Real Estate Investors plc, 2nd Floor, 75/77 Colmore Row, Birmingham B2 2AP.

**BASSINGTHWAIGHTE, His Honour Keith;** a Circuit Judge, 1991–2003; Resident Judge, Guildford Crown Court Centre, 2000–03; a Deputy Circuit Judge, 2003–05; *b* 19 Jan. 1943; *s* of Reginald and Barbara Bassingthwaighte; *m* 1966, Olwyn Burn. *Educ:* Ashford (Middx) County Grammar Sch. Admitted solicitor, 1967. Served RAF Legal Branch as Flt Lt, 1968, Sqdn Ldr 1973, Wing Comdr 1978 and Gp Capt. 1981; retired 1984. Chm., Industrial Tribunals (London Central and S regions), part-time 1984–85, full-time 1985–91; a Recorder of the Crown Court, 1987–91. Pres., Social Security Appeal, Medical Appeal, Disability Appeal, Child Support Appeal and Vaccine Damage Tribunals, 1994–98; a Judge, Employment Appeal Tribunal, 1996. Mem., Parole Bd, 2004. *Recreations:* golf, bridge, opera. *Club:* Oake Manor Golf.

**BASSNETT, Prof. Susan Edna,** PhD; FRSL; writer; Professor of Comparative Literature, University of Glasgow, since 2015; Professor of Comparative Literature, University of Warwick, 1992–2016, now Emerita (Pro-Vice-Chancellor, 1997–2003 and 2005–09); *b* 21 Oct. 1945; *d* of Raymond George Bassnett and Anne Eileen Bassnett (*née* Hardwick); one *s* three *d*. *Educ:* Denmark, Portugal, Italy and UK; Univ. of Manchester (BA 1st Cl. Hons English and Italian 1968); Univ. of Lancaster (PhD French 1975). Lecturer: Univ. of Rome, 1968–72; Univ. of Lancaster, 1972–76; Univ. of Warwick, 1976–2016: estabd Centre for Translation and Comparative Cultural Studies, 1985; Reader, 1989–92. Has held Vis. Prof. posts at univs worldwide; Vis. Lectr, Michigan State Univ., 1974–75. Member: Arts Adv. Bd, British Council, 2002–06; W Midlands Culture, 2002–09; Arts Council England, W Midlands, 2003–10; QAA, 2003–08. Mem. Bd, SOAS, 2003–08. Mem., Adv. Panel, Leverhulme Trust, 2015–. Pres., British Comparative Literature Assoc., 2016–. FCIL (FIL 2000); MAE 2006 (Mem. Council, 2007–14); FRSL 2008. *Publications:* Translation Studies, 1980, 4th edn 2013; Luigi Pirandello, 1983; Sylvia Plath: an introduction to the poetry, 1987, 2nd edn 2004; (jtly) The Actress in Her Time: Bernhardt, Terry, Duse, 1988; Magdalena: women's experimental theatre, 1989; (ed) Knives and Angels: Latin American women's writing, 1990; Shakespeare: the Elizabethan plays, 1993; Comparative Literature: a critical introduction, 1993; (jtly) Three Tragic Actresses: Siddons, Rachel, Ristori, 1996; (with A. Lefèvre) Constructing Cultures, 1998; (ed with H. Trivedi) Postcolonial Translation: theory and practice, 1999; Exchanging Lives, 2002; (ed with P. Bush) The Translator as Writer, 2006; Ted Hughes, 2009; (with E. Bielsa) Translation in Global News, 2009; Reflections on Translation, 2011; Translation, 2014; World Literature and Translation, 2018. *Recreations:* reading, walking with dogs, textiles, writing. *Address:* Modern Languages, University of Warwick, Coventry CV4 7AL. *T:* (024) 7652 3655. *E:* s.bassnett@warwick.ac.uk.

**BASTARRECHE, Carlos,** Hon. KCVO 2017; Ambassador of Spain to the Court of St James's, since 2017; *b* Madrid, 27 Nov. 1950; *s* of Carlos and Ana María Bastarreche; *m* 1976, Rosalía Gómez-Pineda Goizueta; one *s* three *d*. *Educ:* Universidad Complutense de Madrid (Law degree); Spanish Diplomatic Acad. (Dip. Internat. Studies). Gen. Directorate for Foreign Policy for Africa and Asia, Foreign Affairs Min., Spain, 1976; Second Sec., Consular and Commercial Repn of Spain, Bucharest, 1976–79; First Sec., Spanish Mission to EC, Brussels, 1979–84; Foreign Affairs Ministry, Spain: Advr, State Secretariat for Relns with EEC, 1984–85; Dep. Dir-Gen., 1985–89, Dir-Gen., 1990–91, for Eur. Communities Coordination and Instl Relns; Dep. Perm. Rep. to EU, Brussels, 1991–96; Foreign Affairs Ministry, Spain: Sec.-Gen. for Foreign Policy and the EU and Foreign Affairs, 1996–2000; Sec.-Gen. for Eur. Affairs, and Spanish rep. to Intergovtl Conf., 2000–02; Perm. Rep. to EU, Brussels, 2002–10; Ambassador of Spain to France, 2010–14; Hd, Public Affairs Spain, Airbus, 2014–17. Comdr by Number, Order of Civil Merit (Spain); Grand Cross, Order of Isabella the Catholic (Spain); Medal, Order of Constitutional Merit (Spain); Comdr de la Légion d'honneur (France). *Recreations:* golf, reading history books. *Address:* Embassy of Spain, 39 Chesham Place, SW1X 8SB. *E:* emb.londres@maec.es.

**BASTON, Ven. Caroline;** Interim Minister, Benefice of Fawley, Hampshire, since 2019; *b* 17 Oct. 1956; *d* of Dr John Baston, MB ChB, DPM, FRCGP and Dr Daphne Baston, MB ChB, MRCGP. *Educ:* Birmingham Univ. (BSc 1978); Birmingham Poly. (Cert Ed 1979); Ripon Coll., Cuddesdon (Hon. Fellow 2014). Teacher, Shireland High Sch., Smethwick, 1979–87. Ordained deacon, 1989, priest, 1994; Asst Curate, Thornhill St Christopher, Southampton, 1989–95; Rector, All Saints', Winchester, with St Andrew,

Chilcomb, with St Peter, Chesil, 1995–2006; Communications Officer, 1995–98, Dir of Ordinands, 1999–2006, Dio. Winchester; Archdeacon of the Isle of Wight, 2006–11, now Archdeacon Emeritus; Priest-in-charge; St Andrew's, N Swindon, 2011–16. Warden: Community of St Mary the Virgin, Wantage, 2013–; Hopeweavers Community, Southampton, 2015–. Hon. Canon: Winchester Cathedral, 2000–06, now Canon Emeritus; Portsmouth Cathedral, 2006–11. *Address:* 39 Clarendon Road, Shirley, Southampton SO16 4GB.

**BASU, Anil Kanti, (Neil),** QPM 2016; Assistant Commissioner, Specialist Operations, Metropolitan Police Service, and National Police Chiefs Council Lead for Counter Terrorism Policing, since 2018; *b* Stafford, 12 June 1968; *s* of late Dr Pankaj Kumar Basu and of Enid Margaret Basu; *m* 2018, Dr Nina Louise Cope; three *s*. *Educ:* Walton High Sch., Stafford; Univ. of Nottingham (BA Hons Econs 1989). Metropolitan Police Service: police officer, 1992–; Comdr, S London, 2012–13; Comdr for Ops, Weeting, Elveden and Tuleta, 2013–17; Commander: Armed Policing, 2013–14; Gangs and Organised Crime, 2014–15; Dep. Asst Comr, Specialist Ops, 2015–16; Sen. Nat. Coordinator, UK Counter Terrorism Policing, 2016–18. Mem., Adv. Bd, GRIT (formerly Youth at Risk), 2015–. Hon. Pres., Metropolitan Police Service Hindu Soc., 2012–. *Recreations:* family, sport, music, movies, motors. *Address:* Metropolitan Police Service, New Scotland Yard, Westminster, SW1A 2JL. *T:* (020) 7230 1212.

**BASU, Dijendra Bhushan;** QC 2015; a Recorder, since 2010; *b* Solihull, 10 Aug. 1968; *s* of Dr Dipendra Bhushan Basu and late Dr Shashi Kanta Basu; one *d*. *Educ:* Queen Mary's Grammar Sch., Walsall; United Med. and Dental Schs of Guy's and St Thomas's, Univ. of London (MB BS with distinction in Surgery 1991). Called to the Bar, Lincoln's Inn, 1994; in practice as a barrister specialising in police, public and employment law; a Special Advocate, 2009–. *Publications:* technical legal jls. *Recreations:* flying helicopters, sailing, cooking, travelling, laughing. *Address:* Serjeants' Inn Chambers, 85 Fleet Street, EC4Y 1AE. *T:* (020) 7427 5000, *Fax:* (020) 7353 0425. *E:* dbasuqc@serjeantsinn.com.

**BASU, Neil;** *see* Basu, A. K.

**BATCHELAR, Judith Margaret,** OBE 2015; Director, Sainsbury's Brand, J. Sainsbury plc, since 2004; *b* Bournemouth, 6 March 1959; *d* of Frank Troke and Margaret Troke; *m* 1989, Geoffrey Batchelar; twin *d*. *Educ:* Univ. of Surrey (BSc Hons Med. Biochem. 1981); King's Coll. London (PGCE 1982). Regd Nutritionist 2002; Regd Scientist 2013. Personnel and Trng Mgr, Bass Charrington, 1983–87; Nat. Account Mgr, Mars Confectionery, 1987–89; Category Mgr, Marks and Spencer plc, 1989–2001; Dir, Own Brand and Technical, Safeway plc, 2001–04. Chair, Agri-tech Leadership Council, subseq. Agri-food Technol. Leadership Council, 2013–18; non-exec. Dir, Envmt Agency, 2018–. Dep. Chair, Bd of Trustees, Farm Africa, 2013–. Non-exec. Dir, Rugby Players Assoc., 2019. FRSA; FIFST 2017. *Recreations:* family, dog walking, Rugby, ballet, theatre. *Address:* J. Sainsbury plc, 33 Holborn, EC1N 2HT. *T:* (020) 7695 6303. *E:* Judith.Batchelar@sainsburys.co.uk.

**BATCHELOR, Lance Henry Lowe;** Group Chief Executive Officer, Saga plc, 2014–Jan. 2020; *b* London, 9 Jan. 1964; *s* of David Henry Lowe Batchelor and Sarah Ann Batchelor; *m* 1989, Wendy Jane Doran; four *s*. *Educ:* Cranleigh Sch.; Univ. of Wales (BSc Econs 1985); Harvard Business Sch. (MBA 1993). Lieut, Submarines, RN, 1985–90; Procter & Gamble: Asst Brand Manager, Health and Beauty Care, 1991–95; Brand Manager, Skincare, 1995–97; Gen. Manager and Mktg Dir, Beauty Care Div., 1997–2000; amazon.com: Gen. Manager and Product Dir, Books, Music/Video, 2000–01; Hd, Worldwide Mktg, 2001–02; Vodafone plc: Mktg Dir and Mem., UK Bd, 2002–04; Global Mktg Dir, Vodafone Consumer, 2004–06; Tesco plc: Mktg Dir, 2007–08; CEO, Tesco Telecoms, 2008–11; CEO, Domino's Pizza Gp plc, 2011–14. Non-exec. Dir, Royal Navy Bd, 2018–. Trustee, Nat. Gall., 2011–19. Mem., RNSA, 1986. Mem., Council of Mgt, White Ensign Assoc., 2014–; Vice Patron, RN and RM Charity, 2015–. Hon. Comdr, RNR, 2017–. Liveryman, Shipwrights' Co., 2017–; Younger Brother, Trinity House, 2017–. FInstD 2015. Hon. Fellow, Aberystwyth Univ., 2017. *Recreations:* sailing, fine art. *Address:* (until Jan. 2020) Saga plc, Enbrook Park, Sandgate, Kent CT20 3SE. *T:* (01303) 771111, *Fax:* (01303) 771175. *E:* lance.batchelor@saga.co.uk.

**BATCHELOR, Lesley Janet,** OBE 2014; Director General, Institute of Export and International Trade, since 2010; Chief Executive Officer, OpentoExport.com, since 2013; *b* Great Bookham, Surrey, 10 Feb. 1957; *d* of William Hazard Batchelor and Joyce Batchelor; *m* 1991, Robert Collins (marr. diss. 2008); one *s*. *Educ:* Coll. for Distributive Trades, London. Dip. Internat. Trade, Inst. of Export, 1991; Dip. CIM 1994. Mgt trainee, then Export Manager, Ciba-Geigy Pharmaceuticals, 1973–84; Eur. Develt Manager, Fujitsu Europe, 1984–86; Internat. Travel Exec. (Airlines), Coca-Cola Europe Ltd, 1986–89; Mktg Manager, Skytech Distribn, 1989–91; Product Manager, Canon UK Ltd, 1991–92; CEO, CMC Strategy and Trng, 1992–2014; Commercial Dir, Pathfinder Business Ltd, 2000–07; Dir, Internat. Sales and Dealer Mktg, Really Useful Machine Co. Ltd, 2007–08; Dir, TEN (Export Network), 2007–10. Non-executive Director: Internat. Business and Diplomatic Exchange, 2015–; Internat. Assoc. Trade Trng Orgns, 2016–. Mem., Judging Panel for internat. trade, Queen's Awards for Enterprise, 2009–; Judge, Nat. Business Awards, 2017–. Freeman, City of London, 2009; Liveryman, World Traders' Co., 2010. *Recreations:* Artbarge project to float Dutch barge on River Ouse, since 2015; walking spaniel, cooking for friends, attending City Livery Company events. *T:* 07774 264725. *E:* lesley@cmc-marketing.com.

**BATCHELOR, Paul Anthony;** Chairman: Crown Agents Bank, 2008–17; Crown Agents Investment Management Ltd, 2008–17; Crown Agents Group, 2007–15; Vice President, Crown Agents Foundation, since 2017; *b* Ashford, Kent, 4 July 1946; *s* of Joseph John Batchelor and Irene Margaret Batchelor (*née* Shoobridge); *m* 1969, Janet Rowden King; one *s* one *d*. *Educ:* Ashford Grammar Sch.; St John's Coll., Cambridge (BA 1st Cl. Hons 1968). Postgrad. Dip. Develt Econs). Economist, Swaziland Govt, 1969–72; Sen. Economist, then Actg Chief Economist, Malawi Govt, 1972–74; Coopers & Lybrand, later PricewaterhouseCoopers, 1974–2004: Partner, 1982–2004; Chief Exec., Coopers & Lybrand Europe, 1994–98; Mem., Global Mgt Team, 1998–2004. Chm., Oxford Policy Mgt, 2006–13. Mem., UK and Internat. Adv. Councils, Transparency Internat., 1995–. Non-exec. Dir, Abacus Technology (Pvt) Ltd, Pakistan, 2010–. Trustee: Langham Partnership UK and Ireland, 2005–14; OM Ships Internat., 2006–14; Water Aid UK, 2009–15; Rochester Good Stewards Trust, 2018–. Chm., Stour Music Fest. Cttee, 2012–; Mem. Bd, Stour Music Fest. Co., 2013–. *Recreations:* classical music, opera, golf, gardening, mountain walking. *Address:* Crown Agents Foundation, Blue Fin Building, 110 Southwark Street, SE1 0SU. *E:* pauljanetbatchelor@yahoo.co.uk. *Clubs:* Royal Over-Seas League; Hever Castle Golf.

**BATCHEN, Prof. Geoffrey John McCallum,** PhD; Professor of Art History, University of Oxford, from Jan. 2020; *b* Melbourne, 21 Nov. 1956; *s* of David Batchen and Gillian Batchen; one *s* one *d*; partner, Justine Varga. *Educ:* Univ. of New South Wales (BSc Arch. 1979); Univ. of Sydney (BA Hons 1982; PhD 1991). Asst Prof., Visual Arts, UCSD, 1991–96; Associate Prof., Art and Art Hist., Univ. of New Mexico, Albuquerque, 1996–2001; Professor of Art History: CUNY Graduate Center, NY, 2002–10; Victoria Univ. of Wellington, NZ, 2010–19. *Publications:* Burning with Desire: the conception of photography, 1997 (trans. Spanish, Korean, Japanese, Slovenian, Chinese, Italian, Ukrainian); Each Wild Idea: writing, photography, history, 2001 (trans. Chinese); William Henry Fox Talbot, 2008; (ed) Photography Degree Zero: reflections on Roland Barthes's Camera Lucida, 2009; Repetition och Skillnad (Swedish), 2011; (ed jtly) Picturing Atrocity: photography in crisis, 2012; Emanations: the art of the cameraless photograph, 2016; Obraz a diseminace (Czech), 2016; More Wild Ideas, 2017 (trans. Chinese); Apparitions: photography and dissemination, 2018. *Recreation:* collecting photographs. *Address:* Department of History of Art, University of Oxford, Suite 9, Littlegate House, St Ebbe's Street, Oxford OX1 1PT. *E:* admin@hoa.ox.ac.uk.

**BATE, Sir (Andrew) Jonathan,** Kt 2015; CBE 2006; PhD; FBA 1999; FRSL; Professor of English Literature, University of Oxford, since 2011; Senior Research Fellow, Worcester College, Oxford, since 2019 (Provost, 2011–19); *b* 26 June 1958; *s* of Ronald Montagu Bate and Sylvia Helen Bate; *m* 1st, 1984, Hilary Gaskin (marr. diss. 1995); 2nd, 1996, Paula Jayne Byrne; two *s* one *d*. *Educ:* Sevenoaks Sch., Kent; St Catharine's Coll., Cambridge (MA; PhD 1984; Hon. Fellow, 2000). Harkness Fellow, Harvard Univ., 1980–81; Research Fellow, St Catharine's Coll., Cambridge, 1983–85; Fellow, Trinity Hall, Cambridge and Lectr, Trinity Hall and Girton Coll., 1985–90; King Alfred Prof. of English Lit., Univ. of Liverpool, 1991–2003; Research Reader, British Acad., 1994–96; Leverhulme Personal Res. Prof., 1999–2004; Prof. of Shakespeare and Renaissance Literature, Univ. of Warwick, 2003–11. Vis. Prof., UCLA, 1989, 1996; Gresham Prof. of Rhetoric, 2017–19; Dist. Sustainability Scholar, Arizona State Univ., 2019. Vice Pres., Humanities, British Acad., 2011–14. Consultant Curator, Shakespeare: Staging the World, BM, 2012. A Judge, Man Booker Prize, 2014. Mem., AHRC, 2007–11. Gov., 2002–17, Mem. Bd, 2003–11, RSC. FRSL 2004. One-man play for Simon Callow, The Man from Stratford, nat. tour, 2010, retitled as Being Shakespeare, Trafalgar Studios, 2011–12, NY and Chicago, 2012, Harold Pinter, 2014. Hon. Fellow, Shakespeare Birthplace Trust, 2013. Patron, Sevenoaks Sch., 2014–. *Publications:* Shakespeare and the English Romantic Imagination, 1986; (ed) Lamb, Essays of Elia, 1987; Shakespearean Constitutions, 1989; Romantic Ecology, 1991; (ed) The Romantics on Shakespeare, 1992; Shakespeare and Ovid, 1993; The Arden Shakespeare: Titus Andronicus, 1995; (ed) Shakespeare: an illustrated stage history, 1996; The Genius of Shakespeare, 1997; The Cure for Love (novel), 1998; The Song of the Earth, 2000; John Clare: a biography, 2003 (Hawthornden Prize, James Tait Black Meml Prize, 2004); (ed) I Am: the selected poetry of John Clare, 2003; (ed) The RSC Shakespeare: complete works, 2007 (individual works, 34 vols, 2009–12); Soul of the Age: the life, mind and world of William Shakespeare, 2008; English Literature: a very short introduction, 2010; (ed) The Public Value of the Humanities, 2011; (with D. Thornton) Shakespeare: staging the world, 2012; (with E. Rasmussen) Shakespeare and Others: collaborative plays, 2013; (with J. Goodman) Worcester: portrait of an Oxford College, 2014; Ted Hughes: the unauthorised life, 2015 (Biographers Internat. Orgn Award, 2016); (ed jtly) Stressed, Unstressed: classic poems to ease the mind, 2016; The Shepherd's Hut: poems, 2017; How the Classics Made Shakespeare, 2019. *Recreations:* tennis, fine art, opera, walking. *Address:* Worcester College, Oxford OX1 2HB.

**BATE, Anthony John; His Honour Judge Bate;** a Circuit Judge, since 2007; *b* Leamington Spa, 30 Nov. 1961; *er s* of Terence and Mary Bate; *m* 1988, Sally Trower; two *s*. *Educ:* Queen Elizabeth's Grammar Sch., Blackburn; Christ's Coll., Cambridge (BA 1983; VetMB 1986). MRCVS 1986. Called to the Bar, Lincoln's Inn (Denning Schol.), 1987; in practice as barrister specialising in criminal and common law, E Anglian Chambers, Norwich, 1988–2007; Mem., Regl Civil Panel of Counsel instructed by Treasury Solicitor, 2000–07; a Recorder, 2003–07. Mem., Parole Bd, 2010–. Trustee, Welfare Fund for Companion Animals, 1999–2018. *Recreations:* browsing second-hand bookshops, badminton, rambling, railway, naval and military history. *Address:* c/o Norwich Crown Court, Bishopgate, Norwich NR3 1UR.

**BATE, Prof. (Christopher) Michael,** PhD; FRS 1997; Royal Society Professor of Developmental Neurobiology (formerly Professor of Developmental Neurobiology), University of Cambridge, 1998–2009, now Emeritus; Fellow of King's College, Cambridge, since 1992. *Educ:* Trinity Coll., Oxford (BA 1966); PhD Cantab 1976. Cambridge University: Lectr in Zoology, until 1994; Reader in Develtl Biol., 1994–98. *Address:* Department of Zoology, Downing Street, Cambridge CB2 3EJ. *T:* (01223) 336639, *Fax:* (01223) 336676; King's College, Cambridge CB2 1ST.

**BATE, David Christopher;** QC 1994; a Recorder, since 1991; *b* 2 May 1945; *s* of late Robert Leslie Bate and Brenda Mabel Bate (*née* Price); *m* 2003, Fiona Adele Graham; three *s* one *d* from previous marriage. *Educ:* Hendon Co. Grammar Sch.; Manchester Univ. (LLB Hons). Called to the Bar, Gray's Inn, 1969; VSO (UNA) with Melanesian Mission, 1969–70; Crown Counsel, British Solomon Is Protectorate, 1971. *Recreations:* swimming, cycling, trying to sing in tune with 'Counterpoint' and Cantemus.

**BATE, Jennifer Lucy,** OBE 2008; FRCO; classical concert organist, since 1969; composer, since 1972; *b* 11 Nov. 1944; *d* of Horace Alfred Bate and Dorothy Marjorie Alice Bate (*née* Hunt). *Educ:* Bristol Univ. (BA Hons 1966). ARCM 1961; LRAM 1963; FRCO 1967. Shaw Librarian, LSE, 1966–69. Designer and Lead Tutor, Jennifer Bate Organ Acad., 2004–. Vice-Pres., British Music Soc., 1996–. Vice-Pres., N London Fest., 2003. Has played in over 40 countries, incl. tours in S America, France and Italy; first organist to open a BBC Prom Concert with solo performance, 1974; world expert on organ works of Olivier Messiaen; has lectured worldwide, incl. A Guide to the King of Instruments (an educn prog. for all age gps); masterclasses and teaching projects for British Council; TV appearances and performances; has made numerous recordings, incl. world première recording of Messiaen's Livre du Saint Sacrement, 1987 (Grand Prix du Disque; Record of Year, Sunday Times; Pick of Year, Times), complete organ works of Mendelssohn, 2005, complete organ works of Peter Dickinson, 2008, Messiaen's La Nativité du Seigneurs, 2010. FRSA 2002. Hon. DMus Bristol, 2007. Personnalité de l'Année (France), 1989; Award for Early Instrumental Music, Music Retailers' Assoc., 1991. Officier de l'ordre des Arts et des Lettres (France), 2011; Chevalier, Ordre National de la Légion d'Honneur (France), 2011. *Compositions:* Toccata on a theme of Martin Shaw, 1979; Four Reflections: No 3 1981, No 2 1982, No 1 1986, No 4 1986; Homage to 1685, 1985; Lament, 1995; An English Canon, 1996; Variations on a Gregorian Theme, 1998; Four Handel-inspired Miniatures, 2007; Five Hymn-Tune Preludes, 2008; Suite on Veni Creator, for organ, 2010. *Publications:* (contrib.) Grove's Dictionary of Music and Musicians, 6th edn 1974– (incl. New Grove's Dictionary of Music and Musicians, 1998–99). *Recreation:* gardening. *Address:* 35 Collingwood Avenue, Muswell Hill, N10 3EH. *T:* (020) 8883 3811, *Fax:* (020) 8444 3695. *E:* jenniferbate@classical-artists.com.

**BATE, Sir Jonathan;** *see* Bate, Sir A. J.

**BATELY, Prof. Janet Margaret, (Mrs L. J. Summers),** CBE 2000; FBA 1990; Sir Israel Gollancz Professor of English Language and Medieval Literature, King's College, University of London, 1995–97, now Emeritus (Professor of English Language and Medieval Literature, 1977–95); *b* 3 April 1932; *d* of late Alfred William Bately and Dorothy Maud Bately (*née* Willis); *m* 1964, Leslie John Summers (*d* 2006), sculptor; one *s*. *Educ:* Greenhead High Sch., Huddersfield; Westcliff High Sch. for Girls; Somerville Coll., Oxford (Shaw

Lefevre Scholar; Eileen Gonner Meml Prize, 1953; BA 1st cl. hons English 1954, Dip. in Comparative Philology (with distinction) 1956, MA 1958; Hon. Fellow, 1997); FKC 1986. Asst Lectr in English, Birkbeck Coll., Univ. of London, 1955–58, Lectr, 1958–69, Reader, 1970–76. Lectures: Sir Israel Gollancz Meml, British Acad., 1978; Toller Meml, Manchester Univ., 1987; Dark Age, Univ. of Kent, 1991; Kemble, Trinity Coll., Dublin, 2012. Chm., Scholarships Cttee, Univ. of London, 1988–91. Member: Council, EETS, 1981–; Exec. Cttee, Fontes Anglo-Saxonici, 1985–2008; Adv. Cttee, Internat. Soc. of Anglo-Saxonists, 1986–91; Adv. Cttee, Sources of Anglo-Saxon Lit. and Culture, 1987–; Humanities Res. Bd, British Acad., 1994–95; Adv. Bd, Inst. for Histl Study of Lang., Glasgow Univ., 1998–. Mem. Hon. Develt Bd, Book Trust, 2002–. Governor: Cranleigh Sch., 1982–88; King's Coll. Sch., Wimbledon, 1991–94; Notting Hill and Ealing High Sch., 1998–2002. FRSA 2000. Gen. Ed., King's Coll. London Medieval Studies, 1987–2001. *Publications:* The Old English Orosius, 1980; The Literary Prose of King Alfred's Reign: Translation or Transformation, 1980; (ed) The Anglo-Saxon Chronicle: MS.A, 1986; The Anglo-Saxon Chronicle: texts and textual relationships, 1991; The Tanner Bede, 1992; Anonymous Old English Homilies: a preliminary bibliography, 1993; (ed jtly) Ohthere's Voyages: a late 9th century account of voyages along the coast of Norway and Denmark and its cultural context, 2006; contribs to: England Before the Conquest, 1971; Saints, Scholars and Heroes (ed M. H. King and W. M. Stevens), 1979; Five Hundred Years of Words and Sounds (ed E. G. Stanley and Douglas Grey), 1983; Learning and Literature in Anglo-Saxon England (ed M. Lapidge and H. Gneuss), 1985; Medieval English Studies (ed D. Kennedy, R. Waldron and J. Wittig), 1988; Words for Robert Burchfield's Sixty-Fifth Birthday (ed E. G. Stanley and T. F. Hoad), 1988; From Anglo-Saxon to Early Middle English (ed M. Godden *et al.*), 1994; Medieval English Language Scholarship (ed A. Oizumi and T. Kubouchi), 2005; (ed A. Cowie) Oxford History of English Lexicography, 2008; Companion to King Alfred the Great (ed N. Discenza and P. Szarmach), 2015; The Kemble Lectures on Anglo-Saxon Studies 2009–12 (ed A. Jorgensen *et al.*), 2015; Leeds Studies in English, Reading Medieval Studies, Eichstätter Beiträge, Medium Aevum, Rev. of English Studies, Anglia, English Studies, Essays and Studies, Classica et Mediaevalia, Scriptorium, Studies in Philology, Mediev. Arch., Notes and Queries, Archaeologia, Anglo-Saxon England, The Dickensian, Jl Soc. of Archivists, Bull. John Rylands Library, Jl of English and Germanic Philology, etc. *Recreations:* music, gardening. *Address:* 86 Cawdor Crescent, W7 2DD. *T:* (020) 8567 0486.

**BATEMAN, Alastair;** Chief Executive Officer, Church Mission Society, since 2019; *b* Frimley, Surrey, 20 May 1974; *s* of Peter and Jean Bateman; *m* 2006, Justine Hyde; one *s* one *d*. *Educ:* Brunel Univ. (BSc 1996); Univ. of Bath (MSc 1999). Mgt Consultant, BearingPoint, 2004–09; Tearfund: Hd of Fundraising, 2011–14; Interim Global Fundraising Dir, 2014–15; Dir of Marketing Strategy, 2016; Chief Operating Officer, Resurgo Trust, 2016–19. *Recreations:* cricket, music. *Address:* 78 Railway Road, Teddington, Middx TW11 8RZ. *E:* ali_bateman@hotmail.com.

**BATEMAN, Prof. Ian,** OBE 2013; PhD; FRSB; Professor of Environmental Science and Economics, since 2015 and Director, Land, Environment, Economics and Policy Institute, since 2016, University of Exeter; Director, South West Partnership for Environment and Economic Prosperity, since 2017; *b* Birmingham, 1961; *s* of Ken and Anne Bateman; *m* Fiona; one *s* two *d*. *Educ:* Handsworth Grammar Sch.; Birmingham Univ. (BSc); Manchester Univ. (MA); Nottingham Univ. (PhD 1997). FRSB (FSB 2014). Prof. of Envmtl Scis, UEA, 2002–15; Dir, Centre for Social and Econ. Res. on the Global Envmt, 2010–15. Principal Investigator: Valuing Nature Network, NERC; Social, Economic and Envmtl Res. Large Grant Award, ESRC. Econs lead, UK Nat. Ecosystem Assessment, DEFRA, 2009–11. Mem., Sci. Adv. Council, DEFRA, 2011–16. Mem. Cttee, Natural Capital, 2012–. FRSA 2013. Wolfson Merit Award, Royal Soc., 2011. *Publications:* Applied Environmental Economics, 2003. *Recreation:* family. *Address:* Land, Environment, Economics and Policy Institute, Business School, University of Exeter, Lazenby House, Rennes Drive, Exeter, Devon EX4 4RJ.

**BATEMAN, Mary-Rose Christine, (Mrs R. D. Farley),** MA; Headmistress, Perse School for Girls, Cambridge, 1980–89; *b* 16 March 1935; *d* of late Comdr G. A. Bateman, RN, and Mrs G. A. Bateman; *m* 1990, Richard Dashwood Farley (*d* 1996). *Educ:* The Abbey, Malvern Wells, Worcs; St Anne's Coll., Oxford (MA); CertEd Cambridge. Assistant English Mistress: Westonbirt Sch., Tetbury, Glos, 1957–60; Ashford Sch., Kent, 1960–61; Lady Eleanor Holles Sch., Middx, 1961–64; Head of English Department: Westonbirt Sch., Glos, 1964–69; Brighton and Hove High Sch., GPDST, 1969–71; Headmistress, Berkhamsted School for Girls, Herts, 1971–80. Administrator, Women's Nat. Cancer Control Campaign, 1989. *Address:* 3 Compton Court, Long Compton, Shipston on Stour, Warwickshire CV36 5JW. *T:* (01608) 684127.

**BATEMAN, Paul Terence;** Chairman, JP Morgan Asset Management, since 2007 (Chief Executive Officer, 2002–07); *b* 28 April 1946; *s* of Nelson John Bateman and Frances Ellen (*née* Johnston); *m* 1970, Moira (*née* Burdis); two *s*. *Educ:* Westcliff High Sch. for Boys; Univ. of Leicester (BSc). Save and Prosper Gp Ltd, 1967: graduate, secretarial dept, 1967–68; asst to Gp Actuary, 1968–73; Marketing Manager, 1973–75; Gp Marketing Manager, 1975–80; Gp Marketing and Develt Manager, 1980–81; Exec. Dir, Marketing and Develt, 1981–88; Chief Exec., 1988–95; Chm., Robert Fleming Asset Mgt, 1995–2001; Hd, Asset Mgt for Europe, Asia and Japan, JP Morgan Fleming Asset Mgt, 2001–02. Chm., Barts City Lifesavers, 1998–2011. *Recreation:* yachting. *Address:* JP Morgan Asset Management, 60 Victoria Embankment, EC4Y 0JP.

**BATEMAN, Peter;** HM Diplomatic Service, retired; Ambassador to Azerbaijan, 2011–13; Clerk and Chief Executive Officer, Armourers and Brasiers' Co., since 2014; *b* 23 Dec. 1955; *s* of late Sqdn Ldr Ralph Edwin Bateman, MBE and of Alma Bateman (*née* Laws); *m* 1985, Andrea Henriette Subercaseaux; two *s* one *d*. *Educ:* Carre's Grammar Sch., Sleaford, Lincs; St Peter's Coll., Oxford (MA). Conf. interpreter, EC, 1979–84; joined HM Diplomatic Service, 1984: First Secretary: Tokyo, 1986–90; FCO, 1991–93; (Commercial), Berlin, 1993–97; FCO, 1997–98; Commercial Counsellor, Tokyo, 1998–2002; Counsellor, FCO, 2002–03; on secondment as Dep. Chief Exec., Internat. Financial Services, 2003–05; Ambassador to: Bolivia, 2005–07; Luxembourg, 2007–11. *Recreations:* theatre, family life, golf, travel. *Address:* 46 Erpingham Road, SW15 1BG.

**BATEMAN, Richard George Saumarez La T.;** *see* La Trobe-Bateman.

**BATEMAN, Richard Mark,** PhD, DSc; Visiting Professor, Reading University, since 2000; Hon. Research Fellow, Royal Botanic Gardens, Kew, since 2003; *b* Bradford, 27 May 1958; *s* of William Horace Roy Bateman and Joan Mary Lund (*née* Laban); *m* (marr. diss. 2002); *m* 2016, Prof. Paula Jane Rudall. *Educ:* Luton Coll. of Higher Educn (BSc (Commendation) 1982); Birkbeck Coll., London (BSc 1st Cl. Hons 1984); PhD (Palaeozoic Palaeobotany) London 1988; DSc (Systematic Botany) London 2001. Asst SO, Sect. for Quaternary Studies, Rothamsted Exptl Station, 1977–84; Lindemann Res. Fellow and Vis. Scientist, Dept of Paleobiol., Smithsonian Instn, Washington, 1988–91; Sen. NERC Res. Fellow (Palaeobotany), Depts of Earth and Plant Scis, Oxford Univ., 1991–94; PSO, Royal Botanic Gdn, Edinburgh, and Nat. Museums of Scotland, 1994–96; Dir of Sci. and SPSO, Royal Botanic Gdn, Edinburgh, 1996–99; Keeper of Botany, 1999–2004, Individual Merit Researcher (Evolution), 2005–06, Natural History Mus.; Hd of Policy, Bioscis Fedn, 2006–07 (Mem., Exec. Council, 2004–06); Sen. Res. Fellow, Dept of Geog., Earth and Envmtl Scis, Univ. of Birmingham, 2007–11. Hon. Res. Fellow, Edinburgh Univ., 1997–2002. Member, Council: Systematics Assoc., 1992–2009 (Pres., 2006–09); UK Systematics Forum, 1997–2001; Linnean Soc., 1999–2010 (Vice-Pres., 2004–08); Bot. Soc. Br. Isles, 2002–08 (Vice-Pres., 2004–08); Vice Pres., Eur. Soc. for Evolutionary Develtl Biol., 2009–13. Mem., Awards Cttee III, Royal Soc., 2003–09. Pres., UK Hardy Orchid Soc., 2000–. President's Award, Geol Soc. of GB, 1988; Bicentenary Medal, Linnean Soc., 1994. *Publications:* (jtly) Molecular Systematics and Plant Evolution, 1999; (jtly) Developmental Genetics and Plant Evolution, 2002; contrib. over 155 papers to scientific jls, over 200 other articles. *Recreations:* natural history, travel, film, folk music, pontificating while drinking decent beer. *Address:* c/o Jodrell Laboratory, Royal Botanic Gardens Kew, Richmond, Surrey TW9 3DS. *T:* (020) 8948 2350.

**BATEMAN, Richard Montague;** Executive Secretary, Geological Society, 1980–97; *b* 27 Nov. 1943; *s* of late Gordon Montague Bateman and Joan Rhoda Bateman (*née* Puddifoot); *m* Gillian Elizabeth, *er d* of late Noel Leslie Costain, OBE; one *d*. *Educ:* Lyme Regis Grammar Sch.; Greenwich Maritime Inst., Univ. of Greenwich (MA 2002). Entered Civil Service, 1964, MoD (Air), 1965–69; Chamber of Shipping of UK, 1969–75, Asst Sec., 1973–75; Gen. Council of British Shipping, 1975–80. Sec., Assoc. of European Geol Socs, 1987–92. Mem., Envmt Council, 1994–97. Mem. Council, Haslemere Educnl Mus., 1998–2010. Member: Ocean Liner Soc., 1992; Sci., Technol., Engrg and Med. PR Assoc., 1993; Geologists' Assoc., 1997–2004, 2008–17 (Mem. Council, 2008–10); Soc. for Nautical Res., 1997 (Mem. Council, 2003–07, 2008–12 and 2013–; Fellow, 2015); British Titanic Soc., 1998; Steamship Historical Soc. of America, 1999–2010; Council, Greenwich Forum, 2008–. Associate, ACENVO, then ACEVO, 1998–2001. MInstD 2017 (Associate 1989). *Recreations:* maritime history, classical music. *Club:* Royal Naval and Royal Albert Yacht.

**BATES;** *see* Baker-Bates.

**BATES,** family name of **Baron Bates**.

**BATES,** Baron *cr* 2008 (Life Peer), of Langbaurgh in the County of North Yorkshire; **Michael Walton Bates;** PC 2015; *b* 26 May 1961; *s* of John Bates and Ruth Walton; *m* 1st, 1983, Carole Whitfield (marr. diss 2008); two *s*; 2nd, 2012, Xuelin Li. *Educ:* Heathfield Sen. High Sch.; Gateshead Coll.; Wadham Coll., Oxford (MBA 1998). Young Conservatives: Mem., Nat. Adv. Cttee, 1984–87; Chm., Northern Area, 1984–87. Sen. Vice-Pres., later Dir of Consultancy and Res., 1998–2006, Sen. Advr, 2006–07, Oxford Analytica Inc.; Man. Dir, Walton Bates Associates Ltd, 2006–11. Director: estandardsforum.com Inc., 2001–07; Financial Standards Foundn (Bermuda) Ltd, 2001–03; non-executive Director: Congregational & General plc, 2001–06; Vardy Gp of Cos, 2006–10; non-exec. Chm., Scholes & Brown Asset Management, 2008–11. Assoc. Chm., Northern Area Develt Initiative, 1990–92. Contested (C): Tyne Bridge, 1987; Langbaurgh, Nov. 1991. MP (C) Langbaurgh, 1992–97; contested (C) Middlesbrough South and Cleveland East, 1997. PPS to Minister of State, DSS, 1992–93, NI Office, 1994; an Asst Govt Whip, 1994–95; a Lord Comr, HM Treasury, 1995–96; HM Paymaster Gen., 1996–97. Shadow Minister for Cabinet Office, Communities and Local Govt, Energy and Climate Change, Children, Schs and Families, 2009–10; Dep. Speaker, H of L, 2013; a Lord in Waiting (Govt Whip), 2013–14; Parly Under-Sec. of State, 2014–15, Minister of State, 2015–16, Home Office; Minister of State, DFID, 2016–19; spokesman for HM Treasury, H of L, 2017–. Member: Select Cttee on Social Security, 1992; Select Cttee on Health, 1994. Dep. Chm., Cons. Party (North), 2007–10. Shell Fellow, Industry and Parlt Trust, 1997–. Mem., RIIA, 1998–2005. Member: Business Adv. Forum, Saïd Business Sch. (formerly Mem. Council, Sch. of Mgt Studies), Oxford Univ., 2000–10; Caux Round Table, 2001– (Trustee, 2006–08; Fellow, 2008–); European Ideas Network, 2002–05; Bd, Internat. Olympic Truce Foundn, 2016–. Vice Chairman: Emmanuel Schs Foundn, 2009–10; Emmanuel Coll., 2008–10; King's Acad., 2008–10; Trinity Acad., 2008–10; Bede Acad., 2008–10. *Address:* House of Lords, SW1A 0PW.

**BATES, Anthony John;** Director, GoPro, since 2014 (President, 2014–16); *b* Isleworth, 29 April 1967; *s* of David Bates and Valerie Bates; *m* 2009, Corica; four *s*. Sen. Network Manager, Univ. of London Computer Centre, 1986–92; Sen. Engr, RIPE Network Coordination Centre, 1992–94; Sen. Network Architect, MCI Telecommunications, 1994–96; Senior Vice President and General Manager: Service Provider Gp, Cisco Systems Inc., 1996–2009; Enterprise, Commercial and Small Business Gp, Cisco, 2009–10; CEO, Skype, 2010–11; Exec. Vice Pres., Business Develt and Evangelism Gp, Microsoft, 2011–14; CEO of Growth, Social Capital, 2017–18. Member, Board of Directors: YouTube, 2006–07; LOVEFILM, 2006–08; Bubble Motion, 2008–09; TokBox, 2008–09; eBay, 2015–; VMware, 2016–. *Recreations:* ski-ing, tennis.

**BATES, Air Vice-Marshal Brian Lawrence,** CBE 2005; Divisional Marketing Director, Communications and Security Division, Ultra Electronics, 2015–17 (Divisional Strategy Director, Tactical Systems Division, 2013–15); *b* Nicosia, Cyprus, 15 June 1957; *s* of David Bates and Sylvia Bates (*née* Payne); *m* 1st, 1981, Melinda Lawler (marr. diss. 1998); three *s* two *d*; 2nd, 1998, Joanne Saunders; one *s* one *d*. *Educ:* Wellington Sch., Somerset; Portsmouth Poly. (BA Hons Econs). Navigator and qwi, F4 Phantom, 1980–91; staff duties, HQ UK Air, 1991–92; RAF Staff Coll., 1993; PSO to AOC 11 Gp, 1993–95; staff duties, MoD, 1995–97; OC Ops Wing, RAF Leeming, 1998–2000; Hd RAF Presentation Team, 2000–01; Comdr British Forces Middle E, 2001; OC RAF Leeming, 2002–04; Asst Dir Strategic Plans, MoD, 2004–05; CDS Liaison Officer to Chm. of US Jt Chiefs of Staff, 2005–06; Dir Jt Capability, MoD, 2006–08; ACOS Capability HQ Air Comd, 2008–09; Sen. Directing Staff (Air), RCDS, 2009–12. Chm., RAF Club, 2011–12. *Recreations:* golf, tennis, squash.

**BATES, Clive David Nicholas;** Director, Counterfactual, since 2013; *b* 16 Feb. 1961; *s* of David and Patricia Bates; *m* 2014, Catriona Wendy Campbell Laing, *qv*. *Educ:* Wilmslow Grammar Sch., Cheshire; Emmanuel Coll., Cambridge (BA Hons Engrg 1983); Imperial Coll., London (MSc Envmtl Technol. 1992). Marketing computers for IBM (UK) Ltd, 1983–91; envmtl campaigner, Greenpeace, 1992–95; Programme Manager, Internat. Inst. for Energy Conservation, 1996–97; Dir, ASH, 1997–2003; Team Leader, Prime Minister's Strategy Unit, Cabinet Office, 2003–05; Head: Envmtl Policy, EA, 2005–07; UN Envmt Programme, Sudan, 2007–09; Dir Gen., Sustainable Futures, Welsh Assembly Govt, later Welsh Govt, 2009–12; Special Projects Advr, DECC (on secondment), 2012. *Publications:* reports and papers for campaigning groups. *Recreations:* cycling, mountains. *Address:* 4 Pentney Road, SW12 0NX. *Club:* Black's.

**BATES, Daniel;** Chief Executive Officer, Sheffield Theatres, since 2009; *b* London, Feb. 1965; *s* of Mark and Barbara Smith; adopted Bates as professional name. *Educ:* Central Sch. of Speech and Drama. Stage Manager, then Exec. Dir, W Yorks Playhouse, 1987–2005; CEO, York Th. Royal, 2005–09. *Recreation:* theatre. *Address:* Sheffield Theatres Trust, 55 Norfolk Street, Sheffield S1 1DA. *T:* (0114) 201 3804. *E:* d.bates@sheffieldtheatres.co.uk.

**BATES, Air Vice-Marshal David Frank,** CB 1983; RAF retired; *b* 10 April 1928; *s* of late S. F. Bates, MusB, FRCO, and N. A. Bates (*née* Story); *m* 1954, Margaret Winifred (*née* Biles); one *s* one *d*. *Educ:* Warwick Sch.; RAF Coll., Cranwell. Commnd, 1950; served Egypt, Innsworth, UKSLS Australia, HQ Transport Comd, RAF Technical Coll., Staff Coll., Lyneham, El Adem, Staff Coll., Jt Services Staff Coll., Innsworth, and RCDS, 1950–73; Stn Comdr, Uxbridge, 1974–75; Dir of Personnel Ground, 1975–76; Dir of Personnel Management (ADP), 1976–79; AOA, RAF Support Comd, 1979–82. Bursar, Warwick Sch., 1983–85. Pres., Adastrian Cricket Club, 1977–82. *Recreations:* cricket, most sports, gardening, model railways. *Address:* Meadow Cottage, Calf Lane, Chipping Campden, Glos GL55 6JQ.

**BATES, Prof. David Richard,** PhD; FRHistS, FSA; Professor of Medieval History, University of East Anglia, 2008–10, now Emeritus; *b* 30 April 1945; *s* of Jack Bates and Violet Anne Bates (*née* Swain); *m* 1971, Helen Mary Fryer; one *s* one *d*. *Educ:* King Edward VI Grammar Sch., Nuneaton; Univ. of Exeter (BA 1966; PhD 1970). FRHistS 1985; FSA 1993. Lectr, then Sen. Lectr and Reader in Hist., UC, Cardiff, subseq. Univ. of Wales, Cardiff, 1973–94; Edwards Prof. of Medieval Hist., Univ. of Glasgow, 1994–2003; Prof. of Hist. and Dir, Inst. of Historical Res., Univ. of London, 2003–08 (Hon. Fellow, 2008). Huntington Library Fellow, 1984; Prof. Invité, Ecole Nat. des Chartes, Paris, 1999; British Acad. Marc Fitch Res. Reader, 2001–03; Vis. Fellow Commoner, Trinity Coll., Cambridge, 2002–03; Dir d'Etudes Invité, Ecole Pratique des Hautes Etudes, Paris, 2003; Vis. Prof., Univ. de Caen-Basse-Normandie, 2009–12; James Ford Lectr in British Hist., Univ. of Oxford, 2009–10. Dir, Battle Conf. on Anglo-Norman Studies, 2010–13. A Vice-Pres., RHistS, 2003–06. Founding Fellow, Inst. of Contemp. Scotland, 2000; Centenary Fellow, Historical Assoc., 2006; Leverhulme Trust Emeritus Fellow, 2013–15. Life Mem., Clare Hall, Cambridge, 2009. MAE 2009. FRSA 2018. Dr *hc* Caen, 2000. *Publications:* Normandy before 1066, 1982; A Bibliography of Domesday Book, 1986; William the Conqueror, 1989; Bishop Remigius of Lincoln 1067–1092, 1992; (ed jtly) England and Normandy in the Middle Ages, 1994; (ed jtly) Conflict and Coexistence, 1997; Regesta Regum Anglo-Normannorum: the Acta of William I 1066–1087, 1998; Reordering the Past and Negotiating the Present in Stenton's First Century (Stenton Lect.), 2000; (ed jtly) Domesday Book, 2001; (ed jtly) Writing Medieval Biography 750–1250: essays in honour of Frank Barlow, 2006; (ed jtly) Liens personnels, réseaux, solidarités en France et dans les îles britanniques, 2006; (ed jtly) The Creighton Century, 1907–2007, 2009; (ed) Anglo-Norman Studies: XXXIV–XXXVI, 2012–14, Proceedings of the Battle Conferences, 2011–13; (ed jtly) East Anglia and its North Sea World in the Middle Ages, 2013; The Normans and Empire, 2013; (ed jtly) Penser les mondes normands médiévaux, 2016; William the Conqueror, 2016 (trans. French, 2019); (ed jtly) People, Texts, Artefacts, 2018; (ed) 1066 in Perspective, 2018; contribs to various books and many articles in historical jls incl. English Historical Rev., Speculum, Histl Res. and Annales de Normandie. *Recreation:* opera. *Address:* 11 Thomas Christian Way, Bottisham, Cambridge CB25 9DX.

**BATES, Django Leon;** jazz keyboardist, E flat hornist and composer; *b* 2 Oct. 1960; *s* of Ralf Bates and Frances Sinker (*née* Roseveare); *m* 2015, Sophie Schudel; one *s* three *d*. *Educ:* ILEA Centre for Young Musicians; Morley Coll. A founder mem., Loose Tubes; band leader: Humans, subseq. Human Chain, 1980–; Delightful Precipice, 1991–; stoRMchaser, 2005–; Belovèd (trio), 2010–. Performances worldwide. Artistic Dir, Fuse Fest., Leeds, March 2004; Prof. of Rhythmic Music, Rhythmic Music Conservatory, Copenhagen, 2005–11; Prof. of Jazz, Bern Univ. of the Arts, 2011–. Resident composer: Molde Internat. Jazz Fest., 1995; European City of Culture, Copenhagen, 1996; Harrogate Internat. Fest., 1997. ALCM; Fellow, Leeds Coll. of Music, 2005; Hon. RAM 2000. Danish Jazzpar Prize, 1997. *Compositions include:* Out There (music theatre prodn), 1993; What it's Like to be Alive (piano concerto), 1996; Interval Song, 1996; 1 in a Million, 1997; 2000 Years Beyond Undo (electronic keyboard concerto), 2000; Umpteenth Violin Concerto, 2004; The Study of Touch, 2013. *Recordings include:* Music for the Third Policeman, 1990; summer fruits (and unrest), 1993; autumn fires (and green shoots), 1994; winter truce (and homes blaze), 1995; Good Evening…here is the news, 1996; Like Life, 1998; Quiet Nights, 1998; You Live and Learn (apparently), 2004; Spring is Here (Shall We Dance?), 2008; Belovèd Bird, 2010; Confirmation, 2012. *Address:* c/o Jeremy Farnell, 21 St Johns Church Road, E9 6EJ. *E:* management@djangobates.co.uk.

**BATES, Prof. Gillian Patricia,** PhD; FRS 2007; FMedSci; Professor of Molecular Neuroscience, Huntington's Disease Centre, Department of Neurodegenerative Disease and Dementia Research Institute (formerly Sobell Department of Motor Neuroscience and Movement Disorders), Institute of Neurology, University College London, since 2016; *b* 19 May 1956; *d* of Alan Richard Bates and Joan Mabel Bates. *Educ:* Kenilworth Grammar Sch.; Sheffield Univ. (BSc 1979); Birkbeck Coll., London (MSc 1984); St Mary's Hosp. Med. Sch., Univ. of London (PhD 1987). Postdoctoral Fellow, ICRF, 1987–93; Sen. Lectr in Molecular Biology, UMDS of Guy's and St Thomas' Hosps, 1994–98; Prof. of Neurogenetics, 1998–2016, Hd, Div. of Genetics and Molecular Medicine, 2011–16, Guy's, King's Coll. and St Thomas' Hosps Sch. of Medicine, later KCL Sch. of Medicine. Mem., EMBO, 2002. FMedSci 1999. Hon. DSc Sheffield 2009. Nat. Med. Res. Award, Nat. Health Council, USA, 1993; Milton Wexler Award for Res. into Huntington's Disease, Huntington's Disease Soc. of America, 1998; Glaxo Wellcome Gold Medal, Royal Soc., 1998; Pius XI Medal, 1998; Klaus Joachim Zulch Prize, 2001; Leslie Brenner Gehry Prize for Innovation in Sci., Hereditary Disease Foundn, 2011. *Publications:* papers in genetics, molecular biology, and neurosci. jls; contribs to scientific and med. reference books. *Recreations:* reading, contemporary arts and design. *Address:* Department of Neurodegenenerative Disease, UCL Institute of Neurology, Room 605, Queen Square House, Queen Square, WC1N 3BG. *T:* (020) 3448 4522. *E:* gillian.bates@ucl.ac.uk.

**BATES, Rt Rev. Gordon;** an Hon. Assistant Bishop, Diocese of York, since 2010; *b* 16 March 1934; *s* of Ernest and Kathleen Bates; *m* 1960, Betty (*née* Vaux) (*d* 2014); two *d*. *Educ:* Kelham Theological Coll. (SSM). Curate of All Saints, New Eltham, 1958–62; Youth Chaplain in Gloucester Diocese, 1962–64; Diocesan Youth Officer and Chaplain of Liverpool Cathedral, 1965–69; Vicar of Huyton, 1969–73; Canon Residentiary and Precentor of Liverpool Cathedral and Diocesan Director of Ordinands, 1973–83; Bp Suffragan of Whitby, 1983–99. Hon. Asst Bp, Dios of Carlisle and Blackburn, 1999–2010. Mem., House of Bishops, Gen. Synod, 1988–99. Hon. Chaplain, Friarage Hosp., Northallerton, 2015–18. Mem., Central Religious Adv. Council to BBC and ITV, 1990–93. Chm., Cumbria, RSCM, 2002–04. Trustee, Sandford St Martin Trust, 1990–93. *Recreations:* music, writing. *Address:* 19 Fernwood Close, Brompton, Northallerton DL6 2UX. *T:* (01609) 761586.

**BATES, Sir James Geoffrey,** 7th Bt *cr* 1880, of Bellefield, co. Lancaster; *b* 14 March 1985; *s* of Richard Geoffrey Bates, *yr s* of 5th Bt and Diana Margaret Rankin; *S* uncle, 2007. *Heir: kinsman* Hugh Percy Bates [*b* 9 Jan. 1953; *m* 1977, Angela Roberta Wall; one *s* one *d*].

**BATES, John Gerald Higgs;** Solicitor, Office of Inland Revenue, 1990–96; *b* 28 July 1936; *o s* of Thomas William Bates and Winifred Alice Higgs; *m* 1971, Antoinette Lotery (*d* 1984); two *s*; *m* 1992, Alba Heather Phyllida Whicher. *Educ:* Kettering Grammar Sch.; St Catharine's Coll., Cambridge (MA); Harvard Law Sch. (LLM). Called to the Bar, Middle Temple, 1959. Practised at the Bar, 1962–66; Office of Solicitor of Inland Revenue, 1966–96: Under Sec. (Legal), 1990. *Recreations:* cooking, wine, music.

**BATES, Kenneth;** President, Leeds United Football Club, 2013 (Chairman, 2005–13); *b* 4 Dec. 1931; *m* Suzannah. Ready-mix concrete business; dairy farmer; Chairman: Oldham Athletic FC; Wigan Athletic FC, 1981; Chelsea FC, 1982–2004; Wembley Nat. Stadium Ltd, until 2000 (Dir, 1997–2001).

**BATES, Laura Carolyn,** BEM 2015; FRSL; Founder, Everyday Sexism Project, 2012; *b* Oxford, 27 Aug. 1986; *d* of Adrian Keith Bates and Diane Elizabeth Bates; *m* 2014, Nicholas Taylor. *Educ:* King's Coll., Taunton; St John's Coll., Cambridge (BA Eng. Lit.). Writer for Internat. Business Times, Guardian, TIME Mag, NY Times. Patron, Somerset and Avon Rape and Sexual Abuse Support, 2014. FRSL 2018. *Publications:* Everyday Sexism, 2014; Girl Up, 2016; Misogynation: the true scale of sexism, 2018; The Burning, 2019. *E:* laura@everydaysexism.com.

**BATES, Meg;** *see* Munn, M.

**BATES, Michael, (Mick);** farmer; Member for Montgomeryshire, National Assembly for Wales, 1999–2011 (Lib Dem 1999–2010, Ind 2010–11); *b* 24 Sept. 1947; *s* of George William Bates and Lilly (*née* Stevens); *m* 1972, Buddug Thomas; one *s* one *d*. *Educ:* Open Univ. (BA Educn and Sci. 1970). Science teacher, Humphrey Perkins Jun. High Sch., Barrow on Soar, and Belvidere Secondary Sch., Shrewsbury, 1970–75; Head of Gen. Sci., Grove Sch., Market Drayton, 1975–77; farmer, 1977–99. Mem. (Lib Dem) Powys CC, 1994–95. National Farmers' Union: Chm., Llanfair Caereinion Br., 1983–85; Chm., Co. Livestock Cttee, 1988–91; Mem., Co. Public Affairs Cttee, 1990–97; County Chm., Powys, 1991; NFU delegate, 1995. Lib Dem Br. Sec., 1988, Election Sub Agent, 1992. Mem., Eisteddfod Finance Cttee, 1989. Gov., Llanfair Co. Primary Sch., 1994–95. Chm., Llanfair Forum Community Regeneration Project. *Recreations:* all sports, especially Rugby, charity work, painting, walking, music.

**BATES, Michael Charles,** OBE 1994; HM Diplomatic Service, retired; Consul-General, Atlanta, 2001–05; *b* 9 April 1948; *s* of late Stanley Herbert Bates and Winifred Bates (*née* Watkinson); *m* 1971, Janice Kwan Foh Yin; one *s* one *d*. *Educ:* Stratton Grammar Sch. Joined HM Diplomatic Service, 1966: Attaché, New Delhi, 1971–74; Third Sec., Moscow, 1974–77; FCO, 1977–79; Second, later First Sec., Singapore, 1979–83; First Sec., Brussels, 1983–87; Press Officer to Prime Minister, 1987–89; Head, Parly Relns Unit, FCO, 1989–91; Dep. Head of Mission, Riga, 1991–92; Chargé d'Affaires, Bratislava, 1993–94; Ambassador, Slovak Republic, 1994–95; Dep. Head, News Dept, FCO, 1995–96; Dep. High Comr, Bombay, 1996–2001. *Recreations:* music, reading, travel, rambling.

**BATES, Michael David;** Regional Managing Partner, UK, Clifford Chance, since 2018; *b* Leeds, 24 Aug. 1967; *s* of David John Bates and June Lesley Bates; *m* 2001, Kate Gibbons; two *s* one *d*. *Educ:* Leeds Grammar Sch.; Berkhamsted Sch.; Exeter Univ. (LLM); Coll. of Law. Admitted as solicitor, 1993; Clifford Chance: Solicitor, 1993–; Partner, 2001–; Finance Practice Hd, 2010–18. *Recreations:* golf, ski-ing, music. *Address:* Clifford Chance, 10 Upper Bank Street, E14 5JJ. *T:* (020) 7006 1000. *E:* michael.bates@cliffordchance.com.

**BATES, Patricia Ann;** *see* Stewart, P. A.

**BATES, Prof. Paul David,** CBE 2019; PhD; Professor of Hydrology, University of Bristol, since 2003; *b* Leamington Spa, 29 May 1967; *s* of Robert John Bates and Joyce Bates; *m* 1995, Dr Alison Matthews; two *s*. *Educ:* Univ. of Southampton (BSc Geog. 1989); Univ. of Bristol (PhD 1993). Postdoctoral Researcher, Univ. of Bristol and Laboratoire Nat. d'Hydraulique, Paris, 1993–95; University of Bristol: Lectr, 1995–2000; on sabbatical at Princeton Univ. and EU Jt Res. Centre, 2000; Reader, 2000–03; on sabbatical at NASA Jet Propulsion Lab. and Univ. of Messina, 2007; Dir, Cabot Inst., 2010–13; Hd, Sch. of Geographical Scis, 2013–17. Chm., Fathom Global (formerly SSBN) Ltd, 2013–. Fellow, Amer. Geophysical Union, 2015. Royal Soc. Wolfson Res. Merit Award, 2017. *Publications:* (ed jtly) Floodplain Processes, 1996; (ed jtly) High Resolution Flow Modelling in Hydrology and Geomorphology, 2000; (ed jtly) Model Validation: perspectives in hydrological science, 2001; (ed jtly) Computational Fluid Dynamics, 2005; (ed jtly) Global Flood Hazard: applications in modeling, mapping and forecasting, 2018 (PROSE Award for Best Earth Scis Book, Assoc. of Amer. Publrs, 2019); over 200 articles in internat. scientific jls. *Recreations:* running, windsurfing, ski-ing, bass guitarist with the Grateful Dad. *Address:* School of Geographical Sciences, University of Bristol, University Road, Bristol BS8 1SS. *T:* (0117) 928 9954. *E:* paul.bates@bristol.ac.uk.

**BATES, Sir Richard (Dawson Hoult),** 3rd Bt *cr* 1937, of Magherabuoy, co. Londonderry; *b* 12 May 1956; *er s* of Sir Dawson Bates, 2nd Bt, MC and of Mary Murray (*née* Hoult); *S* father, 1998; *m* 2001, Harriet Domenique, *yr d* of Domenico Scaramella; one *s* one *d*. *Heir: s* Dominic Dawson Bates, *b* 21 Jan. 2006.

**BATES, Sarah Catherine;** Chair: Polar Capital Technology Trust, since 2017 (Director, since 2011); Merian Global Investors, since 2018; *b* Hants, 30 Jan. 1959; *d* of Ralph White and Judy White; *m* 1982, Steve Bates; one *d*. *Educ:* Manchester High Sch. for Girls; Trinity Hall, Cambridge (BA Hons 1980); London Business Sch. (MBA 1984). Food Retailing Analyst, Simon and Coates, 1980–82; Analyst and Fund Manager, National Provident Instn, 1982–85; Invesco: Fund Manager, 1985–89; Hd, UK Equities, 1989–94; Jt Chief Investment Officer, 1989–94; Man. Dir, Specialist Funds, 1994–99; CEO, UK Institutional, 1999–2003; Chair: Witan Pacific Investment Trust, 2004–17 (non-exec. Dir, 2004–17); JP Morgan American Investment Trust plc, 2005–17 (non-exec. Dir, 2005–17); St James's Place plc, 2013–18 (non-exec. Dir, 2004–13); non-executive Director: Invesco English and International plc, 1999–2010; New India Investment Trust, 2004–13; MTI Partners, 2007–10; U+I plc, 2010–17 (Chair, Audit Cttee, 2010–17); Worldwide Healthcare Trust, 2013–. Lay Advr, Royal Coll. of Surgeons, 2004–13; Advisor: Merseyside Pension Fund, 2005–10; East Riding Pension Fund, 2005–17; Chair, Investment Cttee, CRUK Pension Fund, 2006–15; Chair, Stena Line (UK) Pension Fund, 2007–13; Member, Investment Committee: Univs Superannuation Scheme, 2013–; BBC Pension Scheme, 2018–. Dir, Assoc. of Investment Cos, 2006–15 (Chair, 2011–13). Chair: Kings Corner Proj., 2007–13; Diversity Proj. Charity, 2018–. Fellow, CFA UK, 2018. *Recreations:* theatre, Twitter, reading, keeping show on the road. *Address:* 12 Alwyne Place, N1 2NL. *E:* sarah@sbates.co.uk.

**BATES, Simon Philip;** broadcaster; *b* Birmingham, 17 Dec. 1947; *s* of Henry Edward Bates and Marjorie Joan (*née* Garside); *m* 1978, Carolyn Miller (marr. diss. 2001); one *d*. *Educ:* Adams Grammar Sch., Shropshire. Announcer and commentator, New Zealand Broadcasting Corp., 1966–69; News/Features, Australian Broadcasting Commn, 1969–73; BBC, 1973–93; Breakfast programme presenter: London Broadcasting, 1993–97; Classic FM, 1997–2010; Smooth Radio, 2011–; presenter, various radio stations, incl. BBC, 2006–17. Commentator, CBS News, 1993–. DUniv Open, 2010. Pater Award for Excellence in Broadcasting, Australia, 1987; Sony Gold Award and NY Fest. Award for Radio series, Around the World in 80 Days, 1989; Radio Personality of Year, Variety Club, 1993; Argiva Commercial Radio Special Award, 2006. *Publications:* Simon Bates, My Tune:

an autobiography, 1993. *Recreations:* history, cinema, countryside, travel. *Address:* c/o Qtalent Ltd, 2nd Floor, 161 Drury Lane, Covent Garden, WC2B 5PN. *T:* (020) 7430 5400. *E:* pdale@qtalent.co.uk. *Clubs:* Ivy; Cricketers'.

BATES, Wendy Elizabeth; *see* Sudbury, W. E.

BATESON, John Swinburne, FCIHT; Chairman, Country Holiday Parks Ltd, since 2002; *b* 11 Jan. 1942; *s* of William Swinburne Bateson and Katherine Urquart (*née* Lyttle); *m* Jean Vivien Forsyth; one *s* two *d*. *Educ:* Appleby Grammar Sch.; Lancaster Royal Grammar Sch. FCIHT (FIHT 1986). Family business and associated activities, 1959–61; Harbour & General Works Ltd: Trainee Quantity Surveyor, 1961; Quantity Surveyor, 1966; Site Quantity Surveyor, Marples Ridgway Ltd, 1966–68; Leonard Fairclough Ltd: Site Quantity Surveyor, 1969; Contracts Surveyor, 1971; Chief Quantity Surveyor, Scotland, 1974; Fairclough Civil Engineering Ltd: Asst to Chief Exec., 1977; Man. Dir, Southern Div., 1979; Fairclough Construction Group Ltd: Asst to Chief Exec., 1980; Dir, 1981–95; AMEC plc: Dir, 1982–86; Dep. Chief Exec., 1986–88; Gp Chief Exec., 1988–95. Chairman: Bateson's Hotels (1958) Ltd, 1986–2002; Ind. Radio Gp, 1995–99; Merewood Gp Ltd, 1997–2003. *Recreations:* gardening, reading, chess, antiques, Spain.

BATEY, Peter Graham, CMG 2015; OBE 1997; Chairman: Vermilion Partners Ltd, since 2005; Great Britain China Centre, 2004–14; *b* Consett, Co. Durham, 1 July 1958; *s* of Frederic Surtees Batey and Eleanor Graham Carr. *Educ:* Dame Allan's Boys' Sch., Newcastle upon Tyne; Keble Coll., Oxford (BA 1981; Pres., OU Student Union, 1979–80). Exec. trainee, Citibank NA, 1981–82; Political Sec. to Rt Hon. Sir Edward Heath, KG, MBE, 1982–86; Chief Rep. in China, Arthur Andersen & Co., 1986–89; Chairman: Batey Burn & Co. Ltd, 1989–2004; Apco Asia Ltd, 1999–2004. Chm., China Index Fund, 1997–2007; Director: Sichuan Shuijingfang, 2006–13; Lim China Opportunities Fund, 2006–12. Chm., British Chamber of Commerce in China, 1994–96; Pres., EU Chamber of Commerce in China, 2001–02; Sen. Advr to Lord Mayor and Corp. of City of London in China, 2006–08; Vice Chm., China Britain Business Council, 2012–. Trustee, Sir Edward Heath Charitable Foundn, 2013–. *Recreations:* history, politics, reading, travel. *Address:* c/o Vermilion Partners Ltd, 31st Floor, China World Tower 2, 1 Jianguomenwai Dajie, Beijing 100004, People's Republic of China. *T:* (10) 65058008, *Fax:* (10) 65056586; c/o Vermilion Partners Ltd, 42 Brook Street, W1K 5DB. *T:* (020) 3178 7320, *Fax:* (020) 7958 9090. *E:* p.batey@vermilion-partners.com. *Clubs:* Athenæum; China (Beijing); China (Hong Kong).

BATH, 7th Marquess of, *cr* 1789; **Alexander George Thynn;** Bt 1641; Viscount Weymouth and Baron Thynne, 1682; Director: Cheddar Caves, 1956–2010; Longleat Enterprises, 1964–2010; *b* 6 May 1932; *s* of 6th Marquess of Bath and his 1st wife, Hon. Daphne Winifred Louise (*d* 1997), *d* of 4th Baron Vivian; *S* father, 1992; *m* 1969, Anna Gael Gyarmathy; one *s* one *d*. *Educ:* Eton College; Christ Church, Oxford (BA, MA). Lieutenant in the Life Guards, 1951–52, and in Royal Wilts Yeomanry, 1953–57. Contested (Wessex Regionalist): Westbury, Feb. 1974; Wells, 1979; contested (Wessex Regionalist and European Federal Party) Wessex, European Election 1979. Permanent exhibn of paintings since 1949 and murals since 1964, first opened to the public in 1962 in private apartments at Longleat House. Record, I Play the Host, singing own compositions, 1974. *Publications:* (as Alexander Thynn) (before 1976 Alexander Thynne) The Carry-cot, 1972; Lord Weymouth's Murals, 1974; A Regionalist Manifesto, 1975; The King is Dead, 1976; Pillars of the Establishment, 1980; The New World Order of Alexander Thynn, 2000; A Plateful of Privilege, vol. 1, the Early Years, vol. 2, Top Hat and Tails, vol. 3, Two Bites of the Apple, 2003, vol. 4, A Degree of Instability: the Oxford years, 2005. *Heir: s* Viscount Weymouth, *qv. Address:* Longleat House, Warminster, Wilts BA12 7NN. *T:* (01985) 844300.

BATH, Archdeacon of; *see* Youings, Ven. A.

BATH, Rear Adm. Michael Anthony William; Naval Secretary, Assistant Chief of Naval Staff (Personnel) and Flag Officer Reserves, since 2018; *b* Birmingham, 1966; *s* of William Bath and Theresa Bath; *m* 1994, Antonia Barton. *Educ:* King Edward VI Five Ways Grammar Sch.; Univ. of Leicester (BSc Geol. 1987); King's Coll. London (MA Defence Studies 2002). Joined RN 1987; ACOS J1/J4, PJHQ, 2009–11; New Employment Model Prog. Manager and Dir, Personnel Strategy, 2012–15; Cdre Naval Personnel Strategy, 2015–17; ACOS People Capability, 2017–18. *Recreations:* cricket, golf, ski-ing, reading, cinema. *Address:* c/o Naval Secretary, Navy Command Headquarters, Leach Building, Whale Island, Portsmouth PO2 8BY. *Clubs:* Naval, MCC; Broadhalfpenny Brigands Cricket.

BATH AND WELLS, Bishop of, since 2014; **Rt Rev. Peter Hancock;** *b* 26 July 1955; *s* of Kenneth and Jean Hancock; *m* 1979, (Elizabeth) Jane Sindall; two *s* two *d*. *Educ:* Price's Sch., Fareham; Selwyn Coll., Cambridge (BA 1976; MA 1979); Oak Hill Theol Coll. (BA 1980); Nottingham Univ. (MA 2008). Ordained deacon 1980, priest 1981; Curate: Christ Church, Portsdown, 1980–83; Radipole and Melcombe Regis Team Ministry, 1983–87; Vicar, St Wilfrid, Cowplain, 1987–99; RD of Havant, 1993–98; Archdeacon of The Meon, 1999–2010; Diocesan Dir of Mission, Portsmouth, 2003–07; Bishop Suffragan of Basingstoke, 2010–14. Hon. Canon, Portsmouth Cathedral, 1997–99. *Recreations:* walking, reading, watching sport. *Address:* The Bishops' Office, The Bishop's Palace, Wells, Som BA5 2PD.

BATHERSBY, Most Rev. John Alexius, AO 2008; STD; Archbishop of Brisbane, (RC), 1992–2011, now Archbishop Emeritus; *b* 26 July 1936; *s* of John Thomas Bathersby and Grace Maud Bathersby (*née* Conquest). *Educ:* Pius XII Seminary, Banyo, Qld, Australia; Gregorian Univ., Rome (STL, STD). Priest, 1961; Asst Priest, Goondiwindi, 1962–68; Spiritual Dir, Banyo Seminary, 1973–86; Bishop of Cairns, 1986–92. *Recreation:* bush walking.

BATHO, Sir Peter (Ghislain), 3rd Bt *cr* 1928, of Frinton, Essex; *b* 9 Dec. 1939; *s* of Sir Maurice Benjamin Batho, 2nd Bt and Antoinette Marie (*d* 1994), *d* of Baron d'Udekem d'Acoz; *S* father, 1990; *m* 1966, Lucille Mary, *d* of Wilfrid F. Williamson; three *s*. *Educ:* Ampleforth Coll.; Writtle Agricl Coll. Career in agriculture. Member: Suffolk CC, 1989–93; Suffolk Coastal DC, 2003–15. *Heir: s* Rupert Sebastian Ghislain Batho [*b* 26 Oct. 1967; *m* 1995, Jo-Anne Louise, *e d* of Rodney Frank Hellawell]. *Address:* Park Farm, Saxmundham, Suffolk IP17 1DQ. *T:* (01728) 602132.

BATHURST, family name of **Earl Bathurst** and **Viscount Bledisloe**.

BATHURST, 9th Earl *cr* 1772; **Allen Christopher Bertram Bathurst;** Baron Bathurst, 1712; Baron Apsley, 1771; *b* 11 March 1961; *s* of 8th Earl Bathurst and Judith Mary Bathurst (*née* Nelson); *S* father, 2011; *m* 1st, 1986, Hilary (marr. diss. 1995), *d* of John F. George, Weston Lodge Albury, Guildford; one *s* one *d*; 2nd, 1996, Sara, *d* of Christopher Chapman. *Educ:* Harrow Sch.; Wye Coll., London Univ.; RAC, Cirencester. Gov., 2003–14, Vice Pres., 2014–, Royal Agricl Coll., Cirencester. Chm., NFU, Glos Co., 2003–04; President: Glos Farming Wildlife Adv. Gp, 2006–; Cirencester Park Polo Club, 2011–. Patron, Glos CCC, 2015–. *Heir: s* Lord Apsley, *qv. Address:* Cirencester Park, Cirencester, Glos GL7 2BT.

BATHURST, Maj. Gen. Benjamin John, CBE 2015 (OBE 2005); General Officer Commanding London District and Major General Household Division, since 2016; *b* Haslemere, 15 April 1964; *s* of Admiral of the Fleet Sir (David) Benjamin Bathurst, *qv*; *m* 1996, Katherine Ellison; one *s* one *d*. *Educ:* Eton; Univ. of Bristol (BSc 1986); Cranfield Univ. (MA 1996). Commnd Welsh Guards, 1987; CO, 1st Bn Welsh Guards, 2004–06; Dir, Army PR, 2006–08; Dep. Dir, Strategy, Baghdad, Iraq, 2008–09; Comdr, Initial Trng Gp, 2010; Dir, Army Trng, 2011–14; UK Nat. Contingent Comdr, Kabul, Afghanistan, 2014. Comdt, Royal Army Physical Trng Corps, 2011–13; Dir, MoD Ministerial Adv. Gp, HQ ISAF—Afghanistan, 2014–15; rcds 2015–16. *Recreations:* shooting, fishing, ski-ing. *Address:* c/o Headquarters Welsh Guards, Wellington Barracks, Birdcage Walk, SW1E 6HQ. *Club:* Boodle's.

BATHURST, Admiral of the Fleet Sir (David) Benjamin, GCB 1991 (KCB 1987); First Sea Lord and Chief of Naval Staff, and First and Principal Naval Aide-de-Camp to the Queen, 1993–95; Vice Lord-Lieutenant, Somerset, 1999–2011; *b* 27 May 1936; *s* of late Group Captain Peter Bathurst, RAF and Lady Ann Bathurst; *m* 1959, Sarah Peto; one *s* three *d*. *Educ:* Eton College; Britannia RN College, Dartmouth. Joined RN, 1953; qualified as Pilot, 1960, as Helicopter Instructor, 1964; Fleet Air Arm appts incl. 2 years' exchange with RAN, 723 and 725 Sqdns; Senior Pilot, 820 Naval Air Sqdn; CO 819 Naval Air Sqdn; HMS Norfolk, 1971; Naval Staff, 1973; CO, HMS Ariadne, 1975; Naval Asst to First Sea Lord, 1976; Captain, 5th Frigate Sqdn, HMS Minerva, 1978; RCDS 1981; Dir of Naval Air Warfare, 1982; Flag Officer, Second Flotilla, 1983–85; Dir-Gen., Naval Manpower and Training, 1985–86; Chief of Fleet Support, 1986–89; C-in-C Fleet, Allied C-in-C Channel, and C-in-C Eastern Atlantic Area, 1989–91; Vice Chief of Defence Staff, 1991–93. Younger Brother, Trinity House. Liveryman, Hon. Co. of Air Pilots (formerly GAPAN); Hon. Liveryman, Fruiterers' Co. DL Somerset, 1996. *Recreations:* gardening, shooting, fishing. *Address:* c/o National Westminster Bank, 9 York Buildings, Cornhill, Bridgwater TA6 3BA. *Clubs:* Boodle's, Army and Navy, MCC.

*See also* Maj. Gen. B. J. Bathurst.

BATHURST, Sir Frederick William John H.; *see* Hervey-Bathurst.

BATHURST NORMAN, His Honour George Alfred; a Senior Circuit Judge, 1997–2004 (a Circuit Judge, 1986–2004); *b* 15 Jan. 1939; *s* of Charles Phipps Bathurst Norman and Hon. Doreen Albinia de Burgh Norman (*née* Gibbs); *m* 1973, Susan Elizabeth Ball; one *s* one *d*. *Educ:* Harrow Sch.; Magdalen Coll., Oxford (BA). Called to the Bar, Inner Temple, 1961; SE Circuit, 1962; Dep. Circuit Judge, 1975; a Metropolitan Stipendiary Magistrate, 1981–86; a Recorder, 1986. Mem., Home Office Working Party on Coroners Rules, 1976–81. Mem., Gen. Council of the Bar, 1968–70. Mem., Middlesex Probation Cttee, 1994–99. Chm., Lord Chancellor's Adv. Cttee on JPs for Middlesex, 1996–2004 (Dep. Chm., 1994–96). *Publications:* research papers on drugs and drug smuggling. *Recreations:* wildlife, ornithology, cricket, travel. *Club:* MCC.

BATISTE, Simon Anthony; His Honour Judge Batiste; a Circuit Judge, since 2018; *b* Sheffield; *s* of Spencer Lee Batiste, *qv*; *m* 2004, Juliet Everson; three *d*. *Educ:* Leeds Grammar Sch.; Univ. of Newcastle (LLB Law). Called to the Bar, Lincoln's Inn, 1995; a Fee-paid Judge of First-tier Tribunal, Immigration and Asylum Chamber, 2006–18; a Recorder, 2012–18. Law Clerk to Sheffield Assay Office, 2000–18; Mem., British Hallmarking Council, 2000–18. *Recreations:* ski-ing, mixed martial arts, cinema, running and walking in Yorkshire Dales. *Address:* Newcastle upon Tyne Combined Court Centre, The Law Courts, The Quayside, Newcastle upon Tyne NE1 3LA.

BATISTE, Spencer Lee; solicitor, since 1970; a Judge of the Upper Tribunal (Immigration and Asylum Chamber) (formerly a Vice-President, Immigration Appeal Tribunal, later a Senior Immigration Judge, Asylum and Immigration Tribunal), 2002–10 (Immigration Adjudicator, 1997–2002); *b* 5 June 1945; *m* 1969, Susan Elizabeth (*née* Atkin); one *s* one *d*. *Educ:* Carmel Coll.; Sorbonne, Paris; Cambridge Univ. (MA). MP (C) Elmet, 1983–97; contested (C) same seat, 1997. PPS to Minister of State for Industry and IT, 1985–87, to Minister of State for Defence Procurement, 1987–89, to Sir Leon Brittan, Vice-Pres. of EC Commn, 1989–97. Member: Select Cttee on Energy, 1985; Select Cttee on Information, 1991–97; Select Cttee on Sci. and Technology, 1992–97; Vice-Chairman: Cons. Space Cttee, 1986–97 (Sec., 1983–85); Cons. Trade and Industry Cttee, 1989–97. Pres., Yorks Cons. Trade Unionists, 1984–87 (Nat. Pres., 1990). Vice-Chm., Small Business Bureau, 1983–92. Law Clerk to Sheffield Assay Office, 1974–2000. Mem., British Hallmarking Council, 1988–2000. *Recreations:* travel, genealogy, gardening, photography.

*See also* S. A. Batiste.

BATSON, Philip David; HM Diplomatic Service; Head of Programming, Overseas Territories Department, Foreign and Commonwealth Office, since 2019; *b* Woolwich, 26 June 1968; *s* of David and Margaret Batson; *m* 2006, Joanna Samuels-Watson; one *s*. *Educ:* Dartford Grammar Sch. for Boys. Entered FCO, 1987; Entry Clearance Officer, Bombay, 1991–94; Third Sec. (Pol), Paris, 1995–97; Second, later First Sec., FCO, 1997–2004; Dep. Hd of Mission, Tunis, 2004–08; Dep. Hd, Corporate Services Prog., FCO, 2008–11; Games-time co-ordinator and crisis planner, London 2012 Olympic and Paralympic Games, 2011–12; Ambassador to Republic of Moldova, 2013–16; Gp Head, Africa Regl Dept, DFID, 2017–19. *Recreations:* cricket, gardening, family. *Address:* c/o Foreign and Commonwealth Office, King Charles Street, SW1A 2AH. *E:* phil.batson@fco.gov.uk.

BATT, Dr Christopher, OBE 1998; Chief Executive, Museums, Libraries and Archives Council, 2003–07; *b* 3 July 1947; *s* of Charles and Ethel Batt; *m* 2004, Adrienne Billcliffe. *Educ:* Henry Thornton Grammar Sch.; Open Univ. (BA 1st Cl. Hons); University Coll. London (PhD 2015). FCLIP (FLA 1985; Hon. Fellow 1998). London Borough of Croydon: Dep. Chief Librarian, 1978–91; Bor. Libraries and Mus Officer, 1991–96; Dir, Leisure Services, 1996–99; Chief Network Advr, Liby and Inf. Commn, 1999–2000; Dir, Libraries and Inf. Soc. Team, Resource: Council for Mus, Archives and Libraries, 2000–03. Dir, Chris Batt Consulting Ltd, 2007–10. Trustee, Ralph Vaughan Williams Soc. FRSA 2001. *Publications:* Information Technology in Public Libraries, 1985, 6th edn 1998; contribs to Public Liby Jl. *Recreations:* flying light aircraft, photography, history of science and technology, music. *E:* cbatt@mac.com.

BATTARBEE, Prof. Richard William, DPhil, DSc; FRS 2006; Professor of Environmental Change, University College London, 1991–2007, now Emeritus; *b* 30 May 1947; *s* of Halstead and Ethel Battarbee; *m* 1972, Gill Parkes. *Educ:* University Coll. London (BA; Hon. Fellow 2011); DPhil NUU 1973; DSc London 1997. Royal Soc. Eur. Res. Fellow, Uppsala Univ., 1971–73; Res. Fellow, NUU, 1973–76; University College London: Lectr, 1976–82, Reader, 1982–91, in Geog.; Dir, Envmtl Res. Centre, 1991–2007. Foreign Mem., Norwegian Acad. of Sci. and Letters, 1991. Hon. Prof., Nanjing Inst. for Geog. and Limnology, 2002–, Einstein Prof., 2012, Chinese Acad. of Scis. FAAAS 2018. Hon. DSc: Ulster, 2007; Queen's Univ., Kingston, Ont. 2015. Research medals: (and Rector's Guest) Univ. of Helsinki, 1994; Moscow State Univ., 1995. Back Award, 1989, Victoria Medal, 2010, RGS; Ruth Patrick Award, Amer. Soc. for Limnology and Oceanography, 2009; James Croll Medal, Quarternary Res. Assoc., 2013. Lifetime Achievement Award, Internat. Paleolimnology Assoc., 2015. Civic Pride Award, Addingham Civic Soc., 2018. *Publications:* Palaeolimnology and Lake Acidification, 1990;

Global Change in the Holocene, 2003; Past Climate Variability through Europe and Africa, 2004; Natural Climate Variability and Global Warming, 2008; Climate Change Impacts on Freshwater Ecosystems, 2010. *Recreations:* piano, environmental citizen science. *Address:* 9 Main Street, Addingham, W Yorks LS29 0PD. *E:* r.battarbee@ucl.ac.uk.

**BATTEN, Gerard;** Member (UK Ind) London Region, European Parliament, 2004–19; Leader, UK Independence Party, 2018–19; *b* 27 March 1954. Hand bookbinder, 1972–76; Manager, BT, 1976–2004. UK Independence Party: Founder Mem., 1993–; Mem., NEC, 1993–97, 2002–06; Party Sec., 1994–97. Contested (UK Ind): Romford, 2015; London Reg., EP, 2019.

**BATTEN, Stephen Duval;** QC 1989; a Recorder, 1988–2010; *b* 2 April 1945; *s* of Brig. Stephen Alexander Holgate Batten, CBE and of Alice Joan Batten, MBE, *d* of Sir Ernest Royden, 3rd Bt; *m* 1976, Valerie Jean Trim; one *s* one *d*. *Educ:* Uppingham; Pembroke Coll., Oxford (BA). Called to the Bar, Middle Temple, 1968, Bencher 1998. *Recreations:* planter gardening, kitchen bridge and other puzzles.

**BATTEN, Tracey Leigh;** non-executive Director, Medibank, Australia, since 2017; *b* Melbourne, Australia, 30 April 1966; *d* of Jeffrey and Judith Batten; *m* 2002, Simon Blair; one step *s* one step *d*. *Educ:* Firbank Anglican Sch.; Univ. of Melbourne (MB BS 1989); Univ. of New South Wales (MHA 1995); Harvard Univ. (MBA 2001). CMO, St Vincent's Hosp., Melbourne, 1995–97; Chief of Health Progs, Inner and Eastern Healthcare Network, Vic, 1998–99; Chief Executive: Dental Health Services, Vic, 2001–03; Eastern Health, Melbourne, 2004–08; St Vincent's Health Australia, 2009–13; Chief Exec., Imperial Coll. Healthcare NHS Trust, 2014–17. FRACMA 1996; FAICD 2006. *Recreations:* gourmet cooking, food and wine, travel, paddle boarding. *Club:* Harvard (Australia).

**BATTERBURY, His Honour Paul Tracy Shepherd,** TD 1972 (2 bars); DL; a Circuit Judge, 1983–99; *b* 25 Jan. 1934; *o s* of late Hugh Basil John Batterbury and Inez Batterbury (*née* Shepherd); *m* 2018, Norma, *d* of Norman Tweedy Bratt; one *s* one *d* by a previous marriage. *Educ:* St Olave's Grammar Sch., Southwark; Univ. of Bristol (LLB). Served RAF, 1952–55, TA, 1959–85 (Major, RA). Called to Bar, Inner Temple, 1959; practising barrister, 1959–83. Councillor: Chislehurst and Sidcup UDC, 1960–62; London Borough of Greenwich, 1968–71 (Chm., Housing Cttee, 1970–71). Founder Trustee, St Olave's Sch., SE9, 1970–2001; Founder Chm., Gallipoli Meml Lects, 1986–89. Vice-Pres., SE London, SJAB, 1988–91. DL Greater London, 1986–2001; rep. DL, London Borough of Havering, 1989–95. *Recreations:* walking, caravanning. *Address:* 5 Paper Buildings, Temple, EC4Y 7HB. *T:* (020) 7583 9275.

**BATTERHAM, Prof. Robin John,** AO 2004; PhD; FREng; FTSE; FAA; Kernot Professor of Engineering, University of Melbourne, since 2009; *b* 3 April 1941; *s* of Maurice Samuel and Marjorie Kate Batterham. *Educ:* Brighton Grammar Sch.; Melbourne Univ. (BEng; PhD 1969). AMusA 1975; FTSE 1988; FAustIMM 1989; FIChemE 1989; FIEAust 1989; FAIM 1999; FAICD 1999; FAA 2001; FREng 2004; CEng; CPEng; CSci. Res. Scientist, later Chief Res. Scientist and Chief of Minerals Res. Div., CSIRO, 1970–88; various positions incl. Man. Dir, R&D, then Global Practice Leader, Innovation, 1988–2006, Gp Chief Scientist, 2006–09, Rio Tinto; Chief Scientist of Australia, 1999–2005. Professorial Fellow, Univ. of Melbourne, 2004–10. President: IChemE, 2004; Australian Acad. of Technol Scis and Engrg, 2005–12. Corresp. Mem., Swiss Acad. Engrg Scis, 2002; Foreign Associate: NAE, US, 2004; Chinese Acad. of Engrg, 2013. Hon. DLitt Melbourne, 2004; Hon. DSc Sydney Univ. of Technol., 2006; Hon. DEng Queensland, 2011. Centenary Medal (Australia), 2001. *Publications:* The Chance to Change, 2000; jl, conf. and patent pubns. *Recreations:* music (organist Scots Ch, Melbourne), ski-ing, cycling. *Address:* 153 Park Drive, Parkville, Vic 3052, Australia. *T:* (3) 8344 9737, 0417 351776. *E:* robin.batterham@unimelb.edu.au.

**BATTERS, Minette Bridget;** beef and sheep farmer, since 1998; President, National Farmers' Union, since 2018 (Deputy President, 2014–18); *b* Salisbury, 28 May 1967; *d* of Richard James and Bridget Irene Hill; *m* Malcolm Batters; one *s* one *d*. *Educ:* Godolphin Sch.; Salisbury Coll.; Cordon Bleu Dip., London. Asst to racehorse trainers, David Elsworth and James Toller, 1985–90; freelance catering business, 1990–, and wedding venue, 2012–. Co-Founder, Ladies in Beef, 2010–. *Publications:* contribs to Farmers' Weekly, Salisbury Jl. *Recreations:* running marathons, horse riding, reading, gardening, family. *Address:* Barford Park Farm, Downton, Salisbury, Wilts SP5 3QF. *T:* (01725) 513393. *E:* minette.batters@nfu.org.uk.

**BATTISCOMBE, Christopher Charles Richard,** CMG 1992; Director General (formerly Secretary General), Society of London Art Dealers, since 2001; Secretary, British Art Market Federation, since 2001; *b* 27 April 1940; *s* of late Lt-Col Christopher Robert Battiscombe and Karin Sigrid (*née* Timberg); *m* 1972, Brigid Melita Theresa Lunn; one *s* one *d*. *Educ:* Wellington Coll.; New Coll., Oxford (BA Greats). Entered FO, 1963; ME Centre for Arabic Studies, Shemlan, Lebanon, 1963–65; Third/Second Sec., Kuwait, 1965–68; FCO, 1968–71; First Secretary: UK Delegn, OECD, Paris, 1971–74; UK Mission to UN, New York, 1974–78; Asst Head, Eastern European and Soviet Dept, FCO, 1978–80; Commercial Counsellor: Cairo, 1981–84; Paris, 1984–86; Counsellor, FCO, 1986–90; Ambassador to Algeria, 1990–94; Asst Under-Sec. of State, then Dir (Public Depts), FCO, 1994–97; Ambassador to Jordan, 1997–2000. Chm., Anglo Jordanian Soc., 2002–09. JP Wimbledon, 2002–07. *Recreations:* golf, ski-ing, tennis. *Clubs:* Kandahar; Temple Golf.

**BATTISHILL, Sir Anthony (Michael William),** GCB 1997 (KCB 1989); Chairman, Board of Inland Revenue, 1986–97 (Deputy Chairman, 1985); *b* 5 July 1937; *s* of William George Battishill and Kathleen Rose Bishop; *m* 1961, Heather Frances Lawes; one *d*. *Educ:* Taunton Sch.; Hele's Sch., Exeter; London Sch. of Economics (BSc (Econ); Hon. Fellow 2013). 2nd Lieut, RAEC, 1958–60. Inland Revenue, 1960–63; HM Treasury, 1963–65; Inland Revenue, 1965–76, Asst Sec., 1970; Central Policy Review Staff, 1976–77; Principal Private Sec. to Chancellor of the Exchequer, HM Treasury, 1977–80; Under Sec., HM Treasury, 1980–82, 1983–85, Inland Revenue, 1982–83. Chm., Student Loans Co. Ltd, 1998–2001. Mem. Ct of Governors, LSE, 1987–2012, now Emeritus (Vice-Chm., 2003–09). *Recreations:* gardening, old maps. *Address:* 4 Highfield Close, West Byfleet, Surrey KT14 6QR.

**BATTLE, Dennis Frank Orlando;** Commissioner, 1990–98, and Director of Personnel and Finance, 1994–98, Customs and Excise; *b* 17 Dec. 1942; *s* of Frank William Orlando and Marion Kathleen Battle; *m* 1965, Sandra Moule (*d* 2017); one *s* one *d*. *Educ:* Bedford Modern School. Joined Customs and Excise as Exec. Officer, 1962; Higher Exec. Officer, NBPI, 1967; Sen. Exec. Officer, CS Coll., 1972; returned to Customs and Excise, 1975: Grade 7 1978, Asst Sec. 1985; Comr, 1990–98; Dir of Personnel, 1990–94. Consultant on public sector reform and human resource mgt, 1998–2014. Non-exec. Dir, Sentinel Housing Assoc. (formerly Sentinel Housing Group), 1998–2010. FCIPD (FIPD 1998). *Recreations:* lunching with friends, watching Aldershot FC and Sussex CCC, watercolour painting.

**BATTLE, Rt Hon. John Dominic;** PC 2002; Pro-Chancellor, Leeds Trinity University, since 2018; *b* 26 April 1951; *s* of John and late Audrey Battle; *m* 1977, Mary Meenan; one *s* two *d*. *Educ:* Leeds Univ. (BA Hons (1st cl.) 1976). Training for RC Priesthood, Upholland Coll., 1969–72; Leeds Univ., 1973–77; Res. Officer to Derek Enright, MEP, 1979–83; Nat. Co-ordinator, Church Action on Poverty, 1983–87. MP (Lab) Leeds W, 1987–2010. Opposition front-bench spokesman on housing, 1992–94, on science and technology, 1994–95, on energy, 1995–97; Minister of State: (Minister for Energy and Industry), DTI, 1997–99; FCO, 1999–2001. Mem., Internat. Develt Select Cttee, 2001–10. Chairman, All Party Parliamentary Group: on Overseas Develt, 2005–10 (Vice-Chm., 1992–97); on Poverty, 2006–10. Chair: Leeds Dio. Justice and Peace Commn, 2010–; Bramley Baths Community Ltd, 2012–; Project Bonhoeffer, 2014–. Trustee, Citizens UK, 2018–. Fellow, Blackfriars Coll., Oxford, 2010–. KSG 2009. *Recreations:* walking, poetry, supporting Leeds United FC. *Address:* Leeds Trinity University, Horsforth, Leeds LS18 5HD. *E:* johnbattle.leedswest@gmail.com.

**BATTLE, Susan, (Sue),** CBE 2006 (OBE 1995); Chief Executive, Birmingham Chamber of Commerce and Industry, 1999–2006; *b* 7 Aug. 1946; *d* of Harry and Beryl Sagar; *m* 1969, George Henry Battle. *Educ:* Old Hall Sch., Norfolk; Newcastle upon Tyne Coll. of Commerce (HND Business Studies). Statistical Asst to Sales Dir, Procter & Gamble Ltd, 1967–72; Adminr, M & R Internat., Riyadh, 1972–75; Birmingham Chamber of Commerce and Industry: Asst Sec., 1977–80; Head of Home and Economic Dept, 1980–84; Asst Dir, 1984–88; Dep. Chief Exec., 1989–99. Hon. Dr Central England in Birmingham, 2007. *Recreations:* ornithology, the countryside, Islamic history and culture. *Address:* 8 Brookfield House, Hackmans Gate Lane, Belbroughton, Stourbridge, Worcs DY9 0DL.

**BATTY, Christopher Michael;** His Honour Judge Christopher Batty; a Circuit Judge, since 2009; *b* Leeds, 13 Oct. 1966; *s* of Michael Batty and Joyce Batty; *m* 2005, Kate Martha Rayfield; one *s* one *d*. *Educ:* Abbey Grange C of E Sch., Leeds; Liverpool Poly. (LLB Hons). Called to the Bar, Gray's Inn, 1989; in practice as a barrister, 1989–2009; a Recorder, 2005–09. *Recreations:* watching sport, Leeds United, Hunslet Hawks, reading, cooking.

**BATTY, Prof. (John) Michael,** CBE 2004; PhD; FRS 2009; FBA 2001; FRTPI, FCILT, FAcSS; Bartlett Professor (formerly Professor of Spatial Analysis and Planning, then Bartlett Professor of Planning), since 1995, and Chairman, Centre for Advanced Spatial Analysis, since 2010 (Director, 1995–2010), University College London; *b* 11 Jan. 1945; *s* of Jack Batty and Nell Batty (*née* Marsden); *m* 1969, Susan Elizabeth Howell; one *s*. *Educ:* Quarry Bank Grammar Sch., Liverpool; Univ. of Manchester (BA 1966); UWIST (PhD 1984). FRTPI 1983; FCILT (FCIT 1990). Asst Lectr, Univ. of Manchester, 1966–69; University of Reading: Res. Asst, 1969–72; Lectr, 1972–74 and 1975–76; Reader, 1976–79; Prof. of City and Regl Planning, 1979–90, Dean, Sch. of Envmtl Design, 1983–86, UC Cardiff; Prof. of Geog., 1990–95, Dir, Nat. Center for Geographic Inf. and Analysis, 1990–95, SUNY, Buffalo. Vis. Asst Prof., Univ. of Waterloo, Ont, 1974; Vis. Fellow, Univ. of Melbourne, 1982; Croucher Fellow, Univ. of Hong Kong, 1986; Vis. Prof., Univ. of Illinois at Urbana-Champaign, 1986; Sir Edward Youde Meml Foundn Vis. Prof., Univ. of Hong Kong, 2001. Ed., Envmt and Planning B, 1981–. Mem., Res. Bd, 1980–82, Chm., Planning Cttee, 1980–82, SSRC; Vice-Chm., Envmt and Planning Cttee, ESRC, 1982–84; Mem., Jt Transport Cttee, 1982–85, Mem., Scientific Computing Adv. Panel, 1989–90, SERC; Mem., Cttee on Scientific Computing, NERC, 1988–90; Mem., Computer Bd for Univs and Res. Councils, 1988–90. FAcSS (AcSS 2001). FRSA 1983. Hon. LHD SUNY Buffalo, 2008; Hon. LLD Leicester, 2015. Award for Technol Progress, Assoc. Geographic Inf., 1998; Back Award, RGS, 1999; Alonso Prize, Regl Sci. Assoc., 2011; Univ. Consortium of Geographic Information Sci. Award, 2012; Vautrin-Lud Prize for Geographical Sci., 2013; Founders Medal, RGS, 2015; Gold Medal, RTPI, 2016; Sen. Scholar Award, Complex Systems Soc. 2016; Alonso Prize, Regl Sci. Assoc., 2017; Waldo Tobler GIScience Prize, Austrian Acad. of Scis, 2019. *Publications:* Urban Modelling, 1976; (ed) Systems Analysis in Urban Policy-Making and Planning, 1983; (ed) Optimization and Discrete Choice in Urban Systems, 1985; (ed) Advances in Urban Systems Modelling, 1986; Microcomputer Graphics, 1987; (ed) Cities of the 21st Century, 1991; Fractal Cities, 1994; (ed) Cities in Competition, 1995; (ed) Spatial Analysis, 1996; (ed) Advanced Spatial Analysis, 2003; Cities and Complexity, 2005; (ed) Virtual Geographic Environments, 2009; (ed) Agent Based Models of Geographical Systems, 2012; The New Science of Cities, 2013; Inventing Future Cities, 2018. *Recreations:* discovering America, reading, Indian food, Georgian architecture. *Address:* Centre for Advanced Spatial Analysis, University College London, 90 Tottenham Court Road, W1T 4TJ. *T:* 07768 423656; 9 White Horse House, 1 Little Britain, EC1A 7BX. *T:* (020) 7600 8186.

**BATTY, Paul Daniel;** QC 1995; His Honour Judge Batty; a Circuit Judge, since 2003; *b* 13 June 1953; *s* of late Vincent Batty and Catherine Batty; *m* 1986, Angela Jane Palmer; one *d*. *Educ:* St Aidan's Grammar Sch., Sunderland; Newcastle upon Tyne Univ. (LLB). Called to the Bar, Lincoln's Inn, 1975, Bencher, 2003; Junior, NE Circuit, 1985; Bar Mess Junior, 1982–85; Asst Recorder, 1991; a Recorder, 1994–2003; Hon. Recorder: Carlisle, 2012–15; York, 2015–. Freeman, City of Carlisle, 2016. *Recreations:* boating, angling, Rugby. *Address:* York Crown Court, The Castle, York YO1 9WZ. *T:* (01904) 645121.

**BATTY, Peter Wright;** television and film producer, director and writer; Chief Executive, Peter Batty Productions, since 1970; *b* 18 June 1931; *s* of late Ernest Faulkner Batty and Gladys Victoria Wright; *m* 1959, Anne Elizabeth Stringer (*d* 2000); two *s* one *d*. *Educ:* Bede Grammar Sch., Sunderland; Queen's Coll., Oxford. Feature-writer, Financial Times, 1954–56; freelance journalist, USA, 1956–58; Producer, BBC TV, 1958–64: mem. original Tonight team, other prodns incl. The Quiet Revolution, The Big Freeze, The Katanga Affair, Sons of the Navvy Man; Editor, Tonight, 1963–64; Exec. Producer and Associate Head of Factual Programming, ATV, 1964–68: prodns incl. The Fall and Rise of the House of Krupp (Grand Prix for Documentary, Venice Film Fest., 1965; Silver Dove, Leipzig Film Fest., 1965), The Road to Suez, The Suez Affair, Vietnam Fly-in, Battle for the Desert; freelance work for BBC TV, ITV and Channel 4, 1968–. Progs dir., prod and scripted incl. The Plutocrats, The Aristocrats, Battle for Cassino, Battle for the Bulge, Birth of the Bomb, Farouk: last of the Pharaohs, Operation Barbarossa, Superspy, Sunderland's Pride and Passion, A Rothschild and his Red Gold, Search for the Super, Spy Extraordinary, Story of Wine, World of Television, The Rise and Rise of Laura Ashley, The Gospel According to St Michael, Battle for Warsaw, Battle for Dien Bien Phu, Nuclear Nightmares, A Turn Up in a Million, Il Poverello, Swindle!, The Algerian War, Fonteyn and Nureyev: the perfect partnership, The Divided Union, A Time for Remembrance, Swastika over British Soil, Tito: Churchill's man?, Tito: his own man; prod and scripted 6 episodes (incl. pilot) World at War series. *Publications:* The House of Krupp, 1966; (with Peter Parish) The Divided Union, 1987; La Guerre d'Algérie, 1989; Hoodwinking Churchill: Tito's great confidence trick, 2011. *Recreations:* walking, reading, listening to music. *Address:* Claremont House, Renfrew Road, Kingston, Surrey KT2 7NT. *T:* (020) 8942 6304. *E:* peterbatty31@outlook.com. *Club:* Garrick.

**BATTY, Wendy;** *see* Darke, W.

**BATY, Robert John,** OBE 2002; CEng, FREng, FICE; Chief Executive, South West Water Ltd, 1996–2006; *b* 1 June 1944; *s* of late Robert George Baty and of Sarah Baty (*née* Hall); *m* 1975, Patricia Fagan; two *d*. *Educ*: Calday Grange Grammar Sch.; Liverpool Coll. of Building. CEng 1970; FCIWEM 1981; FIWO 1990; FICE 1992; FREng 2000. North West Water: Resident Engr, then Principal Engr, 1974–83; Area Manager, 1983–85; Regl Manager, 1985–88; Engrg and Scientific Dir, SW Water Ltd, 1988–96. Exec. Dir, Pennon plc, 1996–2006. Non-exec. Dir, Royal Devon and Exeter NHS Foundn Trust, 2004–10. Registered Comr, Infrastructure Planning Commn, 2010–12. CCMI 2001. *Recreations*: Rugby and sport generally, recreational flying, classic car restoration. *Address*: Hillcot, 78 Oldfield Drive, Heswall, Wirral CH60 9HA. *T*: (0151) 348 4921.

**BAUCHER, Heather Anne; Her Honour Judge Baucher;** a Circuit Judge, since 2009; *b* Crosby, 2 June 1962; *d* of Keith Robertson and Margaret Patricia Robertson; *m* 1987, Gerald Marsh Baucher (*d* 2012); one *s* one *d*. *Educ*: Formby High Sch., Formby; Sheffield Univ. (LLB 1st Cl. Hons; Jacqueline Falconer Prize); Chester Law Coll. Davis Campbell, later Hill Dickinson: articled clerk, 1984–86; Asst Solicitor, 1986–89; Salaried Partner, 1989–91; Equity Partner/Mem., 1991–2008; Recorder, 2004–09. Mem., Solicitors Disciplinary Tribunal, 2002–09. *Recreations*: walking, swimming, Liverpool FC, church, theatre, art and museum exhibitions, member of Ladies Joggers. *Address*: County Court at Central London, Royal Courts of Justice, Strand, WC2A 2LL. *T*: (020) 7947 7490. *E*: hhjudge.baucher@ejudiciary.net.

**BAUCKHAM, Ian Roger,** CBE 2017; Executive Headteacher, Bennett Memorial Diocesan School, since 2004; Chief Executive Officer, Tenax Schools Trust, since 2015; *b* Hornchurch, 7 March 1962; *s* of Alan and Irene Bauckham. *Educ*: Downing Coll., Cambridge (BA 1st Cl. Modern and Medieval Langs 1984); Univ. of Nottingham (PGCE 1985); Inst. of Educn, Univ. of London (MA Educn 1994); Heythrop Coll., Univ. of London (MA Philosophy 1997). Teacher of modern foreign languages: Cardinal Newman Sch., Hove, 1985–90; abroad, 1990–91; Kingsbury High Sch., Brent, 1992–96; Hd of Sixth Form, 1996–2001, Dep. Headteacher, 2001–04, Bennett Meml Diocesan Sch. Member: Headteacher Bd, SE and S London Regl Schs Comr, 2014–17; Bd, Ofqual, 2018– (Mem., Standards Adv. Gp, 2015–). Pres., Assoc. of Sch. and Coll. Leaders, 2013–14. *Recreations*: walking, theatre, ski-ing. *Address*: 19A Great Bounds Drive, Southborough, Tunbridge Wells, Kent TN4 0TR.

**BAUCKHAM, Prof. Richard John,** PhD; FBA 1998; FRSE; Professor of New Testament Studies, 1992–2007, and Bishop Wardlaw Professor, 2000–07, St Mary's College, University of St Andrews, now Emeritus Professor; Senior Scholar, Ridley Hall, Cambridge, since 2007; *b* 22 Sept. 1946; *s* of John Robert Bauckham and Stephania Lilian Bauckham (*née* Wells). *Educ*: Enfield GS; Clare Coll., Cambridge (BA Hons Hist. 1st cl. 1969; MA 1972; PhD 1973). FRSE 2002. Fellow, St John's Coll., Cambridge, 1972–75; Lectr in Theol., Leeds Univ., 1976–77; Lectr, 1977–87, Reader, 1987–92, in Hist. of Christian Thought, Manchester Univ. Member: Doctrine Commn, C of E, 1990–2003; Doctrine Cttee, Scottish Episcopal Ch, 1997–2002. *Publications*: Tudor Apocalypse, 1978; Jude, 2 Peter (commentary), 1983; Moltmann: Messianic theology in the making, 1987; The Bible in Politics, 1989, 2nd edn 2010; Word Biblical Themes: Jude, 2 Peter, 1990; Jude and the Relatives of Jesus in the Early Church, 1990; The Theology of the Book of Revelation, 1993; The Climax of Prophecy, 1993; The Theology of Jürgen Moltmann, 1995; The Fate of the Dead, 1998; James: Wisdom of James, Disciple of Jesus the Sage, 1999; God Crucified: monotheism and Christology in the New Testament, 1999; (with Trevor Hart) Hope Against Hope: Christian eschatology in contemporary context, 1999; Gospel Women, 2002; God and the Crisis of Freedom, 2002; Bible and Mission, 2003; The MacBears of Bearloch, 2006; Jesus and the Eyewitnesses, 2006 (expanded edn 2017); The Testimony of the Beloved Disciple, 2007; Jesus and the God of Israel, 2008; The Jewish World around the New Testament, 2008; Bible and Ecology: rediscovering the community of creation, 2010; Jesus: a very short introduction, 2011; Living with Other Creatures, 2011; Gospel of Glory, 2015; The Bible in the Contemporary World, 2015; The Christian World Around the New Testament, 2017; *edited*: (jtly) Scripture, Tradition and Reason, 1988; (jtly) The Nuclear Weapons Debate: theological and ethical issues, 1989; The Book of Acts in its Palestinian Setting, 1995; The Gospels for All Christians, 1997; God will be All in All: the eschatology of Jürgen Moltmann, 1999; Magdala of Galilee, 2018; many articles in books and learned jls. *Recreations*: novels, poetry, allotment. *Address*: 11 Archway Court, Barton Road, Cambridge CB3 9LW.

**BAUGH, John Robert;** Headmaster, Dragon School, Oxford, 2002–17; *b* Kampala, Uganda, 1956; *s* of late Michael Baugh, LVO, MBE, QPM and Iris Baugh; *m* 1984, Wendy; two *d*. *Educ*: Aldenham Sch.; St Luke's Coll., Exeter (BEd 1978). Teacher, Haileybury Coll., 1980–87; Headmaster: Solefield Sch., Sevenoaks, 1987–97; Edge Grove Sch., Herts, 1997–2002. *Recreations*: most sports, music, reading, travel.

**BAUGH, (John William) Matthew,** OBE 2013; HM Diplomatic Service; Director, Negotiation Coordination Unit, Department for Exiting the European Union, since 2016; *b* Ndola, Zambia, 24 July 1973; *s* of David Baugh and Nicola Baugh; *m* 2001, Dr Caroline; one *s* two *d*. *Educ*: Oratory Sch.; Univ. of Bristol (BA Hons Hist. 1994; MSc Internat. Policy 1996). Fast Stream, MoD and DFID, 1997–99; Department for International Development: Head: Kosovo Crisis Unit, 1999–2000; Humanitarian Policy and Global Emergencies, 2000–02; Afghanistan Crisis Unit, 2001–02; First Sec., Khartoum, 2002–04; Head: UK Post-Conflict Reconstruction Unit, 2005–06; Iraq Dept, DFID, 2006–07; Principal Private Sec. to the Sec. of State for Internat. Develt, 2008–09; HCSC 2010; UK Rep. to Somalia, 2010–11; Ambassador (non-res.) to Somalia, 2012–13; Head, Central and Southern Africa Dept, 2013–14, E and W Africa Dept, 2014–16, FCO. *Recreations*: ski-ing, walking, mountaineering, family. *Address*: Department for Exiting the European Union, 9 Downing Street, SW1A 2AS.

**BAUGHAN, Julian James;** QC 1990; a Recorder, 1985–2014; *b* 8 Feb. 1944; *s* of late Prof. E. C. Baughan, CBE, and Mrs E. C. Baughan. *Educ*: Eton Coll. (King's Schol.); Balliol Coll., Oxford (Brassey Italian Schol.; BA History). Called to Bar, Inner Temple, 1967 (Profumo Schol., Philip Teichman Schol., Major Schol.); Prosecuting Counsel to DTI, 1983–90.

**BAUGHEN, Rt Rev. Michael Alfred;** Bishop of Chester, 1982–96; Assistant Bishop, diocese of Guildford, since 2006; *b* 7 June 1930; *s* of Alfred Henry and Clarice Adelaide Baughen; *m* 1956, Myrtle Newcomb Phillips (*d* 2014); two *s* one *d*. *Educ*: Bromley County Grammar Sch.; Univ. of London; Oak Hill Theol Coll. BD (London). With Martins Bank, 1946–48, 1950–51. Army, Royal Signals, 1948–50. Degree Course and Ordination Trng, 1951–56; Curate: St Paul's, Hyson Green, Nottingham, 1956–59; Reigate Parish Ch., 1959–61; Candidates Sec., Church Pastoral Aid Soc., 1961–64; Rector of Holy Trinity (Platt), Rusholme, Manchester, 1964–70; Vicar of All Souls, Langham Place, W1, 1970–75; Rector, 1975–82; Area Dean of St Marylebone, 1978–82; a Prebendary of St Paul's Cathedral, 1979–82; Asst Bp, dio. of London, 1996–2006; Priest-in-charge, St James's, Clerkenwell, 1997–98. Hon. LLD Liverpool, 1994; Hon. DD Chester, 2017. *Publications*: Moses and the Venture of Faith, 1979; The Prayer Principle, 1981; II Corinthians: a spiritual health-warning to the Church, 1982; Chained to the Gospel, 1986; Evidence for Christ, 1986; Getting through to God, 1992; (with Myrtle Baughen) Your Marriage, 1994; Grace People: rooted in God's covenant love, 2006; The One Big Question: the God of love in a world of suffering, 2010; Centred on Christ: Lent 2014 study guide, 2013; My Beloved Son: Advent study guide, 2015; 2 Timothy: 30-day devotional, 2016; Editor: Youth Praise, 1966; Youth Praise II, 1969; Psalm Praise, 1973; consultant editor, Hymns for Today's Church, 1982; gen. ed, Sing Glory, 1999. *Recreations*: music, railways, touring, watercolour painting. *Address*: 23 The Atrium, Woolsack Way, Godalming, Surrey GU7 1EN.

**BAULCOMBE, Prof. Sir David (Charles),** Kt 2009; PhD; FRS 2001; FMedSci; Regius Professor of Botany, 2009–19, now Emeritus, and Royal Society Research Professor, since 2007, Department of Plant Sciences, University of Cambridge (Professor of Botany, 2007–09); Fellow of Trinity College, Cambridge, 2009–19; *b* 7 April 1952; *s* of William (Jim) and Joan Baulcombe; *m* 1976, Rose Eden; one *s* three *d*. *Educ*: Leamington Coll., Leamington Spa; Leeds Univ. (BSc Botany); Edinburgh Univ. (PhD 1977). Postdoctoral Fellow: McGill Univ., Montreal, 1977–78; Univ. of Georgia, Athens, 1979–80; res. scientist, Plant Breeding Inst., Cambridge, 1981–88; Sen. Scientist, Sainsbury Lab., John Innes Centre, Norwich, 1988–2007; Prof., Dept of Biological Scis, UEA, 2002–07 (Hon. Prof., 1998–2002). Mem., BBSRC, 2009–16. Mem. Bd, NIAB, 2008–. President: Internat. Soc. of Plant Molecular Biology, 2003–04; Biochemical Soc., 2015–17. Mem., EMBO, 1998; MAE, 2003; For. Associate Mem., Nat. Acad. of Scis, USA, 2005. Mem., Lawes Agricl Trust, 2009–. For. Fellow, Nat. Acad. of Scis, India, 2011. FMedSci 2010. Hon. FRSE 2015. Corresp. Mem., Royal Acad. of Arts and Scis, Barcelona, 2013. Hon. DSc: Wageningen Agricl Univ., 2008; UEA, 2011; Birmingham, 2011; Edinburgh, 2014; Helsinki, 2014; Leeds, 2015; Hon. LLD Dundee, 2014. Prix des Céréalières de France, 1990; Kumho Sci. Internat. Award, Kumho Cultural Foundn, S Korea, 2002; (jtly) Wiley Internat. Prize in Biomedicine, 2003; Beijerinck Prize for Virology, Royal Dutch Acad. Arts and Scis, 2004; Royal Medal, Royal Soc., 2006; (jtly) Franklin Medal, Franklin Inst., USA, 2008; (jtly) Albert Lasker Basic Med. Res. Award, 2008; Harvey Prize, Technion Univ., Israel, 2010; Wolf Prize for Agric., Israel, 2010; Balzan Prize, Rome, 2012; (jtly) Gruber Genetics Prize, Gruber Foundn, 2014; McClintock Prize for Plant Genetics and Genome Studies, Maize Genetics Exec. Cttee, 2013; Mendel Medal, Genetics Soc., 2017. *Publications*: contrib. res. papers and articles on plant genetics, virology and genetic engrg in Nature, Science, Cell, and specialist jls. *Recreations*: sailing, hill-walking, music, running. *Address*: Department of Plant Sciences, University of Cambridge, Cambridge CB2 3EA. *T*: (01223) 339386. *Club*: Norfolk Punt (Barton, Norfolk).

**BAUM, Prof. Michael,** ChM; FRCS; Professor of Surgery, 1996–2000, now Emeritus, and Visiting Professor of Medical Humanities, since 2000, University College London (Director, Clinical Trials Group, Division of Surgery, 2008–13); Consultant Surgeon, UCL Hospitals NHS Trust, 1996–2001; *b* 31 May 1937; *s* of Isidor and Mary Baum; *m* 1965, Judith (*née* Marcus); one *s* two *d*. *Educ*: Univ. of Birmingham (MB, ChB; ChM). FRCS 1965. Lecturer in Surgery, King's College Hosp., 1969–72; Research Fellow, Univ. of Pittsburgh, USA, 1971–72; Reader in Surgery, Welsh National Sch. of Medicine, Cardiff, 1972–78; Hon. Cons. Surgeon, King's College Hosp., 1978–80; Professor of Surgery: KCH Med. Sch., London, 1980–90; Inst. of Cancer Res., Royal Marsden Hosp., 1990–96, Prof. Emeritus, 1996–; Vis. Prof., UCL, 1995–96. Chairman: SE Thames Regional Cancer Organisation, 1988–90; British Breast Gp, 1989–91; Breast Cancer Cttee, UK Coordinating Cttee for Cancer Research, 1989–96; Psychosocial Oncology Cttee, Nat. Cancer Res. Network, 2004–06; Mem., Adv. Cttee on Breast Cancer Screening, DHSS, 1987–95; Specialist Advr, Select Cttee on Health, 1996–98. President: British Oncological Assoc., 1996–98; Eur. Breast Cancer Conf., 2000–02. Chm., Med. Cttee, AVMA, 2000–05. Karl Popper Meml Lect., LSE, 2007. FRSA 1998. Hon. FRCR 1998. Hon. MD Göteborg, 1986. Gold Medal, Internat. Coll. of Surgeons, 1994; Celebrating Survival award, Univ. of Texas, San Antonio, 2000; William McGuire Prize, Univ. of Texas, 2002; Internat. Soc. for Breast Cancer Res. Prize, 2003; St Gallen Prize, Switzerland, 2007; Galen Medal for Therapeutics, Soc. of Apothecaries, 2008. *Publications*: Breast Cancer—The Facts, 1981, 3rd edn 1994; Classic Papers in Breast Disease, 2003; Breast Beating: one man's odyssey in the search for the cure for breast cancer, the meaning of life and other easy questions, 2010; The Scepticaemic Surgeon, 2014; *fiction*: The First Tablet of the Holy Covenant, 2013; Aaron's Rod, 2017; multiple pubns on breast cancer, cancer therapy, cancer biology and the philosophy of science. *Recreations*: painting, theatre, reading, philosophizing. *Address*: 4 Corringway, NW11 7ED. *Club*: Royal Society of Medicine.

**BAUMANN, Paul David,** CBE 2018; Chapter Clerk and Receiver General, Westminster Abbey, since 2018; *b* Shoreham-by-Sea, 29 May 1962; *s* of Michael David Baumann and Barbara Ellen Baumann; *m* 1985, Diana Rosemary Guthrie (*née* Henderson); two *s* one *d*. *Educ*: Hardye's Sch., Dorchester; St Catharine's Coll., Cambridge (Posener Schol.; BA Modern and Medieval Langs 1984; MA 1988; Tasker Prize 1984). FCMA 1992; CGMA. Unilever: joined as mgt trainee, latterly Divl Controller, 1984–93; Financial Controller, Langnese-Iglo GmBH, 1993–96; Finance Dir, Unilever Ireland plc, 1996–2000; Finance and IT Dir, UDL GmBH, 2000–01; Vice-Pres., Finance Excellence, Unilever plc, 2001–07; Dir, Finance and Investment, NHS London, 2007–12; Chief Financial Officer, NHS England, 2012–18. Mem., Howard Partnership Trust, 2017–. Mem., Guildford Cathedral Council, 2009–18; Mem. Bd, Acad. of Ancient Music, 2018–. *Publications*: (contrib.) Creating Value in a Regulated World: CFO perspectives, 2006. *Recreations*: organist, family accompanist, member of several chamber choirs, concert and opera goer, foreign travel, culture and cuisine. *Address*: Chapter Office, Westminster Abbey, 20 Dean's Yard, SW1P 3PA. *T*: (020) 7654 4860. *E*: Paul.Baumann@westminster-Abbey.org.

**BAUMBERG, Prof. Jeremy John,** DPhil; FRS 2011; FInstP; Professor of Nanoscience, University of Cambridge, since 2007; Fellow, Jesus College, Cambridge, since 2007; *b* 4 March 1967; *s* of late Prof. Simon Baumberg, OBE and of Ruth Elizabeth Baumberg; *m* 1994, Melissa Murray; two *d*. *Educ*: Jesus Coll., Cambridge (BA Hons Natural Scis 1988); Jesus Coll., Oxford (DPhil 1993). FInstP 1999. Jun. Res. Fellow, Jesus Coll., Oxford, 1992–94; IBM Res. Fellow, UCSB, USA, 1994–95; Researcher, Hitachi Cambridge Lab., 1995–98; Prof. of Nano-scale Physics, Univ. of Southampton, 1998–2007. Founder, Mesophotonics Ltd, 2001–08. Fellow: Inst. of Nanotechnology, 1999; Optical Soc. of America, 2006. *Recreations*: fell walking, pianist, drinking saké, stone carving, kinetic sculptures, tennis, choral singing, clock making. *Address*: Cavendish Laboratory, University of Cambridge, J. J. Thompson Avenue, Cambridge CB3 0HE. *T*: (01223) 337429. *E*: j.j.baumberg@phy.cam.ac.uk.

**BAUME, Jonathan Edward;** General Secretary, FDA (formerly Association of First Division Civil Servants), 1997–2012; a Civil Service Commissioner, 2012–17; *b* 14 July 1953; *s* of late George Frederick Baume and Mary Louisa Baume (*née* Hardwick). *Educ*: Queen Elizabeth Grammar Sch., Wakefield; Keble Coll., Oxford (BA Hons 1974; MA). Oxfordshire CC, 1974–76; Dept of Employment Gp, 1977–87; Orgn and Indust. Relns Dept, TUC, 1987–89; Asst Gen. Sec., 1989–94, Dep. Gen. Sec., 1994–97, FDA. Member: TUC Gen. Council, 2001–; Council, ACAS, 2011–15. Member: Ministerial Adv. Gp on Openness in Public Sector, 1998–99; Ministerial Adv. Gp on Implementation of Freedom of Information Act, 2001–04; Age Adv. Gp, DTI, 2004–10; Adv. Cttee on Business Appts, 2018–. Mem. Bd, HSE. Non-executive Director: Office of Nuclear Regulation; Criminal Cases Review Commn, 2014–. *Recreations*: yoga, post-war jazz, world music, rambling. *Club*: Athenæum.

**BAUMGARTNER, Tony Alan Walter;** His Honour Judge Baumgartner; JP; a Circuit Judge, since 2019; *b* Bundaberg, 9 Aug. 1971; *s* of Alan Walter Baumgartner and Maree Elaine Baumgartner (*née* Gott); *m* 2018, Dennis Noel Kavanagh. *Educ:* Griffith Univ. (BCom 1992); Queensland Univ. of Technol. (LLB 1997); University Coll. London (LLM 1998). Dip. Internat. Arbitration CIArb 2018, FCIArb 2018. Admitted solicitor: Supreme Court of Qld, 1999; Fed. Courts of Australia, 1999; England and Wales, 2001 (Solicitor Advocate, 2011); Courts of Ireland, 2017; articled law clerk, Bedford & Associates, 1993–97; caseworker, CPS, 1997–98; articled law clerk, 1998–99, Solicitor, 1999, Allen, Allen & Hemsley; Solicitor, Mayer, Brown, Rowe & Maw LLP, 1999–2005; Clyde & Co. LLP: Sen. Associate, 2005–09; Legal Dir, 2009–11; Partner, 2011–19; a Recorder, 2009–19; a Fee-paid Judge, First-tier Tribunal, Health, Educn and Social Entitlement Chamber (Restricted Patients Panel), 2018–. Court Examnr, 2017–. Mem., Spoliation Adv. Panel, 2013– (Dep. Chm., 2016–). Hon. Legal Advr, Royal Courts of Justice CAB, 2005–19. Instructor, Inst. of Art and Law, 2005–; Vis. Lectr, LLM in Art Business and Law, QMUL, 2017–. Gov., John Ball Primary Sch., 2002–08 (Chm. of Govs, 2005–07). FRAS 2015. Freeman, City of London, 2014; Liveryman, City of London Solicitors' Co., 2015. JP Qld 1994. *Publications:* Halsbury's Laws of England, 4th edn reissue 1999, Vol. 45(2); various articles on art and law. *Recreations:* reading, international Rugby, surfing, swimming, fine art and antiques.

**BAUR, Christopher Frank;** storyteller and editor; *b* 28 May 1942; *s* of Mrs Marty Stewart (*née* Sigg) and Frank Baur; *m* 1965, Jaqueline Gilchrist; four *s. Educ:* Dalhousie Prep. Sch.; Strathallan Sch., Perthshire. Joined Scotsman as copy boy, 1960; trained as journalist; Scotsman's Industrial Reporter, 1963, additionally Scottish Politics, 1972; Financial Times, Scottish corresp., 1973; Scottish political corresp., BBC, 1976; The Scotsman: Asst Editor, 1978, writing on politics and economic affairs; Dep. Editor, 1983–85; Editor, 1985–87; Editor, Scottish Business Insider, 1990–94; Dir, Insider Gp, 1994–2003; Man. Dir, Insider Custom Publishing, 1997–99; Editl/Man. Dir, Insider Pubns, 1999–2003; Exec. Chm./Editl Dir, Editions Publishing Ltd, 2004–13. *Recreation:* creating. *Address:* 4 Roman Court, Pathhead, Midlothian EH37 5AH. *T:* (01875) 320476.

**BAVEYSTOCK, Nicholas Guy;** DL; Director General, Institution of Civil Engineers, since 2012; *b* Horsham, W Sussex, 14 April 1962; *s* of late Robert Harold Baveystock and of Anne Mary Baveystock; *m* 1993, Christine Mary Shardlow. *Educ:* Windlesham House Sch., Washington, Sussex; Collyers' Grammar Sch., Horsham; King's Coll. London (MA). Joined Army, 1985; mentioned in despatches, 1989; CO 35 Engr Regt, 2002–04; Comdr, 1st Armd Div., RE, 2004–06; COS Multinat. Div. (S) Iraq, 2005–06; rcds 2007; Comdt, RSME, 2008–11; retired in rank of Brig. Non-executive Director: Engrg UK, 2012–; WISE, 2013–17; Mid Kent Coll. Trng Services, 2018–. Mem. Bd, E4E, ETF, 2012–. Mem., Construction Industry Council, 2012–. Vice Pres., Instn of Royal Engrs, 2015–. Mem. Adv. Bd, Services Sound and Vision Corp., 2018–. Mem., Smeatonian Soc. DL Kent, 2019. QCVS 2006. *Publications:* Lessons from Post Conflict Reconstruction, 2007; A History of the Royal Engineers in Iraq: 2003–10, 2011. *Recreations:* golf, travel, deputy assistant under-groom to my wife's horse, chief carer to a recalcitrant spaniel. *Address:* Institution of Civil Engineers, One Great George Street, SW1P 3AA. *Clubs:* Army and Navy; Blythe Sappers.

**BAVIN, Rt Rev. Timothy John,** FRSCM; OSB; Hon. Assistant Bishop: Diocese of Portsmouth, since 2012; Diocese of Winchester, since 2013; *b* 17 Sept. 1935; *s* of Edward Sydney Durrance and Marjorie Gwendoline Bavin. *Educ:* Brighton Coll.; Worcester Coll., Oxford (2nd Cl. Theol., MA); Cuddesdon Coll. Curate, St Alban's Cathedral Pretoria, 1961–64; Chaplain, St Alban's Coll., Pretoria, 1965–68; Curate of Uckfield, Sussex, 1969–71; Vicar of Good Shepherd, Brighton, 1971–73; Dean and Rector of Cathedral of St Mary the Virgin, Johannesburg, 1973–74; Bishop of Johannesburg, 1974–84; Bishop of Portsmouth, 1985–95; monk, OSB, 1996–. Mem., OGS, 1987–97; FRSCM 1991. ChStJ 1975. *Publications:* Deacons in the Ministry of the Church, 1987. *Recreations:* music, gardening. *Address:* Alton Abbey, Alton, Hants GU34 4AP.

**BAWA, Prof. Kamaljit,** PhD; FRS 2015; Distinguished Professor of Biology, University of Massachusetts Boston, since 1996. *Educ:* Punjab Univ., Chandigarh (BS 1958; BS Hons 1960; MS Hons 1962; PhD 1967). Grad. Res. Asst, Botany Dept, Punjab Univ., Chandigarh, 1962–67; Postdoctoral Res. Associate and Instructor, Coll. of Forest Resources, Univ. of Washington, Seattle, 1967–72; Res. Fellow, Gray Herbarium, Harvard Univ., 1973–74; Department of Biology, University of Massachusetts Boston: Asst Prof., 1974–77; Associate Prof., 1977–81; Prof., 1981–96; Res. Prof., 1991–94; Chm., Biol. Dept, 1989–92. Giorgio Ruffolo Fellow in Sustainability Sci., Harvard Univ., 2009–10. Ed. in Chief, Conservation and Society, 2001–; Associate Editor: Conservation Biol., 1987–93; Econ. Botany, 1997–; Ecol. and Society, 2009–; Acad. Ed., PLoS One, 2011–. Founder Pres., Ashoka Trust for Res. in Ecol. and Envmt, 1996–; Pres., 2000, Hon. Fellow, 2003, Assoc. Tropical Biol. and Conservation. FAAAS 2007; Fellow: Amer. Acad. Arts and Scis, 2012; Royal Norwegian Soc. Letters and Scis, 2012. Hon. DSc Alberta, 2014. *Publications:* (ed jtly) Tropical Ecosystems: structure, diversity and human welfare, 2001; (with S. Kadur) Sahyadris: India's Western Ghats, 2005; (jtly) Conservation Biology: a primer for South Asia, 2010; (with S. Kadur) Himalaya: mountains of life, 2013; contrib. learned jls. *Address:* Department of Biology, University of Massachusetts Boston, Boston, MA 02125–3393, USA.

**BAWTREE, Rear Adm. David Kenneth,** CB 1993; CEng, FIMechE, FIET; Flag Officer, and Naval Base Commander, Portsmouth, 1990–93; *b* 1 Oct. 1937; *s* of Kenneth Alfred Bawtree and Dorothy Constance Bawtree (*née* Allen); *m* 1962, Ann Cummins; one *s* one *d. Educ:* Christ's Hospital; Royal Naval Engineering College. BSc(Eng). Served in HM Ships Maidstone, Jutland, Diamond, Defender, Rothesay, Bristol, and MoD, 1965–76; Staff of C-in-C Fleet, 1979, of DG Weapons, 1981; Dep. Dir, Naval Analysis, 1983; RCDS 1985; Dep. Dir, Op. Requirements (Navy), 1986; Dir, Naval Engrg Training, 1987–90. Civil Emergencies Advr, Home Office, 1993–97. Advr in Civil Emergencies, Visor Consultants, 1998–; Project Manager: MMI (Research), 2001–02; Stargate Technologies, 2002–04; SeaCell, 2004–07. Dir, Portsmouth Healthcare NHS Trust, 1993–96; Chm., Portsmouth Hosps NHS Trust, 1996–2001. Chm. and Chief Exec., 2001–12, Pres., 2012–15, Future Ship Proj. for 21st Century, later UK Flagship, Univ. of the Oceans. Pres., Portsmouth Model Boats Display Team, 1992–. Past President: Royal Naval and Royal Albert Yacht Club, Portsmouth; Naval Home Club; RN & RM Children's Home; Royal Naval Squash Rackets Assoc. Chm., Portsmouth Dockyard Industries, 1997; Past Member: Victory Technical Adv. Cttee; Mary Rose Trust; Royal Naval Mus.; Trustee, HMS Warrior 1860, 1993– (Chm., 1997–2015); Dir, Portsmouth Historic Dockyard (formerly The Flagship Portsmouth Trust), 1997–2012 (Chm., 2000–05). Trustee: St Mary's Music Foundn, 1990–2001 (Chm., 1990–2001); Portsmouth News Snowball Appeal, 1992–94; Chm., Hants Foundn for Young Musicians, 1993–2003. Patron, CP Centre, 2002–13; former Patron, Portsmouth MacMillan Appeal; volunteer, Spear, 2015–. Almoner, Christ's Hospital, 1998–2004. Governor: Portsmouth Grammar Sch., 1990– (Chm., 1994–2009); Penhale First Sch., 1991–2002. Guildsman, St Bride's, Fleet St, 1997– (Mem. Court, 2013–18); Consultant to Bishop of London, 1998–2006. Mem. Court, Royal Soc. of St George Westminster, 2014–17. Mem., Past Overseers' Soc., 2014–. Pres., Rugby Fives Assoc., 2019– (Dep. Pres., 2016–18). Freeman, City of London; Liveryman, Engineers' Co. (Master, 2007–08); Mem. Cttee, 007 Past Masters' Assoc., 2010– (Mem., 2007–10); Mem., Soc. of Past Overseers. FRSA 2006–09. DL Hants, 1997. City of Portsmouth Merit Award, 2013. *Recreations:* fives (Nat. Masters' Champion, 2003–09, 2011), racket ball, organs and their music, miniature furniture, tropical fish. *Clubs:* Pilgrims, Victory Services.

**BAX, Martin Charles Owen,** DM; FRCP; FRSL; Senior Lecturer, Imperial College School of Medicine, 1997–2001, now Emeritus Reader; *b* 13 Aug. 1933; *s* of Cyril E. O. Bax and E. C. M. Bayne; *m* 1956, Judith Mary Osborn (*d* 2015); three *s. Educ:* Dauntsey's Sch., Wilts; New Coll., Oxford (MA, BM BCh, DM); Guy's Hosp., London. Lectr, Guy's Med. Sch., 1961–74; Res. Paediatrician, Thomas Coram Res. Unit, St Mary's Hosp., London, 1974–82; Dir, Community Paediatric Res. Unit, St Mary's Hosp. Med. Sch., 1982–85; Med. Dir, Community Paediatric Res. Unit, Westminster Hosp. Med. Sch., later Charing Cross and Westminster Med. Sch., subseq. Imperial Coll. Sch. of Medicine, 1985–2003. Pres., Soc. for the Study of Behavioural Phenotypes, 1978–. Editor, Ambit Literary & Arts Magazine, 1959–; Sen. Ed., Mac Keith Press, 1978–2004. Folke Bernadette Lectr, Sweden, 1984. FRSL 2002. Anderson-Aldrich Award, Amer. Acad. of Paediatrics, 1990; Dist. Service Award, Amer. Acad. for Cerebral Palsy & Develt Medicine, 1994. *Publications:* The Hospital Ship (novel), 1975; Edmond Went Far Away (for children), 1990; (jtly) Child Development and Child Health, 1990; Love on the Borders (novel), 2005; Memoirs of a Gone World (short stories), 2010. *Recreations:* tennis, walking. *Address:* 17 Priory Gardens, Highgate, N6 5QY. *T:* (020) 8340 3566. *Clubs:* Chelsea Arts, Royal Society of Medicine.

**BAXENDALE, Denise B.;** see Barrett-Baxendale.

**BAXENDALE, Presiley Lamorna, (Mrs R. K. FitzGerald);** QC 1992; *b* 31 Jan. 1951; *d* of late Geoffrey Arthur Baxendale and Elizabeth (*née* Stevenson); *m* 1978, Richard Kieran FitzGerald; one *s* one *d. Educ:* St Mary's Sch., Wantage; St Anne's Coll., Oxford (BA). Called to the Bar, Lincoln's Inn, 1974, Bencher, 1999; Jun. Counsel to Crown, Common Law, 1991. Member: ICSTIS, 1986–90; Council, Justice, 1994–2002. Mem., Ct of Govs, LSE, 1988–2007. Counsel to Scott Inquiry, 1992–95. Hon. Fellow, LSE, 2008.

**BAXENDELL, Sir Peter (Brian),** Kt 1981; CBE 1972; FREng; FIC; Director, Shell Transport and Trading Co., 1973–95 (Chairman, 1979–85); *b* 28 Feb. 1925; *s* of Lesley Wilfred Edward Baxendell and Evelyn Mary Baxendell (*née* Gaskin); *m* 1949, Rosemary (*née* Lacey); two *s* two *d. Educ:* St Francis Xavier's, Liverpool; Royal School of Mines, London (ARSM, BSc; FIC 1983). FREng (FEng 1978). Joined Royal Dutch/Shell Group, 1946; Petroleum Engr in Egypt, 1947, and Venezuela, 1950; Techn. Dir, Shell-BP Nigeria, 1963; Head of SE Asia Div., London, 1966; Man. Dir, Shell-BP Nigeria, 1969; Chm., Shell UK, 1974–79; Man. Dir, 1973, Chm., Cttee of Man. Dirs, 1982–85, Royal Dutch/Shell Gp of Cos; Chm., Shell Canada Ltd, 1980–85; Dir, Shell Oil Co., USA, 1982–85; Chm., Hawker Siddeley Gp, 1986–91 (Dir, 1984–91; Dep. Chm., Jan.–April 1986); Director: Sun Life Assurance Co. of Canada, 1986–97; Inchcape, 1986–93. Mem., UGC, 1983–89. Mem., Governing Body, Imperial Coll., London, 1983–99 (Vice Chm., 1991–99). Hon. DSc: Heriot-Watt, 1982; QUB, 1986; London, 1986; Loughborough, 1987. Commander, Order of Orange-Nassau, 1985. *Publications:* articles on petroleum engrg subjects in scientific jls. *Recreations:* watching sport, reading. *Address:* c/o Shell Centre, SE1 7NA.

**BAXTER, Bernadette;** Her Honour Judge Baxter; a Circuit Judge, since 2016; *b* Kingston-upon-Hull; *d* of Anthony Baxter and Margaret Baxter; *m* 1997, Malcolm Henry Rogerson; two *s. Educ:* St Mary's High Sch., Hull; London Sch. of Econs (LLB). Called to the Bar, Middle Temple, 1987; barrister, 211 Deansgate Chambers, 1987–92, Lincoln House Chambers, 1992–2016; a Recorder, 2006–16. *Recreations:* travel, theatre, cinema, reading, walking. *Address:* Manchester Crown Court, The Court House, Minshull Street, Manchester M1 3FS. *T:* (0161) 954 7500. *E:* hhj.bernadette.baxter@ejudiciary.net.

**BAXTER, Canon Dr Christina Ann,** CBE 2005; Principal, St John's College, Nottingham, 1997–2012 (Dean, 1988–97); Chairman of House of Laity, General Synod of Church of England, 1995–2010 (Vice-Chairman, 1990–95); *b* 8 March 1947; *d* of late Leslie John David and Madge Adeline Baxter. *Educ:* Walthamstow Hall, Sevenoaks, Kent; Durham Univ. (BA, PhD); Bristol Univ. (Cert Ed). Asst Teacher, 1969–73, Head of Religious Educn, 1973–76, John Leggott Sixth Form Coll., Scunthorpe; part-time tutor, St John's Coll., Durham, and Durham research student, 1976–79; Lectr in Christian Doctrine, St John's Coll., Nottingham, 1979–2012. Canon Theologian, Coventry Cath., 1996–2006; Lay Canon, Southwell Minster, 2000–13, now Canon Emeritus. Mem., Archbishops' Council, 1998–2010. Hon. DTheol Chester, 2013. *Publications:* Wounds of Jesus, 2005. *Recreation:* swimming. *Address:* 18 St Michael's Square, Bramcote, Nottingham NG9 3HG. *T:* (0115) 922 4087.

**BAXTER, Glen;** artist; *b* 4 March 1944; *s* of Charles Baxter and Florence Baxter; *m* 1991, Carole Suzanne Elsa Agis; one *s* one *d. Educ:* Leeds Coll. of Art. *Exhibitions:* Gotham Book Mart, NYC, 1974, 1976, 1979; Anthony Stokes Gall., London, 1978, 1980; ICA, 1981; Mus. of Modern Art, Oxford, 1981; Nigel Greenwood Gall., London, 1983, 1985, 1990; Holly Solomon Gall., NY, 1985; Sydney Biennale, Australia, 1986; Samia Saouma, Paris, 1987, 1991; Musée de l'Abbaye Sainte-Croix, Les Sables d'Olonne, France, 1987; Seita Mus., Paris, 1990; Adelaide Fest., 1992; Tanya Rumpff Galerie, Haarlem, 1992; Ginza Art Space, Tokyo, 1994; Wilkinson Fine Art, London, 1994; Les Entrepôts Laydet, Paris, 1995; Nagy Fine Art, Sydney, 1996; Modernism, San Francisco, 1998, 2002, 2006, 2008; Galerie de la Châme, Paris, 1998, 2004, 2008; Artothèque Gal., Angoulême, and Gal. de la Châtre, Palais de Congrès, Paris, Chris Beetles Gall., and Anthony Wilkinson Gall., London, 1999; Lombard Freid Fine Arts, NY, 2001; Galerie Daniel Blau, Munich, 2001, 2009; Le Salon d'Art, Brussels, 2003, 2008, 2015; Wetering Galerie, Amsterdam, 2004; Flowers Central Gall., London, 2004, 2006, 2009, 2011, 2015; Galerie Martine et Thibault de la Châtre, Paris, 2006, 2008, 2010–11; Espace Ecureuil Fondation d'Art, Toulouse, 2009; Poitiers, 2010; Advent Calendar, Meymac Contemporary Art Centre, 2010; Cognac, 2011; La Station, Nice, 2013; Galerie Isabelle Gounod, Paris 2016, 2018; Fondation Fernet-Branca, Saint Louis, France, 2018; Castello di Potentino, Tuscany, 2018; Vernon Street Gall., Leeds, 2019. *Works in collections:* Tate Gall.; De Young Mus., San Francisco; V&A; Arts Council; NY Public Liby; Southampton Univ.; FRAC Poitou-Charentes; FRAC Picardie; Centre Georges Pompidou, Paris; Chase Manhattan Bank, NY. Histl tapestry (commnd by French Min. of Culture, 1999), Contemporary Art Mus., Rochechouart, France. Chevalier des Arts et des Lettres (France), 2013. *Publications:* The Works, 1977; Atlas, 1979; The Impending Gleam, 1981; Glen Baxter: his life, 1983; Jodhpurs in the Quantocks, 1986; The Billiard Table Murders, 1990; Returns to Normal, 1992; The Wonder Book of Sex, 1995; 1936 at the Hotel Furkablick, 1997; Glen Baxter's Gourmet Guide, 1997; Blizzards of Tweed, 1999; Trundling Grunts, 2002; Loomings over the Suet, 2004; (with Clark Coolidge) Speech with Humans, 2007; Ominous Stains, 2009; (with Alberto Manguel) Le safari historico-gastronomique en Poitou Charentes, 2010; Colonel Baxter's Dutch Safari, 2012; Almost Completely Baxter, 2016. *Recreations:* marquetry, snood retrieval. *Clubs:* Chelsea Arts, Academy; Ale and Quail (New York).

**BAXTER, Gregory David;** Chief Digital Officer, MetLife, since 2017; *b* Australia, 8 Aug. 1967. *Educ:* Monash Univ. (BAppSc); Univ. of Melbourne (MBA). Sen. Project Manager, IBM, 1989–97; Booz Allen Hamilton, later Booz & Co., 1998–2011 (Partner, 2006–11);

Man. Dir and Global Hd, Citi Digital Strategy, 2011–17. Guest Lectr, NY Univ. Mem. Council, RIIA, 2011–17. *Recreations:* triathlon (Australian representative), running (elite marathon qualification). *Address:* 220 Riverside Boulevard, Apt 41D, New York, NY 10069, USA. *E:* greg.d.baxter@gmail.com.

BAXTER, (James) Neil; writer and editor, since 2018; Secretary and Treasurer, Royal Incorporation of Architects in Scotland, 2008–18; *b* Bellshill, 3 May 1960; *s* of Andrew Baxter and Elizabeth Baxter (*née* McCardle); civil partnership 2007, John, (Josh), McGuire. *Educ:* Lenzie Acad.; Glasgow Univ. (MA Hons Eng. Lit. and Hist. of Fine Art 1982). Co-ordinator, Thirties Study and Competitions Officer, RIAS, 1982–83; Asst Editor, Architectural Design, 1984; Asst Sec., RIAS, 1984–88; Principal, Neil Baxter Associates, 1988–2008. Tutor (pt-time), Mackintosh Sch. of Architecture, 1987–89; Guest Tutor (pt-time), Sch. of Urban Studies, Glasgow Univ., 2003. Develt Dir (pt-time), Glasgow Building Preservation Trust, 2004–07. Sec., Alexander Greek Thomson Trust, 1998–2008; Vice Chairman: Tron Th., 2002–04; Glasgow Film Th., 2010–14; Dir, St Andrew's in the Square Trust, 2003; Member: Adv. Bd, Common Purpose Glasgow, 2004–07; Glasgow Health Commn, 2008; Lord Provost of Edinburgh's Commn on Civic Bldgs, 2016–17; Trustee: N Highland Connections, 2008–11; Martin Jones Educn Trust, 2008; Secretary: Scottish Building Contracts Cttee, 2009–17; Cross-Party Gp on Architecture and the Built Envmt, Scottish Parlt, 2016–17. Curator, Festival of Architecture, 2016. Dir, Cuba Conservation Trust, 2012–13. Life Member: Saltire Soc., 2003 (Mem. Council, 1984–86); Charles Rennie Mackintosh Soc., 1991 (Mem. Bd, 1988–91); Architectural Heritage Soc. of Scotland, 1995. FRSA; MCIPR. Hon. FRIAS 2013; Hon. FRIBA 2017. Mem., Eur. Urban Res. Assoc. Glasgow Lord Provost's Medal, 2008. *Publications:* (with Pat Lally) Lazarus Only Done it Once: the story of my lives, 2000; (ed) A Tale of Two Towns: a history of Medieval Glasgow, 2007, 2nd edn 2008; The Wee Green Book: the extraordinary story of Glasgow Green, 2007; Re-Designing Scotland's Cities: the first 25 years of the Burrell Company, 2007; (jtly) Glasgow's Greatest Exhibition, 2008; (ed) A Life in Cities: an architectural autobiography, 2009; (ed) The Architectural Tourist, 2012; (ed) On Life and Architecture, 2013; (ed jtly) Scotstyle: 100 years of Scottish architecture, 2016; (ed) RIAS Centenary: 100th birthday contributions from the RIAS' honorary fellows, 2016; Adventures in Space, 2016. *Recreations:* reading, writing, running (12 marathons to date), ruins, being walked by the dog (Lily). *Club:* Scottish Arts (Edinburgh) (Hon. Mem.).

BAXTER, Jayne; Member (Lab) Mid Scotland and Fife, Scottish Parliament, Dec. 2012–2016; *b* Mansfield, 5 Nov. 1955; *d* of Denis and Annabel Knight; two *s. Educ:* Napier Univ. (BA Business Studies). Houseparent, Social Work Dept, Fife Regl Council, 1976–81; Chief Exec.'s Unit, Dunfermline DC, 1988–95; Corporate Policy Officer, Fife Council, 1995–2011; Sen. Parly Asst, Office of Rt Hon. Gordon Brown, MP, 2011–12.

BAXTER, John, CBE 2016; FREng; FRSE; FIMechE, FIET; Group Engineering Director, BP plc, 2004–15; *b* 26 March 1951; *s* of late Robert Baxter and Ruth Baxter (*née* Baxter); *m* 1996, Margaret Helen Carnell; two *s* from a previous marriage. *Educ:* Queen's Park Sch., Glasgow; Strathclyde Univ. (BSc Hons); RNC, Greenwich (Postgrad. Dip.). FIMechE 1993; FIET (FIEE 2001); FREng 2003. Hd, Nuclear Reactors, Harwell, 1988–90; Director: Engrg, UKAEA, 1990–94; Dounreay, 1994–96; Mem., UKAEA, 1994–98; Chief Engr, 1998–2001, Gp Engrg Dir, 2001–04, Powergen plc. President: IMechE, 2007–08; Welding Inst., 2011–14. Vice Pres., RedR, 2010–15. Director: Sovereign Living Ltd, 2011–14; Florin Living Ltd, 2011–14; Thane Ltd, 2012–; non-exec. Dir, Sellafield Ltd. Chm., AHRC, Strathclyde Univ., 2016–. Vis. Prof. of Nuclear Engrg, Strathclyde Univ. FRSE 2008. Hon. FIChemE 2013; Hon. FIWeldE. Lt Col, 2003–07, Col, 2007–, Engr & Logistic Staff Corps, RE (V). Liveryman: Co. of Engrs, 2001; Tallow Chandlers' Co., 2010 (Master, 2018–19); Master, Engineers' Co., 2014. Hon. DTech Robert Gordon, 2008; Hon. DSc Strathclyde, 2011. *Recreations:* sailing, shooting, walking. *Address:* c/o Royal Academy of Engineering, 3 Carlton House Terrace, SW1Y 5DG.

BAXTER, John Lawson; Vice Lord-Lieutenant of County Londonderry, 2002–14; *b* 25 Nov. 1939; *s* of John Lawson Baxter and Enid Maud Taggart; *m* 1967; three *s. Educ:* Trinity Coll., Dublin; Queen's Univ., Belfast; BA, BComm, LLB; LLM Tulane Univ., New Orleans. Solicitor. Mem. (U) N Ireland Assembly, for N Antrim, 1973–75; Minister of Information, N Ireland Executive, 1974. Chm. (part-time), Industrial Tribunals (NI), 1980–83; Member: Northern Health and Social Services Board, 1982–88; Criminal Injury Appeals Panel, 2002–12. Mem. Council, Ulster Univ., 2002–09. DL Co. Londonderry, 1988. *Recreations:* golf, fishing. *Address:* Beardville, Cloyfin, Coleraine, N Ireland. *T:* (028) 2073 1552.

BAXTER, John Stephen; Head Master, Wells Cathedral School, 1986–2000; *b* 7 Sept. 1939; *s* of George Baxter and Muriel (*née* Firman); *m* 1965, Priscilla Candy; two *s. Educ:* Magdalen Coll. Sch., Oxford; Merton Coll., Oxford; Grey Coll., Durham. BA Modern History, Durham; DipEd Oxford. Assistant Master: Cranleigh Sch., 1964–67; Christ's Coll., NZ, 1967–70; Westminster Sch., 1971–86 (Hd of Hist., 1974–79; Hse Master, 1979–86). Educn Consultant, Emergent Dynamics (formerly Breakthrough), 2000–05. Ecclesiastical Insce Gp Scholar, 1993; Korea Foundn Fellow, 1993. Res. Asst, H of C, 1971–79; Reader, Edward Arnold, 1980–83. Mem., Admiralty Interview Bd, 1988–2005. Chairman: SW Div., HMC, 1991; Choir Schs Assoc., 1995–97; Nat. Assoc. of Music and Ballet Schs, 1998–2000; Mem., Music and Dance Scheme Adv. Gp, DfES, 2001–07. Governor: St Aubyn's Sch., 1978–95; Truro Sch., 2000–07 (Chm., 2002–07); Trustee: Commonwealth Linking Trust, 1972–95; Wells Cath. Sch. Foundn, 2007–17; Member, Board of Management: MusicSpace, 1988–2000; British Sch. of Brussels, 2000–10 (Trustee, 2006–); Ind. Mem., SW Cttee, NT, 2008–12. Mem. (ex-officio), NYO, 1986–2000. Page Schol., 1998, Chm., Cornwall Br., 2003–10, ESU. Trustee, Cornwall Music Therapy Trust, 2009–. MCMI (MIMgt 1991); FRSA 1990 (Mem., SW Region Cttee, 2001–04). Freeman, City of London, 1991; Liveryman, Musicians' Co., 1991–. *Publications:* (contrib.) History of Lords and Commons Cricket, 1989; The Three Churches of St Minver, 2003, 2nd edn 2013; papers and articles in educn jls. *Recreations:* music, Cornish history, golf, sport (GB Olympic Hockey Squad, Oxon; Capt., Oxon U19 Rugby; Minor Counties Cricket, Cornwall Veterans Cricket). *Address:* Boscarne, Rock, Wadebridge, Cornwall PL27 6LP. *T:* (01208) 863613. *Clubs:* MCC (Mem., Indoor Sch. Cttee, 1976–86); Vincent's (Oxford); St Enodoc Golf (Cornwall) (Capt., 2011–13).

BAXTER, Kenneth Peter; Director, Baxter & Associates Pty Ltd, since 2000; Chairman, Papua New Guinea Sustainable Energy Development Ltd, since 2006; Productivity Commissioner, since 2015; Commissioner, NSW Natural Resources Commission, since 2018; *b* 23 Oct. 1943; *s* of P. F. Baxter and R. L. Baxter; *m* 1973, Pamela Annabel Marr; two *s* one *d. Educ:* Fort St Boys' High Sch.; Univ. of Sydney (BEc). Industrial Advocate and Research Officer, Graziers' Assoc. of NSW, 1965–70; consultant, 1970–73; farming columnist and press sec., 1973–80; Develt Manager, Versatile Farm Machinery Pty Ltd, 1973–76; Dir, Corporate Affairs and Asst Man. Dir, Philip Morris Aust. Ltd, 1981–82; Manager, Adv. Services, Capel Court Corp. Ltd, 1982–83; Cllr, Aust. Rural Adjustment Unit, 1982–87; Mem., Aust. Egg Bd, 1983–85; Man. Dir, NSW Egg Corp., 1983–88; Advr, Mackay Mill Merger Cttee, 1986–87; Chairman: Aust. Dairy R&D Corp. (formerly Res. Council), 1986–92; Good Food Products Aust. Pty Ltd, 1986–88; Privest Rural Ltd, 1987–88; Darling Harbour Authy, 1989–90; Austdairy Ltd, 1992–98; Aust. Dairy Corp., 1992–98; Thai Dairy Ind. Co. Ltd, 1996–99 (Dir, 1992–98); Computronics Ltd, 2002–07; AVT Plasma Ltd, 2003–06; PNG Sustainable Infrastructure Ltd, 2006–14; XRF Scientific Ltd, 2006–15; InfraCo Asia, 2012–16; Director: Grain Handling Authy, NSW, 1986–89; KPMG Nat. Office, 1996–2000; Hydro Tas (formerly Hydro Electric Corp. of Tasmania), 1996–2007; VRI Biomedical Ltd, 2000–03; TFG International Pty Ltd, 2001–; non-exec. Dir, Air Niugini Ltd, 2004–07 (PNG Govt Rep., 2002–04). Private Sec. to Hon. K. S. Wriedt, 1976–80; Special Advr, Senate Standing Cttee on Finance and Govt Admin, 1980–81; Dep. Dir-Gen., Premier's Dept, NSW, 1988–92; Sec., Dept of the Premier and Cabinet, Vic, 1992–95 (Chm., Public Service Bd; Mem., State Superannuation Bd); Dir-Gen., Premier's Dept, NSW, 1995–96; Policy Advr to Chief Sec., PNG, 1999–2007. Chairman: Aust. Govt Electricity Industry Supply Cttee; Hunter District Water Bd Corporatisation Cttee; NSW Grain Corp. Privatisation Cttee; Mem., GIO Aust. Ltd Privatisation Cttee. Member: Sydney Org Cttee for 2000 Olympic Games, 1995–96; Audit Cttee, Tasmania HEC, 1999–2007; Chairman: Audit Cttee, Office of Film and Literature Classification, 2002–07; Audit Cttee, Federal Magistrates Court, 2007–08. Dep. Chm., Aust. Nat. Rlys Commn, 2001–03 (Comr, 1997–98). Director: Multiple Sclerosis Soc. of NSW, 1986–91; Baker Med. Res. Foundn, 1996–98. Adjunct Professor: NSW and Sydney Univs, 1999–2003; Macquarie Univ., 2004–05. Dir, Tasmania Symphony Orch., 2007–09. Mem. Cttee, Boston, Melbourne, Oxford Conversazione. Dir, NSW Inst. of Mgt. FAICD 1980; FAIM 1985; Fellow, American Inst. of Pol Affairs (NY), American Univ., Washington, 2015. *Publications:* Wool Marketing in New Zealand, 1967, 2nd edn 1972; Statutory Marketing Authorities, 1988; Failure, Chaos and Leadership, 1994. *Recreations:* sailing, rowing, political science. *Address:* Baxter & Associates, Level 5, 16 O'Connell Street, Sydney, NSW 2000, Australia. *T:* (2) 92232224. *Clubs:* Melbourne (Victoria); Royal Sydney Yacht Squadron (Sydney); Mosman Rowing.

BAXTER, Prof. Murdoch Scott, PhD, CChem, FRSC; FRSE; scientific consultant; Founding Editor: Journal of Environmental Radioactivity, since 1983; Radioactivity in the Environment book series, since 1999; *b* 12 March 1944; *s* of John Sawyer Napier Baxter and Margaret Hastie Baxter (*née* Murdoch); *m* 1968, Janice Henderson; one *s. Educ:* Univ. of Glasgow. BSc Hons Chem. 1966, PhD Geochem. 1969. Research Fellow, State Univ. of NY (Noble gas history of lunar rocks and meteorites), 1969–70; Lectr, Dept of Chemistry, Univ. of Glasgow (geochem., radiochem. and envmtl radioactivity), 1970–85; Vis. Consultant, IAEA (nuclear waste disposal), 1981–82; Dir, Scottish Univs Res. and Reactor Centre, 1985–90; Dir, Marine Envmt Lab. (formerly Internat. Lab. of Marine Radioactivity), IAEA, 1990–97; Personal Chair, Univ. of Glasgow, 1985–95. Member: Challenger Soc. for Marine Sci., 1975–; Scottish Assoc. for Marine Sci. (formerly Scottish Marine Biology Assoc.), 1975–. FRSE 1989; Fellow, Internat. Union of Eco-Ethics, 1998; Hon. Mem. and Advr, Internat. Union of Radioecol., 1999–; Advr, Inst. Nuclear Technol., Portugal, 2000–. Mem., Scotch Malt Whisky Soc. Chevalier, Order of St Charles (Monaco), 1997. *Publications:* numerous papers to professional jls. *Recreations:* hill walking, sports, Queen's Park FC, F1, good food, malt whisky. *Address:* Ampfield House, Clachan Seil, Argyll PA34 4TL. *T:* (01852) 300351. *E:* murdochbaxter@gmail.com.

BAXTER, Neil; *see* Baxter, J. N.

BAXTER, Prof. Rodney James, FRS 1982; FAA 1977; Professor in the Department of Theoretical Physics, Institute of Advanced Studies, and in the School of Mathematical Sciences, 1981–2002, Visiting Fellow in the School of Mathematical Sciences, since 2002, Australian National University; *b* 8 Feb. 1940; *s* of Thomas James Baxter and Florence A. Baxter; *m* 1968, Elizabeth Phillips; one *s* one *d. Educ:* Bancroft's Sch., Essex; Trinity Coll., Cambridge; Australian National Univ. Reservoir Engineer, Iraq Petroleum Co., 1964–65; Research Fellow, ANU, 1965–68; Asst Prof., Mathematics Dept, Massachusetts Inst. of Technology, 1968–70; Fellow, ANU, 1970–81; Royal Soc. Res. Prof., 1992, Sen. Fellow, 1992–, Isaac Newton Inst. for Mathematical Scis, Cambridge Univ. Pawsey Medal, Aust. Acad. of Science, 1975; Boltzmann Medal, IUPAP, 1980; Heineman Prize, Amer. Inst. of Physics, 1987; Harrie Massey Medal, Inst. of Physics, 1994; Centenary Medal (Australia), 2003; Onsager Prize, Amer. Physical Soc., 2006; Onsager Medal, Norwegian Univ. of Sci. and Technol., 2006; Royal Medal, Royal Soc., 2013. *Publications:* Exactly Solved Models in Statistical Mechanics, 1982; contribs to Proc. Royal Soc., Jl of Physics A, Physical Rev., Statistical Physics, Annals of Physics. *Recreation:* theatre. *Address:* Centre for Mathematics and its Applications, Building 27, Australian National University, Canberra, ACT 0200, Australia. *T:* (2) 61253511.

BAXTER, Roger George, PhD; UK boarding school consultant; Partner, Select Education (formerly Select Education and Select Consultants), 1995–2014; *b* 21 April 1940; *s* of late Rev. Benjamin George Baxter and Gweneth Muriel Baxter (*née* Causer); *m* 1967, Dorothy Ann Cook; one *s* one *d. Educ:* Handsworth Grammar Sch., Birmingham; Univ. of Sheffield (BSc, PhD). Junior Research Fellow, Univ. of Sheffield, 1965–66, Lectr, Dept of Applied Mathematics, 1966–70; Asst Mathematics Master, Winchester Coll., 1970–81, Under Master, 1976–81; Headmaster, Sedbergh Sch., 1982–95. Governor: Bramcote Sch., Scarborough, 1982–95; Hurworth Hse Sch., Darlington, 1982–95; Cathedral Choir Sch., Ripon, 1984–95; Mowden Hall Sch., Northumberland, 1984–96; Cundall Manor Sch., York, 1988–98; Durham Sch., 1995–2005; Bow Sch., Durham, 1995–2005; Chetwynde Sch., Barrow, 2003–09 (Chm. Govs, 2005–09). Member: HMC Academic Policy Cttee, 1985–90; Common Entrance Board, 1989–94. Mem. Ct, Univ. of Lancaster, 1994–95. Overseas Mem., British Business Gp Dubai & Northern Emirates, 1999–2008. Church Warden, Cartmel Priory, 1997–. Freeman, City of London, 1992; Liveryman, Gunmakers' Co., 1992–. *Publications:* various papers on numerical studies in magnetoplasma diffusion with applications to the F-2 layer of the ionosphere. *Recreations:* opera, music, cooking, wine. *Address:* The Rivelin, Lindale, Grange-over-Sands, Cumbria LA11 6LJ. *T:* and *Fax:* (01539) 535129. *E:* baxterrg@aol.com.

BAXTER, Sarah April Louise; Deputy Editor, since 2013, and columnist, since 2016, Sunday Times; *b* London, 25 Nov. 1959; *d* of George Robert Baxter and Virginia Louise Baxter (*née* Cox); *m* 2001, Jez Coulson; one *s* one *d. Educ:* N London Collegiate Sch.; St Hilda's Coll., Oxford (BA Hons Modern Hist.). News ed., Time Out, 1988–90; Political ed., New Statesman, 1990–94; Asst Ed., Observer, 1995; Presenter, TV progs, Parliament Prog., 1994, The Midnight Hour, 1995; Sunday Times: Ed., News Rev., 1996–2001; NY corresp., 2001–04; Washington corresp., 2004–09; Ed., Sunday Times Magazine, 2009–15. Non-exec. Dir, Times Newspapers Hldgs Ltd, 2010–. *Recreations:* family and children, juggling work and home life. *Address:* The Sunday Times, 1 London Bridge Street, SE1 9GF. *E:* sarah.baxter@sunday-times.co.uk. *Club:* Soho House.

BAY, Rt Rev. Ross; *see* Auckland (NZ), Bishop of.

BAYCROFT, Rt Rev. John Arthur; Bishop of Ottawa, 1993–99; *b* 2 June 1933; *s* of Robert Baycroft and Mary Alice (*née* Williams); *m* 1955, Joan, *d* of Victor Lake and Dora Lake (*née* Harrison); one *s* two *d. Educ:* Sir William Turner Sch.; Christ's Coll., Cambridge (Synge Schol.) (BA 1954; MA 1958); Ripon Hall, Oxford; Trinity Coll., Toronto (BD 1959). Ordained deacon, 1955, priest, 1956; Rector, Loughborough, Ont, 1955–57; Asst Rector, St Matthew's, Ottawa, 1957–62; Rector, Perth, Ont, 1962–67; St Matthias, Ottawa, 1967–84; Christchurch Cathedral, and Dean of Ottawa, 1984–86; Suffragan Bishop of Ottawa, 1985–93; Dir, Anglican Centre in Rome, and Archbp of Canterbury's

Rep. to the Holy See, 1999–2001; Dir, Ecumenical Relns and Studies, Anglican Communion, 2002–03. Mem., ARCIC, 1982–2004. Hon. DD: Montreal Diocesan Theol Coll., 1988; Huron Coll., 1997; Wycliffe Coll., Toronto, 2004; DSLitt (*jur. dig.*) Thornloe Univ., 1991; DUniv St Paul, Ottawa, 2002. Eugene de Mazenod Medal, Univ. St Paul, Ottawa, 2013. *Publications:* The Anglican Way, 1980; The Eucharistic Way, 1982; The Way of Prayer, 1983; numerous articles in jls. *Recreations:* theatre, art, ballet. *Address:* 97 Java Street, Ottawa, ON K1Y 3L5, Canada. *Clubs:* National Press, Rideau (Ottawa).

**BAYES, Rt Rev. Paul;** see Liverpool, Bishop of.

**BAYFIELD, Rabbi Prof. Anthony Michael,** CBE 2011; President, Movement for Reform Judaism, 2011–16 (Head of Movement, 2005–10; Chief Executive, Reform Movement and Reform Synagogues of Great Britain, 1994–2005); Professor of Jewish Theology and Thought, Leo Baeck College, since 2014; *b* 4 July 1946; *s* of Ronald Bayfield and Sheila (*née* Mann); *m* 1969, Linda Gavinia (*née* Rose) (*d* 2003); one *s* two *d*. *Educ:* Royal Liberty Sch.; Gidea Park; Magdalene Coll., Cambridge (MA (Hons) Law); Leo Baeck Coll., London (Rabbinic degree). Rabbi, NW Surrey Synagogue, 1972–82; Dir, Sternberg Centre for Judaism (Manor House Trust), 1983–2010. Dir, Advancement of Jewish Educn Trust, 1987–93; Co-ordinator of Supervisors, 1987–93; Lectr in Homiletics, 1992–96, Lectr in Personal Theol., 2002–13, Leo Baeck Coll. Chairman: Assembly of Rabbis, Reform Synagogues of GB, 1980–82; Council of Reform and Liberal Rabbis, 1984–86. Co-Pres., CCJ, 2004–12. Founder Editor, Manna (Qly Jl of Progressive Judaism), 1983–2011. DD Lambeth, 2006. *Publications:* Churban: the murder of the Jews of Europe, 1981; (ed) Dialogue with a Difference, 1992; Sinai, Law and Responsible Autonomy: Reform Judaism and the Halakhic tradition, 1993; (ed jtly) He Kissed Him and They Wept, 2001; (ed jtly) Beyond the Dysfunctional Family, 2012; (ed) Deep Calls to Deep, 2017; Being Jewish Today: confronting the real issues, 2019; articles in European Judaism, Brit. Jl of Religious Educn, Church Times. *Recreations:* family life, suffering with West Ham United FC. *Address:* Leo Baeck College, Sternberg Centre for Judaism, 80 East End Road, Finchley, N3 2SY.
See also D. Bayfield.

**BAYFIELD, Daniel;** QC 2016; *b* London, 12 Jan. 1975; *s* of Rabbi Prof. Anthony Michael Bayfield, *qv*; *m* 2006, Lisa Goldscheider; three *s*. *Educ:* Latymer Sch.; Magdalene Coll., Cambridge (BA Law 1997; MA). Called to the Bar, Inner Temple, 1998; in practice as a barrister, specialising in restructuring and insolvency, banking and finance, gen. commercial litigation, and sport, South Square, 2000–. *Recreations:* watching and playing football, cricket and tennis with my sons, little time for anything else. *Address:* 3–4 South Square, Gray's Inn, WC1R 5HP. *T:* (020) 7696 9900, *Fax:* (020) 7696 9911. *E:* danielbayfield@southsquare.com.

**BAYLEY, Hagan;** see Bayley, J. H. P.

**BAYLEY, Sir Hugh,** Kt 2015; *b* 9 Jan. 1952; *s* of Michael and Pauline Bayley; *m* 1984, Fenella Jeffers; one *s* one *d*. *Educ:* Haileybury Sch.; Univ. of Bristol (BSc); Univ. of York (BPhil). Dist Officer, 1975–77, Nat. Officer, 1977–82, NALGO; Gen. Sec., Internat. Broadcasting Trust, 1982–86; Lectr in Social Policy, 1986–87, Res. Fellow in Health Econs, 1987–92, Univ. of York. Councillor, London Bor. of Camden, 1980–86. Mem., York HA, 1988–90. MP (Lab) York, 1992–97, City of York, 1997–2010, York Central, 2010–15. PPS to Sec. of State for Health, 1997–98; Parly Under-Sec. of State, DSS, 1999–2001. Dep. Speaker, 2010. Mem., Select Cttee on Health, 1992–97, on Internat. Develt, 2001–15. Chairman: Public Bill Cttees, 2005–15; Africa All Party Parly Gp, 2003–14 (Vice-Chair, 2014–15). UK delegate to: N Atlantic Assembly, 1997–99; NATO Parly Assembly, 2001–15 (Vice-Pres., 2010–12; Pres., 2012–14; Rapporteur, 2006–08, Chm., 2008–11, Econs and Security Cttee). Chairman: Westminster Foundn for Democracy, 2005–08; UK Br., Commonwealth Parly Assoc., 2006–08; Parly Network on the World Bank, 2008–10; UK Bd Mem., Internat. Rescue Cttee, 2016–. Lay Mem., Nursing and Midwifery Council, 2017–. Trustee, Drill2Think, 2018–. *Publications:* The Nation's Health, 1995; Why NATO Matters, 2014. *Address:* 9 Holly Terrace, York YO10 4DS. *E:* hughbayley@live.co.uk.

**BAYLEY, Prof. (John) Hagan (Pryce),** PhD; FRS 2011; Professor of Chemical Biology, University of Oxford, since 2003; Fellow, Hertford College, Oxford, since 2003; *b* 13 Feb. 1951; *s* of David and Nora Bayley; *m* 1988, Orit Braha; two *s*. *Educ:* King's Sch., Chester; Uppingham Sch.; Balliol Coll., Oxford (BA, MA); Harvard Univ. (PhD Chem. 1979). Postdoctoral res., Depts of Chem. and Biol., MIT, 1979–81; Asst Prof. of Biochem., Columbia Univ., 1981–84; Lectr in Organic Chem., and Fellow, Brasenose Coll., Oxford Univ., 1984–85; Columbia University: Asst Investigator, Howard Hughes Med. Inst., 1985–88; Associate Prof., Center for Neurobiol. and Behavior, 1987–88; Sen. Scientist, 1988–94, Principal Scientist, 1994–96, Worcester Foundn; Associate Prof. of Biochem. and Molecular Biol., 1991–96, and of Physiol., 1995–96, Univ. of Mass Med. Center; Associate Prof. of Chem., Clark Univ., 1996; Prof. of Chem., Texas A&M Univ., 1997–2003; Prof. and Hd, Dept of Med. Biochem. and Genetics, Texas A&M Univ. System Health Sci. Center, 1997–2003. *Address:* Department of Chemistry, University of Oxford, Chemistry Research Laboratory, Mansfield Road, Oxford OX1 3TA. *T:* (01865) 285100, *Fax:* (01865) 275708. *E:* hagan.bayley@chem.ox.ac.uk.

**BAYLEY, Nicola Mary;** writer, artist and illustrator; *b* 18 Aug. 1949; *d* of Percy Harold Bayley and Ann Barbara Crowder; *m* 1978, Alan John Howard Hilton, *qv*; one *s*. *Educ:* Farnborough Hill Convent College; St Martin's Sch. of Art (DipAD); Royal College of Art (MA Illus.). *Publications: written and illustrated:* Nicola Bayley's Book of Nursery Rhymes, 1975; One Old Oxford Ox, 1977; Copy Cats (5 books), 1984; As I was Going Up and Down, 1985; Hush-a-bye Baby, 1985; *compiled and illustrated:* The Necessary Cat, 1998; *illustrated:* Tyger Voyage, 1976; Puss in Boots, 1976; La Corona and the Tin Frog, 1979; The Patchwork Cat, 1981; The Mouldy, 1983; Merry Go Rhymes (4 books), 1987; The Mousehole Cat, 1990; (with Jan Mark) Fun with Mrs Thumb, 1993; Katje the Windmill Cat, 2001; The Jungle Book: Mowgli's story, 2005; (with Brian Patten) The Big Snuggle Up, 2011; (with Brian Patten) Can I Come Too?, 2014. *Recreations:* watching the garden, opera, sleeping, cats. *Address:* c/o Caroline Sheldon Literary Agency Ltd, 71 Hillgate Place, W8 7SS. *Club:* Art Workers Guild.

**BAYLEY, Stephen Paul;** critic, consultant, curator, commentator and author; *b* 13 Oct. 1951; *s* of late Donald Sydney Staines Bayley and Anne Bayley; *m* 1981, Flo Fothergill; one *s* one *d*. *Educ:* Quarry Bank Sch., Liverpool; Manchester Univ.; Liverpool Univ. Sch. of Architecture. Lecturer: Hist. of Art, Open Univ., 1974–76; Hist. and Theory of Art, Univ. of Kent, 1976–80; Dir, Conran Foundn, 1981–89; Dir, Boilerhouse Project, in V&A Mus., 1982–86; Founding Dir, later Chief Exec., Design Mus., 1986–89 (Mem., Curatorial Cttee, 2012–16). Occasional critic and regular contributor to Daily Telegraph, The Times, The Independent and consumer, technical and professional jls. Mem., Design Cttee, LRT, 1989–91. Chm., Brit Insurance Design Awards, 2011. Has lectured at: Nat. Inst. of Design, Ahmedabad; India Inst. of Technol., Bombay; Art Gall. of WA, Perth; Nat. Gall. of Victoria, Melbourne; Salon de l'Automobile, Geneva; Sony Design Center, Tokyo; Internat. Expo, Nagoya; Art Coll. Center of Design (Europe), La Tour-de-Peilz, Switzerland; École Supérieure des Sciences et Études Commerciales, Paris; RIBA; RSA; RCA; and at univs, colls and museums throughout Britain and Europe. Trustee, Royal Fine Arts Commn Trust, 2015–. Honorary Fellow: Liverpool Inst. of Performing Arts, 2001; UWIC, 2007; Hon. FRIBA, 2009. Magazine Columnist of the Year, PPA, 1995. Chevalier de l'Ordre des Arts et des Lettres (France), 1989. *Publications:* In Good Shape, 1979; The Albert Memorial, 1981; Harley Earl and the Dream Machine, 1983; The Conran Directory of Design, 1985; Sex, Drink and Fast Cars, 1986; Twentieth Century Style and Design, 1986; Commerce and Culture, 1989; Taste, 1991; Beefeater 2-Day Guide to London, 1993; Labour Camp: the failure of style over substance, 1998; Moving Objects, 1999; General Knowledge, 2000; Sex: an intimate history, 2001; Dictionary of Idiocy (with an Appendix by Gustave Flaubert), 2003; Life's A Pitch, 2007; Intelligence Made Visible, 2007; Cars, 2008; Woman as Design, 2009; La Dolce Vita, 2011; Ugly: the aesthetics of everything, 2012; Charm, 2013; Death Drive: there are no accidents, 2016; Taste: the secret meaning of things, 2017; Signs of Life: why brands matter, 2017; How to Steal Fire, 2019. *Recreations:* indistinguishable from work, but each involves dodging crowds, words, pictures, food, drink, tennis and spending time in sunny places. *Address:* (office) 3 Jubilee Place, SW3 3TD. *T:* (020) 7351 9111. *W:* www.stephenbayley.com. *Clubs:* Athenæum, Hurlingham, Chelsea Arts, Beefsteak.

**BAYLIS, Katharine Mary;** see Davidson, K. M.

**BAYLIS, Prof. Peter Howard,** MD; FRCP, FMedSci; Dean of Medicine, 1997–2005, Provost of Faculty of Medical Sciences, 2002–05, University of Newcastle upon Tyne; *b* 9 Sept. 1943; *s* of late Derek Baylis and of Lore Baylis; *m* 1968, Dr Susan Mary While; one *s* two *d*. *Educ:* Wallington Grammar Sch.; Univ. of Bristol (BSc, MB ChB, MD). FRCP 1983. Trng in medicine, endocrinology and research, Queen Elizabeth Hosp., Birmingham, 1970–76; Clinical Endocrinology Fellow, Univ. of Indiana, 1976–78; Lectr in Medicine, Univ. of Birmingham, 1978–80; Consultant Physician and Sen. Lectr in Medicine, Royal Victoria Infirmary, Newcastle, 1980–90; Prof. of Exptl Medicine and Clinical Sub-Dean, Med. Sch., Univ. of Newcastle upon Tyne, 1990–97. Founder FMedSci, 1998. *Publications:* (with P. Padfield) The Posterior Pituitary: hormone secretion in health and disease, 1985; (jtly) Case Presentations in Endocrinology and Diabetes, 1988; Salt and Water Homeostasis in Health and Disease, 1989; book chapters and over 130 original articles. *Recreations:* long-distance running, classical music, reading. *Address:* 53 The Rise, Darras Hall, Ponteland, Newcastle upon Tyne NE20 9LQ.

**BAYLISS, David,** OBE 1992; FREng; independent consultant, since 2010; Director: Halcrow Consulting (formerly Halcrow Fox), 1999–2009; Blackpool Urban Regeneration Co., 2005–10; *b* 9 July 1938; *s* of Herbert and Annie Esther Bayliss; *m* 1961, Dorothy Christine Crohill; two *s* one *d*. *Educ:* Arnold Sch., Blackpool; UMIST (BSc Tech 1961); Manchester Univ. (Dip TP 1966). FRTPI 1970; FCIHT (FIHT 1972); FCILT (FCIT 1972–2008); CEng, FICE, 1980; FITE 1984; FREng (FEng 1993). Manchester Corp., 1961–66; GLC, 1966–68; Centre for Environmental Studies, 1968–69; GLC, 1969–84 (Asst Divl Engr; Head, Transport Studies; Chief Transport Planner); Dir of Planning, London Transport, 1984–99. Chairman: SERC/DoT LINK Transport Infrastructure and Ops Steering Gp, 1991–96, Inland Surface Transport Prog. Adv. Gp, 1996–; UITP Internat. Commn on Transport Econs, 1996–98; Fifth Framework Expert Adv. Gp on Sustainable Mobility and Intermodality, EC, 1998–2002. Vis. Prof., Imperial Coll. London (formerly ICSTM), 1999–2011. Chm., Regional Studies Assoc., 1978–81; Member Council: CIT, 1978–82; IHT, 1992–94; ICE, 1996–98; Royal Acad. of Engrg, 1999–2002. President: British Parking Assoc., 1987–89; Transport Studies Soc., 1989–90; UK Vice Pres., Internat. Union of Public Transport, 1997–98. Chm., Rees Jeffreys Road Fund, 2004–13. Mem., Transit Res. Analysis Cttee, NAE, 2004–09; Mem., Public Policy Cttee, 2005–, Trustee, 2011–, RAC Foundn. TPP 2010. *Recreations:* writing, travel, wine. *Address:* 37 Ledborough Lane, Beaconsfield, Bucks HP9 2DB. *T:* (01494) 673313.

**BAYLISS, Jeremy David Bagot,** FRICS; Chief Executive, The Foundation, Royal Botanic Gardens, Kew, 1997–2002; President, Royal Institution of Chartered Surveyors, 1996–97; *b* 27 March 1937; *s* of Edmund Bayliss and Marjorie Clare (*née* Thompson); *m* 1962, Hon. Mary Selina Bridgeman (Hon. Mary Selina Bayliss, CVO) (*d* 2019); three *s*. *Educ:* Harrow; Sidney Sussex Coll., Cambridge (MA). ARICS 1962, FRICS 1971. 2nd Lieut, Coldstream Guards, 1956–57. Partner, Gerald Eve, Chartered Surveyors, 1967–97 (Sen. Partner, 1988–97); Chm., Gerald Eve Financial Services, 1989–96. Royal Institution of Chartered Surveyors: Chm., various cttees, 1983–97; Mem., Gen. Council, 1987–97; Pres., Planning and Develt Div., 1989–90. Chm., CBI Land Use Panel, 1992–95. Mem., Adv. Panel to Secs of State for the Envmt and for Wales on Standards for Planning Inspectorate, 1993–96. Hon. Co. Organiser (Berks), Nat. Gardens Scheme, 2002–07. Trustee: Royal Merchant Navy Sch. Foundn, 2003–07; Soc. for Horticl Therapy, 2004–09. Gov., Bearwood Coll., 1999–2008 (Chm., 2003–08). Chm., Reading S Cons. Assoc., 1975–78. *Recreations:* gardening, country pursuits, classic cars. *Address:* Loddon Lower Farm, Swallowfield, near Reading, Berks RG7 1JE. *T:* (0118) 988 3218. *Club:* Boodle's.

**BAYLISS, John;** Deputy Chairman, Abbey National plc, 1991–93; *b* 22 Jan. 1934; *s* of late Athol Thomas Bayliss and Elizabeth Rose Bayliss; *m* 1954, Maureen (*née* Smith); one *d*. *Educ:* Haberdashers' Aske's, Hatcham. Westminster Bank, 1950; Abbey National Building Society, then Abbey National plc, 1957–93: Regional Man., 1969; Personnel Man., 1972; Asst Gen. Man., 1974; General Manager: Field Operations, 1976; Housing, 1981; Marketing, 1983; Man. Dir (Retail Ops), 1983–91. Chairman: Broomleigh Housing Assoc. Ltd, 1990–96; Richmount Mgt Ltd, 1994–2000; Affinity (formerly Broomleigh Charitable) Trust, 1999–2004; Dir, Downland Affinity Gp Ltd, 2003–04. *Recreation:* France. *Address:* Lyndhurst, Broad Oak, Brenchley, Kent TN12 7NN.

**BAYLISS, John Francis Temple;** an Assistant Judge Advocate General, 1996–2010; a Recorder, 1999–2015; *b* 11 Aug. 1942; *s* of Capt. Horace Temple Taylor Bayliss, DSO, RN and Patricia Bayliss (*née* Loftus); *m* 1981, Annelize Kors; one *s* one *d*. *Educ:* Ampleforth Coll.; BRNC, Dartmouth. Joined Royal Navy, 1960; called to the Bar, Gray's Inn, 1974, NSW, 1981; Comd Legal Officer, Sydney, RAN, 1980–82; Captain, 1986; Sec. to C-in-C Fleet, 1986–88; IMS, Brussels, 1988–92; Chief Naval Judge Advocate, 1992–95; an Asst Recorder, 1994–99. Liveryman, Glovers' Co., 2014. *Recreations:* golf, fly-fishing. *Address:* Cedarwood, Warwicks Bench Lane, Guildford, Surrey GU1 3TP. *T:* 07711 261869.

**BAYLISS, Michelle Louise;** see Heeley, M. L.

**BAYLISS, Rev. Roger Owen;** Principal Chaplain, Church of Scotland and Free Churches, and Director, Chaplaincy Services, Royal Air Force, 1998–2001; Chaplain, HM Prison Service; *b* 21 July 1944; *s* of Stanley John Bayliss and Joyce Audrey Bayliss; *m* 1976, Pauline Jones (marr. diss.); two *s*. *Educ:* Westminster Coll., Oxford (DTh 1999); MTh Oxon 2007. RMN 1966; SRN 1969; SRN for Mentally Subnormal, 1975; Dip. Counselling. Nurse training: Saxondale Hosp., 1963–66; Nottingham Gen. Hosp., 1966–69; Lea Castle Inst., 1973–75; ordained, 1981; entered Chaplains' Branch, RAF, 1981: served at stations: Lyneham, Marham, Stanley (Falkland Is), Bruggen, N Luffenham, Cottesmore, Leeming, Coningsby; HQ RAF Germany; 2 Gp HQ; RAF Support Comd; HQ PTC. QHC, 1998–2001. *Recreations:* classic cars, fly fishing, squash, music (rock and blues), reading, golf, aerobic fitness, cooking. *Address:* Best Wishes Tienda, Box No 772, La Piramide, Local 11, Puerto de Mazarron, Murcia 30860, Spain. *Clubs:* Royal Air Force; Parc Golf Centre (Newport); Players (Doddington); Campasol Golf (Spain).

**BAYLISS, Thomas William Maxwell**; QC 2003; **His Honour Judge Bayliss;** a Circuit Judge, since 2012; b 24 June 1954; s of Thomas Maxwell Bayliss and Dorothy Vera Bayliss; m 1977, Caroline Jane Allpress; one s one d. Educ: King's Sch., Gloucester; Leeds Univ. (LLB Hons). Called to the Bar, Inner Temple, 1977, Bencher, 2008; Standing Counsel to Inland Revenue, 1991–2003; a Recorder, 2000–12. Mem., Restricted Patients Panel, First-tier Tribunal (Mental Health), 2012–. Recreations: bridge, golf, tennis, playgoing. Address: Leeds Combined Court Centre, The Courthouse, 1 Oxford Row, Leeds LS1 3BG. Clubs: Alwoodley Golf; Hunstanton Golf.

**BAYLISS, Valerie June,** CB 1996; education and training consultant; Associate Professor of Education, University of Sheffield, 1996–2001; b 10 June 1944; d of George and Ellen Russell; m 1971, Derek Andrew Bayliss; one s. Educ: Wallington County Grammar Sch. for Girls; Univ. of Wales (1st cl. hons History, BA 1965; MA 1967). Research Student, LSE, 1966–68; Dept of Employment, 1968; Manpower Services Commission, subseq. Training Agency: Head of Job Centre Services, 1978–82; Head, YTS Policy, 1982–85; Dir, Field Ops, 1985–87; Under Sec., and Dir, Resources and Personnel, 1987–90; Dir of Educn Progs, later of Youth and Educn Policy, Dept of Employment, subseq. Dept for Educn and Employment, 1991–95. Sheffield University: Mem. Council, 1988–95 and 2002–11 (Chm., Audit Cttee, 2004–11); Dir, Management Sch., 1991–96. Director: Sheffield Futures Ltd (formerly Sheffield Careers Guidance Services Ltd), 1997–2004 (Chm., 1999–2004); Connexions South Yorkshire Ltd, 2001–04. Mem. Bd, Sheffield Develt Corp., 1996–97. Dep. Chm., Nat. Adv. Council for Careers and Educnl Guidance, 1996–2000. Mem. Council, RSA, 2002–07; Director, RSA projects: Redefining Work, 1996–98; Redefining Schooling, 1998–99; Opening Minds, 2000–05. Mem. Council, 1996–2013, Mem. Exec., 1999–2013, Jt Hon. Sec., 2005–09, Vice-Chm., 2009–13, C&G; Gov., Barnsley Coll., 1996–2002. Chm., S Yorks Reg., Victorian Soc., 1997–. Trustee, Brathay Hall Trust, 2001–10; Chair, Friends of Old Town Hall, Sheffield, 2014–; Trustee, Castlegate Preservation Trust, 2016– (Chair, 2016–). Patron, Nat. Youth Agency, 1996–. Hon. Fellow, Inst. of Careers Guidance, 1996. FRSA 1990; FCGI 2005. Publications: Key Views on the Future of Work, 1997; Redefining Work, 1998; Redefining Schooling, 1998; Redefining the Curriculum, 1999; Opening Minds: education for the 21st Century, 1999; What Should Our Children Learn?, 2000; Opening Minds: Taking Stock, 2003. Recreations: walking, reading, listening to music, conservation of heritage buildings. T: (0114) 230 7693.

**BAYLY, Richard Dion;** pig breeder, since 2014; Deputy Regional Director, Government Office for the South West, 2007–11; b 25 Feb. 1951; s of Edward Hugh Bayly and Denise Bayly (née Dudley); m 1986, Dr Lea Diane Jones; two d. Educ: Rugby Sch.; Bristol Univ. (BScEcon). Tutor, Rathkeale Coll., Masterton, NZ, 1970; entered Civil Service, 1974: DoE, 1974–79; Dept of Transport, 1979–97 (on secondment to BRB, as Dir, Privatisation Studies, 1990–91); DETR, 1997–2001 (on secondment to Cabinet Office, 1997–99; Acting Chief Exec., CS Coll., 1998–99); DfT (formerly DTLR), 2001–11; Dir, Devon and Cornwall, Govt Office for SW, 1999–2007. Member: Tavistock Deanery Synod, 2008–13, 2019–; Plymouth Cultural Bd, 2010–14; Exeter Cathedral Council, 2012–18; Dean's Council, Plymouth Univ. Business Sch., 2012–14; Bd, Univ. of St Mark and St John (formerly UC of St Mark and St John), 2013–19; Client Bd, Plymouth Hist. Centre, 2014–17; Dir, Plymouth Barbican Trust, 2012–. Trustee: Peninsula Med. Foundn, 2010–15; SW Film and TV Archive, 2013–. Chair, Sheepstor Welfare Charity, 1980–. Churchwarden, St Leonard's Sheepstor, 2009–. DL Devon, 2012. Hon. DBus Plymouth, 2010. Recreations: sailing, gardening, walking, travel, reading, responsibility without power, being a hopeless parent, giving unlicensed sermons. Address: Blowiscombe Barton, Milton Combe, Yelverton, Devon PL20 6HR.

**BAYNE, Prof. Brian Leicester,** OBE 1998; PhD; FRSB; Visiting Professor, University of Sydney, 2011–12 (Research Professor, 1997–2001, Visiting Professor, 2001–11, Centre for Research on Ecological Impacts of Coastal Cities); b 24 July 1938; s of John Leonard and Jean Leicester Bayne; m 1960, Marianne Middleton; two d. Educ: Ardingly Coll.; Univ. of Wales (BSc, PhD). Post-doctoral res., Univ. of Copenhagen and Fisheries Laboratory, Conwy, 1963–68; Lectr, Sch. of Biology, Univ. of Leicester, 1968–73; Institute for Marine Environmental Research, Plymouth: Res. Scientist, 1973–83; Dir, 1983–88; Plymouth Marine Laboratory, NERC: Dir, 1988–94; Dir, Centre for Coastal and Marine Scis, 1994–97. Fellow, Univ. of Wales, 1996; Hon. Dr Univ. of Basque Country, 2015. Publications: Marine Mussels: ecology and physiology, 1976; The Biology of Oysters, 2017. Recreation: sailing.

**BAYNE, Sir Nicholas (Peter),** KCMG 1992 (CMG 1984); HM Diplomatic Service, retired; High Commissioner to Canada, 1992–96; b 15 Feb. 1937; s of late Captain Ronald Bayne, RN and Elisabeth Ashcroft; m 1961, Diana Wilde; two s (and one s decd). Educ: Eton Coll.; Christ Church, Oxford (MA, DPhil). Entered Diplomatic Service, 1961; served at British Embassies in Manila, 1963–66, and Bonn, 1969–72; seconded to HM Treasury, 1974–75; Financial Counsellor, Paris, 1975–79; Head of Financial, later Economic Relations, Dept, FCO, 1979–82; attached to RIIA, 1982–83; Ambassador to Zaire, 1983–84, also accredited to the Congo, Rwanda and Burundi, 1984; seconded to CSSB, 1985; Ambassador and UK Perm. Rep. to OECD, Paris, 1985–88; Dep. Under-Sec. of State, FCO, 1988–92. Chm., Liberalisation of Trade in Services Cttee, British Invisibles, 1996–2000. Fellow, Internat. Relns Dept, LSE, 1997–. Publications: (with R. D. Putnam) Hanging Together: the Seven-Power Summits, 1984, rev. edn 1987 (trans. German, Japanese, Italian); Hanging in There: the G7 and G8 summit in maturity and renewal, 2000; The Grey Wares of North-West Anatolia and their Relation to the Early Greek Settlements, 2000; (with S. Woolcock) The New Economic Diplomacy, 2003, 4th edn 2017; Staying Together: the G8 summit confronts the 21st century, 2005; Economic Diplomat (memoirs), 2010. Recreations: reading, sightseeing. Address: 2 Chetwynd House, Hampton Court Road, East Molesey, Surrey KT8 9BS. Club: Travellers.

**BAYNE, Shenagh Irvine;** a District Judge (Magistrates' Courts), 2004–18; b 30 April 1953; d of David Morton Bayne and Katherine Clementine Bayne; partner, S. A. Gibson. Educ: English Sch. of Paris; Berkhamsted Sch. for Girls; Edinburgh Univ. (BA). Admitted solicitor, 1980; Trevor Hamlyn & Co., Solicitors, 1980–82; Deacons, Hong Kong, 1982–84; Simmons & Simmons, Solicitors, 1984–85; EMI Music, 1985–86; Freelance Solicitor Advocate, 1986–92, 1997–2004; CPS, 1992–97; Stipendiary Magistrate, subseq. Dep. Dist Judge, 1998–2004. Immigration Adjudicator (pt-time), 2002–04. Recreations: golf, hill-walking, ski-ing, contemporary literature, film and theatre going, travel. Club: Hong Kong Football.

**BAYNES, Sir Christopher (Rory),** 8th Bt cr 1801, of Harefield Place, Middlesex; b 11 May 1956; s of Sir John Baynes, 7th Bt and of Shirley Maxwell Baynes (née Dodds); S father, 2005; m 1992, Sandra Finuala Merriman; two s one d. Heir: s Alasdair William Merriman Baynes, b 3 Dec. 1993.

**BAYNHAM, Prof. Alexander Christopher;** strategic technical consultant, since 1996; Principal, Cranfield University (formerly Cranfield Institute of Technology) (Shrivenham Campus), 1989–96, now Emeritus Professor; b 22 Dec. 1935; s of Alexander Baynham and Dulcie Rowena Rees; m 1961, Eileen May Wilson; two s one d. Educ: Marling Sch.; Reading Univ. (BSc); Warwick Univ. (PhD); Royal Coll. of Defence Studies (rcds). Joined Royal Signals and Radar Estab., Malvern, 1955; rejoined, 1961 (univ. studies, 1958–61); Head, Optics and Electronics Gp, 1976; RCDS, 1978; Scientific Adviser to Asst Chief Adviser on Projects, 1979; Dep. Dir, 1980–83, Dir, 1984–86, RSRE; Dir, RARDE, 1986–89. Publications: Plasma Effects in Semi-conductors, 1971; assorted papers in Jl of Physics, Jl of Applied Physics and in Proc. Phys. Soc. Recreations: church activities, music. Address: c/o Cranfield University, Shrivenham Campus, Swindon, Wilts SN6 8LA.

**BAYS, Rt Rev. Eric;** Bishop of Qu'Appelle, 1986–97; b 10 Aug. 1932; s of Rev. Canon P. C. Bays and Hilda (née Harper); m 1967, Patricia Ann Earle; one s one d. Educ: Univ. of Manitoba (BSc 1955); Univ. of Saskatchewan (BA 1959); Univ. of Emmanuel College (LTh 1959); Christian Theological Seminary (MMin 1974). Flight Lieut, RCAF (Reserve), 1955. Asst Curate, All Saints', Winnipeg, 1959–61; Lecturer, Emmanuel Coll., 1961–62; Priest-in-charge: Burns Lake, BC, 1962–63; Masset, BC, 1963–64; Novice, Community of the Resurrection, Mirfield, 1964–65; Vicar, St Saviour's, Winnipeg with Bird's Hill, 1965–68; Rector, All Saints', Winnipeg, 1968–76; Professor, Coll. of Emmanuel and St Chad, 1976–86, Vice-Principal, 1981–86. Canon of St John's Cathedral, Winnipeg, 1971–86. Hon. DD Coll. of Emmanuel and St Chad, 1987. Publications: Indian Residential Schools: another picture, 2009. Recreations: choral music, reading. Address: 200 Clearview Avenue, Apt 2327, Ottawa, ON K1Z 8M2, Canada.

**BAYTON, Rt Rev. John,** AM 1983; Master Iconographer, St Peter's Icon School, since 1999; b 24 March 1930; s of Ernest Bayton and Jean Bayton (née Edwards); m 1959, Elizabeth Anne, d of Rt Rev. J. A. G. Housden; one s two d. Educ: Aust. Coll. of Theology, ACT (ThL (Hons)); St Francis Theol Coll., Brisbane. Ordained deacon 1956, priest 1957; Rector, Longreach, Qld, 1958–63; Rector and Sub-dean, Thursday Island (Canon in Residence), 1963–65; Rector, Auchenflower, 1965–68; Army Chaplain: CMF, 1967–76; RAA, 1976–84; Dean of St Paul's Cathedral, Rockhampton, 1968–79; Vicar, St Peter's, Eastern Hill, 1980–89; Archdeacon of Malvern, 1986–89; Bishop of Geelong (Asst Bishop, dio. of Melbourne), 1989–95; Episcopal Chaplain, St George's Coll., Jerusalem, 1995–96, 1998 (Chm., Australasian Cttee, 2003–06; Vis. Chaplain and Lectr, 2003–06); Assisting Bishop in Chicago, Chaplain-in-Residence and Vis. Prof., Seabury-Western Seminary, Evanston, 1997; Adminr, St John's Cathedral, Brisbane, 1998–99. Founder, 1981, Patron, 1993–, Inst. for Spiritual Studies, Melbourne; Founder, Rockhampton Regl Art Gall., 1978. Vis. Fellow, Trinity Coll. Theol Sch., Univ. of Melbourne, 2007. Solo Art Exhibitions: Brisbane 1967, 1976, 1978, 1998; Rockhampton 1975, 1976; Melbourne 1981, 1984, 1986, 1987; Jerusalem, 1995, 1996; Chicago, 1997; Raffles Artfolio Gall., Singapore, 1999; Bishopscourt, Melbourne, 2001, 2004, 2006; Malvern Town Hall, 2010. Represented in public and private collections Australia, Chicago, USA, Jerusalem, UK, Singapore, Tokyo, NZ. Prelate, Aust. Priory, Order of St John of Jerusalem and Knights Hospitaler, 1990; GCSJ 1995; ChLJ 2000; OMLJ 2004; Cross of Merit, Order of St John of Jerusalem, 2008. Centenary Medal (Australia), 2001. Publications: Cross over Carpentaria, 1965; Coming of the Light, 1971; The Icon, 1980; (ed) Anglican Spirituality, 1982; Stations of the Cross, 2010; Grampy: the life and times of a blacksmith, 2013. Recreations: painting, sketching, sculpting, reading, walking. Address: 219 Canterbury Road, Blackburn, Vic 3130, Australia. Club: Melbourne (Melbourne).

**BAYVEL, Prof. Polina,** CBE 2017; FRS 2016; FREng; FIEEE, FOSA, FInstP, FIET; Professor of Optical Communications and Networks, University College London, since 2002; b Kharkov, USSR, 14 April 1966; d of Leopold Bayvel and Raisa Bayvel (née Shapiro); two s. Educ: Hasmonean High Sch. for Girls; University Coll. London (BSc(Eng) Electronic and Electrical Engrg 1986; PhD Electronic and Electrical Engrg 1990). FIET (FIEE 2001); FInstP 2002; FREng 2002; FOSA 2008; FIEEE 2010. Royal Soc. Postdoctoral Res. Fellow, Gen. Physics Inst., USSR Acad. of Scis, 1990; Sen. Systems Engr/Area Manager, Europe, Submarine Systems Div., STC plc, Greenwich, 1990–91; Principal Systems Engr, STC Laboratories, later Bell-Northern Res./Nortel Europe Ltd, Harlow, 1991–93 (on secondment to Bell-Northern Res. (Canada), 1991–92); Royal Soc. Univ. Res. Fellow, Dept of Electronic and Electrical Engrg, UCL, 1993–2003. RISE Fellow, EPSRC, 2014. Hon. DSc S Wales, 2014. Paterson Medal and Prize, Inst. of Physics, 2002; Royal Soc. Wolfson Merit Award, 2007; Engrg Achievement Award, IEEE Photonics Soc., 2013; Clifford Paterson Prize Lecture Medal, Royal Soc., 2014; Colin Campbell Mitchell Award and Medal, RAEng, 2015. Publications: contrib. over 350 papers to peer-reviewed internat. jls and confs. Recreations: hiking, swimming, reading, ski-ing, theatre, travelling, opera. Address: UCL Department of Electronic and Electrical Engineering, University College London, Torrington Place, WC1E 7JE. T: (020) 7679 7921, 07803 123559. E: p.bayvel@ucl.ac.uk.

**BAZALGETTE, Hilary Jane, (Lady Bazalgette);** see Newiss, H. J.

**BAZALGETTE, Sir Peter (Lytton),** Kt 2012; Chairman, ITV plc, since 2016 (non-executive Director, since 2013); b 22 May 1953; s of late (Evelyn) Paul Bazalgette and Diana Muriel Bazalgette (née Coffin); m 1985, Hilary Jane Newiss, qv; one s one d. Educ: Dulwich Coll.; Fitzwilliam Coll., Cambridge (Pres., Cambridge Union, 1975; BA Hons Law 1976; Hon. Fellow, 2015). BBC News Trainee, 1977; Man. Dir, Bazal, 1987–98; Creative Dir, GMG Endemol Entertainment, 1998–2002; Chm., Endemol UK plc, 2002–07; Chief Creative Officer, Endemol Gp, 2005–07. Non-exec. Dir, Channel 4, 2001–04. TV formats created, 1984–, incl. Food and Drink, Ready Steady Cook, Changing Rooms, Ground Force; formats sold to 30 countries; UK producer, Big Brother. Dep. Chm., National Film & Television Sch., 2002–09. Chairman: Sony Music Television, 2009–13; Sony Pictures TV UK, 2009–13; MirriAd, 2009–12 (non-exec. Dir, 2013–15); Arts Council England, 2013–17; Lovecrafts, 2018–. Non-executive Director: YouGov, 2005–15 (Mem., Adv. Bd, 2016–); Base79 (formerly MyVideoRights), 2008–13; Nutopia, 2008–16; Mem., Adv. Bd, Bartle Bogle Hegarty, 2009–; DCMS, 2011–12; Mem. Bd, UK Res. and Innovation, 2018–. Mem., Holocaust Commn, 2014–15 (Chm., Expert Gp on Commemoration, 2014–15); Chm., UK Holocaust Meml Foundn, 2015–18. MacTaggart Lectr, Edinburgh TV Fest., 1998; Wheldon Lectr, RTS, 2001. Co-Chm., British Acad. of Gastronomes, 1993–2010. Pres., Crossness Engines Trust, 2009– (Trustee, 1994–; Chm., 1999). Chm., ENO, 2012–13 (Trustee, 2004–09; Dep.-Chm., 2009–12). Mem., English Heritage Blue Plaques Panel, 2014–. Chm., Baillie Gifford Prize for Non-Fiction, 2018–. Trustee, Debate Mate, 2009–12. Fellow, BAFTA, 2000; FRTS 2002 (Pres., 2010–16). Hon. DLitt Warwick, 2015; Hon. DArts: Salford, 2015; Sunderland, 2016; UWE, 2016. Judges Award RTS, 2003. Publications: Billion Dollar Game, 2005; The Empathy Instinct, 2017; (ed) Egon Ronay: the man who taught Britain how to eat, 2011; jointly: BBC Food Check, 1989; The Food Revolution, 1991; The Big Food & Drink Book, 1993; You Don't Have to Diet 1994. Recreation: all arts and popular culture. E: vikki@newbaz.com.
See also V. P. Bazalgette.

**BAZALGETTE, Simon Louis;** Group Chief Executive, Jockey Club, 2008–19 Chairman, Jockey Club Racecourses, 2008–19; b Aylesbury, 28 March 1962; s of John and Jane Bazalgette; m 1990, Elizabeth McInnes; four s. Educ: Warwick Univ. (BSc Hons Maths). Mem., ICAEW 1987. With KPMG London, 1984–93; Founder Dir, Music Choice Europe plc, Chief Exec., 1999–2003; Founder Exec. Chm., Racing UK, 2004–08 Director: Racecourse Media Gp, 2004–; Turf TV, 2007–09. Sen. Ind. Dir, London 2017 World Championships, 2016–; non-exec. Dir, English Football League, 2019–. Chm.

Grubb Inst., 2011–16 (Vice Chm., 2003–11). Trustee, Ragged School Mus., 2017–. *Recreations:* family, music, horse racing, Brentford FC, Harlequins Rugby. *E:* simon@bazalgette.com.

**BAZALGETTE, Vivian Paul;** Chief Investment Officer and Executive Director, M&G plc, 1996–2002; Chairman, Fidelity European Values plc, since 2016; *b* Croydon, 7 May 1951; *s* of late Evelyn Paul Bazalgette and Diana Muriel Bazalgette (*née* Coffin); *m* 1976, Katharine Diana St John-Brooks; one *s* two *d. Educ:* Dulwich Coll.; St John's Coll., Cambridge (BA English Lit. 1973; MA 1977). DTI, 1975–79; stockbroker, James Capel, 1979–83; fund manager, S.G. Warburg & Co., 1983–86; Exec. Dir, Gartmore plc, 1986–95. Advr, BAE Systems Pension Fund, 2003–. Non-executive Director: Brunner Investment Trust plc, 2004–; Henderson High Income Investment Trust plc, 2004–16; Perpetual Income & Growth Investment Trust plc, 2007–18; St James's Place plc, 2011–14 (Chm., Investment Cttee, 2011–14). Advr, Nuffield Foundn, 2008–15. Member: Investment Cttee, St John's Coll., Cambridge, 2000–06; Adv. Bd, Greenwich Hosp., 2008–13. Gov., Dulwich Coll., 2005–15 (Vice-Chm. Govs, 2009–15). Trustee: King's Coll. Hosp. Charity, 2000–10; Dulwich Estate, 2003–12; St Christopher's Hospice, 2017–. *Recreations:* classical music, sport, gardening, bridge. *E:* vivian.bazalgette@btinternet.com. *Clubs:* Dulwich, Royal Over-Seas League.
*See also* Sir P. L. Bazalgette.

**BAZELEY, Victoria Louise;** *see* Hamilton, V. L.

**BAZLEY, Rt Rev. Colin Frederick;** Bishop of Chile, 1977–2000; an Hon. Assistant Bishop, Diocese of Chester, since 2000; *b* 27 June 1935; *s* of Reginald Samuel Bazley and Isabella Davies; *m* 1960, Barbara Helen Griffiths; three *d. Educ:* Birkenhead School; St Peter's Hall, Oxford (MA); Tyndale Hall, Bristol. Deacon 1959, priest 1960; Assistant Curate, St Leonard's, Bootle, 1959–62; Missionary of S American Missionary Society in Chile, 1962–69; Rural Dean of Chol-Chol, 1962–66; Archdeacon of Temuco, 1966–69; Assistant Bishop for Cautín and Malleco, Dio. Chile, Bolivia and Peru, 1969–75; Assistant Bishop for Santiago, 1975–77; Bishop of Chile, Bolivia and Peru, 1977; diocese divided, Oct. 1977; Bishop of Chile and Bolivia until Oct. 1981, when diocese again divided; Presiding Bishop of the Anglican Council for South America, 1977–83; Primate, Province of S Cone of America, 1989–95. Warden of Readers, 2000–05, Rural Dean of Wallasey, 2009–11, dio. of Chester. Mem., Inter-Anglican Theol and Doctrinal Commn, 1994–97. *Recreations:* football (Liverpool supporter), fishing on camping holidays. *Address:* 121 Brackenwood Road, Higher Bebington, Wirral CH63 2LU.

**BAZLEY, Janet Claire, (Mrs I. F. Airey);** QC 2006; a Recorder, since 2000; *d* of John Harold Bazley and Loukia Bazley; *m* 1987, Ian Frank Airey; one *s* two *d. Educ:* Lady Eleanor Holles Sch.; University Coll. London (LLB Hons 1979). Called to the Bar, Lincoln's Inn, 1980; in practice as a barrister, 1980–. Member: Family Law Bar Assoc., 1992–; Resolution; Assoc. of Lawyers for Children. *Publications:* Money Laundering for Lawyers (with David Winch), 2004; (jtly) Applications under Schedule 1 to the Children Act 1989, 2009; contrib. to Halsbury's Laws. *Recreations:* foreign languages and travel, opera, hill walking. *Address:* 1GC Family Law, 10 Lincoln's Inn Fields, WC2A 3BP. *T:* (020) 7797 7900, *Fax:* (020) 7797 7929. *E:* bazley@1gc.com

**BAZLEY, Dame Margaret (Clara),** ONZ 2012; DNZM 1999; Chair of Commissioners, Canterbury Regional Council, 2010–16; *b* 23 Jan. 1938. *Educ:* Registered Comprehensive Nurse; Dip. Nursing, DoH and Victoria Univ.; Dip. Health Admin, Massey Univ. Nursing, 1956–78, including: Matron, Sunnyside Psych. Hosp., Christchurch, 1965–73; Dep. Matron in Chief, Auckland Hosp. Bd, 1974–75; Chief Nursing Officer, Waikato Hosp. Bd, 1975–78; Dir, Div. of Nursing, NZ Dept of Health, 1978–84; State Services Commission: Comr, 1984–87; Dep. Chm., 1987–88; Sec. for Transport, 1988–93; Dir-Gen., Dept of Social Welfare, 1993–99; Chief Exec., Min. of Social Policy, NZ, 1999–2001. Mem., NZ delegns to OECD, ISSA, WHO, Internat. Council of Nursing, etc, in Australia, USA and Europe. Chair, Foundn for Res., Sci. and Technol., 2004–08 (Dep. Presiding Mem., 2002–04). Chair, NZ Fire Service Commn, 1999–2011. Member: Waitangi Tribunal, 2001–10; Commn of Inquiry into Police Conduct, 2004–07; Royal Commn of Inquiry on Auckland Governance, 2007–09; Chair, Fundamental Rev. of Legal Aid System, 2009; Dep. Chair, Canterbury Earthquake Recovery Commn, 2010–11; Registrar of Pecuniary Interests of Members of NZ Parlt, 2006–13; Mem., Adv. Bd, Transition to Long-term Recovery Arrangements, 2014–15. Trustee, Westpactrust Stadium, 2000–05. Hon. DLit Massey, 2008. Business Woman of the Year, More/AirNZ, 1987; Blake Medal, Sir Peter Blake Trust, 2011. *Recreations:* gardening, reading, cooking, music. *Address:* 8B Wharenui Apartments, 274 Oriental Parade, Wellington 6011, New Zealand.

**BEACH;** *see* Hicks Beach, family name of Earl St Aldwyn.

**BEACH, Prof. David Hugh,** PhD; FRS 1996; FMedSci; Professor of Stem Cell Biology, Queen Mary University of London, since 2004; *b* 18 May 1954; *s* of Gen. Sir (William Gerald) Hugh Beach, GBE, KCB, MC. *Educ:* Peterhouse, Cambridge (BA); Univ. of Miami (PhD 1977). Postdoctoral Fellow, Univ. of Sussex, 1978–82; Cold Spring Harbor Laboratory: Postdoctoral Fellow, 1982–83; Jun. Staff Investigator, then Sen. Staff Investigator, 1984–89; Tenured Scientist, 1992–; Sen. Staff Scientist, 1989–97; Investigator, Howard Hughes Med. Inst., 1990–97; Adjunct Investigator, Cold Spring Harbour Lab., 1997–2000; Hugh and Catherine Stevenson Prof. of Cancer Biology, UCL, 1997–2002. Adjunct Associate Prof., SUNY, Stony, 1990–97. Founder, Mitotix Inc., 1992; Founder and Pres., Genetica Inc., 1996–2004. FMedSci 2008. Eli Lilly Research Award, 1994; Bristol-Myers Squibb Award, 2000; Raymond Bourgine Award for cancer research, 2001. *Publications:* numerous papers in reviewed jls, incl. Nature and Cell and Science. *Recreations:* flying, scuba diving, ski-ing, shooting, fly fishing, writing fiction. *Address:* Centre for Cutaneous Research, Blizard Institute, Barts and The London School of Medicine and Dentistry, Blizard Building, 4 Newark Street, E1 2AT. *T:* 07799 620947.

**BEACH, Dr Mark Howard Frances;** Director of Care, The Haven + London, since 2018; *b* Gloucester, 13 Jan. 1962; *s* of John and Frances Beach; *m* 1991, Annabel (separated); one *d. Educ:* Univ. of Kent (BA 1983); Univ. of Nottingham (MA 1995); King's Coll. London (DMin 2011). Ordained deacon, 1987, priest, 1988; Rector, All Hallows, Gedling, 1993–2000; Bishop's Chaplain, Dio. of Wakefield, 2000–03; Team Rector, Rugby, 2003–12; Dean of Rochester, 2012–15; Dir, Blackfriars Settlement, 2015–17. Mem., Pewterers' Co., 1986–. *Publications:* Using Common Worship - Holy Communion, 2000, 2nd edn 2001; (contrib.) Moving on in Ministry, 2013. *Recreation:* music. *Address:* Apt 304, 80 Back Church Lane, E1 1FL. *E:* mark.beach62@gmail.com.

**BEADLE, (John) Nicholas,** CMG 2006; *b* 20 Aug. 1957; *s* of late Lt-Col George Colin Beadle and Gillian Beadle; *m* 1990, Linda Rose Davidson; one *d.* Thomson Newspapers, 1978–83; Proprietor, Accommodation Ltd, 1984–90; Dir, cos of late Jack Calvert, 1990–97; Ministry of Defence, 1997–2007: UK Hydrographic Office, 1997–2001; RCDS 2002; NATO Policy, 2003; EU and UN Policy, 2004; Sen. Advr to Iraqi MoD, Baghdad, 2004–05; Private Sec. to Sec. of State for Defence, 2005–07; Fellow, Harvard Univ., 2007–08; Dir, Govt Afghanistan Strategy and Communications, Cabinet Office, 2008–09; Sen. Advr to the Prime Minister, 2009–10; Advr on Middle East and N Africa, Cabinet Office, 2011. Partner, Lily Partnership (formerly Lily & Co.), 2011–. Non-executive Director: Region Gp, 2006–; Edinburgh Business Sch., 2013–17. Dir, Horns Farm, Castle Bolton, 2017–. Hon. Prof., Univ. of Exeter, 2012–; Sen. Associate Fellow, RUSI, 2012–18. *E:* nicholasbeadle@gmail.com.

**BEADLES, Anthony Hugh,** MA; Headmaster of Epsom College, 1993–2000; *b* 18 Sept. 1940; *s* of late O. H. R. Beadles, OBE and N. K. Beadles; *m* 1970, Heather Iona McFerran; two *s* one *d. Educ:* Epsom Coll.; Christ Church, Oxford (MA). Head of History, Ellesmere Coll., 1963–67; Head of History and Asst Housemaster, Harrow Sch., 1967–85; Headmaster, King's Sch., Bruton, 1985–93. *Recreations:* cricket, mountains, golf. *Address:* Chaff Barn, Downyard, Compton Pauncefoot, Yeovil, Somerset BA22 7EL. *Clubs:* MCC; Vincent's (Oxford).

**BEAKE, Ven. Stuart Alexander;** Archdeacon of Surrey, 2005–17, now Archdeacon Emeritus; *b* 18 Sept. 1949; *s* of Ernest Alexander and Pamela Mary Beake; *m* 1987, Sally Anne Williams; one *s* one *d. Educ:* King's Coll. Sch., Wimbledon; Emmanuel Coll., Cambridge (BA 1972, MA 1975); Cuddesdon Coll., Oxford. Ordained deacon, 1974, priest, 1975; Asst Curate, Hitchin St Mary, 1974–79; Team Vicar, St Mary, Hemel Hempstead, 1979–85; Domestic Chaplain to Bishop of Southwell, 1985–87; Vicar, St Andrew, Shottery, 1987–2000; RD, Fosse Deanery, 1992–99; Diocesan Dir of Ordinands and Hd, Vocations and Trng Dept, Coventry Dio., 1995–2000; Sub-Dean and Canon Residentiary, Coventry Cathedral, 2000–05, now Canon Emeritus, 2005 (Hon. Canon, 1999); Canon Residentiary, 2010–, Sub-Dean, 2017–, Guildford Cathedral (Hon. Canon, 2005). *Recreations:* reading, gardening, music, model railway, old jokes. *Address:* Hollyhocks Barn, Hollyhocks Cottage, High Street, Bramley, Guildford GU5 0HB.

**BEAL, Kieron Conrad;** QC 2012; *b* Portsmouth, 16 Jan. 1971; *s* of Kerry and Pauline Beal; *m* 2002, Dr Isobel Frisken; two *d. Educ:* Chichester High Sch. for Boys; Phillips Exeter Acad., NH, USA; Selwyn Coll., Cambridge (BA 1993); Harvard Law Sch. (LLM). Called to the Bar, Inner Temple, 1995, Bencher, 2016; in practice as barrister, specialising in EU and competition law, 1995–. Mem., Attorney Gen.'s C Panel, 1999–2002, B Panel, 2002–07, A Panel, 2007–12. Chm., Bar European Gp, 2018–. *Publications:* (contrib.) EC Competition Procedure, 1996, 3rd edn 2012; (contrib.) Value Added Tax: Commentary & Analysis, 2010; (contrib.) Employee Competition, 2011, 3rd edn 2016; (contrib.) Britain Alone, 2016; (contrib.) Football and the Law, 2018; (contrib.) Brexit: the legal implications, 2019. *Recreations:* ski-ing, sailing, squash, tennis. *Address:* Blackstone Chambers, Blackstone House, Temple, EC4Y 9BW. *T:* (020) 7583 1770, *Fax:* (020) 7822 7350. *E:* kieronbeal@blackstonechambers.com.

**BEAL, Peter George,** PhD; FBA 1993; FSA; manuscript expert; Database Compiler, Catalogue of English Literary Manuscripts 1450–1700, since 2005; Consultant, Department of Books and Manuscripts, Sotheby's, London, since 2005; *b* Coventry, 16 April 1944; *s* of William George Beal and Marjorie Ena Owen; *m* 1st, 1974, Gwyneth Morgan (marr. diss. 1980); 2nd, 1982, Sally Josephine Taylor (marr. diss. 1994); one step *s*; 3rd, 1998, Grace Janette Ioppolo. *Educ:* King Henry VIII Grammar Sch., Coventry; Leeds Univ. (BA Hons English, 1966; PhD 1974). Res. editor, Bowker/Mansell Publishing, 1974–79; Manuscript Expert, 1980–2005, Dep. Dir, 1990–95, Dir, 1996–2005, Printed Books and MSS, subseq. Dept of Books and MSS, Sotheby's, London. Lyell Reader in Bibliography, Oxford Univ., 1995–96. Vis. Prof., Dept of English, Reading Univ., 2000–02; Sen. Res. Fellow, Inst. of English Studies, Univ. of London, 2002–. FSA 2007. *Publications:* Index of English Literary Manuscripts, vol. I, parts 1 and 2, 1450–1625 (2 vols), 1980, vol. II, parts 1 and 2, 1625–1700 (2 vols), 1987, 1993; (gen. ed.) English Verse Miscellanies of the Seventeenth Century (5 vols), 1990; In Praise of Scribes: manuscripts and their makers in 17th century England, 1998; A Dictionary of English Manuscript Terminology 1450–2000, 2008; (co-founded and co-ed) English Manuscript Studies 1100–1700, annually, 1989–2013; contribs, mainly on 16th and 17th century literary MSS, to learned jls. *Recreations:* reading, films, travel, swimming. *Address:* Institute of English Studies, Senate House, Malet Street, WC1E 7HU. *E:* Peter.Beal@sas.ac.uk.

**BEALE, Prof. Hugh Gurney,** FBA 2004; Professor of Law, University of Warwick, 1987–2018, now Emeritus; *b* 4 May 1948; *s* of Charles Beale and Anne Freeland Beale (*née* Gurney-Dixon); *m* 1970, Jane Wilson Cox; two *s* one *d. Educ:* Leys Sch., Cambridge; Exeter Coll., Oxford (BA Jurisp. 1969). Called to the Bar, Lincoln's Inn, 1971 (Hon. Bencher, 1999). Lecturer in Law: Univ. of Connecticut, 1969–71; UCW, Aberystwyth, 1971–73; Univ. of Bristol, 1973–86; Reader, Univ. of Bristol, 1986–87. Visiting Professor: Univ. of N Carolina, 1982–83; Univ. of Paris I, 1995; Univ. of Utrecht, 1996; Univ. of Oxford, 2007–; Univ. of Amsterdam, 2009–13; Nat. Taiwanese Univ., 2018; Hong Kong Univ., 2018; City Univ., HK, 2019; Sen. Res. Fellow, Harris Manchester Coll., Oxford, 2014–June 2020. A Law Comr, 2000–07. Hon. QC 2002. Hon. LLD: Miskolc, 1995; De Montfort, 2003; Antwerp, 2005; Eötvös Loránd, 2018. *Publications:* Remedies for Breach of Contract, 1980; (jtly) Contract Cases and Materials, 1985, 5th edn 2007; (ed jtly) Principles of European Contract Law, Part I, 1995, Parts I and II, 2000; (Gen. Ed.) Chitty on Contracts, 28th edn 1999 to 33rd edn 2018; (ed jtly) Casebooks on the Common Law of Europe: Contract Law, 2001, 3rd edn 2019; Mistake and Non-disclosure of Facts: models for English contract law, 2012. *Recreations:* fishing, music, walking. *Address:* School of Law, University of Warwick, Coventry CV4 7AL.

**BEALE, Dame Inga (Kristine),** DBE 2017; Chief Executive, Lloyd's of London, 2014–18; *b* Newbury, 15 May 1963; *d* of Raymond John Beale and Astri Beale (*née* Gisholt); *m* 2014, Philippe Henri Pfeiffer. *Educ:* ACII 1987; Chartered Insurer, 2016. Underwriter, Prudential Assurance, 1982–92; Pres., Europe, GE Insurance Solutions, 1992–2006; CEO, Converium Gp, 2006–07; Mem., Gp Mgt Bd, Zurich Insurance, 2008–11; CEO, Canopius Gp, 2012–13. Mem. Bd, London First, 2019–. Patron, Insuring Women's Futures, 2017–. *E:* inga.beale@outlook.com. *Club:* Wasps Rugby.

**BEALE, James Patrick;** Director, Programme Delivery and Resources, Plan International, since 2018 (Director, Institutional Funding, 2012–18); *b* 14 Nov. 1959; *s* of Patrick Ashton Beale and Janet Margaret Beale; *m* 1991, Mary Elizabeth Wilson; two *d. Educ:* Sch. of Oriental and African Studies, Univ. of London (BA Hons Geog.); Univ. of Reading (MSc Agricl Econs 1986). Data analyst, Kestrel Gp, Tripoli, Libya, 1982–84; Project Manager, Agric. and Fisheries Div., Crown Agents, 1986–88; Sight Savers International: Programme Manager, E Asia and Pacific, 1988–93; Regl Dir, Thailand and Bangladesh, 1993–95; Chief Exec., Ockenden Venture, subseq. Ockenden Internat., 1995–2008; Sen. Prog. Manager, Maxwell Stamp plc, 2008; Head, Internat. Partnership Develt, ActionAid Internat., 2008–12. *Address:* Plan International, Block A, Duke Street, Woking, Surrey GU21 5BH.

**BEALE, Lt-Gen. Sir Peter (John),** KBE 1992; FRCP; Hon. Consultant, British Red Cross, since 2000 (Chief Medical Adviser, 1994–2000); *b* 18 March 1934; *s* of Basil and Eileen Beale; *m* 1st, 1959, Julia Mary Winter, MB BS (*d* 2000); four *s* one *d* (and one *d* decd); 2nd, 2001, Mary Elisabeth Williams. *Educ:* St Paul's Cathedral Choir Sch.; Felsted Sch. (Music Schol.); Gonville and Caius Coll., Cambridge (Choral Schol.; BA); Westminster Hosp. MB BChir 1958. DTM&H; FCCM; FFOM. Commissioned RAMC, 1960; medical training, 1964–71; Consultant Physician, Army, 1971; served Far East, Middle East, BAOR; Community Physician, Army, 1981; served BAOR and UK; Comdr

Medical, HQ UKLF, 1987–90; DGAMS, 1990–93; Surg. Gen., MoD, 1991–94. QHP 1987–94. President: Army Squash, 1989–94; Old Felstedian Soc., 1998–2001; Army Officer Golfing Soc., 2001–05; Captain, Old Felstedian Golfing Soc., 2001–03. Gov., Yehudi Menuhin Sch., 1995–2012. OStJ. *Publications:* contribs to professional jls on tropical and military medicine. *Recreations:* music (conductor, tenor, pianist, French Horn player), sport (golf, squash, tennis), bridge. *Address:* The Old Bakery, Avebury, Marlborough, Wilts SN8 1RF. *T:* (01672) 539315. *Club:* Tidworth Garrison Golf (Pres., 1990–2003).
*See also Sir S. R. Beale.*

**BEALE, Sarah Elizabeth;** Chief Executive, Construction Industry Training Board, since 2017; *b* Whitehaven, 3 Oct. 1976; *d* of Gordan Little and Betty Little; partner, Aaron Blake. *Educ:* Workington Acad.; Oxford Brookes Univ. (BSc Applied Accounting). FCCA 2009. Gibbons & Co. Chartered Accountants, 1995–96; J. F. W. Robinson & Co Chartered Accountants, 1996–2000; Harvest Housing Assoc., 2000–02; Bowater Home Improvements, 2002–05; Construction Industry Training Board: Business Area Finance Mgr, Nat. Experienced Worker Assessment Mgr, Hd of Directorate Finance and Planning, then Hd of Customer Services, 2005–12; Interim Corporate Services Dir, 2012–13; Chief Finance Officer and Corporate Performance Dir, 2014–16. Trustee, BRE, 2019–. *Recreation:* walking. *Address:* Construction Industry Training Board, Bircham Newton, King's Lynn, Norfolk PE31 6RH.

**BEALE, Sir Simon Russell, (Sir Simon Russell Beale),** Kt 2019; CBE 2003; actor; *b* 12 Jan. 1961; *s* of Lt-Gen. Sir Peter Beale, *qv. Educ:* St Paul's Cathedral Choir Sch.; Clifton Coll., Bristol; Gonville and Caius Coll., Cambridge (BA 1st Cl. Hons English 1982; Hon. Fellow, 2008); Guildhall Sch. of Music and Drama. Royal Shakespeare Co., 1985–93 (Associate Artist); Royal National Theatre, 1995–98 (Associate Artist). *Theatre:* Look to the Rainbow, Apollo, 1983; Women Beware Women, Royal Court, 1985; Royal Shakespeare Company: A Winter's Tale, The Fair Maid of the West, 1985; Restoration, Man of Mode, 1987; Troilus and Cressida, The Seagull, Edward II, 1989; Richard III, 1990; Ghosts, 1993; The Tempest, 1993–94; Royal National Theatre: Volpone, 1995 (best supporting actor, Olivier Award, 1996); Rosencrantz and Guildenstern are Dead, 1995; Othello, 1997; Candide (best actor in a musical, Olivier Award, 2000), Money, Summerfolk, Battle Royal, 1999; Hamlet (best actor, Evening Standard Award, best Shakespearean perf., Critics' Circle Award), 2000; Humble Boy, 2001; Jumpers, 2003; The Life of Galileo, 2006; The Alchemist, 2006; Much Ado About Nothing, 2007; Major Barbara, 2008; A Slight Ache, 2008; London Assurance, 2010; Collaborators, 2011 (best actor, London Evening Standard Theatre Award, 2012); Timon of Athens, 2012; King Lear, 2014; The Lehman Trilogy, 2018, transf. Piccadilly Th., 2019; Uncle Vanya, Twelfth Night, Donmar Warehouse, 2002 (best actor, Evening Standard Award, Critics' Circle Award, and Olivier Award, 2003); Macbeth, Almeida, 2005; Julius Caesar, Barbican, 2005; The Philanthropist, Donmar Warehouse, 2005 (best actor, Evening Standard Theatre Award, and Critics' Circle Award, 2005); Spamalot, NY, 2005, Palace Th., 2007; The Winter's Tale, The Cherry Orchard, Old Vic, 2009; Deathtrap, Noël Coward Th., 2010; Alice's Adventures in Wonderland, Royal Ballet, Covent Garden, 2011; Privates on Parade, Noël Coward Th., 2012; The Hothouse, Trafalgar Studios, 2013; Temple, Donmar Warehouse, 2015; Mr Foote's Other Leg, Hampstead Th., transf. Th. Royal Haymarket, 2015; The Tempest, RSC, 2016; The Tragedy of King Richard the Second, Almeida, 2018; *television:* Persuasion, 1995; A Dance to the Music of Time, 1997 (best actor, RTS Award, 1997, BAFTA Award, 1998); Spooks, 2010–11; Henry IV, 2012 (best supporting actor, BAFTA, 2013); Penny Dreadful, 2014–16; Vanity Fair, 2018; presenter: Sacred Music, 2008, 2010; Symphony, 2011; *films:* Hamlet, 1997; The Temptation of Franz Schubert, 1997; An Ideal Husband, 1999; The Deep Blue Sea, 2011; Into the Woods, 2014; The Legend of Tarzan, 2016; The Death of Stalin, 2017; Operation Finale, 2018; Mary Queen of Scots, 2019; performances on radio. *Recreations:* music, history, history of religion, crosswords. *Address:* c/o Dalzell & Beresford, Paddock Suite, The Courtyard, 55 Charterhouse Street, EC1M 6HA. *T:* (020) 7336 0351.

**BEALES, Prof. Derek Edward Dawson,** PhD, LittD; FRHistS; FBA 1989; Professor of Modern History, University of Cambridge, 1980–97, now Emeritus; Fellow of Sidney Sussex College, Cambridge, since 1958; *b* 12 June 1931; *s* of late Edward Beales and Dorothy Kathleen Beales (*née* Dawson); *m* 1964, Sara Jean (*née* Ledbury); one *s* one *d. Educ:* Bishop's Stortford Coll.; Sidney Sussex Coll., Cambridge (MA, PhD, LittD). Sidney Sussex College, Cambridge: Research Fellow, 1955–58; Tutor, 1961–70; Vice-Master, 1973–75; Cambridge University: Asst Lectr, 1962–65, Lectr, 1965–80; Chairman: Faculty Board of History, 1979–81; Mgt Cttee, Internat. Studies, 1992–95; Member: Liby Syndicate, 1982–88; Gen. Bd of Faculties, 1987–89. Vis. Lectr, Harvard Univ., 1965; Lectures: Founder's Meml, St Deiniol's Liby, Hawarden, 1990; Stenton, Univ. of Reading, 1992; Birkbeck, Trinity Coll., Cambridge, 1993. Vis. Prof., Central Eur. Univ., Budapest, 1995–. Fellow, Collegium Budapest, 1995; Leverhulme Emeritus Fellowship, 2000. British rep., Humanities Standing Cttee, ESF, 1994–99. Mem. Council, RHistS, 1984–88. Editor, 1971–75, Mem. Editl Bd, Historical Jl, 1976–2002 (Chm., 1990–97). *Publications:* England and Italy 1859–60, 1961; From Castlereagh to Gladstone, 1969; The Risorgimento and the Unification of Italy, 1971, 2nd edn (with E. F. Biagini), 2002; History and Biography, 1981; (ed with Geoffrey Best) History, Society and the Churches, 1985; Joseph II: in the shadow of Maria Theresa 1741–80, 1987; Mozart and the Habsburgs, 1993; (ed with H. B. Nisbet) Sidney Sussex Quatercentenary Essays, 1996; (Gen. Ed.) Cassell's Companions to 18th and 20th Century Britain, 2001; Prosperity and Plunder: European Catholic monasteries in the Age of Revolution, 2003 (Paolucci/Bagehot Book Award, Intercollegiate Studies Inst., 2004); Enlightenment and Reform in the Eighteenth Century, 2005; Joseph II: against the world 1780–1790, 2009; (contrib.) Quincentenary History of St John's Coll., Cambridge, 2011; (ed with Renato Pasta) Relazione di Pietro Leopoldo sullo stato della Monarchia austriaca (1784), 2013; (contrib.) The Man Behind the Queen, 2014; (ed with Renato Pasta) Essai sur la Monarchie autrichienne 1790, 2019; articles in learned jls. *Recreations:* playing keyboard instruments and bridge, walking, not gardening. *Address:* Sidney Sussex College, Cambridge CB2 3HU. *T:* (01223) 338833.

**BEALL, Dr Jo;** Director, Education and Society, and Member, Executive Board, British Council, since 2011; *b* London, 1952; *d* of Gordon R. Adams and Jeanne C. Adams; one *s. Educ:* La Sagesse Convent, Newcastle upon Tyne; Our Lady of Fatima Convent, Durban, SA; Univ. of Natal (BA Hons; MA); London Sch. of Econs and Pol Sci. (PhD). Prof. of Devlt Studies, 2001–09, Dir, Develt Studies Inst., 2004–07, LSE; Dep. Vice Chancellor (Academic, Ext. Relns and Internat.), Univ. of Cape Town, 2009–11. *Publications:* Uniting a Divided City, 2002; Funding Local Governance, 2009; Cities and Development, 2009; Urbanisation and Development: interdisciplinary perspectives, 2010. *Recreations:* walking, reading, music, travel, family. *Address:* British Council, 10 Spring Gardens, SW1A 2BN. *T:* (020) 7389 4238. *E:* jo.beall@britishcouncil.org. *Club:* University Women's.

**BEAMISH, Sir Adrian (John),** KCMG 1999 (CMG 1988); HM Diplomatic Service, retired; Ambassador to Mexico, 1994–99; *b* 21 Jan. 1939; *s* of Thomas Charles Constantine Beamish and Josephine Mary (*née* Lee); *m* 1965, Caroline Lipscomb (marr. diss. 1991); two *d*; *m* 1994, Antonia Cavanagh (marr. diss. 2011; she *d* 2014); one *d*, and one step *s* one step *d. Educ:* Christian Brothers' Coll., Cork; Prior Park Coll., Bath; Christ's Coll., Cambridge (MA); Università per gli Stranieri, Perugia. Third, later Second Secretary, Tehran, 1963–66; Foreign Office, 1966–69; First Sec., UK Delegn, OECD, Paris, 1970–73; New Delhi, 1973–76; FCO, 1976–78; Counsellor, Personnel Operations Dept, FCO, 1978–80; Counsellor (Economic), Bonn, 1981–85; Hd, Falkland Is Dept, FCO, 1985–87; Ambassador to Peru, 1987–89; Asst Under-Sec. of State (Americas), FCO, 1989–94. Lectr, History Dept, University Coll., Cork, 1999–2009; Consultant, BOC Group, 1999–2001. *Recreations:* books, plants. *Address:* 117 Eton Rise, NW3 2DD. *E:* beamishadrian@gmail.com.

**BEAMISH, Sir David (Richard),** KCB 2017; Clerk of the Parliaments, House of Lords, 2011–17; *b* 20 Aug. 1952; *s* of late Richard Ludlow Beamish and Heather Margaret Ensor Beamish (*née* Lock); *m* 1989, (Fiona) Philippa Tudor, *qv;* one *d. Educ:* Marlborough Coll.; St John's Coll., Cambridge (MA, LLM). House of Lords: Clerk, 1974; Sen. Clerk, 1979; Chief Clerk, 1987; Principal Clerk, 1993; seconded to Cabinet Office as Private Sec. to Leader of H of L and Govt Chief Whip, 1983–86; Clerk of the Journals, 1993–95 and 2002–05; Clerk of Cttees and Clerk of Overseas Office, 1995–2002; Reading Clerk, 2003–07; Clerk Asst, 2007–11. Hon. Sen. Res. Associate, Constitution Unit, UCL, 2017–. Trustee: Hansard Soc., 2018–; Friends of Dulwich Picture Gall., 2018–. Member: Southwark Diocesan Synod, 2014–; Southwark Diocesan Bd of Patronage, 2018–; Southwark Diocesan Council of Trustees, 2019–; Sec., Dulwich Deanery Synod, 2015–. Chm., Dulwich Soc. Tree Cttee, 2018–. BBC TV Mastermind Champion, 1988. *Publications:* (ed jtly) The House of Lords at Work, 1993. *Recreations:* church bell ringing, family history, walking. *E:* mail@davidbeamish.uk.

**BEAMISH, (Fiona) Philippa, (Lady Beamish);** *see* Tudor, F. P.

**BEAMISH, Sarah Frances, (Sally);** composer and viola player; *b* 26 Aug. 1956; *d* of William Anthony Alten Beamish and Ursula Mary (*née* Snow); *m* 1988, Robert Irvine (separated 2008); two *s* one *d. Educ:* Camden Sch. for Girls; Nat. Youth Orch.; Royal Northern Coll. of Music (GRNCM); Staatliche Hochschule für Musik, Detmold. Viola player, Raphael Ensemble, Acad. of St Martin-in-the-Fields, London Sinfonietta, Lontano, 1979–90; Composer's Bursary, Arts Council, 1989; Composer-in-Residence: Swedish Chamber Orch., 1998–2002; Scottish Chamber Orch., 1998–2002. Co-Dir, St Magnus Composers' Course. Recordings: River ('Cello, Viola and Oboe Concertos); The Imagined Sound of Sun on Stone (Saxophone Concerto, etc); Bridging the Day ('cello and piano), 2001; String Quartets, 2006; The Seafarer, 2008. *Compositions include:* 1st Symphony (first perf., Iceland SO, 1993); Viola Concerto No 2, 2002; Trumpet Concerto, 2003; Percussion Concerto, 2005; Shenachie (stage musical), 2006; Accordion Concerto, 2006; Under the Wing of the Rock (Viola Concerto No 3), 2006; The Song Gatherer (Cello Concerto No 2), 2009; Spinal Chords (Orch.), 2012; Equal Voices (chorus and orch., settings of poems by Sir Andrew Motion), 2014; Song-cycle; Hafez Songs; The Day Dawn; Cage of Doves; The Tempest (ballet), 2016; The Little Mermaid (ballet), 2017. FRSE 2016. Hon. DMus Glasgow, 2001. *Recreations:* painting, writing, walking. *Address:* Edition Peters, 2-6 Baches Street, N1 6DN.

**BEAN, Sir Charles (Richard),** Kt 2014; Professor, London School of Economics and Political Science, since 2014; Member, UK Budget Responsibility Committee, since 2017; *b* 16 Sept. 1953; *s* of Charles Ernest Bean and Mary (*née* Welsh). *Educ:* Emmanuel Coll., Cambridge (BA 1975); MIT (PhD 1981). Economist, HM Treasury, 1975–79 and 1981–82; London School of Economics: Lectr, 1982–86; Reader, 1986–90; Prof., 1990–2000; Bank of England: Chief Economist and Exec. Dir, 2000–08; Dep. Gov., 2008–14. Conducted Ind. Rev. of Economic Statistics (reported 2016). Visiting Professor: Stanford Univ., 1990; Reserve Bank of Australia, 1999. Pres., Royal Economic Soc., 2013–15. *Publications:* contrib. learned jls. *Recreations:* cricket, opera.

**BEAN, Rt Hon. Sir David (Michael),** Kt 2004; PC 2014; **Rt Hon. Lord Justice Bean;** a Lord Justice of Appeal, since 2014; *b* 25 March 1954; *s* of late George Joseph Bean and Zdenka White; *m* 1st, 1986 (marr. diss. 1996); two *s;* 2nd, 2004, Ruth Thompson (*d* 2016). *Educ:* St Paul's Sch., Barnes; Trinity Hall, Cambridge (1st Cl. Hons Law; Pres., Cambridge Union Soc., 1975; Hon. Fellow, 2017). Called to the Bar, Middle Temple, 1976, Bencher, 2001 (Treas., 2019); a Recorder, 1996–2004; QC 1997; a Presiding Judge, SE Circuit, 2007–10; a Judge of the High Court of Justice, QBD, 2004–14. Chairman: Gen. Council of the Bar, 2002 (Vice-Chm., 2001); Employment Law Bar Assoc., 1999–2001; Immigration Services Tribunal, 2001–04; Law Commn of England and Wales, 2015–18. Lay Mem., GMC, 2003–04; Member: Civil Justice Council, 2003–05; Judicial Appts Commn, 2010–14. Pres., Assoc. of Lancastrians in London, 2011. *Publications:* Injunctions, 1979, 13th edn 2018; (with Anthony Nigel Fricker) Enforcement of Injunctions and Undertakings, 1991; (ed) Law Reform for All, 1996. *Recreations:* opera, hill-walking, books. *Address:* Royal Courts of Justice, Strand, WC2A 2LL. *Clubs:* Athenæum; Reform.

**BEAN, Rev. Canon John Victor;** Vicar, St Mary, Cowes, Isle of Wight, 1966–91, and Priest-in-charge, All Saints, Gurnard, IoW, 1978–91; Chaplain to the Queen, 1980–95; *b* 1 Dec. 1925; *s* of Albert Victor and Eleanor Ethel Bean; *m* 1955, Nancy Evelyn Evans; two *s* one *d* (and one *d* died in infancy). *Educ:* local schools; Grammar Sch., Gt Yarmouth; Downing Coll., Cambridge (MA); Salisbury Theological Coll., 1948. Served War, RNVR, 1944–46; returned to Cambridge, 1946–48. Assistant Curate: St James, Milton, Portsmouth, 1950–55; St Peter and St Paul, Fareham, 1955–59; Vicar, St Helen's, IoW, 1959–66. Rural Dean of West Wight, 1968–73; Clergy Proctor for Diocese of Portsmouth, 1973–80; Hon. Canon, Portsmouth Cathedral, 1970–91, Canon Emeritus, 1991. *Recreations:* drawing and painting, reading, writing, talking and listening, tidying up. *Address:* 23 Queens Road, Ryde, Isle of Wight PO33 3BG. *Club:* Gurnard Sailing (Gurnard).

**BEAN, Marisa;** *see* Robles, M.

**BEAN, Martin George,** CBE 2015; Vice-Chancellor and President, RMIT University, since 2015; *b* Melbourne, Australia, 26 Oct. 1964; *s* of Alfred and Margaret Bean; *m* 1987, Mary Murphy; three *d. Educ:* Univ. of Technol., Sydney (BEd (Adult)). Assoc. Internat. étudiants en science économique et commerciale, 1985–87; Gen. Manager, Asia Pacific, Drake Trng and Technologies, 1990–93; Area Educn Manager, Australasia, Dir, N Amer. Educn, and Vice-Pres., Educn Worldwide Sales and Mkt Develt, Novell Inc., 1993–97; Exec. Vice-Pres., IT Business Unit and Mktg, Pres., Sylvan Prometric, and Chief IT Business Strategist, Thomson Learning, Thomson Corp./Sylvan Learning Systems, 1997–2001; Chief Operating Officer and Mem. Bd of Dirs, New Horizons Computer Learning Centres Inc., 2001–05; Gen. Manager, Worldwide Educn Products Gp, Microsoft Inc., 2005–09; Vice-Chancellor, Open Univ., 2009–14. Member: Digital Adv. Gp, BM, 2012; Strategic Adv. Bd, Internat. Unit, UK Higher Educn, 2013; Leadership Council, Nat. Centre for Univs and Business, 2013. Mem., Bd of Govs, Commonwealth of Learning, 2010–. Trustee, British Council, 2011–14. Ambassador, UKTI, 2014. Learning Leadership Award, Masie Center Learning Conf., 2013; Colin Corder Award for Services to Learning Learning and Perf. Inst., 2014. *Recreations:* sailing, scuba diving, travel. *Address:* Office of the Vice-Chancellor, RMIT University, GPO Box 2476, Melbourne, Vic 3001, Australia. *Club:* Sloane.

**BEAN, Prof. Philip Thomas,** PhD; Professor of Criminology and Director, Midland Centre for Criminology and Criminal Justice, Department of Social Sciences, Loughborough University, 1990–2003, now Emeritus Professor; *b* 24 Sept. 1936; *s* o

Thomas William Bean and Amy Bean; m 1st, 1964, Anne Elizabeth Sellar (marr. diss. 1968); 2nd, 1969, Valerie Winifred Davis (d 1999); two s. Educ: Bedford Modern Sch.; Univ. of London (BSc Soc (ext.), MSc Econ); Univ. of Nottingham (PhD). Probation Officer, Inner London Probation Service, 1963–69; Res. Officer, MRC, 1969–72; Lectr and Sen. Lectr in Social Sci., Univ. of Nottingham, 1972–90; Reader in Criminology, Univ. of Loughborough, 1990. Vis. Prof. at American, Canadian and Australian univs; Vis. Scholar, Univ. of Cambridge, 2014–. Pres., British Soc. of Criminology, 1996–99; Associate, GMC, 2000–05. *Publications:* The Social Control of Drugs, 1974; Rehabilitation and Deviance, 1976; Compulsory Admissions to Mental Hospitals, 1980; Punishment, 1981; Mental Disorder and Legal Control, 1987; Mental Disorder and Community Safety, 2000; Drugs and Crime, 2004, 4th edn 2014; Madness and Crime, 2007; Legalising Drugs, 2010; Probation and Privatisation, 2019; numerous contribs to learned jls. *Recreations:* poetry, music, esp. New Orleans jazz and opera. *Address:* 41 Trevor Road, West Bridgford, Notts NG2 6FT. *T:* (0115) 923 3895.

**BEAN, Richard Anthony;** playwright; b Kingston-upon-Hull, 11 June 1956; s of John and Rita Bean; two d. Educ: Hull Grammar Sch.; Loughborough Univ. (BSc Hons Social Psychol.). Formerly occupational psychologist and stand-up comedian. Stage plays: Toast, Royal Court, 1999; Mr England, Sheffield Crucible, 2000; The Mentalists, NT, 2002; Under the Whaleback, Royal Court, 2003; Smack Family Robinson, Live, Newcastle, 2003, Rose Th., Kingston-upon-Thames, 2013; The God Botherers, Bush, 2003; Honeymoon Suite, Royal Court, 2004; Harvest, Royal Court, 2005; Up on Roof, Truck, Hull, 2006; The English Game, Yvonne Arnaud, Guildford, 2008; England People Very Nice, NT, 2009; Pub Quiz is Life, Truck, Hull, 2009; The Big Fellah, Lyric, Hammersmith, 2010; The Heretic, Royal Court, 2011; One Man, Two Guvnors, NT, 2011; Great Britain, NT, transf. Th. Royal, Haymarket, 2014; Pitcairn, Minerva Th., Chichester, 2014; Made in Dagenham, Adelphi, 2014; The Nap, Sheffield Crucible, 2016; The Hypocrite, Hull Truck, transf. RSC, 2017; (with Clive Coleman) Young Marx, Bridge Th., 2017. *Publications:* Toast, 1999; Mr England, 2000; The Mentalists, 2002; Under the Whaleback, 2003; Smack Family Robinson, 2003; The God Botherers, 2003; Honeymoon Suite, 2004; Harvest, 2005; Up on Roof, 2006; The English Game, 2008; England People Very Nice, 2009; Pub Quiz is Life, 2009; The Big Fellah, 2010; The Heretic, 2011; One Man, Two Guvnors, 2011; (with Clive Coleman) Young Marx, 2017. *Recreations:* chopping logs, wild cooking, chainsaws. *Address:* c/o Rose Cobbe, United Agents, 12–26 Lexington Street, W1F 0LE. *T:* (020) 3214 0800. *Club:* Actors Anonymous Cricket.

**BEAN, Shaun Mark, (Sean);** actor; b Sheffield, 17 April 1959; s of Brian and Rita Bean; m 1st, 1981, Debra James (marr. diss.); 2nd, 1990, Melanie Hill (marr. diss. 1997); two d; 3rd, 1997, Abigail Cruttenden (marr. diss. 2000); one d; 4th, 2008, Georgina Sutcliffe (marr. diss.); 5th, 2017, Ashley Moore. Educ: RADA. Stage début, Tybalt in Romeo and Juliet, Watermill Th., Newbury, 1983; *other theatre includes:* Romeo and Juliet, The Fair Maid of the West, A Midsummer Night's Dream, RSC, 1986–87; Killing the Cat, Royal Court Th., 1990; Macbeth, Albery Th., 2002. *Television includes:* Troubles, 1988; The Fifteen Streets, 1989; Small Zones, Lorna Doone, 1990; Tell Me That You Love Me, My Kingdom for a Horse, Clarissa, Prince, 1991; Fool's Gold, 1992; Lady Chatterley, A Woman's Guide to Adultery, 1993; Sharpe (series), 1993–97; Scarlett, Jacob, 1994; Bravo Two Zero, Extremely Dangerous, 1999; Henry VIII, 2003; Sharpe's Challenge, 2006; Sharpe's Peril, 2008; Red Riding, 2009; Game of Thrones, 2011; Missing, Accused, 2012; Legends, 2014–15; The Frankenstein Chronicles, 2015, 2017; Wasted, 2016; Broken, 2017 (Best Leading Actor, BAFTA, 2018); Curfew, World on Fire, 2019. *Films include:* Caravaggio, 1986; Stormy Monday, 1988; War Requiem, How to Get Ahead in Advertising, 1989; Windprints, The Field, 1990; In the Border Country, 1991; Patriot Games, 1992; Shopping, Black Beauty, 1994; Goldeneye, 1995; When Saturday Comes, 1996; Anna Karenina, 1997; Airborne, Ronin, 1998; Essex Boys, 2000; The Lord of the Rings: The Fellowship of the Ring, 2001; Don't Say a Word, Tom and Thomas, Equilibrium, 2002; The Big Empty, 2003; Troy, National Treasure, 2004; The Island, Flightplan, 2005; North Country, The Dark, Silent Hill, 2006; Outlaw, The Hitcher, Far North, 2007; Black Death, 2010; Cleanskin, Mirror Mirror, 2012; The Martian, 2015; Dark River, 2018. *Address:* c/o Independent Talent Group Ltd, 40 Whitfield Street, W1T 2RH.

**BEANE, Ven. Andrew Mark;** Archdeacon of Exeter, since 2019; b King's Lynn, 9 Nov. 1972; s of Frederick and Rosemary Beane; m 2006, Catherine; one d. Educ: Anglia Poly. Univ. (HNC Business Studies); Nottingham Univ. (BA Hons Theology and Ministry 2002). Ordained deacon, 2002, priest, 2003; Curate, Thorpe Hamlet, 2002–05; Rector, Spixworth and St Faiths, 2005–12; Rector, Aylsham, 2012–19. Hon. Canon, Norwich Cathedral, 2015–. Governor: St Michael's Sch., Aylsham, 2012–; Bure Valley Sch., Aylsham, 2013–; Aylsham High Sch., 2013–. *Recreations:* family, walking, social media. *Address:* Emmanuel House, Station Road, Ide, Exeter EX2 9RS. *T:* (01392) 425577. *E:* archdeacon.of.exeter@exeter.anglican.org.

**BEANEY, Jan, (Mrs S. Udall);** textile artist; author; b 31 July 1938; d of Jack and Audrey Beaney; m 1967, Stephen Udall; one s one d. Educ: Southampton Coll. of Art; W Sussex Coll. of Art (NDD Painting/Lithography); Hornsey Coll. of Art (ATC); City & Guilds of London Inst. (Licentiate). Lecturer in Art and Embroidery: grammar/technical sch., Northolt, 1959–64; Whitelands Coll. of Educn, 1964–68; Associate Lectr in Embroidery and Design, Windsor and Maidenhead Coll., subseq. E Berks Coll., 1976–2000, Artist-in-Residence, 2000–10. Freelance lectr and teacher in design/stitched textiles, UK, USA, Australia, NZ, Canada, Israel and Germany, 1966–. Work exhibited in UK, Europe, USA, Israel and Japan; work in private and public collections, GB and worldwide. Co-founder, Double Trouble Enterprises (publishers), 1997. Presenter, BBC TV series, Embroidery, 1980; contribs to TV progs, 1984–95. Examr, then Jt Chief Examr, Creative Studies, C&G, 1979–95. Member: 62 Gp of Textile Artists, 1962– (Hon. Mem., 1998); Embroiderers' Guild, 1963– (Hon. Mem., 2001; Jt Pres., 2012–18); Hon. Mem., C&G, 1996. Fellow, Soc. of Designer Craftsmen, 2016. MUniv Surrey, 1995. *Publications:* The Young Embroiderer, 1966; Fun with Collage, 1970; Fun with Embroidery, 1975; Landscapes in Picture, Collage and Design, 1976; Buildings in Picture, Collage and Design, 1976; Textures and Surface Patterns, 1978; Embroidery: new approaches, 1978; Stitches: new approaches, 1985; The Art of the Needle, 1988; Vanishing Act, 1997; with Jean Littlejohn: A Complete Guide to Creative Embroidery, 1971; Stitch Magic, 1998; Bonding and Beyond, Transfer to Transform, 1999; Gardens and More, Conversations with Constance, 2000; Trees as a Theme, Giving Pleasure, 2001; New Dimensions, Double Vision, 2002; A Tale of Two Stitches, A Sketch in Time, 2003; No Stone Unturned, Connections, 2004; Colour Explorations, Over the Line, 2005; Grids to Stitch, Seductive Surfaces, 2006; Red, Embellish and Enrich, 2007; Location, Location, Seeing Double, 2008; Fragile Fabrics, Constructions, 2009; Stitchscapes, 2010; Stitch Rhythms and Patterns, 2011; Memory Cloths, 2015; contrib. numerous articles on stitching and textile design. *Recreations:* entertaining friends, travel, reading, painting, gardening. *Address:* Double Trouble Enterprises, 233 Courthouse Road, Maidenhead, Berks SL6 6HF.

**BEAR, Sir Michael (David),** Kt 2012; CEng, FRICS; JP; Managing Director, Michael Bear Developments Ltd, since 1996; Chairman, Turley, since 2017; Lord Mayor of London, 2010–11; b Nairobi, 21 Jan. 1953; s of Lionel Meyer Bear and Rebecca Bear; m 1979, Barbara Anne Sandler; one s one d. Educ: Clifton Coll. Sch.; Univ. of Witwatersrand (BSc Eng 1974); Cranfield Inst. of Technol. (MBA 1981). CEng 1978; MICE 1979, Hon. FICE 2008; FRICS 2009. Aid worker, S African Voluntary Service, 1970–74; Project Engineer: Hawkins Hawkins & Osborne, 1974–78; Sir Frederick Snow Ltd, 1978–81; Business Analyst, Taylor Woodrow, 1981–82; Internat. Business Develt Manager, Balfour Beatty Engrg Ltd, 1982–88; Man. Dir, Iberia Develts Ltd, 1988–89; Dir, LET Europe BV, 1989–93; Chief Exec., Spitalfields Develt Gp, 1991–2011; Man. Dir, Balfour Beatty Property Ltd, 1993–2012; Regeneration Dir, Hammerson UK Properties plc, 2007–12. Director: Avatar Ltd, 1993–2000; White City Centre Ltd, 1994–98; British Urban Develt Ltd, 1995–99; Cityside Regeneration Ltd, 1997–2003; Future Cities Catapult, 2016–; non-exec. Dir, Arup Gp Ltd, 2009–15. Chm., Regeneration Investment Orgn, UKTI, 2013–16; UK Special Envoy for Sustainable Urbanisation, China, 2014–17. Vis. Prof. in Civil Engrg, City Univ., 2011–; Prof. of Sustainable Urbanisation, Univ. of Sheffield, 2016–. Chm., Bethnal Green City Challenge, 1993–97. Director: Spitalfields Music (formerly Spitalfields Fest.), 1991–2006 (Hon. Advr, 2007–); Spitalfields Mkt Community Trust, 1991–2012; Metropolitan Drinking Fountain and Cattle Trough Assoc., 2005–; CRASH, 2006–11; City Arts Trust, 2007–11. MInstD 1997. Governor: London Metropolitan Univ., 2000–03; London South Bank Univ., 2004–10; Christ's Hosp., 2005–; Sir John Cass Primary Sch., 2006–12; Clifton Coll., 2007–14; Sir John Cass Foundn, 2008–12; Coram, 2008– (Pres., 2012–); City Acad., Hackney, 2008–12. Liveryman: Co. of Paviors, 2002– (Mem., Ct of Assts, 2006–; Master, 2012–13); Co. of Chartered Surveyors, 2006– (Mem., Ct of Assts, 2007–16); Co. of Engineers, 2009–. Hon. Liveryman, Co. of Security Professionals, 2010–; Hon. Freeman, Co. of Environmental Cleaners, 2010–. Mem., Guild of Freemen, 2008–. City of London, Portsoken Ward: Councilman, 2003–04; Dep. Alderman, 2004–05; Alderman, 2005–. JP 2005, Sheriff, 2007–08, City of London. Hon. FREng 2010. Hon. DSc: City, 2011; London Southbank, 2012; Cranfield, 2012. KStJ 2011 (SBStJ 2008). *Recreations:* small business ventures, scuba diving, tennis, opera, theatre, international travel, supporting the England Rugby team. *Address:* c/o Turley, Lacon House, 84 Theobald's Road, WC1X 8NL. *T:* 07778 218725, *Fax:* (020) 8346 3991. *E:* michael@thebearsinc.com. *Clubs:* Athenæum, East India.

**BEARD, Alexander Charles,** CBE 2013; Chief Executive, Royal Opera House, since 2013; b London, 14 Oct. 1963; s of Charles Henry and Patricia Anne Beard; m 1993, Katharine Betty Warde-Aldam; one s one d. Educ: Manchester Grammar Sch.; Westminster Sch.; King's Coll. London (BA Classics; FKC 2013). KPMG, London, 1985–86; Arts Council, 1987–93; Tate: Dir, Finance and Admin, 1994–98, Dir, Business, 1998–2002; Dep. Dir, 2002–13. Member: Philanthropy Prog., DCMS, 2010–; WWI Centenary Cultural Prog., 2013–; West End Partnership, 2015–. Trustee: Global Giving UK, 2007–13; Glyndebourne Prodns Ltd, 2008–13; Chm., High House Prodn Park Ltd, 2013–. *Recreations:* cricket, visual arts, opera, ballet, music, cycling, cooking. *Address:* c/o Royal Opera House, Covent Garden, WC2E 9DD. *E:* alex.beard@roh.org.uk. *Clubs:* Garrick; White City Cricket.

**BEARD, Rear Adm. Hugh Dominic;** Assistant Chief of Naval Staff Capability, since 2018; b Birmingham, 28 Dec. 1967; s of John Beard and Merlyn Beard (née Everett, later Lewis); m 1991, Jennifer Lynch; two s one d. Educ: St Anselm's Catholic Comp. Sch., Canterbury; King's Coll. London (MA Defence Studies 2003). Joined RN, 1987; Exec. Officer, HMS Vengeance, 1999–2002; Commanding Officer: HMS Trenchant, 2005–07; HMS Westminster, 2012–14; Defence Advr to Cabinet Office for 2015 Strategic Defence and Security Rev., 2015; Hd, Capability Strategy, MoD, 2016–18. *Recreations:* squash, badminton, athletics, golf, theatre, cinema. *Address:* c/o Naval Secretary, Fleet Headquarters, Whale Island, Portsmouth PO2 8BY.

**BEARD, Mark John;** Headmaster, University College School, since 2013; b Carshalton, 27 Jan. 1971; m 1998, Jacqueline Aspin; two s. Educ: Whitgift Sch.; Corpus Christi Coll., Oxford (BA 1994; PGCE 1995; MA); King's Coll. London (MEd 2002). Teacher of Chemistry and CCF Contingent Comdr, King Edward's Sch., Birmingham, 1995–99; Hd of Chemistry, St Paul's Sch., London, 1999–2006; Hd of Sixth Form, 2006–09, Dep. Headmaster, 2009–13, Brighton Coll. *Publications:* contrib. Tetrahedron. *Recreations:* squash, reading, ancient history and the classics. *Address:* University College School, Frognal, Hampstead, NW3 6XH. *T:* (020) 7435 2215.

**BEARD, Dame Mary;** see Beard, Dame W. M.

**BEARD, Peter Hill;** American photographer; b 22 Jan. 1938; s of Anson Beard; m 1st, 1967, Minnie Cushing (marr. diss. 1971); 2nd, 1978, Cheryl Tiegs (marr. diss. 1984); 3rd, 1986, Nejma Khanum; one d. Educ: Yale Univ. (grad 1961). Career of escapism through collage, books, diaries and anthropology. Major exhibitions include: Blum-Helman, NY, 1975 (first exhibn); ICP, NY, 1977 (first one man exhibn); Diary, 1979, African Wallpaper, 1993, Seibu Mus., Japan; Carnets Africains, Paris, 1996–97; Pettiness and Futility, LA, 1998; 50 Years of Portraits, Toronto, LA, New Orleans, 1998–99; Stress and Density, Berlin, Vienna, 1999; 28 Pieces, Paris, 1999; Living Sculpture, London, 2004–05; Time's Up, London, 2006–07. *Publications:* The End of the Game, 1965, 5th edn 2008, 50th Anniv. edn 2015; Eyelids of Morning: the mingled destinies of crocodiles and men, 1973; Longing for Darkness: Kamante's tales from Out of Africa, 1975; Zara's Tales from Hog Ranch, 2004; Peter Beard, art edn 2006, collector's edn 2007, trade edns 2008 and 2013; Ele Portfolio, 2009; exhibition catalogues: Diary, 1993; Photo poche, 1996; Carnets Africains, 1997; Peter Beard: 50 Years of Portraits, 1999; Stress and Density, 1999. *Address:* Peter Beard Studio, 525 West 20th Street, New York, NY 10011, USA. *Club:* White Rhino (Nyeri, Kenya).

**BEARD, Philip Charles William;** Chief Executive, Queens Park Rangers Football Club, 2011–15; b Liverpool, 4 Jan. 1961; s of Roland and Joan Beard; m 1994, Louise; one s two d. Educ: Langley Park Grammar Sch. Founding Partner, Air Miles, 1988–2001; Dir, London 2012 Olympic and Paralympic Bid, 2003–05; Dir, Mktg and Sponsorship, LOCOG, 2005–06; CEO, AEG the O2, 2006–09; Chm., Sport and Partnerships, AEG Europe, 2006–10. *Recreations:* ski-ing, tennis, golf. *Address:* 4 Earlsfield Road, SW18 3DW. *Club:* St George's Hill Golf.

**BEARD, Dame (Winifred) Mary, (Dame Mary Cormack),** DBE 2018 (OBE 2013); PhD; FBA 2010; FSA; Professor of Classics, University of Cambridge, since 2004; Fellow, Newnham College, Cambridge, since 1984; Professor of Ancient Literature, Royal Academy, since 2013; b 1 Jan. 1955; d of Roy Whitbread Beard and Joyce Emily (née Taylor); m 1985, Robin Sinclair Cormack, qv; one s one d. Educ: Newnham Coll., Cambridge (BA Classics 1977, MA 1980; PhD 1982). FSA 2005. Lectr in Classics, KCL, 1979–83; University of Cambridge: Lectr in Classics, 1984–99; Reader in Classics, 1999–2004. Writer and presenter: Pompeii: Life and Death in a Roman Town, BBC2, 2010; A Point of View, BBC Radio 4, 2011, 2012; Meet the Romans with Mary Beard, BBC2, 2012; Caligula with Mary Beard, BBC2, 2013; Pompeii: new secrets revealed with Mary Beard, BBC1, 2016; Pompeii: life before death, BBC1, 2016; Mary Beard's Ultimate Rome, BBC2, 2016; Civilisations, BBC2, 2018; Julius Caesar Revealed, BBC1, 2018; presenter, Front Row Late, BBC2, 2018–. Mem., First World War Centenary Adv. Gp, 2014–18. For. Mem., Amer. Acad. of Arts and Scis, 2011; Internat. Mem., American Philosophical Soc., 2012. Hon. DLitt: Bristol, 2012; St Andrews, 2013; Buckingham, 2014; London, 2014; Rome, 2014; Kent, 2016; Liverpool, 2016; Open, 2017; Bard Coll., USA, 2017; Northumbria, 2018. Hon. FCollT 2014. Bodley Medal, Bodleian Libraries, 2016;

Princess of Asturias Award for Social Scis, 2016. Classics Ed. (pt-time), TLS, 1992–. *Publications:* (with M. Crawford) Rome in the Late Republic, 1985, 2nd edn 1999; The Good Working Mother's Guide, 1989; (ed jtly) Pagan Priests: religion and power in the ancient world, 1990; (with J. Henderson) Classics: a very short introduction, 1995, 2nd edn 2000; (jtly) Religions of Rome I and II, 1998; The Invention of Jane Harrison, 2000; (with J. Henderson) Classical Art: from Greece to Rome, 2001; The Parthenon, 2002; (with K. Hopkins) The Colosseum, 2005; The Roman Triumph, 2007; Pompeii: the life of a Roman town (Wolfson History Prize), 2008; It's A Don's Life, 2009; All in a Don's Day, 2012; Confronting the Classics, 2013; Laughter in Ancient Rome, 2014; SPQR: a history of ancient Rome, 2015; Women & Power: a manifesto, 2017; Civilisations: how do we look/the eye of faith, 2018. *Address:* Newnham College, Cambridge CB3 9DF. *T:* (01223) 335700. *E:* mb127@cam.ac.uk.

**BEARDER, Catherine Zena;** Member (Lib Dem) South East Region, European Parliament, since 2009 (Quaestor of European Parliament, 2014 and 2017); *b* Broxbourne, Herts, 14 Jan. 1949; *d* of Ernest James Bailey and Joan Irene Clare Bailey; *m* 1974, Prof. Simon Kenneth Bearder; three *s. Educ:* Hawthorn Sch., Frinton on Sea; St Christopher's Sch., Letchworth. Work on family farm, Herts, 1964–66; antique dealer, Hertford, 1966–74; field asst to zool field studies on hyenas and bushbabies, S Africa, 1974–78; work in fundraising office, Berks, Bucks and Oxon Wildlife Trust, 1987–90; Manager, Bicester CAB, 1990–94; Development Officer: NFWI, 1994–97; Witness Service, Oxon Victim Support, 1998–99; Regl Dir, SE, Britain in Europe, 2004–05. Member (Lib Dem): Wendlebury PC, 1986–92; Cherwell DC, 1995–99; Oxon CC, 2003–05. Mem., Police Consultative Cttee, Northern Oxfordshire, 1993–95. Chairman: and Co-founder, Bicester Volunteer Link, 1992–95; Bicester Community Educn Council, 1992–95; Banbury Emergency Accommodation Initiative, 1998–2000. Trustee and Board Member: Oxon Rural Community Council, 2000–08; Oxon Victim Support, 2001–02; Thame CAB, 2002–03. Chm., Banbury Lib Dems, 1997; Vice Pres., Green Lib Dems, 2009–; Vice Chm., Lib Dems' Eur. Gp, 2009–. Chm., Lib Dem conf. cttee, S Central Reg., 2003–08. Chm., Oxon Lib Dems Printing Soc., 2000–08. Contested (Lib Dem): Banbury, 1997; Henley, 2001; SE England, Eur. Parlt, 1999, 2004. Member: IAM; UNA (UK); Eur. Movt. Police Lay Visitor, Bicester and Banbury, 1992–95. Pres., Bicester Friends of the Earth, 1990–94. Gov., St Edburg's C of E Sch., Bicester, 1986–91. FRSA. *Recreations:* painting, gardening. *Address:* (office) Sun House, 2a Stanley Road, Oxford OX4 1QZ. *E:* catherine@bearder.eu, catherine.bearder@europarl.europa.eu. *Club:* National Liberal.

**BEARDMORE, Prof. John Alec,** CBiol, FRSB; Emeritus Professor and Consultant in Aquacultural Genetics, Swansea University (formerly University of Wales, Swansea), since 2000; *b* 1 May 1930; *s* of George Edward Beardmore and Anne Jean (*née* Warrington); *m* 1953, Anne Patricia Wallace; three *s* one *d* (and one *s* decd). *Educ:* Burton on Trent Grammar Sch.; Birmingham Central Tech. Coll.; Univ. of Sheffield. BSc (1st Cl. Botany) 1953, PhD (Genetics) 1956. Research Demonstrator, Dept of Botany, Univ. of Sheffield, 1954–56; Commonwealth Fund Fellow, Columbia Univ., 1956–58; Vis. Asst Prof. in Plant Breeding, Cornell Univ., 1958; Lectr in Genetics, Univ. of Sheffield, 1958–61; Prof. of Genetics and Dir, Genetics Inst., Univ. of Groningen, 1961–66; Nat. Science Foundn Senior Foreign Fellow, Pennsylvania State Univ., 1966; University College of Swansea, subseq. University of Wales, Swansea: Prof. of Genetics, 1966–97; Dean of Science, 1974–76; Vice-Principal, 1977–80; Dir, Inst. of Marine Studies, 1983–87; Hd, Sch. of Biol Scis, 1988–95; Professorial Fellow in Genetics, 1997–2000. Manager, DFID (formerly ODA) Fish Genetics Res. Prog., 1990–2001; Man. Dir, 1995–2005, Chm., 2005–, Fishgen Ltd. Chm., Univ. of Wales Validation Bd, 1994–97; Mem., Univ. of Wales Vice Chancellors' Bd, 1993–96. Vis. Prof., Univ. of Ghent, 1992–2002. Member: NERC Aquatic Life Scis Cttee, 1982–87 (Chm., 1984–87); CNAA: Life Scis Cttee, 1979–85; Cttee for Science, 1985–87; Bd, Council of Sci. and Technology Insts, 1983–85 (Chm., 1984–85); Council, Galton Inst. (formerly Eugenics Soc.), 1980–96, 2002– (Chm., Res. Cttee, 1979–87; Vice-Pres., 2005–08; Treas., 2007–); British Nat. Cttee for Biology, 1983–87; Council, Linnean Soc., 1989–93; Cttee, Heads of Univ. Biol Scis (Treas., 1989–91, Chm., 1991–94); Adv. Bd, Internat. Foundn for Sci., 1992–98; Vice-Pres., Inst. of Biol., 1985–87 (Mem. Council, 1976–79; Hon. Sec., 1980–85); UK rep., Council of European Communities Biologists Assoc., 1980–87. Pres., Gower Soc., 2012–15 (Hon. Treas., 2005–11). FRSA; FAAAS; FRSocMed. Darwin Lectr, Inst. of Biol. and Eugenics Soc., 1984. Univ. of Helsinki Medal, 1980. *Publications:* (ed with B. Battaglia) Marine Organisms: genetics ecology and evolution, 1977; (ed jtly) Artemia: basic and applied biology, 2002; articles on evolutionary genetics, human genetics and applications of genetics to aquaculture. *Recreation:* bridge. *Address:* Heathway Close, Camberley, Surrey GU15 2EP. *T:* (01276) 27713.

**BEARDMORE, Nicola Ann;** Director, Latitude 83, since 2015; *b* Clatterbridge, 6 Dec. 1970; *d* of Edward Rowlinson and Doreen Rowlinson; *m* 1995, Tim Beardmore; two *s. Educ:* Lakelands Sch., Ellesmere; Shrewsbury Coll. MCIM 1996. Information Officer, 1991–94; Customer Develt and Mktg Manager, 1994–98, British Waterways; Managing Director: Shropshire Bridal Centre, 1997–2006; Borderland Tourism, 2002–07; Shropshire Council: Hd, Communications, 2006–13; Dir, Resources and Support, 2013–15. Young Entrepreneur of the Yr, Shell, 1997. *Recreations:* painting, travel, family, proud mum to Ash and Connor. *E:* nicki.beardmore@latitude83.co.uk.

**BEARDSHAW, Christopher Paul;** garden designer and television presenter; Director, Chris Beardshaw Ltd, since 2001; *b* Worcs, 11 Jan. 1969; *s* of George and Gillian Beardshaw; partner, Frances Toase; three *d. Educ:* Cheltenham and Gloucester Coll. of Higher Educn (BA Hons Landscape Architecture; Postgrad. Landscape Architecture). Landscape architect: Cheltenham Landscape Design, 1992; Andrew Davies Partnership, 1993–97; Lectr, Pershore Coll., Worcs, 1997–2001; presenter, BBC TV and radio, 1998–, including: Gardeners' World, 2001–04; The Flying Gardener, 2001–03; Hidden Gardens, 2002–04; Wild About Your Garden, 2009; Ploughs, Cows and Clover, 2010; Hidcote: a garden for all seasons, 2011; Get Up & Grow, 2011–13; Apples: British to the Core, 2012; British Gardens in Time, 2014; Deep Down & Dirty, 2014. Consultant Lectr, Royal Botanic Gdns, Edinburgh, 2007–. Columnist: The English Garden Mag.; Garden News. Hon. Fellow, Univ. of Glos, 2004. 7 RHS Gold Medals; 6 RHS Best in Show Awards. *Publications:* The Natural Gardener, 2003; How Does Your Garden Grow?, 2007; The Secret Life of the Garden, 2009. *Recreations:* diving, cycling. *Address:* c/o Chris Beardshaw Ltd, Staverton Court, Staverton, Cheltenham, Glos GL51 0UX. *E:* info@chrisbeardshaw.com.

**BEARDSHAW, Virginia Zachry,** CBE 2015; Chief Executive Officer, I CAN, 2005–15; *b* Manhattan, 15 June 1952; *d* of David Beardshaw and Charlotte Beardshaw (*née* Zachry); *m* 1976, Sir Andrew Thomas Cahn, *qv*; two *s* one *d. Educ:* Mount Sch., York; New Hall, Cambridge (BA Hons Soc. Anthropol. 1974); London Sch. of Econs and Pol Sci. (Dip Soc. Admin). Researcher, Dept of Regius Prof. of Medicine, Oxford Univ., 1975–76; Stagiaire, EC, Brussels, 1976–77; Social Audit, London, 1977–82; Eur. Co-ordinator, Health Action Internat., The Hague, 1982–86; Founder Fellow, King's Fund Inst., 1987–89; Director: King's Fund London Initiative, 1989–93; Commissioning, Barnet HA, 1993–99;

Modernisation, London Regl Office, NHS, 1999–2002; UK Services, British Red Cross, 2002–05. Vice Chm., ACEVO, 2012–15. Gov., LSE, 2011–17 (Chair, Nominations Cttee, 2013–17). *Recreations:* gardening, choir, walking, theatre, opera.

**BEARE, Stuart Newton;** Consultant, Richards Butler, Solicitors, 1996–2002 (Partner, 1969–96, Senior Partner, 1988–91); *b* 6 Oct. 1936; *s* of Newton Beare and Joyce (*née* Atkinson); *m* 1974, Cheryl Wells. *Educ:* Clifton Coll.; Clare Coll., Cambridge (MA, LLB). Nat. Service, commnd Royal Signals, attached RWAFF, 1956–57. Plebiscite Supervisory Officer, N Cameroons, 1960–61; admitted solicitor, 1964. Clerk, Ward of Portsoken, 1993–96 (Hon. Ward Clerk, 1996–2013). Master, City of London Solicitors' Co. and Pres., City of London Law Soc., 1995–96. *Recreations:* mountain walking, ski-ing. *Address:* 24 Ripplevale Grove, N1 1HU. *T:* (020) 7609 0766. *Clubs:* Alpine, Oriental.

**BEARMAN, Prof. Peter William,** FREng; Professor of Experimental Aerodynamics, Imperial College of Science, Technology and Medicine, 1986–2004, now Emeritus; *b* 8 Oct. 1938; *s* of William Stanley Bearman and Nana Joan Bearman; *m* 1969, Marietta Neubauer; one *s* one *d. Educ:* Jesus Coll., Cambridge (MA 1962; PhD 1965). SSO, Nat. Phys. Lab., 1965–69; Department of Aeronautics, Imperial College, London: Lectr, 1969–81; Reader, 1981–86; Head of Dept, 1989–98; Pro-Rector, Projects, 1999–2001, Dep. Rector, 2001–04, ICSTM. FRAeS 1990; FCGI 1997; FREng (FEng 1997). *Publications:* (ed) Flow-induced Vibration, 1995; around 200 sci. papers. *Recreations:* cycling, gardening, ski-ing. *Address:* Imperial College, SW7 2AZ. *T:* (020) 7594 5055.

**BEARN, Rev. Hugh William;** Vicar, St Anne's Church, Tottington, since 1996; Chaplain to the Queen, since 2006; *b* 31 March 1962; *s* of John Hugh Bearn and Gladys Eileen Bearn (*née* Saint); *m* 1990, Alison Margaret (*neé* Cooper); two *s. Educ:* Oxford Sch.; Manchester Univ. (BA 1984; MA 1998); St John's Coll., Durham (CTh 1988). Schoolmaster, St Edmund's Sch., Canterbury; ordained deacon, 1989, priest, 1990; Asst Curate, Christ Church, Heaton, 1989–92; Chaplain, RAF, 1992–96. Chaplain: RAChD, TA, 1996–2002; Bury Hospice, 1999–2004 and 2010–; Manchester County ACF, 2006; Greater Manchester ACF, 2012–; Chaplain to the Bishop, RBL Fest. of Remembrance, 2002–. Member: Fraternity, CR, Mirfield, 1991–; Sen. Common Room, St Anselm Hall, Univ. of Manchester, 2002– (Hon. Chaplain). Vice-Pres., Manchester Br., Prayer Bk Soc., 2003–. Sec., Old Boys' Soc., Oxford Sch., 1983; Gov., Tottington High Sch., 1996–2001; Foundn Gov., Christ Church Primary Sch., 2015–16. Freeman: City of London, 2009; Clockmakers' Co., 2009 (Chaplain, 2010–). Bk Reviewer, Contact, 1997. *Publications:* History of Tottington St Anne, 1999; On the Way... a journey into faith, 2007; The Royal College of Chaplains 1912–2011: a photographic register, 2012. *Recreations:* family, all things French, marathon running, keep fit, all sport, supporting the varied social, musical and sporting life of my boys, regimental history of the Bearn family. *Address:* The Vicarage, Chapel Street, Tottington, Bury, Lancs BL8 4AP. *T:* (01204) 883713. *E:* hughbearn@aol.com. *Clubs:* Royal Air Force; Royal Irish Officers (Belfast); Manchester Dio. Cricket.

**BEARSTED,** 5th Viscount *cr* 1925, of Maidstone, Kent; **Nicholas Alan Samuel;** Bt 1903; Baron 1921; *b* 22 Jan. 1950; *s* of 4th Viscount Bearsted, MC, TD and Hon. Elizabeth Adelaide (*d* 1983), *d* of Baron Cohen, PC; *S* father, 1996; *m* 1975, Caroline Jane, *d* of Dr David Sacks; one *s* four *d. Educ:* Eton; New Coll., Oxford. *Heir:* *s* Hon. Harry Richard Samuel, *b* 23 May 1988. *Address:* The Estate Office, Farley Hall, Castle Road, Farley Hill, Berks RG7 1UL.

**BEASHEL, His Honour John Francis;** DL; a Circuit Judge, 1993–2008; Resident Judge, Dorchester Crown Court, 1994–2006; *b* 3 Aug. 1942; *s* of late Nicholas Beashel and Margaret Rita Beashel, JP; *m* 1966, Kay Dunning; three *s* one *d. Educ:* Coll. of Law. Called to the Bar, Gray's Inn, 1970, NSW, 1989; Asst Recorder, 1983–89; Recorder, 1989–93; Liaison Judge to Dorset Justices, 1994–2006. Member: Parole Bd for England and Wales, 2007–16; Mental Health Review Tribunal, 2008–12. Pres., Dorset Br., Magistrates' Assoc., 1998–2006. DL Dorset, 2007. *Recreations:* golf, travel, reading, walking, cooking. *Club:* Ferndown Golf (Capt., 2012).

**BEASLEY, Ann, (Ann Beasley Manders),** CBE 2010; Director General for Finance Assurance and Commercial Group, Ministry of Justice, 2013–16; *b* 13 Sept. 1958; *d* of late Albert Beasley and of Joyce Shirley Beasley (*née* Hodgson); marr. diss.; two *s. Educ:* Manchester Univ. (BSc Maths, MSc Stats); Kingston Univ. (MBA). CPFA 2008. Asst Statistician, HM Customs & Excise, 1980–82; Sen. Asst Statistician and Statistician, CAA, 1982–88; joined Metropolitan Police Service, 1988; Hd, Performance Inf., 1988–92; Hd, Equal Opportunities, 1992–94; Area Business Manager, 1994–2000; Hd, Business Develt and Support, then Dir, Business Change, 2000–02; Hd, Planning Gp, HM Prison Service, 2002–03; Dir of Finance, HM Prison Service, later Dir of Finance and Perf., Nat. Offender Mgt Service, 2003–10; Dir Gen. for Finance, later Finance and Corporate Services, MoJ, 2010–13. Ind. Mem., Audit Cttee, ACAS, 2017–. Vice Chair, St George's Univ. Hosps Foundn Trust, 2017– (non-exec. Dir, 2018–); Chair, SW London and St George's Mental Health Trust, 2018–. Trustee, Alzheimer's Soc., 2009–16 (Ind. Mem., Audit Cttee, 2006–09; Vice Chair, 2012–14; Chair, 2014–16). *Recreations:* theatre, original art, DIY, cats, gardening, chocolate.

**BEASLEY, Dame Christine (Joan),** DBE 2008 (CBE 2002); Chief Nursing Officer, Department of Health, 2004–12; *b* 13 June 1944; *d* of Clifford and Muriel de'Ath; *m* 1st, 1967, John Wills; three *s;* 2nd, 1989, Jack Beasley. *Educ:* Royal London Hosp. (SRN); W London Inst. (Registered Dist Nurse; DMS; DipN). Chief Nurse, Riverside Hosps, 1989–94; Regl Dir of Nursing, N Thames and London, 1994–2002; Partnership Develt Dir, Modernisation Agency, 2002–04. Non-exec. Dir and Vice Chair, NHS Trust Develt Authy, 2012–16. Fellow, Queen's Nursing Inst., 2004. Trustee, Marie Curie Cancer Care, 2000–11. Pro-Chancellor, Univ. of W London (formerly Thames Valley Univ.), 2006–12 (Gov., 2000–06); Chairman: Council, Buckinghamshire New Univ., 2012–16; Local Educn and Trng Bd of N and E London, 2012–. Chm. Trustees, Florence Nightingale Mus., 2016–. *Recreations:* theatre, entertaining, travel. *Address:* 80 Mayfield Avenue, Ealing, W13 9UX. *T:* (020) 7210 5598.

**BEASLEY, Rt Rev. Noel Michael Roy;** *see* Hertford, Bishop Suffragan of.

**BEASLEY-MURRAY, Rev. Dr Paul;** ministry consultant; Senior Minister, Central Baptist (formerly Baptist) Church, Victoria Road South, Chelmsford, 1993–2014; *b* 14 March 1944; *s* of late Rev. Dr George R. Beasley-Murray; *m* 1967, Caroline (*née* Griffiths); three *s* one *d. Educ:* Trinity School of John Whitgift; Jesus Coll., Cambridge (MA); Northern Baptist Coll. and Manchester Univ. (PhD); Baptist Theol Seminary, Rüschlikon and Zürich Univ. Baptist Missionary Soc., Zaire (Professor at National Univ., Theol Faculty), 1970–72; Pastor of Altrincham Baptist Church, Cheshire, 1973–86; Principal, Spurgeon's Coll., 1986–92. Chairman: Ministry Today (formerly Richard Baxter Inst. for Ministry), 1994–2018; Coll. of Baptist Ministers, 2013–. Patron: J's Hospice, Essex, 2007–; Soc. of Mary and Martha, Sheldon, Exeter, 2008–. Editor, Ministry Today, 1994–2018 Writer of weekly blog, Church Matters, 2011–. Chair, Cambridge Soc. of Essex, 2019–. *Publications:* (with A. Wilkinson) Turning the Tide, 1981; Pastors Under Pressure, 1989 Dynamic Leadership, 1990; (ed) Mission to the World, 1991; Faith and Festivity, 1991 Radical Believers, 1992; (ed) Anyone for Ordination?, 1993; A Call to Excellence, 1995

Radical Disciples, 1996; Happy Every After?: a guide to the marriage adventure, 1996; Radical Leaders, 1997; Power for God's Sake, 1998; The Message of the Resurrection, 2000; Fearless for Truth, 2002; Building for the Future, 2003; A Loved One Dies, 2005; Joy to the World, 2005; Transform Your Church, 2005; Baptism, Belonging and Breaking Bread, 2010; A Retreat Lectionary, 2012; Living Out the Call: rising to the challenges of ministry today, 4 vols, 2015; (with T. Calkin) The Passionate Leader, 2015; (with T. Calkin) The Visionary Leader, 2016; (with T. Calkin) The Leader with Character, 2018; Retirement Matters for Ministers, 2018; This is My Story: a story of life, faith and ministry, 2018; (with T. Calkin) The Gifted Leader, 2019. *Recreations:* music, parties, cooking, entertaining my eight grandchildren. *Address:* The Old Manse, 3 Roxwell Road, Chelmsford, Essex CM1 2LY. *T:* (01245) 352996. *E:* paulbeasleymurray@gmail.com. *W:* paulbeasleymurray.com. *Club:* Chelmsford Rivermead Rotary (Pres., 2016–17; Paul Harris Fellow, 2018).

**BEASTALL, John Sale,** CB 1995; Head of Local Government Group, HM Treasury, 1993–95; *b* 2 July 1941; *s* of Howard and Marjorie Betty Beastall (*née* Sale). *Educ:* St Paul's School; Balliol College, Oxford (BA 1963). Asst Principal, HM Treasury, 1963–67 (Asst Private Sec. to Chancellor of the Exchequer, 1966–67); Principal: HM Treasury, 1967–68 and 1971–75 (Private Sec. to Paymaster General, 1974–75); CSD, 1968–71; Assistant Secretary: HM Treasury, 1975–79 and 1981–85; CSD, 1979–81; DES, 1985–87; Treasury Officer of Accounts, 1987–93. Receiver, Met. Police Dist, 1995; Develt Dir, St Paul's Sch., 1996–2000. Chairman: Outward Housing, 2002–07; LAMB Health Care Foundn, 2004–10; Feltham Community Chaplaincy Trust, 2008–17. Chm., Standards Cttee, Ealing BC, 2010–. Chm. Govs, Green Sch., Isleworth, 2012–. *Club:* Oxford and Cambridge.

**BEATH, Prof. John Arnott,** OBE 2015; FRSE; FAcSS; Professor, University of St Andrews, 1991–2009, now Emeritus; Vice-President, Royal Economic Society, since 2016 (Secretary General, 2008–15); *b* Thurso, Caithness, 15 June 1944; *s* of James Beath and Marion McKendrick Spence; *m* 1980, Dr Monika Juliana Anna Schröder. *Educ:* Hillhead High Sch., Glasgow; Queen's Coll., Dundee, Univ. of St Andrews (MA 1966); Wye Coll., Univ. of London (MPhil 1968); Univ. of Pennsylvania (AM 1971); St John's Coll., Cambridge (MA 1975). Thouron Scholar, Univ. of Pennsylvania, 1968–71; Res. Officer, Univ. of Cambridge, 1972–79; Lectr, then Sen. Lectr, Univ. of Bristol, 1979–91. Chm., Econ. Res. Inst. of NI, 2003–09; Member: Doctors and Dentists Pay Rev. Body, 2003–09; Prison Service Pay Rev. Body, 2010–16; Competition Appeal Tribunal, 2011–19. Mem. Council, ESRC, 2009–14. FRSE 2007; FRSA 2003; FAcSS 2016. *Publications:* The Economic Theory of Product Differentiation, 1991; articles in learned jls in econs. *Recreations:* golf, gardening, music, travel, walking. *Address:* School of Economics and Finance, University of St Andrews, St Andrews, Fife KY16 9AR. *T:* (01334) 462443, *Fax:* (01334) 462444.

**BEATON, Ailsa Elizabeth,** OBE 2010; JP; non-executive Director: Information Commissioner's Office, since 2013; Airport Coordination Ltd, since 2018; *b* Kettering, 18 Sept. 1957; *d* of Daniel Beaton and Wendy Beaton; partner, David Powell; one *s* one *d*. *Educ:* Northampton High Sch.; Chelsea Coll., Univ. of London (BSc Hons Chem.). CEng 1999. Business Develt Dir, General Electric (USA), 1980–85; Sen. Partner, PA Consulting Gp, 1985–97; Chief Information Officer: ICL plc, 1997–99; Metropolitan Police Service, 2000–13. Ind. non-exec. Dir, Bacs Payment Schemes Ltd, 2013–18. Trustee and Gov., Legal Educn Foundn, 2013–. JP SW London, 2016. Mem., Burmese Cat Club. *Recreations:* photography, house renovation, gardening. *T:* 07872 424572. *E:* ailsa@clapham.com.

**BEATON, James Wallace,** GC 1974; CVO 1992 (LVO 1987); security manager, now retired; Chief Superintendent, Metropolitan Police, 1985–92; *b* St Fergus, Aberdeenshire, 16 Feb. 1943; *s* of J. A. Beaton and B. McDonald; *m* 1965, Anne C. Ballantyne (*d* 2011); two *d*. *Educ:* Peterhead Acad., Aberdeenshire. Joined Metropolitan Police, 1962: Notting Hill, 1962–66; Sergeant, Harrow Road, 1966–71; Station Sergeant, Wembley, 1971–73; Royalty Protection Officer, 'A' Division, 1973; Police Officer to The Princess Anne, 1973–79; Police Inspector, 1974; Chief Inspector, 1979; Superintendent, 1983; Queen's Police Officer, 1983–92. JP E Yorks, 2004. Director's Honor Award, US Secret Service, 1974. *Recreations:* reading, keeping fit, golf, hill walking. *Address:* 6 Finch Park, Beverley, East Yorkshire HU17 7DW.

**BEATON, Prof. Roderick Macleod,** PhD; FBA 2013; Koraes Professor of Modern Greek and Byzantine History, Language and Literature, 1988–2018, now Emeritus, and Director, Centre for Hellenic Studies, 2012–18, King's College London; *b* Edinburgh, 29 Sept. 1951; *s* of late Duncan Beaton and Janet Beaton (*née* Purves); *m* 1978, Fran Downs; two *s*. *Educ:* George Watson's Coll., Edinburgh; Peterhouse, Cambridge (BA Hons English Lit. 1973; PhD Modern Greek 1977). Ouranis Foundn Fellow in Modern Greek, Univ. of Birmingham, 1977–80; King's College London: Lectr in Modern Greek Lang. and Lit., 1981–88; Hd, Dept of Byzantine and Modern Greek Studies, 1988–94, 1995–98. Mem. Council, British Sch. at Athens, 2011–. FKC 2018. *Publications:* Ariadne's Children (fiction), 1995; The Medieval Greek Romance, 1996; Introduction to Modern Greek Literature, 1999; George Seferis: waiting for the angel, 2003; Byron's War: romantic rebellion, Greek revolution, 2013; (ed and trans.) George Sefaris: novel and other poems, 2016; Greece: biography of a modern nation, 2019. *Recreations:* writing, travel, opera, theatre. *Address:* Department of Classics, King's College London, Strand, WC2R 2LS. *T:* (020) 7848 2517. *E:* rod.beaton@kcl.ac.uk. *Club:* Oxford and Cambridge.

**BEATSON, Rt Hon. Sir Jack,** Kt 2003; PC 2013; FBA 2001; a Lord Justice of Appeal, 2013–18; a Judge of the Court of Appeal, Cayman Islands, since 2018; *b* 3 Nov. 1948; *s* of late John James Beatson and Miriam Beatson (*née* White); *m* 1973, Charlotte, *y d* of Lt-Col J. A. Christie-Miller; one *d* (one *s* decd). *Educ:* Whittingehame Coll., Brighton; Brasenose Coll., Oxford (BCL, MA; DCL 2000; Hon. Fellow 2010); LLD Cantab 2001. Called to the Bar, Inner Temple, 1972, Hon. Bencher, 1993; a Law Comr, 1989–94; a Recorder, 1994–2003; QC 1998; a Dep. High Court Judge, 2000–03; a Judge of the High Court of Justice, QBD, 2003–13; Queen's Bench Liaison Judge for Midlands and Wales Circuits, 2009–12. Lectr in Law, Univ. of Bristol, 1972–73; Fellow and Tutor in Law, Merton Coll., Oxford, 1973–94 (Hon. Fellow, 1995); University of Cambridge: Rouse Ball Prof. of English Law, 1993–2003; Fellow, St John's Coll., 1994–2003 (Hon. Fellow, 2005); Dir, Centre for Public Law, 1997–2001; Chm., Faculty of Law, 2001–03. Visiting Professor: Osgoode Hall Law Sch., Toronto, 1979; Univ. of Virginia Law Sch., 1980, 1983, 2016; Univ. of Oxford, 2018–; Vis. Sen. Teaching Fellow, Nat. Univ. of Singapore, 1987; Vis. Fellow, Univ. of WA, 1988; Dist. Vis. Prof., Univ. of Toronto, 2000; Professorial Fellow, Melbourne Law Sch., Univ. of Melbourne, 2018–. Mem., Competition (formerly Monopolies and Mergers) Commn, 1995–2000. Pres., British Acad. Forensic Scis, 2007–09. *Publications:* (ed jtly) Chitty on Contract, 25th edn 1982 to 28th edn 1999; (with M. H. Matthews) Administrative Law: Cases and Materials, 1983, 2nd edn 1989; The Use and Abuse of Unjust Enrichment, 1991; (ed jtly) Good Faith and Fault in Contract Law, 1995; (ed jtly) European Public Law, 1998; Anson's Law of Contract, 27th edn 1998 to 30th edn (jtly) 2016; (jtly) Human Rights: the 1998 Act and the European Convention, 2000; (ed with R. Zimmermann) Jurists Uprooted: German-speaking émigré lawyers in twentieth century Britain, 2004; (jtly) Human Rights: judicial protection in the UK, 2008; articles on administrative law, contract, and restitution in legal jls. *Recreations:* trying to relax, amateur gardening.

**BEATSON, Mark;** Senior Labour Market Analyst, Chartered Institute of Personnel and Development, since 2017; *b* Elsecar, S Yorks, 27 Sept. 1963; *s* of Eric and Brenda Beatson. *Educ:* Swinton Comprehensive Sch.; Univ. of York (BA Hons Econs and Econometrics). Asst Economist, 1985–89, Econ. Advr, 1989–93, Dept of Employment; Econ. Advr, HM Treasury, 1993–95; Chief Economist, HSE, 1995–98; Hd, Employment Mkt Analysis and Res., 1998–2003, Sci. and Innovation Analysis, 2003–08, DTI; Chief Economist, DIUS, 2008–09; Dir of Sci. and Innovation Analysis, BIS, 2009–10; Dir, Econs, FTI Consulting, 2010–12; Chief Economist, CIPD, 2012–16. Hon. Vis. Prof., London Guildhall Faculty of Business and Law, London Metropolitan Univ., 2014–17. FRSA. *Recreations:* Arsenal FC, Yorkshire cricket, Spain, music, cinema. *Address:* Chartered Institute of Personnel and Development, 151 The Broadway, SW19 1JQ. *T:* (020) 8612 6364. *E:* mark.beatson@hotmail.com.

**BEATTIE, Alan Henry;** European Leader Writer, Financial Times, since 2016; *b* Chester, 24 April 1971; *s* of David and Jane Beattie; *m* 2012, Juliane von Reppert-Bismarck; one *d*. *Educ:* Christleton Co. High Sch., Chester; Balliol Coll., Oxford (BA Hons Modern Hist. 1993); Jesus Coll., Cambridge (MPhil Econs 1996). Economist, Bank of England, 1996–98; Financial Times: Currency Corresp., 1998–99; Econs Corresp., 1999–2002; Internat. Econs Corresp., 2002–04; Econs Leader Writer, 2004; World Trade Ed., 2004–10; Internat. Econ. Ed., 2010–14; Econs Leader Writer, 2014–16. Associate Fellow, Chatham House. *Publications:* False Economy, 2009; Who's in Charge Here?, 2012. *Recreations:* fatherhood, Twitter. *Address:* Financial Times, 1 Boulevard Charlemagne, Box 12, 1041 Brussels, Belgium. *E:* alan.beattie@ft.com.

**BEATTIE, Andrew Watt;** Chief Parliamentary Counsel, Scottish Government, since 2012; *b* Aberdeen, 16 Nov. 1972; *s* of Andrew Watt Beattie and Janet Beattie; *m* 1999, Claire Louise Devine; two *s* one *d*. *Educ:* Elgin Acad.; Univ. of Edinburgh (LLB Hons 1994; DipLP 1995). Solicitor, Shepherd & Wedderburn, WS, 1995–99; Depute Scottish Parly Counsel, 1999–2008; Scottish Parly Counsel, 2008–12. *Recreations:* canoeing, camping, hillock-walking. *Address:* 4 Clouds, Duns, Berwickshire TD11 3BB. *T:* (01361) 883745. *E:* andy.beattie@scotland.gsi.gov.uk.

**BEATTIE, Basil,** RA 2006; artist; *b* W Hartlepool, 9 Jan. 1935. *Educ:* W Hartlepool Coll. of Art; Royal Acad. Schs. Lectr, Goldsmiths' Coll., London, until 1998. Solo exhibitions include: Greenwich Th. Gall., 1968; Mayfair Gall., 1971; Goldsmiths' Gall., 1982; Curwen Gall., 1987, 1990; Todd Gall., 1993, 1995, 1996, 1998; Ikon Gall., Birmingham, 1994; Newton Gall., Johannesburg, 1994; Path Galerie, Aalst, Belgium, 1996; Galerie Renate Bender, Munich, 1997; Sadler's Wells Th., 2002; Tate Britain, 2007; Two Rooms Gall., Auckland, NZ, 2008; James Hyman Fine Art, London, 2011; Middlesbrough Inst. of Modern Art, 2016; Royal Acad., 2018; group exhibitions include: Whitechapel Art Gall., 1958–61; Walker Art Gall., Liverpool, 1965, 1987, 1989, 1991, 1997; Royal Acad. bicentenary exhibn, 1968; Hayward Gall., 1970, 1974, 1980, 1982, 1996; Jerwood Gall., 1998, 2001, 2009; Royal Acad. summer exhibn, 2011, 2012, 2013; *work in collections* including: Arts Council; Birmingham City Mus. and Art Gall.; Contemporary Art Soc.; Saatchi; Tate Gall.; Whitworth Art Gall., Manchester. Maj. Arts Council Award, 1976; Athena Award, 1986; Nordstern Print Prize, Royal Acad., 1991.

**BEATTIE, Colin;** Member (SNP) Midlothian North and Musselburgh, Scottish Parliament, since 2011; *b* Forfar, 17 Oct. 1951; *s* of James Watt Beattie and Catherine Beattie; *m* 1987, Lisa Hallinan. *Educ:* Forfar Acad.; MCIBS 1972. Various internat. banking posts, 1972–92; Regl Hd, Custody, Standard Chartered Bank, 1992–95; Vice-Pres., Citigroup, 1995–2006. Mem. (SNP), Midlothian Council, 2007–12. Nat. Treas., SNP, 2003–. Dir/Trustee, Nat. Mining Mus. of Scotland, 2007–. *Recreations:* history, current affairs, gardening (badly), classical music. *Address:* Eskbank House, Glenesk Crescent, Dalkeith, Midlothian EH22 3BL. *T:* (0131) 660 3242. *E:* colin.beattie1@btinternet.com.

**BEATTIE, David,** CMG 1989; HM Diplomatic Service, retired; Personnel Assessor, Foreign and Commonwealth Office, 1998–2008; *b* 5 March 1938; *s* of late George William David Beattie and Norna Alice (*née* Nicolson); *m* 1966, Ulla Marita Alha, *d* of late Allan Alha and Brita-Maja (*née* Tuominen), Helsinki, Finland; two *d*. *Educ:* Merchant Taylors' Sch., Crosby; Lincoln Coll., Oxford (BA 1964, MA 1967). National Service, Royal Navy, 1957–59; Sub-Lieut RNR, 1959; Lieut RNR 1962–67. Entered HM Foreign (now Diplomatic) Service, 1963; FO, 1963–64; Moscow, 1964–66; FO, 1966–70; Nicosia, 1970–74; FCO, 1974–78; Counsellor, later Dep. Head, UK Delegn to Negotiations on Mutual Reduction of Forces and Armaments and Associated Measures in Central Europe, Vienna, 1978–82; Counsellor (Commercial), Moscow, 1982–85; Head of Energy, Science and Space Dept, FCO, 1985–87; Min. and Dep. UK Perm. Rep. to NATO, Brussels, 1987–92; Ambassador to Swiss Confedn, and concurrently (non-resident) to Principality of Liechtenstein, 1992–97. Principal Sec., Royal Stuart Soc., 1997–2002; Vice-Pres., Anglo-Swiss Soc., 2000–06. Hon. Life Mem., British-Swiss Chamber of Commerce, 2000. Trustee, Chiswick House Friends, 1998–2012. Freeman, City of London, 1989; Mem. Ct Assts, Masons' Co., 2000– (Master, 2006–07). Commander's Cross, Order of Merit (Liechtenstein), 2007. *Publications:* Liechtenstein: a modern history, 2004 (trans. German, 2005), 2nd edn 2012 (trans. German, 2015); Benjamin Holland: boatswain and bigamist, 2015. *Recreations:* bridge, walking, history. *Address:* 19 Riverside Place, Colchester, Essex CO1 2ZG. *Club:* Travellers.

**BEATTIE, Dame Heather;** *see* Steel, Dame A. H.

**BEATTIE, Maureen Jane;** actor; President, Equity, since 2018; *b* Bundoran, Co. Donegal, 14 Aug. 1953; *d* of John Gerard Beattie and Catherine Louise McGinley. *Educ:* Notre Dame Primary Sch., Glasgow; Notre Dame High Sch., Glasgow; Royal Scottish Acad. of Music and Dramatic Art (Dip. Dramatic Art 1974; James Bridie Gold Medal 1974). Theatre includes: Medea, Edinburgh Fringe Fest., 2000 (Herald Angel Award, 2000); Jennifer Tremblay Trilogy, Edinburgh Fringe Fest., 2015 (Herald Archangel Lasting Contribution Award, Stage Award for Acting Excellence, 2015); Yerma, Young Vic, transf. NY, 2018. Can You Hear Me? (Pye Radio Award for Best Performance by an Actress, 1981). Outstanding Woman of Scotland Award, Saltire Soc., 2018.

**BEATTIE, Hon. Peter (Douglas),** AC 2012; Queensland Government Trade and Investment Commissioner, The Americas, 2008–10; Chair, Australian Rugby League Commission, since 2018; *b* 18 Nov. 1952; *s* of Arthur and Edna Beattie; *m* 1975, Heather Scott-Halliday; twin *s* one *d*. *Educ:* Atherton High Sch.; Univ. of Queensland (BA, LLB); Queensland Univ. of Technol. (MA). Admitted Solicitor, Supreme Court of Qld, 1978. MLA (ALP) Brisbane Central, 1989–2007; Minister for Health, 1995–96; Leader, State Opposition, 1996–98; Premier of Qld, 1998–2007; Minister for Trade, 2001–07. Adjunct Prof. in Biosci. and Nanotechnol., Aust. Inst. for Bioenrgrg and Nanotechnol. and Inst. for Molecular Biosci., Univ. of Qld, 2010–; pt-time Lecturer, Clemson Univ., S Carolina, 2010–. Chm., Gold Coast 2018 Commonwealth Games Corp., 2016–18; Member, Board: Med. Res. Commercialisation Fund, 2010–; Univ. of Queensland in America Inc.,

2011–13. Chm., Nat. Assoc. of Cinema Operators, 2011–13. Mem., Amer. Bd, Australian American Dialogue, 2010–13. Columnist, The Australian, 2010–; national commentator: Sky News, 2015– (presenter, Beattie and Newman); Sunrise, Channel 7. Hon. DSc Queensland, 2003; DUniv: Griffith, 2004; Qld Univ. of Technol., 2007; Bond, 2007; Hon. DLaws S Carolina, 2007. *Publications:* In the Arena, 1990; The Year of the Dangerous Ones, 1994; Making a Difference: life, leadership and politics, 2006; Where to from here, Australia?, 2016; articles in newspapers. *Recreations:* walking, biotechnology history, reading, swimming, alternative energies, writing, Rugby League, Commonwealth Games.

**BEATTIE, Trevor Stephen;** Creative Director, Beattie McGuinness Bungay, since 2005; *b* 24 Dec. 1958; *s* of late John Vincent Beattie and Ada Alice Beattie. *Educ:* Wolverhampton Poly. (BA Hons). Copywriter, advertising: ABM 1981–83; BMP, 1987–90; joined TBWA/ HKR, 1990; Creative Dir, 1993–2005, Chm., 2001–05, TBWA/London (Advertising). Notable ad campaigns: Labour Party, French Connection (fcuk), Sony PlayStation, Wonderbra. Hon. DA: Wolverhampton, 2000; Birmingham, 2011. *Recreations:* flying, gardening, fighting the forces of conservatism, flying to (and from!) space with Virgin Galactic. *Address:* (office) 2nd Floor, The Crane Building, 22 Lavington Street, SE1 0NZ. *T:* (020) 7632 0400.

**BEATTY,** 3rd Earl *cr* 1919; **David Beatty;** Viscount Borodale of Wexford, Baron Beatty of the North Sea and of Brooksby, 1919; *b* 21 Nov. 1946; *s* of 2nd Earl Beatty, DSC, and of Dorothy Rita, *d* of late M. J. Furey, New Orleans, USA; *S* father, 1972; *m* 1971, Anne (marr. diss. 1983), *d* of A. Please, Wokingham; two *s*; *m* 1984, Anoma Corinne Wijewardene (marr. diss. 2000). *Educ:* Eton. *Heir: s* Viscount Borodale, *qv.*

**BEATTY, Hon. (Henry) Perrin,** OC 2018; PC (Can) 1979; President and Chief Executive Officer, Canadian Chamber of Commerce, since 2007; *b* 1 June 1950; *m* 1974, Julia Kenny; two *s. Educ:* Upper Canada College; Univ. of Western Ontario (BA 1971). MP (Progressive C) Wellington–Grey–Dufferin–Simcoe, Canada, 1972–93; Minister of State for Treasury Bd, 1979; Minister of Nat. Revenue and for Canada Post Corp., 1984; Solicitor General, 1985; Minister of Nat. Defence, 1986–89; Minister of Nat. Health and Welfare, 1989–91; Minister of Communications, 1991–93; Minister for External Affairs, 1993; Pres. and CEO, Canadian Broadcasting Corp., 1995–99; Pres. and CEO, Canadian Manufacturers and Exporters, 1999–2007. Chancellor, Univ. of Ontario Inst. of Technol., 2008–16. Hon. Vis. Prof., Univ. of Western Ontario, 1994–95. *Address:* Canadian Chamber of Commerce, 1700–275 Slater Street, Ottawa, ON K1P 5H9, Canada.

**BEAUCHAMP, Sir Christopher Radstock Proctor-,** 9th Bt *cr* 1744; solicitor with Gilbert Stephens, Exeter, retired; *b* 30 Jan. 1935; *s* of Rev. Sir Ivor Cuthbert Proctor-Beauchamp, 8th Bt, and Caroline Muriel (*d* 1987), *d* of late Frank Densham; *S* father, 1971; *m* 1965, Rosalind Emily Margot (*d* 2014), 3rd *d* of G. P. Wainwright, St Leonards-on-Sea; two *s* one *d. Educ:* Rugby; Trinity College, Cambridge (MA). *Heir: s* Charles Barclay Proctor-Beauchamp [*b* 7 July 1969; *m* 1996, Harriet, *e d* of Anthony Meacock; one *s* twin *d*]. *Address:* The Coach House, 4 Balfour Mews, Sidmouth, Devon EX10 8XL.

**BEAUCHAMP, Brig. Vernon John;** management consultant, 2011–12; International Internal Auditor, World Society for the Protection of Animals, 2008–12; *b* 19 Sept. 1943; *s* of late Herbert George Beauchamp and Vera Helena (*née* Daly); *m* 1971, Annemarie, *d* of Evert Teunis van den Born; two *s. Educ:* Portsmouth Grammar Sch.; RMA Sandhurst. Commnd Royal Warwickshire Fusiliers, 1963; transferred 2nd KEO Gurkha Rifles, 1969; served Germany, Borneo, Hong Kong, Brunei, Malaysia and Nepal; Army Staff Coll., 1976; Dep. Comdr, British Gurkhas, Nepal, 1979; Bde Major, 20 Armoured Bde, 1977–79; NDC, 1981; Comdt, 2 Bn 2nd KEO Gurkha Rifles, 1981–84; sen. staff appts, MoD and HQ BAOR, 1984–87; Comdr, 48 Gurkha Inf. Bde, 1987–89; RCDS, 1990; Comdt, Sch. of Infantry, 1991–93. Chief Executive: Royal Hosp. for Neuro-disability, 1993–2000; Nat. Autistic Soc., 2000–08. *Recreations:* golf, walking, gardening. *Address:* 20 Castle Street, Farnham, Surrey GU9 7JA.

**BEAUCLERK,** family name of **Duke of St Albans.**

**BEAUFORT,** 12th Duke of, *cr* 1682; **Henry John Fitzroy Somerset;** *b* 22 May 1952; *s* of 11th Duke of Beaufort and Lady Caroline Jane Thynne, *d* of 6th Marquess of Bath; *S* father, 2017; *m* 1st, 1987, Tracy Louise (marr. diss. 2018), *yr d* of Hon. Peter Ward and Hon. Mrs Claire Ward; two *s* one *d*; 2nd, 2018, Georgia, *d* of Tristram and Virginia Powell. *Educ:* Eton; Cirencester Agricultural College. *Recreations:* golf, shooting, rock music, selective television watching. *Heir: s* Marquess of Worcester, *qv. Club:* Turf.

**BEAUFOY, Simon Roger Barton;** screenwriter and director; *b* Keighley, 26 Dec. 1966; *s* of Roger and Madeleine Beaufoy; *m* Jane Garwood; one *s* one *d. Educ:* Malsis Prep. Sch., Yorks; Ermysted's Grammar Sch., Skipton; Sedbergh Sch.; St Peter's Coll., Oxford; Bournemouth & Poole Coll. of Art and Design (film course 1992). *Television:* (dir) Shattered Dream, 1993; (dir and writer) Physics for Fish, 1994–95; (writer) Burn Up, 2008; (writer) Trust, 2018; *films:* (co-writer and dir) Yellow, 1996; writer: The Full Monty, 1997 (adapted for stage, 2013); Among Giants, 1998; (and co-dir) The Darkest Light, 1999; This is not a Love Song, 2003; Yasmin, 2004; Miss Pettigrew Lives for a Day, 2008; Slumdog Millionaire (Academy, Golden Globe and BAFTA Awards for Best Adapted Screenplay), 2009; 127 Hours, 2010; Salmon Fishing in the Yemen, 2012; The Hunger Games: Catching Fire, 2013; Everest, 2015; Battle of the Sexes, 2017. *Recreations:* barge-driving, ski-touring, climbing, river swimming. *Address:* c/o Charlotte Knight, Knight Hall Agency, Lower Ground Floor, 7 Mallow Street, EC1Y 8RQ. *T:* (020) 3397 2901. *E:* office@knighthallagency.com.

**BEAUMONT,** family name of **Viscount Allendale.**

**BEAUMONT, Sir Bill;** *see* Beaumont, Sir W. B.

**BEAUMONT, Christopher Michael;** Seigneur of Sark, since 2016; *b* Reigate, Surrey, 4 Feb. 1957; *s* of (John) Michael Beaumont, OBE and Diana Mary La Trobe-Bateman; *m* 1980, Sarah Vivienne Rees; one *s* one *d. Educ:* Clifton Coll.; Royal Mil. Coll. of Sci. (BSc Hons). Commnd RE, 1978; officer, 1978–2002, incl. Comd Depot Regt RE, 1998–99 and SO, Bowman Team, Defence Procurement Agency, 1999–2002. Prog. Manager, General Dynamics, 2002–08; Contract Prog. Manager, 2008–12; Engrg Manager, Rolls-Royce Control Systems, 2012–16. *Recreations:* making music (piano and choral), theatre, art and architecture, nature, environment and sustainability, history, archaeology, despotism. *Heir: s* Hugh John Barber Rees-Beaumont, *b* 17 Dec. 1996. *Address:* La Seigneurie, Sark, Channel Islands GY10 1SF. *T:* (01481) 832017. *E:* seigneur@gov.sark.gg. *Club:* Royal Channel Island Yacht.

**BEAUMONT, David Colin Baskcomb;** HM Diplomatic Service, retired; High Commissioner, Botswana, 1995–98; *b* 16 Aug. 1942; *s* of Colin Baskcomb Beaumont and Denise Heather Smith; *m* 1965, Barbara Enid Morris; two *s* one *d. Educ:* St Benedict's Sch., Ealing. Joined CRO, 1961; Private Sec. to Special Rep. in Africa, Nairobi, 1965; Third Sec., Bahrain, 1967; Second Sec., FCO, 1970; Second Sec. (Commercial), Accra, 1974; First Sec., FCO, 1977; First Sec. (Develt), Kathmandu, 1981; First Sec. and Dep. Head of Mission, Addis Ababa, 1982; First Sec., later Counsellor, FCO, 1986; Head of Protocol Dept, 1989–94, and First Asst Marshal of the Diplomatic Corps, 1993–94, FCO. Dir, Guildford Crossroads Care, 1999–2002. *Recreations:* walking, cooking, playing bridge. *Address:* 42 Harvey Road, Guildford, Surrey GU1 3SE. *T:* (01483) 539577. *Clubs:* MCC; Tudor Bridge.

**BEAUMONT, Rt Rev. Gerald Edward;** Vicar, Parish of St John's, Camberwell, Diocese of Melbourne, 2004–10; *b* 18 Feb. 1940; *s* of John Beaumont and Marjorie Beaumont; *m* 1967, Elsa Lynette Sampson; two *d. Educ:* Australian Coll. of Theology (LTh); Royal Melbourne Inst. of Technology (BA Fine Arts). Ordained deacon 1968, priest 1969, Melbourne; Curate: St Andrew's, Brighton, Vic., 1968–70; Geelong W, 1970–71; Vicar of Mooroolbark, 1971–74; Priest/Pilot, Carpentaria Aerial Mission, Dio. Carpentaria, Qld, 1974–75; Vicar, Armadale-Hawksburn, Vic., 1975–81; Priest-in-Charge, Kooyong, Vic., 1982–86; Vicar, E Melbourne, 1986–92; Canon Pastor, St George's Cathedral, Perth, WA, 1992–94; Rector, Ascension, Alice Springs, NT, and Hon. Canon, Christ Church Cathedral, Darwin, 1995–98; an Asst Bishop, Dio. of Perth, WA (Bp of Goldfields-Country Region), 1998–2004. *Recreations:* painting (exhibiting professional artist), motorcycling. *Club:* Ulysses (Melbourne).

**BEAUMONT, John Richard;** President, Beaumont Partners SL (formerly Beaumont Partners sprl), since 2007; *b* 24 June 1957; *s* of Jim Beaumont and Betty Marie (*née* Jarratt); *m* 2000, Annie Margaret (*née* Jupp); two *d* by a previous marriage. *Educ:* Univ. of Durham (BA Geog.). Res. Asst, Univ. of Leeds, 1978–80; Lectr, Univ. of Keele, 1980–83; Consultant, Coopers & Lybrand (London and NY), 1983–85; Jt Man. Dir, Pinpoint Analysis Ltd, London, 1985–87; ICL Prof. of Applied Management Information Systems and Dir, European Centre for Inf. Resource Management, Univ. of Stirling, 1987–90; Prof. and Hd of Sch. of Management, Bath Univ., 1990–92. Man. Dir, Stratatech, 1986–93; Energis Communications Ltd: Strategy Planning Manager, 1993–94; Head of Corporate Strategy and Affairs, 1994–95; Dir of Marketing, 1995–96; Dir of Strategy and Business Develt, 1996–99; Man. Dir, Planet Online Ltd, subseq. Energis$^2$, 1998–2002; Dir, Energis plc, 2001–02; CEO, UK eUniversities Worldwide Ltd, 2002–04; Partner, Beaumont and Beaumont Ltd, 2004–05; CEO, QA plc, 2005–06; Man. Dir and Hd of UK Public Services, BearingPoint Ltd, 2006–07. Chairman: Ision AG, 2001–02; LifeCash Ltd, 2011–14; LineFactory, 2015–; Mindscape Group Ltd, 2018–; Dep. Chm. Supervisory Bd, Business Online AG, 1999–2000; Dir, Metro Hldgs Ltd, 1998–2002; non-executive Director: WorldPay Ltd, 1999–2002; European Telecommunications and Technology Ltd, 1999–2003; Novia Financial plc, 2007– (Dep. Chm.); Chm., Novia Global Ltd, 2014–. Non-executive Director: Office of Nat. Statistics, 1996–99; UK Health Educn Partnership, 2003–04; Real Club de Golf Las Brisas, 2012–16 (Vice-Pres., 2016–17; Pres., 2017–18); Emergent Capital Partners, 2014–. Hon. Professor: QUB, 1990–93; City Univ., 1994–98. Mem. Council, ESRC, 1989–93. *Publications:* (with P. Keys) Future Cities, 1982; (with A. Gatrell) An Introduction to Q-Analysis, 1982; (with S. Williams) Projects in Geography, 1983; An Introduction to Market Analysis, 1991; (with E. Sutherland) Information Resources Management, 1992; (jtly) Managing our Environment, 1993. *Recreations:* family, good wine and food, travel, golf, watching Rugby (League and Union), reading fiction, author of two novels. *Address:* Las Alamandas, Avenida del Prado, Nueva Andalucia, 29660 Marbella, Spain.

**BEAUMONT, John Richard;** Regional Chairman of Employment Tribunals (North West Region), 1999–2002; *b* 22 June 1947; *s* of late Stanley and Winifred Beaumont; *m* 1986, Susan Margaret (*née* Blowers); one *s* two *d*, and one step *s. Educ:* Wolverhampton Grammar Sch.; Merton Coll., Oxford (BA 1969; MA 1973). Schoolmaster, Buckingham Coll., Harrow, 1969–71; Regl Organiser, W Midlands, 1971–73, Nat. Dir of Projects, 1973–74, Shelter; Senior Legal Officer: Alnwick DC, 1974; Thurrock BC, 1974–75; called to the Bar, Inner Temple, 1976; in practice at the Bar, Northern Circuit, 1976–94; Chm., Industrial, then Employment, Tribunals, subseq. Employment Judge, 1994–2008 (pt-time, 1992–94); Chm., Reserve Forces Appeal Tribunal, 1999–2008. Gov., Knutsford High Sch., 1999 (Vice-Chm., 2000–02; Chm., 2002–07). *Recreations:* walking, reading (especially Victorian history and literature), family picnics, non-league football (League Rep., Unibond Northern Premier League). *Address:* Carlton House, Seymour Chase, Knutsford, Cheshire WA16 9BY.

**BEAUMONT, Martin Dudley,** CVO 2017; FCA; Chairman, Chester Race Course Co. Ltd, since 2011 (Director, since 2007); *b* 6 Aug. 1949; *s* of Patrick Beaumont, DL and late Lindesay Beaumont; *m* 1976, Andrea Wilberforce; three *d. Educ:* Stowe Sch.; Magdalene Coll., Cambridge (MA Econs/Land Economy). FCA 1975. Dir, 1980–83, Partner, 1983–87, Thomson McLintock, subseq. KPMG; Gp Finance Dir, Egmont Publishing Gp, 1987–90; Chief Financial Officer, 1990–92, Chief Exec., 1992–2002, United Co-operatives; Dir, 1996–2007, Dep. Chm., 2000–07, Co-operative Bank; Gp Chief Exec., Co-operative Gp, 2002–07; Dep. Chm., Co-operative Financial Services, 2002–07; Dir, CIS, 2002–07. Chairman: Skillsmart Retail Ltd, 2007–12; Kind Consumer Ltd, 2009–16 (Dir, 2009–). Dir, PBSI Gp, 2010–12. Mem. of Adv. Bd, Kurt Salmon Associates, 2008–14. Dir, 2005–07, Dep. Chm., 2006–07, NW Business Leadership Team. Mem. Council, Duchy of Lancaster, 2007–17. High Sheriff, Cheshire, 2013–14. *Recreations:* family, fishing, shooting, tennis, reading.

**BEAUMONT, His Honour Peter John Luther,** CBE 2013; QC 1986; a Circuit Judge, 1989–2013; *b* 10 Jan. 1944; *s* of S. P. L. Beaumont, OBE, and D. V. Beaumont; *m* 1970, Ann Jarratt; one *s* one *d. Educ:* Peterhouse, Zimbabwe; Univ. of Zimbabwe (BScEcon Hons). Called to the Bar, Lincoln's Inn, 1967 (Bencher, 2001); practised South Eastern Circuit; a Recorder, 1986; Common Serjeant, City of London, 2001–04; Recorder of London, 2004–13. Member: Parole Bd, 1992–97; Criminal Cttee, Judicial Studies Bd, 2000–03; Sentencing Guidelines Council, 2004–09. Governor, Felsted Sch., 1990–2002 (Chm., 1993–98). Master, Cutlers' Co., 2019–20. *Recreations:* golf, tennis, gardening. *Address:* 111 Church Street, Orford, Suffolk IP12 2LL. *T:* (01394) 450 967. *Club:* Travellers.

**BEAUMONT, Prof. Steven Peter,** OBE 2002; PhD; CEng, FREng; FRSE; Professor of Nanoelectronics, since 1989, and Vice Principal for Research and Enterprise, 2005–14, now Emeritus Vice Principal, University of Glasgow; *b* Norwich, 20 Feb. 1952; *s* of Albert Reginald Beaumont and Joyce Margaret Beaumont (later Churchard) and step *s* of Arthur Robert Churchard; *m* 1977, Joanne Mary Beaumont; one *s* two *d. Educ:* Norwich Sch.; Corpus Christi Coll., Cambridge (BA 1974; PhD 1979). CEng 1987, MIET 1987; FREng 2007; FRSE 2000. University of Glasgow: Res. Fellow, 1978–83; Barr & Stroud Lectr, then Sen. Lectr, 1983–89; Hd, Dept of Electronics and Electrical Engrg, 1994–98; Dir, Inst. for System Level Integration, 1999–2004; Academic Lead, Scottish Innovation Centre for Sensors and Imaging Systems, 2013–. Tech. Dir, Intellemetrics Ltd, 1982–90; Director: Photonix Ltd, 2003–10; GU Hldgs Ltd, 2005–15; Kelvin Nanotechnology Ltd, 2005–; Gold Standard Simulations Ltd, 2011–16; Anacail Ltd, 2011–; Clyde Bioscis Ltd, 2012–15; Semiwise Ltd, 2013–; Sannox Therapeutics Ltd, 2013–; SAW Dx Ltd, 2013–; Cronin 3D Ltd, 2014–15; Thermoelectric Conversion Systems Ltd, 2014–. Mem., Scottish Sci. Adv. Cttee, Scottish Govt, 2005–09. Awards Convener, RSE, 2011–15. *Publications:* contrib. papers to learned jls and at major academic confs. *Recreations:* crofting, reading, listening to music. *Address:* QuantIC, University of Glasgow, Glasgow G12 8QQ.

**BEAUMONT, Sir William Blackledge, (Sir Bill),** Kt 2019; CBE 2008 (OBE 1982); DL; Rugby Union footballer, retired; sports broadcaster and writer; Chairman, Bill Beaumont Textiles Ltd, since 2011 (Managing Director, 1998–2011); *b* 9 March 1952; *s* of Ronald Walton Beaumont and Joyce Beaumont; *m* 1977, Hilary Jane Seed; three *s*. *Educ:* Ellesmere Coll., Shropshire. Joined family textile business, 1971; Dir, J. Blackledge & Son Ltd, 1981–98. First played Rugby Union for England, 1975; 34 caps (20 caps as Captain); Mem., British Lions, NZ tour, 1977; Captain, British Lions, S Africa tour, 1980; played for Lancashire Barbarians, retd 1982. Chm., British Lions, NZ tour, 2005. Television includes A Question of Sport (BBC TV), 1982–96. Mem., Internat. Rugby Bd, then World Rugby, 1999– (Chm., 2016–); Chm., RFU, 2012–16. DL Lancs, 2012. *Publications:* Thanks to Rugby, 1982; Bill Beaumont's Tackle Rugby, 1983; Bill Beaumont's Sporting Year Book, 1984; Bill Beaumont: the autobiography, 2003; (with Mark Baldwin) Beaumont's Up and Under, 2005. *Recreations:* tennis, golf, water ski-ing. *Clubs:* East India, MCC; Fylde Rugby Union Football; Royal Lytham St Anne's Golf.

**BEAVAN, Jenny,** OBE 2017; freelance costume designer, since 1976; *b* London, 3 Aug. 1950; *d* of Peter Hargrave Beavan and Molly (Panter) Beavan; partner, 1980–95, Ian Bronson Albery, *qv*; one *d*. *Educ:* Chelsea Froebel Sch.; Kensington High Sch.; Putney High Sch.; Central Sch. of Art and Design. Freelance costume designer for films, incl. Merchant Ivory Films, 1982–95, theatre, ballet, opera, TV and installations. Costume designer for *opera* incl. Carmen, ROH, 1972; *theatre* incl. Private Lives, 2001; *films* including: A Room with a View, 1986 (Academy Award for Best Costume Design (jtly), BAFTA Film Award for Best Costume Design, 1987); White Fang, 1991; The Remains of the Day, 1993; Sherlock Holmes, 2009; The King's Speech, 2011; Mad Max: Fury Road, 2015 (Academy Award for Best Achievement in Costume Design, BAFTA Film Award for Best Costume Design, 2016); A United Kingdom, 2016; Life, 2017; Patrick, 2018; Christopher Robin, 2018; The Nutcracker and the Four Realms, 2018; *television* including: Cranford, 2007–09 (Primetime Emmy for Outstanding Costumes for Miniseries, Movie or Special (jtly), 2010); The Gathering Storm, 2012; Esio Trot, 2015. Hon. Fellow, Rose Bruford Coll., 2014. *Recreations:* family, music, gardening, flea markets.

**BEAVER, Dr Sarah Ann;** Fellow and Bursar, All Souls College, Oxford, 2008–20; *b* 5 Feb. 1952; *d* of John Maurice Wilks and Ida Elizabeth Wilks (*née* Clements); *m* 1979, Rev. Dr William Carpenter Beaver, *qv*; two *s*. *Educ:* Bath High Sch., GPDST; Somerville Coll., Oxford (MA Modern Hist.); Sheffield Univ. (Cert Ed); Wolfson Coll., Oxford (DPhil 1979). Asst Mistress, Lord Williams's Sch., Thame, 1974–76; Jun. Res. Fellow, Wolfson Coll., Oxford, 1978–80; Lectr, Balliol Coll., Oxford, 1979–80; Ministry of Defence, 1980–: Principal, 1985; Hd, Materiel Co-ordination (Navy), 1994; Dir, Procurement Finance, 1995–98; on loan to Nat. Assembly for Wales as Dir, NHS Finance, 1998–2002; Dir, EU and UN, 2002–04; Dir Gen., Internat. Security Policy, 2004–07; Command Sec., Perm. Jt HQ (UK), MoD, 2007–08. Trustee, Marie Curie (formerly Marie Curie Cancer Care), 2007–16; Citizens Advice Oxford, 2019–. *Recreations:* cycling, gardening. *Address:* Townsend Close, 50 Church Way, Iffley, Oxford OX4 4EF. *T:* (01865) 778061. *E:* sarah.beaver@all-souls.ox.ac.uk.

**BEAVER, Rev. Dr William Carpenter,** II; Officiating Chaplain to Household Division and Household Cavalry Mounted Regiment, 2009–15; Curate, St Mary the Virgin, Iffley, Oxford, 2011–18; Chaplain, Light Cavalry, Honourable Artillery Company, since 2016; *b* 17 Sept. 1945; *s* of late William Carpenter Beaver, MD and Margaret Edith Beaver, MD (*née* Nelson); *m* 1979, Sarah Ann Wilks (*see* S. A. Beaver); two *s*. *Educ:* Colorado Coll., USA (BA 1967; Benezet Distinguished Alumnus, 2000); US Army Comd and Staff Coll. (psc 1980); Wolfson Coll., Oxford (Beit Sen. Schol., Rhodes House; DPhil 1976); St Stephen's House, Oxford (CTh 1982). Served US Army, 1967–71 (Bronze Star (valour, thrice); Meritorious Service Medal; Air Medal; Combat Infantry Badge), Reserves, 1971–96. Exec. Dir, Univ. of Oxford Develt Records Project, and Jun. Res. Fellow, Wolfson Coll., Oxford, 1977–80; Dep. Hd, Corporate and Community Communications, J. Walter Thompson, 1980–83; Dir, Publicity, Barnardo's, 1983–89; Group Director: Public Affairs, Pergamon AGB Internat. Res., 1989–90; Corporate Affairs, Nat. Westminster Bank, 1990–92; Dir, Marketing, The Industrial Soc., 1992–97; Dir of Communications, C of E, 1997–2002, BRCS, 2002–03; Office of the Lord Mayor of London, 2003–10. Vice-Chm. (Cadets), Reserve Forces and Cadets Assoc. Gtr London, 2010–15. Ordained deacon, 1982, priest, 1983; Curate: St John the Divine, Kennington, 1982–95; St Mary Redcliffe, Bristol, 1995–2008; St Andrew, Holborn, 2001–04; Univ. Ch of St Mary the Virgin, Oxford, 2010–11; Hon. Priest-in-charge, St Andrew's, Avonmouth, 1995–98. Chaplain, Mercers' Co., 2002–10. Vice Chm., Charles Edward Brooke Sch., Brixton, 1992–2002. Mem., Pilgrim Soc., 2008–. FCIPR (FIPR 2003). Freeman, Art Scholars' Co., 2013–. Editor, Heraldic Craftsman, Soc. of Heraldic Arts, 2012–18. SBStJ 2012. *Publications:* Under Every Leaf, 2012, 2019. *Recreation:* bicycling. *Address:* Townsend Close, 50 Church Way, Iffley, Oxford OX4 4EF.

**BEAVERBROOK,** 3rd Baron *cr* 1917, of Beaverbrook, New Brunswick, and of Cherkley, Surrey; **Maxwell William Humphrey Aitken;** Bt 1916; Chairman, Beaverbrook Foundation, since 1985; *b* 29 Dec. 1951; *s* of Sir (John William) Max Aitken, 2nd Bt, DSO, DFC, and of Violet, *d* of Sir Humphrey de Trafford, 4th Bt, MC; *S* to disclaimed barony of father, 1985; *m* 1974, Susan Angela More O'Ferrall; two *s* two *d*. *Educ:* Charterhouse; Pembroke Coll., Cambridge; RCDS. Beaverbrook Newspapers Ltd, 1973–77; Dir, Ventech, 1983–86; Chm., Ventech Healthcare Corp. Inc., 1986, 1988–92. Govt spokesman for Home Office and DTI, H of L, 1986; a Lord in Waiting (Government Whip), 1986–88; Dep. Treas., 1988–90, Treas., 1990–92, Cons. Party; Treas., European Democratic Union, 1990–92. Chairman: Net Integration Inc., 2000–07; Pine Ventures plc, 2007–10. Chm., Nat. Assoc. of Boys' Clubs, 1989–92. Mem. Council, Homeopathic Trust, 1986–92. Hon. Air Cdre, 4624 Sqn, 2004–09, Hon. Inspector Gen. (Air Vice-Marshal), 2009–16, Comdt Gen., 2016–, RAuxAF; ADC to the Queen, 2017–19. *Recreations:* motor sport (Eur. GT Champion, 1994), offshore powerboat racing (winner, Harmsworth Trophy, 2004). *Heir: s* Hon. Maxwell Francis Aitken [*b* 17 March 1977; *m* 2007, Inés Nieto Gómez-Valencia; one *s* one *d*]. *Address:* Ashlett House, Fawley, Hants SO45 1DT. *Clubs:* White's, Royal Air Force; Royal Yacht Squadron; British Racing Drivers' (Dir, 2015–); British Powerboat Racing (Chm., 2003–10; Vice-Pres., 2010–).

*See also* Duke of Roxburghe.

**BEAVIS, Andrew William,** PhD; Chief Scientific Officer, Vertual Ltd, since 2007; Head, Radiation Physics, Hull and East Yorkshire NHS Hospitals Trust, since 2008; *b* Northampton, 1 Jan. 1966; *s* of Colin Beavis and Gillian Beavis; *m* 1990, Sally Andrew; two *s* one *d*. *Educ:* Longcroft Sch., Beverley; Univ. of Newcastle upon Tyne (BSc Hons 1st Cl 1987; PhD 1990). CPhys 1990; MInstP 1990; CSci 2000; FIPEM 2007; FBIR 2012. Clinical Scientist (Med. Physics), Hull and East Yorks NHS Hosps Trust, 1992–. Vis. Prof., Sheffield Hallam Univ., 2005–; Hon. Prof., Univ. of Hull, 2008–. Member: Amer. Assoc. of Physicists in Medicine, 1998; Inst. of Physics in Medicine, 2000; Eur. Soc. for Radiotherapy and Oncol., 2009. MInstD 2013. *Publications:* scientific articles in jls, 1987–. *Recreations:* music (Hawkwind, Motorhead, etc), Rugby League, Rugby Union, family. *Address:* Vertual Ltd, Anchor House, The Maltings, Silvester Street, Hull HU1 3HD. *E:* andy@vertual.co.uk.

**BEAVIS, Air Chief Marshal Sir Michael (Gordon),** KCB 1981; CBE 1977 (OBE 1969); AFC 1962; Director, Skye Pharma PLC (formerly Tubular Edgington Group, then Black & Edgington Group), 1989–2006; *b* 13 Aug. 1929; *s* of Walter Erle Beavis and Mary Ann (*née* Sarjantson); *m* 1950, Joy Marion (*née* Jones) (*d* 2017); one *s* one *d*. *Educ:* Kilburn Grammar Sch. Joined RAF 1947; commnd 1949; served Fighter Comd Squadrons 1950–54, RNZAF 1954–56; flew Vulcan aircraft, Bomber Comd, 1958–62; Staff Coll., 1963; MoD, 1964–66; OC No 10 Squadron (VC10s), 1966–68; Group Captain Flying, Akrotiri, Cyprus, 1968–71; Asst Dir, Defence Policy, MoD, 1971–73; RCDS, 1974; RAF Germany, 1975–77 (SASO 1976–77); Dir Gen. RAF Training, 1977–80; Comdt, RAF Staff Coll., 1980–81; AOC-in-C, RAF Support Comd, 1981–84; Dep. C-in-C, AFCENT, 1984–86. Dir, Alliance Aircraft Co., USA, 2000–03. CCMI. Freeman, City of London, 1980; Liveryman, Hon. Co. of Air Pilots (formerly GAPAN), 1983. *Recreations:* bridge, sociable lunches. *Address:* c/o Lloyds, 202 High Street, Lincoln LN5 7AP. *Club:* Royal Air Force.

**BEAZER, Brian Cyril;** Chairman and Chief Executive, Beazer (formerly C. H. Beazer (Holdings)) PLC, 1983–91; Chairman, Beazer Homes USA Inc., 1992–2015, now Chairman Emeritus; *b* 22 Feb. 1935; *s* of late Cyril Henry George Beazer and of Ada Vera Beazer; *m* 1958, Patricia (*née* White); one *d*. *Educ:* Wells Cathedral School. Joined C. H. Beazer, 1958; Man. Dir, 1968; apptd Chm. and Chief Exec. on death of his father in 1983. *Recreations:* walking, reading. *Address:* The Weavers House, Castle Combe, Wiltshire SN14 7HX.

**BEAZLEY, Christopher John Pridham;** Member (C) Eastern Region, England, European Parliament, 1999–2009; *b* 5 Sept. 1952; *s* of late Peter George Beazley, CBE; *m* 1978, Christiane Marie Elyane (*née* Dillemann); two *s* one *d*. *Educ:* Shrewsbury; Bristol Univ. Former Nuffield Research Fellow, School of European Studies, Sussex Univ. Vice Chm., Lewes and Eastbourne branch, European Movement, 1980; Wealden DC, 1979–83. MEP (C) Cornwall and Plymouth, 1984–94; contested (C) Cornwall and W Plymouth, Eur. Parly elecns, 1994; European Parliament: spokesman on regl policy, 1984–89, on justice and home affairs, 1992–94, on constitutional affairs, 1999–2001, on educn and culture, 2001; Vice-Chairman: Transport Cttee, 1989–91; Baltic States Delegn, 1991–94; Mem., Foreign Affairs Cttee, 2007–09; Chairman: Estonian Delegn, 2001–04; Baltic States Intergp, 2004–09. Church Warden, Boxgrove Priory, W Sussex, 2017–18. Order of the Cross of Terra Mariana (Estonia), 2009; Comdr of the Order of the Three Stars (Latvia), 2009; Cross of Comdr, Order for Merits to Lithuania, 2010. *Club:* Oriental.

**BEAZLEY, Hon. Kim Christian,** AC 2009; Governor of Western Australia, since 2018; *b* 14 Dec. 1948; *s* of late Hon. Kim Edward Beazley and of Betty Beazley; *m* 1st, 1974, Mary Paltridge (marr. diss. 1989); two *d*; 2nd, 1990, Susanna Annus; one *d*. *Educ:* Univ. of Western Australia (MA); Oxford Univ. (Rhodes Scholar; MPhil). Tutor in Social and Political Theory, Murdoch Univ., WA, 1976–79; Lectr 1980. MP (ALP) Swan, Perth, 1980–96, Brand, Perth, 1996–2007, Australia; Minister of State for Aviation, and Minister Assisting the Minister for Defence, 1983–84; Special Minister of State, 1983–84; Minister of State for Defence, 1984–90; Minister for Transport and Communications, 1990–91, for Finance, 1991, for Employment, Educn and Training, 1991–93, for Finance, 1993–96; Leader of the House of Representatives, 1988–96 (Vice-Pres., Exec. Council, 1988–91); Dep. Prime Minister, 1995–96; Leader of the Opposition, 1996–2001 and 2005–06. Mem., Jt Parly Cttee on Foreign Affairs and Defence, 1980–83, 2002–05, on Aust. Security Intelligence Orgn, ASIS and DSD, 2002–05. Mem. Nat. Exec., ALP, 1991–94, 1996–2001. Australian Ambassador to USA, 2010–16. Pres., Aust. Inst. of Internat. Affairs, 2016–18 (Fellow). Member: Bd, Defence S Australia, 2008–10; Council, Aust. Nat. War Meml, 2009; Co-Chm., Aust. American Leadership Dialogue, 2016–18. Chancellor, ANU, 2009–10. Professorial Fellow, UWA, 2007–10; Distinguished Fellow: Aust. Strategic Policy Inst., 2016–18; Perth USAsia Centre (Mem. Bd, 2016–). Mem. Adv. Bd, Army Jl, 2007–10. KStJ 2019. Hon. LLD Notre Dame Australia, 2014; DUniv Murdoch, 2016. *Publications:* (with I. Clark) The Politics of Intrusion: the Super-Powers in the Indian Ocean, 1979. *Recreations:* swimming, reading. *Address:* Government House, St Georges Terrace, Perth, WA 6000, Australia.

**BEAZLEY, Richard Hugh;** Vice Lord-Lieutenant of Hertfordshire, since 2010; *b* Broxbourne, 16 June 1949; *s* of late John Beazley, DFC and Mary Beazley, MBE; *m* 1977, Violet Bradford; two *s*. *Educ:* Cheltenham Coll.; Exeter Univ. (LLB). Lawyer, economist and Chief Exec. of various Mobil Oil Corp. subsidiaries, living in Norway, Indonesia, Canada, USA and UK, 1976–2000. Chm., E and N Herts NHS Trust, 2002–12. Trustee, Florence Nightingale Foundn, 2008–17 (Vice Chm., 2011–17). Chm., Bd of Govs, Univ. of Hertfordshire, 2013–. DL Herts, 2004. Hon. Col, Beds and Herts ACF, 2014–. *Recreations:* cross-country ski-ing, walking, shooting. *Address:* New Hall, Standon, Herts SG11 1NX. *T:* (01279) 842717. *Club:* Travellers.

**BEAZLEY, Thomas Alan George;** QC 2001; *b* 2 March 1951; *s* of late Derek Edwin George Beazley and of Rosemary Janet Beazley; *m* 1980, Ingrid Ann Marrable; two *d*. *Educ:* Emmanuel Coll., Cambridge (BA; LLB). Called to the Bar, Middle Temple, 1979; Hd of Chambers, Blackstone Chambers, 2004–12; Partner and Hd of Internat. Litigation, Joseph Hage Aaronson LLP, 2013–. *Recreations:* reading, travelling, cooking. *Address:* Joseph Hage Aaronson, 7th Floor, 280 High Holborn, WC1V 7EE.

**BEBB, Gordon Montfort;** QC 2002; a Recorder, since 2001; *b* 1 May 1952; *s* of Simon and Adonia Montfort Bebb; *m* 1978, Rachel Millington; one *s* one *d*. *Educ:* Winchester Coll.; Magdalen Coll., Oxford (MA). Called to the Bar, Middle Temple, 1975; Asst Recorder, 1997–2001. Chm. of Trustees, Blond McIndoe Med. Res. Foundn, 2015–. *Recreations:* theatre, art, music, sport. *Address:* Outer Temple Chambers, The Outer Temple, 222 Strand, WC2R 1BA. *T:* (020) 7353 6381, *Fax:* (020) 7583 1786. *Clubs:* Boodle's, Jesters.

**BEBB, Guto ap Owain;** MP for Aberconwy, since 2010 (C, 2010–19; Ind, since 2019); *b* Wrexham, 9 Oct. 1968; *s* of Owain Bebb and Helen Gwyn; *m* 1993, Esyllt Penri; three *s* two *d* (incl. twin *s*). *Educ:* Univ. of Wales, Aberystwyth (BA Hist. 1990). Founder, Partneriaeth Egin Partnership, econ. develt consultancy, 1993–2010. Business Develt Dir, Innovas Wales. Contested (C): Ogmore, Feb. 2002; Conwy, 2005; Parly Under-Sec. of State for Wales, 2016–18; a Lord Comr of HM Treasury (Govt Whip), 2016–18; Parly Under-Sec. of State, MoD, 2018. *Recreations:* reading, music. *Address:* House of Commons, SW1A 0AA. *T:* (020) 7219 7002. *E:* guto.bebb.mp@parliament.uk.

**BEBBINGTON, Prof. Warren Arthur,** PhD; Vice Chancellor and President, University of Adelaide, 2012–17; Professorial Fellow, University of Melbourne, since 2017; *b* Caulfield, Vic, 1952; *s* of Arthur and Thelma Bebbington; *m* 1st, 1981 (marr. diss. 1989); 2nd, 1991, Barbara Watson (separated 2017); three *s*. *Educ:* Caulfield High Sch.; Univ. of Melbourne (BMus; MMus); City Univ., NY (MA; MPhil; PhD 1983). Conductor of choirs and opera in Australia, 1979–2005. Lectr, Canberra Sch. of Music, 1979–85; res. asst to Prof. Gustave Reese, NY, 1978; Dean of Music, Univ. of Qld, 1985–91; University of Melbourne: Dean of Music, 1991–2005; Pro Vice Chancellor, 2006–10; Dep. Vice Chancellor, 2010–12. *Publications:* Oxford Companion to Australian Music, 1997; A

Dictionary of Australian Music, 1998. *Recreations:* sailing, flying. *Address:* PO Box 6001, Caulfield South, SA 3162, Australia. *E:* warren.bebbington@unimelb.edu.au. *Club:* Melbourne.

**BECHER, Sir John (William Michael) Wrixon-,** 6th Bt *cr* 1831, of Ballygiblin, co. Cork; Chairman, Future Electric Ltd, since 2008; Consultant, Weatherbys Private Bank and Weatherbys Hamilton Insurance Brokers, since 2014; *b* 29 Sept. 1950; *s* of Sir William Fane Wrixon-Becher, 5th Bt, MC and Hon. Vanda Wrixon-Becher (who later *m* 9th Earl of Glasgow), *d* of 4th Baron Vivian; *S* father, 2000. *Educ:* Ludgrove; Harrow; Neuchâtel Univ. G. N. Rouse & Others, 1971–74; Lloyds Broker, Eckersley Hicks Ltd, 1974–82; Hutchison Craft Financial Services Ltd, 1982–87; Dir, Wise Speke Financial Services Ltd, 1987–93; Financial Consultant, HSBC Actuaries and Consultants Ltd, 1993–2000; Partner, Ford Reynolds and Associates Ltd, 2000–05. Director: Old Street Productions Ltd, 2001–03; Wind Energy Ltd, 2002–04. *Recreation:* shooting a line and fishing for compliments. *Address:* The Stables, Garnons, Herefordshire HR4 7JU.

**BECK, Rev. Brian Edgar,** MA; President of the Methodist Conference, 1993–94; Secretary of the Conference, 1984–98; *b* 27 Sept. 1933; *o s* of late A. G. and C. A. Beck; *m* 1958, Margaret Ludlow; three *d*. *Educ:* City of London School; Corpus Christi College, Cambridge (1st Cl. Classical Tripos pts 1 and 2); Wesley House, Cambridge (1st Cl. Theol. Tripos pt 2). BA 1955, MA 1959. Ordained Methodist Minister, 1960; Asst Tutor, Handsworth Coll., 1957–59; E Suffolk Circuit Minister, 1959–62; St Paul's United Theological Coll., Limuru, Kenya, 1962–68; Tutor, Wesley House, Cambridge, 1968–80, Principal 1980–84 (Life Fellow, 2017). Sec., E African Church Union Consultation Worship and Liturgy Cttee, 1963–68; Mem., World Methodist Council, 1966–71, 1981–98; Co-Chm., Oxford Inst. of Methodist Theol. Studies, 1976–2002. Hon. Chaplain, Guild of St Bride, Fleet Street, 1994–. Fernley-Hartley Lectr, 1978; Vis. Prof., Wesley Theol Seminary, Washington, 1999. DD Lambeth, 1998. *Publications:* Reading the New Testament Today, 1977; Christian Character in the Gospel of St Luke, 1989; Gospel Insights, 1998; Exploring Methodism's Heritage, 2004; (ed jtly) Unmasking Methodist Theology, 2004; Methodist Heritage and Identity, 2017; contributor to: Christian Belief, a Catholic-Methodist statement, 1970; Unity the Next Step?, 1972; Suffering and Martyrdom in the New Testament, 1981; Rethinking Wesley's Theology, 1998; Community-Unity-Communion, 1998; Managing the Church?, 2000; Apostolicity and Unity, 2002; Reflections on Ministry, 2004; A Thankful Heart and a Discerning Mind, 2010; The Ashgate Research Companion to World Methodism, 2013; articles in NT Studies, Epworth Review. *Recreations:* walking, DIY, cross-stitch. *Address:* 26 Hurrell Road, Cambridge CB4 3RH. *T:* (01223) 312260.

**BECK, Clive;** *b* 12 April 1937; *s* of Sir Edgar Charles Beck, CBE, and Mary Agnes Beck; *m* 1960, Philippa Flood; three *s* three *d*. *Educ:* Ampleforth College. 2nd Lieut, The Life Guards, 1956–57; John Mowlem & Co., 1957–67; SGB Group, 1967–86; Dep. Chm., John Mowlem & Co., 1986–92. Director: London Management Ltd, 1990–2000; Pioneer Concrete Holdings plc, 1990–97. *Recreations:* golf, travel. *Address:* 8 Atherton Drive, Wimbledon, SW19 5LB. *Clubs:* Royal Wimbledon Golf, Swinley Forest Golf.
*See also* Sir *E. P. Beck.*

**BECK, Sir (Edgar) Philip,** Kt 1988; Chairman: John Mowlem & Co., 1979–95; Railtrack, 1999–2001; *b* 9 Aug. 1934; *s* of Sir Edgar Charles Beck, CBE, and Mary Agnes Beck; *m* 1st, 1957, Thomasina Joanna Jeal (marr. diss.); two *s*; 2nd, 1991, Bridget Cockerell (*née* Heathcoat-Amory). *Educ:* Ampleforth College; Jesus College, Cambridge (MA). Dir, John Mowlem, 1964, Dep. Chm., 1978–79. Chairman: FCEC, 1982–83; Export Group for Constructional Industries, 1986–88. Non-executive Director: Invensys, 1992–2003; Delta, 1993–2004.
*See also C. Beck.*

**BECK, Lydia Helena;** *see* Lopes Cardozo Kindersley, L. H.

**BECK, Peter,** CVO 2016; MD; FRCP; Lord-Lieutenant for South Glamorgan, 2008–16; *b* Leicester, 4 July 1941; *s* of Frank Beck and Kittie Eileen Beck (*née* Clark); *m* 1964, Lyn Davies; one *s* one *d*. *Educ:* Wyggeston Boys' Sch., Leicester; St Mary's Hosp. Med. Sch., London (MB BS Hons 1965; MD 1976); MA Wales 1989. FRCP 1980. VSO Jordan, 1961–62. Jun. posts, St Mary's and Hammersmith Hosps, 1965–67; SHO, then Registrar, Cardiff Royal Infirmary, 1967–70; Lectr, Welsh Nat. Sch. of Medicine, Cardiff, 1970–71; MRC Clin. Res. Fellow, Cardiff, 1971–73; Wellcome Travelling Fellow, Harvard Med. Sch., 1974–75; Consultant Physician, Cardiff Teaching Hosps, 1974–2003. Surgeon Comdr, RNR, 1975–91. President: Cardiff and Vale of Glamorgan Boy Scouts, 2008–16; Cttee, Wales Festival of Remembrance, 2008–16 (Chm., 2007); Vice President: ABF S Glamorgan, 2008–; RFCA S Glamorgan, 2008–16; Chm., Lord Chancellor's Adv. Cttee on JPs, 2008–16; Patron, SSAFA, S Glamorgan, 2011–. DL S Glamorgan, 1994–2008. KStJ 2016 (CStJ 2008, OStJ 2006; Chm., 2006–08, Pres., 2008–, Council, S Glamorgan). *Publications:* contrib. papers on haemophilia, angio-oedema, immuno-assay, diabetes and med. ethics. *Recreations:* golf, kayaking, family, art, ski-ing. *Address:* Tyla Teg, 46 Ty Gwyn Road, Penylan, Cardiff CF23 5JG. *T:* (029) 2048 5982. *E:* pandlbeck@gmail.com. *Clubs:* Army and Navy; Cardiff and County; Royal Porthcawl Golf.

**BECK, Sir Philip;** *see* Beck, Sir E. P.

**BECK, Prof. Stephen Bernard Marcus,** PhD; Professor, since 2012, and Head, Department of Multidisciplinary Engineering Education, since 2014, University of Sheffield; *b* Geneva; *s* of Frank Beck and Louise Beck; *m* 1994, Alison Ward; one *s* one *d*. *Educ:* Dartington Hall Sch.; Univ. of Bath (BSc 1985); Univ. of Sheffield (PhD 1992). CEng 1996; FIMechE 2003. Programmer, Fermilab, 1985–86; University of Sheffield: Programmer, 1990–96; Lectr, 1996–2002; Sen. Lectr, 2002–12. Vice Pres., IMechE, 2016–19. PFHEA. *Publications:* (jtly) The Little Book of Thermofluids, 2006. *Recreations:* hill walking, cycling to work, classical music, cooking. *Address:* Multidisciplinary Engineering Education, University of Sheffield, The Diamond, 32 Leavygreave Road, Sheffield S3 7RD. *E:* s.beck@sheffield.ac.uk.

**BECKE, Prof. Axel Dieter,** PhD; FRS 2006; FRSC; Killam Professor of Computational Science, 2006–15, and Harry Shirreff Professor of Chemical Research, 2012–15, Dalhousie University, now Professor Emeritus; *b* Esslingen, Germany, 10 June 1953. *Educ:* Queen's Univ., Kingston, Ont (BSc 1975); McMaster Univ. (MSc 1977; PhD 1981). FRSC 2000. Postdoctoral Fellow, Dalhousie Univ., 1981–84; NSERC Univ. Res. Fellow, Queen's Univ., 1984–94; Prof. of Chemistry, Queen's Univ., until 2006. Killam Res. Fellow, Canada Council for the Arts, 2005–07. Mem., Internat. Acad. of Quantum Molec. Sci (Medal, 1991). Schrödinger Medal, World Assoc. of Theoretical and Computational Chemists, 2000; Award in Theoretical Chemistry, ACS, 2014; CIC Medal, 2015; Gerhard Herzberg Canada Gold Medal, NSERC, 2015; Killam Prize in Natural Scis, Canada Council, 2016. *Publications:* articles in scientific jls. *Address:* Department of Chemistry, Room 212, Chemistry Building, Dalhousie University, 6274 Coburg Road, PO Box 15000, Halifax, NS B3H 4R2, Canada.

**BECKER, Boris Franz;** former professional tennis player; entrepreneur; Head of Men's Tennis, Germany, since 2017; *b* 22 Nov. 1967; *s* of late Karl-Heinz and Elvira Becker; *m* 1st, Barbara Feltus (marr. diss. 2001); two *s*; one *d*; 2nd, 2009, Lilly Kerssenberg (marr. diss. 2019); one *s*. West German Junior Champion, 1983; wins include: Young Masters' Junior Tournament, 1985; Wimbledon, 1985 (youngest winner), 1986, 1989; US Open, 1989; Australian Open, 1991, 1996; ATP World Champion, 1992, 1995; Davis Cup winner, 1988, 1989; retired as professional tennis player, 1999. Head Coach to Novak Djokovic, 2013–16. *Publications:* Boris Becker – The Player: the autobiography, 2004.

**BECKER, Rashmi;** Founder, Step Change Studios, since 2017; *b* London, 4 July 1973; *d* of Abdul Quddus Choudhury and Kanti Rani Choudhury. *Educ:* Selwyn Coll., Cambridge (MPhil Educn 1996). Account Exec., Hill and Knowlton, WPP, 1997–99; Press Officer, DFEE, 1999–2000; Sen. Press Officer, EC, then EP, Brussels (on secondment), 2000–01; Sen. Inf. Officer, FCO, 2001–02; Hd, EU Communications, FCO, 2003–06; Hd, Stakeholder Communications, Wellcome Trust, 2006–08; Dir, Dubai Healthcare City, 2008–11; Exec. Dir, Dimensions, 2011–13; Strategic Advr, MacIntyre Charity, 2013–16. Dir, English Fedn of Disability Sport, 2013–16; Trustee, Sport England, 2018–. *Recreations:* dance, running, hiking, cycling, film, marathons (London, 1998; San Francisco, 2013; Paris, 2014; New York, 2015). *E:* contact@stepchangestudios.com.

**BECKERLEG, John;** Management Consultant, Management Options Ltd, 2004–06 and 2008–18; Director of Supporting Services, Chief Fire Officers Association, 2014–17; *b* 12 Aug. 1956; *s* of Lewis Beckerleg and Doris (*née* Bundy); *m* 1983, April Cornelia Saunders; two *s* one *d*. *Educ:* Emmanuel Coll., Cambridge (MA 1981); MBA Henley Mgt Coll. 1998. CIPFA 1981. Chief Accountant, Cambs CC, 1985–87; Sen. Asst Co. Treas., Herts CC, 1987–91; Buckinghamshire County Council: Dep. Co. Treas., 1991–93; Dir of Finance, 1993–96; Dir of Corporate Services, 1996–98; Dir of Social Services, 1998–2000; Strategic Manager, 2000–04; Dir of Resources, Nat. Policing Improvement Agency, 2006–08; Hd of Resources, Youth Justice Bd, 2009–10; Director of Corporate Services: S Downs Nat. Park Authy, 2010–11; Hants Fire and Rescue Service, 2011–14. Chm., Jt Audit Cttee, Northants Police, 2014–; Member: Audit Cttee, H of L, 2015–; Finance Cttee, Bar Council, 2016–. Hon. Treas., Citizens Advice Aylesbury Vale, 2017–; Hon. Treas., Milton Keynes Mus. *Recreations:* theatre, genealogy, Rugby, art. *Address:* Daffodil Cottage, Main Street, Grendon Underwood, Bucks HP18 0ST.

**BECKERMAN, Wilfred,** PhD; Fellow of Balliol College, Oxford, 1975–92, now Emeritus; Hon. Visiting Professor of Economics, University College London, since 2005; *b* 19 May 1925; *s* of Morris and Mathilda Beckerman; *m* 1st, 1952, Nicole Geneviève Ritter (*d* 1979); one *s* two *d*; 2nd, 1991, Joanna Pasek; one *d*. *Educ:* Ealing County Sch.; Trinity Coll., Cambridge (MA, PhD). RNVR, 1943–46. Trinity Coll., Cambridge, 1946–50; Lecturer in Economics, Univ. of Nottingham, 1950–52; OEEC and OECD, Paris, 1952–61; National Inst. of Economic and Social Research, 1962–63; Fellow of Balliol Coll., Oxford, 1964–69; Economic Advr to Pres. of BoT (leave of absence from Balliol), 1967–69; Prof. of Political Economy, Univ. of London, and Head of Dept of Political Economy, UCL, 1969–75; Reader in Economics, Oxford Univ., 1978–92. Mem., Royal Commn on Environmental Pollution, 1970–73. Member: Exec. Cttee, NIESR, 1973–96; Council, Royal Economic Soc., 1990–93. Elie Halévy Vis. Prof., Institut d'Etudes Politiques, Paris, 1977; Resident Scholar, Woodrow Wilson Internat. Center for Scholars, Washington, DC, 1982. Consultant: World Bank; OECD; ILO. Pres., Section F (Economics), BAAS, 1978. *Publications:* The British Economy in 1975 (with associates), 1965; International Comparisons of Real Incomes, 1966; An Introduction to National Income Analysis, 1968; (ed and contrib.) The Labour Government's Economic Record, 1972; In Defence of Economic Growth, 1974; Measures of Leisure, Equality and Welfare, 1978; (ed and contrib.) Slow Growth in Britain: causes and consequences, 1979; Poverty and the Impact of Income Maintenance Programmes, 1979; (with S. Clark) Poverty and the Impact of Social Security in Britain since 1961, 1982; (ed and contrib.) Wage Rigidity and Unemployment, 1986; Small is Stupid, 1995; Growth, the Environment and the Distribution of Incomes, 1995; (with J. Pasek) Justice, Posterity and the Environment, 2001; A Poverty of Reason: sustainable development and economic growth, 2003; Economics as Applied Ethics, 2010; articles in Economic Jl, Economica, Econometrica, Review of Economic Studies, Review of Economics and Statistics, World Economics, Oxford Economic Papers, etc. *Recreations:* various. *Address:* 1c Norham Gardens, Oxford OX2 6PS.

**BECKETT,** family name of **Baron Grimthorpe.**

**BECKETT, Frances Mary,** OBE 2006; charity consultant; Chief Executive, Church Urban Fund, 2002–08; *b* 20 Nov. 1951. *Educ:* Trent Poly. (CQSW); LSE (MSc Vol. Sector Orgn). Social Worker, Somerset CC, 1972–76; Student Advr, UCCF, 1976–80; Community Worker, 1981–86; Shaftesbury Society, 1986–2002: Social Work Advr, Community Care Co-ordinator, Urban Action Dir; Chief Exec., 1995–2002. Chairman: ACEVO, 2003–05; Voluntary and Community Sector Adv. Gp, Home Office, 2003–05, Cabinet Office, 2005–08: Get Fair Nat. Poverty Campaign, 2007–10. Member of Board: Faith Based Regeneration Network, 2004–11; NCVO, 2006–07; LDA, 2008–12; Orbit Housing, 2011– (Chm., Orbit SE Assoc., 2011–13; Chm., Orbit Living, 2013–). Trustee: Southwark CAB, 2010–16; Action Tutoring, 2014–; Brighton & Hove Street Pastors, 2018–. Chair: Urban Expression, 2014–16; Friends of Brimmington Park, 2014–16; Release, 2018–. Gov., St Andrew's Primary Sch., Hove, 2018–. FRSA 2000. *Publications:* Called to Action, 1989; Rebuild, 2001; Leading Community Projects, 2014. *Recreations:* Church involvement, theatre, cinema, reading. *Address:* 34 Belfast Street, Hove, E Sussex BN3 3YS.

**BECKETT, Prof. John Vincent,** PhD; FRHistS, FSA; Professor of English Regional History, University of Nottingham, since 1990 (on secondment as Director, Victoria County History, University of London, 2005–10); *b* 12 July 1950; *s* of William Vincent Beckett and Kathleen Amelia Beckett (*née* Reed); *m* 1979, Christine Sylvia Campbell; one *s*. *Educ:* Univ. of Lancaster (BA 1971; PhD 1975). FRHistS 1981. Lord Adams Res. Fellow, Univ. of Newcastle upon Tyne, 1974–76; Lectr in Hist., Wroxton Coll. of Fairleigh Dickinson Univ., Banbury, 1976–78; Lectr in Econ. and Social Hist., Univ. of Hull, 1979; University of Nottingham: Lectr in Hist., 1979–87; Reader in English Regl Hist., 1987–90. Chm., Editl Bd, Midland Hist., 2001–. Chm., British Agricl Hist. Soc., 2001–05. Chairman: Hist. of Lincs Cttee, 1988–; Thoroton Soc. of Notts, 1992–. FSA 1992. Hon. Fellow, Inst. of Historical Res., 2013. *Publications:* Coal and Tobacco: the Lowthers and the economic development of West Cumberland 1660–1760, 1981; The Aristocracy in England 1660–1914, 1986, rev. edn 1989; The East Midlands from AD1000, 1988; A History of Laxton: England's last open-field village, 1989; The Agricultural Revolution, 1990; The Rise and Fall of the Grenvilles, Dukes of Buckingham and Chandos 1710–1921, 1994; (jtly) Agricultural Rent in England 1690–1914, 1997; (ed) A Centenary History of Nottingham, 1997; (jtly) Farm Production in England 1700–1914, 2001; Byron and Newstead: the aristocrat and the Abbey, 2001; (ed) Nottinghamshire Past: essays in honour of Adrian Henstock, 2003; City Status in the United Kingdom 1830–2002, 2005; Writing Local History, 2007; Nottingham: a history of Britain's global university, 2016; contrib. numerous articles and reviews to jls incl. Agricl Hist., Agricl Hist. Rev., Archives, Bull. Inst. Histl Res., Bull. John Rylands Liby, Byron Jl, Econ. Hist. Rev., English Histl Rev., History

Today, Jl British Studies. *Recreations:* sport, walking, local history. *Address:* Department of History, University Park, Nottingham NG7 2RD. *T:* (0115) 951 5936. *E:* John.Beckett@nottingham.ac.uk.

BECKETT, Rear Adm. Keith Andrew, CBE 2014; Chief Strategic Systems Executive, Ministry of Defence, since 2014; *b* Stockport, 7 June 1963; *s* of Charles Beckett and Enid Beckett; *m* 1989, Susan Mary Berry; one *s* three *d*. *Educ:* Holyhead Co. Sec. Sch.; RN Engrg Coll. (BScEng 1985); Royal Mil. Coll. of Sci. (MDA 1999). CEng 2006; FIMarEST 2006. Joined RN, 1981; HMS Trafalgar, 1987–90; HMS Ocelot, 1990–92; Clyde Submarine Base, 1992–94; HMS Triumph, 1994–97; Dept of Naval Sec., 1997–98; Hd, Submarine Nuclear Safety, Defence Procurement, 1999–2002; Devonport Flotilla Submarine Engr, 2002–04; rcds 2004; CSO Engrg (Submarines), 2004–07; UK Tech. Liaison Officer, Naval Sea Systems Comd, Washington, DC, 2007–10; Dir Nuclear Propulsion, Defence Equipment and Support, 2010–13; Naval Base Comdr, Clyde Naval Base, 2013–14. Vice Pres., RNRU, 2011–March 2020.

BECKETT, Rt Hon. Dame Margaret (Mary), DBE 2013; PC 1993; MP (Lab) Derby South, since 1983; *b* 15 Jan. 1943; *d* of late Cyril and Winifred Jackson; *m* 1979, Lionel A. Beckett; two step *s*. *Educ:* Notre Dame High Sch., Norwich; Manchester Coll. of Sci. and Technol. Formerly: engrg apprentice (metallurgy), AEI, Manchester; exptl officer, Manchester Univ.; Labour Party res. asst, 1970–74; political adviser, Minister for Overseas Develt, 1974; Principal Researcher, Granada TV, 1979–83. Contested (Lab) Lincoln, Feb. 1974; MP (Lab) Lincoln, Oct. 1974–1979; PPS to Minister for Overseas Develt, 1974–75; Asst Govt Whip, 1975–76; Parly Under-Sec. of State, DES, 1976–79; Opposition front bench spokesman on health and social security, 1984–89; Mem., Shadow Cabinet, 1989–97; Shadow Chief Sec. to the Treasury, 1989–92; Shadow Leader, H of C, 1992–94; Campaigns Co-ordinator and Dep. Leader, Lab Party, 1992–94; Actg Leader, Lab Party, May–July 1994; opposition front bench spokesman on health, 1994–95, on trade and industry, 1995–97; Pres., BoT, and Sec. of State for Trade and Industry, 1997–98; Pres. of the Council and Leader, H of C, 1998–2001; Secretary of State: for Envmt, Food and Rural Affairs, 2001–06; for Foreign and Commonwealth Affairs, 2006–07; Minister of State (Minister for Housing and Planning), DCLG, 2008–09. Chair: Intelligence and Security Cttee, 2008; Jt Cttee on Nat. Security Strategy, 2011–. Mem. NEC, Labour Party, 1980–81, 1985–86, 1988–97 and 2011–. Mem., Cttee on Standards in Public Life, 2010–. *Recreations:* cooking, reading, caravanning. *Address:* c/o House of Commons, SW1A 0AA.

BECKETT, Nikaila Susan; non-executive Chairman: Technetix Group Ltd, since 2008; NSB Holdings Ltd, since 2013; CTB Systems Ltd, since 2016; *b* 16 June 1961; two *s*. IBM, UK, USA and Europe, 1979–95; Founder, 1995, Chief Exec., 1997–2007, NSB Retail Systems Plc; Man. Dir, NSB Ltd (Grenada), 2013–. Non-executive Chairman: Victoria plc, 2010–12 (non-exec. Dir, 2007–12); Kiala SV, 2011–12 (Sen. Ind. Dir, 2009–11); non-exec. Dir, Unit4 Gp, 2013–. *Recreations:* sailing, scuba diving, tennis, eating out.

BECKETT, Sir Richard (Gervase), 3rd Bt *cr* 1921; QC 1988; barrister; *b* 27 March 1944; *s* of Sir Martyn Gervase Beckett, 2nd Bt, MC, RIBA and Hon. Priscilla, *d* of 3rd Viscount Esher, GBE; *S* father, 2001; *m* 1976, Elizabeth Ann, *d* of Major Hugo Waterhouse; one *s* three *d*. *Educ:* Eton. Diploma in Economics (Oxford). Called to the Bar, Middle Temple, 1965; practice at the Bar, 1966–2009. *Recreation:* landscape. *Heir: s* Walter Gervase Beckett, *b* 16 Jan. 1987. *Address:* 51 Lennox Gardens, SW1X 0DF. *Clubs:* Pratt's, Portland.

BECKETT, Samantha Mary Constance, (Mrs I. D. Mason), OBE 1999; Director General, EU Exit and Analysis (formerly International, Growth and Analysis), Department for Business, Energy and Industrial Strategy, since 2017; *b* Camberley, 19 Dec. 1966; *d* of Bill Beckett and Connie Beckett (*née* McKenna); *m* 1994, Ian David Mason; two *d*. *Educ:* St Wilfrid's RC Comprehensive Sch., Crawley; New Coll., Oxford (BA Hons PPE); London Sch. of Econs (MSc Econs). Joined HM Treasury, 1988; Mem., Econ. Briefing and Analysis teams, 1988–96; Chancellor of the Exchequer's Speechwriter, 1996–98; Sec. to Diana, Princess of Wales Meml Cttee, 1998; Head: Productivity Team, 1999–2000; Competition and Econ. Regulation Team, 2000–04; Director: Ops, 2004–07; Policy and Planning, 2007; Fiscal Policy, 2008–12; Dir, Econ. and Domestic Secretariat, Cabinet Office, 2012–13; Dir Gen., Econs and Markets, BIS, subseq. BEIS, and Dep. Hd, Govt Econ. Service, 2013–17. *Address:* Department for Business, Energy and Industrial Strategy, 1 Victoria Street, SW1H 0ET.

BECKETT, Lt Gen. Sir Thomas (Anthony), KCB 2018; CBE 2010; Executive Director, International Institute for Strategic Studies - Middle East, since 2018; *b* Bahrain, 28 July 1962; *s* of Brendan Beckett and Kathleen Beckett; *m* 1992, Fiona Graham; three *d*. *Educ:* Blackrock Coll., Dublin; Cranfield Univ. (MA Military Studies 1994; MSc Global Security 2002). Commnd QRIH, 1984; psc 1994; SO2 DMO, MoD, 1994–96; 2IC 2nd Bn Parachute Regt, 1998–2000; CO 1st Bn Parachute Regt, 2002–04; hcsc 2005; Dep. Dir, HCSC, 2005–07; Dep. C2 Multi-Nat. Forces Iraq, 2007; Comdr 20th Armoured Bde, 2007–09; Dir Commitments HQ Land Forces, 2009–10; Dep. Comdr, NATO Rapid Deployable Corps (Italy), 2010–12; COS ISAF Jt Comd, 2012–13. Defence Sen. Advr to the Middle E, 2015–18; Security Envoy to Kurdistan Reg. of Iraq, 2015–18. Col, QRH, 2014–; Dep. Col Comdt, Parachute Regt, 2016–. Officer, Legion of Merit (USA), 2007. *Recreations:* surfing, stalking (deer), military history, cycling, chile sauces. *Clubs:* Cavalry and Guards; Capital (Bahrain).

BECKETT, William Cartwright, CB 1978; LLM; Solicitor to the Corporation of Lloyd's, 1985–93; *b* 21 Sept. 1929; *s* of late William Beckett and Emily (*née* Cartwright); *m* 1st, 1956, Marjorie Jean Hoskin; two *s*; 2nd, 1974, Lesley Margaret Furlonger. *Educ:* Salford Grammar Sch.; Manchester Univ. (LLB 1950, LLM 1952). Called to Bar, Middle Temple, 1952. Joined Treasury Solicitor's Dept, 1956; Board of Trade, 1965; Asst Solicitor, DEP, 1969; Under-Sec., DTI, 1972; Dep.-Sec. 1977; Legal Secretary, Law Officers' Dept, 1975–80; Solicitor, DTI, 1980–84. *Recreations:* music, golf. *Address:* Red Rowans, Bethesda Street, Upper Basildon, Pangbourne, West Berkshire RG8 8NU.

BECKFORD, Prof. James Arthur, PhD, DLitt; FBA 2004; Professor of Sociology, University of Warwick, 1989–2007, now Emeritus; *b* 1 Dec. 1942; *s* of late John Henry Beckford and Elisabeth Alice May Beckford; *m* 1965, Julia Carolyn Hanson; one *s* twin *d*. *Educ:* Alma Rd Sch.; Tottenham Grammar Sch.; Univ. of Reading (BA 1965; PhD 1972; DLitt 1985). Lectr in Sociol., Univ. of Reading, 1966–73; Lectr, then Sen. Lectr, Sociol., Univ. of Durham, 1973–87; Prof. of Sociol., Loyola Univ. of Chicago, 1987–89. Directeur d'études invité: Ecole des Hautes Etudes en Sciences Sociales, Paris, 2001; Ecole Pratique des Hautes Etudes, Paris, 2004. F. D. Maurice Lectr, KCL, 2014. Pres., Soc. for the Scientific Study of Religion, 2010–11. FRSA. Dr Sciences Religieuses *hc* Lausanne, 2014. *Publications:* The Trumpet of Prophecy: a sociological study of Jehovah's Witnesses, 1975; Religious Organization: a trend report and bibliography, 1975; Cult Controversies: societal responses to new religious movements, 1985; (ed) New Religious Movements and Rapid Social Change, 1986; (ed jtly) The Changing Face of Religion, 1989; Religion and Advanced Industrial Society, 1989; (ed jtly) Secularization, Rationalism and Sectarianism, 1993; (with S. Gilliat) Religion in Prison: equal rites in a multi-faith society, 1998; (ed jtly) Challenging Religion: essays in honour of Eileen Barker, 2003; Social Theory and Religion, 2003; (jtly) Muslims in Prison: challenge and change in Britain and France, 2005; (ed jtly) Theorising Religion: classical and contemporary debates, 2006; (ed jtly) The Sage Handbook of the Sociology of Religion, 2007; (ed) Migration and Religion, 2 vols, 2015; (ed jtly) New Religious Movements and Counselling, 2018; numerous scholarly articles and chapters. *Recreations:* owls, Japanese language, playing the clarinet and bagpipes, Ancient Greek. *Address:* Department of Sociology, University of Warwick, Coventry CV4 7AL. *T:* (home) (01926) 851252, *Fax:* (024) 7652 3497. *E:* j.a.beckford@warwick.ac.uk.

BECKHAM, David Robert Joseph, OBE 2003; professional footballer, 1992–2013; Captain, England Football Team, 2000–06; *b* Leytonstone, 2 May 1975; *s* of Ted and Sandra Beckham; *m* 1999, Victoria Caroline Adams (OBE 2017); three *s* one *d*. Manchester United Football Club: trainee, 1991; team member, 1992–2003; Premier League début, 1995; member, winning team: FA Premier League, 1996, 1997, 1999, 2000, 2001, 2003; FA Cup, 1996, 1999; Charity Shield, 1996, 1997; UEFA Champions League, 1999; team mem., Real Madrid FC, 2003–07, mem., winning team, La Liga, 2007; team member: Los Angeles Galaxy, 2007–12, mem., winning team, Major League Soccer Championship, 2011; AC Milan, 2009, 2010; Paris Saint-Germain, 2013. Internat. appearances for England, 1996–2006 (115 caps); mem., World Cup team, 1998, 2002 and 2006. Opened David Beckham children's football acad., London and LA, 2005. Owner, Club Internacional de Fútbol Miami, 2018–. Bobby Charlton Soccer Skills Award, 1987; Manchester United Player of the Year, 1996–97; Young Player of the Year, PFA, 1996–97; Sky Football Personality of the Year, 1997; Sportsman of the Year, Sport Writers' Assoc., 2001; BBC Sports Personality of the Year, 2001; Lifetime Achievement Award, BBC Sports Personality of the Year, 2010. *Publications:* (with Neil Harman) David Beckham: my story, 1999; David Beckham: my world (autobiog.), 2000; (with Tom Watt) My Side (autobiog.), 2003; David Beckham, 2013.

BECKINGHAM, Peter; HM Diplomatic Service, retired; Governor, Turks and Caicos Islands, 2013–16; *b* 16 March 1949; *s* of late Rev. Leslie Beckingham and Eileen Beckingham (*née* Grimsey); *m* 1975, Jill Mary Trotman; two *d*. *Educ:* Chigwell Sch.; Selwyn Coll., Cambridge (MA). MIEx 1998. Argo Record Co., 1970–74; BOTB, 1974–79; Dir, British Inf. Services, NY, 1979–84; News Dept, FCO, 1984 (Hd, Press Centre, G7 Summit); Energy, Sci. and Space Dept, FCO, 1984–86; Hd, Horn of Africa Section, E Africa Dept, FCO, 1986–88; First Sec. (Commercial), Stockholm, 1988–92; Hd, Political Section, Canberra, 1992–96; Dir, Jt Export Promotion Directorate, FCO/DTI, 1996–99; Consul Gen., Sydney, and Dir Gen., Trade and Investment Promotion, Australia, 1999–2004; Ambassador to Philippines, 2005–09; FCO, 2009–10; Dep. High Comr, Mumbai, 2010–13. Chair, Philippines British Business Council, 2018–; Adviser: Good Relations India, 2017–; Sandals Resorts Gp, 2018–; London Rep., British Chamber of Commerce Philippines, 2018–; Trustee: West India Cttee, 2018–; UK Overseas Territories Conservation Forum, 2018–. *Publications:* (ed) Australia and Britain: the evolving relationship, 1993; (ed) Our Shared Future, UK-Australia Dialogue, 2004. *Recreations:* music, golf, tennis. *Address:* Garth Lodge, Shepherds Lane, Lodsworth, W Sussex GU28 9BN. *E:* peter.beckingham@hotmail.com.

BECKLAKE, (Ernest) John (Stephen), PhD; CEng; Senior Research Fellow, Science Museum, since 1994; *b* 24 June 1943; *s* of Ernest and Evelyn Becklake; *m* 1965, Susan Elizabeth (*née* Buckle), BSc; two *s*. *Educ:* Bideford Grammar Sch.; Exeter Univ. (BSc, PhD). CEng 1988; FRAeS 1992. Engr, EMI Electronics, Wells, 1967–69; Post-Doctoral Fellow, Victoria Univ., BC, Canada, 1969–70; Sen. Scientist, Marconi Space and Def. Systems, Frimley, 1970–72; Science Museum: Asst Keeper, Dept of Earth and Space Sciences, 1972–80; Keeper, Dept of Elect. Engrg, Communications and Circulation, 1980–85; Keeper, Dept of Engrg, subseq. Head of Technology Gp, 1985–94. Member: Internat. Acad. of Astronautics, 1988– (Chm., Hist. Cttee, 1996); British Interplanetary Soc., 2006. Man. Ed., DERA Hist. Project, DERA Farnborough, 1995–2001. Consultant, German Rocketry, Aerospace Mus., Cosford, 1997–2004. *Publications:* Man and the Moon, 1980; The Climate Crisis, 1989; The Population Explosion, 1990; Pollution, 1990; (ed) History of Rocketry and Astronautics, vol. XVI, 1995; (series editor) Exploration and Discovery, 1980–; technical pubns in Electronics Letters, Jl of Physics D, Jl of British Interplanetary Soc., and Spaceflight. *Recreations:* gardening, golf, Rugby. *Address:* Tree Wood, Robin Hood Lane, Sutton Green, Guildford, Surrey GU4 7QG. *T:* (01483) 766931. *Club:* Puttenham Golf.

BECKMAN, Michael David; QC 1976; *b* 6 April 1932; *s* of Nathan and Esther Beckman; *m*; two *d*. *Educ:* King's Coll., London (LLB (Hons)). Called to the Bar, Lincoln's Inn, 1954. Qualified mediator, CEDR, 2004, ADR, 2006. *Recreations:* various. *Address:* Bullards, Widford, Herts SG12 8SG. *T:* (01279) 842669.

BECKWITH, Sir John (Lionel), Kt 2002; CBE 1996; FCA; Chairman, Pacific Investments, since 1993; Founder Chairman, London & Edinburgh Trust PLC, 1971–92; *b* 19 March 1947; *s* of Col Harold Beckwith and Agnes Camilla McMichael (*née* Duncan); *m* 1975, Heather Marie Robbins (marr. diss. 2001); two *s* one *d*; one *d* with Hélène Aubry. *Educ:* Harrow Sch. FCA 1970; ATII 1970. Arthur Andersen & Co., 1969–71; with London & Edinburgh Trust PLC, 1971–92. Founder Chm., Rutland Trust plc, 1986–91; Chairman: Riverside PLC, 1993–97; Barbican Healthcare PLC, 1996–98; Red River Capital Hldgs, 2006–11. Director: Frontiers Gp, 1996–2011; Harlequin FC, 1996–97. Member: Develt Bd, Cancer Relief Macmillan Fund; NCH Action for Children's 125th Anniversary Appeal Cttee. Vice-President: RNIB; Youth Clubs UK; Founder, and Pres., Youth Sport Trust; Patron, Teenage Cancer Trust. Hon. DLitt Loughborough, 2000. Duke of Edinburgh Arthur Bell Trophy, 1999. *Recreations:* sport, music, ballet. *Address:* (office) 124 Sloane Street, SW1X 9BW. *Clubs:* MCC, Annabel's, Queen's, Harry's Bar; Old Harrovian Football; Rosslyn Park Football; Royal Berkshire Golf; Thurlestone Golf; Sunningdale Golf; Chiswick Riverside Health and Racquet.

See also P. M. *Beckwith*.

BECKWITH, Peter Michael, OBE 2007; Chairman: PMB Holdings Ltd, since 1992; Aspria Holdings BV, since 1992; Director, Ambassador Entertainment Group, 2009–12 (Deputy Chairman, Ambassador Theatre Group Ltd, 1992–2010); *b* 20 Jan. 1945; *s* of Col Harold Andrew Beckwith and Agnes Camilla McMichael Beckwith; *m* 1st, 1968, Paula Gay Bateman (*d* 2011); two *d*; 2nd, 2014, Vivien Louise McLean. *Educ:* Harrow School; Emmanuel College, Cambridge (MA Hons; Hon. Fellow, 1999). Qualified Solicitor, 1970; Asst Solicitor, Norton Rose Botterell & Roche; London & Edinburgh Trust: Joint Founder and shareholder, 1972; Managing Director, 1983–86; Dep. Chm., 1987; Chm., 1992. Pres., Harbour Club, Milan, 1999–. Vice Patron, Cambridge Foundn, 1992– (Trustee, 1997–2002). Gov., Harrow Sch., 1992–2011. Hon. LLD Cantab, 2000. *Recreations:* tennis, ski-ing, Association football, theatre, dogs, cycling. *Address:* PMB Holdings Ltd, 4 Hill Street, W1J 5NE. *Clubs:* Garrick, Riverside Racquets, Chelsea Football; Downhill Only (Wengen); Harbour (Milan); Austria Haus (Vail).

See also Sir J. L. *Beckwith*.

BECTIVE, Earl of; Thomas Rupert Charles Christopher Taylour; *b* 18 June 1989; *s* and *heir* of Marquis of Headfort, *qv*. *Educ:* Dragon Sch.; Radley Coll.; Durham Univ. (BA Hons Econs). With Liberum Capital, 2011–14; with Citi, 2014–. *Recreation:* rowing (Mem., GB Junior Rowing Team, 2007).

**BEDDINGTON, Sir John (Rex)**, Kt 2010; CMG 2004; PhD; FRS 2001; FRSE; FICE; Chief Scientific Adviser to the Government and Head of the Government Office for Science, Department for Business, Innovation and Skills (formerly Department for Innovation, Universities and Skills), 2008–13; b 13 Oct. 1945; s of Harry Beddington and Mildred (née Weale); m 1st, 1968, Sarah West (marr. diss. 1972); one s; 2nd, 1973, Prof. Sally Baldwin (marr. diss. 1979); one d; 3rd, 1990, Caroline Hiller. Educ: Monmouth Sch.; London Sch. of Econs (BSc Econs, MSc); Edinburgh Univ. (PhD). FICE 2010. Res. Asst, Edinburgh Univ., 1968–71; Lectr on Population Biol., York Univ., 1971–84; Imperial College, London: Reader in Applied Population Biol., 1984–91; Prof. of Applied Population Biol., 1991–2007; Dir, Centre for Envmtl Technol., 1994–97; Dir, T. H. Huxley Sch. of Envmt, Earth Scis and Engrg, 1998–2001; Hd, Dept of Envmtl Sci. and Technol., 2001–04. Sen. Fellow, Internat. Inst. for Envmt and Develt, 1980–83; Hd, UK Scientific Delegn, Commn for Conservation of Antarctic Living Marine Resources, 1983–2007; Dir, Fisheries Mgt Sci. Prog., DFID (formerly ODA), 1989–2006; Chairman: Scientific Cttee, Indian Ocean Tuna Commn, 1998; Sci. Adv. Council, DEFRA, 2005–07; Rothamsted Res., 2014–; Mem., NERC, 2000–06 (Mem. Exec. Bd, 2002–05); Pres., Zool Soc. of London, 2014– (Mem. Council, 2003–07). Chairman Trustees: People's Trust for Endangered Species, 1984–2007; Marine Educn and Conservation Trust, 1987–2007; Trustee, Natural History Mus., 2013–. Pres., Resource Modelling Assoc., 1992–94. Sen. Advr, Oxford Martin Sch., 2013–. MAE 2010. FCGI 2011; FRSE 2011. Hon. FREng 2012. DUniv York, 2009; Hon. DSc: Edinburgh, 2011; Aberdeen, 2012; Hon. DCL Newcastle, 2011. Heidelberg Award for Envmtl Excellence, 1997. Publications: articles on ecology, population biol. and fisheries mgt. Recreations: hill-walking, art, birdwatching. Club: Travellers.

**BEDDOE**; see Rowe-Beddoe.

**BEDDOE, Martin William Denton; His Honour Judge Beddoe**; a Circuit Judge, since 2007; b Abyad, Egypt, 7 July 1955; s of late Lt Col Arthur Beddoe and Jane Beddoe; m 1993, Prof. Mary Margaret Anne McCabe, qv; two d. Educ: Peterhouse, Cambridge (BA Hons 1977; MA 1982). Called to the Bar, Gray's Inn, 1979; in practice at the Bar, 1980–2007; Recorder, 2002–07; Standing Counsel to HMRC Prosecutions Office, 2005–07. Diversity and Community Relations Judge, 2016–. Mem., Parole Bd for England and Wales, 2010–. Tutor Judge, Judicial Coll. (formerly Judicial Studies Bd), 2007–. Recreations: golf, cricket, two wheel travel, France. Address: c/o Southwark Crown Court, 1 English Grounds (off Battlebridge Lane), Southwark, SE1 2HU. T: (020) 7522 7200. Clubs: Royal Worlington and Newmarket Golf; Philanderers Cricket.

**BEDELL, Elaine**; Chief Executive, Southbank Centre, since 2017; d of Albert and Iris Bedell; m 1990, Clive Brill; one s one d. Educ: Valentines High Sch., Ilford; Leeds Univ. (BA 1st Cl. Hons English). Producer, BBC, 1987–93 (productions include: Start the Week (radio); Clive James Talk Shows; Clive James on the 90s (BAFTA award 1991); Recording; New Year's Eve Shows; Assignment: Bill Clinton's election campaign); Hd, Factual Entertainment, Tiger Aspect Prodns, and Exec. Producer, Bill Hicks, It's Just a Ride, 1993–94; Managing Director: Watchmaker Prodns, 1994–2000; Chrysalis Entertainment, 2000–02; Exec. Dir, Royal Shakespeare Co. Enterprises, 2002–03; Ind. Exec., 2003–04, Commng Ed., Factual Entertainment, 2004–06, Controller, Entertainment Commng, 2007–09, BBC; Dir, Entertainment and Comedy, ITV, 2009–16. Trustee, V&A Mus., 2015–17. Publications: About That Night, 2019. Recreations: writing, reading, dancing. Address: Southbank Centre, Belvedere Road, Lambeth, SE1 8XX. E: Elaine.Bedell@southbankcentre.co.uk.

**BEDFORD, 15th Duke of**, cr 1694; **Andrew Ian Henry Russell**; Marquess of Tavistock, 1694; Earl of Bedford, 1550; Baron Russell, 1539; Baron Russell of Thornhaugh, 1603; Baron Howland of Streatham, 1695; Partner, Bloomsbury Stud, since 1985; Director: Tattersalls Ltd, since 1992; Woburn Enterprises Ltd, since 2003; Jockey Club Estates, since 2014; b 30 March 1962; e s of 14th Duke of Bedford and of Henrietta, d of late Henry F. Tiarks; S father, 2003; m 2000, Louise, d of late Donald Crammond and of Dowager Lady Delves Broughton; one s one d. Educ: Heatherdown; Harrow; Harvard. Recreation: country pursuits. Heir: s Marquess of Tavistock, qv. Address: Woburn Abbey, Woburn, Beds MK17 9WA. T: (01525) 290333, Fax: (01525) 290191. Clubs: Jockey; AD (Cambridge, Mass).

**BEDFORD, Bishop Suffragan of**, since 2012; **Rt Rev. Richard William Bryant Atkinson**, OBE 2002; b 17 Dec. 1958; s of William and Eileen Atkinson; m 1984, Helen Valerie Bavister (see H. V. Atkinson); one s two d. Educ: St Paul's Sch.; Magdalene Coll., Cambridge (BA 1980; MA 1984); Ripon Coll., Cuddesdon; Birmingham Univ. (MA 2009). Ordained deacon, 1984, priest, 1985; Asst Curate, Abingdon, 1984–87; Team Vicar, 1987–91, Team Rector, 1991–96, Sheffield Manor; Vicar of Rotherham, 1996–2002; Archdeacon of Leicester, 2002–12. Hon. Canon, Sheffield Cathedral, 1998–2002. Mem., Gen. Synod of C of E, 1991–2012; Church Comr, 2001–08. Hon. Tutor, Ripon Coll., Cuddesdon, 1987–92. Mem., Carnegie UK Trust Commn, 2006–09. Dep. Chm., Places for People, 1998–2005; Chairman: Braunstone Community Assoc., 2002–06; Community Resettlement Support Project, 2013–16. Chairman: St Philips Centre for Study and Engagement in a Multi Faith Society, 2005–12; St Albans Diocesan Bd of Educn, 2013–; Eastern Reg. Ministry Course, 2014–; Co-Chair: C of E Mission and Public Affairs Council, 2012–16. Dir, Dio. of St Albans Multi-Acad. Trust, 2016–. Trustee: Church Urban Fund, 2003–08; Near Neighbours, 2010–; Luton Roma Trust, 2015–; Just Finance Foundn, 2019–. Gov., Univ. of Bedfordshire, 2017–. Recreations: cooking, biography and history, walking, watching Rugby Union, housing and regeneration, The Archers. Address: Bishop's Lodge, Bedford Road, Cardington MK44 3SS. T: (01234) 831432. E: bishopbedford@stalbans.anglican.org.

**BEDFORD, Archdeacon of**; see Middlebrook, Ven. D. J.

**BEDFORD, Michael Charles Anthony**; QC 2016; b Shipley, W Riding, 23 Aug. 1962; s of Carl and Julia Bedford; m 1993, Rachel Foot; two s. Educ: Guthlaxton Coll., Leics; King's Coll. London (LLB Hons). Called to the Bar, Gray's Inn, 1985; in practice as barrister, specialising in planning and envmtl law, 1985–. Mem., Maserati Club. Recreations: Italian cars, French wine, English cheese. Address: Cornerstone Barristers, 2–3 Gray's Inn Square, WC1R 5JH. T: (020) 7242 4986. E: clerks@cornerstonebarristers.com.

**BEDFORD, Robin Steven; His Honour Judge Bedford**; a Circuit Judge, since 2013; b Heckmondwike, W Yorks, 1 Feb. 1964; s of Stanley and Anne Patricia Bedford; m 1999, Lynn Janet Ashbee; four s. Educ: Batley Grammar Sch.; Hatfield Poly. (BA Hons); Univ. of Huddersfield (LLM). Admitted as solicitor, 1988; Partner, 1989–2000, Sen. Partner, 2000–07, Jordans Solicitors; Solicitor-Advocate, Higher Courts (Civil), 2000–07; a Dep. Dist Judge, 2002–07; a Dist Judge, 2007–13. Recreations: classic cars, wine, cheese.

**BEDDINGTON, Steuart John Rudolf**, OBE 2016; freelance conductor; Artistic Director, English Sinfonia, 1981–90; b 1939; s of late L. H. Bedford and Lesley Florence Keitley Duff; m 1st, 1969, Norma Burrowes, qv; 2nd, 1980, Celia, er d of Mr and Mrs G. R. Harding; two d. Educ: Lancing Coll., Sussex; Royal Acad. of Music. Fellow, RCO; FRAM; BA. Royal Acad. of Music, 1965; English Opera Gp, later English Music Theatre Co., 1967–80 (Co-Artistic Dir, 1976–79); Artistic Dir, 1974–98, and Exec. Artistic Dir, 1987–98, Aldeburgh Festival. Debut at Metropolitan, NY, 1974 (Death in Venice); new prodn of The Marriage of Figaro, 1975. Has conducted with English Opera Gp, Welsh National Opera, Florentine Opera, Luxembourg Philharmonic, Royal Scottish Nat. Orch., Bordeaux Opera, Opera Theatre of St Louis, NY City Opera, Canadian Opera, Paris Opera, Cologne Opera, San Diego Opera; also at Royal Opera House, Covent Garden (operas incl. Owen Wingrave and Death in Venice, by Benjamin Britten, and Così Fan Tutte); also in Santa Fe, Buenos Aires, France, Belgium, Holland, Canada, Vienna, Denmark, etc. Recordings include a series of works by Benjamin Britten. Recreations: golf, gardening. Address: c/o HarrisonParrott Ltd, The Ark, 201 Talgarth Road, W6 8BJ.

**BEDFORD-JONES, Rt Rev. Michael Hugh Harold**; a Suffragan Bishop of Toronto, 1994–2008 (Area Bishop of York Scarborough, 1994–2006, of Trent-Durham, 2006–08); b 29 Sept. 1942; s of Rev. Canon Hugh Bedford-Jones and Gretchen Flagler Bedford-Jones (née Gray); m 1967, Jeanne Yvonne Soules. Educ: Toronto Univ. (BA 1965; MA 1979); Univ. of Trinity Coll., Toronto (STB 1968). Ordained deacon, 1967, priest, 1968; St James' Cathedral, Toronto: Asst Curate, 1968–70; Dir of Christian Educn, 1970–74; Sen. Asst, 1974–75; Rector, Ch. of the Epiphany, Scarborough, 1976–83; Regl Dean, Scarborough, 1980–83; Rector, St Aidan, Toronto, 1983–88; Regl Dean, Toronto East, 1985–88; Exec. Asst to Bishop of Toronto, 1988–91; Canon, St James' Cathedral, 1990; Dean of Dio. of Ontario and Rector of St George's Cathedral, Kingston, Ont, 1991–94. Hon. DD Univ. of Trinity Coll., Toronto, 1997; Hon. STD Thorneloe, 2004. Recreations: sailing, music, cottage life. Address: 384 Lakebreeze Drive, Newcastle, ON L1B 1P5, Canada. E: michaelbj94@hotmail.com.

**BEDI, Kirsten Frances**; see Oswald, K. F.

**BEDI, Prof. Raman**, DDS; DSc; FDSRCSE, FDSRCS, FFPH, FFGDP(UK); Professor of Transcultural Oral Health, since 2002, and Head, Centre for International Child Oral Health, since 2006, King's College, London; Director, Global Child Dental Health Taskforce, since 2006; b 20 May 1953; s of Satya-Paul Bedi and Raj Bedi (née Kaur); m 1986, Kathryn Jane Walter; three s. Educ: Headlands Sch.; Univ. of Bristol (BDS 1976, DDS 1993; DSc 2003); Trinity Coll., Bristol (DipHE Theol. 1979); Univ. of Manchester (MSc 1986). FDSRCSE 1982; FDSRCS 2002; FFPH 2003; FFGDP(UK) 2004. Lecturer in Paediatric Dentistry: Univ. of Manchester, 1979–82; Univ. of Hong Kong, 1983–86; Univ. of Edinburgh, 1988–91; Sen. Lectr in Paediatric Dentistry, Univ. of Birmingham, 1991–96; Prof. and Head of Dept of Transcultural Oral Health, Eastman Dental Inst., UCL, 1996–2002; Chief Dental Officer for England, DoH, 2002–05. Co-Dir, WHO Collaborating Centre for Disability, Culture and Oral Health, 1998–2008; Chm., Oral Health Gp, World Fedn of Public Health Assocs, 2012–. Member: NHS/DoH Top Team, 2002–05; Strategic Wider Participation Cttee, HEFCE, 2003–09; Bd, Higher Educn Leadership Foundn, 2003–06; Founding Mem., Nat. Health and Social Care Leadership Network, 2004–05. President: British Soc. for Disability and Oral Health, 2002; Educn Res. Gp, Internat. Assoc. for Dental Res., 2002–04 (Chm., Regl Develt Cttee, 2002–04); Chm., British Assoc. of Physicians of Indian Origin, 2006–09; Sec.-Gen., Global Assoc. of Physicians of Indian Origin, 2008–09. Chm., Global Child Dental Fund, 2008–; Trustee, Children's Soc., 2006–09. Mem., Gen. Synod of C of E, 1995–2005. Hon. FDSRCPGlas. Hon. DHL A. T. Still Univ., Arizona, 2009. Public Health Service Medal, USA, 2005. Publications: (ed with P. Jones) Betel-quid and Tobacco Chewing Among the Bangladeshi Community in the United Kingdom: usage and health issues, 1995; (with P. Jones) Embracing Goodwill: establishing healthy alliances with black organisations, 1996; (ed jtly) Dentists, Patients and Ethnic Minorities: towards the new millennium, 1996; (with P. A. Lowe) Best Practise in Primary Healthcare: oral healthcare delivery in a multi-ethnic society, 1997; (with J. Sardo Infirri) The Root Cause: oral health care in disadvantaged communities, 1999; (with E. Davidson and J. J. Liu) Health Care Professionals of Indian Origin: a common agenda, 2012; contribs to scientific jls. Recreations: chess, tennis, travelling. Address: Oak Cottage, 12 Manor Way, Potters Bar, Herts EN6 1EL. Club: Athenæum.

**BEDINGFELD, Sir Henry (Edgar) Paston-**, 10th Bt cr 1661, of Oxburgh, Norfolk; Norroy and Ulster King of Arms, 2010–14; b 7 Dec. 1943; s of Sir Edmund Paston-Bedingfeld, 9th Bt and late Joan Lynette (née Rees); S father, 2011; m 1968, Mary Kathleen, d of Brig. R. D. Ambrose, CIE, OBE, MC; two s two d. Educ: Ampleforth College, York. Chartered Surveyor. Rouge Croix Pursuivant of Arms, 1983–93; York Herald of Arms, 1993–2010. Genealogist, British Assoc. of SMO Malta, 1995–2000. Pres., Norfolk Heraldry Soc., 2006– (Founder, 1975); Vice-President: Cambridge Univ. Heraldic and Genealogical Soc., 1988–; Royal Soc. of St George, 2012–; Mem. Exec. Cttee, Standing Council of the Baronetage, 2012–. Patron, Breckland Soc., 2003–. Rep. of Duke of Norfolk, Commn d'Inf. et de Liaison des Assocs Nobles d'Europe, 1994–2016. Freeman of the City of London; Liveryman: Scriveners' Co. Master, 2012–13). Kt of Sovereign Mil. Order of Malta. Publications: Oxburgh Hall, The First 500 Years, 1982; (jtly) Heraldry, 1993. Heir: s Richard Edmund Ambrose Paston-Bedingfeld, (Father Benedict), b 8 Feb. 1975. Address: Oxburgh Hall, Norfolk PE33 9PS. T: (01366) 328269.

**BEDNORZ, Johannes-Georg**, PhD; Physicist at IBM Research Laboratory, Zürich, since 1982 (IBM Fellow 1987); b 16 May 1950. Educ: Univ. of Münster (Masters 1976); Swiss Federal Institute of Technology, ETH Zürich (PhD 1984). Nobel Prize for Physics (jtly), 1987. Publications: papers in learned jls on new super-conducting materials. Address: IBM Zürich Research Laboratory, Säumerstrasse 4, 8803 Rüschlikon, Switzerland.

**BEECH, Prof. David John**, PhD; FMedSci; Professor of Cardiovascular Science, since 2000, and Director, Cardiovascular Research, since 2008, University of Leeds; b Chesterfield, 5 March 1964; s of John and Valerie Beech; m 1989, Maggie Nicol; two s one d. Educ: Silverdale Comprehensive Sch.; Univ. of Manchester (BSc Pharmacol. 1985); St George's Hosp. Med. Sch., Univ. of London (PhD Pharmacol. 1988). Res. Fellow, Univ. of Washington, 1988–90; Wellcome Trust Fellow, Univs of London and Leeds, 1990–93; Lectr in Pharmacol., Univ. of Leeds, 1993–2000. Reviewing Ed., British Jl Pharmacol., 1997–2001; Reviewing Ed., 1997–2005, Sen. Ed., 2005–06, Jl Physiol. Member: Selection Panel, Wellcome Trust-Dept of Biotechnol. India Alliance, 2009–15; Population and Systems Medicine Bd, MRC, 2010–14. FMedSci 2013. Publications: contribs to Nature. Recreation: running. Address: Leeds Institute of Cardiovascular and Metabolic Medicine, University of Leeds, Leeds LS2 9JT. T: (0113) 343 4323. E: d.j.beech@leeds.ac.uk.

**BEECH, Jacqueline Elaine; Her Honour Judge Beech**; a Circuit Judge, since 2007; Designated Civil Judge for Cumbria and Lancashire, since 2017; b Coventry, 8 Jan. 1958; d of Deric Charles Beech and Maureen Mary Beech (née Clooney). Educ: Wolston High Sch. Sec. Mod.; Tile Hill Coll. of Further Educn; Preston Poly. (BA Hons 1980). Called to the Bar, Middle Temple, 1981; a Recorder, 2002–07. A Judge of the Upper Tribunal (Admin. Appeals Chamber), 2009– (Chairman: Transport Tribunal, 2000–09; London Bus Permits Appeal Panel, 2002–09). Publications: (contrib. transport section) Atkins Court Forms, vol. 39, 2nd edn 2006, 3rd edn 2010. Recreations: fell walking and all things Cumbrian, arts and literature, fine food and wine (Higher Cert. in Wine and Spirits, Wine & Spirit Education Trust). Address: Preston Combined Court Centre, The Law Courts, Openshaw Place, Ringway, Preston, Lancs PR1 2LL. T: (01772) 844700. Club: Reform.

**BEECHAM,** family name of **Baron Beecham**.

**BEECHAM,** Baron *cr* 2010 (Life Peer), of Benwell and Newcastle upon Tyne in the County of Tyne and Wear; **Jeremy Hugh Beecham,** Kt 1994; DL; Member, Newcastle upon Tyne City Council, since 1967 (Leader, 1977–94); Consultant, Beecham Peacock, since 2002; *b* 17 Nov. 1944; *s* of Laurence and Florence Beecham; *m* 1968, Brenda Elizabeth (*née* Woolf) (*d* 2010); one *s* one *d. Educ:* Royal Grammar Sch., Newcastle upon Tyne; University Coll., Oxford (First Cl. Hons Jurisprudence; MA). Chm., OU Labour Club, 1964. Admitted Solicitor, 1968; Partner, Allan Henderson Beecham & Peacock, subseq. Beecham Peacock, 1968–2002. Dir, Northern Develt Co., 1986–91. Newcastle upon Tyne City Council: Chairman: Social Services Cttee, 1973–77; Policy and Resources Cttee, 1977–94; Finance Cttee, 1979–85; Develt Cttee, 1995–97; Newcastle City Challenge, 1992–97. Chairman: AMA, 1991–97 (Dep. Chm., 1984–86; Vice Chm., 1986–91); Local Govt Assoc., 1995–2004 (Vice Chm., 2004–10); Review of Local Public Services in Wales, 2005–06; Vice Chm., Northern Regl Councils Assoc., 1986–91. Labour Party: Member: Local and Regl Govt Sub-Cttee, NEC, 1971–83, 1991–; NEC/Shadow Cabinet Wkg Pty on Future of Local Govt, 1984–87; Domestic and Internat. Policy Cttee, 1992–; Jt Policy Cttee, 1992–; NEC, 1998–2010 (Chm., 2005–06). Opposition spokesman on health, 2010–12, on local govt, 2010–, on justice, 2012–, on housing, 2015–, H of L. Member: RTPI Working Party on Public Participation in Planning, 1980–82; Historic Bldgs and Monuments Commn for England, 1983–87; Local and Central Govt Relns Res. Cttee, Joseph Rowntree Meml Trust, 1987–96; President's Cttee, Business in the Community, 1988–; Bd of Trustees, NE Civic Trust, 1989–92; NHS Modernisation Bd, 2000–04; Community Voluntary and Local Services Honours Cttee, 2005–10. Pres., BURA, 1996–2009. Participant, Königswinter Conf., 1986. Member: Council of Management, Neighbourhood Energy Action, 1987–89; Council, Common Purpose, 1989–; President: Age Concern Newcastle, 1995–2017; Newcastle Choral Soc., 1997–; Newcastle People to People, 1998–2007; Vice President: Community Foundn, 2000–; Newcastle CVS, 2001–. Mem. Adv. Bd, Harold Hartog Sch. of Govt, Tel Aviv Univ., 2005–; Mem. Bd, New Israel Fund, 2007–. Trustee, Trusthouse Charitable Foundn, 1999–2013. Contested (Lab) Tynemouth, 1970. DL Tyne and Wear, 1995. Hon. Freeman Newcastle upon Tyne, 1995. Hon. Fellow, Univ. of Northumbria (formerly Newcastle upon Tyne Poly.), 1989. Hon. DCL Newcastle, 1992. *Recreations:* reading, history, music, very amateur photography, the Northumbrian countryside. *Address:* (office) House of Lords, SW1A 0PW; 39 The Drive, Gosforth, Newcastle upon Tyne NE3 4AJ. *T:* (0191) 285 1888.

**BEECHAM, Sir Robert Adrian,** 5th Bt *cr* 1914, of Ewanville, Huyton, co. Palatine of Lancaster; *b* 6 Jan. 1942; *yr s* of Sir Adrian Welles Beecham, 3rd Bt and Barbara Joyce (*née* Cohen); *S* brother, 2011, but his name does not appear on the Official Roll of the Baronetage; *m* 1969, Daphne Mattinson; one *s* one *d. Educ:* Winchester; Clare Coll., Cambridge (BA 1963; MA 1967). *Heir: s* Michael John Beecham [*b* 1972; *m* 2004, Rachel Smith; two *s*].

**BEECHEY, John,** CBE 2016; arbitrator, in own practice, since 2015; *b* London, 18 June 1952; *s* of Stanley Leonard Beechey and Marjorie Alexandra Beechey; *m* 1982, Jennifer Gibbons; one *s* one *d. Educ:* Dulwich Coll.; Christ Church, Oxford (BA French and German). FCIArb 1982. Admitted solicitor, 1977; Partner, Clifford Chance LLP, 1983–2008; Pres., ICC Internat. Court of Arbitration, 2009–15; Mem., Governing Bd, ICCA, 2018–. Mem. Bd, ICC UK, 2015–. Chm., BVI Internat. Arbitration Centre, 2016–; Mem., Investment Adv. Panel, Woodsford Litigation Funding, 2016–. *Recreations:* arts (especially literature and opera), travel, walking. *Address:* Arbitration Chambers Hong Kong, Chinachem Hollywood Centre Suite 801, 1 Hollywood Road, Central, Hong Kong. *T:* 21406555; Arbitration Chambers, Lamb Building, Temple, EC4Y 7AS. *T:* (020) 7167 2040. *E:* jb@beecheyarbitration.com. *Club:* Garrick.

**BEECHING, Sarah Margaret;** Founder and Executive Director, Oshun Partnership, since 2011; *b* Kingston upon Thames, 9 Sept. 1969; *d* of Richard Kirby Todd and Susan Todd; *m* 1999, Jean-Michel Beeching; one *s* one *d. Educ:* Tiffin Girls' Sch.; City of London Poly. (BA Hons Financial Econs 1991); Birkbeck Coll., Univ. of London (MSc Econs 1994); Diplôme d'Études Française 2005. Research Analyst: London Business Sch., 1994–96; RIIA, 1994–96; Economist, Africa Econs Dept, 1996–98, Hd, Conflict and Security Policy Team, 1998–2001, DFID; sabbatical, Hong Kong and Paris, 2001–05; Cabinet Office: Conflict and Security Strategy Manager, 2006–08; Sen. Policy Advr, Afghanistan Strategy Team, Stabilisation Rev. Team and G20 London Summit, 2008–09; Hd, Campaigns and UN High Level Events, DFID, 2009–11. Chair, Bd of Trustees, Out of the Box Partnerships, 2014–. Gov., Tiffin Girls' Sch., 2016–. FRSA 2019. Mem. RGS. Editor, PHARE and TACIS jls, EC, 1995–2003. *Publications:* (jtly) The Role of Foreign Direct Investment in Central and Eastern Europe: multinationals in transition, 1997. *Recreations:* exploring uncharted corners of the planet and changing the world, one email at a time. *Address:* Oshun Partnership, West End House, 33 Lower Richmond Road, SW14 7EZ. *T:* (020) 8878 8940. *E:* sarah.beeching@oshunpartnership.com.

**BEEDHAM, Trevor,** FRCOG; Consultant Gynaecologist and Obstetrician, The Royal London and St Bartholomew's Hospitals, 1981–2009; Associate Dean, 2006–08, and Hon. Professor, since 2008, Barts and the London (formerly Queen Mary) School of Medicine and Dentistry; *b* 30 July 1942; *s* of Herbert and Olive Beedham (*née* Spikings); *m* 1966, Anne Darnbrough-Cameron; two *s* one *d. Educ:* High Pavement Grammar Sch., Nottingham; Royal Dental Hosp., and London Hosp. Med. Sch., Univ. of London (BDS 1965; MB BS Hons 1972). MRCOG 1977, FRCOG 1989. Barts and The London NHS Trust: Clin. Dir, 2003–08; Dep. Med. Dir, 2006–09; Divl Dir, 2008–09. Examr, MB BS, DRCOG, MRCOG, 1981–; PLAB Part 1 Panel and Med. Sch., 2001–09. Visitor, GMC, 2001–. Asst. Soc. of Apothecaries, 1996– (Chm., Exam. Bd, 2004–09, 2012–19; Master, 2009–10; Dean, 2012–16). Mem., Forensic Adv. Cttee, 2013–17. Advr, UK Assoc. of Forensic Nurses, 2012–18. Pres., Friends of Royal London Hosp., 2015–. Gov., Sons of the Clergy, 2010–18. Hon. DSc Buckingham, 2010. *Publications:* contrib. and ed text books in obstetrics and gynaecology; referee for BJOG, Obstetrician and Gynaecologist, Jl of RSM, etc; contrib. British Jl of Hospital Medicine. *Recreations:* swimming, sailing. *Address:* 15 Lawrie Park Crescent, Sydenham, SE26 6HH. *T:* (020) 3252 1024. *Clubs:* Athenæum, City Livery (Mem. Council, 2014–17).

**BEELS, Jonathan Sidney Spencer,** CMG 1998; HM Diplomatic Service, retired; *b* 19 Jan. 1943; *s* of Sidney Beels and Joan Constance Beels (*née* Groves); *m* 1st, 1966, Patricia Joan Mills (marr. diss. 1982); one *s* one *d*; 2nd, 1983, Penelope Jane Aedy (marr. diss. 1998); 3rd, 2015, Mary Clare Metcalfe. *Educ:* Ardingly Coll.; St John's Coll., Cambridge (MA 1969). Entered Diplomatic Service, 1965; Prague, 1970–73; FCO, 1973–77; on loan to Northern Ireland Office, 1977–78; resigned from Diplomatic Service, 1979; Govt Service, Sultanate of Oman, 1979–83; Man. Dir, Control Risks (GS) Ltd, 1983–88; rejoined Diplomatic Service, 1988; Counsellor, Nicosia, 1992–93; FCO, 1994–98. Consultant, MoD, 1998–99. *Recreations:* shooting, quad-biking, photography using a drone.

**BEENSTOCK, Prof. Michael,** PhD; Pinchas Sapir Professor of Economics, Hebrew University, Jerusalem, 1996–2014, now Emeritus; *b* 18 June 1946; *s* of Sidney and Taubie Beenstock; *m* 1968, Ruchi Hager; one *s* four *d. Educ:* London Sch. of Econs and Political Science (BSc, MSc; PhD 1976). Econ. Advisor, HM Treasury, 1970–76; Economist, World Bank, Washington, DC, 1976–78; Sen. Res. Fellow, London Business Sch., 1978–81; Esmée Fairbairn Prof. of Finance and Investment, City Univ. Business Sch., 1981–87; Prof. of Econs, Hebrew Univ., Jerusalem, 1987–96 (Lady Davis Prof., 1987–89). *Publications:* The Foreign Exchange Market, 1978; A Neoclassical Analysis of Macroeconomic Policy, 1980; Health, Migration and Development, 1980; The World Economy in Transition, 1983, 2nd edn 1984; Work, Welfare and Taxation, 1986; (jtly) Insurance for Unemployment, 1986; (ed) Modelling the Labour Market, 1988; (jtly) Modelling the World Shipping Markets, 1993; Heredity, Family and Inequality, 2012; (jtly) The Econometric Analysis of Non-Stationary Spatial Panel Data, 2019. *Recreation:* music. *Address:* Kefar Etzion 35/4, Jerusalem 93392, Israel. *T:* (2) 6723184.

**BEER, Dame Gillian (Patricia Kempster),** DBE 1998; FBA 1991; FRSL; King Edward VII Professor of English Literature, University of Cambridge, 1994–2002; President, Clare Hall, Cambridge, 1994–2001 (Fellow, 2001–02, Hon. Fellow, 2002); *b* 27 Jan. 1935; *d* of Owen Kempster Thomas and Ruth Winifred Bell; *m* 1962, Prof. John Bernard Beer, FBA; three *s. Educ:* St Anne's Coll., Oxford (MA, BLitt; Hon. Fellow, 1989); LittD Cambridge. Asst Lectr, Bedford Coll., London, 1959–62; part-time Lectr, Liverpool Univ., 1962–64; Cambridge University: Asst Lectr 1966–71, Lectr, subseq. Reader in Literature and Narrative, 1971–89; Prof. of English, 1989–94; Fellow, Girton Coll., 1965–94 (Hon. Fellow, 1994). Andrew W. Mellon Sen. Scholar, Yale Center for British Art, 2009–11. Vice-Pres., British Acad., 1994–96; Pres., Hist. of Science Sect., BAAS, 1998. Trustee, BM, 1992–2002. Chm., Poetry Book Soc., 1992–96; President: British Comparative Lit. Soc., 2003–10; British Lit. and Sci. Soc., 2006–; Modern Humanities Res. Assoc., 2011. Chm. Judges, Booker Prize, 1997. Gen. Ed., Cambridge Studies in Nineteenth Century Lit. and Culture, 1992–. FRSL 2006. Hon. Fellow, Univ. of Wales, Cardiff, 1996. Foreign Hon. Mem., Amer. Acad. of Arts and Scis, 2001; Internat. Mem., Amer. Philosophical Soc., 2010. Hon. LittD: Liverpool, 1995; Anglia Poly., 1997; Leicester, 1999; London, 2001; Sorbonne, 2001; QUB, 2005; Hon. DLitt: Oxford, 2005; Harvard, 2012; St Andrews, 2013; Hon. Dr Ghent, 2018. Rose Mary Crawshay Prize, British Acad., 1983; Truman Capote Prize for Literary Criticism, 2017. *Publications:* Meredith: a change of masks, 1970; The Romance, 1970; Darwin's Plots, 1983, 3rd edn 2009; George Eliot, 1986; Arguing with the Past, 1989; (ed) The Waves by Virginia Woolf, 1992; (ed) Between the Acts by Virginia Woolf, 1992; Open Fields, 1996; Virginia Woolf: the common ground, 1996; (ed) The Origin of Species by Charles Darwin, 1996; (ed) Persuasion by Jane Austen, 1998; (ed) The Wolfman and Other Cases by Sigmund Freud, 2002; (ed) Love and Mr Lewisham by H. G. Wells, 2009; Jabberwocky: collected and annotated edition of the poems of Lewis Carroll, 2012; Alice in Space: the sideways Victorian world of Lewis Carroll, 2016. *Recreations:* music, travel, conversation. *Address:* Clare Hall, Herschel Road, Cambridge CB3 9AL. *T:* (01223) 356384.

**BEER, Ian David Stafford,** CBE 1992; MA; Head Master of Harrow, 1981–91; Chairman of Trustees, RFU Injured Players Foundation, 2008–11 (Founder, 1993, Trustee, 1993–2008, and Chairman of Trustees, 2005–08, SPIRE Rugby Trust (formerly SPIRE); Chairman of Trustees, RFU Charitable Trust, 2005–08); *b* 28 April 1931; *s* of late William Beer and Doris Ethel Beer; *m* 1960, Angela Felce, *d* of Col E. S. G. Howard, MC, RA and F. D. Howard; two *s* one *d. Educ:* Whitgift Sch.; St Catharine's Coll., Cambridge (Exhibitioner; MA, PGCE). ESU Walter Page Scholar, 1968. Second Lieut in 1st Bn Royal Fusiliers, 1950. Bursar, Ottershaw Sch., 1955; Guinness Ltd, 1956–57; House Master, Marlborough Coll., Wilts, 1957–61; Head Master: Ellesmere Coll., Salop, 1961–69; Lancing Coll., Sussex, 1969–81. Chairman: HMC Academic Cttee, 1977–79; HMC, 1980; Physical Educn Working Gp for Nat. Curriculum, 1990–91; ISJC, then ISC, 1997–2001 (Vice-Chm., 1994–97; Chm., Adv. Cttee, 1988–91); Vice-Chm., GBA, 1994–2001; Founder Mem., Gen. Teaching Council, 2000–01. Mem., Sports Council, 1992–94. Chm. Council, Winston Churchill Meml Trust, 1997–2006 (Mem., 1990–2006; Trustee, 1998–2006); Trustee, RMC Group plc Welfare Trust, 1983–2006. Evelyn Wrench Lectr, ESU, 1988, 1990. Governor: Whitgift Sch., 1986–91; Charterhouse Sch., 1991–93; Malvern Coll., 1991–2001; Mem. Council, Univ. of Buckingham, 1992–96; Chm. of Trustees, Lancing Coll. Chapel Trust, 1996–2008. Chm. Editorial Bd, Rugby World and Post (formerly Rugby World, then Rugby Post), 1977–93. JP Shropshire, 1963–69, W Sussex, 1970–81, Middx, 1981–91, Glos, 1992. Hon. FCP 1990. Order of St Ethelbert, Hereford Cathedral, 2016. *Publications:* But Headmaster!, 2001. *Recreations:* Rugby Football Union (Mem. Exec. Cttee, 1984–95; Vice Pres., 1991–93; Pres., 1993–94) (formerly: played Rugby for England; CURFC (Capt.), Harlequins, Bath, Old Whitgiftians), painting, reading, zoology, meeting people. *Address:* Ankerdine House, South Parade, Ledbury, Herefordshire HR8 2HB. *Clubs:* East India, Devonshire, Sports and Public Schools; Hawks (Cambridge).

**BEER, Dame Janet (Patricia),** DBE 2018; PhD; Vice-Chancellor, University of Liverpool, since 2015; *b* 1 Aug. 1956; *d* of Derek Stanley John Beer and Jean Patricia Beer; *m* 1996, David Woodman; one *s* one *d. Educ:* Univ. of Reading (BA Hons); Univ. of Warwick (MA; PhD 1984). Pt-time Lectr, Univ. of Warwick, 1979–80 and 1981–83; Yale Fellow, Yale Univ., 1980–81; Educn Adminr, ILEA, 1983–89; Sen., then Principal Lectr, Univ. of Surrey, Roehampton, later Roehampton Univ., 1989–97; Hd, Dept of English, 1998–2002, Pro Vice-Chancellor and Dean of Faculty, 2002–07, Manchester Metropolitan Univ.; Vice-Chancellor, Oxford Brookes Univ., 2007–15. Specialist Advr, Educn and Skills Select Cttee, H of C, 2000–07; Member of Board: Higher Educn Acad., 2004–09; Equality Challenge Unit, 2008– (Chair, 2011–17); Universities UK, 2009– (Vice-Pres., 2013–17; Pres., 2017–19); UCAS, 2013–17; Nat. Centre for Univs and Business, 2013–17; British Council, 2014–; Mem., Adv. Bd, Higher Educn Policy Inst., 2007–18; Chairman: Higher Educn Public Information Steering Gp (formerly Teaching Quality Information/Nat. Student Survey Steering Gp), 2009–16; University Alliance, 2009–12; Supporting Professionalism in Admissions, 2012–14. Vis. Fellow, Nuffield Coll., Oxford, 2011–15. *Publications:* Edith Wharton: traveller in the land of letters, 1990, 2nd edn 1995; Kate Chopin, Edith Wharton and Charlotte Perkins Gilman: studies in short fiction, 1997, 2nd edn 2005; Edith Wharton, 2002; (ed jtly) Special Relationships: Anglo-American antagonisms and affinities 1854–1936, 2002; (jtly) American Feminism: key source documents 1848–1920, 2002; (ed) The Cambridge Companion to Kate Chopin, 2008; (with Avril Horner) Edith Wharton: sex, satire and the older woman, 2011. *Recreations:* swimming, walking, theatre, family. *Address:* Office of the Vice-Chancellor, University of Liverpool, The Foundation Building, Liverpool L69 7ZX. *T:* (0151) 7942003. *E:* J.P.Beer@Liverpool.ac.uk.

**BEER, Jason;** QC 2011; a Recorder, since 2010; *b* Gillingham, Kent, 11 Nov. 1969; *s* of Barrington Beer and June Patricia Beer; *m* 2007, Samantha Bird; one *s* one *d. Educ:* Gillingham Grammar Sch. for Boys; Warwick Univ. (LLB Hons). Called to the Bar, Inner Temple, 1992; Jun. Counsel to the Crown, 2008–11. *Publications:* Public Inquiries, 2011. *Address:* 5 Essex Court, Temple, EC4Y 9AH. *T:* (020) 7410 2000, *Fax:* (020) 7410 2011. *E:* beer@5essexcourt.co.uk.

**BEER, Ven. John Stuart;** Archdeacon of Cambridge (formerly Ely), 2004–14; Bye Fellow, Fitzwilliam College, Cambridge, since 2001; *b* 15 March 1944; *s* of late John Gilbert Beer and May (*née* Scott); *m* 1970, Susan, *d* of late Gordon and Jessie Spencer; two *s* one *d. Educ:* Roundhay Sch.; Pembroke Coll., Oxford (MA (Theol.) 1968); Westcott House,

Cambridge (MA 1976). Advertising and Finance, Rowntree & Co. Ltd, York, 1965–69; ordained deacon, 1971, priest, 1972; Asst Curate, St John the Baptist, Knaresborough, 1971–74; Fellow and Chaplain, Fitzwilliam Coll., Cambridge, and Chaplain, New Hall, 1974–80; Rector of Toft with Hardwick, Caldecote and Childerley, 1980–87; Dir of Post Ordination Training and Dir of Studies for Readers, dio. of Ely, and Vicar of Grantchester, 1987–97; Dir of Ordinands, 1987–2002, Co-Dir, 1993–2002, dio. Ely; Archdeacon of Huntingdon, 1997–2004, and of Wisbech, 2003–04. Mem., Ethics Cttee, Dunn Res. Inst., 1987–2001. Chm., Cathedral Pilgrims Assoc. Conf., 1987–97. *Publications:* Who is Jesus?, 1982; (contrib.) Sermons from St Benet's, 2010; contribs to theol jls. *Recreations:* tennis, golf, music, wine.

**BEER, Air Vice-Marshal Peter George,** CB 1995; CBE 1987 (OBE 1979); LVO 1974; Fellow and Home Bursar, Jesus College, Oxford, 1997–2006, now Emeritus Fellow; *b* 16 July 1941; *s* of Herbert George Beer and Kathleen Mary Beer; *m* 1975, Fiona Georgina Hamilton Davidson (*d* 2015); two *s*. *Educ:* Hugh Sexey's Sch., Bruton; MA Oxon 1997. Equerry to HM the Queen, 1971–74; Officer Commanding: No 55 Sqdn, 1977–79; RAF Brize Norton, 1984–86; Dir, RAF Plans and Programmes, 1989–91; Comdr British Forces, Falkland Is, 1991–92; Dir-Gen. Training and Personnel, RAF, 1992–94; COS, Personnel and Training Comd, RAF, 1994–95, retd. Non-exec. Dir, Oxford Radcliffe Hosps NHS Trust, 1997–2003. Vice-Pres., RAF Hockey Assoc. *Recreations:* cricket, opera, travel. *Address:* Southfield, Stonehill Lane, Southmoor, Oxon OX13 5HU. *Clubs:* Royal Air Force, MCC.

**BEER, Victoria Louise,** CBE 2013; Regional Schools Commissioner for Lancashire and West Yorkshire, since 2015; *b* Middlesbrough, 22 Oct. 1966; *d* of Robert Littlefair and Margaret Littlefair; *m* 1998, Roger Beer. *Educ:* Northfield Comp. Sch., Billingham; Nottingham Trent Univ. (BA Hons Communication Studies); Univ. of Leicester (PGCE English). NPQH. Teacher of English, Macmillan Coll., Middlesbrough, 1993–98; Head of English, Wright Robinson Sch., Manchester, 1998–2001; Dep. Head, 2001–07, Head, 2007–11, Exec. Principal, 2011–15, Ashton on Mersey Sch.; Exec. Principal, W Trafford Learning Partnership, 2015. Chm., Teaching Schs Council, 2011–15. *Recreations:* gardening, holidays. *Address:* 8 Marple Old Road, Offerton Green, Stockport SK2 5HQ. *E:* vickybeer@yahoo.co.uk.

**BEERLING, Prof. David John,** PhD; FRS 2014; Sorby Professor of Natural Sciences, since 2014, and Director, Leverhulme Centre for Climate Change Mitigation, since 2016, University of Sheffield (Professor of Palaeoclimatology, 2002–14); *b* Tunbridge Wells, 1965; *s* of John William Beerling, *qv*; *m* 2011, Juliette Dawn Fraser; one *s*. *Educ:* University Coll., then Univ. of Wales Coll., Cardiff (BSc Hons 1987; PhD 1990). Post-doctoral research scientist: RHBNC, 1990–91; Univ. of Durham, 1991–93; Royal Soc. Univ. Res. Fellow, 1994–2002. Edward P. Bass Dist. Vis. Envmtl Schol., 2008–09, and Dist. Lectr, 2008, Yale Inst. of Biospheric Studies, Yale Univ. Royal Soc. Wolfson Res. Merit Award, 2009–14. Scientific Consultant, How to Grow a Planet, BBC TV series, 2011–12. Lectures: Eighth Annual Venn, Maths Inst., Univ. of Hull, 2008; Rothamsted, Rothamsted Res., Harpenden, 2012; Holden Botany, Univ. of Nottingham, 2013. Philip Leverhulme Prize in Earth Scis, Leverhulme Trust, 2001. *Publications:* (with F. I. Woodward) Vegetation and the Terrestrial Carbon Cycle: modelling the first 400 million years, 2001; The Emerald Planet: how plants changed Earth's history, 2007, repr. 2012; Making Eden: how plants transformed a barren planet, 2019; contribs to learned jls incl. Philosophical Trans Royal Soc. *Recreations:* fishing (coarse, game, sea), fell running, literature, history of science, food, cinema. *Address:* Department of Animal and Plant Sciences, University of Sheffield, Sheffield S10 2TN. *T:* (0114) 222 4359, *Fax:* (0114) 222 0002. *E:* d.j.beerling@sheffield.ac.uk.

**BEERLING, John William;** freelance media consultant, film director, and writer, since 1994; cruise ship lecturer, since 2008; *b* 12 April 1937; *s* of Raymond Starr and Mary Elizabeth Julia Beerling; *m* 1st, 1959, Carol Ann Reynolds (marr. diss. 1991); one *s* one *d*; 2nd, 1993, Celia Margaret Potter (marr. diss. 1998); 3rd, 1999, Susan Patricia Armstrong. *Educ:* Sir Roger Manwood's Grammar Sch., Sandwich, Kent. National Service, RAF, 1955–57. Joined BBC, 1957; Studio Manager, 1958; Producer, 1962; Head of Radio 1 Programmes, 1983; Controller, Radio 1, 1985–93. Chairman: Radio Data Systems Forum, Geneva, 1993–2015; Radio Skipton CIC, 2012–14; Dir, Stereo Pair, 1997–98; Partner, The Great Outdoor Picture Co., 1998–2002; Man. Dir, Classic Gold Digital Radio, 2000–02. Gov., Brits Sch. for Performing Arts and Technology, 1995–2006. Pres., TRIC, 1992–93. Fellow, Radio Acad., 2005. *Publications:* Emperor Rosko's D. J. Handbook, 1976; Radio 1—The Inside Scene, 2008; Inside Radio 1, 2015. *Recreations:* photography, fishing, ski-ing, watercolour artist. *Address:* White Rose Cottage, 2 Farn Brakes, Church Street, Rudgwick, Horsham RH12 3EJ. *W:* www.johnnybeerling.co.uk.
*See also* D. J. Beerling.

**BEESLEY, Dr Ian Blake;** Chairman: Wisdom of the Ancients Consulting Ltd, since 2003; Postcode Address File Advisory Board, since 2007; Secretary-General, European Chiropractors' Union, since 2015; *b* 11 July 1942; *s* of Frank and Catherine Beesley; *m* 1st, 1964, Birgitte (*née* Smith) (marr. diss. 1982); 2nd, 1983, Elizabeth (*née* Wigley) (marr. diss. 1998); one *s* two *d*; 3rd, 2000, Edna (*née* Chivers) (CBE 2006); one step *s*. *Educ:* Manchester Grammar School; St Edmund Hall, Oxford (PPE 1963; MA; Cert. in Statistics 1964); Queen Mary, Univ. of London (PhD 2013). Central Statistical Office, 1964–76; Chief Statistician, HM Treasury, 1976–78; Dep. Head, Unit supporting Lord Rayner, PM's adviser on efficiency, 1981–83; Under Sec. and Official Head of PM's Efficiency Unit, 1983–86; Partner, Price Waterhouse, subseq. PricewaterhouseCoopers, 1986–2003. Comr for Nat. Statistics, 2004–08. Official Historian, Cabinet Office, 2007–16. Alternate Mem., Jarratt Cttee on efficiency in universities, 1984–85; Mem., Croham Cttee to review function and operation of UGC, 1985–87. Member: Employment Service Adv. Gp, 1992–98; Expert Gp advising Govt on Nat. Experience Corps, 2000–01; Home Sec.'s Expert Gp on compilation and publication of crime statistics, 2006. Mem., Council, Surrey Univ., 1986–92. FSS 1966; FRSA 1990. Freeman: Co. of Mgt Consultants, 2003; City of London, 2003. *Publications:* Policy analysis and evaluation in British Government (RIPA seminar papers), 1983; (contrib.) Straight from the CEO, 1998; (contrib.) The Real Iron Lady: working with Mrs T, 2013; Official History of the Cabinet Secretaries, 2016; contribs to Jl Royal Statistical Soc., BACKspace (Jl Eur. Chiropractors' Union); articles on value for money in the arts. *Address:* (office) 15 Park Lane, Southwold IP18 6HL. *Club:* Savile.

**BEESLEY, Peter Frederick Barton;** Consultant Registrar, Faculty Office of the Archbishop of Canterbury, since 2016 (Registrar, 1981–2012; Joint Registrar, 2012–16); Partner and Consultant, Lee Bolton Monier-Williams, since 2008; *b* 30 April 1943; *s* of Ronald Fitzgerald Barton Beesley and Mary Kurczyn (*née* Parker); *m* 1974, Elizabeth Jane Grahame; one *s* two *d*. *Educ:* King's School, Worcester; Exeter Univ. (LLB); Coll. of Law, Guildford. Articled Clerk and Asst Solicitor, Windeatt & Windeatt, 1965–68; Asst Solicitor, 1968–69, Partner, 1969–2008, Sen. Partner, 2000–08, Lee Bolton & Lee. Jt Registrar, Dio. St Albans, 1969–78; Registrar: Dio. of Guildford, 1981–2013; Woodard Corp., 1987–2011; Dio. of Ely, 2002–13 (Jt, 1978–2002); Dio. of Hereford, 2007–13 (Jt, 1983–2007). Legal Advr, Nat. Soc. (C of E) for Promoting Religious Educn, 1975–2013; Secretary: Ecclesiastical Law Assoc., 1978–98 (Vice-Chm., 1998–2000; Chm., 2000–02); Ecclesiastical Law Soc., 1987–2010; Mem. Legal Adv. Commn, General Synod of C of E, 1992–; Pres., City of Westminster Law Soc., 1991–92. Mem., Glaziers' Trust, 1996–2006 (Vice-Chm., 1998–2000; Chm., 2000–03). Liveryman, Glaziers' and Painters' of Glass Co., 1981 (Mem. Ct Assts, 1995–; Master, 2005–06); Chm., London Stained Glass Repository, 2009–11; View Chm., Glaziers Foundn, 2011–. Trustee, Arbory Trust, 2000–14; Bishopsland Educnl Trust, 2002–. Governor: Hampstead Parochial Sch., 1983–2003 (Chm., 1986–95); Sarum Hall Sch., 1997–. Canterbury Cross for services to C of E, Lambeth Palace, 2016. *Publications:* (contrib. jtly) Encyclopaedia of Forms and Precedents, Vol. 13, Ecclesiastical Law, 1987; Anglican Marriage in England and Wales, a Guide to the Law for Clergy, 1992. *Address:* (office) 1 The Sanctuary, Westminster, SW1P 3JT. *T:* (020) 7222 5381. *Clubs:* Athenæum, MCC.

**BEESLEY, Tracy;** *see* Hussell, T.

**BEESON, Andrew Nigel Wendover;** company director; *b* 30 March 1944; *s* of Nigel Wendover Beeson (killed in action 1944) and Anne Beeson (*née* Sutherland, now Hodges); *m* 1st, 1971, Susan Gerard (marr. diss. 1983); one *s* one *d*; 2nd, 1986, Carrie Martin; one *d*. *Educ:* Eton Coll. Partner, Capel Cure Myers, 1972–85; Director: ANZ Merchant Bank, 1985–87; ANZ McCaughan, 1987–89; Founder, Beeson Gregory Holdings Ltd, 1989; CEO, 1989–2001, Dep. Chm., 2001, Beeson Gregory Gp; Chm., Evolution Gp plc, 2002–03. Non-executive Director: IP2IPO Gp, 2001–04; Woolworths Gp, 2001–08; NB Real Estate Gp (formerly Nelson Bakewell Hldgs), 2001–10; Schroder Gp plc, 2004–16 (Sen. Ind. Dir, 2010–12; Chm., 2012–16); Queen's Club Ltd, 2007–10; Westhouse Hldgs, 2009–12; DataWind UK, 2007–13 (non-exec. Chm., 2007–12). Founding Chm., City Gp for Small Cos, 1992–95; Director: European Assoc. Securities Dealers, 1995–2002; European Assoc. Securities Dealers Automatic Quotations, 1996–2001; Assoc. of Private Client Investment Managers and Stockbrokers, 2002–03. Trustee, Tennis and Rackets Assoc., 1996–2013 (Vice Pres., 2015–). Achievement Award, Coopers & Lybrand, 1995. *Recreations:* Real tennis, shooting, collecting. *Address:* 21 Warwick Square, SW1V 2AB. *T:* (020) 7834 2903. *Clubs:* MCC (Mem. Cttee, 2004–07; Trustee, 2013–17), Pratt's, White's, Queen's (Trustee, 2017–); Swinley Golf (Ascot); Royal West Norfolk Golf.

**BEESON, Very Rev. Trevor Randall,** OBE 1997; writer; Dean of Winchester, 1987–96, now Dean Emeritus; *b* 2 March 1926; *s* of late Arthur William and Matilda Beeson; *m* 1950, Josephine Grace Cope (*d* 1997); two *d*. *Educ:* King's Coll., London (AKC 1950; FKC 1987); St Boniface Coll., Warminster. RAF Met Office, 1944–47. Deacon, 1951; Priest, 1952; Curate, Leadgate, Co. Durham, 1951–54; Priest-in-charge and subseq. Vicar of St Chad, Stockton-on-Tees, 1954–65; Curate of St Martin-in-the-Fields, London, 1965–71; Vicar of Ware, Herts, 1971–76; Canon of Westminster, 1976–87; Treasurer, Westminster, 1978–82; Rector of St Margaret's, Westminster, 1982–87; Chaplain to Speaker of House of Commons, 1982–87. Chaplain of St Bride's, Fleet Street, 1967–84. Television and radio commentator and presenter, 1968–82; Religious Programmes Advr, LWT, 1970–86. Chm., Christian Action, 1988–96. Gen. Sec., Parish and People, 1962–64; Editor, New Christian, and Man. Dir, Prism Publications Ltd, 1965–70; European Corresp. of The Christian Century (Chicago), 1970–83; Chm., SCM Press Ltd, 1978–87. Select Preacher, Oxford, 1980, 1991. Hon. Asst Priest, Romsey Abbey and United Benefice of Braishfield, 1997–. Mem. Council, WWF, 1987–94. MA (Lambeth) 1976; Hon. DLitt Southampton, 1999. *Publications:* New Area Mission, 1963; (jtly) Worship in a United Church, 1964; An Eye for an Ear, 1972; The Church of England in Crisis, 1973; Discretion and Valour: religious conditions in Russia and Eastern Europe, 1974 (trans. French, German, Italian, Finnish, Russian); Britain Today and Tomorrow, 1978; Westminster Abbey, 1981; A Vision of Hope: the churches and change in Latin America, 1984; (contrib.) God's Truth, 1988; A Dean's Diary: Winchester 1987–1996, 1997; Window on Westminster, 1998; Rebels and Reformers, 1999; (contrib.) AD 2000 Years of Christianity, 1999; The Bishops, 2002; (ed) Priests and Prelates, Daily Telegraph Obituaries, 2002; The Deans, 2004; (contrib.) Christianity: a complete guide, 2005; The Canons, 2006; Round the Church in 50 Years: a personal journey, 2007; In Tuneful Accord: the church musicians, 2009; The Church's Folk Songs: a history of hymns ancient and modern, 2011; The Church's Other Half: women's ministry, 2011; Priests and Politics, 2013; contrib. to DNB, Oxford Dictionary of the Church. *Recreation:* gardening. *Address:* 69 Greatbridge Road, Romsey, Hants SO51 8FE. *T:* (01794) 514627.
*See also* Very Rev. C. W. Taylor.

**BEESTON, James,** OBE 2004; Chairman, Invigour Ltd, 2001–09; *b* 2 April 1947; *s* of Richard and Mary Beeston; *m* 1971, Christine, *d* of Barry and Enid Thomas; two *s*. *Educ:* King Edward's, Camp Hill; Birmingham Sch. of Planning. DipTP. Birmingham City Council: Public Works Dept, 1965–74; Central Area Planning Officer, 1974–80; Divl Planning Officer, 1980–85; Asst Dir of Develt, 1985–87; Project Controller, National Indoor Arena; Co-ordinator, first phase, Birmingham Olympics bid; Develt Manager and Dep. Chief Exec., Birmingham Heartlands Ltd, 1987–92; Chief Executive: Birmingham Heartlands Develt Corp., 1992–98; Millennium Point Trust Co., 1997–2001. Dir, Beeston Associates Ltd, 2001–11. Mem., Governing Body, Birmingham City Univ., 2007–17. Governor: King Edward VI Camp Hill Sch. for Boys, Birmingham, 1996– (Chm., 2002–11); Schs of King Edward the Sixth in Birmingham, 2003–17 (Chm., 2011–15; Bailiff, 2016–17). *Publications:* (jtly) Negotiating with Planning Authorities. *Recreations:* family (two sons, Mark and Paul, and two grandchildren, Isabella and Henry), cricket, sport, gardening, travel.

**BEESTON, Kevin Stanley;** Chairman, Taylor Wimpey plc, 2010–Feb. 2020; *b* 18 Sept. 1962; *s* of Denis and Patricia Beeston; *m* 1991, Jayne Anne Knowles; two *s* one *d*. *Educ:* Gorleston Grammar Sch. ACMA 1986, FCMA 1990. Serco Group plc, 1985–2010: Finance Dir, 1996–99; Chief Exec., 1999–2002; Exec. Chm., 2002–07; Chm., 2007–10. Chairman: Partnerships in Care, 2007–14; Infinitas Learning BV, 2007–10; Domestic & General Hldgs, 2008–15; Equiniti, 2011–17; non-executive Director: IMI plc, 2005–12; FA Premier League Ltd, 2015–; Severn Trent, 2016–.

**BEETHAM, Geoffrey Howard,** CB 1992; Legal Adviser to Department of Transport, 1983–93; Principal Assistant Solicitor, Treasury Solicitor's Department, 1983–93; *b* 9 Jan. 1933; *s* of Reginald Percy Beetham and Hetty Lilian Beetham (*née* Redman); *m* 1st, 1956, Valerie Douglass (marr. diss. 1975); three *d*; 2nd, 1977, Carol Ann Dorrell; two step *s*. *Educ:* City of London Sch.; St John's Coll., Oxford (BA Jurisp.). Nat. Service, RAF, 1951–53. Solicitor, 1960; Assistant Solicitor: Metropolitan Borough of Battersea, 1960–65; London Borough of Wandsworth, 1965–70; Sen. Legal Assistant and Asst Solicitor, DoE, 1970–77; Asst Solicitor, Dept of Transport, 1977–83. Legal Mem., Mental Health Review Tribunal, 1994–2005. *Recreations:* throwing pots, music, countryside.

**BEETON, David Christopher,** CBE 1998; Chairman, Roman Baths Foundation, 2015–19; *b* 25 Aug. 1939; *s* of Ernest Beeton and Ethel Beeton; *m* 1968, Brenda Lomax; two *s*. *Educ:* Ipswich Sch.; King's Coll., London Univ. (LLB). Solicitor. Chief Exec., Bath CC, 1973–85; Sec., National Trust, 1985–89; Chief Exec., Historic Royal Palaces, 1989–99; Dir Gen., British Casino Assoc., 2000–04. Chm., Bath World Heritage Site Steering Gp, 2009–13. Hon. MA Bath, 2003. *Recreations:* swimming, historic buildings, cooking, music. *Address:* 61 Lyncombe Hill, Bath BA2 4PH. *T:* (01225) 317026.

**BEEVER, Jane Ann**; Headteacher, Loreto Grammar School, since 2006; Executive Head, St Antony's Catholic College, since 2013; *b* Liverpool, 1 Dec. 1965; *d* of Jeremiah Bryan and Agnes Ann Cullen; *m* 2002, Ron Beever. *Educ*: Bellerive Grammar Sch., Liverpool; Liverpool Univ. (BA Hons); York Univ. (PGCE); Leeds Univ. (MA). Hd of Sixth Form, Prince Henry's GS, 1994–99; Asst Warden, Impington Village Coll., 1999–2002; Dep. Hd, Loreto GS, 2002–06. Gov., St Benedict's Catholic Primary Sch., 2014–; Mem., Bd of Govs, Liverpool Hope Univ., 2017–. *Recreations*: walking, gardening, France, literature. *Address*: Loreto Grammar School, Dunham Road, Altrincham, Cheshire WA14 4AH. *T*: (0161) 928 3703, *Fax*: (0161) 924 1323. *E*: head@loretogrammar.co.uk.

**BEEVERS, Elizabeth Anne**; *see* Smaller, E. A.

**BEEVOR, Sir Antony (James)**, Kt 2017; FRSL; FRHistS; historian; *b* 14 Dec. 1946; *s* of John Grosvenor Beevor and Carinthia Jane Beevor (née Waterfield); *m* 1986, Artemis Clare Antonia Cooper, qv; one *s* one *d*. *Educ*: Winchester Coll.; RMA Sandhurst. Served 11th Hussars (PAO), 1967–70; posts in mktg and advertising, London and Paris, 1971–75; occasional journalism and literary criticism. Mem., Armed Forces into the 21st Century seminars, KCL, 1993–95; Visiting Professor: Sch. of Hist., Classics and Archaeology, Birkbeck Coll., London Univ., 2002–; Sch. of History, Univ. of Kent, 2011–; Lees Knowles Lectr, Cambridge, 2002; Boeing Vis. Fellow, Australian War Meml, 2012. Member: Exec. Council, French Theatre Season, 1996–97; Council, Soc. for Army Historical Res., 2000–03; Council, Soc. of Authors, 2005– (Chm., 2003–05; Mem. Mgt Cttee, 2001–05); Cttee, London Library, 2002–04; Cttee, Waterloo 200, 2011–; Academic Adv. Cttee, European Council on Tolerance and Reconciliation, 2018–. Dir, Ocito Ltd, 2003–. Judge: Shiva Naipaul Meml Prize, 2000; British Acad. Book Prize, 2004; David Cohen Prize, 2005; non-exec. Dir, Baillie Gifford Prize, 2016– (Mem., Steering Cttee, Samuel Johnson Prize, 2004–16). Patron, Nat. Acad. of Writing, 2000–. FRSL 1999; FRHistS 2016. Hon. FKC 2016. Hon. DLitt: Kent, 2004; Bath, 2009; UEA, 2014; York, 2015. Pritzker Mil. Mus. and Liby Lit. Award, 2014; Norton Medlicott Medal for Services to Hist., 2016. Chevalier de l'Ordre des Arts et des Lettres (France), 1997; Order of the Cross of Terra Mariana (Estonia), 2008; Commander, Order of the Crown (Belgium), 2016. *Publications*: four novels; The Spanish Civil War, 1982; Inside the British Army, 1990; Crete: the battle and the resistance, 1991 (Runciman Prize); (with Artemis Cooper) Paris After the Liberation, 1994; Stalingrad, 1998 (Samuel Johnson Prize, Wolfson Prize for History, Hawthornden Prize, 1999); (contrib.) The British Army, Manpower and Society, 1999; Berlin: the downfall 1945, 2002 (Longman-History Today Trustees' Award, 2003); The Mystery of Olga Chekhova, 2004; (ed with L. Vinogradova) A Writer At War: Vasily Grossman with the Red Army 1941–1945, 2005; (contrib.) Russia, War, Peace and Diplomacy: essays in honour of John Erickson, 2005; La Guerra Civil Española, 2005 (La Vanguardia Prize, 2005; UK edn as The Battle for Spain, 2006); D-Day: the battle for Normandy, 2009 (RUSI Duke of Westminster Medal for Mil. Lit., 2010; Prix Henry Malherbe, Assoc. des Écrivains Combattants, 2010); The Second World War, 2012; Ardennes 1944, 2015; Arnhem: the battle for the bridges 1944, 2018. *Address*: 54 St Maur Road, SW6 4DP. *W*: www.antonybeevor.com. *Clubs*: Brooks's; The Brook (New York).

**BEEVOR, Antony Romer**, MBE 2010; Senior Advisor, SG Hambros, 2000–03 (Managing Director, 1998–2000); *b* 18 May 1940; *s* of late Miles Beevor and Sybil (née Gilliat); *m* 1970, Cecilia Hopton; one *s* one *d*. *Educ*: Winchester; New Coll., Oxford (BA). Admitted Solicitor, 1965. Ashurst Morris Crisp & Co., 1962–72 (on secondment as Sec., Panel on Takeovers and Mergers, 1969–71); joined Hambros Bank, 1972; Dir, 1974–98; Exec. Dir, 1985–98; on secondment, as Dir-Gen., Panel on Takeovers and Mergers, 1987–89 (Dep. Chm., 1999–2013); Director: Hambros plc, 1990–98; (non-exec.), Rugby Gp, 1993–2000; Gerrard Group, 1995–2000; Croda International, 1996–2005 (Chm., 2002–05); Helical Bar, 2000–12; Nestor Healthcare Gp, 2000–03 (Chm., 2002–03). Mem. Council, 1970–2009, Chm., 1999–2009, Fairbridge; Chm., Croda Trustees Ltd, 2006–09. Gov., Francis Holland Schs Trust, 2013–18; Mem., Audit Cttee, Compton Verney House Trust, 2013–. *Recreation*: low level golf. *Clubs*: Hurlingham, Brooks's.

**BEEVOR, Christopher David M.**; *see* MacKenzie-Beevor.

**BEEVOR, Sir (Thomas) Hugh (Cunliffe)**, 8th Bt *cr* 1784; Chairman, Orchard Toys Ltd, since 2004; *b* 1 Oct. 1962; *s* of Sir Thomas Agnew Beevor, 7th Bt and Barbara Clare Beevor (née Cunliffe); *S* father, 2017; *m* 1988, Charlotte Louise, *e d* of Keith Ernest Harvey; two *s* one *d*. *Educ*: Radley Coll.; Pembroke Coll., Cambridge (BA 1985); RAC Cirencester. *Heir*: *s* Thomas William Harvey Beevor, *b* 15 April 1990.

**BEFFA, Jean-Louis Guy Henri**, Hon. CBE 2005; Grand Officier de la Légion d'Honneur; Chairman, Board of Directors, Compagnie de Saint-Gobain, 2007–10, now Hon. Chairman (Chairman and Chief Executive Officer, 1986–2007); *b* 11 Aug. 1941; *m* 1967, Marie-Madeleine Brunel; two *s* one *d*. *Educ*: Ecole Polytechnique (Ing. au Corps des Mines); Dip. de l'Inst d'Etudes Politiques de Paris. Compagnie de Saint-Gobain: Vice-Pres., Corporate Planning, 1974–77; Pres., Pipe Div., 1978–82; Chief Operating Officer, 1982–86. Vice Chm. Bd, BNP Paribas, 2000–10. Mem., Supervisory Bd, Siemens, 2008–13; Dir, ENGIE (formerly GDF Suez), 2008–15. Great Officer, Order of Merit (Germany). *Recreations*: opera, ballet. *Address*: c/o Compagnie de Saint-Gobain, Les Miroirs, 18 avenue d'Alsace, 92096 Paris la Défense cedex, France. *T*: 147623310.

**BEGBIE, Rev. Prof. Jeremy Sutherland**, PhD; Thomas A. Langford Distinguished Professor of Theology, and Director, Duke Initiatives in Theology and the Arts, Duke Divinity School, Duke University, USA, since 2009; *b* Bristol, 15 June 1957. *Educ*: George Watson's Coll., Edinburgh; Univ. of Edinburgh (BA 1977); Univ. of Aberdeen (BD 1980; PhD 1987); Ridley Hall, Cambridge. ARCM 1977; LRAM 1981. Hon. Chaplain, Royal Holloway Coll., Univ. of London, 1982–85; Asst Curate, St John's, Egham, 1982–85; ordained deacon, 1982, priest, 1983; Ridley Hall, Cambridge: Chaplain and Tutor, 1985–87; Lectr in Christian Doctrine, 1987–2008; Dir of Studies, 1987–93; Vice-Principal, 1993–2000; Associate Principal, 2000–08; University of Cambridge: Affiliated Lectr, 1994–2008, Dir, Theol. Through the Arts, Centre for Advanced Religious and Theol Studies, 1997–2000, Faculty of Divinity; Affiliated Lectr, Faculty of Music, 2007–; University of St Andrews: Associate Dir, Inst. of Theol., Imagination and the Arts, 2000–08; Dir, Theol. Through the Arts, 2000–08; Hon. Reader, 2000–03, Hon. Prof., 2003–08, Sch. of Divinity. FRSCM 2006. *Publications*: Music in God's Purposes, 1988; Voicing Creation's Praise: towards a theology of the arts, 1991; Theology, Music and Time, 2000; (ed) Beholding the Glory, 2000; (ed) Sounding the Depths: theology through the arts, 2002; Resounding Truth: Christian wisdom in the world of music, 2007; (ed with S. R. Guthrie) Resonant Witness: conversations between music and theology, 2011; Music, Modernity and God: essays in listening, 2013; Redeeming Transcendence, 2018; A Peculiar Orthodoxy, 2018. *Recreations*: mountain walking, violin making.

**BEGENT, Prof. Richard Henry John**, MD; FRCP, FMedSci; Professor of Clinical Oncology, UCL Medical School, University College London (formerly Royal Free Hospital Medical School, then Royal Free and University College Medical School), 1990–2010, now Emeritus Professor of Oncology, University College London; *b* 14 Feb. 1945; *s* of Harry Hawley Begent and Doris Ena Begent; *m* 1969, Nicola Ann Thomerson; one *s* two *d*. *Educ*: Haileybury and Imperial Service Coll.; St Bartholomew's Hosp. Medical Coll. (MB BS; MD 1978). FRCP 1986; FRCR 1999. House Officer, Prince of Wales, St Leonard's, Southend and Royal Marsden Hosps, 1967–71; Registrar in Medicine, Royal Marsden, St George's and Chichester Hosps, 1971–75; Clin. Res. Fellow, ICRF, 1975–77; Charing Cross Hospital Medical School: Lectr in Medical Oncology, 1977–80; Sen. Lectr and Hon. Consultant Physician, 1980–86; Gibb Res. Fellow, CRC, 1986–90; Reader in Med. Oncology, Charing Cross and Westminster Med. Sch., 1986–90; Head, Department of Oncology: Royal Free Hosp. Med. Sch., 1990–97; UCL, 1997–2010; Hon. Consultant Physician, Royal Free Hosp., 1990–. Chm., Nat. Cancer Res. Inst. Informatics Task Force, 2004–10. FMedSci 2000. *Publications*: contribs on antibody targeting of cancer and gastrointestinal oncology. *Recreations*: gardening, ski-ing, ancient woodland. *Address*: 6 St Albans Road, NW5 1RD. *E*: r.begent@ucl.ac.uk.

**BEGG, Dame Anne**; *see* Begg, Dame M. A.

**BEGG, Prof. David**; Chief Executive, Transport Times, since 2003 (Publisher and Contributor, 2005–17); Chairman, Tube Lines, 2006–10; *b* 12 June 1956; *m* 2004, Claire Haigh. *Educ*: Portobello Secondary Sch.; Heriot-Watt Univ. Mgt trainee, British Rail, 1979–81; Lectr in Econs, Napier Poly., then Napier Univ., 1981–97; Prof. of Transport Policy and Dir, Centre for Transport Policy, Robert Gordon Univ., 1997. Chm., UK Commn for Integrated Transport, 1999–2005. Non-executive Director: BRB, 1997–99; Shadow SRA, 1999–2001; SRA, 2001–05; Manchester Passenger Transport Exec., later Transport for Greater Manchester, 2003–13; First Gp, 2005–14; Heathrow (SP) Ltd (formerly BAA), 2010–; Mem. Bd, Transport for London, 2000–05. Chm., Northern Way Transport Compact, 2006–11; non-exec. Chm., EAMS Gp, 2016–; Mem., Adv. Bd, Cubic Transportation Systems, 2015–. Dir, Portobello Partnership, 2003–. Hd, Heathrow Winter Resilience Enquiry, 2010–11. Vis. Prof., Plymouth Univ., 2006–. Member (Lab): Lothian Regl Council (Chm., Finance Cttee, 1990–94); Edinburgh City Council (Chm., Transport Cttee, 1994–99). *Recreations*: golf, watching football (Hibs). *Address*: Transport Times, Unit 27, Beaufort Court, Admirals Way, E14 8XL.

**BEGG, Prof. David Knox Houston**, PhD; FRSE; FCGI; Professor of Economics, Imperial College Business School (formerly Tanaka Business School), Imperial College London, 2003–12, now Emeritus (Principal, 2003–12); *b* 25 June 1950; *s* of late Robert William Begg, CBE and Sheena Margaret Begg (née Boyd); *m* 2002, Jenny Holland. *Educ*: St John's Coll., Cambridge (BA Econs 1972 (double 1st); Adam Smith Prize 1971); Nuffield Coll., Oxford (MPhil 1974); MIT (PhD 1977; Kennedy Schol.). Oxford University: Fellow in Econs, Worcester Coll., and Lectr, 1977–86; Tutor, 1980–82, Sen. Tutor, 1983–86, Business Summer Sch.; Birkbeck College, London: Prof. of Econs, 1987–2002 (Hd of Dept, 1987–90 and 1996–98); Actg Vice Master, 1997. Res. Dir, Centre for Econ. Forecasting, London Business Sch., 1981–83; Centre for Economic Policy Research: Res. Fellow, 1983–2012; Mem., Exec. Cttee, 2002–08. Vis. Asst Prof., Princeton Univ., 1979; Visiting Professor: MIT, 1994; INSEAD, 1995; Visiting Fellow: IMF, 1999; Reserve Bank of Australia, 2000. Econ. Policy Advr, Bank of England, 1986. Chm., Begg Commn on future of UK outside the euro, 2002. Non-executive Director: Trace Gp plc, 2006–07; Touchstone (formerly Imperial) Innovations plc, 2012–17; Senior Ind. Dir, IP Gp, 2017–. FRSE 2004; FCGI 2006. Founding Man. Ed., Econ. Policy, 1985–2000. *Publications*: The Rational Expectations Revolution in Macroeconomics, 1981; (jtly) Economics, 1984, 11th edn 2014 (trans. French, Spanish, Italian, Polish, Vietnamese, Chinese, Greek); Monetarism and Macroeconomics: contributions on the UK policy debate, 1987; (jtly) The Impact of Eastern Europe, 1990; (jtly) The Making of Monetary Union, 1991; (jtly) Making Sense of Subsidiarity, 1993; (jtly) EU Enlargement, 1993; (jtly) Independent and Accountable: a new mandate for the Bank of England, 1993; (jtly) EMU: getting the endgame right, 1997; (ed jtly) EMU: prospects and challenges for the Euro, 1998; (jtly) Monetary and Exchange Rate Policies, EMU, and Central and Eastern Europe, 1999; Safe at Any Speed?: monitoring the European Central Bank, 1999; (jtly) Foundations of Economics, 2000, 4th edn 2009; Global Economics: contemporary issues for 2002, 2002; (jtly) Surviving the Slowdown: monitoring the European Central Bank, 2003; (with D. Ward) Economics for Business, 2003, 5th edn 2016; (jtly) Sustainable Regimes of Capital Movements in Accession Countries, 2003; contribs to learned jls, esp. on exchange rates and monetary policy. *Recreations*: music, crosswords, gardening, all sport. *Address*: Camberlot Place, Camberlot Road, Hailsham BN27 3RQ. *E*: d.begg@imperial.ac.uk.

**BEGG, Prof. Hugh MacKemmie**, PhD; consultant in private practice; *b* 25 Oct. 1941; *s* of Hugh Alexander Begg and Margaret Neil Begg; *m* 1968, Jane Elizabeth Harrison; two *d*. *Educ*: High Sch., Glasgow; Univ. of St Andrews (MA Hons 1964); Univ. of British Columbia (MA 1966); Univ. of Dundee (PhD 1979); Edinburgh Coll. of Art (DipTP 1981). FRTPI 1991. Lectr in Pol Econ., Univ. of St Andrews, 1966–67; Res. Fellow, Tayside Study, 1967–69; Lectr in Econs, Univ. of Dundee, 1969–76; Asst Dir of Planning and Develt, Tayside Regl Council, 1976–79; Prof. and Hd, Sch. of Town and Regl Planning, and Dean, Fac. of Envmtl Studies, Univ. of Dundee, 1979–93. Vis. Prof. of Econs, Abertay Univ. (formerly Univ. of Abertay Dundee), 2000–. Consultant, UNDP, 1986–2000. Mem., Private Legislation Procedure (Scot.) Extra-Parly Panel, 1993–99; Reporter, Scottish Directorate for Planning and Envmtl Appeals (formerly Scottish Exec. Inq. Reporters Unit), 1995–2014; External Complaints Adjudicator, Scottish Enterprise, 1996–2002; Mem., Local Govt Boundary Commn for Scotland, 1999–2007; Convenor, Standards Commn for Scotland, 2002–03; Assessor, Private Bills Unit, 2006–07, Ind. Assessor, Hybrid and Private Bills, 2009–14, Scottish Parlt. Convenor, RTPI in Scotland, 1991. Mem., Bonnetmaker Craft of Dundee. *Publications*: numerous contribs to academic, professional and tech. jls relating mainly to econs, town and regl planning, and monitoring and evaluation of public policy. *Recreations*: hill walking, Guide Dogs for the Blind (puppy walker), watching Rugby. *Address*: 4 The Esplanade, Broughty Ferry, Dundee DD5 2EL. *T*: (01382) 779642. *E*: HughBegg@blueyonder.co.uk. *Club*: Monifieth and District Rotary.

**BEGG, Dame (Margaret) Anne**, DBE 2011; *b* 6 Dec. 1955; *d* of David Begg, MBE and Margaret Catherine Begg (née Ross). *Educ*: Brechin High Sch.; Univ. of Aberdeen (MA); Aberdeen Coll. of Education. English and History Teacher, Webster's High Sch., Kirriemuir, 1978–88; Asst Principal English Teacher, 1988–91, Principal English Teacher, 1991–97, Arbroath Acad. MP Aberdeen S, 1997–2015; contested (Lab) same seat, 2015. Member: Scottish Affairs Select Cttee, 1998–2001; Work and Pensions Select Cttee, 2001–15 (Chm., 2010–15); Speaker's Panel of Chairmen, 2002–10. Vice-Chairman: Labour Party Nat. Policy Forum, 2006–10; Speakers' Conf. on Parly Participation, 2008–10. Mem., NEC, Lab Party, 1998–99. Member: Bd, Scottish Social Services Council, 2016–18; Bd, NHS Grampian, 2016–18; Aberdeen Disability Equity Partnership, 2015–19; Moray Integration Jt Health and Social Care Bd, 2016–18. Mem. Bd, Aberdeen Performing Arts, 2017–. Patron: Cornerstone Community Care, 2015–; Pushing Out the Boat, 2015–; Trustee, Scottish Children's Lottery, 2016–. Hon. DSc Aberdeen, 2016. *Recreations*: reading novels, theatre, cinema, public speaking, watching TV dramas. *E*: anne.annebegg@hotmail.co.uk.

**BEGGS, Prof. Jean Duthie**, CBE 2006; PhD; FRS 1998; FRSE; Professor of Molecular Biology, Wellcome (formerly Wellcome Trust) Centre for Cell Biology, Institute of Cell Biology, University of Edinburgh, 1999–2019 (SHEFC Professor, 1999–2005; Royal

Society Darwin Trust Research Professor, 2005–16); *b* 16 April 1950; *d* of William Renfrew Lancaster and Jean Crawford Lancaster (*née* Duthie); *m* 1972, Dr Ian Beggs; two *s. Educ:* Glasgow High Sch. for Girls; Univ. of Glasgow (BSc Hons 1971; PhD 1974). FRSE 1995. Postdoctoral Fellow: Dept of Molecular Biol., Univ. of Edinburgh, 1974–77; Plant Breeding Inst., Cambridge, 1977–79; Beit Meml Fellow for Med. Res., 1976–79; Lectr, Dept of Biochem., ICSTM, 1979–85; University of Edinburgh: Royal Soc. Univ. Res. Fellow, Dept of Molecular Biol., 1985–89; Royal Soc. EPA Cephalosporin Fund Sen. Res. Fellow, 1989–99, Professorial Res. Fellow, 1994–99, Inst. Cell and Molecular Biol. Vice-Pres. for Life Scis, RSE, 2009–12. Wellcome Trust Sen. Investigator, 2014–18. Mem., EMBO, 1991; MAE 2000. Hon. DSc St Andrews, 2016. Gabor Medal, Royal Soc., 2003; Novartis Medal, Biochemical Soc., 2004; Chancellor's Award, Univ. of Edinburgh, 2005. *Publications:* research papers and reviews on gene cloning in yeast and molecular biology of RNA splicing. *Recreations:* walking my dogs, yoga, scuba diving, listening to classical music.

**BEGGS, John Robert, (Roy),** MBE 2015; Member (UU), Larne Borough Council, 1973–2015; *b* 20 Feb. 1936; *s* of John Beggs; *m* 1959, Wilma Lorimer; two *s* two *d. Educ:* Ballyclare High Sch.; Stranmillis Trng Coll. (Certificate/Diploma in Educn). Teacher, 1957–78, Vice-Principal, 1978–83, Larne High Sch. Mem., 1973–87 and 1988–2015, Chm., 1985–87 and 2007–09, NE Educn and Library Bd; Pres., Assoc. of Educn and Liby Bds, NI, 1984–85 (Vice-Pres., 1983–85). Mayor of Larne, 1978–83; Mem. for N Antrim, NI Assembly, 1982–86. MP (UU) East Antrim, 1983–2005 (resigned seat Dec. 1985 in protest against Anglo-Irish Agreement; re-elected Jan. 1986); contested (UU) same seat, 2005. Mem., H of C Public Accounts Commn, 1984–2005. Mem., NI Drainage Council, 2006–15. Chm., Mid and E Antrim Rural Develt Local Action Gp, 2015–16. Dir, Local (formerly Larne) Enterprise Develt Co., 1985–. Hon. Burgess, Borough of Larne, 2015. *Address:* 171 Carrickfergus Road, Larne, Co. Antrim BT40 3JZ. *T:* (028) 2827 8976, 07711 842550.

*See also* R. Beggs.

**BEGGS, Roy;** Member (UU) Antrim East, Northern Ireland Assembly, since 1998; *b* 3 July 1962; *s* of John Robert Beggs, *qv* and Elizabeth Wilhelmina Beggs (*née* Lorimer); *m* 1989, Sandra Maureen Gillespie; two *s* one *d. Educ:* Larne Grammar Sch.; Queen's Univ., Belfast (BEng Hons Industrial Engrg). Hon. Secretary: Ulster Young Unionist Council, 1986 and 1987; E Antrim UU Assoc., 1992–2002. Northern Ireland Assembly: Dep. Speaker, 2011–16; Member: Higher and Further Educn, Trng & Employment Deptl Cttee, subseq. Employment and Learning Cttee, 1999–2002; Public Accounts Cttee, 1999–2003 (Vice Chm., 2007–11, 2014–16); Cttee of the Centre, 2000–03; Regl Develt Cttee, 2011–12; Assembly and Exec. Review Cttee, 2011–15 (Vice Chm., 2011–15); Health, Social Services and Public Safety Cttee, 2012–14; Social Develt Cttee, 2015–16; Justice Cttee, 2016–17; Vice Chairman: Cttee on Standards and Privileges, 1999–2002; Finance and Personnel Cttee, 2002–03, 2007–08; Envmt Cttee, 2008–10; Agriculture and Rural Develt Cttee, 2010–11; Chm., All Party Assembly Gp on Children and Young People, 2007–09, for Community and Voluntary Sector, 2009–12. Mem. (UU), Carrickfergus BC, 2001–11. Contested (UU) Antrim E, 2015. Vice-Chairman: Carrickfergus Community Safety Partnership, 2004–07; Mem., Carrickfergus Dist Policing Partnership, 2007–11. Mem. Cttee, Raloo Presbyterian Church, 1999– (Elder, 2018–). Gov., Glynn Primary Sch. *Recreations:* walking, cycling; Officer, 1st Raloo Boys' Brigade. *Address:* (office) 3 St Brides Street, Carrickfergus, Northern Ireland BT38 8AF. *T:* (028) 9336 2995. *E:* office@ roybeggs.co.uk.

**BEGLEY, Kim Sean Robert;** tenor; *b* 23 June 1952; *s* of late William Begley and of Elizabeth Begley (*née* Cooke); *m* 1986, Elizabeth Mary, *d* of Charles Collier; two *s. Educ:* Rock Ferry High Sch., Birkenhead; Wimbledon Sch. of Art (costume course); Guildhall Sch. of Music and Drama (theory, piano and voice); Nat. Opera Studio. Early career in theatre: Wardrobe Dept, Gateway Th., Chester; acted in Liverpool, Newbury, London and tours; with RSC, 1977–78; many rôles as principal tenor, Royal Opera House, 1983–89: operas included A Midsummer Night's Dream, King Priam, Florentine Tragedy, Otello, Das Rheingold, Tannhäuser, and Katya Kabanová; début: with Glyndebourne Touring Opera as Don Ottavio in Don Giovanni, 1986; with Glyndebourne Festival Opera as Gastone in La Traviata, 1988; subseq. rôles at Glyndebourne include: Graf Elemer in Arabella, 1989; Boris in Katya Kabanová, 1990; High Priest in Idomeneo, and Pellegrin in New Year, 1991; Laca in Jenůfa, 1992; Albert Gregor in The Makropulos Case, 1995 (also WNO, 1994, and Chicago Lyric Opera (US début), 1995); Florestan in Fidelio, 2001; Polonius in Hamlet, 2017; other rôles include: Male Chorus in The Rape of Lucretia, 1993, Captain Vere in Billy Budd, 2012, ENO; Novagerio in Palestrina, 1997, Drum-Major in Wozzeck, 2002, Edrisi in Król Roger, 2015, Royal Opera House; Laca in Jenufa, 2003, Herod in Salome, 2008, Metropolitan Opera; also appearances at the Proms, at opera houses in Frankfurt, Geneva, Salzburg, Cologne, San Francisco, and at La Scala, Milan. *Address:* c/o HarrisonParrott Ltd, The Ark, 201 Talgarth Road, W6 8BJ.

**BEGLEY, Órfhlaith;** MP (SF) West Tyrone, since May 2018; *b* Carrickmore, Co. Tyrone, 1991; *d* of Seán Begley. *Educ:* Queen's Univ. Belfast (BA Law and Politics). Former Solicitor, Portadown. *Address:* c/o Sinn Féin, 53 Falls Road, Belfast BT12 4PD.

**BEGOVIĆ, Elvira;** General Manager, ONASA Independent News Agency, since 2006 (Executive Manager, 2005–06); *b* 28 Jan. 1961; *d* of Arif and Zejna Dizdarević; *m* 1983, Mirza Begović. *Educ:* Univ. Džemal Bijedić Mostar (BA Econs; postgrad. studies in Mgt and Inf. Technologies). Head Office Manager, Zoitours, Olympic Center, Sarajevo, 1983–95; Exec. Manager, 1995–97, Dir, 1997–98, Futura Media, Mktg and Publishing Agency; Exec. Manager of Internat. Mktg, OSSA Mktg Agency, 1998–99; Dep. Gen. Manager, ONASA Ind. News Agency, 1999–2001; Ambassador of Bosnia and Herzegovina to UK, 2001–05, and, non-resident, to Ireland, 2003–05. First Award, MIT Centre, Sarajevo, 1996; Special Recognition, Orgn of Women in Internat. Trade, USA, 1997. *Publications:* (jtly) Let's Buy Domestic Goods, 1998. *Recreations:* music, walking, reading, theatre, art. *Address:* Dženetića Čikma 10/IV, 71000 Sarajevo, Bosnia and Herzegovina.

**BEHAGG, Prof. Clive,** OBE 2018; PhD; Vice-Chancellor, University of Chichester, 2011–17; *b* 4 July 1950; *s* of Frederick Arthur Behagg and Freda Winifred Behagg; *m* 1974, Christine Robbins; one *s* two *d. Educ:* West Hatch Technical High Sch., Chigwell; Univ. of Birmingham (BA Hons Medieval and Mod. Hist. 1971; PhD 1982). Lectr, Univ. of Birmingham, 1975–76; Bognor Regis Trng Coll., later West Sussex Inst. of Higher Educn, then Chichester Inst. of Higher Educn, subseq. University Coll. Chichester, then Univ. of Chichester: Lectr, 1976–77; Sen. Lectr, 1977–98; Chair in Hist., 1995; Dep. Principal, 1998–2005; Dep. Vice-Chancellor, 2005–10; Actg Vice-Chancellor, 2010–11. Review Chair, QAA, 1998–2010. Mem., Corp., Central Sussex Coll., 2008–. *Publications:* Politics and Production in the Early Nineteenth Century, 1990; Labour and Reform, 1991, 2nd edn 2001; Years of Expansion, 1991, 2nd edn 2002; Chartism, 1993; contrib. articles in Social History and Business History. *Recreations:* listening to rock, classical music and opera, nineteenth century art, following Tottenham Hotspur.

**BEHAN, Sir David,** Kt 2017; CBE 2004; Chair, Health Education England, since 2018; *b* Blackburn, Lancs, 20 Nov. 1955; *s* of Brian Behan and Hilda Behan; *m* 1981, Alison Lamont Connell; two *s. Educ:* St Mary's College RC Grammar Sch. for Boys; Univ. of Bradford (BA Hons, CQSW 1978). Social worker, 1978–80, Team Manager, 1980–84, Wakefield MDC; Proj. Leader, 1984–86, Area Manager, 1986–89, Avon CC; Cleveland County Council: Sen. Asst Dir, 1989–91; Dep. Dir, 1991–94; Dir, Social Services, 1994–96; Dir, Social Services, London Bor. of Greenwich, 1996–2003; Chief Inspector, Commn for Social Care Inspection, 2003–06; Dir Gen. for Social Care, DoH, 2006–12; Chief Exec., Care Quality Commn, 2012–18. Non-exec. Dir, HC-One, 2018–. Pres., Assoc. of Dirs of Social Services, 2002–03. Hon. DLaws Greenwich, 2004; Hon. DH Bradford, 2017. *Publications:* Social Work with Young Offenders, 1981. *Recreations:* cycling, travel, cooking, arts.

**BEHAR, His Honour Richard Victor Montague Edward;** a Circuit Judge, 2000–11; *b* 14 Feb. 1941; *s* of Edward Behar and Eileen Behar, *d* of Montague Evans; *m* 1982, Iwona Krystyna (*née* Grabowska); two *s* one *d. Educ:* Stowe Sch. (Schol.); St John's Coll., Oxford (MA). Called to the Bar, Middle Temple, 1965; in practice at the Bar, 1967–2000; SE Circuit; Asst Recorder, 1991–95; a Recorder, 1995–2000; part-time immigration and asylum adjudicator, 1998–2000. Chairman: Bar European Gp, 1988–90; British-Ukrainian Law Assoc., 1993–2000; Co-opted Mem., Internat. Relns Cttee, Gen. Council of Bar, 1988–2000. Freeman, City of London, 2010; Liveryman, Fanmakers' Co., 2011–. *Recreations:* foreign languages and travel, cinema, theatre, reading. *Address:* c/o Judicial Secretariat, 3rd Floor, 1 Queen Victoria Street, EC4N 4XY. *Clubs:* Oxford and Cambridge, Hurlingham, Polish Hearth.

**BEHARRY, Johnson Gideon,** VC 2005; Lance-Corporal, Princess of Wales's Royal Regiment, since 2006; *b* Grenada, 26 July 1979; *s* of Michael Bolah and Florette Beharry; *m* 2013, Mallissa Venice Noel; one *s. Educ:* Samaratin Presbyterian Sch., Grenada. Joined Princess of Wales's Royal Regt, 2001; Private, 2001–06. Founder, JBVC Foundn. *Publications:* Barefoot Soldier, 2006.

**BEHARRYLAL, Satyanand Sarju, (Anand);** QC 2018; *b* London, 29 Jan. 1975; *s* of Reynold Sirju Beharrylal and Sham Ramasray-Beharrylal; *m* 2011, Angharad Davies; two *d. Educ:* St Benedict's Coll., La Romaine, Trinidad; Univ. of Hertfordshire (LLB Hons 1996); University Coll. London (LLM 1998). Called to the Bar, Lincoln's Inn, 1997; attorney, High Court of Trinidad and Tobago, 2001; in practice as a barrister, specialising in general common law (crime and civil), Bell Yard Chambers, 2002–05, 15 New Bridge Street, 2005–16, 2 Bedford Row, 2016–. *Publications:* contrib. article Counsel Mag. *Recreations:* Caribbean travel, food and wine. *Address:* 2 Bedford Row, WC1R 4BU. *T:* (020) 7440 8888, *Fax:* (020) 7242 1738. *E:* clerks@2bedfordrow.co.uk.

**BEHRENS, His Honour Clive Owen John;** a Circuit Judge, 1996–2016; *b* 14 Sept. 1948; *s* of late Col William Edward Behrens and Dulcie Bella Behrens; *m* 1974, Clemency Anne Susan Butler; one *s* one *d. Educ:* Eton Coll.; Trinity Coll., Cambridge (BA Hons). Called to the Bar, Gray's Inn, 1972; in practice at the Bar, 1974–96; specialised in Chancery and commercial work; a Recorder, 1992–96. *Recreations:* golf, bridge, tennis, walking. *Address:* Birstwith House, Birstwith, Harrogate HG3 2PN. *Club:* Alwoodley (Leeds).

**BEHRENS, Robert Fredrick,** CBE 2016; Parliamentary and Health Service Ombudsman, since 2017; *b* Manchester, 19 Jan. 1952; *s* of Louis Aubrey, (Bill), Behrens and Joan Behrens; *m* 1985, Deborah Sandler; two *s. Educ:* Burnage Grammar Sch., Manchester; Nottingham Univ. (BA Hons 1973); Exeter Univ. (MA 1976). Lectr, then Sen. Lectr in Social and Public Admin, Coventry Poly., 1975–88; Civil Service College: Sen. Lectr, 1988–92; Director: Southern Africa Develt Unit, 1992–97; Internat. Consultancy Gp, 1997–2001; Dir, Internat. Public Service Gp, Cabinet Office, 2001–03; Sec., Cttee on Standards in Public Life, 2003–06; Complaints Comr, Bar Standards Bd for England and Wales, 2006–08; Ind. Adjudicator and CEO, Office of Ind. Adjudicator for Higher Educn in England and Wales, 2008–16. Chm., Eur. Network of Ombudsmen in Higher Educn, 2016–; Mem., Bar Standards Bd, 2011–17. Vis. Prof., Inst. of Educn, UCL, 2016–. Trustee: Fort Hare Foundn, UK, 2008–; UCAS, 2017–. FRSA. *Recreation:* nineteenth and twentieth century history and art. *Club:* Manchester City FC.

**BEHRENS-ABOUSEIF, Prof. Doris,** PhD; Nasser D. Khalili Professor of Islamic Art and Architecture, School of Oriental and African Studies, University of London, 2000–14, now Emerita; *b* 7 Jan. 1946; *d* of Mounir H. Abouseif and Mary Badawy; *m* 1964, Dr Gerhard Behrens; one *s. Educ:* American Univ. of Cairo (MA); Univ. of Hamburg (PhD 1972); Univ. of Freiburg (Habilitation 1992). Privatdozentin: Univ. of Freiburg, 1993–95; Univ. of Munich, 1995–2000. Vis. Prof. at univs incl. Univ. of Bamberg, 1989, Harvard Univ., 1990–91 and 1998–99, Freie Univ., Berlin, 1995–96, Amer. Univ. in Cairo, 2002; Porter Chair Vis. Prof., Univ. of Virginia, 2012; Research Fellow: Annemarie-Schimmel-Kolleg, Univ. of Bonn, 2013; Japan Soc. for the promotion of Science, 2016. Mem., Classic and Oriental Studies, Academia Europaea, 2006–. MAE 2006. *Publications:* The Minarets of Cairo, 1985; Islamic Architecture in Cairo: an introduction, 1989; Egypt's Adjustment to Ottoman Rule: institutions, Waqf and architecture in Cairo (16th & 17th centuries), 1994; Beauty in Arabic Culture, 1999; Cairo of the Mamluks: a history of architecture and its culture, 2007; The Minarets of Cairo, 2010; Practising Diplomacy in the Mamluk Sultanate: gifts and material culture in the Medieval Islamic World, 2014; The Book in Mamluk Egypt and Syria (1250–1517): scribes, libraries and market, 2019; contrib. articles to Encyclopaedia of Islam, Encyclopaedia of the Quran, Annales Islamologiques, Der Islam, Mamluk Studies Rev., Muqarnas. *Recreation:* reading crime novels. *Address:* Department of Art and Archaeology, School of Oriental and African Studies, University of London, Thornhaugh Street, Russell Square, WC1H 0XG. *T:* (020) 7898 4455, *Fax:* (020) 7898 4477. *E:* da30@ soas.ac.uk.

**BEIGHTON, Leonard John Hobhouse,** CB 1992; Deputy Chairman, Board of Inland Revenue, 1992–94 (Director General, 1988–92); *b* 20 May 1934; *s* of John Durant Kennedy Beighton, OBE and Leonora Hobhouse; *m* 1962, Judith Valerie Bridge (decd); one *s* (one *d* decd). *Educ:* Tonbridge Sch.; Corpus Christi College, Oxford (MA PPE). Inland Revenue, 1957; seconded HM Treasury, 1968–69 (Private Sec. to Chief Sec.), and 1977–79. Dir, World Vision UK, 1997–2007 (Vice Chm., 2002–04, Chm., 2004–07). Mem. Council, Shaftesbury Soc., 1995–2007 (Treas., 1998–99). Trustee, Livability (formerly Grooms-Shaftesbury), 2007–16. Hon. Fellow, Chartered Inst. of Taxation, 2011. *Address:* 160 Tilt Road, Cobham, Surrey KT11 3HR.

**BEINART, Prof. William J.,** PhD; FBA 2009; Rhodes Professor of Race Relations, University of Oxford, 1997–2015, now Emeritus (Director, 2002–06, Director of Graduate Studies, 2009–10, African Studies Centre); Fellow, St Antony's College, Oxford, 1997, now Emeritus. *Educ:* Univ. of Cape Town (BA Hist. 1971); Sch. of Oriental and African Studies, Univ. of London (PhD 1979). Res. Officer, Queen Elizabeth House, Oxford, 1978–83; University of Bristol: Lectr, 1983–90, Reader, 1990–95, in Econ. and Pol Hist. Prof. of African History, 1995–97. Leverhulme Sen. Res. Fellow, British Acad., 1995–96 Pres., African Studies Assoc., 2008–10. Mem., Editl Bd, Jl of Southern African Studies (Ed. 1982–87; Chm., 1992–98). *Publications:* The Political Economy of Pondoland 1860–1930 1982; (jtly) Hidden Struggles in Rural South Africa: politics and popular movements in the Transkei and Eastern Cape 1890–1930, 1987; Twentieth-century South Africa, 1994, 2nd edn 2001; (with Peter Coates) Environment and History: the taming of nature in the USA and South Africa, 1995; The Rise of Conservation in South Africa, 2003; (ed with J McGregor) Social History and African Environments, 2003; (with Lotte Hughes

Environment and Empire, 2007; (ed with Marcelle Dawson) Popular Politics and Resistance Movements in South Africa, 2010. *Address*: African Studies Centre, University of Oxford, 13 Bevington Road, Oxford OX2 6LH.

**BEITH,** family name of **Baron Beith**.

**BEITH,** Baron *cr* 2015 (Life Peer), of Berwick upon Tweed in the County of Northumberland; **Alan James Beith,** Kt 2008; PC 1992; *b* 20 April 1943; *o s* of James and Joan Beith, Poynton, Ches; *m* 1st, 1965, Barbara Jean Ward (*d* 1998); one *d* (one *s* decd); 2nd, 2001, Baroness Maddock, *qv*. *Educ*: King's Sch., Macclesfield; Balliol and Nuffield Colls, Oxford (BLitt, MA). Lectr, Dept of Politics, Univ. of Newcastle upon Tyne, 1966–73. Member: Gen. Adv. Council of BBC, 1974–84; Hexham RDC, 1969–74; Corbridge Parish Council, 1970–74; Tynedale District Council, 1973–74; NE Transport Users' Consultative Cttee, 1970–74. MP Berwick-upon-Tweed, Nov. 1973–2015 (L 1973–88, Lib Dem 1988–2015). Mem., House of Commons Commn, 1979–97; UK Rep. to Council of Europe and WEU, 1976–84. Liberal Chief Whip, 1976–85; Deputy Leader: Liberal Party, 1985–88; Liberal Democrats, 1992–2003. Member: Select Cttee on Treasury affairs, 1987–94; Intelligence and Security Cttee, 1994–2008; Chairman: Justice Select Cttee (formerly LCD, then Constitutional Affairs), 2003–15; Liaison Cttee, 2010–15; Mem., Speaker's Cttee on Electoral Commn, 2001–10 (Dep. Chm., 2001–03). Trustee, Historic Chapels Trust, 1993–2014 (Chm., 2002–14; Pres., 2014–). Hon. Bencher, Middle Temple, 2014. Hon. DCL: Newcastle upon Tyne, 1998; Northumbria, 2010; Earlham Coll., Indiana, 2013. Methodist Local Preacher. *Publications*: The Case for the Liberal Party and the Alliance, 1983; (jtly) Faith and Politics, 1987; A View from the North, 2008; chapter in The British General Election of 1964, ed Butler and King, 1965. *Recreations*: walking, music. *Address*: 28 Castle Terrace, Berwick-upon-Tweed TD15 1NZ. *Clubs*: Athenæum, National Liberal (Pres.); Northern Counties (Newcastle).

**BEKER, Prof. Henry Joseph,** PhD; FREng; Visiting Professor of Information Technology, Royal Holloway (formerly Royal Holloway College, then Royal Holloway and Bedford New College), University of London, since 1984; Scientific Collaborator, Plantentuin Meise Botanical Gardens, Belgium, since 2016; *b* 22 Dec. 1951; *s* of late Jozef and Mary Beker; *m* 1976, Mary Louise (*née* Keilthy); two *d*. *Educ*: Kilburn Grammar Sch.; Univ. of London (BSc Maths 1973, PhD 1976); Open Univ. (BA 1982). CEng, FIET (FIEE 1997; MIEE 1984); FIS (MIS 1977); CStat 1993; CMath, FIMA 1994 (AFIMA 1978). Sen. Res. Asst, Dept of Statistics, University Coll. of Swansea, 1976–77; Principal Mathematician, Racal-Comsec Ltd, 1977–80, Chief Mathematician, 1980–83; Dir of Research, Racal Research Ltd, 1983–85; Dir of Systems, Racal-Chubb Security Systems Ltd, 1985–86; Man. Dir, Racal-Guardata Ltd, 1986–88; Chm., Zergo Hldgs, then Baltimore Technologies plc, 1989–2000 (Chief Exec., 1988–99). Chairman: Shopcreator plc, 2000–02; Bladerunner Ltd, 2001–10; Blackthorn Technologies Ltd, 2012–15; RiskLens Inc. (formerly CXOWare Inc.), 2013–15; Director: i-NET VCT plc, 2000–02; Close Finsbury Eurotech Trust plc, 2000–02. Chm., e-Learning Foundn, 2000–03. Mem., Nuffield Health, 2011–14. Mem. Council, British Mycological Soc., 2001–03. Vis. Prof. of IT, Westfield Coll., Univ. of London, 1983–84. Pres., IMA, 1998–99 (Vice Pres., 1988–89). Hon. Fellow: RHBNC, 2000; CABI, 2002; Queen Mary, Univ. of London, 2004. FREng 2000. *Publications*: Cipher Systems, 1982; Secure Speech Communications, 1985; Cryptography and Coding, 1989; (jtly) Fungi Europaei, 14: Hebeloma, 2016. *Recreations*: mycology, natural history, travel. *Address*: Rue Père de Deken 19, 1040 Brussels, Belgium. *E*: henry@hjbeker.com.

**BEKKER, Althea Enid Philippa D.;** *see* Dundas-Bekker.

**BEKOE, Dr Daniel Adzei;** Chairman, Council of State, Republic of Ghana, 2005–08 (Member, 2001–08); *b* 7 Dec. 1928; *s* of Aristocles Silvanus Adzete Bekoe and Jessie Nadu (*née* Awuletey); *m* 1958, Theresa Victoria Anyisaa Annan (marr. diss. 1983); three *s* (and one *s* decd); *m* 1988, Bertha Augustina Ashia Randolph. *Educ*: Achimota Sch.; University Coll. of Gold Coast (BSc London); Univ. of Oxford (DPhil). Jun. Res. Asst, Univ. of Calif, LA, 1957–58; Univ. of Ghana (formerly University Coll. of Ghana): Lectr, 1958–63; Sen. Lectr, 1963–65; Associate Prof., 1965–74; Prof. of Chemistry, 1974–83; Vice-Chancellor, 1976–83; Dir, UNESCO Regl Office for Sci. and Technol. for Africa, 1983–85; Regl Dir, Internat. Develt Res. Centre, Nairobi, 1986–92. Chm., Ghana Atomic Energy Commn, 2001–08; Mem., Bd of Govs, IAEA, 2004–06, 2007–08. Sabbatical year, Univ. of Calif, LA, 1962–63; Vis. Associate Prof., Univ. of Ibadan, 1966–67. Member: UN Univ. Council, 1980–83; UN Adv. Cttee on Science and Technology for Develt, 1980–82. Chm., Presbyterian Univ. Council, 2003–05. President: ICSU, 1980–83; Ghana Acad. of Arts and Scis, 1993–96; African Assoc. of Pure and Applied Chem., 1995–98. *Publications*: articles on molecular structures in crystallographic and chemical jls; gen. articles in Proc. Ghana Acad. of Arts and Sciences. *Recreation*: music. *Address*: PO Box CT 3383, Accra, Ghana. *T*: (30) 2774020, (20) 8147622.

**BELBEN, Michael John;** restaurateur; *b* Swindon, 1952; *s* of John and Rosemary Belben; *m* 1996, Lisa Etherington (marr. diss. 2008); one *s*. *Educ*: Coll. for Distributive Trades, London (HND Business Studies (Advertising and Mktg)). Manager: Peppermint Park Restaurant, 1980–83; Smith's Restaurant, Covent Gdn, 1984–87; Melange Restaurant, Covent Gdn, 1988–90; Proprietor, Eagle Public House, Farringdon, 1991–; Partner: Anchor & Hope, Waterloo, 2003–; Gt Queen St, Covent Gdn, 2007–. London Restaurateur of Year, London Restaurant Awards, 2008. *Recreations*: theatre, contemporary and classical music, art, walking, cycling, car booting! *Address*: 159 Farringdon Road, EC1R 3AL.

**BELBIN, Dr (Raymond) Meredith;** Founding Partner, Belbin Associates, since 1988; Founder and Chairman, Better Together Ltd, since 2011; *b* W Wickham, Kent, 4 June 1926; *s* of Harold Meredith Belbin and Shirley Agnes Belbin (*née* Herbert); *m* 1st, 1949, Eunice Fellows (*d* 2006); one *s* one *d*; 2nd, 2008, Sheila Munds. *Educ*: Sevenoaks Sch.; Royal Grammar Sch., High Wycombe; Clare Coll., Cambridge (BA 1948; MA; PhD 1952). Res. worker, Nuffield Res. Unit into Problems of Ageing, 1949–52; Res. Fellow, Dept of Econs and Prodn, Coll. of Aeronautics, Cranfield, and Lectr, Work Study Sch., 1952–55; self-employed mgt consultant, 1955–; Chm., Industrial Trng Res. Unit, Cambridge, 1959–69; Dir, Employment Develt Unit, Cambridge, 1969–73. Consultant to OECD, US Dept of Labor and EU Commn. Vis. Prof., Mgt Coll., Univ. of Reading, 2008–13. Has made internat. lecture tours and adv. visits to state orgns in Russia and China. Mem. Court, Univ. of Reading, 2008–13. Hon. Fellow, Henley Mgt Coll., 2005–07. *Publications*: Management Teams: why they succeed or fail, 1981, 3rd edn 2010; The Job Promoters, 1990; Team Roles at Work, 1993, 2nd edn 2010; The Coming Shape of Organization, 1996; Changing the Way We Work, 1997; Beyond the Team, 2000; Managing without Power, 2001; The Evolution of Human Behaviour, 2005; Managing Genetic Diversity, 2011; The Long Road to Civilisation, 2015. *Recreations*: landscape gardening, golf. *Address*: 3–4 Bennell Court, West Street, Comberton, Cambridge CB23 7EN. *T*: (01223) 264975. *E*: meredith@belbin.com.

**BELCHER, John William,** CBE 2006; PhD; Chief Executive, Anchor Trust, 1995–2009; *b* 1 May 1947; *m* 1973, Norma Wolffberg; one *s* one *d*. *Educ*: Univ. of Western Ontario (BA); London Sch. of Econs and Pol Sci. (PhD 1998). Dept of Nat. Health and Welfare, Canada, 1973–78; Lewisham LBC, 1978; Hd, Prog. Planning Div., Social Services, Bexley LBC, 1979–84; Dir, Social Services Div., Scope, 1984–88; Dir, Social Services, Health, Housing, Envmtl Health, Trading Standards, Redbridge LBC, 1988–94. Mem., Ind. Safeguarding Authy, 2007–11. Sen. Consultant, deVere Gp, São Paulo, 2011–12; Co. Dir, Five Sciences, 2013–.

**BELCHER, Penelope Mary; Her Honour Judge Penelope Belcher;** a Circuit Judge, since 2006; *b* 27 Aug. 1957; *d* of Arthur John Lucas and Margaret Elizabeth Lucas; *m* 1985, Simon James Belcher; one *s* one *d*. *Educ*: St Hugh's Coll., Oxford (BA, MA Jurisprudence). Called to the Bar, Middle Temple, 1980; barrister, 1980–90; attorney, State Bar of Calif, 1988–89; admitted solicitor, 1993; solicitor: Eversheds, 1993–99, Partner, 1995; Hammonds, 2000–06, Asst Dir for Advocacy. *Recreations*: sailing, racket sports, playing flute, classical music, theatre, reading. *Address*: Leeds Combined Court Centre, The Court House, 1 Oxford Row, Leeds LS1 3BG. *T*: (0113) 306 2800. *E*: hhj.penelope.belcher@ejudiciary.net.

**BELCHER, Prof. Stephen Ernest,** PhD; Chief Scientist, Meteorological Office, since 2017; *b* Wantage, 30 Dec. 1964; *s* of Brian and Margaret Belcher; one *s*. *Educ*: St Bartholomew's Sch., Newbury, Berks; Jesus Coll., Cambridge (BA 1986; MA 1990; PhD 1990). Research Scientist: Stanford Univ., 1990–92; Univ. of Cambridge, 1992–94; Lectr, 1994–2001, Reader, 2001–04, Prof., 2004–16, Univ. of Reading; Dir, Met Office Hadley Centre, 2012–16. *Publications*: contrib. peer-reviewed scientific pubns. *Recreations*: cycling, surfing, playing the drums. *Address*: Meteorological Office, Fitzroy Road, Exeter EX1 3PB. *T*: 07787 294479. *E*: Stephen.belcher@metoffice.gov.uk.

**BELCOURT, Norma Elizabeth, (Mrs Emile Belcourt);** *see* Burrowes, N. E.

**BELDAM, Rt Hon. Sir (Alexander) Roy (Asplin),** Kt 1981; PC 1989; a Lord Justice of Appeal, 1989–2000; *b* 29 March 1925; *s* of George William Beldam and Margaret Frew Shettle (formerly Beldam, *née* Underwood); *m* 1st, 1953, Elisabeth Bryant Farr (*d* 2005); two *s* one *d*; 2nd, 2007, Elizabeth Mary Warren. *Educ*: Oundle Sch.; Brasenose Coll., Oxford. Sub-Lt, RNVR Air Branch, 1943–46. Called to Bar, Inner Temple, 1950; Bencher, 1977; QC 1969; a Recorder of the Crown Court, 1972–81; Presiding Judge, Wales and Chester Circuit, Jan.–Oct. 1985; a Judge of the High Court of Justice, QBD, 1981–89. Chm., Law Commn, 1985–89. *Recreations*: sailing, cricket, naval history. *Address*: 16 The Riverside, Graburn Way, East Molesey, Surrey KT8 9BF.

**BELFALL, David John;** Chairman, Care and Repair Scotland, 2009–15; *b* 26 April 1947; *s* of Frederick Belfall and Ada Belfall (*née* Jacobs); *m* 1972, Lorna McLaughlan; one *s* one *d*. *Educ*: Colchester Royal Grammar Sch.; St John's Coll., Cambridge (BA Hons). Joined Home Office, 1969: Pvte Sec. to Perm. Sec., 1973–74; Sec. to Lord Scarman's Red Lion Square Inquiry, 1974–75; Principal, Police and Prisons Depts, 1975–82; Asst Sec., Police and Immigration Depts, 1982–88; Under-Secretary, Scottish Office: Emergency Services, Home and Health Dept, 1988–91; Health Policy and Public Health Directorate, 1991–95; Head, Housing and Area Regeneration Gp, Scottish Office, then Scottish Exec., Develt Dept, 1995–2002; Chm., Glasgow Council for the Voluntary Sector, 2002–06. Mem., Scottish Criminal Cases Rev. Commn, 2002–09, NHS Lothian Bd, 2004–09.

**BELFAST, Earl of; James Chichester;** *b* 19 Nov. 1990; *s* and *heir* of Marquess of Donegall, *qv*; *m* 2015, Oilbhe, *d* of late Charles Reid and of Dr Margaret Mary Cahill.

**BELFAST, Dean of;** *see* Forde, Very Rev. S. B.

**BELFIELD, Dr Alan James,** FREng; Chairman, Arup Group Ltd, since 2019; *b* Leek, Staffs, 1 May 1956; *s* of Dennis Belfield and Nora Belfield; *m* 2006, Joy Leaman; one *s* one *d*. *Educ*: Univ. of Nottingham (BSc 1st Cl. 1977; PhD 1982); Univ. of Warwick (MBA 1994). FIMechE 2015; FREng 2016. Engr, BR Res., 1978–85; Exec. Engr, Hawtal Whiting, 1985–92; Arup: Sen. Engr, 1992–94; Associate Dir, 1994–96; Dir, 1996–; Bd Dir, 2006–; Chief Operating Officer, Arup Gp, 2017–19. *Recreations*: walking the dog, opera, photography, watching Stoke City FC. *Address*: Arup, 13 Fitzroy Street, W1T 4BQ. *T*: (020) 7755 6701. *E*: alan.belfield@arup.com.

**BELFIELD, Toby James;** Principal, Ruthin School, since 2010; *b* Plymouth, 19 Oct. 1972; *s* of Mark and Catherine Belfield; *m* 2001, Barbara Mary Dean; one *d*. *Educ*: Trinity Coll., Cambridge (BA Maths 1994; MA 1998). Teacher of Maths, Concord Coll., 1995–99; Asst Dir of Studies, Liverpool Coll., 1999–2001; Hd of Sixth Form, Ruthin Sch., 2001–04; Dep. Dir, Capita plc, 2004–08; Bursar and Vice-Principal, Ruthin Sch., 2008–10. *Recreations*: cathedral organist, flying aircraft, piano playing, orchestral conducting, overseas travel. *Address*: Ruthin School, Mold Road, Ruthin, Denbighshire LL15 1EE. *T*: (01824) 702543. *E*: principal@ruthinschool.co.uk.

**BELGRAVE, Sir Elliott (Fitzroy),** GCMG 2012; CHB 1993; Governor General of Barbados, 2012–17; *b* Barbados, 16 March 1931; *s* of Albert Belgrave and Adora Belgrave; *m* 1961, Loretta Rochester; one *d*. *Educ*: Coleridge Secondary Sch., Barbados; University Coll. London (LLB 1962); Darwin Coll., Cambridge (MPhil Criminol. 1979). Called to the Bar, Inner Temple, 1963, Bencher, 2014; Magistrate, Barbados, 1967–69; Sen. Crown Counsel, 1969–76; Principal Crown Counsel, 1976–78; Dep. Dir, Public Prosecutions, 1979–86; Judge, High Court, Barbados, 1987–95. KStJ 2013. *Recreations*: reading, swimming, gardening, travelling. *Address*: c/o Government House, St Michael, Barbados. *E*: elliottfitzroy@caribsurf.com. *Club*: Barbados Yacht.

**BELGROVE, David Raymond,** OBE 2010; HM Diplomatic Service; Ambassador to Liberia, since 2015; *b* Aylesbury, 18 Jan. 1962; *s* of Raymond and Eunice Belgrove; *m* 1985, Mette Ofstad; two *d*. *Educ*: Aylesbury Grammar Sch. Entered FCO, 1982; Third Secretary: Kuwait, 1986–90; (IT), FCO, 1990–93; (Consular/Immigration), Calcutta, 1993–98; First Secretary: (Media and Public Affairs), Ottawa, 1998–2002; (Caribbean), FCO, 2002–04; Team Leader (Peacekeeping and Peacebuilding), FCO, 2004–07; Head: Counter Narcotics Team, Kabul, 2007–09; Afghan Drugs Unit, FCO, 2009–10; Chargé d'Affaires, Monrovia, 2010–12; Dep. Hd of Mission, Khartoum, 2012–15. *Recreations*: hiking, camping, golf, photography. *Address*: c/o Foreign and Commonwealth Office, King Charles Street, SW1A 2AH.

**BELHAVEN and STENTON,** 13th Lord *cr* 1647; **Robert Anthony Carmichael Hamilton;** *b* 27 Feb. 1927; *o s* of 12th Lord Belhaven and Stenton; *S* father, 1961; *m* 1st, 1952, Elizabeth Ann (*d* 2011), *d* of late Col A. H. Moseley, Warrawee, NSW; one *s* one *d*; 2nd, 1973, Rosemary Lady Mactaggart (marr. diss. 1986), *o d* of Sir Herbert Williams, 1st Bt, MP; one *d* (adopted); 3rd, 1986, Malgorzata Maria, *d* of Tadeusz Hruzik-Mazurkiewicz, advocate, Krakow, Poland; one *d*. *Educ*: Eton. Commissioned, The Cameronians, 1947. Commander Cross, Order of Merit (Poland), 1995. *Recreation*: cooking. *Heir*: *s* Master of Belhaven, *qv*. *Address*: 710 Howard House, Dolphin Square, SW1V 3PQ. *Club*: Polish Hearth.

**BELHAVEN, Master of;** Hon. Frederick Carmichael Arthur Hamilton; *b* 27 Sept. 1953; *s* of 13th Lord Belhaven and Stenton, *qv*; *m* 1st, 1981, Elizabeth Anne (marr. diss. 1988), *d* of S. V. Tredinnick, Wisborough Green, Sussex; two *s*; 2nd, 1991, Philippa Martha Gausel Whitehead (marr. diss. 2010), *d* of Sir Rowland Whitehead, 5th Bt; one *d*; 3rd, 2013, Lorna, *d* of James Watson Hurst. *Educ*: Eton.

**BELL, Prof. Andrew John,** PhD; FIMMM; CEng, FREng; Professor of Electronic Materials, University of Leeds, since 2000; *b* Rochdale, Lancs, 3 May 1957; *s* of John Reed Bell and Audrey Holt Bell; *m* 1984, Helen Clare Jurkowski; one *s* one *d*. *Educ*: Bury Grammar Sch., Bury, Lancs; Univ. of Birmingham (BSc 1st Cl. Hons 1978); Univ. of Leeds (PhD Ceramic Sci. and Engrg 1984). FIMMM 1985; CEng 1995. Scientist, Plessey Res. (Caswell) Ltd, 1978–81; Res. Gp Manager, Cookson Res., Perivale, 1984–89; Lectr, Univ. of Leeds, 1989–91; Sen. Scientist, Ecole Polytechnique Fédérale de Lausanne, Switzerland, 1991–95; Res. Manager, Oxley Devtelts Co. Ltd, 1995–2000; University of Leeds: Dir, Inst. for Materials Res., 2003–11; Pro-Dean for Res., Faculty of Engrg, 2003–07; Hd, Sch. of Chem. and Process Engrg, 2011–14. FREng 2016. *Publications*: contrib. papers to scientific jls on topics of ferroelectric and piezoelectric materials. *Recreations*: listening to music, playing guitar (mainly jazz), reading, cycling, walking. *Address*: School of Chemical and Process Engineering, University of Leeds, Woodhouse Lane, Leeds LS2 9JT. *T*: (0113) 343 2370. *E*: a.j.bell@leeds.ac.uk.

**BELL, Andrew Leighton Craig;** Chief Executive Officer, Witan Investment Trust plc, since 2010; *b* UK, 20 July 1955; *m* Yvonne; one *s* one *d*. *Educ*: Queen Elizabeth Grammar Sch., Wakefield; University Coll., Oxford (MA PPE 1976); London Business Sch. (Sloan Fellow 1986). Pres., Oxford Union, 1976. Cons. Res. Dept, 1976–78; Shell Internat., 1978–86; Phillips & Drew, 1987–88; Barclays de Zoete Wedd, 1988–96; Credit Suisse First Boston, 1996–2000; Hd of Res., Carr Sheppards Crosthwaite, 2000–10. Chairman: Assoc. of Investment Trusts, 2013–15; Gabelli Value Plus+ Trust plc, 2015–18. *Recreations*: tennis, ski-ing, scuba, wine. *Address*: Witan Investment Trust plc, 14 Queen Anne's Gate, SW1H 9AA. *T*: (020) 7227 9770. *E*: andrew.b@witan.co.uk.

**BELL, Andrew Montgomery;** Sheriff of Lothian and Borders, 1990–2004; *b* 21 Feb. 1940; *s* of James Montgomery Bell and Mary Bell (*née* Cavaye), Edinburgh; *m* 1969, Ann Margaret Robinson; one *s* one *d*. *Educ*: Royal High Sch., Edinburgh; Univ. of Edinburgh (BL). Solicitor, 1961–74; called to Bar, 1975; Sheriff of S Strathclyde, Dumfries and Galloway at Hamilton, 1979–84; Sheriff of Glasgow and Strathkelvin, 1984–90. Mem., Legal Questions Cttee, Ch of Scotland, 2005–09. Pres., Old Edinburgh Club, 2010–13. *Publications*: (contrib.) Stair Memorial Encyclopaedia of Scots Law, 1995. *Recreations*: reading, listening to music. *Address*: 5 York Road, Trinity, Edinburgh EH5 3EJ. *T*: (0131) 552 3859. *Club*: New (Edinburgh).

**BELL, Anthony Peter,** OBE 1998; Managing Partner, Rothwell Douglas Ltd, 2015–18; *b* Derby, 28 Oct. 1957; *s* of Douglas Bell and Joyce Bell; partner, Elizabeth Carol Rothwell; three *s* one *d*. *Educ*: St Bede's RC Comp. Sch., Ashby, Scunthorpe; Scunthorpe Sch. of Nursing; Charles Frear Sch. of Nursing, Leicester; Univ. of Huddersfield; Liverpool John Moores Univ. (MBA). RN. Dir, Nursing and Quality, University Hosps Aintree, 1990–93; Dir, Jt Commng, Liverpool HA, 1993–2000; Chief Exec., Royal Liverpool Children's NHS Trust, 2000–07; CEO, Royal Liverpool and Broadgreen Univ. Hosps NHS Trust, 2007–12; CEO, Chelsea and Westminster NHS Foundn Trust, 2012–14. Chairman: Standing Nursing and Midwifery Adv. Cttee, 1996–99; Nat. Children's Hosps Alliance, 2003–07. Mem., Adv. Bd, Sch. of Mgt, Univ. of Liverpool, 2008–; Gov., Liverpool John Moores Univ., 2010–. *Publications*: (ed jtly) Placing Ladders: harnessing our leadership potential, 2009. *Recreations*: blues music, guitar, photography, ski-ing, travel. *Address*: 8 Tallow Road, The Island, Brentford TW8 8EU. *E*: tonybellme2@me.com.

**BELL, Prof. Anthony Raymond, (Tony),** PhD; FRS 2017; Professor of Physics, University of Oxford, since 2007; Senior Research Fellow, Somerville College, Oxford, since 2017; *b* Lincoln, 9 June 1952; *s* of Raymond and Muriel Bell; *m* 1975, Irene Barnett; two *s* one *d*. *Educ*: Leeds Modern Sch.; Churchill Coll., Cambridge (BA Natural Scis 1974; PhD Radio Astronomy 1978). Res. Engr, Marconi Radar, 1977–79; Res. Scientist, Rutherford Appleton Lab., 1979–85; Lectr, then Prof., Imperial Coll. London, 1985–2005; Minister, Methodist Church, Oxford, 2005–07. *Recreations*: Methodist local preacher, piano. *E*: Tony.Bell@physics.ox.ac.uk.

**BELL, Catherine Elisabeth Dorcas, (Mrs R. J. Weber),** CB 2003; PhD; Acting Permanent Secretary, Department of Trade and Industry, 2005; *b* 26 April 1951; *d* of late Frank Douglas Howe and of Phyllis (*née* Walsh); *m* 1993, Richard John Weber; one *s*. *Educ*: Balshaw's Grammar Sch., Leyland, Lancs; Girton Coll., Cambridge (MA); Univ. of Kent (PhD). Joined Department of Trade and Industry, 1975; Pvte Sec. to Sec. of State for Trade and Industry, 1980–81; Principal, 1981; Asst Sec., 1986; Under Sec., 1991; Head of Competition Policy Div., 1991–93; maternity leave, 1993–94; Resident Chm., CSSB, 1994–95; Hd of Central Policy Unit, 1995–97; Dir, Utilities Review Team, 1997–99, and Competition Policy, 1998–99; Dir Gen., Corporate and Consumer Affairs, subseq. Competition and Markets Gp, 1999–2002; Dir Gen., Services Gp, 2002–05. Non-executive Director: Swiss Re (UK), 1999–2008; CAA, 2006–14; Ensus Ltd, 2006–11; United Utilities, 2007–16; National Grid Gas plc, 2014–; National Grid Electricity Transmission plc, 2014–; Horder Healthcare, 2016–; Cadent Ltd, 2017–. Non-exec. Mem. Bd, DoH, 2011–16. Mem., Competition Appeal Tribunal, 2017–. Trustee, 2016–, Pension Trustee, 2016–, Charity for Civil Servants (formerly CS Benevolent Fund) (Chm., Investment Cttee, 2008–14). Gov., LSE, 2008–18. *Recreations*: film, ski-ing, gardening.

**BELL, Catherine Jane, (Mrs Paul Moreton);** Co-Group Managing Director, Scholastic UK, since 2012; *b* Airdrie, 22 Oct. 1969; *d* of Edward Bell, *qv*; *m* 2002, Paul Moreton; two *d*. *Educ*: Newstead Wood Sch. for Girls; Richmond Internat. Univ. (BA Hons Eng. Lit. 1992); Drew Univ., NJ; Univ. of Stirling (MPhil Publishing Studies 1993). Penguin Group: Promotions Manager, 1997–98, Mktg Manager, 1998, Penguin Children's Books; Mktg Dir, Ladybird Books, 1998–2000; Mktg Dir, 2000–03, Mktg and PR Dir, 2003–05, DK; Mktg Dir, DK and Penguin Preschool, 2005–09; Sales and Mktg Dir, DK, 2009–12. *Recreations*: family, friends, reading, netball, theatre, Arsenal supporter. *Address*: Scholastic Ltd, Euston House, 24 Eversholt Street, NW1 1DB. *T*: (020) 7756 7760, 07973 257528.

**BELL, (Charles) Trevor;** General Secretary, Colliery Officials and Staffs Area of the National Union of Mineworkers, 1979–89; Member, National Executive Committee of the National Union of Mineworkers, 1979–89; *b* 22 Sept. 1927; *s* of Charles and Annie Bell; *m* 1974, Patricia Ann Tappin. *Educ*: state schools; Technical Coll. (City and Guilds Engrg); Coleg Harlech, N Wales (Trades Union scholarship, 1955). Craftsman in coal mining industry, 1941. Mem., Labour Party, 1946–. *Recreations*: gardening, reading. *Address*: Wakefield, West Yorks.

**BELL, Cressida Iras;** textile designer, illustrator, cake decorator and painter; Director, Cressida Bell Ltd, since 1984; *b* 13 April 1959; *d* of late Prof. Quentin Bell, FRSL and (Anne) Olivier Bell (*née* Popham). *Educ*: St Martin's Sch. of Art (BA Hons Fashion); Royal Coll. of Art (MA). Group exhibitions include: Duncan Grant & Cressida Bell, Sally Hunter Fine Art, 1984; Scarf Show, Liberty's, 1987; Arts & Crafts to Avant-Garde, RFH, 1992; Colour into Cloth, Crafts Council, 1994; Bloomsbury: 3 Generations, NY, 1996. Commissions include: scarf for BM, 1988; scarf for V&A, 1992; book jacket, Song of Love, 1991; interiors, Soho Studios, 1994–2015; carpet for British Consulate, Hong Kong, 1996; for Heal's, RA, Charleston Trust, London Rev. of Books, Art Fund, Heywood Hill, Natural History Mus., Burford Garden Co., British Airways, Dulwich Picture Gall.; major stationery licence with Museums & Galleries Ltd, 2017–. *Publications*: The Decorative Painter, 1996; (illustrated) Arabella Boxer's Book of English Food, 2012; Cressida Bell's Cake Design, 2013. *Recreations*: travel, cookery, dress-making, languages, gardening.

**BELL, Sir David (Charles Maurice),** Kt 2004; Chairman, Financial Times, 1996–2009; Director for People, Pearson plc, 1998–2009; *b* 30 Sept. 1946; *s* of Roderick Martin Bell and Mary Frances Bell (*née* Wade); *m* 1972, Primrose Frances Moran; two *s* one *d*. *Educ*: Worth Sch.; Trinity Hall, Cambridge (BA 2nd Cl. Hons Hist.); Univ. of Pennsylvania (MA Econs and Pol Sci.). Oxford Mail and Times, 1970–72; Financial Times, 1972–2009: Washington Corresp., 1975–78; News Editor, Internat. Edn, 1978–80; Features Editor, 1980–85; Man. Editor, 1985–89; Advertisement Dir, 1989–93; Marketing Dir, 1992–93; Chief Exec., 1993–96. Dir, Pearson plc, 1996–2009. Pres., Les Echos, 2003–07. Mem., UK Council, INSEAD, 1994–2007. Non-exec. Dir, The Economist, 2005–18. Chm., Cambridge Univ. Press, 2012–16 (Sen. Ind. Dir, Press and Assessment Bd, 2017–). Trustee: Common Purpose, 1994–2015 (Chm., 2009–11); Bureau of Investigative Journalism, 2010–15; Esmée Fairbairn Foundn, 2010–16; Chairman: Millennium Bridge Trust, 1997–; Internat. Youth Foundn, 1998–2006; Crisis, 2001–12; Sadler's Wells, 2005–16; Internat. Inst. for War and Peace Reporting, 2006–; London Transport Mus., 2007–16; Transformation Trust, 2009–; Orwell Prize Cttee, 2009–11; Nat. Equality Standard Bd, 2012–; Media Standards Trust, 2014– (Acting Chm., 2006–11). Pres., Coram, 2015–. Chm., Chapel St Community Schools Trust, 2014–. Mem., Leveson Inquiry into culture, practice and ethics of the press, 2011–12. Chm. Council, Roehampton Univ., 2008–. *Recreations*: cycling, theatre, Victorian social history. *Address*: 35 Belitha Villas, N1 1PE. *T*: (020) 7609 4000. *Club*: Garrick.

**BELL, David Mackintosh;** HM Diplomatic Service, retired; *b* 2 Aug. 1939; *s* of late David Little Bell and Kathleen Bell (*née* McBurnie); *m* 1st, 1963, Ann Adair Wilson (marr. diss.); one *s* one *d*; 2nd, 1996, Dominique Van Hille; two *s*. *Educ*: Ayr Acad.; Glasgow Univ. (MA 1959). Commonwealth Relations Office, 1960; served Karachi, Enugu, Havana and Mexico City; FCO, 1968–71; Budapest, 1971–74; 2nd, later 1st Sec., FCO, 1974–77; Commercial Consul, NY, 1977–81; FCO, 1981–86; Press Sec., Bonn, 1986–90; Consul-General, Lille, 1990–95; Consul-Gen., Zürich, and Dir, British Export Promotion in Switzerland and Liechtenstein, 1995–97. Lectr in Internat. Business Studies, Institut Supérieur Européen de Gestion, Lille, 1997–2002. Chm., British Community Assoc., Lille, 2002–05. *Recreations*: reading, crosswords, cooking. *Address*: 6 rue de Wattignies, 59139 Noyelles-lez-Seclin, France. *T*: (3) 20327910. *E*: david.bell59139@orange.fr.

**BELL, Sir David (Robert),** KCB 2011; Vice-Chancellor and Chief Executive, University of Sunderland, since 2018; *b* 31 March 1959; *s* of Robert Bell and Marie Blackie Slater Bell; *m* 1981, Louise Caroline Poole; two *d*. *Educ*: Univ. of Glasgow (MA, MEd); Jordanhill Coll. of Educn (PGCE Primary). Teacher, Cuthbertson Primary Sch., Glasgow, 1982–85; Dep. Headteacher, Powers Hall Jun. Sch., Essex, 1985–88; Headteacher, Kingston Primary Sch., Essex, 1988–90; Asst Dir of Educn, Newcastle CC, 1990–93 and 1994–95; Harkness Fellow, Atlanta, Georgia, 1993–94; Chief Educn Officer, 1995–98, Dir of Educn and Libraries, 1998–2000, Newcastle CC; Chief Exec., Beds CC, 2000–02; HM Chief Inspector of Schs, 2002–05; Perm. Sec., DES, later DCSF, then DFE, 2006–11; Vice-Chancellor, Univ. of Reading, 2012–18. DUniv Strathclyde, 2004. *Publications*: Parents' Guide to the National Curriculum (Primary), 1991; Parents' Guide to the National Curriculum (Secondary), 1991; Inspirations for History, 1992; Bright Ideas: maths projects, 1992. *Recreations*: reading, football, keeping fit. *Address*: University of Sunderland, Edinburgh Building, City Campus, Chester Road, Sunderland SR1 3SD. *T*: (0191) 515 2713. *E*: vice.chancellor@sunderland.ac.uk.

**BELL, Derek,** PhD; independent education consultant, since 2011; Professor of Education, College of Teachers, since 2007; Director, Learnus, since 2013; Head of Education, Wellcome Trust, 2009–11; *b* Hartlepool, 7 Oct. 1950; *s* of Mark Bell and Margaret Bell (*née* Hudson); *m* 1973, Jacqueline Wendy Jackson; twin *d*. *Educ*: Queen Elizabeth's Grammar Sch., Mansfield; Durham Univ. (BSc Hons Botany 1972); Univ. of Liverpool (PGCE 1976; PhD 1976; MEd 1990). Asst teacher, Christleton High Sch., Chester, 1976–80; Hd, Biol. Dept, Grange Comp. Sch., Runcorn, 1980–82; Liverpool Institute of Higher Education, later Liverpool Hope University: Sen. Lectr in Biol., 1983–88, in Professional Studies in Educn, 1988–89 and 1991–92; Admissions Tutor, St Katharine's Coll., 1987–89; on secondment as Res. Fellow, Centre for Res. in Primary Sci., Univ. of Liverpool, 1989–91; Dir, Inservice Educn, 1992–96; Dir, Graduate Studies and Res., 1996–99; Vice Principal, Bishop Grosseteste Univ. Coll., 1999–2002; Chief Exec., Assoc. for Sci. Educn, 2002–08. Co-ordinator, Nuffield Primary Sci. Proj., 1993–99; Chief External Examiner: Modular Prog. in Professional Develt, Bath Spa Univ. Coll., 1998–2000; PGCE Prog., St Martin's Coll. of Higher Educn, Lancaster, 2000–03. Member Board: STEMNET, 2002–13; Engrg UK, 2005–11; Sci. Council, 2005–08; IBM Trust, 2010–; Understanding Animal Res., 2010–16; Member: Inter-Academies Sci. Educn Panel, 2011–16; Judging Panel, Eur. Competition for Young Scientists, 2011–16; Trustee: Centre of the Cell, 2012–14; Primary Sci. Teaching Trust, 2017–; Nat. Educn Trust Academies Trust, 2017–; Sandstone Ridge Trust, 2018–. Hon. DEd Manchester Metropolitan, 2011. Editor, Educn in Science, 2002–09. *Publications*: (ed) Science Co-ordinator's Handbook, 1996; (ed) Understanding Science Ideas: a guide for primary teachers, 1997; (jtly) Science and Literacy: a guide for primary teachers, 1998; (with R. Ritchie) Towards Effective Subject Leadership in the Primary School, 1999; (ed jtly) Teaching the Primary Curriculum, 2002; contrib. chapters in books, articles in jls and res. reports. *Recreations*: ski-ing, walking, theatre-going, active holidays (kayaking, white water rafting and river sledging), resisting growing up. *E*: derek@campanulaconsulting.co.uk.

**BELL, Prof. Derek,** OBE 2018; MD; FRCP, FRCPGlas, FRCPE; Professor of Acute Medicine, Imperial College London, since 2006; Hon. Consultant Physician, Department of Medicine, Chelsea and Westminster Hospital, since 1996; President, Royal College of Physicians of Edinburgh, since 2014. *Educ*: Univ. of Edinburgh (BSc 1st Cl. Pathol.; MB ChB Medicine; MD Inflammatory Response to Myocardial Infarction 1989. FRCPE 1993; FRCP 1996; FRCPGlas 1999. Consultant Chest Physician, Central Middx Hosp. 1990–96; Consultant Physician, Edinburgh Royal Infirmary, 1996–2006; Hon. Sen. Lectr Univ. of Edinburgh, 1998–2006; Med. Dir, Acute Hosps Div., NHS Lothian, 2005–06 Nat. Clin. Lead for Unscheduled Care, NHS Scotland, 2007–10; Dir, NIHR NW London Collaboration for Leadership in Applied Health Res. and Care, 2008–; R&D Dir and Campus Dir, Chelsea and Westminster Hosp. NHS Trust, 2009–; Acute Care Lead, NHS London, 2011–13. Pres., Soc. of Acute Medicine, 2003–07. Mem. Council, RCPE, 2007– *Address*: Royal College of Physicians of Edinburgh, 9 Queen Street, Edinburgh EH2 1JQ *T*: (0131) 247 3638. *E*: president@rcpe.ac.uk.

**BELL, Dr Donald Atkinson**, CEng; Technical Director, Marchland Consulting Ltd, 1991–2004; *b* 28 May 1941; *s* of late Robert Hamilton Bell and Gladys Mildred Bell; *m* 1967, Joyce Louisa Godber; two *s*. *Educ:* Royal Belfast Academical Instn; Queen's Univ., Belfast (BSc); Southampton Univ. (PhD); Glasgow Univ. (MSc). FIMechE; MIET; FBCS. National Physical Lab., 1966–77; Dept of Industry, 1978–82; Dir, Nat. Engrg Lab., 1983–90; Hd of R&D, Strathclyde Inst., 1990–91. *Address:* 32 Elmfield Avenue, Teddington, Middx TW11 8BS. *T:* (020) 8943 1326. *E:* donald@marchland.org.

**BELL, Prof. Donald Munro;** international concert and opera artist; freelance singer; Professor of Music, Calgary University, 1982–2014; private tutor; *b* Burnaby, BC, Canada, 19 June 1934; one *s*; *m* Angela Dowling. *Educ:* South Burnaby High Sch., BC, Canada; Royal Coll. of Music (Associate Bd Scholarship). Made Wigmore Hall (recital) debut, 1958; since then has sung at Bayreuth Wagner Festival, 1958, 1959, 1960; Lucerne and Berlin Festivals, 1959; Philadelphia and New York debuts with Eugene Ormandy, 1959; Israel, 1962; Russia Recital Tour, 1963; Glyndebourne Festival, 1963, 1974, 1982; with Deutsche Oper am Rhein, Düsseldorf, 1964–67; Scottish National Opera, 1974; Scottish Opera, 1978; Basler Kammer Orchestre, 1978; Australian Tour (Musica Viva), 1980. Prof. and Head of Vocal Dept, Ottawa Univ., 1979–82. Worked with mentor, Dr Richard Millar, Oberlin Conservatory, Ohio, 1985–92. Directed Opera Workshop at Univ. of Calgary, 1982–89; Artistic Dir, Univ. of Calgary Celebrity Series, 2004–08; Mem., Univ. of Calgary Senate, 2006–09 (Voting Mem., 2010–14). Member: Nat. Assoc. of Teachers of Singing - Internat., 1985–2014; Nat. Opera Assoc., 1985– (Dir, Alberta Br., 1986–90, for Canada, 1988–90). Has made recordings. Van L. Lawrence Fellowship, Voice Foundn, Philadelphia and NATS, 2009. Judge of various competitions incl. Hynatyshyn and Juno Awards. Arnold Bax Medal, 1955. *E:* tweedlesum@gmail.com.

**BELL, Edward;** Chairman, Bell Lomax Moreton Agency (formerly Bell Lomax Literary and Sport Agency), 2002–14; *b* 2 Aug. 1949; *s* of Eddie and Jean Bell; *m* 1969, Junette Bannatyne; one *s* two *d*. *Educ:* Airdrie High Sch. Cert. of Business Studies. With Hodder & Stoughton, 1970–85; Man. Dir, Collins General Div., 1985–89; launched Harper Paperbacks in USA, 1989; HarperCollins UK: Publisher, 1990–2000; Dep. Chief Exec., 1990–91; Chief Exec., 1991–92; Chm., 1992–2000; Chm., HarperCollins India, 1994–2000. Non-executive Director: beCogent Ltd, 2000–10; Haynes Publishing Gp plc, 2000– (Chm., 2016–); Management Diagnostics Ltd, 2000–14; New Century Media, 2009–. *Recreations:* reading, golf, supporting Arsenal, opera, collecting old books. *Clubs:* Royal Automobile; AutoWink (Epsom); Addington Golf (Croydon).
See also C. J. Bell.

**BELL, Prof. Emily Jane;** Professor of Professional Practice, and Director, Tow Center for Digital Journalism, Graduate School of Journalism, Columbia University, since 2010; *b* 14 Sept. 1965; *d* of Peter Bell and Bridget Bell; *m* 1994, Edmund Hugh Crooks; three *s*. *Educ:* Christ Church, Oxford (BA Juris. 1987). Reporter: Big Farm Weekly, 1987–88; Campaign, 1988–90; The Observer: reporter, 1990–96; Dep. Business Ed., 1996–98; Business Ed., 1998–2000; Founder and Ed., MediaGuardian.co.uk, 2000; Ed.-in-Chief, Guardian Unlimited, 2001–06; Dir of Digital Content, Guardian News and Media, 2006–10. Columnist, Broadcast, 1999–. Vis. Prof., Univ. College Falmouth, 2009–10. Member: Digital Adv. Bd, Digital First Media, 2010–; Bd of Overseers, Columbia Journalism Review, 2010–. Trustee, Grierson Trust, 2009–. *Publications:* (with Chris Alden) The Media Directory, 2004; contrib. to Guardian and Columbia Journalism Review. *Recreations:* child management, cooking, opera and theatre-going, reading, season ticket holder Arsenal FC. *Address:* Graduate School of Journalism, Pulitzer Hall, MC 3801, Columbia University, 2950 Broadway (at 116th Street), New York, NY 10027, USA. *E:* ebell@columbia.edu.

**BELL, Gary Terence;** QC 2012; *b* Nottingham, 9 Nov. 1959; *s* of Terence Bell and Maureen Bell; *m* 1992, Sophia Fitzhugh; two *s* one *d*. *Educ:* Toothill Comp. Sch., Bingham, Notts; Univ. of Bristol (LLB Hons 1987). Coal miner, 1976; lawn mower mechanic, 1976; forklift truck driver, 1976–78; fireman, 1978; pork pie prodn line worker, 1978; homeless drifter, 1978–80; journalist for The Spectator, The Guardian, Mail on Sunday, The Big Issue; presenter, The Legalizer, BBC TV, 2012. Called to the Bar, Inner Temple, 1989; in practice as a barrister, 1989–. *Publications:* Toby and the Great Stink, 2010; Animal QC, 2015; Beyond Reasonable Doubt, 2019. *Recreations:* golf, football, cricket, fishing. *Address:* No5 Chambers, Fountain Court, Steelhouse Lane, Birmingham B4 6DR. *T:* 07710 472059. *E:* garybell2009@googlemail.com.

**BELL, Geoffrey Lakin;** President, Geoffrey Bell and Co., New York, since 1982; Chairman, Guinness Mahon Holdings, 1987–93; *b* 8 Nov. 1939; *s* of Walter Lakin Bell and Ann (*née* Barnes); *m* 1973, Joan Abel; one *d*. *Educ:* Grimsby Technical Sch.; London School of Economics and Political Science. Economic Asst, HM Treasury, 1961–63; Vis. Scholar, Fed. Reserve System, principally with Federal Reserve Bank of St Louis, 1963–64; HM Treasury, also Special Lectr at LSE, 1964–66; Economic Advr, British Embassy, Washington, 1966–69; 1969–82: Asst to Chm., J. Henry Schroder Wagg; Dir, Schroder Wagg; Exec. Vice Pres., Schroder Internat. and Sen. Advr, Schroder Bank and Trust Co., NY; Special Columnist on Econs and Finance, The Times, 1969–74; Exec. Sec. and Mem., Gp of Thirty, 1978–. Chairman: Guyana Americas Merchant Bank, 2001–; ProLogis Eur. Properties, 2007–12; Dir, Axis Capital Hldgs Ltd (Bermuda), 2006–. Mem., Court of Govs, LSE, 1994–2014. Cons. Editor, International Reports, 1983–93. *Publications:* The Euro-Dollar Market and the International Financial System, 1973; numerous articles on internat. econs and finance in UK and USA. *Address:* 17 Abbotsbury House, Abbotsbury Road, W14 8EN. *T:* (020) 7603 9408; 455 East 57th Street, New York, NY, USA. *T:* (212) 8381193. *Club:* Reform.

**BELL, Graham Andrew;** television presenter; Presenter, BBC Ski Sunday, since 2001; *b* Akrotiri, Cyprus, 4 Jan. 1966; *s* of Rod and Jean Bell; *m* 1991, Sarah Edwards; one *s* one *d*. *Educ:* George Watson's Coll. British Alpine Ski Team, 1982–98; British Olympic Team, 1984, 1988, 1992, 1994, 1998; Performance Dir, Snowsport GB, 1999–2003; commentator, Eurosport, 1998–2001. *Recreations:* ski-ing, cycling, triathlon, dangerous stuff, science. *Address:* Champions UK plc, Barrington House, Leake Road, Costock, Loughborough LE12 6XA. *T:* 0845 331 3031. *E:* mail@championsukplc.com. *Club:* Kandahar Ski.

**BELL, Prof. Graham Arthur Charlton**, PhD; FRS 2016; James McGill Professor, Department of Biology, McGill University, since 2002; *b* Leicester, 3 March 1949; *s* of Arthur Charlton Bell and Edna May Bell (*née* Charlton); *m* 1971, Susan Eva Rosinger; three *s*. *Educ:* Wyggeston Grammar Sch., Leicester; St Peter's Coll., Oxford (BA 1970; PhD 1974; Hon. Fellow 2003). Scientist, Fish and Game Dept, Govt of Alberta, 1975–76; McGill University: Vis. Lectr, 1976; Vis. Asst Prof., 1977; Asst Prof., 1978–83; Associate Prof., 1983–89; Prof., 1989–. Visiting Research Fellow: Merton Coll., Oxford, 2016; St Catherine's Coll., Oxford, 2019. *Publications:* The Masterpiece of Nature, 1982; Sex and Death in Protozoa, 1989; Selection: the mechanism of evolution, 2008; The Evolution of Life, 2015; contrib. articles to learned jls. *Recreation:* angling (for anything that swims). *Address:* Biology Department, McGill University, 1205 Avenue Docteur Penfield, Montreal, QC H3A 1B1, Canada. *T:* (514) 3986458. *E:* graham.bell@mcgill.ca.

**BELL, Howard James;** Chief Executive, Provident Financial plc, 1997–2001; *b* 28 March 1944; *m* 1969, Susan Vivienne Fell; one *s* (one *d* decd). *Educ:* Bradford Univ. (MBA). Yorkshire Imperial Metals Ltd, 1963–67; Provident Financial plc, 1967–2001: computer systems analyst, 1967–72; personnel and trng, 1972–80; Line Manager, 1980–89; Dir, 1989–2001; Ops Dir, 1993–95; Man. Dir, 1995–97. Chm., Invocas Gp plc, 2006–11. Chm., Bradford Business Link Ltd, 1993–98; Chm., Bradford Trng and Enterprise Council Ltd, 1998–2001; Bradford Ambassador, 1998. Chm., Meningitis Res. Foundn, 1997–2005. Mem. Council, Univ. of Bradford, 1998–99. *Recreations:* sport, travel.

**BELL, Prof. Ian Frederick Andrew**, PhD; Professor of American Literature, University of Keele, since 1992; *b* 31 Oct. 1947; *s* of Frederick George Bell and Cecilia Bell; three *s*. *Educ:* West Bridgford Grammar Sch.; Univ. of Reading (BA 1970; PhD 1978). Lectr, Sen. Lectr and Reader in Amer. Lit., Univ. of Keele, 1973–92. *Publications:* Critic as Scientist: the modernist poetics of Ezra Pound, 1981; (ed) Ezra Pound: tactics for reading, 1982; (ed) Henry James: fiction as history, 1984; (ed jtly) American Literary Landscapes: the fiction and the fact, 1988; Henry James and the Past: readings into time, 1991; (ed) The Best of O. Henry, 1993; Washington Square: styles of money, 1993. *Recreations:* visual arts, cinema, ferret wrangling. *Address:* Department of American Studies, University of Keele, Staffs ST5 5BG. *T:* (01782) 733012.

**BELL, Rt Rev. James Harold;** Area Bishop of Ripon, 2014–17; an Honorary Assistant Bishop, Diocese of Carlisle, since 2017; *b* 20 Nov. 1950; *s* of James and Melita Jane Bell. *Educ:* St John's Coll., Durham Univ. (BA (Mod. Hist.) 1972); Wycliffe Hall, Oxford (BA (Theol.) 1974, MA 1978). Ordained deacon, 1975, priest, 1976; Chaplain and Lectr, 1976–82; Official Fellow, 1979–82, Brasenose Coll., Oxford; Pro-proctor, Oxford Univ., 1982; Rector, St Mary, Northolt, 1982–93; Area Dean, Ealing, 1991–93; Willesden Area Advr for Ministry, and Dir, Willesden Ministry Trng Prog., 1993–97; Dir of Ministry and Trng, Dio. Ripon, and Res. Canon, Ripon Cathedral, 1997–99; Dir of Mission, Dio. Ripon and Leeds, 1999–2004; Bishop Suffragan of Knaresborough, 2004–14. Mem., Gen. Synod, 2010 (Chm., Rural Affairs Gp, 2009–17). Hon. Canon, Ripon Cathedral, 1999–2004. Dir, Methodist Chapel Aid, 2007–12. Mem. Council, Yorks Ministry Course, 2011– (Chm., 2012–17). Gov., York St John Univ., 2009–17 (Hon. Fellow 2018); Mem., Consultative Gp, Harrogate Coll., 2008–17. Trustee: St Michael's Hospice, Harrogate, 2014–17; Yorks Causeway Schs, 2015–17. *Publications:* (ed jtly) Re-shaping Rural Ministry, 2009. *Recreations:* entertaining (and being entertained), collecting, gardening (as required). *Address:* Stone Croft, Bolton, Appleby-in-Westmoorland, Cumbria CA16 6AL. *T:* (017683) 61649.

**BELL, Janet;** *see* Browne, E. J.

**BELL, Jason;** photographer; *b* London, 19 April 1969; *s* of Peter Alexander Bell and Susan Margaret St Claire Bell (*née* Carruthers, now Laws); civil partnership 2007, Guy Harrington (civil partnership diss. 2019). *Educ:* Westminster Sch.; St Catherine's Coll., Oxford (BA PPE 1990). Self-employed photographer, 1990–. Main editorial clients include Vanity Fair and Vogue UK; work includes numerous film posters; official photographer, christening of Prince George, 2013. Many photographs in NPG collection. Hon. FRPS 2011; Hon. FBIPP 2018. *Publications:* Gold Rush, 2001; Hats Off, 2002; GiveGet, 2004; An Englishman in New York, 2010. *Address:* c/o Soho Management, 2nd Floor, 34 Albert Street, NW1 7NU. *E:* kate@sohomanagement.co; c/o Robbie Feldman, 170 N 11th Street, Suite 6B, Brooklyn, NY 11211, USA. *E:* robbie@sohomanagement.co.

**BELL, Prof. Jeanne Elisabeth, (Mrs D. Rutovitz)**, CBE 2007; MD; FRCPath, FMedSci; FRSE; Professor of Neuropathology, University of Edinburgh, 1999–2009, now Emeritus; Hon. Consultant in Neuropathology, Western General Hospital, Edinburgh, 1999–2007; *b* 10 Aug. 1942; *d* of Rhys and Joan Hall; *m* 1983, Dr Denis Rutovitz, MBE; two step *s* two step *d*, and one *s* from former marr. *Educ:* Univ. of Newcastle upon Tyne (BSc Hons Anatomy 1963; MD 1972); Univ. of Durham (MB BS 1966). FRCPath 1995. Lectr in Anatomy, Univ. of Newcastle upon Tyne, 1967–70; Res. Officer, MRC Human Genetics Unit, Edinburgh, 1974–79; Sen. Registrar in Paediatric Pathology, Royal Hosp. for Sick Children, Edinburgh, 1979–84; Sen. Lectr in Neuropathol., Univ. of Edinburgh, 1984–99. FRSE 1998; FMedSci 2002. *Publications:* (jtly) Colour Atlas of Neuropathology, 1995; contrib. chapters on develt and forensic, psychiatric and neurol medicine; scientific papers and reviews in neurosci. jls. *Recreations:* travel, handicrafts, films, looking after grandchildren, humanitarian aid work (founded Edinburgh Direct Aid with husband, 1992). *Address:* CJD Surveillance Unit, Bryan Matthews Building, Western General Hospital, Crewe Road, Edinburgh EH4 2XU. *T:* (0131) 537 1955, *Fax:* (0131) 343 1404. *E:* Jeannebell76@gmail.com.

**BELL, Dame Jocelyn;** *see* Bell Burnell, Dame S. J.

**BELL, Sir John (Irving)**, GBE 2015; Kt 2008; DM; FRCP; FRS 2008; Regius Professor of Medicine, University of Oxford, since 2002; Student of Christ Church, Oxford, since 2002; *b* 1 July 1952; *s* of Robert Edward Bell and Mary Agnes (*née* Wholey). *Educ:* Univ. of Alberta, Canada (BSc Medicine); Oxford Univ. (BA Hons Physiol Sci.; BM, BCh; DM 1990). FRCP 1992. Rhodes Scholar, Univ. of Alberta and Magdalen Coll., Oxford, 1975. Postgraduate training in medicine, 1979–82 (John Radcliffe Hosp., Hammersmith Hosp., Guy's Hosp., Nat. Hosp. for Neurol Disease); Clinical Fellow in Immunology, Stanford Univ., USA, 1982–87; University of Oxford: Wellcome Sen. Clin. Fellow, 1987–89; University Lectr, 1989–92; Nuffield Prof. of Clin. Medicine, 1992–2002; Fellow, Magdalen Coll., 1990–2002. Mem., MRC, 1996–2002. Chairman: OSCHR, 2006–18; Human Genome Strategy Gp, 2010– (report published 2012). UK Life Sciences Champion, 2011–18. Founder FMedSci 1998 (Pres., 2006–11). Sen. Mem., OUBC, 1996–. *Publications:* scientific papers in immunology and genetics. *Recreations:* rowing, swimming, sailing. *Address:* Christ Church, Oxford OX1 1DP. *Clubs:* Leander (Henley-on-Thames); Vincent's (Oxford).

**BELL, Sir John Lowthian**, 5th Bt *cr* 1885; *b* 14 June 1960; *s* of Sir Hugh Francis Bell, 4th Bt and Lady Bell (*d* 1990) (Mary Howson, MB, ChB, *d* of late George Howson, The Hyde, Hambledon); *S* father, 1970; *m* 1985, Venetia, *d* of J. A. Perry, Taunton; one *s* one *d*. *Recreations:* shooting, fishing. *Heir:* *s* John Hugh Bell, *b* 29 July 1988.

**BELL, Prof. (John) Nigel (Berridge)**, PhD; Professor of Environmental Pollution, Imperial College London, 1989–2011, now Emeritus; *b* 26 April 1943; *s* of John Edward Donald Bell and Dorothy Elise Bell (*née* White); *m* 1st, 1970, Jennifer Margaret Pollard (marr. diss. 1977); 2nd, 1978, Carolyn Mary Davies (marr. diss. 1992); three *s*; 3rd, 2006, Elinor Margaret Lord. *Educ:* County Grammar Sch. of King Edward VII, Melton Mowbray; Univ. of Manchester (BSc Botany 1964; PhD Plant Ecol. 1969); Univ. of Waterloo, Ont. (MSc Biol. 1965; Science Alumnus of Honour 2007). Teaching Fellow, Univ. of Waterloo, 1964–65; Res. Asst, Bedford Coll., Univ. of London, 1968–70; Imperial College, University of London: Res. Asst, 1970–72; Lectr, 1972–83; Sen. Lectr, 1983–87; Reader in Envmtl Pollution, 1987–89; Dir, 1980–2008, Dir, Careers and Alumni, 2008–13, MSc in Envmtl Technol. (formerly MSc Studies); Dir, Centre for Envmtl Technology, 1986–94; Head, Agricl and Envmtl Mgt Sect., Dept of Biology, 1986–2001. Hon. DES Waterloo, 1998. Rector's Medal for Teaching, Imperial Coll. London, 2010. *Publications:* (ed)

Ecological Aspects of Radionuclide Releases, 1983; Air Pollution Injury to Vegetation, 1986; (ed) Acid Rain and Britain's Natural Ecosystems, 1988; Air Pollution and Forest Health in the European Community, 1990; (ed) Air Pollution and Plant Life, 2nd edn 2002; Biosphere Implications of Deep Disposal of Nuclear Waste, 2007; numerous papers in jls on air pollution and radioactive pollution. *Recreations:* classical music, travel, walking, railways. *Address:* Centre for Environmental Policy, Weeks Building, 16 Prince's Gardens, Imperial College London, SW7 2AZ. *T:* (020) 7594 9288; 48 Western Elms Avenue, Reading, Berks RG30 2AN. *T:* (0118) 958 0653.

**BELL, Rev. Prof. John Stephen,** DPhil; FBA 1999; Professor of Law, University of Cambridge, since 2001 (Chair, School of Humanities and Social Sciences, 2005–09); Fellow, Pembroke College, Cambridge, since 2001; *b* 5 May 1953; *s* of Harry Bell and Elsie Bell (*née* Walmsley); *m* 1983, Sheila Brookes; two *s*. *Educ:* Trinity Coll., Cambridge (BA 1974; MA 1978); Gregorian Univ., Rome (Baccalaureus in Philosophy 1976); Wadham Coll., Oxford (DPhil 1980); St Mary's Univ. Coll., London (BA 2013). Asst, Inst de droit comparé, Paris II, 1974–75; Fellow and Tutor in Law, Wadham Coll., Oxford, 1979–89; Leeds University: Prof. of Public and Comparative Law, 1989–2001; Pro-Vice Chancellor for Teaching, 1992–94. Professeur associé: Univs of Paris I and Paris II, 1985–86; Univ. du Maine, 1995–96; Vis. Prof., Katholieke Univ., Brussels, 1993–. Chm., Jt Academic Stage Bd, 2004–09. Mem., Res. Council, Eur. Univ. Inst., Florence, 1997–2003. Pres., SPTL, 1998–99. Ordained deacon, Dio. of East Anglia, 2012. FRSA 1995. Hon. QC 2003. *Publications:* Policy Arguments in Judicial Decisions, 1983; French Constitutional Law, 1992; (with L. N. Brown) French Administrative Law, 4th edn 1993, 5th edn 1998; (with G. Engle) Cross on Statutory Interpretation, 3rd edn 1995; (jtly) Principles of French Law, 1998; (contrib.) New Directions in European Public Law, 1998; French Legal Cultures, 2001; Judiciaries within Europe, 2006; (with D. Ibbetson) European Legal Development: the case of tort, 2012; contribs to learned jls. *Recreation:* learning and speaking foreign languages. *Address:* Faculty of Law, University of Cambridge, 10 West Road, Cambridge CB3 9DZ.

**BELL, Dr Jonathan Richard,** CB 2006; CChem, FRSC; Director, Jon Bell Associates Ltd, since 2006; *b* 12 Nov. 1947; *s* of late Stanley and Marjorie Bell; *m* 1971, Lynne Trezise; one *s*. *Educ:* Cambridge Grammar Sch. for Boys; Univ. of Hull (BSc 1969; PhD 1972). CChem 1973, FRSC 1992. Post doctoral researcher, Dyon Perrins Lab., Univ. of Oxford, 1973–74; Packaging Chemist, Metal Box Co., 1974–75; Ministry of Agriculture, Fisheries and Food, 1975–2000: Head: Food Sci. Div. I, 1989–92; Food Sci. Div. II, 1992–95; Additives and Novel Food Div., 1995–2000; Food Standards Agency: Dir, Food Safety Policy, Chief Scientific Advr and Dep. Chief Exec., 2000–03; Chief Exec. and Chief Scientific Advr, 2003–06. Consultant on agri-food and health matters, crisis mgt and performance mgt, 2006–. *T:* 07905 672760. *E:* jon.bell@jonbellassociates.co.uk.

**BELL, Joshua;** violinist; Music Director, Academy of St Martin in the Fields, since 2011; *b* Indiana, 9 Dec. 1967; *s* of Alan and Shirley Bell. *Educ:* Sch. of Music, Univ. of Indiana (studied with Josef Gingold). Internat. début with Philadelphia Orch., 1981; performances with orchs in Europe, USA, Canada, S America and Asia incl. Royal Philharmonic, London Philharmonic, BBC Symphony, Philadelphia, CBSO, Chicago Symphony, Boston Symphony, LA Philharmonic, NY Philharmonic and Cleveland Orch. Recitals in Europe and USA. Vis. Prof., Royal Acad. of Music, 1997; Sen. Lectr, Jacobs Sch. of Music, Indiana Univ., 2008–. Numerous recordings (Grammy Award, 2001; Billboard Classical CD of Yr 2004). Mercury Music Prize, 2000; Indiana Gov.'s Arts Award, 2003; Golden Plate Award, Acad. of Achievement, 2008; Educn Through Music Man of Yr, 2009; Musical America Instrumentalist of Yr, 2010; Paul Newman Award, Arts Horizons, 2011; Huberman Award, Moment Mag., 2011; Dushkin Award, Music Inst. of Chicago, 2016. *Recreations:* golf, tennis, computers. *Address:* c/o IMG Artists, Capital Tower, 91 Waterloo Road, SE1 8RT.

**BELL, Lindsay Frances;** Director, Local Government Finance, Department for Communities and Local Government (formerly Office of the Deputy Prime Minister), 2004–10; *b* 29 April 1950; one *s* one *d*. *Educ:* University Coll. London (BA 1971); St Anne's Coll., Oxford (BPhil 1973). Department of the Environment, later Department of the Environment, Transport and the Regions, subseq. Office of the Deputy Prime Minister, then Department for Communities and Local Govt, 1975–2010: Head: Finance Deptl Services, 1987–89; Water Regulation Div., 1989–90; Local Govt Reorgn Div., 1990–94; Local Authy Grants, 1994–97; Dir, Regl Policy, 1997–2000; Dep. Hd, Domestic Affairs, Cabinet Office (on secondment), 2000–03; Dir, Strategy, Neighbourhood Renewal Unit, 2003–04.

**BELL, Marcus David John;** Director, Race Disparity Unit, Cabinet Office, since 2016; *b* N Tarrytown, NY, 10 Nov. 1966; *s* of late Colin James Bell and of Kathleen Bell; *m* 1999, Deborah Parkin; twin *s* twin *d*. *Educ:* Winchester Coll. (Schol.); Balliol Coll., Oxford (Markby Schol.; BA Hons Hist. and Mod. Langs). Admin. trainee, DES, 1989–92; Private Sec., Chancellor of Duchy of Lancaster, 1992–93; Principal, DFE, 1993–96; Registrar, Bishop Grosseteste Coll., Lincoln, 1996–98; Principal, DFEE, 1998–2001; Deputy Director: Social Exclusion Unit, Cabinet Office, 2001–04; Young People at Risk Div., DFES, then DCSF, 2004–08; Director: Workforce Strategy, DCSF, 2008–09; Workforce Gp, DCSF, then DFE, 2009–11; Prison Reform, MoJ, 2016; Open Data Projects, Cabinet Office, 2017–18. Chair of Govs, Cranbrook Church of England Primary Sch., 2013–. *Recreations:* cooking, coffee. *Address:* Cabinet Office, 1 Horse Guards Road, SW1A 2HQ.

**BELL, Marian Patricia,** CBE 2005; economist; Member, Monetary Policy Committee, Bank of England, 2002–05; *b* 28 Oct. 1957; *d* of Joseph Denis Milburn Bell and Wilhelmenia Maxwell Bell (*née* Miller). *Educ:* Hertford Coll., Oxford (BA PPE); Birkbeck Coll., London (MSc Econs). Sen. Economist, Royal Bank of Scotland, 1985–89; Econ. Advr, HM Treasury, 1989–91; Sen. Treasury Economist, 1991–97; Hd of Res., Treasury and Capital Mkts, Royal Bank of Scotland, 1997–2000; Consultant, alpha economics, 2000–02, 2005–. Member: Internat. Adv. Council, Zurich Financial Services, 2007–14; Fiscal Policy Panel, States of Jersey, 2007–14, States of Guernsey, 2010–11, CI. Non-exec. Dir, Emerging Health Threats Forum, 2006–12. Governor: Contemporary Dance Trust, The Place, 2005–14 (Vice-Chm., 2008–14); NIESR, 2014–.

**BELL, Martin,** OBE 1992; Ambassador (formerly Special Representative) for Humanitarian Emergencies, UNICEF, since 2001; *b* 31 Aug. 1938; *s* of late Adrian Hanbury Bell and Marjorie H. Bell; *m* 1st, 1971, Nelly Lucienne Gourdon (marr. diss.); two *d*; 2nd, 1985, Rebecca D. Sobel (marr. diss.); 3rd, 1998, Fiona Goddard. *Educ:* The Leys Sch., Cambridge; King's Coll., Cambridge (MA). BBC TV News: Reporter, 1965–77; Diplomatic Correspondent, 1977–78; Chief Washington Correspondent, 1978–89; Berlin Correspondent, 1989–93; E European Correspondent, 1993–94; Foreign Affairs Correspondent, 1994–96; Special Correspondent, BBC Nine O'Clock News, 1997. Pool TV Reporter, 7th Armoured Bde, Gulf War, 1991. MP (Ind.) Tatton, 1997–2001. Contested (Ind.) Brentwood and Ongar, 2001. DUniv Derby, 1996; Hon. MA: East Anglia, 1997; N London, 1997; Hon. DLit Kingston, 2002. RTS Reporter of the Year, 1977, TV Journalist of the Year, 1992. *Publications:* In Harm's Way, 1995; An Accidental MP, 2000; Through Gates of Fire, 2003; The Truth that Sticks: New Labour's breach of trust, 2007; A Very British Revolution, 2009; For Whom the Bell Tolls, 2011; The End of Empire, 2015; War and the Death of News, 2017. *Address:* 71 Denman Drive, NW11 6RA.

**BELL, Martin George Henry;** Senior Partner, Ashurst Morris Crisp, 1986–92; *b* 16 Jan. 1935; *s* of Leonard George Bell and Phyllis Bell (*née* Green); *m* 1965, Shirley Wrightson; two *s*. *Educ:* Charterhouse. Nat. Service, 1953–55. Articles, 1956–61, admitted Solicitor, 1961, Assistant, 1961, Partner, 1963, Ashurst Morris Crisp. Dir, Laird Gp, 1994–2002. *Recreation:* walking.

**BELL, Prof. Martin Guy,** PhD; FBA 2009; FSA; Professor of Archaeological Science, University of Reading, since 2002; *b* Brighton, 28 Oct. 1953; *s* of William and Joy Bell; *m* 1981, Dr Jennifer Foster; two *d*. *Educ:* Cardinal Newman Sch., Hove; Inst. of Archaeol., Univ. of London (BSc, PhD). Res. asst, then Res. Fellow, Bristol Univ., 1980–83; Lectr, then Sen. Lectr, Univ. of Wales, Lampeter, 1983–96; Sen. Lectr, Univ. of Reading, 1996–2002. FSA 1984. *Publications:* Brean Down: excavations, 1983–87, 1990; (with M. J. C. Walker) Late Quaternary Environmental Change, 1992, 2nd edn 2005; (ed with J. Boardman) Past and Present Soil Erosion, 1992; (jtly) The Experimental Earthwork Project, 1996; Prehistoric Intertidal Archaeology, 2000; Prehistoric Coastal Communities, 2007; The Bronze Age in the Severn Estuary, 2013. *Recreations:* swimming, walking, natural history. *Address:* Department of Archaeology, University of Reading, Whiteknights, PO Box 227, Reading RG6 6AB. *T:* (0118) 378 7724, *Fax:* (0118) 378 6718. *E:* m.g.bell@reading.ac.uk.

**BELL, Mary Elizabeth;** *see* Stacey, M. E.

**BELL, Matthew Alexander Charlton,** OBE 2018; Director and Joint Head of Public Policy Practice, Frontier Economics, since 2017; *b* York, 17 May 1975; *s* of Graham and Susan Bell; partner, 2005, Almudena Lara; one *s* one *d*. *Educ:* McGill Univ. (BA); Darwin Coll., Cambridge (MPhil). Dir, Frontier Economics Ltd, 1999–2014; CEO, Cttee on Climate Change, 2014–17. *Publications:* contrib. articles on regulation, public policy and investment decisions. *Recreations:* my family, brief spurts of reading, writing, travel, theatre. *Address:* Frontier Economics, 71 High Holborn, WC1V 6DA. *T:* (020) 7031 7000. *E:* matthew.bell@frontier-economics.com.

**BELL, Prof. Michael,** PhD; FBA 2008; Professor of English, University of Warwick, 1994–2008, now Emeritus; *b* Chelmsford, 21 July 1941; *s* of Michael James Bell and Josephine Bell; *m* 1st (marr. diss.); one *s* one *d*; 2nd, 2016. *Educ:* University Coll. London (BA; PhD 1970). English asst, Lyons, France, 1962–63; teacher of English and French, St Stephen's Sch., Welling, 1963–64; English asst, Erlangen, Germany, 1964–65; Instructor, 1965–69, Lectr, 1969–70, Univ. of Western Ontario; Associate Prof., Ithaca Coll., NY, 1970–73; University of Warwick: Lectr, 1973–81; Sen. Lectr, 1981–92; Reader in English, 1992–94. *Publications:* Primitivism, 1972; (ed) Context of English Literature 1900–1930, 1982; The Sentiment of Reality: truth of feeling in the European novel, 1983; F. R. Leavis, 1988; D. H. Lawrence: language and being, 1992; Gabriel García Márquez: solitude and solidarity, 1993; Literature, Modernism and Myth: belief and responsibility in the Twentieth Century, 1997; Sentimentalism, Ethics and the Culture of Feeling, 2001; Open Secrets: literature and education and authority from J.-J. Rousseau to J. M. Coetzee, 2007. *Recreation:* walking. *Address:* 27 Claremont Road, Leamington Spa, Warks CV31 3EH. *T:* (01926) 312719. *E:* Bell.Michael@talktalk.net.

**BELL, Michael John Vincent,** CB 1992; independent export controls consultant, since 2013; Senior Adviser, MK Trade Compliance Group, since 2013; Associate, Deloitte LLP, since 2018; *b* 9 Sept. 1941; *s* of late C. R. V. Bell, OBE and Jane Bell, MBE; *m* 1983, Mary Shippen, *o d* of late J. W. and Margaret Shippen; one *s* two *d*. *Educ:* Winchester Coll.; Magdalen Coll., Oxford (BA Lit.Hum., MA). Res. Associate, Inst. for Strategic Studies, 1964; Ministry of Defence: Asst Principal, 1965; Principal, 1969; Asst Sec., 1975; on loan to HM Treasury, 1977–79; Asst Under Sec. of State (Resources and Programmes), 1982–84; Dir Gen. of Management Audit, 1984–86; Asst Sec. Gen. for Defence Planning and Policy, NATO, 1986–88; Dep. Under-Sec. of State (Finance), 1988–92, (Defence Procurement), 1992–95; Dep. Chief of Defence Procurement (Support), 1995–96; Project Dir, European Consolidation, BAe (on secondment), 1996–99; Gp Hd of Strategic Analysis, BAe, subseq. BAE Systems, 1999–2003; Gp Export Controls Consultant, BAE Systems, 2004–12. *Recreation:* military history.

**BELL, Nigel;** *see* Bell, J. N. B.

**BELL, Nigel Christopher,** CEng, CITP; Strategy and Development, Government and Health, Atos UK, since 2016; Managing Partner, AllChange Business Advisors Ltd, since 2016; *b* 29 July 1959; *s* of Leonard Bell and Marlene Bell (*née* Gould); *m* 1985, Colette Julia Stein; one *s* one *d*. *Educ:* Kendal Grammar Sch.; Loughborough Univ. (BSc Hons Computer Studies); Sheffield Hallam Univ. (MSc Managing Change). CEng 1990; CITP 2008; FBCS 2008. Analyst Programmer, Comshare, 1981–85; Project Co-ordinator, Honeywell Bull, 1985–87; Project Manager, Boots, 1987–88; Mgt Consultant, Price Waterhouse, 1988–93; Div. Dir, Eur. Inf. Systems, Low & Bonar, 1993–96; Vice-Pres., Inf. Systems and Services, Astra Charnwood, 1996–98; Inf. Systems and Technol. Dir for Drug Develt, Astra AB, 1998–99; Chief Exec., NHS Information Authy, 1999–2001; Dir, Service Transformation, Office of e-Envoy, Cabinet Office, 2001–02; Dir and Principal Consultant, Ophis Ltd, 2002–11; Man. Partner, HP Enterprise Services, 2012–15; Service Transformation Dir, NHS Shared Business Services, 2015–16. *Recreations:* fell-walking, gym, hi-fi, cinema.

**BELL, Sir Peter (Robert Frank),** Kt 2002; MD; FRCS, FRCSGlas; Professor and Head of Department of Surgery, University of Leicester, 1974–2003, now Emeritus; *b* 12 June 1938; *s* of Frank and Ruby Bell; *m* 1961, Anne Jennings; one *s* two *d*. *Educ:* Univ. of Sheffield (MB, ChB Hons 1961; MD 1969). FRCS 1965; FRCSGlas 1968. Postgrad. surg. career in Sheffield hosps, 1961–65; Lectr in Surgery, Univ. of Glasgow, 1965–68; Sir Henry Wellcome Travelling Fellow, Univ. of Colorado, 1968–69; Consultant Surgeon and Sen. Lectr, Western Infirm., Glasgow, 1969–74. President: Surgical Res. Soc., 1986–88; European Soc. of Vascular Surgery, 1994; Vascular Soc. of GB and Ireland, 1998–99; Internat. Soc. of Vascular Surgeons, 2003–; Mem. Council, RCS, 1992– (Vice Pres., 2001–04). Pres., Hope Foundn for Cancer Res.; Chm., Circulation Foundn. Founder FMedSci 1998. Hon. DSc Leicester, 2003; Dr *hc* Lisbon, 2009. *Publications:* Surgical Aspects of Haemodialysis, 1974, 2nd edn 1983; Operative Arterial Surgery, 1982; Arterial Surgery of the Lower Limb, 1991; Surgical Management of Vascular Disease, 1992; 596 pubns on vascular disease, transplantation and cancer in med. and surg. jls. *Recreations:* horticulture, oil painting, bowls, reading.

**BELL, Robert John;** Chief Executive, Royal Brompton and Harefield NHS Foundation Trust, since 2005; *b* Tripoli, Lebanon, 22 July 1950; *s* of Jack R. Bell and May Bell (*née* Dagher); *m* 1973, Patricia L. Neate; one *s* two *d*. *Educ:* Univ. of Toronto (BASc Industrial Engrg 1973); Professional Engr, Ont, 1975; Cornell Univ. (EDP 1978); Queen's Univ., Canada (MPA 1980). Systems engr, Hosp. for Sick Children, Toronto, 1972–74; Planning Officer, Min. of Health, Ont, 1974–75; Treasury Bd Officer, Mgt Bd of Cabinet, Toronto 1975–76; Exec. Dir, Min. of Health, Ont, 1976–80; Vice President: Extendicare Ltd

London, 1980–83; Hilton Universal Hosps, London, 1983–85; Exec. Dir, Min. of Health, Ont, 1985–86; Partner, KPMG (Peat Marwick), Toronto, 1986–90; Ernst & Young, Toronto: Partner and Nat. Dir (Health Care), 1990–2000; Vice Pres., Cap Gemini, 2000–02; Pres. and CEO, William Osler Health Centre, Ont, 2002–05. Non-executive Director: CORDA, 2008–15; Inst. of Cardiovascular Medicine and Sci., 2011–; Imperial Coll. Health Partners, 2012–; Royal Brompton and Harefield Hosps Charity, 2012–15. Vis. Prof., Imperial Coll. London, 2014–. Chm., Assoc. of UK University Hosps, 2017. Freeman, City of London, 2018. *Recreation:* antique collector (Oriental rugs and carpets, commemorative bronze medallions, coins, model soldiers). *Address:* Oak Tree House, Broadway Road, Childswickham, Broadway, Worcs WR12 7HP. *T:* (office) (020) 7351 8652, 07970 296445. *E:* robertbell49@btinternet.com.

**BELL, Hon. Sir Rodger,** Kt 1993; a Judge of the High Court of Justice, Queen's Bench Division, 1993–2006; a Presiding Judge, South Eastern Circuit, 2001–05; *b* 13 Sept. 1939; *s* of John Thornton Bell and Edith Bell; *m* 1969, (Sylvia) Claire Tatton Brown; one *s* three *d*. *Educ:* Moulsham Sch.; Brentwood Sch.; Brasenose Coll., Oxford (BA). Called to the Bar, Middle Temple, 1963, Bencher, 1989; QC 1982; a Recorder, 1980–93; Chm., NHS Tribunal, 1991–93; Legal Mem., Mental Health Review Tribunals, 1983–93; Mem., Parole Board, 1990–93. *Address:* The Mill House, Upton Hellions, Crediton, Devon EX17 4AE.

**BELL, Stephen Ainswood;** Associate Conductor, Hallé Pops, since 2013; *b* Bury, Lancs, 13 July 1962; *s* of Frank Bell and Joan Bell; *m* 2007, Charlotte Lines; three *d*. *Educ:* Bacup and Rawtenstall Grammar Sch.; Royal Coll. of Music (GRSM Hons; ARCM). Sub Principal Horn, 1985–92, Principal Horn, 1992–2015, BBC Concert Orchestra; freelance conductor, 2000–. *Recreations:* travel, cars, food. *Address:* Hallé Concerts Society, Bridgewater Hall, Manchester M1 5HA. *T:* (0161) 237 7000. *E:* stephenbell62@icloud.com.

**BELL, Prof. Stephen David,** PhD; Professor, Molecular and Cellular Biochemistry Department, Indiana University, since 2012; *b* Glasgow, 10 July 1967; *s* of David and Jean Bell; *m* 2007, Rachel Yvonne Samson; one *d*. *Educ:* Glasgow Univ. (BSc Hons Molecular Biol. 1989; PhD 1992). Post-doctoral res., Wellcome Centre for Molecular Parasitology, 1992–95, Gurdon Inst., Cambridge, 1996–2001; Gp Leader, MRC Cancer Cell Unit, Cambridge, 2001–07; Prof. of Microbiol., Univ. of Oxford, 2007–12; Fellow, Wadham Coll., Oxford, 2007–12. Fellow, EMBO, 2006. Tenovus Medal, Tenovus Scotland, 2006. *Publications:* (with Melvin Depamphilis) Genome Duplication, 2010; contrib. scientific jls in fields of transcription, DNA replication and cell division. *Recreations:* climbing, bird watching. *Address:* Molecular and Cellular Biochemistry Department, Indiana University, Simon Hall MSB, Room 405A, 212 S Hawthorne Drive, Bloomington, IN 47405, USA.

**BELL, Steve W. M.;** freelance cartoonist and illustrator, since 1977; *b* 26 Feb. 1951; *m* 1977; four *c*. *Educ:* Slough Grammar Sch.; Teesside Coll. of Art; Univ. of Leeds (BA Fine Art 1974); Exeter Univ. (teaching cert.). Teacher of art, Aston Manor Sch., Birmingham, 1976–77. Contribs to Whoopee!, Cheeky, Jackpot, New Statesman, New Society, Social Work Today, NME, Journalist; Maggie's Farm series, Time Out, then City Limits, 1979; IF…series, Guardian, 1981–. Exhibitions of cartoons: Barbican Gall.; Cartoon Gall.; Cartoon Mus.; Lightbox Gall., Woking; Wilhelm Busch Mus., Hanover. Hon. MLit Teesside, 1995; Hon. DLit: Sussex, 1996; Loughborough, 2006; Leeds, 2007; Brighton, 2011. *Publications:* Maggie's Farm, 1981; Further Down on Maggie's Farm, 1982; The If Chronicle, 1983; (with B. Homer) Waiting for the Upturn, 1986; Maggie's Farm: the last round up, 1987; If…Bounces Back, 1987; If…Breezes In, 1988; (with R. Woddis) Funny Old World, 1991; If…Goes Down the John, 1992; If…Bottoms Out, 1993; Big If…, 1995; (with S. Hoggart) Live Briefs: a political sketchbook, 1996; If…Files, 1997; Bell's Eye, 1999; (with B. Homer) Chairman Blair's Little Red Book, 2001; Unstoppable If…, 2001; Unspeakable If…, 2003; Apes of Wrath, 2004; If…Marches On, 2006; My Vision for a New You, 2006; If…Bursts Out, 2010. *Address:* Belltoons, PO Box 5298, Brighton BN50 8AR. *W:* www.belltoons.co.uk.

**BELL, Trevor;** *see* Bell, C. T.

**BELL, William Bradshaw,** OBE 2005; JP; Member (UU) Lagan Valley, Northern Ireland Assembly, 1998–2007; *b* 9 Oct. 1935; *s* of Robert Bell and Mary Ann Bell; *m* 1969, Leona Maxwell; one *s* three *d*. *Educ:* Fane Street Primary School, Belfast; Grosvenor High School, Belfast. Member: for N Belfast, NI Constitutional Convention, 1975–76; Belfast City Council, 1976–85 (Unionist spokesman on housing, 1976–79; Lord Mayor of Belfast, 1979–80); for S Antrim, NI Assembly, 1982–86 (Dep. Chm., Finance and Personnel Cttee, 1984–86); Lisburn CC (formerly BC), 1989–2005 (Chairman: Police Liaison Cttee, 1991; Finance Cttee, 1993–95; Economic Develt Cttee, 1996–98; Mayor of Lisburn, 2003–04). Chm., NI Public Accounts Cttee, 1999–2002. Contested (UU) Lagan Valley, NI Assembly, 2007. *Recreations:* music, motoring, writing.

**BELL, Sir William Hollin Dayrell M.;** *see* Morrison-Bell.

**BELL BURNELL, Dame (Susan) Jocelyn,** DBE 2007 (CBE 1999); PhD; FRS 2003; FRSE, FRAS; astronomer; Visiting Professor of Astrophysics, University of Oxford, since 2004; Chancellor, University of Dundee, since 2018; *b* 15 July 1943; *d* of G. Philip and M. Allison Bell; *m* 1968, Martin Burnell (separated 1989); one *s*. *Educ:* The Mount Sch., York; Glasgow Univ. (BSc); New Hall, Cambridge (PhD; Hon. Fellow, 1996). FRAS 1969; FRSE 2004. Res. Fellowships, Univ. of Southampton, 1968–73; Res. Asst, Mullard Space Science Lab., UCL, 1974–82; Sen. Res. Fellow, 1982–86, SSO, 1986–89, Grade 7, 1989–91, Royal Observatory, Edinburgh; Prof. of Physics, Open Univ., 1991–2001; Dean, Science Faculty, Univ. of Bath, 2001–04. An Editor, The Observatory, 1973–76. Vis. Fellow, 1999, Vis. Prof. for Distinguished Teaching, 1999–2000, Princeton Univ.; Sackler Vis. Prof., Univ. of Calif, Berkeley, 2000; Philips Visitor, Haverford Coll., Pa, 1999; Tuve Fellow, Carnegie Instn of Washington, 2000; Vainu Bappu Vis. Prof., Indian Inst. of Astrophysics, Bangalore, 2013. Lectures: Marie Curie, Inst. of Physics, 1994; Appleton, Univ., Edinburgh, 1994; Jansky, Nat. Radio Astronomy Observatory, USA, 1995; Royal Instn, 1996; Maddison, Keele Univ., 1997; Flamsteed, Derby Univ., 1997; Royal Soc., 1997; Hamilton, Princeton Univ., 1997; Women in Physics, Aust. Inst of Physics, 1999; Bishop, Columbia Univ. NY, 1999; Elizabeth Spreadbury, UCL, 2001; Flamsteed, Royal Observatory, Greenwich, 2003; Herschel, Bath, 2003; Robinson (and medal), Armagh, 2004; Nuffield, Assoc. of Sci. Educators, 2005; Inst. of Physics, Ireland, 2005; Campbell, Southampton, 2006; Gordon, Cornell, 2006; Athena, Keele, 2006; Kelvin (and Medal), Royal Philosophical Soc., Glasgow, 2007; Compton, Washington Univ., St Louis, Mo, 2008; Sophia, Newcastle, 2008; Dean's, Melbourne, 2008; Lewis, Assoc. of Sci. Educators, 2010; Faraday, Royal Soc., 2011; de Waard, Groningen Univ., 2011; Wood, Mount Allison Univ., 2012; Edinburgh, Royal Soc. of Edinburgh, 2012; Helen Sawyer Hogg Prize and Lect., Royal Astronomical Soc. of Canada, 2012; Sven Berggren Prize and Lect., Kungl Fysiografiska Sällskapet I Lund, Sweden, 2012; Appleton, Rutherford Appleton Lab., 2012; Lise Meitner, German Physical Soc. and Austrian Physical Soc., 2013; Centenary, Indian Inst. of Sci., Bangalore, 2014; J. L. Synge, TCD, 2014; Founder's, Univ. of Bath, 2015; Moon, San Angelo State Univ., Texas, 2015; de Coursey, Trinity Univ., San Antonio, Texas, 2015; Mohler Prize and Lect., Univ. of Michigan, 2016; Allison Levick, Sydney, 2018; Elizabeth Laird Meml, Western Univ., Ont, 2018; Reines, Univ. of Calif, Irvine, 2019. Distinguished Lectr, Internat. Space Univ., 2000, 2002. Mem., IAU, 1979–; Chm., Physics Trng and Mobility of Researchers Fellowships Panel, EC, 1996–98 (Vice Chm., 1995); President: RAS, 2002–04 (Vice-Pres., 1995–97); Inst. of Physics, 2008–11 (Hon. FInstP 2012); British Science Assoc., 2011–12; Royal Soc. of Edinburgh, 2014–18; Mem. Council, Royal Soc., 2004–06; Mem. Panel, Women for Sci., Inter Acad. Council, 2005–06. Mem. Council, Open Univ., 1997–99. Trustee, Nat. Maritime Mus., 2000–09. Chm., Grand Jury, Eur. Commn Marie Curie Excellence Awards, 2005. Foreign Member: Onsala Telescope Bd, Sweden, 1996–2002; Nat. Acad. of Scis, USA, 2005; Amer. Philosophical Soc., 2016; Hon. Member: Sigma-Pi-Sigma, 2000; Royal Irish Acad., 2012; Amer. Astronomical Assoc., 2015; Bilim Akademisi, Turkey, 2016; Internat. Hon. Mem., American Acad. of Arts and Scis, 2018. Hon. Principal, No 35 Sch., Beijing, 2012; Hon. Prof., Xinjiang Astronomical Observatory, China, 2013. FRSA 1999–2011. Honorary Fellow: BAAS, 2006; Glyndwr Univ., 2011. Hon. DSc: Heriot-Watt, 1993; Newcastle, Warwick, 1995; Cambridge, 1996; Glasgow, Sussex, 1997; St Andrews, London, 1999; Leeds, Haverford Coll., Penn, Williams Coll., Mass, 2000; Portsmouth, QUB, 2002; Edinburgh 2003; Keele, 2005; Harvard, Durham 2007; Trinity Dublin, Michigan, Southampton, 2008; Leicester, Loughborough, Lancaster, NUI, 2009; Aberdeen, UCL, 2013; Manchester, 2014; McGill, Edinburgh Napier, Strathclyde, Hull, 2015; Rutgers, Alberta, 2016; DUniv: York, 1994; Open, 2009; Valencia 2017; Hon. DPhil Dublin City, 2015; Hon. LLD Dundee, 2017. Michelson Medal, Franklin Inst., Philadelphia (jtly with Prof. A. Hewish), 1973; J. Robert Oppenheimer Meml Prize, Univ. of Miami, 1978; Rennie Taylor Award, Amer. Tentative Soc., NY, 1978; (first) Beatrice M. Tinsley Prize, Amer. Astronomical Soc., 1987; Herschel Medal, RAS, 1989; Edinburgh Medal, City of Edinburgh, 1999; Targa Giuseppe Piazzi Award, Palermo, Sicily, 1999; Magellanic Premium, Amer. Philos. Soc., 2000; Joseph Priestly Award, Dickinson Coll., Penn, 2002; Faraday Medal, Royal Soc., 2010; Grote Reber Medal, 2011; Lifetime Achievement Award, Women of the Year, 2015; Gold Medal, Consejo Superior de Investigaciones Científicas, Spain, 2015; Royal Medal (Physical Scis), Royal Soc., 2015; President's Medal, Inst. of Physics, 2016; Breakthrough Prize in Fundamental Physics, 2018; Grande Médaille, French Acad. of Scis, 2018. Discovered the first four pulsars (neutron stars), 1967–68. *Publications:* Broken for Life, 1989; (ed jtly) Next Generation Infrared Space Observatory, 1992; (ed with Maurice Riordan) Dark Matter: poems of space, 2008; A Quaker Astronomer Reflects, 2013; papers in Nature, Science, Astronomy and Astrophysics, Jl of Geophys. Res., Monthly Notices of RAS. *Recreations:* Quaker interests, walking. *Address:* University of Oxford, Department of Astrophysics, Denys Wilkinson Building, Keble Road, Oxford OX1 3RH.

**BELLAK, John George;** Chairman, Severn Trent plc (formerly Severn-Trent Water Authority), 1983–94; *b* 19 Nov. 1930; *m* 1960, Mary Prudence Marshall; three *s* one *d*. *Educ:* Uppingham; Clare College, Cambridge. MA (Economics). Sales and Marketing Dir, Royal Doulton, 1968–80, Man. Dir, 1980–83; Chairman: Royal Crown Derby, 1972–83; Lawleys Ltd, 1972–83. President: British Ceramic Manufacturers' Fedn, 1982–83; Fedn of European Porcelain and Earthenware Manufacturers, 1982–83; European Waste Water Group, 1991–93; Dep. Chm., Water Services Assoc., 1992 (Vice-Chm., 1990–91; Chm., 1991). Chm., Aberdeen High Income Trust (formerly Abtrust High Income Investment Trust), 1994–2003; Dir, Ascot Holdings, 1993–96. Mem., Grand Council, CBI, 1984–94. Mem. Court, Keele Univ., 1984–96. *Recreations:* ornithology, field sports, reading. *Address:* 1 Council House Court, Shrewsbury SY1 2AU. *Clubs:* Carlton, Beefsteak.

**BELLAMY, Sir Christopher (William),** Kt 2000; Chairman, Global Competition Practice, Linklaters, since 2011; *b* 25 April 1946; *s* of late William Albert Bellamy, TD, MRCS, LRCP and Vyvienne Hilda, *d* of Albert Meyrick, OBE; *m* 1989, Deirdre Patricia (*née* Turner); one *s* two *d*. *Educ:* Tonbridge Sch.; Brasenose Coll., Oxford (MA). Called to the Bar, Middle Temple, 1968; Bencher, 1994. Taught in Africa, 1968–69; in practice at Bar, 1970–92; QC 1986; Asst Recorder, 1989–92; Judge: Court of First Instance, EC, 1992–99; Employment Appeal Tribunal, 2000–07; a Recorder, 2000–07; a Deputy High Court Judge, 2000–16; President: Appeal Tribunals, Competition Commn, 1999–2003; Competition Appeal Tribunal, 2003–07. President: Assoc. of European Competition Law Judges, 2002–06 (Hon. Pres., 2008); UK Assoc. of European Law, 2004–09. Mem., Adv. Council, British Inst. of Internat. and Comparative Law, 2007– (Mem., Adv. Council, Bingham Centre for the Rule of Law, 2011–). Gov., Ravensbourne Coll. of Design and Communication, 1988–92. Examiner, All Souls Coll., Oxford, 2018. Liveryman, Broderers' Co., 1995 (Master, 2018–19). Commandeur, Ordre Grand-Ducal de la Couronne de Chêne (Luxembourg), 2013. *Publications:* (with G. Child) Common Market Law of Competition, 1973, 8th edn (ed D. Bailey and L. John), 2018; public lectures and articles on legal matters. *Recreations:* history, walking, family life. *Address:* Linklaters, 1 Silk Street, EC2Y 8HQ. *T:* (020) 7456 3457. *Clubs:* Athenæum, Garrick.

**BELLAMY, His Honour Clifford William;** a Circuit Judge, 2004–19; Designated Family Judge for Derby, 2016–19; *b* 20 May 1952; *s* of late William Broughton Bellamy and Joan Ernestine Bellamy; *m* 1976, Christine Ann Hughes; two *s*. *Educ:* Burton upon Trent Grammar Sch.; University Coll. London (LLB); Coll. of Ripon and York St John (MA). Admitted solicitor, 1976; Dist Judge, 1995–2004; Designated Family Judge for Warwickshire and Coventry, 2006–12, for Leicester, 2012–16. Ordained Methodist Minister, 2001. *Publications:* Complaints and Discipline in the Methodist Church, 2000, 3rd edn 2008; (contrib.) What is a Minister?, 2002. *Recreations:* reading, opera, walking along the Promenade des Anglais.

**BELLAMY, David Charles;** Chairman, International Advisory Board, St James's Place PLC, since 2018; Chairman, Weatherbys Bank Ltd and Weatherbys Ltd, since 2018; *b* 15 April 1953; *s* of Percival Leonard Bellamy and Elizabeth Margaret Bellamy; *m* 1970, Janette Godfrey; two *s* one *d*. *Educ:* Sutton High Grammar Sch., Plymouth. Hambro Life Assce, subseq. Allied Dunbar Assce, 1973–91 (Divl Dir, Strategic Res. Unit, 1988–91); Sales Ops, J. Rothschild Assce Gp, 1991–97; Gp Ops Dir, 1997–2000, Man. Dir, 2000–07, CEO, 2007–17, St James's Place. Trustee, St James's Place Foundn (Charitable Trust), 1997– (Chm., 2018–). *Recreations:* family, horse racing, horse racing ownership. *Address:* St James's Place PLC, 1 Tetbury Road, Cirencester, Glos GL7 1FP; Weatherbys, Sanders Road, Wellingborough, Northants NN8 4BX.

**BELLAMY, David James,** OBE 1994; PhD; FLS; CBiol, FRSB; botanist; writer and broadcaster; *b* 18 Jan. 1933; *s* of Thomas Bellamy and Winifred (*née* Green); *m* 1959, Rosemary Froy; two *s* three *d*. *Educ:* London University: Chelsea Coll. of Science and Technology (BSc); Bedford Coll. (PhD). Lectr, then Sen. Lectr, Dept of Botany, Univ. of Durham, 1960–80; Hon. Prof. of Adult and Continuing Educn, 1980–82; Special Prof., then Special Prof. of Geog., Nottingham Univ., 1987–; Vis. Prof. of Natural Heritage Studies, Massey Univ., NZ, 1988–89; Hon. Prof., Univ. of Central Qld, 1999–. Inaugural David Bellamy Lect., 2013. Dir, David Bellamy Associates, envmtl consultants, 1988–95; Associate Dir, P-E Internat., 1993–94; Chm., Greengro Produce Ltd, 2002–; Hon. Dir, Zander Corp., 2004–. Founder Dir, 1982, Pres., 1998, Conservation Foundn; Trustee: WWF, 1985–89; Living Landscape Trust, 1985–; Pensthorpe Conservation Trust Ltd, 2010–; President: WATCH, 1982–2005; YHA, 1983–2004; Population Concern, 1988–2003; Nat. Assoc. of Envmtl Educn, 1989–2010; Assoc. of Master Thatchers, 1991–97; Council, Zool Soc. of London, 1991–94, 2002–; Plantlife, 1994–2005; Wildflower Soc.,

1995–98; Wildlife Trust Partnership, 1996–2005; British Holiday and Home Parks Assoc., 1996–; Camping and Caravanning Club, 2002–13 (Vice-Pres., 2014–); Vice-Pres., Wild Trout Trust, 2005–. Chair: Welsh Fest. of Countryside, 1999–2002; Abela Conservation Foundn, 2003; Cedrus Ltd, 2003–04; Chair of Govs, Mareeba Wetland Foundn, 2002–. Patron: Te Pua O Whirinaki Regeneration Trust, NZ, 2009–; British Chelonia Gp, 2009–; Lower Mole Countryside Trust, 2013–. Governor, Repton Sch., 1983–89. Chief I Spy, 1983. Contested (Referendum) Huntingdon, 1997. Presenter and script writer for television and radio programmes, BBC and ITV; programmes include Longest Running Show on Earth, 1985; main series: Life in our Sea, 1970; Bellamy on Botany, 1973; Bellamy's Britain, 1975; Bellamy's Europe, 1977; Botanic Man, 1979; Up a Gum Tree, 1980; Backyard Safari, 1981; The Great Seasons, 1982; Bellamy's New World, 1983; You Can't See The Wood, 1984; Discovery, 1985; Seaside Safari, 1985; End of the Rainbow Show, 1985; Bellamy's Bugle, 1986; Turning the Tide, 1986; The End of the Rainbow Show, 1986; Bellamy's Bird's Eye View, 1988; Moa's Ark, 1990; Bellamy Rides Again, 1991, 1992; Wetlands, 1991; England's Last Wilderness, 1992; Blooming Bellamy, 1993; Routes of Wisdom, 1993; Bellamy's Border Raids: the Peak District, 1994; Westwatch, 1996; A Welsh Herbal, 1998; Making Tracks, 1998 and 1999; A Celtic Herbal, 1999; Kite Country, Bellamy and the Argonauts, 2000; The Challenge, 2000; Agrissentials, 2006. FCIWEM 1996; FRIN 2005. Hon. Fellow: BICSc 1997; Royal Entomol Soc. of London; Hon. FLS 1997. Hon. Fellow, Univ. of Lancaster, 1997. DUniv Open, 1984; Hon. DSc: CNAA, 1990; Nottingham, 1993; Dunelm, 1995; Bournemouth, 1999; Kingston, 2000; Oxford Brookes, 2004. Frances Ritchie Meml Prize, Rambler's Assoc., 1989; UNEP Global 500 Award, 1990; Environmental Communicator of the Year, British Assoc. of Communicators in Business, 1996; Guild of Travel Writers Award, 1996; Busk Medal, RGS, 2001. Order of the Golden Ark (Netherlands), 1989. *Publications*: Peatlands, 1974; Bellamy on Botany, 1974; Bellamy's Britain, 1975; Bellamy's Europe, 1977; Life Giving Sea, 1977; Botanic Man, 1978; Half of Paradise, 1979; The Great Seasons, 1981; Backyard Safari, 1981; Discovering the Countryside with David Bellamy: vols I and II, 1982, vols III and IV, 1983; The Mouse Book, 1983; Bellamy's New World, 1983; The Queen's Hidden Garden, 1984; Turning the Tide, 1986; The Vanishing Bogs of Ireland, 1986; Bellamy's Changing Countryside, 4 vols, 1989; (with Brendan Quayle) England's Last Wilderness, 1989; England's Lost Wilderness, 1990; (with Jane Gifford) Wilderness in Britain, 1991; How Green Are You?, 1991; Tomorrow's Earth, 1991; (with Andrea Pfister) World Medicine, 1992; Blooming Bellamy, 1993; Poo, You and the Potoroo's Loo, 1997; (contrib.) The Blue UNESCO, 1999; The English Landscape, 2000; (consultant) The Countryside Detective, 2000; The Jolly Green Giant (autobiog.), 2002; (with Piers Browne) The Glorious Trees of Great Britain, 2002; The Bellamy Herbal, 2003; Conflicts in the Countryside, 2005. *Recreations*: family, gardening, ballet. *Address*: 1 Chapelside Meadows, Hamsterley, Co. Durham DL13 3RG.

**BELLAMY, (Kenneth) Rex**; Tennis Correspondent, The Times, 1967–89; *b* 15 Sept. 1928; *s* of Sampson Bellamy and Kathleen May Bellamy; *m* 1st, 1951, Hilda O'Shea (*d* 2000); one step *d*; 2nd, 2006, Wendy Elizabeth Matthews (*d* 2018). *Educ*: Yeovil; Woodhouse Grammar Sch., Sheffield. National Service, RA and RASC, 1946–49. Sports and Feature Writer, Sheffield Telegraph, 1944–46 and 1949–53; Sports Writer: Birmingham Gazette, 1953–56; The Times, 1956–89. World Championship Tennis award for service to tennis, 1988; International Tennis-writing Awards: 5 from Assoc. of Tennis Professionals, 1975–79 (award discontinued); 2 from Women's Tennis Assoc., 1977–78. *Publications*: Teach Yourself Squash (jtly), 1968; The Tennis Set, 1972; The Story of Squash, 1978 rev. edn as Squash—A History, 1988; The Peak District Companion, 1981; Walking the Tops, 1984; Game, Set and Deadline, 1986; Love Thirty, 1990; The Four Peaks, 1992. *Recreations*: hill-walking, table tennis. *Address*: Ashfield Lodge, 68 Petersfield Road, Midhurst, W Sussex GU29 9JR.

**BELLAMY, Martin Clifford**, PhD; Chief Information Officer, Financial Conduct Authority, since 2017; *b* Newcastle, 18 Jan. 1961; *s* of late Frank Bellamy and Mildred Bellamy; *m* 1985, Nicola Hammond; one *s* one *d*. *Educ*: Imperial Coll. London (BSc Hons Engrg 1983); London Business Sch. (MSc (Sloan) 1994); Imperial Coll. London (PhD 2014). Marketing Manager, BT, 1983–87; Dir, Real Time Technol., Reuters, 1987–2000; Partner, KPMG, 2000–01; Mem. Faculty, Ashridge Business Sch., 2001–02; Chief Information Officer, Pension Service, DWP, 2002–08; Hd, NHS Connecting for Health, DoH, 2008–09; G Cloud Dir, Cabinet Office, 2009–10; Dir, Change and ICT, Nat. Offender Mgt Service, MoJ, 2010–14; Crown Rep., Cabinet Office, 2011–14; Dir of Information Services, Univ. of Cambridge, 2014–17. Fellow, 2014–17, By-Fellow, 2017–, Hughes Hall, Cambridge. Non-exec. Dir, Group NBT, 2010–12. Hon. MA Cantab, 2017. FBCS 2005; CITP 2005; FAPM 2013; RPP 2013. *Recreations*: theatre, cinema, gym, walking, travel, family. *Address*: Financial Conduct Authority, 12 Endeavour Square, E20 1JN. *T*: (020) 7066 8524. *Club*: Oxford and Cambridge.

**BELLAMY, Prof. Richard Paul**, PhD; Professor of Political Science, University College London, since 2005 (Director: School of Public Policy, 2005–10; European Institute, 2010–13); Director, Max Weber Programme, European University Institute, Florence, 2014–19; *b* 15 June 1957; *s* of late Edmund Henry Bellamy and Joan Bellamy (*née* Roberts); one *d*; *m* 2017, Sandra Kröger. *Educ*: Trinity Hall, Cambridge (BA 1979; PhD 1982). ESRC Post-doctoral Res. Fellow, Nuffield Coll., Oxford, 1983–86 (Jun. Dean, 1985–86); Lectr, House of Politics, Christ Church, Oxford, 1984–86; Fellow and Coll. Lectr in Hist., Jesus Coll., Cambridge, and Lector, Trinity Coll., Cambridge, 1986–88; Lectr in Politics, Univ. of Edinburgh, 1988–92; Professor: of Politics, UEA, 1992–96; of Politics and Internat. Relns, Univ. of Reading, 1996–2002; of Govt, Univ. of Essex, 2002–05. Acad. Dir, Eur. Consortium for Pol Res., 2002–06; Chair, Britain and Ireland Assoc. for Political Thought, 2009–12. Mem., Politics and Internat. Relns Panel, REF 2014, 2011–. Vis. Prof., Univ. of Exeter, 2012, 2014–20; Visiting Fellow: Nuffield Coll., Oxford, 1995; Nat. Europe Centre, ANU, 2005; Jean Monnet Fellow, Social and Pol Sci. Dept, European Univ. Inst., Florence, 2000–01; Centre for Advanced Study, Oslo, 2010; Sen. Res. Fellow, Hanse Wissenschaft-Kolleg, Delmenhorst, 2013–14. Ed., Critical Rev. of Internat. Social and Political Philosophy, 2002–. FRSA 2002; FAcSS (AcSS 2008). Serena Medal, British Acad., 2012; (with Sandra Kröger) Journal Article Award, PADEMIA, 2016. *Publications*: Modern Italian Social Theory: ideology and politics from Pareto to the present, 1987 (trans. Indonesian); Liberalism and Modern Society: an historical argument, 1992 (trans. Portuguese and Chinese); (with D. Schecter) Gramsci and the Italian State, 1993 (trans. Japanese); Liberalism and Pluralism: towards a politics of compromise, 1999; Rethinking Liberalism, 2000 (trans. Chinese); Political Constitutionalism: a Republican defence of the constitutionality of democracy, 2007 (trans. Spanish; David and Elaine Spitz Prize, 2009); Citizenship, 2008; Croce, Gramsci, Bobbio and the Italian Political Tradition, 2014; A Republican Europe of States: cosmopolitanism, intergovernmentalism and democracy in the EU, 2019; (with D. Castiglione) From Maastricht to Brexit: democracy, constitutionalism and citizenship in the EU, 2019; *editor*: Liberalism and Recent Legal and Social Philosophy, 1989; Victorian Liberalism: nineteenth century political thought and practice, 1990; Theories and Concepts of Politics: an introduction, 1993; (jtly) Democracy and Constitutional Culture in the Union of Europe, 1995; Constitutionalism, Democracy and Sovereignty: American and European perspectives, 1996; (with A. Ross) A Textual Introduction to Social and Political Thought, 1996; (with D. Castiglione) Constitutionalism in Transformation: European and theoretical perspectives, 1996; (with M. Hollis) Pluralism and Liberal Neutrality, 1999; (with A. Warleigh) Citizenship and Governance in the European Union, 2001; (with A. Mason) Political Concepts, 2003; (with T. Ball) The Cambridge History of Twentieth Century Political Thought, 2003 (trans. Arabic, Turkish and Chinese); (jtly) Lineages of European Citizenship: rights, belonging and participation in eleven nation states, 2004; The Rule of Law and the Separation of Powers, 2005; (jtly) Making European Citizens: civic inclusion in a transitional context, 2006; Constitutionalism and Democracy, 2006; Introduction to Citizenship, 2008; Public Ethics, 2010; Citizenship, 2010; (jtly) Representation and Democracy in the EU: does the one come at the expense of the other?, 2014; (jtly) Citizenship: critical concepts, 4 vols, 2014; (jtly) Political Theory and the European Union, 2017; (jtly) European Boundaries in Question?, 2017; *contrib.* chapters in books and numerous articles to jls incl. Political Studies, British Jl Pol Sci., Philosophical Qly, Eur. Law Jl, Law and Philosophy, Eur. Jl Pol Res., Govt and Opposition, Eur. Jl Pol Theory, Hist. of Pol Thought, Philosophical Forum, Jl Modern Italian Studies, Jl Eur. Public Policy. *Recreations*: listening to and playing music of all kinds, reading and writing, walking, talking, cooking, gardening, films and theatre, sex, food and drink, running. *Address*: Department of Political Science, School of Public Policy, University College London, The Rubin Building, 29–31 Tavistock Square, WC1H 9QU. *T*: (020) 7679 4999, *Fax*: (020) 7679 4978. *E*: r.bellamy@ucl.ac.uk.

**BELLAMY-JAMES, Stephen Howard George Thompson**; QC 1996; a Recorder, since 2000; *b* 27 Sept. 1950; *m* 1988, Dr Rita Margaret Mary James, DCHS; one *d*. *Educ*: The Grammar Sch., Heckmondwike; Trinity Hall, Cambridge (MA Hons Law). ACIArb. Called to the Bar, Lincoln's Inn, 1974, Bencher, 2006; Asst Recorder, 1997–2000; Dep. High Court Judge, 2000–. Asst Parly Boundary Comr, 2000–10. Accredited Family Mediator, 2007. Member: Cttee, Family Bar Assoc., 1989–96, 2001–02; General Council of the Bar, 1993–96. Chm., Bar Council Scholarship Trust, 2000–12. Member: British Inst. of Internat. and Comparative Law, 1991–97; Family Mediators' Assoc., 2007–13. Chm., Public Inquiry into Parly Constituencies for Devon, Plymouth, and Torbay, 2003–04. Pres., Nat. Safeguarding Panels, Sport Resolutions (UK), 2012–. Trustee, Wooden Spoon - The Children's Charity of Rugby, 2011–16. Fellow, Inst. of Advanced Legal Studies, 2000. Freeman: City of London, 2002; City of Glasgow, 2012; Master, Fruiterers' Co., 2016–17. *Recreations*: music, opera, ski-ing, sailing, gardening.

**BELLENGER, Dr Dominic Terence Joseph**, FSA; FRHistS; Senior Research Associate, Von Hügel Institute, Cambridge, since 2016; Abbot of Downside, 2006–14; Parish Priest, St Benedict's, Stratton-on-the-Fosse, 1999–2015; *b* 21 July 1950; *s* of Gerald Bellenger and Kathleen Bellenger (*née* O'Donnell). *Educ*: Finchley Grammar Sch.; Jesus Coll., Cambridge (Scholar, MA, PhD); Angelicum Univ., Rome. Res. Student in History, 1972–78 and Lightfoot Schol. in Eccl. Hist., Cambridge, 1975–78; Assistant Master: St Mary's Sch., Cambridge, 1975–78; Downside Sch., 1978–82; Benedictine Monk, Downside Abbey, 1982–2018; Priest, 1988; Housemaster, 1989–91, Head Master, 1991–95, Downside Sch.; Dir of Histl Res., Downside Abbey, 1995–2014; Parish Priest: Little Malvern, 1995–99; St Aldhelm's, Chilcompton, 2002–06; Prior, Downside Abbey, 2001–06; Titular Abbot of St Albans, 2014–18. Member: Cttee, Eccl. Hist. Soc., 1982–85; Cttee, English Benedictine Hist. Commn, 1987–2017; Council, Catholic Record Soc., 1990–99, 2005–11, 2013–; Clifton Diocesan Educn Commn, 1995–2001; Delegate, Benedictine Gen. Chapter, 2001–06. Annalist, English Benedictine Congregation, 2009–18. Trustee: Catholic Family Hist. Soc., 1990–99; Andrew C. Duncan Catholic History Trust, 1993–2018; Friends of Somerset Churches, 1996–2011; Somerset Record Soc., 1998–; Glastonbury Abbey, 2009–15. President: English Catholic Hist. Assoc., 1991–2018; Downside Fisher Club, Bermondsey, 2009–14. Governor: Moor Park Sch., Ludlow, 1991–99; St Antony's, Leweston, Sherborne, 1991–93; St Mary's Sch., Shaftesbury, 1992–96; Moreton Hall, Suffolk, 1995–2001; St Joseph's, Malvern, 1997–99; Downside Sch., 1999–2015 (Chm.); St Gregory's, Bath, 2001–05; Ammerdown Centre, 2006–09. Chaplain, Kts of Malta, 2004–17. Visiting Scholar: Sarum Coll., 2004–14; St Edmund's Coll., Cambridge, 2014–16; Select Preacher, Cambridge Univ., 2014. York Minster Lecture, 2001. Leverhulme Res. Award, 1986. FRSA; FHEA. Editor: South Western Catholic History, 1982–2012; The Downside Review, 2011–18; English correspondent, Rev. d'Hist. de l'Eglise de France, 1982–85. *Publications*: English and Welsh Priests 1558–1800, 1984; The French Exiled Clergy, 1986; (ed) Opening the Scrolls, 1987; (ed jtly) Les Archives du Nord, Calendar of 20 H, 1987; (ed) St Cuthbert, 1987; (ed jtly) Letters of Bede Jarrett, 1989; (ed) Fathers in Faith, 1991; (ed) The Great Return, 1994; (ed) Downside: a pictorial history, 1998; (jtly) Princes of the Church, 2001; (jtly) Medieval Worlds, 2003; (jtly) The Mitre and the Crown, 2005; (jtly) The Medieval Church, 2006; (ed) Downside Abbey: an architectural history, 2011; Time and Place, 2013; St Wulstan's, Little Malvern, 2013; (jtly) St Benedict's Stratton on the Fosse, 2014; (jtly) David Knowles, 2014; Monks with a Mission, 2014; Monastic Identities, 2014; 200 Downside Monks, 2014; Here and There, 2015; Fearless Resting Place, 2015; contributor to many other books; articles in learned jls and periodicals. *Recreations*: books, church architecture, travel, visual arts, writing. *Address*: c/o Downside Abbey, Stratton-on-the-Fosse, Radstock, Bath BA3 4RH.

**BELLEW**; *see* Grattan-Bellew.

**BELLEW**, family name of **Baron Bellew**.

**BELLEW, 8th Baron** *cr* 1848 (Ire.); **Bryan Edward Bellew**; Bt 1688; *b* 19 March 1943; *er s* of 7th Baron Bellew and Mary Elizabeth (*d* 1978), *d* of Rev. Edward Eustace Hill; *S* father, 2010; *m* 1968, Rosemary Sarah, *d* of late Major Reginald Kilner Brasier Hitchcock, MC; one *s* (and one *s* decd). *Educ*: Eton; Royal Military Acad., Sandhurst. Major, Irish Guards, retd. *Heir*: *s* Hon. Anthony Richard Brooke Bellew [*b* 9 Sept. 1972; *m* 2001, Ann Elizabeth, *e d* of Peter Plunkett; three *s* one *d*].

**BELLEW, Patrick John**, RDI 2010; FREng; Principal, Atelier Ten, since 1990; *b* Osmotherly, N Yorks, 12 June 1959; *s* of late James Kevin Bellew and of Judith Ann Bellew (*née* Peckston); *m* 1985, Lois Jane Clay; one *s* two *d*. *Educ*: Stonyhurst Coll.; Univ. of Bath (BSc Hons). Buro Happold, Bath, 1981–87; Dir, Synergy Consulting Engrs, 1988–90 *Major projects include*: Earth Centre, 2000; Baltic Arts Centre, 2002; Fedn Square, Melbourne, 2002; Alpine House, Jodrell Bldg, Shirley Sherwood Gall. and Herbarium Kew Gardens, 2003–10; Savill Bldg, Savill Gardens, 2005; Grand Rapids Art Mus., 2005 Sculpture Sch., Yale, 2006; Kroon Hall, Yale Univ., 2008; Ashmolean Mus., 2009; British Pavilion, Shanghai Expo, 2010; Univ. of the Arts, Kings Cross, 2011; Gardens by the Bay Singapore, 2011–12; Royal Nat. Th. Renovation, 2012–; WWF HQ, 2013; Türkiye Müteahhitler Birliği HQ, Ankara, 2013. Vis. Lectr, Bartlett Sch. of Architecture, 1991–93 Vis. Lectr and Tutor, Sch. of Construction, Reading Univ., 1991–2004; Vis. Lectr 2001–09, Saarinen Vis. Prof., 2010–, Yale Univ. Sch. of Architecture. Gov., Bldg Centre Trust, 1996–2010; Member: Design Rev. Panel, Design Council (formerly CABE) 1999–2003, 2009–; RIBA Awards Panel, 2011–; Trustee, UK Green Bldg Council, 2008–FRSA 1997; FEI 2001; FCIBSE 2001; FREng 2004. Hon. FRIBA 2000. Happold Medal 2008; Silver Medal, CIBSE, 2013. *Publications*: Green:House, Green:Engineering environmental design at Gardens by the Bay (jtly), 2012; (contrib.) Intelligent Building 2013; Invisible Architecture, 2015; articles in Ingenia, Architects Jl, CIBSE Jl, RIBA J

Building Design. *Recreations*: guitar, music, cinema, sailing. *Address*: Atelier Ten, 19 Perseverance Works, 38 Kingsland Road, E2 8DD. *T*: (020) 7749 5950. *E*: patrick.bellew@atelierten.com.

**BELLINGHAM, Sir Henry (Campbell)**, Kt 2016; MP (C) North West Norfolk, 1983–97 and since 2001; *b* 29 March 1955; *s* of late Henry Bellingham; *m* 1993, Emma, *o d* of P. J. H. Whiteley and Lady Angela Whiteley. *Educ*: Eton; Magdalene Coll., Cambridge (BA 1977). Called to the Bar, Middle Temple, 1978; in practice as barrister, 1978–88. Dir of and consultant to companies, 1998–2010. Contested (C) Norfolk North West, 1997. PPS to Sec. of State for Transport, 1990–92, for Defence, 1992–95, for Foreign and Commonwealth Affairs, 1995–97; Opposition spokesman on Trade and Industry, and Shadow Minister for Small Businesses and Employment, 2002–05; Opposition Whip, 2005–06; Shadow Minister for Justice and Legal Services, 2006–10; Parly Under-Sec. of State (Minister for Africa, UN and Overseas Territories), FCO, 2010–12. Member: Select Cttee on the Environment, 1987–90; NI Select Cttee, 2001–02; Trade and Industry Select Cttee, 2003–04; HS2 Select Cttee, 2017. Chm., Cons. Council on Eastern Europe, 1989–94; officer, Cons. back bench cttees, 1983–90. Chm., Westminster Foundn for Democracy, 2013– ; Co-Chm., Global Law Summit, 2014–16. *Address*: c/o House of Commons, SW1A 0AA. *Club*: White's.

**BELLINGHAM, Peter Gordon;** Chief Executive, Sinfonia Cymru, since 2018; *b* 23 Jan. 1956; *s* of Arthur Stanley and Kathleen Bellingham; *m* 1985, Julie Robinson (stage name, Julie Jensen); two *s* one *d*. *Educ*: Royal Northern Coll. of Music. Mgt Trainee, Fulcrum Centre, Slough, 1977–78; Publicity Officer, Torch Th., Milford Haven, 1978–80; PRO, Northern Ballet Th., 1980–81; Festivals Asst, Cheltenham Festivals, 1981–82; Mktg Manager, Northern Ballet Th., 1982–85; Music Officer, 1985–86, Theatres Manager, 1986–87, Bradford CC; Account Dir, sponsorship and events, PRC Communications, 1987–89; Hd, Sales and Mktg, 1989–92, Hd, Planning, 1992–93, Bradford Theatres; freelance arts consultant, 1993–94; Welsh National Opera: Dir of Mktg, 1994–2002; Exec. Dir, 2002–09; Man. Dir, 2009–15; arts consultant, 2015–18. Trustee, Sinfonia Cymru, 2014–18. *Recreation*: tennis (former Chm., Windsor Lawn Tennis Club, Penarth). *Address*: 76 Westbourne Road, Penarth CF64 3HB. *T*: 07971 063213. *E*: peter@sinfoniacymru.co.uk.

**BELLINGHAM, Sir William Alexander Noel Henry**, 9th Bt (2nd creation) *cr* 1796, of Castle Bellingham, co. Louth; *b* 19 Aug. 1991; *s* of Sir Anthony Edward Norman Bellingham, 8th Bt and Denise Marie Bellingham (*née* Moity); *S* father, 2014, but his name does not appear on the Official Roll of the Baronetage.

**BELLIS, Bertram Thomas;** Headmaster, The Leys School, Cambridge, 1975–86; *b* 4 May 1927; *s* of Rev. Thomas J. Bellis and Mary A. Bellis; *m* 1952, Joan Healey; two *s*. *Educ*: Kingswood Sch., Bath; St John's Coll., Cambridge (Exhibr in Maths, MA). Rossall Sch., 1951–55; Highgate Sch., 1955–65; Headmaster, Daniel Stewart's Coll., 1965–72; Principal, Daniel Stewart's and Melville Coll., 1972–75. Founding Dir, Mathematics in Educn and Industry Schools Project, 1963–65. Chm., Scottish Educn Dept Cttee on Computers and the Schools (reports, 1969 and 1972); Member: Council, Inst. of Math., 1975–79; Educational Research Bd, SSRC, 1975–80. Governor: Queenswood Sch., 1980–92; St John's Coll. Sch., 1981–86. Pres., Mathematical Assoc., 1971–72. Schoolmaster Fellow, Balliol Coll., Oxford, 1963; FIMA 1964; FRSE 1972. *Address*: 13 Marlborough Court, Grange Road, Cambridge CB3 9BQ.

**BELLOS, Alexander;** writer and mathematician; *b* Oxford, 22 Nov. 1969; *s* of David Bellos and Ilona Bellos (*née* Roth, now Morison); *m* 2013, Natalie Hunt; two *s*. *Educ*: Hampton Park Comp. Sch., Southampton; Richard Taunton Coll., Southampton; Corpus Christi Coll., Oxford (BA Maths and Philos.); Westminster Press (Dip. Journalism). Reporter, Brighton Evening Argus, 1991–93; The Guardian: reporter, 1994–97; South America corresp., 1998–2003. Maths and puzzles blog, www.theguardian.com, 2012– . Inventor, Loop (pool played on elliptical table), 2015. *Publications*: Futebol: the Brazilian way of life, 2002, rev. edn 2014; (ghostwriter) Pelé: the autobiography, 2006; Alex's Adventures in Numberland, 2010; Alex Through the Looking Glass, 2014; (with Edmund Harriss) Snowflake Seashell Star, 2015; Can You Solve My Problems?, 2016; (with Ben Lyttleton) Football School, 2016; (with Ben Lyttleton) Football School Season 2, 2017; (with Edmund Harriss) Visions of Numberland, 2017; Puzzle Ninja, 2017; (with Ben Lyttleton) Football School: the amazing quiz book, 2018; (with Ben Lyttleton) Football School Season 3, 2018; (with Ben Lyttleton) Football School Star Players, 2019; (with Ben Lyttleton) Football School Season 4, 2019; So You Think You've Got Problems, 2019. *Recreations*: films, music, cycling. *Address*: c/o Rebecca Carter, Janklow & Nesbit, 13a Hillgate Street, W8 7SP. *T*: (020) 7243 2975. *E*: rcarter@janklow.co.uk.

**BELLOS, Linda Ann**, OBE 2007; equality and diversity practitioner, since 2001; Chair, Institute of Equality and Diversity Practitioners, 2009–14; *b* 13 Dec. 1950; *d* of Emmanuel Adebowale and Renee Sackman; *m* 1970, Jonathan Bellos (marr. diss. 1983); one *s* one *d*; civil partnership 2005, Caroline Jones (*d* 2015). *Educ*: Silverthorne Girls' Sec. Mod. Sch.; Dick Shephard Comp. Sch.; Univ. of Sussex (BA Hons 1981). HM Inspector of Taxes, Tax Office, 1972–77; finance worker/journalist, Spare Rib, 1981–83; Community Accountant, Lambeth Inner City Consultancy Gp, 1983–84; Team Leader, Women's Unit, GLC, 1984–86; Mem. (Lab), Lambeth LBC, 1985–88 (Leader, 1986–88); Hd, Women's Unit, 1988–90, Actg Asst Dir, Social Services, 1990–91, Hackney LBC; freelance journalist and consultant, 1992–99; Regl Manager, Focus Consultancy Ltd, 1999–2002; self-employed, 2002–03; Dir, Equality Diversity and Human Rights (formerly Diversity Solutions Consultancy) Ltd, 2003–12. Community activist: Queen's Park Community Assoc., Brighton, 1974–81; Women Against Violence Against Women, 1981–86. Vice-Chm., Black Sections, Labour Party, 1984–87; Treas., African Reparations Movt UK, 1994–97; Chairman: New Initiatives Youth and Community Assoc., 1998–2005; Southwark Anti-Homophobic Forum, 1998–2004; Southwark Action for Voluntary Orgns, 2001–07; Southwark Lesbian, Gay, Bisexual and Transgender network, 2002–06; Bronze Woman Proj., 2002– ; Co-Chm., LGBT Community Adv. Gp, and Mem., Diversity Bd, Metropolitan Police Service, 2000–03. *Publications*: (contrib.) A Vision Back and Forth, 1995; (contrib.) Making Black Waves, 1995; (contrib.) IC3: the Penguin book of new Black writing in Britain, 2000; contrib. papers, essays and articles in books and magazines. *Recreations*: gardening, reading, music. *Address*: 1 Crown Point Drive, Bixley, Norfolk NR14 8RR. *T*: 0345 260 0028. *E*: linda@lindabellos.co.uk.

**BELMAHI, Mohammed;** Founding and Managing Partner, Quattro Group, since 2014; Senior Fellow, Al Alakhawyn University, since 2013; *b* 18 Aug. 1948; *s* of Redouane Belmahi and Aziza Filal Belmahi; *m* 1973, Åse Ask; one *d*. *Educ*: Ecole Nationale d'Architecture, Toulouse (Architect DPLG 1975); New York Univ. (Master of Urban Planning 1975; PhD Prog. in Public Admin 1976; MPhil 1985); Harvard Inst. for Internat. Develt, 1981. London Business Sch. (Sen. Exec. Prog.), 1991. UN Center for Housing, Building and Planning, NY, 1975–76; Min. of Housing and Land Use Planning, and Dir, Land Use Planning, Rabat, 1977–79; Prime Minister's Office, Rabat (Mem., State Owned Enterprise Reform Task Force), 1979–82; Dir of Tourism, Min. of Tourism, 1982–86; Dir Gen., Moroccan Nat. Tourist Bd, 1987–88; Mem., Exec. Cttee, ONA Hldg Gp, Casablanca, 1988–96; Dir Gen. for Real Estate and Tourism, and Dir Gen., Casablanca World Trade Center; Ambassador to India and Nepal, 1996–99; Ambassador to Court of St James's, 1999–2009; Advr to Chm. and CEO, 2009–13, Architect Gen., 2010–13, OCP Gp; Chm., OCP Foundn, 2010–13. Freeman, City of London, 2006. Indira Gandhi Meml Award, 1997; Interfaith Gold Medallion, Three Faiths Forum, 2009. Officer, National Order of Merit (Portugal), 1991; Kt Comdr, Royal Order of Francis I, 2003. *Recreations*: golf, swimming, collecting miniature elephants, drawing portraits. *Address*: Apt 5.03, 3 Columbia Gardens, Lillie Square, SW6 1FU. *E*: mbelmahi@hotmail.com; 1 Rue Beni Mtir, Souissi, 10170 Rabat, Morocco. *Club*: Dar Es Salam Golf (Rabat).

**BELMONT, Abbot of;** see Stonham, Rt Rev. Dom P.

**BELMORE**, 8th Earl of, *cr* 1797; **John Armar Lowry-Corry;** Baron Belmore, 1781; Viscount Belmore, 1789; *b* 4 Sept. 1951; *s* of 7th Earl of Belmore and Gloria Anthea, *d* of late Herbert Bryant Harker, Melbourne, Australia; *S* father, 1960; *m* 1984, Lady Mary Meade, *d* of 6th Earl of Clanwilliam; two *s* one *d*. *Educ*: Lancing; Royal Agricultural Coll., Cirencester. Member: Adv. Bd, PRO, Belfast, 1996–2006; Bd of Govs and Guardians, Nat. Gall. of Ireland, 1998–2003. *Recreation*: fishing. *Heir*: *s* Viscount Corry, *qv*. *Address*: The Garden House, Castle Coole, Enniskillen, N Ireland BT74 6JY. *T*: (028) 6632 2463.

**BELOFF, Hon. Michael Jacob**, MA; QC 1981; barrister and writer; President, Trinity College, University of Oxford, 1996–2006; *b* 18 April 1942; *s* of Baron Beloff, FBA and Helen Dobrin; *m* 1969, Judith Mary Arkinstall; one *s* one *d*. *Educ*: Dragon Sch., Oxford; Eton Coll. (King's Schol.; Captain of Sch. 1960); Magdalen Coll., Oxford (Demy; H. W. C. Davis Prizeman, 1962; BA Hist. (1st cl.) 1963, Law 1965; MA 1967). Pres., Oxford Union Soc., 1962 (Trustee, Oldut, 1996); Oxford Union tour of USA, 1964. Called to the Bar, Gray's Inn, 1967 (Gerald Moody Schol., 1963, Atkin Schol., 1967; Bencher, 1988; Treas., 2008); Jt Head of Chambers, 4–5 Gray's Inn Sq., 1993–2000; a Recorder, 1985–95; a Dep. High Court Judge, 1989–99; a Judge of the Courts of Appeal, Jersey and Guernsey, 1995– , Sen. Ordinary Appeal Judge, 2004–14. Vice-Pres., Interception of Communications (Bailiwick of Guernsey) Tribunal, 1998–2014; a Judge of the First-tier Tribunal (Gen. Regulatory Chamber) (formerly Dep. Chm., Information (formerly Data Protection (Nat. Security)) Tribunal), 2000–13; Chm., Interception of Communications (Bailiwick of Jersey) Tribunal, 2003– ; Pres., Investigatory Powers Tribunal, Guernsey, 2005– . Mem., Singapore Internat. Panel of Mediators, 2009– ; For. Consultant, Law Counsel (Dacca), 1990– . Lectr in Law, Trinity Coll., Oxford, 1965–66. Associate Ed., DNB (Legal), 1996– ; Legal Correspondent: New Society, 1969–79; The Observer, 1979–81; Columnist, San Diego Law Jl, 1999–2001. First Chm., Administrative Law Bar Assoc., 1986–96, now Chm. Emeritus. Member: Bingham Law Reform Cttee on Discovery of Documents and Disclosure, 1982– ; Sen. Salary Review Bd, 1995–2002 (Chm., Judicial Sub-Cttee, 1998–2012); Court of Arbitration for Sport, 1996– (Mem., *ad hoc* Panel, Olympic Games, Atlanta, 1996, Sydney, 2000, Athens, 2004, Beijing, 2008, Rio, 2016, Commonwealth Games, Kuala Lumpur, 1998, Manchester, 2002, Melbourne, 2006); Doping Appeal Panel, Eur. Golf Tour, 2012– ; Ironman Appeal Panel, 2016– ; Ultimate Sports Appeal Panel, 2016– ; Chm., ICC Code of Conduct Commn, 2002– (Chm., Disputes Resolution Cttee, 2015– ); Chairman: Ethics Commn, London 2012; IAAF Ethics Bd, 2014– ; IAAF Disciplinary Tribunal, 2017; Hon. Legal Advr, IAAF World Championships London 2017; Judge, Internat. Court of Appeal, Fédn Internat. de l'Automobile, 2010–17. Chm., Oxford Univ. Tribunal into Alleged Plagiarism, 1990. Gov., Dragon Sch., Oxford, 1995–2003; Mem. Council, Cheltenham Ladies' Coll., 1996–2002. Chm., Jardine Scholarship Foundn, 2000–06. Visiting Professor: Tulane Univ., 2001, 2003; Buckingham Univ., 2006– . Lectures: Statute Law Soc., 1994; Admin. Law Bar Assoc., 1995; John Kelly Meml, UC Dublin, 1997; Lasok, Univ. of Exeter, 1998; Atkin, Reform Club, 1999; K. Ramamani, Madras, 1999; Margaret Howard, Trinity Coll., Oxford, 2000; Bailiff's, Guernsey, 2002; Espeland, Oslo, 2002; Alexander Howard, RCP, 2003; David Hall Meml, Envmtl Law Foundn, Law Soc., 2004; Neill, All Souls Coll., Oxford, 2006; Ben Kingsley, Warwick Sch., 2008; Barnard's Inn, Reading, 2009; Alexander, CIArb, 2009; Birkenhead, Gray's Inn, 2010; Sir David Williams, Cambridge, 2010; Lady Hale, Salford, 2012; Edward Grayson Meml, 2012; MacDermott, QUB, 2014. High Sheriff, Oxford, 2018. Consultant Ed., Judicial Review Bulletin, 1996–2016; Gen. Ed., Internat. Sports Law Review, 2000– ; an Associate Ed., Oxford DNB. Hon. Mem., Internat. Athletes' Club. FRSA 1996. Hon. Fellow, Soc. for Advanced Legal Studies, 1997. FICPD 1998. FAcSS (AcSS 2003). Hon. DLitt Fairleigh Dickinson, 2003; Hon. DLaws: De Montfort, 2010; Buckingham, 2017; Open, 2018. Women's Legal Defence Award (first winner), 1991; Lifetime Achievement Award, Chambers Directory, 2010. *Publications*: A Short Walk on the Campus (ed with J. Aitken), 1966; The Plateglass Universities, 1968; The Sex Discrimination Act, 1976; (jtly) Sports Law, 1999, 2nd edn 2012; contributor to: Halsbury's Laws of England (contribution on Time), 1983, 2nd edn 1999, (contribution on Sports Law) 5th edn 2012; Judicial Safeguards in Administrative Proceedings, 1989; Judicial Review, 1991, 3rd edn 2006; Practitioner's Handbook of EC Law, 1998; Israel Among the Nations, 1998; The Human Rights Act, 1999; The University: international expectations, 2002; Blair's Britain, 1997–2007, 2007; The House of Lords, 2009; Festschriften for: Lord Cooke of Thorndon, 1997; Sir William Wade, 1998; Sir Louis Blom-Cooper, 1999; Sir David Williams, 2000; Lord Slynn of Hadley, 2000; Rolf Ryssdal, 2001; H. M. Seervai, 2002; contrib. Encounter, Minerva, Irish Jurist, Political Qly, Current Legal Problems, Public Law, Statute Law Review, Modern Law Review, British Jl of Sport and Law, Denning Law Jl, Singapore Law Jl, NZ Law Jl, TLS, Spectator, DNB, The Oldie, etc. *Recreation*: running very slowly. *Address*: Blackstone Chambers, Blackstone House, Temple, EC4Y 9BW. *T*: (020) 7583 1770. *E*: michaelbeloff@blackstonechambers.com. *Clubs*: Reform, Royal Automobile (Steward, 1999–2018; Vice-Pres., 2018– ); Vincent's, Gridiron (Oxford); Achilles (Vice Pres., 2013– ).

**BELPER**, 5th Baron *cr* 1856, of Belper, co. Derby; **Richard Henry Strutt;** *b* 24 Oct. 1941; *o s* of 4th Baron Belper and Zara Sophie Kathleen Mary, *y d* of Sir Harry Malinwaring, 5th Bt; *S* father, 1999; *m* 1st, 1966, Jennifer Vivian (marr. diss. 1979), *d* of late Capt. Peter Winser; one *s* one *d*; 2nd, 1980, Judith Mary de Jonge (*née* Twynam). *Educ*: Harrow; RAC Cirencester. *Heir*: *s* Hon. Michael Henry Strutt [*b* 5 Jan. 1969; *m* 2004, Vanessa Hoare; three *d*]. *Address*: The Park, Kingston on Soar, Nottingham NG11 0DH.

**BELSKY, Prof. Jay**, PhD; Robert M. and Natalie Reid Dorn Professor of Human and Community Development, University of California, Davis, since 2011; *s* of Irving and Sylvia Belsky; two *s*. *Educ*: Vassar Coll. (BA Psychology 1974); Cornell Univ. (MS Child Develt 1976; PhD Human Develt and Family Studies 1978). Res. Associate, Prenatal/Early Infancy Proj., Elmira, NY, 1977–78; Asst Prof., 1978–83, Associate Prof., 1983–86, Prof., 1986–96, Distinguished Prof., 1996–2001, of Human Develt, Dept of Human Develt and Family Studies, Penn State Univ.; Prof. of Psychology and Dir, Inst. for Study of Children, Families and Social Issues, Birkbeck, Univ. of London, 1999–2010. *Publications*: (ed) In the Beginning: readings on infancy, 1982; (jtly) The Child in the Family, 1984; (ed jtly) Clinical Implications of Attachment, 1988; (with J. Kelly) The Transition to Parenthood, 1994; (jtly) Childhood, 1995; (ed jtly) Evaluating Sure Start: does area-based early intervention work?, 2007. *Recreations*: swimming, travelling. *Address*: University of California, Davis, One Shields Avenue, Hart Hall, Davis, CA 95616, USA.

**BELTON, Adrian;** Chairman, Stockport NHS Foundation Trust, since 2017; *b* Cheltenham, 29 June 1956; *s* of Michael and Vera Belton; *m* 2009, Helen Mary Phillips, *qv*; one step *s* one step *d*; one *s* two *d* by a previous marriage. *Educ*: King Edward VII Sch., Sheffield; Univ. of Durham (BSc Hons 1977). ACIB 1979; DipFS 1981. Joined Barclays plc Gp, 1977, Dir, Operational Risk, 1998–2000; Risk Dir, Bradford & Bingley plc, 2000–03; Corporate Dir, Nottingham CC, 2004–05; Exec. Dir, Natural England, 2006–08; Chief Exec., Central Sci. Lab., 2008–09; Chief Executive: Food and Envmt Res. Agency, 2009–14; CITB, 2014–16. Chm., Inst. of Envmtl Mgt and Assessment, 2009–13 (Vice Chm., 2007–09); Chm., DSTL, 2019–. Member: Council, Yorkshire Innovation, 2008–11; Bd, Assoc. of Chief Execs, 2009–16. Mem. Council, Sheffield Univ., 2014–. *Recreations*: cycling, mountaineering, ski-ing, sailing, fell running, music (playing piano). *Address*: Stockport NHS Foundation Trust, Stepping Hill Hospital, Stockport SK2 7JE. *T*: 07531 658011. *E*: adrian.belton@stockport.nhs.uk.

**BELTON, Prof. Peter Stanley,** PhD; Professor of Biomaterials Science, 2001–08, now Emeritus, and Associate Dean, Faculty of Science, 2006–07, University of East Anglia (Head of Chemistry, School of Chemical Sciences and Pharmacy, 2004–06); *b* 19 June 1947; *s* of Stanley Belton and Bertha (*née* Lawrence); *m* 1976, Teresa Stutz; three *s*. *Educ*: Cooper's Sch., Bow; Chelsea Coll., Univ. of London (BSc 1st Cl. Hons Chem. 1968; PhD 1972). University of East Anglia: Open Univ. Fellowship, 1971–72; ICI Fellowship, 1972–74; Res. Leader, Unilever Res., Port Sunlight, 1974–79; AFRC, later BBSRC, Institute of Food Research Norwich Laboratory: Hd, Molecular Spectroscopy Gp, 1979–87; Hd, Chem. Physics Dept, 1987–90; Hd, Food Structure & Biopolymer Technol. Dept, 1990–91; Hd, Food Colloid & Biopolymer Sci. Dept, 1991–92; Hd, Norwich Lab., 1992–99; Dep. Dir, Inst. of Food Res., AFRC, later BBSRC, 1994–99; Hd, Food Materials Div., Inst. of Food Res., BBSRC, 1999–2001. Visiting Professor: Univ. of São Paulo, 1976; Centre d'Etudes Nucléaire, 1989. FIFST 1994 (Vice-Pres., 2001–02; Pres., 2003–05). Series Editor, Monographs in Food Analysis, 1994–2005. *Publications*: (jtly) From Arms Race to World Peace, 1991; Food, Science and Society, 2002; Poems: people, places and things, 2017; contrib. books and jls. *Recreations*: coarse fishing, listening to music, making wine. *Address*: School of Chemistry, University of East Anglia, Norwich NR4 7TJ; 45 Jessopp Road, Norwich, Norfolk NR2 3JF. *T*: (01603) 465851.

**BELTRAMI, Adrian Joseph;** QC 2008; a Deputy High Court Judge, since 2018; *b* Glasgow, 8 Nov. 1964; *s* of late Joseph Beltrami and of Brigid Dolores Beltrami (*née* Fallon); *m* 1991, Charlotte Bentley; one *s* two *d*. *Educ*: Stonyhurst; Downing Coll., Cambridge (BA 1987); Harvard Law Sch. (LLM). Called to the Bar, Lincoln's Inn, 1989; in practice at the Bar, specialising in commercial litigation, banking and financial services, insolvency, professional negligence and civil fraud. *Publications*: (principal contributor) Banking Litigation, 1999, 2nd edn 2005. *Recreations*: family, tennis, Dickens, wine, Wiltshire. *Address*: 3 Verulam Buildings, Gray's Inn, WC1R 5NT. *E*: abeltrami@3vb.com. *Club*: Riverside Racquets.

**BEN-TOVIM, Atarah, (Mrs Douglas Boyd),** MBE 1980 (for services to children's music); flute course director, adjudicator and concert presenter; *b* 1 Oct. 1940; *d* of Tsvi Ben-Tovim and Gladys Ben-Tovim; *m*; one *d*; *m* 1976, Douglas Boyd. *Educ*: Royal Acad. of Music, London. ARAM 1967. Principal Flautist, Royal Liverpool Philharmonic Orchestra, 1962–75; children's concerts with Atarah's Band, 1973–88; various TV and radio series incl. Atarah's Music Box, Radio 3, 1976–79; Founder and Artistic Dir, Children's Concert Centre, 1975–95; Creator and Presenter, Children's Classic Orchestral Concerts, 1994–2010; Artistic Dir, Children's Music Foundn, 1995–2005. SW France Rep., Associate Bd of Royal Schs of Music, 1996–. Chm., British Flute Soc., 2005–10. Hon. DMus CNAA, 1991. *Publications*: Atarah's Book (autobiog.), 1976, 2nd edn 1979; Atarah's Band Kits (14 published), 1978–; Children and Music, 1979; (jtly) The Right Instrument For Your Child, 1985, 5th edn 2012; You Can Make Music!, 1986; The Young Orchestral Flautist, Books 1–3, 1990; Queen Eleanor's Legacy, 1994; The Flute Book, 1997. *Recreations*: music, writing, building houses, collecting 1200 flute figures. *Address*: 2 Le Bos, Juillac, 33890 Gensac, France. *T*: 557474428.

**BENDALL, Dr Eve Rosemarie Duffield;** Chief Executive Officer, English National Board for Nursing, Midwifery and Health Visiting, 1981–86; *b* 7 Aug. 1927; *d* of Col F. W. D. Bendall, CMG, MA, and Mrs M. L. Bendall, LRAM, ARCM. *Educ*: Malvern Girls' Coll.; London Univ. (MA, PhD); Royal Free Hosp. (SRN). Ward Sister, Dorset County Hosp., 1953–55; Night Supt, Manchester Babies' Hosp., 1955–56; Nurse Tutor: United Sheffield Hosps Sch. of Nursing, 1958–61; St George's Hosp., London, 1961–63; Principal, Sch. of Nursing, Hosp. for Sick Children, Gt Ormond Street, 1963–69. Registrar, GNC, 1973–77. *Publications*: (jtly) Basic Nursing, 1963, 3rd edn 1970; (jtly) A Guide to Medical and Surgical Nursing, 1965, 2nd edn 1970; (jtly) A History of the General Nursing Council, 1969; So You Passed, Nurse (research), 1975. *Recreation*: auspicious ageing. *E*: evebndll34@gmail.com.

**BENDALL, Vivian Walter Hough;** chartered surveyor and valuer in private practice, 1956–2014; *b* 14 Dec. 1938; *s* of late Cecil Aubrey Bendall and Olive Alvina Bendall (*née* Hough); *m* 1969, Ann Rosalind Jarvis (marr. diss. 1992). *Educ*: Coombe Hill House, Croydon; Broad Green Coll., Croydon. IRRV; FNAEA 1984. Mem. Croydon Council, 1964–78; Mem. GLC, 1970–73; Chm., Greater London Young Conservatives, 1967–68. Contested (C): Hertford and Stevenage, Feb. and Oct. 1974; Ilford North, 1997 and 2001. MP (C) Ilford North, March 1978–1997. Backbench Committees: Vice-Chm., Transport Cttee, 1982–83; Sec., Foreign and Commonwealth Affairs Cttee, 1981–84; Vice-Chm., Employment Cttee, 1984–87 (Jt Sec. 1981–84). Vice Chm., Kensington and Chelsea Cons. Assoc., 2011– (Chm., 2009–11). Former Member: Central Council for Care of the Elderly; South Eastern Area Reg. Assoc. for the Blind; Dr Barnardo's New Mossford Home Fund Raising Cttee. Master, Glass Sellers' Co., 2011–12. AMRSH 1991. Hon. FASI. *Recreations*: cricket, motor sport. *Address*: 57 Basuto Road, SW6 4BL. *T*: (020) 7736 4315. *Club*: Carlton.

**BENDER, Sir Brian (Geoffrey),** KCB 2003 (CB 1998); PhD; Chairman, Water UK, since 2015; *b* 25 Feb. 1949; *s* of late Prof. Arnold Eric Bender; *m* 1974, Penelope Clark; one *s* one *d*. *Educ*: Greenford Grammar Sch.; Imperial Coll., London Univ. (BSc, PhD; FIC 2006). Joined DTI, 1973; Private Sec. to Sec. of State for Trade, 1976–77; First Sec. (Trade Policy), Office of UK Permanent Rep. to EC, 1977–82; Principal (responsible for internat. steel issues), DTI, 1982–84; Counsellor (Industry), Office of UK Permanent Rep. to EC, 1985–89; Under Sec. and Dep. Head of European Secretariat, Cabinet Office, 1990–93; Hd of Regl Develt Div., DTI, 1993–94; Dep. Sec. and Head of European Secretariat, Cabinet Office, 1994–98; Head of Public Service Delivery, Cabinet Office, 1998–99; Permanent Secretary: Cabinet Office, 1999–2000; MAFF, 2000–01; DEFRA, 2001–05; DTI, later BERR, 2005–09. Chm., London Metal Exchange, 2010–19. Non-executive Director: Financial Reporting Council, 2014–; Pool Reinsurance, 2014–. Trustee, Lloyds Register Foundn, 2013–. Gov., Dulwich Coll., 2009–19.

**BENDERSKY, Pamela May H.;** *see* Hudson-Bendersky.

**BENDIGO, Bishop of,** since 2018; **Rt Rev. Dr Matthew Peter Brain;** *b* Sydney, 1975; *s* of Rt Rev. Dr Peter Robert Brain, *qv*; *m* 1997, Rachael Narelle; five *c*. *Educ*: Kingsway Christian Coll.; Curtin Univ. of Technol. (BSc Physiotherapy 1996); Trinity Theol Coll. (BTh Hons 2001); Univ. of Notre Dame, Australia (PThD 2009). Physiotherapist and Project Officer, Cerebral Palsy Assoc. of WA, 1997–99; ordained deacon, 2003, priest, 2004; Asst Minister, Parish of Wanneroo, Perth, 2002–03; Diocesan Youth Minister, Dio. of NW Aust., 2003–04; Minister-in-charge, Parish of Kalbarri, 2005–09; Chaplain, Kalbarri District High Sch., 2007–09; Diocese of Canberra and Goulburn: Dir, Synergy Youth and Children, 2010–13; Dir, Parish Support, Chaplaincy and Mission, 2013–15; Acting Registrar and Gen. Manager, 2014, 2016; Asst Bishop and Dir, Ministry Trng and Develt, 2015–17. Mem., Faculty, St Mark's Nat. Theol Centre, 2010–17 (writer, 'Me Too!' St Mark's Children's Ministry Trng Package, 2011). *Publications*: The Bible Overview, 2001, 2nd edn, 2007; The First Story, 2005; 'Engage!' How the Church can reconnect with young people, 2011; Wise: transforming pastoral ministry, 2019; chapters and articles in texts and learned jls. *Recreations*: reading, guitar, running, cycling. *Address*: PO Box 2, Bendigo, Vic 3552, Australia. *T*: (3) 54434711. *E*: bishop@bendigoanglican.org.au.

**BENEDETTI, Nicola Joy,** CBE 2019 (MBE 2013); violinist; *b* Irvine, Scotland, 20 July 1987; *d* of Gio and Francesca Benedetti. *Educ*: Wellington Sch., Ayr; Yehudi Menuhin Sch. Winner, BBC Young Musician of Year, 2004; has appeared with LSO, San Francisco SO, Pittsburgh SO, Danish Nat. SO, BBC Scottish SO and Scottish Chamber Orch., Orch. Nat. d'Ile de France, Camerata Salzburg, Spanish Nat. Orch., Frankfurt Radio SO, Netherlands Radio Philharmonic Orch., Washington Nat. SO, Leipzig Gewandhaus Orch., Melbourne SO, and BBC SO; has made recordings; chamber musician, in collaboration with cellist, Leonard Elschenbroich and pianist, Alexei Grynyuk, 2008–, incl. tours of Scotland and S America and concerts at LSO, St Luke's, Frankfurt Alte Oper, Bremen, Hong Kong City Hall and at Ravinia Fest., Schloss Elmau Fest., Istanbul Fest., Gstaad Menuhin Fest., Edinburgh Fest., Cheltenham Fest., and BBC Proms. Founder, Benedetti Sessions, 2013. Mem. Bd and teacher, Big Noise project, Scotland, 2010–. Hon. FRSE 2017. Hon. DLitt: Glasgow Caledonian, 2007; Heriot-Watt, 2010; Hon. LLD Dundee; Hon. DMus: Edinburgh, 2011; Royal Conservatoire of Scotland, 2013; Leicester, 2013. FRCM 2014. Young British Classical Performer, 2008, Best Female Artist, 2012, Female Artist of Year, 2013, Classic Brit Awards; Queen's Medal for Music, 2017. *Recreations*: cinema, travel, jazz, yoga. *Address*: c/o Askonas Holt Ltd, 15 Fetter Lane, EC4A 1BW.

**BENEDETTI, Renato Giovanni,** RIBA; architect; Director, Benedetti Architects Ltd, since 2016; *b* 30 Nov. 1962; *s* of Giovanni Benedetti and Giulia (*née* Fugaccia); *m* 2006, Romy Derman. *Educ*: Cobourg Dist Collegiate Inst. East (Ontario Schol. 1981); Univ. of Waterloo Sch. of Architecture, Ontario (BES 1985; BArch 1988). RIBA 1996. Stonemason and bricklayer, 1976–81; Associate, David Chipperfield Architects, 1989–96; with Jonathan McDowell formed McDowell+Benedetti, 1996, Partner, 1996–2016; Dir, McDowell+Benedetti Ltd, 1998–2016; main projects include: Oliver's Wharf Penthouse, Wapping, 1996; Assoc. of Photographers, New Gall. and HQ, London, 1998; Suncourt House, Islington, 2002; Nursing Home for Merchant Taylors' Co., Lewisham, 2002; Springboard Centre, Stokesley, 2005; Castleford Bridge, 2008; JBC Uttoxeter Masterplan, 2008; Scale Lane Bridge, Hull, 2013; Claremont Fan Court Sch. Masterplan, Esher, 2013; BAFTA HQ, 2014; Eleventh Ch of Christ Scientist, London, 2016. Built Envmt Expert, Design Council CABE, 2012–. Dir, The Dance Movement, 1999–2007. Mem. Panel, Art for Architecture Award, RSA, 1999–2004; Client Design Advr and Competitions Judge, 2000–, Competitions Architect Advr, RIBA. Mem. Cttee, Architecture Club, 1997–; Founding Mem. Cttee, London Festival of Architecture, 2003–12; Member: Southwark Design Review Panel, 2006–; Wandsworth Design Rev. Panel, 2011–; Lewisham Design Rev. Panel, 2013–. *Recreations*: travel, arts, sport. *Address*: (office) 34–35 Hatton Garden, EC1N 8DX. *Clubs*: Architecture, Soho House.

**BENEDICT XVI, His Holiness, (Joseph Alois Ratzinger);** His Holiness Pope Benedict XVI, 2005–13, now Pope Emeritus; *b* Markt am Inn, Germany, 16 April 1927; *s* of Joseph Ratzinger and Maria Ratzinger (*née* Peintner). *Educ*: St Michael Seminary, Traunstein; Ludwig-Maximilian Univ., Munich. Military service, 1943–45. Ordained priest, 1951. Professor: Freising Coll., 1958; Univ. of Bonn, 1959; Univ. of Münster, 1963; Univ. of Tübingen, 1966; Univ. of Regensburg, 1969; Archbishop of Munich and Freising, 1977–82; Prefect, Congregation for the Doctrine of the Faith, 1981–2005. Cardinal Priest, 1977, Cardinal Bishop of Velletri-Segni, 1993; Vice-Dean, 1998–2002, Dean, 2002–05, Sacred Coll. of Cardinals; elected Pope, 19 April 2005. *Publications*: God of Jesus Christ, 1978; The Ratzinger Report, 1985; Feast of Faith, 1986; Principles of Christian Morality, 1986; Principles of Catholic Theology, 1987; 'In the Beginning'…: a Catholic understanding of the story of the creation and the fall, 1990; To Look on Christ, 1991; The Meaning of Christian Brotherhood, 1993; A Turning Point for Europe?, 1994; The Nature and Mission of Theology, 1995; Called to Communion, 1996; Gospel, Catechesis, Catechism, 1997; Ad Tuendam Fidem - to Protect the Faith, 1998; Milestones: memoirs 1927–1977, 1998; Many Religions, One Covenant, 1999; The Spirit of the Liturgy, 2000; God is Near Us, 2003; Truth and Tolerance, 2004; The End of Time?, 2005; Pilgrim Fellowship of Faith, 2005; Values in a Time of Upheaval, 2006; Jesus of Nazareth, vol. 1, 2007, vol. 2, 2011, vol. 3, 2012; Great Christian Thinkers: from the Early Church through the Middle Ages, 2011; Last Testament: in his own words, 2016. *Address*: c/o Apostolic Palace, 00120 Vatican City State.

**BENEDICTUS, David Henry;** critic, book writer, director for stage, television and radio, teacher and stamp dealer; *b* 16 Sept. 1938; *s* of late Henry Jules Benedictus and Kathleen Constance (*née* Ricardo); *m* 1971, Yvonne Daphne Antrobus (marr. diss. 2002); one *s* one *d*; and one *s* one *d*. *Educ*: Stone House, Broadstairs; Eton College; Balliol College, Oxford (BA English); State Univ. of Iowa. News and current affairs, BBC Radio, 1961; Drama Director, BBC TV, 1962; Story Editor, Wednesday Play and various series, BBC, 1965; Thames TV Trainee Director, at Bristol Old Vic, 1968; Asst Dir, RSC, Aldwych, 1970; Judith E. Wilson Vis. Fellow, Cambridge, and Fellow Commoner, Churchill Coll., Cambridge, 1981–82; Commissioning Editor, Drama Series, Channel 4 TV, 1984–86 (commissions included: The Manageress, 1987; Porterhouse Blue (Internat. Emmy), 1987); BBC Radio: Readings Editor, 1989–95; Editor, Radio 3 Drama, 1992; Sen. Producer, Serial Readings, 1993 (incl. The Bible, 1992; Arcadia, 1993; Macbeth, 1995); also producer of radio series on Cole Porter, Rodgers and Hart, Glenn Miller, film music, etc. Writer in Residence: Sutton Library, Surrey, 1975; Kibbutz Gezer, Israel, 1978; Bitterne Library, Southampton, 1983–84; Snowsfields Sch., Bermondsey, 2001–02; Head of Drama, Putney High Sch., 2003–04; teaching incl. Creative Writing residentially at Oxford for Oxbridge Academics, 2003–; Royal Lit. Fund Fellow, Goldsmiths Coll., 2007; supply teacher variously. Antiques corresp., Standard, 1977–80; reviewer for books, stage, films, records, for major newspapers and magazines, principally The Economist. Dir, Kingston Books, 1988–90. Member: Amnesty International; Soc. of Authors. Plays include: Betjemania, 1976, 1996; The Golden Key, 1982; What A Way To Run A Revolution!, 1985; You Say Potato, 1992; The Happy Hypocrite (music by S. Hodel); performer, Name Dropping, Old Court Room, Brighton, 2016. *Publications*: The Fourth of June, 1962; You're a Big Boy Now, 1963; This Animal is Mischievous, 1965; Hump, or Bone by Bone Alive, 1967; The Guru and the Golf Club, 1969; A World of Windows, 1971; The Rabbi's Wife, 1976; Junk,

how and where to buy beautiful things at next to nothing prices, 1976; A Twentieth Century Man, 1978; The Antique Collector's Guide, 1980; Lloyd George (from Elaine Morgan's screenplay), 1981; Whose Life is it Anyway? (from Brian Clarke's screenplay), 1981; Who Killed the Prince Consort?, 1982; Local Hero (from Bill Forsyth's screenplay), 1983; The Essential London Guide, 1984; Floating Down to Camelot, 1985; The Streets of London, 1986; The Absolutely Essential London Guide, 1986; Uncle Ernie's System, 1988–2009; Little Sir Nicholas, 1990; (with Prof. Hans Kalmus) Odyssey of a Scientist, 1991; Sunny Intervals and Showers, 1992; The Stamp Collector, 1994; How to Cope When the Money Runs Out, 1998; Dropping Names (memoirs), 2005; Return to the Hundred Acre Wood, 2009; numerous short stories for Radio 4 etc. *Recreations:* chess, tennis, cricket, auctions, table tennis, piano playing, horse racing, car boot sales, eating. *Address:* Flat 1, 39 Sackville Gardens, Hove, E Sussex BN3 4GJ. *T:* (01273) 242477, 07986 041386. *E:* davidbenedictus@hotmail.com.
*See also* J. T. D. Maugham.

**BENEDIKTSSON, Einar,** MA; Knight Commander, Order of the Falcon, Iceland; Ambassador of Iceland, retired 2001; *b* Reykjavík, 30 April 1931; *s* of Stefan M. Benediktsson and Sigridur Oddsdóttir; *m* 1956, Elsa Petursdóttir; three *s* two *d. Educ:* Colgate Univ., NY; Fletcher Sch. of Law and Diplomacy, Mass; London Sch. of Econs and Pol Science; Inst. des Etudes Européennes, Turin. With OEEC, 1956–60; Head of Section, Mins of Econ. Affairs and Commerce, 1961–64, and Min. of For. Affairs, 1964; Counsellor, Paris, 1964–68; Head of Section, Min. of For. Affairs, 1968–70; Perm. Rep. to Internat. Orgns, Geneva, 1970–76; Chm., EFTA Council, 1975; Ambassador to France, also accredited to Spain and Portugal, and Perm. Rep. to OECD and UNESCO, 1976–82; Ambassador to UK and concurrently to The Netherlands, Nigeria and Ireland, 1982–86; Perm. Rep. to N Atlantic Council, 1986–90, and Ambassador to Belgium and Luxembourg, 1986–91; Ambassador to Norway, also to Poland and Czechoslovakia, 1991–93; Ambassador to USA, also accredited to Canada, Mexico, Chile, Argentina, Uruguay, Venezuela and Costa Rica, 1993–97; Exec. Dir, Leifur Eiriksson Millennium Commn of Iceland, 1997–2001; Advr, Office of the Prime Minister and Min. of Foreign Affairs, Reykjavík, 2001–02, Min. of Foreign Affairs, 2009–. Chm., UNICEF Iceland, 2003–08. Holds foreign decorations. *Publications:* Iceland and European Development—A Historical Account from a Personal Perspective, 2003; Ad skilja heiminn: æviminningar sendiherra (memoir), 2009. *Address:* Hvassaleiti 28, 103 Reykjavík, Iceland. *T:* 5681943. *E:* mason@islandia.is.

**BENETTON, Luciano;** industrialist; Executive Chairman and President, Benetton Group SpA, 1978–2012 and since 2018; *b* 13 May 1935. Established Fratelli Benetton (with brothers), 1965; founder and Pres., Benetton, 1978; Benetton Holdings, 1981; Vice-Pres. and Man. Dir, Benetton Group SpA; Mem. Board, Edizione Holding SpA; Pres., Benetton Foundn. Mem., Italian Senate, 1992–94. Awards: Civiltà Veneta, 1986; Premio Creatività, 1992. *Publications:* contribs to La Biblioteca di Harvard, economic and business strategies, 1988. *Address:* Benetton Group SpA, via Villa Minelli 1, 31050 Ponzano Veneto (TV), Italy. *T:* (422) 4491.

**BENFORD, Rt Rev. Steven Charles;** *see* Dunedin, Bishop of.

**BENGER, John Stuart,** DPhil; Clerk of the House of Commons, and Head of the House of Commons Service, since 2019; *b* Stockport, 18 Nov. 1959; *s* of late Kurt Benger and Marian Benger (*née* Hollis); *m* 1986, Susan Elizabeth Irvine; two *s. Educ:* Stockport Grammar Sch.; St Catharine's Coll., Cambridge (BA Hons 1982); Worcester Coll., Oxford (PGCE 1983; DPhil 1989). House of Commons: procedural and cttee posts, 1986–90; Clerk: Cttee of Public Accounts, 1990–94; Table Office, 1994–98; Health Cttee, 1998–2004; Public Bill Office, 2004–08; Treasury Cttee, 2008–09; Principal Clerk: Delegated Legislation, 2009–11; Select Cttees, 2011–12; Dir, Service Delivery, Dept of Information Services, 2012–15; Clerk Asst and Man. Dir, Chamber and Cttees Team (formerly Dir Gen., Dept of Chamber and Cttee Services), 2015–19. *Recreations:* art galleries, Manchester United, coffee, family and friends. *Address:* House of Commons, SW1A 0AA. *T:* (020) 7219 3311. *E:* bengerjs@parliament.uk.

**BENHAM, George Frederick;** Headmaster, Cardinal Hinsley RC High School, 1999–2003; *b* 26 Oct. 1946; *m* 1996, Elizabeth Maria; two *s. Educ:* Queen Mary Coll., London (BA 1969; MPhil 1972); Inst. of Educn, London Univ. (DipEd 1978; MA 1980). Lectr, Univ. of Aberdeen, 1971–75; teacher at various schs in London, 1975–85; Educn Advr, 1985–87; London Borough of Brent: Dep. Dir of Educn, 1987–89, Dir, 1989–95; Chief Exec., 1995–98. FRSA 1978; FCMI (FBIM 1978). *Publications:* contribs on education to learned jls in USA, Holland, UK and Switzerland.

**BENÍTEZ MAUDES, Rafael;** Manager, Dalian Yifang Football Club, China, since 2019; *b* Madrid, 16 April 1960; *s* of Francisco Benítez and Rosario Maudes; *m* 1998, Montserrat Seara; two *d. Educ:* Nat. Inst. of Physical Educn, Madrid (Licenciate Physical Educn 1982; Soccer Master 1982). Soccer player: joined Real Madrid juniors teams aged 13; AD Parla, 1981–85; Linares CF, 1985–86; soccer coach: Real Madrid B Jun., 1986–90; Real Madrid A Jun., 1990–91; Real Madrid U-19, 1990–93; Real Madrid B, 1991–92, 1993–95; (a second coach) Real Madrid, 1993–94; Real Valladolid, SAD, 1995–96; Club Atlético Osasuna, 1996–97; CF Extremadura, 1997–99; Tenerife CF, 1999–2000; Valencia CF SAD, 2000–04 (UEFA Cup, 2004); manager: Liverpool FC, 2004–10 (UEFA Champions League, Eur. Super Cup, 2005; FA Cup, 2006); Inter Milan, 2010–11 (Italian Super Cup, FIFA Club World Cup, 2010); (interim) Chelsea FC, 2012–13 (UEFA Europa League, 2013); head coach, SSC Napoli, 2013–15 (Italian Cup, Italian Super Cup, 2014); coach, Real Madrid, 2015–16; manager, Newcastle Utd FC, 2016–19. Hon. Life Mem., Newcastle Utd Supporters Trust, 2019. Hon. Dr Miguel Hernández, Elche, 2008. UEFA Manager of the Year (jtly), 2003–04, 2004–05; Agustín de Betancourt Medal, Polytechnic Univ., Madrid, 2010; Gold Medal of Hon. Patronage, Univ. Philosophical Soc., TCD, 2012. Silver Medal, Royal Order of Sporting Merit (Spain), 2011. *Publications:* Champions League Dreams, 2012. *Recreations:* playing chess, mus (Spanish card game) and Stratego.

**BENJAMIN,** Baroness *cr* 2010 (Life Peer), of Beckenham in the County of Kent; **Floella Karen Yunies Benjamin,** OBE 2001; DL; actress, independent producer, writer and children's campaigner; Founder, 1987, Chief Executive, since 1998, Floella Benjamin Productions Ltd; *b* 23 Sept. 1949; *d* of Roy Benjamin and Veronica Benjamin (*née* Dryce); *m* 1980, Keith Taylor; one *s* one *d. Educ:* Penge Girls' Sch. Chief Accountants Office, Barclays Bank, 1967–69; Actress: *stage:* Hair, Shaftesbury Th., 1970–72; Jesus Christ Superstar, Palace, 1972–74; Black Mikado, Cambridge Th., 1974–75; The Husband-in-Law, Comedy, 1976; *television* includes: Within These Walls, 1974–75; Playschool, 1976–88; Playaway, 1976–82; Angels, 1978–80; Send in the Girls, Waterloo Sunset, 1980; Maybury, 1981; Kids, 1982; Fast Forward, 1983–85; Lay-on-Five, 1986–87; Line of Beauty, 2006; Mama Mirabelle's Home Movies, 2007; Sarah Jane Adventures, 2007–11; Chuggington, 2010–13; CBeebies Bedtime Stories, 2013–; also produced and starred in: Treehouse, 1987; Playabout, 1990–92; Hullabaloo, 1994; Caribbean Light, 1998; Jamboree, 1998–2001; Caribbean Kitchen, 1999; Taste of Barbados, 2000; Taste of Cuba, 2001; Coming to England, 2003 (RTS Award 2004); *films:* Black Joy, 1977; Run Fatboy Run, 2007. Member: Royal Mail Stamp Adv. Cttee, 1994–2001; Video Consultative Council, 1996–2000, Children's Viewing Adv. Gp, 2000–04, BBFC; Foreign and Commonwealth Caribbean Adv. Gp, 1998–2002; Millennium Commn, 1999–2007; Chairman: Women of Year Lunch, 1996–2000; Pegasus Opera Co., 2007–08; Windrush Commemoration Cttee, 2018–. Member: BAFTA, 1990–2001 (Vice-Chm., 1998–99; Chm., TV, 1999–2000); Content Bd, Ofcom, 2003–06. Chancellor, Univ. of Exeter, 2006–16. Governor: Nat. Film and Television Sch., 1995–2014; Commonwealth Inst., 1998–2006; Dulwich Coll., 2001–11; Chm. Govs, Isle of Sheppey Acad., 2009–11. President: The Ramblers (formerly Ramblers' Assoc.), 2008–10; Soc. of Women Writers and Journalists, 2017–; Patron: Transplant Links, 2015–; Windrush Soc., 2018–. DL Gtr London, 2008. Freeman, City of London, 2018. Hon. Fellow: Shakespeare Birthplace Trust, 2013–; British Kinematograph Sound and Television Soc., 2014–. Hon. DLitt Exeter, 2005. Special Lifetime Achievement Award, BAFTA, 2004; J. M. Barrie Award, Action for Children's Arts, 2012. *Publications:* Caribbean Cookery, 1986; *for children:* Floella's Fun Book, 1984; Why the Agouti Has No Tail, 1984; Floella's Funniest Jokes, 1985; Floella's Favourite Folk Tales, 1986; Fall About with Flo, 1986; Floella's Fabulous Bright Ideas, 1986; Floella's Floorboard Book, 1987; Flo and Aston's Books (series of six books), 1987; Snotty and the Rod of Power, 1987; Floella's Cardboard Box Book, 1987; Exploring Caribbean Food in Britain, 1988; For Goodness Sake, 1994; Skip Across the Ocean, 1995; Coming to England, 1995, 20th Anniv. edn 2016; My Two Grannies, 2007; The Arms of Britannia, 2010; My Two Grandads, 2010; Sea of Tears (novel), 2011. *Recreations:* singing, golf, photography, running. *Address:* House of Lords, SW1A 0PW. *W:* www.floellabenjamin.com.

**BENJAMIN, Sir George (William John),** Kt 2017; CBE 2010; composer, conductor and pianist; Henry Purcell Professor of Composition, King's College, London University, since 2001; *b* 31 Jan. 1960; *s* of late William Benjamin and Susan Benjamin (*née* Bendon). *Educ:* Westminster School (private tuition with Peter Gellhorn); Paris Conservatoire (Olivier Messiaen); King's College, Cambridge (Alexander Goehr; Hon. Fellow, 2014). MA, MusB. First London orchestral performance, BBC Proms, 1980; research at Institut de Recherche et Coordination Acoustique/Musique, Paris, 1984–87; Prince Consort Prof. of Composition, RCM, 1994–2001 (Vis. Prof., 1987–94); ROH, Covent Garden début, Written on Skin, 2013. Artistic consultant, Sounding the Century, BBC R3, 1996–99. Featured composer: Tanglewood Fest., 1999, 2002, 2003, 2012, 2013; LSO Fest., 2002–03; Deutsches Symphonie Orch., Berlin, 2005; Strasbourg Musica, 2005; Carta Blanca, Madrid, 2005; Fest. d'Automne, Paris, 2006; Lucerne Fest., 2008; San Francisco, 2010; Auftakt Fest., Frankfurt, 2011; Aix-en-Provence Fest., 2012; Southbank London, Cultural Olympiad, 2012; Toronto and NY, 2015; Aldeburgh Fest., 2015; Holland Fest., 2018; Berlin Philharmonic Orch. and Elbphilharmonie, Hamburg, 2018–19. Hon. FKC 2016; Hon. FRCM 1993; Hon. RAM 2003; Hon. GSMD 2020. Mem., Bavarian Acad. of Arts, 2000; Hon. Mem., Royal Philharmonic Soc., 2011; Mem., Royal Swedish Acad. of Music, 2018. Lili Boulanger Award, USA, 1985; Gramophone Contemp. Music Award, 1990, 2014, 2017; Schönberg Prize, Berlin, 2002; Royal Philharmonic Soc. Awards, 2003, 2004, 2009, 2014; Composer of the Year, Musical America, 2014; Composition Prize, Prince Pierre de Monaco Foundn, 2015; Golden Lion Award, Venice Biennale, 2019. Commandeur, Ordre des Arts et des Lettres (France), 2014 (Chevalier, 1996). *Publications include: orchestral:* Altitude, 1977; Ringed by the Flat Horizon, 1980; A Mind of Winter, 1981; At First Light, 1982; Jubilation, 1985; Antara, 1987; Sudden Time, 1993; Three Inventions for Chamber Orchestra, 1995; Sometime Voices, 1996; Palimpsests, 2002; Olicantus, 2002; Dance Figures, 2004; Duet, for piano and orch., 2008; Dream of the Song, 2015; Lessons in Love and Violence, 2017; *chamber music:* Violin Sonata, 1977; Piano Sonata, 1978; Octet, 1978; Flight, 1979; Sortilèges, 1981; Three Studies for Solo Piano, 1985; Upon Silence, 1990, 1991; Viola, Viola, 1997; Shadowlines, for solo piano, 2001; Three Miniatures for Violin, 2001; Piano Figures, 2004; *opera:* Into the Little Hill, 2006; Written on Skin, 2012; Lessons in Love and Violence, 2018. *Address:* c/o Faber Music Ltd, Bloomsbury House, 74–77 Great Russell Street, WC1B 3DA.

**BENJAMIN, Jon;** *see* Benjamin, M. J.

**BENJAMIN, Jonathan, (Jon);** HM Diplomatic Service; Director, Diplomatic Academy, Foreign and Commonwealth Office, since 2017; *b* London, 19 Jan. 1963; *s* of late Arthur Benjamin and of Edith Benjamin (*née* Landau); *m* 2014, Carolina Vasquez; one *s. Educ:* Univ. of Surrey (BSc 1st Cl. Hons German, Swedish and Internat. Relns 1985). Telex operator, Skandinaviska Enskilda Banken, Gothenburg, 1983, 1985; joined FCO, SE Asia Section, 1986; Second Sec. (Pol), Jakarta, 1987–91; Hd, Central Asia and Caucasus Section, Eastern Dept, FCO, 1992–93; Private Sec. to Minister for Europe, 1993–95; Hd, Pol Section, Ankara, 1996–99; Hd, Human Rights Policy Dept, FCO, 2002–05; Dep., then Actg Consul Gen., NY, 2005–08; on secondment to AIG, then to Eurasia Gp, NY, 2008–09; Ambassador to Chile, 2009–14; High Comr to Ghana and non-res. Ambassador to Togo, Burkina Faso and Benin, 2014–17. Ed.-in-Chief, Human Rights Annual Report, FCO, 2002–04. Pres., Alexander Selkirk Foundn, 2010–13. *Recreations:* football, languages, Humanism, the role of religion in politics and foreign policy. *Address:* c/o Foreign and Commonwealth Office, King Charles Street, SW1A 2AH. *E:* Jon.Benjamin@fco.gov.uk.

**BENJAMIN, Leanne Faye,** OBE 2005; AM 2015; Principal, Royal Ballet Company, 1993–2013; *b* Rockhampton, Australia, 13 July 1964; *m* 2001, Tobias Round; one *s. Educ:* Royal Ballet Sch. (Adeline Genée Gold Medal). Joined Sadler's Wells Royal Ballet, 1983: Soloist, 1985–87; Principal, 1987–88; Principal: London Fest. Ballet, later English Nat. Ballet, 1988–90; Deutsche Oper Ballet, Berlin, 1990–92; joined Royal Ballet Co., 1992. Numerous leading rôles; *created roles:* Greta in Metamorphosis; Earth in Homage to the Queen; Mr Worldly Wise; Two-Part Invention; Masquerade; Qualia; Tanglewood; Despite; DGV; Children of Adam. Gov. Royal Ballet Cos, 2016–; Patron, Tait Meml Trust. Hon. Dr Performing Arts Central Qld, 2014. Best Female Dancer, Nat. Dance Awards, 2004, 2009; De Valois Award for Outstanding Achievement in Dance, 2013. Prix de Lausanne, 1981. *Address:* c/o Royal Ballet, Royal Opera House, Covent Garden, WC2E 9DD.

**BENJAMIN, Marc Jonathan, (Jon);** Founder and Owner, MJB Consulting, since 2013; *b* 31 Oct. 1964; *s* of Alan and Barbara Benjamin; *m* 1990, Suzanne Nicola Taylor; one *s* one *d. Educ:* Dulwich Coll.; Univ. of Manchester (LLB Hons); Coll. of Law (Dist.). With Denton Hall, 1988–92; admitted solicitor, 1990; solicitor, Teacher Stern Selby, 1993–96; Hd, Business Div., United Jewish Israel Appeal, 1996–99; Chief Exec., British ORT, 1999–2004; Dir Gen. and Chief Exec., Bd of Deputies of British Jews, 2005–13; Chief Operating Officer, World ORT, 2014–15. *Recreations:* family, travel, cycling, reading (histories in particular), ski-ing, Crystal Palace FC, music.

**BENN,** family name of **Viscount Stansgate**.

**BENN, Rt Hon. Hilary (James Wedgwood);** PC 2003; MP (Lab) Leeds Central, since June 1999; *b* 26 Nov. 1953; *s* of Rt Hon. Tony Benn, PC; *m* 1st, 1973, Rosalind Caroline Retey (*d* 1979); 2nd, 1982, Sally Christina Clark; three *s* one *d. Educ:* Holland Park Comprehensive Sch.; Sussex Univ. (BA Hons Russian and East European Studies). Res. Asst, Nat. Referendum Campaign, 1975; Res. Officer, 1975–93, Head of Res., 1993–96, Head of Policy and Communications, 1996–97, ASTMS, then MSF; Jt Sec., Finance Panel, Labour Party Commn of Inquiry, on secondment, 1980; Special Advr to Sec. of State for Educn and Employment, 1997–99. MSF Rep., Labour Party Nat. Policy Forum, 1994–97;

Chair: Educn Cttee, ALA, 1988–90; Unions 21, 1995–99; Member: Educn Cttee, AMA, 1986–90; Envmt Policy Commn, Labour Party, 1994–97; Party into Power Task Force on Labour Party's Democracy, 1996–97. Parliamentary Under-Secretary of State: DFID, 2001–02; Home Office, 2002–03; Minister of State, DFID, 2003; Secretary of State: for Internat. Develt, 2003–07; for Envmt, Food and Rural Affairs, 2007–10; Shadow Sec. of State for Envmt, Food and Rural Affairs, 2010; Shadow Leader, H of C, 2010–11; Shadow Sec. of State for Communities and Local Govt, 2011–15; Shadow Foreign Sec., 2015–16. Chm., Select Cttee on Exiting the EU, 2016–; Member: Envmt, Transport and the Regions Select Cttee, 1999–2001; H of C Commn, 2010–11. Vice-Chair, PLP Educn and Employment Cttee, 2000–01; Mem., Sustainable Communities Policy Commn, Labour Party, 2007–; Co-Convenor, Internat. Policy Commn, Labour Party, 2016–. Pres., Acton CLP, 1979–82. Mem. (Lab) Ealing LBC, 1979–99 (Dep. Leader, 1986–90; Chair, Educn Cttee, 1986–90; Dep. Leader, Labour Gp, 1984–94). Vice-Chm., Commn for Africa, 2004–05. Contested (Lab) Ealing N, 1983, 1987. Minister of the Year, House Mag., 2006 and 2007; Politicians' Politician Award, Channel 4, 2006; Parliamentarian of the Year, Spectator, 2016. *Publications:* (contrib.) Beyond 2002: long-term policies for Labour, 1999; (contrib.) Men Who Made Labour, 2006. *Recreations:* watching sport, gardening. *Address:* House of Commons, SW1A 0AA.
*See also Viscount Stansgate.*

**BENN, Sir (James) Jonathan,** 4th Bt *cr* 1914; Chairman, SCA Pension Trusts Ltd, 1988–98; *b* 27 July 1933; *s* of Sir John Andrews Benn, 3rd Bt, and Hon. Ursula Lady Benn, *o d* of 1st Baron Hankey, PC, GCB, GCMG, GCVO, FRS; *S* father, 1984; *m* 1960, Jennifer Mary, *e d* of late Dr Wilfred Howells, OBE; one *s* one *d*. *Educ:* Harrow; Clare College, Cambridge (MA). Various positions with Reed International PLC (formerly A. E. Reed & Co.), 1957–88; Dir, Reed Paper & Board (UK) Ltd, 1971, Man. Dir 1976; Dir, Reed Group Ltd, 1976; Chm. and Chief Exec., Reed Paper & Board (UK) Ltd, 1977–90; Chm., Reedpack Paper Gp, 1988–90; Dir, Reedpack Ltd, 1988–90. Pres., British Paper and Board Industries Fedn, 1985–87. Dir, Broomhill Trust, 1991–96. *Recreations:* golf, ski-ing, music. *Heir: s* Robert Ernest Benn [*b* 17 Oct. 1963; *m* 1985, Sheila Margaret (marr. diss. 2014), 2nd *d* of Dr Alastair Blain; one *s* one *d*]. *Address:* Fielden Lodge, Tonbridge Road, Ightham, Kent TN15 9AN.
*See also T. J. Benn.*

**BENN, Jeremy Richard,** CEng, FREng, FICE, FCIWEM; Executive Chairman, JBA Group Ltd, since 2013 (Chief Executive, 2006–13); *b* Stockton-on-Tees, Co. Durham, 30 April 1962; *s* of Selwyn Benn and Joan Margaret Benn (*née* Blamires); *m* 1998, Caroline Louise Storey. *Educ:* Archbishop Holgate's Grammar Sch., York; Girton Coll., Cambridge (BA Geog. 1983; MA); Univ. of Newcastle upon Tyne (MSc Engrg Hydrol. 1984). CEng 1995; FICE 1996; CWEM, FCIWEM 1996; CEnv 2000; FREng 2010; MIEI 2010. Grad. Engr, Hydraulics Research Ltd, 1984–85, Hydraulic Engr, Hydraulic Analysis Ltd, 1985–87; Hydrologist, Bullen and Partners, 1987–93; Associate, Bullen Consultants, 1993–95; Dir, JBA Consulting, 1996–2006; Dir, JBA Consulting Engrs and Scientists (Ireland), 2006–. Vis. Prof. in Flood Risk Mgt, Univ. of Sheffield, 2008–. Mem., Modelling and Risk R&D Theme Tech. Adv. Gp, DEFRA/Envmt Agency, 2005–. Advr to NZ Earthquake Commn, 2013. Mem., Scour at Foundns panel, Internat. Assoc. of Hydraulic Engrg, 2001–. Member: British Hydrol Soc., 1997; British Dam Soc., 2004; Engrs Ireland, 2010; MASCE 1997. *Publications:* Floodplain Modelling using HEC-RAS, 2003; Managing Scour and Flood Risk to Railway Infrastructure, 2013; contribs to Jl Forensic Engrg, Jl ICE, Jl Flood Risk Mgt. *Recreations:* walking, industrial history. *Address:* JBA Consulting, South Barn, Broughton Hall, Skipton, N Yorks BD23 3AE. *T:* (01756) 799919, *Fax:* (01756) 799449. *E:* jeremy.benn@jbaconsulting.com.

**BENN, Sir Jonathan;** *see* Benn, Sir J. J.

**BENN, Timothy John;** Chairman, Timothy Benn Publishing Ltd, 1983–97, and other companies; *b* 27 Oct. 1936; *yr s* of Sir John Andrews Benn, 3rd Bt, and Hon. Ursula Helen Alers Hankey; *m* 1982, Christina Grace Townsend. *Educ:* Harrow; Clare Coll., Cambridge (MA); Princeton Univ., USA; Harvard Business Sch., USA (National Marketing Council Course; Scholarship Award). FInstM. 2nd Lieut Scots Guards, 1956–57. Benn Brothers Ltd: Board Member, 1961–82; Managing Director, 1972–82; Dep. Chm., 1976–81; Chm., Benn Brothers plc, 1981–82; Ernest Benn: Board Member, 1967–82; Managing Director, 1973–82; Chairman and Managing Director, 1974–82; Proprietor and Publisher, Creel Press, 1991–. Chairman: Bouverie Publishing Co., 1983–2003; Buckley Press, 1984–97; Henry Greenwood and Co., 1987–98; Dalesman Publishing Co., 1989–2004; The Countryman Publishing Co., 2000–04; Director: Huveaux plc, 2001–06; Country Publications Ltd, 2016–. Chairman: Council, PPA, 1970–73; Nat. Advertising Benevolent Soc., 1970–71; Member: Council, Advertising Assoc., 1962; Special Projects Cttee, Crafts Council, 1979–82. President: Thirty Club of London, 1982–83; Tonbridge Civic Soc., 1982–87. Chm., Kennel Appeal Bd, Battersea Dogs and Cats Home, 2012–14. *Publications:* The (Almost) Compleat Angler, 1985; Images of Angling, 2010. *Recreations:* writing, gardening, flyfishing, toymaking. *Address:* Chase Cottage, Chase Lane, Blackdown, Haslemere, Surrey GU27 3AG. *Clubs:* Flyfishers', Third Guards.
*See also Sir J. J. Benn.*

**BENN, Rt Rev. Wallace Parke;** Bishop Suffragan of Lewes, 1997–2012; *b* 6 Aug. 1947; *s* of William and Lucinda Jane Benn; *m* 1978, Lindsay Develing; one *s* one *d*. *Educ:* St Andrew's Coll., Dublin; UC, Dublin (BA); Trinity Coll., Bristol (external DipTheol London Univ.). Ordained deacon, 1972, priest, 1973; Assistant Curate: St Mark's, New Ferry, Wirral, 1972–76; St Mary's, Cheadle, 1976–82; Vicar: St James the Great, Audley, Stoke-on-Trent, 1982–87; St Peter's, Harold Wood, and part-time Chaplain, Harold Wood Hosp., 1987–97. President: Fellowship of Word and Spirit, 1998–; Church of England Evangelical Council, 2000–14; Church Soc., 2016–. *Publications:* The Last Word, 1996; Jesus our Joy, 2000; (contrib.) Preach the Word, 2007; The Ministry of the Word, 2018; articles in theol jls. *Recreations:* reading, walking with my wife, Rugby, motor sports.

**BENNATHAN, Joel Nathan;** QC 2006; a Recorder, since 2009; *b* 15 July 1961; *s* of late Esra Bennathan and Marion Bennathan, OBE; *m* 2004, Melanie Gingell; one *s* two *d*. *Educ:* Bristol Grammar Sch.; Queen Mary Coll., Univ. of London (LLB). Called to the Bar, Middle Temple, 1985; specialising in criminal law. *Publications:* legal articles in the Times, Solicitors' Jl and New Statesman. *Recreations:* art, theatre, family, socialism. *Address:* Doughty Street Chambers, 54 Doughty Street, WC1N 2LS.

**BENNER, Michael Peter;** Managing Director, Society of Independent Brewers, since 2014; *b* Rotherham, 6 July 1966; *s* of Peter and Anita Benner; *m* 1997, Helen; three *s* one *d*. *Educ:* McAuley Sch., Doncaster; Middlesex Univ. (BA Hons). Lectr in Mktg and Econs, 1992–94; Press Manager, 1994–97, Hd of Campaigns and Communications, 1997–2004, Chief Exec., 2004–14, CAMRA. *Recreations:* running, music, Jaguar cars. *Address:* Society of Independent Brewers, National Brewery Centre, Horninglow Street, Burton-Upon-Trent DE14 1NG.

**BENNET,** family name of **Earl of Tankerville.**

**BENNET, Dr Carey Louise;** National Delivery Director (North and East) (formerly Regional Lead for the East of England), Achievement for All 3As, 2011–15; Art Psychotherapist, Cambridge Art Therapy, since 2019; *b* 10 Jan. 1958; *d* of late Robin Bennet and Ann-Marie Bennet; *m* 1989, Peter James Cunningham; two *s*. *Educ:* Froebel Inst., Roehampton; Jesus Coll., Oxford; Linacre Coll., Oxford (DPhil); Univ. of Herts (MA Art Psychotherapy 2019). Education Officer: Leics CC, 1987–90; Cambs CC, 1990–2000; Asst Dir of Educn, Northants CC, 2000–03; Dir for Schs, 2003–06, Dir for Schs, Children and Families, 2007–08, Essex CC, 2003–06; Dir of Delivery Support, Together for Disabled Children, 2008–10; Strategic Advr, Children and Learners Div., DCSF, later DFE, 2010; Dir, Carey Bennet Associates Ltd, 2010–11. *Publications:* (with P. J. Downes) Help Your Child Through Secondary School, 1997. *Recreations:* psychotherapy, arts and well-being. *Address:* 21 Halifax Road, Cambridge CB4 3QB.

**BENNETT, Alan;** writer and dramatist; *b* 9 May 1934; *s* of Walter Bennett and Lilian Mary Peel; civil partnership 2006, Rupert Thomas. *Educ:* Leeds Modern Sch.; Exeter Coll., Oxford (BA Modern History, 1957; Hon. Fellow, 1987). Jun. Lectr, Modern History, Magdalen Coll., Oxford, 1960–62. Trustee, National Gall., 1993–98. Hon. Freeman: Leeds, 2005; Rousham, 2009. Hon. FRA 2000. Hon. DLitt Leeds, 1990. Co-author and actor, Beyond the Fringe, Royal Lyceum, Edinburgh, 1960, Fortune, London, 1961 and Golden, NY, 1962; author and actor, On the Margin (TV series), 1966; *stage plays:* Forty Years On, Apollo, 1968; Getting On, Queen's, 1971; Habeas Corpus, Lyric, 1973; The Old Country, Queen's, 1977; Enjoy, Vaudeville, 1980; Kafka's Dick, Royal Court, 1986; Single Spies (double bill: A Question of Attribution; An Englishman Abroad (also dir)), NT, 1988; The Wind in the Willows (adapted), NT, 1990; The Madness of George III, NT, 1991, Nottingham Playhouse, 2018; Talking Heads, Comedy, 1992 and 1996; The Lady in the Van, Queen's, 1999; Hymn, Harrogate Fest., 2001; The History Boys, NT, 2004, NY, 2006; The Habit of Art, NT, 2009; People, NT, 2012; Cocktail Sticks, NT, 2012; Allelujah!, Bridge Th., 2018; *BBC TV films:* A Day Out, 1972; Sunset Across the Bay, 1975; *TV Plays for LWT,* 1978–79: Doris and Doreen; The Old Crowd; Me! I'm Afraid of Virginia Woolf; All Day on the Sands; Afternoon Off; One Fine Day; *BBC TV plays:* A Little Outing, A Visit from Miss Prothero, 1977; Intensive Care, Say Something Happened, Our Winnie, Marks, A Woman of No Importance, Rolling Home; An Englishman Abroad, 1983; The Insurance Man, 1986; Talking Heads (series), 1988 (adapted for stage comedy, 1992); 102 Boulevard Haussmann, 1991; A Question of Attribution, 1991; Talking Heads 2 (series), 1998; Telling Tales (series), 2000; *BBC TV documentaries:* Dinner at Noon, 1988; Portrait or Bust, 1994; The Abbey, 1995; Alan Bennett's Diaries, 2016; *Channel 4:* Poetry in Motion, 1990; Poetry in Motion 2, 1992; *feature films:* A Private Function, 1984; Prick Up Your Ears, 1987; The Madness of King George, 1995; The History Boys, 2006; The Lady in the Van, 2015; *radio play:* Denmark Hill, 2014. *Publications:* (with Cook, Miller and Moore) Beyond the Fringe, 1962; Forty Years On, 1969; Getting On, 1972; Habeas Corpus, 1973; The Old Country, 1978; Enjoy, 1980; Office Suite, 1981; Objects of Affection, 1982; A Private Function, 1984; The Writer in Disguise, 1985; Prick Up Your Ears (screenplay), 1987; Two Kafka Plays, 1987; Talking Heads, 1988 (Hawthornden Prize, 1989); Single Spies, 1989; The Lady in the Van, 1990, complete edn 2015; Poetry in Motion, 1990; The Wind in the Willows (adaptation), 1991; The Madness of George III, 1992; (jtly) Poetry in Motion 2, 1992; Writing Home, 1994 (collected articles); The Madness of King George (screenplay), 1995; The Clothes They Stood Up In, 1998; The Complete Talking Heads, 1998; Father! Father! Burning Bright, 2000; Telling Tales (autobiog.), 2000; The Laying On of Hands, 2001; The History Boys, 2004, screenplay, 2006; Untold Stories, 2005; The Uncommon Reader, 2007; A Life Like Other People's (memoir), 2009; The Habit of Art, 2009; Smut: two unseemly stories, 2011; Hymn and Cocktail Sticks, 2012; People, 2012; Six Poets: Hardy to Larkin (anthology), 2014; Keeping On Keeping On, 2016; Allelujah!, 2018. *Address:* c/o United Agents, 12–26 Lexington Street, W1F 0LE.

**BENNETT, Cdre Alan Reginald Courtenay,** DSC 1982; JP; FRAeS; Chief Executive, Royal College of Surgeons of England, 2009–13; *b* Gosport, 11 Feb. 1954; *s* of late Peter Bennett and Joan Bennett; *m* 1979, Sarah Anne Shaw; two *s* one *d*. *Educ:* Bradfield Coll., Berks; BRNC Dartmouth. Royal Navy: officer trng, 1972–75; Warfare Officer, HMS Amazon, 1976–77; helicopter flying trng, 1978–79; pilot, 846 Cdo Sqdn, HMS Bulwark and HMS Hermes, 1979–82; Lynx Flight Comdr, HMS Arrow, 1982–84; RNSC 1985; Principal Warfare Officer, HMS Danae, 1986–87; Sen. Pilot, 846 Cdo Sqdn, 1988–90; CO, HMS Alacrity, 1990–92; Directing Staff, JSDC, Greenwich, 1993; Commander: RN Air Officer Appts, MoD, 1994–95; Air Wing, HMS Illustrious, 1996–97; Hd, Policy and Plans Div., Internat. Mil. Staff, NATO HQ, Brussels, 1997–99; Dir, Personnel/Plans/Communications, Jt Helicopter Comd, Wilton, 1999–2002; JSCSC 2003; CO, RN Air Station Yeovilton, 2003–05; British Naval Attaché, Washington, DC, 2006–08. Comdr 1990; Capt. 1997; Cdre 2003. RYA Yachtmaster Offshore Instructor (pt-time), 2008–13. FRAeS 2003. Mem., RNSA. JP Dorset, 2017. *Recreations:* family, cruising and maintaining a Sweden Yachts 390, enjoying the countryside.

**BENNETT, (Albert) Edward;** Director, G24 Nuclear Safety Assistance Co-ordination Centre, 1992–95, and Directorate of Nuclear Safety, Industry and the Environment, and Civil Protection (formerly of Nuclear Safety and Control of Chemical Pollution), 1987–95, European Commission; *b* 11 Sept. 1931; *s* of Albert Edward and Frances Ann Bennett; *m* 1957, Jean Louise Paston-Cooper; two *s*. *Educ:* University Coll. Sch., Hampstead; London Hosp. Med. Coll. MB BS London; FFCM 1972, FFOM 1984. Surgeon Lieut, RN, 1957–60; Senior Lectr, Dept of Clinical Epidemiology and Social Medicine, St Thomas's Hosp. Med. Sch., 1964–70; Dir, Health Services Evaluation Gp, Univ. of Oxford, 1970–77; Prof. and Head of Dept of Clinical Epidemiology and Social Medicine, St George's Hosp. Med. Sch., Univ. of London, 1974–81; Director: Health and Safety Directorate, EEC, 1981–87. Hon. Editor, Internat. Jl of Epidemiology, 1977–81. *Publications:* Questionnaires in Medicine, 1975; (ed) Communications between Doctors and Patients, 1976; (ed) Recent Advances in Community Medicine, 1978; numerous sci. reports and contribs on epidemiology of chronic disease and evaluation of health services. *Recreations:* opera, gardening, browsing. *Address:* 605 Atlantic Suites, Europort, Gibraltar.
*See also N. E. F. Bennett.*

**BENNETT, Andrew Francis;** retired teacher; *b* Manchester, 9 March 1939; *m;* two *s* one *d*. *Educ:* Birmingham Univ. (BSocSc). Joined Labour Party, 1957; Member, Oldham Borough Council, 1964–74. Member, National Union of Teachers. Contested (Lab) Knutsford, 1970. MP (Lab) Stockport North, Feb. 1974–1983, Denton and Reddish, 1983–2005. An Opposition spokesperson on educn, 1983–88. Jt Chm., Select Cttee on Envmt, Transport and Regl Affairs, 1997–2005 (Chm., Envmt Sub-Cttee, 1997–2005). Interested especially in environment and education. *Recreations:* photography, walking, climbing. *Address:* 28 Brownsville Road, Stockport SK4 4PF.

**BENNETT, Andrew John,** CMG 1998; President, Tropical Agricultural Association, since 2003; *b* 25 April 1942; *s* of Leonard Charles Bennett and Edna Mary Bennett (*née* Harding); *m* 1996, Yin Yin Jackson. *Educ:* St Edward's Sch., Oxford; University Coll. of N Wales (BSc Agr Scis 1965); Univ. of West Indies, Trinidad (DipTA 1967); Univ. of Reading (MSc Crop Protection 1970). VSO Kenya, 1965–66; Agricl Officer (Research), Govt of St Vincent, 1967–69; Maize Agronomist, Govt of Malawi, 1971–74; Crop Develt

Manager, 1976–78, Chief Research Officer, 1978–79, S Region, Sudan; Asst Agricl Adviser, ODA, 1980–83; Natural Resources Adviser (ODA), SE Asia Develt Div., Bangkok, 1983–85; Head, British Develt Div. in Pacific (ODA), Fiji, 1985–87; Chief Natural Resources Advr, ODA, FCO, subseq. DFID, 1987–2002. Dir and Sec., Eynesbury Estates, 1990–2008. Dir, Syngenta Foundn for Sustainable Agriculture, 2002–16 (Exec. Dir, 2002–07). Non-executive Director: CABI, 2009–15; IBO UK, 2015–. Pres., Tropical Agric. Assoc., 2003–. Chairman: Bd Trustees, Sci. Develt Network, 2008–14; Alliance Bd, Consultative Gp on Internat. Agricl Res., 2010–11; Member: Bd Trustees, Centre for Internat. Forestry Res., 2002–10 (Chm., 2006–10); Council, ODI, 2003–08; Interim Panel, Global Crop Diversity Trust, 2003–06; Bd Trustees, Internat. Orgn (formerly Network) on Bamboo and Rattan, 2011–18 (Chair, 2016–18); Trustee: Crop Innovations (formerly Eur. Centre for Underutilised Crops), 2012–; African Fellowship Trust, 2015– (Chair, 2017–). Dir, Doyle Foundn, 2002–. FRSA 2000. Hon. DSc Cranfield, 1999. *Recreations:* walking, gardening. *Address:* Chroyle, Gloucester Road, Bath BA1 8BH. *T:* (01225) 851489. *E:* andrewj.bennett@btinternet.com.

BENNETT, Brian Maurice; HM Diplomatic Service, retired; Ambassador to Belarus, 2003–07; Trustee, Humphrey Richardson Taylor Charitable Trust, since 2019 (Administrator, 2008–18); *b* 1 April 1948; *s* of Valentine and Dorothy Bennett; *m* 1969, Lynne Skipsey; three *s*. *Educ:* Totton Grammar Sch.; Sheffield Univ. (BA Hons Russian). AIL 1988. Joined HM Diplomatic Service, 1971; Prague, 1973–76; Helsinki, 1977–79; Bridgetown, Barbados, 1983–86; Vienna, 1986–88; The Hague, 1988–92; Dep. Hd of Mission, Tunis, 1997–2000. Chm., Anglo-Belarusian Soc., 2014–. *Publications:* The Last Dictatorship in Europe: Belarus under Lukashenko, 2011. *Recreations:* singing, walking, table tennis.

BENNETT, Catherine Elizabeth; see O'Leary, C. E.

BENNETT, Clive Ronald Reath, CBE 2007; Managing Director, Imago Services Ltd, 2008–13; *b* 20 Dec. 1947; *s* of Ron and Betty Bennett; *m* 1970, Pauline Weeks; three *d*. *Educ:* Hatfield Poly. (BSc). CEng 1971. Design Engr, Norton Abrasives Ltd, 1970–71; Industrial Engr, Radiomobile (Smiths Industries), 1971–73; Rank Xerox (UK) Ltd: Technical Service and Supply Dir, 1973–83; Gen. Manager, Supplies Distribn, 1983–84; Gen. Manager, Distribn, Polycell Products, 1984–87; Business Excellence Dir, Sara Lee Household and Personal Care, 1987–94; Gp Ops Dir, Norton Health Care, 1994–99; Chief Exec., DVLA, 2000–07. *Recreations:* music, swimming. *T:* (01243) 261904. *E:* clivebennett20@btinternet.com.

BENNETT, David John, CBE 2015; FCA; Group Chief Executive (formerly Managing Director), Sanctuary Group (formerly Sanctuary Housing Group), 1992–2018; *b* 16 April 1951; *s* of Wing Comdr Donald Albert Bennett, MBE and Eva Mary Bennett; *m* 1987, Katrina Momcilovic; two *d*. *Educ:* De Aston Sch. FCA 1975; CCMI 2007. Payne Stone Fraser, Chartered Accountants, 1969–74; Management Accountant, Beecham Pharmaceuticals, 1974–76; Chief Accountant, Heurtey Petrochem, 1976–80; Financial Controller: Samuel Lewis Trust, 1980–82; Peabody Trust, 1982–85; Finance Dir, 1985–86, Chief Exec., 1986–89, Spiral Housing Assoc.; Dep. Chief Exec., Sanctuary Housing Assoc., 1989–92. Gov., Sutton Community Sch., 2003–08. *Recreations:* music, photography, game fishing.

BENNETT, David Jonathan; Chairman, Ashmore plc, since 2018 (non-executive Director, since 2014); Deputy Chairman, Clydesdale Bank, since 2015; *b* 26 March 1962; *m* 1991, Sue Moss; two *s*. *Educ:* King's Coll. Sch., Wimbledon; Queens' Coll., Cambridge (BA Hons Econs 1983). Grindlays Bank, 1983–85; Money Market Dealer: Chemical Bank, 1985–86; Abbey Nat. Building Soc., 1986–88; Cheltenham & Gloucester plc: Gen. Mgr (Treasury and Investments), 1988–93; Head: of Strategic Planning, 1994; of Sales and Marketing, 1994–95; Finance Dir, 1995–96; Exec. Dir, NBNZ, 1996–98; CEO, Countrywide Bank, Lloyds TSB Gp, 1999; Alliance & Leicester plc: Gp Treas., 1999–2000; Exec. Dir, 2000–01; Gp Finance Dir, 2001–07; Gp Chief Exec., 2007–08; Exec. Dir, Abbey, 2008–09. Dir, David Bennett Adv. Ltd, 2011–15. Chm., HomeServe Membership Ltd, 2012–17; non-executive Director: easyJet plc, 2005–14; Pacnet Ltd, 2009–14; Clarity Commerce Solutions Ltd, 2010–11; CMC Markets, 2010–12; Jerrold Hldgs Ltd, 2011–; Bank of Ireland (UK) plc, 2013–15; PayPal Europe, 2014–. *Recreations:* travel, Rugby supporter.

BENNETT, Dr David William; Chairman: Viapath LLP, since 2016; Four Eyes Insight, since 2016; *b* Wolverhampton, 3 Aug. 1955; *s* of William Edwin Bennett, Halesowen and Irene Joan Bennett (*née* Davis). *Educ:* Halesowen GS; Univ. of Birmingham (BSc; S. W. J. Smith Prize); Trinity Coll., Oxford (DPhil); London Business Sch. (Cert. Corporate Finance). Manager: Shell Research Ltd, 1979–82; Shell Internat. Petroleum Co., 1982–86; Dir, McKinsey & Co. Inc., 1986–2004; Hd, Prime Minister's Policy Directorate and Prime Minister's Strategy Unit, 2005–07; Chm., 10 Partnership Ltd, 2007–10; Interim Chief Exec., 2010–12, Chm., 2011–14, Chief Exec., 2012–15, Monitor, Ind. Regulator of NHS Foundn Trusts. Non-exec. Dir, GHK Hldgs Ltd, 2008–12. Associate Fellow, Inst. for Govt, 2008–15; Vis. Prof., Inst. of Global Heath Innovation, Imperial Coll. London, 2016–. *Publications:* contrib. res. papers to Nuclear Physics, 1977–80. *Recreations:* motor sports, cycling, swimming. *E:* david@bennetts-online.net.

BENNETT, Prof. Dorothy Catherine, PhD; FMedSci; Professor of Cell Biology, since 1999, and Director, Molecular and Clinical Sciences Research Institute, since 2016, St George's, University of London (formerly St George's Hospital Medical School, University of London); *b* Leicester, 16 Feb. 1954; *d* of Herbert Bennett and Eileen Bennett; *m* 1981, Robert Brooks; two *d*. *Educ:* Rawlins Sch., Quorn; King's Coll., Cambridge (BA Nat. Scis 1975); ICRF London Labs and King's Coll. London (PhD 1979). Research Fellow: Salk Inst., La Jolla, 1979–81; ICRF Labs, London, 1981–83; St George's Hosp. Med. Sch., Univ. of London, then St George's, Univ. of London: CRC Investigator, 1983–87; Lectr, 1987–91; Sen. Lectr, 1991–93; Reader in Cell Biol., 1993–99; Hd, Cell Biol. and Genetics Res. Centre, 2014–16. President: Europ. Soc. for Pigment Cell Res., 2000–03; Internat. Fedn of Pigment Cell Socs, 2002–05; Internat. Cell Senescence Assoc., 2013–17. Mem., Internat. Expert Panel for French Govt res. bodies (Agence Nat. de la Recherche, Institut Nat. de la Santé et de la Recherche Médicale, Agence d'Evaluation de la Recherche et de l'Enseignement Supérieur), 2006–; adv. roles for med. charities, UK and Italy. FMedSci 2017. *Publications:* The Colors of Mice: a model genetic network (jtly), 2010; over 150 articles and reviews in scientific jls and textbooks on genetics of pigmentation and skin cancer, and cell senescence. *Recreations:* music (ancient and modern), reading, walking, travel, theatre, art, planetary matters. *Address:* Molecular and Clinical Sciences Research Institute, St George's, University of London, Mailpoint J2A, Cranmer Terrace, SW17 0RE. *T:* (020) 8725 5918, *Fax:* (020) 8725 2992. *E:* dbennett@sgul.ac.uk.

BENNETT, Douglas Simon; child and adolescent psychotherapist; Chief Executive, North London Hospice, 2002–14; *b* 18 Aug. 1958. *Educ:* Bristol Univ. (LLB); Brunel Univ. (MA Public Sector Mgt 1989); Middx Univ. (MA Integrative Child and Adolescent Psychotherapy 2015). Trainee Solicitor, Slaughter & May, 1980–82; admitted Solicitor, 1982; Society of Voluntary Associations: Inner London Co-ordinator, 1982–84; Asst Dir, 1984–86; Dep. Dir, 1986–88; Dir, Age Concern, Brent, 1989; Head of Planning, British Red Cross, 1989–97; Chief Exec., Nat. Soc. for Epilepsy, 1997–2000; Univ. of Salamanca, 2000–01. Mem., UKCP. *Recreations:* meals with friends, walking, concerts, opera, going to cinema and theatre. *E:* londonchildtherapy@hotmail.com.

BENNETT, Edward; see Bennett, A. E.

BENNETT, Elizabeth Martin; see Allen, E. M.

BENNETT, Air Vice Marshal Sir Erik Peter, KBE 1990; CB 1984; CVO 2010; retired from RAF, 1991; Commander, Sultan of Oman's Air Force (in the rank of Air Marshal), 1974–90; *s* of Robert Francis and Anne Myra Bennett. *Educ:* The King's Hospital, Dublin. Air Adviser to King Hussein, 1958–62; RAF Staff College, 1963; Jt Services Staff Coll., 1968; RAF Coll. of Air Warfare, 1971. Order of Istiqlal (Jordan), 1960; Order of Oman, 1980; Order of Merit (Oman), 1989; Order of Sultan Qaboos (Oman), 1985; Medal of Honour (Oman), 1989. *Recreations:* riding, sailing, big game fishing. *Address:* Bait Al Manooma, Seeb-Hail Al Awahir, PO Box 1751, Postal Code 111, Sultanate of Oman. *Clubs:* Royal Air Force, Beefsteak, Pratt's.

BENNETT, Gareth John; Member (UK Ind) South Wales Central, since 2016, and Leader, UK Independence Party, since 2018, National Assembly for Wales; *b* Cardiff, 1 Dec. 1968; *s* of Frederick Keith Bennett and Joan Patricia Bennett (*née* Butcher, now Withers). *Educ:* Llandaff City Primary Sch., Cardiff; Radyr Comprehensive Sch., Cardiff; Middlesex Poly.; Cardiff Inst. of Higher Educn (Cert. Journalism 1992). NCTJ Reporter, Carmarthen Jl Newsletter, 1992–96; admin posts, 1996–98; English lang. teacher, SE Asia, 1998–99; mkt res. interviewer, Cardiff, 1999–2001; adminr and call centre operator, Swindon, 2001–04; property develt, 2004–12; English teacher, China and Thailand, 2012–13; painting, decorating and labouring jobs, 2013–16. *Publications:* with David Collins: Never Mind the Bluebirds: the ultimate Cardiff City quiz book, 2012; Never Mind the Bluebirds 2: another ultimate Cardiff City quiz book, 2013; The Secret Premier League Diary of a Cardiff City Football Fan, 2014; The Little Book of Cardiff, 2015. *Recreations:* football, travel. *Address:* National Assembly for Wales, Cardiff Bay, Cardiff CF99 1NA. *T:* 0300 200 7263. *E:* Gareth.Bennett@assembly.wales.

BENNETT, Hon. Sir Hugh (Peter Derwyn), Kt 1995; DL; Deputy Judge of the High Court of Justice, 2010–18 (a Judge of the High Court of Justice, Family Division, 1995–2010); Nominated Administrative Court Judge, 2004–10; a Lieutenant Bailiff, Guernsey, since 2018; *b* 8 Sept. 1943; *s* of late Peter Ward Bennett, OBE, and Priscilla Ann Bennett; *m* 1969, Elizabeth (*née* Landon); one *s* three *d*. *Educ:* Haileybury and ISC; Churchill College, Cambridge (MA). Called to the Bar, Inner Temple, 1966, Bencher, 1993; an Assistant Recorder, 1987; QC 1988; a Recorder, 1990–95; Family Law (finance) Facilitator, 2010–18; arbitrator, 2012–18. Presiding Judge, NE Circuit, 1999–2002; a Judge, Courts of Appeal of Jersey and Guernsey, 2010–15. Mem., Supreme Court Rule Cttee, 1988–92; Chm. (part-time), Betting Levy Appeal Tribunal, 1989–95. Hon. Legal Advr, Sussex County Playing Fields Assoc., 1988–95. Chm., Sussex Assoc. for Rehabilitation of Offenders, 1998–2004. Fellow of Woodard Corp., 1987–99; Mem. Council, Lancing Coll., 1981–95. MCIArb 2012. DL W Sussex, 2003. *Recreations:* cricket, tennis, shooting, fishing. *Clubs:* Garrick, Pilgrims, MCC; Sussex.
See also Sir H. J. F. S. Cholmeley, Bt.

BENNETT, Prof. James Arthur, PhD; Director, Museum of the History of Science, 1994–2012, and Professor, 2010–12, now Emeritus, University of Oxford; Fellow of Linacre College, Oxford, 1994–2012, now Emeritus; Visiting Keeper, The Science Museum, 2013–15, now Emeritus; *b* 2 April 1947; *s* of James Hutchinson Bennett and Margaret Anna Bennett (*née* McCune); *m* 1st, 1971, France Annie Ramette (marr. diss. 2002); two *d*; 2nd, 2005, Sylvia Sumira. *Educ:* Grosvenor High Sch., Belfast; Clare Coll., Univ. of Cambridge (BA 1969; PhD 1974). FRAS 1976; FSA 1989. Lectr, Univ. of Aberdeen, 1973–74; Archivist, Royal Astronomical Soc., 1974–76; Curator of Astronomy, Nat. Maritime Mus. 1977–79; Curator, Whipple Mus. of Hist. of Sci., Cambridge, 1979–94; Sen. Res. Fellow, 1984–94, Sen. Tutor, 1992–94, Churchill Coll., Cambridge. Member: Cttee, Sci. Mus., 2004–10 (Chm., Maths Gall. Adv. Bd, 2014–16; London Sci. City Adv. Bd, 2017–); Astronomical Heritage Cttee, RAS, 2009–17; Bd, Nobel Mus., Stockholm, 2011–14; Council, Belfast Natural Hist. and Philosophical Soc., 2015–; Liby Cttee, Royal Soc., 2016–18. President: Scientific Instrument Commn, IUHPS, 1998–2002; British Soc. for History of Sci., 2000–02; Hakluyt Soc., 2016– (Mem. Council, 2012–); Vice Pres., Internat. Acad. of History of Sci., 2013–17. Paul Bunge Prize, German Chemical Soc., 2001; PhysicsEstoire Prize, European Phys. Soc., 2018. Member, Editorial Board: Jl for History of Astronomy, 1990–2004; Notes and Records, Royal Soc., 2000–08; Isis, 2001–03; Nuncius, 2001–12; The Northern Mariner, 2016–; Chm., Editl Bd, Sci. Mus. Gp Jl, 2013–16. *Publications:* The Mathematical Science of Christopher Wren, 1982; The Divided Circle, 1987; Church, State and Astronomy in Ireland, 1990; (ed jtly) Making Instruments Count, 1993; (with S. Johnston) The Geometry of War, 1996; (with S. Mandelbrote) The Garden, the Ark, the Tower, the Temple, 1998; (jtly) London's Leonardo, 2003; (ed jtly) Oxford Companion to the History of Modern Science, 2003; (ed jtly) Cabinets of Experimental Philosophy in Eighteenth-Century Europe, 2013; (with M. Hunter) The Image of Restoration Science, 2017; Navigation: a very short introduction, 2017; articles in books and jls, and exhibition catalogues. *Recreations:* music, Rugby, cooking. *Address:* 20 Alma Place, Oxford OX4 1JW. *T:* (01865) 203883.

BENNETT, Jana Eve, OBE 2000; media consultant, since 2017; President and General Manager, History Network, A+E Networks LLC, 2015–17 (President, FYI and LMN channels, 2013–15); *b* 6 Nov. 1956; *d* of Gordon Willard Bennett and Elizabeth (*née* Cushing); *m* 1996, Richard Clemmow; one *s* one *d*. *Educ:* Bognor Regis Comprehensive Sch.; St Anne's Coll., Oxford (BA PPE); London Sch. of Econs (MSc with dist. Internat. Relns); Wharton Sch., Univ. of Penn (AMP). Co-editor, Millennium, jl internat. relns; British Broadcasting Corporation: news trainee, 1978; news daily editor; series producer, then Ed., Antenna, 1987; Ed., Horizon, 1990; Head, BBC Science, 1994–97; Dir and Dep. Chief Exec., BBC Prodn, 1997–99; Exec. Vice-Pres., Learning Channel, US Discovery Communications Inc., 1999–2002; Dir, Television and Mem., Exec. Bd, BBC, 2002–11; Pres., Worldwide Networks and Global iPlayer, and Man. Dir for Latin America, BBC Worldwide, 2011–12 (Mem., Exec. Bd, 2003–11). Member: Bd, UKTV, 2011–12; Bd, Women in Film and TV, 2011–13 (Chm., 2012–13); Exec. Cttee, Internat. Emmys, 2010–13; Bd, Pew Res. Center, 2013– (non-exec. Dir, 2014–). Trustee: Natural Hist. Mus., 1999–2004; British Liby, 2019–. Mem., Visitors Bd, Pitt Rivers Univ. Mus. of Natural History, 2013–. Gov., RSC, 2005–16. Gov., LSE, 2002–07. FRTS 1999. *Publications:* (jtly) The Disappeared: Argentina's dirty war, 1986. *Recreations:* exploration, travel literature, ski-ing, Brazil. *E:* jana@janabennettmedia.com.

BENNETT, Jonathan Simon; His Honour Judge Jonathan Bennett; a Circuit Judge, since 2015; *b* 13 July 1957; *s* of late Leonard Arthur Covil Bennett and Edith Irene Bennett; *m* 1982, Sarah Jayne Blackmore; three *s* one *d*. *Educ:* City of London Sch.; Reading Univ. (LLB Hons). Admitted solicitor, 1982; Dep. Dist Judge, 1998–2003; a Dist Judge (Magistrates' Courts), 2003–15; a Recorder, 2009–15. Chm. (pt-time), Appeals Service,

1997–2003. Chm. of Trustees, Open Hands Project, 2007–. *Recreations:* following Charlton Athletic, lay leader within St Thomas' Church, Philadelphia, Sheffield. *Address:* Derby Combined Court Centre, Morledge, Derby DE1 2XE. *E:* jonathan.bennett57@sky.com.

BENNETT, **Katherine Susan**, CBE 2019 (OBE 2004); FRAeS; Senior Vice President, Airbus in the UK, since 2017; *b* Solihull, 8 Dec. 1967; *d* of Richard Norton Bowes and Diana Margaret Bowes; *m* 1996, Simon Mark Paget Bennett. *Educ:* Greenacre Sch., Banstead; Univ. of Leicester (BA Hons Combined Arts). Account Manager, Hill & Knowlton PR, 1990–95; Corporate Affairs, Corp. of London, 1995–96; Hd, Govt Affairs, Vauxhall Motors, 1996–2004; Airbus: Hd, UK Govt Affairs, 2004–07; Dir, Communications and Govt Affairs, 2007–10; Vice Pres., Public Affairs, 2017–. FRAeS 2016. Hon. DSc Cranfield, 2019. *Recreations:* choral singing, church organist, theatre, community activist. *T:* (020) 7395 7883. *E:* katherine.bennett@airbus.com.

BENNETT, **Linda Kristin**, OBE 2007; Chief Executive, L. K. Bennett, 1990–2008 (non-executive Director, since 2008); *b* 8 Sept. 1962; *d* of Peter and Hafdís Bennett; *m* 2000, Philip W. Harley; one *d*. *Educ:* Haberdashers' Aske's Sch. for Girls; Univ. of Reading (BSc). Founded L. K. Bennett, 1990. Hon. Fellow, Univ. of Arts, London, 2004. Hon. LLD Reading, 2005. Veuve Clicquot Business Woman of Year Award, 2004. *Recreations:* architectural history, British 20th century art, walking, travel, cinema. *Address:* c/o Anthony Pins, Nyman Libson Paul, Regina House, 124 Finchley Road, NW3 5JS. *T:* (020) 7433 2427. *E:* linda.bennett@lkbennett.com.

BENNETT, **Margaret Joan**; Group Finance and Human Resources Director, Good Things Foundation (formerly Online Centres Foundation, then Tinder Foundation) (part-time), since 2011; freelance mentor and consultant, since 2011; *b* 22 Dec. 1960; *d* of Rev. Canon Ian Frederick Bennett and Dr Rachel Bennett; *m* 1987, David Hill (marr. diss. 1994); one *s*. *Educ:* St Anne's Coll., Oxford (BA Hons PPE 1983). Chartered Accountant, KPMG, 1983–87; Finance Officer, West Midlands Arts, 1987–89; Asst Dir, North West Arts, 1989–91; Central Services Dir, Nottingham Community Housing Assoc., 1992–96; Chief Exec., Nat. Liby for the Blind, 1996–2001; Head, Lifelong Learning and Technologies Div., then Lifelong Learning Directorate, DCSF, later DFES, subseq. Dep. Dir, Further Educn and Skills Directorate, DIUS, then BIS, 2001–06; Dep. Chief Exec. and Exec. Dir, Finance and Resources, Learning and Skills Improvement Service, 2006–11. *Recreations:* the arts, reading, walking, music, cooking. *Address:* 23 Endcliffe Rise Road, Sheffield S11 8RU. *T:* (0114) 268 3053.

BENNETT, **Prof. Martin Arthur**, FRS 1995; FRSC, FRACI, FAA; Professor, Research School of Chemistry, Australian National University, 1991–2000, Emeritus Professor, since 2001; *b* 11 Aug. 1935; *s* of late Arthur Edward Charles Bennett and Dorothy Ivy Bennett; *m* 1964, Rae Elizabeth Mathews; two *s*. *Educ:* Haberdashers' Aske's Hampstead Sch.; Imperial Coll. of Science and Technology, London (BSc 1957; PhD 1960; DSc 1974). FRACI 1977; FAA 1980; FRSC 1997. Postdoctoral Fellow, Univ. of S California, 1960–61; Turner and Newall Fellow, 1961–63, Lectr, 1963–67, UCL; Fellow, 1967–70, Sen. Fellow, 1970–79, Professorial Fellow, 1979–91, Res. Sch. of Chem., ANU. Adjunct Prof., RMIT, 2000–. Vis. Prof. and Vis. Fellow, univs in Canada, Germany, USA, Japan, China and NZ. Corresp. Mem., Bayerische Akademie der Wissenschaften, 2005. Numerous awards, Aust. learned instns; Nyholm Medal, RSC, 1991; Max Planck Soc. Res. Award, 1994; Centenary Medal (Australia), 2001. *Publications:* chapters on Ruthenium in Comprehensive Organometallic Chemistry; contribs to learned jls. *Recreations:* golf, reading, foreign languages. *Address:* Research School of Chemistry, Australian National University, Canberra, ACT 2601, Australia. *T:* (2) 61253639; 21 Black Street, Yarralumla, ACT 2600, Australia. *T:* (2) 62824154.

BENNETT, **Prof. Martin Richard**, PhD; FRCP, FAHA; British Heart Foundation Professor of Cardiovascular Sciences, University of Cambridge, since 2000; Hon. Consultant Cardiologist, Cambridge University Hospitals NHS Trust, since 2000; *b* Northampton, 30 Aug. 1962; *s* of Peter and Beryl Bennett; *m* 1991, Catherine Margaret Blaymires; two *s*. *Educ:* Northampton Sch. for Boys; Welsh Nat. Sch. of Medicine, Cardiff (BSc 1st Cl. Hons Anatomy 1983; MB BCh 1st Cl. Hons 1986); PhD Wales 1993; MA Cantab 2001. FRCP 2001. Registrar in Cardiology, Gen. and Sandwell Hosps, Birmingham, 1988–90; BHF Clinician Scientist, 1990–97; BHF Sen. Fellow and Hon. Consultant Cardiologist, Univ. of Cambridge, 1997–2000. Vis. Scientist, Univ. of Washington, Seattle, 1993–95. FAHA 2001; FMedSci 2017. *Publications:* contrib. scientific papers and book chapters on cardiovascular disease, with specialist interest in atherosclerosis, apoptosis, restenosis and cellular senescence. *Recreations:* cricket, classic cars, contemporary film and books, travelling. *Address:* Division of Cardiovascular Medicine, Box 110, Addenbrooke's Centre for Clinical Investigation, Addenbrooke's Hospital, Cambridge CB2 0QQ. *T:* (01223) 331504, *Fax:* (01223) 331505. *E:* mrb@mole.bio.cam.ac.uk.

BENNETT, **Matthew Paul**; Founding Partner, Centrefield LLP, since 2015; *b* Bolton, 16 Oct. 1976. *Educ:* Rivington and Blackrod High Sch.; Univ. of Leeds (LLB Hons 1st Cl. Law). Solicitor, James Chapman & Co., 2001–06; Partner, Brabners LLP, 2006–15. *Address:* Centrefield LLP, 7 Constance Street, Knott Mill, Manchester M15 4QJ. *T:* 07973 741701. *E:* matthewbennett@centrefield.law.

BENNETT, **Natalie Louise**; Leader, Green Party, 2012–16; *b* Sydney, Australia, 10 Feb. 1966; *d* of John and Joy Bennett. *Educ:* Univ. of Sydney (BAgrSc Hons); Univ. of New England, Armidale (BA Hons Asian Studies); Univ. of Leicester (MA Mass Communications). Reporter and sub-editor, Northern Daily Leader, Cootamunda Herald, Eastern Riverina Observer, Australia; volunteer, Office of Nat. Commn on Women's Affairs, Thailand, 1995–96; sub-editor: Bangkok Post, 1996–99; The Times, 2000–04; Independent, 2004–05; Ed., Guardian Weekly, 2007–12. Blogger, 2006–. Contested (Green) Sheffield Central, 2017. Mem., Editl Bd, Green Eur. jl, 2013–15; Contrib. Ed., Left Foot Forward. Founder, Carnival of Feminists, 2005–09. Trustee: Fawcett Soc., 2010–14; Eur. Green Foundn, 2016–. Gov., Netley Primary Sch., 2008–16. *Recreations:* women's history, cycling and walking, baking and crocheting. *Address:* Sheffield Green Party, 73 Eskdale Road, Sheffield S6 1SL. *E:* natalie.bennett@greenparty.org.uk.

*[Created a Baroness (Life Peer), 2019 but title not gazetted at time of going to press.]*

BENNETT, **Neil Edward Francis**; Chief Executive, Maitland, since 2010 (Managing Partner, 2004–08; Vice Chairman, 2008–10); *b* 15 May 1965; *s* of Albert Edward Bennett, *qv*; *m* 1992, Carole Kenyon; two *d*. *Educ:* Westminster Sch.; University Coll. London (BA Medieval Archaeol.); City Univ. (Dip. Journalism). Staff writer, Investors Chronicle, 1987–89; The Times: Banking Corresp., 1989–92; Ed., Tempus column, 1992–94; Dep. Business Editor, 1994–95; City Editor, Sunday Telegraph, 1995–2002; Chief Exec., Gavin Anderson & Co. Ltd, 2002–04. Principal financial columnist, jagnotes-euro.com, 1999–2000. Mem. Bd of Advrs, London Capital Club, 2004–12. Dir, PRCA, 2017–. Trustee: John Schofield Trust, 2011–15; Chailey Heritage Foundn, 2019–. FRSA 2008. Jun. Wincott Foundn Award, 1992; Business Journalist of the Year, British Press Awards, 1998, 1999. *Recreations:* running, antiquarian book collecting, Irish Terriers. *Address:* Maitland, 13 King's Boulevard, N1C 4BU.

BENNETT, **Nicholas**; Public Services Ombudsman for Wales, since 2014; *b* St Asaph, 29 April 1969; *s* of Nicholas Bennett and Catherine Ellen Bennett (*née* Roberts); *m* 1994, Nia Gwenllian Thomas; one *s* two *d*. *Educ:* Llangefni Comprehensive Sch.; University Coll. of Wales, Aberystwyth (BSc Econ Politics 1990; MBA 1991). Wales Eur. Centre, Brussels, 1995–99; Special Advr to Dep. First Minister of Wales, Welsh Assembly Govt, 2000–02; Dir, Bute Communications, 2004–06; Gp Chief Exec., Community Housing Cymru, 2006–14. Chair, Ombudsman Assoc., 2017–19. Dir, Eur. Region, Internat. Ombudsman Inst. (Mem., World Bd). Member: All Wales Convention, Welsh Lang. Bd; Ofcom Adv. Panel, Williams Commn. *Recreations:* running, indie rock, Laugharne, walking. *Address:* (office) 1 Ffordd yr Hen Gae, Pencoed, Bridgend, Glamorgan CF35 5LJ. *T:* (01656) 641152. *E:* nick.bennett@ombudsman-wales.org.uk. *Club:* Glamorganshire Golf.

BENNETT, **Nicholas Jerome**; Managing Director, Kent Refurbishment Ltd, 2002–18; *b* 7 May 1949; *s* of late Peter Ramsden Bennett and Antonia Mary Flanagan; *m* 1995, Ruth, *er d* of late Andrew and Alma Whitelaw, Barnham Broom, Norfolk. *Educ:* Sedgehill Sch.; Polytechnic of North London (BA Hons Philosophy); Univ. of London Inst. of Educn (PGCE Distinction); Univ. of Sussex (MA). Educnl publishing, 1974; schoolmaster, 1976–85; educn officer, 1985–87; Advr on public affairs, Price Waterhouse, 1993–98; Chief Exec., ACE, 1998–2002. Member (C): Lewisham LBC, 1974–82 (Leader of the Opposition, 1979–81); co-opted Mem., ILEA Educn Cttee, 1978–81; Bromley LBC, 2006– (Chm., Educn Cttee, 2012–19; Mayor, 2019–20). Mem., FEFCE, 1992–97. Contested (C): St Pancras N, 1973 and Greenwich, by-elecn 1974, GLC elections; Hackney Central, 1979. MP (C) Pembroke, 1987–92; contested (C): Pembroke, 1992; Reading W, 1997. PPS to Minister of State, Department of Transport, 1990; Parly Under-Sec. of State, Welsh Office, 1990–92. Member: Select Cttee on Welsh Affairs, 1987–90; Select Cttee on Procedure, 1988–90; Vice-Chm. (Wales), Cons. backbench Party Organisation Cttee, 1990. Chm., Beckenham Cons. Assoc., 2006–09. Chm., Nat. Council for Civil Protection, 1990. Mem., Western Front Assoc. Evelyn Wrench Speaker, US ESU, 2011–14. Gov., London SE Coll. of Further and Higher Educn, 2014–18. Trustee, Mytime Active Leisure Trust, 2014–18. JP, SW Div., Greater (formerly Inner) London, 1998. *Publications:* (contrib.) Primary Headship in the 1990s, 1989; (contrib.) 100 Buildings, 100 Years, 2014. *Recreations:* swimming, history, transport, browsing in second-hand bookshops, cinema, small scale gardening, visiting battlefields of First and Second World War, architecture. *Address:* 18 Upper Park Road, Bromley, Kent BR1 3HT. *T:* (020) 8466 1363.

BENNETT, **Nicholas John**, CB 2008; Director General, Strategic Technologies, Ministry of Defence, 2005–09; *b* 30 Sept. 1948; *s* of John Douglas Bennett and Betty Yvonne Bennett (*née* Harker); *m* 1st, 1971, Susan Mary Worthington (*d* 1997); one *s* one *d*; 2nd, 2000, Lesley Ann Davie (*née* Thorpe). *Educ:* Bishop Wordsworth Sch., Salisbury; Brunel Univ. (BTech Hons Electronic Engrg 1971). Ministry of Defence: HQ No 90 (S) Gp, 1971–77; A&AEE, 1977–80; Hd, Engrg Design, RAF Signals Engrg Estabt, 1980–83; Principal D Air Radio, 1983–84; Asst Chief Design Engr, RAF Signals Engrg Estabt, 1984–86; Asst Dir, European Fighter Aircraft, 1986–89; rcds 1990; Hd, Civilian Mgt (Specialists), 2, 1991–92; Dir, Ops and Engrg, NATO European Fighter Aircraft Mgt Agency, 1992–96; Chief Exec., Specialist Procurement Services, 1996–99; Dir Gen., Human Resources, Defence Logistics Orgn, 1999–2001; Dir Gen., Scrutiny and Analysis, 2001–05. Director: SturQuest, 2016–; SturQuest Enterprises, 2016–. *Recreations:* cricket, ski-ing, practical study of wine.

BENNETT, **Vice Adm. Paul Martin**, CB 2016; OBE 2007; Chief of Staff, Supreme Allied Command Transformation, since 2018; *b* Newcastle-under-Lyme, 3 Aug. 1964; *s* of John and Helen Bennett; *m* 1988, Kay Sutherland; two *d*. *Educ:* Hymers Coll., Hull; Univ. of Newcastle upon Tyne (BA Hons Hist. 1985). BRNC, Dartmouth, 1985–86; HMS Hermione, 1986–87; HMS Cygnet, 1987–88; Dep. Ops Officer (Sen. Naval Officer), NI, 1988–89; HMS Birmingham, 1989–92; Commanding Officer: HMS Biter and Manchester Univ. RN Unit, 1992–93; HMS Dryad, 1993–94; HMS Atherstone, 1996–98; HMS Exeter, 1998–2000; Fleet Ops Officer, 2000–02; Hd Maritime, Directorate of Operational Capability, 2002–03; Dep. ACOS, Above Water, 2003–06; hcsc 2007; Multi-nat. Security Transition Team, Baghdad, 2007; Comdg Officer, HMS Daring, 2008–09; Comdr, Amphibious Task Gp, 2009–11; Dir, Naval Personnel Strategy, 2011–13; Dir, Develt Concepts and Doctrine Centre, MoD, 2013; COS Jt Forces Comd, 2013–16; ACNS (Capability) and COS Navy Comd HQ, 2016–17; Comdr, Maritime Forces and Rear Adm. Surface Ships, 2017–18. Younger Brother, Trinity Hse, 2010–. Liveryman, Carpenters' Co., 2012–. *Recreations:* mountain biking, road biking, traditional rowing, sailing. *Address:* Allied Command Transformation, 7857 Blandy Road, Suite 100, Norfolk, VA 23551–2490, USA.

BENNETT, **Penelope Anne**; Commissioner for Health and Social Care, South West Region, Appointments Commission (formerly NHS Appointments Commission), 2003–12; *b* 5 June 1956; *d* of late Peter Atherton Pettican-Runnicles and of Dorothy Isabel Pettican-Runnicles (*née* Grover); *m* 1982, John David Bennett; three *d*. *Educ:* West Hatch, Chigwell; Hatfield Poly. (BSc Hons); Open Univ. (MBA). Admitted as solicitor, 1982; solicitor in private practice, 1982–95; non-exec. Dir and Vice Chm., 1995–98, Chm., 1998–2002, E Glos NHS Trust; non-exec. Dir and Vice Chm., Avon, Glos and Wilts Strategic HA, 2002–04. Ind. Mem., Standards Cttee, Cotswold DC, 2001–10. Gp Bd Dir, Chm., Audit Cttee and Trustee, Hanover Housing Assoc., 2004–11. *Recreations:* family life, travel, walking, reading, gardening. *Address:* 11 St Peters Road, Cirencester, Glos GL7 1RE. *T:* (01285) 640691.

BENNETT, **Peter Gordon**, FRICS; Common Councillor, City of London Corporation, since 2016 (City Surveyor, 2008–16); *m* 1973, Janetta Hall; two *s* one *d*. *Educ:* Fitzwilliam Coll., Cambridge (BA Geog. 1970; MA). Chartered Surveyor, 1977. FRICS 1989. Res. Officer, Wool, Jute and Flax Trng Bd, 1970–72; Valuer, Valuation Office, Bd of Inland Revenue, 1972–76; Valuer, then Sen. Mgt Surveyor, Bradford CC, 1976–85; Dep. City Estate Agent, 1985–88, City Estate Agent and Valuer, 1988–90, Swansea CC; Dep. City Surveyor, Corp. of London, subseq. City of London Corp., 1990–2008. Perm. Mem., Bank of England Property Forum, 2002–. Mem., London Council, CBI, 2004–08. First Chm., London Reg., RICS, 2001–04. Charity Trustee, Royal Grammar Sch., High Wycombe, 2003–. Trustee, City of London Acad. Trust, 2018–. Liveryman, Chartered Surveyors' Co., 2009–; Bridgemaster, City of London, 2011–. *Recreations:* Rugby, opera, gardening. *Address:* City of London Corporation, PO Box 270, Guildhall, EC2P 2EJ. *T:* 07785 301612. *E:* peter.bennett@cityoflondon.gov.uk.

BENNETT, **Gen. Sir Phillip (Harvey)**, AC 1985 (AO 1981); KBE 1983; DSO 1969; Chairman, Australian War Memorial Foundation, 2003–2006; National President, Order of Australia Association, 1997–2000; *b* 27 Dec. 1928; *m* 1955, Margaret Heywood; two *s* one *d*. *Educ:* Perth Modern Sch.; Royal Mil. Coll.; jssc, rcds, psc (Aust.). Served, 1950–57: 3rd Bn RAR, Korea (despatches 1951), Sch. of Infantry (Instr), 25 Cdn Bde, Korea, 1952–53, Pacific Is Regt, PNG, and 16th Bn Cameron Highlanders of WA; Commando training, Royal Marines, England, Malta and Cyprus, 1957–58; OC 2 Commando Co., Melb., 1958–61; Aust. Staff Coll., 1961–62; Sen. Instr, then Chief Instr, Officer Cadet Sch., Portsea, 1962–65; AAG Directorate of Personal Services, AHQ, 1965–67; Co. 1 RAR,

1967–69 (served Vietnam; DSO); Exchange Instr, Jt Services Staff Coll., England, 1969–71; COL Directorate of Co-ordination and Organization, AHQ, 1971–73; COS HQ Fd Force Comd, 1974–75; RCDS, England, 1976; Comdr 1st Div., 1977–79; Asst Chief of Def. Force Staff, 1979–82; Chief of General Staff, 1982–84; Chief of Defence Force, Australia, 1984–87; Governor, Tasmania, 1987–95. Hon. Col, Royal Tasmania Regt, 1987–95. KStJ 1988. Hon. LLD: New South Wales, 1987; Tasmania, 1992. *Recreations:* reading, golf. *Address:* c/o Commonwealth Club, ACT 2600, Australia. *Clubs:* Commonwealth, University House (Canberra).

**BENNETT, His Honour Raymond Clayton Watson;** a Circuit Judge, 1989–2004; *b* 20 June 1939; *s* of Harold Watson and Doris Helena Bennett (previously Watson); *m* 1965, Elaine Margaret Haworth; one *s* one *d. Educ:* Bury Grammar Sch.; Manchester Univ. (LLB). Solicitor, 1964–72; called to the Bar, Middle Temple, 1972; practising barrister, 1972–89; an Asst Recorder, 1984; a Recorder, 1988. Hon. Recorder, Burnley, 1998–2004. *Recreations:* reading, painting, golf.

**BENNETT, Richard Charles;** Deputy Director, High Speed Rail programme, Department for Transport, 2013–16; *b* 8 Sept. 1958; *s* of Ben and Cynthia Bennett. *Educ:* Bristol Grammar Sch.; Christ's Coll., Cambridge (MA). Joined Dept of Transport, 1983; various roles, incl. internat. aviation, streetworks and investigation into King's Cross fire; Private Sec. to Minister of State for Transport, 1984–85; Railways Div., 1993–96, Finance Div., 1996–99, Dept of Transport, later DETR; Divl Manager, 1999–2001, Dir, 2001–03, London Underground Task Gp, DTLR, later DfT; Corporate Dir, Highways Agency, 2003–05; Department for Transport: Shared Services Prog. Manager, 2006–07; Hd of Ports Div., 2007–10; Hd of Maritime Commerce and Infrastructure, 2011–12.

**BENNETT, Richard Ernest Tulloch;** Group Managing Director and General Counsel, HSBC Holdings plc, 2010–12; Consultant, Norton Rose Fulbright, since 2013; *b* at sea on SS Corfu, 20 Sept. 1951; *s* of late Norman Bennett and of June Bennett; *m* 1977, Helen M. Tailby; two *s. Educ:* Haileybury; Univ. of Bristol (LLB 1973). Admitted solicitor, England and Wales, 1976, Hong Kong, 1979, Victoria, Australia, 1984; Asst Solicitor, Stephenson Harwood, 1976–79; Hongkong and Shanghai Banking Corporation, later HSBC Holdings plc: Asst Gp Legal Advr, 1979–88; Dep. Gp Legal Advr, 1988–92; Hd, Legal and Compliance, Asia Pacific, 1993–97; Gp Gen. Manager, Legal and Compliance, 1998–2010. Treas., Assoc. of Gen. Counsel and Co. Secs of FTSE 100, 2005–10. Non-exec. Dir, Aquis Exchange Ltd, 2014–. Member, Organising Committee: Hong Kong Sevens, 1983–96; Rugby World Cup Sevens, 1997; Pres., Penguins Internat. RFC, 2010. *Recreations:* sport (Rugby and golf), wine. *Clubs:* Liphook Golf; Hong Kong (Chm., 1996–97), Hong Kong Golf, Sheko Country (Hong Kong).

**BENNETT, Prof. Robert John,** PhD; FBA 1991; Professor of Geography, University of Cambridge, 1996–2010, now Emeritus; Fellow of St Catharine's College, Cambridge, 1996–2010, now Emeritus; *b* 23 March 1948; *s* of Thomas Edward Bennett and Kathleen Elizabeth Robson; *m* 1971, Elizabeth Anne Allen; two *s. Educ:* Taunton's Sch., Southampton; St Catharine's Coll., Cambridge (BA 1970; PhD 1974). Lecturer: University Coll. London, 1973–78; Univ. of Cambridge, 1978–85; Fellow and Dir of Studies, 1978–85, Tutor, 1981–85, Fitzwilliam Coll., Cambridge; Prof. of Geography, LSE, 1985–96. Leverhulme Personal Res. Prof., 1996–2000. Vis. Prof., Univ. California at Berkeley, 1978; Guest Schol., Brookings Instn, Washington DC, 1978, 1979, 1981; Hubert Humphrey Inst. Fellow, Univ. Minnesota, 1985; Univ. Fellow, Macquarie, 1987; Snyder Lectr, Toronto, 1988. Treas., IBG, 1990–93; Vice Pres., RGS, 1993–95 and 1998–2001 (Mem. Council, 1990–2001); Chm., Council of British Geography, 1995–2000; Vice Pres. and Res. Chm., British Acad., 2001–08. Vice Pres., Inst. of Small Business and Entrepreneurship, 2004–07. Mem., Res. Awards Adv. Panel, Leverhulme Trust, 2000–07. MInstD. Murchison Award, 1982, Founder's Medal, 1998, RGS. Co-editor, Government and Policy, 2008–16 (Gen. Editor, 1982–2008); European Co-Editor, Geographical Analysis, 1985–83. *Publications:* Environmental Systems (with R. J. Chorley), 1978; Spatial Time Series, 1979; Geography of Public Finance, 1980; (ed) European Progress in Spatial Analysis, 1981; (ed with N. Wrigley) Quantitative Geography, 1981; Central Grants to Local Government, 1982; (with K. C. Tan) Optimal Control of Spatial Systems, 1984; Intergovernmental Financial Relations in Austria, 1985; (with A. G. Wilson) Mathematical Methods in Human Geography and Planning, 1985; (ed with H. Zimmermann) Local Business Taxes in Britain and Germany, 1986; (with G. Krebs) Die Wirkung Kommunaler Steuern auf die Steuerliche Belastung der Kapitalbildung, 1987; (with G. Krebs) Local Business Taxes in Britain and Germany, 1988; (ed) Territory and Administration in Europe, 1989; (ed) Decentralisation, Local Governments and Markets, 1990; (with G. Krebs) Local Economic Development Initiatives in Britain and Germany, 1991; (ed with R. C. Estall) Global Change and Challenge, 1991; (with A. McCoshan) Enterprise and Human Resource Development, 1993; (jtly) Local Empowerment and Business Services, 1994; (with G. Krebs and H. Zimmermann) Chambers of Commerce in Britain and Germany, 1994; (ed) Trade Associations in Britain and Germany, 1997; (with D. Payne) Local and Regional Economic Development, 2000; The Voice of Liverpool Business: the first chamber of commerce 1774–1796, 2010; Local Business Voice: the history of chambers of commerce 1760–2011, 2011; Entrepreneurship, Small Business and Public Policy: evolution and revolution, 2014; Documents of the First Chambers of Commerce in Britain and Ireland, 1767–1839, 2018. *Recreations:* the family, genealogy. *Address:* c/o Department of Geography, University of Cambridge, Downing Place, Cambridge CB2 3EN.

**BENNETT, Sir Ronald (Wilfred Murdoch),** 3rd Bt *cr* 1929; *b* 25 March 1930; *o s* of Sir Wilfred Bennett, 2nd Bt, and Marion Agnes, OBE (*d* 1985), *d* of late James Somervell, Sorn Castle, Ayrshire, and step *d* of late Edwin Sandys Dawes; *S* father, 1952; *m* 1st, 1953, Rose-Marie Audrey Patricia, *o d* of Major A. L. J. H. Aubépin, France and Co. Mayo, Ireland; two *d*; 2nd, 1968, Anne Keane, *d* of late Leslie George Tooker; 3rd, 1979, Angela C. Kelly. *Educ:* Wellington Coll.; Trinity Coll., Oxford. *Heir: cousin* Mark Edward Francis Bennett [*b* 5 April 1960; *m* 1995, Jayne M. Jensen (marr. diss. 1998)]. *Clubs:* Kampala, Uganda (Kampala).

**BENNETT, Timothy Mark;** Chairman, Centre of Innovation and Excellence in Livestock, since 2016; *b* Old Hill, Staffs, 18 July 1953; *s* of Roy Bennett and Betty Bennett; *m* 1976, Susan Elizabeth Davies; one *s* one *d. Educ:* Halesowen Grammar Sch.; Seale Hayne Agricultural Coll. (Dip. 1973). Farmer, nr Carmarthen, 1978–. Food Standards Agency: Mem. Bd, 2007–17; Acting Chm., 2013–15; Chm., 2015–16; Dep. Chm., 2012–13, 2016–17. Pres., NFU, 2004–06 (Dep. Pres., 1998–2004); Vice Pres., COPA, 2005–06; Chm., DairyCo, 2007–14. Member: Agricl Land Tribunal (Wales), 1990–; Policy Issues Council, Inst. of Grocery Distribution, 2004–06; Agricl and Horticl Develt Bd, 2007–13; Trustee: Farming and Wildlife Adv. Gp, 2008–10; Organic Res. Centre, 2017–. FRAGS 2010. *Recreations:* reading, gardening, walking, West Bromwich Albion Football Club. *Address:* Derwendeg Farm, Maesybont, Llanelli, Carmarthenshire SA14 7HG. *T:* (01558) 668238. *E:* timbennett238@gmail.com. *Club:* Farmers (Vice Chm., 2016; Chm., 2017).

**BENNETT, Vivienne Jane,** CBE 2016; Chief Nurse, Public Health England, and Principal Adviser to Government on Public Health Nursing, since 2015; *b* London, 24 Sept. 1957; *d* of Anthony and Jean Willis; *m* 1978, Timothy Bennett; one *s* one *d. Educ:* Wheatley Park Sch.; Oxford Sch. of Nursing (RGN); Oxford Poly. (HVCert); Open Univ. (BA); Sch. of Advanced Urban Studies, Bristol Univ. (MSc Health and Social Policy). Nurse, 1979–; Health Visitor, 1981–; Dir of Nursing, S Warks Combined Care Trust, 2000–02, S Warks PCT, 2002–07; Dep. Chief Nursing Officer, 2007–12, Dir of Nursing, 2012–15, DoH; Dir of Nursing, PHE, 2013–15. Vis. Prof., KCL, 2011–. Fellow: Queen's Nursing Inst., 2009; Inst. of Health Visiting, 2013. Hon. FKC 2013. Hon. DBA Coventry, 2012; Hon. LLD Bristol, 2015. *Recreations:* power walking, travel. *Address:* Public Health England, Wellington House, 133–155 Waterloo Road, SE1 8UG.

**BENNETT, William;** QC 2019; *b* Islington, 11 Jan. 1964; *s* of William Percival Bennett and Joyce May Bennett; *m* 1998, Judith Carmel Hagerty; one *s* one *d. Educ:* Bancroft's Sch.; Univ. of Liverpool (BA Hist.). Called to the Bar, Inner Temple, 1994; in practice as a barrister, specialising in libel and privacy law. Pres., Liverpool Univ. Guild of Undergraduates, 1985–86. *Recreations:* walking, cycling. *Address:* 5RB Chambers, 5 Gray's Inn Square, Gray's Inn, WC1R 5AH. *T:* (020) 7242 2902. *E:* williambennett@5rb.com.

**BENNETT, Zai;** Director of Programmes, Sky UK and Ireland, since 2016; *b* London, 5 May 1974; *s* of Alan Bennett and Raesa Nursey (*née* Lycholit); *m* 2007, Penny White; one *s* one *d. Educ:* Goffs Sch., Cheshunt; Queen Mary Coll., Univ. of London (BA Hist. and Politics; MA Contemp. British Hist.). Scheduler: Carlton TV, 1996–97; Channel 5, 1997–98; Planning Manager, ITV2, 1998–2001; Hd of Programme Strategy Digital Channels, ITV, 2001–06; Controller, ITV2, 2006–09; Dir, Digital Channels and Acquisitions, ITV, 2009–11; Controller, BBC Three, 2011–14; Dir, Sky Atlantic, 2014–16. *Recreation:* impersonating primates for children. *Address:* c/o Sky Broadcasting, 1, 8 Sky Central, Grant Way, Isleworth TW7 5QD.

**BENNETT-JONES, Peter,** CBE 2014; Chairman: PBJ Management, since 1988; Burning Bright Productions, since 2012; *b* 11 March 1955; *s* of late Dr Nicholas and of Ruth Bennett-Jones; *m* 1990, Alison E. Watts; two *s* one *d. Educ:* Winchester Coll.; Magdalene Coll., Cambridge (MA Law). Director: Oxford and Cambridge Shakespeare Co. Ltd, 1977–82; Pola Jones Assocs, 1977–82; Managing Director: Talkback, 1982–86; Corporate Communications Consultants Ltd, 1986–88; Chairman: Tiger Television, 1988–2011; Tiger Aspect Prodns, 1993–2011; Tiger Aspect Pictures, 1999–2011. Production credits include: Mr Bean; The Vicar of Dibley; Harry Enfield; Billy Elliot; Our House (Olivier Award, 2003). Chm., Comic Relief, 1998–2013. Member: Council, RADA, 2007–10; Bd, RNT, 2010–18. Gov., Rugby Sch., 2009–17; Trustee: Arnold Foundn, 2007–15 (Chm., 2009–15); Liverpool Playhouse-Everyman, 2014–; Save the Children (UK), 2015–19 (Chm., 2015–19). FRTS 2009. Hon Fellow, Bangor Univ., 2008. Special Award, BAFTA, 2011; Lifetime Achievement Award, RTS, 2011. Hon. Golden Rose of Montreux, 1999. *Recreation:* simply messing about in boats. *Address:* (office) 22 Rathbone Street, W1T 1LG; 8 Rawlinson Road, Oxford OX2 6UE. *T:* (01865) 515414. *Clubs:* Oxford and Cambridge, Groucho, Soho House.

**BENNETTS, Denise Margaret Mary;** Co-Founder and Director, Bennetts Associates Architects, since 1987; *b* 26 Jan. 1953; *d* of James and Agnes Smith; *m* 1974, Robert John, (Rab), Bennetts, *qv*; one *s* one *d. Educ:* Heriot-Watt Univ./Edinburgh Coll. of Art (BArch Hons 1976; DipArch 1977). RIBA 1979. Casson Conder Partnership, 1978–88. Major projects include: Brighton Central Liby; Wessex Water Operations Centre, Bath; BT Headquarters, Edinburgh; Hampstead Th., London. Assessor: Civic Trust Awards, 1997–; RIBA Awards, 2005. *Address:* Bennetts Associates Architects, 1 Rawstorne Place, EC1V 7NL. *T:* (020) 7520 3300, *Fax:* (020) 7520 3333. *E:* denise.bennetts@bennettsassociates.com.

**BENNETTS, Philip James;** QC 2011; a Principal Crown Advocate, since 2009; *b* Weiburg, Germany, 10 June 1962; *s* of Col Michael Bennetts and Bridget Bron-Bennetts; *m* 1994, Jill Mathews; one *s* one *d. Educ:* Kingswood Sch.; Brunel Univ. (LLB Hons). Called to the Bar, Lincoln's Inn, 1986; in practice as a barrister, QEB Hollis Whiteman Chambers, 1988–2009. *Recreations:* riding, shooting, long distance running. *E:* philip.bennetts@cps.gsi.gov.uk.

**BENNETTS, Robert John, (Rab),** OBE 2003; Co-Founder and Director, Bennetts Associates Architects, since 1987; *b* 14 April 1953; *s* of Frank Vivian Bennetts and Frances Mary Bennetts; *m* 1974, Denise Margaret Mary Smith (*see* D. M. M. Bennetts); one *s* one *d. Educ:* Heriot-Watt Univ./Edinburgh Coll. of Art (BArch Hons 1976; DipArch 1977). RIBA 1979. Architect, Arup Associates, 1977–87. Major projects include: Powergen HQ, 1994; Wessex Water Offices, 2000; Hampstead Th., 2003; Brighton Central Liby, 2005; New Street Square, City of London, 2003; Royal Shakespeare Th., Stratford upon Avon, 2005; Edinburgh Univ. Potterrow develt, Informatics Forum, 2008, Data Technol. Inst., 2018; private house, Cumbria, 2016; offices, Chancery Lane, 2016; Woolwich Creative District, 2019; current project: Edinburgh Futures Inst. Member: Movt for Innovation Bd, DTI, 1999–2002; Planning Cttee, Islington LBC, 2000–03; Strategic Forum for Construction, Olympic Task Gp, 2005–; Bd, UK Green Bldg Council, 2007–16; CABE, 2010–11; Trustee, Design Council CABE, 2011–16. Chm., Competitions Cttee, RIBA, 1995–98. Dir, Sadler's Wells Th., 2006–. Contribs to BBC Radio culture progs. *Publications:* (contrib.) The Commercial Offices Handbook, 2003; Bennetts Associates - Four Commentaries, 2005; Bennetts Associates - Five Insights, 2016. *Recreations:* travel (especially with family), drawings, arts generally, watching football (Arsenal) and attempting to play. *Address:* Bennetts Associates Architects, 1 Rawstorne Place, EC1V 7NL. *T:* (020) 7520 3300, *Fax:* (020) 7520 3333. *E:* rab.bennetts@bennettsassociates.com. *Club:* Architecture.

**BENNION, Phillip;** Member (Lib Dem) West Midlands Region, European Parliament, Feb. 2012–2014 and since 2019; *b* Tamworth, 7 Oct. 1954; *m* 2000, Penny Foord. *Educ:* Queen Elizabeth Grammar Sch.; Aberdeen Univ. (BSc Agricl Botany); Newcastle Univ. (PhD Agronomy); Birmingham Univ. (BA 1st Cl. Hist. and Econ. and Social Hist.). Arable farmer, Staffs, 1985–. Member (Lib Dem): Lichfield DC, 1999–2011; Staffs CC, 2002–05. Mem., Oilseeds R&D Cttee, 1996–2002, Combinable Crops R&D Cttee, 2005–11, Cereals and Oilseeds Div., Agriculture and Horticulture Develt Bd. Vice Chm., Staffs Rural Forum, 2003–09; Founding Chm., Staffs Rural Hub, 2004–09. Contested (Lib Dem): W Midlands, EP, 2014; Birmingham Hodge Hill, 2015, 2017. Mem., Exec. Cttee, Liberal Internat. (Chm., British Gp, 2015–18; Mem., Human Rights Cttee, 2016–); Vice Chm., Federal Internat. Relns Cttee, Lib Dems, 2017–19. *Address:* European Parliament, 60 Rue Wiertz, 1047 Brussels, Belgium.

**BENSBERG, Mark;** HM Diplomatic Service; Deputy Head of Mission, Oslo, since 2017; *b* 19 July 1962; *s* of Anthony Charles Bensberg and Ann Bensberg; *m* 1991, Jacqueline Margaret Campbell; one *d. Educ:* Tiffin Sch. Entered FCO, 1980; Paris, 1982–85; Africa/ME floater, 1985–88; Vice-Consul, Vienna, 1988–91; FCO, 1991–94; Accra, 1994–97; Second Sec., Brussels, 1997–2000; FCO, 2000–04; Dep. Hd of Mission, Kinshasa, 2004–06; High Comr, Namibia, 2007–11; Dep. Dir, Estates and Security Directorate, FCO, 2011–14; Ambassador to Côte d'Ivoire, 2014–16. *Recreations:* cooking, photography, ski-ing. *Address:* c/o Foreign and Commonwealth Office, King Charles Street, SW1A 2AH.

**BENSON, Charles Jefferis Woodburn;** QC 2010; barrister; Proprietor: Benson Ingram Law LLP; Praxis Professional Services Ltd; *b* Salisbury, Wilts, 28 Feb. 1962; *s* of Sir Christopher (John) Benson, *qv*; partner, Rachel Elizabeth Temple; one *s*. *Educ:* Cheltenham Coll.; Dundee Univ. (BBA Hons 1985); Wolfson Coll., Cambridge (BA Tripos 1987; LLM 1988). Called to the Bar, Middle Temple, 1990; in practice as barrister, specialising in commercial and quasi criminal law, civil and criminal recovery. Member: Amnesty Internat.; Liberty; Bar Pro Bono Unit. Freeman: City of London; Watermen and Lightermen's Co., 2006. *Publications:* Marine Environmental Law (with John Bates), 1993. *Recreations:* fishing, river restoration, Greek language and culture, boating, travel, literature and poetry (especially Russian), film, cinema, cat lover, being outdoors. *Address:* Benson Ingram Law LLP, 28 Queen Street, EC4R 1BB; Thomas More Chambers, 7 Lincoln's Inn Fields, WC2A 3BP. *E:* charles.bensonqc@bensoningram.com.

**BENSON, Sir Christopher (John),** Kt 1988; DL; FRICS; Chairman, Cross London Rail Links Ltd, 2001–04; *b* 20 July 1933; *s* of Charles Woodburn Benson and Catherine Clara (*née* Bishton); *m* 1960, Margaret Josephine, OBE, JP, DL, *d* of Ernest Jefferies Bundy; two *s*. *Educ:* Worcester Cathedral King's Sch.; Thames Nautical Trng Coll., HMS Worcester. FRICS. Cadet, Union Castle Mail Steamship Co. (Midshipman, RNR, 1949–51); Ordinary Seaman, RN, 1951–52; Sub-Lieut, RNVR, 1952–56. Chartered surveyor and agricl auctioneer, Worcs, Herefords, Wilts, Dorset, Hants, 1953–64; Dir, Arndale Develts Ltd, 1965–69; Chm., Dolphin Develts Ltd, 1969–71; Man. Dir, 1976–88, Chm., 1988–93, MEPC; Chairman: The Boots Company, 1990–94 (Dir, 1989–94); Sun Alliance Gp, 1993–96 (Dir, 1988; Dep. Chm., 1992–93); Costain plc, 1993–96; Albright & Wilson, 1995–99; Dep. Chm., Thorn Lighting Gp, 1994–98. Dir, House of Fraser plc, 1982–86; Chm., Reedpack Ltd, 1989–90. Chairman: LDDC, 1984–88; Housing Corp., 1990–94; Funding Agency for Schs, 1994–97. Pres., British Property Fedn, 1981–83; Chm., Property Adv. Gp to DoE, 1988–90; Pres., London Chamber of Commerce and Industry, 2000–01 (Hon. Vice Pres., 2001–); Mem. Council, CBI, 1990–97; Mem., Takeover Panel, 1994–2002. Mem., Adv. Bd, Cathedral plc, 2013–15. Dir, Royal Opera House, 1984–92. Chm., Britain-Australia Soc., 2007–09 (Chm., Educn Trust, 2012–17; Pres., 2017–). Chm., Civic Trust, 1985–90; Trustee: Metropolitan Police Museum, 1986–2011; Sea Cadets Assoc., 2002–05; Marine Soc. and Sea Cadets, 2005–09 (Hon. Vice Pres., 2009–); Vice Pres., Macmillan Cancer Relief (formerly Cancer Relief Macmillan Fund), 1991–; Pres.'s Rep. Vice Pres., RSA, 1992–97; Pres., Nat. Deaf Children's Soc., 1995–; Chm., Coram (formerly Coram Family), 2005–08 (Hon. Vice Pres., 2008–). Patron: Changing Faces, 1993–; River Bourne Community Farm, 2010–; Friends of Erlestoke Prison, 2012–; Wessex Medical Res., 2016–. Mem. Council, Marlborough Coll., 1982–90; Gov., Inns of Court Sch. of Law, 1996–2001 (Principal, 2000–01). Freeman: City of London, 1975; Co. of Watermen and Lightermen, 1985 (Master, 2004–05); Liveryman: Co. of Gold and Silver Wyre Drawers, 1975; Hon. Co. of Air Pilots (formerly GAPAN), 1981; Co. of Chartered Surveyors, 1984–2017; Mem., Hon. Co. of Master Mariners, 2016 (Associate, 2012–16). High Sheriff of Wilts, 2002. DL Greater London, 2005. Lay Canon, Salisbury Cathedral, 2000–10, now Lay Canon Emeritus. FRSA 1984. Hon. FRCPath 1992; Hon. FCIOB 1992. Hon. Fellow: Wolfson Coll., Cambridge, 1990; Univ. of Southampton, 2014. Hon. Bencher, Middle Temple, 1984. Hon. DSc: City, 2000; Bradford, 2001. *Recreations:* farming, aviation, opera, ballet. *Address:* 2, 50 South Audley Street, W1K 2QE. *T:* (020) 7629 2398. *E:* sircjbenson@me.com. *Club:* Garrick.
*See also C. J. W. Benson.*

**BENSON, David Holford;** Senior Adviser, Stonehage Fleming (formerly Fleming Family & Partners), since 2002; *b* 26 Feb. 1938; *s* of Sir Rex Benson, DSO, MVO, MC, and Lady Leslie Foster Benson; *m* 1964, Lady Elizabeth Mary Charteris, *d* of 12th Earl of Wemyss and March, KT; one *s* two *d*. *Educ:* Eton Coll.; Madrid. CIGEM (CIGasE 1989). Shell Transport & Trading, 1957–63; Kleinwort Benson Gp, subseq. Dresdner Kleinwort Benson Gp, 1963–2004: Vice-Chm., 1989–92; non-exec. Dir, 1992–98; Chm., Charter European Trust, 1992–2003. Non-executive Director: Rouse Co., 1987–2004; BG Group plc (formerly British Gas), 1988–2004; Dover Corp., 1995–2014; Daniel Thwaites plc, 1998–2006; Murray Internat. Investment Trust, 2000–09; Vice Chm., Leach Internat. (formerly Leach Relais), 1992–2004. Chairman: COIF Charities Funds (formerly Charities Official Investment Fund), 1984–2005; Trustees, Edward James Foundn, 2002–09 (Trustee, 1996–2011); Fleming-Wyfold Art Foundn, 2010–; Trustee, UK Historic Bldg Preservation Trust, 1996–2001. Hon. RWS 2018. *Recreation:* painting. *Address:* Stonehage Fleming, 15 Suffolk Street, SW1Y 4HG; Cucumber Farm, Singleton, Chichester, W Sussex PO18 0HG. *Clubs:* White's, English-Speaking Union.

**BENSON, Ven. George Patrick, (Paddy);** Archdeacon of Hereford, 2011–18, now Archdeacon Emeritus; *b* Derby, 26 June 1949; *s* of George and Barbara Benson; *m* 1974, Eleanor Silver; one *s* two *d*. *Educ:* Bemrose Sch., Derby; Leighton Park Sch., Reading; Christ Church, Oxford (BA 1970); Trinity Coll., Bristol (BD Univ. of London 1977); All Nations Christian Coll., St John's Coll., Nottingham; Open Univ. (MPhil 1994). Editl Asst, Marcham Manor Press, 1971–74; Dir of Academic Studies, St Andrew's Coll., Kabare, Kenya, 1979–86; Publications Sec. and Dir of Communications, Dio. of Mt Kenya East, 1987–89; ordained deacon, 1991, priest, 1992; Curate, St Mary Upton, Wirral, 1991–95; Vicar, Christ Church, Barnston, Wirral, 1995–2010. Hon. Canon, Chester, 2009, Emeritus, 2011. *Publications:* (ed) Origen as Apologist by Dora Pym; numerous chapters in works on mission theology and politics in Kenya; contrib. to Expository Times, Evangelical Fellowship in the Anglican Communion Bulletin. *Recreations:* gardening, walking, following Derby County and Tranmere Rovers. *Address:* 26 West Park Drive, Leeds LS16 5BL. *T:* 07946 565697. *E:* muhunjia@aol.com.

**BENSON, Glenwyn;** Controller, BBC Knowledge (formerly Factual TV), 2003–07; *b* 23 Nov. 1947; *d* of late Tudor David, OBE and Nancy David; *m* 1973, Dr Ian Anthony Benson; one *s* one *d*. *Educ:* Nonsuch County Grammar Sch. for Girls, Cheam; Girton Coll., Cambridge (MA); Harvard Univ. (Frank Knox Fellow). Dep. Editor, Weekend World, LWT, 1986–88; BBC: Editor: On the Record, 1990–92; Panorama, 1992–95; Head: of Commng, Adult Educn, 1995–97; of Science, 1997–2000; Controller, Specialist Factual, 2000–01; Jt Dir, Factual and Learning, 2001–03; Mem., Exec. Cttee, 2001–03. Creative Lead, BBC response to OFCOM review of Public Service Broadcasting, 2007–09. Mem., RTS, 2005–. Gov., Nat. Film and Television Sch., 2001–09. FRSA. Hon. FRTS 2008. *Recreations:* gardening, music.

**BENSON, Gordon Mitchell,** OBE 2000; RA 2000; FRIAS; Partner, Benson+Forsyth, architects, established 1978; *b* 5 Oct. 1946; *s* of William Benson and Gavina Dewar (*née* Mitchell); one *s* one *d*. *Educ:* Univ. of Strathclyde; Architectural Assoc. Sch. of Architecture (AA Dip). SADG; FRIAS; ARIBA. London housing projects, Camden Council, 1968–78. Prof. of Architecture, Strathclyde Univ., 1986–90; Vis. Prof., Edinburgh Univ., 1991–96. Mem., Royal Fine Art Commn for Scotland, 1993. *Built work:* Branch Hill Housing, 1974; Mansfield Rd Housing, 1975; Lambie St Housing, 1975; Maiden Lane, 1976; Marico Furniture Workshop and Residence, 1979; Boarbank Oratory, 1985; Physio Room, Cumbria, 1986; Pavilion, Glasgow Garden Fest., 1989; Machi Nakao: The Divided House, Jyohanna Mus., Japan, 1994; Gall. 22 Admin Bldg, Mus. of Scotland, 1997; Mus. of Scotland, 1998; extension, Nat. Gall. of Ireland, 2000. Has won numerous awards and competitions incl. Lifetime Achievement Award, Scottish Design Awards, 2011.

*Publications:* contribs to Scotsman, Daily Telegraph, Sunday Times and professional jls incl. Architectural Rev., Architects Jl, Bldg Design, RIBA Jl, RSA Jl and overseas architectural jls.

**BENSON, Jeremy Keith;** QC 2001; a Recorder, since 1997; *b* 17 Jan. 1953; *s* of Jack Henry Benson and Renee Esther Benson; *m* 1985, Dr Karen Judith Silkoff (marr. diss. 2016); two *s* one *d*; *m* 2017, Anneli Mary Gerran Robins. *Educ:* City of London Sch.; Essex Univ. (BA Hons 1973); St Peter's Coll., Saltley, Birmingham (PGCE 1974); Inns of Court Sch. of Law. Hd of Econs Dept, King's Heath Boys' Sch., 1974–76; called to the Bar, Middle Temple, 1978, Bencher, 2002. Asst Recorder, 1993–97. Member: Cttee, Criminal Bar Assoc., 1997–2003; Qualifications Cttee, Bar Standards Bd, 2006–12. Mem., Political Cartoon Soc., 2001–. *Recreations:* cricket, football, collecting political cartoons. *Address:* 18 Red Lion Court, EC4A 3EB. *T:* (020) 7520 6000.

**BENSON, John Trevor;** QC 2001; a Recorder, since 1998; *b* 22 Jan. 1955; *s* of Trevor Benson and Ruth (*née* Oliver); *m* 1984, Sheila Patricia Riordan; one *s* two *d*. *Educ:* Liverpool Univ. (LLB Hons). Called to the Bar, Middle Temple, 1978. *Recreations:* cookery, Liverpool FC, music, Italy, gardening. *Address:* Atlantic Chambers, 4/6 Cook Street, Liverpool L2 9QU. *T:* (0151) 236 4421; 1MCB Chambers, 15 New Bridge Street, EC4V 6AU.

**BENSON, Hon. Michael D'Arcy,** MBE 2019; Chairman, Ashmore Group, 2006–15; *b* Windsor, 23 May 1943; *s* of Baron Benson, GBE; *m* 1969, Rachel Woods; one *s* two *d*. *Educ:* Eton. Dir, Lazard Bros, 1979–85; CEO, Scimitar Asset Mgt, 1985–92; Dir, Capital House, 1992–94; CEO, Invesco Asia, 1994–97; CEO, 1997–2003, Chm., 2003–05, Invesco Global; Vice Chm., Amvescap, 2001–05. Chm., Hayaat Gp, 2012–14; Director: Border Asset Mgt, 2006–11; Morse plc, 2007–09; Trinity Street Asset Mgt, 2011– (Chm., 2016–). Dir, York Minster Fund, 2007–16; Chief Exec., York Minster Revealed, 2010–16. Trustee, St Catherine's Foundn, Windsor, 1987–94. Mem., Merchant Adventurers of York, 2017–. *Recreations:* sailing, shooting, gardening. *Address:* Grange Farm, Westow, York YO60 7NJ. *T:* (01653) 658296. *E:* mdbenson43@gmail.com. *Clubs:* Brooks's; Newport Sailing (S Wales).

**BENSON, Neil Winston,** OBE 2004; FCA; Senior Partner, Lewis Golden LLP (formerly Lewis Golden & Co.), Chartered Accountants, since 1980; *b* 17 Oct. 1937; *s* of late John William Benson and Rebecca (*née* Winston); *m* 1960, Ann Margery Licht; one *s* one *d*. *Educ:* Clifton Coll. FCA 1961. Articled clerk with Hartleys, Wilkins and Flew, 1955–60; qualified as chartered accountant, 1961; Lewis Golden & Co.: Sen. Clerk, 1961–63; Partner, 1963–. Director: Davis Service Gp (formerly Godfrey Davis) Plc, 1981–2005 (Chm., 1990–2001); Shaftesbury Plc, 1986–2003; Moss Bros Gp Plc, 1989–2001 (Chm., 1990–2001); Business Post Gp Plc, 1993–2001 (Chm., 1995–2001). Royal Shakespeare Company: Gov. and Main Bd Dir, 1997–2008; Hon. Gov., 2011–; Corp. of London Assessor, 1995–97. Hon. Treasurer and Trustee: Cystic Fibrosis Res. Trust, 1990–99; Foundn for Liver Res. (formerly Liver Res. Trust), 1991–2005. *Recreations:* Real tennis, golf, watching Rugby, theatre, my Alvis. *Address:* 40 Queen Anne Street, W1G 9EL. *T:* (020) 7580 7313. *Clubs:* Garrick, MCC, Saints and Sinners (Chm., 1979 and 2009; Life Pres.); Lake Nona Golf (Orlando, Fla).

**BENSON, Ven. Paddy;** *see* Benson, Ven. G. P.

**BENSON, His Honour Peter Charles;** a Circuit Judge, 2001–16; *b* 16 June 1949; *s* of Robert Benson and Dorothy Benson (*née* Cartman). *Educ:* Bradford Grammar Sch.; Birmingham Univ. (Schol.; BSocSc). Called to the Bar, Middle Temple, 1975; in practice at the Bar, Leeds, 1975–2001. A Recorder of the Crown Court, 1995–2001; Liaison Judge: for Calderdale Magistrates' Ct, 2003–16; for Huddersfield Magistrates' Ct, 2003–12. Mem., Parole Bd, 2003–09. Trustee, Internat. Spinal Res., 2019–. *Recreations:* golf, wine, travel. *Clubs:* East India; Bradford; Ilkley Golf (Pres., 2016–17), Ganton Golf, Ilkley Bowling, Bar Golfing Society (Capt., 2018).

**BENSON, Richard Anthony;** QC 1995; a Recorder, 1995–2018; *b* 20 Feb. 1946; *s* of Douglas Arthur Benson and Muriel Alice Benson (*née* Fairfield); *m* 1st, 1967, Katherine Anne Smith (marr. diss. 1997); one *s* two *d*; 2nd, 2000, Sarah Levina Gaunt (marr. diss. 2004); three *s* one *d*; 3rd, 2006, Prof. Alison Jane Simmons; twin *s*. *Educ:* St Piran's Prep. Sch.; Wrekin Coll.; Coll. of Law; Inns of Court Sch. of Law. Sailing and overland expedition to Africa, 1964–65; articled to Bircham & Co. (Solicitors), 1965–67; joined Inner Temple as student, 1968; adventuring in Sudan, 1969–70; called to the Bar, Inner Temple, 1974, Bencher, 2013; in practice on Midland (formerly Midland and Oxford) Circuit, specialising in defending heavyweight criminal cases and courts martial; Asst Recorder, 1990–95. Mem., Steering Cttee for tape recording of police interviews, 1983–84. Consultant, Justice for Agriculture, Zimbabwe, 2003; Personal security aide to Roy Bennett, MP, Zimbabwe, 2003; Inter Univ. Moot advocacy consultant, 2007–; part-time Chm. of disciplinary cttees for political parties, 2014; criminal evidence workshops consultant, Oxford Brookes Univ., 2015–. Trustee, Forgotten Veterans UK, 2017–. *Recreations:* parachuting 1969–75, private pilot's licence 1982, ski-ing poorly but with enthusiasm, the plays of William Shakespeare and his contemporaries, deflating pomposity, writing THAT book! *Address:* The Manse, 18 Temple Street, Brill, Bucks HP18 9SX. *T:* (01844) 237959. *Club:* Bar Yacht.

**BENSON, Prof. Trevor Mark,** PhD, DSc; FREng; Professor of Optoelectronics, University of Nottingham, since 1996; *b* Sheffield, 12 March 1958; *s* of Frank Benson and Kathleen Benson; *m* 1983, Margaret; two *s*. *Educ:* Univ. of Sheffield (BSc Hons Physics 1979; PhD Electronic and Electrical Engrg 1982); Univ. of Nottingham (DSc 2005). CEng 1996; FIET 2001; FInstP 2002; CPhys 2002; FREng 2005. Lectr, Dept of Electrical and Electronic Engrg, University Coll. Cardiff, 1982–89; University of Nottingham: Sen. Lectr, 1989–94, Reader, 1994–96, in Photonics; Hd, Dept of Electrical and Electronic Engrg, 2008–11; Dir, George Green Inst. for Electromagnetics Res., 2011–16. Vis. Prof. of Photonics, Center for Photonics and Smart Materials, Zewail City of Sci. and Technol., Egypt, 2018–. Fellow, Eur. Optical Soc., 2018. *Publications:* (with F. A. Benson) Fields, Waves and Transmission Lines, 1991; (jtly) Non-Stationary Electromagnetics, 2012, 2nd edn 2018; (ed jtly) Recent Trends in Computational Photonics, 2017; over 325 res. articles in jls. *Recreations:* music, gardening, walking. *Address:* Department of Electrical and Electronic Engineering, Faculty of Engineering, University of Nottingham, University Park, Nottingham NG7 2RD. *T:* (0115) 951 5589. *E:* trevor.benson@nottingham.ac.uk.

**BENT, Margaret (Hilda),** CBE 2008; PhD; FBA 1993; musicologist; Senior Research Fellow, All Souls College, Oxford, 1992–2008, now Emeritus Fellow; *b* 23 Dec. 1940; *d* of late Horace Bassington and Miriam (*née* Simpson); *m*; one *s* one *d*; partner, Myles Fredric Burnyeat, *qv*. *Educ:* Haberdashers' Aske's Acton Sch.; Girton Coll., Cambridge (organ schol.; BA 1962; MusB 1963; MA; PhD 1969; Hon. Fellow 2007). Lectr, then Sen. Lectr, Music Dept, Goldsmiths' Coll., London Univ., 1972–75; Vis. Prof., then full Prof. and Chm., Music Dept, Brandeis Univ., 1975–81; Prof., later Chm., Music Dept, Princeton Univ., 1981–92. Guggenheim Fellow, 1983–84; Dist. Sen. Fellow, Sch. of Advanced Studies, London Univ., 2010. Visiting Professor: Univ. of Chicago, 2005; Harvard Univ., 2009; Univ. of Basel, 2009–10. Pres., Amer. Musicological Soc., 1984–86 (Corresp. Mem.,

1995). MAE 1995. FRHistS 1995; FSA 2002. For. Hon. Mem., Amer. Acad. of Arts and Scis, 1994; Corresp. Fellow, Medieval Acad. of America, 2004; Internat. Mem., Amer. Philosophical Soc., 2013; Corresp. Mem., Accademia Olimpica Vicenza, 2017. Hon. DMus Glasgow, 1997; Hon. DFA Notre Dame, 2002; Dr *hc* Montreal, 2010. F. Ll. Harrison Medal, Soc. for Musicol. in Ireland, 2007; Claude V. Palisca Award, Amer. Musicol Soc., 2009; Derek Allen Prize, BA, 2016. *Publications*: (ed jtly) Old Hall Manuscript, vols I and II 1969, vol III 1973; (ed jtly) John Dunstable, Complete Works, 1970; (ed) Four Anonymous Masses, 1979; Dunstaple, 1981; (ed jtly) Ciconia, 1985; (ed) Rossini, Il Turco in Italia, 1988; Fauvel Studies, 1998; Counterpoint, Composition and Musica Ficta, 2002; Bologna Q15: the making and remaking of a musical manuscript, 2008; (ed jtly) A Veneto Liber Cantus, 2012; Magister Jacobus de Ispania, Author of the Speculum musicae, 2015; (contrib.) New Grove Dictionary of Music and Musicians, 1980; contrib. Musica Disciplina, Jl of Amer. Musicol Soc., Early Music Hist. etc. *Address*: All Souls College, Oxford OX1 4AL. *T*: (01865) 279379.

**BENTALL, (Leonard) Edward;** DL; FCA; Chairman, Bentalls, 1982–2001; *b* 26 May 1939; *s* of late Leonard Edward Rowan Bentall and Adelia Elizabeth Bentall (*née* Hawes); *m* 1964, Wendy Ann Daniel; three *d*. *Educ*: Stowe School. Articled Clerk, Dixon Wilson Tubbs & Gillett, 1958–64. Bentalls, 1965–2001: Management Accountant, Merchandise Controller, Merchandise Dir, Man. Dir, Chm. and Man. Dir, Chm. and Chief Exec. Nonexec. Dir, Associated Independent Stores, 1979–82. Pres., Textile Benevolent Assoc., 1991–95. Non-exec. Director: Kingston Hosp. Trust, 1990–98 (Dep. Chm., 1998); Riverside Radio, 1996–99. Governor: Brooklands Tech. Coll., 1981–90; Kingston Coll., 1990; Kingston Grammar Sch., 1992–2002; Patron, Bedelsford Sch. Assoc., 1997–2008. Trustee: Kingston and Dist Sea Cadet Corps TS Steadfast, 1966– (Chm., Unit Mgt Cttee, 1994–2004); Spirit of Normandy Trust, 2000–; Chm. Bd of Trustees, Shooting Star Trust Children's Hospice Appeal, 2000–03. Vice-Pres., Surrey PGA, 1995–. Steward, Nat. Greyhound Racing Club, 1998–2007 (Sen. Steward, 2005–07). Hon. Life Mem., Tamesis Sailing Club, 1997. FInstD. DL Greater London, 1999. *Address*: Heneage Farm, Windlesham Road, Chobham, Woking, Surrey GU24 8QR. *T*: (01276) 858256. *Clubs*: Naval, MCC, Saints and Sinners; Surrey Cricket.

**BENTHALL, Jonathan Charles Mackenzie;** social researcher; Hon. Research Associate, Department of Anthropology, University College London, since 2003 (Hon. Research Fellow, 1994–2003); Director, Royal Anthropological Institute, 1974–2000, Director Emeritus, 2015; *b* Calcutta, 12 Sept. 1941; *s* of Sir Arthur Paul Benthall, KBE and Mary Lucy, (Mollie), Pringle; *m* 1975, Zamira, *d* of Baron Menuhin, OM, KBE; two *s* and one step *s*. *Educ*: Eton (KS); King's Coll., Cambridge (MA). Sec., Inst. of Contemporary Arts, 1971–73. Ed., Anthropol. Today, 1985–2000. Member: UK Adv. Cttee, 1981–87, Overseas Adv. Cttee, 1985–86, 1990–96, Council, 1987–90, Assembly, 1990–98, SCF; Assoc. of Social Anthropologists, 1983; Trustee: Internat. NGO Trng and Res. Centre, 1997–2006 (Chm., 1998–2003); Alliance of Religions and Conservation, 1997–2004. Associate Fellow, Humanitarian and Conflict Response Inst., Univ. of Manchester, 2010–. Co-Dir, Gulf Charities Workshop, Univ. of Cambridge, 2012. Advr, Islamic Charities Project (formerly Montreux Initiative), Swiss Federal Dept of Foreign Affairs, 2005–13. Expert testimony in legal cases, 2006–14. Anthropology in Media Award, Amer. Anthropol. Assoc., 1993; Patron's Medal, RAI, 2001. Chevalier de l'Ordre des Arts et des Lettres (France), 1973. *Publications*: Science and Technology in Art Today, 1972; (ed) Ecology: the Shaping Enquiry, 1972; (ed) The Limits of Human Nature, 1973; (ed jtly) The Body as a Medium of Expression, 1975; The Body Electric: patterns of western industrial culture, 1976; Disasters, Relief and the Media, 1993, 2nd edn 2010; (ed) The Best of Anthropology Today, 2002; (jtly) The Charitable Crescent: politics of aid in the Muslim world, 2003, 2nd edn 2009; Returning to Religion: why a secular age is haunted by faith, 2008; (ed jtly) Gulf Charities and Islamic Philanthropy in the "Age of Terror" and Beyond, 2014; Islamic Charities and Islamic Humanism in Troubled Times, 2016. *Recreations*: listening to music, swimming, mountain walking, books, writing light verse. *Address*: Downingbury Farmhouse, Pembury, Tunbridge Wells, Kent TN2 4AD. *Club*: Athenæum.

**BENTHAM, Howard Lownds;** QC 1996; a Recorder, since 1988; *b* 26 Feb. 1948; *s* of William Foster Bentham and Elsie Bentham; *m* 1978, Elizabeth Anne Owen; one *s*. *Educ*: Malvern Coll.; Liverpool Univ. (LLB). Called to the Bar, Gray's Inn, 1970; Asst Recorder, 1985–88. *Recreations*: motor racing, scuba diving, watching wildlife. *Address*: c/o St Johns Buildings, 24a–28 St John Street, Manchester M3 4DJ. *T*: (0161) 214 1500.

**BENTHAM-MacLEARY, Donald Whyte,** OBE 2004; Guest Principal Répétiteur to the Principal Artists, Royal Ballet (Répétiteur, 1981–94; Senior Répétiteur, 1994–99; Principal Répétiteur, 1999–2002); *b* Glasgow, 22 Aug. 1937; *s* of Donald Herbert MacLeary, MPS, and Jean Spiers (*née* Leslie); adopted surname Bentham-MacLeary, 2006; civil partnership 2006, Trevor Bentham. *Educ*: Inverness Royal Academy; The Royal Ballet School. Principal male dancer, 1959–78, Ballet Master, 1978–81, Royal Ballet. *Classical Ballets*: (full length) Swan Lake, Giselle, 1958; Sleeping Beauty, Cinderella, Sylvia, 1959; Ondine, La Fille Mal Gardée, 1960; (centre male rôle) in Ashton's Symphonic Variations, 1962; Sonnet Pas de Trois, 1964; Romeo and Juliet, 1965; Eugene Onegin, Stuttgart, 1966; Apollo, 1966; Nutcracker, 1968; Swan Lake with N. Makarova, 1972. *Creations*: (1954–74): Solitaire, The Burrow, Danse Concertante, Antigone, Diversions, Le Baiser de la Fée, Jabez and the Devil, Raymonda Pas de Deux (for Frederick Ashton), two episodes in Images of Love; Song of the Earth; Lilac Garden (revival); Jazz Calendar; Raymonda (for Nureyev); The Man in Kenneth MacMillan's Checkpoint; leading rôle in Concerto no 2 (Balanchine's Ballet Imperial, renamed); Elite Syncopations, 1974; Kenneth MacMillan's Four Seasons Symphony; the Prince in Cinderella; Catabutte in Sleeping Beauty, 2003. Toured Brazil with Royal Ballet, Spring 1973. Guest dancer, Scottish Ballet, 1979. *Recreations*: reading, theatre, records (all types), riding, swimming.
See also A. R. MacLeary.

**BENTINCK, Alice Yvonne,** MBE 2016; Co-Founder and Chief Product Officer, Entrepreneur First, since 2011; *b* Salisbury, 23 July 1986; *d* of Mark Bentinck and Miranda Bentinck. *Educ*: Godolphin Sch., Salisbury; Univ. of Nottingham (BA Hons Mgt Studies). Business Analyst, McKinsey & Co., 2009–11. Co-Founder and non-exec. Dir, Code First: Girls, 2011–. Mem., Computer Sci. Industrial Liaison Bd, Imperial Coll. London, 2015–. *Address*: Entrepreneur First, Block L, The Biscuit Factory, Clements Road, SE16 4DG. *T*: 07780 223625. *E*: alice@joinef.com.

**BENTINCK, Timothy;** see Portland, Earl of.

**BENTINCK van SCHOONHETEN, Baron Willem Oswald;** Ambassador of the Netherlands to the Court of St James's, 1999–2003 (and concurrently to Iceland, 1999–2002); *b* 9 March 1940; *s* of late Baron Oswald François Bentinck van Schoonheten and Meta Hendrica Bentinck van Schoonheten (*née* van der Slooten); *m* 1974, Corinne C. Elink Schuurman; two *s* one *d*. *Educ*: Univ. of Utrecht (Master of Law). Entered Netherlands Foreign Service, 1968; Buenos Aires, 1968–71; Rome, 1971–73; Internat. Relns Dept, Min. of Foreign Affairs, 1973–76; Perm. Rep., NY, 1976–79; Economic Counsellor, Moscow, 1979–81; Counsellor and Dep. Hd of Mission, Ottawa, 1981–84; Hd of Political Affairs Section and Dep. Dir, Atlantic Co-operation and Security Affairs Dept, Min. of Foreign Affairs, 1984–87; Minister and Deputy Head of Mission: Moscow, 1987–90; Washington, 1990–94; Ambassador to Madrid, 1994–98. Officer, Order of Orange Nassau (Netherlands), 1992; Kt, Order of Merit (Italy), 1972; Grand Cross, Order of Isabella la Católica (Spain), 1999. *Recreations*: shooting, golf, bridge. *Address*: Delistraat 59, 2585 VX Den Haag, The Netherlands. *Clubs*: Haagsche (Plaats Royaal); Royal Haagsche Golf and Country.

**BENTLEY, (Anthony) Philip;** QC 1991; Barrister, McDermott Will & Emery/Stanbrook (formerly Stanbrook & Hooper), Brussels, since 1980; *b* 5 Dec. 1948; *s* of late Kenneth Bentley and of Frances Elizabeth (*née* Scott); *m* 1980, Christine Anne-Marie Odile Bausier; two *s* two *d*. *Educ*: St George's Coll., Weybridge; St Catharine's Coll., Cambridge (MA); Faculté de droit d'Aix-en-Provence (Dip.). Called to the Bar, Lincoln's Inn, 1970. With ICI, 1973–77; Dilley & Custer, 1977–80. Dir, Bar Mutual Indemnity Fund, 1989–2003. Mem., Fondation Universitaire, Brussels. Oboist and Librarian, Orch. symphonique des étudiants, Catholic Univ. of Louvain. *Publications*: (with C. Stanbrook) Dumping and Subsidies, 2nd edn 1996; (with A. Silberston) Anti-Dumping and Countervailing Action: limits imposed by economic and legal theory, 2007. *Address*: (office) Avenue des Nerviens 9–31, 1040 Brussels, Belgium. *T*: (2) 2305059.

**BENTLEY, Rt Rev. David Edward;** Bishop of Gloucester, 1993–2003; Hon. Assistant Bishop, Diocese of Lichfield, since 2004; *b* 7 Aug. 1935; *s* of William Bentley and Florence (*née* Dalgleish); *m* 1962, Clarice Lahmers; two *s* two *d*. *Educ*: Gt Yarmouth Grammar School; Univ. of Leeds (BA English); Westcott House, Cambridge. Deacon 1960, priest 1961; Curate: St Ambrose, Bristol, 1960–62; Holy Trinity with St Mary, Guildford, 1962–66; Rector: Headley, Bordon, 1966–73; Esher, 1973–86; RD of Emly, 1977–82; Suffragan Bishop of Lynn, 1986–93; Warden, Community of All Hallows, Ditchingham, 1989–93. Hon. Canon of Guildford Cathedral, 1980. Chairman: Guildford dio. House of Clergy, 1977–86; Guildford dio. Council of Social Responsibility, 1980–86; ACCM Candidates Cttee, 1987–91; ABM Recruitment and Selection Cttee, 1991–93; ABM Ministry Develt and Deployment Cttee, 1995–98; Deployment, Remuneration and Conditions of Service Cttee, Ministry Div., Archbishops' Council, 1999–2002. Hon. PhD Gloucestershire, 2002. *Recreations*: music; sport, especially cricket; theatre, travel. *Address*: 19 Gable Croft, Lichfield WS14 9RY. *T*: (01543) 419376. *Club*: MCC.

**BENTLEY, David Jeffrey,** CB 1993; Legal Counsellor, Foreign and Commonwealth Office, 1995–97; *b* 5 July 1935; *s* of late Harry Jeffrey Bentley and Katherine (*née* Barnett). *Educ*: Watford Boys' Grammar School; New College, Oxford (BCL, MA). Called to the Bar, Lincoln's Inn, 1963; University teaching, 1957–79; Asst Parly Counsel, 1965–67; Legal Adviser's Branch, Home Office, 1979–95, Principal Asst Legal Advr, 1988–95. *Recreations*: reading, listening to music, walking. *Address*: 192 Randolph Avenue, W9 1PE. *Club*: Oxford and Cambridge.

**BENTLEY, Ven. Frank William Henry;** Archdeacon of Worcester and Canon Residentiary of Worcester Cathedral, 1984–99, now Emeritus; Chaplain to the Queen, 1994–2004; *b* 4 March 1934; *s* of Nowell and May Bentley; *m* 1st, 1957, Muriel Bland (*d* 1958); one *s*; 2nd, 1960, Yvonne Wilson (*d* 2000); two *s* one *d*; 3rd, 2006, Kathleen M. Gibbs. *Educ*: Yeovil School; King's College London (AKC). Deacon 1958, priest 1959; Curate in Shepton Mallet, 1958–62; Rector of Kingsdon with Podymore Milton and Curate-in-charge, Yeovilton, 1962–66; Rector of Babcary, 1966–82; Vicar of Wiveliscombe, 1966–76; Rural Dean of Tone, 1973–76; Vicar of St John-in-Bedwardine, Worcester, 1976–84; Rural Dean of Martley and Worcester West, 1979–84. Hon. Canon of Worcester Cathedral, 1981. Resident Chaplain, St Oswald's Hosp., Worcester, 1999–2004. *Recreations*: gardening, local history. *Address*: Willow Cottage, Station Road, Fladbury, Pershore, Worcs WR10 2QW. *T*: (01386) 861847.

**BENTLEY, Prof. George,** ChM; DSc; FRCS, FMedSci; Professor of Orthopaedic Surgery at University College London (formerly at Postgraduate Medical Federation), University of London, 1982–2002, now Emeritus Professor and Director, Institute of Orthopaedics; Hon. Consultant Orthopaedic Surgeon, Royal National Orthopaedic Hospital, Stanmore, since 1982; *b* 19 Jan. 1936; *s* of George and Doris Bentley; *m* 1960, Ann Gillian Hutchings; two *s* one *d*. *Educ*: Rotherham Grammar Sch.; Sheffield Univ. (MB, ChB, ChM; DSc 2002). FRCS 1964. House Surgeon, Sheffield Royal Infirmary, 1959–61; Lectr in Anatomy, Birmingham Univ., 1961–62; Surg. Registrar, Sheffield Royal Infirm., 1963–65; Orthopaedic Registrar, Orthopaedic Hosp., Oswestry, 1965–67; Sen. Registrar in Orthopaedics, Nuffield Orthopaedic Centre and Radcliffe Infirm., Oxford, 1967–69; Instructor in Orth., Univ. of Pittsburgh, USA, 1969–70; Lectr, 1970–71, Sen. Lectr and Reader in Orth., 1971–76, Univ. of Oxford; Prof. of Orth. and Accident Surgery, Univ. of Liverpool, 1976–82; Dir, Inst. of Orthopaedics, UC and Middx Sch. of Medicine, Univ. of London, 1982–2002. Hon. Consultant Orthopaedic Surgeon, Middlesex Hosp., 1984–2001. Eur. Ed.-in-Chief, Jl Arthroplasty, 2001–; Member, Editorial Board: Jl Bone and Jt Surgery, 1974–76, 2006–; The Knee, 1993–2004; Clinical Materials, 1993–98; Orthopaedics Internat., 1997–. Numerous lectures including: Hunterian Prof., RCS, 1972; Watson-Jones, 1996, Alan Apley Meml, 2006, Robert Jones, 2007, RCS and BOA. Chairman: Scientific Cttee, EFORT, 1995–2002; Intercollegiate Bd, Exam. in Orthopaedics UK, 1996–99. Vice-Pres., RCS, 2003–04 (Mem. Council, 1992–2004); Mem. Council, British Orthopaedic Assoc. (Pres., 1991–92); Pres., British Orthopaedic Res. Soc., 1985–87; Vice-Pres., 2002–03, Pres., 2004–06, European Fedn of Nat. Assocs of Orthopaedics and Traumatology; Member: Orthopaedic Association: Australia; NZ; SA; Eastern; Argentina; Amer. Orthopaedic and Res. Soc.; Eur. Orthopaedic Res. Soc.; SICOT; ESSKA; ISAKOS. Pres., Seddon Soc., 1996–. FMedSci 1999. FRCSE ad hominem 1999; Hon. FRSocMed 2019. Hon. Mem., French Soc. of Trauma and Orthopaedics, 1999; Hon. Fellow: Educnl Council for Foreign Medical Graduates, 1969; British Orthopaedic Assoc., 2004; Czech Orthopaedic Assoc., 2004; Eur. Fedn of Nat. Assocs of Orthopaedics and Traumatol., 2007. *Publications*: (ed) 3rd edn vols I and II, Rob and Smith Operative Surgery—Orthopaedics, 1979, 4th edn 1991; (ed) Mercer's Orthopaedic Surgery, 8th edn 1983, 9th edn 1996; (ed) European Surgical Orthopaedics and Traumatology, 2014; (jtly) Orthopaedic Study Guide Series, 2018; papers on cell-engineered cartilage grafting of joints, arthritis, accident surgery and scoliosis in leading med. and surg. jls. *Recreations*: golf, tennis, music, horology. *Address*: Royal National Orthopaedic Hospital, Stanmore, Middx HA7 4LP. *T*: (020) 8909 5532. *E*: profg@bentleyoxford.com.

**BENTLEY, Ven. Ian Robert;** Archdeacon of Lynn, since 2018; *b* Southend-on-Sea, 28 April 1955; *s* of Frank and Kathleen Bentley; *m* 1984, Caroline Margaret Hooson; one *s* one *d*. *Educ*: Westcliff High Sch. for Boys, Southend-on-Sea; Sheffield Univ. (BA Hons 1976); Sheffield City Poly. (PGCE 1978); St John's Coll., Durham Univ. (CTM 1995). Deputy Headteacher: St Gilbert's Sch., Stamford, Lincs, 1984–88; Lancaster Service Children's Sch., Minden, Germany, 1988–93; ordained deacon, 1995, priest, 1996; Curate, Mattishall, 1995–98; Rector, Earsham Gp, 1998–2006; Vicar: St Mark's with St Luke's, Oulton Broad, 2006–17; St Peter, Mancroft, Norwich, 2017–18. Hon. Canon and Chapter Canon, Norwich Cathedral, 2013–. *Recreations*: music, films, boating, reading, singing, ballroom and Latin dancing, family, cooking, supporting Norwich City FC. *Address*: Holly Tree House, Whitwell Road, Sparham, Norwich NR9 5PN. *E*: ianbentley241@gmail.com.

**BENTLEY, John Ransome;** entrepreneur, inventor and novelist; *b* 19 Feb. 1940; *m* 1st, 1960, Dorothy (marr. diss. 1969; decd); one *s* one *d*; two *d*; 2nd, 1982, Katherine Susan (marr. diss. 1986; she *d* 2011), *d* of Gerald Percy and the Marchioness of Bute; 3rd, 1990, Honore (marr. diss. 1992); 4th, 2002, Janet. *Educ:* Harrow Sch. Media entrepreneur and financier. Chairman: Barclay Securities plc, 1969–73; Intervision Video (Holdings) plc, 1980–83; Viewcall America Inc., 1995–97; Electronic Game Card Inc., 2002–05. Inventor of Internet TV (Viewcall America, 1996) and digital gaming (Electronic Game Card, 2004). *Publications:* The Royal Secret, 2015; Terrorism: the survival bible handbook, 2015. *Recreations:* living, writing, travel, politics, history. *W:* www.johnbentley.biz.

**BENTLEY, Julie;** Chief Executive, Action for Children, since 2018; *b* Chelmsford, Essex, 21 March 1969; *d* of Donald and Pamela Bentley; partner, Sean Murphy. *Educ:* Open Univ. (MBA). Dir, Corporate Services, ARP, 2000–04; Chief Executive Officer: Suzy Lamplugh Trust, 2004–08; FPA, 2008–12; Chief Exec., Girlguiding, 2012–18. Member: Internat. Women's Forum; Fawcett Soc. *Recreations:* theatre, cinema, walking, cycling. *Address:* Action for Children, 3 The Boulevard, Ascot Road, Watford WD18 8AG. *W:* www.twitter.com/JulieBentley.

**BENTLEY, Philip;** *see* Bentley, A. P.

**BENTLEY, Robert Paul,** FDSRCS, FRCS, FRCS (OMFS); Consultant Craniofacial Surgeon, since 2000, Clinical Director for Major Trauma, since 2007 and Clinical Director for Surgery, since 2013, King's College Hospital; Clinical Director for South East London, Kent and Medway Major Trauma Network, since 2013; *b* Cardiff, 16 Feb. 1963; *s* of Thomas Hamilton Bentley and Dorothy Irene Bentley; *m* 2008, Madelene Jerlmyr; one *s* one *d*. *Educ:* Whitchurch High Sch., Cardiff; Univ. of Wales Coll. of Medicine (BDS 1985; MB ChB 1992). FDSRCS 1988; FRCS 1995; FRCS (OMFS) 1999. Hse Surgeon, University Hosp. of Wales, 1992–93; SHO, Royal Gwent Hosp., 1993–94; Registrar, Queen Elizabeth Hosp., Birmingham, 1994–99; Craniofacial Fellow: Birmingham Children's Hosp., 1999–2000; Univ. of Heidelberg, 2000. *Publications:* over 20 articles in peer-reviewed jls; four book chapters. *Recreations:* cycling, tennis, sailing, football. *Address:* Department of Maxillofacial Surgery, King's College Hospital, Denmark Hill, SE5 9RS. *T:* (020) 3299 1753, *Fax:* (020) 3299 3754. *E:* robert.bentley@nhs.net.

**BENTLEY, Sarah Rosamund Irvine;** *see* Foot, S. R. I.

**BENTLY, Prof. Lionel Alexander Fiennes;** Herchel Smith Professor of Intellectual Property Law, and Director, Centre of Intellectual Property and Information Law, University of Cambridge, since 2004; Professorial Fellow, Emmanuel College, Cambridge, since 2004; *b* 2 July 1964; *s* of Lionel Charles Warwick Bently and Helen Joy Bently (*née* Wright); partner, Clair Milligan. *Educ:* Pembroke Coll., Cambridge (BA Law). Prof. of Law, KCL, 2002–04. Called to the Bar, Inner Temple, 2009. Door Tenant: Hogarth Chambers, Lincoln's Inn, 2004–11; 11 South Square, Gray's Inn, 2011–. *Publications:* with Brad Sherman: The Making of Modern Intellectual Property Law, 1999; Intellectual Property Law, 2001, 3rd edn 2008. *Recreations:* football (Mem., Arsenal FC), punk rock, industrial and related music. *Address:* Centre of Intellectual Property and Information Law, Faculty of Law, University of Cambridge, 10 West Road, Cambridge CB3 9DZ. *T:* (01223) 330081, *Fax:* (01223) 330086. *E:* lb329@cam.ac.uk.

**BENTON, David Michael;** Partner, since 1997, and Global Head, International Capital Markets, since 2018, Allen & Overy LLP (Global Co-Head, International Capital Markets, 2014–18); *b* Leeds, 4 March 1966; *s* of Alan and Jean Benton; *m* 1991, Mary Bull; one *s* one *d*. *Educ:* Monmouth Sch.; Bradford Grammar Sch.; Corpus Christi Coll., Cambridge (BA Hons Law 1987). Admitted as solicitor, 1990; Allen & Overy LLP: Associate, 1990–97; Hd, Derivatives and Structured Finance, 2010–14. Legal Advr to Credit Derivatives Determinations Cttee, Internat. Swaps and Derivatives Assoc., 2009–. *Recreations:* running, spending time in the Yorkshire Dales, Leeds Rhinos and New York Rangers. *Address:* Allen & Overy LLP, One Bishops Square, E1 6AD. *T:* (020) 3088 3118. *E:* david.benton@allenovery.com.

**BENTON, Joseph Edward;** JP; *b* 28 Sept. 1933; *s* of Thomas and Agnes Benton; *m* 1959, Doris Wynne; four *d*. *Educ:* St Monica's Primary and Secondary Sch.; Bootle Technical Coll. Nat. Service, RAF, 1955. Apprentice fitter and turner, 1949; former Personnel Manager, Pacific Steam Navigation Co.; Girobank, 1982–90. Councillor, Sefton Borough Council, 1970–90 (Leader, Labour Gp, 1985–90). MP (Lab) Bootle, Nov. 1990–2015. An Opposition Whip, 1994–97. Mem., Speaker's Panel of Chairmen, 1992–94, 1997–2015. Member: Select Cttee on Educn, 1997–98; NI Affairs Cttee, 2010–15; Sec., All Party Parly Pro-Life Gp, 1992–2015; Member: British/Spanish Parly Gp, 1997–2015; British/Irish Parly Gp, 1997–2015; Parly Assembly of Council of Europe, 2010–. Mem., Bd Visitors, Liverpool Prison (Walton), 1974–81. Chm. of Govs, Hugh Baird Coll. of Technology, 1972–93. Assoc. Mem., IPM, 1965; MIL 1963. JP South Sefton, 1969. KSG 2014.

**BENTON, Margaret Carole;** artist and arts consultant, since 2013; *b* 14 April 1943; *d* of late Lawrence and Mary Benton. *Educ:* The Red Maids Sch., Bristol; Univ. of Wales (BA Hons French). British Broadcasting Corporation: Radio, 1966–67; News, Paris Office, 1967–69; Schools Television, 1969–70; Gen. Features Television, 1970–71; COI (Overseas Documentaries/Co-prodns), 1971–75; BBC Television, Bristol, 1975–85; Nat. Museum of Photography, Film and Television, 1985–90; Director: Theatre Mus., V&A, 1990–2003; The Making, 2003–12. Young People's Mentor, Surrey Care Trust, 2013–16. Estab. Nat. Video Archive of Performance, V&A, 1992. Member: Theatres Adv. Council, 1991–2002; Council of Management (British Centre), Internat. Theatre Inst.; Museums Assoc.; Pres., Société Internationale des Bibliothèques et des Musées des Arts du Spectacle, 1992–96. Trustee, New Ashgate Gall., 2013–; Patron, Stroud Internat. Textiles, 2013–18. Prod and dir. numerous television documentaries and other progs for BBC. *Recreations:* painting, visual arts, theatre, opera, cinema, gardening, rural "idylling". *Address:* Summerden South, Waggoners Wells, Grayshott GU26 6DN.

**BENTON, Prof. Michael James,** PhD; FRS 2014; FGS, FLS; FRSE; Professor of Vertebrate Palaeontology, University of Bristol, since 1997 (Head, School of Biological Sciences, 2016–18); *b* 8 April 1956; *s* of Alexander Charles Benton and Elsie Christine Benton (*née* Taylor); *m* 1983, Mary Monro; one *s* one *d*. *Educ:* Univ. of Aberdeen (BSc Hons Zool. 1978); Univ. of Newcastle upon Tyne (PhD Geol. 1981). FLS 1983; FGS 1987. SO, NCC, 1981–82; Jun. Res. Fellow, Trinity Coll., Oxford, 1982–84; Lectr, QUB, 1984–89; University of Bristol: Lectr, Dept of Geol., 1989–92; Reader in Vertebrate Palaeontol., 1992–97; Hd, Dept of Earth Scis, 2001–08. President: Geologists' Assoc., 2006–08; Internat. Palaeontol Assoc., 2012–14. Edward Bass Dist. Vis. Scholar, Yale Univ., 2009; Dist. Prof., Chinese Acad. of Scis, 2012. FRSE 2008. Lyell Medal, Geol Soc. of London, 2005; T. Neville George Medal, Geol Soc. of Glasgow, 2006. *Publications:* The Phylogeny and Classification of the Tetrapods, 1988; Vertebrate Palaeontology, 1990, 4th edn 2015; Fossil Record 2, 1993; Fossil Reptiles of Great Britain, 1995; The Penguin Historical Atlas of Dinosaurs, 1996; (with D. A. T. Harper) Basic Palaeontology, 1997; Walking with Dinosaurs: the facts, 2000; (jtly) The Age of Dinosaurs in Russia and Mongolia, 2001; (jtly) Permian and Triassic Red Beds and the Penarth Group of Great Britain, 2002; When Life Nearly Died: the greatest mass extinction of all time, 2003, 2nd edn 2015; Mesozoic and Tertiary Fossil Mammals and Birds of Great Britain, 2005; Very Short Introduction to the History of Life, 2008; The Seventy Great Mysteries of the Natural World, 2008; (with D. A. T. Harper) Introduction to Paleobiology and the Fossil Record, 2009, 2nd edn 2019; History of Life, 6th edn, 2019; 45 popular books and over 400 scientific papers. *Recreations:* reading, travelling, swimming, crosswords. *Address:* School of Earth Sciences, Life Sciences Building, University of Bristol, Tyndall Avenue, Bristol BS8 1TQ. *T:* (0117) 394 1208, *Fax:* (0117) 925 3385. *E:* mike.benton@bristol.ac.uk.

**BENTON, Peter Faulkner,** MA; Director-General, British Institute of Management, 1987–92; *b* 6 Oct. 1934; *s* of late S. F. Benton and Mrs H. D. Benton; *m* 1959, Ruth, *d* of late R. S. Cobb, MC, FRIBA and Mrs J. P. Cobb; two *s* three *d*. *Educ:* Oundle; Queens' Coll., Cambridge (MA Nat. Sciences). 2nd Lieut RE, 1953–55. Unilever Ltd, 1958–60; Shell Chemicals Ltd, 1960–63; Berger Jenson and Nicholson Ltd, 1963–64; McKinsey & Co. Inc., London and Chicago, 1964–71 (led reorgn of British gas industry, 1967–71); Gallaher Ltd, 1971, Dir, 1973–77; Man. Dir, Post Office Telecommunications, 1978–81; Dep. Chm., British Telecom, 1981–83. Advr, Stern Stewart Inc., 1995–2002. Chairman: Saunders Valve Ltd, 1972–77; Mono Pumps Group, 1976–77; European Practice, Nolan, Norton & Co., 1984–87; Identica Ltd, 1992–93; Director: Singer and Friedlander, 1983–89; Woodside Communications, 1995–96; Mem., Supervisory Bd, Hiross Holdings AG, Austria, 1992–94. Dir, Turing Inst., 1985–94. Chairman: Enfield Dist HA, 1986–92; Enterprise Support Gp, 1993–96. Chm., Heating, Ventilating, Air Conditioning and Refrigerating Equipment Sector Working Party, NEDO, 1976–79; Member: Electronics Industry EDC, 1980–83; Econ. and Financial Policy Cttee, CBI, 1979–83; Special Adviser to EEC, 1983–84; Nat. Curriculum Science Wkg Gp, 1987–88; Indust. Develt Adv. Bd, DTI, 1988–94; Ind. Mem., British Liby Adv. Council, 1988–93; Internat. Adv. Bd for Science and Technology to Govt of Portugal, 1996–2003. Adviser, Arthur Andersen Société Coopérative, 1993–98. Vice-President: British Mech. Engrg Confedn, 1974–77; European Council of Management, 1989–93. Chairman: Ditchley Conf. on Inf. Technol., 1982; Financial Times Conf., World Electronics, 1983; World Bank Conf. on Catastrophe Avoidance, Washington, 1988, Karlstad, 1989; Vis. Gp, Inst. for Systems Engrg and Informatics, Italy, 1993; Inst. for Systems, Informatics and Safety, 1996; Euromoney Conf., New Delhi, 1998; Jt Chm., European Mgt Congress, Prague, 1990. Royal Signals Instn Lectr, London, 1980; ASLIB Lectr, 1988; Adam Smith Lectr, 1991. Pres., Highgate Literary and Scientific Instn, 1981–88. Chm., N London Hospice Gp, 1985–89. Governor, Molecule Club Theatre, 1985–91. CCMI. *Publications:* Riding the Whirlwind, 1990; articles on management, science and IT. *Recreations:* reading, baroque music, sailing, conversation, looking at buildings. *Address:* Northgate House, 130 Highgate Hill, N6 5HD. *T:* (020) 8341 1122; Dolphins, Hockens Lane, Polruan, Fowey, Cornwall PL23 1PP. *Clubs:* Athenæum, Oxford and Cambridge, The Pilgrims; Blythe Sappers; Royal Fowey Yacht.

**BENTON JONES, Sir James Peter Martin;** *see* Jones, Sir J. P. M. B.

**BENYON, Rt Hon. Richard (Henry Ronald);** PC 2016; MP for Newbury, since 2005 (C, 2005–19; Ind, since 2019); *b* 21 Oct. 1960; *s* of Sir William Richard Benyon; *m* 2004, Zoe Robinson; two *s*, and three *s* from previous marriage. *Educ:* Bradfield Coll.; Royal Agricl Coll. MRICS. Served Army, 1980–84: commnd RGJ; served NI and Far East. Land Agent, 1987–90; farmer, Englefield, Berks, 1990–; Chm., Englefield Estate Trust Corp. Ltd (Rural and Urban Land Hldgs), 2001–10. Parly Under Sec. of State, DEFRA, 2010–13. *Recreations:* walking, conservation, shooting, cooking. *Address:* House of Commons, SW1A 0AA. *Club:* Beefsteak.

**BENYON, Thomas Yates,** OBE 2010; Founder and Director, ZANE: Zimbabwe A National Emergency, since 2000; Co-Founder and Trustee, Community Emergency Foodbank, since 2006; Founder, Zimbabwe Charity Alliance, since 2013; Director of various companies; *b* 13 Aug. 1942; *s* of late Thomas Yates Benyon and Joan Ida Walters; *m* 1968, Olivia Jane (*née* Scott Plummer); two *s* two *d*. *Educ:* Wellington Sch., Somerset; RMA Sandhurst; Wycliffe Hall, Oxford (DBTS 2002). Lieut, Scots Guards, 1963–67. Insurance broking and banking, 1967–79. Chm., Milton Keynes HA, 1989–94; Dir, Bucks Purchasing Authy, 1994–96. Councillor, Aylesbury Vale DC, 1976–79. Contested (C): Huyton, Feb. 1974; Haringey (Wood Green), Oct. 1974; MP (C) Abingdon, 1979–83; Vice Chm., Health and Social Services Cttee, 1982–83; Mem., Social Services Select Cttee, 1980–83. Founder Chm., Assoc. of Lloyd's Members, 1982–87; Founder: Soc. of Names, 1990–; Insurance Insider Publishing plc, 1997–; Guild Acquisitions plc, 2006–; Co-founder, Trendwatch Asset Mgt, 2009. Mem., Gen. Synod of C of E, 2005–10. *Recreations:* family, music. *Address:* Rectory Farm House, Bladon, Oxon OX20 1RS. *Clubs:* Royal Automobile, Pratt's; Third Guards.

**BERAL, Dame Valerie,** DBE 2010; AC 2010; MD; FRCP; FRS 2006; Director, Cancer Epidemiology Unit (formerly ICRF Clinical Trials and Epidemiology, then Cancer Epidemiology, Unit), Oxford, since 1989; Fellow of Green Templeton College (formerly Green College), Oxford, since 1989; Professor of Epidemiology, University of Oxford, since 1996; *b* 28 July 1946; partner, Prof. Paul E. M. Fine; two *s*. *Educ:* Univ. of Sydney (MB BS 1969; MD 2001). MRCP 1971, FRCP 1992. Lectr, Sen. Lectr, then Reader in Epidemiol., LSHTM, 1970–88. Chm., DoH Adv. Cttee on Breast Cancer Screening, 2000. Hon. FFPH (Hon. FFPHM 2000); Hon. FRCOG 2001. *Publications:* articles on causes of breast and other cancers in women. *Address:* 193 Morrell Avenue, Oxford OX4 1NF; Cancer Epidemiology Unit, Richard Doll Building, Roosevelt Drive, Oxford OX3 7LF.

**BERCOW, Rt Hon. John (Simon);** PC 2009; MP Buckingham; Speaker of the House of Commons, since June 2009; *b* 19 Jan. 1963; *s* of late Charles Bercow and of Brenda Bercow (*née* Bailey); *m* 2002, Sally Illman; two *s* one *d*. *Educ:* Finchley Manorhill Sch.; Univ. of Essex (BA 1st Cl. Hons Govt 1985). Nat. Chm., Fedn of Cons. Students, 1986–87; Credit Analyst, Hambros Bank, 1987–88; Public Affairs Consultant, Sallingbury Casey, later Rowland Sallingbury Casey, 1988–95; Dir, Rowland Co., 1994–95; Special Adviser to: Chief Sec. to Treasury, 1995; Sec. of State for Nat. Heritage, 1995–96; free-lance consultant, 1996–97. Councillor (C), Lambeth BC, 1986–90 (Dep. Leader, Opposition Gp, 1987–89). Vice-Chm., Cons. Collegiate Forum, 1987. MP Buckingham, 1997– ((C) 1997–June 2009, when elected Speaker). Opposition spokesman: on educn and employment, 1999–2000; on home affairs, 2000–01; Shadow Chief Sec. to HM Treasury, 2001–02; Shadow Minister for Work and Pensions, 2002; Shadow Sec. of State for Internat. Develt, 2003–04. Member: Trade and Industry Select Cttee, 1998–99; Internat. Develt Select Cttee, 2004–09; Chairmen's Panel, 2005–09. Chair: (ex officio) H of C Commn, 2009–; Speaker's Cttee on Electoral Commn, 2009–; Speaker's Cttee for indep. Parly Standards Authy, 2009–; Speaker's Commn on Digital Democracy, 2014–. President: All-Party Parly Gp for America, 2009–; All-Party Parly Gp for Internet and Communications Technol., 2011–. Contested (C): Motherwell S, 1987; Bristol S, 1992. Leader, Review of Services for Children and Young People with Speech, Language and Communication Needs, 2007–08 (report published 2008). Pres., UK Br., CPA, 2009–. Hon. President: Hansard Soc. for Parly Govt, 2009–; IPU British Gp, 2009–. Co-Dir, Advanced Speaking and Campaigning Course, 1989–97. Chancellor: Bedfordshire Univ., 2014–; Univ. of Essex, 2017–. Hon. Prof. of Politics, Sch. of Social Scis, Univ. of Manchester, 2017. Freedom, City of London, 2016. DUniv Essex, 2010; Hon. Dr of Laws: Buckingham,

2013; De Montfort, 2014; DSc City, 2014. Backbencher to Watch, Spectator Mag., 1998; Opposition MP of the Year, C4/Hansard Soc. Political Awards, 2005; Backbencher of the Year, House Mag., 2005; ePolitix/Dods Health Champion, 2006, Disability Champion, 2007, Internat. Champion, 2007; Politician of the Year, Stonewall Awards, 2010. *Publications:* Tennis Maestros, 2014. *Recreations:* tennis (trying to play and watching Roger Federer), football (Arsenal FC supporter), reading, swimming, music, cinema. *Address:* Speaker's House, Westminster, SW1A 0AA.

**BEREJIKLIAN, Hon. Gladys**; MP (L) Willoughby, New South Wales, since 2003; Premier of New South Wales, Australia, since 2017; *b* Sydney, 22 Sept. 1970; *d* of Krikor Berejiklian and Arsha Berejiklian. *Educ:* North Ryde Public Sch.; Peter Board (formerly North Ryde) High Sch.; Univ. of Sydney (BA 1992; Grad. Dip. Internat. Studies 1996); Univ. of NSW (MCom 2001). Pres., NSW Young Liberals, 1996–97. Exec., Commonwealth Bank of Australia, 1998–2003. Minister for Transport, 2011–15, Treas., 2015–17, NSW. Leader, NSW Liberal Party, 2017–. *Recreations:* reading, walking, gym, golf, film. *Address:* 280 Willoughby Road, Naremburn, NSW 2065, Australia. *T:* (2) 94394199, *Fax:* (2) 94399299. *E:* willoughby@parliament.nsw.gov.au.

**BERESFORD**, family name of **Baron Decies** and **Marquess of Waterford**.

**BERESFORD, Sir (Alexander) Paul**, Kt 1990; dental surgeon; MP (C) Mole Valley, since 1997 (Croydon Central, 1992–97); *b* 6 April 1946; *s* of Raymond and Joan Beresford; *m* Julie Haynes; three *s* one *d*. *Educ:* Richmond Primary Sch., Richmond, Nelson, NZ; Waimea Coll., Richmond; Otago Univ., Dunedin. Mem. (C), Wandsworth BC, 1978–94 (Leader of Council, 1983–92). Mem., Audit Commn, 1991–92. Parly Under-Sec. of State, DoE, 1994–97. *Address:* c/o House of Commons, SW1A 0AA.

**BERESFORD, Marcus de la Poer**, CBE 2003; Chairman, Ricardo plc, 2004–09; non-executive Director, Cobham plc, 2004–13; *b* 15 May 1942; *s* of late Anthony de la Poer Beresford and Mary (née Canning); *m* 1965, Jean Helen Kitchener; two *s*. *Educ:* Harrow Sch.; St John's Coll., Cambridge (MA Mech. Sci.). FIET (FIEE 1986). Man. Dir, Automotive Instrumentation Gp, Smiths Industries, 1978–83; Dir and Gen. Manager, Lucas Electronics Ltd, 1983–85; Man. Dir, Siemens Plessey Controls Ltd, 1985–92; Dir, Siemens plc, 1991–92; Man. Dir, GKN Industrial Services, 1992–2001; Dir, 1992–2002, Chief Exec., 2001–02, GKN plc. Non-executive Director: Camas, then Aggregate Industries, plc, 1994–2000; Spirent plc, 1999–2006. Non-exec. Dir, Engrg and Technol. Bd, 2002–05. Mem. Council, Open Univ., 1997–2000. Freeman, City of London, 1963; Liveryman, Skinners' Co., 1973. *Recreations:* golf, tennis, gardening.

**BERESFORD, Meg**; Manager, Wiston Lodge (formerly YMCA Centre, Wiston Lodge), since 1997 (Assistant Director, 1994–97); *b* 5 Sept. 1937; *d* of late John Tristram Beresford and of Anne Stuart-Wortley; *m* 1959, William Tanner; two *s*. *Educ:* Sherborne School for Girls; Seale Hayne Agricultural Coll., Newton Abbot; Univ. of Warwick. Community worker, Leamington Spa; Organising Sec., European Nuclear Disarmament, 1981–83; Gen. Sec., CND, 1985–90; gardener, 1991–92; Staff Co-ordinator, 1992–94, Iona Community. Mem. Bd, Wiston Lodge, 2014–; Sec., Tinto Music and Arts, 2014–. Campaigner to preserve lives and habitats of bees and other pollinators. *Publications:* Into the Twenty First Century, 1989; contributor to End Jl, Sanity. *Recreations:* walking, reading, camping, music. *Address:* Wiston Lodge, Millrigg Road, Wiston, Biggar ML12 6HT.

**BERESFORD, Sir Paul**; see Beresford, Sir A. P.

**BERESFORD-PEIRSE, Sir Henry (Njerš de la Poer)**, 7th Bt *cr* 1814, of Bagnall, Waterford; *b* London, 25 March 1969; *er s* of Sir Henry Grant de la Poer Beresford-Peirse, 6th Bt and of Jadranka Beresford-Peirse (née Njerš); *S* father, 2013; *m* 2005, Joanna Tamlyn; two *s* one *d*. *Educ:* Harrow Sch. *Recreation:* cricket. *Heir:* *s* Harry Tamlyn de la Poer Beresford-Peirse, *b* 23 Feb. 2007. *Address:* Bedale Manor, Bedale, N Yorkshire DL8 1EP. *T:* (01677) 422811. *Club:* White's.

**BERG, Alan**; District Judge (Magistrates' Courts) (formerly Stipendiary Magistrate), Greater Manchester, 1994–2010; Deputy District Judge, 2010–14; *b* 17 Feb. 1943; *s* of Simon and Esther Berg; *m* 1967, Lorna Lewis; two *s*. *Educ:* King George V Grammar Sch., Southport; Law Coll., Liverpool. Solicitor in private practice, Liverpool, 1967–94; Sen. Partner, Canter Levin & Berg, 1980–93; Asst Stipendiary Magistrate, 1991–94. *Recreations:* grandchildren, reading, worrying, voluntary work.

**BERG, Eddie**; Director, Eddie Berg Projects, since 2014; Chief Executive, Rich Mix, since 2016; *b* 25 Aug. 1958; *s* of Francis and Edith Hollingsworth; *m* 1986, Karen Berg (marr. diss.); one *s*. *Educ:* Open Univ. House Manager, Everyman Th., Liverpool, 1984–87; Dir, Moviola, Liverpool, 1988–96; Chief Exec., Foundn for Art and Creative Technol., Liverpool, 1996–2005; Artistic Dir, BFI Southbank, 2005–11; Dir of Partnerships, BFI, 2011–14. Consultant, Employability and Ind. Engagement, Sch. of Arts and Digital Industries, Univ. of E London, 2014–. Exec. Chm., Gtr Birmingham Film Strategy Bd, 2014–. Chair: Puppetry Develt Steering Cttee, Arts Council England, 2014–; Ext. Adv. Bd, Inst. for Creative Enterprise, Edge Hill Univ., 2014–. Trustee, Culture24, 2014–. FRSA. *Publications:* (contrib.) Empire, Ruins and Networks: the transcultural agenda in art, 2005; Factors: 1988–2005. *Recreations:* films, media art, music, cooking, eating out, discovering new ideas/places/people, football, travel, thinking, soaking up the sun, reading.

**BERG, Geoffrey**, MVO 1976; HM Diplomatic Service, retired; *b* 5 July 1945; *s* of Bertram Lionel Berg and Irene Amelia Berg (née Hunt); *m* 1970, Sheila Maxine Brown; one *s*. *Educ:* Woking County Grammar Sch. for Boys. Joined CRO, 1963; Diplomatic Service Admin, 1965–68; Latin American floater duties, 1968–70; Third Sec. (Vice-Consul), Bucharest, 1970–72; FCO, 1972–75; Second, later First Sec. (Inf.), Helsinki, 1975–79; FCO, 1979–84; First Sec. (Commercial), Madrid, 1984–88; FCO, 1988–90; Counsellor on secondment to DTI, 1990–93; Dep. Head of Mission, Mexico City, 1993–96; Dep. Consul-Gen. and Dir of Trade, NY, 1997–2001; Consul-Gen., Toronto and Dir, Trade and Investment, Canada, 2002–05. Chevalier First Cl., Order of Lion (Finland), 1976; Official Cross, Order of Civil Merit (Spain), 1988. *Recreations:* travel, photography. *Club:* Royal Over-Seas League.

**BERG, Rev. John J.**; see Johansen-Berg.

**BERG, Prof. Maxine Louise**, DPhil; FBA 2004; FRHistS; Professor of History, University of Warwick, since 1998; *b* 22 Feb. 1950; *m* 1977, Prof. John Charles Robertson, *qv*; three *d*. *Educ:* Simon Fraser Univ., BC (BA); Univ. of Sussex (MA); Univ. of Oxford (DPhil 1976). Sir Lewis Namier Jun. Res. Fellow in Hist., Balliol Coll., Oxford, 1974; University of Warwick, 1978–: Lectr, then Sen. Lectr, Dept of Econs; Sen. Lectr, then Reader, Dept of History; Director: Eighteenth Century Centre, 1998–2007; Global History and Culture Centre, 2007–10. Associate Fellow, Centre for Hist. and Econs, Univ. of Cambridge, 2010–. Sen. Mem., Robinson Coll., Cambridge, 2010–. Hon. Fellow, Balliol Coll., Oxford, 2009. *Publications:* (ed) Technology and Toil in Nineteenth Century Britain, 1979; Machinery Question and the Making of Political Economy 1815–48, 1982; (ed jtly) Manufacture in Town and Country Before the Factory, 1983; The Age of Manufactures: industry, innovation and work in Britain 1700–1820, 1985, 2nd edn 1994; Political Economy in the Twentieth Century, 1989; (ed) Markets and Manufacture in Early Industrial Europe, 1991, new edn 2013; A Woman in History: Eileen Power 1889–1940, 1996; (ed with Kristine Bruland) Technological Revolutions in Europe 1760–1860, 1997; (ed with Helen Clifford) Consumers and Luxury in Europe 1650–1850, 1999; (ed with Elizabeth Eger) Luxury in the Eighteenth Century: debates, desires and delectable goods, 2002; Luxury and Pleasure in Eighteenth-Century Britain, 2005; (ed) Writing the History of the Global: challenges for the twenty-first century, 2013; (ed jtly) Goods from the East: trading Eurasia 1600–1800, 2014; contrib. learned jls. *Address:* Department of History, University of Warwick, Coventry CV4 7AL.

**BERG, Prof. Paul**, PhD; Cahill Professor in Cancer Research (Biochemistry), 1994–2000, now Professor Emeritus, and Director, Beckman Center for Molecular and Genetic Medicine, 1985–2000, Stanford University School of Medicine; *b* New York, 30 June 1926; *m* Mildred Levy; one *s*. *Educ:* Pennsylvania State Univ. (BS); Western Reserve Univ. (PhD). Pre-doctoral and post-doctoral med. research, 1950–54; scholar in cancer research, American Cancer Soc., Washington Univ., 1954; Asst to Associate Prof. of Microbiology, Washington Univ., 1955–59; Stanford Univ. Sch. of Medicine: Associate Prof. of Biochem., 1959–60; Prof., Dept of Biochem., 1960, Chm. 1969–74; Willson Prof. of Biochem., 1970–93; Non-resident Fellow, Salk Inst., 1973–83. Editor, Biochemical and Biophysical Res. Communications, 1959–68; Member: NIH Study, Sect. on Physiol Chem.; Editorial Bd, Jl of Molecular Biology, 1966–69; Bd of Sci. Advisors, Jane Coffin Childs Foundn for Med. Res.; Adv. Bds to Nat. Insts of Health, Amer. Cancer Soc., Nat. Sci. Foundn, MIT and Harvard, 1970–80; Council, Nat. Acad. of Scis, 1979. Former Pres., Amer. Soc. of Biological Chemists; Foreign Member: Japan Biochem. Soc., 1978; French Acad. of Scis, 1981; Royal Soc., 1992; Pontifical Acad. of Scis, 1996. Lectures: Harvey, 1972; Lynen, 1977; Weizmann Inst., 1977; Univ. of Pittsburgh, 1978; Priestly, Pennsylvania State Univ., 1978; Shell, Univ. of California at Davis, 1978; Dreyfus, Northwestern Univ., 1979; Jesup, Columbia Univ., 1980; Karl-August-Förster, Univ. of Mainz, 1980; David Rivett Meml, CSIR, Melb., 1980. Hon. DSc: Rochester and Yale Univs, 1978; Washington Univ., St Louis, 1986; Pennsylvania State Univ., 1995; numerous awards include: Eli Lilly Award, 1959; Calif. Scientist of the Year, 1963; Nat. Acad. of Scis, 1966, 1974; Amer. Acad. of Arts and Scis, 1966; Henry J. Kaiser, Stanford Univ. Sch. of Med., 1969, 1972; V. D. Mattia Prize of Roche Inst. for Molec. Biol., 1972; Gairdner Foundn Award, Nobel Prize in Chemistry, New York Acad. of Scis and Albert Lasker Med. Res. awards, 1980; National Medal of Science, 1983. *Publications:* (jtly) Genes and Genomes: a changing perspective, 1990; (jtly) Dealing with Genes: the language of heredity, 1992; (jtly) George Beadle: an uncommon farmer, 2003; many scientific articles and reviews. *Address:* Beckman Center-BO62, Stanford University Medical Center, Stanford, CA 94305–5301, USA.

**BERG, Raymond Jeremy**; Managing Partner, Osborne Clarke LLP, since 2015; *b* London, 30 Dec. 1967; *s* of Emmanuel Berg and Ann Berg; *m* 1994, Catherine Julia Noble; one *s* two *d*. *Educ:* Exeter Coll., Oxford (BA Juris. 1989). Admitted as solicitor, 1992; Lawyer, Allen & Overy, 1992–2001; Partner, Osborne Clarke LLP, 2001–. Trustee, Social Mobility Business Partnership, 2018–; Mem., Steering Cttee, RollOnMonday prog., 2016–. *Recreations:* family, Tottenham Hotspur FC, Ibiza. *Address:* Osborne Clarke LLP, One London Wall, EC2Y 5EB. *Clubs:* h, Ned.

**BERGANZA, Teresa**; singer (mezzo-soprano); *b* Madrid, Spain; *d* of Guillermo and Maria Ascension Berganza; *m*; three *c*. *Educ:* Début in Aix-en-Provence, 1957; début in England, Glyndebourne, 1958; appeared at Glyndebourne, 1959; Royal Opera House, Covent Garden, 1959, 1960, 1963, 1964, 1976, 1977, 1979, 1981, 1984, 1985; Royal Festival Hall, 1960, 1961, 1962, 1967, 1971; appears regularly in Vienna, Milan, Aix-en-Provence, Holland, Japan, Edinburgh, Paris, Israel, America; Carmen, opening ceremonies, Expo 92, Seville; participated opening ceremonies, Barcelona Olympics, 1992. Mem. (first elected woman), Spanish Royal Acad. of Arts, 1994. Prizes: Lucretia Arana; Nacional Lírica, Spain; Lily Pons, 1976; Acad. Nat. du Disque Lyrique; USA record award; Harriet Cohen Internat. Music Award, 1974; Grand Prix Rossini; Médaille d'or, Ville Aix-en-Provence; International Critic Award, 1988. Charles Cross (6 times); Grand Cross, Isabel la Católica, Spain; Gran Cruz al Mérito en las Bellas Artes, Spain; Commandeur, l'Ordre des Arts et des Lettres, France; Cruz de Alfonso X El Sabio, Spain. *Publications:* Flor de Soledad y Silencio, 1984. *Recreations:* music, books, the arts. *Address:* Avenida de Juan de Borbón y Battenberg 16, 28200 San Lorenzo del Escorial, Madrid, Spain.

**BERGER, Luciana Clare**; MP for Liverpool, Wavertree, since 2010 (Lab Co-op, 2010–19; Ind, 2019; Lib Dem, since 2019); *b* Wembley, 13 May 1981; *m* 2015, Alistair Goldsmith; one *s* one *d*. *Educ:* Haberdashers' Aske's Sch. for Girls, Elstree; Univ. of Birmingham (BCom); Birkbeck Coll., Univ. of London (MSc Govt). Govt Strategy Unit, Accenture, 2005–06; Govt and Parly Manager, NHS Confedn, 2006–07. Shadow Minister: for Energy and Climate Change, 2010–13; of Public Health, 2013–15; for Mental Health, 2015–16. Mem., Health and Social Care (formerly Health) Select Cttee, 2016–. Dir, Labour Friends of Israel, 2007–10. Member, Advisory Board: Money and Mental Health Policy Inst.; Growing Up North project, Children's Comr; Advr, Health Policy Res. Unit, UCL and KCL Consortium. Vice Pres., British Assoc. for Counselling and Psychotherapy. FRSA. Hon. Fellow, Mental Health Context res. gp, Heseltine Inst., Univ. of Liverpool. *Address:* House of Commons, SW1A 0AA.

**BERGHUSER, Sir Hugo (Erich)**, Kt 1989; MBE 1981; *b* Germany, 25 Oct. 1935; *m* Christa; one *s* one *d*. *Educ:* Volksschule, Stiepel; Trade School, Bochum. Cabinet-maker. Embarked on ship to emigrate to Australia, 1958; ship (Skaubryn) caught fire and sank in the Indian Ocean; arrived in Papua New Guinea in 1959; active in the building industries, meat trade and timber sawmilling trade, employing over 700. MP, PNG, 1987–92; Minister for Civil Aviation, Tourism and Culture, 1987. Independence Medal, PNG, 1975; Silver Jubilee Medal, 1977; Service Medal, PNG, 1980; Long Service Medal, PNG, 1985. Distinctive Cross, 1st Cl. (Germany), 1986; Grand Cross (Germany), 1991; Hon. Consulate Gen. (Turkey). *Address:* PO Box 1785, Boroko, NCD, Papua New Guinea. *Club:* Papua.

**BERGIN, Prof. Joseph**, LittD; FBA 1996; Professor of History, University of Manchester, 1996–2011, now Emeritus; *b* Kilkenny, 11 Feb. 1948; *s* of Cornelius Bergin and Brigid (née Phelan); *m* 1978, Sylvia Papazian; one *s* one *d*. *Educ:* Rockwell Coll., Co. Tipperary; University Coll., Dublin; Peterhouse, Cambridge; LittD Manchester 2004. Lectr in History, Maynooth Coll., 1976–78; Manchester University: Lectr in History, 1978–88; Sen. Lectr, 1988–92; Reader, 1992–96. Visiting Professor: Lyon Univ., 1991–92; Ecole des Chartes, Paris, 1995; Nancy Univ., 1999; Montpellier, 2004; Sorbonne, 2005. Leverhulme Major Res. Fellow, 2000–03; Fellow, Wissenschaftskolleg, Berlin, 2006–07. Resident, Inst. for Advanced Study, Nantes, 2012–13. Corresp. étranger, Acad. des Inscriptions et Belles-Lettres, Paris, 2011; MAE 2012. Prix Richelieu, Rueil-Malmaison, France, 1995; Medal of Antiquities of France, Acad. Inscriptions et Belles-Lettres, Paris, 2010; Médaille Richelieu, Sorbonne, 2010. Officier, Ordre des Palmes Académiques (France), 2010. *Publications:* Cardinal Richelieu: power and the pursuit of wealth, 1985; Cardinal La Rochefoucauld, 1987; The Rise of Richelieu, 1991; The Making of the French Episcopate 1589–1661, 1996; Seventeenth Century Europe, 2000; Crown, Church and Episcopate under Louis XIV, 2004; Church, Society and Religious Change in France 1580–1730, 2009; The

Politics of Religion in Early Modern France, 2014; A History of France, 2015. *Recreations:* sports, book hunting, music, walking. *Address:* 9 Sibley Road, Heaton Moor, Stockport, Cheshire SK4 4HH. *T:* (0161) 432 4650.

**BERGIN, Terence Edward;** QC 2016; *b* London, 1961; *s* of Edward and Georgina Bergin; partner, Christine Aniszewski; one *s. Educ:* Queens' Coll., Cambridge (BA 1984). Called to the Bar, Inner Temple, 1985. *Recreations:* music, books, film, Arsenal FC. *Address:* 4 Pump Court, Temple, EC4Y 7AN. *T:* (020) 7842 5555. *E:* clerks@4pumpcourt.com.

**BERGIN, Thomas;** correspondent, since 2001, and investigative journalist, since 2012, Reuters; *b* Dublin, 24 Oct. 1971; *s* of Charles J. Bergin and Mary Rose Bergin (*née* O'Doherty); *m* 2005, Sophy Tonder; two *s. Educ:* Clongowes Wood Coll., Ireland; University Coll. Dublin (BA Philosophy and Econs 1992); University Coll., Galway (Dip. Business Studies 1993). Researcher, Foreign Trade Bank of Mexico, 1994–95; Fund Adminr, ING Barings, 1995–97; Energy Broker, HOB (Ireland) Ltd, 1997–98; reporter, Futures & Options World, 1999–2001. Orwell Prize for Journalism, Orwell Trust, 2013; Gerald Loeb Award, UCLA Anderson Sch. of Mgt, 2013; Business Reporter of Year, British Press Awards, 2013; Business Journalist of Year, London Press Club, 2013; Business Reporting Award, NY Press Club, 2013; Business Feature Award, Deadline Club, 2013; Soc. of American Business Editors and Writers Award, 2013; Overseas Press Club of America Award, 2015; Society of Publishers in Asia Award, 2017. *Publications:* Spills & Spin: the inside story of BP, 2011. *Address:* c/o Reuters, 30 South Colonnade, E14 5EP. *T:* (020) 7542 1111. *E:* tom.bergin@reuters.com.

**BERGQUIST, Mats Fingal Thorwald,** Hon. CMG 1983; PhD; Ambassador of Sweden to the Court of St James's, 1997–2004; *b* 5 Sept. 1938; *s* of Thorwald and Ingrid Bergquist; *m* 1st, 1968, Marianne Lübeck (*d* 1979); two *s;* 2nd, 1991, Agneta Lorichs; two *s. Educ:* Univ. of Lund (MA 1960; PhL 1964; PhD 1970). Joined Swedish Diplomatic Service, 1964: served: London, 1964–66; Perm. Mission to UN, NY, 1966–68; First Sec., subseq. Counsellor, Foreign Ministry, 1970–76; Counsellor, Washington, 1976–81; Asst Dep. Under Sec., 1981–85; Dep. Under Sec. for Political Affairs, 1985–87; Ambassador to: Israel, 1987–92; Finland, 1992–97. Chm., Swedish Inst. for Internat. Affairs, 2006–12. Chancellor, Växjö Univ., 2005–09. Commander: Légion d'Honneur (France), 1983; Order of Orange-Nassau (Netherlands), 1987; Grand Cross, Finnish Lion (Finland), 1994. *Publications:* Sweden and the EEC, 1970; War and Surrogate War, 1976; Balance of Power and Deterrence, 1988; Conflict Without End?, 1993; From Cold War to Lukewarm Peace, 1998; The Blair Experiment, 2007. *Recreations:* music, tennis. *Address:* Bergsgatan 16, 11223 Stockholm, Sweden.

**BERINGER, Guy Gibson,** CBE 2016; Chairman, Legal Education Foundation, since 2012; *b* 12 Aug. 1955; *s* of Lt Col Frederick Richard Beringer and Hazel Margaret Beringer (*née* Orr); *m* 1979, Margaret Catherine Powell; three *d. Educ:* Campbell Coll., Belfast; St Catharine's Coll., Cambridge (MA). Admitted Solicitor, 1980; joined Allen & Overy, 1978: Asst Solicitor, 1980–85; Partner, 1985–2008; Managing Partner, Corporate Dept, 1994–99; Sen. Partner, 2000–08. Non-executive Chairman: ATC Gp, 2010–13; SageTech Medical Equipment Ltd, 2018–; non-executive Director: Fleming Family & Partners Ltd, 2008–15; London Irish Hldgs Ltd, 2009–14; BCKR Ltd, 2012–. Chm., Export Credits Guarantee Dept (UK Export Finance), 2010–16; non-exec. Mem. Bd, HM Courts Service, 2008–11. Mem., Law Soc., 1980–. Adjunct Prof., Imperial Coll. Business Sch. (formerly Tanaka Business Sch.), Imperial Coll., London, 2008–. Chm., City Music Services, 2012–; Chm., Temple Music Foundn, 2017–. Gov. and Dep. Chm., Coll. of Law, 2009–12. Co-Chm., Develt Bd, Bingham Centre for the Rule of Law, 2012–. Fellow Commoner, St Catharine's Coll., Cambridge, 2008. Hon. QC 2006; Hon. Bencher, Inner Temple, 2009. *Recreations:* choral singing, golf, boating. *Address:* 2 King's Bench Walk, 2 Pair, Inner Temple, EC4Y 7DE. *T:* (020) 3722 9412. *Clubs:* Athenæum; Hawks (Cambridge).

**BERINGER, Prof. Sir John (Evelyn),** Kt 2000; CBE 1993; Professor of Molecular Genetics, 1984–2005, now Professor Emeritus, and Pro-Vice-Chancellor, 2001–05, University of Bristol; *b* 14 Feb. 1944; *s* of late Group Captain William Beringer and of Evelyn Joan Beringer; *m* 1970, Sheila Murray; three *s. Educ:* Univ. of Edinburgh (Scottish Dip. in Agric. 1965; BSc 1970); Univ. of East Anglia (PhD 1973). Microbial Geneticist, John Innes Inst., 1970–80; Head, Dept of Microbiology, Rothamsted Exptl Station, Harpenden, 1980–84; University of Bristol: Dir, Molecular Genetics Unit, 1984–88; Head, Dept of Microbiology, 1986–90; Head, Dept of Botany, 1990–93; Dean of Science, 1996–2001. Chairman, advisory committees: Genetic Manipulation Planned Release Sub-Cttee, 1987–90; Releases to Envmt, 1990–99; Chm., Main Panel D, 2008 RAE. Member: NERC, 1996–2001; Council for Sci. and Technol., 2004–08. Chairman: Governing Council, John Innes Centre, 2000–09; Inst. of Garden and Landscape History, 2006–08. Fleming Lectr, Soc. for Gen. Microbiology, 1979. Hon. DSc: Exeter, 2006; East Anglia, 2011. *Publications:* sci. contribs to biological jls and proceedings. *Recreations:* gardening, reading, classic cars, golf.

**BERKELEY,** family name of **Baron Berkeley of Knighton.**

**BERKELEY, 18th Baron** *cr* 1421; **Anthony Fitzhardinge Gueterbock,** OBE 1989; Baron Gueterbock (Life Peer) 2000; Chairman, Rail Freight Group, since 1996; *b* 20 Sept. 1939; *o s* of Brig. E. A. L. Gueterbock (*d* 1984) and Hon. Cynthia Ella Gueterbock (*d* 1991), *sister* of Baroness Berkeley, 17th in line; *S* aunt, 1992; *m* 1st, 1965, Diane Christine (marr. diss. 1998), *e d* of Eric William John Townsend; two *s* one *d;* 2nd, 1999, Julia Rosalind (marr. diss. 2011), *d* of Michael Clarke; 3rd, 2017, Marian Bennett. *Educ:* Eton; Trinity Coll., Cambridge (MA). CEng, MICE. Engineering, construction and planning, Sir Alexander Gibb & Partners, 1961–65; multi-disciplinary engineering and construction, planning and business develt, George Wimpey PLC, 1965–81; The Channel Tunnel Group/Eurotunnel, 1981–96. Chm., Piggyback Consortium, 1992–98. Chm., UK Marine Pilots' Assoc., 1998–; Mem. Bd, Eur. Rail Freight Assoc., 2007– (Pres. 2009–11). Trustee, Plymouth Marine Laboratories Ltd, 2011–16. Harbour Comr, Port of Fowey, 2006–13. Hon. DSc Brighton, 1996. *Recreations:* ski-ing, sailing. *Heir: s* Hon. Thomas Fitzhardinge Gueterbock [*b* 5 Jan. 1969; *m* 1995, Helen Ruth, *er d* of Lt-Comdr Brian Walsh, RN retd]. *Address:* c/o House of Lords, SW1A 0PW.

**BERKELEY OF KNIGHTON,** Baron *cr* 2013 (Life Peer), of Knighton in the County of Powys; **Michael Fitzhardinge Berkeley,** CBE 2012; composer and broadcaster; *b* 29 May 1948; *s* of late Sir Lennox Randal Berkeley and Elizabeth Freda (*née* Bernstein); *m* 1979, Deborah Jane Coltman-Rogers (*d* 2014); one *d; m* 2016, Elizabeth Jane West. *Educ:* Westminster Cathedral Choir Sch.; The Oratory Sch.; Royal Acad. of Music (ARAM 1984; FRAM 1996). FRWCMD 2003; FRNCM 2004. Studied privately with Richard Rodney Bennett; rock musician; phlebotomist, St Bartholomew's Hosp., 1969–71; Presentation Asst, LWT, 1973; Announcer, BBC Radio 3, 1974–79; regular presenter of arts programmes for BBC (Meridian, World Service, Private Passions, Radio 3); introduces proms, concerts and festivals for BBC2 and Radio 3, BBC television documentaries and Glyndebourne for C4. Associate Composer: to Scottish Chamber Orch., 1979; to BBC Nat. Orch. of Wales, 2001–08. Jt Artistic Dir, Spitalfields Fest., 1994–97; Artistic Dir, Cheltenham Fest., 1995–2004. Member: Exec. Cttee, Assoc. of Professional Composers, 1982–84; Central Music Adv. Cttee, BBC, 1986–90; Gen. Adv. Council, BBC, 1990–95; New Music Sub-Cttee, Arts Council of GB, 1984–86; Music Panel Adviser to Arts Council, 1986–90; Mem., Bd of Dirs, Royal Opera House, Covent Gdn, 1996–2001 (Mem., 1994–98, Chm., 1998–99, Opera Bd). Vis. Prof., Huddersfield Univ. (formerly Poly.), 1991–94. Governor: NYO, 1994–96; Royal Ballet, 2001– (Chm., 2003–12); Dir, Britten-Pears Foundn, 1996–2009. Hon. DMus UEA, 2007. *Compositions: orchestral music:* Fanfare and National Anthem, 1979; Primavera, 1979; Flames, 1981; Gregorian Variations, 1982; Daybreak and a Candle End, 1985; Gethsemane Fragment, 1990; Secret Garden, 1998; The Garden of Earthly Delights, 1998; Tristessa, 2003; Concerto for Orchestra, 2005; Slow Dawn, 2008; *for chamber or small orchestra:* Meditations, 1977 (Guinness Prize for Composition); Fantasia Concertante, 1978; Uprising: Symphony in one movement, 1980; Suite: the Vision of Piers the Ploughman, 1981; The Romance of the Rose, 1982; Coronach, 1988; Entertaining Master Punch, 1991; Abstract Mirror, 2002; *concertos:* Concerto for Oboe and String Orch., 1977; Concerto for Cello and Small Orch., 1983; Concerto for Horn and String Orch., 1984; Organ Concerto, 1987; Clarinet Concerto, 1991; Viola Concerto, 1994; Violin Concerto, 2016; *chamber music:* String Trio, 1978; American Suite, 1980; Chamber Symphony, 1980; String Quartet No 1, 1981; Nocturne, 1982; Piano Trio, 1982; Music from Chaucer, 1983; Quintet for Clarinet and Strings, 1983; String Quartet No 2, 1984; The Mayfly, 1984; Pas de deux, 1985; For the Savage Messiah, 1985; Quartet Study, 1987; Catch Me if You Can, 1993; Torque and Velocity, 1997; Piano Quintet, 2009; Into the Ravine (oboe quintet), 2011; *strings:* Etude de Fleurs, 1979; Sonata for Violin and Piano, 1979; Iberian Notebook, 1980; Variations on Greek Folk-Songs, 1981; Funerals and Fandangos, 1984; A Mosaic for Father Popieluszko, 1985; *guitar:* Lament, 1980; Worry Beads, 1981; Sonata in One Movement, 1982; Impromptu, 1985; Magnetic Field, 1995; *keyboard:* Passacaglia, 1978; Strange Meeting, 1978; Organ Sonata, 1979; Dark Sleep, 1994; Haiku, 2016; *woodwind:* Three Moods, 1979; Fierce Tears, 1984; Flighting, 1985; Keening, 1987; *vocal music for solo voice:* The Wild Winds, 1978; Rain, 1979; Wessex Graves, 1981; Songs of Awakening Love, 1986; Speaking Silence, 1986; Three Cabaret Sons, 2012 (words by Ian McEwan); *vocal/orchestral:* Love Cries, 1999 (adaptation from the Second Mrs Kong by Harrison Birtwistle); *vocal/chamber:* Three Rilke Sonnets for Soprano and Ensemble, 2011; *choral music:* At the Round Earth's Imagin'd Corners, 1980; The Crocodile and Father William, 1982; Easter, 1982; As the Wind Doth Blow, 1983; Hereford Communion Service, 1985; Pasce Oves Meas, 1985; Verbum Caro Factum Est, 1987; The Red Macula, 1989; Night Song in the Jungle, 1990; Winter Fragments, 1996; Farewell, 1999; Torch Light, 2006; Gabriel's Lament (chorus and orch.), 2009; Anthem: Advent Carol (words by Rowan Williams), 2010; Listen, Listen, O My Child (anthem for Archbishop of Canterbury's enthronement), 2013; Build This House, 2014 (for King's Coll., Cambridge); Magna Carta Te Deum, 2015 (for 800th Anniv. of Magna Carta, Lincoln Cathedral); This Endernight, 2016; *oratorio:* Or Shall We Die?, 1983 (text by Ian McEwan; filmed for Channel 4); *opera:* libretti by David Malouf: Baa Baa Black Sheep, 1993; Jane Eyre, 2000; libretto by Ian McEwan: For You, 2008; *ballet:* Bastet, 1988; Rushes - Fragments from a Lost Story, 2008 (adapted from Prokofiev's film music and subseq. pubd and recorded as Symphonic Suite from The Queen of Spades, 2009); Tetractys - The Art of Fugue (arranged and orchestrated from Bach's Art of Fugue), 2014; *film music:* Captive, 1986; Twenty-one, 1990; Goldeneye, 1991. *Publications:* The Music Pack, 1994; musical compositions; articles in The Observer, The Guardian, The Listener, The Sunday Telegraph, and Vogue. *Recreations:* looking at paintings, reading, walking and hill farming in mid-Wales, tennis, ski-ing. *Address:* c/o Ralph Blackbourn, Artist Manager, Rayfield Allied, Studio 26 China Works, 100 Black Prince Road, SE1 7SJ. *T:* (020) 3176 5502.

**BERKHOUT, Prof. Frans,** DPhil; FAcSS; Professor of Environment, Society and Climate, since 2013, and Executive Dean, Faculty of Social Science and Public Policy, since 2015, King's College London; *b* Dar-es-Salaam, Tanganyika, 21 Oct. 1961; *s* of Joop Berkhout and Katherine Berkhout-Heim; *m* 1992, Diane Moody; one *s* one *d. Educ:* Univ. of Leeds (BSc Geog. 1983); Sussex Univ. (DPhil Sci. and Technol. Policy Studies 1989). Res. Fellow, Sci. Policy Res. Unit, Sussex Univ., 1989–92 and 1994–96; Res. Associate, Center for Energy and Envmtl Studies and Lectr, Woodrow Wilson Sch., Princeton Univ., 1992–94; Sen. Fellow, and Leader, Envmt Prog., SPRU-Sci. and Technol. Policy Res., Univ. of Sussex, 1996–2004; Co-Dir, Global Envmtl Change Prog., 1999–2000, Dir, Sustainable Technologies Prog., 2002–04, UK ESRC; VU University, Amsterdam: Prof. of Innovation and Sustainability, 2004–; Director: Inst. for Envmtl Studies, 2004–12; Amsterdam Global Change Inst., 2010–13; Interim Dir, Future Earth Prog., ICSU, Paris, 2013–15. FAcSS 2017. *Publications:* (with S. M. MacGill) The Politics of Anxiety: Sellafield's cancer-link controversy, 1987; Radioactive waste: politics and technology, 1991; (jtly) World Inventory of Plutonium and Highly-Enriched Uranium, 1992; (ed jtly) Industrial Ecology and Global Change, 1994; (jtly) Plutonium and Highly Enriched Uranium 1996: world inventories, capabilities and possibilities, 1997; (ed jtly) Managing a Material World: perspectives in industrial ecology, 1998; (ed jtly) Negotiating Environmental Change: new perspectives from social science, 2003; (ed jtly) Climate Change Governance in Europe: confronting dilemmas of mitigation and adaptation, 2010; (ed jtly) Innovating Climate Governance: moving beyond experiments, 2018; contrib. articles to learned jls. *Recreations:* distance running, golf, walking. *Address:* King's College London, Strand Campus, WC2R 2LS. *T:* (020) 7848 1306. *E:* frans.berkhout@kcl.ac.uk.

**BERKLEY, David Nahum;** QC 1999; barrister and mediator; a Recorder, since 2001; *b* 3 Dec. 1955; *s* of Elchanan Berkovitz and Doreen Berkley (*née* Wacks); *m* 1978, Deborah Fay Haffner; one *s* four *d. Educ:* Manchester Jewish Grammar Sch.; Gateshead Yeshiva; Univ. of Manchester (LLB (Hons)). Litigation Asst, Halliwell Landau, 1978–79; called to the Bar, Middle Temple, 1979; Founding Head, Merchant Chambers, Northern Circuit, 1996; Hd, Commercial Gp, St Johns Bldgs, 2004–. Dep. Dist Judge, 1998–2001. Chm., N Circuit Commercial Bar Assoc., 2003–08 (Sec. 1997–2003). Hon. Teaching Fellow, Sch. of Law, Manchester Metropolitan Univ., 2012–14. *Recreation:* books. *Address:* St Johns Buildings, 24A–28 St John Street, Manchester M3 4DJ. *T:* (0161) 214 1500, *Fax:* (0161) 835 3929. *E:* david.berkley@stjohnsbuildings.co.uk; 3 Paper Buildings, Temple Lane, EC4Y 7EU. *T:* (020) 7583 8055. *E:* david.berkley@3pb.co.uk.

**BERKLEY, Prof. James Alexander,** MD; FRCPCH; FMedSci; Senior Clinical Research Fellow, since 2005, and Professor of Paediatric Infectious Diseases, since 2015, University of Oxford; Hon. Consultant Paediatrician, John Radcliffe Hospital, Oxford, since 2011; *b* Billericay, Essex, 20 Feb. 1965; *s* of John Barrie Berkley and Jean Chisholm Berkley; *m* 2003, Anne Lynda Diane Willetts; one *s* one *d. Educ:* Univ. of Newcastle upon Tyne (MB BS 1990; MD Invasive Bacterial Infections in African Children 2003; specialist trng in Paediatric Immunol. and Infectious Diseases, 2005); Univ. of Liverpool (MA Tropical Medicine (Dist.) 1993). MRCP 1995; FRCPCH 2010. Specialist Registrar: Gen. and Community Paediatrics, 2001, Neonatology, 2001–02, Paediatric Gastroenterology, 2002, Alder Hey Hosp., Liverpool; Wellcome Trust Trng Fellow, Clin. Tropical Medicine, Univ. of Oxford and KEMRI/Wellcome Trust Res. Prog., Kenya, 2002–03; Specialist Registrar in Paediatric Immunol. and Infectious Diseases, Newcastle Gen. Hosp., 2003–05; Wellcome Trust Intermediate Clin. Fellow, Univ. of Oxford, Kilifi, Kenya, 2005–13; Hd, Clin. Res., KEMRI/Wellcome Trust Res. Prog., Kilifi, Kenya, 2013–15; Associate Prof., Univ. of Oxford, 2014–15. Affiliate Prof. of Global Health, Univ. of Washington, 2016–; FMedSci 2017. *Publications:* contrib. learned articles on causes, risk factors and interventional trials for life-threatening infections among children in developing countries. *Recreations:*

wildlife, photography, wilderness activities, walking, camping, swimming. *Address:* Centre for Tropical Medicine and Global Health, Nuffield Department of Medicine Research Building, University of Oxford, Old Road Campus, Roosevelt Drive, Headington, Oxford OX3 7FZ.

**BERKLEY, Michael Stuart; His Honour Judge Michael Berkley;** a Circuit Judge, since 2018; *b* Colombo, Ceylon, 1966; *s* of Peter and Patricia Berkley; civil partnership 2014, Scott Arrowsmith. *Educ:* Ashlyns Sch., Berkhamsted; City of London Poly. (LLB Hons). Called to the Bar, Middle Temple, 1989; Hd of Chambers, 1999–2018; a Recorder, 2012–18. *Recreations:* theatre, food, walking, wine, opera. *Address:* Salisbury Law Courts, Wilton Road, Salisbury, Wilts SP2 7EP.

**BERKOFF, Ann Carolyn;** *see* Treneman, A. C.

**BERKOFF, Steven;** actor, director and writer; *b* 3 Aug. 1937; *s* of Polly and Al Berks (formerly Berkovitch); *m* (marr. diss.); *m* 2018, Clara Fischer. *Educ:* Raine's Foundation Grammar School, Stepney; Grocers' Co. Sch., Hackney. *Plays acted*, 1965–: Zoo Story; Arturo Ui; Dinner with Saddam; *plays directed/acted/wrote*, 1969–: Metamorphosis (also directed on Broadway, 1989, Japan, 1992); Macbeth (directed and acted); Agamemnon; The Trial; The Fall of the House of Usher; East; Kvetch (Evening Standard Comedy of the Year Award, 1991); season of 3 plays, NT; Hamlet (directed and acted); Decadence (filmed, 1993); Brighton Beach Scumbags; Greek; West; One Man; Shakespeare's Villains (one-man show), Haymarket, 1998; Messiah, Old Vic, 2003; *wrote and directed:* Sink the Belgrano, Mermaid, 1986, Acapulco, 1992; Six Actors in Search of a Director, 2012; *wrote and co-directed:* Religion and Anarchy, Jermyn St Th., 2013; *directed:* Coriolanus, NY, 1988, Munich, 1991; Salomé, Edinburgh Festival, NT (and acted), 1989, Phoenix (and acted), 1990; The Trial, NT, 1991; Coriolanus, Mermaid (and acted), 1996; Massage, LA (and acted), 1997; East, Vaudeville, 1999; Messiah, 2000; The Secret Love Life of Ophelia, 2001; Sit and Shiver, New End, 2006; On the Waterfront, Nottingham Playhouse (and adapted), 2008, transf. Th. Royal, Haymarket, 2009; Oedipus, Liverpool Playhouse (and adapted), 2011; The Hairy Ape, Odyssey Th., LA, 2016; *films acted:* A Clockwork Orange, 1971; Barry Lyndon, The Passenger, 1975; McVicar, 1980; Outland, 1981; Octopussy, 1983; Beverly Hills Cop, 1984; Rambo, Underworld, Revolution, 1985; Under the Cherry Moon, Absolute Beginners, 1986; Prisoner of Rio, 1988; The Krays, 1990; Decadence, 1994; Fair Game, 1995; Another 9½ Weeks (Love in Paris), 1997; Legionnaire, 1998; The Big I Am, Drop Dead Gorgeous, The Tourist, 2010; The Girl with the Dragon Tattoo, 2012; Tell Tale Heart (and wrote), 2017; Shakespeare's Heroes and Villains (and wrote), 2017. Hon. DLitt Brunel, 2010. *Publications:* East, 1977; Gross Intrusion (short stories), 1979; Decadence, 1982; Greek, 1982; West, 1985; Lunch, 1985; Harry's Xmas, 1985; Kvetch, 1987; Acapulco, 1987; Sink the Belgrano, 1987; Massage, 1987; America, 1988; I Am Hamlet, 1989; A Prisoner in Rio, 1989; The Theatre of Steven Berkoff (photographic), 1992; Coriolanus in Deutschland, 1992; Meditations on Metamorphosis, 1995; Free Association (autobiog.), 1996; Graft: tales of an actor (short stories), 1998; Shopping in the Santa Monica Mall, Ritual in Blood, Messiah, Oedipus, 2000; The Secret Love Life of Ophelia, 2001; Tough Acts, 2003; Richard II in New York, 2007; My Life in Food, 2008; You Remind Me of Marilyn Monroe, 2009; Diary of a Juvenile Delinquent (memoir), 2010; Tales from an Actor's Life, 2011; One-Act Plays, 2012; East-End Photographs, 2012; *play adaptations:* The Fall of the House of Usher, 1977; Agamemnon, 1977; The Trial, 1981; Metamorphosis, 1981; In the Penal Colony, 1988. *Recreations:* ping-pong, photography, travelling. *Address:* c/o Joanna Marston, 1 Clareville Grove Mews, SW7 5AH. *T:* (020) 7370 1080. *W:* www.stevenberkoff.com.

**BERKOVIC, Prof. Samuel Frank,** AC 2014 (AM 2005); MD; FRS 2007; FRACP; FAA; FAHMS; neurologist and clinical researcher; Laureate Professor, Department of Medicine, University of Melbourne, since 2007 (Australia Fellow, 2007–12); *b* Melbourne, 13 Oct. 1953; *s* of Alexander and Eva Clara Berkovic; *m* 1977, Helena Makowski; one *s* two *d*. *Educ:* Univ. of Melbourne (MB BS 1977; BMedSci 1977; MD 1985). FRACP 1985. Department of Medicine, University of Melbourne: Sen. Lectr, 1989–94; Associate Prof., 1995–98; Prof., 1998–2007; Scientific Dir, Brain Res. Inst., Melbourne, 2001–; Dir, Epilepsy Res. Centre, 1998–. Adjunct Prof., Dept of Neurol. and Neurosurgery, Faculty of Medicine, McGill Univ., Canada, 1989–. Internat. Mem., Nat. Acad. of Medicine (USA), 2017. FAA 2005; FAHMS 2015. Epilepsy Res. Recognition Award, Amer. Epilepsy Soc., 1995; Novartis Prize for Epilepsy Res., 2001; GlaxoSmithKline Australia Award for Res. Excellence, 2002; Zulch Prize for Basic Neurol Res., Max Planck Soc., Germany, 2005; Curtin Medal, ANU, 2005; Clive and Vera Ramaciotti Medal for Excellence in Biomed. Res., 2006; Bethlehem Griffiths Res. Foundn Medal, 2009; Samuel Gershon Medal for Translational Neurosci., S Australian Health and Med. Res. Inst., 2014; (jtly) Prime Minister of Australia's Award for Sci., 2014; Sen. Australian of Year, Vic, 2015; T.S. Srinivasan Endowment Prize and Oration, India, 2017. *Address:* Department of Medicine, Melbourne Brain Centre, 245 Burgundy Street, Heidelberg, Vic 3084, Australia. *T:* (3) 90357093, *Fax:* (3) 94962291. *E:* s.berkovic@unimelb.edu.au.

**BERKSHIRE, Archdeacon of;** *no new appointment at time of going to press.*

**BERKSON, Simon Nathaniel; His Honour Judge Berkson;** a Circuit Judge, since 2016; *b* Birkenhead, 19 Aug. 1964; *s* of Philip Henry Berkson and Adrienne June Berkson; *m* 1992, Siân Catherine Price; two *s*. *Educ:* Calday Grange Grammar Sch., W Kirby; Bristol Poly. (LLB Hons 1985). Called to the Bar, Gray's Inn, 1986; in practice as barrister, Liverpool, 1986–2016; a Recorder, 2012–16. *Recreations:* walking, swimming. *Address:* Chester Crown Court, The Castle, Chester CH1 2AN.

**BERLUSCONI, Silvio;** Senator, Italian Parliament, 2013; Prime Minister of Italy, 1994, 2001–06 and 2008–11; *b* 29 Sept. 1936; *s* of late Luigi Berlusconi and Rosella Berlusconi (*née* Bossi); *m* 1st, 1965, Carla Elvira Dall'Oglio (marr. diss. 1985); one *s* one *d*; 2nd, 1990, Veronica Lario (marr. diss. 2014), actress; one *s* two *d*. *Educ:* Univ. of Milan (law degree 1961). Founder: Edilnord construction co., 1962; Telemilano, cable TV station, 1974; Fininvest, 1975–94, hldg co. with interests in commercial TV, printed media, publishing, advertising, insurance, financial services, retailing and football; companies created/acquired include: TV networks, Canale 5, 1980, Italia 1, 1982, Rete 4, 1984, La Cinq, 1986, Telefünf, 1987, Telecinco, 1989; cinema chain, Cinema 5, 1985; dept store chain, La Standa, 1988; publg co., Arnoldo Mondadori Editore, 1990; newspaper, Il Giornale; Chm., AC Milan FC, 1986–2004 and 2006–17. MP Italy, 1994 and 1996–2013 (Forza Italy, 1994 and 1996–2009; Popolo della Libertà, 1996–2013). Leader: Forza Italia, 1993–2009, 2013–; Popolo della Libertà, 2009–13; Leader of the Opposition, Italy, 1996–2001; Minister of Foreign Affairs, 2002.

**BERMAN, Charlotte Allegra;** Managing Director and Global Co-Head of Securities Services, HSBC, since 2018 (Global Head of Public Sector Banking, 2013–18; Head of Financial Institutions Group, Europe, Middle East and Africa, 2016–18); *b* London, 12 Aug. 1971; *d* of late Nestor Montague Berman and Ursula Anne Berman (*née* Sharp); civil partnership 2006, *m* 2015, J. E. M. Arnold (marr. diss. 2019); one *d*. *Educ:* Wellington Sch., Som; Rugby Sch.; Magdalen Coll., Oxford (MA Modern Langs). Associate, CS First Boston, 1994–97; Dir, Barclays Capital, 1997–2001; Exec. Dir, 2001–03, Man. Dir, 2003–13, UBS. Non-exec. Dir, HSBC Asset Mgt UK, 2015–18. Mem. Bd, Internat. Capital Mkts Assoc., 2011–13. Trustee: NPG, 2011–; Magdalen Coll. Develt Trust, 2014–. *Recreations:* the arts, travel, scuba diving, ski-ing. *Address:* c/o HSBC, 8 Canada Square, E14 5HQ. *T:* (020) 7992 2651. *Clubs:* Royal Automobile, Soho House.

**BERMAN, Denise Rae;** *see* Osborn, D. R.

**BERMAN, Edward David, (ED BERMAN),** MBE 1979; social entrepreneur and activist, playwright, theatre director and producer; educationalist; Founder, Chief Executive and Artistic Director, Inter-Action, since 1968; *b* 8 March 1941; 2nd *s* of Jack Berman and Ida (*née* Webber); naturalized British citizen, 1976. *Educ:* Harvard (BA Hons); Exeter Coll., Oxford (Rhodes Schol.); Dept of Educnl Studies, Oxford (1978–). *Plays:* 8 produced since 1966; *director: theatre:* (premières) *inter alia* Dirty Linen (London and Broadway), 1976, and The Dogg's Troupe (15 minute) Hamlet, (ed) by Tom Stoppard, 1976 (also filmed, 1976); Dogg's Hamlet, Cahoot's Macbeth, 1979, by Tom Stoppard; *producer: theatre:* 125 stage premières for adults and 170 new plays for children, London, 1967–89; *maker of films:* (educational) The Head, 1971; Two Weeler, 1972; Farm in the City, 1977; Marx for Beginners Cartoon (co-prod., voice dir), 1978; *actor:* over 1200 performances as Prof. Dogg, Otto Première Check, Super Santa. Editor: 18 community arts, action and constructive leisure handbooks, 1972–; 2 anthologies of plays, 1976–78. Trustee and Founder, Inter-Action Trust, 1968; Director and Founder: Ambiance Lunch-Hour Th. Club, 1968; Prof. Dogg's Troupe for Children, 1968; Labrys Trust, 1969; Inter-Action Advisory Service, 1970; Infilms, 1970; The Almost Free Th., 1971; Inprint Publishing Unit, 1972; City Farm 1, 1972; Alternative Education Project, 1973–84; Inter-Action Trust Ltd, 1974; Town and Country Inter-Action (Milton Keynes) Ltd, 1975; Ambiance Inter-Action Inc., 1976; Talacre Centre Ltd, 1977; Co-Founder: Inter-Action Housing Trust Ltd, 1970; NUBS, Neighbourhood Use of Bldgs and Space; Community Design Centre, 1974; Beginners Books Ltd, 1978; Inter-Action Housing Co-operative, 1978; Founder and Artistic Dir, Fun Art Bus I, 1972–73. Founder, Artistic Dir, BARC, British Amer. Rep. Co., 1978. Devised: Inter-Action Creative Game Method, 1967; Super Santa, Father Xmas Union, 1967–82; Chairman: Save Piccadilly Campaign, 1971–80; Talacre Action Gp, 1972; Nat. Assoc. of Arts Centres, 1975–79; Dir, Islington Bus Co., 1974–76; Treas., Fair Play for Children Campaign, 1975–77; Hd of campaign to re-open blocked Thames Walkway, Isle of Dogs, 2010–. Founder: Nat. Fedn of City Farms, 1976; WAC—Weekend Arts Coll., 1979; co-founder: Sport-Space, 1976; FUSION—London and Commonwealth Youth Ensemble, 1981. Founder and Co-Director: Internat. Inst. for Social Enterprise, 1980; Country Wings, 1981; OPS, Occupation Preparation Systems, 1982; Options Training Ltd, 1983; Social Enterprise Projects Ltd, 1984; Founder and Trustee: Inter-Action Social Enterprise Trust Ltd, Social Enterprise Foundn of Inter-Action, 1984; Inter-Action Trust, South Africa, 2001–04; Cdre, Ships-in-the-City, 1988; Pres., HMS President (1918), 1988–2004; Founder and Director: Network Inter-Action; Youth-Tech; Star Dome, 1989; Marketing and Business Services International Ltd, 1992; Artistic Dir, Inter-Action Fun Art Bus II, 2010–. Public Service Special Adviser: on inner city matters to Sec. of State for the Environment, 1982–83; Ministry of Labour, Russia, 1992–94, Min. of Economy, 1993–95. Visiting Professor: of Social Enterprise, Great Lakes Inst. of Mgt, Chennai, 2006–07; in Community Develt, Rose Bruford Coll., 2011–12. Consultant, Res. Books, UEL, 2009–12. Founding Chairman: Rhodes Scholars in Britain, 2014–15 (Trustee, 2014–); FAB Foundn UK, 2015–. Co-Chm., Isle of Dogs Neighbourhood Planning Forum, 2015–. As community artist: created 17 formats for participatory theatre, 1968–85; Community Media Van, 1983; Community Cameos, 1977–83; MIY—Make It Yourself, 1978; RIY—Raise It Yourself, 1981; IES—Instant Enterprise Systems, 1981; Learning Domes, 1993; Public Art Workshop, 1994. Mayor's Community Champion for Canary Wharf Ward, 2014–. Torchbearer, London 2012 Olympics. FRSA 2015. Freeman, City of London, 2003; Mem. Guild of Freemen, City of London. Pearly King of River Thames, 2002–. *Publications:* Prof. R. L. Dogg's Zoo's Who I and II, 1975; Selecting Business Software, 1984; Make a Real Job of It, Breaks for Young Bands, 1985; How to Set Up a Small Business, 1987; Healthy Learning Songs & Activities, 1988; New Game Songs & Activities, 1989; (research paper) The Democracy Handbook, 1999. *Recreations:* solitude, conversation, work, music. *Address:* Inter-Action, 55 Anchorage Point, Chandlers Mews, Isle of Dogs, E14 8NF. *T:* and *Fax:* (020) 7515 4449.

**BERMAN, Sir Franklin (Delow),** KCMG 1994 (CMG 1986); HM Diplomatic Service, retired; barrister and international arbitrator; Visiting Professor of International Law: University of Oxford, since 2000; University of Cape Town, since 2000; *b* 23 Dec. 1939; *s* of Joshua Zelic Berman and Gertrude (*née* Levin); *m* 1964, Christine Mary Lawler; two *s* three *d* (triplets). *Educ:* Rondebosch Boys' High Sch., Cape Town; Univ. of Cape Town; Wadham and Nuffield Colls, Oxford (Hon. Fellow, Wadham Coll., 1995). BA, BSc Cape Town; MA Oxford. Rhodes Scholar, 1961; Martin Wronker Prizeman, 1963; called to Bar, Middle Temple, 1966 (Hon. Bencher, 1997). HM Diplomatic Service, 1965–99: Asst Legal Adviser, FO, 1965; Legal Adviser: British Military Govt, Berlin, 1971; British Embassy, Bonn, 1972; Legal Counsellor, FCO, 1974; Counsellor and Legal Adviser, UK Mission to UN, NY, 1982; FCO, 1985, Dep. Legal Advr, 1988, Legal Advr, 1991–99. *Ad hoc* Judge, Internat. Court of Justice, 2003–05; Member: Perm. Court of Arbitration, The Hague, 2010–; Court of Arbitration under Indus Waters Treaty, 2010–13. Chairman: Diplomatic Service Assoc., 1979–82; Appeals Bd, Internat. Oil Pollution Compensation Fund, 1986–2004; Claims Cttee, General Settlement Fund, Austria, 2001–17; Diplomatic Service Appeal Bd, 2002–06; Appeals Bd, WEU, 2002–05. Member: Council of Mgt, then Bd of Trustees, British Inst. of Internat. and Comparative Law, 1992–2011 (Chm., 2012–17); Council, British Br., Internat. Law Assoc., 1993–; Adv. Council, Centre for Advanced Study of European and Comparative Law, Oxford, 1995–; Adv. Council, Oxford Univ. Law Foundn, 1998–2004; Gov., Inst. of Advanced Legal Studies, Univ. of London, 1992–98. J. C. Smith Vis. Fellow, Nottingham Univ., 1993. Hon. Fellow, Soc. of Advanced Legal Studies, 1997. Trustee: Greenwich Foundn for RNC, 1997–2005; Univ. of Cape Town Trust, 2001– (Chm., 2010–); Whittuck Trust, 2001–. Patron, Pimpernel Trust, 2015–. Hon. QC 1992. Mem. Editl Bd, British Yearbook of Internat. Law, 1994–; Gen. Ed., Oxford Internat. Law Library, 2009–. Grand Decoration of Honour in Gold with Star (Austria), 2007; Grand Croix, Ordre Royal (Cambodia), 2014. *Recreations:* gardening, walking, reading, music, choral singing. *Address:* Essex Court Chambers, 24 Lincoln's Inn Fields, WC2A 3EG.

**BERMAN, Lawrence Sam,** CB 1975; retired; *b* 15 May 1928; *yr s* of late Jack and Violet Berman; *m* 1954, Kathleen D. Lewis (*d* 1996); one *s* one *d*. *Educ:* St Clement Danes Grammar Sch.; London Sch. of Economics. BSc (Econ) 1st cl. hons 1947; MSc (Econ) 1950. Res. Asst, LSE, 1947; Nuffield Coll., Oxford, 1948; Econ. Commn for Europe, 1949; Central Statistical Office: Asst Statistician 1952; Statistician 1955; Chief Statistician 1964; Asst Dir 1968; Dir of Statistics, Depts of Industry and Trade, 1972–83. Statistical Advr, Caribbean Tourism R&D Centre, Barbados, 1984–85. Editor, National Income Blue Book, 1954–60; Member: Council, Royal Statistical Soc., 1970–74 (Vice-Pres., 1973–74); Council, Internat. Assoc. for Research in Income and Wealth, 1980–85; ISI. *Publications:* Caribbean Tourism Statistical Reports; articles and papers in Jl of Royal Statistical Soc., Economica, Economic Trends, Statistical News, etc. *Recreations:* bridge, travel, theatre. *Address:* 10 Carlton Close, Edgware, Middx HA8 7PY. *T:* (020) 8958 6938.

**BERMAN, Paul Richard;** HM Diplomatic Service; Director, Legal Service, Council of the European Union, since 2012; *b* London, 23 Nov. 1964; *s* of Prof. David Solomon Berman and Patricia Denise Berman (*née* Clayman). *Educ:* Westminster Sch. (Queen's Schol.); Balliol Coll., Oxford (BA 1st Cl. Hons PPE); Grad. Inst. of Internat. Studies, Geneva (DES Relns Internationales); City Univ. (DipLaw). Called to the Bar, Gray's Inn, 1990 (Holt Schol.); joined HM Diplomatic Service, 1991; Asst Legal Advr, FCO, 1991–95; Legal Advr, Adv. Service on Internat. Humanitarian Law, Internat. Cttee of Red Cross, Geneva, 1996–98; Sen. Asst Legal Advr, FCO, 1998–2000; Counsellor, Attorney Gen.'s Chambers, 2000–02; Legal Counsellor: UK Perm. Representation to EU, Brussels, 2002–07; FCO, 2007–08; Cabinet Office Legal Advr and Dir, European Div., Treasury Solicitor's Dept, 2008–12. Member: Adv. Bd, Centre for Eur. Law, KCL, 2008–; Internat. Inst. of Humanitarian Law, San Remo, 2009–. Vis. Prof., Coll. of Europe, Bruges, 2013–. *Publications:* (contrib.) Satow's Diplomatic Practice, 6th edn 2009, centenary edn, 2017; (contrib.) EU Law after Lisbon, 2012. *Recreations:* hiking, sailing, music, theatre. *Address:* Council of the European Union, rue de la Loi 175, 1048 Brussels, Belgium. *Club:* Royal Over-Seas League.

**BERMANN, Sylvie-Agnès;** Officer de l'ordre national du mérite, 2008 (Chevalier, 1996); Officier de la Légion d'Honneur, 2012 (Chevalier, 2003); Ambassador of France to the Russian Federation, since 2017; *b* Salins-les Bains, France, 19 Oct. 1953; *d* of Gustave-Guy Bermann and Elisabeth Barbier. *Educ:* Sorbonne Univ. (history degree); Paris Inst. of Political Studies; French Inst. of Oriental Langs and Civilizations (Chinese); Beijing Langs Inst. Vice-Consul, Hong Kong, 1979–80; Second Secretary: Beijing, 1980–82; Asia and Oceania Directorate, 1982–86; Second Counsellor, Moscow, 1986–89; Hd, Southeast Asia Dept, 1989–92; Second Counsellor, French Perm. Mission to UN, 1992–96; Hd, Common Foreign and Security Policy Dept, French Foreign Ministry, 1996–2002; Ambassador to WEU and Political and Security Cttee, EU, Brussels, 2002–05; Hd, Directorate for UN and internat. orgns, human rights and Francophony, French Foreign Ministry, 2005–11; Ambassador: to China, 2011–14; to the Court of St James's, 2014–17. *Recreations:* literature, cinema, theatre, opera.

**BERMINGHAM, Gerald Edward;** barrister; *b* Dublin, 20 Aug. 1940; *s* of late Patrick Xavier Bermingham and Eva Terescena Bermingham; *m* 1st, 1964, Joan (marr. diss.); two *s*; 2nd, 1978, Judith (marr. diss.); 3rd, 1998, Jilly; one *s*. *Educ:* Cotton College, N Staffs; Wellingborough Grammar School; Sheffield University (LLB Hons). Admitted Solicitor, 1967; called to the Bar, Gray's Inn, 1985. Councillor, Sheffield City Council, 1975–79, 1980–82. Contested (Lab) SE Derbyshire, 1979. MP (Lab) St Helens South, 1983–2001. *Recreations:* sport, reading, TV. *Address:* 5 Fountain Court, Steelhouse Lane, Birmingham B4 6DR.

**BERNARD, Beverley Amari;** *see* Blaize, B. A.

**BERNARD, Sir Dallas (Edmund),** 2nd Bt *cr* 1954; Director: Morgan Grenfell (Holdings) Ltd, 1972–79; Italian International Bank plc, 1978–89; *b* 14 Dec. 1926; *o s* of Sir Dallas Gerald Mercer Bernard, 1st Bt, and Betty (*d* 1980), *e d* of late Sir Charles Addis, KCMG; *S* father, 1975; *m* 1st, 1959, Sheila Mary Gordon Robey (marr. diss. 1979; she *d* 2009); two *d* (and one *d* decd); 2nd, 1979, Mrs Monica Montford (*née* Hudson) (marr. diss. 2003); one *d*; 3rd, 2003, Mrs Graciela Scorza, *d* of late Francisco Scorza Fúster and Celmira Leguizamón O'Higgins. *Educ:* Eton Coll.; Corpus Christi Coll., Oxford (MA). FCIS. Director: Dreyfus Intercontinental Investment Fund NV, 1970–91; Morgan Grenfell & Co. Ltd, 1964–77; Dominion Securities Ltd, Toronto, 1968–79; Nat. & Foreign Securities Trust Ltd, 1981–86; Dreyfus Dollar Internat. Fund Inc., 1982–91; Chm., Thames Trust Ltd, 1983–86. Mem. Monopolies and Mergers Commn, 1973–79. Mem. Council, GPDST, 1988–93 (Finance Cttee, 1975–92). *Heir:* none. *Address:* Ivery House, Church Hill, Wroughton, Wilts SN4 9JS. *T:* (01793) 814370. *Club:* Army and Navy.

**BERNARD, Daniel Camille;** Chairman: Kingfisher plc, 2009–17 (Joint Deputy Chairman, 2006–07; Deputy Chairman, 2007–09); Majid Al Futtaim Retail Group, 2010–15; Senior Advisor, TowerBrook Capital Partners, since 2010; *b* 18 Feb. 1946; *s* of Paul Bernard and Simone (*née* Doise); *m* 1968, Chantal Leduc; one *s* two *d*. *Educ:* Lycée Camille Desmoulins, Cateau; Lycée Faidherbe, Lille; HEC Business Sch.; Univ. of Paris. Divl Manager, Mammouth, 1976–81; Chief Exec. Officer, Metro France, 1981–89; Mem. Bd and Chief Operating Officer, Metro Internat., 1989–92; Carrefour Group: CEO, 1992–98; Chm. and CEO, 1998–2005. Pres., Provestis, 2006–; non-executive Director: Alcatel-Lucent (formerly Alcatel), 1997–2014; Cap Gemini, 2005–. Chm., HEC Foundn, 2008–14. *Recreations:* mountains, ski-ing, opera.

**BERNARD, Ralph Mitchell,** CBE 2002; Chairman: Classic FM plc, 2007–12 (Director, 1991–2012; Chief Executive, 1997–2005); British Lung Foundation, 2009–11 (Trustee, since 2011); Public Service Broadcasting Trust, since 2011; Chairman and Chief Executive, Quidem Productions Ltd, since 2011; *b* 11 Feb. 1953; *s* of Reginald and Irene Bernard; *m* 1977, Lisa Anne Susan Kiené; four *d*. *Educ:* Caterham High Sch., Ilford. Copy boy, London News Service, 1970–71; Reporter: Express and Independent, Leytonstone, 1971–72; Stratford Express, 1972–73; Cambridge Evening News, 1973–75; radio journalist, 1975–78, Documentaries Ed., 1978–80, Radio Hallam, Sheffield; News Ed., Hereward Radio, Peterborough, 1980–82; Prog. Controller, 1982–83, Man. Dir, 1983–85, Wiltshire Radio; Pre-launch Manager, Classic FM, 1991; Chief Exec., 1985–2001, Exec. Chm., 2001–05, GWR Gp plc; Chief Exec., GCap Media plc, 2005–07. Chairman: London News Radio (LBC and News Direct), 1996–2001; Digital One Ltd, 1998–2009; Director: Ind. Radio News, 1994–2011; Watermill Th., Newbury, 2005–15; Touch Broadcasting Ltd, 2009–; Screenplay Films, 2016–. Chm., Broadcast Journalists' Trng Council, 2014–. Chm., Central Sch. of Ballet, 2008–. Chm., Campaign Bd, Great Western Hosp., Swindon, 2000–02. Trustee, Shakespeare Birthplace Trust, 2012–. Gov., Dauntsey's Sch., 2007–. Fellow, Radio Acad., 1999. Sony Gold Award, 2000. *Recreations:* music (most), walking, newspaper originals, cricket. *Address:* Quidem Productions Ltd, Spittleborough Farmhouse, Old Swindon Road, Royal Wootton Bassett, Swindon SN4 8ET.

**BERNAYS, Robert Edward John,** OBE 2010; Vice Lord-Lieutenant of Gloucestershire, since 2011; *b* Bristol, 7 Oct. 1944; *s* of Robert Hamilton Bernays, MP and Nancy Bernays (*née* Britton); *m* 1975, Alison Urquhart; three *d*. *Educ:* Eton Coll.; Wye Coll., Univ. of London (Dip. Farm Business Admin). Farmer, 1963–2005. Trustee, Berkeley Estates, 1999–. Chm., Tender LifeCare Ltd, 2015–16. Dir, Fertility Focus, 2008–17. Pres. and Chm., St Monica Trust, 1999–2010. Gov., Dauntsey's Sch., 1995–2005 (Chm., 1999–2005); Chm., Colston's Sch., Bristol, 2013–16. Master, Merchant Venturers' Soc., Bristol, 1996–97. High Sheriff Avon, 1987; DL Glos, 1988. *Recreations:* sailing, ski-ing, walking, gardening and most of all, family. *Address:* Whitecroft, 3A Merlin Haven, Wotton-under-Edge, Glos GL12 7BA. *E:* robertbernays@yahoo.com.

**BERNAYS, Rosamund;** *see* Horwood-Smart, R.

**BERNER, Roger Francis;** a Judge of the Upper Tribunal (Tax and Chancery Chamber), 2011–19; *b* London, 16 March 1952; *s* of John and Doreen Berner; *m* 1st, 1979, Susan Gibbons (marr. diss. 1995); one *s* one *d*; 2nd, 2011, Gay Bateman. *Educ:* Southgate Sch.; Coll. of Law, Guildford (Clements Inn Prizeman 1975). Admitted as solicitor, 1976; Asst Solicitor, Freshfields, 1976–79; Solicitor, 1979–82, Partner, 1982–90, Stevens & Bolton; Solicitor, Freshfields, 1990–93; Partner, Freshfields Bruckhaus Deringer, 1993–2007; Gp Hd of Tax, N. M. Rothschild & Sons Ltd, 2007–09; a Judge, First-tier Tribunal (Tax Chamber), 2009–11. *Publications:* (contrib.) Tolley's Company Law, 1983. *Recreations:* family, sport, theatre, opera, ballet, cinema.

**BERNERD, Elliott;** Co-founder and Chairman, Chelsfield Partners, since 2006; *b* 23 May 1945; *s* of late Geoffrey Bernerd and of Trudie Malawer (*née* Melzack); *m* 1st, 1968, Susan Elizabeth Lynton (marr. diss. 1989); two *d*; 2nd, 1992, Sonia Ramsay (*née* Ramalho) (marr. diss. 2009). Chairman: Chelsfield plc, 1987–2004; Wentworth Group Holdings Ltd, 1990–2004. Chairman: London Philharmonic Trust, 1987–94; South Bank Foundn, 1996–2007; South Bank Bd Ltd, 1998–2002. Chm. Trustees, Facial Surgery Res. Foundn, 2004–. *Recreations:* tennis, ski-ing. *Clubs:* Savile, Cavalry and Guards, Royal Automobile; Wentworth.

**BERNERS, Baroness** (16th in line), *cr* 1455; **Pamela Vivien Kirkham;** *b* 30 Sept. 1929; *er d* of Harold Williams and Baroness Berners, 15th in line (*d* 1992); *S* to Barony of mother (called out of abeyance, 1995); *m* 1952, Michael Joseph Sperry Kirkham (*d* 2017); two *s* one *d*. *Educ:* Bredenbury Court, Hereford; Stonar Sch., Wilts. Radcliffe Infirmary, Oxford (SRN 1951). *Recreations:* painting, drawing, gardening, reading. *Heir:* *s* Hon. Rupert William Tyrwhitt Kirkham [*b* 18 Feb. 1953; *m* 1994, Lisa Carol Judy Lipsey; one *s*].

**BERNERS-LEE, Sir Timothy (John),** OM 2007; KBE 2004 (OBE 1997); RDI 2009; FRS 2001; FREng; 3Com Founders Professor, since 1999, Director, World Wide Web Consortium, and Professor of Engineering, Computer Science and Artificial Intelligence Laboratory, Massachusetts Institute of Technology; Professor of Computer Science, University of Oxford, since 2016; Fellow, Christ Church, Oxford, since 2016; *b* London, 8 June 1955; *s* of late Conway Berners-Lee and Mary Lee Berners-Lee (*née* Woods); *m* 2014, Rosemary Leith; two *c* by a previous marriage. *Educ:* Emanuel Sch., London; Queen's Coll., Oxford (BA 1976; Hon. Fellow, 1999). Plessey Telecommunications Ltd, 1976–78; software engr, D. G. Nash Ltd, 1978; ind. consultant, 1978–80, incl. software consultancy, CERN, Geneva (wrote unpublished prog., Enquire, forerunner of World Wide Web); Founding Dir, responsible for tech. design, Image Computer Systems Ltd, 1981–84; Fellowship, CERN, 1984–94: global hypertext project, 1989, became World Wide Web, 1990 (available on Internet, 1991); designed URL (universal resource locator) and HTML (hypertext markup lang.); joined Lab. for Computer Sci., MIT, 1994. Prof. of Computer Sci., Univ. of Southampton, 2004–16. Founder Dir, Web Science Trust, 2009–. Co-Dir, Open Data Inst., Shoreditch, 2011–. MacArthur Fellow, John D. and Catherine T. MacArthur Foundn, 1998. Distinguished FBCS; FREng 2001. Hon. FBA 2011. Hon. DSc Oxon, 2001. (Jtly) Queen Elizabeth Prize for Engrg, Royal Acad. of Engrg, 2013; A. M. Turing Award, Assoc. for Computing Machinery, 2017. *Publications:* Weaving the Web, 2000. *Address:* Computer Science and Artificial Intelligence Laboratory, Massachusetts Institute of Technology, 77 Massachusetts Avenue, Cambridge, MA 02139, USA.

**BERNEY, Sir Julian (Reedham Stuart),** 11th Bt *cr* 1620; Chairman, Schroders European Real Estate Investment Trust plc; *b* 26 Sept. 1952; *s* of Lieut John Reedham Erskine Berney (killed on active service in Korea, 1952), Royal Norfolk Regt, and Hon. Jean Davina, *d* of 1st Viscount Stuart of Findhorn, PC, CH, MVO, MC; *S* grandfather, 1975; *m* 1976, Sheena Mary, *yr d* of late Ralph Day and Ann Gordon Day; two *s* one *d*. *Educ:* Wellington Coll.; North East London Polytechnic. FRICS 1992. Formerly Internat. Dir, Jones Lang LaSalle, Strutt & Parker, BNP Paribas, Aberdeen Property Investors; Dir and Proprietor, Consulting South East Ltd, 2010. Freeman, Fishmongers' Co. *Recreation:* sailing. *Heir:* *s* William Reedham John Berney [*b* 29 June 1980; *m* 2013, Mariana Cid Tamayo; one *s* one *d*]. *Address:* Reeds House, 40 London Road, Maldon, Essex CM9 6HE. *T:* (01621) 853420. *Clubs:* Royal Ocean Racing; Royal Cruising; Royal Yacht Squadron.

**BERNIE, Philip Robert;** Head of Sport, BBC Television, since 2009; *b* Maidenhead, 22 Feb. 1962; *s* of Ronald Bernie and Yetta Bernie (*née* Zurich); *m* 2010, Pamela Hunnisett. *Educ:* St Paul's Sch., London; University Coll., Oxford (MA Hist.). BBC Sport: asst producer, 1986–90; asst ed., 1990–96; ed., 1996–2005; progs edited incl. Match of the Day, Grandstand, Match of the Day 2, Sports Personality of the Year, Wimbledon, World Cup, Olympics; Head: of Progs, 2005–06; of TV Sport Editorial, 2006–09. *Recreations:* finding and eating good food, travelling, time with our dog and cat, playing football and tennis, swimming, watching comedy, reading. *Address:* BBC Television, Quay House, Media City UK, Salford M50 2QH. *T:* (0161) 335 6261. *E:* philip.bernie@bbc.co.uk. *Clubs:* MCC; Tottenham Hotspur Football.

**BERNSTEIN, David,** CBE 2014; Executive Chairman, Ted Baker plc, since 2019 (non-executive Director, 2003–19; non-executive Chairman, 2013–19); Chairman of Trustees, British Red Cross, since 2014; *b* St Helens, Lancs, 22 May 1943; *s* of Henry Bernstein and Anne Bernstein; *m* 1966, Gillian Davis; four *s*. *Educ:* Christ's Coll. Finchley. FCA 1966. Joined Bright Grahame Murray, chartered accountants, 1968; admitted Partner, 1969; Jt Sen. Partner, 1980–88; Man. Dir, Gp Develt, Pentland Gp plc, 1988–94; Dir, 1994–2003, Chm., 1998–2003, Manchester City plc; Dir, 2003–11, Chm., 2008–11, Wembley National Stadium; Chm., FA, 2011–13. Non-executive Chairman: French Connection Gp plc, 1995–2001; Blacks Leisure Gp plc, 1996–2011; Adams Childrenswear Ltd, 2000–05; Sport and Leisure Gp Ltd, 2006–11; Chm., Orchid Gp Ltd, 2010–12; non-exec. Dir, Carluccio's plc, 2005–10. Pres., Level Playing Field, 2007–; Chm., Centre for Access to Football in Europe, 2008–; Trustee, Sharre Zadek Hosp., Jerusalem. *Recreations:* tennis (Chm., Chandos Lawn Tennis Club), running (completed two London Marathons), golf, theatre, modern history. *Address:* Ted Baker plc, Ugly Brown Building, 6a St Pancras Way, NW1 0TB.

**BERNSTEIN, Sir Howard,** Kt 2003; DL; Chief Executive, Manchester City Council, 1998–2017; *b* 9 April 1953; *s* of Maurice and Miriam Bernstein; *m* 1980, Yvonne Selwyn (marr. diss. 2004); one *s* one *d* (and one *s* decd); *m* 2004, Vanessa. *Educ:* Ducie High Sch., Manchester; London Univ. (ext.). Manchester City Council: Head of Urban Policy, 1980–86; Asst Chief Exec., 1986–90; Dep. Chief Exec., 1990–98; Dep. Clerk, 1986–98, Clerk, 1998–, Gtr Manchester PTA; Chief Exec., Manchester City Centre Task Force, 1996. Sec., Commonwealth Games Organising Cttee, 1996–2002; Mem. Bd, Olympic Delivery Authy, 2006–08. Chm., ReBlackpool, 2008. Hon. FRIBA 2003. Hon. RNCM 2005. Hon. DLitt UMIST, 2003; Hon. LLD Manchester, 2004; Hon. DBA Manchester Metropolitan, 2005. DL Gtr Manchester 2003. *Recreations:* sport, particularly football and cricket.

**BERNSTEIN, Her Honour Ingeborg, (Inge);** a Circuit Judge, 1991–2001; *b* 24 Feb. 1931; *d* of Sarah and Eli Bernstein; *m* 1967, Eric Geoffrey Goldrein; one *s* one *d*. *Educ:* Peterborough County School; St Edmund's College, Liverpool; Liverpool University. Called to the Bar, Inner Temple, 1952; practice on Northern Circuit; a Recorder, 1978–91. Chm., Mental Health Review Tribunal, 1968–91 and 1992–2007; Mem., Mental Health Act Commn, 1984–86. *Recreation:* the domestic arts.

**BERNSTEIN, Rt Hon. Dame Ingrid Ann;** *see* Simler, Rt Hon. Dame I. A.

**BERRAGAN, Maj.-Gen. Gerald Brian,** CB 1988; Chief Executive, Institute of Packaging, 1988–98; b 2 May 1933; s of William James and Marion Beatrice Berragan; m 1956, Anne Helen Kelly; three s. Commissioned REME 1954; attached 7th Hussars, Hong Kong, 1954–55; transf. RAOC 1956; served UK, Belgium, Germany and with 44 Para Bde (TA); Staff College, 1966; Nat. Defence Coll., 1972–73; Comdr RAOC 3 Div., 1973–76; AQMG HQ N Ireland, 1976–78; HQ DGOS, 1978–80; Comdt Central Ordnance Depot, Chilwell, 1980–82; Sen. Management Course, Henley, 1982; Comdt COD Bicester, 1982–83; Dir, Supply Ops (Army), 1983–85; Sen. Internat. Defence Management Course, USA, 1985; Dir Gen. of Ordnance Services, 1985–88. Col Comdt, RAOC, 1988–93, RLC 1993–98. UK Dir, World Packaging Orgn, 1988–98. FInstPkg.

**BERRAGAN, Lt Gen. Sir Gerald William, (Sir Gerry),** KBE 2015; CB 2011; Chief Executive, Institute for Apprenticeships and Technical Education (formerly Institute for Apprenticeships), since 2017. Commnd RA, 1979; Chief Targeting and Information Ops, HQ ARRC, 2002–04; COS Field Army, 2004–06; Dep. Comdr Multi-Nat. Corps Iraq, 2007; Dir Gen. Army Recruiting and Trng, 2007–11; Dir Gen. Personnel, HQ Land Forces, 2011–12; Adjutant Gen., 2012–15. Legion of Merit (USA), 2007.

**BERRESFORD, James Whistler;** Chief Executive Officer, VisitEngland, 2009–16; b Chesterfield, 29 April 1956; s of Michael and Mary Berresford; m 1995, Dawn Mary; one s. Educ: Abbotsholme Sch.; Huddersfield Poly. (BA Hons Humanities); City of London Univ. (Postgrad. Arts). Mktg Manager, Nottingham Playhouse, 1979–82; Nottinghamshire County Council: Tourism Officer, 1982–90; Asst Dir, Leisure, 1990–99; Dir (E), Heart of England Tourist Bd, 1999–2002; Dir, Tourism, NW Regl Develt Agency, 2002–08. Chairman: Buxton Crescent and Thermal Spa Heritage Trust, 2016–; Islands Partnership, Isles of Scilly, 2016–; Trustee, SS Great Britain Trust, 2016–. Associate, Liverpool Inst. Performing Arts, 2007–. Hon. DBA Chester, 2011. Recreations: walking, cycling, English holidays, theatre, football. E: james.berresford@ntlworld.com.

**BERRIDGE,** Baroness cr 2011 (Life Peer), of the Vale of Catmose in the County of Rutland; **Elizabeth Rose Berridge;** a Baroness in Waiting (Government Whip), since 2019; b Oakham, Rutland, 22 March 1972. Educ: Catmose Coll.; Rutland Coll.; Emmanuel Coll., Cambridge (BA 1995); Inns of Court Sch. of Law, London. Called to the Bar, Inner Temple, 1996; barrister, Kings Chambers, Manchester, 1996–2005. Exec. Dir, Conservative Christian Fellowship, 2005–11. Mem., Jt Cttee on Human Rights, H of L 2011–15; Co-Chair, All Party Parly Gp on Internat. Freedom of Religion or Belief, 2012–. Mem., Internat. Panel of Parliamentarians for Freedom of Religion or Belief, 2014–; Co-Dir, Commonwealth Initiative for Freedom of Religion or Belief, 2015–18; Dir, Freedom Declared Foundn, 2018–. Mem., Adv. Council, Theos, 2012–. Trustee: Kainos Community, 2006–14; British Future, 2012–16. Contested (C) Stockport, 2005. Recreations: swimming, Ghana, church, piano, tennis. Address: House of Lords, SW1A 0PW. T: (020) 7219 8943.

**BERRIDGE, Sir Michael (John),** Kt 1998; PhD; FRS 1984; Fellow of Trinity College, Cambridge, since 1972; Head of Signalling Programme, Babraham Institute Laboratory of Molecular Signalling, 1996–2003, now Emeritus Babraham Fellow; b 22 Oct. 1938; s of George Kirton Berridge and Stella Elaine Hards; m 1965, Susan Graham Winter; one s one d. Educ: University Coll. of Rhodesia and Nyasaland (BSc); Univ. of Cambridge (PhD). Post-doctoral Fellow: Univ. of Virginia, 1965–66; Case Western Reserve Univ., Cleveland, Ohio, 1966–69; AFRC Lab. of Molecular Signalling (formerly Unit of Insect Neurophysiology and Pharmacology), Dept of Zoology, Univ. of Cambridge, 1969–90; Babraham Inst. Lab. of Molecular Signalling, 1990–2003. Founder FMedSci 1998. King Faisal Internat. Prize in Sci., 1986; Jeantet Prize in Medicine, 1986; Gairdner Foundn Internat. Award, 1988; Lasker Basic Med. Res. Award, 1989; Dr H. P. Heineken Prize for Biochemistry and Biophysics, 1994; Wolf Foundn Prize in Medicine, 1995; Shaw Prize in Life Sci. and Medicine, Shaw Prize Foundn, 2005. Publications: papers in Jl Exptl Biol., Biochem. Jl and Nature. Recreations: golf, gardening. Address: The Babraham Institute, Babraham Hall, Babraham, Cambridge CB22 3AT. T: (01223) 496621.

**BERRIEDALE, Lord; Alexander James Richard Sinclair;** b 26 March 1981; s and heir of Earl of Caithness, qv. Educ: St David's Coll., Llandudno. Studying to be a commercial pilot. Recreation: outdoor pursuits.

**BERRIMAN, Sir David,** Kt 1990; FCIB; Chairman, Association of Lloyd's Members, 1994–98 (Committee Member, 1993–98); b 20 May 1928; s of late Algernon Edward Berriman, OBE and late Enid Kathleen Berriman (née Sutcliffe); m 1st, 1955, Margaret Lloyd (née Owen) (marr. diss. 1995; she d 1995); two s; 2nd, 1971, Shirley Elizabeth (née Wright) (d 1993); 3rd, 1995, Patricia Ann Salter (née Walker) (d 2013); 4th, 2014, Caryl Ann Ayscough (née Spinks). Educ: Winchester; New Coll., Oxford (MA, Dip. Econ. and Pol Sci.); Harvard Business Sch. PMD course, 1961. First National City Bank of New York, 1952–56; Ford Motor Co. Ltd, 1956–60; AEI Hotpoint, 1960–63; Gen. Manager, United Leasing Corporation Ltd, 1963–64; Morgan Grenfell & Co. Ltd: Manager, 1964; Exec. Dir, 1968–73; Dir, Guinness Mahon & Co. Ltd, 1973–87 (Exec. Dir. 1973–85). Chairman: Bunzl Textile Holdings Ltd, 1981–88 (Dep. Chm., 1980); Alban Communications Ltd, 1988–90 (Dir, 1983–; Dep. Chm., 1987–88); Privatised Public Service Pension Plan Trustees Ltd, 1994–97; Director (non-exec.): Cable and Wireless, 1975–88; Sky Television (formerly Satellite Television), 1981–89 (Chm., 1981–85); Bahrain Telecommunications Corp., 1982–88; Britannia Building Soc., 1983–93; Ashenden Enterprises Ltd, 1983–2001; Videotron Hldgs plc, 1989–97; KDB Bank (UK) Ltd, 1991–98. Chairman: Lewisham and N Southwark DHA, 1981–84; NE Thames RHA, 1984–90. Member: Govt review body on Harland and Wolff diversification, 1980; Corp. of Lloyd's Disciplinary Bd, 1996–2001; Bd of Trade's Interim Action Cttee for the Film Industry, 1977–85; British Screen Adv. Council, 1985–91. Director: British Screen Finance Ltd, 1985–91; Nat. Film Develt Fund, 1985–91. Dep. Chm., Nat. Film and Television School, 1988–92 (Gov., 1977–92). Chairman: MacIntyre Care, 1978–92 (Gov., 1977–92); MacIntyre Charitable Trust, 1986–92; MacIntyre Foundn, 1993–95; Member, Council: Internat. Hosp. Fedn, 1985–86; King Edward's Hosp. Fund for London, 1985–90. Trustee: New Coll., Oxford Development Fund, 1983–95; Kent Community Housing Trust, 1990–2008 (Dep. Chm., 1998–2008). CCMI. Recreations: golf, lawn tennis. Club: Royal Automobile (Mem., Sen. One Hundred Roll).

**BERRUYER, Guy;** Chief Executive, Sage Group plc, 2010–14; b France, 12 Aug. 1951; m 1986, Pascale Laroche; two s one d. Educ: Ecole Poly. Fédérale de Lausanne; Harvard Univ. (MBA). Dir, Mktg and Sales Distribution, Groupe Bull, 1984–89; S Eur. Man. Dir, Claris, 1989–94; Eur. Man. Dir, Intuit, 1994–97; Sage Group plc: joined 1997 to run French operation; Mem. Bd of Dirs and CEO, Mainland Europe business, 2000–10, Asian Ops, 2005–10. Chm., Linaro Ltd, 2015–; non-exec. Dir, Meggitt plc, 2012–. Mem. Council, Univ. of Southampton, 2015–. Recreations: golf, theatre.

**BERRY,** family name of **Viscounts Camrose** and **Kemsley.**

**BERRY, Amanda Sonia,** OBE 2009; Chief Executive, British Academy of Film and Television Arts, since 2000; b Darlington, 20 Aug. 1961; d of Thomas and Anita Berry. Educ: Richmond Sch.; York Coll. of Art and Technol.; Newcastle upon Tyne Poly. Co-dir, Duncan Health Associates, later ICM, 1982–88; researcher, light entertainment and current affairs, LWT, 1989–90; Producer and Develt Exec., Scottish Television Enterprises, 1990–98; Dir, Develt and Events, 1998–99, Dep. Exec. Dir, 1999–2000, BAFTA. Recreations: film, music, art, cycling, holidays. Address: British Academy of Film and Television Arts, 195 Piccadilly, W1J 9LN. T: (020) 7734 0022.

**BERRY, Anthony Charles,** QC 1994; b 4 Oct. 1950; s of Geoffrey Vernon Berry and Audrey Millicent Berry (née Farrar); m 1977, Susan Carmen Traversi; three s one d. Educ: Downside Sch.; Lincoln Coll., Oxford (BA Phil. and Psychol.). Called to the Bar, Gray's Inn, 1976, Bencher, 2002. Sec., Criminal Bar Assoc., 1991–93; Mem., Bar Council, 1993–95. Recreations: tennis, golf. Address: 9 Bedford Row, WC1R 4AZ. T: (020) 7489 2727.

**BERRY, (Anthony) Scyld (Ivens);** cricket correspondent, The Telegraph, since 2014; Editor, Wisden Cricketers' Almanack, 2007–11; b 28 April 1954; s of late Prof. Francis Berry; m 1984, Sunita Ghosh; two s one d. Educ: Westbourne School, Sheffield; Ampleforth College; Christ's College, Cambridge (MA Oriental Studies). Cricket correspondent: The Observer, 1978–89; The Sunday Correspondent, 1989–90; The Independent on Sunday, 1991–93; Sunday Telegraph, 1993–2014. Cricket Journalist of the Year, Sports Journalists' Assoc., 2018. Publications: Cricket Wallah, 1982; Train to Julia Creek, 1984; (ed) The Observer on Cricket, 1987; Cricket Odyssey, 1988; (with Phil Edmonds) 100 Great Bowlers, 1989; (with Rupert Peploe) Cricket's Burning Passion, 2006 (Cricket Soc./MCC Book of the Year, 2006); Cricket: the game of life, 2015 (Book of the Year, Cricket Writers Club, 2016). Recreations: playing village cricket, being at home. Address: c/o The Telegraph, 111 Buckingham Palace Road, SW1W 0DT. Club: Hinton Charterhouse Cricket.

**BERRY, Sir Colin (Leonard),** Kt 1993; DSc; FRCPath; Professor of Morbid Anatomy, University of London, at The London Hospital Medical College, 1976–2002, now Emeritus; Warden of Joint Medical and Dental School, St Bartholomew's and Royal London Hospitals, and Vice-Principal for Medicine and Dentistry, Queen Mary and Westfield College, London University, 1995–96; b 28 Sept. 1937; s of Ronald Leonard Berry and Peggy-Caroline (née Benson); m 1960, Yvonne Waters; two s. Educ: privately, and Beckenham Grammar Sch.; Charing Cross Hosp. Med. Sch. (MB, BS; Governors' Clinical Gold Medal, Llewellyn Schol., Pierera Prize in Clinical Subjects, Steadman Prize in Path.); trained in Histopath. Charing Cross Hosp., 1962–64. MD 1968, PhD 1970, DSc 1993 (London). FRCPath 1979; FFPM 1991; FRCP 1993; FFOM 1995; FRCPE 1997. Lectr and Sen. Lectr, Inst. of Child Health, London, 1964–70; Reader in Pathology, Guy's Hosp. Med. Sch., 1970–76; Dean, London Hosp. Med. Coll., 1994–95. Gillson Scholar, Worshipful Soc. of Apothecaries, 1967–68 and 1970–72; Arris and Gail Lectr, RCS, 1973; Lectures: Bawden, BCPC, 1990; John Hull Grundy, Royal Army Med. Coll., 1992; Simonides, European Soc. of Pathology, 1993; Lucas, RCP, 1994; Sir Michael Davies, Expert Witness Inst., 2005; Sir Roy Cameron, RCPath, 2009; Sir William Paton, British Toxicol. Soc., 2014. Chairman: Cttee on Dental and Surgical Materials, 1982–92 (Vice-Chm., 1979–82); Scientific Sub-Cttee on Pesticides, MAFF, 1984–87; Adv. Cttee on Pesticides, MAFF/DHSS, 1988– (Mem., 1982–87); Bd in Histology and Cytology, Union Européenne des Médecins Spécialistes, 1993–99; Member: Toxicology Review Panel, WHO, 1976–84, 1987–; Scientific Adv. Cttee on Pesticides, EEC, 1981–88; Cttee on Toxicity of Chemicals in Food, Consumer Products and the Environment, 1982–86; Cttee on Safety of Medicines, Dept of Health, 1990–92; Ownership Bd, Pesticides Safety Directorate, 1994–99; Steering Gp on Envmt and Health, ESF, 1995–; Radical Review of Coroner Service, Home Office, 2001–03; MRC, 1990–94; GMC, 1993–96 and 1998–2003; Chm., Physiological Systems and Disorders Bd, MRC, 1990–92 (Mem., 1988–). Member, Advisory Board: Sci. and Policy, American Council on Sci. and Health, 2001–; Sense about Science, 2003–; Scientific Alliance, 2003–; Fundação para Ciência e a Tecnologia, Portugal, 2005–; Agência de Acreditação e Avaliação do Ensino Superior, Portugal, 2008–. Chm., Programme Cttee, Eur. Sci. Open Forum, 2006, 2008. President: Developmental Path. Soc., 1976–79; European Soc. of Pathology, 1989–91 (Pres. elect, 1987–89); British Acad. of Forensic Scis, 2003–05 (Pres. elect, 2001–02). Sec., Fedn of Assocs of Clinical Profs, 1987– (Hon. Fellow, 2007); Chm. Council, 1993–99, Hon. Vice-Pres., 2000–, Res. Defence Soc.; Hon. Sec., ACP, 1982–85 (Meetings Sec., 1979–82). Scientific Advr, BIBRA, 1987–90. Hon. Curator, Deutsches Mus., Munich, 2006–10. Pres., British Medical Golfing Soc., 2016–. Treasurer, RCPath, 1988–93 (Asst Registrar, 1981–84). Asst to Court, Apothecaries' Soc., 1990– (Master, 2003–04; Treas., 2004–14). Knight President, Imperial Soc. of Knights Bachelor, 2019– (Mem. Council, 1997–; Treas. 2006–12; Knight Principal, 2012–19). Founder FMedSci 1998. Hon. Fellow, British Toxicol. Soc., 2006. Corresp. Member: Deutsche Akad. der Naturforscher Leopoldina, 1993 (Hon. Mem., 2005); Nordrhein-Westfälische Akademie, 1993; German Pathol Soc., 2000 (Hon. Mem., 2005). Hon. MD Ioannina, Greece, 2003. Publications: Teratology: trends and applications, 1975; Paediatric Pathology, 1981, 3rd edn 1995; Diseases of the Arterial Wall, 1988; contrib. to many texts; numerous pubns in Jl of Path., Circulation Res. and other path. jls. Recreations: fishing, pond building, golf. Clubs: Reform, Farmers; Dulwich and Sydenham Golf.

**BERRY, Graham;** freelance advisor and consultant on the arts, Singapore, 2007–11; Director, Scottish Arts Council, 2002–07; b 12 Jan. 1945; s of Alexander and Émélie Berry; m 2007, Irene Ng; one s one d by a previous marriage. Educ: Royal High Sch., Edinburgh. ICAS. Chartered accountant, Price Waterhouse, 1968–70; Divl Chief Accountant, Trust House Forte, 1970–74; Company Secretary, 1974–86: Scottish Film Council; Scottish Council for Educn and Technol.; Glasgow Film Th.; Filmhouse, Edinburgh; Scottish Film Prodn Fund; Finance Officer, Univ. of Stirling, 1986–89; Hd of Funding and Resources, Scottish Arts Council, 1989–2002. Publications: From Kilts to Sarongs: Scottish pioneers of Singapore, 2015. Recreations: mountaineering, photography.

**BERRY, (Gwenda) Lynne,** OBE 2006; Chair, Public Benefit, since 2011; b 27 Jan. 1953. Social Worker, Wandsworth LBC, 1976–79; Community Worker, Camden Council of Social Service, 1979–81; Lecturer: PCL, 1981–84; NISW, 1984–88; Social Services Inspector, DoH, 1988–90; Chief Exec., Family Welfare Assoc., 1990–96; Exec. Dir, Charity Commn, 1996–99; Chief Executive: EOC, 1999–2001; Gen Social Care Council, 2001–07; WRVS, 2007–11. Non-exec. Dir, Europe Div., DTI, 1998–2001. Chm., CPAG, 2001–05; Member: Better Regulation Commn (formerly Better Regulation Task Force), 2005–07; Risk and Regulation Commn, 2007–09; Adv. Bd, Office of Third Sector, 2008–12; Lifting the Burdens of Red Tape on Charities and Social Enterprises, Cabinet Office/BIS Task Force, 2010; Bd, Internat. Women's Forum UK, 2012–15. Associate, Civil Exchange, 2011–. Sen. Fellow, Anglia Ruskin Univ., 2010–; Vis. Prof., Cass Business Sch., City Univ., 2014– (Sen. Fellow, 2011–14; Exec. Chair, Cass Global Women's Leadership Prog., 2017–19); Fellow Commoner, Lucy Cavendish Coll., Cambridge, 2015–. Mem. Bd, British Waterways, 2011–12; Vice Chm., Canal and River Trust, 2012–17; Chm., Glandŵr Cymru, 2015–17; Chair: Commn on the Voluntary Sector and Ageing, 2013–17; Breast Cancer Now, 2015–19; Sustrans, 2018–. Trustee: Tomorrow Project, 2001–06; Nat. Centre for Social Res., 2002–09; Cumberland Lodge, 2008–19; Anne Frank Trust, 2010–13; Pro-Bono Economics, 2011–17; Patron's Fund, 2016–17. Non-exec. Dir, Cambridge Univ. Hosp. Trust, 2012–15. Former Member of Council: Inst. of Educn, London Univ.; Franco-British Council. FRSA. Hon. Fellow, Cardiff Univ.,

2012. Hon. Dr Health Scis Anglia Ruskin, 2010; Hon. DSc Bedfordshire, 2011. Merit Award, Social Care Assoc., 2006; Outstanding Achievement Award, Civil Soc., 2017. *Publications:* contrib. books on Europe and social policy, complaints procedures and consumer rights, and jls on social policy and women's issues. *T:* (020) 7697 8446. *E:* lynne@lynneberry.co.uk. *Club:* Reform.

**BERRY, Rt Hon. Jake;** *see* Berry, Rt Hon. J. J. G.

**BERRY, James;** *see* Berry, M. J. E.

**BERRY, Rt Hon. James Jacob Gilchrist, (Rt Hon. Jake);** PC 2019; MP (C) Rossendale and Darwen, since 2010; Minister of State, Cabinet Office and Ministry of Housing, Communities and Local Government, since 2019; *b* Liverpool, 29 Dec. 1978; *s* of John David Gilchrist Berry and Ann Elizabeth Berry (née Curtis); *m* 2018, Alice Molly Radclyffe Robinson; two *s. Educ:* Liverpool Coll.; Sheffield Univ. (BA Hons); Coll. of Law, Chester. Admitted solicitor, 2003; Solicitor: Bremner Sons and Corlett, 2001–02; City Law Partnership, 2002–04; DWF Solicitors, 2004–07; Halliwells, 2007–10. PPS to Minister of State for Housing and Local Govt, 2010–12, to Minister without Portfolio, Cabinet Office, 2012–15, to Chief Secretary to the Treasury, 2015–17; Parly Under-Sec. of State, DCLG, then MHCLG, 2017–19, BEIS, 2019. Mem., Downing Street Policy Unit, 2013–. Consultant Solicitor, Squire Sanders (UK) LLP, 2011–. *Recreations:* sailing, ski-ing, fishing. *Address:* House of Commons, SW1A 0AA. *E:* jake.berry.mp@parliament.uk. *Clubs:* Carlton; St James's (Manchester); Rawtenstall Conservative.

**BERRY, Janette Susan,** QPM 2006; Independent Bureaucracy Advocate, Home Office, 2008–10; *b* Carshalton, 29 Aug. 1954; *d* of Ralph Cooke and Marian (née Hook); *m* 1980, Graham Berry; one *s* one *d. Educ:* Fosse Bank Girls' Sch., Tonbridge; Open Univ. (BA). Kent County Constabulary, 1971–2008: Cadet, 1971–73; Constable, 1973–75; Detective Constable, 1975–77; Sergeant, 1977–79; Sergeant (Instructor), 1979–81; Patrol Sergeant, 1981–84; Inspector, 1984–97; Force Crime Prevention Officer, 1986–2000; Chief Inspector, 1987–2008. Chairman: Kent Police Fedn, 1991–97; Police Fedn of England and Wales, 2002–08. Sec., Inspectors' Central Cttee, 1987–2001. FRSA. Police Long Service and Good Conduct Medal, 1996; Golden Jubilee Medal, 2002. *Recreations:* family, theatre, current affairs, travel, supporting Crystal Palace Football Club, armchair sports fan.

**BERRY, Lynne;** *see* Berry, G. L.

**BERRY, Mary Rosa Alleyne, (Mrs P. J. M. Hunnings),** CBE 2012; cookery writer, since 1966, and television cook, since 1970; *b* Bath, 24 March 1935; *d* of Alleyne and Margery Berry; *m* 1966, Paul John Mack Hunnings; one *s* one *d* (and one *s* decd). *Educ:* Bath High Sch.; Bath Coll. of Home Econs; C&G Teaching; Paris Cordon Bleu. Cookery Editor: Housewife mag., 1966–70; Ideal Home mag., 1970–73; radio and TV series and appearances, 1970–, including: (as judge) The Great British Bake Off, BBC TV, 2010–16; Desert Island Discs, BBC Radio 4, 2012; The Mary Berry Story, BBC TV, 2013; Mary Berry Cooks, BBC TV, 2014; Mary Berry's Absolute Favourites, BBC TV, 2015; The Great British Baking Show, ABC, 2015; Mary Berry's Foolproof Cooking, BBC TV, 2016; Mary Berry's Easter Feast, 2016; Mary Berry Everyday, Mary Berry's Country House Secrets, BBC TV, 2017; Classic Mary Berry, Britain's Best Home Cook, BBC TV, 2018; Mary Berry's Quick Cooking, BBC TV, 2019. *Publications:* Cook Book, 1970; Popular Freezer Cookery, 1972; Popular French Cookery, 1972; Good Afternoon Cookery Book, 1976; One Pot Cooking, 1978; Family Recipes, 1979; Television Cook Book, 1979; Glorious Puds, 1980; Home Cooking, 1980; Cooking with Cheese, 1980; Day by Day Cooking, 1981; Mary Berry's Main Course, 1981; Recipes from Home and Abroad, 1981; New Book of Meat Cookery, 1981; Fruit Fare, 1982; County Cooking, 1982; The Perfect Sunday Lunch, 1982; Crockery Cookery, 1983; Cooking at Home, 1983; Complete Television Cook Book, 1983; Food as Presents, 1983; Fast Desserts, 1983; Family Cooking, 1984; Iceland Guide to Cooking from your Freezer, 1985; Kitchen Wisdom, 1985; Feed Your Family the Healthier Way, 1985; New Freezer Cook Book, 1985; Cooking for Celebrations, 1986; Chocolate Delights, 1987; Mary Berry's Favourite Microwave Recipes, 1988; Mary Berry's Favourite Recipes, 1990; Mary Berry's Desserts and Confections, 1991; Mary Berry's Food Processor Cookbook, 1992; Hamlyn All Colour Cookbook, 1992; Fast Cakes, 1992; Mary Berry's Cookery Course, 1993; Mary Berry's Quick and Easy Cakes, 1993; Mary Berry's Freezer Cookbook, 1994; More Fast Cakes, 1994; Fast Suppers, 1994; Ultimate Cakes, 1994, 2nd edn as Mary Berry's Ultimate Cake Book, 2003; Favourite French Recipes, 1995; Classic Home Cooking, 1995; Mary Berry's Complete Cookbook, 1995, 2nd edn 2003; Mary Berry's Perfect Sunday, 1996; The Aga Book, 1996; Mary Berry Cooks Puddings and Desserts, 1997; The New Cook, 1997; Favourite Cakes, 1997; Mary Berry Cooks Cakes, 1998; Mary Berry's New Aga Cookbook, 1999; Mary Berry at Home, 2001; Mary Berry's Cakes, Puddings and Breads, 2001; Mary Berry's Classic Meat Dishes, 2001; Mary Berry's Soups, Salads and Starters, 2001; Cook Now, Eat Later, 2002; Mary Berry's Foolproof Cakes, 2004; Real Food Fast, 2005; Mary Berry's Christmas Collection, 2006; One Step Ahead with Mary Berry, 2007; Mary Berry's Stress-free Kitchen, 2008; Mary Berry's Baking Bible, 2009; Mary Berry and Lucy Young Cook up a Feast, 2010; Sunday Lunches, 2011; Mary Berry and Lucy Young At Home, 2013; Mary Berry Cooks, 2014; Mary Berry's Absolute Favourites, 2015; Mary Berry's Foolproof Cooking, 2016; Mary Berry Everyday, 2017; Mary's Household Tips and Tricks, 2017; Classic, 2018; Fast Cakes, 2018; Mary Berry's Quick Cooking, 2019. *Recreations:* gardening, tennis, walking. *E:* info@maryberry.co.uk. *W:* www.maryberry.co.uk.

**BERRY, (Michael) James (Ellwood);** barrister; *b* Canterbury, 4 Aug. 1983; *s* of Dr Michael Berry and Margaret Berry; *m* 2013, Nehali Shah; one *d. Educ:* King's Sch., Canterbury; University Coll. London (LLB 1st Cl. Hons 2005); Harvard Law Sch. (LLM 2007). Called to the Bar, Lincoln's Inn, 2006. Associate, Coll. of Policing, 2014–. MP (C) Kingston and Surbiton, 2015–17; contested (C) same seat, 2017. PPS to Minister of State for Health, 2016–17. Mem., Select Cttee on Home Affairs, 2015–17. *Recreations:* hiking in National Parks in UK and USA, US politics, piano (listening). *Address:* Serjeants' Inn Chambers, 85 Fleet Street, EC4Y 1AE.

**BERRY, Sir Michael (Victor),** Kt 1996; FRS 1982; Professor of Physics, Bristol University, 1978–88 and 2006–08, now Emeritus (Royal Society Research Professor, 1988–2006); *b* 14 March 1941; *s* of Jack and Marie Berry; *m* 1st, 1961, Eveline Ethel Fitt (marr. diss. 1970); two *s;* 2nd, 1971, Lesley Jane Allen (marr. diss. 1984); two *d;* 3rd, 1984, Monica Suzi Saiovici; one *s* one *d. Educ:* Univ. of Exeter (BSc; Hon. PhD 1991); Univ. of St Andrews (PhD). Bristol University: Res. Fellow, 1965–67; Lectr, 1967–74; Reader, 1974–78. Bakerian Lectr, Royal Soc., 1987. Mem., Royal Scientific Soc., Uppsala, 1988; Foreign Member: US Nat. Acad. of Sci., 1995; Royal Netherlands Acad. of Arts and Scis, 2000. Hon. FInstP 1999. Maxwell Medal and Prize, Inst. of Physics, 1978; Dirac Medal and Prize, Inst. of Physics, 1990; Lilienfeld Prize, Amer. Physical Soc., 1990; Royal Medal, Royal Soc., 1990; Naylor Prize and Lectureship in Applied Maths, London Math. Soc., 1992; Science for Art Prize, LVMH, Paris, 1994; Hewlett Packard Europhysics Prize, 1995; Dirac Medal, Internat. Centre for Theoretical Physics, 1996; Kapitsa Medal, Russian Acad. of Scis, 1997; Wolf Prize for Physics, Wolf Foundn, Israel, 1998; Ig Nobel Prize for Physics, 2000; Onsager Medal, Norwegian Technical Univ., 2001; 1st and 3rd prizes, Visions of Sci., Novartis/Daily Telegraph, 2002; Polya Prize, London Mathematical Soc., 2005; Chancellor's Medal, Univ. of Bristol, 2005; Richtmyer Award, Amer. Assoc. of Physics Teachers, 2014; Lorentz Medal, Royal Netherlands Acad. Arts and Scis, 2015; Moyal Medal, Macquarie Univ., 2016. *Publications:* Diffraction of Light by Ultrasound, 1966; Principles of Cosmology and Gravitation, 1976; A Half-Century of Physical Asymptotics and Other Diversions, 2017; about 500 research papers, book reviews, etc, on physics. *Recreations:* anything but sport. *Address:* H. H. Wills Physics Laboratory, Royal Fort, Tyndall Avenue, Bristol BS8 1TL. *T:* (0117) 928 8778. *W:* http://michaelberryphysics.wordpress.com.

**BERRY, Paul L.;** Member (Ind Unionist), Armagh, Banbridge and Craigavon Borough Council (formerly Armagh City and District Council); *b* 3 June 1976. *Educ:* Craigavon Coll. of Further Educn. Sales person, hardware warehouse, 1994–96; examr, shoe firm, 1996–98. Northern Ireland Assembly: Mem. (DUP, 1998–2006, Ind., 2006–07) Newry and Armagh; contested (Ind) same seat, 2007; Mem., Health Cttee and Standards and Privileges Cttee. Mem., Health Action Zone. Member: Loyal Orange Instn; Royal Black Perceptory; Apprentice Boys of Derry. Contested (DUP) Newry and Armagh, 2005. *Recreation:* interest in football.

**BERRY, Peter Fremantle,** CMG 1999; Chairman, Crown Agents for Oversea Governments and Administrations, 1998–2007; President, Crown Agents Foundation, 2003–11; *b* St Andrews, Fife, 17 May 1944; *s* of late John Berry, CBE and Hon. Bride Berry, *d* of 3rd Baron Cottesloe, CB; *m* 1972, Paola Padovani; one *s* two *d. Educ:* Eton Coll.; Lincoln Coll., Oxford (MA Hons Mod. History). Harrisons & Crosfield, London, 1966–73: Manager: Kuala Belait, Brunei, 1968; Indonesia, 1970; Anglo Indonesian Corp., London: Gen. Man., 1973; Dir, 1974–82; Crown Agents for Oversea Governments and Administrations, 1982–2007: Director: Asia and Pacific, based Singapore, 1982–84; ME, Asia and Pacific, based London, 1984–88; Man. Dir and Crown Agent, 1988–2002; Chm. of Crown Agents' banking and asset mgt subsidiaries. Director: Thomas Tapling Ltd, 1987– (Chm., 2007–); Anglo-Eastern Plantations Plc, 1991–93; Henderson TR Pacific Investment Trust, 1994–2008; Scottish Eastern Investment Trust, 1995–98; Kier Group plc, 1997–2007; Martin Currie Portfolio Investment Trust plc, later Martin Currie Global Portfolio Trust, 1999–2012 (Chm., 2000–12); Martin Currie Capital Return Trust plc, 1999–2000; Mylnfield Res. Services, 2007–14 (Chm., 2008–11). Member: Management Bd, Resource, 1989–92; Internat. Bd, Transparency Internat., 1993–; Pres., Transparency Internat. (UK), 2003–. Member: Rubber Growers Assoc., 1978–82; UK Task Force on Kuwait, 1991; UK-Japan 21st Century (formerly UK-Japan 2000) Gp, 1992–2007 (Dir, 2000–03); Whitehall Export Promotion Cttee, 1992–98; Internat. Cttee, CBI, 1997–2003; British Trade Internat. Sectors and Projects, subseq. Business Adv., Gp, 1998–2004; Council: Malaysia, Singapore and Brunei Assoc., 1982–87; Indonesia Assoc., 1974–93 (Chm., 1986–89). Advr on econ. develt, City of London Corp., 2003–14. Trustee: CAF, 2000–09 (Chm., Internat. Cttee, 2000–09); Mylnfield Trust, 2007–11; Dir and Trustee, Charity Bank, 2003–09. Mem., Adv. Council, Sch. of Mgt, RHUL, 2005–. Governor, Scottish Crop Res. Inst., 2007–11 (Chm., 2008–11). Liveryman, Musicians' Co., 2008–. FRSA. Order of the Rising Sun (Japan), 2008. *Recreations:* wildlife and country pursuits in Britain and Italy, travel and international development. *Club:* Royal Automobile.

**BERRY, Prof. Peter Jeremy,** FRCP, FRCPath; Professor of Paediatric Pathology, University of Bristol, 1991–2001, now Emeritus; *b* 21 March 1950; *s* of Peter Berry and Marjorie Berry (née Lang). *Educ:* Epsom Coll.; Magdalene Coll., Cambridge (BA, MB, BChir); London Metropolitan Univ. (MA Music Technol. 2010). Kent and Canterbury Hosp., 1975–77; Sen. Registrar in Histopathology, Addenbrooke's Hosp., 1977–81; Research Fellow, Children's Hosp., Denver, 1981–83; Consultant Paediatric Pathologist, Bristol Royal Hosp. for Sick Children, 1983–2001. Hon. FRCPH 2007. *Publications:* chapters and papers on cot death and children's tumours. *Recreations:* walking, fishing, music, canal boating, making period woodwind instruments. *Club:* Royal Society of Medicine.

**BERRY, Dr Roger Leslie;** *b* 4 July 1948; *s* of Mary Joyce Berry and Sydney Berry; *m* 1996, Alison Delyth. *Educ:* Dalton County Jun. Sch.; Huddersfield New Coll.; Univ. of Bristol (BSc); Univ. of Sussex (DPhil). Lectr in Econs and Associate Fellow, IDS, Univ. of Sussex, 1973–74; Lecturer in Economics: Univ. of Papua New Guinea, 1974–78; Univ. of Bristol, 1978–92. Avon County Council: Mem., 1981–93; Chm., Finance and Admin Cttee, 1981–84; Dep. Leader of Council, 1985–86; Leader, Labour Group, 1986–92. Contested (Lab): Weston-super-Mare, 1983; Kingswood, 1987. MP (Lab) Kingswood, 1992–2010; contested (Lab) same seat, 2010. Mem., Trade and Industry Select Cttee, 1995–2010; Sec., 1994–2009, Co-chair, 2009–10, All-Party Disability Gp. Vice-Chair, 2004–07, Chair, 2007–10, British Gp, Occasional Consultant, 2013–, IPU. Chair, Full Employment Forum, 1994–99. Dir, Tribune Publications Ltd, 1997–2003. Vice Pres., Disabled Drivers Assoc., 1997–2010; Trustee: Disabled Law Service, 1997–99; Snowdon Award Scheme, 1997–2003; Disability Alliance, 2010–12; Action on Disability and Work UK (formerly Vassall Centre Trust), 2010–16; Disability Rights UK, 2011–; Avon and Bristol Law Centre, 2014– (Chair, 2015–); Mem., Exec. Cttee, Law Centres Network, 2019–. Chair, Connecting Kingswood, 2013–15. *Publications:* contribs to learned jls; newspaper articles and pamphlets. *Recreations:* travel, cooking, reading, cinema, theatre. *Address:* 9 Manor Road, Bristol BS16 2JD. *T:* 07748 965655.

**BERRY, Scyld;** *see* Berry, A. S. I.

**BERRY, Siân Rebecca;** Member (Green) London Assembly, Greater London Assembly, since 2016; Co-Leader, Green Party, since 2018. *Educ:* Univ. of Oxford (MEng Metallurgy and Sci. Materials 1997). Medical copywriter; PA; website manager; User and Client Support Manager, Symplectic Ltd, 2009–11; Roads and Sustainable Transport campaigner, Campaign for Better Transport, 2011–15. Mem. (Green), Camden LBC, 2014–. Green Party: Principal Speaker, 2006–07; Candidate (Green) for Mayor of London, 2008, 2016; Press Officer, 2008. Contested (Green) Holborn and St Pancras, 2017. *Publications:* 50 Ways to Make Your House and Garden Greener, 2008; 50 Ways to Greener Travel, 2008; 50 Ways to be a Greener Shopper, 2008; 50 Ways to Save Water and Energy, 2008; Mend It!: 400 easy repairs for everyday items, 2009; Junk for Joy, 50 Ways, Mend It!, 2011. *Address:* London Assembly, Greater London Authority, City Hall, Queen's Walk, SE1 2AA.

**BERRY, Simon George Francis Graham,** CVO 2017; writer; Chairman, Berry Bros & Rudd Ltd, 2005–17; *b* London, 26 Nov. 1957; *s* of late Antony Arthur Berry and Sonia Alice Berry (née Graham-Hodgson); *m* 2005, Lucy Hamilton; one step *s* one step *d. Educ:* Eton Coll.; Harvard Business Sch. (OPM). With Berry Bros & Rudd, 1977–2017. Chm., Wine and Spirit Benevolent Soc., 2008. Clerk to Royal Cellars, 2008–. Mem. Council, 2010–, Chm., Develt Bd, 2014–, RADA. *Recreation:* choosing Desert Island Discs while waiting patiently for the BBC to call. *Address:* Lovel House, Upton Lovell, Wilts BA12 0JP. *Clubs:* Pratt's, Garrick.

**BERRY, Thomas Henry Seager S.;** *see* Seager Berry.

**BERTHOIN, Georges Paul;** Officier, Légion d'Honneur, 2006; Médaille militaire, Croix de Guerre, Médaille de la Résistance avec Rosette, France, 1945; Executive Member of the Trilateral Commission (Japan, N America, W Europe), 1973–75, and since 1993

(Chairman, 1975–92, Hon. European Chairman, since 1992); Honorary International Chairman, the European Movement, since 1981 (Chairman, 1978–81); *b* Nérac, France, 17 May 1925; *s* of Jean Berthoin and Germaine Mourgnot; *m* 1st, 1950, Ann White Whittlesey (decd); three *d* (and one *d* decd); 2nd, 1965, Pamela Jenkins (decd); two *s*. *Educ*: Grenoble Univ.; École des Sciences Politiques, Paris; Harvard Univ. Licencié ès Lettres (Philosophie), Licencié en Droit, Laureate for Economics (Grenoble). Lectr, McGill Univ., Montreal, 1948; Private Sec. to French Minister of Finance, 1948–50; Head of Staff of Superprefect of Alsace-Lorraine-Champagne, 1950–52. Joined High Authority of European Coal and Steel Community, and then Principal Private Sec. to its Pres. (Jean Monnet), 1952–53–55. Dep. Chief Rep. of ECSC in UK, 1956–67; Chargé d'Affaires for Commission of the European Communities (ECSC Euratom-Common Market), 1968; Principal Adviser to the Commission, and its Dep. Chief Rep. in London, 1969–70, Chief Representative, 1971–73. Member: Nine Wise Men Gp on Africa, 1988–89; Bd, Aspen Inst., Berlin; Adv. Bd, Johns Hopkins Univ. Bologna Center Sch. of Advanced Studies. Hon. Chm., Jean Monnet Assoc., 2001–. Regular Lectr, RCDS, London. *Recreations*: art, theatre, walking, collecting objects. *Address*: 67 Avenue Niel, 75017 Paris, France.

**BERTHOUD, Sir Martin (Seymour),** KCVO 1985; CMG 1985; HM Diplomatic Service, retired; *b* 20 Aug. 1931; *s* of Sir Eric Berthoud, KCMG and late Ruth Tilston, *d* of Sir Charles Bright, FRSE; *m* 1960, Marguerite Joan Richarda Phayre (*d* 2009); three *s* one *d*. *Educ*: Rugby Sch.; Magdalen Coll., Oxford (MA). Served with British Embassies in: Tehran, 1956–58; Manila, 1961–64; Pretoria/Cape Town, 1967–71; Tehran, 1971–73; Counsellor, Helsinki, 1974–77; Inspector, HM Diplomatic Service, 1977–79; Head of N. American Dept, FCO, 1979–81; Consul-General, Sydney, 1982–85; High Comr, Trinidad and Tobago, 1985–91. EC Monitor, Croatia, 1991. Dir, The Wates Foundn, 1993–2001. Patron: Green Light Trust, 2001–10; Prisoners Abroad, 2002–; Church Housing Trust, 2002–. EC Monitoring Mission Service Medal, 1994. Commander, Order of the Lion (Finland), 1976; Keys of City of San Fernando (Trinidad), 1991. *Publications*: Undiplomatic Episodes (autobiog.), 2017. *Recreations*: keeping fit, entertaining, bird-watching, cooking, grandchildren, grappling with IT. *Address*: Gillyflower Cottage, Stoke by Nayland, Suffolk CO6 4RD. *T*: (01206) 263237. *Club*: Oxford and Cambridge.

**BERTIE,** family name of Earl of Lindsey and Abingdon.

**BERTIN,** Baroness *cr* 2016 (Life Peer), of Battersea in the London Borough of Wandsworth; **Gabrielle Louise Bertin;** *b* Croydon, 14 March 1978; *d* of Claude Bertin and Lynne Jansson (*née* Kewney); *m* 1st, 2007, Chris Glenny (marr. diss. 2011); 2nd, 2013, Michael Grist; one *s* one *d* and one step *d*. *Educ*: Croydon High Sch.; Univ. of Southampton. Trader (Equity), BNP Paribas, 2000–02; Press Officer, Cons. Party, 2002–05; Press Sec. to Rt Hon. David Cameron, MP, Leader of the Opposition and subseq. Prime Minister, 2005–13; Dir, Ext. Relations, Office of the Prime Minister, 2013–16. *Recreations*: tennis, cooking. *Address*: House of Lords, SW1A 0PW. *E*: contactholmember@parliament.uk.

**BERTRAM, Dr Brian Colin Ricardo;** Special Projects Co-ordinator, Bristol Zoo Gardens, 1995–2003; *b* 14 April 1944; *s* of late Dr Colin Bertram and Dr (Cicely) Kate Bertram; *m* 1975, Katharine Jean Gillie; one *s* two *d*. *Educ*: Perse School, Cambridge; St John's Coll., Cambridge (BA 1965; MA 1968); PhD Cambridge, 1969. FIBiol 1981. Research Fellow, Serengeti Res. Inst., Tanzania, 1969–73; Sen. Res. Fellow, King's Coll., Cambridge, 1976–79; Curator of Mammals, 1980–87, and Curator of Aquarium and Invertebrates, 1982–87, Zoological Society of London; Dir-Gen., Wildfowl and Wetlands Trust, 1987–92. Zoo Inspector, Sec. of State's List, 1983–. Mem., Zoos Expert Cttee (formerly Zoos Forum), 2005–15. Vice-Pres., World Pheasant Assoc., 1990–97 (Mem. Council, 2010–); Mem. Council, Zool Soc. of London, 1993–97, 1999–2002, 2004–07, 2010–14, 2015– (Vice Pres., 2011–12). *Publications*: Pride of Lions, 1978; The Ostrich Communal Nesting System, 1992; Lions, 1998. *Recreations*: family, friends, zoology, garden, travel, beekeeping. *Address*: Fieldhead, Amberley, Stroud, Glos GL5 5AG. *T*: (01453) 872796. *Club*: Zoological.
See also J. Bertram.

**BERTRAM, (Charles) William,** RIBA; Founder and Managing Director, William Bertram of Bath Ltd, 2006–13; *b* 2 Oct. 1939; *s* of Lt Col Richard Bertram and Elizabeth Florence Oriana Bertram (*née* Bedwell); *m* 1963, Victoria Harriette Ingle; one *s* two *d*. *Educ*: Sherborne Sch.; AA Sch. of Architecture (AA Dip. Hons 1964). RIBA 1965. Founder: William Bertram Fell (architectural practice), 1970; William Bertram, Consulting Architect, 1996–2006. Architect to the Prince of Wales, 1987–2010; Consultant Architect: to Strangways Estate, 1972–96; to Duchy of Cornwall Eastern Reg., 1987–; to RNLI, 2002–08; Architect to Churchill Graves Trust, 1996–2009; Advr to Theatre Royal, Bath, 2005–13. Major projects include: *conversions and restorations*: Nos 15 and 16 into Royal Crescent Hotel, Bath, 1979; Abbotsbury Village, Dorset, 1980 (UK Council EAHY Award, 1987); St Anne's Place, Bath, 1985 (Bath Conservation Area Adv. Cttee Envmtl Award, 1987); Dower House, Bath (Civic Trust Award for Conservation), 1986; Cliveden into hotel, 1986–89; farm buildings and visitor's extension, Highgrove, Glos, 1988; Perrystone Court, Herefordshire, 1996; Shooting Lodge, Easter Auchintoul, 1998 (Inverness Civic Trust Biennial Award, 1999); Dinmore Manor, 2000–05; Rockley Manor, Wilts, 2000–03; Parnham House, Dorset (re-ordering), 2005; Encombe House, Dorset, 2005 (Georgian Group Award, 2006); Old Rectory, Combe Hay, 2009 (Design Quality Award, Bath and NE Som Council, 2010); *new work*: Stradling House, Somerset, 1979; Angmering Park, Sussex, 1983–85; Cavendish Lodge, Bath, 1986–97 (Stone Fedn Award, 1997); tree house, Highgrove, 1988; Dunley Farmhouse, Hants, 1996; South Kenwood, Devon, 1997; Nos 25, 1997, 57, 1999, 79, 2009, 53 and 53a, 2010, Winnington Rd, Hampstead; *gardens*: Highgrove, Camerton Court, Dinmore Manor, Albemarle House, Va, USA. Trustee, Bath Preservation Trust, 1966–68. Chm., Compton Dando Ch Estate Trust, 1981–2005. *Publications*: An Appreciation of Abbotsbury, 1973; The Architect's Tale, 2009. *Recreations*: garden designing, tennis, golf (badly), walking, writing, sketching. *Address*: Woodrising, Loves Hill, Timsbury, Bath BA2 0EU. *T*: (01761) 470718. *E*: williebertramofbath@gmail.com.

**BERTRAM, Dr Christoph;** Partner, Bernzen Sonntag Attorneys, Hamburg, 2008–18; Steven Müller Chair in German Studies, School of Advanced International Studies, Bologna Center, Johns Hopkins University, 2005–06; *b* 3 Sept. 1937; German national; *m* 1st, 1967, Renate Edith Bergemann (marr. diss. 1980); 2nd, 1980, Ragnhild Lindemann; two *s* two *d*. *Educ*: Free Univ. Berlin and Bonn Univ. (law); Institut d'Etudes Politiques, Paris (political science). Dr of Law 1967. Joined Internat. Inst. for Strategic Studies as Research Associate, 1967, Asst Dir, 1969–74, Dir, 1974–82; Mem. Planning Staff, West German Min. of Defence, 1969–70. Political and Foreign Editor, 1982–85, Diplomatic Correspondent, 1986–98, Die Zeit; Dir, Stiftung Wissenschaft und Politik (Foundn Sci. and Policy), 1998–2005. Chm. of Bd, Berlin Inst. for Population and Develt, 2007–12. *Publications*: (with Alastair Buchan *et al*.) Europe's Futures—Europe's Choices, 1969; Mutual Force Reductions in Europe: the political aspects, 1972; (ed, with Johan J. Holst) New Strategic Factors in the North Atlantic, 1977; Arms Control and Technological Change, 1979; Europe in the Balance, 1995; Rethinking Iran—from Confrontation to Cooperation, 2008. *Recreations*: clocks, sailing.

**BERTRAM, George,** CB 1999; Director, National Services, Board of Inland Revenue, 2000–01; *b* 19 Sept. 1944; *s* of late George Bertram and of Muriel Bertram; *m* 1969, Jean Swales. *Educ*: Houghton-le-Spring Grammar Sch. Nat. Assistance Bd, Sunderland, 1964–70; Department of Health and Social Security, then Department of Social Security: Staff Trng, Billingham, 1970–73; Sunderland, 1973–76; Regl Office, Newcastle upon Tyne, 1976–80; South Shields, 1980–83; Manager: Peterlee, 1983; Hartlepool, 1983–84; Middlesbrough, 1984–89; Sunderland, 1989; Contributions Agency: Head of Field Ops, 1989–92; Dep. Chief Exec., and Dir of Compliance and Educn, 1992–94; actg Chief Exec., 1994–95; Dep. Chief Exec., and Dir of Ops, 1995–97; Chief Exec., 1997–99; Dir, Nat. Insce Contribns, Bd of Inland Revenue, 1999–2000. Mem., CSAB, 2001–12. *Recreations*: golf, Sunderland AFC, cricket, gardening, travel. *Address*: 8 Holmewood Drive, Rowlands Gill, Tyne and Wear NE39 1EL. *Club*: Garesfield Golf.

**BERTRAM, Joanna, (Jo);** Chief Digital and Strategy Officer, Telefonica UK (O2), since 2018; *b* London, 4 Oct. 1981; *d* of Dr Brian Colin Ricardo Bertram, *qv*. *Educ*: Newnham Coll., Cambridge (BA Hons Natural Scis 2003); INSEAD (MBA 2008). Consultant, UK and Australia, Accenture, 2004–07; Engagement Manager, Switzerland and SA, McKinsey & Co., 2009–13; Regl Gen. Manager, UK, Ireland and Nordics, later N Europe, Uber, 2013–17; Exec.-in-Residence, EQT Ventures, 2017–18. *Recreations*: travel, ski-ing.

**BERTRAM, Robert David Darney;** Member, Competition (formerly Monopolies and Mergers) Commission, 1998–2005; *b* 6 Oct. 1941; *s* of late D. N. S. Bertram; *m* 1967, Patricia Joan Laithwaite; two *s*. *Educ*: Edinburgh Academy; Oxford Univ. (MA); Edinburgh Univ. (LLB (Hons), Berriedale Keith Prize). An Assistant Solicitor, Linklaters & Paines, London, 1968–69; Partner: Dundas & Wilson, CS, 1969–92; Shepherd & Wedderburn, WS, 1992–98. Associate, Institute of Taxation, 1970 (Mem., Technical Cttee, 1986); Examiner (pt-time), Law Society of Scotland, 1972–75; Member: Scottish Law Commn, 1978–86; VAT Tribunal, Scotland, 1984–92; Council, UKCC (later Nurses' and Midwives' Council), 1988–2002 (Chm., Audit Cttee, 1998–2002; Lay Panellist, 2002–); Insolvency Practices' Council, 2000–; Audit Adv. Bd, Scottish Parlt Corporate Body, 2002–. Assessor, Edinburgh Univ. Ct, 2000–03. Hon. Prof., Edinburgh and Heriot-Watt Univs, 2000–16. Non-exec. Dir, The Weir Group plc, 1983–2000. Trustee, David Hume Inst., 1998–2011. *Publications*: contribs to professional jls. *Recreations*: books, jazz, browsing. *Clubs*: Royal Over-Seas League; Scottish Arts, New (Edinburgh).

**BERTRAM, William;** see Bertram, C. W.

**BERTSCHINGER, Dame Claire,** DBE 2010; DL; Assistant Professor and Director, Tropical Nursing course, London School of Hygiene and Tropical Medicine, since 2003; author and public speaker, since 2005; *b* Herts; *d* of John William Bertschinger and Rene Bertschinger (*née* White). *Educ*: St Nicholas Prim. Sch., Old Harlow; Fawbert and Barnard Prim. Sch., Sawbridgeworth; Chantry Mount Sch., Bishops Stortford; Loughton Coll. of Further Educn (Pre-Nursing Course); St Mary's Hosp., Paddington (RGN 1975); Hosp. for Tropical Diseases, London (Cert. Tropical Nursing 1978); ICRC (Cours d'Intégration and Cours de Détention 1991); Brunel Univ. (MSc Med. Anthropol. 1998). Nursing appts, UK; medic, Scientific Exploration Soc., Panama, PNG and Sulawesi; work in emergency disaster relief, primarily war zones, with ICRC incl. Afghanistan, Kenya, Lebanon, Sudan, Sierra Leone, Ivory Coast and Liberia; trng officer, Health Div., ICRC, Geneva. Hon. DSSc Brunel, 2008; Hon. DSc De Montfort, 2009; Hon. DEd Robert Gordon, Aberdeen, 2010; DUniv Stafford, 2011; Hon. Dr Health Scis Anglia Ruskin, 2012. Bish Medal, Scientific Exploration Soc., 1985; Florence Nightingale Medal, ICRC, 1991; Window to the World Award, Woman of the Year, 2005; Internat. Human Rights and Nursing Award, Internat. Centre for Nursing Ethics, Univ. of Surrey, 2007; Commemorative Medal, Soka Gakkai Internat., 2010. DL Herts, 2012. *Publications*: Moving Mountains (autobiog.), 2005. *Address*: Faculty of Infectious and Tropical Diseases, London School of Hygiene and Tropical Medicine, Keppel Street, WC1E 7HT. *E*: claire.bertschinger@lshtm.ac.uk.

**BERWICK, Bishop Suffragan of,** since 2016; **Rt Rev. Mark Simon Austin Tanner;** *b* Canada, Nov. 1970; *s* of Prof. Stuart Tanner and Joy Tanner; *m* 1994; two *c*. *Educ*: Loughborough Grammar Sch.; Christ Church, Oxford (BA Hons 1992; MA 1997); St John's Coll., Durham Univ. (BA Hons 1998); Liverpool Univ. (MTh 2002). Youth Pastor, Holy Trinity, Coventry, 1992–95; ordained deacon, 1998, priest, 1999; Asst Curate, St Mary's, Upton, 1998–2001; Vicar: St Mary's, Doncaster, 2001–07; Holy Trinity, Ripon, 2007–11; Area Dean of Ripon, 2009–11; Warden of Cranmer Hall, 2011–16, Vice-Principal, St John's Coll., 2013–16, Durham Univ. Officiating Chaplain to the Military, 2009–13. Regl Network Leader, New Wine, 2009. Series Convenor, Grove Bks, 2005–10. *Publications*: Renewing the Traditional Church, 2002; Developing Visionary Leadership, 2004; How to Write a Good Sermon, 2007; How to Develop Vision in the Local Church, 2009; How to Preach a Good Sermon, 2009; The Introvert Charismatic: the gift of introversion in a noisy Church, 2015; The PCC Member's Essential Guide, 2016. *Club*: Inst. of Advanced Motorists.

**BERWICK, Sir George (Thomas),** Kt 2013; CBE 2007; Executive Principal, Ravens Wood School, 2011–13; Chief Executive Officer, Ravens Wood Learning Trust, 2012–13; *b* Folkestone, 10 Oct. 1948; *m* 1973, Maria; two *d*. *Educ*: Duke of York's Mil. Sch., Dover; Univ. Coll. of Wales, Aberystwyth (BA); Leeds Univ. (MA); Carnegie Sch. of Physical Educn (PGCE); Anglia Univ. (Advanced Dip.); Cambridge Univ. Inst. of Educn (PhD Univ. of East Anglia 1994). Plymouth Coll.; Deanes Sch., Thundersley; Hassenbrook Sch., Stanford-le-Hope; Epping Forest High Sch.; Sen. Educn Officer, Essex LEA, 1989–93; Headteacher, Ravens Wood Sch., Bromley, 1993–2011. Educn Advr to Cabinet Office, 2001–05. Dir, London Leadership Strategy, 2003–08. Chief Exec., Nat. Teaching Schs, 2008–11. CEO, 2005–13, Chm., 2013–, Olevi Ltd; CEO, Challenge Partners, 2011–18. Vis. Professorial Fellow, Inst. of Educn, Univ. of London, 2011–. *Publications*: Building Success, 2001; Engaging in Excellence, Vol. 1, The Approach, 2011, Vol. 2, Moral Capital, 2012. *Recreations*: family life, cycling, piano, gardening, wine.

**BĒRZIŅŠ, Andris;** President of Latvia, 2011–15; *b* 10 Dec. 1944. *Educ*: Nītaure Elementary Sch.; Sigulda No 1 High Sch.; Faculty of Mechanics, Rīga Poly. Inst.; Faculty of Radio Engrg, Rīga Poly. Inst.; Faculty of Econs, Univ. of Latvia. Served Soviet military, 1963–66. Radio engr, then Man. Dir, R/A Elektrons, 1971–88; Dep. Minister for Community Services, 1988–89. Chm., Valmira Dist, Council of People's Deputies, 1989–93; Member: Supreme Council, Republic of Latvia, 1990–93; Saeima, Republic of Latvia, 2010–11; Chm., Econ., Agricl, Envmtl and Regl Policy Cttee, 2010–11. Mem., Supervisory Council, Bank of Latvia, 1990–92; Pres., A/S Latvijas Unibanka, 1993–2004; Chm., Supervisory Council, A/S Latvenergo, 2000–09. Pres., Latvian Chamber of Commerce and Industry, 2006–10. Commemorative pin for participants in 1991 barricades, Latvia, 1996. Comdr, 2000, First Grade, with Chain, 2011, Order of Three Stars (Latvia); Cross of Recognition, First Grade (Latvia), 2011; Order of Viesturs, First Grade (Latvia), 2011.

**BESGROVE, Maj.-Gen. Peter Vincent Ronald,** CBE 1992; CEng, FIET, FCMI; Chief Executive, Haig Homes, 2002–13; *b* 23 Oct. 1948; *s* of Ronald Alfred Besgrove and Josephine Besgrove (*née* Buckley); *m* 1971, Eileen McEwan; two *d*. *Educ*: Magdalen Coll. Sch.; Welbeck Coll.; Royal Military Coll. of Sci. (BSc Eng Hons). CEng 1985; FIET (FIEE

1997). Commnd REME, 1968: served BAOR, NI and England, 1968–79; Staff Coll., 1980; Dep. COS, 6 Armd Bde, 1981–83; Comd, 5 Armd Workshop, BAOR, 1983–84; jsdc 1985; DS, Staff Coll., 1985–87; Comd Maintenance 3 Armd Div., BAOR, 1987–89; Asst COS, HQ NI, 1989–91; Comdt, Sch. of Electrical and Mechanical Engrg, 1991–92; Comd, REME Trng Gp, 1992–93; rcds 1994; Dir of Manning (Army), 1995–97; Dir Gen. Equipment Support (Army), 1997–99; Asst COS J1, HQ Allied Forces S, 1999–2001. Col Comdt, REME, 1999–2004. Co. Sec., Haig Housing Trust, 2008–14. Non-exec. Dir, SCS Ltd, 2002–06. Mem. Bd of Trustees, Treloar Trust, 2002–12; Chm. of Govs, Treloar Coll., 2003–10. Dir, United Services Trustee, 2007–11. FCMI (FIMgt 2001). *Recreations:* painting, fishing, shooting, sailing, DIY. *Address:* c/o Regimental HQ REME, MoD Lyneham, Lyneham, Chippenham SN15 9HB. *Club:* Victory Services.

**BESLEY, Morrish Alexander, (Tim)**, AC 2002 (AO 1992); FTSE; Chairman: Australian Research Council, 2002–06; Co-operative Research Centre for greenhouse gas technology, 2003–09; Wheat Export Authority, 2005–07; *b* New Plymouth, NZ, 14 March 1927; *s* of Hugh Morrish Besley and Isabel (*née* Alexander); *m* 1st, 1952, Nancy Cave (marr. diss. 2001); three *s*; 2nd, 2001, Sarah Harrington; one *s* one *d*. *Educ:* Univ. of New Zealand (BE Civil); Macquarie Univ. (BLegS). Hon. FIEAust 2005 (FIEAust 1982); FTSE (FTS 1985). Engr, Ministry of Works, NZ, 1950; Snowy Mts Hydro-Electric Authy, Australia, 1950–67; First Assistant Secretary: Dept of External Territories, Australia, 1967–73; Dept of Treasury, Australia, 1973–76 (Exec. Mem., Foreign Investment Rev. Bd, 1975–76); Sec., Commonwealth Dept of Business and Consumer Affairs, and Comptroller General of Customs, Australia, 1976–81; Monier Ltd: Man. Dir, 1982–87; Chm. and Chief Exec., 1987; Chairman: Monier Redland Ltd, 1988; Redland Australia, 1988–95; CIG Gp, 1988–93; Commonwealth Banking Corp., 1988–91; Leighton Hldgs Ltd, 1990–2001; Commonwealth Bank of Australia, 1991–99. Director: Amcor Ltd, 1985–97; Fujitsu Australia Ltd, 1988–97; O'Connell Street Associates Pty Ltd, 1990–2017; Clyde Industries Ltd, 1991–96. Chm., NSW Transport Adv. Bd, 2013–16. Mem., NSW Council and Nat. Exec., Metal Trades Industry Assoc. (Pres., 1991–92). Chancellor, Macquarie Univ., 1994–2001. Mem. Bd, Australian Learning and Teaching Council (formerly Carrick Inst. for Teaching and Learning in Higher Educn), 2006–11; Chm., Sci. and Engrg Challenge, Univ. of Newcastle, 2006–18. Chm., Sydney Royal Botanic Gardens Trust, 1988–92; Trustee, Royal Botanic Gdns Sydney Foundn, 1992–99; Governor, Australian Nat. Gall. Foundn, 1992–; Chm., Centenary Inst. Med. Res. Foundn, 1992–96; Mem., Aust. Bd of Reference, World Vision, 1992–. Pres., AATSE, 1998–2002. Mem., Red Shield Appeal Cttee, 1988–99, Sydney Adv. Bd, 1994–99, Salvation Army. Hon. DSc Macquarie, 2002. *Recreations:* reading, gardening. *Address:* PO Box 304, Cammeray, NSW 2062, Australia. *Clubs:* Australian, Union (Sydney); Royal Sydney Yacht Squadron.

**BESLEY, Sir Timothy (John)**, Kt 2018; CBE 2010; DPhil; FBA 2001; School Professor of Economics and Political Science, since 2012, and W. Arthur Lewis Professor of Development Economics, London School of Economics (Professor of Economics and Political Science, 1995–2007; Kuwait Professor of Economics and Political Science, 2007–11); *b* 14 Sept. 1960; *s* of John Besley and June Besley (*née* Turton); *m* 1993, Gillian Nicola Paull; two *s*. *Educ:* Keble Coll., Oxford (BA PPE 1983); All Souls Coll., Oxford (MPhil; DPhil 1987). Prize Fellow, All Souls Coll., Oxford, 1984–91 and 1995–2000; Asst Prof., Princeton Univ., 1988–95; Dir, Suntory Toyota Internat. Centres for Econs and Related Disciplines, LSE, 2001–11. Research Fellow: Inst. for Fiscal Studies, 1995–2011; Inst. for Econ. and Social Res., 1995–2011; Two Year Fellow, All Souls Coll., Oxford, 2016–. Mem., Monetary Policy Cttee, Bank of England, 2006–09. Mem., Nat. Infrastructure Commn, 2015–. Co-Ed., Amer. Econ. Rev., 1999–2004. Chm., Council of Mgt, NIESR, 2008–16. President: European Economic Assoc., 2010; Internat. Economic Assoc., 2014–17; Econometric Soc., 2018 (Fellow, 2000; Vice-Pres., 2017). Foreign Hon. Mem., Amer. Acad. of Arts and Scis, 2011. *Publications:* contribs to Amer. Econ. Rev., Jl Political Econ., Econometrica, Qly Jl Econs and other scholarly jls. *Recreations:* Fulham FC, squash, playing violin, reading. *Address:* London School of Economics, Houghton Street, WC2A 2AE. *T:* (020) 7955 6702.

**BESSANT, Rev. Canon Simon David**; Vicar, St Saviour, High Green, Sheffield, 2012–19; Priest in Charge, St Mark, Grenoside, Sheffield, 2014–19; Mission Development Officer, Sheffield, since 2019; *b* 16 Feb. 1956; *s* of Ernest and Joan Bessant; *m* 1978, Ruth Margaret Hadfield; three *d*. *Educ:* Sheffield Univ. (BMus 1977; MA 2000); Nottingham Univ. (DipTh 1979). Ordained deacon, 1981, priest, 1982; Curate, St John and St James, Liverpool, 1981–84; Vicar: Emmanuel Ch, Holloway, 1984–91; Ch of the Redeemer, Blackburn, 1991–98; RD, Blackburn, 1997–98; Diocesan Dir for Mission, Dio. of Blackburn, 1998–2007; Vicar, All Saints, Ecclesall, Sheffield, 2007–12. Member: Gen. Synod of C of E, 2001–15; Archbishops' Council, 2006–07. Hon. Canon, Blackburn Cathedral, 2006–07, now Canon Emeritus. *Recreations:* listening to Schoenberg, reading counterfactuals, experimental fish cookery.

**BESSBOROUGH, 12th Earl of**, *cr* 1739 (Ire.); **Myles Fitzhugh Longfield Ponsonby**; Baron Bessborough (Ire.) 1721; Viscount Duncannon (Ire.) 1722; Baron Ponsonby (GB) 1749; Baron Duncannon (UK) 1834; *b* 16 Feb. 1941; *e s* of 11th Earl of Bessborough and his 1st wife, Patricia, *d* of Col Fitzhugh Minnigerode; *S* father, 2002; *m* 1972, Alison, *d* of William Storey, OBE; two *s* one *d*. Heir: *s* Viscount Duncannon, *qv*. *Address:* Broadreed, Stansted Park, Rowlands Castle, Hants PO9 6DZ.

**BESSBOROUGH, Madeleine, Countess of; Madeleine Lola Margaret Ponsonby**, OBE 2010; owner and Director, New Art Centre Sculpture Park and Art Gallery, Roche Court and Roche Farm; *b* Aldershot, 8 Nov. 1935; *d* of Maj. Gen. Laurence Douglas Grand, CB, CIE, CBE and Irene Grand (*née* Mathew); *m* 1963, Arthur Mountifort Longfield Ponsonby, 11th Earl of Bessborough; two *s*. *Educ:* St Mary's Sch., St Leonards-on-Sea; Prior's Field, Godalming. Founder: New Art Centre, London, 1957; Roche Court Sculpture Park, 1995; Roche Court Educnl Trust, 2005. Mem. Council, RCA, 1963–72 (Hon. Fellow, 1979). Lay Canon, Salisbury Cathedral, 2008–18, now Canon Emeritus. Patron, Salisbury Hospice, 1999–2007; Vice-Pres., Wilts Historic Churches Trust, 2009. *Recreations:* contemporary architecture, small working farm, gardening. *Address:* Roche Court, East Winterslow, Salisbury, Wilts SP5 1BG. *T:* (01980) 862244, *Fax:* (01980) 862447. *E:* nac@sculpture.uk.com.

**BESSER, Prof. (Gordon) Michael**, MD, DSc; FRCP, FMedSci; Professor of Medicine and Head of Department of Endocrinology and the Medical Professorial Unit, St Bartholomew's and the Royal London School of Medicine and Dentistry, Queen Mary and Westfield College (formerly St Bartholomew's Hospital Medical College), London University, at St Bartholomew's Hospital, 1992–2001, and at Royal London Hospital, 1994–2001, now Professor Emeritus, Queen Mary University of London; Consultant and Lead Clinician, Department of Endocrinology, Bart's and the London (formerly Royal Hospitals) NHS Trust, 1994–2001, now Hon. Consultant Physician; *b* 22 Jan. 1936; *s* of Hyman Besser and Leah Besser (*née* Geller); *m* 1972; one *s* one *d*. *Educ:* Hove County Grammar Sch.; Bart's Med. Coll., Univ. of London (BSc, MB BS, MD, DSc). FRCP 1973. St Bartholomew's Hospital: Lectr in Medicine, 1966–70; Sen. Lectr and Hon. Consultant Physician, 1970–74; Prof. of Endocrinology, Med. Coll., 1974–92; Consultant and Physician i/c Dept of Endocrinology, 1974–2001; Dir of Medicine, 1989–93; Chief Exec., 1992–94. Consultant Endocrinologist: to RN, 1989–2001; The London Clinic Centre for Endocrinology, 2001–14. Vis. Prof., univs and med. estabts in Australasia, Canada, China, Hong Kong, Italy, Malta, S Africa, USA, Yugoslavia. Cttee work for Acad. of Med. Scis, RCP, RSocMed, Soc. for Endocrinology, Jt Cttee on Higher Med. Training; Medical Research Council: former Mem., Physiol. Systems Bd and Grants Cttee (Chm., 1984–86); Chm., Working Party on Hormone Replacement Therapy, 1992–95. Royal College of Physicians: Lectr, 1974, 1993, 1999; Censor, 1990–92; Sen. Vice-Pres. and Sen. Censor, 1995–97; Chm. Clinical Examng Bd, MRCP (UK), 1999–2003. Founder FMedSci 1998. Hon. MD Turin, 1985. Mem. Editl Bd, Clinics in Endocrinology and Metabolism, 1977–92; former Mem. Editl Bd, Jl of Endocrinol., Neuroendocrinol., and Clinical Endocrinol. Trustee: Barts Foundn for Res., 1985–2005; Barlow Collection of Chinese Ceramics, Univ. of Sussex, 2004–11; William Harvey Res. Foundn, 2005–11; St Bartholomew's Hosp. Med. Coll., 2005–17; Willoughby Trust for Inflammatory Res., 2012–17. *Publications:* Fundamentals of Clinical Endocrinology (with R. Hall and J. Anderson), 2nd edn 1978, 3rd edn 1980, (ed with R. Hall) 4th edn 1989; Clinical Neuroendocrinology, 1977; Recent Advances in Medicine, 3 edns, 1981–87; (ed jtly) Endocrinology, 2nd edn 1989, 3rd edn 1994; Clinical Endocrinology, 1986, 3rd edn 2002; Clinical Diabetes, 1988; contribs to learned jls. *Recreations:* early Chinese ceramics, modern European art, opera, ballet, theatre, making ceramics, keeping fit. *Address:* 5 Devonshire Place, W1G 6HL. *Club:* Garrick.

**BEST**, family name of **Barons Best** and **Wynford**.

**BEST, Baron** *cr* 2001 (Life Peer), of Godmanstone in the County of Dorset; **Richard Stuart Best**, OBE 1988; DL; *b* 22 June 1945; *s* of Walter Stuart Best, DL, JP and Frances Mary Chignell; *m* 1st, 1970, Ima Akpan (marr. diss. 1976); one *s* one *d*; 2nd, 1978, Belinda Janie Tremayne Stemp; one *s* one *d*. *Educ:* Shrewsbury School; University of Nottingham (BA). British Churches Housing Trust, 1968–73 (Dir, 1971–73); Director: Nat. Fedn of Housing Assocs, 1973–88; Joseph Rowntree Foundn, 1988–2006. Pres., LGA, 2005–15; Chairman: Hanover Housing Assoc., 2006–14; Hull Partnership Liaison Bd, 2002–04; Westminster Housing Commn, 2004–05; The Giving Forum, 2005–11; Commn on Future of Housing in NI, 2009–10; DCLG/LGA Housing Commn, 2010; The Glazing Ombudsman, 2012–14; Dep. Chm., Westminster CC Standards Cttee, 2008–13; Regulation of Property Agents Wkg Gp, MHCLG, 2018–; Affordable Housing Commn, 2018–; Sec., Duke of Edinburgh's Inquiry into British Housing, 1984–91. Chm., UK Nat. Council for UN City Summit, 1995–96. Trustee: Sutton Housing Trust, 1971–84 (Dep. Chm., 1983–84); Internat. Year of Shelter for the Homeless 1987 Trust; RSA, 2006–12 (Treas., 2009–12); Committee Member: UK Housing Trust, 1976–88; Sutton Hastoe Housing Assoc., 1982–2000. House of Lords: Chm., Audit Cttee, 2005–10; Mem., Econ. Affairs Cttee, 2007–12; Chm., All Party Parly Gp on Housing and Care for Older People, 2009–; Chm., Select Cttee on Communications, 2014–17. Member: Social Policy Cttee, C of E Bd for Social Responsibility, 1986–91; BBC/IBA Central Appeals Cttee, 1989–91; Cttee, Assoc. of Charitable Foundns, 1989–92; Council for Charitable Support, 1995–2005; Housing Minister's Sounding Bd, DETR, 1999–2001; DTI Foresight Panel on Built Envmt, 1999–2001; Minister for Local Govt's Sounding Bd, DTLR/ODPM, 2001–05; NCVO Adv. Council, 2001–16; Commn on Future of Birmingham's Council Housing, 2002; Comr, Rural Develt Commn, 1989–98. A Church Comr, 2018–. Trustee, 2020 Public Services Trust, 2008–11. Mem. Council, Ombudsman for Estate Agents, 2007–09; Chm., The Property Ombudsman, 2009–17. Vice Pres., TCPA, 2007–. Pres., Sustainable Energy Assoc., 2017–. Patron: Nat. Family and Parenting Inst., 2001–; Housing Assocs Charitable Trust, 2007–; Vice-Patron, Servite Houses, 2001–. DL N Yorks, 2012. FAcSS 2015. Hon. FRIBA, 2001. Hon. LittD Sheffield, 2003; DUniv York, 2007. *Publications:* Rural Housing: problems and solutions, 1981; Housing Associations 1890–1990, 1991; Housing After 2000 AD, 1992; The Inclusive Homes of the Future, 1999; Housing Shortages: what councils can do, 2010; (with Jeremy Porteus) Housing our Ageing Population: plan for implementation, 2012. *Address:* House of Lords, SW1A 0PW. *Clubs:* Travellers, Farmers.
*See also* J. L. S. Best.

**BEST, Dr Anthony Bernard**, OBE 2010; Chief Executive, Percy Hedley Foundation, 2008–11; *b* 1 June 1947. *Educ:* Univ. of Leeds (Teacher's Cert.); Univ. of Newcastle upon Tyne (Dip. Special Ed.); Univ. of Birmingham (MEd; PhD 1993). Lectr in Special Educn, Univ. of Birmingham, 1978–90; Educn Develt Consultant, Hilton Perkins, USA, 1990–93; Principal, RNIB, 1993–2001; Chief Exec., Sense, 2001–08. European Rep., Internat. Council for Visually Impaired, 1997–99; Chm., Strategy Cttee, Deafblind International, 2006–09; Mem., Diversity Panel, ITV, 2009–. Trustee: Sightsavers, 1984–87; Signature (Council for Advancement of Communication with Deaf People), 2008–12. Ext. Examr, deafblind studies, Open Univ., 2009–17; Educn Consultant, Scope, 2011–13. Trustee: Henshaws Soc. for Blind People, 2014–; N Tyneside CAB, 2016–. Governor: Whitefields Sch., Waltham Forest, 2005–12; Henshaws Specialist Coll., 2016– (Chm., 2017–). *Publications:* Steps to Independence, 1987; Teaching Children with Visual Impairment, 1992; The Management of Visually Impaired Children, 1993; An International Research Agenda for Conductive Education, 2011. *E:* tonybest987@gmail.com.

**BEST, David William**; Chairman, Medical Marketing International Group plc (formerly Medical Marketing International Ltd), 1996–2008; *b* 1 Dec. 1949; *s* of William Robertson Best and Frances Best; *m* 1972, Margaret Smart Mitchell (marr. diss. 2015); one *s* one *d*. *Educ:* North Manchester Grammar Sch.; Univ. of Edinburgh. Mgt posts in pharmaceutical industry, 1973–88; Co-Founder, Man. Dir, 1988–96, Chief Exec., 1995–96, Medical Marketing Internat. Ltd (first private sector technology mgt co. in Europe); Founder and CEO, Bioscience Innovation Centre plc, 1996–2008; Chairman: BioStarter Initiative, 2001–08; Oncosense Ltd, 2003–08; Viratis Ltd, 2003–08; Genvax Ltd, 2004–08; Founder, Bioscience Venture Capital Trust plc, 2001. Mem., AIM Adv. Panel, London Stock Exchange, 2002–08. Gold Friend, Duke of Edinburgh's Internat. Award, 2000–; Mem., Internat. Fundraising Cttee, British Red Cross, 2001–. Founder Mem., Global Scots, 2003. Ambassador, Med. Emergency Relief Internat., 2002–. *Recreations:* running, hill walking. *E:* best.david@btinternet.com.

**BEST, Harold**; *b* 18 Dec. 1937; *s* of Fred and Marie Patricia Best; *m* 1960, Mary Glyn; two *s* two *d*. *Educ:* Meanwood County Sch.; Leeds Coll. of Technol. Electrical technician; worked for Co-op. Movt, in electrical contracting industry, and in educn (technical support). MP (Lab) Leeds North West, 1997–2005. *Address:* 19 Wynmore Avenue, Bramhope, Leeds LS16 9DD.

**BEST, James Leigh Stuart**; Director, DDB Worldwide, 1991–2008 (Chief Strategy and People Officer, 2002–07); *b* 1 April 1954; *s* of Walter Stuart Best, DL, JP and Frances Mary Best (*née* Chignell), *m* 1979, Priscilla Mary Rose McNeile; two *s* one *d*. *Educ:* Shrewsbury Sch.; New Coll., Oxford (BA, MA). Dir, Boase Massimi Pollitt plc, 1985–89; Chm., BMP DDB, 1989–2000; Gp Chm., DDB UK, 2000–05. Chairman: UK Advertising Assoc., 1997–2002; Credos, 2010–; Cttee of Advertising Practice and Broadcast Cttee of Advertising Practice, 2011–; Mem. Council, ASA, 2007–11. Pres., Eur. Assoc. Communications Agencies, 2003–05. Vice-Chm., Deborah Hutton campaign, 2009–15. Trustee, Hist. of Advertising Trust, 2013– (Dep. Chair, 2017–). Vis.

Prof., Richmond Internat. Univ., 2015–. FIPA 1996. *Publications:* (ed) Scottish Advertising Works, vol. 3 2003, vol. 4 2005. *Recreations:* farming, wildlife. *Address:* Manor Farm House, Godmanstone, Dorset DT2 7AQ.
*See also Baron Best.*

BEST, (Katherine) Jane; *see* Humphries, K. J.

BEST, Keith (Lander), TD 1981; management consultant and lecturer; *b* 10 June 1949; *s* of late Peter Edwin Wilson Best and Margaret Louisa Best; *m* 1990, Elizabeth Margaret Gibson; two *d*. *Educ:* Brighton Coll.; Keble Coll., Oxford (BA (Hons) Jurisprudence; MA). Assistant Master, Summerfields Sch., Oxford, 1967; called to the Bar, Inner Temple, 1971; Lectr in Law, 1973. Served: 289 Parachute Battery, RHA (V), 1970–76; with RM on HMS Bulwark, 1976; Naval Gunfire Liaison Officer with Commando Forces (Major). Councillor, Brighton Borough Council (Chm. Lands Cttee, Housing Cttee), 1976–80. Dir, Prisoners Abroad, 1989–93; Chief Exec., Immigration Adv. Service, 1993–2009. MP (C): Anglesey, 1979–83; Ynys Môn, 1983–87. PPS to Sec. of State for Wales, 1981–84. Former Chm., All Party Alcohol Policy and Services Gp; former Mem., Select Cttee on Welsh Affairs. Chairman: Bow Gp Defence Cttee; British Cttee for Vietnamese Refugees; Internat. Council of Parliamentarians' Global Action; World Federalist Movement, 1987–2018 (Sec., 2018–); Conservative Action for Electoral Reform, 1992–; Vauxhall Conservative Assoc., 1997–99; Electronic Immigration Network, 1998–2008; Electoral Reform Soc., 1998–2003 (Mem. Council, 1996–2013); Assoc. of Regulated Immigration Advrs, 2003–09; Electoral Reform Internat. Services, 2007–14; Wyndham Place Charlemagne Trust, 2013–; Vice Chm., European Council on Refugees and Exiles, 2011–14; Mem., Foreign Secretary's Adv. Sub-Gp on Prevention of Torture, 2010–14. Chief Executive: Med. Foundn for the Care of Victims of Torture, later Freedom from Torture, 2010–14; SurvivorsUK, 2015–17; Chm., Charity 2020, 2015–. Sec. and Trustee, Parly Outreach Trust, 2015–. Vice Chair, London for Europe, 2018– (Hon. Sec., Eur. Movement, 2015–). Member: Conservative Gtr London Area Exec. Cttee, 1997–99; UN Disarmament Cttee. Mem., Young Conservative Nat. Adv. Cttee, 1978. Mem. Cttee, Assoc. of Lloyd's Mems. Pres., Holyhead Leisure Fest. Ltd, 1981–2012. Trustee, Cranstoun Drug Services (formerly Odyssey Trust), 2003–09. Chm. and Trustee, Bangladesh Female Acad., 2009–11. Founder Member: Two Piers Housing Co-operative, 1977; Brighton Housing Trust, 1976; school manager, Downs County First Sch. and Downs Middle Sch., 1976. Dep. Ed., District Councils Rev. FRSA. *Publications:* Write Your Own Will, 1978 (paperback); The Right Way to Prove a Will, 1980 (paperback). *Recreations:* parachuting, walking, photography, travel. *Address:* 15 St Stephen's Terrace, SW8 1DJ. *Clubs:* Royal Artillery Mess (Woolwich); Holyhead Conservative; RSA.

BEST, Matthew Robert; opera singer, conductor, composer, arranger, teacher; Founder/Musical Director, Corydon Singers, since 1973, Corydon Orchestra, since 1991, Artistic Director, since 1996; *b* 6 Feb. 1957; *s* of late Peter Best and of Isabel Mary Best; *m* 1983, Rosalind Sandra Mayes; one *s* one *d*. *Educ:* Sevenoaks Sch.; King's Coll., Cambridge (Choral Schol.; MA Hons Music). Singer: Nat. Opera Studio, 1979–80; Principal bass, Royal Opera, 1980–86; Guest Artist, Royal Opera, Opera North, WNO, ENO, Scottish Opera, Netherlands Opera, Florida Grand Opera, Théâtre du Châtelet (Paris), Opéra de Nancy, Staatstheater Stuttgart, Théâtre de la Monnaie, Brussels, Opéra de Lyon, Santa Fé Opera, Oper Frankfurt, Royal Swedish Opera, Oper Leipzig, Opera de Bilbao and others, 1982–; principal operatic rôles incl. Flying Dutchman, Scarpia, Pizarro, Wotan (complete Ring Cycle, Edinburgh Internat. Fest., 2003), King Mark, Rocco, Commendatore, Amfortas, Kurwenal, King Heinrich, Orest, Jochanaan, Peneios, La Roche; created rôles: Vairochana in Jonathan Harvey's Wagner Dream (world premiere); Tiresias in Julian Anderson's Thebans (world premiere); Tsargo in Kaija Saariaho's Adriana Mater (US premiere); has performed in concerts worldwide and at major European and American fests. Conductor: concert appearances with Corydon Singers and Corydon Orch. at fests throughout UK and Europe, at South Bank and BBC Promenade concerts; Prin. Conductor, The Hanover Band, 1998–99; Guest Conductor with English Chamber Orch., London Mozart Players, City of London Sinfonia, Royal Seville SO, English Northern Philharmonia, New Queen's Hall Orch., Manchester Camerata, RTE Concert Orch., Northern Sinfonia, BBC Nat. Orch. of Wales, Sønderjyllands Symfoniorkester and Royal Liverpool Philharmonic Orch.; has made numerous recordings of choral/orchestral music and opera. *Compositions* include: Alice (operetta) performed at Aldeburgh Fest., 1979; choral and orchestral works performed by King's Coll. Choir, Cambridge, Corydon Singers. Teacher, Sch. of Vocal Studies and Opera, RNCM, 2014–. *Recreations:* reading, hill-walking, crosswords, gardening. *Address:* c/o Intermusica Artists' Management Ltd, 9 Kingsway, WC2B 6XF. *T:* (020) 7608 9900.

BEST, Prof. Serena Michelle, (Mrs A. I. Jaunzens), CBE 2017; PhD; CEng, FREng; Professor of Materials Science, University of Cambridge, since 2009; Fellow, St John's College, Cambridge, since 2000; *b* 24 Jan. 1964; *d* of Anthony and Barbara Best; *m* 1986, Allan Imants Jaunzens; two *s*. *Educ:* Univ. of Surrey (BSc); Queen Mary and Westfield Coll., Univ. of London (PhD 1990). CEng 1995; FREng 2012. Lectr, 1994–99, Reader, 1999–2000, QMW; Lectr, 2000–06, Reader, 2006–09, Univ. of Cambridge. Pres., IMMM, 2019–. *Publications:* contribs to learned jls incl. Jl Royal Soc. Interface, Advanced Materials and Biomaterials. *Address:* Department of Materials Science and Metallurgy, University of Cambridge, 27 Charles Babbage Road, Cambridge CB3 0FS. *E:* smb51@cam.ac.uk.

BEST-SHAW, Sir Thomas (Joshua), 11th Bt *cr* 1665, of Eltham, Kent; *b* Maidstone, 7 March 1965; *s* of Sir John Michael Robert Best-Shaw, 10th Bt and of Jane Best-Shaw (*née* Guthrie); *S* father, 2014; *m* 1992, Emily Susan (*née* Rubin); two *s*. *Educ:* Maidstone Grammar Sch.; Univ. of Reading (BSc Hons Bldg Surveying). Local govt, 1992–2014; portrait artist, 2014–. Liveryman, Vintners' Co., 1994. *Recreations:* walking, classical music. *Heir: s* Joshua John Kirkland Best-Shaw, *b* 17 Jan. 1995. *Address:* South View House, 226 Tonbridge Road, Wateringbury, Maidstone, Kent ME18 5NY. *E:* bestshaw1@gmail.com.

BESTERMAN, Tristram Paul; freelance adviser, speaker, writer and activist on museums, cultural restitution and environmental sustainability; *b* 19 Sept. 1949; *s* of late Dr Edwin Melville Mack Besterman and Audrey (*née* Heald); *m* 1977, Perry Garceau; two *s* one *d*. *Educ:* Stowe Sch.; Trinity Coll., Cambridge (BA 1971, MA 1979). FGS 1978; AMA 1979, FMA 1986. Studio Manager, BBC, 1971–73; Preparator's Asst, Geological and Mining Mus., Sydney, NSW, 1974; jackeroo, cattle station, Qld, 1974; Educn Asst, Sheffield City Museums, 1974–78; Dep. Curator and Keeper of Geology, Warwickshire Museums, 1978–85; City Curator, Plymouth City Museums and Art Gall., 1985–93; Dir, Manchester Mus., 1994–2005. Civil mediator, CMC accredited, 2010. Chm., Ethics Cttee, Museums Assoc., 1994–2001; Mem., Ministerial Working Gp on Human Remains, 2001–03. Trustee: Centre for Contemporary Art and the Natural World, 2008–13 (Chm., 2012–13); Gaia Trust, 2016–. Mem. Cttee, Cornwall Butterfly Conservation, 2015–; Community Leader, Plastic Free Liskeard, 2018–. *Publications:* contribs to museological literature. *Recreations:* music, photography, industrial archaeology, grandchildren and other forms of natural history. *Address:* Hollywell House, Lodge Hill, Liskeard, Cornwall PL14 4EH. *T:* (01579) 349146.

BETEGH, Prof. Gábor Sándor, PhD; Laurence Professor of Ancient Philosophy, University of Cambridge, since 2014; Fellow, Christ's College, Cambridge, since 2014; *b* Budapest, Hungary, 20 June 1968; *s* of Sándor Betegh and Katalin Soltész; *m* 1997, Ágnes Sándor; two *d*. *Educ:* Eötvös Univ., Budapest (MA); École des Hautes Études en Sciences Sociales, Paris (Dip. d'études approfondies; PhD 1999). Jun. Res. Fellow, Center for Hellenic Studies, Harvard Univ., 2000–01; Prof., Central European Univ., 2001–14. Vis. Prof., Cornell Univ., 2007; Fellow, Wissenschaftskolleg Berlin, 2004–05; Topoi Sen. Res. Fellow, 2009–10. *Publications:* The Derveni Papyrus, 2004, 2nd edn 2007. *Recreations:* climbing, music. *Address:* Christ's College, Cambridge CB2 3BU.

BETHEL, Dr Archibald Anderson, CBE 2008 (OBE 1996); CEng, FREng; FIMechE; FRSE; Chief Executive, Babcock International Group plc, since 2016 (Executive Director, 2004–16); *b* High Blantyre, Lanarkshire, 9 Feb. 1953; *s* of Jack and Margaret Bethel; *m* 1984, Doreen; one *s* one *d*. *Educ:* Hamilton Acad.; Univ. of Strathclyde (BSc, MBA, DSc). FREng 2003. Chief Exec., Scottish Enterprise Lanarkshire, 1991–96; Chief Operating Officer, Motherwell Bridge Gp, 1996–2003; Chm., Scottish Enterprise Lanarkshire, 2003–08. Vice Pres., IMechE, 2005–13; Pres., Soc. of Maritime Industries, 2010–. Lay Mem. Court, Univ. of Strathclyde, 2012–. FRSE 2010. *Recreations:* golf, guitar, travel, science. *Address:* 11 Frederick Boulevard, Thorntonhall, Glasgow G74 5DE. *T:* (0141) 644 3883. *E:* aabethel@btinternet.com, archie.bethel@babcockinternational.com.

BETHEL, Martin; QC 1983; a Recorder of the Crown Court, 1979–2015; *b* 12 March 1943; *o s* of late Rev. Ralph Bethel and Enid Bethel; *m* 1974, Kathryn Denby; two *s* one *d*. *Educ:* Kingswood Sch.; Fitzwilliam Coll., Cambridge (MA, LLM). Called to the Bar, Inner Temple, 1965; North-Eastern Circuit (Circuit Junior, 1969); a Dep. High Court Judge, 1995–2015. Member: Criminal Injuries Compensation Bd, 1999–2000; Criminal Injuries Compensation Tribunal (formerly Appeals Panel), 2000–10. Governor, Ashville Coll., Harrogate, 1989–2001. Pres., Runswick Bay Rescue Boat, 2001–04. *Recreations:* walking, travel, golf, croquet. *Address:* c/o St Pauls Chambers, 19–20 Park Row, Leeds LS1 5JF.

BETHEL, Robert George Hankin; Medical Practitioner, since 1972; *b* London, 7 June 1948; *s* of Horace Hankin Bethel and Eileen Maude, (Mollie), Bethel (*née* Motyer). *Educ:* Eastbourne Grammar Sch.; Pembroke Coll., Cambridge (BA 1969; MA 1973); St Mary's Hosp. Med. Sch., London (MB BChir 1972). MRCGP 1979. Hse Physician, Queen Elizabeth II Hosp., Welwyn Garden City, 1972; Hse Surgeon, Nottingham Gen. Hosp., 1973; SHO, Northwick Park Hosp. and Clin. Res. Centre, Harrow, 1974; Registrar, W Middx Univ. Hosp., 1974–76; GP, Englefield Green and Old Windsor, 1976–2005 (Sen. Partner, Runnymede Med. Practice, 1997–2005); Rheumatologist (pt-time), Heatherwood Hosp., Ascot, 1976–92; Hosp. Practitioner, Windsor (Geriatrics), 1980–91. Course Tutor, Open Univ., 1979–80; Approved Trainer for Gen. Practice (Oxford Deanery), 1984–2005; Associate Teacher, ICSTM (formerly St Mary's Hosp. Med. Sch.), 1989–2004; Med. Officer, Brunel Univ., 1993–98. GP Appraiser, NHS England (South, South Central) (formerly Berks E PCT, then Thames Valley Primary Care Agency), 2004–19. GMC Associate (Performance Assessor and Professional and Linguistic Assessments Bd Examr), 2002–18. Adv. Ed., Horizons, 1988–91. Member: Exec. Cttee, E Berks BMA, 1977–93 (Divl Sec., 1983–85); Bd, SW Thames Faculty, RCGP, 1983–92; Med. Mem., Ind. Tribunal Service (disability), 1991–99. Vice Chm., Old Windsor Day Centre, 1989–94. Chm., Middx Province Relief Fund, 2015– (Vice Chm., 2010–15). Life FRSocMed 1975 (Sec., 1993–95; Vice Pres., Sect. of Gen. Practice, 1995–97); FRSPH (FRSH 1990); Fellow, Med. Soc. of London, 1995. Member: Council, Royal Masonic Trust for Girls and Boys, 2002–16; Matthew Wren Soc., 2009–. Cambridge Society: Sec., 1982–85; Chm., 1988–95; Mem. Council, 1991–2009; Vice Pres., Surrey Br., 1995–. Freeman, City of London, 1977 (Mem., Guild of Freemen, 1978–). Society of Apothecaries of London: Freeman, 1977–; Liveryman, 1981–; Court Asst, 1998–; Chm., Charity Cttee, 2007–10; Warden, 2008–10; Master, 2010–11; Hon. Treas., 2014–; Liveryman and Freeman, Curriers' Co., 2011– (Trustee, Millennium Trust, 2003–17; Mem., Charity Cttee, 2014–17). Governor: Corp. of Sons of the Clergy 2011–; Royal Humane Soc., 2011–14 (Life Gov., 2014). Wandsman, St Paul's Cath., 1987–. *Publications:* contrib. scientific papers to med. jls with perst ref. to rheumatol. and gen. practice. *Recreations:* genealogy, books, travel. *T:* (01753) 540411. *E:* robert.bethel@cantab.net. *Clubs:* United Oxford and Cambridge; MCC.

BETHELL, family name of Barons Bethell and Westbury.

BETHELL, 5th Baron *cr* 1922, of Romford, co. Essex; James Nicholas Bethell; Bt 1911; a Lord in Waiting (Government Whip), since 2019; *b* 1 Oct. 1967; *e s* of 4th Baron Bethell and Cecilia Lothian Bethell (*née* Honeyman); *S* father, 2007; *m* 2004, Melissa, *d* of Douglas Wong, Newport Beach, Calif; one *s* two *d*. *Educ:* Harrow; Edinburgh Univ. (MA Hons History). Legislative aide, Office of Sec. of State, US Senate, 1985; Stagière, DG IV, EC, 1989; reporter, Sunday Times, 1990–93; correspondent, The Independent, 1993–94; Ministry of Sound, 1995–2001 (latterly Man. Dir); Capital Radio plc, 2001–05; Man. Partner, Portland, 2005–08; Dir of Communications, Policy Exchange, 2008; Founder and Dir, Westbourne Communications, 2009–18. Contested (C) Tooting, 2005. Elected Mem., H of L, 2018. *Publications:* (ed) A Pub Guide to Edinburgh, 1989; (jtly) Blue Skies Ahead, 1997. *Recreations:* hunting, shooting, clubbing. *Heir: s* Hon. Jacob Nicholas Douglas Bethell, *b* 17 Oct. 2006. *Address:* Lockeridge Down, Lockeridge, near Marlborough, Wilts SN8 4EL. *T:* (01672) 861 192. *Clubs:* Pratt's, Soho House.

BETHELL, Prof. Leslie Michael; Director, Centre for Brazilian Studies, University of Oxford, 1997–2007; Fellow, St Antony's College, Oxford, 1997–2007, now Emeritus; *b* 12 Feb. 1937; *s* of late Stanley Bethell and Bessie Bethell (*née* Stoddart); *m* 1961 (marr. diss. 1983); two *s*. *Educ:* Cockburn High Sch., Leeds; University Coll. London (BA, PhD). Lectr in History, Univ. of Bristol, 1961–66; Lectr 1966–74, Reader 1974–86, in Hispanic Amer. and Brazilian History, UCL; Prof. of Latin Amer. Hist., 1986–92, now Emeritus, and Dir, Inst. of Latin Amer. Studies, 1987–92, London Univ.; Sen. Res. Fellow, St Antony's Coll., Oxford, 1993–97. Visiting Professor: Instituto Universitário de Pesquisas do Rio de Janeiro, 1979; Univ. of California at San Diego, 1985; Woodrow Wilson Internat. Center for Scholars, Washington, 1987, 1996–97, 2008–09, 2010 and 2011 (Sen. Scholar, 2009–14); Univ. of Chicago, 1992–93; Centro de Pesquisa e Documentação de História, Fundação Getúlio Vargas, Rio de Janeiro, 2008–12; Univ. Federal da Integração Latino-Americana, Foz do Iguaçu, 2011; KCL, 2011–17; Univ. São Paulo, 2012. Member: Acad. Brasileira de Ciencias, 2004; Acad. Brasileira de Letras, 2010. Grand Officer, Nat. Order of the Southern Cross (Brazil), 1999 (Comdr, 1994); Comdr, Nat. Order of Scientific Merit (Brazil), 2010. *Publications:* The Abolition of the Brazilian Slave Trade, 1970; (ed) The Cambridge History of Latin America: vols I and II, Colonial Latin America, 1984; vol. III, From Independence to *c* 1870, 1985; vols IV and V, From *c* 1870 to 1930, 1986; vol. VII, Mexico, Central America and the Caribbean since 1930, 1990; vol. VIII, Spanish South America since 1930, 1991; vol. VI, Economy, Society and Politics since 1930, Part 1, Economy and Society, Part 2, Politics and Society, 1994; vol. XI, Bibliographical Essays, 1995; vol. X, Ideas, Culture and Society since 1930, 1995; vol. IX, Brazil since 1930, 2008; (jtly) Latin America between the Second World War and the Cold War 1944–48, 1992; The Paraguayan War (1864–70), 1995; (ed) Brasil. Fardo do Passado, Promessa do Futuro: dez ensaios sobre política e sociedade brasileira, 2002; Brazil by British and Irish authors, 2003; (jtly) Joaquim Nabuco e os abolicionistas ingleses, 2008; (jtly) Joaquim Nabuco: British abolitionists and the end of slavery in Brazil, 2009; Charles Landseer: Desenhos e aquarelas de Portugal e do Brasil 1825–1826, 2010; (ed) Joaquim Nabuco, My Formative Years, 2012; (jtly) Joaquim Nabuco, correspondente internacional, 1882–91, 2 vols, 2013; Joaquim Nabuco no mundo: abolicionista, jornalista e diplomata, 2016; (ed) Viva la Revolución: Eric Hobsbawm on Latin America, 2016; Brazil: essays on history and politics, 2018; articles and chapters on Latin American history, Brazilian history, culture, politics and internat. relns. *Address:* Avenida Aquarela do Brasil 333, Bloco 1, apto 1302, São Conrado, 22610–010 Rio de Janeiro, Brazil. *E:* leslie.bethell@sant.ox.ac.uk; c/o St Antony's College, Oxford OX2 6JF.

**BETHENCOURT, Ulinka Christiane;** *see* Rublack, U. C.

**BETHLEHEM, Sir Daniel (Lincoln),** KCMG 2010; QC 2003; Director: Legal Policy International Ltd, since 2011; Palantir Technologies UK Ltd, since 2013; *b* London, 16 June 1960. *Educ:* Univ. of Witwatersrand (BA 1981); Univ. of Bristol (LLB Hons 1985); Queens' Coll., Cambridge (LLM 1990). Called to the Bar, Middle Temple, 1988, Bencher, 2008; in practice as a barrister specialising in public internat. law, 1990–2006 and 2011–. Lectr in Internat. Law, LSE, 1992–98; Dep. Dir, 1998–2003, Dir, 2003–06, Lauterpacht Res. Centre for Internat. Law, subseq. Lauterpacht Centre for Internat. Law, Univ. of Cambridge; Legal Advr, FCO, 2006–11. Vis. Prof., Dept of War Studies, KCL, 2015–. *Publications:* (ed jtly) The Kuwait Crisis: basic documents, 1991; (ed) The Kuwait Crisis: sanctions and their economic consequences (2 vols), 1991; (ed jtly) The Yugoslav Crisis in International Law: general issues, 1997; (Gen. Ed.; jtly) International Environmental Law Reports, (5 vols), 1999–2007; (ed jtly) The Oxford Handbook of International Trade Law, 2009; contribs to Cambridge Jl of Internat. Law, Am. Jl of Internat. Law, Eur. Jl of Internat. Law. *Address:* 20 Essex Street, WC2R 3AL.

**BETT, Sir Michael,** Kt 1995; CBE 1990; MA; *b* 18 Jan. 1935; *s* of Arthur Bett, OBE and Nina Daniells; *m* 1959, Christine Angela Reid; one *s* two *d*. *Educ:* Aldenham Sch.; Pembroke Coll., Cambridge (Hon. Fellow, 2004). Dir, Industrial Relations, Engrg Employers' Fedn, 1970–72; Personnel Dir, General Electric Co. Ltd, 1972–77; Dir of Personnel, BBC, 1977–81; British Telecom: Bd Mem. for Personnel, 1981–84; Corporate Dir, Personnel and Corporate Services, 1984–85; Man. Dir Local (Inland) Communications Services, 1985–87; Man. Dir, UK Communications, 1987–88; Man. Dir, British Telecom UK, 1988–91; Vice-Chm., 1990–91; Dep. Chm., 1991–94; non-exec. Dir, 1994–96. Chairman: Cellnet, 1991–99; Workhouse Ltd, 1992–95; J2C plc, 2000–02; Pace Micro Technology Plc, 2000–06; Director: Compel Gp plc, 1993–2005 (Chm., 2000–05); KMG Financial Services, 1994–99; Eyretel plc, 1996–2003; non-exec. Dir, Ordnance Survey, 2002–06. Chairman: Nurses Pay Rev. Body, 1990–95; Social Security Adv. Cttee, 1993–95; Armed Forces Ind. Review on Manpower, 1994–95; Nat. Council, TEC, 1994–95; Inspectorate of the Security Industry, 1994–2000; Nat. Security Inspectorate, 2000–07; Pensions Protection and Investment Accreditation Bd, 2000–06; Ind. Review of Pay and Conditions of Service in Higher Educn; Co-Chm., British N Amer. Cttee, 1997–99; Member: Pay Bd, 1973–74; Training Levy Exemption Referee, 1975–82; Civil Service Arbitration Tribunal, 1977–83; Cttee of Inquiry into UK Prison Services, 1978–79; Cttee of Inquiry into Water Service Dispute, 1983; NHS Management Inquiry, 1983; Armed Forces Pay Review Body, 1983–87; Civil Service Coll. Adv. Council, 1983–88; Trng Commn (formerly MSC), 1985–89; First Civil Service Comr, 1995–2000. Member Council: St Christopher's Hospice, 1993–99; Royal Hosp. for Neurodisability, 1996–2005 (Chm., 1998–2005); Cranfield Inst. of Technology, 1982–87; Pro-Chancellor, 1993–2003, Chancellor, 2004–11, Aston Univ.; Vice-Pres., Roffey Park Mgt Inst., 1999–. Chairman: Bromley CABx, 1985–93; SCF, 1992–98. Chm. of Govs, Cranbrook Sch., 1992–2000. Dir, English Shakespeare Co., 1988–95; Chairman: One World Broadcasting Trust, 1996–2002; English Shakespeare Internat., 1997–2000. Chm., Sevenoaks Volunteer Develt Agency, 2005–07. CCIPD (Pres., 1992–98); CCMI; FRSA. Hon. Col, 81 Signal Sqn (Vols), RCS, 1990–96. DBA (*hc*): IMCB, 1986; CNAA/Liverpool Poly., 1991; Hon. DSc Aston, 1996; DUniv Kent, 2013. *Recreations:* television and radio, theatre, music, cooking, gardening, golf. *Address:* Colets Well, The Green, Otford, Kent TN14 5PD.

**BETTEL, Xavier;** Prime Minister of Luxembourg, since 2013; Minister of State, Minister of Communications and Media, and Religious Affairs Minister, since 2013; Minister of Culture, since 2015; *b* Luxembourg, 3 March 1973; *s* of Claude and Aniela Bettel; *m* 2015, Gauthier Destenay. *Educ:* Univ. of Nancy (MA Public and Eur. Law; Postgrad. Dip. Advanced Studies in Pol Scis and Public Law). Lawyer, 2001–13. Parliament of Luxembourg: Mem. (Dem) Chamber of Deputies, 1999–2013; Vice Chairman: Legal Affairs Cttee, 2004–13; Cttee of Inquiry into Intelligence Service, 2012–13. Mem. Council, 2000–05, Alderman, 2005–11, Mayor, 2011–13, Luxembourg City. Chm., Democratic Party, 2013–15 (Chm., Parly Gp, 2009–11). Grand Officier, Order of Orange Nassau (Netherlands), 2012; Grand Cross, Order of Oak Crown (Luxembourg), 2014. *Address:* Office of the Prime Minister, 4 rue de la Congrégation, 1352 Luxembourg. *E:* bureau.premierministre@me.etat.lu.

**BETTERIDGE, Prof. (Denis) John,** MD, PhD; FRCP; Consultant Physician, University College Hospital, London, 1981–2017; Professor of Endocrinology and Metabolism, University College London, 1994–2010; Dean, Royal Society of Medicine, 2011–14, Dean Emeritus, 2015–16; *b* Ashby-de-la-Zouch, Leics, 24 Sept. 1948; *s* of Winston and Annie Betteridge; *m* 1989, Christine Martin; one *s* one *d*. *Educ:* Ashby-de-la-Zouch Boys' Grammar Sch.; King's Coll. Med. Sch. and Guy's Hosp. Med. Sch., London (BSc 1st Cl. Hons Biochem. 1969; MB BS 1972; MD 1979); Bath Univ. (PhD 1981). FRCP 1985. House posts, King's Coll. Hosp., 1972–73; SHO, Hammersmith, Brompton and St Bartholomew's Hosps, 1973–75; Registrar and Res. Registrar, St Bartholomew's Hosp. (Aylwen Bursary); R. D. Lawrence Fellowship, British Diabetic Assoc.; Sen. Registrar, Royal United Hosp., Bath; UK Prin. Investigator and Mem., Internat. Steering Cttee, PROactive. Member: taskforce gp on diabetes and vascular disease, Jt Eur. Soc. Cardiol. and Eur. Assoc. for Study of Diabetes; Steering Cttee for UK Prospective Diabetes Study, MRC. Mem., Grants Cttee, BHF, 2005–09. Past Pres., Council on Lipids in Clin. Medicine, RSocMed. Formerly Chm., Heart UK. Dist. Fellow, Internat. Atherosclerosis Soc. (Sen. Advr to Bd); FAHA. Member: Eur. Diabetes Assoc.; Amer. Diabetes Assoc.; Eur. Atherosclerosis Soc. Governor: City of London Sch. for Girls; City Acad. Islington. *Publications:* Sport for Diabetics, 1987; Lipids: current perspectives, 1996; Lipoproteins in Health and Disease, 1999; Diabetes: current perspectives, 2000; Lipids in Vascular Disease, 2000; Clinicians Guide to Lipids and Coronary Disease, 2003; Case Studies in Diabetes, 2003; Case Studies in Lipid Management, 2007; Hyperlipidaemia, 2011; Lectures in Hypercholesterolaemia, 2013; Managing Cardiovascular Complications in Diabetes, 2014. *Recreations:* music, gardening, cricket, fly fishing, shooting. *Address:* Willesley Park, Outdowns, Effingham, Surrey KT24 5QR. *T:* (01483) 283458. *E:* profdjb66@gmail.com.

**BETTISON, Sir Norman (George),** Kt 2006; QPM 2000; Chief Constable, West Yorkshire Police, 2007–12; *b* 3 Jan. 1956; *s* of George and Betty Bettison; *m* 2004, Gillian. *Educ:* Queen's Coll., Oxford (MA Psychol. and Philosophy); Sheffield Hallam Univ. (MBA). Police officer, 1972–2004: S Yorks Police, 1972–93; W Yorks Police, 1993–98; Chief Constable, Merseyside Police, 1998–2004; Chief Exec., Centrex (nat. trng body to Police Service), 2004–06. Independence Medal (Rhodesia), 1980. *Publications:* Hillsborough Untold, 2016.

**BETTLEY-SMITH, Robert,** FRICS; chartered surveyor; consultant and company director; *b* 27 July 1953; *s* of late Dr Neville Smith and Joyce Bettley, BA; *m* 1980, Judith, (Judy), Patricia Naylor, MA (Cantab); two *s* one *d*. *Educ:* Royal Wolverhampton Sch.; Royal Agricl Coll., Cirencester (Prizeman); Queens' Coll., Cambridge. Surveyor, 1980–83, Sen. Surveyor, 1983–85, ADAS; Principal, 1985–91, Regl Dir, 1992–98, MAFF; Chief Exec., FWAG (on secondment), 1998–2002; Dir, Project Team, DEFRA, 2003–05; Chief Exec., Govt Decontamination Service, DEFRA, 2005–09; Chief Exec. and Sec., Strategic Adv. Bd for Intellectual Property Policy, 2009–10; Sen. Civil Servant, DEFRA, 2010–11. Director: Mercian Mktg Ltd, 1997–2002; Peak Produce Ltd, 2001–05; Camley Estates Ltd, 2002–; Ryan Housing Ltd, 2012–; Betley and District Heritage Ltd, 2013–. Chm., Betley, Balterley and Wrinehill PC, 2007– (Vice Chm., 2005–07). Trustee, Newcastle-under-Lyme Rural Parishes' Transport Scheme, 2010–. Dir, Llangollen Railway plc, 2017–19; Trustee, Llangollen Railway Trust, 2017–19. FCMI. *Publications:* Capital Investment by Landowners 1972–1977; contribs to RASE Jl, Chartered Surveyor, and other professional jls. *Recreations:* Christian faith, village activities, Association Football (referee and spectator), our boat, fruit growing, ski-ing, steam engines, keeping my children in a manner to which they aspire to be accustomed whilst working on heritage railways as a trainee fireman and in other roles. *Address:* Estate Office, Beech Wood, Betley, Crewe, Cheshire CW3 9AB. *T:* (01270) 820137. *E:* r.bettley-smith@talk21.com. *Club:* Farmers.

**BETTRIDGE, Brig. John Bryan,** CBE 1983; Principal, Emergency Planning College (formerly Civil Defence College), 1984–93; *b* 16 Aug. 1932; *s* of Henry George Bettridge and Dorothy Bettridge; *m* 1959, one *s* one *d*. *Educ:* Eastbourne Grammar School. Commissioned RA, 1951; regimental duty, 4 RHA and 52 Locating Regt, 1952–59; Instructor, RMA Sandhurst, 1959–61; Student, Staff Coll., Camberley, 1962; War Office, 1964–66; Bty Comd, 1 RHA, 1968–70; Comd, 3 RHA, 1973–75, Hong Kong; Chief Instructor, Tactics, RSA, 1976; Comd RA 2 Div., 1977–78; RCDS 1979; Dep. Comdt, Staff Coll., 1980–82; Comdt, RSA Larkhill, 1983–84. *Recreations:* golf, carpentry. *Address:* 50 Main Street, Bishopthorpe, York YO23 2RB. *T:* (01904) 704270.

**BETTS, Charles Valentine,** CB 1998; FREng, FRINA; Director General Submarines, and Deputy Controller of the Navy, Ministry of Defence, 1994–98; Head, Royal Corps of Naval Constructors, 1992–98; *b* 10 Jan. 1942; *s* of late Harold Blair Betts and Mary Ellis Betts (*née* France); *m* 1965, Rev. Patricia Joyce Bennett; two *s*. *Educ:* St Catharine's Coll., Cambridge (BA Hons, MA Mech. Scis); Royal Naval Coll., Greenwich (Prof. Cert., Naval Arch.); Univ. of London (MPhil Naval Arch.). CEng; FREng (FEng 1991). Asst Constructor, MoD, 1966–71; Lectr in Naval Arch., UCL, 1971–74; Constructor, HM Dockyard, Portsmouth, 1974–77; Constructor and Chief Constructor, MoD, Bath, 1977–83; Chief Constructor, MoD, London, 1983–85; Prof. of Naval Arch., UCL, 1985–89; Dir, Surface Ships B, MoD, Bath, 1989–92; Dir Gen., Surface Ships, MoD, 1992–94. Director (non-executive): BMT Group Ltd, 1999–2001; BMT Reliability Consultants Ltd, 2000–01; BMT Gp Ltd (formerly British Maritime Technology Ltd, later BMT Ltd), 2001–12. Mem., Nat. Historic Ships Cttee, 2006–06. Mem. Council, RINA, 1985–2002, 2003–09 (Vice-Pres., 2003–09). Trustee: Alpha Internat. Ministries, 1993–2001; The Coverdale Trust, 2001–04 (Vice-Chm.); BMT Gp Employee Benefit Trust, 2006–12 (Chm., 2010–12); Chm. Trustees, BMT Pension and Life Assurance Scheme, 2006–12. Mem. Court, Univ. of Bath, 2007–16. Mem., Moody Owners Assoc. FRSA 1994. *Publications:* (jtly) The Marine Technology Reference Book, 1990; Vanguard to Dreadnought: 30 years of naval construction 1983–2013, 2018; papers in professional jls. *Recreations:* supporting my wife in her rôle as Church of England priest, cruising together under sail, listening to music, amusing our grandchildren, walking, reading. *Clubs:* Royal Naval Sailing Association; Royal Victoria Yacht (IoW).

**BETTS, Clive James Charles;** MP (Lab) Sheffield South East, since 2010 (Sheffield Attercliffe, 1992–2010); *b* 13 Jan. 1950; *s* of late Harold and Nellie Betts. *Educ:* Longley Sch., Sheffield; King Edward VII Sch., Sheffield; Pembroke Coll., Cambridge (BA Econ). Sheffield City Council: Councillor (Lab), 1976–92; Chm., Housing Cttee, 1980–86; Chm., Finance Cttee, 1986–88; Dep. Leader, 1986–87; Leader, 1987–92. Chm., S Yorks Pension Authority, 1989–92; Dep. Chm., AMA, 1988–91 (Chm., Housing Cttee, 1985–89). An Asst Government Whip, 1997–98; a Lord Comr of HM Treasury (Govt Whip), 1998–2001. Member, Select Committee on: HM Treasury, 1995–96; Selection, 1997–2001; Transport, Local Govt and the Regions, 2001–02; MHCLG (formerly ODPM, then DCLG), 2002– (Chm., 2010–); Finance and Services, 2005–15; Finance, 2015–17. Member: Parly Contributory Pension Fund, 2005–; H of C Members' Fund, 2005–. Chm., 1995–96, Sec., 1995–97, Labour's Treasury Deptl Cttee; Labour Ldr's Campaign Team, 1995–96. *Recreations:* Sheffield Wednesday FC, football, squash, walking, real ale. *Address:* House of Commons, SW1A 0AA.

**BETTS, Jane Margaret;** *see* Mordue, J. M.

**BETTS, Lily Edna Minerva, (Mrs John Betts);** *see* Mackie, L. E. M.

**BETTS, Peter George,** CBE 2010; Director, International Climate and Energy, Department for Business, Energy and Industrial Strategy, 2016–18; *b* 3 March 1959; *s* of George Frank Betts and Joyce Ann Betts (*née* Pedder); *m* 2006, Fiona Jane MacGregor. *Educ:* Emanuel Sch., Battersea; Mansfield Coll., Oxford (BA Hist. 1982); Ecole Nationale d'Administration, Paris. Joined Civil Service, 1984; First Sec. (Envmt), Office of UK Perm Rep. to EU, Brussels, 1994–98; Head, Global Atmosphere Div., DETR, 1998–2001; Head, Work and Pensions Team, 2001–02, Pension and Savings Team, 2002–04, Budget and Public Finances Directorate, HM Treasury; Principal Private Sec. to Dep. Prime Minister and Hd, Ministerial Gp, ODPM, 2004–05; Dir, Regl Policy, ODPM, subseq. DCLG, 2005–06; Dir, Fire and Resilience, DCLG, 2006–08; Dir, Internat. Climate Change, DEFRA, later DECC, 2008–09; Actg Dir-Gen., Energy and Climate Change Internat., DECC, 2009–10; Dir, Internat. Climate Change, DECC, later BEIS, 2010–16.

**BETTS, Ven. Steven James;** Archdeacon of Norfolk, since 2012; *b* Nottingham, 22 Nov. 1964; *s* of late Ronald and Mary Betts; *m* 1992, Sarah Taylor; three *s*. *Educ:* Nottingham Bluecoat Grammar Sch.; Univ. of York (BSc Chemistry 1986); Univ. of Oxford (CTh 1990). Ordained deacon, 1990, priest, 1991; Curate, Holy Cross, Bearstead, with St Mary's, Thurnham, 1990–94; Chaplain to Bishop of Norwich, 1994–97; Vicar, Old Catton, Norwich, 1997–2005; Bishop's Officer for Ordinands and Initial Trng, 2005–12. *Recreations:* family, walking (especially in Austria), European travel. *Address:* 8 Boulton Road, Thorpe St Andrew, Norwich NR7 0DF. *T:* (01603) 559199. *E:* archdeacon.norfolk@dioceseofnorwich.org.

**BEUTLER, Prof. Bruce Alan,** MD; Regental Professor, Director, Center for Genetics of Host Defense, and Raymond and Ellen Willie Distinguished Chair in Cancer Research, University of Texas Southwestern Medical Center, since 2011; *b* Chicago, Ill, 29 Dec. 1957; *s* of Ernst Beutler and Brondelle May Beutler (*née* Fleisher); *m* 1980, Barbara Lanzl (marr. diss.); three *s*. *Educ:* Polytechnic Sch., Pasadena, Calif; Univ. of Calif, San Diego (BA

1976); Univ. of Chicago (MD 1981). Residency, Univ. of Texas Southwestern Med. Center, 1981–83; Postdoctoral Fellow, 1983–85, Asst Prof., 1985–86, Rockefeller Univ.; University of Texas Southwestern Medical Center: Asst Prof., 1986–90; Associate Prof., 1990–96; Prof., 1996–2000; Investigator, Howard Hughes Med. Inst., 1986–2000; Prof., Scripps Res. Inst., 2000–11. Member: NAS, 2008; Inst. of Medicine, 2008. Fellow, Amer. Acad. of Arts and Scis, 2013. (Jtly) Robert Koch Prize, 2004; (jtly) Balzan Prize, Internat. Balzan Prize Foundn, 2007; (jtly) Shaw Prize in Life Sci. and Medicine, 2011; (jtly) Nobel Prize for Physiology or Medicine, 2011. *Publications:* over 300 papers. *Address:* Beutler Lab, University of Texas Southwestern Medical Center, 5323 Harry Hines Boulevard, Dallas, TX 75390–8505, USA.

**BEVAN, Alison Claire,** BEM 2013; Director, Royal West of England Academy, since 2013; *b* Singapore, 1 Jan. 1965; *d* of John Edbrooke Lloyd and Barbara Lloyd; *m* 2004, Vince Bevan. *Educ:* Tasker Milward Sch.; Univ. of Nottingham (BA Hons Hist. of Art 1986). Res. Asst, Graham Sutherland Gall., 1987; Gall. Asst, Henry Thomas Gall., 1987–89; Glynn Vivian Art Gallery: Exhibns Asst, 1989–91; Exhibns Officer, 1991–97; Actg Curator, 1997–99; Dir, Penlee House Gall. and Mus., 1999–2013. *Recreations:* choral singing, co-parenting delinquent border collie, holidaying in Ireland, knitting. *Address:* Royal West of England Academy, Queens Road, Bristol BS8 1PX. *T:* (0117) 906 7603. *E:* Alison.Bevan@rwa.org.uk.

**BEVAN, Anthony Richard Van,** RA 2007; artist (painter); *b* Bradford, 22 July 1951; *s* of Adrian Van Christkarken Bevan and Margaret Betty Bevan (*née* Pemberton); *m* 1991, Glenys Johnson; one *d*. *Educ:* Bradford Sch. of Art; Goldsmiths Coll., London (DipAD); Slade Sch. of Fine Art (HDFA). *Solo exhibitions:* Tony Bevan: Paintings 1980–87, ICA, London, Orchard Gall., Londonderry, Kettle's Yard, Cambridge and Cartwright Hall, Bradford, 1987–88; Haus der Kunst, Munich, 1989; Whitechapel Art Gall., 1993; (retrospective) Inst. Valencia d'Art Modern, Valencia, 2005–06; (retrospective) Long Mus., Shanghai, 2014; (retrospective) Cartwright Hall, Bradford, 2016–17. *Relevant publication:* Tony Bevan, 2006. *Recreation:* food and wine. *Address:* 20 Blackheath Park, Blackheath, SE3 9RP. *T:* (020) 8852 0250, *Fax:* (020) 8469 0856. *E:* glenys.johnson@btconnect.com.

**BEVAN, Dianne;** Associate, Global Partners Governance, since 2015; *b* 31 Oct. 1958; *d* of Alan and Brenda Roe; *m* 1986, Nigel Bevan; one *s* one *d*. *Educ:* Selby Grammar Sch., N Yorks; Univ. of Hull (LLB Hons); Chester Coll. of Law (Solicitors' Finals); Cardiff Univ. (MPA). Articled clerk, Surrey CC, 1981–83; admitted solicitor, 1983; Solicitor: W Sussex CC, 1983–85; S Glamorgan CC, 1985–88; Chief Solicitor, 1988–91, Asst Co. Sec., 1991–93, W Glamorgan CC; Director, Legal and Administrative Services: S Glamorgan CC, 1993–96; Cardiff CC, 1996–99; Corporate Manager, Cardiff CC, 1999–2003; Dep. Clerk, 2003–12, Chief Operating Officer, 2007–12, Nat. Assembly for Wales. *Recreations:* travel, theatre, cinema, visual arts.

**BEVAN, (Edward) Julian;** QC 1991; *b* 23 Oct. 1940; *m* 1966, Bronwen Mary Windsor Lewis; two *s* two *d*. *Educ:* Eton. Called to the Bar, Gray's Inn, 1962, Bencher, 1989; Standing Counsel for the Inland Revenue, 1974; Jun. Treasury Counsel, 1977, Sen. Treasury Counsel, 1985, First Sen. Treasury Counsel, 1989–91, Central Criminal Court. *Club:* White's.

**BEVAN, Prof. Hugh Keith;** JP; Professor of Law, University of Hull, 1969–89; *b* 8 Oct. 1922; *s* of Thomas Edward Bevan and Marjorie Avril Bevan (*née* Trick); *m* 1950, Mary Harris; one *d* (one *s* decd). *Educ:* Neath Grammar Sch.; University Coll. of Wales, Aberystwyth. LLB 1949, LLM 1966. Called to the Bar, Middle Temple, 1959. Served RA, 1943–46. University of Hull: Lectr in Law, 1950–61; Sen. Lectr in Law, 1961–69; Pro Vice-Chancellor, 1979–82; Wolfson College, Cambridge: Vis. Fellow, 1986 and 1989–90; Fellow, 1990–92; Hon. Fellow, 1992. Chm., Rent Assessment Cttees, 1982–92. Pres., Soc. of Public Teachers of Law, 1987–88. JP Kingston-upon-Hull, 1972 (Chm. of Bench, 1984–89). Hon. Fellow, Swansea Univ., 2007. Hon. LLD: Hull, 1990; Sheffield, 2000. *Publications:* Source Book of Family Law (with P. R. H. Webb), 1964; Law Relating to Children, 1973; (with M. L. Parry) The Children Act 1975, 1978; Child Law, 1988; numerous articles. *Recreations:* music, golf. *Address:* Wolfson College, Cambridge CB3 9BB. *T:* (01223) 335900.

**BEVAN, Sir James (David),** KCMG 2012 (CMG 2006); HM Diplomatic Service, retired; Chief Executive, Environment Agency, since 2015; *b* 13 July 1959; *s* of late Douglas Bevan and of Diana Bevan; *m* 1984, Janet Purdie; three *d*. *Educ:* Univ. of Sussex (BA Hons Social Anthropology). Joined FCO, 1982; Kinshasa, 1984–86; UK Delegn to NATO, Brussels, 1986–90; FCO, 1990–92; Paris, 1993; Washington, 1994–98; Hd, Africa Dept (Equatorial), FCO, 1998–2000; Hd, EU Dept (Internal), FCO, 2000–01; Director: SE Europe and Gibraltar, FCO, 2002; Africa, FCO, 2003–06; Dir Gen., Change and Delivery, then Chief Operating Officer, FCO, 2007–11; High Comr to India, 2011–15. FCO Vis. Fellow, Harvard Univ., 2006. *Recreations:* music, not worrying.

**BEVAN, His Honour John Penry Vaughan;** QC 1997; a Circuit Judge, 2004–17; a Senior Circuit Judge, 2011–17; *b* 7 Sept. 1947; *s* of late Llewellyn Vaughan Bevan and Hilda Molly Bevan; *m* 1st, 1971, Dinah Nicholson; two *d*; 2nd, 1978, Veronica Aliaga-Kelly; one *s* one *d*. *Educ:* Radley Coll.; Magdalene Coll., Cambridge (BA). Called to the Bar, Middle Temple, 1970, Bencher, 2001. A Recorder, 1988–2004; Sen. Treasury Counsel, CCC, 1989–97. Judicial Mem., Parole Bd, 2018–. *Recreation:* sailing. *Clubs:* Leander (Henley-on-Thames); Aldeburgh Yacht; Orford Sailing.

**BEVAN, John Stuart,** OBE 1995; Further Education Funding Council for England Ombudsman, 1996–2001; *b* 19 Nov. 1935; *s* of Frank Oakland and Ruth Mary Bevan; *m* 1960, Patricia Vera Beatrice (*née* Joyce); two *s* two *d*. *Educ:* Eggars Grammar Sch.; Jesus Coll., Oxford; St Bartholomew's Hosp. Med. Coll. MA, MSc; FInstP. Health Physicist, UK Atomic Energy Authority, 1960–62; Lectr, then Sen. Lectr in Physics, Polytechnic of the South Bank (previously Borough Polytechnic), 1962–73; Inner London Education Authority: Asst Educn Officer, then Sen. Asst Educn Officer, 1973–76; Dep. Educn Officer, 1977–79; Dir of Educn, 1979–82; Sec., NAB, 1982–88; Dir of Educn Services, London Residuary Body, 1989–92; Chief Exec., ACFHE, 1992–93; Sec., Assoc. for Colls, 1993–94. Former Member, National Executive Committees: Nat. Union of Teachers; Assoc. of Teachers in Technical Instns (Pres., 1972–73). Chm., Nat. Youth Agency, 1996–2002. Scout Association: Asst, later Dep. Comr, Kent, 1982–99; Chm., Nat. Activities Bd, 1988–93; Nat. Comr for Activities, 1994–95; Chm., Programme and Trng, 1995–96; Chm., Cttee of Council, 1996–2001; Skills Instructor and Chm. Appts Cttee, Eden Dist, 2000–. Mem., Adventure Activities Industry Adv. Cttee, CCPR (formerly HSC), 1997–2007 (Chm., 2004–07). Co. Sec., Great Asby Broadband CIC, 2007–18; Vice-Chm., Cumbria Local Access Forum, 2001–12. Treas., Appleby Deanery, Carlisle Dio., 2002–13; Local Lay Minister, benefice containing Asby St Peter, Carlisle Dio., 2005–. Hon. Fellow: S Bank Univ. (formerly Poly. of the S Bank), 1987; Westminster Coll., Oxford, 1990. DUniv Surrey, 1990; Hon. LLD CNAA, 1992. *Recreations:* Scouting, foreign travel, hill-walking. *Address:* The Hollies, Great Asby, Appleby, Cumbria CA16 6HD. *T:* (01768) 353433.

See also R. M. Bevan.

**BEVAN, Julian;** see Bevan, E. J.

**BEVAN, Sir Martyn Evan E.;** see Evans-Bevan.

**BEVAN, Melinda;** see Simmons, M.

**BEVAN, Prof. Michael John,** PhD; FRS 1991; Investigator, Howard Hughes Medical Institute, and Professor, Department of Immunology, University of Washington, Seattle, 1990–2015, now Emeritus Professor; *b* 20 Sept. 1945; *s* of Thomas John and Doris Mary Bevan; *m* 1985, Pamela Jean Fink; two *s*. *Educ:* Pontypridd Boys' Grammar Sch.; University Coll. London (BSc Zool. 1967; MSc Biochem. 1968); Nat. Inst. for Med. Research, London (PhD 1972). Postdoctoral Fellow, Salk Inst. for Biol Studies, La Jolla, Calif, 1973–76, Asst Res. Prof., 1976–77; Asst, then Associate, Prof., Dept of Biology, MIT, 1977–82; Associate, then Member, Dept of Immunology, Scripps Res. Inst., La Jolla, Calif, 1982–90. *Publications:* numerous original res. pubns in scientific jls incl. Nature, Science, Cell, Jl Exptl Medicine. *Recreations:* hiking, reading, woodturning.

**BEVAN, Prof. Michael Webster,** OBE 2019; PhD; FRS 2013; Project Leader, Cell and Developmental Biology Department, and Deputy Director, John Innes Centre, Biotechnology and Biological Sciences Research Council, since 2010 (Acting Director, 2009–10); Professor, University of East Anglia, since 1997; *b* Otorohanga, NZ, 5 June 1952; *s* of John Vernon Bevan and Sue (*née* Webster); *m* 1982, Jane Foster; two *s*. *Educ:* Univ. of Auckland (BSc 1973; MSc Hons 1974); Univ. of Cambridge (PhD 1979). Res. Fellow, Washington Univ., St Louis, Mo, 1980; Higher Scientific Officer, 1982–84, SSO, 1984–86, PSO, 1986–88, Plant Breeding Inst., Cambridge; Hd, Dept of Molecular Genetics, then Cell and Develtl Biol., Inst. of Plant Sci. Res., AFRC, subseq. John Innes Centre, BBSRC, 1988–2009. Mem., EMBO, 2001. Rank Prize, Rank Foundn, 1986; Kumho Science Internat. Award in Plant Molecular Biol. and Biotechnol., Kumho Cultural Foundn of Korea, 2001. *Publications:* contrib. numerous chapters in books and articles to learned jls. *Recreations:* reading modern literature, gardening, walking. *Address:* 329 Unthank Road, Norwich NR4 7QA. *T:* (01603) 504181.

**BEVAN, Sir Nicolas,** Kt 2001; CB 1991; Speaker's Secretary, House of Commons, 1993–2003; *b* 8 March 1942; *s* of late Roger Bevan, BM, and Diana Mary Bevan (*née* Freeman); *m* 1982, Christine, *d* of N. A. Berry. *Educ:* Westminster Sch. (Hon. Fellow 2003); Corpus Christi Coll., Oxford (MA LitHum). Ministry of Defence: Asst Principal, 1964; Principal, 1969; Private Sec. to Chief of Air Staff, 1970–73; Cabinet Office, 1973–75; Asst Sec., 1976; RCDS 1981; Asst Under Sec. of State, 1985; Under Sec., Cabinet Office, 1992–93. Freeman, City of London, 2008; Liveryman, Woolmen's Co., 2009. *Recreation:* gardening. *Clubs:* National Liberal, Lansdowne, Victory Services.

**BEVAN, Robert,** MBE 2004; comedian, after-dinner speaker (as Bob "The Cat" Bevan), author, broadcaster, presenter, interviewer, journalist, poet, scriptwriter; *b* 26 Feb. 1945; *s* of Eric and Iris Rose Bevan; *m* 2012, Laura Collins. *Educ:* Wilson's Grammar Sch., Camberwell. MCIPR 1974. Trainee sales rep., Nicholls & Clarke, 1961–62; Asst Chief Reporter, Lloyd's List and Shipping Gazette, 1962–66; PR Manager, Shorthorn Soc. of GB and Ireland, 1966; Dep. Ed., Travel Agency Mag., 1967–69; Hertford Public Relations Ltd: Account Exec., 1969–70; Dir, 1970–72; Man. Dir, 1972–74; Gp Dir of PR, European Ferries Plc, 1974–83; Chm., Bevan PR Ltd, 1983–92. Member: NUJ, 1967–; Soc. of Authors. Hon. Barker, 1990–, Celebrity Ambassador, 2015–, Variety Club of GB; Mem., Grand Order of Water Rats, 2001–. Ambassador for County of Kent, 2011–. President: Old Wilsonians' Assoc., 1995 (Life Mem.); Bells Yew Green CC, 1996–2009; Kent CCC, 2013–14; Nat. Sporting Club, 2014; Vice President: Old Wilsonians' FC, 1970–; Crystal Palace FC, 1986–; Frant CC, 1993–; Middlesex Wanderers FC, 1996–; Dulwich Hamlet FC, 2000–; Tonbridge Angels FC, 2002–. Trustee, Lord's Taverners, 1995–2004, 2009–11, 2015–18. *Publications:* Nearly Famous, 2003. *Recreations:* football, cricket, reading, travel, food, drink. *Address:* Barelands Oast, Bells Yew Green, Kent TN3 9BD. *E:* Bob@bobthecatbevan.co.uk. *W:* www.bobthecatbevan.com. *Clubs:* Les Ambassadeurs; Kent CC.

**BEVAN, Dr Robin Meredith;** Headteacher, Southend High School for Boys, since 2007; *b* Tonbridge, Kent, 14 Aug. 1966; *s* of John Stuart Bevan, *qv*; *m* 1991 (marr. diss. 2015); one *s* two *d*. *Educ:* Judd Sch., Tonbridge (Stamp Leaving School.); Jesus Coll., Oxford (MA Maths 1987); Nottingham Univ. (PGCE Secondary Maths 1989); Trinity Hall, Cambridge (MEd Curriculum 1999; PhD Educn (Computerised Knowledge Mapping) 2007). Teacher of Mathematics: Mill Hill Co. High Sch., Mill Hill, 1989–91; Friends Sch. (Soc. of Friends), Gt Ayton, 1991–94; Hd of Maths, 1994–99, Asst Dir of Studies, 1998–99, Westcliff High Sch. for Boys, Westcliff on Sea; Dep. Headteacher, King Edward VI GS, Chelmsford, 1999–2007. Pubns Ed. and Cttee Chair, Managing Maths, Mathematical Assoc., 2001–05. Mem., Adv. Gp, Support Staff Res., DfES, 2004–07. Member: Res. Rev. Gps, Evidence for Policy and Practice Information Centre, 2001–07; Res. Bulletin Steering Gp, Nat. Educnl Res. Foundn, 2003–05; Nat. Teacher Res. Panel, 2003–16 (Vice Chair, 2008–13; Chair, 2014–16); Steering Gp, Nat. Assoc. of Sch. Partnerships, 2012–14; Res. Use in Educn Adv. Gp, Educn Endowment Foundn, 2013–16; Curriculum and Assessment Quality Cttee, AQA, 2015–; Association of Teachers and Lecturers: Member, National Executive: for Essex, Southend, Thurrock and Germany, 2005–14; representing UK Sch. and Coll. Leadership, 2014–18; Trustee, Pension Scheme, 2012–; Nat. Vice-Pres., 2018; Mem., Nat. Council, Assoc. of Managers in Educn, 2010–18; National Education Union: Mem., Jt Exec. Council, 2017–18; Mem., Nat. Exec., 2019–; Nat. Vice Pres., 2019–. Chair, Consortium for Selective Schs in Essex, 2011–12, 2017–18 (Advr, 1999–; Mem., 2007–); Mem., Southend on Sea Educn Bd (formerly Schs Forum), 2009– (Vice Chair, 2015–). Mem., Fabian Soc., 1995–. Founding Mem., Chartered Coll. of Teaching, 2017 (Fellow, 2018). Trustee, Southend Educn Trust, 2008–; Patron, Inst. of Sch. Business Leadership (formerly Nat. Assoc. of Sch. Business Managers), 2017–. *Publications:* (contrib.) Graded Exercises in Pure Mathematics for AS and A2, 2001; (ed) Managing Mathematics: handbook for heads of mathematics, 2005; contribs to Teacher Develt, Reflecting Educn. *Recreations:* competitive cycling (qualified coach and active competitor, time triallist representing Cambridge University Cycling Club in national student events, 2004, 2005), completing mid-life road cycling challenges (Passo dello Stelvio 2016), vintage (1969) Land Rover owner. *Address:* Southend High School for Boys, Prittlewell Chase, Southend on Sea, Essex SS0 0RG. *T:* (01702) 606200. *E:* enquiries@shsb.org.

**BEVAN, Stephen Mark;** Director, HR Research, Institute for Employment Studies, since 2016; *b* Maidstone, 21 Aug. 1959; *s* of Keith Bevan and Janet Bevan; *m* 1983, Jennifer Karen Bray; three *s* one *d*. *Educ:* Oakwood Park Grammar Sch., Maidstone; Aston Univ. (BSc Hons Mgt 1981); Inst. of Educn, London Univ. (PGCE 1982). Associate Dir, Inst. of Employment Studies, 1983–2001; Dir, Res., 2002–08, Man. Dir, 2008–11, Dir, Centre for Workforce Effectiveness, 2011–16, The Work Foundn. Hon. Prof., Lancaster Univ., 2011–. Global Alliance of Mental Illness Advocacy Networks-Europe Personality Award, 2014. *Publications:* Cracking the Performance Code, 2005; Fit for Work: musculoskeletal disorders in the European workforce, 2009; 21st Century Workforces and Workplaces, 2018; reviewer for Lancet and Jl of Occupational and Organisational Psychol. *Recreations:* walking, reading, current affairs, cycling with Chris. *Address:* Institute for Employment Studies, City Gate, 185 Dyke Road, Brighton BN3 1TL. *T:* (01273) 763400. *E:* stephen.bevan@employment-studies.co.uk.

**BEVAN, Tim**, CBE 2005; film producer; Co-Founder and Co-Chairman, Working Title Films, since 1984; Chairman, UK Film Council, 2009–11; *m* 1st, 1992, Joely Richardson, *qv* (marr. diss. 2001); one *d*; 2nd, Amy Gadney; one *s* one *d*. Formerly runner, Video Arts; co-founder, Aldabra, 1984. Film producer (jointly): A World Apart, 1988; Fools of Fortune, 1990; Drop Dead Fred, 1991; Bob Roberts, 1992; with Sarah Radclyffe: My Beautiful Laundrette, 1986; Sammy and Rosie Get Laid, Personal Services, 1987; Paperhouse, For Queen and Country, 1989; Dark Obsession, The Tall Guy, Chicago Joe and the Showgirl, 1990; London Kills Me, Rubin and Ed, 1992; with Eric Fellner: Posse, Romeo is Bleeding, 1993; Four Weddings and a Funeral, The Hudsucker Proxy, 1994; Loch Ness, Panther, French Kiss, Moonlight & Valentino, Dead Man Walking, 1995; Fargo, 1996; Bean, The Matchmaker, The Borrowers, The Hi-Lo Country, 1997; Elizabeth, The Big Lebowski, What Rats Won't Do, 1998; Notting Hill, Plunkett & Macleane, 1999; O Brother, Where Art Thou?, Billy Elliot, The Man Who Cried, 2000; Bridget Jones's Diary, Captain Corelli's Mandolin, The Man Who Wasn't There, Long Time Dead, 2001; 40 Days and 40 Nights, About a Boy, Ali G Indahouse, The Guru, My Little Eye, 2002; Love Actually, Calcium Kid, Ned Kelly, Shape of Things, Johnny English, Thirteen, 2003; Thunderbirds, Inside I'm Dancing, Wimbledon, Shaun of the Dead, Bridget Jones: The Edge of Reason, 2004; Mickybo and Me, Pride and Prejudice, Nanny McPhee, The Interpreter, 2005; United 93, Hot Stuff, Sixty Six, 2006; The Golden Age, Atonement, Mr Bean's Holiday, Hot Fuzz, Gone, Smokin' Aces, 2007; Definitely Maybe, Wild Child, Burn After Reading, 2008; Frost/Nixon, State of Play, The Soloist, The Boat That Rocked, Hippie Hippie Shake, A Serious Man, 2009; Green Zone, Nanny McPhee and the Big Bang, 2010; Paul, Senna, Johnny English Reborn, Tinker, Tailor, Soldier, Spy, 2011; Anna Karenina, Les Misérables, Big Miracle, Contraband, 2012; I Give it a Year, Closed Circuit, About Time, Rush, The World's End, 2013; Two Faces of January, 2014; The Theory of Everything, Trash, Everest, Legend, We Are Your Friends, The Program, 2015; The Danish Girl, Hail Caesar, Genius, Grimsby, Bridget Jones's Baby, 2016; Baby Driver, Victoria & Abdul, The Snowman, 2017; Darkest Hour, 7 Days in Entebbe, King of Thieves, Johnny English Strikes Again, 2018; Mary Queen of Scots, The Kid Who Would Be King, 2019; sole producer, High Fidelity, 2000. Television includes: Tales of the City, 1993; The Borrowers, 1993; More Tales of the City, 1998; The Tudors, 2007–10; The Borrowers, Birdsong, Love Bites, 2011; True Love, 2012; Yonderland, 2013–16; About a Boy, 2014–15; London Spy, You, Me and the Apocalypse, 2015. *Address*: Working Title Films, 26 Aybrook Street, W1U 4AN.

**BEVAN, Dame Yasmin (Prodhan)**, DBE 2007; Chief Executive, Chiltern Learning Trust, 2013–14 (Executive Principal and Headteacher: Denbigh High School and Challney High School for Boys, 2008–14; Dallow Primary School, 2014; Headteacher, Denbigh High School, 1991–2014); *b* 3 Dec. 1953; *d* of Badiuzzaman and Selima Prodhan. *Educ*: London Sch. of Econs (BSc Hons Govt 1976); Roehampton Inst. (PGCE 1977); Open Univ. (BA 1983); Inst. of Educn, Univ. of London (MA 1990). Teacher of Maths, Greenford High Sch., Ealing, 1977–78; Hd of Sixth Form and Hd of Maths, Pen Park Girls' Sch., Bristol, 1979–86; Dep. Hd, Canons High Sch., Harrow, 1987–91; Adv. headteacher, DCSF (on secondment), 2007–08. Nat. Leader of Educn, 2008–; Member: Practitioners' Gp on Sch. Behaviour and Discipline, DfES, 2005; Sure Start Stakeholders' Gp, DfES, 2006; Ministerial Task Force on Gifted and Talented Educn, 2007–08; Expert Gp on Assessment, 2008–; Ministerial Adv. Gp, DfE, on Role of Local Authy in relation to children and educnl services, 2010–, Nat. Curriculum Review, 2010–; Ofsted Access and Achievement Expert Panel, 2012. Mem., NW London and S Central Headteacher Bd, 2017–. Mem., Governing Council, 2000–04, Adv. Gp on Nat. Leaders of Educn, 2006, Nat. Coll. for Sch. Leadership. Trustee, United Learning, 2014–. Hon. DEd Bedfordshire, 2008. Headteacher of the Year in a Secondary Sch., Eastern Region, Teaching Awards, 2005. *Recreations*: reading, keeping fit, cinema, opera, gardening, spending time with family and friends.

**BEVEN, Prof. Keith John**, PhD; FRS 2017; Professor of Fluid Dynamics, 1991–2015, and Distinguished Professor of Hydrology, 2008–15, Lancaster University, now Emeritus; *b* Barnehurst, Kent, 23 July 1950; *s* of Donald Jack Beven and Vera May Beven (*née* Stone); *m* 1973, Sheila Barkham (separated 1992); one *d*; partner, 2002, Monique Romanens. *Educ*: Chislehurst and Sidcup Grammar Sch.; Univ. of Bristol (BSc 1971); Univ. of East Anglia (PhD 1975). Res. Fellow, Sch. of Geog., Univ. of Leeds, 1975–77; HSO, Inst. of Hydrol., Wallingford, 1977–79; Asst Prof. of Envmtl Scis, Univ. of Virginia, 1979–82; SSO and PSO, Inst. of Hydrol., Wallingford, 1982–85; Lectr, then Reader in Engrg Hydrol., Lancaster Univ., 1985–91. Visiting Professor: UCSB, 1996; École polytechnique fédérale de Lausanne, 1997; Internat. Francqui Chair, Katholieke Universiteit Leuven, 2000–01; King of Sweden's Envmtl Guest Prof., Uppsala Univ. and Swedish Univ. of Agricl Scis, 2006–07. Fellow, Amer. Geophysical Union, 1995; Foreign Mem., NAE, 2017. Hon. DSc Bristol, 2015. Dalton Medal, Eur. Geophysical Union, 2001; Internat. Hydrol. Medal, IAHS/WMO/UNESCO, 2009; Horton Medal, Amer. Geophysical Union, 2012; President's Prize, British Hydrological Soc., 2013. *Publications*: (ed with P. Carling) Floods: hydrological sedimentological and geomorphological implications, 1989; (ed with I. D. Moore) Terrain Analysis and Distributed Modelling in Hydrology, 1992; (ed with M. J. Kirkby) Channel Network Hydrology, 1993; (ed with P. C. Chatwin and J. H. M. Millbank) Mixing and Transport in the Environment, 1994; (ed) Distributed Modelling in Hydrology: applications of TOPMODEL, 1997; Rainfall-Runoff Modelling: the primer, 2001, 2nd edn 2012; Environmental Modelling: an uncertain future?, 2009; (jtly) Hydrology in Practice, 4th edn 2010; (ed with J. W. Hall) Applied Uncertainty Estimation in Flood Risk Management, 2014; over 400 papers in jls. *Recreations*: photography (books: Mallerstang Magic; Mallerstang in Mono; Mallerstang in Panorama), walking. *E*: k.beven@lancaster.ac.uk.

**BEVER, Rosalyn**; Partner, since 2011, and Regional Managing Partner and National Head of Family Law, since 2018, Irwin Mitchell (Head, Manchester Family Law Team, 2011–18); *b* Hyde, Gtr Manchester, 10 Feb. 1971; *d* of John Ralph and Jennifer Smethurst; *m* 1998, Adrian Michael Bever; three *s*. *Educ*: Fairfield High Sch. for Girls; Univ. of Leeds (BSc Hons Construction Mgt/Quantity Surveying). Trainee solicitor, Jones Goodall Solicitors, Wakefield, W Yorks, 1993–98; admitted as solicitor, 1998; Solicitor, Mace & Jones, Manchester, 1998–2011. *Recreations*: keen walker, cooking, reading, book clubs, family. *Address*: Irwin Mitchell, One St Peter's Square, Manchester M2 3AF. *T*: 07909 544677. *E*: ros.bever@irwinmitchell.com.

**BEVERIDGE, Bruce Cameron**; Chief Executive, British Society of Animal Science, 2017–18; *b* Edinburgh, 1966; *s* of Alec Beveridge and Sandra Margaret Moncrieff. *Educ*: High Sch. of Dundee; Edinburgh Acad.; Univ. of Edinburgh (LLB; DipLP). Legal Sec. to Lord Pres. of Court of Session, 2000–04; Dep. Keeper, Registers of Scotland, 2004–09; Dep. Dir, Rural Affairs and Envmt, Scottish Govt, 2009–11; Chair, Centre for Rural Develt, Scottish Land and Estates, 2012. Non-exec. Chm., thinkWhere Ltd, 2015–17. Pres., Law Soc. of Scotland, 2013–14 (Vice Pres., 2012–13). Chair, Professional Services, WS Soc., 2012–17 (formerly Vice Chair). Chm., Edinburgh Academy Foundn, 2014–16. Mem., Editl Bd and Wise Owl, LBC Wise Counsel, 2008–. *Publications*: contrib. articles to Jl Law Soc. of Scotland. *Recreations*: golf, music and the arts, motorsport (spectating). *Clubs*: Western (Glasgow); Royal and Ancient Golf (St Andrews), Golf House (Elie).

**BEVERIDGE, Crawford William**, CBE 1995; FRSE; Chairman, Autodesk Inc., 2009–19; *b* 3 Nov. 1945; *s* of William Wilson Beveridge and Catherine Crawford Beveridge; *m* 1977, Marguerite DeVoe; one *s* one *d*. *Educ*: Edinburgh Univ. (BSc); Bradford Univ. (MSc). Appts with Hewlett Packard in Scotland, Switzerland, USA, 1968–77; European Personnel Manager, Digital Equipment Corp., 1977–81; Vice-Pres., Human Resources, Analog Devices, 1982–85; Vice-Pres., Corporate Resources, Sun Microsystems, 1985–90; Chief Exec., Scottish Enterprise, 1991–2000; Exec. Vice-Pres., People and Places, and Chief Human Resources Officer, 2000–06, Chm., 2006–10, Sun Microsystems Inc. Mem., Scottish Parlt Ind. Budget Review Panel, 2010; Chm., Council of Econ. Advrs, Scotland, 2011–. FRSE 2016. *Recreations*: music, cooking, paperweights.

**BEVERIDGE, John Caldwell**; QC 1979; Recorder, Western Circuit, 1975–96; *b* 26 Sept. 1937; *s* of late Prof. William Ian Beardmore Beveridge; *m* 1st, 1973, Frances Ann Clunes Grant Martineau (marr. diss. 1989); 2nd, 1989, Lilian Adamson (marr. diss. 2003); 3rd, 2005, Rebecca Rosemary Amara Boulos-Hanna. *Educ*: Jesus Coll., Cambridge (MA, LLB). Called to the Bar, Inner Temple, 1963, Bencher, 1985; Western Circuit; called to the Bar, NSW, 1975, QC (NSW), 1980. Mem. (C), Westminster City Council, 1968–72. Director: Barker Poland Financial Mgt Ltd, 2000–06; Onda Life Inc., 2018–. Trustee: Dogs Trust (formerly Nat. Canine Defence League), 1998–; Manchester Dogs Home, 2003–07 (Vice-Pres., 2007–14). Partner, Perfect Pitch, 2008–. Chm., 2003–14, Patron, 2014–, St James's Conservation Trust. Freeman, City of London; Liveryman, Goldsmiths' Co. Jt Master, Westmeath Foxhounds, 1976–79. Comdr, Star of Honour (Ethiopia), 1992. *Recreations*: conversation, travelling. *Address*: Cross Creek House, Stoke Gabriel, Devon TQ9 6RL. *T*: (01760) 444444. *Clubs*: Beefsteak, Pratt's, Turf; Brook (New York).

**BEVERLEY, Bishop Suffragan of**, since 2013; Rt Rev. Glyn Hamilton Webster; Episcopal Visitor for the Northern Province, since 2013; an Honorary Assistant Bishop: Diocese of Chester, since 2013; Diocese of Sheffield, since 2013; Diocese of Liverpool, since 2013; Diocese of Durham, since 2014; Diocese of Manchester, since 2014; Diocese of Leeds (formerly West Yorkshire and the Dales), since 2014; *b* 1951. *Educ*: Cranmer Hall, Durham. SRN, Blackburn Royal Infirmary, 1973; ordained deacon, 1977, priest, 1978; Asst Curate, All Saints, Huntingdon, 1977–81; Vicar, St Luke, York, 1981–92; Sen. Chaplain, York Hosps NHS Foundn Trust, 1992–99; Rural Dean, City of York, 1997–2004; Dir of Ordinands, Dio. of York, 2005–10. Canon and Preb., 1994–99, Canon Res., 1999–2013, York Minster. Member: Gen. Synod, 1995–; Crown Nominations Commn; Archbishops' Council. *Address*: Holy Trinity Rectory, Micklegate, York YO1 6LE. *T*: (01904) 628155.

**BEVERLEY, Lt-Gen. Sir Henry (York La Roche)**, KCB 1991; OBE 1979; Commandant General Royal Marines, 1990–93; Director-General, Winston Churchill Memorial Trust, 1993–2002; *b* 25 Oct. 1935; *s* of Vice-Adm. Sir York Beverley, KBE, CB, and Lady Beverley; *m* 1963, Sally Anne Maclean; two *d*. *Educ*: Wellington College. DS Staff Coll., 1976–78; CO 42 Cdo RM, 1978–80; Comdt CTC RM, 1980–82; Director RM Personnel, MoD, 1983–84; Comd 3 Cdo Bde RM, 1984–86; Maj.-Gen. Trng and Reserve Forces RM, 1986–88; COS to CGRM, 1988–90. Chm. Trustees, Royal Marines Mus., 1997–2007. Pres., Corps of Commissionaires, 2008–11.

**BEVERLEY, Prof. Peter Charles Leonard**, FMedSci; Scientific Head, Edward Jenner Institute for Vaccine Research, 1995–2005; Emeritus Professor, University of Oxford, 2011 (Principal Research Fellow, 2005–11); Visiting Professor, Imperial College London, since 2014; *b* 7 March 1943; *s* of Samuel and Elinor Beverley; *m* 1967, Elisabeth A. Copleston (separated); two *s*; one *d* with Prof. Elizabeth Simpson, *qv*. *Educ*: University Coll. London (BSc, MB BS; DSc 1987). Research Fellow: NIMR, London, 1969–72; Sloan-Kettering Inst., NY, 1972–73; ICRF Tumour Immunology Unit, UCL, 1973–78; permanent staff mem., ICRF, 1978–95; Prof. of Tumour Immunology, UCL, 1988–95; Dep. Dir, 1988–92, Dir, 1992–95, Tumour Immunology Unit, UCL. FMedSci 2003. *Publications*: contribs to immunological, biological and med. jls. *Recreations*: music, reading, writing. *E*: pbeverley347@gmail.com.

**BEVERSTOCK, Rear Adm. Mark Alistair**; Principal Consultant, Frazer Nash Consultancy Ltd, since 2016; *b* Dumfries, 8 Feb. 1964; *s* of Alistair Beverstock and Jane Beverstock; *m* 1984, Morag Hazlett; two *s* one *d*. *Educ*: RNEC Manadon (BScEng 1985). CEng 1996; FIET 2006. Tactical Weapons Engr Officer, 1986–88; Tenth Submarine Sqn, 1988–92; Weapon Engr Officer, HMS Vanguard, 1992–96; Ministry of Defence: Defence Equipment and Support, 1996–98; Naval Staff, 1998–2000; Strategic Systems Proj., Defence Equipment and Support, 2000–03; rcds 2004; MoD, 2005–07; CO HMS Neptune, 2007–09; Ministry of Defence: Dep. Chief Strategic Systems Exec., Defence Equipment and Support, 2009–10; Hd, Underwater Capability, 2010–12; Chief Strategic Systems Exec., Defence Equipment and Support, 2012–14; ACDS (Policy), MoD, 2014–16. Pres., RN and RM Cycling Assoc., 2002–15.

**BEVINGTON, Adrian**; Head of Recruitment Operations, Middlesbrough Football Club, since 2018; *b* Middlesbrough, 14 July 1971; *s* of Graham Bevington and Barbara Bevington; *m* 1996, Andrea Rounce; one *s*. *Educ*: Hustler Sch., Middlesbrough. Trainee reporter, C&P News, ICI Wilton, 1987–89; Clerk: Langbaurgh on Tees BC, 1989–94; Middlesbrough BC, 1994–95; Press Officer, Middlesbrough FC, 1995–97; Football Association: Media Officer, 1997–2000; Sen. Media Officer, 2000–03; Hd, Media, 2003–04; Dir, Communications, 2004–10; Man. Dir, 2010–14, Dir of Communications, 2011–14, Club England; Owner, Adrian Bevington Sport & PR Ltd, 2015–18. Project Consultant, Euro 2016 Tournament, Football Assoc. of Wales, 2015–16. Pt-time writer, Middlesbrough FC, and various pubns, 1989–95. *Publications*: (jtly) Doom to Boom: the most dramatic decade in the life of Middlesbrough FC 1986–1996, 1996; (jtly) Boro's Best: the players' and fans' fabulous fifty, 1997; (jtly) Don't Call Me Happy—John Hendrie: the autobiography, 1997. *Recreations*: reading, football, golf, travelling. *Address*: Middlesbrough Football Club, Rockliffe Park Training Ground, Hurworth Place, Darlington DL2 2DU.

**BEVINGTON, Her Honour Christian Veronica**; a Circuit Judge, 1998–2009; a Deputy Circuit Judge, 2009–11; *d* of late Michael Falkner Bevington and Dulcie Marian Bevington (*née* Gratton); *m* 1961, David Levitt, OBE (marr. diss. 1973); one *s* two *d*. *Educ*: St James's, W Malvern; London Sch. of Econs (LLB Hons). Called to the Bar: Inner Temple, 1961 (Bencher, 1994); Lincoln's Inn, *ad eundem* 1971. Co-Founder, Charitable Housing Trust, 1966: Company Sec. and Housing Manager, Circle 33 Housing Trust, 1966–76; joined Peat Marwick & Co., 1976; returned to full-time practice at the Bar, 1980; Head of Chambers, 1981–98; Recorder, 1994–98. Chm., Independent Inquiry for City and County of Cardiff, 1997. Chm., Mental Health Review Tribunals, 2002–03. Dir, Veronica Grant Centre for Spoken English and Culture Ltd, 2014–. Freeman, City of London, 2016; Liveryman, Fanmakers' Co., 2016–. *Publications*: The Bevington Report, 1997. *Recreations*: music, travel. *Club*: Reform.

*See also* A. F. J. Levitt.

**BEW**, family name of **Baron Bew**.

**BEW**, Baron *cr* 2007 (Life Peer), of Donegore in the County of Antrim; **Paul Anthony Elliott Bew**, PhD; Professor of Irish Politics, Queen's University of Belfast, 1991–2014, now Emeritus; *b* 22 Jan. 1950; *s* of Dr Kenneth Bew and Dr Mary Bew (*née* Leahy); *m* 1977, Prof. Greta Joyce Jones; one *s*. *Educ*: Brackenber House Sch.; Campbell Coll., Belfast; Pembroke Coll., Cambridge (MA; PhD 1974; Hon. Fellow, 2007). Lectr, Sch. of Humanities, Ulster Coll., 1975–79; Queen's University, Belfast: Lectr in Eur. and American Hist., 1979–84; Lectr, 1984–87, Reader, 1987–91, Dept of Politics. Vis. Lectr, Univ. of Pennsylvania, 1982–83; Parnell Fellow, Magdalene Coll., Cambridge, 1996–97; Vis. Prof., Surrey Univ., 1997–; Burns Vis. Schol., Boston Coll., 1999–2000. Historical Advr to Bloody Sunday Tribunal. Chm., Key Stage 2 Assessment Rev., 2010–11. Mem., British/ Irish Interparly Assembly, 2011. Chm., Cttee on Standards in Public Life, 2013–18; Chair, H of L Appts Commn, 2018–. Mem., Select Cttee on London Local Authy Bill, 2008, on Draft Defamation Bill, 2011, on Parly Privilege (both Houses), 2013; Co-Chm., Speaker's Adv. Cttee, 2015; Sec., All Party Gp on Archives and Hist., 2007–. Pres., Irish Assoc. for Econs and Cultural Relns, 1990–92; Exec. Mem., British Irish Assoc., 1995– (Chm., 2007–); Mem., Anglo Israel Assoc. (Chm., 2011). MRIA 2004. Mem., Editl Bd, Parliamentary Affairs, 2012–. Special Recognition Award, Pol Studies Assoc., 2012. *Publications*: Land and the National Question in Ireland 1858–82, 1978; (jtly) The State in Northern Ireland, 1979, 2nd edn 1996; C. S. Parnell, 1980, 2nd edn 1991; (jtly) Seán Lemass and the Making of Modern Ireland, 1983; (jtly) The British State and the Ulster Crisis, 1985; Conflict and Conciliation in Ireland 1890–1910, 1987; (jtly) The Dynamics of Irish Politics, 1989; (ed jtly) Passion and Prejudice, 1993; (jtly) Northern Ireland: a chronology of the Troubles, 1993, rev. edn 1999; Ideology and the Irish Question, 1994; John Redmond, 1996; (jtly) The Northern Ireland Peace Process 1993–96, 1996; (jtly) Between War and Peace, 1997; Ireland: the politics of enmity 1789–2006, 2007; The Making and Re-making of the Good Friday Agreement, 2007; Enigma: a new life of Parnell, 2011; David Gray: a Yankee in de Valera's Ireland, 2012; Churchill and Ireland, 2015; contrib. numerous articles and reviews. *Recreations*: soccer, cinema, theatre. *Address*: Department of Politics, Queen's University of Belfast, 21 University Square, Belfast BT7 1NN. *T*: (028) 9024 5133.

**BEWICK, Dr Michael**, FRCGP, FRCP; Founder and Director, iQ4U Consultants Ltd, since 2015; Senior Medical Advisor, FTI Consulting, since 2015; *b* Workington, Cumbria, 11 Sept. 1956; *m* 1978, Patricia; two *d*. *Educ*: Workington Grammar Sch.; St Mary's Med. Sch., Univ. of London (MB BS 1980). MRCPE 1985; MRCP 1988, FRCP 2010; FRCGP 2004. Jun. hse posts, St Mary's Hosp., Paddington; Asst Lectr, Dept of Oncol., St Bartholomew's Hosp.; SHO, Stoke Mandeville Hosp.; Registrar, then Sen. Registrar, Ninewells Hosp., Dundee, until 1987; GP trng, Cumbria, 1987–89; Principal, Beech Hse Med. Centre, Cumbria, 1987–2007; Medical Director: for Primary Care, NHS Cumbria, 2007–12; N of England, 2012–13; Dep. Med. Dir, NHS England, 2013–15. Teacher and Examr, RCGP (Chair of Assessment, 2005–12). *Recreations*: cycling (slowly), theatre, travel, pursuit of the best taste in food and wine. *Address*: Moat Barn, 17 Redgates Lane, Sewards End, Saffron Walden, Essex CB10 2LW.

**BEWICKE-COPLEY**, family name of **Baron Cromwell**.

**BEWLEY, Thomas Henry**, Hon. CBE 1988; MA; MD; FRCP, FRCPI, FRCPsych; Consultant Psychiatrist, Tooting Bec and St Thomas' Hospitals, 1961–88, now Emeritus Consultant, St Thomas' Hospital; *b* 8 July 1926; *s* of Geoffrey Bewley and Victoria Jane Wilson; *m* 1955, Beulah Rosemary Knox (Dame Beulah Bewley, DBE) (*d* 2018); one *s* three *d* (and one *d* decd). *Educ*: St Columba's College, Dublin; Trinity College, Dublin University (MA; MD 1958). FRCPsych 1972, Hon. FRCPsych 1989. Hon. MD Dublin, 1987. Qualified TCD, 1950; trained St Patrick's Hosp., Dublin, Maudsley Hosp., Univ. of Cincinnati. Hon. Sen. Lectr, St George's Hosp. Med. Sch., 1968–96. Member: Standing Adv. Cttee on Drug Dependence, 1966–71; Adv. Council on Misuse of Drugs, 1972–84; Consultant Adviser on Drug Dependence to DHSS, 1972–81; Consultant, WHO, 1969–88. Pres., RCPsych, 1984–87 (Dean, 1977–82); Jt Co-founder and Mem. Council, Inst. for Study of Drug Dependence, 1967–96. *Publications*: Handbook for Inceptors and Trainees in Psychiatry, 1976, 2nd edn 1980; Madness to Mental Illness, 2008; papers on drug dependence, medical manpower and side effects of drugs. *Clubs*: Reform, London Chapter of Irish Georgian Society.

**BEWSEY, Jane, (Mrs Robert Mocatta)**; QC 2010; *b* Malaysia, 12 Feb. 1964; *d* of Jack and Audrey Bewsey; *m* 1992, Robert Mocatta; two *s* one *d*. *Educ*: Rosebery Sch., Epsom; Jesus Coll., Cambridge (BA 1985). Called to the Bar, Inner Temple, 1986; in practice as barrister, specialising in crime. *Publications*: The Law of Investor Protection, 1996, 2nd edn 2003. *Recreations*: reading, walking. *Address*: 18 Red Lion Court, EC4A 3EB. *T*: (020) 7520 6000.

**BEX, Kate**; QC 2017; a Recorder, since 2018; *b* Sussex; 22 Dec.; *d* of John Bex and Mary Elizabeth Penelope Bex (*née* Poore). *Educ*: Oxford Poly. (BA Hons). Called to the Bar, Middle Temple, 1992; in practice as a barrister, specialising in crime, 2 Hare Court, 1993–2017, Red Lion Chambers, 2017–. *Address*: Red Lion Chambers, 18 Red Lion Court, EC4A 3EB. *E*: kate.bex@18rlc.co.uk.

**BEY, Patricia Mary Alice, (Mrs R. S. L. Woodward)**; Founder and Owner, Barwheys Dairy, since 2009; *b* Lagos, Nigeria, 18 Nov. 1957; *d* of Alex and Mary Bey; *m* 2009, Robert Stanley Laurence Woodward, *qv*. *Educ*: St Joan of Arc Sch., Rickmansworth; Durham Univ. (BSc Hons Engrg Sci. 1979); London Business Sch. (MBA 1987). Editor, Derwent Pubns, 1979–85; Touche Ross, subseq. Deloitte and Touche, then Deloitte Consulting: consulting roles, 1987–94; Partner, 1994–2001; Man. Partner, Deloitte Consulting Netherlands, 1999–2001; Man. Dir, Sch. of Coaching, 2003–07; freelance consultant, 2008. Member: Ayrshire Cattle Soc., 2008–; Specialist Cheesemakers Assoc., 2009–. Trustee: Friends of V&A, 2010–17; Nat. Galleries of Scotland, 2012–. *Recreations*: breeding pedigree Ayrshire cattle, gardening, cooking. *Address*: Crawfordston Farm, Maybole, Ayrshire KA19 7JS. *E*: tricia@pmab.co.uk.

**BEYER, John Charles**; HM Diplomatic Service, retired; Senior Associate Member, St Antony's College, Oxford, since 2009; Tutor, Diplomacy, Department of Continuing Education, University of Oxford, since 2012; *b* 29 April 1950; *s* of William Herbert Beyer and Doris Irene Beyer (*née* Tomline); *m* 1971, Letty Marindin Minns; one *s* one *d*. *Educ*: Abingdon Sch.; Queens' Coll., Cambridge (MA). Vis. Schol., Université de Paris VII, 1973–74; British Council Schol., Beijing Langs Inst., 1974–75; Lectr, Dept of Oriental Langs, Univ. of Calif, Berkeley, 1979–80; Researcher, Dept of Chinese Studies, Leeds Univ., 1980–82; Missions Exec., Sino-British Trade Council, 1983–85; Editor, China-Britain Trade Rev., 1985–90; Dir, Sino-British Trade Council, 1990–91; Dir, China-Britain Trade Gp, 1991–98; Head, Mediterranean Section, EU Dept, FCO, 1999–2002; Dep. Hd of Mission, Luxembourg, 2002–05; Ambassador to Moldova, 2006–09. *Recreation*: family. *Address*: 44 South Hill Park, NW3 2SJ. *T*: (020) 7435 4795.

**BEYFUS, Drusilla Norman**; writer, editor, broadcaster; Tutor, Central St Martin's College of Art, 1989–2007; *d* of Norman Beyfus and Florence Noel Barker; *m* 1956, Milton Shulman (*d* 2004); one *s* two *d*. *Educ*: Royal Naval Sch.; Channing Sch. Woman's Editor, Sunday Express, 1950; columnist, Daily Express, 1952–55; Associate Editor, Queen magazine, 1956; Home Editor, The Observer, 1963; Associate Editor, Daily Telegraph magazine, 1966; Editor, Brides and Setting Up Home magazine, 1972–79; Associate Editor, 1979–87, Contributing Editor, 1987–88, Vogue magazine; Editor, Harrods Magazine, 1987–88; columnist, Sunday Telegraph, 1990–91; Contributing Editor, Telegraph Magazine, 1991–2009; columnist, You magazine (Mail on Sunday), 1994–2002. TV and radio appearances, incl. Call My Bluff, The Big Breakfast and talks programmes. Hon. MA London Inst., 2002. *Publications*: (with Anne Edwards) Lady Behave, 1956, rev. edn 1969; The English Marriage, 1968; The Brides Book, 1981; The Art of Giving, 1987; Modern Manners, 1992; The Done Thing (series): Courtship, 1992; Parties, 1992; Business, 1993; Sex, 1993; The You Guide to Modern Dilemmas, 1997; Vogue On Hubert de Givenchy, 2013; Vogue On Valentino Garavani, 2015; contrib. to Sunday Times, Punch, New Statesman, Daily Telegraph, Daily Mail. *Recreations*: walking, modern art, cooking. *Address*: 51G Eaton Square, SW1W 9BE. *T*: (020) 7235 7162, *T*: 07714 245847.
*See also* Marchioness of Normanby, A. Shulman.

**BEYNON, Ann**, OBE 2008; Director, Wales, BT, 2004–15 (National Manager, 1998–2004); Adviser: Severn Trent Water, since 2015; National Assembly of Wales, since 2018; *b* 14 April 1953; *d* of Roger Talfryn Jones and Margaret Rose Beynon Jones; name changed to Beynon by deed poll, 1984; *m* 1st, 1976, John Trefor (marr. diss. 1983); 2nd, 1986, William Gwenlyn Parry (*d* 1991); one *s* one *d*; 3rd, 1996, Leighton Russell Andrews, *qv*. *Educ*: UCNW, Bangor (BA Hons). Pres., Students' Union, UCNW, 1974–75. Administrator, Yr Academi Gymreig (Welsh Acad.), 1977–81; S4C, 1981–95: Press Officer, 1981–83; Head of Press and PR, 1983–91; Head, Political and Internat. Affairs, 1991–95; Dir of Business Develt, Cardiff Bay Develt Corp., 1995–98. Mem. Bd, BITC UK, 2006–10; Chm., BITC Wales Cttee, 2006–10. Chair: Adv. Bd, Wales Governance Centre, Cardiff Univ., 2015–18; Transition Bd, Cardiff City Region, 2015–17. Member: Royal Commn on H of L Reform, 1999; Welsh Lang. Bd, 1995–2000; Wales Cttee, EOC, 2000–07; Wales Comr, Equality and Human Rights Commn, 2009–16. Non-executive Director: Farmers' Union of Wales Insurance Services, 2016–; Hafren Dyfrdwy, 2018–. Gov., Nat. Film and TV Sch., 1995–2002; Mem. Council, Bangor Univ. (formerly Univ. of Wales, Bangor), 2004–10. Chm., Sgript Cymru Theatre Co., 1999–2007. *Recreations*: reading, languages, tapestry, managing my late husband's literary estate. *Address*: 11 Waungron Road, Llandaff, Cardiff CF5 2JJ. *T*: (029) 2055 5425.

**BEYNON, Prof. Huw**, DSocSc; Professor of Sociology, 1999–2010, Research Professor, 2010–14, now Professor Emeritus, and Founding Director, Wales Institute of Social and Economic Research, Data and Method, 2008–10, Cardiff University; *b* 10 Dec. 1942; *s* of Dewi and Megan Beynon; *m* 1994, Helen Anne Sampson; one *s* from previous *m*. *Educ*: University Coll. of Wales, Aberystwyth (BA 1964); Univ. of Liverpool (Dip. Industrial Admin); Univ. of Manchester (DSocSc 1999). Lectr, Univ. of Bristol, 1968–73; Simon Marks Res. Fellow, Univ. of Manchester, 1973–75; Lectr, then Reader, Durham Univ., 1975–87; Prof. and Res. Dean, Univ. of Manchester, 1987–99; Dir, Sch. of Social Scis, Cardiff Univ., 1999–2009. FAcSS (AcSS 2000); Founding FLSW 2010. Hon. DLitt Durham, 2013. *Publications*: (with R. M. Blackburn) Perceptions of Work: variations within a factory, 1972; Working for Ford, 1973, 2nd edn 1985; (with T. Nichols) Living with Capitalism: class relations in the modern factory, 1977; (with H. Wainwright) The Workers' Report on Vickers Ltd, 1978; (with N. Hedges) Born to Work, 1980; (ed) Digging Deeper: issues in the 1984 miners' strike, 1987; (jtly) A Tale of Two Industries: the decline of coal and steel in the North East of England, 1991; (jtly) A Place Called Teesside: a locality in a global economy, 1994; (with T. Austrin) Masters and Servants: class and patronage in the making of a labour organisation, 1994; (ed with P. Glavanis) Patterns of Social Inequality, 1999; (jtly) Digging Up Trouble: protest and the environment on the coal-fields, 2000; (jtly) Coalfield Regeneration: dealing with the consequences of industrial decline, 2000; (ed with S. Rowbotham) Looking at Class, 2002; (jtly) Managing Employment Change: the new reality of work, 2002; (jtly) Exploring the Tomato: transformations of nature, society and economy, 2002; (ed with T. Nichols) The Fordism of Ford and Modern Management: Fordism and post-Fordism, vols 1 and 2, 2006; (ed with T. Nichols) Patterns of Work in the post-Fordist Era: Fordism and post-Fordism, vols 1 and 2, 2006. *Recreations*: hill-walking, gardening. *Address*: Orchard Farm, Llanellen, Abergavenny NP7 9BU. *T*: (01873) 858307. *E*: beynonh@cardiff.ac.uk.

**BEYNON, Dr John David Emrys**, FREng, FIET; Principal, King's College London, 1990–92; *b* 11 March 1939; *s* of John Emrys and Elvira Beynon; *m* 1964, Hazel Janet Hurley; two *s* one *d*. *Educ*: Univ. of Wales (BSc); Univ. of Southampton (MSc, PhD). FIERE 1977; FIET (FIEE 1978); FREng (FEng 1988). Scientific Officer, Radio Res. Station, Slough, 1962–64; Univ. of Southampton: Lectr, Sen. Lectr and Reader, 1964–77; Prof. of Electronics, UWIST, Cardiff, 1977–79; University of Surrey: Prof. of Elec. Engrg, 1979–90; Head of Dept of Electronic and Elec. Engrg, 1979–83; Pro-Vice-Chancellor, 1983–87; Sen. Pro-Vice-Chancellor, 1987–90. Vis. Prof., Carleton Univ., Ottawa, 1975; Cons. to various cos, Govt estabts and Adviser to British Council, 1964–. Member: Accreditation Cttee, IEE, 1983–89; Adv. Cttee on Engrg and Technology, British Council, 1983–92; Technology Sub-Cttee, UGC, 1984–89; Nat. Electronics Council, 1985–91; Cttee 1, 1990–92, Main Cttee, 1991–94, CICHE; Adv. Cttee, Erasmus, 1990–92; Standing Cttee on Educn and Trng, Royal Acad. of Engrg, 1992–95; Adv. Council, British Liby, 1994–99; ITC, 1995–2000. Engrg Professors' Conference: Hon. Sec., 1982–84; Vice-Chm., 1984–85 and 1987–88; Chm., 1985–87. Chm., Retired Mems Surrey Network, IET, 2015–16 (Sec., 2010–16). Chm., Westminster Christian Council, 1998–2000; Sec., Bloomsbury Central Baptist Church, 2000–14. FRSA 1982; FKC 1990. Hon. Fellow, UC Swansea, 1990. *Publications*: Charge-Coupled Devices and Their Applications (with D. R. Lamb), 1980; papers on plasma physics, semiconductor devices and integrated circuits, and engrg educn. *Recreations*: music, photography, travel. *Address*: 13 Great Quarry, Guildford, Surrey GU1 3XN.

**BEZOS, Jeffrey Preston**; Founder, and Chairman, since 1994, Chief Executive Officer, since 1996, Amazon.com Inc., internet retailer, since 1994; founder, Blue Origin, Seattle, 2000; *b* 12 Jan. 1964; *m* 1993, MacKenzie Tuttle (marr. diss. 2019); four *c*. *Educ*: Princeton Univ. (degree in elec. engrg and computer sci., *summa cum laude*, 1986). Mem. staff, FITEL, NY, 1986–88; Bankers Trust Co., 1988–90 (Vice-Pres., 1990); D. E. Shaw & Co., 1990–94 (Sen. Vice-Pres., 1992–94). Owner, Washington Post, 2013–. *Address*: Amazon.com Inc., 410 Terry Avenue North, Seattle, WA 98109–5210, USA.

**BHADESHIA, Sir Harshad (Kumar Dharamshi Hansraj)**, Kt 2015; PhD; FRS 1998; FREng; TATA Steel Professor of Metallurgy, since 2008, and Director, SKF Steel Technology Centre, since 2009, University of Cambridge; Fellow of Darwin College, Cambridge, since 1993; *b* 27 Nov. 1953; *s* of Dharamshi Hansraj Bhadeshia and Narmda Dharamshi Bhadeshia; *m* 1978 (marr. diss. 1992); two *d*. *Educ*: City of London Poly. (BSc 1976); Univ. of Cambridge (PhD 1979). CEng. Technician: British Oxygen Co., 1970–72; Murex Welding Processes, 1972–73; University of Cambridge: engaged in res., 1976–79; SERC Res. Fellow, 1979–81; Demonstrator, 1981–85; Lectr in Physical Metallurgy, 1985–93; Reader in Physical Metallurgy, 1993–99; Prof. of Physical Metallurgy, 1999–2008. FREng 2002. *Publications*: Geometry of Crystals, 1987; Bainite in Steels, 1992; (with R. W. K. Honeycombe) Steels, 1995; more than 260 res. papers. *Recreation*: squash.

**BHAGWATI, Dr Jaimini;** High Commissioner of India in the United Kingdom, 2012–13; RBI Chair Professor, Indian Council for Research on International Economic Relations. *Educ:* St Columba's High Sch., Delhi; Delhi Univ. (MSc Physics); Sloan Sch., Massachusetts Inst. Technol. (MS Finance); Tufts Univ. (PhD Finance); Harvard Business Sch. (EDP). Entered Min. of External Affairs, India, 1976; Third Sec., then Second Sec., Madrid; Under Sec. (Bangladesh, Sri Lanka and Maldives) and Officer on Special Duty (Ext. Press Relns), New Delhi; First Sec., Chargé d'Affaires, Havana; Dep. Sec., Dept of Atomic Energy, Mumbai; Dep. Sec. (USA and Canada), New Delhi; World Bank Treasury, Washington: Financial Officer, Treasury Tech. Assistance, 1991–93; Sen. Financial Officer, 1993–95, Principal Financial Officer, 1995–96, Funding Dept; Lead Specialist, Derivatives, 1996–98; Hd, Asset-Liability Mgt, 1998–99; Jt Sec. (Capital Mkts, Pension Reforms and Ext. Commercial Borrowings), Min. of Finance, 1999–2002; Chief, Corporate Finance, World Bank, Washington, 2002–05; Jt Sec., later Addnl Sec. (Eurasia), 2005–07, Addnl Sec. (Econ. Relns), 2007–08, Min. of Ext. Affairs; Ambassador to Belgium, Luxembourg and EU, 2008–12. Columnist, Business Standard. *Address:* c/o Indian Council for Research on International Economic Relations, Core 6A, 4th Floor, India Habitat Center, Lodhi Road, New Delhi 110003, India.

**BHALOO, Zia Kurban;** QC 2010; *b* Dar es Salaam, Tanzania, 3 Aug. 1967; *d* of Malek and Kurban Bhaloo; one *d*. *Educ:* Banda Prep. Sch.; Cheltenham Ladies' Coll.; University Coll. London (LLB, LLM). Called to the Bar, Middle Temple, 1990, Bencher, 2014; in practice as barrister, specialising in commercial chancery, property and landlord and tenant. *Address:* Landmark Chambers, 180 Fleet Street, EC4A 2HG.

**BHANJI, Abdul Fazal,** OBE 2017; FCA; Special Advisor to the Senior Partner, PricewaterhouseCoopers, since 2001; Director, Hanson Green, since 2012; *s* of Fazal Bhanji Jessa and Jenabai Karmali Jinah; *m* 1980, Arzina Dhalla; three *s*. *Educ:* Kelly Coll., Tavistock; Univ. of Kent, Canterbury (BA Hons Accounting). FCA 1980. Coopers & Lybrand, then PricewaterhouseCoopers, 1972–: work in audit, accountancy and adv. practice in London, Canada, India and Switzerland; estabd Business Develt practice in UK, 1986–2001; Partner, 1988; Partner-in-Charge, Business Develt in UK, 1988–2001; Chairman: India Desk, 1995–2001; Charity Focus Gp, 1995–2001. Non-exec. Dir, Whitehead Mann plc, 2005–06. Member: FEFC for Gtr London, 1993–99; City of London Early Years Develt and Childcare Partnership, 1999–2000. Mem., Europe Cttee, 2002–, London Reg. Council, 2006–, CBI. Mem. and Chm., Finance Cttee, Marshall Aid Commemoration Commn, 2001–16. Member: Governing Body, SOAS, 2000–10; Council, Open Univ. 2001–02; Trustee, 2008–, Dep. Chm., 2009–, Univ. of London; Bd, Royal Central School of Speech and Drama, 2018–. Mem., Develt Cttee, Asia House, 2000–02. Charter Mem., Indus Entrepreneurs (TiE), 2000–04. Chairman: Aga Khan Econ. Planning Bd, UK, 1990–93; Nat. Cttee, Aga Khan Foundn (UK), 1997–2006; Mem., HH Prince Aga Khan Shia Imami Ismaili Council, UK, 1990–93; Trustee, Prince's Foundn for Children and the Arts, 2008–14. FRSA. Freeman, City of London, 1987; Liveryman: Co. of Glaziers and Painters of Glass, 2003; Barbers' Co., 2009. *Recreations:* cricket, bridge, squash, golf, chess, ski-ing, backgammon. *Address:* PricewaterhouseCoopers LLP, 1 Embankment Place, WC2N 6RH. *Clubs:* Brooks's, Farmers, Mosimann's, Walbrook.

**BHARDWAJA, Neelam;** Management Consultant, Neelam Management Consultancy Ltd, since 2012; one *s*. *Educ:* Univ. of E Anglia (BSc Hons 1978; MA; CQSW 1982). Social worker, Birmingham CC, 1978–80 and 1982–83; various appts, Cambs CC, 1983–2001; Service Manager, Peterborough CC, 2001–03; Hd, Children's and Families, Bor. of Poole, 2003–05; Corporate Director, Opportunities, then Corporate Dir, Adult and Children's Social Services, Educn and Lifelong Learning, Cardiff Council, 2005–12; Asst Dir, Safeguarding and Support, Haringey Council, 2014–16; Dir of Ops, Gloucestershire CC, 2017–18; Service Dir, Plymouth CC, 2018–. Mem., Children and Families Cttee, ADSS, 2003–05; Vice Pres., 2008–09, Pres., 2009–10, ADSS Cymru. *Publications:* various articles. *Recreations:* enjoying Welsh countryside and beaches, enjoying success and achievements to date. *T:* 07837 491589. *E:* n.mc@outlook.com.

**BHARUCHA, Chitra,** MBE 2009; FRCPath; Vice-Chairman, BBC Trust, 2006–10 (Acting Chairman, 2007); Trustee, Marie Curie Cancer Care, 2007–17; *b* 6 April 1945; *d* of late George Gnanadickam and Mangalam Gnanadickam (*née* Ramaiya); *m* 1967, Hoshang Bharucha; two *d*. *Educ:* Ewart Sch., Madras; Christian Med. Coll., Vellore, India (MB BS); Queen's Univ. Belfast (Cert. Commercial Law 1993). Nuffield Schol., 1967; Council of Europe Fellow, 1980. Dep. Dir, NI Blood Transfusion Service, 1981–2000; Consultant Haematologist, Belfast City Hosp., 1981–2000. Non-exec. Dir, UK Transplant, 2000–01. Chm., Adv. Cttee on Animal Feeding Stuffs, Food Standards Agency, 2002–08; Mem. Council, ASA, 2004–07. Mem., Lab. Services Adv. Cttee, DHSS NI, 1995–2000. Mem., Partners' Council, NICE, 1999–2000. UK Blood Transfusion Service: Mem., Standing Adv. Cttee for Selection of Blood Donors, 1995–98; Chm., Standing Adv. Cttee for Transfusion Transmitted Infections, 1998–2000. Member: WHO Expert Adv. Panel for Blood Products, 1988–2000; Blood Safety Adv. Cttee, NI, 1998–2000; Standing Adv. Cttee for Pathology, NI, 1998–2000. Mem., Scientific Cttee, Eur. Sch. of Blood Transfusion, 1996–2000; Co-ordinator of Standardisation for Eur. Cord Blood Banking, 1996–2000. Chm., Adjudication Panels, Med. Practitioners Tribunal Service, 2010–15. Mem., Appts Cttee, Bd of Recognition Panel, 2014. Mem., 1999–2004, Associate Mem., 2004–07, GMC. Royal College of Pathologists: Mem. Council, 1996–2000; Chm., NI Affairs Cttee, 1998–2000; Mem., Patient Liaison Gp, 1998–2001. Pres., Med. Women's Fedn, 1994–95. Mem. Council, Internat. Soc. of Blood Transfusion, 1996–2000. Vice-Chm., NI Council for Postgrad. Med. Educn, 1999–2000. Member: Council, BBC NI, 1996–99; ITC, 2001–03. Mem. Bd, FIT Biotech Oy, 2016–19 (Chm., 2018–19). Member: Adv. Forum (NI), Sargent Cancer Care for Children, 2000–03; NI Council, Leprosy Mission, 1994–2003. Gov., Methodist Coll., Belfast, 1990–93; Mem., Exec. Cttee, Assoc. of Governing Bodies of Voluntary Grammar Schs, 1990–95. FRSA 2002–08; FCGI 2009. Hon. DMedSci QUB, 2008. *Recreations:* opera, theatre, classical music, hill walking. *Club:* Reform.

**BHASKAR, Sanjeev,** OBE 2006; actor and writer; *b* 31 Oct. 1963; *s* of Inderjit and Janak Bhaskar; *m* 2005, Meera Syal, *qv*; one *s*, and one step *d*. *Educ:* Springwell Primary Sch., Heston; Cranford Community Coll.; Univ. of Hertfordshire (BA Hons Business Studies (Mktg). Mktg Exec., IBM, 1987–88; Tour Manager, Arts Council (GB) Project, 1990–92; Mktg Officer, Tom Allen Arts Centre, Stratford, London, 1993–95. Performer and writer: Goodness Gracious Me, Radio 4, 1996–98, BBC TV, 1998–2000; The Kumars at No 42, BBC TV, 2001–06, The Kumars, Sky 1, 2014; Mumbai Calling, ITV, 2009; actor: Life Isn't All Ha Ha Hee Hee, BBC TV, 2005; The Indian Doctor, BBC TV, 2010, 2012, 2013; Unforgotten, ITV, 2015, 2017, 2018; actor in films: Notting Hill, 1999; The Mystic Masseur, 2001; The Guru, 2002; Anita and Me, 2002; Yesterday, 2019; Horrible Histories: the movie, 2019; actor in play, Dinner with Saddam, Menier Chocolate Factory, 2015. Presenter, India with Sanjeev Bhaskar, BBC TV series, 2007. Ambassador, Prince's Trust, 2000–. Chancellor, Univ. of Sussex, 2009–. Hon. DLitt, 2004. *Publications:* India with Sanjeev Bhaskar, 2007. *Recreations:* dreaming, chatting, collecting and watching movies, staying in, anything relating to Elvis Presley/Beatles/film trivia/gadgets. *Address:* c/o United Agents, 12–26 Lexington Street, W1F 0LE.

**BHATIA,** Baron *cr* 2001 (Life Peer), of Hampton in the London Borough of Richmond-upon-Thames; **Amirali Alibhai Bhatia,** OBE 1997; Chairman, Forbes Trust, since 1985; *b* 18 March 1932; *s* of Alibhai Bhatia and Fatma Alibhai Bhatia; *m* 1954, Nurbanu Amersi Kanji; three *d*. Career in manufacturing, Tanzania, 1960–72; Dir, Casley Finance Ltd and Forbes Campbell (Internat.) Ltd, 1973–2001. Chm., SITPRO, 1998–2004; Board Member: E London TEC, 1991–2001; Nat. Lottery Charities Bd, 1995–2000; Local Investment Fund, 1997–; Project Fullemploy, 1997–99 (Chm., 1994–97); Mem., Prime Minister's Adv. Cttee for Queen's Award, 1999–. Chairman: Council of Ethnic Minority Vol. Sector Orgns, 1999–; Ethnic Minority Foundn, 1999–2009; Hon. Treas., Mem. Bd and Exec. Cttee, Internat. Alert, 1994–2000; Trustee: Oxfam, 1985–99 (Chm., Trading Bd, 1986–92); Community Develt Foundn, 1988–97 (Mem., Budget and Finance Cttee); Charities Evaluation Services, 1989–90; Water Aid, 2000–03; St Christopher's Hospice, 1997–2003 (Mem., Audit Cttee); Bd, Diana, Princess of Wales Meml Fund, 2001–03. Trustee, High/Scope Educn Res. Foundn, Mich, 1985–97; Bd Mem., Tower Hamlets Coll., 1991–98. MInstD. Personality of the Year, UK Charity Awards, 2001; Beacon Prize for Leadership, Beacon Fellowship, 2003. *Recreations:* reading, cricket, voluntary work.

**BHATT, Raju;** Partner, Bhatt Murphy Solicitors, since 1998; *b* Kampala, Uganda, 24 Oct. 1957; *s* of Manjula and Batukrai Bhatt; *m* 1987, Pragna Patel; two *d*. *Educ:* Shimoni Primary Sch., Kampala; Kololo Secondary Sch., Kampala; Christ's Coll., Finchley; Worcester Coll., Oxford (BA Hons Oriental Studies (Sanskrit)); City of London Poly. BM Birnberg & Co.: trainee, 1986–88; admitted Solicitor, 1988; Solicitor, 1988–98. Mem., Hillsborough Ind. Panel, 2010–12. *Recreations:* music, walking, reading, family. *Address:* Bhatt Murphy, 10 Tyssen Street, E8 2FE. *T:* (020) 7729 1115, *Fax:* (020) 7729 1117. *E:* r.bhatt@bhattmurphy.co.uk.

**BHATTACHARYA, Satyajit,** LVO 2018; FRCSE, FRCS; Consultant Surgeon, Royal London Hospital, Barts Health NHS Trust (formerly Royal London Hospital and St Bartholomew's Hospital), since 1999 (specialist in liver, biliary and pancreatic surgery); Medical Director, The London Clinic; Serjeant-Surgeon to the Royal Household, since 2016 (Surgeon, 2006–16); *b* Mumbai, 22 Nov. 1962; *s* of Durga Prasanna and Kalpana Bhattacharya; *m* 1988, Dr Shanti Vijayaraghavan; one *d*. *Educ:* Don Bosco Sch. and St Xavier's Coll., Mumbai; Grant Med. Coll., Mumbai (MB BS 1984, MS 1988); Royal Free Hosp. Sch. of Medicine (MPhil 1995). FRCSE 1991; FRCS 1998. Registrar and Lectr, Royal Free and University Coll. Hosps, 1989–95 and 1996–98. Member: Ct of Examrs, RCS, 2005–11; Jt Inter-Collegiate Exam. Bd in Gen. Surgery, 2014–. *Publications:* contrib. chapters to med. textbooks; papers in med. jls incl. Nature Clin. Practice, Hepatology, British Jl Surgery, British Jl Cancer. *Address:* HPB Surgery Unit, Royal London Hospital, Whitechapel, E1 1BB. *T:* (020) 3594 2747, *Fax:* (020) 3594 3255. *E:* satya.bhattacharya@bartshealth.nhs.uk.

**BHATTACHARYA, Prof. Shoumo,** MD; FRCP, FMedSci; Professor of Cardiovascular Medicine, since 2004, and British Heart Foundation Professor of Cardiovascular Medicine, since 2009, University of Oxford; Fellow, Green Templeton College (formerly Green College), Oxford, since 2004; *b* 24 Feb. 1960; *s* of Cdre Asoke Kumar Bhattacharya and Jayashri Bhattacharya; *m* 1989, Dr Jane Caldwell; two *s*. *Educ:* All India Inst. of Med. Sci., New Delhi (MD 1985); King's Coll. London (MSc). FRCP 2003. Jun. Resident in Medicine, All India Inst. of Med. Scis, New Delhi, 1983–85; Registrar in Cardiology and Medicine, Northwick Park Hosp., Harrow, 1987–90; MRC Trng Fellow and Hon. Sen. Registrar, Northwick Park Hosp., Harrow and Hammersmith Hosp., London, 1990–94; BHF Internat. Res. Fellow, 1994–96, Instructor in Medicine, 1996–98, Dana-Farber Cancer Inst. and Harvard Med. Sch., Boston, Mass; Wellcome Trust Sen. Fellow in Clinical Sci., 1998–2008 and Hon. Consultant Cardiologist, 1998–, Dept of Cardiovascular Medicine and Wellcome (formerly Wellcome Trust) Centre for Human Genetics, Univ. of Oxford. FMedSci 2006. *Publications:* articles in Nature, Nature Genetics, Cell, Genes & Develt, Jl Biol Chem. *Recreations:* science, history, theory and practice of the culinary arts. *Address:* Wellcome Centre for Human Genetics, Roosevelt Drive, Oxford OX3 7BN. *T:* (01865) 287771. *E:* sbhattac@well.ox.ac.uk.

**BHOGAL, Rev. Inderjit Singh,** OBE 2005; Officer, Methodist Discipleship and Ministries Learning Network, 2014–18; President, Methodist Conference, 2000–01; *b* Nairobi, 17 Jan. 1953; *m* 1986, Kathryn Anne; one *s* one *d*. *Educ:* Khalsa Sikh Sch., Nairobi; Blue Coat C of E Sch., Dudley; Dudley Tech. Coll.; Hartley Victoria Coll., Manchester (BA Manchester Univ. 1979); Westminster Coll., Oxford (MA 1991); Sheffield Hallam Univ. (MSc 2017). Minister: Darlington Street Circuit, 1979–87; Carver Street Circuit, Sheffield, 1987–94; Sheffield Inner City Ecumenical Mission, 1994–2004. Co-ordinator, Wolverhampton Inter-Faith Gp, 1984–87; Mem., Sheffield Chaplaincy to Higher Educn, 1987–94 (Chm., 1990–94); Dir of Studies, 1994–97, Dir, 1997–2004, Urban Theol. Unit, Sheffield; Consultant Theologian, Christian Aid, 2004–05; CEO (formerly Dir), Yorks and Humber Faiths Forum, 2005–11; Leader, Corrymeela Community, 2011–14. Mem., Home Office Race Equality Adv. Panel, 2003–07. Patron, Race Equality in Employment Prog., 2003–10. Founder, 2005, Pres., 2011–, City of Sanctuary (Chm., 2005–12). DUniv: Oxford Brookes, 2001; Sheffield Hallam, 2002. *Publications:* A Table for All, 2000; On the Hoof: theology in transit, 2001; Unlocking the Doors, 2002; Becoming a City of Sanctuary, 2009; West Highland Way: diary of a walker, 2009; (with Satwant Kaur Rait) Understanding Sikhism, 2010. *Recreations:* walking, cooking, sport, writing.

**BHOGAL, Kiran;** Partner, and Head of Healthcare (London), Hill Dickinson LLP, since 2016; *b* Nairobi, 16 May 1965; *d* of Sarwan Singh Bhogal and Ravinder Kaur Bhogal. *Educ:* Loreto Convent Msongari, Nairobi; Univ. of Buckingham (LLB Hons 1987); Kenya Law Sch. (Dip.); Trent Poly. Admitted solicitor, 1991; Asst Solicitor, then Sen. Solicitor, 1991–97, Partner, 1997–2008, Wansbroughs Willey Hargrave, then Beachcroft Wansbroughs, subseq. Beachcroft LLP; Weightmans LLP, 2009–15; solicitor advocate, 2006; a Dep. Dist Judge, 2006–. *Publications:* (contrib.) Corporate Liability: work related deaths and criminal prosecutions, 2003. *Recreations:* theatre, walking, travel, reading. *Address:* Hill Dickinson LLP, The Broadgate Tower, 20 Primrose Street, EC2A 2EW. *T:* (020) 7280 9344, *Fax:* (020) 7283 1144. *E:* kiran.bhogal@hilldickinson.com.

**BHOWMICK, Prof. Bimal Kanti,** OBE 2001; DL; MD; FRCP; Professor (personal chair), Cardiff University, 2004; Consultant Physician, Intermediate Care, Glan Clwyd Hospital, Rhyl, since 2006; Consultant Physician, Community Care: Isle of Anglesey, since 2011; Powys Teaching Hospital, since 2013; Consultant Physician, Community Care of the Elderly, Warrington and Halton Foundation Trust, since 2015; *b* 13 Feb. 1940; *s* of late Jamini Mohan Bhowmick and of Ashalata Bhowmick; *m* 1969, Dr Aparna Banerjee; two *s* one *d*. *Educ:* Calcutta Univ. (MB BS; MD 1968). FRCP 1987. SHO, Victoria Hosp., Blackpool, 1969–71; SHO, 1971–72, Registrar, 1972–74, Burton Rd Hosp., Dudley; Sen. Registrar, H. M. Stanley Hosp., St Asaph, 1974–76; Consultant Physician, 1976–2005, now Emeritus, Clin. Dir, 1993–2004, Clin. Dir of Integrated Medicine, 2001–02, Care of the Elderly, Glan Clwyd Hosp., Rhyl. Associate Dean for Overseas Doctors in Wales, Sch. of Postgrad. Med. and Dental Educn, Univ. of Wales Coll. of Med., 1997–2006; Hon. Sen. Lectr, Inst. of Res., Univ. of Wales, Bangor, 1998–. Mem. Council, 1998–2001, Censor, 2001–03, RCP. Mem., Bevan Commn, 2011–. Fellow: UWCM, 2003; Glyndwr Univ., Wrexham, 2006. DL Clwyd, 2009. Lifetime Achievement Award, NHS, 2009;

Recognition Achievement Award, Welsh Govt, 2011; Bevan Prize for elderly health and wellbeing, Bevan Foundn, 2014. *Publications:* (contrib.) Parkinson's Disease and Parkinsonism in the Elderly, 2000; numerous contribs to learned jls. *Recreations:* reading, gardening, cinema. *Address:* Jamini, Allt Goch, St Asaph, Denbighshire LL17 0BP.

**BHUGRA, Prof. Dinesh Kumar Makhan Lal,** CBE 2012; PhD; FRCP, FRCPE, FRCPsych; Professor of Mental Health and Cultural Diversity, Institute of Psychiatry, King's College London, 2004–14, now Emeritus; President, Mental Health Foundation, since 2014 (Chair, 2011–14); President, British Medical Association, 2018–19; *b* Yamuna Nagar, India, 8 July 1952; *s* of Makhan Lal and Shanta Bhugra; partner, Michael Bryn Thacker. *Educ:* Univ. of Poona (MB BS 1976); Univ. of Leicester (MPhil Psychiatry 1990); S Bank Univ. (MSc Sociol. 1991); Univ. of London (MA Social Anthropol. 1996; PhD Psychiatry 1999). LMSSA 1980; MRCPsych 1985, FRCPsych 1997, Hon FRCPsych 2012; FRCP 2010; FFPH 2011; FRCPE 2012. Registrar, then SHO, Leics Rotation Scheme, 1981–86; Sen. Registrar, Maudsley Trng Scheme, 1986–89; Lectr, MRC Social Psychiatry Unit, 1989–92; Sen. Lectr, Maudsley Hosp., 1992–2002; Reader, S London and Maudsley NHS Trust, 2002–04; Hon. Consultant, S London and Maudsley Foundn NHS Trust (formerly Maudsley Hosp., then S London and Maudsley NHS Trust), 2004–. President: RCPsych, 2008–11 (Dean, 2003–08); World Psychiatric Assoc., 2014–17 (Pres.-elect, 2011–14). Hon. Member: S African Soc. of Psychiatry, 2016; Asociación Ecuatoriana de Psiquiatría, 2016. Hon. Fellow: Am. Coll. of Psychiatrists, 2010; Hong Kong Coll. of Psychiatrists, 2012; Hon. FKC, 2017. Lifetime Achievement Award, Pakistan Psychiatric Soc., 2012; President's Medal, Indian Psychiatric Soc., 2017. Editor: Internat. Rev. of Psych., 2000–; Internat. Jl of Social Psych., 2000–. *Publications:* Mad Tales from Bollywood: portrayal of mental illness in conventional Hindi cinema, 2006; (ed with K. Bhui) Culture and Mental Health: a comprehensive textbook, 2007; (ed with K. Bhui) Textbook of Cultural Psychiatry, 2007, 2nd edn 2018; (ed jtly) A Selected Annotated Bibliography of Public Attitudes to Mental Health, 1975–2005, 2007; (ed jtly) Workplace-based Assessments in Psychiatry, 2007, 2nd edn 2011; (ed jtly) Management for Psychiatrists, 3rd edn 2007, 4th edn 2016; (ed with O. Howes) Handbook for Psychiatric Trainees, 2007; (ed jtly) Principles of Social Psychiatry, 2010; (ed jtly) Clinical Topics in Cultural Psychiatry, 2010; (ed jtly) Mental Health of Refugees and Asylum Seekers, 2010; (ed jtly) Migration and Mental Health, 2011 (trans. Japanese 2017); (ed jtly) Professionalism in Mental Health Care, 2011; (ed jtly) Workplace-Based Assessments in Psychiatric Training, 2011; (ed jtly) Troublesome Disguises, 2015; (ed jtly) Pluralism in Psychiatry, 2015; (ed jtly) Psychiatry in Practice, 2015; (ed jtly) Routledge Handbook of Psychiatry in Asia, 2016; (ed jtly) Oxford Textbook of Public Mental Health, 2018; Practical Cultural Psychiatry, 2018. *Recreations:* reading crime novels and fiction by Indian authors, cinema (Hitchcock and Billy Wilder), theatre, Hindi film music. *Address:* PO 72, Centre for Affective Disorders, Institute of Psychiatry, Psychology and Neuroscience, King's College London, De Crespigny Park, SE5 8AF. *T:* (020) 7848 0500, *Fax:* (020) 7848 0333. *E:* dinesh.bhugra@dineshbhugra.net. *Club:* Reform.

**BIAGI, Marco;** Senior Counsel, Message Matters, since 2016; *b* Alexandria, W Dunbartonshire, 31 July 1982; *s* of Antonio Biagi and Mary Biagi. *Educ:* Hermitage Acad.; Wadham Coll., Oxford; Univ. of Calif, Berkeley; Univ. of St Andrews (MA Hons Internat. Relns 2005); Univ. of Glasgow (MSc Pol Communication 2010). Vice-Pres. (Representation), Students' Assoc., Univ. of St Andrews, 2002–03. Parly Asst to Keith Brown, MSP, 2007–09; Parly Researcher, SNP Central Staff, 2009–11. Mem. (SNP) Edinburgh Central, Scottish Parlt, 2011–16; Minister for Local Govt and Community Empowerment, 2014–16. Trustee, Nat. Liby of Scotland, 2011–13. *Recreations:* amateur drama, running, retro music, science fiction, musical theatre, real ciders. *Address:* c/o 6 North St Andrew Street, Edinburgh EH2 1HJ. *E:* marco@biagi.scot.

**BIAGINI, Almut;** *see* Hintze, A.

**BIANCHI, Adrian,** MOM 1995; MD; FRCS, FRCSE; Consultant Specialist Paediatric and Neonatal Surgeon, Manchester and North Western Region, 1984–2010; *b* 19 Jan. 1948; *s* of Loris and Yvonne Bianchi (*née* Ganado); *m* 1970, Claire (*née* Sammut); two *s* one *d*. *Educ:* Medical Sch., Royal Univ. of Malta (MD 1969). FRCS 1975; FRCSE 1975. Specialised in paediatric and neonatal surgery through surgical progs, Liverpool and Manchester; Dir, Neonatal Surgery, and Mem., Bd of Mgt, St Mary's Hosp., Manchester, 1987–2002; Paediatric Surgical Rep., Mgt Bd, Royal Manchester Children's Hosp., 1984–90; has developed orig. surgical techniques and new surgical approaches incl. surgical mgt of children with short bowel. Visiting Specialist Neonatal and Paediatric Surgeon: Mater Dei Hospital, Malta, 1987–; Ospedale dei Bambini, Spedali Civili di Brescia, Italy, 2014–. Denis Browne Gold Medal, British Assoc. of Paediatric Surgeons, 2012. *Publications:* contrib. chapters in paediatric surgical operative and gen. surgical textbooks; 78 articles in medical jls. *Recreations:* reproduction of antique furniture, marquetry, ancient civilizations, swimming, gardening (bonsai, carnations). *Address:* 1 Elleray Road, Middleton, Manchester M24 1NY. *T:* (0161) 643 6406. *E:* bianchi54@gmail.com.

**BIBB, Prof. Mervyn James,** PhD; FRS 2013; Project Leader, Molecular Microbiology, John Innes Centre, 1982–2016, now Emeritus Fellow; *m;* two *d*. *Educ:* Univ. of East Anglia (BSc; PhD Streptomyces Genetics 1978). Postdoctoral res., Stanford Univ., Calif, 1978–82; on leave of absence from John Innes Centre with biotechnol. co. in San Diego. Co-founder, Novacta Biosystems. Lepetit Award; Colworth Prize, Microbiol. Soc., 1995; Charles Thom Award, Soc. for Industrial Microbiol. and Biotechnol., 2001; Heatley Medal and Prize, Biochem. Soc., 2013; David Gottlieb Medal, Univ. of Illinois, 2017. *Address:* Department of Molecular Microbiology, John Innes Centre, Norwich Research Park, Colney, Norwich NR4 7UH.

**BIBBY, Dame Enid,** DBE 2004; education consultant; school improvement adviser; Headteacher, Wood Green High School College of Sport, Maths and Computing, Wednesbury, 1998–2006; Chief Executive Officer, DEB Consultants Ltd, 2006–16; *b* 8 Feb. 1951; *d* of Fred and Ivy Kemp; *m* 1999, Dr Bob Bibby (*d* 2014); two step *d*. *Educ:* Lancaster Univ. (BA Hons English); Liverpool Univ. (PGCE); Univ. of Cambridge (AdvDip. Ed). Deputy Headteacher: Lealands Community Sch., Luton, 1986–89; Leon Community Sch., Bletchley, 1989–95; Headteacher, Silverdale Sch., Sheffield, 1995–98. Mem. Council, Specialist Schs and Acads (formerly Special Schs) Trust, 2002–05; Mem. Bd, W Midlands, British Educnl Communications and Technol. Agency, 2004–05; Nat. Challenge Advr, 2008–10. Gov., Ofsted, 2007–08. Dir, Merddyn Court Mgt Ltd, 2015–. Unilever Fellow, London Leadership Centre, 2002. FRSA 1997; FCMI (FIMgt 1998). JP Milton Keynes, 1989–94. Chair, Shropshire Rural Community Council, 2013–15; Sec., Llanfairpg WI, 2017–; Trustee, Anglesey Fedn of WIs, 2017–; Vice Chair, Anglesey Column Trust, 2017–. Editor, W Shropshire Talking Newspaper, 2012–15. *Recreations:* sailing, fell walking, modern literature, Crete.

**BIBBY, Brig. Greville Kenneth,** CBE 2010 (MBE 1999); Clerk to the Grocers' Company, since 2016; *b* Charlwood, Surrey, 13 Aug. 1961; *s* of Derek Graham Bibby and Jeanette Maynard Alister Bibby; *m* 1991, Gillian Ann Ingham; two *s* one *d*. *Educ:* Wellington Coll., Berks; RMA, Sandhurst. Commnd Army, 1981; Served NI, London, Germany, Gulf War 1, Afghanistan; psc 1993; CO, 1st Bn, Coldstream Guards, 2000–02; Dep. Comdr, British Task Force, Helmand Province, 2009; Comdr, 15 (NE) Bde, 2011–14; Regtl Lt Col, Coldstream Guards, 2012–15. Chairman: Kohima Mus. and Welfare Trust, 2011–; Waterloo Uncovered (charity), 2016–. *Recreations:* golf, tennis, Chelsea FC, ski-ing. *Address:* Worshipful Company of Grocers, Grocers' Hall, Princes Street, EC2R 8AD. *T:* (020) 7606 3113. *E:* clerk@grocershall.co.uk. *Clubs:* Berkshire Golf, St Enodoc Golf.

**BIBBY, Sir Michael (James),** 3rd Bt *cr* 1959, of Tarporley, Co. Palatine of Chester; DL; non-executive Director, Bibby Line Group Ltd, since 2018 (Managing Director, 2000–18); *b* 2 Aug. 1963; *e s* of Sir Derek Bibby, 2nd Bt and Christine Maud, *d* of Rt Rev. F. J. Okell, Bishop Suffragan of Stockport; *S* father, 2002; *m* 1994, Beverley, *o d* of Donald Graham; two *s* (twins). *Educ:* Rugby; Trinity Coll., Oxford Univ. Pres., UK Chamber of Shipping, 2018–. FICS. DL Merseyside, 2013. Hon. DLaws Liverpool, 2012. *Heir: s* Alexander James Bibby, *b* 24 Aug. 1997. *Address:* Bibby Line Group Ltd, 105 Duke Street, Liverpool L1 5JQ.

**BICESTER,** 5th Baron *cr* 1938, of Tusmore, co. Oxford; **Charles James Vivian Smith;** Founding Partner, Levantis Wealth Control, Gibraltar, since 2015; *b* Johannesburg, SA, 7 Sept. 1963; *s* of late George Henry Vivian Smith and of June Rose Vivian Smith (*née* Foster Towne, later Hersov); *S* cousin, 2016; *m* 2006, Deborah Michelle James; two *s*. *Educ:* St Bede's Sch., Eastbourne; Milton Abbey Sch., Dorset; Boston Univ./Schiller Internat. Univ., London (BA Internat. Business). Founder, Medran Develts Ltd, 1985–88; Acquisitions Advr, Wilton Securities (London) Ltd, 1988–89; Exec., Rothschild Ventures LLP, 1989–91; Associate, NM Rothschild Asset Mgt Ltd, 1991–93; Founder and CEO, Indochina (Hldgs) Ltd, 1994–2001; Commercial Dir, PeopleNews.com, 2000–01; mgt consultant, 2000–04; Business Develt Dir, Alphasoft Ltd, 2004–06; Founder and investor, America Indochina Mgt Ltd, 2005–17; Founder and CEO, SMyS.com Ltd, 2006–09; owner, Smartfix BV, 2007–09; Consultant, PC30, 2009; Partnership Dir, Adoreum Partners, 2009; CEO, Cempa Investments Ltd, 2009–11. Dir, Maya Cove Resource Partners Ltd, 2011–. *Recreations:* riding, shooting, golf, ski-ing. *Heir: s* Hon. Milo Louis Vivian Smith, *b* 2 Aug. 2007. *Address:* c/o Levantis Wealth Control Ltd, Suite 5.06 World Trade Centre, 6 Bayside Road, Gibraltar GX11 1AA. *T:* 20045568. *E:* Charles@vivian-smith.com. *Clubs:* Turf; La Reserva (Sotogrande, Spain).

**BICHARD,** Baron *cr* 2010 (Life Peer), of Nailsworth in the County of Gloucestershire; **Michael George Bichard,** KCB 1999; Chairman, National Audit Office, since 2015; *b* 31 Jan. 1947. *Educ:* Manchester Univ. (LLB); Birmingham Univ. (MSocSci). Chief Executive: Brent BC, 1980–86; Gloucestershire CC, 1986–90; Social Security Benefits Agency, 1990–95; Perm. Sec., Employment Dept Gp, April–July 1995; Jt Perm. Sec., July–Dec. 1995, Perm. Sec., 1996–2001, DfEE. Rector, London Inst., subseq. Univ. of the Arts London, 2001–08. Dir, 2008–10, Sen. Fellow, 2010–12, Inst. for Govt. Dep. Speaker, H of L, 2012–17. Chm., Soham Murders Inquiry, 2004. Chm., Legal Services Commn, 2005–08. Chairman: Rathbone Training Ltd, 2001–08; RSe Consulting, 2003–08; non-executive Director: Reed Exec. plc, 2002–04; The Key, 2015–. Chm., Design Council, 2008–11. Mem., ESRC, 1989–92. Chm Bd Dirs, ARTIS, 2003–06. Chm. Trustees, Social Care Inst. for Excellence, 2013–18; Dir, River and Rowing Mus. Foundn, 2002–; Trustee, Shakespeare's Globe, 2008– (Chm., 2015–18). Governor: Henley Mgt Coll., 2002–08; Council, Dyslexia Inst., 2003–06. Hon. Fellow, Inst. of Local Govt Studies, Birmingham Univ. FIPD; CCMI; FRSA. DUniv: Leeds Metropolitan, 1992; Middlesex, 2001; Southampton Inst., 2002; Hon. LLD: Birmingham, 1999; Bradford, 2004; Cranfield, 2006; Hon. DBA UWE, 2016.

**BICK;** *see* Moore-Bick.

**BICKELL, Brian;** Chief Executive, Shaftesbury PLC, since 2011; *b* London, 6 Aug. 1954; *m* 2007, Kevin Keogh. *Educ:* FCA 1976. Audit dept, F. W. Stephens, Chartered Accts, 1972–77, Stoy Hayward, Chartered Accts, 1977–82; Gp Financial Accountant, Stock Conversion plc, 1983–86; joined Shaftesbury PLC, 1986: Dir, 1987; Finance Dir, 1987–2011. Chm., UK China Visitor Alliance, 2016–; Member, Board: Freehold, 2012–; Westminster Property Assoc., 2016–. *Address:* Shaftesbury PLC, 22 Ganton Street, W1F 7FD. *T:* (020) 7333 8118, *Fax:* (020) 7333 0660. *E:* brian.bickell@shaftesbury.co.uk.

**BICKET, Harry Alexander Clarence;** Artistic Director, The English Concert, since 2007; Music Director, Santa Fe Opera, since 2018 (Chief Conductor, 2013–18); *b* Liverpool, 15 May 1961; *s* of late Henry Bicket and Katharine Bicket; *m* 2011, Audrey du Cauzé de Nazelle; one *s* one *d*. *Educ:* Radley Coll.; Royal Coll. of Music; Christ Church, Oxford (BA 1983; MA 1985). FRCO 1980. Duke of Edinburgh's Organ Scholar, St George's Chapel, Windsor Castle, 1978–80; Christopher Tatton Organ Scholar, Christ Church, Oxford, 1980–83; Sub-Organist, Westminster Abbey, 1984–88; Chorus Master, ENO, 1988–93; freelance conductor, 1993–. Hon. RAM 2018. *Address:* c/o The English Concert, West Wing, Somerset House, Strand, WC2R 1LA. *T:* (020) 7759 1100.

**BICKFORD, James David Prydeaux,** CB 1995; Chairman, Bickford Associates; author and scriptwriter; *b* 28 July 1940; *s* of late William A. J. P. Bickford and Muriel Bickford (*née* Smythe); *m* 1965, Carolyn Jane, *d* of late Major W. A. R. Sumner, RHA; three *s*. *Educ:* Downside; Law Society's College of Law, London. Admitted to Roll of Solicitors, 1963; Solicitor of the Supreme Court. In practice, J. J. Newcombe, Solicitors, Okehampton, 1963–69; Crown Counsel and Legal Advr to Govt of Turks and Caicos Islands, BWI, 1969–71; Asst Legal Advr, FCO, 1971–79 and 1982–84; Legal Advr, British Mil. Govt, Berlin, 1979–82; Legal Counsellor, FCO, 1984–87; Under Sec., MoD, and Legal Advr to Security and Intelligence Services, 1987–95. Judge Ben C. Green Lectr in Law, Case Western Reserve Univ., USA; Vis. Prof. of Law, Cleveland State Univ., USA. Mem., Panel of Legal Experts, Internat. Telecommunications Satellite Orgn, 1985–87; Chm., Assembly of Internat. Maritime Satellite Orgn, 1985–87. Mem., Law Soc. Hon. Mem., Nat. Security Cttee, Amer. Bar Assoc. Scriptwriter (with wife), infomercial for SOCA, Was Any of This Your Fault?, 2008 (Internat. Visual Commns Silver Award for Best Drama). Bronze Award (with wife), Best Script Magnum Opus, Event and Visual Communication Assoc., 2017. *Publications:* Land Dealings Simplified in the Turks and Caicos Islands, 1971; *fiction:* The Face of Tomorrow, 2004; contribs on intelligence, organised crime and money-laundering issues to symposia, jls, media and internet. *Recreations:* the family, sailing, fishing. *Address:* c/o National Westminster Bank, Torrington, Devon EX38 8HP.

**BICKFORD-SMITH, Margaret Osborne;** QC 2003; a Recorder, since 1997; *b* 4 June 1950; *d* of James Maclean Todd and Janet Gillespie Todd (*née* Holmes); *m* 1970, Stephen William Bickford-Smith; one *s*. *Educ:* Headington Sch.; Lady Margaret Hall, Oxford (MA). MCIArb 2006. Called to the Bar, Inner Temple, 1973, Bencher, 1993; in practice as barrister and mediator. Chair: Inns' Conduct Cttee, 2012–14 (Vice Chair, 2009–12); London Br., CIArb, 2012–15. Mem., Hounslow LBC, 1974–82. Freeman, City of London, 2014; Liveryman, Arbitrators' Co., 2014– (Ct Asst, 2015–; Master, 2019–20). *Recreations:* Italy, art, music. *Address:* Crown Office Chambers, 2 Crown Office Row, Temple, EC4Y 7HJ. *T:* (020) 7797 8100, *Fax:* (020) 7797 8101. *Club:* Royal Automobile.

**BICKLE, Prof. Michael James,** DPhil; FRS 2007; Director of Research, Department of Earth Sciences, University of Cambridge, since 2015 (Professor, 2000–15); *b* 26 Feb. 1948; *s* of Ronald Stancliffe Bickle and René Florence Bickle; *m* 1978, Hazel Joan Chapman; two *d*. *Educ:* Queens' Coll., Cambridge (BA 1970); DPhil Oxon. Lectr, then Sen. Lectr, Univ.

of Western Australia, 1978–83; Lectr, 1983–95, Reader, 1995–2000, in Earth Scis, Univ. of Cambridge. *Recreations:* orienteering, sailing. *Address:* Department of Earth Sciences, Downing Street, Cambridge CB2 3EQ. *T:* (01223) 333400, *Fax:* (01223) 333450. *E:* mb72@esc.cam.ac.uk.

**BICKLER, Simon Lloyd;** QC 2011; a Recorder, since 2012; *b* Leeds, 19 July 1964; *s* of David Bickler and Ruth Bickler; *m* 1990, Tracy Coburn; three *s* one *d*. *Educ:* Allerton High Sch.; Sheffield Univ. (BA Hons Law). Called to the Bar, Inner Temple, 1988; in practice as a barrister, specialising in family and criminal law, 1988–. *Recreations:* Leeds United, golf, reading. *Address:* St Pauls Chambers, Park Row House, 19–20 Park Row LS1 5JF.

**BICKLEY, Susan Rochford;** mezzo soprano, since 1982; *b* Liverpool, 27 May 1955; *d* of Alan Rochford Bickley and Mabel Bickley (*née* Owens); *m* 1984, Anthony Castro; two *s*. *Educ:* Quarry Bank Comp. Sch., Liverpool; City Univ., London (BSc Hons Music 1980); Guildhall Sch. of Music (Cert. Postgrad. Studies 1981, Gold Medal 1981). Mem. (Alto 1), Swingle Singers, 1982–84. Operatic roles include: Kostelnicka in Jenufa, Glyndebourne, WNO, New Israeli Opera, Opera North; Kabanicha in Katya Kabanova, Glyndebourne, ENO, Paris Opera, ROH; Cassandra in Les Troyens, ENO; Dorabella in Così fan tutte, ENO; Marcellina in Figaro, Glyndebourne, ENO, WNO; Donna Elvira in Don Giovanni, Glyndebourne Touring Opera; Dido in Dido and Aeneas, ENO, Opera North; Mrs Sedley in Peter Grimes, Glyndebourne; Florence Pike in Albert Herring, Glyndebourne; Mrs Grose in Turn of the Screw, Glyndebourne; Baba the Turk in Rake's Progress, Glyndebourne, Garsington; Fyodor in Boris Godunov, ROH; Aksinya in Lady Macbeth of Mtsensk, ROH; Babulenka in The Gambler, ROH; Mistress Quickly in Falstaff, Opera North; Meg Page in Falstaff, ENO; Irene in Theodora, Glyndebourne; Storge in Jeptha, WNO, ENO; Juno in Semele, ENO, Scottish Opera; Andromache in King Priam, ENO; Nan in New Year, Glyndebourne; Jezibaba in Rusalka, Opera North; Herodias in Salome, San Francisco Opera; Brangane in Tristan und Isolde, WNO; Ghost in The Last Supper, Berlin Stadtsoper Unter den Linden, Glyndebourne; Mescalina in Grand Macabre, ENO; Countess Geschwitz in Lulu, de Vlaamse Oper; Die Kurfürstin in Prinz vom Homburg, de Vlaamse Oper; Sarah in Roberto Devereux, Buxton Opera; Romeo in i Capuleti e i Montechi, Grange Opera; Waltraute in Götterdämmerung, Halle Orch., Opera North; Josefa Miranda in Of Love and Other Demons, Opera National du Rhin; Louise Michel in Al Gran Sole Carico d'Amore, Salzburg Fest. and Berlin Staatsoper; Fricka in Die Walküre, Halle Orch., Opera North; Fricka in Rheingold, Hallé Orch.; La Nourrice in Ariane et Barbe Bleu, Frankfurt Oper; Tzippy/Mama in Where the Wild Things Are, Aldeburgh Fest. and with LA Phil.; La Messagiera in Orfeo, Royal Opera Hse; Mother in Between Worlds, ENO; Matron in The Nose, ROH; multiple roles, Julietta, ENO; Ortrud in Lohengrin, WNO; Witch in Hänsel und Gretel, Garsington Opera; Eduige in Rodelinda, ENO; Jocasta in Thebans, ENO; Herodias in Salome, Dallas Opera; Paulina in The Winter's Tale, ENO; Genevieve in Pelléas et Mélisande, Garsington; Carmen in The Skating Rink, Garsington Opera; created rôles: Virgie in Anna Nicole, ROH; Anne in Two Boys, ENO; concerts with all major British ensembles, orchs, etc; frequent broadcasts and recitals. Over 40 commercial recordings. RPS Singer's Award, 2010. *Recreations:* walking in Britain, reading, theatre, playing Snatch, planning Xmas parties. *Address:* c/o Intermusica, 9 Kingsway, WC2B 6XF. *T:* (020) 7608 9900, *Fax:* (020) 7490 3263. *E:* jmaynard@intermusica.co.uk.

**BICKMORE, Prof. Wendy Anne,** PhD; FRS 2017; FMedSci; FRSE; Director, MRC Human Genetics Unit, University of Edinburgh, since 2015; *b* Shoreham-by-Sea, 28 July 1961; *d* of Keith and Beryl Bickmore. *Educ:* Chichester High Sch. for Girls; Univ. of Oxford (BA Hons Biochem.); Univ. of Edinburgh (PhD). Fellow, Lister Inst. of Preventive Medicine, 1991–96; Hd, Chromosomes and Gene Expression Section, MRC Human Genetics Unit, 2009–15. Pres., Genetics Soc., 2015–17. FMedSci 2005; FRSE 2005. Mem., Scottish Malt Whisky Soc. *Recreations:* gardening, walking the dog, painting - botanical illustration and watercolour landscape painting, tree-planting. *Address:* MRC Human Genetics Unit, Institute of Genetics and Molecular Medicine, Crewe Road, Edinburgh EH4 2XU. *T:* (0131) 651 8500, *Fax:* (0131) 651 8800. *E:* Wendy.Bickmore@igmm.ed.ac.uk.

**BIDDELL, Christopher William, (Bill);** Vice Lord-Lieutenant of Surrey, since 2016; *b* Wroxall, IoW, 27 April 1960; *s* of Christopher Biddell and Barbara Biddell; *m* 1985, Bridget Thornton; two *d*. *Educ:* Christ's Hospital; Magdalene Coll., Cambridge (BA 1982). MRICS 1985. Chartered surveyor and estate manager, Hampton Estate, 1987–. Non-executive Director: Wealden Hops, 2014–; Stern Farms Ltd, 2014–. President: Disability Initiative, Camberley, 2004–; Guildford Working Gundog Soc., 2010–. Gov., Christ's Hospital, 2005–. Trustee, Surrey Agricl Soc., 2010– (Chm., 2016–18). High Sheriff 2001, DL 2002, Surrey. *Recreations:* fishing, golf, Scotland, cooking. *Address:* Hampton Lodge, Seale, Farnham GU10 1JE. *T:* (01483) 810465. *Club:* Hawks' (Cambridge).

**BIDDER, Neil;** QC 1998; **His Honour Judge Bidder;** a Circuit Judge, since 2004; a Deputy High Court Judge, since 2007; *b* 22 July 1953; *s* of Glyn Turner Bidder and Constance Mabel Bidder; *m* 1978, Madeleine Thomas; two *s*. *Educ:* Ogmore Grammar Sch.; Queens' Coll., Cambridge (BA 1974; MA 1977); Dalhousie Univ., Canada (LLM 1977). Called to the Bar, Lincoln's Inn, 1976, Additional Bencher, 2008; in practice at the Bar, 1976–; an Asst Recorder, 1991–94; a Recorder, 1994–2004; Hd of Chambers, 2001–04. Judicial Mem., Parole Bd, 2007–12. Hon. Sec., Council of HM's Circuit Judges, 2012–15 (Pres., 2017). Founder Chm., Welsh Personal Injury Lawyers Assoc., 1999–2002. *Recreations:* choral singing, opera, gardening, sport. *Address:* Cardiff Crown Court, Cathays Park, Cardiff CF10 3PG.

**BIDDLE, Prof. Martin,** CBE 2014 (OBE 1997); FBA 1985; FSA; Professor of Medieval Archaeology, University of Oxford, 1997–2002, now Emeritus; Astor Senior Research Fellow in Medieval Archaeology, Hertford College, Oxford, 1989–2002, now Emeritus; Director, Winchester Research Unit, since 1968; *b* 4 June 1937; *s* of Reginald Samuel Biddle and Gwladys Florence Biddle (*née* Baker); *m* 1st, 1961, Hannelore Becker (marr. diss. 1966); two *d*; 2nd, 1966, Birthe (*d* 2010), *d* of Landsretssagfører Axel Th. and Anni Kjølbye of Sønderborg, Denmark; two *d*. *Educ:* Merchant Taylors' Sch., Northwood; Pembroke Coll., Cambridge (MA 1965; Hon. Fellow 2006); MA Oxon 1967; MA Pennsylvania 1977. FSA 1964. Second Lieut, 4 RTR, 1956; 1 Ind. Sqn, RTR, Berlin, 1956–57. Asst Inspector of Ancient Monuments, MPBW, 1961–63; Lectr in Medieval Archaeology, Univ. of Exeter, 1963–67; Vis. Fellow, All Souls Coll., Oxford, 1967–68; Dir, University Museum, and Prof. of Anthropology and of History of Art, Univ. of Pennsylvania, 1977–81; Lectr of The House, Christ Church, Oxford, 1983–86. Directed excavations and investigations: Nonsuch Palace, 1959–60; Winchester, 1961–71; (with Birthe Kjølbye-Biddle): Repton, 1974–88, 1993; St Alban's Abbey, 1978, 1982–84, 1991, 1994–95, 2003, 2006; Holy Sepulchre, Jerusalem, 1989–90, 1992, 1993, 1998, 2017; Qasr Ibrim, Egypt, 1990, 1992, 1995, 2000. Archaeological Consultant: Canterbury Cathedral, 1987–2016; St Albans Abbey and Cathedral Church; Eurotunnel, etc. Mem., Faculty Adv. Cttee, Winchester Cathedral, 2011– (Chm., 2013–). Chm., Rescue, Trust for British Archaeology, 1971–75. Mem., Royal Commn on Historical Monuments of England, 1984–95. Chm., Historic Towns Atlas Cttee, 1994–2013; Pres., Soc. for Medieval Archaeology, 1995–98; Vice-Pres., Soc. of Antiquaries, 2006–09. Hon. Mem., British Numismatic Soc., 2008. Hon. Freeman, Winchester, 2010. General Editor, Winchester Studies, 1976–. Hon. DLitt Southampton, 2003. (With Birthe Biddle) Frend Medal, Soc. of Antiquaries, 1986. *Publications:* (with C. Heighway) The Future of London's Past, 1973; (with F. Barlow and others) Winchester in the Early Middle Ages, 1976; (with H. M. Colvin, J. Summerson and others) The History of the King's Works, vol. iv, pt 2, 1982; Object and Economy in Medieval Winchester, 1990; The Tomb of Christ, 1999 (German edn, 1998; Italian edn, 2002); King Arthur's Round Table, 2000; (jtly) Henry VIII's Coastal Artillery Fort at Camber Castle, Rye, Sussex, 2001; Nonsuch Palace: the material culture of a noble restoration household, 2005; (ed) The Winchester Mint, 2012; The Search for Winchester's Anglo-Saxon Minsters, 2018; papers on archaeological, historical and art-historical subjects in learned jls. *Recreations:* travel, esp. Hellenic and Indian travel, reading. *Address:* 19 Hamilton Road, Oxford OX2 7PY. *T:* (01865) 559017, 07880 716915.

**BIDDLECOMBE, Henrietta Catherine;** see Knight, H. C.

**BIDDLESTONE, Prof. Anthony Joseph, (Joe),** PhD; CEng; FIChemE; Professor of Chemical Engineering, 1993–2004, now Professor Emeritus, and University Foundation Fellow, since 2005, University of Birmingham; *b* 8 Aug. 1937; *s* of William Albert and Ivy Evelyn Biddlestone; *m* 1973, Marion Summers; two *s*. *Educ:* George Dixon Grammar Sch., Birmingham; Univ. of Birmingham (BSc 1958; PhD 1961). CEng 1964; FIChemE 1973. University of Birmingham: Lectr, 1965–85; Sen Lectr, 1985–93; Hd, Sch. of Chem. Engrg, 1993–98; Dean of Engrg, 1998–2002. Chm., Accreditation Bd, IChemE, 1992–99. FRSA 1999. *Publications:* numerous contribs to refereed learned jls on aerobic biodegradation of organic wastes. *Recreations:* church music, organist, conductor. *Address:* School of Chemical Engineering, University of Birmingham, Edgbaston, Birmingham B15 2TT. *T:* (0121) 414 5290.

**BIDDULPH,** family name of **Baron Biddulph**.

**BIDDULPH,** 5th Baron *cr* 1903; **Anthony Nicholas Colin Maitland Biddulph;** interior designer; sporting manager; *b* 8 April 1959; *s* of 4th Baron Biddulph and of Lady Mary, *d* of Viscount Maitland (killed in action, 1943) and *gd* of 15th Earl of Lauderdale; *S* father, 1988; *m* 1993, Hon. Sian Diana (marr. diss. 2001), *y d* of Baron Gibson-Watt, MC; two *s*. *Educ:* Cheltenham; RAC, Cirencester. Liveryman, Armourers' and Brasiers' Co., 1995. *Recreations:* shooting, fishing, painting. *Heir: s* Hon. Robert Julian Maitland Biddulph, *b* 8 July 1994. *Address:* 8 Orbel Street, SW11 3NZ; Makerstoun House, Kelso TD5 7PA. *Clubs:* Cavalry and Guards, White's.

**BIDDULPH, Sir Ian D'Olier, (Jack),** 11th Bt *cr* 1664, of Westcombe, Kent; *b* 28 Feb. 1940; *s* of Sir Stuart Royden Biddulph, 10th Bt and Muriel Margaret (*d* 1995), *d* of Angus Harkness, Hamley Bridge, S Australia; *S* father, 1986; *m* 1967, Margaret Eleanor, *o d* of late John Gablonski, Oxley, Brisbane; one *s* two *d*. *Heir: s* Paul William Biddulph [*b* 30 Oct. 1967; *m* 2000, Susan, *d* of late James Adkins; two *d*]. *Address:* 17 Kendall Street, Oxley, Qld 4075, Australia.

**BIDE, Rev. Mary Elizabeth;** Priest Vicar, Wells Cathedral, since 2018; a Chaplain to the Queen, since 2013; *b* Oxford, 10 Feb. 1953; *d* of Norman Ellis and Phyllis Ellis; *m* 1975, Mark Bide; one *s* two *d*. *Educ:* Oxford High Sch. for Girls (GPDST); St Anne's Coll., Oxford (BA 1st Cl. Hons Botany 1974). Teacher of Biol., St Paul's Girls' Sch., 1974–75; Ed., W. B. Saunders, 1976–78; Teacher of Sci., St Bede's, 1978–82; Teacher of Maths, St Catherine's Sch., Bramley, 1989–95; ordained deacon, 1994, priest, 1995; Asst Curate, St Nicholas, St Bookham, 1994–98; Vicar, Frimley Green, 1998–2003; Precentor, Christ Church Cath., Oxford, 2003–07; Team Rector, Parish of Wimbledon, 2007–16. Chair, Oxford Diocesan Liturgical Cttee, 2006–07; Member: Guildford Diocesan Adv. Cttee, 2001–03; Guildford Diocesan Synod, 2002–03; Gen. Synod of C of E, 2005–07; Diocesan Bd of Finance, 2009–12; Bishoprics and Cathedrals Cttee, 2010–. Tutor, Guildford Diocesan Ministry Course, 1996–2003. *Recreations:* walking, singing, wildlife, theatre, music. *Address:* Roselands, Weston Lane, Christon, Axbridge, Som BS26 2XT. *T:* (01934) 827705. *E:* mary.bide@gmail.com.

**BIDEN, Joseph Robinette,** Jr; JD; Vice-President of the United States of America, 2009–16; Benjamin Franklin Presidential Practice Professor, Penn Biden Center for Diplomacy and Global Engagement, University of Pennsylvania, since 2017; Chairman, Biden Institute, School of Public Policy and Administration, University of Delaware, since 2017; *b* Scranton, Penn, 20 Nov. 1942; *s* of late Joseph Robinette Biden and Jean Biden; *m* 1st, 1966, Neilia Hunter (*d* 1972); one *s* (and one *s* one *d* decd); 2nd, 1977, Jill Jacobs; one *d*. *Educ:* Univ. of Delaware (AB 1965); Syracuse Univ. Coll. of Law, NY (JD 1968). Admitted to Delaware Bar, 1968; Trial Attorney, Public Defender's Office, Delaware, 1968; Founding Partner, Biden & Walsh, law firm, Wilmington, 1968–72. Mem. (Democrat), New Castle CC, 1970–72; US Senator (Democrat) from Delaware, 1973–2009. US Senate: Member: Judiciary Cttee, 1981–87 and 1995–97 (Chm., 1987–95); Foreign Relns Cttee, 1997–2009 (Chm., 2001–03 and 2007–09); Chm., Caucus on Internat. Narcotics Control, 2007–09; Co-Chm., NATO Observer Gp. Adjunct Prof., Widener Univ. Sch. of Law, 1991– (on leave of absence). Presidential Medal of Freedom (USA), 2017. *Publications:* Promises to Keep: on life and politics (autobiog.), 2007; Promise Me, Dad: a year of hope, hardship and purpose, 2017.

**BIDWELL, James Richard Philip;** Chairman and Chief Executive Officer, Springwise Intelligence Ltd, since 2015; Co-Founder, Re_Set Advisory, 2017; Partner, CapitalD, since 2017; *b* 19 Jan. 1965; *s* of Sir Hugh Charles Philip Bidwell, GBE; *m* 1995, Rebecca Mathiesen (marr. diss. 2014); three *d*. *Educ:* Eton Coll.; Univ. of Bristol (BA Hons French). Account Mgr, Lowe Howard-Spink Advertising, 1987–92; Marketing Mgr, Walt Disney Attractions, 1992–97; Head of Marketing, Segaworld, 1997–98; Marketing Dir, Carland LP, 1998–99; Marketing Director: eToys Inc., 1999–2001; Selfridges plc, 2001–05; Chief Executive Officer: Visit London, 2005–08; London Unlimited, 2005–08; Man. Dir, Anthropologie, Europe, 2009–11; Man. Dir, subseq. CEO, Cass Art, 2012–13 (non-exec. Dir, 2011–12, 2013–14); non-exec. Chm., 2013, CEO, 2013–14, Easyart Hldgs Ltd. Non-executive Director: Natural Mat Co., 2007–; Goodwood Estate, 2011–12; Invincible Brands, 2018–. Trustee, Cass Sculpture Foundation 2008–13. Liveryman, Co. of Grocers, 1999–. *Publications:* Disrupt!: 100 lessons in business innovation, 2017. *Recreations:* mountain biking, fly fishing, ski-ing, tennis, sea kayaking. *E:* bidwelljames1@gmail.com. *Clubs:* Ivy; Frensham Flyfishers; Steep Lawn Tennis.

**BIDWELL, Robin O'Neill,** CBE 1999; PhD; Chairman, LOC Holdings Ltd, since 2014; *b* 15 Sept. 1944; *s* of late Philip John Bidwell and Ellen O'Neill Bidwell; *m* 1st, 1970, Caroline Margaret Budd (marr. diss. 1993); one *s* one *d*; 2nd, 1995, Veronica Rosemary Lucia Verey. *Educ:* Charterhouse; Christ Church, Oxford (BA 1966; MA 1970); Bradford Mgt Centre (PhD 1974). Founder ERL, now ERM, 1973: Dir, 1974–2011; Man. Dir, 1977–93; Chm., ERM Internat., 1993–2001; Exec. Chm., 2001–08; Gp Pres., 2008–11. Non-executive Director: CU Envmtl Trust plc, 1992–2002; ICE Organisation Ltd, 2010–14; Tiny Totos, Kenya, 2019–; Conservation Alpha, 2019–; Chm., Investment Cttee, Insitor Impact Fund, 2014–. Authy Mem., Ofgem, 2003–10. Advr, Prince of Wales Business Leaders Forum, 1993–2007; Trustee, Heritage Trust, 1987–96; Chm., Adv. Cttee, ZSL Field Conservation, 2009–12. Member: Task Force on envmtl implications of 1992,

EC, 1989–90; Bd, Sustainability Challenge Foundn, Netherlands, 1993–2003; NERC, 1996–2002; Adv. Cttee on Business and the Envmt, 1999–2003; Member Council: World Business Council for Sustainable Develt, 1997–2012; UK Roundtable on Sustainable Develt, 1998–2000; Chairman: Low Carbon Enterprise Fund, 2008–18; Ofgem Low Carbon Network Fund Expert Panel, 2011–16; World Conservation Monitoring Centre, 2016–. Chm., Green Alliance, 2008–14 (Trustee, 1991–2016). Chm., Woodchester Trust, 2012–. *Recreations:* conservation, ski-ing, reading, theatre, gardening. *Address:* Woodchester Park House, Nympsfield, Glos GL10 3UN.

**BIELBY, Catherine Mary;** *see* Markus, C. M.

**BIENZ, Dr Mariann, (Lady Pelham),** FRS 2003; FMedSci; Senior Group Leader, since 1991, and Deputy Director, since 2018, MRC Laboratory of Molecular Biology (Divisional Head of Cell Biology, 2007–08; Divisional Head of Protein and Nucleic Chemistry, 2008–18); *b* 21 Dec. 1953; *d* of Jürg Bienz and Lilly Bienz (*née* Gubler); *m* 1996, Hugh Reginald Brentnall Pelham (*see* Sir Hugh Pelham); one *s* one *d*. *Educ:* Gymnasium Winterthur; Univ. of Zürich (Dip. Zool. and Molecular Biol.; PhD 1981). Postdoctoral res. at MRC Lab. of Molecular Biol., Cambridge; Asst Prof., 1986–90, Associate Prof., 1990–91, Univ. of Zürich. Mem., EMBO, 1989. FMedSci 2006. Friedrich Miescher Prize, Swiss Biochemical Soc., 1990. *Publications:* contribs on cell and molecular biol. to various internat. jls. *Recreations:* classical music, singing, mountain walking. *Address:* MRC Laboratory of Molecular Biology, Francis Crick Avenue, Cambridge CB2 0QH.

**BIERMAN, James;** Producer, Empire Street Productions, since 2016; *b* London, 1971; *m* 2014, Kate Mitchell; one *s* two *d*. Actor; Gen. Manager, Aldwych Th., 2002–06; Gen. Manager, 2006–08, Exec. Producer, 2008–11, Donmar Warehouse; Producer, Michael Grandage Co., 2011–16. *Recreations:* theatre, film, family, Liverpool FC. *Address:* Empire Street Productions, Fourth Floor, 37 Berwick Street, W1F 8RS.

**BIGG, Prof. Martin Geoffrey,** PhD; Professor of Environmental Technology Innovation, University of the West of England, since 2011 (Director, Environmental Innovation Network, 2011–16); *b* Beckenham, 29 Sept. 1955; *s* of Harold Thomas Bigg and Eileen Grace Bigg; *m* 1978, Eileen Frances Winter; one *s* two *d*. *Educ:* Trinity Sch. of John Whitgift, Croydon; Univ. of Bristol (BSc 1977); Univ. of Salford (PhD 1980); Univ. of Manchester (MSc 2003). CSc 2004; CChem 2004; FRSC 2004; FIEMA 2005; CEnv 2006. Prodn Chemist, May and Baker Ltd, 1980–85; Plant Manager, Fine Organics Ltd, 1985–87; Principal Pollution Inspector, HM Inspectorate of Pollution, 1987–88; Hd, Local Authy Unit, DoE, 1988–90; Hd, Integrated Envmtl Mgt, HM Inspectorate of Pollution, 1990–96; Environment Agency: Nat. Regulatory Policy Manager, 1996–99; Head: Industry Regulation, 1999–2008; Industry and Waste, 2008–11. Proj. Lead, World Bank and EU, Jordan, Tajikistan, Mongolia, Russia and China, 2008–. Chair: Bristol Green Capital Partnership, 2011–14 (Mem. Bd and Chm., Evaluation Gp, 2014–16); Strategic Adv. Council, IEMA, 2013– (Mem. Bd, 2013–). CEnv of the Year, Soc. for Envmt, 2015. *Publications:* (contrib.) Environmental Management in Organisations: the IEMA handbook, 2nd edn 2011; (contrib.) Pollution: causes, effects and control, 5th edn 2014; (contrib.) Developments in Environmental Regulation, 2017. *Recreations:* walking, travel, theatre, family, building European and global collaboration, saving the planet. *Address:* University of the West of England, Coldharbour Lane, Bristol BS16 1QY; 12 Folly Close, Radlett WD7 8DR. *T:* 07825 365591. *E:* martingbigg@gmail.com.

**BIGG, Sally Jane Janet;** *see* Gunnell, S. J. J.

**BIGGAM, Sir Robin (Adair),** Kt 1993; Chairman, Independent Television Commission, 1997–2003; *b* 8 July 1938; *s* of Thomas and Eileen Biggam; *m* 1962, Elizabeth McArthur McDougall; one *s* two *d*. *Educ:* Lanark Grammar Sch. Chartered accountant. Peat Marwick Mitchell, 1960–63; ICI, 1964–81; Director: ICL, 1981–84; Dunlop Holdings plc, 1984–85; Man. Dir, 1986–87, Chief Exec., 1987–91, Chm., 1992–96, BICC plc; Chm., Spectris (formerly Fairey Gp), 1996–2001. Non Executive Director: Chloride Group plc, 1985–87; Lloyds Abbey Life plc (formerly Abbey Life Gp), 1985–90; Redland Gp plc, 1991–97; BAE Systems (formerly British Aerospace), plc, 1994–2003; Foreign & Colonial German Investment Trust plc, 1995–98; British Energy plc, 1996–2002. Pres., German-British Chamber of Commerce, 1995–97. Chancellor, Univ. of Bedfordshire (formerly Univ. of Luton), 2001–09. *Recreations:* golf, fishing.

**BIGGAR, Rev. Canon Prof. Nigel John,** PhD; Regius Professor of Moral and Pastoral Theology, since 2007 and Director, McDonald Centre for Theology, Ethics and Public Life, since 2008, University of Oxford; Canon of Christ Church, Oxford, since 2007; *b* 14 March 1955; *s* of Francis and Jeanne Biggar; *m* 1982, Virginia Dunn. *Educ:* Monkton Combe Sen. Sch., Bath; Worcester Coll., Oxford (BA Modern Hist. 1976; MA 1988); Regent Coll., Vancouver (Master of Christian Studies 1981); Univ. of Chicago (AM Religious Studies 1980; PhD Christian Theol. 1986). Librarian, Latimer Hse, Oxford, 1985–91; Lectr in Christian Ethics, Wycliffe Hall, Oxford, 1987–94; ordained deacon, 1990, priest, 1991; Fellow and Chaplain, Oriel Coll., Oxford, 1990–99; Prof. of Theol., Dept of Theol. and Religious Studies, Univ. of Leeds, 1999–2004; Prof. of Theol., Sch. of Religions and Theol., 2004–07, Fellow, 2005–07, TCD; Canon, Christ Ch Cathedral, Dublin, 2004–07. Lectr, Leeds Parish Ch, 1999–2003. Mem., Cttee on Ethical Issues in Medicine, RCP, 2000–14. Pres., Soc. for Study of Christian Ethics, 2003–06. *Publications:* (ed jtly) Cities of Gods: faith, politics and pluralism in Judaism, Christianity and Islam, 1986; (ed) Reckoning with Barth: essays in commemoration of the 100th anniversary of the birth of Karl Barth, 1988; Theological Politics: a critique of Faith in the City, the report of the Archbishop of Canterbury's Commission on Urban Priority Areas (1985), 1988; The Hastening that Waits: Karl Barth's Ethics, 1993, rev. edn 1995; Good Life: reflections on what we value today, 1997; (ed with Rufus Black) The Revival of Natural Law: philosophical, theological and ethical responses to the Finnis-Grisez School, 2000; (ed) Burying the Past: making peace and doing justice after civil conflict, 2001, rev. edn 2003; Aiming to Kill: the ethics of suicide and euthanasia, 2004; (ed with Linda Hogan) Religious Voices in Public Places, 2009; Behaving in Public: how to do Christian ethics, 2011; In Defence of War, 2013; Between Kin and Cosmopolis: an ethic of the nation, 2014. *Recreations:* reading history, walking battlefields, visiting historic cemeteries, playing cards. *Address:* Christ Church, Oxford OX1 1DP. *Club:* Athenæum.

**BIGGS, Dr John,** CChem, FRSC, Moderator, 1992–93, Chairman, 1993–97, Free Church Federal Council; *b* 3 Jan. 1933; *s* of Horace James Biggs and Elsie Alice Biggs, Leicester; *m* 1965, Brenda Muriel Hickleton. *Educ:* Wyggeston Grammar Sch. for Boys, Leicester; Downing Coll., Cambridge (Graystone Scholar). MA, PhD (Cantab). FRSC (FCS 1958); CChem 1979. DSIR Res. Fellow, Cambridge, 1958–60; Lectr in Chemistry, Univ. of Hull, 1960–87. President: Baptist Students' Fedn, 1955–56; Yorkshire Baptist Assoc., 1973–74; Vice-Pres., Baptist Men's Movement, 1995–97. Pres., 1997–98; Baptist Union of GB: Chm., Home Mission Working Gp, 1981–88; Mem. Council, 1978–2013, Chm., 1990–94; Pres., 1989–90; Mem., Scholarships and Ministerial Trng Bursary Cttee, 1978–2001 (Chm., 1995–2001). Examnr in Chem., Cambridge Assessment (formerly UCLES), 1958–2014 (Consultant and Prin. Examnr, 1983–2011). Governor, Northern Baptist Coll., Manchester, 1989–2000; Chm., Relocation Steering Cttee, Baptist Theol Seminary, Prague, 1994–96 (Mem. Bd of Trustees, Rüschlikon, Zürich, 1989–94, Vice-Chm., 1992–94). Member: Envmtl Issues Network, CTBI (formerly CCBI), 1990–2007 (Mem. Steering Cttee and Adv. Panel, Eco-Congregation Prog., 1999–2004); Envmt Gp, Churches Together in Cumbria, 1997–2012; Chm., Sustainable Communities (Cumbria), 2004–08. Dir and Chm., Ambleside Parish Centre, 2012– (Mem., 2005–, Vice Chm., 2009–12, Chm., 2012–, Mgt Cttee); Trustee, Ambleside with Brathay Trust, 2008–. Chm., Cumbria Br., Cambridge Soc., 2011–16. Local Preacher, South Lakes Circuit, Methodist Church, 2001–. *Recreations:* fell-walking, opera, photography. *Address:* Fellcroft, Easedale Road, Grasmere, Ambleside, Cumbria LA22 9QR.

**BIGGS, John Robert;** Executive Mayor of Tower Hamlets, since 2015; *b* 19 Nov. 1957; *s* of late Robert Edmund Biggs and Mary Jeanette Biggs (*née* Phillips); *m* 1993, Christine Sibley (marr. diss. 2015); one *d*. *Educ:* Queen Elizabeth's Boys' Sch., Barnet; Bristol Univ. (BSc Hons Chem. 1979); Birkbeck Coll., London Univ. (Postgrad. Dip. Computer Sci. 1984); Westminster Univ. (Postgrad. Dip. Law 1996, Legal Practice Course 1998). Operating theatre orderly, 1979–80; lab. technician, 1980–83; systems analyst, 1984–91; self-employed computer consultant, 1991–92. Mem. (Lab), Tower Hamlets BC, 1988–2002 (Leader of Opposition, 1991–94; Leader, 1994–95). Mem. (Lab) City and East, London Assembly, GLA, 2000–16. Vice Chm., London Develt Agency, 2004–08; Dep. Chm., London Thames Gateway Develt Corp., 2004–08; Member: London Health Commn, 2008–11; Metropolitan Police Authy, 2000–03, 2009–12; London Legacy Develt Corp., 2015–18. Chair, Gtr London Provincial Council, 2018–; Dep. Chair, Gtr London Employment Forum, 2018–. Non-exec. Dir, Tower Hamlets HAT, 1996–2004 (Vice-Chm., 1999–2004); Dir, Socialist Health Assoc., 1997–2000. Gov., Birkbeck, Univ. of London, 2009–16. Hon. Fellow: QMUL, 2009; Birkbeck, Univ. of London, 2017. *Recreations:* reading, walking. *T:* 07974 918322.

**BIGGS, John Sydney Grainge,** MD; FRCOG, FRANZCOG; Postgraduate Medical Dean, University of Cambridge, and Eastern Region, NHS Executive, 1991–2001; Consultant Emeritus, Canberra Hospital, 2014; *b* 16 Dec. 1935; *s* of Charles V. G. Biggs and Leah M. Biggs (*née* Price); *m* 1960, T. Glyndon Daley; three *s* two *d*. *Educ:* Carey Grammar Sch., Melbourne; Univ. of Melbourne (MB BS 1960); MD Aberdeen 1973; MA Cantab 1994. MRCOG 1966, FRCOG 1980; FRANZCOG 1979; DHMSA 1993. House Officer, Royal Melbourne Hosp., 1961; RMO, Royal Children's Hosp., Melbourne, 1962; RMO and Registrar, Royal Women's Hosp., Melbourne, 1963–64; Lecturer in Obstetrics and Gynaecology: Univ. of Qld, 1965; Univ. of Aberdeen, 1966–69; University of Queensland: Sen. Lectr, 1969–72; Reader, 1973–82; Dean of Medicine and Prof., 1983–91. Vis. Fellow, ANU, 2010–. Adjunct Prof. of Medical Educn, Univ. of Health Scis, Lahore, Pakistan, 2008–. Chairman: Bd, Coast City Country Trng, 2006–10; ACT Health Human Res. Ethics Cttee, 2010–14. Conducted evaluation of postgrad. med. trng for Higher Educn Commn, Pakistan, 2006–07 and survey of performance in hospitals, Lahore for Govt of Punjab, Pakistan, 2008. Hon. Prof., UEA, 1997–2001. Pres., ASME, 1999–2002 (Chm., 1996–99). *Publications:* contrib. to learned jls on ovarian structure and function, 1996–82, and medical educn, 1983–2013. *Recreations:* gardening, walking, reading. *Address:* 21 Conyers Street, Hughes, ACT 2605, Australia. *T:* (2) 61616643. *Club:* Royal Society of Medicine.

**BIGGS, Lewis,** OBE 2011; curator, writer and cultural consultant; Director/Chief Executive, Liverpool Biennial of Contemporary Art, 2000–11 (Trustee and non-executive Director, 1998–2000); *b* 22 April 1952; *s* of Lewis Ian Biggs and Penelope Torre Biggs (*née* Torr); *m* 1983, Ann Margaret Compton (marr. diss. 2002); one *s* one *d*; *m* 2011, Lisa Katharine Milroy, *qv*. *Educ:* New Coll., Oxford (MA Mod. Hist. 1974); Courtauld Inst., Univ. of London (MA Hist. of Art 1979). Gallery Co-ordinator, Arnolfini Gall., Bristol, 1979–84; Exhibns Officer, British Council, 1984–87; Curator of Exhibns, Tate Gall., Liverpool, 1987–90; Curator, then Dir, Tate Gall., Liverpool, 1990–2000. Director: Oriel Mostyn Gall., Llandudno, 1991–98; Art Transpennine Ltd, 1996–2002; Culture Campus Ltd, 2006–11; Another Place Ltd, 2006–. Member: Visual Arts Adv. Cttee, British Council, 1991–2007; Visual Arts Panel, Arts Council of England, 1996–99; NW Arts Bd, 1997–2002; Liverpool Cath. Fabric Adv. Cttee, 1995–98; Liverpool Urban Design and Conservation Panel, 2003–09; Cass Sculpture Foundn, Goodwood, 2010–11; Internat. Council, Rockbund Art Mus., Shanghai, 2011–13. Trustee: Liverpool Architecture and Design Trust, 1997–99; John Moores Liverpool Exhibn Trust, 2011–; Foundn for Art and Creative Technol., 2011–14; Centre for Chinese Contemporary Art (formerly Chinese Arts Centre), Manchester, 2011–15; Situations, Bristol, 2011–13. Dir and Chm., Inst. for Public Art, 2013–. Dir, Internat. Award for Art Criticism Ltd, 2014–. Vis. Prof. of Contemporary Art, Liverpool Art Sch., Liverpool John Moores Univ., 2001–04 and 2011– (Hon. Fellow, 1998); Hon. Prof., Glasgow Sch. of Art, 2011–14; Advr, 2011–15, Prof. of Public Arts, 2015–19, Coll. of Arts, Shanghai Univ. Curator: Aichi Triennale Nagoya, 2013; Folkestone Triennial, 2014, 2017, 2020; Land Art Mongolia Biennial, 2018; Public Art, Kaunas European Capital of Culture 2022, 2017–. Associate Fellow, Univ. of Liverpool, 1992. FRSA. Gen. series Ed., Tate Modern Artists, 2001–14. Hon. MA Univ. for Creative Arts, 2014.

**BIGGS, Matthew John;** gardener, writer and broadcaster; *b* Leicester, 2 June 1960; *s* of Ivan and Marion Biggs; *m* 1991, Gillian Mastemaker; one *s* two *d*. *Educ:* City of Leicester Boys' Grammar Sch.; Charles Keene Coll. of Further Educn (ONC Public Admin 1978); Pershore Coll. of Horticulture (Nat. Cert. Horticulture Nursery and Ornamental 1979); Royal Botanic Gdns, Kew (Dip. Hort. 1986). Educnl guide, 1986–89, garden design and maintenance, 1991–95, Royal Botanic Gdns, Kew; researcher and presenter, Garden Club, Channel 4, 1991–96; expert tour leader, Gardening Cruises and land based tours, 1994–; guest expert, Gardening Phone-In, LBC Radio, 1994–2008; Dir, Grass Roots, Meridian TV, 1997–2002; Panel Mem., Gardeners' Question Time, BBC Radio 4, 2003–; Course Dir, Plants and Plantsmanship, English Gardening Sch., 2009–12. Mem., Woody Plant Cttee, 2015–, Floral Judge, 2016–, RHS. Mem., Plant Conservation Cttee, Plant Heritage, 2015–. Trustee, Perennial, 2016–17. Ambassador, Hardy Plant Soc., 2017–. Feature gardens at Hampton Court Flower Show, 2009, BBC Gardeners' World Live, 2011; conceptual artist, Hampton Court Flower Show, 2014. Journalist: RHS The Garden mag., 1993–; BBC Gardeners' World mag., 1994–. One Man Two Plant Hunters (one man show), 2017–. *Publications:* (contrib.) RHS Dictionary of Gardening, 1990; Practical Guide to Healthy Houseplants, 1996; Matthew Biggs' Complete Book of Vegetables, 1997; (with R. Lancaster) What Houseplant, Where, 1998; (contrib.) Gardeners' Question Time: plant chooser, 2003; (contrib.) Gardeners' Question Time: Gardening Techniques, 2005; Gardening at Eden and how to do it at home, 2006; Allotment Days, 2007; Lessons from Great Gardeners, 2015; (with Thane Prince) RHS Great British Village Show, 2017; (jtly) The Plant Messiah, 2017; Grow Something Different to Eat, 2018; Secrets of Great Botanists, 2018; RHS A Nation in Bloom: celebrating the people, plants and places of the Royal Horticultural Society, 2019. *Recreations:* supporting anything associated with Leicestershire, making cider, church visiting. *Address:* 40 Singlets Lane, Flamstead, St Albans, Herts AL3 8EP. *T:* (01582) 849020. *E:* matthew@biggs-btconnect.com.

**BIGGS, Michael Nicholas;** Chairman: Direct Line Insurance Group plc, since 2012; Close Brothers Group plc, since 2017; *b* 14 Aug. 1952; *s* of Eric Peter and Hilda May Biggs; two *s*. *Educ:* Alleyne's Grammar Sch.; Worcester Coll., Oxford (MA 1974). ACA 1979. Arthur Andersen & Co., 1976–84; HSBC, 1984–87; Gp Financial Controller, Morgan Grenfell &

Co., 1987–91; Norwich Union: Gp Financial Controller, 1991–95; Gen. Manager Internat., 1995–97; Gp Finance Dir, 1997–2000; CGNU, later Aviva: Gp Exec. Dir, 2000–01; Gp Finance Dir, 2001–03; Resolution plc: Gp Finance Dir, 2005–07; Gp Chief Exec., 2007–08; Chm., 2008–13. *Recreations:* gardening, history, antiques. *Club:* Royal Automobile.

BIGGS, Prof. Peter Martin, CBE 1987; PhD, DSc; FRS 1976; Director of Animal Health (formerly Animal Disease Research), Agricultural and Food Research Council, 1986–88, retired; Visiting Professor of Veterinary Microbiology, Royal Veterinary College, University of London, 1982–2008, now Honorary Professor; *b* 13 Aug. 1926; *s* of Ronald Biggs and Cécile Biggs (*née* Player); *m* 1950, Alison Janet Molteno; two *s* one *d*. *Educ:* Bedales Sch.; Cambridge Sch., USA; Queen's Univ., Belfast; Royal Veterinary Coll., Univ. of London (BSc 1953, DSc 1975); Univ. of Bristol (PhD 1958). FRCVS, FRCPath, FRSB, CBiol. Served RAF, 1944–48; Research Asst, Univ. of Bristol, 1953–55, Lectr, 1955–59; Houghton Poultry Research Station: Head of Leukosis Experimental Unit, 1959–74; Dep. Dir, 1971–74; Dir, 1974–86. Andrew D. White Prof.-at-Large, Cornell Univ., 1988–94. Sir William Dick Meml Lectr, Univ. of Edinburgh, 1974 and 1987; E. H. W. Wilmott Guest Lectr, Univ. of Bristol, 1977; Leeuwenhoek Prize Lectr, Royal Soc., 1997. Member: Veterinary Products Cttee, 1973–98; Management Bd, AFRC, 1986–88. President: BVPA, 1974–75; World Vet. Poultry Assoc., 1981–85 (Hon. Life Pres., 1985); Internat. Assoc. for Comparative Res. on Leukemia and Related Diseases, 1981–83; Inst. of Biol., 1990–92; Vice Pres., BVA, 1996–98. Founder FMedSci 1998. Hon. FRASE 1986. Hon. DVM Ludwig-Maximilians Univ., 1976; Dr *hc* Liège, 1991. Tom Newman Meml Award, 1964; Poultry Science Award, British Oil and Cake Mills, 1968; J. T. Edwards Meml Medal, 1969; Dalrymple-Champneys Cup and Medal, 1973; Bledisloe Veterinary Award, 1977; Wooldridge Meml Medal and Lecture, 1978; Joszef Marek Meml Medal, Vet. Univ. of Budapest, 1979; Victory Medal, Central Vet. Soc., 1980; Gordon Meml Medal and Lecture, Robert Fraser Gordon Meml Trust, 1989; Wolf Foundn Prize in Agric., 1989; Chiron Award, BVA, 1999; Poultry Industry Special Merit Award, British Poultry Council, 2011. *Publications:* scientific papers on viruses and infectious disease. *Recreations:* music making, natural history. *Address:* Willows, London Road, St Ives PE27 5ES. *T:* (01480) 463471. *Clubs:* Farmers, Athenæum.

BIGGS, Prof. Simon Richard, PhD; FREng, FTSE; Senior Deputy Vice-Chancellor, University of Western Australia, since 2018; *b* Butleigh, Som, 22 Jan. 1965; *s* of Alan Michael Biggs and Shirley Anne Biggs; *m* 1999, Sarah Jane Gardiner; two *d*. *Educ:* Crispin Comprehensive Sch.; Strode Coll.; Univ. of Bristol (BSc 1986; PhD 1990). FREng 2011; FTSE 2016. Research Fellow: CNRS, Strasbourg, 1990–92; Univ. of Melbourne, 1992–94; University of Newcastle, New South Wales: Lectr, 1994–97; Sen. Lectr, 1998–99; Associate Prof., 2000–02; Prof. of Particle Sci. and Engrg, Univ. of Leeds, 2002–14; Exec. Dean, Faculty of Engrg, Architecture and IT, Univ. of Queensland, 2014–18. CSO, Chamelic Ltd, 2006–14; Mem. Bd, Escubed Ltd, 2009–18. *Address:* Vice-Chancellery, University of Western Australia, 35 Stirling Highway, Crawley, WA 6009, Australia.

BIGHAM, family name of Viscount Mersey.

BIGLAND, Brenda, CBE 2006; education consultant, adviser, trainer and coach, 2011–17; *b* 6 June 1951; *d* of Edwin and Sylvia Francis; *m* 1972, Paul Bigland; one *s*. *Educ:* Calcot Primary Sch., Reading; St Joseph's Convent, Reading; St Osyth's Coll., Essex; British Dyslexia Inst. (Associate Mem.); Bulmershe Coll. (BEd Hons 1989); Reading Univ. (MA Instnl Mgt and Educnl Admin 1993). Teacher: Garland Primary Sch., Berks, 1972–74; Aldermaston Sch., Berks, 1974–75; Francis Bailey Sch., Berks, 1975; Dep. Hd, St John Bosco (Ind.) Sch., Reading, 1978–80; Hd, Prep. Sch., Presentation Coll. (Indep.), Reading, 1980–88; Dep. Hd, Marish Sch., Berks, 1988–92; Headteacher, Lent Rise School, Burnham and Nat. Leader of Educn, 1993–2011. Consultant/Adviser, DFE (formerly DES, then DFES, subseq. DCSF), 2002–; Nat. Coll. of Sch. Leadership, 2002–; Specialist Schs and Academies Trust, 2002–; Consultant, Implementation Rev. Gp (Educn), 2009– (Mem., 2006). Member: Bd, Trng and Develt Agency, 2002–09; Nat. Educn Leadership Gp for Business in the Community, 2002–; Task Force Gp on Employer Engagement in Educn, 2008–10. Ambassador for British Council promoting internat. collaboration across schs nationally and internationally. Judge, Teaching Awards Trust, 2004– (Fellow, 2006); Lifetime Fellow, ICT Register, Schools Network Trust, 2010. Trustee, Reading Football Community Trust, 2015–16. Consultant, Bentley Priory Battle of Britain Trust (Trustee, 2008–09). FBCS 2009. *Publications:* articles on educn subjects, incl. 21st Century learning, employer engagement in educn, internat. collaboration, community cohesion, leadership in educn, inspections and accountability in educn, etc. *Recreations:* travel, theatre, music, reading, spending time with family and friends incl. two grandsons Henry and Arthur, Rotarian. *E:* b.bigland@btinternet.com.

BIGLOU, Liliana, OBE 2003; Director, Ghana, British Council, 2013–17; *b* Jaworzno, Poland, 25 Feb. 1957; *d* of Józef Sztejnbis and Henryka Kowalska; *m* 1977, Conrad Biglou; two *d*. *Educ:* Sch. of Slavonic and E Eur. Studies, Univ. of London (BA Russian and Polish Studies; DipLib; MA Liby and Information Sci.). MCLIP 1991. British Council: Asst Dir, Malawi, 1992–95; Dep. Dir, Ghana, 1995–97; Director: Kazakhstan, 1997–2001; Ukraine, 2001–05; Romania, 2005–09; Kenya, 2009–10; Canada, 2010–13. Medal, Supreme Council of Ukraine, 2005. *Recreations:* gardening, travel, herbal medicine.

BIGNELL, (Francis) Geoffrey; Chairman, Just Employment Ltd, Solicitors, 2009–15 (Founder and Principal, 1999–2009); *b* 7 March 1949; *s* of Ernest Francis John Bignell and Olive Ethel Bignell (*née* Peatson); *m* 1978, Susan Rachel Harrison; two *s* one *d*. *Educ:* Isleworth Grammar Sch.; Trinity Hall, Cambridge (MA); Coll. of Law. Social work in Basildon and Worksop, 1971–74; articled to Notts CC, 1975–78; admitted Solicitor, 1977; Prosecuting Solicitor, Notts Police Authy, 1978–80; Asst and Sen. Asst Solicitor, Leics CC, 1980–83; Prin. Solicitor, Warwicks CC, 1983–87; Asst Sec.-Gen. (Management), Law Soc., 1987–95; Chief Executive: Law Soc. Services Ltd, 1995–97; Solicitors Property Centres Ltd, 1997–98. Non-executive Director: Cheviot Financial Services (formerly Cheviot Personal Pensions) Ltd, 1992–2005; Ambersham Holdings Ltd, 1998–2001; Lawyers Defence Union Ltd, 1999–2002; Peter Honey Publications Ltd, 2000–02. Member: Rail Passengers' (formerly Rail Users' Consultative) Cttee for Southern England, 1997–2005 (Vice-Chm., 2002–05); SW Trains Passenger Panel, 2002–17 (Chm., 2015–17); Chm., SW Railway Customer Council, 2017–. Trustee, Disability Initiative, 2015–. Gov., George Abbot Sch., 1995–2001 (Vice-Chm., 1998–2001); Mem., Corp. of Guildford Coll., 1997–2001 (Vice-Chm., 1998–2001). Chm., Guildford Catholic Parish Finance Cttee, 2018–. *Publications:* contribs to learned jls. *Recreations:* faith, family, friendship and fun. *Address:* Roseland, 13 Lower Edgeborough Road, Guildford, Surrey GU1 2DX.

BIGNELL, Janet Susan; QC 2015; a Recorder, since 2009; *b* Shrewsbury, 31 Jan. 1968; *d* of Richard Bignell and Rosemary Bignell (*née* Jones). *Educ:* King Edward VI Coll., Nuneaton; Downing Coll., Cambridge (BA Hons Law 1990; MA 1994); Hertford Coll., Oxford (BCL Hons 1991); Inns of Court Sch. of Law. FCIArb 2014. Called to the Bar, Lincoln's Inn, 1992, Bencher, 2015. In practice as barrister, Falcon Chambers, London. Qualified Civil and Commercial Mediator, 2016. Mem., Bar Council, 2016–. Mem., Editl Bd, Landlord and Tenant Rev., 1999–. *Publications:* contrib. Auctioneers, Estate Agents and Valuers, in Encyclopaedia of Forms and Precedents, 5th edn, 1985, 1995 and 1999 reissues; The Carers' Directory, 1987; (jtly) Fisher and Lightwood's Law of Mortgage, 11th edn 2000; The Lawyers' Factbook, Landlord and Tenant, 2001–04; (jtly) Registered Land: the new law, 2002; (jtly) Registered Land, Law and Practice under the Land Registration Act 2002, 2004; Lewison's Drafting Business Leases, 7th edn 2007, 8th edn 2013. *Recreations:* theatre, travel. *Address:* Falcon Chambers, Falcon Court, EC4Y 1AA. *E:* bignell@falcon-chambers.com.

BIGNON, Arnaud; Consulting Chef, Trestelis Group, since 2018; *b* Le Mans, 5 Jan. 1974; *s* of Gérard Bignon and Ginette Bignon; *m* 2015, Sophie; two *s*. *Educ:* BeP; Baccalauréat Professionnel. Worked in kitchens in Le Mans, then Paris; Restaurant Drouant, Paris, 1993–96; Restaurant Meridien 25, Paris, 1996–97; sous chef, Hôtel Le Bristol, Paris, 1998–2005; Head Chef, Restaurant Spondi, Athens, 2005–12; Exec. Head Chef, The Greenhouse, Mayfair, London, 2012–18 (two Michelin stars, 2013).

BIGSBY, Prof. Christopher William Edgar, PhD; FRSL; Professor of American Studies, 1984–2018, now Emeritus, and Founder and Director, Arthur Miller Centre for American Studies, since 1989, University of East Anglia; Founder and Director, British Archive for Contemporary Writing, since 2015; *b* Dundee, 27 June 1941; *s* of Edgar and Ivy Bigsby; *m* 1965, Pamela Lovelady; two *s* two *d*. *Educ:* Univ. of Sheffield (BA English 1962; MA 1964); Univ. of Nottingham (PhD 1966). FRSL 2000. Fulbright Schol., 1963–64. Lectr, UC of Wales, Aberystwyth, 1966–69; Lectr, 1969–73, Sen. Lectr, 1973–76, Reader, 1976–84, UEA. *TV plays:* (with Malcolm Bradbury): The After Dinner Game, 1975; Stones, 1976; *BBC radio plays:* (with Malcolm Bradbury): Patterson, 1983; Long Days Journey, 1988; Presenter: BBC Radio: Kaleidoscope, 1982–90; Present Voices, Past Words, 1991; The Index, 1999; First Night; Third Ear; The Archive Hour; Off the Page, 2000–02; Meridian; BBC TV: Bookmark; Edith Wharton; Of Mice and Men. FRSA. *Publications:* Confrontation and Commitment, 1967; Albee, 1969; (ed) Three Negro Plays, 1969; The Black American Writer, 2 vols, 1971; Dada and Surrealism, 1972; (ed) Edward Albee, 1975; (ed) Superculture, 1975; (ed) Approaches to Popular Culture, 1976; Tom Stoppard, 1980; The Second Black Renaissance, 1980; (ed) Contemporary English Drama, 1981; A Critical Introduction to 20th Century American Drama, vol. 1, 1982, vol. 2, 1984, vol. 3, 1985; Joe Orton, 1982; (ed) The Radical Imagination and the Liberal Tradition, 1982; David Mamet, 1985; (ed) Cultural Change in the United States since World War II, 1986; (ed) Plays by Susan Glaspell, 1987; (ed) File on Miller, 1987; (ed) Arthur Miller and Company, 1990; Modern American Drama 1945–1990, 1992; (ed) Nineteenth Century American Short Stories, 1995; (ed) The Portable Arthur Miller, 1995; (ed) The Cambridge Companion to Arthur Miller, 1997; (ed with D. B. Wilmeth) The Cambridge History of American Theatre, vol. 1, 1998, vol. 2, 1999, vol. 3, 2000; Contemporary American Playwrights, 1999; Modern American Drama 1945–2000, 2000; (ed) Writers in Conversation with Christopher Bigsby, vol. 1, 2000, vol. 2, 2001, vols 3 and 4, 2011, vol. 5, 2013, vol. 6, 2017, vol. 7, 2018; (ed) The Cambridge Companion to David Mamet, 2004; Arthur Miller: a critical study, 2004; (ed) Remembering Arthur Miller, 2005; (ed) A New Introduction to American Studies, 2005; Remembering and Imagining the Holocaust: the chain of memory, 2006; (ed) The Cambridge Companion to Modern American Culture, 2006; Neil LaBute, 2007; (ed) The Cambridge Companion to August Wilson, 2007; Arthur Miller: 1915–1962, 2009; Arthur Miller: 1962–2005, 2011; Viewing America: 21st century television drama, 2013; Twenty-first Century American Playwrights, 2018; *novels:* Hester, 1994; Pearl, 1995; Still Lives, 1996; Beautiful Dreamer, 2002; One Hundred Days: One Hundred Nights, 2007; Poe, or the Revenant, 2012; Ballygoran, 2014; Flint, 2015, The Hotel, 2016. *Recreations:* still looking, avoiding questionnaires. *Address:* School of Art, Media and American Studies, University of East Anglia, Norwich NR4 7TJ. *E:* c.bigsby@uea.ac.uk; 3 Church Farm, Watton Road, Colney, Norwich NR4 7TX.

BIJUR, Peter Isaac; Chairman of the Board and Chief Executive Officer, Texaco Inc., 1996–2001; *b* 14 Oct. 1942; *m* 2000, Kjestine M. Anderson; two *s* one *d* from former marriage. *Educ:* Univ. of Pittsburgh (BA Pol Sci. 1964); Columbia Univ. (MBA 1966). Texaco, 1966–2001: Manager, Buffalo sales dist, 1971–73; Asst Manager to Vice-Pres. for public affairs, 1973–75; Staff Co-ordinator, dept of strategic planning, 1975–77; Asst to Exec. Vice-Pres., 1977–80; Manager, Rocky Mountain Refining and Marketing, 1980–81; Asst to Chm. of Bd, 1981–83; Pres., Texaco Oil Trading & Supply Co., 1984; Vice-Pres., special projects, 1984–86; Pres. and Chief Exec., Texaco Canada, 1987–89; Chm., Pres. and Chief Exec., Texaco Canada Resources, Calgary, 1988–89; Chm., Texaco Ltd, 1989–91; Pres., Texaco Europe, 1990–92; Sen. Vice Pres., 1992–96, Vice Chm. Bd, 1996, Texaco Inc. Director: GulfMark Offshore, Inc., 2003; AB Volvo, 2006–14.

BIKAS, Konstantinos; Grand Commander, Order of the Phoenix (Greece); Ambassador of Greece to Israel, since 2016; *b* Athens, 14 March 1955; *s* of Konstantinos Bikas and Aphrodite Gana; *m* 1987, Maria Goga; one *s* one *d*. *Educ:* Varvakeion Exemplary High Sch.; Univ. of Athens (Law degree with Hons 1978); Univ. of Hamburg (Grad. studies in Private Shipping Law and Internat. Law). Mil. Service, Hellenic Navy, 1978–79. Diplomatic Cabinet of Dep. Minister of Foreign Affairs, 1984–85, and of Minister of Foreign Affairs, 1985–88; Consul, Vancouver, 1988–92; First Sec., Algeria, 1992–93; spokesman of Greek Foreign Ministry and Counsellor, 1993–98; Hd of Mission as Chargé D'Affaires en pied), Baghdad, 1998–2002; Consul Gen., Boston, 2002–05; Dir, Private Office of Pres. of Greece and Minister Plenipotentiary 2nd Cl., 2005–09; Head (Dir Gen.), Nat. Intelligence Service and Minister Plenipotentiary 1st Cl., 2009–12; Ambassador to the Court of St James's, 2012–16. Pres., Varvakeion Foundn, 2006–09. Founder and Ed., Thesis (Min. of Foreign Affairs foreign policy pubn), 1996–98. Grand Officer, Order of Merit (Italy); Commander 1st Class: Royal Order of Polar Star (Sweden); Order of Dannebrog (Denmark); Order of Lion (Finland); Comdr, Order of Merit (Germany); Grand Decoration of Honour in Gold with Star (Austria).

BILDT, Carl, Hon. KCMG 1998; Minister of Foreign Affairs, Sweden, 2006–14; *b* Halmstad, 15 July 1949; *s* of Daniel B. Bildt and Kerstin Bildt (*née* Andersson); *m* 1984, Mia Bohman; one *s* one *d*; *m* 1998, Anna Maria Corazza. *Educ:* Stockholm Univ. Mem., Stockholm CC, 1974–77; MP (Moderate Party), Sweden, 1979–2001; Under-Sec. of State for Co-ordination and Planning, Cabinet Office, 1979–81; Member: Parly Standing Cttee in Foreign Affairs, 1982–86; Adv. Council on Foreign Affairs, 1982–99; Submarine Defence Commn, 1982–83; 1984 Defence Cttee, 1984–87; Prime Minister of Sweden, 1991–94; EU Special Rep. to Conflict in Former Yugoslavia, and Co-Chm., Internat. Conf. on Former Yugoslavia, 1995; High Rep. for Peace Implementation in Bosnia and Herzegovina, 1996–97; Special Envoy of UN Sec. Gen., Balkans, 1999–2001. Chm., Moderate Party, 1986–99. Chm., Kreab Gp, Sweden; Sen. Advr, IT Provider, Stockholm; Director: Legg Mason Inc.; HiQ; Lundin Petroleum; Vostok Nafta; Öhmans. Trustee, RAND Corp. Mem., IISS, 1981–. Mem., Nordic Council, 1986 (Chm., Conservative Gp, 1988–91). Chm., Nordic Venture Network. Chm., Internat. Democratic Union, 1992–99. Chm., Global Commn on Internet Governance, 2014–. Advr, Bd of Dirs, LetterOne, 2015–; Sen. Advr, Covington & Burling LLP, 2016–. *Publications:* Landet Som Steg ut Kylan, 1972; Framtid i Frihet, 1976; Hallänning, Svensk, Europé, 1991; Peace Journey, 1998.

**BILGIÇ, Abdurrahman;** Ambassador of Turkey to the Court of St James's, 2014–18; *b* Adiyaman, Turkey, 1963; *m* Esra; one *s* one *d*. *Educ:* Ankara Univ. Dir Gen., Press and Information Dept, Prime Ministry, Turkey, 2003–05; Consul Gen., Munich, 2005–07; Ambassador to Japan, 2011; Dep. Undersec., Prime Ministry, 2011–14. *Club:* Travellers.

**BILIMORIA,** family name of **Baron Bilimoria**.

**BILIMORIA,** Baron *cr* 2006 (Life Peer), of Chelsea in the Royal Borough of Kensington and Chelsea; **Karan Faridoon Bilimoria,** CBE 2004; DL; FCA; Chairman: Cobra Beer Partnership Ltd with Molson Coors, since 2009; Molson Coors Cobra India Private Ltd, since 2011; Cobra Beer Partnership Ltd (formerly Cobra Beer), 2007–09 (Founder, 1989; Chief Executive, 1989–2007); *b* 26 Nov. 1961; *s* of late Lt Gen. Faridoon Noshir Bilimoria, PVSM, ADC and of Yasmin Bilimoria; *m* 1993, Heather Walker; two *s* two *d*. *Educ:* Hebron Sch., Lushington Hall, India; Indian Inst. of Mgt and Commerce, Osmania Univ., Hyderabad (BCom Hons); City of London Poly. (Dip. Acctg 1982); Sidney Sussex Coll., Cambridge (BA Law 1988; half blue polo; MA; Hon. Fellow 2007); Cranfield Univ. (Business Growth Prog. 1998); London Business Sch. (Growing Your Business Presidents Prog. 2008); Harvard Business Sch. (President's Leadership Prog. 2011). ACA 1986, FCA 2002. Trainee articled chartered accountant, Ernst & Young, 1982–86, qualified chartered accountant, 1986; Consulting Accountant, Cresvale Ltd, London, 1988–89; Sales and Mktg Dir, Eur. Accounting Focus Mag., 1989; Founder, Gen. Bilimoria Wines, 1989. Founder and Publg Dir, Tandoori Mag., 1994–2003. Non-executive Director: Brake Bros Ltd, 2004–07; Booker Gp plc, 2007– (Sen. Ind. Dir); Member, Advisory Board: Boston Analytics, 2005–10; Seven Hills, 2013–; Assoc. Mem., BUPA, 2007–. Vis. Entrepreneur, Centre for Entrepreneurial Learning, Cambridge Univ., 2004–; Guest Lecturer: Judge Business Sch., Cambridge; Cranfield Univ. Sch. of Mgt; London Business Sch.; Vis. Prof., London Metropolitan Univ. UK Chm., Indo-British Partnership, UK Trade and Investment, DTI and FCO, 2003–09; Chairman: Indo-British Partnership Network, 2005–07; UK India Business Council, 2007–09 (Pres., 2009–12); Member: UK India Consultative Gp, FCO, 2002–03; Chancellor's Asia Task Force, 2005–10; UK-India Round Table, 2005–; Member: Nat. Employment Panel, DWP, 2001–07 (Chm., Small and Med. Size Enterprise Bd, 2001–05); New Deal Task Force, DfEE, 1999–2001; Neighbourhood Renewal Private Sector Panel, ODPM, 2003–05; RE Council of England and Wales, 2013–. Founding Chm., Zoroastrian All-Party Parly Gp, 2013–; Vice-Chair, All-Party Parly Gp on Indo-British, 2013–, on Trade and Investment, 2015–, on Beer, 2015–; Treas., All-Party Parly Gp on British Curry and Catering Industry, 2014–; Mem., All-Party Parly Gp on Students, 2015–, on Armed Forces, 2015–, on S Africa, 2015–, on Mgt, 2015–, on Maldives, 2015–, on Economy of W Midlands, 2016–, on Gen. Aviation, 2018–; Co-Chair, All-Party Parly Gp on Internat. Students, 2015–. Mentor, Metropolitan Police Jt Mentoring Initiative, 2002–04. Vice-Chm., Asian Business Assoc., 2003–08, Dep. Pres., 2008–10, LCCI; Mem., LCCI/Asian Business Assoc. Panel, Bank of England, 2000–03; Charter Mem., Indus Entrepreneurs, 2002–; Mem. Bd, Indus Entrepreneurs, UK, 2003–06; Founding Pres., UK Zoroastrian Chamber of Commerce, 2003–06. Member: Young Presidents' Orgn, 2000–12 (Chm., London Chapter, 2004–05); Birmingham Business Sch. Adv. Bd, 2005–; Adv. Council, CIDA Foundn UK, 2006–; Duke of York's Business Adv. Council, 2006–09; World Presidents' Orgn, 2012–; CEO World Presidents' Orgn, 2012–; E20 Steering Gp, 2013–; Commn on Future of Mgt, 2014; Enterprise Leader, Prince's Trust, 2008–; Founding Mem., Prime Minister of India's Global Adv. Council, 2010–. Member: Meml Gates Cttee, 2009– (Chm., 2003–09; Vice Patron, Meml Gates Trust, 1999–2004); Special Adv. Panel, UK Nat. Meml to Mahatma Gandhi, 2014. Mem., Pres.'s Cttee, London First, 2002–06; Ambassador: London 2012 Olympic Bid, 2005; Interactive Univ., UK, 2005–; British Liby Business and IP Centre, 2013–. Nat. Champion, Nat. Council for Grad. Entrepreneurship, 2004–; Pres., UK Council for Internat. Student Affairs, 2015–; Pres., CBI, July 2020– (Vice-Pres., 2019–July 2020); Hon. Pres., Training for Life, 2004–10. Chancellor: Thames Valley Univ., 2005–10 (Gov., 2001–04); Univ. of Birmingham, 2014– (Mem., Adv. Bd, Business Sch., 2005–); Mem., Adv. Bd, Cranfield Sch. of Mgt, 2009–; University of Cambridge: Mem., Adv. Bd, Judge Business Sch., 2008–; Chm., India Partnership Adv. Bd, 2009–12; Mem., Vice-Chancellor's Circle of Advrs for India, 2012–. Comr, Royal Hosp. Chelsea, 2006–12. Gov., Ditchley Foundn, 2004– (Mem. Council, 2011–). Trustee: British Cardiovascular Res. Trust, 2006–; St Paul's Cathedral Foundn, 2011–13; Cobra Foundn. Patron: St Andrew's Univ. Cricket Club, 2001–; Thare Machi Starfish Initiative, 2001–; Rethink severe mental illness, 2003–; Thames Community Foundn, 2005–; India Internat. Foundn, 2006–; British Sikh Assoc., 2007; Children in Need Inst. UK, 2008–13; Pratham UK, 2008–; British Consultancy Charitable Trust, 2008–; A-T Foundn, 2012; Global Forum for Indian Leadership, 2014; India Assoc., 2014–; founding Patron, Oxford Entrepreneurs, 2004–; Hon. Patron, Friends of Bedfont Lakes Country Park, 2007; Chm., Adv. Bd, Loomba Foundn, 2001–; Member, Advisory Board: Adab Trust, 2007–; Roundhouse Trust, 2008–; Gov., Jawaharlal Nehru Meml Trust, 2013–. Bynum Tudor Fellow, Kellogg Coll., Univ. of Oxford, 2017–18. Vice-Pres., Cambridge Union. FInstD 2005; CCMI 2005. Hon. Life FRSA 2004 (Council Mem., 2004–07; Patron, India, 2005–). Freeman: City of London; Guild of Entrepreneurs, 2015; Liveryman: Drapers' Co., 2005–; Brewers' Co., 2008–; Chartered Accountants' Co., 2010–. DL Gtr London, 2001–; Rep. DL Hounslow, 2005–10. Hon. DBus: Brunel, 2005; London Metropolitan, 2008; Hon. DLitt: Heriot-Watt, 2005; Univ. of W London, 2012; DUniv Staffs, 2006; Hon. DSc Cranfield, 2009. Numerous awards, including: Outstanding Achievement Award: Execs Assoc. of GB, 2002; ICAEW, 2005; Asian of the Year, Asian Who's Who, 2002; Entrepreneur of the Year: Asian Achievers Awards, 2003; LCCI, 2003; Nat. Business Awards, London and SE England, 2004; Business Person of the Year, LCCI, 2004; Albert Medal, RSA, 2004; Leadership Award, Dir Mag., IoD, 2008; Special Recognition Award, UK Trade and Investment India; Gold Medal, CMI, 2009. Pravasi Bharti Samman (India), 2008. *Publications:* (jtly) Bottled for Business: the less gassy guide to entrepreneurship, 2007; (jtly) Against the Grain: lessons in entrepreneurship from the founder of Cobra Beer, 2009. *Recreations:* reading, current affairs, travel, art, music, theatre, tennis, horse riding, golf, scuba diving, sailing. *Address:* Cobra Beer Partnership Ltd, Welken House, 10–11 Charterhouse Square, Barbican, EC1M 6EH. *T:* (020) 7788 2880. *E:* bilimoria@parliament.uk. *Clubs:* Carlton; Hawks, University Pitt (Cambridge); Guards' Polo; Delhi Gymkhana, Delhi Golf; Secunderabad; Kelvin Grove (Cape Town).

**BILL, Lt Gen. Sir David (Robert),** KCB 2011 (CB 2006); Chairman, FSI Group, since 2016 (Strategy Director, 2014–16); *b* 17 Nov. 1954; *s* of late Robert Bill, DSO, RN and Wendy Jean Bill (*née* Booth); *m* 1981, Gabrielle Catherine Thunder; three *s*. *Educ:* Charterhouse; Welbeck Coll.; RMA Sandhurst; RMCS (BA Hons Eng 1978). Maj., Dir Mil. Ops, 1987–88; 33 Ind. Field Sqn, RE, 1989–90; DS Staff Coll., 1991–92; in Comd, 39 Engr Regt, 1992–94; Col, Army Staff Duties, 1994–97; Comdr Engr, 1997–99, BGS, 1999–2001, HQ Land Comd; rcds, 2002; GOC UK Support Comd (Germany), 2003–06; Dep. Comdr, NATO Rapid Deployable Corps, Italy, 2006–08; UK Mil. Rep. to NATO and EU, 2008–11; Comdt, RCDS, 2012–14. Col, Queen's Gurkha Engrs, 2006–13. Pres., Gurkha Bde Assoc., 2013–. *Recreations:* alpine ski-ing, golf, hockey, bridge. *Address:* Stourcastle Lodge, Gough's Close, Sturminster Newton, Dorset DT10 1BU. *E:* david.gay.bill@gmail.com. *Clubs:* MCC, Oriental.

**BILL, Peter Anthony;** freelance journalist; *b* 14 March 1947; *s* of John Samuel Bill and Margaret Mary Bill; *m* 1969, Elizabeth Allen; one *s* one *d*. *Educ:* St Bartholomew's Grammar Sch., Newbury; Oxford Poly. Surveyor, construction industry: Bance & Sons, Newbury, 1962–64; Kingerlee of Oxford, 1964–69; George Wimpey, Bristol, 1969–75, and Kent, 1977–83; Anglo-American (Zambia), 1975–77; journalist: Contract Jl, 1983–85; Building mag., 1985–96 (Ed., 1990–96); Hd of Pubns, Fleming Securities, 1996–97; Ed., Estates Gazette, 1998–2009; columnist, London Evening Standard (formerly Evening Standard), 2007–15. Pres., Internat. Bldg Press, 1991–95 and 1997–2000. Mem., Develt Cttee, Duke of Edinburgh's Award, 2013–17. *Publications:* Planet Property, 2013; monographs for Smith Institute on housing, building sustainable communities, and environmental policies. *Recreations:* reading, writing. *Address:* Flat 29, 43 Bartholomew Close, EC1A 7HN. *T:* (020) 7600 2871. *E:* peter.bill@me.com. *Club:* Reform.

**BILLARI, Prof. Francesco Candeloro,** FBA 2014; Professor of Demography, and President, Dodena Centre for Research on Social Dynamics and Public Policy, Bocconi University, since 2017; *b* Milan, 13 Oct. 1970; *s* of Giovanni Billari and Vera Billari (*née* Pullara); *m* 1996, Chiara de Florio la Rocca; five *c*. *Educ:* Univ. Bocconi (Laurea Economia Politica 1994); Univ. di Padova (Dottorato di Ricerca (Demografia) 1998). Hd, Res. Gp, Max Planck Inst. for Demographic Res., 1999–2002; Prof. of Demography, 2002–12, Vice-Rector of Develt, 2009–12, Univ. Bocconi. Dist; Hd, Dept of Sociology, 2012–15, Prof. of Sociology and Demography 2012–17, Univ. of Oxford; Fellow, Nuffield Coll., Oxford, 2012–17. Res. Schol., Univ. of Pennsylvania, 2008–09. Ed.-in-Chief, Advances in Life Course Res., 2008–. *Recreations:* family, ski-ing, football. *Address:* Department of Social and Political Sciences, Bocconi University, Via Roentgen, 20136 Milan, Italy.

**BILLER, Prof. Peter Paul Arpad,** DPhil; FBA 2012; FRHistS; Professor of Medieval History, University of York, since 2001; *b* Stanmore, Middx, 9 April 1945; *s* of Victor and Klara Biller; *m* 1973, Margherita, (Miggy), Minio-Paluello (MBE 2016); two *d*. *Educ:* St Benedict's, Ealing; Oriel Coll., Oxford (BA Modern Hist. 1966; MA 1970; DPhil 1974; Hon. Fellow 2017). FRHistS 1987. Temp. Lectr, Univ. of Keele, 1969–70; University of York: Temp. Lectr, 1970–71; Lectr, 1971–93; Sen. Lectr, 1993–2001. Vis. Fellow, All Souls Coll., Oxford, 1990; British Acad. Marc Fitch Sen. Res. Reader, 1993–95; Vis. Prof., Écoles des Hautes Études en Sci. Sociale, Paris, 2001. Antiquary Essay Prize, Denys Hay Seminar in Medieval and Renaissance Hist., Univ. of Edinburgh, 1986–87. *Publications:* (ed with A. Hudson) Heresy and Literacy, 1000–1530, 1994; (ed with A. Minnis) Medieval Theology and the Natural Body, 1997; (ed with A. Minnis) Handling Sin: confessions in the Middle Ages, 1998; (ed with R. B. Dobson) The Medieval Church: universities, heresy and the religious life: essays in honour of Gordon Leff, 1999; The Measure of Multitude: population in Medieval thought, 2000 (Longman/History Today Best Hist. Book of Year (jtly), 2001); (ed with J. Ziegler) Religion and Medicine in the Middle Ages, 2001; The Waldenses 1170–1530: between a religious order and a church, 2001; (ed with C. Bruschi) Texts and the Repression of Medieval Heresy, 2003; (ed jtly) Inquisitors and Heretics in Thirteenth-Century Languedoc: edition and translation of Toulouse inquisition depositions, 1273–1282, 2011; contribs to learned jls incl. Past and Present, Jl Ecclesiastical Hist. *Recreations:* grandchildren, cooking and entertaining, art, cinema, music, theatre. *Address:* Department of History, University of York, Heslington, York YO10 5DD. *T:* (01904) 624783, *Fax:* (01904) 322955. *E:* pete.biller@york.ac.uk.

**BILLEY, Emma Marion;** *see* Ward, E. M.

**BILLINGHAM,** family name of **Baroness Billingham**.

**BILLINGHAM,** Baroness *cr* 2000 (Life Peer), of Banbury in the co. of Oxfordshire; **Angela Theodora Billingham;** JP; *b* 31 July 1939; *d* of late Theodore Vincent Case and Eva Case (*née* Saxby); *m* 1962, Anthony Peter Billingham (*d* 1992); two *d*. *Educ:* Aylesbury GS; London Univ. Teacher, 1960–90; Examiner, 1990–95. Mayor of Banbury, 1976; Member (Lab): Banbury BC, 1970–74; Cherwell DC, 1974–84; Oxfordshire CC, 1993–94. Contested (Lab) Banbury, 1992. MEP (Lab) Northants and Blaby, 1994–99; contested (Lab) E Midlands Reg., 1999. Chief Whip, Party of European Socialists, EP, 1995–99. Opposition spokesman for sport, H of L, 2013–. Member: Cttee on Olympic and Paralympic Legacy, H of L, 2013–; Eur. Sub-Cttee C, EU Russia Relns, H of L, 2014–. Chm., Lords and Commons Tennis Club, 2002–; Mem., H of L Bridge Team, 2001–. Chm., Corby Urban Regeneration Bd, 2001–03. JP N Oxfordshire and Bicester, 1976. *Recreations:* tennis, gardening, bridge, cinema, grandchildren. *Address:* 6 Crediton Hill, NW6 1HP; c/o House of Lords, SW1A 0PW. *Clubs:* All England Lawn Tennis, Cumberland Lawn Tennis (W Hampstead).

*See also* Z. A. Billingham, S. A. Jones.

**BILLINGHAM, Mark Philip David;** writer and comedian; crime novelist, since 2001; *b* Birmingham, 2 July 1961; *s* of Jeff Billingham and Patricia Billingham (*née* Grice, now Thompson); *m* 1994, Claire Winyard; one *s* one *d*. *Educ:* King Edward VI Camp Hill Grammar Sch. for Boys; Birmingham Univ. (BA Hons Drama and Th. Arts). Stand-up comedian, 1987–2012; television actor: Boon, 1984; Dempsey and Makepeace, 1985; Juliet Bravo, 1985; Maid Marian and Her Merry Men, 1989–92 (also writer, 1992); Harry's Mad, 1993–96 (also writer, 1993); Knight School (also writer), 1997–98; writer for television: What's That Noise?, 1995–96 (also presenter); The Cramp Twins, 1998–2000. Writer (with music by My Darling Clementine), touring show, The Other Half, 2015–19. *Publications:* Knight School, 1998; Sleepyhead, 2001; Scaredy Cat, 2002; Lazybones, 2003; The Burning Girl, 2004; Lifeless, 2005; Buried, 2006; Death Message, 2007; In the Dark, 2008; Bloodline, 2009; From the Dead, 2010; Good As Dead, 2011; Rush of Blood, 2012; The Dying Hours, 2013; The Bones Beneath, 2014; Great Lost Albums, 2014; Time of Death, 2015; Die of Shame, 2016; Love Like Blood, 2017; The Killing Habit, 2018; Cut Off, 2018; Their Little Secret, 2019; as Will Peterson: Triskellion, 2008; Triskellion 2: The Burning, 2009; Triskellion 3: The Gathering, 2010. *Recreations:* music, especially country (alt and cheesy), playing the guitar badly, movies, poker, tennis, food, embarrassing my children, supporting Wolverhampton Wanderers in spite of everything, trying to smuggle examples of Victorian taxidermy into the house, murdering songs for fun as a member of Fun Lovin' Crime Writers. *Address:* c/o Lutyens & Rubinstein, 21 Kensington Park Road, W11 2EU. *T:* (020) 7792 4855. *E:* mail@markbillingham.com. *W:* www.markbillingham.com, www.twitter.com/MarkBillingham. *Clubs:* One Alfred Place, Union.

**BILLINGHAM, Zoe Ann, (Mrs Dennis Skinner);** HM Inspector of Constabulary, since 2009 and HM Inspector of Fire & Rescue Services, since 2017; *b* Kings Lynn, Norfolk, 31 Dec. 1964; *d* of late Anthony Peter Billingham and of Baroness Billingham, *qv*; *m* 1997, Dennis Skinner, *s* of Dennis Edward Skinner, *qv*; one *s*. *Educ:* Banbury Comprehensive Sch.; St Hugh's Coll., Oxford (BA Hons PPE 1986); Coll. of Law, London. Policy Advr, London Bor. of Brent, 1987–90; Policy Advr, 1990–93, Solicitor, 1993–2000, London Bor. of Camden; Develt Manager, 2000–02, Dep. Dir, Prime Minister's Office of Public Services Reform, 2002–04, Cabinet Office; Dir, Community Safety and Sustainability, Audit Commn, 2004–09. *Recreations:* losing to 17 year old son at tennis, photography, travel. *Address:* c/o HM Inspectorate of Constabulary and Fire & Rescue Services, 6th Floor, Globe House, 89 Eccleston Square, SW1V 1PN. *T:* (020) 7802 1800. *Clubs:* Cumberland Lawn Tennis; Thorpeness Golf and Country.

**BILLINGS, Rev. Canon Dr Alan Roy**; Police and Crime Commissioner for South Yorkshire, since 2014; *b* Leicester, 7 Oct. 1942; *s* of Paul William Stanley Billings and Dorothy May Billings (*née* Siddons); *m* 1966, Daphne Thomas (marr. diss. 1993); two *s*; *m* 1994, Linda Woodhead (marr. diss. 2002); *m* 2007, Veronica Mary Hardstaff, *qv*. *Educ*: Wyggeston Grammar Sch., Leicester; Emmanuel Coll., Cambridge (BA Theol Tripos 1965; MA 1969); Bristol Univ. (PGCE); Leicester Univ. (MEd); New York Theol Seminary (DMin 1987); Lincoln Theol Coll. Ordained deacon, 1968, priest, 1969; Curate, St Mary, Knighton, Leicester, 1968–72; Vicar, St Silas, Broomhall, Sheffield, 1972–76; Vicar, St Mary the Virgin, Beighton, 1976–77; Hd of RE, Broadway Sch., Barnsley, 1977–81; Vicar, St Mary, Walkley, Sheffield, 1981–86; Vice Principal, and Dir, Oxford Inst. for Church and Society, Ripon Coll., Cuddesdon, Oxford, 1986–92; Principal, W Midlands Ministerial Trng Course, and Actg Principal, Queen's Coll., Birmingham, 1992–94; Vicar, St George, Kendal and St John, Grayrigg, 1994–2007; Hon. Sen. Res. Fellow, and Dir, Centre for Ethics and Religion, Lancaster Univ., 1996–2007. Schs Adjudicator, 1999–2006. Member: Bd, Funding Agency for Schs, 1997–99; Community Cohesion Panel, Home Office, 2002–04; Youth Justice Bd for England and Wales, 2004–10; England Cttee, Big Lottery Fund, 2007–13. Hon. Canon, Carlisle Cathedral, 2005–07, now Canon Emeritus. Mem. (Lab), Sheffield CC, 1975–86 (Dep. Leader, 1980–86). FRSA. *Publications*: Dying and Grieving, 2002; Secular Lives, Sacred Hearts, 2004; God and Community Cohesion, 2009; Making God Possible, 2010; Lost Church, 2013; The Dove, the Fig Leaf and the Sword, 2014. *Recreation*: writing stories for grandchildren. *Address*: 43 Northfield Court, Sheffield S10 1QR. *T*: (0114) 267 6549. *E*: alanbillingsuk@yahoo.co.uk. *Clubs*: Travellers; Trades and Labour (Sheffield).

**BILLINGTON, Brenda May**, OBE 2012; FRCS; Consultant Ophthalmic Surgeon, Royal Berkshire Hospital, Reading, 1985–2011; President, Royal College of Ophthalmologists, 2006–09; *b* 19 Jan. 1951; *d* of Gwynn and Leslie Billington; *m* 1987, James (marr. diss. 1997); one *s*. *Educ*: Queen Anne's Sch., Caversham; Univ. of Birmingham (MB ChB 1974). FRCS 1980; FRCOphth 1989, Hon. FRCOphth 2015. Resident Surgical Officer, Moorfields Eye Hosp., 1978–81; Sen. Registrar in Ophthalmology, St Thomas' Hosp. and Moorfields Eye Hosp., 1982–85. Liveryman, Soc. of Apothecaries, 1989–. Fellow, European Bd of Ophthalmology, 2003. *Publications*: contribs to ophthalmic scientific jls, mainly clinical studies of treatment for patients with retinal detachment. *Recreations*: excursions with nieces and nephew, voluntary work in the community, walking with the dog. *Club*: Royal Society of Medicine.

**BILLINGTON, Brian John, (Bill)**; consultant on roads and transport, since 1998; *b* 25 Feb. 1939; *s* of late Kenneth Jack Billington and Doris Violet Billington; *m* 1965, Gillian Elizabeth Annis; two *d*. *Educ*: Slough Grammar Sch.; The Polytechnic, Regent Street (BSc(Econ)); LSE (MSc). Lectr, The Polytechnic, Regent Street, 1966–68; Min. of Power, later Dept of Energy, 1969–74; Dept of Transport, later Dept of Envmt, Transport and the Regions, 1974–98; Highways Agency, 1994–98; Under Sec., 1991–98. *Address*: 100 Fox Lane, N13 4AX. *T*: (020) 8886 0898.

**BILLINGTON, Kevin**; film, theatre and television director; *b* 12 June 1934; *s* of Richard and Margaret Billington; *m* 1967, Lady Rachel Mary Pakenham (*see* Lady Rachel Billington); one *s* two *d* (and one *s* decd). *Educ*: Bryanston Sch.; Queens' Coll., Cambridge (BA); Open Univ. (MusDip 1999; BA Hons 2002; MA (Mus) 2007). Film dir, BBC prog., Tonight, 1960–63; documentary film dir, BBC, 1963–67; films include: A Sort of Paradise; Many Mexicos; The Mexican Attitude; Twilight of Empire; Mary McCarthy's Paris; These Humble Shores; Matador; A Few Castles in Spain; The English Cardinal; A Socialist Childhood; Madison Avenue, USA; ATV documentary, All The Queen's Men. *Feature Film Director*: Interlude, 1967; The Rise and Rise of Michael Rimmer, 1969; The Light at the Edge of the World, 1970; Voices, 1974; Reflections, 1984. *Television Director*: And No One Can Save Her, 1973; Once Upon a Time is Now (documentary), 1978; The Music Will Never Stop (documentary), 1979; Henry VIII, 1979; The Jail Diary of Albie Sachs, 1980; The Good Soldier, 1981; Outside Edge, 1982; The Sonnets of William Shakespeare, 1984; Heartland, 1989; Small Doses, 1990; A Time to Dance, 1992. *Theatre Director*: Find Your Way Home, 1970; Me, 1973; The Birthday Party, 1974; The Caretaker, 1975; Bloody Neighbours, 1975; Emigrés, 1976; The Homecoming, 1978; Quartermaine's Terms, 1982; The Deliberate Death of a Polish Priest, 1985 (Channel Four, 1986); The Philanthropist, 1986; The Lover, and A Slight Ache (double bill), 1987; The Breadwinner, 1989; Veterans Day, 1989; Quartermaine's Terms, 1993; Old Times, 1994; Six Characters in Search of an Author, 1999; Our Country's Good, 1999; Victory, 2001; Wild Honey, 2002. *Screenplays*: Bodily Harm, 2000; Loving Attitudes, 2001. Chm., BAFTA, 1989–90 and 1990–91. Screenwriters' Guild Award, 1966 and 1967; Guild of TV Producers and Directors Award, 1966 and 1967. *Recreation*: swimming. *Address*: The Court House, Poyntington, Sherborne, Dorset DT9 4LF. *Club*: Garrick.

**BILLINGTON, Michael**, OBE 2013; Drama Critic of The Guardian, since 1971; *b* 16 Nov. 1939; *s* of Alfred Billington and Patricia (*née* Bradshaw); *m* 1978, Jeanine Bradlaugh. *Educ*: Warwick Sch.; St Catherine's Coll., Oxford (BA; Hon. Fellow 2005). Trained as journalist with Liverpool Daily Post and Echo, 1961–62; Public Liaison Officer and Director for Lincoln Theatre Co., 1962–64; reviewed plays, films and television for The Times, 1965–71. Film Critic: Birmingham Post, 1968–78; Illustrated London News, 1968–81; London Arts Correspondent, New York Times, 1978–90; Drama Critic, Country Life, 1987–. Contributor to numerous radio and television Arts programmes, incl. Kaleidoscope, Critics' Forum, The Book Programme, Arena. Presenter, The Billington Interview and Theatre Call, BBC World Service. Writer and Presenter, television profiles of Peggy Ashcroft, Peter Hall and Alan Ayckbourn. Prof. of Drama, Colorado Coll., 1981; Vis. Prof., KCL, 2002–. FKC 2009. Hon. DLitt Warwick, 2009. IPC Critic of the Year, 1974; Pragnell Shakespeare Birthday Award, 2009. *Publications*: The Modern Actor, 1974; How Tickled I Am, 1977; (ed) The Performing Arts, 1980; The Guinness Book of Theatre Facts and Feats, 1982; Alan Ayckbourn, 1983; Tom Stoppard, 1987; Peggy Ashcroft, 1988; (ed) Twelfth Night, 1990; One Night Stands, 1993; The Life and Work of Harold Pinter, 1996; (ed) Stage and Screen Lives, 2001; State of the Nation, 2007; The 101 Greatest Plays, 2015. *Recreations*: work, travel, cricket. *Address*: 15 Hearne Road, W4 3NJ. *T*: (020) 8995 0455.

**BILLINGTON, Lady Rachel (Mary)**, OBE 2012; writer; *b* 11 May 1942; *d* of 7th Earl of Longford, KG, PC, and Elizabeth, Countess of Longford, CBE; *m* 1967, Kevin Billington, *qv*; one *s* two *d* (and one *s* decd). *Educ*: London Univ. (BA English). Work includes: short stories; four BBC radio plays; two BBC TV plays, Don't be Silly, 1979, Life After Death, 1981. Reviewer and feature writer. Co-editor, Inside Time, 1991–. Trustee: Tablet Trust, 1991–; Longford Trust, 2002–; Siobhan Dowd Trust, 2008–. *Publications*: All Things Nice, 1969; The Big Dipper, 1970; Lilacs out of the Dead Land, 1971; Cock Robin, 1973; Beautiful, 1974; A Painted Devil, 1975; A Woman's Age, 1979; Occasion of Sin, 1982; The Garish Day, 1985; Loving Attitudes, 1988; Theo and Matilda, 1990; Bodily Harm, 1992; The Family Year, 1992; The Great Umbilical: mother, daughter, mother, 1994; Magic and Fate, 1996; Perfect Happiness: the sequel to Emma, 1996; Tiger Sky, 1998; A Woman's Life, 2002; The Space Between, 2004; One Summer, 2006; Lies and Loyalties, 2008; The Missing Boy, 2010; Maria and the Admiral, 2012; Glory: a story of Gallipoli, 2015; *for children*: Rosanna and the Wizard-Robot, 1981; The First Christmas, 1983; Star-Time, 1984; The First Easter, 1987; The First Miracles, 1990; Life of Jesus, 1996; Life of St Francis, 1999; Far-out, 2002; There's More to Life, 2006; Poppy's Hero, 2012; Poppy's Angel, 2013. *Recreations*: nature, painting. *Address*: The Court House, Poyntington, near Sherborne, Dorset DT9 4LF. *Clubs*: Society of Authors, PEN (Pres., 1997–2000).

**BILSLAND, Christopher Nigel**, OBE 2014; Chamberlain, City of London Corporation, 2007–14; *b* 5 May 1954; *s* of John Bilsland and Dallas Aileen Bilsland; *m* 1980, Gillian Smith; one *s* one *d*. *Educ*: Doncaster Grammar Sch.; Chesterfield Coll. of Technol. CPFA 1976. Accountant, Doncaster MBC, 1972–79; Chief Auditor, Derby CC, 1979–82; Sen. Manager, Deloitte Haskins & Sells, 1982–87; Asst County Treas., Hampshire CC, 1987–91; County Treas., Somerset CC, 1991–2006. Non-exec. Dir, London Pensions CIV Ltd, 2016–. Mem. Council, CIPFA, 1998–2011 (Pres., 2011–12). Hon. FGS, 2016. *Recreations*: high handicap golfer, horseracing, taking credit for children's achievements. *Address*: Alpenhaus, 3 Laurel Drive, Oxted, Surrey RH8 9DT.

**BILTCLIFFE, Moira Elizabeth**; *see* Buffini, M. E.

**BINDLOSS, Edward Christopher James; His Honour Judge Bindloss**; a Circuit Judge, since 2015; *b* Marlborough, 1967; *s* of late Christopher and Susan Bindloss; *m* 1999, Stephanie; two *s* one *d*. *Educ*: Ipswich Sch.; Univ. of York (BA Philosophy and Politics); City Univ. (DipLaw). Called to the Bar, Gray's Inn, 1993; a Recorder, 2008–15. *Recreations*: cricket, literature, cinema, swimming, philosophy, writing. *Address*: Newcastle-upon-Tyne Combined Court Centre, The Law Courts, The Quayside, Newcastle-upon-Tyne NE1 3LA. *Club*: Yorkshire Gentlemen's Cricket.

**BINDMAN, Sir Geoffrey (Lionel)**, Kt 2007; Consultant, Bindmans LLP (formerly Bindman & Partners), Solicitors, since 2004 (Senior Partner, 1974–2004); *b* 3 Jan. 1933; *s* of Dr Gerald and Lena Bindman; *m* 1961, Lynn Janice Winton; two *s* one *d*. *Educ*: Newcastle upon Tyne Royal Grammar Sch.; Oriel Coll., Oxford (BA 1955; BCL 1956; MA 1959). Admitted Solicitor, 1959; Teaching Fellow, Northwestern Univ., Ill, 1959–60; Partner, Lawford & Co., 1965–74. Legal adviser: Race Relations Bd, 1966–76; CRE, 1976–83. Visiting Professor of Law: UCLA, 1982; UCL, 1990–; London South Bank Univ., 2003–. Hon. Pres., Discrimination Law Assoc., 1999–; Chm., Soc. of Labour Lawyers, 1999–2001. Chm., British Inst. of Human Rights, 2005–13. Pres., Client Interviewing Comp. for England and Wales, 1990–. Columnist, New Law Journal, 2006–. Trustee: Wordsworth Trust, 1997–2013; Helen Bamber Foundn, 2006–13; ATG Trust (Pres., 2010–); Lawyers for Palestinian Human Rights, 2011–; Vice-Pres., One World Trust, 2006–; Pres., John Thelwall Soc., 2012–. Hon. QC 2011. Hon. LLD: De Montfort, 2000; Kingston, 2006. Liberty Award for Lifetime Human Rights Achievement, 1999; Centenary Award for Human Rights, Law Soc. Gazette, 2003. *Publications*: (jtly) Race and Law, 1972; (ed) South Africa: human rights and the rule of law, 1988. *Recreations*: walking, music, book collecting. *Address*: (office) 236 Gray's Inn Road, WC1X 8HB. *T*: (020) 7833 4433.

**BING, His Honour Inigo Geoffrey**; a Circuit Judge, 2000–12; *b* 1 April 1944; *s* of late Geoffrey Henry Cecil Bing, QC and Crystal Frances Bing; *m* 1st, 1980, Shirley-Anne Holmes (*née* Benka) (*d* 2003); three step *c*; 2nd, 2004, Judith Caroline Anne Hughes, *qv* (marr. diss.); 3rd, 2019, Mary Honeyball, *qv*. *Educ*: St Olave's Grammar Sch., Southwark; Birmingham Univ. (LLB); Birkbeck, Univ. of London (BA Hons 1st Cl. Hist. and Philos. 2016; MA 2017). Called to the Bar, Inner Temple, 1967, Bencher, 2012; practised London and SE Circuit; a District Judge (Magistrates' Courts) (formerly a Metropolitan Stipendiary Magistrate), 1989–2000; a Recorder, 1996–2000. Mem., Parole Bd, 2002–09. Mem. (Lab) London Borough of Lambeth, 1971–78 (Chm., F and GP Cttee, 1974–78); Co-founder, Lambeth Community Law Centre. Contested Braintree: (SDP) 1983; (SDP/Alliance) 1987. *Publications*: Criminal Procedure and Sentencing in the Magistrates' Court, 1990, 5th edn 1999. *Recreations*: music, travel, historical research. *Address*: 56 Bedford Court Mansions, Bedford Avenue, WC1B 3AD; 41 rue Fond de Val, Raye-sur-Authie 62140, France. *Club*: Reform (Chm., 2006–07).

**BINGHAM**, family name of **Earl of Lucan** and **Baron Clanmorris**.

**BINGHAM, Andrew Russell**; *b* Buxton, 23 June 1962; *s* of late Anthony Russell Bingham and of Mary Dorothea Bingham. *Educ*: Long Lane Sec. Sch., Chapel-en-le-Frith; High Peak Coll. of Further Educn. Company Dir, A.R.B. Sales Ltd, 1983–2004. Mem. (C) High Peak BC, 1999–2012 (Chm., Social Inclusion Cttee, 2003–07). Contested (C) High Peak, 2005. MP (C) High Peak, 2010–17; contested (C) same seat, 2017. *Recreations*: cricket, football, cooking.

**BINGHAM, Lady Camilla**; QC 2013; *b* London, 30 June 1970; *yr d* of 7th Earl of Lucan and Veronica Mary (*née* Duncan); *m* 1998, Michael Gordon Bloch, *qv*; four *s*. *Educ*: St Swithun's Sch., Winchester; Balliol Coll., Oxford (BA Lit. Hum. 1992). Called to the Bar, Inner Temple, 1996, Bencher, 2015; in practice as barrister, specialising in commercial litigation and arbitration. *Address*: One Essex Court, Temple, EC4Y 9AR. *T*: (020) 7583 2000. *E*: cbingham@oeclaw.co.uk.

**BINGHAM, Hon. Charlotte Mary Thérèse**; playwright and novelist; *b* 29 June 1942; *d* of 7th Baron Clanmorris (John Bingham) and of Madeleine Mary, *d* of late Clement Ebel; *m* 1964, Terence Joseph Brady (*d* 2016); one *s* one *d*. *Educ*: The Priory, Haywards Heath; Sorbonne. *TV series* with Terence Brady: Boy Meets Girl; Take Three Girls; Upstairs Downstairs; Away From It All; Play for Today; No—Honestly; Yes—Honestly; Pig in the Middle; Thomas and Sarah; The Complete Lack of Charm of the Bourgeoisie; Nanny; Oh Madeline! (USA TV); Father Matthew's Daughter; Forever Green; The Upper Hand; *TV films*: Love With a Perfect Stranger, 1986; Losing Control, 1987; The Seventh Raven, 1987; This Magic Moment, 1988; screenwriter with Terence Brady, Riders, 1993; *stage*: with Terence Brady: (contrib.) The Sloane Ranger Revue, 1985; I Wish, I Wish, 1989; (adaptation) The Shell Seekers, 1999; *radio* with Terence Brady: Hear Hear! The Victoria Line. *Publications*: Coronet among the Weeds, 1963; Lucinda, 1965; Coronet among the Grass, 1972; Belgravia, 1983; Country Life, 1984; At Home, 1986; To Hear A Nightingale, 1988; The Business, 1989; In Sunshine or In Shadow, 1991; Stardust, 1992; By Invitation, 1993; Nanny, 1993; Change of Heart, 1994 (Romantic Novel of the Year Award, 1995, Romantic Novelists' Assoc.); Debutantes, 1995; The Nightingale Sings, 1996; Grand Affair, 1997; Love Song, 1998; The Kissing Garden, 1999; The Love Knot, 2000; The Blue Note, 2000; The Season, 2001; Summertime, 2001; Distant Music, 2002; The Chestnut Tree, 2002; The Wind off the Sea, 2003; The Moon at Midnight, 2003; Daughters of Eden, 2004; House of Flowers, 2004; The Magic Hour, 2005; Friday's Girl, 2005; Out of the Blue, 2006; In Distant Fields, 2006; The White Marriage, 2007; Goodnight Sweetheart, 2007; The Enchanted, 2008; The Land of Summer, 2008; The Daisy Club, 2009; Mums on the Run, 2010; A Dip before Breakfast, 2011; The Light on the Swan, 2014; MI5 and Me: a coronet among the spooks, 2018; Spies and Stars: MI5, showbusiness and me, 2019; with Terence Brady: Victoria, 1972; Rose's Story, 1973; Victoria and Company, 1974; Yes—Honestly, 1977. *Recreations*: music, theatre, dogs. *Address*: United Authors Ltd, 11–15 Betterton Street, WC2H 9BP. *Club*: Society of Authors.

**BINGHAM, Sir (Eardley) Max,** Kt 1988; QC (Tas.) 1974; Chairman, Queensland Criminal Justice Commission, 1989–92; *b* 18 March 1927; *s* of Thomas Eardley and Olive Bingham; *m* 1952, Margaret Garrett Jesson; three *s* one *d*. *Educ:* Univ. of Tasmania (LLB (Hons)); Lincoln Coll., Oxford (BCL; Rhodes Schol., 1950); Univ. of California at Berkeley (Harkness Commonwealth Fund Fellow, 1963). RANR, 1945–46. Legal practice, and teaching, Univ. of Tasmania, 1953–69. MHA Tasmania, 1969–84; Attorney-General, 1969–72; Leader of the Opposition, 1972–79, Dep. Leader of the Opposition, 1982; Dep. Premier of Tas., 1982–84. Mem., Nat. Crime Authority, 1984–87. Hon. LLD Tasmania, 1998. *Publications:* contribs to jls. *Recreations:* reading, music. *Address:* Unit 1, Maning Reef, 482 Sandy Bay Road, Sandy Bay, Tas 7005, Australia. *Clubs:* Tasmanian, Royal Yacht of Tasmania (Hobart).

**BINGHAM, James Stewart,** TD 1982; FRCP, FRCPE, FRCOG; Consultant Physician in Genitourinary and HIV Medicine, Guy's and St Thomas' NHS Foundation Trust (formerly St Thomas' Hospital, then Guy's and St Thomas' Hospital Trust), 1992–2011; *b* 31 July 1945; *s* of Dr William Bingham and Nora Mary Bingham (*née* Beckett); *m* 1974, Elizabeth Eleanor Stewart; one *s*. *Educ:* Campbell Coll., Belfast; Queen's Univ., Belfast (MB BCh BAO 1969). MRCOG 1974, FRCOG 1989; FRCPE 1994; FRCP 1999. Initial career in obstetrics and gynaecology in NI, Rhodesia and Canada, 1970–75; Middlesex Hospital: Sen. Registrar in Venereology, 1975–77; Consultant in Genitourinary Med., 1977–92; Consultant Physician in Genitourinary Med., Bromley Hosps, 1992–94. Hon. Consultant in Genitourinary Medicine to the Army, 2000–09. Pres. Exec. Cttee, Internat. Union against Sexually Transmitted Infections, 2001–03 (Mem., 1995–; Hon. Treas., 1995–99; Mem. jt initiative with WHO Europe and Open Soc. Inst. to introduce protocols to Central Asia, 2004–06; Sen. Counsellor, 2005–12); Member: Council, Med. Soc. for Study of Venereal Diseases, 1979–82, 1983–97, 1999–2001 (Hon. Treas., 1986–93; Pres., 1993–95; Hon. Life Fellow, 2007); Cttee, Assoc. for Genitourinary Medicine, 1993–2003 (Chm., 1999–2001); Specialist Adv. Cttee in Genitourinary Medicine, Jt Cttee for Higher Med. Trng, 1988–95, 2003–09 (Sec., 1989–93; Chm., 1993–95); Working Party on Med. Audit in Genitourinary Medicine, 1989–94; Dermatology and Venereology sub-cttee, Central Consultants' and Specialists' Cttee, BMA, 1992–2008 (Chm., 1998–2000); Working Gp on Read Codes (Genitourinary Medicine), 1993–94; Exec. Cttee, British HIV Assoc., 1996–2000 (Founding Hon. Treas., 1996–2000; Hon. Fellow, 2002). Examiner in Genitourinary Medicine: Soc. of Apothecaries, 1982–2007 (Convenor, 1992–95); Univ. of Liverpool, 1996–98; Prince of Songkla Univ., Thailand, 2000–02; UCL, 2005–07. WHO: Consultant, Bulgaria, 1993; Advr, STD interventions for preventing HIV infection, Geneva, 1998; UK rep., Dermatovenereology cttee, Union of European Monospecialties, 2003–09 (Treas., 2005–09). Mem., Editl Bd, Eur. S&D Guidelines, 2008–09. Trustee: BMA Foundn for AIDS, subseq. Med. Foundn for AIDS and Sexual Health, 2000–06; River House, 1996–2002. 257 (NI) Field Ambulance and 217 General Hosp. RAMC(V), TA, 1969–83. Life FRSocMed, 2000. Hon. Life Fellow Oration, 2009, Harrison Lect., 2010, BASHH. Silver Medal Oration, Inst. of Venereology, India, 2000. Freeman, City of London, 2013; Yeoman, 2012, Liveryman, 2017, Apothecaries' Soc. *Publications:* Sexually Transmitted Diseases: a pocket picture guide, 1984, 2nd edn 1989; articles and chapters on aspects of genital tract and HIV infections. *Recreations:* military and medical history, gardening. *E:* james_bingham@outlook.com. *Clubs:* Army and Navy, City Volunteer Officers, Royal Automobile.

**BINGHAM, Col Jeremy David S.;** *see* Smith-Bingham.

**BINGHAM, John,** CBE 1991; FRS 1977; Plant Breeding International, Cambridge, 1981–91; *b* 19 June 1930; *s* of Thomas Frederick Bingham and Emma Maud Lusher; *m* 1983, Jadwiga Anna Siedlecka; one *s*. Mem. of staff, Plant Breeding Inst. of Cambridge, subseq. Plant Breeding Internat. Cambridge Ltd, 1954–91. Has researched in plant breeding, culminating in production of improved winter wheat varieties for British agriculture. Pres., Royal Norfolk Agricl Assoc., 1991. Hon. FRASE, 1983. Hon. ScD UEA, 1992. Res. medal, RASE, 1975; Mullard Medal of Royal Society, 1975; Massey Ferguson Nat. Award for Services to UK Agric., 1984. *Recreations:* farming, conservation of wild life. *Address:* Hereward Barn, Church Lane, Mattishall Burgh, Dereham, Norfolk NR20 3QZ. *T:* (01362) 858354.

**BINGHAM, Judith Caroline;** composer; *b* 21 June 1952; *d* of Jack Bingham and Peggy (*née* McGowan); *m* 1985, Andrew Petrow (marr. diss. 2011). *Educ:* High Storrs Grammar Sch., Sheffield; Royal Acad. of Music (Principal's Prize for Music, 1972; ARAM 1997). Mem., BBC Singers, 1983–95. *Major works:* The Divine Image, 1976; Cocaine Lil, 1977; Flynn, 1979; Chamouni, 1982; Cradle Song of the Blessed Virgin, Scenes From Nature, 1983; Just Before Dawn, 1985; A Cold Spell, 1987; Christmas Past, Christmas Present, 1988; Chartres, 1988; Dove Cottage by Moonlight, 1989; Four Minute Mile, 1991; The Stars Above, The Earth Below, 1991; Unpredictable But Providential, 1991; Irish Tenebrae, The Uttermost, 1992; O Magnum Mysterium, Santa Casa, Beyond Redemption, 1994; Evening Canticles, Epiphany, Salt in the Blood, The Red Hot Nail, 1995; The Mysteries of Adad, The Temple at Karnak, No Discord, 1996; Gleams of a Remoter World, The Waning Moon, Below the Surface Stream, Chapman's Pool, 1997; Missa Brevis, The Clouded Heaven, Bassoon Concerto, Unheimlich, Vorarlberg, Shelley Dreams, 1998; The Shooting Star, Walzerspiele, The Cathedral of Trees, Water Lilies, Otherworld, 1999; Necklace of Light, Annunciation, The Shepherd's Gift, St Bride, Assisted by Angels, These are Our Footsteps, 2000; 50 Shades of Green; The Shadow Side of Joy Finzi, 2001; Beneath these alien stars, 2001; Bright Spirit, 2001; My Father's Arms, 2002; Ave Verum Corpus, enter GHOST, The Mystery of Boranup, Aquileia, Uppon the First Sight of New England, Incarnation with Shepherds Dancing, 2002; Missa Brevis No 2, The Road to Emmaeus, The Moon over Westminster Cathedral, Ancient Sunlight, The Christmas Truce, Bach's Tomb, O Clap Your Hands, 2003; The Ivory Tree, The Secret Garden, The Yearning Strong, Limehouse Nocturne, Lo in the Silent Night, Our Faith is a Light, Margaret Forsaken, Down and Out, Touch'd by Heavenly Fire, In Nomine, 2004; Ghost Towns of the American West, A Formal Order, Down and Out, We Two, Edington Canticles, The Shepheardes Calender, 2005; Hidden City, La Boiteuse, An Ancient Music, Winter's Pilgrimage, My Heart Strangely Warm'd, The Cruelty of the Gods, The Flying Hours, The Morning-Watch, Capriccio, 2006; Missa Brevis, Awake My Soul, The Hired Hand, Ziggurat, Jacob's Ladder, Fantasia, Shakespeare Requiem, 2007; She Walks in Beauty, Byron, violent progress, Harvest, Shadow Aspect, 2008; See and Keep Silent, Billingbear, Actaeon, Annunciation II, Distant Thunder, Tomkat Murr, 2009; Wells Service, A Bird is Singing, The Pilgrim's Travels, Mary Anning, Annunciation III, Now the Magi Arrive, Holy of Holies, 2010; The Everlasting Crown, Corpus Christi Carol, Ave Virgo Sanctissimi, Eden, Celticity, 2011; London Haiku, The Hythe, Leonardo (Bassoon Concerto 2), 2012; In Mary's Love, Angel Fragments, My Heart Laid Bare, 2013; Hymn to St Paul, A Walk with Ivor Gurney, Dürer Portrait, Tableaux Vivants, The Very Distant Days, Altartavla, Les Saintes Maries de la Mer, Oboe Concerto, Solomon and Love, Arcadia, Missa Brevis IV, Ghostly Grace, Glass Beatitude, Fa La Ninna, 2014; Zodiack, The Angel of Mons, 2015; Jesu Dulcis Memoria, The Neglected Child, Adieu Solace, The Colour of Fire, Doth the Moon Shine, Sing O Heavens, The Three Angels, The Linnaeus Garden, I Will Lift Up Mine Eyes, Oriel Magnificat, Piano Trio no 2. BBC Young Composer, 1977; Barlow Prize for choral music, 2004; BASCA British Composer Awards for liturgical music, 2004, for choral music, 2004, 2006 and for Instrumental Music, 2008. FRNCM 2005; FRSCM 2007; FGCM 2014. *Recreations:* films, art, books, friends. *Address:* c/o Peters Edition, 2–6 Baches Street, N1 6DN. *T:* (020) 8660 4766.

**BINGHAM, Sir Max;** *see* Bingham, Sir E. M.

**BINGHAM, Victoria Mary Mayne;** Headmistress, South Hampstead High School, since 2017; *b* London, 23 Feb. 1978; *d* of Julian Richard Currall and Susan Montgomery Currall; *m* 2001, John Bingham; one *d*. *Educ:* European School of Brussels I; Keble Coll., Oxford (MA Lit.Hum.); Homerton Coll., Cambridge (PGCE). Teacher of Classics, Guildford High Sch., 2001–04; Hd, Classics, St Catherine's Sch., Bramley, 2004–10; Dep. Hd, Guildford High Sch., 2010–16. *Recreation:* running (long-distance). *Address:* South Hampstead High School, 1–3 Maresfield Gardens, NW3 5SS. *T:* (020) 7309 6217. *E:* v.bingham@shhs.gdst.net.

**BINI SMAGHI, Lorenzo,** PhD; Chairman, Société Générale, since 2015 (Director, since 2014); *b* Florence, 29 Nov. 1956. *Educ:* Univ. Catholique de Louvain (Lic. Scis Econs 1978); Univ. of Southern Calif (MA Econs 1980); Univ. of Chicago (PhD Econs 1988). Research Department, Banca d'Italia: Economist, Internat. Section, 1983–88; Hd of Exchange Rate and Internat. Trade Div., 1988–94; Hd of Policy Div., EMI, Frankfurt, 1994–98; Dep. Dir Gen. for Res., ECB, Frankfurt, 1998; Dir Gen. for Internat. Financial Relns, Min. of the Economy and Finance, Italy, 1998–2005; Mem., Exec. Bd, European Central Bank, 2005–11. Pres., SNAM, 2012–16. Vis. Scholar, Center for Internat. Affairs, Harvard Univ., 2012–. Pres., Fondazione Palazzo Strozzi, Florence, 2006–. Grande Ufficiale al Merito della Repubblica Italiana, 2006. *Publications:* L'Euro, 1998, 3rd edn 2001; (with D. Gros) Open Issues in European Central Banking, 2000; Chi Ci Salva dalla Prossima Crisi Finanziaria?, 2000; Il Paradosso dell'euro, 2008; Austerity: European democracies against the wall, 2013; 33 false verità sull'Europa, 2014. *Address:* Via Giuseppe Cuboni 2, Rome 00197, Italy.

**BINLEY, Brian Arthur Roland;** *b* 1 April 1942; *s* of Frank Binley and Phyllis Binley (*née* Underwood); *m* 1985, Jacqueline Denise Gibbs; one *s*, and one *s* by a previous marriage. *Educ:* Finedon Mulso (C of E) Sch. Chairman and Founder: BCC Mktg Services Ltd, 1989–; Beechwood House Publishing Ltd, 1993–2001 (publishers of Binley's Directories). Mem. (C) Northants CC, 1997–2009. MP (C) Northampton S, 2005–15. FRSA 1996. *Recreations:* golf, Association football, cricket, opera. *Clubs:* Carlton; Northampton Town and County.

**BINMORE, Prof. Kenneth George,** CBE 2001; PhD; FBA 1995; Professor of Economics, University College London, 1991–2003, now Emeritus; *b* 27 Sept. 1940; *s* of Ernest George Binmore and Maud Alice (*née* Holland); *m* 1968, Josephine Ann Lee; two *s* two *d*. *Educ:* Imperial Coll., London (BSc; PhD 1964). Lectr, Reader and Prof. of Maths, LSE, 1969–88; Prof. of Econs, LSE and Univ. of Michigan, 1988–93; Dir, ESRC Centre for Econ. Learning and Social Evolution, 1994–2002. *Publications:* Mathematical Analysis, 1977, 2nd edn 1982; Logic, Sets and Numbers, 1980; Topological Ideas, 1981; Calculus, 1982; Economic Organizations as Games, 1986; Economics of Bargaining, 1986; Essays on the Foundations of Game Theory, 1991; Fun and Games, 1992; Frontiers of Game Theory, 1993; Game Theory and the Social Contract: vol. I, Playing Fair, 1994; vol. II, Just Playing, 1998; Natural Justice, 2005; Playing for Real, 2007; Does Game Theory Work?, 2007; Very Short Introduction to Game Theory, 2007; Rational Decisions, 2008; papers. *Recreation:* philosophy. *Address:* Newmills, Whitebrook, Monmouth NP25 4TY. *T:* (01600) 860691.

**BINNEY, Prof. James Jeffrey,** DPhil; FRS 2000; FRAS, FInstP; Professor of Physics, University of Oxford, since 1996; Fellow, Merton College, Oxford, since 1981; *b* 12 April 1950; *s* of Harry Augustus Roy Binney and Barbara Binney (*née* Poole); *m* 1993, Lucy Elliot Buckingham; one *s* one *d*. *Educ:* King's Coll. Sch., Wimbledon; Churchill Coll., Cambridge (BA 1971, MA 1975); Albert Ludwigs Univ., Freiburg im Breisgau; Christ Church and Magdalen Coll., Oxford (DPhil 1976). Fellow, Magdalen Coll., Oxford, 1975–79; Vis. Asst Prof., Princeton Univ., 1979–81; Lectr in Theoretical Physics, 1981–90, Reader, 1990–96, Oxford Univ. Lindemann Fellow, Princeton Univ., 1975–76; Fairchild Dist. Schol., CIT, 1983–84; Visiting Fellow: Univ. of Arizona, 1989; Princeton Univ., 1992; ANU, 1995. FRAS 1973; FInstP 2000. Maxwell Medal and Prize, 1986, Dirac Medal, 2010, Inst. of Physics; Brouwer Award, American Astronomy Soc., 2003; Eddington Medal, RAS, 2013; Occhialini Medal, Italian Physical Soc., 2015. *Publications:* A Very Short Introduction to Astrophysics, 2016; jointly: Galactic Astronomy: structure and kinematics, 1981; Galactic Dynamics, 1987; PICK for Humans, 1990; The Theory of Critical Phenomena, 1992; Galactic Astronomy, 1998; The Physics of Quantum Mechanics, 2008. *Recreations:* carpentry, stone and metalwork, walking. *Address:* Rudolf Peierls Centre for Theoretical Physics, Beecroft Building, Parks Road, Oxford OX1 3PU. *T:* (01865) 273979.

**BINNEY, Marcus Hugh Crofton,** CBE 2006 (OBE 1983); FSA; writer, journalist, conservationist; Founder, 1975, and President, since 1984, Save Britain's Heritage (Chairman, 1975–84); *b* 21 Sept. 1944; *s* of late Lt-Col Francis Crofton Simms, MC and of Sonia, *d* of Rear-Adm. Sir William Marcus Charles Beresford-Whyte, KCB, CMG (she m 2nd, Sir George Binney, DSO); *m* 1st, 1966, Hon. Sara Anne Vanneck (marr. diss. 1976), *e d* of 6th Baron Huntingfield; 2nd, 1981, Anne Carolyn, *d* of Dr T. H. Hills, Merstham, Surrey; two *s*. *Educ:* Magdalene Coll., Cambridge (BA 1966). Architectural writer, 1968–77, Architectural Editor, 1977–84, Editor, 1984–86, Country Life; Ed., Landscape, 1987–88; envmt correspondent, Harpers & Queen, 1989–90; architecture correspondent, The Times, 1991–. Sec., UK Cttee, Internat. Council on Monuments and Sites, 1972–81; Mem., Montagu Cttee (report, Britain's Historic Buildings, published 1980); Director: Rly Heritage Trust, 1985–; HMS Warrior; Chm., Save Europe's Heritage, 1995–; President: Friends of City Churches, 1998– (Chm., 1995–98); Save Jersey's Heritage, 1990–. Television series: Co-Presenter, Great Houses of Europe, 1993, 1996, 1997. Exhibitions: (joint organizer) The Destruction of the Country House, V&A Mus., 1974; Change and Decay: the future of our churches, V&A Mus., 1977. FSA 1989. Hon. FRIBA 2004. London Conservation Medal, 1985. *Publications:* (with Peter Burman): Change and Decay: the future of our churches, 1977; Chapels and Churches: who cares?, 1977; (with Max Hanna) Preservation Pays, 1978; (ed jtly) Railway Architecture, 1979; (ed jtly) Satanic Mills, 1979; (ed jtly) Our Past Before Us, 1981; (with Kit Martin) The Country House: to be or not to be, 1982; (with Max Hanna) Preserve and Prosper, 1983; The Architecture of Sir Robert Taylor, 1984; Our Vanishing Heritage, 1984; Country Manors of Portugal, 1987; (jtly) Bright Futures: the reuse of industrial buildings, 1990; Palace on the River, 1991; (with M. Watson-Smyth) The Save Action Guide, 1991; Châteaux of the Loire, 1992; (with R. Runciman) Glyndebourne: building a vision, 1994; The Châteaux of France: photographs by Frederick Evans 1906–7, 1994; Railway Architecture: the way ahead, 1995; (with Patrick Bowe) Houses and Gardens of Portugal, 1998; Town Houses: 800 years of evolution and innovation in urban design, 1998; Airport Builders, 1999; The Ritz Hotel, London, 1999, Centenary edn 2006; (with Graham Byfield) London Sketchbook: a city observed, 2001; Women Who Lived for Danger, 2002; Great Houses of Europe, 2003; Secret War Heroes, 2005; Save Britain's Heritage 1975–2005: thirty years of campaigning, 2005; In Search of the Perfect House: 500 of the best buildings in Britain and Ireland, 2007; The Blandys of Madeira: 1811–2011, 2011. *Address:* Domaine des Vaux, St Lawrence, Jersey JE3 1JG. *T:* (01534) 864424, *Fax:* (01534) 862612. *E:* mbinney@msn.com.

**BINNIE, Frank Hugh,** FCSD; Chairman and Chief Executive, Binnie International, since 1998; *b* 1 March 1950; *s* of Dr Hugh Lawson Binnie and Isobel May Van Dijk (*née* Nairn); *m* 1996, Fiona Margaret Maclean Nicolson (*née* Hart); one *s* one *d*; and three *s* by previous marriage. *Educ*: Loughborough GS; De Montfort Univ., Leicester (Dip. Textile Technol. 1970). ATI 1970. FCSD 1992. Mgt trainee, Corah Textiles, Leicester, 1970–73; Founder Manager, Floreal Knitwear, Mauritius, 1973–76; Sales Manager, Kemptons Knitwear, Leicester, 1976–79; Gen. Manager, Texport Unilever, 1979–82; Manager, Kilspindie Knitwear, Haddington, 1982–85; Dir and Co. Sec., Midlothian Enterprise, 1985–88; Man. Dir, Perkins, Hodgkinson & Gillibrand, 1988–90; Chief Exec., Design Council, Scotland, then Scottish Design, 1990–96. Chief Exec., Caledonian Foundn, 1996–97; Chief Executive Officer: Internet Soc. Scotland, 1998–2003; ScotlandIS, 2000–03; Executive Chairman: Scottish Internet Exchange, 1999–2003; Scotnom Ltd, 2000–05; Broadband Scotland Ltd, 2001–04; Chm., EBusiness Scotland Ltd, 1999–2004; Co-Founder, Ecommerce Exchange (Scotland) Ltd, 1999–2004; Sen. Consultant, Career Associates, 1998–2014; Founder and Dir, Rainbow Cloud Ltd, 2014–15. Vis. Prof., Strathclyde Univ., 1990–96; External Assessor: MBA, Westminster Univ., 1995–97; Design Mgt, De Montfort Univ., 1996–99. Chm., Sector Gp for Design, Scotvec, 1995–96. Mem. Exec. Council, Scottish Council of Develt and Industry, 2001–05. Gen. Manager, Kenilworth Court Assoc., 2005–16. Formerly Mem. Bd, 1996 UK City of Architecture and Design. Trustee, Flatfeet Dance Co. Ltd, 2013–14. Tutor, Chess in Schools and Communities, 2017–. FRSA 1992; MInstD. *Recreations*: sailing (RYA Yachtmaster), motor boating, dog walking, first bloke global travel. *Clubs*: Winchester House (Sec., 2009–10); Hurlingham Yacht.

**BINNIG, Prof. Dr Gerd Karl;** IBM Fellow, since 1986; Honorary Professor of Physics, University of Munich, since 1987; Founder and Chief Technology Officer (formerly Head of Research), Definiens AG, since 1999; *b* 20 July 1947; *m* 2003, Renate; one *s* one *d* by former marriage. *Educ*: J. W. Goethe Univ., Frankfurt/M (DipPhys; PhD). Research staff mem., IBM Zurich Res. Lab., in fields of superconductivity of semiconductors and scanning tunnelling microscopy, 1978–, Gp Leader 1984–; IBM Almaden Res. Center, San José, and collab. with Stanford Univ., 1985–86; Vis. Prof., Stanford Univ., 1985–86. Member: Technology Council, IBM Acad., 1989–92; Supervisory Bd, Mercedes Automobil Holding AG, 1989–95. For. Associate Mem., Acad. of Scis, Washington, 1987. Hon. FRMS 1988. Scanning Tunnelling Microscopy awards: Physics Prize, German Phys. Soc., 1982; Otto Klung Prize, 1983; (jtly) King Faisal Internat. Prize for Science and Hewlett Packard Europhysics Prize, 1984; (jtly) Nobel Prize in Physics, 1986; Elliot Cresson Medal, Franklin Inst., Philadelphia, 1987; Minnie Rosen Award, Ross Univ., NY, 1988. Grosses Verdienstkreuz mit Stern und Schulterband des Verdienstordens (FRG), 1987; Bayerischer Verdienstorden, 1992. *Recreations*: music, tennis, soccer, golf. *Address*: Definiens AG, Bernhard-Wicki-Strasse 5, 80636 Munich, Germany.

**BINNS, Benjamin Edward Noël L.;** *see* Lyster-Binns.

**BINNS, David John,** CBE 1989; Trust Board Secretary, Halton General Hospital NHS Trust, 1995–99 (non-executive Director, 1992–94); *b* 12 April 1929; *s* of Henry Norman Binns, OBE and Ivy Mary Binns; *m* 1957, Jean Margaret Evans; one *s* (one *d* decd). *Educ*: Fleetwood Grammar Sch.; Rossall Sch.; Sheffield Univ. LLB 1951. Solicitor 1954. Articled Clerk, Sheffield City Council, 1949; Asst Solicitor, Warrington County Borough Council, 1954; Dep. Town Clerk, Warrington County Borough Council, 1958; General Manager: Warrington Develt Corp., 1969–81; Warrington and Runcorn Develt Corp., 1981–89. Mem., Warrington DHA, 1990–92. *Address*: 4 Cedarways, Appleton, Warrington, Cheshire WA4 5EW.

**BINNS, Gareth Ian;** Chief Executive, Institute of Imagination, since 2016 (Director, Learning and Content, Institute of Imagination (formerly London Children's Museum), 2011–16); *b* 6 Feb. 1958; *s* of Ian Binns and Mavis Eleanor Binns (*née* Jones); partner, Sally Bacon; one *s*. *Educ*: Southampton Univ. (BA Hons Archaeol. and Geog.); Durham Univ. (MA Anglo-Saxon and Viking Archaeol.); Nottingham Univ. (PGCE Geog. and Hist.); Birkbeck Coll., London (Dip. Multimedia Mgt). Actg Hd of Dept, and Div. Leader, Bilborough Sixth Form Coll., 1984–88; Educn Officer, Council for British Archaeol., 1988–91; Countryside and Envmtl Educn Officer, 1991–98, Hd of Educn and Interpretation, 1998–2000, NT; Educn Dir, NESTA, 2000–03; Keeper of Learning and Inf., BM, 2003–06; Dir of Ops, Personal Finance Educn Gp, 2006–09; Chief Exec., Sorrell Foundn, 2009–10. *Recreations*: museums and galleries, hill-walking, art appreciation and collecting, historic buildings, landscape history, running. *Address*: Institute of Imagination, Second Home, 68 Hanbury Street, E1 5JL.

**BINNS, Jacqueline Sukie, (Mrs W. A. T. Hills);** artist, embroiderer and sculptor, since 1986; *b* 24 May 1963; *d* of Dennis Binns and Eileen (*née* Andrews); *m* 1986, Warwick Alan Theodore Hills. *Educ*: Goldsmiths' Coll., London (BA Textiles 1986). Exhibitions include: Southwark Cathedral, Leicester Mus., Salisbury Cathedral, 1987 and 2007; Gawthorpe Hall, Peterborough Cathedral, 1988; St Alban's Abbey, 1989, 1992; St Paul's Cathedral, 1990; Royal Sch. of Needlework, 1993; Sheffield Cath., Goldsmiths' Coll., 1997; Shrewsbury Abbey, 1998; Wimpole Hall, Cambridge, Winchester Cath., 1999; Guildford Cath., Portsmouth Cath., Alexandra Palace, 2000; De Morgan Centre, 2003; Guildford Cathedral, 2008; works of art in private collections and cathedrals and churches in America, Australia, Europe and UK; works include: St Alban Cope, 1988, and embroideries for 12 copes in St Albans Abbey; Pentecost Panel for Whitelands Coll., London, 1991; Altar Hangings for Warwick Hospital's Chapel: White, 1994; Purple, 1998; Red, 1999; Green, 2001; Travelling Cope and Mitre for Bishop of London, 2003; 1400th Anniversary Cope and Mitre for St Paul's Cathedral, 2004; lifesize Crucifixion sculpture for St Peter's Ch, Plymouth, 2007; Altar sets for All Hallows by the Tower, London: Red 2009; White, 2015; Purple, 2015; Green, 2017; Virgin and Child Sculpture, All Hallows by the Tower, London, 2011; The Unity Sculptures for St Mary the Virgin Ch and Christopher Rawlins Sch., Adderbury, 2013; Altar sets for St Mary's, Stoke D'Abernon: Red, 2014, White, 2018; Coffin Pall for King Richard III, 2015; Cope, Mitre and Stole for Bishop of Aston, 2015; Cope, Mitre and Stole for Bishop of St Davids, 2017; Tower Hill Madonna and Child Sculpture for Dean of Montreal, Canada, 2018; Altarcloths for All Saints, Fulham, London. *Recreations*: walking, the arts, costume. *Address*: 1 Cargill Road, Earlsfield, SW18 3EF. *T*: (020) 8874 0895. *E*: jb@jacquiebinns.com.

**BINNS, James Wallace,** PhD, DLitt; FBA 2004; Lecturer, 1984–91, Reader, 1991–2002, in Latin Literature, Honorary Fellow, since 2002, University of York; *b* 1 Sept. 1940; *s* of Wallace William and Madge Binns. *Educ*: Univ. of Birmingham (BA 1964; MA 1965; PhD 1969; DLitt 1992). Exec. Officer, War Office, 1958–61; Lectr in Later Latin, Univ. of Birmingham, 1965–84. Hon. Lectr, Univ. of Leeds, 1987–. *Publications*: Intellectual Culture in Elizabethan and Jacobean England, 1990; (ed with S. E. Banks) Gervase of Tilbury: Otia Imperialia, 2002. *Recreations*: travel, films, military history. *Address*: Centre for Medieval Studies, University of York, King's Manor, York YO1 7EP. *T*: (01904) 433910, *Fax*: (01904) 433918.

**BINNS, Rev. John Richard,** PhD; Vicar, St Mary the Great with St Michael, Cambridge, 1994–2017; Rural Dean of North Cambridge, 2007–11; *b* 10 Jan. 1951. *Educ*: St John's Coll., Cambridge (MA 1976); King's Coll., London (PhD 1989); Coll. of the Resurrection, Mirfield. Ordained deacon, 1976, priest, 1977; Assistant Curate: Holy Trinity, Clapham, 1976–78; Clapham Old Town, 1978–80; Team Vicar, Mortlake with E Sheen, 1980–87; Vicar, Holy Trinity, Upper Tooting, 1987–94. Dir, Inst. for Orthodox Christian Studies, 1999–. Hon. Canon, Ely Cathedral, 2007–. Chm. Trustees, Partners for Change Ethiopia (formerly St Matthew's Children's Fund, Ethiopia), 2004–. *Publications*: Cyril of Scythopolis: lives of the Monks of Palestine, 1991; Ascetics and Ambassadors of Christ, 1994; Great St Mary's, Cambridge's University Church, 2000; An Introduction to the Christian Orthodox Churches, 2002; The Orthodox Church of Ethiopia: a history, 2017. *Address*: 197 Chase Road, Burntwood WS7 0EB. *T*: (01543) 670217.

**BINNS, Malcolm;** concert pianist; *b* 29 Jan. 1936; *s* of Douglas and May Binns. *Educ*: Bradford Grammar Sch.; Royal Coll. of Music (ARCM, Chappell Gold Medal, Medal of Worshipful Co. of Musicians). London début, 1957; Henry Wood Proms début, 1960; Royal Festival Hall début, 1961; Festival Hall appearances in London Philharmonic Orchestra International series, 1969–; toured with Scottish Nat. Orch., 1989; concerts at Aldeburgh, Leeds, Three Choirs (1975), Bath and Canterbury Festivals; regular appearances at Promenade concerts and broadcasts for BBC Radio; celebrated 60th birthday with series of concerts, 1996; series of recitals for BBC linking Clementi and Beethoven, 1997. First complete recording of Beethoven piano sonatas on original instruments, 1980; première recordings of Sir William Sterndale Bennett's piano concertos with London Philharmonic and Philharmonia Orchs, 1990; première recording of Stanford's re-discovered Third Piano Concerto, with RPO, 1996. *Recreation*: collecting antique gramophone records. *Address*: 233 Court Road, Orpington, Kent BR6 9BY. *T*: (01689) 831056.

**BINNS, Hon. Patrick George;** farm owner and operator, since 2014; Consul General of Canada to Boston, USA, 2010–14; *b* Saskatchewan, 8 Oct. 1948; *s* of late Stan and Phyllis Binns; *m* 1971, Carol MacMillan; three *s* one *d*. *Educ*: Univ. of Alberta (BA, MA 1971). Rural Develt Council, PEI, 1974–78; MLA (PC) 4th Kings, PEI, 1978–84; Minister of: Municipal Affairs, Labour, and Envmt, 1979–80; of Community Affairs, 1980–82; of Fisheries and of Industry, 1982–84; MP (PC) Cardigan, 1984–88; Parly Sec. to Minister of Fisheries and Oceans, 1984–88; MLA (PC) Dist 5, Murray River-Gaspereaux, PEI, 1996–2007; Premier and Pres. of Exec. Council, PEI, 1996–2007; Leader, PC Party, PEI, 1996–2007; Minister responsible for Intergovtl Affairs, 1996–2007; Minister of Agriculture, Fisheries and Aquaculture, 2006–07; Ambassador of Canada to Ireland, 2007–10. President: Island Bean Ltd, 1988–96; Pat Binns & Associates, 1988–96. Silver Jubilee Medal, 1977; Golden Jubilee Medal, 2002; Diamond Jubilee Medal, 2012. *Recreations*: cycling, canoeing, golfing. *Address*: (home) 2896 Grey's Road, Murray River RR#4, PE C0A 1W0, Canada. *T*: (902) 9622196.

**BINNS, Susan May;** Director, Information Society and Media, European Commission, 2005–08; *b* 22 April 1948; *d* of Jack and Mollie Binns. *Educ*: Harrogate Coll.; LSE (BSc Econ Internat. Relations). HM Diplomatic Service, 1968–80: served FCO and Brussels; New Delhi, 1978–80; Cabinet of Ivor Richard, EC Member, Brussels, 1981–84; Counsellor, EC Delegations: Washington, 1985–88; Belgrade, 1988; Dep. Chef de Cabinet of Bruce Millan, EC Mem. resp. for regl policies, 1989–91, Chef de Cabinet, 1991–95; Dir, Internal Market, EC, 1995–2004. *Recreations*: gardening, golf. *Address*: 18 rue du Charnois, 1342 Limelette, Belgium.

**BINSKI, Prof. Paul,** PhD; FSA; FBA 2007; Professor of the History of Medieval Art, University of Cambridge, since 2006 (Head, Department of History of Art, 2014–16); Fellow, Gonville and Caius College, Cambridge, 1983–87 and since 1996; *b* 9 Nov. 1956; *s* of late Eugene and Pamela Binski. *Educ*: Harrow Sch.; Gonville and Caius Coll., Cambridge (BA 1979, MA); PhD 1984. Asst Prof., Dept of History of Art, Yale Univ., and Fellow, Saybrook Coll., 1988–91; Lecturer, Department of History of Art: Univ. of Manchester, 1991–95; Cambridge Univ., 1996–2002 (Hd of Dept, 1999–2001); Reader in Hist. of Medieval Art, Cambridge Univ., 2002–06. Slade Prof. of Fine Art, Univ. of Oxford, 2007. Vis. Mem., IAS, Princeton, 1987–88; Getty Postdoctoral Fellow, Dept of Art and Archaeol., Princeton Univ., 1987–88; Ailsa Mellon Bruce Vis. Sen. Fellow, Center for Advanced Study in Visual Arts, Nat. Gall. of Art, Washington, 1992; British Acad./Leverhulme Trust Sen. Res. Fellow, 2003–04; Leverhulme Trust Major Res. Fellowship, 2011–14. Associate Ed., Art History, 1992–97; Mem., Res. and Pubn Cttee, British Acad. Corpus Vitrearum Medii Aevi, 1995–; Mem., Editl Bd, British Art Jl, 1999–. Member: Peterborough Cathedral Fabric Adv. Cttee, 1996–2006; Westminster Abbey Fabric Commn, 1998–. Mem., Exec. Cttee, Walpole Soc., 1999–2003. Foreign Advr, Internat. Center of Medieval Art, The Cloisters, NY, 2004–07. Presenter, Divine Designs, Channel 5, 2002–04. FSA 1998. Gov., Harrow Sch., 2011–. *Publications*: The Painted Chamber at Westminster, 1986; (jtly) Dominican Painting in East Anglia: the Thornham Parva Retable and the Musée de Cluny Frontal, 1987; (ed with J. Alexander) Age of Chivalry: art in Plantagenet England 1200–1400, 1987; Westminster Abbey and the Plantagenets: kingship and the representation of power 1200–1400, 1995; Medieval Death: ritual and representation, 1996; (ed with W. Noel) New Offerings, Ancient Treasures: essays in medieval art in honour of George Henderson, 2001; Becket's Crown: art and imagination in Gothic England 1170–1300, 2004; (ed with S. Panayotova) The Cambridge Illuminations: ten centuries of book production in the Medieval West, 2005; (with P. Zutshi) Western Illuminated Manuscripts: a catalogue of the collection in Cambridge University Library, 2011; Gothic Wonder: art, artifice and the decorated style 1290–1350, 2014; contrib. articles to learned jls. *Recreations*: organ music, old churches and houses, conversation. *Address*: Gonville and Caius College, Cambridge CB2 1TA.

**BINTLEY, David Julian,** CBE 2001; choreographer; Artistic Director: Birmingham Royal Ballet, 1995–2019; National Ballet of Japan, 2010–14; *b* 17 Sept. 1957; *s* of David Bintley and Glenys Bintley (*née* Ellinthorpe); *m* 1981, Jennifer Catherine Ursula Mills; two *s*. *Educ*: Holme Valley Grammar School. Royal Ballet School, 1974; Sadler's Wells Royal Ballet, 1976; first professional choreography, The Outsider, 1978; first three act ballet, The Swan of Tuonela, 1982; Company Choreographer, 1983–85, Resident Choreographer, 1985–86, Sadler's Wells Royal Ballet; Resident Choreographer and Principal Dancer, Royal Ballet, 1986–93. Ballets created include: Hobson's Choice, 1989, rev. 2019; Carmina Burana, 1995; Far from the Madding Crowd, 1996; The Nutcracker Sweeties; The Protecting Veil, 1998; The Shakespeare Suite; Arthur, Part One, 2000; Arthur, Part Two, 2001; Beauty and the Beast, 2003; Take Five, 2007; Aladdin, 2008; E=mc$^2$, 2009; Cinderella, 2010; The Prince of the Pagodas (new version), 2011; Faster, 2012; The King Dances, 2015; The Tempest, 2016. Evening Standard Award for Ballet, for Choros and Consort Lessons, both 1983; Laurence Olivier Award for Petrushka, 1984; Manchester Evening News Award for Dance, for Still Life at the Penguin Café, 1987, for Edward II, 1998.

**BIRBALSINGH, Katharine;** Headmistress and Co-founder, Michaela Community School, Brent, 2014–19; *b* Auckland, NZ, 16 Sept. 1973; *d* of Frank and Norma Birbalsingh; one *s*. *Educ*: Victoria Park Collegiate Inst., Toronto; New Coll., Oxford (MA French and Philosophy). Teacher of French: Archbishop Tenison's Sch., Kennington, 1999–2002; St Thomas the Apostle Sch., Peckham, 2002–03; Dunraven, Streatham, 2003–10; Teacher of French and Vice Principal, St Michael and All Angels Acad., Camberwell, 2010. *Publications*: To Miss with Love, 2011; Battle Hymn of the Tiger Teachers, 2016. *Recreation*: cinema.

**BIRCH,** family name of **Baroness Young of Hornsey**.

**BIRCH, Prof. Bryan John,** FRS 1972; Professor of Arithmetic, University of Oxford, 1985–98, now Emeritus; Fellow of Brasenose College, Oxford, 1966–98, now Emeritus; *b* 25 Sept. 1931; *s* of Arthur Jack Benjamin Birch and Mary Edith Birch; *m* 1961, Gina Margaret Christ (*d* 2005); two *s* one *d. Educ:* Shrewsbury Sch.; Trinity Coll., Cambridge (MA, PhD; Hon. Fellow, 2016). Harkness Fellow, Princeton, 1957–58; Fellow: Trinity Coll., Cambridge, 1956–60; Churchill Coll., Cambridge, 1960–62; Sen. Lectr, later Reader, Univ. of Manchester, 1962–65; Reader in Mathematics, Univ. of Oxford, 1966–85. Deleg., OUP, 1988–98. Hon. FIMA. Mem., Bd of Sen. Whitehead Prize, 1993, De Morgan Medal, 2007, LMS. *Publications:* articles in learned jls, mainly on number theory; various editorships. *Recreations:* gardening (theoretical), opera, hunting wild flowers. *Address:* Green Cottage, Boars Hill, Oxford OX1 5DQ. *T:* (01865) 735367; Mathematical Institute, University of Oxford, Radcliffe Observatory Quarter, Woodstock Road, Oxford OX2 6GG. *E:* birch@maths.ox.ac.uk.

**BIRCH, Prof. Dinah Lynne,** CBE 2016; DPhil; Professor of English Literature, since 2003, and Pro-Vice Chancellor, since 2011, University of Liverpool; *b* Melton Mowbray, Leics, 4 Oct. 1953; *d* of Edward Neil Baggeley and Rowena Iris Baggeley (*née* Hempshall); *m* 1976, Sidney Ian Birch; one *s* one *d. Educ:* King Edward VII Upper Sch., Melton Mowbray; St Hugh's Coll., Oxford (BA, MA, DPhil 1980). Jun. Res. Fellow, Merton Coll., Oxford, 1980–82; Fixed-term Tutorial Fellow in English, St Hugh's Coll., Oxford, 1982–85; Lectr in Lit., Open Univ., 1986–90; Lectr, Univ. of Oxford, 1990–2003; Stirling Boyd Fellow in English Lit., 1990–2003, Vice-Pres., 2002–03, Trinity Coll., Oxford. Vis. Prof., Lancaster Univ., 2003–; Chancellor's Dist. Lectr, Louisiana State Univ., 2002. Mem., RAE 2008 Sub-Panel 57, English Lang. and Lit., 2008; Chair, Sub-Panel 29, English Lang. and Lit., 2014, Dep. Chair, Main Panel D, Arts and Humanities, 2014, REF 2014; Chair, Main Panel D, Arts and Humanities REF 2021, 2017. Pres., British Assoc. for Victorian Studies, 2018–. Mem., Judging Panel for Man Booker Prize, 2012. Richard Hillary Trust, 1990–. Companion, Guild of St George, 2002–. FEA 2003. *Publications:* Ruskin's Myths, 1988; Ruskin on Turner, 1990; (ed) Anthony Trollope's The Duke's Children, 1995; (ed) George Eliot's The Mill on the Floss, 1996; (ed) Ruskin and the Dawn of the Modern, 1999; (ed) John Ruskin's Fors Clavigera, 2000; (ed jtly) Ruskin and Gender, 2002; (ed) John Ruskin: selected writings, 2004; Our Victorian Education, 2008; (gen. ed.) Oxford Companion to English Literature, 2009; (ed jtly) Conflict and Difference in Nineteenth-Century Literature, 2010; (ed) Elizabeth Gaskell's Cranford, 2011; (ed) Anthony Trollope's Can You Forgive Her?, 2012; (ed jtly) Concise Oxford Companion to English Literature, 2012; (ed) Anthony Trollope's The Small House at Allington, 2014; contrib. articles to essay collections and learned jls; contrib. reviews to London Rev. of Books, TLS, The Times, Guardian, Independent. *Recreations:* reading, music, cinema. *Address:* University of Liverpool, Foundation Building, 765 Brownlow Hill, Liverpool L69 7ZX. *T:* (0151) 794 2003. *Club:* Athenæum.

**BIRCH, Sir John (Allan),** KCVO 1993; CMG 1987; HM Diplomatic Service, retired; Ambassador to Hungary, 1989–95; *b* 24 May 1935; *s* of late C. Allan Birch, MD, FRCP and Marjorie (*née* Bold); *m* 1960, Primula Haselden; three *s* one *d. Educ:* Leighton Park Sch.; Corpus Christi Coll., Cambridge (MA). Served HM Forces, Middlesex Regt, 1954–56. Joined HM Foreign Service, 1959; served: Paris, 1960–63; Singapore, 1963–64; Bucharest, 1965–68; Geneva, 1968–70; Kabul, 1973–76; Royal Coll. of Defence Studies, 1977; Comprehensive Test Ban Treaty Negotiations, Geneva, 1977–80; Counsellor, Budapest, 1980–83; Hd of East European Dept, FCO, 1983–86; Ambassador and Dep. Perm. Rep. to UN, NY, 1986–89. Pres., UN Trusteeship Council, 1987–89. Dir and Chief Exec., British Assoc. for Central and Eastern Europe, 1995–2004. Dir, Schroder Emerging Countries Fund plc, 1996–2004; Directing Staff, RCDS, 2004–18. Chairman, Advisory Board: SSEES, 2006–18; UCL European Inst., 2014–; Member Council: Chatham House (RIIA), 1997–2003; UCL, 1999–2008 (Vice-Chm., 2005–08; Chm., Research Ethics Cttee, 2003–12; Hon. Fellow, 2009). Trustee, Wytham Hall for the Homeless, 1999–2014. *Recreations:* tennis, ski-ing, carpentry. *Address:* 185 Ashley Gardens, Emery Hill Street, SW1P 1PD. *Club:* Athenæum.

**BIRCH, Peter Gibbs,** CBE 1992; Chairman, Land Securities PLC, 1998–2007; Chairman, Legal Services Commission, 2000–03; *b* 4 Dec. 1937; *m* 1962, Gillian (*née* Benge); three *s* one *d. Educ:* Allhallows Sch., Devon. Royal West Kent Regt, seconded to Jamaica Regt, 1957–58 (2nd Lieut). Nestlé Co., UK, Singapore and Malaysia, 1958–65; Sales and Mkting, Gillette, 1965; Gen. Sales Manager, Gillette Australia, 1969; Man. Dir, Gillette, NZ, 1971; Gen. Manager, Gillette, SE Asia (based Singapore), 1973; Gp Gen. Manager, Gillette, Africa, ME, Eastern Europe, 1975; Man. Dir, Gillette UK, 1981; Dir and Chief Exec., Abbey Nat. Building Soc., then Abbey Nat. plc, 1984–98. Chairman: Trinity plc, 1998–99; UCTX, 2000–01; Kensington Gp, 2000–07; Trigold plc, 2007–; Sen. non-exec. Dir, Trinity Mirror plc, 1999–2007; non-executive Director: Hoskyns Gp, 1988–93; Argos, 1990–98; Scottish Mutual Assurance, 1992–98; N. M. Rothschild & Sons, 1998–2004 (Advr, 2004–08); Dalgety, 1993–98; Dah Sing Financial Services, 1997–2011; PIC, 1998–2000; Coca-Cola Beverages, 1998–2000; Travelex plc, 1999–2009; Sainsbury's Bank plc, 2002–06; Lamprell Energy Ltd, 2006–08 (Chm., 2007–08); Banco Finantia, 2007–08; Advr, Cambridge Place Investment Mgt LLP, 2004–. Chm., Council of Mortgage Lenders, 1991–92. Trustee, Cap Gemini, 1993–. FCBSI. Pres., Middlesex Young People's (formerly Middlesex Assoc. of Boys') Clubs, 1988–; Chm., Clubs for Young People, 2010–15. *Recreations:* active holidays, swimming.

**BIRCH, Robin Arthur,** CB 1995; voluntary worker; civil servant, retired; *b* 12 Oct. 1939; *s* of late Arthur and Olive Birch; *m* 1962, Jane Marion Irvine Sturdy; two *s. Educ:* King Henry VIII Sch., Coventry; Christ Church, Oxford (MA). Entered Min. of Health as Asst Principal, 1961; Private Sec. to Charles Loughlin, MP (Parly Sec.), 1965–66; Principal, 1966; seconded to: Interdeptl Social Work Gp, 1969–70; Home Office (Community Develt Project), 1970–72; Asst Sec., DHSS, 1973; Chm., Working Party on Manpower and Trng for Social Services, 1974–76 (HMSO Report, 1976); Principal Private Sec. to Leader of the House of Commons, 1980–81; Under Sec., DHSS, 1982; Asst Auditor Gen., Nat. Audit Office, 1984–86, on secondment; Dir, Regl Orgn, 1988–90; Dep. Sec. (Policy), 1990–95, DSS. Hon. Sec., Friends of Christ Church Cathedral, Oxford, 1978–2006. Vice-Pres., Age Concern England, 1998–2008 (Chm., 1995–98). Chairman: Response Organisation (formerly Oxfordshire Gp Homes), 1995–2014 (Vice-Chm., 2014–17; Chm., Finance Cttee, 2014–17; Patron, 2017–); Low Vision Services Implementation Gp for England, 1999–2005 (Chm. Working Gp, 1998–99; Report, 1999); Oxford Credit Union, 2005–10; Buildings and Glebe Cttees, Dio. of Oxford, 2009–17; Oxford Develt Bd, Crisis UK, 2011–16. Trustee: Oxford CAB, 1996–2004 (Chm., 1997–2002); Oxfordshire Community Foundn, 1996–2002; Lady Nuffield Home (Oxford), 1996–2015; Age Concern Oxfordshire, 1998–2005; Wyndham Housing Assoc., 2001–09; Roman Research Trust, 2002–16; City of Oxford Charity, 2004– (Chm., 2004–19); Oxfordshire Assoc. for the Blind, 2018– (Jt Patron, 2010–18). Mem., Order of St Frideswide, Dio. Oxford, 2015. DL Oxfordshire, 1996. *Recreations:* family and friends, travel, music, byways of classical antiquity, garden railway. *Club:* Oxford Rotary (Pres., 2008–09).

**BIRCH, Sir Roger,** Kt 1992; CBE 1987; QPM 1980; Chief Constable, Sussex Police, 1983–93; *b* 27 Sept. 1930; *s* of John Edward Lawrence Birch and Ruby Birch; *m* 1st, 1954, Jeanne Margaret Head (*d* 2006); one *s*; 2nd, 2011, Susan Elizabeth Raine. *Educ:* King's Coll., Taunton. Cadet, Royal Naval Coll., Dartmouth, 1949–50; Pilot Officer, RAF, 1950–52. Devon Constabulary, 1954–72: Constable, uniform and CID; then through ranks to Chief Supt; Asst Chief Constable, Mid-Anglia Constab., 1972–74; Dep. Chief Constable, Kent Constab., 1974–78; Chief Constable, Warwickshire Constab., 1978–83. Dir, Police Extended Interviews, 1983–91; Pres., Assoc. of Chief Police Officers, 1987–88 (Vice-Pres., 1986–87; Chm., Traffic Cttee, 1983–86; Chm., Internat. Affairs Adv. Cttee, 1988–92); Vice Chm., Internat. Cttee, Internat. Assoc. of Chiefs of Police, 1989–93; Trustee: Police Dependants' Trust, 1981–93; Police Gurney Fund, 1983–91. Mem., St John Ambulance Council, Sussex, 1986–93. UK Vice-Pres., Royal Life Saving Soc., 1985–93 (Chm., SE Region, 1983–93). Mem. Council, IAM, 1984–93. Hon. Fellow, Centre for Legal Studies, 1993. Hon. LLD Sussex, 1991. *Publications:* articles on criminal intelligence, breath measuring instruments and on the urban environment, in learned jls. *Recreations:* walking, music. *Club:* Royal Air Force (Trustee, 2007–16).

**BIRCH, Prof. Sarah,** DPhil, PhD; FBA 2013; Professor of Political Science, King's College London, since 2016; *b* Boston, Mass, 5 Dec. 1963; *d* of David and Louisa Birch. *Educ:* Dartmouth Coll. (AB); Somerville Coll., Oxford (MPhil; DPhil 1992); Univ. of Essex (MA; PhD 1998). Lectr, 1996–2003, Reader, 2003–12, Prof., 2012–13, Univ. of Essex; Prof. of Comparative Politics, Univ. of Glasgow, 2013–16. Ed., British Jl Political Sci., 2002–11. FRSA 2016; FAcSS 2018. *Publications:* Elections and Democratization in Ukraine, 2000; Electoral Systems and Political Transformation in Post-communist Russia, 2003; Full Participation: a comparative study of compulsory voting, 2009; Electoral Malpractice, 2011; Ethics and Integrity in British Politics: how citizens judge their politicians' conduct and why it matters, 2015. *Recreation:* photography. *Address:* Department of Political Economy, King's College London, Aldwych, WC2B 4BG.

**BIRCH, Rt Hon. Dame Sue (Lascelles);** *see* Carr, Rt Hon. Dame S. L.

**BIRCH, Rt Hon. Sir William (Francis),** GNZM 1999; PC 1992; consultant in public policy and affairs; company director; Minister of Finance, 1993–97, Treasurer, 1997–99, New Zealand; *b* 9 April 1934; *s* of Charles William Birch and Elizabeth Alicia (*née* Wells); *m* 1953, Rosa Mitchell; three *s* one *d.* Surveyor. Borough Councillor 1965–74, Dep. Mayor 1968–74, Pukekohe. MP (Nat.) Pukekohe, NZ, 1972–99; Jun. Opposition Whip, 1973–75; Sen. Govt Whip, 1975–78; Minister of: Energy, Science and Technol. and Nat. Develt, 1978–81; Energy, Regl Develt and Nat. Develt, 1981–84; Labour, Immigration and State Services, 1990–93; Employment, 1991–93; Health, 1993; Minister for Pacific Island Affairs, 1990–91. Chm., Internat. Energy Agency, 1983. *Recreations:* fishing, gardening. *Address:* 420 Bremner Road, RD2, Drury, New Zealand. *Clubs:* Rotary; Jaycee International.

**BIRCHALL, Prof. Martin Anthony,** FRCSI; FMedSci; Professor of Laryngology, University College London, since 2009; Programme Director, UCL-Partners, since 2010; *b* Wigan, Lancs, 13 Aug. 1961; *s* of Gerrard and Ruth Birchall; *m* 1989, Tina Pike; three *s* two *d. Educ:* St Edward's Coll., Liverpool; Jesus Coll., Cambridge (BA 1982; BChir 1984; MB 1985; MA Hons 1986; MD 1994). FRCSI 1988; FRCS (Otolaryngol.) 1989; FRCS (Otorhinolaryngol.) 1989. Sen. Lectr and Reader, Univ. of Bristol; Professor of Head and Neck Surgery, Univ. of Liverpool, 2004–05; of Surgery, Univ. of Bristol, 2006–08. FMedSci 2010. *Publications:* contrib. scientific papers to jls incl. Lancet, BMJ and Nature. *Recreations:* running, reading, films. *Address:* Professorial Unit, Royal National Throat, Nose and Ear Hospital, 330 Gray's Inn Road, WC1X 8DA. *T:* (020) 7915 1300, 7915 1308. *E:* m.birchall@ucl.ac.uk.

**BIRD,** family name of **Baron Bird.**

**BIRD,** Baron *cr* 2015 (Life Peer), of Notting Hill in the Royal Borough of Kensington and Chelsea; **John Anthony Bird,** MBE 1995; Founder, and Editor-in-Chief: The Big Issue, since 1991; ITTIA, since 2004; Wedge Card, since 2007; Chapter Catcher, since 2019; *b* 30 Jan. 1946; *s* of Alfred Ernest Bird and Eileen Mary (*née* Dunne); *m* 1st, 1965, Linda Stuart Haston (marr. diss.); one *d*; 2nd, 1973, Isobel Theresa (marr. diss.), *d* of Sir Robert Ricketts, 7th Bt; one *s* one *d*; 3rd, 2004, Parveen Sodhi; one *s* one *d. Educ:* St Thomas More's Secondary Mod. Sch.; Ealing Coll. (BA Hons Hum.). Gardening asst, Royal Borough of Kensington and Chelsea, 1963–64; printer, Acrow Engrg, 1964–73; bean canner, H. J. Heinz, 1973–74; printer: Pictorial Charts Educnl Trust, 1974–75; Broadoak Press, 1978–83; print and publishing consultant, 1983–91. Contested Mayor of London, 2008. Hon. Fellow, Liverpool John Moores Univ., 2000. Hon. Dr Oxford Brookes, 2001. *Publications:* Some Luck (autobiog.), 2003; How to Change Your Life in 7 Steps, 2006; Change Your Life: 10 steps to get what you want, 2008; Necessity of Poverty, 2012; Why Drawing Naked Women is Good for the Soul, 2013. *Recreations:* swimming, cycling, running, drawing, talking, educating. *Address:* The Big Issue, 113–115 Fonthill Road, Finsbury Park, N4 3HH.

**BIRD, Sir Adrian (Peter),** Kt 2014; CBE 2005; PhD; FMedSci; FRS 1989; FRSE; Buchanan Professor of Genetics, Edinburgh University, since 1990; Director, Wellcome Trust Centre for Cell Biology, 1999–2011; *b* 3 July 1947; *s* of Kenneth George Bird and Aileen Mary Bird; *m* 1st, 1976; one *s* one *d*; 2nd, 1993, Prof. Catherine Mary Abbott; one *s* one *d. Educ:* Queen Elizabeth's Grammar School, Hartlebury; Univ. of Sussex (BSc(Hons)); Univ. of Edinburgh (PhD 1971). Damon Runyan Fellow, Yale Univ., 1972–73; postdoctoral fellowship, Univ. of Zurich, 1974–75; Medical Research Council, Edinburgh: scientific staff, Mammalian Genome Unit, 1975–87; Sen. Scientist, Inst. for Molecular Pathol., Vienna, 1988–90. Mem. Bd of Govs, Wellcome Trust, 2000–10. Trustee, Cancer Research UK, 2011–16. FRSE 1994; FMedSci 2001. Louis Jeantet Prize for Med. Res., Switzerland, 1999; Gabor Medal, 1999, GlaxoSmithKline Prize, 2012, Buchanan Medal, 2018, Royal Soc.; Novartis Medal, Biochem. Soc., 2007; Charles Leopold Mayer Prize, French Acad. of Scis, 2008; Gairdner Internat. Award, Gairdner Foundn, Canada, 2011; Frontiers of Knowledge Award, Banco Bilbao Vizcaya Argentaria, Spain, 2014; Shaw Prize for Life Science and Medicine, 2016. *Publications:* articles in Nature, Cell and other jls. *Recreations:* sport, music, food. *Address:* Wellcome Centre for Cell Biology, University of Edinburgh, Michael Swann Building, Max Born Crescent, Edinburgh EH9 3BF. *T:* (0131) 650 5670.

**BIRD, Alan Robert;** Head, City of London School, since 2018; *b* Guildford, 22 July 1977; *s* of Graham Bird and Heather Bird; partner, Geraint Lewis. *Educ:* Trinity Hall, Cambridge (BA Hons 1st Cl. Econs 1999); London Sch. of Econs and Political Sci. (MSc Econs 2002; ESRC Scholar). Tonbridge School: Teacher of Econs and Politics, 2002–04; Hd, Politics, 2004–09; Brighton College: Hd, Sixth Form, 2010–13; Dep. Headmaster, 2013–17. Gov., London Acad. of Excellence, 2014–17. *Recreations:* travel, music, politics, cuisine, family. *Address:* City of London School, 107 Queen Victoria Street, EC4V 3AL. *T:* (020) 3680 6400. *E:* head@cityoflondonschool.org.uk.

**BIRD, Anthony Patrick Michael,** OBE 1991; Chairman, Bird Group of Companies Ltd, since 2002 (Director, since 1958); *b* 28 Dec. 1935; *s* of William Thomas Bird and May Frances Bird; *m* 1985, Janet Eleanor Burns; one *s* six *d. Educ:* Ratcliffe Coll., Leics. Served 4th RTR. Jt Man. Dir, Bird Gp of Cos, 1973–2002. Chm., Nuclear Services Gp Ltd, 1982–91. Member: Minerals, Metals, Materials and Chemicals Requirements Cttee,

1983–85, Industrial Materials and Vehicles Mkt Adv. Cttee, 1985–86, DTI; Lead Waste Cttee, DoE, 1984–85; Adv. Gp on Decommng of North Sea Oil Platforms, 1985–90 (Chm.); Adv. Cttee on Business and the Envmt, 1990–93; Bd, Envmtl Mgt Agency, Welsh Office, 1991–93. Mem. Bd, Warwickshire Police Authy, 1995–2003. Bureau International de la Récupération: Pres., Ferrous Div., 1976–95; Pres., 1995–99 (Pres. of Honour, 1999); Treas., 2000–08; Life Mem. of Honour, 2008. President: Midwest Metals Assoc., 1975–76; British Metals Fedn, 1979–80 (Life Pres., 1992); Fedn of Eur. Recycling Industry, 1981–89 and 2001–03 (Pres. of Honour, 2003). Chm. Trustees, Stoneleigh Abbey Ltd, 1998–; Trustee, Shakespeare Birthplace Trust, 2007–. Gov., 2002–, Chm. Trustees, 2004–, King Edward VI GS, Stratford-upon-Avon. Gov., Stratford-upon-Avon Coll., 2016–. Prince of Wales Award for Prodn and Innovation, 1986. *Recreations:* field sports, Rugby football, agriculture, architecture, fine arts. *Address:* c/o Bird Group of Companies Ltd, The Hunting Lodge, Billesley Road, Stratford-upon-Avon, Warwicks CV37 9RA. *Club:* Carlton.

**BIRD, Prof. Colin Carmichael,** CBE 2000; PhD; FRCPath, FRCPE, FRCSE, FMedSci; FRSE; Dean, Faculty of Medicine and Provost, Faculty Group of Medicine and Veterinary Medicine, University of Edinburgh, 1995–2002; *b* 5 March 1938; *s* of John and Sarah Bird; *m* 1964, Ailsa M. Ross; two *s* one *d. Educ:* Lenzie Acad.; Glasgow Univ. (MB ChB 1961; PhD 1967). FRCPath 1978 (MRCPath 1968); FRCPE 1989; FRCSE 1995; FRSE 1992. Research Fellow and Lectr in Pathology, Univ. of Glasgow, 1962–67; Lectr in Pathology, Univ. of Aberdeen, 1967–72; Sen. Lectr in Pathology, Univ. of Edinburgh, 1972–75; Professor of Pathology: Univ. of Leeds, 1975–86; Univ. of Edinburgh, 1986–2002, now Emeritus. Founder FMedSci 1998. Dr *hc* Edinburgh, 2004. Knight's Cross, Order of Merit (Poland), 2006. *Publications:* contribs to various scientific jls on cancer and cancer genetics. *Recreations:* golf, walking, music, reading. *Address:* 45 Ann Street, Edinburgh EH4 1PL. *T:* (0131) 332 5568. *Club:* New (Edinburgh).

**BIRD, Conrad,** CBE 2016; Director, GREAT Britain Campaign, Department for International Trade, since 2017 (Prime Minister's Office, 2011–17); *b* Coventry, 7 March 1961; *s* of Dr Norman Bird and Danuta Maria Theresa Bird; *m* 1991, Sophie Juliet Cottrell; two *d. Educ:* Marlborough Coll.; St Edmund Hall, Oxford (BA Eng. Lit.). Copywriter, 1983–84; Copy Dir, 1985–88; self-employed 1989–90; Founder, Hunnam Bird Ltd, 1990–98; Planning Dir, Lowe Broadway, 1998–2001; Client Dir, Enterprise IG, 2001–02; Man. Consultant, COI, 2002–05; Dep. Dir, Strategic Communications, Cabinet Office, 2005–08; Hd, Public Diplomacy and Strategic Campaigns, FCO, 2008–11. *Recreations:* marathon running, cartoons. *Address:* 61 Aldbourne Road, W12 0LW. *T:* (020) 8749 9397, 07947 253621. *E:* conradbird@hotmail.com.

**BIRD, Dickie;** *see* Bird, H. D.

**BIRD, Drayton Charles Colston;** Founder, 1991, Chairman, since 1992, Drayton Bird Associates (formerly Partnership); *b* 22 Aug. 1936; *s* of George Freeman Bird and Marjorie Louise Bird; *m* 1st, 1957, Pamela Bland (marr. diss.); two *s* one *d,* 2nd, 1971, Anna Te Paora (marr. diss.); 3rd, 1982, Cece Topley (marr. diss.). *Educ:* Trent Coll.; Manchester Univ. Asst Sec., Manchester Cotton Assoc., 1955–57; with sundry advertising agencies, 1957–68; Founder, Small Business Inst., 1968; publisher, Business Ideas newsletter, 1968–70; Co-Founder, then Man. Dir, Trenear-Harvey, Bird & Watson, 1977–85; Vice Chm., Ogilvy & Mather Direct Worldwide, 1985–91. Inaugural Fellow, Inst. Direct Mktg, 1996. *Publications:* Some Rats Run Faster, 1964; Commonsense Direct Marketing: the printed shop, 1982, 5th edn 2007; How To Write Sales Letters That Sell, 1994, 2nd edn 2002; Marketing Insights and Outrages, 1999; How to Make Direct Marketing Work for Your Law Firm, 2009. *Recreations:* music, reading, wine, writing. *Address:* Drayton Bird Associates, Moyle House, Fleet Hill, Finchampstead, Wokingham, Berks RG40 4LJ.

**BIRD, Harold Dennis, (Dickie),** OBE 2012 (MBE 1986); umpire of first-class cricket, 1970–98, and of Test cricket, 1970–96; foundation Member, Independent International Panel of Umpires, 1993; Founder and Trustee, Dickie Bird Foundation, since 2004; *b* 19 April 1933; *s* of James Harold Bird and Ethel Bird; unmarried. *Educ:* Burton Road Primary Sch.; Raley Sch., Barnsley. Played county cricket for Yorkshire, 1956–60 (highest first-class score, 181 not out *v* Glamorgan, 1959), and Leicestershire, 1960–66; qualified MCC Advanced Cricket Coach, 1966; umpired 159 international matches (world record in 1996): 67 Tests (world record in 1994), incl. Queen's Silver Jubilee Test, Lord's, 1977, Centenary Test, Lord's, 1980, Bi-Centenary Test, Lord's, 1987, 3 in Zimbabwe, and WI *v* Pakistan series, 1993, in NZ, Pakistan and India, 1994, and Australia *v* Pakistan series, 1995; 92 one-day internationals, 1973–96 (world record in 1994); 4 World Cup tournaments, 1975–87, and Final at Lord's, 1975, 1979, 1983; Women's World Cup, and Final, NZ, 1982; finals of Gillette, NatWest, and Benson & Hedges competitions, Lord's, 1974–98; Rest of the World XI *v* World XI, Wembley Stadium, 1983; Centenary of Test cricket, England *v* WI, Old Trafford, 1984; Rothmans Cup, 1983, 1985, Asia Cup, 1984, 1985, Champion's Cup, 1986, and Sharjah Tournament, 1993, UAE. Has travelled worldwide. Guest appearances on TV and radio progs include Down Your Way, Question of Sport, This is Your Life, Breakfast with Frost and Desert Island Discs, Country File, Top Gear; subject of BBC2 documentary, 1996; participant, The Young Ones, 2010. Freeman of Barnsley, 2000. Subject of life-size bronze statue, Barnsley, 2009. Hon. Life Mem., Assoc. of Cricket Officials, 2012. Hon. Fellow, Bradford Coll., 2015. DUniv Sheffield Hallam, 1996; Hon. LLD Leeds, 1997; Hon. DCL Huddersfield, 2008. Yorkshire Personality of the Year, 1977; Yorkshire Man of the Year, 1996; People of the Year Award, RADAR/Abbey Nat., 1996; Special Sporting Award, Variety Club of GB, 1997; Cricket Writer's Award, 1997; English Sports Council (Yorks Reg.) Award, 1998; Special Merit Award, Professional Cricketers' Assoc., 1998; Barnsley Millennium of Merit Award, 2000; Yorkshire Hall of Fame, BBC Yorkshire Sports Awards, 2006. *Publications:* Not Out, 1978; That's Out, 1985; From the Pavilion End, 1988; Dickie Bird, My Autobiography, 1997; White Cap and Bails, 1999; Dickie Bird's Britain, 2002; 80 Not Out, 2012. *Recreations:* watching football, listening to Barbra Streisand, Nat King Cole, Diana Ross and Shirley Bassey records. *Address:* White Rose Cottage, 40 Paddock Road, Staincross, Barnsley, Yorks S75 6LE. *T:* (01226) 384491. *Clubs:* MCC (Hon. Life Mem., 1996), Lord's Taverners; Yorkshire CC (Hon. Life Mem., 1994; Pres., 2014–16); Leicestershire CC (Hon. Life Mem., 1996); Cambridge University Cricket (Hon. Life Mem., 1996); Barnsley Football (Hon. Life Mem., 2003).

**BIRD, John Michael;** actor and writer; *b* 22 Nov. 1936; *s* of Horace George Bird and Dorothy May Bird (*née* Haubitz); *m* Libby Crandon, musician. *Educ:* High Pavement Grammar Sch., Nottingham; King's Coll., Cambridge (BA 1958). Asst Artistic Dir, 1959–61, Associate Artistic Dir, 1961–63, Royal Court Theatre; writer and performer, The Establishment, 1961–64; Joint Founder: New York Establishment, 1963; New Theatre, NY, 1963. *Stage* includes: Luv, tour, 1971; Who's Who?, Arnaud, Guildford, 1972; Habeas Corpus, Lyric, 1973; The Ball Game, Open Space, 1978; Bremner, Bird and Fortune, Albery, 2002; *films:* Take a Girl Like You; The Seven Per Cent Solution; Yellow Pages; A Dandy in Aspic; *television* includes: Not so much a Programme, 1965–66; The Late Show, 1966; BBC3; A Series of Birds; With Bird Will Travel; John Bird/John Wells; Blue Remembered Hills; A Very Peculiar Practice; Travelling Man; El C.I.D., 1990, 1991, 1992; Rory Bremner… Who Else?, 1992–99 (jtly) BAFTA Award for best light entertainment performance, 1997]; The Long Johns, 1996–99; In the Red, 1998; Bremner, Bird and Fortune, 1999–2007; Chambers, 2000, 2001; Absolute Power, 2003, 2005; South Bank Show, 2007; Silly Money, 2008. Hon. DLitt Nottingham, 2002. *Publications:* (with John Fortune) The Long Johns, 1996; (with Rory Bremner and John Fortune) You Are Here, 2004. *Address:* c/o Chatto & Linnit Ltd, 17 Old Park Lane, W1K 1QT.

**BIRD, Judith Pamela;** *see* Kelly, Judith Pamela.

**BIRD, Julian Piers;** Chief Executive: Society of London Theatre, since 2010; UK Theatre Association (formerly Theatrical Management Association), since 2010; *b* Epsom, 3 April 1974; *s* of Colin Miles Dudley Bird and Veronica Mary Bird. *Educ:* Epsom Coll.; Univ. of Exeter (BA Hons Econs). Bank of England, 1995–97; FSA, 1997–2007; Chief Operating Officer, Tate, 2007–10; Exec. Producer, Olivier Awards, 2011–. Chair, Drama UK, 2013–. Mem., Adv. Cttee, American Theatre Wing, NY, 2012–. Trustee: Yvonne Arnaud Th., Guildford, 2005– (Chair, 2013–); De La Warr Pavilion, Bexhill on Sea, 2008– (Chair, 2014–); Southwold and Aldeburgh Th. Trust, 2010–. *Recreations:* theatre, cinema, art, overseas travel, watching Spurs. *Address:* Society of London Theatre, 32 Rose Street, WC2E 9ET. *T:* (020) 7557 6702. *E:* julian@soltukt.co.uk. *Clubs:* Ivy, Groucho, h.

**BIRD, Rt Rev. Michael;** Archdeacon of Pembroke, Ontario, since 2018; *b* Oakville, Ont, 15 Nov. 1957; *m* 1980, Susan Elaine Bailey; two *s* one *d. Educ:* Univ. of Toronto (BSc 1980); Trinity Coll., Toronto (MDiv 1984). Ordained deacon, 1984, priest, 1984; Rector, Burin, Newfoundland, 1984–87; Asst Priest, St George's, St Catharines, 1987–89; Rector: St Paul's, Dunnville and Dunn Parish, 1989–94; St Cuthbert's, Oakville, 1994–98; St Luke's, Burlington, 1998–2007; Coadjutor Bishop of Niagara, 2007. Regl Dean, Trafalgar, 1997; Canon, Christ's Church Cathedral, Hamilton, 1999; Archdeacon of Trafalgar, 2005; Bishop of Niagara, 2008–18.

**BIRD, Michael George,** OBE 2000; Director, Russia, British Council, and Cultural Counsellor, British Embassy, Moscow, since 2015; *b* 5 Jan. 1960; *s* of George Bird and Margaret Bird; *m* 2003, Simone Lees. *Educ:* Bedales Sch.; Emmanuel Coll., Cambridge (BA 1982); Voronezh Univ. (Dip. Russian Studies). Kennedy Schol., Harvard Univ., 1982–83. Teacher, Vienna, 1983–85; British Council: London, 1985–87; Asst Dir, Moscow, 1987–91; Eur. Liaison Officer, Brussels, 1991–93; Director: St Petersburg, 1993–97; Ukraine, 1997–2001; Scotland, 2001–05; Germany, 2005–09; Regional Director: SE Europe, 2009–11; Wider Europe, 2012–15. *Recreations:* music, travel, mountaineering. *Address:* British Council, Moscow, Russia. *T:* 9037971184. *E:* Michael.Bird@britishcouncil.org.

**BIRD, Michael James;** Regional Employment Judge (formerly Chairman of Industrial, later Employment Tribunals) for Wales, 1992–2008; *b* 11 Nov. 1935; *s* of Walter Garfield and Ireen Bird; *m* 1963, Susan Harris (*d* 2008); three *d. Educ:* Lewis Sch., Pengam; King's Coll., Univ. of London (LLB Hons). Solicitor (Hons) 1961. Assistant solicitor, 1961–62; Partner, T. S. Edwards & Son, 1962–67, Sen. Partner, 1967–84. Deputy Registrar of County and High Court, 1976–77; Chairman of Industrial Tribunal, part-time), 1977–83; Chm. of Industrial Tribunal, Bristol, 1984–87, Cardiff, 1987–92. Chm., Gwent Italian Soc., 1978–86 (Sec., 1976–78); Member: Royal Life Saving Soc., 1976– (President's Commendation, 1984); Amateur Swimming Assoc. (Advanced Teacher, 1981–); Newport and Maindee ASC; Crawshays Welsh RFC. *Recreations:* water sports, opera. *Address:* 17 Allt-yr-yn Avenue, Newport, Gwent NP20 5DA. *T:* (01633) 252000.

**BIRD, Richard;** Executive Director, UK Major Ports Group, 2007–14; *b* 12 Feb. 1950; *s* of late Desmond and Betty Bird; *m* 1973, Penelope Anne Frudd; one *s* one *d. Educ:* King's Sch., Canterbury; Magdalen Coll., Oxford. Admin. Trainee, DoE, 1971–73; Asst Private Sec. to Minister for Planning and Local Govt, 1974–75; Principal, Dept of Transport, 1975–78; First Sec., UK Rep. to EC, Brussels, 1978–82; Principal Private Sec. to Sec. of State for Transport, 1982–83; Asst Sec., 1983, Under Sec., 1990, Dept of Transport; Cabinet Office, 1992–94; Dir of Personnel, Dept of Transport, 1994–97; Dir, Urban (later Integrated) and Local Transport, DETR, 1997–2001; Dir of Energy, Envmt and Waste, 2001–03, of Water, 2003–07, DEFRA. Non-exec. Dir, United Utilities Water, 2008–11. Mem., Oxford Univ. Fencing Club, 1969–71 (represented Britain at World Youth Fencing Championship, 1970). FRSA 2006. *Recreations:* choral singing, summer sports. *Address:* c/o UK Major Ports Group, 30 Park Street, SE1 9EZ.

**BIRD, Sir Richard (Geoffrey Chapman),** 4th Bt *cr* 1922; *b* 3 Nov. 1935; *er* surv. *s* of Sir Donald Bird, 3rd Bt, and Anne Rowena (*d* 1969), *d* of late Charles Chapman; *S* father, 1963; *m* 1st, 1957, Gillian Frances (*d* 1966), *d* of Bernard Haggett, Solihull; two *s* four *d*; 2nd, 1968, Helen Patricia, *d* of Frank Beaumont, Pontefract; two *d. Educ:* Beaumont. Heir: *s* John Andrew Bird [*b* 19 Jan. 1964; *m* 1988, Winifred Dixon; two *s* one *d*]. *Address:* 20 Milcote Road, Solihull, W Midlands B91 1JN.

**BIRD, Richard Herries,** CB 1983; Deputy Secretary, Department of Education and Science, 1980–90; *b* 8 June 1932; *s* of late Edgar Bird and Armorel (*née* Dudley-Scott); *m* 1963, Valerie, *d* of Edward and Mary Sanderson; two *d. Educ:* Winchester Coll.; Clare Coll., Cambridge. Min. of Transport and Civil Aviation, 1955; Principal Private Sec. to Minister of Transport, 1966–67; CSD 1969; DoE 1971; DES 1973. *Address:* 15 Pinehurst, Sevenoaks, Kent TN14 5AQ.

**BIRD, Prof. Richard Simpson,** PhD; Professor of Computation, University of Oxford, 1996–2008; Fellow, Lincoln College, Oxford, since 1988; *b* 13 Feb. 1943; *s* of John William Bird and Martha (*née* Solar); *m* 1967, Norma Christine Lapworth. *Educ:* St Olave's Grammar Sch.; Gonville and Caius Coll., Cambridge (MA); Inst. of Computer Sci., Univ. of London (MSc; PhD 1973). Lecturer: in Computer Sci., Reading Univ., 1972–83; Oxford Univ., 1983–88; Dir, Computing Lab., Oxford Univ., 1998–2003. *Publications:* Programs and Machines, 1977; Introduction to Functional Programming, 1988, 2nd edn 1998; Algebra of Programming, 1996; Pearls of Functional Algorithm Design, 2010; Thinking Functionally with Haskell, 2014. *Recreations:* swimming, bridge, poker. *Address:* Stocks, Chapel Lane, Blewbury, Oxon OX11 9PQ. *T:* (01235) 850258; Lincoln College, Oxford OX1 3DR.

**BIRD, Roger Charles;** District Judge, Bristol County Court and District Registry of High Court, 1987–2005; *b* 28 April 1939; *s* of late Bertram Charles Bird and Olive Mary Bird; *m* 1964, Marie-Christine Snow; two *s. Educ:* Millfield Sch.; Univ. of Bristol (LLB Hons). Admitted solicitor, 1965; asst solicitor with various firms, 1965–69; Partner, Wilmot Thompson and Bird, Bristol, 1969–79; Registrar, Yeovil County Court, 1979–86. Member: Matrimonial Causes Rule Cttee, 1986–90; President's Adoption Cttee, Family Div., 1990–2002; Children Act Adv. Cttee, 1993–97; Lord Chancellor's Adv. Gp on Ancillary Relief, 1993–2004; Judicial Adv. Gp, Children and Family Court Adv. Support Service, 2000–01. Chm., Child Protection (later Safeguarding) Commn, dio. of Clifton, 2002–12; Mem., Nat. Catholic Safeguarding Council, 2008–12. Pres., Assoc. of Dist Judges, 1995–96. *Publications:* (with C. F. Turner) Bird and Turner's Forms and Precedents, 1985, 3rd edn 1992; (editor-in-chief) Sweet and Maxwell's Family Law Manual, 1985–96; Child Maintenance: the new law, 1992, 6th edn 2008; Domestic Violence, 1996, 7th edn 2018; (with S. M. Cretney) Divorce: the new law, 1996; Ancillary Relief Handbook, 1998, 12th edn as Financial Remedies Handbook, 2019; Pension Sharing: the new law, 2000; (editor-in-chief) Emergency Remedies in the Family Courts, 2000–09; (editor-in-chief)

Jordan's Precedents Service, 2002–09; numerous articles in legal jls. *Recreations:* wine, listening to music, gardens and gardening, rural walks. *Address:* 38 Downleaze, Sneyd Park, Bristol BS9 1LY.

**BIRD, Rufus Benedict Godfrey;** Surveyor of the Queen's Works of Art, since 2018; *b* Berlin, 16 April 1974; *s* of Derek and Jacina Bird; *m* 2004, Arabella Venetia Jane Hardy; three *d*. *Educ:* Eton Coll.; Peterhouse, Cambridge (BA Hons Hist. of Art 1996). Furniture Specialist, Christie, Manson & Woods Ltd, 1999–2010 (Dir, 2007–10); Dep. Surveyor of the Queen's Works of Art, 2010–17. *Recreations:* yachting, shooting, music, music dramas of Richard Wagner. *Address:* Royal Collection Trust, York House, St James's Palace, SW1A 1BQ. *Clubs:* Beefsteak; University Pitt (Cambridge).

**BIRD, Sheila Macdonald,** OBE 2011; PhD; FRSE; Programme Leader, MRC Biostatistics Unit, Cambridge, 1996–2015, now Visiting Fellow; Visiting Professor, Department of Mathematics and Statistics, University of Strathclyde, since 2002; Hon. Senior Visiting Fellow, Cambridge Institute of Public Health, since 2016; Hon. Professor, College of Medicine and Veterinary Medicine, University of Edinburgh, since 2017; *b* Inverness, 18 May 1952; *d* of Herbert Gore and Isabella Agnes Gordon Gore (*née* Macdonald); *m* 1999, Dr Angus Graham Bird (*d* 2000); one step *s*. *Educ:* Elgin Acad.; Aberdeen Univ. (MA 1974; PhD 1981). CStat 1993; FFPH (by dist.) 2005. Res. Asst in Med. Stats, Edinburgh Univ., 1974–76; Lectr in Stats, Aberdeen Univ., 1976–80; Statistician, 1980–90, Sen. Statistician, 1990–96, MRC Biostats Unit, Cambridge; Statistical Dir, MRC-Biostatistical Initiative for AIDS and HIV Studies in Scotland, 1991–96. Vice-Pres. for Ext. Affairs, Royal Statistical Soc., 2005–09. FRSE 2012; FMedSci 2017. Hon. DSc Edinburgh, 2018. Guy Medal in Bronze, 1989, Bradford Hill Medal, 2000, Chambers Medal, 2010, Howard Medal, 2015, Royal Statistical Soc.; Glaxo Medal, Soc. of Apothecaries, 2001. *Publications:* (with D. G. Altman) Statistics in Practice, 1982; (with B. A. Bradley) Renal Transplantation: sense and sensitization, 1988; contribs to learned jls, incl. Jl Royal Statistical Soc., Lancet, Addiction, BMJ, Jl Statistical Methods in Med. Res. *Recreations:* hill walking, antiques, Scottish paintings, culinary essays. *Address:* MRC Biostatistics Unit, Cambridge Institute of Public Health, Robinson Way, Cambridge CB2 0SR. *T:* (01223) 330300, 07800 639269. *E:* sheila.bird@mrc-bsu.cam.ac.uk; Department of Mathematics and Statistics, University of Strathclyde, Livingstone Tower, 26 Richmond Street, Glasgow G1 1XH.

**BIRD, Simon Christopher;** QC 2009; *b* Felixstowe, 9 Oct. 1963; *s* of John and Christine Bird. *Educ:* Univ. of Reading (LLB). Called to the Bar, Middle Temple, 1987; a Dep. Principal Judge, First-tier Tribunal, Local Govt Standards in England (formerly Dep. Pres., Adjudication Panel for England), 2006–12; a Judge, First-tier Tribunal, General Regulatory Chamber (Envmt), 2012–. *Recreations:* gardening, golf, fly-fishing. *Address:* Francis Taylor Building, Inner Temple, EC4Y 7BY. *Clubs:* East India, MCC.

**BIRD, Steven David;** Managing Director, Birds Solicitors, since 2000; *b* Billericay, 9 Dec. 1963; *s* of David Roy Bird and Diane Christine Rena Bird (*née* Bugg); *m* 1993, Cathryn Mary Williams; two *s* two *d*. *Educ:* Royal Liberty Sch.; Univ. of Birmingham (LLB Hons Law and French 1986; LLM 1988); Univ. de Limoges (Dip. d'Etudes Juridiques Françaises 1985); Coll. of Law, Guildford. Admitted solicitor, 1990. With Simons Muirhead & Burton, 1988–2000. List of Counsel, Internat. Criminal Ct, 2016–. Member, Committee: London Criminal Courts Solicitors' Assoc., 2006–; Criminal Appeal Lawyers' Assoc., 2002– (Chm., 2014–). *Publications:* Police Station Advisers Index, 1995, 4th edn 2010; (contrib.) The Criminal Cases Review Commission: hope for the innocent?, 2010; (contrib.) Taylor on Criminal Appeals, 2nd edn 2012; (contrib.) Human Trafficking and Modern Slavery Law and Practice, 2018; (contrib.) The Drug Offences Handbook, 2018. *Recreations:* football (still playing), Arsenal FC, music, theatre, golf. *Address:* Birds Solicitors, 61 Wandsworth High Street, SW18 2PT. *T:* (020) 8874 7433, *Fax:* (020) 8870 4770. *E:* s.bird@birds.eu.com.

**BIRD, Vivien Mary;** Chief Executive, Booktrust, 2007–15; Senior Policy Adviser and Member, Management Board, since 2015, and Secretary and External Liaison, since 2018, European Literacy Policy Network; *b* Jersey, CI, 29 Nov. 1950; *d* of late Jurat Lester Vivian Bailhache (sometime Lieut Bailiff of Jersey), and Nanette Ross Bailhache (*née* Ferguson); *m* 1974, Brendan John Bird; one *d* (and one *d* decd). *Educ:* Jersey Coll. for Girls; Southbank Poly. (HND Business Studies with Langs). DipM; Dip. Adult Literacy Teaching, RSA; Trainer Dip. (IT) Adult Educn, RSA. Mktg Exec., United Newspapers, 1971–74; Information Officer, Res. Unit, COI, 1974–78; volunteer adult literacy tutor, CRE community literacy project, Hammersmith Reading Centre, 1979–83; Community Outreach Worker, 1983–87 and 1990–94; National Literacy Trust, 1994–2007, posts include: Partnerships Develt Manager, 1999–2002; Ed., Literacy Today, 1995–2002; Project Dir, Literacy and Social Inclusion, 2002–05; Dir, Reading is Fundamental, 2005–07. Contrib. to TV, radio and print media debates on literacy and reading promotion, 2004–; keynote speaker for British Council at confs in Cairo, China and Taiwan, 2009–12. Chair, EU Read, 2009–14. Mem., Brightwells Multi Academy Trust, 2016–; Mem., Arts and Creative Economy Adv. Gp, British Council, 2016–. Dir and Trustee, Think Equal, 2017–. Governor: Horder Rd Nursery Sch., 1980–83 (Chair, 1981–83); Langford Primary Sch., 1980–83; Sulivan Primary Sch., 1983–89 (Chair, 1984–88); Jack Tizard Special Sch., 1985–88; Sacred Heart High Sch., 1989–94; Phoenix High Sch., 1995–2006 (Special Gov.; Vice Chair of Govs, 1995–97, Chair, 1997–2006). FRSA. JP W London, 1989–96. *Publications:* A Literacy Guide for School Governors, 1998; (contrib. with P. Hannon) Handbook of Family Literacy, 2004, repr. 2011; Literacy and Social Inclusion: the handbook, 2005; (contrib.) Literacy and Social Inclusion: closing the gap, 2007. *Recreations:* tennis (player in Middlesex League), reading (especially translated fiction), music (Bruce Springsteen and Mary Black), family, promotion of reading in UK and internationally. *Address:* 1 Sulivan Road, SW6 3DT. *T:* (020) 7736 8722. *E:* viv.bird1@icloud.com. *Club:* Parsons Green Tennis.

See also Sir P. M. Bailhache, Sir W. J. Bailhache.

**BIRDS, Prof. John Richard;** Professor of Commercial Law, University of Manchester, 2006–10, now Emeritus; Hon. Professor: University of Sheffield, since 2011; University of Exeter, since 2017; *b* 20 June 1948; *s* of John Sidney Birds and Katharine Charlotte Birds; *m* 1st, 1973, Margaret Rhona Richardson (marr. diss. 2008); two *s* one *d*; 2nd, 2009, Rachel Jane Williams. *Educ:* Chesterfield Grammar Sch.; University College London (LLB, LLM). Lectr in Law: Newcastle Polytechnic, 1970; QMC, Univ. of London, 1972; University of Sheffield: Lectr in Law, 1978–82; Sen. Lectr, 1982–85; Reader, 1985–89; Hd, Dept of Law, 1987–99 and 2002–05; Prof. of Commercial Law, 1989–2006. Hon. Prof. of Law, Univ. of Manchester, 2010–11. FRSA. Pres., Soc. of Legal Scholars, 2003–04. *Publications:* Modern Insurance Law, 1982, 11th edn 2019; (with A. J. Boyle) Company Law, 1983, 10th edn 2019; (jtly) Secretarial Administration, 1984; (ed jtly) MacGillivray and Parkington on Insurance Law, 8th edn 1988, 9th edn (as MacGillivray on Insurance Law) 1997 to 14th edn 2018; (ed jtly) Principles of European Insurance Contract Law, 2nd edn 2016; General Editor: Encyclopedia of Insurance Law, 2006; Annotated Companies Acts, 2007, 3rd edn 2013; Annotated Companies Legislation, 2010, 2nd edn 2012; articles in learned jls. *Recreations:* music, gardening, walking.

**BIRDSALL, Derek Walter,** RDI; freelance graphic designer; *b* 1 Aug. 1934; *s* of Frederick Birdsall and Hilda Birdsall (*née* Smith); *m* 1954, Shirley Thompson; three *s* one *d*. *Educ:* King's Sch., Pontefract, Yorks; Wakefield Coll. of Art, Yorks; Central Sch. of Arts and Crafts, London (NDD). National Service, RAOC Printing Unit, Cyprus, 1955–57. Lectr in Typographical Design, London Coll. of Printing, 1959–61; freelance graphic designer, working from his studio in Covent Garden, later Islington, 1961–; Founding Partner, Omnific Studios Partnership, 1983. Vis. Prof. of Graphic Art and Design, RCA, 1987–88. Consultant designer, The Independent Magazine, 1989–93; Tutor and designer of housestyle for Prince of Wales's Inst. of Arch., 1991; Design Consultant, NACF, 1992–97; Consultant Designer to C of E, 1999–. Has broadcast on TV and radio on design subjects and his work; catalogue designs for major museums throughout the world have won many awards, incl. Gold Medal, New York Art Directors' Club, 1987. Mem., AGI, 1968–96; FCSD (FSIAD 1964); RDI 1982; FRSA; Hon. FRCA 1988; Hon. FISTD 2005. Prince Philip Designers Prize, 2005; D&AD President's Award, 2012. *Publications:* (with C. H. O'D. Alexander) Fischer v Spassky, 1972; (with C. H. O'D. Alexander) A Book of Chess, 1974; (with Carlo M. Cippola) The Technology of Man—a visual history, 1978; (with Bruce Bernard) Lucian Freud, 1996; Notes on Book Design, 2004. *Recreations:* chess, poker. *Address:* 9 Grange Road, Broadstairs, Kent CT10 3EP. *Club:* Chelsea Arts.

**BIREEDO, Omer Yousif;** President of Reyada for Capacity Building, Studies and Consultations, Sudan, since 2014; *b* 1 Jan. 1939; *s* of Yousif Bireedo and Fatima Hasan; *m* 1978, Kalthoum M. E. Barakat; one *s* two *d*. *Educ:* Univ. of Khartoum (BA); Delhi Univ. (MA). Sudanese Diplomatic Service: Third Sec., New Delhi, 1963–66; London, 1966–69; Dep. Dir, Consular Dept, Min. of Foreign Affairs, Khartoum, 1969–71; Uganda, 1971–73; Mission to UN, NY, 1973–76; Dir, Dept of Internat. Orgns, Min. of Foreign Affairs, Khartoum, 1976–78 and 1986–89; Ambassador and Perm. Rep. to UN and Internat. Orgns, Geneva and Vienna, 1978–83, NY, 1983–86; Ambassador to Saudi Arabia, 1989–92; 1st Under-Sec., Min. of Foreign Affairs, Khartoum, 1992–95; Ambassador to UK, 1995–99; Dir, Political Dept, Palace of Pres. of Sudan, Khartoum, 1999–2004; Nat. Advr, Republican Palace, Sudan, 2004–12. Chairman: UN Exec. Cttee, UNHCR, 1981; Second (Econ.) Cttee, UN Gen. Assembly, 1985. Mem., UN Admin. Tribunal, 2001–04; Pres., UN Assoc. of Sudan, 2009. Pres., Council, Sinnar Univ., 2009–. Republican Order (Sudan), 1972. *Publications:* Villager in the Diplomatic Court (memoirs), 2013. *Recreations:* walking, reading. *Address:* c/o Ministry of Foreign Affairs, Khartoum, Sudan.

**BIRGENEAU, Dr Robert Joseph,** FRS 2001; FRSC 2002; Arnold and Barbara Silverman Distinguished Professor of Physics, Materials Science and Engineering, and Public Policy, University of California, Berkeley, since 2013 (Chancellor, 2004–13); *b* Toronto, 25 March 1942; *m* 1964, Mary Catherine Ware; one *s* three *d*. *Educ:* Univ. of Toronto (BSc 1963); Yale Univ. (PhD 1966). Grad. Student, 1963–66, Instructor, 1966–67, Dept of Engrg and Applied Sci., Yale Univ.; Nat. Res. Council of Canada Postdoctoral Fellow, Oxford Univ., 1967–68; Bell Laboratories, Murray Hill, NJ: Mem., Tech. Staff, Physical Res. Lab., 1968–74; Res. Hd, Scattering and Low Energy Physics Dept, 1975; Consultant, 1977–80; Massachusetts Institute of Technology: Prof. of Physics, 1975–2000; Cecil and Ida Green Prof. of Physics, 1982–2000; Associate Dir, Res. Lab. of Electronics, 1983–86; Head: Solid State, Atomic and Plasma Physics, 1987–88; Dept of Physics, 1988–91; Dean, Sch. of Sci., 1991–2000; Pres. and Prof. of Physics, Univ. of Toronto, 2000–04. Consultant: IBM Res. Labs, NY, 1980–83; Sandia Nat. Labs, Albuquerque, 1985–90. Guest Sen. Physicist, Brookhaven Nat. Lab., NY, 1968–2004; Vis. Scientist, Riso Nat. Lab., Roskilde, Denmark, 1971, 1979. Numerous lectures at univs in USA, Canada, UK and Israel, incl. A. W. Scott Lecture, Cambridge Univ., 2000. Co-Chm., Polaroid Sci. and Technol. Bd, 1998–2002. Mem., Ext. Adv. Cttee, Physics Dept, Oxford Univ., 2000. FAAAS 1982; Fellow: APS, 1980; Amer. Acad. Arts and Scis, 1987 (Co-Chm., Lincoln Project, 2013–18); NAS 2004. Trustee, Boston Mus. of Sci., 1992–2001; Gov., Argonne Nat. Lab., 1992–2001; Mem., Adv. Council, Nippon Electric Co. Res. Inst., 1995–2000. Vannevar Bush Award, NSF, 2016. Holds numerous awards, prizes and hon. degrees. *Publications:* numerous contribs to learned jls on phases and phase transition behaviour of novel states of matter. *Address:* c/o University of California, Berkeley, 366 Le Conte Hall, Berkeley, CA 94720–7300, USA.

**BIRK, Rebecca Alice;** Rabbi, Finchley Progressive Synagogue, since 2011; *b* London, 28 July 1970; *d* of David and Kate Birk; two *s* one *d*. *Educ:* Oxford High Sch.; Bristol Univ. (BA Hons); Harvard Univ. (MA Theol Studies); Leo Baeck Coll. (MA Jewish Studies). Researcher, Sunday and Moral Maze progs, BBC Radio 4, 1996–98; Rabbi, Woodford Liberal Synagogue, 2001–05; Rabbi Educator, Westminster Synagogue, 2005–10; Jewish Chaplain, HMP Holloway, 2004–14. Vis. Rabbi, Progressive Jews of Stockholm, 2004–. *Publications:* contrib. sermons to books. *Recreations:* wild swimming, coffee and cake with friends, female novelists. *E:* rebeccabirk@me.com.

**BIRKENHEAD, Bishop Suffragan of,** since 2007; **Rt Rev. (Gordon) Keith Sinclair;** *b* 3 Dec. 1952; *s* of Donald and Joyce Sinclair; *m* 1989, Rosemary Jones; two *s* one *d*. *Educ:* Christ Church, Oxford (BA, MA 1975); Cranmer Hall, Durham (BA 1984). Ordained deacon, 1984, priest, 1985; Asst Curate, Christ Church, Summerfield, 1984–88; Vicar, St Peter and St Paul, Aston, 1988–2001; Area Dean, Aston, 2000–01; Vicar, Holy Trinity, Coventry, 2001–07. Hon. Canon, Birmingham Cathedral, 2000–01. *Recreations:* walking, cinema, theatre. *Address:* Bishop's Lodge, 67 Bidston Road, Prenton CH43 6TR. *T:* (0151) 652 2741. *E:* bpbirkenhead@chester.anglican.org.

**BIRKETT,** family name of **Baron Birkett**.

**BIRKETT,** 3rd Baron *cr* 1958, of Ulverston; **Thomas Birkett;** *b* 25 July 1982; *o s* of 2nd Baron Birkett and Gloria Birkett (*née* Taylor); *S* father, 2015; *m* 2014, Nathalie Harrison; one *d*.

**BIRKETT, Sir Peter,** Kt 2012; Founder, 2016, and Executive Director, since 2017, Highgate Hill House School, Devon; *b* Scunthorpe, 6 Nov. 1959; *s* of John and Sylvia Birkett; *m* 1997, Julie Nicola Doe; one *s* one *d*. *Educ:* Frederick Gough Comprehensive Sch.; Huddersfield Poly. (Cert Ed 1985); Univ. of Reading (MA). Apprentice engr, 1976–82; engrg work, Australia, 1982–84; Lectr, Basingstoke Coll. of Technol., 1985–96; Dir of Technol., Bristol Coll., 1996–2001; Dep. Principal, Sheffield Coll., 2002–05; Founder and Chief Exec., then Dir Gen., Barnfield Fedn, 2005–13; Dir, Educn Solutions and Support, 2014–17. Mem. Bd, Young People's Learning Agency, 2009–12. *Recreations:* fitness, gym, golf. *Address:* Coles House, Coles Lane, Kinsbourne Green, Harpenden, Herts AL5 3PX. *T:* 07765 182948. *E:* spbirkett@outlook.com. *Club:* Luton Hoo.

**BIRKETT, Peter Vidler;** QC 1989; a Recorder, since 1989; *b* 13 July 1948; *s* of late Neville Lawn Birkett, MA, MB BCh, FRES and Marjorie Joy Birkett; *m* 1976, Jane Elizabeth Fell; two *s*. *Educ:* Sedbergh School; Univ. of Leicester. Called to the Bar, Inner Temple, 1972, Bencher, 1996; practice on SE Circuit, 1973–77, on N Circuit, 1977– (Leader, 1999–2001). Asst Recorder, 1986–89; Deemster, High Ct, IOM, 2000. Mem., General Council of the Bar, 1999–2001. Vice-Chm., Advocacy Trng Council of Eng. and Wales, 2004–08. Hon. Fellow, Manchester Metropolitan Univ., 2007. *Recreations:* golf, conversation, playing the piano. *Address:* 18 St John Street, Manchester M3 4EA. *T:* (0161) 834 9843. *Clubs:* Wilmslow Golf; Seniors Golf Soc.

**BIRKHEAD, Prof. Timothy Robert**, DPhil, DSc; FRS 2004; Professor of Zoology, Department of Animal and Plant Sciences, University of Sheffield, 1992–2018, now Emeritus; *b* 28 Feb. 1950; *s* of Robert Harold and Nancy Olga Birkhead; *m* 1976, Miriam Enid Appleton; one *s* two *d*. *Educ*: Univ. of Newcastle upon Tyne (BSc 1972; DSc 1989); Wolfson Coll., Oxford (DPhil 1976). Department of Animal and Plant Sciences, University of Sheffield: Lectr, 1976–86; Sen. Lectr, 1986–89; Reader, 1989–92. Nuffield Res. Fellow, 1990–91; Leverhulme Res. Fellow, 1995–96. Elliot Coues Medal, Amer. Ornithologists' Union, 2011; Medal, Assoc. for Study of Animal Behaviour, 2012; UK Higher Educn Biosci. Teacher of the Year Award, RSB, 2013; Silver Medal, Zool Soc. of London, 2014; Eisenmann Medal, Linnaean Soc. of New York, 2016; Godman-Salvin Medal, British Ornithologists' Union, 2016; Clarivate Analytics Award for Communicating Zoology, ZSL, 2017; Stephen Jay Gould Prize, Soc. for Study of Evolution, 2017; Nat. Teaching Fellowship, Higher Educn Acad., 2017. *Publications*: (with C. M. Perrins) Avian Ecology, 1983; (with M. E. Birkhead) The Survival Factor, 1989; The Magpies: the ecology and behaviour of black-billed and yellow-billed magpies, 1991; (with A. P. Møller) Sperm Competition in Birds: evolutionary causes and consequences, 1992; Great Auk Islands, 1993; (with A. P. Møller) Sperm Competition and Sexual Selection, 1998; Promiscuity, 2000; The Red Canary, 2003; The Wisdom of Birds, 2008; (ed jtly) Sperm Biology: an evolutionary perspective, 2009; Bird Sense: what it's like to be a bird, 2012; (jtly) Ten Thousand Birds: ornithology since Darwin, 2014; The Most Perfect Thing: inside (and outside) of a bird's egg, 2016; The Wonderful Mr Willughby: the first true ornithologist, 2018. *Recreations*: art, music, walking. *Address*: 47 Whiteley Wood Road, Sheffield S11 7FF. *T*: (0114) 222 4622, *Fax*: (0114) 222 0002. *E*: t.r.birkhead@sheffield.ac.uk.

**BIRKIN, Sir John (Christian William)**, 6th Bt *cr* 1905, of Ruddington Grange, Notts; *b* 2 July 1953; *s* of Sir Charles Lloyd Birkin, 5th Bt and Janet (*d* 1983), *d* of Peter Johnson; *S* father, 1985; *m* 1994, Emma Gage; one *s* one *d*. *Educ*: Eton; Trinity Coll., Dublin; London Film School. *Heir*: *s* Benjamin Charles Birkin, *b* 4 Nov. 1995. *Address*: Place Barton, Ashton, Exeter, Devon EX6 7QP.

**BIRKINSHAW, Prof. Julian Mark**, PhD; FBA 2012; Professor of Strategy and Entrepreneurship, since 2004 and Deputy Dean, since 2017, London Business School; *b* Hexham, 16 Oct. 1964; *s* of John (Ian) and Susan Birkinshaw; *m* 1994, Laura Maclellan; two *s* one *d*. *Educ*: Perse Sch. for Boys; Manchester Grammar Sch.; Durham Univ. (BSc); Univ. of Western Ontario (MBA; PhD 1995). Asst Prof., Stockholm Sch. of Econs, 1995–99; London Business School: Asst Prof., 1999–2000; Associate Prof., 2000–04; Dep. Dean, Progs, 2007–10. Vis. Schol., INSEAD Business Sch., 2006–07. *Publications*: Becoming a Better Boss: why good management is so difficult, 2013; Fast/Forward: make your company fit for the future, 2017. *Recreations*: running, triathlons, orienteering, piano. *Address*: London Business School, Regents Park, NW1 4SA. *T*: (020) 7000 8718. *E*: jbirkinshaw@london.edu.

**BIRKMYRE, Sir James**, 4th Bt *cr* 1921, of Dalmunzie, County of Perth; Director of Championship Management (formerly Tournament Development), PGA European Tour, since 1994; *b* 29 Feb. 1956; *s* of Sir Archibald Birkmyre, 3rd Bt and of Gillian Mary (*née* Downes); *S* father, 2001; *m* 1st, 1990 (marr. diss. 2010); one *s*; 2nd, 2012, Kim Jean Andreolli, *d* of George and Jane Florek, Florida, USA. *Educ*: Radley Coll.; Ecole Supérieure de Commerce, Neuchâtel; Ealing Tech. Coll. (BA Hons). Account Mgr, Collet Dickenson & Pearce Advertising, 1978–82; Account Dir, TBWA Advertising, 1982–87; Sponsorship Dir, The Wight Co., 1987–93; Man. Dir, Birchgrey, 1993–94. Mem., RGS. *Recreations*: tennis, fly-fishing, golf, ski-ing, shooting, mountaineering. *Heir*: *s* Alexander Birkmyre, *b* 24 May 1991. *Address*: 1 Parsonage Farm Cottage, Frilsham, Berks RG18 9UY. *T*: (01635) 201282. *Clubs*: MCC, Lord's Taverners; Sunningdale Golf; Reading Football; Dalmunzie Golf (Hon. Mem.).

**BIRLEY, Prof. Susan Joyce, (Mrs David Norburn)**; Professor of Entrepreneurship, The Business School (formerly Professor of Management), Imperial College, London, 1990–2003; Director, Entrepreneurship Centre, 2000–03; *m* 1st, 1964, Arwyn Hopkins (marr. diss. 1970); 2nd, 1975, Prof. David Norburn, *qv*. *Educ*: Nelson Grammar Sch.; University College London (BSc 1964; Fellow, 2004); PhD London 1974. FSS. Teacher, Dunsmore Sch., 1964–66; Lectr, Lanchester Polytechnic, 1966–68; Lectr and Sen. Lectr, Poly. of Central London, 1968–72; Sen. Res. Fellow, City Univ., 1972–74; London Business School: Sen. Res. Fellow, 1974–79; Lectr in Small Business, 1979–82; University of Notre Dame, USA: Adjunct Associate Prof., 1978–82; Associate Prof. of Strategy and Entrepreneurship, 1982–85; Philip and Pauline Harris Prof. of Entrepreneurship, Cranfield Inst. of Technol., 1985–90. Academic Dir, European Foundn for Entrepreneurship Res., 1988–91. Member: CNAA, 1987–90; NI Economic Council, 1988–94; PCFC, 1988–92; Adv. Panel on Deregulation, DTI, 1989–91; Bd, LEDU, NI, 1992–93. Founder Director and Shareholder: Guidehouse Group, 1980–85; Greyfriars Ltd, 1982–85; Newchurch & Co., 1986–97 (Chm.); Director: NatWest Bank, 1996–2000; Process Systems Enterprise Ltd, 1997–2003; IC Innovations Ltd, 1997–2003; BAE Systems, 2000–07. Mem. Panel, Foresight Steering Gp, 1997–2001. Governor, Harris City Technol. Coll., 1990–92. FCGI 2001; Fellow, British Acad. of Mgt, 1996. Freeman, City of London, 1964. Mem. Editl Bds, various business jls. *Publications*: From Private to Public (jtly), 1977; The Small Business Casebook, 1979; The Small Business Casebook: teaching manual, 1980; New Enterprises, 1982; (contrib.) Small Business and Entrepreneurship, ed Burns and Dewhurst, 1989; (jtly) Exit Routes, 1989; (jtly) The British Entrepreneur, 1989; (ed) European Entrepreneurship: emerging growth companies, 1989; (ed jtly) International Perspectives on Entrepreneurship, 1992; Entrepreneurship Research: global perspectives, 1993; Mastering Enterprise, 1997; Mastering Entrepreneurship, 2000; Franchising: pathway to wealth creation, 2004; numerous contribs to learned jls. *Recreation*: gardening.

**BIRMINGHAM, Archbishop of, (RC)**, since 2009; **Most Rev. Bernard Longley**; *b* 5 April 1955; *s* of Frederick and Audrey Longley. *Educ*: Xaverian Coll., Manchester; RNCM; New Coll., Oxford (MA); St John's Seminary, Wonersh. Ordained priest, 1981; Asst Priest, St Joseph's, Epsom, 1982–85; English Coll., Rome, 1985–87; Theol. Tutor, St John's Seminary, Wonersh, 1987–96; Catholic Bishops' Conference: Nat. Ecumenical Officer, 1996–2003; Asst Gen. Sec. (responsible for Ecumenism and Inter Faith Affairs), 2000–03; Auxiliary Bishop of Westminster, (RC), 2003–09; Titular Bishop of Zarna, 2003–09. Hon. Canon, Worcester Cathedral, 2013–. Co-chair, Anglican RC Internat. Commn, 2011–; Mem., Pontifical Council for Promoting the New Evangelism, 2011–; RC Co-Chm., English Anglican-Roman Catholic Cttee, 2011–17; Chairman: Bishops' Conference Dept for Dialogue and Unity, 2009–; Commn for Overseas Seminaries, 2012–. Surrey Chm., Diocesan Commn for Christian Unity, 1991–96; Moderator, Steering Cttee, CTBI, 1999–2003. *Address*: Archbishop's House, 8 Shadwell Street, Birmingham B4 6EY.

**BIRMINGHAM, Bishop of**, since 2006; **Rt Rev. David Andrew Urquhart**, KCMG 2018; Prelate of the Most Distinguished Order of St Michael and St George, since 2005; *b* 14 April 1952; *s* of late Hector Maconochie Urquhart, FRCSE and Elizabeth Mary Florence Urquhart (*née* Jones). *Educ*: Croftinloan; Rugby Sch.; Ealing Business Sch. (BA Hons); Wycliffe Hall, Oxford. Volunteer in Uganda, 1971; BP plc, 1972–82; ordained deacon, 1984, priest, 1985; Curate, St Nicholas, Kingston upon Hull, 1984–87; Team Vicar, Drypool, 1987–92; Vicar, Holy Trinity, Coventry, 1992–2000; Bp Suffragan of Birkenhead, 2000–06. Hon. Canon, Coventry Cathedral, 1999–2000. Chairman: Hull and E Yorks Faith in the City Gp, 1985–90; CMS, 1994–2007; Chester Dio. Bd of Educn, 2001–06; Wirral Local Strategic Partnership, 2002–06; Council, Ridley Hall, Cambridge, 2010–17; Birmingham Social Inclusion Process, 2012–16; Univ. of Birmingham Commn on Wealth Distribution, 2012–13. Convenor, Lords Spiritual, 2015–. Mem., Banking Standards Bd, 2014–. Director: Coventry City Centre Co., 1997–2000; Hippodrome Theatre, Birmingham, 2009–18; Be Birmingham Strategic Partnership, 2009–12. A Church Comr, 2017–. Archbp of Canterbury's Episcopal Link with China, 2006–. Chm. Governors, Craven (LEA) Primary Sch., 1988–92; Gov., Rugby Sch., 1999–2019. Entered House of Lords, 2010. Hon. Freeman, Metropolitan Borough of Wirral, 2006. Tallow Chandlers Medal, BP, 1977. Hon. DD Birmingham, 2009; DUniv Birmingham City, 2014; DLitt Aston, 2017. *Recreations*: motor-cycling, fives (half blue, Rugby fives, 1984), watching films, collecting books on red deer. *Address*: Bishop's Croft, Old Church Road, Harborne, Birmingham B17 0BG. *T*: (0121) 427 1163. *E*: bishop@cofebirmingham.com. *Club*: Athenæum.

**BIRMINGHAM, Auxiliary Bishops of, (RC);** *see* Kenney, Rt Rev. W.; McGough, Rt Rev. D.

**BIRMINGHAM, Dean of;** *see* Thompson, Very Rev. M.

**BIRMINGHAM, Archdeacon of;** *see* Tomlinson, Ven. J. C.

**BIRMINGHAM, Prof. Richard Walter**, PhD; CEng; FRINA; Professor of Small Craft Design, Newcastle University, since 2002; President, Royal Institution of Naval Architects, since 2018; *b* Cardiff, 21 May 1953; *s* of Walter Birmingham and Maisie Birmingham; one *s* two *d*. *Educ*: Coopers' Co. Sch., London; Newcastle Univ. (BEng 1st Cl. Naval Arch. and Ship Prodn 1991; PhD 1994). CEng 1996; FRINA 2001. Trng Coordinator, Internat. Boatbuilding Centre, Lowestoft, 1985–88; Newcastle University: Lectr, 1994–2000; Sen. Lectr, 2000–02; Hd, Sch. of Marine Sci. and Technol., 2007–13. Member: Bd, Marine Mgt Orgn, 2009–13; Tech. Adv. Bd, RNLI, 2017–. Trustee, Blyth Tall Ship, 2014–. *Publications*: Boatbuilding Techniques Illustrated, 1984; Understanding Engineering Design: context, theory and practice, 1997; over 80 papers in learned jls and confs. *Recreations*: hillwalking, storytelling. *Address*: School of Engineering, Armstrong Building, Newcastle University, Newcastle upon Tyne NE1 7RU. *E*: Richard.Birmingham@ncl.ac.uk.

**BIRNBAUM, Michael Ian;** QC 1992; a Recorder, 1995–2014; *b* 26 Feb. 1947; *s* of Samuel Birnbaum and Anne (*née* Zucker); *m* 1984, Aimee Dara Schachter. *Educ*: Southgate County Grammar Sch.; Christ Church, Oxford (BA Jurisp.). Called to the Bar, Middle Temple, 1969; practice mainly in criminal law, extradition and human rights; Asst Recorder, 1990–95. Chm., W Africa Sub-Cttee, Bar Human Rights Cttee, 2002–07; Mem., Bar Internat. Relns Cttee, 2001–07. Trustee, Redress Trust, 2007–. *Publications*: two reports on the case in Nigeria of Ken Saro-Wiwa and others. *Recreations*: singing, opera, reading. *Address*: Foundry Chambers, Quality House, 5–9 Quality Court, Chancery Lane, WC2A 1HP. *T*: (020) 7400 1800.

**BIRNEY, Dr John Frederick William, (Ewan)**, CBE 2019; FRS 2014; Joint Director and Senior Scientist, European Molecular Biology Laboratory – European Bioinformatics Institute, since 2012; *b* Paddington, 1972; *s* of Jack and Joy Birney; *m* 2003, Barley Laycock; one *s* one *d*. *Educ*: Eton Coll.; Balliol Coll., Oxford (BA Biochem. 1996); St John's Coll., Cambridge (PhD 2000). Res. at Sanger Inst., Univ. of Cambridge, 1996–2000; Team leader, Eur. Bioinformatics Inst., 2000–10; Mem., Associate Faculty, Wellcome Trust Sanger Inst., 2012–; Mem., UKRI-BBSRC, 2019–. FMedSci 2015. Francis Crick Award, Royal Soc., 2003; Overton Prize, Internat. Soc. for Computational Biol., 2005; Benjamin Franklin Award, Bioinformatics Orgn, 2005. *Publications*: contribs to learned jls, incl. Nature, Science, Genome Res. *Recreations*: science, cookery. *Address*: European Bioinformatics Institute, Wellcome Genome Campus, Hinxton, Cambridge CB10 1SD.

**BIRNIE, Dr Esmond;** Senior Economist, Economic Policy, Ulster University, since 2016; *b* 6 Jan. 1965; *s* of Dr James Whyte Birnie and Ruth Alexandra Birnie (*née* Bell). *Educ*: Gonville and Caius Coll., Cambridge (BA 1st Cl. Hons Econs 1986); Queen's Univ., Belfast (PhD Econs 1994). Res. Asst, NI Econ. Res. Centre, 1986–89; Lectr in Econs, 1989–2000, Sen. Lectr in Econs and Mgt, 2000–07, QUB. Northern Ireland Assembly: Mem. (UU) Belfast S, 1998–2007; contested same seat, 2007; Ministerial Special Advr, Dept for Employment and Learning, NI, 2007–10; Chief Economist, NI, PricewaterhouseCoopers LLP, 2010–16. Chm., Cttee for Higher and Further Educn, Trng and Employment, then for Employment and Learning, 1999–2002. UU Party spokesman: on North-South affairs and British-Irish Council, 1999–2003; on Dept of Finance and Family, 2006–07; Talks negotiator, 2006–07. *Publications*: Without Profit or Prophets, 1997; *jointly*: Closing the Productivity Gap, 1990; East German Productivity, 1993; The Competitiveness of Industry in Ireland, 1994; Competitiveness of Industry in the Czech Republic and Hungary, 1995; An Economics Lesson for Irish Nationalists and Republicans, 1995; Environmental Regulation, the Firm and Competitiveness, 1998; The Northern Ireland Economy, 1999; Environmental Regulation and Competitive Advantage, 2000; Can the Celtic Tiger Cross the Border?, 2001; A Brighter Future for Northern Ireland: the case against the Euro, 2002; Government Futures (pamphlet series), 2010–12. *Recreations*: cycling, jogging, art, architecture, music, church choir, active church member. *Address*: 32 Finaghy Road South, Finaghy, Belfast BT10 0DR.

**BIRRELL, Sir James (Drake)**, Kt 1993; FCA; FCBSI; Chief Executive, Halifax Building Society, 1988–93; *b* 18 Aug. 1933; *s* of James Russell Birrell, MA and Edith Marion Birrell, BSc (*née* Drake); *m* 1958, Margaret Anne Pattison; two *d*. *Educ*: Belle Vue Grammar School, Bradford. FCA 1955; FCBSI 1989. Boyce Welch & Co. (articled clerk), 1949–55; Pilot Officer, RAF, 1955–57; chartered accountant, Price Waterhouse, 1957–60; Accountant, ADA Halifax, 1960–61; Management Accountant, Empire Stores, 1961–64; Dir and Co. Sec., John Gladstone & Co., 1964–68; Halifax Building Society, 1968–93. Non-executive Director: Securicor, 1993–2003; Wesleyan Gen. Assce Soc., 1993–2004. Mem., Building Societies Commn, 1994–2001. *Recreations*: golf, gardening, archaeology, local history.

**BIRSE, Peter Malcolm;** Chairman, Birse Group, 1999–2001 (Chairman and Chief Executive, 1970–99); *b* 24 Nov. 1942; *s* of Peter A. M. Birse and Margaret C. Birse; *m* 1969, Helen Searle; two *s* one *d*. *Educ*: Arbroath High Sch.; St Andrews Univ. (BScEng). MICE. Engineer, John Mowlem, 1963–66; Site Manager: Cammon (Ghana), 1966–68; Cammon (UK), 1968–69; Engineer, Foster Wheeler, 1969–70; founded Birse Group, 1970. *Recreations*: sailing, ski-ing. *Address*: c/o Birse Group, Humber Road, Barton-on-Humber, N Lincs DN18 5BW. *Club*: Royal Ocean Racing.

**BIRSS, Hon. Sir Colin (Ian);** Kt 2013; **Hon. Mr Justice Birss;** a Judge of the High Court of Justice, Chancery Division, since 2013; *b* Thurso, 28 Dec. 1964; *s* of Ian and Davina Birss; *m* 1987, Kathryn Squibbs; two *s* one *d*. *Educ*: Downing Coll., Cambridge (BA Natural Sci. 1986); City Univ. (Dip. Law 1989). Called to the Bar, Middle Temple, 1990, Bencher, 2011; in practice at the Bar, 1990–2010; QC 2008; a Specialist Circuit Judge, Patents County Ct, 2010–13. Standing Counsel to Comptroller-Gen. of Patents, 2003–08; Member: Bar Standards Bd Professional Conduct and Complaints Cttee, 2003–09; Civil Procedure Rule Cttee, 2014–; Dep. Chm., 2009–10, Chm., 2010–13, Copyright Tribunal.

Adv. Ed., Civil Procedure, 2013–. *Publications*: Terrell on the Law of Patents, 15th edn, 2000 to 18th edn, 2016. *Recreation*: beekeeping. *Address*: Royal Courts of Justice, Rolls Building, 7 Rolls Buildings, Fetter Lane, EC4A 1NL.

**BIRT**, family name of **Baron Birt**.

**BIRT**, Baron *cr* 2000 (Life Peer), of Liverpool in the County of Merseyside; **John Birt**, Kt 1998; Prime Minister's Strategy Adviser, 2001–05; *b* 10 Dec. 1944; *s* of Leo Vincent Birt and Ida Birt; *m* 1965, Jane Frances (*née* Lake) (marr. diss. 2006); one *s* one *d*; *m* 2006, Eithne Victoria Wallis, *qv*. *Educ*: St Mary's Coll., Liverpool; St Catherine's Coll., Oxford (MA; Hon. Fellow 1992). Producer, Nice Time, 1968–69; Joint Editor, World in Action, 1969–70; Producer, The Frost Programme, 1971–72; Executive Producer, Weekend World, 1972–74; Head of Current Affairs, LWT, 1974–77; Co-Producer, The Nixon Interviews, 1977; Controller of Features and Current Affairs, LWT, 1977–81; Dir of Programmes, LWT, 1982–87; Dep. Dir-Gen., 1987–92, Dir-Gen., 1992–2000, BBC. Adviser: McKinsey & Co., 2000–05; Terra Firma, 2005–; Capgemini, 2006–10. Chairman: Lynx New Media, subseq. Lynx Capital Ventures, 2000–04; Waste Recycling Gp, 2006; Infinis, 2006–07 (non-exec. Dir, 2007–13); Maltby Capital Ltd, 2008–10 (non-exec. Dir, 2007–08); Novera Energy plc, 2010; PayPal (Europe) Ltd, 2010–14 (non-exec. Dir, 2004–10); HEG (formerly Host Europe Gp), 2013–17; CPA Global, 2015–17; JLA, 2018–; Vice-Chm., Eutelsat, 2012– (non-exec. Dir, 2006–12); non-exec. Dir, Shopvolution, 2012–17. Advr to Prime Minister on Criminal Justice, 2000–01; Mem., Cabinet Office Strategy Bd, 2003–05. Vis. Fellow, Nuffield Coll., Oxford, 1991–99. Member: Wilton Park Academic Council, 1980–83; Media Law Gp, 1983–94; Opportunity 2000 (formerly Women's Economic) Target Team, BITC, 1991–98; Internat. Council, Mus. of TV and Radio, NY, 1994–2000; Broadcasting Research Unit: Mem., Working Party on the new Technologies, 1981–83; Mem., Exec. Cttee, 1983–87. Mem. Adv. Bd, GovernUp, 2013–. Vice-Pres., RTS, 1994–2000 (Fellow, 1989). FIET (CompIEE 1998). Hon. Fellow, Univ. of Wales Cardiff, 1997. Hon. DLitt: Liverpool John Moores, 1992; City, 1998; Bradford, 1999; Westminster, 2010. Emmy Award, US Nat. Acad. of Television, Arts and Scis, 1995. *Publications*: The Harder Path (autobiog.), 2002; various articles in newspapers and journals. *Recreations*: football, walking, cinema. *Address*: c/o House of Lords, SW1A 0PW.

**BIRT, Sir Michael (Cameron St John)**, Kt 2012; QC 1995; a Judge of the Court of Appeal of Jersey, since 2000, of Guernsey, since 2009, and of the Cayman Islands, since 2018; a Commissioner, Royal Court of Jersey, since 2015; *b* 25 Aug. 1948; *s* of late St John Michael Clive Birt, OBE, FRCS and Mairi Araminta Birt (*née* Cameron); *m* 1973, Joan Frances Miller; two *s* one *d*. *Educ*: Marlborough Coll.; Magdalene Coll., Cambridge (MA Law). Called to the Bar, Middle Temple, 1970, Bencher, 2009, to Jersey Bar, 1977; in practice: London, 1971–75; as Jersey advocate, with Ogier & Le Cornu, St Helier, 1976–93; Crown Advocate of Jersey, 1987–93; HM Attorney General, Jersey, 1994–2000; Dep. Bailiff, 2000–09, Bailiff, 2009–15, of Jersey; Deemster, Appeal Div., High Ct of Isle of Man, 2015–18. *Recreations*: ski-ing, yachting, golf. *Address*: Bailiff's Chambers, Royal Court House, St Helier, Jersey JE1 1BA. *T*: (01534) 441100, *Fax*: (01534) 441137. *Clubs*: Royal Channel Islands Yacht; Royal Jersey Golf.

**BIRT, Simon Christopher**; QC 2015; *b* Farnborough, Kent, 5 March 1975; *s* of Derek and Theresa Birt; *m* 1999, Gemma Lau; one *s* three *d*. *Educ*: Solihull Sch.; Brasenose Coll., Oxford (MA; BCL). Called to the Bar, Gray's Inn, 1998; in practice as barrister, specialising in commercial litigation, 1998–. *Recreations*: music, family. *Address*: Brick Court Chambers, 7–8 Essex Street, WC2R 3LD.

**BIRTLES, His Honour William Jack**; a Circuit Judge, 2002–14; *b* 27 Oct. 1944; *s* of William George Birtles and Dorothy Louisa Birtles (*née* Martin); *m* 1981, Rt Hon. Patricia Hope Hewitt, *qv*; one *s* one *d*. *Educ*: King's Coll. London (LLB, AKC 1967; LLM 1968); Harvard Law Sch. (Kennedy Schol.; LLM 1971); New York Univ. Law Sch. (Robert Marshall Fellow). Called to the Bar: Gray's Inn, 1970, Bencher, 2008; Lincoln's Inn, 1998; NI, 1998; Lecturer in Law: KCL, 1968–70; UCL, 1972–74; in practice as barrister, 1974–2002. Vis. Fellow, 1993–94, Sen. Associate Mem., 1996–2014, St Antony's Coll. Oxford. Liveryman, Tallow Chandlers' Co., 2011. *Publications*: (with R. Stein) Planning and Environmental Law, 1994; (with A. Forge) Local Government Finance Law, 2000; (jtly) Environmental Liability, 2004; contrib. legal jls. *Recreations*: listening to opera and classical music, reading fiction and poetry, collecting European travel books, international relations, theatre, being in Norfolk. *Club*: Travellers.

**BIRTS, His Honour Peter William**; QC 1990; QC (NI) 1996; a Circuit Judge, 2005–16; *b* 9 Feb. 1946; *s* of late John Claude Birts and Audrey Lavinia Birts; *m* 1st, 1971, Penelope Ann Eyre (marr. diss. 1997); two *d* one *s*; 2nd, 1997, Mrs Angela Forcer-Evans. *Educ*: Lancing College; St John's College, Cambridge (choral scholarship; MA). Called to the Bar, Gray's Inn, 1968, Bencher 1998; a Recorder, 1989–2005; a Dep. High Ct Judge, 2000–05; Mem., Gen. Council of the Bar, 1989–95 (Chm., Legal Aid and Fees Cttee, 1994–95). Member: Judicial Studies Bd (Main Bd and Civil and Family Cttee), 1991–96; County Court Rules Cttee, 1991–99; Legal Member: Mental Health Review Tribunals, 1994–; Parole Bd, 2006–16. Asst Parly Boundary Comr, 1992–95. Gov., Benenden Sch., 1990–93. Freeman, City of London, 1967; Liveryman, Carpenters' Co., 1967– (Master, 2018). *Publications*: Trespass: summary procedure for possession of land (with Alan Willis), 1987; Remedies for Trespass, 1990; (ed and contrib.) Butterworths Costs Service, 1999–2009. *Recreations*: music, tennis, country pursuits. *Club*: Hurlingham.

**BIRTWISTLE, Gordon**; *b* Oswaldtwistle, 6 Sept. 1943; *m* 1986, Kathleen; one *s* one *d*. *Educ*: Accrington Coll. (HNC Prodn Engrg; HNC Mech. Engrg). Apprentice, Howard and Bullough, Accrington; work in engrg industry; owner, Stuart Engrg, 1996–2002. Councillor (Lab), Gt Harwood, Lancs, 1970–74; Mem. (Lib Dem) Burnley BC, 1983– (Mayor, 2002–03; Leader, 2006–10). Contested (Lib Dem) Burnley, 1992, 1997. MP (Lib Dem) Burnley, 2010–15; contested (Lib Dem) same seat, 2015, 2017.

**BIRTWISTLE, Sir Harrison**, CH 2001; Kt 1988; composer; Henry Purcell Professor of Composition, King's College London, 1994–2001; *b* 1934; *m* Sheila; three *s*. *Educ*: Royal Manchester Coll. of Music; RAM (Hon. FRAM). Of Music, Cranborne Chase Sch., 1962–65. Composer-in-residence, London Philharmonic Orch., 1993–. Vis. Fellow, Princeton Univ., 1966–68; Cornell Vis. Prof. of Music, Swarthmore Coll., 1973; Vis. Slee Prof., State Univ. of NY at Buffalo, 1974–75. An Associate Dir, NT, 1975–88. Mem., Akademie der Kunst, Berlin. FKC 1998. Hon. DMus: Sussex; Cambridge, 2010; Hon. DLitt Salford. Evening Standard Award for Opera, 1987, 1991; Ernst von Siemens Foundn Prize, 1995. Chevalier des Arts et des Lettres (France), 1986. *Publications*: Refrains and Choruses, 1957; Monody for Corpus Christi, 1959; Précis, 1959; The World is Discovered, 1960; Chorales, 1962, 1963; Entre'actes and Sappho Fragments, 1964; Three Movements with Fanfares, 1964; Tragoedia, 1965; Ring a Dumb Carillon, 1965; Carmen Paschale, 1965; The Mark of the Goat, 1965, 1966; The Visions of Francesco Petrarca, 1966; Verses, 1966; Punch and Judy, 1966–67 (opera); Three Lessons in a Frame, 1967; Linoii, 1968; Nomos, 1968; Verses for Ensembles, 1969; Down by the Greenwood Side, 1969; Hoquetus David (arr. of Machaut), 1969; Cantata, 1969; Ut Hermita Solvs, 1969; Medusa, 1969–70; Prologue, 1970; Nenia on the Death of Orpheus, 1970; An Imaginary Landscape, 1971; Meridian, 1971; The Fields of Sorrow, 1971; Chronometer, 1971; Epilogue—Full Fathom Five, 1972; Tombeau, 1972; The Triumph of Time, 1972; La Plage: eight arias of remembrance, 1972; Dinah and Nick's Love Song, 1972; Chanson de Geste, 1973; The World is Discovered, 1973; Grimethorpe Aria, 1973; 5 Chorale Preludes from Bach, 1973; Chorales from a Toyshop, 1973; Interludes from a Tragedy, 1973; The Mask of Orpheus, 1973–84 (opera) (Grawemeyer Award, Univ. of Louisville, 1987); Melencolia I, 1975; Pulse Field, Bow Down, Silbury Air, 1977; For O, for O, the Hobby-horse is forgot, 1977; Carmen Arcadiae Mechanicae Perpetuum, 1978; agm, 1979; On the Sheer Threshold of the Night, 1980; Quintet, 1981; Pulse Sampler, 1981; Deowa, 1983; Yan Tan Tethera, 1984; Still Movement, 1984; Secret Theatre, 1984; Songs by Myself, 1984; Earth Dances, 1986; Fanfare for Will, 1987; Endless Parade, 1987; Gawain, 1990 (opera); Four Poems by Jaan Kaplinski, 1991; Gawain's Journey, 1991; Antiphonies, 1992; The Second Mrs Kong, 1994 (opera); Cry of Anubis, 1995; Panic, 1995; Pulse Shadows, 1996; Slow Frieze, 1997; Exody, 1997; Harrison's Clocks, 1998; The Silk House Antiphonies, 1999; The Woman and the Hare, 1999; The Last Supper (opera), 2000; The Axe Manual, 2001; The Shadow of Night, 2002; Theseus Game, 2003; 26 Orpheus Elegies, 2003; Ring Dance of the Nazarene, 2003; The Gleam, 2003; The Io Passion, 2004; Night's Black Bird, 2004; Neruda Madrigales, 2005; The Minotaur, 2008; The Tree of Strings, 2008; The Corridor (opera), 2009; Angel Fighter, 2010, Violin Concerto, 2011; Oboe Quartet, 2011; Piano Trio, 2011; Fantasia Upon All the Notes, 2011; Moth Requiem, 2012; In Broken Images, 2012; Songs from the Same Earth, 2013; Construction with Guitar, 2013; Responses, 2014; The Cure (opera), 2015; The Silk House Sequences, 2015; Five Lessons in a Frame, 2016; Deep Time, 2017; Dear Dusty Moth, 2017; Keyboard Engine, 2018; Intrada, 2018; Three Holy Songs, 2018; Donum Simoni, 2018; Duet for Eight Strings, 2019. *Address*: c/o Rayfield Allied Ltd, Studio 26 China Works, 100 Black Prince Road, SE1 7SJ.

**BIRTWISTLE, Susan Elizabeth, (Lady Eyre)**; film and television producer; writer; *d* of late Frank Edgar Birtwistle and Brenda Mary Birtwistle (*née* Higham); *m* 1973, Richard Charles Hastings Eyre (*see* Sir Richard Eyre); one *d*. Theatre director: Royal Lyceum Th. in Educn Co., 1970–72; Nottingham Playhouse Roundabout Co., 1973–78; freelance TV producer, 1980–: work includes: Hotel du Lac, 1986 (BAFTA Award; Cable/Ace Award); Scoop; 'v' (RTS Award); Or Shall We Die?; Dutch Girls; Ball Trap on the Côte Sauvage; Anna Lee, 1993; Pride and Prejudice, 1995 (TRIC Award, TV Critics of Britain Award, 1995; TV Critics of America Award, Peabody Award, Voice of the Listener and Viewer Award, 1996; BVA Award, English Heritage Award, Banff Award, Banff Victor Ludorum Award); Emma, 1996; King Lear, 1998; Wives and Daughters, 1999; Armadillo, 2001; Cranford, 2007, 2009. Mem., Arts Council Drama Panel, 1975–77. *Publications*: The Making of Pride and Prejudice, 1995; The Making of Jane Austen's Emma, 1996; The Cranford Companion, 2010. *Recreations*: music, books, theatre, gardening. *Address*: c/o Nick Marston, Curtis Brown, 4th Floor, Haymarket House, 28–29 Haymarket, SW1Y 4SP. *T*: (020) 7396 6600.

**BISCHOFF, Dr Manfred**; Chairman, Supervisory Board, Daimler (formerly DaimlerChrysler) AG, since 2007; *b* Calw, Germany, 22 April 1942. *Educ*: Univ. of Tübingen; Univ. of Heidelberg (MEc; Dr rer. pol. 1973). Asst Prof. for Econ. Politics and Internat. Trade, Alfred Weber Inst., Univ. of Heidelberg, 1968–76; joined Daimler-Benz AG, 1976; Project Co-ordinator for Mercedes Benz Cross Country Cars, Corporate Subsids, M & A Dept, 1976–81; Internat. Projects, M & A, Finance Dept, 1981–88 (Vice-Pres., Finance Cos and Corporate Subsids); Member, Board of Management: and Chief Financial Officer, Mercedes do Brasil, 1988–89; and Chief Financial Officer, Deutsche Aerospace AG, later Daimler-Benz Aerospace AG, 1989–95; Daimler-Benz AG, later DaimlerChrysler AG, 1995–2003; and Pres. and CEO, DASA, 1995–2000; Mitsubishi Motors Corp., 2000–03; Chm. Supervisory Bd, MTU Aero Engines, 2000–03; Chm., EADS (European Aeronautic Defence and Space Co.), 2000–07; Mem. several supervisory bds. President: Eur. Assoc. Aerospace Industries, 1995–96; Fedn of German Aerospace Industries, 1996–2000. *Address*: Daimler AG, 70546 Stuttgart, Germany.

**BISCHOFF, Sir Winfried Franz Wilhelm, (Sir Win)**, Kt 2000; Chairman, J. P. Morgan Securities plc, since 2015; *b* 10 May 1941; *s* of late Paul Helmut Bischoff and Hildegard (*née* Kühne); *m* 1972, Rosemary Elizabeth (*d* 2018), *d* of Hon. Leslie Leathers; two *s*. *Educ*: Marist Brothers, Inanda, Johannesburg, S Africa; Univ. of the Witwatersrand, Johannesburg (BCom). Man. Dir, Schroders Asia Ltd, Hong Kong, 1971–82; Dir, 1978–2000, Chm., 1983–94, J. Henry Schroder & Co. Ltd; Dir, 1983–2000, Gp Chief Exec., 1984–95, Chm., 1995–2000, Schroders plc. Dep. Chm., Cable and Wireless, 1995–2003 (non-exec. Dir, 1991–2003); Chairman: Citigroup Europe, 2000–09; Citigroup Inc., 2007–09; Financial Reporting Council, 2014–19; non-executive Director: Land Securities plc, 1999–2008; McGraw-Hill Cos, Inc., 1999–; IFIL, Finanziaria di Partecipazioni SpA, 2000–04; Eli Lilly & Co., 2000–14; Siemens Hldgs plc, 2001–03; Prudential plc, 2007–09; Akbank AS, 2007–08 (Mem., Internat. Adv. Bd, 2009–); Lloyds Banking Gp, 2009–14. Chm., Adv. Council, TheCityUK, 2009–14. Hon. DSc City, 2000. *Recreations*: opera, music, golf. *Address*: J. P. Morgan Securities plc, 25 Bank Street, E14 5JP. *Clubs*: Swinley Forest Golf, Frilford Heath Golf, Loch Lomond Golf; Blind Brook Golf (US).

**BISCOE, Prof. Timothy John**; Visiting Professor, University of Bristol, since 2006; Pro-Provost, China, University College London, 1996–2001; *b* 28 April 1932; *s* of late Rev. W. H. Biscoe and Mrs M. G. Biscoe; *m* 1st, 1955, Daphne Miriam (*née* Gurton) (*d* 2005); one *s* two *d*; 2nd, 2009, Sarah Neale Lawson. *Educ*: Latymer Upper School; The London Hospital Medical College. BSc (Hons) Physiology, 1953; MB, BS 1957; DSc London, 1993; FRCP 1983. London Hospital, 1957–58; RAMC Short Service Commission, 1958–62; Physiologist, CDEE, Porton Down, 1959–62; ARC Inst. of Animal Physiology, Babraham, 1962–65; Res. Fellow in Physiology, John Curtin Sch. of Med. Res., Canberra, 1965–66; Associate Res. Physiologist, Cardiovascular Res. Inst., UC Medical Center, San Francisco, 1966–68; University of Bristol: Res. Associate, Dept of Physiology, 1968–70; 2nd Chair of Physiology, 1970–79; Head of Dept of Physiology, 1975–79. University College London: Jodrell Prof. of Physiology, 1979–92; Vice Provost, 1990–92; Hon. Fellow, 1996; Emeritus Prof., 1996; Dep. Vice-Chancellor, Univ. of Hong Kong, 1992–95. McLaughlin Vis. Prof., McMaster Univ., Ont. 1986; Hooker Distinguished Vis. Prof., McMaster Univ., 1990. Hon. Sec., Physiological Soc., 1977–82; Member Council: Harveian Soc., 1983–86; Research Defence Soc., 1983–90 (Hon. Sec., 1983–86). Mem., Academia Europaea, 1991. *Publications*: papers on neurophysiology in Journal of Physiology, etc. *Recreations*: looking, listening, reading. *Address*: c/o Physiology Department, University of Bristol, Bristol BS8 1TD. *Club*: Garrick.

**BISH-JONES, Trevor Charles**; Co-founder, mypeoplebiz.com, 2009; Chief Operating Officer, United Electronics, 2010–14; *b* 23 April 1960; *m* 1990, Amanda Zeil; two *d*. *Educ*: Varndean Grammar Sch., Brighton; Portsmouth Sch. of Pharmacy (BSc Hons Pharmacy). Res. Chemist, Tosco Corporate, Colorado, 1980–81; Boots plc: Store Manager, 1981–84; EPOS Project Manager, 1984–86; Buying and Marketing Controller for Photo/Sound/Vision/Home, 1987–94; Dixons Group: Marketing Dir, PC World and Dixons, 1994–97; Man. Dir, The Link, then Dixons, then Currys, 1997–2002; CEO, Woolworths Gp plc, 2002–08. *Recreation*: horse riding.

**BISHKO, Roy Colin;** Founder and Chairman, Tie Rack Ltd, 1981–99 (Co-Chairman, 1999–2007); b 2 March 1944; s of Isidore Bishko and Rae Bishko; m 1969, Barbara Eileen (née Hirsch); one s one d. Educ: Grey Coll., Bloemfontein, SA; Univ. of S Africa (Attorney's Admission 1967). With Schlesinger Orgn, 1969–74; Dir, Dorrington Investment Co. Ltd, 1974–76; Man. Dir, Chaddesley Investments, London, 1976–78. FRSA 1992. Recreations: golf, history.

**BISHOP,** family name of **Baroness O'Cathain.**

**BISHOP, Alan John;** Chief Executive, Creative Industries Federation, since 2018; b 2 Aug. 1953; s of Ronald and Betty Bishop. Educ: Queen's Coll., Oxford (BA Hons). With various advertising agencies, incl. Bates & FCB, 1974–85; joined Saatchi & Saatchi, 1985; Chairman: N America, 1994–97; UK, 1997–98; International, 1998–2002; Chief Exec., COI, 2003–09; Chief Exec., Southbank Centre, 2009–17. Recreations: bridge, music. Club: Soho House.

**BISHOP, Ven. (Anthony) Peter,** CB 2001; Associate Priest, Tewkesbury with Walton Cardiff and Twyning, 2001–06; b 24 May 1946; s of Geoffrey Richard Bishop and Dora Annie Bishop; m 1970, Ruth Isabel Jordan; two s. Educ: London Coll. of Divinity; St John's Coll., Nottingham (LTh 1971; MPhil 1983). Civil Servant, MoT, 1963–67; ordained deacon 1971, priest 1972; Curate, Beckenham, 1971–75; RAF Chaplain, 1975–2001: Asst Chaplain-in-Chief, 1991–98; Chaplain-in-Chief, and Archdeacon, RAF, 1998–2001. QHC 1996–2001. Canon of Lincoln, 1998–2001. Mem., Gen. Synod of C of E, 1998–2001. Mem. Council, RAF Benevolent Fund, 1998–2001; Vice-Pres., RAFA, 1998–. Vice-Pres., Friends of St Clement Danes, 1998–. FRSA 1983; FRAeS 1999. Recreations: walking, history, biography, cookery, living in France. Address: La Croix Blanche, 50810 St Germain d'Elle, France.

**BISHOP, Dr Arthur Clive;** Deputy Director, British Museum (Natural History), 1982–89, and Keeper of Mineralogy, 1975–89; b 9 July 1930; s of late Charles Henry Bishop and Hilda (née Clowes); m 1st, 1962, Helen (née Bennison) (d 2005); one d; 2nd, 2008, Kathleen Martha Renfrew (née Hope). Educ: Wolstanton County Grammar Sch., Newcastle, Staffs; King's Coll., Univ. of London (Shell Scholar; FKC 1985). BSc 1951, PhD 1954. Geologist, HM Geological Survey, 1954; served RAF Educn Br., 1955–57; Lectr in Geology, Queen Mary Coll., Univ. of London, 1958; Principal Sci. Officer, British Museum (Natural History), 1969, Deputy Keeper 1972. Geological Society: Daniel Pidgeon Fund, 1958; Murchison Fund, 1970; Vice-Pres., 1977–78; Mineralogical Society: Gen. Sec., 1965–72; Vice-Pres., 1973–74; Pres., 1986–87; Pres., Geologists' Assoc., 1978–80 (Halstead Medallist, 1999); Vice-Pres., Inst. of Science Technology, 1973–82. Mem. d'honneur, La Société Jersiaise, 1983. Publications: An Outline of Crystal Morphology, 1967; (with W. R. Hamilton and A. R. Woolley) Hamlyn Guide to Minerals, Rocks and Fossils, 1974, rev. edn as Philip's Minerals, Rocks and Fossils, 1999; (with B. E. Leake and R. J. Howarth) The Wyley History of the Geologists' Association, 2013; papers in various jls, mainly on geology of Channel Is and Brittany, and on dioritic rocks. Recreation: drawing and painting.

**BISHOP, Hon. Bronwyn Kathleen;** MHR (L) Mackellar, New South Wales, 1994–2016; Speaker, House of Representatives, Australia, 2013–15; b Sydney, NSW, 19 Oct. 1942; d of Thomas Francis Setright and Kathleen Setright (née Congreve); m 1966, Alan Bishop (marr. diss. 1992; he d 2010); two d. Educ: Univ. of Sydney (LLB). Admitted as solicitor, NSW, 1967. Senator (L), NSW, 1987–94. Shadow Minister: for Urban and Regl Strategy, 1994; for Health, 1994–95; for Privatisation and for Commonwealth and State Relns, 1995–96; Minister: for Defence Industries, Sci. and Personnel, 1996–98; for Aged Care, 1998–2001; Shadow Minister: for Veterans' Affairs, 2007–08; for Seniors, 2009–13; Shadow Special Minister of State, 2010–13. Chair: Standing Cttee on Legal and Constitutional Affairs, 2002–04; Hse of Reps Standing Cttee on Family and Human Services, 2004–07; Mem., Speaker's Panel, House of Reps, 2004–07. Dep. Chm., Pacific Democratic Union, 1993–98. Mem., Australian Cttee, Pacific Basin Econ. Council. NSW Division, Liberal Party of Australia: Mem., State Exec., 1980–; Vice-Pres., 1982–85; Pres., 1985–87; Mem., Jt Parly Public Accounts Cttee, 1987–94. Vice-Pres., Asthma Foundn, NSW, 1975–78; Life Member: Royal NSW Inst. for Deaf and Blind Children (former Vice-Pres.); Art Gall. Soc. of NSW. Centenary Medal, 2003. Recreations: family, music, art, football. Clubs: Commonwealth (ACT); Union University and Schools (Sydney).

**BISHOP, Prof. Christopher Michael,** PhD; FRS 2017; FREng; FRSE; Distinguished Scientist, since 2010, and Laboratory Director, since 2015, Microsoft Research Cambridge (Deputy Director, 1997–2008; Chief Research Scientist, 2008–10); Fellow, Darwin College, Cambridge, since 1998; Professor of Computer Science (part-time), University of Edinburgh, since 1997; b Norwich, 7 April 1959; s of Leonard Bishop and Joyce Bishop; m 1988, Jennifer Mary Morris; two s. Educ: Earlham Sch., Norwich; St Catherine's Coll., Oxford (BA Hons Physics 1980; MA 1984); Univ. of Edinburgh (PhD Theoretical Physics 1983). FREng 2004; FRSE 2007. Res. Physicist, Culham Lab., UKAEA, 1983–93; Prof. of Computer Sci., Aston Univ., 1993–97. Trustee, Royal Instn of GB (Vice-Pres., 2010). Publications: Neural Networks for Pattern Recognition, 1995; Pattern Recognition and Machine Learning, 2006. Recreations: flying light aircraft, including aerobatics. Address: Microsoft Research, 21 Station Road, Cambridge CB1 2FB. E: Christopher.Bishop@microsoft.com.

**BISHOP, Prof. David Hugh Langler,** PhD, DSc; FRSB; Fellow, St Cross College, Oxford, 1984–98, now Emeritus; Director, Natural Environment Research Council Institute of Virology and Environmental Microbiology (formerly Institute of Virology), 1984–95; b 31 Dec. 1937; s of late Reginald Samuel Harold Bishop and of Violet Rosina May Langler; m 1st, 1963, Margaret Duthie (marr. diss.); one s one d; 2nd, 1971, Polly Roy (marr. diss.); one s; 3rd, 1999, Margreta Buijs; one s two d. Educ: Liverpool Univ. (BSc Hons Biochem. 1959, PhD 1962); MA 1984, DSc 1988, Oxon. FRSB (FIBiol 1989). Postdoctoral Fellow, CNRS, Gif-sur-Yvette, 1962–63; Research Associate, Univ. of Edinburgh, 1963–66, Univ. of Illinois, 1966–69; Asst Prof., 1969–70, Associate Prof., 1970–71, Columbia Univ.; Associate Prof., 1971–75, Prof., 1975, Rutgers Univ.; University of Alabama at Birmingham: Prof., 1975–84; Sen. Scientist, Comprehensive Cancer Center, 1975–84; Chm., Dept of Microbiology, 1983–84; Adjunct Prof., Dept of Internat. Health, 1996–99. Vis. Fellow, Lincoln Coll., Oxford, 1981–82; Vis. Prof. of Virology, Oxford Univ., 1984–97; Hon. Prof., Dept of Microbiol., Univ. of Qld, 1997–2000. Life Mem., Internat. Cttee for Taxonomy of Viruses, 1997–. Nathaniel A. Young Award in Virology, 1981. Publications: Rhabdoviruses, 1979; numerous contribs to books and jls. Recreation: hill walking. Address: 8 Rosemount Crescent, Glenrothes, Fife KY6 2QQ.

**BISHOP, Prof. Dorothy Vera Margaret,** DPhil; FBA 2006; FRS 2014; FMedSci; Professor of Developmental Neuropsychology, since 1999, and Wellcome Principal Research Fellow, since 1998, University of Oxford; b 14 Feb. 1952; d of Aubrey Francis Bishop and Annemarie Sofia Bishop (née Eucken); m 1976, Patrick Michael Anthony Rabbitt, qv. Educ: St Hugh's Coll., Oxford (BA Hons 1973; MA; DPhil 1978); Inst. of Psychiatry, Univ. of London (MPhil 1975). Res. Officer, Neuropsychology Unit, Dept of Clinical Neurology, Univ. of Oxford, 1975–82; Sen. Res. Fellow, MRC, at Univs of Newcastle upon Tyne and Manchester, 1982–91; Sen. Res. Scientist, MRC Applied Psychology Unit, Cambridge, 1991–98. Adjunct Prof., Univ. of Western Australia, 1998. Mem., ESRC, 1996–2000. FMedSci 2000; Fellow, Assoc. for Psychol Sci., 2010. Hon. DM Lund, 2004; Hon. DSc: Newcastle upon Tyne, 2012; Western Australia, 2012. Publications: (ed with K. Mogford) Language Development in Exceptional Circumstances, 1988; Handedness and Developmental Disorders, 1990; Uncommon Understanding: development and disorders of language comprehension in children, 1997; (ed with L. B. Leonard) Speech and Language Impairments in Children, 2000. Recreations: Victorian novels, pre-1945 films, blogging (http://deevybee.blogspot.com), Twitter (www.twitter.com/deevybee), writing crime fiction under pen-name Deevy Bishop (two Kindle e-books, The Case of the Fremantle Fingers, The Case of the Brothel in the Bush, 2011). Address: Department of Experimental Psychology, Anna Watts Building, Woodstock Road, Oxford OX2 6GG. T: (01865) 271386.

**BISHOP, Edward James;** QC 2011; b London, 13 Sept. 1960; s of late James Drew Bishop; m 1994, Sarah Paneth. Educ: King's Sch., Canterbury; Pembroke Coll., Cambridge (BA 1982); Poly. of Central London (DipLaw). Called to the Bar, Middle Temple, 1985; in practice as a barrister, specialising in clinical negligence, 1 Chancery Lane, 1986–. Publications: (contrib. ed.) Kemp and Kemp on the Quantum of Damages, 2008–; contribs to various other legal books and jls. Recreations: travel, travel writing, football, cricket, music (fiddle player and singer in country folk band Police Dog Hogan). Address: 1 Chancery Lane, WC2A 1LF. T: (020) 7092 2900, Fax: (020) 7404 9876. E: ebishop@1chancerylane.com. Club: MCC.

**BISHOP, Ven. Ian Gregory;** Archdeacon of Macclesfield, since 2011; b Devizes, 13 Nov. 1962; s of John and Lorna Bishop; m 1986, Sue Winton; three s. Educ: Devizes Sch.; Portsmouth Poly. (BSc Urban Land Admin. 1984; ARICS 1986); Oak Hill Theol Coll. (BA Theol and Pastoral Studies 1991); St John's Coll., Durham (MA Theol. and Ministry 2017). Ordained deacon, 1991, priest, 1992; Curate, Christ Church, Purley, 1991–95; Rector: Tas Valley Team Ministry, 1995–2001; St Michael and All Angels, Middlewich, and St John the Evangelist, Byley, 2001–11. Address: 57A Sandbach Road, Congleton, Cheshire CW12 4LH. E: ian.bishop@chester.anglican.org.

**BISHOP, His Honour John Edward;** a Circuit Judge, 1993–2004; b 9 Feb. 1943; s of Albert George Bishop and Frances Marion Bishop; m 1968, Elizabeth Ann Grover; two d. Educ: St Edward's Sch., Oxford. Articled to P. F. Carter-Ruck at Messrs Oswald Hickson Collier & Co., WC2, 1962–66; admitted solicitor, 1966; Partner: Messrs Copley Clark & Co., Sutton, 1969–81; Messrs Tuck & Mann, Epsom, 1981–85; Registrar: Woolwich County Court, 1985–88; Croydon County Court, 1988–93 (District Judge, 1992–93); an Asst Recorder, 1987–90; a Recorder, 1990–93. Pres., Mid-Surrey Law Soc., 1980–81. Recreations: golf, walking, music, reading, garden, family. Clubs: East India; Walton Heath Golf.

**BISHOP, Prof. (John) Michael,** MD; Professor of Microbiology and Immunology, since 1972, and of Biochemistry and Biophysics, since 1982, University Professor, since 1994, Director, G. W. Hooper Research Foundation, since 1981, and Chancellor, 1998–2009, now Chancellor Emeritus, University of California, San Francisco; b 22 Feb. 1936; s of John and Carrie Bishop; m 1959, Kathryn Putman; two s. Educ: Gettysburg Coll., Gettysburg (AB); Harvard Univ., Boston (MD). Intern/Asst Resident in Internal Med., Mass. Gen. Hosp., 1962–64; Res. Associate, NIAID, NIH, 1964–67; Vis. Scientist, Heinrich-Pette Inst., Hamburg, 1967–68; Asst Prof., Microbiology, 1968–70, Associate Prof., Microbiology, 1970–72, Univ. of California. Member: Nat. Acad. of Scis, 1980–; Amer. Acad. of Arts and Scis, 1984–. Foreign Mem., Royal Soc., 2008. Hon. DSc: Gettysburg, 1983; KCL, 2008. Albert Lasker Award for Basic Med. Res., 1982; Passano Foundn Award, 1983; Warren Triennial Prize, 1983; Armand Hammer Cancer Res. Award, 1984; Gen. Motors Cancer Res. Award, 1984; Gairdner Foundn Internat. Award, 1984; ACS Medal of Honor, 1985; (jtly) Nobel Prize in Physiology or Medicine, 1989. Publications: The Rise of the Genetic Paradigm, 1995; Proto-oncogenes and Plasticity in Cell Signaling, 1995; How to Win the Nobel Prize: an unexpected life in science, 2003; over 400 pubns in refereed sci. jls. Recreations: music, reading, theatre. Address: G. W. Hooper Research Foundation, Box 0552, 1542 HSW, University of California, 513 Parnassus Avenue, San Francisco, CA 94143–0552, USA. T: (415) 4763211.

**BISHOP, Kathryn Ann, (Mrs Mark Carden);** Chair, Welsh Revenue Authority, since 2017; Associate Fellow: Saïd Business School, University of Oxford, since 2004; Green Templeton College, Oxford, since 2014; b Binghamton, NY, 2 Aug. 1958; d of Geoffrey and Marjorie Bishop; m 1990, Mark Carden; two s. Educ: City of Worcester Grammar Sch. for Girls; Wellesley Coll., USA (BA Hons summa cum laude 1979); Jesus Coll., Oxford (MPhil 1981). Sen. Manager, Accenture, 1981–90; Asst Dir, 1990–91, Personnel Develt Dir, 1992–94, Allied Dunbar; Change Manager, Eagle Star Life, 1994–96; Prog. Dir, Allied Dunbar/Eagle Star Life, 1996–98; Dir, Business Transformation, Eagle Star, Allied Dunbar and Zurich Gp, 1998–99; Dir, Naughton Consulting Ltd, 1999–; Hd, Planning and Projects, UWE, 2001–04. Non-executive Director: UK Intellectual Property Office, 2000–09; Welsh Assembly Govt, 2003–10; UK Border Agency, 2010–12. Civil Service Comr, 2012–17 (Interim First Civil Service Comr, 2016). Mem., Phi Beta Kappa, 1979. Gov., Horsley C of E (Aided) Primary Sch., 1996–2012; Chm., Bd of Trustees, Dean Close Sch., 2014–; Trustee, Horsley Free Sch. Charities Trust, 1996– (Chm., 2015–). Recreations: singing in choirs, theatre, reading. Address: Saïd Business School, University of Oxford, Egrove Park, Kennington, Oxford OX1 4DY. Club: Lansdowne.

**BISHOP, Malcolm Leslie;** QC 1993; a Recorder, 2000–14; b 9 Oct. 1944; s of late John Bishop and Irene Bishop (née Dunn); civil partnership 2006, Anthony Patrick Vander Woerd, e s of Surg. Comdr Dirk Jan Albert Vander Woerd, Royal Dutch Navy, and Anne Patricia Venise Bowen Vander Woerd (now Kennard). Educ: Ruabon Grammar Sch.; Regent's Park Coll., Oxford Univ. (Samuel Davies Prizeman; Hon. Mods in Theology, BA Jurisprudence, MA; Hon. Fellow 2016). Chm., OU Dem. Lab. Club, 1966. Called to the Bar, Inner Temple, 1968, Bencher, 2003; in practice on Wales and Chester Circuit. A Dep. High Court Judge, Family Div., 1997–2014; an Asst Recorder, 1998–2000. Chm., I of M Legal Services Commn, 2002. Circuit Rep., Bar Council, 1987–92; Mem., Exec. Cttee, Family Law Bar Assoc., 1985–. Contested (Lab), Bath, Feb. and Oct. 1974. Hon. Standing Counsel, Regent's Park Coll., Oxford Univ., 2007–. Publications: St John's Gospel: a lawyer's translation from the original Greek, 2018; Revelation Unveiled St John's Apocalypse: a lawyer's translation from the original Greek, 2019. Recreations: politics, wine. Address: Ely Place Chambers, 13 Ely Place, EC1N 6RY. T: (020) 7400 9600. Clubs: Oxford and Cambridge; Cardiff and County (Cardiff).

**BISHOP, Mark Andrew; His Honour Judge Bishop;** a Circuit Judge, since 2009; Resident Judge, Luton Crown Court, since 2019; b Cambridge, 12 July 1958; s of Robin Bishop and Joyce Bishop; m 1986, Christine Smart; three d. Educ: Leys Sch., Cambridge; Downing Coll., Cambridge (MA 1984). Called to the Bar, Middle Temple, 1981 (Astbury Schol.); in practice as a barrister, 1 Temple Gardens, 1982–2009; Recorder, 2001–09; Fee-paid Tribunal Judge, Mental Health Rev. Tribunal, 2007–, Restricted Patients Panel, 2009–; Sen. Judge, 2017–, Presiding Sen. Judge, 2018–, Sovereign Base Area, Cyprus. Dep. Chancellor, Dio. of Rochester, 2000–16; Chancellor, Dio. of Lincoln, 2007–; Chm., Bishops' Disciplinary Tribunals, 2015–. Ordained deacon, 2002, priest, 2003; Asst Curate,

2002–05, Asst Priest, 2005–, Little St Mary, Cambridge. Pres., Cambridge Union Soc., 1980; ESU debating tour of USA, 1981. Gov., Leys Sch., Cambridge, 1989–2016. *Recreations:* family, holidays, music. *Address:* Luton Crown Court, 7 George Street, Luton LU1 2AA.

**BISHOP, Mark John;** Executive Principal, YK Pao School, Shanghai, China, since 2018; *b* Wimbledon, 4 Feb. 1962; *s* of John and Jean Bishop; *m* 2004, Tymian Brown; one *s* and one step *d. Educ:* Charterhouse Sch.; St Edmund Hall, Oxford (MA); Henley Mgt Coll. (MBA). Teacher of Religious Studies and Philosophy, Royal Grammar Sch., Guildford, 1985–96; Dep. Hd, Caterham Sch., 1996–2005; Dir, Perrett Laver, 2005; Headmaster, Trinity Sch., Croydon, 2006–16; Chief Exec., Perrett Laver, 2016–17. *Recreations:* mountain walking, diving, cycling, golf. *Address:* 5 The Copse, Caterham, Surrey CR3 6DU. *E:* markandtymian@aol.com.

**BISHOP, Michael;** *see* Bishop, J. M.

**BISHOP, Michael William;** JP; Chairman, Heritage Care Ltd, 2001–08; *b* 22 Oct. 1941; *s* of Ronald Lewis William and Gwendoline Mary Bishop; *m* Loraine Helen Jones; two *s* one *d. Educ:* Manchester Univ. (BA (Econs) IIi Hons); Leicester Univ. (CertAppSocStudies). Director of Social Services: Cleveland CC, 1981–89; Manchester City Council, 1989–95. Mem., Derbys Probation Bd, 2004–10. Non-exec. Dir, Derbys NHS PCT, 2007–09. Chm., Derbys Assoc. for Blind People, 2004–08; Trustee, RNID, 1996–2004 (Dep. Chm., 2002–04); Mem., Hearing Aid Council, 2004–10. Mem. Bd, Community Transport for Town and Countary, 2011–18. JP Manchester City, 1996–2000, High Peak, 2000–11.

**BISHOP, Patrick Joseph;** military historian and author, since 2007; *b* Ashford, Kent, 17 Oct. 1952; *s* of Ernest Bishop and Kathleen Bishop (*née* Kelly); *m* 2008, Henrietta Miers; one *d. Educ:* Wimbledon Coll.; Corpus Christi Coll., Oxford (Exhibnr; BA Hons Modern Hist.). Reporter, The Observer, 1979–84 (corresp. with British Forces in Falkland Is War, 1982); reporter and Diplomatic Corresp., Sunday Times, 1985–87; Daily Telegraph: ME Corresp., 1988–92; Sen. Foreign Corresp., 1992–95; Foreign Ed., 1995–97; Associate Ed. (Foreign), 1997–99; Paris Corresp., 1999–2001; Special Corresp., 2002–07. Dir, Médecins sans Frontières UK, 1992–2002 (Chm., 1995–2000). *Publications:* Famous Victory, 1992; The Irish Empire, 1999; Fighter Boys, 2003; Bomber Boys, 2007; 3 Para, 2007; A Good War (novel), 2008; Ground Truth, 2009; The Battle of Britain, 2009; Follow Me Home (novel), 2011; Target Tirpitz, 2012; Wings, 2012; The Reckoning, 2014; The Cooler King: the true story of William Ash - Spitfire pilot, P.O.W. and WWII's greatest escaper, 2015; Air Force Blue, 2017; The Man Who Was Saturday: the extraordinary life of Airey Neave, 2019. *Recreations:* fishing, painting, family. *E:* patrickbishop2001@hotmail.com. *Club:* Savile.

**BISHOP, Ven. Peter;** *see* Bishop, Ven. A. P.

**BISHOP, Prof. Peter Antony;** Professor of Urban Design, Bartlett School of Architecture, University College London, since 2012; Director, Allies and Morrison Urban Practitioners, since 2011; *b* 15 Sept. 1953; *s* of Jack and Audrey Bishop; *m* 1998, Lesley Williams; one *s* one *d. Educ:* Trinity Sch. of John Whitgift; Univ. of Manchester (BA 1st Cl. Hons). Hd of Planning, London Bor. of Tower Hamlets, 1985–87; Dir, Engrg and Property, London Bor. of Haringey, 1987–97; Director of Environment: London Bor. of Hammersmith & Fulham, 1997–2001 (projects included: develt of White City, the BBC, Fulham FC); London Bor. of Camden, with resp. for redevelt of King's Cross, 2001–06; London Development Agency: Dir, Design for London, 2006–09; Gp Dir, Design Develt and Envmt, and Dep. Chief Exec., 2009–11. Mem., London Adv. Cttee, English Heritage, 2007–. Chm., Architecture Centre Network, 2010–. Has lectured and taught extensively. Vis. Prof., Nottingham Trent Univ., 2007–; Dist. Vis. Prof., Univ. of Technol., Sydney, 2017. Hon. Fellow, UCL, 2008; Hon. FRIBA, 2008. Hon. Dr Kingston, 2011. *Publications:* (with Lesley Williams) The Temporary City, 2012; (with Lesley Williams) Planning, Politics and City Making: a case study of King's Cross, 2016. *Recreations:* rock climbing, squash, collecting antiquarian books, European cinema. *Address:* Bartlett School of Architecture, University College London, Wates House, 22 Gordon Street, WC1H 0QB. *E:* peter.bishop@ucl.ac.uk.

**BISHOP, Stephen;** *see* Kovacevich, S.

**BISHOP, Timothy Harper Paul;** QC 2011; *b* Horsham, 16 June 1969; *s* of Hedley Paul Bishop and Marian Dorothy Bishop (*née* German); *m* 1993, Claire Louise Brind; three *s* one *d. Educ:* Maidstone Grammar Sch.; Trinity Coll., Cambridge (BA 1990; MA 1993). Called to the Bar, Inner Temple, 1991; in practice as a barrister specialising in matrimonial finance, 1992–; Hd of Chambers, 2017–. *Publications:* (with Gavin Smith) Enforcing Financial Orders in Matrimonial Proceedings, 2000. *Recreations:* Rugby coaching, ski-ing, tennis. *Address:* 1 Hare Court, Temple, EC4Y 7BE. *T:* (020) 7797 7070, *Fax:* (020) 7797 7435. *E:* bishop@1hc.com. *Club:* Royal Automobile.

**BISHOP-KOVACEVICH, Stephen;** *see* Kovacevich, S.

**BISHOPP, Colin Philip;** a Judge of the Upper Tribunal, 2009–17 (Special Commissioner of Income Tax, 2001–09; Chairman, VAT and Duties Tribunal, 2001–09 (part-time Chairman, 1990–2001)); President, Tax Chamber of the First-tier Tribunal, 2011–17; *b* 10 Oct. 1947; *s* of late Clement Walter Bishopp and of Alison Moray Bishopp (*née* Stewart); *m* 1st, 1970 (marr. diss. 1987); one *s* one *d*; 2nd, 1988 (marr. diss. 2010); three *s. Educ:* Manchester Grammar Sch.; St Catharine's Coll., Cambridge (BA 1968, MA 1971). Admitted solicitor, 1971; Partner: A. W. Mawer & Co., Solicitors, 1973–88; Lace Mawer, Solicitors, 1988–97; Berrymans Lace Mawer, Solicitors, 1997–2001. Chairman: Financial Services and Markets Tribunal, 2001–10; Pensions Regulator Tribunal, 2005–10; Claims Mgt Services Tribunal, 2007–09. *Recreations:* travel, photography, walking, classical music. *Address:* 4 Claremont Close, Winslow, Buckingham MK18 3GG. *T:* (01296) 715994.

**BISIGNANI, Giovanni;** Director General and Chief Executive Officer, International Air Transport Association, 2002–11, now Emeritus (Member, Executive Committee, 1991–94); Chairman, Global Agenda Council on Aviation, Travel and Tourism, World Economic Forum, 2011–12 (Member, since 2012); *b* 10 Dec. 1946; *s* of Renato Bisignani and Vincenza Carpano; *m* 1975, Elena Pasanisi; one *d. Educ:* Rome Univ. (Master of Law); Harvard Business Sch. First National City Bank, NY, 1970; Manager, Res. and Econ. Planning Dept, Ente Partecipazioni e Finanziamento Industria Manifatturiera, Rome, 1973–76; COS to Chair, ENI, Rome, 1976–79; Istituto Ricostruzione Industriale, Rome: COS to Chm., 1979–81, and Rep. on Bds of Finsider, Italstat, SME and Fincantieri, 1979–89; Exec. Vice Pres., Internat., 1981–89; Man. Dir and CEO, Alitalia, Rome, 1989–94; Chm., Galileo Internat., Chicago, 1993–94; Pres., Tirrenia di Navigazione SpA, Rome, 1994–98; SM Logistics-Gruppo Serra Merzario SpA, 1998–2001: Man. Dir and CEO, Milan; Chm., Merzario USA, Inc., NY; Bd Mem., Merzario UK London; Opodo, 2001–02: CEO, London; Man. Dir, Berlin; Man. Dir, Paris. Vis. Prof., Sch. of Engrg, Cranfield Univ., 2012–. Chm., AEA, 1991; Member: Bd, Assolombarda, Milan, 1998–2000; European Adv. Bd, Pratt & Whitney, United Technologies, 1998–2001; Bd, UK NATS Ltd, 2002–12; Bd, Safran, 2011–17; Bd, Aircastle Ltd, 2012–; Bd, Alitalia, 2015–. FR.AeS 2009. Hon. DSc Cranfield, 2010. *Recreations:* golf, tennis, riding. *Address:* International Air Transport Association, Route de l'Aéroport 33, PO Box 416, 1215 Geneva 15 Airport, Switzerland. *E:* bisignanig@gmail.com.

**BISPHAM, Christine; Her Honour Judge Bispham;** a Circuit Judge, since 2018; *b* Whiston, 28 June 1969; *d* of Christopher Bispham and Mavis Bispham. *Educ:* Rainhill High Sch.; Univ. of Leicester (LLB Hons 1990); Coll. of Law, London. Called to the Bar, Lincoln's Inn, 1991; barrister, 1991–2018; a Recorder, 2008–18. Northern Circuit: Mem., 1991–2018; Jun., 1994–95; Crier, 2003–18; Hon. Sec., 2006–08; Ed., In Brief, 2011–13. Bar Council Rep., 1997–2008. Sec., UK Assoc. of Women Judges, 2015–18. *Publications:* (contrib.) Personal Injury Litigation Service, 1990; Domestic Injunctions (with Margaret de Haas), 2nd edn 1998. *Recreations:* walking, music, shopping, films, exploring Scotland, afternoon tea. *Address:* Liverpool Civil and Family Court, 35 Vernon Street, Liverpool L2 2BX. *E:* hhj.christine.bispham@ejudiciary.net. *Club:* Athenæum (Liverpool).

**BISS, Adele, (Mrs R. O. Davies);** businesswoman; a Civil Service Commissioner, 2010–15; *b* 18 Oct. 1944; *d* of Robert and Bronia Biss; *m* 1973, Roger Oliver Davies, *qv*; one *s. Educ:* Cheltenham Ladies' Coll.; University Coll. London (BSc Econ; Fellow, 2008). Unilever, 1968; Thomson Holidays, 1970; Chief Exec., Biss Lancaster, 1978–88; Chm., BTA and English Tourist Bd, 1993–96; Chm., A. S. Biss & Co., 1996–2007. Director: Aegis plc, 1985–90; BR, 1987–92; European Passenger Services, subseq. Eurostar (UK) Ltd, 1990–2010; Bowthorpe plc, 1993–97; Harry Ramsden's, 1995–99; Engine Gp, 2005–10. Gov., Middx Univ., 1995–2007; Member Council: GDST (formerly GPDST), 1996–2003; UCL, 1997–2007. Hon. DBA Lincoln, 2002. *Recreation:* friends and family.

**BISSELL, Frances Mary;** freelance writer; *b* 19 Aug. 1946; *d* of Robert Maloney and Mary Maloney (*née* Kelly); *m* 1970, Thomas Emery Bissell; one step *d. Educ:* Univ. of Leeds (BA Hons French). VSO Nigeria, 1965–66; Assistante, Ecole Normale, Albi, 1968–69; British Council, 1970–87; The Times, 1987–2000; food and cookery writer, cook and consultant, 1983–, TV presenter, 1995–. Guest cook: Mandarin Oriental, Hong Kong, 1987, 1990, 1995; London Intercontinental, 1987, 1988 and 1996; Manila Peninsula, 1989; Colombo Hilton, Sri Lanka, 1991; The Dusit Thani, Bangkok, 1992; George V, Paris, 1994; The Mark, NY, 1997, 1999 and 2000; Rio Suites Hotel, Las Vegas, 1997; guest teacher: Bogotá Hilton, Colombia, 1988; Ballymaloe Cooking Sch., Ireland, 1990; The Times cookery evenings at Leith's Sch. of Food and Wine, 1991; Learning for Pleasure, Spain, 1995 and 1996; Consultant: Ta' Frenc, Gozo, 2004–; Sloane Club, 2006–13; Guest Lecturer: Swan Hellenic, 2001–; Hebridean Internat. Cruises, 2005–09; Hebridean Island Cruises, 2010–; Hebridean River Cruises, 2016–. Member judging panel: THF Hotels Chef of the Year, 1988 and 1990; Annual Catey Award Function Menu, 1989–94; A Fresh Taste of Britain, Women's Farming Union, 1989; UK Finals, Prix Taittinger, 1993, 1994; Roux Diners Club Scholarship, 1995–98; Roux Scholarship, 2000–02; Slow Food, 2003–; Gourmet Voice, 2006–; Shackleton Fund Fellowship, 2001. Founder Mem., Guild of Food Writers, 1985. Chef Mem., Acad. of Culinary Arts (formerly Académie Culinaire de France), 1997, Fellow, 2008. Columnist: Caterer & Hotelkeeper, 1988–94; Hampstead and Highgate Express, 1999–; Sunday Times of Malta, 2003–16; Malta Taste, 2005–. Glenfiddich Cookery Writer of the Year, 1994; James Beard Foundn Award, USA, 1995. *Television:* Frances Bissell's Westcountry Kitchen, 1995; Frances Bissell's Christmas Cooking, 1996. *Publications:* A Cook's Calendar, 1985; The Pleasures of Cookery, 1986; Ten Dinner Parties for Two, 1988; Sainsbury's Book of Food, 1989 (US edn, as The Book of Food, 1994); Oriental Flavours, 1990; The Real Meat Cookbook, 1992; The Times Cookbook, 1993; Frances Bissell's West Country Kitchen, 1996; (with Tom Bissell) An A–Z of Food and Wine in Plain English, 1999; The Organic Meat Cookbook, 1999; Modern Classics, 2000; Entertaining, 2002; Preserving Nature's Bounty, 2006; The Scented Kitchen, 2007, 2nd edn 2012; The Floral Baker, 2014; The Fragrant Pantry, 2017; contrib. to Caterer and Hotelkeeper, Sunday Times Mag., Homes and Gardens, House & Garden, Country Living, Decanter, Country Life. *Recreations:* travelling, reading. *Address:* 2 Carlingford Road, NW3 1RX.

**BISSON, (Anthony) Nicholas,** PhD; Director, HS2 Phase 2, Department for Transport, since 2014; *b* Manchester, 7 July 1972; *s* of Anthony Bisson and Anne Bisson; *m* 2002, Sally Rickards; one *s* one *d. Educ:* St Albans Sch.; Univ. of Durham (BSc Maths 1993); Univ. of Warwick (PhD Stats 1996). Department of the Environment, later DETR, then DTLR, subseq. DfT, 1996–: EC (on secondment), 1999; Downing Street Policy Directorate, 2001–02; Hd, London Transport, 2002–05; Asst Hd, Highways and Transport, W Sussex CC (on secondment), 2006–07; Dir, Regl and Local Transport, 2007–11; Dir, Rail Policy, subseq. Rail Strategy and Funding, 2011–14. *Address:* Department for Transport, 33 Horseferry Road, SW1P 4DR. *T:* (020) 7944 4250. *E:* nick.bisson@dft.gov.uk.

**BISSON, Hon. Claude,** OC 1999; Counsel, McCarthy Tétrault, Montreal, 1996; a Judge of the Court of Appeal, Quebec, 1980–96; Chief Justice of Quebec, 1988–94; *b* 9 May 1931; *m* 1957, Louisette Lanneville; two *s* one *d. Educ:* Univ. de Laval, Quebec (BA 1950; LLL 1953). Called to Bar, Quebec, 1954. Superior Court Judge, Montreal, 1969–80. *Address:* c/o McCarthy Tétrault, 1000 de La Gauchetière Street West, Montreal, QC H3B 0A2, Canada.

**BISSON, Nicholas;** *see* Bisson, A. N.

**BISZTYGA, Jan;** Officer's Cross of the Order of Polonia Restituta 1970; Order of Merit 1973; Senior Advisor to President, Bartimpex, since 2003; *b* 19 Jan. 1933; *s* of Kazimierz Bisztyga; *m* 1956, Otylia; one *s. Educ:* Jagiellonian Univ. (MSc Biochemistry). Asst Professor, Jagiellonian Univ., Cracow, 1954–57; political youth movement, 1956–59; Min. for Foreign Affairs, 1959–63; Attaché, New Delhi, 1963–64; Min. for Foreign Affairs, 1964–69; Head of Planning Dept, Min. for Foreign Affairs, 1969–71; Dep. Foreign Minister, 1972–75; Ambassador in Athens, 1975–78, to UK, 1978–81; Ideology Dept, Polish United Workers' Party; expert in Office of Pres. of Polish Republic, 1990–91; Advr on Foreign Trade Enterprise, Euroamer, 1991–94; Advr to PM's Office, 1994–97; Pol Advr to Minister of Interior and Admin, 1997–2001; Advisor: to PM of Poland, 2001–03; The Foreign Trade Enterprise Bartimpex, 2003–06. *Recreations:* game shooting, fishing, history. *Address:* (home) Jaworzyńska 11–18, Warsaw 00634, Poland; (office) Bartimpex, Al. Szucho 9, Warsaw, Poland. *T:* (622) 2757, 0605 155185, *Fax:* (621) 0943. *E:* biuro@bartimpex.com.pl.

**BITEL, Nicholas Andrew;** Consultant, Kerman & Co., since 2012; Chief Executive, London Marathon, since 1995; Chairman, Sport England, since 2013; *b* 31 Aug. 1959; *s* of Max and Cecilia Bitel; *m* 1982, Sharon Levan; three *s. Educ:* St Paul's Sch., London; Davidson Coll., NC (Dean Rusk Schol.); Manchester Univ. (LLB). Admitted solicitor, 1983; Partner, Max Bitel Greene, 1983–2011. Dir, Olympic Park Legacy Co., then London Legacy Develt Corp., 2009–18. Member: Council, UK Sport, 2005–08 and 2013–; Bd, Sport England, 2010–. Vice-Chm., Wigan Athletic, 1991–95. *Publications:* contribs to Sport and the Law Jl. *Recreations:* sports, theatre. *Address:* Kerman & Co., 200 Strand, WC2R 1DJ. *T:* (020) 7539 7272, *Fax:* (020) 7240 5780. *Club:* MCC.

**BJERREGAARD, Ritt Jytte;** Lord Mayor, City of Copenhagen, 2006–09; *b* Copenhagen, 19 May 1941; *d* of Gudmund Bjerregaard and Rita (*née* Hærslev); *m* 1966, Prof. Søren Mørch. Qualified as teacher, 1964. MP (Social Dem.), Denmark: Otterup (Fyn), 1971–95; Lejre, 1999–2005; Minister for: Educn, 1973 and 1975–78; Social Affairs, 1979–81; Mem., EC, 1995–99; Minister for Food, Agric. and Fisheries, 2000–01. Chm., Social Dem. Parly Gp, 1981–82 and 1987–92 (Dep. Chm., 1982–87). Pres., Danish European Movt, 1992–94. Mem., Trilateral Commn, 1982–2001. Vice-Pres., Danish delegn, CSCE, 1992–94. Vice-Pres., Socialist Internat. Women, 1992–94. *Publications:* books on educn and politics in Denmark, including: Strid, 1979; Til venner og fjender, 1982; I opposition, 1987; (with S. Mørch) Fyn med omliggende oor, 1989; Verden er saa stor, saa stor, 1990; Mine Æbler, 2003; Mit København, 2005; (jtly) Min mor er død, 2010; Ritt: erindringer, 2015; articles in Danish jls. *Recreation:* growing apples.

**BLACK OF BRENTWOOD,** Baron *cr* 2010 (Life Peer), of Brentwood in the County of Essex; **Guy Vaughan Black;** Deputy Chairman, Telegraph Media Group, since 2018 (Corporate Affairs Director, then Executive Director, 2005–18); *b* 6 Aug. 1964; *s* of Thomas Black and Monica Black (*née* Drew); civil partnership 2006, *m* 2015, Mark William Bolland, *qv. Educ:* Brentwood Sch., Essex; Peterhouse, Cambridge (John Cosin Schol.; Sir Herbert Butterfield Prize for History, 1985; MA). Graduate Trainee, Corporate Banking Div., BZW, 1985–86; Desk Officer, Conservative Res. Dept, 1986–89; Special Advr to Sec. of State for Energy, 1989–92; Account Dir, Westminster Strategy, 1992–94; Associate Dir, Lowe Bell Good Relns, 1994–96; Dir, Press Complaints Commn, 1996–2003; Press Sec. to Leader of the Opposition, and Dir of Media, Conservative Central Office, 2004–05. Dir, Advertising Standards Bd of Finance, 2005–; Chm., Press Standards Bd of Finance, 2009–15; Dir, Regulatory Funding Co., 2018–. Mem. (C), Brentwood DC, 1988–92. President: London Press Club, 2012–; Soc. of Old Brentwoods, 2012–13; Printing Charity, 2013–14 (Pres. Emeritus, 2015); Eur. Newspaper Publishers Assoc., 2014–15; Inst. of Promotional Marketing, 2015–. Patron: Peterhouse Politics Soc., 2004–; Rory Peck Trust, 2014–; Internat. Cat Care, 2017–; Terrence Higgins Trust, 2017–; Vice-President: NI Schools Debating Competition, 2011–; Journalists' Charity, 2014–; News Media Europe, 2016–. Chairman: Commonwealth Press Union Trust, 2009–; Hanover Band Foundn, 2014–17; Trustee: Sir Edward Heath's Charitable Foundn, 2006–10; Imperial War Museum, 2007–15; Mayor of London's Fund for Young Musicians, 2011–12; Bloomsbury Network, 2018–; Treas., Imperial War Mus. Foundn, 2015–. Member: Council, RCM, 2009– (Chm., 2017–); Guild of St Bride's, Fleet Street, 2010–. Gov., Brentwood Sch., 2013–. Churchwarden, St Bride's, 2014–17. Liveryman, Stationers' Co., 2016–. FRSA 1997; MCIPR 2007, Hon. FCIPR 2016. *Recreations:* music, cats, reading, Umbria. *Address:* House of Lords, SW1A 0PW. *T:* (office) (020) 7931 3806. *Club:* Athenæum.

**BLACK OF CROSSHARBOUR,** Baron *cr* 2001 (Life Peer), of Crossharbour in the London Borough of Tower Hamlets; **Conrad Moffat Black;** PC (Can.) 1992; Chairman, Conrad Black Capital Corporation, 1978–2014, now Hon. Chairman; *b* 25 Aug. 1944; *m* 1st, 1978, Joanna Catherine Louise Hishon (name changed by deed poll in 1990 from Shirley Gail Hishon) (marr. diss., 1992); two *s* one *d*; 2nd, 1992, Barbara Amiel. *Educ:* Carleton Univ. (BA); Laval Univ. (LLL); MA History McGill, 1973. Chm. and Chief Exec., Ravelston Corp., 1979–2005; Chm., 1979, Chief Exec., 1985–2005, Argus Corp.; Chm., The Telegraph Gp Ltd, 1987–2005 (Dir, 1985–2005); Chm. and CEO, Hollinger International Inc., 1990–2003. Mem., Editl Bd, Nat. Interest, Washington, 1997. Hon. LLD: St Francis Xavier, 1979; McMaster, 1979; Carleton, 1989; Hon. LittD Univ. of Windsor, 1979. KLJ; KCSG 2001. *Publications:* Duplessis, 1977, rev. edn as Render Unto Caesar, 1998; A Life in Progress (autobiog.), 1993; Franklin Delano Roosevelt: champion of freedom, 2003; The Invincible Quest: the life of Richard Milhous Nixon, 2007; A Matter of Principle, 2011; Flight of the Eagle: a strategic history of the United States, 2013; Rise to Greatness, The History of Canada - from the Vikings to the Present, 2014; Backward Glances, 2017; Donald J. Trump: a president like no other, 2018.

**BLACK OF DERWENT, Rt Hon. Lady;** Jill Margaret Black, DBE 1999; PC 2010; a Justice of the Supreme Court of the United Kingdom, since 2017; *b* 1 June 1954; *d* of Dr James Irvine Currie and late Dr Margaret Yvonne Currie; *m* 1978, David Charles Black (marr. diss. 2013); one *s* one *d*; *m* 2013, Rt Hon. Sir Richard George Bramwell McCombe, *qv. Educ:* Penrhos Coll., Colwyn Bay; Durham Univ. (BA Hons Law). Called to the Bar, Inner Temple, 1976; QC 1994; a Recorder, 1999; a Judge of the High Ct of Justice, Family Div., 1999–2010; Family Div. Liaison Judge, N Circuit, 2000–04; a Lady Justice of Appeal, 2010–17; Head, Internat. Family Justice, 2013–17. Chm., Family Cttee, Judicial Studies Bd, 2004–18. Comr, Judicial Appts Commn, 2008–13. *Publications:* Divorce: the things you thought you'd never need to know, 1982, 8th edn 2004; A Practical Approach to Family Law, 1986, 10th edn 2015; (jtly) The Working Mother's Survival Guide, 1988; (jtly) The Family Court Practice, annually, 1993–; (jtly) Family Law: Legal Practice Course guide, 2009. *Address:* Supreme Court of the United Kingdom, Parliament Square, SW1P 3BD.

**BLACK, Dr Aline Mary;** Headteacher, Colchester County High School for Girls, 1987–98; *b* 2 July 1936; *d* of Maurice and Harriet Rose; *m* 1972, David Black. *Educ:* Manchester Univ.; Birkbeck and King's Colls, London (BSc Hons Physics 1957; PGCE 1959; BSc Hons Chemistry 1970; PhD 1973). Res. Physicist, Richard, Thomas & Baldwins, 1957–58; Physics Teacher, Sir William Perkins' Sch., 1959–61; Head of Physics, City of London Sch. for Girls, 1961–71; Science Advr, Waltham Forest LBC, 1973–75; Science and Maths Advr, Bexley LBC, 1975–77; Headteacher: Leyton Sen. High Sch. for Girls, 1977–82; Gravesend Grammar Sch. for Girls, 1982–87. *Recreations:* archaeology, walking. *Address:* 11 Winchester Road, Frinton on Sea, Essex CO13 9JB. *T:* (01255) 852794.

**BLACK, Col Anthony Edward Norman,** OBE 1981; Chief Executive Commissioner, Scout Association, 1987–95; *b* 20 Jan. 1938; *s* of late Arthur Norman Black and Phyllis Margaret Ranicar; *m* 1963, Susan Frances Copeland; two *s. Educ:* Brighton College; RMA Sandhurst. Commissioned RE, 1957; served Kenya, Aden, Germany, Cyprus; Army Staff Course, Camberley, 1970; GSO1 Ghana Armed Forces Staff Coll., 1976–78; CO 36 Engr Regt, 1978–80; Col GS MGO Secretariat, 1980–82; Comd Engrs Falkland Islands, 1983; Comdt, Army Apprentices Coll., Chepstow, 1983–86; retired 1987. *Recreations:* gardening, bird watching. *Address:* National Westminster Bank, 50 High Street, Egham, Surrey TW20 9EU.

**BLACK, His Honour Barrington (Malcolm);** a Circuit Judge, 1993–2005; a Deputy Circuit Judge, 2005–07; a Justice of Supreme Court of Gibraltar, 2012–14; *b* 16 Aug. 1932; *s* of Louis and Millicent Black; *m* 1962, Diana Heller, JP; two *s* two *d. Educ:* Roundhay Sch.; Leeds Univ. (Pres. of Union, 1952; Vice-Pres., NUS, 1953–54; LLB). Admitted Solicitor, 1956. Served Army, 1956–58, commnd RASC. Partner, Walker, Morris & Coles, 1958–69; Sen. Partner, Barrington Black, Austin & Co., 1969–84. An Asst Recorder, 1987–91, a Recorder, 1991–93; a Metropolitan Stipendiary Magistrate, 1984–93. Chairman: Inner London Juvenile Court, 1985–93; Family Court, 1991–93. Mem. Court and Council, Leeds Univ., 1979–84. Councillor, Harrogate Bor. Council, 1964–67; contested (L) Harrogate, 1964. *Publications:* Both Sides of the Bench, 2015. *Recreations:* writing, opera, music.

**BLACK, Benjamin;** *see* Banville, J.

**BLACK, Dame Carol (Mary),** DBE 2005 (CBE 2002); FRCP, FMedSci; Principal, Newnham College, Cambridge, 2012–19; *b* 26 Dec. 1939; *d* of Edgar and Annie Herbert; *m* 1st, 1973, James Black (marr. diss. 1983); 2nd, 2002, Christopher Morley. *Educ:* Univ. of Bristol (BA Hist. 1962; Dip. Med. Social Studies 1963; MB ChB 1970; MD 1974). FRCP 1988; FRCSGlas 2003; FRCPI 2003; FRCPE 2003; FRCPCH 2003. Res. Fellow, Univ. of Bristol Sch. of Medicine, 1971–73; Consultant Rheumatologist: W Middx Univ. Hosp., 1981–89; Royal Free Hampstead NHS Trust, 1989–94; Prof. of Rheumatol., Royal Free and University Coll. Med. Sch., Univ. of London, 1994–2006, now Emeritus; Med. Dir, Royal Free Hampstead NHS Trust, 2000–02; Nat. Dir for Health and Work, DoH and DWP, 2006–11. Member: Nat. Specialist Commng Adv. Gp, DoH, 2000–06; Appraisal Cttee, NICE, 1999–2002; NHS Modernisation Bd, DoH, 2002–04; non-exec. Dir, NHS Inst. for Innovation and Improvement, 2006–. Public Appts Ambassador, Govt Equalities Office, Cabinet Office, 2009–; Chm., Centre for Workforce Intelligence, 2010–; Member: Employee Engagement Task Force, BIS, 2011–16; Life Scis Skills Strategy Bd, Cogent, 2011–. Chm., Nuffield Trust, 2006–16; Mem., Clin. Interest Gp, Wellcome Trust, 1996–2003 (Vice-Chm., 1997); Mem., Scientific Co-ordinating Cttee, Arthritis Res. Campaign, 1999–2004; Founder Member and Chairman: UK Scleroderma Gp, 1985–; Eur. Scleroderma Club, 1989–2003; President: Scleroderma Soc., 2006–; Raynaud's and Scleroderma Assoc., 2007–; British Lung Foundn, 2007–; Treat Trust, Wales, 2009–. Member Council: Section of Clin. Immunol. and Allergy, RSocMed, 1998–2000 (Pres., 1997–99); Acad. Med. Sci. Vice-Pres., 1998–2002, Pres., 2002–06, RCP; Vice-Chm., 2003–05, Chm., 2006–09, Acad. of Med. Royal Colls. Pro-Chancellor, Univ. of Bristol, 2007–. Vice Chm., Imperial Coll. Healthcare Charity, 2008– (Chm., Res. Cttee, 2008–). Trustee: St Mary's and Hammersmith Hosps NHS Charitable Trust, 2008–; NPG, 2010–18; Mem., Main Awards Cttee, Queen's Award for Voluntary Service, 2009–. Chair: British Liby, 2018–; Centre for Ageing Better, 2019–. FMedSci 1999; FRCS; FACP 2002; FRACP 2003; FAMM 2003; FAMS 2003; Mem., Assoc. Physicians, 1997; CCMI 2002. Hon. Member: Italian Soc. Rheumatol., 1995; Turkish Soc. Rheumatol., 1995–. Hon. Fellow: UCL, 2003; Lucy Cavendish Coll., Cambridge, 2004; Hon. FRCPsych 2012. Hon. DSc Bristol, 2003; Leicester, 2006; Sheffield, 2006; Hertfordshire, 2006; Glasgow, 2007; Exeter, 2007; Southampton, 2007; Imperial Coll. London, 2008; Hon. MD Nottingham, 2004. Mem., editl bds, various scientific jls. *Publications:* (with A. R. Myers) Systemic Sclerosis, 1985; (with J. Jayson) Scleroderma, 1988; contrib. scientific and med. papers in learned jls. *Recreations:* music, walking, travel, theatre. *Address:* 28 Cornwall Terrace Mews, NW1 5LL.

**BLACK, Charles Stewart Forbes;** a District Judge (Magistrates' Courts) (formerly a Metropolitan Stipendiary Magistrate), 1993–2012 (Chairman, Youth Courts, 1994–2012); *b* 6 Feb. 1947; *s* of Roger Bernard Black and Mary Agnes (*née* Murray); *m* 1976, Mhairi Shuna Elspeth McNab; one *d. Educ:* Kent Coll., Canterbury; Council of Legal Educn. Called to the Bar, Inner Temple, 1970; ad eundem Gray's Inn, 1973; Head of Chambers, 1981–93. *Recreations:* reading, playing with computers.

**BLACK, Colin Hyndmarsh;** Chairman: Kleinwort Benson Investment Management Ltd, 1988–95; Merchants Trust, 1993–2000 (Director, 1992–2000); *b* 4 Feb. 1930; *s* of Daisy Louise (*née* Morris) and Robert Black; *m* 1955, Christine Fleurette Browne (*d* 2017); one *s* one *d. Educ:* Ayr Acad.; Fettes Coll.; St Andrews Univ. (MA) Edinburgh Univ. (LLB). Subaltern, RA, 1954–56; Brander and Cruickshank, Aberdeen, 1957–71 (Partner in charge of investment management); Globe Investment Trust, 1971–90, Dep. Chm., 1983–90. Chairman: Scottish Widows' Fund and Life Assurance Soc., 1987–95; Assoc. of Investment Trust Cos, 1987–89; non-executive Director: Temple Bar Investment Trust, 1963–2000; Clyde Petroleum, 1976–96; Electra Investment Trust, 1975–94; Kleinwort Benson Gp plc, 1988–95; Scottish Power plc, 1990–95; East German Investment Trust, 1990–96; Govett Asian Smaller Cos Investment Trust, 1994–2000 (Chm., 1994–2000); Postern Fund Management Ltd, 1996–99; PFM Carried Interest Ltd, 1996–2000. *Recreations:* travel, watching cricket, walking Labradors. *Address:* Patney House, Bath Road, Fyfield, Wilts SN8 1PU. *T:* (01672) 861451.

**BLACK, Sir David;** *see* Black, Sir R. D.

**BLACK, Don,** OBE 1999; lyric writer; *b* 21 June 1938; *s* of Betsy and Morris Blackstone; *m* 1958, Shirley Berg; two *s. Educ:* Hackney Central Sch. Professional lyric writer, 1960–; collaborates with Andrew Lloyd Webber, John Barry, Jule Styne, Elmer Bernstein and other leading composers; musicals include: Billy, 1974; Tell Me on a Sunday, 1979; Song and Dance, 1982; Aspects of Love, 1989; Sunset Boulevard, 1993; The Goodbye Girl, 1997; Bombay Dreams, 2002; Dracula, 2002; Romeo and Juliet: The Musical, 2002; Brighton Rock, 2004; Bonnie and Clyde, NY, 2011; Stephen Ward, 2013; Mrs Henderson Presents, 2015; films include: Thunderball, 1965; Diamonds Are Forever, 1971; The Man with the Golden Gun, 1974; Tomorrow Never Dies, 1997; The World is Not Enough, 1999. Fellow, BASCA, 2009. Hon. DArts City, 2005. Numerous awards, UK and USA, including: Academy Award, 1966, for song Born Free; Tony Award, 1995, for Sunset Boulevard (Best Book for a musical, and Best Score, lyrics). *Recreations:* snooker, swimming. *Address:* c/o John Cohen, Clintons, 55 Drury Lane, WC2B 5SQ. *T:* (020) 7379 6080. *Clubs:* Royal Automobile, Groucho.

**BLACK, Gavin MacFarlane,** CBE 2010; FRICS; DL, JP; Senior Partner, Gavin Black & Partners, since 2003; Vice Lord-Lieutenant for Tyne and Wear, since 2013; *b* Gosforth, Newcastle upon Tyne, 19 July 1949; *s* of Joseph Gavin Landells Black and Mildred Mabel Black (*née* Johnston); *m* 1974, Christine Lynne Smith; two *d. Educ:* Rossall Sch., Lancs. FRICS 1986. Founding Partner, Swaisland Black & Partners, 1973–79; Sen. Partner, Gavin Black & Partners, 1979–87; Partner, 1987–94, Dep. Chm. and Dir, 1994–2003, Chesterton Internat. Chm. Govs, Univ. of Northumbria, 1997–2010. High Sheriff, 2009–10, DL, 2010, Tyne & Wear. Fellow, N of England Inst. of Mining and Mech. Engrs, 2017. Hon. DCL Northumbria. *Recreations:* walking, Rugby football, golf, family. *Address:* Garden House, Hawkwell, Stamfordham, Newcastle upon Tyne NE18 0QT. *T:* (01661) 886406. *E:* gavinmblack@gmail.com. *Clubs:* Sloane; Northern Counties.

**BLACK, Air Vice-Marshal George Philip,** CB 1987; OBE 1967; AFC 1962 (Bar 1971); FRAeS; Royal Air Force, retired 1987; Defence Consultant: BAE SYSTEMS, 2001–05; SELEX Galileo Ltd (formerly SELEX (Sensors and Airborne Systems)), 2000–11; *b* 10 July 1932; *s* of William and Elizabeth Black; *m* 1954, Ella Ruddiman (*née* Walker); two *s. Educ:* Hilton Acad., Aberdeen. Joined RAF, 1950; flying trng in Canada, 1951; served, 1952–64; fighter pilot; carrier pilot (on exchange to FAA); Flying Instr; HQ Fighter Comd; commanded No 111 (Fighter) Sqdn, 1964–66; Mem., Lightning Aerobatic Team, 1965; commanded Lightning Operational Conversion Unit, 1967–69; commanded No 5 (Fighter) Sqdn, 1969–70 (Huddleston Trophy); JSSC, 1970; Air Plans, MoD, 1971–72; Stn Comdr, RAF Wildenrath, and Harrier Field Force Comdr, RAF Germany, 1972–74; Gp Captain Ops HQ 38 Gp, 1974–76; RCDS, 1977; Gp Captain Ops HQ 11 (Fighter) Gp, 1978–80; Comdr Allied Air Defence Sector One, 1980–83; Comdt ROC, 1983–84; DCS (Ops), HQ AAFCE, 1984–87. Air ADC to the Queen, 1981–83. Sen. Defence Advr, subseq. Dir, Mil. Marketing, GEC-Ferranti, 1987–93; Dir, Mil. Business Develt, Marconi Electronic Systems, subseq. BAE SYSTEMS, 1993–2000. FCMI (FBIM 1977). FRAeS 2001. *Recreations:* military aviation history, railways. *Club:* Royal Air Force.

**BLACK, Prof. Graeme Charles Mackinlay**, OBE 2017; DPhil; FMedSci; Professor of Genetics and Ophthalmology, University of Manchester, since 2004; *b* Oxford, 6 Sept. 1962; *s* of James Mackinlay Black and Cynthia Miriam Black; *m* 1990, Lucy Seabright; one *s* one *d*. *Educ*: Abingdon Sch.; Jesus Coll., Cambridge (BA 1984); Merton Coll., Oxford (BM BCh 1987); St Catherine's Coll., Oxford (DPhil 1994). FRCOphth 1996. Hon. Consultant in Genetics and Ophthalmol., Manchester Royal Eye Hosp., 2001–; Dir, NIHR Manchester Biomed. Res. Centre, 2008–12; Dir, Inst. of Human Develt, 2012–14, Strategic Dir, Centre for Genomic Medicine, 2014–, Univ. of Manchester. FMedSci 2016. *Recreations*: hill climbing, landscape photography, cycling. *Address*: St Mary's Hospital, Oxford Road, Manchester M13 9WL. *T*: (0161) 276 6269. *E*: graeme.black@manchester.ac.uk.

**BLACK, Helen Mary; Her Honour Judge Black;** a Circuit Judge, since 2007; *b* 14 June 1959; *d* of Dennis and Carole Clifford; *m* 1981, Jonathan Stuart Winterhalter Black, *qv*; two *s*. *Educ*: Ashburton High Sch.; Coll. of Law, Chester. Admitted solicitor, 1982; Partner, Addison Madden, Portsmouth, 1982–2000; Dep. Dist Judge, 1995–2000, Dist Judge, 2000–07, Principal Registry of Family Div.; Recorder, 2005–07. Family Tutor Team Mem., Judicial Studies Bd, 2004–. *Publications*: (ed) Butterworth's Family Law Service: vol. 21, Atkins Court Forms: Husband and Wife and Cohabitation, and civil partnerships, 2004–, new edn, vol. 20, as Family: relationships and their breakdowns, and financial remedies, 2012. *Recreations*: marathon running, ski-ing, mountain biking, having fun, Crystal Palace FC, golf. *Address*: Portsmouth Combined Court Centre, The Courts of Justice, Winston Churchill Avenue, Portsmouth, Hants PO1 2EB. *Club*: Ladies' Ski (Chichester).

**BLACK, His Honour James Walter;** QC 1979; Judge, District Court of New South Wales, 2000–13; *b* 8 Feb. 1941; *s* of Dr James Black and Mrs Clementine M. Black (*née* Robb); *m* 1st, 1964, Jane Marie Keyden; two *s* one *d*; 2nd, 1985, Diana Marjorie Day (*née* Harris); one *d*. *Educ*: Harecroft Hall, Gosforth, Cumbria; Trinity Coll., Glenalmond, Perthshire; St Catharine's Coll., Cambridge (MA). Called to the Bar, Middle Temple, 1964, NSW Bar, 1986; a Recorder, 1976–87. *Recreation*: golf.

**BLACK, Prof. Jeremy Martin**, MBE 1999; PhD; Professor of History, University of Exeter, since 1996; *b* 30 Oct. 1955; *s* of Cyril Alfred Black and Doreen Black (*née* Ellis); *m* 1981, Sarah Elizabeth Hollis; one *s* one *d*. *Educ*: Haberdashers' Aske's Sch.; Queens' Coll., Cambridge (Entrance Schol.; Foundn Schol.; BA Starred First 1978; MA); St John's Coll., Oxford (MA); Merton Coll., Oxford (Harmsworth Schol.); PhD Dunelm 1983. University of Durham: Lectr, 1980–90; Sen. Lectr, 1990–91; Reader, 1991–94; Prof., 1994–95; Dir, Res. Foundn and Soc. of Fellows, 1990–95. Sen. Fellow, 2002–, Templeton Fellow, 2018, Foreign Policy Res. Inst. Member, Council: British Records Assoc., 1989–2005; Royal Historical Soc., 1991–95 and 1996–2000. Mem., Council, Univ. of Exeter, 1999–2003. Ed., Archives, 1989–2005. *Publications*: The British and the Grand Tour, 1985; British Foreign Policy in the Age of Walpole, 1985; Natural and Necessary Enemies: Anglo-French relations in the eighteenth century, 1986; The English Press in the Eighteenth Century, 1987; The Collapse of the Anglo-French Alliance 1727–31, 1987; Culloden and the '45, 1990; The Rise of the European Powers 1679–1793, 1990; Robert Walpole and the Nature of Politics in Early-Eighteenth Century Britain, 1990; Europe in the Eighteenth Century, 1990, 2nd edn 2000; A System of Ambition?: British foreign policy 1660–1793, 1991; A Military Revolution?: military change and European society 1550–1800, 1991; War for America: the fight for independence 1775–1783, 1991; The British Abroad: the Grand Tour in the eighteenth century, 1992; Pitt the Elder, 1992; The Politics of Britain 1688–1800, 1993; History of England, 1993; British Foreign Policy in an Age of Revolution, 1994; European Warfare 1660–1815, 1994; Convergence or Divergence? Britain and the Continent, 1994; A History of the British Isles, 1996, 2nd edn 2003; Illustrated History of Eighteenth Century Britain, 1996; Warfare Renaissance to Revolution 1492–1792, 1996; America or Europe: British foreign policy 1739–63, 1997; Maps and History, 1997; Maps and Politics, 1997; War and the World: military power and the fate of continents 1450–2000, 1998; Why Wars Happen, 1998; From Louis XIV to Napoleon: the fate of a great power, 1999; Britain as a Military Power 1688–1815, 1999; A New History of England, 2000; Historical Atlas of Britain: the end of the Middle Ages to the Georgian era, 2000; War: past, present and future, 2000; Modern British History, 2000; A New History of Wales, 2000; British Diplomats and Diplomacy 1688–1800, 2001; The Politics of James Bond, 2001; War in the New Century, 2001; Eighteenth Century Britain, 2001; The English Press 1621–1861, 2001; Western Warfare 1775–1882, 2001; Western Warfare 1882–1975, 2001; Walpole in Power, 2001; The Making of Modern Britain. The Age of Edinburgh to the New Millennium, 2001; Europe and the World 1650–1830, 2001; European Warfare 1494–1660, 2002; The World in the Twentieth Century, 2002; America as a Military Power 1775–1882, 2002; France and the Grand Tour, 2003; Italy and the Grand Tour, 2003; World War Two: a military history, 2003; Visions of the World: a history of maps, 2003; Britain Since the Seventies: politics and society in the consumer age, 2003; Georgian Devon, 2003; The Hanoverians, 2004; The British Seaborne Empire, 2004; Parliament and Foreign Policy in the Eighteenth Century, 2004; Kings, Nobles and Commoners: states and societies in early modern Europe, 2004; War and the New Disorder in the 21st Century, 2004; Rethinking Military History, 2004; War since 1945, 2004; Using History, 2005; Introduction to Global Military History, 2005; A Subject for Taste: culture in eighteenth century England, 2005; The Continental Commitment: Britain, Hanover and interventionism 1714–1793, 2005; The European Question and the National Interest, 2006; George III, 2006; The Age of Total War 1860–1945, 2006; The Dotted Red Line: Britain's defence policy in the modern world, 2006; A Military History of Britain, 2006; The Slave Trade, 2006; Altered States: America since the Sixties, 2006; War in European History 1494–1660, 2006; Trade, Empire and British Foreign Policy 1689–1815, 2007; European Warfare in a Global Context 1660–1815, 2007; George II, 2007; A Short History of Britain, 2007, 2nd edn 2015; The Holocaust, 2008; The Curse of History, 2008; Great Powers and the Quest for Hegemony: the world order since 1500, 2008; What If?: counterfactualism and the problem of history, 2008; War Since 1990, 2009; Europe Since the Seventies, 2009; War in the Nineteenth Century, 2009; War: a short history, 2009; The War of 1812 in the Age of Napoleon, 2009; Geopolitics, 2009; Ideas for the Universities, 2009; Defence Policy Issues for a New Government, 2009; The Politics of World War Two, 2009; London: a history, 2009; Naval Power, 2009; The Battle of Waterloo, 2010; A History of Diplomacy, 2010; A Brief History of Britain 1851–2010, 2010; The Cold War, 2011; The Great War and the Making of the Modern World, 2011; Beyond the Military Revolutions: war in the seventeenth century world, 2011; A Brief History of Slavery, 2011; Debating Foreign Policy in Eighteenth-Century Britain, 2011; Historiography: contesting the past; claiming the future, 2011; War in the World: a comparative history 1450–1600, 2011; Fighting for America: the struggle for mastery in North America, 2011; War and the Cultural Turn, 2011; Empire Reviewed, 2012; Avoiding Armageddon: from the Great War to the fall of France, 1918–1940, 2012; War in the Eighteenth-Century World, 2012; War and Technology, 2013; The Reign of King George II, 2014; Politics and Foreign Policy in the Age of George I: 1714–1727, 2014; British Politics and Foreign Policy 1727–1744, 2014; A Century of Conflict, War 1914–2014, 2014; The Power of Knowledge: how information technology made the modern world, 2014; Contesting History: narratives of public history, 2014; War in the Modern World 1990–2014, 2015; Rethinking World War Two, 2015; The Cold War, A Military History, 2015; Clio's Battles, 2015; The Atlantic Slave Trade in World History, 2015; Metropolis: mapping the city, 2015; British Politics and Foreign Policy, 1744-57, 2015; Other Pasts, Different Presents, Alternative Futures, 2015; Geopolitics and the Quest for Dominance, 2015; The City on the Hill: a life of the University of Exeter, 2015; Airpower: a global history, 2016; War in Europe: 1450 to the present, 2016; The Holocaust: history and memory, 2016; War and Maps: mapping war across the ages, 2016; Insurgency and Counterinsurgency: a global history, 2016; (jtly) The Little Book of Big History: the story of life, the universe and everything, 2016; The World of James Bond: the lives and times of 007, 2017; Mapping Naval Warfare: a visual history of conflict at sea, 2017; Combined Operations: a global history of amphibious and airborne warfare, 2017; Naval Warfare: a global history since 1860, 2017; A History of Britain: 1945 to brexit, 2017; Geographies of an Imperial Power: the British world, 1688–1815, 2017; Mapping Shakespeare, 2018; English Nationalism: a short history, 2018; Land Warfare since 1860: a global history of boots on the ground, 2018; Fortifications and Siegecraft, 2018; Forts: an illustrated history, 2018; A Brief History of Italy, 2018; Charting the Past: the historical worlds of eighteenth century England, 2018; Exeter's University: a history, 2018; War and its Causes, 2019; Britain and Europe: a short history, 2019; A Brief History of Spain, 2019; Imperial Legacies: the British empire around the world, 2019; England in the Age of Shakespeare, 2019; Mapping World War II, 2019; Strategy, 2020; A Brief History of Portugal, 2020. *Recreations*: pub lunches, country walks, reading detective novels in a hot bath, talking, travel, family and friends. *Address*: Department of History, University of Exeter, Amory Building, Rennes Drive, Exeter EX4 4RJ. *Club*: Athenæum.

**BLACK, Jill Margaret;** *see* Black of Derwent, Rt Hon. Lady.

**BLACK, John Alexander;** QC 1998; *b* 23 April 1951; *s* of late John Alexander Black and Grace Gardiner Black (*née* Cornock); *m* 1st, 1977, Penelope Anne Willdig (marr. diss. 2007); one *s* two *d*; 2nd, 2008, Fiona, *d* of Dr and Mrs G. Jackson. *Educ*: St James' Choir Sch., Grimsby; Hull Univ. (LLB 1974). Called to the Bar, Inner Temple, 1975. Liveryman, Feltmakers' Co., 2016–. *Recreations*: classical music, motor cars, political history. *Address*: 33 Chancery Lane, WC2A 1EN.

**BLACK, Jonathan Stuart Winterhalter; His Honour Judge Jonathan Black;** a Circuit Judge, since 2010; *b* Radcliffe, Lancs, 2 March 1957; *s* of Stuart James Black and Dorothy Mildred Black; *m* 1981, Helen Mary Black, *qv*; two *s*. *Educ*: Burnley Grammar Sch.; Manchester Poly. (Law Soc. Pt 1 1975); Coll. of Law, Chester; Univ. of Portsmouth (Post Graduate Dip. Personnel Mgt 1984); Univ. of Staffordshire (LLM Dist. 1992). Admitted solicitor, 1980; Clerk to the Justices: for NE Hants, 1989–99; for Hants and IoW, 1999–2010; a Dep. District Judge (Magistrates' Courts), 2004–10; a Recorder, 2005–10. Member: Youth Justice Bd for England and Wales, 1998–2002; Criminal Justice Consultative Council, 2001–02. *Publications*: Drinking and Driving: a decade of development, 1999; Drinking and Driving Offences: law and practice, 2004, 2nd edn 2007; (ed jtly) Atkin's Court Forms, Vol. 21, 3rd edn 2012; articles in Criminal Law Rev., New Law Jl, Solicitors Jl. *Recreations*: ski mountaineering, climbing, cricket, Burnley Football Club. *Address*: Guildford Crown Court, Bedford Road, Guildford, Surrey GU1 4ST. *T*: (01483) 468528. *E*: hhj.jonathan.black@ejudiciary.net. *Clubs*: MCC, Alpine.

**BLACK, Prof. Julia**, DPhil; FBA 2015; Professor of Law, since 2006, and Strategic Director of Innovation, since 2019, London School of Economics and Political Science (Interim Director, 2016–17; Pro Director for Research, 2014–19); External Member, Prudential Regulation Authority Committee, since 2018; *b* Waterloo, Lancs, 29 Jan. 1967; *d* of Peter Black and Marilyn Black; *m* 1999, Tim Cross; one *s* one *d*. *Educ*: Lincoln Coll., Oxford (BA Hons Juris. 1st Cl. 1988; DPhil 1994). Lectr, LSE, 1994–2006. Ind. Mem. Bd, Solicitors Regulation Authy, 2014–19 (Chm., Policy Cttee, 2016–19). Mem. Bd, UK Res. and Innovation, 2017–. Gen. Editor, Modern Law Rev., 2013–18. *Publications*: Rules and Regulators, 1997; (ed jtly) Regulatory Innovation, 2005; articles in Modern Law Rev., Oxford Jl of Legal Studies, Regulation and Governance, Jl of Law and Society, Law and Policy. *Recreations*: marathon running, downhill and cross-country ski-ing, mountain walking. *Address*: London School of Economics and Political Science, Houghton Street, WC2A 2AE. *T*: (020) 7955 7684. *E*: j.black@lse.ac.uk.

**BLACK, Rev. Leonard Albert;** Catholic Priest of the Ordinariate of Our Lady of Walsingham in Scotland, since 2011; *b* 19 March 1949; *s* of James Morrison Black and Mary Cruickshanks Black (*née* Walker); *m* 1975, Ruth Catherine (*née* Morrison); two *s* one *d*. *Educ*: Bernard Gilpin Soc., Durham; Edinburgh Theol Coll. (Luscombe Schol. 1972); Allen Hall Seminary, London (Ordinariate Formation for Catholic Priesthood). Ordained deacon, 1972, priest, 1973; Curate, St Margaret of Scotland, Aberdeen, 1972–75; Chaplain, St Paul's Cathedral, and St Martin's, Dundee, with All Souls, Invergowrie, 1975–77; Priest i/c, St Ninian's, Aberdeen, 1977–80; Rector: St John the Evangelist, Inverness, and Priest i/c, Culloden Mission, 1980–87; St Michael and All Angels, Inverness, 1980–2011; ordained RC deacon and priest, 2011, to serve the Ordinariate Gp in Scotland; Sen. Pastor, Ordinariate Mission in Scotland, 2011–; Mem., Ordinariate UK Co-ordinators, 2012–; webmaster, Ordinariate of Our Lady of Walsingham, 2014–. Canon, St Andrew's Cathedral, Inverness, 1992–2011. Area Chaplain (Scotland), Actors' Church Union, 1987–2003; Northern Area Regional Chaplain, Missions to Seamen (Scotland), 1991–2002; Synod Clerk, Dio. of Moray, Ross and Caithness, 1992–2003; Dean of Moray, Ross and Caithness, 2003–09. Mem., SSC, 1979–2011. Regional Dean (Scotland), Forward in Faith, 2001–11. Commissary to Bishop of the Murray, Anglican Church of Australia, 2006–11; permission to officiate, dio. of the Murray, 2006–11. Religious Affairs and Community Progs Producer, 1987–2004, Religious Progs Producer, 2004–14, Moray Firth Radio, Inverness; Religious Progs Producer, Nevis Radio, Fort William, 2007–15. Ed., Diocese of Moray, Ross and Caithness Diocesan Directory, 1985–2003; Mem., Editl Bd, Portal Mag., 2011–. *Publications*: Churches of Diocese of Moray, Ross and Caithness, annually, 1992–2004; Sir Ninian Comper - Liturgical Architect, 1999; The Church that Moved Across the Water, 2003; The Ordinariate of Our Lady of Walsingham in Scotland, 2017. *Recreations*: visiting Baroque churches and ancient archaeological sites, music, theatre, good food, fine wines and exploring malt whisky. *Address*: 49 Laurel Avenue, Inverness IV3 5RR. *T*: (01463) 235597. *E*: fr.len@angelforce.co.uk.

**BLACK, Liam;** Founder and Chief Encouragement Officer, As We Please Ltd, since 2018; Executive Chairman, Big White Wall, since 2018; *b* Reading, 24 Jan. 1961; *s* of John Black and Anne Black (*née* Delaney); *m* 1981, Maggie Sheehan; two *s* one *d*. *Educ*: Roehampton Inst. (BA Hons Eng. and Religious Studies). Volunteer overseas, 1982–84; Archdio. of Liverpool, 1985–91; Crisis, 1991–94; Big Issue, 1995–96; Chief Executive Officer: FRC Gp, Liverpool, 1996–2004; Fifteen Foundn, 2004–08; Co-Founder, Wavelength Companies Ltd, 2008–18. Trustee, NESTA, 2008–12. *Publications*: There's No Business Like Social Business, 2004; The Social Entrepreneur's A to Z, 2014. *Recreations*: drinking, tennis, arguing.

**BLACK, Mhairi;** MP (SNP) Paisley and Renfrewshire South, since 2015; *b* Paisley, 1994; *d* of Alan Black. *Educ*: Univ. of Glasgow (MA 1st Cl. Hons Politics 2015). *Address*: House of Commons, SW1A 0AA.

**BLACK, Hon. Michael Eric John,** AC 1998; Chief Justice, Federal Court of Australia, 1991–2010; *b* 22 March 1940; *s* of Col E. R. E. Black, OBE and Lorna Black (*née* Thwaites); *m* 1963, Margaret Dungan; one *s* one *d. Educ:* St John's on the Hill, Chepstow; Wesley Coll., Melbourne; Univ. of Melbourne (LLB). Practice, Victorian Bar, 1964–90, ACT Bar, 1974–90; QC Victoria 1980, QC Tasmania 1984. Mem. Board, Royal Melbourne Hosp., 1986–90 (Chm., Ethics Cttee); The Defence Force Advocate, 1987–90; Chm., Attorney General's Steering Cttee, Courts Exec. Service, 2011–12. Mem., Dispute Resolution Panels for Nat. Gas and Electricity Mkt Rules, 2012–. Co-Pres., Internat. Assoc. of Supreme Admin. Jurisdictions, 2007–10. Sen. Fellow, Law Sch., Melbourne Univ., 2011–14. Chair: Australian Law Schs Standards Cttee, 2011–; Legal Services Council, 2014–. Mem., Adv. Bd, Social Equity Inst., Melbourne Univ., 2013–. Hon. LLD Melbourne, 2010. Centenary Medal (Australia), 2001. *Address:* PO Box 728, Kew, Vic 3101, Australia.

**BLACK, Michael Jonathan;** QC 1995; a Recorder, 1999–2013; *b* 31 March 1954; *s* of Samuel and Lillian Black; *m* 1984, Ann, *e d* of Keith and Rosa Pentol; two *s. Educ:* Stand Grammar Sch.; University College London (LLB). FCIArb 1991. Called to the Bar, Middle Temple, 1978, Bencher, 2006; an Asst Recorder, 1995–99; a Dep. Judge, Technology and Construction Court, 1999–2013; Dep. High Court Judge, 2008–13. Asst Comr, Parly Boundary Commn for England, 2000–. Admitted to Bar: of Dubai Internat. Financial Centre Court, 2006; of Eastern Caribbean Supreme Court, 2007. Member: Civil Procedure Cttee, 2000–04; Panel of Mediators, Court of Appeal, 2001–03; Civil Justice Council, 2005–09; Court, Casablanca Internat. Mediation and Arbitration Centre, 2016–; UK Mem., ICC Commn on Arbitration and Alternative Dispute Resolution, 2017–. Vis. Res. Fellow, UMIST, 1996–2002; Vis. Prof. of Construction and Engrg Law, Sch. of Mech., Aerospace and Civil Engrg, Manchester Univ. (formerly Manchester Centre for Civil and Construction Engrg), 2002–. FCInstCES (FInstCES 2001). Liveryman, Arbitrators' Co., 2002 (Freeman, 2000). *Publications:* (contrib.) New Horizons in Construction Law, 1998; (contrib.) The Law and Practice of Compromise, 5th edn 2002, 7th edn 2010; (contrib.) Discovery Deskbook for Construction Disputes, 2006; (contrib.) International Construction Law, 2009; (contrib.) The UK Supreme Court Yearbook, vol. 8, 2016–17 Legal Year, 2018. *Address:* 24 Old Buildings, Lincoln's Inn, WC2A 3UP. *T:* (020) 7691 2424, *Fax:* (0845) 280 1950; 11 rue du General-Dufour, 1204 Geneva, Switzerland. *T:* (22) 3222500, *Fax:* (22) 3222515. *E:* mbqc@xxiv.co.uk. *Clubs:* Athenæum; Capital (Dubai).

**BLACK, Neil;** Performance Director, UK Athletics, since 2012; *b* Ashington, Northumberland, 23 May 1959; *s* of Neville and Mary Ann Black; *m* 1988, Ruth Carlyle. *Educ:* Ashington High Sch.; Northumbria Univ. Chartered SRP 1981. Nat. Lead Physiotherapist, English Inst. of Sport, 2003; UK Athletics: Chief Physiotherapist, 2004–12; Lead for Medicine and Sports Sci., 2006–12. *Publications:* (jtly) Sports Injuries Management. *Recreations:* biking, running. *Address:* UK Athletics, Athletics House, Alexander Stadium, Walsall Road, Perry Barr, Birmingham B42 2BE.

**BLACK, Prof. Sir Nicholas (Andrew),** Kt 2017; MD; FRCS, FRCPE; Professor of Health Services Research, London School of Hygiene and Tropical Medicine, since 1995; *b* Bristol, 21 May 1951; *s* of Joseph and Margaret Black; *m* 2005, Philippa Gough. *Educ:* Bristol Grammar Sch.; Univ. of Birmingham (MB BS 1974; MD 1983). DCH 1976; DRCOG 1976; FFPH 1990; FRCS 2002; FRCPE 2013. MO, Save the Children Fund, Nepal, 1977–78; Registrar in Public Health, Oxon, 1978–83; Lectr, Open Univ., 1983–85; Sen. Lectr, 1985–93, Reader, 1993–95, LSHTM. Hon. Consultant in Public Health, NHS London, 2006–13, NHS England, 2013–17. Co-ed., Jl Health Services Res. and Policy, 1995–2017. Chair, Nat. Adv. Gp on Clin. Audit and Enquiries, NHS England (formerly DoH), 2007–16; Chair, Bd, NIHR Kent, Surrey and Sussex Applied Res. Collaboration, 2019–. Founding Chair, UK Health Services Res. Network, 2005–08. Trustee, Intensive Care Nat. Audit and Res. Centre, 2002–18. Mem. Adv. Bd, Kaleidoscope Health and Care, 2019–. FRSA. *Publications:* Understanding Health Services, 2005, 2nd edn 2017; Walking London's Medical History, 2006, 2nd edn 2012. *Recreations:* Arsenal, cooking, gardening, contemporary art, history of healthcare. *Address:* Department of Health Services Research and Policy, London School of Hygiene and Tropical Medicine, 15–17 Tavistock Place, WC1H 9SH. *T:* (020) 7927 2228. *E:* nick.black@lshtm.ac.uk.

**BLACK, Prof. Paul Joseph,** OBE 1983; PhD; FInstP; Professor of Science Education, University of London, 1976–95 (in School of Education, King's College, 1985–95), now Emeritus Professor; *b* 10 Sept. 1930; *s* of Walter and Susie Black; *m* 1957, Mary Elaine Weston; four *s* one *d. Educ:* Rhyl Grammar Sch.; Univ. of Manchester (BSc); Univ. of Cambridge (PhD). FInstP 1986, Hon. FInstP, 2015. Royal Society John Jaffé Studentship, 1953–56. Univ. of Birmingham: Lectr in Physics, 1956–66; Reader in Crystal Physics, 1966–74; Prof. of Physics (Science Education), 1974–76; Dir, Centre for Science and Maths Educn, Chelsea Coll., Univ. of London, 1976–85; subseq., following merger of colls, Head, Centre for Educnl Studies, KCL, 1985–89 (FKC 1990); Dean, Faculty of Educn, Univ. of London, 1978–82. Vis. Prof., Stanford Univ., 1999–2002. Educnl Consultant: to Nuffield Chelsea Curriculum Trust, 1978–93 (Chm., 1992–93); to OECD, 1988–96; Consultant to: World Bank, 1991; US Nat. Sci. Foundn, 1992. Vice-Pres., Royal Instn of Great Britain, 1983–85; Chairman: National Curriculum Task Gp on Assessment and Testing, DES, 1987–88; Internat. Commn on Physics Educn, 1993–99 (Mem., 1987–93); S London Cttee, RC Archdio. of Southwark Schs' Commn, 1996–2006; Dep. Chm., Grubb Inst. for Behavioural Studies, 1990–2002 (Mem. Council, 1983–2002; Chm., 1985–90; Hon. Vice-Pres., 1997); Member: School Curriculum Develt Cttee, 1984–88; Nat. Curriculum Council, 1988–91 (Dep. Chm., 1989–91); Exec., Univs Council for Educn of Teachers, 1982–86; Res. Grants Bd, ESRC, 1987–90; Exec., Editl Cttee for Nat. Sci. Educn Standards, Nat. Res. Council, USA, 1994–95; US Nat. Acad. of Scis Bd on Testing and Assessment, 1995–99. President: Groupe Internat. de la Recherche sur l'Enseignement de la Physique, 1984–91; Educn Section, British Assoc., 1992–93; Vice Pres. and Mem. Council, IUPAP, 1997–99; Member: US Nat. Acad. of Educn, 2010; Phi Delta Kappan, 2010; Hon. Pres., Assoc. for Science Educn, 1986 (Hon. Life Mem., 1986); Hon. Mem., Standing Conf. on Sch. Science and Technol., 1989. Trustee: Nat. Energy Foundn, 1992–2000; One Plus One Marriage and Partnership Research, 1996–2015 (Chair of Trustees, 1996–2013). Hon. Mem., CGLI, 1989; Foreign Mem., US Nat. Acad. of Educn, 2010. FRSA 1990; Osher Fellow, San Francisco Exploratorium, 1993. DUniv: Surrey, 1991; Open, 2002; Hon. DEd Kingston, 2003. Bragg Medal, Inst. of Physics, 1973; Medal, Internat. Commn on Physics Educn, 2000; Dist. Contribs to Sci. Educn Res. Award, Nat. Assoc. for Res. in Sci. Teaching, USA, 2004; Lifetime Achievement Award: Assoc. for Sci. Educn, 2005; Internat. Soc. for Design and Develt in Educn, 2009; John Nisbet Fellowship Award, British Educnl Res. Assoc., 2014. Kt of St Gregory, 1973. *Publications:* (jtly) Nuffield Advanced Physics Project, 1972; (contrib.) Higher Education Learning Project Books, 1977; (jtly) Open Work in Science, 1992; Nuffield Primary Science books (for Key Stages 1 and 2), 1993; (ed jtly) Children's Informal Ideas in Science, 1993; (ed jtly) Teachers Assessing Pupils: lessons from science classrooms, 1995; (jtly) Primary SPACE Project Research Reports: Light, 1990, Electricity, 1991, Processes of Life, 1992, The Earth in Space, 1994; (ed jtly) Changing the Subject, 1996; Testing: friend or foe, 1998; (jtly) Inside the Black Box, 1998; (ed jtly) Classroom Assessment and the National Science Education Standards, 2001; (jtly) Working Inside the Black Box, 2002; (jtly) Standards in Public Examinations, 2002; (jtly) Inside Science Education Reform, 2003; (jtly) Assessment for Learning, 2003; (jtly) Science Inside the Black Box, 2004; (jtly) Inside the Black Box of Assessment: assessment of learning, 2013; (jtly) The Role of Assessment in Pedagory, 2016; papers on crystallography, physics and science, technology education, and assessment in education. *Address:* 70 Abbeyfield Girton Green, Wellbrook Way, Girton, Cambridge CB3 0GQ.

**BLACK, Peter Malcolm,** CBE 2017; Member (Lib Dem) South Wales West, National Assembly for Wales, 1999–2016; *b* 30 Jan. 1960; *s* of John Malcolm and Joan Arlene Black; *m* 1st, 1984, Patricia Mary Hopkin (marr. diss. 1995); 2nd, 2000, Angela Lynette Jones. *Educ:* Wirral Grammar Sch. for Boys; University Coll. of Swansea (BA Hons English and History). Exec. Officer, Land Registry for Wales, 1983–99. Member: (L) Swansea City Council, 1984–96; (Lib Dem) City and County of Swansea Unitary Council, 1996–. Chm., Lib Dem Wales, 1995–97 (Sec., Finance and Admin Cttee, 1996–99). *Recreations:* theatre, poetry, films. *Address:* 115 Cecil Street, Manselton, Swansea SA5 8QL.

**BLACK, Prof. Richard,** PhD; Pro-Vice-Chancellor and Head, College of Social Sciences, University of Birmingham, since 2018; *b* Cambridge, 10 Aug. 1964; *s* of Harold and Dorothy Black; *m* 1998, Martha Walsh (marr. diss. 2016); one *s. Educ:* Perse Sch., Cambridge; Hertford Coll., Oxford (BA Geog. 1986); Royal Holloway and Bedford New Coll., Univ. of London (PhD 1990). Lectr in Geog., KCL, 1989–95; University of Sussex: Lectr, 1995–99, Sen. Lectr, 1999–2001, Reader, 2001–02, in Human Geog.; Prof. of Human Geog., 2003–13; Hd, Sch. of Global Studies, 2009–13; Pro-Dir (Res. and Enterprise), SOAS, Univ. of London, 2013–18. *Publications:* Crisis and Change in Rural Europe, 1992; Geography and Refugees, 1993; Refugees, Environment and Development, 1998; The End of the Refugee Cycle?, 1999; Targeting Development, 2004; (ed jtly) A Continent Moving West?, 2010. *Recreations:* walking, theatre, travel, football, banjo. *Address:* College of Social Sciences, Muirhead Tower, University of Birmingham, Edgbaston, Birmingham B15 2TT. *T:* (0121) 415 8104. *E:* r.black@bham.ac.uk.

**BLACK, Prof. Robert;** QC (Scot.) 1987; FRSE; Professor of Scots Law, University of Edinburgh, 1981–2004, now Emeritus; *b* 12 June 1947; *s* of James Little Black and Jeannie Findlay Lyon. *Educ:* Lockerbie Acad.; Dumfries Acad.; Edinburgh Univ. (LLB); McGill Univ., Montreal (LLM); Lord Pres. Cooper Meml Prize, Univ. of Edinburgh, 1968; Vans Dunlop Scholarship, Univ. of Edinburgh, 1968; Commonwealth Scholarship, Commonwealth Scholarship Commn, 1968. Advocate, 1972; Lectr in Scots Law, Univ. of Edinburgh, 1972–75; Sen. Legal Officer, Scottish Law Commn, 1975–78; in practice at Scottish Bar, 1978–81; Temp. Sheriff, 1981–95. Chm., Inquiry into operations of Monklands DC, 1994–95. Dir, Gannaga Lodge, Agterkop, South Africa, 2005–. Gen. Editor, The Laws of Scotland: Stair Memorial Encyclopaedia, 1988–96 (Dep., then Jt, Gen. Editor, 1981–88). FRSA 1991; FRSE 1992; Founding Fellow, Inst. of Contemporary Scotland, 2000. *Publications:* An Introduction to Written Pleading, 1982; Civil Jurisdiction: the new rules, 1983; articles in UK, US, German and S African legal jls. *Recreation:* seeking to overturn the Lockerbie conviction. *Address:* 6/4 Glenogle Road, Edinburgh EH3 5HW. *T:* (0131) 557 3571, 07717 946917. *E:* rblackqc@gmail.com; Gannaga Lodge, Agterkop, Middelpos 8193, Northern Cape, South Africa. *T:* (027) 0500454, 0647656579.

**BLACK, Sir (Robert) David,** 3rd Bt *cr* 1922; *b* 29 March 1929; *s* of Sir Robert Andrew Stransham Black, 2nd Bt, ED, and Ivy (*d* 1980), *d* of late Brig.-Gen. Sir Samuel Wilson, GCMG, KCB, KBE; *S* father, 1979; *m* 1st, 1953, Rosemary Diana (marr. diss. 1972), *d* of Sir Rupert John Hardy, 4th Bt; two *d* (and one *d* decd); 2nd, 1973, Dorothy Maureen (*d* 2011), *d* of Major Charles R. Eustace Radclyffe and *widow* of A. R. D. Pilkington. *Educ:* Eton. Lieut, Royal Horse Guards, 1949; Captain 1953; Major 1960; retired, 1961. Served with Berkshire and Westminster Dragoons, TA, 1964–67, and Berkshire Territorials, TAVR III, 1967–69; Vice-Chm., Berkshire, Eastern Wessex TAVRA, 1985–92. Joint Master, Garth and South Berks Foxhounds, 1965–73. Hon. Col, 94 (Berks Yeo.) Signal Sqn (TA), 1988–98. DL Caithness, 1991–2004; High Sheriff, Oxfordshire, 1993. *Recreations:* shooting, gardening, fishing. *Heir:* none. *Address:* Beech Farm House, Woodcote, near Reading, Berks RG8 0QB. *T:* (01491) 682234. *Clubs:* Flyfishers', Cavalry and Guards.

**BLACK, Robert William,** CBE 2012; FRSE; Auditor General for Scotland, 2000–12; *b* 6 Nov. 1946; *s* of Robert G. Black and Nell Black (*née* Gray); *m* 1970, Doreen Mary Riach, MBE; three *s* one *d. Educ:* Univ. of Aberdeen (MA Hons Econs); Heriot-Watt Univ. (MSc Town Planning); Univ. of Strathclyde (MSc Public Policy). Planner, Notts CC, 1971–73; Supervisory Planner, Glasgow CC, 1973–75; Gp Leader, Res. and Intelligence, 1975–80, Sen. Exec., Chief Exec.'s Dept, 1980–85, Strathclyde Regl Council; Chief Executive: Stirling DC, 1985–90; Tayside Regl Council, 1990–95; Controller of Audit, Accounts Commn for Scotland, 1995–2000. Chm., Shelter Commn on Housing and Wellbeing in Scotland, 2013–; Chair, Fiscal Affairs Scotland, 2014–. Public Interest Mem., ICAS, 2012–. Mem. Bd, BL, 2012–. Lay Mem. Ct, Univ. of Edinburgh, 2012–. FSS 1984–2012; FRSE 2006. Hon. LLD Aberdeen, 2004; Hon. DBA Queen Margaret UC, Edinburgh, 2006. *Recreations:* the outdoors, the arts. *Address:* Backcroft Cottage, Backcroft, Dunblane FK15 0BL. *T:* 07595 426270. *E:* robertwblack@me.com. *Club:* New (Edinburgh).

**BLACK, Roger Anthony,** MBE 1992; former athlete; presenter, BBC Television, since 1998; corporate motivational speaker; Partner, BackleyBlack; *b* 31 March 1966; *s* of late David Black and of Thelma Black; one *d*; *m* 2002, Julia Burgess; twin *s. Educ:* Portsmouth Grammar Sch. Commonwealth Games: gold medal for 400m and 4 × 400m, 1986; European Championships: gold medal for 400m and 4 × 400m, 1986, 1990; silver medal for 400m, 1994; World Championships: gold medal for 4 × 400m, silver medal for 400m, 1991; Olympic Games: bronze medal for 4 × 400m, 1992; silver medal for 400m and 4 × 400m, 1996. Hon. MA Southampton, 1992. *Publications:* How Long's the Course? (autobiog.), 1998. *Recreations:* guitar, football, dog. *Address:* Chinthurst Cottage, Chinthurst Lane, Shalford GU4 8JR. *E:* roger@rogerblack.co.uk.

**BLACK, Rona McLeod, (Lady Black);** *see* MacKie, R. McL.

**BLACK, Stewart;** *see* Black, C. S. F.

**BLACK, Prof. Dame Susan Margaret, (Prof. Dame Sue Black),** DBE 2016 (OBE 2001); PhD; FRSE; FRCPE, FRAI, FRSB; Pro-Vice-Chancellor, Lancaster University, since 2018; *b* 7 May 1961; *d* of Alasdair John Gunn and Isabel Ann Gunn (*née* Bailey); *m* 1993, Thomas William Black; three *d. Educ:* Univ. of Aberdeen (BSc Hons 1982; PhD 1987). FRCPE 2013. Lectr in Anatomy, UMDS, 1987–92; Consultant Forensic Anthropologist, Univ. of Glasgow, 1995–2001; University of Dundee: Prof. of Anatomy and Forensic Anthropology, 2003–18; Dir, Leverhulme Res. Centre for Forensic Sci. 2016–18; Dep. Principal, Public Engagement, 2013–16. Hd, Forensic Anthropol., Kosovo Mission, FCO, 1999–2000. Founder, 2001, and Pres., 2009, British Assoc. for Human Identification. Dir, Nat. Advanced Training in Disaster Victim Identification, 2007–10. Pres., RAI, 2018–. Hon. Prof. of Anatomy, Royal Scottish Acad., 2014. FRSE 2005; FRAI 2009; FRSB 2014; Hon. FRCPSGlas 2017. Patron, Dundee Women's Science Fest. 2014–. Hon. DSc: Robert Gordon, 2003; Abertay, 2009; Hon. MD St Andrews, 2018. Police Commendation, Disaster Victim Identification, 2008; Lucy Mair Medal, RAI, 2008; Queen's Award for Higher Educn, 2013; Wolfson Res. Merit Award, Royal Soc., 2013.

Fletcher of Saltoun Award, 2014; Jephcott Medal, RSocMed, 2016; Gold Medal, Anatomical Soc., 2018. *Publications:* (jtly) Essential Anatomy for Anaesthesia, 1997; (jtly) Developmental Juvenile Osteology, 2000, 2nd edn 2016; (jtly) The Juvenile Skeleton, 2004; (jtly) Forensic Human Identification: an introduction, 2006; (jtly) Juvenile Osteology: a field and laboratory manual, 2009; (jtly) Disaster Victim Identification: the practitioner's guide, 2010; (jtly) Age Estimation in the Living: the practitioner's guide, 2010; (jtly) Forensic Anthropology 2000 to 2010, 2011; (jtly) Disaster Victim Identification: experience and practice, 2011; (jtly) Forensic Investigation of Dismemberment, 2016; All That Remains: a life in death, 2018. *Recreations:* writing, family. *Address:* Lancaster University, Lancaster LA1 4YW. *T:* (01524) 594282. *E:* sue.black@lancaster.ac.uk.

**BLACKADDER, Dame Elizabeth (Violet),** DBE 2003 (OBE 1982); RA 1976; RSA 1972; artist; Her Majesty's Painter and Limner in Scotland, since 2000; *b* 24 Sept. 1931; *m* 1956, John Houston. *Educ:* Falkirk High Sch.; Univ. of Edinburgh; Edinburgh Coll. of Art. Lectr, Sch. of Drawing and Painting, Edinburgh Coll. of Art, 1962–86. Exhibns, Mercury Gall., London, 1965–; retrospective exhibitions: Scottish Arts Council, 1981; Aberystwyth Arts Centre, 1989; Talbot Rice Gall., Edinburgh, 2000. Work in collections including: Scottish Nat. Gall. of Modern Art; Scottish Nat. Portrait Gall.; Nat. Portrait Gall.; Government Art Collection; Kettle's Yard, Cambridge; Hunterian Art Gall., Glasgow. Hon. FRIAS 1986; Hon. FRSE 1994. Hon. DLitt: Heriot-Watt, 1989; Strathclyde, 1998; Glasgow, 2001; St Andrews, 2003; Dr (*hc*): Edinburgh, 1990; London, 2004; Hon. LLD Aberdeen, 1997; Hon. Dr Stirling, 2002. *Relevant publications:* Elizabeth Blackadder, by Judith Bumpus, 1988; Elizabeth Blackadder, by Duncan Macmillan, 1999; Elizabeth Blackadder Prints, by Christopher Allan, 2003. *Address:* c/o Royal Scottish Academy, The Mound, Edinburgh EH2 2EL.

**BLACKBEARD, Roy Warren;** High Commissioner for Botswana in the United Kingdom, 1998–2018; *b* 16 April 1953. *Educ:* Kimberley Boys' High Sch. Official Learner, Metallurgy, De Beers, 1972–79; Audit Clerk, Price Waterhouse, 1973–74; CEO, Blackbeard & Co. (Pty) Ltd, 1974–89; ranch manager, 1974–96. MP, Serowe N, 1989–98; Asst Minister, 1992–94, Minister, 1994–97, of Agriculture, Botswana. Mem., Central DC, 1979–89 (Member: Gen. Purposes and Finance Cttee, 1979–89; Livestock Industry Adv. Cttee, 1979–89). Treas., Youth Wing, Botswana Democratic Party, 1980–96. Dir, Air Botswana, 1979–89. *Recreations:* sporting, skeet shooting, theatre, cinema, tennis.

**BLACKBOURN, Prof. David Gordon,** PhD; FR.HistS; Cornelius Vanderbilt Distinguished Professor of History, Vanderbilt University, since 2012; *b* 1 Nov. 1949; *s* of Harry Blackbourn and Pamela Jean (*née* Youngman); *m* 1st, 1985, Deborah Frances Langton (marr. diss. 2013); one *s* one *d*; 2nd, 2014, Celia Stewart Applegate. *Educ:* Leeds Modern Grammar Sch.; Christ's Coll., Cambridge (BA Hons Hist. 1970); MA 1974, PhD 1976, Cambridge. Res. Fellow, Jesus Coll., Cambridge, 1973–76; Lectr in History, QMC, Univ. of London, 1976–79; Birkbeck College, University of London: Lectr, 1979–85; Reader, 1985–89; Prof. of Mod. European History, 1989–92; Harvard University: Prof. of Hist., 1992–97; Coolidge Prof. of Hist., 1997–2012; Dir, Center for Eur. Studies, Harvard, 2007–12. Research Fellow: Inst. of European Hist., Mainz, 1974–75; Alexander von Humboldt Foundn, Bonn-Bad Godesberg, 1984–85; John Simon Guggenheim Meml Foundn, NY, 1994–95; Vis. Kratter Prof. of European Hist., Stanford Univ., 1989–90; Walter Channing Cabot Fellow, Harvard Univ., 2003–04; Mem., Inst. for Advanced Study, Princeton Univ., 2017–18. Lectures: Annual, German Histl Inst., London, 1998; Malcolm Wynn, Stetson Univ., Fla, 2002; George C. Windell Meml, Univ. of New Orleans, 2006; Crayenborgh, Leiden, Netherlands, 2007; Jakob and Wilhelm Grimm, Univ. of Waterloo, Ont, 2010. Mem., Editl Bd, Past and Present, 1988–. Sec. 1979–81, Mem. Cttee 1981–86, German Hist. Soc.; Member, Academic Advisory Board: German Hist. Inst., London, 1983–92; Inst. for European Hist., Mainz, 1995–2006; Lichtenbergkolleg, Univ. of Goettingen, 2007–; German Histl Inst., Washington, 2008–15 (Mem., 2004–15, Pres., 2008–13, Bd of Friends); Mem., Vis. Cttee for the Social Scis, MIT, 2009–13; Vice-Pres., 2002, Pres., 2003, Conference Gp on Central European Hist., American Hist. Assoc. Member: Adv. Bd, Edmund Spevack Meml Foundn, 2003–06; Bd of Trustees, Nat. Humanities Center, 2016–. FR.HistS 1987; Fellow, American Acad. of Arts and Scis, 2007. Corresp. FBA 2011. *Publications:* Class, Religion and Local Politics in Wilhelmine Germany, 1980; (with Geoff Eley) Mythen Deutscher Geschichtsschreibung, 1980 (Japanese edn 1983); (with Geoff Eley) The Peculiarities of German History, 1984; Populists and Patricians, 1987; (ed with Richard J. Evans) The German Bourgeoisie, 1991; Marpingen: apparitions of the Virgin Mary in Bismarckian Germany, 1993 (Amer. Historical Assoc. prize for best book in German history); The Fontana History of Germany: the long nineteenth century 1780–1918, 1997, 2nd edn as A History of Germany 1780–1918: the long nineteenth century, 2003; The Conquest of Nature: water, landscape and the making of modern Germany, 2006 (George L. Mosse Prize, Weyerhaeuser Prize, H-Soz-u-Kult Prize); (ed with James Retallack) Localism, Landscape and the Ambiguities of Place, 2007; Landschaften der Deutschen Geschichte: Aufsätze zur Geschichte der Neuzeit, 2016. *Recreations:* reading, jazz and classical music, walking. *Address:* Department of History, Vanderbilt University, PMB 351802, 2301 Vanderbilt Place, Nashville, TN 37235, USA. *E:* david.blackbourn@vanderbilt.edu.

**BLACKBURN, Bishop of,** since 2013; **Rt Rev. Julian Tudor Henderson;** *b* 23 July 1954; *s* of late Ian Tudor Henderson and Susan Blundell Henderson; *m* 1984, Heather Gwenllian Lees; one *s* one *d*. *Educ:* Radley Coll.; Keble Coll., Oxford (MA Theol.). Ordained deacon, 1979, priest, 1980; Curate, St Mary's, Islington, 1979–83; Vicar: Emmanuel and St Mary in the Castle, Hastings, 1983–92; Holy Trinity, Claygate, 1992–2005; Archdeacon of Dorking, 2005–13. Hon. Canon, Guildford Cathedral, 2001–13. *Recreations:* gardening, reading, walking. *Address:* Bishop's House, Ribchester Road, Clayton Le Dale, Blackburn BB1 9EF. *T:* (01254) 248234. *E:* bishop@bishopofblackburn.org.uk.

**BLACKBURN, Dean of;** see Howell-Jones, Very Rev. P.

**BLACKBURN, Archdeacon of;** see Ireland, Ven. M. C.

**BLACKBURN, Dr Bonnie Jean,** FBA 2005; freelance editor, since 1990; *b* 15 July 1939; *d* of John Hall Blackburn and Ruth Blackburn; *m* 1st, 1971, Edward E. Lowinsky (*d* 1985); one *d*; 2nd, 1990, Leofranc Holford-Strevens. *Educ:* Wellesley Coll., Mass (BA 1961); Univ. of Chicago (MA 1963, PhD 1970). Vis. Associate Prof., Univ. of Chicago, 1986; Lectr, Sch. of Music, Northwestern Univ., 1987; Vis. Associate Prof., State Univ. of NY, Buffalo, 1989–90; Mem., Common Room, Wolfson Coll., Oxford, 1993–. Hon. Mem., Faculty of Music, Oxford Univ., 1999–. *Publications:* (ed) Johannis Lupi Opera omnia, 3 vols, 1980–89; (ed jtly) A Correspondence of Renaissance Musicians, 1991; (with L. Holford-Strevens) The Oxford Companion to the Year, 1999; Composition, Printing and Performance: studies in Renaissance music, 2000; (with L. Holford-Strevens) The Oxford Book of Days, 2000; (ed) New Josquin Edition, 21–22: Motets on Non-biblical Texts De Domino Jesu Christo, 2003–07; (ed with L. Holford-Strevens) Florentius de Faxolis, Book on Music, 2010; contribs to volumes of essays and Festschriften; contrib. articles to Basler Jahrbuch für historische Musikpraxis, Early Music Hist., Early Music, Jl Alamire Foundn, Jl Musicol., Jl Amer. Musicol. Soc., Musica disciplina, Musical Qly, Studi musicali, Tijdschrift van de Koninklijke Vereniging voor Nederlandse Muziekgeschiedenis, Recercare, Jl Royal Musical Assoc., Procs British Acad., The Lute, Jl Lute Soc. of America. *Recreation:* travel. *Address:* 67 St Bernard's Road, Oxford OX2 6EJ. *T:* (01865) 552808, *Fax:* (01865) 512237. *E:* bonnie.blackburn@wolfson.ox.ac.uk.

**BLACKBURN, Vice Adm. Sir David Anthony James, (Sir Tom),** KCVO 2004 (LVO 1978); CB 1999; Master of HM Household, 2000–05; an Extra Equerry to the Queen, since 2000; *b* 18 Jan. 1945; *s* of late Lieut J. Blackburn, DSC, RN, and late Mrs M. J. G. Pickering-Pick; *m* 1973, Elizabeth Barstow; three *d*. *Educ:* Taunton Sch. RNC Dartmouth, 1963; HMS Kirkliston (in comd), 1972–73; Equerry-in-Waiting to the Duke of Edinburgh, 1976–78; Exec. Officer, HMS Antrim, 1978–81; MoD (Navy), 1981–83; Comdr, HMS Birmingham, 1983–84; MoD (Navy), 1984–86; HMS York (in comd) and Captain Third Destroyer Sqn, 1987–88; Dir, Naval Manpower and Trng (Seamen), MoD, 1988–90; Cdre, Clyde, and Naval Base Comdr, Clyde, 1990–92; HMS Cornwall (in comd) and Captain, Second Frigate Sqn, 1992–93; Defence Attaché and Hd of British Defence Staff, Washington, 1994–97; COS to Comdr Allied Naval Forces Southern Europe, 1997–99. Mem., Pensions Appeal Tribunal, 2005–15. Chairman: St John Ambulance (London Dist), 2006–10; Marine Soc. & Sea Cadets, 2006–10; Dep. Chm., RYA, 2007–10. Trustee: Mission to Seafarers, 2005–15; Order of St John, 2007–15. *Club:* Royal Cruising.

**BLACKBURN, David Michael;** property project consultant, since 1986, and commercial mediator, since 2004; *b* London, 23 Dec. 1937; *s* of Rudolph Isaac Blackburn and Esther Sybil Blackburn; *m* 1970, Janice Brown (OBE 2011); three *s*. *Educ:* City of London Sch.; St John's Coll., Cambridge (BA 1959; LLM 1960; MA 1962). Registered Mediator, CEDR, 2006–. Admitted solicitor 1962; Partner, Courts & Co., solicitors, 1962–81. Director: Rosehaugh plc, 1979–85; Rosehaugh Stanhope Developments plc, 1983–92; Blackburn Associates Ltd, 1986–2010; QVS Developments Ltd, 1998–2004. Member Board: Nat. Opera Studio, 1994–2012; Design Mus., 2006–11; Olivebrook Ltd, 2011–. *Recreations:* opera, contemporary arts, architecture and design, lively discussion, Indian and other travel.

**BLACKBURN, Elizabeth;** QC 1998; *b* 5 Oct. 1954; *d* of Robert Arnold Parker and Edna Parker (*née* Baines); *m* 1979, John Blackburn, *qv*; two *s*. *Educ:* City of London Sch. for Girls; Manchester Univ. (BA Hons English 1976). Called to the Bar, Middle Temple, 1978 (Harmsworth Schol.), Bencher, 2008; in practice at the Bar, 1978–, specialising in commercial and admiralty law, 1980–; Examr, High Court, 1987–90; Joint Head of Chambers: Stone Chambers, Gray's Inn, 2014–16; London, St Philips Stone, 2016–18; 36 Stone, Gray's Inn, 2018–. Mem., Exec. Cttee, British Maritime Law Assoc., 2003–. Mem., UK delegn, Internat. Oil Pollution Compensation Supplementary Fund Protocol Diplomatic Conf., 2003; Legal Mem., DCMS Adv. Cttee on Historic Wreck Sites, 2004–14; Member, Panel: Lloyd's Form Salvage Arbitrators, 2009–; Singapore Internat. Arbitration Centre, 2015–; Singapore Chamber of Maritime Arbitration, 2015–; Pacific Internat. Arbitration Centre, 2015–; Hong Kong Internat. Arbitration Centre, 2018–; BVI Internat. Arbitration Centre, 2018–; London Court of Internat. Arbitration Centre, 2018–. Mem., Baltic Exchange, 2016–. *Recreations:* cinema, travel. *Address:* 36 Stone, 4 Field Court, Gray's Inn, WC1R 5EF. *T:* (020) 7440 6900.

*See also* R. S. Parker.

**BLACKBURN, Prof. Elizabeth Helen, (Mrs J. W. Sedat),** AC 2010; PhD; FRS 1992; Morris Herzstein Professor in Biology and Physiology, University of California, San Francisco (Professor of Biochemistry and Biophysics, 1990–2014, now Emerita; Chair, Department of Microbiology and Immunology, 1993–99); *b* 26 Nov. 1948; *d* of Harold Stewart Blackburn and Marcia Constance (*née* Jack); *m* 1975, John William Sedat; one *s*. *Educ:* Univ. of Melbourne (BSc Hons 1970; MSc 1972); Cambridge Univ. (PhD 1975). University of California, Berkeley: Asst Prof., Dept of Molecular Biol., 1978–83; Associate Prof., 1983–86; Prof. of Molecular Biology, 1986–90. Pres., Amer. Soc. for Cell Biol., 1998. Mem., Amer. Acad. Arts and Scis; For. Associate, Nat. Acad. of Scis, USA, 1993. Hon. DSc: Yale, 1991; Cambridge, 2009. Award for Molecular Biol., Nat. Acad. Scis, USA, 1990; Australia Prize, 1998; Gairdner Prize, Gairdner Foundn, 1998; General Motors Sloan Prize, 2001; Lasker Prize, 2006; (jtly) Nobel Prize in Physiology or Medicine, 2009. *Publications:* (jtly) The Telomere Effect, 2017; research and review articles in Nature, Science, Cell. *Recreation:* music. *Address:* Department of Biochemistry and Biophysics, University of California, Mission Bay Campus, 600 16th Street, Room GH–S312F, Box 2200, San Francisco, CA 94158–2517, USA. *T:* (415) 4764912.

**BLACKBURN, (Jeffrey) Michael,** CVO 2009; Chief Executive, Halifax Building Society, then Halifax plc, 1993–98; *b* 16 Dec. 1941; *s* of late Jeffrey and Renee Blackburn; *m* 1987, Louise Clair Jouny; two *s*, and one *s* one *d* from a previous marriage. *Educ:* Northgate Grammar Sch., Ipswich. FCIB. Chief Manager, Lloyds Bank Business Adv. Service, 1979–83; Dir and Chief Exec., Joint Credit Card Co. Ltd, 1983–87; Dir and Chief Exec., Leeds Permanent Building Soc., 1987–93. Director: DFS Furniture plc, 1999–2004; George Wimpey PLC, 1999–2005; Town Centre Securities plc, 1999–2002; In Kind Direct, 1999–2009 (Dep. Chm., 2001–09); Freeport plc, 2003–07; Chm., Fairpoint (formerly Debt Free Direct) Gp plc, 2005–08. Pres., CIB, 1998–99. Mem. Court, Leeds Univ., 2001–07. Gov., NYO, 1999–2007; Trustee, Duke of Edinburgh's Award, 1998–2009. DUniv Leeds Metropolitan, 1998; Hon. DLitt Huddersfield, 1998. *Recreations:* music, theatre, opera, sport. *Club:* Oriental.

*See also* T. M. Blackburn.

**BLACKBURN, John;** QC 1984; arbitrator; *b* 13 Nov. 1945; *s* of Harry and Violet Blackburn; *m* 1st, 1970, Alison Nield (marr. diss. 1978); 2nd, 1979, Elizabeth Parker (see E. Blackburn); two *s*. *Educ:* Rugby Sch.; Worcester Coll., Oxford (Scholar, 1967; Gibbs Prize in Law, 1967). Called to the Bar, Middle Temple, 1969 (Astbury Law Scholar), Bencher, 1993. Practising barrister, 1970–2006. *Recreations:* cricket, golf, paintings, wine. *Address:* 1 Atkin Building, Gray's Inn, WC1R 5AT.

**BLACKBURN, Ven. John,** CB 2004; Vicar of Risca, Gwent, 2004–13; *b* 3 Dec. 1947; *m* 1970, Anne Elisabeth Woodcock; two *d*. *Educ:* University Coll., Cardiff (DipTh); St Michael's Coll., Llandaff (DPS 1971); Open Univ. (BA Hons 1988; AdvDipEd; BSc 2004). Deacon 1971, priest 1972; Curate, Risca, 1971–76; Chaplain, HM Forces, 1976–2004: Dep. Chaplain-Gen., 1999–2000, Chaplain-Gen., 2000–04; Archdeacon of HM Land Forces, 1999–2004, now Emeritus. QHC 1996–2004. Hon. Canon, Ripon Cathedral, 2001–04, now Canon Emeritus. Chm., Gwent Br., SSAFA, 2006–. Trustee, League of Mercy, 2013. FRSA 1994. *Recreations:* travelling, game shooting, reading, English watercolours. *Address:* St Hilary, 11 Gelli Avenue, Risca, Newport, Gwent NP11 6QF. *Club:* National.

**BLACKBURN, Michael;** see Blackburn, J. M.

**BLACKBURN, Peter Hugh,** CBE 2003; FCA; Chairman, Northern Foods, 2002–05; *b* 17 Dec. 1940; *s* of Hugh Edward Blackburn and Sarah Blackburn (*née* Moffatt); *m* 1967, Gillian Mary Popple; three *d*. *Educ:* Douai Sch., Reading; Leeds Univ. (BA Hons Philosophy and French); Poitiers Univ. (Dipl. French); Inst. of Chartered Accts; AMP, Harvard Business Sch., 1976. R. S. Dawson & Co., Bradford (articles), 1962–66; various positions within John Mackintosh and Rowntree Mackintosh, 1966–91; Chm., Rowntree

UK, 1985–91; Head, Nestlé Chocolate, Confectionery and Biscuit Strategy Group, 1989–90; Chm. and Chief Exec., Nestlé UK, 1991–96 and 1997–2001; Pres. and Dir Gen., Nestlé France, 1996–97. Non-executive Director: SIG, 2001–09; Compass Gp, 2002–07. President: ISBA, 1998–2000; FDF, 2000–02. Nat. Pres., Modern Languages Assoc., 1987–89; Chm., Council, Festival of Languages Young Linguist Competition, 1985–89; Chm., Harrogate Internat. Fest., 2004–11 (Trustee, 2011–16). Mem., Council of Industry and Higher Educn, 1990–92. Mem. Council, York Univ., 1989–92, 2001–03. York Merchant Adventurers, 1989–2006. FIGD 1991. Hon. FCIL (Hon. FIL 1989). Hon. DLitt Bradford, 1991; Hon. DBA Leeds Metropolitan, 2005. Chevalier du Tastevin, 1984. *Recreations:* fell walking, photography.

**BLACKBURN, Rt Rev. Richard Finn;** Bishop Suffragan of Warrington, 2009–18; an Honorary Assistant Bishop, Diocese of Sheffield, since 2019; *b* 22 Jan. 1952; *s* of William Brow Blackburn and Ingeborg Blackburn (*née* Lerche-Thomsen); *m* 1980, Helen Claire Davies; one *s* three *d*. *Educ:* Aysgarth Sch.; Eastbourne Coll.; St John's Coll., Durham Univ. (BA); Hull Univ. (MA); Westcott House, Cambridge. National Westminster Bank, 1976–81; deacon 1983, priest 1984; Curate, St Dunstan and All Saints, Stepney, 1983–87; Priest-in-charge, St John the Baptist, Isleworth, 1987–92; Vicar of Mosborough, 1992–99; RD of Attercliffe, 1996–99; Hon. Canon, 1998–99, Residentiary Canon, 1999–2005, Sheffield Cathedral; Archdeacon of Sheffield and Rotherham (formerly Archdeacon of Sheffield), 1999–2009; Actg Bp of Sodor and Man, 2016–17. Dignitary in Convocation, 2000–05. Mem., Hse of Bishops and Gen. Synod, 2015–18. Mem., C of E Pensions Bd, 2003–09 (Vice Chm., 2006–09); Chair, Churches Regl Commn for Yorks and the Humber, 2005–08. Member, School Council: Worksop Coll., 2000–09; Ranby House Sch., 2000–09. *Recreations:* rowing, walking, gardening, music. *E:* bishoprichardblackburn@hotmail.co.uk.

**BLACKBURN, Prof. Robert,** PhD, LLD; FRHistS; Professor of Constitutional Law, King's College London, since 1997; *b* London; *s* of Lt Comdr Richard, (Dick), Blackburn and Dulcie Blackburn; *m* 1985, Paula Summerhayes; one *s* two *d*. *Educ:* Rugby Sch.; Univ. of Leeds (BA Hist.; PhD; LLD Law); Coll. of Law (law diplomas); London Sch. of Econs and Political Sci. (MSc Govt). Admitted solicitor, 1979; King's College London: Lectr, 1981–92; Sen. Lectr, 1992–94; Reader in Public Law, 1994–97; Actg Hd, Law Sch., 2006–07; Leverhulme Res. Fellow, 2007–09; Hd of Dept, Inst. of Contemporary British Hist., 2010–14. UK Nat. Corresp., Council of Europe Directorate of Human Rights, 1983–2008. Special Counsel, Inq. into Codifying the UK Constitution, Political and Constitutional Reform Cttee, H of C, 2010–15. FRHistS 1989. Hon. QC 2016. *Publications:* The Meeting of Parliament, 1990; (ed jtly) Human Rights for the 1990s: legal, political and ethical issues, 1991; (ed) Constitutional Studies: contemporary issues and controversies, 1992; (ed) Rights of Citizenship, 1993; (jtly) A Written Constitution for the United Kingdom, 1993; The Electoral System in Britain, 1995; (ed jtly) Human Rights for the 21st Century, 1997; Towards a Constitutional Bill of Rights for the United Kingdom, 1999; (ed jtly) Constitutional Reform: the Labour government's constitutional reform agenda, 1999; (ed jtly) Fundamental Rights in Europe, 2001; (ed jtly) Griffith and Ryle on Parliament: functions, practice and procedures, 2nd edn 2003; King and Country: monarchy and the future King Charles III, 2006; (contrib.) Halsbury's Laws of England: Parliament, Vol. 78, 5th edn 2010; Constitutional and Administrative Law, Vol. 20, 5th edn 2014; Crown and Crown Proceedings, Vol. 29, 2014, rev. edn 2019. *Recreations:* playing guitar, picnics in Richmond Park, holidaying in the French Alps. *Address:* School of Law, King's College London, Strand, WC2R 2LS. *T:* (020) 7848 2516.

**BLACKBURN, Prof. Simon Walter,** PhD; FBA 2002; Bertrand Russell Professor of Philosophy (formerly Professor of Philosophy), University of Cambridge, 2001–11; *b* 12 July 1944; *s* of Cuthbert and Edna Blackburn; *m* 1968, Angela Bowles; one *s* one *d*. *Educ:* Trinity Coll., Cambridge (BA 1965; PhD 1970). Research Fellow, Churchill Coll., Cambridge, 1967–70; Fellow and Tutor in Philosophy, Pembroke Coll., Oxford, 1970–90; Edna J. Koury Dist. Prof. of Philosophy, Univ. of N Carolina, 1990–2000. Visiting Professor: Princeton Univ., 1987; Ohio State Univ., 1988; Adjunct Prof., ANU, 1993–2001. Fellow, Amer. Acad. of Arts and Scis, 2008. Editor, Mind, 1984–90. *Publications:* Reason and Prediction, 1973; Spreading the Word, 1984; Essays in Quasi Realism, 1993; Oxford Dictionary of Philosophy, 1994; Ruling Passions, 1998; Think, 1999; Being Good, 2001; Lust, 2004; Truth: a guide for the perplexed, 2005; Plato's Republic, 2006; How to Read Hume, 2008; The Big Questions: philosophy, 2009; Practical Tortoise Raising, 2011; Mirror, Mirror: the uses and abuses of self-love, 2014. *Recreations:* hill-walking, sailing, photography. *Address:* 141 Thornton Road, Cambridge CB3 0NE. *T:* (01223) 528278.

**BLACKBURN, Prof. Timothy Michael,** DPhil; Professor of Invasion Biology, University College London, since 2014; *b* Chelmsford, 3 July 1966; *s* of (Jeffrey) Michael Blackburn, *qv* and Jill I. Firth; *m* 2010, Noëlle F. Kümpel; one *d*. *Educ:* St Albans Sch.; Leeds Grammar Sch.; Univ. of Manchester (BSc 1st Cl. Hons Zool.); DPhil Zool. Oxon 1990. Lectr, 2000–05, Prof. of Macroecol., 2005–07, Univ. of Birmingham; Dir, Inst. of Zool., 2007–14. *Publications:* with K. J. Gaston: Pattern and Process in Macroecology, 2000; Macroecology: concepts and consequences, 2003; (jtly) Avian Invasions: the ecology and evolution of exotic birds, 2009. *Recreations:* birding, photography, cooking, eating. *Address:* Department of Genetics, Evolution and Environment, Centre for Biodiversity and Environment Research, Darwin Building, University College London, Gower Street, WC1E 6BT.

**BLACKBURN, Vice Adm. Sir Tom;** *see* Blackburn, Vice Adm. Sir D. A. J.

**BLACKBURNE, Alison;** HM Diplomatic Service; Ambassador to the Republic of South Sudan, 2017–19; *b* 20 June 1964. *Educ:* Leeds Univ. (BA Hons French/Russian). Entered FCO, 1987; Third, later Second, Sec. (Chancery), Warsaw, 1989–92; First Secretary: FCO, 1992–96; UKMIS, NY, 1996–2000 (Political), Stockholm, 2000–03; Counsellor and Dep. Hd of Mission, Harare, 2003–06; Political Counsellor, UK Perm. Representation to EU, Brussels, 2006–08; Principal Private Sec. to Lord Chancellor and Sec. of State, MoJ, 2008–10; Dep. Hd of Mission, Indonesia, 2011; Consul-Gen., Washington, DC, 2011–12; High Comr to Uganda, 2012–16.

**BLACKBURNE, Hon. Sir William (Anthony),** Kt 1993; a Judge of the High Court of Justice, Chancery Division, 1993–2009; *b* 24 Feb. 1944; *m* 1996, Vivien, *d* of A. C. Webber. Called to the Bar, Inner Temple, 1966; Bencher, Lincoln's Inn, 1992 (Treas., 2015). QC 1984. Vice-Chancellor of the County Palatine of Lancaster, 1998–2002. Treas., Gen. Council of the Bar, 1988–90. Mem., Haringey LBC, 1974–78, 1986–93. Chm., Pakistan Soc., 2012–. Mem., Bomber Comd Meml Trust, 2010–15. Pres., Madrigal Soc., 2011–13. *Club:* Garrick.

**BLACKETT, Sir Hugh Francis,** 12th Bt *cr* 1673, of Newcastle, Northumberland; *b* 11 Feb. 1955; *e s* of Major Sir Francis Hugh Blackett, 11th Bt and his 1st wife, Elizabeth Eily Barrie (*née* Dennison) (*d* 1982); *S* father, 1995; *m* 1982, Anna, *yr d* of J. St G. Coldwell; one *s* three *d*. *Educ:* Eton. High Sheriff, Northumberland, 2007–08. *Heir: s* Henry Douglas Blackett, *b* 2 Feb. 1992.

**BLACKETT, Jeffrey; His Honour Judge Blackett;** Judge Advocate General of the Armed Forces, since 2004; a Senior Circuit Judge, since 2005; a Deputy High Court Judge, since 2013; *b* 20 May 1955; *s* of Lt Comdr William Blackett and Gwendoline Blackett; *m* 1981, Sally Anne Fulford; one *s* one *d*. *Educ:* Portsmouth Grammar Sch.; University Coll. London (LLB 1976); Council of Legal Educn; St Antony's Coll., Oxford (MSt 2000). Called to the Bar, Gray's Inn, 1983, Bencher, 2008. Served RN, Supply and Secretariat Br., 1973–2004; Comdr, HMS Collingwood, 1995–97; Dir, Pay and Pensions, 1997–99; Chief Naval Judge Advocate, 2000–04. Actg Metropolitan Stipendiary Magistrate, 1995–99; a Recorder, 2000–04. Chm., Inns Conduct Cttee, 2009–12. Special Prof., Univ. of Nottingham, 2010. Mem., Bd of Dirs, RFU, 2014–18 (Hon. Discipline Officer, 2003–13). Trustee, Help for Heroes, 2012–18. *Publications:* (with J. W. Rant) Courts-Martial, Discipline and the Criminal Process in the Armed Services, 2003; Rant on the Court Martial and Service Law, 2009. *Recreations:* Rugby, squash, golf. *Address:* Room TM9.06, Thomas More Building, Royal Courts of Justice, Strand, WC2A 2LL. *T:* (020) 7218 8095, *Fax:* (020) 7218 8094. *E:* HHJ.Jeff.Blackett@ejudiciary.net. *Club:* Royal Automobile.

**BLACKFORD, Rt Hon. Ian;** PC 2017; MP (SNP) Ross, Skye and Lochaber, since 2015; *b* Edinburgh, 1961; *m* Ann. *Educ:* Royal High Sch., Edinburgh. Dir, UBS Philips and Drew, 1989–93; Man. Dir, Nat West Mkts, 1993–99; Man. Dir, Deutsche Bank, 1999–2003; Man. Dir, First Seer, 2003–; Hd, Investor Relns, CSM, 2005–12. Non-executive Director: Edinburgh Bicycle Cooperative, 2008–13; Commsworld, 2006– (Chm., 2014–). Chm., NW Skye Recreational Assoc. Dir, Cuillin FM (community radio stn). Mem. Bd, Golden Charter Trust, 2008–. SNP Leader, H of C, 2017–. Contested (SNP): Ayr, 1997; Paisley, Nov. 1997. *Address:* House of Commons, SW1A 0AA.

**BLACKHAM, Vice-Adm. Sir Jeremy (Joe),** KCB 1999; freelance writer, speaker and mentor; Visiting Lecturer, King's College London, since 2008; *b* 10 Sept. 1943; *s* of Rear-Adm. Joseph Leslie Blackham, CB; *m* 1971, Candy Carter. *Educ:* Bradfield Coll., Berks; Open Univ. (BA 1st Cl. Hons 1979; MA 2009). RN Staff Course, 1974. Joined RN, 1961; Spanish Interpreter, 1966; commanded HM Ships Beachampton, 1969–70, Ashanti, 1977–79, Nottingham, 1984–85; rcds 1986; Commandant, RN Staff Coll., Greenwich, 1987–89; Dir of Naval Plans, 1989–92; Captain, HMS Ark Royal, 1992–93 (Comdr RN Task Group, Adriatic); DG, Naval Personnel Strategy and Plans, 1993–95; ACNS and Adm. Pres., RNC, Greenwich, 1995–97; Dep. Comdr, Fleet, 1997–99; DCDS (Progs and Personnel), 1999; DCDS (Equipment Capability), MoD, 1999–2002. Mem., CDS Strategic Adv. Panel, 2012–. UK Pres., EADS, 2003–06; Chairman: EADS Defence Systems UK, 2004–06; Atmaana Ltd, 2005–08 (Dir, 2003–10); Sarnmere, 2006–16; Director: Condor PM, 2006–; Airbus Helicopters UK (formerly Eurocopter UK), 2008–16. Lectr, RUSI and defence orgns; Vis. Lectr, Kingston Univ., 2014–18. Ext. Examr, Kingston Univ., 2013–17. Chm., Academic Adv. Bd, Aeronautical Engrg Faculty, City Univ., 2004–07; Member: Council, RUSI (Vice Pres., 2003–); RIIA; MInstD. Pres., HMS Cavalier Assoc., 2010–. Chm., Blackheath Conservatoire of Music and Arts, 2000–07. Liveryman, Shipwrights' Co., 1999–. Editor, Naval Review, 2003–17; Mem., Editorial Adv. Bd, Defence Procurement Analysis, 2004–06. Mem., Adv. Bd, City Forum, 2005–08. MInstD. Member: NT; English Heritage. *Publications:* numerous articles on defence, strategic affairs and walking. *Recreations:* cricket, music, theatre, language, travel, walking. *Address:* Monk Frith, Bell Green, Cratfield, Suffolk IP19 0DH. *Clubs:* MCC; Kent County Cricket.

**BLACKHURST, Christopher Charles;** Executive Director, CTF Partners, since 2016; journalist and media adviser, 2015–16; Group Editorial Director, 2012–14, Group Content Director, 2013–15, and Multi-media Head of Business, 2014–15, The Independent and Evening Standard; *b* Barrow-in-Furness, 24 Dec. 1959; *s* of Donald Blackhurst and Rose Bestwick Blackhurst (*née* Wood); *m* 1st, 1986, Lynette Dorothy Wood Grice (marr. diss. 2003); two *s* one *d*; 2nd, 2004, Annabelle Sara Fisher; one *s* one *d*. *Educ:* Barrow-in-Furness Grammar Sch. for Boys; Trinity Hall, Cambridge (BA Hons Law 1982; MA). With Cameron Markby Solicitors, 1983–84; Asst Ed., 1984–85; Dep. Ed., 1985–86, Internat. Financial Law Rev.; Sen. Writer, Business Mag., 1986–89; Business Feature Writer and Dep. Insight Ed., Sunday Times, 1989–90; City Ed., Sunday Express, 1990–92; Sen. Business Writer, Independent on Sunday, 1992–93; Westminster corresp., Independent, 1993–96; Asst Ed., Independent on Sunday, 1996–97; Deputy Editor: Independent and Independent on Sunday, 1997–98; Daily Express and Sunday Express, 1998–2001; City Ed., Evening Standard, 2002–11; Ed., The Independent, 2011–13. Trustee and Director: Kingston Th. Trust, 2004–11 and 2015–17; KIDS, 2017–; Mem., Develt Bd, The Sixteen, 2009–11. Mem., Arts & Business Adv. Bd, 2010–11. Mem., Fund Raising Bd, Maggie's Cancer Care Charity, 2005–07. *Recreations:* golf, tennis, theatre. *Address:* CTF Partners, 6 Chesterfield Gardens, W1J 5BQ. *T:* (020) 7318 5770. *Clubs:* Reform, Soho House, Roehampton (Chm., 2010–11, 2015–17).

**BLACKIE, Jonathan Adam,** CBE 2010; Regional Director, Government Office for the North East, 2002–11; Culture Partnership Manager, Association of North East Councils, since 2013; *b* 29 April 1953; *s* of late James Blackie and Nansie Blackie; *m* 1983, Julie; four *d*. *Educ:* Heriot-Watt Univ./Edinburgh Coll. of Art (BSc Hons Town and Country Planning 1976). Res. Associate, Univ. of Edinburgh, 1976–81; Sen. Policy Officer, Newcastle CC, 1981–87; Principal Policy Officer, Kirklees MDC, 1987–89; Regl Projects Manager, Audit Commn, 1989–92; Dir, Newcastle City Challenge, 1992–96; Regl Dir, English Partnerships (NE), 1996–99; Dir, One NorthEast RDA, 1999–2002. Vis. Prof., Univ. of Northumbria, 2012–. Peer Reviewer, Study of Central and Southern Denmark, OECD, 2011–12. Chair: New Writing North, 2008–15; Governing Body, St Chad's Coll., Univ. of Durham, 2009–17; River Tyne Steering Gp, 2014–; Trustees, Alnwick Garden, 2011–. Trustee, Tyne and Wear Archives and Museums Service, 2017–. *Recreations:* arts, golf, tennis. *Address:* The Coach House, Prestwick Whins Farm, Northumberland NE20 9UD. *E:* jonathanblackie@hotmail.co.uk.

**BLACKISTON, Galton;** chef-patron, Morston Hall, since 1992 (Michelin Star, since 1999); *b* Norwich, 1962; *s* of Bill Blackiston and Ann Blackiston; *m* 1987, Tracy Rowe; two *s*. *Educ:* Hainford Primary Sch.; Homewood Sch., Tenterden; Ashford Technical Coll. Market stall, Rye Market, 1984–85; Head Chef, Miller Howe Hotel and Restaurant, 1985–91. Fellow: Craft Guild of Chefs, 2001; Great British Chefs. Patron, Macmillan Cancer Support. *Publications:* Cooking at Morston Hall, 2002; A Return to Real Cooking, 2006; Summertime, 2009; Hook Line Sinker, 2017. *Recreations:* cricket, golf, shooting. *Address:* Morston Hall, Morston, Holt NR25 7AA. *T:* (01263) 741041 *Fax:* (01263) 740419. *E:* reception@morstonhall.com. *Clubs:* MCC; Norwich City Football (Ambassador Mem.).

**BLACKLEY, Air Vice-Marshal Allan Baillie,** CBE 1983; AFC; BSc; Principal, Emergency Planning College, 1993–97; *b* 28 Sept. 1937. Flight Lieut, 1961; Sqn Leader, 1968; Wing Comdr, 1974; Directorate of Air Staff Plans, Dept of CAS, Air Force Dept, 1977; Gp Capt., 1980; OC RAF Valley and ADC to the Queen, 1980–82; Gp Capt. (Air Defence) RAF Strike Comd, 1982–83; Dir (Air Defence), MoD, 1984–85; Air Cdre, 1985; Comdt, RAF CFS, Scampton, 1985–87; SASO, No 11 Gp, 1987–89; Dep. COS (Ops HQ AFCENT, 1989–91; AO Scotland and NI, 1991–93. Chm., Lincs and Notts Ambulance Charitable Trust, 1998–2001. *Address:* Benameer, 40a Horncastle Road, Woodhall Spa, Lincs LN10 6UZ.

**BLACKLEY, Ian Lorimer;** HM Diplomatic Service, retired; b 14 Dec. 1946; s of late John Lorimer Blackley and Christina Ferrier (née Aitken); m 1981, Pamela Ann Helena Belt; one s. Educ: Sedbergh Sch.; St Catharine's Coll., Cambridge (MA). Joined Diplomatic Service, 1969; MECAS, Lebanon, 1971–72; Third Sec., Tripoli, 1972–73; Second Sec., Berlin, 1973–74; First Sec., Damascus, 1974–77; FCO, 1977–80; Head of Chancery and HM Consul, Beirut, 1980–82; First Sec. (Agric.), The Hague, 1982–86; Asst Head, ME Dept, FCO, 1986–88; Counsellor, Kuwait, 1988–90; British Rep. to Govt of Occupied Kuwait in Exile, Aug. 1990–March 1991; Counsellor, Damascus, 1991–93; Spokesman, EU Electoral Mission, Palestinian Elections, 1995–96; Sen. Observer, British Mission to Yemeni Elections, 1997. Recreations: fly fishing, Islamic art. Address: 63 Northumberland Street, Edinburgh EH3 6JQ.

**BLACKMAN, Elizabeth Marion;** b 26 Sept. 1949; m Derek Blackman (marr. diss.); one s one d. Educ: Carlisle County Sch. for Girls; Prince Henry's Grammar Sch., Otley; Clifton Coll., Nottingham (BEd Hons). Teacher, 1972–93, Hd, 1993–97, Upper Sch., Bramcote Park Comp., Nottingham. Mem. (Lab) Broxtowe BC, 1991–98 (Dep. Leader, 1995–97). MP (Lab) Erewash, 1997–2010. PPS to Sec. of State for Defence, 2000–05, to Leader of the H of C, 2005–06; an Asst Govt Whip, 2006–07; Vice-Chamberlain of HM Household, 2007–08. Mem., Treasury Select Cttee, 1997–2000. Chm., All-Pty Parly Gp on Autism, 2004–06.

**BLACKMAN, Sir Frank (Milton),** KA 1985; KCVO 1985 (CVO 1975); OBE 1969 (MBE 1964); Ombudsman for Barbados, 1987–93; b 31 July 1926; s of late A. Milton Blackman and Winnifred Blackman (née Pile); m 1st, 1958, Edith Mary Knight (d 1994); one s; 2nd, 1995, Norma Cox Astwood (OBE 1997). Educ: Wesley Hall Boys' Sch., Barbados; Harrison Coll., Barbados. Clerical Officer, Colonial Secretary's Office, 1944–56; Sec., Public Service Commn, 1956–57; Asst Sec., Colonial Sec.'s Office, 1957; Cabinet Office/Premier's Office, 1958–66: Clerk of the Legislative Council, 1958–64; Perm. Sec./Cabinet Sec., 1966–86; Head of CS, 1981–86. Address: Lausanne, Rendezvous Hill, Christ Church, BB 15115, Barbados. T: 4273463.

**BLACKMAN, Gilbert Albert Waller,** CBE 1978 (OBE 1973); FREng, CEng, FIMechE; Chairman, Central Electricity Generating Board, Jan.–March 1990, retired; b 28 July 1925; s of Ernest Albert Cecil Blackman and Amy Blackman; m 1948, Lilian Rosay. Educ: Wanstead County High Sch.; Wandsworth Tech. Coll. CEng, FIMechE 1967; Hon. FInstE (FInstF 1964). Commnd RE, 1945–48. Trainee Engr, London Div., Brit. Electricity Authority, 1948–50; various appts in power stns, 1950–63; Central Electricity Generating Board: Stn Supt, Belvedere, 1963–64; Asst Reg. Dir, E Midlands Div., 1964–67; Asst Reg. Dir, Midlands Reg., 1967–70; Dir of Generation, Midlands Reg., 1970–75; Dir Gen., N Eastern Reg., 1975–77; Mem., 1977–90; Dep. Chm. and Prodn Man. Dir, 1986–89; Chm., British Electricity Internat. Ltd, 1988–90; Dir, Nat. Power, 1990–94. Recreations: music, photography, art.
See also L. C. F. Blackman.

**BLACKMAN, Kirsty;** MP (SNP) Aberdeen North, since 2015; b Aberdeen; m Luke Blackman; one s one d. Educ: Robert Gordon's Coll. Mem. (SNP) Aberdeen CC, 2007–15. Address: House of Commons, SW1A 0AA.

**BLACKMAN, Dr Lionel Cyril Francis;** Director, British American Tobacco Co. Ltd, 1980–85 (General Manager, Group Research and Development, 1978–80); b 12 Sept. 1930; s of Mr and Mrs Ernest Albert Cecil Blackman; m 1955, Susan Hazel Peachey (marr. diss 1983); one s one d. Educ: Wanstead High Sch.; Queen Mary Coll., London. BSc 1952; PhD 1955. Scientific Officer, then Senior Research Fellow, RN Scientific Service, 1954–57; ICI Research Fellow, then Lectr in Chemical Physics of Solids, Imperial Coll., London, 1957–60; Asst Dir (London), then Dir, Chemical Research Div., BR, 1961–64; Dir of Basic Research, then Dir Gen., British Coal Utilisation Research Assoc., 1964–71; Director: Fibreglass Ltd (subsid. of Pilkington Bros Ltd), 1971–78; Compocem Ltd, 1975–78; Cemfil Corp. (US), 1975–78; Vice-Pres., Cementos y Fibras SA (Spain), 1976–78. Chm., Hockering Residents Assoc., 1995–2003. CEng; CChem; FRSC; DIC; Sen. FEI. Publications: (ed) Modern Aspects of Graphite Technology, 1970; Athletics World Records in the 20th Century, 1988; Four histories of the development of the Hockering Estate, Woking, 2000, 2004, 2007, 2009; papers in various scientific and technical jls on dropwise condensation of steam, ferrites, sintering of oxides, graphite and its crystal compounds, glass surface coatings, glass reinforced cement. Recreations: gardening, glass, music, wine (Founder Chm., Epping Forest Wine Soc. (Pres., 1971–)). Address: Griffin House, Knowl Hill, The Hockering, Woking, Surrey GU22 7HL. T: (01483) 766328.
See also G. A. W. Blackman.

**BLACKMAN, Malorie,** OBE 2008; FRSL; author, since 1990; b London, 8 Feb. 1962. Educ: Honor Oak Grammar Sch.; Thames Poly. (HNC Computer Sci.); Nat. Film and Television Sch. (Screenwriting). Documentation Asst, 1981–82, Jun. Programmer, 1982–83, Scicon; Systems Programmer, Reuters, 1983–85; Project Manager, Digital Equipt, 1985–87; Database Manager, Reuters, 1987–90. Children's Laureate, 2013–15. Vis. Fellow, LMH, Oxford, 2016–19. FRSL 2009. Eleanor Farjeon Award, Children's Book Circle, 2006. Publications: for young adults: Not So Stupid, 1990; Trust Me, 1997; Impact: Horror, 1997; Words Last Forever, 1998; The Stuff of Nightmares, 2007; (ed) Unheard Voices, 2007; Boys Don't Cry, 2010; Noble Conflict, 2013; Jon for Short, 2013; Dr Who: the ripple effect, 2013; Heart Break Girl, 2014; (ed) Love Hurts, 2015; Chasing the Stars, 2016; Noughts & Crosses series: Noughts & Crosses, 2001 (adapted for stage, 2019); An Eye For an Eye, 2003; Knife Edge, 2004; Checkmate, 2005; Double Cross, 2008; Callum, 2012; Nought Forever, 2019; Crossfire, 2019; for children: That New Dress, 1992; Hacker, 1992; Operation Gadgetman!, 1993; Jack Sweettooth the 73rd, 1995; Whizziwig, 1995; The Space Stowaway, 1995; Thief!, 1996; A.N.T.I.D.O.T.E., 1997; Pig Heart Boy, 1997 (televised 1999); Forbidden Game, 1999; Animal Avengers, 1999; Don't Be Afraid, 1999; Whizziwig Returns, 1999; Hostage, 1999; Tell Me No Lies, 1999; Dangerous Reality, 1999; Dead Gorgeous, 2002; Cloud Busting, 2004; Robot Girl, 2015; Contact, 2015; Peace Maker, 2016; Deadly Dare Mystery series: The Computer Ghost, 1997; Deadly Dare, 1998; Lie Detectives, 1998; for new readers: Elaine, You're a Brat, 1991; Girl Wonder and the Terrific Twins, 1991; Girl Wonder's Winter Adventures, 1992; Betsey Biggalow is Here!, 1992; Betsey Biggalow the Detective, 1992; Hurricane Betsey, 1993; Magic Betsey, 1994; Girl Wonder to the Rescue, 1994; My Friend's a Gris-Quok!, 1994; Rachel versus Bonecrusher the Mighty, 1994; Rachel and the Difference Thief, 1994; (jtly) Crazy Crocs, 1994; Betsey's Birthday Surprise, 1996; Grandma's Haunted Handbag, 1996; The Mellion Moon Mystery, 1996; Peril on Planet Pelia, 1996; Quasar Quartz Quest, 1996; Secret of the Terrible Hand, 1996; Space Race, 1997; Fangs, 1998; Snow Dog, 2001; The Monster Crisp-Guzzler, 2002; Sinclair, Wonder Bear, 2003; Amazing Adventures of Girl Wonder, 2003; Ellie and the Cat, 2005; picture books: That New Dress, 1991; Mrs Spoon's Family, 1995; Marty Monster, 1999; Dizzy's Walk, 1999; I Want a Cuddle, 2002; Jessica Strange, 2002. Recreations: music, reading, theatre, cinema, computer games. Address: c/o The Agency (London) Ltd, 24 Pottery Lane, Holland Park, W11 4LZ. T: (020) 7727 1346. E: hd-office@theagency.co.uk.

**BLACKMAN, Robert;** MP (C) Harrow East, since 2010; b 26 April 1956; m 1988, Nicola Jennings. Educ: Univ. of Liverpool (BSc). Sales trng, 1991–98, Regulatory Compliance Manager, 1998–2010, BT. Mem. (C) Brent BC, 1986–2010 (Leader, 1991–96; Dep. Leader, 2006–10). Mem. (C) Brent and Harrow, London Assembly, GLA, 2004–08. Contested (C): Brent S, 1992; Bedford, 1997; Brent N, 2005. Address: House of Commons, SW1A 0AA.

**BLACKMAN, Prof. Timothy John,** PhD; Vice-Chancellor, Open University, since 2019; b Gravesend, 22 Oct. 1956; s of Frederick and Julia Blackman; m Roberta C. Woods (see R. C. Blackman-Woods); one d. Educ: Durham Univ. (BA Geog.; PhD Social Scis 1987). Merchant seaman, 1975–76; community worker, 1979–80; Lectr in Social Policy, Univ. of Ulster, 1982–90; Hd of Res., Newcastle CC, 1990–95; Dep. Dean, and Prof. of Social Policy, Oxford Brookes Univ., 1995–2000; Dean, and Prof. of Social Policy, Teesside Univ., 2000–04; Dean, and Prof. of Sociol. and Social Policy, Durham Univ., 2004–11; Pro Vice-Chancellor, Open Univ., 2011–15. MInstD 2015. Publications: Planning Belfast: a case study of public policy and community action, 1991; Urban Policy in Practice, 1995; Social Care and Social Exclusion: a comparative study of older people's care in Europe, 2001; Placing Health: neighbourhood renewal, health improvement and complexity, 2006; Studying Health Inequalities: an applied approach, 2014. Recreations: walking, music, reading. Address: Open University, Walton Hall, Milton Keynes MK7 6AA.

**BLACKMAN-WOODS, Roberta C.,** PhD; MP (Lab) City of Durham, since 2005; b 16 Aug. 1957; d of Charles and Eleanor Woods; m Prof. Timothy John Blackman, qv; one d. Educ: Univ. of Ulster (BSc Combined Soc. Scis 1979; PhD 1989). Welfare Rights Officer, Newcastle CC, 1982–85; Lectr in Social Policy, Univ. of Ulster, then Univ. of Newcastle upon Tyne, 1985–95; Dean of Social and Labour Studies, Ruskin Coll., Oxford, 1995–2000; Prof. of Social Policy and Dep. Dean, Sch. of Arts and Social Scis, Univ. of Northumbria, 2000–05. Mem., Child Poverty Action Gp. PPS to Minister of State for Innovation, Univs and Skills, 2008–10; Asst Regl Minister for NE; Shadow Minister: Cabinet Office, 2010–11; BIS, 2010–11; DCLG, 2011–17; Internat. Develt, 2017–18. Chair, Parly Univ. Gp, 2011–; Vice Chair, All Party Parly Gp on Sch. Food, 2010–. Recreation: music. Address: (office) The Miners' Hall, Redhills, Durham DH1 4BD. T: (0191) 374 1915, Fax: (0191) 374 1916. E: mail@roberta.org.uk; House of Commons, SW1A 0AA.

**BLACKMORE, Joanna Melancy Lyndon;** see Prior, J. M. L.

**BLACKMORE, Prof. Stephen,** CBE 2011; PhD; FRSE; CBiol, FRSB; FLS; Her Majesty's Botanist in Scotland, since 2010; Chair, Botanic Gardens Conservation International, since 2014; b 30 July 1952; s of Edwin Arthur and Josephine Blackmore; m 1973, Patricia Jane Melrose Hawley; one s one d. Educ: Univ. of Reading (BSc 1973; PhD 1976). CBiol, FRSB (FIBiol 1993); FLS 1976. Botanist and Administrator, Royal Society Aldabra Research Station, Indian Ocean, 1976–77; Head of Nat. Herbarium and Lectr in Botany, Univ. of Malaŵi, 1977–80; Head of Palynology Section, Dept of Botany, BM (Natural Hist.), 1980–90; Keeper of Botany, 1990–99, Associate Dir, 1992–95, Natural Hist. Mus.; Regius Keeper, Royal Botanic Garden Edinburgh, 1999–2013 (Hon. Fellow, 2014). Visiting Professor: Reading Univ., 1995–; Glasgow Univ., 1999–; Kunming Inst. of Botany, 2004–; Hon. Prof., Univ. of Edinburgh, 2004–. Chm., Darwin Adv. Cttee, DEFRA, 2013–19. Pres., Systematics Assoc., 1994–97; Chm., UK Systematics Forum, 1993–99. Trustee: Little Sparta Trust, 2001–10; Botanic Gardens Conservation Internat., 2000–; Seychelles Islands Foundn, 2007–; Mem., Bd of Govs, Edinburgh Coll. of Art, 2004–10. FRSE 2000. Hon. Fellow, 48 Gp Club 'The Icebreakers', 2005. Scottish Horticl Medal, Royal Caledonian Horticl Soc., 2008; Victoria Medal of Honour, RHS, 2012; Linnean Medal, Linnean Soc. of London, 2012. Publications: Bee Orchids, 1985; Buttercups, 1985; (ed jtly) Pollen and Spores: form and function, 1986; (ed jtly) Evolution, Systematics and Fossil History of the Hamamelidae, 2 vols, 1989; (ed jtly) Microspores: evolution and ontogeny, 1990; (ed jtly) Pollen and Spores: patterns of diversification, 1991; (ed jtly) An Atlas of Plant Sexual Reproduction, 1992; (ed jtly) Systematics Agenda 2000: The Challenge For Europe, 1996; Pollen and Spores: morphology and biology, 2000; Gardening the Earth: gateways to a sustainable future, 2009; Green Universe, 2012; (ed jtly) Plants of China, 2013; (ed jtly) Plant Conservation, Science and Practice, 2017; How Plants Work, 2018; contribs to professional jls. Recreations: hill walking, photography, blues guitar music. Address: Botanic Gardens Conservation International, Descanso House, 199 Kew Road, Richmond, Surrey TW9 3BW. T: (020) 8332 5953.

**BLACKMORE, Timothy John,** MBE 1999; Consultant Editorial Director, 7Digital plc (formerly UBC Media Group), 2004–14; b Hull, 3 July 1944; s of Rev. Harry J. Blackmore and Marjorie Blackmore; m 1967, Margaret Hughes; one s one d. Educ: King's Sch., Pontefract; Blyth Grammar Sch. Producer, Radio One, 1967–77; Hd of Programmes, Capital Radio, 1977–83; freelance producer and artist manager, 1983–87; Dir, Radio Acad., 1987–89; Prog. Dir, Unique Broadcasting, 1989–2004. Manager, Alan, (Fluff), Freeman, 1983–2006; Producer, Ivor Novello Awards, 1986–2005; Chairman: Sony Radio Academy Awards, 1999–2011; Oneword Ltd, 2000–05; Classic Gold Digital Network, 2000–07. Chm., Charles Parker Archive Trust, 2008–14. Chm., Lydiard Millicent Parish Council, 2013–14 (Vice Chm., 2011–13). Fellow, Radio Acad., 1994. Award for Outstanding Contribn to Music Radio, 2012; Lifetime Achievement Award, 2017. Recreations: DIY, music, food and wine. Address: Bayshill View, 21 St Georges Road, Cheltenham, Glos GL50 3DT. E: tim@timblackmore.com.

**BLACKSELL, His Honour Henry Oliver;** QC 1994; a Circuit Judge, 1996–2018; b 28 Nov. 1948; s of James Edward Blacksell, MBE and Joan Simmons Yates Blacksell (née Yates); m 1st, 1971, Diana Frances Mary Burton (marr. diss. 1985; she d 2005); 2nd, 1986, Miranda Jane, d of His Honour W. A. L. Allardice; one s one d. Educ: Barnstaple Grammar Sch.; Exeter Univ. (LLB). Called to the Bar, Inner Temple, 1972; a Recorder, 1993–96. Recreations: family, theatre, ancient humour. Club: Harlequin Rugby Football.

**BLACKSTONE,** Baroness cr 1987 (Life Peer), of Stoke Newington in Greater London; **Tessa Ann Vosper Blackstone;** PC 2001; PhD; Vice-Chancellor, University of Greenwich, 2004–11; b 27 Sept. 1942; d of late Geoffrey Vaughan Blackstone, CBE, GM, QFSM and Joanna Blackstone; m 1963, Tom Evans (marr. diss.; he d 1985); one s one d. Educ: Ware Grammar Sch.; London School of Economics (BScSoc, PhD; Hon. Fellow, 1995). Associate Lectr, Enfield Coll., 1965–66; Asst Lectr, then Lectr, Dept of Social Administration, LSE, 1966–75; Adviser, Central Policy Review Staff, Cabinet Office, 1975–78; Prof. of Educnl Admin, Univ. of London Inst. of Educn, 1978–83; Dep. Educn Officer (Resources), then Clerk and Dir of Education, ILEA, 1983–87; Master, Birkbeck Coll., London Univ., 1987–97 (Fellow, 1998). Fellow, Centre for Studies in Social Policy, 1972–74; Special Rowntree Visiting Fellow, Policy Studies Inst., 1987. Vis. Prof., LSE, 2003–05. Chm., Gen. Adv. Council of BBC, 1987–91; First Chm., Inst. for Public Policy Research, 1988–97. Non-executive Director: Project Fullemploy, 1984–91; Royal Opera House, 1987–97 and 2009–14 (Chm., Ballet Bd, 1991–97); Thames Television, 1991–92; Granada Learning, 2003–06; VT Gp plc, 2004–10; Mott McDonald, 2005–07. Member: Planning Bd, Arts Council of GB, 1986–90; Management Cttee, King Edward's Hosp. Fund for London, 1990–95; Marshall Aid Commemoration Commn, 2005–09; Gov. and

Mem. of Council, Ditchley Foundn, 1990–97; Gov., Royal Ballet, 1991–2001. Vice Pres., VSO, 1992–. Co-Chm., Franco-British Council, 2013–. Chm., RIBA Trust, 2003–10. Opposition spokesman, House of Lords: on educn and science, 1988–92; on foreign affairs, 1992–97; Minister of State, DfEE, 1997–2001; Minister of State (Minister for Arts), DCMS, 2001–03. Trustee: Architecture Foundn, 1991–97; Nat. Hist. Mus., 1992–97. Chairman: Great Ormond St Hosp. Trust Bd, 2009–17; British Library, 2010–18; Orbit Gp, 2013–; British Lung Foundn, 2017–; Bar Standards Bd, 2018–. Honorary Fellow: Canterbury Christchurch, 2009; Inst. of Child Health, UCL, 2016; Hon. FRIBA 2005. Hon. DLitt: Bradford, 1990; Bristol Poly., 1991; Kent, 2011; DUniv: Middlesex, 1993; Strathclyde, Leeds Metropolitan, 1996; QUB, 2007; Greenwich, 2012; Hon. LLD: Aberdeen, 1994; St Andrews, 1995; Hon Dr: Sorbonne, 1998; Rome, 2004; Hon. DSc (SocSci) London, 2016. Légion d'Honneur (France), 2016. *Publications:* Students in Conflict (jtly), 1970; A Fair Start, 1971; Education and Day Care for Young Children in Need, 1973; The Academic Labour Market (jtly), 1974; Social Policy and Administration in Britain, 1975; Disadvantage and Education (jtly), 1982; Educational Policy and Educational Inequality (jtly), 1982; Response to Adversity (jtly), 1983; Testing Children (jtly), 1983; Inside the Think Tank (jtly), 1988; Prisons and Penal Reform, 1990; Race Relations in Britain, 1997. *Address:* House of Lords, SW1A 0PW.

**BLACKWELL**, family name of **Baron Blackwell**.

**BLACKWELL, Baron** *cr* 1997 (Life Peer), of Woodcote in the co. of Surrey; **Norman Roy Blackwell**; Chairman, Lloyds Banking Group, since 2014 (non-executive Director, since 2012); *b* 29 July 1952; *s* of Albert Blackwell and Frances Blackwell (*née* Lutman); *m* 1974, Brenda Clucas; three *s* two *d. Educ:* RAM (Jun. Exhibnr); Trinity Coll., Cambridge (MA); Wharton Business Sch., Univ. of Pennsylvania (AM, MBA; PhD 1976). With Plessey Co., 1976–78; Partner, McKinsey & Co., 1978–95, elected Partner, 1984; Special Advr, Prime Minister's Policy Unit, 1986–87 (on leave of absence); Head, Prime Minister's Policy Unit, 1995–97; Dir, Gp Develt, NatWest Gp, 1997–2000; Special Advr, KPMG Corp. Finance, 2000–08. Chairman: Interserve plc, 2006–16; Scottish Widows Gp, 2012–14; non-executive Director: Dixons Gp, 2000–03; Corporate Services Gp, 2000–06; Centre for Policy Studies, 2000–13 (Chm., 2000–09); Segro (formerly Slough Estates), 2001–10; SmartStream Technologies Ltd, 2001–06; Standard Life Assurance, 2003–12; OFT, 2003–10; OFCOM, 2009–14; Halma, 2010–14; Comr, Postcomm, 2010–11. *Recreations:* classical music, walking. *Address:* c/o House of Lords, SW1A 0PW. *E:* blackwelln@parliament.uk. *Clubs:* Carlton, Royal Automobile.

**BLACKWELL, Rt Rev. Douglas Charles**; an Area (formerly Suffragan) Bishop of Toronto (Area Bishop of Trent-Durham), 1988–2003; *b* 3 June 1938; *s* of late William John Blackwell and Ethel N. Blackwell (*née* Keates); *m* 1963, Sandra Dianne Griffiths; one *s* two *d. Educ:* Wycliffe Coll., Univ. of Toronto (DipTh, LTh). Deacon 1963, priest 1964; Asst Curate, St Stephen's, Calgary, 1964; Vicar, Cochrane Mission, Diocese of Calgary, 1966; Rector, St Paul's, North Battleford, Diocese of Saskatoon, 1969; Regional Dean of Battleford, 1970; Archdeacon of Battlefords-Lloydminster, 1973; Asst Director, Aurora Conf. Centre, Diocese of Toronto, 1974; Executive Asst to Archbishop of Toronto, 1977; Canon of St James's Cathedral, Toronto, 1978; Archdeacon of York, 1986. Hon. DD Wycliffe Coll., Toronto, 1990. *Address:* 63 Glen Dhu Drive, Whitby, ON L1R 1K3, Canada. *T:* (905) 4308460.

**BLACKWELL, Prof. Jenefer Mary**; Professor of Genetics and Health, Telethon Kids Institute (formerly Telethon Institute for Child Health Research), University of Western Australia, since 2007; Affiliated Principal Investigator, Cambridge Institute for Medical Research, since 2007; Senior Scientist, Department of Pathology, University of Cambridge, since 2014; Professorial Fellow, Newnham College, Cambridge, since 1993; *b* 8 Dec. 1948; *d* of Frank Blackwell and Elsie Winifred Broadhurst; *m* 1973, Simon John Miles; one *s* one *d. Educ:* Univ. of Western Australia (BSc 1969 (1st Cl. Hons Zoology); PhD 1974 (Population Genetics)); DSc Cantab, 2010. Cons. Biologist and Res. Officer, WA Govt Depts, 1973–74; Lectr in Biol., Avery Hill Coll. of Educn, London, 1975–76; London School of Hygiene and Tropical Medicine: Res. Fellow, Ross Inst. of Tropical Hygiene, 1976–82; Wellcome Trust Sen. Lectr, Dept of Trop. Hygiene, 1982–88, Dept of Med. Parasitology, 1988–91 (and Head, Immunobiol. of Parasitic Diseases Unit); Reader, Univ. of London, 1989–91; Glaxo Prof. of Molecular Parasitology, Univ. of Cambridge, 1991–2007; Dir, Cambridge Inst. for Med. Res., 1998–2001. Faculty Mem., Molecular Biol. of Parasitism Course, Marine Biol. Labs, Wood's Hole, Mass, 1988. FMedSci 2000; FAA 2015. Hon. DSc Khartoum, 2009. *Publications:* (with D. Wakelin) Genetics of Resistance to Bacterial and Parasitic Infection, 1988. *Recreations:* music, cycling, walking. *Address:* Genetics and Health Laboratory, Telethon Kids Institute, PO Box 855, West Perth, WA 6872, Australia. *T:* (8) 63191000.

**BLACKWELL, Julian, (Toby)**; DL; President, since 1995, and Chairman, 1996–99, Blackwell Ltd; Chairman, The Blackwell Group Ltd, 1980–94; *b* 10 Jan. 1929; *s* of Sir Basil Henry Blackwell and late Marion Christine, *d* of John Soans; *m* 1953, Jennifer Jocelyn Darley Wykeham (*d* 2018); two *s* one *d. Educ:* Winchester; Trinity Coll., Oxford. Served 5th RTR, 1947–49; 21st SAS (TA), 1950–59. Dir and Chm., various Blackwell companies, 1956–2003. Chm. Council, ASLIB, 1966–68 (Vice-Pres., 1982); Co-founder and Chm., Mail Users' Assoc., 1975–78 and 1987–90; Pres., Booksellers' Assoc., 1980–82; Chairman: Thames Business Advice Centre, 1986–97; Heart of England TEC, 1989–94; Fox FM, 1989–98. Chm., Son White Meml Trust, 1991–. DL Oxon 1987, High Sheriff, 1991–92. Hon. DLitt Robert Gordon, 1997; DUniv Sheffield Hallam, 1998; Hon. DBA Oxford Brookes, 1999. *Recreations:* thinking, fighting the Eurocrats. *Address:* c/o 50 Broad Street, Oxford OX1 3BQ. *T:* (01865) 792111. *Clubs:* Special Forces; Royal Yacht Squadron; Leander (Henley); Rock and District Sports.

**BLACKWELL, Nigel Stirling**; Chairman, Blackwell Publishing Ltd, 2001–07; *b* 18 March 1947; *s* of late Richard Blackwell, DSC and Marguerite Brook Blackwell (*née* Holliday); *m* 1st, 1984, Eliza Pumpelly Mauran (*d* 1995), *d* of Frank Mauran III; one *s* one *d*; 2nd, 2005, Christina Lowry, *d* of Rolf Pasold. *Educ:* Dragon Sch., Oxford; Winchester; St Edmund Hall, Oxford (MA). Dep. Chm. and CEO, Blackwell N America, 1979–86; Jt Man. Dir, B. H. Blackwell Ltd, 1980–83 (Dir, 1974–89); Man. Dir, Blackwell Gp, 1983–89; Chm. and Man. Dir, Blackwell Retail Gp, 1983–89; Chairman: Basil Blackwell Ltd, subseq. Blackwell Publishers, 1985–2001; Blackwell Scientific, subseq. Blackwell Science, 1990–2001; Munksgaard Publishers, Copenhagen, 1992–2001. Dir, 1990–2004, Vice Pres., 2003–, Western Provident Assoc.; Chm., Richard Blackwell Scholarship Trust, 1984–2001; Sen. Trustee, Pharsalia Charitable Trust, 2007–. Mem., York Harbor Volunteer Veteran Fireman's Assoc., Maine, 2001. *Recreations:* country pursuits, swimming, boats, collecting. *Clubs:* White's; Vincent's (Oxford); Leander; York Harbor Reading Room (Maine); Dunes (Narragansett, RI).

**BLACKWELL, Tracy**; Chief Executive Officer, Pension Insurance Corporation plc, since 2015; *b* Rockford, Ill, 29 Dec. 1967; *d* of Richard Rasmussen and Mary Kathryn Two; *m* 1st, 1993, Pearse Rutledge (marr. diss. 2003); 2nd, 2004, James Blackwell; one *s. Educ:* Univ. of Illinois, Champaign-Urbana (BS Finance); Nijenrode Univ. (MBA). Goldman Sachs Internat., 1994–2003; Chief Investment Officer, Pension Insurance Corp. plc, 2006–15. Non-exec. Dir, United Trust Bank, 2013–. Hon. Treas. and Trustee, Elton John Aids Foundn, 2017–. FRSA. *Recreations:* sailing, ski-ing, cycling, dogs, gardening. *Address:* Langham, N Norfolk.

**BLACKWOOD**, family name of **Baron Dufferin and Claneboye**.

**BLACKWOOD OF NORTH OXFORD, Baroness** *cr* 2019 (Life Peer). of North Oxford in the County of Oxfordshire; **Nicola Blackwood**; Parliamentary Under Secretary of State, Department of Health and Social Care, since 2019; *b* Johannesburg, 1979; *m* 2016, Paul Bate. *Educ:* home schooled; Trinity Coll. of Music; St Anne's Coll., Oxford (BA 1st Cl. Music); Emmanuel Coll., Cambridge (MPhil Musicology). Political Unit, Cons. Res. Dept, Gen. Election, 2005; Parly researcher to Andrew Mitchell, MP, 2007. MP (C) Oxford W and Abingdon, 2010–17; contested (C) same seat 2017. PPS to Minister for Skills and Enterprise, 2013–14, for Energy, 2014–15; Parly Under-Sec. of State, DoH, 2016–17. Mem., Home Affairs Select Cttee, 2010–15; Chm., Sci. and Technol. Select Cttee, 2015–16; Chair, All Party Gp on Women, Peace and Security, 2010–17. Vice Chm., Cons. Party, 2010–13. Policy Fellow, Public, 2017–. Member: Adv. Bd, Eagle Genomics, 2017–; Bd of Dirs, CaSE, 2017–; Chair, Human Tissue Authy, 2018–.

**BLACKWOOD, (Andrew) Guy**; QC 2014; *b* 5 April 1970; *s* of Roger Arthur Blackwood and Carolyn Mary Blackwood (*née* Crichton, later Markham); *m* 2003, Francesca Muscau; one *d. Educ:* Stowe Sch.; University Coll. London (LLB Laws). Called to the Bar, Inner Temple, 1997; in practice as barrister, specialising in commercial law, insurance, energy and banking, 1997–. *Publications:* (jtly) Chalmers' Marine Insurance Act 1906, 11th edn 2015. *Recreations:* Italian culture, reading, travel, antique books. *Address:* Quadrant Chambers, Quadrant House, 10 Fleet Street, EC4Y 1AU.

**BLAGDEN, Emma Rosemary**; *see* Read, E. R.

**BLAHNIK, Manolo**, Hon. CBE 2007; designer of shoes and furniture, since 1973; Director, Manolo Blahnik International Ltd, since 1973; *b* Canary Is, 28 Nov. 1942; *s* of late E. Blahnik and of Manuela Blahnik. *Educ:* Univ. of Geneva; Louvre Art Sch., Paris. Hon. RDI 2001. Hon. DArts RCA, 2001; Hon. Dr Bath Spa, 2012. Retrospective exhibn, Design Mus., London, 2003. Fashion Council of America Award, 1987, 1990, 1997; Balenciaga Award, 1989; Antonio Lopez Award, Hispanic Inst., Washington, 1990; British Fashion Council Award, 1990, 1999; American Leather New York Award, 1991; Silver Slipper Award, Houston Mus. of Fine Art, 1999 (first awarded to a shoe designer); Neiman Marcus Award, USA, 2000; Golden Needle Award, Spain, 2001; Medalla de Oro al Mérito en las Bellas Artes, Spain, 2002; Medalla de Oro de Canarias, Spain, 2003; Shoe Designer of the Year, Footwear News, 2003; Accessory Designer of the Year, Lycra British Style Awards, 2003; Pinnacle in Art and Design Award, Pratt Inst., NY, 2005; Rodeo Drive Walk of Style Award, Beverly Hills, 2008; Best Internat. Professional Aim Prix, Marie Claire Prix de la Mode, Spain, 2008; Felicidad Duce Fashion Prize, Spain, 2010; André Leon Talley Lifetime Achievement Award, Savannah Coll. of Art and Design, 2011; Lifetime Achievement Award, Footwear News, 2011; Outstanding Achievement in Fashion Award, British Fashion Awards, 2012; Premio Nacional de Diseño de Moda, Spain, 2012; Couture Council Award for Artistry of Fashion, 2015; Luxury Legend Award, Walpole British Luxury Awards, 2018. *Publications:* Manolo Blahnik: Drawings, 2003; Manolo's New Shoes, 2010; (illustrator) Manolo Blahnik and the Tale of the Elves and the Shoemaker, by Camilla Morton; Fleeting Gestures and Obsessions, 2015; *relevant publications:* Manolo Blahnik, by Colin McDowell, 2000; Blahnik by Boman: a photographic conversation, by Eric Boman, 2005. *Recreations:* travel, painting. *Address:* (office) 30 Welbeck Street, W1G 8ER. *T:* (020) 7352 8622.

**BLAIN, Francis Rene**; High Commissioner (formerly Ambassador) of The Gambia to the Court of St James's, since 2017; *b* Banjul, 8 Nov. 1943; *s* of Rene Blain and Christiana Blain; one *s* four *d. Educ:* Univ. of Sierra Leone (BA Educn). Ambassador and Perm. Rep. of The Gambia to the UN, 1982–84; Principal Officer, UNDP Office, Islamabad, 1984–85; UNDP Resident Rep. in Liberia, 1985–89; Dep. Dir, Special Unit for Tech. Cooperation among Developing Countries, 1987–2002; Special Rep. of Econ. Community of W African States, Liberia, 2003–05. *Recreations:* playing lawn tennis, watching movies. *Address:* 35 The Avenue, NW6 7NR. *T:* 07448 836638. *Club:* Fajara (Banjul).

**BLAIN, Prof. Peter George**, CBE 2002; PhD; FRCP, FRCPE, FFOM; CBiol, FRSB; FBTS; Professor of Environmental Medicine, University of Newcastle upon Tyne, and Consultant Physician, Newcastle Hospitals NHS Trust, since 1986; Director: Medical Toxicology Centre, since 2006; Health Protection Research Unit in Chemical and Radiation Threats and Hazards, National Institute of Health Research, since 2014; Consultant in Emergency Response Medicine, Public Health England (formerly Health Protection Agency), since 2009; *b* 15 March 1951; *s* of Reginald Blain and Margaret (*née* Graham); *m* 1977, Patricia Anne Crawford; two *s* one *d. Educ:* Univ. of Newcastle upon Tyne (BMedSci; MB, BS; PhD 1988). MFOM 1990, FFOM 1997; FRCP 1990; FRCPE 1991; CBiol 1986; FRSB (FIBiol 1989). Jun. hosp. doctor, Royal Victoria Infirmary, Newcastle upon Tyne, 1975–79; University of Newcastle upon Tyne: Lectr in Clinical Pharmacol., 1979–80; Wellcome Res. Fellow in Clinical Pharmacol. and Neurology, 1980–81; First Asst in Clinical Pharmacol., 1981–85; Hd, Biomed. Scis and Human Toxicol. Res., ICI plc, 1985–86. Consultant Physician: Freeman Gp of Hosps NHS Trust (formerly Freeman Hosp.), 1988–; Royal Victoria Infirmary NHS Trust (formerly Royal Victoria Inf.), 1988–; Newcastle Hosps NHS Trust, 1998–; Consultant in Envmtl Medicine and Toxicol., Northern and Yorks RHA, 1992–. Hd, Med. Toxicol., HPA, 2004–10. Clin. Advr to Defence Med. Services, MoD, 1995–; UK Expert Advr on Weapons of Mass Destruction to Sec. Gen. of UN, 2010–; UK Delegate to G8 Global Health Security Gp, 2011–. Medical Advisor: to ICRC, 2012–; to WHO, 2013–. Chairman: Chem., Biol, Radiol and Nuclear Defence and Human Scis Bd (formerly Chem., Biol and Human Technologies Bd), MoD, 1994–; Adv. Gp on Military Medicine (formerly Med. Countermeasures), MoD, 1998–; Adv. Gp on Military and Emergency Response Medicine, MoD and DHSC (formerly DoH), 2012–; Member: Defence Scientific Adv. Council, MoD, 1994–; Scientific Adv. Gp on the Medical Implications of Less-Lethal Technologies, 2011–. FBTS 2007. *Publications:* contrib. to textbooks in toxicol. and medicine; res. papers in acad. jls in toxicol. *Recreations:* hill walking, extreme tourism. *Address:* Medical Toxicology Centre, Wolfson Building, Medical School, Newcastle upon Tyne NE2 4AA. *T:* (0191) 222 7195, *Fax:* (0191) 222 6442. *E:* p.g.blain@ncl.ac.uk.

**BLAIN, Sophie Clodagh Mary**; *see* Andreae, S. C. M.

**BLAIR**, family name of **Baron Blair of Boughton**.

**BLAIR OF BOUGHTON, Baron** *cr* 2010 (Life Peer), of Boughton in the County of Cheshire; **Ian Warwick Blair**, Kt 2003; QPM 1999; Chairman, Thames Valley Partnership, 2009–16 (Patron, since 2016); Commissioner, Metropolitan Police, 2005–08 (Deputy Commissioner, 2000–05); *b* 19 March 1953; *yr s* of late Francis James Blair and Sheila Kathleen Blair; *m* 1980, Felicity Jane White; one *s* one *d. Educ:* Wrekin Coll. Harvard High Sch., LA; Christ Church, Oxford (MA; Hon. Student, 2005). Joined Metropolitan Police, 1974; uniform and CID posts, 1974–91; Chief Supt, SO to HM Chief Inspector of Constabulary, 1991–93; Asst Chief Constable, 1994–97, des. Dep. to Chief

Constable, 1997, Thames Valley Police; Chief Constable, Surrey Police, 1998–2000. Mem., Commn on Assisted Dying, 2010–12. Visiting Fellow: Internat. Centre for Advanced Studies, NY Univ., 1998; Nuffield Coll., Oxford, 2001; John Jay Coll., NY, 2009; Hon. Vis. Prof., Univ. of Northampton, 2015–16. Trustee: St Paul's Cathedral Foundn, 2010–13; Shakespeare's Globe Theatre, 2010–18; Woolf Inst. of Abrahamic Faiths, 2010– (Chm., 2016–); Longford Trust, 2010–; Michael Sieff Foundn, 2013–; Chm. of Trustees, Helen and Douglas House, 2018–. Freeman, City of London, 2009. Hon DLaws Lincoln, 2013. *Publications:* Investigating Rape: a new approach for police, 1985; Policing Controversy (memoir), 2009. *Recreations:* tennis, golf, theatre. *Clubs:* Athenæum, MCC.
*See also R. D. Blair.*

**BLAIR, Rt Hon. Anthony Charles Lynton, (Tony);** PC 1994; Senior Advisor, JPMorgan Chase, since 2008; Chairman, European Council on Tolerance and Reconciliation, since 2015; Founder and Chairman, Tony Blair Institute for Global Change, since 2016; *b* 6 May 1953; *s* of late Leo Charles Lynton Blair and Hazel Blair; *m* 1980, Cherie Booth, *qv*; three *s* one *d*. *Educ:* Durham Choristers School; Fettes College, Edinburgh; St John's College, Oxford. Called to the Bar, Lincoln's Inn, 1976; Hon. Bencher, 1994. MP (Lab) Sedgefield, 1983–June 2007. Leader of the Opposition, 1994–97; Prime Minister and First Lord of the Treasury, 1997–2007. Leader of the Labour Party, 1994–2007. Quartet Representative, 2007–15. Founder and Patron: Tony Blair Sports Foundn, 2007–17; Tony Blair Faith Foundn, 2008–; Africa Governance Initiative, 2008–. US Presidential Medal of Freedom, 2009. *Publications:* New Britain: my vision of a young country, 1996; The Third Way, 1998; A Journey (memoirs), 2010. *Address:* PO Box 60519, London, W2 7JU. *Club:* Fishburn Working Men's.
*See also Hon. Sir W. J. L. Blair.*

**BLAIR, Bruce Graeme Donald;** QC 1989; a Deputy High Court Judge, 1990–2016; *b* 12 April 1946; *s* of late Dr Donald Alexander Sangster Blair, MA, MD, DPM and Eleanor Violet Blair (*née* Van Ryneveld); *m* 1970, Susanne Blair (*née* Hartung); three *d* (and one *s* decd). *Educ:* Harrow School; Magdalene College, Cambridge. Called to the Bar, Middle Temple, 1969, Bencher, 1997; Hd of Chambers, 1 Hare Court, 1997–2007. Chm., British Horseracing Authy Appeal Bd, 2000–. Comr, Royal Court of Jersey, 2001–. *Publications:* Practical Matrimonial Precedents (jtly), 1989. *Recreations:* bridge, golf, turf. *Address:* 1 Hare Court, Temple, EC4Y 7BE. *T:* (020) 7797 7070. *Club:* MCC.

**BLAIR, Cherie;** *see* Booth, C.

**BLAIR, Hew David;** Chairman, Justerini & Brooks, since 2007 (Director of Buying, 1986–2012); *b* Surrey, 10 Feb. 1951; *s* of David Arthur Blair and Elizabeth Blair (*née* Morton); *m* 1980, Joanna McCorquodale; three *d*. *Educ:* Harrow Sch.; Bordeaux Univ. Pres., Vignobles Internationaux, 2010–15. Mem., Royal Household Wine Cttee, 2007–; Pres., Royal Warrant Holders Assoc., 2012 (Vice Pres., 2011–12). Mem., Queen's Body Guard for Scotland, Royal Co. of Archers. *Recreations:* fishing, shooting, golf, garden design, wine. *Address:* Leadervale House, Earlston, Berwickshire TD4 6AJ; 15 Thurloe Court, SW3 6SB. *T:* (office) (020) 7484 6400. *E:* hew.blair@justerinis.com. *Clubs:* White's; Honourable Company of Edinburgh Golfers.

**BLAIR, Ian Charles;** non-executive Audit Director, Rushcliffe Clinical Commissioning Group, since 2012; *b* 31 Aug. 1947; *s* of John Blair and Robina Poppy Blair (*née* Carr); *m* 1st, 1974, Jennifer Mary Hodgson (*d* 2007); one *s* one *d*; 2nd, 2015, Veronica Philomena Edkins. *Educ:* Liberton High Sch., Edinburgh; Open Univ. (BA 1995). CPFA (IPFA 1969). Accountant, Midlothian CC, 1964–72; Sen. Accountant, Scottish Special Housing Assoc., 1972–75; Sen. Asst Treas., Lothian Health Bd, 1975–81; City Treasurer: Bath CC, 1981–91; Nottingham CC, 1991–2002; public finance consultant, 2002–12; Chm., Ian and Jennifer Blair & Co. Ltd, 2002–. Treas., Derbys Probation Bd, 2005–11. Advr, ADC, 1992–97. Lay Mem., Nat. Diabetes Footcare Audit, 2017. Chm., S Wales and West, CIPFA, 1991; Pres., Audit Cttee, Eurocities, 1999–2002; Mem., Exec., Soc. Municipal Treasurers, 1999–2002. Sen. Res. Associate, Warwick Business Sch., 2007–13. Internat. develt work for British Council, World Bank, UN. Volunteer researcher, Heritage Res. Proj., Notts CCC, 2015–. *Publications:* contribs to prof. jls, govt research papers. *Recreations:* family, sports (Hearts FC and Bath RFC), theatre. *Address:* 15 Killerton Park Drive, West Bridgford, Notts NG2 7SB.

**BLAIR, John;** *see* Blair, W. J.

**BLAIR, Jonathan Roy,** CBE 2015; film and television producer and director; Founder, Jon Blair Film Co., since 1984; *b* Cape Town, 30 Oct. 1950; *s* of Maurice and Dorothy Blair; *m* 1st, 1978, Judy Graham (marr. diss.); one *s* one *d*; 2nd, 2004, Yvonne Sellins; two *s*. *Educ:* St Stithians Coll., Johannesburg; St Paul's Sch., London; London Sch. of Econs and Political Sci. (BSc Econ)). Journalist, film and TV producer, director and writer; covered wars in Africa, ME and Asia, 1970s and 1980s; Co-founder and Dir, Spitting Image Prodns, 1983–86; *films* include: Schindler, 1984 (BAFTA Flaherty Documentary Award, 1984); Spalding Gray's Monster in a Box, 1992; Anne Frank Remembered, 1995 (Internat. Emmy Award, 1995; Oscar for Best Documentary, 1996; Dist. Achievement Award, Internat. Documentary Assoc., 1996); Dancing with the Devil, 2009; *television* includes: This Week: South Africa There is no Crisis, 1976 (producer); Spitting Image, 1984–86 (co-founder, co-creator, producer and exec. producer); Do You Mean There Are Still Real Cowboys?, 1985; The Kimberley Carlile Inquiry, 1986; The Age of Terror series, 2002; Reporters at War series, 2004 (Emmy Award (jtly), 2005); Ochberg's Orphans, 2007; Bahrain Shouting in the Dark, 2011 (exec. producer) (Amnesty Media Award for Internat. TV and Radio (jtly), Robert F. Kennedy Journalism Award (jtly), 2012); *theatre* includes: writer and dir, The Biko Inquest, NY, 1978, London, 1984. Hon. PhD Stockton, NJ, 1994. *E:* jonrblair@gmail.com.

**BLAIR, Michael Campbell;** barrister in independent practice; *b* 26 Aug. 1941; *s* of Sir Alastair Campbell Blair, KCVO and Catriona Hatchard Blair (*née* Orr); *m* 1966, Halldóra Isabel (*née* Tunnard); one *s*. *Educ:* Rugby Sch.; Clare Coll., Cambridge (MA, LLM); Yale Univ., USA (Mellon Fellow; MA). Called to the Bar, Middle Temple, 1965 (Harmsworth Law Scholar); Bencher, 1995, Dep. Treas., 2007, Treas., 2008. Lord Chancellor's Dept, 1966–87. Securities and Investments Board: General Counsel, 1987–93; Head of Policy and Legal Affairs, 1993–95; Dep. Chief Exec. and Gen. Counsel, 1996–98; Gen. Counsel to Bd, FSA, 1998–2000; Chairman: PIA, 2000–02; IMRO, 2000–02; SFA, 2001–02. Dep. Chm., 2007–08, Chm., 2008–09, SWX Swiss Exchange Europe Ltd. Dir, Financial Services Compensation Scheme Ltd, 2000–05. Mem., Competition Appeal Tribunal, 2000–16; Chm., Review Body on Doctors' and Dentists' Remuneration, 2001–07; Pres., Guernsey Financial Services Tribunal, 2002–08; Member, Board: Dubai FSA, 2003–13; Chicago Mercantile Exchange (London) Ltd, 2013–17. Chairman: Bar Assoc. for Commerce, Finance and Industry, 1990–91; Bar Conf., 1993; Member: Gen. Council of the Bar, 1989–98 (Chm., Professional Standards Cttee, 1994; Treas., 1995–98); Council of Legal Educn, 1992–97. Hon. QC 1996. FRSA 1992. *Publications:* Sale of Goods Act 1979, 1980; Financial Services: the new core rules, 1991; (ed) Blackstone's Guide to the Bank of England Act 1998, 1998; (ed) Blackstone's Guide to the Financial Services and Markets Act 2000, 2001, 2nd edn 2009; (ed) Butterworths Financial Regulation Service, 2002–07; (ed) Financial Services, Halsbury's Laws of England, vol. 18(i), 4th edn 2003; (ed jtly) Financial Services Law, 2006, 4th edn 2018; (ed jtly) Financial Markets and Exchanges Law, 2007, 2nd edn 2012; legal articles in jls. *Address:* 3 Burbage Road, SE24 9HJ. *T:* (020) 7274 7614. *Club:* Athenæum.
*See also R. O. Blair.*

**BLAIR, Capt. Neil;** *see* Blair, Capt. R. N.

**BLAIR, Neil Lyndon Marc;** Founding Partner, The Blair Partnership, since 2011; *b* London, 21 Sept. 1966; *s* of Dennis and Cynthia Blair; *m* Debra; two *s*. *Educ:* Exeter Coll., Oxford (MA Juris. 1989); Coll. of Law, Guildford. Admitted solicitor, 1990; Solicitor, Linklaters & Paines, 1992–96; Hd, Business Affairs, Europe, Warner Bros Prodns, 1996–2001; Partner and Literary Agent, Christopher Little Literary Agency, 2001–11. Dir, Pottermore Ltd, 2011–. Trustee, Lumos, 2010– (Chm., 2014–). *Address:* The Blair Partnership, PO Box 7828, W1A 4GE. *T:* (020) 7504 2520. *E:* neil.blair@theblairpartnership.com.

**BLAIR, Sir Patrick David H.;** *see* Hunter Blair.

**BLAIR, Peter Michael;** QC 2006; **His Honour Judge Blair;** a Circuit Judge, since 2014; a Senior Circuit Judge, since 2017; *b* 24 Aug. 1961; *s* of Michael Blair and Joan (*née* Goodwin); *m* 1984, Sharon Atherton; one *s* two *d*. *Educ:* Princess Sophie Primary Sch.; Addis Ababa; Brocksford Hall; Monkton Combe Sch.; Univ. of Oxford (BA Juris.). Called to the Bar, Inner Temple, 1983, Bencher; in practice as barrister, Guildhall Chambers, Bristol, 1984–2014; Hd of Chambers, 2006–14. Asst Recorder, 1998–2000; Recorder, 2000–14. Mem., Western Circuit Cttee, 1991–97. Mem., Bath CC, 1988–92. *Recreations:* landscape oil painting, poultry and pig keeping, gadgets. *Address:* Bristol Crown Court, The Law Courts, Small Street, Bristol BS1 1DA. *Club:* Royal Ocean Racing.

**BLAIR, Richard David, (Sandy),** CBE 2005; DL; Chair, Remuneration Board, National Assembly for Wales, 2013–15 (Member, 2010–15); *b* Hull, 15 Aug. 1946; *s* of late Francis James Blair and Sheila Kathleen Blair (*née* Law); *m* 1971, Susan Elizabeth Crump; two *s* one *d*. *Educ:* Bromsgrove Sch.; Durham Univ. Admitted as solicitor, 1969; private solicitor, 1969–74; local govt solicitor, 1974–77, local govt manager, 1977–84, Knowsley MBC; Chief Executive: Bassetlaw DC, 1984–92; Newport BC, 1992–96; Newport CC, 1995–2000; Dir, Welsh Local Govt Assoc., 2001–04. Non-exec. Dir, HSE, 2006–12. Chair, Monmouth Diocesan Bd of Finance, 2006–15; Mem., Governing Body and Representative Body, Church in Wales, 2006–17. Gov., UWIC, 2004–10. Pres., Solace, 1999–2000. DL Gwent, 2014. *Recreations:* minor charity trusteeships, watching Rugby. *Address:* Orchard House, Llantrisant, Usk NP15 1LG. *T:* (01291) 673239. *E:* rd_sandyblair@hotmail.com. *Club:* Newport Rugby.
*See also Baron Blair of Boughton.*

**BLAIR, Capt. (Robert) Neil,** RN; CVO 2001 (LVO 1997); Private Secretary, Treasurer and Extra Equerry to the Duke of York, 1990–2001; Private Secretary to Princess Alexandra, the Hon. Lady Ogilvy, 1995–2001; *b* 14 July 1936; *s* of Harley Blair and Jane Blair (*née* Tarr); *m* 1960, Barbara Jane, *d* of Ian and Monica Rankin; two *s* one *d*. *Educ:* St John's Coll., Johannesburg; RNC, Dartmouth. Joined RN, 1954: served HMY Britannia, 1958–59 and 1970–71; FAA, 1961–70; in command: HMS Shavington, 1965–67; HMS Ashanti, 1972–74; HMS Royal Arthur, 1978; Comdr, BRNC, Dartmouth, 1979–80; Naval and Air Attaché, Athens, 1982–85; Defence and Naval Attaché, The Hague, 1986–89. Younger Brother, Trinity House, 1991. *Recreations:* photography, cricket, hill-walking. *Clubs:* Army and Navy, MCC.

**BLAIR, Robin Orr,** CVO 2008 (LVO 1999); Lord Lyon King of Arms and Secretary of the Order of the Thistle, 2001–08, Angus Herald Extraordinary, since 2008; *b* 1 Jan. 1940; *s* of Sir Alastair Campbell Blair, KCVO and Catriona Hatchard Blair (*née* Orr); *m* 1st, 1972, Elizabeth Caroline McCallum Webster (*d* 2000); two *s* one *d*; 2nd, 2005, Lel Simpson. *Educ:* Cargilfield; Rugby; St Andrews Univ. (MA); Edinburgh Univ. (LLB). WS 1965. Partner: Davidson & Syme WS, 1967–72; Dundas & Wilson CS, 1972–97 (Managing Partner, 1976–83, 1988–91); Turcan Connell WS, 1997–2000. Chm., Top Flight Leisure Gp, 1987–98 (non-exec. Dir, 1977–98); non-exec. Dir, Tullis Russell & Co. Ltd, 1977–98. Chm., Scottish Solicitors' Staff Pension Scheme, 1985–91. Hon. Sec., Assoc. of Edinburgh Royal Tradesmen, 1966–91. Purse Bearer to Lord High Comr to Gen. Assembly, C of S, 1988–2002. Chm., Scotland's Churches Scheme, 1997–2013; Pres., Scotland's Churches Trust, 2017– (Chm., 2013–15). Gen. Council Assessor, Ct of Edinburgh Univ., 2003–07. Mem., Royal Co. of Archers. *Address:* 2 Blacket Place, Edinburgh EH9 1RL. *T:* (0131) 667 2906. *Clubs:* New (Edinburgh); Hon. Company of Edinburgh Golfers.
*See also M. C. Blair.*

**BLAIR, Sandy;** *see* Blair, R. D.

**BLAIR, Rt Hon. Tony;** *see* Blair, Rt Hon. A. C. L.

**BLAIR, Hon. Sir William (James Lynton),** Kt 2008; a Judge of the High Court of Justice, Queen's Bench Division, 2008–17; Professor of Financial Law and Ethics, Queen Mary University of London, since 2017; *b* 31 March 1950; *s* of late Leo Charles Lynton Blair and Hazel Elizabeth (*née* Corscadden); *m* 1982, Katy Tse. *Educ:* Fettes Coll., Edinburgh; Balliol Coll., Oxford (BA 1971). Called to the Bar, Lincoln's Inn, 1972, Bencher, 2003; QC 1994; Asst Recorder, 1996–98; Recorder, 1998–2008; Dep. High Court Judge, 2003–08. Vis. Prof. of Law, LSE, 1994–. Part-time Chm., Financial Services and Mkts Tribunal, 2001–10; Chm., Qatar Financial Centre Regulatory Tribunal, 2006–11. Member: Internat. Monetary Law Cttee, 1996– (Chm., 2004–), Council, British Br., 2000–, Internat. Law Assoc.; Financial Mkts Law Cttee, 2008–; Jt Bd of Appeal, European Supervisory Authorities, 2011– (Pres., 2012–). Trustee, British Inst. of Internat. and Comparative Law, 2009–. Hon. Fellow, Soc. for Advanced Legal Studies, 1997. *Publications:* (ed) Encyclopaedia of Banking Law, 1982; (jtly) Banking and the Financial Services Act, 1993, 3rd edn, as Banking and Financial Services Regulation, 2002; (ed) Bullen, Leake and Jacob's Precedents of Pleading, 16th edn, 2008; (ed) Banks and Financial Crime, 2008; contrib. other legal books and jls. *Recreations:* travel, walking. *Club:* Athenæum.
*See also Rt Hon. A. C. L. Blair.*

**BLAIR, Prof. (William) John,** DPhil; FBA 2008; FSA; historian and archaeologist; Fellow and Praelector in History, Queen's College, Oxford, since 1981; Professor of Medieval History and Archaeology, University of Oxford, since 2006; *b* Woking, 4 March 1955; *s* of late Claude Blair, CVO, OBE and Joan Mary Greville Blair (*née* Drinkwater); *m* 2005, (Terttu) Kanerva Heikkinen; one *s* one *d*. *Educ:* St John's Sch., Leatherhead; Brasenose Coll., Oxford (BA 1st Cl. 1976; DPhil 1983). FSA 1983. Freeman, Cutlers' Co., 2004, Liveryman, 2009. *Publications:* (ed) Minsters and Parish Churches, 1988; (ed with N. Ramsay) English Medieval Industries, 1991; Early Medieval Surrey, 1991; (ed with R. Sharpe) Pastoral Care before the Parish, 1992; Anglo-Saxon Oxfordshire, 1994; (ed with B. Golding) The Cloister and the World, 1996; (ed jtly) The Blackwell Encyclopaedia of Anglo-Saxon England, 1999; The Church in Anglo-Saxon Society, 2005; (ed) Waterways and Canal-Building in Medieval England, 2007; Building Anglo-Saxon England, 2018;

contribs to books and jls. *Recreations:* travel, landscape and architecture, reading, listening to music. *Address:* Queen's College, Oxford OX1 4AW. *T:* (01865) 279120. *E:* john.blair@queens.ox.ac.uk.

**BLAIS, Hon. Jean Jacques;** PC (Can.) 1976; QC (Can.) 1978; Counsel, MBM Intellectual Property Law LLP (formerly Marusyk, Miller & Swain), Ottawa, since 1999; *b* 27 June 1940; *m* 1968, Maureen Ahearn; two *s* one *d. Educ:* Secondary Sch., Sturgeon Falls; Univ. of Ottawa (BA, LLB, LLM). Professional lawyer. MP (L) Nipissing, Ontario, 1972, re-elected 1974, 1979, 1980; defeated Sept. 1984; Parliamentary Sec. to Pres. of Privy Council, 1975; Post Master General, 1976; Solicitor General, 1978; Minister of Supply and Services, and Receiver General, 1980; Minister of Nat. Defence, 1983–84. Lectr in Private Internat. Law, Ottawa Univ., 1986–88. Dir, Canada Israel Industrial R & D Foundn, 1994–2008. Mem., Security and Intelligence Review Cttee, 1984–91; Dep. Chm., Provisional Election Commn, Bosnia and Herzegovina, 1998; Head of Mission: Elections Canada/Internat. Foundn of Election Systems mission to Afghanistan, 2003; Internat. Foundn for Electoral Systems, Iraq, 2003. Chm., Canadian Inst. of Strategic Studies, 1993–2003, 2004–05; Chm. Emeritus, Pearson Internat. Peacekeeping Center, 2003– (Chm., 1994–2003); Director: Canadian Parly Center, 2005–13 (Vice-Pres., 2010–13); Conference of Defence Assocs Inst., 2008–12. Chm., Heart Inst., Univ. of Ottawa, 2005–11 (Dir, 1995–2003); Mem. Bd of Dirs, Institut du Savoir, Montfort Hosp., 2016–18. Hon DLitt Nipissing, 2007. *Recreations:* golf, snooker. *Address:* (office) 275 Slater Street, 14th Floor, Ottawa, ON K1P 5H9, Canada. *T:* and *Fax:* (613) 5670762. *E:* jjblais@mbm.com.

**BLAIZE, Beverley Amari;** health practitioner; Deputy Chair, Commission for Racial Equality, 2000–03; *b* 9 Aug. 1949; *d* of Edmund Blaize and Jane John-Baptist; *m* 1974, Leslie Bernard; one *d. Educ:* Univ. of Westminster (BA Hons); De Montfort Univ. (MA). Founder Trustee and CEO, Windsor Fellowship, 1985–95; Advr to Kagiso Trust, 1995–96, Man. Trustee, Nations Trust, 1995–98, RSA. Trustee, Esmée Fairbairn Foundn, 2003–06. *Publications:* The Homecoming: journey of the orphan child, 2006. *Recreations:* writing, yoga, cooking. *Address:* 1 Hydeside Gardens, Lower Edmonton, N9 9RP.

**BLAKE, Alison Mary,** CMG 2018; HM Diplomatic Service; Ambassador to the Islamic Republic of Afghanistan, since 2019; *b* London; *d* of Raymond J. Blake and Barbara M. Blake; *m* Col Peter A. Henry, US Army (retd). *Educ:* Roan Sch. for Girls, Greenwich; Merton Coll., Oxford (MA Jt Hons Ancient and Modern Hist. 1980). Archaeologist with Dept of Urban Archaeol., Mus. of London, English Heritage and GLC, 1983–87; asst to music advr, RNIB, 1987; asst, Centre for Econ. Policy Res., 1988; MoD, 1989–95, incl. Asst Private Sec. to Sec. of State for Defence; entered FCO, 1996; First Sec., UK Delegn to NATO, Brussels, 1996–99; Dep. Hd, Eastern Adriatic Dept, FCO, 1999–2001; First Sec., Washington, 2001–05; Head: Foreign and Develt Policy, Cabinet Office (on secondment), 2006–07; Conflict Gp, FCO, 2007–11; Dep. High Comr, Islamabad, 2011–14; High Comr to Bangladesh, 2016–19. *Address:* c/o Foreign and Commonwealth Office, King Charles Street, SW1A 2AH.

**BLAKE, Prof. Andrew,** PhD; FRS 2005; FREng, FIET, FIEEE; Consultant in Artificial Intelligence, since 2015; Chair, Samsung AI Centre, Cambridge, since 2018; Honorary Fellow, Alan Turing Institute, since 2018 (Director, 2015–18); Fellow, Clare Hall, Cambridge, since 1998; *b* 12 March 1956; *s* of Alan Geoffrey Blake and Judith Anne Blake (*née* Hart); *m* 1982, Fiona Anne-Marie Hewitt; one *s* one *d. Educ:* Rugby Sch.; Trinity Coll., Cambridge (MA); Univ. of Edinburgh (PhD 1983). FIET (FIEE 1994); FREng (FEng 1998); FIEEE 2008. Kennedy Meml Fellow, MIT, 1977–78; Research Scientist, Ferranti Edinburgh, 1978–80; University of Edinburgh: Res. Associate, 1980–83; Lectr in Computer Sci., 1983–87; Royal Soc. Res. Fellow, 1984–87; University of Oxford: Lectr in Image Processing, 1987–96; Fellow, Exeter Coll., 1987–99; Prof. of Engrg Sci., 1996–99; Royal Soc. Sen. Res. Fellow, 1998–99; Vis. Prof. of Engrg, 1999–; Microsoft Research Cambridge: Distinguished Scientist (formerly Sen. Res. Scientist, later Principal Res. Scientist), 1999–2015; Partner, 2005–11; Dep. Man. Dir, 2008–10; Laboratory Dir, 2010–15. Honorary Professor: of Informatics, Univ. of Edinburgh, 2006–07; of Machine Intelligence, Univ. of Cambridge, 2007–. Gibbs Lect., Amer. Math. Soc., 2014. Mem., EPSRC, 2012–16. Mem. Council, Royal Soc., 2010–12. Hon. DSc Edinburgh, 2012; Hon. DEng Sheffield, 2013. Marr Prize, IEEE, 2001; Silver Medal, 2006, (jtly) MacRobert Award, 2011, RAEng; Mountbatten Medal, IET, 2007; Lovelace Medal, BCS, 2016. *Publications:* (with A. Zisserman) Visual Reconstruction, 1987; (with T. Troscianko) AI and the Eye, 1990; (with A. Yuille) Active Vision, 1992; (with M. Isard) Active Contours, 1998; (jtly) Markov Random Fields for Vision and Image Processing, 2011; articles on machine vision, robotics, visual psychology. *Address:* Clare Hall, Herschel Road, Cambridge CB3 9AL.

**BLAKE, His Honour Andrew Nicholas Hubert;** a Circuit Judge, 1999–2016; *b* 18 Aug. 1946; *s* of late John Berchmans Blake and Beryl Mary Blake; *m* 1978, Joy Ruth Shevloff; one *s. Educ:* Ampleforth Coll.; Hertford Coll., Oxford (MA Hist.). Called to the Bar, Inner Temple, 1971; in practice in Manchester, 1972–99. Mem. Cttee, Council of Circuit Judges, 2004–08. *Recreations:* ski-ing, fishing, cycling, the Turf. *Club:* Norbury Fishing.

**BLAKE, Sir Charles Valentine Bruce,** 19th Bt *cr* 1622, *of* Menlough, Galway; *b* 13 July 1994; *s* of Sir Anthony Teilo Bruce Blake, 18th Bt and of Geraldine Blake (*née* Shnaps); *S* father, 2014, but his name does not appear on the Official Roll of the Baronetage. *Heir:* cousin Jonathan Luttrell Blake [*b* 5 Feb. 1953; *m* 1st, 1977, Eleanora Elizabeth Mostert (marr. diss. 1988); three *d;* 2nd, 1990, Valerie Anne Boasman; two *d*].

**BLAKE, Prof. Christopher,** CBE 1991; FRSE; Chairman, Glenrothes Development Corporation, 1987–96; *b* 28 April 1926; *s* of George Blake and Eliza Blake; *m* 1951, Elizabeth McIntyre (*d* 2009); two *s* two *d. Educ:* Dollar Academy; St Andrews Univ. (MA 1950; PhD 1965). Served in Royal Navy, 1944–47. Teaching posts, Bowdoin Coll., Maine, and Princeton Univ., 1951–53; Asst, Edinburgh Univ., 1953–55; Stewarts & Lloyds Ltd, 1955–60; Lectr and Sen. Lectr, Univ. of St Andrews, 1960–67; Sen. Lectr and Prof. of Economics, 1967–74, Bonar Prof. of Applied Econs, 1974–88, Univ. of Dundee. Dir, Alliance Trust plc, 1974–94; Chm., William Low & Co. plc, 1985–90 (Dir, 1980–90). Member: Council for Applied Science in Scotland, 1978–86; Royal Commn on Envmtl Pollution, 1980–86. Treasurer, RSE, 1986–89. *Publications:* articles in economic and other jls. *Recreation:* golf. *Address:* 7 Provost Niven Close, St Andrews, Fife KY16 9BL. *T:* (01334) 473840. *Club:* Royal and Ancient (St Andrews).

**BLAKE, Clifford Douglas,** AO 2002 (AM 1988); PhD; FAIAS; Vice-Chancellor, University of Adelaide, 2001–02; *b* 27 Aug. 1937; *s* of William Oscar Blake and Isobel Florence Blake (*née* Keown); partner, 1988, Stanley Leslie Champley. *Educ:* Muswellbrook High Sch.; Univ. of Sydney (BScAgr 1st Cl. Hons; Univ. Medal); Univ. of London (PhD). University of Sydney: Sir Benjamin Fuller Travelling Schol., 1959–61; Lectr and Sen. Lectr in Plant Pathology, 1963–70; Wilson Fellow, St Andrew's Coll., 1963–71; foundation Principal, Riverina College of Advanced Educn, subseq. renamed Riverina-Murray Inst. of Higher Educn, 1971–90; Vice-Chancellor, Charles Sturt Univ., 1990–2001. Chm., Bd of Dirs, S. P. Jain Sch. of Global Mgt, 2012–. Pres., Aust. Higher Educn Industrial Assoc., 1992–99; Member, Board of Directors: Open Learning Agency of Australia Pty, 1993–96; Australian Vice Chancellors' Cttee, 1994–99; Convenor, NSW Vice Chancellors' Cttee, 1996–98. Member: NSW Bd, Vocational and Tech. Educn, 2001–02; NSW Admin. Appeals Tribunal, 2002–10. Gov., Commonwealth of Learning, 1992–2000; Chm., Nat. Cttee on Distance Educn, 1994–95. Freeman, City of Wagga Wagga, 1996; Hon. Citizen, City of Bathurst, 1998. Hon. Fellow, Commonwealth Learning, 2002. Hon. DEd Admin, Sydney, 2001; DUniv Charles Sturt, 2001; Hon. PhD Econs, HELP Univ., Malaysia 2018; Hon. Dr Central Qld, 2018. Farrer Medallist for contrib to Aust. agriculture, Farrer Meml Trust, 1996; Paul Harris Fellow, Rotary Club, 2001. *Publications:* (ed) Fundamentals of Modern Agriculture, 1967, 3rd edn 1971; 25 scientific papers. *Recreation:* travel. *Address:* 55 Waratah Road, Wentworth Falls, NSW 2782, Australia. *Clubs:* Union, University and Schools (Sydney).

**BLAKE, David Charles,** Eur Ing, CEng, FIMechE; Partner, Bee Services, since 1996; *b* 23 Sept. 1936; *s* of Walter David John Blake and Ellen Charlotte Blake; *m* 1st, 1959, Della Victoria Stevenson (marr. diss. 1996); two *s;* 2nd, 1996, Christine Emmett; one *d. Educ:* South East Essex Technical Sch.; South East Essex Technical Coll. British Transport Commn, later British Railways Board, 1953–96: Engrg apprentice, Stratford Locomotive Works, 1953–57; Technical Management, BR Eastern Reg., 1957–69; Construction Engr, W Coast Main Line Electrification, 1969–74; Area Maintenance Engineer: Motherwell Scottish Reg., 1974–75; Shields Scottish Reg., 1975–76; Rolling Stock Engr, Scottish Reg., 1976–78; Electrical Engr, E Reg., 1978–80; Chief Mechanical and Electrical Engr, Southern Reg., 1980–82; Director: Manufacturing and Maintenance Policy, BRB, 1983–87; Mech. and Elec. Engrg, BRB, 1987–90; Man. Dir, King's Cross Projects Gp, BRB, 1990–93; Man. Dir, Vendor Unit, BRB, 1993–96. Non-executive Director: Engineering Link Ltd, 1999–2003; Leics County and Rutland PCT, 2006–09; Chm., Leics County and Rutland Community Health Services, 2009–11. Gov., St Mary & St John C of E Voluntary Aided Primary Sch., North Luffenham, 2004–08. *Recreations:* gardening, hill walking. *Address:* The Windmill, Morcott, Rutland LE15 9DQ. *T:* (01572) 747000.

**BLAKE, Prof. David Leonard;** composer; Professor of Music, University of York, 1976–2001, now Emeritus; *b* 2 Sept. 1936; *s* of Leonard Blake and Dorothy Blake; *m* 1960, Rita Muir; two *s* one *d. Educ:* Latymer Upper School; Gonville and Caius College, Cambridge (BA 1960, MA 1963); Deutsche Akademie der Künste, Berlin, GDR. School teacher: Ealing Grammar Sch., 1961–62; Northwood Secondary Sch., 1962–63; University of York: Granada Arts Fellow, 1963–64; Lectr in Music, 1964; Sen. Lectr, 1971–76. *Recordings* (own compositions): Violin Concerto: In Praise of Krishna; Variations for Piano; The Almanack. *Compositions* include: String Quartet No 1, 1962; It's a Small War (musical for schools), 1962; Chamber Symphony, 1966; Lumina (text from Ezra Pound's Cantos) (cantata for soprano, baritone, chorus and orch.), 1969; Metamorphoses, for large orch., 1971; Nonet, for wind, 1971; The Bones of Chuang Tzu (cantata for baritone and piano), 1972; In Praise of Krishna: Bengali lyrics, 1973; String Quartet No 2, 1973; Violin Concerto, 1976; Toussaint (opera), 1974–77; From the Mattress Grave (song cycle), 1978; Nine Songs of Heine, 1978; Clarinet Quintet, 1980; String Quartet No 3, 1982; Rise Dove, for bass and orch., 1983; The Plumber's Gift (opera), 1985–88; Cello Concerto, 1992; Three Ritsos Choruses, 1992; The Griffin's Tale, for baritone and orch., 1994; Diversions on Themes of Hanns Eisler, for alto sax. and piano, 1995; The Fabulous Adventures of Alexander the Great, for chorus and orch. of young people, 1996; Scoring a Century (entertainment, text by Keith Warner), 1999; The Shades of Love (Cavafy), for bass and small orch., 2000; The Lonely Wife I and II (poems from the Chinese for soprano and mezzo), 2003; String Quartet No 4, 2004; Rings of Jade (poems by Ho Chi Minh), for medium voice and orch., 2005; The Coming of the Year 'Carol' for SATB chorus and piano, 2008; Four Cabaret Songs for female voice and piano, 2008; On the Autumn Air for oboe, 2009; Ten Gallows Songs of Christian Morgenstern, 2009; String Quartet No 5, 2010; Fanny and Alexander (operatic drama, text by Keith Warner), 2013; Songs and Epigrams, 2014; Icarus (opera, text by Keith Warner), 2015; Medea's Cell, Narcissus Reflects, Persephone's Rounds (monodramas, text by Keith Warner), 2018–19. *Publications:* (ed) Hanns Eisler: a miscellany, 1995. *Address:* Cringley House, Silver Street, Askrigg, Leyburn, N Yorks DL8 3HS. *E:* davidlblake90@gmail.com.

**BLAKE, Sir Francis Michael,** 3rd Bt *cr* 1907; *b* 11 July 1943; *o s* of Sir F. Edward C. Blake, 2nd Bt and Olive Mary (*d* 1946) *d* of Charles Liddell Simpson; *S* father, 1950; *m* 1968, Joan Ashbridge, *d* of F. C. A. Miller; two *s. Educ:* Rugby. High Sheriff, Northumberland, 2002. *Heir: s* Francis Julian Blake [*b* 17 Feb. 1971; *m* 1st, 2000, Dr Jennifer Armstrong (marr. diss. 2007), *o d* of Peter Armstrong; 2nd, 2009, Claire Louise, *d* of James Donald; one *s* one *d*]. *Address:* The Dower House, Tillmouth Park, Cornhill-on-Tweed, Northumberland TD12 4UR. *T:* (01890) 882443.

**BLAKE, Howard David,** OBE 1994; FRAM; composer; *b* 28 Oct. 1938; *s* of Horace C. Blake and Grace B. Blake (*née* Benson); two *s* one *d. Educ:* Brighton, Hove and Sussex Grammar Sch.; Royal Acad. of Music. FRAM 1989. Dir, PRS, 1978–87; Co-founder, Assoc. of Professional Composers, 1980. *Compositions:* concert works: The Song of St Francis, 1976; Benedictus, 1979; Sinfonietta for brass ensemble, 1981; Clarinet Concerto, 1984; Shakespeare Songs, 1987; Festival Mass, 1987; Diversions for Cello and Orchestra, 1989; Four Songs of the Nativity, 1990; Piano Concerto for Princess of Wales, 1990; Violin Concerto for City of Leeds, 1993; The Land of Counterpane, 1995; Charter for Peace (commissioned by FCO for 50th anniv. of UN), 1995; All God's Creatures, 1995; Lifecycle for solo piano, 1996; Flute Concerto, 1996; Still Falls the Rain, 1998; The Passion of Mary, 2002, revised 2006; The Rise of the House of Usher, 2003; Songs of Truth and Glory, 2005; Winterdream, 2006; Violin Sonata, 2007; Spieltreib (String Quartet), 2008; Sleepwalking, 2009; Bassoon Concerto, 2009; Speech after Long Silence (piano), 2010; Cello Sonata, 2010; James Joyce Songs, 2012; Prelude for Vova (for Vladimir Ashkenazy), 2012; *stage works:* Henry V, 1984, As You Like It, 1985, RSC; The Snowman Stageshow (ballet in two acts), 1993; Eva (ballet), Gothenburg Opera House, 1996; Eine Frau Ohne Namen (ballet), Gladbach Opera House, 2016; *film and television scores include:* The Duellists, 1977; The Snowman (TV), 1982; A Month in the Country, 1986 (BFI Anthony Asquith Award); Granpa (TV, 1987; A Midsummer Night's Dream (RSC and Channel 4), 1996; The Bear (TV), 1998; My Life So Far, 1999. Dir and producer, The Land of Counterpane (animated film), 2016. *Recreations:* reading, walking, swimming. *Address:* Studio 6, 18 Kensington Court Place, W8 5BJ. *E:* howard@howardblake.com. *Clubs:* Groucho, Chelsea Arts, Ivy.

**BLAKE, John Michael;** Managing Director: Blake Publishing, 1991–2000; John Blake Publishing, 2000–18; Metro Publishing, 2001–18; Soho Friday Media Ltd, since 2018; *b* Nov. 1948; *s* of late Major Edwin Blake, MBE, and of Joyce Blake; *m* 1968, Dian Sutherland Campbell; one *s* two *d. Educ:* Westminster City Grammar Sch.; North-West London Polytechnic. Reporter: Hackney Gazette, 1966; Evening Post, Luton, 1969; Fleet Street News Agency, 1970; Columnist: London Evening News, 1971; London Evening Standard, 1980; The Sun, 1982; Asst Editor, Daily Mirror, 1985; Editor, The People, 1988–89; Pres., Mirror Group Newspapers (USA), 1989; Exec. Producer, Sky Television, 1990. *Publications:* Up and Down with The Rolling Stones, 1978; All You Needed Was Love, 1981. *Recreations:* messing about in boats, triathlon, scuba diving. *Address:* Soho Friday Media Ltd, The Office, Lindsfields, Chichester Road, West Wittering, Chichester, W Sussex PO20 8QA. *Clubs:* Groucho, Chelsea Arts; Cruising Association.

**BLAKE, Jonathan Elazar;** Head, Investment Funds Strategy, Investment Funds Team, O'Melveny & Myers LLP, 2017–19; *b* 7 July 1954; *s* of late Asher Blake and Nomi Blake; *m* Isabel Horovitz; three *s* one *d*. *Educ:* Haberdashers' Aske's Sch.; Queens' Coll., Cambridge (BA 1975; LLB 1976). CTA; CF. Stephenson Harwood, 1977–82; SJ Berwin, then King & Wood Mallesons LLP: Partner, 1982–2017; Sen. Partner, 2006–12; Hd, Internat. Private Funds Dept, 2012–17. Former Mem. Council, British Venture Capital Assoc.; former Chm., Tax and Legal Cttee, European Private Equity and Venture Capital Assoc. *Recreations:* ski-ing, walking, theatre, travel, family.

**BLAKE, Mary Netterville,** MA; Headmistress, Manchester High School for Girls, 1975–83; *b* 12 Sept. 1922; *d* of John Netterville Blake and Agnes Barr Blake. *Educ:* Howell's Sch., Denbigh; St Anne's Coll., Oxford (MA). Asst Mistress, The Mount Sch., York, 1945–48; Head of Geography Dept, King's High Sch., Warwick, 1948–56; Associate Gen. Sec., Student Christian Movement in Schools, 1956–60; Head Mistress, Selby Grammar Sch., 1960–75. Pres., Assoc. of Headmistresses, 1976–77; first Pres., Secondary Heads Assoc., 1978. *Address:* 11 Baldenhall, Hall Green, Malvern, Worcs WR14 3RZ. *T:* (01684) 564359.

**BLAKE, Hon. Sir Nicholas (John Gorrod),** Kt 2007; a Judge of the High Court of Justice, Queen's Bench Division, 2007–17; a President, Upper Tribunal (Immigration and Asylum Chamber), 2010–13; *b* 21 June 1949; *s* of Leslie Gorrod Blake and Jean Margaret (*née* Ballinger); *m* 1986, Clio Whittaker; one *s* two *d* (and one *s* decd). *Educ:* Cranleigh Sch.; Magdalene Coll., Cambridge (BA Hons Hist.); Inns of Court Sch. of Law. Called to the Bar, Middle Temple, 1974, Bencher, 2002. QC 1994; Asst Recorder, 1999–2000; Recorder, 2000–07; Dep. Judge of the High Court, 2003–07. Chm., Immigration Lawyers Practitioners Assoc., 1994–97. Mem. Council, Justice, 1995–2007. Trustee, NPG, 2005–13. FRSA. *Publications:* Police, Law and the People, 1974; (jtly) Wigs and Workers, 1980; (jtly) New Nationality Law, 1983; (ed jtly) Immigration Law and Practice, 3rd edn 1991, 4th edn 1995; Immigration Asylum and Human Rights, 2002; The Deepcut Review, 2006. *Recreation:* the visual arts. *Address:* Matrix Chambers, Griffin Building, Gray's Inn, WC1R 5LN.

**BLAKE, Sir Peter (Thomas),** Kt 2002; CBE 1983; RDI 1987; ARCA; painter; *b* 25 June 1932; *s* of Kenneth William Blake; *m* 1963, Jann Haworth (marr. diss. 1982); two *d*; *m* 1987, Chrissy Wilson; one *d*. *Educ:* Gravesend Tech. Coll.; Gravesend Sch. of Art; RCA. ARA 1974; RA 1980, resigned 2005; Prof. of Drawing, Royal Acad., 2002–04. Works exhibited: ICA, 1958, 1960; Guggenheim Competition, 1958; Cambridge, 1959; RA, 1960; Musée d'Art Moderne, Paris, 1968; Waddington Galls, 1970, 1972, 1977, 1990, 2005, 2010; Stedelijk Mus., Amsterdam, 1973; Kunstverein, Hamburg, 1973; Gemeentemuseum, Arnhem, 1974; Palais des Beaux-Arts, Brussels, 1974; Galleria Documenta, Turin, 1982; Paul Stolper Gall., London, 2007; Waddington Custot Galleries, 2012, 2015, 2018; Nat. Mus. Wales, 2013; Bohun Gall., Henley-on-Thames, 2018; retrospective exhibitions: Tate Gall., 1983; Gal. Claude Bernard, Paris, 1984, 2009, 2016; Nishimura Gall., Tokyo, 1988; Nat. Gall., 1996; London Inst. Gall., 2003; Wetterling Gall. Stockholm, 2006, 2016; Tate Liverpool, 2007; Paul Morris Gall., NY, 2007; Galerie Thomas Levy, Hamburg, 2008; Chelsea Futurespace, 2013; works in public collections: Trinity Coll., Cambridge; Carlisle City Gall.; Tate Gall.; Arts Council of GB; Mus. of Modern Art, NY; V & A Mus.; Mus. Boymans-van Beuningen, Rotterdam; Calouste Gulbenkian Foundn, London; RCA; Whitworth Art Gall., Univ. of Manchester; Baltimore Mus. of Art, Md; Pallant House Gall., Chichester. Third Associate Artist, Nat. Gall., 1994. *Publications:* Peter Blake's ABC, 2009; Venice Fantasies, 2009; illustrations for: Oxford Illustrated Old Testament, 1968; Roger McGough, Summer with Monica, 1978; cover illustration, Arden Shakespeare: Othello, 1980; Anthony and Cleopatra, 1980; Timon of Athens, 1980; contribs to: Times Educnl Supp.; Ark; Graphis 70; World of Art; Architectural Rev.; House and Garden; Painter and Sculptor; relevant publication: Peter Blake: one man show, by Marco Livingstone, 2009. *Recreations:* sculpture, wining and dining, going to rock and roll concerts, boxing and wrestling matches; living well is the best revenge. *Address:* c/o Waddington Galleries Ltd, 11 Cork Street, W1S 3LT.

**BLAKE, Sir Quentin (Saxby),** Kt 2013; CBE 2005 (OBE 1988); RDI 1981; freelance artist and illustrator, since 1957; Honorary Professor (formerly Visiting Professor), Royal College of Art, since 1989; first Children's Laureate, 1999–2001; *b* 16 Dec. 1932; *s* of William Blake and Evelyn Blake. *Educ:* Chislehurst and Sidcup Grammar Sch.; Downing Coll., Cambridge (MA; Hon. Fellow, 2000); Inst. of Education, Univ. of London (PGCE 1957). Royal College of Art: Tutor, 1965–77; Head, Dept of Illustration, 1978–86; Vis. Tutor, 1986–89; Sen. Fellow, 1988. Exhibitions of watercolour drawings, Workshop Gallery: Invitation to the Dance, 1972; Runners and Riders, 1973; Creature Comforts, 1974; Water Music, 1976; exhibitions of illustration work: Chris Beetles Gall., 1993, 1996, 2004, 2007, 2010, 2011, 2012, 2013; Dulwich Picture Gall., 2004; South Kensington and Chelsea Mental Health Care Centre: The Kershaw Pictures, 2006; Sixty New Drawings, 2006; Our Friends in the Circus, 2009; New Drawings, Etchings and Lithographs, Marlborough Fine Art, 2012; Drawn by Hand, Fitzwilliam Mus., Cambridge, 2013; Quentin Blake: Life Under Water - A Hastings Celebration, Jerwood Gall., 2015; The Roald Dahl Centenary Portraits, BL, 2016 (and UK tour); The BFG in Pictures, House of Illustration, 2016 (and UK tour); Quentin Blake: The Life of Birds, House of Illustration, 2017; The Only Way to Travel, Jerwood Gall., 2017; Quentin Blake: Voyages to the Moon and the Sun, House of Illustration, 2018; 100 Figures: The Unseen Art of Quentin Blake, House of Illustration, 2018; Walking with Birds, Jerwood Gall., 2018; The World of Hats, Jerwood Gall., 2018; Quentin Blake and John Yeoman: Fifty Years of Children's Books, House of Illustration, 2018 (and UK tour); retrospective: Nat. Theatre, 1984; Somerset House, 2003; Museo Luzzati, Genoa, 2009; As Large as Life, Compton Verney, 2011 (and UK tour); Quentin Blake et les Ages de la Vie, Municipal Liby, Angers, France, 2011; Inside Stories, House of Illustration, 2014; KT&G SangSangMadang Gall., South Korea, 2017. Curator: Tell Me A Picture, Nat. Gall., 2001; A Baker's Dozen, Bury St Edmunds, 2001; Magic Pencil, British Council, 2001; In All Directions, Arts Council, 2005; Quentin Blake et les Demoiselles des Bords de Seine, Paris, 2005. Freeman, City of London, 2015. Hon. Fellow, Brighton Univ. Hon. FRA 2001. Hon. Dr: London Inst., 2000; RCA, Northumbria, 2001; Anglia Ruskin, 2007; Inst. of Educn, London, 2008; Hon. LittD Cambridge, 2004; DUniv Open, 2006; Hon. DLitt Loughborough, 2007. Hans Christian Andersen Award, 2002; Prince Philip Designers' Prize, Design Council, 2011; Eleanor Farjeon Award, 2012. Officier, l'Ordre des Arts et des Lettres (France), 2007; Chevalier de la Légion d'Honneur (France), 2014. *Publications:* (author and illustrator) for children: Patrick, 1968; Jack and Nancy, 1969; Angelo, 1970; Snuff, 1973; The Adventures of Lester, 1977; Mr Magnolia, 1980 (Fedn of Children's Bk Gps Award); Kate Greenaway Medal, 1981); Quentin Blake's Nursery Rhyme Book, 1983; The Story of the Dancing Frog, 1984; Mrs Armitage on Wheels, 1987; Quentin Blake's ABC, 1989; All Join In, 1990; Cockatoos, 1991; Simpkin, 1993; Clown, 1995 (Bologna Ragazzi Prize, 1996); Mrs Armitage and the Big Wave, 1997; Dix Grenouilles, 1997; The Green Ship, 1998; Zagazoo, 1998; Fantastic Daisy Artichoke, 1999; Un Bateau dans le Ciel, 2000; Loveykins, 2002; Mrs Armitage Queen of the Road, 2003; Angel Pavement, 2004; Angelica Sprocket's Pockets, 2010; The Five of Us, 2014; author (for children): Three Little Monkeys, 2016; Three Little Monkeys on Holiday, 2019; (editor and illustrator) for children: Custard and Company, by Ogden Nash, 1979; The Quentin Blake Book of Nonsense Verse, 1994; The Quentin Blake Book of Nonsense Stories, 1996; Promenade de Quentin Blake au Pays de la Poésie Française, 2003; (illustrator) for children: Russell Hoban: How Tom Beat Captain Najork and his Hired Sportsmen, 1974 (Whitbread Lit. Award, 1975; Hans Andersen Honour Book, 1975); A Near Thing for Captain Najork, 1976; The Rain Door, 1986; Rosie's Magic Horse, 2012; Hilaire Belloc: Algernon and Other Cautionary Tales, 1991; Michael Rosen: Mind Your Own Business, 1974; Wouldn't You Like to Know, 1977; You Can't Catch Me, 1981; Quick Let's Get Out of Here, 1982; Don't Put Mustard in the Custard, 1985; Michael Rosen's Sad Book, 2005; Roald Dahl: The Enormous Crocodile, 1978; The Twits, 1980; George's Marvellous Medicine, 1981; Revolting Rhymes, 1982; The BFG, 1982; The Witches, 1983; Dirty Beasts, 1984; The Giraffe and the Pelly and Me, 1985; Matilda, 1988; Rhyme Stew, 1989; Esio Trot, 1990; Dahl Diary, 1991; My Year, 1993; Danny the Champion of the World, 1994; Roald Dahl's Revolting Recipes, 1994; Charlie and the Chocolate Factory, 1995; Charlie and the Great Glass Elevator, 1995; James and the Giant Peach, 1995; The Magic Finger, 1995; Fantastic Mr Fox, 1996; Even More Revolting Recipes, 2001; Boy, 2012; Billy and the Minpins, 2017; Matilda, BL 30th Anniv. Edn, 2018; Matilda, World Traveller 30th Anniv. Edn, 2018; Matilda, Astrophysicist 30th Anniv. Edn, 2018; (ed Susan Rennie) Oxford Roald Dahl Dictionary, 2016; John Yeoman: A Drink of Water, 1960, new edn 2017; The Boy Who Sprouted Antlers, 1961, new edn 2018; Featherbrains, 1993; The Singing Tortoise, 1993; The Family Album, 1993; The Do-It-Yourself House that Jack Built, 1994; Mr Nodd's Ark, 1995; Up with Birds!, 1992; The Princes' Gifts, 1997; The Heron and the Crane, 1999; Three Little Owls, 2013; All the Year Round, 2017; John Ruskin, The King of Golden River, 2019; books by Clement Freud, Sid Fleischman, Sylvia Plath, Margaret Mahy, Joan Aiken, Dr Seuss, Michael Morpurgo, David Walliams and Beatrix Potter; (illustrator) for adults: Aristophanes, The Birds, 1971; Lewis Carroll, The Hunting of the Snark, 1976; Stella Gibbons, Cold Comfort Farm, 1977; Evelyn Waugh, Black Mischief, 1980, Scoop, 1981; George Orwell, Animal Farm, 1984; Cyrano de Bergerac, Voyages to the Sun and Moon, 1991, new edn 2018; Cervantes, Don Quixote, 1995; Charles Dickens, A Christmas Carol, 1995; Victor Hugo, The Hunchback of Notre Dame, 1998; Voltaire, Candide, 2011; Fifty Fables of La Fontaine, 2013; The Golden Ass of Lucius Apuleius, 2015; Russell Hoban, Riddley Walker, 2017; Moonlight Travellers, 2019; *non-fiction:* (author) La Vie de la Page, 1995; Woman with a Book (drawings), 1999; (jtly) Drawing for the Artistically Undiscovered, 2000; Words and Pictures, 2000; The Laureate's Party, 2000; Tell me a Picture, 2001; Laureate's Progress, 2002; In All Directions, 2005; Quentin Blake et les Demoiselles des Bords de Seine, 2005; The Life of Birds (drawings), 2005; Vive Nos Vieux Jours!, 2007; Beyond the Page, 2012; Pens Ink and Places, 2018; 100 Figures: The Unseen Art of Quentin Blake, 2018.

**BLAKE, Richard Andrew;** a District Judge (Magistrates' Courts), Westminster (Lincolnshire, 2006–11; Camberwell Green, 2011); *b* 14 March 1955; *s* of late Lionel Henry Blake and of Betty Blake; civil partnership 2006, Jonathan Neil Langston. *Educ:* Magistrates Law Dip. 1980; Poly. of Central London (Dip. Law 1981); Inns of Court Sch. of Law (Bar. Dip. 1982). Magistrates' Courts Service, 1974–83, Sen. Ct Clerk, Willesden Magistrates' Ct, 1982–83; called to the Bar, Gray's Inn, 1982; Avon and Somerset Prosecuting Solicitor's Office, 1983–86; Sen. Crown Prosecutor, Kingston, 1986–89, Principal Crown Prosecutor, 1989–90, CPS; in private practice as a barrister, One Inner Temple Lane, 1990–2006; apptd Dep. Stipendiary Magistrate, later Dist Judge, 1999. *Recreations:* boating, Jaguar motor cars, Isle of Wight, walking the dog. *Club:* Island Sailing (Cowes).

**BLAKE, Robert John William F.;** *see* fFrench Blake.

**BLAKE, Simon Anthony,** OBE 2011; Chief Executive, Mental Health First Aid England, since 2018; *b* 28 Jan. 1974; *s* of John and Margaret Blake; civil partnership 2010, Dr John Swift. *Educ:* Univ. of Wales Coll. of Cardiff (BA Psychol.); Univ. of Wales Coll., Newport (Postgrad. Cert. Counselling); London South Bank Univ. (Postgrad. Dip. Social Res. Methods). Develt Officer, FPA, 1996–99; Dir, Sex Educn Forum, 1999–2002; Asst Dir, Nat. Children's Bureau, 2002–06; on secondment to DoH as Children's Policy Advr, 2004; Chief Exec., Brook, 2006–15; Chief Exec., NUS, 2015–18. Non-exec. Dir, Endsleigh Insce Services Ltd, 2015. Chairman: Compact Voice, 2008–15; Diversity Role Models, 2012–15; Vice Chair: Black Health Agency, 2009–11; Stonewall, 2015–. CMgr, CCMI 2016 (Level 5 Mgt and Leadership). *Publications:* (with J. Laxton) Strides: a practical guide to sex and relationships education with young men, 1998; A Whole School Approach to PSHE and Citizenship, 2000, 2nd edn 2006; (with G. Frances) Just Say No to Abstinence Education!, 2001; (with M. Biddulph) Moving Goalposts: setting a training agenda for sexual health work with boys and young men, 2001; (with Z. Katrak) Faith, Values and Sex and Relationships Education, 2002; Sex and Relationships Education: a step-by-step guide for teachers, 2002; (with P. Power) Teaching and Learning About HIV: a resource for Key Stages 1 to 4, 2003; (with J. Lynch) Sex, Alcohol and Other Drugs: exploring the links in young people's lives, 2004; (with A. Shutt) Be Aware: young people, alcohol and other drugs, 2004; Cards for Life: promoting emotional and social development, 2005; (with S. Plant) Addressing Inequalities and Inclusion through Personal, Social, Health Education and Citizenship, 2005; (with S. Muttock) Assessment and Evaluation in Sex and Relationships Education, 2005; (jtly) Promoting Emotional and Social Development in Schools: a practical guide, 2007; (with P. Baraitser) Involving Young Men in Chlamydia Screening: a practical guide, 2009; (with T. Lloyd) Young Men, Sex and Pregnancy: best practice guidance, 2010; (with Y. Gbajobi) Student Union Stories: issues and trends in students' unions, 2018. *Recreations:* swimming, running, horseriding. *Address:* Mental Health First Aid England, 21 Prescot Street, E1 8BB. *E:* simon.blake@mhfaengland.org.

**BLAKE-JAMES, Linda Elizabeth;** *see* Sullivan, L. E.

**BLAKEBROUGH, Adele Esther,** MBE 2006; Co-Founder and Chief Executive Officer, Social Business Trust, since 2010; *b* Southend, Essex, 11 Feb. 1961; *d* of Eric Blakebrough and Mary Blakebrough; *m* 1st, 1982, Ian Gordon Fairbairn (marr. diss. 1992); one *d*; 2nd, 1993, Prof. Ian Richard Hargreaves, *qv*; two *d*. *Educ:* St Andrew's and St Mark's Primary Sch., Surbiton; Hinchley Wood Comp. Sch.; Convent of the Sacred Hearts, Epsom; Univ. of Manchester (BA Theol. 1983, MA Pastoral Theol. 1993). Ordained minister, Baptist church, 1985; Asst Minister, John Bunyan Baptist Ch, 1985–92; CEO, Kaleidoscope Project, 1992–97; Co-Founder and Jt CEO, Community Action Network, 1998–2008. Non-exec. Dir, Impact Internat., 2008–. Chair, Internat. Adv. Bd, Cardiff Business Sch., 2019–. Sieff Award, community leader, BITC, 2007. *Recreations:* doing up houses, Wales, walking my Cocker Spaniel. *Address:* Social Business Trust, 13 St Swithin's Lane, EC4N 8AL. *T:* (020) 3096 8022. *E:* adele@socialbusinesstrust.org.

**BLAKELEY, Trevor,** CEng; FRINA; FIMarEST; FIMechE; Chief Executive, Royal Institution of Naval Architects, since 1997; *b* 22 Nov. 1943; *m* 1965, Patricia Challenger; one *s* one *d*. *Educ:* Goole Grammar Sch.; BRNC Dartmouth; RNEC Manadon (BSc 1968); BA Open Univ. 1995. CEng 1973; FIMarEST (FIMarE 1996); FIMechE 1996; FRINA 1997. Joined RN, 1963; served as engineering specialist; retired 1996. Chm., Confedn of Eur. Maritime Technology Socs, 2006–. Gov., Horndean Technol. Coll., 2002–. Mem., Shipwrights' Co., 1999–. *Recreations:* theatre, music, horse riding. *Address:* Royal Institution of Naval Architects, 8–9 Northumberland Street, WC2N 5DA. *T:* (020) 7235 4622.

**BLAKEMORE, Sir Colin (Brian)**, Kt 2014; FRS 1992; Professor of Neuroscience, Oxford University, 2007–12, now Emeritus; Fellow of Magdalen College, Oxford, 1979–2012, now Emeritus; Emeritus Professor, Duke-National University of Singapore Graduate Medical School, since 2008; Yeung Kin Man Endowed Chair Professor in Neuroscience, since 2019, and Senior Fellow, Hong Kong Institute for Advanced Study, since 2017, City University of Hong Kong; *b* 1 June 1944; *s* of Cedric Norman Blakemore and Beryl Ann Smith; *m* 1965, Andrée Elizabeth Washbourne; three *d*. *Educ*: King Henry VIII Sch., Coventry; Corpus Christi Coll., Cambridge (Smyth Scholar; BA 1965; MA 1969; ScD 1988; Hon. Fellow, 1994); Univ. of Calif, Berkeley (PhD 1968); Magdalen Coll., Oxford (MA 1979; DSc 1989). FIBiol, CBiol 1996, Hon. FRSB (Hon. FIBiol 2004). Harkness Fellow, Neurosensory Lab., Univ. of Calif, Berkeley, 1965–68; Cambridge University: Fellow and Dir of Medical Studies, Downing Coll., 1971–79; Univ. Demonstr in Physiol., 1968–72; Univ. Lectr in Physiol., 1972–79; Leverhulme Fellow, 1974–75; Royal Soc. Locke Res. Fellow, 1976–79; Oxford University: Waynflete Prof. of Physiol., 1979–2007 (on leave of absence, 2003–07); Prof. of Neurosci., Univ. of Warwick, 2007–11; Prof. of Neurosci. and Philosophy, Sch. of Advanced Study, Univ. of London, 2012–18, now Emeritus; Director: McDonnell-Pew Centre for Cognitive Neurosci., 1990–2003; MRC IRC for Cognitive Neurosci., 1996–2003. Chief Exec., MRC, 2003–07 (Chm., Neurobiology and Mental Health Bd Grants Cttee, 1977–79). Non-exec. Dir, BTG plc, 2007–10. Agency for Science, Technology and Research, Singapore: Mem., Biomed. Scis Internat. Adv. Cttee, 2005–08; Chair, Neurosci. Adv. Cttee, 2006–07; Chairman: UK Stem Cell Funders Forum, 2003–07; Internat. Stem Cell Forum, 2003–07; Hds of Internat. Res. Orgns, 2003–07; Chair, A*STAR, Duke-Nat. Univ. of Singapore Grad. Med. Sch. Neurosci. Res., 2007–10 (Ext. Scientific Advr, 2010–); Gen. Adv. Cttee on Sci., Food Standards Agency, 2007–; Sci. Skills Working Gp, 2009–; Rev. Panel for Neuroscis, Swedish Res. Council, 2009; Inst. of Medicine Workshop on US and Eur. Animal Res. Regulations, 2010–11. Visiting Professor: NY Univ., 1970; Bell Telephone Labs, 1970; MIT, 1971; Royal Soc. Study Visit, Keio Univ., Tokyo, 1974; Lethaby Prof., RCA, 1978–79; Storer Vis. Prof., Univ. of Calif, Davis, 1980; Royal Soc. Exchange Visit, Inst. of Biophysics, Beijing, 1980; Vis. Scientist, Salk Inst., 1982, 1983, 1992; Macallum Vis. Lectr, Univ. of Toronto, 1984; McLaughlin Vis. Prof., McMaster Univ., Ont, 1992; Regents' Prof. and Vis. Prof., Univ. of Calif, Davis, 1995–97; Spinoza Prof., Univ. of Amsterdam, 1996; Dist. Visitor, BioMed. Res. Council, Singapore, 2005. Chm. Council, BAAS, 2001–04 (Pres., Gen. Section, 1989; Pres., 1997–98, Vice-Pres., 1990–97, 1998–2001; Hon. Fellow, 2001); President: British Neurosci. Assoc., 1997–2000; Physiological Soc., 2001–03 (Mem. Council and Exec. Cttee, 2001–03); Bioscis Fedn, 2002–04 (Mem. Exec. Cttee and Council, 2001–04); Assoc. of British Sci. Writers, 2004–15 (Chm., Judging Panel, Assoc. of British Sci. Writers and Irish Sci. Writer Awards, 2010–11); British Biol. Olympiad, 2005–; Internat. Scientific Council, Fondation Neurodis, Lyon, 2009–. Hon. Pres., World Cultural Council, 1983–. Mem., World Fedn of Scientists, 1988–; Fellow: World Econ. Forum, 1994–98; World Innovation Foundn, 2002–. Chairman: Council, Res. Defence Soc., 2007–08; Selection Cttee, Brain Prize, 2010–; Founding Chm. of Council, Understanding Animal Res., 2008–09. Founder Mem., Bd of Govs, Internat. Brain Injury Assoc. (Nat. Head Injury Foundn Inc., Washington), 1993–; Mem. Professional Adv. Panel, and Patron, Headway (Nat. Head Injuries Assoc.), 1997–; Member: BBC Sci. Consultative Group, 1975–79; Scientific Cttee, Bristol Exploratory, 1983–99; British Nat. Cttee for Physiol. Scis, 1985–86; Professional Adv. Cttee, Schizophrenia: A National Emergency, 1989–95 (Trustee, 2001–03; Vice-Patron, 2003–); Adv. Gp on Non-Ionising Radiation, NRPB, 1992–2003 (Chm., Weak Electrical Fields Gp, 2008–09; Mem., Sub-Cttee on MRI, 2003, Working Party on melatonin, 2003); Council, European Neurosci. Assoc., 1998–2000; Council, Fedn of European Neurosci. Socs, 1998–2000; Nat. Cttee for 2000 Forum for European Neurosci., Brighton, 1998–2000; Home Office/DSTL TETRA Health and Safety Study Mgt Cttee, 2002–05; AlphaGalileo Foundn, 2003–; Adv. Bd, Cable Sci. Network, 2003–; Public Educn and Communication Cttee, Soc. for Neurosci., 2004–08; UK Drug Policy Commn, 2006–; Royal Instn, 2008–; Wilton Park Adv. Council, FCO, 2010–. Member: Department of Health: Ind. Expert Gp on Mobile Phones, 1999–2000; Prog. Mgt Cttee, UK Telecoms Health Res. Prog., 2000–03; Res. for Patient Benefits Working Party, 2003–04; Bd, UK Clinical Res. Collaboration, 2004–07; UK Stem Cell Initiative Panel, 2005–07; Department for Business, Innovation and Skills: Co-ordinating Cttee, Foresight project on Cognitive Systems, 2001–04; Stakeholder Gps for Foresight projects on Brain Sci., Addiction and Drugs, 2004–06, and Obesity, 2005–07; Expert Gp on Sci. and Media, Govt Office for Sci., 2009–10; Mem. Bd, OSCHR, 2007. International Brain Research Organization: Member: Council, 1973–2001; Exec. Cttee, 1985–91; Nominating Cttee, 1993–2001 (Chm., 1997–2001); Publications Cttee, 1999–; Cttee on By-Laws, 1999–2001; Chm., Special Cttee, 1984–86; Ed.-in-Chief, IBRO News and website, 1993–2001. Co-Founder, 1992, Mem., 1992–2003, Boyd Gp. Dana Foundation: Mem. Exec. Cttee, Dana Alliance for Brain Initiatives, NY, 1996–; Mem. Adv. Gp for Dana Centre, Sci. Mus., London, 2002–03; Vice-Chm., European Dana Alliance for the Brain, 1996–. Royal Society: Chairman: Wkg Gp, Public Prog., 2001–03; Partnership Grants Cttee, 2001–03; Steering Cttee for Brain Waves project on policy implications of advances in neurosci., 2010–; Member: Hooke Cttee, 1992–2001; Council, COPUS, 2001–02; Sci. in Soc. Cttee, 2001–04; Michael Faraday Prize Cttee, 2001–05; Jt Acad. Med. Scis Wkg Gp on Sci. of Transmissible Spongiform Encephalopathies, 2000; Editl Bd, Phil Trans Royal Soc. B, 2010–; Member: Scientific Adv. Bd, Cognitive Neurosci. Inst., NY, 1981–95; Adv. Bd, WNET TV, NY, 1986–88; Organising Cttee, Child Vision Res. Soc., 1986–; Cttee of Scientific Direction, CNRS Lab de Neuroscis, Marseille, 1989; Review Cttee, Human Sci. Frontier Prog., 1992–95; Scientific Adv. Cttee, Volkswagen Stiftung, 1997–2003; Strategic Adv. Cttee, ProSeed Capital Hldgs, 2000–; Adv. Council, Sense about Sci., 2002–; Exec. Council, Novartis Foundn, 2002–; Sci., Engrg and Envmt Adv. Cttee, British Council, 2003–; Bd, Coalition for Med. Progress, 2003–07 (Chm., 2005–07; Trustee, 2005–07); Adv. Bd, Imaging Sci. Centre, Imperial Coll. London, 2005–; Adv. Gp for Health Res., EC Framework Prog. 7, 2006–08; Council, Med. Genetics Sect., RSocMed, 2007–; Adv. Council, ABPI, 2007–09; Sci. Adv. Bd, Agence Nationale de Recherche, France, 2008–; RIKEN Adv. Council, Japan, 2008– (Vice Chm., 2011); Adv. Bd, Eur. Neuroethics Soc., 2008–; Longevity Sci. Adv. Panel, Legal & General, 2009–; Adv. Council, Campaign for Sci. and Engrg, 2011–; Adv. Bd, RedHill Biopharma Ltd, 2011–; Scientific and Strategic Adv. Gp, ReNeuron, 2011–; Sci. and Technol. Advr, Technol. Develt Cttee, Abu Dhabi, 2010–. Hon. Associate: Rationalist Press Assoc., 1986–; Rationalist Internat., 2000–; Cheltenham Fest. of Sci., 2001–; Nat. Secular Soc., 2010–; Mem. Jury, Sci. Book Prizes, 1989; Founder Mem. Cttee, Dir and Trustee, Harkness Fellowships Assoc., 1997–; Patron: Assoc. for Art, Sci., Engrg and Technol., 1997–; At-Bristol Science Centre, 1997– (Scientific Advr, 1997–; Mem., Adv. Council, 2007–); Clifton Scientific Trust, Bristol, 1999–; Oxford Univ. Scientific Soc., 2000–; Oxford Literary Fest., 2002–; Wrexham Sci. Fest., 2002–; Humanists for a Better World, 2011–. Distinguished Supporter, Humanists UK (formerly British Humanist Assoc.), 1996–. President: Sci. Soc., Dulwich Coll., 1983; Brain Tumour UK, 2010–. Motor Neurone Disease Association: Pres., Oxon Br., 2004–; Patron, 2005–; Pres., 2008–; Hon. Mem., 2005; Vice-Pres., Progressive Supranuclear Palsy Assoc., 2004–; Trustee: Brain Child, 1991–; Bhopal Med. Appeal, 2003–; Pilgrim Trust, 2009–; Patron: Corpal, 1989–; Saferworld, 1991–; Member: Med. Panel, Patients' Voice for Med. Advance (formerly Seriously Ill for Med. Res.), 2002–; Internat. Adv. Council, Louise T. Blouin Foundn, 2005–; Scientific Adv. Bd, Lifeboat Foundn, 2006–; Neurosci. Adv. Bd, Peter and Patricia Gruber Foundn, 2006–09; Supporter, Sense, 2009–; Scientific Advr, Beckley Foundn, 2001–; Consultant: ASPEX Ltd, 1987–89; MMCO Ltd, 1988–95; Bébé Vision Tropique, Paris, 1993–94; Hall of Human Biol., Natural Hist. Mus., 1989; USAF Spatial Orientation Prog., 1994; WHO, 2002–03; Thriving Child Project, Jabadao (Centre for Study of Movt, Learning and Health), 2002–; Adv. Cttee, Progress Educnl Trust, 2008–; Tandent Vision Science, Inc., 2010–. Judge: Debating Matters Competition, Inst. of Ideas, 2008; Grierson Awards, 2009; Nat. Young Scientist and Young Technologist of the Year, 2009–. BBC Reith Lectr, 1976; Presenter: BBC Radio programmes: Science in China, 1981; From Molecules to Mind, 1982; Machines with Minds, 1982; Science in Japan, 1987; You Know it Makes Sense, 1992; BBC TV series: Common Sense, 1982; The Mind Machine, 1988; Imagina, 1995; Moments of Genius, 2000; The Next Big Thing, 2000–02; God and the Scientists, Channel 4, 2009; The Evidence, Vaccine Disputes, BMJ Video series, 2009; Lectures include: Aubrey Lewis, Inst. of Psych., 1979; Lord Charnwood, Amer. Acad. of Optometry, 1980; Vickers, Neonatal Soc., 1981; Harveian, Harveian Soc. of London, 1982; Christmas, Royal Instn, 1982; George Frederic Still, BPA, 1983; Edridge-Green, RCS, 1984; Halliburton, KCL, 1986; Cairns Meml (also Medal), Cambridge Univ., 1986; Bertram Louis Abrahams, RCP, 1986; Norman McAlister Gregg (also Medal), RACO, 1988; Dietrich Bodenstein, Univ. of Va, 1989; Charnock Bradley, Univ. of Edinburgh, 1989; Boda Meml, Oxford Soc., Bombay, 1989; Doyne, Oxford Ophthalmol Congress, 1989 (also Medal); G. L. Brown, Physiol Soc., 1990; Sir Douglas Robb, Univ. of Auckland, 1991; Montgomery (also Medal), RCSI and Irish Ophthalmol Soc., 1991; T. T. Cozzika Foundn, Patras, 1992; Osler (also Medal), RCP, 1993; James Law, Cornell, 1994; Newton, Cos of Spectacle Makers, and Clockmakers and Scientific Instrument Makers, 1997; Cockcroft, UMIST, 1997; David Oppenheimer Meml, Oxford, 2000; Alfred Meyer Meml (also Medal), British Neuropathol Soc., 2001; Dorothy J. Killam, Dalhousie Univ., 2001; Menzies Foundn (and Medal), 2002; F. C. Donders, Nijmegen, 2003; Miller Com, Univ. of Illinois, 2003; Gordon Holmes, Cambridge Univ., 2004; Lord David Sainsbury, Bristol Univ., 2005; Harveian Oration, RCP, 2005; Kenneth Myer, Howard Florey Inst., Univ. of Melbourne, 2006 (also Medal); IBM Hursley, Southampton Univ., 2006; Kavli Distinguished, Yale Univ., 2008; Chief Scientist's, Food Standards Agency, 2008; Bristol, Bristol Univ., 2008; Foundn, RCPath, 2008; Max Cowan, Dana Foundn, 2010; Ida Mann (also Medal), Oxford Eye Hosp., 2010; Humphreys, Univ. of Birmingham, 2011. Hon. Professor: China Acad. of Mgt Sci., 1990–; Peking Union Med. Coll., 2005; Univ. of Warwick, 2010–. Mem., Academia Rodinensis Pro Remediatione, 1988; MAE 1995; Founder FMedSci 1998; FRSocMed 2003. Hon. FRCP 2004. Foreign Member: Royal Netherlands Acad. of Arts and Scis, 1993; Chinese Acad. of Engrg, 2009. Hon. Member: Alpha Omega Alpha Honor Med. Soc., USA, 1996; Physiol Soc., 1998; Internat. Assoc. of Sci. Clubs, 2002–; Cambridge Union Soc., 2003. Freeman, City of London, 1998; Mem., Co. of Spectacle Makers, 1997, Liveryman, 1998–. Foreign Fellow, Nat. Acad. Scis, India, 2008. Hon. Fellow: Cardiff Univ., 1998; Downing Coll., Cambridge, 1999; Indian Acad. of Neuroscis, 2007; Hon. FBPhS (Hon. FBPharmacolS 2007). Hon. DSc: Aston, 1992; Salford, 1994; Manchester, 2005; Aberdeen, 2005; KCL, 2007; Hon. DM Nottingham, 2008; DUniv: Open, 2011; York, 2011. Silver Award, BMA Film Competition, 1972; Silver Award, Padua Internat. Film Fest., 1973; Robert Bing Prize, Swiss Acad. of Med. Sciences, 1975; Copeman Medal, Corpus Christi Coll., Cambridge, 1977; Richardson Cross Medal, S Western Ophthalmol Soc., 1978; Man of the Year, Royal Assoc. for Disability and Rehabilitation, 1978; Phi Beta Kappa Award in Sci., 1978; John Locke Medal, Apothecaries' Soc., 1983; Prix du Docteur Robert Netter, Acad. Nat. de Médecine, Paris, 1984; Norman McAlister Gregg Award, RACO, 1988; Michael Faraday Prize, Royal Soc., 1989; John P. McGovern Science and Soc. Medal, Sigma Xi, USA, 1990; G. L. Brown Prize, Physiol Soc., 1990; Ellison-Cliffe Medal, RSM, 1993; Annual Review Prize, Physiol Soc., 1994; Charles F. Prentice Award, Amer. Acad. of Optometry, 1994; Alcon Prize, Alcon Res. Inst., 1996; Meml Medal, Charles Univ., Prague, 1998; Charter Award, IBiol, 2001; Baly Medal, RCP, 2001; Outstanding Contribn to Neurosci. Award, British Neurosci. Assoc., 2001; BioIndustry Assoc. Award, 2004; Lord Crook Gold Medal, Spectacle Makers' Co., 2004; Edinburgh Medal, City of Edinburgh, 2005; Sci. Educator Award, Soc. for Neurosci., 2005; Kenneth Meyer Medal, Howard Florey Inst., Melbourne, 2006; James Bull Gold Medal, British Soc. of Neuroradiologists, 2009; Ferrier Prize, Royal Soc., 2010; Prize for Sci. Documentaries, Fest. de Film CinéGlobe, Geneva, 2010. *Publications*: Handbook of Psychobiology (with M. S. Gazzaniga), 1975; Mechanics of the Mind, 1977; (with S. A. Greenfield) Mindwaves, 1987; The Mind Machine, 1988, 2nd edn 1994; (with H. B. Barlow and M. Weston-Smith) Images and Understanding, 1990; Vision: coding and efficiency, 1990; (with S. D. Iversen) Gender and Society, 2000; (with S. Jennett) Oxford Companion to the Body, 2001; (with A. Parker and A. Derrington) The Physiology of Cognitive Processes, 2003; (with C. A. Heywood and A. D. Milner) The Roots of Visual Awareness, 2003; res. reports in Jl of Physiol., Jl of Neuroscience, Nature, Lancet, etc; opinion columns in The Times, Guardian, Independent, Daily Telegraph, Sunday Times, Observer, etc. *Recreation*: wasting time. *Address*: Hong Kong Institute for Advanced Study, City University of Hong Kong, Fong Yun-wah Building, Tat Chee Avenue, Kowloon, Hong Kong. *Club*: Chelsea Arts (Hon. Mem., 1991–92).

*See also S.-J. Blakemore.*

**BLAKEMORE, Michael Howell**, AO 2003; OBE 2003; freelance director and writer; *b* Sydney, NSW, 18 June 1928; *s* of late Conrad Blakemore and Una Mary Blakemore (*née* Litchfield); *m* 1st, 1960, Shirley (*née* Bush); one *s*; 2nd, 1986, Tanya McCallin; two *d*. *Educ*: The King's Sch., NSW; Sydney Univ.; Royal Academy of Dramatic Art. Actor with Birmingham Rep. Theatre, Shakespeare Memorial Theatre, etc, 1952–66; Co-dir, Glasgow Citizens Theatre (1st prod., The Investigation), 1966–68; Associate Artistic Dir, Nat. Theatre, 1971–76. Dir, Players, NY, 1978. Resident Dir, Lyric Theatre, Hammersmith, 1980. Best Dir, London Critics, 1972. *Productions include*: A Day in the Death of Joe Egg, Comedy, 1967, Broadway 1968; Arturo Ui, Saville, 1969, Israel, 1969; Forget-me-not Lane, Apollo, 1971; Separate Tables, Apollo, 1976; Privates on Parade, Aldwych (RSC), transf. Piccadilly, 1977; Candida, Albery, 1977; Design for Living, Phoenix, 1977; Knuckle, Comedy, 1978; All My Sons, Wyndham's, 1981; Benefactors, Vaudeville, 1984, NY, 1986; Made in Bangkok, Aldwych, 1986; Lettice and Lovage, Globe, 1987, NY, 1990 (Outer Critics Circle Award, NY, 1990); Uncle Vanya, Vaudeville, 1988; City of Angels, Broadway, 1989 (Outer Critics Circle Award, NY, 1990), Prince of Wales Th., 1993; The Ride Down Mount Morgan, Wyndhams, 1991; Tosca, WNO, 1992; Here, Donmar Warehouse, 1993; The Sisters Rosensweig, Old Vic, 1994; Now You Know, Hampstead, 1995; Alarms and Excursions, Gielgud, 1998; Mr Peter's Connections, Almeida, 2000; Life After George, Duchess, 2002; The Three Sisters, Playhouse, 2003; Embers, Duke of York, 2006; Blithe Spirit, Gielgud Th., 2014; The Life, Southwark Playhouse, 2017 (Offie Award for Best Musical Prodn, 2018); *National Theatre*: The National Health, 1969; Long Day's Journey Into Night, 1971; The Front Page, Macbeth, 1972; The Cherry Orchard, 1973; Grand Manoeuvres, 1974; Plunder, 1976; After the Fall, 1990; Copenhagen, 1998, transf. Duchess, then Montparnasse, Paris, 1999 (Molière Award, Tony Award, Drama Desk Award, 2000), then Sydney Th. Co., 2002 (Helpmann Award, Australia, 2003), revival, Chichester Fest. Th., 2018; Democracy, 2003, transf. Wyndham's, then NY, 2005; Afterlife, 2008; *Royal Court Theatre*: Widowers' Houses, 1968; Don's Party, 1973; Lyric

*Theatre, Hammersmith:* Make and Break, 1980, transf. Haymarket, 1980; Travelling North, 1980; The Wild Duck, 1980; Noises Off, 1982 (transf. to Savoy, 1982, NY, 1983 (Drama Desk Award, NY, 1983–84; Outer Critics Circle Award, NY, 1983; Hollywood Drama-League Award, LA, 1984)); *foreign productions include:* The White Devil, Minneapolis, 1976; Hay Fever, 1976, The Seagull, 1979, Aarhus; Mourning Becomes Electra, Melbourne, 1980; Death Defying Acts, NY, 1995; The Life (musical), Broadway, NY, 1997; Kiss Me Kate, Broadway, NY, 1999 (Tony Award, Drama Desk Award, 2000), transf. Victoria Palace, 2001; Deuce, Is He Dead?, Broadway, NY, 2007; Blithe Spirit, Broadway, NY, 2009, US tour 2015. *Films:* A Personal History of the Australian Surf, 1981 (Standard film award, 1982); Privates on Parade, 1983; The Old Reliable, 1988; Country Life, 1995 (Film Critics Circle of Australia Award, 1994). Inducted American Theatre Hall of Fame, 2010. *Publications:* Next Season (novel), 1969; Australia Fair, 1985; Arguments with England (memoir), 2005; Stage Blood (memoir), 2013 (Sheridan Morley Prize, 2013); contrib. The New Yorker. *Recreation:* surfing.

**BLAKEMORE, Prof. Sarah-Jayne,** PhD; FBA 2018; CPsychol; FRSB; Professor of Psychology in the Social Sciences, University of Cambridge, since 2019; *b* Cambridge, 11 Aug. 1974; *d* of Sir Colin Brian Blakemore, *qv*; *m* 2002, Dr James Kilner; two *s*. *Educ:* St Philip's and St James's Primary Sch., Oxford; Crescent Prep. Sch., Oxford; Oxford High Sch. (GDST), Oxford; St John's Coll., Oxford (BA 1st Cl. Hons Exptl Psychol. 1996); University Coll. London (PhD Neurosci. 2000). Wellcome Trust Internat. Res. Fellow, Neurosci. Res. Centre, Inserm, Lyon, 2001–02; University College London: Wellcome Trust Res. Fellow, 2002–03; Gp Leader, Develtl Cognitive Neurosci. Lab., 2004; Reader in Cognitive Neurosci., 2006–10; Prof. of Cognitive Neurosci., 2010–19; Dep. Dir, Inst. of Cognitive Neurosci., 2014–19; Royal Soc. Dorothy Hodgkin Res. Fellow, 2004–08; Royal Soc. Univ. Res. Fellow, 2008–16. *Publications:* (with U. Frith) The Learning Brain: lessons for education, 2005; Section Ed., The Cognitive Neurosciences, 5th edn, 2014; Inventing Ourselves: the secret life of the teenage brain, 2018; contrib. papers to scientific jls. *Recreations:* family, friends, travel, restaurants, music, walking. *Address:* Department of Psychology, University of Cambridge, Free School Lane, Cambridge CB2 3RQ.

**BLAKENHAM,** 3rd Viscount *cr* 1963, of Little Blakenham; **Caspar John Hare;** Professor of Philosophy, Massachusetts Institute of Technology, since 2015; *b* 8 April 1972; *s* of 2nd Viscount Blakenham and Marcia Persephone (*née* Hare); *S* father, 2018; *m* Melissa Jane Mohr; one *s* one *d*. *Educ:* Wesleyan Univ. (BA 1994); Stanford Univ. (MA 1998); Princeton Univ. (PhD 2004). Massachusetts Institute of Technology: Instructor in Philosophy, 2003–04; Asst Prof. of Philosophy, 2004–07; Associate Prof. of Philosophy, 2007–15. *Publications:* On Myself, and Other, Less Important Subjects, 2009; The Limits of Kindness, 2013; articles in jls. *Heir:* *s* Hon. Inigo Hare, *b* 2006.

**BLAKER, Gary Mark;** QC 2015; *b* London, 20 June 1970; *s* of Marshall Blaker and Philippa Blaker; *m* 1998, Sharon Horwitz; one *d*. *Educ:* Haberdashers' Aske's Sch. for Boys, Elstree; Christ's Coll., Cambridge (BA Law 1992; MA). Called to the Bar, Middle Temple, 1993, Bencher, 2015; in practice as a barrister, specialising in property and chancery, Selborne Chambers. Vice Pres., POhWER, 2012–. Liveryman, Fan Makers' Co., 1992– (Mem., Ct of Assts, 2014–). *Recreations:* opera, theatre, travel, collecting historical autograph letters, watching Arsenal FC. *Address:* Selborne Chambers, 10 Essex Street, WC2R 3AA. *T:* (020) 7420 9500. *E:* gary.blaker@selbornechambers.co.uk.

**BLAKER, Sir John,** 3rd Bt *cr* 1919; *b* 22 March 1935; *s* of Sir Reginald Blaker, 2nd Bt, TD, and Sheila Kellas, *d* of Dr Alexander Cran; *S* father, 1975; *m* 1st, 1960, Catherine Ann (marr. diss. 1965), *d* of late F. J. Thorold; 2nd, 1968, Elizabeth Katherine (*d* 2012), *d* of late Col John Tinsley Russell, DSO. *Address:* Stantons Farm, East Chiltington, near Lewes, East Sussex BN7 3BB.

**BLAKESLEY, Patrick James;** QC 2018; *b* Ashover, Derbyshire, 9 Dec. 1968; *s* of John Blakesley and Rosemary Blakesley (*née* Simms); *m* 2001, Rosalind Polly Gray (*see* R. P. Blakesley); one *s* one *d*. *Educ:* Shrewsbury Sch.; Balliol Coll., Oxford (MA Lit.Hum. 1991); City Univ. (DipLaw 1992). Called to the Bar, Inner Temple, 1993; in practice as a barrister, specialising in personal injury, insurance, professional indemnity. *Recreations:* increasingly painful cricket, over-enthusiastic outdoor cooking, fly fishing, Derbyshire hills. *Address:* Crown Office Chambers, 2 Crown Office Row, Temple, EC4Y 7HJ. *T:* (020) 7797 8100. *E:* blakesley@crownofficechambers.com.

**BLAKESLEY, Rosalind Polly,** DPhil; Professor of Russian and European Art, since 2018 and Head, Department of History of Art, since 2016, University of Cambridge; Fellow of Pembroke College, Cambridge, since 2002; *b* Purley, London, 30 March 1970; *d* of Peter Gray and Mavis Gray (*née* Donaldson); *m* 2001, Patrick James Blakesley, *qv*; one *s* one *d*. *Educ:* Beacon Hill Sch., Hong Kong; Cheltenham Ladies' Coll.; Gonville and Caius Coll., Cambridge (BA 1992); Christ Church, Oxford (DPhil 1997). Leverhulme Study Abroad Student, Moscow State Univ., 1994–95; Laming Jun. Fellow, Queen's Coll., Oxford, 1996–98, Affiliated Res. Fellow, Russian Inst. of Art Hist., Moscow, 1997; Lecturer in History of Art: Univ. of Newcastle upon Tyne, 1998–2000; Univ. of Kent, 2001–02; University of Cambridge: Asst Lectr, 2002–03, Lectr, 2003–05, Sen. Lectr, 2005–13, in Hist. of Art; Reader in Russian and European Art, 2013–18; Leverhulme Res. Fellow, 2009–10; Founder and Co-Dir, Cambridge Courtauld Russian Art Centre, 2011–. Curator: Images of Persuasion: an Exhibn of Soviet Posters, Barbican Centre, London, 1993; Russia and the Arts: the age of Tolstoy and Tchaikovsky, NPG, 2016; Consultant to: A Style of Life, a Style of Art: Nat. Romantic Movements in Eur. Art, State Tretyakov Gall., Moscow, 1999; International Arts and Crafts, V&A Mus., 2005; Consultant Curator, An Imperial Collection: Women Artists from the State Hermitage Mus., Nat. Mus. of Women in Arts, Washington, DC. Ind. Assessor, Reviewing Cttee on Export of Works of Art, DCMS, 2000–01. Syndic, Fitzwilliam Mus., 2016–; Mem. Cttee, Kettle's Yard, 2016–. Trustee, NPG, 2010–18. Gov., Shrewsbury Sch., 2008–12. Mem., Jury, Pushkin House Russian Book Prize, 2018. Member: Editl Adv. Bd, Slavonica Jl, 2007–; Editl Adv. Bd, Jl of Art Historiography, 2016–; Editl Bd, Art History Jl, 2018–. Pushkin Medal (Russia), 2017. *Publications:* Russian Genre Painting in the Nineteenth Century, 2000; (ed jtly) An Imperial Collection: women artists from the State Hermitage Museum, 2003; The Arts and Crafts Movement, 2006; (ed jtly) Russian Art and the West, 2007; (ed jtly) From Realism to the Silver Age: new studies in Russian artistic culture, 2014; The Russian Canvas: painting in Imperial Russia, 1757–1881, 2016 (Pushkin House Russian Book Prize, 2017; Best Book Award, Art Newspaper Russia, 2018); contribs to books, exhibn catalogues and learned jls; book and exhibn reviews. *Recreations:* boats, brunch. *Address:* Pembroke College, Cambridge CB2 1RF.

**BLAKEWAY, Richard Anthony;** Strategic Advisor, EcoWorld International (formerly Willmott Residential), since 2016; *b* Wales, 14 Oct. 1978; *s* of John and Maureen Blakeway; *m* 2011, Joanna Tudor; one *s*. *Educ:* Univ. of Hull (BA Hons British Politics and Legislative Studies). Parly researcher, 2001–08; Ed., Internat. Develt Mag., 2004–08; Mayoral Advr on Housing, 2008–12; Dep. Mayor for Housing, Land and Property, GLA, 2012–16; Special Advr, Prime Minister's Office, 2016. Mem. Bd, Homes and Communities Agency, 2017–. Election Observer: Somaliland, 2005; Ukraine, 2006. Trustee, Chartered Inst. of Housing, 2011–16. Chairman: Homes for London; BexleyCo Ltd. FRSA. *Recreations:* opera, collecting art and artefacts, travel, architecture, writing, Victorian politics. *E:* richard@tudorblakeway.com. *Club:* Surrey County Cricket.

**BLAKEY, David Cecil,** CBE 1998; QPM 1993; DL; HM Inspector of Constabulary, 1999–2004; *b* 1943; *s* of Cecil and Elsie Jane Blakey; *m* 1966, Wendy Margaret Cartwright; one *s* one *d*. *Educ:* Jarrow Grammar Sch.; Univ. of Newcastle upon Tyne (MBA). VSO, Sarawak, 1962; Constable, Durham Constabulary, 1963; Police National Computer, 1972–76; Supt, Durham, 1979; Chief Supt, Northumbria, 1984; Asst Chief Constable, West Mercia, 1986; RCDS, 1989; Deputy Chief Constable: Leics, 1989–90; West Mercia, 1990–91; Chief Constable, W Mercia, 1991–99. Pres., ACPO, 1997–98. DL Worcs, 1999. *Recreations:* books, history. *Address:* c/o HM Inspectorate of Constabulary, Bartleet House, 165a Birmingham Road, Bromsgrove, Worcs B61 0DJ.

**BLAKEY, (Diana) Kristin;** *see* Henry, D. K.

**BLAKISTON, Sir Ferguson Arthur James,** 9th Bt *cr* 1763; entrepreneur and writer; *b* 19 Feb. 1963; *er s* of Sir Arthur Norman Hunter Blakiston, 8th Bt, and Mary Ferguson (*d* 1982), *d* of late Alfred Ernest Gillingham, Cave, S Canterbury, NZ; *S* father, 1977; *m* 1993, Linda Jane, *d* of late Robert John Key, Queenstown, NZ; two *d*. *Educ:* Lincoln Coll., NZ (Diploma in Agriculture 1983); Auckland Inst. of Technology (Cert. in Marketing, 1993); NZ Inst. of Business Studies (Diploma in Travel Writing). *Heir:* *b* Norman John Balfour Blakiston, Executive Officer [*b* 7 April 1964; *m* 1994, Rhonda Maree Hart; three *s* one *d*]. *Address:* 8 Coulter Place, Geraldine, S Canterbury, New Zealand.

**BLAKSTAD, Michael Björn;** External Professor of Digital Media, University of Glamorgan, 2002–12; *b* 18 April 1940; *s* of late Clifford and Alice Blakstad; *m* 1965, Patricia Marilyn Wotherspoon; one *s* twin *d*. *Educ:* Ampleforth Coll.; Oriel Coll., Oxford (MA Lit. Hum.). General trainee, BBC, 1962–68; Producer, Yorkshire Television, 1968–71; freelance TV producer, 1971–74; Programme Editor, BBC, 1974–80; Dir of Programmes, TV South, 1980–84. Founder and Managing Director, Blackrod, 1980 (Chm., 1981–84); Chairman and Chief Executive: Workhouse Productions, 1984–88; Chrysalis Television Ltd, 1988–90; Chm., 1990–2003, Chief Exec., 1990–94, Workhouse Ltd; Chairman: Filmscreen Internat. Ltd, 1984–86; Friday Productions, 1984–88; Blackrod Interactive Services, 1988–90; Winchester Independent Radio Ltd, 1995–98; Moviola, 2009–11; Jt Chief Exec., Videodisc Co., 1984–88; Dir, Chrysalis Gp, 1988–90. Dir, michaelblakstad ltd, 2002–05. Director: IPPA, 1986–90; Internat. Video Communications Assoc., 1988–90, 1999–2001; Winchester Theatre Royal, 1988–95 (Chm., 1990–95). Chairman: Southern Screen, 1998–2004; Exec. Steering Gp, broadbandshow, 2002–04. Chm. Govs, Bedales Schs, 2001–05. Hampshire Ambassador, 2005–13. Chm., East Meon History Gp, 2010–. Awards include: Radio Industries Club, 1975, 1977, 1979; RTS, 1976; BAFTA/Shell Prize, 1976; BIM/John Player, 1976; Nyon, 1978. Hon. MSc Salford, 1983; FRSA; MRI. *Publications:* The Risk Business, 1979; Tomorrow's World looks to the Eighties, 1979; (with Aldwyn Cooper) The Communicating Organisation, 1995; The Liphook Story, 2004. *Recreations:* local history, writing, opera, theatre. *Address:* 15 The Green, East Meon, Petersfield, Hants GU32 1QT.

**BLANC, Christian;** Deputy (Allied UDF, then New Centre) for Yvelines, French National Assembly, 2002–08 and 2010–12; Secretary of State for Development of the Greater Paris Area, 2008–10; *b* Talence, Gironde, 17 May 1942; *s* of Marcel Blanc and Encarna (*née* Miranda); *m* 1st, 1973, Asa Birgitta Hagglund (marr. diss.); two *d*; 2nd, 2003, Ingrid Arion. *Educ:* Institut d'Etudes Politiques, Bordeaux (Dip.). Asst Dir, Sopexa Scandinavia, 1969; Dep. to Controller, Mission for Territorial Equipment, 1970–74; Hd of Bureau, Sec. of State for Youth and Sports, 1974–76; Asst Gen. Delegate, Tech. Interministerial Agency for Leisure and Fresh Air, 1976–80; Dir of Cabinet, Commn of EC, Brussels, 1981–83; Prefect: Commune of Haute-Pyrénées, 1983–84; Govt of New Caledonia, 1985; Seine and Marne, 1985–89; without portfolio, 1989. Pres. and Dir-Gen., Régie Autonome des Transports Parisiens, 1989–92; Pres., Air France, 1993–97; Vice-Chm., Merrill Lynch Europe, 2000–02; Chm., Merrill Lynch France SA, 2000–02. Director: Middle East Airlines, 1998–99; Carrefour; Cap Gemini. Dir, Chancery, Univs of Paris, 1991–2001. Pres. External Selection Cttee for Recruitment of Sen. Treasury Officials, 2000–02. Officer, Légion d'Honneur (France), 1988; Officier, Ordre National du Merite (France), 1994. *Publications:* Pour un Etat Stratège garant de l'intérêt général, 1993; Le Lièvre et la Tortue, 1994; La Croissance ou le Chaos, 2006; Le Grand Paris du XXIe siècle, 2010; Paris, ville monde, 2015.

**BLANC, Raymond René,** Hon. OBE 2007; chef; Patron and Chairman, Blanc Restaurants Ltd, since 1984; Culinary Director, Eurostar, since 2012; *b* 19 Nov. 1949; *m*; two *s*. *Educ:* CEG de Valdahon; Lycée technique de horlogerie, Besançon. Chef de rang, 1971; Manager and chef de cuisine, 1976; proprietor and chef, Les Quat' Saisons, Summertown, 1977; Dir and Chm., Maison Blanc, 1978–88; proprietor, Le Petit Blanc, 1984–88; Chef/patron and Chairman, Le Manoir aux Quat' Saisons, 1984–; co-owner: Brasserie Blanc (formerly Le Petit Blanc) restaurants: Oxford, 1996–; Cheltenham, 1998–; Birmingham, 1999–; Manchester, 2000–09; Tunbridge Wells, 2004–09; Bristol, 2008–; Portsmouth, 2009–; Milton Keynes, 2010–; Chichester, 2010–; Winchester, 2010–; Berkhamsted, 2012–; Beaconsfield, 2014–. TV series: Blanc Mange, 1994; The Restaurant, 2007, 2008, 2009; Raymond Blanc's Kitchen Secrets, 2010, 2011; Raymond Blanc: the very hungry Frenchman, 2012; Raymond Blanc: how to cook well, 2013. Académicien Mentor, Académie Culinaire de France. Master Chef Great Britain. Hon. DBA Oxford Brookes Univ., 1999. Personnalité de l'année, 1990. Commandeur de l'Assoc. Internat. des Maîtres Conseils en Gastronomie Française. Chevalier: Légion d'Honneur (France), 2013; Ordre du Mérite agricole (France), 2013. *Publications:* Recipes from Le Manoir aux Quat' Saisons, 1988; Cooking for Friends, 1991; Blanc Mange, 1994; A Blanc Christmas, 1996; Blanc Vite, 1998; Foolproof French Cookery, 2002; A Taste of My Life, 2008; Kitchen Secrets, 2011; Kew on a Plate with Raymond Blanc, 2015; Le Manoir aux Quat' Saisons, 2016. *Recreations:* reading, tennis, riding, classical and rock music. *Address:* Le Manoir aux Quat' Saisons, Church Road, Great Milton, Oxford OX44 7PD.

**BLANCH, Sir Malcolm,** KCVO 1998 (CVO 1992; LVO 1981; MVO 1968); Clerk Comptroller to Queen Elizabeth the Queen Mother, 1967–98; *b* 27 May 1932; *s* of late John and Louie Blanch; *m* 1957, Jean Harding Richardson (*d* 2007); two *s*. *Educ:* Dinnington Sch., Yorks. Served RN, 1949–56. Asst Keeper and Steward in Royal Yachts, Victoria & Albert, 1953, Britannia, 1954–56; Queen Elizabeth the Queen Mother's Household, 1957–98: Clerk Accountant, 1960–67. Freeman, City of London, 1989. *Recreations:* gardening, music. *Address:* 12 Bishop's Drive, East Harnham, Salisbury, Wilts SP2 8NZ. *T:* (01722) 329862.

**BLANCH, Rev. Dr Michael Dennis,** TD and bar 1990; Member (Lib Dem), East Sussex County Council, 2013–17; non-stipendiary Church of England priest; *b* 22 Oct. 1946; *s* of Harold Clement Blanch and Jane Emily Blanch; *m* 1973, Penelope Ann Worthington; two *s*. *Educ:* William Ellis Sch.; Univ. of Birmingham (BScSoc 1969; DipEd 1970; PhD 1975). AMA 1979. Keeper of Education, Nat. Army Mus., 1973–77; Sen. Museums Keeper, Rotherham MBC, 1977–79; Asst Dir, Libraries, Oldham MBC, 1979–81; Dir of Museums, 1981–84, Dir of Leisure Services, 1984–88, Calderdale MBC; County Leisure Services

Officer, Shropshire CC, 1988–91; Chief Executive: Eastbourne BC, 1991–95; London Borough of Bromley, 1995–2000; Falkland Is Govt, 2000–03 and 2007. Ordained Priest (C of E), 2010; Priest in Charge, St Mary's, Hampden Park and St Peter's The Hydneye, 2013–17; Vicar of Isfield, 2018–. FCMI (FIMgt 1985). *Publications:* War and Weapons, 1976; Soldiers, 1980. *Recreations:* mountain biking, hill walking, sailing, previously Territorial Army. *Address:* 4 Ashburnham Road, Eastbourne, E Sussex BN21 2HU. *T:* (01323) 747944.

BLANCHARD, Claire; QC 2010; *b* Louth, 11 Aug. 1969; *d* of Jeffrey and Judith Blanchard. *Educ:* Liverpool Poly. (LLB Hons 1991). Called to the Bar, Gray's Inn, 1992, Bencher, 2014; in practice as barrister specialising in commercial law. *Recreation:* Arsenal FC. *Address:* Essex Court Chambers, 24 Lincoln's Inn Fields, WC2A 3EG.

BLANCHARD, Rt Hon. Sir Peter, KNZM 2009 (DCNZM 2005); PC 1998; a Judge of the Supreme Court, New Zealand, 2004–12, Acting Judge, 2012–17; *b* 2 Aug. 1942; *s* of Cyril Francis Blanchard and Zora Louis Blanchard (now Parkinson); *m* 1968, Judith Isabel Watts; one *s* one *d. Educ:* King's Coll., Auckland; Univ. of Auckland (LLM 1968); Harvard Univ. (Frank Knox Fellow, 1968; Fulbright Fellow, 1968; LLM 1969). Admitted barrister and solicitor, Supreme Court of NZ, 1966; Partner: Grierson Jackson & Partners, 1968–83; Simpson Grierson, 1983–92; Judge: High Court of NZ, 1992–96; Court of Appeal of NZ, 1996–2003. Comr, Law Commn, 1990–94. *Publications:* Handbook on Agreements for Sale and Purchase of Land, 1978, 4th edn 1987; Company Receiverships in Australia and New Zealand, 1982, 2nd edn (jtly) 1994; (jtly) Private Receivers of Companies in New Zealand, 2008. *Recreations:* reading, music, theatre, walking. *Address:* 1/2 Marine Parade, Herne Bay, Auckland 1011, New Zealand.

BLANCHET, Pauline; *see* Marois, P.

BLANCHETT, Catherine Elise, (Cate), AC 2017; actress; Joint Artistic Director, Sydney Theatre Company, 2008–13; *b* 1969; *d* of late Bob Blanchett and of June Blanchett; *m* 1997, Andrew Upton; three *s* one adopted *d. Educ:* Methodist Ladies' Coll., Melbourne; Melbourne Univ.; Nat. Inst. of Dramatic Art, Sydney. *Theatre includes:* Top Girls, Sydney Th. Co., 1992; Kafka Dances (Newcomer Award, Sydney Th. Critics Circle, 1993); Oleanna, Sydney Th. Co. (Rosemont Best Actress Award); Hamlet, Belvoir Th. Co., 1995; Sweet Phoebe, Sydney Th. Co.; The Tempest, The Blind Giant is Dancing, Belvoir Street Th. Co.; The Seagull, 1996; Plenty, Almeida, 1999; A Streetcar Named Desire, Sydney Th. Co., Sydney, transf. NY, 2009; Gross und Klein, Sydney Th. Co., Sydney, 2011, transf. Barbican, 2012; The Maids, NY City Centre, NY, 2014; The Present, Barrymore Th., NY, 2016; When We Have Sufficiently Tortured Each Other, NT, 2019. *Television includes:* Heartland, GP, Police Rescue, 1994; Bordertown, 1995. *Films include:* Parkland, 1996; Paradise Road, Thank God He Met Lizzie, Oscar and Lucinda, 1997; Elizabeth, 1998 (Best Actress, BAFTA, and Best Actress in a Drama, Golden Globe Awards, 1999); An Ideal Husband, Pushing Tin, 1999; Dreamtime Alice (also co-prod.), The Talented Mr Ripley, The Man Who Cried, 2000; The Fellowship of the Ring, The Gift, Bandits, 2001; Heaven, The Shipping News, Charlotte Gray, Chasing the Dragon, The Two Towers, 2002; Veronica Guerin, The Return of the King, 2003; The Missing, Coffee & Cigarettes, 2004; The Aviator (Academy Award for Best Supporting Actress), The Life Aquatic with Steve Zissou, 2005; Little Fish, Babel, 2006; Notes on a Scandal, The Good German, I'm Not There, The Golden Age, 2007; Indiana Jones and the Kingdom of the Crystal Skull, 2008; The Curious Case of Benjamin Button, 2009; Robin Hood, 2010; Hanna, 2011; The Hobbit: An Unexpected Journey, 2012; Blue Jasmine, 2013 (Best Actress in a Motion Picture, Drama, Golden Globe Awards and Screen Actors Guild Awards, Best Actress, BAFTA and Independent Spirit Awards, Leading Actress, Academy Awards, 2014); The Monuments Men, How to Train Your Dragon 2, 2014; Cinderella, Carol, Truth, 2015; Knight of Cups, 2016; Thor: Ragnarok, Manifesto, 2017; Ocean's 8, The House with a Clock in its Walls, Mowgli: legend of the jungle, 2018; How to Train Your Dragon: The Hidden World, 2019. Hon. DLitt Macquarie, 2014. *Address:* c/o RGM Artist Group, PO Box 128, Surry Hills, NSW 2010, Australia.

BLANCKENHAGEN, Jane Maureen; *see* Kelly, Jane Maureen.

BLAND, Christopher Donald Jack; Lord-Lieutenant of the Isle of Wight, 1995–2006; Chairman, Hovertravel Ltd, 1965–2010; *b* 8 Oct. 1936; *s* of Christopher Donald James Bland and Iris Raynor Bland; *m* 1962, Judith Anne Louise Maynard; one *s* three *d. Educ:* Sandroyd Prep. Sch.; Clayesmore Public Sch. Nat. Service, Gordon Highlanders, later Lieut RE, 1955–57. Rolls Royce Ltd, 1957–61; Britten Norman Aircraft Co., 1961–65; Hovertravel Ltd (world's first hovercraft operator), 1965; Sen. Partner, Norwood, 1981–; Dir, Red Funnel Gp PLC, 1986–2006; Chm., Vectis Transport PLC, 1988–2006. Mem., Albany Prison Bd, 1978–88; Chm., IoW HA, 1988–90. High Sheriff, IoW, 1989–90. *Recreations:* flying vintage aircraft, vintage sports cars, tinkering with water mills. *Address:* Yafford House, Shorwell, Isle of Wight PO30 3LH. *T:* (01983) 740428. *Clubs:* Isle of Wight County; Royal Yacht Squadron (Cowes).

BLAND, Dr Roger Farrant, OBE 2008; Keeper, Department of Britain, Europe and Prehistory, British Museum, 2013–15 (Keeper: Department of Portable Antiquities and Treasure, 2005–13; Department of Prehistory and Europe, 2012–13); *b* London, 3 April 1955; *s* of David Farrant Bland and Mary Elmore Bland; *m* 1987, Dr Lucilla Mary Burn; one *d. Educ:* St Paul's Sch., London; King's Coll. London (BA 1978); Magdalen Coll., Oxford; University Coll. London (PhD 1991). Curator, 1979–2001, Dep. Keeper, 2001–05, Dept of Coins and Medals, BM. Advr, DNH, then DCMS, 1994–2003. Pres., British Numismatic Soc., 2011–16; Pres., Royal Numismatic Soc., 2018– (Vice Pres., 2009–18); Member: Council, Soc. of Antiquaries of London, 1995–98, 2011–14; Treasure Valuation Cttee, 2016–. Vis. Prof., Univ. of Leicester, 2015–; Sen. Fellow, McDonald Inst., Univ. of Cambridge, 2015–; Hon. Res. Fellow, BM, 2015–. Mem. Council, Soc. of Antiquaries of London, 1995–98 and 2011–14. Churchwarden and Treas., St Margaret's, Cley-next-the-Sea; Reader, Dio. of Norwich, 2018–. Joint Editor: Portable Antiquities: Annual Reports, 1997–2006; Reports on the Operation of the Treasure Act, 1997–2006; Portable Antiquities and Treasure: Annual Reports, 2007–09; Editor, Glaven Historian, 2016–. Prix de l'Académie des Inscriptions et Belles-Lettres, 2011; Medal, Royal Numismatic Soc., 2014; President's Medal, British Acad., 2016. *Publications:* Coin Hoards from Roman Britain III: the Blackmoor hoard, 1982; (with E. M. Besly) The Cunetio Treasure, 1983; (ed jtly) Coin Hoards from Roman Britain VI, 1986, and VII, 1987; (with A. M. Burnett) The Normanby Hoard and Other Roman Coin Hoards, 1988; (ed) The Chalfont Hoard and Other Roman Coin Hoards, 1992; (with C. Johns) The Hoxne Treasure: an illustrated introduction, 1993; Portable Antiquities: a discussion document, 1996; (ed jtly) Coin Hoards from Roman Britain X, 1997; The Treasure Act 1996: Code of Practice (England and Wales), 1997; (with K. Leahy) The Staffordshire Hoard, 2009, 2nd edn 2014; (with X. Loriot) Roman and Early Byzantine Gold Coins Found in Britain and Ireland, 2010; (jtly) The Frome Hoard, 2010; (ed jtly) Hoarding and the Deposition of Metalwork, 2015; (ed jtly) Studies in Ancient Coinage in Honour of Andrew Burnett, 2015; Coin Hoards and Hoarding in Roman Britain, 2018; (jtly) The Cunetio and Normanby Hoards, 2018. *Recreations:* walking, sailing, bird watching, Norfolk churches. *Address:* Stallgates, 2 Langham Road, Blakeney, Holt, Norfolk NR25 7PG. *T:* (01263) 740806. *E:* roger.bland@btinternet.com.

BLAND, Lt-Col Sir Simon (Claud Michael), KCVO 1982 (CVO 1973; MVO 1967); Extra Equerry to the Duke and Duchess of Gloucester, since 1989 (Comptroller, Private Secretary and Equerry, 1972–89); Extra Equerry to Princess Alice Duchess of Gloucester, 1989–2004 (Private Secretary and Comptroller, 1974–89); *b* 4 Dec. 1923; *s* of late Sir Nevile Bland, KCMG, KCVO, and Portia (*née* Ottley); *m* 1954, Olivia (DStJ 1999) (*d* 2013), *d* of late Major William Blackett, Arbigland, Dumfries; one *s* three *d. Educ:* Eton College. Served War of 1939–45, Scots Guards, in Italy; BJSM, Washington, 1948–49; 2nd Bn, Scots Guards, Malaya, 1949–51; Asst Mil. Adviser at UK High Commn, Karachi, 1959–60; Asst Private Sec., 1961–63, Comptroller and Private Sec., 1963–74, to late Duke of Gloucester; Private Sec. to late Prince William, 1968–72. Dir, West End Bd, Commercial Union, 1964–95; Vice-Pres., Raleigh Internat. (formerly Operation Raleigh), 1989–96. Chm., Coll. of St Barnabas, 1993–97; Member Council: Pestalozzi Children's Village Trust, 1989–2006, Vice-Pres., 2006–; Elizabeth Finn Trust (formerly DGAA Homelife), 1990–; Order of St John for Kent, 1990–; Pres., Friends of Edenbridge Hosp., 1990–2013. Mem., RBL, 1961–. Freeman, City of London, 1988. KStJ 1988. *Address:* Blossoms, Mead Road, Edenbridge, Kent TN8 5DD. *T:* (01732) 865489. *Club:* Buck's.

BLANDFORD, Marquess of; George John Godolphin Spencer-Churchill; *b* 28 July 1992; *er s* and *heir* of Duke of Marlborough, *qv*; *m* 2018, Camilla Thorp. *Educ:* Harrow.

BLANDFORD, Jacqueline Leigh, (Jay); *see* Hunt, J. L.

BLANDFORD, Prof. Roger David, FRS 1989; Professor of Physics, since 2003, and Luke Blossom Professor, School of Humanities and Sciences, since 2005, Stanford University; *b* 28 Aug. 1949; *s* of Jack George and Janet Margaret Blandford; *m* 1972, Elizabeth Denise Kellett; two *s. Educ:* King Edward's Sch., Birmingham; Magdalene Coll. Cambridge Univ. (BA, MA, PhD; Bye Fellow 1973). Res. Fellow, St John's Coll., Cambridge, 1973–76; Inst. for Advanced Study, Princeton, 1974–75; CIT, 1976–2003, Richard Chace Tolman Prof. of Theoretical Astrophysics, 1989–2003; Pehong and Adele Chen Prof. of Particle Astrophysics and Cosmology, 2003–05, Dir, Kavli Inst. for Particle Astrophysics and Cosmology, 2003–13, Stanford Univ. Mem., Nat. Acad. of Scis, 2005–. Fellow, Amer. Acad. of Arts and Scis, 1993. Gold Medal, RAS, 2013; Crafoord Prize, Royal Swedish Acad. of Scis, 2016. *Address:* Department of Physics, Stanford University, 382 Via Pueblo Mall, Stanford, CA 94305–4060, USA. *T:* (650) 7234233. *E:* rdb3@stanford.edu.

BLANEY, Dr David McAllister; Chief Executive, Higher Education Funding Council for Wales, since 2012; *b* Loughton, Essex, 5 March 1964; *s* of Prof. Walter Blaney and Jane Blaney; *m* 1991, Julia Mallett; two *d. Educ:* St John's Sch., Epping; Manchester Poly. (BA Hons Business Studies); Univ. of Wolverhampton (MBA); Cardiff Univ. (EdD 2006). Lectr, Humberside Coll. of HE, 1986–89; Lectr, 1989–90, Sen. Lectr, 1990–92, Principal Lectr, 1992–93, Univ. of Wolverhampton; University of Wales, Newport: Academic Devel Officer, 1993–95; Hd, Academic Develt, 1995–97; Dep. Asst Principal, 1997–99; Asst Principal, 1999–2003; Dir of Quality, 2003–04; Hd, Funding and Reconfiguration, 2005–08, Dir, Strategic Develt, 2008–12, HEFCW. *Recreations:* music, motor sports, war histories, malt whisky. *Address:* Higher Education Funding Council for Wales, Tŷ Afon, Bedwas Road, Bedwas, Caerphilly CF83 8WT. *T:* (029) 2085 9660. *E:* david.blaney@hefcw.ac.uk.

BLANK, Sir (Maurice) Victor, Kt 1999; Chairman, Lloyds Banking Group (formerly Lloyds TSB Group) plc, 2006–09; *b* 9 Nov. 1942; *s* of Joseph Blank and Ruth Blank (*née* Levey); *m* 1977, Sylvia Helen (*née* Richford); two *s* one *d. Educ:* Stockport Grammar Sch.; St Catherine's Coll., Oxford (MA; Domus Fellow, 1998; Hon. Fellow 2002). Solicitor of the Supreme Court. Joined Clifford-Turner as articled clerk, 1964: Solicitor, 1966; Partner, 1969; Charterhouse Bank: Dir, and Head of Corporate Finance, 1981; Chief Exec., 1985–96; Chm., 1985–97; Chief Exec., 1985–96, Chm., 1991–97, Charterhouse plc; Dir, Charterhouse Eur. Hldg, 1993– (Chm., 1993–97); Chairman: Mirror Group plc, 1998–99; Trinity Mirror PLC, 1999–2006; GUS (formerly The Great Universal Stores) plc, 2000–06 (Dir, 1993–2006; Dep. Chm., 1996–2000). Non-executive Director: Coats Viyella, subseq. Coats, plc, 1989 (Dep. Chm., 1999–2003); Williams (formerly Williams Hldgs) plc, 1995–2000; Sen. Ind. Dir, Chubb plc, 2000–03; Sen. Advr, Texas Pacific Gp. Mem., 1998–2004, Chm., 1998–2004, Industrial Develt Adv. Bd; Mem., Financial Reporting Council, 2003–07; Mem., Adv. Bd, 2011–, Chm., Strategy and Develt Bd, 2015–, Global Leadership Foundn; Chm., Eur. Adv. Bd, Cheung Kong Graduate Sch. of Business, 2012–. UK Business Ambassador, 2008–12. Chairman: Wellbeing, subseq. Wellbeing of Women, 1989–; Social Mobility Foundn, 2013–17 (Dep. Chm., 2017–); Chm., Bd of Trustees, Rothschild Foundn Hanadiv Europe, 2011–; Chm., Develt Bd, British Acad., 2015–. Chm., Union of Jewish Students, 2000–17 (Hon. Pres., 2017–); Vice-Pres., Jewish Leadership Council, 2009–. Mem. Council, Oxford Univ., 2000–07; Trustee, Saïd Business Sch., Univ. of Oxford, 2005–. Mem., RSA. CCMI (CIMgt 2000). Hon. FRCOG 1998. *Publications:* (jtly) Weinberg and Blank on Take-Overs and Mergers, 3rd edn 1971 to 5th edn 1989. *Recreations:* family, cricket, tennis, theatre.

BLANKS, Timothy Seldon; Editor-at-Large, Business of Fashion, since 2015; *b* Auckland, NZ, 8 Sept. 1954; *s* of Keith Owen Blanks and Jill Blanks; partner, 2012, Jeff Lounds. *Educ:* Auckland Grammar Sch.; Univ. of Auckland (BA Eng.). Editor, Toronto Life Fashion, 1987–90; Host, Fashion File, Canadian Broadcasting Corp., 1989–2006; Editor-at-Large, Style.com, 2006–15. Hon. Dr Academy of Art Univ., San Francisco, 2016. Media Award, Council of Fashion Designers of America, 2013. *Publications:* Mind, Body and Soul: the Body Shop book of wellbeing, 1998; The World of Anna Sui, 2017; *contributed to:* The Snippy World of Michael Roberts, 2005; Sample: 100 fashion designers, 2006; 20 Years of Dolce&Gabbana for Men, 2010; Another Portrait Book, 2010; Alexander McQueen: savage beauty, 2011; Anna Bauer: backstage, 2012; New Fashion Photography, 2013; Hair: Guido Palau, 2014; Walter Van Beirendonck: dream the world awake, 2014; Bottega Veneta: art of collaboration, 2015; Reigning Men: fashion in menswear 1715–2015, 2016; Dries Van Noten 0–100, 2017. *Recreations:* fine dining, travel, music. *Address:* 155 Sutherland Avenue, W9 1ES. *T:* 07494 410344. *E:* timblanks@yahoo.co.uk. *Club:* Soho House.

BLANNING, Prof. Timothy Charles William, LittD; FBA 1990; Professor of Modern European History, University of Cambridge, 1992–2009, now Emeritus; Fellow, Sidney Sussex College, Cambridge, since 1965; *b* 21 April 1942; *s* of Thomas Walter Blanning and Gwendolyn Marchant (*née* Jones); *m* 1988, Nicky Jones; one *s* one *d. Educ:* King's Sch., Bruton, Somerset; Sidney Sussex Coll., Cambridge (BA, MA; PhD 1967; LittD 1998). University of Cambridge: Res. Fellow, Sidney Sussex Coll., 1965–68; Asst Lectr in History, 1972–76; Lectr in History, 1976–87; Reader in Modern European History, 1987–92. *Publications:* Joseph II and Enlightened Despotism, 1970; Reform and Revolution in Mainz 1740–1803, 1974; The French Revolution in Germany, 1983; The Origins of the French Revolutionary Wars, 1986; The French Revolution: aristocrats versus bourgeois?, 1987 (trans. Italian, 1989, Portuguese, 1991, 2005); Joseph II, 1994; The French Revolutionary Wars 1787–1802, 1996; (ed) The Oxford Illustrated History of Modern Europe, 1996 (trans. Japanese, 2000, Korean, 2003, Greek, 2013); (ed) The Rise and Fall of the French Revolution, 1996; (ed) History cland Biography: essays in honour of Derek Beales, 1996; The French Revolution: class war or culture clash?, 1998 (trans. Japanese, 2005); (ed) Reform in Great Britain and Germany 1750–1850, 1999; (ed) The Short Oxford History of Europe: the eighteenth century, 2000 (trans. Polish, 2000, Spanish, 2002); (ed) The Short Oxford History of Europe: the nineteenth century, 2000 (trans. Polish, 2000, Spanish, 2002); The Culture of Power and the Power of Culture: old regime Europe 1660–1789, 2002; (ed) Unity and Diversity in European Culture *c* 1800, 2006; The Pursuit of Glory: Europe 1648–1815, 2007 (trans. Italian, 2011, Chinese, 2019); The Triumph of Music: composers, musicians and their audiences, 1700 to the present, 2008 (trans. German, 2010, Portuguese, 2011, Spanish, 2011); The Romantic Revolution, 2009 (trans. Croatian, 2012, Arabic, 2014); Frederick the Great: King of Prussia, 2015 (British Acad. Medal, 2016; trans. German, Chinese, 2019); George I, 2017. *Recreations:* music, football (Tottenham Hotspur FC). *Address:* Sidney Sussex College, Cambridge CB2 3HU. *T:* (01223) 338880. *Club:* Athenæum.

**BLANTERN, Dr Paul Jonathan;** Chief Executive, Northamptonshire County Council, 2010–17; *b* Ketton, Rutland, 10 Feb. 1966; *s* of Edward John and Cynthia Blantern; *m* 1991, Georgina Jane Findlay; two *s*. *Educ:* Stamford Sch.; Southampton Univ. (BSc Hons Envmtl Sci.); Exeter Univ. (PhD 1991); Cass Business Sch. (MBA 1997); Chartered Instn of Water and Envmtl Mgt (Dip. Water and Envmtl Mgt). Prodn Manager, Anglian Water, 1991–98; Business Perf. and Transformation Manager, AWG plc, 1998–2000; Strategy Manager, Fountain GB Ltd, 2000–01; Principal Consultant, 2001–03, Man. Dir, 2003–05, Severn Trent Utility Services; Man. Dir, Complete Credit Mgt, 2003–05; Dir, Customer Services, Solihull MBC, 2005–07; Corporate Dir, Customer and Community Services, Northants CC, 2008–10; Man. Dir, Local Govt Shared Services, 2010–13; Chm., Leadership for Libraries Taskforce, 2015–17. Clerk to Lieutenancy of Northants, 2010–17. Pres., Northants County Assoc. of Local Councils, 2010–17. *Recreations:* table tennis, skiing, canoeing.

**BLASHFORD-SNELL, Col John Nicholas,** CBE 2019 (OBE 1996; MBE 1969); author, lecturer and broadcaster; Ministry of Defence consultant (on staff, 1983–91); *b* 22 Oct. 1936; *s* of late Rev. Prebendary Leland John Blashford Snell and Gwendolen Ives Sadler; *m* 1960, Judith Frances (*née* Sherman); two *d*. *Educ:* Victoria Coll., Jersey, CI; RMA, Sandhurst. Commissioned Royal Engineers, 1957; 33 Ind. Fd Sqdn RE Cyprus, 1958–61; comd Operation Aphrodite (Expedition) Cyprus, 1959–61; Instructor: Junior Leaders Regt RE, 1962–63; RMA Sandhurst, 1963–66; Adjt 3rd Div. Engineers, 1966–67; comd Great Abbai Expedn (Blue Nile), 1968; sc RMCS Shrivenham and Camberley, 1968–69; comd Dahlak Quest Expedn, 1969–70; GSO2 MoD, 1970–72; comd British Trans-Americas Expedn, 1971–72; OC 48 Fd Sqdn RE, service in Belize, Oman, Ulster, 1972–74; comd Zaire River Expedn, 1974–75; CO Junior Leaders Regt RE, 1976–78; Dir of Operations, Operation Drake, 1977–81; on staff (GSO1), MoD, 1978–82; in command, The Fort George Volunteers, 1982–83. Operation Raleigh: Operations Dir, 1982–88; Dir Gen., 1989–91; Leader, Kota Mama expedn, 1995–, and numerous other expedns. Hon. Chm., 1969–2008, Pres., 2008–, Scientific Exploration Soc.; Hon. Chm., Scientific Exploration Soc. Jersey, 2002–; Pres., Just A Drop, 2004– (Hon. Chm., 2001–04); Appeal Dir, Trinity Sailing Trust, 2004–09 (Hon. Vice-Pres., 2009–); Trustee, Operation New World, 1995–; Patron, The Gorilla Orgn, 2019. Hon. Pres., The Vole Club, 1996–; Hon. Life Pres., Centre for Fortean Zoology, 2003–. Hon. Keeper of the Quaich, 2013. Chm., Liverpool Construction Crafts Guild, 2003–05 (Pres., 2005–). FRSGS 1975. Freeman, City of Hereford, 1984. Hon. Fellow, Liverpool John Moores Univ., 2010. Hon. DSc Durham, 1986; Hon. DEng Bournemouth, 1997. Cuthbert Peek Award, RGS, 1970; Darien Medal (Colombia), 1972; Segrave Trophy, 1974; Livingstone Medal, RSGS, 1975; Paul Harris Fellow, Rotary Internat., 1981; Patron's Medal, RGS, 1993; Gold Medal, Instn of RE, 1994; La Paz Medal (Bolivia), 2000; Hon. Worker Medal (1st Cl.) (Mongolia), 2016. *Publications:* Weapons and Tactics (with Tom Wintringham), 1970; (with Richard Snailham) The Expedition Organiser's Guide, 1970, 2nd edn 1976; Where the Trails Run Out, 1974; In the Steps of Stanley, 1975, 2nd edn 1975; (with A. Ballantine) Expeditions the Experts' Way, 1977, 2nd edn 1978; A Taste for Adventure, 1978; (with Michael Cable) Operation Drake, 1981; Mysteries: encounters with the unexplained, 1983; Operation Raleigh, the Start of an Adventure, 1987; (with Ann Tweedy) Operation Raleigh, Adventure Challenge, 1988; (with Ann Tweedy) Operation Raleigh, Adventure Unlimited, 1990; Something lost behind the Ranges, 1994, rev. edn 2014; (with Rula Lenska) Mammoth Hunt, 1996; (with Richard Snailham) Kota Mama, 2000; (with Richard Snailham) East to the Amazon, 2002. *Recreations:* motoring, shooting, food, wine, wildlife studies. *Clubs:* Travellers; Artists' (Liverpool); Galley Hill Shooting (Hon. Pres.); Explorers (New York); Jersey Pistol.

**BLATCHFORD, Sir Ian (Craig),** Kt 2019; Director and Chief Executive, Science Museum Group, and Director, Science Museum, since 2010; *b* Plymouth, 17 Aug. 1965; *s* of late David George Blatchford and of Elizabeth Jayne Cole. *Educ:* Mansfield Coll., Oxford (MA Law); Birkbeck Coll., Univ. of London (MA Renaissance Studies). Bank of England, 1986–88; Barclays de Zoete Wedd, 1988; Dep. Finance Dir, Arts Council, 1989–94; Financial Controller, Cricket Communications, 1994–96; Dir, Finance, RA, 1996–2002; Dir, Finance and Resources, 2002–04, Dep. Dir, 2004–10, V&A Mus. Chm. of Govs, De Montfort Univ., 2011–18. Mem., CIMA. FSA 2011. Pushkin Medal (Russia), 2015. *Recreations:* collecting Russian porcelain, classical music. *Address:* Science Museum, Exhibition Road, SW7 2DD. *E:* ian.blatchford@sciencemuseum.ac.uk. *Club:* Athenæum.

**BLATCHFORD, Roy Terence,** CBE 2016; Founding Director, National Education Trust, 2006–16; *b* Bedfordshire, 14 Oct. 1952; *s* of Don and Barbara Blatchford; *m* 1979, Anne Carter; one *s*. *Educ:* Univ. of Reading (BA English Hons); Inst. of Educn, Univ. of London (MA English (Dist.)). Teacher, London; Headteacher, 1985–2003: William Ellis Sch., London; Bicester Community Coll., Oxon; Walton High, Milton Keynes; HMI, 2003–06. *Publications:* The Restless School, 2014; National Standards of Excellence for Headteachers, 2015; (ed jtly) Self-Improving Schools, 2016; Success is a Journey, 2018. *Recreations:* cricket, cycling, ski-ing. *E:* royb88@gmail.com.

**BLATCHLEY, Geraldine;** *see* James, G.

**BLATHERWICK, Sir David (Elliott Spiby),** KCMG 1997 (CMG 1990); OBE 1973; HM Diplomatic Service, retired; *b* 13 July 1941; *s* of Edward S. Blatherwick; *m* 1964, (Margaret) Clare Crompton; one *s* one *d*. *Educ:* Lincoln Sch.; Wadham Coll., Oxford. Entered FO, 1964; Second Sec., Kuwait, 1968; First Sec., Dublin, 1970; FCO, 1973; Head of Chancery, Cairo, 1977; Head, Pol Affairs Dept, NI Office (Belfast), 1981; Hd, Energy, Science and Space Dept, FCO, 1983; sabbatical leave at Stanford Univ., Calif, 1985–86; Counsellor and Hd of Chancery, UK Mission to UN, NY, 1986–89; Prin. Finance Officer and Chief Inspector, FCO, 1989–91; Ambassador to: Republic of Ireland, 1991–95; Egypt, 1995–99. Chm., British Egyptian Chamber of Commerce, 1999–2015. *Publications:* The International Politics of Telecommunications, 1987. *Recreations:* music, sailing, walking. *Club:* Athenæum.

**BLATT, Prof. Michael Robert,** PhD; FRSE; Regius Professor of Botany, University of Glasgow, since 2001; *b* 9 Sept. 1953; *s* of Frank Blatt and Gloria Blatt (*née* Freeman); *m* 1980, Jane Stroh; one *s* one *d*. *Educ:* Univ. of Wisconsin-Madison (BSc Biochem. and Botany 1975); Univ. Erlangen-Nürnberg (Matricula Natural Scis 1979); Stanford Univ. (PhD Biol Scis 1981). NRSA Res. Fellow, Dept of Physiol., Yale Univ. Sch. of Medicine, 1980–83; NATO Fellow and Sen. Res. Associate, Botany Sch., Univ. of Cambridge, 1983–90; Lectr and Reader in Plant Cell and Membrane Biol., 1990–97, Prof. of Plant Membrane Biol., 1997–2000, Wye Coll., Univ. of London; Prof. of Plant Physiol. and Biophysics, Imperial Coll., London, 2000–01. Ed.-in-Chief, Jl Plant Physiol., 2013–. FRSE 2003. *Publications:* numerous res. articles in fields of biol membrane transport, plant and fungal cell biol. and sensory physiol. *Recreations:* ski-ing, mountaineering, sailing, music. *Address:* Institute of Molecular Cell and Systems Biology, University of Glasgow, Glasgow G12 8QQ. *T:* (0141) 330 4451, *Fax:* (0141) 330 4447. *E:* michael.blatt@glasgow.ac.uk.

**BLATTER, Joseph Sepp;** President, Fédération Internationale de Football Association, 1998–2016; *b* 10 March 1936; *s* of Joseph and Berta Blatter-Nellen; *m* (marr. diss.); one *d*. *Educ:* Univ. of Lausanne (BA Business Admin and Econs). Gen. Sec., Swiss Ice-Hockey Fedn, 1964–66; Press Officer, Swiss Sports Orgn, 1966–68; Dir, Sports Timing and PR, Longines SA, 1968–75; Technical Dir, 1975–81, Gen. Sec. and CEO, 1981–98, FIFA. Mem., IOC, 1999–2015. Hon. Mem., Swiss FA. Hon. PhD Nelson Mandela Metropolitan, SA, 2006. Olympic Order, 1994; American Global Peace Award, 2003. Kt, Sultanate of Pahang, 1990; Order of Good Hope (S Africa), 1998; Chevalier, Légion d'Honneur (France); Grosse Verdienstkreuz (Germany), 2006. *Recreations:* crosswords, tennis, books (detective stories).

**BLAYNEY, David James,** QC 2013; *b* 1969; *s* of Robert and Ann Blayney; *m* 1995, Katherine; two *c*. *Educ:* St Michael's Sch., Jersey; Canford Sch., Dorset; Lincoln Coll., Oxford (BA Juris.). Called to the Bar, Lincoln's Inn, 1992; Intern, Legal Resources Centre, Cape Town, 1992–93; Pupil, 13 Old Sq., Lincoln's Inn, 1993–94; in practice as barrister, 1994–. Trustee, Reigate and Banstead CAB, 2012–. *Recreations:* family, music, windsurfing, running. *Address:* 6 New Square, Lincoln's Inn, WC2A 3QS. *T:* (020) 7242 6105. *E:* dblayney@serlecourt.co.uk.

**BLAZE, Robin Peter;** countertenor; Professor, Royal College of Music, since 1999; *b* 11 Jan. 1971; *s* of Peter Michael and Christine Margaret Blaze; *m* 1999, Lisa Jane Beckley; one *s*. *Educ:* Magdalen Coll., Oxford (MA Hons); Royal Coll. of Music (Postgrad. Dip.). First professional engagements, 1995; recital broadcasts BBC Radio 3, 1999–2002; Proms solo début, 2000; début recital Wigmore Hall, 2001; opera débuts: Glyndebourne Touring Opera, 2001 (Bertarido, in Rodelinda); ENO, 2002 (Arsamene, in Xerxes); Glyndebourne Fest. Opera (Didymus, in Theodora), and Royal Opera, Covent Gdn (Athamus, in Semele), 2003; concert appearances in Australia (Sydney Opera House), Japan (Tokyo Opera City), Argentina, Brazil, USA (Kennedy Centre) and across Europe. Solo recital recordings, 1999– incl. complete Bach series with Bach Collegium Japan. *Recreations:* golf, reading, cricket.

**BLAZWICK, Iwona Maria Anna,** OBE 2008; Director, Whitechapel Art Gallery, since 2001; *b* 14 Oct. 1955; *d* of Wojciech Blaszczyk and Danuta Mondry-Blaszczyk; *m* 2003, Dr Richard Noble; one *d*. *Educ:* Exeter Univ. (BA 1977). Curator, 1980–85, Dir of Exhibns, 1987–93, Inst. of Contemporary Arts, London; Dir, A.I.R. Gall., 1985–87; Commng Editor, Phaidon Press, 1993–97; Curator, then Hd of Exhibns, Tate Gall. of Modern Art, subseq. Tate Modern, 1997–2001. Art critic, lectr and broadcaster on contemporary art, 1985–; Vis. Lectr, RCA, 1993–97. Curator: Ha-Ha: Contemporary British Artists in an 18th Century Park, Univ. of Plymouth and Nat. Trust, 1993; (jtly) On Taking a Normal Situation, Mus. of Contemporary Art, Antwerp, 1993; Now Here, Louisiana Mus., Denmark, 1996; New Tendencies in British and Japanese Art, Toyama Mus. of Modern Art, Japan, 1996. FRCA. Hon. Fellow, Goldsmiths, 2009. Hon. MA London Metropolitan, 2003; Hon. DPhil Plymouth, 2006; Hon. Dr Univ. of the Arts, 2011; Hon. Dr Middlesex, 2014. Officier, Ordre des Arts et des Lettres (France), 2013. *Publications:* An Endless Feast: on British situationism, 1988; Lawrence Weiner, 1993; Ilya Kabakov, 1998; (ed jtly) Tate Modern: the handbook, 2000; (ed) Century City, 2001; Faces in the Crowd, 2004; Alex Katz, 2006; Revolutions: forms that turn, 2008; Elizabeth Peyton, 2008; Gary Hume, 2009; Cornelia Parker, 2014; Adventures of the Black Square, 2015; exhibn catalogues; contribs to jls. *Recreations:* cinema, dancing, travel, photography. *Address:* 77–82 Whitechapel High Street, E1 7QX. *Club:* Blacks.

**BLEARS, Rt Hon. Hazel Anne;** PC 2005; Chairman, Social Investment Business, since 2016; *b* 14 May 1956; *d* of Arthur and Dorothy Blears; *m* 1989, Michael Halsall. *Educ:* Wardley Grammar Sch.; Trent Poly. (BA Hons Law). Trainee Solicitor, Salford Council, 1978–80; in private practice, 1980–81; Solicitor: Rossendale Council, 1981–83; Wigan Council, 1983–85; Principal Solicitor, Manchester City Council, 1985–97. Mem. (Lab) Salford City Council, 1984–92. MP (Lab) Salford, 1997–2010, Salford and Eccles, 2010–15. Parly Under-Sec. of State, DoH, 2001–03; Minister of State, Home Office, 2003–06; Minister without Portfolio and Chair, Labour Party, 2006–07; Sec. of State for Communities and Local Govt, 2007–09. Contested (Lab): Tatton, 1987; Bury S, 1992. Dir, Co-operative Gp, 2015–. *Recreations:* dance, motorcycling.

**BLEASDALE, Alan;** writer and producer; *b* 23 March 1946; *s* of George and Margaret Bleasdale; *m* 1970, Julia Moses; two *s* one *d*. *Educ:* St Aloysius RC Jun. Sch., Huyton; Wade Deacon Grammar Sch., Widnes; Padgate Teachers Trng Coll. (Teacher's Cert.). Schoolteacher, 1967–75. *TV series: writer:* Boys from the Blackstuff, 1982 (BPG TV Award for Best Series, 1982; Best British TV Drama of the Decade, ITV Achievement of the Decade Awards, 1989); Scully, 1984; The Monocled Mutineer, 1986; (also prod) GBH, 1991 (BPG TV Award for Best Drama Series, 1992); (also prod) Jake's Progress, 1995 (Best Writer Award, Monte Carlo Internat. TV Fest., 1996); (also prod) Melissa, 1997; (adapt.) Oliver Twist, 1999 (Best TV Drama Series, TRIC Award, 2000); The Sinking of the Laconia, 2010; *producer:* Alan Bleasdale Presents, 1994; Soft Sand, Blue Sea, 1997. Hon. DLitt Liverpool Poly., 1991. BAFTA Writers Award, 1982; RTS Writer of the Year, 1982. *Publications: novels:* Scully, 1975; Who's been sleeping in my bed, 1977; *play scripts:* No more sitting on the Old School Bench, 1979; Boys from the Blackstuff, 1982; Are you lonesome tonight?, 1985 (Best Musical, London Standard Drama Awards, 1985); Having a Ball, 1986; It's a Madhouse, 1986; The Monocled Mutineer, 1986; On the Ledge, 1993; *film script:* No Surrender, 1986. *Recreation:* rowing. *Address:* c/o The Agency, 24 Pottery Lane, Holland Park, W11 4LZ. *T:* (020) 7727 1346.

**BLEASDALE, Cyril,** OBE 1988; FCILT; Managing Director, Railnews Ltd, since 1996; *b* 8 July 1934; *s* of Frederick and Alice Bleasdale; *m* 1970, Catherine; one *d*. *Educ:* Evered High Sch., Liverpool; Stanford Univ., Calif (Sen. Exec. Program). Man. Dir, Freightliner Ltd, 1975–82; Dir, Inter City British Rail, 1982–86; Gen. Manager, BR London Midland Region, 1986–90; Dir, Scotrail, 1990–94. Dir, 1997–2009, Chm., 2003–09, Hertfordshire Business Incubation Centre Ltd. Dir Gen., Internat. Council, Chartered Inst. (formerly Inst.) of Logistics and Transport, 1999–2009. FCMI. *Recreations:* music, fitness. *Address:* 22 Trafalgar Street, Cheltenham GL50 1UH. *Club:* Royal Automobile.

**BLEASDALE, Marcus;** documentary photographer, since 1998; human rights activist; Managing Director, Wilstar Social Impact, since 2016; *b* Kendal, Cumbria, 7 March 1968; *s* of Terence and Helen Bleasdale; *m* 2007, Karin Beate Nøsterud; twin *d*. *Educ:* Univ. of Huddersfield (BA Hons Business Econs and Finance); London Inst. (London Coll. of Printing Postgrad. Photojournalism); Univ. of Cambridge (MSt Internat. Relns). Investment banker: Schroders, 1990–94; ABN, 1994–96; Bank of America, 1996–98. Member and owner, VII Photo, 2007–15 (Vice Chair, 2007–09). *Publications:* One

Hundred Years of Darkness, 2002; The Rape of a Nation, 2009; The Unravelling, 2015; contribs to Nat. Geographic Mag., New Yorker. *Recreations:* ski-ing, running, photography. *E:* marcus@marcusbleasdale.com. *Clubs:* Frontline, Ivy, Oxford and Cambridge, Conduit.

**BLEASDALE, Paul Edward;** QC 2001; a Recorder of the Crown Court, since 1996; *b* 18 Dec. 1955; *s* of late William Arthur Bleasdale and Dorothy Elizabeth Bleasdale; *m* 1st, 1991 (marr. diss.); one *s* one *d*; 2nd, 2017, Ruth Dooley. *Educ:* Langley Park Sch. for Boys, Beckenham; Queen Mary Coll., London (LLB 1977). Called to the Bar, Inner Temple, 1978, Bencher, 2011; Asst Recorder, 1992–96. Fee Paid Judge, First-tier Tribunal (Property Chamber) (formerly Dep. Chm., Agricl Lands Tribunal), 1994–. Hon. Prof. of Law, Birmingham Univ., 2012–. *Recreations:* outdoor sports, sailing, golf. *Address:* No 5 Chambers, Fountain Court, Steelhouse Lane, Birmingham B4 6DR.

**BLEDISLOE,** 4th Viscount *cr* 1935; **Rupert Edward Ludlow Bathurst;** portrait artist, since 1989; *b* London, 13 March 1964; *s* of 3rd Viscount Bledisloe, QC, and Elizabeth Mary Thompson; *S* father, 2009; *m* 2001, Shera, *d* of Rohinton and Irma Sarosh; one *s* two *d*. *Educ:* Eton (Oppidan Schol.); Univ. of Exeter; Univ. of the West of England (MA Fine Art (Dist.) 2014). *Heir:* s Hon. Benjamin Rohinton Ludlow Bathurst, *b* 28 March 2004. *Address:* Lydney Park Estate, Lydney, Glos GL15 6BT. *Club:* St Moritz Tobogganing.

**BLEE, Catherine, (Kate),** RDI 2015; artist designer; *b* London, 1961; *d* of Anthony Blee and Gillian Blee; *m* 1989, Charles Thomson; three *s*. *Educ:* Channing Sch.; Camden Sch.; Edinburgh Coll. of Art (BA 1st Cl. 1983; Post Grad. Dip. 1984). Set up Studio, Shoreditch, London, 1986. Vis. Tutor in Mixed Media Textiles, RCA, 2010–. Work in public collections: Crafts Council, 1994; V&A Mus., 1997; Contemp. Arts Soc., 2000; commissions for: FSA Art Collection, 1999; Portcullis House, Westminster, 2000; Girton Coll., Cambridge, 2004; Wellcome Trust, 2004; City and Islington Coll., 2005; (Lead Artist) Southmead Hosp. NHS Trust, 2009; Macmillan Cancer Support, Brighton, 2016. Designer, social investment projects: LOSA, rural South Africa design proj., 2002; Illizi Home, rural Algerian design proj., 2002. *Recreation:* I don't like to separate work and recreation. *Address:* 180 Highbury Hill, N5 1AU. *E:* kate@kateblee.co.uk.

**BLENCATHRA,** Baron *cr* 2011 (Life Peer), of Penrith in the county of Cumbria; **David John Maclean;** PC 1995; *b* 16 May 1953. MP (C) Penrith and the Border, July 1983–2010. Asst Govt Whip, 1987–88; a Lord Comr of HM Treasury (Govt Whip), 1988–89; Parly Sec., MAFF, 1989–92; Minister of State: DoE, 1992–93; Home Office, 1993–97; Opposition Chief Whip, 2001–05. Mem. Bd, Natural England, 2018– (Dep. Chair, 2018–). *Address:* House of Lords, SW1A 0PW.

**BLENKINSOP, Dorothy,** CBE 1990; Regional Nursing Officer, Northern Regional Health Authority, 1973–89, retired; *b* 15 Nov. 1931; *d* of late Joseph Henry Blenkinsop, BEM, and Thelma Irene (née Bishop). *Educ:* South Shields Grammar Sch. for Girls. MA (Dunelm) 1978. SRN 1953; SCM 1954; Health Visitors Cert. 1962. Ward Sister, Royal Victoria Infirmary, Newcastle upon Tyne, 1955–61; Health Visitor, S Shields, 1962–64; Dep. Matron, Gen. Hosp., S Shields, 1964–67; Durham Hospital Management Committee: Prin. Nurse, Durham City Hosps, 1967–69; Prin. Nursing Officer (Top), 1969–71; Chief Nursing Officer, 1971–73. Chm., S Tyneside Health Care Trust, 1992–96. Local Preacher, Methodist Church. Hon. MSc CNAA, 1990. *Publications:* (with E. G. Nelson): Changing the System, 1972; Managing the System, 1976; articles in nursing press. *Address:* 143 Temple Park Road, South Shields, Tyne and Wear NE34 0EN. *T:* (0191) 456 1429.

**BLENKINSOP, Thomas Francis;** Operations Director, Community Trade Union, since 2017; *b* Middlesbrough, 14 Aug. 1980; *s* of William Blenkinsop and Barbara Blenkinsop; *m* 2007, Victoria Emtage. *Educ:* Teesside Univ. (BSc PPE); Warwick Univ. (MA Continental Philos.). Constituency Researcher for Dr Ashok Kumar, MP, 2002–08; full-time Regl Official, Community Trade Union, 2008–10. MP (Lab) Middlesbrough S and E Cleveland, 2010–17. An Opposition Whip, 2011–15. *Recreations:* boxing, RMP Reservist. *Address:* Community Trade Union, 465c Caledonian Road, N7 9GX.

**BLENKINSOPP, Prof. Alison,** OBE 2010; PhD; Professor of the Practice of Pharmacy, University of Bradford, since 2011; *b* 22 June 1959; *d* of Ron and Margaret Morley; *m* 1988, John Blenkinsopp. *Educ:* Bradford Univ. (BPharm 1st Cl. Hons); Aston Univ. (PhD 1988). Lecturer in Pharmacy Practice: Aston Univ., 1982–88; Univ. of Bradford, 1988–91; Dir, NHS Centre for Pharmacy Postgrad. Educn, 1991–95; Sen. Lectr, Health Services Res., 1995–99, Prof. of Practice of Pharmacy, 1999–2011, Keele Univ. Ed., Internat. Jl Pharmacy Practice, 1998–2005. Mem., Cttee on Safety of Medicines, 1999–2005. Mem., Jt Nat. Formulary Cttee, 1989–2017 (Dep. Chm., 2008–17). Charter Gold Medal, RPSGB, 2001. *Publications:* Symptoms in the Pharmacy, 1989, 8th edn 2018; Health Promotion for Community Pharmacists, 1991, 2nd edn 2000; Over the Counter Medication, 2005; Supporting Self Care in Primary Care, 2006; Evaluation of Nurse and Pharmacist Independent Prescribing in England, 2011. *Recreations:* travel, reading, contemporary music, Chicago Cubs supporter. *Address:* School of Pharmacy and Medical Sciences, University of Bradford, Richmond Road, Bradford BD7 1DP. *T:* (01274) 236040. *E:* a.blenkinsopp@bradford.ac.uk.

**BLENNERHASSETT, Sir (Marmaduke) Adrian (Francis William),** 7th Bt, *cr* 1809; *b* 25 May 1940; *s* of Lieut Sir Marmaduke Blennerhassett, 6th Bt, RNVR (killed in action, 1940), and Gwenfra (*d* 1956), *d* of Judge Harrington-Maxwell, Co. Kerry, and of Mrs Douglas Campbell; *S* father, 1940; *m* 1972, Carolyn Margaret, *yr d* of late Gilbert Brown; one *s* one *d*. *Educ:* Michael Hall, Forest Row; McGill Univ.; Imperial Coll., Univ. of London (MSc); Cranfield Business Sch. (MBA). FRGS 2000. *Recreations:* sailing, ski-ing, adventure travelling. *Heir:* s Charles Henry Marmaduke Blennerhassett [*b* 18 July 1975; *m* 2014, Katherine, *d* of Brian Selwyn Lloyd]. *Address:* 38 Hugon Road, SW6 3EN. *Club:* Travellers.

**BLESSED, Brian,** OBE 2016; actor, author and climber; *b* 9 Oct. 1936; *s* of William Blessed and Hilda Blessed (née Wall); *m* 1st, Anne Bomann (marr. diss.); one *d*; 2nd, 1978, Hildegard Neil (née Zimmermann); one *d*. *Educ:* Bolton-on-Dearne Sch.; Bristol Old Vic Theatre Sch. *Stage:* worked in rep., Nottingham, Birmingham, etc; Incident at Vichy, Phoenix, 1966; The Exorcism, Comedy, 1967; State of Revolution, NT, 1977; The Devil's Disciple, 1979 and The Eagle has Two Heads, Chichester; Hamlet, Richard III, and Henry V, RSC, 1984–85; The Relapse, RNT, 2001; King Lear, Guildford, 2015; director: The Glass Menagerie, tour 1998; Mill at Sonning: The Hollow Mill, 2016; Spider's Web, 2017; The Unexpected Guest, 2018; Towards Zero, 2019; one-man show, An Evening with Brian Blessed, tours 1992–93, 1995–96; musicals: Old Deuteronomy in Cats, New London, 1981; Metropolis, Piccadilly, 1989; Hard Times, Haymarket, 2000; Chitty Chitty Bang Bang, Palladium, 2002; narrator, Morning Heroes (Arthur Bliss), with LSO, 1991, and other works; *films include:* The Trojan Women, 1971; Man of La Mancha, 1972; Flash Gordon, 1980; Henry V, 1989; Robin Hood, Prince of Thieves, 1991; Much Ado About Nothing, 1993; Hamlet, 1997; Star Wars—The Phantom Menace, 1998; Walt Disney's Tarzan, 1999; Mumbo Jumbo, 2000; Alexander, 2004; The Conclave, The Day of Wrath, 2006; Back in Business, 2007; As You Like It, 2008; *television includes:* series: Fancy Smith, in Z Cars, 1962–78; The Little World of Don Camillo, 1980; The Black Adder, 1983; My Family and Other Animals, 1987; serials: The Three Musketeers, 1966; I, Claudius, 1976;

Return to Treasure Island, 1986; War and Remembrance, 1988; Catherine the Great, 1995; Tom Jones, 1997; documentary, Ascent of Mars Mountain, 2005. Has made expeditions to: Mt Everest, 1991 (film, Galahad of Everest, won Canadian Grand Prix, Banff Fest., 1992), 1993, 1996; N Pole, Mt Aconcagua, 2002; Chile, 1993; Mt Ararat, Turkey, 2004; Mt Kuiten and Malkin, Mongolia; Mt Kilimanjaro, Africa. *Publications:* The Turquoise Mountain, 1991; The Dynamite Kid, 1992; Nothing's Impossible, 1994; Quest for the Lost World, 1999; Absolute Pandemonium (memoirs), 2015; Panther in My Kitchen, 2018. *Address:* c/o AIM LLP, Studio 405, The Print Rooms, 164–180 Union Street, SE1 0LH.

**BLESSLEY, Andrew Charles;** Clerk to the Clothworkers' Co. of the City of London and Chief Executive (formerly Secretary), Clothworkers' Foundation, 2001–15; *b* 20 May 1951; *s* of late Kenneth Harry Blessley, CBE, ED and Gwendeline Blessley; *m* 1979, Linda Kristine Marr; one *s* one *d*. *Educ:* Haberdashers' Aske's Sch., Elstree; St John's Coll., Cambridge (MA); Harvard Business Sch. (AMP). Joined National Westminster Bank, 1972: appointments in UK and USA, including: Dir, Energy and Natural Resources Gp, 1989–90; COS to Gp Chief Exec., 1990–92; Regl Dir, Central London, 1992–94; Dir, Gp Strategy, 1994–95; Vice-Chm. and Chief Operating Officer, NatWest Bancorp USA, 1995–96; Dir, Retail Mktg and Distribution, 1996–2001. Director: Fleet Bank NA, 1996–97; Lombard NatWest Commercial Services, 1996–98. Dir, Banking Ombudsman Bd, 1996–2000. Member: Regeneration Leadership Team, BITC, 1997–2001; HM Treasury Credit Union Taskforce, 1999–2000. Trustee: NatWest Gp Charitable Trust, 1996–2001; South Square Trust, 2009–. Dir, Prostate Centre, 2004–13; Trustee: Prostate Cancer Charity, 2006–12; Gtr London Fund for the Blind, 2013–14; Holly Lodge Centre, 2019–. Director: Brooklyn Acad. of Music, 1995–96; Corporate Culture, 2006–07. Member: Court, Univ. of Leeds, 2001–15; Council, Blind Aid (formerly Metropolitan Soc. for the Blind), 2001–18 (Vice Chm., 2014–17; Chm., 2017–18); HLF SE Cttee, 2016–19. FRSA 1993. *Recreations:* family, art, theatre, cinema, jazz, walking.

**BLETHYN, Brenda Anne,** OBE 2003; actress; *b* 20 Feb. 1946; *d* of William Charles Bottle and Louisa Kathleen Bottle; partner, 1977, *m* 2011, Michael Mayhew. *Educ:* St Augustine's RC Sch., Ramsgate; Thanet Tech. Coll., Ramsgate; Guildford Sch. of Acting. *Theatre* includes: work with NT, 1975–90, incl. Mysteries, 1979, Double Dealer, 1982, Dalliance, 1987, Beaux' Stratagem, 1989, Bedroom Farce; A Doll's House, 1987, Born Yesterday, 1988, An Ideal Husband, 1992, Royal Exchange, Manchester; Steaming, Comedy, 1981; Benefactors, Vaudeville, 1984; Wildest Dreams, RSC, 1993; The Bed Before Yesterday, Almeida, 1994; Habeas Corpus, Donmar Warehouse, 1996; Absent Friends, NY; Mrs Warren's Profession, Strand, 2002; Haunted, Royal Exchange, Manchester, 2009, 59E59 St Th., NY, 2010, Sydney Opera Hse, 2011; *films* include: The Witches; A River Runs Through It, 1992; Secrets and Lies, 1996; Remember Me, 1996; Music From Another Room, 1997; Girls' Night, In the Winter Dark, 1998; Little Voice, Daddy and Them, 1999; Night Train, Saving Grace, 2000; Anne Frank - The Whole Story, 2001; Lovely and Amazing, 2002; Pumpkin, Yellow Bird, Plots with a View, Blizzard, Sonny, A Way of Life, 2003; Piccadilly Jim, Beyond the Sea, 2004; On a Clear Day, Pride and Prejudice, 2005; Atonement, Clubland, 2007; London River, The Calling, Dead Man Running, 2010; *television* includes: Henry VI Part I, 1981; King Lear, 1983; Chance in a Million (3 series), 1983–85; The Labours of Erica, 1987; The Bullion Boys, 1993; The Buddha of Suburbia, 1993; Sleeping with Mickey, 1993; Outside Edge (3 series), 1994–96; First Signs of Madness (Mona), 1996; Between the Sheets (series), 2003; Belonging, 2004; Mysterious Creatures, 2006; War and Peace, 2007; Vera (9 series), 2011–; King of the Teds, 2012; Mary & Martha, 2013. Hon. DLitt: Kent, 1999; Surrey, 2008. Numerous awards incl. Best Actress Awards (for Secrets and Lies): Cannes Film Fest., 1996; Boston Film Critics, 1997; LA Film Critics, 1997; Golden Globe, 1997; London Film Critics, 1997; BAFTA, 1997; Performance of the Year (for Vera), RTS N East and Border Awards, 2017. *Publications:* Mixed Fancies (memoir), 2006. *Recreations:* reading, swimming, cryptic crosswords. *Address:* c/o Independent Talent Group Ltd, 40 Whitfield Street, W1T 2RH. *T:* (020) 7636 6565.

**BLEWETT, Hon. Neal,** AC 1995; DPhil; FRHistS; FASSA; High Commissioner for Australia in the United Kingdom, 1994–98; *b* 24 Oct. 1933; *s* of James and Phyllis Blewett; *m* 1962, Jill Myford (*d* 1988); one *s* one *d*; partner, 1998, Robert John Brain, *s* of Joseph Linley Brain and Dorothy Eleanor Pierce. *Educ:* Launceston High Sch.; Univ. of Tasmania (Dip Ed, MA); Jesus Coll., Oxford (MA; Hon. Fellow, 1998); St Antony's Coll., Oxford (DPhil). FRHistS 1975. Oxford University: Sen. Schol., St Antony's Coll., 1959–61; Lectr, St Edmund Hall, 1961–63; Lectr in Politics, Univ. of Adelaide, 1964–69; Flinders University, S Australia: Reader, 1970–74; Prof., Dept of Pol Theory and Instns, 1974–77. MP (Lab) Bonython, SA, 1977–94; Mem., Jt Hse Cttee on Foreign Affairs and Defence, 1977–80; Deleg. to Australian Constitutional Convention, 1978; Opposition Spokesman on health and Tasmanian affairs, 1980–83; Minister for: Health, 1983–87; Community Services and Health, 1987–90; Trade and Overseas Develt, 1990–91; Social Security, 1991–93. Vis. Prof., Faculty of Medicine, Univ. of Sydney, 1998–2002. Member Council: Univ. of Adelaide, 1972–74; Torrens Coll. of Advanced Educn, 1972–78. Exec. Bd Mem., WHO, 1995–98. Nat. Pres., Australian Inst. of Internat. Affairs, 1998–2005; Pres., Alcohol and other Drugs Council of Australia, 2002–06; Chair, Rev. of Food Labelling Law and Policy, 2010–11. Chm., NSW Film and Television Office, 2006–09. Life Gov., Kirby Inst., Sydney, 2014. Hon. LLD: Tasmania, 1998; ANU, 2003; Hon. DLitt: Hull, 1999; Flinders, 2009; Univ. of Technol., Sydney, 2010. *Publications:* The Peers, the Parties and the People, 1972; (jtly) Playford to Dunstan: the politics of transition, 1971; A Cabinet Diary, 1999. *Recreations:* bush-walking, reading, cinema, gardening. *Address:* 32 Fitzroy Street, Leura, NSW 2780, Australia.

**BLEWITT, Major Sir Shane (Gabriel Basil),** GCVO 1996 (KCVO 1989; CVO 1987; LVO 1981); Keeper of the Privy Purse and Treasurer to the Queen, 1988–96; an Extra Equerry to the Queen, since 1996; *b* 25 March 1935; *s* of late Col Basil Blewitt; *m* 1969, Julia Morrogh-Bernard, *widow* of Major John Morrogh-Bernard, Irish Guards, and *d* of late Mr Robert Calvert; one *s* one *d* (and one step *s* one step *d*). *Educ:* Ampleforth Coll.; Christ Church, Oxford (MA Hons Mod. Languages). Served Irish Guards, 1956–74 (BAOR, NI, Aden, HK); Antony Gibbs and Sons, 1974; Asst Keeper, 1975–85, Dep. Keeper, 1985–88, of the Privy Purse; Receiver-General, Duchy of Lancaster, 1988–96. Gov., King Edward VII Hosp. Sister Agnes, 1988–2010; Mem. Gen. Council, King's Hosp. Fund, 1988–2010. *Address:* South Corner House, Duncton, Petworth, W Sussex GU28 0LT. *T:* (01798) 342143. *E:* blewittshane@aol.com.

**BLIGH,** family name of **Earl of Darnley.**

**BLIGH, Stephen Ernest;** Director and Head of Maritime Services UK, DNV GL Group (formerly Det Norske Veritas), 2008 (Principal Consultant, 2006–08); *b* 13 May 1953; *s* of George and Doreen Bligh; *m* 1977, Susan Jane Duncan; two *d*. *Educ:* Fullbrook Co. Secondary Sch.; Hull Nautical Coll. Master Mariner 1987. Served at sea with various cos, 1970–85; joined P&O, 1985; Fleet Ops Manager, P&O Containers Ltd, 1989–97; Fleet Marine Manager, P&O NedLloyd, 1997–2003; Chief Exec., Maritime and Coastguard Agency, 2003–06. *Recreations:* Rugby, sailing, flying.

**BLIGHT, Dr Denis Geoffrey,** AO 2004; Executive Director, Crawford Fund, 2008–17; Visitor, School of History, Australian National University, since 2017; *b* 20 Feb. 1945; *s* of Geoffrey Ivan Blight and Bernice Ethel Janet Blight; *m* 1970, Sharon Hill; one *s* one *d*. *Educ:*

Univ. of Western Australia (BSC Hons; PhD). Third, then Second Sec., Australian Embassy, Ankara, 1972–73; First Sec., Australian High Commn, Nairobi, 1976–78; First Sec., Australian High Commn, London, 1980–82; Centre Sec., Australian Centre for Internat. Agricultural Res., 1982–84; Asst Dir Gen., AusAID, 1984–86; Dep. Chief Exec., 1986–91, Chief Exec., 1991–2000, IDP Education Australia; Dir Gen., CAB Internat., 2000–05; Chm., LIS Pty Ltd, 2006–10. Advr, India-Australia Grand Challenge Fund, 2010–; Mem., Adv. Cttee, Australia India Strategic Res. Fund, Australian Dept of Industry Innovation, Sci., Res. and Tertiary Educn, 2011–. Member: Commonwealth Scholarship Commn, 2006–09; Commonwealth Round Table (Australia), 2009–; Mem., ACT Br., Royal Commonwealth Soc., 2007–. FRSA. *Publications:* (with Alec Lazenby) Thirty years in International Education and Development: the IDP story, 1999; History of CAB International: 100 years of scientific endeavour, 2011; Doing Well by Doing Good: how Australia benefits from international agricultural research, 2013. *Recreations:* writing, bicycle riding, travelling, bridge.

**BLISHEN, Anthony Owen,** OBE 1968; HM Diplomatic Service, retired; Counsellor, Foreign and Commonwealth Office, 1981–87; *b* 16 April 1932; *s* of Henry Charles Adolphus Blishen, MBE and Joan Cecile Blishen (*née* Blakeney); *m* 1st, 1963, Sarah Anne Joscelyne (marr. diss. 1994); three *s* one *d*; 2nd, 1994, Elizabeth Appleyard (*née* West). *Educ:* Clayesmore Sch., Dorset; SOAS, London Univ. Commnd Royal Hampshire Regt, 1951; Lt 1st Bn: BAOR, 1953; Malaya, 1953–55; Captain, GSO3 HQ 18 Inf. Bde, Malaya, 1955–56; attached HQ Land Forces, Hong Kong (language trng), 1957–59; GSO3 HQ Far East Land Forces, Singapore, 1960–62; FO, 1963–65; First Sec. and Consul, Peking, 1965–67; First Sec., FCO, 1968–70; Chargé d'Affaires (ad interim), Ulan Bator, 1970; Trade Comr (China trade), Hong Kong, 1971–73; First Sec., FCO, 1973–77; First Sec., 1977–78, Counsellor, 1978–81, Tokyo. *Publications:* translations from Chinese: The Art of Attainment, 2011; The Art of Self Cultivation, 2011; All the Tea in China, 2012; Chinese Jade: the spiritual and cultural significance of jade in China, 2012; Chinese Zen: a path to peace and happiness, 2013; The New Analects: Confucius reconstructed, 2013; The Power of Enlightenment: Chinese Zen poems, 2014; Memory and Oblivion, by Wang Zhousheng, 2014; No Sail on the Western Sea, by Ma Yuan, 2015; A Journey to Inner Peace and Joy: tracing contemporary Chinese hermits, 2015; Aroma's Little Garden, by Qin Wenjun, 2016; Reading Chinese Painting, by Sophia Law Suk Mun, 2016; An Illustrated Modern Reader of the Classic of Tea, by Wu Juenong, 2017; Illustrated Myths and Legends of China, by Huang Haide *et al*, 2018; contrib. Oxford DNB; contribs to Asian Affairs. *Recreations:* Renaissance music (founded Aragon Consort, 1990), oriental languages. *Address:* 5 Beechrow, Ham Common, Richmond, Surrey TW10 5HE.

**BLISS, Prof. Christopher John Emile,** PhD; FBA 1988; Nuffield Professor of International Economics, Oxford University, 1992–2007; Fellow of Nuffield College, Oxford, 1977–2007, now Emeritus; *b* 17 Feb. 1940; *s* of John Llewlyn Bliss and Patricia Paula (*née* Dubern); *m* 1983, Ghada (*née* Saqf El Hait); one adopted *s*, and one *s* two *d* by previous marr. *Educ:* Finchley Catholic Grammar Sch.; King's Coll., Cambridge (BA 1962, MA 1964, PhD 1966). Fellow of Christ's Coll., Cambridge, 1965–71; Asst Lectr, 1965–67, and Lectr, 1967–71, Cambridge Univ.; Prof. of Econs, Univ. of Essex, 1971–77; Nuffield Reader in Internat. Econs, Oxford Univ., 1977–92. Dir, General Funds Investment Trust Ltd, 1980–87. Fellow, Econometric Soc., 1978–96. Editor or Asst Editor, Rev. of Econ. Studies, 1967–71; Managing Editor: Oxford Economic Papers, 1989–96; Economic Jl, 1996–2000. *Publications:* Capital Theory and the Distribution of Income, 1975; (with N. H. Stern) Palanpur: the economy of an Indian village, 1982; Economic Theory and Policy for Trading Blocks, 1994; Trade, Growth, and Inequality, 2007; papers and reviews in learned jls. *Recreation:* music. *Address:* Nuffield College, Oxford OX1 1NF. *T:* (01865) 278500.

**BLISS, Dr Timothy Vivian Pelham,** FRS 1994; FMedSci; Head, Division of Neurophysiology, 1988–2006, Visiting Worker, 2006–14, National Institute for Medical Research; Visiting Worker, Francis Crick Institute, since 2014; Adjunct Professor, University of Toronto, since 2018; *b* 27 July 1940; *s* of Pelham Marryat Bliss and Elizabeth Cotton Bliss (*née* Sproule); *m* 1st, 1975, Virginia Catherine Morton-Evans (*née* O'Rorke); one step *s* two step *d*; one *d* by Katherine Sarah Clough; 2nd, 1994, Isabel Frances Vasseur (*née* Wardrop); two step *s*. *Educ:* Dean Close Sch.; McGill Univ. (BSc 1963; PhD 1967); Hatfield Poly. (BSc Maths 1976). Mem., scientific staff, MRC, 1967–2006. Vis. Prof., Dept of Physiology, UCL, 1993–. Croonian Lectr, Royal Soc., 2012. Trustee, Sir John Soane Mus., 2005–09. MAE 2014. Founder FMedSci 1998. Hon. LLD Dalhousie, 2012; Hon. DSc Herts, 2014. (Jtly) Bristol Myers Squibb Award for Neuroscience, 1991; Feldberg Prize, 1994; British Neurosci. Assoc. Award for outstanding services to British neurosci., 2003; (jtly) Ipsen Prize for Neural Plasticity, Ipsen Foundn, 2013; (jtly) Brain Prize, Lundbeck Foundn, 2016. *Publications:* (ed jtly) Long-term Potentiation, 2004; The Hippocampus Book, 2006; numerous papers on the neural basis of memory and other aspects of the neurophysiology of the brain. *Recreations:* wine, Shakespeare, church architecture. *Address:* Holman House, 18 Market Place, Aylsham, Norwich NR11 6EH. *T:* (01263) 734216. *E:* tim.bliss@crick.ac.uk. *Club:* Academy.

**BLIX, Hans,** PhD, LLD; Chairman, Weapons of Mass Destruction Commission, 2004–09; Executive Chairman, UN Monitoring, Verification and Inspection Commission for Iraq, 2000–03; *b* 28 June 1928; *s* of Gunnar Blix and Hertha Blix (*née* Wiberg); *m* 1962, Eva Margareta Kettis; two *s*. *Educ:* Univ. of Uppsala; Columbia Univ.; Univ. of Cambridge (PhD); Stockholm Univ. (LLD). Associate Prof. in International Law, 1960; Ministry of Foreign Affairs, Stockholm: Legal Adviser, 1963–76; Under-Secretary of State, in charge of internat. development co-operation, 1976; Minister for Foreign Affairs, 1978; Under-Secretary of State, in charge of internat. development co-operation, 1979. Dir Gen., IAEA, 1981–97, now Dir Gen. Emeritus. Member: Sweden's delegn to UN General Assembly, 1961–81; Swedish delegn to Conference on Disarmament in Geneva, 1962–78. Hon. doctorates: Moscow State Univ., 1987; Bucharest Univ., 1994; Univ. of Managua, 1996; Vrije Univ. Brussel, 2003; Padova Univ., 2004; Gothenburg Univ., 2004; Cambridge, 2007. Foratom Award, 1994; Fulbright Award, 2014. *Publications:* Treaty Making Power, 1959; Statsmyndigheternas Internationella Förbindelser, 1964; Sovereignty, Aggression and Neutrality, 1970; The Treaty-Maker's Handbook, 1974; Disarming Iraq, 2004; Why Nuclear Disarmament Matters, 2008. *Recreation:* antique rugs.

**BLIZZARD, Robert John;** *b* 31 May 1950; *s* of late Arthur Blizzard and Joan Blizzard; one *s* one *d*. *Educ:* Univ. of Birmingham (BA Hons 1971). Head of English: Crayford Sch., Bexley, 1976–86; Lynn Grove High Sch., Gorleston, 1986–97. Mem. (Lab), Waveney DC, 1987–97 (Leader, 1991–97). MP (Lab) Waveney, 1997–2010; contested (Lab) same seat, 2010, 2015. PPS to Minister of State, MAFF, 1999–2001, to Minister of State for Work, DWP, 2001–03, to Minister of State for Europe, FCO, 2005–06, to Sec. of State for Transport, 2006–07; an Asst Govt Whip, 2007–08; a Lord Comr of HM Treasury (Govt Whip), 2008–10. Mem., Envmtl Audit Select Cttee, 1997–99; Chairman: British-Brazilian All Pty Gp, 1997–2007; British Offshore Oil and Gas Industry All Pty Gp, 1999–2007; British-Latin America All Pty Gp, 2004–07; British-Chile All Pty Gp, 2005–07; Sec., Jazz Appreciation All Pty Gp, 2004–07. Chm., Jazz Services Ltd, 2010–13. Vice-Pres., Nat. Youth Jazz Collective, 2018–. Gov., Lowestoft Coll., 2010–14. *Recreations:* walking, skiing, travel, listening to jazz, watching Lowestoft Town FC. *E:* bob@waveney.co.

**BLOCH, Lady Camilla;** *see* Bingham, Lady C.

**BLOCH, Prof. Maurice Émile Félix,** PhD; FBA 1990; Professor of Anthropology, University of London at London School of Economics, 1984–2005, now Emeritus; *b* 21 Oct. 1939; *s* of late Pierre Bloch and of Claude Kennedy; step *s* of John Stodart Kennedy, FRS; *m*; one *s* one *d*. *Educ:* Lycée Carnot, Paris; Perse Sch., Cambridge; LSE (BA 1962); Fitzwilliam Coll., Cambridge (PhD 1968). Asst Lectr, Univ. of Wales, Swansea, 1968; Lectr, LSE, 1969; Reader, London Univ., 1977. Prof., Collège de France, 2005–06. Corresp. Mem., Académie Malgache, Madagascar, 1965–2017. *Publications:* Placing the Dead, 1971; Marxism and Anthropology, 1983; From Blessing to Violence, 1986; Ritual, History and Power, 1989; Prey into Hunter, 1992; How We Think They Think, 1998; Anthropology and the Cognitive Challenge, 2012. *Recreation:* book binding. *Address:* Department of Anthropology, London School of Economics, Houghton Street, WC2A 2AE.

**BLOCH, Dame Merle Florence;** *see* Park, Dame M. F.

**BLOCH, Michael Gordon;** QC 1998; *b* 18 Oct. 1951; *s* of John and Thelma Bloch; *m* Caroline Williams (marr. diss.); two *d*; *m* 1998, Lady Camilla Bingham, *qv*; four *s*. *Educ:* Bedales Sch.; Corpus Christi Coll., Cambridge (MA); UEA (MPhil). Called to the Bar, Lincoln's Inn, 1979; in practice as a barrister, 1979–. Trustee, ChildLine. *Recreations:* squash, cinema. *Address:* Blackstone Chambers, Blackstone House, Temple, EC4Y 9BW. *Club:* Royal Automobile.

**BLOCH, Selwyn Irving;** QC 2000; *b* 23 Feb. 1952; *s* of Rev. Cecil Maurice Bloch and Esther Bloch; *m* 1983, Brenda Igra; three *d*. *Educ:* Potchefstroom Boys' High Sch.; Witwatersrand Univ. (BA); Stellenbosch Univ. (LLB). Attorney, S Africa, 1977–; called to the Bar, Middle Temple, 1982; in practice at the Bar, 1983–. *Publications:* (jtly) Employment Covenants and Confidential Information, 1993, 4th edn 2018. *Recreations:* listening to music, walking, reading, theatre. *Address:* Littleton Chambers, 3 King's Bench Walk North, EC4Y 7HR. *T:* (020) 7797 8699.

**BLOCK, David Greenberg,** AC 1988 (AO 1983); *b* 21 March 1936; *s* of Emanuel Block and Hannah Greenberg; *m* 1959, Naomi Denfield; one *s* three *d*. *Educ:* King Edward VII Sch., Johannesburg; Univ. of Witwatersrand (BJuris cum laude). Joined Schroder-Darling & Co., 1964, Dir, 1967–72; Chairman: David Block & Associates, 1972–81; Trinity Properties, 1984–90; George Ward Group, 1986–89; Dep. Chm., Concrete Constructions, 1990; Director: CSR, 1977–88; Kalamazoo Holdings, 1986–94; Dep. Chm., Pacific Magazines & Publishing, 1991–95; Dir, Lloyds Bank NZA, Chm., Lloyds Internat., Dir, Lloyds Merchant Bank (UK) and Adviser, Lloyds Merchant Bank Holdings, 1981–86; Consultant, Coudert Brothers, 1986–91; Adviser: Coopers & Lybrand, 1986–93; S. G. Warburg Group, 1987–95. Consultant: to Prime Minister and Cabinet, 1986–89; to govts, cos and instns, 1986–96; to Premier's Dept, NSW, 1987–88; Mem., Cttee of Enquiry into inflation and taxation, 1975; Chm., Efficiency Scrutiny Unit and Admin. Reform Unit, 1986–88. Comr, Aust. Film Commn, 1978–81; Chm., Sydney Opera House Trust, 1981–89; Trustee, Japanese Friends of Sydney Opera House Foundn, 1992–96; Councillor: Asia-Australian Inst., 1991–96; Nat. Heart Foundn, 1994–96; Gov., Aust. Nat. Gall. Foundn, 1992–96. Dir, Univ. of NSW Foundn, 1989–96. Fellow, Senate of Univ. of Sydney, 1983–87. FAICD; FAIM; FSIA. Hon. LLD New South Wales, 1992. *Recreations:* swimming, squash, music, theatre. *Address:* 30 Clarke Street, Vaucluse, NSW 2030, Australia. *T:* (2) 93376211. *Club:* University (Sydney).

**BLOCK, Neil Selwyn;** QC 2002; *b* 24 May 1957; *s* of Ronald Sydney Block and Barbara Block; *m* 1988, Amanda Jane Hatton; four *s*. *Educ:* E Barnet Grammar Sch.; City of London Poly. (BA Hons Law); Exeter Univ. (LLM); Inns of Court Sch. of Law. Called to the Bar, Gray's Inn, 1980, Bencher, 2008; in practice, specialising in law of professional negligence (incl. clinical negligence), personal injury, product liability, material loss claims, insurance related disputes and contract/commercial litigation; Hd of Chambers, 2013–. Accredited mediator, 2006. *Recreations:* tennis, golf, family, friends. *Address:* Naphill House, Naphill, Bucks HP14 4RL; (chambers) 39 Essex Chambers, 81 Chancery Lane, WC2A 1DD.

**BLOCK, Simon Jonathan;** Honorary Secretary, Commonwealth Boxing Council, since 1980; General Secretary, British Boxing Board of Control, 2000–08; *b* 13 Feb. 1950; *s* of Michael Abraham Hyman Block and Winifred Joy Block (*née* Harris); *m* 1998, Annette Mary Clements (*née* Dunphy); one *s*, and one step *d*. *Educ:* Sunbury Grammar Sch.; East Grinstead Grammar Sch.; Crawley Coll. of Further Educn. Boxed, Crawley Amateur Boxing Club, 1965–68; British Boxing Board of Control: joined, 1979; Sec., S Area Council, 1981–96; Asst Gen. Sec., 1986–99. Company Sec., European Boxing Union, 2000–07; Mem. Bd Governors, World Boxing Council, 2000–03, 2007–09 and 2018–. Vice Pres., Hastings Ex-Boxers' Assoc.; Hon. Mem., London Ex-Boxers' Assoc.; Member: St George's Day Club; Soc. of Friends of Ashdown Forest; Royal Commonwealth Soc. *Recreations:* walking, running (London Marathon, 1987, 1995), horse riding, songwriting (record 'He's the Guy' released 1975). *Address:* 22 Bis Rue Du Charme, 76510 Ricarville Du Val, Normandie, France. *E:* sblockcommbc@gmail.com. *Club:* Royal Over-Seas League.

**BLOFELD, Sir John (Christopher Calthorpe),** Kt 1991; DL; a Judge of the High Court of Justice, Queen's Bench Division, 1990–2001; *b* 11 July 1932; *s* of late T. R. C. Blofeld, CBE; *m* 1961, Judith Anne (*d* 2013), *er d* of Alan Mohun and Mrs James Mitchell; two *s* one *d*. *Educ:* Eton; King's Coll., Cambridge. Called to Bar, Lincoln's Inn, 1956, Bencher, 1990; QC 1975; a Recorder of the Crown Court, 1975–82; a Circuit Judge, 1982–90; Presiding Judge, SE Circuit, 1993–96. Inspector, Dept of Trade, 1979–81. Chancellor: Dio. St Edmundsbury and Ipswich, 1973–2009; Dio. of Norwich, 1998–2007. DL Norfolk, 1991. *Recreations:* watching test cricket, gardening.

**BLOHM, Helen;** *see* Mifflin, H.

**BLOHM, Leslie Adrian;** QC 2006; a Recorder, since 2003; a Deputy High Court Judge, since 2008; *b* 27 Feb. 1959; *s* of Albert Blohm and Ann Blohm; *m* 1986, Helen Mifflin, *qv*; two *d*. *Educ:* Christ's Hospital, Horsham; Keble Coll., Oxford (MA 1981). Called to the Bar, Lincoln's Inn, 1982 (Hardwicke and Jenkins Scholar, 1982), Bencher, 2013; barrister, St John's Chambers, Bristol, 1984–; in practice, specialising in Chancery, esp. Real Property law. *Recreations:* cycling, chess, restoring British motor cars of the sixties. *Address:* St John's Chambers, 101 Victoria Street, Bristol BS1 6PU. *T:* (0117) 921 3456, *Fax:* (0117) 921 4821. *E:* leslie.blohm@stjohnschambers.co.uk.

**BLOIS, Sir Charles (Nicholas Gervase),** 11th Bt *cr* 1686; farming since 1965; *b* 25 Dec. 1939; *s* of Sir Gervase Ralph Edmund Blois, 10th Bt and Mrs Audrey Winifred Blois (*née* Johnson) (*d* 1997); *S* father, 1968; *m* 1967, Celia Helen Mary Pritchett (marr. diss. 2004); one *s* one *d*. *Educ:* Harrow; Trinity Coll., Dublin; Royal Agricultural Coll., Cirencester. Australia, 1963–65. Mem., Scientific Exploration Soc., Motcombe, Dorset. FRGS 1992. *Recreations:* motor cycle adventure travel, RIB cruising. *Heir:* *s* Andrew Charles David Blois [*b* 7 Feb. 1971; *m* 2002, Judith, *d* of John Hardy]. *Address:* Red House Farm, Westleton, Saxmundham, Suffolk IP17 3EQ. *Clubs:* Cruising Association; Ocean Cruising.

**BLOKH, Alexandre,** PhD, (pen-name **Jean Blot**); writer, since 1956; Vice President, PEN Club, since 1998 (International Secretary, 1982–98); *b* Moscow, 31 March 1923; *s* of Arnold Blokh, man of letters, and Anne (*née* Berlinrote); *m* 1956, Nadia Ermolaiev. *Educ:* Bromsgrove Public Sch., Worcester; Univ. of Paris (PhD Law, PhD Letters). International Civil Servant, United Nations, 1947–62: New York, until 1956; Geneva, 1956–62; Director, Arts and Letters, UNESCO, Paris, 1962–81. Critic, arts and letters, in reviews: Arche, Preuves, NRF. Prix des Critiques, 1972; Prix Valéry Larbaud, 1977; Prix Cazes, 1982; Grand Prix de la Critique, 1986; Prix International de la Paix, 1990. Citizen of Honour, City of St Petersburg. Officier, Ordre des Arts et des Lettres (France), 1997; Bogwan Order of Cultural Merit (Korea). *Publications: novels:* Le Soleil de Cavouri, 1956; Les Enfants de New York, 1959; Obscur Ennemi, 1961; Les Illusions Nocturnes, 1964; La Jeune Géante, 1969; La Difficulté d'aimer, 1971; Les Cosmopolites, 1976; Gris du Ciel, 1981; Tout l'été, 1985; Sainte Imposture, 1988; Le Juif Margolin, 1998; Roses d'Amérique, 2003; Une vie à deux, 2007; *essays:* Marguerite Yourcenar; Ossip Mandelstam; Là où tu iras; Sporade; Ivan Gontcharov; La Montagne Sainte; Albert Cohen; Si loin de Dieu et autres voyages; Bloomsbury; Retour en Asie; Vladimir Nabokov; Moïse, notre contemporain; Le Soleil se couche à l'Est, 2005; Alexandre Blok: poète de la perspective Nevski, 2007; Mozart, 2008; Le roman poésie de la prose, 2010; Affaire de coeur, 2012; À Saint-Pétersbourg, nous nous retrouverons, 2013; Le rendez-vous de la Marquise, 2014; Tout sera paysage, 2015; En amitié, 2015; L'histoire du passé, vol. 1, L'Egypte, 2016, vol. 2, Le rêve d'une ombre: la Grèce, 2017, vol. 3, Ave César: Rome, 2018. *Address:* 34 Square Montsouris, 75014 Paris, France. *T:* (1) 45893416.

**BLOMEFIELD, Sir (Thomas) Charles (Peregrine),** 6th Bt *cr* 1807; fine art and philatelic consultant; *b* 24 July 1948; *s* of Sir Thomas Edward Peregrine Blomefield, 5th Bt, and of Ginette, Lady Blomefield; *S* father, 1984; *m* 1975, Georgina Geraldine, *d* of late Commander C. E. Over, Lugger End, Portscatho, Cornwall; one *s* two *d. Educ:* Wellington Coll., Berks; Mansfield Coll., Oxford. Christie's, 1971–75; Wildenstein and Co., 1975–76; Director: Lidchi Art Gallery, Johannesburg, 1976–78; Direct Import Ltd, 1985–2012; Man. Dir, Charles Blomefield and Co., 1980–. *Heir: s* Thomas William Peregrine Blomefield, *b* 16 July 1983. *Address:* 42 Simpson Street, SW11 3HW.

**BLOMFIELD, Paul;** MP (Lab) Sheffield Central, since 2010; *b* Chatham, Kent, 25 Aug. 1953; *s* of Henry and Mabel Blomfield; *m* 2000, Linda McAvan, *qv;* one *s* by a previous marriage. *Educ:* Abbeydale Boys' Grammar Sch.; Tadcaster Grammar Sch.; St John's Coll., York (Cert Ed). Mem., NEC and Vice-Pres., NUS, 1976–78. Various roles, Sheffield Univ., 1978–2003; Gen. Manager, Sheffield Univ. Students' Union, 2003–10. Shadow Minister for Exiting the EU, 2016–. Mem. Bd, Sheffield City Trust, 1994–2008 (Chair, 1997–2008). Gov., Sheffield City Poly., 1982–92. Chm., Sheffield Lab Party, 1993–2008. Mem., Exec. Cttee, Anti-Apartheid Movement, 1978–94. *Recreations:* walking, cycling, watching Sheffield United. *Address:* House of Commons, SW1A 0AA. *E:* paul.blomfield.mp@parliament.uk; Unit 4, Edmund Road Business Centre, 135 Edmund Road, Sheffield S2 4ED. *T:* (0114) 272 2882, *Fax:* (0114) 272 2442.

**BLONDEL, Prof. Jean Fernand Pierre;** Professor of Political Science, European University Institute, Florence, 1985–94; *b* Toulon, France, 26 Oct. 1929; *s* of Fernand Blondel and Marie Blondel (*née* Santelli); *m* 1st, 1954, Michèle (*née* Hadet) (marr. diss. 1979); two *d;* 2nd, 1982, Mrs Theresa Martineau. *Educ:* Collège Saint Louis de Gonzague and Lycée Henri IV, Paris; Institut d'Etudes Politiques and Faculté de Droit, Paris; St Antony's Coll., Oxford. Asst Lectr, then Lectr in Govt, Univ. of Keele, 1958–63; Vis. ACLS Fellow, Yale Univ., 1963–64; Prof. of Government, 1964–84, and Dean, Sch. of Comparative Studies, 1967–69, Univ. of Essex. Visiting Professor: Carleton Univ., Canada, 1969–70; Univ. of Siena, 1995–; Vis. Schol., Russell Sage Foundn, NY, 1984–85. Exec. Dir, European Consortium for Political Res., 1970–79. Member: Royal Swedish Acad. of Scis, 1990; Academia Europaea, 1993; Amer. Acad. of Scis, 2005. Hon. DLitt Salford, 1990; Dr *hc:* Essex, 1992; Univ. Catholique de Louvain, 1992; Turku, 1995; Macerata, 2007; Siena, 2008. Johan Skytte Prize, Johan Skytte Foundn, 2004. *Publications:* Voters, Parties and Leaders, 1963; (jtly) Constituency Politics, 1964; (jtly) Public Administration in France, 1965; An Introduction to Comparative Government, 1969; (jtly) Workbook for Comparative Government, 1972; Comparing Political Systems, 1972; Comparative Legislatures, 1973; The Government of France, 1974; Thinking Politically, 1976; Political Parties, 1978; World Leaders, 1980; The Discipline of Politics, 1981; The Organisation of Governments, 1982; (jtly) Comparative Politics, 1984; Government Ministers in the Contemporary World, 1985; Political Leadership, 1987; (ed jtly) Western European Cabinets, 1988; Comparative Government, 1990, 2nd edn 1995; (ed jtly) The Profession of Cabinet Minister in Western Europe, 1991; (ed jtly) Governing Together, 1993; (ed jtly) Party and Government, 1996; (jtly) People and Parliament in the European Union, 1998; (ed jtly) Democracy, Governance and Economic Performance, 1999; (ed jtly) The Nature of Party Government, 2000; (jtly) Cabinets in Eastern Europe, 2001; (jtly) Political Cultures, 2006; (jtly) Governing New Democracies, 2007; (jtly) Citizens and the State, 2007; (jtly) Personalisation of Leadership, Parties and Citizens, 2010; (jtly) Political Parties and Democracy, 2012; The Presidential Republic, 2015; articles in: Political Studies, Parliamentary Affairs, Public Administration, Revue Française de Science Politique, European Jl of Political Research, etc. *Recreation:* holidays in Provence. *Address:* 3 Thornhill Bridge Wharf, Caledonian Road, N1 0RU.

**BLOOD, Baroness** *cr* 1999 (Life Peer), of Blackwatertown in the county of Armagh; **May Blood,** MBE 1995; Information Officer, Great Shankhill Partnership Co. Ltd, since 1994; Founding Member, Northern Ireland Women's Coalition, since 1996; *b* 26 May 1938; *d* of William and Mary Blood. *Educ:* Donegall Road Primary Sch.; Linfield Secondary Sch. Cutter/Supervisor, Blackstaff Linen Mill Co. Ltd, 1952–90; Manager, Cairn Martin Wood Products, 1991–94. Mem., H of L, 1999–2018. DUniv: Ulster, 1998; QUB, 2000; Open, 2001. *Recreations:* home decorating, reading, gardening. *Address:* 7 Black Mountain Place, Belfast BT13 3TT. *T:* (028) 9032 6514.

**BLOOM, Adrian Jonathan Richard,** VMH; Chairman, Blooms Nurseries Ltd, since 2003; *b* Oakington, Cambridge, 22 May 1940; *s* of Alan Bloom, MBE and Doris Bloom; *m* 1966, Rosemary Vaughan; three *s. Educ:* Diss Grammar Sch. Jt Man. Dir, 1970–90, Man. Dir, 1995–2003, Blooms Nurseries Ltd; Jt Man. Dir, 1984–90, Chm., 1990–99, Blooms of Bressingham plc. Owner, Foggy Bottom garden, Bressingham. VMH 1985. Lifetime Achievement Award, Garden Media Guild, 2015. *Publications:* Conifers for your Garden, 1972; A Year Round Garden, 1979; Blooms of Bressingham Garden Plants, 1992; Winter Garden Glory, 1993; Summer Garden Glory, 1996; Gardening with Conifers, 2001; Blooms Best Perennials and Grasses, 2010. *Recreations:* gardening, walking, ski-ing, travelling, cinema. *Address:* Foggy Bottom, Bressingham, Diss, Norfolk IP22 2AA.

**BLOOM, Anthony Herbert;** Chairman, Cineworld (formerly CINE-UK Ltd), 1995–2020; *b* 15 Feb. 1939; *s* of Joseph Bloom and Margaret Roslyn Bloom; *m* 1973, Gisela von Mellenthin; two *s* two *d. Educ:* Univ. of Witwatersrand (BCom, LLB); Harvard Law Sch. (LLM); Stanford Graduate Sch. of Business (Sloan Fellow, 1970). Hayman Godfrey and Sanderson, S Africa, 1960–64; joined Premier Gp Ltd, S Africa, 1966, Dir, 1969; Dep. Chm., 1975–79, Chm., 1979–88; Director: Barclays Nat. Bank, later First Nat. Bank of Southern Africa Ltd, 1980–88; Liberty Life Assoc., 1982–88; South African Breweries Ltd, 1983–89; CNA Gallo Ltd, 1983–88; RIT Capital Partners plc, 1988–97; Dir and Dep. Chm., Sketchley, 1990–95; Director: Rio Narcea Gold Mines Ltd, 1995–2007; Orthoworld plc, 1999–2007. Director: Ballet Rambert, 1995–2001; LSO, 2008–; Mem., British Library Bd, 1995–2000. Hon. LLD Witwatersrand, 2002. *Recreations:* opera, ballet, theatre, music. *Address:* 8 Hanover Terrace, NW1 4RJ. *T:* (020) 7723 3422.

**BLOOM, His Honour Charles;** QC 1987; a Circuit Judge, 1997–2012 (Hon. 2012); *b* 6 Nov. 1940; *s* of Abraham Barnett Bloom and Freda Bloom (*née* Craft); *m* 1967, Janice Rachelle Goldberg; one *s* one *d. Educ:* Manchester Central Grammar School; Manchester University. LLB Hons 1962. Called to the Bar, Gray's Inn, 1963; practised on Northern Circuit, 1963–97; a Recorder, 1983–97; a Dep. High Ct Judge, Family Div., 1990–2012. Chm., Medical Appeal Tribunals, 1979–97. Tutor Judge, Judicial Coll., 2004–11. Mem., Larner Vinifloral Soc., 1996–; Chair, Yeshurun Debating Soc., 2014–. *Recreations:* tennis, creative writing, reading. *Club:* Friedland Postmusaf Tennis (Cheadle).

**BLOOM, Claire,** CBE 2013; *b* London, 15 Feb. 1931; *d* of late Edward Bloom and Elizabeth Bloom; *m* 1st, 1959, Rod Steiger (marr. diss. 1969; he *d* 2002); one *d;* 2nd, 1969; 3rd, 1990, Philip Roth (marr. diss. 1995; he *d* 2018). *Educ:* schs in UK and USA. First work in England, BBC, 1946. Stratford: Ophelia, Lady Blanche (King John), Perdita, 1948; The Damask Cheek, Lyric, Hammersmith, 1949; The Lady's Not For Burning, Globe, 1949; Ring Round the Moon, Globe, 1949–50. Old Vic: 1952–53: Romeo and Juliet; 1953: Merchant of Venice; 1954: Hamlet, All's Well, Coriolanus, Twelfth Night, Tempest; 1956: Romeo and Juliet (London, and N American tour). Cordelia, in Stratford Festival Company, 1955 (London, provinces and continental tour); Duel of Angels, Apollo, 1958; Rashomon, NY, 1959; Altona, Royal Court, 1961; The Trojan Women, Spoleto Festival, 1963; Ivanov, Phoenix, 1965; A Doll's House, NY, 1971; Hedda Gabler, 1971; Vivat! Vivat Regina!, NY, 1971; A Doll's House, Criterion, 1973 (filmed 1973); A Streetcar Named Desire, Piccadilly, 1974; Rosmersholm, Haymarket, 1977; The Cherry Orchard, Chichester Fest., 1981, Cambridge, Mass, 1994; When We Dead Waken, Almeida, 1990; A Long Day's Journey into Night, ART, Cambridge, Mass, 1996; Electra, McCarter Th., Princeton, NJ, 1998, transf. NY, 1999; Conversations After a Burial, Almeida, 2000; A Little Night Music, Seattle, 2001, NY, 2003; Whistling Psyche, Almeida, 2004; Six Dance Lessons in Six Weeks, Haymarket, 2006. One-woman performances: These Are Women, 1981– (US tour, 1981–82); Enter the Actress, 1998–. First film, Blind Goddess, 1947; *films include:* Limelight; The Man Between; Richard III; Alexander the Great; The Brothers Karamazov; The Buccaneers; Look Back in Anger; Three Moves to Freedom; The Brothers Grimm; The Chapman Report; The Haunting; 80,000 Suspects; Alta Infedelta; Il Maestro di Vigevano; The Outrage; The Spy Who Came in From The Cold; Charly; Three into Two won't go; A Severed Head; Red Sky at Morning; Islands In The Stream; The Clash of the Titans, 1979; Always, 1984; Sammy and Rosie Get Laid, 1987; Crimes and Misdemeanors, 1989; Daylight, 1997; The Book of Eve, 2001; Imagining Argentina, 2002; Daniel and the Superdogs, 2003; The King's Speech, 2011; Max Rose, 2013. *Television:* first appearance on television programmes, 1952, since when she has had frequent successes on TV in the US: In Praise of Love, 1975; Anastasia, 1986; Queenie, 1986; BBC: A Legacy, 1975; The Ghost Writer, 1983; Shadowlands, 1985 (BAFTA award Best TV Actress); Time and the Conways, 1985; Oedipus the King, 1986; What the Deaf Man Heard, 1997; Doctor Who, 2009; BBC Shakespeare: Katharine in Henry VIII, 1979; Gertrude in Hamlet, 1980; the Queen in Cymbeline, Lady Constance in King John, 1983; ITV: series: Brideshead Revisited, 1981; Intimate Contact, 1987; Shadow on the Sun, 1988; play, The Belle of Amherst, 1986; Channel Four: series, The Camomile Lawn, 1992; The Mirror Crack'd, 1992; Remember, 1993; A Village Affair, 1994; Family Money, 1996; series, Imogen's Face, 1998; The Lady in Question, 1999; Law and Order, 2003; Doc Martin, 2005 and 2013. Many appearances as narrator in both contemporary and classic repertoire. Distinguished Vis. Prof., Hunter Coll., NY, 1989. *Publications:* Limelight and After (autobiog.), 1982; Leaving a Doll's House (autobiog.), 1996. *Recreations:* opera, music. *Address:* c/o Conway van Gelder Grant, Third Floor, 8/12 Broadwick Street, W1F 8HW.

**BLOOM, Godfrey William,** TD and bar 1988; Member for Yorkshire and North Lincolnshire, European Parliament, 2004–14 (UK Ind, 2004–13; Ind, 2013–14); *b* 22 Nov. 1949; *s* of Alan Bloom and Phylis Bloom; *m* 1986, Katryna Skowronek. *Educ:* St Olave's Sch.; South East London Day Coll.; Royal Military Acad. Sandhurst; Royal Coll. of Defence Studies. Fund Manager, Mercury Asset Mgt, 1988–93; Econ. Res. Dir, TBO Gp of Cos, 1993–2004. European Parliament: Member: Women and Gender Equality Cttee, 2004–14; Econ. and Monetary Affairs Cttee, 2009–14; Reserve Mem., Envmt Cttee, 2009–14. Econ. Advr, Educational Research Associates, 2008–. Member: Campaign against Political Correctness, 2005–; Surtees Soc., 2012–; British Charolais Cattle Soc. Life Mem., War Memls Trust, 2001. Associate Mem., RCDS, 2011. Hon. Life Mem., Cambridge Univ. Women's RFC, 2003. Patron: Assoc. of British Drivers, 2005–; Drivers' Union, 2013–; Victoria Cross Trust, 2013–. Lead Sponsor and Spokesman, Alliance of British Drivers. Contributor, Going Postal. Micropal Award for Fund Mgt, 1992. Graduate, 2005, Postgraduate, 2009, Armed Forces Parly Scheme (Medal), 2014; Sovereign's Medal, 1995; Eur. Parly Silver Medal, 2014. Resident Author, Libertarian Alliance, 2013–15. *Publications:* Beyond the Fridge, 2007; War Aims and the Economic Consequences for the UK, 2010; Billy Nomates: or what he really said, 2013; Guinea a Minute, 2013; A Dinosaur's Guide to Libertarianism, 2014; The Magic of Banking, 2017; contribs to Financial Times pubns and Army Review. *Recreations:* hunting and shooting, cricket, military history, fell walking. *E:* gbloom@outlook.com. *W:* www.godfreybloom.uk. *Clubs:* East India, Royal Over-Seas League, New Frontier; Bentley Drivers, MG Owners'; Royal Cornish (Hawkedon); Diogenes, Pocklington Rugby; Horsehouse Formals Cricket (Londesborough Park); Brocklesbury Tumblers (Brocklesbury Hunt, N Lincs); Gadflys (Strasbourg).

**BLOOM, Louise Anne Harris;** Member: (Lib Dem) Eastleigh Borough Council, 2002–17 (Cabinet Member for Environment and Sustainability, 2002–17); Liberal Democrat Federal Policy Committee, 2011–15; *b* 7 April 1964; *d* of Christopher George Harris and Patricia Rose Harris (*née* Fray, now Cherrill); *m* 1987, Charles Neil Bloom (marr. diss.); two *d. Educ:* Kingston Poly. (BA Hons Applied Soc. Sci. 1985). Worked for various advertising agencies, 1985–90; freelance orgn mgt of press and publicity events, 1991–97; res. and admin assistant to Lib Dem councillors, Royal Bor. of Kingston upon Thames, 1991–93; Asst to Co-ordinator of Ind. Living Scheme, Kingston Assoc. of Disabled People, 1997; Inf. and Volunteer Develt Officer, Richmond Advice and Inf. on Disability, 1998–2000; Advocacy Service Manager (formerly Advocacy Project Manager), Solent Mind, Southampton, 2002–13; Asst Dir, Options Wellbeing Trust, 2013–16; Sessional Support Worker, YOU Trust, 2015–17; Registered Manager: Nat. Autistic Soc., 2017–18; Hft, 2018; Advocacy Manager, Rethink Mental Illness, 2018–. Mem. (Lib Dem), London Assembly, GLA, 2000–02; Vice Chair: SE England Regl Assembly, 2006–10 (Exec. Mem., 2002–10); SE England Councils, 2010–11. Mem., Standards Bd for England, 2004–06. *Recreations:* theatre, music, reading, travelling, history.

**BLOOM, Margaret Janet, (Lady Bloom),** CBE 2003; Visiting Professor, Dickson Poon School of Law (formerly School of Law), King's College London, 2003–15, now Honorary Professor; Senior Consultant, Freshfields Bruckhaus Deringer, since 2003; *b* 28 July 1943; *d* of John Sturrock and Jean Elizabeth Sturrock (*née* Ranken); *m* 1965, Stephen Robert Bloom (see *Prof. Sir S. R. Bloom*); two *s* two *d. Educ:* Sherborne Sch. for Girls; Girton Coll.

Cambridge (MA). Economist, then Dep. Gp Economist, John Laing and Son, 1965–69; Gp Economist, Tarmac, 1969–70; Sen. Project Manager, NEDO, 1970–86; Sci. and Technol. Secretariat, Cabinet Office, 1986–89; Res. and Technol. Policy Div., 1989–91, Competition Policy Div., 1991–93, Finance and Resource Mgt Div., 1993–95, DTI; Head, Agencies Privatisation Team, 1995–96, Dir, Agencies Gp B, 1996, Cabinet Office; Dir of Competition Policy, subseq. Competition Enforcement, OFT, 1997–2003. Dir, Lending Standards Bd, 2012–19. Member: LINK Consumer Council, 2006–; Access to Cash Review Panel, 2018–19. Vice Chair, Professional Standards Council for Asset Based Finance Assoc., 2013–. Pt-time Lectr, 1977–80, Ext. Examr, 1985–88, for MSc in Architecture, UCL. Dep. Chm., Money Advice Trust, 2007–15 (Trustee, 2003–15). *Recreations:* family, foreign travel, eating out, rambling. *Address:* Dickson Poon School of Law, King's College London, Strand, WC2R 2LS. *T:* (020) 7848 2324, *Fax:* (020) 7848 2443. *E:* margaret.bloom@kcl.ac.uk.

**BLOOM, Prof. Sir Stephen (Robert),** Kt 2012; MD, DSc; FRCP, FRCPath, FMedSci; FRS 2013; FRSB; Professor of Medicine, since 1982, and Head of Division of Diabetes, Endocrinology and Metabolism, since 1994, Imperial College Faculty of Medicine (formerly Royal Postgraduate Medical School), London University; Chief of Service for Pathology, Imperial College Healthcare NHS Trust, since 1994; Consultant Physician, Hammersmith Hospital, since 1982; *b* 24 Oct. 1942; *s* of Arnold and Edith Bloom; *m* 1965, Margaret Janet Sturrock (*see* M. J. Bloom); two *s* two *d*. *Educ:* Queens' Coll., Cambridge (MA 1968; MD 1979); Middlesex Hosp. Med. Sch.; DSc London 1982. FRCP 1978; FRCPath 1993; FRSB (FInstBiol 2008). Middlesex Hospital: Gastro House Physician, 1967–68; Cardiology House Physician, 1968; Casualty Med. Officer, 1969; Leverhulme Res. Schol., Inst. of Clin. Res., 1970; Med. Unit Registrar, 1970–72; MRC Clin. Res. Fellow, 1972–74; House Surgeon, Mount Vernon Hosp., 1968–69; Endocrinology House Physician, Hammersmith Hosp., 1969–70; Sen. Lectr, 1974–78, Reader in Medicine, 1978–82, RPMS, Hammersmith Hosp.; Dir, Endocrinol. Clin. Service, 1982–, and Head of Div. of Investigative Sci., 1997–2007, Imperial Coll., London (formerly RPMS). CSO, Thiakis, 2006–09. Lectures: Copp, Amer. Diabetes Assoc.; Goulstonian, and Lumleian, RCP; Amer. Endocrine Soc. Transatlantic; Lawrence, and Arnold Bloom, British Diabetic Assoc.; Wellcome, RSM. Sen. Censor, RCP, 1999–2001. Chm., Soc. for Endocrinology, 2002–06 (Sec., 1999–2002). Founder FMedSci, 1998. Hon. Dr: Warwick; Brunel. Dale Medal, Soc. for Endocrinology, 2003. *Publications:* Toohey's Medicine, 15th edn, 1994; (with J. Lynn) Surgical Endocrinology, 1993. *Recreations:* walking, jogging, travelling, opera. *Address:* Department of Investigative Medicine, Imperial College Faculty of Medicine, 6th Floor Commonwealth Building, Hammersmith Campus, Du Cane Road, W12 0NN. *T:* (020) 8383 3242.

**BLOOMER, Giles;** *see* Bloomer, R. J. G.

**BLOOMER, Jonathan William,** MBE 2017; FCA; Chairman: Arrow Global Group plc, since 2013; SDL Group Ltd (formerly Shepherd Direct Ltd), since 2014; Morgan Stanley International, since 2018; *b* 23 March 1954; *s* of late Derick William Bloomer and Audrey Alexandra Bloomer; *m* 1977, Anne Elizabeth Judith May; one *s* two *d*. *Educ:* Halesowen Grammar Sch.; Imperial Coll., London (BSc, ARCS 1974). FCA 1982. Partner, Arthur Andersen, 1987–94; Gp Finance Dir, Prudential Corp. plc, 1995–99; Prudential plc: Dep. Gp Chief Exec., 1999–2000; Chief Exec., 2000–05; Partner, Cerberus European Capital Advrs LLP, 2006–12; Chief Exec. (formerly Exec. Chm.), Lucida plc, 2006–12. Chairman: Scottish Re, 2007–12; JLT Employee Benefits Gp, 2013–16; Sen. Ind. Dir, Hargreaves Lansdown plc, 2006–13; non-exec. Dir, Autonomy, 2010–11; Dir, Change Real Estate Ltd, 2013–. Bd Mem., ABI, 2001–05; Chm., Financial Services Practitioner Panel, 2003–05 (Dep. Chm., 2001–03). CCMI (CIMgt 1996). Trustee and Treas., NSPCC, 2009–16. Chm. Trustees, Caterham Sch., 2010–15. *Recreations:* sailing, watching Rugby, gardening.

**BLOOMER, Dr (Robert John) Giles,** OBE 1998; Vice Lord-Lieutenant of South Yorkshire, 2010–16; *b* Barnsley, 1943; *s* of Robert and Aileen Bloomer; *m* 1967, Elizabeth Broughton; two *s* one *d*. *Educ:* Rotherham Grammar Sch.; Univ. of Birmingham (BSc 1964; PhD 1967). MICE 1969. Water engr, Cornwall River Authy and Water Resources Bd, 1967–72; Dir, Bramall Construction, later Keepmoat plc, 1972–85; Chm., Aizlewoods Bldg Materials, 1985–2002. Dir, Rotherham Chamber of Commerce and Industry, 1988–2006 (Pres., 1990). Non-exec. Dir, Rotherham Hosp. NHS Foundn Trust, 2005–11. Trustee: Magna Trust, 1998–2013; S Yorks Community Foundn, 2006–16. Feoffee, Common Lands of Rotherham, 1995–. Liveryman, Builders Merchants' Co., 1991–. DL 1999, High Sheriff 2008–09, S Yorks. *Publications:* (with J. R. Sexton) Generation of Synthetic River Flow Data, 1972. *Club:* Rotary (Rotherham).

**BLOOMFIELD,** family name of **Baroness Bloomfield of Hinton Waldrist**.

**BLOOMFIELD OF HINTON WALDRIST,** Baroness *cr* 2016 (Life Peer), of Hinton Waldrist in the County of Oxfordshire; **Olivia Caroline Bloomfield;** a Baroness in Waiting (Government Whip), since 2019; *b* Cardiff, 30 June 1960; *d* of Anthony Provis and Kathleen Mary Provis (*née* Mottram); *m* 1984, Andrew Kenneth Bloomfield; one *s* two *d*. *Educ:* United World Coll. of the Atlantic; St Hugh's Coll., Oxford (BA Hons PPE). Shipping Finance, Bank of America, 1982–86; Exec. Dir, Financial Services Practice, Russell Reynolds Associates, 1986–93; COS to Treas. of Conservative Party, 2006–10; Partner, Atlantic Superconnection Corp., 2011–16. Advr to Chm., London Pensions Fund Authy, 2012–15. Chairman: Wantage Gp, 2002–15; Pump House Proj., 2013–. Mem. Council, Cheltenham Ladies' Coll., 2002–10. JP Oxon, 1997–2007, Cities of London and Westminster, 2007–10. *Recreations:* swimming, music, learning Welsh. *Address:* House of Lords, SW1A 0PW.

**BLOOMFIELD, Keith George,** CMG 2007; HM Diplomatic Service, retired; Ambassador to Nepal, 2002–06; *b* 2 June 1947; *s* of George William Bloomfield and Edith Joan Bloomfield; *m* 1976, Genevieve Charbonneau; three *d*. *Educ:* Kilburn Grammar Sch.; Lincoln Coll., Oxford (MA). Home Civil Service, 1969–80; Office of UK Rep. to EC, Brussels, 1980–85; FCO, 1985–87; Head of Chancery, Cairo, 1987–90; Dep. Head of Mission, Algiers, 1990–94; Counsellor (Political and Mgt), Rome, 1994–96; Minister and Dep. Head of Mission, Rome, 1997–98; Hd, Counter Terrorism Policy Dept, FCO, 1998–2002. *Recreations:* music, tennis, reading.

**BLOOMFIELD, Sir Kenneth Percy,** KCB 1987 (CB 1982); Joint International Commissioner, Commission for Location of Victims Remains, since 1999; President, AQE, since 2011 (Chairman, AQE Ltd, 2008–11); *b* 15 April 1931; *oc* of late Harry Percy Bloomfield and Doris Bloomfield, Belfast; *m* 1960, Mary Elizabeth Ramsey (MBE 2013); one *s* one *d*. *Educ:* Royal Belfast Academical Instn; St Peter's Coll., Oxford (MA; Hon. Fellow, 1991). Min. of Finance, N Ireland, 1952–56; Private Sec. to Ministers of Finance, 1956–60; Dep. Dir, British Industrial Develt Office, NY, 1960–63; Asst and later Dep. Sec. to Cabinet, NI, 1963–72; Under-Sec., Northern Ireland Office, 1972–73; Sec. to Northern Ireland Executive, Jan.–May 1974; Permanent Secretary: Office of the Executive, NI, 1974–75; Dept of Housing, Local Govt and Planning, NI, 1975–76; Dept of the Environment, NI, 1976–81; Dept of Commerce, NI, 1981–82; Dept of Economic Develt, 1982–84; Head, NICS, and Second Perm. Under Sec. of State, NI Office, 1984–91. Nat.

Gov. and Chm. of Broadcasting Council for NI, BBC, 1991–99. Review of Dental Remuneration, 1992; Consultant, Crown Appts Review Gp, 1999–2001. Comr, NI Victims Commn, 1997–98 (report published 1998). Chairman: Chief Executives' Forum for NI Public Services, 1991–97; NI Higher Educn Council, 1993–2001; Review of Criminal Injuries Compensation in NI, 1998–99; Bangor and Holywood Town Centre Mgt Ltd, 2000–06; Legal Services Commn for NI, 2003–04; Vice-Chm., Mus and Galls of NI, 2002–06. Pres., NI Council, Stationery Office, 1998–2000. Mem., NI Adv. Bd, Bank of Ireland, 1991–; Member of Board: Co-operation North, 1991–93; Opera, NI, 1992–97. Member: Statute Law Adv. Cttee, 1993–97; Nat. Steering Cttee, Give as You Earn, 1992–93; Adv. Cttee, Constitution Unit, 1997; Jersey Review of Machinery of Govt, 1999–2000. Chm., Children in Need Trust, 1992–98; Mem. Bd, Green Park Hosp. Trust, 1993–2001; Patron, NI Council for Integrated Educn, 1998–. Senator (Crown nominee), QUB, 1991–93. Bass Ireland Lectr, Univ. of Ulster, 1991. Gov., Royal Belfast Academical Instn, 1984–2011 (Chm., 2004–11). MRIA 2008. Hon. LLD QUB, 1991; DUniv Open, 2000; Hon. DLitt Ulster, 2002. Dr Ben Wilson Trophy for Individual or Corporate Excellence, NI Chamber of Commerce and Industry, 1990. *Publications:* Stormont in Crisis (a memoir), 1994; A Tragedy of Errors, 2007; A New Life, 2008; The BBC at the Watershed, 2008; *contributions to:* Hope and History, 1996; Broadcasting in a Divided Community, 1996; People and Government: questions for Northern Ireland, 1997; Cool Britannia, 1998; various jls and periodicals. *Recreations:* history, travel, swimming, authorship and public speaking. *Address:* 16 Larch Hill, Holywood, Co. Down BT18 0JN. *T:* (028) 9042 8340.

**BLOOR, Prof. David;** Scientific Adviser, Peratech Ltd, 2003–14; Professor of Applied Physics, University of Durham, 1989–2002, now Emeritus (Chairman, Department of Physics, 1993–96); *b* 25 July 1937; *s* of Alfred Edwin Bloor and Gladys Ellen Bloor (*née* Collins); *m* 1960, Margaret E. A. Avery; four *s* (and one *s* decd). *Educ:* Queen Mary College London (BSc, PhD). CPhys, FInstP. Lectr, Dept of Physics, Univ. of Canterbury, NZ, 1961–64; Queen Mary College London: Lectr, Dept of Physics, 1964; Reader, 1980–84; Prof. of Polymer Physics, 1984–89. Humboldt Fellow: Univ. of Stuttgart, 1975–76; Univ. of Bayreuth, 1997–98; Erskine Fellow, Univ. of Canterbury, NZ, 1983; Royal Society SERC Indust. Fellow, GEC Marconi Res. Centre, 1985–86; Sir Derman Christopherson Foundn Fellow, Univ. of Durham, 1996–97. Co-ordinator, DTI/SERC Molecular Electronics Initiative, 1987–93. Mem., Exec. Cttee, Canon Foundn in Europe, 2000–09 (Chm., Selection Cttee, 2005–09; Hon. Mem., 2009–). *Publications:* over 300 articles in professional jls. *Recreations:* cycling, gardening. *Address:* Department of Physics, Durham University, South Road, Durham DH1 3LE. *T:* (0191) 334 3581.

**BLOSSE, Sir Richard Hely L.;** *see* Lynch-Blosse.

**BLOT, Jean;** *see* Blokh, A.

**BLOUNT, Vice Adm. Keith Edward,** CB 2018; OBE 2012; Commander, Maritime Command, NATO, since 2019; *b* Plymouth, 22 June 1966; *s* of Cyril and Ann Blount; *m* 2007, Deborah Reader; two *d*. *Educ:* Plymstock Sch.; King's Coll. London (MA Defence Studies 2004). Joined RN, 1984; qualified as helicopter pilot, 1986; specialised in anti-submarine and search and rescue, subseq. qualified as instructor, 1991–93; Mem., RN Helicopter Display Team, 1993; CO and Principal Warfare Officer, incl. CO, HMS Anglesey and HMS Somerset, 1993–2005; Mem., Directing Staff, JSCSC, 2005–07; Aviation Desk Officer, Directorate of Navy Resources and Plans, MoD, 2007–08; Comdr, Iraqi Maritime Task Gp and COS, Combined Task Force 151, 2008–09; CO, HMS Ocean, 2009–10; COS to Comdr, UK Maritime Forces, 2010–11; MA to VCDS, 2011–13; UK Maritime Component Comdr and Dep. Comdr, Combined Maritime Forces, 2013–15; ACNS (Aviation, Amphibious Capability and Carriers) and Rear Adm., FAA, 2015–19. FRAeS 2016. *Recreations:* ski-ing, shooting, messing about in boats. *Address:* Atlantic Building, Northwood Headquarters, Middlesex HA6 3DP. *Club:* Naval.

**BLOW, Bridget Penelope,** CBE 2014; Chairman (non-executive), GTP3, since 2016; Senior Independent Director, England Netball, since 2015; *b* 1949; *m* Rod Blow (marr. diss.); one *d*. *Educ:* Caistor Grammar Sch. Systems Develt, Grimsby BC, 1968–79; Human Resources Dir, Divl Dir, Dir of Technol., then Exec. Dir, FI Gp, 1979–92; Systems Dir, 1992–94, Chief Exec., 1994–2005, ITNET; Gp Technol. Dir, Serco Gp plc, 2005–06. Dir, Bank of England, 2000–05. Non-executive Chairman: Trustmarque Solutions, 2006–13; Harvard Internat. plc (formerly Alba plc), 2007–12 (Dir, 2005–12); non-exec. Dep. Chm., Coventry Building Soc., 2009–16 (Dir, 2007–16). Non-executive Chairman: Gtr Birmingham and Solihull LEP Develt Bd, 2010–11; CBSO, 2012–18. Non-exec. Dir, Birmingham Hippodrome Theatre Trust, 2006–15. Pres., Birmingham Chamber of Commerce and Industry, 2008–09. Mem. Council, Univ. of Birmingham, 2005–10. CCMI. Hon. DSc Aston, 2015. NatWest Midlands Business Woman of the Year, 1996. *Recreations:* golf, gym, tennis, theatre.

**BLOW, Prof. (John) Julian,** PhD; FRSE; FMedSci; Professor of Chromosome Maintenance, since 2001, and Dean, School of Life Sciences, since 2016, University of Dundee; *b* Cambridge, 23 Feb. 1961; *s* of Prof. David Mervyn Blow, FRS, and of Mavis Blow; *m* 1988, Margret Michalski; one *s* one *d*. *Educ:* Univ. of Edinburgh (BSc Pathol. 1984); Trinity Coll., Cambridge (PhD 1987). Post-doctoral Fellow: Univ. of Cambridge, 1987–88; Univ. of Oxford, 1988–91; Res. Scientist, 1991–96, Sen. Scientist, 1996–97, ICRF Clare Hall Labs; University of Dundee: Sen. Lectr, Dept of Biochem., 1997–2000; Reader, 2000–01; Dep. Hd, Div. of Gene Regulation and Expression, Sch. of Life Scis, 1998–2008; Dep. Dir, 2008–12, 2012–14, Wellcome Centre for Gene Regulation and Expression; Associate Dean, Coll. of Life Scis, 2010–12; Dir of Res., Sch. of Life Scis, 2014–16. FRSE 2002; FMedSci 2012. *Publications:* peer-reviewed pubns, mainly in field of DNA replication. *Recreations:* mountaineering, orienteering, progressive rock. *Address:* School of Life Sciences, University of Dundee, Dow Street, Dundee DD1 5EH. *T:* (01382) 381042. *E:* j.j.blow@dundee.ac.uk.

**BLOW, Joyce;** *see* Blow Darlington, J.

**BLOW, Julian;** *see* Blow, J. J.

**BLOW DARLINGTON, Joyce,** OBE 1994; Chairman, Child Accident Prevention Trust, 1996–2002; *b* 4 May 1929; *d* of late Walter Blow and Phyllis (*née* Grainger); *m* 1974, Lt-Col J. A. B. Darlington, RE retd (*d* 2011). *Educ:* Bell Baxter Sch., Cupar, Fife; Edinburgh Univ. (MA Hons). John Lewis Partnership, 1951–52; FBI, 1952–53; Press Officer, Council of Indust. Design, 1953–63; Publicity and Advertising Manager, Heal & Son Ltd, 1963–65; entered Civil Service on first regular recruitment of direct entry Principals from business and industry: BoT, 1965–67; Monopolies Commn (gen. enquiry into restrictive practices in supply of prof. services), 1967–70; DTI, 1970, Asst Sec. 1972; Dept of Prices and Consumer Protection, 1974–77; Under-Secretary: OFT, 1977–80; DTI, 1980–84; Chairman: Mail Order Publishers' Authy, 1985–92; Direct Marketing Assoc. Authy, 1992–97. Chm., E Sussex FHSA, 1990–96. Pres., Assoc. for Quality in Healthcare, 1991–94; Vice-Pres., Trading Standards Inst., 1985–; Bd Mem., BSI, 1987–97 (Chm., Consumer Policy Cttee, 1987–93). Founder Mem. and Past Pres., Women in Public Relations. Trustee, Univ. of

Edinburgh Develt Trust, 1990–94; Chm., PR Educn Trust, 1992–97. Freeman, City of London. Hon. FCIPR (FIPR 1964); FCMI; FRSA. *Publications:* Consumers and International Trade: a handbook, 1987. *Recreations:* music, art, architecture, travel, France.

BLOXHAM, Prof. Jeremy, PhD; FRS 2007; Mallinckrodt Professor of Geophysics, Harvard University, since 2004; *b* 29 April 1960; *s* of Lawrence Bloxham and Christine Bloxham; *m* 1985, Katharine Jane Everist; two *s*. *Educ:* Portsmouth Grammar Sch.; Pembroke Coll., Cambridge (BA 1982; PhD 1985). Harvard University: Asst Prof. of Geophysics, 1987–90; John L. Loeb Associate Prof. of Natural Scis, 1990–93; Prof. of Geophysics, 1993–2004; Chair, Dept of Earth and Planetary Scis, 2000–06; Prof. of Computational Sci., 2006; Dean of Physical Scis, 2006–08; Dean of Science, 2008–18. *Publications:* over 60 articles in learned jls. *Recreations:* sailing, ski-ing, flying. *Address:* 14 Washington Square, Marblehead, MA 01945, USA. *T:* (office) (617) 4959517, *Fax:* (617) 4957660. *E:* jeremy_bloxham@harvard.edu. *Club:* Eastern Yacht (Marblehead, Mass).

BLOXHAM, Thomas Paul Richard, MBE 1999; Chairman and Co-Founder, Urban Splash Group, since 1993; *b* 20 Dec. 1963; *m* 1987, Jo Speakman; two *s*. *Educ:* Manchester Univ. (BA Hons Politics and Mod. History). Founder, Urban Splash (Properties), 1992; Baa Bar Ltd, 1991–2006 (Chm.). Mem., Property Adv. Gp, DTLR. Chm., Arts Council England (North West) (formerly NW Arts Bd), 1999–2008; Mem., Arts Council England, 2003–08. Dir, Liverpool Cultural Co. Ltd, 2001–08; Chairman: Manchester Internat. Arts Fest., 2005–; IPPR Centre for Cities Think Tank, 2005–. Chancellor, Manchester Univ., 2008–15. Trustee, Tate Gall., 2009–17. Trustee, Manchester Utd Foundn. Hon. RIBA; FRSA. Hon. Fellow: Liverpool John Moores Univ., 2001; Univ. of Central Lancashire, 2003. Hon. DDes: Oxford Brookes, 2004; Bristol, 2007; Hon. LittD Manchester, 2007; Hon. DBus Plymouth, 2009. UK Property Entrepreneur of the Year, 1998; Nat. Young Entrepreneur of the Year, 1999; North Region Young Entrepreneur of the Year, 1999; Northwest Young Entrepreneur of the Year, IoD, 1999. *Address:* (office) Timber Wharf, 16–24 Worsley Street, Castlefield, Manchester M15 4LD. *E:* tombloxham@urbansplash.co.uk.

BLUCK, Rt Rev. John William; Bishop of Waiapu, 2002–08; *b* 22 July 1943; *m* 1969, Elizabeth Anne Frost; one *s* one *d*. *Educ:* Univ. of Canterbury, NZ (MA 1966); Episcopal Theol Sch., Cambridge, Mass, USA (BD *cum laude* 1969). Ordained deacon, 1970, priest, 1971; served Holy Trinity parish, Gisborne, 1970–72; Editor: NZ Methodist, 1972–77; One World, WCC, 1977–80; Dir of Communications, WCC, 1980–84; Prof. of Pastoral Theol. and Communication, Knox Theol Hall, 1984–90; Dean of Christchurch Cathedral, NZ, 1990–2002. *Publications:* Everyday Ecumenism, 1987; Christian Communication Reconsidered, 1989; Canberra Takeaways, 1991; Long, White and Cloudy, 1998; Waking Up in Strange Places, 1999; Killing Us Softly, 2001; The Giveaway God, 2001; Credible Christianity: finding faith here and now, 2008; Praying the Lord's Prayer, 2010; Hidden Country: finding faith in Aotearoa, 2011; Wai Karekare—Turbulent Waters: the Anglican bicultural journey 1814–2014; Preaching Inside Out, 2017; Seeking the Centre: living well in Aotearoa, 2019. *E:* johnbluck22@gmail.com.

BLUGLASS, Prof. Robert Saul, CBE 1995; MD; FRCP, FRCPsych; Professor of Forensic Psychiatry, University of Birmingham, 1979–96, now Emeritus; Hon. Consultant, Reaside Clinic, Birmingham, since 1995; *b* 22 Sept. 1930; *s* of Henry Bluglass and Fay (*née* Griew); *m* 1962, Dr Jean Margaret Kerry (*née* Montgomery); one *s* one *d*. *Educ:* Warwick Sch., Warwick; Univ. of St Andrews (MB, ChB 1957, MD 1967). DPM 1962; MRCPsych 1971, FRCPsych 1976; MRCP 1994, FRCP 1997. Formerly, Sen. Registrar in Psych., Royal Dundee Liff Hosp. and Maryfield Hosp., Dundee; Consultant in Forensic Psychiatry: W Midlands RHA and the Home Office, 1967–94; S Birmingham Mental Health NHS Trust, 1994–95 (Med. Dir, 1995–96); Consultant i/c Midland Centre for For. Psych., All Saints Hosp., Birmingham, 1967–93; Clinical Dir, Reaside Clinic, Birmingham, 1986–95. Birmingham University: Hon. Lectr, 1968–75, Sen. Clin. Lectr in Forensic Psych., 1975–79; Regl Postgrad. Tutor in Forensic Psych., 1967–95; Jt Dir, Midland Inst. of Forensic Medicine, 1975–87. Dep. Regional Advr in Psychiatry, W Midlands RHA, 1985–87, Regional Advr, 1987–92; Specialist Advr, H of C Select Cttee on Social Services, 1985–87, on Health, 2000–01; Consultant Advr in Psych., RAF, 1992–2001, now Hon. Consultant; Advr in Forensic Psych., Bd of Corrections, Health Service, NSW, 1996–97. Member: Adv. Cttee on Alcoholism, DHSS, 1975–80; Adv. Council on Probation, Home Office, 1974–77; Mental Health Review Tribunal, 1979–2004; Mental Health Act Commn, 1983–85; Forensic Psych. Res. Liaison Gp, DHSS; Rev. of Services for Mentally Disordered Offenders (Reed Cttee), DoH, 1991–94; Inquiry into care and mgt of Christopher Edwards and Richard Linford, 1996–98; Judicial Inquiry into Personality Disorder Unit at Ashworth Special Hosp., 1997–99. Royal College of Psychiatrists: Mem., Ct of Electors, 1976–79; Mem. Council, Exec. and Finance Cttees, 1973–76, 1976–79, 1980–86, 1986–91; Vice-Pres., 1983–85; Chm., For. Psych. Specialist Section, 1978–82; Chm., Midlands Div., 1986–91; Chm., Midlands Soc. of Criminology, 1981–95 (Sec., 1970–81); Past Pres., Sect. of Psych., Birmingham Med. Inst.; Vice-Pres., RAF Psych. Soc.; Mem., Brit. Acad. of For. Sciences; Associate Mem., GMC, 1991–2009. Chm., Compton Verney Coach House Mgt Co. Ltd, 2008–. FRSocMed 1975. Baron ver Heyden de Lancey Law Prize, RSocMed, 1983. *Publications:* Psychiatry, The Law and The Offender, 1980; A Guide to the Mental Health Act 1983, 1983; (ed with Prof. Sir Martin Roth) Psychiatry, Human Rights and the Law, 1985, repr. 2009; (ed with Dr Paul Bowden) The Principles and Practice of Forensic Psychiatry, 1990; articles in Brit. Jl of Hosp. Med., BMJ, Brit. Jl of Psych., and Med., Science and the Law. *Recreations:* water-colour painting, cooking, gardening, travelling, genealogy, supporter of St James's Singers (Vice-Pres., 2014–), Compton Verney Gallery, RSC. *E:* robert.bluglass@gmail.com.

BLUM, Heather Anne Elise Lilian M.; *see* Munroe-Blum.

BLUME, Dame Hilary (Sharon Braverman), DBE 2008; Founder and Director, Charities Advisory Trust (formerly Charity Trading Advisory Group), since 1979; *b* 9 Jan. 1945; *d* of Henry and Muriel Braverman; *m* 1st, 1965, Prof. Stuart Blume (marr. diss. 1977); two *s*; 2nd, 1977, Michael Aslan Norton, *qv*; one *d*. *Educ:* London Sch. of Econs (BSc Econ.); Univ. of Sussex (MPhil). Fund raiser: War on Want, 1971–74; SHAC, 1975–79. Founder and Bd Mem., Green Hotel, Mysore, 1983–; Dir, Card Aid, 1984–; Creator: Good Gifts Catalogue, 2003; Peace Oil, 2006; Founder, Knit for Peace, 2007; Knit for Peace UK, 2010. Comr, Nat. Lottery Commn, 1999–2000. Chm. (formerly Co-Chm.), Finnart House Sch. Trust, 2007– (Vice-Chm., 1996–2007). Patron, Trees for London, 2000–18. Member: Volunteering Adv. Gp, Canal and River Trust, 2016–18; Thrupp Canal Cruising Club, 2016–. FRSA 2002 (Mem. Council, 2004–07). *Publications:* Fund-raising: a comprehensive handbook, 1977; (jtly) Accounting and Financial Management for Charities, 1979, 2nd edn 1985; Charity Trading Handbook, 1981; Charity Christmas Cards, 1984; Museum Trading Handbook, 1987; Charity Shops Handbook, 1995. *Address:* Charities Advisory Trust, Radius Works, Back Lane, Hampstead, NW3 1HL.

BLUMENTHAL, Heston, OBE 2006; Chef Proprietor, The Fat Duck, Bray, since 1995; *b* 27 May 1966; *s* of Stephen Jeffrey Blumenthal and Celia Blumenthal; *m* 1991, Susanna Gage (marr. diss. 2017); one *s* two *d*; *m* 2018, Stephanie Gouveia; one *d*. Credit controller, Team Leasing, 1987–95. Proprietor: The Hinds Head, Bray, 2004– (Michelin Star); Dinner by Heston Blumenthal, Mandarin Oriental Hotel, Knightsbridge, 2011– (2 Michelin Stars); Dinner by Heston Blumenthal, Melbourne, 2015–. Chef of the Year: Good Food Guide, 2001; AA Guide, 2002; GQ Mag., 2004; Catey Awards, Caterer & Hotelkeeper Magazine: Restaurateur of the Year, 2003; Chef of the Year, 2004; Food and Wine Personality of Year Award, GQ/Glenfiddich Awards, 2004; The Fat Duck has also received numerous best restaurant awards, incl. 3rd Michelin Star, 2004. BBC TV programmes: In Search of Perfection, 2006; Further Adventures in Search of Perfection, 2007; Channel 4: Heston's Mission Impossible, 2011; How to Cook like Heston, 2012; Heston's Fantastical Food, 2012; Heston's Great British Food, 2013; Heston's Dinner in Space, 2016. Hon. DSc Reading, 2006; Hon. MSc Bristol, 2007. Hon. FRSC 2006. *Publications:* Family Food, 2002, 2nd edn 2004; In Search of Perfection, 2006; Further Adventures in Search of Perfection, 2007; The Big Fat Duck Cookbook, 2008, new edn 2009; In Search of Total Perfection, 2009; Heston Blumenthal at Home, 2011; Historic Heston, 2013. *Recreations:* the study of historical food, nutrition and exercise, sport. *Address:* The Fat Duck, High Street, Bray, Berks SL6 2AQ. *T:* (01628) 580333, *Fax:* (01628) 776188. *E:* heston@thefatduck.co.uk.

BLUMENTHAL, W(erner) Michael, PhD; US Secretary of the Treasury, 1977–79; Director, Jewish Museum Berlin, 1997–2014; *b* Germany, 3 Jan. 1926. *Educ:* Univ. of California at Berkeley; Princeton Univ. Research Associate, Princeton Univ., 1954–57; Vice-Pres., Dir, Crown Cork Internat. Corp., 1957–61; Dep. Asst Sec. of State for Econ. Affairs, Dept of State, 1961–63; Dep. Special Rep. of the President (with rank Ambassador) for Trade Negotiations, 1963–67; Pres., Bendix Internat., 1967–70; Bendix Corp.: Dir, 1967–77; Vice-Chm., 1970–71; Pres. and Chief Operating Officer, 1971–72; Chm. and Chief Exec. Officer, 1972–77; Burroughs Corp. subseq. Unisys: Chief Exec. Officer, 1980–90; Vice-Chm., 1980; Chm., 1981–90; Lazard Frères & Co. LLC, 1990–96. *Publications:* The Invisible Wall: three hundred years of a German Jewish family, 1998; In achtzig Jahren um die Welt: mein Leben, 2010; From Exile to Washington: a memoir of leadership in the twentieth century, 2013. *Address:* Princeton, NJ 08540, USA; Jewish Museum Berlin, Lindenstrasse 9–14, 10969 Berlin, Germany.

BLUMGART, Prof. Leslie Harold, MD; FRCS, FRCSE, FRCSGlas, FACS; Professor of Surgery, Memorial Sloan-Kettering Cancer Center, New York, since 2008 (Enid A. Haupt Professor of Surgery, 1991–2008; Chief, Section of Hepato-Biliary Surgery, and Director, Programme on Hepato-Biliary Diseases, 1995–2007); Professor of Surgery, Cornell University Medical Center, since 1992; *b* 7 Dec. 1931; of S African parentage; *m* 1955, Pearl Marie Navias (decd); *m* 1968, Sarah Raybould Bowen; two *s* two *d*. *Educ:* Jeppe High Sch., Johannesburg, SA; Univ. of Witwatersrand (BDS); Univ. of Sheffield (MB, ChB Hons; MD 1969). Prize Medal, Clin. Med. and Surg.; Ashby-de-la-Zouch Prize, Surg., Med., Obst. and Gynaecol. FRCS 1966; FRCSGlas 1973 (Hon. FRCSGlas 2001); FRCSE 1976. General dental practice, Durban, SA, 1954–59; Sen. Surgical Registrar, Nottingham Gen. Hosp. and Sheffield Royal Infirmary, 1966–70; Sen. Lectr and Dep. Dir, Dept of Surgery, Welsh Nat. Sch. of Med., also Hon. Cons. Surg., Cardiff Royal Inf., 1970–72; St Mungo Prof. of Surgery, Univ. of Glasgow, and Hon. Cons. Surg., Glasgow Royal Inf., 1972–79; Prof. of Surgery, Royal Postgrad. Sch. of London and Dir of Surgery, Hammersmith Hosp., 1979–86; Prof. of Surgery, Univ. of Bern, 1986–91. Moynihan Fellow, Assoc. of Surgs of Gt Brit. and Ire., 1972; Mayne Vis. Prof., Univ. of Queensland, Brisbane, 1976; Vis. Prof., Univ. of Lund, Sweden, 1977; Nimmo Vis. Prof., Adelaide Univ., 1982; Oliver Beahrs Vis. Prof., Mayo Clinic, 2002; Purvis Oration, 1974; President's Oration, Soc. for Surgery of Aliment. Tract, Toronto, 1977; Lectures: Honyman Gillespie, Univ. of Edinburgh, 1978; Walton, RCPGlas, 1984; Monsarrat, Univ. of Liverpool, 1985; Legg Meml, KCH, 1985; Philip Sandblom, Lund Univ., Sweden, 1986; T. E. Jones Meml, Cleveland Clinic, USA, 1986; L. W. Edwards, Vanderbilt Univ., USA, 1987; Ernest Miles, British Assoc. Surg. Oncology, 1995; DeQuervain, Insespital Bern, Switzerland, 2006; Dallas B. Phemister, Univ. of Chicago, 2007; Sabiston, Univ. Hosp., Zurich, 2007; Davis Foundn, RCPSG, 2007; Lumpkin Lect. in Surgery, Dallas, Texas, 2008; Bevan, Chicago Surgical Soc., 2008; William Longmire, UCLA, 2014; Seymour Schwartz, Univ. of Rochester, 2015. Pres., Internat. Biliary Assoc., 1987. Member: BMA, 1963–; Assoc. of Surgs of GB and Ire., 1971–; Surgical Research Soc., 1971–; Brit. Soc. of Gastroenterology, 1972–; Swiss Surg. Soc., 1987–; Internat. Hepato-Pancreato-Biliary Assoc., 1992–; Amer. Surgical Assoc., 1993–; Soc. Surgical Oncology, 1994–. Hon. Member: Soc. for Surgery of Aliment. Tract, USA, 1977; Soc. Amer. Endoscopic Surgeons, 1986–; Danish Surg. Soc., 1988; Yugoslavian Surg. Soc., 1988; French Surg. Soc., 1990; Austrian Surg. Soc., 2007; Hon. Fellow: Italian Surg. Soc., 2002; French Acad. of Surgery, 2008. Hon. FRCSI 2002. Hon. DSc Sheffield, 1998. Acral Medal, Swedish Soc. Surgery, 1990; Alumnus of the Year, Meml Sloan-Kettering Cancer Center, 2012; Lifetime Achievement Award, European Soc. of Surgical Oncology, 2014; Dist. Service Award, Soc. of Surgical Oncology, 2015; Nonie Lowry Distinguished Service Award, Americas Hepato-Pancreato-Biliary Assoc., 2017. Order of Prasidda, Prabala-Gorkha-Dakshin Bahu, Nepal, 1984. *Publications:* (ed with A. C. Kennedy), Essentials of Medicine and Surgery for Dental Students, 3rd edn 1977, 4th edn 1982; (ed) The Biliary Tract, 1982; (ed) Surgery of the Liver and Biliary Tract, vols 1 and 2, 1988, 6th edn as Blumgart's Surgery of the Liver, Biliary Tract and Pancreas, 2017; Video Atlas of Liver, Biliary and Pancreatic Surgery, 2010; (ed) Surgical Management of Hepatobiliary and Pancreatic Disorders, 2003; chapters in books; numerous publications concerned with medical educn, gastrointestinal surgery and aspects of oncology with particular interests in surgery of the liver, pancreas and biliary tract and hepatic pathophysiology in med. and surgical jls. *Recreations:* water colour painting, wood carving, sculpture. *Address:* Memorial Sloan-Kettering Cancer Center, 1275 York Avenue, New York, NY 10021, USA. *T:* (212) 6395531; 447 E 57th Street #3E, New York, NY 10022, USA. *T:* (917) 9727850, (212) 7550836.

BLUNDELL, Prof. Derek John; Professor of Environmental Geology, University of London, 1975–98, now Emeritus Professor of Geophysics; Dean of Research and Enterprise, Royal Holloway, University of London, 1995–98; *b* 30 June 1933; *s* of Frank and Mollie Blundell; *m* 1960, Mary Patricia; *d* of Archibald and Mildred Leonard. *Educ:* Univ. of Birmingham (BSc); Imperial Coll., London (DIC, PhD). Res. Fellow 1957, Lectr 1959, in Geology, Univ. of Birmingham; Sen. Lectr 1970, Reader 1972, in Geophysics, Univ. of Lancaster; Royal Soc. Vis. Prof., Univ. of Ghana, 1974; Prof. of Environmental Geol., Univ. of London, first at Chelsea Coll. (Hd of Geol. Dept), 1975, then at Royal Holloway and Bedford New Coll., 1985–98; Hd of Geol. Dept, 1992–97; Hon. Fellow, Royal Holloway, 2004. Leverhulme Emeritus Fellow, 1998–2000. Pres., Geological Soc., 1988–90. Mem., Academia Europaea, 1990. Coke Medal, Geological Soc., 1993. *Publications:* (jtly) A Continent Revealed: the European geotraverse, 1992; Lyell: the past is the key to the present, 1998; The Timing and Location of Major Ore Deposits in an Evolving Orogen, 2002; Geodynamics and Ore Deposit Evolution in Europe, 2005; contribs to learned jls mainly relating to seismic exploration of the earth's crust, to earthquake hazards and, early on, to palæomagnetism. *Recreation:* travel. *Address:* Earth Sciences Department, Royal Holloway, University of London, Egham, Surrey TW20 0EX. *Club:* Athenæum.

BLUNDELL, Sir Richard (William), Kt 2014; CBE 2006; FBA 1997; Professor of Economics, since 1984, and Ricardo Professor of Political Economy, since 2006, University College London; *b* 1 May 1952; *s* of Horace Leon and Marjorie Blundell; *m* 1984, Anne

Gaynor Aberdeen; one s one d. *Educ:* Univ. of Bristol (BSc 1st cl. Hons Econs with Stats); LSE (MSc Econometrics). Lectr in Econometrics, Univ. of Manchester, 1975–85; University College London: Head, Dept of Economics, 1988–92; Leverhulme Personal Res. Prof., 1999–2004; Res. Dir, 1986–2016, Dir, ESRC Centre for Microecon. Analysis of Public Policy, 1991–, Inst. for Fiscal Studies. Visiting Professor: Univ. of BC, 1980–81; MIT, 1993; Univ. of Calif at Berkeley, 1994, 1999. Member, Council: Econometric Soc., 1991– (Fellow, 1991; Yrjö Jahnsson Prize, 1995; Frisch Medal, 2000; Mem. Exec. Cttee, 2001–; Pres., 2006); European Econ. Assoc., 1997– (Pres., 2004; Fellow 2004); NRC Panel Mem., Nat. Acad. of Scis, 1999–2000; Pres., REconS, 2010–13. Associate Editor: Rev. Econ. Studies, 1984–88; Jl of Human Resources, 1995–97; Co-Editor: Jl of Econometrics, 1991–97 (Mem., Exec. Council, 1997–); Econometrica, 1997–2001. Hon. For. Mem., Amer. Acad. of Arts and Science, 2002; Hon. Mem., AEA, 2001; Hon. FIA 2003. Hon. Dr: St Gallen, Switzerland, 2003; Mannheim, Germany, 2011; Norges Handelshøyskole, Bergen, Norway, 2011; Svizzera italiana, 2016; Bristol, 2017; Ca' Foscari, Venice, 2018. Laffont Prize, Toulouse, 2008; IZA Prize in Labour Econs, Inst. for Study of Labour, Bonn, 2012; Frontiers of Knowledge Award in Econs, BBVA Foundn, Madrid, 2015; Thomson-Reuters Citation Laureate in Econs, 2015; Erwin Plein Nemmers Prize in Econs, Northwestern Univ., 2016. *Publications:* Unemployment, Search and Labour Supply, 1986; The Measurement of Household Welfare, 1994; Mirrlees Review of Tax Reform, 2010; Labor Supply and Taxation, 2016; contrib. Econometrica, Rev. Econ. Studies, Econ. Jl, Jl Econometrics. *Recreations:* saxophone, guitar, jazz music, travel. *Address:* Department of Economics, University College London, Gower Street, WC1E 6BT. *T:* (020) 7679 5863. *E:* r.blundell@ucl.ac.uk.
See also Sir T. L. Blundell.

BLUNDELL, Sir Thomas Leon, (Sir Tom), Kt 1997; FRS 1984; FRSC; FMedSci; Emeritus Professor and Director of Research, Department of Biochemistry, Cambridge University, since 2009 (Sir William Dunn Professor of Biochemistry, 1995–2009); Fellow of Sidney Sussex College, Cambridge, since 1995; Chairman, Biotechnology and Biological Sciences Research Council, 2009–15; President, Science Council, 2011–16; *b* 7 July 1942; *s* of Horace Leon Blundell and Marjorie Blundell; one *s*; *m* 1987, Bancinyane Lynn Sibanda; two *d*. *Educ:* Steyning Grammar Sch.; Brasenose Coll., Oxford (BA, DPhil; Hon. Fellow, 1989). FRSC 2006. Postdoctoral Res. Fellow, Laboratory of Molecular Biophysics, Oxford Univ., 1967–72; Jun. Res. Fellow, Linacre Coll., Oxford, 1968–70; Lectr, Biological Scis, Sussex Univ., 1973–76; Prof. of Crystallography, Birkbeck Coll., Univ. of London, 1976–90; Dep. Chm. and Dir Gen., AFRC, 1991–94; Chief Exec. and Dep. Chm., BBSRC, 1994–96 (on secondment); Hd, Dept of Biochem., 1996–2009, Chm., Sch. of Biol Scis, 2003–09, Univ. of Cambridge. Director: International Sch. of Crystallography, 1981–; Babraham Inst., Cambridge, 1997–2002. Founder, non-exec. Dir and Chm., Scientific Adv. Bd, Astex Therapeutics (formerly Astex Technol.), 1999–2011; Chm., Scientific Adv. Bd, Astex Pharmaceuticals, 2011–13; non-exec. Dir and Chm., Scientific Adv. Bd, Astex Therapeutics (Otsuka), 2013–. Chm., Royal Commn on Envmtl Pollution, 1998–2005. Dep. Chm., Inst. of Cancer Res., 2007–15. Member: Council, AFRC, 1985–90; MRC AIDS Res. Steering Cttee, 1987–90; ACOST, 1988–90; Council, SERC, 1989–90 (Mem., 1979–82, Chm., 1983–87, Biological Scis Cttee; Mem., Science Bd, 1983–87); ABRC, 1991–94; Council, Royal Soc., 1997–99; R&D Bd, SmithKline Beecham, 1997–2000; Bd, Parly OST, 1998–2007. Hon. Dir, ICRF Unit of Structural Molecular Biology, 1989–96. Councillor, Oxford CBC, 1970–73 (Chm. Planning Cttee, 1972–73). Scientific Consultant, Oxford Molecular Ltd, 1996–99; Chm., Scientific Adv. Bd, Bioprocessing Ltd, 1997–2000; Member: UCB Sci. Adv. Bd, 2005–; Utek Sci. Adv. Bd, 2005–09; Industrial Consultant: Celltech, 1981–86 (non-exec. Dir, 1997–2004; Chm., Scientific Adv. Bd, 1998–2004); Pfizer Central Res., Groton, USA and Sandwich, UK, 1984–90, 2015–; Abingworth Management Ltd, 1988–90, 1996–. President: UK Bioscis Fedn, 2004–08; UK Biochemical Soc., 2009–11. Dir, Lawes Agricl Trust, 1998–2010; Trustee, Daphne Jackson Trust, 1996–2011. Governor, Birkbeck Coll., 1985–89. Founder FMedSci 1998. Hon. Fellow, Linacre Coll., Oxford, 1991. Hon. FRASE 1993; Hon. FIChemE 1995; Hon. Fellow, Biochem. Soc., 2011; Hon. FRSB (Hon. FSB 2012). Hon. Mem., British Biophysics Soc., 2006. Associate Mem., Third World Acad. of Scis, 2009–; Corresponding Member: Chilean Acad. of Scis, 2011–; Brazilian Acad. of Scis, 2015–. Hon. DSc: Edinburgh, East Anglia, 1993; Sheffield, Strathclyde, 1994; Warwick, Antwerp, 1995; Nottingham, 1996; UWE, 1997; Stirling, 2000; Sussex, Pavia, 2002; St Andrews, 2002; London, 2003; Dundee, 2007; Liverpool, 2011; Chile, 2011. Alcon Award for Dist. Work in Vision Research, 1985; Gold Medal, Inst. of Biotechnological Studies, 1987; Sir Hans Krebs Medal, Fedn of European Biochemical Socs, 1987; Ciba Medal, UK Biochemical Soc., 1988; Feldberg Prize for Biology and Medicine, 1988; Gold Medal, SCI, 1995; Pfizer Eur. Award for Innovation, 1998; Bernal Medal, Royal Soc., 1998; Biochem. Soc. Award, 2013; Ewald Award, Internat. Union of Crystallog., 2017. Joint Editor: Progress in Biophysics and Molecular Biology, 1979–; Current Opinion in Structural Biology, 1996–; Member Editorial Advisory Board: Biochemistry, 1986–89; Protein Engineering, 1986–2003; Protein Science, 1992–98; Structure, 1993–. *Publications:* Protein Crystallography, 1976; 585 papers in jls incl. Nature, Science, Structure, Jl Molecular Biol. *Recreations:* playing jazz, listening to opera, walking, international travel. *Address:* Department of Biochemistry, Tennis Court Road, Cambridge CB2 1GA.
See also Sir R. W. Blundell.

BLUNDEN, Sir Hubert (Chisholm), 8th Bt *cr* 1766, of Castle Blunden, Kilkenny; *b* 9 Aug. 1948; *s* of Sir Philip Overington Blunden, 7th Bt and Jeannette Francesca Alexandra, *d* of Captain D. Macdonald, RNR; *S* father, 2007; *m* 1975, Ellish O'Brien; one *s* one *d*. *Educ:* Avoca Sch., Blackrock. 1st Bn, Irish Guards. *Heir: s* Edmund Blunden, *b* 31 July 1982.

BLUNDY, Prof. Jonathan David, PhD; FRS 2008; Professor of Petrology, University of Bristol, since 2004; *b* Wallingford, 7 Aug. 1961; *s* of Peter Desmond Blundy and late Jean Dorothy Blundy; *m* 1992, Katharine Melanie Fawcett (separated 2003); one *s* one *d*, and one step *d*. *Educ:* St Paul's Sch., São Paulo; Giggleswick Sch.; Leeds Grammar Sch.; University Coll., Oxford (BA Hons 1983); Trinity Hall, Cambridge (PhD 1989). Jun. Res. Fellow, Hertford Coll., Oxford, 1990–91; University of Bristol: NERC Res. Fellow, 1991–95; Royal Soc. Univ. Res. Fellow, 1995–2002; NERC Sen. Res. Fellow, 2002–07. MAE 2011. *Publications:* over 80 articles in scientific jls. *Recreations:* rambling, cooking, public transport, Leeds United FC. *Address:* c/o School of Earth Sciences, Wills Memorial Building, University of Bristol, Queens Road, Bristol BS8 1RJ.

BLUNKETT, family name of Baron Blunkett.

BLUNKETT, Baron *cr* 2015 (Life Peer), of Brightside and Hillsborough in the City of Sheffield; David Blunkett; PC 1997; *b* 6 June 1947; *m* (marr. diss.); three *s*; one *s*; *m* 2009, Dr Margaret Williams. *Educ:* night sch. and day release, Shrewsbury Coll. of Technol. and Richmond Coll. of Further Educn, Sheffield; Nat. Cert. in Business Studies, E Midlands Gas Bd; Sheffield Univ. (BA Hons Pol Theory and Instns); Huddersfield Holly Bank Coll. of Educn (Tech.) (PGCFE). Tutor in Industrial Relns, Barnsley Coll. of Technol., 1974–87. Elected to Sheffield City Council (at age of 22), 1970; Chm., Family and Community Services Cttee, 1976–80; Leader, 1980–87; Dep. Chm., AMA, 1984–87. Joined Labour Party at age of 16; Chm., Labour Party NEC, 1993–94 (Dep. Chm., 1992–93; Mem., 1983–98); Chm., Labour Party Cttee on Local govt, 1984–92. MP (Lab) Sheffield, Brightside, 1987–2010, Sheffield, Brightside and Hillsborough, 2010–15. Front bench spokesman on the environment, with special responsibility for local govt and poll tax, 1988–92, on health, 1992–94, on educn, 1994–95, on educn and employment, 1995–97 (Mem., Shadow Cabinet, 1992–97); Secretary of State: for Educn and Employment, 1997–2001; for Home Dept, 2001–04; for Work and Pensions, 2005. Prof. of Politics in Practice, Univ. of Sheffield, 2015–. Chair, Bd of Governance, Univ. of Law, 2015–. FAcSS 2015. Hon. LittD Sheffield, 2016; Hon. Dr: Huddersfield, 2017; Open, 2017; Middlesex, 2018; London South Bank, 2018. *Publications:* (jtly) Local Enterprise and Workers' Plans, 1981; (jtly) Building from the Bottom: the Sheffield Experience, 1983; (jtly) Democracy in Crisis: the town halls respond, 1987; On a Clear Day, 1995; Politics and Progress, 2001; The Blunkett Tapes: my life in the bear pit, 2006. *Address:* House of Lords, SW1A 0PW.

BLUNSDON, His Honour Alan James; a Circuit Judge, 2010–13; Deputy Coroner, North West Kent, since 2004; *b* 22 Aug. 1949. Admitted solicitor, 1973; a Dep. Dist Judge, 1983–91; Dist Judge, 1991–2010.

BLUNT, Charles William; Executive Chairman, Carmichael Carrol, since 2005. *Educ:* Sydney Univ. (BEcon). AASA; CPA. Exec. appts in mining, finance and agricultural industries. MP (Nat. Party) Richmond, NSW, 1984–90; Leader, Parly Nat. Party, 1989–90; opposition Minister, 1984–90, variously for: Sport, Recreation and Tourism; Social Security; Transport and Communications; Community Services and Aged Care; Trade and Resources. Former Mem., parly cttees and official delegns. Chm., Permo-Drive Technologies Ltd, 2001–05; Man. Dir, American Business Services Pty Ltd, 2003–13; CEO, American Chamber of Commerce in Australia, 1990–2013. *Recreations:* golf, reading. *Address:* PO Box 66, Wahroonga, NSW 2076, Australia. *Clubs:* Pymble Golf; Royal Hobart Golf.

BLUNT, Crispin Jeremy Rupert; MP (C) Reigate, since 1997; *b* 15 July 1960; *s* of Maj. Gen. Peter Blunt, CB, MBE, GM and Adrienne (*née* Richardson); *m* 1990, Victoria Ainsley Jenkins (separated 2010); one *s* one *d*. *Educ:* Wellington Coll.; RMA, Sandhurst; Durham Univ. (BA 1984); Cranfield Inst. of Technology (MBA 1991). Commnd, 13th/18th Royal Hussars (QMO), 1980; Troop Leader: UK and Cyprus, 1980–81; BAOR, 1984–85; Regtl Signals Officer/Ops Officer, BAOR/UK, 1985–87; Sqn Leader, 2IC UK, 1987–89; resigned commn, 1990; Rep., Forum of Private Business, 1991–92; Consultant, Politics Internat., 1993; Special Advr to Sec. of State for Defence, 1993–95, to Foreign Sec., 1995–97. Opposition spokesman on NI, 2001–02, on trade, energy and science, 2002–03; on security and counter terrorism, 2009–10; Opposition Whip, 2004–09; Parly Under-Sec. of State, MoJ, 2010–12. Member: Select Cttee on Defence, 1997–2000, 2003–04; Select Cttee on Envmt, Transport and the Regions, 2000–01; Chm., Select Cttee on Foreign Affairs, 2015–17. Co-Chm., All Party Parly Gp on Drug Policy Reform, 2017–, London's Green Belt, 2017–, Humanism, 2017–. Sec., Cons. Foreign and Commonwealth Affairs Cttee, 1997–2001; Chm., Cons. Middle East Council, 2004–08. Co-Chm., Council for Advancement of Arab-British Understanding, 2004–09. *Recreations:* cricket, ski-ing, bridge, gardening. *Address:* House of Commons, SW1A 0AA. *T:* (020) 7219 2254. *Clubs:* MCC; Reigate Priory Cricket.
See also O. S. P. Blunt.

BLUNT, David Graeme, CVO 2001 (LVO 1986); HM Diplomatic Service, retired; Senior Advisor, Wood plc (formerly SgurrEnergy), 2015–18; *b* 19 Jan. 1953; *s* of Daryl and Deidre Blunt; *m* 1975, Geirid Bakkeli; three *s*. *Educ:* Cranleigh Sch.; Manchester Univ. (BA Hons). Teacher, Blairmore Sch., Aberdeenshire, 1976–78; joined HM Diplomatic Service, 1978; FCO, 1978–79; Second, later First, Sec., Vienna, 1979–83; First Secretary: Peking, 1983–87; FCO, 1987–89; Canberra, 1989–94; Counsellor, FCO, 1994–97; Dep. Hd of Mission and Consul-Gen., Oslo, 1997–2001; Dep. Gov., Gibraltar, 2002–05; Hd of Office, then Ambassador, Pristina, Kosovo, 2006–08; Ambassador to Croatia, 2008–11. Dir, Public Policy UK and EU Instns, 2012–13, Man. Dir, 2013–15, Gamesa Wind UK. *Recreations:* choral music, sailing, cross-country ski-ing.

BLUNT, David John; QC 1991; a Recorder of the Crown Court, since 1988; a Deputy High Court Judge, since 1992; writer; *b* 25 Oct. 1944; *s* of late Vernon Egerton Rowland Blunt and Catherine Vera Blunt; *m* 1976, Zaibonesa Ebrahim; one *s* one *d*. *Educ:* Farnham Grammar Sch.; Trinity Hall, Cambridge (MA Hons). Called to the Bar, Middle Temple, 1967, Bencher, 2001 (Autumn Reader, 2016; Dir, Advocacy, 2017). Asst Recorder, 1985–88; Dep. Judge, Technol. and Construction Court. Contested (L): Lambeth Central, 1978, 1979; Cornwall SE, 1983. Chm., Hodie Ltd, 1990–. First TV play broadcast, 1976. *Recreations:* walking, running, cycling, reading, writing, old cars.

BLUNT, Sir David Richard Reginald Harvey, 12th Bt *cr* 1720; *b* 8 Nov. 1938; *s* of Sir Richard David Harvey Blunt, 11th Bt and Elisabeth Malvine Ernestine, *d* of Comdr F. M. Fransen Van de Putte, Royal Netherlands Navy (retd); *S* father, 1975; *m* 1969, Sonia Tudor Rosemary (*née* Day) (*d* 2008); one *d*. *Heir:* kinsman Jonathan Stuart Needham (*né* Blunt; has assumed his stepfather's surname), FCA [*b* 10 April 1955; *m* 1976, Margot B. Blackburn; two *s*].

BLUNT, Oliver Simon Peter; QC 1994; a Recorder, since 1995; *b* 8 March 1951; *s* of Maj.-Gen. Peter Blunt, CB, MBE, GM and Adrienne (*née* Richardson); *m* 1979, Joanna Margaret Dixon; one *s* three *d*. *Educ:* Bedford Sch.; Southampton Univ. (LLB 1973). Called to the Bar, Middle Temple, 1974; Asst Recorder, SE Circuit, 1991–95. *Recreations:* cricket, golf, ski-ing, swimming, mini-rugby coach. *Address:* Furnival Chambers, 32 Furnival Street, EC4A 1JQ. *T:* (020) 7405 3232. *Clubs:* Roehampton; Bank of England Sports; Barnes Cricket; Rosslyn Park Rugby.
See also C. J. R. Blunt.

BLY, John; antique dealer, since 1956; *b* Tring, 27 May 1939; *s* of Frank John and Nina Bly; *m* 1967, Virginia Fisher; two *s*. *Educ:* Berkhamsted Sch. Lectr, TV presenter, public speaker, restorer, valuer, fund raiser, editor and columnist, 1956–. Presenter, TV series: Looking At Antiques, 1971–72; Heirloom, 1975–92; Heirs and Graces, 1989–90; furniture expert, Antiques Roadshow, BBC, 1979–. Columnist, Antiques Monthly (USA), 1975–; contribs to magazines incl. Collectors' Guide, Antique Collecting, Chic Chat and lifestyle mags for Fishmedia Gp. Lectures include: Dupont Winterthur Mus.; Art Inst. of Chicago; Univ. of Birmingham, Alabama; New York Histl Soc.; San Francisco Histl Soc.; Mus. of Art Milwaukee; Governor's Mansion, Springfield, Ill; Key West Mus.; Rosary Coll., Chicago; Galesburg Univ., Ill; V&A Mus.; lectr on cruise ships. FRSA. Liveryman, Goldsmiths' Co., 1989. Hon. Citizen, New Orleans; Kentucky Squire. *Publications:* Discovering Hallmarks on English Silver, 1969, 3rd edn 2000; Discovering English Furniture, 1971, 3rd edn 2010, Japanese edn 1993; Discovering Victorian and Edwardian Furniture, 1973; (ed and compiled) Is It Genuine?, 1986, Italian edn 1983, reissued as Miller's Is It Genuine?, 2002; Antiques Guide for the Collector, 1986; (ed and compiled) Heirloom, 1989; Antique Furniture Expert, 1991; Silver and Sheffield Plate Marks, 1993, 2nd edn 2008; (ed and contrib.) Treasures in Your Home, 1993; (jtly) The Pocket Guide to Antiques and Collectables, 1999; John Bly's Antiques Masterclass, 2005; English Furniture, 2010. *Recreations:* jazz historian, playing drums, cooking, mixing proper martinis and manhattans and drinking same. *Address:* Chelsea Gallery, 533 Kings Road, Chelsea, SW10 0TZ. *Club:* Lansdowne.

**BLYTH**, family name of **Barons Blyth** and **Blyth of Rowington**.

**BLYTH**, 5th Baron *cr* 1907; **James Audley Ian Blyth**; Bt 1895; *b* 13 Nov. 1970; *s* of 4th Baron Blyth and of Oonagh Elizabeth Ann, *yr d* of late William Henry Conway, Dublin; *S* father, 2009; *m* 2003, Elodie Bernadette Andrée Odette, *d* of Jean-Georges Cadet de Fontenay; one *s* one *d*. *Educ*: Newtown Sch., Waterford. *Heir: s* Hon. Hugo Audley Jasper Blyth, *b* 9 May 2006.

**BLYTH OF ROWINGTON**, Baron *cr* 1995 (Life Peer), of Rowington in the County of Warwickshire; **James Blyth**, Kt 1985; Chairman: Diageo plc, 2000–08 (Director, 1998–2008); Greycastle Holdings Ltd, since 2014; Senior Advisor, Greenhill & Co., 2000–02 and 2007–14 (Vice Chairman and Partner, 2002–07); *b* 8 May 1940; *s* of Daniel Blyth and Jane Power Carlton; *m* 1967, Pamela Anne Campbell Dixon; one *s* (one *s* decd). *Educ*: Spiers Sch.; Glasgow Univ. Mobil Oil Co., 1963–69; General Foods Ltd, 1969–71; Mars Ltd, 1971–74; General Manager: Lucas Batteries Ltd, 1974–77; Lucas Aerospace Ltd, 1977–81; Head of Defence Sales, MoD, 1981–85; Man. Dir, Plessey Electronic Systems, 1985–86; Chief Exec., The Plessey Co. plc, 1986–87; The Boots Co.: Chief Exec., 1987–98; Dep. Chm., 1994–98; Chm., 1998–2000; Vice Chm., Middlebrook Pharmaceuticals Inc., 2009–10. Non-executive Director: Imperial Gp PLC, 1984–86; Cadbury-Schweppes PLC, 1986–90; British Aerospace, 1990–94; Anixter Internat. Inc., 1995–; NatWest Gp, 1998–2000; Avoca Capital Hldgs, 2013–14. Mem., H of L, 1995–2018. Chm., Adv. Panel on Citizen's Charter, 1991–97. Pres., ME Assoc., 1988–93; Patron, Combined Services Winter Sports Assoc., 1997–2002. Gov., London Business Sch., 1987–96 (Hon. Fellow, 1997). Liveryman, Coachmakers' and Coach Harness Makers' Co. Hon. LLD Nottingham, 1994. *Recreations*: tennis, paintings, theatre, horse racing, golf. *Clubs*: East India, Royal Automobile, Caledonian, Blackwell Golf.

**BLYTH, Sir Charles, (Sir Chay)**, Kt 1997; CBE 1972; BEM 1967; Chairman, First ScotRail Stakeholder Advisory Board, 2007–15; *b* 14 May 1940; *s* of Robert and Jessie Blyth; *m* 1st, 1962, Maureen Margaret Morris (marr. diss. 1992); one *d*; 2nd, 1995, Felicity Rayson. *Educ*: Hawick High School. HM Forces, Para. Regt, 1958–67. Cadbury Schweppes, 1968–69; Dir, Sailing Ventures (Hampshire) Ltd, 1969–73; Managing Dir, The Challenging Business Ltd (formerly Crownfields Ltd), 1989–2006. Chm. and Dir, First Gt Western Ltd, 2006–07. Organiser: British Steel Challenge Round World Yacht Race 1992–93, 1989–93; BT Global Challenge Round the World Yacht Race 1996–97, 1994–97. Rowed North Atlantic with Captain John Ridgway, June–Sept. 1966; circumnavigated the world westwards solo in yacht British Steel, 1970–71; circumnavigated the world eastwards with crew of paratroopers in yacht Great Britain II, and Winner, Elapsed Time Prize Whitbread Round the World Yacht Race, 1973–74; Atlantic sailing record, Cape Verde to Antigua, 1977; won Round Britain Race in yacht Great Britain IV, 1978 (crew Robert James); won The Observer/Europe 1 doublehanded transatlantic race in record time, 1981 (crew Robert James); Number One to Virgin Atlantic Challenge II successful attempt on the Blue Riband, 1986. Pres., Inst. of Professional Sales, 1998. Yachtsman of the Year, 1971, Special Award for outstanding services to yachting, Yachting Journalists Assoc., 1994; Chichester Trophy, RYS, 1971. Freeman of Hawick, 1972. Hon. DLaw Portsmouth, 1997; Hon. DTech Plymouth, 1998. Great Shogun Award, Order of Scottish Samurai, 2017. *Publications*: A Fighting Chance, 1966; Innocent Aboard, 1968; The Impossible Voyage, 1971; Theirs is the Glory, 1974; The Challenge, 1993. *Recreations*: sailing, horse-riding, hunting. *Address*: 23B North Bridge Street, Hawick, Scottish Borders TD9 9BA. *Clubs*: Royal Ocean Racing; Royal Southern Yacht.

**BLYTHE, Mark Andrew**, CB 1999; Principal Assistant Solicitor, Treasury Solicitor's Department, 1989–2003, and Legal Adviser, HM Treasury, 1993–2003; *b* 4 Sept. 1943; *s* of John Jarratt Blythe and Dorothy Kathleen Blythe; *m* 1972, Brigid Helen Frazer (*née* Skemp); two *s* one *d*. *Educ*: King Edward VII Grammar Sch., Sheffield; University Coll., Oxford (BCL, MA; Open Schol. in Classics, 1961; Gibbs Prize in Law, 1963). Called to the Bar, Inner Temple, 1966; Attorney, NY Bar, 1980. Teaching Associate, Univ. of Pennsylvania Law Sch., 1965–66; Chancery Bar, 1967–77; Legal Consultant, NY, 1978–80; Treasury Solicitor's Dept, 1981–2003: Assistant Solicitor, European Div., 1986–89; Hd, Central Adv. Div., 1989–93.

**BLYTHE, Moira**; *see* Gibb, Dame M.

**BLYTHE, Ronald George**, CBE 2017; writer, since 1953; *b* 6 Nov. 1922; *s* of Albert George Blythe and Matilda Elizabeth (*née* Elkins). *Educ*: St Peter's and St Gregory's Sch., Sudbury, Suffolk. Librarian, 1943–54. Soc. of Authors' Travel Scholarship, 1969. Editor, Penguin Classics, 1966–87. Assistant, Aldeburgh Fest., 1955–57; Member: Eastern Arts Lit. Panel, 1975–85; Cttee, Centre of E Anglian Studies, UEA, 1975–80; Soc. of Authors' Management Cttee, 1980–85; Chm., Essex Fest., 1981–84. President: John Clare Soc., 1981–2015; Robert Bloomfield Soc., 2001–; Kilvert Soc., 2006–. Reader, C of E, 1984–; Lay Canon, St Edmundsbury Cathedral, 2003–. FRSL 1969. Hon. MA UEA, 1990; Hon. DLitt: Anglia Poly. Univ., 2001; Essex, 2002; MLitt Lambeth, 2001. Benson Medal for Literature, RSL, 2006. *Publications*: A Treasonable Growth, 1960; Immediate Possession, 1961; The Age of Illusion, 1963; William Hazlitt: selected writings, 1970; Akenfield (Heinemann Award), 1969; Aldeburgh Anthology, 1972; (ed jtly) Works of Thomas Hardy, 1978; The View in Winter, 1979, 2nd edn 2005; (ed) Writing in a War: stories, essays and poems of 1939–45, 1982; Places, 1982; From the Headlands, 1982; The Stories of Ronald Blythe (Angel Prize for Literature), 1985; Divine Landscapes, 1986; Each Returning Day: the pleasure of diaries, 1989; Private Words: letters and diaries of the Second World War, 1991; First Friends, 1998; Going to Meet George and other outings, 1999; Talking About John Clare, 1999; The Circling Year, 2001; Talking to the Neighbours, 2002; (ed) George Herbert, A Priest to the Temple or The Country Parson, 2003; Eight Poems, 2004; A Country Boy, 2004; The Assassin, 2004; A Writer's Day-Book, 2006; A Year At Bottengoms Farm, 2006; Field Work: selected essays, 2007; Outsiders: a book of garden friends, 2008; The Bookman's Tale, 2009; Aftermath: selected writings 1960–2010, 2010; At the Yeoman's House, 2011; At Helpston: meetings with John Clare, 2011; Village Hours, 2012; The Time by the Sea: Aldeburgh 1955–1958, 2013; Under a Broad Sky, 2013; Decadal (poems), 2014; In the Artist's Garden: a Wormingford journal, 2015; Wormingford Trilogy: Word from Wormingford, 1997; Out of the Valley, 2000; Borderland, 2005. *Recreations*: walking, looking, listening. *Address*: Bottengoms Farm, Wormingford, Colchester, Essex CO6 3AP. *T*: (01206) 271308.

**BLYTHMAN, Joanna**; journalist and author specialising in food issues. Mem. Council, Soil Assoc., 2013–14. Caroline Walker Award, Caroline Walker Trust, 1993; Derek Cooper Award, BBC Radio 4 Food and Farming Awards, 2004; Good Housekeeping Award for Outstanding Contribn to Food, 2007. *Publications*: The Food We Eat, 1996, 2nd rev. edn 1998 (Glenfiddich Special Award, 1997); The Food Our Children Eat, 1999; How to Avoid GM Food, 1999; Shopped, 2004 (Glenfiddich Food Book of Year, 2005); Bad Food Britain, 2006; What to Eat: food that's good for your health, pocket and plate, 2013; Swallow This: serving up the food industry's darkest secrets, 2015.

**BOA, Prof. Elizabeth Janet**, PhD; FBA 2003; Professor of German and Head of Department of German, University of Nottingham, 1996–2001, now Emeritus Professor; *b* 20 March 1939. *Educ*: Univ. of Glasgow (MA 1961); Univ. of Nottingham (PhD). Lectr, Sen. Lectr, then Reader in German, Univ. of Nottingham, 1965–94; Prof. of Modern German Literature, Univ. of Manchester, 1994. *Publications*: (with James H. Reid) Critical Strategies: German fiction in the twentieth century, 1972; Sexual Circus: Wedekind's theatre of subversion, 1987; Kafka: gender, class and race in the letters and fictions, 1996; (with Rachel Palfreyman) Heimat—A German Dream: regional loyalties and national identity in German culture 1890–1990, 2000. *Address*: c/o Department of German, University of Nottingham, University Park, Nottingham NG7 2RD.

**BOADEN, Helen**; Director, BBC Radio, 2013–16; *b* 1 March 1956; *d* of William John Boaden and Barbara Mary Boaden; *m* 1994, Stephen Burley. *Educ*: Univ. of Sussex (BA Hons English 1978). Care Asst, Hackney Social Services, 1978; Reporter: Radio WBAI, NY, 1979; Radio Tees and Radio Aire, 1980–83; Producer, BBC Radio Leeds, 1983–85; Reporter: File on 4, Radio 4, 1985–91; Brass Tacks, BBC 2, 1985–91; Presenter: Woman's Hour, Radio 4, 1985–91; Verdict, Channel 4, 1991; Editor, File on 4, Radio 4, 1991–94; Head: Network Current Affairs, BBC Manchester, 1994–97; Business Progs, BBC News, 1997; Current Affairs and Business Progs, BBC, 1998–2000; Controller: BBC Radio 4, 2000–04; BBC7, 2002–04; Director: BBC News, 2004–13; BBC News Group, 2011–13. Chm., Radio Acad., 2003–05; Chair, Audio Content Fund, 2019–. Author, Boaden Review on orchestral provision in Ireland, RTE, 2018. Shorenstein Fellow, Kennedy Sch. of Govt, Harvard Univ., 2017. Ext. Mem., Council, RA, 2017– (Chair, Remuneration Cttee). Non-exec. Bd Mem., UK Statistics Authy, 2019–. Pres., Holiday Fellowship, 2014–. Trustee: Alcohol Res. UK, 2014–; Stephen Joseph Th., Scarborough, 2015– (Chair, 2017–); Out of Joint Th. Co., 2018–; Patron, Books at the Beach, Scarborough Literary Fest., 2016–. Hon. Fellow, Univ. of the Arts, 2011. Hon. Dr: UEA (Suffolk Coll.); Sussex, 2003; York, 2004; DUniv Open, 2011. *Recreations*: walking, food, travel, yoga, theatre.

**BOAG, Shirley Ann**; *see* Robertson, S. A.

**BOAL, His Honour (John) Graham**; QC 1993; a Senior Circuit Judge, and Permanent Judge at Central Criminal Court, 1996–2005; *b* 24 Oct. 1943; *s* of late Surg. Captain Jackson Graham Boal, RN, and late Dorothy Kenley Boal; *m* 1978, Elizabeth Mary East; one *s*. *Educ*: Eastbourne Coll.; King's Coll. London (LLB). Called to the Bar, Gray's Inn, 1966, Bencher, 1991; Junior Treasury Counsel, 1977–85; Sen. Prosecuting Counsel to the Crown, 1985–91; First Sen. Counsel to the Crown at CCC, 1991–93; a Recorder, 1985–96. Vice Chm., Criminal Bar Assoc., 1991–93. Judicial Mem., Parole Bd, 2001–05. Chairman: Orchid Cancer Appeal, 1999–2005; Seventy4, 2012–13. Trustee, Westminster Drug Project/Seventy4 Foundn, 2013–. *Recreations*: theatre, golf, walking, watching cricket. *Clubs*: Garrick, MCC; Royal West Norfolk Golf; Old Bailey Judges Golfing Society (Life Pres.); New Zealand Golf.

**BOAM, Maj.-Gen. Thomas Anthony**, CB 1987; CBE 1978 (OBE 1973); Vice President, Leonard Cheshire, since 2003 (Trustee and Chairman, South Region, 1997–2003); *b* 14 Feb. 1932; *s* of late Lt-Col T. S. Boam, OBE, and of Mrs Boam; *m* 1961, Penelope Christine Mary Roberts (*d* 2016); one *s* two *d*. *Educ*: Bradfield Coll.; RMA Sandhurst. Commissioned Scots Guards, 1952; Canal Zone, Egypt (with 1SG), 1952–54; GSO3, MO4 War Office, 1959–61; psc 1962; Kenya (with 2SG), 1963–64; DAA&QMG 4 Guards Bde, 1964–65; Malaysia (with 1SG), 1966–67; BM 4 Guards Bde, 1967–69; GSO1 (DS) Staff Coll., Camberley, 1970–71; CO 2SG, 1972–74; RCDS 1974–75; Comd BAAT Nigeria, 1976–78; BGS (Trng) HQ UKLF, 1978; Dep. Comdr and COS Hong Kong, 1979–81; Hd of British Defence Staff Washington, and Defence Attaché, 1981–84, Mil. Attaché, 1981–83; Comdr, British Forces Hong Kong, and Maj.-Gen., Brigade of Gurkhas, 1985–87. MEC, Hong Kong, 1985–87. Dir, British Consultants Bureau, 1988–95. Chm., 4Sight, W Sussex Assoc. for the Blind, 2003–06. Gov., Hayes Dashwood Foundn, 1992–2006. Vice-Patron, Queen Alexandra Hosp. Home, 2006–19 (Gov., 1996–2006; Vice-Chm., 1998–2006). *Recreations*: shooting, gardening, sport. *Address*: 5 Sadlers Warehouse, 29 Little London, Chichester, W Sussex PO19 1PB. *Clubs*: MCC; Sussex.

**BOARDMAN, Christopher Miles**, MBE 1993; professional cyclist, retired 2000; Founder, 2004, and Director of Research and Development, Boardman Bikes; Cycling and Walking Commissioner, Greater Manchester, since 2017; *b* 26 Aug. 1968; *s* of Keith and late Carole Boardman; *m* 1988, Sally-Ann Edwards; four *s* two *d*. Gold Medal, Individual Pursuit, Olympic Games, Barcelona, 1992; World Champion: Pursuit, 1994; Time Trial, 1994; Yellow Jersey Holder, Tour de France, 1994, 1997, 1998; Silver Medal, Time Trial, World Championship, 1996; Bronze Medal, Time Trial, Olympic Games, Atlanta, 1996; World Champion, 4,000 Pursuit, 1996; World One Hour Record Holder: 52.270 km, 1993; 56.375 km, 1996; (under new regulations) 49.441 km, 2000. Policy Advr, British Cycling (Elite Coach, 2005–08; Dir of R&D, 2009–12). Mem., Sports Council for England, 1995–96, English Sports Council, 1996. Hon. DSc Brighton, 1997; Hon. MSc Liverpool, 1995. Man of Year Award, Cheshire Life mag., 1997. *Publications*: (with Andrew Longmore) The Complete Book of Cycling, 2000; Triumphs and Turbulence (autobiog.), 2016. *Address*: c/o British Cycling, Stuart Street, Manchester M11 4DQ.

**BOARDMAN, Faith Rosemary**; independent consultant, since 2005; non-executive Director, King's College Hospital NHS Foundation Trust, since 2012 (Senior Independent Director); *b* 21 Aug. 1950; *d* of Kenneth Mills and Vera Mills (*née* Waterson); *m* 1974, David Boardman; one *s* one *d*. *Educ*: Lady Margaret Hall, Oxford (MA Modern Hist.). Sen. Civil Service trainee, 1972–77, VAT Policy, 1977–79, HM Customs and Excise; Fiscal Policy, HM Treasury, 1979–83; HM Customs and Excise: Tobacco Taxation, 1983–86; Personnel Policy, 1986–89; Chief Exec. (Collector), London Central, 1989–95; Chief Exec. (Grade 3), Contributions Agency, DSS, 1995–97; Chief Exec. (Grade 2), CSA, 1997–2000; Exec. Mem., Deptl Bd, DSS, then DWP, 1995–2000; Chief Exec., London Borough of Lambeth, 2000–05. Ind. Mem., Metropolitan Police Authy, 2007–12; non-executive Adviser: Mayor of London's Office for Policing and Crime, 2012–16; Metropolitan Police Service, 2016–. Non-exec. Mem., Audit Cttee, Nat. Offenders Mgt Service, 2005–11. Mem. Bd, Public Mgt and Policy Assoc. (interim Develt Dir, 2010–13). Non-exec. Dir, HM Courts Service, 2006–08; Associate: Whitehall and Industry Gp; SOLACE; College of Policing. Treas., Vauxhall Business Improvement Dist, 2012–. Chair of Trustees: Vauxhall City Farm, 2005–; London Ecumenical Aids Trust, 2005–13; Mem. Bd, Safer Business Network (formerly Safer London Business Partnership), 2016–. Financial Services Woman of Year Award, 1990. *Recreations*: family, friends, community, music, history, public speaking, travelling.

**BOARDMAN, Sir John**, Kt 1989; FSA 1957; FBA 1969; Lincoln Professor of Classical Archaeology and Art, and Fellow of Lincoln College, University of Oxford, 1978–94 (Hon. Fellow, 1995); *b* 20 Aug. 1927; *s* of Frederick Archibald Boardman; *m* 1952, Sheila Joan Lyndon Stanford (*d* 2005); one *s* one *d*. *Educ*: Chigwell Sch.; Magdalene Coll., Cambridge (BA 1948, MA 1951, Walston Student, 1948–50; Hon. Fellow 1984). 2nd Lt, Intell. Corps, 1950–52. Asst Dir, British Sch. at Athens, 1952–55; Asst Keeper, Ashmolean Museum, Oxford, 1955–59; Reader in Classical Archaeology, Univ. of Oxford, 1959–78; Fellow of Merton Coll., Oxford, 1963–78, Hon. Fellow, 1978. Geddes-Harrower Prof., Aberdeen Univ., 1974; Vis. Prof., Australian Inst. of Archaeology, 1987; Prof. of Ancient History Royal Acad., 1989–; Lectures: Andrew W. Mellon, Washington, 1993; Myres Meml Oxford, 1993. Editor: Journal of Hellenic Studies, 1958–65; Lexicon Iconographicum 1972–99; Cambridge Ancient History, 1978–94. Conducted excavations on Chios

1953–55, and at Tocra in Libya, 1964–65. Delegate, OUP, 1979–89. Pres. Fédn Internat. des Assocs d'Etudes Classiques, 1994–97. Corresponding Fellow: Bavarian Acad. of Scis, 1969; Athens Acad., 1997; Fellow, Inst. of Etruscan Studies, Florence, 1983; Hon. Fellow, Archaeol Soc. of Athens, 1989 (Vice Pres., 1998–); Member: Amer. Philosophical Soc., 1999; Accad. dei Lincei, Rome, 1999; Foreign Member: Royal Danish Acad., 1979; Russian Acad. of Scis, 2003; Mem. associé, Acad. des Inscriptions et Belles Lettres, Institut de France, 1991 (Correspondant, 1985); Hon. Mem., Archaeol Inst. of America, 1993. Pres., Soc. of Jewellery Historians, 2010–12. Hon. MRIA, 1986. Hon. Dr: Dept of Archaeology and History, Univ. of Athens, 1991; Sorbonne, 1994. Cromer Greek Prize, 1959, Kenyon Medal, 1995, British Acad.; Onassis Prize for Humanities, 2009. *Publications:* Cretan Collection in Oxford, 1961; Date of the Knossos Tablets, 1963; Island Gems, 1963; Greeks Overseas, 1964, rev. edn 1999; Greek Art, 1964, rev. edns 1973, 1984, 1996, 2016; Excavations at Tocra, vol. I 1966, vol. II 1973; Pre-Classical, 1967, repr. 1978; Greek Emporio, 1967; Engraved Gems, 1968; Archaic Greek Gems, 1968; Greek Gems and Finger Rings, 1970, repr. 2001; (with D. Kurtz) Greek Burial Customs, 1971; Athenian Black Figure Vases, 1974; Athenian Red Figure Vases, Archaic Period, 1975; Intaglios and Rings, 1975; Corpus Vasorum, Oxford, vol. 3, 1975; Greek Sculpture, Archaic Period, 1978; (with M. Robertson) Corpus Vasorum, Castle Ashby, 1978; (with M. L. Vollenweider) Catalogue of Engraved Gems, Ashmolean Museum, 1978; (with D. Scarisbrick) Harari Collection of Finger Rings, 1978; (with E. La Rocca) Eros in Greece, 1978; Escarabeos de Piedra de Ibiza, 1984; La Ceramica Antica, 1984; Greek Sculpture, Classical Period, 1985; (with D. Finn) The Parthenon and its Sculptures, 1985; (jtly) The Oxford History of the Classical World, 1986; Athenian Red Figure Vases, Classical Period, 1989; (jtly) The Oxford History of Classical Art, 1993; The Diffusion of Classical Art in Antiquity, 1994 (Runciman Prize, 1995); Greek Sculpture, Later Classical, 1995; Early Greek Vase Painting, 1998; Persia and the West, 2000; Greek Vases, 2001; Archaeology of Nostalgia, 2002 (Runciman Prize, 2003); Classical Phoenician Scarabs, 2003; A Collection of Classical and Eastern Intaglios, 2003; The World of Ancient Art, 2006; (with K. Piacenti) Gems and Jewels: the Royal Collection, 2008; The Marlborough Gems, 2009; The Relief Plaques of Eastern Eurasia and China, 2010; The Triumph of Dionysos, 2014; The Greeks in Asia, 2015; (jtly) The Guy Ladrière Collection of Gems and Rings, 2015; (jtly) The Beverley Gems of Alnwick Castle, 2016; (jtly) Natter's Museum Britannicum: British gem collections and collectors of the mid-eighteenth century, 2017; (jtly) Masterpieces in Miniature: engraved gems from prehistory to the present, 2018; Alexander the Great: from his death to the present day, 2019; articles in jls. *Address:* 11 Park Street, Woodstock, Oxford OX20 1SJ. *T:* (01993) 811259. *Club:* Athenæum.

**BOARDMAN, Hon. Nigel Patrick Gray;** Partner, Slaughter and May, since 1982; *b* Northampton, 19 Oct. 1950; *s* of Baron Boardman, MC, TD; one *s* five *d. Educ:* Ampleforth Coll.; Bristol Univ. (BA Hons). Joined Slaughter and May, 1973. Non-exec. Dir, BEIS, 2018–. Trustee, British Mus., 2013–. *Recreations:* my children, grandchildren, watching sport. *Address:* Slaughter and May, 1 Bunhill Row, EC1Y 8YY. *T:* (020) 7090 3418, *Fax:* (020) 7090 5000. *E:* nigel.boardman@slaughterandmay.com.

**BOARDMAN, Norman Keith,** AO 1993; PhD, ScD; FRS 1978; FAA; FTSE; Chief Executive, Commonwealth Scientific and Industrial Research Organization, 1986–90 (post-retirement Fellow, 1990–99); *b* 16 Aug. 1926; *s* of William Robert Boardman and Margaret Boardman; *m* 1952, Mary Clayton Shepherd; two *s* five *d. Educ:* Melbourne Univ. (BSc 1946, MSc 1949); St John's Coll., Cambridge (PhD 1954, ScD 1974). FAA 1972; FTSE (FTS 1986). ICI Fellow, Cambridge, 1953–55; Fulbright Scholar, Univ. of Calif, LA, 1964–66. Res. Officer, Wool Res. Section, CSIRO, 1949–51; CSIRO Div. of Plant Industry: Sen. Res. Scientist, 1956; Principal Res. Scientist, 1961; Sen. Prin. Res. Scientist, 1966; Chief Res. Scientist, 1968; Mem. Exec., 1977–85, Chm. and Chief Exec., 1985–86, CSIRO. Member: Aust. Res. Grants Cttee, 1971–75; Council, ANU, 1979–89 and 1990–91; Bd, Aust. Centre for Internat. Agricl Research, 1982–88; Nat. Water Research Council, 1982–85; Prime Minister's Science Council, 1989–90. Director: Sirotech Ltd, 1986–90; Landcare Aust. Ltd, 1990–98. Pres., Aust. Biochem. Soc., 1976–78; Sec. of Sci. Policy, Aust. Acad. of Sci., 1993–97 (Treas., 1978–81). Corresp. Mem., Amer. Soc. of Plant Physiologists; Foreign Mem., Korean Acad. of Sci. and Technology. Hon. DSc Newcastle, NSW, 1988. David Syme Res. Prize, Melbourne Univ., 1967; Lemberg Medal, Aust. Biochem. Soc., 1969. *Publications:* scientific papers on plant biochemistry, partic. photosynthesis and structure, function and biogenesis of chloroplasts; papers on science and technology policy. *Recreations:* reading, tennis, listening to music. *Address:* 6 Somers Crescent, Forrest, ACT 2603, Australia. *T:* (2) 62951746.

**BOARDMAN, Rev. Philippa Jane,** MBE 2011; Priest-in-charge, St Mary Magdalene, Wandsworth Common, since 2017; *b* Harrow, 24 March 1963; *d* of Lionel Boardman and Audrey Boardman. *Educ:* Haberdashers' Aske's Sch. for Girls; Jesus Coll., Cambridge (BA 1985); Ridley Hall, Cambridge. Ordained deacon, 1990, priest, 1994; Parish Deacon, St Mary and St Stephen, Walthamstow, 1990–93; Curate, St Mary of Eton, Hackney Wick, 1993–96; Priest-in-charge, 1996–2003, Vicar, 2003–13, St Paul and St Mark, Old Ford; Canon Treas., St Paul's Cathedral, 2013–17. Mem., Church Bldgs Council, C of E, 2010–14. Chaplain to Sheriff of the City of London, 2014–15. Gov., Ernest Bevin Coll., 2017–. Trustee, Awareness Foundn, 2018–. Freeman, City of London, 2015; Liveryman, Carpenters' Co., 2016.

**BOAS, John Robert Sotheby, (Bob);** Trustee, National Heritage Memorial Fund and Heritage Lottery Fund, 1998–2002; *b* 28 Feb. 1937; *s* of Edgar Henry Boas and Mary Katherine Boas; *m* 1965, Elisabeth Gersted; one *s* one *d* (and one *s* decd). *Educ:* Corpus Christi Coll., Cambridge (BA Maths (Sen. Optimes)). FCA 1964. Price Waterhouse, 1960–65; ICI, 1965–66; S. G. Warburg, 1966–95; Dir, 1971–95; Vice Chm., 1990–95; Man. Dir, SBC Warburg, 1995–97. Non-executive Director: Chesterfield Properties, 1978–99; ENO, 1990–99; Norwich Union, 1998–2000; Invesco Continental Smaller Cos Trust, 1998–2004; Trident Safeguards Ltd, 1998–2003; Land Command Mgt Bd, 1998–2001; Prospect Publishing Co. Ltd, 2000–16; Telecom Italia, 2004–07. Dir, SFA, 1988–96. Trustee: Nat. Life Stories Collection, 1998–; Guildhall Sch. Trust, 2000–09; Fedn of British Artists (Mall Galls), 2001–07 (Chm., 2001–07); Internat. Musicians Seminar, Prussia Cove, 2002–; Paul Hamlyn Foundn, 2002–09; Architectural Heritage Fund, 2003–08; UCL Cancer Inst. Res. Trust, 2005–16; London String Quartet Foundn, 2006–10; Hatfield House Chamber Music Fest., 2013–. *Recreations:* music, art, theatre, reading, travelling. *Address:* 22 Mansfield Street, W1G 9NR.

**BOASE, Anna Jane;** QC 2019; *b* Stroud, 1 April 1978; *d* of Stuart and Rosamund Boase; *m* 2004, (John William) Rupert Reed, *qv*; one *s* two *d. Educ:* Pate's Grammar Sch., Cheltenham; Downing Coll., Cambridge (BA 1st Cl. Hist. 1999); City Univ., London (DipLaw (Commendation) 2001; Inns of Court Sch. of Law (BVC (Outstanding) 2002). Called to the Bar, Middle Temple, 2002; in practice as barrister, 2002–, specialising in commercial litigation. Arbitrator of Commercial Disputes (pt-time), 2017–. *Address:* One Essex Court, Temple, EC4Y 9AR. *T:* (020) 7583 2000. *E:* clerks@oeclaw.co.uk.

**BOASE, Martin;** Chairman, Omnicom UK plc, 1989–95; *b* 14 July 1932; *s* of Prof. Alan Martin Boase and Elizabeth Grizelle Boase; *m* 1st, 1960, Terry Ann Moir (marr. diss. 1971); one *s* one *d*; 2nd, 1974, Pauline Valerie Brownrigg; one *s* one *d. Educ:* Bedales Sch.; Rendcomb Coll.; New Coll., Oxford. MA; FIPA 1976. Executive, The London Press Exchange, Ltd, 1958–60; Pritchard Wood and Partners, Ltd: Manager, 1961–65; Dir, then Dep. Man. Dir, 1965–68; Founding Partner, The Boase Massimi Pollitt Partnership, Ltd, 1968; Chm., Boase Massimi Pollitt plc, 1977–89 (Jt Chm., 1977–79). Chairman: Maiden Outdoor, 1993–2006; Kiss 100 FM, 1993–2000; Herald Investment Trust, 1994–2009; Investment Trust of Investment Trusts, 1995–2005; Heal's, 1997–2000; Global Professional Media plc, 1999–2005; Jupiter Dividend & Growth Investment Trust, 1999–; Director: Omnicom Gp Inc., 1989–93; EMAP plc, 1991–2000; Matthew Clark plc, 1995–98; New Star Investment Trust, 2000–06. Chairman: Advertising Assoc., 1987–92; British Television Advertising Awards Ltd, 1993–2000. Dir, Oxford Playhouse Trust, 1991–97. *Recreation:* the Turf. *Address:* (office) 12 Bishop's Bridge Road, W2 6AA.

**BOATENG,** family name of **Baron Boateng**.

**BOATENG,** Baron *cr* 2010 (Life Peer), of Akyem in the Republic of Ghana and of Wembley in the London Borough of Brent; **Paul Yaw Boateng;** PC 1999; British High Commissioner in South Africa, 2005–09; barrister-at-law; Chairman and Founder, Akyem Law and Advisory Ltd; *b* 14 June 1951; *s* of Eleanor and Kwaku Boateng; *m* 1980, Janet Alleyne; two *s* three *d. Educ:* Ghana Internat. Sch.; Accra Acad.; Apsley Grammar Sch.; Bristol Univ. (LLB Hons); Coll. of Law. Admitted Solicitor, 1976; Solicitor, Paddington Law Centre, 1976–79; Solicitor and Partner, B. M. Birnberg and Co., 1979–87; called to the Bar, Gray's Inn, 1989. Legal Advr, Scrap Sus Campaign, 1977–81. Greater London Council: Mem. (Lab) for Walthamstow, 1981–86; Chm., Police Cttee, 1981–86; Vice-Chm., Ethnic Minorities Cttee, GLC, 1981–86. Chairman: Afro-Caribbean Educn Resource Project, 1978–86; Westminster CRC, 1979–81; Africa Enterprise Challenge Fund, 2015–. Contested (Lab) Herts W, 1983. MP (Lab) Brent South, 1987–2005. Opposition frontbench spokesman: on treasury and economic affairs, 1989–92; on legal affairs, LCD, 1992–97; Parly Under-Sec. of State, DoH, 1997–98; Minister of State, 1998–2001, and Dep. Home Sec., 1999–2001, Home Office; Financial Sec., 2001–02, Chief Sec., 2002–05, HM Treasury. Mem., H of C Environment Cttee, 1987–89. Member: Home Sec.'s Adv. Council on Race Relations, 1981–86; WCC Commn on prog. to combat racism, 1984–91; Police Training Council, 1981–85; Exec., NCCL, 1980–86. Member, Health Policy Advisory Board: Gilead Sciences, 2010–; Syngenta Foundn, 2019–; Ind. non-exec. Dir, Ghana Internat. Bank; Co-Chm., Africa Intellectual Property Trust, 2012–18; non-exec. Dir and Mem., Adv. Bd of various cos. Chairman: Book Aid Internat., 2014–; In Their Lifetime Appeal, Christian Aid, 2014–16; Africa Enterprise Challenge Fund, 2016–; Water and Sanitation for the Urban Poor, 2018–. Chm. Governors, Priory Park Sch., 1978–84; Governor: Police Staff Coll., Bramshill, 1981–84; LSE, 2012–; Mem. Ct, Bristol Univ., 1994–2001. Internat. Trustee, Duke of Edinburgh's Internat. Youth Award, 2009– (Chm., Internat. Council, 2015–); Global Trustee, Unified Bd, Food for the Hungry Inc., 2010–; Governor: Ditchley Park, 2009–12; Mus. of London, 2009–; ESU, 2010– (Chm., 2015–). Mem. Bd, ENO, 1984–97. Broadcaster. Hon. DLaws Lincoln, Penn, 2004; Hon. LLD Bristol, 2007; Hon. DLaws W London, 2018. *Publications:* (contrib.) Reclaiming the Ground, 1993; (contrib.) Complete Novels of Jane Austen, 1993. *Recreations:* opera, swimming. *Address:* House of Lords, SW1A 0PW. *E:* boatengp@parliament.uk. *Club:* none.

**BOATENG, Ozwald,** OBE 2006; Managing Director, Bespoke Couture Ltd, since 1991; *b* London, 22 Feb. 1967. *Educ:* Southgate Coll. First studio, Portobello Rd, 1991; first store opened London, 1995. Best Menswear Designer, British Fashion Awards, 2000. *Address:* Bespoke Couture Ltd, 30 Savile Row, W1S 3PT. *T:* (020) 7440 5242.

**BOBROW, Prof. Martin,** CBE 1995; FRS 2004; FRCP, FRCPath, FMedSci; Professor of Medical Genetics, Cambridge University, 1995–2005, now Emeritus; *b* 6 Feb. 1938; *s* of Joe and Bessie Bobrow; *m* 1963, Lynda Geraldine Strauss; three *d. Educ:* Univ. of the Witwatersrand (BSc Hons 1958; MB BCh 1963; DSc Med 1979). MRCPath 1978, FRCPath 1990; FRCP 1986. Consultant in Clin. Genetics, Oxford, and Mem., MRC Ext. Sci. Staff, Genetics Lab., Oxford Univ., 1974–81; Prof. of Human Genetics, Univ. of Amsterdam, 1981–82; Prince Philip Prof. of Paediatric Res., UMDS of Guy's and St Thomas' Hosps, London Univ., 1982–95. Mem. Council, 1988–92, 1993–94, Chm., Molecular and Cellular Medicine Bd, 1992–95, MRC; Chairman: Cttee on Med. Aspects of Radiation in the Envmt, 1985–92; Unrelated Live Donor Transplant Regulatory Authy, 1990–99; Nat. Council, Muscular Dystrophy Gp, 1995–2011; Expert Adv. Gp on Data Access, 2012–; Member: Black Adv. Gp on Possible Increased Incidence of Cancer in West Cumbria, 1983–84; Cttee to examine the ethical implications of gene therapy, 1989–93; NHS Central R&D Cttee, DoH, 1991–97; Nuffield Council on Bioethics, 1996–2003; Human Genetics Adv. Commn, 1997–99; Steering Cttee, Global Alliance for Genomics and Health, 2013–17 (Vice-Chm., 2013–15); Bd, BioBank UK, 2016–. Non-exec. Dir, Cambridge Univ. NHS Foundn Trust, 2004–13. Governor, Wellcome Trust, 1996–2007 (Dep. Chm., 2004–07). *Publications:* papers in sci. books and jls. *Address:* The Old School, 5 Church Lane, Balsham, Cambridge CB21 4DS.

**BOBZIEN, Prof. Susanne,** DPhil; FBA 2014; Professor of Philosophy, University of Oxford, since 2013; Senior Research Fellow, All Souls College, Oxford, since 2013; *b* Hamburg, Germany, 6 June 1960; *d* of Hans and Hannelore Bobzien; *m* 2012, Nathan A. Schatz. *Educ:* Univ. of Bonn (MA 1985); Univ. of Oxford (DPhil 1993). Tutorial Fellow in Philosophy, Balliol Coll., Oxford, 1989–90; Official Fellow and Praelector in Philosophy, Queen's Coll., Oxford, 1990–2002; Lectr in Philosophy, Univ. of Oxford, 1993–2002; Prof. of Philosophy, Yale Univ., 2002–10. Erasmus Visiting Professor: Padua, 1992; Bern, 1998; British Acad. Res. Reader, 2000–02; Sen. Vis. Fellow, 2001–02, Sen. Res. Scholar, 2010–13, Yale Univ. Mem., Inst. for Advanced Study, Princeton, 2008–09. *Publications:* Die Stoische Modallogik, 1986; (jtly) Alexander of Aphrodisias: on Aristotle prior Analytics 1.1–7, 1991; Determinism and Freedom in Stoic Philosophy, 1998. *Recreations:* piano playing, walking, nature photography, concerts, cinema. *Address:* All Souls College, Oxford OX1 4AL. *E:* susanne.bobzien@all-souls.ox.ac.uk.

**BOCKMUEHL, Prof. Markus Nikolaus Andreas,** PhD; Dean Ireland's Professor of the Exegesis of Holy Scripture, University of Oxford, since 2014; Fellow, Keble College, Oxford, since 2007; *b* Dueren, 29 Dec. 1961; *s* of Klaus Erich and Elisabeth Bockmuehl; *m* 1994, Celia Rosamund Withycombe; two *s* three *d. Educ:* St George's Sch., Vancouver; Univ. of British Columbia (BA Classical Studies 1981); Regent Coll., Vancouver (MA Theol Studies, MDiv 1984); Univ. of Cambridge (PhD 1987); MA Oxon 2007. Res. Asst in Ancient Hebrew Inscriptions, Univ. of Cambridge, 1987–88; Asst Prof., Regent Coll., Vancouver and Sessional Lectr in Hebrew, Univ. of BC, 1988–89; University of Cambridge: Asst Lectr, 1989–94; Lectr, 1994–2000; Reader, 2000–04; Prof. of Biblical and Early Christian Studies, 2004–06; Professor of Biblical and Early Christian Studies: Univ. of St Andrews, 2006–07; Univ. of Oxford, 2007–14. *Publications:* Revelation and Mystery in Ancient Judaism and Pauline Christianity, 1990; This Jesus: Martyr, Lord, Messiah, 1994; The Epistle to the Philippians, 1997; (ed with M. B. Thompson) A Vision for the Church: studies in early Christian ecclesiology in honour of J. P. M. Sweet, 1997; Jewish Law in Gentile Churches, 2000; (ed) The Cambridge Companion to Jesus, 2001; (ed with D. A. Hagner) The Written Gospel, 2005; Seeing the Word: refocusing New Testament study, 2006; (ed with J. Carleton Paget) Redemption and Resistance: the messianic hopes of Jews and Christians in antiquity, 2007; (ed with A. J. Torrance) Scripture's Doctrine and Theology's Bible: how the New Testament shapes Christian dogmatics, 2008; The Remembered Peter in Ancient Reception and Modern Debate, 2010; (with G. G. Stroumsa) Paradise in Antiquity: Jewish and Christian views, 2010; Simon Peter in Scripture and Memory, 2012 (Spanish edn 2014, Italian edn 2017); Ancient Apocryphal Gospels, 2017; (ed with G. A. Anderson) Creation ex Nihilo: origins, development, contemporary challenges, 2017; contribs to jls incl. Expository Times, Horizons in Biblical Theol., Jl Jewish Studies, Jl for Study of New Testament, Jl for Study of Paul and His Letters, Jl Theol Studies, New Testament Studies, Nova et Vetera, Pro Ecclesia, Revue Biblique, Revue de Qumran, Scottish Jl Theol., Theology. *Recreations:* ski-ing, Italy, Mozart, jazz, spy novels, biographies. *Address:* Keble College, Oxford OX1 3PG. *T:* (01865) 272727. *E:* Markus.Bockmuehl@keble.ox.ac.uk.

**BODDINGTON, Prof. Anne Dorothy McLaren;** Professor of Design Innovation, since 2017 and Pro Vice Chancellor, Research, Business and Innovation, since 2018, Kingston University London; *b* Barnet, 5 Dec. 1959; *d* of John Frederick William Boddington and Joyce McLaren Boddington (*née* Dynes). *Educ:* St Albans Girls' Grammar Sch.; Poly. of Central London (BA Hons 1st Cl. Architecture RIBA Pt 1 Exemption; Postgrad. DipArch RIBA Pt 2 Exemption; Professional Practice in Arch., RIBA Pt 3 Exemption); Royal Holloway, Univ. of London (MA Cultural Geog.). Regd Architect 1987. Senior Lecturer: Sch. of Arch. and Landscape, Thames Poly., 1988–90; Sch. of Arch., Oxford Brookes Univ., 1990–98; University of Brighton: Hd, Sch. of Arch. and Design, 1999–2006; Dean, Coll. of Arts and Humanities, 2006–17; Pro Vice Chancellor, Civic Engagement and Dean, Kingston Sch. of Arts, Kingston Univ. London, 2017–18. Trustee, Design Council, 2015–. Trustee: Edward Johnston Foundn, 2007–12; House, Brighton, 2011–19; Ind. Gov., Northbrook Coll., Worthing, 2012–17. Affiliate Mem., RIBA, 2003. FRSA 2000. *Publications:* (ed jtly) Reshaping Learning: a critical reader: the future of learning spaces in post-compulsory education, 2011; (ed jtly) Museums and Higher Education Working Together: challenges and opportunities, 2013; (contrib.) A Reuse Atlas, 2017. *Recreations:* opera, arts, design, travel. *Address:* 6/15 Sussex Square, Brighton BN2 5AA. *E:* anne.boddington@me.com; Vice Chancellor's Office, Kingston University, Holmwood House, Kingston upon Thames KT1 2SG. *Club:* Chelsea Arts.

**BODDINGTON, Caroline Elizabeth;** Archbishops' Secretary for Appointments, since 2004; *b* 23 Feb. 1964; *d* of David Gamgee Boddington and Marianne Boddington; *m* 2006, Rt Rev. Dr Alastair Llewellyn John Redfern, *qv. Educ:* Malvern Girls' Coll.; Keble Coll., Oxford (MA). MCIPD 1989. BG Gp plc, 1986–2003: Human Resources Manager, Learning and Develt, 1997–99; Business Analyst, Mediterranean Region, 2000; Head: Learning and Develt, 2000–01; Human Resources Ops, 2002–03. *Recreations:* music, travel. *Address:* Church House, Great Smith Street, SW1P 3AZ. *T:* (020) 7898 1876. *E:* caroline.boddington@churchofengland.org.

**BODEN, Prof. Margaret Ann,** OBE 2002; ScD, PhD; FBA 1983; Research Professor in Cognitive Science, University of Sussex, since 2002 (Professor of Philosophy and Psychology, 1980–2002); *b* 26 Nov. 1936; *d* of late Leonard Forbes Boden, OBE, LLB and Violet Dorothy Dawson; *m* 1967, John Raymond Spiers, *qv* (marr. diss. 1981); one *s* one *d*. *Educ:* City of London Sch. for Girls; Newnham Coll., Cambridge (Major schol. in Med. Scis; Sarah Smithson Scholar in Moral Scis; MA; Associate, 1981–93; ScD 1990); Harvard Grad. Sch. (Harkness Fellow; AM; PhD in Cognitive and Social Psychology). Asst Lectr, then Lectr, in Philosophy, Birmingham Univ., 1959–65; Sussex University: Lectr, 1965–72; Reader, 1972–80; Founding Dean, Sch. of Cognitive Sciences, later Cognitive and Computing Sciences, 1987. Vis. Scientist, Yale Univ., 1979. Co-founder, Dir, 1968–85, Sec., 1968–79, Harvester Press. Scientific Adviser: Cambridge Centre for Study of Existential Risk, 2012–; Centre for the Future of Intelligence, Cambridge Univ., 2016–. Founding Chm., Hist. and Philosophy of Psychology Sect., BPsS, 1983; Pres., Sect. X, BAAS, 1993; Vice-Pres., and Chm. of Council, Royal Instn of GB, 1993–95 (Mem. Council, 1992–95). Member: Council for Science and Society, 1986–91 (Trustee, 1990–91); ABRC, 1989–90 (Chm., Working Gp on Peer-Review, 1989–90); Animal Procedures Cttee, Home Office, 1994–98; Sci. Policy Wkg Gp on Machine Learning, Royal Soc., 2015–; Adv. Bd, All Party Parly AI Gp, 2016–; Council, Royal Instn of Philosophy, 1987–; Council, British Acad., 1988–91 (Vice-Pres., 1989–91). Mem., Bd of Curators, Sch. of Advanced Study, Univ. of London, 1995–99. Mem., Soc. of Authors, 1982–98. Trustee, Eric Gill Trust, 1993–. Mem., Academia Europaea, 1993; Fellow, Amer. Assoc. for Artificial Intelligence, 1993; Life Fellow, Assoc. for Study of Artificial Intelligence and Simulation of Behaviour, 1997; Fellow, European Co-ord. Cttee for Artificial Intelligence, 1999. FRSA 1992. Hon. DSc: Sussex, 2001; Bristol, 2002; DUniv Open, 2004. Leslie McMichael Premium, IERE, 1977; 50th Anniv. Gold Medal, Univ. of Sussex, 2013; Covey Award, Internat. Assoc. of Computing and Philosophy, 2013; Lifetime Achievement Award, Internat. Soc. for Artificial Life, 2016; Alan Newell Award, ACM/Assoc. for Advancement of Artificial Intelligence, 2017. *Publications:* Purposive Explanation in Psychology, 1972; Artificial Intelligence and Natural Man, 1977; Piaget, 1979; Minds and Mechanisms, 1981; Computer Models of Mind, 1988; Artificial Intelligence in Psychology, 1989; (ed) The Philosophy of Artificial Intelligence, 1990; The Creative Mind: myths and mechanisms, 1990, 2nd edn 2004; (ed) Dimensions of Creativity, 1994; (ed) The Philosophy of Artificial Life, 1996; (ed) Artificial Intelligence, 1996; Mind as Machine, 2006; Creativity and Art, 2010; AI: its nature and future, 2016; (with Ernest Edmonds) From Fingers to Digits, 2018; Artificial Intelligence: a very short introduction, 2018; General Editor: Explorations in Cognitive Science; Harvester Studies in Cognitive Science; Harvester Studies in Philosophy; contribs to philosophical and psychological jls. *Recreations:* dress-making, dreaming about the South Pacific. *Address:* Centre for Cognitive Science, University of Sussex, Brighton BN1 9QJ. *T:* (01273) 678386. *Club:* Reform.

**BODEN, Martin James;** Headmaster, King Edward's School, Bath, since 2008; *b* Bolton, Lancs, 6 Feb. 1970. *Educ:* Bolton Sch.; Jesus Coll., Cambridge (BA 1992; MA; PGCE). Teacher of Modern Foreign Langs, Bolton Sch., 1993–97; Head: of German, Cheadle Hulme Sch., 1997–2001; of Modern Foreign Langs, Bradford Grammar Sch., 2001–05; Dir of Studies, King Edward's Sch., Bath, 2005–08. *Recreations:* football, cricket, art, music and film appreciation. *Address:* King Edward's Senior School and Sixth Form, North Road, Bath BA2 6HU. *T:* (01225) 464313, *Fax:* (01225) 481363. *E:* headmaster@kesbath.com.

**BODEY, Hon. Sir David (Roderick Lessiter),** Kt 1999; a Judge of the High Court of Justice, Family Division, 1999–2017; a Deputy High Court Judge, since 2017; *b* 14 Oct. 1947; *s* of late Reginald Augustus Bodey, FIA and Betty Francis Bodey; *m* 1976, Ruth (*née* MacAdorey); one *s* one *d*. *Educ:* King's Sch., Canterbury; Univ. of Bristol (LLB Hons 1969). Called to the Bar, Middle Temple, 1970 (Harmsworth Scholar, 1970), Bencher, 1998; QC 1991; an Asst Recorder, 1989; a Recorder, 1993–98; a Dep. High Court Judge, 1994–98; Family Div. Liaison Judge for London, 1999–2001, for N Eastern Circuit, 2001–07. Mem., Family Justice Council, 2008; Dir of Family Trng, Judicial Coll. (formerly Judicial Studies Bd), 2008–17. Legal Assessor, 1983–94, Sen. Legal Assessor, 1994–98, UKCC. Mem., Supreme Court Procedure Cttee, 1995–97. Chm., Family Law Bar Assoc., 1997–98 (Sec., 1995–97); Mem., Family Cttee, Justice, 1995–98. Mem. Adv. Bd, Univ. of Bristol Law Sch., 2017–. Hon. Vis. Prof. of Law, UCL, 2017–. Fellow, Internat. Acad. of Matrimonial Lawyers, 1995. *Recreations:* music, sometime marathon running, attempting to keep on road Triumph TR3. *Address:* c/o Royal Courts of Justice, Strand, WC2A 2LL. *Club:* Lansdowne.

**BODINETZ, Gemma;** Artistic Director, Liverpool Everyman and Playhouse Theatres, since 2003; *b* 4 Oct. 1966; *d* of Shirley McCarthy and Tony Bodinetz and adopted *d* of Terry Brown; *m* 1995, Richard Reddrop; one *s*. *Educ:* Trinity Coll., Dublin (BA Hons). Assistant Director: Royal Court Th., 1991–92; NT, 1992–93; freelance director, 1993–: major productions include: Chimps, Hampstead Th., 1997; Caravan, Bush Th., 1997; Guiding Star, Liverpool, transf. NT, 1998; Bristol Old Vic: Hamlet; Yard Girl, Royal Court; Shopping and Fucking, NYT Workshop; Luminosity, RSC, 2001; at Liverpool Everyman and Playhouse: Mayor of Zalamea, The Kindness of Strangers, 2004; Ma Rainey's Black Bottom; Yellowman, 2004, nat. tour 2006; Who's Afraid of Virginia Woolf?, 2005; The Lady of Leisure, 2006; All My Sons, 2006; Intemperance, 2007; Tartuffe, 2008; The Hypochondriac, 2009; The Misanthrope, 2013; Twelfth Night, 2014; Juno and the Paycock, 2014, transf. Bristol Old Vic; Educating Rita, 2015; The Massive Tragedy of Madame Bovary!, 2016; Fiddler on the Roof, 2017; The Sum, 2017; Paint Your Wagon, 2018; Othello, 2018; also at W Yorks Playhouse, Plymouth Th. Royal, and other theatres. Mem. Bd, Headlong Th. Co. Hon. Fellow, Liverpool John Moores Univ., 2014. Merseyside Woman of the Year, 2004, 2017; Best Dir, UK Th. Awards, 2017. *Recreations:* cinema, reading, building theatres, West Ham Utd. *E:* g.bodinetz@everymanplayhouse.com.

**BODINHAM, Susan;** *see* Sowden, S.

**BODMER, Sir Walter (Fred),** Kt 1986; FRCPath; FRS 1974; FRSB; Head, Cancer and Immunogenetics Laboratory, Weatherall Institute of Molecular Medicine, since 1996, and Emeritus Professor, 2014, University of Oxford; Principal, Hertford College, Oxford, 1996–2005; Consulting Professor, Department of Medicine (Oncology), Stanford University, 2007–13; President, Galton Institute, 2008–14; *b* 10 Jan. 1936; *s* of late Dr Ernest Julius and Sylvia Emily Bodmer; *m* 1956, Julia Gwynaeth Pilkington, FMedSci (*d* 2001); two *s* one *d*; partner, Dr Ann Ganesan. *Educ:* Manchester Grammar Sch.; Clare Coll., Cambridge (BA 1956; MA, PhD 1959). FRCPath 1984; FRSB (FIBiol 1990). Research Fellow 1958–61, Official Fellow 1961, Hon. Fellow 1989, Clare Coll., Cambridge; Demonstrator in Genetics, Univ. of Cambridge, 1960–61; Asst Prof. 1962–66, Associate Prof. 1966–68, Prof. 1968–70, Dept of Genetics, Stanford Univ.; Prof. of Genetics, Univ. of Oxford, 1970–79; Dir of Res., 1979–91, Dir Gen., 1991–96, ICRF. Non-exec. Dir, Fisons plc, 1990–96. Chm., BBC Sci. Consultative Gp, 1981–87; Member: BBC Gen. Adv. Council, 1981–91 (Chm., 1987); Council, Internat. Union Against Cancer, 1982–90; Adv. Bd for Res. Councils, 1983–88; Council, Found for Sci. and Technol., 1995–; Chairman: COPUS, 1990–93; Orgn of European Cancer Insts, 1990–93; NRPB, 1998–2003; Med. and Scientific Adv. Panel, Leukaemia Res. Fund, 2003–09; President: Royal Statistical Soc., 1984–85 (Vice-Pres., 1983–84; Hon. Fellow, 1997); BAAS, 1987–88 (Vice-Pres., 1989–2001); Chm., Council, 1996–2001; Hon. Fellow, 2001); ASE, 1989–90; Human Genome Orgn, 1990–92; British Soc. for Histocompatibility and Immunogenetics, 1990–91 (Hon. Mem. 1992); EACR, 1994–96; British Assoc. for Cancer Res., 1998–2002; first Pres., Internat. Fedn of Assocs for Advancement of Sci. and Technol., 1992–94; Vice-President: Royal Instn, 1981–82; Parly and Scientific Cttee, 1990–93; Hertford Soc. 2015–; Hon. Vice-Pres., Res. Defence Soc., 1990–2008. Trustee: BM (Natural History), 1983–93 (Chm., Bd of Trustees, 1989–93); Sir John Soane's Mus., 1982–2003; Foulkes Foundn, 2002–; Porter Foundn, 2006–. Chancellor, Salford Univ., 1995–2005. Chm. Bd of Dirs, Laban Centre, 1998–2005; Mem. Bd, Trinity Laban, 2005–08 (Companion, 2008); Mem. Bd of Patrons, St Mark's Hosp. and Academic Inst., 1996. Lord Phillips Meml Lect., Cardiff Univ., 2014. Founder FMedSci 1998. Hon. MRIA 1998; Hon. Member: British Soc. of Gastroenterology, 1989; Amer. Assoc. of Immunologists, 1985; St Mark's Assoc., 1995; British Transplantation Soc., 2002; British Soc. Immunol., 2006; For. Associate, US Nat. Acad. of Scis, 1981; For. Mem., Amer. Philosophical Soc., 1989; For. Hon. Mem., Amer. Acad. Arts and Scis, 1972; Fellow, Internat. Inst. of Biotechnology, 1989; Hon. Fellow: Keble Coll., Oxford, 1982; Green Coll., Oxford, 1993; Hertford Coll., Oxford, 2005; Hon. FRCP 1985; Hon. FRCS 1986; Hon. FRSE 1992; Hon. FRSocMed 1994. Liveryman, Drapers' Co., 2008–. Hon. DSc: Bath, Oxford, 1988; Hull, Edinburgh, 1990; Bristol, 1991; Loughborough, 1993; Lancaster, Aberdeen, 1994; Plymouth, 1995; London, Salford, 1996; UMIST, 1997; Witwatersrand, 1998; DUniv Surrey, 1990; Laurea *hc* in Medicine and Surgery, Univ. of Bologna, 1987; Dr *hc* Leuven, 1992; Masaryk, 1994; Haifa, 1998; Hon. MD Birmingham, 1992; Hon. LLD Dundee, 1993. William Allan Meml Award, Amer. Soc. Human Genetics, 1980; Conway Evans Prize, RCP/Royal Soc., 1982; Rabbi Shai Shacknai Meml Prize Lectr, 1983; John Alexander Meml Prize and Lectureship, Univ. of Pennsylvania Med. Sch., 1984; Rose Payne Dist. Scientists Lectureship, Amer. Soc. for Histocompatibility and Immunogenetics, 1985; Bernal Lectr, 1986, Faraday Award, 1994, Royal Medal, 2013, Royal Soc.; Neil Hamilton-Fairley Medal, RCP, 1990; Romanes Lectr, Univ. of Oxford, 1995; Harveian Orator, RCP, 1996; Dalton Medal, Manchester Lit. and Philos. Soc., 2002; D. K. Ludwig Award, 2002; Seroussi Foundn Res. Award, 2003; Carter Medal, British Soc. of Genetic Medicine, 2014. *Publications:* The Genetics of Human Populations (with L. L. Cavalli-Sforza), 1971; (with A. Jones) Our Future Inheritance: choice or chance?, 1974; (with L. L. Cavalli-Sforza) Genetics, Evolution and Man, 1976; (with Robin McKie) The Book of Man, 1994; research papers in genetical, statistical and mathematical and medical jls, etc. *Recreations:* playing the piano, riding, swimming, scuba diving. *Address:* Cancer and Immunogenetics Laboratory, Weatherall Institute of Molecular Medicine, John Radcliffe Hospital, Oxford OX3 9DS. *T:* (01865) 222356. *Clubs:* Athenæum, Oxford and Cambridge.

**BODMIN, Archdeacon of;** *see* Elkington, Ven. A. A.

**BODY, Jennifer Mary,** OBE 2010; Head, Research and Technology, Airbus UK, 2008–10; *b* Bristol, 15 Feb. 1953; *d* of Ronald Jones and Evelyn Jones; *m* 1983, Graham Paul Body; one *s*. *Educ:* Bristol Poly. (HND). Joined British Aircraft Corp., later British Aerospace, as undergraduate apprentice, 1971, then engrg roles; Proj. Exec., Res. and Technol., 1993–97; Head: Design, Nimrod, 1997–2000; Projects, Support Engrg, 2000–02; Engrg Prog. Manager, A400M Wing, 2002–05; Govt Affairs Manager, Res. and Technol., 2005–08. Royal Aeronautical Society: Pres., 2013–14; Chair, Educn and Skills Cttee, 2014–. Governor: Heathrow Aviation Engrg University Trng Coll., 2014–; UWE, 2015–. FRAeS 2008; FCGI 2014. Hon. DEng UWE, 2013; Hon. DSc Kingston, 2016. *Recreations:* cooking, gardening, walking, natural history. *Address:* c/o Royal Aeronautical Society, 4 Hamilton Place, W1J 7BQ. *T:* (020) 7670 4300. *Club:* Royal Air Force.

**BOE, Norman Wallace;** Deputy Solicitor to Secretary of State for Scotland, 1987–96; *b* 30 Aug. 1943; *s* of late Alexander Thomson Boe and Margaret Wallace Revans; *m* 1968, Margaret Irene McKenzie; one *s* one *d*. *Educ:* George Heriot's Sch., Edinburgh; Edinburgh Univ. LLB Hons 1965. Admitted Solicitor, 1967. Legal apprentice, Lindsays, WS, 1965–67; Legal Asst, Menzies & White, WS, 1967–70; Office of Solicitor to Sec. of State for Scotland, 1970–96. Volunteer with Ann Edgar Charitable Trust and NET Patient Foundn, 2014–. *Recreations:* gardening, travelling.

**BOEHMER, Prof. Elleke Deirdre**, DPhil; Professor of World Literature in English, University of Oxford, since 2007; Fellow, since 2007 and Deputy Director, Oxford Life Writing Centre, since 2011, Wolfson College, Oxford; Director, Oxford Research Centre in the Humanities, 2015–17; *b* Durban, SA, 14 Nov. 1961; *d* of Antony Gerhardus Boehmer and Fredrika Boehmer (*née* ten Tusschedé); *m* 1994, Steven John Matthews; two *s*. *Educ:* Rhodes Univ. (BA Hons 1984); St John's Coll., Oxford (MPhil 1987; DPhil 1990). Jun. Lectr in English, Vista Univ., Mamelodi Township, SA, 1984–85; Rhodes Scholar, 1985–88; Lecturer: in Commonwealth Lit., Amer. and Commonwealth Arts Studies, Univ. of Exeter, 1987–88; in Nineteenth- and Twentieth-Century Eng. Lit., St John's Coll., Oxford, 1988–90; in Eng. Lit., Univ. of Leeds, 1990–2000; Prof. in Colonial and Postcolonial Studies, Nottingham Trent Univ., 2000–04; Hildred Carlile Prof. in Lits in English, Royal Holloway, Univ. of London, 2004–07. Vis. Prof., Univ. of Adelaide, 2004; Distinguished Visiting Professor: Univ. of the Witwatersrand, 2009; Monash Univ., 2011; Dist. Vis. Fellow, Univ. of Barcelona, 2010; Dist. Scholar in Residence, Univ. of Virginia, 2014; Vis. Fellow, ANU, 2017–18. Mem. Jury, Internat. Man Booker Prize, 2014–15. Trustee: Charlie Perkins Scholarships, 2010–; Rhodes Trust, 2016–. FEA 2004. Hon. DHum Linnaeus, 2009. *Publications: fiction:* Screens Against the Sky (novel), 1990 (trans. German, 1994); An Immaculate Figure (novel), 1993; Bloodlines (novel), 2000; Nile Baby (novel), 2008; Sharmilla and Other Portraits (stories), 2010; The Shouting in the Dark (novel), 2015 (trans. Dutch, 2015); To the Volcano and Other Stories, 2019; *non-fiction:* (ed jtly) Altered State?: writing and South Africa, 1994; Colonial and Postcolonial Literature: migrant metaphors, 1995 (trans. Mandarin 1998), 2nd edn 2005; (ed) Empire Writing: an anthology of colonial literature 1870–1918, 1998, 2nd edn 2009; Empire, the National, and the Postcolonial, 1890–1920: resistance in interaction, 2002; (ed with Naella Grew) India Calling by Cornelia Sorabji, 2004; (ed) Scouting for Boys by Robert Baden-Powell, 2004; Stories of Women: gender and narrative in the postcolonial nation, 2005; Nelson Mandela: postcolonial thinker, 2008, US edn as Nelson Mandela, 2010 (trans. Arabic, Thai, 2011; Brazilian Portuguese, 2012; Portuguese, 2014); (ed jtly) J. M. Coetzee in Context and Theory, 2009; (ed with Stephen Morton) Terror and the Postcolonial, 2010; (ed with Rosinka Chaudhuri) The Indian Postcolonial: a critical reader, 2010; (ed with Sarah de Mul) The Postcolonial Low Countries: literature, colonialism, multiculturalism, 2012; Indian Arrivals: networks of British Empire 1870–1915, 2015 (Prize for Lit. in English, Eur. Soc. for Study of English, 2016); Postcolonial Poetics: 21st century readings, 2018; (ed with Dominic Davies) Planned Violence: Post/Colonial Urban Infrastructure, Literature and Culture, 2018; (ed with Rouven Kunsmann) The Global Histories of Books: Methods and Practices, 2019; articles in jls incl. Papers of Modern Langs Assoc., Interventions, Jl of Postcolonial Writing, Jl of Commonwealth Lit. *Recreations:* swimming, walking, family, theatre, friends. *Address:* English Faculty, University of Oxford, St Cross Building, Oxford OX1 3UL. *T:* (01865) 271040/055, 07881 623840. *E:* elleke.boehmer@ell.ox.ac.uk.

**BOEL, (Else) Mariann Fischer**; *see* Fischer Boel.

**BOEVEY, Sir Thomas (Michael Blake) C.**; *see* Crawley-Boevey.

**BOFFEY, Christopher John**; News Editor, Guardian News and Media, 2010–11; media consultant, since 2011; *b* Manchester, 23 Nov. 1951; *s* of William and Nora Boffey; *m* 1972, Shirley Edwards; two *s*. *Educ:* Xaverian Coll., Manchester. Reporter, Winsford Guardian, Newcastle Jl, Daily Star, Today, News of the World, The Sun, 1971–94; News Ed., Sunday Mirror, 1994–97; Asst Ed., News, Sunday Telegraph, 1998–2001; Special Advr to Sec. of State for Educn, 2001–02; News Ed., Daily Mirror, 2004–05; media consultant, 2005–07; News Ed., The Observer, 2007–10. Columnist, The Drum, 2012–15. Treas., Journalists' Charity, 2014– (Chm., 2008–10; Life Vice-Pres., 2011). *Recreations:* walking, reading, travelling, exploring London pub architecture. *Address:* 7 Berkeley Road, Crouch End, N8 8RU. *T:* 07860 959450. *E:* chris@boffey.london.

**BOGAN, Paul Simon**; QC 2011; *b* London, 6 Oct. 1957; *s* of Ralph Bogan and Jean Bogan; *m* 1991, Kate Rohde; two *s*. *Educ:* Sevenoaks Sch.; City of London Poly. (BA). Called to the Bar, Gray's Inn, 1983; in practice as barrister, specialising in criminal defence. Mem., Bar Council, 2006–11. Mem. Council, Liberty, 2000–06. *Publications:* Identification: investigation, trial and scientific evidence, 2004, 2nd edn 2011; (jtly) Butterworth's Guide to the Proceeds of Crime Act, 2003, 3rd edn 2008; (jtly) Human Rights in the Investigation and Prosecution of Crime, 2009. *Recreations:* theatre, literature, bridge, football. *Address:* 23 Essex Street Chambers, WC2R 3AA. *T:* (020) 7413 0353, *Fax:* (020) 7413 0374. *E:* paulbogan@23es.com.

**BOGDANOR, Prof. Vernon Bernard**, CBE 1998; FBA 1997; Professor of Government, Oxford University, 1996–2010, now Emeritus; Fellow, Brasenose College, Oxford, 1966–2010, now Emeritus; Research Professor, Institute of Contemporary British History, King's College London, since 2010; *b* 16 July 1943; *s* of Harry Bogdanor and Rosa (*née* Weinger); *m* 1st, 1972, Judith Evelyn Beckett (marr. diss. 2000); two *s*; 2nd, 2009, Sonia Margaret Robertson. *Educ:* Bishopshalt Sch.; The Queen's College, Oxford (BA 1st Cl. PPE 1964; MA 1968; Hon. Fellow, 2009). FRHistS 2013. Brasenose College, Oxford: Sen. Tutor, 1979–85, 1996–97; Vice-Principal, 2001–02; Reader in Government, Oxford Univ., 1990–96. Gresham Prof. of Law, 2004–07; Vis. Prof. of Law, KCL, 2009–10; Vis. Prof., Yale Univ., 2019. Special Advr, H of L Select Cttee on European Communities, 1982–83; Advr on Constitutional and Electoral Matters to Czechoslovak, Hungarian, and Israeli Govts, 1988–; Special Advr, H of C Public Service Cttee, 1996; Mem., UK Delegn to CSCE Conf., Oslo, 1991. Mem. Council, Hansard Soc. for Parly Govt, 1981–97. Mem., Internat. Adv. Council, Israel Democracy Inst., 2010. FAcSS (AcSS 2009). Hon. Fellow, Soc. for Advanced Legal Studies, 1997. Hon. Bencher, Middle Temple, 2010. Hon. DLitt Kent, 2010. FRSA 1992. Sir Isaiah Berlin Prize for Lifetime Contribn to Pol Studies, Pol Studies Assoc., 2008. Chevalier de la Légion d'Honneur (France), 2009. *Publications:* (ed) Disraeli: Lothair, 1975; Devolution, 1979; The People and the Party System, 1981; Multi-Party Politics and the Constitution, 1983; (ed) Democracy and Elections, 1983; (ed) Coalition Government in Western Europe, 1983; What is Proportional Representation?, 1984; (ed) Parties and Democracy in Britain and America, 1984; (ed) Constitutions in Democratic Politics, 1988; (ed) The Blackwell Encyclopaedia of Political Science, 1992; (jtly) Comparing Constitutions, 1995; The Monarchy and the Constitution, 1995; Politics and the Constitution: essays on British Government, 1996; Power and the People: a guide to constitutional reform, 1997; Devolution in the United Kingdom, 1999; (ed) The British Constitution in the 20th century, 2003; (ed) Joined-up Government, 2005; The New British Constitution, 2009; (ed) From the New Jerusalem to New Labour: British Prime Ministers from Attlee to Blair, 2010; The Coalition and the Constitution, 2011; Beyond Brexit, 2019; contribs to learned jls. *Recreations:* music, walking, talking. *Address:* 21 Edmunds Walk, East Finchley, N2 0HU.

**BOGDANOVICH, Peter**; American film director, writer, producer, actor; *b* Kingston, NY, 30 July 1939; *s* of Borislav Bogdanovich and Herma (*née* Robinson); *m* 1962, Polly Platt (marr. diss. 1970; she *d* 2011); two *d*; *m* 1988, L. B. Straten (marr. diss. 2001). Owner: Crescent Moon Productions, Inc., LA, 1986; Holly Moon Co. Inc., LA, 1992. Mem. Faculty, Sch. of Filmmaking, Univ. of N Carolina Sch. of the Arts, 2010. Member: Dirs Guild of America; Writers' Guild of America; Acad. of Motion Picture Arts and Sciences. *Theatre:* Actor, Amer. Shakespeare Fest., Stratford, Conn, 1956, NY Shakespeare Fest., 1958; Dir and producer, off-Broadway: The Big Knife, 1959; Camino Real, Ten Little Indians, Rocket to the Moon, 1961; Once in a Lifetime, 1964. *Films include:* The Wild Angels (2nd-Unit Dir, co-writer, actor), 1966; Targets (dir, co-writer, prod., actor), 1968; The Last Picture Show (dir, co-writer), 1971 (NY Film Critics' Award for Best Screenplay, British Acad. Award for Best Screenplay); Directed by John Ford (dir, writer, interviewer), 1971; What's Up, Doc? (dir, co-writer, prod.), 1972 (Writers' Guild of America Award for Best Screenplay); Paper Moon (dir, prod.), 1973 (Silver Shell Award, Spain); Daisy Miller (dir, prod.), 1974 (Brussels Festival Award for Best Director); At Long Last Love (dir, writer, prod.), 1975; Nickelodeon (dir, co-writer), 1976; Saint Jack (dir, co-writer, actor), 1979 (Pasinetti Award, Critics' Prize, Venice Festival); They All Laughed (dir, writer), 1981; Mask (dir), 1985; Illegally Yours (dir, prod.), 1988; Texasville (dir, prod., writer), 1990; Noises Off (dir, exec. prod.), 1992; The Thing Called Love (dir), 1993; The Cat's Meow (dir), 2002; Hustle (dir), 2004; She's Funny That Way, 2015. *Television:* The Great Professional: Howard Hawks, BBC, 1967; CBS This Morning (weekly commentary), 1987–89; Prowler, CBS, 1995; Blessed Assurance, To Sir With Love II, CBS-MOW, 1996; (actor) The Sopranos, 2000–07. *Publications:* The Cinema of Orson Welles, 1961; The Cinema of Howard Hawks, 1962; The Cinema of Alfred Hitchcock, 1963; John Ford, 1968; Fritz Lang in America, 1969; Allan Dwan: the last pioneer, 1971; Pieces of Time: Peter Bogdanovich on the Movies 1961–85, 1973, enlarged 1985; The Killing of the Unicorn: Dorothy Stratten, 1960–1980, a Memoir, 1984; (ed with introd.) A Year and a Day Engagement Calendar, annually, 1991–; This is Orson Welles, 1992; Who The Devil Made It, 1997; Who the Hell's in It?, 2004; features on films in Esquire, New York Times, Village Voice, Cahiers du Cinema, Los Angeles Times, New York Magazine, Vogue, Variety etc, 1961–.

**BOGER, Prof. David Vernon**, PhD; FRS 2007; FAA, FTSE; Professor of Chemical Engineering, 1982–2009, Laureate Professor, 2000–09, Emeritus Professor, 2010, University of Melbourne; Professor of Engineering, Monash University, 2011; *b* Kutztown, Penn, 13 Nov. 1939; *s* of Charles and Edna Boger; *m* 2003, Reba Angstadt; one *s* two *d* by a previous marriage. *Educ:* Bucknell Univ. (BSc 1961; MSc 1964); Univ. of Illinois (PhD 1965). Monash University: Lectr, 1965–71; Sen. Lectr, 1971–80; Reader, 1980–82; University of Melbourne: Dip. Dean Engrg, 1988–90; Associate Dean (Res.) Engrg, 1990–92; Hd, Dept of Chemical Engrg, 1997–99; Dir, Particulate Fluids Res. Centre, 2000–04. Member: Amer. Soc. of Rheology, 1970–; Australian Soc. of Rheology, 1983–; British Soc. of Rheology, 1989–; Inst. of Non-Newtonian Fluid Mechanics, Univ. of Wales, 1996–. FTSE 1989; FAA 1993; FRSV 2008. *Publications:* Thermodynamics: an introduction, 1976, rev. edn 1987; Rheology and Flow of Non-Newtonian Systems, 1976; An Introduction to the Flow Properties of Polymers, 1980; Rheology and Non-Newtonian Fluid Mechanics, 1983; Rheological Phenomena in Focus, 1993; over 360 articles. *Recreations:* fly fishing, farming. *Address:* Department of Chemical and Biomolecular Engineering, University of Melbourne, Parkville, 3010 Vic, Australia. *T:* (home) (3) 97072407, (mobile) 61459323239. *E:* dvboger@unimelb.edu.au.

**BOGGIS, Andrew Gurdon**, MA; Warden of Forest School, 1992–2009; *b* 1 April 1954; *s* of Lt-Col (Edmund) Allan (Theodore) Boggis and Myrtle (Eirene) Boggis (*née* Donald); *m* 1983, Fiona Mary Cocke; two *d* one *s*. *Educ:* Marlborough Coll.; New Coll., Oxford (MA); King's Coll., Cambridge (PGCE). Asst Master, Hitchin Boys' Sch., 1978–79; Eton College: Asst Master, 1979–92; Master-in-College, 1984–92. Chm., HMC, 2006 (Mem., Cttee, 2001–07); Member: Ind. Schs Exam. Bd, 1992–2001 (Chm., Langs Cttee, 1997–2001); Educn Cttee, ESU, 2004–10. Liveryman, Skinners' Co., 1990– (Extra Mem. Ct, 2004–06; Mem. Ct, 2009–; Master, 2011–12; Chm., Educn Cttee, 2013–). Dir, HMC Projects in Central and Eastern Europe, 2012–. Governor: King's Coll. Sch., Cambridge, 1994–99; Skinners' Co.'s Sch. for Girls, 1997–2009; Purcell Sch. for Music, 2008–11; Skinners' Grammar Sch., 2009–13; Skinners' Kent Acad., 2009–13 (Chm., 2009–13); Canford Sch., Dorset, 2012–17; W Buckland Sch., Devon, 2013–. Mem. Ct, Essex Univ., 1997–2004. Trustee, Dorset Historic Churches Trust, 2012–. *Publications:* articles and reviews. *Recreations:* music, cookery, reading, Austria, rearing pigs, playing the organ, old gramophones. *Address:* Church Cottages, Hooke, Beaminster, Dorset DT8 3PA. *T:* (01308) 861176. *Club:* East India.

**BOGGIS, Emma Louise**; Trustee, since 2013, and Senior Independent Director, since 2017, British Paralympic Association; *b* Guildford, 1 April 1973; *d* of Christopher Robert Woodhams and Susan Woodhams; *m* 2005, Mark Andrew Boggis. *Educ:* Chelmsford County High Sch. for Girls; Oriel Coll., Oxford (BA Hons Philos. and Theol. 1995). Officer, British Army, 1996–2001; Ofsted: Private Sec. to HM Chief Inspector of Schs, 2002–05; Hd, Strategic Communications, 2006–07; Dep. Dir, Cabinet Office, 2007–09; Dep. Hd of Mission, Madrid, 2009–11; Private Sec. to the Prime Minister, 2011–12; Hd, Olympic and Paralympic Legacy Unit, Cabinet Office, 2012–14; CEO, Sport and Recreation Alliance, 2014–19. Trustee, Nat. Paralympic Heritage Trust, 2015–; Mem. Bd, Nat. Lottery Community Fund, 2019–. *Recreations:* running, cycling, swimming, travelling by pedal power, good food. *Address:* British Paralympic Association, 60 Charlotte Street, W1T 2NU.

**BOGGIS, His Honour John Graham**; QC 1993; a Circuit Judge, 1996–2010; *b* 2 April 1949; *s* of Robert Boggis and Joyce (*née* Meek); *m* 2011, Jill Fairall. *Educ:* Whitgift Sch.; Univ. of London (LLB); Univ. of Keele (MA). Called to the Bar, Lincoln's Inn, 1972; a Recorder, 1994–96; a Chancery Circuit Judge, 1997–2001. Asst Boundary Comr, 1993–95. Member: Chancery Bar Assoc., 1982–84; Senate of the Inns of Court and Bar, 1984–85. Staff Rep. Gov., Sherborne Sch., 1993–98. *Recreation:* boating (Cdre, Fairey Owners' Club, 2006–08).

**BOGGIS-ROLFE, Richard**, OBE 2019; Chairman, Odgers Berndtson, since 2001; *b* Bury St Edmunds, 5 April 1950; *s* of Paul Boggis-Rolfe and (Anne) Verena Boggis-Rolfe (*née* Collins); *m* Lucy Elizabeth, *d* of Lt Col Stephen Jenkins, MC, DL; one *s* two *d*. *Educ:* Eton; Trinity Coll., Cambridge (MA); London Business Sch. Commnd Coldstream Guards, 1970; retd as Hon. Major, 1980. Dir, Russell Reynolds Associates, 1983; Dir, Norman Broadbent Internat., 1984–97; Man. Dir, Norman Broadbent Hong Kong, 1985–86; Man. Dir, then Chm., NB Selection Ltd, 1987–95; Chm., Barkers Human Resources, 1992–97; Gp Man. Dir, BNB Resources plc, 1995–97. Chm., Nat. Employer Adv. Bd, 2011–18. Chm., Holfords of Westonbirt Trust, 2007–. Mem. Adv. Bd, Cambridge Judge Business Sch., 2018–. Master, Pewterers' Co., 2011. Vice Patron, Poppy Factory, 2013–. *Address:* The Glebe House, Shipton Moyne, Tetbury, Glos GL8 8PW; L'Hermitage, Basse Nouailette, Hautfort, France. *E:* richard.boggis-rolfe@odgersberndtson.com. *Clubs:* Brooks's, Pratt's, Beefsteak.

**BOGLE, Ellen Gray**, CD 1987; consultant on international trade matters, Lascelles de Mercado Co. Ltd, 2002–09; *d* of late Victor Gray Williams and Eileen Avril Williams; *m* (marr. diss.); one *s* one *d*. *Educ:* St Andrew High Sch., Jamaica; Univ. of the West Indies, Jamaica (BA). Dir of For. Trade, Min. of For. Affairs, Jamaica, 1978–81; Dir, Jamaica Nat. Export Corp., 1978–81; High Comr to Trinidad and Tobago, Barbados, E Caribbean and Guyana, and Ambassador to Suriname, 1982–89; High Comr, UK, 1989–93, and Ambassador to Denmark, Norway, Sweden, Spain and Portugal, 1990–93; Perm. Sec., Min. of Industry, Tourism and Commerce, subseq. Industry, Investment and Commerce,

Jamaica, 1993–96; Min. of Foreign Affairs and Foreign Trade, 1996–2002. Special Envoy of Jamaica to Assoc. of Caribbean States and CARICOM, 1997–2001. *Recreations:* gardening, reading, cooking, volunteer services.

BOGLE, Sir Nigel (Peter Cranston), Kt 2013; Founding Partner, Bartle Bogle Hegarty Ltd, since 1982; *b* 1947. Trainee, then Manager, Leo Burnett, 1967–73; Founding Partner, TBWA, London, 1973–82; former Chief Exec. and non-exec. Gp Chm., Bartle Bogle Hegarty Ltd. *Address:* Bartle Bogle Hegarty Ltd, 60 Kingly Street, W1B 5DS.

BOHUON, Olivier Jean; Chief Executive Officer, Smith & Nephew plc, 2011–18; *b* Paris, 3 Jan. 1959; *s* of Claude Jean Joseph Bohuon and Odile Germaine Bohuon (*née* Guinnebault); *m* 1981, Alexandra Florence Michelle Marie Polliot; two *s* one *d. Educ:* Univ. of Paris XI (Dr Pharmacy 1982); HEC (MBA 1985). Mktg Dir, then Ops Dir, Glaxo France, 1991–95; CEO, then Pres., SmithKline Beecham Labs, 1995–2001; Sen. Vice Pres., Eur. Commercial Ops, GlaxoSmithKline, 2001–03; Hd of Eur., Abbott Labs, 2003–06; Pres., Abbott Internat., 2006–09; Exec. Vice Pres., Abbott Pharmaceuticals, 2009–10; Chief Exec., Pierre Fabre, 2010. Non-executive Director: Shire, 2015–; Takeda Pharmaceuticals, 2015–; Smiths Gp plc, 2018–; Vice Chm., Leo Pharma, 2018–. Chevalier, Légion d'Honneur (France), 2007. *Recreations:* golf, sailing. *Clubs:* Royal Automobile; Saint Cloud Golf, Dinard Golf.

BOILEAU, Sir Nicolas Edmond George, 9th Bt *cr* 1838, of Tacolnestone Hall, Norfolk; *b* 17 Nov. 1964; *s* of Sir Guy Francis Boileau, 8th Bt, and Judith Frances, *d* of George Conrad Hannan; *S* father, 2013. *Heir: b* Christopher Guy Boileau [*b* 1969; *m* 2002, Helen Baker; one *d*].

BOISSIER, Martin Scobell; Vice Lord-Lieutenant of Derbyshire, 1992–2001; *b* 14 May 1926; *s* of Ernest Gabriel Boissier, DSC and Doris Mary Boissier (*née* Bingham); *m* 1955, Margaret Jean Blair, JP; one *s* one *d. Educ:* Bramcote Prep. Sch., Scarborough; Royal Naval Coll., Dartmouth. Service in RN, 1943–58; qualified as Pilot, 1947; Lt-Comdr, retired 1958. Aiton & Co., Derby, 1958, Dir, 1976, retired 1988; Gp Personnel Controller and local Dir, Whessoe, 1980–88; former Director: Silkolene; ATV (Midlands). Mem., East Reg. Bd, Central ITV, 1982–92. Chm., Derbys FHSA, 1990–97. Pres., Royal Sch. for the Deaf, Derby, 1977–; Patron, Arkwright Soc., Cromford, 2002–. Freeman, City of London, 1978; Liveryman, Tinplate Workers alias Wire-workers' Co., 1978 (Mem., Ct of Assts, 1994–2005). DL 1977, High Sheriff, 1978–79, Derbys. *Recreations:* gardening, appreciation of art, music and wine; needlework, charity work. *Address:* Ithersay Cottage, Idridgehay, Belper, Derbyshire DE56 2SB. *T:* (01773) 550210. *Clubs:* MCC; County (Derby).

BOISSIER, Vice Adm. Robin Paul, CB 2007; Chief Executive, Royal National Lifeboat Institution, 2009–19; *b* 14 Oct. 1953; *s* of late Peter Clement Boissier and Joan Rosemary Boissier; *m* 1980, Susan Jane Roxanna Stocker. *Educ:* Harrow Sch.; Emmanuel Coll., Cambridge (MA); London Business Sch. (MSc). Joined RN, 1974; in command: HMS Onyx, 1985; HMS Trafalgar, 1989; HMS Chatham, 1994; Asst Dir, Navy Staff Duties, 1996–97; Dir, Navy Plans and Progs, MOD, 1998–99; Portsmouth Naval Base, 2000–02; ADC to the Queen, 2000–02; Dep. Comdr, NATO Striking Forces, Southern Reg., 2002–04; Dep. Chief Exec., Warship Support Agency, 2004–05; Dir Gen. Logistics (Fleet), MoD, 2005–06; Dep. C-in-C Fleet and Chief Naval Warfare Officer, 2006–09. Younger Brother, Trinity House, 2007. *Publications:* Understanding the Rule of the Road, 2003; Learn the Nautical Rules of the Road, 2010; How to Read a Nautical Chart, 2010. *Recreations:* sailing, gardening. *Clubs:* MCC; Royal Yacht Squadron (Cowes).

BOK, Prof. Derek; Professor of Law, since 1961, 300th Anniversary University Professor, since 1991, President, 1971–91, now President Emeritus, and Interim President, 2006–07, Harvard University; *b* Bryn Mawr, Pa, 22 March 1930; *s* of late Curtis and Margaret Plummer Bok (later Mrs William S. Kiskadden); *m* 1955, Sissela Ann Myrdal, *d* of late Prof. Karl Gunnar Myrdal and Alva Myrdal; one *s* two *d. Educ:* Stanford Univ. (BA); Harvard Univ. (JD); Inst. of Political Science, Univ. of Paris (Fulbright Scholar); George Washington Univ. (MA Economics). Served AUS, 1956–58. Asst Prof. of Law, Harvard Univ., 1958–61, Dean of Law Sch., 1968–71. Chairman: Common Cause, 1998–2006; Bd, Spencer Foundn, 2002–12. *Publications:* The First Three Years of the Schuman Plan, 1955; (ed with Archibald Cox) Cases and Materials on Labor Law, 5th edn 1962, 6th edn 1965, 7th edn 1969, 8th edn 1977; (with John Dunlop) Labor and the American Community, 1970; Beyond the Ivory Tower, 1982; Higher Learning, 1986; Universities and the future of America, 1990; The Cost of Talent, 1993; The State of the Nation, 1996; The Shape of the River, 1998; The Trouble with Government, 2001; Universities in the Marketplace, 2003; Our Underachieving Colleges, 2006; The Politics of Happiness, 2010. *Recreations:* gardening, tennis, ski-ing. *Address:* c/o Kennedy School of Government, Harvard University, Mailbox 50, 79 JFK Street, Cambridge, MA 02138-5801, USA.

BOKHARY, Syed Kemal Shah; Hon. Mr Justice Bokhary; a Non-Permanent Judge, Hong Kong Court of Final Appeal, since 2013 (a Permanent Judge, 1997–2013); *b* 25 Oct. 1947; *s* of Syed Daud Shah Bokhary and Halima Bokhary (*née* Arculli); *m* 1977, Verina Saeeda Chung (see V. S. Bokhary); three *d. Educ:* King George V Sch., Hong Kong. Called to the Bar, Middle Temple, 1970 (Hon. Bencher, 2001); QC (Hong Kong) 1983; practised in Hong Kong and before the Judicial Cttee of the Privy Council, London, 1971–89; Judge of High Court, Hong Kong, 1989–93; Justice of Appeal, Supreme Court of Hong Kong, 1993–97. Mem., Law Reform Commn of Hong Kong, 2000–. Mem. Bd, Law Faculty, 1994–, and Chm., Law and Professional Legal Educn Depts Adv. Cttee, 1997–, City Univ., Hong Kong; Chm., Adv. Bd, Centre for Criminology, Dept of Sociology, Univ. of Hong Kong, 1999–; Chm. Academic Bd, Sch. of Law, 2006–, Chm., Adv. Bd, Faculty of Law, Chinese Univ. of Hong Kong. University of Hong Kong: Hon. Lectr, Dept of Professional Legal Educn, 2000–; Hon. Prof., 2012–; Affiliate, Centre of Near and Middle Eastern Studies, SOAS, 2001–. Mem., Acad. of Experts' Judicial Cttee, 2003–. Mem., RSAA, 1988–. FRAI 1998; Fellow, Hong Kong Inst. of Arbitrators, 2012 (Vice-Pres., 2018). Patron, Advocacy and Mooting Soc., Univ. of Hong Kong, 2003–. Chm., Welsh and W of England Bullmastiff Soc.; Life Mem., Southern Bullmastiff Soc. Mem., Editl Adv. Bd, Halsbury's Laws of Hong Kong, 1993– (Chm., 2011–); Editor-in-Chief: Tort Law and Practice in Hong Kong, 2005–; Archbold Hong Kong, 2008–; Bullen & Leake & Jacobs, Hong Kong vol., 2013–; General Editor: Hong Kong Court of Final Appeal Reports, 2013–; Hong Kong Law Reports and Digest, 2013–; Internat. Adv. Ed., Malaysian Civil Procedure, 2013–. Hon. LLD: Hong Kong, 2012; Hong Kong Shue Yan, 2014. Grand Bauhinia Medal (Hong Kong), 2013. *Publications:* Recollections, 2013; The Law is a Crocodile, 2013; Crocodile at Law, 2014; Human Rights: source, content and enforcement, 2015; Croc of Final Appeal, 2017; Habeas Crocodylus, 2018; articles in Hong Kong Law Jl and other learned jls. *Recreations:* dogs, opera, anthropology, reading, walking, travel, shooting. *Address:* Court of Final Appeal, 8 Jackson Road, Hong Kong. *Clubs:* Hong Kong Jockey, Hong Kong Country, Aberdeen Marina, Hong Kong Clay Target Shooting Association, Hong Kong Rifle Association, Hong Kong Kennel (President).

BOKHARY, Verina Saeeda; a Judge of the Court of First Instance of the High Court (formerly Judge of the High Court), Hong Kong, 1996–2015, now Deputy Judge; *b* 5 Feb. 1950; *d* of Chung Hon-Wing and Hung Shui-Chan; *m* 1977, Syed Kemal Shah Bokhary, *qv*; three *d*. Called to the Bar, Lincoln's Inn, 1971; Temp. Asst Registrar, Royal Courts of Justice, Chancery Div., 1972; Legal Asst, HM Customs & Excise, 1972–76; Legal Officer, Unofficial Mems of the Exec. and Legislative Council Office, Hong Kong, 1976–78; in private practice, Hong Kong, 1978–85; Hong Kong Judiciary: Magistrate, 1985–87; Adjudicator, 1987–89; Dist Court Judge, 1989–95. Chm., Release under Supervision Bd, 1998–2003; Dep. Pres., Long-term Prison Sentences Rev. Bd, 1997–2003. Mem., Updating Gp, High Court Criminal Manual Specimen Directions, 1998–2004. Adv. Ed. and reviewer, Archbold HK, 2003–05. Silver Bauhinia Star (Hong Kong), 2015. *Recreations:* homelife, antiques, reading. *Address:* House C, Eden View, 18 Stanley Village Road, Hong Kong. *T:* 25556655, 92856766.

BOKOVA, Irina Gueorguieva; Director General, UNESCO, 2009–17; *b* 12 July 1952; *d* of Georgi and Nadezhda Bokov; *m* Kalin Mitrev; one *s* one *d. Educ:* English Secondary Sch., Sofia; Moscow State Inst. of Internat. Relns (MBA Internat. Relns); Sch. of Public Affairs, Univ. of Maryland, Washington; John F. Kennedy Sch. of Govt, Harvard Univ. (Exec. Prog. in Leadership and Econ. Develt 1999). Third Sec., Min. of Foreign Affairs, Sofia, 1977–82; Perm. Mission of Bulgaria to UN, NY, 1982–84; Second Sec., UN Dept, 1984–86, Advr to Minister, 1986–90, Min. of Foreign Affairs; Ford Foundn Fellow, 1989; Mem., Constituent Nat. Assembly, 1990–91; First Sec., Eur. Security Dept, Min. of Foreign Affairs, 1991–92; NATO Fellow, Prog. for Central and Eastern Europe on democratic instns, 1992–94; State Sec., Eur. Integration, 1995–97; Minister of Foreign Affairs, 1996–97; Advr to Minister of Foreign Affairs, 1997; MP, 2001–05; Ambassador to France and Monaco, Perm. Delegate of Bulgaria and Rep. on Exec. Bd, UNESCO, 2005–09. Hon. doctorates incl. Edinburgh, 2011. Numerous state distinctions. *Publications:* contribs to Mediterranean Qly, Eur. Policy Forum annual pubns, Jl SE and Black Sea Studies and articles on foreign policy and Eur. integration issues, culture, heritage, educn and sci.

BOKSENBERG, Prof. Alexander, CBE 1996; PhD; FRS 1978; FInstP; FRAS; Hon. Professor of Experimental Astronomy, University of Cambridge, since 1991; Research Professor and PPARC Senior Research Fellow, Institute of Astronomy, University of Cambridge 1996–99, now Emeritus; Extraordinary Fellow, Churchill College, Cambridge, 1996–2003, now Emeritus; Director, Royal Observatories, 1993–96: Royal Greenwich Observatory, Herstmonceux and Cambridge; Royal Observatory, Edinburgh; Isaac Newton Group of optical telescopes, Canary Islands; Joint Astronomy Centre, Hawaii; Chairman, UK National Commission for UNESCO, 2004–10; *b* 18 March 1936; *s* of Julius Boksenberg and Ernestina Steinberg; *m* 1960, Adella Coren; one *s* one *d. Educ:* Stationers' Co.'s Sch.; Univ. of London (BSc, PhD); MA Cantab. Dept of Physics and Astronomy, University Coll. London: SRC Res. Asst, 1960–65; Lectr in Physics, 1965–75; Head of Optical and Ultraviolet Astronomy Res. Group, 1969–81; Reader in Physics, 1975–78; SRC Sen. Fellow, 1976–81; Prof. of Physics and Astronomy, 1978–81; Dir, Royal Greenwich Observatory, 1981–96. Sherman Fairchild Dist. Schol., CIT, 1981–82; Visiting Professor: Dept of Physics and Astronomy, UCL, 1978–; Astronomy Centre, Univ. of Sussex, 1981–89. Chm., New Industrial Concepts Ltd, 1969–81. UK Project Scientist: ESA astronomical satellite TD-1A, 1969–73; NASA-ESA-SERC Internat. Ultraviolet Explorer satellite observatory, 1969–79. Inventor, Image Photon Counting System, ESA-NASA Hubble Space Telescope, 1974–76. USA-UK-Canada Gemini Telescopes Project: UK Dir, 1993–96; Chm., Internat. Expert Cttee, 1992; Chm., UK Steering Cttee, 1992–93; Mem., USA Oversight Cttee, 1993–94. Chairman: SRC Astronomy II Cttee, 1980–81; UK-Japan N+N Bd on Co-operation in Astronomy, 1997–2005; PPARC VISTA Review Bd, 1999–2000; Pres., Internat. Scientific Cttee, Canary Is Observatories, 1984–85 (Mem., 1981–96). Member: ESA Hubble Space Telescope Instrument Definition Team, 1973–95; S African Astronomical Observatory Adv. Cttee, 1978–85; British Council Science Adv. Cttee, 1987–91; Anglo-Australian Telescope Bd, 1989–92 (Dep. Chm., 1991–92); Hubble Space Telescope Users Cttee, 1990–91; Fachbeirat, Max Planck Inst. für Astronomie, 1991–95; European Southern Observatory Vis. Cttee, 1993–95; Finance Cttee, IAU, 1997–2000; Wkg Gp on Basic Scis and Basic Res., ICSU, 2004; Mgt Cttee, Language Centre, Univ. of Cambridge, 2003–07; Steering Cttee, Universe Awareness, 2005–07; Scientific Cttee, Starlight Initiative, 2007–08; mem. or chm. of more than 40 other councils, boards, cttees, panels or courts, 1970–. Exec. Ed., Experimental Astronomy, 1995–2007. Mem. Council and Trustee, Royal Soc., 1995–97 (Mem., Technical Support Steering Gp, 1997–98; Chm., Internat. Exchanges Far East Panel, 2000–06; Hughes Medal, 1999); Mem. Council, Trustee and Vice-Pres., Royal Astronomical Soc., 2000–03 (Chm., Awards Cttee A, 2002–03; Mem., Astronomical Heritage Cttee, 2005–07; Jackson-Gwilt Medal, 1998); Mem. Council, Inst. of Physics, 2001–03 (Mem., Women in Physics Cttee, 2002–03; Chm., Ethics Cttee, 2004–08; Glazebrook Medal and Prize, 2000). UK National Commission for UNESCO: Mem., Foundn Cttee, 1999–2000; Mem. Council, 2000–03; Chm., Sci. Cttee, 2000–03; Chm., Steering Cttee, Campaign Gp, 2003–04; Chm. Bd, 2004–10; Chm., Nat. Sci. Cttee, 2004–11; UNESCO Regional Bureau for Science in Europe: Mem., Scientific Council, 2000–08; Mem., Task Force for Reconstruction of Scientific Co-operation in SE Europe, 2000–03; Chm., Wkg Gp on Restoring Human Potential in SE Europe, 2002–03. UNESCO: Mem., Sci. Sector Cttee of Experts on Internat. Basic Scis Prog., 2002–04; Mem., World Heritage Centre Cttee of Internat. Experts on Archaeo-Astronomical Sites and Observatories, 2004–05; Initiator and Leading Mem., Internat. Rev. Cttee of Experts for Overall Review of UNESCO Sci. Sectors, 2006–08. Mem., Adv. Cttee, Commonwealth Day 2010, 2009–10. Member: Internat. Juries of the UNESCO Science Prize, Javed Husain Prize for Young Scientists, and Kalinga Prize for Popularisation of Science, 2004–; Jury, UNESCO-L'Oreal Fellowships for Women in Science (UK and Ireland), 2006–; Chm., Internat. Jury for Latsis Prize, ESF, 2008. Pres., W London Astronomical Soc., 1978–; Hon. Pres., Astronomical Soc. of Glasgow, 1995–. Pres., British Horological Inst., 2000–01. Royal Soc. lecture tours: Russia, 1989; China, 1995; Japan, 1999; British Council lect. tour, India, 1999. Founding Member: Academia Europaea, 1989; European Astronomical Soc., 1990; Mem., Cambridge Philosophical Soc., 1996–; Titular Mem., Eur. Acad. of Arts, Scis and Humanities, 2007. Patron, Hanwell Community Observatory, 2009–12. Member: Council, Churchill Coll. Cambridge, 1998–2003; Adv. Council, Winston Churchill Meml Trust, 2010–19 (Chm., Sci., Technol. and Engrg, 2010–19); Bd of Trustees, Future Univ., Sudan, 2011–. Fellow, UCL, 1991. FRAS 1965; FInstP 1998; FRSA 1984–90. Clockmakers' Co.: Freeman, 1984; Liveryman, 1989; Mem., Court of Assts, 1994–; Master, 2000. Asteroid (3205) Boksenberg, named 1988. Dr *hc* l'Observatoire de Paris, 1982; DSc *hc* Sussex, 1991. Golden Diploma, Eur. Forum of Experts, 2007. *Publications:* (ed jtly) Modern Technology and its Influence on Astronomy, 1990; (dedicatee and contrib.) Hubble Space Telescope and High Redshift Universe, Procs of 37th Herstmonceux Conf., 1996; (ed jtly) The Role of Astronomy in Society and Culture, Procs of 260th Symposium of Internat. Astronomical Union, 2011; over 240 contribs to learned jls. *Recreation:* ski-ing. *Address:* University of Cambridge, Institute of Astronomy, The Observatories, Madingley Road, Cambridge CB3 0HA. *T:* (01223) 337548. *Club:* Athenæum.

BOLADUADUA, Emitai Lausiki; Director, Institute of Indigenous (Fijian) Studies, since 2009; *b* 13 April 1944; *s* of Naibuka Lausiki and Mere Turavono; *m* 1973, Asinate U Taleaua; four *d. Educ:* Queen Victoria Sch., Fiji; Suva Grammar Sch., Fiji; Univ. of New England, Armidale, NSW (BSc, DipEd); Univ. of Reading (DipEd Admin). Ratu Kadavulevu School: asst teacher, 1968–73; Vice Principal, 1973–81; Principal, 1981–84

Principal: Labasa Coll., 1984–87; Fiji Inst. of Technol., 1988–90; Deputy Secretary: for Educn, Youth and Sport, 1990–93; for Foreign Affairs and Civil Aviation, 1993–97; Permanent Secretary: for Inf., Broadcasting, TV and Telecommunications, 1997; for Home Affairs and Immigration, 1997–99; for Educn, 1999; for Foreign Affairs and External Trade, 1999–2000. Mem., Land Transport Authy, Fiji, 2002. High Comr of Fiji in UK, also accredited to Republic of Ireland, Denmark, Germany, the Holy See, Israel and Egypt, 2002–06. Chm., Cakaudrove Provincial Council, 2008–13. Chm. Council, Fiji Inst. of Technol., 1999; Mem. Council, Univ. of S Pacific, 1990–92 and 1999. CS Medal (Fiji), 1995. *Publications:* Na Vuku ni Vanua - Wisdom of the Land: aspects of Fijian knowledge, culture and history, 2013. *Recreations:* watching cricket, tennis, Rugby Union, reading. *Address:* PO Box 4528, Samabula, Fiji Islands.

**BOLAM, James,** MBE 2009; actor; *b* Sunderland, 16 June 1938; *s* of Robert Alfred Bolam and Marion Alice Bolam (*née* Drury); *m* Susan Jameson, actress. *Educ:* Bede Grammar Sch., Sunderland; Bemrose Sch., Derby. First stage appearance, The Kitchen, Royal Court, 1959; later plays include: Events While Guarding the Bofors Gun, Hampstead, 1966; In Celebration, Royal Court, 1969; Veterans, Royal Court, 1972; Treats, Royal Court, 1976; Who Killed 'Agatha' Christie?, Ambassadors, 1978; King Lear (title rôle), Young Vic, 1981; Run for Your Wife!, Criterion, 1983; Arms and the Man, Cambridge; Who's Afraid of Virginia Woolf?, Birmingham, 1989; Victory, Chichester, 1989; Jeffrey Bernard is Unwell, Apollo, 1990; Glengarry Glen Ross, Donmar Warehouse, 1994; Wild Oats, National, 1995; Endgame, Nottingham Playhouse, 1999; Semi-Detached, 1999, How to Succeed in Business Without Really Trying, 2005, Chichester; Bomber's Moon, Park Th., 2014, trans. Trafalgar Studios, 2015; Fracked!, Chichester Th., 2016. *Films:* A Kind of Loving, 1962; The Loneliness of the Long Distance Runner, 1962; Half a Sixpence, 1967; Otley, 1969; Crucible of Terror, 1971; Straight on till Morning, 1972; In Celebration, 1974; Murder Most Foul; The Likely Lads, 1976; The Great Question; Seaview Knights; Clockwork Mice; Stella Does Tricks; Island on Bird Street; End of the Affair, 1999; It Was an Accident, 2000. *Television series:* The Likely Lads, 1965–69; Whatever Happened to the Likely Lads?, 1973; When the Boat Comes In, 1975–77; The Limbo Connection (Armchair Thriller Series); Only When I Laugh; The Beiderbecke Affair; Room at the Bottom; Andy Capp; The Beiderbecke Tapes; The Beiderbecke Connection; Second Thoughts; Eleven Men Against Eleven; Have your Cake, The Missing Postman, 1997; Pay and Display, Dirty Tricks, Close and True, 2000; Born and Bred, Shipman, 2002; New Tricks (9 series), 2003–12; The Plot Against Harold Wilson, 2006; Grandpa In My Pocket, 2009–; Cold Feet, 2016; also As You Like It, Macbeth, in BBC Shakespeare. *Address:* c/o Rebecca Blond, 69A Kings Road, SW3 4NX.

**BOLAND, Leo;** Chief Executive, Greater London Authority, 2009–11; *b* 1 Aug. 1952; *s* of Stephen and Ellen Boland; *m* 1981, Margaret Gibbons; one *s. Educ:* Ushaw Coll., Durham; Bristol Univ. (BSc Hons Social Scis); Open Univ. Business Sch. (MBA). Grad. trainee, Ealing BC, 1974–75; Community Worker, Newham Rights Centre, 1975–79; Improvement Officer, Housing Dept, Islington BC, 1979–89; Newham Borough Council: Capital Prog. Manager, 1989–91; Asst Dir of Social Services, 1991–98; Asst Chief Exec., 1998–2001; Chief Exec., London Borough of Barnet, 2001–09. *Recreations:* walking, reading, film, eating out.

**BOLEAT, Sir Mark (John),** Kt 2017; company director and consultant; *b* 21 Jan. 1949; *s* of Paul Boleat and Peggy Boleat (*née* Still); *m* 1991, Elizabeth Ann Baker (*née* Barker). *Educ:* Victoria College, Jersey; Lanchester Polytechnic and Univ. of Reading (BA Econs, MA Contemp. European Studies). FCIB. Asst Master, Dulwich College, 1972; Economist, Indust. Policy Group, 1973; The Building Societies Association: Asst Sec., 1974; Under Sec., 1976; Dep. Sec., 1979; Dep. Sec.-Gen., 1981; Sec.-Gen., 1986; Dir-Gen. 1987. Sec.-Gen., Internat. Union of Housing Finance Instns (formerly Internat. Union of Building Socs and Savings Assocs), 1986–89; Mem. Bd, Housing Corp., 1988–93; Chm., Circle 33 Housing Trust, 1990–93; Dir-Gen., ABI, 1993–99; Director: Comino Gp, 2000–06; Countryside Properties, 2001–05. Chm., Link Scheme Ltd, 2017–. Mem., Regulatory Policy Cttee, 2009–12; Chairman: Jersey Competition Regulatory Authy, 2010–16; States of Jersey Development Co., 2011–15. Chairman: Hillingdon Community Trust, 2003–08; Green Corridor, 2008–11; Housing and Finance Inst., 2015–19; City of London Acad. Highbury Grove, 2017–. Dep. Chm., TheCityUK, 2012–17. Member: NCC, 2000–05; Gibraltar Financial Services Commn, 2000–09; Chm., Assoc. of Labour Providers, 2004–12. Mem., Ct of Common Council, City of London Corp., 2002– (Chm., Mkts Cttee, 2008–; Dep. Chm., 2009–12, Chm., 2012–17, Policy and Resources Cttee). *Publications:* The Building Society Industry, 1982; National Housing Finance Systems: a comparative study, 1985; Housing in Britain, 1986; (with Adrian Coles) The Mortgage Market, 1987; Building Societies: the regulatory framework, 1988, 3rd edn 1992; Trade Association Strategy and Management, 1996; Models of Trade Association Co-operation, 2000; Good Practice in Trade Association Governance, 2001; Managing Trade Associations, 2003; Housing Development and Housing Finance in Britain, 2008; An Agenda for Better Regulation, 2009; Jersey's Population—a history, 2015; articles on housing, insurance and finance. *Recreation:* golf. *Address:* 26 Westbury Road, Northwood, Middx HA6 3BU. *Club:* Moor Park Golf.

**BOLES, Nicholas Edward Coleridge;** MP for Grantham and Stamford, since 2010 (C, 2010–19; Ind, since 2019); *b* 2 Nov. 1965; *s* of Sir John Dennis, (Sir Jack), Boles, MBE. *Educ:* Winchester; Magdalen Coll., Oxford (BA PPE); John F. Kennedy Sch. of Govt, Harvard Univ. (MPP 1989). Founder, 1995, Chief Exec., 1995–2000, non-exec. Chm., 2000–08, Longwall Hldgs Ltd. Founder and Dir, Policy Exchange, 2002–07; COS to Mayor of London, 2008. Mem. (C) Westminster CC, 1998–2002 (Chm., Housing Cttee, 1999–2001). Contested (C) Hove, 2005. PPS to Minister of State, DfE, 2010–12; Parly Under-Sec. of State (Minister for Planning), DCLG, 2012–14; Minister of State, BIS and DfE, 2014–16. Sen. Fellow, Inst. for Govt, 2010–12. *Publications:* Which Way's Up?: the future for coalition Britain and how to get there, 2010. *Address:* House of Commons, SW1A 0AA.

*See also J. D. Fishburn.*

**BOLES, Sir Richard Fortescue,** 4th Bt *cr* 1922, of Bishop's Lydeard, Somerset; *b* 12 Dec. 1958; *er s* of Sir Jeremy John Fortescue Boles, 3rd Bt and Dorothy Jane Boles (*née* Worswick); *S* father, 2014; *m* 1990, Allison Beverley, *d* of Brian MacDonald; one *s* one *d. Heir: s* James Alexander Fortescue Boles [*b* 25 May 1993; *m* 2016, Brenny Sally Blake, *d* of Kevin Smith; one *s* one *d*].

**BOLGER, Rt Hon. James Brendan, (Jim),** ONZ 1997; PC 1991; Chairman: Kiwibank Ltd, 2001–10; KiwiRail, 2008–10; *b* 31 May 1935; *s* of Daniel Bolger and Cecilia (*née* Doyle); *m* 1963, Joan Maureen Riddell; six *s* three *d. Educ:* Opunake High Sch. Sheep and cattle farmer, Te Kuiti, 1965–72. Federated Farmers: Br. Chm., 1967–72; sub-provincial Chm., 1970–72; Vice-Pres., Waikato, 1971–72; Mem., Dominion Exec., 1971–72. MP (Nat. Party) King Country, 1972–98; Party Under-Sec., Min. of Agric. and Fisheries, Min. of Maori Affairs, then Minister i/c of Rural Banking Finance Corp., 1975–77; Minister of Fisheries and Associate Minister of Agric., 1977–78; Minister of Labour, 1978–84; Minister of Immigration, 1978–81; Leader of Nat. Party, 1986–97; Leader of the Opposition, 1986–90; Prime Minister of NZ, 1990–97; NZ Ambassador to USA, 1998–2002.

Chairman: Adv. Bd, World Agricl Forum, 2002–; Ian Axford (NZ) Fellowship in Public Policy, 2002–15, now Patron. Chairman: New Zealand Post Ltd, 2002–10; Gas Industry Co., 2004–; Express Couriers Ltd, 2004–10; Trustees Executors Ltd, 2006–15; Parcels Direct Gp. Chancellor, Waikato Univ., 2007–. Pres., ILO, 1983. Hon. Dr Agricl Econs Khon Kaen, 1994; Hon. DLitt Massey, 2002. Silver Jubilee Medal, 1977; NZ Commemoration Medal, 1990; NZ Suffrage Centennial Medal, 1993. *Recreations:* hiking, fishing, reading, Rugby, cricket. *Address:* 6 Lavinia Grove, PO Box 305, Waikanae 5250, New Zealand.

**BOLINGBROKE,** 9th Viscount *cr* 1712, **AND ST JOHN,** 10th Viscount *cr* 1716; **Nicholas Alexander Mowbray St John;** Bt 1611; Baron St John of Lydiard Tregoze, 1712; Baron St John of Battersea, 1716; *b* 20 June 1974; *s* of 7th Viscount Bolingbroke and 8th Viscount St John and of Jainey Anne (*née* McRae); *S* half-*b*, 2011; *m* 2012, Helen McDougall (marr. diss. 2014). *Heir:* kinsman Walter Warren St John [*b* 14 Feb. 1921; *m* 1949, Lida Amelia Goicoechea; one *s* one *d*]. *Address:* New Zealand.

**BOLITHO, Col Edward Thomas,** OBE 1994; Lord-Lieutenant of Cornwall, since 2011; *b* Penzance, 30 Dec. 1955; *s* of Maj. Simon Edward Bolitho, MC and Elizabeth Margaret Bolitho (*née* Creswell); *m* 1985, Alexandra Laura Melissa, *d* of Rear-Adm. Sir Morgan Charles Morgan-Giles, DSO, OBE, GM; one *s* twin *d. Educ:* Eton Coll.; Pembroke Coll., Cambridge (BA 1977). Commnd Grenadier Guards, 1978; Comd 1 Bn, 1993–95; Staff Coll., 1995–98. Chairman: CLA Cornwall, 2007–09; CLA SW, 2009–12. Mem., Newlyn Harbour Commn, 2007–10. Regtl Lt Col, Grenadier Guards, 2000–07. Hon. Air Cdre 2625 (Co. of Cornwall) Sqdn, RAuxAF, 2000–06. Mem., HM Bodyguard, Hon. Corps of Gentlemen at Arms, 2008–. Vice Pres., Royal Cornwall Agricl Assoc., 2014–. Trustee, Duke of Cornwall's Benevolent Fund, 2014–. Chm., Assoc. of Lord Lieutenants, 2018–. Hon. Air Cdre 505 (Wessex) Sqn, RAuxAF, 2016–. DL 2008, High Sheriff, 2011–12, Cornwall. CStJ 2018. *Address:* Trengwainton, Penzance, Cornwall TR20 8SA.

**BOLKESTEIN, Frederik, (Frits);** Member, European Commission, 1999–2004; runs one-person political and economic think tank; *b* 4 April 1933; *m* 1988, Femke Boersma; one *s* one *d* (and one *s* decd). *Educ:* Oregon State Coll., USA; Gemeentelijke Univ., Amsterdam; Univ. of Leiden (Master of Law). Shell Group, 1960–76: posts in E Africa, Honduras, El Salvador, UK, Indonesia and France; Dir, Shell Chimie, Paris, 1973–76. Mem. Parliament (VVD), Netherlands, 1978–82, 1986–88 and 1998–99; Minister for Foreign Trade, 1982–86; Minister of Defence, 1988–89; Chm., VVD Parly Gp, 1990–98. Pres., Liberal Internat., 1996–99. Visiting Professor: Univ. of Leiden, 2005–10; Univ. of Delft, 2005–. Member Supervisory Board: Central Bank of the Netherlands, 2005–11; AF/KLM, 2005–. MRIIA. *Publications:* The Limits of Europe, 2004; De twee lampen van de staatsman, 2006; (with Michel Rocard) Peut-on réformer la France?, 2006; Overmoed en Onverstand, 2008; De Intellectuele Verleiding, 2011 (The Intellectual Temptation, 2013); Cassandra tegen wil en dank (memoir), 2013; (ed jtly) De succesvolle mislukking van Europa, 2015. *W:* www.fritsbolkestein.com.

**BOLLAND, Alexander;** QC (Scot.) 1992; *b* 21 Nov. 1950; *s* of James Bolland and Elizabeth Agnes (*née* Anderson); *m* 1973, Agnes Hunter, *d* of Dr George Pate Moffat, Crookedholm; one *s* two *d. Educ:* Kilmarnock Acad.; Univ. of St Andrews (BD 1973); Glasgow Univ. (LLB 1976). Admitted to Faculty of Advocates, 1978; Capt., Directorate of Army Legal Services, later Army Legal Corps, 1978–80; Standing Jun. Counsel to Dept of Employment in Scotland, 1988–92; Temp. Sheriff, 1988–99; part-time Judge (formerly Chm.), Employment (formerly Industrial) Tribunals, 1993–2013; Legal Chm., Pensions Appeal Tribunal (Scotland) (War Pensions), 2008–18; Chm., Dentists' Vocational Trng Appeal Tribunal, 2013–; Member: Judicial Proceedings Panel, C of S, 2013–17; Military Chaplains Cttee, C of S, 2016–. *Recreations:* Hellenistics, walking, reading. *Address:* The Old Dairy, 60 North Street, St Andrews, Fife KY16 9AH. *T:* (01334) 474599. *Club:* New (Edinburgh).

**BOLLAND, (David) Michael;** broadcast consultant, 2007–15; *b* 27 Feb. 1947; *s* of Allan Bolland and Eileen Lindsay; *m* 1987, Katie Lander; one *s* one *d*, and one *s* two *d* by former marrs. *Educ:* Hillhead High School, Glasgow. Film editor, BBC Scotland, 1965–73; TV Producer, BBC TV, 1973–81; Channel Four Television: Commissioning Editor, Youth, 1981–83; Senior Commissioning Editor, Entertainment, 1983–87; Asst Dir of Programmes, and Head of Art and Entertainment Gp, 1987–88; Controller Arts and Entertainment, and Dep. Dir of Progs, 1988–90; Man. Dir, Initial Films and Television, 1990; Man. Dir, Channel X Ltd, 1990–96; Project Dir, Channel X Broadcasting (Scotland) Ltd, 1991–95; BBC Scotland: Hd of Arts and Entertainment, 1996–2001; Hd of Comedy and Entertainment, 2001–04; Dir of Television, 2004–07, Creative Dir, 2006–07, Nat. Film and Television Sch. Chairman: Edinburgh Internat. TV Fest., 1990; Producers' Alliance for Film and Television, 1995. Member: RTS; BAFTA. *Recreation:* catching up with the world. *Address:* 1 Westbourne Gardens, Glasgow G12 9XE.

**BOLLAND, Hugh Westrope;** Vice Chairman, Schroder Investment Management Ltd, 1999–2000; *b* 14 May 1946; *s* of late Gp Capt. Guy Alfred Bolland, CBE; *m* 1972, Marian Wendy Elton; two *s* one *d. Educ:* St Edward's Sch., Oxford; Univ. of Exeter (BA (Hons) Econs). Joined Schroders, 1970; Man. Dir, Schroders Asia Ltd, Hong Kong, 1984–87; Chief Exec., Schroders Australia Ltd, 1987–90; Chm., Schroder Unit Trusts Ltd, 1990–92; Jt Chief Exec., 1995–96, Chief Exec., 1997–99, Schroder Investment Management Ltd (Dir, 1990–2000); Director: Schroder Split Fund plc, 1993–2002; Fidelity Asian Values plc, 2004–14; JP Morgan Indian Investment Trust, 2004–15; Alliance Trust plc, 2007–12. Mem. Supervisory Bd, Eurocommercial Properties NV, 1998–2013. Gov., St Edward's Sch., Oxford, 1999–2012. *Recreations:* sailing, golf, music. *Clubs:* Hong Kong, Hong Kong Jockey (Hong Kong); Royal Motor Yacht.

**BOLLAND, Marc J.;** Head of European Portfolio Operations, Blackstone, since 2016; *b* Netherlands, 28 March 1959; *s* of J. Bolland and M. Bolland-Bronsvoort. *Educ:* Univ. of Groningen (Masters of Business Admin). Heineken: various mktg roles, 1987–95; Man. Dir, Slovakia and E Europe, 1995–99, Heineken Export Worldwide, 1999–2001; Mem. Bd, 2001–05, Chief Finance Officer, 2005–06, Heineken, NV, Netherlands; Chief Executive Officer: Wm Morrison Supermarkets plc, 2006–10; Marks and Spencer plc, 2010–16. Non-executive Director: Manpower Inc., 2004–15; Coca-Cola Co., 2015–; Internat. Airlines Gp, 2016–; DFID, 2018–.

**BOLLAND, Mark William;** communications consultant, since 2002; *b* 10 April 1966; *s* of late Robert Arthur Bolland and of Joan Bolland (*née* Barker); civil partnership 2006, *m* 2015, Guy Vaughan Black (*see* Baron Black of Brentwood). *Educ:* Kings Manor Sch., Middlesbrough; Univ. of York (BSc). Res. Manager, and Advr to Dir Gen., Advertising Standards Authy, 1988–91; Exec. Asst to Chm., 1991–92, Dir, 1992–96, Press Complaints Commn; Asst Private Sec., 1996–97, Dep. Private Sec., 1997–2002, to HRH the Prince of Wales. Columnist, London Evening Standard, 2006–09; Contributing Editor, Tatler, 2011–17. Vice Pres., Journalists' Charity, 2007–. Trustee: Helen Hamlyn Trust, 2008–14; Open Futures Trust, 2010–13; David Ross Foundn, 2011–; Middlesbrough and Teesside Philanthropic Foundn, 2011–14; David Ross Educn Trust, 2012–16; Dir, Bertarelli Foundn, 2013–. Patron, Internat. Cat Care, 2015–. *Address:* 34 Cannon Court, 5 Brewhouse Yard, EC1V 4JQ. *E:* mark@markbolland.com. *Club:* Garrick.

**BOLLAND, Michael;** see Bolland, D. M.

**BOLLOBÁS, Prof. Béla,** PhD, DSc; FRS 2011; Fellow of Trinity College, Cambridge, since 1971; Honorary Professor of Pure Mathematics, University of Cambridge, since 2006; Distinguished Professor of Excellence in Combinatorics, University of Memphis, Tennessee, since 1995; b 3 Aug. 1943; s of Béla Bollobás and Emma Varga; m 1969, Gabriella Farkas; one s. Educ: Univ. of Budapest (BA 1966; Dr rer. nat. 1967); Univ. of Cambridge (PhD 1972; DSc 1984). Res. Scientist, Hungarian Acad. of Scis, 1966–69; Vis. Scientist, Soviet Acad. of Scis, 1967–68; Vis. Fellow, Oxford, 1969; Cambridge University: Res. Fellow, 1970–72, Dir of Studies in Maths, 1972–96, Trinity Coll.; Asst Lectr, 1971–74, Lectr in Maths, 1974–85; Reader in Pure Maths, 1985–96. Foreign Mem., Hungarian Acad. of Scis, 1990. Hon. Dr Adam Mickiewicz Univ., Poznan, 2013. *Publications:* Extremal Graph Theory, 1978; Graph Theory, 1979; Random Graphs, 1985, 2nd edn 2001; Combinatorics, 1986; Linear Analysis, 1990; Modern Graph Theory, 1998; (with O. M. O'Riordan) Percolation Theory, 2006; The Art of Mathematics, 2006; over 450 papers in learned jls. *Recreations:* books, opera, theatre, tennis, swimming, jogging, windsurfing, riding, ski-ing. *Address:* Trinity College, Cambridge CB2 1TQ; 5 Selwyn Gardens, Cambridge CB3 9AX. *T:* (01223) 354872; 1644 Neshoba Trace Cove, Germantown, TN 38138, USA. *T:* (901) 7514162.

**BOLLOM, Air Marshal Sir Simon (John),** KBE 2016; CB 2011; FREng, FRAeS; Chief Executive, Defence Equipment and Support, Ministry of Defence, since 2018; b London, 22 Jan. 1960; s of John and Mary Bollom; m 1988, Kathryn Megraw; one s one d. Educ: Grove Sch., Hastings; Hastings Grammar Sch.; Southampton Univ. (BSc Hons Mech. Engrg). MIMechE 1991; CEng 1991; FREng 2013. Joined RAF, 1981; Sen. Engrg Officer, 72 Sqn, 1992–94; OC Engrg Wing, RAF Odiham, 1998–99; Dir, Tactical Mobility, 2001–03; Team Leader, Tornado project, 2005–08; Dir, Combat Air, 2008–12; Chief of Materiel (Air), Defence Equipment and Support, MoD, 2012–16; RAF Chief Engr, 2012–16; Chief of Materiel (Ships), MoD, 2017–18. *Recreations:* hockey, cricket coach.

**BOLSOVER, George William, (Bill),** CBE 2011; Chairman, Aggregate Industries (HOLCIM), 2010–14; Director, B2 Consulting Ltd, since 2010; b Oxford, 10 Aug. 1950; s of Derrick and Yoma Bolsover; m 1972, Bridget Hope Lupkin; one s two d. Educ: Dragon Sch., Oxford; Worksop Coll., Notts. FRICS 2012. Trainee, Amey plc, 1972–74; Tarmac plc: Prodn Manager, 1974–82; Engrg and Technical Manager, 1982–84; Gen. Manager, 1984–88; Man. Dir, Topmix, 1988–92; Man. Dir, Roadstone East, 1992–95; Chief Operating Officer, Quarry Products, 1995–98; Exec. Dir, Tarmac plc, 1998–2000; Man. Dir, 2000–03, Gp CEO, Eur. and USA, 2003–05, Aggregate Industries plc; CEO, Aggregate Industries (HOLCIM) and Area Manager, HOLCIM Gp, 2005–10. Chairman: Natural World Safaris, 2007–; Cotswold Stone Solutions, 2015–; Hawk Plant Ltd, 2016–; non-exec. Dir, Robert Brett & Sons Ltd, 2013–. Vice Pres., Wildlife Trusts, 2010–15. Lt Col, RE and Logistics Staff Corps, RE (V), 2003. Hon. LLD Leicester, 2009. *E:* bill@b2consulting.co. *Club:* Worcester Rugby (Dir, 2012–; Chm., 2017–).

**BOLSOVER, John Derrick;** Chairman and Chief Executive, Baring Asset Management Holdings Ltd, 1995–2002; Corporate Adviser, Silver Heritage Group; b 21 June 1947; m 1st, 1971, Susan Elizabeth Peacock; two s one d; 2nd, 1994, Kate Woollett. Educ: Repton Sch.; McGill Univ., Canada (BA). Director: Baring Internat. Investment Mgt Ltd (Hong Kong), 1973–85; Baring Asset Mgt (Japan) Ltd, 1986–2002; Baring Asset Mgt Ltd, 1994–2002; Dep. Chm., Baring Hldgs Ltd, 1995–97; Dir, Baring Asset Mgt Hldgs Inc., 1996–98. Chm., Vpar Ltd, 2011–. *Recreation:* sport. *Clubs:* Boodle's, City; Sunningdale Golf; Valderrama Golf.

**BOLT, (Mohan) Paul;** Director, Sport and Leisure, Department for Culture, Media and Sport, 2008–11; b 8 Feb. 1954; s of Sydney Bolt and Jaya Bolt (née Chandran); m 1991, Carol Spekes. Educ: Trinity Coll., Cambridge (BA 1975); Open Univ. (MBA 1995). Joined Home Office as admin trainee, 1975: Principal, 1980–89; Hd, Mgt Div., 1989–92; Department of National Heritage, then Department for Culture, Media and Sport, 1992–2001: Head: Libraries Div., 1992–94; Fundamental Expenditure Rev., 1994–95; Broadcasting Bill Team, 1995–96; Broadcasting Policy Div., 1996–98; Dir, Strategy and Communications, 1998–2001; Dir, Broadcasting Standards Commn, 2001–03; Dir, Olympic Games Unit, DCMS, 2003–05; Interim Dir, Olympic Bd Secretariat, 2005–06; Dir, Capability Reviews Team, Cabinet Office, 2006–07. Non-exec. Dir, Horserace Betting Levy Bd, 2011–14. *Recreations:* cricket, theatre, reading, bridge. *Clubs:* Reform; Lancashire County Cricket.
*See also* R. R. Bolt.

**BOLT, Ranjit Ralph,** OBE 2003; writer and translator, since 1988; b Manchester, 10 Jan. 1959; s of Sydney Bolt and Jaya Bolt (née Chandran). Educ: Perse Sch., Cambridge; Balliol Coll., Oxford (BA Lit. Hum. 1982). Fund Manager: S. G. Warburg, 1982–88; Smith & Williamson, 1988–90; writer and translator, mainly of French verse plays, including: The Liar, 1989, The Illusion, 1990, Old Vic; Arturo Ui, NT 1991; Tartuffe, Playhouse Th., 1991; The Sisterhood, Chichester, 1991; The Venetian Twins, RSC, 1993; Lysistrata, Old Vic, 1993; Le Cid, NT, 1994; The School for Wives, Piccadilly Th., 1996; Cyrano de Bergerac, NY, 2012; co-writer, Hard Times (musical), 2002; lyricist, Merry Wives, The Musical, RSC, 2006. *Publications:* Losing It (novel in verse), 2001, 2nd edn 2012; The Art of Translation, 2010; translations: Corneille, The Liar, The Illusion and Le Cid, 1995; Tartuffe, 1995, 2nd version, 2001; The Sisterhood, 1995; The Venetian Twins, 1996; The School for Wives, 1997; Lysistrata, 2006; La Fontaine, The Hare and the Tortoise, 2006. *Recreations:* fishing, poker.
*See also* M. P. Bolt.

**BOLTON, 8th Baron** cr 1797, of Bolton Castle, co. York; **Harry Algar Nigel Orde-Powlett;** b 14 Feb. 1954; s of 7th Baron Bolton and of Hon. Christine, e d of 7th Baron Forester; S father, 2001; m 1977, Philippa (d 2016), d of Major Peter Tapply; three s. Educ: Eton. Heir: s Hon. Thomas Peter Algar Orde-Powlett, MC [b 16 July 1979; m 2008, Katie, d of Edward Gribble; two s two d]. *Address:* Fothering House, Wensley DL8 4HZ; Bolton Hall, Wensley, Leyburn, N Yorks DL8 4UF. *T:* (01969) 623674.

**BOLTON, Bishop Suffragan of,** since 2016; **Rt Rev. Mark David Ashcroft;** b Rugby, 3 Sept. 1954; s of David Ashcroft and Joan Ashcroft; m 1977, Sally; three s. Educ: Ridley Hall, Cambridge; Fitzwilliam Coll., Cambridge (BA 1981); Worcester Coll., Oxford (MA 1982). Manager, Cairngorm Restaurant, Edinburgh, 1978–79; ordained deacon, 1982, priest, 1983; Curate, St Margaret, Burnage, 1982–85; Tutor, subseq. Principal, St Paul's Theol Coll., Kapsabet, Kenya, 1986–95; Rector, Christ Church, Harpurhey, 1996–2009; Area Dean, N Manchester, 2000–06; Archdeacon of Manchester, 2009–16. Hon. Canon, Manchester Cathedral, 2004–09. *Recreations:* RSPB (Mem.), photography, sport. *Address:* Bishop's Lodge, Walkden Road, Worsley, Manchester M28 2WH.

**BOLTON, Archdeacon of;** see Burgess, Ven. J. A.

**BOLTON, Anthony John;** Senior Adviser, since 2014, and Director, since 2015, Fidelity International (formerly Fidelity International, then Fidelity Worldwide Investment) (President - Investment, 2008–14); b London, 7 March 1950; s of Alwyn and Betty Bolton; m 1979, Sarah Boyce; two s one d. Educ: Stowe Sch.; Trinity Coll., Cambridge (BA 1971; MA). Keyser Ullmann, 1971–76; Schlesinger Investments, 1976–79; Portfolio Manager, 1979–2008, 2010–14, Dir, UK, 1979–2014, Fidelity Internat., then Fidelity Worldwide Investment, later Fidelity Internat. *Publications:* Investing Against the Tide, 2009. *Recreation:* classical music (listening and writing).
*See also* E. J. Bolton.

**BOLTON, Her Honour Beatrice Maud;** a Circuit Judge, 2001–12; b 26 July 1953; d of late Arthur Henry Bolton and of Freda Bolton; divorced; one s. Educ: Newcastle upon Tyne Church High Sch.; Sheffield Univ. (LLB Hons). Called to the Bar, Gray's Inn, 1975; Asst Recorder, 1994–98; a Recorder, 1998–2001. *Recreations:* playing tennis, gardening, watching football, horse riding.

**BOLTON, Catriona;** see Jarvis, C.

**BOLTON, Group Captain David;** Director, Royal United Services Institute, 1981–94 (Deputy Director, 1980–81); b 15 April 1932; o s of late George Edward and Florence May Bolton; m 1955, Betty Patricia Simmonds (d 2019); three d. Educ: Bede Sch., Co. Durham. Commnd RAF Regt, 1953; subsequent service in Egypt, Jordan, Singapore, Aden, Cyprus, Malta and Germany; RAF Staff Coll., 1969; National Def. Coll., 1972; Central Planning Staff, MoD, 1973–75; OC 33 Wing RAF Regt, 1975–77; Comdt RAF Regt Depot, Catterick, 1977–80; retd 1980. Chm., Macbeth Associates, 1994–2000; Vice-Chm., TASC Eur., 1994–97; Dir, Project Constant Endeavour, 2000–04. Member: RUSI Council, 1973–79; IISS, 1964–90; RIIA, 1975–92; Council, British Atlantic Cttee, 1981–91; Bd of War Studies, Univ. of London, 1984–92; a founding Mem., Adv. Bd, British-American Project, 1985–99. Hon. Steward, Westminster Abbey, 1981–2004. Trench Gascoigne Essay Prize, RUSI, 1972. Editor: Brassey's Defence Year Bk, 1982–92; MacMillan-RUSI Defence Studies, 1982–94; RUSI Internat. Security Review, 1992–94. *Publications:* contrib. learned jls. *Recreations:* choral music, international affairs. *Club:* Royal Air Force.

**BOLTON, David Michael William;** education consultant; Head Master, Dame Alice Owen's School, 1981–94; b 29 Feb. 1936; s of William Benedict Bolton and Edith Phyllis Bolton; m 1961, Janet Christine Fleming; two s one d. Educ: St Francis Xavier's Coll., Liverpool; St Edmund Hall, Oxford (BA 1960; MA 1964); DipEd London 1971. Nat. Service, RAF (Coastal Command), 1955–57. Reckitt & Colman Ltd, 1960–62; Alleyn's Sch., Dulwich, 1962–63; Housemaster, Highgate Sch., 1963–72; Dep. Head, Chancellor's Sch., Herts, 1972–74; Headmaster, Davenant Foundn Grammar Sch., 1974–81. OFSTED Inspector, 1995–2000. Mem. Council, Secondary Heads Assoc., 1991–94 (Chm., Area Five). FRSA 1993. Freeman, City of London, 1994. *Publications:* articles and reviews in TES. *Recreations:* reading, music, travel, walking, family history. *Address:* Mayfield, 8 Wykeham Gate, Haddenham, Bucks HP17 8DF.

**BOLTON, Eric James,** CB 1987; Deputy Chairman, New Opportunities Fund, 2001–04 (Member Board, 1998–2004); b 11 Jan. 1935; s of late James and Lilian Bolton; m 1960, Ann Gregory; one s twin d. Educ: Wigan Grammar Sch.; Chester Coll.; Lancaster Univ. MA. English teacher at secondary schs, 1957–68; Lectr, Chorley Teacher Training Coll., 1968–70; Inspector of Schs, Croydon, 1970–73; HM Inspector of Schs, 1973–79; Staff Inspector (Educnl Disadvantage), 1979–81; Chief Inspector of Schools, DES, 1981–83, Sen. Chief Inspector of Schools, 1983–91; Prof. of Teacher Educn, Inst. of Educn, London Univ., 1991–96. Chairman: Book Trust, 1997–2000 (Vice Chm., 1996–97); ITC Schs Adv. Cttee, 1997–2000; Member: Educn Adv. Cttee, LSO, 1997–2013; Educn Cttee, NESTA, 1999–2002; Trustee, Foundn of Young Musicians, 1992–2010. *Publications:* Verse Writing in Schools, 1964; various articles in educnl jls. *Recreations:* reading, music and opera, fly fishing. *Address:* 44 Saffrons Court, Compton Place Road, Eastbourne BN21 1DY.

**BOLTON, Erica Jane,** OBE 2014; Director, Bolton & Quinn Ltd, since 1981; b 29 June 1953; d of Alwyn Bolton and Betty Bolton (née Pile); m 1986, Robert Alwyn Petrie Hewison, qv; two d. Educ: Westonbirt Sch.; Westfield Coll., Univ. of London (BA Hist. and Hist. of Art 1974). Established Erica Bolton and Jane Quinn Ltd, 1981. *Recreations:* walking, going to museums. *Address:* c/o Bolton & Quinn Ltd, 6 Addison Avenue, W11 4QR. *T:* (020) 7221 5000.
*See also* A. J. Bolton.

**BOLTON, Ivor;** conductor; Music Director (formerly Chief Conductor), Dresden Festival Orchestra, since 2012; Music Director: Teatro Real Madrid, since 2015; Basel Symphony Orchestra, since 2016; Chief Conductor (formerly Music Director), Salzburg Mozarteum Orchestra, 2004–16, now Conductor Laureate; b 17 May 1958; s of Cyril John Bolton and Elsie Bolton (née Worthington); m 1984, Tessa Wendy Knighton, qv; one s. Educ: Queen Elizabeth's GS, Blackburn; Clare Coll., Cambridge (MusB, MA); Royal Coll. of Music (schol.); Nat. Opera Studio. FRCO (CHM) 1976; LRAM 1976. Conductor, Schola Cantorum of Oxford, 1981–82; Music Dir, St James's, Piccadilly, 1982–90; Chorus Master, Glyndebourne, 1985–88; Music Director: English Touring Opera, 1990–93; Glyndebourne Touring Opera, 1992–97; Chief Conductor, Scottish Chamber Orchestra, 1993–96. Founder Dir, St James's Baroque Players, 1984–; Founder and Music Dir, Lufthansa Fest. of Baroque Music, 1985–. Bayerische Staatsopen début, 1994; Royal Opera début, world première of Goehr's Arianna, 1995; Salzburg Fest. début, 2000. Has made several recordings. Bayerische Theaterpreis, Bavarian Govt, 1998; Seal of City of Salzburg, 2010; Grosses Verdienstzeichen (Austria), 2016. *Recreation:* football (keen follower of Arsenal and Blackburn Rovers). *Address:* Graben 12, 1010 Vienna, Austria. *Club:* Garrick.

**BOLTON, John Robert,** JD; National Security Advisor, United States of America, 2018–19; b 20 Nov. 1948; s of Edward Jackson Bolton and Virginia Bolton (née Godfrey); m 1986, Gretchen Brainerd; one d. Educ: Yale Coll. (BA 1970); Yale Law Sch. (JD 1974). Associate, 1974–81, Partner, 1983–85, Covington & Burling, Washington; Gen. Counsel, 1981–82, Asst Adminr, 1982–83, US Agency for Internat. Develt; Asst Attorney Gen., Legislative Affairs, 1985–88, Civil Div., 1988–89, US Dept of Justice; Asst Sec. of State, Internat. Orgn, 1989–93; Partner, Lerner, Reed Bolton & McManus, Washington, 1993–99; Of Counsel, Kutak Rock LLP, 1999–2001; Under Sec. of State, Arms Control and Internat. Security, 2001–05; US Perm. Rep. to UN, 2005–06. Sen. Advr, Kirkland and Ellis, 2008–18. Pres. Nat. Policy Forum, 1995–96; Mem., US Commn on Internat. Religious Freedom, 1999–2001. Adjunct Prof., George Mason Univ., Virginia, 1994–2001. Sen. Vice Pres., 1997–2001, Sen. Fellow, 2007–18, American Enterprise Inst.; Sen. Fellow, Manhattan Inst., 1993. *Publications:* Surrender is Not an Option: defending America at the United Nations and Abroad, 2007; contributor: The Bush Presidency, 1997; Delusions of Grandeur: the United Nations and global intervention, 1997; US International Leadership in the 21st Century, 2000; The Oxford Companion to Politics of the World, 2nd edn 2001; contrib. numerous articles to Wall Street Jl, Washington Post, Washington Times, LA Times, and to jls incl. Foreign Policy, Foreign Affairs, Eur. Jl, National Interest, Legal Times.

**BOLTON, Tessa Wendy;** see Knighton, T. W.

**BOMBAY, Archbishop of, (RC),** since 2006; **His Eminence Cardinal Oswald Gracias;** b 24 Dec. 1944; s of Jervis and Aduzinda Gracias. Educ: St Xavier's Coll., Ranchi (BA 1976); Urban Univ., Rome (DCL 1982); Gregorian Univ., Rome (Dip. Jurisprudence 1982). Ordained priest, 1970; Sec. and Chancellor, Dio. of Jamshedpur, 1971–76; Sec. to

Archbp of Bombay, 1982–86; Chancellor, Archdio. of Bombay, 1982–97; Aux. Bishop of Bombay, 1997–2000; Archbishop of Agra, 2000–06. Cardinal, 2007. Judicial Vicar, 1988–98, Vicar Gen., 1998–2000, Archdio. of Bombay. President: Canon Law Soc. of India, 1987–91 and 1993–97; Catholic Bishops' Conf. of India, 2005– (Sec. Gen., 1998–2002). *Address:* Archbishop's House, 21 Nathalal Parekh Marg, Mumbai 400 001, India.

BOMFORD, David Robert Lee; Chairman, Department of Conservation, 2012–19, and Head of European Art, 2015–19, Museum of Fine Arts, Houston, Texas; Secretary-General, International Institute for Conservation, 1994–2003; *b* 31 March 1946; *s* of Donald James Bomford and Margaret Vanstone Bomford (*née* Spalding); *m* 1st, 1969, Helen Graham (marr. diss. 1989); one *s* two *d*; 2nd, 1990, Zahira Véliz; one *s* one *d. Educ:* Merchant Taylors' Sch.; Univ. of Sussex (BSc 1967; MSc 1968). Asst Restorer, 1968–74, Sen. Restorer of Paintings, 1974–2007, National Gall.; Associate Dir for Collections, 2007–10, Acting Dir, 2010–12, J. Paul Getty Mus., LA (Guest Scholar, 2005). Editor, Studies in Conservation, 1981–91. Vis. Prof., Churubusco Nat. Inst. of Conservation, Mexico City, 1987; Slade Prof. of Fine Art, Univ. of Oxford, 1996–97; Edmond J. Safra Vis. Prof., Center for Advanced Study in Visual Arts, Nat. Gall. of Art, Washington, 2018. Trustee, V&A Mus., 2019–. FIIC 1979. DUniv Sussex, 2016. Coll. of Art Assoc./Heritage Preservation Award for Distinction in Scholarship and Conservation, 2010. *Publications:* Art in the Making: Rembrandt, 1988; Art in the Making: Italian painting before 1400, 1989; Art in the Making: Impressionism, 1990; Conservation of Paintings, 1997; Venice through Canaletto's Eyes, 1998; Colour, 2000; Art in the Making: underdrawings in Renaissance paintings, 2002; Art in the Making: Degas, 2004; Readings in Conservation, 2004; Unfinished Paintings: narratives of the Non Finito, 2015; Vincent van Gogh: his life in art, 2019. *Recreations:* walking, travel, theatre. *Address:* Frog Firle Manor, White Way, Alfriston, E Sussex BN26 5TT. *E:* dbomford@hotmail.co.uk.

BOMFORD, Nicholas Raymond, MA; Head Master of Harrow, 1991–99; *b* 27 Jan. 1939; *s* of late Ernest Raymond Bomford and Patricia Clive Bomford (*née* Brooke), JP; *m* 1966, Gillian Mary Reynolds; two *d. Educ:* Kelly Coll.; Trinity Coll., Oxford (MA, Mod. History). Teaching appts, 1960–64; Lectr in History and Contemp. Affairs, BRNC, Dartmouth, 1964–66, Sen. Lectr, 1966–68; Wellington Coll., 1968–76 (Housemaster, 1973–76); Headmaster: Monmouth Sch., 1977–82; Uppingham Sch., 1982–91. Chm., Jt Standing Cttee, HMC/IAPS, 1986–89; Nat. Rep., HMC Cttee, 1990–91; Mem., Exec. Cttee, Assoc. Governing Bodies of Ind. Schs, 2003–08. Mem. Navy Records Soc. (Councillor, 1967–70, 1973–76, 1984–88). Governor: Sherborne Sch. for Girls, 1994–2007 (Chm., 2000–07); Elstree Prep. Sch., 1996–2009 (Chm., 2001–09); Lord Wandsworth Coll., 1999–2006; Kelly Coll., 1999–2008; Malvern Coll., 2000–06. Chm., Usk Rural Life Mus., Monmouthshire, 2002–11 (Vice-Pres., 2011–); Pres., Tregate Anglers, 2010–14. Freeman, Haberdashers' Co., 1992. *Publications:* Documents in World History, 1914–70, 1973; (contrib.) Dictionary of World History, 1973; Brothers in War: letters from the Western Front, 2013; The Long Meadow: a life in schools, 2013; The Bomfords of Atch Lench: four hundred years of a farming family, 2016. *Recreations:* shooting (Captain OURC, 1959–60; England VIII (Elcho match), 1960), fishing, gardening, music, enjoying Welsh border country and travel in the USA. *Address:* Long Meadow House, Millend, Newland, Glos GL16 8NF.

BOMPAS, (Anthony) George; QC 1994; *b* 6 Nov. 1951; *s* of Donald George Bompas, CMG; *m* 1981, Donna Linda (*d* 2018), *d* of J. O. Schmidt; two *s* one *d. Educ:* Merchant Taylors' Sch., Northwood; Oriel Coll., Oxford (Schol., MA). Called to the Bar, Middle Temple, 1975; Bencher, Lincoln's Inn, 2001. Junior Counsel (Chancery), DTI, 1989–94; Ordinary Judge of Courts of Appeal of Guernsey and Jersey, 2014–. Liveryman, Merchant Taylors' Co., 1982–. *Address:* 4 Stone Buildings, Lincoln's Inn, WC2A 3XT. *T:* (020) 7242 5524.

BON, Michel Marie; Chairman, Devoteam, 2006–13; *b* 5 July 1943; *s* of Emmanuel Bon and Mathilde (*née* Aussedat); *m* 1971, Catherine de Sairigné; one *s* three *d. Educ:* Lycée Champollion, Grenoble; Ecole supérieure des scis économiques et commerciales, Paris; Inst. d'Etudes Politiques, Paris; Ecole Nat. d'Administration, Paris. Insp. of Finance, Min. of Finance, 1971–75; Crédit National, 1975–78; Caisse Nat. de Crédit Agricole, 1978–85; Carrefour, 1985–93 (Chm. and CEO, 1990–93); Dir, Agence Nationale pour l'Emploi, France, 1993–95; Chm. and CEO, France Telecom, 1995–2002; Chairman: Editions du Cerf, 1997–2013; Institut Pasteur, 2003–05. Chairman: Fondation Nat. pour l'Enseignement de la Gestion des Entreprises, 2008–17; Fondact, 2009–. *Address:* 4 avenue de Camoëns, 75116 Paris, France.

BONA, Sir Kina, KBE 1993; Judge of the National and Supreme Court, Papua New Guinea, since 2014; Resident Judge, Bougainville, since 2015; *b* 14 Feb. 1954; *m* 1990, Judith Lilian Sharples; one *d. Educ:* Univ. of Papua New Guinea (LLB 1976). Legal Officer, PNG, 1976–78; Teaching Fellow, Univ. of PNG, 1979; Sen. Legal Officer, 1980–82; Asst Sec., Dept of Justice, 1985–87; Public Prosecutor, PNG, 1988–94; High Comr for PNG in the UK, 1996–2002; lawyer in private practice, 2002–07 and 2012–14; Dep. Registrar, 2007–08, Registrar, 2009–12, Integrity of Political Parties and Candidates Commn, PNG. Pres., PNG Law Soc., 2012–14. *Address:* PO Box 58, Waigani, National Capital District, Papua New Guinea.

BONALLACK, Sir Michael (Francis), Kt 1998; OBE 1971; Director, The Old Course Ltd (St Andrews), since 1990; *b* 31 Dec. 1934; *s* of Sir Richard (Frank) Bonallack, CBE; *m* 1958, Angela Ward; one *s* three *d. Educ:* Chigwell; Haileybury. National Service, 1953–55 (1st Lieut, RASC). Joined family business, Bonallack and Sons Ltd, later Freight Bonallack Ltd, 1955, Dir, 1962–74; Dir, Buckley Investments, 1976–84. Sec., 1983–99, Captain, 1999, Royal and Ancient Golf Club of St Andrews. Non-exec. Dir, PGA European Tour, 2000–15. Chairman: Golf Foundn, 1977–83 (Pres., 2000–02); Professional Golfers' Assoc., 1976–82; President: English Golf Union, 1982; PGA of Europe, 2003–04. Hon. Fellow, Myerscough Coll., 2000. DUniv Stirling, 1994; Hon. LLD: Abertay, Dundee, 2000; St Andrews, 2003. *Recreation:* golf (British Amateur Champion, 1961, 1965, 1968, 1969, 1970; English Amateur Champion, 1962–63, 1965–67 and 1968; Captain, British Walker Cup Team, 1969, 1971; Bobby Jones Award for distinguished sportsmanship in golf, 1972). *Address:* The Croft, Blebo Craigs, Cupar, Fife KY15 5UF. *T:* (01334) 850498. *Clubs:* Royal and Ancient Golf Club (St Andrews); Golf House (Elie); Pine Valley, Ocean Forest, Augusta, Frederica (USA); Hermanus (RSA); Chantilly (France).

BOND, Andrew, CEng; Executive Chairman: Euro Garages, 2011; Poundland, 2017; Director, Pepkor UK, 2014; *b* Grantham, 16 March 1965; *s* of Terence and Christine Bond; *m* 1997, Susan Stringfellow; one *s* one *d. Educ:* King's Grammar Sch., Grantham; Salford Univ. (BSc 1st Cl. Hons 1987); Cranfield Sch. of Mgt (MBA 1993); CEng 1992. Grad. prog., British Gas, 1987–88; Product Dir and Mktg Manager, Hopkinsons Plc, 1988–92; Mktg Manager, 1994–97, Corporate Mktg Dir, 1997–99, Asda; Eur. Own Label Dir, Asda and Wal-Mart Germany, 1999–2000; Man. Dir, George at Asda, 2000–04; Chief Operating Officer, Asda, and Man. Dir, Global George, 2004–05; Pres. and CEO, 2005–10, Chm., 2010–11, Asda; Exec. Vice Pres., Walmart, 2010–11; Exec. Chm., Republic, 2011–13. *Recreations:* running, cycling. *E:* andy@woodcliffeassociates.com.

BOND, Prof. Brian James, FRHistS; Professor of Military History, King's College, University of London, 1986–2001, now Emeritus; *b* 17 April 1936; *s* of Edward Herbert Bond and Olive Bessie Bond (*née* Sartin); *m* 1962, Madeleine Joyce Carr. *Educ:* Sir William Borlase's Sch., Marlow; Worcester Coll., Oxford (BA Hist. 1959); King's Coll. London (MA Hist. 1962; FKC 1996). FRHistS 1978. Nat. Service, 1954–56, commnd RA. Tutor in Mod. Hist., Univ. of Exeter, 1961–62; Lectr, Univ. of Liverpool, 1962–66; King's College London: Lectr in War Studies, 1966–78; Reader, 1978–86. Vis. Prof., Univ. of Western Ontario, 1972–73; Visiting Fellow: Brasenose Coll., Oxford, 1992–93; All Souls Coll., Oxford, 2000. Liddell Hart Lectr, KCL, 1997; Lees Knowles Lectr, Cambridge Univ., 2000; War Studies Lectr, KCL, 2001. Mem. Council, RUSI, 1972–84. Pres., British Commn for Mil. Hist., 1986–2006. Member Editorial Board: Jl Contemp. Hist., 1988–2004; Jl Strategic Studies, 1978–2005; Jl Mil. Hist. (USA), 1992–96; War in Hist., 1994–; an Associate Editor, Oxford DNB, 1996–2002. *Publications:* (ed) Victorian Military Campaigns, 1967, 2nd edn 1994; The Victorian Army and the Staff College, 1972, repr. 2015; (ed) Chief of Staff: the diaries of Lt-Gen. Sir Henry Pownall 1933–1944, vol. 1, 1972, vol. 2, 1974; Britain, France and Belgium, 1939–1940, 1975, 2nd edn 1990; Liddell Hart: a study of his military thought, 1977, 2nd edn 1991; British Military Policy between the Two World Wars, 1980; War and Society in Europe 1870–1970, 1984; (ed with S. Robbins) Staff Officer: the diaries of Lord Moyne 1914–1918, 1987; (ed) The First World War and British Military History, 1991; (ed) Fallen Stars: eleven studies of twentieth century military disasters, 1991; The Pursuit of Victory: from Napoleon to Saddam Hussein, 1996; (ed with N. Cave) Haig: a reappraisal 70 years on, 1999; The Unquiet Western Front: Britain's role in literature and history, 2002; (ed) War Memoirs of Earl Stanhope 1914–1918, 2006; Survivors of a Kind: memoirs of the Western Front, 2008; Liddell Hart and the Western Front, 2010; Britain's Two World Wars Against Germany: myth, memory and the distortions of hindsight, 2014; Studies in British Military History, 2015; Military Historian: my part in the birth and development of war studies, 1966–2016, 2018. *Recreations:* gardening, visiting country houses, observing and protecting wild animals (especially foxes). *Address:* Olmeda, Ferry Lane, Medmenham, Marlow, Bucks SL7 2EZ. *T:* (01491) 571293.

BOND, David James; Security and Defence Editor, Financial Times, since 2017 (Media Correspondent, until 2017); *b* London, 6 Aug. 1973; *s* of George and Jacqueline Bond; *m* 2006, Lucy Edwards; two *s* one *d. Educ:* Wallington High Sch. for Boys; Univ. of Southampton (BA Hons 1995); King's Coll. London (Postgrad. Cert. Sports Law 2004). Sports news reporter: Evening Standard, 1998–2002; Sunday Times, 2002–04; Dep. Sports Ed., Evening Standard, 2004–06; Daily Telegraph: sports news corresp., 2006–08; Sports Ed., 2008–10; Sports Ed., BBC, 2010–14. *Recreations:* running, cricket, reading. *Address:* Financial Times, Bracken House, 1 Friday Street, EC4M 9BT. *Club:* MCC.

BOND, Edward; playwright and director; *b* 18 July 1934; *m* 1971, Elisabeth Pablé. Northern Arts Literary Fellow, 1977–79. Hon. DLitt Yale, 1977. George Devine Award, 1968; John Whiting Award, 1968; Obie Award, 1976; City of Lyon Medal, 2007. *Opera Libretti:* We Come to the River (music by Hans Werner Henze), 1976; The English Cat (music by Hans Werner Henze), 1982; Early Morning (music by Laura Bowler), 2019; *ballet libretto:* Orpheus, 1982; *translations:* Chekhov, The Three Sisters, 1967; Wedekind, Spring Awakening, 1974; Wedekind, Lulu—a monster tragedy, 1992. Hon. DLitt Newman, 2013. *Publications:* Theatre Poems and Songs, 1978; Collected Poems 1978–1985, 1987; Notes on Post-Modernism, 1990; Notes on Imagination, 1995; Selected Letters (5 vols), 1994–2004; Selected Notebooks, vol. 1, 2000, vol. 2, 2001; The Hidden Plot: notes on theatre and the state, 2000; My Day, a song cycle for young people, 2005; The Playwright Speaks: interviews with David Tuallion, 2015; *plays:* The Pope's Wedding, 1962; Saved, 1965; Narrow Road to the Deep North, 1968; Early Morning, 1968; Passion, 1971; Black Mass, 1971; Lear, 1972; The Sea, 1973; Bingo, 1974; The Fool, 1976; A-A-America! (Grandma Faust, and The Swing), 1976; Stone, 1976; The Woman, 1978; The Bundle, 1978; The Worlds with The Activist Papers, 1980; Restoration, 1981; Summer: a play for Europe, and Fables (short stories), 1982; Derek, 1983; Human Cannon, 1984; The War Plays (part 1, Red Black and Ignorant; part 2, The Tin Can People; part 3, Great Peace), 1985; Jackets, 1989; In The Company of Men, 1990; September, 1990; Olly's Prison, 1993; Tuesday, 1993; Coffee: a tragedy, 1995; At the Inland Sea: a play for young people, 1996; Eleven Vests, 1997; The Crime of the Twenty-first Century, 1998; The Children: a play for two adults and sixteen children, 2000; Chair, 2000; Have I None, 2000; Existence, 2002; The Balancing Act, 2003; The Short Elektra, 2004; The Under Room, 2005; Born, 2006; People, 2006; Arcade, 2006; Tune, 2007; Innocence, 2009; A Window, 2009; There Will Be More, 2010; The Edge, 2011; The Hungry Bowl, 2011; The Angry Roads, 2016; The Testament of This Day, 2016; Dea, 2016; The Price of One, 2016; Edward Bond Plays (10 vols), 1977–2018. *Address:* c/o Casarotto Ramsay, Waverley House, 7–12 Noel Street, W1F 8GQ. *E:* mel@casarotto.co.uk. *W:* www.edwardbond.org.

BOND, Geoffrey Charles, OBE 2008; DL; FSA; heritage consultant; Chairman, Geoffrey Bond Consultancy, since 1996; *b* 14 Oct. 1939; *s* of Frederick Richard Bond and Dorothy Bond (*née* Gardner); *m* 1963, Dianora Dunnet; one *s* one *d. Educ:* Becket Sch., Nottingham; Univ. of Hull (BSc Econ Hons 1963). FSA 2008. Baring Bros, London, 1963–64; admitted solicitor, 1969; articled to Ashton Hill & Co., Nottingham, later Ashton Bond Gigg, 1964–68, Partner, 1970–85, Sen. Partner, 1985–96. Chairman: Linpack Packaging plc, 1982–89; Old Market Square Securities, 1984–99; non-executive Director: Charles Lawrence Gp plc, 1973–2013; Hooley Gp of Cos, 1976–2016; Regl Bd, Central Ind. TV plc, 1982–92. Hon. Solicitor to: British Sporting Art Trust, London, 1977–2008; Derby Internat. Porcelain Soc., 1985–2011. Mem., E Midlands Cttee, NT, 1988–97; Dep. Chm., Nat. Mus. of Law and Nat. Centre for Citizenship and the Law, 1993–2015; Chairman: Arts & Business Midlands, 1999–2003; Gp for Educn in Museums, 2001–07; London Livery Cos Collections Adv. Gp, 2008–14; Member: Council, MLA, 2006–12 (Chm., MLA London, 2002–09); London Cultural Strategy Gp, 2010–16; Acceptance in Lieu Panel, MLA, then Arts Council England, 2006–12; Council, Soc. of Antiquaries, 2013–. Mem., Editl Bd, Byron Jl (Chm., 1996–2003); Chairman: London Byron Soc., 1996–2003 (Vice Pres., 2004–); Scottish Byron Soc., 2008–. Founder Trustee, Papplewick Pumping Stn Trust, 1976–2015 (Chm., 1999–2015); Norwegian Business Scholars Trust, Bridge Ward Club, 2002–; Chairman: Water Educn Trust, 2005–15; Chizel Trust, 2013–; Founder, 2010, and Chm., Lord Mayor of London's Cultural Scholarships Scheme, 2010–; Chairman: Curatorial Adv. Panel, Guildhall Art Gall., 2010–15; Rolls Bldg Art and Educn Trust, 2011–; Livery Cos King James Bible Educn Project, 2011. Patron, British Red Cross, Notts, 2010–; Trustee of Council, Liby and Mus. of Freemasonry, 2009–. President: Southwell Archaeology Gp, 2013–; Newark and Notts Agricl Soc., 2015–16; Founder and Chm., Midlands Agricl Engrg Traineeship and Apprenticeship Educn Scheme, 2016–. Sponsor, Southwell Music Fest., 2014–. Mem., City of London Gp, St John Ambulance (formerly City of London Cttee, St John Ambulance (Prince of Wales') Dist), 2003–12. Hon. Consul for Norway in Midlands, 1981–2007; Chm., Assoc. of Hon. Norwegian Consuls in British Isles and Ireland, 1997–99. *Radio:* presenter, The Antiques Shop, Radio Nottingham, 1973–80; *television:* Mem., team of experts, Antiques Roadshow, 1979–84; presenter, Something to Treasure (series), 1985–91; *television films:* producer, Byron's Mine, 1994; assistant producer: The Heart of Shelley, 1992; The Sweet Life, 1997. Sheriff, 2003–04, Dep. Gauger, 2004, City of London; Chm., Livery Cttee, 2007–10; Liveryman: Co. of

Glaziers and Painters of Glass, 1973 (Mem., Ct of Assts, 1992; Master, 1997); Co. of Clockmakers, 2010; Member: Guild of Freemen, 2003–16; City of London Sheriffs' Soc., 2004–; Hon. Liveryman (formerly Mem.), Co. (formerly Guild) of Educators, 2002–; Founder Liveryman, Co. (formerly Guild) of Arts Scholars, 2014–; Mem. Court, City of London Solicitors' Co., 2006–08. Hon. DLaws Nottingham, 2013. DL Notts, 1998. OStJ 2004. Lifetime Achievement Award: City Livery Club, 2014; Nottingham Heritage Forum, 2014. Kt First Class, Royal Norwegian Order of Merit, 1989. *Publications:* (contrib.) Byron: the image of the poet, 2008; (contrib.) Sir Walter Scott Club Celebration Edinburgh Edition Waverley novels, 2010; Lord Byron's Best Friends: from bulldogs to Boatswain and beyond, 2013; articles for learned jls incl. Byron Jl, Newstead Byron Soc. Rev., Studies in Romanticism, Sir Walter Scott Club Rev., Keats-Shelley Jl, Collectors Guide, Trans Thoroton Soc. *Recreations:* antiquarian book collecting, gardening, entertaining, music, giving lectures, rowing. *Address:* Burgage Manor, Southwell, Notts NG25 0EP. *T:* (01636) 816855. *E:* consultancy@gbond.demon.co.uk. *Clubs:* Garrick, Bridge Ward; City Pickwick.

See also Sir M. R. Bond.

**BOND, Ian Andrew Minton,** CVO 2006; Director, Foreign Policy, Centre for European Reform, since 2013; *b* 19 April 1962; *s* of Roy and Joan Bond; *m* 1987, Kathryn Joan Ingamells; two *s* one *d*. *Educ:* King Edward VI Sch., Birmingham; Phillips Acad., Andover, Mass; Balliol Coll., Oxford (BA Hons). Joined Diplomatic Service, 1984; FCO, 1984–87; Mem., UK Delegn to NATO, 1987–90; FCO, 1990–93; First Secretary: Moscow, 1993–96; FCO, 1996–2000; Counsellor and Dep. Hd of Mission, UK Delegn to OSCE, Vienna, 2000–04; Ambassador to Latvia, 2005–07; Counsellor, Washington, 2007–12. *Recreations:* music, opera, choral singing, travel, reading. *Address:* Centre for European Reform, 14 Great College Street, Westminster, SW1P 3RX.

**BOND, Jennie, (Mrs James Keltz);** broadcaster and professional speaker; television presenter, since 2003; *b* 19 Aug. 1950; *d* of late Kenneth Bond and Pamela Bond; *m* 1982, James Keltz; one *d*, and one step *s* one step *d*. *Educ:* St Francis' Coll., Letchworth; Univ. of Warwick. Reporter: Richmond Herald, 1972–75; Evening Mail, Uxbridge, 1975–77; News Producer, BBC, 1977–86; News Corresp., 1986–89, Court Corresp., 1989–2003, BBC. *Publications:* Reporting Royalty (autobiog.), 2001; Elizabeth, Fifty Glorious Years, 2002; Elizabeth, 80 Glorious Years, 2006; Elizabeth: a Diamond Jubilee portrait, 2012; Elizabeth: a celebration in photographs of the Queen's life and reign, 2016; Elizabeth and Philip, 2017. *Recreations:* country life, coastal walks, entertaining friends and family, bopping to bands in our local pub. *Address:* c/o Knight Ayton, 29 Gloucester Place, W1U 8HX.

**BOND, Jeremy Viktor, (Jez);** Founder, 2010, and Artistic Director, since 2013, Park Theatre; *b* Kingston upon Thames, Surrey, 25 May 1977; *s* of Jeremy Bond and Viktoria Bond (née Lengyel Rheinfuss); partner, Awsa Bergstrøm; one *d*. *Educ:* Oundle Sch.; Dulwich Coll.; Univ. of Hull (BA Hons Drama). Freelance th. dir, 1998–2009; trained at Watford Palace Th. (Channel Four Th. Dir Bursary), 2002–04; plays directed include: A Season in South Africa, Old Vic, 2000; Big Boys, Warehouse, Croydon, 2002; Canaries Sometimes Sing, Kings Head and France, 2003; Misconceptions, Hong Kong Arts Centre, 2004; I Have Been Here Before, Watford Palace, 2005; Oliver!, Oxford, 2005; Sleeping Beauty, Salisbury Playhouse, 2006; Shot of Genius, Leicester Sq., 2006; The Twits, Switzerland tour, 2007; The Fame Game, tour of Austria, 2010; Park Theatre: Adult Supervision, Sleeping Beauty, 2013; Jack and the Beanstalk, 2014; Hurling Rubble at the Moon, 2015; Rapunzel, 2015; Madame Rubinstein, 2017; Building the Wall, 2018. *Recreations:* singing, composing, dog training, comedy, never having enough time to play tennis. *Address:* Park Theatre, Clifton Terrace, N4 3JP. *T:* (020) 7870 6876. *E:* info@parktheatre.co.uk. *Club:* h.

**BOND, Sir John (Reginald Hartnell),** Kt 1999; Chairman: Glencore Xstrata plc (formerly Xstrata), 2011–13; Vodafone, 2006–11 (non-executive Director, 2005–11); *b* 24 July 1941; *s* of late Capt. R. H. A. Bond, OBE and E. C. A. Bond; *m* 1968, Elizabeth Caroline Parker; one *s* two *d*. *Educ:* Tonbridge Sch., Kent; Cate Sch., Calif, USA (E-SU Scholar). Joined Hongkong & Shanghai Banking Corp., 1961; worked in Hong Kong, Thailand, Singapore, Indonesia and USA; Chief Exec., Wardley Ltd (Merchant Banking), 1984–87; Hongkong & Shanghai Banking Corporation: Exec. Dir, 1988–91; responsible for: Americas, 1988–89; commercial banking, based in Hong Kong, 1990–91; Pres. and Chief Exec., Marine Midland Banks Inc., Buffalo, USA, 1991–92. Chairman: Hongkong Bank of Canada, 1987–98; HSBC Americas Inc., 1997–2003; Marine Midland Bank, then HSBC Bank USA, 1997–2003; British Bank of the Middle East, then HSBC Bank Middle East, 1998–2004; Midland Bank, then HSBC Bank Plc, 1998–2004; Gp Chief Exec., 1993–98, Gp Chm., 1998–2006, HSBC Hldgs plc; Director: Hang Seng Bank Ltd, 1990–96; HSBC Hldgs, 1990–2006; HSBC Bank plc (formerly Midland Bank), 1993–2004 (Dep. Chm., 1996–98); Bank of England, 2001–04; HSBC N Amer. Hldgs Inc., 2005–06; Advr, KKR Asia, 2006–; non-executive Director: London Stock Exchange, 1994–99; British Steel, 1994–98; Orange plc, 1996–99; Ford Motor Co., 2000–08; Shui On Land Ltd, Hong Kong, 2006–; A P Moller-Maersk A/S, 2008–16; non-executive Advisory Director: Northern Trust Corp., 2009–15; Northern Trust Co., 2009–15; Mem., Adv. Cttee, Mitsubishi, 2007–15. Member: Mayor of Shanghai's Internat. Business Leaders' Adv. Council, 1999– (Chm., 2006–07); China Develt Forum, Beijing, 2001–17; Council of Internat. Advrs, China Banking Regulatory Cttee, 2010–14. Mem., Bd of Dirs, Qatar Foundn, 2009–14. Chm., Inst. of Internat. Finance, Washington, 1998–2003. FCIB (FIB 1982). Hon. Fellow, London Business Sch., 2003. Hon. DEc Richmond, American Univ. in London, 1998; Hon. DLitt: Loughborough, 2000; Sheffield, 2002; Hon. DCL South Bank, 2000; Hon. DSc City, 2004; Hon. DBA London Metropolitan, 2004; Hon. LLD: Nottingham, 2005; Bristol, 2005. Foreign Policy Assoc. Medal, NY, 2003; Magnolia Gold Award, Shanghai Municipal People's Govt, 2003. *Recreations:* golf, hiking, reading biography. *Clubs:* MCC; Hong Kong, Shek O Country (Hong Kong); John's Island (Florida).

**BOND, Prof. (John) Richard,** OC 2004; OOnt 2008; PhD; FRS 2001; FRSC; Professor, since 1987, and University Professor, since 1999, Canadian Institute for Theoretical Astrophysics (Director, 1996–2006); *b* 15 May 1950; *s* of Jack Parry Bond and Margaret Bond. *Educ:* Univ. of Toronto (BSc); Calif Inst. of Technol. (MS, PhD 1979). FRSC 1996. Res. Asst, Kellogg Lab., CIT, 1973–78; Postdoctoral Fellow, Univ. of Calif, Berkeley, 1978–81; Res. Fellow, Inst. of Astronomy, Cambridge, 1982–83; Asst Prof., 1981–85, Associate Prof., 1985–87, Stanford Univ.; Associate Prof., 1985–87, Actg Dir, 1990–91, Canadian Inst. for Theoretical Astrophysics. Sen. Fellow, 1988–2017, Dir, 2002–17, Cosmology and Gravity Prog., Sen. Fellow, Gravity and Extreme Universe Prog., 2017–, Canadian Inst. for Advanced Research. Fellow, APS, 1996. Foreign Hon. Mem., American Acad. of Arts and Scis, 2003; Foreign Associate, NAS, 2011. *Address:* Canadian Institute for Theoretical Astrophysics, University of Toronto, 60 St George Street, Toronto, ON M5S 3H8, Canada. *T:* (416) 9786874.

**BOND, Judith Anne; Her Honour Judge Judith Bond;** a Circuit Judge, since 2019; *b* Wigan, 13 June 1970; *d* of Thomas Brian Bond and Joan Bond; *m* 2014, Martin Dermott. *Educ:* Scarisbrick Hall Sch.; Univ. of Central Lancashire (LLB Hons; DipLP). Admitted solicitor, 2002; Higher Courts (all proceedings) qualification, 2004; a Dep. District Judge, 2013–16; a District Judge, 2016–19. *Recreations:* walking, three day eventing, gundog training, crime books, theatre. *Address:* Wolverhampton Combined Court, Pipers Row, Wolverhampton WV1 3LQ. *T:* (01902) 481000.

**BOND, Dr Martyn Arthur;** consultant on European affairs, since 2003; Senior Honorary Fellow, Regent's University (formerly Regent's College), London, since 2014 (Distinguished Visiting Fellow, European Business School, 2009); *b* 10 Oct. 1942; *s* of Jack Bond and Muriel Caroline Janet (née Webb); *m* 1965, Dinah Macfarlane; two *s* one *d*. *Educ:* Portsmouth Grammar Sch.; Peter Symonds Sch.; Winchester Coll.; Queens' Coll., Cambridge (MA); Univ. of Sussex (DPhil 1971); Univ. of Hamburg. Producer, BBC, 1966–70; Lectr in W European Studies, NUU, 1970–73; Press Officer, Gen. Secretariat, Council of Ministers of EC, 1974–81; BBC Rep., Berlin, 1981–83; Principal Adminr, Gen. Secretariat, Council of Ministers of EC, 1983–88; Dir, UK Office of EP, 1989–99; Dir, Federal Trust, 1999–2002; Dir, Information Europe Ltd, 1999–2018; UK Press Correspondent for Council of Europe, 2006–13. Mem. Bd, Europe-China Assoc., 1976–82; Founder Mem., Quaker Council for European Affairs, 1979–. Contested (SDP/Alliance) Hull W, 1987. Chm., Internat. Adv. Council, 1987–94, Sen. Fellow, 1995–, Salzburg Seminar in American/Global Studies. Vis. Prof. of European Politics, RHUL (formerly RHBNC), 1999–2014. Dir, 2000–05, Dep. Chm., 2005–, London Press Club. Vice-Pres., Chartered Inst. of Linguists, 2015–17. FAcSS (AcSS 2009). Dir, English Coll. Foundn, 1993–; Gov., English Coll. in Prague, 1995–2017. FRSA 1992. *Publications:* A Tale of Two Germanies, 1991; (ed) Eminent Europeans, 1996; (ed) The Treaty of Nice Explained, 2001; (ed) Europe, Parliaments and the Media, 2003; The Council of Europe and the European Convention on Human Rights, 2010, 2nd edn 2019; The Council of Europe, 2011; (ed) The UK and Europe: costs, benefits, options, 2013; (ed) The EU and the US: the Transatlantic relationship, 2014; (ed) Europe and its Neighbours, 2015; contrib. to Jl Legislative Studies, German Life and Letters, Parliament Mag., House Mag., Diplomat mag., The World Today. *Recreations:* Europe, travel, chess, fly-fishing.

**BOND, Sir Michael (Richard),** Kt 1995; FRCPsych, FRCPGlas, FRCSE; FRSE; Professor of Psychological Medicine, University of Glasgow, 1973–98, now Emeritus (Vice Principal, 1986–97; Administrative Dean, Faculty of Medicine, 1991–97); *b* 15 April 1936; *s* of Frederick Richard Bond and Dorothy Bond (née Gardner); *m* 1961, Jane Issitt; one *s* one *d*. *Educ:* Magnus Grammar Sch., Newark, Notts; Univ. of Sheffield (MD, PhD). FRSE 1998. Ho. Surg./Ho. Phys., Royal Inf., Sheffield, 1961–62; Asst Lectr/Res. Registrar, Univ. Dept of Surgery, Sheffield, 1962–64; Res. Registrar/Lectr, Univ. Dept of Psychiatry, Sheffield, 1964–67; Sen. Ho. Officer/Res. Registrar, Registrar/Sen. Registrar, Inst. of Neurological Scis, Glasgow, 1968–71; Lectr in Neurosurgery, Univ. Dept of Neurosurgery, Glasgow, 1971–73. Locum Cons. Neurosurgeon, Oxford, 1972; Hon. Cons. Psychiatrist, Greater Glasgow Health Bd, 1973–98. Member: UGC, 1982–91; UFC, 1991–93; SHEFC, 1992–96; Chm., Jt Med. Adv. Cttee, 1992–95. Pres., 1999–2001, Interim Pres., 2009–10, British Pain Soc.; Member Council: Internat. Assoc. for Study of Pain, 1981–93, 1996–2008 (Pres. 2002–05); St Andrews Ambulance Assoc., 1995–2000. Dir, Prince and Princess of Wales Hospice, Glasgow, 1997–2002. Chairman: Head Injuries Trust for Scotland, 1989–99; Fundraising for Capital Med. Projects, Univ. of Glasgow, 1998–2019; Mem., The London Inquiry, 1991–92. Trustee, Lloyds TSB Foundn, 1999–2005. Gov., High Sch., Glasgow, 1990–2006 (Chm., 2001–06). Member: Incorpn of Bakers of Glasgow, 2006– (Mem., Master Ct, 2007–; Collector, 2009–11; Deacon, 2011–12); Merchants House of Glasgow, 2014–. Chm., Bearsden Art Club, 2014–16. FRSA 1992. Hon. DSc Leicester, 1996; DUniv Glasgow, 2001. *Publications:* Pain, its nature, analysis and treatment, 1979, 2nd edn 1984; (co-ed) Rehabilitation of the Head Injured Adult, 1983, 2nd edn 1989; (with K. H. Simpson) Pain: its nature and treatment, 2006; papers on psychological and social consequences of severe brain injury, psychological aspects of chronic pain and cancer pain, 1963–, and others on similar topics. *Recreations:* painting, gardening, walking. *Address:* 33 Ralston Road, Bearsden, Glasgow G61 3BA. *T:* (home) (0141) 942 4391, (work) (0141) 330 3692. *E:* m.bond@admin.gla.ac.uk. *Clubs:* Athenæum; Glasgow Art.

See also G. C. Bond.

**BOND, Richard;** see Bond, J. R.

**BOND, Richard Douglas;** Senior Partner, Herbert Smith, 2000–05; *b* 23 July 1946; *s* of Douglas Charles Bond and Vera Eileen Bond; *m* 1st, 1973, Anthea Mary Charrington (*d* 1996); two *d*; 2nd, 2007, Julie Ann Nicholls. *Educ:* Berkhamsted Sch. Articled Clerk, Halsey, Lightly & Hemsley, 1964–69; joined Herbert Smith, 1969; seconded to BNOC, 1976–78; Partner, 1977; Head of Corporate, 1993–2000. *Recreations:* golf, cricket, theatre. *Club:* MCC.

**BOND, His Honour Richard Henry;** a Circuit Judge, 1997–2015; *b* 15 April 1947; *s* of Ashley Raymond Bond and Hester Mary Bond (née Bowles); *m* 1987, Annabel Susan Curtis; one *s* one *d*. *Educ:* Sherborne Sch. Called to the Bar, Inner Temple, 1970. *Recreations:* architecture, walking, gardening.

**BOND, Richard Ian Winsor; His Honour Judge Richard I. W. Bond;** a Circuit Judge, since 2013; *b* Lapworth, 22 July 1965; *s* of Ian Charles Winsor Bond and Audrey Kathleen Bond; *m* 1997, Emma-Jane Parsons; one *s* two *d*. *Educ:* Warwick Sch.; Manchester Univ. (LLB Hons 1986); Inns of Court Sch. of Law. Called to the Bar, Middle Temple, 1988; a Recorder, 2009–13. *Recreations:* family, walking, racquet sports, cinema, theatre, travel. *Address:* Birmingham Crown Court, 1 Newton Street, Birmingham B4 7NA.

**BOND, Samantha;** actress; *b* 27 Nov. 1961; *d* of late Philip Bond and Pat Bond (then Sandys); *m* 1989, Alexander Hanson; one *s* one *d*. *Educ:* Godolphin and Latymer Sch.; Bristol Old Vic Theatre Sch. Theatre includes: Juliet in Romeo and Juliet, Lyric, Hammersmith, 1986; Beatrice in Much Ado About Nothing, Phoenix, 1988; Hermione in The Winter's Tale, 1992–93, Rosalind in As You Like It, 1992–93, RSC; C in Three Tall Women, Wyndham's, 1995; Amy in Amy's View, RNT, transf. Aldwych, then NY, 1997; Mary in Memory of Water, Vaudeville, 1998; Lady Macbeth in Macbeth, Albery, 2002; title rôle in A Woman of No Importance, Th. Royal, Haymarket, 2003; Lady Driver in Donkey's Years, Comedy, 2006; Arcadia, Duke of York's, 2009; An Ideal Husband, Vaudeville, 2010; What the Butler Saw, Vaudeville, 2012; Passion Play, Duke of York's, 2013; Dirty Rotten Scoundrels, Savoy, 2014; The Lie, Menier Chocolate Factory, 2017; Elizabeth, Barbican, 2018; television includes: The Ginger Tree, Emma, Family Money, Tears Before Bedtime, Morse, Manhunt, The Hunt, Donovan, Distant Shores, Clapham Junction, Wolfenden, Fanny Hill, Midsomer Murders, Outnumbered, Downton Abbey, Home Fires, Moving On; films include: Eric The Viking, 1989; What Rats Won't Do, 1998; Blinded, 2005; Yes, 2005; A Bunch of Amateurs, 2008; rôle of Moneypenny in: Goldeneye, 1995; Tomorrow Never Dies, 1997; The World is Not Enough, 1999; Die Another Day, 2002. Ambassador: The Prince's Trust, 1997–; Macmillan Cancer Support, 2006–; Patron, Shooting Star Children's Hospice, 2006–; Vice-Chm., Royal Theatrical Fund, 2014; Trustee, Mother2Mothers, 2016. *Recreations:* Scrabble, crosswords, gardening, dancing, watching cricket. *Address:* c/o Conway Van Gelder Grant Ltd, 8–12 Broadwick Street, W1F 8HW. *T:* (020) 7287 0077, *Fax:* (020) 7287 1940.

**BONDEVIK, Rev. Kjell Magne**; Executive Chairman, Oslo Center, since 2018 (President, Oslo Center (formerly Oslo Center for Peace and Human Rights), 2006–18); *b* Molde, Norway, 3 Sept. 1947; *s* of Johannes and Margit Bondevik; *m* 1970, Bjørg Rasmussen; two *s* one *d*. *Educ:* Free Faculty of Theology, Oslo (Candidatus Theologiae 1975). Ordained priest, Lutheran Church of Norway, 1979. State Sec., Prime Minister's Office, 1972–73; MP (KrF) Møre og Romsdal, Norway, 1973–2005; Minister of Church and Educn, 1983–86; Minister of Foreign Affairs, 1989–90; Prime Minister of Norway, 1997–2000 and 2001–05. UN Special Humanitarian Envoy for the Horn of Africa, 2006–07. *Publications:* Et liv i spenning (memoir), 2006. *Address:* c/o Oslo Center, Geitmyrsveien 45 B, 0456 Oslo, Norway.

**BONDY, Rupert Mark**; Senior Vice President, General Counsel and Company Secretary, Reckitt Benckiser plc, since 2017; *b* London, 30 June 1961; *s* of Ivo Bondy and Shuna Bondy (*née* Black); one *s* three *d*. *Educ:* King's Coll., Cambridge (BA 1983); Stanford Law Sch. (JSM 1989). Harkness Fellow, Harvard Univ., 1984–85; called to the Bar, Middle Temple, 1987; admitted California Bar, 1990; lawyer: Morrison & Foerster, 1989–94; Lovells, 1994–95; Smith Kline Beecham, later GlaxoSmithKline: Counsel, 1995–2000; Sen. Vice Pres. and Gen. Counsel, 2001–08; Gp Gen. Counsel, BP plc, 2008–16. *Address:* Reckitt Benckiser plc, 103 Bath Road, Slough, Berks SL1 3UH. *T:* (01753) 217800, *Fax:* (01753) 217899. *E:* rupert.bondy@rb.com.

**BONE, Charles**, PPRI, ARCA; President, Royal Institute of Painters in Water Colours, 1979–89; Governor, Federation of British Artists, 1976–81 and since 1983 (Member, Executive Council, 1983–84 and 1986–88); *b* 15 Sept. 1926; *s* of William Stanley and Elizabeth Bone; *m* Sheila Mitchell, FRSS, ARCA, sculptor; two *s*. *Educ:* Farnham Coll. of Art; Royal Coll. of Art (ARCA). FBI Award for Design. Consultant, COSIRA, 1952–70; Craft Adviser, Malta Inds Assoc., Malta, 1952–78; Lecturer, Brighton Coll. of Art, 1950–86; Director, RI Galleries, Piccadilly, 1965–70. Many mural paintings completed, including those in Eaton Square and Meretea, Italy; oils and water colours in exhibns of RA, London Group, NEAC and RBA, 1950–; 50 one-man shows, 1950–; works in private collections in France, Italy, Malta, America, Canada, Japan, Australia, Norway, Sweden, Germany. Designer of Stourhead Ball, 1959–69; produced Ceramic Mural on the History of Aerial Photography. Critic for Arts Review. Mem. Council, RI, 1964– (Vice-Pres. 1974). Hon. Member: Medical Art Soc.; Soc. Botanical Artists. Hon. FCA (Can.). Hunting Gp Prize for a British Watercolour, 1984. *Film:* Watercolour Painting: a practical guide, 1990. *Publications:* author and illustrator: Waverley, 1991; Authors Circle, 1998; Cathedrals, 2000. *Address:* Winters Farm, Puttenham, Guildford, Surrey GU3 1AR. *T:* (01483) 810226.

**BONE, Sir (James) Drummond**, Kt 2008; Master, Balliol College, Oxford, 2011–18; Pro Vice-Chancellor, University of Oxford, 2016–18; *b* 11 July 1947; *s* of William Drummond Bone, ARSA, RSW and Helen Bone (*née* Yuill); *m* 1970, Vivian Clare Kindon. *Educ:* Ayr Acad.; Univ. of Glasgow (MA); Balliol Coll., Oxford (Snell Exhibnr, 1968–72). Lectr, English and Comparative Literature, Univ. of Warwick, 1972–80; University of Glasgow: Lectr, 1980–89, Sen. Lectr, 1989–95, in English Literature; Dean, Faculty of Arts, 1991–95; Vice-Principal, 1995–99; Prof. of English Literature, 1995–2000; Principal, RHBNC, London Univ., 2000–02 (Hon. Fellow, 2004); Pro-Vice-Chancellor, London Univ., 2001–02; Vice-Chancellor, Univ. of Liverpool, 2002–08. Pres., UUK, 2005–07. Chairman: Foundn for Arts and Creative Technol., 2004–10; Liverpool Capital of Culture Bd, 2005–07; UK Library Research Reserve, 2007–16; Internat. Adv. Bd, Laureate Inc., 2008–11; Observatory on Borderless Higher Educn, 2008–; i-graduate, 2009–11; AHRC, 2014–18 (Sen. Ind. Mem., 2018–); Vice Chm., The Northern Way, 2004–08 (Chm., Innovation and Industry Gp, 2007–10). Mem. Council, 2009–13, Hon. Rector, 2015–, City Univ.; Chm. Council, Stamford Internat. Univ., Thailand, 2011–18; Mem., Adv. Council, UK NARIC, 2010–; Bd Dir, Oxford-Suzhou Centre for Advanced Res., 2017–. Mem., Strategy Bd, Nat. Autism Project, 2014–17. President: British and Irish Assoc. of Zoos and Aquaria, 2008–12; Maserati Club, 2018–. Chm., Wordsworth Trust, 2017–. Report author, Internationalisation of Higher Educn: a 10-year view, DIUS, 2008. Mem., Editl Bd, THE (formerly Times Higher Educn Supplement), 2008–16; Jt Editor, 1993–2015, Sen. Adv. Ed., 2015–, Romanticism jl. FRSA 1995; FRSE 2008. Freeman, Coachmakers' Co., 2007. Hon. DLitt: Chester, 2008; Liverpool, 2008; Lancaster, 2009; Bucharest, 2016; DUniv Glasgow, 2010; Hon. DEd Edinburgh, 2012; Hon. DArts, Xi'an Jiaotong-Liverpool, Suzhou, 2016. *Publications:* Writers and their Work: Byron, 2000; Cambridge Companion to Byron, 2004. *Recreations:* music, ski-ing, Maseratis. *Address:* Balliol College, Oxford OX1 3BJ. *Club:* Athenæum.

**BONE, Peter William**, FCA; MP (C) Wellingborough, since 2005; *b* 19 Oct. 1952; *m* 1981, Jeanette Sweeney; two *s* one *d*. *Educ:* Westcliff-on-Sea Grammar Sch. FCA 1976. Financial Dir, Essex Electronics and Precision Engrg Gp, 1977–83; Chief Exec., High Tech Electronics Co., 1983–90; Man. Dir, Palm Travel (West) Ltd, 1990–2002. Mem. (C), Southend-on-Sea BC, 1977–86. Contested (C): Islwyn, 1992; Pudsey, 1997; Wellingborough, 2001. *Address:* House of Commons, SW1A 0AA; (office) 21 High Street, Wellingborough, Northants NN8 4JZ.

**BONE, Quentin**, MA, DPhil; FRS 1984; zoologist; Honorary Research Fellow, Marine Biological Association UK; *b* 17 Aug. 1931; *s* of late Stephen Bone (landscape painter) and Mary Adshead (mural painter); *m* 1958, Susan Elizabeth Smith; four *s*. *Educ:* Warwick Sch.; St John's Coll., Oxon (Hon. Fellow, 1998). Naples Scholarship, 1954; Fellow by examination, Magdalen Coll., Oxford, 1956. Zoologist at Plymouth Laboratory, Marine Biol Assoc., 1959–91. *Publications:* Biology of Fishes (with N. B. Marshall), 1983, 2nd edn (with J. S. Blaxter also), 1994, 3rd edn (with R. Moore), 2008; (ed) Biology of Pelagic Tunicates, 1998; papers on fish and invertebrates, mainly in Jl of Mar. Biol Assoc. UK. *Address:* Marchant House, 98 Church Road, Plymstock, Plymouth PL9 9BG.

**BONE, Sir Roger (Bridgland)**, KCMG 2002 (CMG 1996); HM Diplomatic Service, retired; President, Boeing UK, 2005–14; *b* 29 July 1944; *s* of late Horace Bridgland Bone and Dora R. Bone (*née* Tring); *m* 1970, Lena M. Bergman; one *s* one *d*. *Educ:* William Palmer's Sch., Grays; St Peter's Coll., Oxford (MA). Entered HM Diplomatic Service, 1966; UK Mission to UN, 1966; FCO, 1967; 3rd Sec., Stockholm, 1968–70; 2nd Sec., FCO, 1970–73; 1st Secretary: Moscow, 1973–75; FCO, 1975–78; 1st Sec., UK Perm. Representation to European Communities, Brussels, 1978–82; Asst Private Sec. to Sec. of State for Foreign and Commonwealth Affairs, 1982–84; Vis. Fellow, Harvard Univ. Center for Internat. Affairs, 1984–85; Counsellor, 1985–89, and Head of Chancery, 1987–89, Washington; Counsellor, FCO, 1989–91; Asst Under Sec. of State, FCO, 1991–95; Ambassador to Sweden, 1995–99; Ambassador to Brazil, 1999–2004. Non-executive Chairman: Boeing Commercial Air Services UK Ltd, 2012–14; Over-C Ltd, 2016–; non-executive Director: Foreign and Colonial Investment Trust plc, 2008– (Sen. Ind. Dir, 2016–); Continental Data Graphics Ltd, 2010–14; ITM Power plc, 2014–; Strategic Advr to ARDC(UK) Ltd, 2016–19. Mem. Council, Brazilian Chamber of Commerce, 2005–12. UK Trade & Investment Ambassador for British Business, 2009–15. Mem., Exec. Council, RUSI, 2007– (Trustee, 2012–); Dir and Trustee, Nat. Centre for Univs and Businesses (formerly Mem., Council for Industry and HE), 2011–. Chm., Anglo-Latin America Foundn, 2005–10; Trustee, Nobrega Foundn, 2005–09; Mem. Council, Air League, 2007– (Pres., 2015–). Freeman, City of London, 2011; Liveryman, Coachmakers' and Coach Harness Makers' Co., 2011–. Hon. FIED, 2014; Hon. CRAeS 2016. Hon DEng Sheffield, 2015. *Recreations:* music, wine. *Address:* 5 Roxburghe Mansions, 32 Kensington Court, W8 5BQ. *Club:* Oxford and Cambridge.

**BONE, Prof. Thomas Renfrew**, CBE 1987; Deputy Principal, University of Strathclyde, 1992–96; *b* 2 Jan. 1935; *s* of James Renfrew Bone and Mary Williams; *m* 1959, Elizabeth Stewart; one *s* one *d*. *Educ:* Greenock High Sch.; Glasgow Univ. MA 1st cl. English 1956, MEd 1st cl. 1962, PhD 1967. Teacher, Paisley Grammar Sch., 1957–62; Lecturer: Jordanhill Coll. of Educn, 1962–63; Glasgow Univ., 1963–67; Jordanhill College of Education: Hd of Educn Dept, 1967–71; Principal, 1972–92. FCCEA 1984; FRSGS 1997; FSES 2011. *Publications:* Studies in History of Scottish Education, 1967; School Inspection in Scotland, 1968; *chapters in:* Whither Scotland, 1971; Education Administration in Australia and Abroad, 1975; Administering Education: international challenge, 1975; European Perspectives in Teacher Education, 1976; Education for Development, 1977; Practice of Teaching, 1978; World Yearbook of Education, 1980; The Management of Educational Institutions, 1982; The Effective Teacher, 1983; Strathclyde: changing horizons, 1985; The Changing Role of the Teacher, 1987; Teacher Education in Europe, 1990; Educational Leadership: challenge and change, 1992. *Recreations:* golf, bridge. *Address:* 7 Marchbank Gardens, Paisley PA1 3JD. *Club:* Paisley Burns.

**BONELL, Carlos Antonio**; guitarist; concert artist, since 1969; *b* London, 23 July 1949; *s* of Carlos Bonell and Ana Bravo; two *s* by a former marriage. *Educ:* William Ellis Sch., Highgate; Royal Coll. of Music (Hon. RCM 1973). Lectr, City Lit, 1970; Prof., RCM 1972. Artistic Dir, London Internat. Guitar Fest., 2005. Début as solo guitarist, Purcell Room, 1971; GLAA Young Musician, 1973; resident guitarist, London Contemp. Dance Theatre, 1974; concert tours and recording with John Williams & Friends, 1975; first solo album, 1975; concerto début, RFH, 1977; NY début, 1978; Carlos Bonell Ensemble début, QEH, 1983, and tours in Europe and Far East; soloist with all major UK orchestras; commissioned and first performed Sonata by Stephen Oliver, 1981; first performance of: guitar concertos by Bryan Kelly, 1979, Barrington Pheloung, 1994, Armand Coeck, 1997; recorded Rodrigo's Concierto de Aranjuez, 1981; first recording of Carlos Bonell Ensemble, The Sea in Spring, 1997; interactive DVD, Classical Guitar Performance, 2004; (with Sir Paul McCartney) composition of concerto for guitar and orchestra, 2006–; recording based on music of rock group Queen, 2008; recording of music by Maltese composer Gordon Mizzi, 2010; recording of arrangements of Beatles' songs, 2011; numerous other solo records and awards. Trujamán Prize, Spain, 2008. *Publications:* Spanish folk songs and dances, 1975; Gaspar Sanz airs and dances, 1977; A Tarrega collection, 1980; First Pieces for solo guitar, 1980; The romantic collection, 1983; The classical collection, 1983; Spanish folk songs for 3 guitars, 1984; Purcell: 3 pieces, 1984; Tarrega Fantasia, 1984; Technique Builder, 1998; Carlos Bonell Guitar Series, 1998; Essential Classics for Guitar, 2004. *Recreations:* cinema, reading, history, playing the guitar, listening to music. *E:* info@carlosbonell.com. *W:* www.carlosbonell.com.

**BONES, Prof. Christopher John**; Chairman, Chartered Institute of Legal Executives, since 2018; Founding Partner, Hammersley and Bones Ltd, since 2010; Founding Partner, since 2010, and Chairman, since 2015, Good Growth Ltd; *b* 12 June 1958; *s* of James C. E. and Sydness M. Bones; *m* 1984, Pamela Gail Fawcett; one *s* one *d*. *Educ:* Dulwich Coll.; Aberdeen Univ. (MA Hons). Advr, Employee Relns, 1982–84, Industrial Relns, 1985–87, Shell; Group Management Development Manager: Grand Met Brewing, 1987–89; Grand Met Retailing, 1989; Personnel and Admin Dir, GME, 1990–92; United Distillers: Orgn Develt Manager, 1992–95; HR Dir, Internat., 1995–97; HR Dir, Europe, 1997–99; Gp Compensation and Benefits Dir, Diageo, 1999; Gp Orgn Effectiveness and Develt Dir, Cadbury Schweppes plc, 1999–2004; Principal, Henley Mgt Coll., 2005–08; Dean, Henley Business Sch., 2008–10, now Dean Emeritus; Prof., Univ. of Reading, 2008–10; Prof., Univ. of Manchester, 2011–18, now Emeritus. Member, Advisory Board: Savile plc, 2008–10; Norman Broadbent, 2014–15. Mem. Bd, Govt Skills, 2005–10; non-exec. Ind. Dir, Agric. and Horticulture Develt Bd UK, 2007–13; non-executive Director: The Working Manager Ltd, 2010–12; The Pipeline (formerly MK-LF Partnership), 2013–. Chm., Lib Dem Party Reform Commn, 2008. Contrib., Human Resources mag., 2003–10. Trustee, Terrence Higgins Trust, 2010–15 (Dep. Chair, 2012–13; Chair, 2013–15). CCMI 2007; FCIPD 2002; FRSA 2001. Dr *hc* Aberdeen, 2012. *Publications:* The Self-Reliant Manager, 1993; The Cult of the Leader, 2010 (CMI/British Liby Mgt Bk of the Year, 2012); (with J. Hammersley) Leading Digital Strategy, 2015; (jtly) Optimizing Digital Strategy, 2018. *Recreations:* gardening, theatre, eradicating bullshit. *Club:* Reform.

**BONEY, His Honour Guy Thomas Knowles**; QC 1990; a Circuit Judge, 2003–14; *b* 28 Dec. 1944; *oc* of Thomas Knowles Boney, MD and Muriel Hilary Eileen Long, FRCS; *m* 1976, Jean Harris Ritchie, *qv*; two *s*. *Educ:* Winchester College; New College, Oxford (BA 1966; MA 1987). Called to the Bar, Middle Temple, 1968 (Harmsworth Scholar), Bencher, 1997; in practice on Western Circuit, 1969–2003; Asst Recorder, 1982–85; Head of Pump Court Chambers, 1992–2001; Recorder, 1985–2003; a Dep. High Court Judge, 1994–2003; an Additional Judge, Court of Appeal (Criminal Div.), 2012–14. Chm., Friends of Winchester Coll., 2001–09. Freeman, Clockmakers' Co., 1996 (Liveryman, 2010–). Lord of the Manor, Stockbridge, 2003–. *Publications:* The Road Safety Act 1967, 1971; contribs to: Halsbury's Laws of England, 4th edn (Road Traffic); horological jls. *Recreations:* horology, history, music (Organist, King's Somborne Parish Church, 1980–), amateur theatre, walking Daisy. *Address:* c/o Winchester Combined Court Centre, Winchester SO23 9EL. *Club:* Garrick.

**BONEY, Jean Harris, (Mrs G. T. K. Boney)**; see Ritchie, J. H.

**BONFIELD, Andrew Robert John**; Chief Financial Officer, Caterpillar Inc., since 2018; *b* Wimbledon, 17 Aug. 1962; *s* of Terence and Roberta Bonfield; *m* Sandra Ann Peel; two *s*. *Educ:* Westville Boys High Sch.; Univ. of Natal (BCom; Postgrad. Dip. Accountancy). CA (SA); ACA. Price Waterhouse, 1984–90; SmithKline Beecham plc: Exec. Corporate Planning, 1990–91; Dir and Vice Pres., Corporate Accts, 1991–95; Corporate Controller, 1995–97; Dep. Finance Dir and Sen. Vice Pres., 1997–99; Chief Financial Officer, 1999–2000; Exec. Dir, Finance, BG Gp plc, 2001–02; Chief Financial Officer: Bristol Myers Squibb Co., 2002–08; Cadbury plc, 2009–10; Exec. Dir of Finance, then Chief Financial Officer, Nat. Grid plc, 2010–18. Director: BOC Gp, 2003–06; ImClone Systems, 2007–08; Kingfisher plc, 2010–18 (Chm., Audit Cttee, 2010–18). *Recreations:* golf, watching sports. *Address:* Caterpillar Inc., 501 Southwest Jefferson Avenue, Peoria, IL 61630, USA. *Club:* Wentworth Golf.

**BONFIELD, Dr Astrid Elizabeth**, CBE 2014; Chief Executive, Queen Elizabeth Diamond Jubilee Trust, since 2012; *b* Welwyn Garden City, 21 May 1969; *d* of Prof. William Bonfield, *qv*; partner, 2006, David Godwin; one *s* one *d*. *Educ:* Bishop's Hatfield Girls Sch.; Southampton Univ. (BA Hons Archaeol. 1990); Univ. of Manchester (MA (Econ) Social Anthropol. 1991; PhD Social Anthropol. 1996). Dir, Inter-Country People's Aid (Zimbabwe), 1997–2001; Prog. Develt Specialist, Bernard van Leer Foundn, 2001–04; Dir of Policy, Aga Khan Foundn, 2004–05; Chief Exec., Diana Princess of Wales Meml Fund, 2005–12. Chair, Eur. Funders Gp for HIV/AIDS, 2005–11. Trustee: Assoc. of Charitable Foundns, 2007–10; Big Lottery Fund, 2012–18; Internat. Agency for Prevention of Blindness, 2014–. Mem., Armourers and Brasiers Gauntlet Trust, 2018–. Mem.,

Armourers and Brasiers' Co. *Recreations:* contemporary dance, gardening. *Address:* Queen Elizabeth Diamond Jubilee Trust, 128 Buckingham Palace Road, SW1W 9SA. *T:* (020) 3358 3370. *E:* astrid.bonfield@qejubileetrust.org. *Club:* Athenæum.

**BONFIELD, Sir Peter (Leahy),** Kt 1996; CBE 1989; FREng; international business executive; *b* 3 June 1944; *s* of George and Patricia Bonfield; *m* 1968, Josephine Houghton. *Educ:* Hitchin Boys' Grammar School; Loughborough Univ. (BTech Hons; Hon. DTech, 1988). FIET (FIEE 1990), FBCS 1990, FCIM 1990; FREng (FEng 1993). Texas Instruments Inc., Dallas, USA, 1966–81; Group Exec. Dir, ICL, 1981–84; Chm. and Man. Dir, STC Internat. Computers Ltd, 1984–90; Chm. and Chief Exec., 1985–96, Dep. Chm., 1997–2000, ICL plc; Dep. Chief Exec., STC plc, 1987–90; Chief Exec., BT plc, 1996–2002. Director: BICC PLC, 1992–96; Ericsson, 2002–15; Mentor Graphics Corp., 2002–17; Taiwan Semiconductor Manufacturing, 2002–; Sony Corp., Japan, 2005–14; GlobalLogic Inc., USA, 2014–18 (Chm., 2015–18); Member: Internat. Adv. Bd, Citigroup (formerly Salomon Smith Barney), 1999–2009; Adv. Bd, Sony Corp., 2004–14; New Venture Partners LLP, 2006–14; Adv. Bd, Apax, 2007–13; Adv. Bd, Longreach Gp, Hong Kong; Adv. Bd, Silent Circle, 2014–16; Chm. Supervisory Bd, NXP Semiconductors, 2006–; non-exec. Mem., Supervisory Bd, Actis LLP, 2013–15; non-exec. Dir, Dubai Internat. Capital, 2007–09; Senior Advisor: Rothschild London, 2010–15; Alix Partners LLP, 2015–; G3 Good Governance Gp, 2015–18; Hampton Gp, London, 2017–18; Bd Mentor, CMI, Belgium, 2005–. Chm., Small Business Charter, 2013–15; Dir, EastWest Inst., USA, 2011–, UK, 2013–18; Chm. Bd, EastWest Inst., UK. Member: European Round Table, 1996–2002; EU-Japan Business Dialogue Round Table, 1999–2002; Ambassador for British Business. Mem., British Quality Foundn, 1993–2012 (Vice-Pres.). Mem., CS Coll. Adv. Council, 1993–97. Chm. Council, Loughborough Univ., 2012–. FRSA 1992. Freeman, City of London, 1990; Liveryman, Information Technologists' Co., 1992. Hon. Citizen, Dallas, Texas, 1994. Hon. doctorates from univs of Loughborough, Surrey, Mid Glamorgan, Nottingham Trent, Brunel, Open, Northumbria at Newcastle, Kingston, Cranfield, Essex and London. Mountbatten Medal, Nat. Electronics Council, 1995; Gold Medal, Inst. of Mgt, 1996. Comdr, Order of the Lion (Finland), 1995. *Recreations:* music, sailing, ski-ing. *Address:* PO Box 129, Shepperton, Middx TW17 9WL. *W:* www.sirpeterbonfield.com. *Clubs:* Royal Automobile, Royal Thames Yacht.

**BONFIELD, Prof. William,** CBE 1998; PhD; FRS 2003; FREng; FMedSci; Professor of Medical Materials, University of Cambridge, 2000–05, now Professor Emeritus; Director, Pfizer Institute for Pharmaceutical Materials Science, 2002–05; *b* 6 March 1937; *s* of Cecil William Bonfield and Ellen Gertrude Bonfield; *m* 1960, Gillian Winifred Edith Cross; one *s* two *d*. *Educ:* Letchworth GS; Imperial College, London (Perry Meml and Bessemer Medals; BScEng, PhD, DIC, ARSM). CEng, FIMMM; FREng (FEng 1993); CPhys 2003; FInstP 2003; FRSC 2005; FMedSci 2010. Honeywell Res. Center, Hopkins, Minn, USA, 1961–68; Queen Mary, later Queen Mary and Westfield College, London: Reader in Materials Science, 1968; Prof. of Materials, 1974–99; Head, Dept of Materials, 1980–90; Chm., Sch. of Engineering, 1981–88; Dean of Engineering, 1985–89; Dir, Univ. of London IRC in Biomedical Materials, 1991–99. Visiting Professor: Chulalongkorn Univ., Bangkok, 1988–98; Henry Ford Hosp., Detroit, 1992; Nat. Univ. of Singapore, 2007; OCMR Dist. Vis. Prof., Univ. of Toronto, 1990; Honorary Professor: Univ. of Sichuan, 1992–; UCL, 2007–. Lectures: Royal Microscopical Soc., 1992; Mellor Meml, Inst. of Materials, 1993; Prof. Moore Meml, Univ. of Bradford, 1994; Dist. Scholar, QUB, 1994; C. W. Hall Meml, SW Res. Inst., San Antonio, Texas, 1996; Hatfield Meml, Univ. of Sheffield, 1996; CSE Internat., Royal Acad. of Engrg, 1998; Hawksley Meml, IMechE, 1999; William Mong Dist., Univ. of Hong Kong, 2002; Robert Warner, Founders' Co., 2005; Furlong Christmas, RCS, 2008; Plenary Lectr, World Biomaterials Congress, Chengdu, 2012; R. W. Thomson, Scottish Assoc. Metals, 2012. Project Leader, EEC Concerted Action in Skeletal Implants, 1989–96. Chm., Med Engrg Cttee, 1989, Mem., Materials Cttee, later Materials Commn, 1983–88, SERC; Institute of Materials: Chairman: Biomaterials Cttee, 1989–96; Biomedical Applications Div., 1996–2005; Vice-Pres., 1998–2002; Member: Materials Sci. Bd, 1989–95; Council, 1996–2005; Member: Jt Dental Cttee, 1984–89; DoH Cttee on Dental and Surgical Materials, 1986–90; Directive Council, Internat. Soc. for Bio-analoging Skeletal Implants, 1988–95; Jl Cttee, Internat. Fedn for Med. and Biol Engrg, 1989–2001; Tech. Cttee, BSI, 1992–; Metallurgy and Materials Res. Assessment Panel, HEFC, 1995–96 and 2001–02; Materials Foresight Panel, OST, 1995–98; Chm., UK Focus on Med. Engrg, Royal Acad. of Engrg, 1998–2001. Chm., London Metallurgical Soc., 1991; Sec. Gen., Internat. Soc. for Ceramics in Medicine, 1998–2005. Mem., Adv. Bd, Royal Soc., 2013–. Director: Abonetics Ltd, 1996–; Biocompatibles plc, 2000–02; Apatech Ltd, 2001–10; OrthoMimetics Ltd, 2007–10; AtoCap Ltd, 2011–. Chm., Editl Bd, Materials in Electronics, 1990–2005; Mem., Editl Bd, Jl of Applied Polymer Sci., 1992–2005; Editor: Jl of Materials Science, 1973–2002; Jl Royal Soc.: Interface, 2004–10; Founding Editor: Jl of Materials Science Letters, 1981–2002; Materials in Medicine, 1990–2006. Freeman: Armourers' and Brasiers' Co., 1994 (Liveryman, 1999); Mem., Ct of Assts, 2001–; Master, 2007–08); City of London, 1998; Engrs' Co., 2013. Hon. Member: Canadian Ortho. Res. Soc., 1983; Materials Res. Soc. of India, 1993. FBSE 1995; FCGI 2012. Hon. FIPEM 2003; Hon. Fellow, Queen Mary, Univ. of London, 2007. Hon. DSc: Aberdeen, 2002; Turku, 2011. Griffith Medal, Inst. of Metals, 1991; Royal Soc. Armourers' and Brasiers' Co. Medal, 1991; George Winter Award, Eur. Soc. for Biomaterials, 1994; Kelvin Medal, ICE, 1995; Acta Metallurgica J. Herbert Hollomon Award, 2000; Chapman Medal, Inst. of Materials, Minerals, and Mining, 2003; Japanese Soc. for Biomaterials Medal, 2003; Prince Philip Gold Medal, Royal Acad. Engrg, 2004; President's Prize, UK Soc. for Biomaterials, 2004; Award of Merit, Internat. Union for Physical and Engrg Scis in Medicine, 2009. *Publications:* Bioceramics, 1991; over 500 research papers on biomaterials, biomechanics and physical metallurgy in sci. jls. *Recreation:* cycling. *Address:* Department of Materials Science and Metallurgy, University of Cambridge, 27 Charles Babbage Road, Cambridge CB3 0FS. *Clubs:* Athenæum; North Road Cycling.

See also A. E. Bonfield.

**BONGERS de RATH, Paul Nicholas;** Director, Local Government International Bureau, 1988–95; international relations consultant in urban affairs, 1996–2002; *b* 25 Oct. 1943; *s* of late Henry Bongers and Marjorie Bongers (*née* Luxton); *m* 1968, Margaret Rennie Huddleston Collins; one *s* two *d*. *Educ:* Bradfield Coll.; New Coll., Oxford (MA); DPA Univ. of London (external), 1968. Administrative Trainee, City of Southampton, 1965–68; Personal Asst to Chief Exec., City of Nottingham, 1968–69; Administrator, Council of Europe, Strasbourg, 1969–71; Assistant Secretary: AMC, 1971–74; AMA, 1974–78; Exec. Sec., British Sections, IULA/CEMR, 1978–88. Consultant, UN Human Settlements Prog., City of Barcelona and Bremen Initiative, 1999–2002. Mem., Exec. Cttee, 2005–07, Chm., Som and Dorset Br., 2010–11, European Movt. Member: Aldeburgh Town Plan Steering Cttee, 2013–14; Cttee, Aldeburgh Soc., 2018– (Sec., 2019–). Volunteer: Snape Maltings (formerly Aldeburgh Music), 2012–; Britten-Pears Foundn, 2012–. *Publications:* Local Government and 1992, 1990, 2nd edn as Local Government and the European Single Market, 1992; articles in local govt jls. *Recreations:* family, music, travel, the arts. *Address:* South House, Church Close, Aldeburgh, Suffolk IP15 5DY.

**BONHAM, Sir (George) Martin (Antony),** 5th Bt *cr* 1852; *b* Cirencester, 18 Feb. 1945; *e s* of Major Sir Antony Lionel Thomas Bonham, 4th Bt and Felicity (*d* 2003), *o d* of late Col. Frank L. Pardoe, DSO; *S* father, 2009; *m* 1st, 1979, Nenon Baillieu (marr. diss. 1992), *e d* of R. R. Wilson and Hon. Mrs Wilson; one *s* three *d*; 2nd, 2011, Pamela Elizabeth, *d* of late Reginald Ernest Harding and of Mrs Elizabeth Hazeldine Hyde Clarke (*née* Bent). *Educ:* Heatherdown Prep. Sch.; Eton Coll.; Aston Univ. Area Manager, Calor Gas Ltd, 1987–91; Consultant, Industrial Soc., 1998–2004; Clerk, Firefighters' Co., 2005–14. *Recreations:* sailing, tennis, ski-ing, golf. *Heir: s* Michael Francis Bonham [*b* 24 May 1980; *m* 2008, Louise Gregory; two *s* two *d*]. *Address:* 21 Tonsley Place, Wandsworth, SW18 1BH. *T:* (020) 8874 8896. *E:* martin.bonham@icloud.com. *Clubs:* Telford Park Tennis; Bembridge Sailing.

**BONHAM, Nicholas;** Director, Nicholas Bonham Consultancy, since 2004; *b* 7 Sept. 1948; *s* of late Leonard Charles Bonham and Diana Maureen (*née* Magwood); *m* 1st, 1977, Kaye Eleanor (*née* Ivett) (marr. diss. 1999); two *d*; 2nd, 2003, Susan Angela Chester. *Educ:* Trent College. Joined W. & F. C. Bonham & Sons Ltd, Fine Art Auctioneers, 1966; Dir, 1970; Man. Dir, 1975–87; Dep. Chm., W. & F. C. Bonham & Sons Ltd, subseq. Bonhams & Brooks, then Bonhams, 1987–2004. Chairman: Noble Investments (UK) plc, 2004–08; Corporate Communication Ltd, 2006–08; Sugar Collection Ltd, 2006–12. Director: Montpelier Properties, 1970–95; Bonhams Gp, 1995–2004; Hodie Ltd, 2001–. Master, Pewterers' Co., 2009–10. *Recreations:* sailing, tobogganing, ski-ing, swimming, scuba. *Clubs:* Kennel; Royal Yacht Squadron, Royal Thames Yacht, Seaview Yacht, South West Shingles Yacht; St Moritz Tobogganing.

**BONHAM-CARTER OF YARNBURY,** Baroness *cr* 2004 (Life Peer), of Yarnbury in the County of Wiltshire; **Jane Mary Bonham Carter;** Prime Minister's Trade Envoy for Mexico, since 2012; *b* 20 Oct. 1957; *d* of Baron Bonham-Carter and Leslie Adrienne, *d* of Condé Nast and Leslie Foster; partner, Lord Razzall, *qv*. *Educ:* St Paul's Girls' Sch.; University Coll. London (BA Philosophy). Producer, Panorama and Newsnight, BBC, 1988–93; Ed., A Week in Politics, Channel 4, 1993–96; Dir of Communications, Lib Dem Party, 1996–98; ind. producer, 1998–2004, Associate, 2004–09, Brook Lapping Productions. Member: Lib Dem Campaigns and Communications Cttee, 1998–2006; Council, Britain in Europe, 1998–2005; Referendum Campaign Team, 2004–05. Member: Adv. Cttee, Centre Forum (formerly Centre for Reform), 1998–2015; RAPt (Rehabilitation for Addicted Prisoners Trust), 1999–. Member: H of L sub-cttee on Home Affairs, 2004–07; H of L Select Cttee on BBC Charter Review, 2005–06, on Communications, 2007–10, 2015–; EU Sub-cttee C on Foreign Affairs, Defence and Develt Policy, 2010–15. Dep. Convenor, Lib Dem Peers, 2010–15; Lib Dem spokesperson for culture, media and sport, 2015–. Mem. Bd, Nat. Campaign for the Arts, 2010–12; Trustee, The Lowry, 2011–. Patron, Studio Th., Salisbury. Vis. Parly Fellow, St Antony's Coll., Oxford, 2013–14. *Address:* House of Lords, SW1A 0PW. *Clubs:* Groucho, Electric House, Academicians' Room.

**BONHAM CARTER, Edward Henry;** Executive Vice-Chairman, Jupiter Fund Management plc, since 2014 (Joint Chief Executive, 2000–07; Chief Executive Officer, 2007–14); *b* London, 24 May 1960; *s* of late Raymond Henry Bonham Carter and of Elena Bonham Carter (*née* Propper de Callejón); *m* 1994, Victoria Studd; two *s* one *d*. *Educ:* Harrow Sch.; Manchester Univ. (BA Econs and Politics). With Schroder Investment Mgt; Electra Investment, 1986–94; Jupiter Asset Management Ltd, 1994–: Manager, Jupiter UK Growth Fund, 1995–99; Chief Investment Officer, 1999–2010. Non-exec. Dir, Land Securities, 2014– (Sen. Ind. Dir, 2016–); Sen. Ind. non-exec. Dir, ITV, 2018–. *Recreations:* yoga, table tennis, cycling. *Address:* Jupiter Fund Management plc, The Zig Zag Building, 70 Victoria Street, SW1E 6SQ. *T:* (020) 3817 1000. *Club:* Brooks's.

See also H. Bonham Carter.

**BONHAM CARTER, Helena,** CBE 2012; actress; *b* 26 May 1966; *d* of late Hon. Raymond Henry Bonham Carter and of Elena Bonham Carter (*née* Propper de Callejón); one *s* one *d* with Tim Burton, *qv*. *Educ:* Hampstead High Sch. for Girls; Westminster Sch. *Films include:* Lady Jane, 1985; A Room with a View, 1986; A Hazard of Hearts, The Mask, 1988; St Francis of Assisi, Getting it Right, 1989; Hamlet, Where Angels Fear to Tread, 1990; Howard's End, 1992; Fatal Deception, 1993; Mary Shelley's Frankenstein, 1994; Mighty Aphrodite, Twelfth Night, 1996; Margaret's Museum, Portraits Chinois, Keep the Aspidistra Flying, 1997; The Wings of the Dove, The Theory of Flight, 1998; The Revengers' Comedies, Fight Club, 1999; Planet of the Apes, Women Talking Dirty, 2001; Novocaine, 2002; Til Human Voices Wake Us, Heart of Me, Big Fish, 2003; Charlie and the Chocolate Factory, 2005; Sixty Six, 2006; Conversations With Other Women, Harry Potter and the Order of the Phoenix, 2007; Sweeney Todd: The Demon Barber of Fleet Street, 2008; Terminator Salvation, Harry Potter and the Half-Blood Prince, 2009; Alice in Wonderland, Harry Potter and the Deathly Hallows, Pt 1, 2010, Pt 2, 2011; The King's Speech (Best Supporting Actress, BAFTA), 2011; Great Expectations, Les Misérables, 2012; The Lone Ranger, 2013; The Young and Prodigious T. S. Spivet, 2014; Cinderella, Suffragette, 2015; Alice Through the Looking Glass, 2016; Ocean's 8, 2018; *television includes:* Miami Vice, 1987; The Vision, 1988; Arms and the Man, 1988; Dancing Queen, 1993; A Dark Adapted Eye, 1994; Live from Baghdad, 2002; Henry VIII, 2003; Enid, 2009 (Best Actress, Internat. Emmy Awards, 2010); Burton and Taylor, 2013; Turks & Caicos, Salting the Battlefield, 2014; Love, Nina, 2016; The Crown, The Dark Crystal: Age of Resistance, 2019; *theatre includes:* Woman in White, Greenwich, 1988; The Chalk Garden, Windsor, 1989; House of Bernarda Alba, Nottingham Playhouse, 1991; The Barber of Seville, Palace, Watford, 1992; Trelawney of the Wells, Comedy, 1992; *radio:* The Reluctant Debutante; Marie Antoinette; The Seagull. Fellow, BFI 2012. *Recreation:* reading. *Address:* c/o Conway van Gelder Grant Ltd, 8–12 Broadwick Street, W1F 8HW. *T:* (020) 7287 0077.

See also E. H. Bonham Carter.

**BONINGTON, Sir Christian (John Storey),** Kt 1996; CVO 2010; CBE 1976; DL; mountaineer, writer and photographer; *b* 6 Aug. 1934; *s* of Charles Bonington, journalist, and Helen Anne Bonington (*née* Storey); *m* 1962, Muriel Wendy Marchant (*d* 2014); two *s* (and one *s* decd). *Educ:* University Coll. Sch., London. RMA Sandhurst, 1955–56; commnd Royal Tank Regt, 1956–61. Unilever Management Trainee, 1961–62; writer and photographer, 1962–. Climbs: Annapurna II, 26,041 ft (1st ascent) 1960; Central Pillar Freney, Mont Blanc (1st ascent), 1961; Nuptse, 25,850 ft (1st ascent), 1961; North Wall of Eiger (1st British ascent), 1962; Central Tower of Paine, Patagonia (1st ascent), 1963; Mem. of team, first descent of Blue Nile, 1968; Leader: successful Annapurna South Face Expedition, 1970; British Everest Expedition, 1972; Brammah, Himalayas (1st ascent), 1973; co-leader, Changabang, Himalayas (1st ascent), 1974; British Everest Expedition (1st ascent SW face), 1975; Ogre (1st ascent), 1977; jt leader, Kongur, NW China (1st ascent), 1981; Shivling West (1st ascent), 1983; Mt Vinson, highest point of Antarctica (1st British ascent), 1983; reached Everest summit, 1985; Panch Chuli II (W Ridge), Kumaon, Himalayas (1st ascent), 1992; Mejslen, Greenland (1st ascent), 1993; Rang Rik Rang, Kinnaur, Himalayas (1st ascent), 1994; Drangnag Ri (1st ascent), 1995; Danga II (1st ascent), 2000. President: British Mountaineering Council, 1988–91 (Vice-Pres., 1976–79, 1985–88); British Orienteering Fedn, 1985–; NT Lake Dist Appeal, 1989–; Council for National Parks, 1992–2000 (Life Vice-Pres., 2000); Vice-President: Army Mountaineering

Assoc., 1980–; YHA, 1990–. Non-exec. Chm., Berghaus Ltd, 1998–. Chm., Mountain Heritage Trust, 2000–04; Dep. Patron, Outward Bound, 2010– (Trustee, 1998–2010); Chm., Risk Mgt Cttee, 1998–2007). Ambassador, Cumbrian Scouts, 2012–. Chancellor, Lancaster Univ., 2005–14. Pres., LEPRA, 1983. DL Cumbria, 2004. MInstD 1992. FRGS (Founders' Medal, 1974); FRPS 1991; FRSA 1996. Hon Fellow: UMIST, 1976; Lancashire Polytechnic, 1991; Univ. of Cumbria, 2010. Hon. MA Salford, 1973; Hon. DSc: Sheffield, 1976; Lancaster, 1983; Hon. DCL Northumbria, 1996; Hon. Dr Sheffield Hallam, 1998; Hon. DLitt Bradford, 2002. Lawrence of Arabia Medal, RSAA, 1986; Livingstone Medal, RSGS, 1991. *Publications:* I Chose to Climb (autobiog.), 1966; Annapurna South Face, 1971; The Next Horizon (autobiog.), 1973; Everest, South West Face, 1973; Everest the Hard Way, 1976; Quest for Adventure, 1981, rev. edn 2000; Kongur: China's elusive summit, 1982; (jtly) Everest: the unclimbed ridge, 1983; The Everest Years, 1986; Mountaineer (autobiog.), 1989; The Climbers, 1992; (with Robin Knox-Johnston) Sea, Ice and Rock, 1992; Chris Bonington's Lake District, 1997; (with Charles Clarke) Tibet's Secret Mountain, 1999; Boundless Horizons (autobiog.), 2000; Chris Bonington's Everest, 2002; Ascent: a life spent climbing on the edge (memoir), 2017. *Recreations:* mountaineering, ski-ing, orienteering. *Address:* Badger Hill, Nether Row, Hesket Newmarket, Wigton, Cumbria CA7 8LA. *T:* (01697) 478286. *E:* chris@bonington.com. *Clubs:* Travellers (Hon. Mem., 2004–09), Alpine (Pres., 1996–99), Alpine Ski, Army and Navy; Climbers' (Hon. Mem.), Fell and Rock Climbing (Hon. Mem.), Border Liners, Carlisle Mountaineering (Hon. Mem.), Keswick Mountaineering (Hon. Mem.), American Alpine (Hon. Mem.), Himalayan (Hon. Mem.), East Indian (Hon. Mem.).

**BONINO, Emma;** Minister of Foreign Affairs, Italy, 2013–14; *b* 9 March 1948. *Educ:* Bocconi Univ., Milan (BA 1972). Mem., Italian Chamber of Deputies, 1976–94 and 2006–08; Minister for Internat. Trade and European Affairs, 2006–08; Vice-Pres., Italian Senate, 2008–13; other posts include: Chm., Radical Party Gp, 1979–81; Mem., Bureau of Parlt, 1992–94. MEP, 1979–94 and 1999–2006; Mem., European Commn, 1994–99. Transnational Radical Party: Pres., 1991–93; Sec., 1993–95. Co-Chair, European Council on Foreign Relns, 2015–. *Recreations:* snorkelling, scuba-diving.

**BONNAR, Anne Elizabeth;** Co-founder and Director, Bonnar Keenlyside, since 1991; Chair, Collective Gallery, since 2016; *b* St Andrews, 9 Oct. 1955; *d* of George and Patricia Bonnar; two *s* two *d*. *Educ:* Dumbarton Acad.; Glasgow Univ. (MA); Jordanhill Coll. of Educn (DipEd); City Univ., London (Dip. Arts Admin). Th. Manager, Young Vic, 1979–80; Publicity Officer, Glasgow Citizens' Th., 1980–83; Gen. Manager, Traverse Th., 1986–91. Transition Dir, Creative Scotland, 2008; Leader, Culture Counts, 2010–16. Non-executive Director: Nat. Galls of Scotland, 2002–10; NT of Scotland, 2005–07; Neuro Foundn, 2007–12. FRSA. *Recreations:* arts, running, yoga. *E:* anne@b-k.co.uk.

**BONNER, Mark;** Founder and Creative Director, GBH Design, since 1999; *b* 24 June 1970; *s* of John and Joan Bonner; *m* 2008, Janice Davison; one *s* one *d*. *Educ:* Hounslow Coll. (Nat. Dip. BTEC (Dist.)); Kingston Univ. (BA 1st Cl. Hons 1991); Royal Coll. of Art (MA 1993). The Partners, 1993–95; Carter Wong & Partners, 1995–96; SAS Design, 1997–99. Tutor in Graphic Design: W Bucks Coll., 1995–; Kingston Univ., 1999–; London Coll. of Communication, 2012; Arts Univ. Bournemouth, 2014–. Chm., Consort Royal Awards, 2004. Mem., D&AD, 2000– (Trustee, 2010–; Mem., Exec. Cttee, 2011–13; Vice Pres., 2013–14; Pres., 2014–15); D&AD Trainer, 2016–. Mem. Bd, Kemistry Gall., 2015–16. D&AD Annual Award, 1991, 1993, 1994, 1995, 1996, 1997, 1998, 1999, 2001, 2002, 2003, 2004, 2005, 2007, 2008, 2009, 2011, Silver Award, 2003, 3 Yellow Pencils, 2011; One Show Gold, Silver and Bronze, 2011, NY Art Dirs Club; Design Week Award, 2003, 2005, 2007, 2008, 2011, 2013, 2015, and Best of Show, 2003; Benchmark Award, 2007; Brand Impact Award, 2016, 2017, 2018; Fresh Award, 2017. *Address:* GBH Design, Chiswick Station House, Burlington Lane, Chiswick, W4 3HB. *T:* (020) 8742 2277. *E:* mark@gregorybonnerhale.com.

**BONNER, Paul Max,** OBE 1999; writer; Director, Secretariat, ITV Network Centre, 1993–94; *b* 30 Nov. 1934; *s* of late Jill and Frank Bonner; *m* 1956, Jenifer Hubbard (*d* 2013); two *s* one *d*. *Educ:* Felsted Sch., Essex. National Service commission, 1953–55. Local journalism, 1955; Radio production, BBC Bristol, 1955–57; Television production, BBC Bristol, 1957–59, BBC Lime Grove, 1959–62; Television Documentary prodn and direction, BBC Lime Grove and Kensington House, 1962–74; Editor, Community Programmes for BBC, 1974–77; Head of Science and Features Programmes for BBC, 1977–80; Channel Controller, Channel Four TV, 1980–83; Exec. Dir and Programme Controller, Channel Four TV, 1983–87; Dir, Programme Planning Secretariat, ITVA, 1987–93. A Manager, Royal Instn, 1982–85; Governor, Nat. Film and TV School, 1983–88; Director: Broadcasting Support Services, 1982–93; House of Commons Broadcasting Unit Ltd, 1989–91; Parly Broadcasting Unit, 1991–94; Chm., Sponsorship and Advertising Cttee, EBU, 1991–94; Member: Bd, Children's Film Unit, 1989–97; COPUS, 1986–92 (Chm., Broadcast Trust, 1995–98). FRTS 1989. *Publications:* Independent Television in Britain: Vol. 5, ITV and the IBA 1981–1992, 1998, Vol. 6, New Developments in Independent Television 1981–92: Channel Four, TV-am, cable and satellite, 2002; Memoir of a Medium Man (autobiog.), 2018; *documentaries include:* Strange Excellency, 1964; Climb up to Hell, 1967; Lost: Four H Bombs, 1967; Search for the Real Che Guevara, 1971; Who Sank the Lusitania?, 1972. *Recreations:* photography, the theatre, listening to good conversation. *Address:* Alan Road, Wimbledon, SW19 7PT. *Clubs:* Reform, Chelsea Arts, Garrick.

**BONNET, Maj.-Gen. Peter Robert Frank,** CB 1991; MBE 1975; Colonel Commandant, Royal Regiment of Artillery, 1990–2000; *b* 12 Dec. 1936; *s* of James Robert and Phyllis Elsie Bonnet; *m* 1961, Sylvia Mary Coy; two *s*. *Educ:* Royal Military Coll. of Science, Shrivenham. BSc (Engrg). Commnd from RMA Sandhurst, 1958; RMCS Shrivenham, 1959–62; apptd to RHA, 1962; Staff trng, RMCS and Staff Coll., Camberley, 1969–70; Comd (Lt-Col), 26 Field Regt, RA, 1978–81; Comd RA (Brig.) 2nd Div., 1982–84; attendance at Indian Nat. Defence Coll., New Delhi, 1985; Dir RA, 1986–89 (Maj.-Gen. 1986); GOC Western Dist, 1989–91, retd 1992. Mem., Exec. Cttee, ABF, 1993–99; Gen. Sec., Officers' Pensions Soc., 1995–2000; Dir, OPS Investment Co. Ltd, 1995–2000; Man. Trustee, OPS Widows' Fund, 1995–2000; Vice Patron, Council Officers' Assoc., 1995–2015. Hon. Col, 26 Field Regt RA, 1992–99. Vice-Pres., Nat. Artillery Assoc., 1989–99. Trustee: Kelly Holdsworth Meml Trust, 1996–2004; Council, Age Concern, 1998–99. *Publications:* International Terrorism, 1985; A Short History of the Royal Regiment of Artillery, 1994. *Recreations:* tennis, sculpture, painting. *T:* (01398) 341324. *Club:* Army and Navy.

**BONNETT, Prof. Raymond,** CChem, FRSC; Professor of Organic Chemistry, Queen Mary, then Queen Mary and Westfield, College, University of London, 1974–94, now Professor Emeritus; *b* 13 July 1931; *s* of Harry and Maud Bonnett; *m* 1956, Shirley Rowe; two *s* one *d*. *Educ:* County Grammar Sch., Bury St Edmunds; Imperial Coll. (BSc, ARCS); Cambridge Univ. (PhD); DSc London 1972. Salters' Fellow, Cambridge, 1957–58; Res. Fellow, Harvard, 1958–59; Asst Prof., Dept of Chemistry, Univ. of British Columbia, 1959–61; Queen Mary, subseq. Queen Mary and Westfield, College, London: Lectr in Organic Chem., 1961–66; Reader in Organic Chem., 1966–74; Hd of Dept of Chemistry, 1982–87; Scotia Res. Prof., 1994–2000. George and Christine Sosnovsky Award in Cancer Therapy, RSC, 2012. *Publications:* sci. papers, esp. in Jls of Royal Soc. of Chemistry and Biochemical Soc. *Recreations:* theatre, bookbinding, gardening. *Address:* Elmbank, 19 Station Road, Epping, Essex CM16 4HG. *T:* (01992) 573203.

**BONNEVILLE, Hugh;** see Williams, H. R. B.

**BONNEY, Barbara;** soprano; *b* Montclair, NJ, 14 April 1956; *d* of Alfred Bonney III and Janet Gates; *m* 1989, Håkan Hagegård; *m* Maurice Whitaker. *Educ:* Univ. of New Hampshire; Mozarteum, Salzburg. Performances include: Sophie in Der Rosenkavalier, Royal Opera, Covent Garden, 1984; Pamina in Die Zauberflöte, La Scala, Milan, 1985; Nyade in Ariadne auf Naxos, Falstaff, 1990, Metropolitan Opera, NY; Susanna in The Marriage of Figaro, Royal Opera, 1995; Les Boréades, Salzburg Fest., 1999; Idomeneo, San Francisco, 1999; Orlando, 2003, Zdenka in Arabella, 2004, Royal Opera. Regular lied recitals and concert perfs; numerous recordings. Prof., Mozarteum, Salzburg, 2007–; Jt Dir, Young Singers Prog., Salzburg Festival, 2008. Vis. Prof., Royal Acad. of Music.

**BONNEY, Very Rev. Mark Philip John;** Dean of Ely, since 2012; *b* Welwyn Garden City, 2 March 1957; *s* of John and Patricia Bonney; *m* 1991, Katherine Jarvis; two *d*. *Educ:* Northgate Grammar Sch. for Boys, Ipswich; St Catharine's Coll., Cambridge (PGCE 1979; MA 1981); St Stephen's House, Oxford (MA 1988). Asst Dir of Music, Durham Sch., 1979–82; ordained deacon, 1985, priest, 1986; Asst Curate, St Peters, Stockton on Tees, 1985–88; Chaplain, 1988–90, Precentor, 1990–92, Cath. and Abbey Church of St Alban; Vicar, Eaton Bray with Edlesborough, 1992–96; Rector, Gt Berkhamstead, 1996–2004; Canon Treas., Salisbury Cath., 2004–12. Hon. Chaplain to Fruiterers' Co., 2017–. Hon. Fellow, Harris Manchester Coll., Oxford, 2018. *Recreations:* golf, cooking, art, family, music. *Address:* The Deanery, The College, Ely, Cambs CB7 4DN. *T:* 07811 466517. *E:* mpjbonney@gmail.com. *Club:* Hawks.

**BONNICI;** see Mifsud Bonnici.

**BONO;** see Hewson, P. D.

**BONOMY, Rt Hon. Lord; Iain Bonomy;** PC 2010; a Senator of the College of Justice in Scotland, 1997–2012; a Judge of the International Criminal Tribunal for the former Yugoslavia, 2004–09; *b* 15 Jan. 1946; *s* of late John Bonomy and of Mary Gray Bonomy (*née* Richardson); *m* 1969, Janet (*née* Gray); two *d*. *Educ:* Dalziel High Sch., Motherwell; Univ. of Glasgow (LLB Hons). Apprentice solicitor, East Kilbride Town Council, 1968–70; Asst solicitor, then Partner, Ballantyne & Copland, solicitors, Motherwell, 1970–83; admitted Faculty of Advocates, 1984; Advocate Depute, then Home Advocate Depute, 1990–96; QC (Scot.) 1993. Surveillance Comr, under Pt III Police Act 1997 and Pt II Regulation of Investigatory Powers Act 2000, 1998–2004, 2010–17; Judicial Comr, 2017–; Chair: Infant Cremation Commn, 2013–14; Post-Corroboration Safeguards Review, 2014–15; Protection of Wild Mammals (Scotland) Act 2002 Rev., 2016. Hon. Bencher, Inner Temple, 2010. Hon. LLD Strathclyde, 2006. *Recreations:* golf, travel, football terraces (now stands). *Address:* Parliament House, Parliament Square, Edinburgh EH1 1RQ. *Clubs:* Torrance House Golf, East Kilbride Golf, Motherwell Football and Athletic.

**BONSER-WILTON, Helen;** Chief Executive Officer, Mary Rose Trust, since 2015; *b* Louth, Lincs, 6 Feb. 1970; *d* of Peter Bonser and Mary Bonser; *m* 2005, Rob Bonser-Wilton; one *s*. *Educ:* Lindsey Comp. Sch., Cleethorpes; Univ. of Bradford (BA Hons German and Spanish 1992). Conference Manager, De Vere, 1992–93; Account Manager: BDH Advertising, 1994–96; Brunnings Communications, 1996–97; Gp Brand Manager, Akzo Nobel, 1998–2001; Gp Mktg Manager, Bernstein Gp, 2001–02; National Trust: Mktg and Supporter Develt Manager, 2003–08; Prog. Dir, Tyntesfield, 2008–09; Dir, Ops, South West, 2009–15; Dir, Change Prog. (on secondment), 2010. *Recreations:* family, rescue dogs, baking, cooking, gardening, travel. *Address:* Mary Rose Trust, College Road, HM Naval Base, Portsmouth PO1 3LX. *E:* h.bonser-wilton@maryrose.org.

**BONSEY, Martin Charles Brian,** AO 2005; CVO 2003 (LVO 2000); Official Secretary to the Governor-General of Australia, 1998–2003; *b* 2 May 1948; *s* of late Thory Richmond Bonsey and of Frances Mary Bonsey; *m* 1971, Joan Hair. *Educ:* Univ. of Melbourne (BA Hons Hist. and Pol Sci.); Australian Nat. Univ. (LLB). Public servant, Australia, 1974–2003. Secretary: Order of Australia, 1998–2003; Australian Bravery Decorations Council, 1998–2003. CStJ 1999.

**BONSOR, Sir Nicholas (Cosmo),** 4th Bt *cr* 1925; DL; mediator; *b* 9 Dec. 1942; *s* of Sir Bryan Cosmo Bonsor, 3rd Bt, MC, TD, and of Elizabeth, *d* of late Captain Angus Valdimar Hambro; *S* father, 1977; *m* 1969, Hon. Nadine Marisa Lampson, *d* of 2nd Baron Killearn; two *s* three *d* (including twin *d*). *Educ:* Eton; Keble College, Oxford (MA). Served Royal Buckinghamshire Yeomanry, 1964–69. Called to the Bar, Inner Temple, 1967; in practice at the Bar, 1967–75, 2003–10. Mem., CLA Legal and Parly Sub-Cttee, 1978–82. MP (C) Nantwich, 1979–83, Upminster, 1983–97; contested (C) Upminster, 1997. Minister of State, FCO, 1995–97. Chm., Select Cttee on Defence, 1992–95; Sec., Cons. Tourism Sub-Cttee, 1979–80; Vice-Chairman: Cons. Foreign Affairs Cttee, 1981–83; Cons. Defence Cttee, 1987–90. Mem. Council, RUSI, 1992–95, 1997–2000. Chm., Food Hygiene Bureau, later Checkmate Plc, 1986–95; Pres. and non-exec. Dir, Liscombe Hldgs, 1997–2000; Chairman: Egerton International Ltd, 2005–16; Metallon Corp. plc, 2011–16; Director: London Mining plc, 2007–15 (Dep. Chm., 2010–15); Blue Note Mining Inc., 2007–09. Chairman: Cyclotron Trust for Cancer Treatment, 1984–92 (Pres., 1992–); British Field Sports Soc., 1987–93; Standing Council of the Baronetage, 1990–93 (Vice-Chm., 1987–90); Baronets' Trust, 1993–95 (Trustee, 1986–95); Verdin Home for Mentally Handicapped, 1981–85. Mem., Council of Lloyd's, 1987–92. MCIArb 2004. Hon. Col, 60 Signals Sqdn, Royal Bucks Hussars (V), 2000–10; Vice Chm., SE RFCA, 2000–10. FRSA 1970. Freeman, City of London, 1988. DL Bucks, 2007. *Publications:* political pamphlets on law and trades unions and relations. *Recreations:* sailing, shooting, military history. *Heir: s* Alexander Cosmo Walrond Bonsor [*b* 8 Sept. 1976; *m* 2006, Jane, *d* of James Troughton; two *s* one *d*]. *Club:* White's.

**BONVIN, Her Honour Jane Anne Marie, (Mrs S. M. Poulter);** DL; a Circuit Judge, 1995–2008; *b* 15 Dec. 1946; *d* of Jean Albert Bonvin and Phyllis Margaret (*née* Boyd); *m* 1972, Sebastian Murray Poulter (*d* 1998). *Educ:* Putney High Sch.; Bristol Univ. (LLB Hons). Law Lectr, IVS, Lesotho, 1969–71; called to the Bar, Gray's Inn, 1971; barrister, Western Circuit, 1972–77 and 1979–95. Trustee, St Cross Hospital, Winchester, 2008–13. Editor, Lesotho Law Reports, 1977–79. DL Hampshire, 2003. *Recreations:* gardening, walking, travel, music. *Address:* Old Dairy Cottage, 7 Southdowns, Old Alresford, Hants SO24 9UR.

**BONYNGE, Richard,** AC 2012 (AO 1983); CBE 1977; opera conductor; *b* Sydney, 29 Sept. 1930; *s* of C. A. Bonynge, Epping, NSW; *m* 1954, Dame Joan Sutherland, OM, AC, DBE (*d* 2010); one *s*. *Educ:* Sydney Conservatorium (pianist). Official debut, as Conductor, with Santa Cecilia Orch. in Rome, 1962; conducted first opera, Faust, Vancouver, 1963. Has conducted in most leading opera houses in world, incl. in Edinburgh, Vienna and Florence Fests. Has been Princ. Conductor and Artistic/Musical Dir of cos, incl. Sutherland/Williamson Internat. Grand Opera Co., Aust., 1965; Vancouver Opera, 1974–77; Australian Opera, 1976–85. Many opera and ballet recordings; also recital discs with Sutherland, Tebaldi, Tourangeau and Pavarotti, and many orchestral and ballet anthologies. Socio d'onore, Regia Accademia Filarmonica di Bologna, 2007. Comdr, Ordre des Arts et des Lettres (France), 1989. *Publications*: (with Dame Joan Sutherland) The Joan Sutherland Album, 1986. *Address*: c/o Bircham Dyson Bell, 50 Broadway, SW1H 0BL.

**BOOBIS, Prof. Alan Raymond,** OBE 2003; PhD; Professor of Biochemical Pharmacology, 1996–2017, and Director, Toxicology Unit, Public Health England (formerly Health Protection Agency Toxicology Unit), 2003–17, Imperial College London (formerly Royal Postgraduate Medical School, London), Professor of Toxicology (part-time), since 2017; *b* Glasgow, 15 Jan. 1949; *s* of Samuel Boobis and Esther Boobis; *m* 1975, Susan Wallace; one *s* one *d*. *Educ*: Bellahouston Acad., Glasgow; Univ. of Glasgow (BSc Hons Pharmacol. 1971; PhD Pharmacol. 1974). CBiol 1991–2019; FRSB until 2019 (FIBiol 1991). Fogarty Vis. Fellow, Nat. Inst. of Child Health and Human Develt, NIH, Bethesda, 1974–76; Royal Postgraduate Medical School, London, later Imperial College London: MRC Postdoctoral Res. Fellow, 1976–79, Lectr, 1979–83, Sen. Lectr, 1983–88, Reader, 1988–96, Dept of Clin. Pharmacol.; Dep. Dir, DoH Toxicology Unit, 1998–2003. Member: Sub-cttee on Pesticides, MAFF, 1992–96; UK Adv. Cttee on Pesticides, 1997–2002 (Dep. Chm., 2000–02; Chm.; Med. and Toxicol. Panel, 2000–03); Vet. Residues Cttee, 2001–04; Cttee on Carcinogenicity, 2003–13; Cttee on Toxicity, 2003–12, 2015– (Chm., 2015–); HPA Bd Sub-Cttee for Radiation, Chem. and Envmtl Hazards, 2005–10. Member: WHO Expert Adv. Panel on Food Safety, 1997–; Jt FAO/ WHO Expert Cttee on Food Additives (Residues of Vet. Drugs), 1997– (Chm., 2011, 2013; Vice Chm., 2015); Jt FAO/WHO Meeting on Pesticide Residues, 1999– (Chm./ Vice-Chm., 2003–07, 2011, 2013, 2015, 2016); Scientific Panel on Plant Health, Plant Protection Products and their Residues, 2003–09 (Vice-Chm., 2006–09), Scientific Panel on Contaminants in the Food Chain, 2009–12, Eur. Food Safety Authy; WHO Study Gp on Tobacco Product Regulation, 2012–; Cttee on Med. Effects of Air Pollutants, 2013–. Medical Research Council: Member: Physiol Medicine and Infections Bd, Res. Cttee A, 1992–95; Adv. Bd, 2000–04; Coll. of Experts, 2004–09. Mem. Scientific Adv. Cttee, Assoc. for Internat. Cancer Res., 2001–05. European Cooperation in the field of Scientific and Technical Research: UK Rep., Mgt Cttee, Action B1, 1986–98; UK Rep. and Vice-Chm., Mgt Cttee, Action B15, 1998–2004; UK Rep. and Chm., Action B25, 2005–09. Mem. Bd of Trustees, Internat. Life Scis Inst., 2009– (Chm., 2015–18); Mem. Bd of Trustees, Health and Envmtl Scis Inst., 2001– (Chm., 2008–10); Mem. Bd of Trustees, Internat. Life Scis Inst. Europe, 2010– (Vice-Pres., 2012–16, 2017–18; Interim Pres., 2016–17). Member: Biochem. Soc., 1971–2011; British Toxicology Soc., 1982– (Chm., 1994–96; Fellow, 2006; John Barnes Prize Lectureship, 2013; Hon. Fellow, 2018); British Pharmacol Soc., 1997– (FBPhS 2016); Soc. of Toxicology, USA, 2007–; Pres., Fedn of Eur. Toxicologists and Eur. Socs of Toxicol., 2000–02 (Hon. Mem. 2006; Merit Award, 2009). Member: Sci. Adv. Bd, Swiss Centre for Applied Human Toxicol., Basel, 2009–; Ext. Adv. Cttee, Center for Res. on Ingredient Safety, Michigan State Univ., 2015–; Scientific Adv. Council Evidence-Based Toxicol. Collaboration, Bloomberg Sch. of Public Health, Johns Hopkins Univ., 2016; Long Range Res. Strategy Scientific Adv. Bd, Cosmetics Europe, 2017–; Scientific Adv. Bd, Agency for Innovations in Food and Chem. Safety Prog., Sci., Technol. and Res., Singapore, 2018–; Scientific Adv. Bd, Owlstone Medical, 2018–. Toxicol. Award, RSC, 2013; Arnold J. Lehman Award, Soc. of Toxicology, USA, 2016. Jt Ed.-in-Chief, 2004–10, Emeritus Ed., 2011–, Food and Chemical Toxicology. *Publications*: edited jointly: Microsomes and Drug Oxidations, 1985; European Consensus Conference on Pharmacogenetics, 1990; Therapeutic Drugs, 1991, 2nd edn 1998; Therapeutic Drugs, Supplement 1, 1992; Therapeutic Drugs, Supplement 2, 1994; Proceedings of the Third International Conference on Practical In Vitro Toxicology, 1994; European Conference on Specificity and Variability in Drug Metabolism, 1995; European Symposium on Prediction of Drug Metabolism in Man: progress and problems, 1999; Proceedings of EUROTOX 2000, 2000; approx. 180 book chapters, reviews, procs of meetings, etc; contrib. over 260 articles in scientific jls. *Recreations*: listening to music (classical, jazz, rock, world), reading (especially science fiction), photography, computers. *Address*: Centre for Pharmacology and Therapeutics, Division of Experimental Medicine, Department of Medicine, Imperial College London, Hammersmith Campus, Ducane Road, W12 0NN. *E*: a.boobis@ imperial.ac.uk.

**BOOKBINDER, Alan Peter;** Master, Downing College, Cambridge, since 2018; *b* 16 March 1956; *s* of Geoffrey Ellis Bookbinder and Bridget Mary Bookbinder; *m* 2005, Vicki Ambery-Smith; one *s* one *d*. *Educ*: Manchester Grammar Sch.; St Catherine's Coll., Oxford (BA Modern Hist. and Modern Langs); Harvard Univ. (MA Regl Studies). Producer, 1986–92, Exec. Producer, 1992–2001, BBC Television; Head of Religion and Ethics, BBC, 2001–06; Dir, Sainsbury Family Charitable Trusts, 2006–18. Mem., Marshall Aid Commemoration Commn, 2016–. *Publications*: Comrades, 1985; contribs to Spectator, Listener, The Tablet. *Address*: Downing College, Cambridge CB2 1DQ.

**BOOKER, Gordon Alan,** FIWEM; utility adviser; Deputy Director General of Water Services, 1990–98; *b* 17 Feb. 1938; *s* of Frederick William Booker and Beryl Booker; *m* 1957, Anne Christine Pike; two *s* one *d*. *Educ*: Dronfield Grammar Sch.; Sheffield Univ. (BEng (Hons) 1960). MICE 1963; FIWEM 1966. Sheffield Water, 1960–65; Birmingham Water, 1965–70; W Glam Water, 1970–74; Welsh Water, 1974–80; Chief Exec., E Worcester Water, 1980–89; Managing Director: Biwater Supply, 1987–90; Bournemouth and W Hants Water Cos, 1989–90. Mem., Council, Water Res. Centre, 1985–90; mem. and chm. of several water industry cttees on automation and leakage control. *Publications*: Water Distribution Systems, 1984; Telemetry and Control, 1986; contrib. Procs of ICE and of IWSA, reports for DoE and NWC, and Jls of IWEM and IAWPRC. *Recreations*: walking, painting. *Address*: 106 The Holloway, Droitwich, Worcs WR9 7AH. *T*: (01905) 772432; Sheplegh Court, Blackawton, Devon TQ9 7AH.

**BOOKER, Pamela Elizabeth;** *see* Alexander, P. E.

**BOOMGAARDEN, Georg;** Ambassador of Germany to the Court of St James's, 2008–13; political consultant, since 2013; *b* Emden, Germany, 24 June 1948; *m* 1972, Christiane von Blücher; two *s* one *d*. *Educ*: Univ. of Kiel (Geophysics Dip. 1973). Entered Foreign Service, Germany, 1974; Desk Officer, Cultural Section, Moscow, 1976–80; Press Officer, Buenos Aires, 1980–83; Federal Foreign Office: Desk Officer, Central America Div., 1983–86; Hd, Information Processing Div., 1986–89; Ambassador to Nicaragua, 1989–92; Hd, Economic Service, Moscow, 1992–95; Federal Foreign Office: Hd, Div. responsible for S Latin America, 1995–99; Dir for Latin American Affairs, 1999–2003; Ambassador to Spain, 2003–05; State Sec., Fed. For. Office, 2005–08. Cross, Order of Merit (Germany), 2001; numerous foreign decorations. *Address*: Berlin.

**BOON, (George) Peter (Richard);** HM Diplomatic Service, retired; High Commissioner to Cameroon and non-resident Ambassador to Chad, Central African Republic, Gabon and Equatorial Guinea, 1998–2002; *b* 2 Nov. 1942; *s* of late George Alan James Boon and Enid Monica Boon (*née* Smith); *m* 1971, Marie Paule Calicis; one *s*. *Educ*: Repton Sch., Derbys. Joined CRO, later FCO, 1963; Bombay, 1966–69; Brussels, 1969–71; Vienna, 1971–74; on secondment to DTI, 1974–75; FCO, 1975–78; The Hague, 1978–81; Spokesman, BMG, Berlin, 1981–86; FCO, 1986–90; First Sec. (Political), Dhaka, 1990–93; FCO, 1994–97. Hon. Sec., BACSA, 2014–. *Address*: Barn End, London Road, Blewbury, Didcot, Oxon OX11 9PB.

**BOONE, Russell John H.;** *see* Hamblin-Boone.

**BOORD, Sir Andrew Richard,** 5th Bt *cr* 1896; *b* 23 Oct. 1962; *s* of late Antony Andrew Boord and Anna Christina Boord; *S* uncle, 2019.

**BOORMAN, Anthony John;** Managing Director, Promontory Financial Group (UK) Ltd, since 2016; *b* 14 Nov. 1958; *s* of William Harry and Margaret Boorman; *m* 1984, Alison Drury; two *s*. *Educ*: Kent Coll., Canterbury; New Coll., Oxford (BA). Various posts, Electricity Consumers' Council, 1985–90, Dir, 1989–90; Dir, Office of Electricity Regulation, 1990–98; Dep. Dir Gen., Office of Gas and Electricity Mkts, 1998–2000; Principal Ombudsman and Decisions Dir, 2000–12, Dep. Chief Ombudsman and Dep. Chief Exec., 2012–14, Financial Ombudsman Service. Non-exec. Dir, S Warwicks NHS Foundn Trust, 2007–18. Mem., Commn for Judicial Appts, 2001–06.

**BOORMAN, Lt-Gen. Sir Derek,** KCB 1986 (CB 1982); Chairman, Health Care Projects Ltd, 1998–2010; *b* 13 Sept. 1930; *s* of late N. R. Boorman, MBE, and Mrs A. L. Boorman (*née* Patman); *m* 1st, 1956, Jennifer Jane Skinner (*d* 1991); two *d* (one *s* decd); 2nd, 1992, Mrs Nicola Cox. *Educ*: Wolstanton Grammar Sch.; RMA Sandhurst. Commnd N Staffords, 1950; Adjt 1 Staffords, 1958–59; Staff Coll., 1961; HQ 48 Gurkha Inf. Bde, 1962–64; Jt Services Staff Coll., 1968; CO 1 Staffords, 1969–71; Instr, Staff Coll., 1972–73; Comdr 51 Inf. Bde, 1975–76; RCDS, 1977; Dir, Public Relations (Army), 1978–79; Director of Military Operations, 1980–82; Comdr, British Forces Hong Kong, and Maj.-Gen. Bde of Gurkhas, 1982–85; Chief of Defence Intelligence, 1985–88. Lieut, Tower of London, 1989–92. Colonel: 6th Queen Elizabeth's Own Gurkha Rifles, 1983–88; Staffordshire Regt (Prince of Wales's), 1985–90. Director: Tarmac Construction, 1988–95. Chairman: KCH Trust, 1992–93; Royal Hosps NHS Trust, 1994–97. Mem., Security Commn, 1991–96. Dep. Pro-Chancellor, Univ. of Kent, 2000–05. *Recreations*: gardening, music, taking wife out to dinner.

**BOORMAN, John,** CBE 1994; film director; *b* 18 Jan. 1933; *m* 1st, 1956, Christel Kruse; one *s* three *d*; 2nd, 1997, Isabella Weibrecht; one *s* two *d*. *Educ*: Salesian Coll., Chertsey. Film Editor, ITN, 1955–58; Dir and Producer, Southern TV, 1958–60; Head of Documentaries, BBC Bristol. *Films include*: Catch us if you Can, 1965; Point Blank, 1967; Hell in the Pacific, 1968; Leo the Last, 1969; Deliverance, 1972; Zardoz, 1973; The Heretic, 1976; Excalibur, 1981; The Emerald Forest, 1985; Hope and Glory, 1987; Where the Heart Is, 1989; I Dreamt I Woke Up, 1991; Beyond Rangoon, 1995; Two Nudes Bathing, 1995; The General, 1998; The Tailor of Panama, 2001; The Tiger's Tail, 2007; Queen and Country, 2014. Gov., BFI, 1983–94. BAFTA Fellow, 2004; BFI Fellow, 2014. Lifetime Achievement Award, Irish Film and TV Awards, 2010. Commandeur, Ordre des Arts et des Lettres (France), 2014. *Publications*: The Legend of Zardoz, 1973; Money into Light, 1985; Hope and Glory, 1987; Projections: (ed) no 1, 1992; (joint editor): no 2, 1993; no 3, 1994; nos 4 and 4½, 1995; nos 5 and 6, 1996; no 7, 1997; no 8, 1998; nos 9–12; no 13, 2004; Adventures of a Suburban Boy, 2003. *Address*: Merlin Films Group, 8 Fitzwilliam Place, Dublin 2, Ireland.

**BOORMAN, Steven Robert,** CBE 2013; specialist occupational health physician, since 1990; Director of Employee Health, Empactis, since 2016; *b* London, 10 July 1959; *s* of John Thomas and Joy Theresa Boorman; *m* 1984, Sharon Mary Griffiths; two *d*. *Educ*: Middlesex Hosp. Med. Sch. (MB BS 1983). MRCGP 1988; FRCP 2008; FRSPH 2013. House Officer, then SHO, Middx Hosp., 1983–84; Anatomy Demonstrator and A&E SHO, 1984–85; GP trainee in London and Warwicks, 1985–90; Med. Advr to Sec. of State for Transport, 1988–90; Royal Mail: Occupational Physician, 1990–92; Prin. Med. Officer, 1992–2000; CMO, 2000–03; Dir, Corporate Responsibility, 2003–11; Med. Dir for UK occupational Health Services, Abermed, 2011–13; Chief Med. Advr, Capita PIP Assessment Services, 2013–14; Chief Med. Officer, Optima Health and Nutrition, 2015–16. Chairman: Council for Work and Health, 2018–; Ethics Cttee, Faculty of Occupational Medicine. Author, Report of Ind. NHS Health and Well-being Rev., 2009. Hon. Sen. Clinical Lectr, Univ. of Birmingham, 1990–2014; Hon. Sen. Lectr, Robert Gordon Univ., Aberdeen, 2011–. Chief Examr, Dip. Occupational Medicine, 1998–. FFOM 2000. Hon. FRCN 2011. *Publications*: (contrib.) Well-being Support, 2008; (contrib.) Men's Health, 2013; (contrib.) Fitness for Work, 5th edn 2013, 6th edn 2019. *Recreations*: DIY, car mechanics. *Address*: 3 Queens Lane, Farnham, Surrey GU9 0LU. *E*: steven.boorman@gmail.com.

**BOOTE, Robert Edward,** CVO 1971; first Director General, Nature Conservancy Council, 1973–80; *b* 6 Feb. 1920; *s* of Ernest Haydn Boote and Helen Rose Boote; *m* 1949, Vera (*née* Badian) (*d* 2015); one *s* one *d*. *Educ*: London Univ. (BSc Econ Hons). DPA; FREconS 1953–61; AIPR 1957–61; FCIS 1960–81. War service, 1939–46, Actg Lt-Col, Hon. Major. Admin. Officer, City of Stoke-on-Trent, 1946–48; Chief Admin. Officer, Staffs County Planning and Develt Dept, 1948–54; Principal, 1954–64, Dep. Dir, 1964–73, Nature Conservancy. Sec. 1965–71, formerly Dep. Sec., Countryside in 1970 Confs, 1963, 1965, 1970 and numerous study groups; a Chief Marshal to the Queen, 1970. Mem., Pesticides Cttee, 1958–73; Chm., Broadland Report, 1963–65; UK Deleg. to Council of Europe Cttee for Conservation of Nature and Natural Resources, 1963–71; Mem., Countryside Review Cttee, 1977–79; Various posts in meetings of UN, UNESCO, EEC and OECD, 1968–81; Member, UK Delegations: USA, 1978; USSR, 1978; China, 1982; Chm. Preparatory Gp for Eur. Conservation Year 1970; Chm. Organising Cttee for European Conservation Conf. 1970 (Conf. Vice-Pres.); Chm. European Cttee, 1969–71; Consultant for European Architectural Heritage Year 1975; Advr, H of L Select Cttee on Eur. Communities, 1980–81. A Vice-Pres. and Chm., Euro Fedn of Nature and Nat. Parks, 1980–81; International Union for Conservation of Nature and Natural Resources: Treas., 1975–78; Mem., Governing Council and Bureau, 1975–81; a Vice-Pres., 1978–81; Rep., Internat. Conf. on Antarctic Marine Living Resources, 1980; Chm., Antarctica Resolution, 1981; Election Officer, 1984; Founder and Chm., 1974–80, Mem., 1980–85, UK Cttee. Council Member: FFPS, 1979–83; RGS, 1983–86; BTCV (Vice-Pres.) 1980–; RSNC (Vice-Pres.) 1980–99; RSNC Wildlife Appeal, 1983–87; WWF, 1980–86; Ecological Parks Trust, 1980–85; YPTES (Chm.), 1982–87; Friends of ENO, 1980–87; Common Ground Internat., 1981–85; Cttees for UK Conservation and Develt Prog., 1980–83; HGTAC, Forestry Commn, 1981–87; Conservator, Wimbledon and Putney Commons, 1981–97; Patron, CSV, 1978–85; Chairman: Instn of Environmental Sciences, 1981–84; Seychelles Appeal Cttee, Royal Soc., 1980–87; Chm., Gp A, Ditchley Foundn Anglo/Amer. Conf. on Environment, 1970; Lead Speaker: Eurogespracht, Vienna, 1970; Internat. Conf., Rehovot, Israel, 1971; Mem., Entretiens Ecologiques de Dijon, 1981; UK Officer Rep., Eur. Environment Ministers Conf., 1976; Judge, Berlin world agro/environ films and TV competitions, 1970, 1972, 1974 and 1980. Initiator and Chm., Age Resource, 1988–98, now Chm. Emeritus; a Vice-Pres., Age Concern, later Age UK, 1990–. Trustee and Hon. Treas., New Renaissance Gp, 1995–2002. FRSA 1971–2010. Hon. Vice-Pres., Landscape Inst., 1971; Hon. MRTPI, 1978, Lifetime Hon. MRTPI, 2014. Greek Distinguished Service Medal, 1946; van Tienhoven European Prize, 1980; Merit Award, IUCN, 1984; Alfred Toepfer Prize for European nature protection, Goethe Foundn, 1995. Adviser: Macmillan Guide to Britain's Nature Reserves, 1980–94; Shell Better Britain Campaign,

1980–91. Member Editorial Boards: Internat. Jl of Environmental Studies, 1975–2002; Town Planning Review, 1979–85; Internat. Jl Environmental Educn and Information, 1981–83. Helped to prepare: Pacemaker (film), 1970 (also appeared in); Man of Action, BBC Radio, 1977. *Publications:* (as Robert Arvill) Man and Environment, 1967, 5th edn 1983; numerous papers, articles, addresses, TV and radio broadcasts, over 4 decades in UK and internat. professional confs in 50 countries. *Recreations:* theatre, music. *Address:* 3 Leeward Gardens, Wimbledon, SW19 7QR. *T:* (020) 8946 1551.

**BOOTE, Sarah Joan**; *see* Thomas, S. J.

**BOOTH**; *see* Sclater-Booth, family name of Baron Basing.

**BOOTH, Alan James; His Honour Judge Booth**; a Circuit Judge, since 2009; *b* Stockport, 18 Jan. 1955; *s* of His Honour James Booth and of Joyce Doreen Booth; *m* 1983, Anne Lesley Binns; one *s* one *d*. *Educ:* Bolton Sch., Bolton; Selwyn Coll., Cambridge (BA 1977). Called to the Bar, Gray's Inn, 1978; in practice, Deans Court Chambers, Manchester, 1978–2009; Asst Recorder, 1996–2000; Recorder, 2000–09. Mem. Bd, NW Reg., 2005–13, Chm., Technical Water Polo Cttee, 2008–13, Amateur Swimming Assoc.; Mem., Water Polo Cttee, 2008–13, Chm., GB Men's Water Polo Mgt Gp, 2013–14, British Swimming. *Recreation:* sport. *Clubs:* Hawks (Cambridge); Sale Harriers; City of Manchester Water Polo.

**BOOTH, Prof. Alison Lee**, PhD; FASSA; Professor of Economics, since 2002, and ANU Public Policy Fellow, since 2012, Australian National University; *b* Melbourne, Australia; *d* of Norman Booth and Marjorie Booth; *m* 1986, Timothy James Hatton; two *d*. *Educ:* Pymble Ladies' Coll., Sydney; Univ. of NSW (BArch); Univ. of Sydney (Master of Town and Country Planning); London Sch. of Econs and Pol Sci. (MSc 1980; PhD 1984). Teaching Asst, LSE, 1981–83; Lecturer in Economics: Univ. of Bristol, 1983–84; City Univ., 1984–88; Brunel Univ., 1988–90; Lectr in Econs, 1990–91, Sen. Lectr in Econs, 1991–94, Birkbeck Coll., Univ. of London; Prof. of Econs, Univ. of Essex, 1995–2013. Mem., Exec. Cttee, Royal Econ. Soc., 1999–2003. Pres., Eur. Assoc. of Labour Economists, 2005–08 (Founding Fellow, 2015). FASSA 2005. Ed.-in-Chief, Labour Economics, 1999–2004. Dist. Fellow Award, Econ. Soc. of Australia, 2017. *Publications:* The Economics of the Trade Union, 1995; (ed with D. Snower) Acquiring Skills: market failures, their symptoms and policy responses, 1996; (ed) The Economics of Labor Unions (2 vols), 2002; *fiction:* Stillwater Creek, 2010; The Indigo Sky, 2011; A Distant Land, 2012; A Perfect Marriage, 2018; articles in learned jls. *Recreations:* writing and reading fiction, walking, sleeping, swimming. *Address:* Research School of Economics, ANU College of Business and Economics, Australian National University, Canberra, ACT 0200, Australia. *E:* alison.booth@anu.edu.au.

**BOOTH, Anthony John**, CBE 1993; CEng, FIET; Chairman, Ericsson Ltd, 1994–2002; *b* 18 March 1939; *s* of Benjamin and Una Lavinia Booth; *m* 1965, Elspeth Marjorie (*née* Fraser); one *s* one *d*. *Educ:* Bungay Grammar Sch.; London Univ. (BScEng, DMS). Joined Post Office Res. Dept, 1957; Exec. Engr and Sen. Exec. Engr, Telecom HQ, 1965–71; Asst Staff Engr, Central HQ Appointments, 1971–74; Head of Section and Div., External Telecom Exec., 1974–78; Head of Div., THQ, 1978–79; Dir, Internat. Networks, 1979–80; Regional Dir, London Region, 1980–83; Corporate Dir, British Telecommunications PLC, 1984–94; Managing Director: BT International, 1983–91; Business Communications, 1991–92; Special Businesses and Internat. Affairs Div., 1992–94. Director: Protek Network Mgt Ltd, 2001–04; RB Phusion Ltd, 2001–16; Dir and Trustee, AQA (Assessment and Qualifs Alliance Ltd), 2000–06 (Vice-Chm., 2003–06); Trustee, AQA Pension Scheme, 2006–11. Mem., HEFCE, 1996–2001. Gov., and Chm. Finance Cttee, Polytechnic of W London, 1991–92; Chm. of Govs, Thames Valley Univ., 1993–96; Mem. Council, Univ. of Surrey, 1998–2004. Member, Guild of Freemen of City of London, 1982–. Chm., SE Reg., RLSS, 1997–2001. FInstD 1997 (Chm., 1999–2002, Pres., 2002–11, W Surrey); CCMI (CBIM 1986; Mem. Bd of Companions, 1999–2006); FRSA 1991. Hon. DPhil Thames Valley, 1998. *Recreations:* opera, golf. *Club:* Caledonian.

**BOOTH, Cherie, (Mrs A. C. L. Blair)**, CBE 2013; QC 1995; Founder and Chair, Omnia Strategy LLP, since 2011; *b* 23 Sept. 1954; *d* of late Anthony Booth and Gale Booth; *m* 1980, Rt Hon. Anthony Charles Lynton Blair, *qv*; three *s* one *d*. *Educ:* St Edmund's RC Primary Sch., Liverpool; Seafield Grammar Sch., Crosby; London Sch. of Economics (LLB; Hon. Fellow, 1999). Called to the Bar, Lincoln's Inn, 1976, Bencher, 1999; an Asst Recorder, 1996–99; a Recorder, 1999–2015; barrister specialising in public, employment and EC law; accredited advanced mediator, ADR Chambers/Harvard Legal Project. Dir, Renault Gp, 2015–. Contested (Lab) Thanet North, 1983. Hon. Vice Pres., Barnardo's, 2007–; Vice Pres., 4Children (formerly Kids Club Network), 1998–; Vice Chair, Internat. Council on Women's Business Leadership, 2011; Founder: Cherie Blair Foundn for Women, 2008–; Africa Justice Foundn, 2011–; Patron: Refuge, 1995–; Home Start, Islington, 1997–; Sargent Cancer Care for Children, subseq. CLIC Sargent, 1998–; Breast Cancer Care, 1998–; Islington Music Centre, 1999–; Victim Support, London, 1999–; Patron, SCOPE, 2002–. Trustee, Citizenship Foundn, 1995–. Fellow: Inst. of Advanced Legal Studies, 1998; Internat. Soc. of Lawyers for Public Service, 1999; FRSA. Chancellor Emeritus, Liverpool John Moores Univ. (Fellow, 1997), Chancellor, 1999–2006); Chancellor, Asian Univ. for Women, Bangladesh, 2011–. Hon. Bencher, King's Inns, Dublin, 2002. DUniv Open, 1999; Hon. LLD: Westminster, 1999; Liverpool, 2003; Hon. DLitt UMIST, 2003. Der Steiger, Germany, 2011; Commonwealth Award for Public Service, Delaware, USA, 2011; Trinity Justitia Omnibus Award, Dublin Univ. Law Society, 2012. *Publications:* (with Cate Haste) The Goldfish Bowl: married to the Prime Minister, 2004; (contrib.) Evidence, 2004; The Negligence Liability of Public Authorities, 2006; Speaking for Myself (autobiog.), 2008. *Recreations:* theatre, the arts, keeping fit, enjoying my children. *Address:* Omnia Strategy LLP, PO Box 60519, W2 7JU.

**BOOTH, Sir Clive**, Kt 2003; Vice-Chancellor, Oxford Brookes University, 1992–97, now Professor Emeritus; *b* 18 April 1943; *s* of Henry Booth and Freda Frankland; *m* 1969, Margaret Sardeson. *Educ:* King's Sch., Macclesfield; Trinity Coll., Cambridge (1st cl. Hons Nat Scis Tripos; MA 1969); Univ. of California, Berkeley (Harkness Fellow, 1973; MA 1974; PhD 1976). Joined DES, 1965; Prin. Pvte Sec. to Sec. of State for Educn and Science, 1975–77; Asst Sec., 1977–81; Dep. Dir, Plymouth Polytechnic, 1981–84; Mem., HM Inspectorate, DES, 1984–86; Dir, Oxford Poly., 1986–92. Asst Comr, Nat. Commn on Educn, 1992–94; Chairman: TTA, 1997–2003; Pay Review Body for Nurses, Midwives and Professions Allied to Medicine, 1998–2005; Big Lottery Fund, 2004–10; Dep. Chm., SEEDA, 1999–2004; Chairman: Central Police Trng and Develt Authy, 2002–07; SE Reg. Bd for Reducing Reoffending, 2005–. Member: Governing Council, SRHE, 1981–90; Adv. Cttee, Brunel Univ. Educn Policy Centre, 1986–91; Computer Bd for Univs and Res. Councils, 1987–92; CNAA Cttee for Information and Develt Services, 1987–92; Fulbright Academic Administrators Selection Cttee, 1988–97; British Council Cttee for Internat. Co-operation in Higher Educn, 1988–96 (Chm., 1994–96); Council for Industry and Higher Educn, 1990–97; Fulbright Commn, 1992–97; Royal Soc. Study Gp on Higher Educn, 1991–97; UFC Inf. Systems Cttee, 1991–93; Oxford Science Park Adv. Cttee, 1992–96; Oxford Inst. of Nursing Bd, 1991–95; Commonwealth Scholarships Commn, 1992–96; UK ERASMUS Council, 1992–97 (Chm., 1993–97); Oxford Trust Adv. Council, 1992–97; Bd, British Inst., Paris, 1997–2005; Know How Fund Mgt Cttee, DFID, 1998–2000. Chairman: PCFC Steering Gp on Statistical Information, 1989–93; Heart of England Educn Forum, 1997–2002; Vice-Chm., CVCP, 1992–97. Chairman: Oxfordshire Learning Partnership, 1999–2004; Mgt Cttee, Oxfordshire Connexions, 2000–03; Director: Thames Action Resource Gp for Educn and Trng, 1986–2000; Thames Valley Technology Centre, 1989–93; British Council, 1995–97 (Sen. Advr, 1997–2005). Leverhulme Res. Fellow, 1983. Governor: Headington and Wheatley Park Schs; Westminster Coll., Oxford, 1997–2000; Trustee, Oxford Diocesan Schs Trust, 2016– (Chair, Finance Cttee, 2016–). Trustee, Lloyds Bank (formerly Lloyds TSB) Foundn for England and Wales, 2011–17. Chair, Berks, Bucks and Oxon Wildlife Trust, 2012–17. Pres., Oxford Civic Soc., 2017–; Concert Manager, Summertown Choral Soc., 2012–. Jt Ed., Higher Educn Qly, 1986–97; Member: Editorial Bd, Oxford Review of Educn, 1990–2015; Editorial Adv. Cttee, Peabody Jl of Educn, Vanderbilt Univ., USA, 2005–15. DUniv Oxford Brookes, 2000; Hon. DEd Sunderland, 2002. *Recreations:* gardening, choral singing, contract bridge, opera. *Address:* 43 St John Street, Oxford OX1 2LH. *T:* (01865) 557762. *E:* boothclive99@gmail.com.

**BOOTH, Sir Douglas Allen**, 3rd Bt *cr* 1916; writer and producer for television, writer for films; Associate, Barak Realty, New York City, 2007; *b* 2 Dec. 1949; *s* of Sir Philip Booth, 2nd Bt, and Ethel, *d* of Joseph Greenfield, NY, USA; *S* father, 1960; *m* 1991, Yolanda Marcela (*née* Scantlebury); two *d*. *Educ:* Beverly Hills High Sch.; Harvard Univ. (Harvard Nat. Scholarship, Nat. Merit Scholarship, 1967); BA (*magna cum laude*) 1975. *Recreations:* music, back-packing. *Heir: b* Derek Blake Booth [*b* 7 April 1953; *m* 1st, 1981, Elizabeth Dreisbach (marr. diss. 2000); one *s* one *d*; 2nd, 2006, Stephanie Louise Moret, MS, PhD]. *Address:* New York City, NY, USA.

**BOOTH, Edmund Dwight**, FREng; Principal, Edmund Booth Consulting Engineer, since 1995; *b* Richmond, Surrey, 16 May 1948; *s* of Edmund Booth and Henrietta Booth; *m* 1st, 1983, Sheena Jean Collison (*d* 2002); 2nd, 2009, Anna Mary Le Hair. *Educ:* King's College Sch., Wimbledon; King's Coll., Cambridge (BA Engrg and Econs 1969). CEng 1975; FICE 1992; FIStructE 1993; FREng 2010. Volunteer, VSO, Sierra Leone, 1975–77; joined Ove Arup & Partners, 1977, Associate, 1992–95. Vis. Prof., Univ. of Oxford, 1997–2002; Hon. Sen. Lectr, Imperial Coll. London, 2004–. Chairman: Soc. for Earthquake and Civil Engrg Dynamics, 1985–87; Cttee B/525/8: Eurocode 8, BSI, 2011–17. Mallet-Milne Lect., Soc. for Earthquake and Civil Engrg Dynamics, 2017. Chm., Sheena Booth Music Trust, 2003–10. Mem., Oxford and Cambridge Music Club. *Publications:* (ed) Concrete Structures in Earthquake Regions, 1994; Earthquake Design Practice for Buildings, 2nd edn, 2006, 3rd edn 2014. *Recreations:* violin, opera, house and garden. *Address:* 2 Miswell Cottages, Icknield Way, Tring HP23 4JU. *T:* 07747 698502. *E:* edmund@booth-seismic.co.uk. *W:* www.booth-seismic.co.uk.

**BOOTH, Fiona Irene**; Head, Provider Programmes and Strategy, Healthcode Ltd, since 2018; *b* London, 8 July 1970; *d* of David Carvosso and Marlene Donovan; *m* 1st, 1993, Paul Booth (marr. diss. 1997); 2nd, 2009, Christopher Moody (marr. diss. 2016). *Educ:* Curtin Univ., WA (BEd 1993). Science teacher, Bunbury Cathedral Grammar Sch., 1994–95; Regl Co-ordinator, Australian Red Cross, 1996–97; Services Manager, QUIT, 1998–2000; Science teacher, Grey Coat Hospital, 2000–01; Educn Welfare Officer, Royal Bor. of Kensington and Chelsea, 2001–02; Hd of Educn, Help the Aged, 2002–03; Hansard Society: Dir, Citizenship Educn Prog., 2003–07; Dep. Chief Exec., 2006–07; Chief Exec., 2007–12; Chief Exec., Assoc. of Ind. Healthcare Orgns, 2013–18. FRSA 2007. *Recreations:* reading, cinema, travelling, wine tasting, gourmet cooking. *Address:* Healthcode Ltd, Swan Court, Watermans Business Park, Kingsbury Crescent, Staines Upon Thames TW18 3BA.

**BOOTH, Hartley**, OBE 2010; Chairman, Uzbek British Trade and Industry Council, UK Trade & Investment (formerly British Trade International), 1999–2012; *b* 17 July 1946; *s* of late V. W. H. Booth and Eilish (*née* Morrow); *m* 1977, Adrianne Claire Cranefield; two *s* one *d*. *Educ:* Queen's Coll., Taunton; Bristol Univ. (LLB); Downing Coll., Cambridge (LLM, PhD). Called to the Bar, Inner Temple, 1970 (Schnar); in practice, 1970–84; Special Advr to Prime Minister and Mem., 10 Downing Street Policy Unit, 1984–88; Chief Exec., British Urban Develt, 1988–90; Consultant: Berwin Leighton (Solicitors), 1991–99; Maclay Murray Spens (Solicitors), 2003–06; Pinsent Masons, 2006–08; Dentons (formerly SNR Denton), 2008–14. Director: Canford Gp plc, 1978–2015; Edexcel, 1999–2001. MP (C) Finchley, 1992–97. PPS to Minister of State, FCO, 1992–94, to Minister of State for Educn, 1995–97. Mem. Select Committees: Home Affairs, 1992; European Legislation, 1992; Public Service, 1995–97; Chm., Urban Affairs Select Cttee, 1994–97. Chm., British Uzbek Soc., 2001–. Vice President: Royal Life Saving Soc., 1990–; British Urban Regeneration Assoc., 1991–94 (Chm., 1990–91); AMA, 1992. Pres., Resources for Autism, 2004– (Chm., 1996–2004). European Editor, Current Law Year Books, 1974–84. Dostlik Medal (Uzbekistan), 2011. *Publications:* British Extradition Law and Procedure, vol. I 1979, vol. II 1980; Return Ticket, 1994. *Recreations:* writing, swimming, delving into history, poetry. *Address:* c/o Gregg Latchams, 14 Manchester Square, W1U 3PP.

**BOOTH, Prof. Ian Westerby**, MD; FRCP, FRCPCH; Sir Leonard Parsons Professor of Paediatrics and Child Health, University of Birmingham, 1996–2010, now Emeritus; Honorary Consultant Paediatric Gastroenterologist, Birmingham Children's Hospital, since 1985; *b* 15 Aug. 1948; *s* of William Westerby Booth and Audrey Iris (*née* Corless). *Educ:* Sir George Monoux Grammar Sch., London; King's Coll. Hosp. Med. Sch., Univ. of London (BSc Hons Physiol. 1969; MB BS 1972; MSc with Dist. Biochem. 1982; MD 1987). DRCOG 1974; DCH 1975; MRCP 1977, FRCP 1991; Founder FRCPCH 1997. Eden Res. Fellow, RCP, 1980–83; Lectr, Inst. Child Health, London, 1983–85; University of Birmingham: Sen. Lectr in Paediatrics and Child Health, 1985–92; Prof. of Paediatric Gastroenterology and Nutrition, 1992–96; Dir, Inst. of Child Health, 1993–2010; Associate Dean, 2000–06, Dean, 2007–10, Medical Sch.; Dir of Educn, 1998–2002, Mem. Exec. Bd, 1995–2002, Children's Hosp., Birmingham. Department of Health: Vice-Chm., Adv. Cttee on Borderline Substances, 1990–97; Member: Panel on Novel Foods, 1992–98; Wkg Gp on Nutritional Adequacy of Infant Formulas, 1994–96. Member: Med. and Res. Adv. Gp, HEA, 1994–99; Specialised Health Services Commn for Wales Wkg Gp on Tertiary Services for Children, 2000–02; Food Standards Agency Expert Gp on Choking Hazards, 2002–04; Ind. Drug Monitoring Cttee, MRC/Food Standards Agency, 2009–. Pres., British Soc. Paediatric Gastroenterology and Nutrition, 1995–98 (Sec., 1985–89); Royal College of Paediatrics and Child Health: Chairman: Standing Cttee on Nutrition, 1996–2002; Academic Bd, 1998–2003; Wkg Gp on Intestinal Failure, 1998–2002; Mem., Safety and Efficiency Register of New Interventional Procedures, Acad. of Med. Royal Colls, 1996–2001. GMC Visitor for Quality Assuring Basic Med. Educn, 2004–08. Non-exec. Dir, Birmingham Women's Healthcare Foundn Trust Bd, 2005–11 (Vice Chm., 2008–11). Trustee, Sir Arthur Thomson Charitable Trust, Univ. of Birmingham, 2011– (Chm., 2014–). Associate Ed., Archives of Diseases of Childhood, 1993–96; Member, Editorial Board: Gut, 1996–2000; Internat. Jl of Gastroenterology, 1996–2011. *Publications:* (with E. Wozniak) Pocket Picture Guides in Clinical Medicine: Paediatrics, 1984; (with D. A. Kelly) An Atlas of Paediatric Gastroenterology and Hepatology, 1996; contribs to learned jls on paediatric gastroenterology and nutrition. *Recreations:* walking to restaurants, hill-walking in France. *Address:* 17 Custom House Quay, Weymouth, Dorset DT4 8BG. *T:* (01305) 786284. *E:* i.w.booth@bham.ac.uk. *Club:* Athenæum.

**BOOTH, Jonothan H.;** see Hammond Booth, J.

**BOOTH, Sir Josslyn Henry Robert G.;** see Gore-Booth.

**BOOTH, Kate Elizabeth;** see Varah, K. E.

**BOOTH, Prof. Ken,** PhD; FBA 2006; E. H. Carr Professor of International Politics, 1999–2008, Senior Research Associate, Department of International Politics, since 2009, and President, David Davies Memorial Institute of International Studies, since 2013 (Director, 2010–13), Aberystwyth University (formerly University of Wales, Aberystwyth); Editor, International Relations, since 2003; *b* 29 Jan. 1943; *s* of Fred and Phyllis Booth; *m* 1967, Eurwen Jones; two *s. Educ:* King's Sch., Pontefract; University Coll. of Wales, Aberystwyth (BA 1st Cl. Hons; PhD 1982). Lectr, Sen. Lectr, then Reader, 1967–99, Hd of Dept, 1999–2005, Dept of Internat. Politics, UC of Wales, Aberystwyth, then Univ. of Wales, Aberystwyth. Scholar-in-Residence, US Naval War Coll., Newport, RI, 1977; Sen. Res. Fellow, Dalhousie Univ., Canada, 1979–81; Vis. Fellow, Cambridge Univ., 1992–93. Chm., British Internat. Studies Assoc., 1995–96. FAcSS (AcSS 2002). FRSA 2006. Susan Strange Award, Internat. Studies Assoc., 2004. *Publications:* (ed jtly and contrib.) Soviet Naval Policy, 1975; (jtly) Contemporary Strategy: Vol. I: Theories and Concepts, 1975, 2nd edn 1987, Vol. II: The Nuclear Powers, 1987; Navies and Foreign Policy, 1977; (ed jtly and contrib.) American Thinking About Peace and War, 1978; Strategy and Ethnocentrism, 1979; Law, Force and Diplomacy at Sea, 1985; (with J. Baylis) Britain, NATO and Nuclear Weapons, 1989; (ed and contrib.) Strategic Power: USA/USSR, 1990; (ed and contrib.) New Thinking About Strategy and International Security, 1991; (with E. Herring) Strategic Studies: keyguide to information sources, 1994; (ed jtly and contrib.) International Relations Theory Today, 1995, 2nd edn 2016; (ed jtly and contrib.) International Theory: positivism and beyond, 1996; (ed and contrib.) Statecraft and Security: the Cold War and beyond, 1998; (ed jtly) The Eighty Years' Crisis, 1998; (ed jtly and contrib.) Strategic Cultures in the Asia-Pacific Region, 1999; (ed jtly) The Interregnum: controversies in world politics 1989–1999, 1999; (ed and contrib.) The Kosovo Tragedy, 2001; (ed jtly) How Might We Live?, 2001; (ed jtly) Great Transformations, 2001; (ed jtly and contrib.) Worlds in Collision, 2002; (ed and contrib.) Critical Security Studies in World Politics, 2005; Theory of World Security, 2007 (jt winner of Foster Watson Prize, 2008); (with N. J. Wheeler) The Security Dilemma, 2008; Realism and World Politics, 2011; (with T. Dunne) Terror in Our Time, 2011; International Relations: all that matters, 2014; contrib. articles to Internat. Affairs, Rev. Internat. Studies, Political Qly, etc. *Recreations:* sport, literature, hill-walking. *Address:* Department of International Politics, Aberystwyth University, Penglais, Aberystwyth SY23 3FE. *T:* (01970) 622694, *Fax:* (01970) 622709. *E:* kob@aber.ac.uk.

**BOOTH, Lawrence;** Editor, Wisden Cricketers' Almanack, since 2012; *b* Oxford, 2 April 1975; *s* of Philip John Booth and Verena Booth; *m* 2014, Anjali Doshi; one *d. Educ:* North Hinksey C of E Prim. Sch.; Magdalen College Sch., Oxford; Sidney Sussex Coll., Cambridge (BA 1st Cl. Hons Mod. and Medieval Langs 1998). Freelancer: 1998–2000; Guardian, 1999–2009; wisden.com, 2000–02; Cricket Writer, Daily Mail, 2009–. *Publications:* Cricket: celebrating the modern game around the world, 2004, 2nd edn 2005; Arm-Ball to Zooter, 2005; Cricket, Lovely Cricket?, 2008, 2nd edn 2009; What are the Butchers For?, 2009; Young Wisden, 2011. *Recreations:* Manchester City FC, Northamptonshire CCC, chess, walking, squash, reading, wine. *Address:* 3 Leconfield Avenue, SW13 0LD. *T:* 07818 423429. *E:* lawrencebooth@hotmail.com. *Club:* Cricket Club of India (Mumbai).

**BOOTH, Dame Margaret (Myfanwy Wood),** DBE 1979; President, Family and Parenting Institute, since 2004 (Chairman, 1999–2004); a Judge of the High Court, Family Division, 1979–94; *b* 11 Sept. 1933; *d* of late Alec Wood Booth and Lilian May Booth; *m* 1st, 1982, Joseph Jackson, QC (*d* 1987); 2nd, 1993, Peter Glucksmann (*d* 2002). *Educ:* Northwood Coll.; University Coll., London (LLM; Fellow, 1982). Called to the Bar, Middle Temple, 1956; Bencher, 1979. QC 1976. Chairman: Family Law Bar Assoc., 1976–78; Matrimonial Causes Procedure Cttee, 1982–85; Inner London Adv. Cttee on Justices of the Peace, 1990–93; Children Act Procedure Adv. Cttee, 1990; Children Act 1989 Adv. Cttee, 1991–93 (report published, 1996); Bar Central Selection Bd, 1993–96; Family Law Cttee, Justice, 1993–98. Pres., Family Mediators Assoc., 1994–95; Chm. Govs, UK Coll. of Family Mediators, 1996–99. Vis. Prof. of Law, Liverpool Univ., 1994–99. Trustee: Rowntree Foundn, 1996–2003; Apex Charitable Trust Ltd, 1996–2003 (Chm., 1997–2003; Pres., 2003–06); Trustee and Chm., Communities That Care (UK), 1997–2003 (Pres., 2003–07). Pres., Alone in London, 1998–2018; Vice-Pres., Catch 22 (formerly Rainer), 2007–10; Patron, The Place to Be, 1999–2018; Governor, Northwood Coll., 1975–96; Member, Council: UCL, 1980–84; Liverpool Univ., 1994–99 (Vice-Pres., 1996–99). Hon. LLD Liverpool, 1992; DUniv Open, 2007. *Publications:* (co-ed) Rayden on Divorce, 10th edn 1967, (cons. ed.) 17th edn 1997; (co-ed) Clarke Hall and Morrison on Children, 9th edn 1977, (cons. ed.) 10th edn 1985. *Address:* 15 Wellington House, Eton Road, NW3 4SY. *Club:* Reform.

**BOOTH, Martin Andrew;** Executive Director, Finance, Glasgow City Council, since 2018; *b* Glasgow, 13 Dec. 1966; *s* of Andrew Booth and Eileen Booth; *m* 2018, Anne; two *s*, and three step *s. Educ:* St Aloysius' Coll., Glasgow; Glasgow Caledonian Univ. (BA, MBA). FCPFA. Trainee accountant, Glasgow DC, 1988–94; Sen. Accountant, Central Regl Council, 1994–96; Principal Accountant, Clackmannanshire Council, 1996; Mgt Accountant, E Dunbartonshire Council, 1996–98; Asst Dir, HMP Kilmarnock, 1998–2000; Management Consultant: PricewaterhouseCoopers, 2000–03; IBM, 2003–06; Man. Dir, Isoplan, 2006–08; Hd, Finance, COSLA, 2008–10; Dir, Finance, Glasgow Life, 2010–18. *Recreations:* golf, Rugby, travel. *Address:* Glasgow City Council, City Chambers, Glasgow G2 1DU. *T:* (0141) 287 3837. *E:* martin.booth@glasgow.gov.uk. *Clubs:* Whitecraigs Golf (Capt., 2017); Glasgow Hutchesons' Aloysians Rugby Football.

**BOOTH, Michael John;** QC 1999; *b* Salford, 24 May 1958; *s* of Eric Charles Booth and Iris Booth (*née* Race); *m* 1987; two *s* one *d*; *m* 2015, Geraldine Riley. *Educ:* Manchester Grammar Sch. (Schol.); Trinity Coll., Cambridge (Open Schol.; MA Hons Law). Pres., Cambridge Union Soc., Michaelmas, 1979. Called to the Bar, Lincoln's Inn, 1981, Bencher, 2008. Mem., Manchester GS's winning team, ESU Nat. Schools Public Speaking Comp., 1975. *Recreations:* walking, swimming, reading, watching football, wine. *Address:* New Square Chambers, 12 New Square, Lincoln's Inn, WC2A 3SW.

**BOOTH, Peter John Richard;** National Organiser, Manufacturing, 1999–2007, and Textile National Trade Group Secretary, 1986–2007, T&G Section of Unite (formerly Transport and General Workers' Union); *b* 27 March 1949; *s* of Eric Albert and Edith Booth; *m* 1970, Edwina Ivy; three *s. Educ:* Little London Infant Sch.; Rawdon Littlemore Junior Sch., Rawdon; Benton Park Secondary Modern School. Dyers' Operative, 1964; National Union of Dyers, Bleachers and Textile Workers: District Officer, 1973; Nat. Research Officer, 1975; Nat. Organiser, 1980; transf. to TGWU, 1982; Nat. Trade Group Organiser, 1982. Member: Yorks and Humberside Regl Innovation Strategy, 1998–2000; Manufg Forum, DTI, 2005–; Manufg Task Gp, TUC, 2005–; Exec., Gen. Fedn of Trade Unions. Director: Man-Made Fibres Industry Trng Adv. Bd, 1986–98; Apparel, Knitting & Textiles Alliance, 1989–96; Nat. Textile Trading Orgn, 1998–2000; Skill-Fast UK, 2002–; Member: Internat. Textile, Garment and Leather Workers Fedn, 1986–2008 (Pres., 1996–2004); Confedn of British Wool Textiles Trng Bd, 1986–98; Carpet Industry Trng Council, 1986–95 (Chm.); Nat. Textile Trng Gp, 1989–2000 (Vice Pres.); Textile, Clothing and Strategy Gp; Presidium, European TU Cttee, 1990–2007; Textiles Industry Adv. Cttee, 1994–2007; Cotton & Allied Textiles Industry Adv. Cttee, 1986–94; Chairman: Wool Textile and Clothing Industry Action Cttee, 1996–98; Cotton Industry War Meml Trust, 2010– (Sec., 2014–). FRSA; CCMI 2006–10. *Publications:* The Old Dog Strike, 1985. *Recreations:* walking, gardening, dominoes, chess. *Address:* Unite (T&G Section), Unite House, 128 Theobalds Road, Holborn, WC1X 8TN.

**BOOTH, Richard John;** QC 2013; a Recorder, since 2008; *b* Newport, Mon, 30 May 1969; *s* of Lyndon Parry Booth and Judith Eleanor Booth (*née* Blandford); *m* 1995, Jo Cooper; one *s* one *d. Educ:* Monmouth Sch.; Michaelhouse, Kwazulu Natal; Fitzwilliam Coll., Cambridge (BA 1991); Univ. Libre de Bruxelles (Lic.Spec.Dr.Eur.). Called to the Bar, Middle Temple, 1993; in practice as barrister, specialising in medical law, professional discipline and sports law, 1993–; Jun. Counsel to the Crown, Attorney Gen.'s Regl Panel, 2000–12; Hd of Chambers, 2018–. Freeman, Haberdashers' Co. *Recreations:* sport (especially Rugby), live music. *Address:* 1 Crown Office Row, Temple, EC4Y 7HH. *T:* (020) 7797 7500, *Fax:* (020) 7797 7550. *E:* richard.booth@1cor.com. *Clubs:* East India; Monmouth Rugby Football; Old Monmothian (Pres., 2011–13).

**BOOTH, Roger Hignett;** Royal Academy of Engineering Visiting Professor, Department of Engineering Science, University of Oxford, 1998–2006; *b* 3 May 1940; *s* of David and Elsie Booth; *m* 1st, 1968, Maureen (*née* Howell) (marr. diss. 1996); two *s*; 2nd, 1997, Thelly (*née* Price). *Educ:* Bentham Grammar Sch.; Birmingham Univ. (BSc Chem. Engrg). MIChemE 1966; CEng 1973. Royal Dutch/Shell Gp (posts in UK, Indonesia, USA, Netherlands, Pakistan), 1961–96; Dir, Solar Century Hldgs Ltd, 1999–2003. Mem., Newnham Parish Council, 2004–12. *Publications:* articles on renewable energy and sustainable develt. *Recreations:* walking, reading, dining with friends, listening to music. *Address:* Firtree Cottage, Newnham Road, Newnham, Hook RG27 9AE. *T:* 07777 680734.

**BOOTH, Sarah Ann;** see Hinkley, S. A.

**BOOTH, Vernon Edward Hartley;** see Booth, H.

**BOOTHBY, Sir Brooke (Charles),** 16th Bt *cr* 1660, of Broadlow Ash, Derbyshire; Vice Lord-Lieutenant, South Glamorgan, since 2011; Chairman: Adventure Activities Licensing Service, since 2007; Adventure Activities Licensing Authority, 1996–2007; *b* 6 April 1949; *s* of Sir Hugo Robert Brooke Boothby, 15th Bt and (Evelyn) Ann (*d* 1993), *d* of late H. C. R. Homfray; *S* father, 1986; *m* 1976, Georgiana Alexandra, *o d* of late Sir John Wriothesley Russell, GCVO, CMG; two *d. Educ:* Eton; Trinity Coll., Cambridge (BA Econs). Chm., Associated Quality Services, 1994–2008; Man. Dir, 1979–95, Vice Chm., 1995–2003, Chm., 2004–, Fontygary Parks Ltd (formerly Fontygary Leisure); Dir, Bradford Rural Estates Ltd, 2001–19. Chm., Capital Region Tourism, 2002–03; Dir, Wales Tourism Alliance, 2002–09. Chairman: Nat. Caravan Council Parks Div., 1987–90; Historic Houses Assoc. for Wales, 2009–13. President: Glamorgan Br., CLA, 1992–94; Vale of Glamorgan Nat. Trust, 1998–2019. Hon. Treas., Consular Assoc. in Wales, 2010–12. Hon. Consul for the Republic of Malta in Wales, 2007–19. High Sheriff, 1986–87, DL, 2007, South Glamorgan. Gov., United World Coll. of the Atlantic, 2003–06. *Recreation:* gardening. *Heir: kinsman* George William Boothby [*b* 18 June 1948; *m* 1977, Sally Louisa Thomas; three *d*]. *Address:* Church House, Penllyn, Cowbridge, Vale of Glamorgan CF71 7RQ. *T:* (01446) 775666. *E:* sirbrookeboothby@hotmail.com.

**BOOTHMAN, His Honour Campbell Lester;** a Circuit Judge, 1988–2003; *b* 3 Sept. 1942; *s* of Gerald and Ann Boothman; *m* 1966, Penelope Evelyn Pepe; three *s. Educ:* Oundle; King's College, London. Called to the Bar, Inner Temple, 1965. A Recorder, 1985–88. *Recreations:* ski-ing, squash. *Address:* 13 The Keg Store, Bath Street, Bristol BS1 6HL.

**BOOTHMAN, Nicholas,** CEng; Director of Technology, Metropolitan Police Service, 1992–2000; *b* 16 Dec. 1941; *s* of late Frederick Boothman and Sarah Ellen (*née* Kirk); *m* 1964, Ernestine Carole Jane Billings; one *d. Educ:* Threshfield Sch.; Ermysted's Grammar Sch., Skipton; Univ. of Birmingham (BSc Physics). CEng, MIET (MIEE 1972). Research at GEC Hirst Res. Centre, Wembley, 1963–72; project management of communication systems for RAF, MoD (PE), 1972–77; Project Manager, Metropolitan Police Office, 1977–88; Chief Engr, Metropolitan Police, 1988–92. *Recreations:* amateur musician, watching cricket, railways, unavoidable gardening. *Address:* 57A Wensleydale Road, Hampton, Middx TW12 2LP.

**BOOTHROYD, Baroness** *cr* 2000 (Life Peer), of Sandwell in the co. of West Midlands; **Betty Boothroyd,** OM 2005; PC 1992; Speaker of the House of Commons, 1992–2000; *b* Dewsbury, 8 Oct. 1929; *d* of Archibald and Mary Boothroyd. *Educ:* Dewsbury Coll. of Commerce and Art. Personal/Political Asst to Labour Ministers. Delegate to N Atlantic Assembly, 1974. MP (Lab) West Bromwich, May 1973–1974, West Bromwich West, 1974–92 (when elected Speaker); MP West Bromwich West, 1992–2000. An Asst Govt Whip, Oct. 1974–Nov. 1975; Dep. Chm. of Ways and Means, and Dep. Speaker, 1987–92. Member: Select Cttee on Foreign Affairs, 1979–81; Speaker's Panel of Chairmen, 1979–87; House of Commons Commn, 1983–87. Mem., European Parlt, 1975–77. Mem., Labour Party NEC, 1981–87. Contested (Lab): SE Leicester (by-elec.), 1957; Peterborough (gen. elec.), 1959; Nelson and Colne (by-elec.), 1968; Rossendale (gen. elec.), 1970. Chancellor, Open Univ., 1994–2007. Hon. Bencher, Middle Temple, 2011. Hon. FCOptom 2005. Freeman: Borough of Sandwell, 1992; Borough of Kirklees, 1992; City of London, 1993; Hon. Freeman: Lightmongers' Co., 2003; Grocers' Co., 2005; Hon. Liveryman: Feltmakers' Co., 1993; Glovers' Co., 1997. Hon. LLD: Birmingham, 1992; South Bank, 1992; Leicester, 1993; Cambridge, 1994; St Andrews, 2001; Hon. DLitt Bradford, 1993; DUniv: Leeds Metropolitan, 1993; North London, 1993; Hon. DCL Oxford, 1995. *Publications:* Betty Boothroyd: the autobiography, 2001. *Address:* House of Lords, SW1A 0PW.

**BOOTLE, Roger Paul;** Chairman, Capital Economics Ltd, since 2016 (Executive Chairman, 2014–16; Managing Director, 1999–2014); *b* 22 June 1952; *s* of David Bootle and Florence (*née* Denman); *m* 1st, 1993, Sally Broomfield (marr. diss. 2007); one *s* two *d*; 2nd, 2011, Alya Samokhvalova. *Educ:* Merton Coll., Oxford (BA PPE 1973); Nuffield Coll., Oxford (MPhil Econs 1975). Chief Economist: Capel-Cure Myers, 1982–86; Lloyds Merchant Bank, 1986–89; Greenwell Montagu, 1989–92; HSBC Markets, 1992–96; Gp Chief Economist, HSBC, 1996–98. Vis. Prof., Manchester Business Sch., 1995–2003. Mem., Chancellor of the Exchequer's Panel of Ind. Econ. Advrs, 1997; Specialist Advr, H of C Treasury Cttee, 1998–2017. Econ. Advr, Deloitte, 1999–2011. Columnist: The Times, 1997–99; Sunday Telegraph, 1999–2006; Daily Telegraph, 2006–. Wolfson Prize for Econs, 2012. *Publications:* (with W. T. Newlyn) Theory of Money, 1978; Index-Linked Gilts, 1985; The Death of Inflation, 1996; Money for Nothing, 2003; The Trouble with Markets, 2009; The Trouble with Europe, 2014, 4th edn as Making a Success of Brexit and

Reforming the EU, 2017; The AI Economy: work, wealth and welfare in the robot age, 2019. *Recreations:* squash, horse-racing, classical music, bridge. *Address:* Capital Economics Ltd, 5th Floor, 100 Victoria Street, Cardinal Place, SW1E 5JL. *T:* (020) 7823 5000.

**BOOTLE-WILBRAHAM,** family name of **Baron Skelmersdale**.

**BOPA RAI, Aprampar Apar Jot Kaur, (Joti), (Mrs W. F. Casey);** a District Judge (Magistrates' Courts), since 2004; *b* 18 Feb. 1957; *d* of Manjit Singh Bopa Rai and Swaran Kaur Bopa Rai; *m* 1993, William Francis Casey. *Educ:* Wolverhampton Polytech. (LLB (Law) 1980); Coll. of Law, Guildford. Admitted solicitor, 1984; Asst Solicitor, Partner, Elgoods, Cheltenham, 1984–89; Partner, Tarlings, Cheltenham, 1989–93; sole practitioner, 1993–2004; Dep. Dist Judge, 2000–04. *Recreations:* walking, ski-ing, reading, visiting historic sites.

**BORBIDGE, Hon. Robert Edward,** AO 2006; Chairman: Cedar Creek Cellars, since 2007; ATM, since 2012; LifeFlight Australia (formerly CareFlight Group (Qld)), since 2013; Legacy Committee, 2018 Commonwealth Games, since 2015; Senior Counsel, Govstrat, since 2011; consultant; *b* Ararat, Vic, 12 Aug. 1954; *s* of Edward A. Borbidge and Jean, (Jane), Borbidge; *m* 1984, Jennifer Gooding; one *s* one *d*. *Educ:* Ararat High Sch., Vic; Overberg High Sch., S Africa. Mem. Bd, Gold Coast Visitors' Bureau, 1980. MLA (Nat.) Surfers Paradise, Qld, 1980–2001; formerly Mem., Qld Parly Delegn, Qld Govt Cttees on Transport, Tourism, Nat. Parks, Sport and Arts, Ind. and Commerce, Local Govt, Main Roads and Police; Minister: for Industry, Small Business, Communications and Technol., 1987–89; for Ind., Small Business, Technol. and Tourism, then for Police, Emergency Services and Corrective Services, and subseq. for Tourism and for Envmt, Conservation and Forestry, 1989; Opposition spokesman on Small Business, Manufg and Regl Devlt and Assisting Leader on Econ. and Trade Devlt, 1990–91; Dep. Leader of Opposition, 1989–91, Leader, 1991–95 and 1998–2001; Premier of Qld and Minister responsible for Ethnic Affairs, 1996–98; Leader, Qld Nat. Party-Lib. Party Coalition, 1992–2001. Chair, Study Gold Coast, 2013–. Chairman: Asset Loan Co., 2004; CEC Gp, 2004–08; Early Learning Services, 2007–08; Rotec Design, 2003–14. Chairman: Australian Sports Coll.; Australian Acad. of Sport Ltd. Griffith University: Chm., Bd of Advice (formerly Exec. Task Force), Inst. for Glycomics, 2003–; Member: Univ. Council, 2006–; Univ. Foundn, 2006–; Trustee, Friends of Griffith Univ., USA, 2004–. DUniv Griffith, 2004. Centenary Medal (Australia), 2001. *Recreations:* travel, reading, tourism, swimming. *Address:* PO Box 84, Isle of Capri, Qld 4217, Australia.

**BORCHERDS, Prof. Richard Ewen,** FRS 1994; Professor of Mathematics, University of California at Berkeley, 1993–96 and since 1999; *b* 29 Nov. 1959; *s* of Dr Peter Howard Borcherds and Margaret Elizabeth Borcherds; *m* Ursula Gritsch. *Educ:* Trinity Coll., Cambridge (BA, MA; PhD 1985). Research Fellow, Trinity Coll., Cambridge, 1983–87; Morrey Asst Prof., Univ. of California, Berkeley, 1987–88; Cambridge University: Royal Soc. Univ. Res. Fellow, 1988–92; Lectr, 1992–93; Royal Soc. Prof., Dept of Maths, 1996–99. Fields Medal, Internat. Mathematical Union, 1998. *Publications:* papers in math. jls. *Address:* Department of Mathematics, University of California, 927 Evans Hall # 3840, Berkeley, CA 94720–3840, USA.

**BORDEN, Prof. Iain Michael,** PhD; Professor of Architecture and Urban Culture, Bartlett School of Architecture, since 2002, and Vice-Dean for Education, Bartlett Faculty of the Built Environment, since 2015, University College London; *b* 9 Nov. 1962; *s* of Anthony Ian Borden and Shelagh Mary Borden; *m* 2001, Claire Haywood; one *s*. *Educ:* Univ. of Newcastle upon Tyne (BA Hist. of Art, Arch. and Ancient Hist. 1985); Bartlett Sch., University Coll. London (MSc Hist. of Modern Arch. 1986); Univ. of Calif, LA (MA Hist. of Arch. and Planning 1989); PhD London 1998. Bartlett School of Architecture, University College London: Lectr, 1989–97, Sen. Lectr, 1997–99, in Architectural Hist.; Reader in Arch. and Urban Culture, 1999–2002; Dir, 2001–05; Head, 2005–09; Sub-Dean and Vice-Dean, 1996–2001, Vice-Dean for Communications, 2011–15, Bartlett Faculty of the Built Envmt, UCL. Hon. FRIBA 2003. *Publications:* (ed with D. Dunster) Architecture and the Sites of History: interpretations of buildings and cities, 1995; (ed jtly) Strangely Familiar: narratives of architecture in the city, 1996; (ed jtly) Gender Space Architecture: an interdisciplinary introduction, 1999; (ed jtly) The City Cultures Reader, 2000, 2nd edn 2003; (ed with J. Rendell) InterSections: architectural histories and critical theories, 2000; (with K. Rüedi) The Dissertation: an architecture student's handbook, 2000, 3rd edn as The Dissertation: a guide for architecture students, 2014; (ed jtly) The Unknown City: contesting architecture and social space, 2001; Skateboarding, Space and the City: architecture and the body, 2001; Manual: the architecture and office of Alford Hall Monaghan Morris, 2003; (ed jtly) Bartlett Works, 2004; (ed jtly) Transculturation: cities, spaces and architectures in Latin America, 2005; (ed jtly) Bartlett Designs: speculating with architecture, 2009; Drive: journeys through film, cities and landscapes, 2012; (ed jtly) Forty Ways To Think About Architecture, 2014; Skateboarding and the City: a complete history, 2019. *Recreations:* driving, photography, skateboarding, wandering around cities. *Address:* Bartlett School of Architecture, University College London, 22 Gordon Street, WC1H 0QB. *E:* i.borden@ucl.ac.uk.

**BORDER, Allan Robert,** AO 1989 (AM 1986); journalist and sports commentator; Director: Queensland Cricket, 2001 (Life Member, since 2010); Cricket Australia, 2002–09; *b* 27 July 1955; *s* of John and Sheila Border; *m* 1980, Jane, *d* of John and Eve Hiscox; two *s* two *d*. *Educ:* N Sydney Tech. Sch.; N Sydney High Sch. First class cricket début, for NSW, 1976; professional cricketer, Queensland State, 1977–96 (Captain, 1983–84); Test début, 1978; Captain, Australian cricket team, 1984–94; played 156 Test matches for Australia, with record of 93 as Captain, scored 27 centuries and 2 double centuries, record total of 11,174 Test runs, also took 39 wickets and record 156 catches; in all first-class cricket matches to 1994, had scored 25,551 runs incl. 68 centuries, and taken 102 wickets and 345 catches. Mem., Nat. Cricket Selection Panel, Aust., 1998–2005 and 2006. With Ronald McConnell Hldgs, 1980–84; with Castlemaine Perkins, 1984–98. Columnist, Courier Mail; commentator, Fox Sports TV. *Publications:* Beyond Ten Thousand: my life story, 1994; Cricket As I See It, 2014. *Address:* c/o Cricket Australia, 60 Jolimont Street, Jolimont, Vic 3002, Australia.

**BORE, Sir Albert,** Kt 2002; Member (Lab), Birmingham City Council, since 1980 (Leader, 1999–2004 and 2012–15); Chairman, University Hospital Birmingham NHS Foundation Trust, 2006–13. Former Lectr in Physics, Aston Univ. Chairman: Birmingham Econ. Develt Cttee, 1984–93; Member: Bd, Advantage West Midlands, 1999–2002; Birmingham Marketing Partnership. Director: Aston Sci. Park; Nat. Exhibition Centre Ltd; Birmingham Technol. Ltd; NEC Finance plc; Optima Community Assoc.; non-exec. Dir, Colliers CRE, 2005–. Pres., EU Cttee of the Regions, 2002–04 (Mem., 1994–). *Address:* c/o Birmingham City Council, Council House, Victoria Square, Birmingham B1 1BB.

**BOREEL, Sir Stephan Gerard,** 14th Bt *cr* 1645, of Amsterdam; *b* 9 Feb. 1945; *s* of Gerard Lucas Boreel and Virginia Rae Bright; *S* kinsman, Sir Francis Boreel, 13th Bt, 2001, but his name does not appear on the Official Roll of the Baronetage; *m* 1972, Francien P. Kooijman; one *s*. *Heir: s* Jacob Lucas Cornelis Boreel, *b* 29 Sept. 1974.

**BORELAND-KELLY, Dame Lorna (May),** DBE 1998; JP; Chief Executive Officer, Bokell Associates, since 2013; *b* 9 Aug. 1952; *d* of late James Boreland and Hortence Boreland Swaby (*née* Boyd); *m* Anthony Owen Kelly; three *s* three *d*. *Educ:* North London Univ. (CQSW 1991). Sen. Practitioner, Social Work Children and Families, St Thomas' Hosp., 1997–2000; Team Manager, 2001–01, Hospital Manager, Children and Families, 2001–07, Mayday Hosp., Croydon; Mayday and Permanence Manager, Dept of Children, Young People and Learners, Mayday NHS Trust, Croydon, 2008–09; Strategic Advisor: Social Work Acad., Children, Young People and Learners, Croydon Council, 2010–13; Mgt and Social Devlt Work, Social Work Acad., Medway Councils, 2013–14. Chair, Professional Capabilities Framework Quality Assurance Gp, Coll. of Social Work, 2013– (Mem., Professional (formerly Transitional Professional) Assembly, 2012–13). Mem., Judicial Appts Commn, 2006–12. Chair of Govs, Lambeth Coll., 1992–2013. Mem., Editl Bd, Community Care Inform, 2010–. Mem., Coll. of Social Work, 2011. Mem., Union of Catholic Mothers. FRSA 2000. JP Central London (Westminster), 1991. *Recreations:* reading, writing short stories (never to be published), walking, boxing, swimming. *Address:* c/o Bokell Associates Ltd, 34 Upper Close, Forest Row RH18 5DX.

**BORG, Alan Charles Nelson,** CBE 1991; PhD; FSA; Director, Victoria and Albert Museum, 1995–2001; *b* 21 Jan. 1942; *s* of late Charles John Nelson Borg and Frances Mary Olive Hughes; *m* 1st, 1964, Anne (marr. diss.), *d* of late Dr William Blackmore; one *s* one *d*; 2nd, 1976, Lady Caroline, *d* of late Captain Lord Francis Hill, *yr s* of 6th Marquess of Downshire; two *d*. *Educ:* Westminster Sch.; Brasenose Coll., Oxford (MA); Courtauld Inst. of Art (PhD). Lecteur d'anglais, Université d'Aix-Marseille, 1964–65; Lectr, History of Art, Indiana Univ., 1967–69; Asst Prof. of History of Art, Princeton Univ., 1969–70; Asst Keeper of the Royal Armouries, HM Tower of London, 1970–78; Keeper, Sainsbury Centre for Visual Arts, Univ. of E Anglia, 1978–82; Dir Gen., Imperial War Mus., 1982–95. Vis. Prof., Univ. of Reading, 2010–. Member: British Nat. Cttee for Hist. of Second World War, 1982–95; Bd of War Studies, KCL, 1982–95; COPUS, 1992–95; Council, Museums Assoc., 1992–95; Adv. Cttee on Public Records, 1993–99; Court of Advisers, St Paul's Cathedral, 1996–2000; Bd of Mgt, Courtauld Inst. of Art, 1998–2002; Chm., Nat. Inventory of War Memls, 1988–95; Admin. Council, Louvre Mus., 1999–2001. Chm., Nat. Mus. Dirs' Conf., 1998–2000. President: Elizabethan Club, 1994–2000; Meyrick Soc., 1994–. Trustee: Foundling Museum, 1998–2010 (Chm. Trustees, 2006–09); Vice Pres., 2010–); Handel House, 2002–06; St Paul's Cathedral Foundn, 2002–05; Topolski Memoir, 2007–10. Governor: Thomas Coram Foundn for Children, 1995–2005; Westminster Sch., 1998–2019. Freeman, City of London, 1997; Hon. Liveryman, Painter Stainers' Co., 1997; Hon. Freeman, Cooks' Co., 2011. Librarian and Trustee, Priory of England and the Islands, Order of St John, 2007–. KStJ 2012 (OStJ 2007). Hon. FRCA 1991; Hon. FRIBA 2001. DUniv Sheffield Hallam, 2000. *Publications:* Architectural Sculpture in Romanesque Provence, 1972; European Swords and Daggers in the Tower of London, 1974; Torture and Punishment, 1975; Heads and Horses, 1976; Arms and Armour in Britain, 1979; (ed with A. R. Martindale) The Vanishing Past: studies presented to Christopher Hohler, 1981; War Memorials, 1991; The History of the Worshipful Company of Painter-Stainers, 2005; A History of the Worshipful Company of Cooks, 2011; (with D. Coke) Vauxhall Gardens, 2011; articles in learned jls. *Recreations:* fencing (Oxford blue, 1962, 1963), music, travel. *Address:* 16 Devonshire House, 1 Lindsay Square, Pimlico, SW1V 2HN. *Clubs:* Beefsteak, Special Forces.

**BORG, Björn Rune;** professional tennis player, 1972–83 and 1991–93, now playing on ATP Champions Tour; *b* 6 June 1956; *s* of late Rune Borg and of Margaretha Borg; *m* 1st, 1980, Mariana Simionescu (marr. diss. 1984); one *s* by Jannike Björling; 2nd, 1989, Loredana Berte (marr. diss. 1992); 3rd, 2002, Patricia Östfeldt; one *s*. *Educ:* Blombacka Sch., Södertälje. Started to play tennis at age of 9; won Wimbledon junior title, 1972; became professional player in 1972. Mem., Swedish Davis Cup team, annually 1972–80 (youngest player ever in a winning Davis Cup team, 1975). Championship titles: Italian, 1974, 1978; French, 1974, 1975, 1978, 1979, 1980, 1981; Wimbledon, record of 5 consecutive singles titles, 1976–80; World Champion, 1978, 1979, 1980; Masters, 1980, 1981. Owner, fashion label, Björn Borg. *Publications:* (with Eugene Scott) Björn Borg: my life and game, 1980. *Address:* c/o IMG, Building 6, Chiswick Park, 566 Chiswick High Road, W4 5HR.

**BORG, Joseph,** LLD; Senior Lecturer, 1988–2004 and 2010–17, and Chairman, Mediterranean Academy of Diplomatic Studies, 2010–17, University of Malta; *b* 19 March 1952; *m* Isabelle Agius; one *s* one *d*. *Educ:* Univ. of Malta (NP 1974; LLD 1975); University Coll. of Wales, Aberystwyth (LLM 1988). Legal advr to cos and corporate bodies, Malta and abroad, 1976–98; Lectr in Law, Univ. of Malta, 1979–88. Dir, Central Bank of Malta, 1992–95. MP (Nationalist), Malta, 1995–2004; Parly Sec., Min. of Foreign Affairs, 1998–99; Minister of Foreign Affairs, 1999–2004; Mem., EC, 2004–10. Chm., Malta Maritime Forum, 2015–. Non-exec. Dir, AgriBank plc, 2012– (Chm., 2013–). Hon. DLitt Malta, 2016.

**BÖRJESSON, Rolf Libert;** Chairman: Rexam PLC, 2004–08 (Chief Executive, 1996–2004); Ahlsell AB, 2006–12; *b* 27 Sept. 1942; *s* of Stig Allan Börjesson and Brita Ahlström; *m* 1969, Kristina Ivarsson; two *d*. *Educ:* Chalmers Univ., Gothenburg (MSc Chem. Engrg). With Steenberg & Flygt, 1968–71; ITT Europe, Brussels, 1971–74; President: Sund Akesson/Sundpacma, 1974–77; AB Securitas Industrier, 1977–81; Wayne Europe, 1981–87; PLM AB: Exec. Vice Pres., 1987–88; Chief Operating Officer, 1988–90; Pres. and CEO, 1990–96. Chm., LifeAir (formerly Biolight, then Ascenditur) AB, 2011–; non-executive Director: SCA AB, 2003–15; Avery Dennison, 2005–15; Huhtamaki Gp, 2008–18. *Recreations:* shooting, ski-ing, riding.

**BORLAND, Polly;** photographic artist; *b* E Melbourne, Australia; *d* of Kevin William Borland and Margaret Agnes Aitken; *m* 1989, John Anthony Hillcoat; one *s*. *Educ:* Primary Sch., Preshil; Mitcham High Sch., Tenaden; Royal Melbourne Inst. of Technol. (Dip. Photography with Hons). Self-employed photographic portraiturist and editorial photographic-based artist. Hon. FRPS 2002. *Publications:* (jtly) Australians, 2000; The Babies, 2001; (jtly) Bunny, 2008; (jtly) Smudge, 2010; (jtly) Polly Borland: Everything I Want to Be When I Grow Up, 2012; You, 2013; Morph, 2018. *Address:* 7523 Mulholland Drive, Los Angeles, CA 90046, USA. *T:* (323) 3887657. *E:* pollyborland@hotmail.com. *Club:* Blacks.

**BORLEY, Lester,** CBE 1993; Secretary General, 1993–96, Member Council, since 1990, Europa Nostra, The Hague; Chairman, Europa Nostra UK, since 2009; *b* 7 April 1931; *er s* of Edwin Richard Borley and Mary Dorena Davies; *m* Mary Alison, *e d* of Edward John Pearce and Kathleen Florence Barratt; three *d*. *Educ:* Dover Grammar Sch.; Queen Mary Coll. and Birkbeck Coll., London Univ. Pres. of Union, QMC, 1953; Dep. Pres., Univ. of London Union, 1954; ESU debating team tour of USA, 1955. Joined British Travel Assoc., 1955; Asst to Gen. Manager, USA, 1957–61; Manager: Chicago Office, 1961–64; Australia, 1964–67; West Germany, 1967–69; Chief Executive: Scottish Tourist Bd, 1970–75; English Tourist Bd, 1975–83; Dir, Nat. Trust for Scotland, 1983–93 (Mem. Council, 2002–07). Member: Exec. Cttee, Scotland's Garden Scheme, 1970–75, 1983–93; Council, Nat. Gardens Scheme, 1975–83; Park and Gardens Cttee, Zool Soc. of London, 1979–83; Internat. Cultural Tourism Cttee, ICOMOS, 1990–; Chm., Cultural Tourism Cttee, ICOMOS (UK), 1993–2003. Adviser: World Monuments Fund, NY, 1995–; UNESCO

World Heritage Centre, Paris, 2002–; Mem., Scotland Cttee, Nat. Commn, UNESCO UK, 2008–. Governor, Edinburgh Film House, 1987–96 (Hon. Vice Pres., 1996–2007); Trustee: Cromarty Arts Trust, 1995–2006; Hopetoun House Preservation Trust, 1998–2002. Visiting Lecturer: Acad. Istropolitana Nova, Bratislava, 1993–; Coll. of New Europe, Krakow, 1998–; Faculty Mem., Salzburg Seminar, 1996. Organiser of and speaker at many internat. confs on conservation and cultural heritage. Founder Fellow, Tourism Soc., 1978. FRSA 1982. Hon. FRSGS 1989. DLitt *hc* Robert Gordon Inst. of Technology, Aberdeen, 1991. Honorable Kentucky Col. 1963. *Publications:* English Cathedrals and Tourism, 1979; Historic Cities and Sustainable Tourism, 1995; Sustaining the Cultural Heritage of Europe, 1998; (ed) Dear Maurice: Culture and Identity in late 20th Century Scotland, 1998; (ed) To be a Pilgrim: meeting the needs of visitors to cathedrals and great churches in the UK, 2001; (ed) Hugh Miller in Context, 2002; (ed) Celebrating The Life and Times of Hugh Miller: Scotland in the early 19th century, 2003; (ed) The Grand Tour and its Influence on Architecture, Artistic Taste and Patronage, 2008; contributor to: Patronage of the Arts by Foundations and NGOs in Europe, 1991; Universal Tourism, 1992; Cultural Tourism, 1994; Manual of Heritage Management, 1994; Tourism and Culture, 1996; Il Paesaggio Culturale nelle strategia europee, 1996; Preserving the Built Heritage, 1997. *Recreations:* reading, listening to music, visiting exhibitions, collecting glass and ceramics, gardening. *Address:* 4 Belford Place, Edinburgh EH4 3DH. *Club:* New (Edinburgh).

**BORMAN, Tracy,** PhD; writer and historian, since 2004; Chief Executive, Heritage Education Trust, since 2008; Joint Chief Curator, Historic Royal Palaces, since 2013; *b* Lincoln, 1 Jan. 1972; *d* of John Borman and Joan Borman; *m* 2015, Thomas Ashworth; one *d*. *Educ:* William Farr Sch., Lincoln; Yarborough High Sch., Lincoln; Univ. of Hull (BA, MA; PhD 1997). Hd, Interpretation, Nat. Archives, 1999–2001; Learning Dir, English Heritage, 2001–08. Pres., Marble Hill Soc., 2013–. Trustee: Buccleuch Living Heritage Trust, 2016–; Nat. Archives Trust, 2018–. Hon. DLit Hull, 2017. *Publications:* Henrietta Howard: king's mistress, queen's servant, 2007; Elizabeth's Women: the hidden story of the Virgin Queen, 2009; The Ring and the Crown: a history of royal weddings 1066–2011, 2011; Matilda: Queen of the Conqueror, 2011; Witches: a tale of sorcery, scandal and seduction, 2013; Thomas Cromwell: the hidden story of Henry VIII's most faithful servant, 2014; The Story of the Tower of London, 2015; The Private Lives of the Tudors, 2016; The King's Witch (novel), 2018; Henry VIII and the Men Who Made Him, 2018; The Story of Kensington Palace, 2019; The Devil's Slave (novel), 2019. *Recreations:* walking, cycling, family, seeking out the best coffee and cakes in London. *Address:* Apartment 25, Hampton Court Palace, Surrey KT8 9AU. *T:* 07950 436859. *E:* tracy.borman@googlemail.com.

**BORN, Gary Brian;** Partner, Wilmer Cutler Pickering Hale and Dorr (formerly Wilmer Cutler & Pickering) LLP, since 1988; *b* New York, 14 Sept. 1955; *s* of Clyde Raymond and Eleanor Born; *m* 1986, Beatrix von Wedel; one *s* one *d*. *Educ:* Haverford Coll., Pennsylvania (BA summa cum laude 1978); Univ. of Pennsylvania Law Sch. (JD summa cum laude 1981). Rapporteur, Cttee on Extraterritorial Application of Nat Laws, ICC, 1985–90; Associate Prof. of Law, Univ. of Arizona Coll. of Law, 1987–88; Adjunct Prof. of Law, Georgetown Law Sch., 1987–91; Lectr, Stanford Law Sch., 2007–09; Adjunct Prof., Sch. of Transnat. Law, Peking Univ., 2010; Vis. Prof. of Law and Kwa Geok Choo Dist. Visitor, Nat. Univ. of Singapore, 2011; Lectr, Harvard Law Sch., 2011–12; Hon. Prof. of Law, Univ. of St Gallen, Switzerland, 2012–; Bok Internat. Law Prof., Univ. of Pennsylvania Law Sch., 2013–14; Vis. Prof. of Law, Tsinghua Univ. Sch. of Law, 2014–. Member: Singapore Internat. Arbitration Centre Court of Arbitration, 2013–; Court of Arbitration, Jerusalem Arbitration Center, 2014–. Co-Chair, Cttee on Internat. Aspects of Litigation, Internat. Section, ABA, 1989–92. Member: Bd, Inst. for US Studies, 1996–2001; Amer. Law Inst., 1999–; Acad. Council, Inst. for Transnat. Arbitration, 2009–. Member: Exec. Council, Amer. Soc. of Internat. Law, 1991–94 (Exec. Vice-Pres., 2014–); Adv. Ctttee, Amer. Law Inst. Project on Internat. Commercial Arbitration Law of US, 2009–; Adv. Bd, Africa Internat. Legal Awareness, 2011–; Adv. Cttee, Amer. Law Inst. Restatement (Fourth) Foreign Relations Law of US, 2013–; Internat. Arbitration Cttee, Korean Commercial Arbitration Bd, 2014–; Internat. Adv. Bd, Hong Kong Internat. Arbitration Centre, 2014–; Global Adv. Bd, NY Internat. Arbitration Center, 2014–. Chm., Bd of Trustees, Haverford Coll. Foundn (UK) Ltd, 2012–; Mem., Bd of Trustees, British Inst. of Internat. and Comparative Law, 2010–. Hon. LLD Wayne State, 2012. Member: Adv. Bd, Indian Jl of Arbitration Law, 2012–; Editl Adv. Bd, Jl of World Investment and Trade, 2013–. *Publications:* (jtly) The Extraterritorial Application of National Laws, 1987; International Civil Litigation in United States Courts, 1990, 5th edn 2011; International Commercial Arbitration: commentary and materials, 1996, 2nd edn 2000; International Arbitration and Forum Selection Agreements: drafting and enforcing, 1999, 3rd edn 2010; International Commercial Arbitration, 2009, 2nd edn 2014; International Arbitration: cases and materials, 2011, 2nd edn 2014; International Arbitration: law and practice, 2012. *Recreation:* my children. *Address:* Wilmer Cutler Pickering Hale and Dorr LLP, 49 Park Lane, W1K 1PS. *T:* (020) 7872 1000, *Fax:* (020) 7872 1699. *E:* gary.born@wilmerhale.com.

**BORN, Prof. Georgina Emma Mary,** OBE 2016; PhD; FBA 2014; FRAI; Professor of Music and Anthropology, and Senior Research Fellow, University of Oxford, since 2010; Fellow, Mansfield College, Oxford, since 2012; *b* Wheatley, Oxon, 15 Nov. 1955; *d* of Prof. Gustav Victor Rudolf Born, FRS and Dr Wilfrida Ann Born (later Mully); partner, Prof. Andrew M. Barry; one *s* one *d*. *Educ:* Godolphin and Latymer Sch.; Purcell Sch., London; Dartington Hall Sch., Devon; Royal Coll. of Music (Jun. Exhibnr); Chelsea Sch. of Art; University Coll. London (BSc 1st Cl. Hons Anthropol. 1982; PhD Anthropol. 1989). Cellist and bass guitarist, Henry Cow, Mike Westbrook's Orch., Derek Bailey's Co., 1976–89; Lecturer: Dept of Human Scis, Brunel Univ., 1986–89; Dept of Media and Communications, Goldsmiths' Coll., Univ. of London, 1989–97; Sen. Res. Fellow, King's Coll., Cambridge, 1997–98; Fellow and Dir of Studies in Social and Pol Scis, Emmanuel Coll., Cambridge, 1998–2006; University of Cambridge: Lectr in Social and Pol Scis, 1998–2003; Reader, 2003–06; Prof. of Sociol., Anthropol. and Music, 2006–10; Fellow, Girton Coll., Cambridge, 2008–10. Vis. Prof., Inst. of Musicol., Aarhus Univ., 1996–97; Hon. Prof., Dept of Anthropol., UCL, 2006–11; Schulich Dist. Vis. Prof. and Dean's Chair in Music, McGill Univ., 2013–15; Bloch Dist. Vis. Prof. in Music, Univ. of Calif. Berkeley, 2014; Vis. Prof., Dept of Musicol., Univ. of Oslo, 2014–19; Dist. Vis. Prof., Univ. of Calif. Irvine, 2019; Fellow, Humanities Res. Inst., Univ. of Calif, 2002–03; Vis. Fellow, Centre for Critical and Cultural Studies, Univ. of Qld, 2006; Rayson Huang Lectr, Univ. of Hong Kong, 2018; Sen. Fellow, Inst. of Advanced Studies, Aarhus Univ., 2018–19. Radcliffe-Brown Lectr in Social Anthropol., British Acad., 2015. Advr, H of L Select Cttee on review of BBC's Charter, 2005. Consultant, NESTA, 2005. FRAI 1998. Dent Medal, Royal Musical Assoc., 2007. *Publications:* Rationalizing Culture: IRCAM, Boulez, and the institutionalization of the musical avant-garde, 1995; (ed with D. Hesmondhalgh) Western Music and its Others: difference, representation and appropriation in music, 2000; Uncertain Vision: Birt, Dyke and the reinvention of the BBC, 2004, 2nd edn 2005; (ed with A. Barry) Interdisciplinarity: reconfigurations of the social and natural sciences, 2013; (ed) Music, Sound and Space, 2013; (ed jtly) Improvisation and Social Aesthetics, 2017.

*Recreations:* family, reading, politics, music and sound, film and television, art, walking, travel. *Address:* Faculty of Music, St Aldate's, University of Oxford, Oxford OX1 1DB. *T:* (01865) 286079. *E:* georgina.born@music.ox.ac.uk.

**BORODALE, Viscount; Sean David Beatty;** poet and artist; *b* 12 June 1973; *s* and heir of 3rd Earl Beatty, *qv*; *m* 2002, Susan Jane Hill; two *s*. *Publications:* Notes for an Atlas, 2003; Bee Journal (poetry), 2012; Human Work (poetry), 2015; Asylum (poetry), 2018. *Heir: s* Hon. Orlando Thomas Beatty, *b* 17 Nov. 2003.

**BORRELL, Roger;** Group Editor, Archant Life magazines (North), since 2010; Editor, Lancashire Life magazine, since 2006; *b* 26 May 1954; *s* of Henry and Joy Borrell; *m* 1st, Anne Youngman (marr. diss.); one *s* one *d*; 2nd, 2010, Barbara Waite. *Educ:* Falmouth Grammar Sch. Dep. Ed., Newcastle Evening Chronicle, 1995–99; Editor: Lancs Evening Post, 1999–2001; Birmingham Evening Mail, 2001–05; Ed.-in-Chief, Trinity Mirror Midlands, 2003–05. *Recreations:* fly-fishing, hill-walking. *Address:* Archant Life, The Barn, Elms Farm, Hobb Lane, Daresbury WA4 5LS. *T:* 07841 492724. *E:* roger.borrell@lancashirelife.co.uk.

**BORRELL FONTELLES, Josep;** Minister of Foreign Affairs, European Union and Cooperation, Spain, since 2018; *b* 24 April 1947. *Educ:* Univ. Politécnica, Madrid; Complutense Univ., Madrid (DEconSc); Inst. français du Pétrole, Paris; Stanford Univ. Engr and Dir, Dept of Systems, Compañía Española de Petróleos, 1972–81. Councillor, Madrid, 1979–82; Hd of Finance, Madrid Regl Govt, 1979–82; Under Sec., Budget and Public Spending, 1982–84; Treasury Minister, 1984–91; Mem. (PSOE) for Barcelona, Congress of Deputies, 1986–2004; Minister of Public Works and Transport, 1991–96, of the Envmt, 1993–96. Mem. (PSOE), 2004–09, Pres., 2004–07, Eur. Parlt. Pres., Eur. University Inst., 2010–12. *Address:* Ministry of Foreign Affairs, European Union and Cooperation, Sede Palacio de Santa Cruz, Plaza de la Provincia 1, 28071 Madrid, Spain.

**BORRETT, Neil Edgar;** non-executive Chairman, Forentech Ltd, 2004–11; *b* 10 March 1940; *m* 1965; two *d*. *Educ:* Coll. of Estate Management. FRICS 1969. Dir of property cos, 1963–90; Dir, Property Hldgs, DoE, 1990–96; Chief Exec., Property Advisers to the Civil Estate, 1996–97; Dir, Urban Estate, Crown Estate, 1997–2000. Chm., Matek Business Media, 1994–2004. Governor: London South Bank (formerly S Bank) Univ., 1996–2004; Hillcroft Coll., Surbiton, 2005–14.

**BORRIELLO, Prof. (Saverio) Peter,** PhD; Chief Executive, Veterinary Medicines Directorate, since 2011; *b* 29 Oct. 1953; *s* of Pasquale Borriello and Margaret Rose (née Taylor); partner, Helen Georgina Archer; one *s* one *d*. *Educ:* Oldbury Grammar Sch., W Midlands; University Coll. London (BSc; Fellow 1998); Central Public Health Lab. and St Thomas's Hosp. Med. Sch. (PhD 1981). MRCPath 1987, FRCPath 1998; FFPH 2004–09. MRC Clinical Research Centre: Upjohn Res. Fellow, 1979–82; Res. Scientist, 1982–86; Head of Gp, 1986–92; University of Nottingham: Head of Gp, Dept of Microbiol., 1992–93; personal chair, 1993; Founding Dir, Inst. of Infections and Immunity, 1993–95; Special Prof., 1996–2004; Dir, Central Public Health Lab., 1995–2006, when integrated with Communicable Diseases Surveillance Centre to form Centre for Infections, HPA; Health Protection Agency: Dir, Centre for Infections, 2006–08; Dir, Specialist and Ref. Microbiology Div. and R&D, 2003–08; CEO, Veterinary Laboratories Agency, 2008–11. Vis. Prof., LSHTM, 1997–2004; Hon. Professor: RVC, 2009–; Nottingham Univ., 2013–. Hon. Mem., Soc. of Applied Microbiol., 2009. Oakley Lectr, Pathol Soc. of GB and Ireland, 1990; J. D. Williams Lectr, Fedn of Infection Socs, 2013. Proctor & Gamble Applied Healthcare Microbiol. Award, Soc. of Applied Microbiol., 2010. *Publications:* Antibiotic Associated Diarrhoea and Colitis, 1984; Clostridia in Gastro-intestinal Disease, 1985; Clinical and Molecular Aspects of Anaerobes, 1990; (ed) Topley & Wilson's Microbiology and Microbial Infections, 10th edition, 2005; papers in scientific jls. *Recreations:* antiques and bric a brac, interesting facts, questioning. *Address:* Veterinary Medicines Directorate, Woodham Lane, New Haw, Addlestone, Surrey KT15 3LS. *T:* (01932) 338302.

**BORROW, David Stanley;** Member (Lab): Preston City Council, since 2011; Lancashire County Council, 2013–17 (Deputy Leader, 2013–17); *b* 2 Aug. 1952; *s* of James Borrow and Nancy (née Crawshaw); civil registration 2006, John Garland. *Educ:* Mirfield Grammar Sch., W Yorks; Lanchester Poly. (BA Hons Econs). Trainee, Yorkshire Bank, 1973–75; Lancashire Valuation Tribunal: Asst Clerk, 1975–78; Dep. Clerk, 1978–81; Dep. Clerk, Manchester S Valuation Tribunal, 1981–83; Clerk to Tribunal, Merseyside Valuation Tribunal, 1983–97. Pres., Soc. of Clerks of Valuation Tribunals, 1990–92 and 1996–97. Mem. (Lab) Preston BC, 1987–97 (Leader, 1992–94, 1995–97). MP (Lab) S Ribble, 1997–2010; contested (Lab) same seat, 2010. *E:* davidsborrow@hotmail.com.

**BORROWS, Simon Alexander;** Chief Executive, 3i Group plc, since 2012 (Director, since 2011); *b* Taplow, Bucks, 24 Jan. 1959; *s* of Kenneth Ambrose Borrows and Ailsa Nancy Borrows; *m* 1987, Sally Ann Weston; one *s* two *d*. *Educ:* Rossall Sch.; Queen Mary Coll., Univ. of London (LLB Hons); London Business Sch. (MBA 1985). Executive: Credit Dept, HSBC, Hong Kong, 1980–83; Corporate Finance Div., Morgan Grenfell and Co Ltd, 1985–88; Dir, Baring Bros & Co. Ltd, 1988–98 (Hd, Mergers and Acquisitions, 1995–98); Partner, Greenhill & Co. Inc., 1998–2011: Founding Partner, London Office, 1998; Co-Pres., 2004–07; Co-Chief Exec., 2007–10; Chm., Greenhill Europe, 2010–11. Director: British Land plc, 2011–17; Inchcape plc, 2011–15. *Recreations:* golf, ski-ing, theatre, road cycling. *Address:* 3i Group plc, 16 Palace Street, SW1E 5JD. *T:* (020) 7975 3280, *Fax:* (020) 7975 3543. *E:* simon.borrows@3i.com. *Clubs:* Queenwood Golf, St George's Hill Golf.

**BORSUK, Teresa Anna;** Senior Partner, Pollard Thomas Edwards, Architects, since 2014; *b* Ilford, 9 Nov. 1956; *d* of Jan Borsuk and Agnieszka Borsuk (née Lichwa). *Educ:* Ursuline High Sch., Ilford; Bartlett Sch. of Architecture, University Coll. London (BSc Hons 1st Cl. 1978; DipArch 1981); Kansas Univ., Lawrence. ARB 1983; RIBA 1992. Client Design Advisor. Pollard Thomas Edwards, 1984–: Dir, 1987–99; Exec. Dir, 1999–2014. Woman Architect of the Year, Architects' Jl, 2015. *Recreations:* travel, Africa, literature, theatre, food, ancestry, limestone pavements. *Address:* c/o Pollard Thomas Edwards, Diespeker Wharf, 38 Graham Street, N1 8JX. *T:* (020) 7336 7777. *E:* teresa.borsuk@ptea.co.uk.

**BORTHWICK,** family name of **Baron Borthwick**.

**BORTHWICK, 24th Lord** *cr* 1450 (Scot.); **John Hugh Borthwick of That Ilk;** DL; Baron of Heriotmuir and Laird of Crookston, Midlothian; Hereditary Falconer of Scotland to the Queen; landowner; *b* 14 Nov. 1940; *er twin s* of 23rd Lord Borthwick and Margaret Frances (*d* 1976), *d* of Alexander Campbell Cormack; *S* father, 1996; *m* 1974, Adelaide, *d* of A. Birkmyre; two *d*. *Educ:* Gordonstoun; Edinburgh School of Agriculture (SDA, NDA). DL Midlothian, 2001. *Recreations:* wild trout fishing, stalking, stamp and cigarette card collecting. *Heir:* twin *b* Hon. James Henry Alexander Borthwick, Master of Borthwick [*b* 14 Nov. 1940; *m* 1972, Elspeth, *d* of Lt-Col A. D. MacConachie; one *s*]. *Address:* The Garden Flat, Crookston House, Heriot, Midlothian EH38 5YS. *T:* (01875) 835236. *Club:* New (Edinburgh).

**BORTHWICK, Prof. Alistair George Liam**, PhD, DSc; FREng; FRSE; Professor of Applied Hydrodynamics, University of Edinburgh, since 2013; *b* Meriden, 7 Feb. 1957; *s* of Max and Pamela Borthwick; two *s*; *m* 2014, Gillian Parsons. *Educ*: Univ. of Liverpool (BEng Civil Engrg 1978; PhD 1982); Univ. of Oxford (MA 1990; DSc 2007). FREng 2014. Engr, Brown & Root (UK) Ltd, 1982–83; Lectr, Univ. of Salford, 1984–90; Lectr, 1990–96, Reader, 1996–2002, Prof., 2002–11, Univ. of Oxford; Fellow, St Edmund Hall, Oxford, 1990–2011, now Emeritus; Hd, Dept of Civil and Envmtl Engrg, UC Cork, 2011–13. Adjunct Professor: Peking Univ., 2010–; of Marine Energy, NUI Galway, 2014–. FRSE 2015. Dr *hc* Budapest Univ. of Technol. and Econs, 2016. *Publications*: contribs to scientific jls incl. Water, Bioresource Technol., Jl Hydrol. *Recreations*: literature, art, contemporary music, walking, football (Plymouth Argyle), history of science. *Address*: School of Engineering, University of Edinburgh, King's Buildings, Edinburgh EH9 3JL. *T*: (0131) 650 5588. *E*: alistair.borthwick@ed.ac.uk.

**BORTHWICK, Sir Antony Thomas**, 4th Bt *cr* 1908, of Whitburgh, Humbie, Co. Haddington; *b* 12 Feb. 1941; *e s* of Sir John Borthwick, 3rd Bt and his 1st wife, Irene Sophie (*née* Heller); *S* father, 2002; *m* 1966, Gillian Deirdre Broke Thurston (marr. diss.); one *s* two *d*; *m* 2002, Martha Wheeler Donner (*d* 2017). *Educ*: Eton. *Heir*: *s* Matthew Thomas Thurston Borthwick, *b* 2 July 1968.

**BORWICK**, family name of **Baron Borwick**.

**BORWICK**, 5th Baron *cr* 1922, of Hawkshead, co. Lancaster; **Geoffrey Robert James, (Jamie), Borwick**; Bt 1916; Chairman, Federated Trust Corporation Ltd, since 1987; *b* 7 March 1955; *s* of Hon. Robin Sandbach Borwick (*d* 2003), 3rd *s* of 3rd Baron Borwick, and Hon. Patricia Garnett Borwick (*d* 2009), *d* of Baron McAlpine of Moffat (Life Peer); *S* uncle, 2007; *m* 1981, Victoria Lorne Peta (*née* Poore) (*see* V. L. P. Borwick); three *s* one *d*. *Educ*: Eton Coll. Sir Robert McAlpine & Sons Ltd, 1972–81; Manganese Bronze Holdings plc, 1981–2003 (CEO, 1987–2001; Chm., 2001–03); non-exec. Dir, Hansa Trust plc, 1984–2012. Trustee: Federated Foundn, 1985–; British Lung Foundn, 2001–08, 2011–17; Royal Brompton and Harefield Hosps Charity, 2012–. Elected Mem., H of L, 2013–. *Recreations*: travel, swimming, walking. *Heir*: *s* Hon. Edwin Dennis William Borwick, *b* 14 April 1984. *Address*: 33 Phillimore Gardens, W8 7QG. *T*: 07774 859290, *Fax*: (020) 7937 2656; 15 Great College Street, SW1P 3RX; House of Lords, SW1A 0PW. *E*: jamie@borwick.com. *Club*: Garrick.

**BORWICK, Lady; Victoria Lorne Peta Borwick**; *b* London, 26 April 1956; *d* of late R. Dennis and Peta Poore; *m* 1981, Geoffrey Robert James Borwick (*see* Baron Borwick); three *s* one *d*. *Educ*: Wispers Sch. Dir, Clarion Events, 1976–2002; Dir, Treasurer's Dept, Conservative Central Office, 2002–04; Commercial Dir, ACI, 2004–06; Mem., Adv. Council, Open Europe, 2007–15. Mem. (C), RBK&C Council, 2002–. Greater London Authority: Mem. (C) London Assembly, 2008–Sept. 2015; Member: Transport Cttee, 2008–15; Police and Crime Cttee, 2012–15; Chm., Health Cttee, 2011–12; Dep Mayor of London, 2012–15; Chm., Civil Liberties Panel, Metropolitan Police Authy, 2009–12. MP (C) Kensington, 2015–17; contested (C) same seat, 2017. Mem., Sci. and Technol. Select Cttee, 2015–17. Gov., Golborne Children's Centre (formerly Ainsworth Nursery Sch.), 1990–. Trustee, Federated Foundn, 1985–. FRSA 1989. Freeman, City of London, 1999; Liveryman, Clockmakers' Co., 2000. *Publications*: The Cost of the London Mayor, 2007; Streets Ahead: relieving congestion on Oxford Street, Regent Street and Bond Street, 2010; Responding to G20, 2010. *Recreations*: making fudge, ski-ing, tennis. *Address*: 33 Phillimore Gardens, W8 7QG. *T*: (020) 7376 9262, *Fax*: (020) 7937 2656.

**BORYSIEWICZ, Sir Leszek (Krzysztof)**, Kt 2001; PhD; FRCP, FRCPath, FMedSci; FRS 2008; DL; Vice-Chancellor, Cambridge University, 2010–17; Chairman, Board of Trustees, Cancer Research UK, since 2016; *b* 13 April 1951; *s* of Jan Borysiewicz and Zofia Helena Woloszyn; *m* 1976, Gwenllian Sian Jones; two *d*. *Educ*: Cardiff High Sch.; Welsh Nat. Sch. of Medicine (BSc, MB BCh 1975); Univ. of London (PhD 1986). MRCP 1979, FRCP 1989; FRCPath 2002. Hosp. appts at University Hosp. of Wales, Hammersmith Hosp., Nat. Hosp. for Nervous Diseases and Ealing Hosp., 1975–79; Registrar, Dept of Medicine, Hammersmith Hosp., 1979–80; Royal Postgraduate Medical School: MRC Clinical Trng Fellow, 1980–82; Lister Res. Fellow and Sen. Lectr, 1982–86; Wellcome Trust Sen. Lectr in Infectious Diseases, Addenbrooke's Hosp., Cambridge, 1987–88; Lectr in Medicine, Univ. of Cambridge, 1988–91; Prof. of Medicine, Univ. of Wales Coll. of Medicine, 1991–2001; Principal, Faculty of Medicine, 2001–04, Dep. Rector, 2004–07, Imperial Coll.; Chief Exec., MRC, 2007–10 (Mem., Technol. Bd, 2007–10). Chm., R&D Grants Cttee, NHS (Wales), 1994–98. Non-exec. Dir, NW London Strategic HA, 2003–05. Member: MRC, 1995–2000 (Chm., Molecular and Cell Bd, 1996–2000; Chm., Jt MRC/DoH Spongiform Encephalopathies Cttee, 1996–2002); Cancer Res. UK, 2004– (Mem. Council and Trustee, 2002–05; Chm., Sci. Cttee, 2002–04); Lister Inst., 2004–; Global Sci. and Innovation Forum, 2008–10; Singapore Biomed. Scis Internat. Adv. Council, 2008–; Council, St George's House, 2014–; Siemens Technol. and Innovation Council, 2015–; REF Rev. Panel, 2016–; Bd, UK Res. and Innovation, 2017–; Chairman: Sci. Council, Internat. Agency for Res. on Cancer, WHO, 2002–04; UK Stem Cell Funders' Forum, 2007–10; Hds of Internat. (Biomed.) Res. Orgns, 2007–10. Harveian Orator, RCP, 2009. Gov., Wellcome Trust, 2006–07; Trustee, Nuffield Trust, 2002–07; Inst. for Res. in Schs, 2015–. Founder FMedSci 1998 (Mem. Council, 1997–2002); FCGI 2004. Mem., Polish Acad. Arts and Scis, Krakow, 1996. Hon. Prof., Shanghai Jiao Tong Univ., 2011. DL Cambs, 2012. Fellow, Cardiff Univ., 2006; Hon. Fellow: Wolfson Coll., Cambridge, 2002; Univ. of Wales Inst., Cardiff, 2011. Hon. DSc: Southampton, 2008; Hull, 2008; Glasgow, 2011; Hong Kong, 2012; Peking, 2012; Aberdeen, 2014; Hon. MD Sheffield, 2010; Hon. Dr: Imperial Coll. London, 2017; Bialystok, 2017. Moxon Trust Medal, RCP, 2002; Jephcott Medal, RSM, 2007; Galen Medal in Therapeutics, Soc. of Apothecaries, 2011; Inserm Internat. Prize, 2014. *Publications*: papers on immunology and pathogenesis of virus infection and viral induced cancer. *Recreations*: Rugby football, cricket, painting. *Address*: Chairman's Office, Cancer Research UK, Angel Building, 407 St John Street, EC1V 4AD. *T*: (020) 3469 8177. *Clubs*: Athenæum, Oxford and Cambridge.

**BOSANQUET, Prof. Nicholas**; Professor of Health Policy, Imperial College London (formerly Imperial College, University of London), since 1993; *b* 17 Jan. 1942; *s* of late Lt Col Neville Richard Gustavus Bosanquet and Nancy Bosanquet; *m* 1st, 1974, Anne Connolly (marr. diss. 1993); two *d*; 2nd, 1996, Anna Zarzecka (marr. diss. 2016). *Educ*: Winchester Coll.; Clare Coll., Cambridge (BA Hist.); Yale Univ. (Mellon Fellow); London Sch. of Econs (MSc Econs). Econ. Advr, NBPI, 1967–69; Lecturer in Economics: LSE, 1969–72; King's Fund Coll., 1973–86; City Univ., 1977–84; Sen. Research Fellow, Centre for Health Econs, Univ. of York, 1984–88; Prof. of Health Policy, RHBNC, Univ. of London, 1988–93. Special Advr, Health Cttee, H of C, 1988–90, 2000–. Consultant: WHO, 1989; World Bank, 1993. Arbitrator, ACAS, 1983–90. Non-executive Director: Abbey Health, 1998–2000; Richmond and Twickenham Primary Care Trust, 2001–07; Associate, Volterra Consulting, 2012–. Health Policy Advr, Care UK plc, 1995–2003; Health Policy Advr, 2001–18, Dir, 2015–, Sussex Health Care; Advr on NHS Business Relns, Hosp. Corp. of America, 2002–04. Consultant Dir, Reform, 2005–18; Chm., 2006–12, Dir, 2012–18, TBS (GB). Chm., Health Service Rev. for Cornwall, 2007–08; Mem. Adv. Bd, Cancer Reform Strategy, 2007; Chief Investigator, GlaxoSmithKline, Salford Lung Study, 2013–. Mem., York Central Lib Dems. *Publications*: Industrial Relations in the NHS: the search for a system, 1980; After the New Right, 1983; Family Doctors and Economic Incentives, 1989; (with K. Sikora) The Economics of Cancer Care, 2006; Our Land at War: Britain's key First World War sites, 2014; contrib. to econ. and med. jls. *Recreations*: visiting battlefields, brainstorming with Americans and others about military history. *Address*: 40 Bishophill Senior, York YO1 6DZ.

**BOSCAWEN**, family name of **Viscount Falmouth**.

**BOSE, Mihir**, FICA; freelance writer and broadcaster; *b* 12 Jan. 1947; *s* of Kiran Chandra Bose and Sova Rani Bose; *m* 1st, 1986, Kalpana (marr. diss. 1999); one *d*; 2nd, 2002, Caroline Alison Gascoyne-Cecil. *Educ*: St Xavier's High Sch.; St Xavier's Coll., Bombay (BSc Physics and Maths). Cricket Corresp., LBC, 1974–75; For. Corresp., Sunday Times, Spectator, New Society, 1975–78; freelance writer, 1979; Editor: Property Guide, 1980–81; International Fund Guide, 1980–81; Pensions, 1981–83; Financial Planning Ed. 1983–84; City Ed. 1984–86, Dep. Ed. 1985–86, Financial Weekly; City Features Ed., London Daily News, 1986–87; freelance writer, mainly on regular contract basis, specialising in finance, sports and feature writing for Sunday Times, Spectator, Mail on Sunday, Independent, The Times, Guardian, Daily Telegraph, 1987–2006; Sports Ed., BBC News, 2007–09; contributor, London Evening Standard, Insideworldfootball.biz, Sunday Times, Independent, Financial Times, History Today, Guardian, Daily Telegraph, regular broadcaster for BBC, Sky and other media networks, 2009–. Mem., Gambling Review Body, Home Office, 2000–01. Mem. Council, Nat. Army Mus., 2007–13. Trustee, Sporting Equals, 2009–16. Hon DLitt Loughborough, 2012. *Publications*: Keith Miller, 1979, 2nd edn 1980; The Lost Hero, 1982, 2nd edn 2014; All in a Day's Work, 1983; The Aga Khan, 1984; A Maidan View, 1986; The Crash, 1988, 3rd edn 1989, incl. Jap. edn; Insurance: are you covered?, 1988, 2nd edn 1991; Crash - a new money crisis, 1989; (jtly) Fraud, 1989; Cricket Voices, 1990; How to Invest in a Bear Market, 1990; History of Indian Cricket, 1990, 2nd edn 2002; Michael Grade: screening the image, 1992; (jtly) Behind Closed Doors, 1992; Sporting Colours, 1994; False Messiah: the life and times of Terry Venables, 1996; Sporting Alien, 1996; Sporting Babylon, 1999; Manchester Unlimited: the rise and rise of the world's premier football club, 1999; Raj, Spies, Rebellion, 2004; The Magic of Indian Cricket, 2006; Bollywood - a history, 2006; Manchester Disunited: trouble and takeover at the world's richest football club, 2007; The World Cup: all you need to know, 2010; The Spirit of the Game: how sport has changed the modern world, 2012; Game Changer: how the English Premier League came to dominate the world, 2012; (jtly) William Hill: the man and the business, 2014; Silver, the Spy Who Fooled the Nazis, 2016; From Midnight to Glorious Morning, 2017; Lion and Lamb: a portrait of British moral duality, 2018; (with Moeen Ali) Moeen, 2018. *Recreations*: running his own cricket team, walking, reading, films, travelling. *Clubs*: Reform, MCC.

**BOSHER, Sir Robin**, Kt 2012; Regional Director, South East and Director of Quality and Training, Ofsted, 2014–16; *b* Oxford, 30 Jan. 1957; *s* of Frederick A. and Eileen A. D. Bosher; *m* 1978, Anna Maria Davey; two *d*. *Educ*: Gosford Hill Sch., Oxford; Culham Coll., Abingdon (Cert Ed, BEd Oxon). Teacher, 1978–88: Primary Teacher, Oaklands Junior, Biggin Hill, then New Ash Green First Sch.; Dep. Hd, Wickham Common Sch., Bromley; Headmaster: Clare Hse Primary Sch., Bromley, 1988–93; Perry Hall Primary Sch., Orpington, 1993–99; Hd of Access, Bromley Local Authy, 1999–2002; Headmaster, Fairlawn Primary Sch., Lewisham, 2002–12; Exec. Head, Fairlawn, Kilmorie and Haseltine Primary Schs, Lewisham, 2009–12; Dir, Primary Educn, Harris Fedn, 2012–14. Operational Dir (Primary), London Challenge, 2005–10. *Recreations*: theatre, cinema, travel. *Address*: 64 Constance Crescent, Hayes, Bromley, Kent BR2 7QQ. *T*: (020) 8402 7297, 07909 687959. *E*: robinbosher@hotmail.com.

**BOSHOFF, Dr Christoffer**, FRCP; Vice-President, Early Development and Immuno-Translational Oncology, Pfizer Inc., since 2013; *b* 22 June 1965. *Educ*: Pretoria Univ. (MB ChB 1987); PhD London 1998. MRCP 1991. University College London: Glaxo Wellcome Res. Fellow, 1998–2004; Prof. of Cancer Medicine, 2001–13; Dir, Cancer Inst., 2006–13; Consultant Physician, Dept of Oncology, UCL and University Coll. London Hosps, 2000–13. Adjunct Prof., Yale Univ., 2014–. FMedSci 2005. *Address*: Pfizer Inc., 10555 Science Center Drive, La Jolla, CA 92121, USA. *E*: chris.boshoff@pfizer.com.

**BOSONNET, Paul Graham**, CBE 1995; Deputy Chairman, BOC Group, 1985–92; *b* 12 Sept. 1932; *s* of Edgar Raymond Bosonnet and Sylvia Gladys Cradock; *m* 1958, Joan Colet Cunningham; one *s* two *d*. *Educ*: St John's College, Southsea. FCA. Accountant, British Oxygen Co., 1957; Dir, BOC International, 1976; Dep. Chm., British Telecommunications plc, 1991–95. Chairman: Logica, 1990–95; G. A. Day, 1996–2001; Director: MAM Gp, 1991–98; Lucas Varity (formerly Lucas Industries), 1993–97. Vice Chm., Council, Royal Holloway (formerly RHBNC), Univ. of London, 1986–95 (Hon. Fellow, 2003). *Recreations*: genealogy, walking. *Address*: 2 The Green, Charters Village Drive, East Grinstead, W Sussex RH19 2GX. *T*: (01342) 870717.

**BOSS, Sandra Lynne, (Mrs Ian Lazarus)**; External Member, Prudential Regulation Committee (formerly Prudential Regulation Authority Board), Bank of England, 2014–Aug. 2020; *b* Seattle, Washington, 17 April 1967; *d* of William Boss and Verla Boss; *m* 2011, Ian Lazarus; two *d*. *Educ*: Stanford Univ. (BA Amer. Studies Major and Econs Sec. Major 1989); Harvard Business Sch. (MBA 1994). Financial Analyst, Trammell Crow Co., 1989–92; Associate, Merrill Lynch and Co., 1993; McKinsey and Co.: Consultant, 1994–99; Partner, 2000–05; Sen. Partner, 2005–14; Co-Hd, Corporate and Investment Banking practice, 2003–08; Man. Partner, Boston Office, 2004–07; Hd, Credit and Counterparty Risk service line, 2010–12. Non-executive Director: Enstar Gp, 2015– (Chm., Risk Cttee, 2017–); Elementis plc, 2017–. Bank of England: Ind. Dir, RTGS/CHAPS Bd, 2017– (Chm., Risk Cttee, 2017–); Mem., RTGS Renewal Cttee, Court of Dirs, 2018–. Trustee, McKinsey Master Retirement Trust, 2006–08. Chm., Edith Wharton Restoration, 2006–09. Mem., Wkg Gp, Inst. of Internat. Finance, 2009–14. *Publications*: contributor: McKinsey Qly; McKinsey on Corporate and Investment Banking (also Mem., Editl Bd). *Recreations*: family, reading, yoga, sailing. *Address*: Prudential Regulation Authority, Bank of England, 20 Moorgate, EC2R 6DA. *E*: sandra.boss@bankofengland.co.uk.

**BOSSANO, Hon. Sir Joseph (John)**, KCMG 2018; MP (Gibraltar Socialist Labour Party); Minister for Economic Development, Telecommunications and Gibraltar Savings Bank, since 2014; *b* 10 June 1939; *s* of Maria Teresa and Oscar Bossano; *m* (marr. diss.); three *s* one *d*; *m* 1988, Rose Torrilla. *Educ*: Gibraltar Grammar School; Univ. of London (BScEcon); Univ. of Birmingham (BA). Factory worker, 1958–60; Seaman, 1960–64; Health Inspector, 1964–68; student, 1968–72; building worker, 1972–74; Union leader, 1974–88; MP, Gibraltar, 1972–; Leader of the Opposition, Gibraltar, 1984–88 and 1996–2011; Chief Minister, 1988–96; Minister for Employment, 2011–14. Founder and Leader, Gibraltar Socialist Labour Party, 1976–2010. *Recreations*: thinking, cooking, gardening. *Address*: 2 Gowlands Ramp, Gibraltar.

**BOSSOM, Sir Bruce Charles**, 3rd Bt *cr* 1953; *b* London, 22 Aug. 1952; *s* of Hon. Sir Clive Bossom, 2nd Bt and Lady Barbara Bossom, *sister* of 9th Earl of Guilford; *S* father, 2017; *m* 1985, Penelope Jane, *d* of late Edward Holland-Martin. *Educ*: Eton Coll.; Harvard Business

Sch. (PMD). FRICS 1987. Partner, Jones Lang Wootton, 1972–86; Dir, Phoenix, subseq. Mountleigh, 1986–93; Man. Dir, La Salle Partners, 1993–99; Founding Partner, Orion Capital Managers, 1999–. *Recreation:* country pursuits. *Heir: s* George Edward Martin Bossom, *b* 21 Feb. 1992. *Address:* Overbury Court, Overbury, Glos GL20 7NP. *T:* 07785 220687. *E:* bbossom@orioncapman.com; Orion Capital Managers, 2 Cavendish Square, W1G 0PU. *Club:* White's.

BOSSY, Rev. Michael Joseph Frederick, SJ; Assistant Priest, St Ignatius Church, South Tottenham, since 2005; Rector, Stonyhurst College, 1993–97 (Headmaster, 1972–85); *b* 22 Nov. 1929; *s* of F. J. Bossy and K. Bossy (*née* White). *Educ:* St Ignatius Coll., Stamford Hill; Heythrop Coll., Oxon (STL); Oxford Univ. (MA). Taught at: St Ignatius Coll., Stamford Hill, 1956–59; St Francis Xavier's Coll., Liverpool, 1963–64; Stonyhurst Coll., 1965–85; Asst Priest, 1986–88, Rector and Parish Priest, 1988–92, Parish of St Aloysius, Glasgow; Actg Parish Priest, St Mary of the Angels, Liverpool, 1998; Asst Priest, Corpus Christi Church, Brixton, 1998–2005. *Recreation:* watching games on TV. *Address:* St Ignatius Church, 27 High Road, N15 6ND.

BOSTOCK, Prof. Christopher John, PhD; Director, BBSRC Institute for Animal Health, 1997–2002; *b* 29 May 1942; *s* of John Major Leslie Bostock and Mildred Lilian Bostock; *m* 1st, 1963, Yvonne Pauline Kendrick (marr. diss. 1990); one *s* two *d*; 2nd, 1992, Patricia Roberts. *Educ:* Univ. of Edinburgh (BSc Hons; Sir Ramsay Wright Post-Grad. Schol., 1965; PhD 1968). Univ. Demonstr, Univ. of Edinburgh, 1965–69; Vis. Fellow, Univ. of Colorado, 1969–71; Res. Fellow, Univ. of St Andrews, 1971–72; Res. Scientist, MRC Clin. and Population Cytogenetics Unit, Edinburgh, 1972–77; Res. Scientist, 1977–83, Asst Dir, 1983–85, MRC Mammalian Genome Unit; Head of Molecular Biology: Animal Virus Res. Inst., AFRC, 1985–89; Inst. for Animal Health, AFRC, then BBSRC, 1989–97. Visiting Professor: Univ. of Wisconsin, 1985; Dept of Clin. Veterinary Sci., Univ. of Bristol, 1998–; Sch. of Animal and Microbial Scis, Univ. of Reading, 2000–. Hon. FRAgS 2002. *Publications:* (with Adrian Sumner) The Eukaryotic Chromosome, 1978; scientific res. papers on chromosomes, tumour cell drug resistance, infectious disease agents. *Recreations:* French country life, walking, building.

BOSTOCK, Prof. Hugh, PhD; FRS 2001; Professor of Neurophysiology, Institute of Neurology, University College London, 1996–2009, now Emeritus; *b* 25 Aug. 1944; *s* of Edward and Alice Bostock; *m* 1975, Kate Shaw; two *s* one *d*. *Educ:* Merton Coll., Oxford (BA); University Coll. London (MSc, PhD 1974). Institute of Neurology, London University, 1974–2009: Lectr, 1976–87; Sen. Lectr, 1987–92; Reader, 1992–96. *Publications:* contrib. papers to Jl Physiol., Brain and similar jls. *Address:* Newton House, 24 Bridge Street, Olney, Bucks MK46 4AB.

BOSTOCK, Kate Margaret; founder and owner, Angel & Rocket, since 2014; *b* Burton-on-Trent, 8 Sept. 1956; *d* of George and Ruth Parker; *m* 1991, Neil Andrew Bostock; two *s*. *Educ:* Ashby Grammar Sch. Work in design, 1982–92; Dir, Buying to Buying, 1992–95; Product Dir, Next, 1995–2001; Clothing Dir, George @ Asda, 2001–04; Womenswear Dir, 2004–08, Exec. Dir, Clothing, 2008–09, Exec. Dir, Gen. Merchandise, 2009–12, Marks & Spencer; Exec. Dir, Product and Trading, ASOS plc, 2013; Chief Exec., Coast, 2013–15. Hon. DA De Montfort, 2008; Hon. Dr Business Studies Manchester, 2008; Hon. DArts Leicester, 2008. *Recreations:* music, art, theatre, travel, shopping!

BOSTON, 11th Baron *cr* 1761; George William Eustace Boteler Irby; Bt 1704; derivatives broker, since 1993; *b* 1 Aug. 1971; *s* of 10th Baron Boston and Rhonda Anne (*née* Bate); *S* father, 2007; *m* 1998, Nicola Sydney Mary (*née* Reid); two *s* two *d*. *Educ:* Eton; Bristol Univ. (BSc Hons Psychology). *Heir: s* Hon. Thomas William George Boteler Irby, *b* 9 Dec. 1999. *Address:* Hookers Farm, Hartley Wespall, Hook, Hants RG27 0AP.

BOSTON, Archdeacon of; see Allain Chapman, Ven. J. P. H.

BOSTON, David Merrick, OBE 1976; MA; Director (formerly Curator), Horniman Public Museum and Public Park Trust (formerly Horniman Museum and Library), London, 1965–93; Hon. Curator, and tenant, Home Museum, 2006, Hon. Archivist and Librarian, since 2006, Quebec House, National Trust; *b* Salisbury, Wilts, 15 May 1931; *s* of late Dr H. M. Boston; *m* 1961, Catharine, *d* of late Rev. Prof. (Edward) Geoffrey (Simons) Parrinder; one *s* two *d*. *Educ:* Rondebosch, Cape Town; Bishop Wordsworth's, Salisbury; Selwyn Coll., Cambridge; Univ. of Cape Town. BA History Cantab 1954; MA 1958. RAF, 1950–51; Adjt, Marine Craft Trng School. Field survey, S African Inst. of Race Relations, 1955; Curator, King's Regt Collection, and Keeper of Ethnology, Liverpool Museums, 1956–62; Asst Keeper, British Museum, New World archaeology and ethnography, 1962–65. Chm., British Nat. Cttee of Internat. Council of Museums, 1976–80; Vice-Chm., Internat. Cttee for Museums of Ethnography, 1989–95; Member, Council: Museums Assoc., 1969–70; Royal Anthropological Inst., 1969 and 1998–2001 (Vice-Pres., 1972–75, 1977–80, 1995–98, Hon. Sec., 1985–88, Hon. Librarian, 1992–2001). Visiting Scientist: National Museum of Man, Ottawa, 1970; Japan Foundation, Tokyo, 1986. Consultant, Prog. for Belize, 1994–. Gov., Dolmetsch Foundn, 1983–. Vice President: Dulwich Decorative & Fine Arts Soc., 1987–2001; Friends of the Horniman, 1995–2002; Mem. Cttee, Wolfe Soc., 1999–. Trustee, Haslemere Museum, 1996–2012. FMA; FRAI; FRGS; FRSA. Ordenom Jugoslavenske Zastave sa zlatnom zvezdom na ogrlici (Yugoslavia), 1981. *Publications:* Pre-Columbian Pottery of the Americas, 1980; contribs to learned jls and encyclopaedias and on Pre-European Americas, in World Ceramics (ed R. J. Charleston). *Address:* 14 The Green, Westerham, Kent TN16 1AS. *T:* (01959) 565812. *Club:* Royal Air Force.

BOSTON, Kenneth George, AO 2001; PhD; Chief Executive, Qualifications and Curriculum Authority, UK, 2002–09; *b* 9 Sept. 1942; *s* of Kenneth Frances and Enid Beatrice Boston; *m* 1978, Yvonne Roep; one *d*. *Educ:* Univ. of Melbourne (MA; PhD 1981). Director-General: of Educn, SA, 1988–91; of Educn and Trng, NSW, 1991–2002. Pres., Australian Coll. of Educn, 2001–02. Member: Expert Panel for School Funding Review, Australia, 2010–11; Australian Qualifications Framework Council, 2010–12. Member, Board: Musica Viva Australia, 2012–14; Stewart House, 2012. *Club:* Sydney Cricket.

BOSTRIDGE, Dr Ian Charles, CBE 2004; singer and writer; *b* 25 Dec. 1964; *s* of late Leslie John Bostridge and of Lilian Winifred (*née* Clark); *m* 1992, Lucasta Miller; one *s* one *d*. *Educ:* Dulwich Coll. Prep. Sch.; Westminster Sch. (Queen's Schol.); St John's Coll., Oxford (MA, DPhil Hist. 1990; Hon. Fellow, 2010); St John's Coll., Cambridge (MPhil Hist. and Philosophy of Sci.). North Sen. Schol., St John's Coll., Oxford, 1988–90; Jun. Res. Fellow, and British Acad. Postdoctoral Res. Fellow, Corpus Christi Coll., Oxford, 1992–95 (Hon. Fellow, 2001). Humanitas Vis. Prof. of Classical Music and Music Educn, Univ. of Oxford, 2014–15. Professional début as Young Sailor in Tristan, RFH/LPO, 1993; operatic stage début as Lysander, Midsummer Night's Dream, Australian Opera at Edinburgh Fest., 1994; Royal Opera House début, in Salome, 1995; début: with ENO, as Tamino, 1996; with Munich State Opera, as Nerone in Poppaea, 1998; Vienna State Opera, as Ottavio, 2006; with Opéra de Paris, as Jeptha, 2018; other rôles include: Belmonte, Die Entführung aus dem Serail; Vasek, The Bartered Bride; Quint, The Turn of the Screw; title rôle, Orfeo (Monteverdi); Caliban, The Tempest (world première, 2004); Jupiter, Semele; Vere, Billy Budd; Aschenbach, Death in Venice. Wigmore Hall recital début, 1995; Carnegie Hall début, 1999; recitals include: Edinburgh Fest., Aldeburgh Fest., Munich, Salzburg, Schubertiade Fests; Vienna Konzerthaus and Musikverein; Châtelet; Champs Elysées; Lincoln Center; Carnegie Hall; La Scala; own Carte Blanche series, Concertgebouw, 2005; own Perspectives series, Carnegie Hall, 2006 and Barbican Centre, 2007–08; programmed own series at Schubertiade, Vienna Konzerthaus and Wigmore Hall; première (Cologne) and dedicatee, Hans Werner Henze, Sechs Gesänge aus dem Arabischen; The Dark Mirror: Zender's Winterreise, Barbican Centre, 2016. Television includes: Schubert's Winterreise, Channel 4, 1997 (Prague TV Award); Britten Serenade, and as presenter, Janacek documentary, BBC; subject of S Bank Show profile. Has made numerous recordings. Patron: Music Libraries Trust; Macmillan Carol Concert; Ambassador, Youth Music. Edinburgh Fest. Univ. Lect., 2000; Breakspear Lect., Univ. of Trondheim, 2015; Lect., Bristol Inst. for Res. in Humanities and Arts, Univ. of Bristol, 2015. Inaugural Artist-in-Residence, Seoul Philharmonic, 2018. Hon. Fellow, Wolfson Coll., Oxford, 2016. Hon RAM 2002. Hon. DMus St Andrews, 2003. NFMS award, 1990; Young Concert Artists' Trust award, 1992; Début Award, Royal Philharmonic Soc., 1995; Solo Vocal Award, Gramophone, 1996, 1998, 2003; Classical Music Award, South Bank Show, 1996; Echo Award, 1997, 1999, 2003, 2013, 2014, 2017; Munich Fest. Prize, 1998; Choc de l'Année Award, 1998, 2004; Edison Award, 1999, 2002; Grammy Award (opera), 1999, 2010 (solo vocal recital) 2017; Brit Critics Award, 2000; Preis der Deutschen Schallplattenkritik, 2001, 2006; Acad. Charles Cros, Grand Prix du Disque, 2001; Japanese Recording Acad. Prize, 2004, 2007, 2017. *Publications:* Witchcraft and its Transformations c. 1650–c. 1750, 1997; (contrib.) Civil Histories: essays presented to Sir Keith Thomas, 2000; A Singer's Notebook, 2011; Schubert's Winter Journey: anatomy of an obsession, 2014 (Duff Cooper Prize for non-fiction, 2015) (trans. French 2018, Essay Book Prize, Assoc. Professionnelle de la Critique de Théâtre, Musique et Danse, 2018, Grand Prix, France Musique des Muses awards, 2019); reviews and articles in The Times, TLS, Wall St Jl, Guardian, NY Rev. of Books, etc. *Recreations:* reading, cooking, looking at pictures. *Address:* c/o Askonas Holt Ltd, 15 Fetter Lane, EC4A 1BW. *T:* (020) 7400 1700, *Fax:* (020) 7400 1799. *Club:* Garrick.
See also M. A. Bostridge.

BOSTRIDGE, Mark Andrew; writer; *b* London, 28 June 1961; *s* of late Leslie John Bostridge and of Lilian Winifred, (Sandy), (*née* Clark). *Educ:* Dulwich College Prep. Sch.; Westminster Sch.; St Anne's Coll., Oxford (Gladstone Meml Prize; BA). Political res. asst, 1985–86; researcher/asst producer, BBC, 1990–94; Literary Executor, Vera Brittain Estate, 1999–. Consultant on feature film, Testament of Youth, 2008–14. *Publications:* Vera Brittain: a life (with Paul Berry), 1995; (ed jtly) Letters from a Lost Generation, 1998; (ed) Lives for Sale, 2004; Florence Nightingale: the woman and her legend, 2008 (Elizabeth Longford Prize for Histl Biog., 2009); (ed) Because You Died, 2008; The Fateful Year: England 1914, 2014; Vera Brittain and the First World War, 2014; articles and reviews in nat. press. *Recreations:* diary-keeping, ghost-watching. *Address:* c/o United Agents, 12–26 Lexington Street, W1F 0LE. *T:* (020) 3214 0800.
See also I. C. Bostridge.

BOSTRÖM, Antonia; Director of Collections, Victoria and Albert Museum, since 2018; *b* London, 10 Sept. 1957; *d* of Jan Boström and Eliette Boström (*née* von Tschirschky und Boegendorff, now Lady Hulbert); *m* 1999, Dean Baker; two *d*. *Educ:* Bousfield Primary Sch., London; Cours St Louis (French Lycée), Stockholm; Glendower Girls' Sch., London; Peers Sch., Cowley, Oxon; Courtauld Inst. of Art, Univ. of London (BA Hons 1979; PhD 1996). Asst Curator (Archives), NPG, 1980; Mus. Asst (Liby and Sculpture Dept), V&A Mus., 1980–85; Area Ed., Grove Dictionary of Art, 1985–88; Actg Curator, Perm. Collection of Paintings and Sculpture, Royal Acad. of Arts, 1995–96; Res. Schol., 1996–98, Asst Curator, 1998–2004, Detroit Inst. of Arts; Sen. Curator and Hd, Sculpture and Decorative Arts Dept, J. Paul Getty Mus., LA, 2004–13; Dir, Curatorial Affairs, Nelson-Atkins Mus. of Art, Kansas City, 2013–16; Keeper of Sculpture, Metalwork, Ceramics and Glass, V&A, 2016–18. Member: Adv. Bd, Brice Charitable Foundn, LA, 2009–; Adv. Council, Vistas, NY, 2012–. Trustee: Gilbert Collection, V&A Mus., 2016–; Museums Sheffield, 2016–. *Publications:* (jtly) Catalogue of Italian Sculpture in the Detroit Institute of Arts, 2002; (ed) The Encyclopedia of Sculpture, 2004; The Fran and Ray Stark Collection of 20th Century Sculpture at the J. Paul Getty Museum, 2008; (ed and contrib.) A Labyrinth for the Park: celebrating the twenty-fifth anniversary of the Donald J. Hall Sculpture Park, 2014; contribs to jls incl. Burlington Mag., Apollo Mag., Sculpture Jl. *Recreations:* travel, music, cinema, theatre, walking, gardening, food. *Address:* Victoria and Albert Museum, Cromwell Road, SW7 2RL. *T:* (020) 7942 2611. *E:* a.bostrom@vam.ac.uk.

BOSTROM, Prof. Nick, PhD; Professor of Applied Ethics, since 2008, Director, Future of Humanity Institute, since 2005, and Director, Governance of AI Program, University of Oxford; *b* Helsingborg, Sweden, 10 March 1973. *Educ:* Univ. of Gothenburg (BA Philos.); Univ. of Stockholm (MA Philos. and Phys); King's Coll. London (MSc Computational Neurosci.); London Sch. of Econs and Pol Sci. (PhD Philos. 2000). Co-Founder, World Transhumanist Assoc., 1997; Lectr, Yale Univ., 2000–02; British Acad. Postdoctoral Fellow, Univ. of Oxford, 2003–05. Co-Founder, Inst. for Ethics and Emerging Technols, 2004. *Publications:* Anthropic Bias, 2002, 2010; (ed jtly) Global Catastrophic Risks, 2008, 2011; (ed jtly) Human Enhancement, 2009, 2010; Superintelligence, 2014, 2016; articles in Nature, Ethics, Jl of Philos., Mind, Philos. Qly, Bioethics, Utilitas. *Address:* Future of Humanity Institute, University of Oxford, Faculty of Philosophy, Suite 1, Littlegate House, 16/17 St Ebbe's Street, Oxford OX1 1PT.

BOSVILLE MACDONALD OF SLEAT, Sir Ian Godfrey, 17th Bt *cr* 1625; Premier Baronet of Nova Scotia; DL; MRSPH; 25th Chief of Sleat; *b* 18 July 1947; *er s* of Sir (Alexander) Somerled Angus Bosville Macdonald of Sleat, 16th Bt, MC, 24th Chief of Sleat and Mary, Lady Bosville Macdonald of Sleat; *S* father, 1958; *m* 1970, Juliet Fleury, *o d* of late Maj.-Gen. J. M. D. Ward-Harrison, OBE, MC; one *s* one *d* (and one *d* decd). *Educ:* Pinewood Sch.; Eton Coll.; Royal Agricultural Coll. ARICS 1972; FRICS 1986. Member (for Bridlington South), Humberside CC, 1981–84. MRSPH (MRSH 1972); Mem., Econ. Res. Council, 1979–. Chairman: Rural Develt Commn, Humberside, 1988–95; Rural Partnership ER of Yorks Council, 2000–; President: Humber and Wolds Rural Community Council, 1996–2012; British Food and Farming in Humberside, 1989; Humberside Young Farmers, 1989–96; British Red Cross: Mem. Council and Trustee, 1995–97; Nat. Trustee, 2001–06; Chairman: N of England Reg., 2000–04; Nat. Assembly, 2002–07; Chm., Clan Donald Lands Trust, Armadale Castle, Isle of Skye, 2008–. President: Humberside Br., 1988–96; Hull and ER Br., 1996–2003. High Sheriff, Humberside, 1988–89; DL ER of Yorks, 1997. *Recreation:* ornithology. *Heir: s* Somerled Alexander Bosville Macdonald, younger of Sleat [*b* 30 Jan. 1976; *m* 2003, Charlotte, *yr d* of Richard Perkins; two *s*]. *Address:* Hazel Bush House, Hazel Bush Lane, York YO32 9TR. *T:* (01904) 468239, 07733 413527. *Clubs:* Lansdowne, White's; New, Puffin's (Edinburgh).

BOSWALL, Sir (Thomas) Alford H.; see Houstoun-Boswall.

BOSWELL, family name of Baron Boswell of Aynho.

BOSWELL OF AYNHO, Baron *cr* 2010 (Life Peer), of Aynho in the County of Northamptonshire; Timothy Eric Boswell; *b* 2 Dec. 1942; *s* of late Eric New Boswell and of Joan Winifred Caroline Boswell; *m* 1969, Helen Delahay (*d* 2019), *d* of Rev. Arthur

Rees; three d. *Educ:* Marlborough Coll.; New Coll., Oxford (MA; Dip. Agricl Econs). Conservative Res. Dept, 1966–73 (Head of Econ. Section, 1970–73); managed family farming business, 1974–87; part-time Special Adviser to Minister of Agriculture, Fisheries and Food, 1984–86. Chm., Leics, Northants and Rutland Counties Br., NFU, 1983; Mem. Council, 1966–90, Pres., 1984–90, Perry Foundn (for Agricl Res.); Mem., AFRC, 1988–90. MP (C) Daventry, 1987–2010. PPS to Financial Sec. to the Treasury, 1989–90; an Asst Govt Whip, 1990–92; a Lord Comr of HM Treasury (a Govt Whip), 1992; Parly Under-Sec. of State, DFE, 1992–95; Parly Sec., MAFF, 1995–97; Opposition frontbench spokesman on Treasury matters, 1997, on trade and industry, 1997–99, on further and higher educn and disabilities, 1999–2001, 2002–03, on pensions and disabilities, 2001–02, on home, constitutional and legal affairs, 2003–04; Shadow Minister for Work, 2004–07; PPS to Chm., Cons. Party, 2005–07. Member Select Cttee for: Agriculture, 1987–89; Innovation, Univs and Skills, 2007–09; for Sci. and Technol., 2009–10; Sec., Cons. Backbench Cttee on Agriculture, 1987–89; Chm., All-Party Charity Law Review Panel, 1988–90. Treas., 1976–79, Chm., 1979–83, Daventry Constituency Cons. Assoc. Contested (C) Rugby, Feb. 1974. Principal Dep. Chm. of Cttees, H of L, 2012–; Chair, EU Select Cttee, H of L, 2012–. Pres., Nat. Energy Action, 2012–13. Chairman: Friends of Torres Vedras, 2011–12; Northants VCH Trust, 2011–. Governor: Cardiff Metropolitan Univ. (formerly Univ. of Wales Inst.), 2007–12 (Vice-Chm., 2010–12); Northampton Univ., 2010–12 (Hon. Fellow, 2010). FSA 2016. DL Northants, 2010. *Recreations:* the countryside, shooting, snooker, poetry. *Address:* House of Lords, SW1A 0PW. *Club:* Farmers.

See also Hon. V. M. B. Prentis.

**BOSWELL, Alexander;** Vice Lord-Lieutenant for Buckinghamshire, since 2011; Founder and Chief Executive Officer, MK Investors Group, since 2015; b North Crawley, 26 Jan. 1951; s of Ian Boswell and Vera Boswell; m 1977, Jane Elizabeth Ratcliffe; one s one d. *Educ:* Radley Coll.; Corpus Christi, Oxford (MA Mod. Hist.). Working landowner and farmer, 1977–; small business entrepreneur, 1977–. Dir, BW Foods Ltd, 1996–. Country Land & Business Association: Chairman: London Council, 2011; London Policy Cttee, 2011–15; Bucks Br., 2012–15; Mem. Council, 2012–. Chm., Bucks Honours Cttee, 2014. Pres., Milton Keynes Community Foundn, 2009; Patron: Willen Hospice, 2007; Bletchley Park, 2011; Trustee, Milton Keynes Parks Trust, 2009–17; organiser, Treasures in MK art exhibn, 2014. Bucks Ambassador, 2005. High Sheriff 2006–07, DL 2008, Bucks. *Recreations:* beautiful places, collecting and racing historic cars, wildlife conservation, game shooting, art, music, Italy. *Address:* Quakers House, North Crawley MK16 9HW. *T:* (01234) 391203. *E:* ab@quakershouse.com. *Club:* Royal Automobile.

**BOSWELL, Lt-Gen. Sir Alexander (Crawford Simpson),** KCB 1982; CBE 1974 (OBE 1971; MBE 1962); DL; Lieutenant-Governor and Commander-in-Chief, Guernsey, 1985–90; b 3 Aug. 1928; s of Alexander Boswell Simpson Boswell and Elizabeth Burns Simpson Boswell (née Park); m 1956, Jocelyn Leslie Blundstone Pomfret, d of Surg. Rear-Adm. A. A. Pomfret, CB, OBE; five s. *Educ:* Merchiston Castle Sch.; RMA, Sandhurst. Enlisted in Army, 1947; Commnd, Argyll and Sutherland Highlanders, Dec. 1948; regimental appts, Hong Kong, Korea, UK, Suez, Guyana, 1949–58; sc Camberley, 1959; Mil. Asst (GSO2) to GOC Berlin, 1960–62; Co. Comdr, then Second in Comd, 1 A and SH, Malaya and Borneo, 1963–65 (despatches 1965); Directing Staff, Staff Coll., Camberley, 1965–68; CO, 1 A and SH, 1968–71; Col GS Trng Army Strategic Comd, 1971; Brig. Comdg 39 Inf. Bde, 1972–74; COS, 1st British Corps, 1974–76; NDC (Canada), 1976–77; GOC 2nd Armd Div., 1978–80; Dir, TA and Cadets, 1980–82; GOC Scotland and Governor of Edinburgh Castle, 1982–85. Chairman: Scottish Veterans' Residences, 1991–2001; Officers Assoc. (Scottish Br.), 1991–98. Col, Argyll and Sutherland Highlanders, 1972–82; Hon. Col, Tayforth Univs OTC, 1982–86; Col Comdt, Scottish Div., 1982–86; Hon. Col, Scottish Transport Regt RLC(V), 1993–96. Captain of Tarbet, 1974–82. Pres., Friends of St Mary's Haddington, 1992–2003. KStJ 1985. DL East Lothian, 1993. *Address:* c/o Bank of Scotland, 44 Court Street, Haddington EH41 3NP.

**BOSWELL, (Andrew) Timothy;** a District Judge (Magistrates' Courts), since 2018; b Chesterfield, 30 April 1981; s of Andrew Boswell and Margaret Boswell; m 2017, Helen Laura Woolley. *Educ:* Brookfield Community Sch., Chesterfield; Hertford Coll., Oxford (BCL). Called to the Bar, Gray's Inn, 2004; barrister: 13 King's Bench Walk, 2004–14; Cornwall Street Chambers, 2014–17; a Dep. Dist Judge (Magistrates' Courts), 2012–18. *Recreations:* reading, cricket, football, travel. *Address:* North Staffordshire Justice Centre, The Court House, Ryecroft, Newcastle under Lyme, Staffordshire ST5 2AA.

**BOSWELL, Lindsay Alice;** QC 1997; b Nairobi, 22 Nov. 1958; d of Graham Leonard William Boswell and Erica Boswell; m 1987, Jonathan James Acton Davis, qv; one s. *Educ:* St Mary's, Ascot; Brooke House; University Coll. London (BSc Econ Hons); City Univ. (Dip. Law). Called to the Bar, Gray's Inn, 1982, Bencher, 2004. *Recreations:* open water swimming, walking, beekeeping, counting sheep. *Address:* Quadrant Chambers, 10 Fleet Street, Temple, EC4Y 1AU. *Clubs:* Royal Air Force; Dolphin Swimming and Boating (San Francisco).

**BOSWELL, Philip John;** Director, Asia Pacific, Systech International, since 2018; b Bellshill, 23 July 1963; s of Peter and Joan Boswell; m Anne; one s two d. *Educ:* Glasgow Caledonian Univ. (BSc Quantity Surveying 1989); Univ. of Reading (Dip. Arbitration 2007). FCIArb 2007. Sen. Contracts Engr, Qatar Petroleum, 2003–06; Sen. Contracts Engr and Project Services Engr, 2006–08, Lead Contracts Engr, 2008–11, BP; Contracts and Procurement Specialist, Shell, 2011–14; Contracts Engr, Premier Oil, 2014–15; Oil and Gas Consultant, Turner & Townsend, 2017. MP (SNP) Coatbridge, Chryston and Bellshill, 2015–17. *Recreations:* family, music, cycling, walking, reading.

**BOSWELL, Timothy;** see Boswell, A. T.

**BOSWOOD, Anthony Richard;** QC 1986; international arbitrator; b 1 Oct. 1947; s of late Noel Gordon Paul Boswood and of Cicily Ann Watson; m 1973, Sarah Bridget Alexander; three d. *Educ:* St Paul's Sch.; New Coll., Oxford (BCL, MA). Called to Bar, Middle Temple, 1970, Bencher, 1995. *Recreations:* music and opera, hunting, gardening, theology, singing. *Address:* Fountain Court, Temple, EC4Y 9DH. *T:* (020) 7583 3335; Podere Casanuova, Pieveasciata, Castelnuovo Berardenga (SI), Italy; South Hay House, Binsted, Alton, Hants GU35 9NR. *E:* aboswood@fountaincourt.co.uk. *Club:* Athenæum.

**BOTHAM, Sir Ian (Terence),** Kt 2007; OBE 1992; broadcaster, commentator and writer; b 24 Nov. 1955; s of Leslie and Marie Botham; m 1976, Kathryn Waller; one s two d. *Educ:* Milford Junior Sch.; Buckler's Mead Secondary Sch., Yeovil. Bowler and batsman for County Cricket Clubs: Somerset, 1974–87 (Captain, 1983–85; Hon. Life Mem., 1993); Worcestershire, 1987–91; Durham, 1992–93 (Hon. Life Mem.); England Test cricketer, 1977–92 (Captain, 1980–81); scored 1,000 runs and took 100 wickets in 21 Tests at age 23, 1979; scored 3,000 runs and took 300 wickets in Tests to 1982; first player to score a century and take 10 wickets in a Test match, Bombay, 1979; made 100 runs and took 8 wickets in 3 Tests, 1978, 1980, 1984; made 5,200 runs, took 383 wickets and 120 catches in 102 Tests; played cricket for Queensland, football for Scunthorpe and Yeovil. Chm., Mission Sports Mgt (formerly Mission Logistics) Ltd, 2000–12. Marathon walks for leukaemia research incl. Land's End to John o'Groats and Alps; Pres., Leukaemia and Lymphoma Res. (formerly Leukaemia Res. Fund), 2003–. Columnist, Daily Mirror. Team captain, A Question of Sport, BBC, 1989–96. Mem., Sky cricket commentary team, 1995–. Launched Botham wines, 2018. *Publications:* Ian Botham on Cricket, 1980; (with Ian Jarrett) Botham Down Under, 1983; (with Kenneth Gregory) Botham's Bedside Cricket Book, 1983; (with Peter Roebuck) It Sort of Clicks, 1986, rev. edn 1987; (with Jack Bannister) Cricket My Way, 1989; Botham: my autobiography, 1994; (with Peter Hayter) The Botham Report, 1997; Botham's Century, 2001; My Illustrated Life, 2007; Head On: the autobiography, 2007; Ian Botham on Fishing, 2008; My Sporting Heroes, 2009; Beefy's Cricket Tales, 2013. *Address:* North Yorkshire. *Club:* MCC (Hon. Mem. 1994).

**BOTHAMLEY, John Peter,** CBE 2013; Managing Director, John Newlands Ltd, since 1970; b Bramley, Guildford, 31 May 1944; s of Stanley Vincent Bothamley and Ethel Florence Bothamley (née Ingall); partner, Elizabeth Lloyd. *Educ:* Purley Grammar Sch.; Thames Poly. (BA Hons Architecture). Res. Exec., Economist Intelligence Unit, 1962–65; Econ. Researcher, Transport Hldg Co., 1965–66; Man. Dir's Asst, Ayling Industries Ltd, 1967–69. Associate, Creating Buildings, 1991–. Founder Trustee: Four Acre Trust, 1996–; Talk the Talk, 2013–; Trustee: Assoc. of Charitable Foundns, 2002–06; First Give, 2013–18. Chair, Hereford Civic Soc., 2011–18; Mem., Civic Voice. Gov., Univ. of Worcester, 2017–. FRSA 1998. *Recreations:* contemporary architecture, education, drawing, cycling, democracy, travel, journalism. *Address:* Treferanon, St Weonards, Hereford HR2 8QF. *T:* (01981) 580002. *E:* john@johnbothamley.co.uk.

**BOTHROYD, Shirley Ann;** barrister. Called to the Bar, 1982; Second Prosecuting Counsel, 1989–91, First Prosecuting Counsel, 1991–93, to Inland Revenue at CCC and Inner London Crown Ct. *Recreations:* wine, organizing others.

**BOTÍN-SANZ DE SAUTUOLA Y O'SHEA, Ana,** Hon. DBE 2015; Executive Chairman, Banco Santander, since 2014; b Santander, Spain, 4 Oct. 1960; d of late Emilio Botín and of Paloma O'Shea, 1st Marquise of O'Shea; m 1983, Guillermo Morenès Mariátegui; three s. *Educ:* St Mary's, Ascot; Bryn Mawr Coll. (BA Econs). JP Morgan, 1981–88 (Vice Pres., 1985–88); Banco Santander, 1988–99: Dep. Man. Dir, then Man. Dir, Banco Santander, later Chief Exec., Banco Santander de Negocios; Founder and CEO, Suala, private equity fund and IT web consultancy firm, 1999–2002; Chair, Banesto, 2002–10; CEO, Santander UK, 2010–14. Non-exec. Dir, Coca Cola Co., 2013–. *Recreations:* family, golf, reading, music, social responsibility and philanthropic work as a Founder and Chair of CyD Foundn for higher education and Empieza por Educar (Spanish affiliate of Teach for All). *Address:* Santander Group City, Av. de Cantabria s/n 28660, Boadilla del Monte, Madrid, Spain.

**BOTT, Catherine Jane;** singer and broadcaster; b 11 Sept. 1952; d of Maurice Bott and Patricia Bott (née Sherlock). *Educ:* King's High Sch. for Girls, Warwick; Guildhall Sch. of Music and Drama (GGSM). Concert, oratorio and recital singer; worldwide concert engagements, incl. world premières of Francis Grier's Five Joyful Mysteries, 2000, Joe Duddell's Not Waving but Drowning, 2002; first public performance of Jonathan Dove's Five Am'rous Sighs, 2002; radio broadcasts; numerous recordings with leading ensembles and orchestras, recital recordings and recordings of operatic roles, incl. Purcell's Dido, Messaggiera (l'Orfeo), Drusilla (l'Incoronazione di Poppaea), and Mandane (Artaxerxes). Co-Presenter, The Early Music Show, BBC Radio 3, 2003–13; presenter, Everything You Ever Wanted to Know About Classical Music, The Full Works Concert, Classic FM, 2013–; regular contrib. to music and arts progs on Radio 4. Patron, Portsmouth Festivities, 2005–. FGS (FGSM 2009). *Recreations:* exploring London, going to the ballet, learning Spanish rather slowly. *Address:* c/o MAS, Ranmore House, 19 Ranmore Road, Dorking, Surrey RH4 1HE.

**BOTT, Dr David Charles,** FRSC; Chairman, Oxford Biomaterials, since 2004; Director of Innovation Programmes and Communications, Technology Strategy Board, since 2007; b Gosport, Hants, 25 Nov. 1953; s of Kenneth Charles and Mary Lewis Bott; m 1981, Connie Ramsay; three s. *Educ:* Univ. of Sussex (BSc 1975; PhD 1979). Res. scientist, British Petroleum Res., 1979–87; Res. Manager, Courtaulds, 1987–95; Res. Dir, ICI Acrylics, 1995–99; Divl Vice Pres. of Res., National Starch, 1999–2001; Dir of Res., ICI, 2001–04; CEO, Materials UK, 2004–07. Dir, Oxford Advanced Surfaces, 2010–. FRSA. Hon. PhD Sheffield, 2011. *Publications:* contrib. chapters in books and papers to jls. *Recreations:* keeping an old car on the roads, trying to play guitar. *Address:* 10 Mansion House, Norton Grange, Little Kineton, Warks CV35 0DP. *T:* (01926) 642099. *E:* david.bott@mac.com.

**BOTT, Ian Bernard,** FREng; Director, Admiralty Research Establishment, Ministry of Defence, 1984–88, retired; consultant engineer, since 1988; b 1 April 1932; s of late Edwin Bernard and Agnes Bott; m 1955, Kathleen Mary (née Broadbent) (d 2016); one s one d. *Educ:* Nottingham High Sch.; Southwell Minster Grammar Sch.; Stafford Technical Coll.; Manchester Univ. BSc Hons Physics. FIEE, FInstP; FREng (FEng 1985). Nottingham Lace Industry, 1949–53. Royal Air Force, 1953–55. English Electric, Stafford, 1955–57; Royal Radar Estabt, 1960–75 (inventor of millimetre wavelength Relativistic Electron Cyclotron Maser, 1963 (patent holder); pioneer of the Gyrotron; Head of Electronics Group, 1973–75); Counsellor and Dep. Hd of Defence Research and Development Staff, British Embassy, Washington DC, 1975–77; Ministry of Defence: Dep. Dir Underwater Weapons Projects (S/M), 1977–79; Asst Chief Scientific Advr (Projects), 1979–81; Dir Gen., Guided Weapons and Electronics, 1981–82; Principal Dep. Dir, AWRE, MoD, 1982–84. Mem. Council, Fellowship of Engrg, 1987–90. Hon. Chm., Portsmouth Area Hospice, subseq. The Rowans Hospice, 1989–94 (Hon. Life Vice Pres., 1998). Trustee, Panasonic Trust, 1993–96. Freeman, City of London, 1985; Liveryman, Co. of Engineers, 1985. *Publications:* papers on physics and electronics subjects in jls of learned socs. *Recreations:* walking, horology, music. *Address:* The Lodge, Brand Lane, Ludlow, Shropshire SY8 1NN. *E:* ianbbott@tiscali.co.uk. *Club:* Royal Automobile.

**BOTT, Susan Mary,** CBE 2014; Deputy Chief Executive, Disability Rights UK (Director, Policy and Development, 2012); b Faversham, Kent, 23 Aug. 1956; d of E. R. Bott and E. Bott; one s one d. *Educ:* Exhall Grange Special Sch., Coventry; Univ. of Sheffield (BSc); Aston Univ. (MSc). Shropshire Disability Consortium: develt worker; Chief Exec., 1995–2005; Chief Exec., Nat. Centre for Independent Living, 2006–12. Chm., Think Local Act Personal Partnership, 2011–13. *Recreations:* enjoying the great outdoors, especially the sea. *T:* 07725 511562. *E:* suembott@gmail.com.

**BOTTING, Maj.-Gen. David Francis Edmund,** CB 1992; CBE 1986; Director General of Ordnance Services, Ministry of Defence, 1990–93; b 15 Dec. 1937; s of Leonard Edmund Botting and Elizabeth Mildred Botting (née Stacey); m 1962, Anne Outhwaite; two s. *Educ:* St Paul's School, London. National Service, RAOC, 1956; commissioned Eaton Hall, 1957; Regular Commission, 1958; regtl appts, Kineton, Deepcut, Borneo, Singapore and Malaya, 1957–67; sc 1968; BAOR, 1972–74; 1 Div., 1974–75; 3rd Div., 1981–82; Col AQ 1 Div., 1982–85; Comd Sup. 1 (BR) Corps, 1987; ACOS HQ UKLF, 1987–90. Rep. Col Comdt, RAOC, 1993; Col Comdt, RLC, 1993–2002. Trustee, Army Benevolent Fund, 1997–2007; Chm., RLC Mus. Trust, 2000–04; Pres., RAOC Charitable Trust, 2002–07.

FILDM 1991; MInstPS 1991. Freeman, City of London, 1990; Liveryman, Co. of Gold and Silver Wyre Drawers, 1991–2008. *Recreations:* golf, philately, furniture restoration. *Clubs:* Army and Navy; Tidworth Golf.

BOTTING, (Elizabeth) Louise, CBE 1993; Chairman, Douglas Deakin Young, 1988–2005 (Managing Director, 1982–88); *b* 19 Sept. 1939; *d* of Robert and Edith Young; marr. diss.; two *d*; *m* 1989, Leslie Arthur Carpenter, *qv. Educ:* Sutton Coldfield High School; London Sch. of Economics (BSc Econ.). Kleinwort Benson, 1961–65; Daily Mail, 1970–75; British Forces Broadcasting, 1971–83; Douglas Deakin Young, financial consultancy, 1975–2005. Director: Trinity International, 1991–99; CGU (formerly General Accident), 1992–2000; London Weekend Television, 1992–94; 102, Stratford-upon-Avon Radio Station, 1996–2001; Camelot plc, 1999–2010. Presenter, BBC Moneybox, 1977–92. Mem. Top Salaries Review Body, 1987–94.

*See also J. R. C. Young.*

BOTTOMLEY, family name of **Baroness Bottomley of Nettlestone**.

BOTTOMLEY OF NETTLESTONE, Baroness *cr* 2005 (Life Peer), of St Helens, in the county of Isle of Wight; **Virginia Hilda Brunette Maxwell Bottomley**; PC 1992; JP; DL; *b* 12 March 1948; *d* of late W. John Garnett, CBE and of Barbara (*née* Rutherford-Smith); *m* Sir Peter James Bottomley, *qv*; one *s* two *d. Educ:* London Sch. of Econs and Pol Science (MSc). Research for Child Poverty Action Gp, 1971–73; behavioural scientist, 1973–84. Partner, Odgers Berndtson (formerly Odgers, Ray and Berndtson), 2000– (Dir, Odgers Gp Ltd, 2000–); Member: Supervisory Bd, AkzoNobel NV, 2000–12; Internat. Adv. Council, Chugai Pharmaceutical Co. Ltd, 2012–. Non-executive Director: BUPA, 2006–12; Smith & Nephew, 2012–. Mem., MRC, 1987–88. Contested (C) IoW, 1983. MP (C) Surrey SW, May 1984–2005. PPS: to Minister of State for Educn and Science, 1985–86; to Minister for Overseas Develt, 1986–87; to Sec. of State for Foreign and Commonwealth Affairs, 1987–88; Parly Under-Sec. of State, DoE, 1988–89; Minister for Health, 1989–92; Secretary of State: for Health, 1992–95; for Nat. Heritage, 1995–97. Fellow, Industry Parlt Trust, 1987 (Trustee, 2002–05); Ind. Trustee, Economist newspaper, 2005–. Vice-Chm., British Council, 1998–2001. Pro-Chancellor, Univ. of Surrey, 2005–16; Chancellor, Univ. of Hull, 2006–. Mem. Bd, Prince of Wales Internat. Business Leaders Forum, 2002–10; Pres., Farnham Castle, Centre for Internat. Briefing, 2003–10. Mem., UK Adv. Bd, ICC, 2005–. Nat. Pres., Abbeyfield Soc., 2003–09. Mem., Court of Govs, LSE, 1985–2016; Mem. Council, Ditchley Foundn, 2005– (Gov., 1991–2005); Gov., Univ. of the Arts (formerly London Inst.), 2000–06; Mem., Bd of Internat. Overseers, Sabanci Univ., 2015–. JP Inner London, 1975 (Chm., Lambeth Juvenile Court, 1981–84). DL Surrey, 2006. Sheriff, Kingston-upon-Hull, 2013–. Freeman, City of London, 1988. Lay Canon, Guildford Cathedral, 2002–15. *Recreations:* work, grandchildren. *Address:* House of Lords, SW1A 0PW. *Clubs:* Athenæum; Seaview Yacht.

BOTTOMLEY, Sir Peter (James), Kt 2011; MP (C) Worthing West, since 1997 (Greenwich, Woolwich West, June 1975–1983, Eltham, 1983–97); *b* 30 July 1944; *er s* of Sir James Reginald Alfred Bottomley, KCMG; *m* 1967, Virginia Garnett (*see* Baroness Bottomley of Nettlestone); one *s* two *d. Educ:* comprehensive sch.; Westminster Sch.; Trinity Coll., Cambridge (MA). Driving, industrial sales, industrial relations, industrial economics. Contested (C) GLC elect., Vauxhall, 1973; (C) Woolwich West, gen. elecns, 1974. PPS to Minister of State, FCO, 1982–83, to Sec. of State for Social Services, 1983–84, to Sec. of State for NI, 1990; Parly Under Sec. of State, Dept of Employment, 1984–86, Dept of Transport, 1986–89, NI Office, 1989–90. Member, Select Committee: on Violence in the Family, 1976–77; on Overseas Develt, 1978–79; on Constitutional Affairs, 2003–05; on HS2, 2014–16; Member: Transport Cttee, 1992–97; Ecclesiastical Cttee, 2002–05, 2010–. Sec., Cons. Parly For. and Commonwealth Cttee, 1979–81; Leader, UK Delegn to Parly Assembly, OSCE, 2010–15. Pres., Cons. Trade Unionists, 1978–80; Vice-Pres., Fedn of Cons. Students, 1980–82. Chairman: British Union of Family Orgns, 1973–80; Family Forum, 1980–82; Church of England Children's Soc., 1983–84. Member Council: MIND, 1981–82; NACRO, 1997–2004; Trustee, Christian Aid, 1978–84. Parly Swimming Champion, 1980–81, 1984–86; Captain, Parly Football Team; occasional Parly Dinghy Sailing Champion; Parly Warden, St Margaret's Church, Westminster, 2010–. Mem., Ct of Assts, Drapers' Co. Castrol/Inst. of Motor Industry Road Safety Gold Medal, 1988. *Recreations:* children, book reviewing, canoeing. *Address:* House of Commons, SW1A 0AA. *E:* bottomleyp@parliament.uk.

BOTTOMS, Sir Anthony Edward, Kt 2001; FBA 1997; Wolfson Professor of Criminology, 1984–2006, now Emeritus, and Director of the Institute of Criminology, 1984–98, University of Cambridge; Fellow of Fitzwilliam College, Cambridge, 1984–2006, now Life Fellow (President, 1994–98); Professorial Fellow in Criminology, University of Sheffield, 2002–07, now Honorary Professor; *b* 29 Aug. 1939; *yr s* of James William Bottoms, medical missionary, and Dorothy Ethel Bottoms (*née* Barnes); *m* 1962, Janet Freda Wenger; one *s* one *d. Educ:* Eltham Coll.; Corpus Christi Coll., Oxford (MA; Hon. Fellow, 2012); Corpus Christi Coll., Cambridge (Dip. Criminol. 1962; MA); Univ. of Sheffield (PhD). Probation Officer, 1962–64; Research Officer, Inst. of Criminology, Univ. of Cambridge, 1964–68; Univ. of Sheffield: Lecturer, 1968–72; Sen. Lectr, 1972–76; Prof. of Criminology, 1976–84; Dean of Faculty of Law, 1981–84. Canadian Commonwealth Vis. Fellow, Simon Fraser Univ., BC, 1982; Vis. Prof., QUB, 1999–2000. Member: Parole Bd for England and Wales, 1974–76; Home Office Res. and Adv. Gp on Long-Term Prison System, 1984–90. Specialist Advr, NI Cttee, H of C, 1998, 2003–04, 2007. Chm. of Trustees, Westminster Coll., Cambridge, 2008–14. Editor, Howard Journal of Penology and Crime Prevention, 1975–81. Hon. LLD: QUB, 2003; Sheffield, 2009; Edinburgh, 2015; Hederdoktor, Malmö, 2014. Sellin-Glueck Award, Amer. Soc. of Criminology, 1996; Eur. Criminology Award, Eur. Soc. of Criminology, 2007. *Publications:* (jtly) Criminals Coming of Age, 1973; (jtly) The Urban Criminal, 1976; (jtly) Defendants in the Criminal Process, 1976; The Suspended Sentence after Ten Years (Frank Dawtry Lecture), 1980; (ed jtly) The Coming Penal Crisis, 1980; (ed jtly) Problems of Long-Term Imprisonment, 1987; (jtly) Social Inquiry Reports, 1988; (jtly) Intermediate Treatment and Juvenile Justice, 1990; Crime Prevention facing the 1990s (James Smart Lecture), 1990; Intensive Community Supervision for Young Offenders, 1995; (jtly) Prisons and the Problem of Order, 1996; (jtly) Criminal Deterrence and Sentence Severity, 1999; (ed jtly) Community Penalties, 2001; (ed jtly) Ideology, Crime and Criminal Justice, 2002; (ed jtly) Alternatives to Prison, 2004; (ed jtly) Hearing the Victim, 2010; (ed jtly) Young Adult Offenders, 2012; (ed jtly) Global Perspectives on Desistance, 2016; The Sentencing Council in 2017, 2018; (ed jtly) Penal Censure, 2019; various articles and reviews. *Address:* Institute of Criminology, Sidgwick Avenue, Cambridge CB3 9DA. *T:* (01223) 335360.

BOTTONE, Bonaventura; tenor; *s* of Bonaventura Bottone and Kathleen; *m* Jennifer Dakin; two *s* two *d. Educ:* Lascelles Secondary Mod. Sch., Harrow; Royal Acad. Music (ARAM 1984; FRAM 1998). Has appeared at numerous international venues, including: Nice Opera (début 1982); Houston Opera (début 1987); Royal Opera House, Covent Garden (début 1987); London Coliseum; Glyndebourne Fest. (début 1990); Bavarian State Opera, Munich (début 1991); Fundação de São Carlos, Lisbon (début 1994); Chicago Lyric Opera (début 1994); New Israeli Opera, Tel Aviv (début 1995); Metropolitan Opera, NY (début 1998); Opera del Teatro Municipal, Santiago (début 1998); Paris Opéra Bastille (début 2000); Atlanta Opera (début 2001); Brisbane SO (début 2002); Deutsches SO Berlin (début 2002); La Fenice, Venice (début 2003); La Scala, Milan (début 2007); Los Angeles Opera (début 2008). Has performed with Philharmonia Orch., Edmonton SO, ENO, Royal Opera Co., Scottish Opera, Opera North, Welsh Opera, City of Birmingham SO and BBC Concert Orchestra; rôles include: Alfredo in La Traviata, Italian Tenor in Der Rosenkavalier, Governor General in Candide, Nanki-Poo in Mikado, Lenski in Eugene Onegin, Alfred in Die Fledermaus, Narraboth in Salome, Duke of Mantua in Rigoletto, Pinkerton in Madam Butterfly, Turridù in Cavalleria Rusticana, title rôle, Damnation of Faust, title rôle, Doctor Ox's Experiment (world première), Rodolfo in La Bohème, Riccardo in Un Ballo in Maschera, Troilus in Troilus and Cressida, Loge in Das Rheingold, Torquemada in L'heure Espagnole, Nick in La Fanciulla del West, L'Abate in Adriana Lecouvreur, Basilio in Le Nozze di Figaro, Benda in The Jacobin, Arturo in Lucia di Lammermoor, Nick in La Fanciulla del West, Tzar Berendey in The Snowmaiden, Emperor Altoum in Turandot, Don Ottavio in Don Giovanni, Pepe in Rita. Has made numerous recordings. Patron, Bampton Opera, 2014–; Hd, Bd of Adjudicators, Bampton Young Singers' Competition, 2017–. *Recreations:* gardening, boating. *Address:* c/o Rayfield Allied, Studio 26 China Works, 100 Black Prince Road, SE1 7SJ. *T:* (020) 3176 5500, *Fax:* 0700 602 4143. *E:* info@rayfieldallied.com.

BOTWOOD, Richard Price; Director-General, Chartered Institute of Transport, 1989–98; *b* 1 June 1932; *s* of Allan Bertram and Hilda Amelia Botwood; *m* 1964, Victoria Sanderson; one *s* one *d. Educ:* Oundle School. Sec., Tozer Kemsley & Millbourn, 1952–56; Dir, International Factors, 1956–61; Asst Man. Dir, Melbray Group, 1961–73; Chm. and Man. Dir, W. S. Sanderson (Morpeth), wine and spirit merchants, 1973–85; Dir-Gen., Air Transport Users' Cttee, 1986–89. *Recreations:* opera, gardening, embroidery, golf. *Address:* 54 Bute Gardens, W6 7DX. *T:* (020) 8748 8875.

BOUCHARD, Hon. Lucien; GOQ 2008; PC (Can.) 1988; Senior Partner, Davies Ward Phillips & Vineberg LLP, since 2001; President, Quebec Oil and Gas Association, 2011–13; *b* 22 Dec. 1938; *m* 1989, Audrey Best (marr. diss; she *d* 2011); two *s. Educ:* Collège de Jonquière; Université Laval (BA, BSocSc, LLB 1964). Called to the Bar, Quebec, 1964; in private practice, Chicoutimi, 1964–85. Pres., Saguenay Bar, 1978; Mem., Admin Cttee and Chm., Specialisation Cttee, Quebec Bar. Ambassador to France, 1985–88; MP (C), 1988–90, (Ind), 1990–91, (Bloc Québécois), 1991–96, Lac-St-Jean; Secretary of State, 1988–89; Minister of the Envmt, 1989–90; Chm. and Leader, Bloc Québécois, 1991–96; Leader of Federal Opposition, 1993–96; Mem. for Jonquière, Quebec Nat. Assembly, 1996–2001; Prime Minister of Quebec, 1996–2001; Leader, Parti Québécois, 1996–2001. Director: Transcontinental Inc.; Saputo Inc.; TransForce Inc. Commandeur, Légion d'Honneur (France), 2002. *Publications:* (jtly) Martin-Bouchard Report, 1978; A visage découvert, 1992 (trans. English 1994); specialised articles in legal and labour relns jls. *Address:* Davies Ward Phillips & Vineberg LLP, 1501 McGill College Avenue, 26th Floor, Montreal, QC H3A 3N9, Canada.

BOUCHER, Prof. Bruce Ambler, PhD; FSA; Director, Sir John Soane's Museum, since 2016; *b* Birmingham, Ala, 5 Nov. 1948; *s* of John Boucher and Louise Boucher (*née* Kean); *m* 1st, 1974, Gillian Moore (marr. diss. 1981); 2nd, 1982, Isabel Carlisle (marr. diss. 1996); two *d*; 3rd, 1999, Diane Michaels (*née* Radley). *Educ:* Harvard Univ. (AB 1970); Magdalen Coll., Oxford (Rhodes Scholar; BA 1972; MA 1977); Courtauld Inst. of Art, Univ. of London (MA 1974; PhD 1987). University College London: Lectr, 1976–92, Reader, 1992–98, in Hist. of Art; Prof. of Hist. of Art, 1998–2002, now Emeritus; Curator, European Sculpture and Decorative Arts and Ancient Art, Art Inst. of Chicago, 2002–09; Dir, Art Mus., Univ. of Virginia, 2009–16. *Publications:* The Sculpture of Jacopo Sansovino, 1991; Andrea Palladio: the architect in his time, 1994, 3rd edn 2007; Italian Baroque Sculpture, 1998; (ed) Earth and Fire: Italian terracotta sculptures from Donatello to Canova, 2001. *Recreations:* opera, travel, Wigmore Hall. *Address:* Sir John Soane's Museum, 13 Lincoln's Inn Fields, WC2A 3BP. *T:* (020) 7440 4263, *Fax:* (020) 7831 3957. *E:* bboucher@soane.org.uk. *Clubs:* Athenæum; Harvard of New York.

BOUCHIER, Prof. Ian Arthur Dennis, CBE 1990; Professor of Medicine, University of Edinburgh, 1986–97; Chief Scientist, Scottish Office Department of Health (formerly Home and Health Department), 1992–97; *b* 7 Sept. 1932; *s* of E. A. and M. Bouchier; *m* 1959, Patricia Norma Henshilwood; two *s. Educ:* Rondebosch Boys' High Sch., Cape Town; Univ. of Cape Town. MB, ChB, MD, FRCP, FRCPE, FFPH; FRSE, FRSB. Groote Schuur Hospital: House Officer, 1955–58; Registrar, 1958–61; Asst Lectr, Royal Free Hosp., 1962–63; Instructor in Medicine, Boston Univ. Sch. of Medicine, 1964–65; Sen. Lectr 1965–70, Reader in Medicine 1970–73, Univ. of London; Prof. of Medicine, 1973–86, and Dean, Faculty of Medicine and Dentistry, 1982–86, Univ. of Dundee. Pres., World Organisation of Gastroenterology, 1990–98 (Sec. Gen., 1982–90); British Society of Gastroenterology: Mem. Council, 1987–90; Chm. Educn Cttee, 1987–90; Pres., 1994–95. Member: Chief Scientist Cttee, Scotland, 1980–97; MRC, 1982–86; Council, RCPE, 1984–90. Goulstonian Lectr, RCP, 1971; Sydney Watson Smith Lectr, RCPE, 1991. Visiting Professor of Medicine: Michigan Univ., 1979; McGill Univ., 1983; RPMS, 1984; Shenyang Univ., Hong Kong Univ., 1988. FRSA. Hon. FCP (SoAf); Founder FMedSci 1998. Hon. Mem., Japanese Soc. Gastroenterology; Correspl. Member: Soc. Italiana di Gastroenterologia; Royal Catalonian Acad. of Medicine. Chm., Editl Bd, Current Opinion in Gastroenterology, 1987–91; Member, Editorial Board: Baillière's Clinical Gastroenterology, 1987–98; Hellenic Jl of Gastroenterology, 1988–98; Internat. Gastroenterology, 1988–98. Hon. MD Iasi, 2001. *Publications:* (ed jtly) Bilirubin Metabolism, 1967; (ed) Clinical Investigation of Gastrointestinal Function, 1969, 2nd edn 1981; (ed) Seventh Symposium on Advanced Medicine, 1971; (ed) Diseases of the Biliary Tract, vol. 2, 1973; Gastroenterology, 1973, 3rd edn 1982; (jtly) Aspects of Clinical Gastroenterology, 1975; (ed jtly) Clinical Skills, 1976, 2nd edn 1982; (ed) Recent Advances in Gastroenterology 3, 1976, 4, 1980, 5, 1983; (ed jtly) Textbook of Gastroenterology, 1984; (ed jtly) Inflammatory Bowel Disease, 1986, 2nd edn 1993; (ed jtly) Davidson's Principles and Practice of Medicine, 15th edn 1987 to 17th edn 1995; (ed jtly) Clinical Investigations in Gastroenterology, 1988; (ed) Jaundice, 1989; (ed jtly) Infectious Diarrhoea, 1993; (ed jtly) Gastroenterology Clinical Science and Practice, vols 1 and 2, 2nd edn 1993; (ed jtly) Quality Assurance in Medical Care, 1993; (ed jtly) French's Index of Differential Diagnosis, 13th edn 1996; 600 scientific papers and communications. *Recreations:* history of whaling, music of Berlioz, cooking.

BOUGH, Francis Joseph; broadcaster; *b* 15 Jan. 1933; *m*; three *s. Educ:* Oswestry; Merton College, Oxford (BA). With ICI, 1957–62; BBC, 1962–89; presenter of Sportsview, 1964–67, of Grandstand, 1967–82, of Nationwide, 1972–83, of breakfast television, 1983–87, of Holiday, 1987–88; presenter: 6 o'clock Live, LWT, 1989–92; Sky TV, 1989–90; LBC Radio, 1992–96; Travel Live, on Travel TV (cable and satellite), 1996–. Richard Dimbleby Award for Factual Television, BAFTA, 1976. Former Oxford soccer blue, Shropshire sprint champion. *Publications:* Cue Frank! (autobiog.), 1980; Frank Bough's Breakfast Book, 1984.

BOUGHEY, Sir John (George Fletcher), 11th Bt *cr* 1798; medical practitioner; *b* 12 Aug. 1959; *s* of Sir Richard James Boughey, 10th Bt, and of Davina Julia (now Lady Loch), *d* of FitzHerbert Wright; *S* father, 1978; *m* 2004, Hebote Bishaw (marr. diss. 2006). *Educ:* Eton

Univ. of Zimbabwe (MB ChB 1984); LRCPE; LRCSE; LRCPSGlas 1990; MRCPI 1994. *Heir*: *b* James Richard Boughey [*b* 29 Aug. 1960; *m* 1989, Katy Fenwicke-Clennell; two *s* two *d*].

**BOULDING, Dame Hilary,** DBE 2017; President, Trinity College, Oxford, since 2017; *b* 25 Jan. 1957; *d* of James Frederick Boulding and Dorothy Boulding (*née* Watson). *Educ*: Heaton Sch., Newcastle upon Tyne; St Hilda's Coll., Oxford (BA Hons Music). TV Dir, 1981–85, TV Producer, 1985–92, BBC Scotland; Head of Arts and Music, BBC Wales, 1992–97; Commissioning Editor, Music (Policy), BBC Radio 3, 1997–99; Dir of Music, Arts Council of England, subseq. Arts Council England, 1999–2007; Principal, RWCMD, 2007–17. Mem. Bd, WNO, 2008–17; Chm., Conservatoires UK, 2014–17. *Recreations*: music, gardening. *Address*: President's Lodgings, Trinity College, Oxford OX1 3BH.

**BOULDING, Philip Vincent;** QC 1996; *b* 1 Feb. 1954; *s* of Vincent Fergusson Boulding and Sylvia Boulding; *m* 1988, Helen Elizabeth Richardson; one *s* one *d*. *Educ*: Downing Coll., Cambridge (Scholar; BA Law 1st Cl. Hons 1976; LLM 1977; MA 1979; Rugby Blue). Called to the Bar, Gray's Inn, 1979, Bencher, 2004; practice in London and South East; internat. arbitration practice in FE, based in Hong Kong; regular arbitrator, adjudicator and mediator in commercial contract disputes, esp. in engrg and construction law; admitted to Hong Kong Bar, 1997; Mem., Panel of Arbitrators, 2016–, Dir, Accredited Adjudicator Trng Course, 2016–, HK Internat. Arbitration Centre. Approved Arbitrator and Approved Mediator, Kuala Lumpur Regl Centre for Arbitration; rights of audience, Dubai Internat. Finance Centre Court. Pres., Cambridge Univ. Amateur Boxing Club, 1990–94 (Vice-Pres., 1994–2000); Sen. Pres., Downing Coll. Griffins' Club, Cambridge, 2004–. Gov., Hills Road VI Form Coll., Cambridge, 1997–2000. Consultant Ed., Construction Law Reports, 2007–. *Publications*: (contrib.) Keating on Construction Contracts, 8th edn, 2008 to 10th edn, 2016, (contrib.) Keating Supplement, 2013, 2018, 2019. *Recreations*: Rugby, tennis, swimming, shooting. *Address*: c/o Keating Chambers, 15 Essex Street, WC2R 3AA. *Clubs*: Royal Automobile; Hawks (Cambridge).

**BOULT, Geoffrey Pattisson;** education consultant, since 2014; Director, Juniper Barn Ltd, since 2017; Headmaster, Giggleswick School, 2001–14; *b* 6 June 1957; *s* of late Peter and Jane Boult; *m* 1984, Katharine Goddard; four *d*. *Educ*: Durham Univ. (BA Hons; PGCE). Teacher, Canford Sch., Dorset, 1980–87; Hd of Humanities, Geelong GS, 1984–85; Hd of Geog., Cranleigh Sch., 1987–92; Housemaster, St Edward's Sch., Oxford, 1992–2001. Sec., Oxford Conf. in Educn, 1982–86; Dir, Boarding Schs Assoc., 2003–09 (Chm., 2007–08); Sec. and Chm. (NE), HMC, 2010–12. Chm., Suffolk Coastal Filling Station, 2017. *Recreations*: golf, fireworks, reading, lay evangelist. *Address*: Church Farm, Rendham, Suffolk IP17 2AZ.

**BOULTON, Adam;** see Boulton, T. A. B.

**BOULTON, His Honour David John;** a Circuit Judge, 2001–12; Liaison Judge, St Helens Justices, 2004–11; *b* 2 July 1945; *s* of late John Ellis and Hilda May Boulton; *m* 1971, Suzanne Proudlove. *Educ*: Quarry Bank High Sch., Liverpool; Liverpool Univ. (LLB). Called to the Bar, Middle Temple, 1970; specialised in crime; Standing Counsel for DTI, 1989–99, Customs and Excise, 1993–99, Inland Revenue, 1997–99; an Asst Recorder, 1984–89; a Recorder, 1989–2001. Mem., Bar Council, 1995–2001. Tutor Judge, Judicial Studies Bd, 2007–12. *Recreations*: wine, gardens, travel. *Address*: c/o Queen Elizabeth II Law Courts, Derby Square, Liverpool L2 1XA. *Clubs*: Athenæum (Liverpool); Lancashire CC.

**BOULTON, Fiona Jane;** Headmistress, Guildford High School, since 2002; *b* 11 April 1964; *d* of Michael Harry Lockton and (Elizabeth) Iona Lockton; *m* 1994, Richard Edward Stanley Boulton, *qv*; one *s* two *d*. *Educ*: University Coll., Cardiff (BSc Hons); Exeter Coll., Oxford (PGCE); Inst. of Educn, Univ. of London (MA; NPQH). Housemistress: Stowe Sch., 1989–91; Marlborough Coll., 1991–95; Dep. Head, Guildford High Sch., 1996–2002. Nat. Leader of Educn, 2013–. Chm., HMC, 2019–Sept. 2020. *Recreations*: cooking, walking, art, theatre, reading. *Address*: Waterton, Cleardown, The Hockering, Woking, Surrey GU22 7HH. *E*: fiona.boulton@guildfordhigh.co.uk. *Club*: Lansdowne.

**BOULTON, Prof. Geoffrey Stewart,** OBE 2000; FRS 1992; FRSE; Regius Professor of Geology and Mineralogy, 1986–2008, and Vice-Principal, 1999–2008, University of Edinburgh, now Senior Hon. Professorial Fellow and Regius Professor of Geology Emeritus; General Secretary, Royal Society of Edinburgh, 2007–11; *b* 28 Nov. 1940; *s* of George Stewart and Rose Boulton; *m* 1964, Denise Bryers Lawns; two *d*. *Educ*: Longton High Sch.; Birmingham Univ. BSc, PhD, DSc. FGS 1961; FRSE 1989. British Geol Survey, 1962–64; Demonstrator, Univ. of Keele, 1964–65; Fellow, Univ. of Birmingham, 1965–68; Hydrogeologist, Kenya, 1968; Lectr, then Reader, Univ. of E Anglia, 1968–86; Provost and Dean, Faculty of Sci. and Engrg, Univ. of Edinburgh, 1994–99. Prof., Amsterdam Univ., 1980–86. Mem., Royal Commn on Envmtl Pollution, 1994–2000. NERC: Chairman: Polar Sci. Bd, 1992–95; Earth Sci. and Technol. Bd, 1994–98; Mem. Council, 1993–98; Royal Society: Chm., Sect. Cttee 5 for Earth Sci. and Astronomy, 1993–95; Mem., Council, 1997–99, 2013–16; Chair, Policy Advisory Gp, 2012–16. Member: NCC Scotland, 1991–92; SHEFC, 1997–2003 (Chm., Res. Policy Cttee, 2000–03); Council, Scottish Assoc. for Marine Sci., 1997–2003 (Pres., 2013–18; Vice Pres.); Scottish Sci. Adv. Cttee, 2003–07; Council for Sci. and Technol., 2004–12. Pres., Cttee on Data for Sci. and Technol., 2014–18, Mem. Governing Bd, 2018–, Internat. Sci. Council (formerly Internat. Council for Sci.). UK Deleg. to IUGS, 1996–99. President: Geol Soc. of Edinburgh, 1991–93; Quaternary Res. Assoc., 1991–94; Chm., Council, Univ. of Heidelberg, 2007–; Mem., Strategic Council, Univ. of Geneva, 2009–. Hon. DTech Chalmers, Sweden, 2002; Hon. DSc: Birmingham, 2007; Keele, 2007; Heidelberg, 2008. Kirk Bryan Medal, Geol Soc. of America, 1976; Seligman Crystal, Internat. Glaciol. Soc., 2001; Lyell Medal, Geol Soc., 2006; Tedford Sci. Medal, Inst. for Contemp. Scotland, 2006; James Croll Medal, Quaternary Res. Assoc., 2011; Polar Medal, 2015. Commandeur, Ordre des Palmes Académiques (France), 2009. *Publications*: numerous articles in learned jls on glaciology, quaternary, marine and polar geology. *Recreations*: violin, mountaineering, sailing. *Address*: Old Barn Farm, 13 Long Street, Belton, Leics LE12 9TP.

**BOULTON, Sir John Gibson,** 4th Bt *cr* 1944, of Braxted Park, co. Essex; *b* 18 Dec. 1946; *o s* of Sir William Whytehead Boulton, 3rd Bt, CBE, TD, and Margaret Elizabeth, *o d* of late Brig. H. N. A. Hunter, DSO; *S* father, 2010. *Educ*: Stowe. *Heir*: none.

**BOULTON, Richard Edward Stanley;** QC 2011; FCA; *b* London, 3 May 1959; *s* of Sir Clifford John Boulton, GCB; *m* 1994, Fiona Jane Lockton (*see* F. J. Boulton); one *s* two *d*. *Educ*: Marlborough Coll.; Oriel Coll., Oxford (MA Modern Hist.); Coll. of Law, Guildford (Postgrad. DipLaw (Dist.) 2002); BPP Law Sch. (BVC (Outstanding) 2003). ACA 1986, FCA 1996. With Arthur Andersen, 1981–2001: Partner, 1990–2001; UK Head of Econ. and Financial Consulting Gp, 1994–95, of Business Consulting, 1995–97; Worldwide Managing Partner: Strategy and Service Categories, 1997–2000; Business Consulting, 2000–01; Chief Information Officer, 2000–01; LECG LLC: Global Hd of Finance and Accounting Services, 2005; Sen. Man. Dir, 2007–11; Bd Mem., 2008–10. Called to the Bar, Inner Temple, 2003; in practice as barrister, specialising in commercial litigation, 2004–. Treas., Tate Members, 1993–2006. Fellow, Academy of Experts, 1994. *Publications*: (jtly) Cracking the Value Code: how successful businesses are creating wealth in the new economy, 2000. *Recreations*: running, golf, theatre, wine, cricket, travel. *Address*: One Essex Court, Temple, EC4Y 9AR. *E*: rboulton@oeclaw.co.uk; Waterton, Cleardown, Woking, Surrey GU22 7HH. *T*: (01483) 760258, 07785 396954. *E*: richardeboulton@hotmail.com. *Clubs*: MCC; Wisley Golf.

**BOULTON, (Thomas) Adam (Babington);** broadcaster; Editor at Large, Sky News, since 2014; *b* 15 Feb. 1959; *s* of late Dr Thomas B. Boulton, OBE and Helen C. Boulton; *m* 1st, 1985, Kerena Mond (marr. diss. 2004); three *d*; 2nd, 2006, Angela Margaret Jane Hunter, *qv*. *Educ*: Tower Hse Sch., Sheen; St Andrew's Sch., Pangbourne; Westminster Sch.; Christ Church, Oxford (MA); Sch. of Advanced Internat. Studies, Johns Hopkins Univ. (MA). Stringer, Inter Press, Washington, 1981–82; Talks Writer, BBC External Services, 1982; TV Journalist, 1982–84, Political Editor, 1984–89, TV-am; Political Ed. and Presenter, Sky News, 1989–2014. Columnist, Sunday Times, 2013–. Chm., Parly Lobby, 2007. Editl Adv. Bd, Reaction, 2019–. Gov., Sevenoaks Sch., 2013–. Mem. Council, KCL, 2004–13; FKC 2013. Hon. Dr Sheffield Hallam, 2008; Hon. DBus Plymouth, 2013. *Publications*: (contrib.) Political Communications: why Labour won the general election of 1997, 2000; (contrib.) Political Communications: the general election campaign of 2005, 2007; Tony's Ten Years, 2008; (contrib.) 20 Years of Breaking News, 2009; (with Joey Jones) Hung Together, 2010; (contrib.) Political Communication in Britain, 2011. *Recreations*: arts, gardening. *Address*: c/o Sky News, 2nd Floor, 4 Millbank, SW1P 3JA. *T*: (020) 7032 2820, *Fax*: (020) 1900 7028. *E*: adam.boulton@sky.uk. *W*: www.twitter.com/adamboultonsky. *Clubs*: Beefsteak, Pilgrims.

**BOUNDS, (Kenneth) Peter,** CBE 2013; Chief Executive, Liverpool City Council, 1991–99; *b* 7 Nov. 1943; *s* of Rev. Kenneth Bounds and Doris Bounds; *m* 1965, Geraldine Amy Slee; two *s*. *Educ*: Ashville College, Harrogate. Admitted Solicitor, 1971. Dir of Admin, Stockport MBC, 1973–82; Chief Exec., Bolton MBC, 1982–91. A Civil Service Comr, 2001–07. Pres., Assoc. of Dist Secs, 1980–81; Chm., Soc. of Metropolitan Chief Execs, 1997; Company Secretary: Greater Manchester Econ. Develt Ltd, 1986–91; NW Tourist Bd, 1986–91; Royal Liverpool Philharmonic Soc., 2000–07, 2008–11 (Dir, 1993–2000; Dep. Chm., 1997–2000; Chm., 2007–08). Chair: Liverpool City Challenge, 1991–95; Liverpool City of Learning, 1994–97; Liverpool Partnership Gp, 1994–99; Renew N Staffs (Housing Market Renewal Partnership), 2002–11; Liverpool Cathedral Council, 2004–; Centre of Refurbishment Excellence Ltd, 2011–13. Non-executive Director: Mgt Bd, Government Office for SE, 2008–09, for NW, 2009–11; N Staffs Regeneration Partnership, 2007–10. Chair, Relate Cheshire and Merseyside, 2010–18. Member: President's Council, Methodist Church, 1981–84; Bd of Trustees for Methodist Church Purposes, 1983–2008. Mem. Council, Liverpool Inst. of Performing Arts, 2009–11. Patron, Centre for Tomorrow's Company, 1997–2010. Hon. Sec., Mary Jane Cross Charity, 2016–. Hon. Fellow, Bolton Inst. of Higher Educn, 1991. FRSA 1994. Hon. LLD Liverpool, 2009; DUniv Bolton, 2010. *Recreations*: music, theatre. *Address*: 44 Reynolds Court, Vale Road, Woolton, Liverpool L25 7RZ.

**BOURDEAUX, Rev. Canon Michael Alan;** Director, 1969–99, President, since 2003, Keston Institute, Oxford (formerly Keston College, Kent); *b* 19 March 1934; *s* of Richard Edward and Lillian Myra Bourdeaux; *m* 1st, 1960, Gillian Mary Davies (*d* 1978); one *s* one *d*; 2nd, 1979, Lorna Elizabeth Waterton; one *s* one *d*. *Educ*: Truro Sch.; St Edmund Hall, Oxford (MA Hons Mod. Langs); Wycliffe Hall, Oxford (Hons Theology); BD Oxon 1969. Moscow State Univ., 1959–60; Deacon, 1960; Asst Curate, Enfield Parish Church, Middx, 1960–64; researching at Chislehurst, Kent, on the Church in the Soviet Union, with grant from Centre de Recherches, Geneva, 1965–68. Vis. Prof., St Bernard's Seminary, Rochester, NY, 1969; Vis. Fellow, LSE, 1969–71; Research Fellow, RIIA, Chatham House, 1971–73; Dawson Lectr on Church and State, Baylor Univ., Waco, Texas, 1972; Chavasse Meml Lectr, Oxford Univ., 1976; Kathryn W. Davis Prof. in Slavic Studies, Wellesley Coll., Wellesley, Mass, 1981; Moorhouse Lectr, Melbourne, 1987; Vis. Fellow, St Edmund Hall, Oxford, 1989–90; Vis. Prof., Inst. for Econ., Political and Cultural Develt, Notre Dame Univ., Ind., 1993; Croall Lectr, Univ. of Edinburgh, 2002; Paul G Manolis Dist. Lectr, Patriarch Athenagoras Inst., Berkeley, CA, 2009. Mem., High-Level Experts' Gp on For. Policy and Common Security, EC, 1993–94. Hon. Canon, Rochester Cathedral, 1990–99, now Canon Emeritus; Artistic Dir (formerly Hon. Dir), Iffley Music Soc., 1996–2013. Founded Keston College, a research centre on religion in the Communist countries, 1969. Founder of journal, Religion in Communist Lands, 1973, retitled Religion, State and Society: the Keston Jl, 1992. Mem. Council, Britain-Russia Centre, 1991–2000. DD Lambeth, 1996; Hon. DHL Wittenberg, Ohio, 2009; Hon. DD Evangelical Theol Faculty, Osiek, Croatia, 2009. Templeton Prize for Progress in Religion, 1984. Order of Grand Duke Gediminas, 1999, Order of Vytautas the Great, 2005 (Lithuania). *Publications*: Opium of the People, 1965, 2nd edn 1977; Religious Ferment in Russia, 1968; Patriarch and Prophets, 1970, 2nd edn 1975; Faith on Trial in Russia, 1971; Land of Crosses, 1979; Risen Indeed, 1983; (with Lorna Bourdeaux) Ten Growing Soviet Churches, 1987; Gorbachev, Glasnost and the Gospel, 1990, rev. US edn, The Gospel's Triumph over Communism, 1991; (ed) The Politics of Religion in Russia and the New States of Eurasia, 1995; (ed jtly) Proselytism and Orthodoxy in Russia, 1999; Religion and Society: essays on religious life in Russia today, 2002; (ed jtly) Contemporary Religious Life in Russia, vol. 1, 2003, vol. 2, 2003, vol. 3, 2005; (ed jtly) Atlas of Contemporary Religious Life in Russia, vol. 1, 2005, vol. 2, 2006, vol. 3, 2008, vol. 4, 2009. *Recreations*: choral singing, Member, Assoc. of British Tennis Officials. *Address*: 101 Church Way, Iffley, Oxford OX4 4EG. *T*: (01865) 777276. *Club*: Athenæum.

**BOURDILLON, Peter John,** FRCP; Medical Awards Administrator, Association of Commonwealth Universities, since 2001; *b* 10 July 1941; *s* of John Francis Bourdillon and Pamela Maud Bourdillon (*née* Chetham); *m* 1964, Catriona Glencairn-Campbell, FGA, *d* of Brig. W. Glencairn-Campbell, OBE and Lady Muir-Mackenzie; one *s* two *d*. *Educ*: Rugby Sch.; Middlesex Hosp. Med. Sch. (MB BS 1965). MRCP 1968, FRCP 1983. House physician and surgeon posts in London, 1965–68; Med. Registrar, Middlesex Hosp., 1969–70; Hammersmith Hospital: Med. Registrar, 1970–72; Sen. Registrar in Cardiol., 1972–74; Consultant in Clin. Physiol. (Cardiol.), subseq. in Cardiovascular Disease, 1975–2006. Part-time MO, 1975–81, part-time SMO, 1981–91, Hd of Med. Manpower and Educn Div., 1991–93, DHSS, then DoH; Head (Grade 3), Health Care (Med.), then Specialist Clin. Services, Div., DoH, 1993–97; on secondment from DoH to Academy of Med. Royal Colls, 1997–2001. Cardiologist (part-time), Hertford Cardiology (formerly Quantum Res.) Ltd, 2002–07. Medical Awards Administrator, ACU, 2001–. Hon. Sen. Lectr, RPMS, later ICSM, London Univ., 1979–. QHP 1996–99. *Publications*: contrib. to med. jls incl. Drug Information Jl and Annals of Noninvasive Electrocardiol. *Recreations*: writing software, walking, ski-ing, renaissance art history. *Address*: 13 Grove Terrace, NW5 1PH. *T*: (020) 7485 6839. *E*: pbourdillon@msn.com.

**BOURDON, Derek Conway,** FIA; Director, 1981–84, and General Manager, 1979–84, Prudential Assurance Co. Ltd; Director, London and Manchester Group PLC, 1986–94; *b* 3 Nov. 1932; *s* of late Walter Alphonse Bourdon and Winifred Gladys Vera Bourdon; *m* Uta Margrit Bourdon. *Educ*: Bancroft's School. FIA 1957. RAF Operations Research (Flying Officer), 1956–58. Joined Prudential, 1950; South Africa, 1962–65; Dep. General

Manager, 1976–79. Chairman, Vanbrugh Life, 1974–79. Member, Policyholders Protection Board, 1980–84; Chm., Industrial Life Offices Assoc., 1982–84 (Vice-Chm., 1980–82). *Recreations:* golf, bridge. *Club:* Barton-on-Sea Golf.

**BOURKE,** family name of **Earl of Mayo**.

**BOURKE, Hon. Dame (Elizabeth) Shân (Josephine) L.;** *see* Legge-Bourke, Hon. Dame E. S. J.

**BOURKE, Evelyn Brigid;** Group Chief Executive Officer, Bupa, since 2016; *b* Tipperary, Ireland, 31 Jan. 1965; *d* of Michael Bourke and Mary Bourke (*née* Troy); *m* 2015, Seamus Creedon. *Educ:* London Business Sch. (MBA 1999). FIA 1988. Trainee Actuary, New Ireland Assurance, 1982–86; managerial roles, Bank of Ireland, 1986–90; Consultant and Principal, Tillinghast Towers Perrin, 1991–2001; Strategy Consultant, St James's Place, 2001–03; CEO, Chase de Vere, 2004; Strategy Dir, Gp Actuarial Dir, Finance Dir, Standard Life Assurance, 2005–09; Chief Financial Officer and CEO, Heritage Business, Friends Provident, then Friends Provident Hldgs UK, later Friends Life Gp, 2009–12; Chief Financial Officer, Bupa, 2012–16. Non-exec. Dir, Bd, Bank of Ireland Gp plc, 2018–. *Recreations:* Rugby, Munster fan, food, wine, travel. *Address:* Bupa, 1 Angel Court, EC2R 7HJ. *T:* 07912 181481. *E:* evelyn.bourke@bupa.com. *Club:* Athenæum.

**BOURKE, Prof. Joanna,** PhD; FBA 2014; FRHistS; Professor of History, Birkbeck, University of London; *b* Blenheim, NZ. *Educ:* Auckland Univ. (BA; MA); Australian Nat. Univ. (PhD). Held posts at ANU, then Emmanuel Coll., Cambridge; Birkbeck Coll., Univ. of London, 1992–. *Publications:* Husbandry to Housewifery: women, economic change and housework in Ireland, 1890–1914, 1993 (Ronald Tress Prize, 1993); Working Class Cultures in Britain, 1890–1960: gender, class and ethnicity, 1993; Dismembering the Male: men's bodies, Britain and the Great War, 1996; An Intimate History of Killing: face-to-face killing in 20th century warfare, 1999 (Fraenkel Prize in Contemp. Hist., 1998; Wolfson Hist. Prize, 2000); (ed) Edward Casey: misfit soldier, 1999; The Second World War: a people's history, 2001; (ed jtly) The Penguin Atlas of British and Irish History: from earliest times to the present day, 2001; Fear: a cultural history, 2005; Rape: a history from 1860s to the present, 2007; What it Means to be Human: reflections from 1791 to the present, 2011; The Story of Pain: from prayer to painkillers, 2014; Wounding the World: how the military and war-play invade our lives, 2014; (ed) War and Art: a visual history of modern conflict, 2017. *Address:* Department of History, Classics and Archaeology, Birkbeck, University of London, 28 Russell Square, WC1B 5DQ.

**BOURKE, Martin;** HM Diplomatic Service, retired; Deputy High Commissioner, New Zealand, 2000–04; *b* 12 March 1947; *s* of late Robert Martin Bourke and Enid Millicent Bourke (*née* Love); *m* 1973, Anne Marie Marguerite Hottelet; four *s*. *Educ:* Stockport Grammar Sch.; University Coll. London (BA Hons 1969); King's Coll. London (MA 1970). Joined FCO, 1970; Brussels, 1971–73; Singapore, 1974–76; Lagos, 1978–80; on loan to DTI, 1980–84; Consul (Commercial), Johannesburg, 1984–88; Asst Head, Envmt, Sci. and Energy Dept, FCO, 1990–93; Gov., Turks and Caicos Islands, 1993–96; Area Manager, Prince's Trust (on secondment), 1996–99. *Recreations:* walking, reading, theatre, amateur dramatics.

**BOURKE, Rt Rev. Michael Gay;** Bishop Suffragan of Wolverhampton, 1993–2006; an Honorary Assistant Bishop, Diocese of Hereford, since 2007; *b* 28 Nov. 1941; *s* of Gordon and Hilda Bourke; *m* 1968, Elizabeth Bieler; one *s* one *d*. *Educ:* Hamond's Grammar Sch., Swaffham, Norfolk; Corpus Christi Coll., Cambridge (Mod. Langs, MA); Univ. of Tübingen (Theology); Cuddesdon Theological Coll. Curate, St James', Grimsby, 1967–71; Priest-in-charge, Panshanger Conventional Dist (Local Ecumenical Project), Welwyn Garden City, 1971–78; Vicar, All Saints', Southill, Beds, 1978–86; Archdeacon of Bedford, 1986–93. Course Dir, St Albans Diocese Ministerial Trng Scheme, 1975–87. Anglican Co-Chm., Meissen Commn, 1997–2006. Hon. Canon, Lichfield Cathedral, 1993–2006. *Recreations:* astronomy, railways, European history, Welsh language. *Address:* The Maltings, Little Stretton, Church Stretton SY6 6AP.

**BOURKE, Patrick Francis John O'D.;** *see* O'Donnell Bourke.

**BOURKE, Prof. Richard Edmund,** PhD; FBA 2018; Professor of the History of Political Thought, University of Cambridge, since 2019; Fellow, King's College, Cambridge. *Educ:* University Coll. Dublin (BA); Birkbeck Coll., Univ. of London (BA); King's Coll., Cambridge (PhD 1993). Lectr, UCD, 1990–93; Lectr, 1993, Prof., 2012–18, QMW, subseq. QMUL. *Publications:* Peace in Ireland: the war of ideas, 2003; Empire and Revolution: the political life of Edmund Burke, 2015. *Address:* King's College, Cambridge CB2 1ST.

**BOURN, Sir John (Bryant),** KCB 1991 (CB 1986); Comptroller and Auditor General, 1988–2008; Independent Adviser to Prime Minister on Ministers' Interests, 2006–08; *b* 21 Feb. 1934; *s* of late Henry Thomas Bryant Bourn and Beatrice Grace Bourn; *m* 1959, Ardita Ann Fleming (decd); one *s* (one *d* decd). *Educ:* Southgate County Grammar Sch.; LSE. 1st cl. hons BScEcon 1954, PhD 1958. Air Min. 1956–63; HM Treasury, 1963–64; Private Sec. to Perm. Under-Sec., MoD, 1964–69; Asst Sec. and Dir of Programmes, Civil Service Coll., 1969–72; Asst Sec., MoD, 1972–74; Under-Sec., Northern Ireland Office, 1974–77; Asst Under-Sec. of State, MoD, 1977–82; Dep. Sec., Northern Ireland Office, 1982–84; Dep. Under Sec. of State (Defence Procurement), MoD, 1985–88; Auditor General for Wales, 1999–2005. Visiting Professor: LSE, 1983–2013; Bournemouth Univ., 2009–18. Chairman: Accountancy Foundn Review Bd, 2000–03; Professional Oversight Bd (formerly Professional Oversight Bd for Accountancy), 2003–08. Chm., Multi-Lateral Audit Adv. Gp, World Bank, 1999–2008; Member: Financial Reporting Council, 1990–2008; Financial Reporting Review Panel, 1991–2008; Foundn for Governance Res. and Educn, 2008–. FCIPS 1995; CCMI (CIMgt 1994). Freeman, City of London, 1996. Hon. Fellow: Brighton Univ., 1989; LSE, 1995. Hon. LLD Brunel, 1995; DUniv Open, 1998; Hon. DBA West of England, 2011. *Publications:* Public Sector Audit: is it value for money, 2007; articles and reviews in professional jls. *Recreations:* swimming, tennis.

**BOURNE OF ABERYSTWYTH,** Baron *cr* 2013 (Life Peer), of Aberystwyth in the County of Ceredigion and of Wethersfield in the County of Essex; **Nicholas Henry Bourne;** *b* 1 Jan. 1952; *s* of late John Morgan Bourne and Joan Edith Mary Bourne. *Educ:* King Edward VI Sch., Chelmsford; UCW, Aberystwyth (LLB 1st Cl. Hons; LLM 1976); Trinity Coll., Cambridge (LLM). Called to the Bar, Gray's Inn, 1976. Supervisor in Law: Corpus Christi Coll., Cambridge, 1974–80; St Catharine's Coll., Cambridge, 1974–82; LSE, 1975–77; Principal, Chart Univ. Tutors Ltd, 1979–88; Co. Sec. and Dir, Chart Foulks Lynch plc, 1984–88; Dir, Holborn Gp Ltd, 1988–91; Swansea Institute: Prof. of Law, 1991–96; Dean of Law, 1992–96; Asst Principal, 1996–98. Lectr in Co. Law, Univ. of London Ext. Degree Prog. at UCL, 1991–96; Sen. Lectr in Law, South Bank Univ., 1991–92; Vis. Lectr, Hong Kong Univ., 1996–2008. Member: Editl Bd, Malaysian Law News, 1991–2008; Editl Adv. Bd, Business Law Rev., 1991–. Member: NE Thames RHA, 1990–92; W Glamorgan HA, 1994–97; Doctors' and Dentists' Review Body, 1998–99. Mem. (C) Mid and W Wales, and Leader of Conservatives, Nat. Assembly for Wales, 1999–2011; contested (C) same seat, 2011. A Lord in Waiting (Govt Whip), 2014–16; Parly Under-Sec. of State, DECC, 2015–16, Wales Office, 2015–17 and 2017–19, NI Office,

2017, DCLG, then MHCLG, 2016–19. Mem., Delegated Powers and Regulatory Reform Cttee, H of L, 2014–15. Hon. Fellow, Aberystwyth Univ., 2015. Hon. LLD UWTSD, 2018. *Publications:* Duties and Responsibilities of British Company Directors, 1982; British Company Law and Practice, 1983; Business Law for Accountants, 1987; Lecture Notes for Company Law, 1993, 3rd edn 1998; Essential Company Law, 1994, 2nd edn 1997; Business Law and Practice, 1994; (with B. Pillans) Scottish Company Law, 1996, 2nd edn 1999; Bourne on Company Law, 1993, 7th edn 2016; contrib. to business and co. law jls. *Recreations:* walking, tennis, badminton, squash, theatre, cricket, travel, cinema. *Address:* House of Lords, SW1A 0PW. *Club:* Oxford and Cambridge.

**BOURNE, Charles Gregory;** QC 2014; a Recorder, since 2009; a Deputy High Court Judge, since 2016; *b* London, 4 July 1964; *s* of Stanford Bourne and Judith Bourne; *m* 1995, Catherine Chadwick; one *s* one *d*. *Educ:* University College Sch., Hampstead; Trinity Coll., Cambridge (BA English 1986); Université de Paris IV (Maîtrise Lettres Modernes 1987). Called to the Bar, Middle Temple, 1991; in practice as barrister, specialising in public and employment law, 11 King's Bench Walk, 2012–. Mediator, CEDR, 2000–. *Publications:* (jtly) Civil Advocacy: a practical guide, 1997, 2nd edn 2001; Going Back, 2013; (contrib.) The Civil Court Practice, 2007–; (contrib.) Tolley's Employment Handbook, 2013–. *Recreations:* literature, music, tennis, cookery. *Address:* 11 King's Bench Walk, Temple, EC4Y 7EQ. *T:* (020) 7632 8500, *Fax:* (020) 7583 9123. *E:* clerks@11kbw.com.

**BOURNE, Prof. (Frederick) John,** CBE 1995; Professor of Animal Health, University of Bristol, 1988–2007, now Emeritus; *b* 3 Jan. 1937; *s* of Sidney John Bourne and Florence Beatrice Bourne; *m* 1959, Mary Angela Minter; two *s*. *Educ:* Univ. of London (BVetMed); Univ. of Bristol (PhD). MRCVS 1961. Gen. vet. practice, 1961–67; University of Bristol: Lectr in Animal Husbandry, 1967–76; Reader in Animal Husbandry, 1976–80; Prof. and Hd of Dept of Veterinary Medicine, 1980–88; Dir, AFRC, subseq. BBSRC, Inst. for Animal Health, 1988–97. Vis. Prof., Univ. of Reading, 1999. Chm., Govt Ind. Scientific Gp for Control of Cattle TB, 1998–2007. For. Mem., Polish Acad. of Sci., 1994. Hon. Fellow: Edward Jenner Inst. for Vaccine Res., 2001; Pirbright Inst., 2015. *Publications:* over 250 contribs to variety of jls, incl. Immunology, Vet. Immunology and Immunopath., Res. in Vet. Sci., Infection and Immunity, Nature, Procs of US Nat. Acad. of Scis, Internat. Jl of Infectious Diseases, Animal Welfare, Jl of Applied Ecology, Jl of Zoology. *Recreations:* gardening, fishing, golf, cricket, music. *Address:* Westlands, Jubilee Lane, Langford, Bristol BS40 5EJ. *T:* (01934) 852 464.

**BOURNE, Ian Maclean;** QC 2006; **His Honour Judge Bourne;** a Circuit Judge, since 2016; *b* 19 Jan. 1954; *s* of late Ian Bourne and Jean Talbot (*née* Scarrott); *m* 1993, Lucy Pollock; one *s* three *d*. *Educ:* Marlborough; Exeter Univ. (LLB). Called to the Bar, Inner Temple, 1977; in practice, S Eastern Circuit; an Asst Recorder, 1997–2000; a Recorder, 2000–16. *Recreations:* cricket, gardening, photography. *Address:* Harrow Crown Court, Hailsham Drive, off Headstone Drive, Harrow HA1 4TU. *T:* (020) 8424 2294. *Club:* Hurlingham.

**BOURNE, John;** *see* Bourne, F. J.

**BOURNE, Lisa;** *see* Roberts, L.

**BOURNE, Margaret Janet,** OBE 1982; Chairman, CORDA Ltd, 1992–2001; *b* 18 Aug. 1931; *d* of Thomas William Southcott and Nora Annie Southcott (*née* Pelling); *m* 1960, George Brian Bourne. *Educ:* Twickenham Grammar Sch.; Royal Holloway Coll. (BSc). MRAeS 1962; CEng, FIET (FIEE 1997). Fairey Engineering, 1953–62; Army Operational Res. Estabt, 1962–65; Defence Operational Analysis Estabt, 1965–76; Asst Dir, Scientific Adv. Gp Army, 1976–80; Hd of Assessments Div., ASWE, 1980–82; Hd of Weapon Dept, ASWE, 1982–84; Dep. Dir, Admiralty Res. Estabt, 1984–87; Asst Chief Scientific Advr (Capabilities), MoD, 1987–91. *Recreations:* playing early music, gardening, natural history. *T:* (01428) 714329.

**BOURNE, Sir Matthew (Christopher),** Kt 2016; OBE 2001; director and choreographer; Founder Director, New Adventures, since 2002; *b* 13 Jan. 1960; *s* of Harold Jeffrey, (Jim), Bourne and June Lillian Bourne (*née* Handley); partner, Arthur Pita, *qv*. *Educ:* Laban Centre for Movement and Dance (BA Hons Dance and Theatre 1986; Hon. Fellow 1997). Artistic Dir and Jt Founder Mem., Adventures in Motion Pictures, 1987–2002. Dir, Spitfire Trust, 1996; Mem. Bd, Laban Centre for Movt and Dance, 1999; Mem., Hon. Cttee, Dance Cares, 1995. *Works include:* for *Adventures in Motion Pictures*, created and directed: Overlap Lovers, 1987; Spitfire, 1988; The Infernal Galop, 1989; Green Fingers, 1990; Town and Country, 1991; Deadly Serious, 1992; Nutcracker, 1992 (revised 2002); The Percys of Fitzrovia, 1992; Highland Fling, 1994 (revised 2005); Swan Lake, 1995 (Olivier Award, 1996; LA Drama Critics Award, 1997; 2 Tony Awards, 1999; 3 Drama Desk Awards, 1999; 2 Outer Critics' Circle Awards, 1999; Astaire Award, 1999); Cinderella, 1997; The Car Man (Evening Standard Award), 2000; Lord of the Flies, 2014; *for other companies*, choreographed: As You Like It, RSC, 1989; Leonce and Lena, Crucible, Sheffield, 1989; Children of Eden, Prince Edward Theatre, 1991; A Midsummer Night's Dream, Aix-en-Provence Fest., 1991; The Tempest, NYT, 1991; Show Boat, Malmö Stadsteater, 1991; Peer Gynt, Ninagawa Co., Oslo, Barbican, 1994; Watch with Mother, Nat. Youth Dance Co., 1994; Oliver!, London Palladium, 1994, (and co-dir) Th. Royal, 2009; My Fair Lady, South Pacific, RNT, 2001; dir, Play Without Words, NT, 2002, Sadler's Wells, 2012; co-dir and choreographer, Mary Poppins, Prince Edward Th., 2004, Bristol Hippodrome, 2015; director and choreographer: Edward Scissorhands, Sadler's Wells, 2005; Dorian Gray (tour), 2009; Lord of the Flies, Th. Royal, Glasgow, 2011; Sleeping Beauty, Sadler's Wells, 2012; The Red Shoes, Th. Royal, Plymouth, 2016 (Best Th. Choreographer, Olivier Awards, 2017); Romeo and Juliet, Curve Th., Leicester, 2019 (and UK tour); as performer, created numerous rôles in AMP prodns on stage and in films; *films choreographed* include: Late Flowering Lust, 1993; Drip: a narcissistic love story, 1993; *television film:* Matthew Bourne's Christmas, 2011. Hon. Dr: Open; De Montfort; Plymouth; Kingston; Roehampton; Royal Conservatoire of Scotland; Hon. DLitt Oxford, 2018. De Valois Award, Nat. Dance Awards, 2014; Queen Elizabeth II Coronation Award, 2016; Trailblazer in Dance and Theatre, Inst. of Dance and Theatre, 2017; Special Olivier Award, 2019. *Recreations:* old movies, theatre and music, reading obituaries. *Address:* c/o Jessica Sykes, Independent Talent Group Ltd, 40 Whitfield Street, W1T 2RH. *T:* (020) 7636 6565; New Adventures, Sadler's Wells, Rosebery Avenue, EC1R 4TN. *Club:* Soho House.

**BOURNE, (Rowland) Richard,** OBE 2002; Head, Commonwealth Policy Studies Unit, Institute of Commonwealth Studies, London University, 1999–2005, Senior Research Fellow, 2006–16; *b* 27 July 1940; *s* of late Arthur Brittan and Edith Mary Bourne; *m* 1966, Juliet Mary, *d* of John Attenborough, CBE; two *s* one *d*. *Educ:* Uppingham Sch., Rutland; Brasenose Coll., Oxford (BA Mod. Hist.). Journalist, The Guardian, 1962–72 (Education correspondent, 1968–72); Asst Editor, New Society, 1972–77; Evening Standard: Dep. Editor, 1977–78; London Columnist, 1978–79; Founder Editor, Learn Magazine, 1979; Dep. Editor, Commonwealth Inst., 1983–89; Dir, Commonwealth Human Rights Initiative, 1990–92 (Chm., Trustee Cttee, 1994–2003); consultant, 1993–94; Co-Dir, Commonwealth Values in Educn Project, Inst. of Educn, London Univ., 1995–98; Dir, Commonwealth Non-Govtl Office for S Africa and Mozambique, 1995–97; Sec., Ramphal Inst. (formerly Ramphal Centre), 2007–14. Chm., Editl Bd, Round Table, 2005–11.

Consultant: Internat. Broadcasting Trust, 1980–81; Adv. Council for Adult and Continuing Educn, 1982. Chm., Survival Internat., 1983–98. Chm., Brazilian Contemporary Arts, 1995–98; Acting Chair of Corporation, Greenwich Community Coll., 2014–15. Treas., Anglo-Portuguese Foundn, 1985–87. Dep. Chm., Royal Commonwealth Soc., 2001–07. *Publications*: Political Leaders of Latin America, 1969; (with Brian MacArthur) The Struggle for Education, 1970; Getulio Vargas of Brazil, 1974; Assault on the Amazon, 1978; Londoners, 1981; (with Jessica Gould) Self-Sufficiency, 16–25, 1983; Lords of Fleet Street, 1990; News on a Knife-Edge, 1995; Britain in the Commonwealth, 1997; (ed) Universities and Development, 2000; (ed) Where Next for the Group of 54?, 2001; Invisible Lives, 2003; Lula of Brazil: the story so far, 2008; (ed) Shridath Ramphal: the Commonwealth and the world, 2008; (ed with Mark Collins) From Hook to Plate, 2009; Catastrophe: what went wrong in Zimbabwe, 2011; Nigeria: a new history of a turbulent century, 2015; (ed) Behind the Scenes in the Vintage Years, 2016. *Recreations*: theatre, fishing, supporting Charlton Athletic. *Address*: 26 Bennett Park, SE3 9RB. *T*: (020) 8297 4182. *Club*: Royal Automobile.

**BOURNE, Sam;** *see* Freedland, J. S.

**BOURNE, Stephen Robert Richard;** Chapter Clerk and Administrator, since 2013 and Lay Canon, since 2017, Ely Cathedral; Fellow, 2001–19, now Emeritus, and Vice-President, 2015–18, Clare Hall, Cambridge; *b* 20 March 1952; *s* of Colyn M. Bourne and Kathleen Bourne (*née* Turner); *m* 1978, Stephanie Ann Bickford; one *s* one *d*. *Educ*: Berkhamsted Sch.; Univ. of Edinburgh (MA 1974); MA Cantab 2001. ACA 1977. Deloitte Haskins and Sells, London and Hong Kong, 1974–80; Exxon Chemical Asia-Pacific, Hong Kong, 1980–86; Dow Jones Telerate, Hong Kong and London: Financial Dir Asia, 1986–89; Gen. Manager, N Europe, 1989–94; Man. Dir, Financial Printing Div., St Ives plc, 1994–96; Cambridge University Press: Development Dir, 1997–2000; Chm., Printing, 2000–02; University Printer and Chief Exec., 2002–12; Pres., 2012–13; Pres., Cambridge Internat. Connections, 2012–13. Director: Britten Sinfonia, 2003–15 (Chm., 2010–15); Wine Soc., 2004–15; Th. Royal, Bury St Edmunds, 2012–16 (Chm., 2012–16). Mem. Council, CBI East, 2007–14 (Chm., 2010–12). Prince of Wales' Ambassador, E of England, BITC, 2009. Governor: Perse Sch. for Girls, 1998–2004; Berkhamsted Sch., 2010–12. Treas. and Vice-Chm., RSPCA Hong Kong, 1981–86. Chm., Hong Kong Water Ski Assoc., 1980–85. Hon. Vice-President: Cambridge Univ. Lawn Tennis Club, 2005–; Burwell and Exning Cricket Club, 2006–. Pres., Old Berkhamstedians, 2011–13. Liveryman: Stationers' Co.; Educators' Co. FRSA 2002. *Recreations*: performing arts, ski-ing, cricket-watching, fine wines. *Address*: Falmouth Lodge, Snailwell Road, Newmarket CB8 7DN. *T*: (01353) 660308. *E*: stephenrrbourne@gmail.com. *Clubs*: Athenæum; Royal Scots (Edinburgh); Kent CC, Cambridge University Cricket; Hong Kong, Aberdeen Boat (Hong Kong).

**BOURNE, Dame Susan (Mary),** DBE 2013; Headteacher, The Avenue School, Reading, 2003–17; *b* Penwortham, 2 Feb. 1953; *d* of William Fiddler and Ruth Fiddler; *m* 1987, Roger Bourne; one *s* one *d*. *Educ*: Balshaw's Grammar Sch., Leyland; Bath Coll. of Educn (Cert Ed Home Econs); Reading Coll. (Dip. Special Educn). NPQH. Nat. Leader of Educn, 2009–17. Mem., Headteacher Bd for NW London and S Central England, 2017–. *Recreations*: sailing, sewing, cooking, art, bonsai.

**BOURNE, Prof. Thomas Holland,** PhD; FRCOG; Consultant Gynaecologist, Queen Charlotte's and Chelsea Hospital, Imperial College NHS Trust, London, since 2008; Consultant, Department of Obstetrics and Gynaecology, University Hospitals Leuven, since 2007; Professor of Practice, Imperial College London, since 2018 (Adjunct Professor and Research Team Leader, 2013–18); *b* Kendal, 19 Dec. 1959; *s* of Douglas Holland Bourne and Lilian Anne Bourne; *m* 2010, Vicky Cripps; two step *d*. *Educ*: Cheadle Hulme Sch.; Middlesex Hosp. Med. Sch., London (MS BS 1984); Univ. of Göteborg (PhD 1995). MRCOG 1990, FRCOG 2003. House Officer: Gen. Medicine, Cheltenham Gen. Hosp., 1984–85; Surgery, Middlesex Hosp., London, 1984; Senior House Officer: Accident and Emergency and Orthopaedics, Bristol Royal Inf., 1985; Obstetrics and Gynaecol., St Mary's Hosp., Manchester, 1986; (and Registrar) Obstetrics and Gynaecol., Gloucester Royal Hosp., 1987; Neonatal Unit, John Radcliffe Hosp., Oxford, 1988; Sen. Clin. Res. Fellow in Gynaecol., 1989–91, Lectr and Hon. Sen. Registrar in Obstetrics and Gynaecol., 1991–95, King's Coll. Hosp., London; Swedish MRC Vis. Scientist Fellow, Sahlgrenska Univ. Hosp., Univ. of Göteborg, 1995–96; St George's, University of London: Sen. Lectr in Obstetrics and Gynaecol., 1996–99; Reader in Acute Gynaecol. and Gynaecol Ultrasound, 2005–07; Consultant Obstetrician and Gynaecologist, St George's Hosp., London, 1999–2007. Visiting Professor: Katholieke Univ. Leuven, 2007–; Imperial Coll. London, 2008–. Dir, Women's Ultrasound Centres Ltd, 1998–. Member: Steering Cttee, Internat. Ovarian Tumor Analysis trial, 1993–; consensus gp on pregnancy viability, Soc. of Radiologists in Ultrasound, USA, 2012; consensus panel on criteria to diagnose ovarian cancer, American Inst. of Ultrasound in Medicine, 2014–15; world conference cttee, 2014–, Scientific Adv. Cttee, 2015–, Supporting Our Doctors Task Force, 2017–, RCOG; Refining Ovarian Cancer Test Accuracy Scores and UK Early Pregnancy Surveillance Service study trial cttees, 2015–; consensus panel on classifying ovarian masses, American Coll. of Radiologists, 2015–; H of C All Party Parly Gp on Baby Loss, 2016–18. Trustee and Med. Advr, Ectopic Pregnancy Trust, 2005–; Mem. Bd, Assoc. of Early Pregnancy Units, 2005–11; Mem., Mgt Gp, and Dir, Early Pregnancy Res., Tommy's Nat. Centre for Miscarriage Res., 2016–. Expert Advr to NICE, 2011–. Treas., Internat. Soc. of Ultrasound in Obstetrics and Gynecol., 2015– (Mem. Bd and Dir, 2006–14; Pres. Elect, 2018; Dir, ISUOG Courses and Conferences Ltd, 1997–2003); Pres., UK Assoc. of Early Pregnancy Units, 2015–. Mem., Chelsea Clinical Soc. Hon. Fellow, Amer. Inst. of Ultrasound in Medicine, 2015; Hon. Mem., Australasian Soc. for Ultrasound in Medicine, 2016–. Mem. Editl Bd, Australasian Jl of Ultrasound in Medicine, 2015–. *Publications*: (ed) Transvaginal Colour Doppler: a scientific basis to the use of transvaginal colour Doppler in gynaecology, 1995; (ed) Ultrasound and Endoscopic Surgery in Obstetrics and Gynaecology: a combined approach to diagnosis and treatment, 2002; (ed) Ultrasound in Gynaecology, 2004; (ed) Handbook of Early Pregnancy Care, 2006; (ed) Acute Gynaecology: early pregnancy complications, 2009; (ed) Acute Gynaecology: infection, uterine and ovarian pathology, 2009; (ed) Dewhurst's Textbook of Obstetrics and Gynaecology, 9th edn, 2017; over 330 articles in academic jls; h-index of 77. *Recreations*: family, cricket, cycling, drumming, sailing, theatre, cinema, visual arts. *Address*: 25 Harley Street, W1G 9QW. *T*: (020) 7636 6765. *E*: womensultrasound@btinternet.com. *Clubs*: MCC; Armadillos Cricket; Bembridge Sailing, Royal Solent Sailing, St Lucia Yacht.

**BOURNE, Valerie Iris;** organic gardener; garden writer, since 1995; *b* Southall, Middx, 28 July 1950; *d* of Albert Edward Teall and Iris Mary Teall (*née* Bosanquet); partner, Dr Jolyon Kirby; two *d* by a previous marriage. *Educ*: Greenford Co. Grammar Sch.; Bordesley Coll. of Educn (Teaching Cert. 1971). Vegetable res., Nat. Vegetable Res. Stn, Wellesbourne, 1971–75; teacher specialising in literacy, 1971–95; internat. lectr and photographer, 1995–; freelance writer for newspapers and jls, incl. Daily Telegraph, Country Living, Gardens Illustrated, English Garden, Saga, Amateur Gardening, Garden Answers, 1995–. Mem., Herbaceous Cttee, RHS, 2006–. Ambassador, Hardy Plant Soc., 2017–. Journalist of the Year, 2014, News Story of the Year, 2016, Columnist of the Year, 2018, Garden Media Guild. *Publications*: Seeds of Wisdom, 2004; The Natural Gardener, 2005; The Winter Garden, 2006; Ten Minute Gardener's Vegetable Growing Diary, 2011; Ten Minute Gardener's Flower Growing Diary, 2011; Colour in the Garden, 2011; Ten Minute Gardener's Fruit Diary, 2011; The Living Jigsaw, 2016; Ten Minute Fruit and Vegetable Handbook, 2018. *Recreations*: organic gardening, conservation and wildlife, snowdrops, cricket, crosswords, grandchildren. *Address*: Spring Cottage, Cold Aston, Cheltenham, Glos GL54 3BJ. *E*: info@valbourne.co.uk. *W*: www.valbourne.co.uk.

**BOURNE-ARTON, His Honour Simon Nicholas,** QC 1994; a Senior Circuit Judge, 2012–19; *b* 5 Sept. 1949; *s* of late Major Anthony Temple Bourne-Arton, MBE; *m* 1974, Diana Carr-Walker; two *s* one *d*. *Educ*: Aysgarth Prep. Sch.; Harrow; Teesside Poly. (HND Bus. Studies); Leeds Univ. (LLB Hons). Called to the Bar, Inner Temple, 1975, Bencher, 2003. An Asst Recorder, 1989–93; a Recorder, 1993–2012; Leader, North Eastern Circuit, 2006–09; Hon. Recorder of Middlesbrough, 2012–19. *Recreations*: living in the country, golf, tennis, being with family and friends, drinking wine.

**BOURNE-MAY, Jonathan James Seaburne;** Clerk to Vintners' Company, since 2012; *b* Dumfries, 4 July 1958; *s* of late Geoffrey and Josephine Bourne-May; *m* 1986, Karen Laver; two *s*. *Educ*: Eton; RMA, Sandhurst. Joined Coldstream Guards, 1977; psc 1990; jsdc 1996; MA to C-in-C, 1997–98; i/c 1st Bn Coldstream Guards, 1998–2001; COS HQ London Dist, 2004–06; i/c 143 (W Midlands) Bde, 2006–09; Brig., HQ Land, 2009–12. Regtl Lieut Col, Coldstream Guards, 2002–12. Chm., Mgt Bd, Guards Mus., 2013–17 (Mem., 2012–17). Dir, Livery Cos' Mutual Ltd, 2014–. *Recreations*: music, history, travel, hill walking. *Address*: Vintners' Company, Upper Thames Street, EC4V 3BG. *T*: (020) 7651 0744. *E*: theclerk@vintnershall.co.uk.

**BOURNEMOUTH, Archdeacon of;** *see* Rouch, Ven. P. B.

**BOURNS, Robert Henry Glanville;** DL; Consultant, TLT LLP, since 2018 (Partner, 2000–18; Senior Partner, 2002–15); Chair, Board, Law Society of England and Wales, since 2018 (Vice-President, 2015–16; President, 2016–17); *b* Bristol, 11 May 1956; *s* of Herbert Kitchener Bourns and (Grace) Joan (Valerie) Bourns; *m* 1983, Fiona Mary Spencer; three *s* one *d*. *Educ*: Clifton Coll., Bristol; University Coll., Cardiff (LLB). Admitted as solicitor, 1980; solicitor, Osborne Clarke, 1980–83; solicitor, 1983–86, Partner, 1986–96, Man. Partner, 1996–2000, Trumps; Man. Partner, TLT LLP, 2000–02. Pres., Bristol Law Soc., 2005–06. Trustee: St Peter's Hospice, 2005–11 (Chm., 2011–14); ABLAZE (Bristol Learning Action Zone), 2009–; Dir, Friends of Room 13 (Hareclive) Ltd, 2011–; Chairman: Quartet Community Foundn, 2014–18; Bannerman Road Primary Acad., Bristol. Pres., Dolphin Soc., 2014–15; Mem., Soc. of Merchant Venturers, 2015–. DL Bristol, 2014. Hon. LLD UWE, 2016. *Recreations*: walking, ski-ing, gardening. *Address*: TLT LLP, 20 Gresham Street, EC2V 7JE. *T*: 0333 006 0266. *E*: robert.bourns@tltsolicitors.com.

**BOURS, Louise;** Member for North West Region, European Parliament, 2014–19 (UK Ind, 2014–18; Ind, 2018–19); *b* Congleton, Cheshire, 23 Dec. 1968; *d* of Terence Bours and Mavis Bours; two *d*. *Educ*: Mountview Conservatoire for the Performing Arts; Blackburn Coll. (BA Hons Social Sci. (Lancaster Univ.) 2014). Actor in TV progs, Grown Ups, 1996, Peak Practice, 1997, Band of Gold, 1997, Brookside, 2000; Mem., D'Oyly Carte Opera Co., 2000. Mem., Congleton Town Council, 2003–15 (Mayor, 2006–07); Mem. (C, then Ind, later UKIP) Congleton BC, 2007–09. Health spokesman, UKIP, 2015–16. Contested (UK Ind) Knowsley, 2015. Musical Dir, Centre Stage Youth Th., Congleton, 2015–.

**BOUSHER, Stephen;** lawyer; Principal Assistant Solicitor, HM Revenue and Customs (formerly Board of Inland Revenue), 2000–13; *b* 13 Feb. 1952; *s* of Leslie Arthur and Clare Bousher; *m* 1974, Jan Townsend; one *s* one *d*. *Educ*: Bec Grammar Sch., Tooting; Southampton Univ. (LLB). Called to the Bar, Gray's Inn, 1975; Board of Inland Revenue, later HM Revenue and Customs, 1976–2013: Asst Solicitor, 1988–2000; Team Leader, Tax Simplification, then Tax Law Rewrite, Project, 1996–2000. Sen. Consultant Lawyer, Joseph Hage Aaronson LLP, 2014–. *Recreations*: cinema, watching sport, arguing with Holden, listening to The Grateful Dead, travelling.

**BOUSTED, Dr Mary Winefride;** Joint General Secretary, National Education Union, since 2017 (General Secretary, Association of Teachers and Lecturers, 2003–17); *b* 15 Sept. 1959; *d* of Edward and Winefride Bleasdale; *m* 1983, Donald Bousted; one *d*. *Educ*: Hull Univ. (BA Hons); Inst. of Educn, London Univ. (MA Dist.); York Univ. (PhD 1999). English teacher, Bentley Wood High Sch., Harrow, 1982–87; Hd of English, Whitmore High Sch., Harrow, 1988–91; Lectr, 1991–95, Dir, Initial Teacher Trng, 1995–97, Univ. of York; Head: Secondary Educn, Edge Hill Coll., 1997–99; Sch. of Educn, Kingston Univ., 1999–2003. Pres., TUC, 2016–17. *Publications*: contrib. English in Educn, Changing English, Educnl Rev. *Recreations*: walking, reading, film, music. *Address*: National Education Union, Hamilton House, Mabledon Place, WC1H 9BD.

**BOUVERIE;** *see* Pleydell-Bouverie, family name of Earl of Radnor.

**BOUVERIE, Juliet Pleydell-;** Chief Executive, Stroke Association, since 2016; *b* Oxford, 2 May 1968; *d* of late Simon and Vivien Pleydell-Bouverie. *Educ*: Queen Anne's Sch., Caversham; St Hugh's Coll., Oxford (BA Hons Modern Langs (French and German) 1990); Univ. of Westminster (Dip. Mgt Studies (Dist.) 1997). Strategic Planner, British Red Cross, 1994–99; Macmillan Cancer Support: Hd, Planning and Policy, 1999–2008; Dir, Corporate Develt, 2008–11; Exec. Dir, Services and Influencing, 2011–15. Chm., Patient Experience Bd, UCL Hosps, 2011–14. Trustee, Long-Term Conditions Alliance, 2005–08. *Recreations*: gardening, yoga, walking, travel, literature. *Address*: Stroke Association, Stroke Association House, 240 City Road, EC1V 2PR. *T*: (020) 7566 0301, 07515 596919. *E*: juliet.bouverie@stroke.org.uk.

**BOVEY, Kathleen Margaret;** *see* Wales, K. M.

**BOVEY, Philip Henry;** Director, Company Law Reform Project, Department of Trade and Industry, 2004–07; *b* 11 July 1948; *s* of late Norman Henry Bovey and Dorothy Yvonne Kent Bovey; *m* 1974, Jenet Alison, *d* of late Rev. Canon J. M. McTear and Margaret McTear; one *s* one *d*. *Educ*: Rugby; Peterhouse, Cambridge (schol.; MA). Solicitor. 3rd Sec., FCO, 1970–71; with Slaughter and May, 1972–75; Legal Assistant, 1976; Sen. Legal Assistant, 1976; Depts of Trade and Industry, 1976–77; Cabinet Office, 1977–78; Depts of Trade, Industry, Prices and Consumer Protection, later DTI, 1978–2007; Asst Solicitor, 1982; Under-Sec., 1985; Dir, Legal Services, 1996–2004. Companies Act Inspector, 1984–88 (report published 1988); Legal Advr to Deregulation, subseq. Better Regulation, then Regulatory Impact Unit, Cabinet Office, 1995–2002. ARPS 2008. *Recreation*: photography. *Address*: 102 Cleveland Gardens, Barnes, SW13 0AH. *T*: (020) 8876 3710.

**BOWATER, Sir Euan David Vansittart,** 3rd Bt *cr* 1939, of Friston, Suffolk; *b* 9 Sept. 1935; *s* of Sir Noël Vansittart Bowater, 2nd Bt, GBE, MC, and Constance Heiton, *d* of David Gordon Bett; *S* father, 1984; *m* 1964, Susan Mary Humphrey, *d* of late A. R. O. Slater, FCA; two *s* two *d*. *Educ*: Eton; Trinity Coll., Cambridge (BA). *Recreations*: travel, golf, music. *Heir*: *s* Moray David Vansittart Bowater [*b* 24 April 1967; *m* 1993, Mandana Firoozan; two *d*].

**BOWATER, Sir Michael Patrick,** 5th Bt *cr* 1914, of Hill Crest, Croydon; *b* 18 July 1949; *s* of Sir J(ohn) Vansittart Bowater, 4th Bt, and Joan Kathleen Bowater (*née* Scullard); *S* father, 2008; *m* 1968, Alison, *d* of Edward Wall; four *d*. *Heir*: none.

**BOWCOCK, John Brown,** FICE; consulting engineer; Senior Consultant, Sir Alexander Gibb & Partners Ltd, 1996–99 (Director, 1989–96; Chairman, 1993–95); *b* 25 Oct. 1931; *s* of John Brown Bowcock and Mabel Bowcock; *m* 1955, Pauline Mary Elizabeth Dalton; three *d*. *Educ*: Hastings Grammar Sch.; St Catherine's Coll., Oxford (MA). FICE 1971. Nat. service, RAF, 1954–56. Joined Sir Alexander Gibb & Partners, 1957: worked on water resource projects overseas incl. Kariba (Zimbabwe), Roseires (Sudan) and Latiyan (Iran), 1957–70; responsible for major dam projects and Drakensberg pumped storage project, SA, 1970–78; Partner, 1978–89; Chief Exec., 1989–93. Chairman: British Dam Soc., 1992–93; British Consultants Bureau, 1991–92; ACE, 1995–96. *Recreations*: golf, music, reading. *Address*: Lothlorien, Crowsley Road, Shiplake, Oxon RG9 3JU. *T*: (0118) 940 4443. *Clubs*: Royal Air Force; Huntercombe Golf (Henley).

**BOWDEN, Rev. Canon Andrew,** *see* Bowden, Rev. Canon R. A.

**BOWDEN, Sir Andrew,** Kt 1994; MBE 1961; International Consultant, Global Equities Corp., 2004–10; *b* 8 April 1930; *s* of William Victor Bowden, Solicitor, and Francesca Wilson; *m* 1970, Benita Napier; one *s* one *d*. *Educ*: Ardingly College. Paint industry, 1955–68; Man. Dir, Personnel Assessments Ltd, 1969–71; Man. Dir, Haymarket Personnel Selection Ltd, 1970–71; Director: Sales Education & Leadership Ltd, 1970–71; Jenkin and Purser (Holdings) Ltd, 1973–77. Mem., Wandsworth Borough Council, 1956–62. Contested (C): N Hammersmith, 1955; N Kensington, 1964; Kemp Town, Brighton, 1966. MP (C) Brighton, Kemptown, 1970–97; contested (C) same seat, 1997. Jt Chm., All Party Old Age Pensioners Parly Gp, 1972–97; Chm., All Party BLESMA Gp, 1975–97; Mem. Select Cttee on Expenditure, 1973–74, on Abortion, 1975, on Employment, 1979–83. Mem., Council of Europe, 1987–97. Nat. Chm., Young Conservatives, 1960–61. Internat. Chm., People to People, 1981–83. Nat. Pres., Captive Animals Protection Soc., 1978–98. Mem., Chichester Dio. Synod, 1998–2003. Mem. School Council, Ardingly Coll., 1982–97. *Publications*: (jtly) Dare We Trust Them? - a new vision for Europe, 2005. *Recreations*: birdwatching, chess, poker. *Address*: 35 Wanderdown Road, Ovingdean, Brighton BN2 7BT. *T*: (01273) 552136. *Club*: Carlton.

**BOWDEN, Dawn Alison Louise;** Member (Lab) Merthyr Tydfil and Rhymney, National Assembly for Wales, since 2016; *b* Bristol, 14 Feb. 1960; *d* of Graham Bowden and Christine Bowden; two *s*; *m* 2011, Martin Eaglestone. *Educ*: St Bernadette's Catholic Secondary Sch., Bristol; Soundwell Tech. Coll. Organiser, NALGO, 1983–94; Sen. Manager, 1996–2016, Hd, Health, 2012–16, UNISON Cymru/Wales. *Recreations*: Bristol City supporter, season ticket holder Merthyr Town FC, travel (particularly to Italy), food, wine, reading, music, family. *Address*: National Assembly for Wales, Cardiff Bay, Cardiff CF99 1NA. *T*: 0300 200 7170. *E*: dawn.bowden@assembly.wales; 110 High Street, Merthyr CF47 8AP. *T*: (01685) 386672.

**BOWDEN, Gerald Francis,** TD 1971; barrister, chartered surveyor and university lecturer; *b* 26 Aug. 1935; *s* of Frank Albert Bowden and Elsie Bowden (*née* Burrill); *m* 1967, Heather Elizabeth Hill (*née* Hall) (*d* 1984); one *d* (and one *d* decd), and one step *s* one step *d*. *Educ*: Battersea Grammar School; Magdalen College, Oxford (MA); Coll. of Estate Mgt, London. FRICS 1984. Called to the Bar, Gray's Inn, 1962. Worked in advertising industry, 1964–68; property marketing and investment, 1968–72; Principal Lecturer in Law, Dept of Estate Management, Polytechnic of the South Bank, 1972–83; Vis. Lectr, Kingston Univ., 1993–2004. Chm. Panel, Examination in Public of Suffolk Co. Structure Plan, 1993. Mem. of Delegacy, KCL, 1978–84. Mem. GLC for Dulwich, 1977–81; a co-opted Mem., ILEA, 1981–84. MP (C) Dulwich, 1983–92; contested (C) Dulwich, 1992. PPS to Minister for Arts, 1990–92. Mem., Select Cttee on Educn, Sci. and Arts, 1990–92. Vice-Chairman: Cons. Backbench Educn Cttee, 1987–89; Cons. Backbench Arts and Heritage Cttee, 1987–92. Pres., Greater London Conservative Trade Unionists, 1985–88. Pres., Southwark Chamber of Commerce, 1986–89. Chairman: Walcot Educn Foundn, 1978–2001; Lambeth and Southwark Housing Assoc. (formerly Soc.), 1973–84; London Rent Assessment Panel, 1994–2006; Leasehold Valuation Tribunal, 1994–2006; Pres., Appeal Tribunal on Building Regulation, 1995–2005. Chm., Magdalen Soc., 1991–2001; Trustee, Magdalen Coll. Develt Trust, 1991–2009. Mem. Council, Royal Albert Hall, 1994–2019. Estates Gov., Alleyn's Coll. of God's Gift, Dulwich, 1992–2003 (Chm.). After Nat. Service, continued to serve in TA until 1984 (Lt-Col). Vice Pres., London City Hall Br., RBL, 2010–. *Publications*: An Introduction to the Law of Contract and Tort, 1977; The Housing Act, 1988. *Recreations*: gardening, books, pictures, renovating old houses. *Address*: 130 Kennington Park Road, SE11 4DJ. *T*: (020) 7582 7361. *Clubs*: Oxford and Cambridge (Chm., 1994–96; Trustee, 2002–11), Chelsea Arts, Garrick.

**BOWDEN, James Nicholas Geoffrey,** CMG 2012; OBE 2002; MVO 2017; HM Diplomatic Service; Ambassador to Chile, since 2018; *b* 27 May 1960; *s* of Geoffrey Bowden and Gillian (*née* Mathieson); *m* 1st, 1986, Alison Hulme (marr. diss. 1999); one *s* one *d*; 2nd, 1999, Sarah Peaslee; twin *s* one *d*. *Educ*: Eton. Served RGJ, 1980–86. Entered HM Diplomatic Service, 1986; Second Sec., FCO, 1986–90; Dep. Consul Gen., Aden, 1990–91; Second Sec., Khartoum, 1991–93; First Secretary: FCO, 1993–96; Washington, 1996–99; Riyadh, 1999–2000; FCO, 2000–03; Deputy Head of Mission: Kuwait, 2003–04; Baghdad, 2004–05; Kuwait, 2005–06; Ambassador: to Bahrain, 2006–11; to Oman, 2011–14; Dep. Private Sec. to the Prince of Wales and the Duchess of Cornwall, 2014–17. *Recreations*: hunting, walking. *Address*: c/o Foreign and Commonwealth Office, King Charles Street, SW1A 2AH.

**BOWDEN, Mark Rainer,** CMG 2017; Assistant Secretary General, United Nations, UN Assistance Mission to Afghanistan, 2012–17; *b* Edgware, 11 June 1951; *s* of Roland and Regine Bowden; *m* (marr. diss.); two *d*. *Educ*: Brunel Univ. (BSc Hons 1973). Mem., econ. planning staff, ODM, 1973–76; Res. Fellow, Dept of Nutrition, Queen Elizabeth Coll., Univ. of London, 1976–79; Save the Children Fund: Field Dir, Bangladesh, 1979–81; Hd, Regl Office for E Africa, 1981–84; Africa Dir, 1984–99; Conflict Mgt Advr, FCO, 1999–2001; Hd of Policy, UN Office for Coordination of Humanitarian Affairs, 2001–06; Dir, Civil Affairs, UN Mission in Sudan, 2006–12; UN Resident Rep. and UN Humanitarian Coordinator for Somalia, 2008–12. Mem. Bd, Afghan Aid, 2017–. FRSA. *Recreations*: bird watching, photography. *Address*: 4 Devonshire House, 29 Lindsay Square, SW1V 2HN. *T*: 07505 079891. *E*: markrbowden@gmail.com.

**BOWDEN, Sir Nicholas Richard,** 4th Bt *cr* 1915, of City of Nottingham; farmer, now retired; *b* 13 Aug. 1935; *s* of Sir Frank Bowden, 3rd Bt and his 1st wife, Marie-José Stiénon De Messey; *S* father, 2001. *Educ*: Millfield Sch. Asst to horse-trainer; farmer. *Recreation*: riding. *Heir*: *half-nephew* Alexander Gordan Houston Bowden [*b* 14 May 1972; *m* 2009, Nicola Judy Fleming; one *s* two *d*]. *Address*: 4 Hensting Farm Cottages, Fishers Pond, Eastleigh, Hants SO50 7HH. *Club*: Lansdowne.

**BOWDEN, Rev. Canon (Robert) Andrew;** Chaplain to the Queen, 1992–2008; Associate Priest, Thameshead benefice, diocese of Gloucester, 2004–08; *b* 13 Nov. 1938; *s* of Charles Bowden and Miriam (*née* Howard-Tripp); *m* 1966, Susan (*née* Humpidge); three *d*. *Educ*: Clifton Coll., Bristol; Worcester Coll., Oxford (Scholar; BA 1962; DipTh 1963; MA 1967; BDQ 1968); Cuddesdon Coll., Oxford. Ordained deacon, 1965, priest, 1966. Curate: St George, Wolverhampton, 1965–69; St Luke's, Duston, 1969–72; Rector: Byfield, 1972–79; Coates, Rodmarton and Sapperton with Frampton Mansell, 1979–2004. Chaplain, Royal Agricl Coll., Cirencester, 1979–93; Rural Advr, 1981–93, Local Ministry Officer, 1993–2008, dio. of Gloucester; Mem., Archbp's Commn on Rural Areas, 1988–90; Chm., Churches Rural Gp, 2004–07. Hon. Canon, Gloucester Cathedral, 1990–2008, Canon Emeritus, 2008–. *Publications*: Ministry in the Countryside, 1994; (with M. West) Dynamic Local Ministry, 2000; (ed) Ordained Local Ministry in the Church of England, 2012. *Recreation*: breeding Andalusian poultry and Shetland sheep. *Address*: Washbrook Cottage, Caudle Green, Cheltenham, Glos GL53 9PW. *T*: (01285) 821067. *E*: randrewbowden@gmail.com.

**BOWDERY, Martin Howard;** QC 2000; a Recorder, since 2003; Deputy Judge, Technology and Construction Court, since 2004; *b* 2 July 1956; *s* of Ray Bowdery and Beryl Bowdery (*née* Porter); *m* 1st, 1982 (marr. diss. 1999); two *s* four *d*; 2nd, 2002, Lindsay Moffat, *d* of Ted and Joan Moffat. *Educ*: Trinity Sch. of John Whitgift; Pembroke Coll., Oxford (BA PPE 1978). Called to the Bar, Inner Temple, 1980; practising Barrister, 1982–. Ed., Internat. Construction Law Rev., 1983–87. *Publications*: contributor to: Construction Contract Reform: a plea for sanity, 1999; Construction Law Handbook, 2000; Hudson's Building and Engineering Contracts, 12th edn, 2010. *Address*: 1 Atkin Building, Gray's Inn, WC1R 5AT. *T*: (020) 7404 0102. *Clubs*: Garrick; Isle of Purbeck Golf.

**BOWDLER, Timothy John,** CBE 2006; *b* 16 May 1947; *s* of Henry Neville Bowdler and Barbara Mary Bowdler (*née* Richardson); *m* 1976, Brita Margaretha Eklund; two *d*. *Educ*: Wrekin Coll.; Birmingham Univ. (BSc Engrg Prodn 1969); London Business Sch. (MBA 1975). Graduate mgt trainee, subseq. branch admin. manager, GKN Sankey Ltd, 1969–73; General Bearings Division, RHP Bearings Ltd: Commercial Manager, 1975–77; Gen. Manager, Business Ops, 1977–81; Sandvik Ltd: Dir and Gen. Manager, Sandvik Steel, 1981–84; Man. Dir, Spooner Industries Ltd, 1984–87; Man. Dir, Chloride Motive Power, Chloride Gp plc, 1987–88; Dir N Div., Tyzack & Partners Ltd, 1989–90; Divl Man. Dir, Cape Architectural Products, 1990–92, Cape Building and Architectural Products, 1992–94, Cape plc; Gp Man. Dir, 1994–97, Chief Exec., 1997–2009, Johnston Press plc. Chm., Press Standards Bd of Finance Ltd, 2005–09 (Dir, 2000–09). Non-executive Director: ABP Hldgs plc, 2001–06; PA Group, 2001–10 (non-exec. Chm., 2009–10); Miller Gp, 2004–12; Tullis Russell, 2010–14; Chm., Laidlaw Interiors Gp, 2012–15. Council Mem., Newspaper Soc., 1994–2008 (Pres., 2002–03). *Recreations*: golf, fishing, Swedish summerhouse. *E*: timbowdler@gmail.com. *Clubs*: Bruntsfield Links Golfing Society, Hon. Company of Edinburgh Golfers.

**BOWDON, Humphrey Anthony Erdeswick B.;** *see* Butler-Bowdon.

**BOWE, Dame Colette,** DBE 2014; PhD; Chairman, Banking Standards Board (formerly Banking Standards Review Council), 2014–19; *b* 27 Nov. 1946; *d* of Philip Bowe and Norah (*née* Hughes). *Educ*: Notre Dame High Sch., Liverpool; Queen Mary Coll., Univ. of London (BSc Econs, PhD); LSE (MSc Econs). Research Officer, LSE, 1969–70; Econ. Advr, Nat. Ports Council, 1971–73; Department of Industry: Econ. Advr, 1975–78; Principal, 1979–81; Department of Trade and Industry: Asst Sec., 1981–84; Dir of Information, 1984–87; Controller of Public Affairs, IBA, 1987–89; Dir, SIB, 1989–93; Chief Exec., PIA, 1994–97; Exec. Chm., Save & Prosper and Fleming Fund Mgt (Luxembourg), 1998–2001; Chm., Telecoms Ombudsman Service Council, 2002–03. Chm., OFCOM, 2009–14 (Chm., Consumer Panel, 2007; non-exec. Dir, 2008–09); Member: Statistics Commn, 2000–08; UK Statistics Authy, 2010–18; non-exec. Dir, DfT, 2014–17. Chm., Electra Private Equity plc, 2010–14 (non-exec. Dir., 2007–14); non-executive Director: Thames Water Utilities Ltd, 2001–06 (Dep. Chm., 2002–06); Yorkshire Building Soc., 2003–06; Framlington Gp, 2003–05; Axa Framlington, 2005–09; Morgan Stanley Bank Internat., 2005–10; Morgan Stanley Internat., 2010–11; Goldfish Bank, 2007–08; London and Continental Railways, 2008–11; Mem., Supervisory Bd, Axa Deutschland GmbH, 2009–14; Mem. Bd, Axa IM, 2012–14. Ext. Mem., Financial Policy Cttee, Bank of England, 2019–. Trustee, Internat. Financial Reporting Standards Foundn, 2018–. Chm., Alcohol Concern, 2002–06. Chm., Associated Bd of the Royal Schs of Music, 2012–18. Chm. Council, Queen Mary, Univ. of London, 2003–09; Gov. and Mem. Council of Mgt, NIESR, 2002–10; Vis. Fellow, Nuffield Coll., Oxford, 2013–. Governor: Bancroft's Sch., 2009–16; City of London Acad. Highbury Grove, 2018–. Trustee: Camden People's Theatre, 2002–11; Wincott Foundn, 2004–11; Tablet Trust, 2010–; Nuffield Foundn, 2012–; Mountview Acad. of Theatre Arts, 2016–19; Pres., VLV, 2015–19. Liveryman, Drapers' Co., 2008–. Hon. Fellow, Liverpool John Moores Univ., 1995. Hon. DSc QMUL, 2010; Hon. Dr: Wolverhampton, 2018; Liverpool Hope, 2018. *Recreations*: music, London, watching football. *E*: info@redrock23.com.

**BOWE, David Robert;** public affairs consultant; Member (Lab) Yorkshire and the Humber Region, European Parliament, 1999–2004 (Cleveland and Yorkshire North, 1989–94; Cleveland and Richmond, 1994–99); *b* Gateshead, 19 July 1955; *m* 1978, Helena Scattergood; one *s* one *d*. *Educ*: Sunderland Polytechnic; Bath Univ. BSc; PGCE. Former science teacher. Mem., Middlesbrough Borough Council, 1983–89 (Chm., Monitoring and Review Cttee). European Parliament: Mem., Cttee on Envmt, Public Health and Consumer Protection, 1989–2004; substitute Member: Cttee on Econ. and Monetary Affairs, 1994–99; Industry Cttee, 1999–2004. Mem., UNISON. *Address*: 4 Silverdale Mount, Guiseley, Leeds LS20 8PY. *E*: mail@davidbowe.co.uk.

**BOWEN, Anthony John,** PhD; Lector, Faculty of Classics, 1990–2003, and Orator, 1993–2007, University of Cambridge; Fellow, Jesus College, Cambridge, 1995–2007, now Emeritus Fellow (President, 2003–05); *b* 17 May 1940; *s* of Dr Reginald Bowen and Dorothy Bowen (*née* Jinks). *Educ*: Bradfield Coll., Berks; St John's Coll., Cambridge; PhD Cantab 2016. Teacher: Bradfield Coll., 1963–67 (producer of Greek play, 1961, 1964, 1967); Shrewsbury Sch., 1967–90. Contested (L/Alliance) Shrewsbury and Atcham, 1983. Member: (L, then Lib Dem) Shropshire CC, 1981–89; (Lib Dem) Cambridgeshire CC, 1997–2005. *Publications*: Aeschylus, Cheophori, 1986; The Story of Lucretia, 1987; Plutarch, the Malice of Herodotus, 1992; Xenophon, Symposium, 1998; (with Peter Garnsey) Lactantius, Divine Institutes, 2003; Cambridge Orations 1993–2007: a selection, 2008; Aeschylus, Suppliant Women, 2013. *Recreations*: travel, politics, music, food and wine. *Address*: Jesus College, Cambridge CB5 8BL. *T*: (01223) 323722.

**BOWEN, Maj.-Gen. Bryan Morris,** CB 1988; Paymaster-in-Chief and Inspector of Army Pay Services, 1986–89, retired; *b* 8 March 1932; *s* of Frederick Bowen and Gwendoline Bowen (*née* Morris); *m* 1955, Suzanne Rowena (*née* Howell); two *d*. *Educ*: Newport High Sch.; Exeter Univ. FCMA; ndc, psc†, sq, pfc. Joined RE, 1953, served UK and BAOR; transf. RAPC, 1958: Paymaster 1/6 QEO Gurkha Rifles, Malaya and UK, 1960–63; Army Cost and Management Accounting Services, 1963–68; DAAG, MoD, 1968–70; Exchange Officer, US Army, Washington, DC, 1970–72; Nat. Defence Coll., 1972–73; DS, RMCS Shrivenham, 1973–76; AAG, MOD, 1976–79; Col (Principal), MoD F4(AD), 1979–81; Chief Paymaster, Army Pay Office (Officers Accounts), 1981–82; Dep. Paymaster-in-Chief, 1982–85. Col Comdt, RAPC, 1990–92; Dep. Col Comdt, AGC, 1992–93. Mem. Council, CIMA, 1990–94; Chm., Oxfordshire Cttee, Army Benevolent Fund, 1990–92;

Special Comr, Duke of York's Royal Mil. Sch., Dover, 1990–2000 (Chm., 1992–2000); Dir, United Services Trustee, 1990–2000; Pres., Nat. Service Veterans' Assoc., 2003–15. Freeman, City of London, 1987. *Address:* Foxlea, Yew Tree Farm, Goodworth Clatford, Andover, Hants SP11 7QY.

**BOWEN, Carolyn Elizabeth Cunningham;** *see* Sinclair, C. E. C.

**BOWEN, Prof. (David) Keith,** DPhil; FRS 1998; FREng; Visiting Professor of Physics, University of Durham, since 2003; Professor of Engineering, University of Warwick, 1989–97, now Emeritus; consultant in X-ray science and technology and in technical due diligence for investors and M&A, since 2010; *b* 10 May 1940; *s* of Harold Lane Bowen and Muriel Bowen; *m* 1968, Beryl Lodge; one *s*. *Educ:* Christ's Hosp.; St Edmund Hall, Oxford (MA 1966; DPhil Metallurgy 1967; Hon. Fellow 2006); Open Univ. (Dip. Music 2006; MA Music 2009). FREng (FEng 1997); FIMMM (FIM 1983); CPhys 1998, FInstP 1998. SRC Res. Fellow, Oxford Univ., 1966–68; Department of Engineering, University of Warwick: Lectr, 1968–78; Sen. Lectr, 1978–85; Reader, 1985–89. Vis. Prof., MIT, 1987. Pres., Bede Scientific Inc., 1996–2002; Gp Dir of Technology, 2000–05, Chief Scientist, 2005–08, Bede plc. Pres., Kammermusik Workshops Inc., USA, 2004–15; Chm., Spires Music Ltd, 2007–15. Non-exec. Dir, Circadian Solar (formerly AdvanceSis) Ltd, 2005–10; Chm., goHDR, 2011–15 (non-exec. Dir, 2010–15). Royal Coll. of Music Doctoral Scholar supported by Pamela Weston Award, 2012–19. *Publications:* (with C. R. Hall) Microscopy of Materials, 1975; (with B. K. Tanner) High Resolution X-Ray Diffractometry and Topography, 1998; X-Ray Metrology in Semiconductor Manufacturing, 2006; more than 150 articles in learned jls; 8 patents; pubns in clarinet organology. *Recreations:* music (orchestral and chamber clarinet player, conductor and coach), clarinet restoration, woodwork, gardening. E: d.k.bowen@warwick.ac.uk.

**BOWEN, Desmond John,** CB 2009; CMG 2002; Staff Counsellor, Security and Intelligence Services, 2009–16; *b* 11 Jan. 1949; *s* of John and Deborah Bowen; *m* 1979, Susan Brandt; one *s* one *d*. *Educ:* Charterhouse; University Coll., Oxford (MA). Parachute Regt, 1970–73; joined MoD, 1973; seconded to FCO, 1978–81, 1987–91; Private Sec. to Permanent Under Sec. of State, 1982–85; Dir Gen. of Mktg, Defence Export Services Orgn, 1995–97; Fellow, Center for Internat. Affairs, Harvard Univ., 1997–98; Asst Under Sec. of State (Service Personnel Policy), 1998–99; Dir, Private Office of Sec. Gen., NATO, 1999–2001; Dir Gen. Operational Policy, MoD, 2001–02; on secondment as Dep. Dir, Overseas and Defence Secretariat, Cabinet Office, 2002–04; Policy Dir, MoD, 2004–08. Mem., UN Sec.-Gen.'s Adv. Bd on Disarmament Matters, 2009–13. Vis. Prof., Reading Univ., 2010–17. Trustee, Imperial War Mus, 2017–. Associate Fellow, IISS, 2018–. *Publications:* (contrib.) British Generals in Blair's Wars, 2013; contrib. Conflict and Terrorism jl, Survival jl, RUSI's Afghan Papers. *Recreation:* mountains.

**BOWEN, Edward Farquharson,** CBE 2010; TD 1976; QC (Scot.) 1992; Temporary Judge, Court of Session, 2000–14; *b* 1 May 1945; *s* of late Stanley Bowen, CBE; *m* 1975, Patricia Margaret Brown, *y* d of Rev. R. Russell Brown, Perth; two *s* two *d*. *Educ:* Melville Coll., Edinburgh; Edinburgh Univ. (LLB 1966). Enrolled as Solicitor in Scotland, 1968; admitted to Faculty of Advocates, 1970. Standing Jun. Counsel: to Scottish Educn Dept, 1977–79; to Home Office in Scotland, 1979; Advocate-Depute, 1979–83; Sheriff of Tayside Central and Fife, 1983–90; Partner, Thorntons, WS, 1990–91; Sheriff-Principal of Glasgow and Strathkelvin, 1997–2005, of Lothian and Borders, 2005–11. Chm. (part-time), Industrial Tribunals, 1995–97; Mem. Criminal Injuries Compensation Bd, 1996–97. Chm., Ind. Rev. of Sheriff and Jury Procedure, 2009–10. Chm., Northern Lighthouse Bd, 2003–05 (Comr of Northern Lights, 1997–2011). Chancellor's Assessor, Edinburgh Univ. Court, 2011–19. Served RAOC (TA and T&AVR), 1964–80. *Recreation:* golf. *Address:* The Old Manse, Lundie, Angus DD2 5NW. *Clubs:* New (Edinburgh); Royal & Ancient Golf (St Andrews); Hon. Company of Edinburgh Golfers; Panmure Golf.

**BOWEN, Sir George Edward Michael,** 6th Bt *cr* 1921, of Colworth, Co. Bedford; *b* 27 Dec. 1987; *s* of Sir Mark Edward Mortimer Bowen, 5th Bt and of Kerry Tessa Bowen (née Moriarty); *S* father, 2014. *Heir:* cousin Michael Edward Bowen [*b* 14 Dec. 1944; *m* 1968, Gillian Margaret Garside; three *d*].

**BOWEN, Geraint Robert Lewis,** FRCO; Organist and Director of Music, Hereford Cathedral, since 2001; *b* 11 Jan. 1963; *s* of late Kenneth John Bowen and of Angela Mary Bowen (née Evenden); *m* 1987, Catherine Lucy Dennis; two *s*. *Educ:* Haverstock Sch.; William Ellis Sch.; Jesus Coll., Cambridge (organ schol.; BA 1986, MA 1989); Trinity Coll., Dublin (MusB 1987). FRCO 1987. Assistant Organist: Hampstead Parish Ch and St Clement Danes Ch, 1985–86; St Patrick's Cathedral, Dublin, 1986–89; Hereford Cathedral, 1989–94; Organist and Master of the Choristers, St Davids Cathedral, and Artistic Dir, St Davids Cathedral Fest., 1995–2001. Conductor, Hereford Choral Soc., 2001–; Associate Conductor, Three Choirs Fest. at Gloucester and Worcester, 2002–; Conductor, Three Choirs Fest. at Hereford, 2003–. Hon. FGCM 2012. *Recreations:* growing vegetables, railways, travel, typography, walking. *Address:* 7 College Cloisters, Cathedral Close, Hereford HR1 2NG. *T:* (01432) 374238. *E:* organist@herefordcathedral.org.

**BOWEN, Janet Margaret,** CVO 2018; Lord-Lieutenant of Ross and Cromarty, Skye and Lochalsh, 2007–19; *b* 12 July 1944; *d* of Capt. Alexander Matheson, RN and Mary Matheson; *m* 1972, Christopher Richard Croasdaile Bowen; one *s* one *d*. *Educ:* Butterstone House Sch.; North Foreland Lodge. Sec., British Red Cross HQ and volunteer, British Red Cross VSO scheme, 1965–68; Sec., Church Soc., 1969–72; Mem., Children's Panel, 1986–2004. Pres., Red Cross, Highland and Western Isles, 2007–12 (Chm., Volunteer Council, 2000–07). *Recreations:* cherishing husband and family, gardening, cooking, countryside, five grandchildren. *Address:* Kinellan House, Strathpeffer, Ross-shire IV14 9ET. *T:* (01997) 421476. *E:* janet@kinellan.org.

**BOWEN, Jeremy Francis John;** Middle East Editor, BBC, since 2005; *b* 6 Feb. 1960; *s* of (David) Gareth (Francis) Bowen and (Margaret Frances) Jennifer Bowen (née Delany); partner, Julia Williams; one *s* one *d*. *Educ:* Cardiff High Sch.; University Coll. London (BA Hons Hist.; Fellow 2005); Johns Hopkins Univ. Sch. of Advanced Internat. Studies, Washington and Bologna, Italy (MA Internat. Affairs). Joined BBC, 1984: news trainee, 1984–85; financial news reporter, 1986–87; Foreign Correspondent, 1987–2000: Radio Corresp., Geneva, 1987; Foreign Affairs Corresp., TV, 1988–95; Middle East Corresp., 1995–2000; Presenter, BBC Breakfast, 2000–02; foreign correspondent and television presenter, 2002–05; Rome Corresp., 2005. Hon. Fellow: Cardiff Univ., 2009; Univ. of S Wales, 2013; Cardiff Metropolitan Univ., 2015; Aberystwyth Univ., 2015. Hon. DSocSci Nottingham Trent, 2014. Journalism award: NY TV Fest., 1993; Monte Carlo TV Fest., 1994; RTS, 1996; BAFTA Award for BBC team coverage of Kosovo Crisis, 1999; Sony Gold Award for coverage of Saddam Hussein's arrest, 2004; Internat. Emmy, BBC Team Award for coverage of 2006 war in Lebanon and Israel, 2007; Bayeux War corresp. prize for coverage of Gaza war, 2009, for radio report covering Syrian war, 2012; Charles Wheeler Award for excellence in broadcast journalism, British Journalism Rev., 2010; (jtly) Peace Through Media Award, Next Century Foundn, 2012; Specialist Journalist of the Year, 2013, Television Journalist of the Year, 2014, RTS; BAFTA Cymru Siân Phillips Award, 2014; Emmy Award, 2014, Peabody Award, 2014, for Syria coverage; RTS interview of the year, 2015, for Pres. Bashar al Assad; Nick Clarke Award, 2015, for Pres. Bashar al Assad; James Cameron Prize, 2015; Frontline Award, 2015, Bayeux Award for War Correspondents, 2016, for Yemen. *Publications:* Six Days: how the 1967 war shaped the Middle East, 2003; War Stories, 2006; The Arab Uprisings: the people want the fall of the regime, 2012. *Recreations:* sport, cooking, not travelling. *Address:* c/o BBC News, Broadcasting House, Portland Place, W1A 1AA.
*See also* N. J. H. Bowen.

**BOWEN, Keith;** *see* Bowen, D. K.

**BOWEN, Most Rev. Michael George;** Archbishop and Metropolitan of Southwark, (RC), 1977–2003, now Archbishop Emeritus; *b* 23 April 1930; *s* of late Major C. L. J. Bowen and Maisie Bowen (who *m* 1945, Sir Paul Makins, 4th Bt). *Educ:* Downside; Trinity Coll., Cambridge; Gregorian Univ., Rome. Army, 1948–49, 2nd Lieut Irish Guards; Wine Trade, 1951–52; English Coll., Rome, 1952–59; ordained 1958; Curate at Earlsfield and at Walworth, South London, 1959–63; taught theology, Beda Coll., Rome, 1963–66; Chancellor of Diocese of Arundel and Brighton, 1966–70; Coadjutor Bishop with right of succession to See of Arundel and Brighton, 1970–71; Bishop of Arundel and Brighton, 1971–77. Pres., Bishops' Conf. of England and Wales, 1999–2000 (Vice-Pres., 1996–98). *Recreations:* golf, tennis. *Address:* c/o Archbishop's House, St George's Road, SE1 6HX. *T:* (020) 7928 2495.

**BOWEN, Nicholas James Hugh;** QC 2009; *b* Cardiff, 18 Aug. 1961; *s* of (David) Gareth (Francis) Bowen and (Margaret) Jennifer Bowen (née Delany); *m* 1990, Maryanne St Clare; two *s* one *d*. *Educ:* Cardiff High Sch.; Univ. of Sussex (BA Law 1983); Council of Legal Educn. Called to the Bar, Gray's Inn, 1984; in practice as a barrister, 29 Bedford Row, 1988–2005, Doughty Street, 2005–, specialising in public and admin. law, human rights and civil liberties, state liability in tort, actions against the police, inquest law and professional negligence. *Recreations:* gardening, sailing, walking the Black Mountains, building sheds. *Address:* 53–54 Doughty Street, WC1N 2LS. *T:* (020) 7404 1313, *Fax:* (020) 7404 2283/4.
*See also* J. F. J. Bowen.

**BOWEN, Paul Edward;** QC 2012; a Recorder, since 2018; *b* Oslo, 17 July 1967; *s* of Brig. Derek Harvey Bowen, OBE and Juliet Aymée Bowen; *m* 2000, Michèle, (Mimi), Spencer; one *s* one *d*. *Educ:* Tonbridge Sch.; Univ. of Exeter (LLB 1989). Clifford Chance, 1991–93; admitted Solicitor, 1993; called to the Bar, Inner Temple, 1993; in practice as a barrister, specialising in human rights and public law, Doughty Street Chambers, 1993–2014, Brick Court Chambers, 2014–. Special Advocate, 2007–12. Member: Adv. Bd, Children's Comr, 2010–; A Panel of Counsel, Equality and Human Rights Commn, 2015–. Gov., Wildlesham House Sch., 2007–10. *Publications:* Blackstone's Guide to the Mental Health Act 2007, 2008. *Recreations:* family life, sailing, the great outdoors. *E:* paul.bowen@brickcourt.co.uk. *Club:* Penn.

**BOWEN, Thomas Edward Ifor L.;** *see* Lewis-Bowen.

**BOWEN-BRAVERY, Katy Louise;** Editorial Director, Both Barrels Media Ltd, since 2017; *b* Cosford, Salop, 27 June 1959; *d* of late Kenyon Bowen-Bravery and of Mary Bowen-Bravery; *m* (marr. diss.); one *s*. *Educ:* Francis Bacon Sch., St Albans; Univ. of Wales Inst. of Sci. and Technol. (BA Hons); Cardiff Sch. of Journalism (Dip. Journalism); PPA Dip. Publishing. Reporter, sub-ed., Western Daily Press, 1983–85; freelance feature writer, Daily Mail and sub-ed., Mail on Sunday, 1985; Mem., launch team, Today newspaper, then Ed., Saturday mag., Male and Female, 1985–89; Commng Ed., Good Weekend mag., Sydney Morning Herald, 1989–94; Editor: Boulevard, subseq. Express on Sunday Mag., Sunday Express, 1994–96; Sunday Mirror mag., 1996–2002; Dep. Ed., 2002–08, Ed., 2008–17, Saga Mag. *Recreations:* lepidoptery, windsurfing, VW campervanning. *Club:* Union.

**BOWEN-SIMPKINS, Peter,** FRCOG; Consultant Obstetrician and Gynaecologist: Singleton Hospital, Swansea, 1979–98; Swansea NHS Trust, 1999–2002; Executive Medical Director: London Women's Clinic, since 2018 (Medical Director, London Women's Clinic at Singleton Hospital (formerly Cromwell IVF and Fertility Centre), Swansea, 1992, later Medical Director, London Women's Clinic, Wales and London); JD Healthcare, since 2005; *b* 28 Oct. 1941; *s* of late Horace John Bowen-Simpkins and Christine Dulce Bowen-Simpkins (née Clarke); *m* 1967, Kathrin Ganguin; two *d*. *Educ:* Malvern Coll.; Selwyn Coll., Cambridge (BA 1963); MA 1966, MB BChir 1966, Cambridge; Guy's Hosp. Med. Sch. LRCP, MRCS 1966; FRCOG 1985; FFSRH (FFFP 2005; MFFP 1993). Leader, Cambridge expedn to Eritrea, 1963; Resident MO, Queen Charlotte's Maternity Hosp., London, 1971; Resident Surg. Officer, Samaritan Hosp. for Women, London, 1972; Sen. Registrar and Lectr, Middlesex Hosp. and Hosp. for Women, Soho Square, 1972–78; Inspector of Nullity for Wales, 1980. Lectr, Margaret Pyke Centre for Family Planning, 1973–2003. Royal College of Obstetricians and Gynaecologists: Mem. Council, 1993–2005; Hon. Treas., 1998–2005; Mem. Foundn Bd, Fac. of Family Planning, 1995–98; Trustee and Bd Mem., WellBeing, 1998–2012. Chm. Mgt Bd, BJOG, 1998–2005. Pres., Victor Bonney Soc., 2002–05. Hon. Treas., Royal Med. Benevolent Fund, 2008–14. Freeman, City of London, 1980; Liveryman: Soc. of Apothecaries, 1976; Livery Co. of Wales (formerly Welsh Livery Guild), 1995. Handcock Prize for Surgery, RCS, 1966. *Publications:* Pocket Examiner in Obstetrics and Gynaecology, 1983, 2nd edn 1992; A Practice of Obstetrics and Gynaecology, 2000; papers on obstetrics and gynaecol. in BMJ, BJOG, BJA, Fertility and Sterility, etc. *Recreations:* flyfishing, walking, ski-ing, opera, classical music, golf. *Address:* Quaker Cottage, 19–21 College Street, Petersfield GU31 4AG. *E:* pbs@reynoldston.com. *Club:* Gynaecological Travellers.

**BOWER, Cynthia;** Chief Executive, Care Quality Commission, 2009–12; *b* Worksop, Notts, 6 July 1955; *d* of Harold and Clariss Bower; one *s* by Roger William Shannon. *Educ:* Univ. of Birmingham (BA Hons English Lang. and Lit. 1976; DipSW 1979; MScSoc 1994). Various posts with Birmingham CC, 1979–95, incl. Asst Dir of Social Services, 1992–95; Chief Executive: Birmingham Specialist Community Health Trust, 2000–02; S Birmingham PCT, 2002–05; NHS W Midlands, 2006–08. Chm., Gateway Family Services, 2006–08; Mem. Bd, Skills for Health, 2007–13. Non-exec. Dir, John Taylor Hospice, 2012–19; Dir, Salad City Social Enterprise, 2015–. Trustee, Ibba Girls Boarding Sch., S Sudan, 2015–. Guardian, Growing Points, 2012–17. Mem., Lunar Soc. Hon. PhD: Birmingham, 2009; Aston, 2009. FRSA 2012. *Recreations:* music, literature, art, cinema, running, swimming, dining, yoga, travel.

**BOWER, Thomas Michael;** writer and journalist; *b* 28 Sept. 1946; *s* of George Bower and Sylvia Bower; *m* 1st, 1971, Juliet Ann Oddie (marr. diss. 1981); two *s*; 2nd, 1985, Veronica Judith Colleton Wadley, *qv*; one *s* one *d*. *Educ:* William Ellis Sch.; London Sch. of Econs (LLB). Called to the Bar, Gray's Inn, 1969; with BBC TV, 1970–95: researcher, 24 Hours, 1970–72; producer, Midweek, 1972–76; Dep. Ed. and Producer, Panorama, 1976–86; Producer, Documentaries, 1986–95; contributor, Daily Mail, The Times and Sunday Times. Queen Victoria Bronze Medal, RSPCA, 1975; Award for Excellence in Broadcasting, Ohio State Univ., 1979; Best TV Documentary, Fest. dei Popoli, 1987; Fipa d'Or, Cannes, for best TV documentary, The Confession, 1991; Chairman's Award, BPA, 1991; Special Award, Outstanding Achievement for a Body of Work, Spear's Book Awards,

2011. *Publications:* Blind Eye to Murder, a Pledge Betrayed, 1981; Klaus Barbie, Butcher of Lyons, 1984; The Paperclip Conspiracy, 1987; Maxwell the Outsider, 1988; The Red Web, 1989; Tiny Rowland, a Rebel Tycoon, 1993; The Perfect English Spy, Sir Dick White, 1995; Heroes of World War 2, 1995; Maxwell: the Final Verdict, 1995; Blood Money: the Swiss, the Nazis and the looted billions, 1997; Fayed: the unauthorised biography, 1998; Branson, 2000, reissued, 2008; The Paymaster: Geoffrey Robinson, Maxwell and New Labour, 2001; Broken Dreams: vanity, greed and the souring of British football (William Hill Sports Book of the Year), 2003; Gordon Brown, 2004, reissued as Gordon Brown, Prime Minister, 2007; Conrad & Lady Black: dancing on the edge, 2006; The Squeeze: oil, money and greed in the twenty-first century, 2009; No Angel: the secret life of Bernie Ecclestone, 2011; Sweet Revenge: the intimate life of Simon Cowell, 2012; Branson: behind the mask, 2014; Broken Vows: Tony Blair: the tragedy of power, 2016; Rebel Prince: the power, passion and defiance of Prince Charles, 2018; Dangerous Hero: Corbyn's ruthless plot for power, 2019. *Recreations:* walking, ski-ing, shooting. *Address:* 10 Thurlow Road, NW3 5PL. *T:* (020) 7435 9776. *Clubs:* Garrick, Beefsteak.

**BOWER, Veronica Judith Colleton;** *see* Wadley, V. J. C.

**BOWER-EASTON, Helen Alice,** CBE 2016; Director of Communication, Foreign and Commonwealth Office, 2017–18; *b* Birmingham, 30 Aug. 1978; *d* of John and Diana Bower; *m* 2016, Mark Easton; one *d*. *Educ:* Edgbaston High Sch. for Girls; Cardiff Univ. (BSc Econ EU Studies with French and Italian 2001). Asst to Spokesperson, Office of Rt Hon. Christopher Patten, EC, 2003–04; press office, Home Office, 2004–07; Dep. Spokesperson, 2007–09, Spokesperson, 2009–11, UK Representation to EU; Chief Press Officer, Foreign and Defence Affairs, No 10 Downing St, 2011–15; Prime Minister's Official Spokesperson, 2015–17. *Recreations:* tennis, scuba diving, photography, cooking, travel, Raleigh venturer. *Address:* Foreign and Commonwealth Office, King Charles Street, SW1A 2AH. *T:* (020) 7008 1500.

**BOWERING, Christine,** DL; MA; Chairman, Nottingham City Hospital NHS Trust, 1998–2006; Headmistress, Nottingham High School for Girls (GPDST), 1984–96; *b* 30 June 1936; *d* of Kenneth Soper and Florence E. W. Soper; *m* 1960, Rev. John Anthony Bowering (*d* 2014); one *s* one *d*. *Educ:* St Bernard's Convent, Westcliff-on-Sea; Newnham Coll., Cambridge (MA). Assistant Teacher: St Bernard's Convent; Ursuline Convent, Brentwood; Sheffield High Sch. (GPDST). Mem., Engineering Council, 1988–91. Dir, Queen's Med. Centre, Nottingham, 1993–98. Chairman: Educn Cttee, GSA, 1989–93; Ind. Schs Curriculum Cttee, 1992–94; Mem., Educn Cttee, Goldsmiths' Co., 1992–2009. Governor: Nottingham Trent Univ. (formerly Nottingham Poly.), 1989–96 (Mem., 1990–, Chm., 1990–96, Employment Cttee); Minster Sch., Southwell, 2004– (Chair, Strategic Develt and Pupil Cttee). Assoc. Mem., Newnham Coll., Cambridge, 1991–2002. Trustee, Southwell Dio. Council for Family Care, 1998– (Chm., 2007–12). DL Notts, 2000. Freeman, Goldsmiths' Co., 2005. Hon. DLitt Nottingham, 1996. *Address:* Linthwaite Cottage, Main Street, Kirklington, Newark NG22 8ND. *T:* (01636) 816995.

**BOWERS, John Simon;** QC 1998; a Recorder, since 2003; a Deputy High Court Judge, since 2010; Principal, Brasenose College, Oxford, since 2015; *b* 2 Jan. 1956; *s* of late Alfred and Irene Bowers; *m* 1982, Prof. Suzanne Franks; one *s* two *d*. *Educ:* Matthew Humberstone Comp. Sch., Cleethorpes; Lincoln Coll., Oxford (MA, BCL). Called to the Bar, Middle Temple, 1979, Bencher, 2004; in practice at the Bar, 1979–. Chairman: Employment Appeal Tribunal Users' Gp, 1995–99; (part-time), Employment Tribunals, 2001–02; Mediator, Centre for Dispute Resolution, 1998–. Chairman: Employment Law Bar Assoc., 2001–03; Bar Disciplinary Tribunal, 2001–10; Member: Liaison Cttee, Govt Human Rights Task Force, 1999–2001; Bar Council Race Relations Cttee, 1999–2002; Standards Bd for England, 2000–05; Standards Bd, Metropolitan Police Authy, 2010–12. Mem. Council, Univ. of Kent, 2012–15; Chair, Legal Panel, Oxford Conf. of Colls, 2016–; Member: Bd of Friends, Neve Shalom village, 2009–; Bd, Kessler Foundn, 2011–14. *Publications:* Bowers on Employment Law, 1980, 9th edn as Practical Approach to Employment Law, 2017; (jtly) Atkin's Court Forms, vol. 38, 1986, 2003; (jtly) Modern Law of Strikes, 1987; Industrial Tribunal Procedure, 1987, 2nd edn, as Employment Tribunal Procedure, 1998; (jtly) The Employment Act 1988, 1988; Termination of Employment, 1988, 3rd edn 1995; (jtly) Transfer of Undertakings: the legal pitfalls, 1989, 6th edn 1996; (jtly) Basic Procedure in Courts and Tribunals, 1990; (jtly) Textbook on Employment Law, 1990, 9th edn 2006; (jtly) Employment Law Update, 1991; Transfer of Undertakings Encyclopaedia, 1998; Whistleblowing: the new law, 2000, 3rd edn 2017; Employment Law and Human Rights, 2000; The Law of Industrial Action and Trade Union Recognition, 2011, 3rd edn 2019; (contrib.) Bullen & Leake on Pleadings; many articles in legal jls. *Recreations:* football, tennis. *Address:* Brasenose College, Radcliffe Square, Oxford OX1 4AJ.

**BOWERS, Dr Keith Henry,** CEng, FREng; Head of Profession, Civil Engineering and Built Environment, Transport for London, since 2017; *b* Wokingham, 24 Nov. 1965; *s* of Dr Brian Peter Bowers and Faith Wendy Bowers; *m* 1987, Donna Hoult; three *s*. *Educ:* Wilson's Sch., Wallington; Univ. of Wales, Swansea (BSc 1987); Queen Mary Coll., Univ. of London (MSc 1988); Univ. of Leeds (PhD 1997). CEng 1997; FGS 1991; FICE 2003; FIMMM 2017; FREng 2017. Materials testing consultant, Technotrade Ltd, 1988–89; Proj. Manager and team leader, Ground Engrg Div., TRL, 1990–2001; ARUP: Sen. Engr, 2001–03; Associate, 2003–05; Associate Dir, 2005–06, seconded to Rail Link Engrg as an Engrg Manager on construction of Channel Tunnel Rail Link, Thameslink and Kings Cross station tunnels, London, 2001–05; Principal Civil Engr and Hd of Tunnels, London Underground, TfL, 2006–17. *Publications:* academic papers related to tunnelling and underground transport infrastructure. *Address:* 66 Lambardes, New Ash Green, Longfield, Kent DA3 8HU. *T:* 07909 682706. *E:* keith@kbowers.co.uk.

**BOWERS, His Honour Peter Hammond;** a Circuit Judge, 1995–2015; *b* 22 June 1945; *s* of Edward Hammond Bowers and Elsie Bowers; *m* 1970, Brenda Janet Burgess; two *s* one *d*. *Educ:* Acklam Hall, Middlesbrough. Admitted solicitor, 1966; in private practice, 1966–70; Prosecuting Solicitor, 1970–72; called to the Bar, Inner Temple, 1972; barrister, N Eastern Circuit, 1972–95. *Recreations:* cricket, aspiring artist, antiques, paintings, armchair sportsman.

**BOWERS, Roger George,** CMG 1997; OBE 1984; PhD; Chief Executive, Trinity College, London, 1998–2006 (Member Council, 1997–98); *b* 23 May 1942; *s* of George Albert Bowers and Hilda Mary Bowers (*née* Wells); *m* 1st, 1963, Gweneth Iris Pither (marr. diss.); one *s* one *d*; 2nd, 2009, Jennifer Ann Pugsley. *Educ:* Royal Grammar Sch., Guildford; Wadham Coll., Oxford (BA); Reading Univ. (MPhil; PhD). Joined British Council, 1964; Tutor to Overseas Students, Univ. of Birmingham, 1965; Asst Regl Dir, Cape Coast, Ghana, 1965–69; seconded to Eng. Lang. Trng Inst., Allahabad, 1971–73; Asst Regl Educ. Advr, Calcutta, 1973–76; Eng. Lang. Consultancies Dept, 1978–80; seconded to Ain Shams Univ., Cairo, 1980–84; Dir, Eng. Lang. Services Dept, 1984–85; Dep. Controller, 1985–89, Controller, then Dir, 1989–93, Eng. Lang. and Lit. Div.; Asst Dir-Gen. (Manchester), and Dir of Professional Services, 1993–96. Director: R. G. Bowers & Associates, 1996–2009; World of Language Ltd, 1997–2009. Jt Editor, Cambridge Handbooks for Language Teachers, 1985–92; Member: Editorial Cttee, ELT Documents, 1984–93; Bd of Management, ELT Jl, 1985–96. Mem. Corp., Trinity Coll. of Music,

1999–2006. Trustee, A. S. Hornby Educnl Trust, 1997–2016 (Chm., 2007–14). FRSA 1993. Hon. FTCL 2007. *Publications:* In Passing, 1976; Talking About Grammar, 1987; Word Play, 1990. *Recreations:* fishing, cooking, eating, travel in France. *Address:* 25 Hillbrow, Richmond Hill, Surrey TW10 6BH.

**BOWERS, Rupert John;** QC 2015; *b* New York, 29 Jan. 1971; *s* of John Robert Bowers and Patricia Ann Maureen Bowers; *m* 1999, Olivia Charlotte Eliott Lockhart; three *d*. *Educ:* Oundle Sch.; Univ. of Newcastle upon Tyne (BA Hons Psychol. 1992); Coll. of Law, London (DipLaw); Inns of Court Sch. of Law. Called to the Bar, Gray's Inn, 1995; in practice as barrister, specialising in search and seizure, white collar crime, extradition and sports law. *Publications:* Blackstone's Guide to the Terrorism Act 2006, 2006. *Recreations:* mountaineering, ski-ing, playing football (knees permitting), attending the village pub and La Grange in St Gervais. *Address:* Doughty Street Chambers, 53/54 Doughty Street, WC1N 2LS. *T:* (020) 7404 1313. *E:* r.bowers@doughtystreet.co.uk. *Club:* Offham Tennis.

**BOWERS-BROADBENT, Christopher Joseph St George;** organist and composer; *b* 13 Jan. 1945; *s* of late Henry W. Bowers-Broadbent and Doris E. Bowers-Broadbent (*née* Mizen); *m* 1970, Deirdre Ann Cape; one *s* one *d*. *Educ:* King's Coll., Cambridge (Chorister); Berkhamsted Sch.; Royal Acad. of Music (Rec.Dip.; FRAM 1983). Organist and Choirmaster, St Pancras Parish Church, 1965–88; début recital, 1966; Organist, 1973–, and Dir of Music, W London Synagogue, 2012–; Organist and Choirmaster, Hon. Soc. of Gray's Inn, 1983– (Fellow, 2012). Prof., RAM, 1975–92. Numerous recordings. *Publications:* numerous sacred and secular compositions; chamber operas: The Pied Piper, 1972; The Seacock Bane, 1979; The Last Man, 1983, 2nd edn 2003; The Face, 2012. *Recreations:* sketching, silence. *Address:* 94 Colney Hatch Lane, N10 1EA. *T:* (020) 8883 1933.

**BOWES, Michael Anthony;** QC 2001; a Recorder, since 2000; Deputy High Court Judge, since 2010; *b* 22 Dec. 1956; *s* of late Michael Philip Bowes and of Patricia Bowes; *m* 1987, Amanda Wissler; two *d*. *Educ:* St George's Coll., Weybridge; Manchester Univ. (LLB). Called to the Bar, Middle Temple, 1980, Bencher, 2007; in practice, Western Circuit, 1996–; specialising in criminal and civil fraud, corporate white collar and financial regulatory work; Jt Hd, Outer Temple Chambers, 2012–. Fellow, Goodenough Coll., 2015–. Trustee: Bloomsbury Art Fair Ltd, 2011–; Transparency Internat. UK, 2015–; Not1More, 2018–. Gov., Knighton House Sch., Dorset, 2008–15. *Recreations:* ski-ing, riding, sailing. *Address:* Outer Temple Chambers, 222 Strand, WC2R 1BA. *T:* (020) 7353 6381.

**BOWES, Roger Norman;** Managing Director and Proprietor, Global Information Management Services Ltd, 2005–10; *b* 28 Jan. 1943; *s* of late Russell Ernest Bowes and Sybil Caroline Rose Bowes (*née* Bell); *m* 1st, 1961, Denise Hume Windsor (marr. diss. 1974); one *d*; 2nd, 1977, Ann Rosemary O'Connor (*née* Hamstead) (marr. diss. 1988). *Educ:* Chiswick and Dorking Grammar Schools. Advertisement Executive: Associated Newspapers, 1962–67; IPC/Mirror Gp Newspapers, 1967–70; Marketing Exec./Sales Manager, Mirror Gp, 1970–75; Media Dir, McCann Erickson Advertising, 1976–78; Mirror Gp Newspapers: Adv. Dir, 1978–81; Dep. Chief Exec., 1982–83; Chief Exec., 1984; Man. Dir, Guinness Enterprises, 1985; Chief Executive: Express Gp Newspapers, 1985–86; Aslib, 1989–2004; Chm., Citybridge, 1987–97. *Recreations:* political and military history, cookery, architectural restoration, classic cars.

**BOWES LYON,** family name of **Earl of Strathmore and Kinghorne**.

**BOWES LYON, Sir Simon (Alexander),** KCVO 2005; FCA; director of investment companies; farmer; Lord-Lieutenant of Hertfordshire, 1986–2007; *b* 17 June 1932; *s* of Hon. Sir David Bowes Lyon, KCVO, and Rachel Bowes Lyon (*née* Spender Clay) (*d* 1996); *m* 1966, Caroline, *d* of Rt Rev. Victor Pike, CB, CBE, DD, and of Dorothea Pike; three *s* one *d*. *Educ:* Eton; Magdalen Coll., Oxford (BA). Hon. LLD Herts, 2007. KStJ 1997. *Recreations:* botany, gardening, shooting, music. *Address:* St Paul's Walden Bury, Hitchin, Herts SG4 8BP. *T:* (01438) 871218; 12 Morpeth Mansions, SW1P 1ER. *T:* (020) 7828 8057. *E:* spw@boweslyon.demon.co.uk.
*See also* R. P. Glazebrook.

**BOWEY, Prof. Angela Marilyn,** PhD; Director, Glassencyclopedia.com and Glass-time.com, since 1997; Professor of Business Administration, Strathclyde Business School, University of Strathclyde, Glasgow, 1976–87; *b* 20 Oct. 1940; *d* of Jack Nicholas Peterson and Kathleen (*née* Griffin); *m* 1st, 1960, Miklos Papp; two *s* one *d*; 2nd, 1965, Gregory Bowey (marr. diss. 1980); one *s* one *d*; 3rd, 2001, Prof. Andrew William John Thomson, OBE (*d* 2014). *Educ:* Withington Girls' Sch., Manchester; Univ. of Manchester (BA Econs, PhD). Technical Asst, Nuclear Power Gp, 1961–62; Asst Lectr, Elizabeth Gaskell Coll. of Educn, 1967–68; Manchester Business School: Res. Associate, 1968–69; Res. Fellow, 1969–72; Lectr, 1972–76; Dir, Pay Advice Res. Centre, Glasgow, 1977–86, Gibraltar, 1987–97. Vis. Professor: Admin. Staff Coll. of India, 1975; Western Australian Inst. of Technology, 1976; Univ. of WA, 1977; Prahran Coll. of Advanced Educn, Australia, 1978; Massey Univ., NZ, 1978. ACAS Arbitrator, 1977–92; Dir, Pay and Rewards Res. Centre, 1978–85; Comr, Equal Opportunities Commn, 1980–86; Member: Scottish Econ. Council, 1980–83; Police Adv. Bd (Scotland) (formerly Adv. Panel on Police), 1983–88. Gov., Scottish Police Coll., 1985–88. Owner/operator, Paihia Gym, 1992–; Chair, Rotary Oceania Med. Aid for Children, NZ, 2014–16. Paul Harris Fellow. Editor, Management Decision, 1979–82. Website Ed., Paperweight Collectors' Assoc. Inc., USA, 2007–. *Publications:* Job and Pay Comparisons (with Tom Lupton), 1973, 2nd edn 1974; A Guide to Manpower Planning, 1974, 2nd edn 1977; (with Tom Lupton) Wages and Salaries, 1974, 2nd edn 1982; Handbook of Salary and Wage Systems, 1975, 2nd edn 1982; The Sociology of Organisations, 1976; (with Richard Thorpe and Phil Hellier) Payment Systems and Productivity, 1986, repr. 2015; Managing Salary and Wage Systems, 1987; (jtly) Bagley Glass, 2004, 4th edn 2017; New Zealand Glass, 2005, 2nd edn 2013; London Lampworkers: Pirelli, Bimini and Komaromy glass, 2013; (with Bob Martin) Pirelli Glass, 2016; articles in Brit. Jl of Indust. Relations, Jl of Management Studies, and Management Decision. *Address:* Paihia, Bay of Islands, New Zealand. *Clubs:* Rotary (Bay of Islands), Waitangi Golf (New Zealand).

**BOWEY, Olwyn,** RA 1975 (ARA 1970); practising artist (painter); *b* 10 Feb. 1936; *o d* of James and Olive Bowey. *Educ:* West Hartlepool Sch. of Art; Royal Coll. of Art. One-man shows: Zwemmer Gall., 1961; New Grafton Gall., 1969; also exhibited at Leicester Gall., Royal Academy; work purchased through Chantrey Bequest for Tate Gall., Royal Academy, Min. of Works, etc.

**BOWHAY, Rosalind Louise;** *see* Smyth, R. L.

**BOWIE, Andrew Campbell;** MP (C) West Aberdeenshire and Kincardine, since 2017; *b* Arbroath, 28 May 1987; *s* of Donald Alexander Bowie and Karen Fiona Bowie; *m* 2015, Madeleine Josephine Clarke. *Educ:* Inverurie Acad.; BRNC; Univ. of Aberdeen (MA Hons Hist. and Politics 2013). Jun. Warfare Officer, RN, 2007–10. Mil. Projects Manager, Divex, 2013; Campaign Manager, Cons. Party, 2014–15; Sen. Parly Asst, EP, 2015–16; Hd of Office, Scottish Parlt, 2016–17. PPS, DCMS, 2018, to Prime Minister, 2018–19.

Mem., Work and Pensions Cttee, H of C, 2017–18. *Recreations:* running, football, violin. *Address:* House of Commons, SW1A 0AA. *T:* (020) 7219 2791. *E:* andrew.bowie.mp@parliament.uk.

**BOWIE, Graham Maitland,** CBE 1992; Chief Executive, Lothian Regional Council, 1986–94; *b* 11 Nov. 1931; *s* of John Graham Bowie and Agnes Bowie; *m* 1962, Maureen Jennifer O'Sullivan; one *s* two *d*. *Educ:* Alloa Academy; Univ. of St Andrews (MA); Univ. of Glasgow (LLB). National Service, 1956–58. Asst Sec., Glasgow Chamber of Commerce, 1958–60; Product Planner, Ford Motor Co., 1960–64; Edinburgh Corp. Educn Dept, 1964–69; ILEA, 1969–75; Dir of Policy Planning, Lothian Regional Council, 1975–86. Mem., Nat. Lotteries Charities Bd, 1994–97. *Recreations:* walking, travel, the arts. *Address:* 8 Keith Crescent, Edinburgh EH4 3NH.

**BOWIS, John Crocket,** OBE 1981; Patron, Health First Europe, since 2018 (Chairman, 2009–18); adviser and consultant on health, since 2009; *b* 2 Aug. 1945; *s* of late Thomas Palin Bowis and Georgiana Joyce (*née* Crocket); *m* 1968, Caroline May (*née* Taylor); two *s* one *d*. *Educ:* Tonbridge Sch.; Brasenose Coll., Oxford (MA). Tutor, Cumberland Lodge, Windsor Great Park, 1966–67; Cons. Party Agent, Peterborough, Derby, Harborough and Blaby, 1968–72; Conservative Central Office: National Organiser, Fedn of Cons. Students, 1972–75; Nat. Organiser, Cons. Trade Unionists, 1975–79; Dir of Community Affairs, 1979–81; Campaign Dir, 1981–82, Public Affairs Dir, 1983–87, British Insurance Brokers Assoc.; Press and Parly Consultant, Nat. Fedn of Self-employed and Small Firms, 1982–83. Councillor (C) Royal Bor. of Kingston upon Thames, 1982–86 (Chm. of Educn, 1985–86). MP (C) Battersea, 1987–97; contested (C) same seat, 1997. PPS to Minister for Local Govt and Inner Cities, DoE, 1989–90, to Sec. of State for Wales, 1990–93; Parly Under-Sec. of State, DoH, 1993–96, Dept of Transport, 1996–97. Mem., Select Cttee on Members' Interests, 1987–90; Vice-Chm., All Party Gp on Social Sci., 1988–93; Chm., All Party Somali Gp, 1991–97. Secretary: Cons. Inner Cities Cttee, 1987–89; Cons. Educn Cttee, 1988–89; Cons. Arts and Heritage Cttee, 1988–89; Parliamentary Adviser to: ACFHE, 1987–93; Assoc. for Coll. Management, 1990–93; ATL (formerly AMMA), 1992–93. MEP (C) London Region, 1999–2009. European Parliament: Party spokesman on envmt, health and consumer affairs, 1999–2009; Rapporteur: on food safety, 2000–01; on health and enlargement, 2000–04; on European Centre for Disease Control, 2005–09; on patient mobility, 2005–09; on mental health, 2006–09; on cross border healthcare, 2007–09; Dep. Leader, Cons. MEPs, 2002–04. Special Advr, FIPRA Internat., 2009–19; Member, Advisory Board: Instinctif (formerly Policy Action), 2010–18; Eli Lilley, 2013–; Chm., Health Adv. Bd, GlaxoSmithKline, 2009–; Vice-Pres., Eur. Health Forum Gastein, 2009–; Co-Chair, EGIDE (Sanofi) European Diabetes Experts, 2018–. Chm., Nat. Council for Civil Protection, 1992–93. Advr to WHO for global campaigns on mental health and epilepsy, 1987–99; Internat. Policy Advr to WHO at Inst. of Psychiatry, 1997–2009; Board Member: Inst. of Psychiatry, 1997–99; Internat. Social Service, 1997–2000; Internat. Inst. for Special Needs Offenders, 1998–2008; Churches Educn and Develt Partnership for SA, 1998–2005; SANE and Saneline, 2000–; European Men's Health Forum, 2001–; Mental Disability Advocacy Center - UK, 2008–15; Global Initiative on Psychiatry, 2009–; Gamian Europe, 2009–; TB Vaccine Initiative, 2009–; World Fedn for Mental Health, 2011–. Trustee and Vice-Pres., Share Community, 1990–; Ambassador: Nat. Aids Trust, 1997–; Alzheimer's Soc., 2009–; Patron: Epilepsy Res. UK, 1997–; Dame Vera Lynn Trust, 2009–; President: Torche, 1999–2009; Battersea Cons. Assoc., 2000–; Kingston and Surbiton Cons. Assoc., 2011–; Vice Pres., Parkinson's Disease Soc., 2003–. Director: Battersea Arts Centre, 1991–99; Royal Nat. Theatre, 1992–95; South Bank Centre, 1992–95; Royal Acad. of Dancing, 1992–99. Fellow, Industry and Parlt Trust, 1992. Hon. FRCPsych 2003; Hon. FRCP 2009. Eur. Public Health Alliance Award for Service to Public Health, 2009. *Recreations:* theatre, music, art, sport, watching AFC Wimbledon. *Address:* 44 Howard Road, New Malden KT3 4EA. *E:* johnbowis@aol.com.

**BOWKER, Prof. John Westerdale;** Hon. Canon of Canterbury Cathedral, since 1985; Adjunct Professor of Religion, North Carolina State University, since 1986; Adjunct Professor of Religious Studies, University of Pennsylvania, since 1986; *b* 30 July 1935; *s* of Gordon Westerdale Bowker and Marguerite (*née* Burdick); *m* 1963, Margaret Roper; one *s*. *Educ:* St John's Sch., Leatherhead; Worcester Coll., Oxford (MA); Ripon Hall, Oxford. National Service, RWAFF, N Nigeria, 1953–55. Henry Stephenson Fellow, Sheffield Univ., 1961; Deacon, St Augustine's, Brocco Bank, Sheffield, 1961; Priest and Dean of Chapel, Corpus Christi Coll., Cambridge, 1962; Asst Lectr, 1965, Lectr, 1970, Univ. of Cambridge; Prof. of Religious Studies, Univ. of Lancaster, 1974–85; Dean, 1984–91 and Fellow, 1984–93, Trinity Coll., Cambridge. Gresham Prof. of Divinity, 1992–97; Fellow, Gresham Coll., London, 1997. Lectures: Wilde, Univ. of Oxford, 1972–75; Staley, Rollins Coll., Florida, 1978–79; Public, Univ. of Cardiff, 1984; Riddell, Newcastle Univ., 1985; Boutwood, Univ. of Cambridge, 1985; Harris Meml, Toronto, 1986; Boardman, Univ. of Pa, 1988; Montefiore, Univ. of Southampton, 1989; Scott Holland, London Univ., 1989; Bicentenary, Univ. of Georgetown, Washington, 1989; Heslington, York, 1997: Member: Durham Commn on Religious Educn, 1967–70; Root Commn on Marriage and Divorce, 1967–71; Archbps' Commn on Doctrine, 1977–86; Patron, Marriage Research Inst.; Hon. Pres., Stauros; Vice-President: Inst. on Religion in an Age of Science, 1980; Culture and Animals Foundn, 1984–92; Pres., Christian Action on AIDS, 1987–91. *Publications:* The Targums and Rabbinic Literature, 1969, 2nd edn 1979; Problems of Suffering in Religions of the World, 1970, 3rd edn 1987; Jesus and the Pharisees, 1973; The Sense of God, 1973, 2nd edn 1995; The Religious Imagination and the Sense of God, 1978; Uncle Bolpenny Tries Things Out, 1973; Worlds of Faith, 1983; (ed) Violence and Aggression, 1983; Licensed Insanities: religions and belief in God in the contemporary world, 1987; The Meanings of Death, 1991 (HarperCollins Religious Book Prize, 1993); A Year to Live, 1991; Hallowed Ground: the religious poetry of place, 1993; (ed jtly) Themes in Religious Studies, 1994; Voices of Islam, 1995; Is God a Virus? Genes, Culture and Religion, 1995; World Religions, 1997; The Oxford Dictionary of World Religions, 1997; The Complete Bible Handbook: an illustrated companion, 1998 (Benjamin Franklin Award, 1999); The Concise Oxford Dictionary of World Religions, 2000; The Cambridge Illustrated History of Religions, 2002; God: a brief history, 2002; The Sacred Neuron, 2005; Beliefs that Changed the World, 2007; The Aerial Atlas of the Holy Land, 2008; Conflict and Reconciliation: the contribution of religions, 2008; Knowing the Unknowable: science and religions on God and the universe, 2008; An Alphabet of Animals, 2009; Before the Ending of the Day, 2010; The Message and the Book, 2011; God: a very short introduction, 2014; Why Religions Matter, 2015; Religion Hurts: why religions do harm as well as good, 2018. *Recreations:* books, painting, poetry. *Address:* 14 Bowers Croft, Cambridge CB1 8RP.

**BOWKER, (Steven) Richard,** CBE 2005; FCILT; FCMA; Senior Independent non-executive Director, Football League Ltd, 2012–18; Chair, UK Athletics, 2017–19; *b* 23 April 1966; *s* of Roger William Bowker and Dr Sylvia Grace Bowker; *m* 2002, Madeline Victoria Ivemy; two *s* one *d*. *Educ:* Queen Elizabeth's Grammar Sch., Blackburn; Univ. of Leicester (BA Upper 2nd Cl. Hons Econs and Econ. and Social Hist. 1988). ACMA 1993, FCMA 2003; FCILT (FCIT, FILT 2001); CGMA 2012. Professional musician, 1988–89; Manager, London Underground Ltd, 1989–96; Principal, Babcock & Brown Ltd, 1996–99; Dir, Quasar Associates Ltd, 1999–2000; Gp Commercial Dir, Virgin Gp, 2000–01; Co-Chm., Virgin Rail Gp Ltd, 2000–01 (non-exec. Dir, 1999–2001); Dir, Virgin Atlantic Airways, 2000–01; Chm. and Chief Exec., Strategic Rail Authy, 2001–04; Chief Executive: Partnerships for Schs, 2005–06; Etihad Rail (formerly Union Railway), UAE, 2009–12; Gp Chief Exec., Nat. Express Gp plc, 2006–09. Exec. Advr, Arcadis (formerly Sen. Advr, EC Harris), 2013–16. Non-executive Director: British Waterways, 2004–09 (Vice Chm., 2008–09); Super League (Europe) Ltd, 2014–16; Founder Dir, Criterium Cycles, 2013– (Chm., 2016–); Dir, London Marathon Events Ltd, 2015–17. Mem., Internat. Adv. Council, Assoc. of MBAs, 2003–07. Mem. Council, 2012–17, Mem. Internat. Cttee, 2014–16, FA; Comr, Football Regulatory Authy, 2013–17. Mem. Bd, Countryside Alliance, 2006–09. Vice-President: London Internat. Piano Competition, 2002–; Settle and Carlisle Railway Trust, 2009– (Trustee, 2004–09); Friends of Nat. Railway Mus., York, 2009–; Dep. Pres., Heritage Railway Assoc., 2005–18. Chair, Govs, S. Anselm's Prep. Sch., Bakewell, 2018–. *Recreations:* hill walking, piano, canal boating, wine, Blackburn Rovers FC, running, cycling.

**BOWKETT, Alan John;** venture capitalist and organic farmer; *b* 6 Jan. 1951; *er s* of John and Margaret Bowkett; *m* 1975, Joy Dianne Neale; three *s* two *d*. *Educ:* King Charles I Grammar Sch., Kidderminster; University College London (BSc Econ); London Business Sch. (MSc Econ). Corporate Planning Manager, Lex Service, 1977–83; Corporate Develt Manager, BET, 1983–85; Man. Dir, Boulton & Paul, 1985–87; Chief Executive: United Precision Industries, 1987–91; Berisford Internat., then Berisford plc, 1992–99. Director: Anglian Group, 1992–94; Pallasinvest SA (Luxembourg), 1992–98; Greene King, 1993–2006 (Chm., Audit Cttee, 1997–2006); Chairman: Calder Gp Ltd, 1994–96; Acordis BV, 2000–04; Metzeler APS SA, 2000–05; Doncaster Gp Ltd, 2003–06; Britax plc, 2004–08; Redrow plc, 2007–09; Strix Ltd, 2008–17; Gladedale Gp Ltd, 2009–12; Norwich City FC plc, 2009–15; McCarthy & Stone plc, 2010–13; Avio Gp SpA, 2010–17; Euromedic Bv, 2012–15; Diaverum BV, 2016; Integrated Dental Hldgs Ltd, 2017–; Cambridge Educn Gp Ltd, 2017–. Councillor (C) London Borough of Ealing, 1978–82 (Chm., Social Services); Dep. Chm., Ealing Acton Cons. Assoc., 1982–84. Chm., Univ. of Law, 2012–15; Council Mem., UEA, 1988–94 (Treasurer, 1990–94; Hon. Fellow, 1997). FRSA 1993. *Recreations:* growing vegetables, shooting, opera, Italy, listening to Archers, salmon fishing, watching Norwich City. *Clubs:* Carlton, Royal Automobile, Farmers.

**BOWLBY, Prof. Rachel Helena,** FBA 2007; Professor of Comparative Literature and English, University College London, since 2014; *b* 29 Jan. 1957; *d* of Rt Rev. Ronald Oliver Bowlby, *qv*; two *d*. *Educ:* St Anne's Coll., Oxford (1st Cl. Hon. Mods Latin and Greek Lit. 1977; BA 1st Cl. Hons English 1979); Yale Univ. (PhD Comparative Lit. 1983). University of Sussex: Lectr in English, 1984–90; Sen. Lectr, 1990–92; Reader, 1992–94; Prof., 1994–97; Oxford University: Fellow, St Hilda's Coll., 1997–99; Prof. of English, 1998–99; Prof. of English and Related Lit., Univ. of York, 1999–2004; Lord Northcliffe Prof. of Modern English Lit., UCL, 2004–14; Prof. of Comparative Lit., Princeton Univ., 2013–16. Leverhulme Major Res. Fellow, 2011–13. Lectures: Bateson, Oxford, 2006; Gauss Seminars, Princeton Univ., 2008; Churchill, Univ. of Bristol, 2013; Richard Hoggart, Goldsmiths, Univ. of London, 2018. *Publications:* Just Looking, 1985; Virginia Woolf, 1988; Still Crazy After All These Years: women, writing and psychoanalysis, 1992; Shopping with Freud, 1993; Feminist Destinations and Further Essays on Virginia Woolf, 1997; Carried Away: the invention of modern shopping, 2000; Freudian Mythologies: Greek tragedy and modern identities, 2007; A Child of One's Own: parental stories, 2013; Everyday Stories, 2016; Talking Walking: essays in cultural criticism, 2018. *Address:* School of European Languages, Culture and Society, University College London, Gower Street, WC1E 6BT. *E:* r.bowlby@ucl.ac.uk.

**BOWLBY, Sir Richard Peregrine Longstaff,** 3rd Bt *cr* 1923, of Manchester Square, St Marylebone; *b* 11 Aug. 1941; *s* of Edward John Mostyn Bowlby, CBE, MD (*d* 1990), 2nd *s* of Sir Anthony Alfred Bowlby, 1st Bt, KCB, KCMG, KCVO, and Ursula, *d* of Dr T. G. Longstaff; *S* uncle, 1993; *m* 1963, Xenia, *o d* of R. P. A. Garrett; one *s* one *d*. *Heir*: *s* Benjamin Bowlby [*b* 2 Nov. 1966; *m* 1992, Mylanna Sophia, *er d* of M. C. Colyer; two *s* one *d*]. *Address:* Boundary House, Wyldes Close, NW11 7JB.

**BOWLBY, Rt Rev. Ronald Oliver;** Bishop of Southwark, 1980–91; *b* 16 Aug. 1926; *s* of Oliver and Helena Bowlby; *m* 1956, Elizabeth Trevelyan Monro (*d* 2015); three *s* two *d*. *Educ:* Eton Coll.; Trinity College, Oxford (MA; Hon. Fellow, 1991); Westcott House, Cambridge. Curate of St Luke's, Pallion, Sunderland, 1952–56; Priest-in-charge and Vicar of St Aidan, Billingham, 1956–66; Vicar of Croydon, 1966–72; Bishop of Newcastle, 1973–80; Asst Bishop, Dio. of Lichfield, 1991–2010. Chairman: Hospital Chaplaincies Council, 1975–82; Social Policy Cttee, Bd for Social Responsibility, 1986–90; Mem., Anglican Consultative Council, 1977–85. President: Nat. Fedn of Housing Assocs, 1988–94; Churches' Nat. Housing Coalition, 1991–94. Hon. Fellow, Newcastle upon Tyne Polytechnic, 1980. *Publications:* contrib. Church without Walls, ed Lindars, 1969; contrib. Church and Politics Today, ed Moyser, 1985. *Recreation:* reading. *Address:* Swan Hill House, Swan Hill, Shrewsbury SY1 1NQ.

See also R. H. Bowlby.

**BOWLER, Prof. Peter John,** PhD; FBA 2004; Professor of the History of Science, Queen's University, Belfast, 1992–2009, now Emeritus; *b* 8 Oct. 1944; *s* of Wallace Bowler and Florence Edith Bowler (*née* Moon); *m* 1966, Sheila Mary Holt; one *s* one *d*. *Educ:* King's Coll., Cambridge (BA 1966, MA 1971); Univ. of Sussex (MSc 1967); Univ. of Toronto (PhD 1971). Lectr in Humanities, Science Univ. of Malaysia, Penang, 1972–75; Asst Prof. of Hist., Univ. of Winnipeg, 1975–79; Lectr, 1979–87, Reader, 1987–92, in Hist. and the Philos. of Sci., Queen's Univ., Belfast. MRIA 1993. *Publications:* The Eclipse of Darwinism, 1983, 2nd edn 1992; The Non-Darwinian Revolution, 1988; The Invention of Progress, 1990; Charles Darwin: the man and his influence, 1990; The Fontana History of the Environmental Sciences, 1992; Life's Splendid Drama, 1996; Reconciling Science and Religion, 2001; Monkey Trials and Gorilla Sermons, 2007; Science for All, 2009; Darwin Deleted, 2013; A History of the Future, 2017. *Recreations:* collecting antiquarian science books, walking (when I can find the time). *Address:* School of History and Anthropology, Queen's University, Belfast BT7 1NN. *E:* p.bowler@qub.ac.uk.

**BOWLER, Tim(othy);** novelist and writer; *b* 14 Nov. 1953; *yr s* of Norman and Doreen Bowler; *m* 1st, 1977, Rachel (marr. diss. 2017); 2nd, 2017, Vanessa. *Educ:* Chalkwell Hall Primary Sch.; Westcliff High Sch. for Boys; Univ. of E Anglia (BA Hons Swedish and Scandinavian Studies); Kingston Poly. (PGCE French and German). Forester, 1977; EFL teacher, 1978–79; timber salesman, 1979–82; French and German teacher, 1983–90; Swedish translator, 1990–97; full-time writer, 1997–. Speaker on writing at confs, fests, schs, writers' circles and on radio. Mem., Judging Panel, Costa Book Award, 2010. 15 book awards, both regl and from USA and Europe. *Publications:* Midget, 1994; Dragon's Rock, 1995; River Boy, 1997 (Carnegie Medal, 1998); Shadows, 1999; Storm Catchers, 2001; Starseeker, 2002; Apocalypse, 2004; Blood on Snow, 2004; Walking with the Dead, 2005; Frozen Fire, 2006; Bloodchild, 2008; Buried Thunder, 2011; Sea of Whispers, 2013; Night Runner, 2014; Game Changer, 2015; Blade series: Playing Dead, Book 1, 2008; Closing In, Book 2, 2008; Breaking Free, Book 3, 2009; Running Scared, Book 4, 2009; Fighting Back, Book 5, 2009; Mixing It, Book 6, 2010; Cutting Loose, Book 7, 2010; Risking All, Book 8, 2010; Blade series re-issued as four book series: Enemies, Book 1, 2012; Flight, Book 2, 2012; Firestorm, Book 3, 2012; Endgame, Book 4, 2012. *Recreations:* reading, music, theatre, ballet, cinema, yoga, squash, walking, thinking, dreaming, meditating. *Address:* c/o David Higham Associates, 7th Floor, Waverley House, 7–12 Noel Street, W1F 8GQ. *E:* tim@timbowler.co.uk. *W:* www.timbowler.co.uk.

**BOWLES OF BERKHAMSTED,** Baroness *cr* 2015 (Life Peer), of Bourne End in the County of Hertfordshire; **Sharon Margaret Bowles;** Member (Lib Dem) South East Region, European Parliament, May 2005–2014; non-executive Director, London Stock Exchange plc, since 2014 (non-executive Director, London Stock Exchange Group plc, 2014–16); *b* 12 June 1953; *d* of late Percy Bowles and Florence Bowles; *m* 1981, Andrew Horton; two *s*. *Educ:* Our Lady's Convent, Abingdon; Univ. of Reading (BSc Hons Chem. Physics with Maths 1974); Lady Margaret Hall, Oxford (res. into semiconductors). Chartered Patent Attorney; European Patent Attorney. Trng as patent agent, 1978–81; in practice as Patent Attorney and Trade Mark Attorney, 1981–2014, founded professional practice, subseq. Bowles Horton partnership, 1981. Contested (Lib Dem): Aylesbury, 1992, 1997, Parly elecns; Buckinghamshire and Oxford East, 1994, South East Reg., 1999, 2004, EP elecns. European Parliament: Member: Cttee on Econ. and Monetary Affairs, 2005–14 (Chm., 2009–14); Cttee of Inq. into collapse of Equitable Life Assce Soc., 2006–07; Cttee for Legal Affairs, 2007–14; Special Cttee on Financial and Econ. Crisis, 2009–11; Delegn for relns with countries of SE Asia and ASEAN, 2005–09; Delegn for relns with USA, 2009–14. Mem., Economic Cttee, H of L, 2016–. Chair, Ownership Effect Inquiry, 2017–18 (Report, 2018). Liberal Democrats: Sec., Chilterns Reg., 1990–95; Co-Chm., Internat. Relns Cttee, 2002–06. Vice President: ELDR, 2004–10; Liberal Internat., 2005–07. Hon. LLD Herts, 2018. *Recreation:* music. *Address:* House of Lords, SW1A 0PW. *Club:* National Liberal (Trustee, 2014–).

**BOWLES, Prof. Dianna Joy,** OBE 2003; PhD; Professor of Biochemistry, Centre for Novel Agricultural Products, Department of Biology, University of York, 2008–12, now Emerita; *b* 1 May 1948; *d* of Bertie James Bowles and Cicely (*née* Mee). *Educ:* Univ. of Newcastle upon Tyne (BSc Hons 1970); New Hall, Cambridge (PhD 1973). Research Fellow: Univ. of Kaiserslautern, 1973–75; Univ. of Regensburg, 1975; Weizmann Inst., 1976; Univ. of Cambridge, 1976–77; EMBL, 1978; University of Leeds, 1979–93, Prof., 1991–93; University of York: Prof. of Biochemistry and Co-Founder, Plant Lab., 1994–2000; Weston Prof. of Biochem. and Dir, Centre for Novel Agricultural Products, 2001–08. Scientific Advr, Ownership Bd, MAFF Central Science Lab., 1995–2001. Member: ODA Scientific Adv. Gp, Plant Scis Prog., 1993–97; BBSRC Cttees, 1993–2007; EU Framework 5 External Adv. Gp, 1998–2002; EC DGX11 Directorate Ext. Adv. Gps, 1998–2008; Chair: Theme 2 of Framework 7 Work Prog., Food, Agriculture and Biotechnol., EC, 2006–08; Technol. Strategy Bd, Knowledge Transfer Network, Biosci. for Business, 2006–08; Dir, EPOBIO, EU Sci. to Support Policy, 2005–07; Mem. Bd and Chm., Plant Sector Adv. Gp, Bioscience KTN, 2008–12. Mem., EMBO, 2001. Founder, 2001, Chm. Bd of Trustees, 2002–, Heritage GeneBank, subseq. Sheep Trust. Bill Gates Grantee and project leader for establishing robust supply chain of artemisinin, 2006–12. Founding Ed., and Ed.-in-Chief, Plant Jl, 1991–2002. *Publications:* primary res. articles, reviews, and gen. sci. articles for non-specialist audiences. *Recreations:* Upper Nidderdale, Wasdale Head, Herdwick sheep (Pres., Herdwick Sheep Breeders Assoc., 2003). *Address:* Department of Biology (Area 9), University of York, Heslington, York YO10 5DD.

**BOWLES, Huw Martin Richard;** non-executive Finance Director and Growth Coach, Trecelyn Ltd, since 2012; *b* Tredegar, 27 Nov. 1966; *s* of late Donald Bowles and of Pauline Bowles; *m* 1999, Emma Foster; two *s*. *Educ:* Newbridge Comp. Sch.; Pontypool Coll.; Univ. of Reading (BSc Agric. 1989). Mem., ICAEW, 1993. Auditor: Hays Allan, 1990–95; KPMG, 1995–96; Sen. Consultant, KPMG Financial Mgt, 1996–2000; Finance Director: bEurope Ltd, 2000–01; Investis Ltd, 2001–03; Chief Operating Officer, Organic Milk Suppliers Co-operative Ltd, 2004–12; Finance Dir, Eccentric Gin Co. Ltd, 2014–16. Chm., 2009–12, Co. Sec., 2013–15, Organic Trade Bd; Mem. Council, Soil Assoc., 2009–12. Mem., Somerset Rugby Referees Soc. Gov., Sherston C of E Primary Sch., 2008–11. *Recreations:* Rugby coaching, refereeing and watching, music watching, listening and playing. *E:* huw@bowles.net.

**BOWLES, Peter;** actor; *b* 16 Oct. 1936; *s* of Herbert Reginald Bowles and Sarah Jane (*née* Harrison); *m* 1961, Susan Alexandra Bennett; two *s* one *d*. *Educ:* High Pavement Grammar Sch., Nottingham; RADA (schol.; Kendal Prize 1955). London début in Romeo and Juliet, Old Vic, 1956; *theatre* includes: Happy Haven, Platonov, Royal Court, 1960; Bonne Soupe, Wyndham's, 1961; Afternoon Men, Arts, 1962; Absent Friends, Garrick, 1975; Dirty Linen, Arts, 1976; Born in the Gardens, Globe, 1980; Some of My Best Friends Are Husbands, nat. tour, 1985; The Entertainer, Shaftesbury, 1986; Canaries Sometimes Sing, Albery, 1987; Man of the Moment, Globe, 1990; Otherwise Engaged (also dir), nat. tour, 1992; Separate Tables, Albery, 1993; Pygmalion, Chichester, 1994; Present Laughter, nat. tour, 1994, Aldwych, 1996; In Praise of Love, Apollo, 1995; Gangster No 1, Almeida, 1995; The School for Wives, Piccadilly, 1997; Major Barbara, The Misanthrope, Piccadilly, 1998; Sleuth, tour, 1999; Hedda Gabler, tour, 1999; The Beau, The Royal Family, Th. Royal, Haymarket, 2001; Sleuth, Apollo, 2002; Our Song, nat. tour, 2003; Wait Until Dark, Garrick, 2003; The Old Masters, Comedy, 2004; The Unexpected Man, nat. tour, 2005; Joe & I, King's Head, 2005; Hay Fever, Th. Royal, Haymarket, 2006; The Waltz of the Toreadors, Chichester, 2007; Relatively Speaking, nat. tour, 2008; Loves Labour's Lost, Rose Th., Kingston, 2008; Swan Song, The Browning Version, Bath Th. Royal, 2009; The Rivals, Bath Th. Royal, 2010, transf. Th. Royal, Haymarket, 2011; The Governess, UK tour, 2013; The Exorcist, Birmingham Rep, 2016, transf. Phoenix, 2017; *films* include: Blow Up, 1966; The Charge of the Light Brigade, 1967; Laughter in the Dark, 1968; A Day in the Death of Joe Egg, 1970; The Steal, 1994; The Hollywood Ten, 2000; Gangster No 1 (Exec. Producer); Colour Me Kubrick, 2004; Freebird, 2008; The Bank Job, 2008; Lilting, 2014; Together, 2018; *TV films* include: Shadow on the Sun, 1988; Running Late (also co-prod), 1992; Little White Lies, 1998; Love and War in the Apennines, 2001; Ballet Shoes, 2007; *television series* include: Rumpole of the Bailey, 1976–92; To the Manor Born, 1979–82, 2007; Only when I Laugh, 1979–82; The Bounder, 1982–83; The Irish RM, 1983–85; Lytton's Diary, 1984–86 (also co-created series); Executive Stress, 1987–88; Perfect Scoundrels, 1990–92 (also co-created series); Jericho, 2005; The Life of Rock with Brian Pern, 2016; Murder, 2016; Victoria, 2016–17, 2019. Comedy Actor of the Year, Pye Awards, 1984; ITV Personality of the Year, Variety Club of GB, 1984. Hon. DLitt Nottingham Trent, 2002. *Publications:* (autobiog.) Ask Me If I'm Happy, 2010; Behind the Curtain: the job of acting, 2012. *Recreations:* British art, physical jerks. *Address:* c/o Conway Van Gelder Grant Ltd, 3rd Floor, 8–12 Broadwick Street, W1F 8HW.

**BOWLES, Thomas Henry Charles P.;** *see* Parker Bowles.

**BOWLES, Timothy John;** Master of the Senior (formerly Supreme) Court, Chancery Division, 1999–2018; *b* 20 March 1951; *s* of late Arthur Ernest Bowles and of Elizabeth Mary Bowles; *m* 2018, Jane O'Hare. *Educ:* Downside Sch.; Durham Univ.; Inns of Ct Sch. of Law. FCIArb 1994. Called to the Bar, Gray's Inn, 1973 (Mould Schol.); Mem. (*ad eund.*), Lincoln's Inn, 1990, Bencher, 2016; in practice at the Bar, 1973–99; Dep. Chancery Master, 1996–99, 2018–. Legal Chairman: South and South Eastern Rent Assessment Panel, 1994–2001; London Rent Assessment Panel, 1997–2001; Dep. Chm., Agricl Land Tribunal, 1995–2013. Regl Judge, First-tier Property Chamber, Agric. and Drainage Div., 2013–. Gov., King Edward VI Grammar Sch. (The Royal Grammar Sch.), Guildford, 2001–04. *Publications:* (ed) Civil Court Practice, annually 2001–. *Recreations:* sailing, cricket. *Clubs:* Bar Yacht; Merrow Cricket, Buccaneers Cricket.

**BOWLEY, Martin Richard;** QC 1981; a Recorder of the Crown Court, 1979–88; *b* 29 Dec. 1936; *s* of late Charles Colin Stuart Bowley and Mary Evelyn Bowley; partner, 1976, Julian Marquez Bedoya (*d* 1990). *Educ:* Magdalen Coll. Sch., Oxford; Queen's Coll., Oxford (Styring Exhibnr, 1955; MA; BCL 1961). National Service, 1955–57: commnd Pilot Officer as a Fighter Controller; served 2nd Tactical Air Force, 1956–57. Called to the Bar, Inner Temple, 1962 (Bencher, 1994; Master of the Revels, 2002–10); Midland and Oxford Circuit, 1963–2002; Member: Senate and Bar Council, 1985–86; Gen. Council of Bar, 1987–88, 1989–94 (Treas., 1992–94); Chm., Bar Cttee, 1987. Dir, Barco, 2001–05. Member: Lord Chancellor's Standing Commn on Efficiency, 1986–87; Marre Cttee on Future of Legal Profession, 1987–88; Home Office Steering Gp on Sexual Offences Law Reform, 1999–2000; CPS Wkg Pty on Prosecuting Homophobic Hate Crimes, 2002. Pres., Bar Lesbian and Gay Gp, 1994–. Stonewall Lectr, 1994. Trustee, Bar Representation Unit, 1997–2001. Chm., Questors Theatre, 1972–84 and 1988–93 (Sec., 1963–72; Hon. Life Mem., 1986); Mem. Standing Cttee, Little Theatre Guild of GB, 1974–84 (Vice-Chm., 1979–81, Chm., 1981–84; Hon. Associate, 1997). Mem., Stonewall Gp, 1999–. Mem. Editl Bd, Counsel, 1992–2009. *Publications:* (contrib.) Advising Gay and Lesbian Clients, 1999; Friends and Families (memoir), 2009; contrib. to nat. and legal periodicals. *Recreations:* playing at theatre, watching cricket, island hopping, supporting Stonewall and Terrence Higgins Trust. *Address:* Flat E, 23/24 Great James Street, WC1N 3ES. *T:* (020) 7831 1674. *Clubs:* Garrick, MCC, Surrey CC.

**BOWLING, Frank,** OBE 2008; RA 2005; artist; *b* 26 Feb. 1934; *s* of Richard Sheridan Bowling and Agatha Elizabeth Franklin Bowling; *m* 2013, Rachel Scott; two *s* and two step *d* (and one *s* decd). *Educ:* Royal Coll. of Art (ARCA); Slade Sch., Univ. of London. Tutor, Camberwell Sch. of Arts and Crafts, 1968–83; Lectr, Reading Univ., 1964–66; Instructor, Columbia Univ., NY, 1968–69; Assistant Professor: Douglass Coll., Rutgers Univ., NJ, 1969–70; Massachusetts Coll. of Art, Boston, 1970–71; Artist-in-residence, Rhode Is. Sch. of Design, 1974–75; Lectr, Sch. of Visual Arts, NY, 1975–76; Tutor, Byam Shaw Sch. of Painting and Sculpture, 1975–86; Artist-in-residence, Skowhegan Sch. of Painting and Sculpture, Maine, 1984. John Simon Guggenheim Meml Fellow, 1967 and 1973. *Solo exhibitions:* Grabowski Gall., London, 1962, 1963; Whitney Mus. of Amer. Art, NY, 1971; Gall. Center for Inter-Amer. Relations, 1973–74; Tibor de Nagy, NY, freq. exhibns 1976–89; Serpentine Gall., 1986; Bowling Through the Decade, RWEA, 1989; Nat. Acad. of Scis, Washington, 1993; Bowling Through the Century, De La Warr Pavilion, Bexhill, 1997; Center for Art and Culture, Brooklyn, 1997; Aljira Center for the Arts, Newark, 2003; Frank Bowling: 4 Decades with Color, Phillips Mus. of Art, Lancaster, Pa, 2004; Arts Club, London, 2007; Rollo Contemporary Art, 2010; Tate Britain, 2012; Spanierman Gall., NY, 2012; Hales Gall., London, 2012; Traingone, Spritmuseum, Stockholm, 2014; Map Paintings, Dallas Mus. of Arts, Texas, 2015; Mappa Mundi, monumental paintings, Haus der Kunst, Munich, 2017; Irish Mus. of Modern Art, Dublin, 2018; Sharjah Foundn, UAE, 2018; Tate Britain (retrospective), 2019. Contributing Ed., Artsmagazine, 1969–72. Jt Founder, Young Commonwealth Artists Gp, 1958–63; Chm., London Gp, 1962–66. Shakespeare Quarto Centenary Commn, 1963. Hon. Fellow: Arts Inst., Bournemouth, 2006; UAL, 2013. Hon. DA Wolverhampton, 2007. Grand Prize for Contemporary Art, First World Fest. of Negro Art, Dakar, Senegal, 1966; Pollock Krasner Award, 1992, 1998. *Recreations:* cricket, athletics. *Address:* 8A John Islip Street, SW1P 4PY. *T:* (020) 7821 7065; PO Box 023703, Brooklyn, NY 11202, USA. *T:* (718) 6252579. *Clubs:* Chelsea Arts, Royal Over-Seas League.

**BOWMAN, Prof. Alan Keir,** PhD, DLitt; FBA 1994; Camden Professor of Ancient History, University of Oxford, 2002–10; Fellow, 2002–10, Emeritus Fellow, 2015, and Principal, 2011–15, Brasenose College, Oxford (Acting Principal, 2010–11); *b* Manchester, 23 May 1944; *s* of late Cyril Bowman and Freda (*née* Bowman); *m* 1966, Jacqueline Frayman; one *s* one *d*. *Educ:* Manchester Grammar Sch.; Queen's Coll., Oxford (MA; Hon. Fellow, 2006); Univ. of Toronto (MA, PhD 1969); DLitt Oxon 2012. Canada Council Postdoctoral Fellow, 1969–70; Asst Prof. of Classics, Rutgers Univ., 1970–72; Lectr in Ancient Hist., Manchester Univ., 1972–77; Oxford University: Official Student, Christ Church, 1977–2002, Emeritus Student, 2002; Sen. Censor, Christ Church, 1988–90; Lectr in Ancient Hist., 1977–2002; Dir, Centre for Study of Ancient Documents, 1995–. Vis. Mem., Inst. for Advanced Study, Princeton, 1976, 1981; British Acad. Res. Reader, 1991–93. Chm., Roman Res. Trust, 2000–2009; Pres., Soc. for the Promotion of Roman Studies, 2001–05; Vice-Pres. (Humanities), British Acad., 2014–18. FSA 1999–2017. *Publications:* The Town Councils of Roman Egypt, 1971; (with J. D. Thomas) The Vindolanda Writing-Tablets, 1983, vol. II 1994, vol. III 2003; Egypt after the Pharaohs, 1986, 3rd edn 1996; Life and Letters on the Roman Frontier: Vindolanda and its people, 1994, 2nd edn 1998 (British Archaeological Book Award, 1998), 3rd edn 2003; (jtly) Literacy and Power in the Ancient World, 1994; (ed jtly) The Cambridge Ancient History, 2nd edn, Vol. X 1996, Vol. XI 2000, Vol. XII 2005; (ed jtly) Agriculture in Egypt from Pharaonic to modern times, 1998; (ed jtly) Quantifying the Roman Economy, 2009; (ed jtly) Settlement, Urbanization and Population, 2011; (ed jtly) The Roman Agricultural Economy, 2013; contrib. learned jls. *Recreations:* photography, music, cricket, tennis, walking. *Address:* Brasenose College, Oxford OX1 4AJ. *T:* (01865) 288293, 288255.

**BOWMAN, Sir Charles (Edward Beck),** Kt 2019; Partner, PricewaterhouseCoopers LLP (formerly Price Waterhouse), since 1995; Lord Mayor of London, 2017–18; *b* London, 8 Dec. 1961; *s* of John Bowman and Jenny Bowman; *m* 1996, Samantha Kemball; two *d*. *Educ:* Uppingham Sch.; Univ. of Bristol (BA Arch.). Chartered Accountant 1986; FCA 1996. Joined Price Waterhouse, 1983. Alderman, City of London, 2013–; Sheriff, City of London, 2015–16. *Recreations:* art, architecture, golf, tennis. *E:* charles.bowman@pwc.com. *Clubs:* MCC, Canning; Royal St George's Golf, Royal Worthington and Newmarket Golf, Royal and Ancient Golf.

**BOWMAN, Claire Margaret;** *see* Makin, C. M.

**BOWMAN, Edward Thomas K.;** *see* Kellett-Bowman.

**BOWMAN, Sir (Edwin) Geoffrey,** KCB 2004 (CB 1991); First Parliamentary Counsel, 2002–06; *b* Blackpool, Lancs, 27 Jan. 1946; *er s* of late John Edwin Bowman and Lillian Joan Bowman (*née* Nield); *m* 1969, Carol Margaret, *er d* of late Alexander Ogilvie and Ethel Ogilvie; two *s* one *d*. *Educ:* Roundhay Sch., Leeds; Trinity Coll., Cambridge (Senior Scholar; BA 1st cl., LLB 1st cl., MA, LLM). Called to Bar, Lincoln's Inn (Cassel Scholar), 1968, Bencher, 2002; in practice, Chancery Bar, 1969–71; joined Parliamentary Counsel Office, 1971 (seconded to Law Commission, 1977–79, 1996–98); Dep. Parly Counsel, 1981–84; Parly Counsel, 1984–2002. Hon. QC 2006. Hon. LLD London, 2007. *Publications:* The Elements of Conveyancing (with E. L. G. Tyler), 1972; contrib. legal jls. *Recreations:* music (bassoon, curtal, recorder), history. *Address:* c/o Parliamentary Counsel Office, 1 Horse Guards Road, SW1A 2HQ. *T:* (020) 7276 6572. *Club:* Les Amis du Basson Français (Paris).

**BOWMAN, Eric Joseph;** consultant, since 1986; *b* 1 June 1929; *s* of late Joseph John Bowman and Lilley Bowman; *m* 1951, Esther Kay; one *d. Educ:* Stationers' Company's School; College of Estate Management. FRICS. Private practice, 1945–51; Royal Engineers, 1951–53; private practice, 1953–54; Min. of Works, 1954–63; Min. of Housing and Local Govt, 1963–73; Directorate of Diplomatic and Post Office Services, MPBW, later DoE, 1973–80; Directorate of Quantity Surveying Services, DoE, 1980–83; Dir of Building and Quantity Surveying Services, PSA, DoE, 1983–86. *Recreations:* fly fishing, walking, swimming, gardening, reading, crown green bowls. *Address:* Mearsons Farm, Hubbersty Head, Crosthwaite, near Kendal, Cumbria LA8 8JB. *T:* (01539) 568400.

**BOWMAN, Sir Geoffrey;** *see* Bowman, Sir E. G.

**BOWMAN, James Thomas,** CBE 1997; counter-tenor; *b* Oxford, 6 Nov. 1941; *s* of Benjamin and Cecilia Bowman (*née* Coote). *Educ:* Ely Cathedral Choir Sch.; King's Sch., Ely; New Coll., Oxford (MA (History) 1967; DipEd 1964; Hon. Fellow, 1998). Lay Vicar, Westminster Abbey, 1969–75; Teacher of Voice, GSM, 1983–92; Gentleman in Ordinary, HM Chapel Royal, St James's Palace, 2000–09. Many concert performances with Early Music Consort, 1967–76; operatic performances with: English Opera Gp, 1967; Sadler's Wells Opera, 1970–; Glyndebourne Festival Opera, 1970–; Royal Opera, Covent Gdn, 1972; Sydney Opera, Australia, 1978; Opéra Comique, Paris, 1979; Le Châtelet, Paris, 1982; Geneva, 1983; Scottish Opera, 1985; La Scala, Milan, 1988, 1991; La Fenice, Venice, 1991; Paris Opera, 1991; Badisches Staatstheater, Karlsruhe, 1984; in USA at Santa Fe and Wolf Trap Festivals, Dallas and San Francisco Operas; at Aix-en-Provence Fest., 1979; operatic roles include: Oberon, in A Midsummer Night's Dream; Endymion, in La Calisto; the Priest, in Taverner; Polinesso, in Ariodante; Apollo, in Death in Venice; Astron, in The Ice Break; Ruggiero in Alcina; title rôles: Giulio Cesare; Tamerlano; Xerxes; Scipione; Giustino; Orlando; Ottone. Extensive discography of opera, oratorio and contemporary music. Pres., Holst Singers, 1997–; Vice-Pres., Bach Choir, 2006–. Mem., Royal Soc. of Musicians, 2004. Hon. FRSCM 2012. Hon. DMus Newcastle, 1996. Medal, City of Paris, 1992. Officier, Ordre des Arts et des Lettres (France), 1995. *Recreations:* ecclesiastical architecture, collecting records. *Club:* Athenæum.

**BOWMAN, Sir Jeffery (Haverstock),** Kt 1991; FCA; Chairman: Mid Essex Hospital Services NHS Trust, 1993–99; Masthead Insurance Underwriting PLC, 1993–99; *b* 3 April 1935; *s* of Alfred Haverstock Bowman and Doris Gertrude Bowman; *m* 1963, Susan Claudia Bostock; one *s* two *d. Educ:* Winchester Coll. (schol.); Trinity Hall, Cambridge (major schol.; BA Hons 1st cl. in Law). Served RHG, 1953–55 (commnd, 1954). Price Waterhouse: articled in London, 1958; NY, 1963–64; admitted to partnership, 1966; Mem., Policy Cttee, 1972–91; Dir of Tech. Services, 1973–76; Dir, London Office, 1979–81; Sen. Partner, 1982–91; Chm., Price Waterhouse Europe, 1988–93; Jt Chm., Price Waterhouse World Firm, 1992–93. Dir, Gibbs Mew, 1995–97. Auditor, Duchy of Cornwall, 1971–93. Vice-Pres., Union of Ind. Cos, 1989–93; Member: Council, ICAEW, 1986–90 (Mem., Accounting Standards Cttee, 1982–87); Council, Industrial Soc., 1985–93; Economic and Financial Policy Cttee, CBI, 1987–93; City Capital Markets Cttee, 1989–93; Council, Business in the Community, 1985–91. Chairman: Court of Appeal (Civil Div.) Review, 1996–97; Crown Office Review, 1999–2000. Trustee, 1995–2003, Queen's Trustee, 1998–2003, Royal Botanic Gdns, Kew. Gov., Brentwood Sch., 1985–97. FRSA 1989. Hon. Bencher, Inner Temple, 1998. *Recreations:* golf, opera, gardening, sailing. *Address:* Leeze House, 74 East Street, Coggeshall, Colchester CO6 1SL. *T:* (01376) 793938. *Club:* Garrick.

**BOWMAN, Dr John Christopher,** CBE 1986; PhD; FRSB; independent environmental consultant, 1993–2001; Managing Director (Europe and Africa), Brown & Root Environmental, 1991–93; *b* 13 Aug. 1933; *s* of M. C. Bowman and C. V. Simister; *m* 1961, S. J. Lorimer; three *d. Educ:* Manchester Grammar Sch.; Univ. of Reading (BSc); Univ. of Edinburgh (PhD). Geneticist, later Chief Geneticist, Thornbers, Mytholmroyd, Yorks, 1958–66. Post-doctoral Fellow, North Carolina State Univ., Raleigh, NC, USA, 1964–65; University of Reading: Prof. of Animal Production, 1966–81; Head of Dept of Agric., 1967–71; Dir, Univ. Farms, 1967–78; Dir, Centre for Agricl Strategy, 1975–81; Sec., NERC, 1981–89; Chief Exec., NRA, 1989–91. Dir, Certa Foundn, 1998–2001. Chm., Sonning Parish Council, 1994–98. Mem., Cannington Coll. Corp., 2002–04. Trustee, Somerset Community Foundn, 2005–14. FRSA 1976 (Chair, Forum for Envmtl and Sustainable Develt Awards, 2005–11). Hon. DSc Cranfield, 1990. *Publications:* An Introduction to Animal Breeding, 1974; Animals for Man, 1977; (with P. Susmel) The Future of Beef Production in the European Community, 1979; (jtly) Hammond's Farm Animals, 1983. *Recreations:* golf, gardening, bridge. *Address:* 3 Nut Tree Farm, 2 Lower Street, Merriott, Som TA16 5NG.

**BOWMAN, Mark;** Director General, International Finance, HM Treasury, since 2013; *b* Chelmsford, 23 Sept. 1970; *s* of Jeffery and Susan Bowman; *m* 2004, Tabitha Jay; two *s* one *d. Educ:* Winchester Coll.; Univ. of Bristol (BSc); Univ. of Warwick (MSc). ODI Fellow, Min. of Planning and Finance, Mozambique, 1993–95; HM Treasury, 1995–2011: Principal Private Sec. to Chancellor of Exchequer, 2001–04; Hd, Internat. Poverty Reduction Team, 2005; Director: Internat. Finance, 2006–08; Budget and Tax, 2008–10; Strategy, Planning and Budget, 2010–11; Dir Gen., W Africa, ME, Security and Humanitarian Response, then Humanitarian, Security, Conflict and Internat. Finance, DFID, 2011–13. *Recreations:* sailing, tennis, photography, family. *Address:* 34 Boscombe Road, W12 9HU; HM Treasury, 1 Horse Guards Road, SW1A 2HQ. *E:* mark.bowman@hmtreasury.gsi.gov.uk.

**BOWMAN, Pamela Margaret Munro;** Sheriff at Glasgow, 2003–10; *b* 1 Aug. 1944; *d* of late James M. Wright and Jean Wright; *m* 1967, Bernard Neil Bowman; two *d. Educ:* Beacon Sch., Bridge of Allan; St Andrews Univ. (LLB). Admitted as solicitor and NP, 1967; Partner, Bowman, Solicitors, Dundee and Forfar, 1980–97; Temp. Sheriff, 1995–97; Floating Sheriff, 1997–99; Sheriff of Glasgow and Strathkelvin, 1999–2001; Sheriff of Grampian, Highland and Islands at Aberdeen, 2001–03. Mem. Bd, Scottish Children's Reporter Admin, 2003–10. *Recreations:* theatre, dancing.

**BOWMAN, Penelope Jill;** *see* Watkins, P. J.

**BOWMAN, Philip,** FCA; Chief Executive, Smiths Group plc, 2007–15; *b* Melbourne, Australia, 14 Dec. 1952; *s* of late Thomas Patrick Bowman and Norma Elizabeth (*née* Deravin). *Educ:* Westminster Sch.; Pembroke Coll., Cambridge (MA). FCA 1983. Price Waterhouse, London, 1974–78; Gibbs Bright & Co. Pty Ltd, Melbourne, 1978–83; Granite Industries Inc., Atlanta, 1983–85; Bass plc, London, 1985–95: Finance Dir, 1991–94; Chief Exec., Retail Div., 1994–95; Finance Dir, Coles Myer Ltd, Melbourne, 1995; Chm., Liberty plc, 1998–2000; Chief Executive: Allied Domecq plc, 1999–2005; Scottish Power plc, 2006–07. Chairman: Coral Eurobet Hldgs, 2004–05; Miller Gp Ltd, 2012–14; Miller Gp (UK) Ltd, 2014; non-executive Director: BSkyB Gp plc, 1994–2003; Berry Bros & Rudd, 2006–16; Better Capital Ltd, 2009–; Sen. Ind. Dir, Burberry Gp plc, 2002–17; Dir, Scottish & Newcastle plc, 2006–08. Mem. Adv. Bd, Alchemy Partners, 2000–09. *Recreations:* scuba diving, entomology, opera, computers and electronics. *Clubs:* Victoria Racing, Royal Automobile of Victoria, National Golf (Vic).

**BOWMAN, Richard Alan;** Master of the Supreme Court, Chancery Division, 1996–2004; *b* 3 Oct. 1943; *s* of Harry Bowman and Gladys Bowman (*née* Croft); *m* 1970, Joanna Mary Lodder; two *s* one *d. Educ:* Clifton; St George's Sch., Newport, RI; Keble Coll., Oxford (MA). FCIArb 1995. Admitted solicitor, 1970; Dep. Chancery Master, 1988–96. Chm., Legal Aid Commn, General Synod of C of E, 1996–2011. Accredited Mediator, 2005–12. *Recreations:* Trollope, lunch. *Address:* Smithy House, Tormarton, Badminton, S Glos GL9 1HU.

**BOWMAN, Sarah Meredith;** District Judge, Principal Registry (Family Division), 1993–2014; *b* 24 May 1949; *d* of late Alexander Dennis Bowman and Jean Bowman; *m* 1984, Jake Downey (marr. diss. 2012); three *s. Educ:* Notting Hill and Ealing High Sch.; Leeds Univ. (BA). Called to the Bar, Middle Temple, 1976; Barrister, 1976–93. *Recreations:* my sons, my grandchildren, walking, bridge.

**BOWMAN, Dr Sheridan Gail Esther,** FSA; Keeper, Department of Conservation, Documentation and Science, British Museum, 2002–05; *b* Westlock, Alta, Canada, 11 March 1950; *o d* of Otto and Eva Bowman. *Educ:* Whitehaven County Grammar Sch., Cumbria; St Anne's Coll., Oxford (Open Scholar; MA; DPhil Physics, 1976); Chelsea Coll., London (MSc Maths, 1981); (extramural) London Univ. (Dip. in Archaeol., 1985). FSA 1987 (a Vice Pres., 1993). British Museum: Scientific Officer, 1976; Keeper, Dept of Scientific Res., 1989–2002. *Publications:* Radiocarbon Dating, 1990; (ed) Science and the Past, 1991; papers on scientific techniques, particularly dating, applied to archaeology. *Recreations:* heath and fell walking, gardening, theatre.

**BOWMAN, Victoria Jane, (Vicky);** Director, Myanmar Centre for Responsible Business, since 2013; *b* 12 June 1966; *d* of Dr Frank Neville Hosband Robinson and Daphne Isabel (*née* Coulthard); *m* 1st, 1991, Mark Andrew Bowman (marr. diss. 2001); 2nd, 2006, Htein Lin; one *d. Educ:* Oxford High Sch. for Girls; Pembroke Coll., Cambridge (BA Hons Natural Scis; Hon. Fellow 2016); Univ. of Chicago. Entered FCO, 1988; Third, later Second, Sec., Rangoon, 1990–93; FCO, 1993–96; Spokeswoman, UK Repn to EU, 1996–99; Mem., Cabinet of Eur. Comr for Ext. Relns, 1999–2002; Ambassador to Burma (Union of Myanmar), 2002–06; Hd, Africa Dept (Southern), FCO, 2006–08; Jt Dir, Global and Econ. Issues, FCO, 2008–11; Global Practice Leader Ext. Affairs, Rio Tinto, 2011–13. DUniv Bradford, 2017. *Publications:* On the Road to Mandalay: translation of writings by Mya Than Tint, 1996. *Recreations:* travel, art, languages, translating Burmese fiction and poetry. *Address:* Myanmar Centre for Responsible Business, 6(a) Shinsawpu Road, Kayinchan Qtr, Ahlone, Yangon, Myanmar.

**BOWN, Prof. Lalage Jean,** OBE 1977; FRSE; FAcSS; FEIS; CCIPD; Director, Department of Adult and Continuing Education, University of Glasgow, 1981–92, now Professor Emeritus; *b* 1 April 1927; *d* of late Arthur Mervyn Bown, MC and Dorothy Ethel (*née* Watson); two foster *d. Educ:* Wycombe Abbey Sch.; Cheltenham Ladies' Coll.; Somerville Coll., Oxford (MA); Oxford Post-grad. Internship in Adult Education. FEIS 1990; FRSE 1991; CCIPD (FIPD 1993). Resident Tutor: University Coll. of Gold Coast, 1949–55; Makerere University Coll., Uganda, 1955–59; Asst Dir, then Dep. Dir, Extramural Studies, Univ. of Ibadan, Nigeria, 1960–66; Dir, Extramural Studies and Prof. (*ad personam*), Univ., of Zambia, 1966–70; Prof. of Adult Educn, Ahmadu Bello Univ., Nigeria, 1971–76, Univ. of Lagos, Nigeria, 1977–79; Dean of Educn, Univ. of Lagos, 1979–80; Vis. Fellow, Inst. of Development Studies, 1980–81. Hon. Professor: Internat. Centre for Educn in Develt, Warwick Univ., 1992–97; Inst. of Educn, Univ. of London, 1998–99; James Coleman Meml Lectr, UCLA, 1991; UNESCO Internat. Literacy Lectr, 2009. Member: Bd, British Council, 1981–89; Scottish Community Educn Council, 1982–88; Exec. Cttee, Scottish Inst. of Adult and Continuing Educn, 1982–88; Bd, Network Scotland, 1983–88; Bd of Trustees, Nat. Museums of Scotland, 1987–97; Council, Insite Trust, 1987–95; Bd of Trustees, Womankind Worldwide, 1988–96; Interim Trustee, Books for Develt, 1987–90; British Mem., Commonwealth Standing Cttee on Student Mobility and Higher Educn Co-operation, 1989–94; Trustee, Education Action (formerly World Univ. Service, UK), 1997–2003; Mem. Bd, Council for Educn in the Commonwealth, 2000–07 (Chm., Wkg Gp on Student Mobility, 1998–2000; Jt Dep. Vice-Chair, 2003–06); Governor, Inst. of Develt Studies, 1982–91; President: Develt Studies Assoc., 1984–86; British Comparative and Internat. Educn Soc., 1985–86; Vice-President: WEA, 1989–95 (Hon. Vice-Pres., 1984–88); Commonwealth Assoc. for Educn and Trng of Adults, 1990–93; Hon. Pres., British Assoc. for Literacy in Develt, 1993–98. Patron: African Families Foundn, 2001–; Adult Educn 100, 2019; Trustee, Britain Nigeria Educnl (formerly Alhaji Tafawa Balewa Meml) Trust, 2005–17. Hon. Vice-Pres., Townswomen's Guilds, 1984–2005. Hon. Life Member: People's Educnl Assoc., Ghana, 1973; African Adult Educn Assoc., 1976; NIACE, 2007. FAcSS (AcSS 2002); Paul Harris Fellow, RIBI, 2015. DUniv: Open, 1975; Paisley, 1993; Stirling, 1994; Dr (*hc*) Edinburgh, 1993; Hon. DLitt: Glasgow, 2002; University Centre Shrewsbury, 2018. William Pearson Tolley Medal, Syracuse Univ., USA, 1975; Meritorious Service Award, Nigerian Nat. Council for Adult Educn, 1979; Symons Medal, ACU, 2001; World Teachers' Day Award, Commonwealth Secretariat, 2003; Internat. Adult and Continuing Educn Hall of Fame, 2009; Distinguished Africanist Award, African Studies Assoc. (UK), 2012. *Publications:* Report of the Tongu Rural Survey, 1953; (ed with Michael Crowder) Proceedings of First International Congress of Africanists, 1964; (ed) Two Centuries of African English, 1973; (ed) Adult Education in Nigeria: the next 10 years, 1975; A Rusty Person is Worse than Rusty Iron, 1976; Lifelong Learning: prescription for progress, 1979; (ed with S. H. O. Tomori) A Handbook of Adult Education for West Africa, 1980; (ed with J. T. Okedara) An Introduction to Adult Education: a multi-disciplinary and cross-cultural approach for developing countries, 1980; Preparing the Future: women, literacy and development, 1991; (ed) Towards a Commonwealth of Scholars, 1994; (ed) Education in the Commonwealth: the first 40 years, 2003; (ed) Maintaining Universal Primary Education: lessons from Commonwealth Africa, 2009; numerous articles in academic jls. *Recreations:* travel, reading, entertaining friends. *Address:* 1 Dogpole Court, Dogpole, Shrewsbury SY1 1ES. *T:* (01743) 356155. *E:* lalagebown@tiscali.co.uk. *Club:* Royal Over-Seas League (Life Mem.).

**BOWNE, Anthony Doran;** lighting designer; Director, Laban, since 2003; Principal, Trinity Laban Conservatoire of Music and Dance, since 2010 (Joint Principal, 2006–10); *b* 23 April 1956; *s* of Tony Alfred Bowne and Kathleen Bowne (*née* Doran); *m* 2005, Emma Redding; one *s* one *d. Educ:* Princethorpe Coll.; Kenilworth Grammar Sch.; Univ. of Southampton (BSc Econs 1977); Bartlett Sch. of Architecture, University Coll. London (MSc Arch. 1992). Sen. Financial Analyst, Rover Cars, 1978–81; Laban: Lectr in Lighting Design, 1983–86; Sen. Lectr, 1987–94; Exec. Dir, Transitions Dance Co., 1992–2002; Dep. Chief Exec., 1994–2003. Dep. Chair, Conservatoires UK, 2011–. Sen. Lectr in Th. Lighting Design, Hong Kong Acad. for Performing Arts, 1996–98; Prof. of Dance, Lasalle Coll., Singapore, 2004–; Hon. Vis. Prof., City Univ., London, 2010–. Lighting Designer, 1993–: Carmina Burana, Taiwan, Silent Tongues, Set the Night on Fire, RFH, 1993; Metalcholica, Forgotten Voices, Silence the Pestle Sound, Taiwan, 1994; Swinger, Car, Fierce/Pink/House, 1995; Spring Dance, Hong Kong, 1996; Una Cosa Rara (opera), Dance!! Dance!! Dance!!, Hong Kong, 1997; Vast Desert, Taiwan, 2000; Rite of Spring, Hong Kong, 2001; Now Blind Yourself, Place, London, 2002; Slow-Still-Divided, Place, London, Rite of Spring, Hong Kong Ballet tour, 2003; architectural: G's Club, Shanghai, 1997; Joyce, Dusk 'til Dawn, Hong Kong, 1998; World Finance Centre, Shanghai, 1999;

Chijmes, Singapore, 2001. Chair, Cholmondeleys and Featherstonehaughs Dance Co., 2000–08; Board Member: Bonnie Bird Choreography Fund, 1995–; Dance Forum, DCMS, 2006–; Member: London Cultural Strategy Gp, 2013–16; Teaching Quality and Student Experience Strategic Cttee, then Teaching Excellence and Student Opportunity Strategic Cttee, HEFCE, 2013–18. Board Member: Deptford Creative Village Consortium, 2007–; Creative Process, 2008–. Board Member: Granada/Univ. of Calif Davis, 2002–07; Bird Coll., 2006–16; London Higher, 2008–; One Dance UK, 2016–. Gov., Finnish Inst., London, 2006–. FRSA 2002. Designer for the 90s, Lighting Dimensions mag., USA, 1990; London Dance and Performance Award, Time Out mag., 1992. *Recreations:* wine, food, skiing, theatre. *Address:* Trinity Laban Conservatoire of Music and Dance, King Charles Court, Old Royal Naval College, Greenwich, SE10 9JF. *T:* (020) 8305 4444. *E:* a.bowne@trinitylaban.ac.uk.

**BOWNES, Prof. Mary**, OBE 2007; DPhil; CBiol, FRSB, FRES; FRSE; Professor of Developmental Biology, University of Edinburgh, 1994–2014, now Emerita (Vice Principal, 2003–12; Senior Vice Principal 2012–14; Vice Principal for Community Development, 2015–16); *b* Drewsteignton, 14 Nov. 1948; *d* of Frederick and Florence Bownes; *m* 1973, Michael John Greaves; one *d*. *Educ:* Univ. of Sussex (BSc 1970; DPhil 1973); CBiol, FRSB (FIBiol 2001); FRES 2001; FRSE 2004. Postdoctoral Associate, Univ. of Freiberg and Univ. of Calif, Irvine, 1973–76; Lectr in Genetics and Develt Biol., Univ. of Essex, 1976–79; University of Edinburgh: Lectr, 1979–89, Sen. Lectr, 1989–91, Reader, 1991–94, in Molecular Biol.; Associate Dean for Postgrads, Faculty of Sci. and Engrg, 1997–98; Hd, Inst. of Cell and Molecular Biol., 1998–2001; mem. of numerous univ. cttees and gps. Dir, Scottish Initiative for Biotechnol. Educn, 2002–18. External Examiner: Univ. of Sussex, 1996–2000; Univ. of Oxford, 2001–03; Univ. of York, 2004–06; Univ. of Glasgow, 2005–09; Univ. of Leicester, 2007–09. Chairman: Steering Cttee, Sci. and Plants for Schs Biotechnol. Scotland Proj., 2000–09 (Mem., 1998–); Bd, Edinburgh Consortium for Rural Res., 2003–11 (Mem., 1999–; Mem. Exec. Cttee, 2000–03); Strategy Bd, BBSRC, 2004–07; Studentships and Fellowships Strategy Panel, BBSRC, 2004–07; Young People's Cttee, RSE, 2008–11 (Mem., 2004–07); Member: Bd, Genetics Soc., 1980–83; Cttee, Brit. Soc. for Develtl Biol., 1982–87 (Treas., 1984–89); Adv. Bd, MRC, 2002–03; Meetings Cttee, 2000–08, Cell and Molecular Biol. Section Cttee, 2004–07, RSE; Skills Cttee, SFC, 2006–10; Bd, Scottish Assoc. for Marine Scis, 2009–14; Sci. Adv. Cttee, Nat. Mus Scotland, 2013–; Bd, RZSScot, 2014–; Dir, Edinburgh Beltane, 2008–14. Mem. Bd, Highlands and Is Enterprise, 2007–11. FRSA. Mem., Editl Bd, Jl of Endocrinol., 2000–11. *Publications:* (ed jtly) Metamorphosis, 1985; (ed) Ecdysone: from metabolism to regulation of gene expression, 1986; (with J. Grier) Private Giving, Public Good: the impact of philanthropy at the University of Edinburgh, 2014; over 100 papers in scientific jls and numerous book chapters. *Recreations:* photography, walking, lapidary. *Address:* University of Edinburgh, Charles Stewart House, Room 1.9, 9–16 Chambers Street, Edinburgh EH1 1HT. *E:* mary.bownes@ed.ac.uk.

**BOWNESS**, family name of **Baron Bowness**.

**BOWNESS**, Baron *cr* 1995 (Life Peer), of Warlingham in the County of Surrey and of Croydon in the London Borough of Croydon; **Peter Spencer Bowness**, Kt 1987; CBE 1981; DL; NP; Consultant, Streeter Marshall, Solicitors, Croydon, Purley and Warlingham, 2002–11; *b* 19 May 1943; *s* of Hubert Spencer Bowness and Doreen (Peggy) Bowness; *m* 1969, Marianne Hall (marr. diss.); one *d*; *m* 1984, Mrs Patricia Jane Cook; one step *s*. *Educ:* Whitgift Sch., Croydon. Admitted Solicitor, 1966; NP 1977; Partner, Horsley, Weightman, Richardson and Sadler, subseq. Weightman, Sadler, then Streeter Marshall, 1970–2002. Croydon Council: Mem. (C), 1968–98: Leader, 1976–94; Leader of the Opposition, 1994–96; Mayor of Croydon, 1979–80; Chm., London Boroughs Assoc., 1978–94; Dep. Chm., Assoc. of Metropolitan Authorities, 1978–80. Opposition spokesman on the envmt, transport and the regions, H of L, 1997–98; Member: H of L Select Cttee on EU, 2003–07, 2009– (Chairman: Foreign Affairs, Defence and Develt Policy Sub Cttee, 2003–06; Law and Instnl Sub Cttee, 2009–13); Jt Cttee on Human Rights, 2003–07, 2008–12; Agric., Fisheries, Envmt and Energy Sub-cttee, 2013–; Secondary Legislation Scrutiny Cttee, 2015–; Co-Chm., 2001–12, Vice-Chm., 2015–, All-Party Parly Gp on Lithuania; Vice-Chm., All-Party Parly Gp on Romania, 2006–, on Mongolia, 2015–; Sec., All-Party Parly Gp on Moldova, 2007–; Mem., All-Party Parly Gp on Kosovo, 2012–15, on Serbia, 2012–15, on Latvia, 2015–, on Estonia, 2015–; Mem., Ministerial Bd on Deaths in Custody, 2009–12. Member: Audit Commn, 1983–95; London Residuary Body, 1985–93; Nat. Training Task Force, 1989–92; UK Delegn, CLRAE (Council of Europe), 1990–98; UK Mem., Mem. Bureau, and Mem. Transportation and Telecommunications Commn, EC Cttee of the Regions, 1994–98; Member: UK Delegn to EU Charter of Fundamental Rights Drafting Convention, 1999–2000; Parly Assembly, OSCE, 2007– (Leader of UK Delegn, 2014–17; Vice Pres., 2015–). Gov., Whitgift Foundn, 1982–94. Hon. Col, 151 (Greater London) Transport Regt RCT (V), 1988–93. DL Greater London, 1981; Freeman, City of London, 1984; Hon. Freeman, London Borough of Croydon, 2002. *Recreations:* travel, gardening, our two dachshunds. *Address:* House of Lords, SW1A 0PW.

**BOWNESS, Sir Alan**, Kt 1988; CBE 1976; Director of the Tate Gallery, 1980–88; Director, Henry Moore Foundation, 1988–94 (Member, Committee of Management, 1984–88 and 1994–2003); *b* 11 Jan. 1928; *er s* of George Bowness and Kathleen (*née* Benton); *m* 1957, Sarah Hepworth-Nicholson, *d* of Ben Nicholson, OM, and Dame Barbara Hepworth, DBE; one *s* one *d*. *Educ:* University Coll. Sch.; Downing Coll., Cambridge (Hon. Fellow 1980); Courtauld Inst. of Art, Univ. of London (Hon. Fellow 1986). Worked with Friends' Ambulance Unit and Friends' Service Council, 1946–50; Reg. Art Officer, Arts Council of GB, 1955–57; Courtauld Institute, University of London: Lectr, 1957–67; Reader, 1967–78; Prof. of Hist. of Art, 1978–79; Dep. Dir, 1978–79. Vis. Prof., Humanities Seminar, Johns Hopkins Univ., Baltimore, 1969. Exhibitions arranged and catalogued include: 54:64 Painting and Sculpture of a Decade (with L. Gowing), 1964; Dubuffet, 1966; Sculpture in Battersea Park, 1966; Van Gogh, 1968; Rodin, 1970; William Scott, 1972; French Symbolist Painters (with G. Lacambre), 1972; Ceri Richards, 1975; Courbet (with M. Laclotte), 1977; Post-Impressionism, 1979. Private collection featured in Generation Painting 1955–65: British Art from Collection of Sir Alan Bowness, Heong Gall., Downing Coll., Cambridge, 2016. Mem. Internat. Juries: Premio Di Tella, Buenos Aires, 1965; São Paulo Bienal, 1967; Venice Biennale, 1986; Lehmbruck Prize, Duisburg, 1970; Rembrandt Prize, 1979–88; Heiliger Prize, 1998. Arts Council: Mem., 1973–75 and 1978–80; Mem., Art Panel, 1960–80 (Vice-Chm., 1973–75, Chm., 1978–80); Mem., Arts Film Cttee, 1968–77 (Chm., 1972–75). Member: Fine Arts Cttee, Brit. Council, 1960–69 and 1970–92 (Chm., 1981–92); Exec. Cttee, Contemp. Art Soc., 1961–69 and 1970–86; Kettle's Yard Cttee, Univ. of Cambridge, 1970–99; Cultural Adv. Cttee, UK National Commn for UNESCO, 1973–82. Governor, Chelsea Sch. of Art, 1965–93; Hon. Sec., Assoc. of Art Historians, 1973–76; Dir, Barbara Hepworth Museum, St Ives, Cornwall, 1976–88. Mem. Council, RCA, 1978–99 (Hon. Fellow 1984). Trustee: Yorkshire Sculpture Park, 1979–; Handel House, 1994–2001 (Chm., 1997–2001). Hon. Fellow, Bristol Polytechnic, 1980. Hon. FRIBA 1994. Hon. DLit Liverpool, 1988; Hon. DLitt: Leeds, 1995; Exeter, 1996. Chevalier, l'Ordre des Arts et des Lettres, France, 1973. *Publications:* William Scott Paintings, 1964; Impressionists and Post Impressionists, 1965;

(ed) Henry Moore: complete sculpture 1955–64 (vol. 3) 1965, 1964–73 (vol. 4) 1977, 1974–80 (vol. 5) 1983, 1949–54 (vol. 2) 1987, 1980–86 (vol. 6) 1988; Modern Sculpture, 1965; Barbara Hepworth Drawings, 1966; Alan Davie, 1967; Recent British Painting, 1968; Gauguin, 1971; Barbara Hepworth: complete sculpture 1960–70, 1971; Modern European Art, 1972; Ivon Hitchens, 1973; (contrib.) Picasso 1881–1973, ed R. Penrose, 1973; (contrib.) The Genius of British Painting, ed D. Piper, 1975; The Conditions of Success, 1989; Bernard Meadows, 1994; articles in Burlington Magazine, TLS, Observer, and Annual Register. *Recreations:* going to concerts, theatre, opera. *Address:* 91 Castelnau, SW13 9EL. *T:* (020) 8846 8520; 16 Piazza, St Ives, Cornwall TR26 1NQ. *T:* (01736) 795444.

**BOWRING, Prof. Richard John**; Professor of Japanese Studies, University of Cambridge, 1985–2012, now Emeritus; Master, Selwyn College, Cambridge, 2000–13, now Emeritus Fellow; *b* 6 Feb. 1947; *s* of late Richard Arthur Bowring and Mabel Bowring (*née* Eddy); *m* 1970, Susan (*née* Povey); one *d*. *Educ:* Blundell's Sch.; Downing Coll., Cambridge (PhD 1973; LittD 1997). Lectr in Japanese, Monash Univ., 1973–75; Asst Prof. of Japanese, Columbia Univ., NY, 1978–79; Associate Prof. of Japanese, Princeton Univ., NJ, 1979–84; Cambridge University: Lectr in Japanese, 1984; Chm., Faculty Bd of Oriental Studies, 1987–89, 1998–2000; Fellow, Downing Coll., 1985–2000; Hon. Fellow, 2000; Chm., Bd of Scrutiny, 2010–11; Hd, Dept of E Asian Studies, 2010–12. British Acad. Reader, 1995–97. Trustee: Cambridge Foundn, 1989–98; Daiwa Anglo-Japanese Foundn, 2013–. Advr, UFC, subseq. HEFCE, 1992–94. Gov., SOAS, 1994–99. Order of Rising Sun, 3rd Cl. (Japan), 2013. *Publications:* Mori Ogai and the Modernization of Japanese Culture, 1979; trans., Murasaki Shikibu: her diary and poetic memoirs, 1982; Murasaki Shikibu: The Tale of Genji, 1988, 2nd edn 2004; (jtly) An Introduction to Modern Japanese, 1992; (ed) Cambridge Encyclopedia of Japan, 1993; The Diary of Lady Murasaki, 1996; (jtly) Cambridge Intermediate Japanese, 2002; The Religious Traditions of Japan 500–1600, 2005; (jtly) The Myotei Dialogues: a Japanese Christian critique of native traditions, 2015; In Search of the Way: thought and religion in Early-Modern Japan, 1582–1860, 2017; (ed jtly) Brill Encyclopedia of Buddhism, vol. II, 2019.

**BOWRON, Margaret Ruth, (Mrs A. T. Davy)**; QC 2001; *b* 8 July 1956; *d* of late John Lewis Bowron, CBE and Patricia (*née* Cobby); *m* 1988, Anthony Tallents Davy; two *d*. *Educ:* Convent of Our Lady of Sion, Worthing; Brighton and Hove High Sch., Brighton; King's Coll., London (LLB 1977). Called to the Bar, Inner Temple, 1978, Bencher, 2008; in practice as barrister, specialising in clinical negligence and related work, 1978–. *Recreations:* walking, theatre, travel. *Address:* (chambers) 1 Crown Office Row, Temple, EC4Y 7HH. *T:* (020) 7797 7500.

**BOWRON, Michael**, QPM 2007; Chief Officer of Police, States of Jersey Police, 2011–17; *b* 8 Sept. 1957; *s* of Ronald and Christina Bowron; *m* 1994, Karen Elizabeth Purkiss. *Educ:* Ernest Bevin Comprehensive Sch., Tooting; Sussex Univ. (BA Hons (Sociol.) 1989); Nat. Exec. Inst., FBI Acad. 2007. Sussex Police: Constable 1980; Sergeant 1984; Insp. 1985; Bramshill Schol., Sussex Univ., 1986–89; Chief Insp. 1990; Supt 1991; Asst Chief Constable, Kent Police, 1997–2002; Asst Comr, 2002–06, Comr, 2006–11, City of London Police. Comr of Lieutenancy, City of London, 2007–11. Vis. speaker, Windsor Leadership Trust. Volunteer ranger, Jersey Zoo. FRSA. Hon. DSc City, 2008. OStJ 2012. *Recreations:* athletics, cross-country running, travel, cycling, sea swimming, motorcycling.

**BOWSHER, Brian Robert**, OBE 2018; PhD; FRSC, FInstP; Chief Executive, Science and Technology Facilities Council, 2016–18; *b* Birmingham, 12 July 1957; *s* of Robert Newman Bowsher and Patricia Mary Bowsher; *m* 1987, Sally Smith; one *s*. *Educ:* Handsworth Grammar Sch., Birmingham; Fosters Grammar Sch., Sherborne; Univ. of Southampton (BSc Hons 1978; PhD Chem. 1982). FRSC 2003; CSci 2004; FInstP 2009. Proj. and Sect. Manager, UKAEA, 1981–96; Dept Manager, AEA Technology, 1996–2002; AWE: Hd, Materials Sci., 2002–03; Dir, Res. and Applied Sci., 2003–07; Dir, Systems Engrg, 2007–09; Man. Dir, NPL, 2009–15. Mem., STFC, 2013–18. Mem. Bd, DSTL, 2018–. Hon. FInstMC 2015. Hon. DSc Southampton, 2018. *Publications:* approx. 200 tech. articles. *Recreations:* fly fishing, ski-ing, walking, gardening, playing piano.

**BOWSHER, Michael Frederick Thomas**; QC 2006; *b* 22 Nov. 1963; *s* of His Honour Peter Charles Bowsher, *qv*; *m* 1990, Haylee Fiona, *d* of Terrence and Mary O'Brien, Aberdare; two *s* one *d*. *Educ:* St George's Sch., Windsor Castle; Radley Coll.; Brasenose Coll., Oxford (BA). FCIArb 2000; Chartered Arbitrator, 2002. Called to the Bar: Middle Temple, 1985, Bencher, 2014; NI, 2000; Republic of Ireland, 2012; in practice, Chambers of Donald Keating, QC, then Keating Chambers, 1986–88 and 1992–2001; Associate, Cleary, Gottlieb, Steen & Hamilton (Brussels), 1988–92; in practice, Monckton Chambers, 2001–. Vis. Lectr in EU Public Procurement Law, 2013–16, Vis. Prof., Dickson Poon Sch. of Law, 2016–, KCL. Co-Chm., ICC Task Force on Public Procurement, 2007–13. Mem., Bar Council, 2010–14 (Chair, EU Law Cttee, 2012–14; Mem., Gen. Mgt Cttee, 2012–14). Mem., Contract and Procurement Special Interest Gp, Chartered Inst. of Building, 2018–. Chair, Internat. Sub-Cttee, Middle Temple, 2019–. Fellow: Eur. Law Inst., 2012–; Centre of Eur. Law, KCL, 2014–. Freeman, Arbitrators' Co., 2011– (Liveryman, 2014–). Mem. Editl Bd, Eur. Procurement and Public Private Partnership Law Rev., 2018–. *Publications:* (contrib.) Keating on Building Contracts, 5th edn 1991 to 7th edn 2001; (contrib.) Ward & Smith, Competition Litigation in the UK, 2005; (contrib.) Current Competition Law, 2005; (contrib.) Public Procurement Law, 2011; articles on public procurement and competition law in Public Procurement Law Rev., Current Competition Law and Internat. Construction Law Rev. *Address:* Monckton Chambers, 1 & 2 Raymond Buildings, Gray's Inn, WC1R 5NR. *T:* (020) 7405 7211, *Fax:* (020) 7405 2084. *E:* mbowsher@monckton.com.

**BOWSHER, His Honour Peter Charles**; QC 1978; FCIArb; arbitrator; a Judge of the Technology and Construction Court of the High Court, 1998–2003 (an Official Referee, 1987–98); *b* 9 Feb. 1935; *s* of Charles and Ellen Bowsher; *m* 1960, Deborah Ann, *d* of Frederick Wilkins and Isobel Wilkins (*née* Copp), Vancouver; two *s*. *Educ:* St George's Sch., Windsor Castle; Ardingly; Oriel Coll., Oxford (MA). FCIArb 1990; Chartered Arbitrator, 2000–. Commnd Royal Artillery, 1954; Territorial Army XX Rifle Team, 1957. Called to the Bar, Middle Temple, 1959, Bencher, 1985. Harmsworth Scholar; Blackstone Entrance Scholar. A Legal Assessor to GMC and GDC, 1979–87; a Recorder, 1983–87; a Deputy High Court Judge, Queen's Bench and Chancery Divs, 1985–87. Ind. Review Body, Modified Colliery Review Procedure, 1986–87; Adjudicator, Crown Prosecution Service (Transfer of Staff) Regulations, 1985, 1986–87. Member: IT and the Courts Cttee, 1991–2003; Judicial Cttee, British Acad. of Experts, 1992–2003; Arbrix, 2004–. Member: Soc. for Computers and Law, 1990–; Soc. of Construction Arbitrators, 2005–. Liveryman, Arbitrators' Co., 2010–. *Recreations:* photography, music. *Address:* 150 Clifford's Inn, Fetter Lane, EC4A 1BY. *Clubs:* Brooks's, Royal Automobile.
*See also* M. F. T. Bowsher.

**BOWTELL, Dame Ann (Elizabeth)**, DCB 1997 (CB 1989); PhD; Permanent Secretary, Department of Social Security, 1995–99; *b* 25 April 1938; *d* of John Albert and Olive Rose Kewell; *m* 1961, Michael John Bowtell; two *s* two *d*. *Educ:* Kendrick Girls' Sch., Reading; Girton Coll., Cambridge (MA; Hon. Fellow, 2000); Royal Holloway, Univ. of London (MA 2001; PhD 2010). Asst Principal, Nat. Assistance Board, 1960; Principal: Nat. Assistance Board, 1964; Min. of Social Security, 1966; DHSS, 1968; Asst Sec., 1973, Under

Sec., 1980, DHSS; Dep. Sec., DHSS, later DSS, 1986; Principal Establishment and Finance Officer, DoH (on secondment), 1990–93; First Civil Service Comr and Dep. Sec., Cabinet Office, 1993–95; Dep. Sec., DSS, 1995. Trustee: Joseph Rowntree Foundn, 2001–11; Research Autism, 2012–18. Hon. Dr Middlesex, 1996. *Recreations:* bird watching, medieval history, music, walking. *Address:* 26 Sidney Road, Walton-on-Thames, Surrey KT12 2NA.

**BOWYER**, family name of **Baron Denham**.

**BOWYER, Gordon Arthur,** OBE 1970; RIBA; FCSD; Partner, Bowyer Langlands Batchelor (formerly Gordon Bowyer & Partners), Chartered Architects, 1948–92; *b* 21 March 1923; *s of* Arthur Bowyer and Kathleen Mary Bowyer; *m* 1950, Ursula Meyer; one *s* one *d*. *Educ:* Dauntsey's Sch.; Polytechnic of Central London. Architect and designer in private practice, in partnership with Ursula Bowyer, Iain Langlands and Stephen Batchelor, 1948–92. Practice started with design of Sports Section, South Bank Exhibn, Fest. of Britain, 1951; schs and hostel for handicapped children in Peckham, Bermondsey and Dulwich, 1966–75; housing for Southwark, GLC, Family Housing Assoc., London & Quadrant Housing Assoc. and Greenwich Housing Soc., 1969–83; numerous office conversions for IBM (UK), 1969–89; Peckham Methodist Church, 1975; new offices and shops for Rank City Wall at Brighton, 1975 and Folkestone, 1976; Treasury at Gloucester Cathedral, 1976; conservation at Vanbrugh Castle, Greenwich, 1973, Charlton Assembly Rooms, 1980, Hill Hall, Essex, 1982; lecture theatre, library and accommodation, Jt Services Defence Coll., RNC, Greenwich, 1983; Cabinet War Rooms Museum, Whitehall (with Alan Irvine), 1984; refurbishment of Barry Rooms at Nat. Gall., Stuart & Georgian Galls at Nat. Portrait Gall. and East Hall of Science Museum; new Prints & Drawings and Japanese Gall. at BM; gall. for Japanese prints, Fitzwilliam Mus. Advisory architect: Science Mus., 1992–96; Trustees' Buildings Cttee, Nat. Maritime Mus., 1993–96. Hon. Sec., SIAD, 1957–58. Mem. Council, Friends of the Nat. Maritime Mus., 1985–2003; Trustee, Nat. Maritime Museum, 1977–93. *Address:* 111 Maze Hill, SE10 8XQ.

**BOWYER, Katharine Ann, (Ms Kate Sherwood);** Chief Financial Officer, The Crown Estate, since 2016; a Crown Estate Commissioner, since 2017; *b* Stamford, 14 Oct. 1969; *d* of (Neil) Christopher Bowyer and Peta Margaret Bowyer; *m* 1995, Robert Harry Sherwood; one *s* one *d*. *Educ:* Univ. of Southampton (BSc Hons Geog. 1991). ACA 1995. Various roles to Sen. Manager, Coopers & Lybrand, subseq. PricewaterhouseCoopers, 1991–99; Gp Financial Controller, Liberty International plc, 2000–08; Capital Shopping Centres Group plc, subseq. intu Properties plc: Hd, Investor Relns, 2008–14; Dir, Finance, 2014–16. Trustee, Westminster Amalgamated Charity, 2013–. *Recreations:* jazz trumpet, fly fishing, running and cycling in the hills.

**BOWYER, (Sir) Thomas Weyland,** (15th Bt *cr* 1661); *b* 25 June 1960; *s of* Captain Sir Philip Weyland Bowyer-Smyth, 14th Bt, RN, and Veronica Mary, *d* of Captain C. W. Bower, DSC, RN; relinquished surname of Smyth by deed poll, 1997; *S* father, 1978, but does not use the title; *m* 1st, 1992, Sara Louise Breinlinger (marr. diss. 1997); 2nd, 1998, Mary Rose Helen Giedroyc; one *s* one *d*, and one step *s*. *Heir: kinsman* John Jeremy Windham, MBE [*b* 22 Nov. 1948; *m* 1976, Rachel Mary Finney; one *s* two *d*].

**BOX, (Mary) Tamara;** Managing Partner, Europe and Middle East, Member, Senior Management Team and Member, Board, Reed Smith, since 2016; *b* Lubbock, Texas, USA, 13 Sept. 1967; *d of* Lyndon Box and Patricia Dixon; *m* 1997, James Hugo Lester; one *s*. *Educ:* London Sch. of Economics and Political Sci. (BSc Hons 1989); Georgetown Univ. Law Center (JD 1992). Associate, Coudert Brothers, NY and Singapore, 1992–96; Associate, 1996–99, Partner, 1999–2000, Orrick, Singapore and London; Partner, and Hd, Finance, Tite & Lewis, London, 2000–03; Partner, Lovells, London, 2003–06; Partner, and Hd, Structured Finance, Berwin Leighton Paisner, London, 2006–12; Reed Smith: Partner, 2012–; Hd, Structured Finance, 2012–; Chair, Global Financial Industry Gp, 2014–16. Founder Mem., 30% Club, 2010–. *Recreations:* classic car rallies, ski-ing. *Address:* Reed Smith, The Broadgate Tower, 20 Primrose Street, EC2A 2RS. *T:* (020) 3116 3658. *E:* tbox@reedsmith.com.

**BOXER, Anna;** *see* Ford, Anna.

**BOXER, Charles Ian;** *b* 11 Feb. 1926; *s of* Rev. William Neville Gordon Boxer and Margaret Boxer; *m* 1968, Hilary Fabienne Boxer. *Educ:* Glasgow High Sch.; Edinburgh Univ. (BL). Church of England ministry, 1950–54; apprentice to solicitors, 1954–58; Mem., Dominican Order (RC), 1958–67; Sen. Community Relations Officer for Wandsworth, 1967–77; Dir, Community Affairs and Liaison Div., Commn for Racial Equality, 1977–81. Communicator of the Year, BAIE Awards, 1976. *Recreation:* music. *Address:* Parish Farmhouse, Hassell Street, Hastingleigh, near Ashford, Kent TN25 5JE. *T:* (01233) 750219.

**BOXER, Prof. David Howell,** PhD; Director, Institute of Food Research, 2009–15; Professor of Microbial Metabolism, University of East Anglia, 2009–15; *b* Aberdare, 11 June 1947; *s of* W. H. S. Boxer and S. M. Boxer; *m* 1978, Maureen; one *s* two *d*. *Educ:* Aberdare Boys' Grammar Sch.; Bristol Univ. (BSc Hons Biochem. 1969; PGCE 1973; PhD Biochem. 1974). Dundee University: Nuffield Res. Fellow, 1983–84; Hd, Biochem. Dept, 1988–94; Dean, Sci. Engrg Faculty, 1994–99; Dep. Principal, 2000–02; Vice Principal (Res. and Enterprise), 2002–09. Chm., Scottish Inst. for Res. in Policing, 2007–09; Member: Bd, Scottish Crop Res. Inst., 2004–11; Bd, James Hutton Inst., 2011–15. *Publications:* numerous scientific articles. *Recreations:* ski-ing, cycling.

**BOXER, Graham;** Head of Museums, Canal and River Trust, since 2015; *b* Chingford, London, 26 Aug. 1957; *s of* Charles Boxer and Kathleen Boxer (*née* Webber); *m* 1992, Angela Scholes; two *s*. *Educ:* Univ. of Nottingham (BA Jt Hons Ancient Hist. and Hist.); Univ. of Leicester (Grad. Cert. Mus. Studies); Univ. of Lancaster (Postgrad. Dip. Public Service Collaborative Leadership). Liverpool City Council: Curator, King's Regiment Collection, Regl Hist. Dept, 1990–93, HM Customs and Excise Nat. Mus., 1993–98, Hd, Regl Hist., 1998–2000, Nat. Mus Liverpool; Dir, St George's Hall, 2000–04; Hd, Heritage Develt, Liverpool Culture Co., 2004–09; Hd, Arts, Heritage and Participation, 2009–12; Dir, Imperial War Mus. North, 2012–15. Trustee, Collective Encounters, 2016–. Parent Gov., Ellenbrook Community Prim. Sch., 2003–10; Chm., Interim Exec. Bd, Marlborough Rd Prim. Sch., 2009–11; Foundn Gov., St Andrew's Prim. Sch., 2013–15. Mem., St Mary's Dist Church Council, 2013–. *Address:* Canal and River Trust, Station House, 500 Elder Gate, Milton Keynes MK9 1BB. *E:* graham.boxer@canalrivertrust.org.uk.

**BOXSHALL, Dr Geoffrey Allan,** FRS 1994; Merit Researcher (Band 1), Natural History Museum, 2014–17, now a Scientific Associate; *b* 13 June 1950; *s of* John Edward Boxshall and Sybil Irene Boxshall (*née* Baker); *m* 1972, Roberta Gabriel Smith; one *s* three *d*. *Educ:* Churcher's Coll., Petersfield; Leeds Univ. (BSc, PhD). British Museum (Natural History), subseq. Natural History Museum: Higher SO, 1974–76; SSO, 1976–80; PSO, 1980–91; SPSO, 1991–97; DCSO, 1997–2014. *Publications:* (jtly) Dictionary of Ecology, Evolution and Systematics, 1982, 2nd edn 1998; (jtly) Cambridge Illustrated Dictionary of Natural History, 1987; (ed jtly) Biology of Copepods, 1988; (jtly) Copepod Evolution, 1991; (ed jtly) Pathogens of Wild and Farmed Fish: sea lice, 1993; An Introduction to Copepod Diversity, 2004; numerous papers in scientific jls. *Recreations:* tennis, reading, lexicography, travel. *Address:* Department of Life Sciences, Natural History Museum, Cromwell Road, SW7 5BD. *T:* (020) 7942 5749.

**BOYACK, Sarah;** Member (Lab) Lothian, Scottish Parliament, since 2019; *b* 16 May 1961; *d of* late Jim Boyack. *Educ:* Royal High Sch., Edinburgh; Glasgow Univ. (MA); Heriot-Watt Univ. (DipT&CP). MRTPI. Planning Asst, London Borough of Brent, 1986–88; Sen. Planning Officer, Central Regl Council, 1988–92; Lectr in Planning, Edinburgh Coll. of Art, 1992–99. MSP (Lab) Edinburgh Central, 1999–2011, Lothian, 2011–16; contested (Lab) Edinburgh Central, Scottish Parlt, 2016. Scottish Executive: Minister for Transport and the Envmt, 1999–2000, for Transport, 2000–01, for Transport and Planning, 2001; Dep. Minister for Envmt and Rural Develt, 2007. Scottish Parliament: shadow spokesperson on rural affairs, environment and climate change, 2008–11; Shadow Cabinet Sec. for Local Govt and Planning, 2011–14; Shadow Cabinet Sec. for Rural Affairs, Food, Climate Change and Envmt, 2014–16; Convener, Envmt and Rural Develt Cttee, 2003–07. Hd of Public Affairs, Scottish Fedn of Housing Assocs, 2017–19. *Address:* Scottish Parliament, Edinburgh EH99 1SP.

**BOYCE,** family name of **Baron Boyce**.

**BOYCE,** Baron *cr* 2003 (Life Peer), of Pimlico in the City of Westminster; **Admiral of the Fleet Michael Cecil Boyce,** KG 2011; GCB 1999 (KCB 1995); OBE 1982; DL; Lord Warden and Admiral of the Cinque Ports, and Constable of Dover Castle, since 2004; Bath King of Arms, 2009–18; *b* 2 April 1943; *s of* late Comdr Hugh Boyce, DSC, RN and Madeleine Boyce (*née* Manley); *m* 1st, 1971, Harriette Gail Fletcher (separated 1994; marr. diss. 2005); one *s* one *d*; 2nd, 2006, Fleur Margaret Anne (*née* Smith) (*d* 2016), *widow of* Vice Adm. Malcolm Rutherford, CBE. *Educ:* Hurstpierpoint Coll.; BRNC, Dartmouth. Joined RN, 1961; qualified Submarines, 1965 and TAS, 1970; served in HM Submarines Anchorite, Valiant, and Conqueror, 1965–72; commanded: HM Submarines: Oberon, 1973–74; Opossum, 1974–75; Superb, 1979–81; HMS Brilliant, 1983–84; Captain (SM), Submarine Sea Training, 1984–86; RCDS, 1988; Sen. Naval Officer, ME, 1989; Dir Naval Staff Duties, 1989–91; Flag Officer: Sea Training, 1991–92; Surface Flotilla, 1992–95; Comdr, Anti-Submarine Warfare Striking Force, 1992–94; Second Sea Lord, and C-in-C Naval Home Comd, 1995–97; C-in-C Fleet, C-in-C Eastern Atlantic Area and Comdr Naval Forces N Western Europe, 1997–98; First Sea Lord and Chief of Naval Staff, and First and Principal Naval ADC to the Queen, 1998–2001; Chief of the Defence Staff, 2001–03; ADC to the Queen, 2001–03. Col Comdt, SBS, 2003–. Non-executive Director: VT Gp plc, 2004–10; W. S. Atkins plc, 2004–13. Chm., HMS Victory Preservation Co., 2012–. President: Officers' Assoc., 2003–12; London Br., St John Ambulance, 2003–11; RN Submarine Mus., 2005–; Pilgrims' Soc., 2010–15 (Vice Pres., 2015–); Member of Council: White Ensign Assoc., 2003–13 (Chm., 2007–10; Vice Pres., 2013–); RNLI, 2004–13 (Trustee, 2006–13; Chm., 2008–13; Vice Pres., 2013–); Chm. Adv. Bd, RBL Centre for Blast Injury Studies, 2011–; Trustee, Nat. Maritime Mus., 2005–13; Patron: Sail4Cancer, 2003–; Submariners Assoc., 2003–; Forces in Mind Trust, 2012–. Governor: Alleyn's Sch., 1995–2005; Sir John Hawkins Hosp., 2004–. Freeman, City of London, 1999; Master, Drapers' Co., 2013–14 (Hon. Freeman, 2005; Liveryman, 2009–11; Mem. Ct, 2011–). Elder Brother, Trinity House, 2006 (Yr Brother, 1999–2006). Hon. Bencher, Middle Temple, 2012. DL Greater London, 2003. Hon. LLD Portsmouth, 2005; Hon. Dr Canterbury Christ Church, 2011; Hon. DCL Kent, 2013; Hon. DSc Imperial Coll. London, 2016. KStJ 2002. Comdr, Legion of Merit (US), 1999 (Bronze Oak Leaf, 2003). *Recreations:* squash, tennis, Real tennis, sailing, windsurfing, opera. *Address:* House of Lords, SW1A 0PW. *Clubs:* Garrick, Naval and Military (Dir, 2003–08; Vice Chm., 2005–08; Trustee, 2012–; Vice Pres., 2014–), Queen's.

*See also* Sir G. H. *Boyce*.

**BOYCE, Frank C.;** *see* Cottrell-Boyce.

**BOYCE, Sir Graham (Hugh),** KCMG 2001 (CMG 1991); HM Diplomatic Service, retired; Senior Adviser, Bank of America (formerly Bank of America Merrill Lynch), since 2013; *b* 6 Oct. 1945; *s of* late Comdr Hugh Boyce, DSC, RN and Madeleine Boyce (*née* Manley); *m* 1970, Janet Elizabeth Spencer; one *s* three *d*. *Educ:* Hurstpierpoint Coll.; Jesus Coll., Cambridge (MA). VSO, Antigua, 1967; HM Diplomatic Service, 1968; Ottawa, 1971; MECAS, 1972–74; 1st Sec., Tripoli, Libya, 1974–77; FCO, 1977–81; Kuwait, 1981–85; Asst Hd of ME Dept, FCO, 1985–86; Counsellor and Consul-Gen., Stockholm, 1987–90; Ambassador and Consul-Gen., Doha, 1990–93; Counsellor, FCO, 1993–96; Ambassador to Kuwait, 1996–99; Ambassador to Egypt, 1999–2001. Chairman, Middle East Board: Invensys, 2005–10; Lehman Brothers, 2006–08; MEC Internat., 2011–13; Chairman: Common Purpose Internat., 2012–18; NYA Internat., 2016–18; Adv. Bd, GTS, 2018–; Vice Chairman: VT Internat. Services, 2002–06; EMEA Adv. Bd, Nomura Internat., 2009–13; Adviser to Emir of Qatar, 2001–02; to Shell, 2001–06; to Air Products, 2003–14; Mem., Adv. Bd, Kuwait Investment Office, 2004–; Senior Adviser: Nomura, 2009–13; DLA Piper, 2009–14; various consultancies. Trustee, Dakhleh Oasis Trust, 2001–14. *Recreations:* tennis, golf, walking. *Club:* Oxford and Cambridge.

*See also* Baron *Boyce*.

**BOYCE, Peter John,** AO 1995; PhD; Vice-Chancellor, Murdoch University, Western Australia, 1985–96, now Emeritus Professor; Hon. Research Fellow, University of Tasmania, since 2004 (Visiting Professor, 1996–2000); Hon. Professor of Political Science, 2000–04); *b* 20 Feb. 1935; *s of* Oswald and Marjorie Boyce; *m* 1962, Lorinne Peet; one *s* two *d*. *Educ:* Wesley Coll., Perth, WA; Univ. of Western Australia (MA); Duke Univ., USA (PhD). Res. Fellow, then Fellow, Dept of Internat. Relns, ANU, 1964–66; Nuffield Fellow, St Antony's Coll., Oxford, 1966–67; Sen. Lectr, then Reader, in Political Science, Tasmania Univ., 1967–75; Prof. of Pol Science and Hd, Dept of Govt, Queensland Univ., 1976–79; Prof. of Politics and Hd of Dept, Univ. of W Australia, 1980–84. Visiting Fellow: Corpus Christi Coll., Cambridge, 1989; Merton Coll., Oxford, 1996; Christ Church, Oxford, 1997. Interim Principal, Aust. Maritime Coll., 2005–06. Exec. Mem., Aust.-NZ Foundn, 1979–83; Member: Aust. Human Rights Commn, 1981–86; Consultative Cttee on Relns with Japan, 1983–85; Asia Business Council of WA, 1993–96. Lay Canon of St George's Cath., Perth, 1986–96. Editor, Australian Outlook, 1973–77. Hon. LLD Tasmania, 2006. *Publications:* Malaysia and Singapore in International Diplomacy, 1968; Foreign Affairs for New States, 1977; (co-ord. ed.) Dictionary of Australian Politics, 1980; (co-ord. ed.) Politics in Queensland, 1980; (co-ord. ed.) The Torres Strait Treaty, 1981; (ed) Independence and Alliance, 1983; Diplomacy in the Market Place, 1991; Honest and Unsullied Days, 2001; The Queen's Other Realms, 2008; God and the City, 2012. *Recreations:* gardening, walking, church music. *Address:* #1, 13 Rose Court, Lower Sandy Bay, Tas 7005, Australia. *T:* (03) 62252009.

**BOYCE, Most Rev. Philip,** DD; Bishop of Raphoe, (RC), 1995–2017; *b* 25 Jan. 1940; *s of* Joseph Boyce and Brigid Gallagher. *Educ:* Downings, Co. Donegal; Castlemartyr Coll., Co. Cork; Carmelite House of Studies, Dublin; Pontifical Theol Faculty (Teresianum), Rome (DD). Entered Discalced Carmelites, 1958; studied philosophy in Dublin and theology in Rome; ordained priest, 1966; on teaching staff of Pontifical Theol Faculty (Teresianum), Rome, 1972–95. Mem., Congregation for Divine Worship and Discipline of Sacraments, 1999–2010. *Publications:* The Challenge of Sanctity: a study of Christian perfection in the writings of John Henry Newman, 1974; Spiritual Exodus of John Henry Newman and Thérèse of Lisieux, 1979; (ed) Mary: the Virgin Mary in the life and writings of John Henry Newman, 2001; articles on themes of spiritual theology.

**BOYCE, Sir Robert (Leslie),** 3rd Bt *cr* 1952; FRCSEd (Ophth); Consultant Ophthalmic and Oculoplastic Surgeon, Sunderland Eye Infirmary, since 2003; Managing Director, Minor Ops Ltd, since 2007; *b* 2 May 1962; *s* of Sir Richard (Leslie) Boyce, 2nd Bt, and of Jacqueline Anne (who *m* 2nd, 1974, Christopher Boyce-Dennis), *o d* of Roland A. Hill; *S* father, 1968; *m* 1985, Fiona, second *d* of John Savage, Whitmore Park, Coventry; one *s* one *d*. *Educ*: Cheltenham Coll.; Salford Univ. (BSc 1984, 1st cl. hons); Nottingham Univ. (BMedSci 1991, 1st cl. hons; BM BS 1993). FRCSEd (Ophth) 1998. Sen. House Officer, Manchester Royal Eye Hosp., 1995–98; Specialist Registrar in Ophthalmology, Royal Victoria Infirmary, Sunderland Eye Infirmary and N Riding Infirmary, 1998–2003. *Heir*: *s* Thomas Leslie Boyce, *b* 3 Sept. 1993.

**BOYCE, William;** QC 2001; a Recorder, since 1997; *b* 29 July 1951. *Educ*: St Joseph's Acad. Grammar Sch., Blackheath; Univ. of Kent (BA). Called to the Bar, Gray's Inn, 1976, Bencher, 2007; Jun. Treasury Counsel, 1991–97, Sen. Treasury Counsel, 1997–2001, CCC. *Address*: QEB Hollis Whiteman Chambers, 1–2 Laurence Pountney Hill, EC4R 0EU.

**BOYCOTT,** Baroness *cr* 2018 (Life Peer), of Whitefield in the County of Somerset; **Rosie Boycott;** Chair, London Food Board, since 2008; *b* 13 May 1951; *d* of late Charles Boycott and of Betty Boycott; *m* 1983, David Leitch (marr. diss. 1998; he *d* 2004); one *d*; *m* 1999, Charles Anthony Frederick Howard, *qv. Educ*: Cheltenham Ladies' Coll.; Kent Univ. (pure maths). Has worked on: Frendz mag., 1971; Spare Rib (Founder and Editor), 1971–72; Luka (Buddhist Jl of America), 1973–75; Osrati (Kuwait), 1976–79; Honey mag., 1979–81 (Dep. Ed.); Daily Mail, 1984–85; Sunday Telegraph, Harpers & Queen, 1989–92; Editor: Esquire, 1992–96; Independent on Sunday, 1996–98; The Independent, 1998; The Express, 1998–2001. Regular appearances on Newsnight Review (BBC2) and The Moral Maze (BBC Radio 4). Dir, Dillington Park Nurseries, 2005–09; non-exec. Dir, Eden Project. Bd Mem., Old Vic, 2002–05; Trustee, Hay-on-Wye Literary Fest., 2000–. Trustee, Street Smart. Editor of Year (Magazines), 1994, 1995. *Publications*: Batty, Bloomers & Boycott, 1982; A Nice Girl Like Me, 1984; All for Love, 1987; Our Farm, 2007. *Recreations*: riding, ski-ing, tennis, reading, arts. *Club*: Groucho.

**BOYCOTT, Sir Geoffrey,** Kt 2019; cricket commentator; *b* 21 Oct. 1940; *s* of late Thomas Wilfred Boycott and Jane Boycott; *m* 2003, Rachael Swinglehurst; one *d*. *Educ*: Kinsley Modern Sch.; Hemsworth Grammar Sch. Played cricket for Yorkshire, 1962–86, received County Cap, 1963, Captain of Yorkshire, 1970–78. Played for England, 1964–74, 1977–82; scored 100th first-class hundred, England v Australia, 1977, 150th hundred, 1986; passed former world record no of runs scored in Test Matches, Delhi, Dec. 1981. Mem., General Cttee, 1984–93, Bd, 2005–11, Yorks CCC. Commentator: BBC TV; Trans World Internat.; Channel 9; SABC; Talk Radio; ESPN Star; Channel 4, 2004–05; BBC Radio, 2004–; Ten Sports, 2006–; Five (formerly Channel 5), 2006–; BT Sport, 2017–18. Columnist, Daily Telegraph. Pres., Yorks CCC, 2012–14. *Publications*: Geoff Boycott's Book for Young Cricketers, 1976; Put to the Test: England in Australia 1978–79, 1979; Geoff Boycott's Cricket Quiz, 1979; On Batting, 1980; Opening Up, 1980; In the Fast Lane, 1981; Master Class, 1982; Boycott, The Autobiography, 1987; Boycott on Cricket, 1990; Geoffrey Boycott on Cricket, 1999; The Best XI, 2008; Play Cricket the Right Way, 2010; Corridor of Certainty, 2014. *Recreation*: golf. *Address*: c/o Yorkshire County Cricket Club, Headingley Cricket Ground, Leeds, Yorks LS6 3DP.

**BOYCOTT, Kay Elizabeth;** Chief Executive, Asthma UK, since 2013; *b* Manchester, 3 Dec. 1969; *d* of Alan Boycott and Elizabeth Boycott; one *s* one *d*. *Educ*: Manchester High Sch. for Girls; Univ. of Durham (BA Econs and Hist. 1991). Brand Asst, Nestlé Rowntree, 1991–93; Brand Manager, 1994–95, Account Manager, 1996–97, Gp Controller, 1998–99, Johnson & Johnson; Consultant, 1999–2004, Dir, 2005–09, Oxford Strategic Mktg; Dir, Communications, Policy and Campaigns, Shelter, 2009–13. Non-exec. Dir, Hammersmith and Fulham PCT, 2004–09. Trustee: Gingerbread, 2011–15; Assoc. of Med. Res. Charities, 2018–. Mem., Gen. Adv. Council, King's Fund, 2017–. Lay Mem., Council, Durham Univ., 2018–. *Address*: Asthma UK, 18 Mansell Street, E1 8AA. *T*: (020) 7786 4900. *E*: kboycott@asthma.org.uk.

**BOYD;** *see* Lennox-Boyd.

**BOYD,** family name of **Barons Boyd of Duncansby** and **Kilmarnock**.

**BOYD OF DUNCANSBY,** Baron *cr* 2006 (Life Peer), of Duncansby in Caithness; **Colin David Boyd;** PC 2000; a Senator of the College of Justice in Scotland, since 2012; *b* 7 June 1953; *s* of Dr David Hugh Aird Boyd and Betty Meldrum Boyd; *m* 1979, Fiona Margaret MacLeod; two *s* one *d*. *Educ*: Wick High Sch.; George Watson's Coll., Edinburgh; Manchester Univ. (BA Econ); Edinburgh Univ. (LLB). WS 2007. Solicitor, 1978–82 and 2007–12; called to the Bar, Scotland, 1983; Legal Associate, Royal Town Planning Inst., 1990; Advocate Depute, 1993–95; QC (Scot.) 1995; Solicitor Gen. for Scotland, 1997–99; Solicitor Gen., 1999–2000, Lord Advocate, 2000–06, Scottish Exec. Consultant, Dundas & Wilson LLP, 2007–12. Member: Commn on Scottish Devolution, 2008–09; Scottish Civil Justice Council, 2016–. Vice-Pres., Investigatory Powers Tribunal, 2019– (Mem., 2019–). Hon. Prof. of Law, Univ. of Glasgow, 2008–12. Chm., Northern Lighthouse Heritage Trust, 2009–13. *Publications*: (contrib.) The Legal Aspects of Devolution, 1997. *Recreations*: walking, reading, watching Rugby. *Address*: Supreme Courts, Parliament Square, Edinburgh EH1 1RQ. *T*: (0131) 225 2595.

**BOYD OF MERTON,** 2nd Viscount *cr* 1960, of Merton-in-Penningham, Co. Wigtown; **Simon Donald Rupert Neville Lennox-Boyd;** *b* 7 Dec. 1939; *e s* of 1st Viscount Boyd of Merton, CH, PC, and Lady Patricia Guinness, *d* of 2nd Earl of Iveagh, KG, CB, CMG, FRS; *S* father, 1983; *m* 1962, Alice Mary (JP, DL, High Sheriff of Cornwall, 1987–88), *d* of late Major M. G. D. Clive and of Lady Mary Clive; two *s* two *d*. *Educ*: Eton; Christ Church, Oxford. Dep. Chm., Arthur Guinness & Sons, 1981–86. Chairman: SCF, 1987–92 (Vice-Chm., 1979–82); Stonham Housing Assoc., 1992–99; Iveagh Trustees Ltd, 1992–2003; Trustee, Guinness Trust, 1974–2004. *Heir*: *s* Hon. Benjamin Alan Lennox-Boyd [*b* 21 Oct. 1964; *m* 1993, Sheila Carroll; two *s* one *d*]. *Address*: Voss, Trematon, Saltash PL12 4RX. *T*: (01752) 844359.
See also Baron Spens.

**BOYD, Alan Robb;** Consultant, Pinsent Masons LLP (formerly McGrigors LLP, solicitors), 2010–14 (Director, Public Law, 1997–2010, McGrigor Donald, subseq. McGrigors LLP, solicitors); *b* 30 July 1953; *er s* of Alexander Boyd and Mary Herd Boyd; *m* 1973, Frances Helen Donaldson; two *d*. *Educ*: Irvine Royal Acad.; Univ. of Dundee (LLB 1974); Open Univ. (BA 1985). Admitted solicitor, 1976; Principal Legal Asst, Shetland Is Council, 1979–81; Principal Solicitor, Glenrothes Develt Corp., 1981–84; Legal Advr, Irvine Develt Corp., 1984–97. Mem. Council, Law Soc. of Scotland, 1985–97 (Vice-Pres., 1994–95; Pres., 1995–96); Bd Mem., 1988–94, Pres., 1992–94, European Company Lawyers' Assoc.;

Chm., Assoc. for Scottish Public Affairs, 1998–2000. *Recreations*: golf, music, gardening. *Address*: 26 Hannah Wynd, St Quivox, Ayr KA6 5HB. *T*: (01292) 521936. *Club*: Prestwick St Nicholas Golf.

**BOYD, Andrew Jonathan Corrie,** CMG 2005; OBE 1992; DPhil; HM Diplomatic Service, retired; Director, Special Projects, QinetiQ plc, 2005–11; Senior Research Fellow, University of Buckingham, since 2015 (Flick Research Fellow, 2012–15); *b* 5 May 1950; *s* of John Ronald Boyd and Jane Rhiain Boyd (*née* Morgan); *m* 1979, Ginette Anne Vischer; two *s* one *d*. *Educ*: Tonbridge Sch.; BRNC Dartmouth; St John's Coll., Oxford (BA Hons PPE); Univ. of Buckingham (DPhil Naval Hist. 2015). Served RN, Submarine Service, 1968–80. Entered FCO, 1980; First Secretary: FCO, 1980; (Econ.), Accra, 1981–84; (Chancery), Mexico City, 1988–91; Political Counsellor, Islamabad, 1996–99; Counsellor, FCO, 1999–2005. Dir, Special Projects, QinetiQ plc, 2005–11. *Publications*: The Royal Navy in Eastern Waters: linchpin of victory 1935–1942, 2017. *Recreations*: mountain walking, sea swimming, military history. *Address*: c/o Humanities Research Institute, University of Buckingham, Hunter Street, Buckingham MK18 1EG.

**BOYD, Aparna;** *see* Nathan, A.

**BOYD, Atarah, (Mrs Douglas Boyd);** *see* Ben-Tovim, A.

**BOYD, (David) John;** QC 1982; arbitrator; accredited mediator; Chairman, Axxia Systems Ltd, 1995–2008; *b* 11 Feb. 1935; *s* of David Boyd and Ellen Jane Boyd (*née* Gruer); *m* 1960, Raija Sinikka Lindholm, Finland (*d* 2011); one *d* (one *s* decd). *Educ*: Eastbourne Coll.; St George's Sch., Newport, USA (British-Amer. schoolboy schol.); Gonville and Caius Coll., Cambridge (MA). FCIArb 1979. Various secretarial posts, ICI, 1957–62; Legal Asst, Pfizer, 1962–66; called to the Bar, Gray's Inn, 1963, Bencher, 1988; Sec. and Legal Officer, Henry Wiggin & Co., 1966; Asst Sec. and Sen. Legal Officer (UK), Internat. Nickel, 1968; Dir, Impala Platinum, 1972–78; Sec. and Chief Legal Officer, 1972–86, and Dir, 1984–86, Inco Europe; practising barrister, 1986; Director: Legal Services, 1986–93, Public Affairs and Communications, 1993–95, Digital Equipment Co.; Digital Equipment Scotland, 1987–95. Gen. Comr of Income Tax, 1978–83; Immigration Adjudicator, 1995–2005; Immigration Judge, 2005–08; Vice-Pres., Council of Immigration Judges, 1998–2000. Chm., Bar Assoc. for Commerce, Finance and Industry, 1980–81; Mem., Senate of Inns of Court and Bar, 1978–81. Sec. Gen., Assoc. des Juristes d'Entreprise Européens (European Company Lawyers Assoc.), 1983–84. Dir, Centre for European Dispute Resolution, 1991–94. Legal Advisor to Review Bd for Govt Contracts, 1984–91. Chm., CBI Competition Panel, 1988–93; Mem., Electricity Panel, Monopolies and Mergers Commn, 1991–98. Mem., Exec. Cttee, Royal Acad. of Dancing, 1991–98; Chm., The Place Th. and Contemp. Dance Trust, 1995–98; Dir, Oxford Orch. da Camera, 1996–2001. Treas., Upton Bishop PCC, 2003–19. *Recreations*: holidaying in France, viticulture. *Address*: Beeches, Upton Bishop, Ross-on-Wye, Herefordshire HR9 7UD. *T*: (01989) 780214. *E*: email@johnboyd.net.

**BOYD, Sir Ian (Lamont),** Kt 2019; DSc; FRSB; FRSE; Professor of Biology, since 2001, and Adviser to the Principal's Office, since 2012, University of St Andrews; *b* 9 Feb. 1957; *s* of late Dr John Morton Boyd, CBE, FRSE and Winifred Isobel Boyd; *m* 1982, Sheila M. E. Aitken; one *s* two *d*. *Educ*: George Heriot's Sch., Edinburgh; Univ. of Aberdeen (BSc 1st Cl. Hons 1979; DSc 1996); St John's Coll., Cambridge (PhD 1983). FRSB (FSB 2011). RAF Volunteer Reserve, 1975–78. Churchill Fellow, 1980; SSO, Inst. of Terrestrial Ecol., 1982–87, SPSO, British Antarctic Survey, 1987–2001, NERC; Dir, NERC Sea Mammal Res. Unit, 2001–12, Dir, Scottish Oceans Inst., 2009–12, Univ. of St Andrews; Chief Exec., SMRU Ltd, 2006–09. Chief Scientist, US Navy Behavioral Response Study, 2007–08; Chief Scientific Advr, DEFRA, 2012–19. Mem., Scottish Govt Enquiry into future of Common Fisheries Policy, 2008–10. Hon. Prof., Univ. of Birmingham, 1997–2001. Chairman: Marine Alliance for Sci. and Technol. for Scotland, 2005–10; UK Food Res. Partnership, 2014–16; Member, Council of Management: Hebridean Trust, 1990–2012 and 2015–; Seamark Trust, 1993–2012; Scottish Sustainable Seas Task Force, 2008; Member: Council, Scottish Assoc. for Marine Sci., 2004–08; Adv. Council, Nat. Oceanography Centre, Southampton, 2008–10; Lenfest Forage Fish Task Force, 2009–11; Scottish Science Adv. Council, 2010–15; Adv. Cttee, British Geological Survey, 2012–15; NERC, 2013–18; Sci. Policy Adv. Gp, Royal Soc., 2015–; Chm., Scientific Adv. Bd on Decommissioning, Oil & Gas UK, 2010–12; Co-Chm., Internat. Quiet Oceans Experiment, 2010–12. Director: Fera Science Ltd, 2015–; Hebridean Trust Ltd, 2015–. Ed., 2000–06, Ed.-in-Chief, 2006–07, Jl of Zoology; Mem. Bd, Reviewing Eds, Science, 2011–. FRSE 2002. Hon. DSc Exeter, 2017. US Antarctic Medal, 1995; Bruce Medal, RSE, 1996; Scientific Medal, Zool Soc. of London, 1998; Marsh Award for Marine & Freshwater Conservation, Zool Soc. of London, 2006; Polar Medal, 2017. *Publications*: The Hebrides: a natural history, 1990; Marine Mammals: advances in behavioural and population biology, 1993; The Hebrides: a mosaic of islands, 1996; The Hebrides: a natural tapestry, 1996; The Hebrides: a habitable land, 1996; Conserving Nature: Scotland and the wider world, 2005; Top Predators in Marine Ecosystems, 2006; Marine Mammal Ecology and Conservation: a handbook of techniques, 2010; contrib. numerous papers to scientific jls. *Recreations*: walking, sailing, photography, Rugby. *Address*: University of St Andrews, College Gate, North Street, St Andrews, Fife KY16 9LB. *T*: (01334) 463230. *E*: ilb@st-andrews.ac.uk.

**BOYD, John;** *see* Boyd, D. J.

**BOYD, Sir John (Dixon Iklé),** KCMG 1992 (CMG 1985); HM Diplomatic Service, retired; Fellow, Churchill College, Cambridge, since 2006 (Master, 1996–2006); Chairman, Asia House, 2010–17 (Hon. President, since 2018; Member, International Advisory Council, 2001–); *b* 17 Jan. 1936; *s* of Prof. James Dixon Boyd and late Amélie Lowenthal; *m* 1st, 1968, Gunilla Kristina Ingegerd Rönngren; one *s* one *d*; 2nd, 1977, Julia Daphne Raynsford; three *d*. *Educ*: Westminster Sch. (Hon. Fellow, 2003); Clare Coll., Cambridge (BA; Hon. Fellow, 1994); Yale Univ. (MA). Joined HM Foreign Service, 1962; Hong Kong, 1962–64; Peking, 1965–67; Foreign Office, 1967–69; Washington, 1969–73; 1st Sec., Peking, 1973–75; secondment to HM Treasury, 1976; Counsellor: (Economic), Bonn, 1977–81; (Economic and Soc. Affairs), UK Mission to UN, 1981–84; Asst Under-Sec. of State, FCO, 1984; Political Advr, Hong Kong, 1985–87; Dep. Under-Sec. of State, FCO, 1987–89; Chief Clerk, FCO, 1989–92; Ambassador to Japan, 1992–96. Non-exec Dir, BNFL, 1997–2000. UK Rep., ASEM Vision Gp, 1998–2000; Mem., All Nippon Airways Adv. Gp, 2003–09. Co-Chm., Nuffield Langs Inquiry, 1998–2000. Syndic, Fitzwilliam Mus., 1997–2002. Advr, Iran Heritage Foundn, 2008–. Trustee: Sir Winston Churchill Archive Trust, 1996–2006; Wordsworth Trust, 1997–2013 (Fellow, 2014–) Margaret Thatcher Archive Trust, 1997–2016; Cambridge Foundn, 1997–2005; GF Sasakawa Foundn, 2001–; RAND Europe (UK), 2001–12 (Mem., Council of Advrs 2012–18; Trustee Emeritus, 2018); Huang Hsing Foundn, 2001–; British Mus., 1996–2006 now Trustee Emeritus (Chm., 2002–06); Joseph Needham Res. Inst., 2005– (Chm. 2008–16). Gov., RSC, 1996–2005. Member: Council, Cambridge Univ. Senate, 2001–04 Bd, and Advr, E Asia Inst., Cambridge Univ., 1998–2006; Bd, UK-Japan 21st Century Gp 2006–15; Adv. Council, LSO, 2008–. Emeritus Fellow, British Assoc. for Japanese Studies 2007–. Chairman: Bd of Govs, Bedales Sch., 1996–2001; David Davies Meml Inst. 1997–2001; Trustees, Cambridge Union Soc., 1997–2006. Vice-Chm., Menuhin

Competition (formerly Yehudi Menuhin Internat. Violin) Trust Ltd, 1996–2017. Vice Pres., Lakeland Housing Trust, 2007–16. Hon. Fellow, Inst. of Linguists, 1998–. Fellow, 48 Gp Club, 2008–. Grand Cordon, Order of the Rising Sun (Japan), 2007. *Recreations:* music, fly fishing. *Clubs:* Athenæum, Beefsteak.
*See also Sir R. D. H. Boyd.*

**BOYD, John MacInnes**, CBE 1990; QPM 1984; HM Chief Inspector of Constabulary for Scotland, 1993–96; *b* 14 Oct. 1933; *s* of late F. Duncan Boyd and M. Catherine MacInnes; *m* 1957, Sheila MacSporran; two *s*. *Educ:* Oban High School. Paisley Burgh Police, 1956–67; Renfrew and Bute Constabulary, 1967–75; Strathclyde Police, 1975–84 (Asst Chief Constable, 1979–84); Chief Constable, Dumfries and Galloway Constabulary, 1984–89; HM Inspector of Constabulary for Scotland, 1989–93. Pres., Scotland, ACPO, 1988–89. *Address:* Beechwood, Lochwinnoch Road, Kilmacolm PA13 4DZ.

**BOYD, Sir (John) Michael**, Kt 2012; Artistic Director, Royal Shakespeare Company, 2002–12 (Associate Director, 1996–2002); *b* 6 July 1955; *s* of John Truesdale Boyd and Sheila Boyd; one *s* one *d* by Marcella Evaristi; one *d* by Caroline Hall. *Educ:* Latymer Upper Sch.; Daniel Stewart's Coll.; Univ. of Edinburgh (MA English Lit.). Trainee Dir, Malaya Bronnaya Th., Moscow, 1980; Asst Dir, Belgrade Th., Coventry, 1980–82; Associate Dir, Crucible Th., Sheffield, 1982–84; Founding Artistic Dir, Tron Th., Glasgow, 1985–96. Hon. Prof., Univ. of Michigan, 2001–04. *Productions:* for Tron Theatre: The Guid Sisters, 1989, Tremblay's The Real World, 1991 (also Toronto, NY and Montreal); (with I. Glen) Macbeth, 1993; The Trick is to Keep Breathing (also Royal Court and World Stage Fest., Toronto), 1995; for Royal Shakespeare Co.: The Broken Heart, 1994; The Spanish Tragedy, 1996; Measure for Measure, 1997; Troilus and Cressida (also Tel Aviv and USA), 1999; A Midsummer Night's Dream (also NY), 1999; Romeo and Juliet, 2000; Henry VI, Parts 1, 2 and 3, and Richard III (also USA), 2001; The Tempest, 2002; Hamlet, transf. Albery, 2004; Twelfth Night, transf. Novello, 2005; The Histories, 2006–08, transf. Roundhouse, 2008; As You Like It, 2009, transf. Roundhouse, 2010 (also NY, 2011); The Grain Store, 2009; Antony and Cleopatra, 2010, transf. Roundhouse, 2010, Swan, 2011; Macbeth, 2011; Boris Godunov, 2012; Tamburlaine, 2018; West End: Miss Julie, Haymarket, 2000; other productions: The Big Meal, Ustinov Studio, Th. Royal Bath, 2014; Tamburlaine, NY, 2014; Orfeo, ROH/Roundhouse, 2015; The Intelligent Homosexual's Guide to Capitalism and Socialism with a Key to the Scriptures, Hampstead Th., 2016; Right Now, Traverse Th., Edinburgh, Th. Royal Bath, Bush Th., 2016; Eugene Onegin, Garsington Opera, 2016; The Open House, Ustinov Studio, Th. Royal Bath, 2017; The Cherry Orchard, Bristol Old Vic, 2018. Hon. DLitt Edinburgh, 2009. *Recreations:* cooking, walking, swimming, reading, music. *Address:* c/o Casarotto Ramsay & Associates, Waverley House, 7–12 Noel Street, W1F 8GQ. *T:* (020) 7287 4450.

**BOYD, Sir Kyle Robert Rendell**, 4th Bt *cr* 1916; *b* 15 Feb. 1987; *s* of late Ian Walter Rendell Boyd and LeeAnn Boyd (*née* Dillon); *S* grandfather, 2018; *m* 2015, Nicole Bloudoff; one *s*. *Heir: s* Jack William Cameron Boyd, *b* 20 Dec. 2016.

**BOYD, Morgan Alistair**, CMG 1990; Adviser, Commonwealth Development Corporation, 1994–2000; *b* 1 May 1934; *s* of Norman Robert Boyd and Kathleen Muriel Boyd; *m* 1959, Judith Mary Martin. *Educ:* Marlborough College; Wadham College, Oxford (BA, MA 1955). FRGS 1957. Commonwealth Development Corporation: Management trainee, 1957; Exec., Malaysia, 1958–66; Manager, East Caribbean Housing, Barbados, 1967–70; Gen. Manager, Tanganyika Develt Finance Co., 1970–74; Advr, Industrial Develt Bank, Kenya, 1975; Regl Controller, Central Africa, 1976–80, East Africa, 1981–82; Dep. Gen. Manager, Investigations, London, 1983–84; Dir of Ops, 1985–89; Dep. Gen. Manager, 1989–91; Dep. Chief Exec., 1991–94. Director: EDESA Management, Switzerland, 1995–97; Laxey (formerly Tea Plantations) Investment Trust PLC, 1998–2009; AMREF UK, 1999–2007 (Chm., 2001–07); Douglas Bay Capital PLC, 2009–12; Chm., Gateway to Growth Ltd, 2005–08. Chm., Southern Africa Business Assoc., 1995–2007. Member: RSA, 1990–; Council, Royal African Soc., 1992– (Vice-Chm., 1996–); Management Council, Africa Centre, 1995–2002; Trustee, African Fellowship Trust, 2009–. *Publications:* Royal Challenge Accepted, 1962; Get Up and Go, 2009. *Recreations:* music, sailing, travel. *Address:* 7 South Hill Mansions, South Hill Park, NW3 2SL. *T:* (020) 7435 1082. *Clubs:* Naval, English-Speaking Union.

**BOYD, Norman Jonathan;** Member, Antrim South, Northern Ireland Assembly, 1998–2003 (UKU, 1998–99, NIU, 1999–2003); *b* 16 Oct. 1961; *s* of William and Jean Boyd; *m* 1984, Sylvia Christine (*née* Brindley); one *s* one *d*. *Educ:* Belfast High Sch.; Newtownabbey Technical Coll. (BEC Nat. Cert. in Business Studies with Distinction, 1982). Joined Halifax Bldg Soc., later Halifax plc, 1980: posts included Deptl Manager, Asst Branch Manager, and Manager. NIUP Whip, NI Assembly, 1999–2002. Member: Kilroot True Blues Loyal Orange Lodge, 1988–; Kilroot Royal Arch Purple Chapter, 1989–; Royal Black Instn, Carrickfergus, 1993–. Formerly Mem., Boys' Bde (President's Badge, 1979; Queen's Badge, 1980). *Recreations:* sport - soccer, caravanning, theatre, cinema, programme collecting. *Address:* 18 Woodford Park, Newtownabbey, Co. Antrim BT36 6TJ. *T:* (028) 9084 4297, *Fax:* (028) 9083 6644.

**BOYD, Sir Robert (David Hugh)**, Kt 2004; FRCP, FFPH, FRCPCH, FMedSci; Principal, St George's Hospital Medical School, University of London, 1996–2003; Professor of Paediatrics, 1996–2003, Pro-Vice Chancellor (Medicine), 2000–03, and Deputy Vice-Chancellor, 2002–03, University of London; *b* 14 May 1938; *s* of James Dixon Boyd and Amélie Boyd; *m* 1966, Meriel Cornelia Talbot; one *s* two *d*. *Educ:* Leys Sch.; Clare Coll., Cambridge (MA; MB, BChir); University Coll. Hosp., London. FRCP 1977; FFPH (FFPHM 1997); FRCPCH 1997, Hon. FRCPCH 2004. Jun. med. posts, Hosp. for Sick Children, Gt Ormond St, Brompton Hosp., UCH, 1962–65; Sir Stuart Halley Res. Fellow and Sen. Registrar, UC Hosp. and Med. Sch., 1966–71; Goldsmith's MRC Travelling Fellow, Univ. of Colo Med. Center, 1971–72; Sen. Lectr and Hon. Consultant, UCH Med. Sch., 1972–80; Asst Registrar, RCP, 1980–81; University of Manchester Medical School: Prof. of Paediatrics, 1981–96; Dean, 1989–93; Vis. Prof., 1996–; Hon. Consultant: St Mary's Hosp., Manchester and Booth Hall Children's Hosp., Manchester, 1981–96; St George's Healthcare NHS Trust, 1996–2003. Chm., Nat. Primary Care R&D Centre, Manchester, Salford and York Univs, 1994–96. Vis. Prof., Oregon Health Sci. Univ., 1988. Ed., Placenta, 1989–95. Chm., Manchester HA, 1994–96. Member: Standing Med. Adv. Cttee, 1988–92; Standing Cttee on Postgrad. Med. and Dental Educn, 1995–99; Jt Med. Adv. Cttee, HEFCs, 1994–99; Univs UK (formerly CVCP), 1997–2003 (Mem. Health Cttee, 1997–2003); Scientific Adv. Cttee, AMRC, 1996–2003; Council, RVC, 1999–2004; Chm., Council of Heads of UK Med. Schs, 2001–03; Dir, Gtr Manchester Res. Alliance, 2004–08. Chair: Lloyds TSB Foundn for England & Wales, 2003–09; Council for Assisting Refugee Academics, 2004–10. Non-exec. Chm., Nuovoprobe, 2007–15. Mem., Taskforce supporting R & D in NHS (Culyer Cttee), 1994. Sec., 1977–80, Chm., 1987–90, Acad. Bd, BPA. Co-opted Gov., Kingston Univ., 1998–2003; Gov., Univ. of Manchester, 2004–09. Pres., 1942 Club, 1998–99. Hon. Mem., Amer. Pediatric Soc., 2006. Founder FMedSci 1998. Churchwarden, St Peter's, Prestbury, 2013–17; Chm., Friends of St Peter's, Prestbury, 2017–. Hon. DSc: Kingston, 2003; Keele, 2005. *Publications:* (jtly) Paediatric Problems in General Practice, 1982, 3rd edn 1996; contribs to Placental and Fetal Physiol. and Paediatrics. *Recreations:* flute, cooking, reading, holidays. *Address:* The Stone House, Adlington, Macclesfield, Cheshire SK10 4NU. *T:* (01625) 872400.
*See also Sir J. D. I. Boyd.*

**BOYD, Stewart Craufurd**, CBE 2005; QC 1981; international commercial arbitrator; a Recorder, 1994–2013; *b* 25 Oct. 1943; *s* of late Leslie Balfour Boyd, CBE, and Wendy Marie Boyd; *m* 1970, Catherine Jay; one *s* three *d*. *Educ:* Winchester Coll.; Trinity Coll., Cambridge (MA). Called to the Bar, Middle Temple, 1967, Bencher, 1989. Dep. Chm., FSA, 1999–2005. *Publications:* (ed) Scrutton, Charterparties, 18th edn, 1972 to 21st edn, 2009; (with Sir Michael Mustill) The Law and Practice of Commercial Arbitration, 1982, 1989, 2001; contrib. jls on maritime law, internat. arbitration law, etc. *Recreations:* children and grandchildren, playing the piano and guitar, travel with friends and family, reading and learning. *Address:* 43 Downshire Hill, NW3 1NU. *T:* (020) 7431 1581.

**BOYD, William Andrew Murray**, CBE 2005; FRSL; author; *b* 7 March 1952; *s* of Dr Alexander Murray Boyd and Evelyn Boyd; *m* 1975, Susan Anne (*née* Wilson). *Educ:* Gordonstoun Sch.; Glasgow Univ. (MA Hons English and Philosophy); Jesus Coll., Oxford (Hon. Fellow, 2007). Lecturer in English, St Hilda's Coll., Oxford, 1980–83; Television Critic, New Statesman, 1981–83. *Screenplays:* Good and Bad at Games (TV), 1983; Dutch Girls (TV), 1985; Scoop (TV), 1987; Stars and Bars, 1988; Aunt Julia and the Scriptwriter, 1990; Mr Johnson, 1990; Chaplin, 1992; A Good Man in Africa, 1994; The Trench, 1999 (also Dir); Sword of Honour (TV), 2001; Armadillo (TV), 2001; Man to Man, 2005; A Waste of Shame (TV), 2005; The Three Kings (TV), 2009; Any Human Heart (TV), 2010; Restless (TV), 2012. *Plays:* Longing, 2013, the Argument, 2016, Hampstead Th. FRSL 1983. Hon. DLitt: St Andrews, 1997; Stirling, 1997; Glasgow, 2000; Dundee, 2008. Officier de l'Ordre des Arts et des Lettres (France), 2005. *Publications:* A Good Man in Africa, 1981 (Whitbread Prize 1981, Somerset Maugham Award 1982); On the Yankee Station (short stories), 1981; An Ice-Cream War, 1982 (John Llewellyn Rhys Prize, 1982); Stars and Bars, 1984; School Ties (screenplays: Good and Bad at Games; Dutch Girls), 1985; The New Confessions, 1987; Brazzaville Beach, 1990 (James Tait Black Meml Prize, 1990; McVitie's Prize, 1991); The Blue Afternoon, 1993 (Sunday Express Book of the Year Award, 1993; LA Times Book Award for Fiction, 1995); The Destiny of Nathalie X (short stories), 1995; Armadillo, 1998; Nat Tate: an American artist, 1998; Any Human Heart, 2002 (Prix Jean Monnet, 2003); Fascination (short stories), 2004; Bamboo, 2005; Restless (Costa Novel Award), 2006; The Dream Lover (short stories), 2008; Ordinary Thunderstorms, 2009; Waiting for Sunrise, 2012; Longing (play), 2013; Solo, 2013; The Vanishing Game (novella), 2014; Sweet Caress, 2015; The Argument (play), 2016; The Dreams of Bethany Mellmoth (short stories), 2017; Love is Blind, 2018; Trio, 2020. *Recreation:* strolling. *Address:* c/o The Agency, 24 Pottery Lane, Holland Park, W11 4LZ.

**BOYD-CARPENTER, Sir (Marsom) Henry**, KCVO 2002 (CVO 1994); Senior Partner, Farrer & Co., Solicitors, 2000–02 (Partner, 1968–2002); Private Solicitor to the Queen, 1995–2002; *b* 11 Oct. 1939; *s* of Francis Henry Boyd-Carpenter and Nina Boyd-Carpenter (*née* Townshend); *m* 1971, Lesley Ann Davies; one *s* one *d*. *Educ:* Charterhouse; Balliol Coll., Oxford (BA 1962; MA 1967). Admitted solicitor, 1966; Solicitor to Duchy of Cornwall, 1976–94; Private Solicitor: to Prince of Wales, 1994–96; to Queen Elizabeth the Queen Mother, Duke of York and Prince Edward, later Earl of Wessex, 1995–2002. Law Society: Mem., 1966–; Hon. Auditor, 1979–81. Member: Council, Prince of Wales's Inst. of Architecture, 1995–99; Bd, British Library, 1999–2007 (Dep. Chm., 2003–07); Mem. Council, Friends, 2005–07). Hon. Steward, Westminster Abbey, 1980–; Hon. Legal Advr, Canterbury Cathedral Trust Fund, 1994–2001. Mem. Governing Body, Charterhouse, 1981–2004 (Chm., 2000–04); Governor: St Mary's Sch., Gerrards Cross, 1967–70; Sutton's Hosp. in Charterhouse, 1994–2005. Member: RHS Governance Wkg Party, 2000–01; Council, Chelsea Physic Garden, 1983–2002; Trustee: Nat. Gardens Scheme, 1998–2003; Merlin Trust, 1998–2003; BL Trust, 2012–16; UK Flagship Project, 2012–13. Mem., Bd of Trustees, Inst. of Cancer Res., 2001–07. Pres., Wood Green, The Animals Charity (formerly Wood Green Animal Shelters), 2001–18. Ritterkreuz des Herzoglich Sachsen-Coburg und Gotha'schen Hausordens, 2010. *Recreations:* reading, gardening, listening to music, hill-walking. *Address:* Georgian Wing, Williamscot House, Williamscot, Oxon OX17 1AE.

**BOYD-CARPENTER, Hon. Sir Thomas (Patrick John)**, KBE 1993 (MBE 1973); Chairman, Moorfields Eye Hospital NHS Foundation Trust, 2001–08; senior consultant, 1996–2010, and Director, 1997–2010, People in Business; *b* 16 June 1938; *s* of Baron Boyd-Carpenter, PC; *m* 1972, Mary-Jean (*née* Duffield); one *s* two *d*. *Educ:* Stowe. Commnd 1957; served UK, Oman, Malaya, Borneo and Germany; Instr, Staff Coll., 1975–77; Defence Fellowship, Aberdeen Univ., 1977–78; CO 1st Bn Scots Guards, 1979–81; Comdr 24 Inf. Brigade, 1983–84; Dir, Defence Policy, 1985–87; COS, HQ BAOR, 1988–89; ACDS (Programmes), 1989–92; DCDS (Progs and Personnel), 1992–96; retd in rank of Lt-Gen. Chairman: Social Security Adv. Cttee, 1995–2004; Kensington & Chelsea and Westminster HA, 1996–2001; Adv. Bd on Family Law, 1997–2002. *Publications:* Conventional Deterrence: into the 1990s, 1989. *Recreations:* reading, gardening.
*See also Baroness Hogg.*

**BOYD-LEE, Paul Winston Michael;** Director, Bible Truth Publishers, since 1974; *b* 3 May 1941; *s* of Harry William Lee and Violet Cynthia (*née* Cabrera); *m* 1962, Jean Warburton; one *s*. *Educ:* Brighton Coll.; Open Univ. (BA); Exeter Univ. (DipTh). Entertainments manager, 1963–66; credit controller, 1966–72; farmer, 1973–88; publisher, 1988–. Member: Dir's Bd, Church Army, 1999–2012; Church Army Investment Cttee, 2000–. Member: Gen. Synod of C of E, 1991–; Archbp's Council, 2006–16; Audit Cttee, C of E, 2006–16; Ethical Investment Adv. Gp, C of E, 2006–16. *Publications:* Israel and the New Testament, 1981, 2nd edn 1996; Bible Study Guide to the Israel Peoples, 2012; The Significance of Biblical Israel Today, 2013. *Recreations:* fruit culture, canal drawing, travel. *Address:* Manor Barn, Horsington, Som BA8 0ET. *T:* (01963) 371137, 07710 604777. *E:* pbl2@btinternet.com.

**BOYDE, Prof. Patrick**, PhD; FBA 1987; Serena Professor of Italian, 1981–2002, and Fellow of St John's College, since 1966, University of Cambridge; *b* 30 Nov. 1934; *s* of late Harry Caine Boyde and Florence Colonna Boyde; *m* 1956, Catherine Taylor; four *s*. *Educ:* Braintree County High Sch.; Wanstead County High Sch.; St John's Coll., Cambridge. BA 1956, MA 1960, PhD 1963. Nat. service, commnd RA, 1956–58. Research, St John's Coll., Cambridge, 1958–61; Asst Lectr in Italian, Univ. of Leeds, 1961–62; Asst Lectr, later Lectr, Univ. of Cambridge, 1962–81. Corresp. Fellow, Accademia Nazionale dei Lincei, 1986. *Publications:* Dante's Lyric Poetry (with K. Foster), 1967; Dante's Style in his Lyric Poetry, 1971; Dante Philomythes and Philosopher: Man in the Cosmos, 1981; Perception and Passion in Dante's Comedy, 1993; Human Vices and Human Worth in Dante's Comedy, 2000. *Recreations:* staging plays in Ancient Greek, music.

**BOYDEN, Dame Peggy K.;** *see* Koopman-Boyden.

**BOYE-ANAWOMAH, Margo Ciara Essi; Her Honour Judge Boye;** a Circuit Judge, since 2013; *b* Bromsgrove, 10 Nov. 1963; *d* of late Michael and of Marjorie Boye-Anawomah; *m* 2008, Martin Soorjoo. *Educ:* Ghana Internat. Sch., Ghana; Greycoats,

Westminster; South Bank Univ. (LLB Hons); Inns of Court Sch. of Law. Called to the Bar, Inner Temple, 1989; in practice as barrister, 1989–2013; Dep. Dist Judge, Principal Registry of Family Div., 2003–13; a Family Recorder, 2009–13. Member: Bd, CAFCASS, 2003–10; Professional Adv. Gp, Nat. Youth Advocacy Service, 2007–; Children's Adv. Panel, BBFC, 2010–. *Recreations*: cinema, theatre, music, travel. *Address*: Central London Family Court, First Avenue House, 42–49 High Holborn, WC1V 6NP. *T*: (020) 7421 8594.

**BOYLAN, Prof. Patrick John**, PhD; FMA; FGS; Professor of Heritage Policy and Management, Department of Cultural Policy and Management, City University, 1996–2004, now Emeritus; *b* 17 Aug. 1939; *s* of Francis Boylan and Mary Doreen (*née* Haxby), Hull, Yorks; *m* 1st, Ann Elizabeth, *o d* of late Alfred William and Elizabeth Worsfold (marr. diss.); four *s*; 2nd, Pamela Mary, *o d* of late Rev. Robert William Jack and Mary Inder; three *s*. *Educ*: Marist Coll., Hull; Univ. of Hull (BSc 1960; PGCE 1961); Univ. of Leicester (PhD 1985); Museums Diploma (with Distinction), Museums Assoc., 1966. FMA 1972; FGS 1973; FCMI (FBIM 1990; MBIM 1975). Asst Master, Marist Coll., Hull, 1961–63; Keeper of Geology and Natural History, Kingston upon Hull Museums, 1964–68; Dir of Museums and Art Gallery, Exeter City Council, 1968–72; Dir of Museums and Art Gall., Leicester City Council, 1972–74; Dir of Museums and Arts, Leics County Council, 1974–90; Prof. of Arts Policy Mgt and Hd, Dept of Cultural Policy and Mgt, City Univ., 1990–96. Visiting Professor: UCL, 1995; Univ. of Buckingham, 1997–2002; Fed. Univ. of Rio de Janeiro, 1998. International Council of Museums: Chm., Internat. Cttee for Training of Personnel, 1983–89 and 1998–2004; Chm., UK Nat. Cttee, 1987–93; Mem., Adv. Cttee, 1983–93; Chm., Ethics Cttee, 1984–90; Mem., Exec. Council, 1989–92; Vice-Pres., 1992–98; Chm., Legal Affairs Cttee, 2004–08; Hon. Mem., 2004. Councillor, Museums Assoc., 1970–71 and 1986–92 (Centenary Pres., 1988–90); Sec., Soc. of County Museum Dirs, 1974–78; Chm., Library Cttee, Geol Soc., 1984–87. Chm., William Pengelly Cave Studies Trust, 2007–15 (Hon. Pres., 2015–); Pres., 2012–14, Vice Pres., 2015–17, Yorks Geol Soc. Consultant: UNESCO; Jt UN/UNESCO World Commn on Culture and Develt; Council of Europe; World Bank; British Council, etc. Freeman, City of London, 1991; Liveryman, Framework Knitters' Co., 1991–. FCMI (FBIM 1990; MBIM 1975). Advocacy Award, Internat. Inst. of Conservation, 2012. High Order of Merit 'Danica' (Croatia) 1997. Ed.-in-Chief, Internat. Jl of Intangible Heritage, 2005–09. *Publications*: Ice Age in Yorkshire and Humberside, 1983; The Changing World of Museums and Art Galleries, 1986; Museums 2000: politics, people, professionals and profit, 1991; Review of Convention on Protection of Cultural Property in the Event of Armed Conflict, 1993; Running a Museum: a practical handbook, 2005 (trans. Arabic, French, Spanish, Russian, Chinese, Vietnamese); (with A. V. R. Woollard) Trainer's Manual: for use with Running a Museum: a practical handbook, 2006 (trans. Arabic, French, Spanish, Chinese, Vietnamese); Exchanging Ideas Dispassionately and without Animosity: the Leicester Literary and Philosophical Society 1835–2010, 2010; over 200 papers in learned jls, professional pubns and chapters in books on museums, cultural policy, mgt, prof. training, geology, natural history, history of science and history of music. *Recreations*: the arts (especially opera and contemporary arts and crafts), research on history of science and music, Rotary (Pres., Rotary Club of Leicester, 2009–10; Paul Harris Fellow, 2012). *Address*: 2A Compass Road, Leicester LE5 2HF. *T*: (0116) 220 5496. *E*: p.boylan@city.ac.uk.

**BOYLE**, family name of **Earls of Cork, Glasgow**, and **Shannon**.

**BOYLE, Alan Gordon**; QC 1991; *b* 31 March 1949; *s* of late Dr Michael Morris Boyle and of Hazel Irene Boyle; *m* 1981, Claudine-Aimée Minne-Vercruysse; two *d*. *Educ*: Royal Shrewsbury Sch.; St Catherine's Coll., Oxford (MA). Called to the Bar, Lincoln's Inn, 1972, Bencher, 2003; Head of Chambers, 2008–. *Recreations*: walking, music. *Address*: Serle Court Chambers, 6 New Square, Lincoln's Inn, WC2A 3QS. *T*: (020) 7242 6105.

See also Sir R. M. Boyle.

**BOYLE, (Anthony) Mark**; non-executive Chairman, The Pensions Regulator, since 2014; *b* Caerleon, 5 July 1960; *s* of Anthony Boyle and Rosemary Boyle; *m* 1990, Laura Peckham; one *s* one *d*. *Educ*: St Joseph's High Sch., Newport, Mon; Durham Univ. (BA Hons Econ. Hist. 1981). Lloyds Bank Internat., 1982–86; Kleinwort Benson Ltd, 1986–96; Gp Corporate Develt Dir, Compass Gp plc, 1996–2004; Gp Strategy and Develt Dir, Rentokil Initial plc, 2004–08; Chief Operating Officer, Shareholder Exec., BIS, 2008–13. Non-exec. Chm., Land Registry, 2011–16. *Recreations*: golf, tennis, classical music. *Address*: The Pensions Regulator, Napier House, Trafalgar Place, Brighton BN1 4DW. *E*: mark.boyle@thepensionsregulator.gov.uk. *Club*: Royal Mid-Surrey Golf.

**BOYLE, Christopher Alexander David**; QC 2013; *b* Helensburgh, Scotland, 1970; *s* of Paul A. D. Boyle, MRCVS and Helen A. M. F. Boyle (*née* Lindsay, later Artwell-Dawes); *m* 1998, Ilona Scrymsoure, *d* of Robert Steuart Fothringham of Pourie, DL; two *s* one *d*. *Educ*: Sedbergh Sch.; Merton Coll., Oxford (BA Hons Juris.). Called to the Bar, Lincoln's Inn, 1994; in practice as barrister, specialising in town and country planning, envmtl and infrastructure. Dep. Commissary Gen. and Dep. Vicar Gen., Dio. Canterbury, 2012–13. Sec., Planning and Envmtl Bar Assoc., 2006–13. Chm., Georgian Group, 2015–. Mem., Founding Cttee, Compulsory Purchase Assoc., 2005. Trustee: Prince's Foundn for Building Community, 2009–14 (Chm., Adv. Bd, 2014–17); Cumbria Building Preservation Trust, 2012–. Mem. Council, 2007–12, Mem., Rural Enterprise Panel, 2009–15, Nat. Trust. *Recreations*: farming, restoring ruins, designing gardens. *Address*: Mallsgate Hall, Rowelltown, Carlisle CA6 6LX; Landmark Chambers, 180 Fleet Street, EC4A 2HG. *T*: (020) 7430 1221. *Clubs*: Travellers', Brooks's.

**BOYLE, Rt Rev. Christopher John**; Assistant Bishop of Leicester, 2009–17, now Honorary Assistant Bishop; *b* Birmingham, 8 Nov. 1951. *Educ*: King's Coll. London (AKC). Ordained deacon, 1976, priest, 1977; Asst Curate, Emmanuel, Wylde Green, 1976–80; Bishop's Chaplain, Dio. of Birmingham, 1980–83; Rector, St Mary and St Margaret, Castle Bromwich, 1983–2001; Bishop of N Malawi, 2001–09. Area Dean, Coleshill, 1992–99; Priest-in-charge, All Saints, Shard End, 1996–97; Hon. Canon, Birmingham Cathedral, 1996–2001.

**BOYLE, Danny**; director and producer; Artistic Director, Isles of Wonder, opening ceremony of London Olympic Games 2012, 2010–12; *b* Bury, Lancs, 20 Oct. 1956; one *s* two *d*. With Joint Stock Th. Co.; Artistic Dir, Royal Court Th., 1982–87; also dir prodns for RSC; dir, Frankenstein, NT, 2011. *Films* include: director: Shallow Grave, 1994; Trainspotting, 1996; A Life Less Ordinary, 1997; The Beach, 2000; Alien Love Triangle, 2002; 28 Days Later, 2002; Millions, 2005; Sunshine, 2007; Slumdog Millionaire, 2008 (Academy, BAFTA and Golden Globe Awards for Best Dir, 2009); 127 Hours, 2010; Trance, 2013; Yesterday, 2019; executive producer: Twin Town, 1996; 28 Weeks Later, 2007; Steve Jobs, 2015; T2: Trainspotting, 2017; *television* includes: producer, Elephant, 1989; director: Inspector Morse (2 episodes), 1990–92; The Greater Good, 1991; Arise and Go Now, 1991; Not Even God is Wise Enough, 1993; Mr Wroe's Virgins, 1993; Vacuuming Completely Nude in Paradise, 2001; Strumpet, 2001; Babylon, 2014; Trust (3 episodes), 2018. Beyond Theatre Award, London Evening Standard Theatre Award, 2012. *Address*: c/o Independent Talent Group Ltd, 40 Whitfield Street, W1T 2RH.

**BOYLE, Gerard James**; QC 2017; *b* Belfast, 1 May 1970; *s* of Gerard Boyle and Pamela Boyle; *m* 1994, Rebecca Whalley; one *s* two *d*. *Educ*: St Mary's Christian Brothers Grammar Sch., Belfast; Trinity Hall, Cambridge (BA Hons Law 1991). Called to the Bar: Gray's Inn, 1992; NI, 2008; in practice as a barrister, Serjeants' Inn Chambers.

**BOYLE, Gillian Anne McGregor**; see Watson, G. A. McG.

**BOYLE, James**, FRSE; Founder and Trustee, Edinburgh UNESCO City of Literature, 2004–12 (Chairman, 2004–07); *b* 29 March 1946; *s* of James Boyle and Margaret Halliday Crilly; *m* 1969, Marie Teresa McNamara; three *s*. *Educ*: Strathclyde Univ. (BA Hons (1st cl.) 1969); Univ. of East Anglia (MA 1971). Adult educn lectr, 1971–75; BBC: Educn Officer, 1975–83; Head of Educnl Broadcasting, then Sec. and Head of Press, Scotland, 1983–93; Hd, BBC Radio Scotland, 1992–96; Chief Advr, Editorial Policy, 1996; Controller, Radio 4, 1996–2001; Chm., Scottish Arts Council, 2001–04. A CS Comr, 2001–04, 2007–08. Non-exec. Dir, Franklin Rae Communications, 2004–. Hon. Lectr, Stirling Univ., 1994. Founder Mem., Glasgow UNESCO City of Music, 2008. Chm., Adv. Cttee, British Council Scotland, 2009–14; Trustee, British Council, 2011–13; Chm., Bd of Trustees, Nat. Library of Scotland, 2012–16. Mem. Council and Fellowship Sec., RSE, 2019. FRSE 2016. Hon. DArts: Napier, 2002; Edinburgh, 2005; Hon. LLD Aberdeen, 2005. *Publications*: extensive writing for newspapers; six TV plays for school children; radio scripts. *Recreations*: collecting modern first editions, World War I memorabilia. *Address*: 69 Morningside Drive, Edinburgh EH10 5NJ. *T*: (0131) 447 2121. *E*: james@theboylefamily.com.

**BOYLE, Mark**; see Boyle, A. M.

**BOYLE, Michael David**; Director of Strategy, National Probation Directorate, Home Office, 2002–04; *b* 23 Jan. 1954; *s* of Robert Brian Boyle and Kathleen Boyle; *m* 1977, Clare Gillard. *Educ*: Regent House Grammar Sch., Newtownards, Co. Down; Univ. of St Andrews (MA 1976). Home Office, 1976–2004: Private Sec. to Parly Under-Sec. of State, 1980–81; Prison Dept, 1981–85; Immigration and Nationality Dept, 1985–89; Criminal Policy Dept, 1989–90; Grade 5, Police Dept, 1990–93; Establt Dept, 1993–96; Criminal Dept, 1996–2001; Actg Dir, Community Policy, 2001; Dir, Criminal Law and Policy, 2001–02. *Recreations*: dog-walking, foreign travel, Crystal Palace Football Club. *Address*: Killerby House, 31 West End, Walkington, Beverley, E Yorks HU17 8SX.

**BOYLE, Prof. Nicholas**, LittD; FBA 2001; Schröder Professor of German, University of Cambridge, 2006–13, now Emeritus (Director of Research, 2013); Fellow of Magdalene College, Cambridge, since 1968 (President, 2006–11); *b* 18 June 1946; *e s* of late Hugh Boyle and Margaret Mary Faith (*née* Hopkins, then Mrs R. G. Boothroyd); *m* 1983, Rosemary Angela Devlin; one *s* three *d*. *Educ*: King's Sch., Worcester; Magdalene Coll., Cambridge (schol.; BA 1967; MA; PhD 1976; LittD 2004). University of Cambridge: Res. Fellow in German, Magdalene Coll., 1968–72; Lectr in German, Magdalene and Girton Colls, 1972–74; Univ. Asst Lectr in German, 1974–79; Lectr, 1979–93; Reader, 1993–2000; Hd of Dept, 1996–2001; Prof. of German Literary and Intellectual History, 2000–06; Sec., Faculty Bd of Mod. and Medieval Langs, 1982–85; Tutor, Magdalene Coll., 1984–93. Scholar, Alexander von Humboldt Foundn, 1978, 1980–81; British Acad. Res. Reader in Humanities, 1990–92; Res. Fellow, John Rylands Res. Inst., Univ. of Manchester, 1993; Fellow, Wissenschaftskolleg, Berlin, 1994–95; Erasmus Lectr, Univ. of Notre Dame, 2002–03. Corresp. Fellow, Göttingen Acad. of Scis, 2010. Hon. DHL Georgetown, 2004. W. Heinemann Prize, RSL, 1992; J. G. Robertson Meml Prize, Univ. of London, 1994; Goethe Medal, 2000; Annibel Jenkins Prize, Amer. Soc. for Eighteenth Century Studies, 2002; Friedrich Gundolf Prize, Deutsche Akademie für Sprache und Dichtung, 2009; Gold Medal, Goethe-Gesellschaft, 2017. *Publications*: (ed with M. Swales) Realism in European Literature: essays in honour of J. P. Stern, 1986; Goethe: Faust, Part One, 1987; Goethe: the poet and the age, Vol. 1, 1991 (trans. German 1995), Vol. 2, 2000 (trans. German, 1999); Who Are We Now?: Christian humanism and the global market from Hegel to Heaney, 1998; (ed) Goethe: selected works, 1999; (ed with J. Guthrie) Goethe and the English-Speaking World, 2002; Sacred and Secular Scriptures: a Catholic approach to literature, 2004; German Literature: a very short introduction, 2008, enlarged German edn 2009; 2014: how to survive the next world crisis, 2010; (Gen. Ed.) The Impact of Idealism: the legacy of post-Kantian German thought (4 vols), 2013; articles in The Tablet, New Blackfriars, German Life and Letters, French Studies, etc. *Recreation*: enjoying other people's gardens. *Address*: Magdalene College, Cambridge CB3 0AG. *T*: (01223) 332137; 20 Alpha Road, Cambridge CB4 3DG. *T*: (01223) 364310.

**BOYLE, Prof. Paul Joseph**, CBE 2016; PhD; FBA 2013; FRSE; FRSGS; Vice-Chancellor, Swansea University, since 2019; *b* Felixstowe, Suffolk, 16 Nov. 1964. *Educ*: Deben High Sch., Felixstowe; Lancaster Univ. (BA Hons Geog. 1986; PhD 1991); Univ. of Colorado, Boulder. Lecturer: Univ. of Wales, Swansea, 1991–95; Univ. of Leeds, 1995–99; Prof. of Human Geog., 1999–2014, and Hd, Sch. of Geog. and Geosciences, 2007–10, Univ. of St Andrews; Chief Exec., ESRC, 2010–14; Pres. and Vice-Chancellor, Univ. of Leicester, 2014–19. Hon. Prof., Univ. of Dundee, 2003–. Founding Dir, Social Dimensions of Health Inst., 2003–07. Dep. Dir, Census Interaction Data Service, 2001–05; Dir, ESRC Longitudinal Studies Centre, Scotland, 2001–10; Co-Dir, ESRC Centre for Population Change, 2009–10; Co-Investigator: Wellcome Trust Scottish Health Informatics Prog., 2008–10; ESRC Admin. Data Liaison Service. Chm., Scottish Sci. Adv. Council, 2016–. Pres., Science Europe, 2011–14. Pres., British Soc. for Population Studies, 2007–09 (Vice-Pres., 2005–07). FRSE 2006; FRSGS 2010; FAcSS (AcSS 2013). *Publications*: contribs to learned jls. *Address*: Swansea University, Singleton Park, Swansea SA2 8PP.

**BOYLE, Paul Vincent**, OBE 2010; CA; Chairman, Public Concern at Work, since 2017; *b* Glasgow, 27 July 1959; *s* of Gerrard Boyle and Joan Boyle (*née* O'Donnell); *m* 1991, Claire Andrews; two *d* and one step *s*. *Educ*: Univ. of Glasgow (BAcc 1st Cl. Hons 1980). CA 1983. Coopers & Lybrand, 1980–88; Gp Financial Controller, W H Smith Gp plc, 1988–90; posts with Cadbury Schweppes plc, 1991–98; Chief Operating Officer, FSA, 1998–2004; Chief Exec., Financial Reporting Council, 2004–09; Chief Audit Officer, Aviva plc, 2010–17. Non-exec. Dir, Plus500 Ltd, 2015–. Hon. Prof., Accounting and Finance, Univ. of Glasgow, 2010–14. *Recreations*: golf, tennis. *Clubs*: Caledonian; Denham Golf.

**BOYLE, Prof. Peter**, PhD, DSc; FRCPSGlas, FFPH, FRCPE, FRCPI, FMedSci; FRSE; President, International Prevention Research Institute, since 2009; Professor of Global Public Health, University of Strathclyde, and Director, University of Strathclyde Institute for Global Public Health at International Prevention Research Institute, since 2013; President, World Prevention Alliance, since 2011; *b* 8 June 1951; *s* of Simon and Brigid Boyle; *m* 1976, Helena Mary McNicol; three *d*. *Educ*: Glasgow Univ. (BSc 1974; PhD 1985, DSc (Med) 2006). FRCPSGlas 2003; FFPH 2004; FRCPE 2006; FRCPI 2016. Res. Asst, Dept of Medicine, Univ. of Glasgow, 1974–77; Sen. Statistician, W Scotland Cancer Surveillance Unit, Glasgow, 1977–84; Instructor and Asst Prof., Depts of Biostats and Epidemiol., Harvard Sch. of Public Health, 1984–86; Sen. Scientist, Internat. Agency for Res. on Cancer, Lyon, 1986–91; Dir, Div. of Epidemiol. and Biostats, Eur. Inst. Oncology, Milan, 1991–2004; Dir, Internat. Agency for Res. on Cancer, WHO, 2004–08. Hon.

Professor: of Cancer Epidemiol., Birmingham Univ., 1996–2002; of Cancer Prevention and Control, Oxford Univ., 2003–09; Dundee Univ., 2009–12; Vis. Prof., Glasgow Univ., 2000–; Adjunct Prof., Yale Univ., New Haven, 2010–. Mem., Eur. Acad. of Cancer Sci., 2010. MAE 2013. Hon. Mem., Hungarian Acad. of Sci., 2010. FRSE 2000; FMedSci 2006. Hon. DSc Aberdeen, 2006; Hon. LLD Dundee, 2012. Kt's Cross, Order of Merit (Poland), 2000; Medaille de la Ville de Dardilly, 2016; Royal Medal, RSE, 2017; Chancellor's Medal, Univ. of Strathclyde, 2018. *Publications: jointly:* Cancer Incidence in Scotland: atlas and epidemiological perspective, 1985; Textbooks for General Practitioners, II: Breast Cancer, 1990; Cancer Mortality Atlas in Central Europe, 1996; Nutrition and Cancer, 1996; Tobacco: science, policy and public health, 2004, 2nd edn 2010; *edited jointly:* Cancer Mapping, 1989; Cancer Epidemiology: vital statistics through prevention, 1990; Cancer Mortality Atlas of EEC, 1993; Statistical Methods in Cancer Research, 1996; Textbook of Benign Prostatic Hyperplasia, 1996 (Ipertrofia Prostatica Benigna, vol. I–II, 1997); Monographs in Oncology, vol. I, Colorectal Cancer, 2000; Cancer Incidence in Five Continents, 2008; World Cancer Report 2008, 2008; Cancer Mortality Atlas of Europe, 1993–98, 2009; Textbook of Epidemiology and Biostatistics, 2011; World Breast Cancer Report, 2013; Alcohol: science, policy and public health, 2013; State of Oncology 2013, 2013; State of Oncology in Africa, 2016; contribs to scientific jls. *Recreations:* family, music, football. *Address:* International Prevention Research Institute, 95 cours Lafayette, 69006 Lyon, France. *T:* (4) 72171180. *E:* peter.boyle@i-pri.org. *Clubs:* Celtic (Glasgow); LYINC (Lyon).

**BOYLE, Dr Philip David**; HM Diplomatic Service; Ambassador to Madagascar, since 2017, and (non-resident) to Comoros, since 2018; *b* Birkenhead, 7 May 1976; *s* of David and Valerie Boyle; *m* 2016, Liosliath Mairghraid McGilchrist; one *s*. *Educ:* Whitby High Sch., Ellesmere Port; Univ. of Manchester Inst. of Sci. and Technol. (BSc 1st Cl. Hons Chem. 1997; PhD Inorganic Chem. 2000). Postdoctoral researcher, Inorganic Chem. Lab., Univ. of Oxford, 2001–02; entered FCO, 2002; Desk Officer for Falkland Is, FCO, 2002–03; Arabic trng, FCO, 2004–05; Second Sec. (Pol), Sana'a, 2005–08; Consul Gen., Lille, 2008–11; First Sec. (Pol) Islamabad, 2011–12; Ambassador to Mali and (non-resident) to Niger, 2012–14; Dep. Head, Intelligence Policy Dept, FCO, 2014–17. *Publications:* contrib. papers to peer-reviewed chem. jls. *Recreations:* birding, wildlife photography, hiking, Land Rovers, cricket. *Address:* c/o Foreign and Commonwealth Office, King Charles Street, SW1A 2AH. *E:* philip.boyle@fco.gov.uk.

**BOYLE, Sir Roger (Michael)**, Kt 2011; CBE 2004; FRCP; Consultant Cardiologist, York District Hospital, 1983–2011; National Director for Heart Disease, 2000–11, and for Stroke, 2006–11; *b* 27 Jan. 1948; *s* of late Dr Michael Maurice Boyle and of Hazel Irene Boyle; *m* 1975, Susan Scutt (marr. diss.); three *s*; *m* 2002, Margo Bispham Cox; one *d*. *Educ:* Shrewsbury Sch.; London Hosp. Med. Sch., London Univ. (MB BS 1972). House physician and surgeon, then SHO, London Hosp., 1972–75; Registrar, Chelmsford Hosp., 1975–78; Res. Fellow, Wythenshawe Hosp., Manchester, 1978–80; Lectr in Cardiovascular Studies, Univ. of Leeds, 1980–83. Co-Dir, Nat. Centre for Cardiovascular Prevention and Outcomes, UCL, 2011–13. Hon. Prof., Dept of Surgery, UCH, 2005–08; Hon. Prof. of Cardiol., UCL, 2007. Hon. Consultant Cardiologist, St Mary's Hosp., London, 2004–07. FRSA. Hon. FFPH. *Publications:* contribs to cardiovascular jls on coronary heart disease and trng in cardiology. *Recreations:* sailing, playing the piano, walking. *Address:* Lanhoose Barn, Portscatho, Truro TR2 5EP. *Club:* St Mawes Sailing.
*See also* A. G. Boyle.

**BOYLE, Sir Simon (Hugh Patrick)**, KCVO 2015; Lord-Lieutenant for Gwent, 2001–16; *b* 22 March 1941; *s* of late Lt Col P. J. S. Boyle (killed in action 1944) and Mary Elizabeth Boyle (later Mrs Charles Floyd); *m* 1970, Catriona Gordon; four *d*. *Educ:* Eton Coll. Industrial career with: Stewarts & Lloyds, Australia and UK, 1959–65; Avon Rubber Co. Ltd, 1966–69; British Steel, 1970–2001. Chm., Gwent Criminal Justice Bd, 2003–05. Chm., Monmouth Diocesan Parsonage Bd, 1997–2008; Vice Chm., Monmouth Diocesan Bd of Finance, 2001–12. Vice Chm. of Trustees, St David's Hospice, 1999–. Pres., Gwent Assoc. of Voluntary Orgns, 2006–16. DL 1997, JP 2002, Gwent. CStJ 2002. *Recreations:* gardening, sailing. *Address:* Penpergwm Lodge, Abergavenny, Gwent NP7 9AS. *T:* (01873) 840208. *E:* boyle@penpergwm.co.uk.

**BOYLE, Sir Stephen Gurney**, 5th Bt *cr* 1904; *b* 15 Jan. 1962; *s* of Sir Richard Gurney Boyle, 4th Bt, and of Elizabeth Ann, *yr d* of Norman Dennes; *S* father, 1983. Chm., Co-operative Property Services Ltd. *Recreations:* play, make, fix, and set up guitars, singing, playing piano and synthesizers, making/listening to music, watching cricket and football, cooking, reading, writing (lyrics mainly). *Heir: b* Michael Desmond Boyle, *b* 16 Sept. 1963. *Address:* 38 Partridge Court, Barn Mead, Harlow, Essex CM18 6SH.

**BOYLING, Very Rev. Mark Christopher;** Dean of Carlisle, since 2004; *b* 14 Oct. 1952; *s* of Denis and Margaret Boyling; *m* 1991, Helen Mary (*née* Enoch); one *s* one *d*. *Educ:* Keble Coll., Oxford (BA (Modern Hist.) 1974, BA (Theol.) 1976; MA 1978); Cuddesdon Theol Coll. Ordained deacon, 1977, priest, 1978; Asst Curate, Kirkby, 1977–79; Priest i/c, 1979–80, Team Vicar, 1980–85, St Mark, Kirkby; Chaplain to Bp of Liverpool, 1985–89; Vicar, St Peter, Formby, 1989–94; Canon Residentiary, Liverpool Cathedral, 1994–2004. *Recreations:* travel, cooking. *Address:* The Deanery, Carlisle CA3 8TZ. *T:* (01228) 523335, *Fax:* (01228) 547049. *E:* dean@carlislecathedral.org.uk.

**BOYNE**, 11th Viscount *cr* 1717 (Ire.); **Gustavus Michael Stucley Hamilton-Russell;** DL; Baron Hamilton 1715; Baron Brancepeth (UK) 1866; *b* 27 May 1965; *o s* of 10th Viscount Boyne and of Rosemary Anne, *d* of Sir Dennis Stucley, 5th Bt; *S* father, 1995; *m* 1st, 1991, Lucy (marr. diss. 2012), *d* of George Potter; three *s* one *d* (incl. twin *s*); 2nd, 2013, Julia Howard, *d* of Sir John Philip Howard-Lawson, Bt, *qv*. *Educ:* Harrow; RAC Cirencester. Dip. Rural Estate Management; MRICS (ARICS 1991). Chartered Surveyor with Carter Jonas. DL Shropshire, 2009. *Recreations:* country sports, tennis, ski-ing. *Heir: s* Hon. Gustavus Archie Edward Hamilton-Russell, *b* 30 June 1999. *Address:* Burwarton House, Bridgnorth, Shropshire WV16 6QH. *T:* (01746) 787221. *Club:* Turf.

**BOYNE, Maj.-Gen. John**, CB 1987; MBE 1965; CEng, FIMechE; *b* 7 Nov. 1932; *s* of John Grant Boyne and Agnes Crawford (*née* Forrester); *m* 1956, Norma Beech (*d* 2002); two *s*. *Educ:* King's Sch., Chester; Royal Military Coll. of Science, Shrivenham (BScEng 1st Cl. Hons). CEng, FIMechE 1975. Served in Egypt, Cyprus, Libya and UK, 1951–62; Staff Coll., Camberley, 1963; DAQMG(Ops) HQ MEC, Aden, 1964–66; OC 11 Infantry Workshop, REME, BAOR, 1966–67; Jt Services Staff Coll., 1968; GSO2 MoD, 1968–70; GSO1 (DS), Staff Coll., 1970–72; Comdr REME, 2nd Div., BAOR, 1972–73; AAG MoD, 1973–75; CSO (Personnel) to CPL, MoD, 1975–76; Dep. Dir Elec. and Mech. Engrg, 1st British Corps, 1976–78; RCDS, 1979; Dep. Dir Personal Services (Army), MoD, 1980–82; Vice Adjutant Gen. and Dir of Manning (Army), MoD, 1982–85; Dir Gen., Electrical and Mechanical Engrg, Logistic Executive (Army), MoD, 1985–88. Col Comdt, REME, 1988–93 (Rep. Col Comdt, 1989–90). Trustee, Army Benevolent Fund, 1986–2005. Vice Pres., Army Football Assoc., 1988–2017. FCMI (FBIM 1975). *Recreations:* music, philately, football. *Address:* c/o HSBC, 48 High Street, Runcorn, Cheshire WA7 1AN.

**BOYNE, John;** author; *b* Dublin, 30 April 1971; *s* of Seán and Helen Boyne. *Educ:* Trinity Coll. Dublin (BA); Univ. of E Anglia (MA). Hon. DLitt E Anglia, 2015. *Publications:* The Thief of Time, 2000; Congress of Rough Riders, 2001; Crippen, 2004; Next of Kin, 2006; Mutiny on the Bounty, 2008; The House of Special Purpose, 2009; The Absolutist, 2011; This House is Haunted, 2013; A History of Loneliness, 2014; Beneath the Earth (short stories), 2015; The Heart's Invisible Furies, 2017; A Ladder to the Sky, 2018; for young adults: The Boy in the Striped Pyjamas, 2006; Noah Barleywater Runs Away, 2010; The Terrible Thing That Happened to Barney Brocket, 2012; Stay Where You Are and Then Leave, 2013; The Boy at the Top of the Mountain, 2015; My Brother's Name is Jessica, 2019. *Address:* 5 The Dell, Marley Grange, Rathfarnham, Dublin 16, Ireland. *E:* johnboyne71@gmail.com.

**BOYS, Rt Hon. Sir Michael H.;** *see* Hardie Boys.

**BOYS, Penelope Ann, (Mrs D. C. H. Wright),** CB 2005; Member: Water Services Regulation Authority, 2006–14; Consumers' Committee, National House Builders Council, since 2013; non-executive Director, Office for Nuclear Regulation, since 2016; *b* 11 June 1947; *d* of late Hubert John Boys and Mollie Blackman Boys; *m* 1977, David Charles Henshaw Wright. *Educ:* Guildford County Sch. for Girls. Exec. Officer, DES, 1966–69; Asst Principal, Min. of Power, 1969–72; Private Sec., Minister without Portfolio, 1972–73; Principal, Dept of Energy, 1973–78; seconded to BNOC, 1978–80; Head of Internat. Unit, Dept of Energy, 1981–85; seconded to HM Treasury as Head, ST2 Div., 1985–87; Dir of Personnel, Dept of Energy, 1987–89; Dep. Dir Gen., Office of Electricity Regulation, 1989–93; Head of Personnel, DTI, 1993–96; Sec., Monopolies and Mergers Commn, later Competition Commn, 1996–2000 (Mem. Council, 2012–14); Dep. Dir Gen., 2000–03, Exec. Dir, 2003–05, OFT. Mem., 2006–08, Dep. Chm., 2008–11, Horserace Betting Levy Bd; Mem., Membership Selection Panel, Network Rail, 2011–15. *Recreations:* entertaining, racing, music.

**BOYS-GREENE, Jenny;** *see* Greene, J.

**BOYS SMITH, Stephen Wynn**, CB 2001; Joint Secretary, Independent Monitoring Commission, Northern Ireland, 2004–11; *b* 4 May 1946; *s* of late Rev. Dr John Sandwith Boys Smith and Gwendolen Sara Boys Smith (*née* Wynn); *m* 1971, Linda Elaine Price; one *s* one *d*. *Educ:* Sherborne Sch.; St John's Coll., Cambridge (MA); Univ. of British Columbia (MA). Home Office, 1968; Asst Private Sec. to Home Sec., 1971–73; Central Policy Review Staff, Cabinet Office, 1977; Home Office, 1979; Private Sec. to Home Sec., 1980–81; NI Office, 1981; Principal Private Sec. to Sec. of State for NI, 1981–82; Home Office, 1984; Principal Private Sec. to Home Sec., 1985–87; Asst Under Sec. of State, Home Office, 1989–92; Under Sec., HM Treasury, 1992–95; Home Office: Dep. Sec. and Head of Police Dept, 1995–96; Dir, Police Policy, 1996–98; Dir-Gen., Immigration and Nationality Directorate, 1998–2002; Dir-Gen., Organised Crime, Drugs and Internat. Gp, 2002–03. Mem., Civil Service Appeal Bd, 2004–12. Associate Consultant, Public Admin Internat., 2009–12. Chm., Bedfordshire Gardens Trust, 2004–15. *Recreations:* gardening, reading, history of the Levant. *Address:* 23 Church Street, Ampthill, Beds MK45 2PL. *T:* (01525) 403800. *E:* boyssmith@ntlworld.com. *Club:* Reform.

**BRABAZON**, family name of **Earl of Meath**.

**BRABAZON OF TARA**, 3rd Baron *cr* 1942; **Ivon Anthony Moore-Brabazon;** PC 2013; DL; *b* 20 Dec. 1946; *s* of 2nd Baron Brabazon of Tara, CBE, and Henriette Mary (*d* 1985), *d* of late Sir Rowland Clegg; *S* father, 1974; *m* 1979, Harriet Frances, *o d* of Mervyn P. de Courcy Hamilton, Salisbury, Zimbabwe; one *s* one *d*. *Educ:* Harrow. Mem., Stock Exchange, 1972–84. A Lord in Waiting (Govt Whip), 1984–86; Parly Under-Sec. of State, Dept of Transport, 1986–89; Minister of State: FCO, 1989–90; Dept of Transport, 1990–92; Opposition spokesman on Transport, H of L, 1998–2001; elected Mem., H of L, 1999; Principal Dep. Chm. of Cttees, 2001–02; Chm. of Cttees, 2002–12, H of L; Chm., EU Select Cttee, H of L, 2001–02. Mem., RAC Public Policy Cttee, 1992–99. President: UK Warehousing Assoc., 1992–2018; British Internat. Freight Assoc., 1997–99; Inst. of the Motor Industry, 1998–2004. DL Isle of Wight, 1993. *Recreations:* golf, sailing, Cresta Run. *Heir: s* Hon. Benjamin Ralph Moore-Brabazon [*b* 15 March 1983; *m* 2011, Molly Claire Parish; two *s*]. *Address:* House of Lords, SW1A 0PW. *Clubs:* Royal Yacht Squadron; Bembridge Sailing, St Moritz Tobogganing.

**BRABBINS, Martyn Charles;** freelance orchestral and opera conductor; Music Director, English National Opera, since 2016; *b* 13 Aug. 1959; *s* of Herbert Henry Brabbins and Enid Caroline Brabbins; *m* 1985, Karen Maria Evans; two *s* one *d*. *Educ:* Goldsmiths' Coll., Univ. of London (BMus, MMus; Hon. Fellow, 2004); Leningrad State Conservatoire. Professional début with Scottish Chamber Orch., 1988; Associate Conductor, 1992–94, Associate Prin. Conductor, 1994–2005, BBC Scottish SO; Principal Conductor, Sinfonia 21, 1994–2001; Conducting Consultant, RSAMD, 1996–2002; Huddersfield Choral Society: Principal Conductor, 1998–2006; Conductor Laureate, 2006–13; Music Dir, 2013–; Artistic Dir, Cheltenham Fest., 2005–07; Principal Guest Conductor, Royal Flemish Philharmonic Orch., 2009–15; Chief Conductor, Nagoya Philharmonic Orch., 2013–16; has conducted most major British orchestras, and orchestras abroad, incl. Lahti SO, Tapiola Sinfonietta, St Petersburg Philharmonic, Bergen Philharmonic, Ensemble Intercontemporain, Amsterdam Concertgebouw; Tokyo Metropolitan SO, Deutsches SO Berlin, Adelaide SO; also conducted: Don Giovanni, Kirov Opera, 1988; Magic Flute, ENO, 1995; Montpellier Opera, 1999; Netherlands Opera, 2001; Deutsche Oper, 2001; Frankfurt Opera, 2003, 2007, 2011; Hamburg State Opera, 2006; The Pilgrim's Progress, ENO, 2012; Bavarian State Opera, 2013; Marnie, ENO, 2017; Salome, ENO, 2018; War Requiem, ENO, 2018; Remembering World War One: Vaughan Williams and beyond, BBC SO, 2018; The Kingdom, Hallé Orch., 2019. Founding Dir, Orkney Conducting Course, 2002–; BBC Nat. Orch. of Wales Conducting Course, 2018–. Has made over 120 recordings. Hon. DMus Bristol, 2013. Winner, Leeds Conductors Competition, 1988; BASCA Gold Badge Award, 2018. *Recreation:* family. *Address:* c/o Intermusica, 9 Kingsway, WC2B 6XF. *T:* (020) 7608 9900.

**BRABEN, David John**, OBE 2014; Founder and Chief Executive Officer, Frontier Developments plc, since 2013 (Founder and Chairman, Frontier Developments Ltd, 1994–2013); *b* 2 Jan. 1964; *s* of Prof. Don Braben and Shirley Braben; *m* 1st, 1993, Kathy Dickinson (marr. diss. 1996); 2nd, 2014, Wendy Irvin. *Educ:* Stockton Heath Primary Sch.; Royal Kent Primary Sch.; Buckhurst Hill Co. High Sch.; Jesus Coll., Cambridge (BA 1985; MA Hons Electrical Scis; Dip. Computer Sci.). FIET 2012; FREng 2012. Freelance software designer and writer, 1982–94: Elite, Zarch, Virus, Frontier. Non-exec. Dir, Phonetic Arts Ltd, 2008–10. Chm., Skillset Univ. Accreditation Panel, 2009–14; Mem. Bd, BAFTA Games Cttee, 2009–13. Member: Cambridge Angels, 2006–; Adv. Panel, Cambridge Innovation Capital, 2016–. Founder Trustee and Mem. Bd, Raspberry Pi, 2008–. Hon. DTech Abertay, 2013; Hon. PhD: Open, 2014; York, 2015. Hon. Fellow, BAFTA, 2015. *Recreations:* sailing, movies, board games, computer games, the family, I loved walking my dog before she died. *Address:* c/o Frontier Developments plc, 26 Science Park, Milton Road, Cambridge CB4 0FP. *T:* (01223) 394300. *E:* dbraben@frontier.co.uk.

**BRABIN, Tracy Lynn;** MP (Lab Co-op) Batley and Spen, since Oct. 2016; *b* 9 May 1961; *d* of Terry Brabin and Betty Brabin; *m* 2005, Richard Platt; two *d. Educ:* Heckmondwike Grammar Sch.; Loughborough Univ. (BA Drama); London Coll. of Communication (MA Screenwriting). Actor in television series: A Bit of a Do, 1989; Outside Edge, 1994–96; Coronation Street, 1994–97; EastEnders, 2001; Emmerdale, 2014; writer. Shadow Minister for Educn, 2017–. Mem., BAFTA. *Address:* House of Commons, SW1A 0AA. *E:* tracy.brabin.mp@parliament.uk.

**BRABOURNE, Lord; Nicholas Louis Charles Norton Knatchbull;** *b* 15 May 1981; *s* and *heir* of Earl Mountbatten of Burma, *qv.*

**BRACADALE, Rt Hon. Lord; Alastair Peter Campbell;** PC 2013; a Senator of the College of Justice in Scotland, 2003–17; *b* 18 Sept. 1949; *s* of Rev. Donald Campbell and Margaret Campbell (*née* Montgomery); *m* 1973, Flora Beaton; one *s* two *d. Educ:* George Watson's Coll.; Aberdeen Univ. (MA); Strathclyde Univ. (LLB). Teacher of English, 1973–75; Solicitor, Procurator Fiscal Service, 1979–84; Advocate, 1985; Advocate Depute, 1990–93; called to the Bar, Inner Temple, 1990; QC (Scot.) 1995; Standing Jun. Counsel in Scotland to HM Customs and Excise, 1995; Home Advocate Depute, 1997–98; Crown Counsel, Scottish Court in the Netherlands, 2000–02. Member: Criminal Justice Forum, 1996–97; Scottish Criminal Rules Council, 1996–98; Criminal Injuries Compensation Bd, 1997; Judicial Mem., Parole Bd for Scotland, 2008–11; Judicial Comr, Investigatory Powers Commn, 2016–. Conducted Ind. Rev. of hate crime in Scotland, 2017–18. Hon. LLD: Strathclyde, 2005; Aberdeen, 2012. *Recreations:* walking, sailing, golf. *Address:* Cerna, 69 Dirleton Avenue, North Berwick EH39 4QL. *T:* (01620) 894288.

**BRACE, Christopher James;** Chief Executive, Office of the Police and Crime Commissioner for Hertfordshire, since 2017; *b* Wimbledon, 21 Dec. 1975; *s* of Paul Spencer Brace and Lisa Anne Brace (*née* Corteen); *m* 2004, Jennifer Elinor Walters; three *d. Educ:* King's Coll., Sch., Wimbledon; Univ. of York (MSc Hons Psychol.); Goldsmith's Coll., Univ. of London (MA Hons Contemp. British Politics). Policy and Communications Manager, Centre for Econ. and Social Inclusion, 2002–05; Campaigns Dir, RADAR, 2005–08; Chief Executive: Peter Bedford Housing Assoc., 2008–11; Magistrates' Assoc., 2012–17. *Publications:* (jtly) Counselling in Schools, 2002; (ed with W. Somerville) Welfare to Work Handbook, 2004. *Recreations:* family, current affairs, reading, climbing, piano. *Address:* 29 Gainsborough Avenue, St Albans, Herts AL1 4NJ.

**BRACE, Gary;** Chief Executive, General Teaching Council for Wales, 2000–14; *b* Cardiff, 4 Feb. 1954; *s* of Eric and Irene Brace; *m* 2003, Dawn Morley; two *s* one *d. Educ:* Canton High Sch.; University Coll., Cardiff (BA Hons Hist. 1975; PGCE 1976). Teacher: Lady Mary High Sch., Cardiff, 1976–87; St David's Sixth Form Coll., Cardiff, 1987–91; Curriculum Field Officer, Curriculum Council for Wales, 1991–94; Hist. Subject Officer, Curriculum and Assessment Authy for Wales, 1994–97; Asst Chief Exec., Qualifications, Curriculum and Assessment Authy for Wales, 1997–2000. Mem. Bd, UK Nat. Commn for UNESCO, 2011–18 (Vice Chm., 2013–17). Gov., Herbert Thompson Primary Sch., 2009–16 (Vice Chm., 2014–16). Writer: BBC and Channel 4 Teachers' Guides; Official Guidance for National Curriculum and Assessment. Trustee, Cynnal Cymru-Sustain Wales, 2014– (Vice Chm., 2016–18; Chm., 2018–). Fellow, Internat. Professional Develt Assoc., 2013; FRSA. Hon. Fellow, Univ. of Wales Trinity Saint David, 2018. Chancellor's Medal, Univ. of Glamorgan, 2009. *Recreations:* rowing (Llandaff Rowing Club), travel, music, general aviation.

**BRACE, Michael Thomas,** CBE 2009 (OBE 2005); DL; Chief Executive: VISION 2020 UK, 2001–12; OPSIS, 2002–09; Chairman, British Paralympic Association, 2001–08; *b* 19 June 1950; *s* of late Thomas Brace and Rosina Brace (later Taylor); *m* 1972, Maureen Browne. *Educ:* Poly. of North London (DipSW 1976); CETSW (CQSW 1976); Inst. of Management (DipMgt 1996). Tower Hamlets BC, 1976–81; Hackney BC, 1981–83; Area Manager, Islington BC, 1983–89; Service Manager, RBK&C, 1989–2001. Non-exec. Dir, Nemisys, 2008–. Mem. Bd, London 2012, 2003–08; Dir, UK Anti Doping, 2009–16; Chm., City of London Sport and Physical Activity Network, 2010–12; Mem., Disabled Persons' Advce Cttee, DfT, 2017–. Trustee: Primary Club, 1998–; British Judo Council Foundn, 2010–19; British Wireless for the Blind Fund, 2018–. Gov., UEL, 2006–15. DL Gtr London, 2016. Hon. FCOptom 2005; Hon. FRCOphth 2011. Hon. DPhil London Metropolitan, 2009; Hon. DBA Anglia Ruskin, 2011; Hon. DSSc E London, 2015. *Publications:* Where There's a Will, 1980; Don't Ask Me, Ask the Dog, 2017. *Recreations:* playing cricket, after dinner speaking, ski-ing, reading, music, keep fit (gym), assistive technology. *Address:* 80 Elms Farm Road, Hornchurch, Essex RM12 5RD. *T:* (01708) 456832. *E:* mike@mikebrace.co.uk. *W:* www.mikebrace.co.uk.

**BRACEWELL, Julia Helen,** OBE 1999; Partner, McCarthy Denning Ltd, since 2015; Director, Bracewell Consultancy Ltd, since 2005; *b* 26 April 1964; *d* of Herbert and Joan Bracewell; one *s* one *d. Educ:* Bristol Univ. (LLB). Called to the Bar, Lincoln's Inn, 1997 (non-practising barrister); admitted solicitor, 1998. Partner, Brobeck Hale & Dorr, 1997–2000; Morrison & Foerster, 2000–02; Counsel, WilmerHale, 2013–15. Mem., Sports Council, GB, 1993–96, Sport England, 1996–2001; Chair, sportscotland, 2005–08; Chm., Scottish Steering Gp for 2012 Olympic Games, 2005–08; Board Director: Scottish Inst. of Sport, 2005–08; UK Sport, 2005–08; Dir, British Fencing, 2012–13; Dep. Chair, Scottish Athletics, 2009–13; non-exec. Dir, Scottish Rugby Union, 2019–. Fencing competitor: Commonwealth Championships, 1986 (Bronze Medal), 1990 (Bronze Medal); Olympic Games, Barcelona, 1992. Sailed across Atlantic, 1995. *Recreations:* ski-ing, sailing, racket sports, fencing. *Club:* British Olympians.

**BRACEWELL-SMITH, Sir Charles,** 4th Bt *cr* 1947, of Keighley; *b* 13 Oct. 1955; *s* of Sir George Bracewell Smith, 2nd Bt, MBE, and Helene Marie (*d* 1975), *d* of late John Frederick Hydock, Philadelphia, USA; *S* brother, 1983; *m* 1977, Carol Vivien Hough (*d* 1994); *m* 1996, Nina Kakkar. Former Dir, Park Lane Hotel Ltd. Founder, Homestead Charitable Trust, 1990. *Recreations:* mysticism, theology, philosophy, psychology, poetry, writing, music. *Heir:* none. *Address:* The Hermitage, 7 Clarence Gate Gardens, Glentworth Street, NW1 6AY. *Clubs:* Royal Automobile, Arsenal Football.

**BRACK, Ian;** Chief Executive and Registrar, General Dental Council, since 2016; *b* London, 8 July 1962. *Educ:* BA (Hons) Town Planning; MSc Politics. Dir, Policy, Millennium Commn, 2001–06; Policy Dir, 2006–10, Chief Exec., 2010–13, Olympic Lottery Distributor; Interim CEO, Legal Ombudsman, 2014–15. FRGS. *Recreations:* silence, solitude, travelling, literature. *Address:* General Dental Council, 37 Wimpole Street, W1G 8DQ. *T:* (020) 7167 6000.

**BRACK, Rodney Lee,** CBE 2006; Chief Executive, Horserace Betting Levy Board, 1993–2005; *b* 16 Aug. 1945; *s* of Sydney William Brack and Mary Alice Brack (*née* Quested); *m* 1973, Marilyn Carol Martin; two *s* one *d. Educ:* Whitgift Sch. FCA 1979. Chartered Accountant, 1963–68; Finance Manager, Daily Mirror Gp, 1969–75; Man. Dir, Leisure Div., EMI, 1976–80; Dir, Leisure Div., Lonrho, 1981–84; Financial Controller and Dep. Chief Exec., Horserace Betting Levy Bd, 1985–92. Dir, Horseracing Forensic Lab., 1986–2005. Mem., Lord Donoughue's Future Funding of Racing Review Gp, 2005–06. *Recreations:* music, theatre, cricket, golf. *Address:* 2 Dempster Close, Long Ditton, Surbiton, Surrey KT6 5EZ. *T:* (020) 3624 5047. *E:* rodneybrack@hotmail.com. *Clubs:* MCC, Royal Automobile.

**BRACK, Terence John,** CB 1994; Assistant Under-Secretary of State (General Finance), Ministry of Defence, 1989–94; *b* 17 April 1938; *s* of late Noël D. J. Brack and Tertia Brack; *m* 1983, Christine Mary, *d* of late Douglas and Evelyn Cashin. *Educ:* Bradfield Coll., Berkshire; Caius Coll., Cambridge Univ. (BA Hist. (1st cl. Hons), MA). Pilot Officer, Secretarial Br., RAF, 1956–58. Entered Air Ministry, subseq. MoD, 1961; Private Sec. to Parly Under-Sec. of State for Defence (RAF), 1964–66; Principal, 1966; seconded to HM Treasury, 1968–72; Asst Sec., 1973; Head, Finance and Sec. Div. for Controller of the Navy, 1975–78; Head, Defence Secretariat Div. for Equipment Requirements, 1978–81; RCDS, 1982; Head, Finance and Sec. Div. (Air Launched Guided Weapons and Electronics), 1983–84; Asst Under-Sec. of State (Naval Personnel), 1985–89. Vice-Chm., Management Bd, Royal Hosp. Sch., Holbrook, 1985–89. Pres., London Manx Soc., 2001–02. *Recreations:* walking, travel, family history projects.

**BRACKEN, Michael Thomas,** CBE 2014; Partner, Public Digital, since 2015; *b* St Helens, 10 Dec. 1968; *s* of Thomas Francis and Valerie Bracken; *m* 2009, Abigail Susan Billinghurst (marr. diss. 2019); two *d. Educ:* W London Inst., Brunel Univ. (BA American Studies and Hist. 1991); Liverpool Univ. (MA Latin American Studies 1993); Henley Mgt Coll. (MBA 2006). Internet researcher, journalist and entrepreneur, 1994–97; Vice Pres., Interactive Products, UPC Media/Chello, 1999–2002; Dir, mySociety.org, 2002–05; Commercial Dir, Wavex Technol., 2005–08; Dir, Digital Develt, Guardian News and Media, 2008–11; Exec. Dir, Digital, Cabinet Office, 2011–15; Chief Digital Officer, Co-op Gp, 2015–17. Mem. Bd, Lloyd's of London, 2018–. Vis. Prof., Inst. for Innovation and Public Purpose, UCL, 2018–. *Recreations:* football, golf. *Address:* 86 Oldfield Road, N16 0RP. *E:* mike@mikebracken.com. *W:* www.twitter.com/mtbracken. *Clubs:* Liverpool Football, Sporting Hackney Football (Chm., 2007–14); Hadley Wood Golf.

**BRACKENBURY, (Frederick Edwin) John (Gedge),** CBE 2000; Chairman, Brackenbury Leisure Ltd, since 1996; *b* 9 Feb. 1936; *s* of Claude Russell Brackenbury and Florence Edna Brackenbury; *m* 1st, 1958, Pauline Hinchliffe (marr. diss. 1977); one *s* two *d*; 2nd, 1978, Desiree Sally Taylor; one *s. Educ:* Mercers' Sch., London. Justerini & Brooks Ltd, 1954–62 (Dir, 1958–62); Man. Dir, City Cellars, 1962–65; Chm., Morgan Furze, 1965–67; Dir, IDV Ltd, 1967–72; Founder, Brackenbury consultancy co., 1972–75; Exec. Dir, G. & W. Walker, 1975–83 (Gp Operational Dir, Brent Walker, 1976–83); Man. Dir, All Weather Sports Activities Ltd, 1983–88; Exec. Dir, Brent Walker Gp Plc, 1988–96. Chm., 1991–2002, Dep. Chm., 2002–03, Pubmaster Gp Ltd; Chairman: Active Media Capital Ltd, 2000–07; Avanti Screenmedia Gp plc, 2003–07; Avanti Communications Gp, 2007–14 (Vice Chm., 2014–16); non-executive Director: Western Wines Ltd, 1997–2002; Aspen Gp Plc, 1997–99; Hotel and Catering Trng Co., 1998–2002; SFI Gp Plc, 1998–2005; Holsten (UK) Ltd, 2000–04; Isle of Capri Casinos Inc. (USA), 2004–10; The Isle Casinos Ltd, 2004–09 (Chm.); Blue Chip Casinos, 2006–09. Chairman: Business in Sport & Leisure, 1985–2005 (Life Pres., 2005–13); Hospitality Trng Foundn, 1997–2004; People 1st, 2004–05; Dir, Springboard (formerly Tourism & Hospitality) Educn Trust, 1999–; Trustee and Vice Pres., GamCare, 2009–. *Recreations:* golf, tennis, viticulture, shooting. *Address:* 8 Moore Street, SW3 2QN. *Clubs:* Carlton, Hurlingham.

**BRACKENBURY, Air Vice-Marshal Ian,** CB 2000; OBE 1987; CEng, FIMechE; Director, Rolls-Royce Defence Aerospace (Europe), 2001–06; *b* 28 Aug. 1945; *s* of late Capt. D. E. Brackenbury and of R. Brackenbury (*née* Grant). Directorate of Aircraft Engrg, 1975; Engrg Staff, Strike Comd, 1981; joined Dept for Supply and Orgn, 1986, Dir of Support Mgt, 1993; Dir of Support Mgt, HQ Logistics Comd, 1994; Dir, Helicopter Support, Chief of Fleet Support, 1995–97; Air Officer Engrg and Supply, Strike Comd, 1997–98; Dir Gen. Defence Logistics (Ops and Policy), MoD, 1998–2000. Trustee, Cornwall Air Ambulance Trust, 2009–. *Club:* Royal Air Force.

**BRACKENBURY, John;** *see* Brackenbury, F. E. J. G.

**BRACKENBURY, Ven. Michael Palmer;** Archdeacon of Lincoln, 1988–95, now Emeritus; *b* 6 July 1930; *s* of Frank Brackenbury and Constance Mary (*née* Palmer); *m* 1953, Jean Margaret, *d* of Oscar Arnold Harrison and May (*née* Norton). *Educ:* Norwich School; Lincoln Theological Coll. ACII 1956. RAF, 1948–50. Asst Curate, South Ormsby Group, 1966–69; Rector of Sudbrooke with Scothern, 1969–77; RD of Lawres, 1973–78; Diocesan Dir of Ordinands, Lincoln, 1977–87; Personal Assistant to Bishop of Lincoln, 1977–88; Canon and Prebendary of Lincoln, 1979–95; Diocesan Lay Ministry Adviser, Lincoln, 1986–87. Mem., Gen. Synod of C of E, 1989–95. Mem., Ecclesiastical Law Soc., 1988–. Chm. Lincs Award Bd, Prince's Trust, 1996–2001. *Recreations:* music, reading, travel. *Address:* 18 Lea View, Ryhall, Stamford, Lincs PE9 4HZ. *T:* (01780) 752415.

**BRACKLEY, Rt Rev. Ian James;** Bishop Suffragan of Dorking, 1996–2015; Hon. Assistant Bishop, Diocese of Portsmouth, since 2016; *b* 13 Dec. 1947; *s* of Frederick Arthur James Brackley and Ivy Sarah Catherine (*née* Bush); *m* 1971, Penny Saunders; two *s. Educ:* Westcliff High Sch.; Keble Coll., Oxford (MA); Cuddesdon Coll., Oxford. Ordained deacon, 1971, priest, 1972; Asst Curate, Lockleaze, Bristol, 1971–74; Asst Chaplain, 1974–76, Chaplain, 1976–80, Bryanston Sch., Dorset; Vicar, East Preston with Kingston, 1980–88; Team Rector, St Wilfrid, Haywards Heath, 1988–96. Rural Dean: Arundel and Bognor, 1982–87; Cuckfield, 1989–95. Commissary Bishop of Guildford, 2003–04, 2013–14, of Portsmouth, 2009–10. Chm., Retired Clergy Assoc., 2017–. *Recreations:* golf, classical music, pipe organs. *Address:* 1 Bepton Down, Petersfield, Hants GU31 4PR. *T:* (01730) 266465. *E:* ijbrackley@gmail.com.

**BRACKS, Hon. Stephen (Phillip),** AC 2010; Senior Adviser: to Prime Minister of East Timor, since 2007; to KPMG, 2007–12; Premier of Victoria, and Minister for Multicultural Affairs, 1999–2007; *b* 15 Oct. 1954; *m* 1983, Terry Horsfall; two *s* one *d. Educ:* St Patrick's Coll., Ballarat; Ballarat Univ. (Dip. Business Studies, Grad. DipEd). Secondary commerce teacher, 1976–81; employment project worker and municipal recreation officer, 1981–85; Exec. Dir, Ballarat Educn Centre, 1985–89; Statewide Manager, Victoria's Employment Progs, 1989–93 (on secondment as Ministerial Advr to Premiers of Victoria, 1990); Principal Advr to Fed. Parly Sec. for Transport and Communications, 1993; Exec. Dir Victorian Printing Industry Trng Bd, 1993–94. MLA (ALP) Williamstown, Vic 1994–2007; Shadow Minister for Employment, Industrial Relns and Tourism, 1994–96; Shadow Treas. and Shadow Minister for Finance and Industrial Relns, 1996–99; Dep Chm., Public Accounts and Estimates Cttee, 1996–99; Shadow Treas. and Shadow Ministe for Multicultural Affairs, March–Oct. 1999; Treas., 1999–2000. Leader, State Parly Labo Party, March–Oct. 1999. Chm., United Super Pty Ltd, 2009–; Non-executive Director Jardine Lloyd Thompson Australia, 2007–; Bank of Sydney, 2013–; Maurice Blackburn Lawyers, 2018–; Vice Chm., Adv. Bd, AIMS Financial Gp, 2007–09. Aust. Automotive Industry Envoy, 2009–13. Chairman: Aust. Subscription TV and Radio Assoc., 2009–13 Melbourne Cricket Ground Trust, 2017–; Cycling Australia, 2017–. Hon. Professoria Fellow, Univ. of Melbourne, 2007. Hon. Dr Ballarat. *Recreations:* camping, distance swimming, tennis, football supporter, cycling. *Address:* Old Treasury Building, 20 Sprin Street, Melbourne, Vic 3000, Australia. *E:* info@stevebracks.com.au.

**BRADBURY,** family name of **Baron Bradbury**.

**BRADBURY,** 3rd Baron *cr* 1925, of Winsford, Co. Chester; **John Bradbury;** *b* 17 March 1940; *s* of 2nd Baron Bradbury and of his 1st wife, Joan, *o d* of W. D. Knight; *S* father, 1994; *m* 1968, Susan, *d* of late W. Liddiard; two *s*. *Educ:* Gresham's Sch.; Univ. of Bristol. *Heir: s* Hon. John Timothy Bradbury, *b* 16 Jan. 1973.

**BRADBURY, Anita Jean, (Mrs Philip Bradbury);** *see* Pollack, A. J.

**BRADBURY, His Honour Anthony Vincent;** a Circuit Judge, 1992–2006; Resident Judge, Bow County Court, 1998–2006; *b* 29 Sept. 1941; *s* of late Alfred Charles Bradbury, OBE and Noreen Vincent Bradbury; *m* 1966, Rosalie Anne Buttrey; one *d*. *Educ:* Kent College, Canterbury; Univ. of Birmingham (Sir Henry Barber Law Scholar; LLB). Solicitor 1965; Principal, Bradbury & Co., 1970–81; Registrar, then Dist Judge, Ilford County Court, 1981–91, Chelmsford County Court, 1991–92; a Recorder of the Crown Court, 1990–92; authorised to sit as a Judge of the High Court, Queen's Bench, Chancery and Family Divs, 1998–2006. Chm., SE Circuit Dist Judges, 1989–92. Wandsworth Mem., GLC and ILEA, 1967–70. Contested (C): N Battersea, 1970; S Battersea, Feb. 1974. Chairman of Governors: Putney Coll. for Further Educn, 1968–74; St John's C of E Sch., Buckhurst Hill, 1989–96. Hon. Treas., British Assoc. for Cemeteries in S Asia, 2010–16. *Publications:* Early London County Courts, 2010; Frank Mitchell - Imperial Cricketer, 2014; Rev. E. S. Carter - Yorkshire Cricketing Cleric, 2018; contribs to cricketing periodicals. *Recreations:* reading, Yorkshire cricket, writing for pleasure. *Clubs:* Reform, MCC; Yorkshire CC (Chm., Southern Gp, 1985–87); Cricket Writers'.

**BRADBURY, David Anthony Gaunt;** Director of Libraries, Archives and Guildhall Art Gallery, City of London Corporation (formerly Corporation of London), 2005–09; *b* 1 Nov. 1947; *s* of late Peter Bradbury and Iris Bradbury (*née* Tweedale); *m* 1974, Ellen Williams; three *s* one *d*. *Educ:* Repton Sch.; Univ. of Sussex (BA Russian Studies 1970, MA Contemp. Eur. Studies 1972). MCLIP. Grad. trainee, BM liby, 1972–73; British Library: Lending Div., 1975–86; Dep. Dir (Services), 1986–89, Dir, 1989–95, Document Supply Centre; Dir-Gen., Collections and Services, 1996–2001; Mem. Bd, 1996–2001; Dir, Libraries and Guildhall Art Gall., Corp. of London, 2002–05. Member: Bd, London Univ. Sch. of Advanced Study, 2000–01; Adv. Cttee, Univ. of London Centre for Metropolitan Hist., 2005–09. Mem. Conseil, Projet d'Etablissement de la Bibliothèque nationale de France, 1999–2000. Chm., Saga Trust, 1996–2001. Trustee, London Jl, 2005–09. *Publications:* contrib. jl articles on future of libraries, library co-operation, publishing, digital information. *Recreations:* languages, walking, Scrabble, history of Saddleworth. *Address:* 25 Britton Street, EC1M 5NY. *T:* (020) 7250 3907.

**BRADBURY, Julia Michelle;** television presenter and broadcaster; *b* Dublin, 24 July 1970; *d* of Michael Bradbury and Chrissi Bradbury; partner, Gerard Cunningham; one *s* two *d* (incl. twin *d*). *Educ:* King Edward VII Sch., Sheffield. Reporter, Live TV, 1995; LA Corresp., GMTV, 1996–97; anchor and launch face, Channel 5 TV, 1997, presenter, Exclusive, 1997–99; Presenter: Top Gear, 1998–99; Moral Dilemmas, 2000; Wish You Were Here, 2001–03; Moto GP, Speedway, 2002–04; Watchdog, 2004–09; Wainwright Walks, 2007; Kill It, Cook It, Eat It, 2007–11; Rough Guide To..., 2008; Railway Walks, 2008; Countryfile, 2009–14; Coast to Coast, 2009; South Africa Walks, German Wanderlust, 2010; Canal Walks, 2011; Planet Earth Live, 2013; Take on the Twisters, 2013; Wonders of Britain, 2014–15; Best Walks with a View, 2016; Famous, Rich and Homeless, 2016; Britain's Best Walks, 2017; Britain's Favourite Walks: Top 100, 2018; Australia with Julia Bradbury, 2019. Pres., Camping and Caravanning Club, 2013–; Co-Founder, The Outdoor Guide, 2015–. Ambassador: Scouts, 2011–; Outdoor Trust, 2013–; Keep Britain Tidy, 2018–. DUniv Sheffield Hallam, 2013. *Publications:* Railway Walks, 2010; Canal Walks, 2011; Julia Bradbury's Wainwright Walks, 2012; Julia Bradbury's Wainwright Walks, Coast to Coast, 2013; Unforgettable Walks, 2016. *Recreations:* walking, travel, dancing, family, charity, conservationist and environmentalist supporter. *Address:* The Outdoor Guide, PO Box 71931, NW2 9RA. *T:* (020) 3393 5084. *E:* info@juliabradbury.com.

**BRADBURY, Richard Edward,** CBE 2008; Chief Executive, River Island, 2008–11; non-executive Director, Boden, since 2012; *b* Bedford, 4 Feb. 1956; *s* of Albert Edward and Lily Bradbury; *m* 1981, Susan Price; two *d*. *Educ:* Bedford Modern Sch.; Luton Poly. Mgt trainee, Barnaby Rudge, 1975–76; Merchandiser, Harry Fenton Menswear, 1977–79; Burton Group: Merchandiser, 1979–81; Buyer, 1981–84; Buying and Merchandising Controller, 1984–86; Buying Dir, 1986–89; River Island: Man. Dir, Womenswear, 1989–98; Gp Man. Dir, 1998–2007. Mem., Develt Bd, Chickenshed, 2014–; Patron, Scope, 2012 (Chm., Appeal Bd). Worked with NHS on Patient Revolution Initiative, 2012; assists at local hospice. Beacon Fellowship for Pioneering Philanthropy, 2013. *Recreations:* travel, golf, music, wine, eating out, retail.

**BRADBURY, Susan Alison, (Mrs J. C. Whitley),** OBE 2010; Director, Folio Holdings Ltd, 2010–16; *b* 15 June 1947; *d* of John Donovan and Mary Alison Bradbury; *m* 1984, John Christopher Whitley (*d* 2014); one step *s*. *Educ:* Nottingham High Sch. for Girls (GPDST); Bretton Hall Coll. of Educn; Leeds Univ. (BEd Hons). Teacher: British Sch., Gran Canaria, Canary Is, 1969–71; Haydon Rd Jun. Sch., Nottingham, 1971–72; Governess, Seville, 1972–73; Folio Society: Membership Sec., Production Asst, Picture Researcher, Asst Editor, then Sen. Editor, 1973–83; Associate Editl Dir, 1983–84; Editl Dir, 1984–2006; Dep. Man. Dir, 1991–2006; Acting Man. Dir, 1992–96; Ed.-in-Chief, 2006–09. Trustee: John Hodgson Theatre Trust, 2005–; Keats-Shelley Meml Assoc., 2010–; Bankside Gall., 2010–15. Hon. Sec., Soc. of Bookmen, 2000–04 and 2007–13. Freeman, 2010, Liveryman, 2013, Barbers' Co. *Publications:* (trans.) Three Tragedies, by Federico Garcia Lorca, 1977; (ed and transcribed) Sir Thomas Malory's Chronicles of King Arthur, 1982; (with Urgunge Onon) Chinggis Khan, 1993; Midnight Madonna (novel), 1995; anthologies: (with John Letts) A Few Royal Occasions, 1977; Fifty Folio Epigrams, 1996; Christmas Crime Stories, 2004; Christmas Ghost Stories, 2005; A Traveller's Christmas, 2006; (with Robert Fox) Eyewitness to History, 2008; Joanna, George and Henry: a Pre-Raphaelite tale of art, love and friendship, 2012; Winter: a folio anthology, 2016; Spring: a folio anthology, 2017; Summer: a folio anthology, 2018; (ed) The Boyce Papers, 2019; selected and introduced: Short Stories by Somerset Maugham, 1985; Dream Street: short stories by Damon Runyan, 1989; Love Poems by Robert Graves, 1990. *Recreations:* travel, drawing, reading, opera, playing flamenco guitar, riding elderly motorbike. *Address:* 9 Edna Street, SW11 3DP. *T:* (020) 7228 9534. *E:* suewhitley44@gmail.com.

**BRADBURY, Rear-Adm. Thomas Henry,** CB 1979; *b* 4 Dec. 1922; *s* of Thomas Henry Bradbury and Violet Buckingham; *m* 1st, 1945, Beryl Doreen Evans (marr. diss. 1979; she *d* 1985); one *s* (one *d* decd); 2nd, 1979, Sarah Catherine, *d* of Harley Hillier and Mrs Susan Hillier. *Educ:* Christ's Hosp. CO HMS Jufair, 1960–62; Supply Officer, HMS Hermes, 1965–67; Sec. to Controller of Navy, MoD, 1967–70; CO HMS Terror, 1970–71; RCDS, 1972; Dir, Naval Admin. Planning, MoD, 1974–76; Flag Officer, Admiralty Interview Bd, 1977–79. Gp Personnel Dir, Inchcape Gp of Cos, 1979–86; Gp Personnel Exec., Davy Corp., 1987–91. Non-exec. Dir, Eastbourne HA, 1990–93.

**BRADBY, Thomas;** Presenter, ITV News at Ten, since 2015; *b* 13 Jan. 1967; *s* of late Daniel James Bradby and Sarah Ley Bradby; *m* 1994, Claudia Hill-Norton; two *s* one *d*. *Educ:* Sherborne Sch.; Edinburgh Univ. (MA Hons Hist.). ITN trainee, 1990–92; ITV News: political producer, 1992–93; Ireland Corresp., 1993–96; Political Corresp., 1996–98; Asia Corresp., 1998–2001; Royal Corresp., 2001–03; UK Ed., 2003–05; Political Ed., 2005–15. Scriptwriter, TV series, The Great Fire, 2014. *Publications:* novels: Shadow Dancer, 1998 (screenplay for film, 2012); The Sleep of the Dead, 2001; The Master of Rain, 2002; The White Russian, 2003; The God of Chaos, 2005; Blood Money, 2009; Secret Service, 2019. *Recreations:* ski-ing, writing, walking, soccer. *Address:* c/o ITV News, 200 Gray's Inn Road, WC1X 8XZ. *T:* (020) 7430 4991. *E:* tom.bradby@itn.co.uk. *Clubs:* Royal Automobile, Soho House.

**BRADDICK, Janette;** *see* Atkinson, J.

**BRADDICK, Katharine Mary;** Director General, Financial Services, HM Treasury, since 2016; *b* Wendover, 2 June 1974; *d* of William Braddick and Ann Braddick (*née* Bower); *m* 2001, John Tanter; one *s* two *d*. *Educ:* Univ. of Warwick (BA Hons Hist. 1995); Newnham Coll., Cambridge (MPhil Medieval and Modern Langs 1996). Policy advr, health and safety policy, DoE, 1996–97; Department of the Environment, Transport and the Regions: Policy advr, waste policy, 1997–98, integrated transport, 1998–99; Pte Sec. to Minister for London, 1999–2000; Manager, Consumer Awareness, 2000–01; Hd, Personal Lines Insurance, Assoc. of British Insurers, 2001–03; Financial Services Authority: Manager, Communication and Mgt Inf., High Street Firms Div., 2003–05; Manager, Insurance Supervision, 2005; Exec. Asst to Chief Exec., 2005–07; Hd of Dept, Regulatory Strategy, 2007–08; Hd of Dept, Internat. Div., 2008–11; Hd, Prudential Banking Policy, 2011–12; Dir, Prudential Policy, FSA, then Bank of England, 2012–13; Dir for Financial Services (Internat.), HM Treasury, 2014–16. *Recreations:* cultural activities, gardening, food. *Address:* HM Treasury, 1 Horse Guards Road, SW1A 2HQ.

*See also* M. J. Braddick.

**BRADDICK, Prof. Michael Jonathan,** PhD; FBA 2013; Professor of History, since 2001, and Director, Global Humanities Initiative, since 2016, University of Sheffield; *b* Hayling Island, Hants, 29 Aug. 1962; *s* of William and Ann Braddick; *m* 2002, Karen Louise Harvey (marr. diss. 2017); two *d*. *Educ:* Ashlyns Sch., Berkhamsted; King's Coll., Cambridge (BA Hons 1984; PhD 1988). FRHistS 1995. Asst Prof., Birmingham Southern Coll., Ala, 1988–90; University of Sheffield: Temp. Lectr, 1990–91; British Acad. Postdoctoral Fellow, 1991–92; Lectr, 1992–98; Sen. Lectr, 1998–2001; Pro-Vice-Chancellor, 2009–13. Vis. Fellow, Max Planck Inst. for Eur. Legal Hist., Frankfurt, 1999; Mem., Sch. of Histl Studies, Inst. for Advanced Study, Princeton, 2006; Prof. associé, École des Hautes Études en Sciences Sociales, Paris, 2011; Dist. Vis. Fellow, Aust. Res. Council Centre for Hist. of Emotions, Univ. of Adelaide, 2013. *Publications:* Parliamentary Taxation in Seventeenth-Century England: local administration and response, 1994; The Nerves of State: taxation and the financing of the English State, 1558–1714, 1996 (trans. Japanese 2000); (ed with M. Greengrass) The Letters of Sir Cheney Culpeper, 1641–1657, 1996; State Formation in Early Modern England, c. 1550–1700, 2000; (ed with J. Walter) Negotiating Power in Early Modern Society: order, hierarchy and subordination in Britain and Ireland, 2001; (ed with D. Armitage) The British Atlantic World, 1500–1800, 2002, 2nd edn 2009; Political Culture in Later Medieval England: essays by Simon Walker, 2006; God's Fury, England's Fire: a new history of the English civil wars, 2008; The Politics of Gesture: historical perspectives, 2009; The Experience of Revolution in Stuart Britain and Ireland: essays for John Morrill, 2011; (ed) The Oxford Handbook of the English Revolution, 2015; The Common Freedom of the People, 2018; contrib. articles to jls and edited vols. *Recreations:* walking, cinema, football, cricket, Rugby, family. *Address:* Department of History, University of Sheffield, Jessop West, 1 Upper Hanover Street, Sheffield S3 7RA. *E:* m.braddick@sheffield.ac.uk.

*See also* K. M. Braddick.

**BRADDICK, Prof. Oliver John,** PhD; FBA 2012; FMedSci; Professor of Psychology and Head, Department of Experimental Psychology, Oxford University, 2001–11, now Emeritus Professor; Fellow, Magdalen College, Oxford, since 2001; *b* 16 Nov. 1944; *s* of Henry John James Braddick and Edith Muriel Braddick; *m* 1979, Prof. Janette Atkinson, *qv*; two *s* two *d*. *Educ:* Trinity Coll., Cambridge (MA; PhD 1968). Cambridge University: Lectr, 1969–86; Reader in Vision, 1986–93; Fellow, Trinity Coll., 1968–72; University College London: Prof. of Psychol., 1993–2001; Hd of Dept, 1998–2001. Associate, Brown Univ., USA, 1968–69. FMedSci 2001. MAE 2008. Trustee, Assoc. for Res. in Vision and Ophthalmol., 1999–2004. Koffka Medal, Univ. of Giessen, 2009. Ed.-in-Chief, Oxford Res. Encyclopaedia of Psychol., 2014–. *Publications:* numerous articles on vision and its develt in scientific jls and books. *Recreations:* family life including five grandchildren, the arts. *Address:* Department of Experimental Psychology, Radcliffe Observatory Quarter, University of Oxford, Oxford OX2 6GG. *T:* (01865) 512025.

**BRADES, Susan Deborah F.;** *see* Ferleger Brades.

**BRADFORD, 7th Earl of,** *cr* 1815; **Richard Thomas Orlando Bridgeman;** Bt 1660; Baron Bradford, 1794; Viscount Newport, 1815; *b* 3 Oct. 1947; *s* of 6th Earl of Bradford, TD, and Mary Willoughby (*d* 1986), *er d* of Lt-Col T. H. Montgomery, DSO; *S* father, 1981; *m* 1st, 1979, Joanne Elizabeth (marr. diss. 2006), *d* of B. Miller; three *s* one *d*; 2nd, 2008, Dr Penelope Law. *Educ:* Harrow; Trinity College, Cambridge. Owner: Porters English Restaurant of Covent Garden, 1979–2015; Covent Garden Grill, until 2015; Porters Restaurant and Bar, Berkhamsted, 2015–18. Chm., Restaurant Assoc., 2010–14; Bd Mem., Nat. Restaurant Assoc. (USA), 2006–14. *Publications:* (compiled) My Private Parts and the Stuffed Parrot, 1984; The Eccentric Cookbook, 1985; Stately Secrets, 1994; (with Carol Wilson) Porters English Cookery Bible: Ancient and Modern, 2004; (with Carol Wilson) Porters Seasonal Celebrations, 2007. *Heir: s* Viscount Newport, *qv*. *Address:* 46 Sutton Court Road, Chiswick, W4 4NL. *T:* (020) 8994 4846. *E:* bradfordr@porters.uk.com.

**BRADFORD, Area Bishop of,** since 2014; **Rt Rev. Dr Toby Matthew Howarth;** *b* 12 July 1962; *m* 1994, Henriette De Greef; three *d*. *Educ:* Yale Univ. (BA 1986); Wycliffe Hall, Oxford; Birmingham Univ. (MA 1991); Free Univ. of Amsterdam (PhD 2001). Ordained deacon, 1992, priest, 1993; Curate, St Augustine, Derby, 1992–95; Res. Student, Henry Martyn Centre for Reconciliation and Inter Faith Relns, Hyderabad, India, 1995–2000; Evangelist, Pilgrim Father's Church, Rotterdam, 2000–02; Vice Principal and Tutor, Crowther Hall CMS Trng Coll., Selly Oak, 2002–04; Priest-in-charge, St Christopher, Springfield, 2004–11; Bishop's Advr on Inter-faith Relns, 2005–11; Archbishop of Canterbury's Sec. for Inter-religious Affairs, 2011–14. Hon. Canon: All Saints Cathedral, Cairo, 2013–; Ripon Cathedral, 2015–; Bradford Cathedral, 2015; Wakefield Cathedral, 2015. *Publications:* The Twelver Shi'a as a Muslim Minority in India: pulpit of tears, 2005. *Address:* 47 Kirkgate, Shipley, W Yorks BD18 3EH.

**BRADFORD, Dean of;** *see* Lepine, Very Rev. J. J.

**BRADFORD, Archdeacon of;** *see* Jolley, Ven. A. J.

**BRADFORD, Barbara Taylor,** OBE 2007; author; *b* Leeds, 10 May; *d* of late Winston and Freda Taylor; *m* 1963, Robert Bradford. Jun. Reporter, 1949–51, Women's Editor, 1951–53, Yorkshire Evening Post; Fashion Editor, Woman's Own, 1953–54; columnist, London Evening News, 1955–57; Exec. Editor, London American, 1959–62; moved to USA, 1964; Editor, National Design Center Magazine, 1965–69; syndicated columnist, 1968–81. Member, Board of Directors: Literacy Partners of NY, 2001–; Police Athletic League, NY, 2002–; Reporters Without Borders, Washington DC, 2015–. Hon. Ambassador, Nat. Literacy Trust (UK), 2014–. Hon. DLitt: Leeds, 1989; Bradford, 1995; Hon. DHL Teikyo Post, Conn, 1996. *Publications:* Complete Encyclopedia of Homemaking Ideas, 1968; A Garland of Children's Verse, 1968; How to be the Perfect Wife, 1969; Easy Steps to Successful Decorating, 1971; How to Solve Your Decorating Problems, 1976; Decorating Ideas for Casual Living, 1977; Making Space Grow, 1979; Luxury Designs for Apartment Living, 1981; *novels:* A Woman of Substance, 1979 (televised, 1985); Voice of the Heart, 1983; Hold the Dream, 1985 (televised, 1986); Act of Will, 1986; To Be the Best, 1988; The Women in His Life, 1990; Remember, 1991; Angel, 1993; Everything to Gain, 1994; Dangerous to Know, 1995; Love in Another Town, 1995; Her Own Rules, 1996; A Secret Affair, 1996; Power of a Woman, 1997; A Sudden Change of Heart, 1999; Where You Belong, 2000; The Triumph of Katie Byrne, 2001; Emma's Secret, 2003; Unexpected Blessings, 2004; Just Rewards, 2005; The Ravenscar Dynasty, 2006; Heirs of Ravenscar, 2007; Being Elizabeth, 2008; Breaking the Rules, 2009; Playing the Game, 2010; Letter from a Stranger, 2011; Cavendon Hall, 2014; The Cavendon Women, 2015; The Cavendon Luck, 2016; Secrets of Cavendon, 2017; Master of His Fate, 2018. *Address:* Bradford Enterprises, 505 Park Avenue, New York, NY 10022–2605, USA. *T:* (212) 308 7390, *Fax:* (212) 935 1636.

**BRADFORD, (Sir) Edward Alexander Slade,** 5th Bt, *cr* 1902 (but does not use the title); *b* 18 June 1952; *s* of Major Sir Edward Montagu Andrew Bradford, 3rd Bt (*d* 1952) and his 2nd wife, Marjorie Edith (*née* Bere); *S* half-brother, Sir John Ridley Evelyn Bradford, 4th Bt, 1954; *m* 1990, Jacqueline W. Bolton. *Heir: cousin* Andrew Edward Hanning Bradford [*b* 6 Jan. 1955; *m* 1978, Nicola Barbara Smythe; two *s* one *d*].

**BRADFORD, Hon. Max(well Robert);** Associate, Oxford Policy Management Ltd, UK, 2012–14; Principal, 2001–15, and Director, 2005–15, Bradford & Associates Ltd; *b* 19 Jan. 1942; *s* of Robert and Ella Bradford; *m* 1st, 1967, Dr Janet Grieve (marr. diss. 1988); 2nd, 1991, Rosemary Young; two step *d*. *Educ:* Christchurch Boys' High Sch.; Univ. of Canterbury, NZ (MCom Hons); Melbourne Business Sch. (AMP 1978). NZ Treasury, 1966–69, 1973–78; Economist, IMF, Washington, 1969–73; Dir of Advocacy, Employers' Fedn, 1978–85; Chief Exec., Bankers Assoc., 1985–87; Sec.-Gen., Nat. Party, 1987–89; MP (Nat. Party): Tarawera, 1990–96; Rotorua, 1996–99; List, 1999–2002; Minister of Defence, Enterprise, Commerce, Business Develt, Labour, Energy, Revenue, and Immigration, 1996–99; Minister of Defence, 1997–99; Minister for Tertiary Educn, 1999. Dir, Castalia Advisors, 2001–05; Consultant to World Bank and internat. organisations, 2002–15. *Recreations:* sailing, music, reading, fishing, ski-ing, boatbuilding. *Club:* Wellington.

**BRADFORD, Sarah Mary Malet Ward, (Viscountess Bangor);** historian and biographer, critic, broadcaster and journalist; *b* 3 Sept. 1938; *d* of late Brig. Hilary Anthony Hayes, DSO, OBE, and Mary Beatrice de Carteret (*née* Malet), who *m* 2nd, Keith Murray; *m* 1st, 1959, Anthony John Bradford (marr. diss. 1976); one *s* one *d*; 2nd, 1976, Viscount Bangor, *qv. Educ:* St Mary's Convent, Shaftesbury; Lady Margaret Hall, Oxford (schol.). Manuscript Expert, Christies, 1974–77; Consultant, Manuscript Dept, Sotheby's, 1979–81. *Publications:* The Englishman's Wine, 1969, new edn as The Story of Port, 1978, 2nd edn 1983; Portugal and Madeira, 1969; Portugal, 1973; Cesare Borgia, 1976, 2nd edn 2001; Disraeli, 1982, 2nd edn 1996; Princess Grace, 1984; King George VI, 1989, revised edn 2001; Sacheverell Sitwell, 1993; Elizabeth, A Biography of Her Majesty The Queen, 1996, revised edn 2001; America's Queen, The Life of Jacqueline Kennedy Onassis, 2000, 2nd edn 2013; Lucrezia Borgia: life, love and death in Renaissance Italy, 2004; Diana, 2006, 20th anniv. rev. edn 2017; Queen Elizabeth II: her life in our times, 2011. *Recreations:* reading biographies, diaries and letters, gardening, travelling, watching Liverpool FC. *Address:* c/o Aitken Alexander Associates, 291 Gray's Inn Road, WC1X 8EB. *T:* (020) 7373 8672, *Fax:* (020) 7373 6002.

**BRADING, Prof. David Anthony,** PhD, LittD; FBA 1995; Professor of Mexican History, University of Cambridge, 1999–2004; Fellow of Clare Hall, Cambridge, 1995–2004; *b* 26 Aug. 1936; *s* of Ernest Arthur Brading and Amy Mary (*née* Driscoll); *m* 1966, Celia Wu; one *s*. *Educ:* Pembroke Coll., Cambridge (BA 1960; LittD 1991; Hon. Fellow 2008); UCL (PhD 1965). Asst Prof., Univ. of Calif, Berkeley, 1965–71; Associate Prof., Yale Univ., 1971–73; Cambridge University: Lectr, 1973–92; Reader in Latin American Hist., 1992–99. Hon. Prof., Univ. of Lima, 1993. Order of the Aztec Eagle (Mexico), 2003; Medal of the Congress (Peru), 2011. *Publications:* Miners and Merchants in Bourbon Mexico, 1971; Haciendas and Ranchos in the Mexican Bajío, 1979; The Origins of Mexican Nationalism, 1985; The First America, 1991; Church and State in Bourbon Mexico, 1994; Mexican Phoenix, 2001. *Recreations:* music, walking. *Address:* 28 Storey's Way, Cambridge CB3 0DT. *T:* (01223) 352098. *Club:* Oxford and Cambridge.

**BRADLEY,** family name of **Baron Bradley**.

**BRADLEY, Baron** *cr* 2006 (Life Peer), of Withington in the County of Greater Manchester; **Keith John Charles Bradley;** PC 2001; *b* 17 May 1950; *m* 1987, Rhona Graham; two *s* one *d*. *Educ:* Manchester Polytechnic (BA Hons); York Univ. (MPhil). Former health service administrator, North West RHA. Mem., Manchester City Council, 1983–88. MP (Lab) Manchester, Withington, 1987–2005; contested (Lab) same seat, 2005. Opposition spokesman on social security, 1991–96, on transport, 1996–97; Parly Under-Sec. of State, DSS, 1997–98; Treasurer of HM Household (Dep. Chief Whip), 1998–2001; Minister of State, Home Office, 2001–02. Joined Labour Party, 1973; Mem., Manchester Withington Co-op Party. Ind. Review of Mental Health, Learning Disabilities and Criminal Justice System, 2009. Chm., Christie NHS Foundn Trust, 2011–14; non-exec. Dir, Pennine Care NHS Foundn Trust, 2015–18; Trustee: Centre for Mental Health, 2012–; Prison Reform Trust, 2012–. Associate Vice-Pres., 2010–13, Hon. Special Advr, 2013–, Univ. of Manchester; Chair, Council, Univ. of Salford, 2018–. *Address:* House of Lords, SW1A 0PW.

**BRADLEY, Prof. Allan,** PhD; FRS 2002; Director, Wellcome Sanger Institute (formerly The Sanger Centre, then Wellcome Trust Sanger Institute), Hinxton, Cambridge, 2000–10, now Director Emeritus. *Educ:* Trinity Coll., Cambridge (BA Hons 1981; PhD 1986). Baylor College of Medicine, Houston, Texas: Asst Prof., 1987–92, Associate Prof., 1992–95, Cullen Prof. of Genetics, 1995–2000, Dept of Molecular and Human Genetics; Associate Investigator, Howard Hughes Med. Inst., 1993–2000. Mem., EMBO, 2006. *Publications:* articles in jls. *Address:* Wellcome Sanger Institute, Genome Campus, Hinxton, Cambridge CB10 1SA.

**BRADLEY, Andrew;** *see* Bradley, J. A.

**BRADLEY, Andrew,** PhD; Chief Engineer, Hawk Advanced Jet Trainer Aircraft, BAE Systems, 2004–13; *b* Blackburn, Lancs, 20 Jan. 1955; *s* of John Bradley and Margaret Elizabeth Bradley; one *s* two *d*; *m* 2012, Kairen Dods. *Educ:* St Mary's Coll., Blackburn; Durham Univ. (BSc Jt Hons Maths and Phys; PhD Particle Physics 1978). CEng 2009; FIET 2009; FRAeS 2009; FREng 2010. Res. Fellow, Univ. of Manchester, 1978–81; Systems Engr, Nat. Nuclear Corp., 1981–87; British Aerospace, subseq. BAE Systems, 1987–2013: Hd, Software Engrg, 1989–95; Dir, Systems Engrg, 1995–2004. RAEng Vis. Prof. in Applied Systems Engrg, Univ. of Loughborough, 2008–19. *Publications:* articles on particle physics in learned jls. *Recreations:* computer games—writing software (games published from 1980 onwards), golf, squash, music. *Address:* Sandrigg Laithe, Gildersleets Lane, Giggleswick, N Yorks BD24 0JZ. *T:* (01729) 822395. *E:* drandrewbradley@msn.com.

**BRADLEY, Anna Louise;** Chairman, Rail Safety Standards Board, 2015–18; *b* 29 July 1957; *d* of Donald Bradley and Angela Lucy Bradley (*née* Bradley, now Ratcliffe); *m* 1995, Norman Howard Jones; one *s* one *d*. *Educ:* Camden Sch. for Girls; Warwick Univ. (BA Phil, 1978; MBA 1994). Sen. Sub-Editor, Marshall Cavendish Partworks Ltd, 1978–82; Consumers' Association: Sen. Project Leader, 1982–87; Project Manager, Food and Health, 1987–88; Head, Food and Health, 1988–91; Dep. Research Dir, 1991–93; Exec. Dir and Co. Sec., Inst. for the Study of Drug Dependence Ltd, 1993–98; Dir, Nat. Consumer Council, 1999–2002; Dir of Consumer Affairs, then of Retail Themes and Consumer Sector Leader, Financial Services Authy, 2002–05. Chair: Organic Standards Bd, 2006–10; Soil Assoc. Certification Ltd, 2010–13 (non-exec. Dir, 2007–10); Consumer Panel, Office of Communications, 2008–11; Gen. Optical Council, 2010–12 (Mem., 2009–10); Council of Licensed Conveyancers, 2010–15; Southern Water Customer Challenge Gp, 2012–; Healthwatch England, 2012–16; SRA, 2019–; Comr, Care Quality Commn, 2012–16. Member: Adv. Council on the Misuse of Drugs, 1996–98; Agriculture, Envmt and Biotechnol. Commn, 2000–05; Sci. Adv. Council, 2004–05; Ind. Governance Cttee, Zurich UK Life, 2015– (Chair); Ind. non-exec. Dir and Chair, End-user Council, Pay.uk (formerly New Payments System Operator), 2017–. Adv. Consultant, Fishburn Hedges, 2006–10. Trustee, Addaction, 2006–12; Trustee and Mem. Bd, Age UK, 2017–; non-exec. Dir, Life Trust Foundn, 2008–09. Non-exec. Mem. Bd, Colchester Univ. Foundn Trust, 2010–12. Mem., Mgt Cttee, Patients' Assoc., 1985–88. *Publications:* Healthy Eating, 1989; (ed) Understanding Additives, 1988; acad. and research papers in Lancet, Jl Human Nutrition, Dietetics, etc.

**BRADLEY, Anne;** *see* Smith, Anne.

**BRADLEY, Prof. Anthony Wilfred;** constitutional lawyer; *b* 6 Feb. 1934; *s* of David and Olive Bradley (*née* Bonsey); *m* 1959, Kathleen Bryce; one *s* three *d*. *Educ:* Magdalen Coll. Sch., Oxford; Dover Grammar Sch.; Emmanuel Coll., Cambridge (BA 1957, LLB 1958, MA 1961). Solicitor of the Supreme Court, 1960 (Clifford's Inn Prize); called to the Bar, Inner Temple, 1989; in practice as a barrister, 1990–2010. Asst Lectr, 1960–64, Lectr, 1964–68, Cambridge, and Fellow of Trinity Hall, 1960–68; Prof. of Constitutional Law, 1968–89, Dean, Faculty of Law, 1979–82, Prof. Emeritus, 1990, Univ. of Edinburgh. Vis. Reader in Law, UC, Dar es Salaam, 1966–67; Vis. Prof. of Public Law, Univ. of Florence, 1984; Res. Fellow, Inst. of European and Comparative Law, Univ. of Oxford, 2003–. Chairman: Edinburgh Council for Single Homeless, 1984–88; Social Security Appeal Tribunal, 1984–89; Member: Wolfenden Cttee on Voluntary Orgns, 1974–78; Social Scis and Law Cttee, SSRC, 1975–79; Social Studies Sub-Cttee, UGC, 1985–89; Cttee of Inquiry into Local Govt in Scotland, 1980; Cttee to review local govt in Islands of Scotland, 1983–84. Mem. Exec. Cttee, Internat. Assoc. of Constitutional Law, 1999–2007. Legal Advr, H of L Select Cttee on the Constitution, 2002–05; Alternate Mem. (UK), Venice Commn for Democracy Through Law, 2003–10. Ed., Public Law, 1986–92. Hon. QC 2011. Hon. LLD: Staffordshire, 1993; Edinburgh, 1998. *Publications:* (ed with M. Adler) Justice, Discretion and Poverty, 1976; (ed) Wade and Bradley, Constitutional and Administrative Law, 9th edn 1978 to 11th edn 1993, subseq. Bradley and Ewing, Constitutional and Administrative Law, 12th edn 1997 to 16th edn 2014; (with D. Christie) The Scotland Act 1978, 1979; Administrative Law (in Stair Meml Encyc. of the Laws of Scotland), 1987, 2nd edn (with C. Himsworth) 2000; (ed with J. S. Bell) Governmental Liability, 1995, 3rd edn 2008; (ed with K. S. Ziegler and D. Baranger) Constitutionalism and the Role of Parliaments, 2007; contrib. to legal jls and collaborative books. *Recreations:* music (playing and listening), family history. *Address:* 20 Abingdon Road, Cumnor, Oxford OX2 9QN.

**BRADLEY, Averil Olive, (Mrs J. W. P. Bradley);** *see* Mansfield, A. O.

**BRADLEY, Ben;** MP (C) Mansfield, since 2017; *b* Derby, 11 Dec. 1989; *s* of Chris Bradley and Sally Bradley; *m* 2015, Shanade; two *s*. *Educ:* Derby Grammar Sch., Littleover; Mill Hill Sch., Derby; Univ. of Bath; Nottingham Trent Univ. (BA Hons 1st Cl. Politics 2013). Adminr, Open Univ., 2008–11; landscape gardener, Peach Tree, Belper, 2009–10; store asst, Aldi, 2011–12; Campaign Manager, Cons. Party, 2013–15; Office Manager, Mark Spencer, MP, 2015–17; Sen Asst, Nicholas Boles, MP, 2016–17. Member (C): Ashfield DC, 2015–; Notts CC, 2017–. *Publications:* Crossing the Floor: defection and the new Labour phenomenon, 2016. *Recreations:* hockey (field), Rugby, family. *Address:* House of Commons, SW1A 0AA. *T:* (020) 7219 3594. *E:* ben.bradley.mp@parliament.uk.

**BRADLEY, Prof. Benjamin Arthur de Burgh,** PhD; FRCP, FRCPath; Professor of Transplantation Sciences, and Director, Department of Transplantation Sciences, University of Bristol, 1992–2004; *b* 17 Sept. 1942; *s* of Reuben Stephen Bradley and Elsie Marjorie Bradley (*née* Burke); *m* 1968, Anne White; four *d*. *Educ:* Silcoates Sch., Wakefield; Bilston Grammar Sch.; Birmingham Univ. Med. Sch. (MB ChB 1965); Birmingham Univ. (MSc 1967; PhD 1970). FRCPath 1986 (MRCPath 1974); FRCP 1999. House surgeon and house physician, United Birmingham Hosps, 1965–66; MRC Res. Fellow, Dept of Surgery and Exptl Pathology, Univ. of Birmingham, 1967–70; Asst Dir of Res., Dept of Surgery, Univ. of Cambridge, 1970–75; Asst Prof., Dept of Immunohaematology, Univ. of Leiden, 1975–79; Dir, UK Transplant Service, 1979–92. Prof. of Transplantation Immunology, Univ. of Bristol, 1988. Dir of Immunol., Ximerex Inc., 2006–07. Dir, Shannon Applied Biotechnol. Centre, Ireland, 2008–10. Member: Scientific Policy Adv. Cttee, Nat. Inst. for Biol Standards, 1991–96; Bd, Jenner Educnl Trust, 1992–2000; Scientific Cttee, Foundn for Nephrology, 1992–2004. President: Eur. Foundn for Immunogenetics, 1988–89; British Soc. for Histocompatibility and Immunogenetics, 1996–98. Hon. Consultant in Transplantation Scis, N Bristol NHS Trust, 1979–; Hon. Prof., Faculty of Medicine, Nat. Univ. of Ireland, Galway, 2013–. Chm., Editl Bd, European Jl Immunogenetics, 1989–2004. Hon. MA Cantab, 1974. Thomas Pocklington Meml Lect. and Medal, 1985. *Publications:* (with S. M. Gore) Renal Transplantation: sense and sensitization, 1986; Editor and contributor to annual reports of: UK Transplant Service, 1979–90; Transplantation Services and Statistics in UK and Eire, 1991; contrib. textbooks and med. jls on clinical organ and tissue transplantation and immunology, genetics of transplantation and blood transfusion and post-traumatic immunosuppression; articles in scientific jls, chapters in books and papers in conf. procs. *Recreations:* mountain walking, cycling, motorhoming, singing, swimming. *Address:* 3 Cromwell Court, Olveston, Bristol BS35 4BW. *T:* (01454) 201077. *E:* benjaminbzone-whoswho2009@yahoo.co.uk.

**BRADLEY, Catherine Annick Caroline**, CBE 2019; Independent Board Member, Financial Conduct Authority, since 2014; *b* Lyon, 20 April 1959; *d* of Didier Rougeron and Yvette Lafaure Rougeron; *m* 1984, Stephen John Bradley; one *s* two *d. Educ:* HEC Grande Ecole Paris. Vice Pres., Merrill Lynch, NY and London, 1981–91; Exec. Dir, Swiss Bank Corp., London, 1991–94; Eur. Strategy Equity Advisory, Paribas, London, 1994–2000; Man. Dir, Dresdner Kleinwort Wasserstein, London, 2000–03; Credit Suisse, 2003–12: Man. Dir, London; Hd, Equity Linked Solutions Gp for Asia-Pacific, Hong Kong; Hd, Equity Advisory, Asia Pacific, Société Générale Hong Kong, 2013–14. Non-exec. Dir, WS Atkins, 2015–17; Mem. Bd, Peugeot-Citroën, 2016– (Chm., Audit Cttee, 2016–). Mem., Fixed Income, Currencies and Commodities Mkts Standards Bd, 2015–. Visiting Lecturer: Saïd Business Sch., Univ. of Oxford, 2008–10; Internat. Swaps and Derivatives Assoc., 2010; Securities Industry Council, Monetary Authy of Singapore, 2011; Hong Kong Univ. of Sci. and Technol., 2011; LSE Asia, 2012. Trustee, British Sch. of Brussels, 2016–. *Recreations:* mountain walking, bridge, ceramics, family. *Address:* West London and Isle of Wight. *T:* (020) 8742 0633. *E:* cabradley@gmail.com. *Clubs:* Athenæum (Mem., Investment Cttee); Seaview Yacht (IoW), Hong Kong Royal Yacht (life absent mem.).

**BRADLEY, Dr (Charles) Clive;** Managing Director, 1990–99, and Consultant, 1999–2000, Sharp Laboratories of Europe Ltd; *b* 11 April 1937; *s* of late Charles William Bradley and Winifred Smith; *m* 1965, Vivien Audrey Godley (*d* 2017); one *s* one *d. Educ:* Longton High Sch.; Birmingham Univ. (BSc Hons in Physics, 1958); Emmanuel Coll., Cambridge (PhD 1962). CPhys 1997; FInstP 1997. Nat. Phys. Lab., 1961–67; MIT, USA, 1967, 1969; Nat. Bureau of Standards, USA, 1968; Nat. Phys. Lab., 1969–75; DoI, 1975–82, SPSO and Head of Energy Unit, 1978–82; Counsellor (Science and Technology), British Embassy, Tokyo, 1982–88; DCSO and Head of Secretariat, ACOST, Cabinet Office, 1988–90. Dir, Birds Hill Oxshott Estate Co., 2000–08. Vis. Prof., Univ. of Oxford, 1999–2002. Chm., Industrial Energy Conservation Cttee, Internat. Energy Agency, 1980–82. Dep. Comr Gen. for Britain, Sci. Expo Tokyo, 1985. Mem., Oxford Univ. Adv. Council on Continuing Educn, 1993–2001. Treas. and Mem. Council, Japan Soc., 2001–07. A. F. Bulgin Prize, IERE, 1972. Japanese Ambassador's Commendation, 2010. *Publications:* High Pressure Methods in Solid State Research, 1969; contribs to jls on lasers, metals and semiconductors, and speed of light determination. *Recreations:* tennis, gardening. *Address:* 39B The Ridgeway, Fetcham, Leatherhead, Surrey KT22 9BE. *Clubs:* Athenæum; St George's Hill Lawn Tennis; Probus (Mole Valley).

**BRADLEY, (Charles) Stuart,** CBE 1990; Managing Director, Associated British Ports, 1988–95; Director, Associated British Ports Holdings, 1988–2001; *b* 11 Jan. 1936; *s* of Captain Charles Bradley, OBE and Amelia Jane Bradley; *m* 1959, Kathleen Marina (née Loraine); one *s* one *d* (and one *s* decd). *Educ:* Penarth County Sch.; University Coll. Southampton (Warsash). Master Mariner, 1961; FCILT (FCIT 1978). Deck Officer, P&OSN Co., 1952–64; joined British Transport Docks Bd, subseq. Associated British Ports, 1964; Dock and Harbour Master, Silloth, 1968–70; Dock Master, 1970–74, Dock and Marine Superintendent, 1974–76, Plymouth; Docks Manager, Lowestoft, 1976–78; Port Manager, Barry, 1978–80; Dep. Port Manager, 1980–85, Port Manager, 1985–87, Hull; Asst Man. Dir (Resources), 1987–88; Chm., Red Funnel Gp, 1989–2000. Younger Brother, Trinity House, 1994–. *Recreations:* Welsh Rugby, walking by the sea, reading. *Club:* Honourable Company of Master Mariners.

**BRADLEY, Clive;** *see* Bradley, Charles C.

**BRADLEY, Clive,** CBE 1996; Chief Executive, The Publishers Association, 1976–97; Convenor, Confederation of Information Communication Industries, 1984–2014; *b* 25 July 1934; *s* of late Alfred and Kathleen Bradley. *Educ:* Felsted Sch., Essex; Clare Coll., Cambridge (Scholar; MA); Yale Univ. (Mellon Fellow). Called to the Bar, Middle Temple. Current Affairs Producer, BBC, 1961–63; Broadcasting Officer, Labour Party, 1963–64; Political Editor, The Statist, 1965–67; Gp Labour Adviser, IPC, 1967–69; Dep. Gen. Man., Daily and Sunday Mirror, 1969–71; Controller of Admin, IPC Newspapers, 1971–72; i/c IPC ind. radio applications, 1972–73; Dir i/c new prodn arrangements, The Observer, 1973–75. Dep. Chm., Central Valuation Tribunal, 1973–2006. Chairman: Soc. of Bookmen, 1998–2000; Book Power Ltd, 2009–11. Director: Organising Cttee, World Congress on Books, London, 1982; Don't Tax Reading campaign, 1984–85; Organiser, IPA Congress, London, 1988; Mem., DTI Inf. Age Partnership, 1997–2001. Pres., Richmond upon Thames Arts Council, 2015 (Chair, 2003–09; Vice Pres., 2010–15); Pres., U3A Richmond upon Thames, 2011–15. Trustee: Age Concern, Richmond, 1998–2011 (Chm., 2001–03; Treas., 2010–11); Garrick's Temple to Shakespeare, Hampton, 2006–. Gov., Felsted Sch., 1973–2008. *Publications:* Which Way?, 1970; (ed) The Future of the Book, 1982; articles on politics, economics, the press, television, industrial relations. *Recreations:* arts, reading, discussion. *Address:* 8 Northumberland Place, Richmond, Surrey TW10 6TS. *T:* (020) 8940 7172. *E:* bradley_clive@btopenworld.com.

**BRADLEY, Clodagh Maria, (Mrs Julian Alexander);** QC 2016; *b* Brussels, Oct. 1973; *d* of David Bradley and Mary Bradley; *m* 2006, Julian Alexander; one *s* one *d. Educ:* British Sch. of Brussels; Magdalene Coll., Cambridge (BA Law 1995). Called to the Bar, Middle Temple, 1996 (Astbury Major Scholar, 1995–96; Harmsworth Major Entrance Exhibnr, 1995–96); in practice as a barrister, 3 Serjeants' Inn, 1997–2012, One Crown Office Row, 2012–; Attorney Gen.'s C Panel of Jun. Counsel to the Crown, 2000–06. *Recreations:* family, ski-ing, cycling, travel, scuba diving. *Address:* One Crown Office Row, Temple, EC4Y 7HH. *T:* (020) 7797 7500, *Fax:* (020) 7797 7550. *E:* clodagh.bradley@1cor.com.

**BRADLEY, Prof. David John,** DM; FRCP, FRCPath, FFPH, FMedSci; FRSB; Director, Ross Institute, London School of Hygiene and Tropical Medicine, and Professor of Tropical Hygiene, University of London, 1974–2000, now Ross Professor Emeritus of Tropical Public Health; *b* 12 Jan. 1937; *s* of late Harold Robert and of Mona Bradley; *m* 1961, Lorne Marie, *d* of late Major L. G. Farquhar and Marie Farquhar; two *s* two *d. Educ:* Wyggeston Sch., Leicester; Selwyn Coll., Cambridge (Scholar); University Coll. Hosp. Med. Sch. (Atchison Schol., Magrath Schol., Trotter Medal in Surgery, Liston Gold Medal in Surgery, BA Nat. Scis Tripos, Med. Scis and Zoology, 1st cl. Hons, Frank Smart Prize Zool.; MB, BChir, MA 1960); DM Oxon 1972. FRSB (FIBiol 1974); FFPH (FFCM 1979); FRCPath 1981; FRCP 1985. Med. Res. Officer, Ross Inst. Bilharzia Res. Unit, Tanzania, 1961–64; Lectr, 1964–66, Sen. Lectr, 1966–69, Makerere Univ. of East Africa, Uganda; Trop. Res. Fellow of Royal Soc., Sir William Dunn Sch. of Pathology, Oxford, 1969–73; Sen. Res. Fellow, Staines Med. Fellow, Exeter Coll., Oxford, 1971–74; Clinical Reader in Path., Oxford Clinical Med. Sch., 1973–74; Chm., Div. of Communicable and Tropical Diseases, LSHTM, 1982–88. Vis. Prof., Univ. of Wales Coll. of Medicine, 1994. Co-Director, Malaria Ref. Lab., HPA (formerly PHLS), 1974–2003; Hon. Consultant in Public Health Medicine, HPA (formerly PHLS) and to Westminster PCT (formerly to Kensington, Chelsea and Westminster), 1974; Hon. Consultant in Trop. and Communicable Diseases, Bloomsbury DHA, 1983–2001; Dir, WHO Collaborating Centre Envmtl Control of Vectors, 1983; Mem., Bd of Trustees, Internat. Centre for Diarrhoeal Disease Res., Bangladesh, 1979–85 (Chm., 1982–83); Consultant Advisor to Dir, Royal Tropical Inst., Amsterdam, 1980–90; Advr, Ind. Internat. Commn on Health Res.; Member: WHO Expert Adv. Panel on Parasitic Diseases, 1972; Tech. Adv. Gp, Diarrhoea Programme, 1979–85; Panel of Experts on Envmtl Management, 1981; External Review Gp on Trop. Diseases Programme, 1987; Task Force on Health Res. for Develt, 1991–93; Chm., Rev. Cttee, Swiss Tropical Inst., 1994. Editor, Jl of Trop. Med. and Hygiene, 1981; Founding Ed., Tropical Medicine and Internat. Health. Pres., RSTM&H, 1999–2001. FMedSci 1999; For. Corresp. Mem., Royal Belgian Acad. of Medicine, 1984; Corresp. Mem., German Tropenmedizininingesellschaft, 1980; Hon. FIWEM (Hon. FIPHE, 1981). Hon. DSc Leicester, 2004. Chalmers Medal, 1980, Macdonald Medal, 1996, RSTM&H; Harben Gold Medal, RIPH, 2002. *Publications:* (with G. F. and A. U. White) Drawers of Water, 1972; (with E. E. Sabben-Clare and B. Kirkwood) Health in Tropical Africa during the Colonial Period, 1980; (with R. G. Feachem, D. D. Mara and H. Garelick) Sanitation and Disease, 1983; (jtly) Travel Medicine, 1989; (jtly) The Impact of Development Policies on Health, 1990; (jtly) The Malaria Challenge, 1999; papers in learned jls. *Recreations:* natural history, landscape gardens, travel. *Address:* London School of Hygiene and Tropical Medicine, Keppel Street, WC1E 7HT. *T:* (020) 7927 2216.

**BRADLEY, David John;** actor, since 1968; Associate Artist, Royal Shakespeare Co., since 1992; *b* York, 17 April 1942; *s* of George and Hilda Bradley; *m* 1978, Rosanna Baldaccini; two *s* one *d. Educ:* St George's Secondary Modern Sch., York; Royal Acad. of Dramatic Art. Joined National Theatre Co., Old Vic, 1972: The Front Page, Tis a Pity She's a Whore, Twelfth Night, The Cherry Orchard; Royal Shakespeare Co., 1978–, including: The Merchant of Venice, 1979; The Merry Wives of Windsor, 1986; Twelfth Night, Cymbeline, 1988; Dr Faustus, 1989; The Alchemist, 1992; Henry IV, Part 2, 1992; Hamlet, 1993 (Clarence Derwent Award, Equity); The Tempest, 1993; (title rôle) Titus Andronicus, 2003; Royal National Theatre, includes: Richard III, 1990; King Lear, 1990 (Laurence Olivier Award, 1991); Mother Courage; The Homecoming, 1997; The Mysteries, 1999; The Night Season, 2004; Henry IV, Parts 1 and 2, 2005; other performances include: York Mystery Plays, 1976; Britannicus/Phaedra (double-bill) Albery, 1998, transf. NY; Twelfth Night, Donmar, 2004, transf. NY; Vanya, Donmar, 2004, transf. NY; The Caretaker, Crucible Th., Sheffield, 2007, transf. Tricycle; No Man's Land, Duke of York's, 2009; Moonlight, Donmar, 2011; *television* includes: A Family at War, 1971; Martin Chuzzlewit, 1994; Our Friends in the North, 1996; Reckless, 1997; Our Mutual Friend, 1998; Vanity Fair, 1998; The Way We Live Now, 2002; Wild West, 2002–04; Blackpool, 2004; Ideal, 2006–08; True Dare Kiss, 2007; Game of Thrones, 2011–13; World Without End, 2012; Dr Who, 2012; Mount Pleasant, 2012–13; Prisoner's Wives, 2012–13; Broadchurch, 2013 (BAFTA Award for Best Supporting Actor, 2014); The Strain, 2014; Trollhunters, 2017; Les Misérables, 2018; After Life, 2019; *films* include: Tom's Midnight Garden, 1999; The King is Alive, 2000; Harry Potter and the Sorcerer's Stone, 2001; Harry Potter and the Chamber of Secrets, 2002; Nicholas Nickleby, 2002; Harry Potter and the Prisoner of Azkaban, 2004; Harry Potter and the Goblet of Fire, 2005; Harry Potter and the Order of the Phoenix, 2007; Hot Fuzz, 2007; Harry Brown, 2009; Harry Potter and the Half-Blood Prince, 2009; Another Year, 2010; Harry Potter and the Deathly Hallows: Part 2, 2011; Captain America: the First Avenger, 2011; The World's End, 2013; An Adventure in Space and Time, 2013. Pres., Shakespeare Hospice, Stratford-upon-Avon, 2010–. Hon. DLitt: Warwick, 2012; York St John's, 2015. *Recreations:* ski-ing, football (watching), family dinners, singing (frontman for The Crisps), all things Italian. *Address:* c/o Ruth Young, United Agents, 12–26 Lexington Street, W1F 0LE. *T:* (020) 3214 0800.

**BRADLEY, David Rice;** Director of Development, King's College School, Wimbledon, 2000–07; *b* 9 Jan. 1938; *s* of George Leonard Bradley and Evelyn Annie Bradley; *m* 1962, Josephine Elizabeth Turnbull Fricker (née Harries); two *s. Educ:* Christ Coll., Brecon; St Catharine's Coll., Cambridge (Exhibnr; MA English); Edinburgh Univ. (Dip. in Applied Linguistics). Nat. service commn, S Wales Borderers. British Council: served: Dacca, 1962–65; Allahabad, 1966–69; New Delhi, 1969–70; Dir of Studies, British Inst., Madrid, 1970–73; Department of the Environment: Principal, Res. Admin, 1973–76; Planning, Develt Control, 1976–78; Inner Cities, 1978–79; Rayner Study (develt of Management Inf. System for Ministers), 1979–80; Central Policy Planning Unit, 1980–81; Study of Local Govt Finance (Grade 5), 1981–82; on special leave, Gwilym Gibbon Res. Fellow, Nuffield Coll., Oxford, 1982–83; Finance, Envmtl Servs, 1983–86; London Urban Develt, sponsorship of LDDC, 1986–88; Dir (G3), Merseyside Task Force, DoE, 1988–90; Chief Exec., London Borough of Havering, 1990–95; Mgt Consultant, CSC Computer Scis Ltd, 1995–96; Head, Corporate Funding, Univ. of Oxford, 1997–2000. Vis. Fellow, Nuffield Coll., Oxford, 1993–2001. Mem., DoE Adv. Panel on appointments to Sponsored Bodies, 1996–98; non-exec. Dir, E Thames Housing Gp, 1997–98. Mem. Mgt Bd, Bankside Gall., 2002–03. Mem. Council, Sch. of Mgt Studies, Oxford Univ., 1995–98. Hon. Sec., London Planning and Develt Forum, 1990–2003. *Recreations:* painting, gardening. *Address:* 29 York Court, Albany Park Road, Kingston upon Thames, Surrey KT2 5ST. *T:* (020) 8547 1573.

**BRADLEY, Prof. Denise Irene,** AC 2008 (AO 1995); Vice Chancellor and President, University of South Australia, 1997–2007, now Emeritus Professor; *b* 23 March 1942; *d* of Richard Francis Haren and Lillian Irene (née Ward); *m* 1st, 1962, Michael Charles Bradley (marr. diss. 1985); four *s*; 2nd, 1987, Bruce Simpson King. *Educ:* Sydney Univ. (BA); Adelaide Univ. (DipEd 1964); Univ. of NSW (DipLib 1973); Flinders Univ. (MSocAdmin 1986). Women's Advr, Dept of Educn, S Australia, 1977–80; South Australia College of Advanced Education: Dean, Faculty of Educn and Humanities, 1983–86; Dir (Academic), 1986–88; Dep. Principal, 1988–90; Principal, 1990; University of South Australia: Dep. Vice Chancellor, 1991–92; Dep. Vice Chancellor (Academic), 1992–95; Dep. Vice Chancellor and Vice Pres., 1995–96. Chairman: Expert Panel, Nat. Rev. of Higher Educn, 2008; Aust. Health Workforce Adv. Council, 2010–12; Interim Chief Comr, Tertiary Educn Quality and Standards Agency, 2010–11; Member: UNESCO Nat. Commn, 2008–13; Educn Infrastructure Fund Adv. Council, 2009–14; NSW Skills Bd, 2013–; Dep. Chair, Nat. Sch. Resourcing Bd, 2018–. Chm., VERNet Pty Ltd, 2008–15; Dir, SEEK Ltd, 2010–. SA Great, 2005 South Australian of the Year. *Recreation:* reading. *Address:* University of South Australia, GPO Box 2471, Adelaide, SA 5001, Australia.

**BRADLEY, Dominic;** Member (SDLP) Newry and Armagh, Northern Ireland Assembly, 2003–16; *b* 18 Nov. 1954; *s* of William J. Bradley and Sarah McKeown; *m* Mary McManus; one *s. Educ:* St Paul's High Sch., Bessbrook; Abbey Christian Brothers Grammar Sch., Newry; Queen's Univ. Belfast (BA Hons); Univ. of Ulster (MA). Teacher, St Paul's High Sch., Bessbrook, 1978–89 and 1991–2003; Southern Educn and Library Bd, 1989–91. Northern Ireland Assembly: SDLP spokesperson on finance; Mem., Culture, Arts and Leisure Cttee, 2006–16; Mem., Finance and Personnel Cttee, 2011–16. Contested (SDLP) Newry and Armagh, 2010. *Recreations:* walking, swimming, reading. *E:* dominicobrolchain@btinternet.com. *Club:* St Patrick's Gaelic Athletic (Carrickcruppen, Co. Armagh).

**BRADLEY, Prof. Donal Donat Conor,** CBE 2010; PhD; FRS 2004; CEng; Vice President for Research, King Abdullah University of Science and Technology, since 2019; *b* 3 Jan. 1962; *s* of Prof. Daniel Joseph Bradley, FRS and of Winefride Marie-Therese Bradley; *m* 1989, Beverley Diane Hirst; one *s* two *d. Educ:* Wimbledon Coll., London; Imperial Coll., Univ. of London (BSc 1st Cl. Hons 1983; ARCS); Cavendish Lab., Univ. of Cambridge (PhD 1987). MInstP 1990, FInstP 2005; FIET 2013; CEng 2015. Unilever

Res. Fellow in Chem. Physics, Corpus Christi Coll., Cambridge, 1987–89; Toshiba Res. Fellow, Toshiba R&D Center, Kawasaki, Japan, 1987–88; Asst Lectr in Physics, Univ. of Cambridge, 1989–93; Churchill College, Cambridge: Lectr and Fellow, 1989–93 (Hon. Fellow, 2018); Dir of Studies, 1992–93; Tutor, 1992–93; University of Sheffield: Reader in Physics, 1993–95; Warden, Tapton Hall, 1994–99; Prof. of Physics, 1995–2000; Dir, Centre for Molecular Materials, 1995–2000; Royal Soc. Amersham Internat. Sen. Res. Fellow, 1996–97; Leverhulme Trust Res. Fellow, 1997–98; Imperial College, University of London: Prof. of Exptl Solid State Physics, 2000–06; Lee-Lucas Prof. of Experimental Physics, 2006–15; Dep. Dir, Centre for Electronic Materials and Devices, and Hd of Exptl Solid State Gp, 2001–05; Hd, Dept of Physics, 2005–08; Dir, Centre for Plastic Electronics, 2009–15; Dep. Principal, Faculty of Natural Scis, 2008–11; Pro-Rector (Res.), 2011–13; Vice-Provost (Res.), 2013–15; Vis. Prof. of Physics, 2015–; Prof. of Engrg Sci. and Physics, and Hd, Math., Phys. and Life Scis Div., Univ. of Oxford, 2015–19; Fellow, Jesus Coll., Oxford, 2015–19. Adjunct Prof., Hong Kong Baptist Univ., 2012–15; Hon. Prof., Nanjing Univ. of Technol., 2013–; 1000-talent Plan Researcher, Key Lab. for Organic Electronics and Inf. Display, Nanjing Univ. of Posts and Telecoms, 2014–18. Member: SERC/EPSRC Laser Facility Cttee Panel, 1991–95; EPSRC Functional Materials Coll., 1995–2016; ESF EUROCORES Cttee, 2006; Jury Cttee, Degussa European Sci. to Business Award, 2006; RCUK Rev. of UK Physics Panel, 2008; Optoelectronics Adv. Cttee, Rank Prize Funds, 2010–13 (Chair and Trustee, 2013–); Sub-panel 9: Physics, 2014 REF, 2010–14; Scientific and Med. Adv. Bd, Abingdon Health Gp, 2015–17; Special Advr to UK Parlt IUSS cttee inquiry on plastic electronics engrg, 2008–09. Co-inventor, conjugated polymer electroluminescence; co-founder: Cambridge Display Technol. Ltd; Molecular Vision Ltd (Dir, 2001–12); C-Change llp, 2008–15; Director: Imperial Coll. London Consultants Ltd, 2005–06; Solar Press UK Ltd, 2009–16; Advanced Res. Centres Ltd, 2017–19. Lectures: Weissberger-Williams, Eastman Kodak, 2004; Frolich, Univ. of Liverpool, 2009; Chau Wai-yin Meml, Hong Kong Poly. Univ., 2009; Mott, Inst. of Physics, 2009; Bakerian, Royal Soc., 2010; Dist. Lect. in Physics, Hong Kong Baptist Univ., 2011; Global Vision, Nanjing Univ. of Technol., 2013; Founders Prize Lect., Polymer Physics Gp, 2013; Dist. Lect., Inst. for Advanced Study, Hong Kong Univ. of Sci. and Technol., 2015; Centenary Global Lect., Zhejiang Univ., Hangzhou, 2017; Dist. Lect., Hong Kong Baptist Univ., 2017; E-MRS Czochralski, 2019. Editor: Organic Electronics, 2000–05; NPJ Flexible Electronics, 2016–. Member: Physical Soc. Club, 2005–; Royal Soc. Club, 2009–. FRSA 1987. Hon. DSc: Sheffield, 2014; Hong Kong Baptist, 2017. RSA Silver Medal, Outstanding Grad., RCS, 1983; Daiwa Award for Anglo-Japanese Collaboration, 1994; Descartes Prize, EU, 2003; Jan Rajchman Prize, Soc. for Inf. Display, 2005; European Latsis Prize, ESF, 2005; Res. Excellence Award, Imperial Coll., London, 2006; Brian Mercer Award for Innovation, 2007, Bakerian Medal, 2010, Royal Soc.; Faraday Medal, Inst. of Physics, 2009; Faraday Medal, IET, 2010; Founders Prize, Polymer Physics Gp (Inst. of Physics/RSC/IMMM), 2013; Governor's Award for Outstanding Contribn in Internat. Cooperation, Jiangsu Province, China, 2016; E-MRS Czochralski Gold Medal, 2019. Publications: numerous papers in learned jls and 16 patents on polymer optoelectronics. Recreations: dog walking, cinema, music, military history. Address: King Abdullah University of Science and Technology, Room 4206, Level 4, Building 16, Thuwal, 23955–6900, Saudi Arabia.

BRADLEY, Prof. (John) Andrew, PhD; FRCSGlas; Professor of Surgery, University of Cambridge, 1997–2016, now Emeritus; Hon. Consultant Surgeon, Addenbrooke's Hospital, Cambridge, 1997–2016; b 24 Oct. 1950; s of Colin Bradley and Christine Bradley (née Johnstone Miller); m 1987, Eleanor Mary Bolton; two s. Educ: Salendine Nook Secondary Sch., Huddersfield; Huddersfield Coll. of Technol.; Univ. of Leeds (MB ChB 1975); Univ. of Glasgow (PhD 1982). FRCSGlas 1979. Lectr in Surgery, Glasgow Univ., 1978–84; Cons. Surgeon, Western Infirmary, Glasgow, 1984–94; Prof. of Surgery, Univ. of Glasgow, 1994–97; Hon. Cons. Surgeon, Western Infirmary, Glasgow, 1994–97. President: British Transplantation Soc., 1999–2002; Soc. of Academic and Res. Surgery, 2011–13. Founder FMedSci 1998; FRCS ad eundem 1999. Publications: articles in sci. jls, mainly in the field of organ transplantation and immunology. Recreations: hill-walking, art. Address: University Department of Surgery, Box 202, Level 9, Addenbrooke's Hospital, Cambridge CB2 0QQ.

BRADLEY, Dr John Richard, CBE 2015; Consultant Physician and Nephrologist, since 1994, and Director of Research and Development, since 1999, Cambridge University Hospitals NHS Foundation Trust; Fellow and Director of Studies in Medicine, Trinity Hall, Cambridge, since 2001; b 28 March 1958; s of late Frank Leonard Bradley and of Joan Mary Phyllis Bradley (née Hurst); m 1985, Jane Alyson Fletcher; one s one d. Educ: Nottingham High Sch.; Univ. of Nottingham (BMedSci 1979; BM BS 1981; DM 1990); MA Cantab 2001. Sen. Registrar (Gen. and Renal Medicine), Addenbrooke's Hosp., Cambridge, 1988–90; Vis. Res. Associate, Harvard Med. Sch., 1990–91; Res. Schol., Molecular Cardiol. Prog., Yale Univ., 1991–92; Dir, NIHR Cambridge Biomed. Res. Centre, 2007–; Sen. Investigator, NIHR, 2010–; Dir of Res., Cambridge Univ. Health Partners, 2014–. Hon. Prof. of Exptl Medicine, Univ. of Cambridge, 2015–. Pres., Nephrology Section, RSocMed, 2012–13. Ed., British Jl Renal Medicine, 1996–. Publications: (jtly) Lecture Notes on Clinical Medicine, 1976, (contrib.) 5th edn 1997 to 8th edn 2018; contrib. articles on renal and vascular biol. Recreation: comedy. Address: Box 118, Cambridge University Hospitals NHS Foundation Trust, Cambridge Biomedical Campus, Hills Road, Cambridge CB2 0QQ. T: (01223) 217828. E: jrb1000@cam.ac.uk.

BRADLEY, Rt Hon. Karen (Anne); PC 2016; MP (C) Staffordshire Moorlands, since 2010; b Newcastle-under-Lyme, 12 March 1970; d of Kenneth and Olive Howarth; m 2001, Neil Austin Bradley; two s. Educ: Buxton Girls' Sch., Derbys; Imperial Coll., London (BSc Hons Maths). Tax Manager, Deloitte & Touche (formerly Touche Ross), 1991–98; Sen. Tax Manager, KPMG, 1998–2004; self-employed fiscal and economic consultant, 2004–07; Sen. Tax Manager, KPMG, 2007–10. An Asst Govt Whip, 2012–13; a Lord Comr of HM Treasury (Govt Whip), 2013–14; Parly Under-Sec. of State, Home Office, 2014–16; Sec. of State for Digital, Culture, Media and Sport (formerly Culture, Media and Sport), 2016–18; Sec. of State for NI, 2018–19. Associate Mem., ICAEW, 1995; Mem., Chartered Inst. of Taxation, 1996. Recreations: travel, wine tasting, cooking, puzzles, walking. Address: House of Commons, SW1A 0AA. T: (020) 7219 7215. E: karen.bradley.mp@parliament.uk.

BRADLEY, Martin Eugene Joseph, OBE 2013; FRCN; DL; Chairman, Northern Ireland Association for Mental Health, 2011–14; b Belfast, 23 June 1950; s of Edward and Elizabeth Bradley; m 1986, Nuala Mooney; one s one d. Educ: Univ. of London (Dip. Nursing 1976); Univ. of Ulster (BSc Hons Educn 1981; MSc Educn 1985); Queen's Univ. Belfast (Dip. Health Econs 1996). Nursing student, St Olave's and Guy's Hosps, 1968–71; Postgrad. nursing student, Maudsley Hosp., 1973–74; Staff Nurse, 1974–75, Charge Nurse, 1975–76, Whiteabbey Hosp.; Nurse Tutor, Central Sch. of Psychiatric and Special Care Nursing, 1977–80; Sen. Tutor, Belfast Northern Gp Sch. of Nursing, 1980–82; Sen. Tutor, 1982–86, Dir of Nurse Educn, 1986–89, Belfast Northern Coll. of Nursing; Dir of Nurse Educn, Eastern Area Coll. of Nursing, Belfast, 1989–91; Dep. Chief Nursing Officer, Dept of Health and Social Services, NI, 1991–97; Chief Nurse, 1997–2000, Dir of Health Care, 2000–03, Western Health and Social Services Bd, Londonderry; Dir, RCN, NI, 2003–05; Chief Nursing Officer, DoH, Social Services and Public Safety, NI, 2005–11. Chair: Ministerial Review of Undergraduate Nursing and Midwifery Educn, Dept of Health and Children, Ireland, 2011–12; Rev. of Nurse and Midwifery Prescribing, Health Service Exec., Ireland, 2015–16. Chair, Down and Connor Irish Bishops' Drug Initiative, 2010–; Dep. Chair, Belfast Health and Social Care Trust, 2015–. Mem. Bd, UK Bd of Healthcare Chaplaincy, 2011–18. Vis. Prof. of Nursing, Univ. of Ulster, 1998–. Mem. Council, Pharmaceutical Soc. of NI, 2012–. Trustee, Florence Nightingale Foundn, 2010–18. Mem. Court, Univ. of Ulster, 2014–17. FQNI 2011. DL Belfast, 2015. MUniv Open, 2018. Recreations: gardening, music, theatre, opera, walking, reading. E: martinbradley06@hotmail.com. Club: Royal Society of Medicine.

BRADLEY, Michael Paul, CB 2017; Chief Financial Officer, High Speed Two Ltd, since 2018; b Burnley, 5 July 1963; s of John A. Bradley and Dorothy B. Bradley; m 1985, Julie; three s. Educ: Lancashire Poly. (BA Hons Business Studies 1985). FCMA. Finance Director: Alstom Transport, 1995–2003; Enterprise plc, 2004–11; Dir Gen. Resources, Defence Equipment and Support, MoD, 2012–18. Recreations: cricket with Nelson Cricket Club, football. Address: Heirs House Farm, Heirs House Lane, Colne, Lancs BB8 9TA. E: michaelbradley.home@gmail.com.

BRADLEY, Prof. Patrick James, FRCSI, FRCSE, FRCS; Consultant Head and Neck Oncologic Surgeon, Nottingham University Hospitals, Queen's Medical Centre Campus, 1982–2009, now Emeritus Consultant; Special Professor of Head and Neck Oncologic Surgery, University of Nottingham Medical School, 2007–09, now Emeritus Hon. Professor; b Thurles, Co. Tipperary, 10 May 1949; s of Gerry Bradley and Nan Bradley (née O'Leary); m 1974, Sheena Kelly; three s two d. Educ: Glenstal Abbey Sch., Limerick; University Coll. Dublin (MB BCh, BAO 1973; DCH 1975); Univ. of Nottingham (MBA Public Health 2002). FRCSI 1977; FRCSE 1979; FRCS (ad eundem) 1999, Hon. FRCS 2015. Registrar, then Sen. Registrar, Royal Liverpool Hosp., 1977–82. Nat. Clinical Lead for Head and Neck Cancer (NHS England and Wales), 2003–08. Hon. Sen. Lectr, 2003–07, Hon. Prof., Faculty of Medicine and Social Scis, 2007–, Middlesex Univ. Ed., Oncol. News (UK), 2008–11 (Associate, Editl Bd, 2006–11); Jt Ed., Current Opinions ORL-HNS (USA), 2008– (Ed., Head and Neck Cancer Section, 1999–2008; Mem., Editl Bd, 2007–08); Series Ed., Advances in ORL-HNS (Switzerland); Member, Editorial Board: Jl Laryngology and Otology (UK), 1996–2011; ENT News (UK), 1997–2011 (Chm., 2002–11); Head and Neck (USA), 2001–; ORL Otolaryngol. (USA), 2003–; Oral Oncol. (UK), 2003–; Clin. Otolaryngol. (UK), 2006–11; Acta Otolaryngologica (Scandinavia), 2006–; Eur. Archives ORL-HNS, 2008–. Hunterian Prof., RCS, 2007–08. British Association of Head and Neck Oncologists: Mem., Nat. Council, 1986–93 and 2001–06; Hon. Sec., 1989–93; Pres., 2003–05; British Association of Otorhinolaryngologists, Head and Neck Surgeons: Mem. Council, 1994–95; Chm., Educnl Cttee, 1999–2002, Cancer Cttee, 1999–2009; Mem., Nat. Exec. Council, British Assoc. Surgical Oncologists, 1998–2000; Pres., 2004–06, Hon. Pres., 2008–, Eur. Laryngological Soc.; Founding Mem. Bd, Eur. Head and Neck Soc., 2004–11; Mem., Foundn Exec. Bd, 2005–11, Vice-Pres., 2006–09, Eur Acad. of Otorhinolaryngology, Head and Neck Surgery; Founding Mem. Bd, 2006, Pres., 2007–09, Eur. Salivary Gland Soc.; Founding Mem., 2005, Chm., Nominating Cttee, 2009–11, Internat. Acad. Oral Oncol. Trustee and Chm. Bd, Head and Neck Foundn, 1998–; Trustee, Nottingham Rhinological Res. Fund, 1999–. FACS 2007. Hon. FRCSLT 2006; Hon. FRACS 2007; Hon. Fellow, Hong Kong Coll. of Otolaryngol., Head and Neck Surgery, 2007. Alumni Award, Sch. of Medicine, UCD Foundn Day, 2015. Publications: contrib. book chapters and articles to learned jls on topics related to clin. activity, head and neck cancers, salivary gland diseases and disorders, rehabilitation, hosp. mgt and med. educn. Recreations: golf, wine tasting, travel. Address: 10 Chartwell Grove, Mapperley Plains, Nottingham NG3 5RD. T: (0115) 920 1611. E: pjbradley@zoo.co.uk. Clubs: Royal Automobile, Royal Society of Medicine; Dooks Golf; Notts Golf.

BRADLEY, Peter Charles Stephen; Director, Speakers' Corner Trust, since 2007; b 12 April 1953; s of Fred and Trudie Bradley; m 2000, Annie Hart; one s one d (twins). Educ: Abingdon Sch.; Univ. of Sussex (BA Hons 1975); Occidental Coll., LA. Res. Dir, Centre for Contemporary Studies, 1979–85; Dir, Good Relations Ltd, 1985–93; Man. Dir, Millbank Consultants Ltd, 1993–97. Mem. (Lab), Westminster CC, 1986–96 (Dep. Leader, Labour Gp, 1990–96). MP (Lab) The Wrekin, 1997–2005; contested (Lab) same seat, 2005. PPS to Minister of State for Rural Affairs, 2001–05. Mem., Select Cttee on Public Admin, 1997–99; Chm., Rural Gp of Labour MPs, 1997–2001. Member: Affordable Rural Housing Commn, 2005–06; Rural Housing Adv. Gp, 2007–09. Fellow, Crick Centre for Public Understanding of Politics, Univ. of Sheffield, 2015. Hon. Patron, ALC Telford Utd, 2004–. FRSA 2006. Recreations: playing/watching cricket, supporting Aston Villa, walking and reading (both slowly). Address: Old Roslyn House, Roslyn Road, Wellington, Telford TF1 3AX. Club: Warwickshire County Cricket.

BRADLEY, Ven. Peter David Douglas; Archdeacon of Warrington, 2001–15, now Archdeacon Emeritus; b 4 June 1949; m 1970, Pat Dutton; three s. Educ: Brookfield Comp. Sch., Kirkby; Lincoln Theol Coll.; Ian Ramsey Coll., Brasted; Nottingham Univ. (BTh 1979). Ordained deacon, 1979, priest, 1980; Curate, Upholland Team, 1979–83; Vicar, Holy Spirit, Dovecot, Liverpool, 1983–94; Dir, Continuing Ministerial Educn, dio. Liverpool, 1989–2001; Team Rector, Upholland, 1994–2011. Mem., Gen. Synod of C of E, 1990–2010. Hon. Canon, Liverpool Cathedral, 2000–15. Recreations: walking, reading. Address: 30 Sandbrook Road, Orrell, Wigan WN5 8UD. T: (01695) 624131.

BRADLEY, Very Rev. Peter Edward; DL; Dean of Sheffield, since 2003; b 26 June 1964; s of William Charles Basil Bradley and Elizabeth Alexandra Bradley. Educ: Royal Belfast Academical Instn; Trinity Hall, Cambridge (BA Theol. and Religious Studies 1986, MA 1989); Ripon Coll., Cuddesdon. Ordained deacon, 1988, priest, 1989; Chaplain, Gonville and Caius Coll., Cambridge, 1990–95; Team Vicar: St Michael and All Angels, Abingdon, 1995–98; All Saints', High Wycombe, 1998–2003; Team Rector, High Wycombe, 2003. DL S Yorks, 2016. Recreations: sculpture, contemporary art, being Irish, hypochondria. Address: The Cathedral, Church Street, Sheffield S1 1HA. T: (0114) 263 6063, Fax: (0114) 279 7412. E: enquiries@sheffield-cathedral.org.uk.

BRADLEY, Peter Richard, CBE 2005; Chief Executive Officer, St John Ambulance Service, New Zealand, since 2012; b 28 Dec. 1957; s of John and Mary Bradley; m 1978, Mary Elisabeth Verhoeff (marr. diss.); one s two d. Educ: Temple Moor Grammar Sch., Leeds; Otago Univ., NZ (MBA). With Commercial Bank of Australia, Auckland, 1973–76; St John Ambulance Service, Auckland, 1976–95; qualified paramedic, 1986; Chief Ambulance Officer, 1993–95; joined London Ambulance Service NHS Trust, 1996; Dir of Ops, 1998–2000; Chief Exec., 2000–12, and Nat. Ambulance Dir, DoH, 2004–12. FNZIM 1999. CStJ 2017 (OStJ 1994; SBStJ 1992). Recreations: reading, sport, music. Address: St John National Headquarters and Northern Region HQ, 2 Harrison Road, Private Bag 14902, Panmore, Auckland 1741, New Zealand.

BRADLEY, Prof. Richard John, FSA, FSAScot; FBA 1995; Professor of Archaeology, Reading University, 1987–2014, now Emeritus; b 18 Nov. 1946; s of John Newsum Bradley and Margaret Bradley (née Saul); m 1976, Katherine Bowden. Educ: Portsmouth Grammar Sch.; Magdalen Coll., Oxford (MA). MCIfA. Lectr in Archaeology, 1971–84, Reader, 1984–87, Reading Univ. Mem., Royal Commn on Historical Monuments of

England, 1987–99. Hon. FSAScot 2007. Hon. Dr Univ. of Lund, 2002. *Publications:* (with A. Ellison) Rams Hill: a Bronze Age Defended Enclosure and its Landscape, 1975; The Prehistoric Settlement of Britain, 1978; (ed with J. Barrett) Settlement and Society in the British Later Bronze Age, 1980; The Social Foundations of Prehistoric Britain, 1984; (ed with J. Gardiner) Neolithic Studies, 1984; The Passage of Arms: an archæological analysis of prehistoric hoards and votive deposits, 1990, rev. edn 1998; (with J. Barrett and M. Green) Landscape, Monuments and Society, 1991; (ed with J. Barrett and M. Hall) Papers on the Prehistoric Archaeology of Cranborne Chase, 1991; Altering the Earth: the origins of monuments in Britain and Continental Europe, 1993; (with M. Edmonds) Interpreting the Axe Trade: production and exchange in Neolithic Britain, 1993; (jtly) Prehistoric Land Divisions on Salisbury Plain: the work of the Wessex Linear Ditches Project, 1994; Rock Art and the Prehistory of Atlantic Europe, 1997; The Significance of Monuments, 1998; An Archaeology of Natural Places, 2000; The Good Stones: a new investigation of the Clava Cairns, 2000; The Past in Prehistoric Society, 2002; The Moon and the Bonfire: an investigation of three stone circles in north-east Scotland, 2004; Ritual and Domestic Life in Prehistoric Europe, 2005; The Prehistory of Britain and Ireland, 2007, rev. edn 2019; Image and Audience: rethinking prehistoric art, 2009; Stages and Screens: an investigation of four henge monuments in northern and north-eastern Scotland, 2011; (ed jtly) Development-led Archaeology in Northwest Europe, 2012; The Idea of Order: the circular archetype in Prehistoric Europe, 2012; (jtly) The Later Prehistory of Northwest Europe: the evidence of development-led fieldwork, 2016; (jtly) The Use and Reuse of Stone Circles: fieldwork at five Scottish monuments and its implications, 2016; A Geography of Offerings, 2017; contribs to learned jls. *Recreations:* literature, contemporary classical music, antiquarian bookshops, twentieth century art and literature. *Address:* Department of Archaeology, University of Reading, Whiteknights, Reading RG6 6AB. *T:* (0118) 378 8130.

**BRADLEY, Robin Alistair,** CBE 2000; CEng; Chief Executive, Atomic Weapons Establishment, Aldermaston, 1997–2000; *b* 3 Aug. 1938; *s* of Cyril Robert Bradley and Phyllis Mary (*née* Stalham); *m* 1964, Marguerite Loftus; one *s* two *d.* MIMechE 1972; CEng 1972. MoD, 1962–65; Hunting Engrg, Ampthill, 1965–72; Manager, Defence Progs (Australia), Hunting Systems, S Australia, 1972–75; Chief Project Engr, Project Manager, then Divl Manager Engrg, Hunting Engrg, Ampthill, 1975–90; Ops Director, AWE/Hunting Brown Root/AEA, Aldermaston (originally on secondment), 1990–96. *Recreations:* athletics, climbing, gardening. *Address:* c/o Hunting plc, 3 Cockspur Street, SW1Y 5BQ.

**BRADLEY, Stephen Edward;** HM Diplomatic Service, retired; Vice Chairman, Wanlian Development, Beijing, since 2014; Senior Consultant, NEX (formerly ICAP (Asia Pacific)), since 2011; *b* 4 April 1958; *s* of Maj.-Gen. Peter Edward Moore Bradley, CB, CBE, DSO; *m* 1982, Elizabeth Gomersall (marr. diss. 2011); one *s* one *d*; *m* 2013, Tara Wang. *Educ:* Marlborough Coll.; Balliol Coll., Oxford; Fudan Univ., Shanghai. South Asian Dept, FCO, 1982; Tokyo, 1983–87; Guinness Peat Aviation, 1987–88; Dep. Political Advr, Hong Kong Govt, 1988–93; Lloyd George Investment Management, 1994–95; Near East and North Africa Dept, FCO, 1995–97; West Indian and Atlantic Dept, FCO, 1997–98; New Millennium Experience Co., 1998–99; Paris, 1999–2002; Minister, Beijing, 2002–03; Consul-Gen., Hong Kong, 2003–08. Director: Husky Energy Inc., 2010–; Swire Properties Ltd, 2011–; China Heritage Fund; Broad Lea Gp. *Recreations:* books, gardens, travel. *Address:* PO Box 10153, General Post Office, Hong Kong, China. *Clubs:* Athenæum; Hong Kong.

**BRADLEY, Stuart;** *see* Bradley, C. S.

**BRADLEY-HOLE, Christopher James,** RIBA; architect and landscape designer; Principal, Christopher Bradley-Hole Landscape; Landscape Director, Spink Property; *b* Hove, 3 Feb. 1951; *s* of John Sidney Bradley-Hole and Joanna Margaret Bradley-Hole. *Educ:* Brighton Coll.; Brighton Poly. (DipArch 1975). Projects completed include: Bury Court, Hants, 2002; Governor's Garden, Portland Castle, 2003; BBC Media Village, White City, 2004; Hortus conclusus, Munich Botanic Garden, 2005; Schloss Ippenburg Garden Fest., 2006; Singapore Garden Fest., 2006; Pallant House Gall., 2007; Stringfellow Hall, Cranfield Univ., 2008; Royal Mile, Appeldoorn, Holland, 2008; Highbury Sq., 2009; Sainsbury Lab., Cambridge Botanic Garden, 2010; Stanislavsky Th., Moscow, 2013. Lectures in UK, USA, Australia, Germany, Italy, Russia, Sweden. Gold Medal, 1997, 2000, 2003, 2004, 2005, 2013, Best in Show, 1997, 2004, Chelsea Flower Show; Lifetime Achievement Award, Soc. of Garden Designers, 2016. *Publications:* The Minimalist Garden, 1999, 2005 (Garden Writers' Guild Award, 2000); Making the Modern Garden, 2007. *Recreations:* gardening, drawing. *Address:* Greystone House, Sudbrook Lane, Richmond TW10 7AT. *T:* (020) 8939 1749. *E:* cbradley-hole@christopherbradley-hole.co.uk.

**BRADLEY-JONES, Luke;** Chief Marketing Officer, Sky UK and Ireland, since 2017 (Brand Director, TV, BSkyB, 2012–15; Director, TV and Content Products, Sky, 2015–17); *b* Malmesbury, 1 April 1976; *s* of Rhodri and Sue Bradley-Jones; *m* 2007, Charlotte; two *d. Educ:* Malvern Coll., Worcs; Balliol Coll., Oxford. Manager, Spectrum Strategy Consultants, 1999–2006; BBC Worldwide: Hd of Strategy, 2006–07; Exec. Vice Pres., Digital Media, US, 2007–09; Man. Dir, BBC.com and Global iPlayer, 2009–11. Gov., Haverstock Sch., 2010–. *Recreations:* music, art, squash, golf, watching cricket, spending time with my beautiful wife and daughters. *E:* lbj1476@yahoo.co.uk.

**BRADMAN, Godfrey Michael,** FCA; company director; *b* 9 Sept. 1936; *s* of William I. Bradman and Anne Bradman (*née* Goldsweig); *m* 1975, Susan Bennett; two *s* three *d.* FCA 1961. Sen. Partner, Godfrey Bradman and Co. (Chartered Accountants), 1961–69; Chm. and Chief Exec., London Mercantile Corp. (Bankers), 1969; Chm., Rosehaugh plc, 1979–91; Joint Chairman: Broadgate Develts, 1984–91; Victoria Quay Ltd, 1993; Chairman: Eur. Land & Property Corp. plc, 1992; Ashpost Finance, 1993; Pondbridge Europe Ltd, 1994; Dep. Chm., Kyp Hldgs plc, 2003–10; Director: Property & Land Investment Corp. plc, 2001–11; Midatech Ltd, 2004–13; Metropolitan & Suburban, 2006–09. Founder and Mem., CLEAR (Campaign for Lead-Free Air) Ltd, 1981–91; Jt Founder, 1983, and Hon. Pres., Campaign for Freedom of Information, 1983; Founder and Chm., Citizen Action and European Citizen Action, 1983–91 (Dir, AIDS Policy Unit, 1987–90); Chm., Friends of the Earth Trust, 1983–91; Council Mem., UN Internat. Year of Shelter for the Homeless, 1987; Pres., Soc. for the Protection of Unborn Children Educnl Res. Trust, 1987; Trustee, Right To Life Charitable Trust; Founder and Jt Chm., Parents Against Tobacco Campaign; Founder, Opren Victims Campaign. Mem. governing body, LSHTM, 1988–91. Hon. Fellow, Downing Coll., Cambridge, 1997 (Wilkins Fellow, 1999); Hon. FKC. Hon. DSc Salford. *Recreation:* reading. *E:* gb@godfreybradman.com.

**BRADNEY, John Robert;** HM Diplomatic Service, retired; *b* 24 July 1931; *s* of Rev. Samuel Bradney, Canon Emeritus of St Alban's Abbey, and Constance Bradney (*née* Partington); *m* 1st, Jean Marion Halls (marr. diss. 1971); one *s* two *d*; 2nd, 1974, Sandra Cherry Smith, JP, *d* of Richard Arthur Amyas Smith, MC. *Educ:* Christ's Hospital. HM Forces, 1949–51; commnd Herts Regt and RWAFF Nigeria Regt; Colonial Police, Nigeria, 1953–65; HM Diplomatic Service, 1965–86: First Sec., Lagos, 1974; FCO, 1977–86 (Counsellor, 1985); Advr, Govt of Oman, 1986–89. Trustee, Carlisle Cathedral Develt Trust, 2007–13 (Chm., 2007–09). DSM Oman, 1989. *Recreations:* salmon and trout fishing, gardening, ornithology. *Address:* Barclays Bank PLC, Penrith, Cumbria CA11 7YB. *Clubs:* Royal Over-Seas League; Yorks Fly Fisher's.

**BRADSHAW,** family name of **Baron Bradshaw**.

**BRADSHAW, Baron** *cr* 1999 (Life Peer), of Wallingford in the county of Oxfordshire; **William Peter Bradshaw;** Senior Visiting Research Fellow, Centre for Socio-Legal Studies, Wolfson College, Oxford, 1985–2000; Honorary Fellow, Wolfson College, Oxford, since 2004 (Supernumerary Fellow, 1988–2003); *b* 9 Sept. 1936; *s* of Leonard Charles Bradshaw and Ivy Doris Bradshaw; *m* 1st, 1957, Jill Hayward (*d* 2002); one *s* one *d*; 2nd, 2003, Diana Mary Ayris. *Educ:* Univ. of Reading (BA Pol Economy, 1957; MA 1960). FCIT 1987 (MCIT 1966). Joined Western Region of British Railways as Management Trainee, 1959; various appts, London and W of England Divs; Divl Manager, Liverpool, 1973; Chief Operating Man., LMR, 1976, Dep. Gen. Man. 1977; Chief Ops Man., BR HQ, 1978; Dir, Policy Unit, 1980; Gen. Man., Western Region, BR, 1983–85; Prof. of Transport Mgt, Univ. of Salford, 1986–92; Chm., Ulsterbus and Citybus Ltd, 1987–93. Member: Thames Valley Police Authority, 1997–2008 (Vice Chm., 1999–2003); BRB, later Strategic Rail Authy, 1999–2001; Commn for Integrated Transport, 1999–2001; Chm., Bus Appeals Body, 1998–2000. Mem. (Lib Dem) Oxfordshire CC, 1993–2008. Special Advr to Transport Select Cttee, H of C, 1992–97; Lib Dem spokesman on transport, H of L, 2001–15. *Recreation:* growing hardy plants. *Address:* House of Lords, SW1A 0PW. *Club:* National Liberal.

**BRADSHAW, Gen. Sir Adrian (John),** KCB 2013 (CB 2009); OBE 1998; DL; Deputy Supreme Allied Commander Europe, 2014–17; *b* 1958; *m* Sally; two *s* one *d. Educ:* Univ. of Reading (BSc Agric. 1979); King's Coll. London (MSc Defence Studies 1991; MA Internat. Relns 2005). Oxford Univ. OTC, 1977–79; RMA, 1979–80; Tank Troop Leader, 14/20th King's Hussars, 1980–82; Intelligence Officer, Nuclear, Biol, Chem. Warfare Officer, 1982–84; army pilots course, 1984; helicopter pilot and AAC Flight Sqdn Dep. Comd, 1984–87; Troop Comdr, 1987–89; acsc, 1990; Ops Officer, UK Special Forces Gp, 1990–92; Sqdn Comdr, 1992–94; Armd Sqdn Leader, 1994–95, CO, Armd Regt, 1995–97, King's Royal Hussars; Instructor, JSCSC, 1998–2000; Dep. Comdr, Combined Jt Special Ops Task Force, Kosovo, 2000; Col, Mil. Ops, MoD, 2000–01; hcsc 2001; Mil. Advr, 3rd (US) Army, Kuwait, 2002–03; Dep. Comdr, US Task Force W, Iraq theatre of ops, 2003; Comdr, 7th Armd Bde, Iraq and Germany, 2003–05; rcds, 2005; Dir Special Forces, MoD, 2005–09; GOC, 1st (UK) Armd Div., 2009–11; US Army Strategic Leadership Prog. (Advanced), 2011; Dep. Comdr, ISAF and UK Nat. Contingent Comdr, Afghanistan, 2011–13; Comdr, Land Forces, 2013–14. Vis. Defence Fellow, Balliol Coll., Oxford, 2011. Chief of Gen. Staff's Liaison Officer and Advr to Jordan. Chm. of Trustees, Blesma, The Limbless Veterans, 2017–; Gov., Royal Hosp. Chelsea, 2018–. DL Gtr London, 2019. NATO Meritorious Service Medal, 2017. Officer, Legion of Merit (US), 2003; Bundeswehr Cross of Honour (Germany), 2011.

**BRADSHAW, Prof. Alexander Marian,** CBE 2007; PhD; FRS 2008; Scientific Member, Max-Planck-Institut für Plasmaphysik, Garching und Greifswald, 1999–2011, now Retired Scientific Member (Scientific Director, 1999–2008, now Emeritus Director); *b* 12 July 1944. *Educ:* Queen Mary Coll., London (BSc 1965; PhD 1969). Scientific Mem., Fritz-Haber Institute of Max-Planck Soc., Berlin, 1980–98. Adjunct Professor of Physics: Technical Univ. of Berlin, 1997; Technical Univ. of Munich, 2000. Pres., German Physical Soc., 1998–2000. Fellow, German Nat. Acad. of Scis (formerly German Acad. of Scis Leopoldina), 2002. Hon. FInstP 2006. *Publications:* articles in learned jls. *Address:* Max-Planck-Institut für Plasmaphysik, Boltzmannstrasse 2, 85748 Garching, Germany. *T:* (89) 32992123, (30) 84134860, *Fax:* (89) 32991001. *E:* alex.bradshaw@ipp.mpg.de.

**BRADSHAW, Rt Hon. Benjamin (Peter James);** PC 2009; MP (Lab) Exeter, since 1997; *b* 30 Aug. 1960; *s* of late Canon Peter Bradshaw and Daphne Bradshaw (*née* Murphy); civil partnership 2006, *m* 2014, Neal Thomas Dalgleish. *Educ:* Thorpe St Andrew Sch., Norwich; Univ. of Sussex (BA Hons). Reporter: Express and Echo, Exeter, 1984–85; Eastern Daily Press, Norwich, 1985–86; BBC Radio Devon, Exeter, 1986–89; BBC Radio Corresp., Berlin, 1989–91; reporter, World At One and World This Weekend, BBC Radio 4, 1991–97. Parly Under-Sec. of State, FCO, 2001–02; Parly Sec., Privy Council Office, 2002–03; Parly Under-Sec. of State, 2003–06, Minister of State, 2006–07, DEFRA; Minister of State, DoH, 2007–09; Minister for the SW, 2007–09; Sec. of State for Culture, Media and Sport, 2009–10; Shadow Sec. of State for Culture, Media and Sport, 2010. Member: European Legislation Select Cttee, 1997–2001; Ecclesiastical Cttee, 1997–2001, 2010–; Culture, Media and Sport Select Cttee, 2012–15; Health and Social Care (formerly Health) Select Cttee, 2015–. Member: Christians on the Left (formerly Christian Socialist Movement), 1997–; Lab. Campaign for Electoral Reform, 1997–. Mem., Inst. of Internat. and Foreign Affairs. Consumer Journalist of Year, Argos, 1988; Journalist of Year, Anglo-German Foundn, 1990; Sony News Reporter Award, 1993. *Recreations:* cycling, walking in Devon, classical music, cooking, gardening. *Address:* House of Commons, SW1A 0AA. *T:* (020) 7219 6597, (constituency office) (01392) 424464. *Club:* Whipton Labour (Exeter).
*See also* J. R. Bradshaw.

**BRADSHAW, Prof. Jonathan Richard,** CBE 2005; DPhil; FBA 2010; Professor of Social Policy, University of York, 1981–2013, now Emeritus; Professor of Social Policy (part-time), Durham University, 2013–15; *b* Windsor, 15 Feb. 1944; *s* of late Canon Peter Bradshaw and Daphne Jessica Bradshaw (*née* Murphy); *m* 1st, 1967, Nora Cook (marr. diss. 1986); two *s* one *d*; 2nd, 1995, Carol Stimson (*d* 1997); two step *s*; 3rd, 2004, Prof. Karen Bloor. *Educ:* Lancing Coll.; Trinity Coll., Dublin (BSS 1st Cl. 1967; MA 1967); Univ. of York (MPhil 1969; DPhil 1978). University of York: Lectr, 1968–73; Founding Dir, Social Policy Res. Unit, 1973–88; Hd, Dept of Social Policy and Social Work, 1988–94 and 2003–07; Dir, Inst. for Res. in the Social Scis, 1994–98. Hon. Vis. Prof., Univ. of Oxford, 2008–; Hon. Res. Fellow, Human Scis Res. Council, SA, 2008–. Chair, Mgt Cttee, York Welfare Benefits Unit, 1969–2014; Dir, Family Budget Unit, 2001–11. Pres., Foundn for Internat. Studies in Social Security, 1999–2003. Member: Res. Cttee, Internat. Social Security Assoc., 1998–; Bd, Internat. Soc. for Child Indicators, 2007–13; Bd, Child Poverty Action Gp, 2012–. FAcSS (AcSS 1996). Hon. FFPHM 1996. DUniv: Turku, 2011; Bath, 2015. *Publications:* The Financial Needs of Disabled Children, 1975; Found Dead, 1978; (jtly) Issues in Social Policy, 1979; Equity and Family Incomes, 1980; The Family Fund: an initiative in social policy, 1980; (jtly) Child Support in the European Community, 1980; (jtly) Energy and Social Policy, 1983; (jtly) Reserved for the Poor: the means test in British social policy, 1983; (jtly) Lone Mothers, Paid Work and Social Security, 1984; (jtly) Budgeting on Benefits, 1987; (jtly) Public Support for Private Residential Care, 1988; Social Security Parity in Northern Ireland, 1989; Lone Parents: policy in the doldrums, 1989; (jtly) Living on the Edge, 1989; Child Poverty and Deprivation in the UK, 1990; (jtly) Lone Parent Families in the UK, 1990; (ed) Budget Standards for the United Kingdom, 1993; (jtly) Support for Children: a comparison of arrangements in fifteen countries, 1993; (jtly) The Employment of Lone Parents: a comparison of policy in 20 countries, 1996; (jtly) Social Assistance in OECD Countries, 1996; (jtly) Using Child Benefit in the Family Budget, 1997; (jtly) Comparative Social Assistance: localisation and discretion, 1997; (jtly) Absent Fathers?, 1999; (ed jtly) Experiencing Poverty, 2000; (ed jtly)

Researching Poverty, 2000; (jtly) Poverty and Social Exclusion in Britain, 2000; (ed) Poverty: the outcomes for children, 2001; (jtly) A Comparison of Child Benefit Packages in 22 Countries, 2001; (ed) The Well-being of Children in the UK, 2002, 4th edn 2016; (jtly) Gender and Poverty in Britain, 2003; (jtly) The Drivers of Social Exclusion, 2004; (jtly) Routes out of Poverty, 2004; (ed jtly) Social Policy, Family Change and Employment in Comparative Perspective, 2006; (jtly) Child Poverty in Large Families, 2006; (jtly) A Minimum Income Standard for Britain, 2008; (jtly) Understanding Children's Well-being, 2010; (jtly) The Measurement of Extreme Poverty in the European Union, 2011; (jtly) Child Benefits in Central and Eastern Europe, 2016; Social Justice for children, 2017; (jtly) Cash Benefits and Poverty in Single-Parent Families, 2017; (jtly) Impact of the Recession on Children in the United Kingdom, 2017; (jtly) Improving lives? Child poverty and social exclusion, 2017; (jtly) The Multi-Dimensional Analysis of Social Exclusion, 2017; (jtly) Inequality in the UK in Comparative Perspective, 2018; contrib. articles to Jl Social Policy, Jl Eur. Social Policy, Poverty, Jl Poverty and Social Justice, Jl Child Indicators Res., Jl Social Indicators, Children and Youth Services Rev., Children and Society, Jl Children's Services, Family Matters, Social Policy and Society. *Recreation:* gardening. *Address:* Department of Social Policy and Social Work, University of York, Heslington, York YO10 5DD. *T:* (01904) 321329. *E:* jrb1@york.ac.uk.
*See also* Rt Hon. B. P. J. Bradshaw.

**BRADSHAW, Martin Clark**; Planning consultant, MB Consultants, 1995–2005; Director, Civic Trust, 1987–95; *b* 25 Aug. 1935; *s* of late Cyril Bradshaw and Nina Isabel Bradshaw; *m* 1st, 1959, Patricia Anne Leggatt (*d* 1981); two *s* one *d*; 2nd, 1986, Gillian Rosemary Payne; three step *s* one step *d*. *Educ:* King's Sch., Macclesfield; St John's Coll., Cambridge (MA); Univ. of Manchester (DipTP); MRTPI. Staff Surveyor, Lands and Surveys Dept, Uganda Protectorate, 1958–63; Asst Planning Officer, Planning Dept, City of Manchester, 1963–67; Asst Dir, City of Toronto Planning Bd, 1967–70; Asst Chief Planner, Cheshire CC, 1970–72; Asst County Planning Officer, Leics CC, 1972–73; Exec. Dir, Planning and Transport, 1973–81, Dir of Planning, 1981–86, W Yorks MCC; DoE Local Plans Inspectorate, 1986–87. Mem. Council, 1989–2001, Pres., 1993, RTPI. Gen. Comr for Income Tax, Bedford, 1987–96, Oxford, 2000–09. Hon. FRIBA 1995. *Recreations:* theatre, art, golf.

**BRADSHAW, Paula Jane**; Member (Alliance), Belfast South, Northern Ireland Assembly, since 2016; *b* Carrickfergus, 1 Nov. 1972; *d* of James and Susan Bradshaw; *m* 2011, Ian Parsley; one *s* one *d*. *Educ:* Belfast High Sch., Newtownabbey; Univ. of Ulster (LLB Law and Govt 2002). Develt Officer, Belfast Traders Assoc., 1997–2000; Econ. Develt Officer, Belfast Partnership, 2000–03; Dir, Greater Village Regeneration Trust, 2003–16. Mem. (Alliance), Belfast CC, 2014–16. *Address:* Alliance Party Northern Ireland, 88 University Street, Belfast BT7 1HE. *T:* 07875 763979. *E:* paula.bradshaw@allianceparty.org.

**BRADSHAW, Prof. Peter**, FRS 1981; Thomas V. Jones Professor of Mechanical Engineering, Department of Mechanical Engineering, Stanford University, 1988–95, now Emeritus; *b* 26 Dec. 1935; *s* of Joseph W. N. Bradshaw and Frances W. G. Bradshaw; *m* 1968, Sheila Dorothy (*née* Brown). *Educ:* Torquay Grammar Sch.; St John's Coll., Cambridge (BA). Scientific Officer, Aerodynamics Div., National Physical Lab., 1957–69; Imperial College, London: Sen. Lectr, Dept of Aeronautics, 1969–71; Reader, 1971–78; Prof. of Experimental Aerodynamics, 1978–88. *Publications:* Experimental Fluid Mechanics, 1964, 2nd edn 1971; An Introduction to Turbulence and its Measurement, 1971, 2nd edn 1975; (with T. Cebeci) Momentum Transfer in Boundary Layers, 1977; (ed) Topics in Applied Physics: Turbulence, 1978; (with T. Cebeci and J. H. Whitelaw) Engineering Calculation Methods for Turbulent Flow, 1981; (with T. Cebeci) Convective Heat Transfer, 1984; author or co-author of over 100 papers in Jl of Fluid Mechanics, AIAA Jl, etc. *Recreations:* ancient history, walking. *Address:* c/o Department of Mechanical Engineering, Stanford University, Stanford, CA 94305–3030, USA.

**BRADSHAW, Peter Nicholas**; author; chief film critic, The Guardian, since 1999; *b* 19 June 1962; *s* of late Albert Desmond Bradshaw and Mollie Bradshaw (*née* Fine); *m* 2007, Dr Caroline Hill; one *s*. *Educ:* Haberdashers' Aske's Sch., Elstree; Pembroke Coll., Cambridge (BA 1st Cl. Hons 1984; PhD 1989). Evening Standard: reporter, Londoner's Diary, 1989–92; leader writer and columnist, 1992–99. Radio: The Skivers, 1995; For One Horrible Moment, 1999; Heresy, 2003; Listener, They Wore It, 2011; In Praise of Powell and Pressburger, 2013; From Fact to Fiction, 2014; television: What The Papers Say; BBC Breakfast; Film: Baddiel's Syndrome, 2001. *Publications:* Not Alan Clark's Diaries, 1998; Lucky Baby Jesus, 1999; Dr Sweet and His Daughter, 2003; Night Of Triumph, 2013; The Films That Made Me…, 2019. *Recreation:* swimming. *Address:* The Guardian, Kings Place, 90 York Way, N1 9AG. *Club:* Soho House.

**BRADTKE, Hon. Robert Anthony**; United States Ambassador to Croatia, 2006–09; Senior Advisor for Partner Engagement on Syria Foreign Fighters, US Department of State, 2014–15; *b* 11 Oct. 1949; *s* of Albert Bradtke and Lucille Bradtke (*née* Gale); *m* 1983, Marsha Barnes. *Educ:* Univ. of Notre Dame; Bologna Center; Johns Hopkins Univ.; Univ. of Virginia. Joined Foreign Service, US Dept of State, 1973; served in: Georgetown, 1973–75; Zagreb, 1976–78; Office of Eastern European Affairs, Dept of State, 1978–81; Moscow, 1983–86; Bonn, 1986–90; Office of Congressional Affairs, Dept of State, 1990–94 (Dep. Asst Sec. of State, 1992–94); Exec. Asst to Sec. of State, 1994–96; Minister and Dep. Chief of Mission, London, 1996–99; Exec. sec., Nat. Security Council, 1999–2001; Dep. Asst Sec. of State for European and Eurasian Affairs, 2002–05. Co-Chair, Minsk Gp, OSCE, 2009–12. Superior Honor Award, Dept of State, 1988, 1996. *Recreations:* hiking, reading, baseball.

**BRADWELL, Area Bishop of**, since 2018; **Rt Rev. Dr John Perumbalath**; *b* 1966. *Educ:* Calicut Univ. (BA 1986); Union Bible Seminary, Pune (BD 1990); Osmania Univ., Hyderabad (MA 1993); Serampore Theol Coll. (MTh 1993); NW Univ., S Africa (PhD 2007). Ordained deacon, 1994, priest, 1995; Curate, St John's, Calcutta, 1994–95; Vicar, St James', Calcutta, 1995–2001; Curate, St George's, Beckenham, 2002–05; Team Vicar, Northfleet and Rosherville, 2005–08; Vicar, All Saints, Northfleet, 2008–13; Diocesan Link Officer, Church Urban Fund, 2008–13; Archdeacon of Barking, 2013–18. *Address:* Bishop's House, Orsett Road, Horndon-on-the-Hill, Essex SS17 8NS. *T:* (01375) 673806.

**BRADY**, Baroness *cr* 2014 (Life Peer), of Knightsbridge in the City of Westminster; **Karren Rita Brady**, CBE 2014; Vice Chairman, West Ham United Football Club, since 2010; *b* 4 April 1969; *d* of Terry and Rita Brady; *m* 1995, Paul Peschisolido; one *s* one *d*. *Educ:* Aldenham Sch. Saatchi & Saatchi, 1987–88; LBC, 1988–89; Sport Newspapers Ltd, 1989–93; Man. Dir, Birmingham City FC, 1993–2009. Non-executive Director: Kerrang! Radio Ltd, 2001–08; Mothercare, 2003–12; Arcadia, 2010–19 (Chm., 2017–19); Syco Entertainment. Co-presenter, The Apprentice, BBC TV, 2010–; Presenter, Give It A Year, ITV, 2018. Mem., Women in Sport Adv. Bd, DCMS. Small Business Ambassador, Cons. Party. DUniv Birmingham, 2010. *Publications:* Brady Plays the Blues, 1997; Playing to Win, 2004; Strong Woman (autobiog.), 2012. *Address:* c/o West Ham United Football Club, Boleyn Ground, Green Street, Upton Park, E13 9AZ.

**BRADY, Alessandra**; *see* Buonfino, A.

**BRADY, Angela Maria**, Hon. OBE 2015; RIBA; Director (formerly Partner), Brady Mallalieu Architects Ltd, since 1987; architect and television broadcaster; glass artist; President, Royal Institute of British Architects, 2011–13; *d* of late Peter Gerard Brady, FRCSI and of Deirdre Brady (*née* Rowan); *m* 1987, Robin Mallalieu, *s* of late Edward Mallalieu and Rita Mallalieu (*née* Shaw); one *s* one *d*. *Educ:* Dublin Sch. of Architecture (BArch Sc; DipArch); Royal Danish Acad., Copenhagen; Univ. of Westminster. MRIAI 1984 (Hon. FRIAI 1999); RIBA 1986; ARB 1986. Work with: William Strong and Associates, Toronto, 1981; Arthur Erikson Architects, Toronto, 1982; Brady, Shipman Martin Architects, Dublin, 1983; GMW Partnership, 1983–84; Lewis and Hickey Architects, London, 1985–87; Shepherd, Epstein and Hunter, 1987–91. Brady Mallalieu projects include: 200 homes in sustainable develt by Ballymore Property, London E14 (RIAI Award, Evening Standard award, 2010); Barra Park Open Air Th. (RIAI Award); new Sch. of Architecture for Metropolitan Univ., London (RIAI Award); St Catherine's Foyer and sports centre, Dublin (Brick Award, Brick Develt Assoc.) housing and healthcare projects for the private and public sector in UK and Ireland. Curator: DiversCity Exhibn, touring UK and world cities, 2003–10; 7 Hands Crafts exhibn, touring London, Cork, Dublin, 2015; Irish 10 Hands Crafts, Hangzhou Craftweek, 2018, Nanjing and London Craft Week, 2019; exhibited glass art in West Cork Creates, 2015, 2016, 2017. Designer and co-presenter, Building the Dream, ITV, 2004; presenter, The Home Show, Channel 4, 2008–09; co-writer and presenter, Designing Ireland, RTÉ One, 2015. Member: CABE/English Heritage Urban Panel, 2001–08; Bd, London Develt Agency, 2006–08 (Design Champion); CABE Enabler, 2009–11; Design Council/CABE Built Envmt Expert, 2015–. Chair, Women in Architecture, RIBA, 2000–05; Co-Founder, 1986, Chair, 2007–, RIAI London Forum; Mem. Council, RIAI, 2007–11. Chm., Finsbury Park Community Forum, 2001–03; Chair, Croydon Council Place Rev. Panel, 2017–; Co-Chair, Bexley Design Rev. Panel, 2017–. Trustee Dir, Building Exploratory, Hackney, 1998–2008. STEMnet Ambassador, 2004–10; Ambassador, Govt Equalities Office, 2009–11. Vice Chair, Civic Trust Awards, 2000–10. Ext. Examr, Brighton Univ., Liverpool Univ., Dublin Sch. of Architecture and Mackintosh Sch. of Architecture, 2009–10. Member: Women's Irish Network, 2003–18; Chelsea Arts Club, 2013–18. Pres., Architects Benevolent Soc., 2015–18. Hon. PhD Dublin Sch. of Architecture, 2011; Hon. DLitt Westminster, 2018. Hon. FRSA 2003; Hon. FRIAS 2013. Greenwich Business Partnership Award, 2008; Women of Outstanding Achievement, WISE Awards, 2012; Lifetime Achievement Award, Women in Construction, 2012; President's Dist. Service Award (Ireland), 2017; Lifetime Achievement Award, Univ. of Westminster Alumni Awards, 2018. *Publications:* (with R. Mallalieu) Dublin: a guide to recent architecture, 1997; (ed) The British Papers, 2015; (ed) The Cork Papers, 2018; articles on architecture and sustainable architecture; contribs to RIBA Jl. *Address:* Brady Mallalieu Architects Ltd, Studio D, 400 Caledonian Road, N1 1DN. *E:* angela@bradymallalieu.com. *W:* www.angelabradydesigns.co.uk, www.brady mallalieu.com, www.twitter.com/AngelaBradyRIBA, www.linkedin.com/AngelaBrady.

**BRADY, Sir Graham (Stuart)**, Kt 2018; MP (C) Altrincham and Sale West, since 1997; *b* 20 May 1967; *s* of John Brady and Maureen Brady (*née* Birch); *m* 1992, Victoria Anne Lowther; one *s* one *d*. *Educ:* Altrincham Grammar Sch.; Univ. of Durham (BA Hons Law 1989); Chm., Durham Univ. Cons. Assoc., 1987; Chm., Northern Area Cons. Collegiate Forum, 1987–89. Shandwick plc, 1989–90; Centre for Policy Studies, 1990–92; Public Affairs Dir, Waterfront Partnership, 1992–97. PPS to Chm. Cons. Party, 1999–2000; an Opposition Whip, 2000; Opposition frontbench spokesman on educn and employment, 2000–01, on educn, 2001–03; PPS to Leader of the Opposition, 2003–04; Shadow Minister for Europe, 2004–07. Member: Educn and Employment Select Cttee, 1997–2001; Treasury Select Cttee, 2007–10; Select Cttee on Party Reform, 2009–10; Jt Chm., All Party Railfreight Gp, 1998–99; Vice-Chm., All Party Gp on Advertising, 1999–2008. Sec., Cons. backbench Educn and Employment Cttee, 1997–2000; Chm., 1922 Cttee, 2010–19 (Mem. Exec., 1998–2000, 2007–10). Associate Ed., The House mag., 2010–. Mem. Council, Alliance of Eur. Conservatives and Reformists, 2015–. Vice-Chm., E Berks Cons. Assoc., 1992–95. Mem. Bd, 2016–, Dep. Chm., 2017–, Centre for Policy Studies. Patron, Counselling and Family Centre (formerly Family Contact Line), 2006–; Vice Patron, Friends of Rosie, 1997–; Trustee, Jubilee Centre, 2008–. Mem., Hamblin Educnl Trust, 2016–. Associate: GMC, 2011–12; Medical Practitioners' Tribunal Service, 2012–. Sport England Party Champion for Lacrosse, 2012–. NW Ambassador for British Mus., 2015–; Pres., Garrick Theatre Soc., 2017–. Vice Pres., Gtr Altrincham Chamber of Commerce, 1997–. Ind. Gov., Manchester Metropolitan Univ., 2008–11. Freeman of Altrincham, 2016. Hon. DSocSc Bolton, 2018. Backbencher of the Year, Spectator, 2010. *Recreations:* family, friends, garden. *Address:* House of Commons, SW1A 0AA.

**BRADY, Prof. Hugh**, PhD, MD; FRCPI; Vice-Chancellor and President, University of Bristol, since 2015; *b* Dublin, 9 Aug. 1959; *m*; three *c*. *Educ:* University Coll., Dublin (MB BCh, BAO 1982; BSc Pharmacol. 1984; PhD Physiol. 1993; MD 1994). MRCPI 1985, FRCPI 1991; Dip. Amer. Bd Internal Medicine, 1992; Dip. Amer. Bd Nephrology, 1993. Intern, then SHO, St Vincent's and St Laurence's Hosp., Dublin, 1982–86; Lectr in Pharmacol., UCD Med. Sch., 1983–84; Clin. Fellow, Univ. of Toronto, 1986–87; Fellow, 1987–89, Attending Physician, 1990–96, Brigham and Women's Hosp., Boston; Harvard Medical School: Instructor in Medicine, 1989–91; Asst Prof. of Medicine, 1991–94; Associate Prof., 1994–96; Chief, Renal Section, Brockton-W Roxbury VA Med. Center, Boston, 1993–96; University College Dublin: Prof. of Medicine and Therapeutics, 1996–2003; Associate Dean of Res., Faculty of Medicine, 1999–2001; Dir, Conway Inst. of Biomolecular and Biomed. Res., 1999–2000; Hd, Dept of Medicine and Therapeutics, 2000–03; Pres., 2004–13, now Pres. Emeritus; Prof. of Medicine and Healthcare Strategy, 2014–15; Pro-Vice-Chancellor, 2004–13, Vice-Chancellor, 2010–11, NUI. Non-executive Director: Kerry Gp plc, 2014–; ICON plc, 2014–. MRIA 2009. FMedSci 2002–04. Hon. FCAI, 2008. Hon. DSc Queen's, Belfast, 2008. Robert Menzies Medal, Univ. of Melbourne, 2012. *Address:* University of Bristol, Senate House, Tyndall Avenue, Bristol BS8 1TH.

**BRADY, Sir (John) Michael**, Kt 2004; FRS 1997; FREng; FMedSci; BP Professor of Information Engineering, Oxford University, 1985–2010, now Emeritus Professor of Oncological Imaging; Fellow of Keble College, Oxford, since 1985; *b* 30 April 1945; *s* of late John and of Priscilla Mansfield; *m* 1967, Naomi Friedlander; two *d*. *Educ:* Manchester Univ. (BSc (1st Cl. Hons Mathematics) 1966; Renold Prize 1967; MSc 1968); Australian National Univ. (PhD 1970). FREng (FEng 1992); FIET (FIEE 1992), Hon. FIET; FInstP 1997. Lectr, Computer Science, 1970, Sen. Lectr 1979, Essex Univ.; Sen. Res. Scientist, MIT, 1980; EPSRC Sen. Fellow, 1994–99. Member: ACOST, 1990–93; Bd, UKAEA, 1994–95; Nat. Technology Foresight Steering Gp, 1994–97; Royal Commn for Exhibn of 1851, 2007–; Chm., IT Adv. Bd, 1989–94. Member Board: Guidance Ltd, 1991–; Oxford Instruments, 1995–2014; AEA Technology, 1995–2003; Surgistec, 1997–2002; Mirada Solutions, 2001–05 (Oxford Med. Image Analysis, 1997–2001; OXIVA, 1999–2001); IXICO, 2006–11; Dexela, 2006–11; Volpara (formerly Matakina), 2008–; Mirada Medical, 2008–; Acuitas Medical, 2009–; Colwiz, 2010–16; IRISS Medical Technologies, 2012–15; ScreenPoint bv, 2014–. FMedSci 2008; Assoc. Mem., Académie des Scis, 2015. DU Essex, 1996; Hon. DSc: Manchester, 1998; Southampton, 1999; Hon. DEng Liverpool, 1999; Dr (*hc*) Univ. Paul Sabatier, Toulouse, 2000; Oxford Brookes, 2006. Faraday Medal, IEE,

2000; Millennium Medal, IEEE, 2000. *Publications:* Theory of Computer Science, 1975; Computer Vision, 1981; Robot Motion, 1982; Computational Theory of Discourse, 1982; Robotics Research, 1984; Artificial Intelligence and Robotics, 1984; Robotics Science, 1989; Mammographic Image Analysis, 1999; Images and Artefacts of the Ancient World, 2004; Digital Mammography, 2006; contribs to jls on computer vision, medical image analysis, robotics, artificial intelligence, computer science. *Recreations:* hiking, music, crosswords.

**BRADY, Mickey;** MP (SF) Newry and Armagh, since 2015; *b* Ballybot, Newry. Project Manager and worker, Newry Welfare Rights Centre. Mem. (SF) Newry and Armagh, NI Assembly, 2007–15. Mem. Bd, Confederation of Community Gps. Gov., Abbey Primary Sch. *Address:* (office) 1 Kilmorey Terrace, Patrick Street, Ballinlare, Newry BT35 8DW.

**BRADY, Dr Paul A.;** Head of International Communications Group, Scottish Executive, 2004–05; *b* 28 July 1949; two *s* one *d*. *Educ:* St Mungo's Acad., Glasgow; Univ. of Glasgow (BSc Hons; PhD 1974). Joined Scottish Office, 1974; Hd, electricity privatisation team, 1988–90; leader, higher educn reforms, 1991–92; Dir of Policy, SHEFC, 1992–93; Hd, Finance Div., Scottish Office, 1993–94; Dir, Finance and Planning, Scottish Enterprise, 1994–98; Dir of Finance, Mgt Exec., NHS in Scotland, 1998–99; Hd, Fisheries and Rural Develt Gp, Envmt and Rural Affairs Dept, Scottish Exec., 1999–2003. Various non-exec. positions incl. Registers of Scotland and Glasgow Univ., 2006–10. *Recreations:* walking, music, family. *Address:* 32 Grange Road, Edinburgh EH9 1UL. *E:* pabrady@gmail.com.

**BRADY, Robin James;** non-profit consultant, since 2009; Chief Executive, Crusaid, 2003–09; *b* 26 June 1971; *s* of Peter Robin Brady and Brenda Patricia Brady (*née* Worth). *Educ:* Univ. of Witwatersrand, Johannesburg (BA (Dramatic Art) 1992). Singer and dancer, 1990–94; Asst Dept Manager, Harrods, 1994–96; retail consultant, 1996–99; Capital Services Officer, Arts Council England, 2000–03. Consultant (pt-time), Crusaid, 2001–03. Dir, Robin's Trading Co. Ltd, 2009–; Member: Adv. Bd, Galeforce Capital, 2009–15; Experience Network, 2015–; EU Consult, 2016 (Vice-Chair, 2017–18; Chair, 2018–). Certified Mem., Inst. of Fundraising, 2006; Mem., SROI Network, 2010–. FRSA 2003. *Recreations:* theatre, opera, film, literature, wine. *E:* robinbrady@me.com.

**BRADY, Scott;** QC (Scot.) 2000; *b* 31 Oct. 1962; *s* of late John Brady and Miriam Cameron Brady (*née* Brown). *Educ:* Ardrossan Acad., Ayrshire; Edinburgh Univ. (LLB); Glasgow Univ. (DipLP). Admitted Advocate, Scottish Bar, 1987; Advocate Depute, 1993–97; called to the Bar, Middle Temple, 1998. *Address:* c/o Advocates' Library, Parliament House, Edinburgh EH1 1RF. *T:* (0131) 226 5071; 3 Temple Gardens, EC4Y 9AU. *Clubs:* Caledonian; Scottish Arts (Edinburgh).

**BRADY, His Eminence Cardinal Seán;** Archbishop of Armagh, (RC), and Primate of All Ireland, 1996–2014; *b* 16 Aug. 1939. *Educ:* St Patrick's Coll., Cavan; St Patrick's Coll., Maynooth (BA 1960; HDipEd 1968); Irish Coll., Rome; Lateran Univ., Rome (STL 1964; DCL 1967). Ordained priest, 1964; teacher, High Sch., St Patrick's Coll., Cavan, 1967–80; Vice Rector, 1980–87, Rector, 1987–93, Pontifical Irish Coll., Rome; Parish Priest, Castletara, Co. Cavan, 1993–95; Coadjutor Archbishop of Armagh, 1995–96. Cardinal, 2007. *Address:* c/o Ara Coeli, Cathedral Road, Armagh BT61 7QY.

**BRADY, Stephen Christopher,** AO 2015; CVO 2011; Ambassador of Australia to France, and (non-resident) to Morocco, Monaco, Algeria and Mauritania, 2014–17; *b* London, 11 June 1959; *s* of Geoffrey Brady and Susanne Brady; partner, Peter Stephens. *Educ:* Canberra Grammar Sch.; Australian National Univ. (BA Hons Internat. Relns). Joined Australian Foreign Service as diplomatic trainee, 1982; Foreign Policy Advr to Leader of the Opposition, 1986–90; Chargé d'Affaires, Dublin, 1990–91; Sen. Advr to Prime Minister of Australia, 1996–98; Ambassador to Sweden and (non-resident) to Finland, Estonia, Latvia and Lithuania, 1998–2003, to Denmark, Norway and Iceland, 1999–2001; Sen. Advr to Prime Minister of Australia, 2003–04; Ambassador to the Netherlands, and Perm. Rep. to OPCW, The Hague, 2004–08; Diplomatic Rep. to Internat. Ct of Justice, Internat. Criminal Ct, Internat. Ct on Former Yugoslavia, and Perm. Ct of Arbitration, 2004–08; Official Sec. to Gov.-Gen. of Australia, 2008–14; Secretary: Council, Order of Australia, 2008–14; Australian Bravery Decorations Council, 2008–14. Mem., European-Australian Business Council; Board Member: Australian Strategic Policy Inst.; Nat. Gall. of Australia; Bangarra Dance Th.; Ethics Centre. Hon. Adjunct Prof., Internat. Relns, Bond Univ. Kt Comdr, Order of Orange Nassau (Netherlands), 2009; Comdr, Order of the Crown (Tonga), 2010; Comdr, Légion d'Honneur (France), 2017. CStJ 2010. *Address:* Potts Point, NSW 2011, Australia. *Club:* Commonwealth (Canberra).

**BRAGG,** family name of **Baron Bragg**.

**BRAGG, Baron** *cr* 1998 (Life Peer), of Wigton in the co. of Cumbria; **Melvyn Bragg,** CH 2018; DL; writer; Presenter and Editor, The South Bank Show, for Sky Arts, since 2011 (for ITV, 1977–2010); Controller of Arts, London Weekend Television, 1990–2010 (Head of Arts, 1982–90); *b* 6 Oct. 1939; *s* of late Stanley Bragg and of Mary Ethel (*née* Parks); *m* 1st, 1961, Marie-Elisabeth Roche (*d* 1971); one *d*; 2nd, 1973, Catherine Mary Haste (marr. diss. 2018); one *s* one *d*. *Educ:* Nelson-Thomlinson Grammar Sch., Wigton; Wadham Coll., Oxford (MA; Hon. Fellow, 1995). BBC Radio and TV Producer, 1961–67; writer and broadcaster, 1967–. Novelist, 1964–. Presenter: BBC TV series: 2nd House, 1973–77; Read all About It (also editor), 1976–77; Reel History of Britain, 2011; Melvyn Bragg on Class and Culture, 2012; The Mystery of Mary Magdalene, 2013; ITV series: Two Thousand Years, 1999; Who's Afraid of the Ten Commandments?, 2000; The Apostles, 2001; (also writer) The Adventure of English, 2003; Not Just on Sunday, 2004; The Big Idea, Channel 4 series, 2001; BBC Radio 4: writer/presenter: Start the Week, 1988–98; On Giants' Shoulders, 1998; In Our Time, 1998–; Routes of English, 1999–2001; Voices of the Powerless, 2002. Dep. Chm., 1985–90, Chm., 1990–95, Border Television. Mem. Arts Council, and Chm. Literature Panel of Arts Council, 1977–80. President: Northern Arts, 1983–87; Nat. Campaign for the Arts, 1986–96; Nat. Acad. of Writing, 2000–04. Pres., MIND, 1999–2011; Appeal Chm., RNIB Talking Books Appeal, 2000–03. Chancellor, Leeds University, 1999–2017. Domus Fellow, St Catherine's Coll., Oxford, 1990. DL Cumbria, 2003. FRSL; FRTS; Fellow, BAFTA, 2010. Hon. FCLIP (Hon. FLA 1994); Hon. FRS 2010; Hon. FBA 2010. Hon. Fellow: Lancashire Polytechnic, 1987; Univ. of Wales, Cardiff, 1996. Hon. DLitt: Liverpool, 1986; Lancaster, 1990; CNAA, 1990; South Bank, 1997; DUniv: Open, 1987; Keele, 2016; Hon. LLD St Andrews, 1993; Hon. DCL Northumbria, 1994. *Plays:* Mardi Gras, 1976 (musical); Orion (TV), 1977; The Hired Man, 1984 (musical); King Lear in New York, 1992; *screenplays:* Isadora; Jesus Christ Superstar; The Music Lovers; Clouds of Glory; Play Dirty. *Publications:* Speak for England, 1976; Land of the Lakes, 1983 (televised); Laurence Olivier, 1984; Rich: the life of Richard Burton, 1988; The Seventh Seal: a study on Ingmar Bergman, 1993; On Giants' Shoulders, 1998; The Adventure of English 500AD–2000, 2003; 12 Books that Changed the World, 2006; In Our Time, 2009; The South Bank Show: final cut, 2010; The Book of Books: the radical impact of the King James Bible 1611–2011, 2011; *novels:* For Want of a Nail, 1965; The Second Inheritance, 1966; Without a City Wall (John Llewellyn Rhys Award), 1968; The Hired Man, 1969 (Time/Life Silver Pen Award, 1970); A Place in England, 1970; The Nerve, 1971; Josh Lawton, 1972; The Silken Net, 1974; A Christmas Child, 1976; Autumn Manoeuvres, 1978; Kingdom Come, 1980; Love and Glory, 1983; The Maid of Buttermere, 1987; A Time to Dance, 1990 (televised 1992); Crystal Rooms, 1992; Credo, 1996; The Soldier's Return, 1999 (W. H. Smith Lit. Award, 2000); A Son of War, 2001; Crossing the Lines, 2003; Remember Me, 2009; Grace & Mary, 2013; Now is the Time, 2015; William Tyndale: a very brief history, 2017; Love Without End: a story of Heloise and Abelard, 2019; articles for various English jls. *Recreations:* walking, books. *Address:* 12 Hampstead Hill Gardens, NW3 2PL. *Clubs:* Garrick, Chelsea Arts.

**BRAGG, Billy;** *see* Bragg, S. W.

**BRAGG, Heather Jean;** *see* Williams, H. J.

**BRAGG, Stephen William, (Billy);** singer and songwriter; *b* Barking, Essex, 20 Dec. 1957; partner, Juliet de Valero Wills; one *s*. *Educ:* Barking Abbey Comprehensive Sch. Singer with Riff Raff, 1977–81, The Blokes, 1999–2008; perf. Pressure Drop, Wellcome Collection, 2010. *Recordings include:* Life's a Riot with Spy vs Spy, 1983; Brewing Up with Billy Bragg, 1984; Between the Wars, 1985; Talking with the Taxman about Poetry, 1986; Back to Basics, 1987; Workers Playtime, 1988; Help Save the Youth of America, 1988; The Internationale, 1990; Don't Try This at Home, 1991; William Bloke, 1996; (with Wilco) Mermaid Avenue, vol. 1, 1998, vol. 2, 2000; Reaching to the Converted, 1999; (with The Blokes) England, Half English, 2002; Mr Love & Justice, 2008; The Complete Mermaid Avenue Sessions, 2012; Tooth & Nail, 2013; (with Joe Henry) Shine A Light, 2016; Bridges Not Walls, 2017. *Publications:* The Progressive Patriot: a search for belonging, 2006; A Lover Sings, 2015; Roots, Radicals and Rockers: how skiffle changed the world, 2017; The Three Dimensions of Freedom, 2019. *Recreations:* reading, beachcombing, reforming the House of Lords. *Address:* c/o Bragg Office, PO Box 6830, Bridport, Dorset DT6 9BH. *W:* www.billybragg.co.uk.

**BRAGGE, Nicolas William;** Master of the Senior (formerly Supreme) Court, Chancery Division, 1997–2014; Acting Chief Chancery Master, 2013–14; *b* Ashford, Kent, 13 Dec. 1948; *o s* of late Norman Bragge and Nicolette Hilda Bragge (*née* Simms); *m* 1973, Pamela Elizabeth Brett; three *s*. *Educ:* S Kent Coll. of Technol., Ashford; Holborn Coll. of Law and Inns of Court Sch. of Law (LLB Hons London). Called to the Bar, Inner Temple, 1972; in practice, Intellectual Property and Chancery Bars, 1974–97; Dep. Chancery Master, 1993–97. Chm. (part-time), Social Security and Disability Appeal Tribunals, 1990–97; Dep. Social Security Comr, 1996–98. Mem. Cttee, Barristers' Benevolent Assoc., 1995–2008. Mem. Council, City of London Br., Royal Soc. of St George, 2008–12. Master, Cutlers' Co., 2003–04; Mem. Court, Guild of Freemen, City of London, 2005–14. Jt Ed., Civil Procedure, 2001–14; an Ed., Atkin's Court Forms, 2011. *Address:* The Towers, Brabourne, Ashford, Kent TN25 6RA.

**BRAGGINS, Peter Charles Deverell;** Senior Lecturer, and Professional Tutor for Teach First, Canterbury Christ Church University, 2006–14; *b* 10 July 1945; *s* of Charles and Hilda Braggins; *m* 1968, Julia Cox; three *d*. *Educ:* Bedford Sch.; Christ's Coll., Cambridge (Open Award; BA Hons Hist. 1967). Teacher, Royal Grammar Sch., Newcastle upon Tyne, 1968–72; Head of History: Bootham Sch., York, 1972–77; Bedford Sch., 1977–82; Dep. Headmaster, Wilson's Sch., Sutton, 1982–91; Headmaster, Skinners' Sch., Tunbridge Wells, 1991–2005. *Recreations:* walking, swimming, music, historical research, football.

**BRAHAM, Edward Charles;** Partner, since 1995, and Senior Partner, since 2016, Freshfields Bruckhaus Deringer LLP (formerly Freshfields) (Global Corporate Practice Group Leader, 2009–14); *b* 17 July 1961; *s* of late David Gerald Henry Braham, QC and (Margaret) Louise Hastings (*née* Treves); *m* 1988, Isabel Dorothy Gurney; two *s* one *d*. *Educ:* Worcester Coll., Oxford (BA 1983; BCL 1984; Vinerian Scholar 1984). Freshfields: articled clerk, 1985; admitted solicitor, 1987. Mem., Adv. Bd, Lord Mayor's Appeal, 2016–; Chair, Mutual Market Access Wkg Gp, Professional and Business Services Council, 2017–; Mem., PM's Financial and Professional Business Services Council, 2019. Dir, TheCityUK, 2018–. Mem., Lowtonian Soc., 2006–. Trustee, Goldsmiths' Centre, 2012– (Chm. 2016–). Liveryman: Goldsmiths' Co., 2004 (Asst, 2011); Solicitors' Co., 2011. *Recreations:* photography, wine, outdoors. *Address:* Fittleworth House, Fittleworth, Pulborough, W Sussex RH20 1JH. *T:* (01798) 865305. *E:* edward.braham@freshfields.com. *Club:* Athenæum.

**BRAID, Caroline Philippa;** *see* Haughey, C. P.

**BRAIDEN, Prof. Paul Mayo,** PhD; FREng, FIMechE, FIET; CPhys; Sir James Woodeson Professor of Manufacturing Engineering, 1983–2006, now Emeritus Professor of Engineering, and Head, Department of Mechanical, Materials and Manufacturing Engineering, 1992–97, University of Newcastle upon Tyne (Postgraduate Dean, Faculty of Engineering, 1985–88); *b* 7 Feb. 1941; *s* of late Isaac Braiden and of Lilian Braiden (*née* Mayo); *m* 1st, 1967, Elizabeth Marjorie Spensley (marr. diss. 1993); 2nd, 1993, Lesley Howard. *Educ:* Univ. of Sheffield (BEng, MEng, PhD). CEng, FIMechE 1978; FIET (FIEE 1983); FREng (FEng 1994); CPhys, MInstP 1973. Asst Prof., Carnegie Mellon Univ., Pittsburgh, 1968–70; Atomic Energy Research Establishment, Harwell: SSO, 1970–73; PSO, 1973–76; Lectr, then Sen. Lectr, Dept of Engrg, Univ. of Durham, 1976–83. Science and Engineering Research Council: Chm., Engrg Design Cttee, 1990–94; Member: Engrg Bd, 1990–91; Engrg Res. Commn, 1991–94; Cttee on Electro-Mechanical Engrg, 1989–91; Automotive Design Prog., 1989–91; Panel on the Innovative Manufg Initiative, 1993–94. Chm., DTI Working Party on Advanced Mfg Technol., 1987–89. Chm., Northern Reg. and Council Mem., IProdE, 1988–90; Hon. Sec. for Mechanical Subjects, Royal Acad. Engrg, 1999–2000. Mem. Bd, Entrust, 1984–91. Mem., Nat. Cttee for Revision of Methodist Hymn Book, 1979–82. *Publications:* articles on materials behaviour, stress analysis, manufacturing technol. and systems in various jls. *Recreations:* music, especially opera/oratorio (trained singer, tenor voice), cycling, ski-ing. *Address:* 34 Eastern Way, Ponteland, Northumberland NE20 9PF. *T:* (01661) 871810.

**BRAILSFORD, Hon. Lord; (Sidney) Neil Brailsford;** a Senator of the College of Justice in Scotland, since 2006; *b* 15 Aug. 1954; *s* of Sidney James Brailsford and Jean Thelma Moar Leighton or Brailsford; *m* 1984, Elaine Nicola Robbie; three *s*. *Educ:* Daniel Stewart's Coll., Edinburgh; Stirling Univ. (BA); Edinburgh Univ. (LLB). Admitted Faculty of Advocates, 1981, Treasurer, 2000; QC (Scot.) 1994; called to the Bar, Lincoln's Inn, 1990. DUniv Stirling, 2010. *Recreations:* travel, food and wine, American history, fishing. *Address:* Court of Session, Parliament House, Parliament Square, Edinburgh EH1 1RQ; 29 Warriston Crescent, Edinburgh EH3 5LB. *T:* (0131) 556 8320; Kidder Hill Road, Grafton, VT 05146, USA. *T:* (802) 8432120. *Club:* New (Edinburgh).

**BRAILSFORD, Sir David (John),** Kt 2013; CBE 2009 (MBE 2005); National Performance Director, British Cycling, 2003–14; Team Principal, Team Ineos (formerly Team Sky), since 2010; *b* Derby, 29 Feb. 1964; *s* of John and Barbara Brailsford; partner, Lisa Buckle; one *d* and one step *d*. *Educ:* Liverpool Univ. (BA Hons Sports Sci. and Psychol.); Sheffield Business Sch. (MBA). Dir, Planet X, 1998–2000; Commercial and Mktg Consultant, BDJ Consultancy Ltd, 1999–2003. Coach of the Year, BBC Sports Personality of the Year Awards, 2008, 2012. *Recreations:* cycling, music, family. *Address:* c/o Team Ineos, National Cycling Centre, Stuart Street, Manchester M11 4DQ.

**BRAILSFORD, (Sidney) Neil;** *see* Brailsford, Hon. Lord.

**BRAIN,** family name of **Baron Brain**.

**BRAIN,** 3rd Baron *cr* 1962, of Eynsham; **Michael Cottrell Brain,** DM; FRCP, FRCPC; Bt 1954; Professor of Medicine, McMaster University, Canada, 1969–94, now Emeritus; *b* 6 Aug. 1928; *yr s* of 1st Baron Brain, DM, FRS, FRCP and Stella Brain (*née* Langdon-Down); *S* brother, 2014; *m* 1960, Dr the Hon. Elizabeth Ann Herbert, *e d* of Baron Tangley, KBE; one *s* two *d*. *Educ:* Leighton Park Sch., New Coll., Oxford (BA 1950; BM BCh 1953; MA 1955; DM 1963). MRCP 1955, FRCP 1968; FRCPC 1972. Hon. Prof. of Biochemistry and Molecular Biol., Calgary Univ., 1995–. *Heir: s* Hon. Thomas Russell Brain, *b* 23 Oct. 1965.

**BRAIN, Charlotte;** *see* Atkins, C.

**BRAIN, David;** President and Chief Executive Officer, Edelman Asia Pacific, Middle East and Africa, 2013–17; *b* Worcs, 15 June 1962; *s* of Denis Brain and Hilda Brain; *m* 1997, Susan Fraser; one *s* one *d*. *Educ:* Univ. of East Anglia (BA Eng. Lit.). Man. Dir, Baldwin Boyle Shand, Singapore, 1994–96; Strategic Planner, Batey ADS, Singapore, 1996–98; Man. Dir, Burson-Marsteller, UK, 1998–2000; Jt CEO, Weber Shandwick, UK, 2000–03; President and Chief Executive Officer: Edelman EMEA, 2003–10; Edelman Asia-Pacific, 2011–13. *Publications:* Crowd Surfing, 2008. *Recreations:* sailing, following Manchester City. *Clubs:* Ivy, Groucho.

**BRAIN, Dame Margaret Anne,** DBE 1994 (OBE 1989); FRCOG; President, Royal College of Midwives, 1987–94 (Member Council, 1970–96); *b* 23 April 1932; *d* of late Charles and Leonora Brain; *m* 1985, Peter Wheeler (*d* 1988), MBE, FRCS, FRCOG. *Educ:* Northampton High Sch.; Westminster Hosp. (SRN 1953); Northampton and Epsom Hosps (SCM 1956); Sheffield Hosp. (MTD 1966). FRCOG *ad eund* 1991. Med. Missionary, USPG St Columba's Hosp., Hazaribagh, Bihar, India, 1959–65; Dep. Matron, Barratt Maternity Home, Northampton, 1966–68; Prin. Midwifery Officer, Reading HMC, 1968–73; Dist Nursing Officer, W Berks DHA, 1974–77; Chief Admin. Nursing Officer, S Glamorgan HA, 1977–88, retd. Member: Nat. Staff Cttee for Nurses and Midwives, 1978–86; Maternity Services Adv. Cttee, 1981–85; Standing Midwifery Cttee, Welsh Nat. Bd, 1982–87; Perinatal Mortality Initiative Steering Gp for Wales, 1983–85; Standing Nursing and Midwifery Adv. Cttee, 1987–93; Women's Nat. Commn, 1990–92; Alternate Treas., 1972–78, Treas., 1978–90, Internat. Confedn of Midwives. Reader, C of E, 2001–. Hon. DSc City, 1995. *Address:* Squirrels, Castle Farm, Lower Broad Oak Road, West Hill, Ottery St Mary, Devon EX11 1UF. *T:* (01404) 812958.

**BRAIN, Rt Rev. Matthew Peter;** *see* Bendigo, Bishop of.

**BRAIN, Rt Rev. Dr Peter Robert;** Bishop of Armidale, 2000–12; Rector, Rockingham - Safety Bay, Perth, 2012–17; *b* 2 April 1947; *s* of Paul W. and Doris J. Brain; *m* 1973, Christine Lesley Charlton; three *s* one *d*. *Educ:* North Sydney Tech. High Sch.; Moore Theol Coll. (ThL, DipA, DipRE); Fuller Seminary, Pasadena (DMin 1994). Worked in Accounts, and Investments, Australian Mutual Provident Soc., 1963–70. Ordained deacon and priest, 1975; Curate: Sans Souci, Sydney, 1975–76; Holy Trinity, Adelaide, 1977–80; Rector: Maddington, Perth, 1980–88; Wanneroo, Perth, 1988–99. *Publications:* Going the Distance in Ministry, 2004; Jesus, Only and Always: studies in Hebrews, 2004; Jesus, Hope Realised: studies in Romans, 2011. *Recreations:* golf, walking, woodwork. *Address:* 48 Abingdon Crescent, Wellard, WA 6170, Australia. *T:* (8) 94393793.

*See also* Bishop of Bendigo.

**BRAIN, Rt Rev. Terence John;** Bishop of Salford, (RC), 1997–2014, now Emeritus; *b* 19 Dec. 1938; *s* of Reginald John Brain and Mary Cooney. *Educ:* Cotton Coll., North Staffordshire; St Mary's Coll., Oscott, Birmingham. Ordained priest, 1964; Asst Priest, St Gregory's, Longton, 1964–65; mem. of staff, Cotton Coll., 1965–69; Hosp. Chaplain, St Patrick's, Birmingham, 1969–71; Archbishop's Secretary, Birmingham, 1971–82; Parish Priest: Bucknall, Stoke-on-Trent, 1982–88; St Austin's, Stafford, 1988–91; Auxiliary Bishop of Birmingham, 1991–97. RC Bishop for Prisons, 1994–2013. Chm., RC Bishops' Social Welfare Cttee, 1992–2002. Episcopal Advr, Nat. Council of Lay Assocs, 1993–2006. Trustee, Caritas Social Action Network, 2002– (Chm. of Trustees, 2007–14). *Recreations:* crossword puzzles, water colour painting.

**BRAISBY, Prof. Nicholas Richard,** PhD; Vice-Chancellor and Chief Executive, Buckinghamshire New University, since 2019 (Deputy Vice-Chancellor, 2017–18); *b* Swansea, 26 Feb. 1965; *s* of Dennis Edward Braisby and Brenda Margaret Braisby; *m* 2010, Ian Colin Hodges. *Educ:* Queens' Coll., Cambridge (BA Natural Scis (Psychol.) 1986); Centre for Cognitive Sci., Univ. of Edinburgh (PhD 1990). Pro Vice-Chancellor, Univ. of West London, 2013–17. *Publications:* (ed jtly) Cognitive Psychology, 2005, 2nd edn 2012; (ed) Cognitive Psychology: a methods companion, 2005. *Recreation:* gardening. *Address:* Buckinghamshire New University, High Wycombe HP11 2JZ; Woodlands, Churchill, Axminster, Devon EX13 7LZ. *T:* 07941 710706. *E:* nick@ianandnick.plus.com.

**BRAITHWAITE, Julian Nicholas,** CMG 2019; HM Diplomatic Service; UK Permanent Representative to World Trade Organisation and to the United Nations in Geneva (with rank of Ambassador), since 2015; *b* Rome, 25 July 1968; *s* of Sir Rodric (Quentin) Braithwaite, *qv*; *m* 1999, Biljana Njagulj; two *d*. *Educ:* Bryanston Sch.; St Catharine's Coll., Cambridge (BA Hist. and Nat. Scis 1990); Harvard Univ. (MPA). Bank of England, 1992–94; joined HM Diplomatic Service, 1994; First Sec., Belgrade, 1996–98; Press Officer, then speechwriter, 10 Downing Street (on secondment), 1998–2002; Special Advr to Supreme Allied Comdr Europe, NATO, 1999; Dir of Communications for High Rep. of Internat. Community, Bosnia and Herzegovina, 2002–04; Counsellor for Global Issues, Washington, DC, 2004–08; Dir, Consular Services, FCO, 2008–11; Hd, Libya Communications Team, 10 Downing Street, 2011; Ambassador to Pol and Security Cttee, EU, 2011–15. *Recreations:* cycling, ski-ing, Montenegro, my family. *Address:* c/o Foreign and Commonwealth Office, King Charles Street, SW1A 2AH.

**BRAITHWAITE, Sir Rodric (Quentin),** GCMG 1994 (KCMG 1988 CMG 1981); HM Diplomatic Service, retired; freelance writer; Senior Advisor and Managing Director, Deutsche Bank (formerly Deutsche Morgan Grenfell), 1994–2002; *b* 17 May 1932; *s* of Henry Warwick Braithwaite and Lorna Constance Davies; *m* 1961, Gillian Mary Robinson (*d* 2008); three *s* one *d* (and one *s* decd). *Educ:* Bedales Sch.; Christ's Coll., Cambridge (1st cl. Mod. Langs, Pts I and II; Hon. Fellow, 1989). Mil. Service, 1950–52. Joined Foreign (subseq. Diplomatic) Service, 1955; served Djakarta, Warsaw and FO, 1957–63; Moscow, 1963–66; Rome, 1966–69; FCO, 1969–72; Vis. Fellow, All Souls Coll., Oxford, 1972–73; Head of European Integration Dept (External), FCO, 1973–75; Head of Chancery, Office of Permanent Rep. to EEC, Brussels, 1975–78; Head of Planning Staff, FCO, 1979–80; Asst Under Sec. of State, FCO, 1981; Minister Commercial, Washington, 1982–84; Dep. Under-Sec. of State, FCO, 1984–88; Ambassador to Soviet Union and Russia, 1988–92; Prime Minister's foreign policy advr, and Chm., Jt Intelligence Cttee, 1992–93. Member: European Strategy Bd, ICL plc, 1994–99; Adv. Bd, Sirocco Aerospace, 1999–2003; Bd, OMZ (Moscow), 2002–03. Vis. Fellow, Wilson Center, Washington, 2005. Mem., Adv. Council on Nat. Records and Archives, 2005–09. Chm. Council, Britain-Russia Centre, 1995–99; Mem. Council, VSO, 1994–99. Dir, ENO, 1992–99. Chm., Internat. Adv. Bd, Moscow Sch. of Political Studies, 1998–2012. Governor: RAM, 1993–2002 (Chm. of Govs, 1998–2002; Hon. FRAM 1996); Wilton Park, 2002–09; Ditchley Park, 2003–. Trustee, BBC Marshall Plan for the Mind, 1995–98. Hon. LLD, 1997, Hon. Prof., 1999, Birmingham; Hon. LLD Buckingham, 2014. *Publications:* (jtly) Engaging Russia, 1995; Russia in Europe, 1999; Across the Moscow River, 2002; Moscow 1941: a city and its people at war, 2006; Afgantsy: the Russians in Afghanistan 1979–1989, 2011; Coming of Age in Warsaw: a Cold War story, 2014; Armageddon and Paranoia: the nuclear confrontation, 2017; various articles.

*See also* J. N. Braithwaite.

**BRAITHWAITE, William Thomas Scatchard;** QC 1992; a Recorder, 1993–99; *b* 20 Jan. 1948; *s* of late John Vernon Braithwaite and Nancy Phyllis Braithwaite; *m* 1972, Sheila Young; one *s* one *d*. *Educ:* Gordonstoun Sch.; Liverpool Univ. (LLB Hons). Called to the Bar, Gray's Inn, 1970; joined chambers in Liverpool, 1970; Asst Recorder of the Crown Court, 1990. Consultant Editor, Kemp and Kemp, The Quantum of Damages, 1995–2004. *Publications:* Medical Aspects of Personal Injury Litigation (ed jtly), 1997; Brain and Spine Injuries: the fight for justice, 2001, 2nd edn 2010. *Recreations:* cars, wine, photography. *Address:* Exchange Chambers, Pearl Assurance House, 1 Derby Square, Liverpool L2 9XX; Exchange Chambers, 7 Ralli Court, West Riverside, Manchester M3 5FT; Exchange Chambers, Oxford House, Oxford Row, Leeds LS1 3BE.

**BRAKA, Ivor Isaac;** art dealer in 20th century and contemporary art; owner, The Gunton Arms, Norfolk, since 2009; *b* Manchester, 19 Dec. 1954; *s* of Joseph Braka and Elizabeth Braka (*née* Dodds); *m* 1st, 1991, Camilla Mary Davidson (marr. diss. 1998); one *s*; one *s* by former partner, Elizabeth de Stanford; 2nd, 2009, Sarah Caroline Graham (marr. diss. 2013); 3rd, 2016, Kristen McMenamy. *Educ:* Oundle Sch.; Pembroke Coll., Oxford (BA Hons English). *Recreations:* animals, alcohol, planting trees. *Address:* 63 Cadogan Square, SW1X 0DY.

**BRAKE, Rt Hon. Thomas (Anthony);** PC 2011; MP (Lib Dem) Carshalton and Wallington, since 1997; *b* 6 May 1962; *s* of Michael and Judy Brake; *m* 1998, Candida Goulden; one *s* one *d*. *Educ:* Imperial Coll., London (BSc Hons Physics); Lycée International, France (Internat. Baccalauréat). Formerly Principal Consultant, Cap Gemini, (IT services). Lib Dem spokesman: on envmt, 1997–2001; on transport, local govt and the regions, 2001–02; on transport and London, 2002–03; on internat. develt, 2003–05; on transport, 2005–06; on local govt, 2006–07; on the Olympics, 2007–10; on London, 2007–10; on foreign affairs, 2015–17; on Exiting the EU and Internat. Trade, 2017–; a Lib Dem Whip, 2000–01; Parly Sec. (Dep. Leader), Office of the Leader of the H of C, 2012–15; an Asst Govt Whip, 2014–15; Lib Dem Chief Whip, 2015–17. Mem., Select Cttee on Transport, 2002–03. Mem., Accommodation and Works Cttee, H of C, 2001–02; Co-Chair, Lib Dem backbench cttee on Home Affairs, Justice and Equalities, 2010–12 (Lib Dem spokesman on home affairs, 2008–10). *Publications:* (jtly) Costing the Earth, 1991. *Recreations:* running, swimming, cycling. *Address:* House of Commons, SW1A 0AA.

**BRAKEFIELD, Prof. Paul Martin,** PhD; FRS 2010; Professor of Zoology, and Director, University Museum of Zoology, University of Cambridge, since 2010; Fellow, Trinity College, Cambridge, since 2011; *b* Woking, 31 May 1952. *Educ:* Univ. of Oxford (BSc Hons Zool.); Univ. of Liverpool (PhD 1979). Formerly Prof. of Evolutionary Biol., Univ. of Leiden. Hon. Prof., Univ. of Sheffield. Pres., Linnean Soc. of London, 2015–18. *Publications:* contribs to jls incl. Amer. Naturalist, Proc. Royal Soc., Proc. NAS, Evolution and Develt, Ecol Entomology. *Address:* Department of Zoology, University of Cambridge, Downing Street, Cambridge CB2 3EJ.

**BRAMALL,** family name of **Baron Bramall**.

**BRAMALL,** Baron *cr* 1987 (Life Peer), of Bushfield in the County of Hampshire; **Field Marshal Edwin Noel Westby Bramall,** KG 1990; GCB 1979 (KCB 1974); OBE 1965; MC 1945; JP; HM Lord-Lieutenant of Greater London, 1986–98; Chief of the Defence Staff, 1982–85; *b* 18 Dec. 1923; *s* of late Major Edmund Haselden Bramall and Mrs Katherine Bridget Bramall (*née* Westby); *m* 1949, Dorothy Avril Wentworth Vernon (*d* 2015); one *s* one *d*. *Educ:* Eton College. Commnd into KRRC, 1943; served in NW Europe, 1944–45; occupation of Japan, 1946–47; Instructor, Sch. of Infantry, 1949–51; psc 1952; Middle East, 1953–58; Instructor, Army Staff Coll., 1958–61; on staff of Lord Mountbatten at MoD, 1963–64; CO, 2 Green Jackets, KRRC, Malaysia during Indonesian confrontation, 1965–66; comd 5th Airportable Bde, 1967–69; idc 1970; GOC 1st Div. BAOR, 1971–73; Lt-Gen., 1973; Comdr, British Forces, Hong Kong, 1973–76; Gen., 1976; C-in-C, UK Land Forces, 1976–78; Vice-Chief of Defence Staff (Personnel and Logistics), 1978–79; Chief of the General Staff, 1979–82; Field Marshal, 1982. ADC (Gen.), 1979–82. Mem., H of L, 1987–2013. Col Comdt, 3rd Bn Royal Green Jackets, 1973–84; Col, 2nd Goorkhas, 1976–86; President: Greater London TAVRA, 1986–98; Gurkha Bde Assoc., 1987–97. Hon. Life Vice Pres., MCC, 1997 (Mem. Cttee, 1985–94; Pres., 1988–89; Trustee, 1994–97). Trustee, Imperial War Museum, 1983–98 (Chm., 1989–98). JP London 1986. KStJ 1986. *Publications:* (jtly) The Chiefs, 1993; The Bramall Papers, 2017. *Recreations:* cricket, painting, travel. *Address:* House of Lords, SW1A 0PW. *Clubs:* Travellers, Army and Navy, Pratt's, MCC, I Zingari, Free Foresters.

**BRAMLEY, Prof. Sir Paul (Anthony),** Kt 1984; FRCS, FDSRCS; Professor of Dental Surgery, University of Sheffield, 1969–88, now Emeritus; *b* 24 May 1923; *s* of Charles and Constance Bramley; *m* 1952, Hazel Morag Boyd, MA, MB ChB (*d* 2017); one *s* three *d*. *Educ:* Wyggeston Grammar Sch., Leicester; Univ. of Birmingham. MB ChB, BDS. FDSRCS 1953; FRCS 1982. HS, Queen Elizabeth Hosp., Birmingham, 1945; Capt., RADC, 224 Para Fd Amb., 1946–48; MO, Church of Scotland, Kenya, 1952; Registrar, Rooksdown House, 1953–54; Consultant Oral Surgeon, SW Region Hosp. Bd, 1954–69; Dir, Dept of Oral Surgery and Orthodontics, Plymouth Gen. Hosp. and Truro Royal Infirmary, 1954–69; Civilian Consultant, RN, 1959–88, now Emeritus; Dean, Sch. of Clinical Dentistry, Univ. of Sheffield, 1972–75. Consultant Oral Surgeon, Trent Region, 1969–88. Chm., Dental Protection Ltd, 1989–95. Member: General Dental Council, 1973–89; Council, Medical Protection Soc., 1975–95; Council, RCS 1975–83 (Tomes Lectr, 1980; Dean of Faculty of Dental Surgery, 1980–83; Colyer Gold Medal, 1988); Royal Commission on NHS, 1976–79; Dental Strategy Review Group; Chm., Standing Dental Adv. Cttee; Consultant Adviser, DHSS, 1970–80; Hon. Sec., British Assoc. of Oral Surgeons, 1968–72, Pres., 1975; President: S Yorks Br., British Dental Assoc., 1975; Oral Surgery Club of GB, 1985–86; Inst. of Maxillofacial Technol., 1987–89; Nat. Pres., BDA, 1988–89. Adviser, Prince of Songkla Univ., Thailand, 1982–94; External Examiner to RCS, RCSI, RCSG, RACDS, Univs of Birmingham, Baghdad, Hong Kong, London, Singapore, Trinity College Dublin, Cardiff, NUI. Pres., Norman Rowe Educnl Trust, 1993–95; Chm., Cavendish Br., NADFAS, 1996–99. Lay Reader, dio. of Winchester, 1953–68. Hon. FRACDS. Hon. DDS: Birmingham, 1987; Prince of Songkla Univ., 1989; Hon. MD Sheffield, 1994. Fellow, Internat. Assoc. of Oral and Maxillofacial Surgeons. Bronze Medal, Helsinki Univ., 1990. *Publications:* (with J. Norman) The Temporomandibular Joint: disease, disorders, surgery, 1989; (ed) Doing Anything After Work?… What About Retirement?, 2010; chapters in textbooks; scientific articles in British and foreign medical and dental jls. *Recreation:* 12 grandchildren and 11 great-grandchildren. *Address:* 7 The Roost, Heather Lane, Hathersage S32 1DQ.

**BRAMLEY, Steven Michael Stuart,** CBE 2014; Director of Legal Services, Metropolitan Police, since 2018; *b* 18 March 1961; *s* of Michael Frank Rayner Bramley and Patricia Anne Bramley (*née* Easter); *m* 1990, Ann Weir; three *s*. *Educ:* Royal Grammar Sch., High Wycombe; UCL (LLB Hons). Called to the Bar, Gray's Inn, 1983, Bencher, 2013; Legal Advr's Br., Home Office, 1986–93 and 1996–2003 (Asst Legal Advr, 1997–2003); NI Office, 1993–96; Dep. Legal Sec. to the Law Officers, 2003–04; Dep. Legal Advr, Home Office, 2004–14; Legal Advr, NI Office, 2009–14; Legal Dir, DCLG, then MHCLG, 2014–18. Member: Bar Council, 2016–17 (Mem., Employed Bar Cttee, 2016–17); Election Information Cttee, Gray's Inn, 2018–. Trustee, 2013–, Vice-Chm., 2014–17, Chm., 2017–, Carers Network. Parish cllr, 2016–.

**BRAMMA, Harry Wakefield,** FRCO; Organist and Director of Music, All Saints', Margaret Street, 1989–2004; Director, Royal School of Church Music, 1989–98; *b* 11 Nov. 1936; *s* of late Fred and Christine Bramma. *Educ:* Bradford Grammar Sch.; Pembroke Coll. Oxford (MA). FRCO 1958 (Harding Prize). Organist, All Saints, Bingley, WR Yorks, 1954–55; Dir of Music, King Edward VI Grammar Sch., Retford, Notts, 1961; Asst Organist, Worcester Cathedral, 1963; Dir of Music, The King's Sch., Worcester, 1965; Organist, Southwark Cathedral, 1976. Vis. Music Supervisor, King's Coll., Cambridge, 1998–2000; Vis. Music Tutor, Christ Church, Oxford, 2000–05. Organist, St Saviour's, E Retford and St Michael's, W Retford, 1961; Asst Conductor and Accompanist, Worcester Fest. Choral Soc., 1963; Organist, Worcester Three Choirs Fest., 1966, 1969, 1972 and 1975; Conductor, Kidderminster Choral Soc., 1972–79. Examr, Associated Bd of Royal Schs of Music, 1978–89. Mem. Council, RCO, 1979–96, Hon. Treas., 1987–96; Mem., Archbishops' Commn on Church Music, 1989–92; Organ Advr, Dio. of Southwark, 1976–93 and 1999–2016, now Emeritus; Mem., Ct of Advrs, St Paul's Cathedral, 1993–99. Hon. Sec., Cathedral Organists' Assoc., 1989–98; Pres., Southwark and S London Soc. of Organists, 1976–; Vice Pres., Church Music Soc.; Mem. Cttee, Organists Charitable Trust (formerly Organists' Benevolent League), 1989–2011. Patron, Herbert Howells Soc., 1987–. Liveryman, Musicians' Co., 1985–. FGCM 1988; FRSCM 1994. Hon. Mem., Assoc. of Anglican Musicians, USA. Hon. DLitt Bradford, 1995. Lancelot Andrewes Medal, Dio. Southwark, 2017. *Recreations:* travel, walking. *Address:* 3 Shepheard's House, Manor Park Road, Chislehurst, Kent BR7 5FT. *Club:* Athenæum.

**BRAMSON, David;** Consultant, Nabarro Nathanson, 2001–06 (Senior Partner, 1995–2001); *b* 8 Feb. 1942; *s* of late Israel Bramson and Deborah Bramson (*née* Warshinsky); *m* 1966, Lilian de Wilde; one *s* one *d*. *Educ:* Willesden Co. Grammar Sch.; University Coll. London (LLB). Solicitor: Mobil Oil Co. Ltd, 1966–68; Nabarro Nathanson, 1968–2006 (Partner, 1969–2001). Member, Policy Cttee, British Property Fedn, 1995–2001; Trustee, Investment Property Forum Educnl Trust, 1997–2001. Lectr on commercial property, 1996–2000. Non-exec. Dir, Liberty Internat. plc, 2001–06. Gov. and Vice Chm., Coram Family, 2002–07. Chairman: Home-Start Camden, 2003–08; Westminster Advocacy Service for Sen. Residents, 2006–10; Advocacy Plus (London) Ltd, 2010–13. Trustee, U3A London, 2014–. *E:* dbramson@blueyonder.co.uk.

**BRAMWELL, Prof. Steven Thomas,** DPhil; Professor of Physics, London Centre for Nanotechnology, and Department of Physics and Astronomy, University College London, since 2009; *b* Norwich, 7 June 1961; *s* of William Bramwell and Mary Bramwell; *m* 2008, Sandra Batten; one *d*. *Educ:* King Edward VI Sch., Southampton; Oriel Coll., Oxford (MA Chem. 1984); Pembroke Coll., Oxford (DPhil Chem. 1989). FInstP 2012. Jun. Res. Fellow, Lincoln Coll., 1986–89; Res. Scientist, Institut Laue-Langevin, Grenoble, 1989–94; University College London: Lectr in Physical Chem.; Prof. of Physical Chem., Dept of Chem., 2000–09. FD *hc* Uppsala, 2019. Holweck Prize, Inst. of Physics and French Physical Soc., 2010; Europhysics Prize, Eur. Physical Soc., 2012. *Publications:* articles in Science, Nature, Nature Physics incl. on discovery and naming of 'spin ice'. *Recreations:* skiing, hill walking, jazz, watercolour painting, cycling, skating, swimming. *Address:* London Centre for Nanotechnology, University College London, 17–19 Gordon Street, WC1H 0AH. *T:* (020) 7679 9963. *E:* s.t.bramwell@ucl.ac.uk.

**BRANAGH, Sir Kenneth (Charles),** Kt 2012; actor and director; *b* 10 Dec. 1960; *s* of William and Frances Branagh; *m* 1st, 1989, Emma Thompson, *qv* (marr. diss. 1997); 2nd, 2003, Lindsay Brunnock. *Educ:* Meadway Comprehensive Sch., Reading; Royal Academy of Dramatic Art (Bancroft Gold Medalist). Pres., RADA, 2015–. *Theatre:* Another Country, Queen's, 1982 (SWET Award, Most Promising Newcomer; Plays and Players Award); The Madness; Francis; Henry V, Golden Girls, Hamlet, Love's Labours Lost, 1984–85; Tell Me Honestly (also author); Across the Roaring Hill; The Glass Maze; Hamlet, RSC, 1992; Edmond, NT, 2003; Ivanov, Wyndham's, 2008; The Painkiller, Lyric Th., Belfast, 2011, Garrick Th., 2016; Macbeth (also dir), Manchester Internat. Fest., 2013, NY 2014; directed: The Play What I Wrote, Wyndham's, 2001, NY, 2003; Ducktastic, Albery, 2005; founder dir, Renaissance Theatre Company, 1987–93: Romeo and Juliet (also dir); Public Enemy (also author); Much Ado About Nothing; As You Like It; Hamlet; Look Back in Anger (also televised); A Midsummer Night's Dream (also dir); King Lear (also dir); Coriolanus; Richard III; directed: Twelfth Night (also televised); The Life of Napoleon; (with Peter Egan) Uncle Vanya; actor-manager, Kenneth Branagh Th. Co., Garrick Th., 2015–, prodns incl. The Winter's Tale (actor and co-dir), Harlequinade (actor and co-dir), All On Her Own (dir), 2015, Romeo and Juliet (co-dir), 2016, The Entertainer (actor), 2016. *Films include:* A Month in the Country, 1987; High Season, 1987; Henry V (also dir), 1989 (Evening Standard Best Film of the Year, 1989; Oscar, Best Costume Design, 1990; BFI Award, Best Film and Technical Achievement, 1990; Young European Film of the Year, 1990; NY Critics Circle Award, Best New Dir; European Actor of the Year, 1990); Dead Again (also dir), 1991; Peter's Friends (also dir), Swan Song (dir), 1992; Swing Kids, Much Ado About Nothing (also dir), 1993; Mary Shelley's Frankenstein (also dir), 1994; (writer and dir) In the Bleak Midwinter, 1995; Othello, 1995; Hamlet (also dir), 1997; The Proposition, 1997; The Gingerbread Man, 1998; The Theory of Flight, 1998; Celebrity, 1999; Wild Wild West, 1999; Love's Labour's Lost (also dir), 2000; How to Kill Your Neighbor's Dog, 2002; Rabbit-Proof Fence, 2002; Harry Potter and the Chamber of Secrets, 2002; Five Children and It, 2004; As You Like It (dir), 2006; The Magic Flute (dir), 2006; Sleuth 2007; Valkyrie, 2009; The Boat that Rocked, 2009; Thor (dir), 2011; My Week with Marilyn, 2011 (Best Supporting Actor, London Critics' Circle Film Awards, 2012); Jack Ryan (also dir), 2013; Cinderella (dir), 2015; Dunkirk, 2017; Murder on the Orient Express (also dir and prod.), 2017; All is True (also dir and prod.), 2019; *television includes:* Billy Trilogy, 1982; Fortunes of War, 1987; Boy in the Bush; To the Lighthouse; Strange Interlude; Ghosts, 1987; The Lady's Not for Burning; Shadow of a Gunman, 1995; Shackleton, Conspiracy (Emmy Award), 2002; Warm Springs, 2005; Wallander, 2008, 2010, 2012, 2016 (Best Actor: BAFTA, 2010; Internat. Emmy Awards, 2017); *radio includes:* Hamlet, and Romeo and Juliet (both also co-dir); King Lear; Anthem for the Doomed Youth; Diaries of Samuel Pepys; Mary Shelley's Frankenstein; Bequest to the Nation, 2005; Cyrano De Bergerac, 2008; Life and Fate, 2011; Antony and Cleopatra, 2014. *Publications:* Public Enemy (play), 1988; Beginning (autobiog.), 1989; *screenplays:* Henry V; Much Ado About Nothing; Hamlet; In the Bleak Midwinter. *Recreations:* reading, playing guitar. *Address:* Longcross Film Studios, Building 124, Chobham Road, Chertsey, Surrey KT16 0EE.

**BRANCH, Jeffrey John;** JP; Vice Lord-Lieutenant of Berkshire, since 2016; *b* Bangor, 4 Aug. 1945; *s* of Jack and Beryl Branch; *m* 1974, Penelope Bailhache; one *s* (and one *s* decd). *Educ:* Buxton Coll.; Balliol Coll., Oxford (BA 1st Cl. English Lang. and Lit. 1967; MA 1971). Housemaster, 1984–97, Hd of English, 1998–2005, Eton Coll. Chm., Upton Hse Sch., 1994–2007. Chm., E Berks Bench, 2005–07. Trustee: Slough Public Hall Trust, 2001–; Charles Davis Trust, 2016–. Vice-Patron, Sail 4 Cancer, 2017–. JP 1992, DL 2010, Berks. *Publications:* contribs to Keats Shelley Rev., Use of English. *Recreations:* theatre, opera, ballet, walking. *T:* (01628) 780708. *E:* jjpa@btinternet.com. *Club:* Athenæum.

**BRANCH, Lynda;** *see* Thomas, L.

**BRANCH, Prof. Michael Arthur,** CMG 2000; PhD; Director, School of Slavonic and East European Studies, 1980–2001, and Professor of Finnish, 1986–2001, London University, at University College London; Fellow, University College London, since 2001; *b* 24 March 1940; *s* of Arthur Frederick Branch and Mahala Parker; *m* 1963, Ritva-Riitta Hannele, *d* of Erkki Kari, Heinola, Finland; three *d*. *Educ:* Shene Grammar Sch.; Sch. of Slavonic and East European Studies, Univ. of London (BA 1963; PhD 1967). School of Slavonic and East European Studies: Asst Lectr and Lectr in Finno-Ugrian Studies, 1967–72; Lectr, 1972–77, and Reader in Finnish, 1977; Chm., Dept of East European Language and Literature, 1979–80. Corresponding Member: Finno-Ugrian Soc., 1977; Finnish Literature Soc. (Helsinki), 1980. Hon. PhD Oulu (Finland), 1983. Comdr, Lion of Finland, 1980; Comdr, Polish Order of Merit, 1992; Comdr, Estonian Terra Mariana Cross, 2000; Officer, Order of Lithuanian Grand Duke Gediminas, 2002. *Publications:* A. J. Sjögren, 1973; (jtly) Finnish Folk Poetry: Epic, 1977; (jtly) A Student's Glossary of Finnish, 1980; (ed) Kalevala, 1985; (jtly) Edith Södergran, 1992; (jtly) The Great Bear, 1993; (jtly) Uses of Tradition, 1994; (jtly) Finland and Poland in the Russian Empire, 1995; (ed) The Writing of National History and Identity, 1999; (ed) Defining Self: essays on emergent identities in Russia, seventeenth to nineteenth centuries, 2010. *Recreation:* walking.

**BRANCH, Sonya Judith Clara;** General Counsel, Bank of England, since 2015; *b* Essex, 19 June 1974; *d* of David and Martina McNulty; *m* 2003, David Henry Branch; two *s* two *d*. *Educ:* St Paul's Girls Sch., Hammersmith; Magdalen Coll., Oxford (MA Hons Juris.); Coll. of Law, London (DipLP); King's Coll. London (Postgrad. Dip. Eur. Competition Law). Corporate Partner, Clifford Chance LLP; Sen. Dir, OFT, 2007–12; Dir, Triennial Rev., DEFRA, 2012; Exec. Dir, Enforcement and Mergers, and Mem. Bd, OFT, 2012–14; Exec. Dir, Enforcement, and Mem. Bd, CMA, 2014–15. Trustee: Target Ovarian Cancer, 2011–18 (Dir Emeritus, 2018); British Inst. of Internat. and Comparative Law, 2017–. *Recreations:* wishing for more time for far-flung travels and theatre, but focussed now on Brexit (too much), family and friendships. *Address:* Bank of England, Threadneedle Street, EC2R 8AH. *E:* sonya.branch@bankofengland.co.uk.

**BRAND,** family name of **Viscount Hampden.**

**BRAND, Prof. Andrea Hilary,** PhD; FRS 2010; FMedSci; Herchel Smith Professor of Molecular Biology, since 2007, and Head of Wellcome Trust Laboratories, since 2015, Wellcome Trust/Cancer Research UK Gurdon Institute and Department of Physiology, Development and Neuroscience, University of Cambridge; Wellcome Trust Senior Investigator, since 2014; Royal Society Darwin Trust Research Professor, since 2016; Fellow, Jesus College, Cambridge, since 2009; *b* 9 March 1959; *d* of Howard and Marlene Brand (*née* Nykerk); partner, Prof. Jim Haseloff; one *d*. *Educ:* UN Internat. Sch., NY; Brasenose Coll., Oxford (BA Hons Biochem. 1981; Hon. Fellow, 2014); MRC Lab. of Molecular Biol. and King's Coll., Cambridge (PhD Molecular Biol. 1986). SERC Post Doctoral Fellow, 1986–87, Helen Hay Whitney Fellow, 1987–89, Harvard Univ.; Leukemia Soc. Special Fellow, Harvard Med. Sch., 1990–93; Cancer Research Campaign Gurdon Institute, subseq. Wellcome Trust/Cancer Research UK Gurdon Institute, University of Cambridge: Wellcome Trust Sen. Fellow in Basic Biomed. Res., 1993–2003; Dir of Res. in Develt Neurobiol., 2003–07; Sen. Gp Leader, 2005–; Res. Fellow, King's Coll., Cambridge, 1999–2003. Invited Prof., Ecole Normale Supérieure, Paris, 2002; Dietrich Bodenstein Lectr, Univ. of Virginia, 2002; Vis. Prof., Univ. of Sydney, 2011. Member, Editorial Board: Bioessays, 2003–07; Neural Develt, 2006–; Fly, 2006–. Mem., Internat. Scientific Adv. Bd, Promega Corp., 1999–2004. Mem., Academic Careers Cttee, 2003–06, Sectional Cttee, 2008–10, Acad. Med. Scis. Mem. Council, Royal Soc., 2013–16. Founding Bd Mem., Rosalind Franklin Soc., 2006–. Mem., EMBO, 2000. FMedSci 2003. Hooke Medal, British Soc. for Cell Biol., 2002; (jtly) William Bate Hardy Prize, Cambridge Philosophical Soc., 2004; Rosalind Franklin Award, Royal Soc., 2006. *Publications:* contrib. articles on cell and develtl biol. in scientific jls. *Recreations:* contemporary dance, decorative arts, reading, ballet, theatre. *Address:* Wellcome Trust/Cancer Research UK Gurdon Institute, University of Cambridge, Tennis Court Road, Cambridge CB2 1QN.

**BRAND, Dr Carlton Michael;** Executive Director (Director Adult Social Services, Electoral Registration Officer, Returning Officer), Wiltshire Council, since 2011 (Corporate Director, Resources, 2007–11, Environment and Place, 2012–17); Owner and Coach, LeadershipMentor.co.uk (Executive Coaching), 2011–16; *b* Maldon, Essex, 12 Oct. 1966; *s* of Michael Brand and Gloria Brand; *m* 2000, Tracy; two *s*. *Educ:* Plume Sch., Maldon; Univ. of East London (BA Hons Business Studies 1993); Univ. of Hertfordshire (MSc Advanced Automotive Engrg, Manuf. and Mgt 1998; EngD 2005); Univ. of West of England (Adv. Cert. Exec. Coaching 2011); Inst. of Leadership and Mgt (Level 7 Exec. Coaching and Leadership Mentoring, 2011). Ford Motor Company: apprentice, 1983–87; test engr, 1987–89; develt engr, 1989–92; Manager: Powertrain Systems Engrg, 1993–95; Strategy Planning, 1995–97; Body Engrg, 1997–2003; Dir, Resources, St Edmundsbury BC, 2004–06. Member: SOLACE, 2005–; Assoc. for Coaching, 2011–. Chartered Manager 2011. FCMI 2010; FRSA 2013. *Publications:* (contrib.) Public and Third Sector Leadership: experience speaks, 2014; contribs to Mgt Jl for local govt, Local Govt Chronicle, Jl of Automotive Engrg and Public Money and Management. *Recreations:* executive coaching and leadership mentoring, fishing, cricket, road and time trial cycling with Frome and District Wheelers, motorsport, challenging public sector thinking through systems thinking, being a frustrated academic, amateur astronomy (observing), researching the history of big telescopes. *Address:* Wiltshire Council, County Hall, Trowbridge, Wilts BA14 8JN. *T:* 07500 808307. *E:* drcarltonbrand@aol.co.uk.

**BRAND, Geoffrey Arthur;** Under-Secretary, Department of Employment, 1972–85; *b* 13 June 1930; *s* of late Arthur William Charles Brand and Muriel Ada Brand; *m* 1954, Joy Trotman (*d* 2014); two *d*. *Educ:* Andover Grammar Sch.; University Coll., London. Entered Min. of Labour, 1953; Private Sec. to Parly Sec., 1956–57; Colonial Office, 1957–58; Private Sec. to Minister of Labour, 1965–66; Asst Sec., Industrial Relations and Research and Planning Divisions, 1966–72. Mem., Archbishop of Canterbury's (later Bishops') Adv. Gp on Urban Priority Areas, 1986–98. FRSA 1985. *Address:* Cedarwood, Seer Green, Beaconsfield, Bucks HP9 2UH. *T:* (01494) 676637.

**BRAND, Helen Joanna,** OBE 2011; Chief Executive, Association of Chartered Certified Accountants, since 2008; *b* Rawtenstall, 22 April 1965; *d* of Colin Anthony and Judith Anne Brand; two *d*. *Educ:* Rainford High Sch.; Univ. of Exeter (BA Hons Politics). Pres., Exeter Univ. Guild of Students, 1986–87. Dir, Internat. Affairs, CIMA, 1987–96; Association of Chartered Certified Accountants: Hd of Corporate Develt, 1996–2002; Chief Operating

Officer, 2002–07; Man. Dir, Strategy, 2007–08. *Recreations:* family activities, cooking, beach life in N Devon, Liverpool FC, modern literature. *Address:* Association of Chartered Certified Accountants, The Adelphi, 1–11 John Adam Street, WC2N 6AU. *T:* (020) 7059 5731.

**BRAND, Jo;** writer and comedian; *m;* two *d.* Formerly psychiatric nurse. Comedy includes stand-up. Television series: Jo Brand Through the Cakehole, 1995; A Big Slice of Jo Brand, 1996; Jo Brand's Commercial Breakdown, 1999; Head on Comedy with Jo Brand, 2000; Nobody Likes a Smartass, 2003; QI, 2003–; Getting On, 2009, 2010, 2012 (Best Female Performance in a Comedy Role, BAFTA, 2011); Jo Brand's Big Splash, 2011; Jo Brand's Winter Warm Up, 2012; The Great British Bake Off - An Extra Slice, 2013–; Splash!, 2013–14; Jo Brand's Hell of a Walk, 2016; Going Forward, 2016; (also writer) Damned, 2016, 2018; Jo Brand's Cats and Kittens, 2017, 2018; Britain's Best Junior Doctor, 2018. Radio series: Windbags (with Donna McPhail); Seven Ages of Man, 2000; VIP RIP, 2019. Theatre, The Pirates of Penzance, Gielgud, 2008. Pantomime début as the Genie of the Lamp, Aladdin, New Wimbledon Th., 2013. Film, The More You Ignore Me (also writer), 2018. Former columnist, The Independent; columnist, Nursing Times, 2000. Best Comedy Club Performer, 1992, Best Female Comedian, 2010, British Comedy Awards. *Publications:* Load of Old Balls: ranking of men in history, 1995; Load of Old Ball Crunchers: women in history, 1996; (with Helen Griffin) Mental (play), 1996; Sorting Out Billy (novel), 2004; It's Different for Girls (novel), 2005; The More You Ignore Me (novel; filmed 2018), 2009; Look Back in Hunger (autobiog.), 2009; Can't Stand Up for Sitting Down (autobiog.), 2010; Born Lippy, 2018. *Address:* c/o Vivenne Clore, Suite 3, De Walden Court, 85 New Cavendish Street, W1W 6XD.

**BRAND, Dr Michael;** Director, Art Gallery of New South Wales, Sydney, since 2012; *b* 9 Jan. 1958; *s* of Lindsay and Betty Brand; *m* 1988, Tina Gomes; two *d. Educ:* Canberra Grammar Sch.; Maret Sch., Washington, DC; Emerson Prep. Sch., Washington; Australian Nat. Univ. (BA Hons Asian Studies); Harvard Univ. (MA; PhD 1987). Curator, Asian Art, Mus. of Art, Rhode Is. Sch. of Design, 1985–87; Res. Fellow, Arthur M. Sackler Gall., Smithsonian Instn, 1987; Co-Dir, Smithsonian Instn Mughal Garden Project, Lahore, Pakistan, 1988–93; Curator, Asian Art. Gall., Australia, 1988–96; Asst Dir, Qld Art Gall., Brisbane, 1996–2000; Director: Virginia Mus. of Fine Arts, USA, 2000–05; J. Paul Getty Mus., 2005–10; Consulting Dir, Aga Khan Mus., Toronto, 2010–12. *Publications:* (ed with G. D. Lowry) Fatehpur-Sikri: a sourcebook, 1985; (with G. D. Lowry) Akbar's India: art from the Mughal City of Victory, 1985; (ed with G. D. Lowry) Studies on Fatehpur-Sikri, 1987; (jtly) Shalamar Garden Lahore: landscape, form and meaning, 1990; (with C. Phoeurn) The Age of Angkor: treasures from the National Museum of Cambodia, 1992; (ed and contrib.) Traditions of Asian Art (traced through the Collection of the National Gallery of Australia), 1995; The Vision of Kings: art and experience in India, 1995; (ed with C. Roberts) Earth, Spirit, Fire: Korean masterpieces of the Choson Dynasty, 2000; contrib. numerous articles to art catalogues, books and jls. *Address:* Art Gallery of New South Wales, Art Gallery Road, The Domain, Sydney, NSW 2000, Australia. *T:* (2) 92251725.

**BRAND, Prof. Paul Anthony,** DPhil; FBA 1998; Professor of English Legal History, University of Oxford, 2010–14; Senior Research Fellow, 1999–2014 and Senior Dean, 2011–14, now Emeritus Fellow, All Souls College, Oxford; *b* 25 Dec. 1946; *s* of Thomas Joseph Brand and Marjorie Jean Brand (*née* Smith); *m* 1st, 1970, Vanessa Carolyn Alexandra Rodrigues (*d* 2009); 2nd, 2016, Susanne Jenks. *Educ:* Hampton Grammar Sch.; Magdalen Coll., Oxford (BA 1967; DPhil 1974). Asst Keeper, Public Record Office, 1970–76; Lectr in Law, UCD, 1976–83; research, 1983–93; Res. Fellow, Inst. of Historical Res., Univ. of London, 1993–99; Fellow, All Souls Coll., Oxford, 1997–99. Vis. Fellow, All Souls Coll., Oxford, 1995; Vis. Prof., Columbia Univ. Law Sch., 1995, 2003; Dist. Vis. Prof., Arizona Center for Medieval and Renaissance Studies and Merriam Vis. Prof. of Law, Arizona State Univ., 2000; Cook Global Law Prof., Univ. of Michigan Law Sch., 2013. Hon. Bencher, Middle Temple, 2014. *Publications:* The Origins of the English Legal Profession, 1992; The Making of the Common Law, 1992; The Earliest English Law Reports, vol. I, vol. II, 1996, vol. III, 2005, vol. IV, 2007; Kings, Barons and Justices: the making and enforcement of legislation in thirteenth century England, 2003; The Parliament Rolls of Medieval England, vols I and II, 2005; Plea Rolls of the Exchequer of the Jews, vol. VI, 2005. *Recreations:* travelling, visiting old buildings and interesting cities. *Address:* All Souls College, Oxford OX1 4AL. *T:* (01865) 279286; The Old Rectory, Church Street, Fenny Compton CV47 2YE. *T:* 01295 770457.

**BRAND, Dr Peter;** General Practitioner, Brading, Isle of Wight, 1977–2006; *b* 16 May 1947; *s* of L. H. Brand and J. Brand (*née* Fredricks); *m* 1972, Jane Vivienne Attlee; two *s. Educ:* Thornbury Grammar Sch., Glos; Birmingham Univ. Med. Sch. MRCS; LRCP; DObstRCOG; MRCGP. Chm., IoW Div., BMA, 1980–84. Contested (Lib Dem) Isle of Wight, 1992, 2001; MP (Lib Dem) Isle of Wight, 1997–2001. *Recreations:* boating, building, choral singing (Mem., Ryde Chorus). *Address:* Chain Ferry House, 3 Ferry Road, East Cowes, Isle of Wight PO32 6RA. *Clubs:* Island Sailing, E Cowes Sailing.

**BRAND, Ven. Richard Harold Guthrie;** Archdeacon of Winchester, since 2016; *b* Oxted, 20 Feb. 1965; *s* of Dick and Chuck Brand; *m* 1996, Sarah Shackleton; one *s* two *d. Educ:* Sherborne Sch.; Durham Univ. (BA Theology 1987; MA Theology and Ministry 2016); Ripon Coll. Cuddesdon. Ordained deacon, 1989, priest 1990; Asst Curate, St Margaret's, King's Lynn, 1989–93; Sen. Curate, Croydon Parish Church, 1993–96; Companion Team Priest, St Barnabas, Christchurch, NZ, 1996–98; Priest-in-charge, St Peter and St Paul, Hambledon, 1998–2006; Diocesan Dir of Ordinands, Dio. of Portsmouth, 1998–2006; Team Rector, Harborough Anglican Team, 2006–16; Area Dean, Gartree Deaneries, Leicester, 2013–16. Chair, Mgt Cttee and Trustees, Launde Abbey, Leics, 2008–13. Honorary Canon: Leicester Cathedral, 2015–16; Winchester Cathedral, 2016–. *Recreations:* trying to sketch, tennis (Real or Lawn), golf, reading. *Address:* Diocesan Office, Wolvesey, Winchester, Hants SO23 9ND. *T:* (01962) 710960. *E:* richard.brand@winchester.anglican.org.

**BRANDIS, Hon. George Henry;** QC (Aust.) 2013; SC 2006; High Commissioner for Australia in the United Kingdom, since 2018; *b* Sydney, Australia, 22 June 1957; *s* of George Henry Francis Brandis and Elaine Marie Brandis (*née* McKinnon); one *s* one *d. Educ:* Villanova Coll., Brisbane; Univ. of Qld (BA 1st Cl. Hons Govt; LLB 1st Cl. Hons); Magdalen Coll., Oxford (BCL; Sir Rupert Cross Prize, 1983). Called to the Australian Bar, 1981; in practice as barrister, 1985–2000. Senator for Qld, Parlt of Australia, 2000–18; Minister for Arts and Sport, 2007; Shadow Attorney Gen., 2007–13; Dep. Leader of Opposition, 2010–13; Attorney Gen., 2013–17; Minister for Arts, 2013–15; Vice Pres., Exec. Council, 2013–17; Dep. Leader, 2013–15, Leader, 2015–17, of Govt in Senate. Comr, CWGC, 2018–; Trustee, Imperial War Mus., 2018–. Hon. Bencher, Lincoln's Inn, 2019. *Publications:* (jtly) Liberals Face the Future, 1985; (jtly) Australian Liberalism: the continuing vision, 1987; contrib. jl articles on legal, political and histl topics. *Recreations:* reading, music. *Address:* High Commission of Australia, Australia House, The Strand, WC2B 4LA. *Clubs:* Athenæum, Garrick, Travellers; Tattersalls (Brisbane); Union (Sydney); Savage (Melbourne).

**BRANDON, Bishop of,** since 2016; **Rt Rev. William Grant Cliff;** *b* Sarnia, Ont, 26 April 1966; *s* of Peter Howard Cliff and Marie Grace Cliff (*née* Macleod). *Educ:* Wyoming Public Sch.; Lambton Central Collegiate and Vocational Inst.; Univ. of Western Ontario (BA 1989; MDiv 1992; MA Theology 2009). Ordained deacon and priest, 1992; Asst Curate, Trinity Church, Simcoe, Ont, 1992–95; Rector: St James's, Hanover and Trinity Church, Durham, 1995–98; St John the Evangelist, Strathroy and St Ann's, Adelaide, 1998–2002; Rector, Collegiate Chapel of St John the Evangelist, and Chaplain, Huron Univ. Coll., 2002–15; Anglican Chaplain to Univ. of Western Ont, 2002–15. Diocesan Liturgical Officer, 2004–15; Diocese of Huron: Clerical Sec. of Synod, 2008–15; Canon Precentor, 2008–15. Canon, Cathedral Chapter, St Paul's Cath. London, Ont, 2003. Hon. DD Huron Univ. Coll., 2013. Queen's Diamond Jubilee Medal, 2012. *Publications:* contrib. Jl of Catholic Biblical Assoc. of Canada. *Recreations:* cooking, entertaining, travel, museums, reading, heraldry. *Address:* (office) 403 13th Street, Brandon, MB R7A 4P9, Canada. *T:* (204) 7272380, *Fax:* (204) 7274135. *E:* bishop@brandon.anglican.ca.

**BRANDON, Louise Ann; Her Honour Judge Brandon;** a Circuit Judge, since 2019; *b* Lancashire, 28 Nov. 1979; *d* of Edward Brandon and Julie Elizabeth Brandon; partner, 2005, Daniel John Fox. *Educ:* Leyland St Mary's RC High Sch., Leyland; Univ. of Manchester (BA Hons Govt and Law 2001; MA Health Care Ethics and Law 2018); Manchester Metropolitan Univ. (Postgrad. DipLS at the Bar 2003). Called to the Bar, Middle Temple, 2003; in practice on Northern Circuit, 2003–19; a Recorder, 2016–19. Chair, Police Misconduct Tribunals, 2016–19. Lay Advr, Health Educn NW, 2014–19. *Recreations:* running, surfing, dog walking, knitting, vegan cookery. *Address:* Liverpool Crown Court, Queen Elizabeth II Law Courts, Derby Square, Liverpool L2 1XA. *E:* HHJ.Louise.Brandon@ejudiciary.net.

**BRANDON, Prof. Nigel Peter,** OBE 2011; PhD; CEng, FREng; Professor of Sustainable Development in Energy, since 2004 (Shell Professor, 2004–09), Dean, Faculty of Engineering, since 2017, and Director, Sustainable Gas Institute, since 2014, Imperial College London (Director, Energy Futures Laboratory, 2005–14); *b* Birmingham, 3 May 1960; *s* of Jeffrey Brandon and Anne Elizabeth Brandon; *m* 1986, Janet Mary Reeves; two *s. Educ:* Arthur Terry Sch.; Imperial Coll., London (BSc Engr 1981; PhD 1984). CEng 2006; FREng 2008. Res. Scientist, BP, 1984–92; Staff Technologist, Rolls-Royce, 1992–98; Sen. Lectr, Imperial Coll. London, 1998–2004. Ceres Power: Founder and CEO, 2001–03; Chief Tech. Officer, 2003–06; Chief Scientist, 2006–09. Sen. Fellow to Res. Councils UK Energy Prog., 2006–14. BIS (formerly DIUS) UK Focal Point in climate change, energy and envmt with China, 2007–11. FEI 2006; FIMMM 2006; FRSA 2007; FHEA 2007; FCGI 2008. Silver Medal, Royal Acad. of Engrg, 2007; Francis Bacon Medal, ASME, 2014. *Publications:* Fuel Cells Compendium, 2005; papers on fuel cell science, energy storage science and engrg and hydrogen systems in jls. *Recreations:* reading science fiction, rolling icosahedra. *Address:* Imperial College London, SW7 2AZ. *T:* (020) 7594 5704, *Fax:* (020) 7594 7444. *E:* n.brandon@imperial.ac.uk.

**BRANDON, Prof. Peter Samuel,** OBE 2010; FRICS; Professor of Quantity and Building Surveying, University of Salford, 1985–2010, now Emeritus; *b* 4 June 1943; *s* of Samuel Brandon and Doris Eileen Florence Brandon (*née* Downing); *m* 1968, Mary Ann Elizabeth Canham; one *s* two *d. Educ:* Bournemouth Grammar Sch.; Bristol Univ. (MSc Architecture); Salford Univ. (DSc 1996). Private practice and local govt, 1963–69; Lectr, Portsmouth Poly., 1969–73; Prin. Lectr, Bristol Poly., 1973–81; Head of Dept, Portsmouth Poly., 1981–85; Salford University: Chm., Surveying Dept, 1985–93; Pro-Vice-Chancellor, 1993–2001; Dir, Res. and Grad. Coll., 1993–2001; Dir of Strategic Progs, 2001–10. Royal Institution of Chartered Surveyors: Chm., Res. Cttee, 1987–91; Mem. Gen. Council representing Gtr Manchester, 1989–93; Mem., Exec. Bd, QS Div., 1991–; Science and Engineering Research Council: Chm., Construction Cttee, 1991–94; Chm., Building Design Technology and Management Sub-Cttee, 1990–91; Member: Engrg Res. Commn, 1991–94; DTI Technology Foresight Panel for Construction, 1994; Chm., Built Envmt Panel for HEFCE RAE, 1996 and 2001. Hon. Mem., ASAQS, 1994. Hon. DEng Heriot-Watt, 2006; DUniv Salford, 2011. *Publications:* Cost Planning of Buildings, 1980, 8th edn 2007; (ed) Building Cost Techniques, 1982; Microcomputers in Building Appraisal, 1983; (ed) Quality and Profit in Building Design, 1984; Computer programs for Building Cost Appraisal, 1985; Building, Cost Modelling and Computers, 1987; Expert Systems: the strategic planning of construction projects, 1988; (ed) Investment, Procurement & Performance in Construction, 1991; (ed) Management, Quality and Economics in Building, 1991; (ed) Integration of Construction Information, 1995; (ed) Client Centered Approach to Knowledge Based Systems, 1995; Evaluation of the Built Environment Sustainability, 1997; (ed) Cities and Sustainability, 2000; (ed) Evaluating Sustainable Development in the Built Environment, 2005, 2nd edn 2010; (ed) Virtual Futures for Design, Construction and Procurement, 2008; (ed) Clients Driving Innovation, 2008; (ed) Future Challenges in Managing and Evaluating Sustainable Development in the Built Environment, 2017. *Recreations:* mountain biking alongside canals, walking, travel, modern art, water colour painting. *Address:* School of the Built Environment, Maxwell Building, University of Salford, Salford M5 4WT. *T:* (0161) 295 5164, 07798 534495.

**BRANDRETH, Benet Xan;** QC 2018; a Recorder, since 2019; writer and performer, since 2011; rhetor, since 2005; *b* London, 13 March 1975; *s* of Gyles Daubency Brandreth, *qv; m* 2005, Kosha Danielle Engler; two *s. Educ:* St Paul's Sch., London; Magdalene Coll., Cambridge (MA Hons); Coll. of Law (CPE); Inns of Court Sch. of Law (BVC). Called to the Bar, Middle Temple, 1999; in practice as barrister specialising in intellectual property rights; A Panel, Attorney-Gen.'s Panel of Counsel, 2015. Trustee, Camden CAB, 2007 (Chair, Trustees, 2008–12). Rhetoric coach to RSC, 2005–. Officer cadet, 1st Bn RHR, 1993–94; 2nd Lieut, 4th Bn (V) RGJ, 1997–98. *Publications:* The Spy of Venice (novel), 2015; The Assassin of Verona (novel), 2017. *Recreations:* reading, walking, Filipino knife-fighting, riddles. *Address:* 11 South Square, Gray's Inn, WC1R 5EY. *W:* www.benetbrandreth.com. *Club:* Garrick.

**BRANDRETH, Gyles Daubeney;** author, broadcaster; *b* 8 March 1948; *s* of late Charles Brandreth and Alice Addison; *m* 1973, Michèle Brown; one *s* two *d. Educ:* Lycée Français de Londres; Betteshanger Sch., Kent; Bedales Sch., Hants; New Coll., Oxford (Scholar). Pres. Oxford Union, Editor of Isis. Chairman: Archway Productions Ltd, 1971–74; Victorama Ltd, 1974–93; Complete Editions Ltd, 1988–93; Director: Colin Smythe Ltd, 1971–73; Newarke Wools Ltd, 1988–92; J. W. Spear & Sons, 1992–95. Dep. Chm., Unicorn Heritage, 1987–90; children's publisher, André Deutsch Ltd, 1997–2000; consultant ed., Whitaker's Almanack, 1997–2002. Freelance journalist, 1968–: contrib. Observer, Guardian, Express, Daily Mail, Daily Mirror, Daily Telegraph, Evening Standard, Spectator, Punch, Homes & Gardens, She, Woman's Own; Columnist: Honey, 1968–69; Manchester Evening News, 1971–72; Woman, 1972–73, 1986–88; TV Times, 1989–92; The Oldie, 2017–; Press Assoc. weekly syndicated column in USA, 1981–85; Ed., Puzzle World, 1989–92; Ed.-at-Large, Sunday Telegraph Review, 1999–2004. MP (C) City of Chester, 1992–97; contested (C) same seat, 1997. PPS to Financial Sec. to Treasury, 1993–94, to Sec. of State for Nat. Heritage, 1994–95, to Sec. of State for Health, 1995; an Asst Govt Whip, 1995–96; a Lord Comr, HM Treasury, 1996–97. Sponsor, 1994 Marriage Act. Broadcaster, 1969–: TV series incl.: Child of the Sixties, 1969; Puzzle Party, 1977; Chatterbox, 1977–78; Memories, 1982; Countdown, 1983–90 and 1997–; TV-am,

1983–90; Railway Carriage Game, 1985; Catchword, 1986; Discovering Gardens, 1990–91; CBS News, 1992–2002; Have I Got News For You, 1997–; Home Shopping Network, 2002–05; This Is Your Life, 2003; Public Opinion, 2004; The One Show, 2007–; (with Hinge and Bracket) Dear Ladies (TV scripts); radio: A Rhyme in Time, Radio 4, 1971; Just A Minute, Radio 4, 1981–; Wordaholics, Radio 4, 2012–; theatrical producer, 1971–86: Through the Looking-Glass, 1972; Oxford Theatre Fest., 1974, 1976; The Dame of Sark, Wyndham's, 1974; The Little Hut, Duke of York's, 1974; Dear Daddy, Ambassador's, 1976; Cambridge Fest., 1986; also Son et Lumière; writer: (with Julian Slade) Now We Are Sixty (play), 1986; (and performer) Zipp! (musical), Edinburgh Fest., 2002 (Most Popular Show award), Duchess, 2003, UK tour, 2004; (with Susannah Pearse) Wonderland (play), 2010; performer: Baron Hardup in Cinderella, Guildford, 1989, Wimbledon, 1990; Malvolio in Twelfth Night The Musical!, Edinburgh Fest., 2005; The One to One Show, Edinburgh Fest., 2010, tour, 2010–11; Lady Bracknell in The Importance of Being Earnest (musical), Riverside Studios, 2011; Looking for Happiness, Edinburgh Fest., 2013, tour, 2013–14; Word Power!, Edinburgh Fest., 2015, tour 2016; Hamlet, Park Th., 2017; Break a Leg!, Edinburgh Fest., 2018, tour 2019. Chancellor, Univ. of Chester, 2017–. Founder: National Scrabble Championships, 1971; British Pantomime Assoc., 1971; Teddy Bear Mus., 1988. Dir, Eur. Movement's People for Europe campaign, 1975; Mem., Better English Campaign, 1995–97. Pres., Oscar Wilde Soc., 2015–. Appeals Chm., 1983–89, Chm., 1989–93, Vice-Pres., 1993–, NPFA. Co-curator, NPG exhibition of children's writers, 2002. Three times holder, world record for longest-ever after-dinner speech (4 hrs 19 mins, 1976; 11 hrs, 1978; 12 hrs 30 mins, 1982). *Publications*: over fifty books since Created in Captivity, 1972; most recent: Under the Jumper (autobiog.), 1993; Who is Nick Saint? (novel), 1996; Venice Midnight (novel), 1998; Breaking the Code (diaries), 1999; John Gielgud, 2000; Brief Encounters: meetings with remarkable people, 2001; Philip and Elizabeth: portrait of a marriage, 2004; Charles and Camilla: portrait of a love affair, 2005; Oscar Wilde and the Candlelight Murders (novel), 2007; Oscar Wilde and the Ring of Death, 2008; Oscar Wilde and the Dead Man's Smile, 2009; Something Sensational to Read in the Train: the diary of a lifetime, 2009; Oscar Wilde and the Nest of Vipers, 2010; Oscar Wilde and the Vatican Murders, 2011; Oscar Wilde and the Murders at Reading Gaol, 2012; (ed) Oxford Dictionary of Humorous Quotations, 2013; The 7 Secrets of Happiness, 2013; (with S. Brandreth) The Lost Art of Having Fun, 2013; (with Saethryd Brandreth) Novelty Knits, 2014; Breaking the Code: 1990–2007, 2014; Word Play, 2015; Jack the Ripper: case closed, 2017; On Christmas, 2017; Have You Eaten Grandma?, 2018; over seventy books for children. *Address*: c/o Curtis Brown, Haymarket House, 28–29 Haymarket, SW1Y 4SP. *W*: www.gylesbrandreth.net.
*See also* B. X. Brandreth.

**BRANDRICK, David Guy,** CBE 1981; Secretary, British Coal Corporation (formerly National Coal Board), 1972–89, retired; Director: Coal Staff Superannuation Scheme Trustees Ltd (formerly British Coal Staff Scheme Superannuation Trustees Ltd), 1989–2002; CMT Pension Trustee Services Ltd, 1993–2002; *b* 17 April 1932; *s* of Harry and Minnie Brandrick; *m* 1956, Eunice Fisher (*d* 1999); one *s* one *d*. *Educ*: Newcastle-under-Lyme High Sch.; St John's Coll., Oxford (MA). Joined National Coal Board, 1955; Chairman's Office, 1957; Principal Private Secretary to Chairman, 1961; Departmental Sec., Production Dept, 1963; Dep. Sec. to the Bd, 1967. *Recreation*: walking.

**BRANDT, Peter Augustus;** Chairman, Atkins Fulford Ltd, 1977–2006; *b* 2 July 1931; *s* of late Walter Augustus Brandt and late Dorothy Gray Brandt (*née* Crane); *m* 1962, Elisabeth Margaret (*née* ten Bos) (*d* 2018); two *s* one *d*. *Educ*: Eton Coll.; Trinity Coll., Cambridge (MA). Joined Wm Brandt's Sons and Co. Ltd, Merchant Bankers, 1954; Mem. Bd, 1960; Chief Executive, 1966; resigned, 1972. Director: London Life Assoc., 1962–89; Corp. of Argentine Meat Producers (CAP) Ltd and affiliates, 1970; Edward Bates (Holdings) Ltd, 1972–77; Edward Bates and Sons Ltd, 1972–77 (Chm., 1974–77). Mem., Nat. Rivers Authy (formerly Nat. Rivers Adv. Cttee), 1988–95. *Recreations*: sailing, rowing, steam engines, wild fowl, English water colours. *Address*: Spout Farm, Boxford, Suffolk CO10 5HA. *Clubs*: Boodle's; Leander (Henley-on-Thames).

**BRANIGAN, Kate Victoria;** QC 2006; *b* 3 Sept. 1961; *d* of late Cyril and of Patricia Branigan; *m* 1983, Robert Solomon; one *s* one *d*. *Educ*: Coopers' Company and Coborn Sch., Upminster; Univ. of Southampton (LLB 1983). Called to the Bar, Inner Temple, 1984; in practice as a barrister specialising in family law, 1984–. Family Mediator, 2011–. *Recreations*: church, entertaining, classical music, reading, theatre, France, walking, ski-ing, being with my family. *Address*: 4 Paper Buildings, Temple, EC4Y 7EX. *T*: (020) 7583 0816, *Fax*: (020) 7353 4979. *E*: kb@4pb.com.

**BRANKIN, Rhona;** Member (Lab) Midlothian, Scottish Parliament, 1999–2011; *b* 19 Jan. 1950; *d* of Edward and Joyce Lloyd; *m* 1998, Peter Jones; two *d* by former marriage. *Educ*: Aberdeen Univ. (BEd 1975); Moray House Coll. (Dip. Special Educnl Needs 1989). Teacher, 1975–94; Lectr in Special Educnl Needs, Northern Coll., Dundee, 1994–99. Scottish Executive: Deputy Minister: for Culture and Sport, 1999–2001; for Envmt and Rural Develt, 2000–01 and 2005–07; for Health and Community Care, 2004–05; Minister for Communities, 2007; Shadow Cabinet Sec. for Educn and Lifelong Learning, 2007–09. Former Chair, Scottish Labour Party. Mem. Bd, Arts and Business Scotland, 2011–18; Public Interest Mem., ICAS, 2011–18. Trustee, Leuchie House Respite Centre, 2011–; Chair, Mavisbank House, 2011–. Hon. FRIBA. *Recreations*: the arts, golf, France.

**BRANNAN, Micheline Hadassah;** Head, Civil and International Group, Scottish Executive Justice Department, 2005–07; Head, Social Justice Group, Scottish Executive Development Department, 2006–07; staff nurse, NHS Lothian, 2011–15; *b* 23 Oct. 1954; *d* of Israel and Halina Moss; *m* 1986, Michael Neilson Brannan (*d* 2008); two *s*. *Educ*: St Hilda's Coll., Oxford (BA 1976, MA Lit. Hum. 1978); Edinburgh Napier Univ. (BNSc 2011). Scottish Office: admin. trainee, 1976–78; HEO(D), 1978–82; Principal, 1982–91; Head: Parole and Lifer Rev. Div., 1991–95; Civil Law Div., 1995–2001; Hd, Criminal Justice Gp, Scottish Exec. Justice Dept, 2001–05. Chair, BEMIS (formerly Black and Ethnic Minority Infrastructure in Scotland), 2014– (Co. Sec., 2011–14). Mem. Bd, Barony Housing Assoc., 2008–12. Member: Scottish Council of Jewish Communities, 2007– (Chair, 2018–); Bd of Mgt, Edinburgh Hebrew Congregation, 2013–16 (Vice-Chair, 2014–16); Exec., Confedn of Friends of Israel, Scotland, 2017–18; Scottish Regl Fundraiser, United Jewish Israel Appeal, 2017–. Jewish Rep., Edinburgh Inter Faith Assoc., 2007–10. Treas., Edinburgh Jewish Literary Soc., 2007–. Editor, Edinburgh Star, mag. for Edinburgh Jewish community, 2011–. *Recreations*: Jewish cultural activities, India. *Address*: 0/2 3 Braidholm Crescent, Glasgow G46 6HH. *E*: michelinehbrannan@msn.com.

**BRANNEN, Paul;** Member (Lab) North East Region, European Parliament, 2014–19; *b* Peterborough, 13 Sept. 1962; *s* of Colin and Joyce Brannen; *m* 1999, Angela Acton Davis; one *s* one *d* and one step *d*. *Educ*: Walbottle Comprehensive Sch., Newcastle upon Tyne; Leeds Univ. (BA Theol. and Religious Studies); Durham Univ. (MBA). Pres., Leeds Univ. Students' Union, 1987–88; Campaigns Officer, Anti-Apartheid Movt, London, 1988–91; press officer, Labour Party, 1991–92; Hd of Campaigns, Christian Aid, 1992–97; Sen. Manager, Hobsbawm Macaulay Communications, 1997–98; Campaigns and Press Officer, Labour Party, 1998–99; Sen. Prog. Dir, Sunderland and Durham Co., Common Purpose, 1999–2005; Hd, Company and Sector Communications, Global Res. Corporate, HSBC, 2005–06; Hd of Advocacy, 2006–12, Hd of England N and Central, 2012–14, Christian Aid. Mem. (Lab), Newcastle upon Tyne CC, 1999–2004. Contested (Lab): Berwick upon Tweed, 1997; Hexham, 2001; NE Reg., EP, 2019. Chair, NE England Nature Partnership, 2019–.

**BRANNEN, Peter;** Visiting Professor in Management, Southampton University, 2000–09; Director, International Labour Office, London, 1992–2003; *b* 1 Dec. 1941; *s* of Joseph Brannen and Monica Brannen (*née* Cairns); *m* 1966, Julia Mary Morgan; two *s*. *Educ*: Ushaw Coll., Durham; Univ. of Manchester (BA Hons Econs 1964). Account Exec., McCann Erickson Advertising, 1964; Sen. Res. Asst, Univ. of Durham, 1966–69; Senior Research Fellow: Univ. of Bradford, 1969–72; Univ. of Southampton Med. Sch., 1973; Department of Employment: Special Advr, 1974; Chief Res. Officer, 1975–86; Head of Internat. Relns, 1989–91. Visiting Fellow: ANU, 1987; Nuffield Coll., Oxford, 1988; Sen. Vis. Fellow, PSI, 1988. Advr, Solidar, Sri Lanka, 2005–10. Mem., Mgt, Indust. Relns and other cttees, SSRC, 1975–81; Chm., British Workplace Indust. Relns Surveys, 1980–89; Member: Admin. Bd, European Foundn, 1986–92 (Dep. Chm., 1991); Employment Labour and Social Affairs Cttee, OECD, 1990–92; Employment Cttee, Council of Europe, 1990–92. FRSA 2000. Editl Bd, Work, Employment and Society, 1986–90. *Publications*: Entering the World of Work, 1975; The Worker Directors, 1976; Authority and Participation in Industry, 1983; various contribs to anthologies and learned jls on economic sociology. *Recreations*: sailing, gardening, music. *Club*: Royal Southampton Yacht.

**BRANSON, Sir Richard (Charles Nicholas),** Kt 2000; Founder and Chairman, Virgin Retail Group, Virgin Communications, Virgin Travel Group, Virgin Hotels Group, Virgin Direct Ltd, Virgin Bride Ltd, Virgin Net Ltd, Virgin Express Holdings Plc and Virgin Mobile; Life President, Virgin Music Group (sold to Thorn-EMI, 1992); *b* 18 July 1950; *s* of late Edward James Branson and of Evette Huntley Branson (*née* Flindt); *m* 1st, 1969 (marr. diss.); 2nd, 1989, Joan Templeman; one *s* one *d*. *Educ*: Stowe. Editor, Student magazine, 1968–69; set up Student Advisory Centre (now Help), 1970. Founded Virgin Mail-Order Co., 1969, followed by Virgin Retail, Virgin Record Label, Virgin Music Publishing, Virgin Recording Studios; estabd Virgin Record subsids in 25 countries, 1980–86; founded Virgin Atlantic Airways, 1984; Voyager Gp Ltd formed 1986, encompassing interests in travel, clubs and hotels; Virgin Records launched in US, 1987; founded: Virgin Radio, 1993; Virgin Rail Gp Ltd, 1996; Virgin Games, 2004; Virgin Care, 2010; Virgin Sport, 2015. Pres., UK 2000, 1988– (Chm., 1986–88); Dir, Intourist Moscow Ltd, 1988–90. Launched charity, The Healthcare Foundn, 1987. Captain, Atlantic Challenger II, winner Blue Riband for fastest crossing of Atlantic by a ship, 1986; with Per Lindstrand, first to cross Atlantic in hot air balloon, 1987, and Pacific, 1991 (longest flight in hot air balloon, 6700 miles, and fastest speed, 200 mph, 1991). *Publications*: Losing My Virginity: the autobiography, 1998; Business Stripped Bare: adventures of a global entrepreneur, 2008; The Virgin Way, 2014; Finding My Virginity (autobiog.), 2017. *Address*: c/o Virgin Group Ltd, The Battleship Building, 179 Harrow Road, W2 6NB.

**BRANSTON, Gareth Philip;** a District Judge (Magistrates' Courts), since 2013; a Recorder, since 2012; *b* Leicester, 25 March 1973; *s* of Julian Rex Branston and Patricia Mary Branston (*née* Spencer); *m* 2008, Patricia Anne Louise Travers; one *d*. *Educ*: Loughborough Grammar Sch.; Episcopal High Sch., Baton Rouge; Queens' Coll., Cambridge (BA 1995, MA 1999); Inns of Court Sch. of Law. Called to the Bar, Gray's Inn, 1996 (Prince of Wales Schol.; Lionel Blundell Award); in practice as a barrister specialising in criminal law and regulatory law, 1997–2013; Tenant, 23 Essex St, 1999–2013 (Sec. of Chambers, 2005–12); a Dep. Dist Judge (Magistrates' Courts), 2009–13. Pegasus Schol., NZ, 2001. Magistrates' Courts Judicial Engagement Gp, 2015–18; Case Officer Wkg Gp, 2016–17. Tutor, Judicial Coll., 2017–. Member: Cttee, Criminal Bar Assoc., 2001–04; Inns' Conduct Cttee, 2013–17; Panel Mem. of Bar Tribunals and Adjudication Service, 2013; Treas., Thames Valley Bar Mess, 2007–13. *Publications*: (Contrib. Ed.) Archbold Magistrates' Court Criminal Practice, 2016–. *Recreations*: swimming, cycling, badminton, cricket, Leicester Tigers, Toblerone, trance, dance, France. *Address*: c/o Thames Magistrates' Court, 58 Bow Road, E3 4DJ. *Club*: Leicester Tigers Rugby Football.

**BRASH, Dr Donald Thomas;** economic policy consultant and director, since 2007; *b* 24 Sept. 1940; *s* of late Rev. Alan Anderson Brash, OBE and Eljean Ivory Brash; *m* 1st, 1964, Erica Beatty; one *s* one *d*; 2nd, 1989, Je Lan Lee; one *s*. *Educ*: Christchurch Boys' High Sch.; Canterbury Univ., NZ (BA Hist. and Econs 1961; MA 1st Cl. Hons Econs 1962); Australian Nat. Univ. (PhD 1966). IBRD, Washington, 1966–71; Gen. Manager, Broadbank Corp. Ltd, 1971–81; Managing Director: NZ Kiwifruit Authy, 1982–86; Trust Bank Gp, 1986–88; Gov., Reserve Bank of NZ, 1988–2002. MP (Nat.) NZ, 2002–07. Leader of Opposition, and Leader, Nat. Party, NZ, 2003–06. Director: ANZ Nat. Bank, 2007–11; Oceania Dairy, 2009–13; Transpower NZ, 2009–11; Chm., Industrial and Commercial Bank of China (NZ), 2013–. Adjunct Prof. of Banking, Auckland Univ. of Technol., 2009–11. Chm., 2025 Taskforce, 2009–11. Member: Monetary and Econ. Council, 1974–76; NZ Planning Council, 1976–80; Cttee of Inquiry on Inflation Accounting, 1976–77; chaired tax cttees incl. cttee which designed NZ's Goods and Services Tax, 1985–88. Hon. Dr Canterbury, 1999. NZIER–Qantas Econs Award, 1999. *Publications*: New Zealand's Debt Servicing Capacity, 1964; American Investment in Australian Industry, 1966; Incredible Luck, 2014. *Recreation*: growing kiwifruit. *Address*: Apt 311, 184 Symonds Street, Auckland 1010, New Zealand. *W*: www.donbrash.com.

**BRASLAVSKY, Dr Nicholas Justin;** QC 1999; a Recorder, since 2001; a Deputy High Court Judge, Queen's Bench Division, since 2008; *b* 9 Feb. 1959; *s* of late Rev. Cyril and Stella Braslavsky; *m* 1990, Jane Margolis; two *s* one *d*. *Educ*: Blackpool Grammar Sch.; High Pavement Grammar Sch., Nottingham; Univ. of Birmingham (LLB Hons 1979; PhD 1982). Called to the Bar, Inner Temple, 1983; in practice at the Bar, 1983–; Hd, Kings Chambers, Manchester, Birmingham and Leeds, 2010–17. Accredited Mediator, 2013. Hon. Lectr of Law, Univ. of Manchester, 2012–; Hon. Prof. of Law, Univ. of Birmingham, 2016–. *Address*: Kings Chambers, 36 Young Street, Manchester M3 3FT; 5 Park Square East, Leeds LS1 2NE; 3 Paper Buildings, Temple, EC4Y 7EU; Embassy House, 60 Church Street, Birmingham B3 2DJ.

**BRASNETT, John,** CMG 1987; HM Diplomatic Service, retired; Deputy High Commissioner, Bombay, 1985–89; *b* 30 Oct. 1929; *s* of late Norman Vincent Brasnett and of Frances May Brasnett (*née* Hewlett); *m* 1956, Jennifer Ann Reid; one *s* one *d*. *Educ*: Blundell's Sch.; Selwyn Coll., Cambridge (BA). Served Royal Artillery, 1948–49. Colonial Administrative Service, Uganda, 1953–65; retired from HM Overseas CS as Dep. Administrator, Karamoja District, 1965; entered HM Diplomatic Service, 1965; 1st Sec., OECD Delegn, 1968; Dep. High Comr, Freetown, 1970; FCO, 1973; Olympic Attaché, Montreal, 1975–76; Dep. High Comr, Accra, 1977–80; Counsellor (Econ. and Commercial), Ottawa, 1980–85. *Recreations*: reading, photography. *Address*: 8 Croft Way, Sevenoaks, Kent TN13 2JX.

**BRASON, Paul,** PPRP (RP 1994); RWA 2001; artist, portrait painter; President, Royal Society of Portrait Painters, 2000–02; *b* 17 June 1952; *s* of John Ainsley Brason and Audrey (*née* Wheldon). *Educ*: King James I Grammar Sch., Newport, IoW; Camberwell Coll. of Art. Work in many public and private collections incl. NPG, Royal Collection, Windsor

Castle, Bodleian Library, Eton Coll., Mus and Galls Commn, Duke of Westminster, Goodwood House, etc. *Recreation:* early period houses and gardens. *Address:* Blakeleys House, Beechen Cliff, Bath BA2 4QT. *T:* 07799 417255. *Clubs:* Arts, Chelsea Arts.

**BRASSARD, Prof. Gilles,** OC 2013; PhD; FRS 2013; FRSC; Professor of Computer Science, since 1988, and Canada Research Chair in Quantum Information Processing, since 2001, University of Montréal; *b* Montréal, 1955. *Educ:* Univ. of Montréal (BSc Computer Sci. 1972; MSc Computer Sci. 1975); Cornell Univ. (PhD Computer Sci. 1979). University of Montréal: Asst Prof., 1979–83; Associate Prof., 1983–88; Founding Dir, Transdisciplinary Inst. for Quantum Information. E. W. R. Steacie Meml Fellow, Chem. Inst. Canada, 1992; Killam Res. Fellow, 1997; Sen. Fellow, Canadian Inst. for Advanced Res., 2002. Ed.-in-Chief, Jl Cryptol., 1991–97. FRSC 1996; Fellow, Internat. Assoc. Cryptologic Res., 2006. Hon. Dr ETH Zurich, 2010. Steacie Prize, E. W. R. Steacie Meml Fund, Canada, 1994; Prix Marie-Victorin, 2000; (jtly) Rank Prize in Optoelectronics, 2006; Award of Excellence, Natural Scis and Energy Res. Council of Canada, 2006; Gerhard Herzberg Canada Gold Medal for Sci. and Engrg, 2009; Killam Prize for Natural Scis, 2011; (jtly) Wolf Prize in Physics, 2018. *Publications:* (with P. Bratley) Algorithmics: theory and practice, 1987; Modern Cryptology, 1988; (with P. Bratley) Fundamentals of Algorithmics, 1996; contribs to learned jls, incl. Physical Rev. Letters, Jl Cryptol., Jl Computer and Systems Scis, Scientific American, Science. *Address:* Department of Computer Science and Operations Research, University of Montréal, PO Box 6128, Centre-Ville STN, Montréal, QC H3C 3J7, Canada.

**BRASSE, Gillian Denise; Her Honour Judge Gillian Brasse;** a Circuit Judge, since 2008; a Deputy High Court Judge, since 2011; *b* London, 19 June 1953; *d* of late Robert Brasse and Iris Brasse; *m* 1986, Patrick Michael Joseph O'Connor, *qv*; two *d. Educ:* Varndean Sch. for Girls, Brighton; Liverpool Univ. (BA Hons 1975). Called to the Bar, Gray's Inn, 1977, Bencher, 2018; Dep. Dist Judge, 1996–2004; Recorder, 2002–08. Jt Hd of Chambers, 14 Gray's Inn Sq., 2004–08. *Recreations:* cinema, theatre, music, pilates, travel. *Address:* Central Family Court, First Avenue House, 42–49 High Holborn, WC1V 6NP.

**BRASSE, His Honour Glenn Clifford;** a Circuit Judge, 2006–16; *b* 16 June 1949; *s* of late Robert Brasse and Iris Brasse; *m* 1974, Valerie Hauser, PhD; three *s. Educ:* Brighton, Hove and Sussex Grammar Sch.; LSE (LLB Hons). Called to the Bar, Middle Temple, 1972; Actg Stipendiary Magistrate, 1989–94; a Dep. Dist Judge, 1995; a Dist Judge, Principal Registry, Family Div., High Ct of Justice, 1995–2006; a Recorder, SE Circuit, 2002–06; Judge, Mental Health Rev. Tribunal (and Restricted Patients Panel), 2011–17. Writer (screenplay), Sanhedrin, 2002. *Publications:* (contrib.) Evidence in Family Proceedings, 1999; (contrib.) Family Law in Practice, 2006; contrib. numerous articles to Family Law. *Recreations:* sport (cycling, squash, mountain walking, ski-ing), classical guitar, drawing and painting, reading, cinema, opera.

**BRASSEY,** family name of **Baron Brassey of Apethorpe**.

**BRASSEY OF APETHORPE,** 4th Baron *cr* 1938, of Apethorpe; **Edward Brassey**; Bt 1922; *b* 9 March 1964; *o s* of 3rd Baron Brassey of Apethorpe, OBE and Myrna Elizabeth Brassey (*née* Baskervyle-Glegg); *S* father, 2015; *m* 2003, Joanna Clare Pardoe; one *s* one *d. Educ:* Eton. Grenadier Guards. Partner, Strutt & Parker, 2013–. *Heir: s* Hon. Christian Brassey, *b* 23 Dec. 2003.

**BRATHWAITE, James Everett,** CBE 2001; Executive Chairman, DRENL Ltd, since 2011; *b* 31 March 1953; *s* of James and Louise Brathwaite; *m* 1977, Barbara Worby; one *s* four *d. Educ:* Sheffield Univ. (BSc Hons Physiol. and Zool.); Open Univ. (Dip. Competent Mgt). Graduate trainee acct, then Sales Trainer, Beecham Pharmaceuticals UK Ltd, 1975–79; a Product Manager, then a Mktg Manager, Antibiotic Mktg Strategy gp, Bayer Pharmaceuticals UK Ltd, 1979–82; founder and Chief Exec., VPS, subseq. Epic Multimedia Group plc, 1982–97; founder Dir and Chief Exec., XL Entertainment plc, 1997–2012; consultant and CEO, Future Gp Ltd, 1997–98; Chairman: Floella Benjamin Productions Ltd, 1997–2002 (Dir, 1997–2002); Renga Media Ltd, 2001–09; SE England Develt Agency, 2002–09; Community Alerts Ltd, 2002–12; Morgan Everett Ltd, 2003–12; Splash FM, 2004–; Brighton and Hove Radio Ltd, 2005–12; non-exec. Chairman: Business Link Sussex Ltd, 1995–2002; X-Tension Ltd, 1996–98 (Dir); Citizen TV Ltd, 1998–2002; BookLines plc, 2000–01; SEAL Ltd, 2000–08; consultant and non-exec. Dir, Amplicon LiveLine Ltd, 1997–99; non-executive Director: Sussex TEC Ltd, subseq. Sussex Enterprise Ltd, 1994–2002; Nat. Business Angels Network, 2003–04; Dir, RSTV, 2007–. Advr on multimedia industry to DTI, 1989; Member: Caribbean Adv. Gp, FCO, 1998–2003 (Treas., 1998–2003); Nat. Business Link Accreditation Adv. Bd, 1999–2000; Small Business Council, 2000–04; Americas Advrs Gp, Trade Partners UK, subseq. UK Trade and Investment, 2001–03; Bd, Envmt Agency, 2005–11. Founder Director: Brit. Interactive Media Assoc. (formerly Brit. Interactive Video Assoc.), 1985–90 (Chm., 1989–90); Wired Sussex, 1996–2002; Dir, Internat. CD-i Assoc., 1993–96. Council Member: Univ. of Sussex, 1995–2001 (Mem. of Ct, 2002–07); Univ. of Greenwich, 2002–12; C&G, 2006–; Business Rep., Bd, Brighton & Hove Sixth Form Coll., 1995–99 (Chm., Finance Cttee, 1995–99). Board Member: Rockinghorse Charity, 1994–96; Arundel Fest., 1998–2002 (Chm., 1999–2002); Farnham Castle Trustees Ltd, 2004–13; Bd of Trustees, Public Catalogue Foundn, 2006–10. Mem., World Traders' Co., 2007–. Hon. Consul for S Africa in SE England, 2007–. Hon. Fellow, UC Chichester, 2003. Mem., BAFTA; MInstD. Hon. FCGI 2006. Hon. Dr Business Southampton Solent, 2008. *Recreations:* the arts, music, ski-ing, watching cricket, football (Manchester United) and Rugby. *Address:* Church Farm House, Rectory Lane, Angmering, W Sussex BN16 4JU. *T:* (01903) 772648, *Fax:* (01903) 859863. *E:* james@brathwaite.net.

**BRATTON, Prof. Jacqueline Susan,** DPhil; Professor of Theatre and Cultural History, Royal Holloway, University of London, 1992–2013, now Emeritus (Head of Drama and Theatre, 1994–2001); *b* 23 April 1945; *d* of Jack Stanley Bratton and Doris Nellie Bratton (*née* Reynolds); partner, Gilli Bush-Bailey. *Educ:* St Anne's, Coll., Oxford (BA 1966; DPhil 1969). Lectr, 1969–83, Reader in English Literature, 1983–84, Bedford Coll., Univ. of London; Reader in Theatre and Cultural History, RHBNC, 1984–92. Series Editor, Shakespeare in Production, 1994–2009; Editor, Nineteenth Century Theatre, 1996–2001. Hon. Fellow, RHUL, 2016. *Publications:* The Victorian Popular Ballad, 1975; The Impact of Victorian Children's Fiction, 1981; (ed) Music Hall: Performance and Style, 1986; King Lear: a stage history edition, 1987; Acts of Supremacy, 1991; (ed) Melodrama: stage picture screen, 1994; New Readings in Theatre History, 2003; The Victorian Clown, 2006; The Making of the West End Stage: marriage, management and the mapping of gender in London, 1830–1870, 2011; (ed) Dickensian Dramas, 2017. *Address:* Department of Drama, Royal Holloway, University of London, Egham TW20 0EX.

**BRATZA, Sir Nicolas (Dušan),** Kt 1998; a Judge of the High Court, Queen's Bench Division, 1998–2012; Judge, 1998–2012, and President, 2011–12, European Court of Human Rights (Section President, 1998–2000, and 2001–07; Vice-President of the Court, 2007–11); *b* 3 March 1945; *s* of late Milan Bratza, concert violinist, and Hon. Margaret Bratza (*née* Russell). *Educ:* Wimbledon Coll.; Brasenose Coll., Oxford (BA 1st Cl. Hons, MA; Hon. Fellow 2011). Instructor, Univ. of Pennsylvania Law Sch., 1967–68; called to Bar, Lincoln's Inn, 1969 (Hardwicke and Droop Schol.), Bencher, 1993; Jun. Counsel to the Crown, Common Law, 1979–88; QC 1988; a Recorder, 1993–98; UK Mem., European Commn of Human Rights, 1993–98. Member: Bd, British Inst. of Human Rights, 2004– (Gov., 1985–2004; Vice-Chm., 1989–98; Pres., 2013–14; Chm. Bd, 2014–); Adv. Council, British Inst. of Internat. and Comparative Law, 2006– (Mem., Bd of Mgt, 1999–2006); Bd, Internat. Service for Human Rights, 2013–19; Internat. Commn of Jurists, 2013– (Mem., Exec. Cttee, 2018–); Bd, Helen Bamber Foundn, 2015–. Chairman: Internat. Adv. Panel on Ukraine, 2014–15; Parly Assembly Investigation Body against Corruption, 2017–18. Patron: Peace Brigade Internat. UK, 2013–; Centre for Study of Human Rights, Univ. of Strathclyde, 2014–. Mem. Editl Bd, European Human Rights Law Review, 1996–2016. Hon. Bencher, King's Inns, Dublin, 2012. Hon. Prof., Sch. of Law, Univ. of Nottingham, 2013–16. Mem. Bd, Surrey Hills Internat. Music Fest., 2013–17. Ambassador, Toynbee Hall 2013–. DU Essex, 2005; Hon. LLD Glasgow, 2007. *Publications:* (jtly) Contempt of Court, and Crown Proceedings, in Halsbury's Laws of England, 4th edn. *Recreations:* music, cricket. *Clubs:* Garrick, MCC.

**BRAUDE, Prof. Peter Riven,** OBE 2015; PhD; FRCOG; FMedSci; FRSB; Professor and Head of Department of Women's Health (formerly Division of Women's and Children's Health), King's College London School of Medicine (formerly Guy's, King's and St Thomas' School of Medicine, King's College, London) (formerly Head of Department of Obstetrics and Gynaecology, United Medical and Dental Schools of Guy's and St Thomas' Hospitals), 1991–2011, now Professor Emeritus of Obstetrics and Gynaecology; *b* Johannesburg, 29 May 1948; *s* of Dr Barnett Braude and Sylvia (*née* Grumberg); *m* 1973, Beatrice Louise Roselaar; two *s. Educ:* Univ. of Witwatersrand (BSc 1968; MB BCh 1972); Jesus Coll., Cambridge (MA 1975; PhD 1981). DPMSA 1983; MRCOG 1982, FRCOG 1993; FRSB (FSB 2011). Lectr in Physiology and Pharmacology, Univ. of Witwatersrand Med. Sch., 1973; Demonstrator, Dept of Anatomy, Univ. of Cambridge, 1974–79; sen. house officer appts, St Mary's Hosp., London and Addenbrooke's Hosp., Cambridge, 1979–81; Sen. Res. Associate, Dept of Obstetrics and Gynaecol., Univ. of Cambridge, 1981–83; Registrar in Obstetrics and Gynaecol., Rosie Maternity Hosp., Cambridge, 1983–85; University of Cambridge: Clinical Lectr in Obstetrics and Gynaecol., 1985–88; MRC Clinical Res. Consultant, Clinical Sch., 1988–89; Consultant and Sen. Lectr, Dept of Obstetrics and Gynaecol., 1989–90; Clinical Dir for Women's Services, 1993–94, Dir, Assisted Conception Unit and Fertility Service, 1993–99, Dir, Centre for Pre-implantation Genetic Diagnosis, 1999–2011, Guy's and St Thomas' Hosp. NHS Trust. Member: HFEA, 1999–2004 (Inspector, 1991–99; Mem., expert panel review of scientific methods to avoid mitochondrial disease, 2011, 2013, 2014, 2015); Mgt Cttee, UK Stem Cell Bank, 2008–10; Adv. Bd on the Safety of Blood Tissues and Organs, DoH, 2008–14; Nuffield Council on Bioethics wkg gp on Novel techniques for prevention of mitochondrial DNA disorders, 2012; Internat. Panel of Experts, Bioethics Adv. Cttee, Singapore, 2014–; Chairman: Sci. Adv. Cttee, 2004–07, Expert Gp on Umbilical Cord Blood Banking, 2006, RCOG; Expert Adv. Gp on multiple births after IVF, HFEA (report, One Child at a Time), 2006. Exec. Sec., Assoc. Profs of Obstetrics and Gynaecol., 1993–95. Mem., Med. Adv. Bd, Tommy's Campaign, 1993–99. Member, Editorial Board: Molecular Human Reproduction, 1992–98; Stem Cells, 2005–08. FMedSci 2006. *Publications:* Obstetric and Gynaecologic Dermatology, 1995, 2nd edn 2002; ABC of Subfertility, 2004; (jtly) Preimplantation Genetic Diagnosis in Clinical Practice, 2014; contribs to scientific jls on develt of the human embryo *in vitro*, assisted conception techniques, treatment of infertility, ethics and politics of new reproductive technologies and preimplantation diagnosis, human embryonic stem cells and mitochondrial replacement technology. *Recreations:* narrowboater (The Slowgoose), Egyptology, geology, ski-ing, music, Apple Macs. *Address:* King's College London Division of Women's Health, 10th Floor NW, St Thomas' Hospital, Westminster Bridge Road, SE1 7EH. *T:* (020) 7188 4138. *E:* peter.braude@kcl.ac.uk.

**BRAVERMAN, Sue-Ellen Cassiana, (Suella);** MP (C) Fareham, since 2015; *b* London, 3 April 1980; *d* of Chris Fernandes and Uma Fernandes; *m* 2018, Rael Braverman. *Educ:* Heathfield Sch., Pinner; Queens' Coll., Cambridge (BA Hons Law 2002); Panthéon-Sorbonne Univ., Paris (LLM 2003); BVC 2005. Called to the Bar, Middle Temple, 2005; admitted to State Bar, NY, 2006; in practice as barrister specialising in planning, judicial review, immigration, No5 Chambers; Mem., Attorney Gen.'s C Panel of Treasury Counsel, 2010–15. PPS to HM Treasury, 2017–18; Parly Under-Sec. of State, Dept for Exiting the EU, 2018. Mem., Educn Select Cttee, 2015–17. Parly Patron, Westminster Strategic Studies Gp, 2015–. Founder and Trustee, Africa Justice Foundn, 2010–14. Co-Founder and Gov., Michaela Community Sch., 2011–. *Address:* House of Commons, SW1A 0AA. *T:* (020) 7219 3000. *E:* suella@suellabraverman.co.uk.

**BRAVERY, Katy Louise B.;** *see* Bowen-Bravery.

**BRAVINER ROMAN, Stephen Thomas;** Director General, Government Legal Department (formerly Treasury Solicitor's Department), since 2014; *b* Leeds, 25 Oct. 1968; *s* of Dennis Braviner and Elizabeth Ann Braviner (*née* Kench); *m* 2001, Veronica Roman; two *d. Educ:* Harrington High Sch., Leeds; Bradford Coll. (BA Hons 1st Cl. Orgn Studies); Leeds Poly. (CPE (Law)); London Sch. of Econs (LLM). Called to the Bar, Gray's Inn, 1992, Bencher, 2017; Legal Advr, EC Litigation, Treasury Solicitor's Dept, 1994–96, DfT, then DETR, 1996–99; Legal Advr, 1999–2001, Dep. Dir, NI Office Team, 2001–02, Legal Advrs' Br., Home Office; Sen. Legal Advr, Attorney Gen's Office, 2002–05; Dep. Dir, Border Control and Counter-terrorism, Legal Advrs' Br., Home Office, 2005–08; Dir of Legal Services (Business, Consumers, Employment and Skills), BERR, later BIS, 2008–11; Legal Adviser: SOCA, 2011–13; DCLG, 2013–14. Co. Sec. and Trustee, Bliss, 2009–13. *Recreations:* spending time with my family, a good read, history. *Address:* Government Legal Department, 102 Petty France, SW1H 9AJ.

**BRAY, Angela Lavinia;** *b* 13 Oct. 1953; *d* of Benedict and Patricia Bray. *Educ:* Downe House, Newbury; St Andrews Univ. (MA Hons Medieval Hist.). Presenter, British Forces Broadcasting, Gibraltar, 1979–80; presenter, producer and reporter, LBC Radio, 1980–88; Hd, Broadcasting Unit, Cons. Central Office, 1989–91; Press Officer, Rt Hon. John Major's Leadership Campaign, Nov. 1990; Press Sec. to Chm., Conservative Party, 1991–92; Public Affairs Consultant, 1992–2000. Mem. (C) West Central, London Assembly, GLA, 2000–08. Contested (C) E Ham, 1997. MP (C) Ealing Central and Acton, 2010–15; contested (C) same seat, 2015. PPS to Minister for Cabinet Office and Paymaster Gen., 2010–12. Mem., Culture, Media and Sport Select Cttee, 2012–15. Pres., Kensington and Chelsea Cons. Pol Forum, 2000–03; Vice Pres., Hammersmith and Fulham Cons. Assoc., 2000–08. Mem. Bd, VisitBritain, 2016–19. *Recreations:* tennis, music, history, walking my dogs. *Club:* Carlton.

**BRAY, Prof. Julia Margaret,** DPhil; FRAS; Laudian Professor of Arabic, University of Oxford, since 2012; Fellow, St John's College, Oxford, since 2012; *b* Cambridge, 28 Sept. 1952; *yr d* of John Bray and Barbara Bray (*née* Jacobs). *Educ:* Coll. Sévigné, Paris; St Hilda's Coll., Oxford (BA Oriental Studies 1974); St Cross Coll., Oxford (DPhil 1984). Archivist, India Office Liby and Records, British Acad. Oriental Documents Cttee, 1976–82; Lecturer in Arabic: Univ. of Manchester, 1983–87; Univ. of Edinburgh, 1989–92; Sen. Lectr in Arabic, Univ. of St Andrews, 1996–2003; Professeur de littérature arabe médiévale, Univ. Paris 8 Vincennes-St Denis, 2003–12. Vis. Lectr, St Antony's Coll. ME Centre, Oxford, 1994–95; James Mew Sen. Res. Fellow in Arabic, Faculty of Oriental Studies, Univ. of

Oxford, 1994–96; Dir de Recherches invitée, Ecole des Hautes Etudes en Sciences Sociales, Paris, 2003. Member and Associate Member: UMR 8167 Orient et Méditerranée, 2004–; EA 1571 Centre de recherches historiques: histoire des pouvoirs, savoirs, sociétés, 2009–. Mem., Union Européenne des Arabisants et Islamisants; Sch. of 'Abbasid Studies. FRAS 1976; Fellow, Amer. Oriental Soc. *Publications:* The Arabic Documents in the Archives of the British Political Agency, Kuwait, 1904–1949, 1982; (ed jtly) The Cambridge History of Arabic Literature: 'Abbasid Belles-Lettres, 1990; Media Arabic, 1993; (ed) Writing and Representation in Medieval Islam, 2006. *Recreations:* the arts, the country, family and friends, Middle Eastern textiles. *Address:* St John's College, Oxford OX1 3JP.

**BRAY, Prof. Kenneth Noel Corbett,** PhD; FRS 1991; CEng; Hopkinson and Imperial Chemical Industries Professor of Applied Thermodynamics, 1985–97, now Emeritus, and Fellow of Girton College, 1985–97, Cambridge University; *b* 19 Nov. 1929; *s* of Harold H. Bray and Effie E. Bray; *m* 1958, Shirley Maureen Culver; two *s* one *d*. *Educ:* Univ. of Cambridge (BA); Univ. of Southampton (PhD); MSE Princeton; CEng; MRAeS; MAIAA. Engr in Research Dept, Handley Page Aircraft, 1955–56; University of Southampton, 1956–85: Dean, Faculty of Engrg and Applied Science, 1975–78; Head, Dept of Aeronautics and Astronautics, 1982–85. Vis. appt, Avco-Everett Res. Lab., Mass, USA, 1961–62; Vis. Prof., MIT, 1966–67; Vis. Res. Engr, Univ. of California, San Diego, 1975, 1983. *Publications:* on topics in gas dynamics, chemically reacting flows, molecular energy transfer processes and combustion. *Recreations:* walking, wood carving, gardening. *Address:* 23 De Freville Avenue, Cambridge CB4 1HW.

**BRAY, Michael Peter;** Partner, Grimaldi Studio Legale, since 2015; *b* 27 March 1947; *s* of William Charles Bray and Ivy Isobel (*née* Ellison); *m* 1st, 1970, Elizabeth Ann Harrington (marr. diss. 2007); two *d*; 2nd, 2010, Gabrielle Taylo. *Educ:* Caterham Sch.; Liverpool Univ. (LLB 1969). Joined Coward Chance, subseq. Clifford Chance, 1970, Partner, 1976–2012; Global Head, Clifford Chance Finance and Capital Markets Practice, 1995–2000; CEO, 2000–03; Consultant, 2012–15. Junior Achievement Worldwide: Mem. Bd, 2003–; Vice-Chair, 2007–10; Chair, 2010–13; Gov., 2010–; Chm., Governance and Nominations Cttee, 2015–. *Recreations:* golf, ski-ing, opera, theatre. *Address:* Nuthurst, Woodland Drive, Ockley, Surrey RH5 5HZ. *T:* 07785 700185. *E:* mike.b.1@hotmail.co.uk.

**BRAY, His Honour Richard Winston Atterton;** a Circuit Judge, 1993–2014; *b* 10 April 1945; *s* of late Winston Bray, CBE and Betty Atterton Bray (*née* Miller); *m* 1978, Judith Elizabeth Margaret Ferguson; one *s* three *d*. *Educ:* Rugby Sch.; Corpus Christi Coll., Oxford (BA). Called to the Bar, Middle Temple, 1970; practised on Midland and Oxford Circuit; Asst Recorder, 1983–87; Recorder, 1987–93. *Recreations:* Real tennis, golf, gardening, bell-ringing. *Clubs:* MCC; Leamington Real Tennis; Aspley Guise Golf.

**BRAY, Dr Xavier;** Director, Wallace Collection, since 2016; *b* 1 May 1972; *s* of Nicholas Bray and Josette Dacosta; *m* 2004, Minna Moore Ede; two *s* one *d*. *Educ:* Trinity Coll., Dublin (PhD 1999). Asst Curator, Nat. Gall., London, 1998–2000; Curator of Paintings, Mus. of Fine Arts, Bilbao, 2000–02; Asst Curator of 17th and 18th Century Eur. Paintings, Nat. Gall., 2002–10; Holly and Arturo Melosi Chief Curator, Dulwich Picture Gall., 2011–16. *Publications:* (contrib.) Oxford Dictionary of Art and Artists, 1997; (contrib.) Goya and 18th Century Spanish Painting, 1999; (contrib.) Goya, 2000; (contrib.) Folio Society Book of the 100 Greatest Paintings, 2001; contribs to Burlington Mag., Master Drawings, L'Objet d'Art, Dossier de l'Art, Apollo, Ars Mag. *Recreations:* opera singing, flamenco and Basque singing, travelling, dance, mime, yoga. *Address:* Wallace Collection, Hertford House, Manchester Square, W1U 3BN. *T:* (020) 7563 9512. *E:* xavier.bray@wallacecollection.org.

**BRAYBROOKE, 11th Baron** *cr* 1788; **Richard Ralph Neville;** company director; *b* London, 10 June 1977; *s* of late George Neville and of Patricia Bernadette Neville (*née* Quinn); *S* kinsman, 2017; *m* 2015, Selina Anne Kelway-Bamber; one *s* one *d*. *Educ:* St Edward's Sch., Oxford. Hereditary Visitor of Magdalene College, Cambridge. Patron of one living. *Recreations:* gardening, gastronomy, genealogy. *Heir: s* Edward Alfred Neville, *b* 1 Dec. 2015. *Address:* London, SW14. *E:* richard@brandlink.co.uk.

**BRAYBROOKE, Rev. Marcus Christopher Rossi;** Joint President, World Congress of Faiths, since 1997 (Chairman, 1978–83 and 1992–99; Vice-President, 1986–97); *b* 16 Nov. 1938; *s* of late Lt-Col Arthur Rossi Braybrooke and Marcia Nona Braybrooke; *m* 1964, Mary Elizabeth Walker, JP, BSc, CQSW; one *s* one *d*. *Educ:* Cranleigh School; Magdalene College, Cambridge (BA, MA); Madras Christian College; Wells Theological College; King's College, London (MPhil). Curate, St Michael's, Highgate, 1964–67; Team Vicar, Strood Clergy Team, 1967–73; Rector, Swainswick, Langridge, Woolley, 1973–79; Dir of Training, Dio. of Bath and Wells, 1979–84; Hon. priest-in-charge, Christ Church, Bath, 1984–91; Exec. Director, Council of Christians and Jews, 1984–87; Preb., Wells Cathedral, 1990–93; Chaplain, Chapel of St Mary Magdalene, Bath, 1992–93; non-stipendiary priest, Marsh and Toot Baldon, Dorchester Team Ministry, Oxford, 1993–2005. Chm., Internat. Interfaith Orgns Co-ordinating Cttee, 1990–93, World Congress of Faiths. Trustee: Interfaith Centre, 1993–2000 (Patron, 2001–12); Internat. Peace Council, 1995–2000; Council for Parlt of World Religions, 1995–2001; Three Faiths Forum, 2001–12; Sir Sigmund Sternberg Charitable Foundn, 2006–; Patron, Utd Religions Initiative, 2001–12. Peace Councillor, 2000–14. Examng Chaplain to Bishop of Bath and Wells, 1984–88. Editor: World Faiths Insight, 1976–91; Common Ground, 1987–93. DD Lambeth, 2004. Sir Sigmund Sternberg Award for contributions to Christian-Jewish relations, 1992; Kashi Humanitarian Award, Kashi Ashram, Fla, 2001; Interfaith Visionary Award, Temple of Understanding, NY, 2010; Man of the Year Award, Ramanuja Mission Trust, Chennai, 2013. *Publications:* Together to the Truth, 1971; The Undiscovered Christ of Hinduism, 1973; Interfaith Worship, 1974; Interfaith Organizations: a historical directory, 1980; Time to Meet, 1990; Wide Embracing Love, 1990; Children of One God, 1991; Pilgrimage of Hope, 1992; Stepping Stones to a Global Ethic, 1992; Be Reconciled, 1992; (ed with Tony Bayfield) Dialogue with a Difference, 1992; Love Without Limit, 1995; Faith in a Global Age, 1995; How to Understand Judaism, 1995; A Wider Vision: a history of the World Congress of Faiths, 1996; The Wisdom of Jesus, 1997; (contrib.) The Miracles of Jesus, 1997; (ed with Jean Potter) All in Good Faith, 1997; (contrib.) The Journeys of St Paul, 1997; The Explorers' Guide to Christianity, 1998; (ed with Peggy Morgan) Testing the Global Ethic, 1999; Christian-Jewish Dialogue: the next steps, 2000; Learn to Pray, 2001; (ed) Bridge of Stars, 2001; What Can We Learn from Hinduism, 2002; What Can We Learn from Islam, 2002; (ed) Lifelines, 2002; (ed) One Thousand World Prayers, 2003; 365 Meditations for a Peaceful Heart and a Peaceful World, 2004; (with Kamran Mofid) Sustaining the Common Good, 2005; A Heart for the World: the interfaith alternative, 2006; (ed) 365 Meditations and Inspirations on Love and Peace, 2006; Beacons of the Light, 2009; Meeting Jews, 2010; Peace in our Hearts, Peace in our World, 2012; Hinduism: a Christian approach, 2012; Islam: a Christian approach, 2012; Christians and Jews Building Bridges, 2012; Widening Vision: the World Congress of Faiths and the Interfaith Movement, 2013; Christianity: an explorer's guide, 2014; Sikhism: a Christian approach, 2018; Faiths Together for the Future, 2018; contrib. to various theol books and jls incl. Theology, Modern Believing (formerly The Modern Churchman), The Tablet, Expository Times, Church Times, Church of England Newspaper, Faith and Freedom, Interreligious Insight, Jl Ecumenical Studies, The Interfaith Observer, Dialogue and Alliance. *Recreations:* gardening, swimming, travel, photography. *Address:* 17 Courtiers Green, Clifton Hampden, Abingdon OX14 3EN.

**BRAYE, Baroness** (8th in line), *cr* 1529, of Eaton Braye, Co. Bedford; **Mary Penelope Aubrey-Fletcher;** DL; *b* 28 Sept. 1941; *d* of 7th Baron Braye and Dorothea (*d* 1994), *yr d* of late Daniel C. Donoghue, Philadelphia; *S* father, 1985; *m* 1981, Lt-Col Edward Henry Lancelot Aubrey-Fletcher, Grenadier Guards. *Educ:* Assumption Convent, Hengrave Hall; Univ. of Warwick. Pres., Blaby Cons. Assoc., 1986–; Dep. Pres., Northants Red Cross, 1983–92; Chm. School Cttee, St Andrew's Occupational Therapy School, 1988–93. Governor: St Andrew's Hosp., Northampton, 1978–; Three Shires Hosp., Northampton, 1983–. High Sheriff of Northants, 1983; JP South Northants, 1981–86; DL Northants 1998. *Heir:* cousin Linda Kathleen Fothergill [*b* 2 May 1930, *née* Browne; *m* 1965, Comdr Christopher Henry Fothergill (*d* 2014), RN; two *s*]. *Address:* The Garden House, The Avenue, Flore, Northampton NN7 4LZ.

**BRAYFIELD, Celia Frances;** author; Associate Reader in Creative Writing, Brunel University, since 2015 (Senior Lecturer, 2005–06; Reader, 2007–15); Senior Lecturer in Creative Writing, Bath Spa University, since 2010; *d* of Felix Francis Brayfield and Helen (Ada Ellen) Brayfield; one *d*. *Educ:* St Paul's Girls' Sch.; Univ. of Grenoble; Brunel Univ. (PhD 2016). Feature writer, Daily Mail, 1969–71; media columnist, Evening Standard, 1974–82; TV critic, The Times, 1984–88; columnist, Sunday Telegraph, 1988–90; feature writer, The Times, 1998–; contrib. to other pubns. Mem., Cttee of Mgt, NCOPF, 1989–2006. Mem., Cttee of Mgt, Soc. of Authors, 1995–98; Dir, Nat. Acad. Writing, 1999–2003; Chm., Higher Educn Cttee, Nat. Assoc. of Writers in Educn, 2015–16. Mem., Benchmark Statement Gp Creative Writing, QAA, 2015–16. SFHEA 2016. *Publications:* Glitter: the truth about fame, 1985; Bestseller, 1996; Deep France, 2004; Arts Reviews, 2008; Writing Historical Fiction, 2013; Rebel Writers: the accidental feminists, 2019; *fiction:* Pearls, 1986; The Prince, 1990; White Ice, 1993; Harvest, 1993; Getting Home, 1998; Sunset, 1999; Heartswap, 2000; Mister Fabulous and Friends, 2003; Wild Weekend, 2004. *Recreations:* family life, the arts. *Address:* c/o Curtis Brown Ltd, Haymarket House, 28/29 Haymarket, SW1Y 4SP. *T:* (020) 7396 4400. *Club:* Chelsea Arts.

**BRAYNE, Prof. Carol Elspeth Goodeve,** CBE 2017; MD; FRCP, FFPH, FMedSci; Professor of Public Health Medicine, since 2001, and Director, Cambridge Institute of Public Health, since 2008, University of Cambridge; Fellow, Darwin College, Cambridge, since 1995; *b* 6 July 1957; *d* of Thomas and Audrey Brayne; *m* 1984, Paul Calloway; two *s* two *d*. *Educ:* Royal Free Hosp. Sch. of Medicine, London Univ. (MB BS, MD); London Sch. of Hygiene and Tropical Medicine (MSc). FFPH (FFPHM 1998); FRCP 2000. Lectr in Epidemiology, Cambridge Univ., 1991–2001. Hon. Consultant in Public Health Medicine: Cambs HA, 1991–2002; Cambs (formerly Hunts) PCT, 2002–13; Public Health England, 2013–. FMedSci 2014. *Address:* Cambridge Institute of Public Health, Forvie Site, Cambridge Biomedical Campus, Cambridge CB2 0SR; Darwin College, Cambridge CB3 9EU.

**BRAZIER, Helen;** Head of RNIB National Library Service, 2007–13; *b* 15 Feb. 1957; *d* of late John David Brazier and Nancy (*née* Lloyd); *m* Paul Sutcliffe. *Educ:* Newnham Coll., Cambridge (MA); Sheffield Univ. (MA). FCLIP. Various posts, 1981–97, incl. UN Volunteer Librarian, 1990–92; Liby Services Dir, 1997–2001, Chief Exec., 2002–06, Nat. Liby for the Blind. Co-ordinator, Share the Vision, 2007–13 (Dir, 2001–07). Non-exec. Dir, Henshaws Soc. for Blind People, 2014–. *Publications:* contrib. various articles to jls. *Recreations:* walking, studio pottery, travel, reading.

**BRAZIER, Prof. John Edward,** PhD; Professor of Health Economics, since 1999, and Dean, School of Health and Related Research, since 2017, University of Sheffield; *b* Caterham, Surrey, 30 Aug. 1961; *s* of Ronald Edward Brazier and Betty Margaret Brazier; three *s*; partner, Cindy Louise Cooper. *Educ:* Purley High Sch. for Boys; Woodcote High Sch.; Univ. of Exeter (BA Econs); Univ. of York (MSc Health Econs); Univ. of Sheffield (PhD 1998). Res. Asst, Dept of Community Medicine, St Thomas' Hosp., United Med. and Dental Sch., Univ. of London, 1984–87; Res. Fellow, York Health Econ. Consortium, Univ. of York, 1987–89; University of Sheffield: Lectr, Med. Care Res. Unit, 1989–93; Dir, Sheffield Health Econs Gp, 1993–2004, Dep. Dir, Res., 2004–10, Dir, Res., 2010–17, Sch. of Health and Related Res. *Publications:* (jtly) Methods for Health Services Research: a state of the art guide, 1998; (jtly) Methods in Health Technology Assessment, 2001; (jtly) Measuring and Valuing Health for Economic Evaluation, 2007, 2nd edn 2017; over 250 scientific papers. *Recreations:* Buddhism, gardening, walking in hills of Derbyshire. *Address:* School of Health and Related Research, University of Sheffield, Regent Court, 30 Regent Street, Sheffield S1 4DA. *T:* (0114) 222 0726. *E:* j.e.brazier@sheffield.ac.uk.

**BRAZIER, Sir Julian (William Hendy),** Kt 2017; TD; non-executive Chairman, Pathway Risk Management, since 2017; *b* 24 July 1953; *s* of Lt-Col P. H. Brazier; *m* 1984, Katharine Elizabeth, *d* of Brig. P. M. Blagden; three *s* (incl. twins). *Educ:* Wellington Coll.; Brasenose Coll., Oxford (schol. in maths; MA); London Business Sch. Chm., Oxford Univ. Cons. Assoc., 1974. Charter Consolidated, 1975–84, Sec., Exec. Cttee of Bd, 1981–84; management consultant to industry, H. B. Maynard, internat. management consultants, 1984–87. Contested (C) Berwick-upon-Tweed, 1983. MP (C) Canterbury, 1987–2017. PPS to Minister of State, HM Treasury, 1990–92, to Sec. of State for Employment, 1992–93; an Opposition Whip, 2001–02; Opposition front bench spokesman: for work and pensions, 2002–03; for internat. devel and overseas trade, 2004–05; for transport (aviation and shipping), 2005–10; Parly Under-Sec. of State, MoD, 2014–16. Mem., Defence Select Cttee, 1997–2001 and 2010–14; Chm., All-Party Reserves and Cadets Gp, 2008–14; Co-Chairman: All-Party Adoption and Fostering Gp, 2000–10; All-Party Adventure and Recreation in Society Gp, 2003–10; All-Party Ports and Maritime Gp, 2010–14; Vice Chm., Cons. Backbench Defence Cttee, 1993–97; Sec., Cons. Backbench Finance Cttee, 1990. Vice-Chm., Ind. Commn on Reserve Forces, 2010–11. Served 13 yrs as an officer in TA, incl. 5 yrs with 21 SAS. *Publications:* pamphlets on defence, economic policy, social security and family issues. *Recreations:* history, science, philosophy, bicycling.

**BRAZIER, Prof. Margaret Rosetta,** OBE 1997; FMedSci; FBA 2014; Professor of Law, University of Manchester, 1990–2018, now Emeritus; *b* 2 Nov. 1950; *d* of Leslie Jacobs and Mary Jacobs (*née* Pickering); *m* 1974, Rodney John Brazier, *qv*; one *d*. *Educ:* Univ. of Manchester (LLB 1971). Called to the Bar, Middle Temple, 1973. University of Manchester: Lectr, 1971–83, Sen. Lectr, 1983–89, Reader, 1989–90, in Law; Dir of Legal Studies, Centre for Social Ethics and Policy, 1987; a founder Dir, Inst. of Medicine, Law and Bioethics, 1996. Chairman: Animal Procedures Cttee, 1993–98; Review of Surrogacy, DoH, 1997–98; Chair: NHS Retained Organs Commn, 2001–04; Nuffield Council Working Pty Critical Care Decision Making in Fetal and Neonatal Medicine, 2004–06; Mem., Nuffield Council on Bioethics, 1995. Leverhulme Emeritus Fellow, 2018–Sept. 2020. FMedSci 2007. Hon. QC 2008. *Publications:* Medicine, Patients and the Law, 1987, (with E. Cave) 6th edn 2016; (jtly) Protecting the Vulnerable: autonomy and health care, 1991; (Gen. Ed.) Clerk & Lindsell on Torts, 17th edn 1995; (ed) Street on Torts, 8th edn to 10th edn 1998; (jtly) Bioethics and Medicine in the Theatre of the Criminal Process, 2013. *Recreations:* literature, theatre, cooking. *Address:* School of Law, University of Manchester, Manchester M13 9PL. *T:* (0161) 275 3593.

**BRAZIER, Dr Patrick Charles;** Chief Executive, Education Development Trust (formerly CfBT Education Trust), since 2017 (International Director, 2013–16; Education Services Director, 2016–17); *b* 2 Aug. 1960; *s* of Kenneth and Judith Brazier. *Educ:* Univ. of Liverpool (MSc (Microbiol.) 1981); PCL (PhD (Microbial Genetics) 1987). Consultant in Biotechnol., Inst. of Technol., Bandung, Indonesia, 1987–88; Sci. Policy Res. Officer, Royal Soc., London, 1989–90; British Council, 1990–: Project Officer, London, 1990–91; Dep. Dir, Uganda, 1991–94; Director: Swaziland, 1994–96; Durban, 1996–97; Dep. Regl Dir, Southern Africa, Johannesburg, 1997–2001; Director: Syria, 2001–03; Indonesia, 2003–04; Governance and Develt, Manchester, 2004–07; Contracts and Projects, Manchester, 2007–08; Middle East, 2008–11; Mem. Mgt Bd, 2011–13; Regl Dir, ME and N Africa, 2011–13. *Address:* Education Development Trust, Highbridge House, 16–18 Duke Street, Reading RG1 4RU. *T:* (0118) 902 1689. *E:* pbrazier@educationdevelopmenttrust.com.

**BRAZIER, Rev. Canon Raymond Venner;** Vicar, St Matthew and St Nathanael, Kingsdown, Bristol, 1984–2005; Chaplain to the Queen, 1998–2010; *b* 12 Oct. 1940; *s* of Harold and Doris Brazier; *m* 1964, Elizabeth Dawn Radford; three *d*. *Educ:* Brockley County Sch., London; Bishop Otter Coll., Chichester; Wells Theol Coll. Assistant teacher: St Martin's County Secondary Boys' Sch., Shenfield, Essex, 1963–66; Kingswood Secondary Boys' Sch., Kingswood, Bristol, 1966–68; ordained deacon 1971, priest 1972; Curate, St Gregory the Great, Horfield, Bristol, 1971–75; Priest-in-charge, 1975–79, Vicar, 1979–84, St Nathanael with St Katharine, Bristol; also Priest-in-charge, St Matthew, Kingsdown, Bristol, 1980–84; Rural Dean of Horfield, 1985–91; Priest-in-charge, Bishopston, Bristol, 1993–97. Asst Advr for Licensed Ministry, Bristol, 2007–. Canon Emeritus, Bristol Cathedral, 2006 (Hon. Canon, 1994–2006); Hon. Chaplain, Colston's Girls Sch., Bristol, 1976–2005; Supplementary Chaplain, HM Prison Bristol, 2006–10. *Recreations:* reading, listening to music, watching sport, cooking, walking, theatre. *Address:* 51 Chalks Road, St George, Bristol BS5 9EP. *T:* (0117) 329 4611.

**BRAZIER, Prof. Rodney John,** MVO 2013; LLD; FRHistS; Professor of Constitutional Law, University of Manchester, 1992–2013, now Emeritus; *b* 13 May 1946; *s* of late Eric Brazier and Mildred Brazier (*née* Davies); *m* 1974, Margaret Rosetta Jacobs (*see* M. R. Brazier); one *d*. *Educ:* Buckhurst Hill County High Sch.; Univ. of Southampton (LLB 1968; LLD 2008). Called to the Bar, Lincoln's Inn, 1970, Bencher, 2000, Emeritus Bencher, 2011. University of Manchester: Asst Lectr, 1968–70; Lectr, 1970–78; Sen. Lectr in Law, 1978–89; Reader in Constitutional Law, 1989–92; Dean, Faculty of Law, 1992–94. Chm., Consumer Credit Appeals Tribunal, 1992–2006. Specialist Adviser: H of C Public Admin Select Cttee, 2003–04; Jt Select Cttee on Draft Constitnl Renewal Bill, 2007–08. Mem., Lord Chancellor's Adv. Council on Nat. Records and Archives, 2014–17. JP Manchester, 1982–89. FRHistS 1994. *Publications:* Constitutional Practice, 1988, 3rd edn 1999; Constitutional Texts, 1990; Constitutional Reform: reshaping the British political system, 1991, 3rd edn 2008; Ministers of the Crown, 1997; (jtly) Constitutional & Administrative Law, 8th edn 1998; articles in legal jls. *Address:* School of Law, University of Manchester, Oxford Road, Manchester M13 9PL. *T:* (0161) 275 3575.

**BREADALBANE AND HOLLAND,** Earldom of, *cr* 1677; dormant since 1995.

**BREADEN, Very Rev. Robert William;** Priest-in-charge, St Columba's, Portree, Isle of Skye, 2007–12; licence to officiate, Diocese of Moray, Ross and Caithness; *b* 7 Nov. 1937; *s* of Moses and Martha Breaden; *m* 1970, Glenice Sutton Martin; one *s* four *d*. *Educ:* The King's Hospital, Dublin; Edinburgh Theological Coll. Deacon 1961, priest 1962; Asst Curate, St Mary's, Broughty Ferry, 1961–65; Rector: Church of the Holy Rood, Carnoustie, 1965–72; St Mary's, Broughty Ferry, 1972–2007; Canon of St Paul's Cathedral, Dundee, 1977; Dean of Brechin, 1984–2007. OStJ 2001. *Recreations:* gardening, horse riding, Rugby enthusiast. *Address:* 6 Chapel Road, Evanton, Dingwall IV16 9XT. *T:* (01349) 830490. *E:* ateallach@gmail.com.

**BREAKWELL, Prof. Dame Glynis (Marie),** DBE 2012; DL; President and Vice Chancellor (formerly Vice Chancellor), University of Bath, 2001–18, Emeritus Professor, 2019; *b* 26 July 1952; *d* of Harold and Vera Breakwell; partner, Colin Rowett. *Educ:* Univ. of Leicester (BA Hons 1973); Univ. of Strathclyde (MSc 1974); Univ. of Bristol (PhD 1976); Nuffield Coll., Oxford (MA 1978; DSc 1995). FBPsS 1987 (Hon. FBPsS 2006); CPsychol 1988. Prize Fellow, Nuffield Coll., Oxford, 1978–82; University of Surrey: Lectr in Psychol., 1981–87; Sen. Lectr, 1987–88; Reader, 1988–91; Prof., 1991–2001; Pro-Vice Chancellor, 1994–2001. Res. Advr to MAFF and Food Standards Agency, 1991–2001. Member: Coll. of Postgrad. Trng Assessors, 1996–2001, Council, 2011–18, ESRC (Chm., Res. Cttee, 2011–17); CVCP/HEFCE Steering Gp on costing and pricing, 1997–2001; HEFCE Leadership Governance and Mgt Cttee, 2004–14; Social Scis Panel, Finnish RAE, 2005; Bd, Higher Educn Career Services Unit, 2007–10; Financial Sustainability Strategy Gp, HEFCE, 2008–14; HEFCE Accountability Burden Proj. Steering Gp, 2008–10; Task Force on HE, CBI, 2009; Res. Councils UK Panel on Public Engagement in Sci., 2009–13; Bd, Leadership Foundn for Higher Educn, 2013–16 (Chair, Res. Panel, 2013–16); Chairman: Nat. Cataloguing Unit for Archives of Contemp. Scientists, 2001–09; HEFCE Widening Participation Rev. Gp, 2004–06; Director: UUK, 2005–18 (Chm., Funding and Mgt Policy Gp, subseq. Funding Policy Network, 2008–17; Chm., HE Funding Task Gp, 2010–11); Universities Superannuation Scheme, 2009–18; Student Loans Co. Ltd, 2011–17; Sen. Ind. Dir, NHS Improvement Bd, 2016–19; Chm., HERDA-SW, 2006–08. Pres., Psychol. Section, BAAS, 1994–95. Mem. Bd, 2001–12, Exec. Cttee, 2010–12, 1994 Gp. Royal Society: Mem., Internat. Policy Cttee, 2002–05, Fruits of Curiosity Report, 2009–10; Advr, Res. on Public Communication of Sci., 2005; Mem., Royal Soc./Acad. of Med. Scis Cttee on Pandemic Influenza, 2006; Mem., Sci. and Technol. Honours Cttee, 2016–. Member: SW Sci. and Industry Council, 2006–10; West of England Local Econ. Partnership, 2011–14; Chair, Council, GW4, 2015–17 (Mem., 2017–). Dir, New Swindon Co., 2002–07. Dir, Theatre Royal, Bath, 2001–06; Trustee, Holburne Mus., Bath, 2001–04; Chairman: Bath Fests, 2006–09; Daphne Jackson Trust, 2009–15. Mem. Council, Cheltenham Ladies' Coll., 2009–15. Mem., Cttee, World Cultural Council, Mexico, 2010–; Chm., Adv. Bd, Inst. of Social Scis, Univ. of Lisbon, 2010–14. DL Somerset, 2010. FRSA 1997; FAcSS 2014 (AcSS 2002); PFHEA 2016. Hon. Prof., Univ. of Shandong, China, 2004. Hon. Fellow, Soc. of Sports and Exercise Medicine Malaysia, 2013. Hon. LLD Bristol, 2004; Hon. DPhil Stellenbosch, 2018. *Publications:* (jtly) Social Work: the social psychological approach, 1982; The Quiet Rebel, 1985; Coping with Threatened Identities, 1986, reprint 2016; Facing Physical Violence, 1989; Interviewing, 1990; (jtly) Managing Violence at Work, 1992; (jtly) Careers and Identities, 1992; (jtly) Basic Evaluation Methods, 1995; Coping with Aggressive Behaviour, 1997; The Psychology of Risk, 2007, 2nd edn 2014; *edited:* (jtly) Social Psychology: a practical manual, 1982; Threatened Identities, 1983; (jtly) Doing Social Psychology, 1988; Human Behavior: encyclopedia of personal relationships, vol. 17, shaping your life, vol. 18, coping with change, 1990; Social Psychology of Political and Economic Cognition, 1991; Social Psychology of Identity and the Self Concept, 1992; (jtly) Empirical Approaches to Social Representations, 1993; (jtly) Research Methods in Psychology, 1995, 5th edn 2020; (jtly) Changing European Identities: social psychological analyses of change, 1996; Doing Social Psychology Research, 2004; (jtly) Identity Process Theory: identity, social action and social change, 2014. *Recreations:* racket sports, painting. *Address:* University of Bath, Bath BA2 7AY. *E:* g.breakwell@bath.ac.uk. *Club:* Athenæum.

**BREALEY, Maj. Gen. Bruce,** CB 2012; Director General Capability, 2011–13; *b* Burton upon Trent, Staffs, 8 Feb. 1959; *s* of Trevor Graham Brealey and Judith Brealey; *m* 1986, Susan Margaret Harrison; one *d*. *Educ:* St Olave's Grammar Sch.; RMA, Sandhurst. Sen. military command and staff appts; Dep. Comdg Gen., Multi Nat. Corps, Iraq, 2007–08; GOC Theatre Troops, 2008–11. *Recreations:* golf, travel, music, theatre, gardening. *Club:* Wentworth.

**BREALEY, Mark Philip;** QC 2002; barrister; *b* 26 Jan. 1960; *s* of Leonard and Shirley Brealey. *Educ:* Reading Univ. (LLB); University Coll. London (LLM). Called to the Bar, Middle Temple, 1984. *Publications:* (with M. Hoskins) Remedies in EC Law, 1994, 2nd edn 1998. *Address:* Monckton Chambers, 1 & 2 Raymond Buildings, Gray's Inn, WC1R 5NR. *Clubs:* Royal Ascot Racing; Tottenham Hotspur Football.

**BREALEY, Prof. Richard Arthur,** FBA 1999; Special Adviser to the Governor, Bank of England, 1998–2001; Professor of Finance, London Business School, 1974–98, Professor Emeritus, since 2001; *b* 9 June 1936; *s* of late Albert Brealey and Irene Brealey; *m* 1967, Diana Cecily Brown Kelly; two *s*. *Educ:* Queen Elizabeth's, Barnet; Exeter Coll., Oxford (MA, 1st Cl. Hons PPE). Sun Life Assce Co. of Canada, 1959–66; Keystone Custodian Funds of Boston, 1966–68; London Business School: Prudential Res. Fellow, 1968–74; Sen. Lectr, 1972–74; Barclaytrust Prof. of Investment, 1974–82; Midland Bank Prof. of Corporate Finance, 1982–91; Tokai Bank Prof. of Finance, 1993–98; Dep. Prin., 1984–88; Governor, 1984–88. Director: Swiss Helvetia Fund Inc., 1987–96, 2009–18; Sun Life Assurance Co. of Canada UK Hldgs plc, 1994–97; Tokai Derivative Products, 1995–97. Trustee, HSBC Investor Family of Funds, 2005–08. Pres., European Finance Assoc., 1975; Dir, Amer. Finance Assoc., 1979–81. *Publications:* An Introduction to Risk and Return from Common Stocks, 1969, 2nd edn 1983; Security Prices in a Competitive Market, 1971; (with J. Lorie) Modern Developments in Investment Management, 1972, 2nd edn 1978; (with S. C. Myers) Principles of Corporate Finance, 1981, (with S. C Myers and F. Allen) 13th edn 2019; (with S. C. Myers and A. J. Marcus) Fundamentals of Corporate Finance, 1995, 10th edn 2019; articles in professional jls. *Recreations:* trekking, horse riding. *Address:* Haydens Cottage, The Pound, Cookham, Berks SL6 9QE. *T:* (01628) 520143.

**BREAM, Julian,** CBE 1985 (OBE 1964); guitarist and lutenist; *b* 15 July 1933; *e s* of Henry G. Bream; *m* 1st, Margaret Williamson; one adopted *s*; 2nd, 1980, Isabel Sanchez. *Educ:* Royal College of Music (Junior Exhibition Award, 1945 and Scholarship, 1948). Began professional career at Cheltenham, 1947; London début, Wigmore Hall, 1951; subsequently has appeared in leading world festivals in Europe, USA, Australia and Far East. A leader in revival of interest in Elizabethan Lute music, on which he has done much research; has encouraged and commissioned many contemporary compositions for the guitar including works by Walton, Britten, Tippett, Henze and Takemitsu. Formed Julian Bream Consort, 1960; inaugurated Semley Festival of Music and Poetry, 1971. DUniv Surrey, 1968. Villa-Lobos Gold Medal, 1976; Gramophone Lifetime Achievement Award, 2013. *Recreations:* walking, gardening, cricket, table tennis, backgammon. *Address:* c/o Hazard Chase, 25 City Road, Cambridge CB1 1DP.

**BREARLEY, Christopher John Scott,** CB 1994; DL; Director General (formerly Deputy Secretary), Planning, Roads and Local Transport, Department of Environment, Transport and the Regions, 1997–2000; *b* 25 May 1943; *s* of Geoffrey Brearley and Winifred (*née* Scott); *m* 1971, Rosemary Stockbridge; two *s*. *Educ:* King Edward VII Sch., Sheffield; Trinity Coll., Oxford. MA 1964, BPhil 1966. Entered Ministry of Transport, 1966; Private Sec. to Perm. Sec., 1969–70; Principal, DoE, 1970; Sec. to Review of Develt Control Procedures (Dobry), DoE, 1973–74; Private Sec. to the Secretary of the Cabinet, Cabinet Office, 1974–76; Asst Sec., 1977; Under Sec., 1981; Dir of Scottish Services, PSA, 1981–83; Cabinet Office, 1983–85; Department of the Environment, 1985–97: Deputy Secretary: Local Govt, 1990–94; Local Govt and Planning, 1994–95; Local and Regl Develt, 1996–97. Mem. (Lib Dem), Three Rivers DC, 2003–07; Chm., SW Herts Lib Dems, 2005–08, 2009–11. Sec., Review of Child Protection in the Catholic Ch, 2000–01. Chm., Nat. Retail Planning Forum, 2005–13. Member: Policy Cttee, CPRE, 2001–07 (Chm., Herts Soc., CPRE, 2004–09); Chiltern Conservation Bd, 2005–07. Governor, Watford Grammar Sch. for Boys, 1988–2004 (Chm. of Govs, 1998–2004); Trustee, Watford Grammar Schs Foundn, 1992–2004, 2011–19 (Chm., 2015–19). Trustee: Motability Tenth Anniv. Trust, 2001–; Motorway Archive Trust, 2001–09; Governor: Oxfordshire and Bucks Mental Health Foundn Trust, 2008–11; Herts Partnership Foundn Trust, later Herts Partnership Univ. NHS Foundn Trust, 2011–17 (Lead Gov., 2013–16). Freeman, City of London, 1998. DL Herts, 2007. Hon. Fellow, Sch. of Public Policy, Birmingham Univ., 2001–03. *Recreation:* meeting friends. *Address:* 3 Mitchell Close, Thame, Oxon OX9 2ET.

**BREARLEY, (John) Michael,** OBE 1978; psychoanalyst; *b* 28 April 1942; *s* of late Horace and Midge Brearley; lives with Mana Sarabhai; two *c*. *Educ:* City of London Sch.; St John's Coll., Cambridge (MA; Hon. Fellow, 1998). Lectr in Philosophy, Univ. of Newcastle upon Tyne, 1968–71. Middlesex County Cricketer, intermittently, 1961–82, capped 1964, Captain, 1971–82; played first Test Match, 1976; Captain of England XI, 1977–80, 1981. Fellow, British Psychoanalytical Soc. (Associate Mem., 1985; Mem., 1991; Pres., 2008–10). Hon. LLD Lancaster, 1999; DUniv Oxford Brookes, 2006. *Publications:* (with Dudley Doust) The Return of the Ashes, 1978; (with Dudley Doust) The Ashes Retained, 1979; Phoenix: the series that rose from the ashes, 1982; The Art of Captaincy, 1985, 2nd edn 2001; (with John Arlott) Arlott in Conversation with Mike Brearley, 1986; On Form, 2017; On Cricket, 2018; articles for The Times. *Club:* MCC (Hon. Life Mem.; Pres., 2007–08; Mem., 2007–17, Chm., 2011–17, World Cricket Cttee).

**BREARLEY, Jonathan;** Chief Executive, Office of Gas and Electricity Markets, from Feb. 2020 (Senior Partner, 2016–18; Executive Director, Systems and Networks, 2018–Feb. 2020); *b* Buckie, Scotland, 23 July 1973; *s* of David William Brearley and Gillian Rose Brearley; *m* 2009, Sumita Dutta. *Educ:* Gillingham Comprehensive Sch., Dorset; Sexey's Sch., Bruton; Glasgow Univ. (BSc Hons Maths and Physics 1995); Girton Coll., Cambridge (MPhil Econs 2000). Analyst, Bain & Co., 2000–02; Sen. Policy Advr, Prime Minister's Strategy Unit, 2002–06; Hd, Local Govt White Paper, DCLG, 2006; Director: Office of Climate Change, 2006–09; Energy Strategy and Futures, then Energy Markets and Networks, DECC, 2009–13; Dir, Brearley Economics, 2013–16. *Recreations:* walking, travel, scuba diving, refurbishing houses, home swapping, reading, cooking, watching DVD box sets. *Address:* Hill Meadows, Radnage, High Wycombe, Bucks HP14 4BU. *T:* 07961 441081. *E:* jonathan.brearley@live.com.

**BREARLEY, Michael;** *see* Brearley, J. M.

**BREARLEY-SMITH, Anne Margaret;** *see* Luther, A. M.

**BREARS, Peter Charles David,** FMA, FSA; writer and museums consultant, since 1994; *b* 30 Aug. 1944; *s* of Charles Brears and Mary (*née* Fett). *Educ:* Castleford Technical High Sch.; Leeds Coll. of Art (DipAD 1967). FMA 1980; FSA 1980. Hon. Asst, Wakefield City

Museum, 1957–66; Keeper of Folk Life, Hampshire CC, 1967–69; Curator: Shibden Hall, Halifax, 1969–72; Clarke Hall, Wakefield, 1972–75; Castle Museum, York, 1975–79; Dir, Leeds City Museums, 1979–94. Founder, 1975, and Mem., 1975–, Group for Regional Studies in Museums, subseq. Social Hist. Curators Gp, 1975; Mem., Social History and Industrial Classification Wkg Party, 1978–; Pres., Soc. for Folk Life Studies, 1995–96. Sophie Coe Prize for food writing, Oxford Symposium for Food History, 1997. *Publications*: The English Country Pottery, 1971; Yorkshire Probate Inventories, 1972; The Collectors' Book of English Country Pottery, 1974; Horse Brasses, 1981; The Gentlewoman's Kitchen, 1984; Traditional Food in Yorkshire, 1987; North Country Folk Art, 1989; Of Curiosities and Rare Things, 1989; Treasures for the People, 1989; Images of Leeds, 1992; Leeds Describ'd, 1993; Leeds Waterfront, 1994; The Country House Kitchen, 1996; Ryedale Recipes, 1998; A Taste of Leeds, 1998; The Old Devon Farmhouse, 1998; All the King's Cooks, 1999, 2nd edn 2011; The Compleat Housekeeper, 2000; The Boke of Kervynge, 2003; A New and Easy Method of Cookery, 2005; Cooking and Dining in Medieval England, 2008 (Andre Simon Award, 2009); Traditional Food in Shropshire, 2009; Jellies and their Moulds, 2010; Cooking and Dining with the Wordsworths, 2011; Traditional Food in Northumbria, 2013; A Leeds Life, 2013; Traditional Food in Yorkshire, 2014; Cooking and Dining in Tudor and Early Stuart England, 2015; The Petworth Book of Country House Cookery, 2015; (with S. Wood) The Real Wuthering Heights, 2016; Traditional Food in Cumbria, 2017; Malton Goes to Market: the recipes, 2017; The Folly, Settle, 2018; articles in Folk Life, Post-Medieval Archaeology, etc; museum guides and catalogues. *Recreations*: hill walking, drawing, cookery. *Address*: 4 Woodbine Terrace, Headingley, Leeds LS6 4AF. *T*: (0113) 275 6537.

**BRECHIN, Bishop of,** since 2018; **Rt Rev. Andrew Christopher Swift**; *b* Aberdeen, 10 Jan. 1968; *s* of Dr Bernard Swift and Christine Swift; *m* 1991, Mary Calvert; one *s* two *d*. *Educ*: Univ. of Edinburgh (BEng Electrical and Mech. Engrg 1990); Univ. of Aberdeen (MSc Mech. Engrg 1997); Ripon Coll., Cuddesdon (BTh Theol. 2008). CEng 1995. RAF, 1986–90; Admiralty Res. Scientist, 1991–97; Naval Consultant, YARD Glasgow, 1997–2000; Engrg Manager, Type 45 Destroyer Prime Contract, 2000–03; Business Develt Exec., BAE Systems/Atkins, 2003; Engrg Manager, Aircraft Carrier Alliance, 2003–05; ordained deacon, 2007, priest, 2008; Asst Curate, St Catharine's, Gloucester, 2007–10; Priest-in-charge, St Martin's, Tighnabruaich, 2010–11; Priest-in-charge, 2010–16, Rector, 2016–18, Holy Trinity, Dunoon, and St Paul, Rothesay; Dean of Argyll and the Isles, 2012–18. Honorary Chaplain: ATC, 2011–18; Mission to Seafarers, 2013–18. DL Argyll and Bute, 2016–18. *Recreations*: narrow boating, cooking, social media, collie walking, reading. *Address*: Diocesan Centre, 38 Langlands Street, Dundee DD4 6SZ. *T*: (01382) 459569.

**BRECHIN, Dean of;** *see* Bridger, Very Rev. F. W.

**BRECHT, Air Vice-Marshal Malcolm Andrew Brian,** CB 2017; CBE 2009; Director, C-17 International Field Services and Program Integration, Boeing Global Services, since 2017; *b* Pembroke, 19 Feb. 1965; *s* of Terence Brian Brecht and Hazel Mary Brecht (*née* Fletcher); *m* 1987, Barbara Joan Corrigan; two *s*. *Educ*: Kingham Hill Sch., Oxfordshire; Univ. of Hull (BA Hons Operational Res. and Mgt Scis 1986); King's Coll. London (MA Defence Studies 2000). Joined RAF, 1983; pilot on HS125, BAe146 and Tristar with 32 Sqdn, Queen's Flight and 216 Sqdn, 1988–98; PSO to AOC 2 Gp, 1998–99; OC 99 Sqdn, introducing Boeing C-17 into service, 2000–03; Air Resources and Plans, 2003–05; Comdr Basrah Air Station, 2005–06; Station Comdr, RAF Brize Norton, 2006–08; Comdr, Kandahar Airfield, 2009–10; on secondment to Cabinet Office to lead Joint Defence and Security Rev. Defence Team, 2010; Air Staff, MoD, 2010–12; COS Capability, 2012–17. CO, 601 (Co. of London) Sqdn, RAuxAF, 2018–. Mem., Gen. Synod, 2014–17. FRAeS 2006. Freeman, Coachmakers' and Coach Harness Makers' Guild, 2012–. QCVS 2006. *Recreations*: cycling and keeping fit, keen Rugby follower, member of local church. *Address*: C-17 International Field Services, Brize Norton, 300 Globemaster Road, RAF Brize Norton OX18 3LX.

**BRECKELL, Paul Anthony;** Director of Strategy and Transformation, Ambitious about Autism, since 2018; *b* Rugby, Warks, 18 Jan. 1971; *s* of Trevor Harry Breckell and Janice Marion Breckell; *m* 1995, Chantal Phillips; one *s*. *Educ*: Ashlyn's Sch., Berkhamsted; Univ. of Sheffield (BA 1st Cl. Hons Econs); London South Bank Univ. (MSc with Dist. Charity Accounting and Financial Mgt). CPFA 1997. Sen. Auditor, Audit Commn, 1992–97; Hd of Finance, Mildmay, 1997–2000; Finance Dir, Church Mission Soc., 2000–07; Man. Dir, 2007–12, Chief Exec., 2012–18, Action on Hearing Loss. Chm., Charity Finance Gp, 2003–07. Trustee: CIPFA, 2009–13; Roffey Park Inst., 2013–. FRSA. *Recreations*: reading, gardening, watching and playing sport. *Address*: Ambitious about Autism, Pears National Centre for Autism Education, Woodside Avenue, N10 3JA. *E*: pbreckell@ambitiousaboutautism.org.uk.

**BRECKENRIDGE, Sir Alasdair (Muir),** Kt 2004; CBE 1995; MD; FRCP, FRCPE; FRSE; FMedSci; Chairman, Medicines and Healthcare Products Regulatory Agency, 2003–12; Professor of Clinical Pharmacology, University of Liverpool, 1974–2002; *b* 7 May 1937; *s* of Thomas and Jane Breckenridge; *m* 1967, Jean Margaret Boyle; two *s*. *Educ*: Bell Baxter Sch., Cupar, Fife; Univ. of St Andrews (MB, ChB Hons 1961); Univ. of London (MSc 1968); Univ. of Dundee (MD Hons 1974). FRCP 1974; FRCPE 1988; FRSE 1991. House Phys. and Surg., Dundee Royal Infirm., 1961–62; Asst, Dept of Medicine, Univ. of St Andrews, 1962–63; successively House Phys., Registrar, Sen. Registrar, Tutor, Lectr and Sen. Lectr, Hammersmith Hosp. and RPMS, 1964–74. Non-exec. Dir, The, 1990–94, Vice Chm., 1993–94, Mersey RHA (Chm., Jan.–July 1993; Chm., Res. Cttee, 1987–91); Vice Chm., NW RHA, 1994–96 (Dir of R & D, 1994–96); Chm., NW Reg., NHS Exec., 1996–99. NHS Advr in Clin. Pharm. to CMO, 1982–94; Mem., NHS Adv. Cttee on Drugs, 1985–98 (Vice Chm., 1986–98). Committee on Safety of Medicines: Mem., 1982–2003 (Vice Chm., 1996–98; Chm., 1999–2003); Chm., Adverse Reactions Subgroup, 1987–92; Chm., Adverse Reactions to Vaccination and Immunisation Sub Cttee, 1989–92; Chm., Sub Cttee on Safety and Efficacy, 1993–95. Medical Research Council: Mem., 1992–96; Member: Clin. Trials Cttee, 1983–; Physiol Systems and Disorders Bd, 1987–91 (Vice Chm., 1990–91); AIDS Therapeutic Cttee, 1989– (Chm., 1993–). Royal College of Physicians: Mem. Council, 1983–86; Mem., Res. Cttee, 1983–88; Mem., Clin. Pharm. Cttee, 1990–95; Mem. Adv. Res. Cttee, 1993–98; Goulstonian Lectr, 1975; William Withering Lectr, 2006. British Pharmacological Society: Mem., 1972–; Foreign Sec., 1984–91; Chm., Clin. Section, 1988–93; Lilly Medal, 1994; Chm. Editl Bd, British Jl of Clin. Pharmacol., 1983–87. Member: Panel on Tropical and Infectious Disease, Wellcome Trust, 1984–87; Res. Cttee, British Heart Foundn, 1977–82; Steering Cttee for Chemotherapy of Malaria, WHO, 1987–91; Exec. Cttee, Internat. Union of Pharm., 1981–87; Central R&D Cttee, NHS, 1991–94; Jt Med. Adv. Cttee, HEFCE, 1995–2002 (Chm., 1998–2002); Cttee on Proprietary Medicinal Products of EU, 2001–02. Chm., Scientific Adv. Bd, Singapore Govt Centre of Regulatory Excellence, 2013–. Mem., Assoc. of Physicians, 1975–. Founder FMedSci 1998. Hon. DSc: St Andrews, 2005; Keele, 2005; Hon. LLD Dundee, 2005; Hon. MD Liverpool, 2007. Paul Martini Prize in Clin. Pharm., Paul Martini Foundn, 1974; Poulson Medal, Norwegian Pharmacol Soc., 1988. Exec. Editor, Pharmacology and Therapeutics, 1982–98. *Publications*: papers on clinical pharmacology in various jls. *Recreations*: hill-walking, golf, music. *Address*: Cree Cottage, Feather Lane, Heswall, Wirral CH60 4RL. *Club*: Athenæum.

**BRECKNOCK, Earl of; James William John Pratt;** *b* 11 Dec. 1965; *s* and *heir* of Marquess Camden, *qv*. *Educ*: Eton; Univ. of Edinburgh.

**BRECON, Dean of;** *see* Shackerley, Very Rev. A. P.

**BREED, Colin Edward;** *b* 4 May 1947; *s* of Alfred Breed and Edith Violet Breed; *m* 1968, Janet Courtiour; one *s* one *d*. *Educ*: Torquay GS. ACIB. Junior, to Area Manager, Midland Bank plc, 1964–81; Manager, Venture Capital Fund, later Man. Dir, Dartington & Co. Ltd, 1981–91; Consultant, Corporate Finance, Allied Provincial Stockbrokers, 1991–92; Dir, Gemini Abrasives Ltd, 1992–97. MP (Lib Dem) SE Cornwall, 1997–2010. Mem., GMC, 1999. *Recreations*: golf, watching live sport. *Address*: 10 Dunheved Road, Saltash, Cornwall PL12 4BW.

**BREEDON, Timothy James,** CBE 2013; Group Chief Executive, Legal & General Group plc, 2006–12; *b* 14 Feb. 1958; *s* of Peter and Ruth Breedon; *m* 1982, Susan Hopkins; three *s*. *Educ*: Worcester Coll., Oxford (MA); London Business Sch. (MSc). Standard Chartered Bank, 1981–85; Legal & General Group, 1987–2012: Gp Dir (Investments), 2002–05; Dep. Chief Exec., 2005. Chm., Northview Gp, 2017–19. Non-exec. Chm., Apax Global Alpha, 2015–; non-exec. Dir, Barclays plc, 2012–; Lead non-exec. Dir, MoJ, 2012–15. Dir, Financial Reporting Council, 2004–07; Chm., ABI, 2010–12. Hon. Treas., Marie Curie Cancer Care, 2014–.

**BREEN, Mary;** Headmistress, St Mary's School Ascot, since 1999; *b* Lancs, 4 Jan. 1964; *d* of Gerard Hayes and Mary Hayes; *m* 1988, James Breen. *Educ*: Univ. of Exeter (BSc Hons 1985); Univ. of Manchester (MSc 1987). Teacher of Physics: Wellington Coll., 1988–89; Abbey Sch., Reading, 1989–91; Eton Coll., 1991–92; St Mary's Sch. Ascot, 1992; Eton Coll., 1992–98, Head of Physics, 1996–98. *Recreations*: travel, cooking, reading, racing, walking, wine. *Address*: St Mary's School Ascot, St Mary's Road, Ascot, Berks SL5 9JF. *T*: (01344) 296600. *E*: mbreen@st-marys-ascot.co.uk. *Club*: Athenæum.

**BREEN, Prof. Richard James,** PhD; FBA 1999; Nuffield Professor of Sociology, University of Oxford, since 2015; Fellow, Nuffield College, Oxford, since 2015; *b* 25 Aug. 1954; *s* of Edward Francis Breen and Emily Breen (*née* Wolstenholme); *m* 1st, 1981, Eleanor Burgess (marr. diss. 1993); 2nd, 1997, Mary Christine O'Sullivan. *Educ*: St Thomas Aquinas Grammar Sch., Leeds; Fitzwilliam Coll., Cambridge (BA 1976; MA 1979; PhD 1981). Research Officer, then Sen. Research Officer, Economic and Social Research Inst., Dublin, 1980–91; Professor of Sociology: QUB, 1991–2000; European Univ. Inst., Florence, 1997–2001; Official Fellow, Nuffield Coll., Oxford, 2000–06; Prof. of Sociology, 2007–15, William Graham Sumner Prof., 2010–15, Yale Univ. MRIA 1998. *Publications*: Understanding Contemporary Ireland, 1990; Social Class and Social Mobility in the Republic of Ireland, 1996; Social Mobility in Europe, 2004; numerous contribs to learned jls. *Recreations*: music, tennis, reading, hill walking. *Address*: Nuffield College, 1 New Road, Oxford OX1 1NF. *T*: (01865) 278589.

**BREEZE, Alastair Jon,** CMG 1990; HM Diplomatic Service, retired; Counsellor, Foreign and Commonwealth Office, 1987–94; *b* 1 June 1934; *s* of Samuel Wilfred Breeze and Gladys Elizabeth Breeze; *m* 1st, 1960, Helen Burns Shaw (*d* 2011); two *s* one *d*; 2nd, 2011, Sarah Elizabeth Fausset. *Educ*: Mill Hill School; Christ's College, Cambridge (Scholar; MA 1959). Served Royal Marines, 1953–55. Foreign Office, 1958; 3rd Sec., Jakarta, 1960–62; FO, 1962–64; 2nd Sec., seconded to Colonial Office for service in Georgetown, 1964–66; 1st Sec., Tehran, 1967–71; FCO, 1971–72; 1st Sec., Islamabad, 1972–75, Lagos, 1976–79; FCO, 1979–83; Counsellor, UK Mission to UN, NY, 1983–87. *Recreations*: sailing, ornithology. *Address*: La Vieille Boucherie, Puntous 65230, France.

**BREEZE, Dr David John,** OBE 2009; FSA, FSAScot, FRSE; Chief Inspector of Ancient Monuments, 1989–2005, Head, Special Heritage Projects, 2005–08, Historic Scotland; Co-ordinator, Antonine Wall World Heritage Site, 2008–09; *b* Blackpool, 25 July 1944; *s* of Reginald C. Breeze and Marian (*née* Lawson); *m* 1972, Pamela Diane Silvester; two *s*. *Educ*: Blackpool Grammar Sch.; University Coll., Durham Univ. (BA; PhD 1970). FSAScot 1970 (Hon. FSAScot 2005); FSA 1975; FRSE 1991; MIFA 1990; Hon. MCIfA (Hon. MIFA 2006). Inspector of Ancient Monuments, Scotland, 1969–88, Principal Inspector, 1988–89. Vis. Prof., Durham Univ., 1994–; Hon. Professor: Edinburgh Univ., 1996–; Newcastle Univ., 2003–; Stirling Univ., 2016–. Chairman: Hadrian's Wall Pilgrimage, 1989, 1999 and 2009; Internat. Congress of Roman Frontier Studies, 1989–2015; British Archaeol Awards, 1993–2009; Mem., Hadrian's Wall Adv. Cttee, English Heritage, 1977–97; President: South Shields Archaeol and Historical Soc., 1983–85; Soc. of Antiquaries of Scotland, 1987–90; Soc. of Antiquaries of Newcastle upon Tyne, 2008–11; Royal Archaeol Inst., 2009–12 (Vice-Pres., 2002–07); Cumberland and Westmorland Antiquarian and Archaeol Soc., 2011–14 (Vice-Pres., 2003–11). Trustee, Senhouse Museum Trust, 1985– (Chm., 2013–18). Corresp. Mem., German Archaeol Inst., 1979. Hon. DLitt Glasgow, 2008. Eur. Archaeol Heritage Prize, Eur. Assoc. of Archaeologists, 2010. *Publications*: (with Brian Dobson) Hadrian's Wall, 1976, 4th edn 2000; (with D. V. Clarke and G. Mackay) The Romans in Scotland, 1980; The Northern Frontiers of Roman Britain, 1982; Roman Forts in Britain, 1983, 2nd edn 2002; (ed) Studies in Scottish Antiquity, 1984; Hadrian's Wall, a Souvenir Guide, 1987, 2nd edn 2003; A Queen's Progress, 1987; The Second Augustan Legion in North Britain, 1989; (ed) Service in the Roman Army, 1989; (with Anna Ritchie) Invaders of Scotland, 1991; (with Brian Dobson) Roman Officers and Frontiers, 1993; Roman Scotland: frontier country, 1996, 2nd edn 2006; (with G. Munro) The Stone of Destiny, 1997; Historic Scotland, 1998; Historic Scotland: peoples and places, 2002; (ed with R. Welander and T. Clancy) The Stone of Destiny: artefact and icon, 2003; (with Sonja Jilek and Andreas Thiel) Frontiers of the Roman Empire, 2005; Handbook to the Roman Wall, 14th edn 2006; The Antonine Wall, 2006; Roman Frontiers in Britain, 2007; Edge of Empire, Rome's Scottish frontier, The Antonine Wall, 2008; (ed with Sonja Jilek) Frontiers of the Roman Empire: the European dimension of a world heritage site, 2008; Frontiers of the Roman Empire: the Antonine Wall, 2009; Frontiers of the Roman Empire: Hadrian's Wall, 2011; The Frontiers of Imperial Rome, 2011; (ed) The First Souvenirs: enamelled vessels from Hadrian's Wall, 2012; (ed) 200 Years: the Society of Antiquaries of Newcastle upon Tyne 1813–2013, 2013; (with M. C. Bishop) The Crosby Garrett Helmet, 2013; Hadrian's Wall: a history of archaeological thought, 2014; (ed with R. H. Jones and I. Oleteans) Understanding Roman Frontiers, 2015; The Roman Army, 2016; Hadrian's Wall: paintings by the Richardson family, 2016; Bearsden: a Roman fort on the Antonine Wall, 2016; Bearsden: life in a Roman fort, 2016; Maryport: a Roman fort and its community, 2018; (ed) The Crosby Garrett Helmet, 2018; Hadrian's Wall: a study in archaeological exploration and interpretation, 2019; contribs to British and foreign jls. *Recreations*: reading, walking, travel.

**BREEZE, Stevan William;** Chief Executive, BSI Group, 2002–08; *b* 4 June 1951; *s* of William and Gwendoline Breeze; *m* 1993, Diana Julie Farthing; one *s* one *d.* Man. Dir, Tefal UK Ltd, 1984–87; Divl Dir, Polly Peck Internat., 1987–90; Divl Gp Man. Dir, BTR plc, 1990–98; Divl Man. Dir, Jarvis plc, 1999–2002. *Recreations:* tennis, ski-ing, travel. *E:* stevanbreeze@yahoo.co.uk.

**BREHONY, Dr John Albert Noel,** CMG 1991; Chairman, Menas Associates, since 2001; *b* 11 Dec. 1936; *s* of Patrick Paul Brehony and Agnes Maher; *m* 1961, Jennifer Ann (*née* Cox); one *s* one *d. Educ:* London Oratory Sch.; Univ. of Durham (BA, PhD). Tutor, Durham Univ., 1960; Economist Intell. Unit, 1961; Res. Fellow, Jerusalem (Jordan), 1962; Lectr, Univ. of Libya, 1965–66; FO, 1966; Kuwait, 1967–69; Aden, 1970–71; Amman, 1973–77; Cairo, 1981–84; Counsellor, FCO, 1984–92; Dir of Middle East Affairs, 1992–99, Advr to Bd on ME Affairs, 1999–2013, Rolls-Royce PLC. Chm., Middle East Assoc., 1996–97; Pres., British Soc. of ME Studies, 2000–06; Mem. Council, Brit. Egyptian Soc., 2003–13; Chairman: Anglo-Jordanian Soc., 2009–13; British Yemeni Soc., 2010–15, 2018–. Chairman: British Inst. at Amman for Archaeol. and Hist., 1992–99; Council for British Res. in the Levant, 2004–09, 2013–16; Mem. Council, British Foundn for the Study of Arabia, 2011–17. Mem. Adv. Bd, London Middle East Inst., SOAS, 1999–; Internat. Advr to Gaza 2010 Project, Harvard Univ., 2005–08. Mem., Algerian British Business Council, 2013–. Trustee, Altajir Trust, 2009–. *Publications:* (ed with Ayman El-Desouky) British-Egyptian Relations from Suez to the Present Day, 2007; Yemen Divided: a failed state in South Arabia, 2011; (ed with Saud al-Sarhan) Rebuilding Yemen, 2015; (ed) Hadhramaut and its Diaspora, 2017. *Recreations:* Middle Eastern history, theatre, opera. *Address:* (office) 32 Bedford Row, WC1R 4HE. *Club:* Athenæum.

**BREHONY, Rosemary;** *see* Deem, R.

**BREMER de MARTINO, Juan José,** Hon. CVO 1975; Ambassador of Mexico to Cuba, since 2013; *b* 22 March 1944; *s* of Juan José Bremer Barrera and Cristina de Martino Noriega; *m* Marcela Sánchez de Bremer Science; two *s. Educ:* Nat. Autonomous Univ. of Mexico (law degree 1966). Private Sec. to Pres. of Mexico, 1972–75; Dep. Sec., Ministry of the Presidency, 1975–76; Hd, Nat. Fine Arts Inst., Mexico, 1976–82; Dep. Sec. for Cultural Affairs, Ministry of Educn, 1982; Ambassador to Sweden, 1982; Mem., Mexican Legislature, 1985–88 (Pres., Foreign Affairs Cttee, Chamber of Deputies); Ambassador to: Soviet Union, 1988–90; FRG, 1990–98; Spain, 1998–2000; USA, 2000–04; Court of St James's, 2004–09. Mem., Commn to Study the Future of Mexican-Amer. Relns, 1986–88. Pres., Cervantino Internat. Fest., 1983; guest lectr at US, Mexican and European univs. *Address:* c/o Mexican Embassy, Calle 12 No. 518, esq. Avenida 7ma, Reparto Miramar, Municipio Playa, Habana, Cuba.

**BREMNER, Jonathan Sinclair Grant;** QC 2018; *b* London, 24 Nov. 1981; *s* of late David Bremner and of Barbara Bremner; partner, 2009, Hui Ling Sarita McCarthy, *qv. Educ:* Belmont House Sch., Glasgow; Hertford Coll., Oxford (BA, BCL). Called to the Bar, Inner Temple, 2005; a barrister, Pump Court Tax Chambers, 2006–. *Recreations:* golf, ski-ing, tennis. *Address:* Pump Court Tax Chambers, 16 Bedford Row, WC1R 4EF. *T:* (020) 7414 8080. *E:* clerks@pumptax.com. *Clubs:* Royal Automobile; Royal Mid-Surrey Golf.

**BREMNER, Myles Ironside;** Chief Executive, Bremner Consulting, since 2016; *b* London, 9 Nov. 1971; *s* of Andrew Bremner and Elaine Bremner (*née* Arkle); *m* 2001, Stephanie Turner; one *s. Educ:* Haileybury Coll.; Univ. of Leeds (BA Hons Hist. 1993). Mktg contracts, 1993–97; Appeals Manager, RNLI, 1997–99; Mktg Manager, British Olympic Assoc., 1999–2001; Hd, Ops, St John Ambulance, 2001–03; Dir, Fundraising, CLIC Sargent Cancer Care for Children, 2003–06; Interim Dir, Fundraising, NCH (Action for Children), 2006–07; Chief Exec., Garden Organic, 2007–13; Dir, Sch. Food Plan, 2013–16 (Mem., Expert Panel, 2012–13). Chairman: Capital Growth, 2008–12; Food Growing in Schs Taskforce, 2012; Member: London Food Bd, 2010–; Warwickshire Local Nature Partnership, 2012–13; Trustee: Sustain, 2008–13; Chefs Adopt a Sch., Royal Acad. of Culinary Arts, 2016–. Gov., Kineton Primary Sch., 2015–. FRSA. *Recreations:* cooking, vegetable growing, amassing my bicycle collection, unenthusiastic triathlete. *Address:* Fighting House, Fighting Close, Kineton, Warwicks CV35 0LS. *T:* 07985 170737. *E:* mylesbremner@mac.com.

**BREMNER, Rory Keith Ogilvy;** satirical impressionist, writer and presenter; *b* 6 April 1961; *s* of late Major Donald Stuart Ogilvy Bremner and Anne Ulithorne Bremner (*née* Simpson); *m* 1987, Susan Shackleton (marr. diss. 1994); *m* 1999, Tessa Campbell Fraser; two *d. Educ:* Wellington Coll.; King's Coll. London (BA Hons French and German 1983; FKC 2005; Hon. Fellow 2006). Television: Now… Something Else, 1986–87; Rory Bremner, 1988–92; Rory Bremner… Who Else?, 1993–99; Bremner, Bird and Fortune, 1999–2010 (also stage version, Albery, 2002); Between Iraq and a Hard Place, 2003; Rory Bremner's Coalition Report, 2015; Rory Bremner's Election Report, 2015. Opera translations: Silver Lake (Weill), 1999; Carmen (Bizet), 2001; Orpheus in the Underworld (Offenbach), 2011; trans. Brecht, A Respectable Wedding, Young Vic, 2007. Theatre, Relative Values, Th. Royal, Bath, 2013, transf. Harold Pinter Th., 2014. British Comedy Award, 1993; BAFTA Award for Best Light Entertainment Performance, 1995, 1996; RTS Awards for Best Television Perf., 1995, 1999, 2000; Channel 4 political humorist of the year, 1998, 2000. *Publications:* (with John Bird and John Fortune) You Are Here, 2004. *Recreations:* cricket, opera, travel. *Address:* c/o PBJ Management, 22 Rathbone Street, W1T 1LG. *T:* (020) 7287 1112. *Club:* Lord's Taverners.

**BRENDEL, Alfred,** Hon. KBE 1989; concert pianist, 1948–2008; writer; *b* 5 Jan. 1931; *s* of Albert Brendel and Ida Brendel (*née* Wieltschnig); *m* 1960, Iris Heymann-Gonzala (marr. diss. 1972); one *d*; *m* 1975, Irene Semler (marr. diss. 2012); one *s* two *d. Educ:* Studied piano with: S. Deželić, 1937–43; L. V. Kaan, 1943–47; also under Edwin Fischer, P. Baumgartner and E. Steuermann; composition with Artur Michl, harmony with Franjo Dugan, Zagreb. Vienna State Diploma, 1947; Premio Bolzano Concorso Busoni, 1949. Concerts: most European countries, North and Latin America, Australia and New Zealand, also N and S Africa and Near and Far East. Many appearances Vienna and Salzburg Festivals, 1960–. Other Festivals: Athens, Granada, Bregenz, Würzburg, Aldeburgh, York, Cheltenham, Edinburgh, Bath, Puerto Rico, Barcelona, Prague, Lucerne, Dubrovnik, etc. Many long playing records (Bach to Schoenberg) incl. first complete recording of Beethoven's piano works (Grand Prix du Disque, 1965). Cycle of Beethoven Sonatas: London, 1962, 1977, 1982–83, 1992–95; Copenhagen, 1964; Vienna, 1965–66; Puerto Rico, 1968; BBC and Rome, 1970; Munich and Stuttgart, 1977; Amsterdam, Paris and Berlin, 1982–83; New York, 1983; 14 Eur. and 4 N Amer. cities, 1992–96; Cycle of Schubert piano works 1822–28 in 19 cities, incl. London, Paris, Amsterdam, Berlin, Vienna, New York, Los Angeles, 1987–88. Television (series): Schubert Piano Music (13 films), Bremen, 1978; Alfred Brendel Masterclass, BBC, 1983; Liszt Années de Pèlerinage, BBC, 1986; Schubert Last Three Sonatas, BBC, 1988. Hon. RAM; FRNCM 1999; Hon. RCM 1999; Hon. Mem., Amer. Acad. of Arts and Sciences, 1984; Korrespondierendes Mitglied, Bayer. Akad. der Wissenschaften (Orden pour le Mérite für Wissenschaften und Künste, 1991); Mitglied, Deutschen Akad. für Sprache und Dichtung, 2009; Hon. Fellow, Exeter Coll., Oxford, 1987; Hon. DMus: London, 1978; Sussex, 1981; Oxford, 1983; Warwick, 1991; Yale, 1992; Dublin UC, 1997; Exeter, 1998; RCM, 1999; Southampton, 2002; Boston New England Conservatoire, 2009; Hochschule Franz Liszt Weimar, 2009; Sheffield, 2010; Bucharest Musikuniv., 2011; McGill, 2011; Juilliard Sch., 2013; Bristol, 2016; York, 2018; DPhil Cologne, 1995; DLit Bari, 2011. Busoni Foundn Award, 1990; Hans von Bülow Medal, Kameradschaft der Berliner Philharmoniker eV, 1992; Gold Medal, Royal Philharmonic Soc., 1993; Ehrenmitgliedschaft der Wiener Philharmoniker, 1998; Léonie Sonnings Musikpris, Denmark, 2002; Ernst von Siemens Musikpreis, 2004; A Life for Music, Artur Rubinstein Prize, Venice, 2007; South Bank Show Award, 2009; Praemium Imperiale, Japan Art Assoc., 2009; Herbert von Karajan Music Prize, 2008; Musikpreis Duisburg, 2010; Franz Liszt Ehrenpreis Weimar, 2011; Goldene Mozart-Medaille Salzburg, 2014. Commandeur des Arts et des Lettres, 2004. *Publications:* Musical Thoughts and Afterthoughts (Essays), 1976; Music Sounded Out, 1990; Fingerzeig, 1996; Störendes Lachen während des Jaworts, 1997; One Finger Too Many, 1998; Kleine Teufel, 1999; Ausgerechnet Ich, 2000; Alfred Brendel on Music: collected essays, 2001; The Veil of Order: Alfred Brendel in conversation with Martin Meyer, 2002; Spiegelbild und schwarzer Spuk (poems), 2003; Cursing Bagels (poems), 2004; Complete Poems, 2005; Friedrich Hebbel, Weltgericht mit Pausen, 2008; Nach dem Schlussakkord, 2010; Playing the Human Game, 2010; A Pianist's A–Z, 2013; Wunderglaube und Misstonleiter (essays), 2014; Music, Sense and Nonsense: collected essays, 2015; Die Dame aus Arezzo, 2018; essays on music in: HiFi Stereophonie, Music and Musicians, Phono, Fono Forum, Österreichische Musikzeitschrift, Gramophone, Die Zeit, New York Rev. of Books, Frankfurter Allgemeine, Neue Zürcher Zeitung, etc. *Recreations:* literature, art galleries, architecture, unintentional humour, "kitsch". *Address:* Maestro Arts, One Eastfields Avenue, SW18 1FQ. *T:* 07496 480040.

**BRENNAN,** family name of **Baron Brennan**.

**BRENNAN,** Baron *cr* 2000 (Life Peer), of Bibury in the co. of Gloucestershire; **Daniel Joseph Brennan;** QC 1985; a Recorder of the Crown Court, since 1982; a Deputy High Court Judge, since 1994; *b* 19 March 1942; *s* of late Daniel Brennan and Mary Brennan; *m* 1968, Pilar, *d* of late Luis Sanchez Hernandez; four *s. Educ:* St Bede's Grammar Sch., Bradford; Victoria University of Manchester (LLB Hons). President, University Union, 1964–65. Called to the Bar: Gray's Inn, 1967 (Bencher, 1993); King's Inns, Dublin, 1990; NI, 2001. Mem., Criminal Injuries Compensation Bd, 1989–97; Ind. Assessor to MoD and MoJ (formerly to Home Sec.) on miscarriages of justice, 2001–11. Chm., Gen. Council of the Bar, 1999 (Vice Chm., 1998). President: Catholic Union of GB, 2001–14; Canning House, 2008–13 (Vice Pres., 2002–07). Patron, UK Consortium for Street Children, 2003–. Chm., Caux Round Table, 2005–10. FRSA 2000. Hon. LLD: Nottingham Trent, 1999; Manchester, 2000; Bradford, 2007; Nat. Inst. for Penal Scis, Mexico, 2008. Delegate for GB and Ireland, Sacred Military Constantinian Order of St George, 2006–10. Cross of St Raimond de Penafort (Spain), 2000; Order of Bernardo O'Higgins (Chile), 2005; Knight Commander of St Gregory (Vatican), 2008; Grand Cross of Order of Isabel la Católica (Spain), 2009. *Publications:* (gen. ed) Bullen and Leake, Precedents of Pleading, 14th edn 2001 to 18th edn 2015. *Address:* Matrix Chambers, Gray's Inn, WC1R 5LN. *T:* (020) 7404 3447, *Fax:* (020) 7404 3448. *Club:* Garrick.

**BRENNAN, Archibald Orr, (Archie),** OBE 1981; designer, weaver, teacher and lecturer, since 1984; *b* 7 Dec. 1931; *s* of James and Jessie Brennan; *m* 1956, Elizabeth Hewitt Carmichael (marr. diss.); three *d. Educ:* Boroughmuir Sch., Edinburgh; Edinburgh College of Art (DA). Training as tapestry weaver/student, 1947–62; Lectr, Edinburgh College of Art, 1962–78; Dir, Edin. Tapestry Co., 1962–77; co-ordinator/designer of all embellishment, new Nat. Parlt Bldg, PNG, 1978–84; Artist in residence, 1977, established production dept, 1978–84, Nat. Arts Sch., PNG. Pres., Soc. of Scottish Artists, 1977–78; Chm., British Craft Centre, 1977–78; travelling lectr, UK, USA, Canada, Australia, PNG, 1962–. Fellow, ANU, 1974–75. *Publications:* articles in various jls.

**BRENNAN, Denis,** CVO 2012; Head, Honours and Appointments Secretariat (formerly Ceremonial Officer), Cabinet Office, 2005–11; *b* 4 Nov. 1951; *s* of Michael and Mary Brennan; *m* 1975, Ursula Mary Brennan (see Dame Ursula Brennan). *Educ:* Gonville and Caius Coll., Cambridge (BA Philos. 1973). Ministry of Defence, 1973–94: Private Sec. to Parly Sec., RAF, 1977–78; policy posts incl. secondment to Cabinet Office, 1978–84; Private Sec. to Sec. of State, 1984–86; Head: Air Staff Secretariat, 1987–90; Housing Task Force, 1990–94; Cabinet Office: Hd, Infrastructure, Defence and Overseas Secretariat, 1994–2002; on loan to DEFRA, 2003–04. *Club:* Reform.

**BRENNAN, Denis Anthony James;** a District Judge (Magistrates' Courts), since 2011; *b* Hammersmith, 27 May 1959; *s* of Jeremiah and Kathleen Brennan; *m* 1995 (marr. diss. 2005); two *d. Educ:* Cardinal Vaughan Grammar Sch.; King's Coll., London (LLB Hons 1980). Babington Browne & Co.: articled clerk, 1982–84; admitted solicitor, 1984; asst solicitor, 1984–87; Geo. J. Dowse & Co.: asst solicitor, 1987–90; Salaried Partner, 1990–92; Equity Partner, 1992–2008; Associate Solicitor, Sonn, Macmillan Walker, 2008–11; a Dep. Dist Judge (Magistrates' Courts), 2003–11. *Recreations:* tennis, badminton, reading, spraffing, cinema, listening to The Pogues, The Lurkers and Tom Waits, going to Ireland. *Address:* c/o Hendon Magistrates' Court, The Court House, The Hyde, Hendon, NW9 7BY.

**BRENNAN, Hon. Sir (Francis) Gerard,** AC 1988; KBE 1981; GBS 2013; Non-Permanent Judge, Court of Final Appeal of Hong Kong, 2000–12; Chancellor, University of Technology, Sydney, 1998–2004; *b* 22 May 1928; *s* of Hon. Mr Justice (Frank Tenison) Brennan and Mrs Gertrude Brennan; *m* 1953, Dr Patricia (*née* O'Hara); three *s* four *d. Educ:* Christian Brothers Coll., Rockhampton, Qld; Downlands Coll., Toowoomba, Qld; Univ. of Qld (BA, LLB). Called to the Queensland Bar, 1951; QC (Australia) 1965. Judge, Aust. Indust. Court, and Additional Judge of Supreme Court of ACT, 1976–81; Judge, Fed. Court of Australia, 1977–81; Justice of the High Court, 1981–95; Chief Justice of Australia, 1995–98; Foundn Scientia Prof. of Law, Univ. of NSW, 1998–99; external Judge, Supreme Court, Republic of Fiji, 1999–2000. President: Admin. Appeals Tribunal, 1976–79; Admin. Review Council, 1976–79; Bar Assoc. of Qld, 1974–76; Aust. Bar Assoc., 1975–76; National Union of Aust. Univ. Students, 1949. Member: Exec. Law Council of Australia, 1974–76; Aust. Law Reform Commn, 1975–77. Hon. LLD: TCD, 1988; Queensland, 1996; ANU, 1996; Melbourne, 1998; UTS, 1998; NSW, 2005; Aust. Catholic Univ., 2017; Hon. DLitt Central Queensland, 1996; DUniv: Griffith, 1996; UTS, 2005. *Address:* (office) Suite 3003, Piccadilly Tower, 133 Castlereagh Street, Sydney, NSW 2000, Australia. *T:* (2) 92618704. *Club:* Australian (Sydney).

**BRENNAN, Kevin Denis;** MP (Lab) Cardiff West, since 2001; *b* 16 Oct. 1959; *s* of Michael John Brennan and Beryl Marie Brennan (*née* Evans); *m* 1988, Amy Lynn Wack; one *d. Educ:* St Alban's R C Comprehensive Sch., Pontypool; Pembroke Coll., Oxford (BA); UC, Cardiff (PGCE); Univ. of Glamorgan (MSc). Volunteer organiser/news ed., Cwmbran Community Press, 1982–84; Hd, Econs and Business Studies, Radyr Comprehensive Sch., 1985–94; Res. Officer for Rhodri Morgan, MP, 1995–2000; Special Advr to First Minister, Nat. Assembly for Wales, 2000. An Asst Govt Whip, 2005–06; a Lord Comr of HM Treasury (Govt Whip), 2006–07; Parly Under-Sec. of State, DCSF, 2007–08; Parly Sec. and Minister for the Third Sector, Cabinet Office, 2008–09; Minister for E Midlands, 2008–10; Minister of State, BIS and DCSF, 2009–10; Shadow Schs Minister, 2010–15; Shadow Minister for: Trade, Industry and Intellectual Property,

2015–16; Arts and Heritage, 2016–. *Recreations:* Rugby (watching now), music (Mem., parly rock gp MP4). *Address:* House of Commons, SW1A 0AA; 395 Cowbridge Road East, Canton, Cardiff CF5 1JG.

**BRENNAN, Dame Maureen,** DBE 2005; Chief Executive Officer, Matrix Academy Trust, since 2017 (Director, since 2013); *b* 26 March 1954; *d* of Joseph and Elizabeth Eddy; *m* 1989, Denis Brennan; one *s*. *Educ:* St Agnes' RC Grammar Sch. for Girls; Newman Coll., Birmingham (BEd). Teacher, St Chad's RC Comprehensive Sch., Birmingham, 1976–80; Hd of Dept, Ladywood Sch., 1980–85; Staff Develt Tutor, Equal Opportunities Co-ordinator, Birmingham Adv. Service, 1985–90; Dep. Hd, Great Barr Sch., 1990–2000; Principal, Hillcrest Sch. and Community Coll., Dudley, 2000–07; Headteacher, Barr Beacon School (formerly Language Coll.), 2007–14; Executive Headteacher: Barr Beacon Language Coll. and Sneyd Community Sch., 2010–11; Barr Beacon Sch., Walsall and Etone Coll., Nuneaton, 2014–17; Bloxwich (formerly Mirus) Acad., Walsall, 2015–17. Nat. Leader of Educn, 2015; Mem., W Midlands Headteacher Bd, Sch. Comrs Gps, 2017–. Fellow, Worcester Univ., 2012. *Address:* Matrix Academy Trust, Leamore Lane, Bloxwich, Walsall WS2 7PS. *T:* (01922) 211264. *E:* mbrennan@matrixacademytrust.org.uk.

**BRENNAN, Nicola Jayne Maria Louise;** *see* Thorp, N. J. M. L.

**BRENNAN, Sarah,** OBE 2017; Chief Executive, YoungMinds Trust, since 2008 (Interim Chief Executive, 2007–08); *b* London, 31 March 1958; *d* of James and Christine Brennan; partner, Sophie Arnold. *Educ:* Univ. of York (BA Hons Philosophy/Sociol. 1980); London Sch. of Econs and Pol Sci. (MSc Voluntary Sector Orgn 1994); Richmond Coll. (Dip. Counselling 1990). Youth worker, 1982–89; Student Counsellor, Roehampton Art Coll., 1989–91; Develt Manager, St Giles Trust, 1991–94; Dir Services, Centrepoint, 1994–2001; CEO, Motiv 8, 2001–06. *Recreations:* mountain trekking, good wines (WSET Level 3 qualif.), ski-ing, cinema, day skipper. *Address:* Tythe Barn, Greenways, Ovingdean, E Sussex BN2 7BA. *T:* 07813 876268. *E:* sarah.brennan@youngminds.org.uk.

**BRENNAN, (Stephen) Patrick C.;** *see* Cracroft-Brennan.

**BRENNAN, Timothy Roger;** QC 2001; a Recorder, since 2000; a Deputy High Court Judge, since 2008; *b* 11 April 1958. *Educ:* Olchfa Sch., Swansea; Balliol Coll., Oxford (BCL, MA). Called to the Bar, Gray's Inn, 1981 (Atkin Schol. 1981; Bencher, 2006; Mem., Mgt Cttee, 2013–15); in practice as barrister specialising in tax, public, commercial and employment law; Addnl Jun. Counsel to Inland Revenue (Common Law), 1991–97, Jun. Counsel, 1997–2001; Asst Recorder, 1997–2000; a Judge of the Employment Appeal Tribunal, 2002–04. Elected Hd of Chambers, 2013–. Mem., Gen. Council of the Bar, 1987, 1988 (Mem., Conduct Cttee, 1989, 1995–98 and 2005; Mem., Professional Practice Cttee, 2010–13; Vice-Chm., 2014); Vice-Chm., Complaints Cttee, Bar Standards Bd, 2006–09. *Publications:* contribs to various tech. legal pubns. *Address:* Devereux Chambers, Queen Elizabeth Building, Temple, EC4Y 9BS. *T:* (020) 7353 7534.

**BRENNAN, Dame Ursula (Mary),** DCB 2013; Permanent Secretary, Ministry of Justice, 2012–15; Clerk of the Crown in Chancery, 2012–15; *b* 28 Oct. 1952; *d* of Philip and Mary Burns; *m* 1975, Denis Brennan, *qv*. *Educ:* Univ. of Kent at Canterbury (BA Hons English and Amer. Lit). ILEA, 1973–75; Department of Health and Social Security, later of Social Security, 1975–2001; Head, Disability Benefits Policy, 1990–93; Dir, IT Services Agency, 1993–95; Dir, Change Management, Benefits Agency, 1995–97; Gp Dir, Working Age Services, 1997–2001; Gp Dir, Working Age and Children Strategy, DWP, 2001–04; Dir Gen., Natural Resources and Rural Affairs, DEFRA, 2004–05; Chief Exec., Office for Criminal Justice Reform, 2006–08; Dir Gen., Corporate Performance, MoJ, 2008; Second Perm. Under-Sec. of State, 2008–10, Perm. Under-Sec. of State, 2010–12, MoD. Mem. Bd, Nat. Th., 2011–19. Mem. Council, Univ. of Kent, 2015–.

**BRENT, Prof. Leslie Baruch,** CBiol; FRSB; Professor Emeritus, University of London, since 1990; *b* Köslin, Germany, 5 July 1925; *s* of Charlotte and Arthur Baruch; arrived UK in Kindertransport, 1938; *m* 1st, 1954, Joanne Elisabeth Manley (marr. diss. 1991); one *s* two *d*; 2nd, 1991, Carol Pamela Martin. *Educ:* Bunce Court Sch., Kent; Birmingham Central Technical Coll.; Univ. of Birmingham; UCL. BSc Birmingham, PhD London. FRSB (FIBiol 1962). Laboratory technician, 1941–43; Army service, 1943–47, Captain; Lectr, Dept of Zoology, UCL, 1954–62; Rockefeller Res. Fellow, Calif Inst of Technology, 1956–57; Res. scientist, Nat. Inst. for Med. Res., 1962–65; Prof. of Zoology, Univ. of Southampton, 1965–69; Prof. of Immunology, St Mary's Hosp. Med. Sch., London, 1969–90. European Editor, Transplantation, 1963–68; Gen. Sec., British Transplantation Soc., 1971–75; Pres., The Transplantation Society, 1976–78; Mem., ONE Study on internat. clin. trial on immuno-regulatory cells in kidney transplantation, 2012–17; Chairman: Wessex Br., Inst. of Biol., 1966–68; Organising Cttee, 9th Internat. Congress of The Transplantation Soc., 1978–82; Fellowships Cttee, Inst. of Biol., 1982–85; Art Cttee, St Mary's Hosp. Med. Sch., 1988–92. Pres., Guild of Undergrads, Birmingham Univ., 1950–51. Chairman: Haringey Community Relations Council, 1979–80; Haringey SDP, 1981–83. Governor: Creighton Sch., 1974–79; Yerbury Sch., 1999–2006; Mem., Islington Schs Ind. Appeals Panel, 2001–06. Trustee, British Scholarship Trust for Former Yugoslavian Territories, 1997–2014. Mem., Eur. Acad. for Scis and Arts (Salzburg), 2002. Hon. MRCP 1986; Hon. Mem., Koszalin Regl Chamber of Physicians (Poland), 2005. Hon. Member: British Transplantation Soc., 1988; Eur. Soc. for Organ Transplantation, 2011; hon. mem. of several foreign scientific socs. FZS 2007. Vice-Chancellor's Prize, Birmingham Univ., 1951; Scientific Medal, Zool Soc., 1963; Peter Medawar Medal and Prize, Internat. Transplantation Soc., 1994. Played hockey for UAU and Staffs, 1949–51. Co-editor, Immunology Letters, 1983–90. *Publications:* (ed with L. Holborow) Progress in Immunology, 5 vols, 1974; (ed jtly) Organ Transplantation: current clinical and immunological concepts, 1989; History of Transplantation Immunology, 1997; (ed jtly) Verstörte Kindheiten. Das Jüdische Waisenhaus in Pankow als Ort der Zuflucht, Geborgenheit und Vertreibung, 2008; Sunday's Child?: a memoir, 2009 (trans. German); articles in scientific and med. jls on transplantation immunology, and obituaries and book reviews. *Recreations:* music, novels, politics. *Address:* Flat 8, Jarman Mansions, 3 Olmstead Close, N10 3FB.

**BRENT, Michael Leon;** QC 1983; a Recorder, 1990–2000; a Deputy High Court Judge, 1994–2000; *b* 8 June 1936; *m* 1965, Rosalind Keller; two *d*. *Educ:* Manchester Grammar Sch.; Manchester Univ. (LLB Hons). Called to the Bar, Gray's Inn, 1961; practised on: Northern Circuit, 1961–67 (Circuit Junior, 1964); Midland and Oxford Circuit, 1967–2000; Hd of Chambers, 1988–97. Mem. Bd, Criminal Injuries Compensation Appeals Panel, 1999–2002. Pres., St John's Wood Soc., 2009–18. *Address:* 9 Gough Square, EC4A 3DG.

**BRENT, Dr Richard,** FRHistS; QC 2017; *b* Crumlin, Gwent, 14 July 1959; *s* of Ernest and Jean Brent; *m* 1992, Clare Batten; one *s* one *d*. *Educ:* City of London Sch.; Peterhouse, Cambridge (BA 1980); Harvard Univ.; Nuffield Coll., Oxford (DPhil 1985). FRHistS 2004. Kennedy Schol., Choate Meml Fellow, Harvard Univ., 1980–81; Res. Student, Nuffield Coll., Oxford, 1981–84; Res. Fellow, St John's Coll., Cambridge, 1985–89; trainee, then asst solicitor, Slaughter & May, 1989–94; called to the Bar, Middle Temple, 1995. Mem., Bar Council, 2014–18. Vis. Fellow, LSE, 2017–18. *Publications:* Liberal Anglican Politics, 1987; Directives: rights and remedies in English and community law, 2001; Banks and Financial Crime, 2008, 2nd edn 2017. *Recreations:* reading, walking, sailing, history. *Address:* 3 Verulam Buildings, Gray's Inn, WC1R 5NT. *T:* (020) 7831 8441. *E:* clerks@3vb.com.

**BRENT, Prof. Richard Peirce,** PhD, DSc; Emeritus Professor, Mathematical Sciences Institute and Research School of Computer Science, Australian National University, since 2011; Conjoint Professor, University of Newcastle, New South Wales, since 2011; *b* 20 April 1946; *s* of Oscar and Nancy Brent; *m* 1st, 1969, Erin O'Connor (*d* 2005); two *s*; 2nd, 2007, Judy-anne Osborn; one *s*. *Educ:* Melbourne Grammar Sch.; Monash Univ. (BSc 1968; DSc 1981); Stanford Univ. (PhD 1971). FAA 1982; FIEEE 1991. IBM Res., Yorktown Heights, NY, 1971–72; Australian National University: Res. Fellow, 1972–73; Fellow, 1973–76; Sen. Fellow, 1976–78; Foundation Prof. of Computer Science, 1978–98; Prof. of Computing Sci., Univ. of Oxford, and Fellow of St Hugh's Coll., Oxford, 1998–2005; Fedn Fellow, Mathematical Scis Inst., 2005–10, Distinguished Prof., 2010–11, ANU. Visiting Professor: Stanford Univ., 1974–75; Univ. of Calif at Berkeley, 1977–78; Harvard Univ., 1997. Fellow, ACM, 1994. Aust. Math. Soc. Medal, 1984; Hannan Medal, Aust. Acad. of Sci., 2005. *Publications:* Algorithms for Minimization without Derivatives, 1973, repr. 2002; Computational Complexity and the Analysis of Algorithms, 1980; (with P. Zimmermann) Modern Computer Arithmetic, 2010. *Recreations:* music, chess, bridge. *Address:* Mathematical Sciences Institute, Australian National University, ACT 2601, Australia.

**BRENTFORD,** 4th Viscount *cr* 1929, of Newick; **Crispin William Joynson-Hicks;** Bt of Holmbury, 1919; Bt of Newick, 1956; Partner, Taylor Joynson Garrett (formerly Joynson-Hicks), 1961–95; *b* 7 April 1933; *s* of 3rd Viscount Brentford and Phyllis (*d* 1979), *o d* of late Major Herbert Allfrey, Tetbury, Glos; *S* father, 1983; *m* 1964, Gillian Evelyn Schluter (*see* Viscountess Brentford); one *s* three *d*. *Educ:* Eton; New College, Oxford. Admitted solicitor, 1960. Master, Girdlers' Co., 1983–84. *Heir: s* Hon. Paul William Joynson-Hicks [*b* 18 April 1971; *m* 2006, Catharine, *d* of Richard James Kay Muir, *qv*; two *s* (one *d* decd)]. *Address:* 5 Birchfield, Church Road, Sundridge, Kent TN14 6DQ. *T:* (01959) 565846.

**BRENTFORD, Viscountess; Gillian Evelyn Joynson-Hicks,** OBE 1996; FCA; Third Church Estates Commissioner, 1999–2005; *b* 22 Nov. 1942; *d* of Gerald Edward Schluter, OBE; *m* 1964, Crispin William Joynson-Hicks (*see* Viscount Brentford); one *s* three *d*. *Educ:* West Heath Sch. FCA 1965. Director: Edward Schluter & Co. (London) Ltd, 1971–88; M. A. F. Europe, 1990–97. Mem., General Synod of C of E, 1990–2005; a Church Comr, 1991–98 (Mem., Bd of Govs, 1993–98); Chm., House of Laity, Dio. of Chichester, 1991–99; Mem., Crown Appts Commn, 1995–2002. Pres., CMS, 1998–2007. Chm., Café Africa Internat., 2006–12. High Sheriff, E Sussex, 1998–99. *Recreations:* family, gardens, travel. *Address:* 5 Birchfield, Church Road, Sundridge, Kent TN14 6DQ.

**BRENTON, Sir Anthony Russell,** KCMG 2007 (CMG 2001); HM Diplomatic Service, retired; Senior Fellow, Department of Politics and International Studies, University of Cambridge, since 2011; *b* 1 Jan. 1950; *s* of Ivan Bernard Brenton and Jean Sylvia (*née* Rostgard); *m* 1981, Susan Mary Penrose; one *s* two *d*. *Educ:* Queens' Coll. Cambridge (BA); Open Univ. (MPhil). Joined HM Diplomatic Service, 1975; Cairo, 1978–81; European Communities Dept, FCO, 1981–85; with UK Perm. Repn to EC, 1985–86; Dep. Chef de Cabinet, EC, 1986–89; Counsellor, 1989; Head: UN Dept, FCO, 1989–90; Envmt, Sci. and Energy Dept, FCO, 1990–92; Fellow, Centre for Internat. Affairs, Harvard Univ., 1992–93; Counsellor, Moscow, 1994–98; Dir, FCO, 1998–2001; Minister, Washington, 2001–04; Ambassador to Russia, 2004–08. Dir, Russo-British Chamber of Commerce, 2008–; Advr, Lloyd's Insce Mkt, 2008–13; Mem., Adv. Bd, EU/Russia Centre, 2010–. Chm., Leys and St Faith's Foundn, 2010–. Extraordinary Fellow, Wolfson Coll., Cambridge, 2009–18; Fellow Commoner, Queens' Coll., Cambridge, 2014–; Hon. Fellow, Strategy and Security Inst., Exeter Univ., 2013–. *Publications:* The Greening of Machiavelli, 1994; Historically Inevitable?: turning points of the Russian Revolution, 2016; press and mag. articles on Russia. *Recreations:* history, Russia. *Address:* Wolfson College, Cambridge CB3 9BB.

**BRENTON, Howard,** FRSL; playwright; *b* 13 Dec. 1942; *s* of Donald Henry Brenton and Rose Lilian (*née* Lewis); *m* 1970, Jane Fry; two *s*. *Educ:* Chichester High Sch. for Boys; St Catharine's Coll., Cambridge (BA Hons English). Hon. DLit: North London; Westminster, 2002; Portsmouth, 2008. FRSL 2016. *Full-length stage plays:* Revenge, 1969; Hitler Dances, and Measure for Measure (after Shakespeare), 1972; Magnificence, 1973; The Churchill Play, 1974; Government Property, 1975; Weapons of Happiness, 1976 (Evening Standard Award); Epsom Downs, 1977; Sore Throats, 1979; The Romans in Britain, 1980; Thirteenth Night, 1981; The Genius, 1983; Bloody Poetry, 1984; Greenland, 1988; H. I. D. (Hess is Dead), 1989; Berlin Bertie, 1992; Kit's Play, 2000; Bacchae/Backup, 2001; Paul, 2005; In Extremis, 2006; Never So Good, 2008; Anne Boleyn, 2010; The Ragged Trousered Philanthropists (stage adaption), 2010; 55 Days, 2012; Dances of Death (adaptation), 2013; #aiww: The Arrest of Ai Weiwei, 2013; Drawing the Line, 2013; Doctor Scroggy's War, 2014; Lawrence After Arabia, 2016; The Blinding Light, 2017; Miss Julie (adaptation), 2017; The Shadow Factory, 2018; Jude, 2019; *one-act stage plays:* Gum and Goo, Heads, The Education of Skinny Spew, and Christie in Love, 1969; Wesley, 1970; Scott of the Antarctic, and A Sky-blue Life, 1971; How Beautiful with Badges, 1972; Mug, 1973; The Thing (for children), 1982; Ransomed, 2015; To the Hacienda, 2016; *collaborations:* (with six others) Lay-By, 1970; (with six others) England's Ireland, 1971; (with David Hare) Brassneck, 1973; (with Trevor Griffiths, David Hare and Ken Campbell), Deeds, 1978; (with Tony Howard) A Short Sharp Shock, 1980; (with Tunde Ikoli) Sleeping Policemen, 1983; (with David Hare) Pravda, 1985 (London Standard Award); Playing Away (opera), 1994 (score by Benedict Mason); *with Tariq Ali:* Iranian Nights, 1989; Moscow Gold, 1990; Ugly Rumours, 1998; *with Tariq Ali and Andy de la Tour:* Collateral Damage, 1999; Snogging Ken, 2000; *television plays:* Lushly, 1971; Brassneck (adaptation of stage play), 1974; The Saliva Milkshake, 1975 (also perf. theatre); The Paradise Run, 1976; Desert of Lies, 1984; *television series:* Dead Head, 1986; (with David Wolstencroft and Simon Mirren) Spooks, 2002–03 (BAFTA award for Best TV Drama series); *radio play:* Nasser's Eden, 1998; *versions of classics:* Bertolt Brecht, The Life of Galileo, 1980; Georg Buchner, Danton's Death, 1982, 2010; Bertolt Brecht, Conversations in Exile, 1982; Goethe, Faust, 1995; Strindberg: Dances Of Death, 2013; Miss Julie, 2017; Creditors, 2019. *Publications:* Diving for Pearls (novel), 1989; Hot Irons: diaries, essays, journalism, 1995; many plays published. *Recreation:* painting. *Address:* c/o Casarotto Ramsay Ltd, Waverley House, 7–12 Noel Street, W1F 8GQ. *T:* (020) 7287 4450.

**BRENTON, Jonathan Andrew,** PhD; Principal Policy Advisor, EU Negotiations, Confederation of British Industry, since 2018; *b* Kampala, Uganda, 24 Dec. 1965; *s* of Prof. David Brenton and Anne Brenton; *m* 2001, Sayana Sarbaa; one *s* two *d*. *Educ:* Bristol Univ. (MA English Lit.); Boston Univ. (MA English Lit.); PhD Cantab 1998. Entered FCO, 1994; Asst Desk Officer, EU Dept Internal, 1994–95; Russian lang. trng, 1995–96; Second Sec. (Commercial), 1996–98, Hd, Econ. Sect., 1998–2000, Moscow; Hd of Sect., EU Dept External, 2000–02; German lang. trng, 2002–03; Press Sec., Berlin, 2003–06; Dep. Hd, Africa Dept Equatorial, FCO, 2006–08; Hd, Jt Mgt Office, Brussels, 2008–10; Ambassador to Belgium, 2010–14; Hd, Campaigns and Engagement Dept, FCO, 2014–15; Minister Counsellor (Prosperity), Moscow, 2015–17; Europe Directorate, FCO, 2017–18. *Recreation:* reading. *Address:* Confederation of British Industry, 78 Cannon Place, EC4N 6HN.

**BRENTON, Timothy Deane;** QC 1998; *b* 4 Nov. 1957; *s* of late Comdr R. W. Brenton, RN and of P. C. D. Brenton; *m* 1981, Annabel Louisa Robson; one *s* one *d*. *Educ:* King's Sch., Rochester; BRNC, Dartmouth; Bristol Univ. (LLB 1st cl. Hons 1979). RN, 1975–79; Lectr in Law, King's Coll. London, 1980; called to the Bar, Middle Temple, 1981; in practice at the Bar, 1981–. Mem., Editl Bd, International Maritime Law, 1994–2001. Hon. Counsel and Trustee, Seafarers UK (formerly King George's Fund for Sailors), 2000–09. *Recreations:* golf, country pursuits, ski-ing, music. *Address:* 7 King's Bench Walk, Inner Temple, EC4Y 7DS. *T:* (020) 7910 8300.

**BRENTWOOD, Bishop of, (RC),** since 2014; **Rt Rev. Alan Williams;** *b* Oldham, 15 March 1951. *Educ:* Durham Univ. (BSc); Univ. of Hull (MA); London Univ. (PhD Psychol.); Univ. of Cambridge (BA); Allen Hall Seminary. Final vows, Soc. of Mary (Marist Fathers), 1981, ordained priest, 1983; Parish Priest, St Lawrence of Canterbury, Sidcup; Superior, Marist Fathers in Eng., 2000–08; Dir, Nat. Shrine of Our Lady at Walsingham. Catholic Chaplain, Sheffield Hallam Univ. *Address:* Cathedral House, Ingrave Road, Brentwood, Essex CM15 8AT.

**BRERETON, Donald,** CB 2001; Vice-President, Carers UK, since 2013 (Chairman, 2005–13); *b* 18 July 1945; *s* of Clarence Vivian and Alice Gwendolin Brereton; *m* 1969, Mary Frances Turley; one *s* two *d*. *Educ:* Plymouth Coll.; Univ. of Newcastle upon Tyne (BA Hons Pol. and Soc. Admin). VSO, Malaysia, 1963–64. Asst Principal, Min. of Health, 1968; Asst Private Sec. to Sec. of State for Social Services, 1971; Private Sec. to Perm. Sec., DHSS, 1972; Prin., Health Services Planning, 1973; Private Sec. to Sec. of State for Social Services, 1979–82; Asst Sec., DHSS Policy Strategy Unit, 1982–83; Sec. to Housing Benefit Rev. Team, 1984; Asst Sec., Housing Benefit, 1985–89; Under Sec., Head of Prime Minister's Efficiency Unit, 1989–93; Under Sec., Social Security Policy Gp, DSS, 1993–2000; Dir, Disability, DSS, then Gp Dir, Disability and Carers, DWP, 2000–03. Dir, 2004–09, Chm. Pension Trustees, 2010–, Motability. Member: Standing Commn on Carers, 2008–15; NHS Nat. Quality Bd, 2009–15. *Recreations:* tennis, holidays, books, gardening, bridge, theatre. *Address:* Carers UK, 20 Great Dover Street, SE1 4LX. *Clubs:* Walthamstow Cricket, Tennis and Squash (Treas., 2012–).

**BRERETON, Jack Edgar;** MP (C) Stoke-on-Trent South, since 2017; *b* Stoke-on-Trent, 13 May 1991; *m* 2016, Laura. *Educ:* Stoke-on-Trent Sixth Form Coll.; Keele Univ. (BA Politics and Internat. Relns); University Coll. London (MSc Democracy and Comparative Politics). Mem. (C), Stoke-on-Trent CC, 2011– (Cabinet Mem. for Regeneration, Transport and Heritage, 2015–17). Contested (C) Stoke-on-Trent Central, Feb. 2017. *Address:* House of Commons, SW1A 0AA.

**BRESLAND, (David) Allan;** Member (DemU) West Tyrone, Northern Ireland Assembly, 2007–11; *b* 16 Aug. 1945; *s* of Hugh and May Bresland; *m* 1966, Mary Elizabeth Martin; four *d*. *Educ:* Ballylaw Primary Sch. Lorry driver: R. J. Hemphill, 1967–76; Water Service, 1976–2001. UDR (pt-time), 1970–85. Mem. (DemU), Strabane DC, 1993–. Contested (DemU) W Tyrone, NI Assembly, 2011. *Recreation:* watching and following cricket. *Address:* 41 Millhaven, Sion Mills, Co. Tyrone BT82 9FG. *T:* (028) 8165 8579, *Fax:* (028) 8165 9177. *E:* a.bresland@btconnect.com.

**BRESLIN, Theresa,** OBE 2019; writer; former librarian; *b* Scotland; *d* of Thomas Green and Sarah Green; *m* Tom Breslin; one *s* three *d*. *Educ:* St Ninian's High Sch., Kirkintilloch; Aston Univ., Birmingham. ALA, then MCILIP. Former mobile librarian, community librarian and Principal Asst, Liby Youth Services, E Dunbartonshire Council. Former Mem., Public Lending Right Adv. Cttee. Manager, Scottish Writers' Proj.; Founder, W of Scotland Children's Book Gp; former Pres., Strathkelvin and Allander Writers' Gp; former Chm., Scottish Youth Librarians Forum; Pres., Trustee Bd, Chartered Inst. of Liby and Inf. Professionals in Scotland, 2016; Member: Fedn of Children's Book Gps; IBBY; Cttee, Soc. of Authors (Scotland); Scottish Children's Writers' Gp; Youth Strategy; Focus Gp, Nat. Year of Reading. Former Dir, Scottish Book Trust. Hon. Mem., Scottish Liby Assoc. 2000. Civic Award, Strathkelvin DC. *Publications:* novels: Simon's Challenge, 1988 (Fidler Award, Young Book Trust, 1988; Best of the Decade Award, Scottish Book Trust, 1992); Different Directions, 1989; A Time to Reap, 1991; New School Blues, 1992; Bullies at School, 1993; Kezzie, 1993; Whispers in the Graveyard, 1994 (Carnegie Medal, 1995); Alien Force, 1995; Missing, 1995; A Homecoming for Kezzie, 1995; Name Games, 1996; Death or Glory Boys, 1996 (Sheffield Book Award, 1997); Blair the Winner!, 1997; Across the Roman Wall, 1997; Body Parts, 1997; The Dream Master, 1999; Starship Rescue, 1999; Blair Makes a Splash, 1999; Duncan of Carrick, 2000; Dream Master: Nightmare!, 2000; Remembrance, 2002 (Best Book for Young Adults, Amer. Liby Assoc., 2003); (ed jtly) My Mum's a Punk, 2002; Dream Master: Gladiator, 2003; Saskia's Journey, 2004; Prisoner in Alcatraz, 2004; Dream Master: Arabian Nights, 2004; Divided City, 2005 (Catalyst Book Award, N Lanarkshire Council, 2005, RED Book Award, Falkirk Council, 2008); Mutant, 2005; The Medici Seal, 2006; Cold Spell, 2007; Midsummer Magic, 2007; Trick or Treat?, 2007; Alligator, 2008; The Nostradamus Prophecy, 2008; Prisoners of the Inquisition, 2010; Ghost Soldier, 2014; Caged, 2016; The Rasputin Dagger, 2017; *plays:* Alligator: the play, 2009; Whispers in the Graveyard: the play, 2009; *non-fiction:* Power Pack: the active guide to using libraries; contrib. short stories in collections; contribs to professional jls on children's literacy and literature. *Recreations:* reading, walking, exploring ancient standing stones, burial grounds and graveyards, old children's books, theatre, film. *W:* www.theresabreslin.com.

**BRETHERTON, James Russell;** Secretary, 1989–2003, and Director of Corporate Services, 1998–2003, United Kingdom Atomic Energy Authority; *b* 28 March 1943; *y s* of Russell Frederick Bretherton, CB and Jocelyn Nina Mathews; *m* 1968, Harriet Grace Drew, *d* of Sir Arthur Charles Walter Drew, KCB; two *s*. *Educ:* King's Sch., Canterbury; Wadham Coll., Oxford (MA History). Voluntary Service as Asst Dist Officer, Nigeria, 1965–66; Asst Principal, Min. of Fuel and Power, 1966–70; Principal, Min. of Technol. 1970–76; Principal Private Sec. to Sec. of State for Energy, 1976–78; Head of Oil Industry Div., Internat. Energy Agency, Paris, 1980–82; Asst Sec., Dept of Energy, 1983–86; United Kingdom Atomic Energy Authority: Principal Finance and Programmes Officer, 1986–89; Commercial and Planning Dir, 1990–94; Dir, Property Mgt and Services, 1994–98. *Recreations:* gardening, walking, bassoon playing (St Giles Orch.), bridge. *Address:* Highview, 15 Hid's Copse Road, Oxford OX2 9JJ. *T:* (01865) 863388.

*See also* P. C. Drew.

**BRETON, Guy,** CM 2014; MD; Rector, University of Montreal, since 2010; *b* Saint-Hyacinthe, Quebec, 1 April 1950; *s* of Gérard Breton and Jeannette Morin; *m* 1974, Andrée Despins; one *d*. *Educ:* Univ. of Sherbrooke (MD 1974); Coll. des Médecins du Québec (Cert. specialist in diagnostic radiol. 1978); Royal Coll. of Canada (Cert. specialist in diagnostic radiol. 1978); Amer. Coll. of Radiol. (Cert. specialist in diagnostic radiol. 1978). FRCPC 1978. University of Montreal: Associate Clinical Prof., 1979–94, Prof. of Radiology, 1994–, Chm., 1996–2003, Dept of Radiol., Radio-oncology and Nuclear Medicine, Faculty of Medicine; Exec. Vice Dean, Faculty of Medicine, 2003–06; Exec. Vice-Rector, 2006–10; University of Montreal Hospital Centre: Hd, Radiol. Dept, 1997–2000; Special Advr to Chm. of Bd and to Exec. Dir, 2008; Vice-Pres., Planning—Health and Services, Teaching and Res., Implantation Soc. for Univ. of Montreal Hosp. Centre, 2001–03. Hon. Prof., China Univ. of Political Sci. and Law, 2013. Hd, Radiol. Dept, Saint-Luc Hosp., 1983–97; Pres. and CEO, Radiologie Varad, 1983–97. President: Quebec Assoc. of Radiologists, 1987–97 (Sec., 1979–87); Canadian Heads of Academic Radiol. of Canada, 1998–2000. Ambassador, Univ. of Sherbrooke, 2010. Hon. Dr: Shanghai Jiao Tong Univ., 2013; Univ. des Technologies de Compiègne, 2013. Albert-Jutras Prize, 2009, Personality of the Year, 2011, Société Canadienne Française de Radiologie. Chevalier, Ordre des Palmes Académiques (France), 2013. *Recreations:* family, golf, walking, music. *Address:* University of Montreal, PO Box 6128, Downtown Branch, Montreal, QC H3C 3J7, Canada. *T:* (514) 3436991. *E:* guy.breton@umontreal.ca.

**BRETSCHER, Barbara Mary Frances, (Mrs M. S. Bretscher);** *see* Pearse, B. M. F.

**BRETSCHER, Mark Steven,** PhD; FRS 1985; Visitor, Division of Cell Biology, Medical Research Council Laboratory of Molecular Biology, Cambridge, 2005–12 (Member of Scientific Staff, 1965–2005; Head of Division, 1984–95); *b* 8 Jan. 1940; *s* of late Egon Bretscher, CBE and Hanni (*née* Greminger). *m* 1978, Barbara Mary Frances Pearse, *qv*; one *s* one *d*. *Educ:* Abingdon Sch., Berks; Gonville and Caius Coll., Cambridge (MA, PhD). Res. Fellow, Gonville and Caius Coll., Cambridge, 1964–70. Vis. Professor: Harvard Univ., 1975; Stanford Univ., 1984. Friedrich Miescher Prize, Swiss Biochemical Soc., 1979. *Publications:* papers in scientific jls on protein biosynthesis, membrane structure and cell locomotion. *Recreation:* gardening. *Address:* Ram Cottage, Commercial End, Swaffham Bulbeck, Cambridge CB25 0ND. *T:* (01223) 811276. *E:* msb@mrc-lmb.cam.ac.uk.

**BRETT,** family name of **Viscount Esher.**

**BRETT, Michael John Lee;** freelance financial journalist, part-time lecturer and writer, since 1982; *b* 23 May 1939; *s* of late John Brett and Margaret Brett (*née* Lee). *Educ:* King's Coll. Sch., Wimbledon; Wadham Coll., Oxford (BA Modern Langs). Investors Review, 1962–64; Fire Protection Assoc., 1964–68; Investors Chronicle, 1968–82: Dep. Editor, 1973–77; Editor, 1977–82. Past Director: Throgmorton Publications; Financial Times Business Publishing Div. *Publications:* Finance for Business: private sector finance; (contrib.) Valuation and Investment Appraisal; How to Read the Financial Pages; Property and Money, 1990; How to Figure Out Company Accounts, 2003. *Recreations:* travelling, reading.

*See also* S. A. L. Brett.

**BRETT, Natalie Anne;** Head, London College of Communication and Pro-Vice-Chancellor, International, University of the Arts, London, since 2013; *b* Pinner, 3 July 1961; *d* of Kenneth and Hazel Tomlin; *m* 2000, Terrence Brett. *Educ:* The Poly., Wolverhampton (BA Hons Graphic Design 1983). Illustrator and graphic designer, 1983–2003 (clients included Penguin, Guardian, BBC, New York Times, IPC mags, and Saatchi and Saatchi); University of the Arts, London: Course Dir, Foundn Art and Design, 2003–06, Dean, 2006–08, Chelsea Coll. of Art and Design; Dean, Camberwell Coll. of Arts, 2008–13. Ext. Gov., Brighton Metropolitan (formerly City) Coll., 2015–. Trustee, Global Univ. Tech. Coll., 2016–. *Recreations:* collecting, travelling, fishing. *Address:* London College of Communication, Elephant and Castle, SE1 6SB. *T:* (020) 7514 8013. *E:* n.brett@lcc.arts.ac.uk.

**BRETT, Richard John;** General Manager, Age UK Torbay, 2011–15; Consultant, Aston Group UK, since 2002 (Director, 2000–01; Joint Managing Director, 2001–02); *b* 23 Oct. 1947; *s* of Henry William Brett and Dorothy Ada Brett; *m* 1st, 1972, Alison Elizabeth Lambert (marr. diss. 1991); one *d*; 2nd, 1991, Maria Antoinette Brown. *Educ:* Univ. of Bradford (MSc). FCA; Associate, Inst. of Taxation. Leonard C. Bye, Chartered Accountants, Middlesbrough, 1964; ICI Petro-chemicals, 1971; Finance Director: Chloride Shires, 1976; Chloride Automotive Batteries, 1979; Westpark, 1981; Thorn EMI Datatech, 1985–88; Gp Dir, Finance and Mgt Services, CAA, 1988–96; Man. Dir, Solution Partners Ltd, 1996–2000. Finance Manager, Age UK (formerly Age Concern) Torbay, 2005. Non-exec. Chair, Age UK Devonwide Enterprises Ltd, 2015–. Trustee: Homeyards Botanical Gardens, 2014–; Pavilions Teignmouth, 2013– (Chair, 2016–); Dir, Pavilions Teignmouth Enterprises Ltd, 2015–. *Recreation:* music.

**BRETT, Simon Anthony Lee,** OBE 2016; writer; *b* 28 Oct. 1945; *s* of late Alan John Brett and Margaret Agnes Brett (*née* Lee). *m* 1971, Lucy Victoria McLaren; two *s* one *d*. *Educ:* Dulwich College; Wadham College, Oxford (BA Hons). Department store Father Christmas, 1967; BBC Radio Producer, 1968–77; LWT Producer, 1977–79. Chm., Adv. Cttee, PLR, 2003–. Chm., Soc. of Authors, 1995–97; Pres., Detection Club, 2001–. Radio and television scripts, incl. After Henry, No Commitments, Smelling of Roses. *Publications: Charles Paris crime novels:* Cast, In Order of Disappearance, 1975; So Much Blood, 1976; Star Trap, 1977; An Amateur Corpse, 1978; A Comedian Dies, 1979; The Dead Side of the Mike, 1980; Situation Tragedy, 1981; Murder Unprompted, 1982; Murder in the Title, 1983; Not Dead, Only Resting, 1984; Dead Giveaway, 1985; What Bloody Man Is That?, 1987; A Series of Murders, 1989; Corporate Bodies, 1991; A Reconstructed Corpse, 1993; Sicken And So Die, 1995; Dead Room Farce, 1997; A Decent Interval, 2013; The Cinderella Killer, 2014; A Deadly Habit, 2018; *Mrs Pargeter crime novels:* A Nice Class of Corpse, 1986; Mrs, Presumed Dead, 1988; Mrs Pargeter's Package, 1990; Mrs Pargeter's Pound of Flesh, 1992; Mrs Pargeter's Plot, 1996; Mrs Pargeter's Point of Honour, 1998; Mrs Pargeter's Principle, 2015; Mrs Pargeter's Public Relations, 2016; *other crime novels:* A Shock to the System, 1984; Dead Romantic, 1985; The Three Detectives and the Missing Superstar, 1986; The Three Detectives and the Knight-in-Armour, 1987; The Christmas Crimes at Puzzel Manor, 1991; Singled Out, 1995; The Body on the Beach, 2000; Death on the Downs, 2001; The Torso in the Town, 2002; Murder in the Museum, 2003; The Hanging in the Hotel, 2004; The Witness at the Wedding, 2005; The Stabbing in the Stables, 2006; Death Under the Dryer, 2007; Blood at the Bookies, 2008; The Poisoning in the Pub, 2009; Blotto, Twinks and the Ex-King's Daughter, 2009; The Shooting in the Shop, 2010; Blotto, Twinks and the Dead Dowager Duchess, 2010; Bones under the Beach Hut, 2011; Blotto, Twinks and the Rodents of the Riviera, 2011; Guns in the Gallery, 2011; Blotto, Twinks and the Bootlegger's Moll, 2012; The Corpse in the Court, 2012; Blotto, Twinks and the Riddle of the Sphinx, 2013; The Strangling on the Stage, 2013; The Tomb in Turkey, 2014; Blotto, Twinks and the Heir to the Tsar, 2015; The Killing in the Café, 2015; (ed) The Sinking Admiral, 2016; The Liar in the Library, 2017; *crime short stories:* A Box of Tricks, 1985; Crime Writers and Other Animals, 1998; *humorous books:* The Child-Owner's Handbook, 1983; Molesworth Rites Again, 1983; Bad Form, 1984; People-Spotting, 1985; The Wastepaper Basket Archive, 1986; How to Stay Topp, 1987; After Henry, 1987; The Booker Book, 1989; How to be a Little Sod, 1992; Look Who's Walking, 1994; Not Another Little Sod!, 1997; The Penultimate Chance Saloon, 2006; On Second Thoughts, 2006; Seriously Funny and other Oxymorons, 2017; *anthologies:* The Faber Book of Useful Verse, 1981; (with Frank Muir) The Book of Comedy Sketches, 1982; Take a Spare Truss, 1983; The Faber Book of Parodies, 1984; The Faber Book of

Diaries, 1987; *stage play:* Silhouette, 1998. *Recreations:* writing, reading, Real tennis, unreal fantasies. *Address:* Frith House, Burpham, Arundel, West Sussex BN18 9RR. *T:* (01903) 882257. *Clubs:* Garrick, Groucho.
See also M. J. L. Brett.

**BRETT, Simon Baliol,** RE 1991 (ARE 1986); wood engraver, printmaker and illustrator; writer on wood engraving; *b* 27 May 1943; *s* of late Antony Baliol Brett and Bay Helen (*née* Brownell); *m* 1974, Juliet Shirley-Smith (*née* Wood); one *d*, and three step *s* one step *d*. *Educ:* Ampleforth Coll.; St Martin's Sch. of Art (NDD 1964). Teacher, Marlborough Coll. Art Sch., 1971–89; publisher, under own Paulinus Print imprint, 1981–88. Editl Advr, Printmaking Today, 1994–. Society of Wood Engravers: Mem., 1984–; Chm., 1986–92; Treas., 1990–2002. Presentation print commnd by Medical Household for Golden Wedding of the Queen and Duke of Edinburgh, 1997. Retrospective exhibns incl. Bankside Gall., Holburne Mus., 2013. Exhibitions curated: Wood Engraving Then and Now, 1987; Out of the Wood, 1991; Wood Engraving Here and Now, 1995. *Publications:* Engravers, 1987; Engravers Two, 1992; Mr Derrick Harris, 1999; An Engraver's Globe, 2002; Wood Engraving - How to Do it, 1994, rev. edn 2010; Simon Brett—An Engraver's Progress, 2013; *books illustrated include:* The Animals of St Gregory (Francis Williams/V&A/NBL Illustration Award), 1981; To the Cross, 1984; Shakespeare's Sonnets, 1989; The Reader's Digest Illustrated Bible, 1990; Clarissa, 1991; Jane Eyre, 1991; The Confessions of Saint Augustine, 1993; Amelia, 1995; Shakespeare, The Classical Plays, 1997; (also picture ed.) The Folio Golden Treasury, 1997; Middlemarch, 1999; The Poetry of John Keats, 2001; The Meditations of Marcus Aurelius, 2002; Legends of the Ring, 2004; The Gypsies, 2006; Legends of the Grail, 2007; Shelley, 2008; Pericles, Prince of Tyre, 2010. *Address:* 12 Blowhorn Street, Marlborough, Wilts SN8 1BT. *T:* (01672) 512905. *E:* woodengraver@icloud.com.

**BRETT, Timothy Edward William;** Member (Lib Dem), Fife Unitary Council, since 2003 (Leader, Lib Dem Group, since 2012); *b* 28 March 1949; *s* of Reuben Brett and Edna Brett (*née* Waterman); *m* 1972, Barbara Jane Turnbull; two *s* one *d* (and one *s* decd). *Educ:* Gravesend GS for Boys; Bristol Univ. (BSc Hons). CIHM; FCIPD 2005. VSO Teacher, Min. of Educn, Sierra Leone, 1971–73; Nat. Admin. Trainee, Leeds RBH, later Yorks RHA, 1973–75; Sen. Admin. Asst (Planning & Personnel), Leeds AHA, 1975–76; Business Manager, Nixon Meml Hosp., Methodist Church-Overseas Div., Segbwema, Sierra Leone, 1976–78; Community Services Adminr, Humberside AHA, 1978; Dep. Adminr, Derbyshire Royal Infirmary, 1979–80; Unit Adminr, Plymouth Gen. Hosp., 1981–85; Unit Adminr, 1985–87, Unit Gen. Manager, 1987–93, Dundee Gen. Hosps Unit; Chief Exec., Dundee Teaching Hosps NHS Trust, 1993–98; Gen. Manager, then Chief Exec., Tayside Health Board, 1998–2001; Dir, Health Protection Scotland, 2002–07. Chm., Social Work and Health Cttee, Fife Council, 2007–12. Contested (Lib Dem) Fife NE, 2015. *Recreations:* hill-walking, swimming, theatre, church activities. *Address:* Woodend Cottage, Hazelton Walls, Cupar, Fife KY15 4QL. *T:* (01382) 330629.

**BRETT-HOLT, Alexis Fayrer;** Legal Adviser, Health and Safety Executive, 2004–10; *b* 7 March 1950; *d* of late Raymond Arthur Brett-Holt and Jacqueline Fayrer Brett-Holt (*née* Fayrer Hosken); *m* 1980, (John) Gareth Roscoe, *qv*; one *s* one *d*. *Educ:* Wimbledon High Sch.; St Anne's Coll., Oxford (BA). Called to the Bar, Lincoln's Inn, 1973, Bencher, 2007; Department of the Environment: Legal Asst, 1974–78; Sen. Legal Asst, 1978–85; Asst Solicitor, 1985–89; Assistant Solicitor: DoH, 1989–93; DoE, 1993–97; Dir, Legal Services C, 1997–2001, Legal Services B, 2001–04, DTI. Pres., Assoc. of First Div. Civil Servants, 1987–89. *Recreation:* bell-ringing. *Club:* CWIL.

**BRETT-SMITH, Adam de la Falaise Brett;** Managing Director, Corney & Barrow Ltd, since 1988; Chairman, Corney & Barrow Hong Kong Ltd, since 2019; *b* Olney, Maryland, USA, 4 June 1956; *s* of Captain Richard Brett-Smith and (Patricia) Karen Brett-Smith (later Lady Beeley). *Educ:* Dragon Sch., Oxford; Westminster Sch.; St Edmund Hall, Oxford (MA Hons English Lang. and Lit.). Corney & Barrow Ltd, 1981–. Mem. Council, Royal Warrant Holders' Assoc., 1996– (Pres., 2001–02). Chm., Queen Elizabeth Scholarship Trust, 2003–05. Clerk of the Prince of Wales's and Duchess of Cornwall's Cellars, Royal Household, 2003–. *Recreations:* motorcycling, shooting, opera, ballet. *Address:* c/o Corney & Barrow, 1 Thomas More Street, E1W 1YZ. *T:* (020) 7265 2400, *Fax:* (020) 7265 2444. *E:* adam.brett-smith@corneyandbarrow.com. *Clubs:* Brooks's, Groucho, Pitt.

**BRETTEN, George Rex;** QC 1980; barrister-at-law; *b* 21 Feb. 1942; *s* of Horace Victor Bretten and Kathleen Edna Betty Bretten; *m* 1965, Maureen Gillian Crowhurst; one *d*. *Educ:* King Edward VII Sch., King's Lynn; Sidney Sussex Coll., Cambridge (MA, LLM). Lectr, Nottingham Univ., 1964–68; Asst Director, Inst. of Law Research and Reform, Alberta, Canada, 1968–70; called to the Bar, Lincoln's Inn, 1965, a Bencher 1989; in practice, 1971–2013. *Publications:* Special Reasons, 1977. *Recreations:* gardening, walking, tennis. *Address:* Sundial House, Weston Road, Edith Weston, Rutland LE15 8HQ. *T:* (01780) 729282. *Club:* Athenæum.

**BREW, David Allan;** Head of Fisheries (formerly Head of Sea Fisheries), Marine Scotland, 2009–11; *b* 19 Feb. 1953; *s* of Kenneth Frederick Cecil Brew and Iris May (*née* Sharpe). *Educ:* Kettering Grammar Sch.; Heriot-Watt Univ. (BA 1st Cl. Hons 1974; Pres., Students' Assoc., 1974–75); Univ. of Strathclyde (MSc 1976); European Univ. Inst., Florence. Scottish Office, 1979–81; Adminr, Directorate-Gen. V, EC, Brussels, 1981–84; Scottish Office: Principal, Glasgow, 1984–88, Edinburgh, 1988–90; Head: Electricity Privatisation Div., 1990–91; Eur. Funds and Co-ordination Div., 1991–95; Sea Fisheries Div., 1995–98; Devolution Team, Constitution Secretariat, Cabinet Office, 1998–2000; Chief Exec., ICAS, 2000–03; Hd, Cultural Policy Div., Scottish Exec., 2004–06; Hd, Rural Communities Div., Scottish Exec., then Scottish Govt, 2006–09. Mem. Bd, MG ALBA, 2012–; Public Mem., Network Rail, 2012–15. Mem. Bd, Creative Scotland, 2015–. Member: Court, Heriot-Watt Univ., 1985–91, 2000–06; Bd, Robert Gordon Univ. 2012–15. *Publications:* (contrib.) Changing Patterns of Relations between the National Parliaments and the European Parliament, 1979; (contrib.) European Electoral Systems Handbook, 1979; (contrib.) The European Parliament: towards a uniform procedure for direct elections, 1981. *Recreations:* languages, music, film, gastronomy. *Address:* 1 Dundas Street, Edinburgh EH3 6QG. *T:* (0131) 556 4692.

**BREWER, Sir David (William),** KG 2016; Kt 2007; CMG 1999; CVO 2015; Lord-Lieutenant of Greater London, 2008–15; Chair of Council, St Paul's Cathedral, since 2015; Vice-President, GB-China Centre, since 2004 (Chairman, 1997–2004); Lord Mayor of London, 2005–06; *b* 28 May 1940; *s* of Dr H. F. Brewer and Elizabeth Brewer (*née* Nickell-Lean); *m* 1985, Tessa Suzanne Mary Jordá (OBE 2015); two *d*. *Educ:* St Paul's Sch.; Univ. of Grenoble. FCII 1966. Joined Sedgwick Group, 1959: Rep., Japan, 1976–78; Director: Sedgwick Far East Ltd, 1982–99 (Chm., 1993–97); Develt Cos, 1982–98; Sedgwick Internat. Risk Mgt Inc., 1990–99; Chairman: Sedgwick Insce and Risk Mgt Consultants (China) Ltd, 1993–97; Sedgwick Japan Ltd, 1994–97. Dir, Sumitomo Marine & Fire Insce Co. (Europe) Ltd, 1985–98; non-executive Director: Tullett Prebon SITICO (China) Ltd, 2007–15; Nat. Bank of Kuwait Internat. Ltd, 2008–18; Senior Adviser: Travelex, 2012–14; DealGlobe Ltd, 2014–; ECO Capacity Exchange, 2015–. UK Business Ambassador, 2010–12. Mem. Bd and Hon. Treas., 1991–2007, Chm., 2007–13, China-Britain Business Council; Chm., Financial Services Cttee, TheCityUK (formerly International Financial Services, London)/China-Britain Business Council, 1993–2013; Chief Advr, Assoc. of Chinese Financial Professionals in UK, 2013–. Pres., City of London Br., IoD, 2008– (Chm., 1999–2008; Life Fellow, 2010); Pres., Insce Inst. of London, 2006–07 (Vice-Pres., 2005–06). Mem., Adv. Council, LSO, 1999–. Pres., City of London Br., RNLI, 2007– (Chm., 1997–2007); Vice-Pres., City of London Sector, BRCS, 1986–. Gov. and Trustee, Sons and Friends of the Clergy, 1993–2015 (Treas., 2008–09; Sen. Treas., 2010–13). Trustee, Daiwa Anglo-Japanese Foundn, 2008–12; Dir, Guildhall Sch. Trust, 1999–. Chm., Royal Over-Seas League, 2016–19. Alderman, City of London, Ward of Bassishaw, 1996–2009 (Mem. Ct of Common Council, 1992–96); Sheriff, City of London, 2002–03; HM Comr of Lieutenancy, City of London, 2005–09. Liveryman: Merchant Taylors' Co., 1968– (Mem., Ct of Assts, 1985–; Master, 2001–02); Mem., Ct of Assts, Blacksmiths' Co., 2007– (Hon. Mem., 2001–07; Prime Warden, 2009–10); Hon. Liveryman: Security Professionals' Co., 2008 (Hon. Freeman, 2003–08); Insurers' Co., 2010. President: London Cornish Assoc., 2005–13; Camel Valley and Bodmin Moor Protection Soc., 2015–. JP City of London, 1979. Hon. Bencher, Gray's Inn, 2004–. Hon. FCSI 2006. Hon. DPhil London Metropolitan, 2005; Hon. DSc City, 2006; Hon. LLD Exeter, 2008; Hon. DSc (Econs) London, 2008; Hon. DLaws Nottingham, 2013. Magnolia Gold Award, Mayor of Shanghai, 2006; Order of the Rising Sun (Japan), 2006. *Recreations:* music (especially opera and choral music), golf, mechanical gardening, chocolate, paronomasia. *Address:* 16 Cowley Street, SW1P 3LZ. *T:* (020) 7222 5481. *E:* david.brewer@dwbrewer.com; Orchard Cottage, Hellanbridge, Bodmin, Cornwall PL30 4QR. *T:* (01208) 841268. *Clubs:* Garrick, MCC; St Enodoc Golf; New Zealand Golf.

**BREWER, Prof. John,** PhD; Interim Deputy Vice Chancellor, Buckinghamshire New University, since 2019; *b* Plymouth, 30 Dec. 1961; *s* of Peter and Marguerite Brewer; *m* 1988, Caroline Rule; two *d*. *Educ:* Knowles Hill Sch.; Loughborough Univ. (BSc, MPhil); Univ. of Bedfordshire (PhD 2015). Head: Human Performance, FA, 1988–93; Lilleshall Human Performance Centre, 1993–2004; Dir, Sports Sci., GlaxoSmithKline, 2004–09; Prof. of Sport and Dir of Sport, Univ. of Bedfordshire, 2009–14; Prof. of Applied Sport Sci., 2014–19, Pro Vice Chancellor for Global Engagement, 2019, St Mary's Univ. Mem. Bd, UK Anti-Doping, 2009–17. Chair: British Handball Assoc., 2008–12; British Ski and Snowboard, 2013–15. Mem. Bd, British Univs and Colls Sport, 2011–15. Chair of Govs, RMS Sch. for Girls, Rickmansworth. *Publications:* London 2012 Training Guide: Athletics - Track Events, 2010; Pocket Anatomy of the Moving Body, 2016; Run Smart, 2017; Running Science, 2017; Sport in 30 Seconds, 2019. *Recreations:* running, ski-ing, hiking. *Address:* Buckinghamshire New University, High Wycombe, Bucks HP11 2JZ. *E:* john.brewer@bucks.ac.uk.

**BREWER, Dame Nicola (Mary), (Dame Nicola Gillham),** DCMG 2011 (CMG 2002); PhD; Vice-Provost (International), University College London, since 2014; *b* 14 Nov. 1957; *d* of late Trevor James Brewer and Mary Margaret Eleanor Brewer (*née* Jones); *m* 1991, Geoffrey Charles Gillham, *qv*; one *s* one *d*. *Educ:* Univ. of Leeds (BA 1980; PhD 1988). Entered FCO, 1983: Second Sec., Mexico City, 1984–87; First Secretary: FCO, 1987–91; (Econ.), Paris, 1991–94; Counsellor: FCO, 1995–98; New Delhi, 1998–2001; Dir, Global Issues, FCO, 2001–02; Dir Gen., Regl Progs, DFID, 2002–04 (on secondment); Dir Gen., Europe, FCO, 2004–07; Chief Exec., Equality and Human Rights Commn, 2007–09; High Comr, S Africa (also accredited to Swaziland and Lesotho), 2009–13. Member: Adv. Panel on Judicial Diversity, MoJ, 2009–10; Trilateral Commn, 2017–. Non-executive Director: Aggreko plc, 2016–; ScottishPower, 2017–. Trustee, Sentebale, 2014–. Hon. Bencher, Middle Temple, 2011. Hon. LLD Leeds, 2009. *Recreations:* reading novels, walking, riding. *Address:* c/o University College London, Gower Street, WC1E 6BT.

**BREWER, Richard John,** FSA; Research Keeper of Roman Archaeology, Amgueddfa Cymru - National Museum Wales, 2010–13, now Honorary Research Fellow; *b* 23 Oct. 1954; *s* of Kenneth Arthur Brewer and Constance Brewer (*née* Crooks). *Educ:* Birchgrove Primary Sch., Cardiff; Cathays High Sch., Cardiff; Inst. of Archaeol., Univ. of London (BA Hons Archaeol. 1976); City & Guilds (Dip. in Health and Social Care (Level 3) 2013). National Museum of Wales: Res. Asst, 1978–85; Asst Keeper, Roman Archaeol., 1985–96; Keeper of Archaeol. & Numismatics, 1996–2010. Chm., Ancient Monuments Adv. Bd for Wales, 2005–10 (Mem., 1997–2010). Mem. Council, 2004–14, and Ed., Britannia, 2009–14, Soc. for Promotion of Roman Studies. Chm., Adv. Cttee, Young Archaeologists' Club, 2002–10. Chm., Diocesan Adv. Cttee, Llandaff, 2011–17. FSA 1986. *Publications:* Corpus of Sculpture of the Roman World: Great Britain, Wales, 1986; Caerwent Roman Town, 1993, 3rd edn 2006; Roman Fortresses and Their Legions, 2000; Caerleon and the Roman Army, 2000; The Second Augustan Legion and the Roman Military Machine, 2002; The Romans in Gwent, 2004. *Recreations:* ultra distance and marathon running, crime fiction, travel, Association Football (Cardiff City), tap dancing. *Address:* Department of Archaeology & Numismatics, Amgueddfa Cymru - National Museum Wales, Cathays Park, Cardiff CF10 3NP. *E:* richard.brewer@museumwales.ac.uk.

**BREWERTON, Prof. Andrew John;** Principal, since 2010, and Professor, since 2018, Plymouth College of Art; Honorary Professor of Fine Art, Shanghai University, since 2000; Distinguished Professor, Shanghai Academy of Fine Arts, since 2018; Chairman: Plymouth Arts Centre, since 2010; Plymouth School of Creative Arts, since 2012; *b* 8 Feb. 1958; *s* of Peter John Thomas Brewerton and Jean Patricia Brewerton (*née* Cameron); *m* 1983, Jan Beaver; two *d*. *Educ:* Wolverhampton Grammar Sch.; Sidney Sussex Coll., Cambridge (R. E. Hentsch Schol.; BA Hons English, MA). Lettore in English, Univ. dell' Aquila, Italy, 1980–82; Glasshouse, Ops, and Prodn Manager, Stuart Crystal, 1984–89; Head of Design and Develt, Dartington Crystal, 1989–94; University of Wolverhampton: Principal Lectr and Hd of Glass, Sch. of Art and Design, 1994–96; Dean, Art and Design, and Prof. of Glass, 1996–2004; Principal, Dartington Coll. of Arts, 2004–08. Visiting Professor: Plymouth Univ., 2004–08; Sch. of Fine Arts, Nanjing Normal Univ., 2017–. Director: Plymouth Sch. of Creative Arts Trust, 2012– (Chair, 2012–); GuildHE, 2012– (Vice-Chair, 2013–); Plymouth Area Business Council, 2015–; Makers HQ CIC, 2017–. Mem., Inspire Multi-Acad. Trust, Ernesettle Community Sch., 2016–. Exec. Mem., Council for Higher Educn in Art and Design, 2001–06; Member: Strategic Adv. Cttee (Business and Community), HEFCE, 2005–08; Bd, Higher Educn Stats Agency, 2006–08; UK Adv. Council, Creative Industries Fedn, 2016–; Adv. Gp (formerly Steering Gp), Cultural Learning Alliance, 2016–; Adv. Gp, Crafts Council, 2017–; Higher Educn Sector Agencies Chairs' Forum, 2017–; Adv. Bd, Shanghai Internat. Art City Res. Inst., 2018–. Stakeholder Bd Mem., The Box, Plymouth, 2015–; Mem., Plymouth Growth Bd, 2015–; Bd Mem., Plymouth Waterfront Partnership Business Improvement District, 2018–. Vice-Chair, Prime Minister's Initiative Higher Educn Adv. Gp, 2006–08. Mem. Council and SW Regl Chm., Arts Council England, 2007–09. Chair, Jury Panel, British Glass Biennale Exhibn, 2004. Dep. Chair, UK Arts and Design Instns Assoc., 2016–; Mem. Bd, Assoc. of Ind. Colleges of Art and Design, USA, 2018–. Chair, Foundn for Higher Educn in Art & Design, 2005– (Trustee, 1999–); Trustee: New Art Gall., Walsall, 1997–2004; Millfields Inspired, 2013–. Hon. MEd St Mark and St John, Plymouth, 2013. *Publications: poetry:* Sirius, 1995; Cade l'uliva, 2003; Raag Leaves for Paresh Chakraborty, 2008; Via, 2010; Glass Tantra: the Art of Loretta H Yang, 2012; contrib. numerous jl articles and catalogue essays on contemporary art. *Recreation:* fresh air. *T:* 07977 462370. *E:* ajbrewerton@gmail.com.

**BREWIN, Prof. Christopher Ray**, PhD; FBA 2012; FBPsS; FAcSS; FMedSci; Professor of Clinical Psychology, University College London, 1999–2018, now Emeritus; Consultant Clinical Psychologist, Camden and Islington NHS Foundation Trust, 1999–2018; *b* London, 16 Oct. 1953; *s* of Denis and Kathleen Mary Brewin; *m* 1989, Bernice Andrews; one step *s* one step *d*. *Educ*: Merchant Taylors Sch.; St John's Coll., Oxford (BA; MSc); Sheffield Univ. (PhD 1981). CPsychol; FBPsS 1988. Lectr in Psychol., Leeds Univ., 1980–83; non-clin. scientist, MRC Social Psychiatry Unit, London, 1983–92; Prof. of Psychol., RHUL, 1992–99. Hon. Civilian Consultant Advr in Clin. Psychol. to AMS, 2010–18. Trustee, Centre for Study of Emotion and Law, 2007–19. FAcSS (AcSS 2001); FMedSci 2016. *Publications*: (ed jtly) Attributions and Psychological Change, 1982; Cognitive Foundations of Clinical Psychology, 1988; (ed jtly) Measuring Mental Health Needs, 1992; Post-traumatic Stress Disorder: malady or myth?, 2003; (ed jtly) The Neuropsychology of PTSD, 2005. *Recreations*: duplicate bridge, tennis, wine. *Address*: Research Department of Clinical Educational and Health Psychology, University College London, Gower Street, WC1E 6BT.

**BREWSTER, (Elsie) Yvonne**, OBE 1993; Artistic Director, Talawa Theatre Co., 1986–2003; *b* 7 Oct. 1938; *d* of Claude Noel Clarke and Kathleen Vanessa Clarke; *m* 1st, 1961, John Roger Francis Jones (marr. diss. 1965); 2nd, 1971, Starr Edmund Francis Home Brewster; one *s*. *Educ*: Rose Bruford Coll. of Speech and Drama (Dip.; Fellow, 2004). ARAM 2018. Stage, TV and radio actress, 1960–; theatre, film, TV and radio director, 1965–; Drama Officer, Arts Council of GB, 1982–84. Mem., London Arts Bd, 1993–99; Trustee, Theatres Trust, 1992–; Patron, Rose Bruford Coll., 1994–. Non-executive Director: Riverside Mental Health NHS Trust, 1994–99; Kensington, Chelsea, Westminster and Brent NHS Trust, 1999–2001. Juror, Commonwealth Writers' Prize, 2005. Fellow: Rose Bruford Coll., 2004; Central Sch. of Speech and Drama, 2005. FRSA 1992. DUniv Open, 2002. *Publications*: Black Plays, Vol. 1, 1987, Vol. 2, 1989, Vol. 3, 1995; The Undertaker's Daughter (autobiog.), 2004; (ed) For The Reckord: a collection of plays by Barry Reckord, 2010; (ed) Mixed Company: three early Jamaican plays, 2012; Vaulting Ambition: Jamaica's Barn Theatre, 2017. *Recreations*: reading, London. *Address*: 41B Dyne Road, NW6 7XG. *T*: (020) 7328 9306.

**BREWSTER, Richard Philip**; Executive Director, National Center on Nonprofit Enterprise, Alexandria, USA, 2003–15; *b* 25 May 1952; *s* of Peter and Patricia Brewster; *m* 1975, Lindy Udale; three *s* one *d*. *Educ*: Leeds Grammar Sch.; Trinity Coll., Oxford (BA Hons). ICI, 1976–86: Sales Rep., 1976–79; Product Manager, 1979–81; Purchasing Manager, 1981–83; Marketing Manager, 1983–86; Nat. Appeals Manager, Oxfam, 1986–89; Dir of Mkting, Spastics Soc., then Scope, 1989–95; Chief Exec., Scope, 1995–2003. *Recreations*: arts, watching sport. *Address*: 10717 Oldfield Drive, Reston, VA 20191, USA.

**BREWSTER, Yvonne**; see Brewster, E. Y.

**BREYER, Stephen Gerald**; Associate Justice, Supreme Court of the United States, since 1994; *b* 15 Aug. 1938; *s* of Irving Breyer and Anne (*née* Roberts); *m* 1967, Joanna Hare; one *s* two *d*. *Educ*: Stanford Univ. (AM 1959); Magdalen Coll., Oxford (Marshall Schol.; BA 1st Cl. Hons PPE 1961; Hon Fellow 1995); Harvard Law Sch. (LLB 1964). Law Clerk, US Supreme Court, 1964–65; Special Asst to Asst Attorney Gen., US Dept of Justice, 1965–67; Harvard University: Asst Prof. of Law, 1967–70; Prof. of Law, Harvard Law Sch., 1970–80, Lectr, 1981–; Prof., Kennedy Sch. of Govt, 1977–80; Asst Special Prosecutor, Watergate Special Prosecution Force, 1973; US Court of Appeals for First Circuit: Circuit Judge, 1980–94; Chief Judge, 1990–94. US Senate Judiciary Committee: Special Counsel, Admin. Practices Subcttee, 1974–75; Chief Counsel, 1979–80; Mem., US Sentencing Commn, 1985–89. Vis. Lectr, Coll. of Law, Sydney, Aust., 1975; Vis. Prof., Univ. of Rome, 1993. Fellow: Amer. Acad. of Arts and Scis; Amer. Bar Foundn. *Publications*: (with P. MacAvoy) The Federal Power Commission and the Regulation of Energy, 1974; (with R. Stewart) Administrative Law and Regulatory Policy, 1979, 3rd edn 1992; Regulation and its Reform, 1982; Breaking the Vicious Circle: toward effective risk regulation, 1993; Active Liberty, 2005; Making Our Democracy Work, 2010; The Court and the World, 2015; contrib. chapters in books; numerous articles in law jls and reviews. *Address*: Supreme Court Building, One First Street NE, Washington, DC 20543–0001, USA. *T*: (202) 4793000.

**BRIANCE, Richard Henry**; Chairman, PMB Capital Ltd, since 2015; *b* Nicosia, Cyprus, 23 Aug. 1953; *s* of John and Prunella Briance; *m* 1979, Lucille Hardin de Zalduondo; two *s* two *d*. *Educ*: Eton Coll.; Jesus Coll., Cambridge (BA Hons 1974). Credit Suisse First Boston, 1975–91, Man. Dir, 1983–91; Vice-Chm., UBS Ltd, 1991–97; Chief Exec., West Merchant Bank, 1997–98; Chief Exec. and Dep. Chm., Hawkpoint Partners, 1999–2010; Chief Exec., Edmond de Rothschild UK, 2010–15. Chm., Trinity Hospice, 2004–11; Trustee: London Children's Ballet, 1994–; Legatum Inst., 2015–; Chm., Kensington and Chelsea Foundn, 2018. *Recreations*: music, golf, ski-ing. *Address*: 13 Holland Street, W8 4NA. *Clubs*: Brooks's, Hurlingham, Royal Automobile; Queenwood Golf; Nantucket Yacht; Sankaty Head Golf.

**BRIAULT, Clive Bramwell**; Managing Director, Risk and Regulation Consulting Ltd, since 2008; *b* 19 Sept. 1957. *Educ*: Merton Coll., Oxford (BA PPE 1978); Nuffield Coll., Oxford (MPhil Econs 1980). Bank of England, 1980–98; FSA, 1998–2008, Man. Dir, Retail Markets, 2004–08.

**BRICE, (Ann) Nuala**, OBE 2011; PhD; a Judge of the Upper Tribunal and of the Tax Chamber of the First Tier Tribunal, 2009 (Special Commissioner of Taxes, 1999–2009 (Deputy Special Commissioner, 1992–99); Chairman, VAT and Duties Tribunals (formerly VAT Tribunals), 1999–2009 (part-time Chairman, 1992–99)); Chairman: Financial Services and Markets Tribunal, 2001–09; Pensions Regulator Tribunal, 2005–09; Claims Management Services Tribunal, 2007–09; *d* of William Connor and Rosaleen Gertrude Connor; *m* 1963, Geoffrey James Barrington Groves Brice, QC (*d* 1999); one *s*. *Educ*: Loreto Convent, Manchester; University Coll. London. LLB (Hons), LLM 1976, PhD 1982, London. Admitted Solicitor of the Supreme Court, 1963 (Stephen Heelis Gold Medal and John Peacock Conveyancing Prize, 1963). The Law Society: Asst Solicitor, 1963; Asst Sec., 1966; Sen. Asst Sec., 1973; Deptl Sec., 1982; Asst Sec.-Gen., 1987–92. Sec., Revenue Law Cttee, 1972–82. Vis. Associate Prof. of Law, Tulane Univ., 1990–99; Vis. Prof. of Law, Univ. of Natal, 1999. MRI 1965. Hon. FIIT 2010. *Recreations*: reading, music, gardening.

**BRICKELL, Christopher David**, CBE 1991; VMH 1976; Director General, Royal Horticultural Society, 1985–93; *b* 29 June 1932; *s* of Bertram Tom Brickell and Kathleen Alice Brickell; *m* 1963, Jeanette Scargill Flecknoe; two *d*. *Educ*: Queen's College, Taunton; Reading Univ. (BSc Horticulture). Joined Royal Horticultural Society Garden, Wisley, 1958: Asst Botanist, 1958; Botanist, 1960; Sen. Scientific Officer, 1964; Dep. Dir, 1968; Dir, 1969–85. Chm., Internat. Commn for the Nomenclature of Cultivated Plants, 1980–2016. Pres., Internat. Soc. for Horticl Sci., 1998–2002. George Robert White Medal of Honor, Mass Hort. Soc., 1988; Inst. of Horticulture Award, 1997; Life Time Achievement Award, Garden Media Guild, 2014. Ed., The RHS Encyclopedia of Practical Gardening, 8 vols, 1979–86. *Publications*: Daphne: the genus in cultivation, 1976; Pruning, 1979, reissued as Pruning and Training, 2011, rev. edn 2017; The Vanishing Garden, 1986; An English Florilegium, 1987; (ed and contrib.) The Gardener's Encyclopaedia of Plants and Flowers, 1989, 6th edn 2019; (ed and contrib.) The RHS Encyclopaedia of Gardening, 1992, 4th edn 2012; Garden Plants, 1995; (ed and contrib.) The RHS A–Z of Garden Plants, 1996, 4th edn 2016; botanical papers in Flora Europaea, European Garden Flora, and Flora of Turkey; horticultural and botanical papers in RHS Jl, The New Plantsman and Alpine Garden Soc. Bulletin. *Recreation*: gardening. *Address*: The Camber, The Street, Nutbourne, Pulborough, West Sussex RH20 2HE.

**BRICKNELL, Lt Gen. Martin Charles Marshall**, CB 2019; Professor of Conflict, Health and Military Medicine, King's College London, since 2019; *b* Malta, 14 Dec. 1963; *s* of Colin Alan Bricknell and Margaret Anne Bricknell; *m* 1987, Kathryn Margaret Fellbaum; three *d*. *Educ*: Christ's Hosp., Horsham; Univ. of Southampton (BM; MD; PhD; MA; MBA; MMEdSci). UK Defence Medical Services, 1984–2018; Hd, Med. Ops and Capability, 2012–15; Dir, Med. Policy and Operational Capability, 2015–17; Acting Surgeon Gen., 2017–18; Surgeon Gen., 2018. Prof. in conflict, health and mil. medicine. OStJ 2015. *Publications*: over 75 acad. articles on mil. med. subjects. *Recreation*: triathlon. *E*: martin.bricknell@gmail.com.

**BRIDEN, Prof. James Christopher**, PhD, DSc; FGS; Professor of Environmental Studies and Director of the Environmental Change Institute, University of Oxford, 1997–2003, now Professor Emeritus; Fellow, Linacre College, Oxford, 1997–2003, now Fellow Emeritus; *b* 30 Dec. 1938; *s* of late Henry Charles Briden and Gladys Elizabeth (*née* Jefkins); *m* 1968, Caroline Mary (*née* Gillmore); one *s* one *d*. *Educ*: Royal Grammar Sch., High Wycombe; St Catherine's Coll., Oxford (MA); ANU (PhD 1965; DSc 1994). FGS 1962; CGeol 1990. Research Fellow: Univ. of Rhodesia, 1965–66; Univ. of Oxford, 1966–67; Univ. of Birmingham, 1967–68; University of Leeds: Lectr, 1968–73; Reader, 1973–75; Prof. of Geophysics, 1975–86; Head, Dept of Earth Sciences, 1976–79 and 1982–85; Dir of Earth Scis, NERC, 1986–94; Vis. Prof. (NERC Res. Prof.), Univ. of Oxford, 1994–96. Canadian Commonwealth Fellow and Vis. Prof., Univ. of Western Ontario, 1979–80; Hon. Prof., Leeds Univ., 1986–94. Mem., NERC, 1981–86; Chairman: Jt Assoc. for Geophysics, 1981–84 (Chm., Founding Cttee, 1978–79); Exec. Cttee, Ocean Drilling Prog., 1994–96; Member: Science and Engrg (formerly Science) Cttee, British Council, 1990–96; Governing Council, Internat. Seismol Centre, 1978–83; Council: Eur. Geophysical Soc., 1976–84; RAS, 1978–79 (FRAS 1962); Geol Soc., 1992–95. Fellow, Amer. Geophysical Union, 1994. Murchison Medal, Geol. Soc., 1984. Editor, Earth and Planetary Science Letters, 1971–97; Ed.-in-chief, Envmtl Sci. and Policy, 2001–10. *Publications*: (with A. G. Smith) Mesozoic and Cenozoic Palaeocontinental World Maps, 1977; (with A. G. Smith and A. M. Hurley) Phanerozoic Palaeocontinental World Maps, 1981; over 90 papers on palaeomagnetism, palaeoclimates, tectonics and aspects of geophysics. *Recreations*: music- and theatre-going, gentle walking, bad golf, mild gardening. *Address*: Stoneleigh House, 1 Paternoster Court, Cassington Road, Yarnton, Oxon OX5 1QB.

**BRIDEN, Timothy John**; Vicar-General, Province of Canterbury, since 2005; *b* 29 Oct. 1951; *s* of Thomas Dan Briden, MA, DPA and Joan Briden (*née* Garratt); *m* 1989, Susanne. *Educ*: Ipswich Sch.; Downing Coll., Cambridge (BA 1974, MA 1978; LLB 1975, LLM 2016). Called to the Bar, Inner Temple, 1976; Chancellor: Dio. Bath and Wells, 1993–; Dio. Truro, 1998–; Deputy Chancellor: Dio. Bristol, 2004–; Dio. Salisbury, 2013–17; Commissary to Bishop of Chichester, 2018–19. Mem. ex officio, Gen. Synod of C of E, 2005– (Mem., Legal Adv. Commn, 1986–). Chm., Ecclesiastical Judges Assoc., 2008– (Sec., 1997–2008). Pres., Old Ipswichian Club, 2010. Ed., Macmorran's Handbook for Church Wardens and Parochial Church Councillors, 1989–. *Publications*: (ed) Moore's Introduction to English Canon Law, 4th edn 2013. *Address*: Lamb Chambers, Elm Court, Temple, EC4Y 7AS. *T*: (020) 7797 8300, *Fax*: (020) 7797 8308.

**BRIDGE, Beverley Jane**; see Glover, B. J.

**BRIDGE, Dame Jill**; see Macleod Clark, Dame J.

**BRIDGE, John Neville**, PhD; Chairman: Endeavour-SCH plc, 2001–11; Agricultural and Horticultural Development Board (formerly Levy Board (UK)), 2006–11; *b* 18 Sept. 1942; *s* of Tom and Eunice Bridge; *m* 1966, Rosalind Forrester; one *s* one *d*. *Educ*: Lancaster Royal Grammar Sch.; Durham Univ. (BA Geog. 1964; PhD Econs 1974); Indiana Univ. (MA Econs 1965). Lectr in Econs and Fellow, Centre for Middle Eastern and Islamic Studies, 1966–74; Hd of Industrial Develt, N of England Develt Council, 1975–84; Chief Executive: Yorks and Humberside Develt Agency, 1984–88; Northern Develt Co., 1988–98; Chm., One Northeast, 1998–2003. Consultant, PricewaterhouseCoopers, 2004–07. Non-executive Director: Tanfield Gp (formerly Comeleon) plc, 2001–12; Kenmore (UK) Ltd, 2001–05; Watson Burton LLP, 2004–06. Member: Bd, English Partnerships, 2000–03; Urban Sounding Bd, 2001–03; Bd, UK Trade and Investment, 2001–03; Treas. Adv. Council, Partnerships UK, 2001–03; Rural Climate Change Forum, 2008–11. Chairman: Northern Sights, 1996–2012; Council, Durham Cathedral, 2001–11; NE Seedcorn Fund, 2001–04; Alnwick Garden Trust, 2003–10; Yorks and NE Reg., Nat. Trust, 2003–12; Land Restoration Trust, 2004–10; Calvert Trust Kielder, 2004–09 (Trustee, 1992–); Spirit of Enterprise Trust, 2004–09; Durham Local Educn Partnership, 2010–18; Bradford Local Educn Partnership, 2011–13; Integrated Bradford SPV1 Ltd, 2011–13; Integrated Bradford SPV2 Ltd, 2011–13; S Tyneside and Gateshead Local Educn Partnership, 2013–18; Victorious (formerly Carillion) Acads Trust, 2017–; Mem. Bd, Community Ventures, 2014–19; Dir, Hexham Community Partnership, 2017–. Consultant, Northumbrian Leisure, 2007–. Res. Fellow, Smith Inst., 2009–; Mem., Food Res. Partnership, 2009–11. Visiting Professor: Newcastle Business Sch., 1996–2010; Durham Univ. Business Sch., 1998–2008. Member: Adv. Bd, Durham Business Sch., 2003–08; Hatfield Coll. Council and Trust, 2006–11. Hon. Fellow, Univ. of Sunderland, 1993. Hon. DCL: Durham, 2005; Northumbria, 2005. *Recreations*: walking, gardening, travel. *Address*: 3 Chains Drive, Corbridge, Northumberland NE45 5BP. *T*: (01434) 634740. *E*: john@bridgedev.co.uk. *Club*: Reform.

**BRIDGE, Keith James**, CBE 1997; consultant, 1989–2000; *b* 21 Aug. 1929; *s* of late James Henry Bridge and Lilian Elizabeth (*née* Nichols); *m* 1960, Thelma Ruby (*née* Hubble); three *d* (and one *s* decd). *Educ*: Sir George Monoux Grammar Sch., Walthamstow; Corpus Christi Coll., Oxford (MA); Univ. of Hull (BTh 2001). CIPFA 1959; CCMI (CBIM 1978). Local govt service, 1953; Dep. City Treasurer, York, 1965; Borough Treas., Bolton, 1967; City Treas., Manchester, 1971; County Treasurer, Greater Manchester Council, 1973; Chief Exec., Humberside CC, 1978–83. Mem., W Yorks Residuary Body, 1985–91. Financial Adviser to Assoc. of Metrop. Authorities, 1971–78; Mem. Council, 1972–84, Pres., 1982–83, Chartered Inst. of Public Finance and Accountancy; Pres., Soc. of Metropolitan Treasurers, 1977–78. Member: Audit Commn for Local Authorities in Eng. and Wales, 1983–86; Exec. Council, Business in the Community, 1987–92; Bd, Public Finance Foundn, 1984–90; Educn Transfer Council (formerly Educn Assets Bd), 1988–2000 (Chm., 1996–2000); Football Licensing Authy, 1990–96. Dir, Phillips & Drew, 1987–89. Chm., York Diocesan Pastoral Cttee, 1989–94. Governor: Univ. of Lincolnshire and Humberside (formerly Humberside Poly.), 1989–98; E Yorks Coll., 2000–01. Hon. LLD Lincs and

Humberside, 1999. Freeman, City of London, 1986. *Publications:* papers in professional jls. *Recreations:* gardening, literature, music. *Address:* 1 Fairlawn, Molescroft, Beverley, E Yorks HU17 7DD. *T:* (01482) 887652.

**BRIDGE, Prof. Michael Greenhalgh,** FBA 2013; Cassel Professor of Commercial Law, London School of Economics, 2009–17, now Emeritus (Professor of Law, 2007–09); Professor of Law, National University of Singapore, since 2013; Senior Research Fellow, Harris Manchester College, Oxford, since 2017; *b* 3 Nov. 1947; *s* of Louis and Sarah Bridge; *m* 1971, Rowena Austin; one *s* one *d*. *Educ:* LSE (LLB 1969; LLM 1970). Called to the Bar, Middle Temple, 1975, Bencher, 2014; Associate Prof., 1977–86, Prof. of Law, 1987–88, McGill Univ., Montreal; Hind Prof. of Commercial Law, Univ. of Nottingham, 1988–2000; Prof. of Commercial Law, UCL, 2001–07. Vis. Prof., QMUL, 2017–. Hon. QC 2018. *Publications:* Sales and Sales Financing in Canada, 1981; Sale of Goods, 1988, (English edn) 1997, 3rd edn as The Sale of Goods, 2014; (jtly) The Companies Act 1989, 1989; Personal Property Law, 1993, 4th edn 2015; The International Sale of Goods, 1999, 4th edn 2017; (with R. Stevens) Cross-Border Security and Insolvency, 2001; (jtly) International Sale of Goods in the Conflict of Laws, 2005; (jtly) Personal Property Security, 2007, new edn as The Law of Security and Title-Based Financing, 2012, 3rd edn 2018; (gen. ed.) Benjamin's Sale of Goods, 8th edn 2010 to 10th edn 2017; (jtly) The Law of Personal Property, 2013, 2nd edn 2017. *Recreations:* travel, wine, music (opera, orchestral, chamber), art. *Address:* Department of Law, London School of Economics, Houghton Street, WC2A 2AE. *T:* (020) 7955 6255, *Fax:* (020) 7955 7366. *E:* m.g.bridge@lse.ac.uk.

**BRIDGE, Stuart Nigel; His Honour Judge Bridge;** a Circuit Judge, since 2012; *b* 12 Aug. 1958; *s* of Albert and Nora Bridge; *m* 1st, 1982, Anabelle Jane Baker (marr. diss. 2001); one *s* one *d*; 2nd, 2003, Prof. Beverley Jane Glover, *qv*; one *s* one *d*. *Educ:* Lawnswood Sch., Leeds; Queens' Coll., Cambridge (BA 1980, MA 1984). Called to the Bar, Middle Temple, 1981, Bencher, 2009; Recorder, 2004–12; Lecturer in Law: Univ. of Leeds, 1985–89; Univ. of Cambridge, 1990–2012; Fellow, Queens' Coll., Cambridge, 1990–2012, now Life Fellow; a Law Comr, 2001–08; Vis. Prof., Cornell Law Sch., 1994. *Publications:* Residential Leases, 1994; Assured Tenancies, 1999; (ed) Theobald on Wills, 16th edn 2001; (jtly) Megarry and Wade's Law of Real Property, 7th edn 2008, 9th edn 2019; (jtly) Snell's Equity, 33rd edn 2014. *Recreations:* walking, football, music, literature, gardening, family and other animals. *Address:* Cambridge Crown Court, 83 East Road, Cambridge CB1 1BT.

**BRIDGE, Timothy John Walter;** DL; Chairman, Greene King plc, 2005–16; *b* 1 Feb. 1949; *s* of late Walter John Blencowe Bridge and Susan Mary Bridge (*née* Rushbrooke). *Educ:* Twyford Sch.; Repton Sch.; Univ. of Exeter (BA). Joined Greene King plc, 1970: Dir, 1977–2016; Man. Dir, 1990–94; Chief Exec., 1994–2005. Non-executive Director: Weatherbys Ltd (formerly Weatherbys Ventures Ltd), 2006–10; William Ransom & Son plc, 2006–10; Chm., Didlington Fisheries Ltd, 2007–. Pres., Gentlemen of Suffolk CC, 1996–. DL Suffolk, 2004. *Recreations:* fishing, shooting, racing. *Address:* Priory Farm, Shudy Camps, Cambs CB21 4RE.

**BRIDGELAND, Prof. Tom Andrew,** PhD; FRS 2014; Professor of Pure Mathematics, University of Sheffield, since 2013; Quondam Fellow, All Souls College, Oxford, since 2013. *Educ:* Shelley High Sch., Huddersfield; Christ's Coll., Cambridge (BA 1st Cl. Hons Maths 1994); Univ. of Edinburgh (PhD 1998). EPSRC Res. Asst, 1998–2000, EPSRC Res. Fellow, 2001–03, Royal Soc. Res. Fellow, 2003–04, Univ. of Edinburgh; Reader and Royal Soc. Res. Fellow, 2004–06, Prof. of Maths, 2006–10, Sheffield Univ.; Sen. Res. Fellow, All Souls Coll., Oxford, 2011–13. Whittemore Lectr, Yale Univ., 2006. Berwick Prize, London Math. Soc., 2003; Whittaker Prize, Edinburgh Math. Soc., 2005; Adams Prize, Univ. of Cambridge, 2007. *Publications:* (jtly) Dirichlet Branes and Mirror Symmetry, 2009; contribs to jls incl. Bull. London Math. Soc., Jl Amer. Math. Soc., Jl Algebra, Duke Math. Jl, Annals of Maths. *Address:* School of Mathematics and Statistics, University of Sheffield, Hicks Building, Hounsfield Road, Sheffield S3 7RH; All Souls College, Oxford OX1 4AL.

**BRIDGEMAN,** family name of **Earl of Bradford** and **Viscount Bridgeman**.

**BRIDGEMAN, 3rd Viscount** *cr* 1929, of Leigh; **Robin John Orlando Bridgeman,** CA; *b* 5 Dec. 1930; *s* of Hon. Geoffrey John Orlando Bridgeman, MC, FRCS (*d* 1974) (2nd *s* of 1st Viscount) and Mary Meriel Gertrude Bridgeman (*d* 1974), *d* of Rt Hon. Sir George John Talbot; S uncle, 1982; *m* 1966, (Victoria) Harriet Lucy Turton (*see* V. H. L. Bridgeman); three *s* (and one *s* decd). *Educ:* Eton. CA 1958. 2nd Lieut, Rifle Bde, 1950–51. Partner: Fenn & Crosthwaite, 1973; Henderson Crosthwaite & Co., 1975–86; Director: Nestor-BNA plc, 1988–94; Guinness Mahon & Co. Ltd, 1988–90; Chm., Asset Management Investment Co. plc, 1994–2001. Opposition Whip, H of L, 1999–2010; elected Mem., H of L, 1999. Dir, Bridgeman Art Library Ltd, 1972–; Chm., Friends of Lambeth Palace Liby, 1992–2008. Chairman: Hosp. of St John and St Elizabeth, 1999–2007; CORESS, 2006–12; Special Trustee, Hammersmith Hosp., 1986–99; Treasurer, Florence Nightingale Aid in Sickness Trust, 1995–2006. Trustee, Music at Winchester, 1995–2006. Gov., Reed's Sch., 1994–2002 (Chm.; Jt Life Pres., 2002). Mem. Court, New England Co., 1986–2015 (Treas., 1996–2007). *Recreations:* music, gardening, travel. *Heir:* s Hon. Luke Robinson Orlando Bridgeman [*b* 1 May 1971; *m* 1996, Victoria Rose, *y d* of late Henry Frost; two *s* one *d*]. *Address:* 19 Chepstow Road, W2 5BP. *T:* (020) 7727 5400; Watley House, Sparsholt, Winchester SO21 2LU. *T:* (01962) 776297. *Clubs:* Beefsteak, Pratt's, MCC; Pitt.

**BRIDGEMAN, John Stuart,** CBE 2001; TD 1995; DL; Chairman, Recovery Career Services, 2014–17; *b* 5 Oct. 1944; *s* of late James Alfred George Bridgeman, Master Mariner, and Edith Celia (*née* Watkins); *m* 1967, Lindy Jane Fillmore; three *d*. *Educ:* Whitchurch Sch., Cardiff; University Coll., Swansea (BSc) (Hon. Fellow, Univ. of Wales, Swansea, 1997); McGill Univ., Montreal. Alcan Inds, 1966–69; Aluminium Co. of Canada, 1969–70; Alcan Australia, 1970; Commercial Dir, Alcan UK, 1977–80; Vice-Pres. (Europe), Alcan Basic Raw Materials, 1978–82; Dir, Saguenay Shipping, 1979–82; Divl Man. Dir, Alcan Aluminium (UK) Ltd, 1981–82; Managing Director: Extrusion Div., Brit. Alcan Aluminium plc, 1983–87; Brit. Alcan Enterprises, 1987–91; Chm., Luxfer Hldgs, 1988–91; Dir, Corporate Planning, Alcan Aluminium Ltd, Montreal, 1992–93; Man. Dir, British Alcan Aluminium plc, 1993–95; Dir-Gen. of Fair Trading, 1995–2000; Chm., GPC Europe, 2000–01; Dir, Regulatory Impact Unit, Cardew & Co., 2001–03. Chm., HRA, 2005–07 (Chm., Regulatory Cttee, 2006–07); Regulatory Dir, 2008–12, Pension Fund Trustee, 2009–, British Horseracing Authy; Member: British Airways NE Consumer Council, 1978–86; Monopolies and Mergers Commn, 1990–95; Adv. Council, Consumer Policy Inst., 2000–04; Canal and River Trust (formerly British Waterways): Mem. Bd, 2006–12, Vice Chm., 2009–12; Pension Trustee, 2007–14; Chm., Fair Trading Cttee, 2007–12; Chm., Audit Cttee, 2007–14; Mem., Ombudsman Cttee, 2007–14; Chm., Wales Adv. Gp, 2008–12; Trustee, 2011–14. Ind. Appeals Comr, Direct Marketing Authy, 2007– (Chm., 2000–06; Roll of Honour, 2006); Ind. Complaints Adjudicator, Assoc. for Television On-Demand, 2007–11. Vis. Prof. of Mgt, Keele Univ., 1992–2011; Vis. Prof., Univ. of Surrey, 2004–07. Ind. Consultant in corporate governance, competition policy and consumer affairs, 2000–. Vice-President: Aluminium Fedn, 1995; Trading Standards Inst., 2001–. Chairman: N Oxon Business Gp, 1984–92; Enterprise Cherwell Ltd, 1985–91; Oxfordshire Economic Partnership, 2000–06; Dir, Heart of England TEC, 1989–2002 (Chm., 2000–02). Chm., Audit and Standards Cttee, Warwicks CC, 2000–. Chm., Regulatory Cttee, Jockey Club, 2005–06. Commnd TA and Reserve Forces, 1978; QOY, 1981–84; Maj. REME (V), 1985–94; Staff Coll., 1986; SO2 Employer Support SE Dist, 1994–95. Hon. Col, 5 (QOOH) Sqdn, 39 (Skinners), later 31 (City of London) Signal Regt (V), 1996–2009; Hon. Col, Queen's Own Oxfordshire Hussars, 1996–. Mem., TAVRA Oxon and E Wessex, 1985–2000. Member: Defence Science Adv. Council, 1991–94; Nat. Employer Liaison Cttee for Reserve Forces, 1992–2002 (Chm., 1998–2002); SE RFCA, 2001–11. Member: UK-Canada Colloquium, 1993– (Treas., 2005); UK-Canada Chamber of Commerce, 1993–2007 (Vice-Pres., 1995–96; Pres., 1997–98); Canada Club, 1994–. Gov., N Oxon Coll., 1985–99 (Chm., 1989; Vice Chm., 1997–99). Trustee: Oxfordshire Community Foundn, 1995–2002; Oxford Orch. da Camera, 1996–2001; Foundn for Canadian Studies, 1996–2010 (Vice-Chm., 2005–06; Chm., 2007–10); Oxfordshire Yeomanry Trust, 1997–2012; Soldiers of Oxfordshire Trust, 2010–; Chm., Oxfordshire Yeomanry Assoc., 2008–12 (Pres., 2017–). Chm. Trustees, Banbury Sunshine Centre, 2002–. Pres., Oxfordshire Gliding Club, 1998–2009. CCMI; FInstD, FRGS, FRSA. Master, Turners' Co., 2014–15 (Liveryman, 2000; Court Asst, 2004–12). DL Oxon, 1989; High Sheriff, Oxon, 1995–96. Hon. Dr Sheffield Hallam, 1996. US Aluminium Assoc. Prize, 1988. *Recreations:* military history, inland waterways, equestrian sports, gardening, family history, ski-ing, shooting. *Clubs:* Reform, MCC; Glamorgan County Cricket.

**BRIDGEMAN, Mrs June,** CB 1990; Deputy Chair, Equal Opportunities Commission, 1991–94; *b* 26 June 1932; *d* of Gordon and Elsie Forbes; *m* 1958, (John) Michael Bridgeman, CB (*d* 2013); one *s* four *d*. *Educ:* variously, England and Scotland; Westfield Coll., London Univ. (BA; Fellow, QMW, 1993–2001). Asst Principal, BoT, 1954; subseq. served in DEA, NBPI, Min. of Housing and Local Govt, DoE; Under Secretary: DoE 1974–76; Central Policy Review Staff, Cabinet Office, 1976–79; Dept of Transport, 1979–90. Mem., BSE Inquiry, 1998–2000. Mem., Central Bd of Finance, C of E, 1979–83; Bishops Selector for ACCM, 1974–89. Member of Council: PSI, 1984–90; NCOPF, 1994–2001; GDST (formerly GPDST), 1995–2002. Vice-Pres., Fawcett Soc., 1994–. Trustee, Rees Jeffreys Road Fund, 1992–2008. FRSA 1991. *Recreations:* assisting and representing local voluntary organisations, local history and heritage research projects and publications. *Address:* Bridge House, Culverden Park Road, Tunbridge Wells TN4 9QX. *T:* (01892) 525578.

**BRIDGEMAN, (Victoria) Harriet Lucy, (Viscountess Bridgeman),** CBE 2014; Founder and Chairman: Bridgeman Art Library, since 1972; Artists' Collecting Society, since 2006; *b* Low Middleton Hall, Co. Durham, 30 March 1942; *d* of Ralph Meredyth Turton and Mary Turton; *m* 1966, Robin John Orlando Bridgeman (*see* Viscount Bridgeman); three *s* (and one *s* decd). *Educ:* private educn with governess; Darlington High Sch., Co. Durham; St Mary's Sch., Wantage; Trinity Coll., Dublin (MA). Exec. Ed., The Masters, 1966–68; Ed., Discovering Antiques, 1968–70. Founder Mem., British Assoc. of Picture Libraries and Agencies, 1974–; Mem., British Copyright Council, 2010–. Trustee: British Sporting Art Trust, 2005–17; Nat. Open Art Competition, 2014–; Eur. Catalogue Raisonné Assoc., 2017–; Mem., Art Cttee, Imperial Healthcare Trust, 2003–15. FRSA. Eur. Women of Year Award (Arts Section), 1997; Internat. Business Women of Year, 2005; Alumni Award, TCD, 2010. *Publications:* with Elizabeth Drury: The Encyclopedia of Victoriana, 1975; Society Scandals, 1977; Needlework: an illustrated history, 1978; Visiting the Gardens of Europe, 1979; Guide to Gardens of Britain and Europe, 1979; The Last Word, 1982. *Recreations:* reading, family, travelling. *Address:* 19 Chepstow Road, W2 5BP. *T:* (home) (020) 7727 5400, (work) (020) 7727 4065. *E:* harriet@bridgemanimages.com. *Clubs:* Chelsea Arts, Academy, Soho.

**BRIDGEN, Andrew;** MP (C) North West Leicestershire, since 2010; *b* Burton upon Trent, Staffs, 28 Oct. 1964; *s* of Alan and Ann Bridgen; *m* 2000, Jacqueline Cremin (marr. diss. 2014); two *s*; *m* 2017, Nevena Pavlovic; one *s*. *Educ:* Pingle Sch., Swadlincote; Nottingham Univ. (BSc Biol Scis 1986). Officer trng, RM, 1987–88; Officer, Staffords (TA), 1989–91. Non-exec. Chm., AB Produce plc, 2010–14 (Man. Dir, 1988–2010). Business Mem., E Midlands Regl Assembly, 1999–2000. Chm., Regulatory Reform Select Cttee, 2015–17 (Mem., 2010–15). *Address:* House of Commons, SW1A 0AA.

**BRIDGER, Very Rev. Dr Francis William;** Rector, St Mary's, Broughty Ferry, since 2012; Dean of Brechin, since 2013; *b* 27 May 1951; *s* of Harry Edward George Bridger and Harriet Rose Bridger; *m* 1st, 1975, Renee Winifred (*d* 2003); one *s* two *d*; 2nd, 2004, Helen Foster. *Educ:* Pembroke Coll., Oxford (BA 1973; MA 1978); Trinity Coll., Bristol; Bristol Univ. (PhD 1981). Ordained deacon, 1978, priest, 1979; Asst Curate, St Jude, Mildmay Park and St Paul, Canonbury, 1978–82; Lectr and Tutor, St John's Coll., Nottingham, 1982–90; Vicar, St Mark, Woodthorpe, 1990–99; Principal, Trinity Theol Coll., Bristol, 1999–2005; Exec. Dir, Center for Anglican Communion Studies, 2006–12, Prof. of Anglican Studies, 2006–15, Fuller Theol Seminary, Calif; Principal, E Midlands Ministry Trng Course, 2009–12. Vis. Prof. of Pastoral Care and Counselling, 1999–2005, of Practical Theol., 2005–06, Fuller Theol Seminary, Calif. Member: Gen. Synod of C of E, 1998–2005; Gen. Synod of Scottish Episcopal Church, 2013–. Theol Advr to Archbishop of Burundi, 2007–10. *Publications:* (ed and contrib.) The Cross and the Bomb, 1983; Videos, Permissiveness and the Law, 1984; Children Finding Faith, 1988, 2nd edn 2000 (trans. French and German 1995); Counselling in Context, 1995, 3rd edn 2005; Celebrating the Family, 1995; Why Can't I have Faith?, 1998; The Diana Phenomenon, 1998; Christian Counselling and the Challenge of Postmodernism, 1999; A Charmed Life: the spirituality of Potterworld, 2001; Opening Windows into Heaven, 2001; 23 Days: a story of love, death and God, 2004; (ed and contrib.) Conversations at the Edges of Things, 2012; contrib. to Tyndale Bull., Anvil, Theology, Jl of Christian Educn, Church Times. *Recreations:* politics, current affairs, media. *Address:* St Mary's Scottish Episcopal Church, Queen Street, Broughty Ferry, Dundee DD5 1AJ.

**BRIDGER, Rev. Canon Gordon Frederick;** Principal, Oak Hill Theological College, 1987–96; *b* 5 Feb. 1932; *s* of late Dr John Dell Bridger and Hilda Bridger; *m* 1962, Elizabeth Doris Bewes; three *d*. *Educ:* Christ's Hospital, Horsham; Selwyn Coll., Cambridge (MA Hons Theology); Ridley Hall, Cambridge. Curate, Islington Parish Church, 1956–59; Curate, Holy Sepulchre Church, Cambridge, 1959–62; Vicar, St Mary, North End, Fulham, 1962–69; Chaplain, St Thomas's Episcopal Church, Edinburgh, 1969–76; Rector, Holy Trinity Church, Heigham, Norwich, 1976–87; RD Norwich (South), 1981–86; Exam. Chaplain to Bishop of Norwich, 1981–86; Hon. Canon, Norwich Cathedral, 1984–87, now Hon. Canon Emeritus. Dir, Open Theol Coll., 1993–97; Mem. Court, Middlesex Univ., 1996–2000. Trustee, Jerusalem Trust, 1998–2006. Fellow, 1996–98, Associate Fellow, 1999–, Coll. of Preachers. Hon. MA Middlesex, 1996. *Publications:* The Man from Outside, 1969, rev. edn 1978; A Day that Changed the World, 1975; A Bible Study Commentary (I Corinthians—Galatians), 1985; The Message of Obadiah, Nahum and Zephaniah, 2010; reviews in The Churchman, Anvil and other Christian papers and magazines. *Recreations:* music, sport, reading. *Address:* The Elms, 4 Common Lane, Sheringham, Norfolk NR26 8PL.

**BRIDGER, Timothy Peter M.;** *see* Moore-Bridger.

**BRIDGES,** family name of **Baron Bridges** and **Baron Bridges of Headley**.

**BRIDGES,** 3rd Baron *cr* 1957; **Mark Thomas Bridges,** KCVO 2019 (CVO 2012); Private Solicitor to the Queen, 2002–18; *b* 25 July 1954; *er s* of 2nd Baron Bridges, GCMG and Rachel Mary Bridges; *S* father, 2017; *m* 1978, Angela Margaret, *er d* of late John Leigh Collinson; three *d* (one *s* decd). *Educ:* Eton Coll.; Corpus Christi Coll., Cambridge (Choral Exhibition). Partner, Farrer & Co., 1985–; Solicitor, Duchy of Lancaster affairs, 1998–2012. Mem. Council, RSCM, 1989–97; Treas., Bach Choir, 1992–97; Chm., Music in Country Churches, 2006–; Trustee: UCL Hospitals Charity, 1992–2010; Leeds Castle Foundn, 2007–. Chm. Govs, Hanford Sch., 2004–13; Governor: Purcell Sch., 2000–12 (Fellow, 2012); Sherborne Sch. for Girls, 2001–11. Academician, Internat. Acad. of Estate and Trust Law, 2005. Mem., Court of Assistants, Goldsmiths' Co., 2006–. *Publications:* (ed) International Succession Laws, 2001. *Recreations:* music, sailing, book collecting. *Heir: b* Hon. Nicholas Edward Bridges [*b* 29 March 1956; *m* 1985, Susan Guggenheim; one *s* one *d* (and one *d* decd)]. *Address:* Farrer & Co., 66 Lincoln's Inn Fields, WC2A 3LH. *T:* (020) 3375 7000, *Fax:* (020) 7242 9899. *E:* mark.bridges@farrer.co.uk. *Clubs:* Brooks's, House of Lords Yacht, Noblemen and Gentlemen's Catch.

**BRIDGES OF HEADLEY,** Baron *cr* 2015 (Life Peer), of Headley Heath in the County of Surrey; **James George Robert Bridges,** MBE 1997; *b* Wimbledon, 15 July 1970; *s* of late Hon. Robert Oliver Bridges, *s* of 1st Baron Bridges, and (Rosamund) Theresa Bridges; *m* 2007, Alice Mary Hickman; one *s* two *d* (incl. twin *s* and *d*). *Educ:* Eton Coll.; Exeter Coll., Oxford (Stapledon Schol.; MA 1st cl. Hist.); Fels Center of Govt, Univ. of Pennsylvania (Thouron Schol.). Cons. Res. Dept, 1992–93; Asst Pol Sec. to Prime Minister, 1994–97; Dir of Communications, British Digital Broadcasting, 1997–98; leader writer, The Times, 1998–2000; Consultant, Quiller Consultants, 2000–04; Chm., Cons. Res. Dept, 2004–05; Campaign Dir, Cons. Party, 2006–07; Consultant, Quiller Consultants, 2007–09; Campaign Co-ordinator, Cons. Party, 2010; Chief Exec., Quiller Consultants, 2010–13; Sen. Advr to Gp Exec. Chm., Santander, 2014–15, 2017–. Parly Sec., Cabinet Office, 2015–16; Parly Under-Sec. of State, DExEU, 2016–17. Trustee, Foundation Years Trust, 2014–. Liveryman, Fishmongers' Co., 2011. *Recreations:* family, walking, history. *Address:* House of Lords, SW1A 0PW. *Clubs:* Beefsteak, White's.

**BRIDGES, Alastair;** Director of Finance and Corporate Services, Independent Parliamentary Standards Authority, since 2016; *b* London, 1964; *s* of Roy Charles Bridges and Jill Margaret Bridges; *m* 1997, Melanie Knight; one *s* one *d*. *Educ:* Aberdeen Grammar Sch.; Univ. of Edinburgh (MA); London Sch. of Econs and Pol Sci. (MSc). CPFA 2010. HM Treasury, 1988–2001: various posts incl. Hd, Health Team, 1999–2001; Cabinet Office, 1995–97 (on secondment); Sen. Manager, Corporate Finance, KPMG, Moscow, 1997–99; Home Office, 2001–14: various posts incl. Dir of Finance, Crime and Policing, 2005–09; Dir, Finance and Corporate Services, HM Passport Office, 2009–14; Dir of Finance and Performance, DEFRA, 2014–15. Hon. Treas., Brook Young People, 2012–. *Recreations:* music, sailing.

**BRIDGES, Andrew Michael,** CBE 2007; independent advisor on making probation work, with RRP, Seetec and others, since 2014; Associate, G4S Care and Justice, 2011–14; *b* Bath, 2 June 1951; *s* of Michael and Peggy Bridges; partner, Lesley Corina; two *s*. *Educ:* City of Bath Boys' Sch.; Univ. of York (BA Hist. 1972); Univ. of Leicester (DipSW 1975); Bristol Poly. (MA 1984); Univ. of Bath (MPhil 1991); Univ. of York (Postgrad. Dip. Railway Studies 2018). Probation Officer, Wilts, 1975–83; Sen. Probation Officer, Gwent, 1983–89; Asst Chief Probation Officer, 1989–98, Chief Probation Officer, 1998–2001, Berks; HM Inspector of Probation, 2001–03; HM Dep. Chief Inspector of Probation, 2003–04; HM Chief Inspector of Probation, 2004–11. Res. Fellow (pt-time), Univ. of Oxford, 1996. Chm., Interdeptl Nat. Offender Employment Forum, 1998–2001. Associate, G4S Care and Justice, 2011–14; Advr to Victims Comr, 2014–19. *Publications:* Increasing the Employability of Offenders: an inquiry into Probation Service effectiveness, 1998. *Recreations:* early morning running (slowly), travelling to sometimes unusual destinations, occasionally continuing to enjoy the Grateful Dead, periodic Railway Studies, and persistently using a Reading FC season ticket since 1995. *W:* andrewbridgesprobation.com.

**BRIDGES, Prof. James Wilfrid;** Professor of Toxicology and Environmental Health, University of Surrey, 1979–2003, Professor Emeritus, since 2004; *b* 9 Aug. 1938; *s* of Wilfrid Edward Seymour Bridges and Mary Winifred Cameron; *m* Olga Vorozhbitova. *Educ:* Bromley Grammar Sch.; Queen Elizabeth Coll., London Univ.; St Mary's Hosp. Med. Sch., London Univ. (BSc, DSc, PhD). Lectr, St Mary's Hosp. Med. Sch., 1962–68; University of Surrey: Senior Lectr then Reader, Dept of Biochemistry, 1968–78; Res. Dir, Robens Inst. of Industrial and Envmtl Health and Safety, 1978–95; Dean, Faculty of Science, 1988–92; Hd, European Inst. of Health and Med. Scis, 1995–2000; Dean for Internat. Strategy, 2000–03. Visiting Professor: Univ. of Texas at Dallas, 1973, 1979; Univ. of Rochester, NY, 1974; Mexico City, 1991; Sen. Scientist, Nat. Inst. of Envmtl Health Scis, N Carolina, 1976. Chm., British Toxicology Soc., 1980–81; First Pres., Fedn of European Toxicology Socs, 1985–88. Member: Vet. Products Cttee, 1982–96; HSE WATCH Cttee, 1982–2005; EC Scientific Cttee on Animal Nutrition, 1991–97; EU Scientific Steering Cttee (Public Health), 1997–2004; EU Mirror Gp, 2006–; DG SANCO Scientific Cttee Co-ordination Gp, 2004–13; Expert, DG Res., 2008–; mem. of various EFSA working gps, 2004–; Mem., Animal Welfare Adv. Gp, Shell Internat., 2014–; former Member: Novel and Irradiated Foods Cttee; Med. Aspects of Water Quality Cttee; Adv. Cttee on Toxic Substances; Chairman: Vet. Residues Cttee, 2001–04; EU Harmonisation of Risk Assessment Working Party, 1998–2004; EU Scientific Cttee on Emerging and Newly Identified Health Risks, 2004–13; IDEA project supervisory gp, 2013–; President: EU Scientific Adv. Cttee on Toxicology, Ecotoxicology and the Envmt, 1997–2004; EU Scientific Cttee on Emerging and Newly Identified Health Risks, 2004–. Founder, Eur. Drug Metabolism Workshops. Foreign Mem., Spanish Royal Acad. of Veterinary Scis. Hon. Member: Soc. of Occupnl Med.; British Toxicol. Soc.; Hon. Fellow, Eur. Soc. of Toxicol. Hon. DSc Baptist Univ. of Hong Kong. *Publications:* (ed jtly) Progress in Drug Metabolism, 10 vols, 1976–88; (with Dr Olga Bridges) Losing Hope: the environment and health in Russia, 1996; over 400 research papers and reviews in scientific jls. *Recreations:* theatre going, various sports. *Address:* Liddington Lodge, Liddington Hall Drive, Guildford GU3 3AE.

**BRIDGES, Dame Mary (Patricia),** DBE 1981; *b* 6 June 1930; *d* of Austin Edward and Lena Mabel Fawkes; *m* 1951, Bertram Marsdin Bridges; (one step *s* decd one step *d* decd). Chm., Honiton Div. Cons. Assoc., 1968–71; Pres., Western Provincial Area, Nat. Union of Cons. and Unionist Assocs, 1987–. Women's Section of Royal British Legion: Pres., Exmouth Br., 1965–; Chm., Devon County Women's Section, 1979–91; County Vice Pres., 1991; County Pres., 1997–2010; SW Area Rep. to Central Cttee, 1985–89; Nat. Vice-Chm., 1989–92; Nat. Chm., 1992–95; Nat. Life Vice-Pres., 1999; Mem. House Cttee, Dunkirk Meml House, 1994–99. Mem., SW Electricity Consultative Council, 1982–90 (Chm., Devon Cttee, 1986–90). Former Mem., Exe Vale HMC; Pres., Exmouth Council of Voluntary Service (Founder Chm., 1975). Member: Exec., Resthaven, Exmouth, 1970–2001 (Chm., League of Friends, 1971–90); Devon FPC, 1985–91; President: Exmouth Br., Royal British Legion Women's Section, 1965–2012; Exmouth and Budleigh Salterton Br., CRUSE, 1980–88; Exmouth Campaign Cttee, Cancer Research, 1981– (Chm., 1975–81); Founder Pres., Exmouth Br., British Heart Foundn, 1984–2004. Mem., Exmouth Cttee, LEPRA, 1962–87 (Hon. Sec., 1964–87); Dir, Home Care Trust, 1988–90; Co-optative Trustee, Exmouth Welfare Trust, 1979–2005; Co-founder, and Trustee, Exmouth and Lympstone Hospiscare, 1986– (Pres., 1994–2004); founder Trustee, Exmouth Adventure Trust for Girls, 1987–90 (Patron, 1990–); Exec. Mem., St Loye's Coll. Foundn for Trng the Disabled for Commerce and Industry, 1988–2001; Governor, Rolle Coll., Exmouth, 1982–88. Hon. Life Member: Retford Cricket Club, 1951; Exmouth Cricket Club, 1997 (Hon. Vice-Pres., 1981; Pres., 1992–2001). *Recreations:* cricket, reading. *Address:* Walton House, 3 Fairfield Close, Exmouth, Devon EX8 2BN. *T:* (01395) 265317.

**BRIDGES, Hon. Simon Joseph;** MP (Nat.) Tauranga, New Zealand, since 2008; Leader of the Opposition, and Leader of the National Party, New Zealand, since 2018; *b* Auckland, 12 Oct. 1976; *s* of Heath Bridges and Ruth Bridges; *m* 2005, Natalie Eaves; two *s* one *d*. *Educ:* Rutherford Coll.; Univ. of Auckland (LLB Hons; BA); St Catherine's Coll., Oxford (BCL 2005). Kensington Swan: Litigation Lawyer, 2000–08; Crown Prosecutor, 2001–08. Minister for Consumer Affairs, 2012–13; Associate Minister: of Transport, 2012–13; for Climate Change Issues, 2012–16; Minister: of Labour, 2013–14; of Energy and Resources, 2013–16; of Transport, 2014–17; Associate Minister of Justice, 2014–16; Minister for Econ. Develt, 2016–17; Associate Minister of Finance, 2016–17. *Address:* Parliament Buildings, Wellington 6160, New Zealand.

**BRIDGES, Stephen John,** LVO 1998; Managing Director, Grant Thornton (USA) LLP, since 2017; *b* 19 June 1960; *s* of Gordon Alfred Richard Bridges and Audrey Middleton; *m* 1990, Kyung Mi. *Educ:* Devonport High Sch.; London Univ. (International Relations); Univ. of Leeds (MA East Asian Studies 2010). Joined FCO, 1980; Third Sec., Luanda, 1984–87; Third, later Second, Sec., Seoul, 1987–91; Second, later First, Sec., UN and SE Asia Dept, FCO, 1991–96; First Sec., and Head, Political Section, Kuala Lumpur, 1996–2000; Ambassador to Cambodia, 2000–05; Dep. High Comr, Dhaka, Bangladesh, 2005–07; Man. Dir, Greater Mekong Resources Co. Ltd, 2008–11; Dir, BSW Energy PTE Ltd, 2009–11; Hd of Workforce, Appts and Services, HR Directorate, FCO, 2011–13; Consul Gen., Chicago, 2013–17. Dir, Soi Dog Foundn (UK). Mem. Bd, British American Business Council, Chicago. DUniv Birmingham, 2016. *Recreations:* sports, food and wine, Montague - the dog. *Address:* c/o Grant Thornton USA, Suite 200, 171 N Clark Street, Chicago, IL 60601, USA.

**BRIDGEWATER, Emma,** CBE 2013; pottery designer; Chairman, Emma Bridgewater Ltd; *b* Cambridge, 23 Dec. 1960; *d* of Adrian Bridgewater and Charlotte Stroud; *m* 1987, Matthew Rice; one *s* three *d*. *Educ:* Oxford High Sch.; Bedford Coll., London Univ. (BA Hons English Lit.). Started Emma Bridgewater Ltd, 1984. Pres., CPRE, 2016–. *Publications:* Toast & Marmalade, and Other Stories, 2014; Pattern & the Secrets of Lasting Design, 2016. *Address:* Emma Bridgewater Ltd, 739 Fulham Road, SW6 5UL.

**BRIDGEWATER, Peter,** PhD; FLS; Chair, National Landcare Network, Australia, since 2017; *b* Bristol, 31 Dec. 1945; *s* of late Denis Henry Bridgewater and Winifred May Bridgewater; one *d*. *Educ:* Univ. of Durham (BSc 1st Cl. Hons; PhD). Consultant, Forestry Canada, 1969, 1970; Lectr in Botany, Monash Univ., 1970–75; Lectr in Plant Biol., 1976–77, Sen. Lectr in Envmtl Sci., 1977–82, Murdoch Univ.; Dir, Aust. Bureau of Flora and Fauna, 1982–88; First Asst Sec., Aust. Dept of Arts, Sport, the Envmt, Tourism and Territories, 1988–89; Chief Scientist, UK Nature Conservancy Council, 1989–90; Chief Exec., Aust. Nature Conservation Agency, incl. Dir, Nat. Parks and Wildlife Service, 1990–97; Chief Sci. Advr, Envmt Australia, incl. Supervising Scientist, Alligator Rivers Reg., 1997–99; Sec., Man and the Biosphere Prog. and Dir, Div. of Ecol Scis, UNESCO, Paris, 1999–2003; Sec. Gen., Ramsar Convention, Gland, 2003–07. Visiting Professor: Beijing Forestry Univ., 2008–; United Nations Univ., Tokyo, 2010–; Vis. Fellow, ANU, 2015–16; Adjunct Prof., Univ. of Canberra, 2016–; Hon. Prof., Univ. of Wollongong. Chairman: Standing Cttee Convention on Migratory Species, 1994–97; Internat. Whaling Commn, 1995–97 (Vice Chm., 1992–94); Inter-govt Coordinating Council, Man and Biosphere Prog., UNESCO, 1995–98; 6th meeting, Conf. of Parties for Convention on Wetlands, 1996; Wkg Gp for Starlight Initiative, 2006–; Jt Nature Conservation Cttee, 2007–14; Eur. Platform for Biodiversity Res. Strategy consultation on Biodiversity, 2009; Pew Whales Commn, 2009; Member: Aust. Nat. Commn for UNESCO, 1993–99; Ind. World Commn on the Oceans, 1995–98; Parks and Wildlife Commn, Northern Territory, 1997–99; Commn on Genetic Diversity, 1998–2000; Sci. and Technol. Adv. Panel to Global Envmt Facility, 1998–2000; Bd, Millennium Ecosystem Assessment, 2000–05; Total Petroleum Bd, Fondation pour biodiversité et la mer, 2002–09; Internat. Steering Cttee, Internat. Mechanism for Scientific Expertise or Biodiversity, 2005–08; Internat. Model Forest Prog. Adv. Council, 2007–. Trustee, Parks Forum, 2003–. Member: Screening Cttee, Cosmos Prize, Japan, 2003–04; Jury, Ramon Margalef Prize for Envmtl Scis, Govt of Catalonia, 2005–08; judging panel, St Andrews Prize, 2010–. MAICD. FLS 2000. Hon. Dr Res. Mgt New England, 1997. *Publications:* over 250 academic papers on sustainable develt, envmtl governance, biodiversity. *Recreations:* cooking, gardening. *Address:* 7/143 Port Jackson Circuit, Phillip, ACT 2606, Australia. *T:* (61) 42325 2967; 2 The Wharfside, Station Place, Isle of Man IM5 1AT. *E:* peter@global-garden.net. *Club:* University House (Canberra).

**BRIDGWATER, Prof. John,** FREng, FIChemE; Shell Professor of Chemical Engineering, Cambridge University, 1993–2004, now Professor Emeritus; Professorial Fellow, 1993–2004 and Senior Tutor, 2004, St Catharine's College, Cambridge; *b* 10 Jan. 1938; *s* of Eric and Mary Bridgwater; *m* 1962, Diane Louise Tucker; one *s* one *d*. *Educ:* Solihull Sch.; St Catharine's Coll., Cambridge (Major Scholar; MA, PhD, ScD); Princeton Univ. (MSE). FREng (FEng 1987). Chemical Engineer, Courtaulds, 1961–64; University of Cambridge: Demonstrator in Chem. Engrg, 1964–69; Univ. Lectr in Chem. Engrg and Fellow, St Catharine's Coll., 1969–71; Esso Res. Fellow in Chem. Engrg, Hertford Coll., Oxford, 1971–73; Univ. Lectr in Engrg Sci., Univ. of Oxford and Lubbock Fellow in Engrg, Balliol Coll., 1973–80; University of Birmingham: Prof., 1980–93; Head, Sch. of Chem. Engrg, 1983–89; Dean, Faculty of Engrg, 1989–92; Gp Leader in Inter-Disciplinary Res. Centre in Materials for High Performance Applications, 1989–93; Hd, Deptof Chemical Engrg, Cambridge Univ., 1993–98. Dir, Tunkhu Abdul Rahman Fund, St Catharine's College, Cambridge, 2004–06. Vis. Associate Prof., Univ. of British Columbia, 1970–71; Vis. Prof., Univ. of Calif at Berkeley, 1992–93; Erskine Vis. Fellow, Univ. of Canterbury, NZ, 2002; Vis. Fellow, Univ. of NSW, 2004–. Mem., Engrg Bd, SERC, 1986–89; Chm., Process Engrg Cttee, SERC, 1986–89. Pres., IChemE, 1997–98 (Vice-Pres., 1995–97). Chm., Editl Bd, Chem. Engrg Science, 1996–2003 (Exec. Editor, 1983–96). *Publications:* (with J. J. Benbow) Paste Flow and Extrusion, 1993; papers on chem. and process engineering in professional jls. *Address:* St Catharine's College, Cambridge CB2 1RL.

**BRIDPORT,** 4th Viscount *cr* 1868; **Alexander Nelson Hood;** Baron Bridport, 1794; 7th Duke of Bronte in Sicily (*cr* 1799); Managing Partner, Bridport & Cie SA, since 1991; *b* 17 March 1948; *s* of 3rd Viscount Bridport and Sheila Jeanne Agatha (*d* 1996), *d* of Johann van Meurs; *S* father, 1969; *m* 1st, 1972, Linda Jacqueline Paravicini (marr. diss.), *d* of Lt-Col and Mrs V. R. Paravicini; one *s*; 2nd, 1979, Mrs Nina Rindt-Martyn (marr. diss. 1999); one *s*.

*Educ:* Eton; Sorbonne. *Heir: s* Hon. Peregrine Alexander Nelson Hood [*b* 30 Aug. 1974; *m* 2013, Serena, *e d* of Shahrokh Nikkhah]. *Address:* 1 Place Longemalle, 1204 Geneva, Switzerland. *T:* (22) 8177000, *Fax:* (22) 8177050. *Club:* Brooks's.

**BRIDSON, Prof. Martin Robert,** PhD; FRS 2016; President, Clay Mathematics Institute, since 2018; Whitehead Professor of Pure Mathematics, University of Oxford, since 2007 (Head of Mathematics, 2015–18); Fellow, Magdalen College, Oxford, since 2007; *b* Douglas, I of M, 22 Oct. 1964; *s* of late Gerald Patrick Bridson and Lilian Mary Bridson (*née* Stuart); *m* 1995, Julie Ann Lynch; two *s* one *d*. *Educ:* Douglas High Sch., I of M; Hertford Coll., Oxford (BA 1986); Cornell Univ. (MS 1988; PhD 1991). Instructor, 1991–92, Asst Prof., 1992–96, Princeton Univ.; CUF Lectr, 1994–96, Reader, 1996–99, Prof. of Topology, 1999–2001, Univ. of Oxford; Tutorial Fellow, Pembroke Coll., Oxford, 1994–2001; Prof. of Pure Maths, Imperial Coll. London, 2001–06. Advanced Fellow, 1997–2002, Sen. Fellow, 2007–12, EPSRC. Visiting Professor: Univ. de Genève, 1992–93 and 2006–07; Ecole Poly. Fédérale de Lausanne, 2007. Forder Lectr, NZ, 2005; Jankowski Lectr, Gdansk, 2008; Marker Lectr, Penn, 2009; Abel Prize Lectr, Oslo, 2009; Schrödinger Lectr, Vienna, 2011; Britton Lectr, Ont, 2012; Pollack Lectr, Israel, 2014. Clay Sen. Scholar, Park City Maths Inst., 2012; Wolf Lectr, Texas, 2018. Mem. Council, LMS, 1999–2006 (Vice Pres., 2004–06). Fellow, American Math. Soc., 2015. Whitehead Prize, LMS, 1999; Wolfson Award, Royal Soc., 2006. Ed. of various mathematical jls. *Publications:* (with A. Haefliger) Metric Spaces of Non-positive Curvature, 1999; (ed with S. M. Salamon) Invitations to Geometry and Topology, 2002; (ed jtly) Geometric and Cohomological Methods in Group Theory, 2009; (with D. Groves) The Quadratic Isoperimetric Inequality for Mapping Tori of Free-group Automorphisms, 2010; contrib. articles to learned jls. *Recreations:* family life, poetry, ball games, chess. *Address:* Mathematical Institute, University of Oxford, Andrew Wiles Building, Radcliffe Observatory Quarter, Woodstock Road, Oxford OX2 6GG.

**BRIEGEL, (Geoffrey) Michael (Olver);** Deputy Master of the Court of Protection, 1977–83; *b* 13 July 1923; *s* of late Roy C. Briegel, TD, and Veria Lindsey Briegel; *m* 1947, Barbara Mary Richardson; three *s* one *d*. *Educ:* Highgate Sch. Served War, RAF, 1942–46 (514 Sqdn Bomber Command). Called to Bar, Lincoln's Inn, 1950; Public Trustee Office, 1954; Clerk of the Lists, Queen's Bench Div., and Legal Sec. to Lord Chief Justice of England, 1963; Dep. Circuit Administrator, South Eastern Circuit, 1971. Legacy Officer, Inst. of Cancer Res., Royal Cancer Hosp., 1983–97; Legacy Consultant, Cancer Res. UK (formerly Imperial Cancer Res. Fund), 1998–2011. *Recreations:* theatre, cinema, music, all sports. *Clubs:* Royal Air Force; Middlesex County Cricket; Armadillos Cricket.

**BRIERLEY, Fiona Jillian,** FRGS; Teacher of Geography, since 1983, and Headteacher, since 2014, Southend High School for Girls; *b* Chadderton, Lancs, 31 March 1957; *d* of Kenneth Brierley and Greta Brierley (*née* Tanner). *Educ:* Chadderton Grammar Sch. for Girls; Blyth Grammar Sch.; Hull Univ. (BA Hons Geog. and Sociol. 1978; PGCE Geog. 1979); Open Univ. (Advanced DipEd 1992; MA Mgt 1993). FRGS 1995. Teacher of Geog., Cramlington High Sch., 1979–82; Hd of Geog., Coquet High Sch., 1982–83; Pastoral Lead, 1987–91, Sen. Teacher and Asst Headteacher, 1991–2013, Dep. Headteacher, 2013–14, Southend High Sch. for Girls. Chair, Southend Sch.-centred initial teacher trng, 2014–. Mem., Daws Heath Histl Soc. *Recreations:* travel, family, friends, walking with Duncan, reading, theatre, photography, quilting and unpicking quilting, art and art history, watching the garden grow, good food, good wine, watching the world go by. *Address:* Southend High School for Girls, Southchurch Boulevard, Southend-on-Sea, Essex SS2 4UZ. *T:* (01702) 588852. *E:* fbrierley@shsg.org.

**BRIERLEY, Sir Ronald (Alfred),** Kt 1988; Chairman, Mercantile Investment Company Ltd, since 2015; *b* Wellington, 2 Aug. 1937; *s* of J. R. Brierley. *Educ:* Wellington Coll. Editor, New Zealand Stocks and Shares, 1957–63; Chairman: Brierley Investments Ltd, 1961–89 (Founder, 1961; Founder Pres. 1989–); Industrial Equity Ltd, 1966–89; Bank of New Zealand, 1987–88 (Dir, 1985–88; Dep. Chm., 1986); GPG, then Guinness Peat Gp plc, 1990–2010 (non-exec. Dir, 2010–15). *Address:* Mercantile Investment Company Ltd, Level 11, 139 Macquarie Street, Sydney, NSW 2000, Australia.

**BRIERS, Rear Adm. Matthew Peter;** Director, Carrier Strike, since 2018; *b* London, 10 Jan. 1966; *s* of Phillips Briers and Maureen Briers; *m* 2012, Pietruszka Motykiewicz. *Educ:* Torpoint Community Sch.; Saltash Sixth Form Coll.; King's Coll. London (MA Defence Studies 2002). Joined RN, 1984; CO 845 Naval Air Sqdn, 2006–08; HCSC 2011; CO Cdo Helicopter Force, 2011–14; Cdre Fleet Air Arm, 2014–16; rcds 2016. Trustee, SkillForce, 2018. President: RN and RM Freefall Parachuting Assoc., 2016–; RN Gliding and Soaring Assoc., 2019–. *Recreations:* fly fishing, modern history, hillwalking, ancient building restoration. *E:* matt.briers978@mod.gov.uk.

**BRIGDEN, Susan Elizabeth,** PhD; FBA 2014; FRHistS; Reader in History, University of Oxford, until 2016; Fellow, Lincoln College, Oxford (formerly Langford Fellow and Tutor in History). *Educ:* Univ. of Manchester (BA); Clare Coll., Cambridge (PhD 1979); MA Oxon. Darby Fellow in Hist., Lincoln Coll., Oxford, 1980; Lectr in Hist., Univ. of Oxford, 1984. *Publications:* London and the Reformation, 1989; New Worlds, Lost Worlds: the rule of the Tudors, 1485–1603, 2000; Thomas Wyatt: the Heart's Forest, 2012 (Wolfson Hist. Prize, 2013); (contrib.) Henry VIII and the Court: art, politics and performance, 2013; contribs to jls incl. Past and Present, Histl Jl, English Histl Rev. *Address:* Lincoln College, Turl Street, Oxford OX1 3DR.

**BRIGGS OF WESTBOURNE, Rt Hon. Lord; Michael Townley Featherstone Briggs,** Kt 2006; PC 2013; a Justice of the Supreme Court of the United Kingdom, since 2017; *b* 23 Dec. 1954; *s* of late Capt. James William Featherstone Briggs, RN and Barbara Nadine Briggs (*née* Pelham Groom); *m* 1981, Beverly Ann Rogers; three *s* one *d*. *Educ:* Charterhouse; Magdalen Coll., Oxford (BA History). Called to the Bar, Lincoln's Inn, 1978, Bencher, 2001; Jun. Counsel to Crown Chancery, 1990–94; QC 1994; Attorney Gen., Duchy of Lancaster, 2001–06; a Judge of the High Ct of Justice, Chancery Div., 2006–13; Vice Chancellor, County Palatine of Lancaster, 2011–13; a Lord Justice of Appeal, 2013–17; Dep. Hd of Civil Justice, 2016–17. *Recreations:* sailing, singing (solo and choral), cooking, classic cars, garden railways. *Address:* Supreme Court of the United Kingdom, Parliament Square, SW1P 3BD. *Clubs:* Bar Yacht; British Classic Yacht; Royal Yacht Squadron.

**BRIGGS, Andrew;** *see* Briggs, G. A. D.

**BRIGGS, David;** *see* Briggs, T. D.

**BRIGGS, David John,** FRCO; freelance composer and concert organist, since 2002; Artist-in-Residence, Cathedral of St John the Divine, New York, since 2017; *b* 1 Nov. 1962; *s* of late J. R. Briggs and of J. A. Briggs (*née* Jones); *m* 1st, 1986, Elisabeth Anne Baker; two *d*; 2nd, 2004, Madge Nimocks. *Educ:* Solihull Sch. (Music Schol.); King's Coll., Cambridge (Organ Schol.; John Stewart of Rannoch Schol. in Sacred Music; MA 1987). FRCO 1980; ARCM 1986. Studied with Jean Langlais in Paris, 1984–86; Asst Organist, Hereford Cathedral, 1985–88; Organist: Truro Cathedral, 1989–94; Gloucester Cathedral, 1994–2002. Vis. Tutor in Improvisation, RNCM, 1995–; Vis. Prof. of Improvisation, RAM, 2001–. Artist-in-Residence, St James Cathedral, Toronto, 2012–17. Festival Conductor, Gloucester Three Choirs Fest., 1995, 1998, 2001. Recital tours, Australia, NZ, S Africa, Russia, Finland, Sweden, France, Belgium, Luxembourg, Germany, Italy, Ireland, Canada and USA. Has made numerous recordings. FRSA 1993. 5 prizes and Silver Medal, Co. of Musicians. *Publications: compositions:* Truro Eucharist, 1990; The Music Mountain, 1991; Te Deum Laudamus, 1998; Creation, 2000; Messe pour Notre-Dame, 2002; Magnificat and Nunc Dimittis, 2004; Symphony Missa pro Defunctis, 2004; Four Concert Etudes, 2005; Toccata Labyrinth, 2006; Cross of Nails, 2009; Hommage à Marcel Dupré, 2009; The Sounding Sea, 2010; *transcriptions:* Cochereau, Improvisations on Alouette, gentille Alouette, 1993; Cantem toto la Gloria, 1997; Suite de Danses improvisées, 1998; Improvisations sur Venez, Divin Messie, 1998; Triptique Symphonique, 1998; for organ: Mahler, Symphony No 5 and No 6; Schubert, Symphony No 8; Tchaikovsky, Symphony No 4; Elgar, Symphony No 1; Ravel, Daphnis et Chloe. *Recreation:* training for private pilot's licence.

**BRIGGS, Prof. Derek Ernest Gilmor,** PhD; FRS 1999; G. Evelyn Hutchinson Professor of Geology and Geophysics, since 2010 (Professor of Geology and Geophysics, since 2003), Curator in Charge of Invertebrate Paleontology, since 2003, and Curator of Invertebrate Zoology, since 2016, Peabody Museum, Yale University; *b* 10 Jan. 1950; *s* of John Gilmor Briggs and Olive Evelyn Briggs (*née* Scanlon); *m* 1972, Jennifer Olive Kershaw; three *s*. *Educ:* Sandford Park Sch., Dublin; Trinity Coll., Dublin (Foundn Scholar; BA Geology); Sidney Sussex Coll., Cambridge (MA, PhD). Res. Fellow, Cambridge, 1974–77; Goldsmiths' College, London University: Department of Geology: Lectr, 1977; Sen. Lectr, 1980; Principal Lectr and Dep. Dean of Sci. and Maths, 1982–85; Department of Earth Sciences, Bristol University: Lectr, 1985; Reader, 1988; Prof. of Palaeontol., 1994–2002; Head of Dept, 1997–2001; Asst Dir, Biogeochemistry Res. Centre, 1990–97; Dir, Yale Inst. for Biospheric Studies, 2004–07; Frederick William Beinecke Prof. of Geology and Geophysics, 2006–10, Dir, Yale Peabody Mus. of Nat. History, 2009–14, Yale Univ. Res. Associate, Royal Ontario Mus., Toronto, 1983–; Vis. Scientist, Field Mus. of Nat. History, Chicago, 1993; Dist. Vis. Scholar, Univ. of Adelaide, 1994; Vis. Prof., Univ. of Chicago and Field Mus. of Nat. History, Chicago, 2001–02; Vis. Scholar, Stanford Univ., 2015. Lectures: Benedum, Univ. of W Virginia, 1994; Case Meml, Michigan Univ., 2004; Darwin, Duquesne Univ., 2006; Walther Arndt Meml, Berlin, 2008; Bownocker, Ohio State Univ., 2009; Clara Jones Langston, Univ. of Texas, Austin, 2013. Editor, Palaeontology and Special Papers in Palaeontology, 1982–86. President: Palaeontol Assoc., 2002–04; Paleontol Soc., 2006–08. Hon. MRIA 2003. Hon. DSc TCD, 2010. Lyell Medal, Geol Soc., 2000; Boyle Medal, Royal Dublin Soc./Irish Times, 2001; Premio Capo d'Orlando, Italy, 2000; Humboldt Res. Award, Alexander von Humboldt Foundn, Univ. of Bonn, 2008; Paleontol Soc. Medal, 2015; Graduate Student Mentor Award in Nat. Scis, Yale Univ., 2017. *Publications:* (ed with K. C. Allen) Evolution and the Fossil Record, 1989; (ed with P. R. Crowther) Palaeobiology: a synthesis, 1990; (ed with P. A. Allison) Taphonomy: releasing the data locked in the fossil record, 1991; (jtly) The Fossils of the Burgess Shale, 1994; The Fossils of the Hunsrück Slate, 1998; (ed with P. R. Crowther) Palaeobiology II, 2001; (jtly) Evolution, 2007; Visions of a Vanished World, 2012; contribs to learned jls. *Recreations:* the outdoors, natural history, golf. *Address:* Department of Geology and Geophysics, Yale University, PO Box 208109, New Haven, CT 06520–8109, USA. *T:* (203) 4328590; Flat 4, 65 Pembroke Road, Clifton, Bristol BS8 3DW.

**BRIGGS, Prof. (George) Andrew (Davidson),** PhD; FInstP; Professor of Nanomaterials, University of Oxford, and Fellow, St Anne's College, Oxford, since 2002; *b* 3 June 1950; *s* of John Davidson Briggs and Catherine Mary Briggs (*née* Lormer); *m* 1981, Diana Margaret Ashley Johnson; two *d*. *Educ:* King's Coll. Sch., Cambridge; Leys Sch., Cambridge; St Catherine's Coll., Oxford (Clothworkers' Schol.; BA, MA); Queens' Coll., Cambridge (PhD 1977); Ridley Hall, Cambridge. FInstP 2004. Physics and RE, House Tutor, Canford Sch., 1971–73; Res. Asst, Engrg Dept, Univ. of Cambridge, 1979; University of Oxford: Res. Fellow, Dept of Metallurgy, 1980–82; Lectr in Physics, 1981–93, Res. Associate, 1982–84, St Catherine's Coll.; Royal Soc. Res. Fellow in Physical Scis, 1983–84; Lectr in Metallurgy and Sci. of Materials, 1984–96; Fellow, Wolfson Coll., 1984–96, now Emeritus; Reader in Materials, 1996–99; Prof. of Materials, 1999–2002. Dir, Quantum Inf. Processing Interdisciplinary Res. Collaboration, and Professorial Res. Fellow, EPSRC, 2002–09. Founding Dir and Vice-Chm., OxLoc Ltd, 2000–08. Vis. Faculty, Center for Quantized Electronic Structures, Univ. of Calif, Santa Barbara, 1990, 1993; Prof. invité, Ecole polytechnique fédérale de Lausanne, 1992–2002; Vis. Scientist, Hewlett-Packard Labs, Palo Alto, 1997–98; Vis. Prof., Univ. of NSW, 2002; Guest Prof., State Key Lab., Wuhan Univ. of Technol., 2005–. Member, Editorial Board: Sci. and Christian Belief, 2001–; Current Opinion in Solid State and Materials Sci., 2002–09; Nanotechnology, 2005–06; Jl of Physics D: Applied Physics, 2009–12. Member: Sci. and Engrg Fellowships Cttee, Royal Commn for the Exhibn of 1891, 2006–; Peer Rev. Coll., EPSRC, 2006–; Internat. Soc. for Sci. and Religion, 2013–; Adv. Council, McDonald Centre for Theology, Ethics and Public Life, 2008–. Dir, Oxford Toppan Centre, 1996–2006; Member: Bd of Mgt, Ian Ramsey Centre, 2001–15; Internat. Bd of Advrs, John Templeton Foundn, 2007–09, 2011–13; Engrg Panel, Newton Internat. Fellowships, 2008–. MAE 2012. Fellow, Cambridge Philosophical Soc., 1973; Hon. Fellow, Royal Microscopical Soc. (Chm. Materials Section, Council, 1986–91; Hon. Treas., 1989–91). Liveryman, Clothworkers' Co., 2005–. Holliday Prize, Inst. of Metals, 1986; (jtly) Metrology for World Class Manufg Award, 1999. *Publications:* An Introduction to Scanning Acoustic Microscopy, 1985; Acoustic Microscopy, 1992, 2nd edn 2010; (ed) The Science of New Materials, 1992; (ed) Advances in Acoustic Microscopy 1, 1995, 2, 1996; The Penultimate Curiosity, 2016; It Keeps Me Seeking, 2018; The Curious Science Quest (series), 2018, 2019; numerous contribs to learned jls. *Recreations:* Christian theology, opera, ski-ing, sailing, flying. *Address:* 5 Northmoor Road, Oxford OX2 6UW. *T:* (01865) 273725, *Fax:* (01865) 273730. *E:* andrew.briggs@materials.ox.ac.uk.

**BRIGGS, Very Rev. George Peter N.;** *see* Nairn-Briggs.

**BRIGGS, Isabel Diana, (Mrs Michael Briggs);** *see* Colegate, I. D.

**BRIGGS, Martin Paul;** Chief Executive, East Midlands Development Agency, 1999–2004; *b* 17 April 1948; *s* of late Maurice William John Briggs and Beryl Edna Briggs; *m* 1999, Angela Byrne; three *s* one *d* and two step *s* one step *d*. *Educ:* Forest Sch., Snaresbrook; Univ. of E Anglia (BA Hons Social Studies). Department of Trade and Industry: Res. Officer and other res. posts, 1970–82; Hd, Location/Inward Investment, E Midlands, 1982–87; Dir, Industry, W Midlands, 1987–91; Director: English Unit, Investment in Britain Bureau, 1991–93; Trade and Industry, Govt Office for E Midlands, 1994–98; Business Links, DTI, 1998–99. Special Prof., Nottingham Univ. *Recreations:* recorded music, tastes catholic, travel, philosophy/theology, family pursuits.

**BRIGGS, Dr (Michael) Peter,** OBE 2010; educational consultant, since 2009; Pro Vice-Chancellor, Roehampton University (formerly Pro-Rector, University of Surrey Roehampton), 2002–07; Special Adviser to Vice-Chancellor, 2007–09; Principal, Southlands College, 2002–09; *b* 3 Dec. 1944; *s* of late Hewieson Briggs and of Doris (*née* Habberley); *m* 1969, Jennifer Elizabeth Watts; one *s* one *d*. *Educ:* Abbeydale Boys' Grammar Sch., Sheffield; Univ. of Sussex (BSc, DPhil). Jun. Res. Fellow in Theoretical Chem., Univ. of Sheffield, 1969–71; Res. Assistant, Dept of Architecture, Univ. of Bristol, 1971–73; Deputation Sec., Methodist Church Overseas Div., 1973–77; Area Sec. (Herts and Essex),

Christian Aid, BCC, 1977–80; British Association for the Advancement of Science: Educn Manager, 1980–86; Public Affairs Man., 1986–88; Dep. Sec., 1988–90; Exec. Sec., then Chief Exec., 1990–2002; Hon. Fellow, 2002. Chairman: Management Cttee, Methodist Church Div. of Social Responsibility, 1983–86; Methodist Youth World Affairs Management Cttee, 1984–92; Mem. Bd, Internat. Assoc. of Methodist Schs, Colls and Univs, 2008–11. Trustee: Central Foundn Schs of London, 2009–15; Wesley House, Cambridge, 2011–; Dulwich Estate, 2013–15. Master, Educators' Co., 2011–12. FRSA 1990. Hon. DSc Leicester, 2002. *Recreation:* walking. *Address:* 42 The Lawns, Pinner HA5 4BL.

**BRIGGS, Michael Townley Featherstone;** *see* Briggs of Westbourne, Rt Hon. Lord.

**BRIGGS, Miles Edward Frank;** Member (C) Lothian, Scottish Parliament, since 2016; *b* Lancs, 30 March 1983; *s of* James Edward Briggs and Joan Briggs (*née* Halliwell). *Educ:* Perth Grammar Sch.; Robert Gordon Univ. (BA Politics, Mgt and Econs). Researcher, Exec. Council, PEI, Canada, 2004–05; Political Advr to Nanette Milne, MSP, 2005–16, and Elizabeth Smith, MSP, 2007–16. Shadow Cabinet Sec. for Health and Sport. Contested (C) Edinburgh SW, 2017. *Recreations:* hill walking, Rugby, Scottish history and music. *Address:* Scottish Parliament, Edinburgh EH99 1SP. *T:* (0131) 348 5944. *E:* miles.briggs.msp@parliament.scot.

**BRIGGS, Nicholas Norman;** Chief Insolvency and Companies Court Judge (formerly Chief Bankruptcy Registrar), since 2017; *b* Bristol, 7 March 1964; *s of* Geoffrey Briggs and Diane Briggs (*née* Rawlins); *m* 1988, Leona Jane Hinde; two *s*. *Educ:* Univ. of Bristol (LLM); Inns of Court Sch. of Law; Univ. of W of England (CPE; Dip. Estate Mgt and Valuation). Called to the Bar, 1994; Dep. Registrar in Bankruptcy, 2007–15; Insolvency and Cos Court Judge, 2015–17. General Editor: Tolley's Insolvency Law; Insolvency Legislation Annotations and Commentary. GSM, RM, 1983; Peacekeeping Force in Cyprus Medal, 1984. *Publications:* (jtly) Insolvency and Enterprise Act, 2002; (jtly) Modern Law of Meetings, 2013. *Recreations:* reading history and novels, theatre, music, all sport, time spent with family and friends. *Club:* Ronnie Scott's.

**BRIGGS, Patrick David,** MA; Principal, Kolej Tuanku Ja'afar, Malaysia, 1997–2005; *b* 24 Aug. 1940; *s of* late Denis Patrick Briggs and of Nancy Sylvester (*née* Jackson); *m* 1968, Alicia Dorothy O'Donnell; two *s* one *d*. *Educ:* Pocklington Sch.; Christ's Coll., Cambridge (MA). Bedford Sch., 1965–87 (Sen. Housemaster, 1983–87); Head Master, William Hulme's GS, 1987–97. Rugby Blue, Cambridge, 1962; England Rugby triallist, 1968 and 1969; Mem. Barbarians, 1968–69; RFU staff coach, 1973–95; England Under-23 Rugby coach, 1975–80; Team Manager, England Students Rugby, 1988–95. *Publications:* The Parents' Guide to Independent Schools, 1979. *Recreations:* cricket, Rugby, golf, fell walking, poetry, theatre, canal-boating. *Address:* 1A Gresham Road, Cambridge CB1 2EP. *T:* (01223) 309405. *Clubs:* East India, Devonshire, Sports and Public Schools, XL; Hawks (Cambridge); Quidnuncs, Cheshire County Cricket, Lancashire County Cricket; Royal Selangor (Kuala Lumpur).

**BRIGGS, Peter;** *see* Briggs, M. P.

**BRIGGS, Raymond Redvers,** CBE 2017; DFA; FCSD; FRSL; freelance illustrator, since 1957; author, since 1961; *b* 18 Jan. 1934; *s of* late Ernest Redvers Briggs and Ethel Bowyer; *m* 1963, Jean Taprell Clark (*d* 1973). *Educ:* Rutlish Sch., Merton; Wimbledon School of Art; Slade School of Fine Art. NDD; DFA London. Part-time Lecturer in Illustration, Faculty of Art, Brighton Polytechnic, 1961–87. FRSL 2005. *Publications:* The Strange House, 1961; Midnight Adventure, 1961; Ring-A-Ring O'Roses, 1962; Sledges to the Rescue, 1963; The White Land, 1963; Fee Fi Fo Fum, 1964; The Mother Goose Treasury, 1966 (Kate Greenaway Medal, 1966); Jim and the Beanstalk, 1970; The Fairy Tale Treasury, 1972; Father Christmas, 1973 (Kate Greenaway Medal, 1973); Father Christmas Goes On Holiday, 1975; Fungus The Bogeyman, 1977 (adapted for BBC TV, 2004); The Snowman, 1978 (animated film, 1982); Gentleman Jim, 1980 (play, Nottingham Playhouse, 1985); When the Wind Blows, 1982 (play, BBC Radio and Whitehall Th., 1983; text publd 1983; cassette 1984; animated film, 1987); Fungus the Bogeyman Plop-Up Book, 1982; The Tin-Pot Foreign General and the Old Iron Woman, 1984; The Snowman Pop-Up, 1986; Unlucky Wally, 1987; Unlucky Wally Twenty Years On, 1989; The Man, 1992; The Bear, 1994; Ethel & Ernest, 1998 (animated film, 2016); UG, Boy Genius of the Stone Age, 2001; Blooming Books, 2003; The Puddleman, 2004; Notes from the Sofa, 2015. *Recreations:* gardening, reading, walking, second-hand bookshops. *Address:* Weston, Underhill Lane, Westmeston, Hassocks, Sussex BN6 8XG.

**BRIGGS, Robin,** FBA 2009; FRHistS; FRSL; Senior Research Fellow, All Souls College, Oxford, 1978–2009, now Emeritus Fellow; *b* Braintree, Essex, 26 May 1942; *s of* Donald Frederick Briggs and Kathleen Ann Briggs; *m* 1st, 1969, Julia Ruth Ballam (marr. diss. 1989); two *s*; 2nd, 1989, Daphne Elizabeth Mariner Nash. *Educ:* Felsted Sch.; Balliol Coll., Oxford (BA 1st Cl. Modern Hist. 1964). Fellow by Exam., 1964–71, Jun. Res. Fellow, 1971–78, All Souls Coll., Oxford; Jun. Proctor, 1972–73, Special Lectr in Modern Hist., 1976–2009, Univ. of Oxford. Visiting Professor: Univ. of Paris IV, Sorbonne, 1981; Coll. de France, Paris, 1995. FRHistS 1969; FRSL 2002. *Publications:* The Scientific Revolution of the Seventeenth Century, 1969; Early Modern France, 1560–1715, 1977, 2nd edn 1998; Communities of Belief, 1989; Witches and Neighbours, 1996, 2nd edn 2002 (trans. German, Dutch and Chinese); The Witches of Lorraine, 2007; contrib. articles to learned jls. *Recreations:* painting, music (listening), golf, woodwork, geology. *Address:* All Souls College, High Street, Oxford OX1 4AL. *T:* (01865) 279379, *Fax:* (01865) 279299. *E:* robin.briggs@all-souls.ox.ac.uk.

**BRIGGS, (Thomas) David,** MBE 2009; Lord-Lieutenant of Cheshire, since 2010; *b* Huddersfield, 25 Aug. 1946; *s of* Thomas and Winnifred Briggs; *m* 1984, Michelle; one *d*. *Educ:* Charterhouse Sch.; St Andrews Univ. (LLB 1st Cl. Hons 1969); Wharton Sch., Univ. of Pennsylvania (MBA 1972). Called to the Bar, Lincoln's Inn, 1970; Man. Dir, Hansons Transport Gp, 1973–74; with Hepworth Ceramics Gp, latterly Man. Dir, Hepworth Plastics Ltd, 1976–79; Managing Director: Dawsons Music Ltd, 1979–2018; Maxilin Ltd, 2002–18. Chm. Council, Cheshire, Order of St John, 2002–10. High Sheriff of Cheshire, 2006–07. Chairman: Chester Cathedral Council; Chester Cathedral Develt Trust; Mem. Council, Chester Univ. Hon. MA Chester, 2009. KStJ 2011. *Recreations:* tennis, ski-ing. *Address:* Dukenfield Hall, Mobberley, Knutsford, Cheshire WA16 7PT. *Clubs:* Army and Navy, Royal Automobile; St James' (Manchester).

**BRIGGS, Prof. Timothy William Roy,** CBE 2018; MD; FRCS; FRCSE; Professor of Orthopaedic Surgery, University College London, since 2011; Consultant Orthopaedic Surgeon, Royal National Orthopaedic Hospital NHS Trust, since 1992 (Medical Director, 1999–2014); National Director of Clinical Quality and Efficiency, NHS, since 2015; *b* Leighton Buzzard, 29 Dec. 1957; *s of* Roy Alexander Briggs and Kathleen Mavis Briggs; *m* 1989, Rhiannon Burridge; one *s* one *d*. *Educ:* Bedford Sch.; Luton VI Form Coll.; London Hosp. Med. Coll. (MB BS Hons 1982); Univ. of Liverpool (MChOrth 1991); University Coll. London (MD Res. 2008). FRCSE 1987; FRCS 1988. Hon. Consultant, St Mark's Hosp., Northwick Park, 2010–. Mem. Council, RCS, 2013–19. Pres., British Orthopaedic Assoc., 2014. Chm., GIRFT Prog., NHS, 2015–. *Publications:* over 170 papers in jls.

*Recreations:* sailing, farming. *Address:* Royal National Orthopaedic Hospital NHS Trust, Brockley Hill, Stanmore, Middx HA7 4LP. *T:* (020) 8909 5532. *E:* rachel.godfrey2@nhs.net.

**BRIGHOUSE, Sir Timothy Robert Peter,** Kt 2009; Chief Adviser for London Schools, Department for Education and Skills, 2003–07; *b* 15 Jan. 1940; *s of* Denison Brighouse and Mary Howard Brighouse; *m* 1st, 1962, Mary Elizabeth Demers (marr. diss. 1988); one *s* one *d*; 2nd, 1989, Elizabeth Ann (formerly Kearney). *Educ:* St Catherine's College, Oxford (MA Modern History); DipEd. Head of History Dept, Cavendish Grammar Sch., Buxton, 1962–64; Dep. Head and Warden, Chepstow Comm. Coll., 1964–66; Asst Educn Officer, Monmouthshire Educn Dept, 1966–69; Sen. Asst Educn Officer, Bucks Educn Dept, 1969–74; Under-Sec., Educn, ACC, 1974–76; Dep. Educn Officer, ILEA, 1976–78; Chief Educn Officer, Oxon, 1978–89; Prof. of Educn and Hd of Dept, Keele Univ., 1989–93; Chief Educn Officer, Birmingham CC, 1993–2002. Jt Vice-Chm., Standards Task Force, 1997–99. Visiting Professor: Keele Univ., 1993–2002; London Univ. Inst. of Educn, 2002; Hon. Prof., Birmingham Univ., 1996. Non-exec. Dir, RM Education plc, 2005–11. Hon. DEd (CNAA) Oxford Poly., 1989; Hon. PhD UCE, 1996; Hon. DLitt: Exeter, 1996; Birmingham, 1999; Sheffield Hallam, 2001; Hon. MA Open Univ., 1997; Hon. EdD UWE, 2002; Hon. Dr: Greenwich, 2003; Middlesex 2004; Wolverhampton, 2006; Sunderland, 2007. *Publications:* Revolution in Education and Training (jt editor and author), 1986; Managing the National Curriculum (jt editor and author), 1990; What Makes a Good School, 1991; Successful Schooling, 1991; (jtly) How to Improve Your School, 1999. *Recreations:* gardening, politics, golf. *Address:* Institute of Education, 20 Bedford Way, WC1H 0AL; Willowbank, Old Road, Headington, Oxford OX3 8TA. *T:* (01865) 766995.

**BRIGHT, Andrew John;** QC 2000; **His Honour Judge Bright;** a Circuit Judge, since 2007; *b* 12 April 1951; *e s of* late J. H. Bright and of Freda Bright (*née* Cotton); *m* 1976, Sally Elizabeth Carter; three *s* one *d*. *Educ:* Wells Cathedral Sch.; University Coll. London (LLB Hons). Called to the Bar, Middle Temple, 1973; in practice at the Bar in field of criminal law, S Eastern Circuit, 1975–2007; Recorder, 2000–07; Resident Judge, St Albans Crown Ct, 2010–18. Co-opted Mem. Cttee, Criminal Bar Assoc., 1993–95; Chm., Herts and Beds Bar Mess, 2003–07. Hon. LLD Herts. *Recreation:* singing in a male voice choir. *Address:* c/o Luton Crown Court, 7 George Street, Luton LU1 2AA.

**BRIGHT, Colin Charles;** HM Diplomatic Service, retired; Counsellor, Foreign and Commonwealth Office, 2006; *b* 2 Jan. 1948; *s of* William Charles John Bright and Doris (*née* Sutton); *m* 1st, 1978, Helen-Anne Michie; 2nd, 1990, Jane Elizabeth Gurney Pease, *d* of Sir (Joseph) Gurney Pease, 5th Bt, *qv*; one *s* one *d* (and one *d* decd). *Educ:* Christ's Hospital; St Andrews Univ. (MA Hons 1971). FCO, 1975–77; Bonn, 1977–79; FCO, 1979–83; seconded to Cabinet Office, 1983–85; British Trade Develt Office, NY, 1985–88; Dep. Head of Mission, Berne, 1989–93; Consul Gen., Frankfurt, 1993–97; Hd of Commonwealth Co-ordination Dept, FCO, 1998–2002; Counsellor, FCO, 2002–03; Consul Gen., Lyon, 2004–06.

**BRIGHT, Sir Graham (Frank James),** Kt 1994; Police and Crime Commissioner (C) for Cambridgeshire, 2012–16; *b* 2 April 1942; *s of* late Robert Frank Bright and Agnes Mary (*née* Graham); *m* 1972, Valerie, *d of* late E. H. Woolliams; one *s*. *Educ:* Hassenbrook County Sch.; Thurrock Technical Coll. Marketing Exec., Pauls & White Ltd, 1958–70; Man. Dir, 1970–2012, Chm., 1977–2012, Dietary Foods Ltd. Dir, Internat. Sweeteners Assoc., 1997– (Chm., 2002–09); Dir, Mother Nature Ltd, 2012–. Contested (C): Thurrock, 1970 and Feb. 1974; Dartford, Oct. 1974. MP (C) Luton East, 1979–83, Luton South, 1983–97; contested (C) Luton South, 1997; contested (C) Eastern Region, EP elecns, 1999. PPS to Ministers of State, Home Office, 1984–87, DoE, 1988–89, to Paymaster Gen., 1989–90, to Prime Minister, 1990–94. Mem. Select Cttee on House of Commons Services, 1982–84. Jt Sec. to Parly Aviation Gp, 1984–90; Chm., Cons. Backbench Smaller Businesses Cttee, 1983–84, 1987–88 (Vice-Chm., 1980–83; Sec., 1979–80); Vice-Chairman: Cons. Backbench Food and Drink Sub-Cttee, 1983 (Sec., 1983–85); Backbench Aviation Cttee, 1987–88; former Sec., Space Sub-Cttee; Introduced Private Member's Bills: Video Recordings Act, 1984; Entertainment (Increased Penalties) Act, 1990. Trustee, Parly Pension Fund, 2008–; Chm., Former MPs Assoc., 2010–15. Member: Thurrock Bor. Council, 1966–79; Essex CC, 1967–70. Chm., Eastern Area CPC, 1977–79; Mem., Nat. CPC, 1980–87; Vice Chm., YC Org., 1970–72; Pres., Eastern Area YCs, 1981–98; Conservative Party: a Vice-Chm., 1994–97; Chm., Eastern Reg., 2006–. Vice-Chm., Small Business Bureau, 1980–89, and 1991–97 (Dir, 1989–91). Chm., 2008–13, Trustee, 2010–14, Hassenbrook Acad. *Publications:* pamphlets on airports, small businesses, education. *Recreations:* golf, gardening. *Address:* 69 St James's Street, SW1A 1PJ. *E:* graham@grahambright.com. *Club:* Carlton.

**BRIGHT, Jonathan Steven Noel;** Director, Citizens Advice Oxfordshire South and Vale, since 2016; *b* Gloucester, 26 Dec. 1951; *s of* Stanley and Suzanne Bright; *m* 1990, Suzanne Lingard; two *s* one *d*. *Educ:* Hardye's Grammar Sch.; Magdalene Coll., Cambridge (BA Social and Pol Sci. 1974); Leicester Univ. (PGCE). Dir, Safe Neighbourhood Unit, NACRO, 1981–90; Dir of Ops, Crime Concern, 1990–97; Deputy Director: Social Exclusion Unit, Cabinet Office, 1997–2000; Neighbourhood Renewal Unit, ODPM, 2001–06; Dir of Policy, Birmingham CC, 2006–07; Regl Dir, Govt Office for the SW, 2008–11; Dir of Homelessness, Support, Climate Change and Bldg Regulations, DCLG, 2011–14; Chief Exec., Community First Oxon (formerly Oxon Rural Community Council), 2014–16. Harkness Fellow, Univ. of Michigan, 1990–91. Fellow, Australian Inst. Criminol., 1996. FRSA. *Publications:* Crime Prevention in the United States: a British perspective, 1993; Turning the Tide: crime, prevention and neighbourhoods, 1997. *Recreations:* wild swimming, cycling, mountain-walking, architecture. *Address:* Citizens Advice, Abbey House, Abbey Close, Abingdon, Oxon OX14 3JD. *T:* 07715 829900. *E:* jon.bright@osavcab.org.uk.

**BRIGHT, Robert Graham;** QC 2007; barrister; a Recorder, since 2018; *b* 22 Aug. 1964; *s of* John and Elizabeth Bright; *m* Susan; three *d*. *Educ:* St Paul's Sch.; St John's Coll., Oxford (BA Juris., BCL). Called to the Bar, Gray's Inn, 1987. *Recreation:* horticulture. *Address:* 7 King's Bench Walk, Temple, EC4Y 7DS.

**BRIGHT, Roger Martin Francis,** CB 2009; Second Commissioner and Chief Executive, The Crown Estate, 2001–11; *b* 2 May 1951. *Educ:* Christ's Hosp.; Trinity Hall, Cambridge (BA 1973). Joined DoE, 1973; posts held include: Hd, Envmtl Policy Co-ordination Div.; Hd, Housing Policy Studies Div.; Hd, Local Govt Review Div.; Principal Private Sec. to Sec. of State for the Envmt, 1989–90; Dir of Information, 1990; Dep. Chief Exec., Housing Corp., 1991–95; Dir of Ops and Finance, 1995–97, Chief Exec., 1998, PIA; Hd of Investment Business Dept (PIA firms), FSA, 1998–99; Dir of Finance and Admin, 1999–2001, a Comr, 2000–11, Crown Estate. Mem., Royal Parks' Bd, 2012–. Non-executive Director: London First, 2008–; Heritage of London Trust, 2008–. Chm., Adv. Bd, Curtin & Co., 2012–. Member: Governing Council, City Univ., 2008– (Dep. Pro-Chancellor, 2012–); Council, RCVS, Univ. of London, 2013–.

**BRIGHTMAN, Dr David Kenneth,** CBiol, FRSB; FRAgS; sole trader, Brightman Farms, since 2010 (Partner, 1982–2010); *b* 12 Aug. 1954; *s of* late Brian George Brightman and Dorothy Brightman; partner, Gillian Theresa Bolton; two *s*. *Educ:* Univ. of Reading;

Univ. of Newcastle upon Tyne (BSc Hons (Agric.) 1977); Univ. of Nottingham (PhD 1983). CBiol, FRSB (FIBiol 2005); ARAgS 2005, FRAgS 2011. Lectr in Crop Prodn, Brooksby Coll., 1980–82. Dir and Co. Sec., Arable Crop Storage Ltd, 1995–2012; Co. Sec., Arable Crop Services Ltd, 1995–2010. Mem. Council, BBSRC, 2003–09 (Mem., Audit Bd, 2009–12). Ministry of Agriculture, Fisheries and Food, later Department for Environment, Food and Rural Affairs: Chm., MAFF/ADAS Drayton Experimental Husbandry Farm Adv. Cttee, 1990–92; Member: Pesticides Forum, 1995–98; Sustainable Arable LINK Prog. Mgt Cttee, 1997–2003; Sub-gp on Biodiversity, Adv. Cttee on Releases to the Envmt, 1999–2001; Agricl Forum, 2008–16. Mem., NFU Pesticides Wkg Gp, 1991–2003 (Chm., 1993–2003). Dir, Rothamsted Res. Assoc., 1990–2005 (Chm., 2001–03); Dir and Trustee, Rothamsted Res. Ltd, 2005–13 (Mem., Audit Cttee, 2013); Dir and Mem., Audit Cttee, Centaur Producers Ltd and Centaur Grain Marketing Ltd, 2006–09; Technol. Strategy Bd Assessor, Agri-Tech Catalyst Fund, 2013–17; Mem., Cereals and Oilseeds Res. and Knowledge Exchange Cttee (formerly Res. and Knowledge Transfer Cttee), HGCA, 2014–. Former Dir, Mid-Tak/CMR Ltd Machinery Rings. Formerly Chairman: Warks Farm Mgt Assoc.; Southam Agricl Discussion Club; Chm., Fenny Compton NFU, 1988–90; mem., various cttees, panels and wkg gps. *Publications*: Dietary Nitrogen Requirements of Entire Male Cattle, 1983; conf. papers in Animal Prodn and for BCPC annual conf., and articles in farming press. *Recreations*: watching sport, watching people.

**BRIGHTON, Wing Comdr Peter**, BSc; CEng, FIET, FRAeS; *b* 26 March 1933; *s* of late Henry Charles Brighton and Ivy Irene Brighton (*née* Crane); *m* 1959, Anne Maureen Lewis Jones (*d* 2007); one *d* (one *s* decd). *Educ*: Wisbech Grammar Sch.; Reading Univ. (BSc); RAF Technical Coll. and Staff Coll. CEng 1966; FIET (FIEE 1980); FRAeS 1981. Pilot, Engr and Attaché, RAF, 1955–71. Man. Dir, Rockwell-Collins UK, 1974–77; Regional Man. Dir, Plessey Co., 1977–78; Man. Dir, Cossor Electronics Ltd, 1978–85; British Aerospace PLC: Divl Man. Dir, 1985–87; Co. Dir of Operations, 1988; Dir Gen., EEF, 1989–91. Chm., Princess Alexandra Hosp. NHS Trust, 1996–97. Pres., Electronic Engineering Assoc., 1984–85. Mem. Ct, Cranfield Inst. of Technology, 1989–92. CCMI (CBIM 1984). Liveryman, Coachmakers and Coach Harness Makers Co., 1989; Freeman of City of London, 1989. *Publications*: articles on aviation topics in learned jls. *Recreations*: music, theatre, crosswords, wining and dining with friends. *Address*: 18 Riverside Wharf, Riverside, Bishop's Stortford CM23 3GN. *T*: (01279) 757440. *Club*: Royal Air Force.

**BRIGHTON AND LEWES, Archdeacon of**; *see* Lloyd Williams, Ven. M. C.

**BRIGHTY, (Anthony) David**, CMG 1984; CVO 1985; HM Diplomatic Service, retired; Ambassador to Spain, and concurrently (non-resident) to Andorra, 1994–98; *b* 7 Feb. 1939; *s* of C. P. J. Brighty and Winifred Brighty; *m* 1963, Diana Porteous (marr. diss. 1979; she *d* 1993); two *s* two *d*; *m* 1997, Susan Olivier. *Educ*: Northgate Grammar Sch., Ipswich; Clare Coll., Cambridge (BA). Entered FO, 1961; Brussels, 1962–63; Havana, 1964–66; FO, 1967–69, resigned; joined S. G. Warburg & Co., 1969; reinstated in FCO, 1971; Saigon, 1973–74; UK Mission to UN, NY, 1975–78; RCDS, 1979; Head of Personnel Operations Dept, FCO, 1980–83; Counsellor, Lisbon, 1983–86; Dir, Cabinet of Sec.-Gen. of NATO, 1986–87; Resident Chm., CSSB, 1988; Ambassador to Cuba, 1989–91; Ambassador to Czech and Slovak Fed. Republic, later to Czech Republic and (non-resident) to Slovakia, 1991–94. Non-executive Director: EFG Private Bank Ltd, 1999–2005; Henderson EuroMicro Investment Trust, 2000–04. Chairman: Co-ordinating (formerly Consultative) Cttee on Remuneration (NATO, OECD, etc), 1999–2006; Anglo Spanish Cultural Foundn/Cañada Blanch Centre for Contemporary Spanish Studies, LSE (formerly Cañada Blanch Foundn (UK)), 2006–. Robin Humphreys Fellow, Inst. for Latin Amer. Studies, London Univ., 2003. Chairman: Anglo-Spanish Soc., 2001–07; Friends of British Liby, 2004–07. Comendador, Order Infante Dom Henrique (Portugal), 1985. *Address*: 18 Gatcombe Road, N19 4PT.

**BRIGNALL, Rt Rev. Peter Malcolm**; *see* Wrexham, Bishop of, (RC).

**BRIGSTOCKE, Dr Hugh Nicholas Andrew**; freelance writer and art historian; *b* 7 May 1943; *s* of late Rev. Canon George Edward Brigstocke and Mollie (*née* Sandford); *m* 1969, Anthea Elizabeth White; one *s* one *d*. *Educ*: Marlborough Coll., Wilts; Magdalene Coll., Cambridge (MA Modern Hist.); Univ. of Edinburgh (PhD Art Hist. 1976). Asst to Hans Hess and John Ingamells, York City Art Gall., 1965–68; Curator, Italian, Spanish and French Paintings, National Gall. of Scotland, Edinburgh, 1968–83; Editor-in-Chief, 1983–87, Consulting Ed., 1987–89, Hon. Consulting Ed., 1989–96, Grove Dictionary of Art; Old Master Paintings, Sotheby's, London, 1989–95: Dir, 1990–95; Hd of Dept, 1993–94; Sen. Expert, 1994–95; Ed. (freelance), Oxford Companion to Western Art, 1995–2001. Guest Curator, Getty Mus., Calif, 1983–84; Paul Mellon Fellow, British Sch. at Rome, 2001. Ed., Walpole Soc., 2000–12. *Publications*: A Critical Catalogue of the Italian and Spanish Paintings, National Gallery of Scotland, 1978, 2nd edn 1993; William Buchanan and the 19th Century Art Trade: 100 letters to his agents in London and Italy, 1982; (ed) Oxford Companion to Western Art, 2001; (jtly) John Flaxman and William Young Ottley in Italy, 2010; British Travellers in Spain 1766–1849, 2015; (jtly) Giulio Cesare Procaccini: life and work with a catalogue of his paintings, 2019; *exhibition catalogues*: (jtly) Poussin Bacchanals and Sacraments, 1981; A Loan Exhibition of Poussin Drawings from British Collections, 1990; (jtly) Masterpieces from Yorkshire Houses: Yorkshire families at home and abroad 1700–1850, 1994; (jtly) Italian Paintings from Burghley House, 1995; (jtly) En Torno a Velázquez, 1999; (jtly) A Poet in Paradise: Lord Lindsay and Christian Art, 2000; (jtly) Procaccini in America, 2002; contrib. articles to various jls incl. Burlington Mag., Apollo, Walpole Soc., British Art Jl, Revue de l'Art, Paragone, Revue du Louvre, Jahrbuch der Berliner Mus., Münchner Jahrbuch, etc. *Recreations*: opera, theatre, wine, horse-racing. *Address*: 118 Micklegate, York YO1 6JX. *T*: (01904) 626013. *E*: hugh.brigstocke@gmail.com.
*See also* Adm. Sir J. R. Brigstocke.

**BRIGSTOCKE, Adm. Sir John (Richard)**, KCB 1997; DL; Judicial Appointments and Conduct Ombudsman, 2006–16; *b* 30 July 1945; *s* of late Rev. Canon George Edward Brigstocke and Molly Brigstocke (*née* Sandford); *m* 1979, Heather, *d* of late Dennis and Muriel Day (*née* Glossop); one *s* (and one *s* decd). *Educ*: Marlborough Coll.; BRNC, Dartmouth; RNC Greenwich; RCDS. Joined RN, 1962; trng, 1962–66; HMS Caprice, 1966–69; HMY Britannia, 1969; HMS Whitby, 1969–70; i/c HMS Upton, 1970–71; long gunnery course, HMS Excellent, 1971–72; HMS Minerva, 1972–74; RNSC Greenwich, 1974; Staff, BRNC Dartmouth, 1974–76; First Lieut, HMS Ariadne, 1976–78; i/c HMS Bacchante, 1978–79; Directorate of Naval Plans, MoD, 1980–81 and 1982–84; Comdr Sea Trng, Portland, 1981–82; i/c HMS York and Capt. (D) 3rd Destroyer Sqn, 1986–87; Capt., BRNC Dartmouth, 1987–88; i/c HMS Ark Royal, 1989–90; FO, 2nd Flotilla, 1991–92; Comdr, UK Task Gp, 1992–93; ACNS and Mem. Admiralty Bd, 1993–95; Adm. Pres. RNC, Greenwich, 1994–95; Flag Officer, Surface Flotilla, 1995–97; Second Sea Lord, Mem. Admiralty Bd, C-in-C Naval Home Comd, and Flag ADC to the Queen, 1997–2000. Chief Exec., St Andrew's Gp of Hosps (med. charity), 2000–04; Director: Ind. Healthcare Assoc., 2000–03; Three Shires Hosp. Ltd, 2000–04; Chm., NHS E Midlands (E Midlands Strategic HA), 2006–10. Trustee, Nuffield Trust for the Forces of the Crown, 2003–. Vice Pres., Northants Sea Cadet Unit (TS Laforey), 2003–. Mem. Council, Univ. of Buckingham, 2005–08 (Mem., 2004–05). Younger Brother, Trinity House, 1981. Freeman, City of London, 1995. DL Northants, 2010. DUniv Buckingham 2009. *Address*: c/o Naval Secretary, Sir Henry Leach Building, Whale Island, Portsmouth PO2 8BY.
*See also* H. N. A. Brigstocke.

**BRIGSTOCKE, Timothy David Alexander**, MBE 2008; FRSB; Managing Partner, Tim Brigstocke Associates, since 1993; Executive Director, Cattle Health Certification Standards, since 2001; Policy Director, Royal Association of British Dairy Farmers, since 2007; *b* Guildford, 2 Sept. 1951; *s* of Alexander Julian Brigstocke, DL and late Diana Mavis Brigstocke (*née* Evershed); *m* 1977, Celia Comber (*d* 2018); three *d*. *Educ*: Wellington Coll.; Bicton Coll. of Agric. (Advanced Nat. Cert. in Agric. 1975); Seale-Hayne Coll. (Dip. Farm Mgt 1976); Open Univ. (BA 1980); Univ. of Aston, Birmingham (MPhil 1984). CBiol 1983; FRSB (FIBiol 2008); CEnv 2008; Professional Agriculturist, 2011. Chief Agricl Advr, BOCM Pauls (formerly Silcock) Ltd, 1984–93; Inst. Business Manager, Inst. of Grassland and Envmtl Res., 1993–96; Chief Exec., Holstein Friesian Soc./Holstein UK & Ireland, 1996–99; Executive Chairman: Royal Assoc. of British Dairy Farmers, 2000–07; Rare Breeds Survival Trust, 2008–11. Vis. Fellow, RAU (formerly RAC), Cirencester, 2002– (Dairy Crest Fellowship, 2005). Non-executive Director: Cogent Breeding Ltd, 2003–11; Grosvenor Farms Ltd, 2003–06; Lantra, 2007–13 (Dep. Chm., 2014–15). Member: Pre-Movement Testing Gp, 2004–06; Adv. Gp on Responsibility and Cost Sharing for Animal Health, 2009–10; Nat. Steering Cttee for Farm Animal Genetic Resources, 2003–06; DEFRA: England Implementation Gp, UK Govt's Animal Health and Welfare Strategy, 2005–09; Adv. Cttee on Animal Feedstuffs, Food Standards Agency, 2005–14; RSPCA/ Freedom Foods Cattle Health and Welfare Gp, 2005–; Sustainable Agric. Strategy Panel, BBSRC, 2008–11; Veterinary Residues Cttee, Veterinary Medicines Directorate, 2009–15; Chairman: GB Cattle Health and Welfare Gp, 2010–; Nat. Equine Forum, 2013–; UK Farm Animal Genetic Resources Cttee, DEFRA, 2014–; British Horse Council (formerly Equine Sector Council for Health and Welfare), 2017–. Director: Soc. of Dairy Technol. Ltd, 2001–14; Soc. for the Envmt, 2006–. Vice Pres., Sci. Policy, Inst. of Biol., 2006–09. Chair, Coll. of Elected Mems, Soc. of Biol., later Royal Soc. of Biol., 2010–16. Chm. Adv. Bd, Sch. of Agric., Royal Agricl Univ. (formerly RAC), Cirencester, 2008–17. FIAgrM 1992; FRAgS 1996. Harvard Agri-Business Seminar, 1998. Trustee: Inst. of Agricl Mgt, 1999– (Chm., 2010–14); Harper Adams UC Develt Trust Ltd, 2006–15; Chm., Bd of Trustees, John Bradburne Meml Soc., 2003–. Princess Royal Award, Royal Assoc. of British Dairy Farmers, 2007; Farm Mgt Award, Inst. of Agricl Mgt, 2014. *Publications*: (with P. N. Wilson) Improved Feeding of Cattle and Sheep, 1982; contrib. papers to scientific and tech. jls. *Recreations*: sport, gardening, reading, modern jazz, modern railways. *Address*: Brick House, Risbury, Leominster, Herefordshire HR6 0NQ. *T*: (01568) 760632. *E*: timbrigstocke@hotmail.com. *Clubs*: Farmers, MCC.

**BRIKHO, Samir Yacoub**; Chief Executive, Amec Foster Wheeler (formerly AMEC) plc, 2006–16; *b* 3 May 1958; *s* of Jacob and Victoria Brikho; two *s*. *Educ*: Royal Inst. of Technols, Stockholm (MSc Thermal Technol.); INSEAD (Young Managers Prog.); Stanford Univ. (Sen. Exec. Prog. 2000). Sen. Vice Pres., ABB, 1993–95; Sen. Vice Pres. and Man. Dir, ABB Kraftwerke, 1995–99; CEO, ABB Alstom Kraftwerke, 1999–2001; Sen. Vice Pres., Internat. Business and Chief Internat. Ops Officer, Alstom Power, 2000–03; Chief Exec., ABB Lummus Global, Switzerland, 2003–05; Mem. Exec. Bd, ABB, Hd, Power Systems Div. and Chm., ABB Lummus Global, 2005–06. Chm., UK Energy Excellence, 2008–10; Co-Chm., UK-UAE CEO Forum, 2011–; Member: Internat. Adv. Bd, SOAS, 2007–; Adv. Bd, Stena Offshore, 2011–; Adv. Bd, Asia House, 2012–; Bd, SEB, 2012–; Dir, UK Japan 21st Century Gp, 2007–; Co-chair, UK-Korea Global CEO Forum, 2013–. Chm., Disaster Resource Partnership Steering Bd, WEF, 2010–; Mem., UK Nat. Cttee, World Petroleum Congress, 2010–. Founder, Palestine Internat. Business Forum, 2005. UK Business Ambassador, 2010–. Chm., Step Change Foundn UK, 2011–. FREng 2013. *Recreations*: sports, music, dance. *Clubs*: Arts, Royal Automobile; Wentworth Golf.

**BRILL, Elaine**; *see* Bedell, E.

**BRILL, Patrick**, OBE 2017; RA 2014; artist, as Bob and Roberta Smith; *b* London, 3 Feb. 1963; *s* of Fredrick Brill and Deirdre Brill (*née* Borlase); *m* 1990, Jessica Voorsanger; one *s* one *d*. *Educ*: Wandsworth Comp. Sch.; Univ. of Reading (BA 1st Cl. Fine Art); British Sch. at Rome (Schol.); Goldsmiths Coll. (MA Fine Arts 1993). Harkness Fellow, Cooper Union Sch. of Arts and Scis, NY, 1988–90. Group exhibitions include: Altermodern, 2009, Rude Britannia, 2010, Tate Britain; solo exhibitions include: The Gotham Golem, Pierogi Gall., NY, 2011; I should be in Charge, Hales Gall., London, 2011; The Aldwincle Golem, The Salisbury Golem, All Saints, Aldwincle, 2011. Poster design for 2012 Olympics. Trustee, Tate, 2009–13. Patron, Nat. Soc. for Educn in Art and Design, 2012. Contested (Ind) (as Bob Smith) Surrey Heath, 2015. Hon. Fellow, Univ. of Creative Arts, Bournemouth, 2011. *Publications*: as Bob and Roberta Smith: Make Your Own Damn Art, 2005; Art U Need, 2008; I Should be in Charge (monograph), 2011. *Recreation*: work all the time - no days off! *Address*: 49 Rhodesia Road, Leytonstone, E11 4DF. *E*: bobsmith.lcca@ntlworld.com.

**BRIMACOMBE, Prof. John Stuart**, FRSE, FRSC, FRSB; Roscoe Professor of Chemistry, University of Dundee, 1969–2002; *b* Falmouth, Cornwall, 18 Aug. 1935; *s* of Stanley Poole Brimacombe and Lillian May Kathleen Brimacombe (*née* Candy); *m* 1959, Eileen (*née* Gibson); four *d*. *Educ*: Falmouth Grammar Sch.; Birmingham Univ. (DSc); DSc Dundee Univ. FRSC 1966; FRSB (FIBiol 2000). Lectr in Chemistry, Birmingham Univ., 1961–69. FRSE 1973. Meldola Medallist, 1964, Haworth Lect. and Medal, 2007, RSC. *Publications*: (co-author) Mucopolysaccharides, 1964; numerous papers, reviews, etc., in: Jl Chem. Soc., Carbohydrate Research, etc. *Recreations*: sport, reading. *Address*: 29 Dalhousie Road, Barnhill, Dundee DD5 2SP. *T*: (01382) 779214.

**BRIMELOW, Alison Jane**, CBE 2005; President, European Patent Office, 2007–10 (President-elect, and Vice-Chair of Administrative Council, 2004–07); *b* 6 June 1949. HM Diplomatic Service, 1973–76; DTI, 1976–2003; Comptroller Gen. and Chief Exec., Patent Office, 1999–2003. Associate Fellow, Green Templeton Coll. (formerly Templeton Coll.), Oxford, 2005–13; Chm., Intellectual Property Inst., QMUL, 2011–13. Chair: Hartlebury Castle Preservation Trust, 2010–13 (Vice Pres., 2013–16); CREATe Prog. Adv. Council, 2014–16; Mem. Bd, Scottish Opera, 2017–. Trustee, Nicholas John Trust, 2010. Gov., Bromsgrove Sch., 2010–13. Mem. Council, Worcester Cath., 2011–16. Hon. LLD Wolverhampton, 2007; Hon. DSc Aston, 2015. Bundesverdienstkreuz (Germany), 2011. *Club*: New (Edinburgh).

**BRIMELOW, (Janine) Kirsty**; QC 2011; *b* Preston, 5 Aug. 1969; *d* of Ron Brimelow and Jean Brimelow (*née* Stockley). *Educ*: Univ. of Birmingham (LLB Hons 1990). Called to the Bar, Gray's Inn, 1991, Bencher, 2015; in practice as a barrister, specialising in criminal, internat. and human rights law. Bar Council: spokesperson, 1998–2008; Member: Bar Public Affairs Gp, 2000–07; Central London Bar Mess Cttee, 2004–07; Bar Conf. Organising Bd, 2006–08; Bar Human Rights Committee: Mem., 2007–11; Vice-Chm., 2007–12; Chm., 2012–18; Rep. for Bar Human Rights Cttee on Euro-Med. Human Rights Network, 2005–10; Member: Pro Bono Bar Caribbean Cttee, 2005–08; Child Rights Unit, 2009–12. Member: Cttee, Criminal Bar Assoc., 2004–10; Attorney Gen. Pro Bono Cttee, 2012–. Member: Opinion Leader Res. Panel, 2005–08; Populus Res. Panel, 2006–08; The Times Law Panel, 2007–09. Barrister of the Year Inspirational Women in

Law Award, 2018; Internat. Pro Bono Barrister of the Year, 2018. *Recreations:* martial arts, mountain climbing, ski-ing, theatre, music, salsa. *Address:* Doughty Street Chambers, 54 Doughty Street, WC1N 2LS. *T:* (020) 7404 1313. *E:* k.brimelow@doughtystreet.co.uk.

**BRIMS, Lt Gen. Robin Vaughan,** CB 2007; CBE 1999 (OBE 1991; MBE 1986); DSO 2003; DL; consultant on military matters and education, since 2010; *b* 27 June 1951; *s* of late David Vaughan Brims and of Eve Georgina Mary Brims. *Educ:* Winchester Coll. Commissioned LI, 1970; sc 1982–83; CO 3rd Bn LI, 1989–91; Comdr, 24 Airmobile Bde, 1995–96; COS, NI, 1997–98; Dir, Army Resources and Plans, 1999; Comdr, Multinat. Div. (South West), 2000; GOC 1 (UK) Armoured Div., 2000–03; Dep. Chief of Jt Ops, MoD, 2003–05; Dep. Commanding Gen., Multinational Force, Iraq, 2005 (on detachment); Comdr, Field Army, Land Comd, 2005–07. Col, Light Infantry, 2001–06; Col Comdt, Light Div., 2005–07; Dep. Col Comdt, AGC, 2001–06. Hon. Colonel: Northumbrian Univs OTC, 2008–13; 72 Engr Regt (Vols), 2008–14. President: Army Cricket, 2003–05; Army Football Assoc., 2005–07. Chm., N of England, 2010–18, Chm., Council, 2011–18, RFCA. Rector, Univ. of Kurdistan Hawler, Iraq, 2008–09. Patron, Finchale Trng Coll., 2012– . Trustee: Dickon Trust, 1994–2014; Ski 2 Freedom, 2008–14; Oswin Project, 2012– (Chm., 2016–); The Key, 2018– ; Director: Norcare, 2010–14; Thirteen Care and Support, 2014–16; Royal Edinburgh Military Tattoo, 2015– . Chm., Northumbria Historic Churches Trust, 2011– . DL, 2009, High Sheriff, 2017–18, Tyne and Wear. Officer, Legion of Merit (USA), 2006. *Recreation:* sport. *Address:* c/o RHQ The Rifles, Peninsula Barracks, Romsey Road, Winchester, Hants SO23 8TS.

**BRIMSON-LEWIS, Stephen John;** freelance theatre designer, since 1985; Associate Artist, since 2013, and Director of Design, since 2014, Royal Shakespeare Company; *b* 15 Feb. 1963; *s* of David and Doris Lewis; adopted stage name Brimson-Lewis. *Educ:* Central Sch. of Art and Design (BA Hons). Designer of productions: for RNT, incl. Les Parents Terribles (Olivier Award for Best Set Design), 1995, A Little Night Music, 1996; for RSC, 1999–, incl. A Midsummer Night's Dream, 2005, Antony and Cleopatra, 2006, Richard II, 2013, Henry IV, 2014, Death of a Salesman, Volpone, Henry V, 2015, King and Country (transf. China, NY), The Tempest, 2016; Design for Living (Olivier Award for Best Set Design), Donmar Warehouse, 1995; Dirty Dancing, Aldwych and world tour, 2006; Waiting for Godot, Haymarket, 2009; Ghosts, Duchess, 2010; Master Builder, Minerva Th., Chichester, 2010; An Ideal Husband, Vaudeville, 2010; Flare Path, The Lion in Winter, The Tempest, Haymarket, 2011; La Bohème, WNO, 2012; Heartbreak House, Chichester, 2012; Waiting for Godot, No Man's Land, Broadway, 2013; Relative Values, Th. Royal, Bath, 2013, transf. Harold Pinter Th., 2014; No Man's Land, Wyndham's, 2016; Love in Idleness, Menier Chocolate Factory, 2017; A Christmas Carol, RSC, 2017; As You Like It, Measure for Measure, RSC, 2019; also for maj. internat. opera and ballet cos. *Address:* c/o Clare Vidal-Hall, 184 Shepherds Bush Road, W6 7NL. *T:* (020) 8741 7647. *E:* cvh@clarevidalhall.com.

**BRINCKMAN, Sir Theodore (George Roderick),** 6th Bt *cr* 1831; retired antiquarian bookseller; *b* 20 March 1932; *s* of Col. Sir Roderick Napoleon Brinckman, 5th Bt, DSO, MC, and Margaret Wilson Southam; *S* father, 1985; *m* 1st, 1958, Helen Mary Anne Cook (marr. diss. 1983), *d* of Arnold Cook; two *s* one *d*; 2nd, 1983, Hon. Sheira Murray (marr. diss. 2001), formerly wife of Christopher Murray, and *d* of Baron Harvington, AE, PC; 3rd, 2001, Margaret Kindersley (*d* 2015), formerly wife of Gay Kindersley, and *d* of Hugh Wakefield. *Educ:* Trinity College School, Port Hope, Ontario; Millfield; Christ Church, Oxford; Trinity Coll., Toronto (BA). *Heir: s* Theodore Jonathan Brinckman, *b* 19 Feb. 1960. *Address:* 25 Milbrook Walk, Woodchester Valley Village, Inchbrook, Nailsworth, Glos GL5 5HE. *T:* (01453) 836756.

**BRIND, (Arthur) Henry,** CMG 1973; HM Diplomatic Service, retired; *b* 4 July 1927; *o s* of late T. H. Brind and late N. W. B. Brind; *m* 1954, Barbara Harrison (*d* 2012); one *s* one *d*. *Educ:* Barry; St John's Coll., Cambridge. HM Forces, 1947–49. Colonial Administrative Service: Gold Coast/Ghana, 1950–60; Regional Sec., Trans-Volta Togoland, 1959. HM Diplomatic Service, 1960–87: Acting High Comr, Uganda, 1972–73; High Comr, Mauritius, 1974–77; Ambassador to Somali Democratic Republic, 1977–80; Vis. Research Fellow, RIIA, 1981–82; High Comr, Malawi, 1983–87. Grand Comdr, Order of Lion of Malawi, 1985. *Publications:* Lying Abroad (memoirs), 1999. *Recreations:* walking, swimming, books. *Address:* 20 Grove Terrace, NW5 1PH. *T:* (020) 7267 1190. *Club:* Reform.

**BRINDED, Malcolm Arthur,** CBE 2002; FREng; Member of the Board, 2003–12, and Executive Director, Upstream International, 2009–12, Royal Dutch/Shell plc; *b* 18 March 1953; *s* of Cliff and Gwen Brinded; *m* 1975, Carola Telford; three *s*. *Educ:* Churchill Coll., Cambridge (MA Engrg). Shell Internat., The Hague, 1974–75; Project Engr, Brunei Shell Petroleum, 1975–80; Facilities Engr, Shell UK Exploration and Prodn, 1980–82; on secondment to Dept of Energy as Policy Advr, 1982–84; Nederlands Aardolie MIJ, 1984–86; Shell Gp, 1987–88; Business Unit Dir, Petroleum Develt, Shell Oman, 1988–92; Shell UK Exploration and Prodn, 1993–2001 (Man. Dir, 1998–2001); Country Chm., Shell UK Ltd, 1999–2002; Dir, Planning, HSE and External Affairs, Shell Internat., 2001–02; Gp Man. Dir, 2002–03, Vice Chm., Cttee of Man. Dirs, 2003, Royal Dutch/Shell Gp of Cos; CEO, Shell Gas & Power, 2003; Exec. Dir, Shell Exploration and Prodn, 2004–09. Non-executive Director: Network Rail, 2010–16; BHP Billiton, 2014–17. Chm., Bd of Trustees, Shell Foundn, 2009. Pres., Energy Inst., 2017–19. FICE; FREng 2002. Hon. FIMechE 2003. Alec Buchanan Smith Award for contrib. to Scottish oil and gas industry, 2001. *Recreations:* music, mountain biking, Rugby.

**BRINDLE, Ian;** Deputy Chairman, Financial Reporting Review Panel, 2001–08; *b* 17 Aug. 1943; *s* of John Brindle and Mabel Brindle (*née* Walsh); *m* 1967, Frances Elisabeth Moseby; two *s* one *d*. *Educ:* Blundell's School; Manchester Univ. (BA Econ). FCA 1969. Price Waterhouse: articled in London, 1965; Toronto, 1971; admitted to partnership, 1976; Mem., Supervisory Cttee, 1988–98; Dir, Audit and Business Advisory Services, 1990–91; Mem., UK Exec., 1990–98; Sen. Partner, 1991–98; company merged with Coopers & Lybrand, 1998; UK Chm., PricewaterhouseCoopers, 1998–2001. Sen. Ind. Dir, Elementis plc, 2008–14 (non-exec. Dir, 2005–08; Chm., 2013–14); non-exec. Dir, Electra Private Equity, 2015– . Member: Auditing Practices Cttee, CCAB, 1986–90 (Chm., 1990); Accounting Standards Bd, 1993–2001 (Mem. Urgent Issues Task Force, 1991–93); Council, ICAEW, 1994–97; Financial Reporting Council, 1995–2008. Auditor, Duchy of Cornwall, 1993– . *Recreations:* tennis, golf. *Address:* Milestones, Packhorse Road, Bessels Green, Sevenoaks, Kent TN13 2QP.

**BRINDLE, Jane;** *see* Cox, Josephine.

**BRINDLE, Prof. Kevin Michael,** DPhil; FMedSci; Professor of Biomedical Magnetic Resonance, University of Cambridge, since 2005; Senior Group Leader, Cancer Research UK Cambridge Institute, since 2006; *b* Oxford, 27 Aug. 1955; *s* of late Cecil Brindle and of Anne Spencer Brindle (*née* Kilbee, now Hale); *m* 1985, Alexandra Mary Fulton. *Educ:* Gosford Hill Comprehensive Sch., Kidlington, Oxford; Oriel Coll., Oxford (BA; MA; DPhil 1982). Royal Society 1983 University Research Fellow: Dept of Biochem., Univ. of Oxford, 1986–90; Dept of Biochem. and Molecular Biol., Univ. of Manchester, 1990–91; Lectr, Univ. of Manchester, 1991–93; Lectr, 1993–2001, Reader, 2001–05, Univ. of Cambridge. FMedSci 2012. *Publications:* contribs to peer-reviewed jls. *Recreations:* cycling, gardening. *Address:* Department of Biochemistry, University of Cambridge, Tennis Court Road, Cambridge CB2 1GA. *T:* (01223) 333674; Cancer Research UK Cambridge Institute, Li Ka Shing Centre, Robinson Way, Cambridge CB2 0RE. *T:* (01223) 769647. *E:* kmb1001@cam.ac.uk.

**BRINDLE, Michael John;** QC 1992; a Recorder, since 2000; a Deputy High Court Judge, since 2001; *b* 23 June 1952; *s* of John Arthur Brindle and Muriel Jones; *m* 1st, 1988, Heather Mary (*née* Pearce) (marr. diss. 2005); one *s* two *d*; 2nd, 2007, Alison Jane (*née* Slann). *Educ:* Westminster Sch.; New Coll., Oxford (Ella Stephens Schol. in Classics; 1st Cl. Hons Mods, 1972; 1st Cl. Jurisprudence, 1974; MA). Called to the Bar, Lincoln's Inn, 1975 (Hardwicke Scholar), Bencher, 2002. Chairman: Commercial Bar Assoc., 2001–02 (Treas., 1999–2001); Bar Educn and Trng Cttee, 2003–05; Bar Council Internat. Cttee, 2008–09. Member: Financial Reporting Review Panel, 1998–2007; Financial Markets Law Cttee, 2004. Chm. Adv. Council, Public Concern at Work, 2001– (Chm. Trustees, 1997–2001). *Recreations:* classical music, travel, bridge. *Address:* Fountain Court, Temple, EC4Y 9DH.

**BRINDLE, Dr Michael John,** CBE 1998; FRCP, FRCR, FRCPC, FRCPE, FRCSE; Consultant Radiologist, The Queen Elizabeth Hospital, King's Lynn, 1972–98; President, Royal College of Radiologists, 1995–98; *b* 18 Nov. 1934; *s* of Dr W. S. Brindle and P. M. Brindle; *m* 1st, 1960, Muriel Eileen Hayward (*d* 2012); one *s* two *d* (and one *s* decd); 2nd, 2014, Diana Sarah Fox. *Educ:* Liverpool Univ. (MB ChB 1958; MD 1967; MRad 1971). FRCPC 1972; FRCR 1989; FRCP 1998; FRCPE 1999; FRCSE 1999. Surgeon Lieut, RN, 1959–62. Consultant, Royal Alexandra Hosp., Edmonton, Alberta, 1966–72. Treas., RCR, 1990–95. LRPS 2007. Hon. FRCGP 1998; Hon. FFSEM 2009. *Recreation:* photography.

**BRINDLEY, Christopher Charles,** MBE 2018; Managing Director, Metro Bank, 2011–15; *b* Manchester, 19 July 1964; *s* of Donald Brindley and Ethel Veronica Brindley; *m* 1986, Elaine Da Costa; one *s* one *d*. *Educ:* Chorlton High Sch. Natwest: Hd of Service and Sales, 1994–96; Area Manager, 1996–99; Regl Retail Manager, 1999–2002; Regl Business Manager, 2002–03; Special Projects Manager (People), 2003–04; Man. Dir, Natwest North, 2004–10; Dir, British Gas, 2010–11. Sen. Associate and Speaker, Raise the Bar, 2008– . Chair: GreaterSport, 2007–18; Sport and Dance, 2014– ; Brand New Moves, 2017– ; non-executive Director: Manchester Co. Football Assoc., 2012– ; Goodson Thomas, 2014– ; Switch the Play, 2015– ; Rugby Football League, 2016– ; Rugby League World Cup 2021, 2018– . *Recreations:* watching sport, Manchester United, family, travel, volunteering, gardening. *E:* chris.brindley@icloud.com.

**BRINDLEY, Very Rev. David Charles;** Dean of Portsmouth, 2002–18; *b* 11 June 1953; *m* 1975, Gillian Griffin; one *s* two *d*. *Educ:* Wednesfield Grammar Sch.; King's Coll., London (BD, AKC 1975; MTh 1976; MPhil 1980); Open Univ. (MA 2016). VSO, Lebanon, 1971–72. Ordained deacon, 1976, priest, 1977; Curate, Epping, 1976–79; Lectr, Coll. of St Paul and St Mary, Cheltenham, 1979–82; Vicar, Quorn, and Dir of Clergy Trng, dio. Leicester, 1982–86; Principal, W of England Ministerial Trng Course, 1987–94; Team Rector, Warwick, 1994–2002. *Publications:* Stepping Aside, 1993; Story, Song and Law, 1996; Richard Beauchamp: medieval England's greatest knight, 2001; *for children:* (with Gillian Brindley): Moses, 1985; Joseph, 1985. *Recreations:* folk music, modern literature, theatre. *Address:* 8 Rookwood Gardens, Fordingbridge SP6 1TA. *E:* davidbrindley3@gmail.com. *Clubs:* Athenæum, Royal Naval.

**BRINDLEY, Prof. Giles Skey,** MA, MD; FRS 1965; FRCP; Professor of Physiology in the University of London at the Institute of Psychiatry, 1968–91, now Emeritus; *b* 30 April 1926; *s* of late Arthur James Benet Skey and Dr Margaret Beatrice Marion Skey (*née* Dewhurst), later Brindley; *m* 1st, 1959, Lucy Dunk Bennell (marr. diss.); 2nd, 1964, Dr Hilary Richards; one *s* one *d*. *Educ:* Leyton County High School; Downing College, Cambridge (Hon. Fellow, 1969); London Hospital Medical College. Various jun. clin. and res. posts, 1950–54; Russian lang. abstractor, British Abstracts of Medical Sciences, 1953–56; successively Demonstrator, Lectr and Reader in Physiology, Univ. of Cambridge, 1954–68; Fellow: King's Coll., Cambridge, 1959–62; Trinity Coll., Cambridge, 1963–68. Hon. Dir, MRC Neurological Prostheses Unit, 1968–92; Hon. Consultant Physician, Maudsley Hosp., 1971–92. Chm. of Editorial Board, Journal of Physiology, 1964–66 (Mem., 1959–64). Visiting Prof., Univ. of California, Berkeley, 1968. Hon. FRCS 1988; Hon. FRCSE 2000. Liebrecht-Franceschetti Prize, German Ophthalmological Soc., 1971; Feldberg Prize, Feldberg Foundn, 1974; St Peter's Medal, British Assoc. of Urological Surgeons, 1987. *Publications:* Physiology of the Retina and Visual Pathway, 1960, 2nd edn 1970; papers in scientific, musicological and medical journals. *Recreations:* designing, making and playing various musical instruments (inventor of the logical bassoon), composing chamber music, songs and short orchestral pieces; formerly cross-country and track running (silver medallist, 2000m steeplechase and 800m (men over 65), World Veterans' Track and Field Championships, Finland, 1991). *Address:* 102 Ferndene Road, SE24 0AA. *T:* (020) 7274 2598.

**BRINDLEY, John Frederick,** CB 1996; Circuit Administrator, South Eastern Circuit, 1995–97; *b* 25 Sept. 1937; *s* of Harold and Eva Brindley; *m* 1960, Judith Ann Sherratt (*d* 2017); one *d*. *Educ:* Leek Grammar Sch. Lord Chancellor's Department: Court Business Officer, Midland and Oxford Circuit, 1971; HQ Personnel Officer, 1976; Courts Administrator, Exeter Group, 1981; Head, Civil Business Div. HQ, 1987; Court Service Management Gp, 1988; Court Service Business Gp, 1991. Chm., CSSB, 1998–2004. *Publications:* Court in the Act, 2009; Music for a While, 2014; The Summer of 1932, 2015; Sport Mainly, 2016. *Recreations:* hockey, cricket, amateur theatricals, choral and solo singing. *Address:* Sidmouth, Devon. *Club:* Athenæum.

**BRINDLEY, Kate Victoria;** Director of Collections and Exhibitions, Chatsworth and the Devonshire Collections, since 2017; *b* Sheffield, 27 May 1970; *d* of Roger and Carol Manning. *Educ:* Silverdale Sch., Sheffield; Univ. of Leeds (BA Jt Hons Hist. of Art and Religious Studies); Univ. of Manchester (Dip. Mus and Gall. Studies). AMA 1996. Curatorial asst, Mead Gall., Warwick Univ., 1992–96; Exhibns Officer, Leamington Spa Art Gall., 1994–98; Art and Exhibns Officer, Rugby Art Gall. and Mus., 1998–2000; freelance curator and consultant, 2000–02; Hd of Arts and Mus., Wolverhampton CC, 2002–05; Dir of Mus, Galleries & Archives, Bristol CC, 2005–09; Director: Middlesbrough Inst. of Modern Art, 2009–14; Arnolfini, Bristol, 2014–16. Advr, Visual Art, Arts Council England, W Midlands, 1996–2002. Lead, SW Hub for Mus, 2005–09. Arts Advr, Paul Hamlyn Foundn, 2008–16 (Chair, Mus & Galls Special Initiative, 2010–16). Trustee: Craftspace Touring, 2002–05; AV Fest. NE, 2010–14 (Vice Chair, 2011–14). *Recreation:* seeking the sun and good coffee. *Address:* Chatsworth, Bakewell, Derbyshire DE45 1PP. *E:* kate.brindley@devonshiregroup.co.uk.

**BRINDLEY, Dame Lynne (Janie),** DBE 2008; Master, Pembroke College, Oxford, 2013–April 2020; *b* 2 July 1950; *d* of Ivan Blowers and Janie Blowers (*née* Williams); adopted *d* of Ronald Williams and Elaine Williams (*née* Chapman), 1958; *m* 1972, Timothy Stuart Brindley. *Educ:* Truro High Sch.; Univ. of Reading (BA 1971); UCL (MA 1975; Hon. Fellow, 2002). FIInfSc 1990; FCLIP (FLA 1990). Head of Mktg and of Chief Exec.'s Office, British Library, 1979–85; Dir of Library and Information Services, and Pro-Vice Chancellor, Aston Univ., 1985–90; Principal Consultant, KPMG, 1990–92; Librarian and

Dir of Information Services, LSE, 1992–97; Librarian and Pro-Vice Chancellor, Univ. of Leeds, 1997–2000; Chief Exec., British Library, 2000–12. Visiting Professor: Knowledge Mgt, Univ. of Leeds, 2000–09; City Univ., 2002–. Member: Lord Chancellor's Adv. Cttee on Public Records, 1992–98; Jt Inf. Systems Cttee, HEFCs, 1992–98 (Chair, Electronic Libraries Prog., 1993–98); Review of Higher Educn Libraries, HEFCs, 1992–93; Internat. Cttee on Social Sci. Inf., UNESCO, 1992–97; Res. Resources Bd, 1994–2001, Communications and Inf. Cttee, 2004–08, ESRC; Liby and Inf. Commn, DCMS, 1999–2000; Stanford Univ. Adv. Council for Libraries and Inf. Resources, 1999–; AHRC, 2008–14; Strategic Adv. Bd for Intellectual Property, 2008–10; Bd, Ofcom, 2011–17; Arts Panel, Wolfson Trust, 2012–. Trustee, Thackray Med. Mus., Leeds, 1999–2001. FRSA 1993. CCMI 2004. Freeman, City of London, 1989; Liveryman, Goldsmiths' Co., 1993– (Mem., Court of Assts, 2006–). Honorary Fellow: Univ. of Wales, Aberystwyth, 2007; LSE, 2008; Hon. FBA 2015. Hon. DLitt: Nottingham Trent, 2001; Oxford, Leicester, London Guildhall, 2002; Reading, Sheffield, 2004; Aston, 2008; Loughborough, Manchester, 2011; TCD, 2012; Hon. DSc: City, 2005; Leeds, 2006; DUniv Open, 2006; Hon. DArts de Montfort, 2011; Hon. DLit London, 2012; Hon. DLaws Durham, 2013. *Publications*: numerous articles on electronic libraries and information mgt. *Recreations*: classical music, theatre, modern art, hill walking. *Address*: Pembroke College, Oxford OX1 1DW. *Club*: Reform.

**BRINE, Stephen Charles**; MP for Winchester, since 2010 (C, 2010–19; Ind, since 2019); *b* 28 Jan. 1974; *s* of Clive Charles Brine and late Gloria Elizabeth Brine; *m* 2003, Susie Toulson; one *s* one *d*. *Educ*: Bohunt Comprehensive Sch.; Highbury Coll., Portsmouth; Liverpool Hope UC (BA Hist. Liverpool Univ. 1997). Journalist: BBC Radio Surrey; BBC Southern Counties Radio; WGN Radio, Chicago; work in consultancy firm specialising in customer care; former Dir, Azalea Gp. Area Campaign Dir, Hants and IoW, Cons. Party, 2001–05. An Asst Govt Whip, 2016–17; Parly Under-Sec. of State, DoH, then DHSC, 2017–19. *Address*: House of Commons, SW1A 0AA.

**BRINK, Prof. Christoffel Hendrik**, CBE 2018; PhD, DPhil; Vice-Chancellor, Newcastle University, 2007–16, now Emeritus; *b* Upington, CP, S Africa, 31 Jan. 1951; *s* of Petrus Johannes Brink and Hester Brink; *m* 1981, Tobea du Preez; one *s* two *d*. *Educ*: Upington Primary and Secondary Sch., SA; Rand Afrikaans Univ., Johannesburg (BSc Maths and Computer Sci. 1972; DPhil 1992); Rhodes Univ. (BSc Hons Maths 1973; MSc Maths 1974; MA Phil. 1975); PhD Algebraic Logic Cambridge 1978. Mil. trng, Army Gymnasium Heidelberg, 1969 (2nd Lt). Lectr in Maths, 1979–80, Sen. Lectr, 1980–86, Univ. of Stellenbosch; Associate Prof. of Maths, Univ. of Cape Town, 1987–92; Sen. Res. Fellow, ANU, 1988–90; University of Cape Town: Hd, Dept of Maths, 1991–94; Prof. of Maths, 1993–99; Hd, Dept of Maths and Applied Maths, 1995–99; Dir, Lab. for Formal Aspects and Complexity in Computer Sci., 1994–99; Coordinator of Strategic Planning, 1997; Pro Vice-Chancellor (Res.) and Prof. of Maths, Univ. of Wollongong, NSW, 1999–2001; Vice-Chancellor and Rector, Stellenbosch Univ., 2002–07. Member, Board: Russell Gp, 2007–16; N8, 2007–16; Equality Challenge Unit, 2008–13; QAA, 2009–13; NE LEP, 2011–13; UUK, 2012–15. Founder Mem., Acad. of Sci. of SA, 1995; FRSSAf 1995. Freedom, City of Newcastle upon Tyne. Hon. Col, Mil. Acad. of SA, 2004–07. Hon. DCL Newcastle upon Tyne, 2017. *Publications*: (jtly) Wiskunde vir Wetenskapstudente (Mathematics for Science Students), 1983; (ed jtly) Relational Methods in Computer Science, 1997; (with I. M. Rewitzky) A Paradigm for Program Semantics: power structures and duality, 2001; No Lesser Place: the taaldebat at Stellenbosch, 2006; The Soul of a University: why excellence is not enough, 2018. *E*: chris.brink@newcastle.ac.uk.

**BRINK, Prof. David Maurice**, DPhil; FRS 1981; Professor of History of Physics, University of Trento, Italy, 1993–98; *b* 20 July 1930; *s* of Maurice Ossian Brink and Victoria May Finlayson; *m* 1958, Verena Wehrli; one *s* two *d*. *Educ*: Friends' Sch., Hobart; Univ. of Tasmania (BSc); Univ. of Oxford (DPhil). Rhodes Scholar, 1951–54; Rutherford Scholar, 1954–58; Lectr, 1954–58, Fellow and Tutor, 1958–93, Balliol Coll., Oxford; Univ. Lectr, 1958–89, H. J. G. Moseley Reader in Physics, 1989–93, Oxford Univ., retd. Instructor, MIT, 1956–57. Foreign Mem., Royal Soc. of Scis of Uppsala, 1992. Rutherford Medal and Prize, Inst. of Physics, 1982; Lise Meitner Prize for Nuclear Physics, Eur. Physical Soc., 2006. *Publications*: Angular Momentum, 1962, 3rd edn 1993; Nuclear Forces, 1965; Semi-classical Methods in Nucleus-Nucleus Scattering, 1985; (with R. Broglia) Nuclear Superfluidity, 2004. *Recreations*: birdwatching, walking. *Address*: 34 Minster Road, Oxford OX4 1LY. *T*: (01865) 246127.

**BRINKLEY, Robert Edward**, CMG 2006; HM Diplomatic Service, retired; *b* 21 Jan. 1954; *s* of Thomas Edward Brinkley and Sheila Doris Brinkley (*née* Gearing); *m* 1982, (Frances) Mary Webster (*née* Edwards); three *s*. *Educ*: Stonyhurst Coll.; Corpus Christi Coll., Oxford (MA). Entered HM Diplomatic Service, 1977: FCO, 1977–78; Mem., UK Delegn to Comprehensive Test Ban Negotiations, Geneva, 1978; Second Sec., Moscow, 1979–82; First Secretary: FCO, 1982–88; Bonn, 1988–92; FCO, 1992–95; Counsellor and Head, Fundamental Expenditure Rev. Unit, FCO, 1995–96; Political Counsellor, Moscow, 1996–99; Head, FCO/Home Office Jt Entry Clearance Unit, 2000–02; Ambassador to Ukraine, 2002–06; High Comr to Pakistan, 2006–09; Business Develt Manager, Associated British Foods plc (on secondment), 2010–11. Member, Advisory Board: Sch. of E Eur. and Slavonic Studies, UCL, 2018– (Chm., 2018–); Andrei Sakharov Centre for Democratic Develt, Vytautas Magnus Univ., Kaunas, Lithuania, 2018–. Vis. Fellow, 2012–, Senator, 2013–, Ukrainian Catholic Univ. Mem., RIIA, 2012–. Chm., Steering Cttee, Ukraine Forum, 2015–; Trustee: Karachi Educn Initiative (UK), 2010–11; BEARR Trust, 2011–18 (Chm., 2012–18; Patron, 2018–); Keston Inst., 2014–; Ukrainian Inst., London, 2016– (Chm., 2018–). Patron, Child Aid Eastern Europe, 2018–. *Recreations*: walking, swimming, reading, music (violin). *Club*: Athenæum.

**BRINLEY JONES, Robert**; *see* Jones, Dr R. B.

**BRINSDEN, Peter Robert**, FRCOG; FRGS; Consultant, Bourn Hall Clinic, Cambridge, since 2016 (Consultant Gynaecologist and Medical Director, 1989–2005; Consultant Medical Director, 2005–10 and 2013–16); Medical Director, Clane Fertility Unit, County Kildare, 1995–2015; Group Medical Director, Bourn Hall International, 2010–13; *b* 2 Sept. 1940; *s* of Dudley and Geraldine Brinsden; *m* 1967, Gillian Susan Heather; two *s*. *Educ*: Rugby Sch.; King's Coll. London; St George's Hosp., London (MB BS 1966). MRCS 1966; LRCP 1966; FRCOG 1989; FRGS 2017. House officer appts, 1967; Medical Officer, Royal Navy, 1966–82: appointments: HMS Glamorgan, 1967–68; RN Hosps, Haslar, Plymouth, Malta and Gibraltar, 1968–78; civilian hosps, Southampton and Portsmouth, 1972–74; Surgeon Comdr, 1976; Consultant Obstetrician and Gynaecologist, RN Hosps, Portsmouth and Plymouth, 1978–82; retd 1982; Consultant: King Fahd Hosp., Riyadh, 1982–84; Bourn Hall and Wellington Hosp., 1985–89. Affiliated Lectr, Univ. of Cambridge Clinical Sch., Addenbrooke's Hosp., 1992–2007. Vis. Prof. in Gynaecology and Fertility, Capital Medical Univ., Beijing, 2001–; Hon. Prof., Peking Union Medical Coll., Beijing, 2003–; Guest Prof., Southern Medical Univ., Guangzhou, 2008–. Inspector, HFEA, 1997–2010. Pres., British Fertility Soc., 2009–12; Trustee: British Fertility Soc. Educnl Trust, 2014–; Abbeyfield Tavistock Soc., 2014–. Gov., Newton Primary Sch., Cambs, 1998–2001. *Publications*: (ed) A Textbook of In-Vitro Fertilization and Assisted Reproduction, 1992, 3rd edn 2005; (ed jtly) A Manual of Intrauterine Insemination and Ovulation Induction, 2010; (ed jtly) In-Vitro Fertilisation: the pioneers' history, 2018; contrib. numerous medical articles and book chapters on infertility and assisted reproduction. *Recreations*: sailing, sub-aqua diving, computing, photography. *Address*: Mapledurham, 116b Whitchurch Road, Tavistock, Devon PL19 9BQ. *E*: peter@brinsden.net.

**BRINSMEAD, Christopher David**, CBE 2015; independent director and adviser; Adviser on Life Sciences to Prime Minister, Department of Health, and Department for Business, Energy and Industrial Strategy (formerly Department of Business, Innovation and Skills), 2010–16; *b* Rochford, Essex, 27 March 1959; *s* of Peter Brinsmead and Anne Brinsmead; *m* 1980, Lisa Hemeter; two *d*. *Educ*: Wells Cathedral Sch.; Nottingham Univ. (BSc 1980); Manchester Business Sch. (MSc 1985). Various commercial roles, ICI, later Zeneca, 1980–97, Regl Vice-Pres. Asia, 1997–99; Vice Pres., Product Strategy, AstraZeneca, 1999–2001; Pres., AstraZeneca UK, 2001–08; Pres., 2002–08, Chm., 2008–10, AstraZeneca Pharma UK; Chairman: Proteus Digital Health Europe (formerly Proteus Biomedical Europe), 2011–17; Bamburgh Capital (formerly Diagnostic Capital) Ltd, 2011–19; Proveca Ltd, 2013–. Non-executive Director: Domino Printing Sciences, 2008–15; Datapharm, 2008–10; UDG Healthcare (formerly United Drug) plc, 2010– (Sen. Ind. Dir, plc, 2017–); Wesleyan Assce Soc., 2010–19; Kinapse Ltd, 2010–16; Cambian Gp plc, 2014–17; Collagen Solutions plc, 2018–; Consort Medical plc, 2019– (Chm., 2019–). Chm., Life Scis Bd, 2008–. Pres., ABPI, 2008–10. Mem. Council, Imperial Coll. London, 2013–. *Recreations*: golf, sailing, walking, running, ski-ing. *Clubs*: Royal Automobile; New Golf (St Andrews).

**BRINTON**, Baroness *cr* 2011 (Life Peer), of Kenardington in the County of Kent; **Sarah Virginia, (Sal), Brinton**; Executive Director, Association of Universities in the East of England, 2006–11; *b* Paddington, 1 April 1955; *d* of late Timothy Denis Brinton and of Jane-Mari Brinton (now Shearing); *m* 1983, Tim Whittaker; two *s* one *d*. *Educ*: Churchill Coll., Cambridge (BA 1984; MA 1992). BBC: Prodn Sec., Radio 3, 1974–76, Radio Drama, 1976–77; Floor Manager, London and Glasgow, 1977–81; Manager: New Cambridge Research Ltd (venture capital), 1984–87; Cambridge Venture Mgt Ltd, 1987–91; Dir, Cambridge Venture Capital Ltd, 1987–91; Bursar: Lucy Cavendish Coll., Cambridge, 1992–97; Selwyn Coll., Cambridge, 1997–2002. Chm., Learning and Skills Council, Cambs, 2000–06; Mem. Bd, E of England Develt Agency, 1999–2004 (Dep. Chm., 2002–04). Mem. (Lib Dem), Cambs CC, 1993–2004 (Leader, Lib Dem Gp, 1997–2004). Contested (Lib Dem): Cambs SE, 1997, 2001; Watford, 2005, 2010. Liberal Democrat Party: Mem., Federal Policy Cttee, 2004–08 and 2010– (Vice Chm., 2006–08); Pres., 2015–; Vice Chair, Federal Conference Cttee; Chair, Diversity Engagement Gp. Dir and Trustee, Christian Blind Mission UK Ltd, 2003–14; Trustee, University for Industry Charitable Trust, 2003–. *Address*: House of Lords, SW1A 0PW.

**BRINTON, Helen Rosemary**; *see* Clark, H. R.

**BRISBANE, Archbishop of**, and Metropolitan of the Province of Queensland, since 2002; **Most Rev. Dr Phillip John Aspinall**; Primate of Australia, 2005–14; *b* 17 Dec. 1959; *m* 1982, Christa Schmitt; two *s*. *Educ*: Univ. of Tasmania (BSc 1980); Brisbane Coll. of Advanced Educn (Grad. DipRE 1985); Ecumenical Inst., Geneva (Cert. 1987); Trinity Coll., Melbourne Coll. of Divinity (BD (Hons) 1988); Monash Univ. (PhD 1989); Deakin Univ. (MBA 1998). Field Officer, C of E Boys' Soc., 1980; Diocesan Youth and Educn Officer, 1981–84; Dep. Warden, Christ Coll., Dio. Tasmania, 1983–84; Dir, Parish Educn, St Stephen's, Mt Waverley, Dio. Melbourne, 1985–88; ordained deacon, 1988, priest, 1989; Asst Curate, St Mark-on-the-Hill, 1988–89; Asst Priest, Brighton, 1989–91; Priest in charge, Bridgewater-Gagebrook, 1991–94; Dir, Anglicare, Tasmania, 1994–98; Acting Archdeacon of Clarence, 1997; Archdeacon for Church and Society, Dio. Tasmania, 1997–98; Asst Bp, Dio. Adelaide, 1998–2002. Chm., Ecumenical Relns Commn, Gen. Synod, 2016–. Member: Standing Cttee, Primates' Meeting of the Anglican Communion, 2007–10; (ex-officio) ACC, 2007–10. *Address*: GPO Box 421, Brisbane, Qld 4001, Australia.

**BRISBANE, Archbishop of, (RC)**, since 2012; **Most Rev. Mark Benedict Coleridge**; *b* 25 Sept. 1948; *s* of Bernard Coleridge. *Educ*: Rostrevor Coll., Adelaide; St Kevin's Coll., Melbourne; Melbourne Univ. (BA 1980); Corpus Christ Coll., Melbourne; Pontifical Biblical Inst., Rome (LSS 1984; DSS 1991). Ordained priest, 1974; Asst Priest, E Doncaster, Ashburton, Pascoe Vale, Melbourne, 1975–80; Catholic Theological College, Melbourne: Lectr in Biblical Studies, 1985–88 and 1991–97; Master, 1995–97; Official, First Section, Secretariat of State, Vatican, 1998–2002; Aux. Bishop of Melbourne, 2002–06; Archbishop of Canberra and Goulburn, (RC), 2006–12. Member: Pontifical Council for Culture, 2004; Bishops' Commission: for Liturgy, 2006, for Doctrine and Morals, 2006. Chairman: Roman Missal Editl Commn, 2004–; Internat. Commn for the Preparation of an English-language Lectionary, 2005–. *Publications*: The Birth of the Lukan Narrative, 1993; Words from the Wound: selected addresses, letters and homilies of Archbishop Mark Coleridge, 2014. *Address*: GPO Box 282, Brisbane, Qld 4001, Australia.

**BRISBANE, Assistant Bishops of**; *see* Venables, Rt Rev. C. D.; Roundhill, Rt Rev. A. J.; Greaves, Rt Rev. J. D.

**BRISBY, John Constant Shannon McBurney**; QC 1996; a Deputy High Court Judge, since 2004; *b* 8 May 1956; *s* of late Michael Douglas James McBurney Brisby and Liliana Daneva-Hadjikaltcheva Drenska; *m* 1985, Claire Alexandra Anne, *d* of Sir Donald Arthur Logan, KCMG. *Educ*: Westminster Sch.; Christ Church, Oxford (Schol.; MA). 2nd Lieut, 5th Royal Inniskilling Dragoon Guards, 1974. Called to the Bar, Lincoln's Inn, 1978 (Mansfield Schol.; Bencher, 2005); in practice as barrister, 1980–. Member, Executive Council: Friends of Bulgaria, 1991– (Chm., 2010–); British-Bulgarian Legal Assoc., 1991–2001. *Publications*: (contrib.) Butterworth's Company Law Precedents, 4th edn; Konstantin Hadjikaltchoff 1856–1940, 2006. *Recreations*: hunting, shooting, ski-ing, tennis, music, reading, art and architecture. *Address*: 4 Stone Buildings, Lincoln's Inn, WC2A 3XT. *T*: (020) 7242 5524. *Clubs*: Beefsteak, Travellers.

**BRISCO, Sir Campbell Howard**, 9th Bt *cr* 1982, of Crofton Place, Cumberland; livestock farmer and manager, retired; *b* 11 Dec. 1944; *s* of Gilfred Rimington Brisco (*d* 1981) and Constance Freda Brisco (*d* 1980), 2nd *d* of Charles John Polson, Masterton, NZ; *S* cousin, 1995, but his name does not appear on the Official Roll of the Baronetage; *m* 1969, Kaye Janette, *d* of Ewan William McFadzien; two *s* one *d*. *Educ*: Southland Boys' High Sch. *Recreation*: sport. *Heir*: *s* Kent Rimington Brisco [*b* 24 Sept. 1972; *m* 2003, Shannon, *d* of Wayne Leahy]. *Address*: 134 Park Street, Winton, Southland 9720, New Zealand. *T*: (3) 2369068.

**BRISCOE, Sir Brian (Anthony)**, Kt 2002; Chairman, Garden City Developments CIC Ltd, since 2013; *b* 29 July 1945; *s* of Anthony Brown Briscoe and Lily Briscoe; *m* 1969, Sheila Mary Cheyne; three *s*. *Educ*: Newcastle Royal Grammar Sch.; St Catharine's Coll., Cambridge (MA); Trent Poly. (DipTP). MRTPI, MRICS. Asst Planner, Derbyshire CC, 1967–71; Section Head, Herefordshire CC, 1971–74; Asst Chief Planner, W Yorks CC, 1974–79; Dep. County Planning Officer, Herts CC, 1979–88; County Planning Officer, Kent CC, 1988–90; Chief Executive: Herts CC, 1990–96; LGA, 1996–2006. Chm., Task

Gp on Gypsies and Travellers, DCLG, 2006–09. Board Member: Visit England, 2007–11; Land Data, 2007–; High Speed Two Ltd, 2009–14 (Chm., 2010–12). Chair, Ind. Transport Commn for Reading, 2007–08, for Cambs, 2008–09. Trustee, TCPA, 2006–16. Hon. DLaws Herts, 2004. FRSA; CCMI. *Publications:* contribs to planning and property jls; chapter in English Structure Planning, 1982. *Recreations:* family, 8 grandchildren, golf, Newcastle United FC. *Address:* Temple House, 257 Boxley Road, Maidstone, Kent ME14 2AS.

BRISCOE, Constance; a part-time Recorder, 1996; author, since 2003; b London, 18 May 1957; d of George and Carmen Briscoe; one s one d. *Educ:* Sacred Heart Sch., Camberwell; Univ. of Newcastle upon Tyne (LLB Hons Law); Council of Legal Educn (Bar Finals). Called to the Bar, Inner Temple, 1983. *Publications:* Ugly, 2006; Beyond Ugly, 2008; The Accused (novel), 2011. *Recreations:* gardening, reading, Billie Holliday, writing, running. *E:* constance.briscoe@googlemail.com.

BRISCOE, Dr James Michael, FRS 2019; FMedSci; Senior Group Leader, Developmental Dynamics Laboratory, Francis Crick Institute, since 2015; b W Sussex, 18 June 1970; s of Kelvin Briscoe and Ann Margaret Briscoe; partner, Melanie Smallman. *Educ:* Univ. of Warwick (BSc Hons Microbiol. and Virol. 1992); Univ. of London (PhD 1996). Res. Fellow, Columbia Univ., 1996–2000; Prog. Leader, 2000–11, Hd of Div., 2011–15, MRC-NIMR. Ed.-in-Chief, Development, Co. of Biologists, 2018–. FMedSci 2019. *Publications:* contrib. scientific papers to jls and scientific pubns. *Recreations:* cinema, theatre, tennis, school governor (secondary). *Address:* Francis Crick Institute, 1 Midland Road, NW1 1AT. *E:* james.briscoe@crick.ac.uk.

BRISCOE, Sir John Geoffrey James, 6th Bt cr 1910, of Bourn Hall, Bourn, Cambridge; b (posthumously) 4 Nov. 1994; o s of Sir (John) James Briscoe, 5th Bt and of Felicity Mary (now Mrs Christopher Edward Whitley), e d of David Melville Watkinson; S father, 1994. *Heir:* uncle Edward Home Briscoe [b 27 March 1955; m 1st, 1979, Anne Lister (marr. diss. 1989); one s one d; 2nd, 1994, Sandy Elizabeth Key (née Lloyd)].

BRISCOE, John Hubert Daly, LVO 1997; FRCGP; Apothecary to HM Household, Windsor, and to HM the Queen Mother's Household at Royal Lodge, 1986–97; Master, Worshipful Society of Apothecaries of London, 2000–01; b 19 March 1933; o s of late Dr Arnold Daly Briscoe and Doris Winifred Briscoe (née Nicholson); m 1958, Janet Anne Earlam; one s three d (and one d decd). *Educ:* St Andrew's Sch., Eastbourne; Winchester Coll.; St John's Coll., Cambridge (MA); St Thomas's Hosp. (MB BChir); DObstRCOG 1959; MRCGP 1968, FRCGP 2006. MO, Overseas CS, Basutoland, 1959–62; Asst in gen. practice, Aldeburgh, 1963–65; Principal in gen. practice, Eton, 1965–97; Medical Officer: Eton Coll., 1965–97; St George's Sch., Windsor Castle, 1976–97. Fellow, MOs of Schs Assoc., 2002 (Pres., 1989–91). FRSocMed 1995–2012. Hon. MO, Guards' Polo Club, 1966–83. Hon. Mem., Windsor and Dist Med. Soc., 1999. Hon. Auditor, Eur. Union of Sch. and Univ. Health and Medicine, 1981–89. Lay Steward, St George's Chapel, Windsor Castle, 1999. Bridgemaster, Baldwin's Bridge Trust, Eton, 1988–89 and 2002–03. Pres., Omar Khayyam Club, 2005. Hon. Licentiate, Apothecaries' Hall, Dublin, 2001. *Publications:* contrib. papers on influenza vaccination and adolescent medicine. *Recreations:* growing vegetables, pictures. *Address:* Wistaria House, 54/56 Kings Road, Windsor, Berks SL4 2AH. *T:* (01753) 855321. *Club:* Athenæum.

BRISE, Sir Timothy Edward R.; see Ruggles-Brise.

BRISON, Ven. William Stanley; Team Rector, Pendleton, Manchester, 1994–98; permission to officiate, diocese of Manchester, since 1999; b 20 Nov. 1929; s of William P. Brison and Marion A. Wilber; m 1951, Marguerite, (Peggy), Adelia Nettleton; two s two d. *Educ:* Alfred Univ., New York (BS Eng); Berkeley Divinity School, New Haven, Conn (STM, MDiv). United States Marine Corps, Captain (Reserve), 1951–53. Engineer, Norton Co., Worcester, Mass, 1953–54. Vicar, then Rector, Christ Episcopal Church, Bethany, Conn, 1957–69; Archdeacon of New Haven, Conn, 1967–69; Rector, Emmanuel Episcopal Church, Stamford, Conn, 1969–72; Vicar, Christ Church, Davyhulme, Manchester, 1972–81; Rector, All Saints', Newton Heath, Manchester, 1981–85; Area Dean of North Manchester, 1981–85; Archdeacon of Bolton, 1985–92, then Archdeacon Emeritus; CMS Missionary, Nigeria, 1992–94; Lectr, St Francis of Assisi Theol Coll., Zaria, 1992–94. Chairman: Bury Christian Aid, 2002–; Goshen and Blackford Bridge Tenants' and Residents' Assoc., 2003–. *Publications:* (with Peggy Brison) A Tale of Two Visits to Chechnya, 2005; Judas, Beloved Disciple, 2013; (with Peggy Brison) Saints and Sinners. *Recreation:* nine grandchildren. *Address:* 2 Scott Avenue, Bury, Lancs BL9 9RS. *T:* (0161) 764 3998.

BRISTOL, 8th Marquess of, cr 1826; Frederick William Augustus Hervey; Baron Hervey of Ickworth, 1703; Earl of Bristol, 1714; Earl Jermyn of Horningsheath, 1826; Hereditary High Steward of the Liberty of St Edmund; b 19 Oct. 1979; s of 6th Marquess of Bristol and of his 3rd wife, Yvonne Marie, d of Anthony Sutton; S half-brother, 1999; m 2018, Meredith Dunn, Boston, Mass. *Educ:* Eton Coll.; Edinburgh Univ. (BCom). Director: Bristol & Stone Real Estate Investment Co., 2004–09; Bristol Estates Ltd (formerly Bristol Settled Estates Ltd), 2010–; CEO, Brickowner, 2015–. Trustee, Gen. Hervey's Charitable Trust, 1999–; Trustee and Chm., Ickworth Church Conservation Trust, 2006–. Patron: Gwrych Castle Preservation Trust, 2002–; Athenaeum, Bury St Edmunds, 2006–; Friends of W Suffolk Hosp., 2013–. *Recreations:* emerging markets, reading, travel. *Address:* Bristol Estates Ltd, 2 Eaton Gate, SW1W 9BJ. *E:* fb@bristolestates.co.uk. *Clubs:* Turf, White's.

BRISTOL, Bishop of, since 2018; Rt Rev. Vivienne Frances Faull; b 20 May 1955; d of William Baines Faull and Pamela June Faull (née Dell); m 1993, Dr Michael Duddridge. *Educ:* Queen's Sch., Chester; St Hilda's Coll., Oxford; St John's Coll., Nottingham; Open Univ. Teacher, N India, 1977–79; youth worker, Everton, 1979. Ordained deaconess, 1982, deacon, 1987, priest, 1994; Deaconess, St Matthew and St James, Mossley Hill, 1982–85; Chaplain: Clare Coll., Cambridge, 1985–90; Gloucester Cathedral, 1990–94; Canon Pastor, 1994–2000, Vice Provost, 1995–2000, Coventry Cathedral; Dean of Leicester, 2000–12; Dean of York, 2012–18. A Church Comr, 2019–. Mem., Gen. Synod of C of E, 2003–12. Chairman: Assoc. of English Cathedrals, 2009–15; Deans' Conf., 2015–18. Hon. Fellow, Clare Coll., Cambridge, 2012. Hon. DPhil Gloucester, 2014; Hon. DLitt Chester, DUniv York, 2015. *Address:* Bishop's Office, Church Lane, Winterbourne, Bristol BS36 1SG.

BRISTOL, Dean of; no new appointment at time of going to press.

BRISTOW, Sir Laurence (Stanley Charles), KCMG 2019 (CMG 2015); HM Diplomatic Service; Ambassador to Russia, 2016–19; b 23 Nov. 1963; s of Stanley and Hilary Bristow; m 1988, Fiona MacCallum; two s. *Educ:* Colchester Royal Grammar Sch.; Trinity Coll., Cambridge (BA 1986; PhD 1991); Open Univ. (MBA 2001). Entered FCO, 1990; Second Sec., Bucharest, 1992–95; First Secretary: FCO, 1995–99; Ankara, 1999–2002; NATO Defence Coll., Rome, 2002–03; FCO, 2003; Ambassador to Azerbaijan, 2004–07; Dep. Hd of Mission, Moscow, 2007–10; Director: Eastern Europe and Central Asia, FCO, 2010–12; Nat. Security, FCO, 2012–15. *Address:* c/o Foreign and Commonwealth Office, King Charles Street, SW1A 2AH.

BRITNELL, Mark Douglas; Global Chairman and Senior Partner for Healthcare, Government and Infrastructure (formerly Partner and Global Head of Healthcare), KPMG, since 2009; b 5 Jan. 1966; s of late Robert Britnell and of Veronica Britnell, now Leigh; m 2005, Stephanie Joy; one s one d. *Educ:* Univ. of Warwick (BA Hons 1988). NHS Mgt Trng Scheme, 1989–92; Gen. Manager, St Mary's Hosp., London, 1992–95; Exec. Dir, Central Middlesex Hosp., London, 1995–98; Chief Executive: Univ. Hosp. Birmingham NHS, then NHS Foundn, Trust, 1998–2006; NHS S Central Strategic HA, 2006–07; Dir Gen., Commissioning, System Mgt and Commercial Directorate, DoH, 2007–09. Non-executive Director: Dr Foster Ltd, 2004–07; Prostate Cancer UK, 2012–15. Sen. Associate, King's Fund, 2004–. *Publications:* In Search of the Perfect Health System, 2015; Human: solving the global workforce crisis in healthcare, 2019. *Recreations:* sport, current affairs, family. *Address:* KPMG, 15 Canada Square, Canary Wharf, E14 5GL. *Club:* Reform.

BRITTAIN, Barbara Jane; see Moorhouse, B. J.

BRITTAIN, Clive Edward; racehorse trainer, 1972–2015; b 15 Dec. 1933; s of Edward John Brittain and Priscilla Rosalind (née Winzer); m 1957, Maureen Helen Robinson. *Educ:* Calne Secondary Mod. Sch. Winning horses trained include: Julio Mariner, St Leger, 1978; Pebbles, 1000 Guineas, 1984; Eclipse, Dubai Champion and Breeders Cup Turf, 1985; Jupiter Island, Japan Cup, Tokyo, 1986; Mystiko, 2000 Guineas, 1991; Terimon, Juddmonte Internat., 1991; User Friendly, Oaks, Irish Oaks, Yorkshire Oaks, St Leger, 1992; Sayyedati, 1000 Guineas, and Jacque le Marois, 1993, Sussex Stakes, 1995; Luso, Hong Kong Vase, 1996 and 1997; Crimplene, Irish 1000 Guineas, 2000; Var, Prix de l'Abbaye, Longchamp, 2004; Warrsan, Coronation Cup, 2003 and 2004, and Grosser Prix von Baden, 2004 and 2005; Rajeem, UAE Equestrian and Racing Fedn Falmouth Stakes, 2006; Hibaayeb, Meon Valley Stud Fillies' Mile, 2009; Rizeena, Moyglare Stud Stakes, 2013. *Recreation:* shooting. *Address:* Carlburg, 49 Bury Road, Newmarket, Suffolk CB8 7BY. *T:* (01638) 664347. *Club:* Jockey Club Rooms (Newmarket).

BRITTAIN, Louise Mary; Partner, Wilkins Kennedy, since 2013; b London, 19 June 1966; d of Michael Brittain and Deborah Balding-Brittain; one s one d. *Educ:* Wycombe High Sch.; Portsmouth Poly. (BSc Hons Math. Scis); Coll. of St Paul and St Mary (PGCE). Licensed Insolvency Practitioner 1999; Law of Property Act Receiver; Nat. Coll. of Ireland (Cert. Personal Insolvency Practice 2014). Deloitte Haskins & Sells, subseq. Coopers & Lybrand Deloitte, then Coopers & Lybrand, 1989–96; Baker Tilly LLP, 1996–2009: Partner, 2001–09; Hd, Special Investigations, 2003–09; Partner and Hd, Contentious Insolvency, Deloitte LLP, 2009–13. Non-exec. Dir, Insolvency Service Steering Bd, 2006–10. Mem., Nat. Cttee, Assoc. of Business Recovery Professionals, 2009–. *Publications:* contrib. Recovery mag. of Assoc. of Business Recovery Professionals, Accountancy Age. *Recreations:* riding, the arts, family. *Address:* Wilkins Kennedy, Bridge House, SE1 9QR. *T:* (020) 7403 1877. *E:* Louise.Brittain@wilkinskennedy.com. *Club:* Le Beaujolais.

BRITTAIN, Paul Delery; Head, Corporate Finance, Norfolk County Council, 2007–13; b Ruislip, Middx, 12 Sept. 1953; s of Reginald William and Corinne Dorothy Brittain; m 2015, Julia Weaver; two s one d. *Educ:* St George's Coll., Weybridge; Exeter Univ. (BA Combined Hons Hist. and Politics 1975). CIPFA 1980. Local government finance roles: Southend BC, 1976–82; S Yorks CC, 1982–86; Sheffield CC, 1986; Lincs CC, 1986–2000; HBS Business Services Ltd, 2000–02; Hd, Financial Mgt, Norfolk CC, 2003–07. Mem., Great Easton Parish Council, 2016– (Vice Chm., 2016–). *Recreations:* walking, travelling, tennis, gardening, ski-ing, sailing. *Address:* 2 Ford Bank, Great Easton, Market Harborough LE16 8SL. *T:* (01536) 772504. *E:* Paulbrittain905@gmail.com.

BRITTAN OF SPENNITHORNE, Lady; Diana Brittan, DBE 2004 (CBE 1995); Chairman: The Connection at St Martin's, 2005–16 (Trustee, 2005–16); Independent Age, 2009–17; b 14 Oct. 1940; d of Leslie Howell Clemetson and Elizabeth Agnes Clemetson (née Leonard); m 1st, 1965, Dr Richard Peterson (marr. diss. 1979); two d; 2nd, 1980, Leon Brittan (Baron Brittan of Spennithorne, PC, QC) (d 2015). *Educ:* Westonbirt Sch., Tetbury. Man. Editor, Eibis Internat., London, 1977–88. Deputy Chairman: HFEA, 1990–97; EOC, 1994–96 (Comr, 1989–94); Mem., Lord Chancellor's Adv. Cttee on Legal Educn and Conduct, 1997–99. Chairman: Rathbone Training, 1991–2002; Nat. Lottery Charities Bd, later Community Fund, 1999–2004; Nat. Family Mediation, 2001–07; Trustee: Action on Addiction, 1993–98; Runnymede Trust, 1995–2006 (Chm., 1998–99); Open Univ. Foundn, 1996–2000; Multiple Birth Foundn, 1998–2001; Carnegie UK Trust, 2009– (Dep. Chm., 2018–); Chm., Carnegie Commn for Rural Community Develt, 2006–07 (Vice-Chm., 2004–06); President: Townswomen's Guild, 1996–; Nat. Assoc. of Connexions Partnerships, 2005–08. Mem., Bd of Mgt, British Sch. of Brussels, 1989–99. JP City of London, 1984–2010. Distinguished Associate, Darwin Coll., Cambridge, 1998. *Recreations:* botany, travel, cinema, cards, walking.

BRITTAN, Sir Samuel, Kt 1993; columnist, Financial Times, 1966–2014 (Assistant Editor, 1978–95); b 29 Dec. 1933; s of late Joseph Brittan, MD, and Rebecca Brittan (née Lipetz). *Educ:* Kilburn Grammar Sch.; Jesus Coll., Cambridge (Hon. Fellow, 1988). 1st Class in Economics, 1955; MA Cantab. Various posts in Financial Times, 1955–61; Economics Editor, Observer, 1961–64; Adviser, DEA, 1965. Fellow, Nuffield Coll., Oxford, 1973–74, Vis. Fellow, 1974–82; Vis. Prof. of Economics, Chicago Law Sch., 1978; Hon. Prof. of Politics, Warwick Univ., 1987–92. Mem., Peacock Cttee on Financing the BBC, 1985–86. Pres., David Hume Soc., 1996–99. Hon. DLitt Heriot-Watt, 1985; DU Essex, 1994. Financial Journalist of the Year Award 1971; George Orwell Prize (for political journalism), 1980; Ludwig Erhard Prize (for economic writing), 1988. Chevalier de la Légion d'Honneur, 1993. *Publications:* The Treasury under the Tories, 1964, rev. edn Steering the Economy, 1969, 1971; Left or Right: The Bogus Dilemma, 1968; The Price of Economic Freedom, 1970; Capitalism and the Permissive Society, 1973, rev. edn as A Restatement of Economic Liberalism, 1988; Is There an Economic Consensus?, 1973; (with P. Lilley) The Delusion of Incomes Policy, 1977; The Economic Consequences of Democracy, 1977; How to End the Monetarist Controversy, 1981; The Role and Limits of Government, 1983; Capitalism with a Human Face, 1995; Essays: Moral, Political and Economic, 1998; Against the Flow, 2005; articles in various jls.

BRITTIN, Matthew John; President, Europe, Middle East and Africa, Google, since 2014; b Walton-on-Thames, 1 Dec. 1968; s of Sid and Shirley Brittin; m 1995, Kate Betts; two s. *Educ:* Hampton Sch.; Robinson Coll., Cambridge (BA 1989); London Business Sch. (MBA Dist. 1997). Chartered Surveyor, Connell Wilson, 1989–95; Consultant, McKinsey & Co. Inc., 1997–2004; Commercial Dir and Digital Dir, Trinity Mirror, 2004–06; Country Dir, 2007–09, Man. Dir, 2009–11, Google UK and Ireland; Vice Pres., Northern and Central Europe, Google, 2011–14. Non-exec. Dir, J. Sainsbury plc, 2011–. Trustee: Media Trust, 2010–; Climate Gp, 2010–16. Chm., Cambridge Univ. Boat Club, 1990–95. Steward, Henley Royal Regatta, 2014–. *Recreations:* former Member of GB Olympic and World Rowing Team (Silver Medal, 1985, Bronze Medal, 1986, World Championship), international dinghy sailing, now Masters' Rowing, cycling and attempting to keep up with teenage sons. *Address:* Google, 1 St Giles High Street, WC2H 8AG.

BRITTON, Alison Claire, OBE 1990; ceramic artist, writer and curator, since 1973; tutor, 1984–2017, and Senior Tutor, 1998–2017, Royal College of Art (Research Coordinator, 2005–15); b 4 May 1948; d of Prof. James Nimmo Britton and Jessie Muriel Britton (née

Robertson); two d. *Educ:* N London Collegiate Sch.; Leeds Coll. of Art; Central Sch. of Art and Design (DipAD); Royal Coll. of Art (MA 1973). FRCA 1990. Solo exhibitions: Crafts Council, 1979; Miharudo Gall., Tokyo, 1985; Contemp. Applied Arts, 1987, 1990; Craft Centre Gall., Sydney, 1988; Marianne Heller Galerie, Sandhausen, Germany, 1995; Australian tour, 1996; Barrett Marsden Gall., later Marsden Woo Gall., London, 1998, 2000, 2003, 2005, 2007, 2009, 2012, 2014, 2018; Crafts Study Centre, Univ. of Creative Arts, Farnham, 2012; Galleri Format, Oslo, 2017; retrospective exhibn (tour), 1990–91; Alison Britton Content and Form (retrospective), V&A Mus., 2016; Guest artist, Shigaraki Cultural Ceramic Park, Japan, 2010; dual exhibn (with Misha Stroj) Stereo Exchange, Copenhagen, 2018; gp exhibn, Contenu: Contained, Musée Ariana, Geneva, 2018. Work in internat. public and private collections. Co-curator, The Raw and the Cooked, MOMA, Oxford and tour, 1993. Peter Dormer Meml Lecture, RCA, 2016. Member: Craft Acquisitions Panel, Contemp. Arts Soc., 2016–; Peter Dormer Meml Lect. Cttee, 2015–. Trustee, Crafts Study Centre, Univ. of Creative Arts, Farnham, 2006– (Chair, 2015–). Hon. MA, Univ. Coll. for the Creative Arts, 2007; Hon. Fellow, Univ. of the Arts, London, 2008. *Publications:* Seeing Things: collected writing on art, craft and design, 2013; essays and reviews in art and craft magazines and books, UK and internat. *Recreations:* film, walking, novels. *Address:* c/o Marsden Woo Gallery, 229 Ebury Street, Belgravia, SW1W 8UT. *T:* (020) 7336 6396.
See also C. M. Britton.

**BRITTON, Andrew James Christie;** Chairman, Finance Committee, Archbishops' Council, 2007–13; b 1 Dec. 1940; s of late Prof. Karl William Britton and Sheila Margaret Christie; m 1963, Pamela Anne, d of His Honour Edward Sutcliffe, QC; three d. *Educ:* Royal Grammar Sch., Newcastle upon Tyne; Oriel Coll., Oxford (BA); LSE (MSc). Joined HM Treasury as Cadet Economist, 1966; Econ. Asst, 1968; Econ. Adviser, 1970; Senior Economic Adviser: DHSS, 1973; HM Treasury, 1975; London Business Sch., 1978–79; Under Sec., HM Treasury, 1980–82; Dir, NIESR, 1982–95 (Hon. Fellow, 2016). Mem., Treasury Panel of Ind. Forecasters, 1993–95. Vis. Prof., Univ. of Bath, 1998–2001. Reader, Dio. of Southwark, 1986–; Lay Canon, Southwark Cathedral, 2004–16. Mem., Bd of Finance, Dio. of Southwark, 1998–2007 (Vice Chm., 1999–2000; Chm., 2000–07). Exec. Sec., Churches' Enquiry into Unemployment and the Future of Work, 1995–97. *Publications:* (ed) Employment, Output and Inflation, 1983; The Trade Cycle in Britain, 1986; (ed) Policymaking with Macroeconomic Models, 1989; Macroeconomic Policy in Britain 1974–87, 1991; Monetary Regimes of the Twentieth Century, 2001; (jtly) Economic Theory and Christian Belief, 2003. *Address:* 2 Shabden Park, High Road, Chipstead, Surrey CR5 3SF.

**BRITTON, Prof. Celia Margaret,** PhD; FBA 2000; Professor of French, University College London, 2003–11, now Emeritus; b 20 March 1946; d of Prof. James Nimmo Britton and Jessie Muriel Britton. *Educ:* New Hall, Cambridge (MA Mod. and Medieval Langs 1969; Postgrad. Dip. Linguistics 1970); Univ. of Essex (PhD Literary Stylistics 1973). Temp. Lectr in French, KCL, 1972–74; Lectr in French Studies, Univ. of Reading, 1974–91; Carnegie Prof. of French, Univ. of Aberdeen, 1991–2002. Chair, RAE French Panel, 2001. Pres., Soc. for French Studies, 1996–98. Chevalier, Ordre des Palmes Académiques (France), 2003. *Publications:* Claude Simon: writing the visible, 1987; The Nouveau Roman: fiction, theory and politics, 1992; Edouard Glissant and Postcolonial Theory, 1999; Race and the Unconscious, 2002; The Sense of Community in French Caribbean Fiction, 2008; Language and Literary Form in French Caribbean Writing, 2014; Perspectives on Culture and Politics in the French Antilles, 2018; numerous articles on French and Francophone literature and film. *Recreations:* travel, cinema, cookery, photography.
See also A. C. Britton.

**BRITTON, Prof. John Richard,** CBE 2013; MD; FRCP; Professor of Epidemiology, University of Nottingham, since 2000; Hon. Consultant in Respiratory Medicine, Nottingham City Hospital, since 1990; b Saltburn-by-Sea, Yorks, 24 Jan. 1955; s of Douglas and Dorothy Britton; m 1980, Ros Hill; two s two d (and one d decd). *Educ:* Watford Grammar Sch.; Guy's Hosp. Med. Sch., Univ. of London (BSc Pharmacol. 1975; MB BS 1978; MD 1987; MSc Epidemiol. 1988). MRCP 1981, FRCP 1994; FFPH 2003. Jun. Hse Officer, then SHO, Guy's and London Chest Hosp., 1978–82; Med. Registrar, Royal S Hants Hosp., then Basingstoke Gen. Hosp., 1982–84; Res. Fellow, then Lectr, City Hosp., Nottingham, 1984–90; Sen. Lectr in Respiratory Medicine, 1990–98, Prof. of Respiratory Medicine, 1998–2000, Univ. of Nottingham. *Publications:* (ed) ABC of smoking cessation, 2004; contrib. papers to learned jls; editor of RCP reports on smoking prevention. *Recreations:* time with family, golf, watching Nottingham Forest, cycling. *Address:* Division of Epidemiology and Public Health, University of Nottingham Clinical Sciences Building, City Hospital, Nottingham NG5 1PB. *T:* (0115) 823 1708. *E:* j.britton@outlook.com.

**BRITTON, John William;** independent consultant, since 1993; b 13 Dec. 1936; s of John Ferguson and Dinah Britton; m 1961, Maisie Rubython; one s one d. *Educ:* Bedlington Grammar Sch.; Bristol Univ. (BScEng 1st Cl. Hons). Royal Aircraft Establishment, Bedford, 1959–83: Hd, Flight Res. Div., 1978–80; Chief Supt and Hd, Flight Systems Bedford Dept, 1981–83; RCDS 1984; Dir, Avionic Equipment and Systems, MoD PE, 1985–86; Science and Technology Assessment Office, Cabinet Office, 1987; Dir Gen. Aircraft 3, MoD PE, 1987–90; Asst Chief Scientific Advr (Projects), MoD, 1990–92, retd. *Recreations:* wine, painting, motor racing (watching), gardening (especially dahlias and fuchsias). *Address:* 6 The Drive, Sharnbrook, Bedford MK44 1HU.

**BRITTON, Mark Gordon,** MD; FRCP; Consultant Physician in respiratory medicine, Ashford and St Peter's Hospitals NHS Trust (formerly St Peter's Hospital, Chertsey), 1983–2011; b 23 Nov. 1946; s of late Capt. Gordon Berry Cowley Britton, CBE and Vera Britton (née Hyman); m 1972, Gillian Vaughan Davies; three s. *Educ:* Ipswich Sch.; Med. Coll. of St Bartholomew's Hosp., London; London Univ. (MB BS 1970, MSc 1981, MD 1982). DIH 1981; FRCP 1990. Surg. Lt Comdr, RNR, 1970–90. Hon. Consultant, King Edward VII's Hosp., London, 1980–2014; Hon. Consultant and Sen. Lectr, St George's Hosp., London, 1983–2011; Med. Dir, St Peter's Hosp. NHS Trust, 1994–97; Hon. Sen. Lectr, Imperial Coll., London, 2001–11. Vis. Prof., Faculty of Health and Med. Scis (formerly Faculty of Medicine), 2006–11, Chm., Adv. Council, Postgraduate Med. Sch., 2008–11. Univ. of Surrey. Member: Med. Reference Panel (Coal Bd), DTI, 2000–11; Industrial Injuries Adv. Council, 2003–13. Chm., Bd of Trustees, 1999–2005, Mem. Council, 2005–08, Vice Pres., 2006–, British Lung Foundn. Trustee: Nat. Confidential Enquiry into Patient Outcome and Death, 2005–13; Whiteley Homes Trust, 2012–18. Freeman, City of London, 1983; Mem., Soc. of Apothecaries, 1979–. Master, Fountain Club, 2010. *Publications:* contrib. various chapters and papers in learned jls on mgt and treatment of asthma, chronic obstructive airways disease and asbestos related diseases. *Recreations:* Rugby football, golf, sailing, gardening, British stamps, Pembrokeshire cottage. *Address:* Woodham House, 92 Ashley Road, Walton-on-Thames, Surrey KT12 1HP. *T:* (01932) 225472, 07850 428748. *E:* markbritton@btinternet.com. *Clubs:* Burhill Golf; Newport Links Golf; New Zealand Golf.

**BRITTON, Sir Paul (John James),** Kt 2010; CB 2001; CVO 2014; Head, Economic and Domestic Affairs Secretariat, 2001–09, and Director General, Domestic Policy and Strategy Group, 2006–09, Cabinet Office; Appointments Secretary to the Prime Minister for senior ecclesiastical appointments, 2008–14; b 17 April 1949; s of Leonard Britton and Maureen Britton; m 1972, Pauline Bruce; one s one d. *Educ:* Clifton Coll.; Magdalene Coll., Cambridge (BA 1971; MA 1974). Department of the Environment: Admin. trainee, 1971–75; Private Sec. to Second Perm. Sec., 1975–77; Principal, 1977; Dept of Transport, 1979–81; DoE, 1981–97: Private Sec. to Minister for Housing and Construction, 1983–84; Asst Sec., 1984; Grade 4, 1991; Dir of Local Govt Finance Policy, 1991–96; Under Sec., 1992; Dir, Envmt Protection Strategy, 1996–97; Dep. Hd, Constitution Secretariat, 1997–98, Dep. Head, Econ. and Domestic Affairs Secretariat, 1998–2001, Cabinet Office; Dir, Town and Country Planning, DTLR, 2001. Member: Crown Nominations Commn, 2008–14; Exec. Cttee, Better Govt Initiative, 2009–. Trustee: Nat. Assoc. for Mental Health, 2010–16 (Vice Chm., 2013–16); Friends of Friendless Churches, 2012–; Nat. Churches Trust, 2015–; Friends of Kent Churches, 2019; Chm., Trustees, Coll. of St Barnabas, Lingfield, 2012–; Vice Chm., Cathedrals Fabric Commn for England, 2016–. Gov., Clifton Coll., 2012–. *Recreations:* architectural history, photography, topography. *Address:* 54 Dry Hill Park Road, Tonbridge, Kent TN10 3BX. *T:* (01732) 365794.

**BRITZ, Lewis;** Executive Councillor, Electrical, Electronic, Telecommunication & Plumbing Union, 1984–95; Member, Industrial Tribunals, 1990–2003; b 7 Jan. 1933; s of Alfred and Hetty Britz; m 1960, Hadassah Rosenberg; four d. *Educ:* Hackney Downs Grammar Sch.; Acton Technical Coll. (OND Elec. Engrg); Nottingham Univ. (BSc (Hons) Engrg); Birkbeck Coll., London Univ. (BA Hons Eng 2002). Head of Research, 1967–71, Nat. Officer, 1971–83, EETPU. Director: LEB, 1977–87; British Internat. Helicopters, 1987–92; Esca Services, 1990–; Chm., Blue Sky Pensions Co. (formerly JIB Pension Scheme Trustee Co. Ltd), 1997–. Mem., Monopolies and Mergers Commn, 1986–92. Sat in Restrictive Practices Court, 1989. *Recreation:* philately. *Address:* 30 Braemar Gardens, West Wickham, Kent BR4 0JW. *T:* (020) 8777 5986.

**BRIXWORTH, Bishop Suffragan of,** since 2011; **Rt Rev. John Edward Holbrook;** b 14 June 1962; s of Edward George Holbrook and Ann Holbrook; m 1985, Elizabeth Mighall; one s one d. *Educ:* Bristol Cathedral Sch.; St Peter's Coll., Oxford (BA 1983; MA 1987); Ridley Hall, Cambridge. Ordained deacon, 1986, priest, 1987; Assistant Curate: St Mary's, Barnes, 1986–89; St Mary's, Bletchley, 1989–93; Vicar, St Mary's, Adderbury, 1993–2002; Rural Dean, Deddington, 2000–02; Rector, Wimborne Minster, 2002–11; Priest-in-charge: St Mary and St Cuthberga and All Saints, Witchampton, 2002–11; St Wolfrida, Horton, 2006–11; Rural Dean, Wimborne, 2004–11; Acting Bishop of Leicester, 2015–16. Chaplain, South and East Dorset PCT, 2002–11; Canon and Preb., Salisbury Cathedral, 2006–11; Canon, Peterborough Cathedral, 2011–. *Address:* Orchard Acre, 11 North Street, Mears Ashby, Northampton NN6 0DW. *T:* (01604) 810721. *E:* bishop.brixworth@peterborough-diocese.org.uk.

**BROAD, Rev. Canon Hugh Duncan;** Permission to officiate: Diocese of Europe, since 2013; Diocese of Gloucester, since 2013; Priest-in-charge, Costa Almeria and Costa Calida, Spain, 2003–13; Area Dean, Gibraltar, 2008–13; b 28 Oct. 1937; s of Horace Edward Broad and Lucy Broad; m 1988, Jacqueline Lissaman; two d. *Educ:* Shropshire Inst. of Agriculture; Bernard Gilpin Soc., Durham Univ.; Lichfield Theol Coll.; Hereford Coll. of Education. Curate, Holy Trinity, Hereford, 1967–72; Asst Master, Bishop of Hereford's Bluecoat Sch., 1972–74; Curate, St Peter and St Paul, Fareham, 1974–76; Vicar, All Saints with St Barnabas, Hereford, 1976–90; Rector, Matson, 1990–97; Vicar, St George, Gloucester and St Margaret, Whaddon, 1997–2003. Chaplain: Victoria Eye Hosp., Hereford, 1976–90; Selwyn Sch., Gloucester, 1990–97. Member: Gen. Synod, C of E, 1995–2003; Crown Appts Commn, 1997–2003. Hon. Canon: Gloucester Cathedral, 2002–03, now Emeritus; Gibraltar Cathedral, 2013. *Recreations:* theatre, music, cricket. *Address:* 44 Vensfield Road, Quedgeley, Gloucester GL2 4FX. *T:* (01452) 541078. *E:* hugh.broad@yahoo.co.uk.

**BROADBENT, Adam Humphrey Charles;** Chairman, Emap plc, 2001–06; b 21 June 1936; s of Harold and Celia Broadbent; m 1963, Sara Peregrine (née Reade); four s. *Educ:* Stonyhurst Coll.; Magdalen Coll., Oxford (MA); London Sch. of Economics (MSc Econ); Queen Mary, Univ. of London (MA 2008). 2nd Lieut, 1st RTR, 1957–59. Bank of London and South America, 1960–63; COI, 1963–66; NIESR, 1966–68; Schroders plc, 1968–96: Dir, J. Henry Schroder Wagg & Co. Ltd, 1984–96; Dir, 1990–96; Group Managing Director: Corporate Finance, 1990–96; Investment Banking, 1994–96; Chm., Arcadia Gp plc, 1998–2002. Director: Carclo, 1997–2003; REL Consultancy Gp, 1997–2005; Capital One Bank (Europe), 2000–10. Chm., Dover Harbour Bd, 1996–2000. Gov., NIESR, 2002–. Dir, Acad. of Ancient Music, 2003–12. *Clubs:* Brooks's, Boodle's.
See also B. R. H. Broadbent.

**BROADBENT, Sir Andrew George,** 5th Bt *cr* 1893, of Brook Street, co. London and Longwood, co. Yorkshire; b 26 Jan. 1963; s of Sqn Ldr Sir George Broadbent, AFC, RAF, 4th Bt and Valerie Anne, o d of Cecil Frank Ward; S father, 1992, but his name does not appear on the Official Roll of the Baronetage. *Educ:* Oakley Hall Prep. Sch., Cirencester; Monkton Combe Sch.; RMA, Sandhurst. Capt., PWO Regt Yorks, 1984; retd 1994. *Recreations:* music, reading, walking, following sport. *Heir:* uncle Robert John Dendy Broadbent, b 4 Nov. 1938.

**BROADBENT, Benjamin Robert Hamond,** PhD; a Deputy Governor, Bank of England, since 2014 (Member: Monetary Policy Committee, since 2011; Financial Policy Cttee, since 2014; Prudential Regulation Committee, since 2017); b Morston, Norfolk, 1 Feb. 1965; s of Adam Humphrey Charles Broadbent, qv; one s. *Educ:* St Paul's Sch., London; Ecole Normale Supérieure de la Musique, Paris (Dip. Performance); Trinity Hall, Cambridge (BA 1988); Harvard Univ. (PhD 1997). Econ. Advr, HM Treasury, 1988–91, 1993–96; Asst Prof., Columbia Univ., 1997–2000; Sen. Economist, Goldman Sachs, 2000–11. *Recreations:* piano, violin. *Address:* Bank of England, Threadneedle Street, EC2R 8AH.

**BROADBENT, Christopher Joseph St George B.;** see Bowers-Broadbent.

**BROADBENT, James, (Jim);** actor, since 1972; b Lincoln, 24 May 1949; s of late Roy Broadbent and Dee (née Findlay); m 1987, Anastasia Lewis; two step s. *Educ:* Leighton Park Sch., Reading; Hammersmith Coll. of Art; LAMDA. Joined Nat. Theatre of Brent, 1983, appeared in: The Messiah, 1983; (jt writer) The Complete Guide to Sex, 1984; (jt writer) The Greatest Story Ever Told, 1987; Founder Member, Science Fiction Theatre of Liverpool: Illuminatus!, 1976; The Warp, 1978; other theatre includes: Hampstead Theatre: Ecstasy, 1979; Goose Pimples, 1980; Royal Shakespeare Co.: Our Friends in the North, Clay, 1981; National Theatre: The Government Inspector, 1984; A Place with the Pigs, 1988; The Pillowman, 2003; Theatre of Blood, 2005; Royal Court: Kafka's Dick, 1986; The Recruiting Officer, Our Country's Good, 1988; Old Vic: A Flea in Her Ear, 1989; Donmar: Habeas Corpus, 1996; Noel Coward Theatre: A Christmas Carol, 2015; A Very Very Very Dark Matter, Bridge Th., 2018; films include: The Time Bandits, 1981; Brazil, 1985; The Good Father, 1986; Life is Sweet, Enchanted April, 1991; A Sense of History (also writer), The Crying Game, 1992; Widow's Peak, 1993; Princess Caraboo, Bullets over Broadway, Wide Eyed and Legless, 1994; Richard III, 1995; The Borrowers, 1997; The

Avengers, Little Voice, 1998; Topsy-Turvy, 1999 (Best Actor, Venice Film Fest., Evening Standard British Film Awards, London Film Critics' Circle, 2001); Bridget Jones's Diary, Moulin Rouge, 2001 (Best Supporting Actor, Nat. Bd of Review, LA Film Critics Assoc., 2001, BAFTA, 2002); Iris, 2002 (Best Supporting Actor, Nat. Bd of Review, LA Film Critics Assoc., 2001, Golden Globe, Acad. Award, 2002); Gangs of New York, Nicholas Nickleby, Bright Young Things, 2003; Around the World in 80 Days, Bridget Jones: The Edge of Reason, Vera Drake, 2004; Vanity Fair, The Chronicles of Narnia: The Lion the Witch and the Wardrobe, 2005; Art School Confidential, 2006; And When Did You Last See Your Father?, Hot Fuzz, Inkheart, 2007; The Young Victoria, The Damned United, Harry Potter and the Half-Blood Prince, 2009; Another Year, 2010; Harry Potter and the Deathly Hallows, Pt 2, 2011; The Iron Lady, 2012; Cloud Atlas, Filth, Le Weekend, Closed Circuit, 2013; Paddington, Get Santa, 2014; Brooklyn, 2015; Bridget Jones's Baby, 2016; The Sense of an Ending, Paddington 2, 2017; King of Thieves, Black '47, 2018; *television series* include: Victoria Wood as Seen on TV; Blackadder; Only Fools and Horses; Gone to the Dogs; Gone to Seed; The Peter Principle; The Gathering Storm, 2002; The Street, 2006, 2007 (Emmy Award, 2007); Longford, 2006 (Best Actor, BAFTA, 2007; Golden Globe Award, 2008); Any Human Heart, 2010; The Great Train Robbery, 2013; London Spy, 2015; War and Peace, 2016; Game of Thrones, 2017; King Lear, 2018. *Publications:* Dull Margaret, 2018. *Recreations:* walking, cooking, golf, wood carving, cinema, reading. *Address:* c/o Independent Talent Group Ltd, 40 Whitfield Street, W1T 2RH. *T:* (020) 7636 6565. *Club:* Two Brydges.

**BROADBENT, (John) Michael;** wine writer; Senior Consultant, Christie's Wine Department, since 1993; *b* 2 May 1927; *s* of late John Fred Broadbent and Hilary Louise Broadbent; *m* 1954, Daphne Joste (*d* 2015); one *s* one *d*; *m* 2019, Valerie Smallwood. *Educ:* Rishworth Sch., Yorks; Bartlett Sch. of Architecture, UCL (Cert. in Architecture 1952). Commissioned RA, 1945–48 (Nat. Service). Trainee, Laytons Wine Merchants, 1952–53; Saccone & Speed, 1953–55; John Harvey & Sons, Bristol, 1955–66 (Dir, 1963); Head, Wine Dept, Christie's, 1966–92. Chm., Christie's S Kensington, 1978–79; Director: Christie Manson & Woods, 1967–99; Christie's Fine Art Ltd, 1998–2001; Christie's Internat. (UK) Ltd, 2001–07. Wine Trade Art Society: Founder Mem., 1954; Chm., 1972–2006; Institute of Masters of Wine: MW 1960; Mem. Council, 1966–78; Chm., 1971–72. Distillers' Company: Liveryman, 1964–80; Mem. Council, 1981–90; Master, 1990–91; Vintners' Company: Freeman *hc*, 2001; Liveryman, 2005–. International Wine and Food Society: Life Mem.; Mem. Council, 1969–92; Internat. Pres., 1985–92; Gold Medal, 1989; Confrérie des Chevaliers du Tastevin: Mem., 1973; Officier-Commandeur, 1993; Grand Officier, 2006; Chm., Wine and Spirit Benevolent Soc., 1991–92. Hon. Pres., Wine and Spirit Educn Trust, 2007–09. Numerous awards from wine socs and other instns. Chevalier, l'Ordre National du Mérite, 1979; La Médaille de la Ville de Paris, Echelon Vermeil, 1989; Wine Spectator Annual Lifetime Achievement Award, 1991; Man of the Year, Decanter magazine, 1993; Glenfiddich Wine Writer of the Year, 2001. *Publications:* Wine Tasting, 1st edn 1968 (numerous foreign edns); The Great Vintage Wine Book, 1980 (foreign edns); Pocket Guide to Wine Tasting, 1988; The Great Vintage Wine Book II, 1991; Pocket Guide to Wine Vintages, 1992; The Bordeaux Atlas, 1997; Vintage Wine, 2003 (also German edn; four top internat. awards); Wine Tasting, 2003; Wine Vintages, 2003; Michael Broadbent's Pocket Vintage Wine Companion, 2007; lead monthly contributor to Decanter, 1978–2014. *Recreations:* piano, painting. *Address:* 87 Rosebank, Holyport Road, SW6 6LJ. *T:* (020) 7381 9283. *Clubs:* Brooks's, Saintsbury.

*See also E. L. Arbuthnot.*

**BROADBENT, Miles Anthony Le Messurier;** Chairman, The Miles Partnership, 1996–2007; *b* 1936; *m* 1980, Robin Anne Beveridge (*d* 2011); two *s* two *d*. *Educ:* Shrewsbury Sch.; Magdalene Coll., Cambridge Univ. (MA); Harvard Business Sch. (MBA). Non-exec. Dir, Roux Waterside Inn Ltd, 1972–. Chm., Magdalene Coll. Assoc., 2004–14; Trustee, Nat. Playing Fields Assoc., 2008–14. *Recreations:* tennis, golf. *Address:* Brackendene, Golf Club Road, St George's Hill, Weybridge, Surrey KT13 0NJ. *T:* (01932) 844159. *Clubs:* St George's Hill Tennis; St George's Hill Golf, Royal Cape Golf (Cape Town).

**BROADBENT, Rt Rev. Peter Alan;** *see* Willesden, Area Bishop of.

**BROADBENT, Sir Richard (John),** KCB 2003; Chairman, Tesco plc, 2011–14; *b* 22 April 1953; *s* of John Barclay Broadbent and Faith Joan Laurie Broadbent (*née* Fisher); *m* 2007, Jill (*née* McLoughlin). *Educ:* Queen Mary Coll., Univ. of London (BSc); Univ. of Manchester (MA). HM Treasury, 1975–86; Harkness Fellow, Stanford Business Sch., 1983–84; Schroders plc, 1986–99: Head, European Corporate Finance, 1995–99; Gp Man. Dir, Corporate Finance, and Mem., Gp Exec. Cttee, 1998–99; Chm., HM Customs and Excise, 2000–03; Barclays plc: Dir, 2003–11; Sen. Ind. Dir, 2005–11; Dep. Chm., 2010–11; Chm., Arriva plc, 2004–10. Trustee, Relate, 2011–14. Partner, Centre for Compassionate Communication, 2009–. MCSI (MSI 1995).

**BROADBENT, Simon Hope;** Visiting Fellow, National Institute of Economic and Social Research, 1994–2013; *b* 4 June 1942; *s* of late Edmund Urquhart Broadbent, CBE and Doris Hope; *m* 1966, Margaret Ann Taylor; two *s* one *d*. *Educ:* University College School; Hatfield College, Durham (BA); Magdalen College, Oxford (BPhil). Malawi Civil Service, 1964; FCO, 1971; UK Treasury and Supply delegn, Washington, 1974; seconded to Bank of England, 1977; Joint Head, Economists Dept, FCO, 1978; Centre for Econ. Policy Res., and Graduate Inst. of Internat. Studies, Geneva, 1984. Hd of Econ. Advrs, later Chief Econ. Advr, FCO, 1984–93. Chm., Friends of Malawi Assoc., 2008–; Trustee, Anglo-German Foundn, 1994–2010. *Recreation:* boating. *Address:* Manor House, Dorchester-on-Thames, Oxon OX10 7HZ. *T:* (01865) 340101.

**BROADBERRY, Prof. Stephen Noel,** DPhil; FBA 2016; Professor of Economic History, University of Oxford, since 2015; Fellow, Nuffield College, Oxford, since 2015; *b* Cambridge, 8 Dec. 1956; *s* of Noel Broadberry and Mabel Broadberry; one *s* one *d*. *Educ:* King Edward VI Sch., Southampton; Univ. of Warwick (BA Hons); Univ. of Oxford (MPhil; DPhil 1982). Jun. Res. Fellow, Queen's Coll., Oxford, 1981–83; Lectr, University Coll., Cardiff, 1983–86; Asst Prof., Univ. of British Columbia, 1986–87; University of Warwick: Lectr, 1987–92; Sen. Lectr, 1992–95; Prof. of Econ. Hist., 1995–2011; Prof. of Econ. Hist., LSE, 2011–15. President: Eur. Histl Econs Soc., 2011–13; Econ. Hist. Soc., 2016–19. Editor: Eur. Rev. of Econ. Hist., 1999–2002; Econ. Hist. Rev., 2010–15. *Publications:* The British Economy Between the Wars: a macroeconomic survey, 1986; The Productivity Race: British manufacturing in international perspective, 1850–1990, 1997; Market Services and the Productivity Race, 1850–2000: Britain in international perspective, 2006; (ed with Kevin O'Rourke) The Cambridge Economic History of Modern Europe, 2 vols, 2010; (jtly) British Economic Growth, 1270–1870, 2015. *Recreations:* organ and piano. *Address:* Nuffield College, Oxford OX1 1NF. *T:* (01865) 288688. *E:* stephen.broadberry@nuffield.ox.ac.uk.

**BROADBRIDGE,** family name of **Baron Broadbridge**.

**BROADBRIDGE,** 4th Baron *cr* 1945, of Brighton, co. Sussex; **Martin Hugh Broadbridge;** Bt 1937; *b* 29 Nov. 1929; *s* of Hon. Hugh Broadbridge and Marjorie Broadbridge; *S* cousin, 2000; *m* 1st, 1954, Norma Sheffield (marr. diss. 1967); one *s* one *d*; 2nd, 1968, Elizabeth Trotman (*d* 2007). *Educ:* St George's Coll., Weybridge; Univ. of Birmingham (BSc 1954). Dist Officer, Northern Nigeria, HMOCS, 1954–63; Dir and Manager, specialist road surface treatments co., 1963–92; consultant, 1992–95. *Recreations:* game fishing, natural history. *Heir:* s Air Vice-Marshal the Hon. Richard John Martin Broadbridge, *qv*. *Address:* 23A Westfield Road, Barton-on-Humber, North Lincolnshire DN18 5AA. *T:* (01652) 632895.

**BROADBRIDGE, Air Vice-Marshal the Hon. Richard John Martin,** CB 2018; FRAeS; FRCGP; Director Healthcare Delivery and Training, Defence Medical Services, 2014–18 (Acting Surgeon General, 2017); *b* Jos, Nigeria, 20 Jan. 1959; *s* and heir of 4th Baron Broadbridge, *qv*; *m* 1980, Jacqueline Roberts; one *s* one *d*. *Educ:* Moseley Sch.; Middlesex Hosp. Med. Sch. (MB BS 1982); Univ. of Bath Sch. of Mgt (MBA). FRAeS 2003; FRCGP 2014. ACOS Health, HQ Air Comd, 2009–11; Hd of Healthcare, Defence Med. Services, 2011–13; Hd, Strategy and Integration, Defence Primary Healthcare, 2013–14. QHS 2009–18. FCMI 2006. *Recreations:* golf, woodturning, cycling, woodland management. *Address:* The Long Barn, Alstone, Tewkesbury, Glos GL20 8JD.

**BROADFOOT, Prof. Patricia Mary,** CBE 2006; DSc, PhD; Professor of Education, University of Bristol, 2010–14, now Emerita; *b* 13 July 1949; *d* of late Norman John Cole, VRD, sometime MP and Margaret Grace Cole (*née* Potter); *m* 1971, John Ledingham Broadfoot (marr. diss. 1977); *m* 1980, David Charles Rockey, *yr s* of Prof. Kenneth Rockey; two *s* one *d*. *Educ:* Queen Elizabeth's Girls' Grammar Sch., Barnet; Leeds Univ. (BA 1970); Edinburgh Univ. (MEd 1977); Open Univ. (PhD 1984); PGCE London 1971; DSc Univ. of Bristol 2000. Teacher, Wolmer's Boys' Sch., Jamaica, 1971–73; Researcher, Scottish Council for Res. in Educn, 1973–77; Lectr and Sen. Lectr, Westhill Coll., Birmingham, 1977–81; University of Bristol: Lectr, 1981–90; Reader, 1990–91; Prof. of Educn, 1991–2006; Hd, Sch. of Educn, 1993–97; Dean of Social Scis, 1999–2002; Pro-Vice-Chancellor, 2002–05, Sen. Pro-Vice-Chancellor, 2005–06; Vice-Chancellor, Univ. of Gloucestershire, 2006–10. Visiting Scholar: Macquarie Univ., Aust., 1987; Univ. of Western Sydney, 1992; Vis. Prof., Univ. of Winchester, 2010–13. Member: Conseil Scientifique de l'Institut Nat. de Recherche Pedagogique, 1998–99; Council, ESRC, 2001–06 (Mem., Res. Grants Bd, 1998–99; Chair, Internat. Cttee, 2002–03; Chair, Research Resources Bd, 2003–06; Chm., Gov. Bd, UK Household Longitudinal Study, 2007–15); UUK/SCOP Burgess Steering Gp, 2005–10; Quality Assessment Learning and Teaching Cttee, HEFCE, 2005–10; DEFRA and DECC Social Sci. Expert Panel, 2012–15; Chair: Adv. Bd, What Works, Paul Hamlyn Foundn/HEFCE nat. project, 2008–17; Pearson/Edexcel Expert Panel on Educnl Assessment, 2011–16. Director: HEA, 2007–09; UCEA, 2007–10; Mem. Bd, UUK, 2008–10; Acad. of Social Scis, 2015–18. Comr, Marmot Review on Health Inequalities, 2009–10. Member: Res. Adv. Bd, ETS, Princeton, USA, 2006–08; Adv. Bd, Cabot Inst. for Study of Envmtl Change, Bristol Univ., 2010–16; Chair, CPRE Glos, 2017–. Director: ViTaL Partnerships Professional Services Ltd, 2011–; Pathways to Learning, 2016– (Chm., 2016–). President: British Educnl Res. Assoc., 1987–88; British Assoc. for Internat. and Comparative Educn, 1997–98. Trustee: St Monica Trust, 2005–09; Lloyds (formerly Lloyds TSB) Foundn, 2011–18 (Vice-Chair, 2012–18). Founding Mem., Assessment Reform Gp, 1989–2003; FAcSS (Founding AcSS 1999) (Mem., Commn on Social Scis, 2001–03). Mem., Governance First, 2006–09. Mem., Adv. Panel, Leverhulme Trust, 2013–. Governor: Gloucestershire Coll., 2006–09; RAU (formerly RAC) Cirencester, 2010–18; Univ. of St Mark and St John Plymouth, 2014–17; Mem. Council, Dean Close Sch., 2007–11. Licensed Reader, C of E, 2014–. Mem., Gloucester Diocesan Synod, 2012–; Chair, Gloucester Diocesan Internat. Partnerships Gp, 2011–17; Reader and Mem., Bishop's Council, Dio. of Gloucester, 2015–. Hon. Canon, Gloucester Cath., 2007–12, now Emeritus. Mem. Court, Hon. Co. of Gloucestershire, 2009–11. Hon. DLitt Bristol, 2010. Editor: Comparative Education, 1993–2004; Assessment in Education, 1994–2002. *Publications:* Assessment, Schools and Society, 1979; (with J. D. Nisbet) The Impact of Research on Education, 1981; (with H. D. Black) Keeping Track of Teaching, 1982; (ed) Selection, Certification and Control, 1984, repr. 2018; (ed) Profiles and Records of Achievement, 1986; Introducing Profiling, 1987; (with M. Osborn) Perceptions of Teaching, 1993; (jtly) The Changing English Primary School, 1994; Education, Assessment and Society, 1996; (ed jtly) Learning from Comparing, 1999; (jtly) Promoting Quality in Learning, 2000; (jtly) What Teachers Do, 2000; (jtly) Assessment: what's in it for schools?, 2002; (jtly) A World of Difference, 2003; An Introduction to Assessment, 2007. *Recreations:* gardening, horse-riding, swimming, walking.

**BROADFOOT, Samantha Louise;** QC 2017; a Recorder, since 2018; *b* The Netherlands, 1972; *d* of Guy Broadfoot and Glen Broadfoot; *m* 2001, Martin Daniel Chamberlain (*see* Hon. Sir M. D. Chamberlain); one *s* two *d*. *Educ:* various schs across Europe; Univ. of Kent at Canterbury (LLB English and French Law); Univ. Pierre Mendes-France, Grenoble (Diplôme de Droit Français); Univ. of Exeter (LLM Eur. and Human Rights Law). Called to the Bar, Middle Temple, 1997. *Recreations:* frontwoman of a rock band, music, outdoor adventures with my family, hill walking, reading. *Address:* Landmark Chambers, 180 Fleet Street, EC4A 2HG. *T:* (020) 7430 1221. *E:* Sbroadfoot@ landmarkchambers.co.uk.

**BROADHURST, Rt Rev. Mgr John Charles;** Bishop Suffragan of Fulham, 1996–2010; *b* 20 July 1942; *s* of late Charles Harold Broadhurst and of Dorothy Sylvia (*née* Prince); *m* 1965, Judith Margaret Randell; two *s* two *d*. *Educ:* Owen's Sch., Islington; King's Coll., London (AKC 1965); St Boniface Coll., Warminster; STh Lambeth, 1982. Ordained deacon, 1966, priest, 1967; Asst Curate, St Michael-at-Bowes, 1966–70; Priest-in-charge, 1970–75, Vicar, 1975–85, St Augustine, Wembley Park; Team Rector, Wood Green, 1985–96. Area Dean: Brent, 1982–85; E Haringey, 1985–91; ordained RC priest, 2012; Prelate of Honour, 2012. Member: Gen. Synod of C of E, 1972–96 (Mem., Standing Cttee, 1988–96); ACC, 1991–96. Chm., Forward in Faith, 1992–2012; Vice-Chm., Church Union, 1997–2012. Hon. DD Nashotah House, Wisconsin, 2003. *Publications:* (ed and contrib.) Quo Vaditis, 1996; numerous contribs to jls. *Recreations:* gardening, history, travel. *Address:* 19 Spencelayh Close, Wellingborough NN8 4UU. *E:* frjohnbroadhurst@ btinternet.com.

**BROADHURST, Norman Neill,** FCA, FCT; Chairman, Chloride Group plc, 2001–10; *b* 19 Sept. 1941; *s* of Samuel Herbert and Ruth Broadhurst; *m* 1964, Kathleen Muriel Joyce; two *d*. *Educ:* Cheadle Hulme Sch. FCA 1975; FCT 1995. Divl Manager, Finance and Admin, China Light Power Co. Ltd, Hong Kong, 1981–86; Finance Dir, United Engineering Steels Ltd, Sheffield, 1986–90; Finance Dir, VSEL plc, Barrow, 1990–94; Finance Dir, Railtrack plc, 1994–2000. Chairman: Freightliner Ltd, 2001–08; Cattles plc, 2006–09 (non-exec. Dir, 2000–09; Dep. Chm., 2006); non-executive Director: Old Mutual, 1999–2008; United Utilities, 1999–2008; Taylor Woodrow, 2000–03; Tomkins, 2000–06. *Recreation:* golf. *Address:* Hobroyd, Pennybridge, Ulverston, Cumbria LA12 7TD. *T:* (01229) 861226. *E:* norman.hobroyd@btinternet.com. *Club:* Ulverston Golf.

**BROADHURST, Robin Shedden,** CVO 2010; CBE 2003; FRICS; non-executive Chairman, Grainger plc, 2007–15 (Director, 2004–15); *b* Cambridge, 7 June 1946; *s* of late Alan Broadhurst and Joan Broadhurst; *m* 1972, Penelope Alison Usher; three *s* one *d*. *Educ:* Felsted Sch.; Coll. of Estate Management. Jones Lang Wootton, later Jones Lang LaSalle: chartered surveyor, 1969–2004; Partner, 1973–2004; Eur. Chm., 1999–2004. Trustee and non-exec. Dir, Grosvenor, 2000–11; non-executive Director: SableKnight, 2001– (Chm., 2006–); Invista Real Estate Investment plc, 2006–09; Regeneration Gp, 2016–; Partner, Chelsfield Partners, 2006–19; Senior Adviser: Credit Suisse, 2004–10; Resolution Partners, 2010–15; Real Estate Advr, SHL Ltd, 2016–; Consultant: Sir Robert McAlpine, 1999–2015; Fishmongers' Co., 2004–13. Chm., Property Advisory Gp, 1997–2002 (Mem., 1990–2002). Mem., Prince's Council, Duchy of Cornwall, 1999–2010. Trustee: Orchid Cancer Appeal, 1999–2013 (Chm., 2005–13); LandAid, 2008–15 (Chm., 2008–15); CBF Funds Trustee Ltd (CCLA), 1999–2014 (Chm., 2006–14); Gerald Palmer Eling Trust, 2000–; SSAFA, 2006–13; King Edward VII Hosp., 2006– (Chm., 2013–19); Royal Marsden Cancer Charity, 2010–19; Englefield Estate, 2011–; Handel House Trust, 2012–; Black Stork Charity (Defence and Nat. Rehabilitation Centre), until 2019; Member: Develt Bd, Royal Opera House, 1991–2000; Council, RNLI, 2006–15; non-exec. Dir, British Liby, 2004–11. Gov., Rugby Sch., 1996–2006. Liveryman: Chartered Surveyors' Co., 1977– (Master, 1997–98); Drapers' Co., 2004–; Fishmongers' Co., 2014–. *Recreations:* theatre, opera, Rugby, sailing, ski-ing, family life. *Address:* 21 Addison Avenue, W11 4QS. *T:* (020) 7603 1143. *Clubs:* Boodles; Honourable Artillery Company.

**BROADIE, Prof. Sarah Jean,** OBE 2019; PhD; FBA 2003; FRSE; Professor of Philosophy, University of St Andrews, since 2001; *b* 3 Nov. 1941; *d* of Prof. John Conrad Waterlow, CMG, FRS; *m* 1984, Frederick Broadie. *Educ:* Somerville Coll., Oxford (BA, BPhil); Univ. of Edinburgh (PhD 1978). Lectr in Philosophy, Univ. of Edinburgh, 1967–84; Professor of Philosophy: Univ. of Texas, Austin, 1984–86; Yale Univ., 1987–91; Rutgers Univ., 1991–93; Princeton Univ., 1993–2001. Pres., Aristotelian Soc., 2012–13; Vice-Pres., British Acad., 2006–08. MAE 2006. FRSE 2002; Fellow, Amer. Acad. of Arts and Scis, 1991. *Publications:* Nature, Change and Agency, 1982; Passage and Possibility, 1982; Ethics with Aristotle, 1991; (with C. Rowe) Aristotle: the Nicomachean ethics, 2002; Nature and Divinity in Plato's Timaeus, 2012; numerous articles on Ancient Greek philosophy. *Recreation:* playing under the auspices of all nine muses. *Address:* Department of Philosophy, University of St Andrews, Edgecliffe, The Scores, St Andrews KY16 9AL. *T:* (01334) 462486, *Fax:* (01334) 462485. *E:* sjb15@st-andrews.ac.uk.

**BROADLEY, Ian R.;** *see* Rank-Broadley.

**BROADLEY, John Kenneth Elliott,** CMG 1988; HM Diplomatic Service, retired; Ambassador to the Holy See, 1988–91; *b* 10 June 1936; *s* of late Kenneth Broadley and late Rosamund Venn (*née* Elliott); *m* 1961, Jane Alice Rachel (*née* Gee); one *s* two *d*. *Educ:* Winchester Coll.; Balliol Coll., Oxford (Exhibnr, MA). Served Army, 1st RHA, 1954–56. Entered HM Diplomatic Service, 1960; Washington, 1963–65; La Paz, 1965–68; FCO, 1968–73; UK Mission to UN, Geneva, 1973–76; Counsellor, Amman, 1976–79; FCO, 1979–84; Dep. Governor, Gibraltar, 1984–88. Trustee: SAT-7 (UK) Trust, 1999–2009 (Chm., 2003–09); Zimbabwe A Nat. Emergency (ZANE), 2012–. Chm. of Govs, Ballard Sch., 1998–2002. *Recreations:* golf, tennis. *Address:* 2 Lovegrove Acre, Dinton, Salisbury, Wilts SP3 5DX.

**BROCK, Deidre Leanne;** MP (SNP) Edinburgh North and Leith, since 2015; *b* Western Australia; partner, Dougie; two *d*. *Educ:* Curtin Univ. (BA English); WA Acad. of Performing Arts. Manager, office of Rob Gibson, MSP. Mem. (SNP) Edinburgh CC, 2007–15; Depute Lord Provost of Edinburgh, until 2015. Member, Board: Edinburgh Internat. Fest. Council; Centre for the Moving Image; Creative Edinburgh. *Address:* House of Commons, SW1A 0AA.

**BROCK, George Laurence;** Professor of Journalism, City, University of London (formerly City University), 2009–17, now Visiting Professor, Cass Business School (Head of Journalism, 2009–14); *b* 7 Nov. 1951; *s* of late Michael George Brock, CBE; *m* 1978, Katharine Sandeman (*see* K. Brock); two *s*. *Educ:* Winchester Coll.; Corpus Christi Coll., Oxford (MA). Reporter: Yorks Evening Press, 1973–76; The Observer, 1976–81; The Times: feature writer and ed., 1981–84; Opinion Page Ed., 1984–87; Foreign Ed., 1987–90; Bureau Chief, Brussels, 1991–95; Eur. Ed., 1995–97; Managing Ed., 1997–2004; Saturday Ed., 2004–08; Internat. Ed., 2008–09. Mem., Defence, Press and Broadcasting Adv. Cttee, 1998–2004. World Editors Forum: Bd Mem., 2001–14; Pres., 2004–08. Mem., British Exec., Internat. Press Inst., 2000–15 (Chm., 2011–15; Mem. Bd, 2011–15). Trustee: Nat. Acad. of Writing, 2008–16; Bureau of Investigative Journalism, 2010–; Internat. News Safety Inst. (UK), 2011–13. Gov., Ditchley Foundn, 2003–12 (Mem., Prog. Cttee, 1995–2003). Mem. Council, Gresham Coll., 2012–. Mem., Editl Bd, The Conversation UK, 2013–17. Judge, Olivier Th. Awards, 2004. FRSA 2004. *Publications:* (jtly) Siege: six days at the Iranian Embassy, 1980; (with N. Wapshott) Thatcher, 1983; Out of Print: newspapers, journalism and the business of news in the digital age, 2013; The Right to Be Forgotten: privacy and media in the digital age, 2016. *Recreations:* theatre, cities, walking, music.

**BROCK, Katharine, (Kay),** CBE 2016; LVO 2002; DL; Chief of Staff to the Archbishop of Canterbury, 2013–16 (Secretary for Public Affairs, 2012–13); *b* 23 May 1953; *d* of George Roland Stewart Sandeman and Helen Stewart Sandeman (*née* McLaren); *m* 1978, George Laurence Brock, *qv*; two *s*. *Educ:* Sherborne Sch. for Girls; Somerville Coll., Oxford (BA Hons 1975); London Business Sch. (MBA 1988). MAFF, 1975–85 (Private Sec. to Perm. Sec., 1980–81); consultant in internat. trade, 1985–88; Spicers Consulting Gp, 1988–89; Dir, PDN Ltd, 1990–91; Ext. Relns Directorate, EC, 1992–95; Advr to UK Knowhow Fund and EBRD, 1995–99; Asst Private Sec. to the Queen, 1999–2002; Private Sec. and COS (formerly Private Sec.) to the Lord Mayor of London, 2004–09; Dir, Ashridge Strategic Mgt Centre, 2010. Mem., Ind. Monitoring Bd, Wandsworth Prison, 2003–04. Pres., Somerville Coll. alumni, 2004–08. Chm., Dance United, 2008–12. Trustee, Acad. of Ancient Music, 2009–13; Mem., Adv. Council, LSO, 2009–16. Gov., Sherborne Girls, 2011–18. Liveryman, Founders' Co., 2005–; Freeman, Merchant Taylors' Co., 2009–. DL Gtr London, 2009. *Recreations:* music, Italy, cycling. *Club:* Farmers.

**BROCK, Dr Sebastian Paul,** FBA 1977; Reader in Syriac Studies, University of Oxford, 1990–2003, now Emeritus; Fellow of Wolfson College, Oxford, 1974–2003, now Emeritus; *b* 24 Feb. 1938; *m* 1966, Helen M. C. (*née* Hughes). *Educ:* Eton College; Trinity Coll., Cambridge (BA 1962, MA 1965); MA and DPhil Oxon 1966. Asst Lectr, 1964–66, Lectr, 1966–67, Dept of Theology, Univ. of Birmingham; Fellow, Selwyn Coll., Cambridge, 1967–72; Lectr, Hebrew and Aramaic, Univ. of Cambridge, 1967–74; Lectr in Aramaic and Syriac, Univ. of Oxford, 1974–90. Corresp. Mem., Syriac Section, Iraqi Acad., 1979. Editor, JSS, 1987–90. Hon. Dr: Pontificio Istituto Orientale, Rome, 1992; St Ephrem Ecumenical Res. Inst., Mahatma Gandhi Univ. of Kottayam, India, 2004; Univ. Saint Esprit, Kaslik, Lebanon, 2004; Hon. DD: Heythrop Coll., Univ. of London, 2016; Craiova, Romania, 2016; Hon. DLitt Birmingham, 1998; Hon. Dr École Pratique des Hautes Études, Paris, 2018. Leverhulme Medal for Humanities and Social Scis, 2009, Ullendorff Medal, 2016, British Acad. *Publications:* Pseudepigrapha Veteris Testamenti Graece II; Testamentum Iobi, 1967; The Syriac Version of the Pseudo-Nonnos Mythological Scholia, 1971; (with C. T. Fritsch and S. Jellicoe) A Classified Bibliography of the Septuagint, 1973; The Harp of the Spirit: Poems of St Ephrem, 1975, 3rd edn 2013; The Holy Spirit in Syrian Baptismal Tradition, 1979, 2nd edn 2008; Sughyotho Mgabyotho, 1982; Syriac Perspectives on Late Antiquity, 1984; Turgome d'Mor Ya'qub da-Srug, 1984; The Luminous Eye: the spiritual world vision of St Ephrem, 1985, 2nd edn 1992; (with S. A. Harvey) Holy Women of the Syrian Orient, 1987; Vetus Testamentum Syriace III. 1: Liber Isaiae, 1987; The Syriac Fathers on Prayer and the Spiritual Life, 1987; Malpanuto d-abohoto suryoye d-'al sluto, 1988; St Ephrem: Hymns on Paradise, 1990; Studies in Syriac Christianity, 1992; Luqoto d-Mimre, 1993; Bride of Light: hymns on Mary from the Syriac churches, 1994; Isaac of Nineveh: the second part, ch. IV–XLI, 1995; Catalogue of Syriac Fragments (New finds) in the Library of the Monastery of St Catherine, Mount Sinai, 1995; The Recensions of the Septuaginta Version of I Samuel, 1996; A Brief Outline of Syriac Literature, 1997, 2nd edn 2009; From Ephrem to Romanos: interactions between Syriac and Greek in late antiquity, 1999; (with D. G. K. Taylor and W. Witakowski) The Hidden Pearl: the Syrian Orthodox Church and its Ancient Aramaic Heritage (3 vols), 2001; (with G Kiraz) Ephrem the Syrian: select poems, 2006; Fire from Heaven: studies in Syriac theology and liturgy, 2006; The Bible in the Syriac Tradition, 2006; An Introduction to Syriac Studies, 2006, 3rd edn 2018; (ed with A. Butts, G. A. Kiraz and L. van Rompay) The Gorgias Encyclopedic Dictionary of the Syriac Heritage, 2011; Mary and Joseph, and other Dialogue Poems, 2011; Treasurehouse of Mysteries: explorations of the Sacred Text through poetry in the Syriac tradition, 2012; (with B. Fitzgerald) Two Early Lives of Severos, Patriarch of Antioch, 2013; The Martyrdom of St Phokas of Sinope, 2013; (with L. van Rompay) Catalogue of the Syriac Manuscripts and Fragments in the Library of Deir al-Surian (Egypt), 2014; Syriac Studies: a classified bibliography, vol. 2 (1991–2010), 2014; (with G. A. Kiraz) The Gorgias Concise Syriac-English, English-Syriac Dictionary, 2015; contrib. Jl of Semitic Studies, JTS, Le Muséon, Oriens Christianus, Orientalia Christiana Periodica, Parole de l'Orient, Revue des études arméniennes. *Address:* Wolfson College, Oxford OX2 6UD; Oriental Institute, Pusey Lane, Oxford OX1 2LE.

**BROCK, Timothy Hugh C.;** *see* Clutton-Brock.

**BROCKDORFF, Prof. Neil,** PhD; FMedSci; FRS 2018; FRSB; Professor of Biochemistry, and Wellcome Trust Principal Research Fellow, Department of Biochemistry, University of Oxford, since 2007; *b* London, 2 Nov. 1950; *s* of Clive Brockdorff and Luiza Brockdorff; *m* 2007, Danielle Hainaver; three *d*. *Educ:* Hampstead Sch.; Univ. of Sussex (BSc Hons); Univ. of Glasgow (PhD 1985). Post-doctoral Scientist, St Marys Hosp., London, 1985–88; Post-doctoral Scientist, 1988–92, MRC Principal Investigator, 1992–94, MRC Clinical Res. Centre, Harrow; MRC Principal Investigator, MRC Clinical Scis Centre, Hammersmith Hosp., 1994–2007. FMedSci 2007; FRSB 2011. *Publications:* reviews and book chapters; over 100 papers in learned jls. *Recreations:* flamenco guitar, gardening, cookery. *Address:* Department of Biochemistry, University of Oxford, South Parks Road, Oxford OX1 3QU. *T:* (01865) 613217. *E:* neil.brockdorff@bioch.ox.ac.uk.

**BROCKES, Prof. Jeremy Patrick,** PhD; FRS 1994; MRC Research Professor, Institute for Structural and Molecular Biology (formerly Department of Biochemistry and Molecular Biology), University College London, 1997–2016, now Emeritus Professor; Member, Ludwig Institute for Cancer Research, 1991–97; *b* 29 Feb. 1948; *s* of Bernard A. Brockes and Edna (*née* Heaney). *Educ:* Winchester Coll.; St John's Coll., Cambridge (BA 1969); Edinburgh Univ. (PhD 1972). Muscular Dystrophy Assoc. of America Postdoctoral Fellow, Dept of Neurobiology, Harvard Med. Sch., 1972–75; Research Fellow, MRC Neuroimmunology Project, UCL, 1975–78; Asst, then Associate, Prof., Div. of Biology, CIT, 1978–83; Staff Mem., MRC Biophysics Unit, KCL, 1983–88; scientific staff, Ludwig Inst. for Cancer Res., UCL/Middlesex Hosp. Br., 1988–97; Prof. of Cell Biology, UCL, 1991–97. Mem. Scientific Adv. Bd, Cambridge Neuroscience Inc., 1987–2000. Brooks Lectr, Harvard Med. Sch., 1997. MAE 1989. Scientific Medal: Zool Soc. of London, 1986; Biol Council, 1990; Newcomb Cleveland Prize, AAAS, 2008. *Publications:* Neuroimmunology, 1982; papers in scientific jls. *Recreations:* soprano saxophone, video-filming and editing, chess. *Address:* Institute for Structural and Molecular Biology, University College London, Gower Street, WC1E 6BT. *T:* (020) 7679 4483.

**BROCKET, 3rd Baron *cr* 1933; Charles Ronald George Nall-Cain;** Bt 1921; *b* 12 Feb. 1952; *s* of Hon. Ronald Charles Manus Nall-Cain (*d* 1961), and of Elizabeth Mary (who *m* 2nd, 1964, Colin John Richard Trotter), *d* of R. J. Stallard; *S* grandfather, 1967; *m* 1st, 1982, Isabell Maria Lorenzo (marr. diss. 1994), *o d* of Gustavo Lorenzo, New York; two *s* one *d*; 2nd, 2006, Harriet Victoria, *d* of James Warren; two *d*. *Educ:* Eton. 14/20 Hussars, 1970–75 (Lieut). Pres., Herts Chamber of Commerce and Industry, 1992; Chm., Business Link Hertfordshire, 1994. Chm., Trust for Information and Prevention (drug prevention initiatives), 1993. Chm., British Motor Centenary Trust; Dir, De Havilland Museum Trust; Patron, Guild of Guide Lectrs, 1992. *Publications:* Call Me Charlie (autobiog.), 2004. *Heir:* *s* Hon. Alexander Christopher Charles Nall-Cain, *b* 30 Sept. 1984. *E:* pa@lordbrocket.com.

**BROCKLEBANK, Sir Aubrey (Thomas),** 6th Bt *cr* 1885; ACA; director of various companies; *b* 29 Jan. 1952; *s* of Sir John Montague Brocklebank, 5th Bt, TD, and Pamela Sue, *d* of late William Harold Pierce, OBE; *S* father, 1974; *m* 1st, 1979, Dr Anna-Marie Dunnet (marr. diss. 1989); two *s*; 2nd, 1997, Hazel Catherine, *yr d* of Brian Roden; (one *s* decd). *Educ:* Eton; University Coll., Durham (BSc Psychology). With Guinness Mahon & Co., 1981–86; Director: Venture Founders, 1986–90; Dartington & Co., 1990–92; Manager, Avon Enterprise Fund, 1990–97. *Recreations:* deep sea tadpole wrestling, shooting, motor racing. *Heir:* *s* Aubrey William Thomas Brocklebank [*b* 15 Dec. 1980; *m* 2012, Kerry Ann Angus; one *d*]. *Club:* Brooks's.

**BROCKLEBANK, Edward;** freelance journalist and broadcaster, since 2011; *b* 24 Sept. 1942; *s* of Fred Brocklebank and Nancy Mitchell Ainslie Brocklebank; *m* 1st, 1965, Lesley Beverley Davidson (marr. diss. 1978); two *s*; 2nd, 2011, Frances Isabel Finlay. *Educ:* Madras Coll.; Univ. of St Andrews (MA). Trainee journalist, D. C. Thomson, Dundee, newspaper publishers, 1960–63; freelance journalist, Fleet St, 1963–65; press officer, Scottish TV, Glasgow, 1965–70; Grampian TV, Aberdeen: reporter, 1970–76; Head: News and Current Affairs, 1977–85; Documentaries and Features, 1985–95; Man. Dir, Greyfriars Prodns, St Andrews, 1995–2001. MSP (C) Mid Scotland and Fife, 2003–11. *Recreations:* ornithology, oil painting, walking, Rugby football. *Club:* Royal & Ancient Golf (St Andrews).

**BROCKLEBANK, James William;** QC 2018; *b* Guisborough, 18 Aug. 1976; *s* of Stephen and Christine Brocklebank; *m* 2001, Kumiko Tateno; one *d*. *Educ:* Cranleigh Sch.; Pembroke Coll., Cambridge (BA Hist. 1997). Called to the Bar, Middle Temple, 1999; in practice as barrister, specialising in commercial law, 2000–. *Recreations:* music, reading, wine. *Address:* 7 King's Bench Walk, Temple, EC4Y 7DS. *T:* (020) 7910 8300.

**BROCKLEBANK-FOWLER, Christopher;** certified management consultant; *b* 13 Jan. 1934; 2nd *s* of Sidney Straton Brocklebank Fowler, MA, LLB Cantab and Iris (*née* Beechey); *m* 1st, 1957, Joan Nowland (marr. diss. 1975; she *d* 2006); two *s*; 2nd, 1975, Mrs Mary Berry (marr. diss. 1986); 3rd, 1996, Mrs Dorothea Rycroft (marr. diss. 2000). *Educ:* Perse Sch., Cambridge; DipAgr Agricl Corresp. Coll., Oxford, 1952. Farm pupil on farms in Suffolk, Cambridgeshire and Norfolk, 1950–55. National service (submarines), Sub-Lt, RNVR, 1952–54. Farm Manager, Kenya, 1955–57; Lever Bros Ltd (Unilever Cos Management Trainee), 1957–59; advertising and marketing consultant, 1959–79; Chm., Overseas Trade and Develt Agency Ltd, 1979–83; Man. Dir, Cambridge Corporate Consultants Ltd,

1985–87. Mem. Bow Group, 1961–81 (Chm., 1968–69; Dir, Bow Publications, 1968–71). Mem. London Conciliation Cttee, 1966–67; Vice-Chm. Information Panel, Nat. Cttee for Commonwealth Immigrants, 1966–67; Mem. Exec. Cttee, Africa Bureau, 1970–74; Chm., SOS Children's Villages, 1978–84. MP King's Lynn, 1970–74, Norfolk North West, 1974–83 (C, 1970–81, SDP, 1981–83); Chm., Conservative Parly Sub-Cttee on Horticulture, 1972–74; Vice-Chairman: Cons. Parly Cttee on Agriculture, 1974–75; Cons. Parly Foreign and Commonwealth Affairs Cttee, 1979 (Jt Sec., 1974–75, 1976–77); Cons. Parly Trade Cttee, 1979–80; SDP Agriculture Policy Cttee, 1982–83; Chairman: UN Parly Gp, 1979–83 (Jt Sec., 1971–78); Cons. Parly Overseas Develt Sub-Cttee, 1979–81; SDP Third World Policy Cttee, 1981–87; Member: Select Cttee for Overseas Develt, 1973–79; Select Cttee on Foreign Affairs, 1979–81; SDP Nat. Steering Cttee, 1981–82; SDP Nat. Cttee, 1982; SDP Parly spokesman on Agriculture, 1981–82, on Overseas Develt, 1981–83, on Foreign Affairs, 1982–83. Contested: (C) West Ham (North), 1964; (SDP) 1983, (SDP/Alliance) 1987, Norfolk North West; (Lib. Dem.) Norfolk South, 1992. Mem., Labour Party, 1996–. Vice Chm., Centre for World Develt Educn, 1980–83; Governor, Inst. of Develt Studies, 1978–81. Vice Pres., Inst. of Mgt Consultancy, 1999. Fellow, De Montfort Univ., 1992. Hon. Fellow IDS. *Publications:* pamphlets and articles on race relations, African affairs, overseas development.

**BROCKLEHURST, Prof. Peter,** FRCOG, FFPH; FMedSci; Professor of Women's Health, and Director, Birmingham Clinical Trials Unit, University of Birmingham, since 2016; *b* Oldham, 23 April 1962; *s* of Albert and Helen Brocklehurst; civil partnership 2007, Dr Guy Rooney. *Educ:* Marple Hall Sch., Marple; Dundee Univ. (MB ChB 1985); London Sch. of Hygiene and Tropical Medicine, Univ. of London (MSc Epidemiol. 1994). MRCOG 1991, FRCOG 2004. Junior House Officer: Gen. Surgery and Urology, Southern Gen. Hosp., Glasgow, 1985–86; Renal and Gen. Medicine, Withington Hosp., Manchester, 1986; Senior House Officer: Obstetrics, Whittington Hosp., London, 1986–87; Gynaecology, Royal Northern Hosp., London, 1987; Genitourinary Medicine, Middx Hosp., 1988; Obstetrics and Gynaecology, Hillingdon Hosp., 1988–89; Lectr, UCL, 1989–92; Registrar, UCH, 1992–93; Consultant Clin. Epidemiologist, 1996–2002, Dir, 2002–11, Nat. Perinatal Epidemiol. Unit, Univ. of Oxford; Prof. of Women's Health, and Dir, Inst. for Women's Health, UCL, 2011–16. FFPH 2007; FMedSci 2015. Mem., Gynaecol Visiting Soc., 2006–. *Publications:* contribs to med. jls, incl. New England Jl Medicine, Lancet, BMJ. *Address:* Birmingham Clinical Trials Unit, Institute of Applied Health Research, Public Health Building, University of Birmingham, Edgbaston, Birmingham B15 2TT.

**BROCKLESBY, Prof. David William,** CMG 1991; FRCVS; Professor of Tropical Animal Health and Director of Centre for Tropical Veterinary Medicine, Royal (Dick) School of Veterinary Studies, University of Edinburgh, 1978–90, now Emeritus; *b* 12 Feb. 1929; *s* of late David Layton Brocklesby, AFC, and Katherine Jessie (*née* Mudd); *m* 1957, Jennifer Mary Hubble, MB, BS (*d* 2012); one *s* three *d*. *Educ:* Terrington Hall Sch.; Sedbergh Sch.; Royal Vet. Coll., Univ. of London; London Sch. of Hygiene and Tropical Med. MRCVS 1954; FRCVS (by election) 1984; MRCPath 1964, FRCPath 1982; DVetMed Zürich 1965. Nat. Service, 4th Queen's Own Hussars (RAC), 1947–49. Vet. Res. Officer (Protozoologist), E Afr. Vet. Res. Org., Muguga, Kenya, 1955–66; Hd of Animal Health Res. Dept, Fisons Pest Control, 1966–67; joined ARC Inst. for Res. on Animal Diseases, Compton, as Parasitologist, 1967; Hd of Parasitology Dept, IRAD, 1969–78. Member: Senatus Academicus, Univ. of Edinburgh, 1978–90; Governing Body, Animal Virus Res. Inst., Pirbright, 1979–86; Bd, Edinburgh Centre of Rural Economy, 1981–88; Council, RCVS, 1985–89. Mem. Editorial Board: Research in Veterinary Science, 1970–88; Tropical Animal Health and Production, 1978–90; British Vet. Jl, 1982–90. *Publications:* papers in sci. jls and chapters in review books, mainly on tropical and veterinary protozoa. *Recreations:* formerly squash and golf, now TV and The Times.

**BROCKLISS, Prof. Laurence William Beaumont,** PhD; FBA 2019; Professor of Early Modern French History, University of Oxford, 2002–17, now Emeritus; Tutor and Fellow in Modern History, Magdalen College, Oxford, 1984–2017, now Emeritus (Vice-President, 2014–15); *b* 20 March 1950; *s* of Henry Richard Brockliss and Rosemary Brockliss (*née* Beaumont); *m* 1974, Alison Jane Gordon; one *s* two *d*. *Educ:* Dulwich Coll.; Gonville and Caius Coll., Cambridge (BA 1971; PhD 1976). Lectr in Hist., Univ. of Hull, 1974–84; CUF Lectr in Mod. Hist., 1984–97, Reader, 1997–2002, Univ. of Oxford. Sarton Prof. in Hist. of Scis, Univ. of Ghent, 1996–97 (Sarton Medal, 1996); Jean Leclerc Prof. of Sociol., Univ. of Louvain-la-Neuve, 2000–01. Ed., Hist. of Univs, 1988–93. *Publications:* French Higher Education in the Seventeenth and Eighteenth Centuries, 1987; (ed with J. Bergin) Richelieu and His Age, 1992; (with C. Jones) The Medical World of Early Modern France, 1997; (ed with D. Eastwood) A Union of Multiple Identities: the British Isles *c* 1750–*c* 1850, 1997; (ed with Sir John Elliott) The World of the Favourite, 1999; Calvet's Web: enlightenment and the republic of letters in eighteenth-century France, 2002; (jtly) Nelson's Surgeon: William Beatty, naval medicine, and the Battle of Trafalgar, 2005; (jtly) Advancing with the Army: medicine, the professions, and social mobility in the British Isles 1790–1850, 2006; (ed) Magdalen College, Oxford: a history, 2008; (ed with H. Montgomery) Childhood and Violence in the Western Tradition, 2010; (ed with N. Sheldon) Mass Education and the Limits of State-Building, *c.* 1870–1920, 2012; The University of Oxford: a history, 2016; (ed with R. Robertson) Isaiah Berlin and the Enlightenment, 2016; (ed) From Provincial Savant to Parisian Naturalist: the recollections of Pierre-Joseph Amoreux (1741–1824), 2017; The University of Oxford: a brief history, 2019. *Recreations:* walking, gardening, amateur dramatics. *Address:* 85 Whitecross, Wootton, Abingdon, Oxon OX13 6BS. *T:* (01235) 529214. *E:* laurence.brockliss@magd.ox.ac.uk.

**BRODIE, Rt Hon. Lord; Philip Hope Brodie;** PC 2013; a Senator of the College of Justice in Scotland, since 2002; *b* 14 July 1950; *s* of Very Rev. Peter Philip Brodie and Constance Lindsay Hope; *m* 1983, Carol Dora McLeish; two *s* one *d*. *Educ:* Dollar Academy; Edinburgh Univ. (LLB Hons); Univ. of Virginia (LLM). Admitted Faculty of Advocates, 1976; QC (Scot.) 1987; called to the Bar, Lincoln's Inn, 1991–2012, Bencher, 2013; Standing Junior Counsel, MoD (Scotland) PE, and HSE, 1983–87; Advocate-Depute, 1997–99. Mem., Mental Welfare Commn for Scotland, 1985–96. Part-time Chairman: Industrial Tribunals, 1987–91; Medical Appeal Tribunals, 1991–96; Employment Tribunals, 2002; Chm., Judicial Studies Cttee, 2006–12. Chm., Cockburn Assoc., 2008–16. Chancellor's Assessor, Edinburgh Napier Univ., 2013–. Pres., Franco-Scottish Soc., 2015. *Recreations:* walking, reading. *Address:* 2 Cobden Crescent, Edinburgh EH9 2BG; Court of Session, Parliament House, Parliament Square, Edinburgh EH1 1RQ.

**BRODIE, Sir Benjamin David Ross,** 5th Bt *cr* 1834; *b* 29 May 1925; *s* of Sir Benjamin Collins Brodie, 4th Bt, MC, and Mary Charlotte (*d* 1940), *e d* of R. E. Palmer, Ballyheigue, Co. Kerry; *S* father, 1971, but his name does not appear on the Official Roll of the Baronetage; *m;* one *s* one *d*. *Educ:* Eton. Formerly Royal Corps of Signals. *Heir: s* Alan Ross Brodie [*b* 7 July 1960; *m* 1993, Jutta Maria Herrmann].

**BRODIE, Charles Gilchrist, (Chic);** Member (SNP) Scotland South, Scottish Parliament, 2011–16; *b* Dundee, 8 May 1944; *s* of Charles and Eileen Brodie; partner, Mary Ann Mann; one *s* two *d*. *Educ:* Morgan Acad., Dundee; St Andrews Univ. (BSc). Grad. trainee, IBM (UK) Ltd, 1966–67; N. C. R. (Manufg) Ltd, 1967–76; Logistics Manager, Sidlaw Industries Ltd, 1976–79; Business Manager, Europe Digital Equipment Manufg Ltd, 1979–83; Wang UK Ltd, 1983–88; Financial Dir, Tandem Computers, 1988–94; Gen. Manager, Twinsoft Europe, 1994–99; Chm. and CEO, Sionet Internat. Ltd, 1999–2002; owner/Dir, Caledonian Strategy (Scotland) Ltd, 2001–10. *Recreations:* golf, reading autobiographies. *Address:* 23 Maybole Road, Ayr KA7 2PZ. *T:* (01292) 294603.

**BRODIE of Lethen, Ewen John,** CVO 2015; Lord-Lieutenant of Nairnshire, 1999–2017; *b* 16 Dec. 1942; *s* of Major David J. Brodie of Lethen, OBE and Diana, *d* of Maj. Gen. Sir John Davidson, KCMG, CB, DSO; *m* 1967, Mariota, *yr d* of Lt-Col Ronald Steuart-Menzies of Culdares; three *d*. *Educ:* Harrow. Lieut, Grenadier Guards, 1961–64; IBM (UK) Ltd, 1965–74; estate mgt, 1975–. Dir, John Gordon & Son, 1992–2011. Vice Chm., Timber Growers Scotland, 1979–82; Chm., Findhorn Dist Salmon Fishing Bd, 2001–07. Mem., N Scotland Regl Adv. Cttee, Forestry Commn, 1977–89. DL Nairn, 1980. *Recreation:* countryside sports. *Address:* The Dower House, Lethen, Nairn IV12 5PR. *T:* (01667) 452123. *Club:* New (Edinburgh).

**BRODIE, Huw David;** Director of Culture and Sport, Welsh Government, 2013–15; *b* 20 July 1958; *s* of John Handel James Brodie and June Brodie; *m* 1985, Benita Humphries (*d* 2003); one *s; m* 2006, Anna Wigley. *Educ:* Trinity Coll., Cambridge (MA Hist.). Joined Dept of Employment, 1980; MSC and Trng Agency, 1983–90; Head of Policy Analysis Br., Trng Agency, 1987; TEC Policy Team, 1988; Asst Dir, Trng Agency, Wales, 1990–92; joined Welsh Office, 1992: Trng, Educn and Enterprise Dept, 1992–94; Head of Industrial and Trng Policy Div., Industry and Trng Dept, 1994–97; Agriculture Dept, 1997–99; Dir, Agric. Dept, Nat. Assembly for Wales, 1999–2003; Welsh Assembly Government, later Welsh Government: Dir, Strategy and Communications, subseq. Strategy, Equality and Communications, 2003–07; Dir for Rural Affairs and for Heritage, 2007–09; Dir of Policy Integration, 2010–11; Dir of Strategic Planning and Equality, 2011–13. *Recreations:* history, archaeology, hill walking.

**BRODIE, Judith Anne;** charity leader; interim executive and consultant, Leadership for Social Change, since 2013; *b* England; *d* of Hilary and Morris Brodie; *m* 2014, William Mumford. *Educ:* Newlands Sch., Maidenhead; University Coll. of N Wales, Bangor (BA Jt Hons Accounting and Maths 1981); Univ. of Southampton (MSc Social Stats 1984); Univ. of Portsmouth Business Sch. (MBA Dist. 1995). Accounting trainee, Ellerman City Liners, 1981–82; Jun. Res. Fellow, Dept of Accounting and Mgt Sci., Univ. of Southampton, 1984–85; Res. Officer, then Sen. Res. Officer, Social Services Dept, Hants CC, 1985–90; Sen. Strategy and Res. Officer, Southampton CC, 1990; Planning Co-ordinator, Social Services Dept, Hants CC, 1991–95; Mgt Consultant, C. A. G. Consultants, 1995; Policy and Communications Manager, Age Concern London, 1995–98; Hd, Cancer Support Service, Cancerbackup, 1998–2003; Chief Exec., Impetus Trust, 2003–06; Dir, VSO UK, 2006–10; Global Funding and Brand Dir, VSO, 2010–11; Chief Exec., Arthritis Care, 2012; Dep. CEO, then interim CEO and Dir of Services, Beating Bowel Cancer, 2015–18; interim CEO, Bond, 2018–19. Mem. (Lab), Lambeth LBC, 1998–2002 (Lead Mem. for Social Services and Health, 1998–2002). Vice-Chair, 2003–07, Trustee, 2003–09, Turning Point. Non-executive Director: S-E London SHA, 2002–06 (Chair, Audit Cttee, 2002–06); Royal Nat. Orthopaedic Hosp., 2011–13. Chair, Expert Adv. Cttee, NHS Digital. Trustee: Royal Nat. Orthopaedic Hosp. Charity, 2011–13; Assoc. of Coloproctol. of GB and Ire., 2017–18. Mem., London and SE Bd, CMI, 2013–15. CMgr, FCMI 2013. *Recreations:* theatre, cinema, current affairs, swimming, art, eating out.

**BRODIE, Philip Hope;** *see* Brodie, Rt Hon. Lord.

**BRODIE, Stanley Eric;** QC 1975; a Recorder of the Crown Court, 1975–89, and Deputy Official Referee, 1984–89; farmer; *b* 2 July 1930; *s* of late Abraham Brodie, MB, BS and Cissie Rachel Brodie; *m* 1956, Gillian Rosemary Joseph; two *d; m* 1973, Elizabeth Gloster (*see* Hon. Dame E. Gloster) (marr. diss. 2005); one *s* one *d*. *Educ:* Bradford Grammar Sch.; Balliol Coll., Oxford (MA). Pres., Oxford Univ. Law Soc., 1952. Called to Bar: Inner Temple, 1954 (Bencher, 1984, Reader, 1999, Treas., 2000); Belize, 1973; BVI, 2009; Mem. NE Circuit, 1954; Lectr in Law, Univ. of Southampton, 1954–55. Mem., Bar Council, 1987–89. Mem., River Doon Fishery Bd, 1990–2017. *Publications:* (jtly) Inner Temple Millennium Lectures, 2002; The Cost to Justice: government policy and the magistrates' courts, 2011. *Recreations:* opera, boating, winter sports, fishing. *Address:* Balgreen Lodge, Hollybush, Ayrshire KA6 7EB. *T:* (01292) 560546; 9 King's Bench Walk, Temple, EC4Y 7DX. *T:* (020) 7353 3428. *Clubs:* Athenæum, Flyfishers', Beefsteak.

**BRODRICK,** family name of **Viscount Midleton**.

**BRODRICK, Dawn Margaret,** CB 2015; Executive Director, Workforce Development, King's College Hospital NHS Foundation Trust, since 2015; *b* Woking, Surrey, 17 June 1964; *d* of Desmond and Margaret Ellis. *Educ:* Winston Churchill Secondary Sch.; Kingston Business Sch. (MA Human Resource Mgt). Hd, Organisational Develt, Jobcentre Plus, 2003–06; Dir for Leadership and Learning, DWP, 2006–09; HR Dir, Personal Tax, HMRC, 2009–12; Dir for People, Capability and Change, DCLG, 2012–15. *Recreations:* Member of Chobham Golf Course, Guide Leader of 1st Bisley Guide Company. *Address:* King's College Hospital NHS Foundation Trust, King's College Hospital, Denmark Hill, SE5 9RS.

**BRODRICK, His Honour Michael John Lee;** a Senior Circuit Judge, 2002–08 (a Circuit Judge, 1987–2008); Resident Judge, Winchester Combined Court, 1999–2008; *b* 12 Oct. 1941; *s* of His Honour Norman John Lee Brodrick, QC and Kate Ruth, *d* of Sir Stanley Unwin, KCMG; *m* 1969, Valerie Lois Stroud; one *s* one *d*. *Educ:* Charterhouse; Merton Coll., Oxford (2nd Jurisp.). Called to the Bar, Lincoln's Inn, 1965, Bencher, 2000; Western Circuit; a Recorder, 1981–87; Liaison Judge to SE Hants Magistrates, 1989–93, to IoW Magistrates, 1989–94, to NE and NW Hants Magistrates, 1999–2007; Hon. Recorder of Winchester, 2005–09. Pres., Transport Tribunal, 2012–16 (Judicial Mem., 1986–2012); a Judge of the Upper Tribunal, 2009–16; Principal Judge for Traffic Comr and Transport Appeals, 2009–15. Member: Senate of Inns of Court and Bar, 1979, served 1979–82; Wine Cttee, Western Circuit, 1982–86; Cttee, Council of Circuit Judges, 1990–2003 (Pres., 2003). Mem., Lord Chancellor's Adv. Cttee for the Appointment of Magistrates, for Portsmouth, 1990–93, for SE Hants, 1993–2000. Chm., Area Judicial Forum for Hants, 2004–08. Counsellor to Dean and Chapter, Winchester Cathedral, 1993–; Churchwarden, St John the Evangelist, Northington, 1995–2001, 2011–19. *Recreation:* gardening.

**BRODY, Prof. Neville,** RDI 2011; graphic designer and typographer; Founder and Director, Brody Associates (formerly Neville Brody Studio, then Research Studios), since 1990; Principal, Brody Associates, since 2013; Professor of Communication, Royal College of Art, since 2018 (Dean, School of Communication, 2011–18); *b* London. *Educ:* Hornsey Sch. of Art; London Coll. of Printing. Designer: Rocking Russian, 1979–80; Stiff Records, 1980–81; Art Director: Fetish Records; The Face mag., 1981–86; Arena mag., 1986–90; Partner, FontShop, 1990–2000; Co-Ed., FUSE, 1991–. Pres., D&AD, 2012–13. Exhibitions include: V&A, 1988; Rocket Gall., Tokyo, 2009. Hon. Fellow, Univ. of the Arts, 2010. *Relevant publication:* The Graphic Language of Neville Brody, by Jon Wozencroft, vol. 1, 1988, vol. 2, 1994. *Publications:* G1: new dimensions in graphic design, 1997. *Address:* Brody Associates, 94 Islington High Street, N1 8EG.

**BRODY, William Ralph**, PhD, MD; FIEEE; President, Salk Institute for Biological Studies, California, 2009–15, now Professor Emeritus; *b* 4 Jan. 1944; *m* Wendyce H.; one *s* one *d*. *Educ*: Massachusetts Inst. of Technol. (BS Electrical Engrg 1965; MS 1966); Stanford Univ. Sch. of Medicine (MD 1970); Stanford Univ. (PhD Electrical Engrg 1972). Dip. Amer. Bd Radiol., 1977. Stanford University School of Medicine: Fellow, Dept of Cardiovascular Surgery, 1970–71; Intern, Dept of Surgery, 1971–72; Resident, Dept of Cardiovascular Surgery, 1972–73; Clin. Associate, Nat. Heart, Lung and Blood Inst., Bethesda, Md, 1973–75; Resident, Dept of Radiol., Univ. of Calif, San Francisco, 1975–77; Stanford University School of Medicine: Dir, Res. Labs, Div. of Diagnostic Radiol., 1977–84; Associate Prof. of Radiol., 1977–82; Dir, Advance Imaging Techniques Lab., 1978–84; Prof. of Radiol., 1982–86 (on leave of absence, 1984–86); Radiologist-in-Chief, Johns Hopkins Hosp., 1987–94; Johns Hopkins University School of Medicine: Martin Donner Prof. and Dir, Dept of Radiol., 1987–94; secondary appt in biomed. engrg and jt appt in electrical and computer engrg, 1987–94; Prof. of Radiol., Univ. of Minn, 1994–96; Pres., Johns Hopkins Univ., 1996–2009. Founder, Resonex Inc., 1983: Consultant, 1983–84; Pres., 1984–86; Pres. and CEO, 1986–87; Chm., 1987–89. Mem., Inst. of Medicine, NAS. Founding Fellow, Amer. Inst. Med. and Biol Engrg; Fellow: Amer. Coll. Cardiol.; Amer. Coll. Radiol.; Council on Cardiovascular Radiol., Amer. Heart Assoc.; Internat. Soc. Magnetic Resonance in Medicine. *Publications*: (ed) Digital Radiography: proceedings of the Stanford Conference on digital radiography, 1981; Digital Radiology, 1984; (ed with G. S. Johnston) Computer Applications to Assist Radiology, 1992; contrib. numerous book chapters and to conf. proceedings and tech. reports; contrib. numerous articles to jls, incl. Radiol., Jl Thoracic Cardiovascular Surgery, Med. Phys., IEEE Trans Biomed. Engrg, Investigative Radiol., Amer. Jl Radiol. *Address*: Salk Institute for Biological Studies, 10010 N Torrey Pines Road, La Jolla, CA 92037, USA.

**BROERS**, family name of **Baron Broers**.

**BROERS**, Baron *cr* 2004 (Life Peer), of Cambridge in the County of Cambridgeshire; **Alec Nigel Broers**, Kt 1998; PhD, ScD; FRS 1986; FREng; FIET; FInstP; President, Royal Academy of Engineering, 2001–06; Professor of Electrical Engineering, Cambridge University, 1984–96, now Emeritus; Vice-Chancellor, Cambridge University, 1996–2003, now Emeritus; Fellow, Churchill College, Cambridge, since 1980 (Master, 1990–96); *b* 17 Sept. 1938; *s* of late Alec William Broers and of Constance Amy (née Cox); *m* 1964, Mary Therese Phelan; two *s*. *Educ*: Geelong Grammar School; Melbourne Univ. (BSc Physics 1958, Electronics 1959); Gonville and Caius College, Cambridge (BA Mech Scis 1962; PhD Mech Scis 1966; ScD 1991; Hon. Fellow, 1996). FIET (FIEE 1984); FREng (FEng 1985); FInstP 1991. IBM Thomas Watson Research Center: Research Staff Mem., 1965–67; Manager, Electron Beam Technology, 1967–72; Manager, Photon and Electron Optics, 1972–80; IBM Fellow, 1977; IBM East Fishkill Laboratory: Manager, Lithography Systems and Technology Tools, 1981–82; Manager, Semiconductor Lithography and Process Develt, 1982–83; Manager, Advanced Develt, 1983–84; Mem., Corporate Tech. Cttee, IBM Corporate HQ, 1984; Cambridge University: Hd of Electrical Div., 1984–92, and of Dept of Engrg, 1992–96; Fellow, Trinity Coll., 1985–90 (Hon. Fellow, 1999). Louis Matheson Prof., Monash Univ., 2010–16. BBC Reith Lectures, 2005. Non-executive Director: Lucas Industries, 1995–97; Vodafone (then Vodafone AirTouch, subseq. reverted to Vodafone) plc, 1998–2007; Mears Technol., 2004–12; FlexEnable Ltd, 2015–. Mem., EPSRC, 1994–2000. Chairman: H of L Sci. and Technol. Select Cttee, 2004–07; Judging Panel, Queen Elizabeth Prize for Engrg, 2012–15. Chairman: Bd of Dirs, Plastic Logic Ltd, 2004–06 (Dir, 2006–07); Bd of Dirs, Diamond Light Source, 2008–14; Bio Nano Consulting, 2010–15. Trustee: BM, 2004–12; Needham Res. Inst., 2009–; St Andrews Prize for the Envmt, 2009– (Chm., 2015–). Mem. Council, Univ. of Melbourne; Trustee, American Univ. of Sharjah, 1997–. Mem. Council, Royal Acad. of Engineering, 1993–96. Pres., Australian Music Foundn, 2013–. Foreign Associate, Nat. Acad. of Engrg, USA, 1994; Mem., Amer. Philosophical Soc., 2001; Foreign Mem., Chinese Acad. Engrg, 2006. DL Cambs, 2000. Hon. Fellow: Univ. of Wales, Cardiff, 2001; St Edmund's Coll., Cambridge, 2003; FIC 2004. Hon. FIEE 1996; Hon. FTSE 2002; Hon. FIMechE 2004; Hon. FMedSci 2004. Hon. DEng: Glasgow, 1996; Trinity Coll., Dublin, 2005; Sheffield, 2007; Durham, 2007; Tufts, 2007; Hon. DSc: Warwick, 1997; UMIST, 2002; London, 2006; Hon. LLD: Melbourne, 2000; Cambridge, 2004; Hon. DTech Greenwich, 2000; DUniv: Anglia Polytech. Univ., 2000; Sheffield Hallam, 2008; Hon. PhD Peking, 2002; Hon. DLaws Monash, 2009. Prize for Industrial Applications of Physics, Amer. Inst. of Physics, 1982; Cledo Brunetti Award, IEEE, 1985; Prince Philip Medal, Royal Acad. Engrg, 2001. *Publications*: The Triumph of Technology (Reith Lectures), 2005; patents and papers on electron microscopy, electron beam lithography, integrated circuit fabrication and nanotechnology. *Recreations*: music, sailing, ski-ing. *Address*: House of Lords, SW1A 0PW.

**BROGAN, Melanie Henrietta;** *see* Dawes, M. H.

**BROKE;** *see* Willoughby de Broke.

**BROKE, Col (George) Robin (Straton),** CVO 2016 (LVO 1977); Director, Association of Leading Visitor Attractions, 1996–2011; Equerry-in-Waiting to the Queen, 1974–77; *b* 31 March 1946; *s* of Maj.-Gen. Robert Straton Broke, CB, OBE, MC; *m* 1978, Patricia Thornhill Shann, *d* of Thomas Thornhill Shann; one *s*. *Educ*: Eton. Commissioned into Royal Artillery, 1965; CO 3 RHA, 1987–89. Mem., HM Bodyguard, Hon. Corps of Gentlemen-at-Arms, 1997–2016. Mem. Bd of Management, King Edward VII's Hosp., London, 1994–96. Trustee, Hedley Foundn, 1998–2018. Gov., Queen Elizabeth Hosp., Kings Lynn, 2010–19. *Recreation*: country pursuits. *Address*: St Mary's Lodge, Bircham, King's Lynn, Norfolk PE31 6QR. *T*: (01485) 578402. *Clubs*: Cavalry and Guards, Queen's.

**BROKENSHIRE, Rt Hon. James (Peter);** PC 2015; MP (C) Old Bexley and Sidcup, since 2010 (Hornchurch, 2005–10); *b* 8 Jan. 1968; *m* 1999, Cathrine Anne Mamelok; one *s* two *d*. *Educ*: Davenant Foundn Grammar Sch.; Cambridge Centre for Sixth Form Studies; Univ. of Exeter (LLB). Solicitor with Jones Day Gouldens, 1991–2005. Opposition front bench spokesman on home affairs, 2006–10. Parly Under-Sec. of State, 2010–14, Minister of State (Minister for Immigration and Security), 2014–16, Home Office; Sec. of State for NI, 2016–18; Sec. of State for Housing, Communities and Local Govt, 2018–19. *Address*: House of Commons, SW1A 0AA.

**BROMFIELD, Sonia Maxine;** *see* Watson, S. M.

**BROMHEAD, (Sir) John Desmond Gonville,** (6th Bt *cr* 1806); S father, 1981, but does not use title. *Heir*: cousin John Edmund de Gonville Bromhead [*b* 10 Oct. 1939; *m* 1965, Janet Frances, *e d* of Harry Vernon Brotherton, Moreton-in-Marsh, Glos; one *s* one *d*].

**BROMILOW, Richard Bruce Davies; His Honour Judge Bromilow;** a Circuit Judge, since 2005; *b* 6 May 1954; *s* of late Comdr Frank Bromilow and of Joyce Bromilow (née Davies); *m* 1985, Alison Nina Whitaker Bell; one *s* one *d*. *Educ*: Aldwickbury Sch., Harpenden; Bedford Sch.; Southampton Univ. (LLB). Inns of Court Sch. of Law. Called to the Bar, Gray's Inn, 1977; in practice as barrister, St John's Chambers, Bristol, 1985–2005; Asst Recorder, 1998–2000; Recorder, 2000–05. *Recreations*: bridge, cricket, cycling, golf, classical music and opera. *Address*: Bristol Civil and Family Justice Centre, 1 Redcliff Street, Bristol BS1 6NP. *Club*: Bristol and Clifton Golf.

**BROMLEY AND BEXLEY, Archdeacon of;** *see* Wright, Ven. P.

**BROMLEY, Sir Charles Howard,** 11th Bt *cr* 1757; *b* 31 July 1963; *s* of Sir Rupert Charles Bromley, 10th Bt and Priscilla Hazel Bromley (née Bourne); *S* father, 2018, but his name does not appear on the Official Roll of the Baronetage; *m* 1998, Marie, *d* of W. J. Taylor; one *s* one *d*. *Heir*: *s* Robert Charles Bromley, *b* 12 Feb. 1999.

**BROMLEY, Sir Michael (Roger),** KBE 1998; Director, Steamships Trading Co. Ltd, 1986–96 and since 2000; *b* 19 July 1948; *s* of Harry and Joan Margaret Bromley; *m* 1st, 1972, Thierrine Brands (marr. diss. 1976); one *d*; 2nd, 1982, Peta Lynette Baynes (marr. diss. 1998); one *s* three *d*. *Educ*: Kikori Bush Sch., PNG, by corresp.; Mount Hagen Park Sch., PNG; Southport Sch., Qld, Australia. Collins & Leahy: Merchandise Operator, then Night Security, then truck driver, 1966–73; Man. Dir, 1982–98; Chm. and CEO, Collins & Leahy Pty Ltd, 1998–2000; Gen. Manager, Bromley & Manton, 1973–82. Chm., Waratah Resources Ltd, 2012–13; Former Chm., Air Niugini. *Recreations*: polocrosse, flying (pilot), scuba diving, sailing. *Club*: Goroka Polocrosse.

**BROMLEY-DAVENPORT, John;** QC 2002; a Recorder of the Crown Court, since 1989; actor, speaker and writer; *b* 13 March 1947; *s* of Togo and Elizabeth Bromley-Davenport; *m* 1971, Judy Francis; one *s* two *d*. *Educ*: Eton Coll.; LAMDA; College of Law. Called to the Bar, Gray's Inn, 1972; Attorney Gen., Northern Circuit, 2007–. *Publications*: Sober in the Morning (anthology of drink and drinking), 2004, 2015; Space Has No Frontier: the biography of Bernard Lovell, 2013; contrib. articles to The Times, Daily Telegraph, Daily Mail, Carmarthen Jl, Country Life. *Recreations*: acting, cricket, shooting, fishing, golf, wine and food. *E*: brommersqc@btinternet.com. *Clubs*: Pratt's, White's; Tarporley Hunt (Pres. 2016); Delamere Forest Golf.

**BROMLEY-DAVENPORT, Sir William (Arthur),** KCVO 2010; landowner; chartered accountant; Lord-Lieutenant of Cheshire, 1990–2010; *b* 7 March 1935; *o s* of Lt-Col Sir Walter Bromley-Davenport, TD, DL and Lenette, *d* of Joseph Y. Jeanes, Philadelphia; *m* 1962, Elizabeth Watts, Oldwick, NJ; one *s* one *d*. *Educ*: Eton; Cornell Univ., NY. Mem. ICA, 1966. National Service, 2nd Batt. Grenadier Guards, 1953–54; Hon. Col 3rd (Vol.) Batt. 22nd (Cheshire) Regt, 1985. Owns land in UK and Norway. Mem. Cttee Cheshire Br., CLA, 1962 (past Chm.). Pres., Cheshire Scout Council, 1990– (Chm., 1981–90). Chm. of Govs, King's Sch., Macclesfield, 1986–2005. JP 1975, DL 1982, High Sheriff 1983–84, Cheshire. Hon. DLitt Chester, 2006. *Address*: Capesthorne Hall, Macclesfield SK11 9JY; Fiva, Aandalsnes, Norway.

**BROMLEY-DERRY, Kim Daniel,** CBE 2017; DL; Group Director, Strategic Partnerships, McLaren Construction, since 2018; *b* London, 22 Feb. 1961; *s* of Daniel Bromley-Derry and Joan Bromley-Derry; *m* 1990, Deborah; two *d*. *Educ*: Anglia Poly. (CSS Social Care 1986); Anglia Business Sch., Cambridge (DMS Mgt 2004; MBA 2006). Residential social worker, Cambs CC, 1982–86; team leader, then Asst Resource Centre Manager, Beds CC, 1986–89; Resource Centre Manager, 1989–91, Policy and Service Develt Manager, 1991–92, Cambs CC; Gp Manager, Beds CC, 1992–94; Ops Manager, Cities in Schs (UK), 1994–96; Area Manager, then County Manager, Lincs CC, 1996–2000; Service Dir, Children and Families, Leicester CC, 2000–05; Exec. Dir, Children and Young People, S Tyneside Council, 2005–07; Exec. Dir, Children and Young People, 2007–10, Chief Exec., 2010–18, London Bor. of Newham. Chm., Nat. Libraries Taskforce, 2017–; Mem., Social Work Taskforce, DoH/DCSF, 2009. Chairman: Children's Inter-Agency Gp, 2008–10; Nat. Advisory on Family Intervention, 2010–12; Mem., Adoption Leadership Bd, 2014–. Mem., London 2017 World Athletics Bd, 2013–18. Non-exec. Dir, Creative and Cultural Skills, 2015–. Pres., Assoc. of Dirs of Children's Services, 2009–10. Governor: Newham Coll. of FE, 2014–; Nat. Coll. of Creative and Cultural Skills, 2016–. Hon. Dr E London, 2017. DL Gtr London, 2019. *Recreations*: family, football, cricket. *Address*: McLaren Construction, 4th Floor, 10 Chiswell Street, EC1Y 4UQ.

**BROMLEY-MARTIN, Michael Granville;** QC 2002; a Recorder of the Crown Court, since 2003; *b* 27 April 1955; *s* of late Captain David Eliot Bromley-Martin, RN, and Angela Felicity Bromley-Martin (née Hampden-Ross); *m* 1983, Anna Frances Birley; one *s* two *d*. *Educ*: Eton; Southampton Univ. (BSc Civil Eng). Called to the Bar, Gray's Inn, 1979. Inspector, DTI, 1989, 1990. The W Wittering Estate PLC, 2016–. Chm. and Trustee, Elms Lane Tennis Club, 1994–. *Recreations*: sailing, shooting, fishing, arts. *Address*: 3 Raymond Buildings, Gray's Inn, WC1R 5BH. *T*: (020) 7400 6400, *Fax*: (020) 7400 6464. *E*: clerks@3rblaw.com. *Clubs*: Garrick, Royal Ocean Racing; Itchenor Sailing.

**BROMPTON, Michael John;** QC 2003; a Recorder, since 2006; *b* 6 Sept. 1950; *s* of late Harry and Lena Brompton; *m* 1st, 1983, Sally Elizabeth Mary O'Brien (marr. diss. 1997); two *d*; 2nd, 2003, Clare Elizabeth Gilbert. *Educ*: Stowe Sch., Buckingham; Univ. of Sussex (BA Hons Hist.); Coll. of Law, London. Called to the Bar, Middle Temple, 1973; in practice, specialising in law of crime, fraud, money-laundering and confiscation of assets; Jt Head of Chambers, 2009–14. Standing Counsel to HM Customs and Excise (Crime), S Eastern Circuit, 1994–2003. *Recreations*: theatre, cricket and Rugby (spectating), modern history, walking. *Address*: 5 Paper Buildings, Temple, EC4Y 7HB. *T*: (020) 7583 6117, *Fax*: (020) 7353 0075.

**BROMWICH, Prof. Michael;** CIMA Professor of Accounting and Financial Management, London School of Economics and Political Science, 1985–2006, now Emeritus; *b* 29 Jan. 1941; *s* of William James Bromwich and Margery (née Townley); *m* 1972, Christine Margaret Elizabeth Whitehead (OBE 1991). *Educ*: Wentworth High Sch., Southend; London School of Economics (BScEcon 1965); FCMA. Ford Motor Co., 1958–62 and 1965–66; Lectr, LSE, 1966–70; Professor of Accounting: UWIST, 1971–77; Univ. of Reading, 1977–85. Mem. Council, ICMA, 1980–85; Vice Pres., ICMA, later CIMA, 1985–87, Pres., CIMA, 1987–88. Accounting Advr, OFT, 2001–08. Mem., Accounting Standards Cttee, 1981–84; Additional Mem., Monopolies and Mergers Commn, 1992–2000; Research Grants Bd, ESRC, 1992–96; Mem., Pension Adv. Gp, LSE, 2012–. Hon. Treas., Disability Alliance, 2007–11; Foundn Trustee and Hon. Treas., Disability Rights UK, 2012–. Hon. DEcon Lund Univ., Sweden, 1993. *Publications*: Economics of Capital Budgeting, 1976; Economics of Accounting Standard Setting, 1985; (jtly) Management Accounting: evolution not revolution, 1989; (jtly) Housing Association Accounting, 1990; Financial Reporting, Information and Capital Markets, 1992; Management Accounting: pathways to progress, 1994; Accounting for Overheads: critique and reforms, 1997; (jtly) Following the Money: the Enron failure and the state of corporate disclosure, 2003; (jtly) Worldwide Financial Reporting: the development and future of accounting standards, 2006; (jtly) Management Accounting: retrospect and prospect, 2009; co-ed others, incl. Essays in British Accounting Research; many articles. *Recreation*: working and eating in restaurants. *Address*: 14 Thornhill Road, N1 1HW. *T*: (020) 7607 9323.

**BRON, Prof. Anthony John,** FRCS, FCOphth, FMedSci; Head, Nuffield Laboratory of Ophthalmology, 1973–2003, and Clinical Professor of Ophthalmology, 1989–2003, University of Oxford, now Professor Emeritus; Fellow of Linacre College, Oxford, 1975–2003; Professor of Experimental Ophthalmology, Vision and Eye Research Unit, Anglia Ruskin University, 2013–17; *b* 3 Feb. 1936; *s* of late Sydney and Fagah Bron; *m* 1st,

1961, Sandra Ruth Shoot (*d* 1976); one *s* one *d* (and one *s* decd); 2nd, 1981, Diana S. Shortt; one step *s* three step *d*. *Educ*: London Univ. (BSc 1957; MB BS 1961); Guy's Hosp. (DO 1964). LRCP 1960; MRCS 1960, FRCS 1968; FCOphth 1989. Guy's Hosp., 1961–63; Clin. Fellow in Ophthalmol., Wilmer Inst., Johns Hopkins Univ., 1964–65; Res. Assistant, Inst. of Ophthalmol., 1965; Moorfields Eye Hospital: Chief Clin. Assistant, 1965; Resident Surg. Officer, 1965–68; Lectr, 1968–70; Sen. Lectr and Hon. Consultant, 1970–73; Margaret Ogilvie's Reader in Ophthalmol., Oxford Univ., 1973–2003; Hon. Consultant, Oxford Eye Hosp., 1989–. Pres., Ophthalmic Section, RSM, 1986; Vice Pres., Jt Eur. Res. Meetings in Ophthalmol. and Vision, 1994–95; Chm., Assoc. for Eye Res., 1993–95; Chm. Cornea Sect., 1998–2002, Pres., 2002–03, Eur. Assoc. for Vision and Eye Res. Mem., Soc. of Scholars, Johns Hopkins Univ., 1991; Chm. and Co-organiser, Internat. Dry Eye Workshop, 2007; Consultant, Internat. Workshop on Meibomian Gland Dysfunction, 2011; Member: Workshop on Contact Lens Discomfort, 2013; Steering Cttee, Tear Film and Ocular Service Workshop, 2017 (Chm., Pathophysiol. subcttee, 2017). ARVO Gold Fellow 2010. Founder FMedSci 1998. Hon. MA Oxon, 1973. *Publications*: (contrib.) The Inborn Errors of Metabolism, 1974; The Unquiet Eye, 1983, 2nd edn 1987; (jtly) Lens Disorders, 1996; (ed and contrib.) Wolff's Anatomy of the Eye and Orbit, 1997; (jtly) Lecture Notes in Ophthalmology, 12th edn 2017; papers on the cornea, tears and crystalline lens. *Recreations*: drawing, photography, musing on Life. *Address*: Nuffield Department of Clinical Neurosciences, Nuffield Laboratory of Ophthalmology, 6th Floor, John Radcliffe Hospital, Headly Way, Oxford OX3 9DU. *T*: 07768 807735. *E*: anthony.bron@ eye.ox.ac.uk. *Club*: Athenæum.

*See also* E. *Bron*.

**BRON, Eleanor**; actress and writer; *d* of late Sydney and Fagah Bron. *Educ*: North London Collegiate Sch., Canons, Edgware; Newnham Coll., Cambridge (BA Hons Mod. Langs). De La Rue Co., 1961. Director: Actors Centre, 1982–93; Soho Theatre Co., 1993–2000. Appearances include: revue, Establishment Nightclub, Soho, 1962, and New York, 1963; Not so much a Programme, More a Way of Life, BBC TV, 1964; several TV series written with John Fortune, and TV series: Making Faces, written by Michael Frayn, 1976; Pinkerton's Progress, 1983; Absolutely Fabulous, 1992; Fat Friends, 2002; Casualty 1909, 2009; Foyle's War, 2010; Midsomer Murders, 2011; Life in Squares, 2015; *TV plays and films include*: Nina, 1978; My Dear Palestrina, 1980; A Month in the Country, 1985; Quartermaine's Terms, 1987; Changing Step, 1989; The Hour of the Lynx, 1990; The Blue Boy, 1994; Vanity Fair, 1998; Gypsy Girl, Randall & Hopkirk (Deceased), 2001; Ted and Alice, 2002. *Stage roles include*: Jennifer Dubedat, The Doctor's Dilemma, 1966; Jean Brodie, The Prime of Miss Jean Brodie, 1967, 1984; title role, Hedda Gabler, 1969; Portia, The Merchant of Venice, 1975; Amanda, Private Lives, 1976; Elena, Uncle Vanya, 1977; Charlotte, The Cherry Orchard, 1978; Margaret, A Family, 1978; On Her Own, 1980; Goody Biddy Bean; The Amusing Spectacle of Cinderella and her Naughty, Naughty Sisters, 1980; Betrayal, 1981; Heartbreak House, 1981; Duet for One, 1982; The Duchess of Malfi, 1985; The Real Inspector Hound, and The Critic (double bill), 1985; Jocasta and Ismene, Oedipus and Oedipus at Colonus, 1987; Infidelities, 1987; The Madwoman of Chaillot, 1988; The Chalk Garden, 1989; The Miser, and The White Devil, 1991; opera, Die Glückliche Hand, Nederlandse Oper, Amsterdam, 1991; Desdemona—if you had only spoken! (one-woman show), 1992; Gertrude, Hamlet, 1993; Agnes, A Delicate Balance, 1996; A Perfect Ganesh, 1996; Doña Rosita: the Spinster, 1997; Be My Baby, 1998; Making Noise Quietly, 1999; Tuppence to Cross the Mersey, 2005; The Clean House, 2006, tour, 2008; In Extremis, 2007; All about my Mother, 2008; The Late Middle Classes, 2010; Forget Me Not, 2015; A Woman of No Importance, Vaudeville Th., 2017; opera, Ariadne auf Naxos, Scottish Opera, 2018. *Films include*: Help!; Alfie; Two for the Road; Bedazzled; Women in Love; The National Health; The Day that Christ Died, 1980; Turtle Diary, 1985; Little Dorrit, 1987; The Attic, 1988; Deadly Advice, 1994; Black Beauty, A Little Princess, 1995; The House of Mirth, 2000; The Heart of Me, 2001; Love's Brother, 2003; Wimbledon, 2004; Streetdance, 2010; Hyde Park on Hudson, 2012. *Radio*: The Archers, BBC Radio 4, 2014–. Author: song-cycle with John Dankworth, 1973; verses for Saint-Saens' Carnival of the Animals, 1975 (recorded). *Publications*: Is Your Marriage Really Necessary (with John Fortune), 1972; (contrib.) My Cambridge, 1976; (contrib.) More Words, 1977; Life and Other Punctures, 1978; The Pillow Book of Eleanor Bron, 1985; (trans.) Desdemona—if you had only spoken!, by Christine Brückner, 1992; Double Take, 1996; (ed jtly) Cedric Price: retriever, 2005. *Address*: c/o Rebecca Blond Associates, 69A King's Road, SW3 4NX.

*See also* A. J. *Bron*.

**BRONNERT, Deborah Jane**, CMG 2012; HM Diplomatic Service; Ambassador to Russia, from Jan. 2020; *b* Stockport, 31 Jan. 1967; *d* of Rev. Preb. Dr David Bronnert and Beryl Bronnert; *m* 2006, Alfonso Torrents; two *s*. *Educ*: Featherstone High Sch., Southall; Univ. of Bristol (BSc Hons Maths); University Coll. London (MA Pol Econ. of Russia and E Europe). DoE, 1989–91; Second Sec., Envmt, UK Repn to EC, Brussels, 1991–93; DoE, then FCO, 1993–95; Mem. of Cabinet, EC, Brussels, 1995–99; Dep. Hd, S Eur. Dept, FCO, 1999–2001; Econ. and Trade Counsellor, Moscow, 2002–05; Hd, Future of Europe Gp, then Hd, Europe Delivery Gp, FCO, 2006–08; Jt Dir, Global and Economic Issues, FCO, 2008–11; Dir, Prosperity, FCO, 2011; Ambassador to Zimbabwe, 2011–14; Chief Operating Officer, FCO, 2014–16; Dir Gen., Econ. and Consular, FCO, 2016–17; Dir Gen., Economic and Global Issues, FCO, 2017–19. Mem. Bd, Merlin, 2010–13. Trustee, British Council, 2015–19. *Publications*: Making Government Policy: the G8 and G20 in 2010; (contrib.) The New Economic Diplomacy: decision-making and negotiation in international economic relations, 3rd edn, 2011. *Recreations*: travel, running, hill walking, politics. *Address*: Foreign and Commonwealth Office, King Charles Street, SW1A 2AH.

**BRONS, Andrew Henry William**; Member for Yorkshire and Humber, European Parliament, 2009–14 (BNP, 2009–13; British Democratic, 2013–14); *b* Hackney, London, 17 June 1947; *s* of Ronald Brons and Alice Elizabeth Brons (*née* Spenner); *m* 1969, Susan Firth (marr. diss. 1985); two *d*. *Educ*: Harrogate Grammar Sch.; Univ. of York (BA Politics). Lectr, Harrogate Coll. of Further Educn, later Harrogate Coll., 1970–2005. Contested (BNP) Keighley, 2010. *Recreations*: dogs, horse riding, family history, clay pigeon shooting.

**BROODBANK, Prof. Cyprian**, PhD; FBA 2015; John Disney Professor of Archaeology and Director, McDonald Institute for Archaeological Research, University of Cambridge, since 2014; Fellow, Gonville and Caius College, Cambridge, since 2014; *b* London, 26 Dec. 1964; *s* of Denis Arthur Broodbank and Hanna Broodbank (*née* Altmann); *m* 2006, Dr Lindsay Close Spencer; one *s* one *d*. *Educ*: Westminster Sch.; Christ Church, Oxford (BA Mod. Hist. 1986); Univ. of Bristol (MA Aegean and Anatolian Prehist. 1987); King's Coll. and Girton Coll., Cambridge (PhD Classics 1996). J. A. Pye Jun. Res. Fellow, University Coll., Oxford, 1991–93; Institute of Archaeology, University College London: Lectr, 1993–2001; Sen. Lectr, 2001–09; Reader, 2009–10; Prof. of Mediterranean Archaeol., 2010–14. Vis. Fellow, All Souls, Oxford, 2005. Samuel H. Kress Fellow, 2007; British Acad. Mid-Career Fellowship, 2012. FSA 2007. Runciman Prize, Anglo-Hellenic League and Bank of Greece, 2001; James R. Wiseman Prize, Archaeol Inst. of Amer., 2002. *Publications*: An Island Archaeology of the Early Cyclades, 2000 (trans. Greek 2008); The Making of the Middle Sea, 2013 (Wolfson History Prize, 2014). *Recreations*: travel, parenthood, art, cooking, Cornwall and Mediterranean, natural history, dogs. *Address*: McDonald Institute for Archaeological Research, Downing Street, Cambridge CB2 3ER. *T*: (01223) 333538.

**BROOK, Anthony Donald**, FCA; Chairman, Ocean Radio Group Ltd, 1994–2000; *b* 24 Sept. 1936; *s* of Donald Charles Brook and Doris Ellen (*née* Emmett); *m* 1st, 1965, Ann Mary Reeves (*d* 2000); two *d*; 2nd, 2005, Jean Curtis (*d* 2018). *Educ*: Eastbourne Coll. FCA 1970 (ACA 1960). Joined Associated Television Ltd, 1966; Financial Controller, ATV Network Ltd, 1969; Dir of External Finance, IBA, 1974; Finance Dir/Gen. Man., ITC Entertainment Ltd, 1978; Dep. Man. Dir, Television South plc, 1981; Man. Dir (Television), TVS Entertainment, 1984–89, Man. Dir Broadcasting, 1989–91; Man. Dir, TVS Television Ltd, 1986–89; Dep. Chm. and Man. Dir, TVS Entertainment plc, 1991–93; Chairman: SelecTV, 1993–95; Advanced Media Gp plc, 1994–95; Southern Screen Commn, 1996–99. *Recreations*: sailing, travel, golf. *Address*: 9 High Street, Rowledge, Farnham GU10 4BS. *Club*: Tamesis (Teddington, Middx).

**BROOK, Prof. Charles Groves Darville**, MD; FRCP, FRCPH; JP; Professor of Paediatric Endocrinology, University College London, 1989–2000, now Emeritus; Consultant Paediatrician, Middlesex Hospital, 1974–2000, and Gt Ormond Street Hospital, 1994–2000, now Hon. Consulting Paediatric Endocrinologist; Director, London Centre for Paediatric Endocrinology, 1994–2000; *b* 15 Jan. 1940; *s* of Air Vice-Marshal William Arthur Darville Brook, CB, CBE, and Marjorie Jean Brook (*née* Grant, later Hamilton); *m* 1963, Hon. Catherine Mary Hawke, *d* of 9th Baron Hawke; two *d*. *Educ*: Rugby Sch.; Magdalene Coll., Cambridge (MA); St Thomas's Hosp. Med. Sch. (MD 1964). FRCP 1979; FRCPCH 1997. Resident posts at St Thomas' and Gt Ormond St Hosps, 1964–74; Res. Fellow, Kinderspital, Zurich, 1972; University College London: Sen. Lectr in Paediatric Endocrinology, 1983–89; Academic Dir of Endocrinology, 1997–2000. Fellow, UCL Hosps, 2000. Vice Pres., 2004–06, Trustee, 2006–14, St Margaret's Somerset Hospice. Member: Pitcombe Parish Council, 2001–07 (Chm., 2003–07); Pitcombe PCC, 2002–11, 2013– (Sec., 2003–05; Church Warden, 2007–11, 2013–19). JP Avon and Som, 2002–10. Andrea Prader Prize, European Soc. for Paediatric Endocrinology, 2000. *Publications*: Practical Paediatric Endocrinology, 1978; Clinical Paediatric Endocrinology, 1981, 7th edn as Brook's Clinical Pediatric Endocrinology, 2019; Essential Endocrinology, 1982, 4th edn 2001 (trans. French, Polish, Greek); Growth Assessment in Childhood and Adolescence, 1982; All About Adolescence, 1985; Current Concepts in Paediatric Endocrinology, 1987; The Practice of Medicine in Adolescence, 1993; A Guide to the Practice of Paediatric Endocrinology, 1993; Handbook of Clinical Pediatric Endocrinology, 2008 (trans. Russian), 2nd edn 2012; numerous papers on endocrinology in med. jls. *Recreations*: gardening, DIY. *Address*: Hadspen Farm, Castle Cary, Som BA7 7LX. *T*: (01963) 351492. *E*: c.brook@ucl.ac.uk.

*See also* Air Vice-Marshal D. C. G. *Brook*.

**BROOK, Air Vice-Marshal David Conway Grant**, CB 1990; CBE 1983; *b* 23 Dec. 1935; *s* of late Air Vice-Marshal William Arthur Darville Brook, CB, CBE and Jean Brook (later Jean Hamilton); *m* 1961, Jessica (*née* Lubbock); one *s* one *d*. *Educ*: Marlborough Coll.; RAF Coll. Pilot, Nos 263, 1 (Fighter) and 14 Sqdns, 1957–62 (Hunter aircraft; fighter combat leader); ADC to AOC-in-C Near East Air Force, 1962–64; CO No 1 (Fighter) Sqdn, 1964–66 (Hunter Mk 9); RN Staff Course, 1967 (psc); RAF Adviser to Dir Land/ Air Warfare (MoD Army), 1968–69; Wing Comdr Offensive Support, Jt Warfare Estab., 1970–72; CO No 20 (Army Cooperation) Sqdn, 1974–76 (Harrier); Station Comdr, RAF Wittering, 1976–78 (Harrier); RCDS, 1979 (rcds); Principal Staff Officer to Chief of Defence Staff, 1980–82; SASO, HQ RAF Germany, 1982–85; Air Officer Scotland and NI, 1986–89. Civil Emergencies Advr, Home Office, 1989–93. Mem., Lord Chancellor's Panel of Ind. (Highway) Inspectors, 1994–2003. Mem., Chipping Camden Town Council, 1992–94; Chm., Broad Campden Village Hall Cttee, 1993–2006. QCVSA 1962. *Publications*: contrib. to Brasseys Annual, RAF Histl Assoc. Jl. *Recreations*: golf, music, walking. *Address*: Darby's Cottage, Back Ends, Chipping Campden, Glos GL55 6AU. *Club*: Royal Air Force.

*See also* Prof. C. G. D. *Brook*.

**BROOK, Air Vice-Marshal John Michael**, CB 1993; FRCGP; Director General, Royal Air Force Medical Services, 1991–94, retired; RAF civilian medical practitioner, 1994–2008; *b* 26 May 1934; *s* of late Norman Brook and Nellie Brook (*née* Burns); *m* 1959, Edna Kilburn; one *s* three *d*. *Educ*: Mirfield Grammar Sch.; Leeds Univ. (MB ChB 1957). MRCGP 1972, FRCGP 1992; Dip AvMed RCP 1974; MFOM 1981. Commissioned 1959; served Laarbruch, Stafford, Muharraq, Watton, Linton-on-Ouse, MoD; SMO, RAF Finningley, 1974–76; MoD, 1976; SMO RAF Brize Norton, 1978–81; OC RAF Av. Med. Trng Centre, 1981–83; RAF Exchange Officer, USAF HQ Systems Command, 1983–86; OC Defence Services Med. Rehabilitation Unit, 1986–87; OC Central Med. Estabt, 1987–89; Dep. Principal MO, MoD Strike Comd, 1989–91; Dep. Surgeon Gen., Health Services, 1991–93. QHS 1991–94. OStJ 1981. *Recreations*: all music, travel, walking. *Address*: 2 Vicarage Fields, Hemingford Grey, Cambs PE28 9BY. *Club*: Royal Air Force.

**BROOK, Peter Stephen Paul**, CH 1998; CBE 1965; producer; Co-Director, The Royal Shakespeare Theatre; *b* 21 March 1925; 2nd *s* of Simon and Ida Brook; *m* 1951, Natasha Parry (*d* 2015), stage and film star; one *s* one *d*. *Educ*: Westminster; Gresham's; Magdalen College, Oxford (MA; Hon. Fellow, 1991). Productions include: The Tragedy of Dr Faustus, 1942; The Infernal Machine, 1945; Birmingham Repertory Theatre: Man and Superman, King John, The Lady from the Sea, 1945–46; Stratford: Romeo and Juliet, Love's Labour's Lost, 1947; London: Vicious Circle, Men Without Shadows, Respectable Prostitute, The Brothers Karamazov, 1946; Director of Productions, Royal Opera House, Covent Garden, 1947–50: Boris Godunov, La Bohème, 1948; Marriage of Figaro, The Olympians, Salome, 1949. Dark of the Moon, 1949; Ring Round the Moon, 1950; Measure for Measure, Stratford, 1950, Paris, 1978; The Little Hut, 1950; The Winter's Tale, 1951; Venice Preserved, 1953; The Little Hut, New York, Faust, Metropolitan Opera House, 1953; The Dark is Light Enough; Both Ends Meet, 1954; House of Flowers, New York, 1954; The Lark, 1955; Titus Andronicus, Stratford, 1955; Hamlet, London, Moscow, 1955, Paris 2000, London, 2001; The Power and the Glory, 1956; Family Reunion, 1956; The Tempest, Stratford, 1957; Cat on a Hot Tin Roof, Paris, 1957; View from the Bridge, Paris, 1958; Irma la Douce, London, 1958; The Fighting Cock, New York, 1959; Le Balcon, Paris, 1960; The Visit, Royalty, 1960; King Lear, Stratford, Aldwych and Moscow, 1962; The Physicists, Aldwych, 1963; Sergeant Musgrave's Dance, Paris, 1963; The Persecution and Assassination of Marat..., Aldwych, 1964 (New York, 1966); The Investigation, Aldwych, 1965; US, Aldwych, 1966; Oedipus, National Theatre, 1968; A Midsummer Night's Dream, Stratford, 1970, NY, 1971; Timon of Athens, Paris, 1974 (Grand Prix Dominique, 1975; Brigadier Prize, 1975); The Ik, Paris, 1975, London, 1976; Ubu Roi, Paris, 1977; Antony and Cleopatra, Stratford, 1978, Aldwych, 1979; Ubu, Young Vic, 1978; Conference of the Birds, France, Australia, NY, 1980; The Cherry Orchard, Paris, 1981, NY, 1988; La tragédie Carmen, Paris, 1981, NY, 1983 (Emmy Award, and Prix Italia, 1984); The Mahabharata, Avignon and Paris, 1985, Glasgow, 1988, televised, 1989 (Internat. Emmy Award 1990); Woza Albert, Paris, 1988; Carmen, Glasgow, 1989; The Tempest, Glasgow and Paris, 1990; Impressions de Pelléas, Paris, 1992; L'Homme Qui, Paris, 1993, The Man Who, Nat. Theatre, 1994, New York, 1995; Qui Est Là, Paris, 1995;

Oh les Beaux Jours, Lausanne, Paris, Moscow, Tbilisi, 1995, London, 1997; Don Giovanni, Aix, 1998; Je Suis un Phenomène, Paris, 1998; Le Costume, Paris, 1999, Young Vic, 2001; The Tragedy of Hamlet, Paris, 2000, Young Vic, 2001; La Tragédie d'Hamlet, Paris, 2002; Far Away, Paris, 2002; La Mort de Krishna, Paris and tour, 2002; Ta Main dans la Mienne, Paris and tour, 2003; Tierno Bokar, Paris and NY, 2004; Le Grand Inquisiteur, Paris, 2005, world tour and (as The Grand Inquisitor) Barbican Pit, 2006; Fragments, Paris, 2006, Young Vic, 2007, internat. tour (in French and English), 2008; Sizwe Banzi, internat. tour, 2007; Warum Warum, world tour (in German), 2008; Love is my Sin, internat. tour, 2009; 11 and 12, Paris and Barbican, internat. tour, 2009; Une Flute Enchantée (opera), world tour, 2010; The Suit, Paris, 2012, internat. tour, 2013, world tour, 2014; The Valley of Astonishment, Young Vic and world tour, 2014; Battlefield, Young Vic and world tour, 2015; The Prisoner, Paris, 2018, and world tour; work with Internat. Centre of Theatre Research, Paris, Iran, W Africa, and USA, 1971, Sahara, Niger and Nigeria, 1972–73. *Directed films*: The Beggar's Opera, 1952; Moderato Cantabile, 1960; Lord of the Flies, 1962; The Marat/Sade, 1967; Tell Me Lies, 1968; King Lear, 1969; Meetings with Remarkable Men, 1979; The Tragedy of Carmen, 1983; (TV film) The Tragedy of Hamlet, 2001. Hon. DLitt: Birmingham; Strathclyde, 1990; Oxford, 1994; Hon. DDra Acad. of Performing Arts, Hong Kong; Dr *hc*: Adam Mickiewicz Univ., Poznan, Poland; New Sorbonne Paris 3; Laurea *hc*, Letters/Th. and Performing Arts, Rome. SWET award, for outstanding contrib by UK theatre artist to US theatre season, 1983. Freiherr von Stein Foundn Shakespeare Award, 1973; Medaille Vermeil de la Ville de Paris, 2011. Commandeur de l'Ordre des Arts et des Lettres; Officer of the Legion of Honour (France), 1995. *Publications*: The Empty Space, 1968; The Shifting Point (autobiog.), 1988; Le Diable c'est l'Ennui, 1991; There Are No Secrets, 1993; Threads of Time: a memoir, 1998; Evoking Shakespeare, 1999; Between Two Silences, 1999; Climate de Confiance, 2007; With Grotowski, 2009; The Quality of Mercy, 2013; Tip of the Tongue: reflections on language and meaning, 2017. *Recreations*: painting, piano playing. *Address*: Centre International de Recherche Théâtrale, 37 bis Boulevard de la Chapelle, 75010 Paris, France.

**BROOK, Richard;** Chief Executive, Orchard Vale Trust, 2013–18; *b* 22 Nov. 1956; *s* of Ralph Brook and Doris May Brook; *m* 1979, Sheena Ward; two *d*. *Educ*: Keele Univ. (BSc Hons Biol. 1978); University Coll., Cardiff (CQSW and Dip. Social Work 1981); Essex Univ. (MA Social Service Planning 1992). Asst Dir, Thames Reach Housing Assoc., 1991–94; Dir of Care, Heritage Care, 1994–96; Dir of Care and Community Services, Shaftesbury Soc., 1996–99; Chief Executive: Christian Alliance Housing Assoc., 1999–2001; Mind (Nat. Assoc. for Mental Health), 2001–06; Chief Exec., Public Guardianship Office and Public Guardian designate, 2006–07; Chief and Public Guardian, Office of the Public Guardian, 2007–08; Chief Executive: Sense, 2008–10; Crossroads Care, Bucks and Milton Keynes, 2011–13. *Recreations*: computing, home restoration, walking.

**BROOK, Sir Richard (John),** Kt 2002; OBE 1988; ScD; FREng; Chairman, ERA Foundation, 2012–15 (non-executive Director and Board Member, 2002–11); Professor of Materials Science, Oxford University, 1995–2003, now Professor Emeritus; Professorial Fellow, St Cross College, Oxford, 1991–2003, now Hon. Fellow; *b* 12 March 1938; *s* of Frank Brook and Emily Sarah (*née* Lytle); *m* 1961, Elizabeth Christine Aldred; one *s* one *d*. *Educ*: Univ. of Leeds (BSc Ceramics); MIT (ScD Ceramics). FREng (FEng 1998). Res. Asst, MIT, 1962–66; Asst Prof. of Materials Science, Univ. of S California, 1966–70; Gp Leader, AERE, 1970–74; Prof. and Head of Dept of Ceramics, Univ. of Leeds, 1974–88; Scientific Mem., Max Planck Soc. and Dir, Max Planck Inst. Metallforschung, Stuttgart, 1988–91; Cookson Prof. of Materials Sci., 1991–95, and Head, Dept of Materials, 1992–94, Oxford Univ.; Chief Exec., EPSRC, 1994–2001; Dir, Leverhulme Trust, 2001–11. Chairman, Materials Cttee, 1985–88, Materials Commn, 1992–94, SERC; Ext. Mem., Res. Cttee, British Gas, 1989–98; Mem., ESTA, 1994–98; Chm., EU Res. Orgns Hds of Res. Councils, 1997–99. Non-exec. Dir and Bd Mem., Carbon Trust, 2002–11. Mem., Royal Commn for Exhibn of 1851, 2009–19. Mem., Res. Cttee, BM, 2012–. Mem., Curatorium, Körber Award, 1995–2003. Editor, Jl of European Ceramic Soc., 1989–2010. Pres., British Ceramic Soc., 1984–86; Vice-Pres., Inst. of Materials, 1993–95; Fellow, Inst. of Ceramics, 1978 (Pres., 1984–86); Dist. Life Fellow, American Ceramic Soc., 1995; Mem. d'Honneur, Soc. Française Métallurgie Matériaux, 1995–. Mem. Senate, Max Planck Soc., 1999–2011. Hon. Prof., Univ. of Stuttgart, 1990–. Mellor Meml Lectr, Swansea, 1989; Stuijts Meml Lectr, Maastricht, 1989. Mem., Deutsche Akad. der Naturforscher Leopoldina, 2002. Hon. FRAM, 2008; Hon. FBA 2011. Dr *hc*: Aveiro, 1995; Limoges, 2003; Hon. DSc: Bradford, 1996; Loughborough, 2000; Brunel, Nottingham Trent, 2001; Strathclyde, 2002. *Publications*: papers in publications of Inst. of Materials, Amer. Ceramic Soc., European Ceramic Soc. *Recreation*: Europe. *Address*: Department of Materials, University of Oxford, Parks Road, Oxford OX1 3PH.

**BROOK, (Rowland) Stuart;** Managing Director, Community and Social Services, States of Jersey, 2010–12; *b* 17 Nov. 1949; *s* of Geoffrey Brook and Eileen Brook; *m* 1971, Susan Heward; two *s* two *d*. *Educ*: Warwick Univ. (BSc; MBA); Hull Univ. (CQSW; DipASS); Bradford Univ. (MA). Probation Officer, Humberside Probation Service, 1973–77; Humberside County Council: Sen. Social Worker, 1977–81; Area Manager, 1981–84; Principal Officer, Dyfed CC, 1984–87; Asst Dir (Ops), Rotherham MBC, 1987–89; Asst Dir, Bradford MBC, 1989–92; Dep. Dir, 1992–94, Dir, 1995–2005, Notts CC Social Services Dept; Dir of Consulting, Tribal Consulting, 2006–07; Dir, Family Care, Notts, 2007–10; Chm., Man. Bd, Notts Community Health, 2008–10. Non-exec. Dir, Notts County NHS PCT, 2007–09. Chm., Nat. Homecare Council, 2003–05. JP Notts 2007–15. *Recreations*: family, running, cycling, garden. *Address*: Orchard Barn, Bradmore Lane, Plumtree, Notts NG12 5EW.

**BROOK, Prof. Timothy James,** PhD; FRSC; Republic of China Chair, Department of History, University of British Columbia, since 2010 (Professor, since 2004); *b* 6 Jan. 1951; *s* of John and Barbara Brook; *m* 1989, Fay Sims; two *s* two *d*. *Educ*: Univ. of Toronto (BA 1973); Harvard Univ. (AM 1977; PhD 1984). Mactaggart Fellow, Dept of Hist., Univ. of Alberta, 1984–86; Professor: Dept of Hist., Univ. of Toronto, 1986–97, 1999–2004; Dept of Hist., Stanford Univ., 1997–99; Principal, St John's Coll., UBC, 2004–09; Shaw Prof. of Chinese, Univ. of Oxford, 2007–09. Getty Foundn Sen. Scholar, 2013–14. Guggenheim Meml Fellowship, 2006; FRSC 2013. Hon. DLitt Warwick, 2010. François-Xavier Garneau Medal, 2005, Wallace K. Ferguson Prize, 2009, Canadian Histl Assoc.; Mark Lynton Prize in History, Columbia Sch. of Journalism and Neiman Foundn, Harvard Univ., 2009; Prix Auguste Pavie, Acad. des Scis d'Outre-mer, 2010. *Publications*: Geographical Sources of Ming-Qing History, 1988, 2nd edn 2002; The Asiatic Mode of Production, 1989; Quelling the People: the military suppression of the Beijing democracy movement, 1992; Praying for Power: Buddhism and the formation of gentry society in Late-Ming China, 1993; (with Hy Van Luong) Culture and Economy: the shaping of capitalism in Eastern Asia, 1997; (with B. Michael Frolic) Civil Society in China, 1997; The Confusions of Pleasure: commerce and culture in Ming China, 1998; Documents on the Rape of Nanking, 1999; (with Gregory Blue) China and Historical Capitalism: genealogies of Sinological knowledge, 1999; (with Andre Schmid) Nation Work: Asian elites and national identities, 2000; (with Bob Tadashi Wakabayashi) Opium Regimes: China, Britain, and Japan, 2000; The Chinese State in Ming Society, 2005; Collaboration: Japanese agents and Chinese elites in wartime China, 2005; (with Jérôme Bourgon and Gregory Blue) Death by a Thousand Cuts, 2008; Vermeer's Hat: the seventeenth century and the dawn of the global world, 2008; The Troubled Empire: China in the Yuan and Ming dynasties, 2010; Mr Selden's Map of China: the spice trade, a lost chart and the South China Sea, 2014; (ed jtly) Sacred Mandates: Asian international relations since Chinggis Khan, 2018; Great State: China and the world, 2019. *Recreations*: music, travel, poetry, sailing. *Address*: Department of History, University of British Columbia, 1873 East Mall, Vancouver, BC V6T 1Z1, Canada.

**BROOK SMITH, Philip Andrew;** QC 2002; a Recorder, since 2006; *b* 6 March 1957; *s* of Alan and Beryl Smith; adopted surname Brook Smith, 1981; *m* 1981, Charlotte Brook; two *s* one *d*. *Educ*: London Sch. of Econs (BSc 1st Cl. Hons Maths; MSc Maths Dist.). Called to the Bar, Middle Temple, 1982; in practice at the Bar, specialising in commercial law, 1983–. *Address*: (chambers) Fountain Court, Temple, EC4Y 9DH. *T*: (020) 7583 3335, *Fax*: (020) 7353 0329. *E*: pbs@fountaincourt.co.uk.

**BROOKE,** family name of **Viscount Brookeborough,** and **Baron Brooke of Sutton Mandeville**.

**BROOKE, Lord; Charles Fulke Chester Greville;** *b* 27 July 1982; *s* and *heir* of Earl of Warwick, *qv*. *Educ*: Eton; Univ. of S Calif; University Coll. London.

**BROOKE OF ALVERTHORPE,** Baron *cr* 1997 (Life Peer), of Alverthorpe in the co. of West Yorkshire; **Clive Brooke;** Joint General Secretary, Public Services Tax and Commerce Union, 1996–98; *b* 21 June 1942; *s* of Mary Brooke (*née* Colbeck) and John Brooke; *m* 1967, Lorna Hopkin Roberts. *Educ*: Thornes House School, Wakefield. Asst Sec., 1964–82, Dep. Gen. Sec., 1982–88, Gen. Sec., 1988–95, Inland Revenue Staff Fedn. Trade Union Congress: Member: Gen. Council, 1989–96; Exec. Cttee, 1993–96. Govt Partnership Dir, NATS Ltd, 2001–06; Sen. Strategic Advr, Accenture UK plc, 1997–2010; Advr, Liverpool Victoria Friendly Soc., 2002–08. Member: Council of Civil Service Unions, 1982–97 (Chm., Major Policy Cttee, 1996–97); H of C Speaker's Commn on Citizenship, 1988; Exec. Cttee, Involvement and Participation Assoc., 1991–97; Council, Inst. for Manpower Studies, 1994–2001; Pensions Compensation Bd, 1996–2006. Member: H of L EU Select Cttee, 1999–2002, and Chm., Sub-Cttee B (Energy, Industry and Transport), 1998–2002; Jt Cttee on H of L Reform, 2002–03; H of L EU Select Cttee D (Agriculture, Environment and Fisheries), 2007–10; H of L Select Cttee on Crossrail Bill, 2008; H of L EU Select Cttee B (Internal Market, Energy and Transport), 2010–15; H of L Inf. Cttee, 2015–16; H of L Select Cttee on Rev. of Licensing Act 2003, 2016–17; Chm., All Party Parly Gp Against Alcohol Harm, 2014–15 (Vice Chair, 2016–). Mem., Labour Party. Mem., Churches Enquiry on Employment and Future of Work, 1995–96. Trustee: Duke of Edinburgh Study Conf., 1993–2010 (Mem., Canada Conf., 1980); Community Services Volunteers, 1989–2012; IPPR, 1997–; Action on Addiction, 2002–13. Jt Patron, Neighbourhood Initiatives Foundn, 1999–2007; Patron: European Assoc. for the Treatment of Addiction (UK), 2001–; Fedn of Drug and Alcohol Professionals, 2002–; Sparrow Schs Foundn, 2005–; Kenward Trust, 2006–; Everyman Project, 2010–; Tax Help For Older Persons, 2011–; British Liver Trust, 2013–. *Recreations*: painting, reading, watching soccer and Rugby League, walking, gym exercise, fellowship with recovering alcohol addicts, yoga. *Address*: House of Lords, SW1A 0PW. *T*: (020) 7219 0478.

**BROOKE OF SUTTON MANDEVILLE,** Baron *cr* 2001 (Life Peer), of Sutton Mandeville in the County of Wiltshire; **Peter Leonard Brooke,** CH 1992; PC 1988; *b* 3 March 1934; *s* of Lord Brooke of Cumnor, PC, CH and Lady Brooke of Ystradfellte, DBE; *m* 1st, 1964, Joan Margaret Smith (*d* 1985); three *s* (and one *s* decd); 2nd, 1991, Lindsay Allinson. *Educ*: Marlborough; Balliol College, Oxford (MA); Harvard Business School (MBA). Vice-Pres., Nat. Union of Students, 1955–56; Chm., Nat. Conf., Student Christian Movement, 1956; Pres., Oxford Union, 1957; Commonwealth Fund Fellow, 1957–59. Research Assistant, IMEDE, Lausanne, 1960–61; Spencer Stuart & Associates, Management Consultants, 1961–79 (Director of parent company, 1965–79, Chairman, 1974–79); worked in NY and Brussels, 1969–73. Dir, Hambros plc, 1997–98. Mem., Camden Borough Council, 1968–69. Chm., St Pancras N Cons. Assoc., 1976–77. Contested (C) Bedwellty, Oct. 1974; MP (C) City of London and Westminster South, Feb. 1977–1997, Cities of London and Westminster, 1997–2001. Mem., H of L, 2001–15. An Asst Govt Whip, 1979–81; a Lord Comr of HM Treasury, 1981–83; Parly Under Sec. of State, DES, 1983–85; Minister of State, HM Treasury, 1985–87; Paymaster Gen., 1987–89; Chm., Conservative Party, 1987–89; Secretary of State: for NI, 1989–92; for Nat. Heritage, 1992–94. Chm., H of C Select Cttee on NI, 1997–2001. Mem., British Irish Parly Body, 1997–2007. Chm., Assoc. of Cons. Peers, 2004–06. Chm., Building Socs Ombudsman Council, 1996–2001. President: IAPS, 1980–83; British Antique Dealers Assoc., 1995–2005; British Art Market Fedn, 1996–2014; Friends of Wilts Churches, 2009–14; Patron, Wilts Heritage Mus., Devizes, 2012–. Mem. Council, Marlborough Coll., 1977–83, 1992–95; Lay Mem., Univ. of London Council, 1994–2006 (Dep. Chm., 2001–02; Chm. and Pro-Chancellor, 2002–06). Chm., Churches Conservation Trust, 1995–98. Trustee: Wordsworth Trust, 1974–2001; Cusichaca Project, 1978–98; Conf. on Trng in Archtl Conservation, 1994–97 (Pres., 1997–). Pres., St Andrew's Youth Club, 1998–2006. Founding Master, Guild of Art Scholars, Dealers and Collectors, 2006. FSA 1998. Sen. Fellow, RCA, 1987; Presentation Fellow, KCL, 1989; Hon. Fellow: QMW, 1996; Univ. of Wales, Lampeter, 2008. Hon. DLitt: Westminster, 1999; London Guildhall, 2001; Hon. LLD London, 2006. *Recreations*: churches, conservation, cricket, visual arts. *Clubs*: Beefsteak, Brooks's, Grillions, MCC, I Zingari.
*See also* D. R. V. Brooke.

**BROOKE, Sir Alistair Weston,** 4th Bt *cr* 1919, of Almondbury; *b* 12 Sept. 1947; *s* of Major Sir John Weston Brooke, 3rd Bt, TD, and Rosemary (*d* 1979), *d* of late Percy Nevill, Birling House, West Malling, Kent; *S* father, 1983; *m* 1982, Susan Mary, *d* of Barry Charles Roger Griffiths, MRCVS, Church House, Norton, Powys; one *d*. *Educ*: Repton; Royal Agricultural Coll., Cirencester. *Recreations*: shooting, farming, racehorse training. *Heir*: *b* Charles Weston Brooke [*b* 27 Jan. 1951; *m* 1984, Tanya Elizabeth, *d* of Antony Thelwell Maurice; one *s* two *d*].

**BROOKE, Rt Hon. Dame Annette (Lesley),** DBE 2015 (OBE 2013); PC 2014; *b* 7 June 1947; *m* Mike Brooke; two *d*. *Educ*: Romford Tech. Sch.; LSE (BSc Econ); Hughes Hall, Cambridge (Cert Ed). Teacher of econs and social scis in schs and colls in Reading, Aylesbury and Poole; Hd of Econs, Talbot Heath Sch., Bournemouth, 1984–94; Tutor, Open Univ., 1971–91. Partner, Broadstone Minerals. Poole Borough Council: Mem. (Lib Dem), 1986–2003; Chairman: Planning Cttee, 1991–96; Educn Cttee, 1996–2000; Dep. Gp Leader, 1995–97, 1998–2000; Mayor, 1997–98. MP (Lib Dem) Mid Dorset and N Poole, 2001–15. Lib Dem spokesman on children, 2004–10. Mem., Panel of Chairs, 2010–15. Chm., Lib Dem Parly Party, 2013–15.

**BROOKE, Sir Christopher;** *see* Brooke, Sir R. C.

**BROOKE, Daniel Roderick Villaret;** Chief Marketing and Communications Officer, 2010–19, and Board Champion for Diversity and Inclusion, Channel 4 Television Corporation; *b* Hammersmith, 1 June 1967; *s* of Baron Brooke of Sutton Mandeville, *qv*; *m*

2004, Juliet Soskice (marr. diss. 2013); two s. *Educ:* Marlborough Coll.; Newcastle Poly. (BA Hons Graphic Design 1989); Univ. of Stirling (MBA 1990). Dir of Mktg, Paramount Comedy Channel, 1996–98; Head of Marketing and Development: Film4, 1998–2000; Digital Channels, Channel 4, 2000–01; Gen. Manager, E4, 2001–03; Managing Director: Digital Channels, Channel 4, 2003–05; Discovery Networks UK, 2005–09; Rare Day Prodns, 2009–10. Trustee, Mass Extinction Monitoring Observatory.

**BROOKE, David Michael Graham;** QC 2017; a Recorder, since 2019; *b* London, 11 June 1966; *s* of Peter Brooke and Muriel Brooke; *m* 1997, Lucy Allum. *Educ:* Lancing Coll.; Durham Univ. (BA Hons); City Univ. (DipLaw). Called to the Bar, Inner Temple, 1990; Hd of Chambers, KBW, 2017–. Licensed Reader, C of E, 2016–. *Recreations:* walking, fishing, travelling. *Address:* KBW Chambers, The Engine House, 1 Foundry Square, Leeds LS11 5DL. *T:* (0113) 297 1200. *E:* dbqc@kbwchambers.com.

**BROOKE, Sir Francis (George Windham),** 4th Bt *cr* 1903; Director, Troy Asset Management Ltd, since 2004; *b* 15 Oct. 1963; *s* of Sir George Cecil Francis Brooke, 3rd Bt, MBE, and of Lady Melissa Brooke, *er d* of 6th Earl of Dunraven and Mount-Earl, CB, CBE, MC; *S* father, 1982; *m* 1989, Hon. Katharine Elizabeth, *o d* of Baron Hussey of North Bradley and of Lady Susan Hussey, *qv*; one *s* two *d*. *Educ:* Eton; Edinburgh University (MA Hons). CFA (AIIMR 1993). Investment Analyst, Kleinwort Benson Securities, 1986–88; Fund Manager, 1989–94, Dir, 1994–97, Foreign & Colonial Mgt Ltd; Dir, Mercury Asset Mgt, subseq., Merrill Lynch Investment Managers, 1997–2004. Trustee, Ascot Authy, 2011–; Chm., Ascot Authy Hldgs Ltd, 2018–. *Heir: s* George Francis Geoffrey Brooke, *b* 10 Sept. 1991. *Address:* Flat 8, 34 Elm Park Gardens, SW10 9NZ; Glenbevan, Croom, Co. Limerick, Ireland. *Clubs:* Turf, White's, Pratt's, Jockey; Royal St George's (Sandwich); Swinley Forest; Brook (New York).

**BROOKE, Prof. George John,** PhD; DD; Rylands Professor of Biblical Criticism and Exegesis, University of Manchester, 1998–2016, now Emeritus; *b* 27 April 1952; *s* of Comdr Henry John Allen Brooke, MBE, DSC, and Lesley Mary Brooke (*née* Noble); *m* 1976, (Rosemary) Jane Peacocke; two *s* one *d*. *Educ:* Wellington Coll.; St Peter's Coll., Oxford (BA 1973; MA 1978; DD 2010); St John's Coll., Cambridge (PGCE 1974); Claremont Graduate Sch., Claremont, Calif (PhD 1978). Fulbright Scholar, 1974–77; Jun. Fellow, Oxford Univ. Centre for Postgrad. Hebrew Studies, 1977–78; Lectr in New Testament Studies, 1978–84, Vice-Principal, 1982–84, Salisbury and Wells Theol Coll.; University of Manchester: Lectr in Intertestamental Lit., 1984–94, Sen. Lectr, 1994–97; Prof. of Biblical Studies, 1997–98. Res. Scholar, Ecumenical Inst., Tantur, 1983; Sen. Res. Fellow, Annenberg Inst., Philadelphia, 1992; Guest Professor: Univ. of Aarhus, 2007; Yale Univ., 2015; Vis. Prof., Univ. of Chester, 2016–; Dirk Smilde Fellow, Univ. of Groningen, 2018. President: British Assoc. of Jewish Studies, 1999; SOTS, 2012. Founding Editor, Dead Sea Discoveries, 1994–; Editor: Jl of Semitic Studies, 1991–2019; SOTS Book List, 2000–06; Studies on the Texts of the Desert of Judah, 2013–. Hon. DèsSc Religions Lausanne, 2018. *Publications:* Exegesis at Qumran: 4QFlorilegium in its Jewish context, 1985; The Allegro Qumran Collection, 1996; (jtly) The Complete World of the Dead Sea Scrolls, 2002, 2nd edn 2011; Qumran and the Jewish Jesus, 2005; The Dead Sea Scrolls and the New Testament: essays in mutual illumination, 2005; Reading the Dead Sea Scrolls: essays in method, 2013; The Dead Sea Scrolls and German Scholarship, 2018; edited: Temple Scroll Studies, 1989; Women in the Biblical Tradition, 1992; New Qumran Texts and Studies, 1994; The Birth of Jesus, 2000; Jewish Ways of Reading the Bible, 2000; edited jointly: Septuagint, Scrolls and Cognate Writings, 1992; Ugarit and the Bible, 1994; Narrativity in Biblical and Related Texts, 2000; Copper Scroll Studies, 2002; Studia Semitica, 2005; Ancient and Modern Scriptural Historiography, 2007; The Significance of Sinai, 2008; The Mermaid and the Partridge, 2011; The Scrolls and Biblical Traditions, 2012; Goochem in Mokum-Wisdom in Amsterdam, 2016; On Prophets, Warriors and Kings, 2016; Jewish Education from Antiquity to the Middle Ages, 2017; Hā-ish Mōshe: studies in honor of Moshe J. Bernstein, 2017; Near Eastern and Arabian Essays, 2018; T&T Clark Companion to the Dead Sea Scrolls, 2019. *Recreations:* cooking, hill walking. *Address:* 3 Bridge Place, Chester CH1 1SA. *T:* (01244) 351432. *E:* george.brooke@manchester.ac.uk.

**BROOKE, Ian Richard,** CB 2002; various posts with Ministry of Defence, 1971–2003; *b* 14 Aug. 1946; *s* of Richard Leslie Frederick Brooke and Betty Margaret (*née* Holliday); *m* 1970, Rachel Grace Wade; two *s*. *Educ:* St Clement Danes Grammar Sch.; Southampton Univ. (BSc(Eng)). FCO, 1967–71. Mem., St Albans Diocesan Synod, 2000–03; Churchwarden, 2003–07; Treas., PCC, 2014–16. *Recreations:* genealogy, walking, visiting cathedrals.

**BROOKE, Prof. John Hedley,** PhD; Andreas Idreos Professor of Science and Religion, and Director, Ian Ramsey Centre, Oxford University, 1999–2006; Fellow of Harris Manchester College, Oxford, 1999–2006, now Fellow Emeritus; *b* 20 May 1944; *s* of Hedley Joseph Brooke and Margaret Brooke (*née* Brown); *m* 1972, Janice Marian Heffer. *Educ:* Fitzwilliam Coll., Cambridge (MA; PhD 1969). Res. Fellow, Fitzwilliam Coll., Cambridge, 1967–68; Tutorial Fellow, Univ. of Sussex, 1968–69; Lancaster University: Lectr, 1969–80; Sen. Lectr, 1980–91; Reader in History of Science, 1991–92; Prof. of History of Science, 1992–99. Co-ordinator, ESF Network on Sci. and Human Values, 2000–04; Co-Dir, Templeton Project on Sci. and Religion in Schs, 2002–06. Vis. Prof., Leeds Univ., 2013–. Lectures: (jtly) Gifford, Glasgow Univ., 1995–96; Alister Hardy Meml, Oxford Univ., 2000; Dist., Amer. Hist. of Sci. Soc., 2001; Darwin Fest., Cambridge Univ., 2009; Boyle, St Mary-le-Bow, 2010; Dimaras, Nat. Hellenic Res. Foundn, Athens, 2016; James Gregory, St Andrews Univ., 2018; Select Preacher, Oxford Univ., 2001. Member: Adv. Bd, Boyle Lectureship, 2010–; Internat. Adv. Bd, Faraday Inst., 2019–. Foundn Fellow, Inst. for Advanced Studies, Durham Univ., 2007. President: Historical Section, BAAS, 1996–97; British Soc. for History of Science, 1996–98; Science and Religion Forum, 2006–; Foundn Mem. and Mem. Exec. Cttee, Internat. Soc. for Sci. and Religion, 2001–08 (Pres., 2008–11; Hon. Fellow, 2017); Corresp. Mem., 1993, Effective Mem., 2013, Internat. Acad. of History of Science. Ed., British Jl for the History of Science, 1989–93. *Publications:* Science and Religion: some historical perspectives, 1991, 2014; Thinking about Matter: studies in the history of chemical philosophy, 1995; (jtly) Reconstructing Nature: the engagement of science and religion, 1998; (ed jtly) Science in Theistic Contexts, 2001; (ed jtly) Heterodoxy in Early Modern Science and Religion, 2005; (ed jtly) Religious Values and the Rise of Science in Europe, 2005; (ed jtly) Science and Religion around the World, 2011; many articles on history of chemistry and history of natural theology. *Recreations:* music (opera), foreign travel, chess, walking, rhododendrons. *Address:* c/o Harris Manchester College, Oxford OX1 3TD. *T:* (01865) 271006.

**BROOKE, John Stephen P.;** *see* Pitt-Brooke.

**BROOKE, Sir (Richard) Christopher,** 12th Bt *cr* 1662, of Norton Priory, Cheshire; *b* London, 10 July 1966; *er s* of Sir Richard Christopher David Brooke, 11th Bt and of Carola Marion (*née* Erskine-Hill, now Countess Cowley); *S* father, 2012; *m* 2002, Sarah Anne Louise Montague, *qv*; three *d*, and one *d* from previous marriage. *Educ:* Eton Coll.; Edinburgh Univ. (MA Hons). Man. Dir, Hillbrooke Hotels Ltd, 2006–. *Recreations:* ski-ing, shooting, fishing, gardening. *Heir: b* Edward Marcus Brooke [*b* 24 March 1970; *m* 1995, Catherine Janet Corbett; one *s* one *d*]. *Address:* 16 St Peter's Square, W6 9AJ. *T:* 07770 268359. *E:* christoph@hillbrooke.co.uk. *Club:* Boodle's.

**BROOKE, Sir Rodney (George),** Kt 2007; CBE 1996; DL; Chairman: Quality Assurance Agency for Higher Education, 2009–14; Leeds Playhouse (formerly West Yorkshire Playhouse), since 2011; *b* 22 Oct. 1939; *s* of George Sidney Brooke and Amy Brooke; *m* 1967, Dr Clare Margaret Cox; one *s* one *d*. *Educ:* Queen Elizabeth's Grammar Sch., Wakefield. Admitted solicitor (hons), 1962. Rochdale County Bor. Council, 1962–63; Leicester CC, 1963–65; Stockport County Bor. Council, 1965–73; West Yorkshire Metropolitan County Council: Dir of Admin, 1973–81; Chief Exec. and Clerk, 1981–84; Clerk to W Yorks Lieutenancy, 1981–84; Chief Exec., Westminster City Council, 1984–89; Clerk to Gtr London Lieutenancy, 1987–89; Sec., AMA, 1990–97. Chm., Bradford HA, 1989–90; Director: Riverside Health Trust, 2000–02; Westminster PCT, 2002–06. Secretary: Yorks and Humberside Tourist Board, 1974–84; Yorks and Humberside Develt Assoc., 1974–84; Hon. Sec., London Boroughs Assoc., 1984–90; Dir, Foundn for IT in Local Govt, 1988–92; Chairman: Electricity Consumers' Cttee (Yorks), 1997–2000; National Electricity Consumers Council, 1999–2000; General Social Care Council, 2002–08. Associate: Local Govt Mgt Bd, 1997–2000; Politics Internat., 1998–2000. Member: Action London, 1988–90; Exec., SOLACE, 1981–84, 1987–89; CS Final Selection Bd, 1991–2000; Ethics Standards Bd for Accountants, 2001–03; Nat. Inf. Governance Bd for Health Records, 2007–13; GMC, 2009. Chm., Durham Univ. Centre for Public Management Res., 1994–97; Vis. Res. Fellow, RIPA, 1989–92; Vis. Fellow, Nuffield Inst. for Health Studies, Leeds Univ., 1989–96; Sen. Vis. Res. Fellow, Sch. of Public Policy, Birmingham Univ., 1997–. Dir, Dolphin Square Trust, 1987–2011 (Chm., 2002–11); Mem. Bd, Capacitybuilders, 2008–11; Chairman: London NE, Royal Jubilee and Prince's Trusts, 1984–91; Ilkley Manor House Trust, 2016–18 (Pres., 2018–). Trustee: Community Develt Foundn, 1996–2000; Dolphin Square Charitable Foundn, 2005–11; Internet Watch Foundn, 2007–13; RNID, 2008–14; Royal Coll. of Pathologists, 2015–17. Associate, Ernst & Young, 1989–90. Editl Advr, Longman Gp, 1989–90. Mem. Council, Tavistock Inst., 2006–12. Gov., Pimlico Sch., 2000–07 (Chm., 2003–05). Hon. Fellow, Inst. of Govt Studies, Birmingham Univ. FRSA. Freeman, City of London, 1993. DL Greater London, 1989. National Order of Merit (France), 1984; Nat. Order of Aztec Eagle (Mexico), 1985; Medal of Merit (Qatar), 1985; Order of Merit (Germany), 1986; Legion of Merit (Senegal), 1988. *Publications:* Managing the Enabling Authority, 1989; The Environmental Role of Local Government, 1990; (jtly) City Futures in Britain and Canada, 1990; (jtly) The Public Service Manager's Handbook, 1992; (jtly) Strengthening Local Government in the 1990s, 1997; (jtly) Ethics in Public Service for the New Millennium, 2000; The Consumers-Eye View of Utilities, 2000; The Councillor: victim or vulgarian, 2005; articles on local govt and social care. *Recreations:* ski-ing, opera, Byzantium, theatre. *Address:* 41 Kings Road, Ilkley, W Yorks LS29 9AR. *T:* (01943) 601869; 706 Grenville House, Dolphin Square, SW1V 3LR. *T:* (020) 7798 8086. *Clubs:* Athenæum, Ski Club of Great Britain.

**BROOKE, Sarah Anne Louise, (Lady Brooke);** *see* Montague, S. A. L.

**BROOKE-BALL, Patricia Ann;** *see* Hitchcock, P. A.

**BROOKEBOROUGH,** 3rd Viscount *cr* 1952, of Colebrooke; **Alan Henry Brooke,** Bt 1822; KG 2018; farmer; a Personal Lord in Waiting to the Queen, since 1997; Lord-Lieutenant of Co. Fermanagh, Northern Ireland, since 2012; *b* 30 June 1952; *s* of 2nd Viscount Brookeborough, PC and Rosemary Hilda (*née* Chichester); *S* father, 1987; *m* 1980, Janet Elizabeth, *d* of J. P. Cooke, Doagh, Ballyclare. *Educ:* Harrow; Millfield. Commissioned 17th/21st Lancers, 1971; transferred 4th (County Fermanagh) Bn, UDR, 1977; Company Commander, 1981–83; Royal Irish Regt (Co. Comdr, 1988–93); Lt-Col, 1993, transf. to RARO. Now farms and runs an estate with a shooting/fishing tourist enterprise. Member: EEC Agricl Sub-Cttee, H of L, 1988–92, 1993–97; EC Select Cttee and Sub-Cttee B (energy, industry and transport), H of L, 1998–2002; Sub-Cttee D, H of L, 2006–10; Sub-Cttee A (EU finance and econs), H of L, 2012–15; Ad hoc Cttee on Financial Exclusion, 2016–17; elected Mem., H of L, 1999. Non-exec. Director: Green Park Unit Hosp. Trust, 1993–2001; Basel International (Jersey), 2000–13 (Chm., 1996–2000). Mem., NI Policing Bd, 2001–06. Hon. Col, 4th/5th Bn, Royal Irish Rangers, 1997–2008. Pres., ABF Soldiers' Charity (formerly ABF), NI, 1995–. Dl 1987, High Sheriff 1995, Co. Fermanagh. *Recreations:* shooting, fishing. *Heir: b* Hon. Christopher Arthur Brooke [*b* 16 May 1954; *m* 1990, Amanda Hodges; four *s* one *d*]. *Address:* Colebrooke Park, Brookeborough, Co. Fermanagh, N Ireland BT94 4DW. *T:* (01365) 531402. *Club:* Cavalry and Guards.

**BROOKER, Alan Bernard;** JP, DL; FCA; Chairman: Kode International, 1988–98; E. T. Heron & Co., 1991–96; *b* 24 Aug. 1931; *s* of late Bernard John Brooker and of Gwendoline Ada (*née* Launchbury); *m* 1957, Diana (*née* Coles); one *s* two *d*. *Educ:* Chigwell School, Essex. FCA 1954. Served 2nd RHA (2nd Lieut), 1954–56. Articled, Cole, Dickin & Hills, Chartered Accountants, 1949–54, qualified 1954; Manager, Cole, Dickin & Hills, 1956–58; Accountant, Independent Dairies, 1958–59; Asst Accountant, Exchange Telegraph Co., 1959–64; Dir, 1964–87, Chm. and Chief Exec., 1980–87, Extel Group. Chm., Serif Cowells, then Serif, 1990–93; Vice-Chairman: Provident Financial, 1983–94; James Martin Associates, 1987–89; non-executive Director: Pauls plc, 1984–85; Aukett Associates, 1988–2002; Plysu, 1988–99; PNA Holdings, 1988–89; Addison Worldwide, 1990–94; Eastern Counties Newspapers (formerly East Anglian Daily Times), 1990–96; ACAL plc, 1996–2002. Member: Council, CBI London Region, 1980–83; Companies Cttee, CBI, 1979–83; Council, CPU, 1975–88. Appeal Chm., Newspaper Press Fund, 1985–86. Governor: Chigwell School, 1968–2006 (Chm., 1978–99); Felixstowe Coll., 1986–94. Essex Pres., RBL, 2002–05. Freeman, City of London; Liveryman, Stationers' and Newspapermakers' Co. (Court Asst, 1985–2007; Master, 1995–96). Churchwarden, St Bride's, Fleet Street, 1986–2002. JP Essex 1972 (Chm. of Bench, Epping and Ongar, 1995–99); DL Essex 1982. FRSA 1980. *Recreations:* cricket, golf. *Address:* Silkwater, East Hill, Evershot, Dorset DT2 0LB. *Clubs:* East India, MCC; Royal Worlington and Newmarket Golf.

**BROOKER, David;** Director of Sport, Department for Culture, Media and Sport, 2011–14; *b* Epping, Essex, 12 July 1952; *s* of Victor Richard Joseph Brooker and Betty Brooker (*née* Pearson); *m* 1976, Jacqueline Pine; two *s* one *d*. *Educ:* Magee Univ. Coll.; Univ. of Ulster (BA Hons English 1974). Northern Ireland Office, 1975–84: Private Sec. to Minister of State, 1979–81, to Perm. Under-Sec., 1982–83; Police Dept, Home Office, 1984–87; Northern Ireland Office: Security Directorate, 1987–90; Pol Directorate, 1991–2000; rcds 1996; Hd, HR, 2001–02; Principal Private Sec. to Sec. of State for NI, 2003–04; Dir of Communications, 2005–08; Dir of Legacy, Govt Olympic Exec., DCMS, 2008–12. Non-exec. Dir, NI Office, 2016–. Mem., ind. assessment panel for UK host-city for 2022 Commonwealth Games (awarded to Birmingham), 2017. Mem., Appts Cttee, CSSC Sports and Leisure, 2014–. Trustee, HighGround, 2015–16 (Chm., 2015–16). *Recreations:* cricket, golf, tennis. *Address:* c/o Northern Ireland Office, 1 Horse Guards Road, SW1A 2HQ. *Clubs:* Travellers; MCC, Buckinghamshire County Cricket.

**BROOKES, James Robert;** ICT consultant, since 1998; non-executive Chairman, HomeWorkBase Ltd, 2005–14; non-executive Director, RMS Ltd, 2007–14; *b* 2 Sept. 1941; *s of* James Brookes and Hettie Brookes (*née* Colley); *m* 1964, Patricia Gaskell (*d* 2011); three *d*. *Educ*: Manchester Grammar Sch.; Corpus Christi Coll., Oxford (MA Maths). FBCS; CEng 1990; Eur Ing, 1991. Various posts as systems and applications programmer in develt, tech. support and sales; Northern Branch Manager, Univs and Nat. Research Region, Ferranti/Internat. Computers, 1962–67; Computer Services Manager, Queen's Univ. Belfast, 1967–69; Operations Manager, Univ. of Manchester Regional Computer Centre, 1969–75; Director: SW Univs Regional Computer Centre, 1975–87; Bath Univ. Computer Service, 1983–87; Inf. Services Orgn, Portsmouth Univ., 1992–95; Head of Information Systems, Avon and Somerset Constabulary, 1995–98. Co-founder and non-exec. Chm., Praxis Systems, 1983; Chief Exec., 1986–91, Consultant, 1991–92, Mem. Council, 2016–19, BCS; non-executive Director: The Knowledge Gp, 1998–2002; Smart South West, 1999–2004; Consultant, SOCITM, 1998–. Vis. Prof., Business Sch., Strathclyde Univ., 1991–98. Mem. Council, PITCOM, 1989–2011 (Prog. Exec., 1997–2000); Mem., PICTFOR, 2011–; Hon. Sec., Council of European Professional Information Socs, 1991–93. Trustee, Young Electronic Designer Awards, 1994–2005. Mem., Bd of Dirs, Marshfield Community Land Trust. FRSA 1988. Freeman, City of London, 1989; Liveryman, Information Technologists' Co. (Mem., 1988). *Recreations*: sailing, fell-walking, cycling, bridge, reading, theatre. *Address*: 29 High Street, Marshfield, Chippenham, Wilts SN14 8LR. *T*: (home) (01225) 891294. *E*: jr.brookes@btinternet.com. *Club*: Oxford and Cambridge.

**BROOKES, Michael John Patrick;** General Secretary, National Association of Head Teachers, 2005–10; Director, Mick Brookes Leadership Associates, 2010–16; *b* 12 May 1948; *s of* Percival John Brookes and Joan Brookes; *m* 2000, Karen Jane Mann; one *s*. *Educ*: King Alfred's Coll., Winchester (Cert Ed); Open Univ. (BA); Nottingham Univ. (MEd). Teacher: Kanes Hill First Sch., Southampton, 1969–70; Liss Jun. Sch., Hants, 1971–74; Dep. Hd, Gosberton Primary Sch., Lincs, 1975–78; Head: Gosberton Clough & Risegate Sch., Lincs, 1978–85; Sherwood Jun. Sch., Notts, 1985–2005. Chm. Govs, Bolton Primary Sch., 2013. *Recreations*: walking, motorcycling, music.

**BROOKES, Nicholas Kelvin,** FCA; Chairman, De La Rue plc, 2004–12 (non-executive Director, 1997–2012); *b* 19 May 1947; *s of* Stanley Brookes and Jean (*née* Wigley); *m* 1968, Maria Rosa Crespo; two *s* one *d*. *Educ*: Harrow Sch. FCA 1971. Articles for ACA, Hart Bros Reddall & Co., London, 1965–69; joined Texas Instruments, 1975; Man. Dir, Canada, 1980–85; Man. Dir, Europe, 1985–92; Vice-Pres., Texas Instruments Inc. and Pres., Materials and Controls Gp, 1992–95; Chief Exec., Bowthorpe, then Spirent, plc, 1995–2004. Non-executive Director: Corp. Financiera ALBA SA, Spain, 1999; Axel-Johnson Inc., Sweden, 2005. Non-exec. Dir, Inst. of Directors, 2007. FInstD. *Recreations*: tennis, badminton, opera. *Club*: Reform.

**BROOKES, Peter C.;** *see* Cannon-Brookes.

**BROOKES, Peter Derek,** CBE 2017; RDI 2002; Political Cartoonist, The Times, since 1993; *b* 28 Sept. 1943; *s of* George Henry Brookes and Joan Elizabeth Brookes; *m* 1971, Angela Harrison; two *s*. *Educ*: Heversham Grammar Sch., Westmorland; RAF Coll., Cranwell (BA London Ext.); Central School of Art and Design (BA). Freelance illustrator, 1969–; Cover Artist, The Spectator, 1986–98, 2005–; stamp designs for Royal Mail, 1995, 1999 and 2003; contributor to: The Times, Sunday Times, Radio Times, New Statesman, The Listener, Spectator, TLS and Glyndebourne Fest. Opera Books. Illustration Tutor: Central Sch. of Art and Design, 1977–79; RCA, 1979–89. Mem., AGI, 1988–. FRSA 2000. Political Cartoonist of the Year, 1996, 1998, 2006, 2010 and 2013, Lifetime Achievement Award, 2017, Cartoon Art Trust Awards; Cartoonist of Year, British Press Awards, 2002, 2007, 2010, 2011, 2012, 2014, 2015 and 2017; Cartoonist of the Year, What the Papers Say Awards, 2005; Cartoonist of the Year, 2006, 2009, 2010 and 2014, Cartoon of the Year, 2015, 2016, 2018, Political Cartoon Soc. *Publications*: Nature Notes, 1997; Nature Notes: the new collection, 1999; Nature Notes III, 2001; Peter Brookes of The Times, 2002; Nature Notes IV, 2004; The Best of Times, 2009; Hard Times, 2011; Sign of the Times, 2013; Testing Times, 2015; Interesting Times, 2017; Critical Times, 2019. *Recreations*: music, QPR, arguing. *Address*: 30 Vanbrugh Hill, Blackheath, SE3 7UF. *T*: (020) 8858 9022, 07540 463854.

**BROOKING, Barry Alfred,** MBE 1972; Chief Executive, British Psychological Society, 2000–04; *b* 2 Feb. 1944; *s of* Alfred Brooking and Winifred Joan Brooking; *m* 1978, Julia Irene McBride (marr. diss. 1993). *Educ*: Milford Haven GS; Sir Joseph Williamson's Math. Sch., Rochester; Birkbeck Coll., London Univ. (BA 1976, MA 1980). ACP. Royal Navy, 1965–81: BRNC Dartmouth, 1965; HMS Pembroke, 1966–67; HMS Diamond, 1968–69; CTC RM, Lympstone, 1969; 41 Cdo RM, 1969–70; 40 Cdo RM, 1970–72; HMS Raleigh, 1972–75; RN Sch. of Educnl and Trng Technol., 1976–78; ARE, 1978–81. Business Adminr, Med. Protection Soc., 1981–91; Regl Dir, St John Ambulance, 1992–95; Chief Exec., Parkinson's Disease Soc., 1995–99. Member: Surrey Magistrates' Soc., 1985–2000; Surrey Magistrates' Courts Cttee, 1993–95; Surrey Probation Cttee, 1993–95; Plymouth District Magistrates' Assoc., 2014–; Dep. Chm., North and East PSD, Surrey, 1995–97. Pres., Brooking Soc., 2004–14 (Mem., 1980–; Chm., 1993–2004). JP Surrey, 1985–2000, Leics, 2001–04, S and W Devon (formerly Plymouth and Dist), 2004–14. Business Develt Award, Surrey TEC, 1994. *Publications*: Naval Mathematics Self-Tuition Text, 1966; Naval English Self-Tuition Text, 1966; Naval Mathematics Programmed-Learning Text, 1967; Royal Navy CCTV Production Techniques Handbook, 1977; (contrib.) Educational Technology in a Changing World: aspects of educational technology Vol. XII, 1978; ARE reports, booklets, articles in jls. *Recreations*: travel, theatre, cinema, music, history, sport. *Address*: 9 Hawkmoor Parke, Bovey Tracey, Devon TQ13 9NL.

**BROOKING, Sir Trevor (David),** Kt 2004; CBE 1999 (MBE 1981); football broadcaster, since 1984; Director of Football Development, Football Association, 2004–14; *b* 2 Oct. 1948; *s of* Henry and Margaret Brooking; *m* 1970, Hilkka Helina Helakorpi; one *s* one *d*. *Educ*: Ilford County High Sch. Professional footballer with West Ham United, 1965–84: played 642 games; scored 111 goals; FA Cup winner, 1975, *v* Fulham, 1980, *v* Arsenal (scoring only goal); won Football League Div. 2, 1980–81; 47 appearances for England, 1974–82. Chm., Eastern Council for Sport and Recreation, 1986–95; Sports Council, then English Sports Council, subseq. Sport England: Mem., 1989–2002; Vice-Chm., 1994–96; Chm., 1998–2002. *Publications*: Trevor Brooking (autobiog.), 1981; Trevor Brooking's 100 Great British Footballers, 1988; My Life in Football, 2014. *Recreations*: golf, tennis.

**BROOKMAN,** family name of **Baron Brookman**.

**BROOKMAN,** Baron *cr* 1998 (Life Peer), of Ebbw Vale in the co. of Gwent; **David Keith Brookman;** General Secretary, Iron and Steel Trades Confederation, 1993–99; *b* 3 Jan. 1937; *s of* George Henry Brookman, MM and Blodwin Brookman (*née* Nash); *m* 1958, Patricia Worthington; three *d*. *Educ*: Nantyglo Grammar Sch., Gwent. Nat. Service, RAF, 1955–57. Steel worker, Richard Thomas & Baldwin, Ebbw Vale, 1953–55 and 1957–73; Iron & Steel Trades Confederation: Organiser, 1973–85; Asst Gen. Sec., 1985–93. Trades Union Congress: Member: Educn Adv. Cttee for Wales, 1976–82; Steel Cttee, 1985–90; Gen. Council, 1992–99. Member: Brit. Steel Jt Accident Prevention Adv. Cttee, 1985–93; Brit. Steel Adv. Cttee on Educn and Trng, 1986–93; Nat. Steel Co-ordinating Cttee, 1991–99 (Chm., 1993–99); Consultative Cttee, ECSC, 1993–2002; Operatives' Security: Jt Ind. Council for Slag Ind., 1985–93; Brit. Steel Long Products portfolio of cos Jt Standing Cttee, 1993–98; Brit. Steel Strip Trade Bd, 1993–98; Mem. Bd, UK Steel Enterprise (formerly Brit. Steel (Ind.) Ltd), 1993–; Jt Sec., European Works Council, British Steel, 1996–98. Member Executive Council: European Metalworkers' Fedn, 1985–95 (Mem., Steel Cttee, 1994–99); CSEU, 1989–93; International Metalworkers' Federation: Hon. Sec., Brit. Section, 1993–99; Pres., Iron and Steel and Non-Ferrous Metals Dept, 1993–99. Labour Party: Member: Exec. Cttee, Wales, 1982–85; Nat. Constitutional Cttee, 1987–91; NEC, 1991–92. Trustee, Julian Melchett Trust, 1985–95. Gov., Gwent Coll. of HE, 1980–84. *Recreations*: cricket, Rugby, reading, golf.

**BROOKMYRE, Christopher John;** author; *b* Glasgow, 6 Sept. 1968; *s of* Jack and Grace Brookmyre; *m* 1991, Dr Marisa Haetzman; one *s*. *Educ*: St Luke's Secondary Sch., Barhead, Glasgow; Univ. of Glasgow (MA Hons). Sub.-ed., Screen Internat., 1989–93; freelance sub-ed., The Scotsman and Edinburgh Evening News, 1993–95. *Publications*: Quite Ugly One Morning, 1996; Country of the Blind, 1997; Not the End of the World, 1998; One Fine Day in the Middle of the Night, 1999; Boiling a Frog, 2000; A Big Boy Did It and Ran Away, 2001; The Sacred Art of Stealing, 2002; Be My Enemy, 2003; All Fun and Games Until Somebody Loses an Eye, 2005; A Tale Etched in Blood and Hard Black Pencil, 2006; Attack of the Unsinkable Rubber Ducks, 2007; A Snowball in Hell, 2008; Pandaemonium, 2009; Where the Bodies Are Buried, 2011; When the Devil Drives, 2012; Bedlam, 2013; Flesh Wounds, 2013; Dead Girl Walking, 2015; Black Widow, 2016; Want You Gone, 2017; Places in the Darkness, 2017; Fallen Angel, 2019; *as Ambrose Parry*: (with Marisa Haetzman) The Way of All Flesh, 2018; The Art of Dying, 2019. *Recreations*: music, walking, tennis, watching St Mirren FC. *Address*: 1 Hamilton Drive, Bothwell, Glasgow G71 8RR. *E*: chrisbrookmyre@live.co.uk.

**BROOKS,** family name of **Baron Crawshaw**.

**BROOKS, Alan;** Director, Horace Clarkson plc, 1993–2001; *b* 30 Dec. 1935; *s of* Charles and Annie Brooks; *m* 1959, Marie Curtis; one *s* two *d*. *Educ*: Leeds Univ. (BSc 1st Cl. Mining Engineering; 1st Cl. Cert. of Competency, Mines and Quarries). CEng. Asst Mine Manager, Winsford Salt Mine, ICI, 1961–66; British Gypsum: Dep. Mines Agent, 1966–71; Dir, Midland Region, 1971–74; Production Dir, 1974–77; Dep. Man. Dir, 1977–85; Man. Dir, 1985–88; Chm., 1988; Gp Man. Dir, Gypsum Products, BPB Industries, subseq. BPB Gypsum Industries, 1988–93; Chm., Anglo United plc, 1993–98. Chairman: Westroc Industries, Canada, 1988; Inveryeso, Spain, 1991; Dir, Falkland Is Hldgs, 1998–2000. *Recreation*: fell walking.

**BROOKS, Barry Philip Stewart,** CEng, FIET; CMarEng, FIMarEST; Director, Wychcote Ltd, since 2003; President, Institution of Engineering and Technology, 2013–14 (Deputy President, 2011–13); *b* Salisbury, Southern Rhodesia, 1 Nov. 1948; *s of* Peter and Kathleen Brooks; *m* 1971, Linda Seaman; three *s*. *Educ*: Chichester High Sch. for Boys; Imperial Coll. London (BSc(Eng) 1971); Royal Naval Coll., Greenwich (postgrad. Dip. Nuclear Reactor Technol. 1973). CEng, CMarEng 2003; FIET 2003; FIMarEST 2003. Served RN, 1968–2002: Nuclear Engr, HMS Courageous, 1974–77; Admiralty Underwater Weapons Estabt, 1977–79; Submarine Tactics and Weapons Gp, 1979–82; Weapons Engr Officer, HMS Spartan, 1982–84; ARE, 1985–87; MoD and FO Submarines, 1987–92; Cabinet Office, 1992–94; MoD, 1994–96; Ship Support Agency, 1996–98; Defence Logistics Orgn, 1998–2002; retired in rank of Cdre. Sen. Consultant, IBM, 2002–03; Dir, Consulting Services, Hitachi Consulting Ltd, 2006–08. Professional Engr Registration and Fellowship Assessor and interviewer, IET, 2003–. Co-ordinator, Hawley Engrg Innovation for a Better Envmt Award, Engrs' Co., then Engrs' Trust, 2008–16. Trustee and Vice Pres., IEE, then IET, 2005–09; Trustee: Inst. of Marine Engrg, Sci. and Technol., 2017–; Engrs' Trust, 2018–. Pres., City and Guilds Coll. Assoc., 2005–06. FInstLM 2010; FCGI 2003. Liveryman, Engrs' Co., 2004– (Mem., Ct of Assts, 2007–; Master, 2019–April 2020). *Recreations*: family, walking, international travel, public speaker, Livery Company, mentoring. *Address*: 26 Late Broads, Winsley, Bradford-on-Avon, Wilts BA15 2NW. *T*: (01225) 722714. *E*: bpsbrooks@gmail.com.

**BROOKS, Prof. David James,** MD, DSc; FRCP, FMedSci; Professor of PET Clinical Science, Division of Neuroscience, University of Newcastle upon Tyne, since 2015; Professor of Neurology (part-time), Institute of Clinical Medicine, Aarhus University, since 2012; *b* 4 Dec. 1949; *s of* late Prof. James Leslie Brooks and Doris Margaret Adeline Brooks (*née* Welply); *m* 1987, Prof. Gillian Patricia Rowlands; two *s*. *Educ*: Newcastle Royal Grammar Sch.; Christ Church and Wolfson Coll., Oxford (BA 1st Cl. Hons Chem. 1972); University Coll. London (MB BS 1979, MD 1986; DSc Medicine 1998). MRCP 1982, FRCP 1993. Hon. Sen. Lectr, Inst. of Psychiatry, London, 1993; Hammersmith Hospital: Hd, Neurol. Gp, MRC Clinical Scis Centre, 1993–2010; Hon. Consultant, 1993–2016; Imperial College London University Hammersmith Hospital: Hartnett Prof. of Neurol., Faculty of Medicine, 1993–2017; Hd, Centre for Neurosci., 2010–11; Dep. Hd, Div. of Brain Scis, 2011–14; Vis. Prof. of Neurol., Faculty of Medicine, 2017–; Clin. Prof., Hammersmith Imanet (formerly Imaging Res. Solutions Ltd), 2001–12. Sen. Neurologist, 2003–13, Hd of Neurol., 2007–13, Medical Diagnostics, GE Healthcare. Chm., Neurosci. Panel (Advanced Grants), Eur. Res. Council, 2017–20. Chm., Scientific Issues Cttee, Movt Disorder Soc., 1998–2002; Member: Med. Adv. Panel, UK Huntington's Disease Assoc., 1996–98; Med. Adv. Bd, 1997–2000, Neurosci Bd, 2004–06, MRC; Wellcome Trust Neurosci. Panel, 2000–03; Biomedical Res. Adv. Panel, 2012–, Scientific Adv. Bd, 2014–, Grant Adv. Panel, 2014–18, Alzheimer UK; Grant Adv. Bd, Alzheimer Res. UK, 2016–; UK Parkinson's Disease Association: Mem., Res. Adv. Panel, 1995–2001 (Chm., 1996–97); Trustee, Council of Mgt, 1996–99 (Chm., 1997–98). Member: Internat. Adv. Panel, Michael J. Fox Foundn for Parkinson's Disease Res., 2002–06; Adv. Bd, Eur. Soc. for Clinical Neuropharmacol., 2004–; Internat. Adv. Bd for German Parkinson Network, 2001–05; Internat. Adv. Bd for German Dementia Network, 2006–08; Chm., Singapore Nat. Univ. Health System Adv. Panel, 2016. Patron, Alzheimer's Soc., 2006–. FMedSci 2001; FEAN. *Publications*: contrib. 997 peer-reviewed pubns to learned jls; h index 116. *Recreations*: music, supporting Arsenal FC. *Address*: Clinical Ageing Research Unit, Newcastle University, Campus for Ageing and Vitality, Newcastle upon Tyne NE4 5PL. *E*: david.brooks@imperial.ac.uk, dbrooks@clin.au.dk, david.brooks@newcastle.ac.uk. *Club*: Athenæum.

**BROOKS, Dorothy Catherine;** *see* Bennett, D. C.

**BROOKS, Edwin,** PhD; FAIM, FCIM; Deputy Principal, Charles Sturt University, 1988–89; *b* Barry, Glamorgan, 1 Dec. 1929; *s of* Edwin Brooks and Agnes Elizabeth (*née* Campbell); *m* 1956, Winifred Hazel Soundie; four *s* two *d*. *Educ*: Barry Grammar Sch.; St John's Coll., Cambridge; PhD Cantab 1958. National Service, Singapore, 1948–49. MP (Lab) Bebington, 1966–70. Univ. of Liverpool: Lectr, Dept of Geography, 1954–66 and 1970–72; Sen. Lectr, 1972–77; Dean, College Studies, 1975–77; Riverina College of Advanced Education, later Riverina-Murray Institute of Higher Education, then Charles Sturt University: Dean of Business and Liberal Studies, 1977–82; Dean of Commerce, 1982–88; Dir, Albury-Wodonga Campus, 1982, Dean Emeritus, 1990. Wagga Wagga Base Hospital: Dir, 1989–96; Dep. Chm., 1989–93; Chm., 1995–96; Riverina Dist Health

Service: Dir and Dep. Chm., 1994–96; Treas., 1995–96. Councillor, Birkenhead, 1958–67. Mem., Courses Cttee, Higher Educn Bd of NSW, 1978–82; Dir, Australian Business Educn Council, 1986–89. Pres., Wagga Wagga Chamber of Commerce, 1988–90. FAIM 1983; FCIM 1989; ACIS 1995. *Publications:* This Crowded Kingdom, 1973; (ed) Tribes of the Amazon Basin in Brazil, 1973. *Recreations:* gardening, listening to music, computing. *Address:* Inchnadamph, 4 Gregadoo Road, Wagga Wagga, NSW 2650, Australia. *T:* (2) 69226798.

**BROOKS, James Wallace**; Owner and Director, Jim Brooks Consulting Ltd, since 2010; *b* 15 Sept. 1952; *s* of Leslie Duncan Brooks and Elizabeth June Brooks; *m* 1999, Kim Campbell; one *d*. *Educ:* Bolton Sch.; Univ. of Nottingham (BA); Liverpool Poly. CIPFA 1977. Dep. Dir of Finance, Bolton MBC, 1985–89; City Treasurer, Manchester CC, 1989–93; Chief Executive: Poole BC, 1993–2002; Kingston upon Hull CC, 2002–03; Exec. Dir, Sector Treasury Ltd, 2004–10. Independent Board Member: Dept of Envmt, NI, 2011–16; Dept of Agriculture, Envmt and Rural Affairs, NI, 2016–; Chairman: Audit Cttee, Envmt Agency, NI, 2014–; Audit and Risk Cttee, NI Assembly, 2017–. *Recreations:* family, music, classic Mercedes sports car, bridge, walking Charlie the labradoodle.

**BROOKS, Prof. John Stuart,** PhD, DSc; FInstP; Vice-Chancellor, Manchester Metropolitan University, 2005–15; *b* 8 March 1949; *s* of Ernest and Maude Brooks; *m* 1971, Jill Everil (*née* Pusey); two *s*. *Educ:* Cheshunt Grammar Sch.; Sheffield Univ. (BSc; PhD 1973; DSc 1998). CPhys, FInstP 1985; CEng 1992. Lectr, Sheffield City Poly., 1973–84; Head of Applied Physics Dept, 1984–90; Dir, Materials Res. Inst., 1990–92; Asst Principal, Sheffield Hallam Univ., 1992–98; Vice-Chancellor, Univ. of Wolverhampton, 1998–2005. Hon. FRIBA 2016. *Publications:* 75 papers on materials and spectroscopy in learned jls. *Recreations:* travel, walking, music, bridge.

**BROOKS, Louise Méarie;** *see* Taylor, L. M.

**BROOKS, Mel;** producer, writer, director, actor; *b* Brooklyn, 28 June 1926; *m* Florence Baum; two *s* one *d*, *m* 1964, Anne Bancroft (*d* 2005); one *s*. TV script writer for series: Your Show of Shows, 1950–54; Caesar's Hour, 1954–57; (co-created) Get Smart, 1965. Films: (cartoon) The Critic (Academy Award), 1964; writer and director: The Producers (Academy Award), 1968 (adapted for stage, NY, 2001 (3 Tony Awards), Th. Royal, London, 2004 (Critics' Circle Award, Olivier Award, 2005), Royal Exchange, Manchester, 2018); Young Frankenstein, 1974 (adapted for stage, Garrick, London, 2017); writer, director and actor: The Twelve Chairs, 1970; Blazing Saddles, 1974; Silent Movie, 1976; writer, director, actor and producer: High Anxiety, 1977; History of the World Part 1, 1981; Spaceballs, 1987; Life Stinks, 1991; Robin Hood: Men in Tights, 1993; Dracula: Dead and Loving It, 1995; actor, producer: To Be Or Not To Be, 1983. Film productions include: The Elephant Man, 1980; The Fly; Frances; My Favorite Year; 84 Charing Cross Road. Several album recordings. Kennedy Center Honor, 2009. BFI Fellowship, 2015; BAFTA Fellowship, 2017. *Address:* c/o The Culver Studios, 9336 W Washington Boulevard, Culver City, CA 90232–2600, USA.

**BROOKS, Michael James;** Deputy Chair, LifeArc (formerly MRC Technology), 2014–16 (Director and Trustee, 2006–16); *b* Edgware, Middx, 16 July 1946; *s* of late James Brooks and Doreen Brooks (*née* Cornwall); *m* 1973, Susan Elizabeth Dickens; two *d*. *Educ:* Harrow Weald Grammar Sch.; Bushey Grammar Sch.; Portsmouth Coll. of Technol. (Dip. Business Studies 1967); London Sch. of Econs and Pol Sci. (MSc Accounting and Finance 1987). Internal Auditor, BP, 1967–70; Mgt Accountant, ICL, 1970–72; Chief Accountant, Santa Fe Drilling Co., Saudi Arabia and Australia, 1972–77; Consultant, Coopers & Lybrand, 1977–79; Royal Dutch Shell Group: Financial Reporting Manager, Shell UK, 1980–81; Budget Controller, Shell UK Expro, 1981–84; Accounting Res., Shell Internat., and Sec., Oil Industry Accounting Cttee, 1984–87; Hd of Financial Forecasts and Appraisals, Shell Internat., 1987–89; Hd of Finance, Shell Gas, 1989–92; Treas., Nigeria LNG, 1992–96; Sen. Finance Rep., M&A Team, Shell Chemicals, 1996–99; Finance Dir, Trinity Energy Ltd, 2001–04. Non-exec. Dir, DVLA, 2009–15; Chair, Audit Cttee, DVA NI, 2010–16. Non-exec. Dir and Dep. Chair, NW Surrey NHS Clin. Commng Gp, 2012–15. Mem., Gp Audit Cttee, DfT, 2010–15. Mem., MRC, 2005–09; Trustee, Med. Res. Foundn, 2006–12. Gov., Univ. of Portsmouth, 2005–14; Mem., Adv. Bd, Portsmouth Business Sch., 2007–15. Trustee and Hon. Treasurer: Histl Assoc., 2018–; Guildford U3A, 2018–. FCMA; FInstD. *Publications:* contrib. numerous articles to professional accounting jls. *Recreations:* watching and talking about cricket, listening to classical music and Blondie, wine, food, history, reading, walking. *Address:* 10 St Omer Road, Guildford, Surrey GU1 2DB. *T:* 07711 132224. *E:* mb4188368@gmail.com. *Clubs:* MCC, Naval; Middlesex County Cricket, Surrey County Cricket.

**BROOKS, Peter Malcolm;** non-executive Director, Genting UK plc, since 2007 (Executive Deputy Chairman, 2007–11; President and Chief Operating Officer, 2011–15); *b* 12 Feb. 1947; *s* of Roger Morrison Brooks and Phyllis Fuller Brooks (*née* Hopkinson); *m* 1987, Patricia Margaret Garrett; one *s*; and one *s* by a previous marriage. *Educ:* Marlborough Coll.; Southampton Univ. (LLB). Solicitor, Macfarlanes, 1970–84 (Partner, 1977–84); Clifford Chance: Partner, 1984–96; Hd of Corporate Practice, 1992–96; General Counsel, Deutsche Morgan Grenfell, 1997–99; Chm., Enodis plc, 2000–08. *Recreations:* opera, theatre, travel, cricket, rackets. *Address:* c/o Genting UK plc, 31 Curzon Street, W1J 7TW. *Club:* Brooks's.

**BROOKS, Rebekah;** Chief Executive, News UK, since 2015; *b* 27 May 1968; *d* of late Robert Wade and of Deborah Wade; *m* 2002, Ross Kemp (marr. diss. 2009); *m* 2009, Charles Brooks; one *d*. *Educ:* Appleton Hall, Cheshire; Sorbonne, Paris. Features Editor, then Associate Editor, subseq. Dep. Editor, News of the World, 1989–98; Dep. Ed., The Sun, 1998–2000; Editor: News of the World, 2000–03; The Sun, 2003–09; Chief Exec., News Internat., 2009–11. Founder Mem. and Pres., Women in Journalism. *Address:* News UK & Ireland Ltd, 1 London Bridge Street, SE1 9GF.

**BROOKS, Richard John;** Arts Editor, Sunday Times, since 1999; *b* 5 Feb. 1946; *s* of late Peter John Brooks and Joan Brooks; *m* 1978, Jane Mannion; two *d*. *Educ:* University College Sch.; Bristol Univ. (BA). Reporter, Bristol Evening Post, 1968–71; Journalist: BBC Radio, 1972–79; Economist, 1979–80; Sunday Times, 1980–85; Media and Culture Editor, Observer, 1986–99. *Recreations:* playing golf and tennis, supporting Arsenal, watching films. *Address:* Sunday Times, 1 London Bridge Street, SE1 9GF. *T:* (020) 7782 5735.

**BROOKS, Robert;** Chairman, Bonhams, 2000–18; *b* 1 Oct. 1956; *s* of late William Frederick Brooks and of Joan Patricia (*née* Marshall); *m* 1981, Evelyn Rachel Durnford; two *s* one *d*. *Educ:* St Benedict's Sch., Ealing. Joined Christie's South Kensington Ltd, 1975, Dir, 1984–87; Dir, Christie Manson and Woods Ltd, 1987–89; established Brooks (Auctioneers) Ltd, 1989; acquired W. & F. C. Bonham and Sons Ltd, 2000. Mem., Adv. Bd, Combat Stress, 2019–. FIA (Gp N Internat. Special Car Series) European Touring Car Champion, 1999. *Recreations:* motor racing, golf, cricket. *Clubs:* Savile; British Racing Drivers' (Chm., 2007–11).

**BROOKS, Roderick Hilary, (Rory),** CBE 2015; Chairman, MML Capital Partners LLP (formerly Mezzanine Management), since 1988; *b* Liverpool, 7 Jan. 1954; *s* of Walter Thomas Brooks and Sheila Ann Brooks (*née* Tobin); *m* 1978, Elizabeth Fairclough; one *s* one *d*. *Educ:* Douai Sch.; Univ. of Manchester Inst. of Sci. and Technol. (BSc Mgt Sci. 1975). First National Bank of Boston, London, Boston and NY, 1975–88: joined as trainee, latterly Vice Pres. Dir, Rory and Elizabeth Brooks Foundn, 2006–. Chm., Global Leadership Bd, Univ. of Manchester, 2007–. Chm., Educn and Ethics, Giving Summit, 2012; Mem. Bd, Centre for Social Justice, 2013–16 (Chm., 2016). Vice Chm., Feadship Heritage Fleet Assoc., 2014– (Chm., 2017). Hon. DLit Manchester, 2010. *Recreations:* family, fitness, travel, motor yachts, art, wine. *Address:* MML Capital Partners LLP, Orion House, 5 Upper St Martins Lane, WC2H 9EA. *T:* (020) 7024 2200. *E:* rbrooks@mmlcapital.com.

**BROOKS, Simon Jeremy,** CB 2006; Honorary Vice-President, European Investment Bank, since 2013 (Vice-President, 2006–12); *b* 1 Aug. 1954; *s* of Stanley William Brooks and Jane Brooks; *m* 1990, Caroline Turk; one *s* one *d*. *Educ:* Queen's Coll., Oxford (BA PPE 1975); Nuffield Coll., Oxford (BPhil Econs 1977). NIESR, 1978–85; HM Treasury, 1985–2006: Econ. Advr, 1985–92; Head: Econ. Analysis 2 Div., 1992–94; Regl and Country Analysis/World Econ. Issues Teams, 1994–98; EU Finance Team, 1998–2000; Dir of Macroeconomics, 2000–06. *Address:* 13 Woodhurst Lane, Oxted RH8 9HN.

**BROOKS, Stuart Armitage,** CMG 2001; OBE 1991; HM Diplomatic Service; Counsellor, Foreign and Commonwealth Office, 1997–2001; *b* 15 May 1948; *s* of Frank and Audrey Brooks; *m* 1975, Mary-Margaret Elliott; two *d*. *Educ:* Churchill Coll., Cambridge (MA). Entered FCO, 1970: Vice-Consul, Rio de Janeiro, 1972–74; Second Sec., on secondment to Home CS, 1974–75; Second, later First, Sec., Lisbon, 1975–78; First Secretary: FCO, 1978; Moscow, 1979–82; FCO, 1982–87; Stockholm, 1987–91; FCO, 1991–93; Counsellor, Vienna, 1993–97. *Recreations:* music, horticulture. *Address:* c/o Foreign and Commonwealth Office, King Charles Street, SW1A 2AH.

**BROOKS, Prof. Thomas Alan Kieran,** PhD; Professor of Law and Government, since 2014 and Dean (formerly Head), Durham Law School, since 2016, Durham University; *b* New Haven, Conn, 14 Oct. 1973; *s* of Alan Brooks and Kathleen Brooks; *m* 2011, Claire Hobson; one *d*. *Educ:* Xavier High Sch., Middletown, Conn; William Paterson Univ. (BA Music and Pol Sci. 1997); Arizona State Univ. (MA Pol Sci. 1999); University Coll. Dublin (MA Philos. 2000); Univ. of Sheffield (PhD Philos. 2004). Newcastle University: Lectr in Pol Thought, 2004–07; Reader in Pol and Legal Philos., 2007–12; Durham University: Reader in Law, Sch. of Law, 2012–14; Associate Member: Philos. Dept, 2012–; Sch. of Govt and Internat. Affairs, 2015–; Fellow, University Coll., Durham, 2018–. Visiting Fellow: Univ. of St Andrews, 2004–05; Uppsala Univ., 2011; Yale Law Sch., Yale Univ., 2015; Academic Visitor, Fac. of Philos., Univ. of Oxford, 2010–11; Vis. Schol., St John's Coll., Oxford 2012. Academic Bencher, Inner Temple, 2018. Columnist, The Journal, Newcastle, 2015–17; freelance columnist: Daily Telegraph, 2016–; The Times, 2017–; Independent, 2017–; The Guardian, 2018–. Founder and Editor: Rev. Jl of Political Philosophy, 2003; Jl of Moral Philosophy, 2003–12 (Associate Ed., 2013–); Adv. Ed., Univ. of Bologna Law Rev., 2016–. FAcSS 2009; FRHistS 2010; FRSA 2012; FHEA 2014. *Publications:* (ed) Rousseau and Law, 2005; (ed jtly) The Legacy of John Rawls, 2005; Hegel's Political Philosophy: a systematic reading of the philosophy of right, 2007, 2nd edn 2013; (ed) Locke and Law, 2007; (ed) The Global Justice Reader, 2008; (ed) The Right to a Fair Trial, 2009; (ed) Ethics and Moral Philosophy, 2011; (ed) New Waves in Ethics, 2011; Punishment, 2012; (ed) Global Justice and International Affairs, 2012; (ed) Hegel's Philosophy of Right, 2012; (ed) Justice and the Capabilities Approach, 2012; (ed) Rawls and Law, 2012; (ed) Just War Theory, 2013; (ed) Ethical Citizenship: British idealism and the politics of recognition, 2014; (ed) Law and Legal Theory, 2014; (ed) Deterrence, 2014; (ed) Juvenile Offending, 2014; (ed) New Waves in Global Justice, 2014; (ed) Retribution, 2014; (ed) Sentencing, 2014; (ed) Shame Punishment, 2014; (ed) Alcohol and Public Policy, 2015; (ed jtly) Rawl's Political Liberalism, 2015; (ed) Current Controversies in Political Philosophy, 2015; Becoming British: UK citizenship examined, 2016; (ed jtly) Hegel's Political Philosophy: on the normative significance of method and system, 2017; (ed) The Oxford Handbook of Global Justice, 2019; (ed) Political Emotions: towards a decent public sphere, 2020; approx. 400 papers in learned jls. *Recreations:* music, travel. *Address:* Durham Law School, Durham University, Durham DH1 3LE. *T:* (0191) 334 4365. *E:* thom.brooks@durham.ac.uk.

**BROOKS, Timothy Stephen;** Chief Executive Officer, BMJ Group, 2012–16; *b* Kingston, Jamaica, 30 Sept. 1957; *s* of Michael and Mavis Brooks; *m* 1997, Catherine Ann Jenkins; one *s* one *d*. *Educ:* St John's Coll., Cambridge (BA Hons English Lang. and Lit. 1979). Reporter: McGraw-Hill, 1979–80; Haymarket Publishing, 1981–84; Founder and Ed., Media Week Ltd, 1984–90; Hd, Corporate Planning, Emap plc, 1991–95; Director: Emap Business Communications, 1996–99; Emap Digital, 1999–2000; IPC Media Ltd, 2000–06; Man. Dir, Guardian News & Media Ltd, 2006–11; Principal, 2Riders Consulting, 2011–12; Exec. Fellow, Dept of Strategy and Entrepreneurship, London Business Sch., 2011–12, 2017–. Director: Guardian Media Gp, 2006–11; Audit Bureau of Circulations Ltd, 2010–11, 2012–13; Professional Publishers Assoc., 2016–18; Pharmaceutical Press, 2017–; Public Digital Ltd, 2018–; Chairman: Knowledge Engineers, 2011–16; NLA Media Access Ltd, 2014–; RCNi, 2018–. Chm., NPA, 2008–10. Member: Digital Adv. Gp, Cabinet Office, 2012–16; Adv. Council, British Liby, 2014– (Chm., 2017–). Chm. Trustees, Open-City, 2011–14. *Recreations:* reading, running, Arsenal Football Club. *E:* timbrooks100@gmail.com.

**BROOKS-WARD, Simon Howe,** CVO 2012 (LVO 2002); OBE 2005; TD 2005; Chairman and Chief Executive, HPower Group, since 1990; *b* London, 30 Sept. 1963; *s* of Raymond Shirley Brooks-Ward and Denise Howe Brooks-Ward; *m* 2010, Annabel Jane Nash; one *s* two *d* and one step *s* one step *d*. *Educ:* Heath Mt Prep. Sch.; Haileybury. Account Manager: Quentin Bell Orgn, 1984–88; Interaction, 1988–90; Director: Pavarotti Internat. Horse Show, 1992–2002; London Internat. Horse Show, Olympia, 1992–; Royal Windsor Horse Show, 1995–; Diamond Jubilee Pageant, 2012; HM the Queen's 90th Birthday Celebrations, 2016. Lt Col, CO, Royal Yeomanry, 2002–05; Brig. Army Reserve; Asst Divl Comdr, 3 (UK) Div., 2012–15; Dep. Dir, Army Reserve Strategy, Army HQ, 2015; Dep. Comdr, Field Army, 2015–18; ACDS (Reserves and Cadets), 2019–. Regtl Hon. Col, Royal Yeomanry, 2017–; Hon. Col, King's Troop, RHA, 2019–. VRSM 2016. *Recreations:* hunting, shooting, sailing, ski-ing. *Address:* HPower Group, Stable House, St Albans Street, Windsor, Berks SL4 1UT. *T:* (01753) 847900, *Fax:* (01753) 847901. *E:* simonbw@hpower.co.uk. *Clubs:* Cavalry & Guards, Ivy; St Mawes Sailing.

**BROOKSBANK, Sir (Edward) Nicholas,** 3rd Bt *cr* 1919; with Christie's, 1974–97; *b* 4 Oct. 1944; *s* of Sir Edward William Brooksbank, 2nd Bt, TD, and of Ann, 2nd *d* of Col T. Clitherow; *S* father, 1983; *m* 1970, Emma, *d* of Rt Hon. Baron Holderness, PC; one *s* one *d*. *Educ:* Eton. Royal Dragoons, 1963–69; Blues and Royals, 1969–73; Adjutant, 1971–73. *Heir: s* (Florian) Tom (Charles) Brooksbank, *b* 9 Aug. 1982. *Address:* Menethorpe Hall, Malton, North Yorks YO17 9QX.

**BROOM, Ven. Andrew Clifford;** Archdeacon of East Riding, since 2014; *b* Norwich, 1965; *m* Tina; two *c*. *Educ:* Keele Univ. (BSocSc 1986); Trinity Coll., Bristol (BA 1992). Youth worker; ordained deacon, 1992, priest, 1993; Assistant Curate: All Saints, Wellington, 1992–96; St Thomas the Martyr, Brampton, 1996–2000; Vicar, St John,

Walton, 2000–09; Dir of Mission and Ministry, Dio. of Derby, 2009–14; Hon. Canon, Derby Cathedral, 2011–14. *Address:* c/o Diocesan House, Aviator Court, Clifton Moor, York YO30 4WJ.

**BROOM, Prof. Donald Maurice;** Colleen Macleod Professor of Animal Welfare, University of Cambridge, 1986–2009, now Emeritus; Fellow, St Catharine's College, Cambridge, 1987–2009, now Emeritus (President, 2001–04); *b* 14 July 1942; *s* of late Donald Edward Broom and Mavis Edith Rose Broom; *m* 1971, Sally Elizabeth Mary Riordan; three *s*. *Educ:* Whitgift Sch.; St Catharine's Coll., Cambridge (MA, PhD, ScD). Lectr, 1967, Sen. Lectr, 1979, Reader, 1982, Dept of Pure and Applied Zoology, Univ. of Reading. Vis. Asst Prof., Univ. of California, Berkeley, 1969; Vis. Lectr, Univ. of W Indies, Trinidad, 1972; Vis. Scientist, CSIRO Div. of Animal Prodn, Perth, WA, 1983. Mem., EEC Farm Animal Welfare Expert Gp, 1981–89; Chm., EU Scientific Veterinary Cttee on Animal Welfare, 1990–97; Vice-Chairman: EU Scientific Cttee on Animal Health and Animal Welfare, 1997–2003; Eur. Food Safety Authy Scientific Panel on Animal Health and Welfare, 2003–09 (Mem., 2009–12); Scientific Advisor: Council of Europe Standing Cttee of Eur. Convention for Protection of Animals kept for Farming Purposes, 1987–2000; EU Delegn to WTO on EC Measures Prohibiting the Importation and Marketing of Seal Products, 2013; EU Rep., Quadripartite Wkg Gp on Humane Trapping Standards, 1995–96. Hon. Res. Associate, BBSRC Inst. of Grassland and Envmtl Res. (formerly AFRC Inst. for Grassland and Animal Production), 1985–. Member: Council, Assoc. for Study of Animal Behaviour, 1971–83 (Hon. Treas., 1971–80); Internat. Ethological Cttee, 1976–79; Council, Soc. for Vet. Ethology, 1981–89 (Vice-Pres., 1986–87, 1989–91; Pres., 1987–89); Animal Welfare Cttee, Zool Soc., 1986–95; NERC Special Cttee on Seals, 1986–96; Farm Animal Welfare Council, MAFF, 1991–99; BSI Panel on ISO Animal (Mammal) Traps, 1993–98; Animal Procedures Cttee, Home Office, 1998–2006; Rural Affairs Cttee, BBC, 2007–18; Fellowship and Grant Selection Panels, Nat. Centre for Replacement, Refinement and Reduction of Animals in Res., MRC, 2012–14; REF Vet., Agricl and Food Panel, HEFCE, 2013–14. Chm., Gp on Land Transport, World Orgn for Animal Health, 2003–06. Trustee, Farm Animal Care Trust, 1986–2009 (Chm., 1999–2009). Author of report, Animal Welfare in the EU, for Policy Dept for Citizens' Rights and Constitutional Affairs, EP, 2017; Irish Govt Scientific Rev. Panel, 2018. Hon. Coll. Fellow, Myerscough Coll., Univ. of Central Lancs, 1999; Hon. Prof., Univ. Salvador, Buenos Aires, 2004; Hon. Fellow, Internat. Soc. for Applied Ethol., 2009. Hon. Socio Corrispondenti, Accad. Peloritana dei Pericolanti Messina, 2005. Vice-Pres., Old Whitgiftian Assoc., 2000–; Vice-Pres., 2004–05, Pres., 2005–06, St Catharine's Soc. FZS 1986. Hon. DSc De Montfort, 2000; Dr *hc* Buenos Aires, 2016; Hon. Dr, Norwegian Univ. of Life Scis, 2005; Hon. Dip. of Recognition, Univ. Nacional Autónoma de México, 2010. George Fleming Prize, British Vet. Jl, 1990; British Soc. of Animal Sci./ RSPCA Award for Innovative Develts in Animal Welfare, 2000; Eurogroup Medal, 2001; Michael Kay Award, RSPCA, 2007; Sir Patrick Moore Award, RSPCA, 2014; Award for Services to Animal Welfare, UFAW, 2016; Lifetime Res. Achievement Award, Confedn of Mexican Univs, 2018. *Publications:* Birds and their Behaviour, 1977 (trans. French, Portuguese); Biology of Behaviour, 1981; (ed jtly) The Encyclopaedia of Domestic Animals, 1986; (ed) Farmed Animals, 1986 (trans. Japanese, Italian); (with A. F. Fraser) Farm Animal Behaviour and Welfare, 1990; (with K. G. Johnson) Stress and Animal Welfare, 1993; (ed) Coping with Challenge: welfare in animals including humans, 2001; The Evolution of Morality and Religion, 2003; (with A. F. Fraser) Domestic Animal Behaviour and Welfare, 2007, 5th edn 2015 (trans. Portuguese, Chinese); Sentience and Animal Welfare, 2014; (with N. Carr) Tourism and Animal Welfare, 2018; over 400 papers in behaviour, psychol, zool, ornithol, agricl and vet. jls. *Recreations:* squash, water-polo, modern pentathlon, ornithology. *Address:* Department of Veterinary Medicine, University of Cambridge, Madingley Road, Cambridge CB3 0ES. *T:* (01223) 337697. *E:* dmb16@cam.ac.uk. *Club:* Hawks (Cambridge).

**BROOM, Peter David;** HM Diplomatic Service, retired; Deputy Director and Head of Trade and Investment, Riyadh, 2010–13; *b* 7 Aug. 1953; *s* of Albert Leslie Broom and Annie Myfannwy Broom; *m* 1976, Vivienne Louise Pyatt; five *d*. *Educ:* Hillside Sch., Finchley. Entered FCO, 1970; Attaché: Oslo, 1974–77; Jedda, 1977–79; Islamabad, 1979–81; FCO, 1981–84; Mbabane, 1984–87; New Delhi, 1987–89; Second Sec., FCO, 1989–91; Consul (Commercial) and Dep. Consul Gen., Brisbane, 1991–97; Consul and Dep. High Comr, Yaoundé, 1997–2000; Consul Gen., Cape Town, 2000–02; Dep. Consul Gen., San Francisco, 2003–07; Consular Directorate, FCO, 2007–10. *Recreations:* sport, history. *Address:* 7 Sunny Hill, Waldringfield, Suffolk IP12 4QS.

**BROOMAN, Thomas Sebastian,** CBE 2008; music consultant, music mentor; *b* Bristol, 1 April 1954; *s* of Frederick Spencer Brooman and Beatrice Lily Brooman; *m* 2004, Amanda Emily Budd; three *s*. *Educ:* Bristol Grammar Sch.; Exeter Coll., Oxford (BA Hons Eng. Lang. and Lit.). Editor, Bristol Recorder, 1979–81; Artistic Dir, WOMAD Festival, 1982–2008; Trustee and Dir, WOMAD Foundn, 1984–2008; Dir, Real World Records, 1988–2008; Artistic Advr, Dartington Hall, 2009–12; Kingswood Foundation, then Creative Youth Network: Music Advr, 2010–17; Associate Artist for Music, 2011–12; Trustee, 2011–17; Music Programmer, Salisbury Arts Centre, 2012–16; radio presenter, BCfm, 2018–. Mentor, South West Music Sch., 2009–. *Publications:* My Festival Romance, 2017. *Recreations:* music, drumming, film and cinema, fictional writing, travel, photography. *Address:* 82 Charlton Road, Kingswood, Bristol BS15 1HF. *T:* (0117) 909 5820. *E:* thomas@heavenlyplanet.com.

**BROOME, Adam Edward;** Director, Adam Broome Ltd, since 2014; *b* Cheltenham, 11 Nov. 1968; *s* of Alan John Broome and Boleslawa Anna Broome; *m* Caron Lindsey Reeves; two *s*. *Educ:* Howard Sch., Rainham, Kent; Bristol Univ. (BSc Maths); Univ. of W of England. CIPFA. Avon County Council: trainee and accountant, 1990–95; Mgt Accountant, 1995–96; Hd, Local Mgt of Schs, Bristol CC, 1995–96; Stoke-on-Trent City Council: Hd, Educn Finance, 1997–98; Asst Dir, 1998–2002; Associate Dir, Audit Commn, 2002–04; Plymouth City Council: Director: for Corporate Resources, 2004–09; for Corporate Support, 2009–11; for Corporate Services, 2012–13; Dir of Resources, Nursing and Midwifery Council, 2016–18. Non-exec. Dir, Royal Cornwall Hosps NHS Trust, 2014–16. *Recreations:* family, friends, walking, cinema, Bristol Rovers, Polish history and language, allotment.

**BROOME, Almira D.;** *see* Delibegović-Broome.

**BROOME, David McPherson,** CBE 1995 (OBE 1970); farmer; British professional show jumper; *b* Cardiff, 1 March 1940; *s* of Fred and Amelia Broome, Chepstow, Gwent; *m* 1976, Elizabeth, *d* of K. W. Fletcher, Thirsk, N Yorkshire; three *s*. *Educ:* Monmouth Grammar Sch. for Boys. European Show Jumping Champion (3 times); World Show Jumping Champion, La Baule, 1970; Olympic Medallist (Bronze) twice, 1960, 1968; King George V Gold Cup 6 times (a record, in 1990). Mounts include: Sunsalve, Aachen, 1961; Mr Softee, Rotterdam, 1967, and Hickstead, 1969; Beethoven, La Baule, France, 1970, as (1st British) World Champion; Sportsman and Philco, Cardiff, 1974; Professional Champion of the World. Pres., British Showjumping Assoc., 2013–. *Publications:* Jump-Off, 1971; (with S. Hadley) Horsemanship, 1983. *Recreation:* shooting. *Address:* Mount Ballan Manor, Port Skewett, Caldicot, Monmouthshire, Wales NP26 5XP.

**BROOME, Prof. John,** PhD; FBA 2000; FRSE; White's Professor of Moral Philosophy, University of Oxford, 2000–14, now Emeritus; Fellow, Corpus Christi College, Oxford, 2000–14, now Emeritus; *b* 17 May 1947; *s* of Richard and Tamsin Broome; *m* 1970, Ann Rowland; one *s* one *d*. *Educ:* Trinity Hall, Cambridge (BA; Hon. Fellow, 2015); Bedford Coll., Univ. of London (MA); Massachusetts Inst. Technol. (PhD 1972). Lectr in Econs, Birkbeck Coll., London Univ., 1972–78; Reader in Econs, 1979–92, Prof. of Econs and Philosophy, 1992–95, Univ. of Bristol; Prof. of Philosophy, Univ. of St Andrews, 1996–2000. Visiting posts: Univ. of Va, 1975; All Souls Coll., Oxford, 1982–83; ANU, 1986, 1993, 2001, 2007, Adjunct Prof., 2008–17, Hon. Prof., 2017–; Princeton Univ., 1987–89; Univ. of Washington, 1988; Univ. of BC, 1993; Swedish Collegium for Advanced Study, Uppsala, 1997–98, 2004, 2008, 2011, 2014 (Mem., Senate, 2014–); Univ. of Canterbury, NZ, 2005; Stanford Univ., 2015–. Lead Author, 5th Assessment Report, Intergovtl Panel on Climate Change, 2011–14. Ed., Economics and Philosophy, 1994–99. Mem., Royal Swedish Acad. of Scis, 2007; Hon. Foreign Mem., American Acad. of Arts and Scis, 2014. FRSE 1999. Hon Dr Lund, 2013. *Publications:* The Microeconomics of Capitalism, 1983; Weighing Goods, 1991; Counting the Cost of Global Warming, 1992; Ethics Out of Economics, 1999; Weighing Lives, 2004; Climate Matters, 2012; Rationality Through Reasoning, 2013. *Recreation:* sailing. *Address:* Corpus Christi College, Oxford OX1 4JF.

**BROOME, John Lawson,** CBE 1987; Founder and Chairman, Alton Towers Theme Park, since 1980 (Chief Executive, 1980–90); *b* 2 Aug. 1943; *s* of late Albert Henry and Mary Elizabeth Broome; *m* 1972, Jane Myott Bagshaw; one *s* two *d*. *Educ:* Rossall School. School master, 1960–65; Dir, JLB Investment Property Group, 1961–, and numerous other companies; Chm. and Chief Exec., Adventure World Theme Park, 1997–99; Chairman: London Launch Ltd, 2000–09; Launch Hldgs, 2005–09; Exec. Chm., Camel Creek Ltd, 2015–. Member: ETB and BTA, 1982–92; Internat. Assoc. of Amusement Parks and Attractions, USA, 1986–89 (Chm., Internat. Cttee; Chm., Internat. Council, 1986–89). Vice-Pres., Ironbridge Gorge Museum Trust. Governor, Staffordshire Univ. (formerly N Staffs Poly.), 1984–95. Vis. Prof., Sunderland Univ., 1996–. Freeman, City of London, 1988. *Recreations:* ski-ing, travelling, antiques, old paintings, objets d'art, fine gardens, restoration of historic properties.

**BROOMFIELD, Alexander Bryan;** property investor; Chairman, Aberdeen Royal Hospitals NHS Trust, 1992–96; *b* 13 Jan. 1937; *s* of late William P. Broomfield, OBE and Eliza M. Broomfield; *m* 1960, Morag Carruthers. *Educ:* Aberdeen Grammar Sch. 26 years with Town & County Motor Garage Ltd; Man. Dir, retired 1992. Member: Grampian Health Bd, 1990–92; Bd, Scottish SHA, 1980–88; Council, Aberdeen Chamber of Commerce, to 1995 (Pres., 1978–79); Vice-Chm., Aberdeen Airport Consultative Cttee, 1990–2015; Chm., Aurora Private Equity Ltd, 2009–11. *Recreations:* walking, fishing, golf. *Address:* 5 Carnegie Gardens, Aberdeen AB15 4AW. *Clubs:* Royal Northern and University (Aberdeen); Royal Aberdeen Golf.

**BROOMHEAD, Pauline,** CBE 2017; Founder and Chief Executive Officer, Foundation for Social Improvement, since 2007; *b* Halifax, W Yorks, 1955; *d* of Alan and Catherine; *m* Stephen Broomhead; two *s*. *Educ:* J. H. Whitley Secondary Sch.; Percival Whitley Coll. Comr for Camping, Girl Guides Assoc., Kenya, 1978–80. Campaign Manager, NSPCC, 1995–2007. Chairman, Trustees: BIGKID Foundn, 2009–13; Bottletop Foundn, 2013–; Trustee, Peter Alan Dickson Foundn, 2010–; non-exec. Dir, Benefacto, 2017–. *E:* admin@thefsi.org.

**BROOMHEAD, Steven John;** Professor of Entrepreneurial Education and Chief Director of Institutional Advancement, Liverpool Hope University, since 2011, on leave of absence as Chief Executive (part-time), Warrington Borough Council, since 2012; *b* 15 Jan. 1956; *s* of Brian and Hazel Broomhead; *m* 1st, 1990, Linda Whelan (marr. diss. 2014); one *d*; 2nd, 2016, Carolyn Williams; one step *s*. *Educ:* W Glam Inst. of HE (BEd (Hons) Wales); Univ. of Leicester (MA); UC Swansea (CertEd). Lectr in Social Sciences, W Bridgford Coll., Nottingham, 1979; Sen. Lectr, Arnold and Carlton Coll., Nottingham, 1981; Vice-Principal, Skelmersdale Coll., Lancashire, 1986; Principal: Peterlee Coll., 1990–94; Warrington Collegiate Inst., 1994–97; Chief Executive: Warrington BC (Unitary), 1997–2003; NW Develt Agency, 2003–10. Chm., Nat. Libraries Task Force, 2018. Chm., NW Chamber of Commerce, 2002–; Board Member: Basic Skills Agency, 1996–2002; Learning and Skills Develt Agency, 2001–; Lancs Enterprise Partnership, 2011–14; Central and W Lancs Chamber of Commerce, 2011–; Mem., Nat. Skills Alliance, 2003–; Policy Advr to DfES, 2000–03. Chairman: Connexions, Chester and Warrington, 2001–05; Recycling Lives (Lancs), 2011–; Warrington and Co., 2013–; Wire Regeneration, 2014–. Chm., 2009–17, Vice Chm., 2018–, Warrington Wolves RLFC. Mem. NW Regl Exec., Prince's Trust, 2001–; Trustee, Nat. Football Mus., 2009–. Advr, E Lancs Rlwy, 2012. Governor: Univ. of Central Lancs, 2005–; Skelmersdale Coll. (Chm., 2006); Warrington and Vale Royal Coll., 2017–. CCMI; FCGI; FRSA. Patron, Campaign for Learning, 2001. *Recreations:* railway history, walking, Notts County FC, Warrington RL FC (Chm., 2010–). *Address:* 5 Heyes Lodge, Dark Lane, Whittle-le-Woods, Chorley PR6 8AH. *E:* Stevebrooms@i.cloud.com.

**BROPHY, Michael John Mary,** CBE 2014; Chief Executive, Charities Aid Foundation, 1982–2002; *b* 24 June 1937; *s* of Gerald and Mary Brophy; *m* 1962, Sarah Rowe; three *s* one *d*. *Educ:* Ampleforth Coll.; Royal Naval Coll., Dartmouth. Entered Royal Navy, 1955; Exec. Br.; Fleet Air Arm pilot; Air Warfare Instructor; gunnery specialist; retired as Lt-Comdr, 1966. Associate Dir, J. Walter Thompson, 1967–74; Appeals Dir, Spastics Soc., 1974–82. Dir, European Foundn Centre, 1989–98 (Chm., 1994–95); Chm., Euro Citizens Action Service, 1996–2002. Trustee: The London (formerly Capital) Community Foundn, 2006–13 (Chm., 2010–13); Charity Employees Benevolent Fund, 2007–12; Chm., United Trusts, 2006–08. Fellow, Inst. of Fundraising, 1990; CBIM 1989–94; FRSA. Hon. DBA Greenwich, 2010. *Publications:* Citizen Power, 2005. *Address:* 8 Oldlands Hall, Herons' Ghyll, Uckfield, E Sussex TN22 3DA. *E:* the.brophys@btinternet.com.

**BROSNAN, Pierce,** Hon. OBE 2003; actor; *b* Navan, Co. Meath, 16 May 1953; *s* of Tom Brosnan and Mary Smith; *m* 1977, Cassandra Harris (*d* 1991), one *s*, and one step *s* (one step *d* decd); *m* 2001, Keely Shaye Smith; two *s*. *Educ:* Drama Centre, London. Asst stage manager, Theatre Royal, York; *stage* appearances include: Red Devil Battery Sign; Filumena; Wait Until Dark; *television* includes: The Manions of America series, 1981; Remington Steele series (title rôle), 1982–87; Nancy Astor, 1984; Noble House 1988; Around the World in 80 Days, 1989; Robinson Crusoe, 1996; Bag of Bones, 2012; The Son, 2017–18; *films* include: Nomads, 1986; The Fourth Protocol, 1987; The Deceivers, 1988; Mr Johnson, 1991; Lawnmower Man, 1992; Mrs Doubtfire, 1993; Love Affair, 1994; The Mirror has Two Faces, Mars Attacks!, 1996; Dante's Peak, 1997; The Nephew, 1998 (also prod); The Thomas Crown Affair, 1999 (also prod); Grey Owl, 2000; The Taylor of Panama, 2001; Evelyn, 2003; Laws of Attraction, After the Sunset, 2004; The Matador, 2006; Seraphim Falls, 2007; Mamma Mia!, Married Life, 2008; Percy Jackson & the Olympians: The Lightning Thief, Remember Me, The Ghost, The Greatest, 2010; Love Is All You Need, 2013; Love Punch, A Long Way Down, The November Man, 2014; Some Kind of Beautiful, No Escape, Survivor, 2015; Urge, 2016; I.T., A Christmas Star, 2017; Mamma Mia! Here We Go Again, 2018; Final Score, 2018; rôle of James Bond in:

GoldenEye, 1995; Tomorrow Never Dies, 1997; The World is Not Enough, 1999; Die Another Day, 2002. *Address:* c/o Guttman Associates, 118 South Beverly Drive, Suite 201, Beverly Hills, CA 90212, USA.

**BROTHERSTON, Leslie William, (Lez);** freelance production designer, since 1984; Associate Artist, New Adventures; *b* 6 Oct. 1961; *s* of L. Brotherston and Irene Richardson. *Educ:* Prescot Grammar Sch., Prescot, Liverpool; Central Sch. of Art and Design (BA Hons Th. Design 1984). First design for Letter to Brezhnev (film); work with Northern Ballet Theatre includes: The Brontes, Strange Meeting, Romeo and Juliet; Giselle, 1997; Dracula, 1997; The Hunchback of Notre Dame, 1998; Carmen (Barclays Th. Award for Outstanding Achievement in Dance, TMA Award), 1999; A Christmas Carol, 2001; designs for *dance* include: for Adventures in Motion Pictures: Highland Fling, 1994; Swan Lake, Piccadilly, 1995, transf. NY (Tony Award for Best Costume Design, Drama Desk Awards for Best Costume Design and Best Set Design, Outer Critics Award for Outstanding Costume Design, 1999); Cinderella, Piccadilly, 1997 (Olivier Award for Outstanding Achievement in Dance, 1998); The Car Man, 2000; Greymatter, Rambert; for Scottish Ballet: Just Scratchin' the Surface, Nightlife, 1999; The Nutcracker, 2012; 6 Faces, K-Ballet, Japan; Bounce, Eur. tour, 2000; Play Without Words, NT, 2002; for Adam Cooper Co.: Les Liaisons Dangereuses (also Co-Dir and writer), Japan, then Sadler's Wells, 2005; for New Adventures: Edward Scissorhands, Sadler's Wells, 2005; Dorian Gray, Edinburgh Fest. and UK tour, 2008; Sleeping Beauty, Sadler's Wells, 2012 (Best Costume Design, Los Angeles Drama Critics Circle Award, 2013); Lord of the Flies, Theatre Royal, Glasgow and UK tour, 2014; *theatre* includes: Jane Eyre, tour; Greenwich: Prisoner of Zenda, 1992; The Sisters Rosensweig, 1994, transf. Old Vic; Handling Bach, 1995; The Last Romantics, Northanger Abbey, 1996; David Copperfield, 1997; Neville's Island, Apollo, 1994; Rosencrantz and Guildenstern are Dead, RNT, 1995; Alarms and Excursions, Gielgud, 1998; Spend, Spend, Spend, Piccadilly, 1999; A Midsummer Night's Dream, Albery, 2000; French and Saunders Live, UK tour, 2000; Little Foxes, Donmar Warehouse, 2001; Victoria Wood - At It Again, Royal Albert Hall, 2001; Bedroom Farce, Aldwych, 2002; Royal Exchange, Manchester: A Woman of No Importance, 2000; Sex, Chips and Rock 'n' Roll, Design for Living, 2002; Volpone, 2004; The Vortex, 2007; Much Ado About Nothing, RSC, 2006; Women Beware Women, NT, 2010; French and Saunders—Still Alive, UK tour, 2008; Under the Blue Sky, Duke of York's 2008; Duet for One, Almeida 2009, transf. Vaudeville; Dancing at Lughnasa, 2009, The Real Thing, 2010, Old Vic; Really Old Like 45, NT, 2010; Measure for Measure, 2010, My City, 2011, Almeida; The Umbrellas of Cherbourg, Gielgud, 2011; The Day We Sang, Manchester Internat. Fest., 2011; Hedda Gabler, Old Vic, 2012; Long Day's Journey into Night, Apollo, 2012; Hysteria, Hampstead Th., 2013; The Duck House, Vaudeville, 2013; The Empress, RSC, 2013; Dawn French: 30 Million Minutes tour, 2014; Seminar, Hampstead Th., 2014; Pride and Prejudice, Show Boat, Sheffield Crucible, 2015; Twelfth Night, Shakespeare's Globe, 2017; Me and My Girl, Flowers for Mrs Harris, Chichester Fest. Th., 2018; The Merry Wives of Windsor, RSC, 2018; Malory Towers, Passenger Shed, Bristol, 2019; Romeo and Juliet, Curve Th., Leicester, 2019 (and UK tour); *opera* includes prodns for Opera Zuid, Hong Kong Arts Fest., Opera North, Glyndebourne Touring Opera, Teatro Bellini, Royal Danish Opera, Opera NI, Buxton Fest., Scottish Opera, WNO; *musicals* include: Side by Side by Sondheim, Greenwich, 1997; Cabaret, Sheffield Crucible; Maria Friedman by Special Arrangement, Donmar Warehouse; My One and Only, Piccadilly, 2002; Brighton Rock, Almeida, 2004; Acorn Antiques, Haymarket, 2005; The Far Pavilions, Shaftesbury, 2005; Sister Act, London Palladium, 2009; Oh What a Lovely War, Th. Royal Stratford East, 2014. Critics Circle Award for Outstanding Achievement in Dance. *Address:* c/o Tracey Elliston, Judy Daish Associates, 2 St Charles Place, W10 6EG. *T:* (020) 8964 8811. *Club:* Soho House.

**BROTHERTON, Ven. (John) Michael;** Archdeacon of Chichester and Canon Residentiary of Chichester Cathedral, 1991–2002; *b* 7 Dec. 1935; *s* of late Clifford and Minnie Brotherton; *m* 1963, Daphne Margaret Yvonne, *d* of Sir Geoffrey Meade, KBE, CMG, CVO; three *s* one *d*. *Educ:* St John's Coll., Cambridge (MA); Cuddesdon Coll., Oxford; Univ. of London Inst. of Educn (PGCE). Ordained: deacon, 1961; priest, 1962; Asst Curate, St Nicolas, Chiswick, 1961–64; Chaplain, Trinity Coll., Port of Spain, Trinidad, 1965–69; Rector of St Michael's, Diego Martin, Trinidad, 1969–75; Vicar, St Mary and St John, Oxford, and Chaplain, St Hilda's Coll., Oxford, 1976–81; Rural Dean of Cowley, 1978–81; Vicar, St Mary, Portsea, 1981–91; permission to officiate, Dio. of London, 2002–. Mem., Legal Adv. Commn, C of E, 1996–2001. Hon. Canon, St Michael's Cathedral, Kobe, Japan, 1986. Proctor in Convocation, 1995–2002. *Recreations:* travel, reading. *Address:* Flat 2, 23 Gledhow Gardens, SW5 0AZ. *T:* (020) 7373 5147. *E:* jmbrotherton@yahoo.co.uk.

**BROTHERTON, Michael Lewis;** Michael Brotherton Associates, Parliamentary Consultants, 1986–2012; *b* 26 May 1931; *s* of late John Basil Brotherton and Maud Brotherton (*née* Parker); *m* 1968, Julia, *d* of late Austin Gerald Comyn King and Katherine Elizabeth King (*née* Barnard Hankey); three *s* one *d*. *Educ:* Prior Park; RNC Dartmouth. Served RN, 1949–64: qual. Observer 1955; Cyprus, 1957 (despatches); Lt-Comdr 1964, retd. Times Newspapers, 1967–74. Chm., Beckenham Conservative Political Cttee, 1967–68; contested (C) Deptford, 1970; MP (C) Louth, Oct. 1974–1983. Pres., Hyde Park Tories, 1975. Mem., Select Cttee on violence in the family, 1975–76. Chm., Friends, 1995–99, Chm., Library Cttee, 1997–99, Boston Parish Church. *Recreations:* cricket, cooking, travel, talking. *Address:* Ava Cottage, 46 The Butts, Chippenham, Wilts SN15 3JS. *T:* (01249) 651783. *Clubs:* Conservative Working Men's, Louth; Castaways; Cleethorpes Conservative; Immingham Conservative.

**BROUCHER, David Stuart;** HM Diplomatic Service, retired; Chairman, Foreign and Commonwealth Association, since 2015 (Vice Chairman, 2009–15); *b* 5 Oct. 1944; *s* of late Clifford Broucher and Betty Broucher (*née* Jordan); *m* 1st, 1971, Marion Monika Blackwell (marr. diss. 2014); one *s*; 2nd, 2014, Lorela Viorica Corbeanu. *Educ:* Manchester Grammar School; Trinity Hall, Cambridge (MA Modern Languages). Foreign Office, 1966; British Military Govt, Berlin, 1968; Cabinet Office, 1972; Prague, 1975; FCO, 1978; UK Perm. Rep. to EC, 1983; Counsellor, Jakarta, 1985–89; Economic Counsellor, Bonn, 1989–93; Counsellor, FCO, 1994; Asst Under Sec. of State, FCO, 1995–97; Ambassador to Czech Republic, 1997–2001; UK Perm. Rep. to Conf. on Disarmament, Geneva (with personal rank of Ambassador), 2001–04. Advr to Pres. of Romania on EU accession, 2005; Advr on EU enlargement to Birmingham Univ., 2006–08. Vis. Fellow, Southampton Univ., 2006–11. *Recreations:* music, golf, sailing. *E:* dbroucher@btinternet.com.

**BROUGH, Dr Colin,** FRCPE; FFCM; Chief Administrative Medical Officer, Lothian Health Board, 1980–88; *b* 4 Jan. 1932; *s* of Peter Brough and Elizabeth C. C. Chalmers; *m* 1957, Maureen Jennings; four *s* one *d*. *Educ:* Bell Baxter Sch., Cupar; Univ. of Edinburgh (MB ChB 1956). DPH 1965; DIH 1965; FFCM 1978; MRCPE 1981; FRCPE 1982. House Officer, Leicester General Hosp. and Royal Infirmary of Edinburgh, 1956–57; Surg.-Lieut, Royal Navy, 1957–60; General Practitioner, Leith and Fife, 1960–64; Dep. Medical Supt, Royal Inf. of Edinburgh, 1965–67; ASMO, PASMO, Dep. SAMO, South-Eastern Regional Hosp. Board, Scotland, 1967–74; Community Medicine Specialist, Lothian Health Board, 1974–80. *Recreations:* golf, shooting, fishing, first aid. *Address:* The Saughs, Gullane, East Lothian EH31 2AL. *T:* (01620) 842179.

**BROUGH, Jonathan;** Head, Hurlingham School, since 2010; *b* Bedford, 2 Feb. 1971; *s* of George Ernest Brough and Amy Elizabeth Brough; civil partnership 2006, *m* 2015, Harry Small. *Educ:* Walmsley House Sch.; Bedford Sch.; Colyton Grammar Sch.; Homerton Coll., Cambridge (BEd Hons 1994); Nat. Coll. for Sch. Leadership (NPQH 2002); Univ. of Roehampton (MA Children's Literature 2016). Head of English: York House Sch., Rickmansworth, 1994–96; Cumnor Hse Sch., Croydon, 1996–99; Dep. Hd (Dir of Studies), Bute Hse Prep. Sch. for Girls, Hammersmith, 1999–2004; Hd, Prep. Dept, City of London Sch. for Girls, 2004–10. Team Inspector, ISI, 2006–. Gov., Fairley Hse Sch., Pimlico, 2006–. FCollT 2013. *Recreations:* believing a book in the hand is worth two on the shelf, getting lost in hidden corners of London, New York and San Francisco, hexadecimal sudoku puzzles, enjoying fine wine, good food and good company. *Address:* Hurlingham School, 122 Putney Bridge Road, Putney, SW15 2NQ. *T:* (020) 8874 7186, *Fax:* (020) 8875 0372. *E:* jonathan.brough@hurlinghamschool.co.uk.

**BROUGHAM,** family name of **Baron Brougham and Vaux**.

**BROUGHAM AND VAUX, 5th Baron** *cr* 1860; **Michael John Brougham,** CBE 1995; *b* 2 Aug. 1938; *s* of 4th Baron and Jean (*d* 1992), *d* of late Brig.–Gen. G. B. S. Follett, DSO, MVO; *S* father, 1967; *m* 1st, 1963, Olivia Susan (marr. diss. 1968; she *d* 1986), *d* of Rear-Admiral Gordon Thomas Seccombe Gray, CB, DSC; one *d*; 2nd, 1969, Catherine Gulliver (marr. diss. 1981), *d* of late W. Gulliver; one *s*. *Educ:* Lycée Jaccard, Lausanne; Millfield School. Dep. Chm. of Cttees, H of L, 1992–; a Dep. Speaker, H of L, 1995–; elected Mem., H of L, 1999; Member: Select Cttee on H of L Officers, 1997–99, on Hybrid Instruments, 1999–2001; Statutory Instruments Jt Cttee, 2001–07; Information Cttee, 2006–08; Catering Cttee, 2008–12; Admin and Works Cttee, 2010–14; Vice-Chm., Assoc. of Cons. Peers, 1998–2002, 2003–07. President: RoSPA, 1986–89; Safety Gps UK (formerly Nat. Health and Safety Gps Council), 1994–. Chm., Tax Payers Soc., 1989–91. Chm., European Secure Vehicle Alliance, 1992–2017. *Heir: s* Hon. Charles William Brougham [*b* 9 Nov. 1971; *m* 2010, Nicola, *y d* of David Moore; one *s* one *d*]. *Address:* 11 Westminster Gardens, Marsham Street, SW1P 4JA.

**BROUGHAM, Christopher John;** QC 1988; *b* 11 Jan. 1947; *s* of late Lt-Comdr Patrick Brougham and Elizabeth Anne (*née* Vestey); *m* 1974; one *s* three *d*. *Educ:* Radley Coll.; Worcester Coll., Oxford (BA Hons). Called to the Bar, Inner Temple, 1969, Bencher, 2007; Dep. High Court Bankruptcy Registrar, 1984. Dep. Churchwarden, Christ Church, Kensington, 1980–95. *Publications:* (contrib.) Encyclopedia of Financial Provision in Family Matters, 1998–; (jtly) Muir Hunter on Personal Insolvency, 2000–2016; (contrib.) Jackson's Matrimonial Finance and Taxation, 2008; (contrib.) Jackson's Matrimonial Finance, 2012. *Recreations:* music, crossword puzzles. *Address:* 3–4 South Square, Gray's Inn, WC1R 5HP. *T:* (020) 7696 9900.

**BROUGHER, Kerry;** Director, Academy of Motion Picture Arts and Sciences Museum, Los Angeles, since 2014; *b* 25 Sept. 1952; *s* of Russell Brougher and Margaret Brougher (*née* Smith); *m* 1987, Nora Halpern; two *d*. *Educ:* Univ. of Calif at Irvine (BA 1974); UCLA (MA 1978). Museum of Contemporary Art, Los Angeles: Asst Curator, 1982–87; Associate Curator, 1987–93; Curator, 1993–97; Dir, MOMA, Oxford, 1997–2000; Hirshhorn Museum and Sculpture Garden: Dep. Dir and Chief Curator, 2001–14; Dir of Art and Progs, 2001–07; Acting Dir, 2007–09 and 2013–14. Co-Artistic Dir, Gwangju Biennale, Korea, 2004. Visitor, Ashmolean Mus., Univ. of Oxford, 1998–; Vis. Fellow, Nuffield Coll., Oxford, 1999–. Mem. Bd of Advrs, Filmforum, Los Angeles, 1994–. FRSA 2000. *Publications:* The Image of Abstraction, 1988; The Beatrice and Philip Gersh Collection, 1989; Wolfgang Laib, 1992; Robert Irwin, 1993; Hiroshi Sugimoto, 1993; Hall of Mirrors: art and film since 1945, 1996; Jeff Wall, 1997; Gustav Metzger, 1998; Notorious: Alfred Hitchcock and contemporary art, 1999; Ed Ruscha, 2000; Enclosed and Enchanted, 2000; Open City: street photographs since 1950, 2001; Visual Music, 2005; Hiroshi Sugimoto, 2005; The Cinema Effect: illusion, reality and the moving image, 2008; Yves Klein: with the void, full powers, 2010. *Address:* Academy of Motion Picture Arts and Sciences Museum, 8949 Wilshire Boulevard, Beverly Hills, CA 90211, USA.

**BROUGHTON,** family name of **Baron Fairhaven**.

**BROUGHTON, Sir David (Delves),** 13th Bt *cr* 1660, of Broughton, Staffordshire; *b* 7 May 1942; *s* of Lt-Comdr P. J. D. Broughton, RN, *gggs* of Rev. Sir Henry Delves Broughton, 8th Bt, and of his 1st wife, Nancy Rosemary, *yr d* of J. E. Paterson; *S* kinsman, 1993, but his name does not appear on the Official Roll of the Baronetage; *m* 1969, Diane, *d* of R. L. Nicol. *Heir:* half *b* Geoffrey Delves Broughton [*b* 1962; *m* 1986, Karen Louise Wright; two *s* two *d*]. *Address:* 31 Mayfield Court, Sandy, Beds SG19 1NF.

**BROUGHTON, Hugh Giles Keyworth;** Founder and Director, Hugh Broughton Architects, since 1995; *b* Worcester, 10 Feb. 1965; *s* of Col Ronnie Broughton and Anne Broughton; *m* 1994, Melanie Ashton; three *s*. *Educ:* Wellington Coll.; Univ. of Edinburgh (MA Hons 1989; DipArch 1990). RIBA 1991. Architect, Troughton McAslan, 1990–94; researcher, YRM plc, Spain, 1994–95. Major projects include: East Wing, Maidstone Mus., 2012; Halley VI Antarctic Res. Station, 2013; Portland Collection, Welbeck, 2016; conservation, Painted Hall, Greenwich, 2019. *Publications:* Madrid: a guide to recent architecture, 1997. *Recreations:* running, walking, kayaking, art, football, family, travel. *Address:* Hugh Broughton Architects, 41 Beavor Lane, W6 9BL. *T:* (020) 8735 9959. *E:* hugh.broughton@hbarchitects.co.uk.

**BROUGHTON, Sir Martin (Faulkner),** Kt 2011; FCA; Chairman and Managing Partner, Sports Investment Partners LLP, since 2010; Chairman, Supponor Ltd, since 2019; *b* 15 April 1947; *m* 1974, Jocelyn Mary Rodgers; one *s* one *d*. *Educ:* Westminster City Grammar Sch. FCA 1969. Career in BAT Group: British-American Tobacco Co.: travelling auditor, 1971–74; Head Office, 1974–80; Souza Cruz, Brazil, 1980–85; Eagle Star, 1985–88 and (Chm.) 1992–93; Chm., Wiggins Teape Gp, 1989–90; Finance Dir, 1988–92; Man. Dir, Financial Services, 1992–98; Gp Chief Exec. and Dep. Chm., BAT Industries, 1993–98; Chm., 1998–2004. Chm., British Airways, 2004–14 (non-exec. Dir, 2000–04); Dep. Chm., Internat. Airlines Gp, 2010–16; non-exec. Dir, Whitbread, 1993–2000. Ind. Dir, 1999–2007, Chm., 2004–07, British Horseracing Bd; Chm., Liverpool FC, 2010. Member: Takeover Panel, 1996–99; Financial Reporting Council, 1998–2004. Co-Chm., TransAtlantic Business Dialogue, 2006–08. Pres., CBI, 2007–09. *Recreations:* theatre, golf, horseracing, football. *Club:* Tandridge Golf.

**BROUGHTON, Dr Peter,** FREng; Director, Marine Engineering Energy Solutions Ltd, since 2013; *b* 1944; *s* of late Thomas Frederick Broughton and Mary Theodosia Broughton; *m* 1968, Jan Mary, *d* of late Ronald George Silveston and Molly Silveston; two *s*. *Educ:* Rowlinson Technical Sch., Sheffield; Manchester Univ. (BSc 1966; PhD 1970). FICE; FIStructE; FIMarEST; FRINA; FREng (FEng 1996). Engrg Surveyor, Lloyd's Register of Shipping, 1971–74; Partner, Campbell Reith and Partners, 1974–75; Sen. Structural Engr, Burmah Oil Development, 1975–76; Supervising Structural Engr, BNOC, 1977–79; Phillips Petroleum Co., 1979–2003: Sen Structl Engr, 1979–82, Civil Engrg Supervisor, 1982–86, UK; Project Engr and Co. Rep., Ekofisk Protective Barrier Project, Norway, 1986–90; Engrg and Procurement Project Manager, Judy/Joanne Develt Project, UK, 1990–94; Project Manager: for Substructures, Ekofisk II Develt Project, Norway, 1994–98;

Maureen Platform Re-Float and Decommng Project Manager, UK, 1998–2003; Consultant, NIRAS Fraenkel (formerly Peter Fraenkel and Partners), 2003–13. Vis. Prof., Dept of Civil Engrg, ICSTM, 1991–2005; Royal Acad. of Engrg Vis. Prof., Oxford Univ., 2004–07. Stanley Grey Award, IMarE, 1992; George Stephenson Medal, 1993, Bill Curtin Medal, 1997, Overseas Premium, 1998, David Hislop Award, 1999, Contribution to Institution Activity Award, 2002, ICE. *Publications:* The Analysis of Cable and Catenary Structures, 1994; numerous technical papers on offshore structures. *Recreations:* walking, fishing, swimming. *Address:* Appletrees, 30 Portsmouth Road, Camberley, Surrey GU15 1JX.

**BROUN, Sir Wayne (Hercules),** 14th Bt *cr* 1686 (NS) of Colstoun, Haddingtonshire; 30th Chief of the Clan Broun/Brown; Chief Executive Officer, Australian Asian Pacific Services Pty Ltd, since 2002; Chairman: BrounBrown.com, since 2011; New Vision Media, since 2015; *b* Inverell, NSW, Australia, 23 Jan. 1952; *s* of Hulance Haddington Broun and Joy Maude Broun (*née* Stack); *S* uncle, 2007; *m* 1st, 1976 (marr. diss. 1998); one *s* one *d*; 2nd, 2001, Caroline Mary Lavender; one *d*. *Educ:* Sydney Grammar Sch.; Wagga Agricl Coll. Queen's Commn (Army), OTU; Lieut, Royal Australian Regt, 1973. Dist Mgr, G. M. Holden, 1976; Man. Dir, Lorimar Telepictures, 1985; Man. Dir and Vice Pres., Warner Bros Internat. Television, Australia/NZ Asia Pacific, 1990; Chairman: Warner Bros Australia, 1991; Movie Network, 1999. Nat. Service Medal, 2004; Australian Defence Medal, 2006. *Recreations:* sport, reading, travel. *Heir:* s Richard Haddington Broun, *b* 3 May 1984. *Address:* 112 Narrabeen Park Parade, Warriewood Beach, NSW 2102, Australia. *T:* (2) 99974175. *E:* aapswayne@bigpond.com. *Clubs:* Royal Automobile of Australia (Sydney); RSL (Pittwater); Royal Motor Yacht (Broken Bay); Bayview Golf; Millbrook Golf (NZ).

**BROUSSE, Olivier,** Chevalier, Ordre du Mérite (France), 2005; Chief Executive Officer, John Laing plc, since 2014; *b* Paris, 28 Feb. 1965; *s* of J. P. Brousse and M. C. Brousse (*née* Chambon); *m* 1991, Isabelle Leven; two *s* one *d*. *Educ:* École Polytechnique, France; École Nationale Ponts et Chaussées, France. Commercial Dir, Unic Systèmes, 1990–94; COS, Compagnie Générale des Eaux, 1994–98; Man. Dir, Connex UK, 1998–2003; Chief Executive Officer, Veolia Transportation, USA, 2004–07; Saur, Paris, 2008–14. *Recreations:* golf, photography. *Address:* 83–85 Onslow Gardens, SW7 3BU. *T:* 07500 553449. *E:* olivier.brousse@me.com. *Clubs:* St Cloud Golf, Polo (Paris).

**BROWN;** see Malloch-Brown, family name of Baron Malloch-Brown.

**BROWN,** family name of **Baron Brown of Eaton-under-Heywood.**

**BROWN OF CAMBRIDGE,** Baroness *cr* 2015 (Life Peer), of Cambridge in the County of Cambridgeshire; **Julia Elizabeth King,** DBE 2012 (CBE 1999); PhD; FRS 2017; CEng, FREng, FIMMM, FRAeS, FIMarEST; FInstP; FEI; Vice Chancellor, Aston University, Birmingham, 2006–16; Fellow, Churchill College, Cambridge, 1987–94 and since 2002; *b* 11 July 1954; *d* of Derrick Arthur King and Joan (*née* Brewer); *m* 1984, Dr Colin William Brown. *Educ:* Godolphin and Latymer Girls' Sch.; New Hall, Cambridge (BA 1975; MA 1978; PhD 1979). CEng 1985. Rolls-Royce Res. Fellow, Girton Coll., Cambridge, 1978–80; Univ. Lectr, Nottingham Univ., 1980–87; Cambridge University: British Gas/FEng Sen. Res. Fellow, 1987–92; Univ. Lectr, 1992–94; Asst Dir, Univ. Technology Centre for Ni-Base Superalloys, 1993–94; Hd of Materials, Rolls-Royce Aerospace Gp, 1994–96; Dir of Advanced Engrg, Rolls-Royce Industrial Power Gp, 1997–98; Man. Dir, Fan Systems, Rolls-Royce plc, 1998–2000; Dir, Engrg and Technology-Marine, Rolls-Royce plc, 2000–02; Chief Exec., Inst. of Physics, 2002–04; Principal, Faculty of Engrg, Imperial Coll. London, 2004–06. Dir, Birmingham Technology Ltd, 2007–; Chair, STEM Learning Ltd, 2016–; non-executive Director: Green Investment Bank, 2012–17; Angel Trains, 2012–15. Mem., Green Commn, 2012–15, Smart City Commn, 2013–, Birmingham CC. Chm., DSAC, 2003–07; Member: Technology Strategy Bd, 2004–09; BIS (formerly BERR) Ministerial Adv. Gp on Manufacturing, 2007–09; Higher Educn Statistics Agency Bd, 2007–12 (Chair, 2011–12); DIUS Strategic Bd, 2008–09; Cttee on Climate Change, 2008– (Chair, Adaption Sub Cttee, 2017–); Automotive Industry Council (formerly Global Agenda Council on Future of Transportation), World Economic Forum, 2008–12; Low Carbon Vehicle Partnership Bd, 2008–11; Interim Nat. Security Forum, 2009–10; BIS Mgt Bd, 2009–12; Independent Rev. Panel for Higher Educn Funding and Student Finance, 2009–10; Bd, Universities UK, 2011–15 (Chair, Innovation and Growth (formerly Employability, Business and Industry) Policy Network, 2011–15); UK Airports Commn, 2012–15; Council, Innovate UK, 2017–. UK Low Carbon Business Ambassador, 2009–. Member: Council, and Hon. Sec. for Educn and Trng, Royal Acad. of Engrg, 2003–06; Council, Energy Inst., 2009–12; Nat. Centre for Univs and Business (formerly Council for Industry and Higher Educn), 2011–15 (Mem., Bd of Dirs, 2013–); EPSRC, 2012–16 (Chm., Fusion Adv. Bd, 2012); Gtr Birmingham and Solihull LEP, 2013–14; Chair, Henry Royce Inst. for Advanced Materials, 2016–. Mem., Governing Body, Institute of Innovation and Technol., 2008–12. Member: Internat. Sci. Cttee, L'Oréal-UNESCO For Women in Science Awards, 2007–13; Sci. and Technol. Honours Cttee, 2012–18. Mem., Bd of Trustees, Cumberland Lodge, 2013–15. Hon. Fellow: New Hall (later Murray Edwards Coll.), Cambridge, 2003; Cardiff Univ., 2003; Soc. for the Envmt, 2011; British Sci. Assoc., 2011; Polymer Processing Acad., India, 2012; Churchill Coll., Cambridge, 2018. FIMMM (FIM 1993); FREng (FEng 1997); FInstP 2002. Hon. FIE 2011; Hon. FIET 2015. Freeman, City of London, 1998; Liveryman, Co. of Goldsmiths, 2005–. Hon. DSc: QMUL, 2008; Manchester, 2014; Exeter, 2015; Brunel, 2017; Hon. DLaws Nottingham, 2016. Grunfeld Medal, 1992, (jtly) Bengough Medal, 1995, Inst. of Materials; Kelvin Medal, ICE, 2001; John Collier Medal, IChemE, 2010; Lunar Soc. Medal, 2011; Constance Tipper Medal, ICF-World Acad. Structural Integrity, 2012; Erna Hamburger Prize, Swiss Federal Inst. Technol., 2012; President's Prize of Engrg, Professors' Council, 2012; LowCVP Low Carbon Champions Award, 2014; Leonardo da Vinci Medal, SEFI, 2014. *Publications:* (ed) Aerospace Materials and Structures, 1997; Educating Engineers for the 21st Century, 2007; King Review of Low Carbon Cars: part I, the potential for CO$_2$ reduction, 2007; part 2, recommendations for action, 2008; over 150 papers on fatigue and fracture in structural materials, aeroengine materials and marine propulsion technology. *Recreations:* people, growing orchids, collecting modern prints, gardening, walking. *Address:* House of Lords, SW1A 0PW.

**BROWN OF EATON-UNDER-HEYWOOD,** Baron *cr* 2004 (Life Peer), of Eaton-under-Heywood in the county of Shropshire; **Simon Denis Brown,** Kt 1984; PC 1992; a Justice of the Supreme Court of the United Kingdom, 2009–12 (a Lord of Appeal in Ordinary, 2004–09); *b* 9 April 1937; *s* of late Denis Baer Brown and Edna Elizabeth (*née* Abrahams); *m* 1963, Jennifer Buddicom; two *s* one *d*. *Educ:* Stowe Sch.; Worcester Coll., Oxford (Hon. Fellow, 1993). Commnd 2nd Lt RA, 1955–57. Called to the Bar, Middle Temple, 1961 (Harmsworth Schol.); Master of the Bench, Hon. Soc. of Middle Temple, 1980; a Recorder, 1979–84; First Jun. Treasury Counsel, Common Law, 1979–84; a Judge of the High Court of Justice, QBD, 1984–92; a Lord Justice of Appeal, 1992–2004; Vice-Pres., Court of Appeal (Civil Div.), 2001–03. President: Security Service Tribunal, 1989–2000; Intelligence Services Tribunal, 1995–2000; Intelligence Services Comr, 2000–06. Chm., Sub-Cttee E (Law and Instns), H of L Select Cttee on EU, 2005–07; Chm., Sub-Cttee on Lords' Conduct, H of L Cttee for Privileges and Conduct, 2013–. Visitor: Pembroke Coll., Cambridge, 2010–19; St Hugh's Coll., Oxford, 2011–; High Steward, Oxford Univ., 2011–12. *Recreations:* golf, theatre, reading. *Address:* House of Lords, SW1A 0PW. *Clubs:* Garrick; Denham Golf; Church Stretton Golf.

**BROWN, Alan;** MP (SNP) Kilmarnock and Loudoun, since 2015; *b* Newmilns, 12 Aug. 1970; *s* of Eric and Irene Brown; *m* 2007, Cyndi Aukerman; two *s*. *Educ:* Loudoun Acad.; Glasgow Univ. (BEng Hons). Engineer: West of Scotland Water, then Strathclyde Regl Council, later Scottish Water, 1993–2007; Grontmij, 2007–15. Mem. (SNP), E Ayrshire Council, 2007–15. *Address:* House of Commons, SW1A 0AA; (office) 31A Titchfield Street, Kilmarnock KA1 3QW.

**BROWN, Hon. Alan John,** AM 2018; Chairman: Apprenticeships Plus, Victoria, 2000–18; IntoWork Australia, 2014–18; *b* Wonthaggi, Vic, 25 Jan. 1946; *m* 1972, Paula McBurnie; three *s* one *d*. Councillor, Wonthaggi BC, 1970–78, Mayor, 1974–77; MLA (L): Westernport, Vic, 1979–85; Gippsland W, Vic, 1985–96; Victorian Shadow Minister for: Youth, Sport and Recreation, 1982; Aboriginal Affairs and Housing, 1982–85; Correctional Services, 1984–85; Resources, 1985; Tspt, 1985–89; Dep. Leader of Opposition, 1987–89; Leader of Opposition, 1989–91; Shadow Minister for Transport, 1991–92; Minister for Transport, 1992–96; Agent-Gen. for Victoria in UK, 1997–2000. Chm., Work & Trng Ltd, Tasmania, 2004–17. Bd Mem., Traffic Technologies Ltd, 2004–17. Chm., Victorian Bushfire Community Adv. Cttee, 2011–12. Silver Jubilee Medal, 1977; Centenary Medal, Australia, 2002. *Recreations:* motor cycle riding, vintage cars, farming. *Address:* Bridgewater Park, Wattle Bank, Vic 3995, Australia.

**BROWN, Alan John,** FCMA; barrister-at-law; Group Chief Executive Officer, Vistra Group, since 2019; *b* Belfast, 8 Nov. 1956; *s* of John and Sallie Brown; *m* 1986, Radhika Edwards (marr. diss. 2016); two *s* one *d*; one *d* by Suzy Black. *Educ:* Methodist Coll., Belfast; Liverpool Univ. (LLB 1978); Council of Legal Educn. CIMA 1983; FCMA 1994. Called to the Bar, Gray's Inn, 1981. Unilever: various posts in UK, 1980–91; Chief Financial Officer, Birds Eye Wall's, 1991–94; Chief Financial Officer, Foods Europe, 1994–97; Chairman: Unilever Taiwan, 1998–2001; Unilever China, 2001–05; Chief Financial Officer, ICI, 2005–08; Chief Executive Officer: Rentokil-Initial plc, 2008–13; ASCO Gp Ltd, 2014–18. Non-exec. Dir, Intertek, 2011–17. *Recreations:* sports, motor racing, vintage and classic cars.

**BROWN, Alan Thomas,** CBE 1978; DL; Chief Executive, Oxfordshire County Council, 1973–88; *b* 18 April 1928; *s* of Thomas Henry Brown and Lucy Lilian (*née* Betts); *m* 1962, Marie Christine East; two *d*. *Educ:* Wyggeston Grammar Sch., Leicester; Sidney Sussex Coll., Cambridge (Wrangler, Maths Tripos 1950, MA 1953). Fellow CIPFA, 1961. Asst, Bor. Treasurer's Dept, Wolverhampton, 1950–56; Asst Sec., IMTA, 1956–58; Dep. Co. Treas., Berks CC, 1958–61; Co. Treas., Cumberland CC, 1961–66; Town Clerk and Chief Exec., Oxford City Council, 1966–73. Member: SE Econ. Planning Council, 1975–79; Audit Commn, 1989–95. DL Oxon 1978. *Recreations:* television, music, reading. *Address:* 4 Malkin Drive, Beaconsfield, Bucks HP9 1JN. *T:* (01494) 677933.

**BROWN, Alan Winthrop,** CB 1992; Head of Health Policy Division, Health and Safety Executive, 1992–94; *b* 14 March 1934; *s* of James Brown and Evelyn V. Brown (*née* Winthrop); *m* 1959, Rut Berit (*née* Ohlson); two *s* one *d*. *Educ:* Bedford Sch.; Pembroke Coll., Cambridge (BA Hons); Cornell Univ., NY (MSc). Joined Min. of Labour, 1959; Private Sec. to Minister, 1961–62; Principal, 1963; Asst Sec., 1969. Dir of Planning, Employment Service Agency, 1973–74; Under-Sec. and Head of Incomes Div., DoE, 1975; Chief Exec., Employment Service Div., 1976–79, Trng Services Div., 1979–82, MSC; Hd Electricity Div., Dept of Energy, 1983–85; Dir, Personnel and Management Services, Dept of Employment, 1985–89; Dir, Resources and Planning, HSE, 1989–92. Chm., Godalming Trust, 1999–2005. Lay Mem., Waverley Primary Care Gp, 2000–02; Patient Rep., Surrey PCT, 2007–13. *Publications:* papers on occupational psychology and industrial training. *Recreations:* history of art, literature, gardening, walking, opera. *Address:* 16 Milford House, Portsmouth Road, Milford, Surrey GU8 5HJ.

**BROWN, Alastair Nigel,** PhD; Sheriff of Tayside, Central and Fife at Dunfermline, since 2019; *b* Kirkcaldy, 3 May 1955; *s* of Kenneth and Evelyn Jean Brown; *m* 1977, Susan Harrison; two *s* one *d*. *Educ:* Royal Grammar Sch., Newcastle upon Tyne; Univ. of Edinburgh (LLB Hons 1977; PhD 1999). Admitted as solicitor, 1979; in practice as solicitor, 1979–2009; with Balfour + Manson Solicitors, Edinburgh, 1979–81, Procurator Fiscal Service, 1981–2003; Advocate Depute, 2004–09; admitted as Advocate, 2010; in private practice at Scots Bar, 2010–11; All-Scotland Floating Sheriff, 2011–14; Sheriff of Tayside, Central and Fife at Dundee, 2014–19. Expert Evaluator, Gp of States Against Corruption, Council of Europe, 2000–19. *Publications:* Criminal Evidence and Procedure: an introduction, 1996, 3rd edn 2011; Regulation of Investigatory Powers in Scotland, 2003; Proceeds of Crime, 2004; Money Laundering, 2009; Sexual Offences (Scotland) Act 2009, 2009, 2nd edn 2015; Bribery Act 2010, 2011. *Recreations:* Church, walking, reading, bluegrass mandolin and guitar, gardening, wood carving. *Address:* c/o Sheriff Court, Carnegie Drive, Dunfermline KY12 7HJ.

**BROWN, Prof. Alice,** CBE 2010; PhD; FRCPE; FRSE; FAcSS; Chairman, Scottish Funding Council, 2013–17; Scottish Public Services Ombudsman, 2002–09; Professor of Politics, University of Edinburgh, 1997–2008, now Emeritus; *b* 30 Sept. 1946; *d* of Robert Wilson and Alice (*née* Morgan); *m* 1965, Alan James Brown; two *d*. *Educ:* Boroughmuir High Sch., Edinburgh; Stevenson Coll., Edinburgh; Univ. of Edinburgh (MA 1983; PhD 1990). FRCPE 2012. Lectr in Econs, Univ. of Stirling, 1984–85; University of Edinburgh: Lectr, 1985–92; Sen. Lectr in Politics, 1992–97; Hd, Dept of Politics, 1995; Hd, Planning Unit, 1996; Co-Dir, Governance of Scotland Forum, subseq. Inst. of Governance, 1998–2002; Vice-Principal, 1999–2002. Chm., Community Planning Task Force (Scotland), 2001–02; Member: SHEFC, 1998–2002 (Chm., Mergers Cttee, 2001–02); Cttee on Standards in Public Life, 1999–2003; Res. Grants Bd, ESRC; Adv. Gp, EOC, Scotland, 1995–2002; Adv. Bd, CRE, Scotland, 2003–07; Bd, ARB, 2006–09; Council, Admin. Justice and Tribunals Council, 2008–13; Adv. Bd, Inst. for Advanced Studies in the Humanities, Univ. of Edinburgh, 2011–13; Steering Cttee, Scottish Resource Centre, Edinburgh Napier Univ., 2011–13. Gen. Sec., RSE, 2011–13. Chancellor, Abertay Univ., 2019–. Founder Member: Engender (women's res. and campaigning gp), 1991–; Scottish Women's Co-ordination Gp, 1999; Mem., Strategic Gp on Women and Work, Scottish Govt, 2013–17. Board Member: Centre for Scottish Public Policy (formerly John Wheatley Centre), 1992–99; Scottish Low Pay Unit; Chm., Lay Adv. Gp, RCPE (Mem., 2003–13). Chair, Nominations Gp for Young Candidates, 2018–. Mem., Educn Cttee, 2018–, RSE. Mem., Scotland Cttee, British Council. Board Member: British and Irish Ombudsman Assoc.; Hansard Soc. Scotland; Political Studies Assoc. Mem., Bd of Govs, Public Policy Inst. for Wales, 2014–. Trustee, David Hume Inst., 2009–17. Asst Ed., Scottish Affairs jl, 1992–2002. Fellow: Stevenson Coll., Edinburgh, 2006; Sunningdale Inst., 2008–12. FRSE 2002; FRSA 2007; FAcSS (AcSS 2002); Hon. Mem., CIPFA, 2004. DUniv: Stirling, 2004; Strathclyde, 2018; Hon. DLaws: Edinburgh Napier, 2009; Aberdeen, 2016; Dr *hc*: Edinburgh, 2010; Robert Gordon, 2018; Hon. DLitt Glasgow Caledonian, 2012; Hon. DSc (SocSci) QUB, 2014. Special Recognition Award, Pol Studies Assoc., 2009; Higher Educn Lifetime Achievement Award, The Herald, 2017; Lifetime

Achievement Award, Holyrood Mag. Public Service Awards, 2017. *Publications*: (co-ed) The Scottish Government Yearbook, 1989–91; The Changing Politics of Gender Equality in Britain, 2002; jointly: A Major Crisis?, 1996; Politics and Society in Scotland, 1996, 1998; Gender Equality in Scotland, 1997; The Scottish Electorate, 1999; New Scotland, New Politics?, 2001. *E*: alajbrown@hotmail.com.

**BROWN, Amanda Margaret B.**; *see* Barrington Brown.

**BROWN, Ven. Andrew**; Archdeacon of Man, since 2011; Chaplain, House of Keys, since 2016; *b* Haslingden, Lancs, 18 Sept. 1955; *s* of Jack Maxwell Brown and Jean Brown; *m* 1982, Jane Rosanne Shakespeare; three *d*. *Educ*: Haslingden Grammar Sch.; St Peter's Coll., Oxford (MA 1982); Ridley Hall, Cambridge. Ordained deacon, 1980, priest, 1981; Asst Curate, Burnley Parish Church, 1980–83; Priest-in-charge, St Francis, Brandlesholme, 1983–86; Vicar: St Peter, Ashton-under-Lyne, 1986–96; St Luke's, Halliwell, 1996–2003; Canon Theologian and Continuing Ministerial Educn Officer, Derby Cathedral, 2003–11. *Publications*: Preaching at Baptisms, 2008. *Recreations*: supporting Burnley FC, reading detective stories, walking, cooking, camping, birding. *Address*: The Archdeacon's House, 16 Devonshire Road, Douglas, Isle of Man IM2 3RB. *T*: (01624) 675430. *E*: archdeacon@sodorandman.im.

**BROWN, Andrew Charles**, FRICS; Secretary and Chief Executive of the Church Commissioners, 2003–Jan. 2020; *b* 30 Oct. 1957; *s* of Gordon Charles Brown and Joan Finch Trail Brown (*née* Tomlin); *m* 1983, Marion Denise Chamberlain (MBE 2016; DL); one *s* one *d*. *Educ*: Ashmole Sch.; South Bank Poly. (BSc Hons). FRICS 1994; Accredited Mediator, CEDR, 2012. Property Negotiator, Healey and Baker, 1981–84; Investment Surveyor, 1984–87, Associate Partner, 1987–91, Partner, 1991–94, St Quintin; Chief Surveyor, Church Commissioners, 1994–2003. Mem. Council, Westminster Property Owners' Assoc., 1997–2003; Member: LionHeart Administration, Investment and Finance Cttee, 2006–14; LionHeart Investment Cttee, 2014–18; Dir, William Leech Foundn, William Leech (Investments) Ltd, 2007–; Chair of Trustees: 2:67 Project, 2007–10; CMS Pension Trust, 2013–18; Trustee, Mediation Herts, 2015–. Mem., PCC, St Paul's Church, St Albans, 2013–17. Hon. Sec., Christians in Property, 1991–2003; Hon. Sec. and Treas., 1894 Club, 2006–11. *Recreations*: family, local church, golf, sport, Chelsea FC, gardening. *Address*: (until Jan. 2020) Church Commissioners, Church House, Great Smith Street, SW1P 3AZ. *T*: (020) 7898 1000. *E*: andrew.brown@churchofengland.org.

**BROWN, Dr Andrew Edward**, CBE 2013; Chief Executive, English Nature, 2003–06; Deputy Chairman, Environment Agency, 2009–12 (Board Member, 2006–09); *b* 9 May 1954; *s* of James Andrew Brown and Gwyneth Brown (*née* Watkins); *m* 1980, Christina Joyce Binks; two *d*. *Educ*: University Coll., Cardiff (BSc Zool. and Envmtl Studies); Leicester Poly. (PhD Freshwater Ecol.). Res. Officer and Tutor, Sussex Univ., 1980–81; Lectr, Bayero Univ., Kano, Nigeria, 1981–83; Nature Conservancy Council: Asst Regl Officer, Cheshire, 1983–86; Develt Officer, Scotland, 1986–89; Sen. Officer, York, 1989–90; English Nature: Strategic Planner, 1990–94; Corporate Manager, 1994–96; Chief Officer, Jt Nature Conservation Cttee, 1996–98; a Dir, English Nature, 1998–2002. Dir, Eur. Forum for Nature Conservation and Pastoralism, 2012–14. Mem., Broads Authority, 1999–2005. Chairman: UK Cttee, IUCN, 2005–07; Policy Cttee, CPRE, 2006–09; Yorkshire Dales Rivers Trust, 2014–18 (Trustee, 2013–); Mem. Council, RSPB, 2006–15; Trustee, Wildfowl and Wetlands Trust, 2008–15. Mem. Council, Linnean Soc., 2007. FLS 2007. *Publications*: contrib. to books on freshwater ecology; papers in scientific jls. *Recreations*: reading, DIY, walking, travel, ski-ing. *Address*: Sunny Bank Farm, Carperby, Leyburn, N Yorks DL8 4DR. *T*: (01969) 662601.

**BROWN, Andrew Edwin**, FRCS; FDSRCS, FDSRCPSGlas; Consultant Maxillofacial Surgeon, Queen Victoria Hospital, East Grinstead, 1981–2008, now Hon. Consultant Surgeon; *b* 22 Aug. 1945; *s* of Edwin and Kathleen Brown; *m* 1969, Joan Elizabeth Phillips; one *s* two *d*. *Educ*: Sir Joseph Williamson's Mathematical Sch., Rochester; Guy's Hosp., Univ. of London (BDS Hons 1969; MB BS 1973). LDSRCS 1968, FDSRCS 1975; LRCP, MRCS 1973, FRCS 1986; FDSRCPSGlas 1975. Registrar, Dept of Oral and Maxillofacial Surgery, Eastman Dental Hosp. and Inst. of Dental Surgery, Univ. of London, 1974–76; Sen. Registrar, Dept of Oral and Maxillofacial Surgery, Queen Victoria Hosp., E Grinstead, 1976–81. Hon. Civil Consultant in Oral and Maxillofacial Surgery, RAF, 2000–09. Chm., Specialist Adv. Cttee in Oral and Maxillofacial Surgery, 2003–05. President: Inst. of Maxillofacial Prosthetists and Technologists, 2002–03; BAOMS, 2006–07. *Publications*: (with P. Banks) Fractures of the Facial Skeleton, 2001, 2nd edn (with M. Perry and P. Banks) 2015; chapters in: Operative Maxillofacial Surgery, 1998, 2nd edn 2010; Maxillofacial Surgery, 1999, 2nd edn 2007; papers on facial trauma, reconstruction, etc in learned jls. *Recreations*: art and graphic design, travel, swimming, medical history, reading history and biography. *Address*: Langleys, West Lane, East Grinstead, W Sussex RH19 4HH.

**BROWN, Andrew Gibson**, CBE 2003; QPM 1997; HM Chief Inspector of Constabulary for Scotland, 2004–07; *b* 11 April 1945; *s* of Alexander Brown and Euphemia Brown; *m* 1988, Fiona McMillan; one *s* one *d*. *Educ*: Kelso High Sch. Police Cadet, 1961; Police Constable, 1964; Detective Chief Supt, 1992; Asst Chief Constable (Crime), Lothian and Borders Police, 1993–98; Chief Constable, Grampian Police, 1998–2004. *Recreations*: spectating Rugby, Prince's Trust, Common Purpose, golf. *Clubs*: Melrose Rugby Football; Broomieknowe Golf.

**BROWN, Andrew Lawson**; QC (Scot.) 2010; *b* Glasgow, 31 May 1966; *s* of late Prof. Al Brown and of Dr Jenny Brown (*née* Tannahill, now Wormald); *m* 1993, Alison Margaret Shiach; one *s* one *d*. *Educ*: Glasgow Acad.; Aberdeen Univ. (LLB Hons). Solicitor, 1989–94; called to the Scottish Bar, 1995; Convenor, Mental Health Tribunal, Scotland, 2005–; ad hoc Advocate Depute, 2006–11, Advocate Depute, 2011–17. Gov., The Burn, Goodenough Coll., 2009–. *Publications*: Wheatley's Road Traffic Law in Scotland, 4th edn, 2007, 5th edn 2014. *Recreations*: flying, military history, orkney. *Address*: Advocates' Library, Parliament House, Edinburgh EH1 1RF. *T*: (0131) 226 5071. *E*: andrew.brown@advocates.org.uk.

**BROWN, Andrew William**, CBE 2012; Director General, Advertising Association, 1993–2006; *b* 3 March 1946; *s* of Harry Brown and Geraldine (*née* O'Leary); *m* 1977, Shelby Ann Hill. *Educ*: St Edmund's Coll., Ware, Herts. J. Walter Thompson Co. Ltd, 1965–93, Board Dir, 1982–93. Chm., CAM Foundn, 1994–96. Director: Advertising Standards Bd of Finance, 1993–2011; Broadcast Advertising Standards Bd of Finance Ltd, 2004–11; Chairman: Cttee of Advertising Practice, 1999–2011; Broadcast Cttee of Advertising Practice, 2004–11 (Mem., Advertising Adv. Cttee, 2004–06); Mem., ITC Advertising Adv. Cttee, 1999–2003. *Recreations*: cricket, theatre, London, Bodmin Moor. *Clubs*: Reform, MCC; XL.

**BROWN, (Anthony) James; His Honour Judge James Brown;** a Circuit Judge, since 2016; *b* Carleton-in-Craven, 16 Feb. 1968; *s* of Brian Brown and Kathleen Brown; *m* 1996, Clare Lindsay; four *d*. *Educ*: Ermysted's Grammar Sch., Skipton; Univ. of Newcastle upon Tyne (LLB Hons 1989). Called to the Bar, Lincoln's Inn, 1990; a Recorder, 2008–16; a Fee-paid Judge, First-tier Tribunal (Mental Health) (Restricted Patients Panel), 2014–16. *Recreations*: sport, walking, books, food, family. *Address*: Teesside Combined Court Centre, Russell Street, Middlesbrough, Cleveland TS1 2AE. *T*: (01642) 340000.

**BROWN, Prof. Archibald Haworth**, CMG 2005; FBA 1991; Professor of Politics, University of Oxford, 1989–2005, now Professor Emeritus; Fellow, St Antony's College, Oxford, 1971–2005, now Fellow Emeritus (Sub-Warden, 1995–97); Director, Russian and East European Centre, St Antony's College, 1991–94 and 1999–2001; *b* 10 May 1938; *s* of late Rev. Alexander Douglas Brown and Mary Brown (*née* Yates); *m* 1963, Patricia Susan Cornwell; one *s* one *d*. *Educ*: Annan Acad.; Dumfries Acad.; City of Westminster Coll.; LSE (BSc Econs, 1st Cl. Hons 1962). MA Oxon 1972. Reporter, Annandale Herald and Annandale Observer, 1954–56. National Service, 1956–58. Lectr in Politics, Glasgow Univ., 1964–71; British Council exchange scholar, Moscow Univ., 1967–68; Lectr in Soviet Instns, Univ. of Oxford, 1971–89. Visiting Professor: of Political Science, Yale Univ. and Univ. of Connecticut, 1980; Columbia Univ., NY, 1985; Univ. of Texas, Austin, 1990–91; INSEAD, 1991; Distinguished Vis. Fellow, Kellogg Inst. for Internat. Studies, Univ. of Notre Dame, 1998. Lectures: Henry L. Stimson, Yale Univ., 1980; Lothian European, Edinburgh, 1999; Alexander Dallin Meml, Stanford, 2006; City of Aberdeen Gorbachev, 2007; James Chace Meml, NY, 2010; BEARR Trust, 2014; Winston Churchill Meml, Cascais, Portugal, 2015. Member, Council: SSEES, Univ. of London, 1992–98; British Acad., 2014–. Founder AcSS 1999. For. Hon. Mem., Amer. Acad. of Arts and Scis, 2003. Diamond Jubilee Lifetime Achievement Award, Pol Studies Assoc., 2010; Dist. Contribs to Slavic, E Eur. and Eurasian Studies Award, ASEEES, 2015. *Publications*: Soviet Politics and Political Science, 1974; (ed jtly and contrib.) The Soviet Union since the Fall of Khrushchev, 1975, 2nd edn 1978; (ed jtly and contrib.) Political Culture and Political Change in Communist States, 1977, 2nd edn 1979; (ed jtly and contrib.) Authority, Power and Policy in the USSR: essays dedicated to Leonard Schapiro, 1980; (ed jtly and contrib.) The Cambridge Encyclopedia of Russia and the Soviet Union, 1982; (ed jtly and contrib.) Soviet Policy for the 1980s, 1982; (ed and contrib.) Political Culture and Communist Studies, 1984; (ed and contrib.) Political Leadership in the Soviet Union, 1989; (ed and contrib.) The Soviet Union: a biographical dictionary, 1990; (ed and contrib.) New Thinking in Soviet Politics, 1992; (ed jtly and contrib.) The Cambridge Encyclopedia of Russia and the Former Soviet Union, 1994; The Gorbachev Factor, 1996 (W. J. M. Mackenzie Prize, Pol Studies Assoc., 1997; Alexander Nove Prize, British Assoc. for Slavonic and E Eur. Studies, 1998); (ed jtly and contrib.) The British Study of Politics in the Twentieth Century, 1999; (ed and contrib.) Contemporary Russian Politics: a reader, 2001; (ed jtly and contrib.) Gorbachev, Yeltsin and Putin: political leadership in Russia's transition, 2001; (ed and contrib.) The Demise of Marxism-Leninism in Russia, 2004; Seven Years that Changed the World: Perestroika in perspective, 2007; The Rise and Fall of Communism, 2009 (Alexander Nove Prize, British Assoc. for Slavonic and E Eur. Studies, 2009; W. J. M. Mackenzie Prize, Pol Studies Assoc., 2010); The Myth of the Strong Leader: political leadership in the modern age, 2014; The Human Factor: Gorbachev, Reagan and Thatcher and the end of the Cold War, 2020; papers in academic jls and symposia; *Festschriften*: Leading Russia – Putin in Perspective: essays in honour of Archie Brown, ed Alex Pravda, 2005; Political Culture and Post-Communism, ed Stephen Whitefield, 2005; Institutions, Ideas and Leadership in Russian Politics, ed Julie Newton and William Tompson, 2010. *Recreations*: novels and political memoirs, opera and ballet, watching football, cricket and tennis. *Address*: St Antony's College, Oxford OX2 6JF.

**BROWN, Sir (Austen) Patrick**, KCB 1995; Chairman, Oil and Gas Authority, 2015–18; *b* 14 April 1940; *m* 1966, Mary (*née* Bulger); one *d*. *Educ*: Royal Grammar School, Newcastle upon Tyne; School of Slavonic and East European Studies, Univ. of London. Carreras Ltd, 1961–69 (Cyprus, 1965–66, Belgium, 1967–68); Management Consultant, Urwick Orr & Partners, UK, France, Portugal, Sweden, 1969–72; DoE, 1972; Asst Sec., Property Services Agency, 1976–80, Dept of Transport, 1980–83; Under Sec., Dept of Transport, 1983–88; Dep. Sec., DoE, 1988–90; Second Perm. Sec., and Chief Exec., PSA, DoE, 1990–91; Perm. Sec., Dept of Transport, 1991–97. Chairman: Go-Ahead Gp, 2002–13 (Dir, 1999–2013); Amey plc, 2004–08; Dep. Chm., Kvaerner Corporate Develt, 1998–99; Director: Hunting PLC, 1998–2001; Arlington Securities plc, 1999–2004; Northumbrian Water Gp plc, 2003–12; Camelot UK Lotteries plc, 2010–18; Chm., Adv. Bd, Alexander Proudfoot Ltd, 2010–12. Chm., Ind. Transport Commn, 1999–2008. Leader, Way Ahead Study into Ex-Service Charities, 2001–02. Trustee, Charities Aid Foundn, 1998–2006; Chm. Trustees, Mobility Choice, 1998–2008. Vis. Prof., later Mem. Court, Newcastle Univ., 1998–2013.

**BROWN, Barry;** *see* Brown, James B. C.

**BROWN, Benjamin Robert**; Presenter, BBC News; *b* 26 May 1960; *s* of late Antony Victor Brown and of Sheila Mary Brown; *m* 1991, Geraldine Anne Ryan; one *s* two *d*. *Educ*: Sutton Valence Sch., Kent; Keble Coll., Oxford (BA Hons PPE); Centre for Journalism Studies, UC, Cardiff. Reporter: Radio Clyde, 1982; Radio City, 1982–85; Independent Radio News, 1985–88; BBC Television News: Corresp., 1988–91; Moscow Corresp., 1991–94; Foreign Affairs Corresp., 1994–98; Special Corresp., 1998–2006; Presenter, BBC News 24, 2006. *Publications*: All Necessary Means: inside the Gulf War (with D. Shukman), 1991; Sandstealers (novel), 2009. *Recreations*: reading, cinema, following Liverpool Football Club. *Address*: c/o BBC News Centre, Broadcasting House, Portland Place, W1A 1AA.

**BROWN, Adm. Sir Brian (Thomas)**, KCB 1989; CBE 1983; Chairman, P-E International plc, 1995–98; Director: Cray Electronics plc, 1991–96; Lorien plc, 1996–2007; *b* 31 Aug. 1934; *s* of late Walter Brown and Gladys (*née* Baddeley); *m* 1959, Veronica, *d* of late Wing Comdr and Mrs J. D. Bird; two *s*. *Educ*: Peter Symonds' School. Joined RN 1952; pilot in 898 and 848 Sqdns, 1959–62; Dep. Supply Officer, HMY Britannia, 1966–68; Supply Officer, HMS Tiger, 1973–75; Secretary: to VCNS, 1975–78; to First Sea Lord, 1979–82; rcds 1983; CO HMS Raleigh, 1984–85; DGNPS, 1986; Dir Gen., Naval Manpower and Trng, 1986–88, and Chief Naval Supply and Secretariat Officer, 1987–88; Chief of Naval Personnel, Second Sea Lord and Admiral Pres., RNC, Greenwich, 1988–91, retired. Chairman: King George's Fund for Sailors, 1993–2003; Exec. Cttee, Nuffield Trust for the Armed Forces of the Crown, 1996–2003; Michael May Young Cricketers Foundn, 1993–2008; President: Victory Services Assoc., 1993–2002; Friends of RN Mus. and HMS Victory, 1993–2003; Portsmouth Services Fly Fishing Assoc., 2005–15; CPRE Hants, 2008–13. Churchwarden, Froxfield with Privett, 1999–2008. CCMI (CBIM 1989); FIPD (FIPM 1990). Hon. DEd CNAA, 1990. Freeman, City of London, 1989; Liveryman, 1991–2012, Freeman, 2012–, Gardeners' Co. Jt Master, Clinkard Meon Valley Beagles, 2003–09. *Recreations*: cricket, gardening, fishing. *Address*: Apartment 1, Blenheim Court, Farnham Road, Liss, Hants GU33 6JA. *Club*: Army and Navy.

**BROWN, Bruce;** *see* Brown, John B.

**BROWN, Prof. Bruce;** Professor of Design, 1989–2016, and Pro-Vice Chancellor (Research) 2006–16, University of Brighton; *b* 14 June 1949; *s* of George and Grace Brown; *m* 1976, Morag Ross; two *d*. *Educ*: Liverpool Coll. of Art (Foundn Cert. 1968); Canterbury Coll. of Art (DipAD 1971); Royal Coll. of Art (MA 1978). Industrial Design Bursary, RSA 1971. Lectr, RCA, 1978–81; Head, Department of Graphic Design: Norwich Sch. of Art,

1981–84; Brighton Poly., 1984–89; Dean, Faculty of Arts and Architecture, Univ. of Brighton, 1989–2006. Dir, Subject Centre for Art, Design & Media, Higher Educn Acad., York, 1999–. Visiting Professor: RCA, 2016–; Goldsmiths, Univ. of London, 2018. Ind. design consultant and Art Dir, Crafts mag., Crafts Council, 1978–84; Mem., Point, Art and Design Res. Jl, 1998–2002. Mem., Panel 64 Art and Design, 2001 RAE, 1997–2001; Chairman: Main Panel O, 2008 RAE, 2005–08; Main Panel D (Arts and Humanities) 2014 RAE, 2010–14; Panel for Visual Arts, Design, Creative Media, other Creative Arts and Creative Writing, Hong Kong RAE 2020, 2018–19. Member: CNAA Bd for Art and Design, 1981–94; Bd, PCFC, 1989–92; CNAA Review Gp of Graphic Design Studies in Polys and Colls, 1990; CNAA and BTEC Jt Review Gp, 1990–92; Hong Kong Council for Acad. Accreditation, 1991–; AHRB Postgrad. Panel for Visual Arts, 1998–2000; Bd of Dirs, SE Arts Bd, Arts Council for England, 1998–2000; RSE and British Acad. Jt Review Gp, 1999–2000; Council for Higher Educn in Art and Design Res. Strategy Gp, 1999–2001; Exec. Cttee, UK Council for Grad. Educn, 2001–04; Exec. Cttee, UK Arts and Humanities Data Service, 2001–07; Steering Cttee, AHRB ICT in Arts and Humanities Res. Prog., 2003–08; HEFCE Cttee for allocation of Res. Capability Funding, 2003, 2005; AHRB Selection Cttees for Peer Review Coll., and for Res. Proposals to ICT Methods Network, 2004; Council, UK Higher Educn Acad., 2004–08 (Mem., Res. Strategy Cttee, 2004–07; Mem., Res. Informed Teaching Gp, 2004–07); Jt Inf. Systems Cttee Selection Cttee, Awareness and Training Prog., Arts and Humanities Researchers in UK, 2004; AHRC/HEFCE Res. Metrics Working Gp for RAE, 2006, 2008; QAA Gp for Qualifs Benchmarks for Masters degrees in UK univs, 2007; Qatar Nat. Res. Fund and Undergrad. Res. Experience Prog., 2007–; Steering Cttee, Handbook for Res. in the Arts, Riksbankens Jubileumsfond, Sweden, 2009–; Internat. Panel of Experts, Review of Nat. Provision in Arts and Culture Higher Educn, Portuguese Min. of Sci., Technol. and Higher Educn, 2009; HEFCE Expert Adv. Gp for the Res. Excellence Framework, 2009–; Adv. Bd, AHRC, 2009–; Scientific Cttee for Humanities, Science Europe, 2013–16; Accreditation Panels, Kosovo Accreditation Agency, 2018; Chair, Accreditation Panels for PhD degree awarding powers, Estonian Accreditation Agency, 2018. Specialist Advr, NZ Quals Authy, 1998. Chairman: Res. Grants Panel, Portuguese Foundn for Sci. and Technol., 2010–; Selection Cttee, UK Nat. Teaching Fellowship Scheme (Projects), 2010–12. Mem., Bd of Dirs, Brighton Photographic Biennale, 2001–04. Member, Board of Trustees: Ditchling Mus., 2006–12; Edward Johnston Foundn, 2006–09; Crafts Council, 2014–. MAE 2015 (Life Fellow, 2018). FRSA 1973 (Life Fellow, 2016). Hon. FRCA 2004; Hon. Fellow, Kent Inst. of Art & Design, 2005. Sanderson Award and Herbert Read Award, RCA, 1978. Ed., Design Issues, 2006–. *Publications*: Brown's Index to Photocomposition Typography, 1983; Graphic Memory, 2000; (contrib.) Art and Design at Brighton 1859–2009, 2009; (contrib.) Shaping Virtue, 2012; contribs to jls incl. Design Jl, Information Design Jl, POINT Art + Design Res. Jl, RCA Papers, Eur. Rev. *Recreations*: music, travel, food, wine, playing classical guitar, portrait painting. *E*: bgb@brucebrown.plus.com. *Clubs*: Savile, Chelsea Arts, Double Crown, Wynkyn de Worde Society.

**BROWN, Bruce Neil C.;** *see* Carnegie-Brown.

**BROWN, Catherine;** Chief Executive, Food Standards Agency, 2012–17; *b* Oxford, 3 Jan. 1967; *d* of David and Juliet Brown; civil partnership 2006, Lesley Meagher. *Educ*: St Paul's Girls' Sch.; New Hall, Cambridge (BA Hons English 1988). Commercial trainee and manager, Unilever, 1989–94; Dir of Finance, then Dep. Chief Exec., Newham Community NHS Trust, 1994–97; Hosp. Manager and Regl Manager, BUPA Hosps, 1997–2001; Man. Dir, BUPA Wellness, 2001–06; Dir of Change and Prog. Mgt, BUPA Membership, 2006–07; Chief Operating Officer, 2007–08, Chief Exec., 2008–11, Animal Health and Vet. Labs Agency, DEFRA. Mem., Legal Services Bd, 2019–. *Recreations*: gardening, horse riding, learning Welsh.

**BROWN, Catherine Roberta; Her Honour Judge Catherine Brown;** a Circuit Judge, since 2018; *b* Lichfield, Staffs, 2 Jan. 1967; *d* of Robert Dunbar Brown and Dorothy May Brown (*née* Ledward); partner, Julian Warrick Moses. *Educ*: Range High Sch., Formby; Nonsuch High Sch. for Girls, Cheam; Univ. of Birmingham (BCom Hons); Poly. of Central London (DipLaw). Called to the Bar, Middle Temple, 1990; barrister, 12 King's Bench Walk, 1990–2018; a Recorder, 2008–18. *Recreations*: retired greyhounds, equality issues, travel. *Address*: Canterbury Crown Court, The Law Courts, Chaucer Road, Canterbury, Kent CT1 1ZA.

**BROWN, Cedric Harold,** FREng, FIGEM, FICE; consultant; Chairman, CB Consultants, since 1996; *b* 7 March 1935; *s* of late William Herbert Brown and Constance Dorothy Brown (*née* Frances); *m* 1956, Joan Hendry; one *s* two *d* (and one *d* decd). *Educ*: Sheffield, Rotherham and Derby Colleges of Technology. Pupil Gas Distribution Engineer, E Midlands Gas Bd, 1953–58, Tech. Asst, 1958–59; Engineering Asst, Tunbridge Wells Borough Council, 1959–60; engineering posts, E Midlands Gas Bd, 1960–75 (Chief Engineer, 1973–75); Dir of Engineering, E Midlands Gas, 1975–78; British Gas Corp., subseq. British Gas plc: Asst Dir (Ops) and Dir (Construction), 1978–79; Dir, Morecambe Bay Project, 1980–87; Regl Chm., British Gas W Midlands, 1987–89; Dir, Man. Dir, Exploration and Production, 1989; Man. Dir, Regl Services, 1989–91; Sen. Man. Dir, 1991–92; Chief Exec., 1992–96. Chairman: Business Champions-E Midlands Devvelt Agency, 2001–04; Lachesis Investment Adv. Cttee, 2002–07. Pres., IGasE, 1996–97. FREng (FEng 1990). Liveryman, Engineers' Co., 1988–. *Publications*: tech. papers to professional bodies. *Recreations*: sport, countryside, places of historic interest.

**BROWN, (Cedric Wilfred) George E.;** *see* Edmonds-Brown.

**BROWN, Charles Dargie,** FREng; consulting engineer, retired; Joint Chairman, Mott, Hay & Anderson, later Mott MacDonald, Consulting Engineers, 1980–89; *b* 13 April 1927; *s* of William Henry Brown and Jean Dargie; *m* 1952, Sylvia Margaret Vallis; one *s* one *d*. *Educ*: Harris Acad., Dundee; St Andrews Univ. (BScEng, 1st Cl. Hons.). FICE; FREng (FEng 1981). Joined staff of Mott, Hay & Anderson, 1947; engaged on highways, tunnels and bridge works, incl. Tamar Bridge, Forth Road Bridge, George Street Bridge, Newport, Kingsferry and Queensferry Bridges, 1947–65; Partner and Director, 1965. Principally concerned with planning, design and supervision of major works, 1965–89, incl. Mersey Queensway tunnels and new London Bridge, and projects in Hong Kong (Tsing Ma Bridge), Malaysia (Pahang River Bridges), highway and bridge works in Indonesia and USA; participated in develt of underground rly systems in Melbourne and Singapore. Member, Smeatonian Soc. of Civil Engrs, 1984–. Hon. LLD Dundee, 1982. *Publications*: papers to Instn of Civil Engrs, on Kingsferry Bridge, George St Bridge, London Bridge and Mersey tunnels; also various papers to engrg confs. *Recreations*: golf, gardening, bird watching, reading. *Address*: 31 Heathfield Road, Petersfield, Hants GU31 4DG. *T*: (01730) 267820. *Club*: Royal Automobile.

**BROWN, Christina Hambley, (Lady Evans);** *see* Brown, Tina.

**BROWN, Christopher;** Director and Chief Executive, National Society for Prevention of Cruelty to Children, 1989–95; *b* 21 June 1938; *s* of Reginald Frank Greenwood Brown and Margaret Eleanor Brown; *m* 1968, Helen Margaret, *d* of George A. Woolsey and Hilda M. Woolsey; three *s* one *d*. *Educ*: Hertford Grammar Sch.; King's Coll., London (AKC); Heythrop Coll., London (MA 2005). Home Office Cert. in Probation. Ordained deacon, 1963, priest, 1964; Assistant Curate, Diocese of Southwark: St Hilda's, Crofton Park, 1963; St Michael's, Wallington, 1964–67. Probation Officer, Nottingham, 1968–72; Sen. Probation Officer, W Midlands, 1972–74; Asst Dir, Social Services, Solihull, 1974–76; Asst Chief Probation Officer, Hereford and Worcester, 1976–79; Chief Probation Officer: Oxfordshire, 1979–86; Essex, 1986–89. Member: Parole Bd, 1985–87; Trng Cttee, Inst. for Study and Treatment of Delinquency, 1986–89; Professional Adv. Cttee, NSPCC, 1986–89; Chm., Social Issues Cttee, Assoc. of Chief Officers of Probation, 1985–87; Founding Trustee, Friends of the Poor in S India, 2008– (Sec., 2008–18). Mem., Green Coll., Oxford, 1981–86. Licensed to officiate, Dio. Chelmsford, 1986–. *Publications*: contribs to various jls on social work practice and community issues, 1971–, to Christian/Islamic studies and dialogues, 2005–, and on Christian/Muslim relations, 2008–. *Recreations*: walking, reading, music, conversation, gardening. *Address*: 7 Baronia Croft, Colchester, Essex CO4 9EE. *E*: chribrow@yahoo.co.uk.

**BROWN, Lt Gen. Christopher Charles,** CBE 1999; Director, Bellerophon Consulting Ltd, since 2014; *b* 26 Oct. 1955; *s* of Philip Alexander George Brown and Gladys Maud Brown; *m* 1983, Leigh Margaret Kennedy; two *s*. *Educ*: University Coll. Cardiff (LLB 1977); Peterhouse, Cambridge (MPhil 2007). Battery Comdr, Chestnut Troop, RHA, 1990–91; UN Mil. Observer, Western Sahara, 1991–92; Directing Staff, Staff Coll., 1992–94; CO, 7th Parachute Regt, RHA, 1994–96; ACOS Plans, HQ ARRC, 1996–99; Comdr RA, 1st Armd Div., 1999–2002; Dep. Sen. British Mil. Advr, US Central Comd, 2002; ADC to the Queen, 2002–03; Director: RA, 2002–03; Mil. Ops, MoD, 2003; COS, Allied Comd Europe RRC, 2004–06; COS, NATO Internat. Security and Assistance Force, Afghanistan, 2006–07; GOC NI, 2007–09; Dep. Comdg Gen. Multi Nat. Force Iraq and Sen. British Mil. Rep. (Iraq), 2009; Iraq Compendium Study Team Leader, 2009–10; Sen. Security Advr, Assessment and Evaluation Commn and African Union High-Level Implementation Panel for Sudan, 2011. Chief Operating Officer, Equilibrium Gulf Ltd, 2014–15. QCVS 2007. *Recreations*: cross-country ski-ing (Bd Mem., British Biathlon Union, 2006–09), orienteering, mountaineering, fishing, sailing (Cdre, British Kiel Yacht Club, 2004–06). *Clubs*: Royal Artillery Yacht, Royal Lymington Yacht.

**BROWN, Christopher David,** MA; Headmaster, Norwich School, 1984–2002; *b* 8 July 1944; *s* of E. K. Brown; *m* 1972, Caroline Dunkerley; two *d*. *Educ*: Plymouth College; Fitzwilliam College, Cambridge (MA). Assistant Master: The Leys School, Cambridge, 1967–71; Pangbourne College, 1971–73; Radley College, 1973–84 (Head of English, 1975–84). Chairman: Choir Schs Assoc., 1997–99; HMC, 2001; Dep. Chm., ISC, 2003–06.

**BROWN, Christopher Ledwith,** OBE 2004; FRGS; Country Director, Vietnam, British Council, 2013–14; *b* 15 March 1953; *s* of Peter and Joanna Brown; *m* 1977, Elizabeth Varrall; one *s* two *d*. *Educ*: Leicester Univ. (BSc Geol.). Served RN, 1974–79; with British Council, 1979–: posts in Nigeria, Nepal, Spain and UK, 1979–95; Dir, Peru, 1995–99; Regl Dir, Western and Southern Europe, 1999–2003; Dir, Turkey, 2003–08; Dir Progs, Sub-Saharan Africa, 2008–13. FRGS 1978. *Recreations*: bricklaying, herding penguins, gundog training.

**BROWN, Prof. Christopher Paul Hadley,** CBE 2011; PhD; Director, Ashmolean Museum, 1998–2014, now Emeritus; Senior Research Fellow, Worcester College, Oxford, since 2014 (Fellow, 1998–2014); Professor of Netherlandish Art, University of Oxford, since 2013; *b* 15 April 1948; *s* of late Arthur Edgar Brown and of Florence Marjorie Brown; *m* 1975, Sally Madeleine Stockton; one *s* one *d*. *Educ*: Merchant Taylors' Sch.; St Catherine's Coll., Oxford (BA Hons Modern History, Dip. History of Art; Hon. Fellow, 2010); Courtauld Inst. of Art, Univ. of London (PhD). National Gallery: Asst Keeper, 1971, with responsibility for Dutch and Flemish 17th cent. paintings; Dep. Keeper, 1979; Keeper, then Chief Curator, 1989–98. Trustee, Dulwich Picture Gall., 1993–2001. Visiting Professor: Univ. of St Andrews, 1996–2008; Centre for Golden Age Studies, Univ. of Amsterdam, 2002. Lectures: Ferens Fine Art, Univ. of Hull, 1980; Cargill, Univ. of Glasgow, 1987; Jasper Walls, Pierpont Morgan Library, NY, 1991; Visual Arts, QUB, 1999; Allard Pierson, Univ. of Amsterdam, 2010; Alex Gordon, Frick Mus., NY, 2011. Fellow, Netherlands Inst. for Advanced Study, Wassenaar, 1993–94. Member: Consultative Cttee, Burlington Mag., 1994–; Cttee of Mgt, Royal Mus. of Fine Arts, Antwerp, 1997–2009; Trustee, Barber Inst. of Fine Arts, Univ. of Birmingham, 2010–. Hon. DLitt: Birmingham, 2012; St Andrews, 2013. *Publications*: Carel Fabritius, 1981; Van Dyck, 1982; Scenes of Everyday Life: seventeenth-century Dutch genre painting, 1984; Dutch Landscape (catalogue), 1986; The Drawings of Anthony van Dyck, 1991; (jtly) Rembrandt: the master and his workshop (catalogue), 1991; Making and Meaning: Rubens's landscapes, 1996; (jtly) Van Dyck 1599–1641, 1999; National Gallery catalogues, incl. The Dutch School 1600–1900, 1990; The Ashmolean: Britain's First Museum, 2009; contribs to art magazines, UK and overseas. *Address*: Ashmolean Museum, Oxford OX1 2PH. *E*: christopher.brown@ashmus.ox.ac.uk.

**BROWN, Colin James;** Principal, Experiential Consultancy Ltd, since 2011; Chairman, Iron Box Capital, since 2015; *b* 27 Nov. 1950; *s* of Gordon and Jeanne Brown; *m* 1st, 1972, Marie-Laure Delvaux (marr. diss. 1984); one *d*; 2nd, 1985, Benedicte Marie Granier; two *s*. *Educ*: George Watson's Boys' Coll., Edinburgh; RMA, Sandhurst; Reading Univ. (BA Hons Hist.). Served RWF, 1971–80 (Captain). Alexander Proudfoot, Paris, 1980–81; Rank Xerox, 1981–82; Bell and Howell, 1982–84; Rank Cintel Ltd, 1984–86; Exec. Vice Pres., Rank Cintel Inc., 1986–89; Man. Dir, Molinare, 1989–92; Divl Man. Dir, Eur. Television Networks, 1992–94; Man. Dir, Cinesite Europe Ltd, 1994–2000; CEO, Cinesite Worldwide, 2000–07; British Film Comr, 2007–11; Gen. Manager, Lucasfilm Singapore, 2014–15. Member: Bd, UK Film Council, 2003–07; Bd, Nat. Film and TV Sch., 2005–11; BAFTA 1993– (Voting Mem.). *Recreations*: travelling, sailing, gastronomy. *Address*: 27 Ennismore Avenue, W4 1SE. *T*: (020) 7861 7905; 4 Rue du Vieux Village, Souvignargues 30250, France. *E*: cjbexperiential@gmail.com, colinxyzbrown@gmail.com. *Clubs*: Chelsea Arts, Soho House.

**BROWN, Craig;** *see* Brown, J. C.

**BROWN, Craig Edward Moncrieff;** freelance writer, since 1977; *b* 23 May 1957; *s* of Peter Brown and Jennifer (*née* Bethell); *m* 1987, Frances Welch; one *s* one *d*. *Educ*: Farleigh House; Eton Coll.; Bristol Univ. Drama Dept. Columnist on: Sunday Telegraph, Daily Telegraph, Daily Mail, Private Eye, Independent on Sunday, Guardian (as Wallace Arnold, and Bel Littlejohn); specialising in parody and satire. What the Papers Say Gen. Pleasure Award, 1996. *Publications*: The Marsh-Marlow Letters, 1984; A Year Inside, 1989; The Agreeable World of Wallace Arnold, 1990; Rear Columns, 1992; Welcome to My Worlds!, 1993; Craig Brown's Greatest Hits, 1993; The Hounding of John Thomas, 1994; The Private Eye Book of Craig Brown Parodies, 1995; (ed jtly) Colin Welch, The Odd Thing About the Colonel and Other Pieces, 1997; Hug Me While I Weep (For I Weep For the World): the lonely struggles of Bel Littlejohn, 1998; This is Craig Brown, 2003; Craig Brown's Imaginary Friends, 2005; 1966 and All That, 2005; The Tony Years, 2006; The Lost Diaries, 2010; One on One, 2012; Ma'am Darling: 99 glimpses of Princess Margaret, 2017. *Recreations*: swimming in the sea, drinking, shopping. *Address*: c/o Private Eye, 6 Carlisle Street, W1D 3BN.

**BROWN, Damian Robert**; QC 2012; b Birkenhead, 30 Jan. 1966; s of Terrence and Elizabeth Brown. Educ: St Anselm's Coll., Birkenhead; Queen Mary Coll., Univ. of London (BA Law and Politics); Inns of Court Sch. of Law. Called to the Bar, Inner Temple, 1989; in practice as barrister, 1989–, specialising in employment, commercial and sports law and professional regulation and discipline. Lectr (pt-time) in Internat. Labour Law, KCL, 1995–98. Mem., Professional Conduct Cttee, Bar Standards Bd, 2006–11; Chm., Employment Law Bar Assoc., 2011. Publications: contributor: Blackstone's Employment Law Practice, 2012–; Tolley's Employment Law, 2012–; Employment Precedents and Company Policy Documents, 2012–; Terminations of Employment, 2012–. Recreations: sport, cooking. Clubs: Milk and Honey; Arsenal Football.

**BROWN, David Allen**; Chief Executive, Go-Ahead Group, since 2011; b Northolt, Middx, 31 Dec. 1960; s of Alan and Pamela Brown; m 1990, Gretchen Fisher; one s one d. Educ: Greenford High Sch.; Reading Univ. (BA Hons Geog.); Univ. of London (Dip. Transport). Various posts, then District Manager, London Transport and London Buses Ltd, 1983–88; Gen. Manager, CentreWest, Mgt Employee Buyout, 1988–96; Man. Dir, Berks Bucks Bus Co., 1996–98; London General and London Central: Ops Dir, 1998–99; Man. Dir, 1999–2003; Chief Exec., 2003–06; Main Bd Advr, Go-Ahead Gp, 2003–06; Man. Dir, Surface Transport, TfL, 2006–11. Non-exec. Dir, Renew Hldgs Ltd, 2017–. MCILT 1985, FCILT 2009; FCIHT 2009. Recreations: trekking, squash, football, family. Address: Go-Ahead Group, 1st Floor, 4 Matthew Parker Street, SW1H 9NP. E: david.brown@go-ahead.com.

**BROWN, Prof. David Anthony**, PhD; FRS 1990; FRSB; Research Professor, Department of Neuroscience, Physiology and Pharmacology (formerly Department of Pharmacology), University College London, since 2005; b 10 Feb. 1936; s of Alfred William and Florence Brown; m Susan Hames; two s one d. Educ: Univ. of London (BSc, BSc, PhD). FRSB (FInstBiol) 1980. University of London: Asst Lectr 1961–65, Lectr 1965–73, Dept of Pharmacology, St Bart's Hosp. Med. Coll.; Dept of Pharmacology, School of Pharmacy: Sen. Lectr, 1973–74; Reader, 1974–77; Professor, 1977–79; Wellcome Professor, 1979–87; Prof. of Pharmacol., Middx Hosp. Med. Sch., then University Coll. and Middx Sch. of Medicine, UCL, 1987–2005 (Hd, Dept of Pharmacol., 1987–2002). Visiting Professor: Univ. of Chicago, 1970; Univ. of Iowa, 1971, 1973; Univ. of Texas, 1979, 1980, 1981; Univ. of Kanazawa, 1987, 1990; Vis. Scientist, Armed Forces Radiobiology Res. Inst., Bethesda, Md, 1976; Fogarty Schol.-in-Residence, NIH, Bethesda, 1985–86. Member: Physiological Soc., 1970–2004 (Hon. Mem., 2004); British Pharmacological Soc., 1965– (Hon. Fellow 2005); Biochemical Soc., 1969–; Academia Europaea, 1990. Dist. Hon. Dr Kanazawa, 1993. Publications: contribs to Jl of Physiology, British Jl of Pharmacology, etc. Recreation: filling in forms. Address: Department of Neuroscience, Physiology and Pharmacology, University College London, Gower Street, WC1E 6BT. E: d.a.brown@ucl.ac.uk.

**BROWN, Dr David John**, CPhys, CEng, FInstP, FIChemE, FRSC; consultant; Director, Trihelica Ltd, since 2016; b 10 March 1956; s of Colin and Patricia Brown; m 1985, Vivienne Burges; two s one d. Educ: Aylesbury Grammar Sch.; Queens' Coll., Cambridge (BA Natural Scis 1978; PhD 1982). CPhys 2001; FInstP 2001; CSci 2004; FIChemE 2011; CEng 2011; FRSC 2013. Various posts, ICI PLC, 1983–93; Dir, Warwick Res. Inst., Univ. of Warwick, 1992–97; Arthur D. Little Ltd, 1997–2006 (Dir and Hd, Technol. and Innovation, 2002–06); Chief Exec., IChemE, 2006–16. Dir, Chemistry Innovation Ltd, 2007–16. Mem. Bd, W Midlands in Europe, 2006–11 (Chm., 2008–11); Member: Bd, Advantage W Midlands, 2006–12 (Dep. Chm., 2009–12); Bd, Central Technol. Belt, 2006–11; W Midlands Innovation and Technol. Council, 2006–11; Bd, Birmingham Sci. City, 2007–; Bd, Science Council, 2008–12; Bd, EngineeringUK, 2009–12. Advr, Nottingham Univ., 2017–; Special Advr, Partnerships, Aston Univ., 2017–. MInstKT 2009. Non-executive Director: Coventry Refugee Centre, 2007–13; Univ. of Birmingham Enterprise, 2016–. Trustee: St Christopher's Fellowship, 2013–; Carers Trust Solihull, 2016–; Kings Heath Christadelphian Ch, 2018–. Publications: various, on scientific, religious and mgt subjects. Recreations: cooking, Church activities, walking. Address: 10 Nailsworth Road, Dorridge, Solihull B93 8NS. T: 07979 658321. E: dbrown@cantab.net, davidbrown.solihull@gmail.com.

**BROWN, David-Joseph**; Co-Founder and Chief Executive Officer, Ve Interactive Ltd, 2009–17; b London, 19 Aug. 1972; s of Joseph Edward Brown and Carol Anne Brown (née Liddle). Educ: Birmingham Conservatoire of Music (Dip. Piano and Composition). ABSM. Pianist and composer, classical and alternative music; Co-Founder, Pres. and Chief Exec., Serious, 1997–2007; Founder and Director: Thinkers HQ Ltd, 2011–15; Clerkenwell Collection Ltd, 2013–15. Speaker on entrepreneurialism and technol. Entrepreneur of the Year, LCCI, 2014; Digital Entrepreneur of the Year, Great British Entrepreneurs Awards, 2014. Recreations: piano, composition, scuba diving, snooker, swimming, ski-ing, arts. Club: Ivy.

**BROWN, Sir David (Martin)**, Kt 2001; FREng; Chairman, British Standards Institution, 2012–18 (non-executive Director, 2010–12); b 14 May 1950; s of Alan Brown and Laura Marjorie Brown (née Richardson); m 1975, Denise Frances Bowers; two s. Educ: Portsmouth Poly. (BSc Electrical Engrg). CEng 1980; FIET (FIEE 1985; Hon. FIET 2008); FREng 1999. With Standard Telephones and Cables, 1979–91; joined Motorola, 1991: Director: UK Ops, Cellular Infrastructure, 1991–93; GSM Product Mgt, 1993–95; Sen. Dir, Radio Access, 1995–97; Chm., Motorola Ltd, 1997–2008. Non-executive Director: P&OSN Co., 2002–06; Domino Printing Scis plc, 2008–15; TTG Global Gp (formerly Siatel Hldgs Ltd), 2010–18; Sen. Ind. Dir, Ceres Power Hldgs plc, 2008–12; Chm., DRS Data & Res. Services plc, 2009–15 (Dep. Chm., 2008–09). Mem., Industrial Develt Adv. Bd, 1998–2004; Vice Chm., UK Trade and Investment, 2000–04. President: ASE, 1998; Fedn of Electronics Industry, 1999–2000; IEE, 2003–04 (Mem. Council, 1986–90, 1997–2001; Dep. Pres., 2001–03); CQI, 2007–08 (Hon. FCQI 2007). Chairman: Qualifications Cttee, QCA, 1997–2003; Ofcom Spectrum Adv. Bd, 2004–10; Ofcom Spectrum Clearance Finance Cttee, 2009–14. Chm., Bletchley Park Trust Ltd, 2019–. Mem. Council, 2008–11, Mem. Court, 2011–16, Cranfield Univ. Vis. Fellow, Kellogg College, Oxford, 2007–. Fellow, St George's House, Windsor Castle, 2008–. CCMI (MBIM 1976). DUniv Surrey, 2004; Hon. DEng Bath, 2004; Hon. DSc Portsmouth, 2005; Hon. DTech Kingston, 2006. Mountbatten Medal, IEE, 2005. Recreations: literature, art, theatre. Address: Bridleway Cottage, Stanmore, Newbury, Berks RG20 8SR. Club: Athenæum.

**BROWN, David Rodney H.**; see Heath-Brown.

**BROWN, Rev. Prof. David William**, DLitt; FBA 2002; FRSE; Wardlaw Professor of Theology, Aesthetics and Culture, University of St Andrews, 2007–15, now Emeritus; b 1 July 1948; s of David William Brown and Catherine Smith. Educ: Keil Sch., Dumbarton; Edinburgh Univ. (MA 1st cl. Classics 1970; DLitt 2012); Oriel Coll., Oxford (BA 1st cl. Phil. and Theol. 1972); Clare Coll., Cambridge (PhD 1976); Westcott House, Cambridge. Fellow, Chaplain and Tutor in Theol. and Phil., Oriel Coll., Oxford and Univ. Lectr in Theol., 1976–90; Van Mildert Prof. of Divinity, Univ. of Durham and Canon of Durham Cathedral, 1990–2007. Vice-Chm., Doctrine Commn of C of E, 1990–95. FRSE 2012. Publications: Choices: ethics and the Christian, 1983; The Divine Trinity, 1985; Continental Philosophy and Modern Theology, 1987; Invitation to Theology, 1989; (ed) Newman: a man for our time, 1990; The Word To Set You Free, 1995; (ed jtly) The Sense of the Sacramental, 1995; (with D. Fuller) Signs of Grace, 1995; (ed jtly) Christ: the Sacramental Word, 1996; Tradition and Imagination: revelation and change, 1999; Discipleship and Imagination: Christian tradition and truth, 2000; God and Enchantment of Place, 2004; Through the Eyes of the Saints, 2005; God and Grace of Body, 2007; God and Mystery in Words, 2008; La tradition kénotique dans la théologie britannique, 2010; Divine Humanity: Kenosis explored and defended, 2011; (contrib.) Theology, Aesthetics, & Culture: responses to the work of David Brown, 2012; (ed) Durham Cathedral: history, fabric and culture, 2015; God in a Single Vision: integrating philosophy and theology, 2016; Divine Generosity and Human Creativity, 2017; (with G. Hopps) The Extravagance of Music, 2018; relevant publication: Christian Theology and the Transformation of Natural Religion: essays in honour of David Brown, ed C. R. Brewer, 2018. Recreations: dog and cat, art, listening to music. Address: Mansfield, 1A Grey Street, Tayport, Fife DD6 9JF. T: (01382) 550063.

**BROWN, Hon. Dean Craig**, AO 2008; company director, since 2006; Chairman, Hillgrove Resources Ltd, 2006–17; b Adelaide, 5 Aug. 1943; m 1979, Rosslyn Judith Wadey; one s one d. Educ: Unley High Sch.; Univ. of New England, NSW (BRurSc, MRurSc); Australian Admin. Staff Coll.; S Australian Inst. of Technol. (Fellowship Dip. in Business Admin). Parliament of South Australia: MP (L) Davenport, 1973–85; Shadow Minister for Industrial Affairs, 1975–79; Minister for Industrial Affairs and for Public Works, 1979–82; Shadow Minister, 1982–85, for: Public Works; Transport; Technology; agricl consultant, 1986–92; MP (L) Alexandra, 1992–93, Finniss, 1993–2006; Leader of Opposition, 1992–93; Shadow Minister for Multicultural and Ethnic Affairs, 1992–93; Premier of SA, and Minister for Multicultural and Ethnic Affairs, 1993–96; Minister: for IT, 1995–96; for Industrial Affairs, Aboriginal Affairs, and Inf. and Contract Services, 1996–97; for Human Services, 1997–2002; Dep. Premier of SA, 2001–02; Dep. Leader of the Opposition, 2002–05. Dir, Scantech Ltd, 2007–17; Chm., InterMet Resources Ltd, 2008–13. Community Liaison Manager for River Murray, SA Govt, 2006–11; Premier's Special Advr on Drought, SA, 2007–11. Chm., Strategic Mgt Cttee, Low Carbon Living CRC Node, UniSA, 2016–. A Dir of state and federal govt bds, company bds and community bds; Director: Foodbank SA, 2007–; Mission Australia Bd, 2012–18. Chm., Playford Meml Trust, SA Govt, 2011–; Chm., SkillsIQ, 2016–. Participant, Duke of Edinburgh Commonwealth Industrial Study Conf., 1980. Patron: Charles Sturt Mus. Trust, 2007–; S Adelaide FC, 2010–; Mates in Construction, SA, 2017–. Hon. DSc New England. Centenary Medal (Australia), 2001; Dist. Alumni Award, Univ. of New England, 1999; Australian Rotary Health Medal, 2014; Alumni Award, Univ. of SA, 2016. Publications: contribs to political, technical and scientific jls. Recreations: walking, fishing, gardening. Address: 11 Leonard Terrace, Torrens Park, SA 5062, Australia.

**BROWN, Douglas Allan**; Sheriff of South Strathclyde, Dumfries and Galloway at Hamilton, since 2008; b 18 June 1951; s of Thomas T. Brown and Thelma R. Cheney or Brown; m 1978, Elaine Ann Currie; one s one d. Educ: Glasgow Univ. (LLB Hons). Procurator Fiscal Depute, Dumbarton and Glasgow, 1977–87; Sen. Procurator Fiscal Depute, Edinburgh, 1987–91; Asst Solicitor, Crown Office, 1991–94; Procurator Fiscal, Ayr, 1994–96; Sen. Asst Procurator Fiscal, Glasgow, 1996–99; Regl Procurator Fiscal, S Strathclyde, Dumfries and Galloway, 1999–2002; Area Procurator Fiscal, Lothian and Borders, 2002–04; all-Scotland floating Sheriff, 2004–08. Recreations: music, tennis, swimming, gardening. Address: Hamilton Sheriff Court, Beckford Street, Hamilton ML3 0BT. T: (01698) 282957, Fax: (01698) 284403. E: sheriffdbrown@scotcourts.gov.uk.

**BROWN, Edmund Gerald, Jr, (Jerry Brown)**; lawyer, writer and politician; Governor of California, 2011–19; b 7 April 1938; s of late Edmund Gerald Brown and of Bernice (née Layne); m 2005, Anne Gust. Educ: Univ. of California at Berkeley (BA 1961); Yale Law School (JD 1964). Admitted to California Bar, 1965; Research Attorney, Calif. Supreme Court, 1964–65; with Tuttle & Taylor, LA, 1966–69; Sec. of State, Calif, 1970–74; Gov. of California, 1975–83; Attorney with Fulbright Jaworski, 1986–91. Democratic Candidate for US Senator from California, 1982; Chm., California Democratic Party, 1989–91; Candidate for Democratic Presidential Nomination, 1992; Mayor of Oakland, Calif, 1999–2006; Attorney Gen. of Calif, 2006–11. Founder and Chm., We the People Legal Foundn, 1992. Trustee, Los Angeles Community Colls, 1969–70.

**BROWN, Edmund Walter F.**; see Fitton-Brown.

**BROWN, Edward Francis Trevenen**; QC 2008; Senior Treasury Counsel, Central Criminal Court, 2007–14; a Recorder, since 2000; b 17 Jan. 1958; s of late Francis Brown, CMG and Ruth Brown; m 1989, Victoria Bell; one s two d. Educ: Eton Coll.; University Coll. at Buckingham (LLB). Caelt Gall., London, 1978–80; Pres., Weighouse Gall., LA, 1979–80. Called to the Bar, Gray's Inn, 1983, Bencher, 2016; Jun. Treasury Counsel, 2001–06. Mem., UN Detention Commn, Kosovo, 2001. Recreations: paintings, architecture. Address: QEB Hollis Whiteman, 1–2 Laurence Pountney Hill, EC4R 0EU. T: (020) 7933 8855, Fax: (020) 7929 3732. E: edward.brown@qebholliswhiteman.co.uk.

**BROWN, Prof. Edwin Thomas**, AC 2001; PhD, DSc Eng; FTSE; FIMMM; Senior Consultant, Golder Associates Pty Ltd, 2001–18; Director, Port of Brisbane Corporation, 2005–11; Senior Deputy Vice-Chancellor, University of Queensland, Australia, 1996–2001 (Deputy Vice-Chancellor, 1990–96; Dean of Engineering, 1987–90); b 4 Dec. 1938; s of George O. and Bessie M. Brown. Educ: Castlemaine High Sch.; Univ. of Melbourne (BE 1960, MEngSc 1964); Univ. of Queensland (PhD 1969); Univ. of London (DSc Eng 1985). MICE 1976; MASCE 1965; FIMMM (FIMM 1980); MIEAust 1965, FIEAust 1987, Hon. FIEAust 2014; FTSE (FTS 1990). Engr, State Electricity Commn of Victoria, 1960–64; James Cook Univ. of North Queensland (formerly UC of Townsville): Lectr, 1965–69; Sen. Lectr, 1969–72; Associate Prof. of Civil Engrg, 1972–75; Imperial College, Univ. of London: Reader in Rock Mechanics, 1975–79; Prof. of Rock Mechanics, 1979–87; Dean, RSM, 1983–86; Hd, Dept of Mineral Resources Engrg, 1985–87. Res. Associate, Dept of Civil and Mineral Engrg, Univ. of Minnesota, 1970; Sen. Visitor, Dept of Engrg, Univ. of Cambridge, 1974; Vis. Prof., Dept of Mining and Fuels Engrg, Univ. of Utah, 1979. Dir, Queensland Rail, 2001–05. Editor-in-Chief, Internat. Jl of Rock Mechanics and Mining Sciences, 1975–82. Chm., British Geotechnical Soc., 1982–83; Pres., Internat. Soc. for Rock Mechanics, 1983–87; Mem. Council, AATSE, 1997–98 and 2002–03. Foreign Mem., Royal Acad. (formerly Fellowship) of Engrg, 1989. Institution of Mining and Metallurgy: Consolidated Gold Fields Gold Medal, 1984; Sir Julius Wernher Meml Lecture, 1985; John Jaeger Meml Award, Aust. Geomechanics Soc., 2004; Müller Award, Internat. Soc. for Rock Mechanics, 2007; Rock Mechanics Award, Soc. for Exploration, Mining and Metallurgy, 2010; Douglas Hay Medal, IMMM, 2013. Publications: (with E. Hoek) Underground Excavations in Rock, 1980; (ed) Rock Characterization, Testing and Monitoring, 1981; (with B. H. G. Brady) Rock Mechanics for Underground Mining, 1985, 3rd edn 2004; (ed) Analytical and Computational Methods in Engineering Rock Mechanics, 1987; Block Caving Geomechanics, 2003, 2nd edn 2007; papers on rock mechanics in civil engrg and mining jls. Recreations: cricket, jazz. Address: 5121 Bridgewater Crest, 55 Baildon Street, Kangaroo Point, Qld 4169, Australia. Club: Queensland (Brisbane).

**BROWN, Elizabeth, (Mrs Ray Brown);** see Vaughan, E.

**BROWN, Sir Ewan,** Kt 2014; CBE 1996; FRSE; Chairman, IMPACT Scotland, since 2016; *b* Perth, 23 March 1942; *s* of John Moir Brown and Isobel Brown; *m* 1966, Christine Lindsay; one *s* one *d. Educ:* Perth Acad.; Univ. of St Andrews (MA 1963; LLB 1964). CA 1967. Exec. Dir, Noble Grossart, 1971–2003. Non-executive Director: Pict Petroleum, 1973–95; Scottish Business Sch., 1974–80; Scottish Transport Gp, 1983–88; Scottish Develt Finance, 1983–93; Wood Gp, 1983–2006; Stagecoach Gp, 1988–; Scottish Widows Bank, 1994–97; Dunedin Income Growth Investment Trust, 1995–96 (Chm., 1996–2001); Lloyds TSB Gp, 1999–2009; Harrison Lovegrove, 2002–08; Noble Grossart Hldgs, 2003–18; Entrepreneurial Scotland, 2014–18; Chairman: Scottish Knowledge, 1996–2001; Lloyds TSB Scotland, 1998–2008; Transport Initiatives Edinburgh, 2002–06; Creative Scotland 2009, 2008–10; James Walker (Leith) Ltd, 2012–; Scottish Financial Enterprise, 2012–16. Hon. Prof. of Finance, Heriot-Watt Univ., 1988–2010. Dep. Chm., Edinburgh Internat. Fest., 2006–14. Chm., Court, Heriot-Watt Univ., 1996–2002; Sen. Gov., Court, St Andrews Univ., 2006–16; Governor: Edinburgh Coll. of Art, 1986–89; George Watson's Coll., 1990–91. Treas., RSE, 2008–12. Member: Council, ICAS, 1988–91; Council, Assembly of C of S, 2003–06. Master, Merchant Co. of City of Edinburgh, 1994–95; Lord Dean of Guild, 1995–97. Trustee, Carnegie Trust for Univs of Scotland, 1996–2006. FRSE 2001; FCIBS 2008. Hon. FRZSScot, 2013. DUniv Heriot-Watt, 2003; Hon. LLD St Andrews, 2016. *Recreations:* golf, the arts, grandchildren, mah jongg. *T:* 07710 390361. *E:* eb80@st-andrews.ac.uk. *Clubs:* New (Edinburgh); Royal and Ancient (St Andrews).

**BROWN, Hon. Dr Ewart Frederick;** JP; MP (PLP), Bermuda, 1993–2010; Premier and Minister of Tourism and Transport, Bermuda, 2006–10; Leader, Progressive Labour Party, 2006–10; *b* 17 May 1946; *s* of Ewart D. A. Brown and Helene A. Brown; *m* 2003, Wanda Henton; four *s* from previous marr. *Educ:* Howard Univ. (BSc, MD); Univ. of Calif, Los Angeles (MPH). Med. Dir, Vermont-Century Med. Clinic, Calif, 1974–93; Med. Dir, 1993–2006, Pres. and Chm. Bd, 1993–, Bermuda Healthcare Services. Minister of Transport, 1998–2004, of Tourism and Transport, 2004–06; Dep. Premier, 2003–06. *Recreation:* golf.

**BROWN, Frank Henry,** OBE 1975; HM Diplomatic Service, retired; *b* 6 Sept. 1923; *s* of late Thomas Henry Brown and Ada Katherine Brown (*née* Clifton); *m* 1943, Sheila Desiree (*d* 1997), *d* of late Rev. Canon John Rees and Elsie Rees; one *s* three *d. Educ:* LCC Bonneville Road, Clapham; Bec Sch., Tooting Bec. C. & E. Morton Ltd, 1940; Colonial Office, 1940–42; RN, 1942–46; Colonial Office, subseq. Commonwealth Office, then Foreign and Commonwealth Office, 1946–83: St Helena, 1948–50; Gold Coast/Ghana, 1954–57; Financial Sec., New Hebrides, 1971–75; Dep. High Comr, Guyana, 1978–80; Asst Head, Nationality and Treaty Dept, FCO, 1980–83. *Recreations:* Christian service, family solidarity, happy great-great-grandfather, appreciating creation. *Address:* Woodcote Grove House, Woodcote Park, Meadow Hill, Coulsdon, Surrey CR5 2XL. *T:* (020) 8660 0939. *Club:* Civil Service.

**BROWN, Gavin Lindberg;** Managing Director, Speak With Impact Ltd, since 2002; *b* 4 June 1975; *s* of William and Jacqueline Brown; *m* 2006, Hilary Fergus; two *s* one *d. Educ:* Boundary Jun. Sch., Hong Kong; Fettes Coll.; Univ. of Strathclyde (LLB Hons 1997; DipLP 1998). Trainee solicitor, 1998–2000, solicitor, 2000–02, McGrigor Donald. MSP (C) Lothians, 2007–11, Lothian, 2011–16. Shadow spokesman for enterprise, energy and tourism, 2007–11, for finance, 2011–16, Scottish Parlt. *Recreation:* tae kwon-do (black belt). *E:* gavin@speakwithimpact.com.

**BROWN, Geoffrey Howard;** journalist, The Times; film historian; *b* 1 March 1949; *s* of John Howard Brown and Nancy (*née* Fardoe); *m* 1985, Catherine Ann Surowiec. *Educ:* King Henry VIII Grammar Sch., Coventry; Pembroke Coll., Cambridge (BA); Royal Coll. of Art (Sch. of Film and TV, MA). Dep. Film Critic, Financial Times, 1977–81; Film Critic, Radio Times, 1981–89; Dep. Film Critic, 1981–90, Film Critic, 1990–98, Music Critic, 1999–, The Times. *Publications:* Walter Forde, 1977; Launder and Gilliat, 1977; Der Produzent: Michael Balcon und der Englische Film, 1981; (contrib.) Michael Balcon: the pursuit of British cinema, 1984; The Common Touch: the films of John Baxter, 1989; (contrib.) The British Cinema Book, 1997; (contrib.) The Unknown 1930s, 1998; (contrib.) British Cinema of the 90s, 2000; (contrib.) The Cinema of Britain and Ireland, 2005; (Associate Ed.) Directors in British and Irish Cinema: a reference guide, 2006; (ed) Alistair Cooke at the Movies, 2009; (contrib.) Ealing Revisited, 2012; (contrib.) The Translation of Films 1900–1950, 2019. *Recreations:* art exhibits, children's books. *Address:* The Times, 1 London Bridge Street, SE1 9GF. *T:* (020) 7782 5167.

**BROWN, Sir Geoffrey Robert C.;** see Clifton-Brown.

**BROWN, Sir George (Francis) Richmond,** 5th Bt *cr* 1863, of Richmond Hill; *b* 3 Feb. 1938; *o s* of Sir Charles Frederick Richmond Brown, 4th Bt and of Audrey Baring; *S* father, 1995; *m* 1978, Philippa Willcox; three *s. Educ:* Eton. Served Welsh Guards, 1956–70; Extra Equerry to HRH The Duke of Edinburgh, 1961–63; ADC to Governor of Queensland, 1964–66; Adjt, 1st Bn Welsh Guards, 1967–69. *Heir:* s Sam George Richmond Brown, *b* 27 Dec. 1979. *Address:* Mas de Sudre, 81600 Gaillac, France. *T:* 563410132. *Clubs:* Pratt's, Cavalry and Guards.

**BROWN, Prof. George William,** OBE 1995; FBA 1986; Honorary Senior Research Fellow (formerly Honorary Professor), Institute of Psychiatry, King's College London, since 2000; *b* 15 Nov. 1930; *s* of late William G. Brown and Lily Jane (*née* Hillier); *m* 1st, 1954, Gillian M. Hole (marr. diss. 1970); one *s* one *d*; 2nd, 1978, Seija T. Sandberg (marr. diss. 1987); one *d*; 3rd, 1990, Elizabeth A. Davies; one *s* one *d. Educ:* Kilburn Grammar Sch.; University Coll. London (BA Anthropol. 1954); LSE (PhD 1961). Scientific Staff, DSIR, 1955–56; MRC Social Psychiatry Res. Unit, Inst. of Psychiatry, 1956–67; joined Social Res. Unit, Bedford Coll., London Univ., 1967; Prof. of Sociology, London Univ. and Jt Dir, Social Res. Unit, Bedford Coll., 1973–80; Mem., Ext. Scientific Staff, MRC, 1980–2000; Hon. Prof. of Sociol., RHBNC, London Univ., 1980–2000, now Emeritus Prof. Mem., Inst. Medicine, 2005. Mem., Academia Europaea, 1990. Founder FMedSci 1998. Hon. FRCPsych, 1987. *Publications:* (jtly) Schizophrenia and Social Care, 1966; (with J. K. Wing) Institutionalism and Schizophrenia, 1970; (with T. O. Harris) Social Origins of Depression, 1978; Life Events and Illness, 1989; numerous contribs to jls. *Address:* 1 Redberry Grove, SE26 4DA. *T:* (020) 8699 0120.

**BROWN, Prof. Gillian,** CBE 1992; Professor of English as an International Language, University of Cambridge, 1988–2004, now Emeritus; Fellow of Clare College, Cambridge, 1988–2007, now Emeritus; *b* 23 Jan. 1937; *d* of Geoffrey Rencher Read and Elsie Olive Chapman; *m* 1959, Edward Keith Brown; three *d. Educ:* Perse Sch. for Girls; Girton Coll., Cambridge (MA); Univ. of Edinburgh (PhD 1971); LittD Cantab 1997. Lectr, University Coll. of Cape Coast, Ghana, 1962–64; Lectr, 1965–81, Reader, 1981–83, Univ. of Edinburgh; Prof., Univ. of Essex, 1983–88 (Dean of Social Scis 1985–88); Dir, Res. Centre for English and Applied Linguistics, Univ. of Cambridge, 1988–2004. Mem., ESRC Educn and Human Develt Cttee, 1983–87; Chm., Research Grants Board, ESRC, 1987–90; Member: Kingman Cttee, 1987–88; UGC, subseq. UFC, 1988–91; Council, Philological Soc., 1988–93; British Council English Teaching Adv. Cttee, 1989–94; Cttee of Mgt, British Inst. in Paris, 1990–2004. Curator, Sch. of Advanced Studies, Univ. of London, 1994–2005. Gov., Bell Educnl Trust, 1987–92. Dr *hc* Univ. of Lyon, 1987. *Publications:* Phonological Rules and Dialect Variation, 1972; Listening to Spoken English, 1977; (with George Yule) Discourse Analysis, 1983; Speakers, Listeners and Communication, 1995; articles in learned jls. *Address:* Clare College, Cambridge CB2 1TL.

**BROWN, Prof. Godfrey Norman;** Director, Institute of Education and Professor of Education, University of Keele, 1967–80, now Emeritus; Director, Betley Court Gallery, 1980–94; *b* 13 July 1926; *s* of Percy Charles and Margaret Elizabeth Brown; *m* 1960, Dr Freda Bowyer (*d* 2015); three *s. Educ:* Whitgift Sch.; School of Oriental and African Studies, London; Merton Coll., Oxford (MA, DPhil). Army service, RAC and Intelligence Corps, 1944–48. Social Affairs Officer, UN Headquarters, NY, 1953–54; Sen. History Master, Barking Abbey Sch., Essex, 1954–57; Lectr in Educn, University Coll. of Ghana, 1958–61; Sen. Lectr, 1961, Prof., 1963, Univ. of Ibadan, Nigeria. Visiting Prof., Univ. of Rhodesia and Nyasaland, 1963; Chm., Assoc. for Recurrent Educn, 1976–77; Mem., Exec. Cttee and Bd of Dirs, World Council for Curriculum and Instruction, 1974–77. OECD Consultant on teacher education, Portugal, 1980. Vice-Pres., Community Council of Staffs, 1984–. Collector of the Year Award, Art and Antiques, 1981; Newcastle-under-Lyme Civic Award for Conservation, 1990. *Publications:* An Active History of Ghana, 2 vols, 1961 and 1964; Living History, 1967; Apartheid, a Teacher's Guide, 1981; Betley Through the Centuries, 1985; This Old House: a domestic biography, 1987; Betley's Cultural Heritage, 2002; edited: (with J. C. Anene) Africa in the Nineteenth and Twentieth Centuries, 1966; Towards a Learning Community, 1971; (with M. Hiskett) Conflict and Harmony in Education in Tropical Africa, 1975; Eccentric Harmony, 2003; contrib. educnl and cultural jls. *Recreations:* family life, art history, conservation, writing. *Address:* Betley Court, Betley, near Crewe, Cheshire CW3 9BH. *T:* (01270) 820652.

**BROWN, Rt Hon. Gordon;** see Brown, Rt Hon. J. G.

**BROWN, Hannah Beatrice, (Mrs M. J. Sullivan);** QC 2017; *b* Marlow, 19 Nov. 1968; *d* of Robert Brown and Jane Brown; *m* Michael Jerome Sullivan, QC; one *s*, and three step *s. Educ:* Queens' Coll., Cambridge (BA 1st Cl. Law 1991). Called to the Bar, Inner Temple, 1992; barrister practising in commercial law, One Essex Court.

**BROWN, (Harold) Vivian (Bigley),** CB 2004; Business Adviser, Traidlinks, Uganda, 2013; *b* 20 Aug. 1945; *s* of late Alec Sidney Brown and Joyce Brown (*née* Bigley); *m* 1970, Jean Josephine Bowyer, yr *d* of Sir Eric Bowyer, KCB, KBE and Lady Bowyer; two *s. Educ:* Leeds Grammar Sch.; St John's Coll., Oxford (BA); St Cross Coll., Oxford (BPhil Islamic Philosophy). Min. of Technology, 1970; DTI, 1972–74 (Private Sec. to Permanent Sec., 1972–73); FCO, 1975–79 (First Sec. Commercial Jeddah); DTI, 1979–86; Hd of Sci. and Technol. Assessment Office, Cabinet Office, 1986–89; Hd of Competition Policy Div., 1989–91; Hd of Investigations Div., 1991–92, of Deregulation Unit, 1992–94, of Small Firms and Business Link, 1994–96, DTI; Dep. Dir Gen. and Dir, Business Link, DTI, 1996–97; Chief Exec., ECGD, 1997–2004; Advr to Minister of Finance, Bahrain, 2004–06; Micro-credit Advr, Lea Toto Prog., Nairobi, 2007–09. *Publications:* (with S. M. Stern and A. Hourani) Islamic Philosophy and the Classical Tradition, 1972. *Recreations:* playing piano, cycling, cooking.

**BROWN, Prof. Harvey Robert,** PhD; FBA 2007; Professor of Philosophy of Physics, University of Oxford, 2006–17; Fellow of Wolfson College, Oxford, 1984–2017, now Emeritus; *b* 4 April 1950; *s* of Harvey C. Brown and M. Katrine Brown; *m* 1980, Maria Rita Kessler; one *s* one *d. Educ:* Univ. of Canterbury, NZ (BSc Hons 1971); Univ. of London (PhD 1978). Asst Prof., Dept of Philos. and Mem., Centro de Lógica, Epistemologia e História da Ciência, São Paulo State Univ. at Campinas, 1978–84; Lectr in Philos. of Physics, 1984–96, Reader in Philos., 1996–2006, Univ. of Oxford. Long-term Visitor, Perimeter Inst. for Theoretical Physics, Waterloo, Ont, 2007–08. Pres., British Soc. for the Philos. of Sci., 2007–09. *Publications:* Albert Einstein. Um simples homem de visão, 1984; Physical Relativity: space-time structure from a dynamical perspective, 2005 (Lakatos Award in the Philosophy of Science (jtly), 2006); numerous contribns to learned jls. *Recreations:* drawing, swimming, motorcycles, cooking, things Brazilian. *Address:* Wolfson College, Linton Road, Oxford OX2 6UD. *E:* harvey.brown@philosophy.ox.ac.uk.

**BROWN, Hazel Christine P.;** see Parker-Brown.

**BROWN, Col Hugh Goundry,** TD 1968; FRCS; Vice Lord-Lieutenant, Tyne & Wear, 1993–2002; *b* 25 Feb. 1927; *s* of Charles Frank Brown and Edith Temple Brown (*née* Smithson); *m* 1961, Ann Mary Crump; one *s* two *d. Educ:* Durham Univ. (MB BS 1949). FRCS 1958. Nat. Service, RMO, 1 (Nyasaland) Bn, KAR, 1950–52. TA 1 (N) Gen. Hosp., 1952–73; OC, 201 (N) Gen. Hosp., 1970–73, Hon. Col, 1982–87. Consultant Plastic Surgeon, Royal Victoria Inf., Newcastle upon Tyne and Sen. Lectr in plastic surgery, Univ. of Newcastle upon Tyne, 1968–92. President: Brit. Soc. for Surgery of the Hand, 1985; Brit. Assoc. Plastic Surgeons, 1988; Brit. Assoc. Clinical Anatomists, 1989. QHS 1972. Tyne & Wear: DL 1986; High Sheriff, 1992. *Publications:* contrib. Brit. Jl Plastic Surgery, Hand, Brit. Jl Anaesthesia. *Recreations:* family, fell-walking. *Address:* 12 Lindisfarne Road, Jesmond, Newcastle upon Tyne NE2 2HE. *T:* (0191) 281 4141. *Club:* Northern Counties (Newcastle).

**BROWN, Prof. Ian James Morris,** PhD, DLitt; playwright; poet; Professor of Drama, Kingston University, 2010–14, now Emeritus; *b* 28 Feb. 1945; *s* of Bruce Beveridge Brown and Eileen Frances Scott Carnegie; *m* 1st, 1968, Judith Ellen Sidaway (marr. diss. 1997); one *s* one *d*; 2nd, 1997, Nicola Dawn Axford. *Educ:* Dollar Academy; Edinburgh Univ. MA Hons, MLitt, DipEd; Crewe and Alsager Coll. (PhD); Glasgow Univ. (DLitt). Playwright, 1969–; poet, 1978–; Schoolmaster, 1967–69, 1970–71; Lectr in Drama, Dunfermline Coll., 1971–76; British Council: Asst Rep., Scotland, 1976–77; Asst Regional Dir, Istanbul, 1977–78; Crewe and Alsager College: Head of Drama, 1978–79; Head of Performance Arts, 1979–82; Programme Leader, BA Hons Drama Studies, 1982–86; Programme Dir, Alsager Arts Centre, 1980–86; Drama Dir, Arts Council of GB, 1986–94; Queen Margaret College, subseq. Queen Margaret University College, Edinburgh: Reader, 1994–95; Prof. of Drama, 1995–2002; Head, Dept of Drama, 1995–99; Dir, Scottish Centre for Cultural Mgt and Policy, 1996–2002; Dean of Arts, 1999–2002; Proprietor, Ian Brown Consultancy, 2002–10. Vis. Prof. (Hon. Sen. Res. Fellow), Dept of Scottish Lit., Univ. of Glasgow, 2007–; Vis. Prof., Centre for the Study of Media and Culture in Small Nations, Univ. of Glamorgan, 2007–13. Vice-Chair, Standing Cttee of Univ. Drama Depts, 2013–16. Chm., Scottish Soc. of Playwrights, 1973–75, 1984–87, 1997–99, 2010–13 (Mem. Council, 1999–2007); convenor, NW Playwrights' Workshop, 1982–85; Member: NW Arts Assoc. Drama panel, 1980–83, General Arts panel, 1983–86; Arts Council of GB Drama panel, 1985–86; British Theatre Institute: Vice-Chm., 1983–85; Chm., 1985–87. Chairman: Dionysia World Fest. of Contemp. Theatre, Chianti, Italy, 1991–94; Highlands and Islands Theatre Network, 2005–09; Drama Na h-Alba, Scotland's Internat. Theatre Fest. and Forum, 2006–09. Cultural consultant, Rose Th., Kingston, 2011–14. Mem. Council, 2010–16, Mem., Exec. Bd, 2011–16, Convener, 2014–16, Saltire Soc.; Assoc. for Scottish Literary Studies, 2010–15 (Convener, Publications Bd, 2012–). Productions: Antigone, 1969; Mother Earth, 1970; The Bacchae, 1972; Positively the Last Final Farewell Performance (ballet), 1972; Rune (choral work), 1973; Carnegie, 1973; The Knife, 1973;

Rabelais, 1973; The Fork, 1976; New Reekie, 1977; Mary, 1977; Runners, 1978; Mary Queen and the Loch Tower, 1979; Pottersville, 1982; Joker in the Pack, 1983; Beatrice, 1989; (jtly) First Strike, 1990; The Scotch Play, 1991; Bacchai, 1991; Wasting Reality, 1992; Margaret, 2000; A Great Reckonin, 2000; An Act o Love, 2011; Translating Lies, 2018; Ane Satyre of the Thrie Estaitis (Edinburgh Fest. workshop), 2018. FRSA 1991; FHEA 2010. Series Editor: The Edinburgh Companions to Scottish Literature, 2007–13; The Internat. Companions to Scottish Lit., 2013–. *Publications:* (ed) An Anthology of Contemporary Scottish Drama (in Croatian), 1999; (ed) Cultural Tourism: the convergence of culture and tourism at the start of the 21st century (in Russian), 2001; Poems for Joan, 2001; (ed) Journey's Beginning: the Gateway Theatre building and company 1884–1965, 2004; (ed) The Edinburgh History of Scottish Literature, 2007; (ed) Changing Identities – Ancient Roots: the history of West Dunbartonshire from earliest times, 2006; (ed) The Edinburgh Companion to Twentieth-Century Scottish Literature, 2009; (ed) From Tartan to Tartanry: Scottish culture, history and myth, 2010; (ed) The Edinburgh Companion to Scottish Drama, 2011; (ed) Literary Tourism, the Trossachs and Walter Scott, 2012; (with A. Riach) Lion's Milk: Turkish poems by Scottish poets, 2012; Scottish Theatre, Diversity, Language, Continuity, 2013; (ed jtly) Roots and Fruits: Scottish identities, history and contemporary literature, 2014; Collyshangles in the Canopy, 2015; History as Theatrical Metaphor: history, myth and national identities in modern Scottish drama, 2016; (ed jtly) Taking Liberties: Scottish literature and expressions of freedom, 2016; articles on drama, theatre and arts policy. *Recreations:* theatre, sport, travel, cooking. *Address:* 34 Dalmeny Avenue, Giffnock, Glasgow G46 7QF.

**BROWN, Jack A.;** Sheriff of Grampian, Highland and Islands at Aberdeen, since 2016; *b* Dundee, 8 June 1959; *s of* Elizabeth Brown; *m* 2014, Nadine Robertson; three *d*. *Educ:* Morgan Acad., Dundee; Univ. of Dundee (LLB, DipLP). NP. Admitted solicitor, 1985; solicitor advocate, 2003; Part-time Sheriff, 2005–16. Vice Pres., Part-Time Sheriffs' Assoc., 2014–16. *Recreations:* golf, reading, art deco pottery and arts. *Address:* Sheriff Court House, Castle Street, Aberdeen AB10 1WP. *T:* (01224) 657241. *E:* sheriffjabrown@scotcourts.gov.uk.

**BROWN, Col James,** CVO 1985; RNZAC (retd); *b* 15 Aug. 1925; *y s of* late John Brown and Eveline Bertha (*née* Cooper), Russells Flat, North Canterbury, NZ; *m* 1952, Patricia Sutton; two *d*. *Educ:* Christchurch Boys' High Sch., NZ; Royal Military Coll., Duntroon, Australia (grad 1947). NZ Regular Army, 1947–71: active service, Korea, 1951–52; Comptroller of Household to Gov.-Gen. of NZ, 1961–62; Reg. Comr of Civil Defence, Dept of Internal Affairs, NZ, 1971–77; Official Sec. to Gov.-Gen. of NZ, 1977–85; Gen. Sec., Duke of Edinburgh's Award Scheme in NZ, 1986–94. Col Comdt, RNZAC, 1982–86; Pres., NZ Army Assoc., 1986–94. *Recreations:* fishing, shooting. *Address:* Apt B8, Huntleigh Apartments, 221 Karori Road, Wellington 6012, New Zealand. *Club:* Wellington (Wellington).

**BROWN, James;** see Brown, Anthony J.

**BROWN, James Anthony, (Tony),** OBE 2013; Chief Minister, Isle of Man, 2006–11; MHK Castletown, 1981–2011 (Speaker, House of Keys, 2001–06); *b* 5 Jan. 1950; *s of* Margaret Brown; *m* 1979, Rachel (*née* Smith); one *s* one *d*. *Educ:* Victoria Road Primary Sch., Castletown; Castle Rushen High Sch., Castletown. Apprentice electrician, 1965–70, electrician, 1970–80, IOM Electricity Bd; self-employed electrician, 1980–81; Proprietor, Tony Brown Electrics, 1981–2010. Mem., Castletown Town Commn, 1976–81 (Chm., 1980–81). Manx Government: Minister: for Health and Social Security, 1986–89; for Local Govt and Envmt, 1989–94; for Tourism and Leisure, 1994–96; for Transport, 1996–2001; Dep. Pres., Tynwald, 2002–06. Pres., Castletown Chamber of Trade and Commerce, 1987–2011; Mem., Castletown Chamber of Commerce, 2014–15. Pres., 1982, Pres. and Chm., 1990–, Castletown and Dist Over 60s Club; Vice-Pres., 1994–2018, Pres., 2018–, Castletown Rifle Club; Pres., Friends of Castletown (Historic) Railway Station, 2014–; Mem., 1990–, Mem. Exec. Cttee, 2014–, Vice Pres., 2015–, Castletown and Dist Br., RBL. Chairman: Castletown Metropolitan Silver Band, 2014–; Castletown Legion Hall Restoration Gp, 2015–; Exec. Cttee, 3rd Castletown Scouts, 2017–. Chm. Trustees, Queen Street Mission Trust, 1993–; Trustee, Castletown Scout and Guide Bldg, 2016–17. Pres., Castletown Fest., 2016–. *Recreations:* photography, history, historic architecture, motorcycle racing, heritage. *Address:* 20 Kissack Road, Castletown, Isle of Man IM9 1NW. *T:* (01624) 824393.

**BROWN, Dr (James) Barry (Conway),** OBE 1978; Subject Assessor, Higher Education Funding Council for England, 1995–97; *b* 3 July 1937; *s of* Frederick Clarence and Alys Brown; *m* 1963, Anne Rosemary Clough (*d* 2007); two *s* one *d*. *Educ:* Cambridge Univ. (BA Nat. Sci 1959; MA 1963); Birmingham Univ. (MSc 1960; PhD 1963). Research Officer, CEGB, Berkeley Nuclear Labs, 1963–67; British Council: Sen. Sci. Officer, Sci. Dept, 1967–69; Sci. Officer, Madrid, 1969–72, Paris, 1972–78; Head, Sci. and Technology Group, 1978–81; Rep. and Cultural Counsellor, Mexico, 1981–85; Dep. Controller (Higher Educn Div.), 1985–89; Dir, EC Liaison Unit (Higher Education), Brussels, 1989–91; Dir, Poland, 1992–94. Treas., St Mary's Church, Purley-on-Thames, 1994–2000. Mem., Pangbourne Choral Soc., 2001–. *Recreations:* music, travel in (and study of) countries of posting, singing, reading. *Address:* 42 Hazel Road, Purley-on-Thames, Reading RG8 8BB. *T:* (0118) 941 7581.

**BROWN, (James) Craig,** CBE 1999; International Team Manager, 1993–2001, and Technical Director, 1993–2002, Scottish Football Association; *b* 1 July 1940; *s of* Hugh and Margaret Brown; *m* 1964 (separated 1981); two *s* one *d*. *Educ:* Scottish Sch. of Physical Educn (DipPE (Distinction)), Strathclyde Univ. BEd (Hons); BA Open Univ. 1976. Teacher of PE, City of Dundee, Teacher, High Blantyre Primary Sch., Dep. Hd Teacher, Belvidere Primary Sch., Hd Teacher, Burnhead Primary Sch., 1962–69; Lectr in Primary Educn, Craigie Coll. of Educn, 1969–86. Professional footballer: Rangers FC, 1958–60; Dundee FC, 1960–65; Falkirk FC, 1965–67; Asst Manager, Motherwell FC, 1974–77; Manager, Clyde FC, 1977–86; Asst Nat. Coach and Asst Technical Dir, Scottish FA, 1986–93; Manager: Preston North End FC, 2002–04; Motherwell, 2009–10; Aberdeen, 2010–13. Football Consultant: Fulham FC, 2006–07; Derby FC, 2007–08. Non-exec. Dir, Aberdeen FC, 2013–. Patron: Scottish Disability Sport, 1999–; Sports Chaplaincy (Scottish Football), 2013–. DUniv Paisley, 1998; Hon. DArts Abertay Dundee, 2000. *Publications:* Craig Brown (autobiog.), 1998, repr. as The Game of My Life, 2001. *Recreations:* golf, reading, travel. *Address:* 36 Queens Crescent, Aberdeen AB15 4BE.

**BROWN, Rt Hon. (James) Gordon;** PC 1996; Special Envoy for the UN Secretary-General for Global Education, since 2012; *b* 20 Feb. 1951; *s of* late Rev. Dr John Brown and J. Elizabeth Brown; *m* 2000, Sarah Jane Macaulay; two *s* (one *d* decd). *Educ:* Kirkcaldy High Sch.; Edinburgh Univ. MA 1972; PhD 1982. Rector, Edinburgh Univ., 1972–75; Temp. Lectr, Edinburgh Univ., 1976; Lectr, Glasgow Coll. of Technology, 1976–80; Journalist and Current Affairs Editor, Scottish TV, 1980–83. Mem., Unite (formerly TGWU). Chm., Labour Party Scottish Council, 1983–84. Contested (Lab) S Edinburgh, 1979. MP (Lab) Dunfermline E, 1983–2005, Kirkcaldy and Cowdenbeath, 2005–15. Opposition Chief Sec. to the Treasury, 1987–89; Opposition Trade and Industry Sec., 1989–92; Opposition Treasury Sec., 1992–97; Chancellor of the Exchequer, 1997–2007; Prime Minister and First Lord of the Treasury, 2007–10. Leader of the Labour Party, 2007–10. Advr, Global Adv. Bd, Pimco, 2015–. Hon. FRSE 2018. DUniv Glasgow, 2015. *Publications:* (ed) The Red Paper on Scotland, 1975; (with H. M. Drucker) The Politics of Nationalism and Devolution, 1980; (ed) Scotland: the real divide, 1983; Maxton, 1986; Where There is Greed, 1989; (with J. Naughtie) John Smith: Life and Soul of the Party, 1994; (with T. Wright) Values, Visions and Voices, 1995; Speeches 1997–2006, 2006; Moving Britain Forward: selected speeches 1997–2006, 2006; Courage: eight portraits, 2007; Britain's Ordinary Heroes, 2007; The Change We Choose: speeches 2007–09, 2010; Beyond the Crash: overcoming the first crisis of globalisation, 2010; My Scotland, Our Britain: a future worth sharing, 2014; My Life, Our Times, 2017. *Recreations:* reading and writing, football and tennis.

**BROWN, Jane;** see Finnis, J.

**BROWN, Janet Marjorie,** PhD; FInstP; FRSE; Chief Executive, Scottish Qualifications Authority, 2007–19; *b* Sheffield, 31 July 1951. *Educ:* High Storrs Grammar Sch. for Girls, Sheffield; Univ. of Birmingham (BSc; PhD 1979). FInstP 2005. Vis. Asst Prof., Univ. of Illinois, Urbana, 1981–84; Mem. Tech. Staff, Bell Laboratories, AT&T, Murray Hill, 1984–90; Dir, Process Architecture and Characterisation, SEMATECH, Austin, 1990–93; Motorola: Dir, Reliability and Quality Assurance, Austin, 1993–97; Eur. Ops Dir, Smartcard Div., E Kilbride, 1997–98; Dir of Ops, Networking Systems Memories, Austin, 1998–2000; Man. Dir, Scottish Enterprise, Glasgow, 2000–07. FRSE 2008. FRSA.

**BROWN, Janice Margaret;** Managing Director and Chief Financial Officer, SOCO International, since 2017; *b* Glasgow, 9 June 1955; *d of* Alex and Phyllis Tinto; *m* 1997, Antony Brown; one *s* one *d*. *Educ:* Trinity Acad., Edinburgh; Edinburgh Univ. (MA Hist. 1978); Heriot Watt Univ. (Dip. Accounting 1987). Senior Tax Manager: KPMG, 1987–97; Deloitte & Touche, 1997–98; Cairn Energy plc: Gp Tax Manager, 1998–99; Gp Financial Controller, 1999–2006; Finance Dir, 2006–11; Man. Dir and Chief Financial Officer, Cairn Energy PLC, 2011–14. Sen. Ind. Dir, Hansen Transmissions Internat., 2008–11; non-executive Director: Cairn India Ltd, 2006–11; Troy Income & Growth Trust, 2013–; Mem. Bd, Edinburgh Printmakers, 2004–06; non-exec. Chm., Audit Cttee, John Wood Gp plc, 2014–. Member: ICAS, 1990 (Mem. Council, 2009–; Dep. Pres., 2013–14; Pres., 2014–15); Chartered Inst. of Taxation, 1991. Chm., Audit Cttee, Scottish Ballet, 2015–. Mem. Exec., Pipeline Steering Gp, 30% Club, 2012–; Trustee, Univ. of Edinburgh Develt Trust, 2011–15. Hon. Dr Edinburgh Napier, 2016. *Recreations:* arts, reading, theatre, literature, walking, travel.

**BROWN, Jayne;** see Brown, M. J.

**BROWN, Jennifer,** FRSE; literary agent; Founder and Owner, Jenny Brown Associates, since 2002; *b* Manchester, 13 May 1958; *d of* William Byers and Pauline Brown; *m* 1992, Alexander Richardson; four *s* (and one *s* decd). *Educ:* George Watson's Coll., Edinburgh; Univ. of Aberdeen (MA Hons 1980). Dir, Edinburgh Internat. Book Fest., 1982–91; Co-ordinator, Readiscovery Campaign, 1994–96; Lit. Dir, Scottish Arts Council, 1996–2002. Mem., Press Complaints Commn, 1993–98. Presenter of book progs, Scottish TV, 1989–94. Mem. Bd, Edinburgh Internat. Book Fest., 2004–. Chair, Bloody Scotland Crime Writing Fest., 2012–. Gov., George Watson's Coll., 2000–05. FRSE 2019. DUniv Open, 2015; Hon. DLitt: Aberdeen, 2017; St Andrews, 2018. *Recreations:* hill walking, theatre, art, family. *Address:* Jenny Brown Associates, 31 Marchmont Road, Edinburgh EH9 1HU. *T:* (0131) 229 5334. *E:* jenny@jennybrownassociates.com.

**BROWN, Jennifer Anne;** Headmistress, City of London School for Girls, since 2019; *b* Finchley, London, 17 Aug. 1969; *d of* Dr Barry Cullen and Margaret Cullen; *m* 1996, Ben Brown; one *s* one *d*. *Educ:* N London Collegiate Sch.; St Anne's Coll., Oxford (MA Hons English Lit. and Lang.). Editl asst, Pergamon Press, 1990–92; English teacher: Cranleigh Sch., 1992–95; Highgate Sch., 1995–2000; English teacher, Second in Dept, then Actg Hd of Dept, S Hampstead High Sch., 2000–08; Hd of English, Channing Sch., 2008–11; Dir, Sen. Sch., St Paul's Girls' Sch., 2011–14; Headmistress, St Albans High Sch. for Girls, 2014–19. Member: Educn Cttee, Adv. Bd, New Coll. of Humanities, 2013–; Professional Develt Cttee, GSA, 2015–; Membership Cttee, HMC, 2016–. Gov., Cranleigh Sch., 2016–. *Recreations:* reading, theatre, writing poetry, ski-ing, wild swimming. *Address:* City of London School for Girls, St Giles Terrace, Barbican, EC2Y 8BB.

**BROWN, Jerry;** see Brown, E. G.

**BROWN, Joe,** CBE 2011 (MBE 1975); freelance guide and climber, and film maker for television and cinema; *b* 26 Sept. 1930; *s of* J. Brown, Longsight, Manchester; *m* 1957, Valerie Gray; two *d*. *Educ:* Stanley Grove, Manchester. Started climbing while working as plumber in Manchester; pioneered new climbs in Wales in early 1950s; gained internat. reputation after climbing West Face of Petit Dru, 1954; climbed Kanchenjunga, 1955; Mustagh Tower, 1956; Mt Communism, USSR, 1962; Trango Tower, 1976; Cotaphxi, 1979; Mt Kenya, 1984; Mt McInley, 1986; other expedns: El Torro, 1970; Bramah 2, 1978; Thalaysagar, 1982; Everest NE Ridge, 1986 and 1988. Climbing Instructor, Whitehall, Derbs, 1961–65; opened climbing equipment shops, Llanberis, 1965, Capel Curig, 1970; Leader of United Newspapers Andean Expedn, 1970; Roraima Expedn, 1973. Hon. Fellow, Manchester Polytechnic, 1970. *Publications:* (autobiog.) The Hard Years, 1967. *Recreations:* mountaineering, ski-ing, fishing. *Address:* Allandale, Llanberis, Gwynedd LL55 4TF. *T:* (01286) 870727. *Clubs:* Alpine (Hon. Mem.), Climbers' (Hon. Mem.); American Alpine (Hon. Mem. 2011).

**BROWN, John,** CBE 1982; FREng; Part-time Dean of Technology, Brunel University, 1988–91; *b* 17 July 1923; *s of* George Brown and Margaret Ditchburn Brown; *m* 1st, 1947, Maureen Dorothy Moore (*d* 1991); one *d*; 2nd, 1992, Dr Helen Crawford Gladstone. *Educ:* Edinburgh University. Radar Research and Development Estabt, 1944–51; Lectr, Imperial Coll., 1951–54; University Coll., London: Lectr, 1954–56; Reader, 1956–64; Prof., 1964–67; seconded to Indian Inst. of Technology as Prof. of Electrical Engrg, 1962–65; Prof. of Elect. Engineering, Imperial Coll. of Science and Technology, 1967–81 (Head of Dept, 1967–79); Tech. Dir, Marconi Electrical Devices Ltd, 1981–83; Dir, Univ. and Schs Liaison, GEC, 1983–88. Mem., SRC, 1977–81 (Chm., Engrg Bd, 1977–81); Chm., Joint ESRC-SERC Cttee, 1988–91; Member: Engrg Group, Nat. Advisory Bd, 1983–84; Engrg Cttee, CNAA, 1985–87; Accreditation Cttee, CNAA, 1987–89. Pres., IEE, 1979–80 (Vice-Pres., 1975–78; Dep. Pres., 1978–79); Pres., IEEIE, 1981–85 (Treasurer, 1989–99). Treas., Church Monuments Soc., 2000–07. Governor: S Bank Polytechnic, 1985–90; Willesden Coll. of Technology, 1985–86. FREng (FEng 1984). Hon. FIET (Hon. FIEIE 1986). Hon. DLitt Nanyang Technol Univ., Singapore, 1996. *Publications:* Microwave Lenses, 1953; (with H. M. Barlow) Radio Surface Waves, 1962; Telecommunications, 1964; (with R. H. Clarke) Diffraction Theory and Antennas, 1980; papers in Proc. IEE, etc. *Recreation:* gardening. *Address:* 28 Dale Side, Gerrards Cross, Bucks SL9 7JE.

**BROWN, (John) Bruce,** FRICS; Chairman, Lambert Smith Hampton, 1988–2008; *b* 15 June 1944; *s of* late Bruce Brown and Margaret Mary (*née* Roberts); *m* 1967, Daphne Jane Walker; one *s* two *d*. *Educ:* Acton Park, Wrexham; Grove Park, Wrexham; Coll. of Estate Management, London Univ. (BSc). FRICS 1977. Surveyor, Samuel Walker & Son, 1967–68; Estates Surveyor, Bracknell Develt Corp., 1968–69; Sen. Develt Surveyor, Town

& City Properties, 1969–71; Sen. Partner, Anthony Brown Stewart, 1971–88. *Recreations:* motor-racing, vintage and veteran cars. *Address:* Radmore Farm, Wappenham, Towcester, Northants NN12 8SX.

**BROWN, Prof. John Campbell,** OBE 2016; PhD; DSc; FRSE; FInstP, FRAS; Regius Professor of Astronomy, University of Glasgow, 1996–2010, now Professor Emeritus and Hon. Senior Research Fellow; Astronomer Royal for Scotland, since 1995; *b* 4 Feb. 1947; *s* of John Brown and Jane Livingston Stewart Brown (*née* Campbell); *m* 1972, Dr Margaret Isobel Logan; one *s* one *d*. *Educ:* Hartfield Primary; Dumbarton Acad.; Glasgow Univ. (BSc 1st Cl. Hons Physics and Astronomy 1968; PhD 1973; DSc 1984). University of Glasgow: Research Asst, 1968–70; Lectr, 1970–78; Sen. Lectr, 1978–80; Reader, 1980–84; Prof. of Astrophysics, 1984–96; Leverhulme Emeritus Fellow, 2012–16. Fellow: Univ. of Tubingen, 1971–72; Univ. of Utrecht, 1973–74; Vis. Fellow, Nat. Center for Atmospheric Res., Colorado, 1977; NASA Associate Prof., Univ. of Md, 1980; Nuffield/NSF Fellow, UCSD and Univ. of Amsterdam, 1984; Brittingham Prof., Univ. of Wisconsin-Madison, 1987; Visiting Fellow, 1999: Univ. of Amsterdam; ETH Zürich; Observatoire de Paris; NASA Goddard SFC; Univ. of Wisconsin-Madison, 2003; Univ. of Alabama-Huntsville; Univ. of Calif, Berkeley, 2006. Hon. Professor: Univ. of Edinburgh, 1996–; Univ. of Aberdeen, 1998–; Guest Res. Fellow, Nat. Center for Atmospheric Res. High Altitude Observatory, Boulder, Colo, 2010, TCD, 2011. Marlar Lectr, Rice Univ., Texas, 2006. Time & Space Project Astronomer, Royal Observatory, Greenwich, 2004–06. Pres., Physics Section, BAAS, 2001. Patron, Scottish Dark Skies Observatory, 2011–14. Trustee, Brisbane Observatory Heritage Trust, 2011–. FRAS 1973 (Vice Pres., 1986–87); FRSE 1984 (Mem. Council, 1997–2000); FInstP 1996; Associate Mem., Brazilian Acad. of Scis, 1988. Kelvin Prize and Medal, Univ. of Glasgow, 1984; Kelvin Medal, Royal Philosophical Soc., Glasgow, 1996; Robinson Lectr and Medal, Armagh Observatory, 1998; Promotion of Physics Award, Inst. of Physics, 2003; Gold Medal, RAS, 2012. *Publications:* (with I. J. D. Craig) Inverse Problems in Astronomy, 1986; (ed with J. T. Schmeltz) The Sun: a laboratory for astrophysics, 1992; (with R. Wilson) Oor Big Braw Cosmos, 2019; around 300 papers in Astrophysical Jl, Astronomy and Astrophysics, Solar Physic, Nature, etc. *Recreations:* oil-painting, lapidary and silvercraft, woodwork, photography, conjuring, reading, cycling, hiking, alto saxophone. *Address:* School of Physics and Astronomy, University of Glasgow, Glasgow G12 8QQ. *T:* (0141) 330 5182; 21 Bradfield Avenue, Glasgow G12 0QH. *T:* (0141) 581 6789, 07976 270904.

**BROWN, John Domenic Weare;** Chairman: John Brown Enterprises; John Brown Publishing Ltd, 1987–2004 (Managing Director, 1987–99); John Brown Citrus Publishing, 2002–04; Bob Books Ltd, since 2006; Co-proprietor, The Watch House, St Mawes, since 2010; *b* 29 May 1953; *s* of Sir John Gilbert Newton Brown, CBE and Virginia (*née* Braddell); *m* 1987, Claudia Zeff; one *s* one *d*. *Educ:* Westminster Sch.; London Coll. of Printing. Managing Director: Eel Pie Publishing, 1982; Virgin Books, 1983–87; Founder, John Brown Publishing Ltd (magazine publisher), 1987. Director: John Wisden and Co., 2003–08; Wisden Gp, 2003–08; The Watch House Ltd, 2011–; non-executive Director: Wanderlust Ltd, 2003–13; Oldie Pubns, 2003–; Aurenis, 2007–14; Pippa Small Jewellery, 2011– (Chm., 2013–); Punk Publishing, 2010–; Songlines Magazine, 2013–15; Eaglemoss, 2015–; Capitalize, 2015–; non-executive Chairman: Wild Frontiers, 2008–; Camara UK, 2010–. Chm., Portobello Centre, 2006–08 (Dir, 1997–2009). Gov. (formerly non-exec. Dir), Notting Hill Prep. Sch., 2003–11; Gov., Kensington Aldridge Acad., 2016–; Trustee, Sch. of Social Entrepreneurs, 2009–. Marcus Morris Award, PPA, 1997. *Recreations:* music (ukulele, a bit of singing but mainly listening), dogs, cars and boats. *Address:* 241a Portobello Road, W11 1LT. *T:* (020) 7243 7402. *Clubs:* Soho House, MCC.

**BROWN, (John) Michael,** CBE 1986; HM Diplomatic Service, retired; *b* 16 Nov. 1929; *m* 1955, Elizabeth Fitton; one *s* one *d*. *Educ:* Sch. of Oriental and African Studies, London. MECAS, 1953. Served at: Cairo, 1954–55; Doha, 1956–57; FO, 1957–60; Havana, 1960–62; FO, 1962–64; Jedda, 1965–66; Maseru, 1966–67; Bogotá, 1967–69; FCO, 1969–71; Ankara, 1971–73; Counsellor, Tripoli, 1973–75; FCO, 1976–79; Ambassador to Costa Rica and Nicaragua, 1979–82; Consul-Gen., Geneva, 1983–85. *Address:* 26 Silchester Place, Winchester, Hants SO23 7FT.

**BROWN, Dr John Michael,** FRS 1996; Lecturer and Tutor in Chemistry, Chemical Research Laboratory, 1974–2008, Leverhulme Emeritus Fellow, 2008–10, Oxford University; Fellow of Wadham College, Oxford, 1974–2007, now Emeritus; *b* 24 Dec. 1939; *s* of John Caulfield Brown and Winefride Brown; *m* 1963, Una Horner; one *s* one *d*. *Educ:* Manchester Univ. (BSc 1960; PhD 1963). Various postdoctoral appts, 1963–66; Lectr in Chemistry, Warwick Univ., 1966–74. Tilden Lectr, RSC, 1991. Hon. DSc UCD, 2016. Organometallic Prize, RSC, 1993; (jtly) Descartes Prize, EU, 2001; Horst Pracejus Prize, German Chem. Soc., 2005; Robert Robinson Award, RSC, 2013. *Publications:* (jtly) Mechanism in Organic Chemistry, 1971; *c* 310 articles and reviews in UK, US and European jls. *Recreations:* countryside (UK, France and Spain), good writing, grandchildren, Man Utd. *Address:* Chemistry Research Laboratory, Mansfield Road, Oxford OX1 3TA. *T:* (01865) 275642, *Fax:* (01865) 285002. *E:* john.brown@chem.ox.ac.uk.

**BROWN, John Michael;** Chairman and Chief Executive, William Hill Organisation, 1989–2004; *b* 17 Sept. 1942; *s* of John Lawrence Brown and Iris May Brown; *m* 1st, 1964, Jennifer Kathleen Dixon (*d* 1993); one *d*; 2nd, 2002, Christine Shine. *Educ:* Stratford Grammar Sch., London. Joined William Hill Orgn, 1959. Dir, Brent Walker, 1991–98. Non-exec. Dir, Satellite Inf. Services, 1989–2004. Dep. Chm., Bookmakers' Cttee, 2000. *Recreation:* horse racing. *Address:* Milford Court, Milford Road, South Milford, Leeds LS25 5AD. *T:* (01997) 689703, 07803 233722. *E:* johnbrown@milfordcourt.com.

**BROWN, Rev. Prof. Judith Margaret, (Mrs P. J. Diggle),** FR.HistS; Beit Professor of Commonwealth History, University of Oxford, 1990–2011; Fellow of Balliol College, Oxford, 1990–2011, now Emeritus; *b* India, 9 July 1944; *d* of late Rev. Wilfred George Brown and Joan M. Brown; *m* 1984, Peter James Diggle (*d* 2015); one *s*. *Educ:* Sherborne Sch. for Girls; Girton Coll., Cambridge (BA 1965; PhD 1968; MA 1969); MA, DPhil Oxon 1990. Research Fellow, Official Fellow and Dir of Studies in History, Girton Coll., Cambridge, 1968–71; Lectr, Sen. Lectr, Reader Elect in History, Univ. of Manchester, 1971–90. Mem., Scholars' Council, Liby of Congress, 2000–09. Trustee, Charles Wallace (India) Trust, 1996–2008; Chm. Trustees, Friends of Delhi Brotherhood Soc., 1997–99. Governor: Bath Spa Univ. (formerly UC), 1997–2011; SOAS, London Univ., 1999–2006; Sherborne Sch. for Girls, 2003–13. Ordained deacon, 2009, priest, 2010. Interim Chaplain, Brasenose Coll., Oxford, 2017. MAE 2011. Hon. DSocSc Natal, 2001. *Publications:* Gandhi's Rise to Power: Indian politics 1915–1922, 1972; Gandhi and Civil Disobedience: the Mahatma in Indian politics 1928–1934, 1977; Men and Gods in a Changing World, 1980; Modern India: the origins of an Asian democracy, 1984, 2nd edn 1994; Gandhi: prisoner of hope, 1989, 2nd edn 1998 (trans. Italian 1995); (ed with F. Foot) Migration: the Asian experience, 1994; (ed with M. Prozesky) Gandhi and South Africa: principles and politics, 1996; (ed with R. Foot) Hong Kong's Transitions 1842–1997, 1997; Nehru, 1999; (ed with W. R. Louis) The Oxford History of the British Empire, vol. IV: the twentieth century, 1999; (ed with R. E. Frykenberg) Christians, Cultural Interactions and India's Religious Traditions, 2002; Nehru: a political life, 2003; Global South Asians: introducing the modern diaspora, 2006; (ed) The Essential Writings of Mahatma Gandhi, 2008;

Windows into the Past: life histories and the historian of South Africa, 2009; (ed with A. Parel) Cambridge Companion to Gandhi, 2011. *Recreations:* classical music, gardening, walking. *Address:* Balliol College, Oxford OX1 3BJ.
See also P. W. H. Brown.

**BROWN, Julian Francis,** RDI 1998; Owner and Creative Director, StudioBrown; *b* 8 Sept. 1955; *s* of Oliver and Barbara Brown; *m* 1986, Louise Mary Aron; two *s* one *d*. *Educ:* Leicester Poly. (BA Hons Industrial Design 1978); RCA (MDes 1983). Designer: David Carter Associates, 1979–80; Porsche Design, Austria, 1983–86; Partner, Lovegrove & Brown, 1986–90; Owner, StudioBrown, 1990–2011. Guest Professor: Hochschule der Künste, Berlin, 1991–92; Essen-Duisburg Univ., 2003–04. External Examiner in Industrial Design: RCA, 1997–99; Glasgow Sch. of Art, 1998–2003. *Address:* Flat F, Portland Lofts, Wilson Street, Bristol BS2 9HE.

**BROWN, June Marion;** *see* Venters, J. M.

**BROWN, Karen Veronica;** Chair of Trustees, Oxfam Great Britain, 2011–17 (Trustee, Oxfam International, 2011–17); *b* Crawley, Sussex, 13 July 1952; *d* of John David Jennings and Katharine Veronica Mary Jennings (*née* Pollok); *m* 1st, 1978, Mark Brown (marr. diss. 1998); 2nd, 1999, John Harrison Blake. *Educ:* Bristol Univ. (LLB Hons 1974); Camberwell Coll. of Arts (BA Hons Fine Art, Drawing, 2011). CEDR Mediation 2001. Asst Ed., WIB Publications, 1975–79; Researcher, then producer, Granada TV, 1979–87; Channel 4 Television: Dep. Commng Ed., News and Current Affairs, 1987–91; Commng Ed., Educn, 1992–96; Controller, Factual Progs, 1996–97; Dep. Dir of Progs, 1997–2001; Dir, Television Corp. plc, 2002–06; Learning Champion, Royal Botanical Gdns, Kew, 2006–07. Associate, Prime Minister's Delivery Unit, 2002–09. Chair, Mines Adv. Gp, 2017–. Chair, ActionAid UK, 2004–09; Vice-Chair, ActionAid Internat., 2009–10; Chair of Trustees: Booktrust, 2014–18; MAG Internat. Gov., Ravensbourne Coll., 2014–. *Recreations:* theatre, reading, art, walking, canoeing. *E:* kvbrown@blueyonder.co.uk.

**BROWN, Keith James;** Member (SNP) Clackmannanshire and Dunblane, Scottish Parliament, since 2011 (Ochil, 2007–11); *b* 20 Dec. 1961; *s* of Atholl Brown and Carole Brown; *m* 1990, Tammy Joyce (separated 2006); two *s* one *d*. *Educ:* Univ. of Dundee (MA Hons 1988); Univ. of Prince Edward Is. (MA Hons). Royal Marines, 1980–83. Clerk, Edinburgh DC, 1988–90; Admin. Officer, 1990–96, Civic Officer, 1996–2007, Stirling DC, then Stirling Council. Scottish Parliament: Minister for Skills and Lifelong Learning, 2009–10, for Transport and Infrastructure, 2010–11, for Housing and Transport, 2011–12, for Transport and Veteran Affairs, 2012–14; Cabinet Sec. for Infrastructure, Investment and Cities, 2014–16, for the Economy, Jobs and Fair Work, 2016–18. Mem. (SNP), Clackmannanshire Council, 1996–2007. Mem., European Cttee of the Regions, 1999–2006, 2008–. *Recreations:* smoking Cuban cigars, Hibernian FC. *Address:* c/o Scottish Parliament, Edinburgh EH99 1SP. *T:* (constituency office) (01259) 219333. *E:* Keith.Brown.msp@parliament.scot.

**BROWN, (Laurence Frederick) Mark; His Honour Judge Mark Brown;** a Circuit Judge, since 2000; a Senior Circuit Judge and Resident Judge, Lancashire Crown Courts, since 2015; Honorary Recorder of Preston, since 2016; *b* 16 March 1953; *s* of late Rt Rev. Ronald Brown and Joyce Brown; *m* 1978, Jane Margaret Boardman; one *s*. *Educ:* Bolton Sch.; St John's Coll., Univ. of Durham (BA Jt Hons Law/Econs; Adam Smith Prize in Econs). Called to the Bar, Inner Temple, 1975, Bencher, 2009; practised, Northern Circuit, 1976–2000; Asst Recorder, 1993–97, a Recorder, 1997–2000; Asst Boundary Comr, England and Wales, 2000. Ethnic Minority Liaison Judge, Liverpool, 2002–05; Magistrates' Liaison Judge: Knowsley Bench, 2002–11; Wirral Bench, 2012–15. Pt-time tutor in Law, Univ. of Liverpool, 1977–82; Lectr and Tutor Judge, Judicial Coll., 2008–16. Criminal Justice Strategy Cttee, Merseyside Area, 1997–2000; Parole Bd, 2003–10; Panel for Judicial Appts, 2004–08. *Recreations:* golf, walking. *Address:* Preston Crown Court, Openshaw Place, Ring Way, Preston, Lancs PR1 2LL. *Club:* Royal Liverpool Golf.

**BROWN, Prof. Lawrence Michael,** ScD; FRS 1982; Professor of Physics, University of Cambridge, 1990–2001, now Emeritus; Founding Fellow, Robinson College, Cambridge, since 1977; *b* 18 March 1936; *s* of Bertson Waterworth Brown and Edith Waghorne; *m* 1965, Susan Drucker; one *s* two *d*. *Educ:* Univ. of Toronto (BASc); Univ. of Birmingham (PhD); ScD Cantab 1992. Athlone Fellow, Univ. of Birmingham, 1957; W. M. Tapp Research Fellow, Gonville and Caius Coll., Cambridge, 1963; University Demonstrator, Cavendish Laboratory, 1965; Lectr, 1970–83, Reader, 1983–90, Cambridge Univ.; Lectr, Robinson Coll., Cambridge, 1977–90. *Publications:* many papers on dislocation plasticity and on structure and properties of materials and electron microscopy in Acta Metallurgica and Philosophical Magazine. *Address:* 74 Alpha Road, Cambridge CB4 3DG. *T:* (01223) 337336; SMF Group, Cavendish Laboratory, J. J. Thompson Avenue, Cambridge CB3 0HE. *T:* (01223) 337200.

**BROWN, Canon Dr Lydia Akrigg, (Mrs Stephen Robbins),** MBE 2011; FRCVS; FRSB; Chairman, Alphavet International Ltd, 2015–17; *b* 28 June 1954; *d* of late Tom Brown and of Barbara Brown (*née* Blackmore); *m* 1st, 1988, John Heckford Seamer (*d* 2007); 2nd, 2011, Ven. Stephen Robbins, *qv*. *Educ:* Childwall Valley High Sch. for Girls, Liverpool; Univ. of Liverpool (BVSc 1978); Univ. of Stirling (PhD 1983); BA Open 1992; Univ. of Warwick (MBA 2002). MRCVS 1978, FRCVS 1987; CBiol, FRSB (FIBiol 2002). Wellcome Trust res. schol., 1978–81; Technical Manager: Ewos Aquaculture, 1982–83; Willows Francis, 1984–85; Asst Prof., Coll. of Veterinary Medicine, Mississippi State Univ., 1985–87; Man. Dir, Biological Labs (UK) Ltd, 1987–89; Eur. Tech. Manager, then UK Country Manager, Abbott Labs, 1989–2000; Man. Dir, 2000–10, Exec. Dir, 2011, PHARMAQ Ltd (formerly Alpharma Animal Health Ltd). Sen. Ind. Dir, 2008–16, Vice Chm., 2010–16, Salisbury NHS Foundn Trust. Dir, Strameno Ltd, 2018–. Hon. Lectr, Univs of Liverpool and London. Mem., Medicines Commn, 2000–05. RCVS specialist in fish health and prodn, 1989–94, 2007–. Royal College of Veterinary Surgeons: Mem. Council, 1991–2007; Chm., various cttees; Pres., 1998–99; Mem., Parly and Scientific Cttee, 1998–2003, Ind. Mem., Planning and Resources Cttee, 2010–; Chm., RCVS Trust, 1998–2004; Pres. Veterinary Benevolent Fund, 2006–14; RCVS rep., Fedn of Veterinarians in Europe, 1998–2000. Mem. Council, Univ. Fedn of Animal Welfare, 2005–14 (Dep. Chm., 2010–12; Chm., 2012–14). Founder Trustee, Veterinary Surgeons Health Support Prog., 1999–2014; Trustee, Humane Slaughter Assoc., 2005–14 (Dep. Chm., 2010–12; Chm., 2012–14; Hon. Pres., 2015–). Mem., Steering Cttee, Vet Helpline, 1993–98, 2008–14. Pres., Southern Counties Veterinary Assoc., 1994–95; Hon. Pres., UFAW, 2015–. MInstD 2001. Gov., Salisbury Cathedral Sch., 2005–. Lay Canon, 2007–13, Emeritus Lay Canon, 2014, Salisbury Cathedral. Liveryman, Farriers Co., 2014–. Dalrymple Champneys Silver Cup and Medal, British Vet. Assoc., 2014. *Publications:* (ed) Rearing Healthy Fish under Primitive Conditions, 1987; The Aquaculture Market, 1989; (ed) Aquaculture for Veterinarians, 1993; contrib. papers and chapters on surgical techniques, anaesthesia, pharmacology and husbandry related to aquaculture. *Recreations:* travel, photography, walking, good food and fine wine. *Address:* Mill Leat, W Gomeldon, Salisbury, Wilts SP4 6JY. *T:* (01980) 611438. *E:* drlydiabrown@gmail.com. *Clubs:* Farmers, Victory Services.

**BROWN, Lyn Carol;** MP (Lab) West Ham, since 2005; *b* 13 April 1960; *m* 2008, John Cullen. *Educ:* Univ. of London (BA). Residential Social Worker, Ealing, 1984–85, Newham, 1985–87, Waltham Forest, 1988–2005. Mem. (Lab) Newham BC, 1988–2005. Founder and Chm., London Libraries Develt Agency, 2000–06. Contested (Lab) Wanstead and Woodford, 1992. An Asst Govt Whip, 2009–10; an Opposition Whip, 2010–13; Shadow Fire and Communities Minister, 2013–15; Shadow Minister for Policing, 2016–17, for the Treasury, 2018–. *Address:* House of Commons, SW1A 0AA.

**BROWN, Malcolm Archibald Halliday;** President, Geological Society of London, 2016–18; *b* Dartford, Kent, 3 May 1953; *s* of James Dallas and Gladys Virtue Brown; *m* 1983, Frances Collins; two *s* one *d*. *Educ:* Kingston Poly. (BSc Geol.); Imperial Coll. London (MSc Petroleum Geol.). Mudlogger, Gibraltar Co., Tripoli, Libya, 1977–79; Subsurface Surveyor, Eastman Whipstock, Dahran, Saudi Arabia, 1979–81; Geologist, 1982–89, Exploration Manager, 1989–96, British Gas Exploration, London and Houston; BG plc: Exploration Dir, 1996–2000; Gen. Manager, 2000–05; Sen. Vice Pres., Exploration, 2005–13; Exec. Vice Pres., Exploration, 2013–16. Hon. DSc Kingston, 2007. *Recreation:* cycling.

**BROWN, Rev. Dr Malcolm Arthur;** Director of Mission and Public Affairs, Church of England, since 2007; *b* 17 Sept. 1954; *s* of Arthur Leslie and Gwendolen Mary Brown; *m* 1983, Angela Josephine; one *s*, and one step *s*. *Educ:* Eltham Coll.; Oriel Coll., Oxford (BA 1976; MA 1982); Westcott House; Univ. of Manchester (PhD 2000). Ordained deacon, 1979, priest, 1980; Asst Curate, Riverhead with Dunton Green, 1979–83; Team Vicar and Industrial Missioner, Southampton City Centre, 1983–90; Exec. Sec., William Temple Foundn, 1990–2000; Principal, E Anglian Ministerial Trng Course, then Eastern Reg. Ministry Course, 2000–07. Honorary Lecturer: Univ. of Manchester, 1993–2000; Univ. of Wales, Bangor, 2000–06; Anglia Ruskin Univ., 2005–; Sen. Associate, Cambridge Theol Fedn, 2007–. Hon. Distinguished Canon, Manchester Cathedral, 2014–; Hon. Canon, Ely Cathedral, 2014–. FHEA 2007; FRSA 2012. *Publications:* After the Market, 2004; (with P. Ballard) The Church and Economic Life, 2006; Tensions in Christian Ethics, 2010; (ed) Anglican Social Theology, 2014; contrib. numerous essays and articles in academic jls. *Recreations:* driving steam trains, metal bashing, rowing. *Address:* Church House, Great Smith Street, SW1P 3NZ. *T:* (020) 7898 1468. *E:* malcolm.brown@churchofengland.org.

**BROWN, Prof. Malcolm Watson,** PhD; FRS 2004; Professor of Anatomy and Cognitive Neuroscience, University of Bristol, 1998–2010, now Emeritus (Research Director, Faculty of Medicine and Veterinary Sciences, 2003–10); *b* 24 Feb. 1946; *s* of Denis and Vivian Irene Brown; *m* 1974, Geraldine Ruth Hassall; one *s* one *d*. *Educ:* Crewkerne Sch., Som.; St John's Coll., Cambridge (BA 1st Cl. Natural Scis Tripos, Theoretical Physics 1968; MA 1972; PhD 1974). Asst in Res., Dept of Anatomy, Univ. of Cambridge, 1972–74; Res. Fellow, Downing Coll., Cambridge, 1973–74; Department of Anatomy, University of Bristol: Lectr, 1975–91; Sen. Lectr, 1991–94; Reader in Anatomy and Cognitive Neurosci., 1994–98; Dep. Hd, 1996–98; Hd, 1998–2006. Special Res. Fellow, AFRC, 1991–92. Exec. Mem., Mgt Cttee, MRC Centre for Synaptic Plasticity, 1999–2010. Member: Brain Res., subseq. British Neurosci., Assoc., 1970–2017; Eur. Brain and Behaviour Soc., 1984–2011; Anatomical Soc. of GB and Ireland, 2000–10. *Publications:* (contrib.) A Textbook of Head and Neck Anatomy, 1988; contrib. scientific papers and reviews to learned jls. *Recreations:* foreign travel, local church responsibilities. *Address:* University of Bristol, School of Physiology, Pharmacology and Neuroscience, Medical Sciences Building, Bristol BS8 1TD. *T:* (0117) 331 1909, *Fax:* (0117) 331 2288. *E:* M.W.Brown@bris.ac.uk.

**BROWN, (Margaret) Jayne,** OBE 2004; Director, Jayne Brown Strategic Solutions, since 2013; Chair, Sheffield Health and Social Care NHS Foundation Trust, since 2016; *b* Oldham, 2 Jan. 1963; *d* of James Seddon and Margaret Seddon; *m* 1992, Kevin Brown; one *d*. *Educ:* Univ. of Manchester (BA Hons Politics and Mod. Hist. 1984); Univ. of Nottingham (MPH 1997). Senior appts, NHS, 1990–2006; Chief Executive: NHS Doncaster, 2006–08; NHS N Yorks and York, 2008–13. Non-executive Director: St Leger Homes, Doncaster, 2010–14; Christie Hosp., 2014–15. Sen. Associate, Good Governance Inst., 2014–16. *Recreations:* reading, theatre, genealogy, food (eating and cooking).

**BROWN, Prof. Margaret Louise,** OBE 2015; PhD; FAcSS; Professor of Mathematics Education, King's College, London, 1990–2013, now Emeritus; *b* 30 Sept. 1943; *d* of (Frederick) Harold Seed and Louisa Seed (*née* Shearer); *m* 1970, Hugh Palmer Brown; three *s*. *Educ:* Merchant Taylors' Sch. for Girls, Liverpool; Newnham Coll., Cambridge (BA Math. 1965; MA 1968); Inst. of Education, London Univ. (PGCE 1966); Chelsea Coll., Univ. of London (PhD 1981). Math. Teacher, Cavendish Sch., Hemel Hempstead, 1966–69; Lectr in Math. Educn, 1969–83, Sen. Lectr, 1983–86, Chelsea Coll., Univ. of London; Reader in Math. Educn, 1986–90, Head of Sch. of Educn, 1992–96, KCL; FKC 1996. Member: Nat. Curriculum Math. Wkg Gp, 1987–88; Numeracy Task Force, 1997–98; Adv. Cttee on Maths Educn, 2005–08; Educn Cttee, Royal Soc., 2013–16; Chair: Jt Math. Council of UK, 1991–95; Trustees, School Math. Project, 1996–2006; Educn Sub-Panel, RAE 2008, 2004–08; Jt Chair, MathsWorldUK, 2015–; President: Math. Assoc., 1990–91; British Educnl Res. Assoc., 1997–98. FAcSS (AcSS 2000). Hon. EdD Kingston, 2002; Hon. DSc Loughborough, 2010. Lifetime Achievement Award, KCL, 2008, Mathematical Assoc., 2009, British Soc. for Res. in Learning Math., 2015; Kavli Medal, Royal Soc., 2013. *Publications:* (jtly) Statistics and Probability, 1972, 2nd edn 1977; (jtly) Low Attainers in Mathematics 5–16, 1982; (jtly) Children Learning Mathematics, 1984; Graded Assessment in Mathematics, 1992; (jtly) Intuition or Evidence?, 1995; (jtly) Effective Teachers of Numeracy, 1997; (jtly) Primary Mathematics and the Developing Professional, 2004; papers in jls and contribs to books on math. educn. *Recreations:* walking, music. *Address:* (home) 34 Girdwood Road, SW18 5QS. *T:* (020) 8789 4344.

**BROWN, (Marion) Patricia;** Under-Secretary (Economics), Treasury, 1972–85; *b* 2 Feb. 1927; *d* of late Henry Oswald Brown and Elsie Elizabeth (*née* Thompson). *Educ:* Norwich High Sch. for Girls; Newnham Coll., Cambridge. Central Economic Planning Staff, Cabinet Office, 1947; Treasury, 1948–54; United States Embassy, London, 1956–59; Treasury, 1959–85. Mem. Council, Royal Holloway and Bedford New Coll., London Univ., 1985–98 (Hon. Fellow, 1999). *Recreations:* bird watching, walking.

**BROWN, Mark;** *see* Brown, L. F. M.

**BROWN, Mark C.;** *see* Cuthbert-Brown.

**BROWN, Martin;** independent consultant on strategic management of public sector organisations, customs and indirect taxation; Member, panel of fiscal experts, International Monetary Fund, since 2008; *b* 26 Jan. 1949; *s* of late Clarence and Anne Brown; *m* 1971, Frances Leithead; two *s*. *Educ:* Bolton Sch.; New Coll., Oxford (MA). Joined Customs and Excise as Admin. Trainee, 1971; Private Sec. to Minister of State and to Financial Sec., HM Treasury, 1974–76; Principal, HM Customs and Excise, 1976; Customs adviser to Barbados Govt, 1984–86; HM Customs and Excise (later HM Revenue and Customs): Asst Sec., 1987; Comr, 1993–2002; Director: Customs, 1993; Central Ops, 1994–96; VAT Policy, 1996–2000; Customs and Tax Practice, 2001–02; Dir, Eurocustoms, Paris (on secondment), 2002–08. *Recreations:* theatre, walking, gardening, pottering. *E:* martin.brown@live.com.

**BROWN, Martin;** a District Judge (Magistrates' Courts), since 2005; *b* 31 Aug. 1958; *s* of Raymond Brown and Beryl Brown (*née* Yorath); *m* 1983, Anne Elizabeth Pooley; one *d*. *Educ:* Univ. of Wales, Aberystwyth (LLB 1979). Admitted solicitor, 1982; High Court (Criminal) Advocate, 1994–2005; Actg Stipendiary Magistrate, subseq. Dep. Dist Judge, 1999–2004. Mem., Test Bd, Centre for Professional Legal Studies, 1998–2005 (Duty Solicitor accreditation scheme). *Recreations:* hill-walking, running, bird-watching, Christian.

**BROWN, Sir Mervyn,** KCMG 1981 (CMG 1975); OBE 1963; HM Diplomatic Service, retired; *b* 24 Sept. 1923; *m* 1949, Elizabeth Gittings (*d* 2013). *Educ:* Ryhope Gram. Sch., Sunderland; St John's Coll., Oxford. Served in RA, 1942–45. Entered HM Foreign Service, 1949; Third Secretary, Buenos Aires, 1950; Second Secretary, UK Mission to UN, New York, 1953; First Secretary, Foreign Office, 1956; Singapore, 1959; Vientiane, 1960; again in Foreign Office, 1963–67; Ambassador to Madagascar, 1967–70; Inspector, FCO, 1970–72; Head of Communications Operations Dept, FCO, 1973–74; Asst Under-Sec. of State (Dir of Communications), 1974; High Comr in Tanzania, 1975–78, and concurrently Ambassador to Madagascar; Minister and Dep. Perm. Representative to UN, 1978; High Comr in Nigeria, 1979–83, and concurrently Ambassador to Benin. Chairman: Visiting Arts Unit of GB, 1983–89; Council, King's Coll., Madrid, 1995–2003; Vice-Pres., Commonwealth Youth Exchange Council, 1984–87. Pres., Britain-Nigeria Assoc., 2000–03; Chm., Anglo-Malagasy Soc., 1986–2008. Associate Mem., Acad. Malgache. Officier, Ordre National (Madagascar). *Publications:* Madagascar Rediscovered, 1978; A History of Madagascar, 1995; War in Shangri-La, 2001. *Recreations:* music, tennis, history, cooking. *Address:* 195 Queen's Gate, SW7 5EU. *Clubs:* Royal Over-Seas League, Hurlingham, All England Lawn Tennis.

**BROWN, Michael;** *see* Brown, John M.

**BROWN, Prof. Michael Alan,** CBE 2008; DL; PhD; CPhys, CEng; Vice-Chancellor and Chief Executive, Liverpool John Moores University, 2000–11, now Ambassador Fellow; Chairman: Procure Plus Holdings, since 2014; Wirral Community NHS Foundation Trust, since 2017; *b* 19 May 1946; *s* of Reginald Leslie Brown and Barbara Evelyn Brown; *m* 1966, Andrea Kathleen Evans; one *s* one *d*. *Educ:* Bridgend Boys' Tech./Grammar Sch.; Nottingham Univ. (BSc Physics; PhD 1971). Eur Ing 1991; MInstP 1980, FInstP 2003; CPhys 1980; MIEE 1984, FIET (FIEE 2002); CEng 1984. Demonstrator, Nottingham Univ., 1967–71; Royal Soc. Post-doctoral Eur. Fellow, Grenoble, 1971–72; Lectr, then Sen. Lectr, in Physics, Loughborough Univ., 1972–86; Gen. Manager, Loughborough Consultants Ltd, 1986–87; Pro Vice-Chancellor, Leicester Poly., then De Montfort Univ., 1987–2000. Dir, UCAS, 2001–05. Mem., Cttee for S African Trade, DTI, 1995–2001. Eur. Trng Consultant to Intel Corp., 1981–87. Mem. and Dir, De Montfort Expertise Ltd, 1989–2000 (Man. Dir, 1989–96); Mem., Dir and Co. Sec., E Midlands Regl Technol. Network Ltd, 1989–96; Mem. and Dir, E Midlands Regl Mgt Centre Ltd, 1991–92; Man. Dir, Flexible Learning Systems Ltd, 1992–2000; Dir, Higher Educn Subscription Fund Ltd, 1994–2000; Dir, Leicester Promotions Ltd, 1996–2000; Exec. Chm., De Montfort Univ., S Africa, 1998–2000; Member: Internat. Sub-Cttee, 2002–07; Finance Sub-Cttee, 2003–07, UUK; Steering Gp for Jt Masters Progs, European Univs Assoc., 2002–05. Ind. Chm., Forum for a Better Leics, 1995–2000; Vice-Pres., Personal Service Soc., Liverpool, 2000–11; Member: Bd, Liverpool First, 2001–11; Liverpool Capital of Culture Ltd, 2003–07; Mem., Monitoring Cttee, Merseyside Objective One Prog., 2002–09 (Chairman: Strategy Sub-Cttee, 2002–05; Strategy and Monitoring Sub-Cttee, 2005–08; Closure Cttee, 2008–09); Director: Merseyside Partnership Ltd, 2002–10; Liverpool Vision, 2003–08; Liverpool Ventures Ltd, 2004–05; Alder Hey Promotions, 2012–18; OSCO Homes Ltd, 2015–; Re:allies Ltd, 2015–; Hardleeys Ltd, 2015–18; Dir and Trustee, Re:vision North Ltd, 2014–; Chairman: Merseyside and Liverpool Theatres Trust Ltd, 2002–13; Liverpool Science Park, 2003–11; Liverpool Strategic Innovation and Improvement Gp, 2008–09; Liverpool Democracy Commn, 2008–09; Alder Hey Children's Charity, 2012–18. Advr, Thinspace Ltd, 2012–15. Vice-Pres., ESU, Merseyside, 2009–12. Mem. and Trustee, Africa Now, 1997–2002; Trustee, Rights and Humanities, 2009–10. CCMI (FIMgt 1991); FCIM 2000; FInstD 2009. FRSA 1996. Freeman, City of London, 2007; Liveryman, Engineers' Co., 2007–. DL Merseyside, 2005. Mem. Editl Bd, Laboratory Microcomputer, 1988–93. Hon. DLaws Liverpool, 2011. *Publications:* (contrib.) Collaboration between Business and Higher Education, 1990; (contrib.) The Funding of Higher Education, 1993; (contrib.) Preparing Students for Career Employment, 1998; numerous contribs to learned jls and internat. conf. proc. on physics, mktg and higher educn mgt. *Recreations:* cinema, theatre, travel, spending time with my wife. *Address:* Dawstone Croft, Dawstone Road, Heswall, Wirral, Merseyside CH60 0BU. *Clubs:* Institute of Directors; Athenaeum (Liverpool).

**BROWN, Michael Russell;** journalist; *b* 3 July 1951; *s* of Frederick Alfred Brown and Greta Mary Brown, OBE (*née* Russell). *Educ:* Andrew Cairns Secondary Modern Sch., Sussex; Univ. of York (BA (Hons) Economics and Politics). Graduate Management Trainee, Barclays Bank Ltd, 1972–74; Lecturer and Tutor, Swinton Conservative Coll., 1974–75; part-time Asst to Michael Marshall, MP, 1975–76; Law Student, 1976–77, Member of Middle Temple; Personal Asst to Nicholas Winterton, MP, 1976–79. MP (C) Brigg and Scunthorpe, 1979–83, Brigg and Cleethorpes, 1983–97; contested (C) Cleethorpes, 1997. PPS to Hon. Douglas Hogg, Minister of State, DTI, 1989–90, FCO, 1990–92; PPS to Sir Patrick Mayhew, Sec. of State for NI, 1992–93; an Asst Govt Whip, 1993–94. Mem., Energy Select Cttee, 1986–89; Sec., 1981–87, Vice-Chm., 1987–89, Conservative Parly N Ireland Cttee. Political columnist, The Independent, 1998–. *Recreations:* cricket, walking. *Address:* 78 Lupus Street, SW1V 3EL. *T:* (020) 7630 9045. *Club:* Reform.

**BROWN, Prof. Michael Stuart,** MD; Regental Professor, University of Texas; Paul J. Thomas Chair in Medicine, Jonsson Center for Molecular Genetics, since 1977, and W. A. Moncrief Distinguished Chair in Cholesterol and Arteriosclerosis Research, since 1989, University of Texas Southwestern Medical School at Dallas; *b* 13 April 1941; *s* of Harvey and Evelyn Brown; *m* 1964, Alice Lapin; two *d*. *Educ:* Univ. of Pennsylvania (AB 1962, MD 1966). Resident in Internal Medicine, Mass. Gen. Hosp., Boston, 1966–68; Research Scientist, NIH, Bethesda, 1968–71; Asst Prof., Univ. of Texas Southwestern Med. Sch. at Dallas, 1971–74; Associate Prof., 1974–76. Member Board of Directors: Regeneron Inc., 1991–; Pfizer Inc., 1996–2012. For. Mem., Royal Soc., 1991. Lounsbery Award, 1979; Albert D. Lasker Award, 1985; (jtly) Nobel Prize in Medicine or Physiology for the discovery of receptors for Low Density Lipoproteins, a fundamental advance in the understanding of cholesterol metabolism, 1985; US Nat. Medal of Science, 1987. *Publications:* numerous papers to learned jls. *Address:* Department of Molecular Genetics, University of Texas Southwestern Medical School, 5323 Harry Hines Boulevard, Dallas, TX 75390–9046, USA.

**BROWN, Michael William Tuke,** MVO 2002; FCILT; Commissioner, Transport for London, since 2015; *b* Belfast, 14 April 1964; *s* of Dr William Aiken Brown and Margaret Elisabeth Brown (*née* Tuke); *m* 2000, Barbara Elizabeth McKelvey; one *s*. *Educ:* Brackenber House; Campbell Coll.; Queen's Univ., Belfast (BSc (Econ); MBA). Chief Operating Officer, London Underground, 2003–08; Man. Dir, Heathrow Airport, BAA, 2008–10; Man. Dir, London Underground and London Rail, TfL, 2010–15. Mem., British Transport

Police Authy, 2004–08. Chair, Transport Infrastructure Efficiency Taskforce, 2019–. FRSA. Hon. LLD QUB, 2016. *Recreations:* gym, family, friends, running. *E:* mikebrown@tfl.gov.uk.

BROWN, Moira; *see* Brown, Susanne M.

BROWN, Prof. Morris Jonathan, FRCP; Professor of Endocrine Hypertension, William Harvey Research Institute, Queen Mary University of London, since 2016; *b* 18 Jan. 1951; *s* of Arnold and Irene Brown; *m* 1977, Diana Phylactou; three *d. Educ:* Harrow; Trinity College, Cambridge (MA, MD); MSc London. FRCP 1987. Lectr, Royal Postgraduate Medical School, 1979–82; Senior Fellow, MRC, 1982–85; Prof. of Clin. Pharmacol., 1985–2016, Dir of Clin. Studies, 1989–2016, Univ. of Cambridge; Fellow, Gonville and Caius Coll., Cambridge, 1989–2016, now Emeritus; Hon. Consultant Physician, Addenbrooke's Hosp., 1985–2016. Oliver-Sharpey Lectr, RCP, 1992. Chm., Med. Res. Soc., 1991–97; Pres., British Hypertension Soc., 2005–07. FMedSci 1999; FAHA 2002; FBPhS (FBPharmacolS 2012); FBHS 2014. Hospital Doctor of the Year, Elsevier Press, 2003; Lilly Gold Medal, British Pharmacol Soc., 2002; Walter Somerville Medal, British Cardiac Soc., 2006; Award for Outstanding Res., Lancet/RCP, 2016; Robert Tigerstedt Lifetime Achievement Award, Internat. Soc. for Hypertension, 2018. *Publications:* Advanced Medicine 21, 1985; (jtly) Clinical Pharmacology, 8th edn 1996 to 12th edn 2018; articles on causes and treatment of hypertension, with special interest in adrenal tumours. *Recreations:* violin and oboe playing, tennis. *Address:* 104 Grange Road, Cambridge CB3 9AA. *Club:* Athenæum.

BROWN, Nageena; *see* Khalique, N.

BROWN, Dr Nicholas David; Principal, Linacre College, Oxford, since 2010; *b* Brockworth, Glos, 4 Dec. 1962; *s* of Ray and Avril Brown; one *s* three *d*; *m* Roosa Leimu. *Educ:* United World Coll. of Atlantic; Churchill Coll., Cambridge (BA Hons Geog. 1985); Aberdeen Univ. (MSc Ecol.); DPhil Oxon. Lectr, Manchester Univ., 1989–92; Res. Officer, Oxford Forestry Inst., 1992–94; Lectr, Oxford Univ., 1994–2010; Sen. Tutor and Dean, Linacre Coll., Oxford, 2006–10. Commonwealth Scholarship Comr, 2013–19. Trustee: Sylva Foundn, 2009–17; Tertiary Educn Scholarship Trust for Africa, 2009– (Chm.); Hill End Outdoor Educn Trust, 2017–. Vice-Patron, Anjali Dance Co., 2015–. *Publications:* contrib. papers to learned jls on tropical and temperate forest ecol. *Recreations:* viola, sailing, cycling, Finnish. *Address:* Linacre College, Oxford OX1 3JA. *T:* (01865) 271662. *E:* nick.brown@linacre.ox.ac.uk.

BROWN, Rt Hon. Nicholas (Hugh); PC 1997; MP (Lab) Newcastle upon Tyne East, since 2010 (Newcastle upon Tyne East, 1983–97; Newcastle upon Tyne East and Wallsend, 1997–2010); *b* 13 June 1950; *s* of late R. C. Brown and G. K. Brown (*née* Tester). *Educ:* Swattenden Secondary Modern Sch.; Tunbridge Wells Tech. High Sch.; Manchester Univ. (BA 1971). Trade Union Officer, GMWU Northern Region, 1978–83. Mem., Newcastle upon Tyne City Council, 1980–84. Opposition front-bench spokesman: on legal affairs, 1984–87; on Treasury affairs, 1987–94; on health, 1994–95; Dep. Chief Opposition Whip, 1995–97; Parly Sec. to HM Treasury (Govt Chief Whip), 1997–98 and 2008–10; Minister, Agriculture, Fisheries and Food, 1998–2001; Minister of State (Minister for Work), DWP, 2001–03; Treasurer of HM Household (Dep. Chief Whip), 2007–08; Minister for NE of England, 2007–10; Shadow Parly Sec. to HM Treasury (Govt Chief Whip), 2010; Opposition Chief Whip, 2016–. House of Commons: Chm., Finance Cttee, 2015–16; Member: Members Estimate Cttee, 2015–16; Liaison Cttee (Commons), 2015–16; H of C Commn, 2015–16; Public Accounts Commn, 2015–; Speaker's Cttee for Ind. Parly Standards Authy, 2010–17. Freeman, City of Newcastle, 2001. *Address:* House of Commons, SW1A 0AA. *Clubs:* Newcastle Labour (Newcastle); Lindisfarne (Wallsend).

BROWN, Nicolas Jerome Danton; Director, Neal Street Productions, since 2013; *b* 11 Sept. 1965; *s* of Simon and Rosemary Brown; *m* 1998, Sarah Barker; two *s. Educ:* Portswood Primary Sch., Southampton; St John's Sch., Leatherhead; Choate Rosemary Hall, Conn.; Clare Coll., Cambridge (BA Hist. 1987). Trainee, Central TV, 1987–89; Develt Exec., 1989–91, Production Exec., 1991–94, Central Films; freelance producer, 1995–2006; Dir, UK Drama Prodn, BBC, 2006–12. *Television:* producer: Insiders, 1997; London Bridge, 1998; Hope and Glory, 1999; Deceit, 1999; Nicholas Nickleby, 2000; White Teeth, 2001–02; Friends and Crocodiles, 2003; Gideon's Daughter, 2004; Bradford Riots, 2005; executive producer: Capturing Mary, 2008; Joe's Palace, 2008; Isles of Wonder, Happy and Glorious, 2012 (London Olympic Games Opening Ceremony films); The Hollow Crown, 2016; Britannia, 2018; *film:* producer, Ladies in Lavender, 2004. *Recreation:* sailing. *Address:* c/o Sara Putt Associates, The Old House, Shepperton Studios, Shepperton, Middx TW17 0QD.

BROWN, Prof. Nigel Leslie, OBE 2014; PhD; FRSE, FRSC, FRSB; Professor of Molecular Microbiology, University of Edinburgh, 2008–12, now Emeritus; Director, Blackah-Brown Consulting, since 2013; *b* 19 Dec. 1948; *s* of Leslie Charles and Beryl Brown; *m* 1971, Gayle Lynnette Blackah; three *d. Educ:* Beverley Grammar Sch.; Univ. of Leeds (BSc 1971; PhD 1974). CBiol, FRSB (FIBiol 1989); FRSC 1990; FRSE 2011. ICI Fellow, MRC Lab. of Molecular Biology, Cambridge, 1974–76; University of Bristol: Lectr in Biochemistry, 1976–81; Royal Soc. EPA Cephalosporin Fund Sen. Res. Fellow, 1981–88; University of Birmingham: Prof. of Molecular Genetics and Microbiol., 1988–2008; Hd, 1994–99, Dep. Hd, 1999–2000, Sch. of Biol Scis; Hd, Sch. of Chemistry, 2003–04; Dir of Sci. and Technol., BBSRC, 2004–08 (Mem., Strategy Bd, 1997–2004); Edinburgh University: Vice-Principal and Hd, Coll. of Sci. and Engrg, 2008–11; Sen. Vice-Principal, Planning and Res. Policy, 2011–12. Chm., Earlham Inst. (formerly Genome Analysis Centre), 2013–17. Member: Scottish Sci. Adv. Council, 2010–15; REF sub-panel, 2012–14; Sêr Cymru II Panel, 2015–; Council, Royal Soc. of Biol., 2016–; Chairman: Deans of Sci. and Engrg in Scotland, 2010–12; Scottish Consortium for Rural Res., 2011–12; NERC Training Adv. Bd (formerly NERC Training Adv. Gp), 2014–19. Vis. Fellow in Genetics, Univ. of Melbourne, 1987–88; Leverhulme Trust Res. Fellow, 2000–01. Hon. Professor: Univ. of Nottingham, 2011–; Univ. of Swansea, 2012–15, 2018–. Pres., Microbiology Soc. (formerly Soc. for Gen. Microbiol.), 2012–15. Chief Ed., Fedn of Eur. Microbiology Socs Microbiology Reviews, 2000–04. Hon. DSc Edinburgh, 2014. *Publications:* contribs to scientific jls, books and magazines and public engagement magazines and blogs. *Recreations:* walking, DIY, gardening, family. *E:* nigel.brown@ed.ac.uk.

BROWN, Pamela; *see* Cameron, P.

BROWN, Patricia; *see* Brown, M. P.

BROWN, Patricia Ann; *see* Heywood, P. A.

BROWN, Patricia Ann; Director, Central Futures Ltd, since 2008; *b* Liverpool, 5 Sept. 1957; *d* of Frederick Brown and Jane Brown (*née* Gallagher). *Educ:* Queen Mary High Sch., Liverpool. CAM Cert. Communications; CAM Dip. PR. Publicity officer, GLC, 1985–86; PR Manager, London Res. Centre, 1986–94; Dir of Information, London First Centre, 1994–97; Chief Exec., Central London Partnership, 1998–2008. Dir, Newlyn Art Gall., 2012– (Vice-Chair, 2014–17). Mem., Strategic Adv. Bd, Gt Western Railway, 2014–.

Trustee: Interchange Trust, 1995–2000; London Internat. Fest. of Th., 2001–13; Borough Mkt Trust, 2007–10; Geffrye Mus., 2009–14; Thames Fest. Trust, 2017–; Chair, London Fest. of Architecture, 2013–16; Mem., Regl Adv. Bd, London and SE, Nat. Trust, 2012–; Deputy Chair, Mayor's Design Adv. Gp, 2012–16; Vice Chair, Develt Cttee, British Property Fedn, 2015–. Hon. FRIBA 2017. *Recreations:* art, architecture and design, walking, swimming, Cornwall. *Address:* 26 Alma Grove, SE1 5PY.

BROWN, Sir Patrick; *see* Brown, Sir A. P.

BROWN, Paul Campbell, CBE 2003; Director, Wightlink Ltd, 2012–14 (Project Manager, 2009–11); *b* 6 Nov. 1945; *s* of James Henry Brown and Edna May Brown (*née* Howell); *m* 1970, Sarah Hunter Bailey; two *s. Educ:* Portsmouth Grammar Sch.; RMA Sandhurst; Balliol Coll., Oxford (BA Hons). Served Army, as Officer, 1966–74. British Forces Broadcasting Service, 1974–78; Ops Manager, BRMB Radio, 1979–81; Prog. and News Dir, Radio Victory, 1981–84; Hd, Radio Programming, IBA, 1984–90; Dep. Chief Exec., Radio Authy, 1990–95; Chief Exec., Commercial Radio Cos Assoc., 1995–2006; Chm., RadioCentre, 2006–08. Director: Rajar, 1996–2006; Skillset, 2004–08. Chm., UK Digital Radio Forum, 2000–01; Pres., Assoc. of European Radios, 1998–2000; Vice Pres., World DAB Forum, 2000–05. FRA 1996 (Chm. Council, 2001–04); FRSA 2000–18. Hospice at Home visitor, Rosemary Foundn, Petersfield, 2017. *Recreations:* sailing, tennis, walking, reading, music presentation. *E:* paul@westernparade.co.uk. *Clubs:* Army and Navy; Thorney Island Sailing (Vice Commodore, 2005–07, Commodore, 2007–09); Emsworth Sailing; Avenue Lawn Tennis and Squash (Havant).

BROWN, Paul G.; Executive Director, UK Retail Banking, Lloyds Bank plc, 1991–97, retired; *b* 10 Sept. 1942; *s* of Col E. G. Brown and Alice Brown (*née* Van Weyenberghe); *m* 1969, Jessica Faunce; one *s* two *d. Educ:* Belgium, Germany and UK. Management appts with Lloyds Bank plc in Germany, Switzerland, USA and UK, 1960–97. *Recreations:* sailing, ski-ing.

BROWN, Sir Peter (Randolph), Kt 1997; Conservative Constituency Agent for Huntingdon, 1985–2009; *b* 30 Aug. 1945; *s* of Stanley Percival Brown and late Dorothy Ida Brown (*née* Bagge); *m* 1983, Antonia Brenda Taylor; one *s* one *d. Educ:* Bushey Sch., New Malden, Surrey. With Inland Revenue, 1961–67; Conservative Constituency Agent: London Bor. of Newham, 1967–70; Lambeth, Norwood, 1970–74; Kingston upon Thames, 1974–85; Cons. Eur. Constituency Agent, Cambridge and N Beds, 1987–90. Dir, PRB Consultancy Services Ltd, 2002–09. Mem. (C), Cambs CC, 2005–17 (Cabinet Mem. for economy, envmt and climate change, 2008–09, for communities, 2009–11). Mem., Cambs and Peterborough Fire Authy, 2011–17. Qualified Mem., Nat. Soc. of Cons. and Unionist Agents, 1968. Freeman, City of London, 1992. *Recreations:* reading, following international tennis, gardening. *Address:* 39 Hartford Road, Huntingdon, Cambs PE29 3RF.

BROWN, Prof. Peter Robert Lamont, FBA 1971; FRHistS; Rollins Professor of History, 1986–2011, now Emeritus, and Director, Program in Hellenic Studies, 2002–09, Princeton University (Visiting Professor, 1983–86); *b* 26 July 1935; *s* of James Lamont and Sheila Brown, Dublin; *m* 1st, 1959, Friedl Esther (*née* Löw-Beer); two *d*; 2nd, 1980, Patricia Ann Fortini; 3rd, 1989, Elizabeth Gilliam. *Educ:* Aravon Sch., Bray, Co. Wicklow, Ireland; Shrewsbury Sch.; New Coll., Oxford (MA). Harmsworth Senior Scholar, Merton Coll., Oxford and Prize Fellow, All Souls Coll., Oxford, 1956; Junior Research Fellow, 1963, Sen. Res. Fellow, 1970–73, All Souls Coll.; Fellow, All Souls Coll., 1956–75; Lectr in Medieval History, Merton Coll. Oxford, 1970–75; Special Lectr in late Roman and early Byzantine History, 1970–73, Reader, 1973–75, Univ. of Oxford; Prof. of History, Royal Holloway Coll., London Univ., 1975–78; Prof. of History and Classics, Univ. of Calif. at Berkeley, 1978–86. Fellow, Amer. Acad. of Arts and Scis, 1978. Hon. DTheol Fribourg, 1975; Hon. DHL: Chicago, 1978; S Methodist Univ., 2004; Hon. DLitt: TCD, 1990; Wesleyan Univ., Conn, 1993; Columbia Univ., NY, 2001; Pisa, 2001; Oxford, 2006; St Andrews, 2014; Hon. DLaws Harvard, 2002; Hon. Dr: Cambridge, 2004; Central Eur. Univ., 2005; Notre Dame, 2008; Aristotle Univ., Thessaloniki, 2010; Hon. DH: Yale, 2006; KCL, 2008; Hon. Dr Humane Studies Amherst Coll., 2009; Hon. DPhil Hebrew Univ., Jerusalem, 2010; Hon. DD St Vladimir's Orthodox Seminary, 2013. Kluge Prize for Lifetime Achievement in Study of Humanity, Liby of Congress, 2008; Balzan Prize, 2011; Jacques Barzun Prize, Amer. Philosophical Soc., 2013; Philip Shaff Prize for Church Hist., American Soc. for Church Hist., 2014. *Publications:* Augustine of Hippo: a biography, 1967; The World of Late Antiquity, 1971; Religion and Society in the Age of St Augustine, 1971; The Making of Late Antiquity, 1978; The Cult of the Saints: its rise and function in Latin Christianity, 1980, reprint 2014; Society and the Holy in Late Antiquity, 1982; The Body and Society: men, women and sexual renunciation in Early Christianity, 1989, rev. edn 2008; Power and Persuasion in Late Antiquity: towards a Christian Empire, 1992; Authority and the Sacred: aspects of the christianization of the Roman world, 1995; The Rise of Western Christendom: triumph and diversity, AD 200–1000, 1996, rev. edn 2013; Poverty and Leadership in the Later Roman Empire, 2002; Through the Eye of a Needle: wealth, the fall of Rome, and the making of Christianity in the West, 340–550 AD, 2012; The Ransom of the Soul, 2015; Treasure and Heaven, 2016. *Address:* Department of History, 129 Dickinson Hall, Princeton University, Princeton, NJ 08544–1017, USA.

BROWN, Peter Wilfred Henry, CBE 1996; Secretary of the British Academy, 1983–2006; *b* 4 June 1941; *s* of late Rev. Wilfred George Brown and Joan Margaret (*née* Adams); *m* 1968, Kathleen Clarke (marr. diss.); one *d. Educ:* Marlborough Coll.; Jesus Coll., Cambridge (Rustat Schol.). Assistant Master in Classics, Birkenhead Sch., 1963–66; Lectr in Classics, Fourah Bay Coll., Univ. of Sierra Leone, 1966–68; Asst Sec., School of Oriental and African Studies, Univ. of London, 1968–75; Dep. Sec., British Academy, 1975–83 (Actg Sec., 1976–77). Mem. Council, British Inst. in Eastern Africa, 1983–2013 (Hon. Treas., 2011–13; Hon. Vice Pres., 2014–). Fellow, National Humanities Center, N Carolina, 1978; Hon. Fellow, British Sch. at Rome, 2007. Hon. DLitt: Birmingham, 1995; Sheffield, 2007. Kt Grand Cross, Order of Merit (Poland), 1995. *Recreation:* the enjoyment of books and classical music. *Address:* 34 Victoria Road, NW6 6PX. *Club:* Athenæum.

*See also* Rev. J. M. Brown.

BROWN, Philip Anthony Russell, CB 1977; Director of Policy, Investment Management Regulatory Organisation, 1985–93; *b* 18 May 1924; *e s* of late Sir William Brown, KCB, KCMG, CBE, and of Elizabeth Mabel (*née* Scott); *m* 1954, Eileen (*d* 1976), *d* of late J. Brennan; *m* 1976, Sarah Elizabeth Dean (*see* S. E. Brown). *Educ:* Malvern; King's Coll., Cambridge. Entered Home Civil Service, Board of Trade, 1947; Private Sec. to Perm. Sec., 1949; Principal, 1952; Private Sec. to Minister of State, 1953; Observer, Civil Service Selection Board, 1957; returned to BoT, 1959; Asst Sec., 1963; Head of Overseas Information Co-ordination Office, 1963; BoT, 1964; Under-Sec., 1969; Head of Establishments Div. 1, BoT, later DTI, 1969; Head of Cos Div., DTI, 1971; Dep. Sec., Dept of Trade, 1974–83. Head of External Relations, Lloyd's of London, 1983–85; Dir, NPI, 1985–90. Mem., Disciplinary Cttee, ICA, 1985–96. Mem., London Adv. Bd, Salvation Army, 1982–92. *Publications:* (contrib.) Multinational Approaches: corporate insiders, 1976; Poems from Square Mile, 1992; articles in various jls. *Recreations:* reading, gardening, music. *Address:* Christmas Croft, Hopgarden Lane, Sevenoaks, Kent TN13 1PX. *Club:* Oxford and Cambridge.

**BROWN, Rev. Raymond**; see Brown, Rev. Robert R.

**BROWN, Rev. Raymond**, PhD; Senior Minister, Victoria Baptist Church, Eastbourne, 1987–93, retired; b 3 March 1928; s of Frank Stevenson Brown and Florence Mansfield; m 1966, Christine Mary Smallman; one s one d. Educ: Spurgeon's Coll., London (BD, MTh); Fitzwilliam Coll., Cambridge (MA, BD, PhD). Minister: Zion Baptist Church, Cambridge, 1956–62; Upton Vale Baptist Church, Torquay, 1964–71; Tutor in Church History, Spurgeon's Coll., London, 1971–73, Principal 1973–86. Pres., Evangelical Alliance, 1975–76; Trustee, Dr Daniel Williams's Charity, 1980–2014; Nat. Chaplain, Girls' Brigade, 1986–90. Publications: Their Problems and Ours, 1969; Let's Read the Old Testament, 1971; Skilful Hands, 1972; Christ Above All: the message of Hebrews, 1982; Bible Study Commentary: 1 Timothy-James, 1983; The English Baptists of the Eighteenth Century, 1986; The Bible Book by Book, 1987; Be My Disciple, 1992; The Message of Deuteronomy: not by bread alone, 1993; Collins Gem Bible Guide, 1993; Four Spiritual Giants, 1997 (US edn as Giants of the Faith, 1997); The Message of Nehemiah: God's servant in a time of change, 1998; The Message of Numbers: journey to the promised land, 2002; Spirituality in Adversity: English nonconformity in a period of repression, 1660–1689, 2012; (ed) The 1662 Diary of Philip Henry (1631–1696), 2014; contribs to: What the Bible Says, 1974; Dictionary of Christian Spirituality, 1983; My Call to Preach, 1986; Encyclopedia of World Faiths, 1987; New Dictionary of Theology, 1988; The Empty Cross, 1989; Dictionary of Evangelical Biography, 1995; Oxford Dictionary of World Religions, 1997; Oxford Dictionary of the Christian Church, 1998; Called to One Hope, 2000; A Protestant Catholic Church of Christ: essays on the history and life of New Road Baptist Church, Oxford, 2003; Challenge to Change: dialogues with a radical Baptist theologian, 2009; The Quakers (1656–1723): the evolution of an alternative community, 2018. Recreations: music, walking. Address: 200B Perne Road, Cambridge CB1 3NX. T: (01223) 700110.

**BROWN, Rebecca Jane; Her Honour Judge Brown**; a Circuit Judge, since 2012; b Singapore, 1966; d of William and Pamela Brown. Educ: York Univ. (BA Hons 1987); City Univ. (DipLaw 1988); Inns of Court Sch. of Law. Called to the Bar, Inner Temple, 1989; in practice at the Bar, 1989–2012; a Recorder, 2004–12 (Family Courts, 2008–12). Recreations: swimming, walking, pilates, cooking, writing, travelling. Address: Milton Keynes County Court, 351 Silbury Boulevard, Witan Gate East, Milton Keynes MK9 2DT; Watford County Court, Cassiobury Court, Cassiobury House, 11–19 Station Road, Watford, Herts WD17 1EZ.

**BROWN, His Honour Richard George**; DL; a Circuit Judge, 1992–2013, a Senior Circuit Judge, 2007–13; b Durham, 10 April 1945; m 1969, Ann Patricia Bridget Wade; one s one d (and one s decd). Educ: Bournville Grammar Sch.; Technical Sch., Birmingham; London Sch. of Economics (LLB Hons); Inns of Court Sch. of Law. Insurance clerk, 1961–62; shop assistant, 1962–63; bus conductor, 1963–64; Trainee Radio Officer, Merchant Navy, 1964–65; taxi driver, 1965–66; assistant, school for children with special needs, 1966–67; bus driver, 1967–68. Called to the Bar, Middle Temple, 1972 (Blackstone Entrance Exhibnr). Asst Recorder, 1986–90; a Recorder of the Crown Court, 1990–92. Resident and Liaison Judge, Crown Courts in E Sussex, 1996–2013. Vice Pres., E Sussex Magistrates' Assoc., 1997–2013. Hon. Recorder, Brighton and Hove, 2008–13. Chm., Bd of Govs, Farney Close Sch., 1984–86; Dir, Deepdene Schs Ltd, Hove, 2014–15. DL E Sussex, 2004. Recreations: watching sport, travel, being with the family and being a grandpa. Club: Armadillos Cricket.

**BROWN, His Honour Robert**; a Circuit Judge, 1988–2011; a Deputy Circuit Judge; b 21 June 1943; s of Robert and Mary Brown. Educ: Arnold Sch., Blackpool; Downing Coll., Cambridge (Exhibnr; BA, LLB). Called to Bar, Inner Temple, 1968 (Major Schol.); a Recorder, 1983–88. Chm., Parole Bd for Life and Imprisonment for Public Protection Prisoners. Recreation: golf. Club: Royal Lytham St Annes Golf.

**BROWN, Robert Edward**, CBE 2014; Member (Lib Dem) South Lanarkshire Council, since 2012; b 25 Dec. 1947; s of Albert Edward Brown and Joan Brown; m 1977, Gwen Morris; one s one d. Educ: Gordon Schools, Huntly; Univ. of Aberdeen (LLB 1st Cl. Hons). Legal Apprentice and Asst, Edmonds and Ledingham, Solicitors, Aberdeen, 1969–72; Procurator Fiscal, Dumbarton, 1972–74; Asst, 1974–75, Partner, 1975–99, Consultant, 1999–2004, Ross Harper and Murphy, Solicitors, Glasgow. Dep. Minister for Educn and Young People, Scottish Exec., 2005–07. Scottish Parliament: Mem. (Lib Dem) Glasgow, 1999–2011; Lib Dem spokesman on communities and housing, 1999–2003, on education, 2003–05, on justice and civil liberties, 2008–11; Convenor, Educn and Young People Cttee, 2003–05; Business Manager, Lib Dem Gp, 2007–08. Convenor: Scottish Lib Dem Policy Cttee, 2002–07; Assoc. of Scottish Lib Dem Councillors and Campaigners, 2018–. Recreations: history, science fiction. Address: 90b Blairbeth Road, Burnside, Rutherglen, Glasgow G73 4JA.

**BROWN, Robert Alan; His Honour Judge Robert Alan Brown**; a Circuit Judge, since 2008; b 29 Sept. 1956; s of late Norman Brown and Elizabeth Ruby Brown (née Watkins); m 1979, Frances Mary Warren; one s. Educ: Northgate Grammar Sch., Ipswich; Queen Mary Coll., Univ. of London (LLB Hons 1978). Called to the Bar, Inner Temple, 1979; in practice as barrister, Leicester, 1980–97, Nottingham, 1997–2008; Recorder, 2001–08. Treasury Counsel for Civil (Provincial), 1992–97. Midland Circuit: Educn and Trng Officer, 2004–08; Rep. on Trng for the Bar Cttee, Bar Council, 2005–06. Recreations: skiing, golf, vegetable gardening, supporting The Tractor Boys. Address: Midland Circuit Secretariat, The Priory Courts, 33 Bull Street, Birmingham B4 6DW.

**BROWN, Robert Iain Cameron**; Chief Executive Officer, AXA Corporate Solutions, since 2016; b Auckland, 8 Jan. 1966; s of Fredrick John Brown and Jessie Denise Yvonne Brown; m 1994, Julia Adler; one s one d. Educ: Felsted, Essex. Chief Multiline Underwriting Officer, Winterthur Internat., Switzerland, 1998–99; Regl Broking Dir, Winterthur Internat., Hong Kong, 1999–2001; Aon, 2001–15: CEO, Aon Corporate and Affinity; Bd Dir, Aon Ltd, 2009–15; Mem., Global Exec. Cttee, Aon Risk Services, 2009–14; CEO, Aon Ltd, 2009–12; CEO, Aon Risk Solutions EMEA, 2012–15. Chm., AXA Insurance Co., 2016–; Director: SLE Worldwide Ltd, 2008–15; Supercover Ltd, 2009–11; Centurion Safety Products Ltd, 2009–. Dir, BIBA, 2009–11. MInstD. Liveryman, Tobacco Pipe Makers' and Tobacco Blenders' Co. (Freeman, 2006). Recreations: golf, Rugby. Address: AXA Corporate Solutions, 4 rue Jules Lefebvre, 75009 Paris, France; AXA Corporate Solutions, 6 Bevis Marks, EC3A 7BA. Clubs: Mosimann's; Gosfield Lake Golf.

**BROWN, Rev. (Robert) Raymond**; Methodist Minister, responsible for lay training and development, Melton Mowbray, 1994–99; Supernumerary Methodist Minister, since 1999; b 24 March 1936; s of Robert Brown and Elsie (née Dudson); m 1959, Barbara (née Johnson); three s (one d decd). Educ: Stockport Sch.; Univ. of Leeds (BA Hons Philosophy); Univ. of Manchester (BD Hons Theology). Ordained Methodist minister, 1959; Minister: Luton Industrial Coll. and Mission, 1959–64; Heald Green and Handforth, 1964–67; commnd RAF Chaplain, 1967; Vice Principal, RAF Chaplains' Sch., 1978–83; Comd Chaplain, RAF Germany, 1983–87; Asst Prin. Chaplain, 1987–90, Prin. Chaplain, 1990–94, Ch of Scotland and Free Churches, RAF. QHC 1990–94. Recreations: music and drama (amateur singer and actor), writing for pleasure; fund-raising for crèche, Sally's Place, set up in remote rural S Africa, in memory of daughter, to look after and feed pre-school children and vulnerable youngsters, managed by World Vision. Address: Flat 1, Hamon Court, St Edmunds Terrace, Hunstanton, Norfolk PE36 5EH. T: (01485) 779762. E: ray.brown980@ntlworld.com. Club: Royal Air Force.

**BROWN, Robert Timothy James**; Consultant, since 2001, and Partner, since 2007, Corker Binning; b Marlborough, Wilts, 22 Nov. 1957; s of John and Lily Brown; m Kristiina Reed; three d. Educ: St Bartholomew's Sch., Newbury; Fitzwilliam Coll., Cambridge (BA Law 1979). Admitted as solicitor, 1983; trainee, then Partner, 1985–2001, Darlington and Parkinson. Dir of Develt, 2000–03, Co-Ed., 2001–03, Juvenile Justice in Russian Fedn. Member: Acad. Rev. Bd, Law Prog., Open Univ., 2002–13; Times Law Panel. Mem. Council, Law Soc., 2004–06. London Criminal Courts Solicitors' Association: Hon. Sec., 1997–2002; Vice-Pres., 2002–03; Pres., 2004–05; Exec. Officer, 2005–06. Mem., British Russian Law Assoc., 1992– (Chm.). Chm., Citizen's Watch Internat. Pres. and Chm., British Acad. of Forensic Sci. Mem., Judging Panel, Legal Aid Lawyer of Year award, Legal Aid Practitioners' Gp, 2007– (Chm.). Publications: (jtly) Archbold Magistrates' Courts Practice, 2005, 12th edn 2016; contribs to The Times, Sunday Times, New Law Jl, FT, Spear's Mag. Recreations: theatre, music, sport, keen walker and runner (incl. London Marathon, 2002). Address: Corker Binning, Cursitor Building, 38 Chancery Lane, WC2A 1EN. T: (020) 7353 6000, 07770 368692, Fax: (020) 7353 6008. E: rb@corkerbinning.com.

**BROWN, Prof. Roger John**, PhD; Professor of Higher Education Policy, Liverpool Hope University, 2007–13, now Emeritus; b 26 June 1947; s of John Richard Brown and Beatrice Anne (née Clamp); m 1st, 1971, Mary Elizabeth George (see M. E. Francis) (marr. diss. 1991); 2nd, 1992, Josephine Ann Titcomb. Educ: St Olave's Grammar Sch., Bermondsey; Queens' Coll., Cambridge (Haynes Exhibnr in History; MA); Inst. of Educn, Univ. of London (PhD). Admin. Officer, ILEA, 1969–75; Sec., William Tyndale Schs' Inquiry, 1975–76; Principal, Dept Industry, Dept Trade, Cabinet Office, OFT, DTI, 1976–84; Assistant Secretary: DoE, 1984–86; DTI, 1986–90; Sec., PCFC, 1990–91; Chief Exec., Cttee of Dirs of Polytechnics, 1991–93; Chief Exec., HEQC, 1993–97; Principal, Southampton Inst., 1998–2005; Prof. of Higher Educn Policy, Southampton Inst., subseq. Southampton Solent Univ., 2004–07; Vice-Chancellor, Southampton Solent Univ., 2005–07. Visiting Professor: Univ. of London Inst. of Educn, 1996–98; Middx Univ., 1997–99; Goldsmiths' Coll., 1997–99; Univ. of Surrey Roehampton (formerly Roehampton Inst.), 1997–; Univ. of East London, 2000–; City Univ., 2001–; Univ. of Southampton, 2006–; Edinburgh Napier Univ. (formerly Napier Univ., Edinburgh), 2007–; Open Univ., 2009–; Univ. of W London (formerly Thames Valley Univ.), 2009– (Gov., 2010–15). Vis. Fellow, Oxford Centre for Higher Educn Policy Studies, 2007–; Hon. Vis. Fellow, Inst. for Policy Studies in Educn, London Metropolitan Univ., 2007–. Vice-Chm., Standing Conf. of Principals, 1999–2003; Vice-Pres., SRHE, 2007–. Chm., Barton Peveril Coll., Eastleigh, 2009–17. Hon. Fellow, AUA, 2010. DUniv: Southampton Solent, 2007; Southampton, 2007; Hon. DLitt W London, 2014; Hon. DEd Liverpool Hope, 2015. Lifetime Achievement Award, Times Higher Educn, 2013. Publications: Educational Policy Making: an analysis, 1983; The Post-Dearing Quality Agenda, 1998; Quality Assurance in Higher Education: the UK experience since 1992, 2004; Higher Education and the Market, 2010; (with Helen Carasso) Everything for Sale?: the marketisation of UK higher education, 2013; The Inequality Crisis: what are the facts and what do we do about it?, 2017; contribs to educnl jls. Recreations: opera, cinema, jazz, collecting books about music. Address: 9 Blenheim Avenue, Southampton SO17 1DW.

**BROWN, Rosemary Jean, (Rosie)**; see Atkins, R. J.

**BROWN, Roswyn Ann H.**; see Hakesley-Brown.

**BROWN, Roy Drysdale**, CEng, FIMechE, FIET; Chairman, GKN plc, 2004–12 (Director, 1996–2012); b 4 Dec. 1946; s of late William Andrew Brown and Isabelle Drysdale (née Davidson); m 1978, Carol Wallace; two s. Educ: Tonbridge Sch.; UCL (GEC Schol.; BSc Mech. Eng); Harvard Business Sch. (MBA). CEng, FIMechE 1983; FIET (FIEE 1990). Commercial Gen. Manager, Vosper Thorneycroft Ltd, 1972–74; Unilever plc, 1974–2001: various financial, mktg and tech. posts, 1974–82; Chairman: Pamol Plantations Sdn Bhd, Malaysia, 1982–86; PBI Cambridge Ltd, 1987–88; Tech. Dir, Birds Eye Walls Ltd, 1988–90; Chm., Lever Bros Ltd, 1991–92; Regional Director: Africa, ME, Central and Eastern Europe, 1992–96; Foods and Beverages Europe, 1996–2001; Dir, Unilever plc and NV, 1992–2001; retd, 2001. Non-executive Director: Brambles Industries Ltd & plc, 2001–06; BUPA, 2001–07; Lloyds Franchise Bd, 2003–08; Alliance & Leicester plc, 2007–10 (Vice-Chm., 2007–08); Abbey National plc, 2008–10; Santander UK plc, 2010–15. Gov., and Chm Develt Gp and Foundn, Tonbridge Sch., 2007–12. Recreations: military history, wild life photography, classical music, opera, woodworking. Clubs: Royal Automobile; Leander (Henley).

**BROWN, Russell Leslie**; b 17 Sept. 1951; s of Howard Russell Brown and Muriel Brown (née Anderson); m 1973, Christine Margaret Calvert; two d. Educ: Annan Acad. With ICI, 1974–97, Plant Operative, 1992–97. Member: Dumfries and Galloway Regl Council, 1986–96 (Chm., Public Protection Cttee, 1990–94); Annandale and Eskdale DC, 1988–96; Dumfries and Galloway UA, 1995–97. MP (Lab) Dumfries, 1997–2005, Dumfries and Galloway, 2005–15; contested (Lab) same seat, 2015. PPS to Sec. of State for Scotland, 2005–10; Shadow Defence Minister, 2010–15. Recreations: walking, football. Address: 46 Northfield Park, Annan DG12 5EZ. T: (01461) 205365.

**BROWN, Prof. Sara Ann, (Sally)**, OBE 2002; PhD; FRSE; Professor of Education, 1990–2001, now Emeritus, and Deputy Principal, 1996–2001, University of Stirling; b 15 Dec. 1935; d of Fred Compigné-Cook and Gwendoline Cook (née Barrett); m 1959, Charles Victor Brown (d 1991); two s. Educ: Bromley High Sch.; University College London (BSc Hons 1957); Smith Coll., Mass (MA 1958); Jordanhill Coll., Glasgow (Teaching Cert. 1966); Univ. of Stirling (PhD 1975). Lectr in Physics, Univ. of Ife and Nigerian Coll. of Tech., 1960–64; Principal Teacher of Science, Helensburgh, 1964–70; Sen. Res. Fellow, Univ. of Stirling, 1970–80; Consultant and Adviser, Scottish Educn Dept, 1980–84; Dir, Scottish Council for Res. in Educn, 1986–90 (Fellow, 1992). Chair: Univs' Assoc. for Continuing Educn (Scotland), 2000–02; Educn Panel, 2001 RAE; Teacher Support Scotland Forum, 2002–10 (Vice Chair, Trustees, 2002–10); Scottish Arts Council Educn Forum, 2003–04; Educn Cttee, RSE, 2011–16 (Vice Convener, 2009–11); Learned Socs' Gp on Scottish Sci. Educn, 2012–16; Professional Adv. Gp on computer sci. in Scottish educn, 2012–16; Vice-Chair, ESRC Teaching and Learning Res. prog., 1998–2005. Chair Adv. Bd, Leirsinn Gaelic res. centre, 2000–03; Member: Academic Council, UHI Millennium Inst., 2001–09; Vision Cttee, Royal Soc., 2011–14. Trustee, RSE Scotland Foundn, 2013–16. Chair, Alcohol Commn, SLP, 2010. Gov., Queen Margaret Univ. (formerly Queen Margaret UC), Edinburgh, 1999–2008 (Vice Chm., 2005–08). FRSA 1989; FRSE 1996; FEIS 1997; AcSS 2000. Hon. Fellow UHI Millennium Inst., 2005. DUniv: Stirling, 2002; Open, 2004; Queen Margaret, 2009; Hon. DEd Edinburgh, 2003. Publications: What Do They Know?, 1980; Making Sense of Teaching, 1993; Special Needs Policy in the 1990s, 1994; numerous academic works. Recreations: theatre, music, opera, current affairs. Address: 30A Chalton Road, Bridge of Allan, Stirling FK9 4EF. T: (01786) 833671. E: s.a.brown@stir.ac.uk.

**BROWN, Sarah Elizabeth,** OBE 2004; Member, General Pharmaceutical Council, 2010–17; *b* 30 Dec. 1943; *d* of Sir Maurice Dean, KCB, KCMG and Anne (*née* Gibson); *m* 1976, Philip Anthony Russell Brown, *qv. Educ:* St Paul's Girls' Sch.; Newnham Coll., Cambridge (BA Nat. Sci.). Joined BoT as Asst Principal, 1965; Private Sec. to Second Perm. Sec., 1968; Principal, 1970; DTI, 1971–96: Asst Sec., 1978; Sec. to Crown Agents Tribunal, 1978–82; Personnel Management Div., 1982–84; Head of Financial Services Bill team, 1984–86; Under Sec., 1986; Head of Companies Div., 1986–91; Head of Enterprise Initiative Div., 1991–93, and Small Firms Div., 1992–93; Head of Small Firms and Business Link Div., 1993–94; Head of Companies Div., 1994–96; Dir, Company Law, 1996. Comr, Friendly Socs Commn, 1997–2001; Mem., Competition (formerly Monopolies and Mergers) Commn, 1998–2007. Dir, Remploy Ltd, 1997–2000; Mem. Bd, Look Ahead Housing Assoc., 1996–2008; Associate Mem., Kensington & Chelsea and Westminster HA, 1996–99; non-executive Director: Kent and Sussex Weald NHS Trust, 1999–2000; Financial Services Compensation Scheme, 2000–07; SW Kent Primary Care Trust, 2001–06; Accountancy and Actuarial Discipline (formerly Accountants Investigation and Discipline) Bd Ltd, 2001–10; Revenue and Customs Prosecutions Office, 2005–09. Member: Civil Service Appeals Bd, 1998–2004; Disciplinary Panel, Taxation Discipline Bd, 2010–18; Lay Mem., Bar Standards Bd, 2006–11 (Special Advr, 2012–15); Mem., Investigations Cttee, RPSGB, 2007–09. Chair, Audit Cttee, Parkinson's UK, 2007–14. Trustee: Horder Healthcare (formerly Horder Centre), 2007–19; Tower Hamlets friends and neighbours, 2013– (Chm., 2013–18). Gov. Dunton Green Primary Sch., 2014– (Chm., 2017–). *Recreations:* travel, theatre, gardening. *Address:* Christmas Croft, Hopgarden Lane, Sevenoaks, Kent TN13 1PX.

**BROWN, Sarah Elizabeth;** writer and broadcaster; Flexible Learning Co-ordinator, Christ's School, Richmond, 2004–17; *b* 13 Sept. 1952; *d* of Lewis William Brown, OBE and Gweneth Elizabeth Brown (*née* Richards); *m* 1989, Paul Malcolm Street; two *s. Educ:* Brighton and Hove High Sch.; I. M. Marsh Coll., Liverpool (Cert Ed Dance and Drama 1973); London Sch. of Contemporary Dance. TV and theatre work, 1976–78; restaurateur and wholefood shop proprietor, 1978–88; Presenter, Vegetarian Kitchen (series), BBC TV, 1983; vegetarian cookery writer and broadcaster, 1984–. Mem. steering gp, Focus on Food, RSA/Waitrose, 1998–2003. Mem., Guild of Food Writers, 1986–2006. Manager, England Over 35s Orienteering Team, 1998–. Egon Ronay Cellnet Award, 1987; Glenfiddich Special Award for Writing, 1988. *Publications:* Vegetarian Kitchen, 1984; Sarah Brown's Vegetarian Cookbook, 1984; Sarah Brown's Healthy Living Cookbook, 1986; Sarah Brown's Vegetarian Microwave Cookbook, 1987; Sarah Brown's New Vegetarian Kitchen, 1987; Sarah Brown's Quick and Easy Vegetarian Cookery, 1989; Secret England, 1989; Outdoor London, 1991; Sarah Brown's Healthy Pregnancy, 1992; Sarah Brown's Fresh Vegetarian Cookery, 1995; No Fuss Vegetarian Cooking, 1998; The Complete Vegetarian Cookbook, 2002; Sarah Brown's World Vegetarian Cookbook, 2004; Parents and Carers Guide to Options 14–16, 2008. *Recreations:* orienteering, listening to TMS, playing German board games.

**BROWN, Rev. Scott James,** CBE 2014; Chaplain of the Fleet (formerly Chaplain of the Fleet and Director General), Naval Chaplaincy Service, 2010–14; Director and Trustee, Cambodian Community Dream Organisation UK, 2016–18; *b* Bellshill, Lanarkshire, 16 May 1968; *s* of James Brown and Margaret Brown (*née* Bryson); *m* 2006, Colin A Fleming. *Educ:* Hamilton Grammar Sch.; Bell Coll. of Technol.; Univ. of Aberdeen (BD 1992). Ordained C of S, 1993; Chaplain, 1993–2007, Principal Chaplain, 2007–10, RN. QHC 2007–14. Trustee, Kilmarnock Old Kirk Trust, 2017–. *Recreations:* travel, interior design, good wine. *Address:* Braeside, 5 Main Street, Drymen, Glasgow G63 0BP. *T:* (01360) 660989, 07824805888. *E:* scott16568@gmail.com.

**BROWN, His Honour Simon Staley;** QC 1995; an Additional High Court Judge, Senior Circuit Judge and a Specialist Mercantile Judge, Midland Circuit, 2006–16; *b* 23 Aug. 1952; *s* of late Peter Brown and Celia Rosamond Brown; *m* 1981, Kathleen Margaret Wain, PhD (Kathy Brown, garden owner, writer and designer); one *s* one *d. Educ:* Harrow Sch.; Queens' Coll., Cambridge (MA). Called to the Bar, Inner Temple, 1976 (Bencher and former Master of the Garden). A Recorder, 2000. Asst Boundary Comr, 2000–05. Mem., Bar Assocs of Professional Negligence, Technology and Construction, London Common and Commercial Law. Formerly: Chm. of Govs, Bedford Sch.; Trustee, The Bedford Charity (The Harpur Trust). *Recreation:* gardening.

**BROWN, Rt Hon. Sir Stephen,** GBE 1999; Kt 1975; PC 1983; a Lord Justice of Appeal, 1983–88; President of the Family Division, 1988–99; *b* 3 Oct. 1924; *s* of Wilfrid Brown and Nora Elizabeth Brown, Longdon Green, Staffordshire; *m* 1951, Patricia Ann, *d* of Richard Good, Tenbury Wells, Worcs; two *s* (twins) three *d. Educ:* Malvern College; Queens' College, Cambridge (Hon. Fellow, 1984). Served RNVR (Lieut), 1943–46. Barrister, Inner Temple, 1949; Bencher, 1974; Treas., 1994. Dep. Chairman, Staffs QS, 1963–71; Recorder of West Bromwich, 1965–71; QC 1966; a Recorder, and Honorary Recorder of West Bromwich, 1972–75; a Judge of the High Court, Family Div., 1975–77, QBD, 1977–83; Presiding Judge, Midland and Oxford Circuit, 1977–81. Member: Parole Board, England and Wales, 1967–71; Butler Cttee on mentally abnormal offenders, 1972–75; Adv. Council on Penal System, 1977; Chm., Adv. Cttee on Conscientious Objectors, 1971–75. Chm. Council, Malvern Coll., 1976–94; President: Edgbaston High Sch., 1989–2014; Malvernian Soc., 1998–. Hon. FRCPsych 2000. Hon. LLD: Birmingham, 1985; Leicester, 1997; UWE, 2000. Chevalier, Légion d'Honneur (France), 2015. *Recreation:* sailing. *Address:* 27 Gabriel Place, 2 Church Road, Birmingham B15 3SH. *Club:* Garrick.

**BROWN, Prof. Stephen David Macleod,** PhD; FMedSci; FRS 2015; Director, Mammalian Genetics Unit, Medical Research Council Harwell Institute (formerly Medical Research Council Mammalian Genetics Unit), since 1998; *b* Dumfries, 3 May 1955; *s* of David Brown and Pamela Brown; *m* 2009, Dr Heena Lad; one *s* one *d*; two *d* by a previous marriage. *Educ:* Belfast Royal Acad.; St Catharine's Coll., Cambridge (BA 1977; PhD 1981). EMBO Res. Fellow, 1981; Lectr, St Mary's Hosp. Med. Sch., 1982–92; Reader, 1992–94, Prof. of Genetics, 1994–98, Imperial Coll. London. Mem., Nuffield Council for Bioethics, 2009–12; Chm., Steering Cttee, Internat. Mouse Phenotyping Consortium, 2010–. Member, Scientific Advisory Board: Mouse Genome Database, Jackson Lab., 2002–05; Wellcome Trust Trypanotolerance Prog., 2003–08; Centre Integratif de Genomique, Lausanne, 2009–; Helmholtz Centrum, Munich, 2009–17; Institut Clinique Souris, Strasbourg, 2013–; GENCODE proj., 2014–16; Mem., Adv. Council, Nat. BioResource Centre, Japan, 2003–. FMedSci 2001; Mem., EMBO, 2005. Editor: Mammalian Genome, 1997–; Current Protocols in Mouse Biology, 2010–. Genetics Soc. Medal, 2009. *Publications:* res. papers in biol., genetics and molecular genetics in jls incl. Nature and Nature Genetics. *Recreations:* wine, reading, cooking. *Address:* MRC Harwell Institute, Oxon OX11 0RD. *T:* (01235) 841053. *E:* s.brown@har.mrc.ac.uk.

**BROWN, Sir Stephen (David Reid),** KCVO 1999; HM Diplomatic Service, retired; advisor to Vermilion Partners, since 2006; Associate, The Ambassador Partnership (formerly ADRg Ambassadors), since 2017 (Co-Chairman, 2010–17); *b* 26 Dec. 1945; *s* of Albert Senior Brown and Edna Brown; *m* 1966, Pamela Denise Gaunt; one *s* one *d. Educ:* Leeds Grammar Sch.; RMA Sandhurst; Univ. of Sussex (BA Hons). Served HM Forces, RA, 1966–76; FCO, 1976–77; 1st Sec., Nicosia, 1977–80; 1st Sec. (Commercial), Paris, 1980–85; FCO, 1985–89; DTI, 1989; Consul-Gen., Melbourne, 1989–94; Commercial Counsellor and Dir of Trade Promotion, Peking, 1994–97; Ambassador, Republic of Korea, 1997–2000; High Comr, Singapore, 2001–02; Chief Exec. (Permanent Sec.), British Trade Internat., then UK Trade & Investment, 2002–05. Gov., Grammar Sch. at Leeds, 2013–. Mem., Cook Soc., 2006–; Jt Pres., British Korean Soc., 2018. *Recreations:* reading, ski-ing, motor sport.

**BROWN, Stephen Paul;** Chief Executive Officer, Rugby Football Union, 2017–18; *b* Ashford, Kent, 14 Feb. 1965; *s* of Paul Henry Brown and Brenda Veronica Brown; *m* 1986, Karen Sue Jefferies; three *d. Educ:* ACCA 2001, FCCA 2006. Gp Hd of Finance, 1998–99, Business Support Manager, 1999–2001, British Energy plc; Abbott Laboratories: Financial Controller, 2001–03; Eur. Area Demand Manager, 2004–05; Finance Dir, UK, 2005–11; Chief Financial Officer, RFU, 2011–17; Man. Dir, England Rugby 2015, 2015–16. *Recreations:* musician, motor sport, art, travel, Rugby.

**BROWN, Stuart Christopher;** QC 1991; a Recorder, 1992–2018; a Deputy High Court Judge, 1994–2018; *b* 4 Sept. 1950; *s* of late Geoffrey Howard Brown and Olive Baum; *m* 1973, Imogen Lucas; two *d. Educ:* Acklam High Sch., Middlesbrough; Worcester Coll., Oxford (BA, BCL); Leeds Beckett Univ. (BA Italian). Called to the Bar, Inner Temple, 1974, Bencher, 1998. Practises on NE Circuit (Leader, 2009–11). Pres., later Judge, Mental Health Rev. Tribunal, 2000–. *Recreations:* family, theatre, walking. *Address:* The Gatehouse, Copgrove, Harrogate HG3 3SZ; Park Lane Plowden, 19 Westgate, Leeds LS1 2RD.

**BROWN, Very Rev. Susan Marjory;** Minister, Dornoch Cathedral, since 1998; Chaplain in Ordinary to the Queen, since 2010; Moderator of the General Assembly of the Church of Scotland, 2018–19; *b* Edinburgh, 12 Dec. 1958; *d* of James S. C. Attwell and Margaret R. Attwell (*née* Brown); *m* 1981, Derek G. Brown; one *s* one *d. Educ:* Penicuik High Sch., Midlothian; Edinburgh Univ. (BD 1981; DipMin 1983). Asst Minister, St Giles' Cathedral, Edinburgh, 1983–85; ordained Minister, 1985; Minister, Killearnan Parish Church, Ross-shire, 1985–98; Moderator: Presbytery of Ross, 1993–94: Presbytery of Sutherland, 2001–02, 2016–17. Vice-Convener: Cttee on Ecumenical Relns, 1999–2001; World Mission Council, 2014–18 (Convener, Europe and Americas Cttee, 2012–18). *Publications:* contrib. to Expository Times. *Recreations:* walking, cooking, golf. *Address:* Cathedral Manse, Dornoch IV25 3HN. *T:* (01862) 810296. *E:* Susan.Brown@churchofscotland.org.uk. *Club:* Royal Dornoch Golf.

**BROWN, Susan Mary;** *see* Spindler, S. M.

**BROWN, Prof. (Susanne) Moira,** OBE 2007; PhD; FRCPath; FRSE; Director, Crusade Laboratories Ltd, Glasgow, 2000–11 (Chief Scientist, 2000–08); *b* 21 March 1946; *d* of Edmund and Elizabeth Mitchell; *m* 1970, Alasdair MacDougall Brown. *Educ:* Queen's Univ., Belfast (BSc 1968); Univ. of Glasgow (PhD 1971). FRCPath 1997. Sen. Scientist, MRC Virology Unit, Glasgow, 1972–95; Prof. of Neurovirology, Univ. of Glasgow, 1995–2004, Prof. Emeritus, 2004. Chm., Med. Res. Scotland (formerly Scottish Hosp. Endowments Res. Trust), 2001–09. FRSE 1999 (Convener, Cell and Molecular Biol Fellowships Cttee, 2001–06). *Publications:* Methods in Molecular Medicine: herpes simplex virus, 1998. *Recreations:* walking, travel, reading, Christian faith, Scottish painters, beagles. *Address:* Kilure, The Steading, Croy Cunninghame, Killearn G63 9QY. *T:* (01360) 551715, *Fax:* (01360) 551716. *E:* s.m.brown@btconnect.com. *Club:* Athenæum.

**BROWN, Rt Rev. Dr Thomas John;** Bishop of Wellington (NZ), 1998–2012; *b* 16 Aug. 1943; *s* of Ernest Robert Brown and Abby Brown; *m* 1965, Dwyllis Lyon; one *s* two *d. Educ:* Otago Univ.; St John's Theol Coll., Auckland (LTh, STh); Graduate Theol Union, Berkeley, Univ. of California (DMin). Curate: St Matthew, Christchurch, NZ, 1972–74; St James the Greater, Leicester, UK, 1974–76; Vicar: Upper Clutha, 1976–79, St John, Roslyn, 1979–85, Dio. Dunedin, NZ; St James, Lower Hutt, Dio. Wellington, 1985–91; Archdeacon of Belmont, 1987–91; Asst Bishop and Vicar General, Diocese of Wellington, 1991–98. *Publications:* Ministry At The Door, 1981; Learning From Liturgy, 1984; (contrib.) Growing in Newness of Life, 1993; (contrib.) Designer Genes, 2000; (contrib.) Gene Technology in New Zealand: scientific issues and implications, 2000. *Recreations:* golf, fly-fishing, reading, swimming.

**BROWN, Timothy Andrew;** Managing Director, TAB Business Solutions Ltd, since 2011; Chief Executive, Jersey Post, since 2014 (non-executive Director, 2011–14); *b* Yorkshire, 27 Sept. 1959; *s* of Ronald Sydney Brown and Marjorie Brown; *m* 1981, Susan Frances Waters; two *s* one *d. Educ:* Cheshunt Sch.; Southampton Univ. (BSc Hons Pol. and Internat. Studies). Asst Auditor, later Sen. Auditor, Nat. Audit Office, 1981–86; KPMG, latterly Principal Consultant, 1986–94; with Royal Mail, 1994–2005: Commercial Dir, 1999–2001; Business and Commercial Strategy Dir, 2001–02; Sales and Mktg Dir, Parcelforce, 2003–05; Sales and Mktg Dir, DHL Express (UK), 2006–07; CEO, Postal Services Commn, 2008–11; Sales and Mktg Dir, City Link, 2012–14. *Recreations:* horse riding, antiques.

**BROWN, Timothy Charles;** Fellow, since 1979, and Director of Music, 1979–2010, Clare College, Cambridge; *b* 9 Dec. 1946; *s* of Roland Frederick John Brown and Ruth Margery Brown (*née* Dawe). *Educ:* Westminster Abbey Choir Sch.; Dean Close Sch., Cheltenham; King's Coll., Cambridge (alto choral schol.; MA); Westminster Coll., Oxford (DipEd). Music Master, Hinchingbrooke Sch., Huntingdon, 1969–72; Dir of Music, Oundle Sch., 1972–79. Mem., Scholars' Vocal Ensemble, 1969–72. Director: Choir of Clare Coll., Cambridge, 1979–2010; Cambridge Univ. Chamber Choir, 1986–2000; English Voices, 1995–; Vis. Dir of Chapel Music, Robinson Coll., Cambridge, 2010–15; Artistic Dir, Zürcher Sing Akademie, 2011–16. *Publications:* (ed) William Walton: shorter choral works, 1999; Choral Works with Orchestra, 2009. *Recreations:* foreign travel, gardens and gardening, walking. *Address:* c/o Clare College, Cambridge CB2 1TL. *T:* (01832) 358431.

**BROWN, Timothy William Trelawny T.;** *see* Tatton-Brown.

**BROWN, Tina, (Christina Hambley Brown), (Lady Evans),** CBE 2000; writer and journalist; founder and Chief Executive Officer: Tina Brown Live Media; Women in the World Media, since 2014; *b* 21 Nov. 1953; *d* of late Bettina Iris Mary Kohr Brown and George Hambley Brown; *m* 1981, Sir Harold Matthew Evans, *qv*; one *s* one *d. Educ:* Univ. of Oxford (MA). Columnist for Punch, 1978; Editor, Tatler, 1979–83; Editor in Chief, Vanity Fair Magazine, 1984–92; Editor, The New Yorker, 1992–98; Chm. and Editor in Chief, Talk magazine, 1998–2002; Partner and Chm., Talk Media, 1998–2002; founder and Ed.-in-Chief, The Daily Beast, 2008–13; Ed.-in-Chief, Newsweek Global (formerly Newsweek), 2010–13. Columnist: The Times, 2002; Washington Post, 2003–. Catherine Pakenham Prize, Most Promising Female Journalist (Sunday Times), 1973; Young Journalist of the Year, 1978. Plays: Under the Bamboo Tree (Sunday Times Drama Award), 1973; Happy Yellow, 1977. *Publications:* Loose Talk, 1979; Life as a Party, 1983; The Diana Chronicles, 2007; The Vanity Fair Diaries: 1983–1992, 2017.

**BROWN, Tom C.;** *see* Cross Brown, T.

**BROWN, Tony;** *see* Brown, J. A.

**BROWN, Prof. Valerie Kathleen**, PhD; agro-ecology science consultant, since 2005; Director, Centre for Agri-Environmental Research, and Research Professor in Agro-Ecology, University of Reading, 2000–04; *b* 11 May 1944; *d* of Reginald Brown and Kathleen (*née* Southerton); *m* 1970, Dr Clive Wall. *Educ*: Imperial Coll., London Univ. (BSc Zoology 1966; ARCS 1966; PhD Entomology 1969; DIC 1969). Lectr, Royal Holloway Coll., London Univ., 1969–74; Imperial College of Science, Technology and Medicine: Lectr, 1975–84; Sen. Lectr, 1984–89; Reader, 1989–94; CAB International: Dir, Internat. Inst. of Entomology, 1994–98; Dir, CABI Bioscience: Environment, 1998–2000. Member: Council, NERC, 2002–04; Sci. Adv. Gp, 2002–03; Res. and Priorities Bd, 2003–04, DEFRA; Nat. Scis Adv. Gp, English Nature, 2002–06; Panel, Govt on the Wildlife Network in England, 2009–; Panel, Govt Rev., Making Space for Nature, 2009–11; Special Advr, Grasslands, DEFRA, 2000–09; Ind. Sci. Advr, DEFRA/Natural England Envmtl Stewardship Res. Prog., 2009–11. Member: Bd, Internat. Assoc. for Ecology, 1997–2006; Nat. Cttee, Internat. Geosphere-Biosphere Prog., 2001–04; Council, RSPB, 2005–09; Council, Nat. Trust, 2013– (Mem., SW Regl Adv. Bd, 2016–); Mem., Strategic Adv. Bd, 2012–17, Trustee, 2017–, Som Wildlife Trust; Chair, Nat. Moth Recording Scheme Steering Gp, 2006–11. *Publications*: Grasshoppers, 1983, 2nd edn 1992; (ed) Insect Life History Strategies, 1983; Multitrophic Interactions, 1997; (ed) Herbivores between Plants and Predators, 1999; over 200 scientific pubns. *Recreations*: bird watching, cultivation of alpine plants, wine tasting, overseas travel. *Address*: Woodpeckers, Stawley, Wellington, Som TA21 0HN. *T*: and *Fax*: (01823) 672063. *E*: valeriekbrown2@gmail.com.

**BROWN, Vivian**; *see* Brown, H. V. B.

**BROWN, Sir William Brian P.**; *see* Pigott-Brown.

**BROWN, William Charles Langdon**, CBE 1992 (OBE 1982); Deputy Group Chief Executive and Deputy Chairman, Standard Chartered PLC, 1988–91 (Director, 1987–94); Deputy Chairman, Standard Chartered Bank, 1989–91; *b* 9 Sept. 1931; *s* of Charles Leonard Brown and Kathleen May Tizzard; *m* 1959, Nachiko Sagawa; one *s* two *d*. *Educ*: John Ruskin Sch., Croydon; Ashbourne Grammar Sch., Derbyshire. Joined Westminster Bank, 1947; transf. to Standard Chartered Bank (formerly Chartered Bank of India, Australia and China, the predecessor of Chartered Bank), 1954; Standard Chartered Bank: Tokyo, 1954–59; Bangkok, 1959–62; Hong Kong, 1962–69; Man., Singapore, 1969–72; Country Man., Bangkok, 1972–75; Area Gen. Man., Hong Kong, 1975–87. Various additional positions in Hong Kong, 1975–87, include: MLC Hong Kong; Chm., Hong Kong Export Credit Insce Corp. Adv. Bd; Mem. Council, Hong Kong Trade Develt Council; Chm., Hong Kong Assoc. of Banks; Director: Mass Railway Corp.; Wing Lung Bank Ltd. Director: Hong Kong Investment Trust, 1991–96; Kexim Bank (UK) Ltd, 1992–2002; Arbuthnot Latham & Co. Ltd, 1993–99; Chm., Atlantis Japan Growth Fund Ltd, 1996–2002. Treas., Royal Commonwealth Soc. and Commonwealth Trust, 1991–96. FCIB 1984; FInstD 1988. Hon. DSSc Chinese Univ. of Hong Kong, 1987. *Recreations*: mountain walking, snow ski-ing, yoga, philately, photography, calligraphy, classical music. *Address*: Appleshaw, 11 Central Avenue, Findon Valley, Worthing, Sussex BN14 0DS. *T*: (01903) 873175; Penthouse B, 15 Portman Square, W1H 6LJ. *T*: (020) 7487 5741, *Fax*: (020) 7486 3005. *Clubs*: Oriental; Hong Kong, Shek-O, Ladies Recreation (Hong Kong).

**BROWN, Yasmin A.**; *see* Alibhai-Brown.

**BROWNBILL, David John**; QC 2008; *b* 26 Sept. 1951; *s* of late Joseph Brownbill and Veronica Brownbill; *m* 1974, Carol Ann Allen; two *d*. *Educ*: Univ. of Nottingham (LLB). Admitted solicitor, 1980; called to the Bar: Gray's Inn, 1989; Lincoln's Inn, 2007; E Caribbean Supreme Court, 2005. Editor: Jl of Internat. Trust and Corporate Planning; International Trust Laws. *Address*: (chambers) XXIV Old Buildings, Lincoln's Inn, WC2A 3UP. *T*: (020) 7691 2424, *Fax*: (020) 7405 1360.

**BROWNBILL, Timothy Patrick**; HM Diplomatic Service; Deputy Director, Security, Foreign and Commonwealth Office, since 2014; *b* 6 Feb. 1960; *s* of George and Helen Brownbill. *Educ*: Sandbach Sch. MIL. Entered HM Diplomatic Service, 1979; Commercial Attaché, Lagos, 1982–86; Vice Consul, Madrid, 1986–90; Dep. Hd of Mission, Vilnius, 1992–94; Commercial Sec., Havana, 1996–98; Internat. Trade Dir, Trade Partners UK, 2000–02; Ambassador to Nicaragua, 2002–04; Dir for Trade Promotion, subseq. Dep. Hd of Mission, Düsseldorf, 2004–08; Hd of Mission, Ho Chi Minh City, Vietnam, 2008–11; Gp Leader for Communications and Asset Mgt, Estates Directorate, FCO, 2012–14. *Recreations*: music, literature, sports, film, languages (French, Spanish, German and some Lithuanian, Vietnamese and Arabic). *Address*: Foreign and Commonwealth Office, King Charles Street, SW1A 2AH.

**BROWNE**, family name of **Marquess of Sligo**, and **Barons Kilmaine** and **Oranmore and Browne**.

**BROWNE OF BELMONT**, Baron *cr* 2006 (Life Peer), of Belmont in the County of Antrim; **Wallace Hamilton Browne**; Member (DemU) Belfast East, Northern Ireland Assembly, 2007–11; *b* 29 Oct. 1947; *s* of Gerald and Phyllis Hamilton Browne. *Educ*: Campbell Coll., Belfast; QUB (BSc (Hons) Zoology 1970). Biology teacher, Raney Endowed Sch., Magherafelt, 1970–2000. Mem. (DemU), Belfast City Council, 1985–2011; Lord Mayor of Belfast, 2005–06. Trustee, Somme Assoc., NI. High Sheriff, Belfast, 2002. *Address*: House of Lords, SW1A 0PW.

**BROWNE OF LADYTON**, Baron *cr* 2010 (Life Peer), of Ladyton in Ayrshire and Arran; **Desmond Henry Browne**; PC 2005; *b* 22 March 1952; *s* of Peter and Maureen Browne. *Educ*: St Michael's Acad., Kilwinning; Univ. of Glasgow. Apprentice Solicitor, Jas Campbell & Co., 1974–76; Solicitor, 1976; Asst Solicitor, 1976–80, Partner, 1980–85, Ross Harper & Murphy; Partner, McCluskey Browne, 1985–92; admitted, Faculty of Advocates, 1993. Contested (Lab) Argyll and Bute, 1992. MP (Lab) Kilmarnock and Loudoun, 1997–2010. Parly Under-Sec. of State, NI Office, 2001–03; Minister of State: (Minister for Work), DWP, 2003–04; Home Office, 2004–05; Chief Sec. to HM Treasury, 2005–06; Secretary of State: for Defence, 2006–08; for Scotland, 2007–08; Special Envoy for Sri Lanka, 2009–10. Vice-Chair, Nuclear Threat Initiative, 2014–. *Recreations*: football, reading.

**BROWNE OF MADINGLEY**, Baron *cr* 2001 (Life Peer), of Cambridge in the County of Cambridgeshire; **Edmund John Phillip Browne**, Kt 1998; FRS 2006; FREng, FIMMM, FInstPet; FInstP; Chairman, L1 Energy, since 2015 (non-executive Director, since 2013); *b* 20 Feb. 1948; *s* of late Edmund John Browne and Paula (*née* Wesz). *Educ*: King's Sch., Ely; St John's Coll., Cambridge (MA Hons; Hon. Fellow, 1997); Stanford Grad. Sch. of Business (MS Business). FIMMM (FIMM 1987); FREng (FEng 1993); FInstPet 1992; FInstP 1992. Joined British Petroleum Co., 1966; Gp Treasurer and Chief Exec., BP Finance Internat., 1984–86; Executive Vice-President and Chief Financial Officer: Standard Oil Co., 1986–87; BP America, 1987–89; Chief Exec. Officer, Standard Oil Prodn Co., 1987–89; Man. Dir and CEO, BP Exploration Co., 1989–95; Man. Dir, 1991–2007, and Gp Chief Exec., 1995–2007, British Petroleum Co. plc, subseq. BP Amoco, later BP plc; Partner, Riverstone Hldgs LLC, 2007–15. Chairman, Advisory Board: Apax Partners, 2007; Stanhope Capital, 2009–; Mubadala Oil and Gas, 2009–14; Chm., Huawei Technologies (UK), 2015–; non-executive Director: SmithKline Beecham, 1995–99; Intel Corp.,

1997–2006; Goldman Sachs, 1999–2007; Foster + Partners, 2007; Cuadrilla Resources, 2010–15 (Chm., 2011–15); Fairfield Energy, 2012–15; Pattern Energy, 2013–; Riverstone Energy Ltd, 2013–15; IHS Markit, 2018–; Mem. Supervisory Bd, DaimlerChrysler AG, 1998–2001; Mem., Climate Change Adv. Bd, Deutsche Bank, 2007–; Chm., Global Energy Adv. Bd, Accenture, 2007–; Mem. Bd, UK Res. and Innovation, 2017–. Govt Lead non-exec. Bd Mem., 2010–15. Chm., Ind. Review of Higher Educn Funding and Student Finance, 2010 (report published 2010). Trustee: BM, 1995–2005; Cicely Saunders Foundn, 2001–08; Tate Gall., 2007–17 (Chm., 2009–17); Chm., Trustees, Queen Elizabeth II Prize for Engrg, 2011–. President: BAAS, 2006–07; RAEng, 2006–11. Chairman: Adv. Bd, Stanford Grad. Sch. of Business, 1995–97, now Chm. Emeritus; Adv. Bd, Judge Business Sch., Cambridge (Judge Inst. of Mgt Studies), 2002–10; Adv. Bd, Sch. of Econs and Mgt, Tsinghua Univ., 2003–07, now Hon. Mem.; Internat. Adv. Bd, Blavatnik Sch. of Govt, Oxford Univ., 2011–; Bd, Donmar Warehouse, 2015–; Francis Crick Inst., 2017–; Governing Bd, Courtauld Inst., 2017–; Mem. Governing Body, London Business Sch., 1996–2000. Hon. Trustee, Chicago SO; Hon. Counsellor, Conference Bd Inc. CCMI (CIMgt 1993). Hon. FIChemE; Hon. FIMechE 2001; Hon. FRSC 2002; Hon. FGS 1999; Foreign Fellow, Amer. Acad. Arts and Scis, 2003. Hon. degrees from Heriot-Watt, Robert Gordon, Dundee, Warwick, Hull, Cranfield, Sheffield Hallam, Buckingham, Belfast, Surrey, Imperial Coll. London, Aston, Leuven, Notre Dame, Thunderbird, Colorado Sch. of Mines, Medeleyev, Arizona State and Swansea. Prince Philip Medal, Royal Acad. of Engrg, 1999; Ernest C. Arbuckle Award, Stanford Univ., 2001; Gold Medal, Inst. of Mgt, 2001. *Publications*: Beyond Business, 2010; Seven Elements that Changed the World, 2013; The Glass Closet, 2014; Connect: how companies succeed by engaging radically with society, 2015; Make, Think, Imagine - Engineering the Future of Civilisation, 2019. *Recreations*: opera, photography, books, pre-Columbian art, 18th century Venetian books and works on paper. *Address*: L1 Energy, Devonshire House, 1 Mayfair Place, W1J 8AJ. *Clubs*: Garrick, Savile.

**BROWNE, Anthony Edward Tudor**; author and illustrator of children's books, since 1976; Children's Laureate, 2009–11; *b* 11 Sept. 1946; *s* of Jack and Doris Browne; *m* 1980, Jane Franklin; one *s* one *d*. *Educ*: Whitcliffe Mount GS, Cleckheaton; Leeds Coll. of Art (BA 1967). Medical Artist, Manchester Royal Infirmary, 1969–71; designer of greetings cards, Gordon Fraser Gall., 1972–86. Hon. DEd: Kingston, 2005; Canterbury Christ Church, 2013. Silver Medal, US Soc. of Illustrators, 1994; Hans Christian Andersen Award, 2000. *Publications*: author and illustrator: Through the Magic Mirror, 1976; Walk in the Park, 1977; Bear Hunt, 1979; Bear Goes to Town, 1982; Gorilla, 1983 (Kurt Maschler Award, 1983; Kate Greenaway Medal, 1984; Boston Globe Horn Book Award, 1986; Netherlands Silver Pencil Award, 1989); Willy the Wimp, 1984; Piggybook, 1985; Willy the Champ, 1985; I Like Books, 1988; The Tunnel, 1989 (Netherlands Silver Pencil Award, 1990); Changes, 1990; Willy and Hugh, 1991; Zoo, 1992 (Kate Greenaway Medal, 1992); Big Baby, 1993; Willy the Wizard, 1995; Look What I've Got!, 1996; Things I Like, 1997; Willy the Dreamer, 1997; Voices in the Park, 1998 (Kurt Maschler Award, 1998); Willy's Pictures, 1999; My Dad, 2000; The Shape Game, 2003; Into the Forest, 2004; My Mum, 2005; Silly Billy, 2006; My Brother, 2007; Little Beauty, 2008; Me and You, 2010; Play the Shape Game, 2010; Bear's Magic Pencil, 2010; (with Joe Browne) Playing the Shape Game: a life in picture books with the Children's Laureate, 2011; How Do You Feel?, 2011; One Gorilla: a counting book, 2012; What If…?, 2013; Willy's Stories, 2014; (with Hanne Bartholin) Frida and Bear, 2015; Willy and the Cloud, 2016; Hide and Seek, 2017; Little Frida, 2019; *illustrator*: Hansel and Gretel (adapted from trans. by Eleanor Quarrie), 1981; Annalena McAfee, The Visitors Who Came to Stay, 1984; Sally Grindley, Knock, Knock!, Who's There?, 1985; Annalena McAfee, Kirsty Knows Best, 1987; Lewis Carroll, Alice's Adventures in Wonderland, 1988 (Kurt Maschler Award, 1988); Gwen Strauss, Trail of Stones (poems), 1990; Gwen Strauss, The Night Shimmy, 1991; Janni Howker, The Topiary Garden, 1993; King Kong (from story by Edgar Wallace and Merian C. Cooper), 1994; Ian McEwan, The Daydreamer, 1994; Animal Fair (traditional), 2002. *Recreations*: walking, looking, reading, going to the cinema, being with my children and grandchildren. *Address*: c/o Walker Books Ltd, 87 Vauxhall Walk, SE11 5HJ. *T*: (020) 7793 0909.

**BROWNE, Anthony Howe**; Chairman, Regulatory Policy Committee, since 2018; *b* Cambridge, 19 Jan. 1967; *s* of Patrick and Gerd Browne; *m* 2003, Paula Higgins; one *s* one *d*. *Educ*: Trinity Hall, Cambridge (BA Hons Maths 1988). Ed., Ford Communications Network, 1991–93; BBC: researcher, Money Prog., 1993–94; broadcast journalist, Business Breakfast, 1994–95; Business Reporter, Radio, 1995–97; Econs corresp., TV and Radio, 1997–98; The Observer: Econs corresp., 1998; Dep. Business Ed., 1999; Health Ed., 1999–2002; The Times: Envmt Ed., 2002–03; Brussels corresp., 2003–06; Chief Political corresp., 2006–07; Dir, Policy Exchange, 2007–08; Policy Dir, London Mayor's Office, 2008–11; Manifesto Dir, Mayor of London's Re-election Campaign, 2011–12; Hd, Govt Relns for Europe, Middle East and Africa, Morgan Stanley, 2012; Chief Exec., BBA, 2012–17. *Publications*: The Euro: should Britain join?, 2001; Do we Need Mass Immigration?, 2002. *Recreations*: walking, running, climbing, eating, drinking, helping caterpillars turn into butterflies.

**BROWNE, Anthony Percy Scott**; Chairman, British Art Market Federation, since 1996; *b* 8 Jan. 1949; *s* of late Percy Browne and Pamela Browne (*née* Exham); *m* 1976, Annabel Louise Hankinson; three *d*. *Educ*: Eton Coll.; Christ Church, Oxford (MA Modern Hist.). Dir, Christie's, 1978–96; Sen. Consultant, Christie's Internat., 1996–. Member: Cultural Industries Export Adv. Gp, 1998–2001; Ministerial Adv. Panel on Illicit Trade, 1999–2003; Adv. Panel, Goodison Review, 2003 (report, Securing the Best for our Museums). Member: Bd, Eur. Fine Art Foundn, 1999–; Council, Amer. Mus. in Britain, 2011–18. Hon. Associate, Soc. of Fine Art Auctioneers, 2005. Vice Chm., Art Fortnight London, 2004–05. Trustee, Raise from the Ruins, 1978–80. *Publications*: (contrib.) Who Owns the Past?, 2005; (contrib.) Fine Art and High Finance, 2010. *Recreations*: fishing, gardening. *Address*: British Art Market Federation, 10 Bury Street, SW1Y 6AA. *T*: (020) 7389 2148. *Clubs*: Turf, Grillion's.

**BROWNE, Benjamin James**; QC 1996; a Recorder, since 2000; *b* 25 April 1954; *s* of late Percy Basil Browne and Jenefer Mary Browne; *m* 1987, Juliet Mary Heywood; one *s* one *d*. *Educ*: Eton Coll.; Christ Church, Oxford (MA). Called to the Bar, Inner Temple, 1976; Hd of Chambers, 2 Temple Gdns, 2005–15. An Asst Recorder, 1998–2000. *Recreations*: country pursuits, gardening. *Address*: 2 Temple Gardens, Temple, EC4Y 9AY. *T*: (020) 7822 1200. *Club*: Boodle's.

**BROWNE, Dr (Brendan) Mark**; Director of Strategic Policy, Equality and Good Relations Directorate, Executive Office (formerly Director of Finance, Strategic Planning and Social Change Directorate, Office of the First Minister and Deputy First Minister), Northern Ireland, since 2015; *b* Belfast, 17 Aug. 1958; *s* of Brendan and Marie Browne; *m* 1984, Maureen Patricia Caldwell; two *s* one *d*. *Educ*: St Patrick's Coll., Knock, Belfast; Queen's Univ. Belfast (BA Hons Econ. and Social Hist. 1980; PhD Econ. and Social Hist. 1989). Statistician, Dept of Finance and Personnel, NI, 1985–91; Department of Education, Northern Ireland: Head: Stats and Res., 1991–96; Sch. Policy, 1996–99; Sch. Funding and Admin, 1999–2002; Post-Primary Rev. Team, 2002–03; Finance Dir and Hd, Strategic Planning, 2003–06; Prog. Dir, Educn and Skills Authy Implementation Team, 2006–09; Dep. Sec., Policy, Dept of Agriculture and Rural Develt, NI, 2009–13; Dir of Resources,

Regeneration, Internat. Relns and Instnl Rev. Directorate, Office of First and Dep. First Minister, NI, 2013–15. *Recreations:* soccer (coaching and watching) (University Blue), golf, walking, gardening, cycling, reading, foreign travel. *Address:* Executive Office, Castle Buildings, Belfast BT4 3SR.

BROWNE, Carolyn, CMG 2017; HM Diplomatic Service; Director, Verification Division, Organisation for the Prohibition of Chemical Weapons, since 2019; *b* 19 Oct. 1958; *d* of late Brig. C. C. Ll. Browne and Margaret Browne (*née* Howard). *Educ:* Godolphin Sch.; S Wilts Grammar Sch., Salisbury; Bristol Univ. (BSc Hons Microbiol.); Linacre Coll., Oxford (DPhil Bacterial Genetics 1985). Joined HM Diplomatic Service, 1985; Second, later First, Sec., Moscow, 1988–91; FCO, 1991–93; UKMIS to UN, NY, 1993–97; FCO, 1997–99; Hd, Human Rights Policy Dept, FCO, 1999–2002; Counsellor (External Relns), UK Perm. Repn to EU, Brussels, 2002–05; FCO, 2005–07; Ambassador to Azerbaijan, 2007–11; Ambassador to Kazakhstan, 2013–17; Sen. Advr, Cabinet Office, 2018. *Address:* c/o Foreign and Commonwealth Office, King Charles Street, SW1A 2AH.

BROWNE, Colin; *see* Browne, J. C. C.

BROWNE, Most Rev. Denis George, CNZM 2001; Bishop of Hamilton (NZ), (RC), 1994–2014; *b* 21 Sept. 1937; *s* of Neville John Browne and Catherine Anne Browne (*née* Moroney). *Educ:* Holy Name Seminary, Christchurch, NZ; Holy Cross College, Mosgiel, NZ. Assistant Priest: Gisborne, 1963–67; Papatoetoe, 1968–71; Remuera, 1972–74; Missionary in Tonga, 1975–77; Bishop of Rarotonga, 1977–83; Bishop of Auckland, 1983–94. Hon. DD; DUniv Waikato, 2016. *Recreation:* golf.

BROWNE, Desmond John Michael; QC 1990; Recorder, 1994–2008; *b* 5 April 1947; *s* of Sir Denis John Browne, KCVO, FRCS and Lady Moyra Blanche Madeleine Browne, DBE; *m* 1973, Jennifer Mary Wilmore; two *d*. *Educ:* Eton College; New College, Oxford (Scholar). Called to the Bar, Gray's Inn, 1969, Bencher, 1999 (Vice-Treas., 2014, Treas., 2015). Asst Recorder, 1991–94. Mem., Investigatory Powers Tribunal, 2018–. Chm., Bar Council, 2009 (Vice-Chm. 2008). Pres., Council of the Inns of Court, 2016–. Hon. Mem., Australian Bar Assoc., 2009. *Recreations:* Australiana, Venice, Sussex Downs. *Address:* 5 Gray's Inn Square, Gray's Inn, WC1R 5AH. *T:* (020) 7242 2902. *Clubs:* Brooks's, Beefsteak.

BROWNE, Prof. (Elizabeth) Janet, (Janet Bell), PhD; FLS; Aramont Professor of the History of Science, Harvard University, since 2006; *b* 30 March 1950; *d* of Douglas Maurice Bell and Elizabeth Mary Bell (*née* Edelsten); *m* 1972, Nicholas Browne; two *d*. *Educ:* Trinity Coll., Dublin (BA Hons 1972); Imperial Coll., London (MSc 1973; PhD 1978). Antiquarian bookseller, 1973–75; Wellcome Inst. for Hist. of Medicine, 1979–83 and 1993–2006, Lectr, then Reader, 1993–2002; Prof. in Hist. of Biology, Wellcome Trust Centre for Hist. of Medicine at UCL, 2002–06. Associate Ed., Correspondence of Charles Darwin, 1983–91. Vis. Sen. Res. Fellow, King's Coll., Cambridge, 1996–97. Member: Blue Plaque Panel, English Heritage, 1999–2006; Liby Cttee, Royal Soc., 2001–05. President: British Soc. for Hist. of Sci., 2002–04; Hist. of Sci. Soc., 2015–17; Section L, AAAS, 2016–17. Mem., Acad. Internat. d'histoire des Scis, 2005. Dibner Dist. Fellow, Huntington Liby, Calif, 2017. FLS 2003; Corresp. FBA 2010. Hon. DSc TCD, 2009. Ed., British Jl for Hist. of Sci., 1993–99. Founders' Medal, Soc. for Hist. of Natural Hist., 2003. *Publications:* The Secular Ark: studies in the history of biogeography, 1983; (jtly) Dictionary of the History of Science, 1981; Charles Darwin: voyaging, 1995; Charles Darwin: the power of place, 2002 (winner, Biog. Section, Nat. Book Critics Circle, 2002; W. H. Heinemann Award, RSL, 2003; James Tait Black Prize (Biog.), Pfizer Prize, Hist. of Sci. Soc., 2004); Darwin's Origin of Species: a biography, 2006; The Quotable Darwin, 2017. *Recreation:* gardening. *Address:* Science Center 371, Department of the History of Science, Harvard University, 1 Oxford Street, Cambridge, MA 02138, USA.

BROWNE, Gillian Brenda B.; *see* Babington-Browne.

BROWNE, Graham David; Associate, National College for Teaching and Leadership (formerly National College for School Leadership); Education Consultant, Brown and Grey Ltd; *b* 6 July 1953; *s* of Edwin and Pamela Browne; *m* 1977, Janet Manning; two *d*. *Educ:* Coll. of St Mark and St John, Plymouth (BEd Geog., Educn, Geol.). Teacher, Prendergast Sch., Catford, 1975–80; with Murdo Maclean & Sons Ltd, Stornoway, 1980–84; Hd of Year, Barnwell Sch., Stevenage, 1984–88; Sen. Teacher, John Bunyan Upper Sch., Bedford, 1988–91; Dep. Hd, Beaumont Sch., St Albans, 1991–95; Principal, Estover Community Coll., Plymouth, 1995–2009; Exec. Principal, Estover Fedn, later Tor Bridge Partnership, Plymouth, 2009. Regl Leader, Nat. Coll. Sch. Leadership, 2006–07; Associate Headteacher, Specialist Schs and Academies Trust; Chairman: Plymouth Assoc. of Secondary Headteachers, 2005–06; Wise Adv. Gp, Plymouth CC, 2007. Advr, Letts Publishers, 1986–87. Teacher of Year Award, SW Reg., Leadership, 2002. *Recreations:* building, orchards, soccer (West Ham United supporter), travel, writing, film, music, member of Chagford Gospel Church.

BROWNE, Very Rev. Dr Herman Beseah; President, Cuttington University, since 2016; *b* 11 March 1965; *s* of George D. Browne and Clavender Railey Browne; *m* 2008, Trokon Lisa Chea; two *d*, and one *s* decd by a previous marriage. *Educ:* Cuttington UC, Liberia (BA Theol.); King's Coll., London (BD; AKC); Heythrop Coll., London (DPhil 1994). Ordained priest, 1987; Co-ordinator of Studies, Simon of Cyrene Theol Inst., London, 1994–96; Archbp's Asst Sec. for Anglican Communion and Ecumenical Affairs, 1996–2001; Archbishop of Canterbury's Sec. for Anglican Communion Affairs, 2001–05; Hd of Theology Dept, Cuttington Univ. Graduate Sch., Liberia, 2005–08; Vice-Pres. for Academic Affairs, African Methodist Episcopal Univ., Liberia, 2008–10; Dean, Trinity Cathedral, Episcopal Ch of Liberia, 2010–16. Canon of Canterbury Cathedral, 2001–05, now Emeritus. Chm., Liberian Community Orgn, UK, 1995–96. *Publications:* Theological Anthropology: a dialectic study of the African and Liberian traditions, 1996, 2nd edn 1998; (ed with G. Griffith-Dickson) Passion for Critique: essays in honour of F. J. Laishley, 1997. *Recreations:* photography, table tennis, movies, music… and often upsetting those I love most. *Address:* Cuttington University, Suokoko Bong County, PO Box 10–0277, 1000 Monrovia 10, Liberia. *T:* 6912417. *E:* herman_gblayon@yahoo.com.

BROWNE, J. B.; *see* Saxton, J. H. C.

BROWNE, His Honour (James) Nicholas; QC 1995; a Circuit Judge, 2006–17; *b* 25 April 1947; *o s* of late James Christopher Browne, MC and Winifred Browne (*née* Pirie); *m* 1981, Angelica Elizabeth Mitchell, a Circuit Judge (*d* 2006); two *d*. *Educ:* Cheltenham Coll.; Liverpool Univ. (LLB 1969). Called to the Bar, Inner Temple, 1971 (Duke of Edinburgh Entrance Schol.); Bencher 2002; Midland (formerly Midland and Oxford) Circuit, 1971–2006; Asst Recorder, 1990–93; a Recorder, 1993–2006. Mem., Bar Council, 1992–94 (Mem., Professional Conduct Cttee, 1993–94). Chairman, Code of Practice Appeal Board: Prescription Medicines Code of Practice Authy, 2000–05; Assoc. of British Pharmaceutical Industry, 2000–05. *Recreations:* cricket, squash, theatre, spending time with family and friends. *E:* nickbrowneqc@hotmail.com. *Clubs:* MCC, Garrick; Cumberland Lawn Tennis.

BROWNE, Janet; *see* Browne, E. J.

BROWNE, Jeremy Richard; International Business Ambassador, Aberdeen Standard Investments, since 2018; *b* 17 May 1970; *s* of Sir Nicholas Walker Browne, KBE, CMG and of Diana (*née* Aldwinckle); *m* 2004, Charlotte (*née* Callen) (marr. diss. 2008); partner, Rachel Binks; one *s* one *d*. *Educ:* Univ. of Nottingham (BA 1992). Pres., Students' Union, Univ. of Nottingham, 1992–93. Dewe Rogerson Ltd, 1994–96; Dir of Press and Broadcasting, Lib Dem Party, 1997–2000; Edelman Communications Worldwide, 2000–02; Associate Dir, Reputation Inc., 2003–04. MP (Lib Dem) Taunton, 2005–10, Taunton Deane, 2010–15. Lib Dem spokesman on foreign affairs, 2005–06; Lib Dem dep. spokesman on home affairs, 2006–07; Lib Dem Shadow Chief Sec. to Treasury, 2007–10; Minister of State: FCO, 2010–12; Home Office, 2012–13. Member: Home Affairs Select Cttee, 2005–08; Political and Constitutional Affairs Select Cttee, 2013–14. Contested (Lib Dem) Enfield Southgate, 1997. Mem. Adv. Bd, Reform, 2005–16. Special Rep. to Europe, City of London, 2015–18. Hon. Prof. of Politics, Univ. of Nottingham, 2015–18 (Internat. Advr, 2015–17). Hon. Vice Pres., Canning House, 2016–. *Publications:* Race Plan, 2014; Why Vote Liberal Democrat, 2014. *Recreations:* Queens Park Rangers, Somerset CCC, American politics, travel, 20th century art.

BROWNE, John Anthony; a District Judge (Magistrates' Courts) (formerly Stipendiary Magistrate), S Yorkshire, 1992–2013; *b* 25 Aug. 1948; *s* of George Henry Browne and Margaret Browne (now Wheeler); *m* 1971, Dr Jill Lesley Atfield; one *s* three *d*. *Educ:* St Peter's de la Salle, Bournemouth; Sheffield Univ. (LLB Hons). Admitted solicitor, 1975; in private practice with Elliot Mather Smith, Chesterfield and Mansfield, 1975–92. *Recreations:* tennis, hill-walking, ski-ing, running (slowly), reading, supporting Sheffield Wednesday.

BROWNE, (John) Colin (Clarke); Founder and Chief Executive Officer, Colin Browne Strategic Communications Ltd, since 2010; Chairman, Voice of the Listener and Viewer, since 2012; Partner, The Maitland Consultancy, 2000–09; *b* 25 Oct. 1945; *s* of late Ernest Browne, JP and Isobel Sarah Browne (*née* McVitie); *m* 1984, Karen Lascelles Barr; one *s*. *Educ:* Wallace High Sch., Lisburn, Co. Antrim; Trinity Coll., Dublin (BA). Post Office, then British Telecommunications, 1969–94: Dir, Chairman's Office, 1980–85; Chief Exec., Broadband Services, 1985–86; Dir, Corporate Relations, 1986–94; Dir of Corporate Affairs, BBC, 1994–2000. Non-exec. Dir, Centre for Effective Dispute Resolution, 2012–17. Member: HDA (formerly HEA), 1996–2003; Spongiform Encephalopathy Cttee, 2003–04; Govt Communications Review Gp, 2003; Communications Consumer Panel, 2008–12. Trustee: BBC Children in Need, 1994–2000; One World Broadcasting Trust, 1997–2003; Inst. of Internat. Communications, 1998–2000; Edinburgh Unesco City of Literature, 2009–14. FCIPR. *Recreations:* sport, music, reading.

BROWNE, John Ernest Douglas Delavalette; Senior Investment Strategist, Euro-Pacific Capital (New York), since 2008; Op-ed Columnist, Pittsburgh Tribune Review, since 2008; Visiting Fellow, Heritage Foundation, Washington DC, since 2008; *b* Hampshire, 17 Oct. 1938; *s* of late Col Ernest Coigny Delavalette Browne, OBE, and Victoria Mary Eugene (*née* Douglas); *m* 1st, 1965, Elizabeth Jeannette Marguerite Garthwaite (marr. diss.); 2nd, 1986, Elaine Margaret Schmid Boylen (marr. diss. 2003). *Educ:* Malvern; RMA Sandhurst; Cranfield Inst. of Technology (MSc); Harvard Business Sch. (MBA). Served Grenadier Guards, British Guiana (Battalion Pilot), Cyprus, BAOR, 1959–67; Captain 1963; TA, Grenadier Guards (Volunteers), 1981–91, Major 1985. Associate, Morgan Stanley & Co., New York, 1969–72; Pember & Boyle, 1972–74; Dir, ME Ops, Eur. Banking Co., 1974–78; Man. Dir, Falcon Finance Mgt Ltd, 1978–95; Vice Pres., Investments, Salomon Smith Barney, subseq. Smith Barney Inc., 1995–2004. Editor, Financial Intelligence Report, Newswax Media Inc., 2006–08. Director: Worms Investments, 1981–83; Scansat (Broadcasting) Ltd, 1988–93; Internat. Bd, World Times (Boston), 1988–2001; Tijari Finance Ltd, 1989–92; Adviser: Barclays Bank Ltd, 1978–84; Trustees Household Div., 1979–83. Director: Churchill Private Clinic, 1980–91; Drug Free America, 1998–2003; Greater Palm Beach Symphony, 1998–2003; World Affairs Council, Palm Beaches, 2003–09. Councillor (C), Westminster Council, 1974–78. MP (C) Winchester, 1979–92; introduced: Trades Description Act (Amendment) Bill, 1988; Protection of Animals (Amendment) Act, 1988; Protection of Privacy Bill, 1989; Armed Forces (Liability for Injury) Bill, 1991. Member: H of C Treasury Select Cttee, 1982–87; Social Services Select Cttee, 1991–92; Secretary: Conservative Finance Cttee, 1982–84; Conservative Defence Cttee, 1982–83; Chairman: Conservative Smaller Business Cttee, 1987–90 (Sec., 1984–87); Lords and Commons Anglo-Swiss Soc., 1979–92 (Treas., 1984–87; Sec., 1987–92); UK deleg. to N Atlantic Assembly, 1986–92 (rapporteur on human rights, 1989–92). Contested: (Ind C) Winchester, 1992; (Ind Against a Federal Europe) Hampshire South and Wight, EP election, 1994; (UK Ind): Falmouth and Camborne, 2001; NE, EP election, 2004; N Devon, 2005. Mem., NFU, 1980–90. Mem., Winchester Preservation Trust, 1980–90; Patron, Winchester Cadets Assoc., 1980–90; Trustee, Winnall Community Assoc., 1981–94; President: Winchester Gp for Disabled People, 1982–92; Hursley Cricket Club, 1985–90. Mem. Court, Univ. of Southampton, 1979–90; Governor, Malvern Coll., 1982–. Liveryman, Goldsmiths' Co., 1982–. OStJ 1979 (Mem., Chapter Gen., 1985–90). Interests include: economics, gold and internat. monetary affairs, defence, broadcasting. *Publications:* Tarantula: an Anglo American Special Forces hunt for bin Laden, 2003; Grenadier Grins, 2006; Hidden Account of the Romanovs, 2013; various articles on finance, gold (A New European Currency—The Karl), defence, Middle East, Soviet leadership. *Recreations:* golf, riding, sailing, shooting, ski-ing. *E:* johnbrowne@post.harvard.edu. *Clubs:* Boodle's, Turf, Special Forces; Fishers Island Yacht (New York); Palm Beach Yacht.

BROWNE, Air Vice-Marshal John Philip Ravenscroft, CBE 1985; *b* 27 April 1937; *s* of late Charles Harold Browne and Lorna Browne (*née* Bailey); *m* 1962, Gillian Dorothy Smith; two *s*. *Educ:* Brockenhurst County High Sch.; Southampton Univ. (BSc(Eng)). CEng, FICE. Commissioned Airfield Construction Branch, RAF, 1958; appts in NEAF and UK, 1959–66; transf. to Engineer Branch, 1966; RAF Coll., Cranwell, 1966–67; aircraft engineering appts, RAF Valley and MoD, 1967–71; RAF Staff Coll., 1972; OC Engrg Wing, RAF Valley, 1973–75; staff appts, MoD and HQ RAF Germany, 1975–82; MoD (PE), 1982–89: Asst Dir, Harrier Projects, 1982–85, Dir, Electronics Radar Airborne, 1985–86, Dir, Airborne Early Warning, 1986–89; Dir Gen. Support Services (RAF), MoD, 1989–92; RAF retd, 1992; Dir Engrg, 1992–95, Dir Systems, 1995–96, NATS, CAA. Pres., RAF Airfield Construction Officers' Assoc., 1991–2017. Trustee, Bletchley Park Trust, 1999–2009. *Publications:* (with M. T. Thurbon) Electronic Warfare, 1998. *Recreations:* family, aviation, military history and a good glass of wine. *Club:* Royal Air Force.

BROWNE, Mark; *see* Browne, B. M.

BROWNE, Nicholas; *see* Browne, J. N.

BROWNE, Robert W.; *see* Woodthorpe Browne.

BROWNE, Robert William M.; *see* Moxon Browne.

BROWNE, Simon Peter Buchanan; QC 2011; *b* Birkenhead, 5 Nov. 1959; *s* of late John Browne and Marcelle Browne; *m* 1991, Amanda Jane Gillett; two *d*. *Educ:* King Edward VI Sch., Southampton; Univ. of East Anglia (LLB Hons 1981); Inns of Court Sch. of Law (Dist.). Called to the Bar, Middle Temple, 1982; in practice as a barrister, specialising in catastrophic injuries, professional regulation, and costs litigation; Barrister Assessor in High Court, 2007–. Accredited Mediator, 2015; Qualified Arbitrator, 2015. Chm., Bar Tribunals and Adjudication Service, 2013–18; Member: Bar Council and Law Soc. Jt Tribunal, 2013–; Civil Justice Council, 2013–18. Chm., Topsy Ojo Testimonial Cttee, 2013–14. *Recreations:* mountains (incl. ski-ing and crofting in Scotland), tennis (lawn and padel - playing and spectating), Rugby, cocker spaniels. *Address:* Temple Garden Chambers, 1 Harcourt Buildings, Temple, EC4Y 9DA. *T:* (020) 7583 1315. *Clubs:* Reform, Hurlingham, Ivy; London Irish Rugby Football.

**BROWNE-CAVE, Sir John Robert Charles C.;** *see* Cave-Browne-Cave.

**BROWNE-WILKINSON, Simon;** QC 1998; barrister; *b* 18 Aug. 1957; *s* of Baron Browne-Wilkinson, PC; *m* 1988, Megan Tresidder (*d* 2001); one *s* one *d*. *Educ:* City of London Sch.; Magdalen Coll., Oxford (BA Jurisprudence 1979). Called to the Bar, Lincoln's Inn, 1981, Bencher, 2008; in practice at the Bar, 1981–2018. *Recreation:* sailing.

**BROWNING,** family name of **Baroness Browning**.

**BROWNING, Baroness** *cr* 2010 (Life Peer), of Whimple in the County of Devon; **Angela Frances Browning**; *b* 4 Dec. 1946; *d* of late Thomas Pearson and Linda Pearson (later Chamberlain); *m* 1968, David Browning; two *s*. *Educ:* Westwood Girls' Grammar Sch.; Reading Coll. of Technol.; Bournemouth Coll. of Technol. FInstSMM. Management Consultant. MP (C) Tiverton, 1992–97, Tiverton and Honiton, 1997–2010; Dep. Chm., Cons. Party, 2006–10. Parly Sec., MAFF, 1994–97; Opposition spokesman: on educn and disability, 1997–98; on trade and industry, 1999–2000; Shadow Leader, H of C, 2000–01. Minister of State for Crime Prevention and Anti-social Behaviour Reduction, Home Office, 2011. Mem., Electoral Commn, 2010–11; Chair, Adv. Cttee on Business Appts, 2015–Jan. 2020. Vice Pres., InstSMM, 1997–2011. Mem. and Vice Pres., Nat. Autistic Soc.; Nat. Vice Pres., Alzheimer's Disease Soc., 1997–. *Recreations:* theatre, opera. *Address:* House of Lords, SW1A 0PW.

**BROWNING, Very Rev. Dr Derek;** Parish Minister, Morningside Parish Church, Edinburgh, since 2001; *b* Edinburgh, 24 May 1962; *s* of late John Browning and Mary Browning (*née* Shanks). *Educ:* N Berwick High Sch.; Corpus Christi Coll., Oxford (MA Hons); St Mary's Coll., Univ. of St Andrews (BD Hons); Princeton Theol Seminary (DMin 1997). Ordained 1987; Parish Minister, Cupar Old Parish Church, 1987–2001. Moderator of the Gen. Assembly of the Church of Scotland, 2017–18. *Recreations:* reading, theatre, cooking, croquet, opera, film, writing. *Address:* 20 Braidburn Crescent, Edinburgh EH10 6EN. *T:* (0131) 447 1617. *E:* derek.browning@churchofscotland.org.uk. *Club:* New (Edinburgh).

**BROWNING, Rt Rev. George Victor;** Convenor, Anglican Communion Environment Network, 2005–11; Bishop of Canberra and Goulburn, 1993–2008; *b* 28 Sept. 1942; *s* of John and Barbara Browning; *m* 1965, Margaret Rowland; three *s*. *Educ:* Ardingly Coll.; Lewes County Grammar Sch., Sussex; St John's Coll., Morpeth, NSW (ThL 1st cl. Hons 1965); Charles Sturt Univ. (BTh Hons 2011; PhD 2015). Curate: Inverell, 1966–68; Armidale, 1968–69; Vicar, Warialda, 1969–73; Vice Warden and Lectr in Old Testament Studies and Pastoral Theol., St John's Coll., Morpeth, 1973–75 (Acting Warden, 1974); Rector of Singleton, Rural Dean and Archdeacon of the Upper Hunter, 1976–84; Rector of Woy Woy and Archdeacon of the Central Coast, 1984–85; Bishop of the Northern Reg., Brisbane, 1985–92; Principal, St Francis' Theol Coll., 1988–92; Bishop of the Coastal Reg., and Asst Bishop, dio. of Brisbane, 1992–93; Priest-in-charge, Wriggle Valley, Salisbury, 2008–09. President: Australia Palestine Advocacy Network, 2013–; Christians for an Ethical Soc., 2014–. Hon. DLitt Charles Sturt Univ., 2007. *Publications:* Sabbath and the Common Good: prospects for a new humanity, 2015. *Recreations:* reading, beekeeping, landcare. *Address:* 24 Henry Place, Long Beach, NSW 2536, Australia. *T:* (2) 4472 7470. *W:* georgebrowning.com.au.

**BROWNING, Helen Mary,** OBE 1998; DL; farmer and business woman; Chairman, Eastbrook Farms Organic Meat, since 1997; Director, Soil Association, since 2011; *b* 22 Nov. 1961; *d* of late Robert Roland Browning and Sheila Mary Browning (*née* Harris); *m* 1989, Henry George Stoye (separated); one *d*. *Educ:* Harper Adams Agricl Coll. (BSc Agricl Technol.). Chairman: British Organic Farmers, 1991–97; Soil Assoc., 1997–2001 (Dir, Food and Farming, 2004–09); Dir of External Affairs, NT, 2010–11. Member: MLC, 1998–2008; Agric. and Envmt Biotechnol. Commn, 1998–2005; Policy Commn on Future of Food and Farming, 2001–02; Chairman: Food Ethics Council, 2000–16 (Mem. Council, 1998–); Animal Health and Welfare England Implementation Gp, 2005–09; Comr, Food, Farming and Countryside Commn, RSA, 2017–. Member: Steering Cttee, Food Chain Centre, 2002–05; Bd, Organic Milk Suppliers Co-op., 2002–11. Trustee, RSPB, 2016–. MInstD 2000. DL Wilts, 2015. *Publications:* (with T. Finney) Pig: tales from an organic farm, 2018. *Recreations:* sport, especially squash, walking, food, reading, travel. *Address:* Eastbrook Farm, Bishopstone, Swindon, Wilts SN6 8PW. *T:* (01793) 792042, *Fax:* (01793) 791239. *Club:* Farmers.

**BROWNING, Prof. Keith Anthony,** PhD; FRS 1978; FRMetS; Director, Joint Centre for Mesoscale Meteorology, 1992–2003, and Professor in Department of Meteorology, 1995–2003, now Professor Emeritus, University of Reading; *b* 31 July 1938; *s* of late Sqdn Ldr James Anthony Browning and Amy Hilda (*née* Greenwood); *m* 1962, Ann Muriel (*née* Baish), BSc, MSc; one *s* two *d*. *Educ:* Commonweal Grammar Sch., Swindon, Wilts; Imperial Coll. of Science and Technology, Univ. of London. BSc, ARCS, PhD, DIC. FRMetS 1962 (Hon. FRMetS 2006); CMet 1994–2015. Research atmospheric physicist, Air Force Cambridge Research Laboratories, Mass, USA, 1962–66; in charge of Meteorological Office Radar Research Lab., RSRE, Malvern, 1966–85; Dep. Dir (Phys. Res.), 1985–89, Dir of Res., 1989–91, Met. Office, Bracknell; Principal Research Fellow, 1966–69; Principal Scientific Officer, 1969–72; Sen. Principal Scientific Officer, 1972–79; Dep. Chief Scientific Officer, 1979–89; Chief Scientific Officer, 1989–91. Director: NERC Univs Weather Res. Network, 2000–03; NERC Univs Facility for Atmospheric Measurements, 2001–03. Ch. Scientist, Nat. Hail Res. Experiment, USA, 1974–75. Visiting Professor: Dept of Meteorology, Reading Univ., 1988–94; Leeds Univ., 2006–. World Climate Research Programme: Member: British Nat. Cttee, 1988–89; Scientific Steering Gp, Global Energy and Water Cycle Expmt, 1988–96 (Chm., Cloud System Sci. Study, 1992–96); WMO/ICSU Jt Scientific Cttee, 1990–94; World Weather Research Programme: Mem., WMO Interim Sci. Steering Cttee, 1996–98; Mem., Sci. Steering Cttee, 1998–2005. Royal Meteorological Society: Mem. Council, 1971–74, 1979–81, 1987–91 and 1994–99 (Vice-Pres., 1979–81, 1987–88 and 1990–91; Pres., 1988–90); Mem., Accreditation Bd, 1993–99; Chm., 1994–99; Member: Editing Cttee, Qly Jl RMetS, 1975–78; Inter-Union Commn on Radio Meteorology, 1975–78; Internat. Commn on Cloud Physics, 1976–84; British Nat. Cttee for Physics, 1979–84; British Nat. Cttee for Geodesy and Geophysics, 1983–89 (Chm., Met. and Atmos. Phys. Sub-Cttee, 1985–89, Vice-Chm., 1979–84); NERC, 1984–87; British Nat. Cttee for Space Res., 1986–89 (Remote Sensing Sub-Cttee, 1986–89); Royal Soc. Interdisciplinary Sci. Cttee for Space Res., 1990–91. MAE, 1989; For. Associate, US Nat. Acad. of Engrg, 1992. UK Nat. Correspondent, Internat. Assoc. of Meteorology and Atmospheric Physics, 1991–94. L. F. Richardson Prize, 1968, Buchan Prize, 1972, William Gaskell Meml Medal, 1982, Symons Gold Medal, 2001, RMetS; L. G. Groves Meml Prize for Meteorology, Met. Office, 1969; Meisinger Award, 1974, Jule Charney Award, 1985, Carl-Gustaf Rossby Research Medal, 2003, Amer. Met. Soc. (Fellow of the Society, 1975; Hon. Mem., 2010); Charles Chree Medal and Prize, Inst. of Physics, 1981. *Publications:* (ed) Nowcasting, 1982; (ed jtly) Global Energy and Water Cycles, 1999; over 200 meteorological papers in learned jls, mainly in Britain and USA. *Recreations:* photography, playing piano, walking, meteorological research.

**BROWNING, Prof. Martin James,** PhD; FBA 2008; Professor of Economics, University of Oxford, 2006–17, now Emeritus; Senior Research Fellow, Nuffield College, Oxford (Fellow, 2006); *b* Loughborough, 27 Aug. 1946; *s* of George and Daisy Browning; *m* 1969, Lisbeth Hammer; two *s* one *d*. *Educ:* London School of Econs (MSc 1979); Tilburg Univ. (PhD 1993). Lectr, Bristol Univ., 1979–84; Prof. of Econs, McMaster Univ., 1984–97; Prof. of Econs, 1997–2006, Dir, Centre for Applied Microeconometrics, 2001–08, Univ. of Copenhagen. Fellow, Econometric Soc., 1996. John Rae Prize, Canadian Econs Assoc., 1996. *Publications:* (jtly) Economics of the Family, 2014; over 60 articles. *Address:* Slotsgade 18, Fredensborg, Denmark. *E:* martin.browning@econ.ku.dk.

**BROWNING, Philip Harold Roger;** a District Judge (Magistrates' Courts), Norfolk, 2004–11; *b* 25 Aug. 1946; *s* of late Harold and Barbara Browning; *m* 1972, Linda; two *s*. *Educ:* Hele's Sch., Exeter; Surbiton County Grammar Sch.; Windsor Grammar Sch.; Coll. of Law. Articled T. W. Stuchbery & Son, Windsor and Maidenhead, 1964–69; admitted solicitor, 1969; Asst Solicitor, Baily, Williams & Lucas, Saffron Walden, 1969–71; Prosecuting Solicitor, Devon, 1972–81; Clerk to Justices: Axminster, Exmouth, Honiton and Wonford, 1981–85; Norwich, 1985–94; a Stipendiary Magistrate, subseq. Dist Judge (Magistrates' Courts), Shropshire, 1994–2000; a District Judge (Magistrates' Courts): West Mercia, 2000–03; Wolverhampton, 2003–04. Course Dir, continuation trng for Dist Judges (Magistrates' Courts), Judicial Studies Bd, 1997–2004. *Recreations:* books, music. *Address:* 46A Forton Road, Newport, Shropshire TF10 7JR. *T:* (01952) 876306.

**BROWNJOHN, Alan Charles;** poet, novelist and critic; *b* 28 July 1931; *s* of Charles Henry Brownjohn and Dorothy Brownjohn (*née* Mulligan); *m* 1st, 1960, (Kathleen) Shirley Toulson (marr. diss. 1969; she *d* 2018); one *s*, and one step *s* one step *d*; 2nd, 1972, Sandra Lesley Willingham (marr. diss. 2005). *Educ:* Brockley County Sch.; Merton Coll., Oxford (BA Hons Mod. Hist. 1953; MA 1961). Asst Master, Beckenham and Penge Boys' Grammar Sch., 1958–65; Lectr, then Sen. Lectr, Battersea Coll. of Educn, subseq. S Bank Poly., 1965–79. Visiting Lecturer: in Poetry, Polytechnic of North London, 1981–83; in Creative Writing, Univ. of N London, then London Metropolitan Univ., 2000–03. Poetry Critic: New Statesman, 1968–74; Encounter, 1978–82; Sunday Times, 1990–2013. Special Award, Writers' Guild Bks Cttee, 2007. *Publications: poetry:* The Railings, 1961; The Lions' Mouths, 1967; Sandgrains on a Tray, 1969; Warrior's Career, 1972; A Song of Good Life, 1975; A Night in the Gazebo, 1980; Collected Poems, 1983, 3rd edn 2006; The Old Flea-Pit, 1987; The Observation Car, 1990; In the Cruel Arcade, 1994; The Cat Without E-Mail, 2001; The Men Around Her Bed, 2004; Ludbrooke, And Others, 2010; The Saner Places: selected poems, 2011; A Bottle, 2015; *novels:* The Way You Tell Them, 1990 (Authors' Club prize, 1991); The Long Shadows, 1997; A Funny Old Year, 2001; Windows on the Moon, 2009; Enjoyment, 2016; *translations:* Goethe, Torquato Tasso (with Sandra Brownjohn), 1986; Corneille, Horace, 1995. *Recreations:* walking, listening to music, left-wing censoriousness. *Address:* 2 Belsize Park, NW3 4ET. *T:* (020) 7794 2479.

**BROWNLEE, Derek Scott;** Director, Scotland, Commercial and Private Banking, Royal Bank of Scotland, since 2014 (Head of Research and Briefing, 2011–13; Director, Corporate Banking Division, 2013–14); *b* 10 Aug. 1974; *s* of David Melville Brownlee and Jean Chisholm Brownlee. *Educ:* Selkirk High Sch.; Univ. of Aberdeen (LLB 1st Cl. Hons). CA 1999. Ernst & Young: Accountant, 1996–99; Consultant, 1999–2001; Sen. Consultant, 2001–02; Hd, Taxation and Pensions Policy, Inst. Dirs, 2002–04; Manager, Deloitte, 2004–05. Contested (C) Tweeddale, Ettrick and Lauderdale, Scottish Parlt, 2003, 2007; MSP (C) S of Scotland, June 2005–2011; contested (C) E Lothian, Scottish Parlt, 2011. Scottish Parliament: Member: Finance Cttee, 2005–11; Scottish Commn for Public Audit, 2007–11. Mem. Adv. Bd, Reform Scotland, 2011–. Dir, Essential Edinburgh Ltd, 2016–. *Club:* Selkirk Conservative.

**BROWNLEE, Prof. George Gow,** PhD; FMedSci; FRS 1987; E. P. Abraham Professor of Chemical Pathology, Sir William Dunn School of Pathology, University of Oxford, 1980–2008; Fellow of Lincoln College, Oxford, since 1980; *b* 13 Jan. 1942; *s* of late Prof. George Brownlee; *m* 1966, Margaret Susan Kemp; one *d* (one *s* decd). *Educ:* Dulwich College; Emmanuel Coll., Cambridge (MA, PhD). Scientific staff of MRC at Laboratory of Molecular Biology, Cambridge, 1966–80. Fellow, Emmanuel Coll., Cambridge, 1967–71. Founder FMedSci 1998. Colworth Medal, 1977, Wellcome Trust Award, 1985, Biochemical Soc.; Owren Medal (Norway), 1987; Haemophilia Medal (France), 1988. *Publications:* Determination of Sequences in RNA (Vol. 3, Part I of Laboratory Techniques in Biochemistry and Molecular Biology), 1972; Fred Sanger - Double Nobel Laureate: a biography, 2014; scientific papers in Jl of Molecular Biology, Nature, Cell, Nucleic Acids Research, etc. *Recreations:* gardening, cricket.

**BROWNLIE, Albert Dempster;** Vice-Chancellor, University of Canterbury, Christchurch, New Zealand, 1977–98; *b* 3 Sept. 1932; *s* of Albert Newman and Netia Brownlie; *m* 1955, Noelene Eunice (*née* Meyer) (*d* 2012); two *d*. *Educ:* Univ. of Auckland, NZ (MCom). Economist, NZ Treasury, 1954–55. Lecturer, Sen. Lectr, Associate Prof. in Economics, Univ. of Auckland, 1956–64; Prof. and Head of Dept of Economics, Univ. of Canterbury, Christchurch, 1965–77. Chairman: Monetary and Economic Council, 1972–78; Australia-NZ Foundn, 1979–83; UGC Cttee to Review NZ Univ. Educn, 1980–82; NZ Vice-Chancellors' Cttee, 1983–84, 1993; Member: Commonwealth Experts Group on New Internat. Economic Order, 1975–77; Commonwealth Experts Gp on Econ. Growth, 1980; Wage Hearing Tribunal, 1976. Silver Jubilee Medal, 1977. *Publications:* articles in learned jls. *Address:* 66 Clyde Road, Ilam, Christchurch 8041, New Zealand. *T:* (3) 3518925.

**BROWNLOW,** 7th Baron *cr* 1776; **Edward John Peregrine Cust;** Bt 1677; Chairman and Managing Director of Harris & Dixon (Underwriting Agencies) Ltd, 1976–82; *b* 25 March 1936; *o s* of 6th Baron Brownlow and Katherine Hariet (*d* 1952), 2nd *d* of Sir David Alexander Kinloch, 11th Bt, CB, MVO; *S* father, 1978; *m* 1964, Shirlie Edith, 2nd *d* of late John Yeomans, The Manor Farm, Hill Croome, Upton-on-Severn, Worcs; one *s*. *Educ:* Eton. Member of Lloyd's, 1961–88, and 1993–96; Director: Hand-in-Hand Fire and Life Insurance Soc. (branch office of Commercial Union Assurance Co. Ltd), 1962–82; Ermitage International Ltd, 1988–99; Vice Chm., Ermitage Global Wealth Mgt Jersey Ltd, 2007–08. High Sheriff of Lincolnshire, 1978–79. CStJ 1999 (Chm. Council, Jersey, 1996–2005). *Heir: s* Hon. Peregrine Edward Quintin Cust [*b* 9 July 1974; *m* 2010, Vanessa Monica Threapleton-Horrocks (marr. diss. 2018)]. *Address:* La Maison des Prés, St Peter, Jersey JE3 7EL. *Club:* White's.

**BROWNLOW, Air Vice-Marshal Bertrand, (John),** CB 1982; OBE 1967; AFC 1962; FRAeS; aviation consultant, since 1997; *b* 13 Jan. 1929; *s* of Robert John Brownlow and Helen Louise Brownlow; *m* 1958, Kathleen Shannon (*d* 2018); one *s* one *d* (and one *s* decd). *Educ:* Beaufort Lodge Sch. Joined RAF, 1947; 12 and 101 Sqdns, ADC to AOC 1 Gp, 103

Sqdn, 213 Sqdn, Empire Test Pilots' Sch., OC Structures and Mech. Eng Flt RAE Farnborough, RAF Staff Coll., Air Min. Op. Requirements, 1949–64; Wing Comdr Ops, RAF Lyneham, 1964–66; Jt Services Staff Coll., 1966–67; DS RAF Staff Coll., 1967–68; Def. and Air Attaché, Stockholm, 1969–71; CO Experimental Flying, RAE Farnborough, 1971–73; Asst Comdt, Office and Flying Trng, RAF Coll., Cranwell, 1973–74; Dir of Flying (R&D), MoD, 1974–77; Comdt, A&AEE, 1977–80; Comdt, RAF Coll., Cranwell, 1980–82; Dir Gen., Trng, RAF, 1982–83, retired 1984. Exec. Dir, Marshall of Cambridge (Engineering), subseq. Dir, Marshall Aerospace, 1987–94. Mem., CAA, 1994–96. Gov., Papworth Hosp. NHS Foundn Trust, 2004–08. FRAeS 1981. Silver Medal, Royal Aero Club, 1983, for servs to RAF gliding; Sword of Honour, GAPAN, 2000. *Recreations:* squash, tennis, golf, gliding (Gold C with two diamonds). *Address:* Woodside, Abbotsley Road, Croxton, St Neots PE19 6SZ. *T:* (01480) 880663. *E:* john.brownlow1@btinternet.com. *Club:* Royal Air Force.

**BROWNLOW, Kevin;** author; film director; *b* 2 June 1938; *s* of Thomas and Niña Brownlow; *m* 1969, Virginia Keane; one *d*. *Educ:* University College School. Entered documentaries, 1955; became film editor, 1958, and edited many documentaries; with Andrew Mollo dir. feature films: It Happened Here, 1964; Winstanley, 1975; dir. Charm of Dynamite, 1967, about Abel Gance, and restored his classic film Napoleon (first shown London, Nov. 1980, NY, Jan. 1981), then Advr to digital restoration and BFI release, 2016. Directed TV documentaries: Universal Horror, 1998; Lon Chaney: a thousand faces, 2000; Cecil B. DeMille: American Epic, 2003; with David Gill: Hollywood, 1980; Thames Silents, 1981–90 (incl. The Big Parade); Channel Four Silents, 1991–99 (incl. Sunrise); Unknown Chaplin, 1983; Buster Keaton: a Hard Act to Follow, 1987; Harold Lloyd—The Third Genius, 1990; D. W. Griffith, Father of Film, 1993; Cinema Europe—The Other Hollywood, 1995; with Michael Kloft: The Tramp and the Dictator, 2002; with Christopher Bird: Buster Keaton—So Funny It Hurt, 2004; Garbo, 2005; I'm King Kong!—The Exploits of Merian C. Cooper, 2005; prod., British Cinema—Personal View, 1986. Hon. Academy Award, 2011. *Publications:* The Parade's Gone By…, 1968; How it Happened Here, 1968; The War, the West and the Wilderness, 1978; Hollywood: the Pioneers, 1979; Napoleon: Abel Gance's classic film, 1983, 2nd edn 2004; Behind The Mask of Innocence, 1991; David Lean: a biography, 1996, 2nd edn 2008; Mary Pickford Rediscovered, 1999; The Search for Charlie Chaplin, 2010; (ed) The Screen of Change, by Peter Hopkinson, 2007; Winstanley, Warts and All, 2009; many articles on film history. *Recreation:* motion pictures. *E:* kevin@photoplay.co.uk.

**BROWNRIGG, Sir Michael Gawen,** 6th Bt *cr* 1816; *b* 11 Oct. 1961; *s* of Sir Nicholas Gawen Brownrigg, 5th Bt and Linda Louise Brownrigg (*née* Lovelace); *S* father, 2018, but his name does not appear on the Official Roll of the Baronetage; *m* 1990, Margaret Dillon, *d* of Dr Clay Burchell; three *s* one *d*. *Heir: s* Nicholas James Brownrigg, *b* 7 July 1993.

**BROWNSWORD, Andrew Douglas,** CBE 2014; DL; Chairman and Chief Executive, Andrew Brownsword Group, since 1993; Chairman: Bath Priory Group Ltd, since 1992; Paxton & Whitfield Ltd, since 2002; Andrew Brownsword Hotels Ltd; *s* of Douglas and Eileen Brownsword; *m* 1983, Christina Brenchley; two *d*. *Educ:* Harvey Grammar Sch., Folkestone. Formed A. Brownsword and Co., wholesale distributors of greetings cards and stationery, 1971; formed the Andrew Brownsword Collection Ltd, 1975; acquired Gordon Fraser Gallery, 1989; greetings cards business acquired by Hallmark Cards, 1994. Chairman: Bath Rugby plc, 1996–2011; Snow & Rock Ltd, 2004–11. Dir, Queensquare Farming Ltd, 2010–. DL Somerset, 2015. *Recreations:* shooting, sailing, ski-ing, hill-walking. *Address:* 4 Queen Square, Bath BA1 2HA.

**BROWNSWORD, Prof. Roger;** Professor of Law (part-time), King's College London, since 2010; Professor of Law (part-time), Bournemouth University, since 2014; Chair, UK Biobank Ethics and Governance Council, 2011–15; *b* Bangor, N Wales, 22 June 1946; *s* of Henry Walley Brownsword and Barbara Kathleen Brownsword; *m* 1971, Susan Elizabeth Marsh; two *s*. *Educ:* Friars Sch., Bangor; London Sch. of Econs and Pol Sci. (LLB 1st Cl. 1968). University of Sheffield: Asst Lectr in Law, 1968–71; Lectr in Law, 1971–80; Sen. Lectr in Law, 1980–88; Reader in Law, 1988–90; Prof. of Law, 1990–2003; Hd, Law Dept, 1999–2002; Hon. Prof., 2003–; Prof. of Law, 2003–10 and Dir, Centre for Technol., Ethics and Law in Society, 2005–10, KCL. Mem., Nuffield Council on Bioethics, 2004–10. *Publications:* (with D. Beyleveld) Law as a Moral Judgement, 1986; (with J. N. Adams) Understanding Contract Law, 1992, 4th edn 2006; (with J. N. Adams) Understanding Law, 1992, 4th edn 2006; (with D. Beyleveld) Mice, Morality and Patents, 1993; (ed jtly) Welfarism in Contract Law, 1994; (with J. N. Adams) Key Issues in Contract, 1995; (ed jtly) Law and Human Genetics: regulating a revolution, 1998; (ed jtly) Good Faith in Contract: concept and context, 1999; Contract Law: themes for the twenty-first century, 2000, 2nd edn 2006; (with D. Beyleveld) Human Dignity in Bioethics and Bio-Law, 2001; Human Rights, 2004; (with D. Beyleveld) Consent in the Law, 2007; Rights, Regulation and the Technological Revolution, 2008; (ed with K. Yeung) Regulating Technologies: legal futures, regulatory frames and technological fixes, 2008; Smith and Thomas: a casebook on contract, 12th edn, 2009, 13th edn 2015; (ed jtly) The Foundations of European Private Law, 2011; (with M. Goodwin) Law and the Technologies of the Twenty-First Century, 2012; (ed jtly) Cambridge Handbook of Human Dignity, 2014; (ed jtly) Oxford Handbook on Law, Regulation and Technology, 2017; (ed jtly) Contract and Regulation: a handbook on new methods of law making in private law, 2017; Law, Technology and Society: re-imagining the regulatory environment, 2019. *Recreations:* exploring the South-West coastline, jazz guitar and piano, Manchester City Football Club. *Address:* 6 Welbeck Close, Dronfield Woodhouse, Dronfield, Derbys S18 8ZT. *T:* (01246) 410460; Flat 2, Eversleigh, 48 West Cliff Road, Bournemouth BH4 8BB. *T:* (01202) 757455. *E:* roger.brownsword@kcl.ac.uk.

**BRUCE;** *see* Hovell-Thurlow-Cumming-Bruce.

**BRUCE,** family name of **Earl of Elgin, Barons Aberdare** and **Bruce of Bennachie** and **Lord Balfour of Burleigh.**

**BRUCE, Lord; Charles Edward Bruce;** DL; board director, not-for-profit sector; *b* 19 Oct. 1961; *s* and *heir* of 11th Earl of Elgin, *qv; m* 1st, 1990, Amanda (marr. diss. 2000), *yr d* of James Movius; two *s* one *d*; 2nd, 2001, Dr Alice Enders; one *s*. *Educ:* Eton College; Univ. of St Andrews (MA Hons); Univ. of Dundee (MSc). A Page of Honour to HM the Queen Mother, 1975–77. Dep. Chm., Assoc. for Protection of Rural Scotland, 1998–2001; former Dir, Ashra Gp Ltd (Envmtl Consultants); Director: Scottish Lime Centre Trust, 1994–; Environmental Trust for Scotland, 1996–. Mem., Internat. Adv. Council, Internat. Academic Forum, 2010–; Pres., Democracy Forum, 2016–. Trustee, Historic Scotland Foundn, 2001–; Chm. Patrons, Nat. Galls of Scotland, 2006–11; Patron: Scottish Centre of Tagore Studies, Edinburgh Napier Univ., 2011–; Clans and Scottish Societies of Canada, 2017–; Mem. Council, Standing Council of Scottish Chiefs, 2017–; Chm., Kolkata Scottish Heritage Trust, 2008–. Dir, Canadian Friends of Scotland Foundn, 2006–; Hon. Pres., St Andrew Soc. (formerly Hon. Vice Pres.), 2007–12; Hon. Patron, Japan Soc. of Scotland, 2008–; Hon. Keeper, Keepers of the Quaich, 2009; Pres., Dunfermline United Burns Club, 2011 (Chm., 2005–10). Mem., Queen's Bodyguard for Scotland, Royal Co. of Archers, 2003. DL Fife, 1997. Hon. Major, 31 Combat Engr Regt (The Elgins), Canadian Forces, 2007; Officer, 78th Fraser Highlanders, Fort St Helen Garrison, Montreal. FSAScot. Paolozzi Gold Medal, Nat. Galls of Scotland, 2012. *Heir: s* Hon. James Andrew Charles Robert Bruce, Master of Bruce, *b* 16 Nov. 1991. *Address:* The Abbey House, Culross, Fife KY12 8JB. *T:* (01383) 880333, *Fax:* (01383) 881218.

**BRUCE OF BENNACHIE,** Baron *cr* 2015 (Life Peer), of Torphins in the County of Aberdeen; **Malcolm Gray Bruce,** Kt 2012; PC 2006; *b* 17 Nov. 1944; *s* of David Stewart Bruce and Kathleen Elmslie (*née* Delf); *m* 1st, 1969, Veronica Jane Wilson (marr. diss. 1992); one *s* one *d*; 2nd, 1998, Rosemary Vetterlein; one *s* two *d*. *Educ:* Wrekin Coll., Shropshire; St Andrews Univ. (MA 1966); Strathclyde Univ. (MSc 1970). Liverpool Daily Post, 1966–67; Buyer, Boots Pure Drug Co., 1967–68; A. Goldberg & Son, 1968–69; Res. Information Officer, NE Scotland Develt Authority, 1971–75; Marketing Dir, Noroil Publishing House (UK), 1975–81; Jt Editor/Publisher/Dir, Aberdeen Petroleum Publishing, 1981–84. Called to the Bar, Gray's Inn, 1995. MP Gordon, 1983–2015 (L 1983–88, Lib Dem, 1988–2015). Dep. Chm., Scottish Liberal Party, 1975–84 (Energy Spokesman, 1975–83); Liberal Parly Spokesman on Scottish Affairs, 1983–85, on Energy, 1985–87, on Trade and Industry, 1987–88; Alliance Parly Spokesman on Employment, 1987; Lib Dem Spokesman on Natural Resources (energy and conservation), 1988–90, on Trade and Industry, 1992–94, 2003–05, on Treasury affairs, 1994–99; Chm., Parly Lib Dems, 1999–2001; Lib Dem Spokesman on envmt, food and rural affairs, 2001–02. Member: Select Cttee on Trade and Industry, 1992–94, Treasury, 1994–98; Standards and Privileges Cttee, 1999–2001; EP rapporteur on recognition of sign languages, 2001–05, on political prisoners in Azerbaijan, 2003–05; Chair, Select Cttee on Internat. Develt, 2005–15. Leader, Scottish Liberal Democrats, 1988–92; Dep. Leader, Liberal Democrats, 2014–15. Mem. Bd, Britain in Europe, 2004–05. Rector of Dundee Univ., 1986–89. Vice-Pres., Nat. Deaf Children's Soc., 1990– (Pres., Grampian Br., 1985–); Trustee, RNID, 2004–10. *Publications:* A New Life for the Country: a rural development programme for West Aberdeenshire, 1978; Putting Energy to Work, 1981; (with others) A New Deal for Rural Scotland, 1983; (with Paddy Ashdown) Growth from the Grassroots, 1985; (with Ray Michie) Toward a Federal UK, 1997. *Recreations:* theatre, music, travel, fresh Scottish air. *Address:* House of Lords, SW1A 0PW. *E:* brucem@parliament.uk.

**BRUCE, Hon. Adam Robert;** WS; Marchmont Herald of Arms, since 2012; *b* Edinburgh, 18 Jan. 1968; *s* of 11th Earl of Elgin, *qv; m* 2003, Maria Sofia, *yr d* of Angelo Granito Pignatelli di Belmonte, 13th Principe di Belmonte; two *s*. *Educ:* Glenalmond Coll.; Balliol Coll., Oxford (BA (Hons) 1989; MA 1994; Pres., Oxford Union, 1989); Univ. of Edinburgh (LLB 1992). Admitted: Solicitor, 1993; WS, 2001; solicitor in private practice, 1993–2006; Dir, Public Policy, McGrigors, 1998–2006; CEO, Airtricity UK Ltd, 2006–08; Global Hd of Corporate Affairs, Mainstream Renewable Power, 2008–. Chairman: British Wind Energy Assoc., subseq. RenewableUK, 2007–10; Offshore Wind Prog. Bd, 2012–15; Seastar Offshore Wind Industrial Alliance, 2014–15; Vice-Pres., European Wind Energy Assoc., 2012–14; Member: Exec. Bd, Global Wind Energy Council, 2017–; Steering Bd, IRENA Coalition for Action, 2019–. Mem., Arbuthnott Commn, 2004–06. Mem., Maths, Phys and Life Scis Develt Bd, Univ. of Oxford, 2010–. Trustee: Policy Inst., 2006–08; St Andrew's Trust for Scots Heraldry, 2007–; Mitsubishi UFJ Trust Oxford Foundn, 2014–; Nat. Mus of Scotland, 2017–. Finlaggan Pursuivant, 2006–08; Unicorn Pursuivant, 2008–12. Mem., Queen's Bodyguard for Scotland, Royal Co. of Archers, 2006–. Mem. Council, WS Soc., 2016–. FRSA; FSA (Scot) 2014. OStJ 2014. *Address:* Mainstream Renewable Power, Arena House, Arena Road, Sandyford, Dublin 18, Ireland. *Clubs:* Pratt's; New (Edinburgh).
*See also* Lord Bruce.

**BRUCE, Prof. Alistair Cameron,** PhD; Associate Dean for Research and Professor of Risk and Governance, Nottingham Business School, Nottingham Trent University, since 2018; *b* 21 May 1955; *s* of Ian Paterson Bruce and Margaret Muriel Bruce; *m* 1989, Gillian Amy Tinker; one *s* two *d*. *Educ:* Univ. of St Andrews (MA Hons Econs 1977); Heriot-Watt Univ. (PhD Econs 1982). Lectr, Heriot-Watt Univ., 1980–81; University of Nottingham: Lectr, 1981–94; Sen. Lectr, 1994–99; Prof. of Decision and Risk Analysis, 1999–2018; Dir, 2003–07, Dir of Research, 2008–10 and 2011–14, Dep. Dean, 2010–15, Dean, 2015–17, Nottingham Univ. Business Sch. Chair, Res. Cttee, Chartered Assoc. of Business Schs. *Publications:* Decisions: risk and reward (with J. E. V. Johnson), 2008; articles in learned jls in areas of econs, mgt, finance, organisational behaviour, decision making, psychology and business history. *Recreations:* horseracing, football (especially supporting Derby County FC), visiting pubs, gardening, cooking, wine, railway history. *Address:* Nottingham Business School, Nottingham Trent University, 50 Shakespeare Street, Nottingham NG1 4FQ. *T:* (0115) 848 6867. *E:* Alistair.bruce@ntu.ac.uk.

**BRUCE, Christopher,** CBE 1998; dancer, choreographer, opera producer; Artistic Director, Rambert Dance Company, 1994–2002; Associate Choreographer, Houston Ballet, since 1997 (Resident Choreographer, 1989–97); *b* Leicester, 3 Oct. 1945; *m* Marian Bruce; two *s* one *d*. *Educ:* Ballet Rambert Sch. Joined Ballet Rambert Company, 1963; leading dancer with co. when re-formed as modern dance co., 1966; Associate Dir, 1975–79; Associate Choreographer, 1979–87; Associate Choreographer, London Fest. Ballet, later English Nat. Ballet, 1986–91. Leading roles include: Pierrot Lunaire, The Tempest (Tetley); L'Après-Midi d'un Faune (Nijinsky); Cruel Garden (also choreographed with Lindsay Kemp); choreographed: for Ballet Rambert: George Frideric (1st work), 1969; For Those Who Die as Cattle, 1971; There Was a Time, 1972; Weekend, 1974; Ancient Voices of Children, 1975; Black Angels, 1976; Cruel Garden, 1977; Night with Waning Moon, 1979; Dancing Day, 1981; Ghost Dances, 1981; Berlin Requiem, 1982; Concertino, 1983; Intimate Pages, 1984; Sergeant Early's Dream, 1984; Ceremonies, 1986; Crossing, 1994; Meeting Point, 1995; Quicksilver, 1996; Stream, 1997; Four Scenes, 1998; God's Plenty, 1999; Grinning in Your Face, 2001; A Steel Garden, 2005; Hush, 2009 (Best Choreography Award, Critics' Circle, 2010); Some Sort of Island Dance, 2015; for London Festival Ballet, later English National Ballet: Land, 1985; The World Again, 1986; The Dream is Over, 1987; Swansong, 1987; Symphony in Three Movements, 1989; for Tanz Forum, Cologne: Wings, 1970; Cantata, 1981; for Nederlands Dans Theater: Village Songs, 1981; Curses and Blessings, 1983; Moonshine, 1993; for Houston Ballet: Gautama Buddha, 1989; Journey, 1990; Nature Dances, 1992; Hush, 2005; for Geneva: Rooster, 1991 (restaged for London Contemporary Dance Theatre, 1992); Kingdom, 1993; for London Contemporary Dance Theatre, Waiting, 1993; for Royal Ballet, Three Songs, Two Voices, 2005; for Ballet Central: Shift, 2007; Für Alina, 2011; Morning and Moonlight, 2015; Mya, 2016; for Ballet Mainz, Dance at the Crossroads, 2007; for Ballet Kiel, Ten Poems, 2009; for Nat. Dance Co. Wales, Dream, 2012; for Phoenix Dance Th., Shadows, 2014; works for Batsheva Dance Co., Munich Opera Ballet, Gulbenkian Ballet Co., Australian Dance Theatre, Royal Danish Ballet, Royal Swedish Ballet. Kent Opera: choreographed and produced: Monteverdi's Il Ballo delle Ingrate, 1980; Combattimento di Tancredi e Clorinda, 1981; chor. John Blow's Venus and Adonis, 1980; co-prod Handel's Agrippina, 1982. Choreographed Mutiny (musical), Piccadilly, 1985. TV productions: Ancient Voices of Children, BBC, 1977; Cruel Garden, BBC, 1981–82; Ghost Dances, Channel 4, 1982, Danmark Radio, 1990; Requiem, Danish-German co-prodn, 1982; Silence is the end of our Song, Danish TV, 1984. Hon. Vis. Prof., Exeter Univ., 2009. Hon. Life Mem., Amnesty Internat., 2002. Hon. DArt De Montfort, 2000; Hon. DLitt Exeter, 2001. Evening Standard's inaugural Dance Award, 1974; Internat. Theatre Inst. Award, 1993;

Evening Standard Ballet Award for outstanding artistic achievement, 1996; de Valois Award, Critics' Circle Nat. Dance Awards, 2003. *Address:* c/o Rambert Dance Co., 99 Upper Ground, SE1 9PP; Houston Ballet, 601 Preston, Houston, TX 77002, USA.

**BRUCE, Fiona;** Presenter: BBC Television News, since 1999; Antiques Roadshow, since 2008; Fake or Fortune?, since 2011; Question Time, since 2019; *b* 25 April 1964; *d* of John and Rosemary Bruce; *m* 1995, Nigel; one *s* one *d*. *Educ:* Hertford Coll., Oxford (MA French/Italian). Joined BBC, 1989: researcher, Panorama, 1989–91; reporter: Breakfast News, 1991–92; First Sight, 1992–93; Public Eye, 1993–95; Newsnight, 1995–98; Presenter: Antiques Show, 1998–2000; Six O'Clock News, 1999; Ten O'Clock News, 1999–; Crimewatch UK, 2000–08; Real Story, 2003–07; Call My Bluff, 2003–05; The Queen's Palaces, 2011; Hive Minds, 2015. *Recreation:* horse riding. *Address:* c/o BBC News, Broadcasting House, Portland Place, W1A 1AA.

**BRUCE, Fiona Claire;** MP (C) Congleton, since 2010; *b* Wick, 26 March 1957; *d* of late Allan Stewart Riley and Greta Riley (*née* Scott); *m* 1990, Richard John Bruce; two *s*. *Educ:* Burnley High Sch.; Howell's Sch., Llandaff; Manchester Univ. (LLB); Chester Law Coll. (LLB). Admitted solicitor, 1981; Founder and Sen. Partner, Fiona Bruce & Co. LLP, 1988–. Mem. (C) Warrington BC, 2004–10 (Exec. Mem. for Value for Money and Finance, 2006–09). Contested (C) Warrington S, 2005. Mem., Internat. Develt Select Cttee, 2012–17 (Chm., Sub-Cttee on Work of Ind. Commn for Aid Impact, 2016–17); Mem., Jt Cttee on Human Rights, 2015–; Vice Chm., All Party Parly Dying Well Gp, 2012–15; Chairman, All Party Parliamentary Group: on ProLife, 2013–; on Supporting Couple Relationships, 2014–; on Alcohol Harm, 2015–; on Religious Educn, 2015–; Co-Chairman, All Party Parliamentary Group: on N Korea, 2013– (Vice Chm., 2012–13); on Foetal Alcohol Syndrome, 2015–; Chm., Cons. Party Human Rights Commn, 2014–. Mem. Bd, Lawyers' Christian Fellowship, 1996–2004; Pres., Warrington Law Soc., 2009. Lay Canon, Chester Cathedral, 2018–. *Publications:* (contrib.) There is Such a Thing as Society, 2002. *Recreations:* family, countryside. *Address:* House of Commons, SW1A 0AA.

**BRUCE, Sir (Francis) Michael Ian;** *see* Bruce, Sir M. I.

**BRUCE, George John Done,** PPRP (RP 1959); painter of portraits, landscapes, still life, flowers; *b* 28 March 1930; *s* of 11th Lord Balfour of Burleigh, Brucefield, Clackmannan, Scotland and Violet Dorothy, *d* of Richard Henry Done, Tarporley, Cheshire; *b* of 12th Lord Balfour of Burleigh, *qv*. *Educ:* Byam Shaw Sch. of Drawing and Painting; by his portrait sitters. Pres., Royal Soc. of Portrait Painters, 1991–94 (Hon. Sec., 1970–84; Vice-Pres., 1984–89). *Recreations:* ski-ing, windsurfing. *Address:* 6 Pembroke Walk, W8 6PQ. *T:* (020) 7937 1493. *Club:* Athenæum.

**BRUCE, Rt Rev. George Lindsey Russell;** Bishop of Ontario, 2002–11; *b* 20 June 1942; *s* of late Harold George Bruce and Helen Florence (*née* Wade); *m* 1965, Theodora Youmatoff; three *s* two *d*. *Educ:* Coll. Militaire Royal de St Jean; Royal Military Coll., Kingston (BA Hons 1964); Canadian Land Forces Command and Staff Coll., Kingston (psc 1970); Montreal Diocesan Coll. (LTh, Dip. Min. 1987; Hon. DD, 2003). Served in staff appts, Canadian Army, 1959–86; retd with rank of Colonel. Ordained deacon, 1987, priest, 1987; Diocese of Ottawa: Asst Curate, St Matthew's, Ottawa, 1987–90; Rector: Parish of Winchester, 1990–96; St James, Perth, 1996–2000; Dean of Ontario, Rector of Kingston, and Incumbent, St George's Cathedral, Ontario, 2000–02. Regional Dean: Stormont, 1994–96; Lanark, 1998–2000. Regtl Chaplain to Gov. Gen.'s Foot Guards (Militia), 1988–97. *Recreations:* golf, coaching soccer. *Address:* 855 Gainsborough Place, Kingston, ON K7P 1E1, Canada.

**BRUCE, Sir Hamish;** *see* Bruce-Clifton, Sir H. H. P.

**BRUCE, Ian Cameron;** Chairman, Ian Bruce Associates Ltd, management consultancy and property co., since 1975; Member (L), Weymouth and Portland Borough Council, 2006–07 and 2012–19 (Leader, 2015–16); *b* 14 March 1947; *s* of Henry Bruce and Ellen Flora Bruce (*née* Bingham); *m* 1969, Hazel Bruce (*née* Roberts); one *s* three *d*. *Educ:* Chelmsford Tech. High Sch.; Bradford Univ.; Mid-Essex Tech. Coll. Mem., Inst. of Management Services. Student apprentice, Marconi, 1965–67; Work Study Engineer: Marconi, 1967–69; Pye Unicam, 1969–70; Haverhill Meat Products, 1970–71; Factory Manager and Work Study Manager, BEPI (Pye), 1971–74; Factory Manager, Sinclair Electronics, 1974–75; Chm. and Founder, gp of employment agencies and management consultants, 1975–. Contested (C) Burnley, 1983; MP (C) Dorset South, 1987–2001; contested (C): same seat, 2001. PPS to Social Security Ministers, 1992–94. Member, Select Committee: on Employment, 1990–92; on Science and Technol., 1995–97; on Information, 1997–2001; Vice-Chm., PITCOM, 1997–2001; Jt Chm., All Party Street Children Gp, 1992–2001; Vice Chairman: Cons. Employment Cttee, 1992; Cons. Social Security Cttee, 1995–97 (Sec., 1991–92); Cons. Educn and Employment Cttee, 1995–2001; Cons. Trade and Industry Cttee, 1999–2001; Pres., Cons. Technol. Forum, 1999–2001. Jt Chm., British Cayman Island Gp, 1995–2001; Vice Chm., British-Nepal Gp, 1993–2001; Secretary: British-Finnish Gp, 1995–2001; British-Romanian Gp, 1995–2001; Chm., European Informatics Market, 1993–2002. Parly Consultant to Telecommunication Managers Assoc., 1989–2001, to Trevor Gilbert Associates, 1993–2002, to Fedn of Recruitment and Employment Services, 1996–97. Contested (C) Yorks W, 1984, Yorks, 2004, Eur. Parlt. ICT Consultant, Engrg Manufg Trng Authy, 2001–05; Employment Expert Witness, TGA, 2001–04. Chm., Weymouth Harbour Bd, 2017–18. FCMA 2001. Foster parent, 1974–77 and 2006–08. Knight, First Class, Order of Lion of Finland, 2001. *Publications:* numerous articles in press and magazines, both technical and political. *Recreations:* swimming, scuba diving, snorkelling, writing, wind surfing, sailing, camping, walking, RYA Day Skipper, politics. *Address:* 14 Preston Road, Weymouth, Dorset DT3 6PZ. *T:* (01305) 833320. *E:* iancbruce@tiscali.co.uk.

**BRUCE, Ian Waugh,** CBE 2004; Vice-President, Royal National Institute of Blind People, since 2003 (Director-General, 1983–2003); Founder Director, 1991–2010, Visiting Professor, since 1991 and President, since 2010, Centre for Charity Effectiveness, Sir John Cass Business School, City, University of London (formerly VOLPROF, the Centre for Voluntary Sector and Not-for-Profit Management, City University Business School, then City University London); *b* 21 April 1945; *s* of Thomas Waugh Bruce and Una (*née* Eagle); *m* 1971, Anthea Christine, (Tina), *d* of Dr P. R. Rowland, FRSC; one *s* one *d*. *Educ:* King Edward VI Sch., Southampton; Central High Sch., Arizona; Univ. of Birmingham (BSocSc Hons 1968). Apprentice Chem. Engr, Courtaulds, 1964–65; Marketing Trainee, then Manager, Unilever, 1968–70; Appeals and PR Officer, then Asst Dir, Age Concern England, 1970–74; Dir, The Volunteer Centre UK, 1975–81; Controller of Secretariat, then Asst Chief Exec., Bor. of Hammersmith and Fulham, 1981–83. Chm., Coventry Internat. Centre, 1964; spokesman, Artists Now, 1973–77. Consultant, UN Div. of Social Affairs, 1970–72; Mem., Prime Minister's Gp on Voluntary Action, 1978–79; Founding Sec., Volonteurope, Brussels, 1979–81; Adviser, BBC Community Progs Unit, 1979–81. Member: Art Panel, Art Film Cttee and New Activities Cttee, Arts Council of GB, 1967–71; National Good Neighbour Campaign, 1977–79; Exec. Cttee, 1978–81, 1990–94, Adv. Council, 1998–, NCVO; Council, Retired Executives Action Clearing House, 1978–83; Adv. Council, Centre for Policy on Ageing, 1979–83; Educn Adv. Council, IBA, 1981–83; Disability Alliance Steering Cttee, 1985–93; Exec. Cttee, Age Concern England,

1986–92, 2002–04; Nat. Adv. Council on Employment of People with Disabilities, 1987–98; DHSS Cttee on Inter-Agency Collaboration on Visual Handicap, 1987–88; Bd, Central London TEC, 1990–97 (Dep. Chm., 1996–97); Council for Charitable Support, 1994–2005; Bd, Focus TEC, 1997–99; Founding Co-Chair, Disability Benefits Consortium, 1988–2001; Chair: Nat. Adv. Cttee, Johns Hopkins Univ. Comparative Non Profit Study, 1996–99; Res. Cttee, Nat. Giving Campaign, 2001–04; Internat. Bd, Internat. Soc. for Low Vision Res., 2002–05; Centre Dirs' Gp, Internat. Soc. of Third Sector Res., 2008–10; Sec., World Nonprofit Academic Centres' Council, 2008–10; Advr, Soweto Kliptown Youth Project, 2007–; Co-founder and Sen. Advr, KnowHow NonProfit, 2009–. Vice Pres., Internat. Council of Voluntarism, Civil Soc. and Social Economy Researcher Assocs, 2012–; Chm., Richmond Soc., 2012–17 (Patron, 2017–); founder Chair, Charities' Gp, CIM, 2013–. Patron, Nat. Fedn of the Blind, 2007–. FCIM 2012; CCMI (CIMgt 1991); FRSA 1991. Hon. DSocSc Birmingham, 1995. Sir Raymond Priestley Expeditionary Award, Univ. of Birmingham, 1968; UK Charity Lifetime Achievement Award, 2001 and 2003. *Publications:* Public Relations and the Social Services, 1972; (jtly) Patronage of the Creative Artist, 1974; Blind and Partially Sighted Adults in Britain, 1991; Meeting Need: successful charity marketing, 1994, 4th edn 2011; The Art of Raising Money, 2010; Communicating Causes, 2018; papers on vision impairment, voluntary and community work, older people, contemporary art, management and marketing. *Recreations:* the arts, the countryside. *Address:* Ormond House Cottage, Ormond Road, Richmond, Surrey TW10 6TH. *Club:* ICA.

**BRUCE, Karen;** choreographer and director; *b* 25 March 1963; *d* of George and Elizabeth Bruce. *Educ:* Betty Laine Theatre Arts. *Theatre:* assistant director: Annie, Crucible, Sheffield; Hello Dolly!, My One and Only, Palladium; Dir and Associate Choreographer, Fame, Cambridge Th. and tour, 1996–2007, Aldwych, 2006; Associate Dir and Choreographer: Grease, Dominion, 1993; Saturday Night Fever, Palladium, UK and world tour, 1998–99, NY, 1999–2000; Choreographer: Chorus Line, 2003, Sweet Charity, 2004, Crucible, Sheffield; Pacific Overtures, Donmar Warehouse, 2004 (Olivier Award for Best Choreography); Annie Get Your Gun, tour, 2005; Brighton Rock, Almeida, 2005; Far Pavilions, Shaftesbury, 2005; Doctor Dolittle, UK tour, 2007; Never Forget, Savoy, 2008; The Bodyguard, Dominion and US tour, 2016; Director and Choreographer: Footloose, Novello and tour, 2006; Love Me Tender, UK tour, 2015; Dir, Midnight Tango, Phoenix and UK tour, 2013; Dir and Co-choreographer, Dance 'Til Dawn, Aldwych, 2014; The Last Tango, Phoenix, 2016; has also choreographed for TV, incl. Strictly Come Dancing; choreographer, opening ceremony for Commonwealth Games, Manchester, 2002. *Address:* 2 Lavell Street, N16 9LS. *T:* (020) 7249 9180.

**BRUCE, Sir Michael Ian,** 12th Bt *cr* 1628; partner, Gossard-Bruce Co., since 1953; President, Newport Sailing Club Inc. and Academy of Sail, Newport Beach, 1978–2000; *b* 3 April 1926; *s* of Sir Michael William Selby Bruce, 11th Bt and Doreen Dalziel, *d* of late W. F. Greenwell; *S* father 1957; holds dual UK and US citizenship; has discontinued first forename, Francis; *m* 1st, 1947, Barbara Stevens (marr. diss., 1957), *d* of Frank J. Lynch; two *s*; 2nd, 1961, Frances Keegan (marr. diss., 1963); 3rd, 1966, Marilyn Ann (marr. diss., 1975), *d* of Carter Mulally; 4th, Patricia Gail (marr. diss. 1991), *d* of Frederich Root; 5th, 1994, Alessandra Conforto, MD. *Educ:* Forman School, Litchfield, Conn; Pomfret, Conn. Served United States Marine Corps, 1943–46 (Letter of Commendation); S Pacific area two years, Bismarck Archipelago, Bougainville, Philippines. Master Mariner's Ticket, 1968; Pres., American Maritime Co., 1981–2000. Mem., US Naval Inst. *Recreations:* sailing, spear-fishing. *Heir: s* Michael Ian Richard Bruce (*né* Bruce; later assumed his stepfather's surname Ross; reverted to Bruce, 2018) [*b* 10 Dec. 1950; *m* 2005, Sandra Salemi; one adopted *s*]. *Clubs:* Rockaway Hunt; Lawrence Beach; Balboa Bay (Newport Beach).

**BRUCE, Michael Stewart Rae;** *see* Marnoch, Rt Hon. Lord.

**BRUCE, Prof. Peter George,** PhD; FRS 2007; FRSE; FRSC; Wolfson Professor of Materials, University of Oxford, since 2014; Fellow, St Edmund Hall, Oxford, since 2014; *b* 2 Oct. 1956; *s* of George H. Bruce and Gladys I. Bruce; *m* 1982, Margaret Duncan; one *s* one *d*. *Educ:* Aberdeen Grammar Sch.; Univ. of Aberdeen (BSc 1978; PhD 1982). FRSC 1994; FRSE 1995. Postdoctoral Res. Fellow, Univ. of Oxford, 1982–85; Lectr, Heriot-Watt Univ., 1985–91; University of St Andrews: Reader, 1991–95; Founder and Dir, Centre for Advanced Materials, 1994–97; Prof. of Chemistry, 1995–2007; Hd, Sch. of Chemistry, 1997–2002; Wardlaw Prof. of Chemistry, 2007–13. RSE Res. Fellow, 1989–90; Royal Soc. Pickering Res. Fellow, 1990–95; Leverhulme Res. Fellow, 1995–98; Vice Pres. and Physical Sec., Royal Soc. Tilden Lect., RSC, 2009. Award for Achievements in Materials Chem., 1999, Beilby Medal, 2003, Interdisciplinary Award, 2003, John Jeyes Lect. and Medal, 2004, Solid State Chem. Award, 2005, Barker Medal, 2014, RSC; Wolfson Merit Award, Royal Soc., 2001; Gunning Victoria Jubilee Prize Lect., RSE, 2004; Battery Div. Res. Award, 2008, Carl Wagner Award, 2011, Electrochem. Soc.; Arfvedson-Schlenk Award, German Chem. Soc., 2011; Galileo Galilei Medal, 2012; Internat. Medal for Materials Sci. and Technol., Materials Res. Soc. of India, 2015; Liversidge Award, RSC, 2016; Hughes Medal, Royal Soc., 2017. *Publications:* Solid State Electrochemistry, 1994; articles in Nature, Science, Jl of ACS, Angewandte Chemie. *Recreations:* thinking, dining, music, running. *Address:* Department of Materials, University of Oxford, Parks Road, Oxford OX1 3PH.

**BRUCE, Maj. Gen. Robert Bernard,** CBE 2016; DSO 2013; Military Secretary, 2017–19; General Officer Scotland, 2017–19; *b* Lisburn, 21 Jan. 1965; *s* of John and Edith Bruce; *m* 1995, Lorna McIntyre; one *s* one *d*. *Educ:* Aberdeen Univ. (MA); Cranfield Univ. (MA); Open Univ. (MBA). Commnd Royal Scots, 1987; Commanding Officer: Royal Scots, 2006; Royal Scots Borderers, 2006–08; Comdr, 4th Mechanized Bde, 2011–13; deployed from Perm. Jt HQ, 2014–15; Dir, Capability, Army HQ, 2015–16. *Recreations:* fly-fishing, golf, military history. *Address:* c/o Army Personnel Centre, Kentigern House, 65 Brown Street, Glasgow G2 8EX. *T:* (0141) 224 3010. *Clubs:* Caledonian; Royal Scots, New (Edinburgh).

**BRUCE, Prof. Steve,** PhD; FBA 2003; FRSE; Professor of Sociology, University of Aberdeen, since 1991 (Head, School of Social Science, 2002); *b* 1 April 1954; *s* of George Bruce and Maria (*née* Ivanova-Savova); *m* 1988, Elizabeth Struthers Duff; one *s* two *d*. *Educ:* Queen Victoria Sch., Dunblane; Univ. of Stirling (BA 1976; PhD 1980). Queen's University, Belfast: Lectr in Sociol., 1978–87; Reader in Sociol., 1987–89; Prof. of Sociol. and Hd, Dept of Sociol., 1989–91. FRSE 2005. *Publications:* No Pope of Rome: militant Protestantism in modern Scotland, 1985; God Save Ulster!: the religion and politics of Paisleyism, 1986; The Rise and Fall of the New Christian Right: Protestant politics in America, 1988; A House Divided: Protestantism, schism and secularization, 1990; Pray TV: televangelism in America, 1990; The Red Hand: loyalist paramilitaries in Northern Ireland, 1992; The Edge of the Union: the Ulster Loyalist political vision, 1994; Religion in Modern Britain, 1995; Religion in the Modern World: from cathedrals to cults, 1996; Conservative, Protestant Politics, 1998; Sociology: a very short introduction, 1999; Choice and Religion: a critique of rational choice theory, 1999; Fundamentalism, 2001; God is Dead: secularization in the West, 2002; Politics and Religion, 2003; (with Steven Yearley) A Dictionary of Sociology, 2004; (jtly) Sectarianism in Scotland, 2004; Paisley, 2007;

Secularization: in defence of an unfashionable theory, 2011. *Recreation:* shooting. *Address:* School of Social Science, University of Aberdeen, Aberdeen AB24 3QY. *T:* (01224) 272729, *Fax:* (01224) 273442.

**BRUCE, Dame Victoria Geraldine,** DBE 2015 (OBE 1997); PhD; CPsychol, FBPsS; FRSE; FBA 1999; Professor of Psychology, Newcastle University, since 2015 (Head, School of Psychology, 2008–15); *b* 4 Jan. 1953; *d* of late Charles Frederick Bruce and of Geraldine Cordelia Diane (*née* Giffard). *Educ:* Newcastle upon Tyne Church High Sch.; Newnham Coll., Cambridge (BA Nat. Scis 1974; MA, PhD Psychol. 1978). CPsychol, FBPsS 1989. University of Nottingham: Lectr, 1978–88; Reader, 1988–90; Prof. of Psychology, 1990–92; Prof. of Psychology, 1992–2002, Dep. Principal (Res.), 1995–2001, Stirling Univ.; Vice Principal and Hd, Coll. of Humanities and Social Sci., Univ. of Edinburgh, 2002–08. Member: Neuroscis Bd, MRC, 1989–92; ESRC, 1992–96 (Chm., Res. Progs Bd, 1992–); SHEFC, 1995–2001 (Chm., Res. Policy Adv. Cttee, 1988–2001); Chairman: Psychology Panel, RAE, 1996, 2001, HEFCE; Main Panel K, 2008 RAE, HEFCE. President: Eur. Soc. for Cognitive Psychology, 1996–98; BPsS, 2001–02; EPsS, 2010–12. Editor, British Jl of Psychology, 1995–2000. FRSE 1996. Hon. Fellow: Cardiff Univ., 2005; Edinburgh Coll. of Art, 2008. Hon. DSc: London, 2002; St Andrews, 2006; York, 2010; Hon. ScD East Anglia, 2017. *Publications:* (with P. R. Green) Visual Perception: physiology, psychology and ecology, 1985, 4th edn (with P. R. Green and M. Georgeson) 2003; Recognising Faces, 1988; (with G. W. Humphreys) Visual Cognition: computational, experimental and neuropsychological perspectives, 1989; (ed) Face Recognition (special edn of European Jl of Cognitive Psychology), 1991; (ed jtly) Processing the Facial Image, 1992; (ed with A. M. Burton) Processing Images of Faces, 1992; (ed with G. W. Humphreys) Object and Face Recognition (special issue of Visual Cognition), 1994; (with I. Roth) Perception and Representation: current issues, 2nd edn 1995; (ed) Unsolved Mysteries of the Mind: tutorial essays in cognition, 1996; (with A. Young) In the Eye of the Beholder: the science of face perception, 1998; (with A. Young) Face Perception, 2011; numerous articles in learned jls and edited books. *Recreations:* dogs, walking, games. *Address:* School of Psychology, Newcastle University, Ridley Building, Newcastle upon Tyne NE1 7RU. *T:* (0191) 208 6579.

**BRUCE-CLIFTON, Sir (Hervey) Hamish (Peter),** 8th Bt *cr* 1804, of Downhill, Londonderry; *b* 20 Nov. 1986; *s* of Sir Hervey James Hugh Bruce-Clifton, 7th Bt and of Charlotte Sara Jane, *e d* of Jack Temple Gore; *S* father, 2010. *Educ:* Harrow Sch.; Univ. of Northumbria (BSc Hons Estate Mgt). *Recreations:* tennis, golf, polo. *Heir:* half *b* Louis William Sinclair Bruce, *b* 3 Aug. 1993.

**BRUCE-GARDNER, Sir Edmund Thomas Peter,** 4th Bt *cr* 1945, of Frilford, Berks; osteopath; *b* 28 Jan. 1982; *s* of Sir Robert Henry Bruce-Gardner, 3rd Bt and Veronica Ann Bruce-Gardner (*née* Hand Oxborrow); *S* father, 2017; *m* 2013, Dr Claire Terese Ahern; one *s* one *d*. *Educ:* Univ. of Kent, Canterbury (BA Hons Social Anthropology 2004); British Sch. of Osteopathy (BOst Practical Osteopathy 2009). *Heir: s* Henry Francis Bruce-Gardner, *b* 12 Oct. 2017.

**BRUCE-GARDYNE, Lucinda Emma Kate,** FRSE; Founder, 2008 and Board Director, since 2017, Genius Foods Ltd (Executive Research and Development Director, 2008–17); *b* Stoke Mandeville, 29 April 1971; *d* of Richard Monbiot and Margaret Monbiot; *m* 1997, Hew Bruce-Gardyne; three *s*. *Educ:* Queen Mary and Westfield Coll., Univ. of London (BSc Hons Physiol. 1993); Leiths Sch. of Food and Wine (Adv. Dip. 1994). Chef de Partie, Bibendum Restaurant, 1994–95; private caterer, Tuscany and London, 1995–98; Sen. Teacher and Demonstrator, Leiths Sch. of Food and Wine, 1998–2000; cookery writer and product pioneer, 2000–08. Non-executive Director: Nat. Skills Acad. for Food and Drink, 2014–; ScaleUp Inst., 2018–; Trustee, Bd, SCI 2019–. Royal Soc. Entrepreneur in Residence, Univ. of Edinburgh, 2018–. FRSE 2017. *Publications:* Leiths Techniques Bible (jtly), 2003; How to Cook for Food Allergies, 2007; The Genius Gluten Free Cook Book, 2016. *Recreations:* mountain walking, running, classical concerts, gardening, entertaining, family, travel. *Address:* Genius Foods, 22 Northumberland Street, South West Lane, Edinburgh EH3 6JD. *T:* (0131) 285 3105. *E:* lucinda.bruce-gardyne@geniusglutenfree.com.

**BRUCE LOCKHART, Logie,** MA; Headmaster of Gresham's School, Holt, 1955–82; *b* 12 Oct. 1921; *s* of late John Harold Bruce Lockhart; *m* 1944, Josephine Agnew (*d* 2009); two *s* two *d* (and one *d* decd). *Educ:* Sedbergh School; St John's College, Cambridge (Schol. and Choral Studentship). RMC Sandhurst, 1941; served War of 1939–45; 9th Sherwood Foresters, 1942; 2nd Household Cavalry (Life Guards), 1944–45. Larmor Award, 1947; Asst Master, Tonbridge School, 1947–55. Sponsor, Nat. Council for Educnl Standards. *Publications:* The Pleasures of Fishing, 1981; Stuff and Nonsense, 1996; Now and Then, This and That, 2014; Now We are Very Old, 2015. *Recreations:* fishing, writing, music, natural history, games; Blue for Rugby football, 1945, 1946, Scottish International, 1948, 1950, 1953; squash for Cambridge, 1946. *Address:* Mead Barn, New Road, Blakeney, Norfolk NR25 7PA. *T:* (01263) 740588.

**BRUDENELL-BRUCE,** family name of **Marquess of Ailesbury**.

**BRUDNIZKI, Martin;** interior designer; Founder and Principal, Martin Brudnizki Design Studio, London and New York, since 2000; Founder, And Objects, 2015; *b* Stockholm, 1966; *s* of Andre Brudnizki and Karin Brudnizki Gamrell. *Educ:* Stockholm Univ. (BA Econ.); American Univ., London (BA Interior Design). Wolfson Design, 1993–94; David Gill Gall., 1995; David Collins Studio, 1995–99. Patron, Sir John Soane's Mus., 2016–. *Recreations:* theatre, ballet, opera, art, walking, charity work. *Address:* Martin Brudnizki Design Studio, 1G Chelsea Reach, 79–89 Lots Road, SW10 0RN. *T:* (020) 3736 7555. *E:* studio@mbds.com; 227 West 29th Street, 13th Floor, New York, NY 10001, USA. *Clubs:* Soho House, Academicians' Room, Ivy, 5 Hertford Street.

**BRUINVELS, Canon Peter Nigel Edward;** Principal, Peter Bruinvels Associates, media management and public affairs consultants, founded 1986; Managing Director, Bruinvels News & Media, since 1992; news broadcaster, political commentator and freelance journalist; *b* 30 March 1950; *er s* of late Stanley and Ninette Maud Bruinvels; *m* 1980, Alison Margaret, *o d* of Major David Gilmore Bacon, RA retd; two *d*. *Educ:* St John's Sch., Leatherhead; London Univ. (LLB Hons); Council of Legal Educn. Co. Sec., BPC Publishing, 1978–81; Sec./Lawyer, Amari PLC, 1981–82; Management Consultant and company director, 1982–. Mem., Cons. Nat. Union Exec., 1976–81. MP (C) Leicester E, 1983–87; contested (C): Leicester E, 1987; The Wrekin, 1997. Jt Chm., British Parly Lighting Gp; Vice-Chairman: Cons. Backbench Cttee on Urban Affairs and New Towns, 1984–87; Cons. Backbench Cttee on Education, 1985–87; Sec., Anglo-Netherlands Parly Gp, 1983–87; Chm., British-Malta Parly Gp, 1984–87; Member: Cons. Backbench Cttee on Home Affairs, 1983–87; Cons. Backbench Cttee on NI, 1983–87; Life Mem., British-Amer. Parly Gp, 1983. Promoter, Crossbows Act, 1987. Campaign Co-ordinator, Eastbourne, gen. election, 1992. Pres., Dorking Conservatives, 1995–2013 (Chm., 1992–95). Director: Aalco Nottingham Ltd, 1983–88; Radio Mercury and Allied Radio, 1994–97. Special Advr, DTI Deregulation Task Force on Pharmaceuticals and Chemicals, 1993. Ind. Lay Chm., NHS Complaints Procedure, 1999–2006; Member: Social Security Appeals Tribunal, 1994–99; Child Support Appeals Tribunal, 1995–99. Non-exec. Dir, E Elmbridge and Mid Surrey PCT, 2002–07. Mem., Surrey LEA, 1997–2007 (Admissions Adjudicator). Inspector, 1994–2009, Sen. Inspector, 2009–, Denominational Ch Schs, OFSTED; Mem., Dearing Implementation Gp for Ch Schs, 2001–10. Church Comr, 1992– (Member: Mission and Pastoral Cttee, 1993– (Dep. Chm., 2015–); Bd of Govs, 1998–; Mgt Adv. Cttee, 1999–2009; Assets Cttee, 2014–; Dep. Chm., Nominations and Governance Cttee, 2009–12); Dir, Church Army, 1999–2004 (Chm., Remuneration Cttee, 1999–2004); Member: Guildford Dio. Synod, 1974– (Vice-Pres., 2003–13); Chm., House of Laity, 2003–13); Gen. Synod, 1985– (Mem., 1991–96 and 2000–, Dep. Chm., 2011–, Legislative Cttee); Guildford Diocesan Bd of Educn, 1994– (Chm., 2005–08; Dep. Chm., 2008–); Gen. Synod Bd of Educn, 1996–2006; Clergy Discipline (Doctrine) Gp, 1999–2010; Guildford Crown Nominations Commn, 2003–; Lay Canon, 2002–; Mem. Coll. of Canons, 2002–. Mem. Council, 2006–, Guildford Cathedral; Dir, Guildford Diocesan Educn Trust, 2012–. Mem., Cathedrals Fabric Commn for England, 2006–16. Mem., SE England Veterans Adv. and Pensions Cttee (formerly War Pensions Cttee), 2003– (Dep. Chm., 2013–19); Chairman: Surrey Jt Services' Charities Cttee, 2004–; Queen Victoria Clergy Fund, 2016–; Hon. Sec., Surrey Military Appeals Cttee (formerly Surrey County Appeals Cttee), 2002–; Military Liaison Advr, Surrey CC, 2013–, Kent CC, 2016–, Civilian-Military Partnership Bd; Project Officer, Guildford Nat. Armed Forces Day, 2015; Mem., Surrey Standing Adv. Council for Religious Educn, 2013–. Dir, SE Reserve Forces' and Cadets' Assoc., 2016–. Accredited MoD Trainer, Forces Connect SE, 2018–. Mem., Jersey Wildlife Preservation Trust. Chm., Surrey Schs Orgn Cttee, 2000–07. Governor: York St John Univ. (formerly Ripon and York St John, then UC of York St John), 1999–2007; Whitelands Coll., Roehampton Univ., 2007– (Chm. of Govs, 2009–12); Mem. Council, Roehampton Univ., 2009–12; Mem. Ct, Univ. of Sussex, 2000–08. County Field Officer, Surrey, 2002–12, County Manager, Sussex, 2011–12, RBL. Regl Fundraiser - SE, ABF The Soldiers' Charity, 2013–. Armed Forces Champion, 11 Infantry Brigade SE, 2016–. MCIPR (MIPR 1981); FRSA 1986; FCIM 1998 (Hon. MCIM 1987; Pres., Norwest Midlands, 1997–98); MCIJ (MJI 1988); Fellow, Industry and Parliament Trust. Granted Freedom, City of London, 1980. Canterbury Cross for services to C of E, Lambeth Palace, 2017. *Publications:* Zoning in on Enterprise, 1982; Light up the Roads, 1984; Sharing in Britain's Success—a Study in Widening Share Ownership, Through Privatisation, 1987; Investing in Enterprise—a Comprehensive Guide to Inner City Regeneration and Urban Renewal, 1989. *Recreations:* political campaigning, military liaison, the media, Church of England. *Address:* 4 Dunkeld Place, Roman Road, Dorking, Surrey RH4 3EU. *T:* (01306) 887082, (mobile) 07721 411688, (office) 07535 396188. *Clubs:* Carlton, Inner Temple, Corporation of Church House.

**BRUMBY, Hon. John Mansfield,** AO 2017; Chairman: Motor Trades Association of Australia Superannuation Fund Pty Ltd, since 2011; BioCurate Pty Ltd, since 2016; Enterprise Fellow, Faculty of Business and Economics, University of Melbourne, since 2017 (Professorial Fellow, 2011–17); National President, Australia China Business Council, since 2014; *b* Melbourne, 21 April 1953; *s* of late Malcolm Mansfield Brumby and of Alison Jessie Brumby; *m* 1985, Rosemary McKenzie; one *s* two *d*. *Educ:* Ivanhoe Grammar Sch.; Melbourne Grammar Sch.; Univ. of Melbourne (BCom 1974); State Coll. of Victoria (DipEd 1975). Grad. Australian Inst. of Superannuation Trustees (Adv.) 2014. Secondary sch. teacher, 1976–80; Union Organiser, Victorian Teachers' Union, 1981–83. Consultant to finance and banking industry, 1990; COS to Federal Minister for Tourism and Resources, 1991–92. MHR (ALP) Bendigo, 1983–90; Chm., Parly Standing Cttee on Employment, Educn and Trng, 1986–90. MLA (ALP) Broadmeadows, Vic, 1993–2010; Shadow Minister for Arts and Ethnic Affairs, 1993–94; Shadow Treas., 1994–96; Shadow Minister: for Agric. and Rural Affairs, 1996–99; for Racing, 1996–99; for Multicultural and Ethnic Affairs, 1997–99; for Primary Industries, 1999; for State and Regl Develt, 1999; of Finance, 1999; Leader of the Opposition, Victoria, 1993–99; Minister: for Finance, and Asst Treas., 1999–2000; for State and Regl Develt, 1999–2006; for Regl and Rural Develt, 2006–07; for Innovation, 2002–07; Treas. of Victoria, 2000–07; Premier of Victoria, and Minister for Veterans' Affairs and for Multicultural Affairs, 2007–10. Director: Huawei Technologies (Aust.) Pty Ltd, 2011–19; Citywide Service Solutions Pty Ltd, 2012– (Chm., 2015–). Chairman: Centre for Workplace Leadership, 2014–; Olivia Newton-John Cancer Res. Inst., 2014–; Melbourne Convention and Exhibn Trust, 2017–; Director: US Studies Centre, 2013–17; Fred Hollows Foundn, 2013– (Chm., 2016–). Vice Chancellor's Fellow, Monash Univ., 2011–16; Chancellor, La Trobe Univ., 2019–. FAICD 2016. Hon. DLitt La Trobe, 2016. Centenary Medal, 2001. *Publications:* Bendigo Almanac and Tourist Guide, 1981; Restoring Democracy, 1999; The Long Haul: lessons in public life, 2015. *Recreations:* tennis, Australian football, Australian film.

**BRUMMELL, David,** CB 2005; Legal Secretary to the Law Officers, 2000–04; *b* 18 Dec. 1947; *s* of late Ernest Brummell and Florence Elizabeth Brummell (*née* Martin). *Educ:* Nottingham High Sch.; Queens' Coll., Cambridge (MA Law 1973); Inst. of Linguistics (Dips in French, German and Spanish). Articled clerk, 1971–73, Asst Solicitor, 1973–75, Simmons & Simmons, Solicitors, London; Legal Adviser: Devon CC, 1975–77; W Sussex CC, 1977–79; Legal Asst, then Sen. Legal Asst, OFT, 1979–84; Treasury Solicitor's Department: Sen. Legal Asst, 1984–86, Grade 6, 1986, Central Adv. Div.; Grade 5, 1986–89; Litigation Div., 1989–2000, Head, 1995–2000. *Recreations:* tennis, walking, music, languages, poetry. *Address:* 14A The Gateways, Park Lane, Richmond, Surrey TW9 2RB. *T:* (020) 8948 1247. *Clubs:* Athenæum; Thames Hare and Hounds.

**BRUMMELL, Paul,** CMG 2016; HM Diplomatic Service; Head, Soft Power and External Affairs Department, Foreign and Commonwealth Office, since 2018; *b* 28 Aug. 1965; *s* of late Robert George and June Brummell; *m* 2012, Adriana Mitsue Ivama; one *s*. *Educ:* St Albans Sch.; St Catharine's Coll., Cambridge (BA Hons Geog.). Joined HM Diplomatic Service, 1987; Third, later Second, Sec., Islamabad, 1989–92; FCO, 1993–94; First Sec., Rome, 1995–2000; Dep. Hd, Eastern Dept, FCO, 2000–01; Ambassador: to Turkmenistan, 2002–05; to Kazakhstan and (non-resident) to Kyrgyz Republic, 2005–09; High Comr to Barbados and (non-resident) to Antigua and Barbuda, Commonwealth of Dominica, Grenada, St Kitts and Nevis, St Lucia, and St Vincent and Grenadines, 2009–13, and concurrently Perm. Rep. to the Orgn of Eastern Caribbean States and Plenipotentiary Rep. to the Caribbean Community, 2010–13, and Consul-Gen. to the Dutch Caribbean, 2011–13; Ambassador to Romania, 2014–18. *Publications:* Turkmenistan—The Bradt Travel Guide, 2005; Kazakhstan—The Bradt Travel Guide, 2008; (jtly) Transylvania—The Bradt Travel Guide, 3rd edn 2018. *Recreations:* travel writing, glam rock. *Address:* c/o Foreign and Commonwealth Office, King Charles Street, SW1A 2AH.

**BRUMMER, Alexander;** City Editor, Daily Mail, since 2000; *b* 25 May 1949; *s* of Michael Brummer and Hilda (*née* Lyons); *m* 1975, Patricia Lyndsey Magrill; two *s* one *d*. *Educ:* Univ. of Southampton (BSc Econ. Politics); Univ. of Bradford Mgt Centre (MSc Business Admin). The Guardian: Financial Corresp., 1973–79; Washington Ed., 1979–89; Foreign Ed., 1989–90; Financial Ed., 1990–99; Associate Ed., 1998–99; Consultant Ed., Mail on Sunday, 1999. Vice-Pres., Bd of Deputies of British Jews, 2012–15. Chm., Abraham Fund Initiatives, 2015–. DUniv Bradford, 2014. Awards include: Financial Journalist of Year, British Press Awards, 1999; Best City Journalist, Media Awards, 2000; Wincott Award for Sen. Financial Journalist of Year, 2001; Newspaper Journalist of Year, 2002, Columnist of the Year, 2007, Lifetime Achievement, 2010, Workworld Media Awards; Business

Journalist of Year, World Leadership Forum, 2006; Business Journalist of the Year, London Press Club, 2009; Financial Journalist of the Year, City of London Corp., 2013; Best Financial Print Journalist, Internat. Financial Awards, 2018. *Publications:* Hanson: a biography, 1994; Weinstock: the life and times, 1999; The Crunch, 2008; The Great Pensions Robbery, 2010; Britain for Sale, 2012; Bad Banks: greed, incompetence and the next global crisis, 2014. *Recreations:* reading, antiques, football. *Address:* Daily Mail, City Office, Northcliffe House, 2 Derry Street, W8 5TT. *T:* (020) 7938 6906. *E:* alex.brummer@dailymail.co.uk. *Club:* Athenæum.

BRUNDIN, Clark Lannerdahl, PhD; Founding Peter Moores Director, School of Management Studies, University of Oxford, 1992–96; President, Templeton College, Oxford, 1992–96; *b* 21 March 1931; *s* of late Ernest Walfrid Brundin and Elinor Brundin (*née* Clark); *m* 1959, Judith Anne (*née* Maloney); two *s* two *d*. *Educ:* Whittier High Sch., California; California Inst. of Technology; Univ. of California, Berkeley (BSc, PhD); MA Oxford. Electronics Petty Officer, US Navy, 1951–55. Associate in Mech. Engrg, UC Berkeley, 1956–57; Demonstr, Dept of Engrg Science, Univ. of Oxford, 1957–58; Res. Engr, Inst. of Engrg Res., UC Berkeley, 1959–63; Univ. Lectr, Dept of Engrg Sci., Univ. of Oxford, 1963–85, Vice-Chm., Gen. Bd of the Faculties, 1984–85; Jesus College, Oxford: Fellow and Tutor in Engrg, 1964–85; Sen. Tutor, 1974–77; Estates Bursar, 1978–84; Hon. Fellow, 1985; Vice Chancellor, Univ. of Warwick, 1985–92. Vis. Prof., Univ. of Calif Santa Barbara, 1978; Vis. Schol., Center for Studies in Higher Educn, UC Berkeley, 1997–. Member: Engrg Bd, CNAA, 1976–82; CICHE, British Council, 1987–96; Adv. Bd, Oxford Centre for Higher Educn Studies, 2000–. Director: Cokethorpe Sch. Educnl Trust, 1983–96; Heritage Projects (Oxford) Ltd, 1985–97; Blackwell Science Ltd, 1990–98; Finsbury Growth Trust plc, 1995–2000; CAF America, 1997–2000 (Pres., 1998–2000); Chm., Anchor Housing Assoc., 1985–91 (Bd Mem., 1985–94). Mem. (Lib Dem) Oxford City Council, 2004–12. Governor: Oxford Poly., 1979–84; Magdalen College Sch., 1987–99; Coventry Sch. Foundn, 1991–99. Chancellor, Oxonia Univ. Network, 2014–. Freeman, City of Oxford, 2012. Hon. Fellow, Green Templeton Coll., Oxford, 2010. Hon. LLD Warwick, 2005. *Publications:* articles on rarefied gas dynamics and higher education. *Recreations:* sailing, mending old machinery, music of all sorts. *Address:* 28 Observatory Street, Oxford OX2 6EW.

BRUNDLE, Martin John; racing driver; presenter and commentator, Formula One, Sky Sports F1, since 2012; *b* 1 June 1959; *s* of late Alfred Edward John Brundle and of Alma Brundle; *m* 1981, Elizabeth Mary Anthony; one *s* one *d*. *Educ:* King Edward VII Grammar Sch., King's Lynn; Norfolk Coll. of Arts and Technol. Formula One racing driver, 1984–96 (158 Grands Prix): World Sportscar Champion, 1988; winner: Daytona 24 hours, 1988; Le Mans 24 hours, 1990. Presenter and commentator: Formula One, ITV, 1997–2008 (Best Sports Prog., BAFTA, 2006, 2007, 2008, 2010); Formula One, BBC, 2009–11. Chm., British Racing Drivers' Club, 2000–03. Grovewood Award, 1982; Segrave Trophy, 1988; RTS Sports Award, 1998, 1999, 2005 and 2006. DCL UEA, 2007. *Publications:* Working the Wheel, 2004; The Martin Brundle Scrapbook, 2013. *Recreations:* helicopter flying, motor biking. *E:* office@mb-f1.com. *Club:* British Racing Drivers' (Silverstone).

BRUNDTLAND, Gro Harlem, MD; Prime Minister of Norway, Feb.–Oct. 1981, 1986–89 and 1990–96; United Nations Special Envoy for Climate Change, 2007–10; Director General, World Health Organisation, 1998–2003; *b* 20 April 1939; *d* of Gudmund and Inga Harlem; *m* 1960, Arne Olav Brundtland; two *s* one *d* (and one *s* decd). *Educ:* Oslo and Harvard Univs. MPH. MO, Directorate of Health, 1966–68; Asst Med. Dir, Oslo Bd of Health, 1968–74; Minister of Environment, 1974–79; MP (Lab) Oslo, 1977–96; Dep. Leader, Labour Party, 1975–81; Dep. Leader, Labour Parly Gp, 1979–81, Leader, 1981–92. Member: Ind. (Palme) Commn on Disarmament and Security Issues, 1979–82; Internat. Commn on Nuclear Non-Proliferation and Disarmament, 2008–10; UN Sec. Gen.'s High Level Panel on Global Sustainability, 2010–12; Chm., UN World Commn on Envmt and Develt, 1983–87. Member: Bd, UN Foundn, 2003–; The Elders, 2007– (Dep. Chm.). Vice-Pres., Socialist Internat. Hon. DCL Oxon, 2001. Third World Prize; Indira Gandhi Prize; Blue Planet Prize. *Publications:* articles on preventive medicine, school health and growth studies, internat. issues. *Recreation:* cross-country ski-ing.

BRUNEI, HM Sultan of; *see* Negara Brunei Darussalam.

BRÜNJES, Emma Jacqueline; Founder and Director, ebp, since 2013; *b* Brighton, 8 Oct. 1981; *d* of Dr Henry Otto Brunjes, *qv*. *Educ:* Brighton and Hove High Sch. for Girls; Lancing Coll.; London Sch. of Econs and Pol Sci. (BSc Govt and Hist. 2003). Hd, Avalon Promotions, 2004–10; Gen. Manager, Nimax Theatres, 2010–13. Chair, Bd, Nabokov Th. Co., 2010–; Member: Bd, League of Ind. Producers, 2017–; Council, Stage One, 2017–. *Recreations:* theatre, opera, ballet, golf, travel, cooking, running, walking the dog. *Address:* ebp, 44 Maiden Lane, Covent Garden, WC2E 7LN. *T:* (020) 7820 9332. *E:* emma@ebpuk.com. *Clubs:* Ivy, Soho House.

BRÜNJES, Dr Henry Otto; Chairman: Premier Medical Group, since 2007; Lancing College, since 2009; English National Opera, since 2015 (Member, Board, since 2010); Medicals Direct Group, since 2018; *b* Norwich, 15 Oct. 1954; *s* of late Henry Otto Brünjes and Ellen Jane Brünjes (*née* McColl); *m* 1980, Jacqueline Mary Storey; three *s* one *d*. *Educ:* Bedford Modern Sch.; St Thomas's Hosp. Med. Sch. (BSc Anatomy 1977); Guy's Hosp. Med. Sch. (MB BS 1980). DRCOG 1982. Jun. hosp. posts, Guy's Hosp. and Royal Sussex County Hosp., 1980–85; GP and Partner, then Sen. Partner, Rottingdean, Sussex, 1985–95; CEO, Premier Med. Gp, 1995–2006; Medical Dir, Capita, 2010–16. Chairman: Rapid Trauma Assessment, 2000–06; Personal Injury Forum, BUPA, 2004–07; Newmans Clinics, 2011–; Warp Technologies, 2016–; Kuro Healthcare, 2016–; Folkington Finance, 2017–. Non-executive Director: Good Care Gp, 2011–16; Equity Syndicate Mgt Ltd, 2013–19. Pres., Sussex Medico-Chirurgical Soc., 2007. FRSocMed 1995; Fellow and Gov., Expert Witness Inst., 2002–; Fellow, Woodard Corp., 2004–; Vice-Pres., Coll. of Medicine, 2009–. Member: Develt Council, Ovingdean Hall Sch. for the Deaf, 1996–2003; Lancing Develt Council, 2009–; Council, Southwark Cathedral Develt Trust, 2012–. Gov., Bedford Modern Sch., 2004–07; Chm., Mowden Sch., 2004–08. *Recreations:* golf, soccer, piano, public speaking. *Address:* Folkington Manor, Folkington, E Sussex BN26 5SD; Flat 37, Peninsula Heights, 93 Albert Embankment, SE1 7TY. *Clubs:* Garrick, Ivy, Reform; Royal St George's Golf; Valderrama Golf (Sotogrande, Spain).

*See also* E. J. Brunjes.

BRUNNER, Adrian John Nelson; QC 1994; *b* 18 June 1946; *s* of late Comdr Hugh Brunner, DSC, RN and Elizabeth Brunner; *m* 1970, Christine Anne Hughes; one *s* four *d*. *Educ:* Ampleforth Coll.; Coll. of Law. Served RN, 1963–66. Called to the Bar, Inner Temple, 1968 (Major Schol., 1967), Bencher, 2006. Recorder, 1990–2010. *Recreations:* yachting, travel. *Address:* Furneaux Pelham Hall, Buntingford, Herts SG9 0LB; Holborn Head Farm, Scrabster, Caithness KW14 7UW. *Clubs:* Royal Yacht Squadron, Bar Yacht.

*See also* C. J. Brunner.

BRUNNER, Catherine Jane; QC 2015; a Recorder, since 2012; *b* Paddington, 5 Aug. 1972; *d* of Adrian John Nelson Brunner, *qv*; *m* 2004, Robin Pargeter; two *d*. *Educ:* St Paul's Girls' Sch.; Edinburgh Univ. (MA Hons Psychol. 1994); City Univ. (DipLaw 1995); Inns of Court Sch. of Law. Called to the Bar, Inner Temple, 1997; in practice as barrister, 1997–. Judge (pt-time) of Upper Tribunal (Admin. Appeals Chamber), 2014–. *Recreations:* painting, travelling. *Address:* Albion Chambers, Broad Street, Bristol BS1 1DR. *T:* (0117) 927 2144.

BRUNNER, Sir Hugo (Laurence Joseph), KCVO 2008; JP; Lord-Lieutenant of Oxfordshire, 1996–2008; *b* 17 Aug. 1935; *s* of Sir Felix Brunner, 3rd Bt and late Dorothea Elizabeth (*née* Irving); *m* 1967, Mary Rose Pollen; five *s* one *d*. *Educ:* Eton; Trinity Coll., Oxford (MA Hons; Hon. Fellow, 1994). With OUP, 1958–65 (First Rep., Hong Kong, 1960–62); Sales Dir, Chatto & Windus, publishers, 1966–76; Dep. Gen. Publisher, OUP, 1977–79; Man. Dir, then Chm., Chatto & Windus, 1979–85. Director: Caithness Glass Ltd, 1966–96 (Chm., 1984–91); Brunner Investment Trust PLC, 1987–99; SCM Press Ltd, 1991–97. Contested (L) Torquay, 1964 and 1966. Chm., Oxford DAC for Care of Churches, 1985–98. Governor: St Edward's Sch., Oxford, 1991–2005; Ripon Coll. Cuddesdon, 1992–2005. Dep. Steward, Univ. of Oxford, 2001–11. Pres., Oxford Civic Soc., 2010–17. High Sheriff, 1988–89, DL 1993, JP 1996, Oxon. Mem., Order of St Frideswide, 2006. Hon. LLD Oxford Brookes, 1999. *Recreations:* hill-walking, being Swiss, study of animal-powered engines. *Address:* 26 Norham Road, Oxford OX2 6SF. *T:* and *Fax:* (01865) 316431. *Clubs:* Reform, Chelsea Arts.

BRUNNER, Sir Nicholas Felix Minturn, 5th Bt *cr* 1895, of Druids Cross and Winnington Old Hall; *b* 16 Jan. 1960; *er s* of Sir John Henry Kilian Brunner, 4th Bt and of Jasmine Cecily Brunner (*née* Wardrop Moore); *S* father, 2015, but his name does not appear on the Official Roll of the Baronetage. *Heir: b* (Mark) Jonathan Irving Brunner, *b* 28 June 1962.

BRUNNING, His Honour David Wilfrid; a mediator, since 2009; a Circuit Judge, 1988–2008; a Deputy High Court Judge, Queen's Bench Division and Family Divisions, 1995–2008; *b* 10 April 1943; *s* of Wilfred and Marion Brunning; *m* 1967, Deirdre Ann Shotton; three *s*. *Educ:* Burton upon Trent Grammar Sch.; Worcester Coll., Oxford (BA (Modern History) 1965; DPA 1966). Called to the Bar, Middle Temple, 1969; Midland and Oxford Circuit, 1970–88; Assigned Judge, Designated Family Judge and Designated Civil Judge, Nottingham, 1994–2004; Judge of the Technology and Construction Court at Nottingham, 1995–2004; Designated Family Judge, Leicester County Court, 2004–08. Judge, Mental Health Rev. Tribunal, 1998–. Mem. Council, Leicester Univ., 2003–11. Lay Reader, Dio. of Leicester. *Recreations:* campanology, walking, wine, military history. *Address:* c/o Mr M. Brunning, No 5 Chambers, Fountain Court, Birmingham B4 6DR.

BRUNO, Franklin Roy, (Frank), MBE 1990; professional boxer, 1982–96; after dinner speaker and mental health campaigner; *b* 16 Nov. 1961; *s* of late Robert Bruno and of Lynette Bruno (*née* Campbell); *m* 1990, Laura Frances Mooney (marr. diss. 2001); one *s* two *d*; one *d* by Yvonne Clydesdale. *Educ:* Oak Hall Sch., Sussex. Amateur boxer, Sir Philip Game Amateur Boxing Club, 1977–80: 21 contests, 20 victories; London ABA and Nat. ABA Heavyweight Champion, 1980; professional career, 1982–96: 45 contests, 40 victories; European Champion, 1985–86; WBC World Heavyweight Champion, 1995. Pantomime appearances: Aladdin, Dominion, 1989, Nottingham, 1990, Wycombe, 2003; Robin Hood, Bristol, 1991; Jack and the Beanstalk, Bradford, 1996; Goldilocks, Birmingham, 1997, Southampton, 1999, Wolverhampton, 2001; UK theatre tour with Ricky Hatton, 2004–06. Sports Personality of Year, Stars Orgn for Spastics, 1989, 1990. *Publications:* Know What I Mean?, 1987; Eye of the Tiger, 1992; From Zero to Hero, 1996; Frank: fighting back, 2005. *Recreations:* swimming, training, driving, eating, shopping for good clothes. *E:* frank@frankbruno.co.uk.

BRUNSDEN, Prof. Denys, OBE 2004; PhD; Professor of Geography, Department of Geography, King's College, University of London, 1983–96, now Emeritus; *b* 14 March 1936; *s* of Francis Stephen Brunsden and Mabel Florence (*née* Martin); *m* 1961, Elizabeth Mary Philippa (*née* Wright); one *s* one *d*. *Educ:* Torquay Grammar Sch. for Boys; King's Coll., Univ. of London (BSc Hons Geography; PhD 1963; FKC 1998). King's College, London: Tutorial Student, 1959–60; Asst Lectr, 1960–63; Lectr, 1963–75; Reader, 1975–83. Vis. Lectr, 1964–65, Erskine Fellow, 1988, Univ. of Canterbury, NZ; Vis. Associate Prof., Louisiana State Univ., 1971; Visiting Professor: Univ. of Durham, 1996–2002; Bournemouth Univ., 1999–2005. Founder Consultant, Geomorphological Services Ltd, 1972. Chairman: British Geomorphol Res. Gp, 1985–86; Wkg Pty for Collaboration in Internat. Geomorphology, 1985–; President: Geographical Assoc., 1986–87 (Hon. Mem., 1996); Internat. Assoc. of Geomorphologists, 1989–93 (Sen. Past Pres., 1993–97; Hon. Fellow 1997); Vice-Pres., RGS, 1984–87; Hon. Mem., Polish Assoc. of Geomorphologists, 1993. Member: St George's House Consultation, 1989; Nat. Curriculum Wkg Party for Physical Educn, 1990–92. Mem. Steering Cttee, successful bid for World Heritage Site status for Dorset and E Devon Coast, 1993–; Chm., Dorset Coast Forum, 1995–2005; Trustee, Jurassic Coast Trust, 2005–. Hon. DSc: Plymouth, 2000; Bournemouth, 2002. Gill Meml Award, RGS (for contribs to study of mass movement and fieldwork), 1977; Republic of China Award Lectr, 1988–89; Assoc. of American Geographers Honours, 1991; Linton Award, British Geomorphol Res. Gp, 1993; William Smith Medal, 2000, R. H. Worth Prize, 2010, Geol Soc. of London; Glossop Lect. and Medal, Geol Soc., 2001. *Publications:* Dartmoor, 1968; Slopes, Forms and Process, 1970; (with J. C. Doornkamp) The Unquiet Landscape, 1971 (USA 1976, Australia 1976, Germany 1977); (with J. B. Thornes) Geomorphology and Time, 1977; (with C. Embleton and D. K. C. Jones) Geomorphology: present problems, future prospects, 1978; (with J. C. Doornkamp and D. K. C. Jones) The Geology, Geomorphology and Pedology of Bahrain, 1980; (with R. U. Cooke, J. C. Doornkamp and D. K. C. Jones) The Urban Geomorphology of Drylands, 1982; (with D. B. Prior) Slope Instability, 1984; (with R. Gardner, A. S. Goudie and D. K. C. Jones) Landshapes, 1989; Natural Disasters, 1990; (with A. S. Goudie) The Environment of the British Isles: an Atlas, 1995; (with R. Dikau) Landslide Recognition, 1996; (jtly) The History of the Study of Landforms, vol. 4, 2008. *Recreations:* making walking sticks and shepherd's-crooks, painting, reading thrillers, enjoying dinner parties and fine wine, talking, travelling to exotic places. *Address:* Department of Geography, King's College London, Strand, WC2R 2LS. *Club:* Geographical.

BRUNSDON, Norman Keith, AM 2000; Chairman and Senior Partner, Price Waterhouse, Australia, 1982–86; *b* 11 Jan. 1930; *s* of late G. A. Brunsdon; *m* 1953, Ruth, *d* of late W. Legg; one *s* one *d*. *Educ:* Wagga Wagga High Sch., NSW. FCA. Price Waterhouse, Australia: joined, 1951; Partner, 1963; Mem. Policy Cttee (Bd), 1970–86; Partner-in-Charge, Sydney, 1975–81; Mem., World Firm Policy Cttee (Bd) and Council of Firms, 1979–86; Agent Gen. for NSW in London, 1989–91. Dir, Arthur Yates & Co. Ltd, 1993–2001. Chm., Aust. Govt's Taxation Adv. Cttee, 1979–83; Trustee, Econ. Develt of Aust. Cttee, 1977–86. Vice-Pres., Thai-Aust. Chamber of Commerce & Industry, 1982–85; Member: Pacific Basin Econ. Council, 1982–86; Aust. Japan Business Co-op. Cttee, 1982–86. Member: Standing Cttee, C of E Dio. Sydney, 1969–74; C of E Children's Homes Cttee, 1974–84 (Treasurer, 1969–75; Acting Chm., 1972–73); Chairman: Anglican Retirement Villages, dio. Sydney, 1991–98; Anglican Foundn for Aged Care, 1993–2001. Governor, King's Sch., Parramatta, 1977–86; Trustee, Bark Endeavour Foundn Pty Ltd,

1992–2001. Hon. Mem., Cook Soc. Freeman, City of London, 1989. *Recreations:* music, opera, theatre, reading. *Address:* PO Box 675, Northbridge, NSW 1560, Australia. *T:* 0404318677. *Club:* Australian (Sydney).

**BRUNSON, Michael John,** OBE 2000; broadcaster and journalist; Political Editor, ITN, 1986–2000; *b* 12 Aug. 1940; *s* of Geoffrey Brunson and Ethel (*née* Mills); *m* 1965, Susan Margaret Brown; two *s*. *Educ:* Bedford Sch.; Queen's Coll., Oxford (BA Theol. 1963; MA). VSO, Sierra Leone, 1963–64; BBC General Trainee, 1964–65; Reporter, BBC SE Radio News, 1965–66; Asst Producer, BBC TV Current Affairs, 1966–68; Independent Television News: Reporter, 1968–72; Washington Corresp., 1972–77; Reporter, 1977–80; Diplomatic Editor, 1980–86; Campaign Reporter with Mrs Thatcher, 1979 and 1983 Gen. Elections. Chairman: Parly Lobby Journalists, 1994; Parly Press Gall., 1999. Member: Govt Adv. Gp on Citizenship Educn, 1997–98; Preparation for Adult Life Gp, QCA, 1998; Adult Learning Cttee, Learning and Skills Council, 2001–03. Trustee, Citizenship Foundn, 2000–06. Chm., Norfolk br., Oxford Univ. Soc. (formerly Oxford Soc.), 2007–15. Mem. Council, Friends of Norwich Cathedral, 2008–14. Vice Pres., Livability, 2013–16. Columnist: The House Mag. (H of C), 1989–90, 1997–99; Saga Magazine, 2000–05. Hon. LittD UEA, 2003. RTS News Event Award, 1994; RTS Judges' Award for lifetime achievement, 2000. *Publications:* A Ringside Seat (autobiog.), 2000. *Recreations:* choral singing, gardening. *Address:* Hill House, Holt Road, Letheringsett, Holt, Norfolk NR25 7YB. *E:* michael.brunson@btinternet.com. *Clubs:* Oxford and Cambridge; Norfolk (Norwich).

**BRUNT, Rev. Prof. Peter William,** CVO 2001; OBE 1994; MD, FRCP, FRCPE; Physician to the Queen in Scotland, 1983–2001; Consultant Physician and Gastroenterologist, Grampian Health Board, Aberdeen, 1970–2001; Clinical Professor of Medicine, University of Aberdeen, 1996–2001; Non-Stipendiary Minister, Diocese of Aberdeen, Scottish Episcopal Church, 1996–2007; *b* 18 Jan. 1936; *s* of late Harry Brunt and Florence J. J. Airey; *m* 1961, Dr Anne Lewis, *d* of Rev. R. H. Lewis; three *d*. *Educ:* Manchester Grammar Sch.; Cheadle Hulme Sch.; King George V Sch.; Univ. of Liverpool (MB, ChB 1959; MD 1967). FRCP 1976; FRCPE 1981. Gen. Med. training, Liverpool Royal Infirmary and Liverpool Hosps, 1959–64; Research Fellow, Johns Hopkins Univ. Sch. of Medicine, Baltimore, USA, 1965–67; Lectr in Medicine, Edinburgh Univ., 1967–68; Senior Registrar, Gastrointestinal Unit, Western Gen. Hosp., Edinburgh, 1968–69; Clin. Sen. Lectr in Medicine, Aberdeen Univ., 1970–96. Hon. Lectr in Medicine, Royal Free Hosp. Sch. of Medicine, Univ. of London, 1969–70. Medical Dir, Scottish Adv. Cttee on Distinction Awards, 2000–05; Chairman: Med. Council on Alcohol, 2004–11; Alcohol Focus Scotland, 2005. Mem., Assoc. of Physicians of GB and Ireland (Pres., 1995–96); Jt Vice-Pres., RCPE, 2005–08. Ordained deacon, 1996, priest, 1997, Scottish Episcopal Church. Hon. FRCSE 2009. *Publications:* (with M. Losowsky and A. E. Read) Diseases of the Liver and Biliary System, 1984; (with P. F. Jones and N. A. G. Mowat) Gastroenterology, 1984. *Recreations:* mountaineering, music, operatics. *Address:* 81 Wansdyke, Morpeth, Northumberland NE61 3QY. *T:* (01670) 519473.

**BRUNTISFIELD,** 3rd Baron *cr* 1942, of Boroughmuir; **Michael John Victor Warrender;** Bt 1715; *b* 9 Jan. 1949; *s* of 2nd Baron Bruntisfield and Anne Moireen, 2nd *d* of Sir Walter Campbell, KCIE; *S* father, 2007; *m* 1978, Baroness Walburga von Twickel; one *s*. *Educ:* Downside; RMA Sandhurst; Durham Univ. (BA 1972). Major, Irish Guards, 1967–86. Director: Robert Fleming Investment Mgt, 1986–2001; Jardine Fleming Investment Mgt, 1986–2001; JP Morgan Asset Mgt, 2000–01; Atlas Capital, 2001–06; Concordia Advisors, 2006–13; Mariner Investment Gp, 2013–14; CIM Investment Mgt, 2014–15; Ruffer LLP, 2016–. *Heir:* s Hon. John Michael Patrick Caspar Warrender, *b* 1 June 1996.

**BRUNTON, Sir James (Lauder),** 4th Bt *cr* 1908, of Stratford Place, St Marylebone; MD; FRCPC; Professor of Medicine, now Emeritus, and former Head of Division of Infectious Diseases, Department of Medicine, University of Toronto; *b* 24 Sept. 1947; *s* of Sir (Edward Francis) Lauder Brunton, 3rd Bt, physician, and Marjorie, *o d* of David Sclater Lewis, MSc, MD, CM, FRCPC; *S* father, 2007, but his name does not appear on the Official Roll of the Baronetage; *m* 1st, 1967, Susan Elizabeth (marr. diss. 1983), *o d* of Charles Hons; one *s* one *d*; 2nd, 1984, Beverly Anne Freedman; one *s*. *Educ:* Bishop's Coll. Sch., Montreal; McGill Univ. (BSc 1968); MD. *Heir:* s Douglas Lauder Brunton [*b* 23 Jan. 1968; *m* 2004, Prof. Susan Jennifer Leat].

**BRUNTON, Sean Alexander McKay;** QC 2018; *b* London, 13 Nov. 1966; *s* of David Brunton and Terry Brunton; *m* 1995, Erica Elizabeth Sylvia Cousins; two *s* one *d*. *Educ:* Pilgrims' Sch., Winchester; Oundle Sch.; Christ's Coll., Cambridge (BA Law 1989; MA 1993). Called to the Bar, Middle Temple, 1990; Mem., Western Circuit, 1992; Attorney Gen.'s List of Approved Counsel, 2010. *Recreations:* writing, sailing, singing. *Address:* Sherford Lodge, Haines Hill, Taunton TA1 4HW. *T:* (01392) 274898. *E:* seanbrunton@colletonchambers.co.uk. *Club:* Royal Vicomté Yacht.

**BRUNTON, Rear Adm. Steven Buchanan,** CBE 2014; Director and owner, Adjuvo Associates Ltd, since 2014; *b* Portsmouth, 26 Sept. 1959; *s* of Thomas Brunton and June Brunton; *m* 1984, Andrea Stacey; two *s*. *Educ:* Portsmouth Northern Grammar Sch.; Mayfield Sch.; RNEC Manadon (BSc, MSc); Internat. Project Mgt Assoc. (Certified Projects Dir 2011). CEng 1990; FIET 2004. Joined RN 1978; Dep. Weapons Engr Officer, HMS Sceptre, 1984–85, HMS Courageous, 1985–87; Weapon Engrg Officer, HMS Superb, 1990–92; Submarine Sea Trng Staff, 1992–94; Project Manager, Defence Information Infrastructure, 2002–05; Team Leader: Crypto and Secure Systems Integrated Project, 2005–06; Sustaining Surface Combatant Capability, 2006–07; Head: Capability (Above Water), 2007–10; Destroyers Project Team, 2010–11; Capital Ships, 2011–12; Dir Ship Acquisition, Defence Equipment and Support, 2012–14. Ind. Advr to Canadian Govt on Nat. Shipbuilding Strategy, 2016–. MCGI 1990. FCMI 2014. *Recreations:* golf, genealogy, gardening.

**BRUTON, Dr Alison Elizabeth;** Head Teacher, Queen Mary's High School, Walsall, since 2009; *b* Plymouth, 28 July 1960; *d* of William and Mildred Dart; *m* 1981, Jonathan Bruton; one *s* two *d*. *Educ:* Plymouth High Sch. for Girls; Royal Holloway Coll., Univ. of London (BSc Hons Maths 1981); Wolverhampton Poly. (PGCE 1982); Univ. of Birmingham (MEd Mgt and Policy Studies 1999; EdD Leadership in Educn 2013). NPQH 2003. Physics teacher, King Edward VI Sixth Form Coll., 1982–88; Hd of Sci., 1992–2000, Hd of Sixth Form, 1998–2000, Dep. Hd, 2000–09, Wolverhampton Girls' High Sch. Nat. Leader of Educn, 2015–. *Recreations:* church, Wolverhampton Wanderers, Star Trek, chair of academy council (primary). *Address:* Queen Mary's High School, Upper Forster Street, Walsall, W Midlands WS4 2AE. *T:* (01922) 721013. *E:* a.bruton@qmhs.org.uk. *Club:* Lansdowne.

**BRUTON, Jane;** see Bruton, V. J.

**BRUTON, John (Gerard);** company director; President, International Financial Services Centre, 2010–15; European Union Ambassador to Washington, 2004–09; *b* 18 May 1947; *s* of Matthew Joseph Bruton and Doris Bruton (*née* Delany); *m* 1981, Finola Gill; one *s* three *d*. *Educ:* St Dominic's Coll., Dublin; Clongowes Wood Coll., Co. Kildare; University Coll., Dublin (BA, BL). King's Inns, Dublin; called to the Bar, 1972. National Secretary, Fine Gael Youth Group, 1966–69. TD (Fine Gael), Meath, 1969–2004. Mem., Dáil Committee of Procedure and Privileges, 1969–73, 1982; Fine Gael Spokesman on Agriculture, 1972–73; Parliamentary Secretary: to Minister for Education, 1973–77; to Minister for Industry and Commerce, 1975–77; Fine Gael Spokesman: on Agriculture, 1977–81; on Finance, Jan.–June 1981; Minister: for Finance, 1981–82, for Industry and Energy, 1982–83, for Industry, Trade, Commerce and Tourism, 1983–86, for Finance, 1986–87; Fine Gael Spokesman on Industry and Commerce, 1987–89, on education, 1989; Leader of the House, 1982–86; Taoiseach (Prime Minister of Ireland), 1994–97; Leader of the Opposition, 1997–2001. Dep. Leader, 1987–90, Leader, 1990–2001, Fine Gael. Pres., EEC Industry, Research and Internal Market Councils, July–Dec. 1984. Member: Parly Assembly, Council of Europe, 1989–90; British-Irish Parly Body, 1993–94; Parly Assembly, WEU, 1997–98; Præsidium, Convention on the Future of Europe, 2002–04. Chm., European Sustainable Materials Platform, 2012–14. Member: Bd, Centre for European Policy Studies, 2010–; Academic Council, Martens Centre, 2012–; Bd, Co-operation Ireland, 2012–. Vice President: Christian Democrat Internat., 1998–2001; EPP, 1999–2005. Director: Ingersoll Rand, 2010–; Montpelier Reinsce, 2010–15; Pimco Irish Funds, 2018–. Dist. Fellow, Centre for Internat. Relns, Johns Hopkins Univ., 2010–; Vis., Fellow, Eur. Inst., LSE, 2010–12. Hon. DLaw: Memorial Univ., Newfoundland, 2002; NUI, 2005; Missouri, 2009. Schumann Medal, 1998. Comdr, Grand Cross of the Royal Order of Polar Star (Sweden), 2008. *Publications:* Faith in Politics: a collection of essays on politics, economics, history and religion, 2015. *Recreation:* reading history. *W:* www.johnbruton.com.

**BRUTON, (Victoria) Jane;** Deputy Editor and Director of Lifestyle, Daily Telegraph, since 2015; *b* Billinge, Wigan, 21 March 1968; *d* of Roger and Glynis Bruton; *m* 1996, Johnathan Paul Whitehead; two *s*. *Educ:* Byrchall High Sch., Ashton-in-Makerfield; Winstanley Coll., Wigan; Nottingham Univ. (BA 1st Cl. Hons English); City Univ. (Postgrad. Dip. Periodical Journalism). Sub-Editor, Chat, 1991–92; Features Editor, then Dep. Editor, Wedding and Home, 1993–96; Associate Editor, Prima, 1997; Editor: LivingEtc, 1998–2001; Eve, 2001–04; Editor-in-Chief, Grazia, 2005–15. Founder Mem., 1993–, and Trustee, 1997–2014, Trees for Cities (formerly Trees for London). *Recreations:* running, charity work. *Address:* Daily Telegraph, 111 Buckingham Palace Road, SW1W 0DT. *T:* (020) 7931 2000.

**BRUZZI, Prof. Stella, (Mrs Mick Conefrey),** PhD; FBA 2013; Dean, Faculty of Arts and Humanities, University College London, since 2017; *b* Florence, Italy, 28 Jan. 1962; *d* of Dr Stefano Bruzzi and late Zara Bruzzi; *m* 1993, Mick Conefrey; one *s* one *d*. *Educ:* St Paul's Girls' Sch., London; Univ. of Manchester (BA 1st Cl. Hons English and Drama); Univ. of Bristol (PhD 1993). Lectr, Drama Dept, Manchester Univ., 1992–93; Royal Holloway, University of London: Lectr, 1993–2000; Sen. Lectr, 2000–02; Reader, 2002–03; Prof. of Film, 2003–06; University of Warwick: Prof. of Film and TV Studies, 2006–17; Chair, Faculty of Arts, 2008–11. Leverhulme Maj. Res. Fellow, 2011–13; Plumer Vis. Res. Fellow, St Anne's Coll., Oxford, 2011–12; Vis. Prof., Univ. of Chile, 2012. *Publications:* Undressing Cinema: clothing and identity in the movies, 1997; New Documentary, 2000, rev. edn 2006 (Chinese edn 2013); (ed with Pamela Church Gibson) Fashion Cultures: theories, explorations and analysis, 2000; Bringing Up Daddy: fatherhood and masculinity in post-war Hollywood, 2005; Seven Up, 2007; Men's Cinema: masculinity and mise-en-scene in Hollywood, 2013; (ed with Pamela Church Gibson) Fashion Cultures Revisited, 2013. *Recreations:* going to cinema and theatre, reading, swimming, being with family and friends. *Address:* Department of English, University College London, Gower Street, WC1E 6BT. *T:* (home) (01865) 553251.

**BRYAN OF PARTICK,** Baroness *cr* 2018 (Life Peer), of Partick in the City of Glasgow; **Pauline Christina Bryan;** author and campaigner. Mem., Labour Party. Founding Mem., Keir Hardy Soc. *Publications:* (jtly) Class, Nation and Socialism, 2013; (ed) What Would Keir Hardie Say?, 2015; Keir Hardie and 21st Century Socialism, 2019. *Address:* House of Lords, SW1A 0PW.

**BRYAN, Ven. Christopher Paul;** Archdeacon of Malmesbury, since 2019; *b* Oxford, 10 July 1975; *s* of Robert William Bryan and Janet Patricia Bryan; *m* 2001, Chantal Louise Suffield-Jones; one *s* two *d*. *Educ:* Royal Grammar Sch., High Wycombe; University Coll., Oxford (BA Biol Scis 1996); St John's Coll., Durham (BA Theology 1999); Cranmer Hall, Durham (DipMin). Ordained deacon, 2000, priest, 2001; Curate, Old Swinford, 2000–04; Priest-in-charge, Lechlade, 2004–10; Rector, Gauzebrook, 2010–19; Area Dean, N Wilts, 2017–19. Trustee, Teach us Too, 2018–. *Recreations:* growing vegetables, rural walking. *Address:* c/o Diocese of Bristol, Hillside House, 1500 Parkway North, Stoke Gifford, Bristol BS34 8YU. *T:* (0117) 9060100. *E:* christopher.bryan@bristoldiocese.org.

**BRYAN, Katharine Ann;** Chief Executive, Northern Ireland Water (formerly Water Service, Northern Ireland), 2004–08; *b* 25 Nov. 1952; *d* of John and Dorothy Ludlow; *m* 1974, Michael Bryan; two *d*. *Educ:* Univ. of Durham (BSc Jt Hons Botany and Geog.); Univ. of Aston in Birmingham (MSc Biol. of Water Mgt). National Rivers Authority: Manager, Regl Fisheries, Conservation and Recreation, Severn-Trent Reg., 1988–92; Regl Gen. Manager (SW), 1992–95; Regl Dir (SW), Envmt Agency, 1995–2000; Chief Exec., N of Scotland Water Authy, 2000–02; Chm., Jt Nature Conservation Cttee, 2002–03; Chief Exec., Northern Ireland Water (formerly Water Service, NI), 2004–08. Comr, Infrastructure Planning Commn, 2010–11; Non-exec. Dir, Defence Infrastructure Orgn (formerly Defence Estates), 2009–11. Mem. Bd, and Chm., Remuneration Cttee, Audit Scotland, 2011–14.

**BRYAN, Kenneth John;** Chairman, Southampton University Hospitals NHS Trust, 1996–2001; *b* 22 July 1939; *s* of late Patrick Joseph Bryan and Elsie May Bryan; *m* 1st, 1962 (marr. diss. 1999); one *d*; 2nd, 2007, Gillian Silvester. *Educ:* De La Salle Coll.; Farnborough GS. Insurance Broker, Lloyds, 1957–59; Major, British Army, 1959–78; Sen. Mgt Cons., KPMG, 1978–79; Hongkong and Shanghai Banking Corporation: Financial Controller, Hong Kong office, 1979–86; Sen. Manager, Banking Services, 1986–88; Hd of Gp Finances, 1988–93; Chief Financial Officer, Midland Bank, 1993–96; Dir Gen., Southampton and Fareham Chamber of Commerce and Industry, 2001–04. Chm. Trustees, Hampshire Autistic Soc., 2001–02 (Trustee, 1996–2002). Gov., Barton Peverill Coll., 1998–2002. Mem., Pangbourne Parish Council, 2007–08. *Recreations:* golf, fly fishing, vegetable growing, scuba diving, bridge, hiking. *Club:* Army and Navy.

**BRYAN, Margaret,** CMG 1988; HM Diplomatic Service, retired; Ambassador to Panama, 1986–89; *b* 26 Sept. 1929; *d* of James Grant and Dorothy Rebecca Galloway; *m* 1952, Peter Bernard Bryan (marr. diss. 1981). *Educ:* Cathedral Sch., Shanghai; Croydon High Sch.; Girton Coll., Cambridge (MA Modern Languages). Second, later First, Secretary, FCO, 1962–80; Head of Chancery and Consul, Kinshasa, 1980–83; Counsellor, Havana, 1983–86. *Recreations:* theatre, travel, opera. *Club:* Royal Over-Seas League.

**BRYAN, Robert Patrick,** OBE 1980; Police Adviser to Foreign and Commonwealth Office, and Inspector General of Dependent Territories Police, 1980–85, retired; security consultant; *b* 29 June 1926; *s* of Maurice Bryan and Elizabeth (*née* Waite); *m* 1948, Hazel Audrey (*née* Braine) (*d* 1990); three *s*. *Educ:* Plaistow Secondary Sch.; Wanstead County

High Sch. Indian Army (Mahratta LI), 1944–47. Bank of Nova Scotia, 1948–49; Metropolitan Police: Constable, 1950; seconded Security Service, 1967–68; Dep. Asst Commissioner, 1977, retired 1980. National Police College: Intermediate Comd Course, 1965; Sen. Comd Course, 1969; occasional lecturer. RCDS 1974. Non-exec. Dir, Control Risks Internat. Ltd, 1986–87; Corporate Security Advr, Unilever, 1986–99; Chm., Los Zapateros (cobblers), 1998–99. Chm., Food Distribn Security Assoc., 1988–99. Gov., Corps of Commissionaires, 1993–97. Gov., Hampton Sch., 1978–97. *Publications:* contribs to police and related pubns, particularly on community relations and juvenile delinquency. *Address:* 28 Bolton Gardens, Teddington, Middx TW11 9AY.

**BRYAN, Hon. Sir Simon James,** Kt 2017; **Hon. Mr Justice Bryan;** a Judge of the High Court, Queen's Bench Division, since 2017; Presiding Judge, South Eastern Circuit, from Jan. 2020; *b* 23 Nov. 1965; *s* of late James Bryan and Dorothy Bryan; *m* 1989, Katharine Hilton; one *s* one *d*. *Educ:* Arnold Sch.; Magdalene Coll., Cambridge (Schol.; Maxwell Prize, George Long Prize; BA Double 1st Law Tripos 1987). Council of Legal Educn Studentship, 1986; called to the Bar, Lincoln's Inn, 1988 (Denning Schol.), Bencher, 2013; Supervisor in Law, Magdalene Coll., Cambridge, 1988–89; in practice as a barrister specialising in commercial law, 1989–2017; QC 2006; a Recorder, 2009–17; a Dep. High Court Judge, 2013–17; Chief Justice of Falkland Is, S Georgia and S Sandwich Islands, British Antarctic Territory and British Indian Ocean Territory, 2015–17. CEDR Accredited Mediator, 2006; MCIArb 2007. Mem., Herts Community Foundn Develt Council, 2011–15. Mem. Court, Univ. of Hertfordshire, 2011–15. Freeman, City of London, 2002; Liveryman, Co. of Gardeners, 2002–; Freeman, Arbitrators' Co., 2017–. *Publications:* (Asst Ed. and contrib.) Encyclopedia of International Commercial Litigation (annually), 2008–. *Recreations:* winter sports, travel, gardening, dogs. *Address:* Royal Courts of Justice, Rolls Building, Fetter Lane, EC4A 1NL. *Clubs:* Travellers, Alpine (Associate).

**BRYANT, Christopher John;** MP (Lab) Rhondda, since 2001; *b* 11 Jan. 1962; *s* of Rees Bryant and Anne Gracie Bryant (*née* Goodwin); civil partnership 2010, Jared Cranney. *Educ:* Cheltenham Coll.; Mansfield Coll., Oxford (MA); Ripon Coll., Cuddesdon (MA, DipTh). Ordained deacon, 1986, priest, 1987; Asst Curate, All Saints, High Wycombe, 1986–89; Youth Chaplain, Dio. Peterborough, 1989–91; Organiser, Holborn & St Pancras Lab. Party, 1991–93; Local Govt Develt Officer, Lab. Party, 1993–94. London Manager, Common Purpose, 1994–96; freelance writer, 1996–98; Hd, Eur. Affairs, BBC, 1998–2000. Dep. Leader, H of C, 2008–09; Parly Under-Sec. of State (Minister for Europe and Latin America), FCO, 2009–10; Shadow Minister for Immigration, 2011–13; for Welfare Reform, 2013–14, for Culture, Media and Sport, 2014–15; Shadow Sec. of State for Culture, Media and Sport, 2015; Shadow Leader, H of C, 2015–16. *Publications:* (ed) Reclaiming the Ground, 1993; (ed) John Smith: an appreciation, 1995; Possible Dreams, 1996; Stafford Cripps: the first modern Chancellor, 1997; Glenda Jackson: the biography, 1998; Parliament: the biography, 2 vols, 2014; Entitled: a critical history of the British aristocracy, 2017. *Recreations:* theatre, modern art, Spain. *Address:* House of Commons, SW1A 0AA. *T:* (020) 7219 8315. *E:* bryantc@parliament.uk. *Club:* Ferndale Rugby Football (Vice-Pres.) (Rhondda).

**BRYANT, David John,** CBE 1980 (MBE 1969); international bowler, 1958–92; *b* 27 Oct. 1931; *s* of Reginald Samuel Harold Bryant and Evelyn Claire (*née* Weaver); *m* 1960, Ruth Georgina (*née* Roberts); two *d*. *Educ:* Weston Grammar Sch.; St Paul's Coll., Cheltenham; Redland Coll., Bristol (teacher training colls). National Service, RAF, 1950–52; teacher trng, 1953–55; schoolmaster, 1955–71; company director, sports business, 1971–78; Dir, Drakelite Ltd (Internat. Bowls Consultant), 1978–97. Hon. Pres., English Bowling Assocs (formerly Assoc.) Charity Trust, 2002–. World Singles Champion, 1966, 1980 and 1988; World Indoor Singles Champion, 1979, 1980 and 1981; World Indoor Pairs Champion, 1986, 1987, 1989, 1990, 1991 and 1992; Kodak Masters International Singles Champion, 1978, 1979 and 1982; Gateway International Masters Singles Champion, 1984, 1985, 1986, 1987; Woolwich International Singles Champion, 1988, 1989; World Triples Champion, 1980; Commonwealth Games Gold Medallist: Singles: 1962, 1970, 1974 and 1978; Fours: 1962. Numerous national and British Isles titles, both indoor and outdoor. England Indoor Team Captain, 1993, 1994. *Publications:* Bryant on Bowls, 1966; Bowl with Bryant, 1984; Bryant on Bowls, 1985; The Game of Bowls, 1990; Bowl to Win, 1994. *Recreations:* angling, gardening. *Address:* 47 Esmond Grove, Clevedon, Somerset BS21 7HP. *Clubs:* Clevedon Bowling, Clevedon Conservative, Clevedon Promenade Bowling.

**BRYANT, His Honour David Michael Arton;** a Circuit Judge, Teeside Combined Court Centre, 1989–2007; Designated Family Judge, 1995–2007; *b* 27 Jan. 1942; *s* of Lt-Col and Mrs A. D. Bryant; *m* 1969, Diana Caroline, *d* of Brig. and Mrs W. C. W. Sloan; two *s* one *d*. *Educ:* Wellington Coll.; Oriel Coll., Oxford (Open Scholar; MA). Called to the Bar, Inner Temple, 1964; practised North Eastern Circuit, 1965–89. Recorder, 1985–89. Mem., Parole Bd, 2007–17. *Recreations:* gardening, shooting, tennis, Byzantine history. *Address:* Park Cottage, Sleningford Park, North Stainley, Ripon, N Yorks HG4 3JA. *Club:* Carlton.

**BRYANT, Air Vice-Marshal Derek Thomas,** CB 1987; OBE 1974; Air Officer Commanding, Headquarters Command and Staff Training and Commandant, Royal Air Force Staff College, 1987–89, retired; *b* 1 Nov. 1933; *s* of Thomas Bryant and Mary (*née* Thurley); *m* 1956, Patricia Dodge (*d* 2014); one *s* one *d*. *Educ:* Latymer Upper Grammar Sch., Hammersmith. Fighter pilot, 1953; Qualified Flying Instructor, 1957; Sqdn Comdr, 1968–74; OC RAF Coningsby, 1976–78; SASO HQ 38 Gp, 1982–84; Dep. Comdr, RAF Germany, 1984–87; various courses and staff appts. *Recreations:* gardening, golf. *Address:* The Granary, 1 Pitt Court, Curry Rivel, Somerset TA10 0PF. *Club:* Royal Air Force.

**BRYANT, Prof. Greyham Frank,** PhD; FREng, FIET; FIMA; Professor of Control, Imperial College, London University, 1982–98, now Professor Emeritus and Senior Research Fellow; *b* 3 June 1931; *s* of Ernest Noel Bryant and Florence Ivy (*née* Russell); *m* 1955, Iris Sybil Jardine; two *s*. *Educ:* Reading Univ.; Imperial Coll. (PhD). FIMA 1973; FIET (FIEE 1987); FREng (FEng 1988). Sen. Scientific Officer, Iron and Steel Res., London, 1959–64; Imperial College: Res. Fellow, 1964–67; Reader in Industrial Control, 1975–82. Chm., Broner Consultants, 1979–88; Director: Greycon Consultants, 1985–2000; Circulation Research, 1989–2008. *Publications:* Automation of Tandem Mills (jtly), 1973; (with L. F. Yeung) Multivariable Control and System Design Techniques, 1996; papers on design of management control schemes, multivariable control and modelling, in learned jls. *Recreations:* music, oil painting. *Address:* 18 Wimborne Avenue, Norwood Green, Middlesex UB2 4HB. *T:* (020) 8574 5648.

**BRYANT, Jayne Kathryn,** FREng; CEng, FIET; Engineering Director, BAE Systems Applied Intelligence, since 2018; *b* Maidstone, 14 July 1958; *d* of Alan Henry Wood and Marjorie Lorna Wood (*née* Cook); *m* 1987, Gary Bryant; two *s* one *d* (triplets). *Educ:* Maidstone Girls' Grammar Sch.; Medway Coll. (HNC Computing 1987). FIET 2005; CEng 2007. Marconi Avionics Ltd: Software Project Leader, 1979–83, Software Manager, 1983–87, Airborne Displays Div.; Chief Engr, Maritime Aircraft Systems Div., 1987–91; Prog. Mgt Exec. and Systems Consultant, Hd Office, 1991–2005; Hd, Engrg Strategy, Selex Sensors and Airborne Systems, 2005–06; BAE Systems: Engrg Dir, Platform Solutions, 2006–09; Engrg Dir, Engr Process Wkg Gp, Performance Excellence, 2009–11; Engrg and Technol. Dir, Defence Information, 2011–18. Vice Pres., IET, 2017–Sept. 2020. FREng 2010; FWES 2015. *Recreation:* horse riding. *Address:* BAE Systems Applied Intelligence, Waterside House, 170 Priestley Road, Surrey Research Park, Guildford, Surrey GU2 7RQ.

**BRYANT, John Martin,** FREng, FIMMM; Joint Chief Executive, Corus Group plc, 1999–2000; *b* 28 Sept. 1943; *s* of William George Bryant and Doris Bryant; *m* 1965, Andrea Irene Emmons; two *s* one *d*. *Educ:* West Monmouth Sch.; St Catharine's Coll., Cambridge (BA Nat. Sci. 1965; MA). CEng 1977; FIMMM (FIM 1993). Trainee, Steel Co. of Wales, 1965; British Steel, 1967–99: Production/Technical Mgt, Port Talbot works, 1967–78; Works Manager, Hot Rolled Products, Port Talbot, 1978–87; Project Manager, Hot Strip Mill Develt, 1982–87; Works Manager, Cold Rolled Products, Shotton, 1987–88; Dir, Coated Products, 1988–90; Dir, Tinplate, 1990–92; Man. Dir, Strip Products, 1992–96; Exec. Dir, 1996–99; Chief Exec., 1999. Director: ASW plc, 1993–95; Bank of Wales plc, 1996–2001; Welsh Water plc, 2001–14; Glas Cymru Ltd, 2001–14; Costain Gp plc, 2002–13; Chm., Actoris Property, 2009–13. Mem., Occupational Health Adv. Cttee, 1988–94. Trustee, Ogmore Centre, 2003–08. FREng 2000. Hon. DSc Wales, 2000. *Recreations:* Rugby, cricket, theatre, opera, family. *Address:* Broadway Farm, 24 Rogers Lane, Laleston, Bridgend CF32 0LA.

**BRYANT, John William;** journalist, author and broadcaster; Editor-in-Chief, The Daily Telegraph and The Sunday Telegraph, 2005–06; *b* 25 April 1944; *s* of late James Douglas John Bryant and Mollie Bryant; *m* 1968, Carol Leffman; two *s*. *Educ:* Sexey's Sch., Bruton; Queen's Coll., Oxford (BA Hons 1966). Edinburgh Evening News, 1967–70; Daily Mail, 1971–86, Exec. Editor, 1980–86; The Times: Man. Editor, 1986–88; Dep. Editor, 1988–90; Editor: Sunday Correspondent, 1990; The European, 1991; Dep. Editor, The Times, 1991–2000; Consultant Editor, Daily Mail, 2000–05. Chm., Evening Standard Editl Cttee, 2009–12. Chm., Press Assoc. Trust, 2008–16. Vice Pres., London Marathon Charitable Trust, 2015– (Vice Chm., 2007–10, Chm. Trustees, 2010–15). *Publications:* Jogging, 1979; 3:59.4: The Quest to Break the Four Minute Mile, 2004; The London Marathon, 2005; The Marathon Makers, 2008; Aubrey's Official Register of London Marathon Runners, 2010; Chris Brasher: the man who made the London Marathon, 2012. *Recreations:* athletics, cross-country and road running, singing (scrumpy'n western). *Address:* 18 Wonford Close, Coombe Lane, Kingston-upon-Thames, Surrey KT2 7XA. *Clubs:* Garrick; Vincent's (Oxford); Thames Hare and Hounds (Pres., 2010–).

**BRYANT, Judith Marie, (Mrs H. M. Hodkinson),** RGN; retired; Fellow, King's Fund College, 1990–94 (part-time Fellow, 1986–90); *b* 31 Dec. 1942; *d* of Frederic John Bryant and Joan Marion; *m* 1986, Prof. Henry Malcolm Hodkinson, *qv*. *Educ:* City of London Sch. for Girls; The London Hosp. (RGN 1964); Brunel Univ. (MPhil 1983). Ward Sister, UCH, 1965–69; Nursing Officer, subseq. Sen. Nursing Officer, Northwick Park Hosp., Harrow, 1969–75; Divl Nursing Officer, Harrow, 1975–78; Dist Nursing Officer, Enfield, 1978–82, Victoria, 1982–85; Chief Nursing Officer and Dir of Quality Assurance, Riverside HA, 1985–86; Regl Nursing Officer, NE Thames RHA, 1986–90. Florence Nightingale Meml Scholar, USA and Canada, 1970. Adviser, DHSS Res. Liaison Cttee for the Elderly, 1977–83; Member: SW Herts DHA, 1981–86; NHS Training Authority, Nurses and Midwives Staff Training Cttee, 1986–89; 1930 Fund for Dist Nurses, 1985–2004; Cttee, Nurseline, 1996–2000. Mem., Criminal Injuries Compensation Tribunal (formerly Appeals Panel), 1999–2012. *Publications:* (with H. M. Hodkinson) Sherratt? A Natural Family of Staffordshire Figures, 1991. *Recreations:* opera, gardening. *Address:* 8 Chiswick Square, Burlington Lane, W4 2QG.

**BRYANT, Julius John Victor,** FSA; Keeper of Word & Image, Victoria & Albert Museum, since 2005; *b* 17 Dec. 1957; *s* of late Robert Bryant and of Dena Bryant (*née* Bond); *m* 1984, Barbara Ann Coffey; one *s*. *Educ:* St Albans Sch.; University College London; Courtauld Inst. of Art; Getty Mus. Mgt Inst. Paintings Cataloguer, Sotheby's, 1980–81; Mus. Asst, V&A Mus., 1982–83; Asst Curator, 1983–88, Curator, 1989–90, Iveagh Bequest, Kenwood; English Heritage: Hd of Museums Div. and Dir of London Historic Properties, 1990–95; Dir of Museums and Collections, 1995–2002; Chief Curator, 2003–05. Visiting Fellow: Yale Center for British Art, 1985, 2009; Huntington Liby and Art Gall., Calif, 1992; British Council Res. Scholar, Leningrad, 1989, Lahore, 2014; Sen. Res. Fellow, Bard Graduate Center, NY, 2013–14. Guest Curator, Sir John Soane's Mus., 2002–05. Member: London Museums Consultative Cttee, 1989–99; Exec. Council, Area Museums Service for SE England, 1992–95; Art Museum Directors' Conf. (formerly Conf. of Nat. and Regl Mus. Dirs), 1998–2005; Hampstead Heath Mgt Cttee, 1990–95; Council, Furniture History Soc., 1998–2000; Mgt Cttee, AHRC (formerly AHRB) Centre for Study of the Domestic Interior, 2002–05; Anglo Sikh Heritage Trail Adv. Gp, 2003–18; Adv. Council, Paul Mellon Centre for Studies in British Art, Yale Univ., 2004–09; Apsley House Adv. Panel, 2004–09; Strawberry Hill Conservation Steering Cttee, 2008–11; Houses of Parlt Curator's Office Steering Gp, 2010–19; Dep. Chm., Cttee for Historic House Museums, ICOM, 2002–08 (Mem., 1999–); Expert Advr on architectural designs, Adv. Council on Export of Works of Art and Objects of Cultural Interest, 2005–16; Pres., Internat. Adv. Cttee of Keepers of Public Collections of Graphic Art, 2012–14 (Mem., 2006–). Pres., Arts Soc. Hampstead Heath (formerly Hampstead Heath DFAS), 1989–. Trustee: Chevening House and Estate, 2011–; William Morris Gall. and Brangwyn Gift, 2013–16. FSA 1999. Editor, Collections Review, 1997–2003. *Publications:* Marble Hill: the design and use of a Palladian estate, 1986; Finest Prospects, 1986; The Victoria and Albert Museum Guide, 1986; Marble Hill House, 1988; Mrs Howard: a woman of reason, 1988; (jtly) The Landscape of Kenwood, 1990; The Iveagh Bequest, Kenwood, 1990; Robert Adam, 1992; London's Country House Collections, 1993; (jtly) The Trojan War: sculptures by Anthony Caro, 1994, 3rd edn 1998; Turner: painting the nation, 1996; Marble Hill, 2002; The Wernher Collection, 2002; (ed) Decorative Arts from the Wernher Collection, 2002; Catalogue of Paintings in the Iveagh Bequest, Kenwood, 2003; Anthony Caro: a life in sculpture, 2004; Thomas Banks (1735–1805): Britain's first modern sculptor, 2005; Apsley House: the Wellington Collection, 2005; The English Grand Tour, 2005; The Complete Works of Barry Martin, 2007; Anthony Caro: the figurative and narrative sculptures, 2009; (ed) Art and Design for All: the Victoria and Albert Museum, 2011; (jtly) Caro: close up, 2012; (jtly) Gainsborough, Rembrandt, Van Dyck: the treasures of Kenwood, 2012; Alec Cobbe: designs for historic interiors, 2013; (contrib.) William Kent: designing Georgian Britain, 2013; Magnificent Marble Statues: British sculpture in The Mansion House, 2013; (jtly) Word and Image: art, books and design from the National Art Library, 2015; Anthony Caro: first drawings, last sculptures, 2016; (jtly) John Lockwood Kipling: arts and crafts in the Punjab and London, 2017; Designing the V&A: the museum as a work of art, 1857–1909, 2017; Chevening: a seat of diplomacy, 2017; Creating the V&A: Victoria and Albert's Museum, 1851–1861, 2019; contribs to Oxford DNB, Grove Dictionary of Art; exhibn catalogues; articles in jls. *Recreations:* running around Hampstead Heath, family life. *Address:* Victoria & Albert Museum, Knightsbridge, SW7 2RL.

**BRYANT, Keith;** QC 2013; *b* Minster, Kent, 23 June 1965; *s* of Keith Furnival and Margaret Edith Bryant; *m* 1994, Kate Morrogh-Bernard; one *s* two *d*. *Educ:* King's Sch., Rochester; Clare Coll., Cambridge (BA Hons Natural Scis 1986; MA); King's Coll., Cambridge (Dip. Comp. Sci.). Called to the Bar, Middle Temple, 1991; in practice as barrister, specialising in pensions and employment law, 1991–; fee-paid Employment

Judge, 2005–. *Recreations:* singing, cooking (and eating), ski-ing, walking. *Address:* Outer Temple Chambers, 222 Strand, WC2R 1BA. *T:* (020) 7353 6381. *E:* keith.bryantqc@outertemple.com. *Club:* Garrick.

**BRYANT, Laurence Charles;** Managing Director, Lapley Enterprises, since 2015; *b* Bath, 4 Oct. 1957; *s* of Philip and Hilary Bryant; *m* 1983, Jean Young; two *s. Educ:* Ralph Allen Sch., Bath; Chippenham Tech. Coll. (HND Electrical Engrg 1988); Cranfield Univ. (MSc 1995). MIET 2004, FIET 2016; MAPM 2006; Registered Project Professional 2010. Technician, RN Store Depot, Copenacre, 1978–85; Test Engr, Towed Array Sonar, RN Supply and Transport Service, Colerne, 1985–89; Engrg Consultant, Copenacre Reprovisioning Study Team, 1989–91; Quality Manager, RN Armament Depot, Beith, 1991–95; Project Manager: Seawolf, Procurement Exec., Portsmouth, 1996–99; Naval Systems, Matra BAe Dynamics, Stevenage, 2000–02; Defence Procurement Agency: Dep. Team Leader Ground Based Air Defence, Bristol, 2002–04; Team Leader Flight Simulation, Bristol, 2004–06; Defence Equipment and Support: Hd, UK Mil. Flying Trng System, Bristol, 2006–09; Dep. Dir Combat Air, Bristol, 2009–12; Dir Weapons, Bristol, 2012–15. Dir and Trustee, Cotswold Canals Trust, 2018–. *Recreations:* sailing, gardening, pianist. *E:* lapley.cottage@gmail.com.

**BRYANT, Rt Rev. Mark Watts;** Bishop Suffragan of Jarrow, 2007–18; *b* 8 Oct. 1949; *s* of Douglas William and Kathleen Joyce Bryant; *m* 1976, Elisabeth Eastaugh; two *s* one *d. Educ:* St John's Sch., Leatherhead; St John's Coll., Univ. of Durham (BA); Cuddesdon Theol Coll. Ordained deacon, 1975, priest, 1976; Curate, Addlestone, 1975–79; Asst Priest, 1979–83; Vicar, 1983–88, St John Studley, Trowbridge; Chaplain, Trowbridge FE Coll., 1979–83; Dir of Ordinands and Hd, Vocations and Trng Dept, Dio. Coventry, 1988–96; Team Rector, Caludon, Coventry, 1996–2001; Archdeacon of Coventry, 2001–07; Residentiary Canon, Coventry Cathedral, 2006–07. *Recreations:* music, walking, popular television.

**BRYANT, Martin Warwick;** Director, Wesleyan Assurance Society, since 2011; *b* 30 June 1952; *s* of Douglas and Marjorie Bryant; *m* 1979, Hilary Mary Southall; one *s* two *d. Educ:* Christ Church, Oxford (MA Hist. and Econs 1975); Univ. of Leeds (MA Econs 1978); Cranfield Sch. of Mgt (MBA 1983). Planning Manager, BOC Gp, 1983–87; Dir of Corporate Develt, Charles Barker plc, 1987–89; Dir of Corporate Develt, Boots Co. plc, 1989–95; Man. Dir, Boots Opticians Ltd, 1995–97; Ops Dir, Boots The Chemists, 1997–2000; Man. Dir, Boots Retail Internat., 2000; Dir of Business Develt, Boots Co. plc, 2000–02; Chief Operating Officer, BP Retail (UK), 2002–04; Dir of Strategy, Home Office, 2004–06; Chief Exec., Shareholder Executive, 2006–07. Non-executive Director: Fire Service Coll., 2008–13; E Midlands Develt Agency, 2009–12; Buying Solutions, 2009–12; non-exec. Advr, Polbita s.p.a., 2007–13. Trustee, Vision Aid Overseas, 2009–; Gov., Nuffield Health, 2013–. *Recreations:* golf, ski-ing, vintage motor cars. *Address:* Upton Grange, Upton, Newark, Notts NG23 5SY. *T:* (01636) 812901. *E:* martinwbryant@aol.com.

**BRYANT, Prof. Peter Elwood,** FRS 1991; Watts Professor of Psychology, Oxford University, 1980–2004; Fellow of Wolfson College, Oxford, 1980–2004, now Emeritus; *b* 24 June 1937; *s* of Michael Bryant; *m* (marr. diss.); one *s* two *d; m* 1995, Prof. Terezinha Nunes, *qv. Educ:* Blundell's Sch.; Clare College, Cambridge (BA 1963; MA 1967); London Univ. (PhD). University Lecturer in Human Experimental Psychology, Oxford, 1967–80; Fellow, St John's Coll., Oxford, 1967–80. Vis. Prof., Oxford Brookes Univ. Editor: British Jl of Developmental Psychol., 1982–88; Cognitive Development, 2000–06. President's award, BPsS, 1984; Dist. Scientific Contribn Award, Soc. for Scientific Study of Reading, 1999. *Publications:* Perception and Understanding in Young Children, 1974; (with L. Bradley) Children's Reading Problems, 1985; (with U. Goswami) Phonological Skills and Learning to Read, 1990; with T. Nunes: Children Doing Mathematics, 1996; Learning & Teaching Mathematics: an international perspective, 1997; Improving Literacy Through Teaching Morphemes, 2006; Children's Reading and Spelling: beyond the first steps, 2009. *Address:* Wolfson College, Oxford OX2 6UD.

**BRYANT, Peter George Francis;** Under Secretary, Department of Trade and Industry, 1989–92; *b* 10 May 1932; *s* of late George Bryant, CBE and Margaret Bryant; *m* 1961, Jean (*née* Morriss); one *s* one *d. Educ:* Sutton Valence Sch.; Birkbeck Coll., London Univ. (BA). Min. of Supply, 1953–55; BoT, 1955–69; 1st Sec. (Commercial), Vienna (on secondment), 1970–72; Dir of British Trade Drive in S Germany, 1973; Department of Trade (later Department of Trade and Industry), 1974–85; seconded to HM Diplomatic Service as Consul-Gen., Düsseldorf, 1985–88, and Dir-Gen. of Trade and Investment Promotion, FRG, 1988.

**BRYANT, Air Chief Marshal Sir Simon,** KCB 2011; CBE 2005; Vice President (Oman), BAE Systems, since 2013; *b* 20 June 1956; *s* of Robert Francis and Audrey Ethel Ashby Bryant; *m* 1984, Helen Burns; one *s* one *d. Educ:* Stamford Sch.; Nottingham Univ. (BA Hons Geog. 1977); King's Coll. London (MA Defence Studies 1993); Cranfield Univ. (DSc 2012). CDir 2010; FCIPD 2010; FRAeS 2012; FRIN 2012. Joined RAF, 1974; served with Fighter Sqdns Nos 19, 56 and 23, 1979–89, and VF-101 USN, 1984–87; RAF Personnel Mgt Centre, 1989–91; RAF Staff Coll., 1992; MoD, 1992–95; OC No 43 (Fighter) Sqdn, 1996–99; Personal Staff Officer to Dep. Comdr, SHAPE, 1999–2001; Sen. British Officer Oman, 2002; AO Scotland and CO, RAF Leuchars, 2003–05; Dir, Jt Capability, 2005–06; COS Personnel and Air Sec., 2006–09; Dep. C-in-C (Personnel) and Air Mem. for Personnel, HQ Air Comd, 2009–10; C-in-C Air Comd and Air ADC to the Queen, 2010–12. Mil. Advr Combat Air, BAE Systems, 2012–13. *Recreations:* tennis (Real and lawn), squash, golf, ski-ing, diving, trekking, bridge.

**BRYANT-HERON, Mark Nicholas;** QC 2014; a Recorder, since 2005; *b* London, 29 Nov. 1961; *s* of Thomas Michael Edward Bryant and Janet Bryant-Heron; *m* 1989, Elizabeth Pratt; one *s* twin *d. Educ:* Netherhall Sch., Cambridge; Clare Coll., Cambridge (BA Law 1984). Called to the Bar, Middle Temple, 1986; in practice as barrister, 1988–, specialising in criminal law, particularly corporate fraud and business crime, bribery and corruption, money laundering and asset forfeiture, revenue and accountancy fraud. *Recreations:* music, cycling, ski-ing, good wine and good company. *Address:* Foundry Chambers, Quality House, 5–9 Quality Court, Chancery Lane, WC2A 1HP. *T:* (020) 7400 1800. *E:* m.bryantheron@foundrychambers.com.

**BRYARS, Donald Leonard;** Commissioner of Customs and Excise, 1978–84 and Director, Personnel, 1979–84, retired; *b* 31 March 1929; *s* of late Leonard and Marie Bryars; *m* 1953, Joan (*née* Yealand); one *d. Educ:* Goole Grammar Sch.; Leeds Univ. Joined Customs and Excise as Executive Officer, 1953, Principal, 1964, Asst Sec., 1971; on loan to Cabinet Office, 1976–78; Director, General Customs, 1978–79. Dir (non-exec.), The Customs Annuity Benevolent Fund Inc., 1986–2004. Trustee, Milton's Cottage Trust, 1993–2002. *Address:* 15 Cedars Walk, Chorleywood, Rickmansworth, Herts WD3 5GD. *T:* (01923) 446752. *Club:* Civil Service (Chm., 1981–85).

**BRYARS, (Richard) Gavin;** composer; *b* 16 Jan. 1943; *s* of Walter Joseph Bryars and Miriam Eleanor Bryars (*née* Hopley); *m* 1st, 1971, Angela Margaret Bigley (marr. diss. 1993); two *d*; 2nd, 1999, Anna Tchernakova; one *s* one *d. Educ:* Goole Grammar Sch.; Sheffield Univ. (BA Hons Philosophy). Freelance bassist, 1963–66; Mem. trio, Joseph Holbrooke (improvising), 1964–66, 1998–2005; Lecturer: Northampton Tech. Coll. and Sch. of Art, 1966–67; Portsmouth Coll. of Art, 1969–70; Sen. Lectr, Leicester Poly., 1970–85; Prof. of Music, Leicester Poly., later De Montfort Univ., 1985–96 (part-time, 1994–96). Visiting Professor: Univ. of Victoria, BC, 1999–2001; Univ. of Hertfordshire, 1999–2004; Associate Res. Fellow, Dartington Coll. of Arts, 2005–08. Founder and Dir, Gavin Bryars Ensemble, 1979–. Mem., Collège de Pataphysique, France, 1974– (Pres., sous-commn des Cliques Claques, 1984–; Regent, 2002–; Transcendent Satrap, 2016). *Compositions* include: The Sinking of the Titanic, 1969; Jesus' Blood Never Failed Me Yet, 1971; Out of Zaleski's Gazebo, 1977; My First Homage, 1978; The Cross Channel Ferry, 1979; The Vespertine Park, The English Mail-Coach, 1980; Les Fiançailles, Allegrasco, 1983; On Photography, Effarene, 1984; String quartet No 1, 1985; Pico's Flight, Sub Rosa, 1986; By the Vaar, The Old Tower of Löbenicht, 1987; Invention of Tradition, Glorious Hill, Doctor Ox's Experiment (Epilogue), 1988; Incipit Vita Nova, 1989; Cadman Requiem, 1989, revd 1996; Alaric I or II, 1989; After the Requiem, String Quartet No 2, 1990; The Black River, The Green Ray, 1991; The White Lodge, 1991; (with Juan Munoz) A Man in a Room Gambling, Die Letzen Tage, 1992; The War in Heaven, The North Shore, 1993; Three Elegies for Nine Clarinets, One Last Bar Then Joe Can Sing, The East Coast, 1994; The South Downs, In Nomine (after Purcell), After Handel's Vesper, Cello Concerto, 1995; The Adnan Songbook, 1996; The Island Chapel, And so ended Kant's travelling in this world, 1997; String Quartet no 3, 1998; First Book of Madrigals, 1998–99; The Porazzi Fragment, 1999; Violin Concerto, 2000; Second Book of Madrigals, 2002; Double Bass Concerto, 2002; Laude Cortonese, vols I, II and III, 2002–09; Third Book of Madrigals, 2003–04; New York (concerto for percussion quintet and orch.), 2004; Lachrymae (viol consort), 2004; From Egil's Saga, 2004; Eight Irish Madrigals, 2004; Creamer Etudes, 2005; Nine Irish Madrigals, 2006; Silva Caledonia, 2006; The Paper Nautilus, 2006; Nothing Like the Sun, 2007; The Church Closest to the Sea, 2007; Sonnets from Scotland, 2008; Ian in the Broch, 2008; Anail De, 2008; Trondur i Gotu, 2008; A Family Likeness, 2008; Laude 35–38, 2008–09; Lauda: the flower of friendship, 2009; Piano Concerto, 2009; The Apotheosis of St Brendan, 2009; Four Songs from the North, 2009; Four Villa I Tatti Madrigals, 2009; Piano Concerto (The Solway Canal), 2010; Ramble on Cortona, 2010; It Never Rains, 2010; Two Love Songs, 2010; Morrison Songbook, 2010; Fifth Book of Madrigals (I Tatti), 2011; Lauda 40–42, 2011–12; Four Battiferri Madrigals, 2011; Underworlds and Overworlds (installation, Leeds), 2012; Four Children's Songs from the Overworld, 2012; Psalm 141, 2012; Song of the Open Road, 2012; The Beckett Songbook, 2012–14; Three Choral Pieces from the Faroe Islands, 2012; Through the Halls, 2012; Dancing with Pannonica, 2012; The Open Road, 2012; The Voice of St Columba, 2012; The Fifth Century, 2014; Sixth Book of Madrigals, 2015; De Profundis Aquarum, 2015; The Other Side of the River (percussion quartet), 2016; (with texts by Caroline Bergvall) Raga Dawn (for two voices and electronics), 2016; The Stopping Train, 2016; Burroughs, 2016; Lauda 43–46, 2017; Mistral (setting Occitan text), 2019; String Quartet 4, 2019; *opera:* Medea, for Opéra de Lyon, 1982, revd 1984, 1995; Doctor Ox's Experiment, for ENO, 1998; G, for Staatstheater Mainz, 2002; Marilyn Forever, Victoria BC, 2013; The Collected Works of Billy the Kid, Lyon, 2018; *ballet:* Four Elements, 1990; Wonderlawn, 1994; 2, 1995; BIPED, 2000; Writings on Water, 2002; Amjad, 2007; The Third Light, Reverence, 2010; Dido-Orfeo, 2011; Pneuma, Bordeaux, 2014; Four Seasons, Sao Paolo, 2014; 11th Floor, Cullberg, 2014; Peer Gynt, Bielefeld, 2014; Laude, Munich 2014; The Heat of August, Flanders, 2017–18; Requiem, Dutch Nat. Ballet, 2019; *theatre:* To Define Happiness, Tallinn, 2007; *film music:* Last Summer, 2000; Sea and Stars, 2002; Season of Mists, 2008; Our Chekhov, 2010; Proezd Serova, 2013; Jili-byli my, 2017; *radio:* (with Blake Morrison) The Pythagorean Comma, BBC Radio 3, 2012. Has made recordings. Hon. Fellow: Bath Spa Univ., 2008; Birmingham Conservatoire, 2015. Hon. DArts Plymouth, 2006. *Recreations:* supporting Yorkshire CCC and Nottingham Forest FC; dalmatians. *Address:* c/o Schott Music, 48 Great Marlborough Street, W1F 7BB. *T:* (020) 7534 0750. *W:* www.gavinbryars.com.

**BRYCE, Gordon Craigie,** RSA 1993 (ARSA 1976); RSW 1976; painter; Head of Fine Art, Gray's School of Art, Aberdeen, 1986–95; *b* 30 June 1943; *s* of George and Annie Bryce; *m* 1st, 1966, Margaret Lothian (marr. diss. 1976); two *s*; 2nd, 1984, Hilary Duthie; one *s* two *d. Educ:* Edinburgh Acad.; George Watson's Coll., Edinburgh; Edinburgh Coll. of Art. Dip. in Art. Exhibited widely in UK, Europe and USA, 1965–, esp. Scottish Gall., Edinburgh and Thackeray Gall., London; 50 one-man exhibns of painting, UK and overseas; paintings in public and private collections, UK, Europe, USA, Canada. *Recreation:* fly fishing. *Address:* Sylva Cottage, 2 Culter House Road, Milltimber, Aberdeen AB13 0EN. *T:* (01224) 733274.

**BRYCE, Hon. Dame Quentin Alice Louise,** AD 2014 (AC 2003; AO 1988); CVO 2011; Governor-General of Australia, 2008–14; *b* 23 Dec. 1942; *d* of Norman Walter Strachan and Edwina Naida Strachan (*née* Wetzel); *m* 1964, Michael John Strachan Bryce, AM, AE; three *s* two *d. Educ:* Moreton Bay Coll., Queensland; Univ. of Queensland (BA 1962; LLB 1965). Admitted to Qld Bar, 1965; Lectr and Tutor, Law Sch., Univ. of Qld, 1968–82; Dir, Women's Inf. Service Qld, Dept of PM and Cabinet, 1984–87; Qld Dir, Human Rights and Equal Opportunity Commn, 1987; Fed. Sex Discrimination Comr, 1988–93; Chm. and CEO, Nat. Childcare Accreditation Council, 1993–96; Principal and CEO, The Women's Coll., Univ. of Sydney, 1997–2003; Governor of Qld, 2003–08. Chm., Special Taskforce on Domestic and Family Violence (report publd 2015). US State Dept Visitor, 1978; Mem., Aust. Delegn to UN Human Rights Commn, Geneva, 1989–92. Nat. Pres., Assoc. for Welfare of Children in Hosp., 1978–81; Vice Pres., Qld Council for Civil Liberties, 1979–80; Pres., Women's Cricket Australia, 1999–2003; Director: Aust. Children's TV Foundn Bd, 1982–92; YWCA, Sydney, 1997–2000; Bradman Foundn, 2002–03; Convener, Nat. Women's Adv. Council, 1982–83 (Mem., 1978–81); Chairman: Jessie Street Nat. Women's Liby, 1996–98; Nat. Breast Cancer Centre Adv. Network, 1996–2003; Member: Internat. Yr for Disabled Persons Legal Cttee, Qld, 1981; Family Planning Council, Qld, 1981–92; Nat. Cttee on Discrimination in Employment and Occupation, 1982–86; Bd, Schizophrenia Foundn Aust., 1987–90; Bd, Abused Child Trust, Qld, 1988–89; Bd, Mindcare Mental Health Foundn, 1990–95; Nat. Alternative Dispute Resolution Adv. Council, 1995–97; Bd, Plan Internat., 1996–2003; Sydney IVF Ethics Cttee, 2000–03. Presiding Mem., Bd of Mgt, Dip. of Policing Practice, NSW, 1998–2001. Mem. Council, Central Qld Univ., 1999–2001. Patron, Nat. Alliance of Girls' Schs, 2001–. Hon. LLD: Macquarie, 1998; Qld, 2006; Sydney, 2010; Melbourne, 2012; Hon. DLitt: Charles Sturt, 2002; Western Sydney, 2012; DUniv: Griffith, 2003; Qld Univ. of Technol., 2004; James Cook, 2008. *Publications:* Dear Quentin: letters of a Governor General, 2017. *Address:* GPO Box 2434, Brisbane, Qld 4001, Australia.

**BRYDEN, David John,** PhD; FSA; Property Manager, Felbrigg Hall and Sheringham Park, National Trust, 1997–2001; *b* 23 Nov. 1943; *s* of George Bryden and Marion (*née* Bellingham); *m* 1964, Helen Margaret Willison; two *s. Educ:* Univ. of Leicester (BScEng); Linacre Coll., Oxford (Dip. in Hist. and Philos. of Sci.); Gonville and Caius Coll., Cambridge (MA 1973); St Edmund's Coll., Cambridge (PhD 1993). FSA 1993. Asst Keeper II, Royal Scottish Mus., 1966–70; Curator, Whipple Mus. of Hist. of Sci., Univ. of Cambridge, 1970–78; Fellow and Steward, St Edmund's House, 1977–78; Asst Keeper I, Science Mus. Library, 1979–87; Academic Administrator, Gresham Coll., 1987–88;

Keeper, Dept of Sci., Technol. and Working Life, Nat. Museums of Scotland, 1988–96. Medal Lectr, Scientific Instrument Soc., 1998; Somerville Meml Lectr, British Sundial Soc., 2010. Pershore Abbey Flagmaster, 2011–; Percy Dawson Medal, Antiquarian Horological Soc., 2016. *Publications:* Scottish Scientific Instrument Makers 1600–1900, 1972; Napier's Bones: a history and instruction manual, 1992; (jtly) A Classified Bibliography on the history of scientific instruments, 1997; articles on early scientific instruments, history of science and technology, printing history and bibliography, numismatics. *Address:* 11 Pensham Hill, Pershore, Worcs WR10 3HA.

**BRYDEN, Prof. Harry Leonard,** PhD; FRS 2005; Professor of Physical Oceanography, University of Southampton, since 2000; *b* 9 July 1946; *s* of Harry L. and Ruth F. Bryden; *m* 1988, Mary E. Woodgate-Jones; four *s*. *Educ:* Dartmouth Coll. (AB Maths 1968); Massachusetts Inst. of Technol. and Woods Hole Oceanographic Instn (PhD Oceanography 1975). Postdoctoral Res. Associate, Oregon State Univ., 1975–77; Woods Hole Oceanographic Institution: Asst Scientist, 1977–80; Associate Scientist, 1980–88; Sen. Scientist, 1988–92; Physical Oceanographer: Inst. of Oceanographic Scis, Surrey, 1993–95; Southampton Oceanography Centre, 1995–2000. Vis. Fellow, Wolfson Coll., Oxford Univ., 1988–89. Henry Stommel Res. Medal, American Meteorol Soc., 2003; Prince Albert I Medal, IAPSO, 2009; Fridtjof Nansen Medal, Eur. Geoscis Union, 2013; Challenger Medal, Challenger Soc. for Marine Science, 2014. *Publications:* numerous refereed scientific pubns on role of the ocean in climate, ocean heat and freshwater transports, exchange between Atlantic and Mediterranean through the Strait of Gibraltar. *Recreation:* walking in the country. *Address:* Ocean and Earth Science, University of Southampton, Empress Dock, Southampton SO14 3ZH. *T:* (023) 8059 6437, *Fax:* (023) 8059 6400.

**BRYDEN, William Campbell Rough, (Bill Bryden),** CBE 1993; director and writer; Head of Drama Television, BBC Scotland, 1984–93; *b* 12 April 1942; *s* of late George Bryden and of Catherine Bryden; *m* 1st, 1971, Hon. Deborah Morris (marr. diss.), *d* of 3rd Baron Killanin, MBE, TD; one *s* one *d*; 2nd, 2008, Angela Douglas. *Educ:* Hillend Public Sch.; Greenock High Sch. Documentary writer, Scottish Television, 1963–64; Assistant Director: Belgrade Theatre, Coventry, 1965–67; Royal Court Th., London, 1967–69; Associate Director: Royal Lyceum Th., Edinburgh, 1971–74; National Th., subseq. RNT, 1975–85; Dir, Cottesloe Theatre (Nat. Theatre), 1978–80. Director: *opera:* Parsifal, 1988, The Cunning Little Vixen, 1990, 2003, Royal Opera House, Covent Garden; The Silver Tassie, Coliseum, 2000; *stage:* Bernstein's Mass, GSMD, 1987; A Life in the Theatre, Haymarket, 1989; The Ship, Harland and Wolff Shipyard, Glasgow, 1990; Cops, Greenwich, 1991; A Month in the Country, Albery, 1994; The Big Picnic, Harland and Wolff Shipyard, Glasgow (also writer), 1994 (televised 1996); Son of Man, RSC, 1995; Uncle Vanya, Chichester, 1996; Three Sisters, Birmingham, 1998; The Good Hope, NT, 2001; The Creeper, Playhouse, 2006; Small Craft Warnings, Arcola, 2008. *Television:* Exec. Producer: Tutti Frutti, by John Byrne, 1987 (Best Series, BAFTA awards); The Play on 1 (series), 1989; Dir, The Shawl, by David Mamet, 1989. *Radio:* includes, 2000–: HMS Ulysses, Daisy Miller, The Plutocrat, Charge of the Light Brigade, The Last Tycoon. Member Board, Scottish Television, 1979–85. Dir of the Year, Laurence Olivier Awards, 1985, Best Dir, Brit. Th. Assoc. and Drama Magazine Awards, 1986, and Evening Standard Best Dir Award, 1985 (for The Mysteries, NT, 1985). Hon. FGSM; Hon. Fellow: Rose Bruford Coll.; Queen Margaret Coll., Edinburgh. DUniv Stirling 1991. *Publications:* (with Nobby Clark) Bryden & Clark: lives in the theatre, 2014; *plays:* Willie Rough, 1972; Benny Lynch, 1974; Old Movies, 1977; *screenplay:* The Long Riders, 1980; *films:* (writer and director) Ill Fares The Land, 1982; The Holy City (for TV), 1985; Aria, 1987. *Recreation:* music.

**BRYDIE, Isobel Gunning,** CVO 2017; MBE 1997; Lord-Lieutenant for West Lothian, 2002–17; *b* 20 Sept. 1942; *d* of Thomas and Sarah Hardie; *m* 1965, John Lawrie Brydie; one *s* one *d* (and one *s* decd). *Educ:* Broxburn High Sch. Mem. Bd, Livingston Develt Corp., 1982–96; Mem. Bd, 1996, Chm., 1997–99, W Lothian NHS Trust. *Recreations:* walking, curling, equestrian. *Address:* Limekilns, 29 Main Street, East Calder, West Lothian EH53 0ES. *T:* (01506) 880800. *Club:* Edinburgh Ladies Curling.

**BRYDON, Sir Donald (Hood),** Kt 2019; CBE 2004 (OBE 1993); Chairman: Sage Group, since 2012 (non-executive Director, since 2012); Chance to Shine Foundation, since 2014; Science Museum Foundation, since 2016; *b* 25 May 1945; *s* of late James Hood Brydon and Mary Duncanson (*née* Young); *m* 1st, 1971, Joan Victoria (marr. diss. 1995); one *s* one *d*; 2nd, 1996, Corrine Susan Jane Green. *Educ:* George Watson's Coll., Edinburgh; Univ. of Edinburgh (BSc). Econs Dept, Univ. of Edinburgh, 1967–70; British Airways Pension Fund, 1970–77; Barclays Investment Manager's Office, 1977–81; Dep. Man. Dir, Barclays Investment Mgt Ltd, 1981–86; BZW Investment Management Ltd: Dir, 1986–88; Man. Dir, 1988–91; BZW Asset Management Ltd: Chm. and Chief Exec., 1991–94; non-exec. Chm., 1994–95; Barclays de Zoete Wedd: Dep. Chief Exec., 1994–96; Acting Chief Exec., 1996; AXA Investment Managers SA: Chief Exec., 1997–2002; Chm., 1997–2006. Chairman: London Metal Exchange, 2003–10; Smiths Gp plc, 2004–13; Taylor Nelson Sofres plc, 2006–08; AXA Framlington, 2006–08; Royal Mail, 2009–15; MRC, 2012–18; London Stock Exchange, 2015–19 (Dir, 1991–98). Director: Edinburgh Inca Investment Trust, 1996–2001; Allied Domecq, 1997–2005; Amersham (formerly Nycomed Amersham), 1997–2004 (Chm., 2003–04); Edinburgh UK Tracker Trust, 1997–2006; AXA UK (formerly Sun Life and Provincial Hldgs), 1997–2007; AXA Investment Managers SA, 2006–12. Chairman: Financial Services Practitioner Panel, 2001–04; Code Cttee, Panel on Takeovers and Mergers, 2002–06. Leader, Ind. Rev. into Quality and Effectiveness of Audit, 2019–. Pres., Eur. Asset Mgt Assoc., 1999–2001; Dep. Pres., Inst. for Financial Services, 2005–06; Chm., *ifs* Sch. of Finance, 2006–09. Chairman: Eur. Children's Trust, 1999–2001; EveryChild, 2003–08; David Rattray Meml Trust (UK), 2007–10; LifeSight Ltd, 2015–17. *Publications:* (jtly) Economics of Technical Information Services, 1972; (jtly) Pension Fund Investment, 1988. *Recreations:* golf, Reading FC, deltiology. *Clubs:* Caledonian; Golf House (Elie); Highgate Golf.

**BRYDON, Robert,** MBE 2013; actor and writer; *b* Swansea, 3 May 1965; *s* of Howard Jones and Joy Brydon Jones; *né* Robert Brydon Jones; surname changed to Brydon by deed poll, 2006; *m* 1st; one *s* two *d*; 2nd, 2008, Claire Holland; two *s*. *Educ:* St John's Sch., Porthcawl; Dumbarton House Sch., Swansea; Porthcawl Comp. Sch.; Royal Welsh Coll. of Music and Drama (Hon. Fellow, 2004). Radio and TV presenter, BBC Wales, 1986–92. *Television:* actor and writer: Marion and Geoff, 2000–03; Human Remains, 2000; Director's Commentary, 2004; The Keith Barret Show, 2004–05; Rob Brydon's Annually Retentive, 2006–07; Rob Brydon's Identity Crisis, 2008; The Rob Brydon Show, 2010–12; The Guess List, 2014; actor: The Way We Live Now, 2001; Cruise of the Gods, 2002; Little Britain, 2005; Kenneth Tynan, In Praise of Hardcore, 2005; Supernova, 2005–06; Gavin and Stacey, 2007–09; Heroes & Villains: Napoleon, 2007; The Gruffalo, 2009; The Trip (series), 2010; The Best of Men, 2012; Room on the Broom (voice), 2012; Gangsta Granny, 2013; The Trip to Italy (series), 2014; The Trip to Spain (series), 2017; presenter: Would I Lie to You?, 2009–; Neil Diamond: One Night Only (Sunday Night at the Palladium), 2014; *radio:* I'm Sorry I Haven't a Clue, 2006–; *films:* First Knight, 1995; Lock, Stock and Two Smoking Barrels, 1998; 24 Hour Party People, 2002; MirrorMask, 2005; A Cock and Bull Story, 2005; Early Man (voice), 2018; Swimming with Men, 2018; Blinded by the Light, 2019; *stand-up shows:* Rob Brydon, UK tour, 2009; Rob Brydon: I am standing up…, UK tour, 2017; Brydon, Mack and Mitchell: town to town, UK tour, 2019; *theatre:* The Painkiller, Lyric, Belfast, 2011, Garrick Th., 2016; A Chorus of Disapproval, Harold Pinter Th., 2012; Future Conditional, Old Vic, 2015; *recording:* Islands in the Stream, with Ruth Jones and Sir Tom Jones for Comic Relief, 2009. *Publications:* Making Divorce Work (as Keith Barret), 2004; Small Man in a Book (autobiog.), 2011. *Recreations:* playing the guitar badly, Apple gadgets, country walks, drinking milk and eating biscuits, thinking about Sydney. *Address:* c/o United Agents, 12–26 Lexington Street, W1F 0LE. *E:* mvincent@unitedagents.co.uk.

**BRYER, Dr David Ronald William,** CMG 1996; Director, Oxfam, 1992–2001; Chairman, Oxfam International, 2003–07; *b* 15 March 1944; *s* of Ronald Bryer and Betty Bryer (*née* Rawlinson); *m* 1980, Margaret Isabel, *e d* of Sir Eric Bowyer, KCB, KBE and Elizabeth (*née* Nicholls); one *s* one *d*. *Educ:* King's Sch., Worcester; Worcester Coll., Oxford (MA, DPhil); Manchester Univ. (Dip. Teaching English Overseas). Teaching and research, Lebanon and Britain, 1964–65, 1967–74 and 1979–81; Asst Keeper, Ashmolean Museum, 1972–74; Oxfam, 1975–2001: Field Dir, Middle East, 1975–79; Co-ordinator, Africa, 1981–84; Overseas Dir, 1984–91; Sen. Advr, Henry Dunant Centre for Humanitarian Dialogue 2001–03. Vis. Fellow, British Acad., 1972. Chm., Steering Cttee for Humanitarian Response, Geneva, 1995–97; Mem., Sen. Adv. Bd, DFID Humanitarian Emergency Response Rev., 2010–11. Chairman: Eurostep, 1993–94; British Overseas Aid Gp, 1998–2000; Home-Start Internat., 2008–11. Mem., UN High Level Panel on financing for develt, 2001. Member: Council, VSO, 1992–2008; Wilton Park Academic Council, 1999–2008; Court, Oxford Brookes Univ., 1999–2003. Lay Canon and Mem. Chapter, Worcester Cathedral, 2013–. Board Member: Save the Children UK, 2002–10; Oxfam America, 2003–07; WWF-UK, 2009–14. Chm., Malvern Hills DFAS, 2012–15; Mem., Malvern Hills Trust (formerly Malvern Hills Conservators), 2014–. *Publications:* The Origins of the Druze Religion, in Der Islam, 1975; articles on humanitarian and development issues. *Recreations:* family and friends, travel, esp. Eastern Mediterranean, walking. *Address:* Bracken Lodge, Eaton Road, Malvern Wells, Worcs WR14 4PE.

**BRYER, Ven. Paul Donald;** Archdeacon of Cornwall, since 2019; *b* Worthing, 21 June 1958; *s* of Maurice Bryer and Janine Bryer; *m* 1985, Fiona Mary Linnell; two *s* one *d*. *Educ:* Worthing Boy's High Sch.; Bishop Otter Coll., Chichester (BEd Sussex Univ. 1980); St John's Coll., Nottingham (DipTh 1990); Nottingham Univ. (MA 1996). Teacher: Midhurst Grammar Sch., 1980–82; Therfield Sch., Leatherhead, 1982–88; ordained deacon, 1990, priest, 1991; Curate, St Stephen, Tonbridge, 1990–94; Team Vicar, St Paul, Camberley, 1994–99; Vicar, St Mary, Camberley, 1999–2001; Locum Priest, St John, Trentham, Dio. of Wellington, NZ, 2000; Vicar, St Paul, Dorking, 2001–14; Rural Dean, Dorking, 2009–14; Archdeacon of Dorking, 2014–19. Mem., Gen. Synod, 2015–. Hon. Canon, Guildford Cathedral, 2014–19. *Recreations:* squash, long distance walks, mountain biking, running, sea kayaking, theatre, contemporary art, Southampton FC. *Address:* The Vicarage, 2 Devoran Lane, Devoran, Truro TR3 6PA. *T:* 07734 498565. *E:* Paul.Bryer@truro.anglican.org. *W:* www.twitter.com/paulbcornwall.

**BRYN, Kare;** Secretary-General, European Free Trade Association, 2006–12; *b* 12 March 1944; *m*; four *c*. *Educ:* Norwegian Sch. of Econs and Business Admin. Joined Norwegian Foreign Service, 1969; served in London, Belgrade, Oslo, Geneva, 1971–84; Hd of Div., 1984, Asst Dir Gen., 1985–89, Multilateral Econ. Co-operation; Dir Gen., Dept for Natural Resources and Envmtl Affairs, 1989–99; Ambassador: to WTO and EFTA, Geneva, 1999–2003; to Netherlands, 2003–06. Comdr, Order of St Olav (Norway), 1998. *Address:* c/o European Free Trade Association, 9–11 rue de Varembé, 1211 Geneva 20, Switzerland.

**BUBB, Sir Stephen (John Limrick),** Kt 2011; JP; Chief Executive, Charity Futures, since 2016; Acting Director, Oxford Institute of Charity, since 2018; *b* 5 Nov. 1952; *s* of John William Edward Bubb and Diana Rosemary Bubb (*née* Willatts); civil partnership 2006, William Anthony Vetters. *Educ:* Gillingham Grammar Sch.; Christ Church, Oxford (MA PPE 1975). FCIPD 2004. Economist, NEDO, 1975–76; Res. Officer, TGWU, 1976–80; Negotiations Officer, NUT, 1980–87; Hd, Pay Negotiations for Local Govt, AMA, 1987–95; Founding Dir, Nat. Lottery Charities Bd, 1995–2000; Chief Exec., Assoc. of Chief Execs of Voluntary Orgns, 2000–16; Sec. Gen., Euclid, Eur. Third Sector Leaders Network, 2006–15. Chairman: Adventure Capital Fund, 2006–16; Social Investment Business (formerly Future Builders England), 2008–16. Pt-time tutor, Open Univ., 1982–87. Founder Dir, Metropolitan Authorities Recruitment Agency, 1990–95. Mem. (Lab), Lambeth Council, 1982–86 (Chief Whip). Mem., W Lambeth HA, 1982–89; non-exec. Mem., Lambeth, Lewisham and Southwark HA, 1998–2002. Ind. Assessor for Govt Appts, 1999–2010; Public Appointment Assessor, 2012–16. Member: Tyson Task Force on Non-exec. Dir Appts, 2002; Honours Cttee, Cabinet Office, 2005–11; Civil Soc. Cttee, Commonwealth Foundn, 2008–12; Dir, Big Society Trust, 2011–14. Chm., Strategy Cttee, Govs of Guy's and St Thomas' Trust, 2004–07. Founding Mem., Pakistan Develt Network, 2006–07. Youth Court Magistrate for Inner London, 1980–2000. Founder Chair, Lambeth Landmark, 1982–88. Chm., City of Oxford Orch., 1993–95. Mem., Court, Southbank Univ., 2012–. Trustee: Helen and Douglas House Hospice, 2014–; Oxford Inst. for the Study of Charity and Philanthropy, 2017–18; Patron, Muslim Charities Forum, 2016–. JP 1980. FRSA 1998. *Publications:* People are Key?, 2003; And Why Not?: tapping the talent of not-for-profit chief executives, 2004; Only Connect: a leader's guide to networking, 2005; Choice and Voice: Third Sector role in service delivery, 2006; Public Matters, 2007; Castles in the Air, 2007; At Tipping Point, 2009; The Big Society: moving from romanticism to reality, 2010; Rediscovering Charity: defining our role with the state, 2010; The History of Charity, 2017. *Recreations:* genealogy, travel, fine art and fine wine, the Anglican church, making a difference. *Address:* 4 Lyham Close, SW2 5QE. *Club:* Oxford and Cambridge.

**BUBBEAR, Theresa Bernice;** HM Diplomatic Service; Ambassador to Estonia, since 2016; *b* London, 14 Dec. 1962; *d* of Stanley Allen and Bernice Allen; *m* 1988, Alan Keith Bubbear; three *d*. *Educ:* Blackheath High Sch.; Girton Coll., Cambridge (BA Mod. and Med. Langs 1985). Joined FCO, 1985; OECD Desk Officer, Econ. Relns Dept, FCO, 1985–87; Third Sec., Moscow, 1987–89; Vice Consul, Johannesburg, 1990–93; Information Dept, FCO, 1993–95; lang. trng, 1995–96; Second Sec., Helsinki, 1996–2000; Hd, Crisis Mgt Team, Counter Terrorism Policy Dept, 2000–02, Hd, Policy and Projects, Human Resources Directorate, 2002–04, Guidance Editor, Internal Communications Team, 2004–07, FCO; Migration Officer, Pretoria, 2007–08; Dep. Hd, HR Ops, FCO, 2008–10; lang. trng, 2011–12; Dep. Hd of Mission, 2012–15, Chargé d'Affaires, 2015–16, Budapest. *Recreations:* family, languages, walking, early music. *Address:* British Embassy, Wismari 6, 10136 Tallinn, Estonia. *E:* theresa.bubbear@fco.gov.uk.

**BUCCLEUCH, 10th Duke of,** *cr* 1663, **AND QUEENSBERRY,** 12th Duke of, *cr* 1684; **Richard Walter John Montagu Douglas Scott,** KT 2017; KBE 2000; FRSE, FRSGS, FSA; Baron Scott of Buccleuch, 1606; Earl of Buccleuch, Baron Scott of Whitchester and Eskdaill, 1619; Earl of Doncaster and Baron Tynedale (Eng.), 1662; Earl of Dalkeith, 1663; Marquis of Dumfriesshire, Earl of Drumlanrig and Sanquhar, Viscount of Nith, Torthorwold and Ross, Baron Douglas, 1684; Lord-Lieutenant of Roxburgh, Ettrick and Lauderdale, since 2016; Lord High Commissioner, General Assembly, Church of Scotland,

2018 and 2019; *b* 14 Feb. 1954; *e s* of 9th Duke of Buccleuch, KT, VRD and Jane (*née* McNeill); *S* father, 2007; *m* 1981, Lady Elizabeth Kerr (*see* Duchess of Buccleuch); two *s* two *d*. *Educ*: Eton; Christ Church, Oxford. Dir, Border Television, 1989–90, 2000. Member: Nature Conservancy Council, 1989–91; Scottish Natural Heritage, 1992–95 (Chm., SW Reg., 1992–95); ITC, 1991–98 (Dep. Chm., 1996–98); Millennium Commn, 1994–2003. Trustee: Nat. Heritage Meml Fund, 2000–05; Royal Collection Trust, 2011–; President: RSGS, 1999–2005; NT for Scotland, 2002–12; Royal Scottish Agricultural Benevolent Inst., 2007–; Royal Blind and Scottish Nat. Inst. for War Blinded, 2007–. Mem. Council, Winston Churchill Meml Trust, 1993–2005. Dist Councillor, Nithsdale, 1984–90. DL Nithsdale and Annandale and Eskdale, 1987, Roxburgh, Ettrick and Lauderdale, 2011. Hon. Col, 52nd Lowland 6th Bn, Royal Regt of Scotland, 2010. FRSGS 2006; FRSE 2007; FSA 2014. Hon. Fellow, UHI, 2002. *Heir: s* Earl of Dalkeith, *qv*. *Address*: Bowhill, Selkirk TD7 5ET. *T*: (01750) 20732.

**BUCCLEUCH, Duchess of; Elizabeth Marian Frances Montagu Douglas Scott;** *b* 8 June 1954; *y d* of 12th Marquess of Lothian, KCVO and of Antonella (*née* Newland), OBE; *m* 1981, Earl of Dalkeith (*see* Duke of Buccleuch and Queensberry); two *s* two *d*. *Educ*: London Sch. of Economics (BSc 1975). Radio journalist, BBC R4, 1977–81. Chairman: Scottish Ballet, 1990–95; Heritage Educn Trust, 1999. Mem. Council, National Trust, 2000. Trustee: Nat. Museums of Scotland, 1991–99; British Mus., 1999. Chm. Council of Mgt, Arts Educnl Schs, London, 1999–2003. *Recreations*: reading, theatre, music, gardening. *Address*: 24 Lansdowne Road, W11 3LL. *T*: (020) 7727 6573, *Fax*: (020) 7229 7279.
*See also Earl of Dalkeith*.

**BUCHAN,** family name of **Baron Tweedsmuir**.

**BUCHAN, 17th Earl of,** *cr* 1469; **Malcolm Harry Erskine;** Lord Auchterhouse, 1469; Lord Cardross, 1610; Baron Erskine, 1806; *b* 4 July 1930; *s* of 16th Earl of Buchan and Christina, Dowager Countess of Buchan (*d* 1994), *d* of late Hugh Woolner and adopted *d* of late Lloyd Baxendale; *S* father, 1984; *m* 1957, Hilary Diana Cecil, *d* of late Sir Ivan McLannahan Power, 2nd Bt; two *s* two *d*. *Educ*: Eton. JP Westminster, 1972–2000. *Heir: s* Lord Cardross, *qv*. *Address*: 6 Richmond Hill, Bath BA1 5QT. *Club*: Carlton.

**BUCHAN, Prof. Alastair Mitchell,** DSc; FRCP, FRCPC, FRCPE, FMedSci; Professor in Stroke Medicine, since 2009, Dean of Medicine and Head, Medical Sciences Division, since 2008, Director, Acute Vascular Imaging Centre (formerly Unit), since 2006, and Hon. Consultant Neurologist, since 2004, University of Oxford; Professorial Fellow of Corpus Christi College, Oxford, since 2009; Senior Investigator, National Institute for Health Research, 2008–19, now Senior Investigator Emeritus; *b* 16 Oct. 1955; *s* of Prof. Alan Robson Buchan and Dorothy Mitchell; *m* 1999, Angelika S. Kaiser; two *d*. *Educ*: Repton Sch.; Sidney Sussex Coll., Cambridge (BA 1977; MA 1981); University Coll., Oxford (BM BCh 1980; MA 2008; DSc 2008). FRCPC 1986; FRCPE 1997; FRCP 2001. Radcliffe Travelling Fellow, UC, Oxford, 1983–85; MRC Centennial Fellow, Cornell Univ., NY, 1985–88; Asst Prof. of Neurol., Univ. of Western Ontario, 1988–91; Associate Prof. of Medicine and Anatomy, Univ. of Ottawa, 1991–95; Prof. of Neurol. and Heart and Stroke Foundn Prof. of Stroke Res., Univ. of Calgary, 1995–2004; Professor of Clinical Geratol., Oxford Univ., 2004–09. R&D Chair, Canadian Stroke Consortium, 1993–2006; Director: Canadian Stroke Network, 1999–2004; UK Stroke Network, 2005–08. Member: Stroke Strategy Cttee, DoH, 2006; Stroke Bd, Charité Hosp., Berlin, 2008–. Dir, Oxford Univ. Hosps NHS Trust Strategic Partnership Bd, 2008– (formerly Strategic Partnership Bd and NHS Trust, John Radcliffe Hosp.). Member: American Acad. of Neurol., 1983–; Canadian Neurol Assoc., 1986–; Internat. Soc. of Cerebral Flow and Metabolism, 1987–; Internat. Stroke Soc., 1988; Soc. for Neurosci., 1988–; Assoc. of British Neurologists, 2000–; American Neurol Assoc., 2002–; Stroke Soc. of Australia, 2005–. Nuffield Med. Trustee, 2008–. Mem. Council, Oxford Univ., 2008–. Gov., Repton Sch., Derbys, 2005–. FMedSci 2007. Hon. LLD Calgary, 2009. *Publications*: Maturation Phenomenon of Cerebral Ischaemic Injury, 2003; contrib. Lancet, New England Jl of Medicine, Nature, Nature Medicine, Jl of Cerebral Blood Flow and Metabolism, Stroke, Jl of Neurosci., Annals of Neurol., Trends in Pharmacol Scis. *Recreations*: archaeology, antiquities, art and world history. *Address*: University of Oxford, John Radcliffe Hospital, Headington, Oxford OX3 9DU. *T*: (01865) 224304, *Fax*: (01865) 221354. *E*: alastair.buchan@medsci.ox.ac.uk; Ashtree House, Waterperry Road, Worminghall, Bucks HP18 9JN. *Clubs*: Athenæum; Osler House (Oxford).

**BUCHAN, Brian John;** Vice Lord-Lieutenant of Oxfordshire, since 2019; *b* Glasgow, 23 May 1952; *s* of James Buchan and Winifred Buchan; *m* 1973, Frances Swaffield; two *s* one *d*. *Educ*: Croesyceiliog Sch.; Jesus Coll., Oxford (BA Chem.). Procter & Gamble, 1974–2000: Gen. Manager, Germany, 1991–94; Regl Vice-Pres., 1995–98; Gp Vice-Pres., 1998–2000; CEO, SSL Internat. plc, 2001–04. Chairman: R&R Ice Cream, 2006–11; Burton's Foods, 2008–13. Chairman: Finance Cttee, Story Mus., Oxford, 2015–; Trustees, OXSRAD, 2018–. FRSA. DL Oxon, 2018. *Recreations*: golf, music, ski-ing. *Club*: Oxford and Cambridge.

**BUCHAN, Dennis Thorne,** RSA 1991 (ARSA 1975); painter; *b* 25 April 1937; *s* of David S. Buchan and Mary Buchan (*née* Clark); *m* 1965, Elizabeth Watson (marr. diss. 1977); one *s* one *d*. *Educ*: Arbroath High Sch.; Dundee Coll. of Art; Patrick Allan Fraser Coll., Arbroath; Dundee Coll. of Art (DA 1958). Nat. Service, RAEC, 1960–62. Lectr in Drawing and Painting, Duncan of Jordanstone Coll. of Art, 1965–94. Mem., SSA, 1961–74. *Solo exhibitions*: Douglas and Foulis Gall., 1965; Saltire Soc., Edinburgh Fest., 1974; Compass Gall., 1975, 2006, A Span of Shores, 1994; Traquair House, Peebles, 1996; Pentacle Business Centre, Glasgow, 2002; The Meffan, Forfar, 2005; *group exhibitions* include: Six Coastal Artists, Demarco Gall., Edinburgh, 1965; Seven Painters in Dundee, Scottish Nat. Gall. of Modern Art, and tour, 1972; Compass Contribution, Tramway, Glasgow, 1990; Scottish Contemporary Painting, Flowers East, London, 1993; Five Scottish Artists, Centre d'Art en l'Ile, Geneva, 1994; Brechin Arts Fest., 2008; Scottish Painters, Kinblethmont House, Arbroath, 2009; work in private and public collections throughout UK and USA. Keith Prize, 1962, Latimer, 1973, William McCauley Award, 1988, Gillies Bequest, 1991, Royal Scottish Acad. *Recreations*: non specific. *Address*: 2 Manor Gardens, Carnoustie, Angus DD7 6HY.

**BUCHAN, Hon. Ursula Margaret Bridget, (Hon. Mrs Wide);** author and journalist; *b* 25 June 1953; twin of 3rd Baron Tweedsmuir and Barbara (*née* Ensor); *m* 1979, Charles Thomas Wide, *qv*; one *s* one *d*. *Educ*: Littlemore Grammar Sch.; Oxford High Sch. for Girls; New Hall, Cambridge (MA); Royal Botanic Gardens, Kew (Dip. Hort.). Freelance journalist, 1980–; gardening columnist: Spectator, 1984–2011; Observer, 1987–93; Sunday Telegraph, 1993–97; Independent, 1998–2003; Daily Telegraph, 2004–11. Gardening and social history author and lectr, 1986–. JP 2004–14. Garden Writer of the Year, 1992, Gardening Columnist of the Year, 2011, Garden Media Guild. *Publications*: An Anthology of Garden Writing, 1986; The Pleasures of Gardening, 1987; (with Nigel Colborn) The Classic Horticulturist, 1987; Foliage Plants, 1988, 2nd edn 1993; The Village Show, 1990; Wall Plants and Climbers, 1992; (with David Stevens) The Garden Book, 1994; Gardening for Pleasure, 1996; Plants for All Seasons, 1999, 2nd edn 2004; Good in a Bed: garden writings from The Spectator, 2001; Better Against a Wall, 2003; The English Garden, 2006; Garden People, 2007; Back to the Garden, 2009; A Green and Pleasant Land: how England's gardeners fought the Second World War, 2013; (ed) The Garden Anthology, 2014; Beyond the Thirty-Nine Steps: a life of John Buchan, 2019. *Recreations*: gardening, fell walking, watching Rugby Union and cricket, choral singing. *Address*: c/o Felicity Bryan Literary Agency, 2a North Parade Avenue, Oxford OX2 6LX.

**BUCHAN-HEPBURN, Sir (John) Alastair (Trant Kidd),** 7th Bt *cr* 1815, of Smeaton Hepburn, Haddingtonshire; *b* 27 June 1931; *s* of John Trant Buchan-Hepburn (*d* 1953), *g g s* of 2nd Bt, and Edith Margaret Mitchell (*née* Robb) (*d* 1980); *S* cousin, 1992; *m* 1957, Georgina Elizabeth, *d* of late Oswald Morris Turner, MC; three *d* (one *s* decd). *Educ*: Charterhouse; St Andrews Univ.; RMA, Sandhurst. 1st King's Dragoon Guards, 1952–57; Captain, 1954; ADC to GOC-in-C, Malaya, 1954–57. Arthur Guinness & Son Co. Ltd, 1959–86; Director: Broughton Brewery Ltd, 1987–95; Broughton Ales Ltd, 1995–2001; Chairman: Valentine Marketing Ltd, 2002–03; Valentine Holdings Ltd, 2002–03. Mem. Cttee, St Andrews Br., RBL. Life Mem., St Andrews Preservation Trust, 1984–; Mem., Baronets' Trust, 1992–; UK Rep., European Commn of the Nobility, 2015–. Trustee, Dundee Industrial Heritage Trust, 1999–2006. Vice-Pres., Maritime Volunteer Service, 2001–07. Member: Regtl Assoc., 1st Queen's Dragoon Guards, 1958–; Vestry, All Saints Scottish Episcopal Ch, St Andrews, 2002–06. Mem., Royal Stuart Soc., 2005. Mem., St Andrews Loches Alliance—La Nouvelle Alliance, 2005–. Mem., Kate Kennedy Club, 1950–, After Many Days Club, 2002–, St Andrews Univ. Member: St Andrews Shoot, 1990–2005; Logiealmond Shoot, 2004–07. Chief Marshal: Dunhill Championship, St Andrews, 1999–2005; Open Championship, St Andrews, 2000 and 2006. Leader, European and Scottish campaign for repatriation from Denmark to Scotland for Christian burial of remains of James Hepburn, 4th Earl of Bothwell and 3rd husband of Mary, Queen of Scots, 2000; remains laid to rest in sarcophagus in crypt of Dragsholm Church, Denmark. *Publications*: trans. from French, Lord James, by Catherine Hermary Vieille, 2010 (also trans. film and TV script). *Recreations*: golf, fishing, shooting, tennis, badminton, travel in Europe (especially France), USA and other parts of the world, antiquities, Buchan and Hepburn genealogical history. *Heir: g s* John James Christopher Thomas Buchan-Hepburn, *b* 1 Dec. 1992. *Address*: Chagford, 60 Argyle Street, St Andrews, Fife KY16 9BU. *T*: and *Fax*: (01334) 472161, *T*: 07939 139545. *E*: alastairbh@gmail.com. *Clubs*: New, Royal Scots (Edinburgh); Royal and Ancient Golf (St Andrews).

**BUCHANAN, Alistair George,** CBE 2009; FCA; Chair and Partner, KPMG, 2013–18; *b* 22 Dec. 1961; *s* of late Colin Buchanan and of Isobel Buchanan; *m* 1988, Linda Pollock; one *s* two *d*. *Educ*: Malvern Coll.; Durham Univ. (BA Hons). FCA 1986. Chartered Accountant, KPMG, 1983–87; Head: UK Utilities Res., Smith New Court, 1987–94; UK, European and Global Res. Div., BZW, 1994–97; USA Utilities Res., Salomon Smith Barney, NY, 1997–2000; European Res., London, Donaldson, Lufkin & Jenrette (DLJ), 2000–01; ABN AMRO, 2001–03; Chief Exec., Ofgem, 2003–13. Non-executive Director: Scottish Water, 2008–09; Thames Water, 2018–; Electricity NW, 2018–. Mem. Council and Chair, Remuneration Cttee, Durham Univ., 2010–; Mem. Council, Royal Holloway, Univ. of London, 2018–. *Recreations*: season ticket holder Harlequins, classical music, all sports.

**BUCHANAN, Sir Andrew (George),** 5th Bt *cr* 1878; KCVO 2011; farmer; Lord-Lieutenant and Keeper of the Rolls for Nottinghamshire, 1991–2012; *b* 21 July 1937; *s* of Major Sir Charles Buchanan, 4th Bt, and Barbara Helen (*d* 1986), *o d* of late Lt-Col Rt Hon. Sir George Stanley, PC, GCSI, GCIE; *S* father, 1984; *m* 1966, Belinda Jane Virginia (*née* Maclean), JP, DL, *widow* of Gresham Neilus Vaughan; one *s* one *d*, and one step *s* one step *d*. *Educ*: Eton; Trinity Coll., Cambridge; Wye Coll., Univ. of London. Nat. Service, 2nd Lieut, Coldstream Guards, 1956–58. Chartered Surveyor with Smith-Woolley & Co., 1965–70. Chm., Bd of Visitors, HM Prison Ranby, 1983 (Vice-Chm. 1982). Commanded A Squadron (SRY), 3rd Bn Worcs and Sherwood Foresters (TA), 1971–74; Hon. Col, B Sqn (SRY), Queen's Own Yeo., 1989–94; Hon. Col, Notts ACF, 2001–07. Pres., E Midlands Reserve Forces and Cadets Assoc., 1999–. High Sheriff, Notts, 1976–77; DL Notts, 1985. KStJ 1991. *Recreations*: ski-ing, walking, forestry. *Heir: s* George Charles Mellish Buchanan [*b* 27 Jan. 1975; *m* 2002, Katharine, *d* of late Tom Price]. *Address*: Hodsock Priory Farm, Blyth, Worksop, Notts S81 0TY. *T*: (01909) 591227. *E*: andrew.buchanan@hodsockpriory.com. *Club*: Boodle's.

**BUCHANAN, Prof. Ann Hermione,** MBE 2012; PhD; FAcSS; Professor of Social Work, 2003–08, now Emeritus, and Senior Research Associate, Department of Social Policy and Intervention, since 2008, University of Oxford; Fellow of St Hilda's College, Oxford, since 1994; *b* Winchester, 1941; *d* of late Raymond Alexander Baring and Margaret Fleetwood (*née* Campbell-Preston, later Countess of Malmesbury); *m* 1964, Alistair John Buchanan; three *d*. *Educ*: Univ. of London (Dip Soc. Studies (Dist.) 1968); Univ. of Bath (Dip Applied Soc. Studies 1980); Univ. of Southampton (PhD 1990). Research Assistant: to Henry Kempe, NSPCC, 1969–71; Burderop Hosp., Wilts, 1973–79; Psychiatric Social Worker Child Guidance, 1980–89; Lecturer: Bracknell Coll., 1989–91; Univ. of Southampton, 1991–94; University of Oxford: Lectr, 1994–2000; Reader, 2000–; Dir, Centre for Res. into Parenting and Children, 1996–2008. Vis. Prof., Univ. of St Petersburg, 1996. Member: ESRC, 2008–13 (Chm., Cttee for updating Framework for Res. Ethics, 2009; Chm., Evaluation Cttee, 2010–13); Council, Acad. of Social Scis, 2010–17. Trustee: Baring Foundn, 2000–12; Family Action, 2000–08; Oxfordshire Community Foundn, 2008–16; Grandparent Plus, 2012–18. FAcSS (AcSS 2009). Hon. MA Oxon 1994; Hon. LLD Bath, 2013. *Publications*: Child Maltreatment: facts, fallacies and interventions, 1996; (ed with B. L. Hudson) Parenting, Schooling and Children's Behaviour, 1998; (with B. L. Hudson) Promoting Children's Emotional Well-being, 2000; (jtly) Families in Conflict: perspectives of children and parents on the Family Court Welfare Service, 2001; What Works for Troubled Children, 1999, rev. edn (with Charlotte Ritchie) 2004; (ed) Major Themes in Health and Social Welfare, 4 vols, 2008; (ed with A. Rotkirch) No Time for Children? Fertility Rates and Population Decline, 2013; (ed with A. Rotkirch) Grandfathers: global perspectives, 2016; over 70 articles on child well-being, grand-parenting, fathering, impact of divorce on children, children at risk of social exclusion, child abuse and children in care. *Recreations*: family, flowers, travel. *Address*: 11 London Place, Oxford OX4 1BD. *T*: (01865) 424576. *E*: ann.buchanan@spi.ox.ac.uk.
*See also Sir J. F. Baring*.

**BUCHANAN, Rt Rev. Colin Ogilvie;** Area Bishop of Woolwich, 1996–2004; an Hon. Assistant Bishop: Diocese of Bradford, 2004–14; Diocese of Leeds (formerly West Yorkshire and The Dales), since 2014; *b* 9 Aug. 1934; *s* of late Prof. Robert Ogilvie Buchanan and of Kathleen Mary (*née* Parnell); *m* 1963; two *d*. *Educ*: Whitgift Sch., S Croydon; Lincoln Coll., Oxford (BA, 2nd Cl. Lit. Hum., MA). Theological training at Tyndale Hall, Bristol, 1959–61; deacon, 1961; priest, 1962; Curate, Cheadle, Cheshire, 1961–64; joined staff of London Coll. of Divinity (now St John's Coll., Nottingham), 1964; posts held: Librarian, 1964–69; Registrar, 1969–74; Director of Studies, 1974–75; Vice-Principal, 1975–78; Principal, 1979–85; Hon. Canon of Southwell Minster, 1982–85; Bishop Suffragan of Aston, 1985–89; Hon. Asst Bishop, Dio. of Rochester, 1989–96; Vicar, St Mark's, Gillingham, Kent, 1991–96. Member: Church of England Liturgical Commn, 1964–86; Doctrinal Commn, 1986–91; House of Clergy, 1970–85, House of Bishops, 1990–2004, General Synod of C of E; Assembly of British Council of Churches, 1971–80; Steering Cttee, CCBI, 1990–92; Council for Christian Unity, 1991–2001; Steering Gp, Internat.

Anglican Liturgical Consultations, 1995–2001. Mem., Lambeth Conf., 1988, 1998 (Mem., Chaplaincy Team, 1998). Chm., Millennium Dome Chaplaincy Gp, 1999–2000. Pres., Movt for Reform of Infant Baptism, 1988–. Vice-Pres., 1987–2005, Pres., 2005–12, Electoral Reform Soc. Grove Books: Proprietor, 1970–85; Hon. Manager, 1985–93; Editorial Consultant, 1993–. DD Lambeth, 1993. *Publications:* (ed) Modern Anglican Liturgies 1958–1968, 1968; (ed) Further Anglican Liturgies 1968–1975, 1975; (jtly) Growing into Union, 1970; (ed jtly) Anglican Worship Today, 1980; (ed) Latest Anglican Liturgies 1976–1984, 1985; (jtly) Reforming Infant Baptism, 1990; Open to Others, 1992; Infant Baptism and the Gospel, 1993; Cut the Connection, 1994; Is the Church of England Biblical?, 1998; (ed) Michael Vasey—Liturgist and Friend, 1999; (ed) The Savoy Conference Revisited, 2002; Historical Dictionary of Anglicanism, 2006 (reissued as The A to Z of Anglicanism, 2009), 2nd edn 2015; Taking the Long View, 2006; (consultant ed.) Oxford Guide to the Book of Common Prayer, 2006; (jtly) A History of the International Anglican Liturgical Consultations, 2007; (ed) Justin Martyr on Baptism and Eucharist, 2007; An Evangelical among the Anglican Liturgists, 2009; The Hampton Court Conference and the 1604 Book of Common Prayer, 2009; (ed) Anglican Eucharistic Liturgies 1985–2010, 2011; St John's College Nottingham: from Northwood to Nottingham—a history of 50 years 1963–2013, 2013; Did the Anglicans and Roman Catholics Agree With Each Other?, 2018; editor: Grove Booklets on Ministry and Worship, 1971–2002; Grove Liturgical Studies, 1975–86; Alcuin/GROW Joint Liturgical Studies, 1987– (regular author in these series); News of Liturgy, 1975–2003; contrib. learned jls. *Recreations:* interested in electoral reform, sport, etc.

**BUCHANAN, Prof. David Alan**, PhD; Professor of Organizational Behaviour, School of Management, Cranfield University, 2005–13, now Emeritus; *b* 26 July 1949; *s* of David Stewart and Harriet Buchanan; *m* 1974, Lesley Fiddes Fulton; one *s* one *d*. *Educ:* Heriot-Watt Univ. (BA Hons); Univ. of Edinburgh (PhD). Personnel Asst, Lothian Regl Council, Edinburgh, 1976–77; Lecturer in Organizational Behaviour: Napier Poly., Edinburgh, 1977–79; Univ. of Glasgow, 1979–86, Sen. Lectr, 1986–89; Prof. of Human Resource Management, Loughborough Univ. of Technology, 1989–95; Dir, Loughborough Univ. Business Sch., 1992–95; Prof. of Organizational Behaviour, Leicester Business Sch., De Montfort Univ., 1995–2005. Vis. Prof. of Organizational Behaviour, Nottingham Business Sch., Nottingham Trent Univ., 2014–. FCIPD; FRSA; FBAM; FAcSS. Hon. FIES. *Publications:* The Development of Job Design Theories and Techniques, 1979; (with A. A. Huczynski) Organizational Behaviour: an introductory text, 1985, Student Workbook, 1994, Instructor's Manual, 1994, 9th edn 2016; (ed jtly) The New Management Challenge: information systems for improved performance, 1988; (with J. McCalman) High Performance Work Systems: the digital experience, 1989; (with R. Badham) Power, Politics, and Organizational Change, 1999, 2nd edn 2008; (ed jtly) The Sustainability and Spread of Organizational Change, 2007; (with A. Bryman) The Sage Handbook of Organizational Research Methods, 2009; with D. Boddy: Organizations in the Computer Age: technological imperatives and strategic choice, 1983; Managing New Technology, 1986; The Technical Change Audit: action for results, 1987; Take the Lead: interpersonal skills for project managers, 1992; The Expertise of the Change Agent: public performance and backstage activity, 1992; (jtly) Managing Organizational Change: a multiple perspectives approach, 2016; (ed jtly) Unconventional Methodology in Organization and Management Research, 2018; numerous contribs to learned jls. *Recreations:* music, reading, photography, diving, fitness, six grandchildren. *Address:* 18 Ascott Gardens, West Bridgford, Nottingham NG2 7TH.

**BUCHANAN, Sir Gordon Kelly McNicol L.;** *see* Leith-Buchanan.

**BUCHANAN, Isobel Wilson, (Mrs Jonathan King)**; soprano; *b* 15 March 1954; *d* of Stewart and Mary Buchanan; *m* 1980, Jonathan Stephen Geoffrey King (otherwise Jonathan Hyde, actor); two *d*. *Educ:* Cumbernauld High Sch.; Royal Scottish Academy of Music and Drama (DRSAMD 1974). Australian Opera principal singer, 1975–78; freelance singer, 1978–; British debut, Glyndebourne, 1978; Vienna Staatsoper debut, 1978; American debut: Santa Fé, 1979; Chicago, 1979; New York, 1979; German debut, Cologne, 1979; French debut, Aix-en-Provence, 1981; ENO debut, 1985; Paris Opera debut, 1986. Performances also with Scottish Opera, Covent Garden, Munich Radio, Belgium, Norway, etc. Various operatic recordings, notably with Solti, Carlos Kleiber and Bonynge. *Recreations:* reading, cooking, walking.

**BUCHANAN, Michael;** Executive Director, Headmasters' and Headmistresses' Conference, since 2018; *b* Brisbane, Australia. *Educ:* King's Coll. London (BSc). Royal Grammar Sch., Guildford, 1984–94; Principal Dep. Hd, Highgate Sch., 1995–2005; Head, Ashford Sch., Kent, 2005–18. Reporting Inspector, 2010–. Nat. Leader of Educn, 2014–. Chm., HMC, 2016–17. *Recreation:* wannabe farmer. *Address:* Headmasters' and Headmistresses' Conference, 12 The Point, Rockingham Road, Market Harborough, Leics LE16 7QU.

**BUCHANAN, Prof. Robert Angus**, OBE 1993; PhD; FSA; FRHistS; Founder and Director, Centre for the History of Technology, Science and Society, 1964–95, Professor of the History of Technology, 1990–95, University of Bath, now Emeritus Professor; Director, National Cataloguing Unit for the Archives of Contemporary Scientists, 1987–95; *b* 5 June 1930; *s* of Roy Graham Buchanan and Bertha (*née* Davis); *m* 1955, Brenda June Wade; two *s*. *Educ:* High Storrs Grammar Sch. for Boys, Sheffield; St Catharine's Coll., Cambridge (MA, PhD). FRHistS 1978; FSA 1990. Educn Officer to Royal Foundn of St Katharine, Stepney, 1956–60 (Co-opted Mem., LCC Educn Cttee, 1958–60); Asst Lectr, Dept of Gen. Studies, Bristol Coll. of Science and Technol. (now Univ. of Bath), 1960; Lectr, 1961, Sen. Lectr, 1966, Head of Humanities Gp, Sch. of Humanities and Social Scis, 1970–95, Reader in Hist. of Technol., 1981–90, Univ. of Bath. Vis. Lectr, Univ. of Delaware, USA, 1969; Vis. Fellow, ANU, Canberra, 1981; Vis. Lectr, Huazhong (Central China) Univ. of Science and Tech., Wuhan, People's Repub. of China, 1983; Jubilee Chair in History of Technol., Chalmers Univ., Göteborg, Sweden, Autumn term, 1984. Royal Comr, Royal Commn on Historical Monuments (England), 1979–93; Sec., Res. Cttee on Indust. Archaeology, Council for British Archaeology, 1972–79; President: (Founding) Bristol Indust. Archaeological Soc., 1967–70; Assoc. for Indust. Archaeology, 1974–77 (Hon. Pres., 2004–10); Newcomen Soc. for History of Engrg and Technol., 1981–83; Internat. Cttee for History of Technol., 1993–97 (Sec.-Gen., 1981–93); Vice Pres., Soc. of Antiquaries, 1995–99; Chm., Water Space Amenity Commn's Working Party on Indust. Archaeology, 1982–83; Member: Properties Cttee, National Trust, 1974–2002; Technol Preservation Awards Cttee, Science Museum, 1973–81. FRSA 1993–99. Hon. Fellow, Science Mus., 1992. Hon. DSc (Engrg) Chalmers Univ., Göteborg, Sweden, 1986. Leonardo da Vinci Medal, Soc. for Hist. of Technol., 1989. *Publications:* Technology and Social Progress, 1965; (with Neil Cossons) Industrial Archaeology of the Bristol Region, 1969; (with Neil Cossons) Industrial Archaeology in Britain, 1972, 2nd edn 1982; (with George Watkins) Industrial Archaeology of the Stationary Steam Engine, 1976; History and Industrial Civilization, 1979; (with C. A. Buchanan) Industrial Archaeology of Central Southern England, 1980; (with Michael Williams) Brunel's Bristol, 1982; The Engineers: a history of the engineering profession in Britain, 1989; The Power of the Machine, 1992; Brunel: the life and times of I. K. Brunel, 2002; (ed and contrib.) Landscape with Technology: essays in honour of L. T. C. Rolt, 2011; (ed and contrib.) The Engineering Revolution: how the modern world was changed by technology, 2019. *Recreations:* Cambridge Judo half-blue, 1955; rambling, travelling, exploring. *Address:* 13 Hensley Road, Bath BA2 2DR. *T:* (01225) 311508.

**BUCHANAN, Robin William Turnbull**, FCA; *b* 2 April 1952; *s* of Iain Buchanan and Gillian Pamela Buchanan (*née* Hughes-Hallett); *m* 1986, Diana Tei Tanaka; one *s* one *d*. *Educ:* Harvard Business Sch. (MBA, Baker Scholar). Mann Judd Landau, subseq. Deloitte & Touche, 1970–77; American Express Internat. Banking Corp., 1979–82; Bain & Company Inc., 1982–: Bain Capital, 1982–84; Man. Partner, London, 1990–96; Sen. Partner, London, 1996–2007; Sen. Advr, 2007–. Dean, then Pres., London Business Sch., 2007–09. Chm., Page Gp (formerly Michael Page Internat.), 2014–15; non-executive Director: Liberty Internat. plc, 1997–2008; Shire plc (formerly Shire Pharmaceuticals Gp plc), 2003–08; Schroders, 2010–; LyondellBasell NV, 2011–. Mem. Bd, Trees for Life, 2014–. Mem., Highland Soc. of London. Fellow, Salzburg Seminar. Mem., Northern Meeting. FRSA. Liveryman, Co. of Ironmongers. *Recreations:* farming, forestry, shooting, collecting old children's books. *Club:* Pilgrims.

**BUCHANAN-DUNLOP, Col Robert Daubeny, (Robin)**, CBE 1987 (OBE 1982); Clerk, Goldsmiths' Company, 1988–2004; *b* 11 Aug. 1939; *o s* of late Col Robert Arthur Buchanan-Dunlop of Drumhead, OBE, The Cameronians (Scottish Rifles) and Patricia Buchanan-Dunlop (*née* Upton); *m* 1972, Nicola Jane Goodhart; two *s*. *Educ:* Loretto Sch. William Thomson & Co., Managers Ben Line, 1958–59. National Service, The Cameronians (Scottish Rifles), 1959–61; Regular Commission, 1961; transf. to Scots Guards; served Kenya, Aden, Sharjah, Germany, NI (despatches); Staff Coll., 1971; HQ 1 Div., 1973–75; Armed Forces Staff Coll., USA, 1978; Directing Staff, Canadian Land Forces Staff Coll., 1978–79; CO 8th (Co. Tyrone) Bn, UDR, 1979–81; COS 52 Lowland Bde, 1982–84; COS NI, 1984–86; Dep. Dir, UK C-in-C Cttees, 1987; retired. Mem., Queen's Body Guard for Scotland (Royal Company of Archers), 1987–. Chm., Lead Body, Jewellery and Allied Industries, 1994–98; Dir, Livery Cos Mutual Ltd, 1999–2014. Mem., British Hallmarking Council, 1988–2004. Member: Council, Goldsmiths' Coll., 1989–2004; Governing Body: Imperial Coll., 1989–2001; London Guildhall Univ., 1997–2002. Chm., Adv. Cttee, Deptford City Challenge, 1992–97. Hon. MA London Guildhall, 1994. *Publications:* Ham: the story of a Wiltshire village, 2011. *Recreations:* walking, gardening, visual arts, writing. *Address:* Ham Green Cottage, Ham, Marlborough, Wilts SN8 3QR. *T:* (01488) 668846. *Club:* Army and Navy.

**BUCHANAN-JARDINE, Sir John (Christopher Rupert)**, 5th Bt *cr* 1885, of Castle Milk, co. Dumfries; *b* 20 March 1952; *o s* of Sir Rupert Buchanan-Jardine, 4th Bt, MC and of Jane Fiona, *d* of Sir Charles Edmondstone, 6th Bt; *S* father, 2010; *m* 1975, Pandora Lavinia, *d* of Peter Murray Lee; one *s* five *d*. *Educ:* Harrow; RAC Cirencester. *Heir: s* James Rupert Buchanan-Jardine, *b* 28 July 1994.

**BUCK, Emma Louise L.;** *see* Lewell-Buck, E. L.

**BUCK, John Stephen;** HM Diplomatic Service, retired; Founding Partner, Ambassador Partnership (formerly ADRgAmbassadors), since 2010; *b* 10 Oct. 1953; *s* of Frederick George Buck and Amelia Ellen Buck (*née* Stevens); *m* 1980, Jean Claire Webb; one *s* one *d*. *Educ:* East Ham GS; York Univ. (BA History 1975); Wolfson Coll., Oxford (MSc Applied Social Studies, 1979; CQSW 1979). Middlesex Probation Service, 1975–77; social worker, Oxfordshire Social Services, 1979–80; joined HM Diplomatic Service, 1980; Second Sec., Sofia, 1982–84; First Sec., FCO, 1984–88; Head of Chancery, Lisbon, 1988–92; FCO, 1992–94; Counsellor, on loan to Cabinet Office, Prin. Private Sec. to Chancellor of the Duchy of Lancaster, 1994–96; Counsellor and Dep. High Comr, Republic of Cyprus, 1996–2000; Head, Public Diplomacy, FCO, 2000–03; Head, Govt Information and Commns Centre, 10 Downing Street/FCO, 2003; Dir, Iraq, FCO, 2003–04; Ambassador to Portugal, 2004–07. Gp Dir, Govt and Public Affairs, BG Gp plc, 2007–09. Chm. Trustees, Musequality, 2013–15. *Recreations:* music, books, art, swimming, cycling, travel. *E:* john.buck@ambassadorllp.com.

**BUCK, Karen Patricia;** MP (Lab) Westminster North, since 2010 (Regent's Park and Kensington North, 1997–2010); *b* 30 Aug. 1958; partner, Barrie Taylor; one *s*. *Educ:* Chelmsford High Sch.; LSE (BSc, MSc, MA). R&D worker, Outset, 1979–83; London Borough of Hackney: Specialist Officer, Developing Services and Employment for Disabled People, 1983–86; Public Health Officer, 1986–87; Lab. Party Policy Directorate (Health), 1987–92; Co-ordinator, Lab. Party Campaign Strategy, 1992–96. Parly Under-Sec. of State, DfT, 2005–06; PPS to Leader of the Opposition, 2013–15. Member: Social Security Select Cttee, 1997–2001; Work and Pensions Select Cttee, 2001–05, 2015–17; Home Affairs Select Cttee, 2006–09; Jt Cttee on Human Rights, 2015–17; Panel of Chairs, 2015–. Chm., London Gp of Labour MPs, 1998–2005. *Address:* House of Commons, SW1A 0AA.

**BUCK, Prof. Kenneth William**, PhD, DSc; Professor of Plant and Fungal Virology, and Head, Microbiology and Plant Pathology Section, then Plant and Microbial Sciences Section, 1986–2005, and Director of Research, Department of Biological Sciences, 2001–05, Imperial College of Science, Technology and Medicine, University of London; *b* 16 Feb. 1938; *s* of William Buck and Nellie Sebra (*née* Turner); *m* 1961, Gwendoline Maureen Patterson; three *d*. *Educ:* Univ. of Birmingham (BSc 1st Cl. Hons 1959; PhD 1962; DSc 1983). Res. Fellow, Univ. of Birmingham, 1962–65; Imperial College, University of London: Lectr, Dept of Biochem., 1965–81; Reader, Dept of Biol., 1981–86; Chairman: Sub-Bd of Examrs in Microbiol., 1981–98; Bd of Examrs in Biol., 2000–05; Panel of Vis. Examrs in Microbiol., London Univ., 1988–96. Sec., Cttee on Non-Specific Immunity, MRC, 1968–71; Member: Plants and Envmt Res. Grants Bd, AFRC, 1992–94; Plant and Microbial Scis Cttee, BBSRC, 1994–97. International Committee on Taxonomy of Viruses: Mem., Exec. Cttee, 1981–93; Mem., 1975–2005, Chm., 1981–87, Fungal Virus Sub-cttee; Sec., 1984–90; Vice-Pres., 1990–93; Mem., Plant Virus Sub-cttee, 1999–2005; Chm., Narnaviridae Study Gp, 2000–05. Chm. of workshops on fungal virol. and plant virus replication, Internat. Congress of Virology, triennially, 1981–93, 1999, 2002, 2005; Mem., Internat. Adv. Cttee, XII Internat. Congress of Virology, Paris, 2002, XIII, San Francisco, 2005. Mem., Soc. for Gen. Microbiol., 1975–2005. Editor, Jl of Gen. Virology, 1991–96 (Mem., Editl Bd, 1985–90, 1997–2001); Mem., Editl Bd, Virology, 1998–2005. *Publications:* (ed) Fungal Virology, 1986; over 200 papers in scientific jls and books. *Recreations:* genealogy, walking, chess, theatre, cinema, opera, ballet, musical concerts, gardening, Member of Probus Club, RHS and English Heritage.

**BUCK, Linda B.**, PhD; Member, Division of Basic Sciences, Fred Hutchinson Cancer Research Center, since 2002; Affiliate Professor of Physiology and Biophysics, University of Washington, since 2003; *b* 29 Jan. 1947. *Educ:* Univ. of Washington (BS 1975); Univ. of Texas (PhD 1980). Associate, Howard Hughes Med. Inst., Columbia Univ., 1984–91; Asst Prof., 1991–96, Associate Prof., 1996–2001, Prof., 2001–02, Dept of Neurobiol., Harvard Med. Sch.; Asst Investigator, 1994–97, Associate Investigator, 1997–2000, Investigator, 2001–, Howard Hughes Med. Inst. Dir, International Flavors & Fragrances Inc., 2007–. Foreign Mem., Royal Soc. 2015. (Jtly) Nobel Prize in Physiology or Medicine, 2004. *Publications:* articles in learned jls. *Address:* Division of Basic Sciences, Fred Hutchinson Cancer Research Center, 1100 Fairview Avenue North, PO Box 19024, Seattle, WA 98109–1024, USA.

**BUCK, Prof. Margaret Ann,** OBE 2008; artist, designer; arts and design consultant; *b* 23 Nov. 1948; *d* of late William Ewart Buck and Winifred Annie Buck; *m* 1985, David Martin Burrows; one *s* one *d* (twins). *Educ:* Pate's Grammar Sch. for Girls, Cheltenham; Gloucestershire Coll. of Art and Design (DipAD Fine Art); Royal Coll. of Art (MA Furniture Design). Head of Dept, then Dep. Head of Sch., Central Sch. of Art and Design, 1982–86; Dep. Head of Sch., Camberwell Sch. of Arts and Crafts, 1987–89; London Institute, then University of the Arts, London: Head, Camberwell Coll. of Arts, 1989–91; Asst Rector, 1989–2006; Head of Coll., Central St Martins Coll. of Art & Design, 1991–2006; Mem., Conferments Panel, 1995–2006; Emeritus Prof., 2007; exhibitions: Proj. Dir and Curator, Theatre Design and Interpretation, 1986; Proj. Dir, A Century in the Making, 1999; conceived and designed, The Innovation Centre: Arts, Communication, Fashion, Design, Central St Martins Coll. of Art & Design, 2003. Represented by Updown Gall., Ramsgate, 2012–16. Lectr, Wimbledon Sch. of Art, 1978–82; lectr at internat. confs incl. Saga Internat. Design Conf., Japan, 1993 and Handwerkskammer für München, 1994; various appts as vis. lectr and ext. examr. Advr on strategic develt of arts and design to Ruler of Sharjah and to Coll. of Fine Arts and Design, Univ. of Sharjah, UAE, 2006–10; ext. consultant, Univ. for the Creative Arts, 2013–. Exhibitor, Design of the Times exhibn, RCA, 1996. Director: Develts at London Inst., later London Artscom, Ltd, 1989–2006; Cochrane Th. Co., 1990–2006; Design Lab Ltd, 1999–2006; Connecting Creativity, 2006–11. Chair: London and SE, Nat. Standing Conf. for Foundn Educn in Art and Design, 1981–87; Nat. Council for Foundn Educn in Art and Design, 1987–92. Trustee: Arts Foundn, 1998–2012; V&A Mus., 2000–06 (Mem. Collections Cttee, 2000–06, Remuneration Cttee, 2004–06, Theatre Mus.). Mem. English Lang. Council, ESU, 2003–16 (Chm., Pres.'s Award for Innovation Design and Excellence in the Use of New Freestanding Technologies in the Teaching and Learning of English, 2003–16). Ext. Mem., Profs' and Readers' Conferments Panel, Liverpool John Moores Univ., 2004. Member: Internat. Adv. Cttee, Fashion Fringe, 2004–06; Internat. Adv. Gp, Shanghai Inst. of Visual Arts, Univ. of Fudan, China, 2005–07 (Hon. Prof., 2007). Governor, GSMD, 2000–09. Ext. Examr, Acad. of Visual Arts, Ljubljana, 2015–. Hon. Associate, Altagamma Internat. Hon. Council, Italy, 2005. Sanderson Art in Industry Award, 1976, Radford Design Award, 1977, Furniture Makers' Co. *E:* mbuck@connectingcreativity.co.uk. *Club:* Chelsea Arts.

**BUCK, Prof. Martin,** PhD; FRS 2009; FRSB; Professor of Molecular Microbiology, Imperial College London, since 1999; *b* London, 16 Oct. 1955; *s* of Geoffrey Edward Buck and Alice Eva Buck (*née* Alexander); *m* 1996, Madeleine Henrietta Moore; two *s*. *Educ:* Bedford Coll., London (BSc Biochem. 1977); MRC-Nat. Inst. for Med. Res. (PhD Biochem. 1980). Postdoctoral Fellow, Univ. of Calif, Berkeley, 1980–83; Higher Scientific Officer, 1983–89, Sen. Scientific Officer, 1989–91, Grade 7, 1991–94, AFRC-BBSRC Nitrogen Fixation Lab., Univ. of Sussex; Imperial College London: Sen. Lectr, 1994–96; Reader, 1996–99; Hd, Dept of Biol Scis, 2001–04. Fellow, Amer. Acad. Microbiol., 2006; FRSB (FSB 2010). *Publications:* contrib. articles to jls on mechanisms governing bacterial gene expression. *Address:* Department of Life Sciences, SAF Building, Imperial College London, SW7 2AZ. *T:* (020) 7594 5442. *E:* m.buck@imperial.ac.uk.

**BUCK-HONOUR, Simon John Langdale;** JP; Chief Executive, British Air Transport Association, 2010–14; *b* Otley, W Yorks, 13 Dec. 1957; *s* of Michael Bernard Langdale Buck and Brenda Buck; civil partnership 2006, *m* 2014, Andrew Mark Honour. *Educ:* Leeds Grammar Sch.; Leeds Poly. (BA 1981). MCILT 1997; MCIPR 2010. Civil servant, Dept of Transport, 1983–95; Hd, Industry Affairs, Air 2000 Ltd, 1995–2002; Gp Hd, Industry Affairs, First Choice Holidays plc, 2002–06; Principal Manager, PR, AQA, 2006–10. JP N Sussex, 2000. *Publications:* various articles on aviation issues. *Recreations:* travel, classic motor cars (Member, Rolls-Royce Enthusiasts and Jaguar Enthusiasts Clubs), company of good friends.

**BUCKBY, Anthony Jonathan,** MBE 1996; education and arts programming consultant, Venice, since 2018; *b* Birmingham, 1 Sept. 1951; *s* of Gordon Buckby and Muriel Buckby (*née* Darby); *m* 1996, Giuliana Salvagno. *Educ:* King's Sch., Worcester; Univ. of Nottingham (BA Hons English Lang. and Lit.); Univ. of Essex (MA Applied Linguistics). Academic Advr, 1982–86, Sch. Dir, 1986–90, British Inst. of Florence; British Council: Director: Bologna, 1990–96; Lang. Services, Italy, Rome, 1996–2000; Deputy Director: Italy, 2000–04; English Lang., London, 2004–07; Dir, Bulgaria, 2007–11; Dir, Greece, 2011–18.

**BUCKELS, Prof. John Anthony Charles,** CBE 2002; MD; FRCS; Professor of Hepatobiliary and Transplant Surgery, University of Birmingham, since 2005; Consultant Hepatobiliary and Liver Transplant Surgeon, Queen Elizabeth Hospital, Birmingham, 1986–2011, now Honorary Consultant Surgeon; Volunteer Surgeon, Médecins sans Frontières; *b* 4 Jan. 1949; *s* of Noel and Loretta Buckels; *m* 1975, Carol Ann Francis; one *s* four *d*. *Educ:* Birmingham Univ. (MB ChB 1972; MD 1986). FRCS 1977. Raine Vis. Prof., Univ. of Western Australia, 1998; Margery Budd Prof., Univ. of Bristol, 2000; Penman Vis. Prof., Univ. of Cape Town, 2007; Mary Weston Vis. Prof., Univ. of KwaZulu Natal, Durban, 2012. *Publications:* numerous contribs on general surgery and transplantation topics to scientific jls. *Recreations:* French home, fishing, sailing. *Address:* 87 Reddings Road, Moseley, Birmingham B13 8LP. *T:* (0121) 449 3310.

**BUCKERIDGE, Frances Mary Theresa;** *see* Hughes, F. M. T.

**BUCKHURST, Lord; William Herbrand Thomas Sackville;** with Quilter Cheviot Investment Management (formerly Cheviot Asset Management), since 2006; *b* 13 June 1979; *s* and *heir* of Earl De La Warr, *qv*; *m* 2010, Countess Xenia, *y d* of Count and Countess Tolstoy-Miloslavsky; one *s* one *d*. *Educ:* Eton; Newcastle Univ. *Recreations:* racing, shooting, cricket, football. *Heir:* *s* Hon. William Lionel Robert Sackville, *b* 24 Jan. 2014. *Address:* Buckhurst Park, Withyham, E Sussex TN7 4BL.

**BUCKINGHAM, Area Bishop of,** since 2003; **Rt Rev. Alan Thomas Lawrence Wilson,** DPhil; *b* 27 March 1955; *s* of Alan Thomas Wilson and Anna Maria Magdalena Wilson; *m* 1984, Lucy Catherine Janet (*née* Richards); two *s* three *d*. *Educ:* Sevenoaks Sch.; St John's Coll., Cambridge (BA 1977, MA 1981); Balliol Coll., Oxford (DPhil 1989); Wycliffe Hall, Oxford. Ordained deacon, 1979, priest, 1980; Hon. Curate, 1979–81, Curate, 1981–82, Eynsham; Priest i/c, St John's, Caversham, and Asst Curate, Caversham and Mapledurham, 1982–89; Vicar, St John's, Caversham, 1989–92; Rector, Sandhurst, 1992–2003. Anglican Substitute Chaplain, HMP Reading, 1990–92; Area Dean, Sonning, 1998–2003; Hon. Canon, Christ Church, Oxford, 2002–03. Chair: Oxford Diocesan Bd of Educn, 2010–; Art Beyond Belief, 2010–16; Oxford Diocesan Bucks Schs Trust, 2017–; Chair of Trustees, Christians Aware, 2011–15; Co-founding Trustee, Oxford Nandyal Educn Foundn, 2012–19. Member: C of E Pensions Bd, 2015–; LGBTI Mission, 2015–. Visitor, Piper's Corner Sch., 2004–; Mem. Council, Wycombe Abbey Sch., 2008–; Governor: Cressex Community Sch., 2008–; Chiltern Hills Acad., 2011–18. Vis. Prof., Univ. of Buckingham, 2009–. *Recreations:* modern history, art and design, photography, singing, running, France. *Address:* Sheridan, Grimms Hill, Great Missenden, Bucks HP16 9BG. *T:* (01494) 862173, *Fax:* (01494) 890508. *E:* bishopbucks@oxford.anglican.org.

**BUCKINGHAM, Archdeacon of;** *see* Elsmore, Ven. G. C.

**BUCKINGHAM, Amyand David,** CBE 1997; FRS 1975; FAA; Professor of Chemistry, University of Cambridge, 1969–97; Fellow of Pembroke College, Cambridge, 1970–97 (Hon. Fellow, 2005); *b* 28 Jan. 1930; 2nd *s* of late Reginald Joslin Buckingham and late Florence Grace Buckingham (formerly Elliot); *m* 1965, Jillian Bowles; one *s* two *d*. *Educ:* Barker Coll., Hornsby, NSW; Univ. of Sydney; Corpus Christi Coll., Cambridge (Shell Postgraduate Schol.). Univ. Medal 1952, MSc 1953, Sydney; PhD 1956, ScD 1985, Cantab. 1851 Exhibn Sen. Studentship, Oxford Univ., 1955–57; Lectr and subseq. Student and Tutor, Christ Church, Oxford, 1955–65; Univ. Lectr in Inorganic Chem. Lab., Oxford, 1958–65; Prof. of Theoretical Chem., Univ. of Bristol, 1965–69. Vis. Lectr, Harvard, 1961; Visiting Professor: Princeton, 1965; Univ. of California (Los Angeles), 1975; Univ. of Illinois, 1976; Univ. of Wisconsin, 1978; ANU, 1996; Vis. Fellow, ANU, 1979 and 1982; Vis. Erskine Fellow, Univ. of Canterbury, NZ, 1990. FRACI 1961 (Masson Meml Schol. 1952; Rennie Meml Medal, 1958); FRSC (formerly FCS) (Harrison Meml Prize, 1959; Tilden Lectr, 1964; Theoretical Chemistry and Spectroscopy Prize, 1970; Faraday Medal and Lectr, 1998; Mem., Faraday Div. (Pres., 1987–89; Mem. Council, 1965–67, 1975–83, 1987–99)); FInstP (Harrie Massey Medal and Prize, 1995); Fellow: Optical Soc. of America (C. H. Townes Medal, 2001); Amer. Phys. Soc.; Mem., Amer. Chem. Soc.; For. Associate, Nat. Acad. Scis, USA, 1992; Foreign Member: Amer. Acad. of Arts and Scis, 1992; Royal Swedish Acad. Scis, 1996; FAA (Corresp. Mem., 2008). Editor: Molecular Physics, 1968–72; Chemical Physics Letters, 1978–99; Internat. Reviews in Physical Chemistry, 1981–89. Member: Chemistry Cttee, SRC, 1967–70; Adv. Council, Royal Mil. Coll. of Science, Shrivenham, 1973–87; Council, Royal Soc., 1999–2001. Senior Treasurer: Oxford Univ. Cricket Club, 1959–64; Cambridge Univ. Cricket Club, 1977–90 (Pres., 1990–2009). Trustee, Henry Fund, 1977–2006. Hon. Dr: Univ. de Nancy I, 1979; Sydney, 1993; Antwerp, 2004. Hughes Medal, Royal Soc., 1996; Ahmed Zewail Prize in Molecular Scis, Elsevier/Chem. Physics Letters, 2007. *Publications:* The Laws and Applications of Thermodynamics, 1964; Organic Liquids, 1978; Principles of Molecular Recognition, 1993; papers in scientific jls. *Recreations:* walking, woodwork, cricket, travel. *Address:* 11 Urwin Gardens, Cambridge CB2 0AP.

**BUCKINGHAM, David Anthony,** AM 2015; Vice-President Marketing, Communications and Student Recruitment, 2012, and Principal Advisor (formerly Senior Co-ordinator), Office of the Vice-Chancellor, 2009, Monash University; *b* 30 March 1946; *s* of Donald Buckingham and Joyce (*née* Craven); *m* 2001, Kiren Mason; one *s* three *d*. *Educ:* Australian National Univ. (BEc 1st Cl. Hons). Aust. Foreign Service, 1972–83; Advr to Prime Minister, Bob Hawke, 1983–86; Dir, Internat. Educn, 1986–89; First Asst Sec., Aviation Div., Aust. Dept of Transport, 1989–92; Dep. Sec., Aust. Dept of Envmt, 1992–94; Exec. Dir, Minerals Council of Australia, 1994–96; Chief Exec., Business Council of Australia, 1996–2001; CEO, Turnbull Porter Novelli, 2001; Man. Dir, Stratpol Consultants, 2002–04; Agent Gen. for Victoria, Australia, in London, 2004–09; Chm., Linking Melbourne Authy, 2009–12. *Recreations:* fishing, walking. *Club:* Sandringham Anglers' (Melbourne).

**BUCKINGHAM, Prof. David Dennis,** PhD; FBA 2015; FAcSS; Professor of Media and Communications, Loughborough University, 2012–14, now Emeritus; *b* London, 6 Oct. 1954; *s* of Dennis Buckingham and Dorothy Buckingham; *m* 1984, Celia Greenwood; two *s*. *Educ:* Latymer Upper Sch., London; Clare Coll., Cambridge (BA Eng. 1975); Central London Poly. (MA Film Studies 1982); Inst. of Educn, Univ. of London (PhD 1993). Media Resources Officer, ILEA, 1978–84; Institute of Education, University of London: Lectr, 1984–96; Reader, 1996–99; Prof. of Educn, 1999–2011; Founder and Dir, Centre for the Study of Children, Youth and Media, 2000–12. Vis. Prof. in USA, Australia, Italy, Norway, Hong Kong, South Africa. FAcSS (AcSS 2011). *Publications:* 30 books incl. Children Talking Television, 1993; Moving Images, 1996; The Making of Citizens, 2000; After the Death of Childhood, 2000; Media Education, 2003; Beyond Technology, 2007; The Material Child, 2011; The Media Education Manifesto, 2019; 250 book chapters and articles in jls. *Recreations:* playing jazz saxophone, swimming, cinema, visual art, walking. *Address:* Department of Social Sciences, Loughborough University, Loughborough LE11 3TU. *T:* (020) 8340 1389. *E:* d.buckingham@lboro.ac.uk. *W:* www.davidbuckingham.net.

**BUCKINGHAM, Ven. Hugh Fletcher;** Archdeacon of the East Riding, 1988–98, now Archdeacon Emeritus; *b* 13 Sept. 1932; *s* of Rev. Christopher Leigh Buckingham and Gladys Margaret Buckingham; *m* 1967, Alison Mary Cock; one *s* one *d*. *Educ:* Lancing College; Hertford Coll., Oxford (MA Hons). Curate: St Thomas', Halliwell, Bolton, 1957–60; St Silas', Sheffield, 1960–65; Vicar of Hindolveston and Guestwick, dio. Norwich, 1965–70; Rector of Fakenham, 1970–88. Hon. Canon of Norwich Cathedral, 1985–88. *Publications:* How To Be A Christian In Trying Circumstances, 1985; Feeling Good, 1989; Happy Ever After, 2000. *Recreations:* pottery, gardening. *Address:* Orchard Cottage, Rectory Corner, Brandsby, York YO61 4RJ.

**BUCKINGHAM, Prof. Julia Clare, (Mrs S. J. Smith),** CBE 2018; PhD, DSc; FRSB; FCGI; Vice-Chancellor and President, Brunel University London, since 2012; *b* 18 Oct. 1950; *d* of late Jack William Harry Buckingham and Barbara Joan Buckingham; *m* 1974, Simon James Smith. *Educ:* St Mary's Sch., Calne; Univ. of Sheffield (BSc Zool. 1971); Royal Free Hosp. Sch. of Medicine, Univ. of London (PhD Pharmacol. 1974; DSc Neuroendocrine Pharmacol. 1987). Res. Fellow, 1974–80, Sen. Lectr in Pharmacol., 1980–87, Royal Free Hosp. Sch. of Medicine, London; Prof. of Pharmacol., Charing Cross and Westminster Med. Sch., 1987–97 (Pre-clinical Dean, 1992–97); Imperial College London: Prof. of Pharmacology, 1997–2012; Head, Dept of Neuroendocrinology, 1997–2003; Dean for Non-clinical Medicine, 2000–03; Hd, Div. of Neurosci. and Mental Health, 2003–07; Pro-Rector (Educn), 2007–10, (Educn and Academic Affairs), 2010–12. Dir, Imperial College Health Partners, 2014–. Mem., Council, Sch. of Pharmacy, London Univ., 2000–05. Pres., British Pharmacol Soc., 2004–05 (Fellow, 2004); Pres., Soc. for Endocrinol., 2011–12 (Treas., 1996–2001; Gen. Sec., 2005–09; Chm., 2009–12); Mem. Council, Bioscis Fedn, 2008–09; Mem. Council and Trustee, Soc. of Biol., later Royal Soc. of Biol., 2009–17. Trustee and Chm., Sci. and Educn Cttee, Royal Instn of GB, 2011–16; Chairman: Science Community Representing Educn, 2013–16; Res. Concordat Strategy Gp, 2017–; Mem. Bd, 2014–, Treas., 2016–, Universities UK; Trustee, STEMNET, 2015–19; Dir, Nat. Centre for Univs and Business, 2016–. Dir, Bioscientifica, 1996–2012 (Chm., 2001–05). Ed., Jl of Neuroendocrinology, 2004–08. Governor: King's Coll. Sch., Wimbledon, 1991–94; St Mary's Sch., Calne, 2003–16. FRSA 1987; FCGI 2009; FRSB (FSB 2009). Hon. FBPhS (Hon. FBPharmacolS 2015). Hon. DSc Sheffield, 2012. *Publications:* Stress, Stress Hormones and the Immune System, 1997; contribs to endocrinol. and pharmacol. jls. *Recreations:* music, ski-ing, sailing. *Address:* Brunel University London, Kingston Lane, Uxbridge, Middx UB8 3PH. *T:* (01895) 274000. *E:* julia.buckingham@brunel.ac.uk. *Clubs:* Athenæum; Riverside.

**BUCKINGHAM, Kathleen Rosemary Bernadette; Her Honour Judge Buckingham;** a Circuit Judge, since 2009; *b* Stoke-on-Trent, 16 June 1958; *d* of late James Donnellan and Mary Donnellan; *m* 1981, William Buckingham; two *d*. *Educ:* St Dominic's High Sch., Stoke-on-Trent; Leeds Univ. (BA Hons; PhD Linguistics); City Univ. (Dip.

Law). Called to the Bar, Middle Temple, 1986; in practice as barrister, North Eastern Circuit, 1986–2009; a Recorder, 2002–09. *Address*: Great Grimsby Combined Court Centre, Town Hall Square, Grimsby, Lincs DN31 1XH.

**BUCKINGHAM, Sarah Jayne; Her Honour Judge Buckingham;** a Circuit Judge, since 2016; *b* Norwich, 10 July 1965; *d* of Cyril Morris and Barbara Buckingham; *m* 1996, Paul Selby; one *s* one *d. Educ*: Newcastle Upon Tyne Poly. (LLB Hons). Called to the Bar, Inner Temple, 1991; a Recorder, 2010–16. *Recreations*: cinema, walking, family. *Address*: Nottingham Crown Court, 60 Canal Street, Nottingham NG1 7EL. *E*: hhj.sarah.buckingham@ejudiciary.net.

**BUCKINGHAMSHIRE,** 10th Earl of, *cr* 1746; **George Miles Hobart-Hampden;** Bt 1611; Baron Hobart 1728; Partner, Watson Wyatt LLP (formerly Watson Wyatt Partners), consulting actuaries, 1995–2004; *b* 15 Dec. 1944; *s* of Cyril Langel Hobart-Hampden (*d* 1972) (*ggs* of 6th Earl), and Margaret Moncrieff Hilborne Hobart-Hampden (*née* Jolliffe) (*d* 1985); *S* cousin, 1983; *m* 2nd, 1975, Alison Wightman, JP, DL (*née* Forrest); two step *s. Educ*: Clifton College; Exeter Univ. (BA Hons History); Birkbeck Coll. and Inst. of Commonwealth Studies, Univ. of London (MA Area Studies). Asst Archivist, Hudson Bay Co., 1968–70; with Noble Lowndes and Partners Ltd, 1970–81; Dir, Scottish Pension Trustees Ltd, 1979–81, resigned; Director: Antony Gibbs Pension Services Ltd, 1981–86; Wardley Investment Services (UK) Ltd, 1986–91; Wardley Investment Services International Ltd (Man. Dir, 1988–91), and of various subsidiaries of Wardley; Gota Global Selection, 1988–95; Korea Asia Fund, 1990–91; Wyatt Co. (UK) Ltd, 1991–95; Russian Pension Trust Co. Ltd, 1994–2001; Trustee Exec. (formerly Associate), 2004 and 2014–, Dir, 2005–14, BESTrustees plc. House of Lords, 1984–99: Member: Sub-Cttee C, 1985–90, Sub-Cttee A, 1990–93, H of L Select Cttee on European Affairs; H of L Sub-Cttee on Staffing of Community Instns, 1987–88. Pres., Buckingham Cons. Constituency Assoc., 1989–2013. President: John Hampden Soc., 1993–; Friends of the Vale of Aylesbury, 1994–2010; Downend Police Community Boxing Club, 2003–. Dir, Britain-Australia Soc., 2004–11 (Dep. Chm., 2006–08; Chm., 2008–10; Dep. Chm., 2010–11); Chairman: Cook Soc., 2007; Aylesbury Vale Community Trust, 2009–13. Mem. Council, Buckinghamshire New Univ. (formerly Buckinghamshire Chilterns UC), 2001–09 (Hon. Fellow, 2009). Gov., Clifton Coll., Bristol, 1991–; Pres., Old Cliftonian Soc., 2000–03. Patron, Chiltern MS Centre, 2005–. Affiliate, Inst. of Actuaries, 2001. Patron: Hobart Town (1804) First Settlers Assoc., 1984–; Sleep Apnoea Trust, 1997. Goodwill Ambassador, City of Hobart, Tasmania, 2009. Liveryman, Glovers' Co., 2007; Freeman: City of Geneva, USA, 1987; Glasgow, 1991. Hon. DLitt Hampden-Sydney Coll., Va, 2015. *Recreations*: fishing, Real tennis, Rugby football, trekking. *Heir: kinsman* Sir John Vere Hobart, Bt, *qv. Address*: The Old Rectory, Church Lane, Edgcott, near Aylesbury, Bucks HP18 0TU. *Clubs*: Leamington Tennis, Hatfield Tennis (Dir, 2001–06), Bristol and Bath Tennis, Radley Tennis, Hobart Tennis.

**BUCKLAND, David John;** artist, designer and film-maker; Creator and Director, Cape Farewell project, since 2000; *b* London, 15 June 1949; *s* of Dennis and Valerie Buckland; one *s* one *d* with Susan, (Siobhan), Davies, *qv. Educ*: Hardye's Sch., Dorchester; London Coll. of Communication, Univ. of the Arts. Works exhibited in galleries in London, Paris and NY; works in collections including: NPG; Centre Georges Pompidou, Paris; Metropolitan Mus., NY; Getty Collection, LA; one-man show of digitally mastered portraits of performers, NPG, 1999; work shown and toured worldwide in UN Exhibn for World Envmt Day; video work, Arctic, Millennium Park, Chicago, 2007; *films* include: Dwell Time, 1996; Art in a Changing Climate; Burning Ice, 2010. Cape Farewell project: exhibn, Art & Climate Change, Natural Hist. Mus., 2006, Kampnagel, Hamburg, 2007, Fundación Canal, Madrid, Mirakain, Tokyo, 2008; TV film, Art from the Arctic, 2006. Curator: EARTH for Royal Acad., 2009; Shift Festival, South Bank, 2010. Designer of stage sets and costumes for Royal Ballet, Rambert Dance Co., Second Stride, Compagnie Cré-Ange, Siobhan Davies Dance Co. *Publications*: (with G. Ehrlich) Arctic Heart: a poem cycle, 1992; (jtly) Burning Ice: art and climate change, 2006. *Recreations*: sailing in the High Arctic, cultural activity, love of theatre and dance, keen hill/mountain walker. *E*: davidbuckland@capefarewell.com.

**BUCKLAND, Nicholas Brian,** OBE 2009; Eur Ing; Chair, CSW Group, since 2015; Peninsula Community Health Community Interest Company, since 2015; *b* Windsor, 21 Feb. 1951; *s* of William Walter and Eileen Doris Buckland; *m* 1986, Deborah Gaynor Lewis Jeffreys; one *s. Educ*: Univ. of Bath (BSc Math. Studies 1973). CEng 1991; CITP 1996; CMgr 2010; Eur Ing 2003. Researcher, BISRA, 1977–80; Support Manager: ICL, 1977–80; Data General, 1980–82; Business Devel Manager, Prime Computer, 1982–87; Sales Manager, Convex, 1987–94; Business Devel Manager, Silicon Graphics, 1994–96. Chair: Tamar Sci. Park, 2006–10; Doctor Communications Solutions, 2008–10; Centre for Modelling and Simulation, 2010–14; Mem. Bd and Dep. Chm., SW RDA, 2001–11; Member, Board: Technol. Strategy Bd, 2004–11; Cornwall Enterprise, 2004–08; Plymouth City Devel Co., 2008–10; TravelWatch SW, 2016– (Trustee, 2017–). Plymouth University: Mem., Bd of Govs, 2002–12 and 2015– (Chm., 2009–12); Pro Chancellor, 2012–16. Chm., Engrg Develt Trust, 2012–; Trustee: Plymouth Th. Royal, 2010– (Chm., 2016–); Karst, 2015–. Governor: Shebbear Coll., 2010–; Slough and Eton Business Acad., 2012–18; Chairman, Governors: UTC Plymouth, 2016–; St Petroc's Sch., 2017–. Mem., Governance Community, Nat. Trust, 2012–17. Chm., Plymouth Waterfront Partnership, 2017–; Dep. Chm., WaterShare, 2015–17, Chm., WaterFutures, 2016–, South West Water. Chm. and Trustee, Riverford Organics Trust, 2018–. Trustee: Peninsula Medical Foundn, 2016–; Plymouth Marine Lab., 2017–; MIST, 2018–. MInstD 1997; MRI 2002. FRSA 2003; FBCS 2003; FIMA 2006; FCMI 2007; FIET 2018. Hon. DTech Plymouth, 2013. *Recreations*: gardening, cricket, Rugby, theatre, music, farming. *Address*: Ditchen Farm, Boyton, Launceston, Cornwall PL15 9RN. *T*: 07768 682683. *E*: buckland01@aol.com. *Clubs*: Farmers, MCC (Associate Mem.); Bude Rugby.

**BUCKLAND, Rt Hon. Robert (James);** QC 2014; PC 2019; MP (C) South Swindon, since 2010; Lord Chancellor and Secretary of State for Justice, since 2019; *b* Llanelli, 22 Sept. 1968; *s* of Roger Buckland and Barbara Buckland; *m* 1997, Sian Reed; one *s* one *d* (twins). *Educ*: St Michael's Sch., Bryn; Durham Univ. (BA Hons Law 1990). Called to the Bar, Inner Temple, 1991, Bencher, 2015; in practice as a barrister, 1992–; a Recorder, 2009–. Mem. (C) Dyfed CC, 1993–96. Contested (C): Islwyn, Feb. 1995; Preseli Pembrokeshire, 1997; S Swindon, 2005. Solicitor General, 2014–19; Minister of State, MoJ, 2019. Member: Justice Select Cttee, 2010–13 and 2014; Cttee on Standards, 2012–14; Cttee on Privileges, 2012–14; Jt Cttee on Human Rights, 2013–15; Chairman: Autism All Party Parly Gp, 2011–14; Cons. Party Human Rights Commn, 2011–14; Vice Pres., Tory Reform Gp, 2010–; Jt Sec., 1922 Cttee, 2012–14; Chm. Exec. Cttee, Soc. of Cons. Lawyers, 2013–14. Mem., Funding Review Panel for Wales, Legal Services Commn, 2000–09. Gov., Ridgeway Sch., Wroughton, 2005–09; Co-ordinator, Swindon Special Educnl Needs Network, 2006–. *Recreations*: music, gentle running, political and military history, architecture, Rugby, cricket, books. *Address*: House of Commons, SW1A 0AA. *T*: (020) 7219 7168. *E*: robert.buckland.mp@parliament.uk. *Clubs*: Carlton; Llanelli Conservative, Swindon Conservative; Crawshays Welsh Rugby Football.

**BUCKLAND, Sir Ross,** Kt 1997; Chief Executive and Director, Unigate plc, 1990–2001; *b* 19 Dec. 1942; *s* of William Arthur Haverfield Buckland and Elizabeth Buckland; *m* 1966, Patricia Ann Bubb; two *s. Educ*: Sydney Boys' High Sch. Various positions in cos engaged in banking, engrg and food ind., 1958–66; Dir, Finance and Admin, Elizabeth Arden Pty Ltd, 1966–73; Kellogg (Australia) Pty Ltd, 1973–77, Man. Dir, 1978; Pres. and Chief Exec., Kellogg Salada Canada Inc., 1979–80; Chm., Kellogg Co. of GB Ltd and Dir, European Ops and Vice-Pres., Kellogg Co., USA, 1981–90. Director: RJB Mining, 1997–99; Allied Domecq, 1998–2004; Nat. Australia Bank Europe, 1999–2002; Mayne Gp Ltd, 2001–04; Goodman Fielder Ltd, 2001–03; Clayton Utz, 2002–08. FCPA; FCIS; FIGD. *Recreation*: walking. *Address*: GPO Box 511, Sydney, NSW 2001, Australia. *Clubs*: Royal Sydney Golf (Sydney), Bonnie Doon Golf (Sydney).

**BUCKLAND, Dame Yvonne Helen Elaine, (Dame Yve),** DBE 2003; Chair, Royal Orthopaedic Hospital NHS Foundation Trust, Birmingham, since 2014; Pro-Chancellor, and Chair of Council, Aston University, since 2017; *b* 29 Nov. 1956; *d* of late George Robert Jones and Margaret Ann Jones (*née* O'Hanlon); *m* 1999, Stephen Freer; two *d. Educ*: Our Lady of Mercy Grammar Sch., Wolverhampton; Leeds Univ. (BA Hons 1977); Univ. of Liverpool (DipArch 1978); Univ. of Central Lancashire (DMS 1984). FFPH (FFPHM 2001). Archivist, 1979–83, Dep. County Archivist, 1983–85, Cheshire CC; Team Leader, Mgt Effectiveness Unit, 1985–88, Asst Dir, Social Services, 1988–92, Birmingham CC; Dep. Chief Exec., Nottingham CC, 1992–99; Chm., Health Educn Authy for England, 1999–2000; Chair: HDA, 2000–05; NHS Inst. for Innovation and Improvement, 2005–11. Non-exec. Dir, S Warwicks Primary Care Trust, 2003–05. Dir, Health Partnership, Warwick Business Sch., 2003–05. Chm., Consumer Council for Water, 2005–15. Fellow, Warwick Inst. of Govt and Public Mgt, 2001. FRSA 2002; FInstD 2015. Hon. Fellow, Soc. for Envmt, 2015. *Recreations*: reading, dancing, all things French. *Address*: Royal Orthopaedic Hospital NHS Foundation Trust, Northfield, Birmingham B31 2AP.

**BUCKLE, Alan Arthur;** independent adviser; *b* 19 May 1959; partner, Adèle; three *s. Educ*: Durham Univ. (BA). ACA 1986. A Sen. Partner and Chief Exec., KPMG Advisory, 2008–11; Dep. Chm. and CEO, KPMG International, 2011–13. Mem., Bd of Trustees, British Council, 2005–12 (Dep. Chm.). Chm. Trustees, CPAG UK, 2016–. *Recreations*: family, small mountains, running, reading and the usual things.

**BUCKLE, Simon James,** CMG 2007; DPhil; FInstP; Head of Climate Change, Biodiversity and Water Division, Organisation for Economic Co-operation and Development, since 2014; *b* 29 Feb. 1960; *s* of Roy Thomas Buckle and Muriel May Buckle; *m* 1990, Dr Rajeshree Bhatt; one *d. Educ*: Univ. of Bristol (BSc 1st Cl. Jt Hons Physics and Philosophy 1982); Univ. of Sussex (DPhil Theoretical Physics 1985); Univ. of London (MSc Financial Econs 1999). Res. Asst, Dept of Physics, Imperial Coll., London, 1985–86; joined HM Diplomatic Service, 1986; Far East Dept, FCO, 1986–88; MoD, 1988–91; Head of Iran Section, Middle East Dept, FCO, 1992–94; First Sec., Dublin, 1994–97; Political Counsellor and Consul Gen., Seoul, 1997–98; Bank of England, 1998–2000, Sen. Manager (Res.), Market Infrastructure Div., 2001–02; Hd, Res. Analysts, FCO, 2003–04; Political Counsellor, Baghdad, 2004–05; Dep. Hd of Mission, Kabul, 2005–06; Counsellor, Global Issues, Paris, 2006–07; Policy Dir, Grantham Inst. for Climate Change, 2007–14, Pro Rector for Internat. Affairs, 2011–13, Imperial Coll. London. *Recreations*: hill walking, music. *Address*: Organisation for Economic Co-operation and Development, 2 rue André Pascal, 75775 Paris Cedex 16, France.

**BUCKLE, Most Rev. Terrence Owen;** Bishop of Yukon, 1995–2010, now Bishop Emeritus; Metropolitan of British Columbia and Yukon, 2005–09; Archbishop of Yukon, 2005–10; Founder and Leader, Street Hope Whitehorse; *b* 24 Aug. 1940; *m* 1963, Moyra Blanche Cooke; two *s* two *d. Educ*: Church Army Training Coll., Canada; Wycliffe Coll., Toronto. Commnd as Church Army Evangelist, 1962; Parish Assistant, St Philip's, Etobicoke, Ont, 1962–64; Dir of Inner Parish, Little Trinity, Toronto, 1964–66; Church Army Incumbent: Ch of the Resurrection, Holman, 1966–70; St George's Anglican Mission, Cambridge Bay, 1970–72; Incumbent, St David's Anglican Mission, Fort Simpson, 1972–75; ordained deacon, May 1973, priest, Nov. 1973; Priest i/c, Ch of the Ascension, Inuvik, and Regl Dean, Lower Mackenzie, 1975–82; Archdeacon of Liard, dio. of Yukon, 1982–88; Rector: St Mary Magdalene, Fort Nelson, 1982–88; Holy Trinity, Yellowknife, 1988–93; Co-Founder and Evangelist, New Life Evangelism Ministries, 1984–94; Bishop Suffragan, dio. of the Arctic, 1993–95. Hon. Canon, St Jude's Cathedral, Iqaluit, 1978. *Recreations*: out-of-door activities, canoeing, camping, hiking.

**BUCKLER, Very Rev. Philip John Warr;** Dean of Lincoln, 2007–16, now Emeritus; *b* 26 April 1949; *s* of Ernest and Cynthia Buckler; *m* 1977, Linda Marjorie; one *d. Educ*: Highgate Sch.; St Peter's Coll., Oxford (BA, MA); Cuddesdon Theol Coll. Ordained deacon, 1972, priest, 1973; Asst Curate, St Peter's, Bushey Heath, 1972–75; Chaplain, Trinity Coll., Cambridge, 1975–81; Sacrist and Minor Canon, St Paul's Cathedral, 1981–86; Vicar of Hampstead, 1987–99; Area Dean of N Camden, 1993–98; Canon Residentiary, 1999–2007, Treas., 2000–07, St Paul's Cathedral. Chaplain, Actors' Church Union, 1983–92; Hon. Chaplain: Scriveners' Co., 1984–2007; Merchant Taylors' Co., 1986–87; Spectacle Makers' Co., 2000–01; Mem. Court, Corp. of Sons of Clergy, 1996–2004. DUniv Bishop Grosseteste, 2015. *Recreations*: cricket, walking, gardening. *Address*: Green Acre, Whelp Street, Preston St Mary, Suffolk CO10 9NL. *T*: (01787) 249760. *Clubs*: Athenæum, MCC.

**BUCKLES, Nicholas Peter;** Chief Executive, G4S (formerly Group 4 Securicor), 2005–13; *b* 1 Feb. 1961; *s* of Ronald Peter Buckles and Sylvia Mary Buckles; *m* 1988, Loraine Salter; one *s* two *d. Educ*: Coventry Univ. (BA Hons Business Studies). Dowty Engrg Gp, 1979–83; Business Analyst, Avon Cosmetics, 1983–85; joined Securicor, 1985: Project Accountant, 1985–88; Commercial Manager, 1988–91; Dir, Securicor Cash Services, 1991–93; Dep. Man. Dir, Securicor Guarding, 1993–96; Man. Dir, Securicor Cash Services, 1996–98; Chief Executive: Securicor Europe, 1998–99; Security Div., 1999–2002; Securicor, 2002–04. *Recreations*: soccer, tennis, walking.

**BUCKLEY,** family name of **Baron Wrenbury.**

**BUCKLEY, Edgar Vincent,** CB 1999; PhD; independent defence and security consultant, since 2014; *b* 17 Nov. 1946; *s* of Michael Joseph Buckley and Mary Buckley; *m* 1972, Frances Jacqueline Cheetham; two *s* three *d. Educ*: St Ignatius Coll., London; North-Western Poly., London (BA Hons 1967); Birkbeck Coll., London (PhD 1974). Teacher, Redbridge, 1970–73; joined MoD, 1973; Administration Trainee, 1974–76; Private Sec. to Vice Chief of Air Staff, 1976–78; Principal, 1978–79; Assistant Director: Strategic Systems Finance, 1980–84; Nuclear Policy, 1984–85; Head of Resources and Programmes (Navy), 1985–89; rcds, 1990; Efficiency Study, Cabinet Office, 1991 (on secondment); Head of Defence Arms Control Unit, 1991–92; Defence Counsellor, UK Delegn to NATO, 1992–96 (on secondment); Asst Under-Sec. of State (Home and Overseas), 1996–99; Asst Sec. Gen. for Defence Planning and Operations, NATO, 1999–2003; Sen. Vice-Pres., European Marketing and Sales, 2003–11, Sen. Consultant, 2011–13, Thales. *Recreations*: running, swimming, reading, home maintenance. *Address*: 9 Forester Road, Bath BA2 6QF.

**BUCKLEY, Sir George (William),** Kt 2011; PhD; FREng; Chairman, Stanley Black & Decker, since 2017 (Director, since 2010); b 1947. Educ: Huddersfield Poly. (BSc Electrical and Electronic Engrg 1972); Huddersfield Poly. and Univ. of Southampton (PhD Engrg 1976). FREng 2018. General Motors; GEC; Man. Dir, Central Services Div., British Railways, 1989–93; Emerson Electric Co., 1993–97: Chief Technol. Officer; President: Electric Motors Div.; Automotive and Precision Motors Div.; Brunswick Corporation, 1997–2005: Pres., Mercury Marine, 1997; Chm. and CEO, 2000–05; Chm., Pres. and CEO, 3M, 2005–12. Non-executive Chairman: Arle Capital LLP, subseq. Smithfield Gp LLP, 2012–15; Expro, 2012–; Ownership Capital, 2013–; Smiths Gp, 2013–; non-executive Director: Archer Daniels Midland Co., 2006; PepsiCo, 2012–; Hitachi, 2012–; Technogym, 2012–; Mem. Adv. Bd, Deutsche Bank; Sen. Advr, Rothschild America, 2012–. Hon. DSc: Huddersfield, 2003; Southampton, 2012.

**BUCKLEY, James;** Chief Executive, Baltic Exchange, 1992–2004; b 5 April 1944; s of late Harold Buckley and of Mabel Buckley; m 1972, Valerie Elizabeth Powles; one d. Educ: Sheffield City Grammar Sch.; Imperial College of Science and Technology (BSc, ARCS). RAF Operational Res., 1965. Principal Scientific Officer, 1971; Asst Sec., CSD; Private Secretary: to Lord Privy Seal, Lord Peart, 1979; to Lord President of Council, Lord Soames, 1979; to Chancellor of Duchy of Lancaster, Baroness Young, 1981; Sec., Civil Service Coll., 1982; Chief Exec., BVA, 1985–87; Dep. Dir Gen., GCBS, 1987–91. Recreations: photography, tennis. Address: 1 Aldenholme, Weybridge, Surrey KT13 0JF.

**BUCKLEY, Martin Howard;** Chairman, Multichem Ltd, 2009–14 (non-executive Director, 2008–14); non-executive Director, Yorwaste Ltd, since 2009; b 10 Aug. 1945; s of Charles and Elma Buckley; m 1972, Kay Lesley Rowson; one s one d. FCA 1969. Man. Dir, packaging subsid., Rexam plc, 1976–79; CEO, NY and Philadelphia Box Plants, LINPAC Containers Internat. Ltd, 1979–85; Waddington plc: Divl Chief Exec., 1985–90; Man. Dir, 1990–92; Chief Exec., 1992–2000. Chm., Leeds Teaching Hospitals NHS Trust, 2003–09. Non-exec. Dir, Magnadata Internat. Ltd, 2002–04. Recreations: walking, clay-pigeon shooting. T: 07836 292633.

**BUCKLEY, Sir Michael (Sydney),** Kt 2002; Parliamentary Commissioner for Administration, and Health Service Commissioner for England, Scotland and Wales, 1997–2002; Scottish Parliamentary Commissioner for Administration and Welsh Administration Ombudsman, 1999–2002; b 20 June 1939; s of Sydney Dowsett Buckley and Grace Bew Buckley; m 1st, 1972, Shirley Stordy (d 1991); one s one d; 2nd, 1992, Judith Cartmell (née Cobb); two step s one step d. Educ: Eltham College; Christ Church, Oxford (MA; Cert. of Stats); Open Univ. (BSc; Dip. Physical Scis). Asst Principal, Treasury, 1962; Asst Private Sec. to Chancellor of Exchequer, 1965–66; Principal: Treasury, 1966–68 and 1971–74; CSD, 1968–71; Assistant Secretary: Treasury, 1974–77 and 1980–82; DoI, 1977–80; Under Secretary: Cabinet Office, 1982–85; Dept of Energy, 1985–91; Chm., Dartford and Gravesham NHS Trust, 1995–96. Member: CS Appeal Bd, 1991–96; GMC, 2003–08. Recreations: photography, listening to music, reading. Address: 1 Manor Court, Bearsted, Maidstone, Kent ME14 4BZ.

**BUCKLEY, Prof. Peter Jennings,** OBE 2012; PhD; FBA 2014; Professor of International Business, University of Leeds, since 1995; b Ashton-under-Lyne, 11 July 1949; s of Robert and Florence Buckley; m 1978, Ann Patricia Kelland; one s one d. Educ: Ashton-under-Lyne Grammar Sch.; Univ. of York (BA Hons Social Scis 1970); Univ. of E Anglia (MA Develt Econs 1971); Univ. of Lancaster (PhD Econs 1975). Esmée Fairbairn res. asst, Univ. of Reading, 1973–74; University of Bradford: Lectr in Internat. Business, 1974–80; Sen. Lectr in Internat. Business, 1980–84; Prof. of Managerial Econs, 1984–95. Cheung Kong Schol. Chair Prof., Univ. of Internat. Business and Econs, Beijing, 2010–. Dr hc Uppsala, 2010; Hon. DSc Lappeenranta, Finland, 2012. Series Ed., New Horizons in Internat. Business, 1992–. Publications: (jtly) The Future of the Multinational Enterprise, 1976 (trans. Japanese, 1993; Korean, 1995), 25th anniv. edn, 2002 (trans. Chinese, 2005); (jtly) Going International, 1978, 2nd edn as Foreign Direct Investment by Smaller UK Firms, 1988; (jtly) European Direct Investments in the USA before World War I, 1982; (jtly) Direct Investment in the UK by Smaller European Firms, 1983; (jtly) The Industrial Relations Practices of Foreign-Owned Firms in British Manufacturing Industry, 1985; (jtly) The Economic Theory of the Multinational Enterprise, 1985; (jtly) Die Multinationalen Unternehmen und der Arbeitsmarkt, 1986; (jtly) North-South Direct Investment in the European Communities, 1987; The Theory of the Multinational Enterprise, 1987; (ed jtly) Handbook of International Trade, 1988; The Multinational Enterprise: theory and applications, 1989; (ed) International Investment, 1990; (jtly) The Management of International Tourism, 1991, 2nd edn 1995; (jtly) International Aspects of UK Economic Activities, 1991; (ed jtly) Multinational Enterprises in Less Developed Countries, 1991; (jtly) Servicing International Markets, 1992; (jtly) International Business Studies: an overview, 1992 (trans. Japanese, 1994); Studies in International Business, 1992; (ed) New Directions in International Business, 1992; (ed jtly) Multinational Enterprises in the World Economy, 1992; (ed jtly) The Internationalisation of the Firm, 1993, 2nd edn 1999; (ed jtly) The Economics of Change in East and Central Europe and its Impact on International Business, 1994; (ed) Cooperative Forms of TNC Activity, 1994; (jtly) Canada–UK: bilateral trade and investment relations, 1995; Foreign Direct Investment and Multinational Enterprises, 1995; (ed jtly) Firms, Organizations and Contracts, 1996; (ed jtly) Multinational Firms and International Relocation, 1997; (ed jtly) Technology Transfer by Small and Medium Sized Enterprises, 1997; International Business: economics and anthropology, theory and method, 1998; International Strategic Management and Government Policy, 1998; (ed jtly) Globalization and Regionalization, 1998; (ed jtly) The Strategy and Organisation of International Business, 1998; (ed jtly) The Global Challenge for Multinational Enterprises, 1999; Multinational Firms, Cooperation and Competition in the World Economy, 2000; (ed jtly) International Mergers and Acquisitions, 2002; The Changing Global Context of International Business, 2003; (ed) International Business, 2003; (jtly) Strategic Business Alliances, 2004; The Challenge of International Business, 2004; (ed) What is International Business?, 2004 (trans. Chinese, 2009); The Multinational Enterprise and the Globalization of Knowledge, 2006; Foreign Direct Investment, China and the World Economy, 2009; (jtly) The Multinational Enterprise Revisited: the essential Buckley and Casson, 2010; Business History and International Business History, 2011; (ed) Globalization and the Global Factory, 2011; Innovations in International Business, 2012; The Multinational Enterprise and the Emergence of the Global Factory, 2014. Recreations: cricket, cartography, football, history, theatre, walking, complaining about the Church of England. Address: Leeds University Business School, Maurice Keyworth Building, Leeds, W Yorks LS2 9JT. T: (0113) 343 4646, Fax: (0113) 343 4754. E: pjb@lubs.leeds.ac.uk.

**BUCKLEY, Lt-Comdr Sir (Peter) Richard,** KCVO 1982 (CVO 1973; MVO 1968); b 31 Jan. 1928; 2nd s of late Alfred Buckley and Mrs E. G. Buckley, Crowthorne, Berks; m 1958, Theresa Mary Neve; two s one d. Educ: Wellington Coll. Cadet, RN, 1945. Served in HM Ships: Mauritius, Ulster, Contest, Defender, and BRNC, Dartmouth. Specialised in TA/S. Invalided from RN (Lt-Comdr), 1961. Private Sec. to the Duke and Duchess of Kent, 1961–89; Extra Equerry to the Duke of Kent, 1989–. Director: Vickers Internat., 1981–89; Malcolm McIntyre Consultancy, 1989–92. Governor: Wellington Coll.,

1989–98; Eagle House Sch., 1989–98 (Chm. of Govs, 1992–98). FRGS 1999. Recreations: fishing, sailing, bee keeping. Address: Coppins Cottages, Iver, Bucks SL0 0AT. T: (01753) 653004. Clubs: Army and Navy; All England Lawn Tennis and Croquet.

**BUCKLEY, Hon. Sir Roger (John),** Kt 1989; a Judge of the High Court of Justice, Queen's Bench Division, 1989–2004; b 26 April 1939; s of Harold and Marjorie Buckley; m 1965, Margaret Gillian, d of Robert and Joan Cowan; one s one d. Educ: Mill Hill Sch.; Manchester Univ. (LLB (Hons)). Called to the Bar, Middle Temple, 1962 (Harmsworth Schol.); Bencher, Middle Temple, 1987; QC 1979; a Recorder, 1986–89; a Judge of the Employment Appeal Tribunal, 1994–2004; Pres., Restrictive Practices Court, 1994–2001. Mem., Investment Adv. Panel, Woodsford Litigation Funding Ltd, 2011–16. Chm., British Horseracing Authy Disciplinary Appeal Bd (formerly Jockey Club Appeal Bd), 2005–14. Mem. Bd, Painshill Park Trust Ltd, 2007– (Trustee, 2005–). Recreations: golf, theatre, breeding and racing thoroughbreds. Address: Brick Court Chambers, 2–8 Essex Street, WC2R 3LD. E: roger@thebuckleys.co.uk. Club: Old Millhillians.

**BUCKMAN, Dr Laurence,** FRCGP; Chairman, General Practitioners Committee, British Medical Association, 2007–13 (Deputy Chairman, 2004–07); General Practitioner, Temple Fortune Health Centre, London, 1993–2019; b London, 19 March 1954; s of Allan Buckman and Toni Buckman; m 1978, Elise Sider; two s. Educ: University College Sch.; University Coll. Hosp. Med. Sch. (MB BS 1977). FRCGP 2001. Jun. Hosp. posts, UCH, Hertford Co. Hosp., Edgware Gen., St Bartholomew's Hosp., Royal Marsden Hosp., 1977–81; Med. Registrar, Mount Vernon Hosp., 1981–83; GP, Borehamwood, Herts, 1983–93. Tutor, Gen. Practice, UCL Med. Sch., 1985–2018. Publications: contrib. articles on medicine and med. politics. Recreations: photography, music, travel, model railways. Address: 21 Southover, Woodside Park, N12 7JG. T: (020) 8446 4667.

**BUCKMASTER,** family name of **Viscount Buckmaster**.

**BUCKMASTER,** 4th Viscount cr 1933, of Cheddington, Buckinghamshire; **Adrian Charles Buckmaster;** Baron 1915; Chairman, GMS Estates Ltd; s of Hon. Colin John Buckmaster and May Buckmaster (née Gibbon); S uncle, 2007; m 1975, Dr Elizabeth Mary Mark; one s two d. Educ: Charterhouse; Clare Coll., Cambridge (BA 1970; MA 1974). Heir: s Hon. Andrew Nicholas Buckmaster [b 1980; m 2014, Dr Helen R. Murray].

**BUCKNALL, Lt Gen. Sir James (Jeffrey Corfield),** KCB 2013; CBE 2004 (MBE 1994); Chief Executive, Weybourne Ltd, since 2013; b 29 Nov. 1958; s of Captain Robin Bucknall and Diana Bucknall, MBE; m 1986, Tessa Jane Freemantle (née Barrett); two s. Educ: Winchester Coll. Joined Army, 1977; commnd Coldstream Guards, 1978; served with 2nd Bn in GB, Germany, NI and Cyprus; Staff Coll., 1990; co. comd NI, 1991 (despatches, 1992); on staff, HQ NI, 1992–96; CO, 1st Bn, Germany and England, 1996–98; COS, 1st (UK) Armd Div., Bosnia and Germany, 1998–2001; HCSC 2001; Comdr, 39 Inf. Bde, Belfast, 2001–03; Dir, Counter Terrorism and UK Ops, MoD, 2004–06; served with HQ Multi-National Force Iraq, Baghdad, 2006; COS, ARRC, Afghanistan, then Germany, 2006–09; Asst Chief of Gen. Staff, 2009–10; Dep. Comdr, ISAF Afghanistan, 2010–11; Comdr Allied Rapid Reaction Forces, 2011–13. Col, Coldstream Guards, 2009–. QCVS 2011. Officer, Legion of Merit (USA), 2009. Recreations: shooting, cricket, military history, long suffering supporter of Newcastle United. Clubs: Pratt's, MCC, Cavalry and Guards.

**BUCKNELL, Bruce James;** HM Diplomatic Service; Deputy High Commissioner, Kolkata, since 2016; b Reading, 15 April 1962; s of John and Mary Bucknell; m 1993, Henrietta Dorrington-Ward; two s. Educ: Taunton Sch.; Durham Univ. (BA Hons Modern Hist. 1984). Entered FCO, 1985; Third Sec., Chancery, Amman, 1988–91; on secondment to EBRD, 1992; Desk Officer, Africa Dept (Equatorial), FCO, 1992–93; Policy Co-ordinator, Africa Comd, FCO, 1993–94; Italian lang. trng, 1994–95; Consul (Press and Public Affairs), Milan, 1995–99; Desk Officer, NATO Section, Security Policy Dept, FCO, 1999–2001; Hd, Central Europe Section, Central and NW Europe Dept (later EU Internal), FCO, 2001–03; Spanish lang. trng, 2003; First Sec., Madrid, 2003–07; Deputy Head: Sudan Unit, FCO/DFID, 2007–09; Estates and Security Directorate, 2009–12; Ambassador to Belarus, 2012–16. Recreations: family, culture, sport, countryside. Address: c/o Foreign and Commonwealth Office, King Charles Street, SW1A 2AH. E: bruce.bucknell@fco.gov.uk.

**BUCKNILL, Thomas Michael,** RD 1983; FRCS; Consultant Orthopaedic Surgeon, St Bartholomew's Hospital, 1977–2011 and Royal London Hospital, 1995–2011; b 11 Jan. 1942; m 1st, 1968, Rachael Offer (marr. diss. 1998); one s three d; 2nd, 1999, Annie Marshall. Educ: Douai Sch.; St Bartholomew's Hosp. Med. Coll., London (MB BS 1964). FRCS 1970. House Surgeon, 1965–66, Anatomy Demonstrator, 1966–67, St Bartholomew's Hosp.; Surgical Registrar, St Stephen's Hosp., Chelsea, 1968–70; Registrar, Royal Nat. Orthopaedic Hosp., Stanmore, 1970–76; Clin. Fellow, Harvard Med. Sch., 1976; Cons. Orthopaedic Surgeon, King Edward VII Hosp., London, 1981–. MO, RNR London Div., 1967–93; Surgeon Comdr, RNR, 1987–93, retd; PMO, Royal Marines Reserve, London, 1988–91. FRSocMed 1995. Publications: (contrib.) Textbook of General Surgery, 1980. Recreations: sailing, golf. Clubs: Naval; Moor Park Golf, Royal Southampton Yacht.

**BUCKWELL, Prof. Allan Edgar;** Senior Research Fellow, Institute for European Environmental Policy, since 2012; b 10 April 1947; s of George Alfred Donald Buckwell and Jessie Ethel Buckwell (née Neave); m 1967, Susan Margaret Hopwood (marr. diss. 1990); two s; m 1997, Dr Elizabeth Gay Mitchell (marr. diss. 2017). Educ: Wye Coll., Univ. of London (BSc Agric.); Manchester Univ. (MA Econ.). Research Associate, Agricl Adjustment Unit, Newcastle Univ., 1970–73; Lectr in Agricl Economics, Newcastle Univ., 1973–84; Prof. of Agricl Econs, Wye Coll., Univ. of London, 1984–99; Policy Dir, Country Land and Business Assoc., 2000–11. Kellogg Res. Fellow, Univ. of Wisconsin, Madison, 1974–75; Vis. Prof., Cornell Univ., 1983. Auxiliare, DG VI, EC, 1995–96. Publications: (jtly) The Cost of the Common Agricultural Policy, 1982; Chinese Grain Economy and Policy, 1989; Privatisation of Agriculture in New Market Economies: lessons from Bulgaria, 1994; articles in Jl Agricl Economics. Recreations: cycling, walking, DIY. Address: 43 Ivy Lane, Canterbury, Kent CT1 1TU. T: 07717 004938. E: allan.buckwell@gmail.com.

**BUCZACKI, Dr Stefan Tadeusz;** biologist; broadcaster, author, expert witness, public speaker and consultant, since 1984; b 16 Oct. 1945; o s of Tadeusz Buczacki and Madeleine Mary Cato Buczacki (née Fry); m 1970, Beverley Ann Charman; two s. Educ: Ecclesbourne Sch., Duffield; Univ. of Southampton (BSc 1st cl. Hons Botany, 1968); Linacre Coll., Oxford (DPhil 1971). CHort, FCIHort (FIHort 1986); CBiol, FRSB; ARPS; FLS. Research Biologist, Nat. Vegetable Res. Station, 1971–84; Partner, Stefan Buczacki Associates, landscape and garden design, 2001–12. Gardening Correspondent: The Guardian, 1986–95; Sunday Mirror, 1993–96; Manchester Evening News, 1997–2009; New Statesman, 2018–; Weekly Columnist: Amateur Gardening 1974–97; Garden News 1997–2016. Radio: Gardeners' Question Time, 1982–94; Classic Gardening Forum, 1994–97; The Gardening Quiz (originator and writer), 1988–93; television: Gardeners' Direct Line, 1983–85; That's Gardening, 1989–90, 1992; Bazaar, 1989–93; Gardeners' World, 1990–91; Chelsea Flower Show, 1990–91; Good Morning,

1992–96; Stefan Buczacki's Gardening Britain, 1996; At Home, 1997–98; Stefan's Garden Roadshow, 1998–2000; Open House, 1998–2002; Learn to Garden with Stefan Buczacki, 1999; Stefan's Ultimate Gardens, 2001; Gardens of Kent, 2009; guest appearances on progs incl. Christmas University Challenge, 2013; *stage*: lecture on mushrooms, John Cage's Musicircus, Barbican, 2004, ENO, 2012. President: W Midlands ASE, 1996–97; British Mycological Soc., 1999–2000 (Vice-Pres., 1994, Press Officer, 2002–08; Mem. Council, 2009–16); Mem. Council, Gardeners' Royal Benevolent Soc., 1990–98. Trustee: Brogdale Horticultural Trust, 1990–95; Hestercombe Gardens Trust, 1996–2006 (Chm., Estates Cttee, 2003–06); North of England Zool Soc./Chester Zoo, 2009–16. Chm., Pershore Forward, 2007–. Patron: Parrs Wood Rural Trust, 1990–; Dawlish Gardens Trust, 1990–; Southport Flower Show, 1991–2018; Warwick Castle Gdns Trust, 1992–; Friends of Hestercombe Gardens, 1994–2006; Nat. Amateur Gardening Show, 1996–98; Caring for God's Acre, 2019–. Mem., Scriptwriters' (formerly Broadcasting) Cttee, Soc. of Authors, 2016–. Hon. Prof., Biol Scis (formerly Plant Pathology), Liverpool John Moores Univ., 1994–. Honorary Fellow: CABI Bioscience, 2003; Warwicks Coll., 2007. Benefactors' Medal, British Mycological Soc., 1996; Veitch Gold Meml Medal, RHS, 2010; Lifetime Achievement Award, Garden Media Guild, 2013. DUniv Derby, 2002; Hon. DLitt Southampton, 2016. *Publications*: (jtly) Collins Guide to the Pests, Diseases and Disorders of Garden Plants, 1981 (shorter Guide, 1983), 4th edn 2014; Gem Guide to Mushrooms and Toadstools, 1982; (ed) Zoosporic Plant Pathogens, 1983; Beat Garden Pests and Diseases, 1985; Gardeners' Questions Answered, 1985; (jtly) Three Men in a Garden, 1986; Ground Rules for Gardeners, 1986; Beginners Guide to Gardening, 1988; Creating a Victorian Flower Garden, 1988; Garden Warfare, 1988; New Generation Guide to the Fungi of Britain and Europe, 1989; A Garden for all Seasons, 1990; Understanding Your Garden, 1990; The Essential Gardener, 1991; Dr Stefan Buczacki's Gardening Hints, 1992; Mushrooms and Toadstools of Britain and Europe, 1992; The Plant Care Manual, 1992; (ed) The Gardener's Handbook, 1993; The Budget Gardening Year, 1993; Best Climbers, 1994; Best Foliage Shrubs, 1994; Best Shade Plants, 1994; Best Soft Fruit, 1994; (jtly) Classic FM Garden Planner, 1995; Best Water Plants, 1995; Best Herbs, 1995; Best Geraniums, 1998; Best Roses, 1996; Best Container Plants, 1996; Stefan Buczacki's Gardening Britain, 1996; Best Garden Doctor, 1997; Best Summer Flowering Shrubs, 1997; Best Winter Plants, 1997; Best Clematis, 1998; Best Pruning, 1998; Stefan Buczacki's Gardening Dictionary, 1998; Stefan Buczacki's Plant Dictionary, 1998; Best Fuchsias, 1999; Best Evergreens, 1999; First Time Gardener, 2000; Best Water Gardens, 2000; Best Kitchen Herbs, 2000; Essential Garden Answers, 2000; Best Ground Cover, 2000; Best Rock Garden Plants, 2000; Plant Problems: prevention and treatment, 2000; Hamlyn Encyclopaedia of Gardening, 2002; Fauna Britannica, 2002; The Commonsense Gardener, 2004; (jtly) Young Gardener, 2006; Garden Natural History, 2007; Collins Wildlife Gardener, 2007; Churchill and Chartwell: the untold story of Churchill's houses and gardens, 2007; National Trust Chartwell Guide, 2010; Collins Fungi Guide, 2012; The Herb Bible, 2015; My darling Mr Asquith: the extraordinary life and times of Venetia Stanley, 2016; Earth to Earth: a natural history of churchyards, 2018; From Blenheim to Chartwell, 2018; contrib. chapters in books and to Oxford DNB; articles in magazines and newspapers; numerous scientific papers in professional jls. *Recreations*: my own garden, photography, my classic Jaguars, fishing, natural history, book collecting, theatre, kippers, Derbyshire porcelain, fine music, travelling and then returning to appreciate the British countryside. *Address*: Prospect House, Clifford Chambers, Stratford-upon-Avon, Warks CV37 8HX. *T*: (01789) 298106. *E*: info@stefanbuczacki.co.uk. *W*: www.stefanbuczacki.co.uk. *Club*: Garrick.

**BUD, Dr Robert Franklin;** Research Keeper, Science Museum, 2014–18, now Emeritus Keeper (Keeper of Science and Medicine, 2011–14); *b* 21 April 1952; *s* of Martin Bud and Hanna Bud (*née* Loebl); *m* 1979, Lisa Frierman; one *s*. *Educ*: University Coll. Sch.; Univ. of Manchester (BSc 1st Cl. Liberal Studies in Sci. 1973); Univ. of Pennsylvania (PhD 1980). Science Museum: Asst Keeper, Industrial Chem., 1978–85; Dep. Keeper, Dept of Physical Scis, 1985–89; Hd, Collections Services, 1989–91; Hd, Life and Envmtl Scis, 1991–94; Manager, Life and Commns Technols, and Res. (Collections), subseq. Information and Res., then Electronic Access, 1994–2007; Principal Curator of Medicine, 2002–11. Associate Sen. Res. Fellow, Centre for Evaluation of Public Policy and Practice, Brunel Univ., 1990–95; Adjunct Prof., Univ. of Va, 1993; Associated Scholar, Dept of History and Philosophy of Sci., Univ. of Cambridge, 2002–; Honorary Senior Research Fellow: Dept Sci. and Technol. Studies, UCL, 2003–; Dept History, Classics and Archaeology, Birkbeck Coll., London, 2003–12; Hon. Professorial Fellow, Dept History, QMUL, 2008–13; AHRC Science in Culture Res. Fellow, 2011–12; Sarton Prof. of History of Sci., Univ. of Ghent, 2012–13; AHRC Leadership Fellow, 2014–16. Associate Editor, Outlook on Sci. Policy, 1989–91; Member Editorial Board: Brit. Jl for Hist. of Sci., 1982–2005; History and Technol., 1993–2009; New Genetics and Society, 1999–; Notes and Records of Royal Soc., 2016–; Mem., Editl Adv. Bd, Oxford Companion to the History of Science, 1998–. Member of Council: Brit. Soc. for Hist. of Sci., 1985–88; Soc. for Hist. of Technol., 1996–98; Mem. Steering Cttee, Hist. of Twentieth Century Medicine Gp, Wellcome Trust, 1998–. Trustee, RN Submarine Mus., 1994–99. FWAAS 1989; FRHistS 1999. (Jtly) Bunge Prize, Hans Jenemann Stiftung, 1998. *Publications*: (with G. K. Roberts) Science versus Practice: chemistry in Victorian Britain, 1984; (jtly) Chemistry in America 1876–1976: historical indicators, 1984; The Uses of Life: a history of biotechnology, 1993 (trans. German 1995); edited jointly: Invisible Connections: instruments, institutions and science, 1992; Guide to the History of Technology in Europe, 1992, 3rd edn 1996; Instruments of Science: an historical encyclopedia, 1998; Manifesting Medicine: bodies and machines, 1999; Cold War, Hot Science: applied research in British defence laboratories 1945–1990, 1999; (jtly) Inventing the Modern World: technology since 1750, 2000; Penicillin: triumph and tragedy, 2007; (ed jtly) Being Modern: the cultural impact of science in the early twentieth century, 2018; articles in learned jls. *Recreations*: family life, walking, second-hand bookshops. *Address*: Science Museum, Exhibition Road, SW7 2DD. *T*: (020) 7942 4200. *E*: robert.bud@sciencemuseum.ac.uk.

**BUDD, Sir Alan (Peter),** GBE 2013; Kt 1997; *b* 16 Nov. 1937; *s* of late Ernest and Elsie Budd; *m* 1964, Susan (*née* Millott); three *s*. *Educ*: Oundle Sch. (Grocers' Co. Schol.); London School of Economics (Leverhulme Schol.; BScEcon); Churchill Coll., Cambridge (PhD). Lectr, Southampton Univ., 1966–69; Ford Foundn Vis. Prof., Carnegie-Mellon Univ., Pittsburgh, 1969–70; Sen. Economic Advr, HM Treasury, 1970–74; Williams & Glyn's Sen. Res. Fellow, London Business Sch., 1974–78; High Level Cons., OECD, 1976–77; Special Advr, Treasury and CS Cttee, 1979–81; Dir, Centre for Economic Forecasting, 1980–88, Prof. of Econs, 1981–91, Fellow, 1997, London Business Sch.; Gp Economic Advr, Barclays Bank, 1988–91; Chief Economic Advr to HM Treasury, and Head of Govt Economic Service, 1991–97; Mem., Monetary Policy Cttee, Bank of England, 1997–99; Sen. Advr, Credit Suisse, 1999–2012. Provost, The Queen's Coll., Oxford, 1999–2008; Chm., Office for Budget Responsibility, 2010. Reserve Bank of Aust. Vis. Prof., Univ. of New South Wales, 1983. Member: Securities and Investments Board, 1987–88; ABRC, 1991; Chairman: Gambling Rev. Body, 2000–01; Tax Law Review Cttee, 2006–12. Member: Council, Inst. for Fiscal Studies, 1988–91, 2004–; Council, REconS, 1988–93. Chairman: British Performing Arts Medicine Trust, 1998–2005; Schola Cantorum of Oxford, 2002–08. Governor: LSE, 1994–2002; NIESR, 1998–. Econs columnist, The Independent, 1991. Hon. Fellow, Queen's Coll., Oxford, 2008. Hon. DSc Salford, 2009. *Publications*: The Politics of Economic Planning, 1978; articles in professional jls. *Recreations*: music, gardening. *Club*: Reform.

**BUDD, Sir Colin (Richard),** KCMG 2002 (CMG 1991); HM Diplomatic Service, retired; Ambassador to the Netherlands, 2001–05; *b* 31 Aug. 1945; *s* of Bernard Wilfred Budd, QC and Margaret Alison Budd, MBE (*née* Burgin); *m* 1971, Agnes Smit; one *s* one *d*. *Educ*: Kingswood Sch., Bath; Pembroke Coll., Cambridge. Entered HM Diplomatic Service, 1967; CO, 1967–68; Asst Private Sec. to Minister without Portfolio, 1968–69; Warsaw, 1969–72; Islamabad, 1972–75; FCO, 1976–80; The Hague, 1980–84; Asst Private Sec. to Sec. of State for Foreign and Commonwealth Affairs, 1984–87; European Secretariat, Cabinet Office, 1987–88; Counsellor (Political), Bonn, 1989–92; Chef de Cabinet to Sir Leon Brittan, Vice Pres. of EC, 1993–96; Dep. Sec., Cabinet Office (on secondment), 1996–97; Dep. Under-Sec. of State, FCO, 1997–2001. Member: Commn for Racial Equality, 2006–07; QC Selection Panel, 2009–13; Prime Minister's Adv. Cttee on Business Appts, 2010–14. *Recreations*: running, mountains, music (Mozart, chansons, Don McLean). *E*: acbudd@hotmail.com.

**BUDD, Rt Rev. Mgr Hugh Christopher;** Bishop of Plymouth, (RC), 1986–2014, now Emeritus; *b* 27 May 1937; *s* of John Alfred and Phyllis Mary Budd. *Educ*: St Mary's Primary School, Hornchurch, Essex; Salesian Coll., Chertsey, Surrey; Cotton Coll., North Staffs; English Coll., Rome. PhL; STD. Ordained Priest, 1962; post-ordination studies, 1963–65; Tutor, English Coll., Rome, 1965–71; Lectr at Newman Coll., Birmingham and part-time Asst Priest, Northfield, Birmingham, 1971–76; Head of Training, Catholic Marriage Advisory Council, National HQ, London, 1976–79; Rector, St John's Seminary, Wonersh, Surrey, 1979–85; Administrator, Brentwood Cathedral, Essex, Nov. 1985–Jan. 1986. *Recreations*: walking, cricket (watching), music (listening). *Address*: The Presbytery, Silver Street, Lyme Regis, Dorset DT7 3HS.

**BUDD, Prof. Malcolm John,** PhD; FBA 1995; Grote Professor of Philosophy of Mind and Logic, University College London, 1998–2001, now Emeritus; *b* 23 Dec. 1941; *s* of Edward Charles Budd and Hilare (*née* Campbell). *Educ*: Latymer Upper Sch.; Jesus Coll., Cambridge (BA 1964; MA 1967; PhD 1968). William Stone Research Fellow, Peterhouse, Cambridge, 1966–70; University College London: Lectr in Philosophy, 1970–87; Reader, 1987–90; Prof. of Philosophy, 1990–98. Pres., British Soc. of Aesthetics, 2004–13. Editor, Aristotelian Soc., 1989–94. Hon. Fellow, Peterhouse, Cambridge, 2011. *Publications*: Music and the Emotions, 1985; Wittgenstein's Philosophy of Psychology, 1989; Values of Art, 1995; The Aesthetic Appreciation of Nature, 2002; Aesthetic Essays, 2008. *Address*: 12 Hardwick Street, Cambridge CB3 9JA.

**BUDENBERG, Robin Francis,** CBE 2015; London Chairman, Centerview Partners, since 2014; First Commissioner and Chairman, The Crown Estate, since 2016; *b* 8 May 1959; *m* 1989, Jacqueline; two *s* two *d*. *Educ*: Rugby Sch.; Exeter Univ. Price Waterhouse, 1980–84; with S. G. Warburg, subseq. SBC Warburg, then Warburg Dillon Read, then UBS Warburg, later UBS Investment Bank, 1984–2009; CEO, 2009–12, Chm., 2012–13, UK Financial Investments.

**BUDGE, Keith Joseph;** Headmaster, Bedales Schools, 2001–18; *b* 24 May 1957; *s* of William and Megan Budge; *m* 1983, Caroline Ann Gent; two *s* one *d*. *Educ*: Rossall Sch.; University Coll., Oxford (MA Hons English; PGCE). Asst Master, Eastbourne Coll., 1980–84; Marlborough College: Asst Master, 1984–88 and 1989–91; Housemaster, Cotton Hse, 1991–95; Instructor in English, Stevenson Sch., Pebble Beach, CA, 1988–89; Headmaster, Loretto Sch., 1995–2000. *Recreations*: hill-walking, trout-fishing, gadgets, theatre.

**BUDGEN, Keith Graham,** CBE 2012; Chair and Panel Member, Judicial Appointments Commission, since 2012; Regional Director, South East, HM Courts Service, 2006–11; *b* 14 Oct. 1950; *s* of Victor Charles Budgen and Norma Budgen (*née* Day); *m* 1980, Penelope Ann Lane; one *s* two *d*. *Educ*: Claygate Primary Sch.; Waynflete Sch., Esher. Lord Chancellor's Department, then Department for Constitutional Affairs, later MoJ, 1967–2011: Group Manager: Newcastle upon Tyne Gp of Courts, 1990–98; London Gp of Crown Courts, 1998–2002; Dir, Criminal Justice Improvement, 2002–06. Asst Comr, Boundary Commn for England, 2011–12. Trustee: Nasio Trust, 2015– (Chair, 2017–); Youth Challenge Oxfordshire, 2017–. *Recreations*: renovating houses, gardening, walking, socialising.

**BUDGETT, Richard Gordon McBride,** OBE 2003; Medical and Scientific Director, International Olympic Committee, since 2012; *b* 20 March 1959; *s* of Robert and Fiona Budgett; *m* 1987, Sue Moore; one *s* two *d*. *Educ*: Radley Coll.; Selwyn Coll., Cambridge (BA 1980, MA 1984); Middlesex Hosp., London (MB BS 1983); London Hosp. (Dip. Sports Medicine 1989); DCH RCP 1986; DRCOG 1987. MRCGP 1988; FISM 2001; FFSEM 2003. Won Gold Medal for rowing (coxed fours), Los Angeles Olympic Games, 1984. Principal in General Practice, Acton, 1989–2004; CMO, Olympic Medical Centre, 1989–2009; Dir of Med. Services, British Olympic Assoc., 1994–2008; Sports Physician, English Inst. of Sport, 2003–12; Chief Med. Officer, LOCOG, 2007–12. MO, Governing Body, British Bobsleigh Assoc., 1989–2007; Dr, Bobsleigh Team, Olympic Winter Games, 1992, 1994; CMO, British Team at Olympic Games, 1996, 1998, 2000, 2002, 2004, 2006; Mem., IOC Med. Commn at Olympic Games, 2008, 2010. Chm., British Assoc. of Sports Exercise Medicine, 2008–11; Mem., List Cttee, World Anti-Doping Agency, 2005– (Chm., 2011–12); Bd Mem., then Chm., Nat. Sports Medicine Inst., 1994–2000; Examiner, Intercollegiate Academic Bd of Sports and Exercise Medicine, 2000. Vis. Prof., Univ. of Surrey, 2016–. Hon. FRCP 2011. *Publications*: articles on sports and exercise medicine in med. jls, mainly on 'Unexplained Underperformance Syndrome'. *Recreations*: sailing, ski-ing and ski-touring, cycling, rowing. *Address*: International Olympic Committee, Château de Vidy, PO Box 356, 1001 Lausanne, Switzerland.

**BUEHRLEN, Veronique Eira;** QC 2010; a Deputy High Court Judge, since 2017; *b* Watford, Dec. 1965; *m* 1998, Timothy Michael Wormington; one *s* one *d*. *Educ*: Ashford Sch. for Girls; St Andrews Univ. (MA 1st Cl. Hons French and Internat. Relns); City Univ. (CPE Dist.). Called to the Bar, Middle Temple, 1991; in practice at the Bar, 1991–, specialising in commercial law. *Address*: Keating Chambers, 15 Essex Street, WC2R 3AA. *T*: (020) 7544 2600.

**BUENFELD, Prof. Nicholas Robert,** PhD; CEng, FREng, FICE, FIStructE; Professor of Concrete Structures, since 2000 and Head, Department of Civil and Environmental Engineering, since 2011, Imperial College London; *b* Kent, 4 Oct. 1956; *s* of Robert William Buenfeld and Patricia Dorothy Buenfeld (*née* Hart); two *s*. *Educ*: Dulwich Coll.; Univ. of Leeds (BSc Hons Civil Engrg 1978); Imperial Coll. London (MSc, DIC 1981; PhD 1984). CEng 1984; MICE 1984, FICE 2011; FREng 2011; FIStructE 2012. Graduate Engr, Mott, Hay and Anderson, 1978–80; Imperial College London: Res. Asst, 1981–84; SERC Res. Fellow, 1984–87; Lectr, 1987–98; Reader in Concrete Structures, 1998–2000 Consultant to William J. Marshall & Partners, Mott MacDonald, Arup, Amec, Bouygues London Underground, Hong Kong Govt, Sri Lanka Govt. Hon. FICT. *Publications*: 20

papers in learned jls and internat. confs. *Recreations:* sport, the arts, restoration of old buildings. *Address:* Department of Civil and Environmental Engineering, Imperial College London, SW7 2AZ. *E:* n.buenfeld@imperial.ac.uk. *Clubs:* Alleyn; Chiswick Riverside; Campden Hill Lawn Tennis.

**BUENO, Antonio de Padua Jose Maria;** QC 1989; a Recorder, 1989–2015; *b* 28 June 1942; *s* of late Antonio and Teresita Bueno; *m* 1966, Christine Mary Lees; three *d*. *Educ:* Downside School; Salamanca Univ. Called to the Bar: Middle Temple, 1964 (Harmsworth Scholar), Bencher, 1998; NSW, Ireland and Gibraltar. An Asst Recorder, 1984–89. *Publications:* (ed jtly) Banking section, Atkin's Encyclopaedia of Court Forms, 2nd edn 1976; (Asst Editor, 24th edn 1979 and 25th edn 1983, Jt Editor, 26th edn 1988) Byles on Bills of Exchange; (Asst Editor) Paget's Law of Banking, 9th edn 1982. *Recreations:* fishing, shooting. *Address:* Hammoon House, Hammoon, Sturminster Newton, Dorset DT10 2DB. *T:* (01258) 861704; Equity House, Blackbrook Park Avenue, Taunton, Somerset TA1 2PX. *T:* 0845 083 3000. *E:* tonybuenoqc@gmail.com. *Clubs:* Athenæum, MCC; Kildare Street (Dublin).

**BUERK, Michael Duncan;** journalist and broadcaster, television; *b* 18 Feb. 1946; *s* of Betty Mary Buerk and Gordon Charles Buerk; *m* 1968, Christine Lilley; two *s*. *Educ:* Solihull School. Thomson Newspapers, Cardiff, 1967–69; reporter, Daily Mail, 1969–70; producer, BBC radio, 1970–71; reporter: HTV (West), 1971–72; BBC TV (South), 1972–73; BBC TV London, 1973–76; correspondent, BBC TV: industrial, 1976–77; energy, 1977–79; Scotland, 1979–81; special corresp. and newscaster, 1981–83; Southern Africa, 1983–87; presenter, BBC TV News, 1988–2002; Chm., The Moral Maze, R4, 1991–; presenter Inside the National Trust, 2013–14; Royal Recipes, 2017–18. Hon. MA Bath, 1991; Hon. LLD Bristol, 1994; Hon. DSc Aston, 2000; DUniv Surrey, 2013. RTS TV Journalist of the Year and RTS News Award, 1984; UN Hunger Award, 1984; numerous other awards, UK and overseas, 1984, 1985; BAFTA News Award, 1985; James Cameron Meml Award, 1988; Science Writer of the Year Award, 1989; Mungo Park Award, RSGS, 1994; Jephcott Medal, Royal Soc. of Medicine, 2013. *Publications:* The Road Taken (autobiog.), 2004. *Recreations:* travel, oenophily, sailing. *Address:* c/o Knight Ayton Management, 29 Gloucester Place, W1U 8HX. *Clubs:* Reform, Garrick.

**BUFFINI, Moira Elizabeth;** playwright and screenwriter; *b* Middlewich, Cheshire, 29 May 1965; *d* of John Buffini and Susan Buffini (*née* Clay); *m* 1995, Martin Biltcliffe; one *s* one *d*. *Educ:* Leftwich High Sch.; St Mary's Coll., Rhos-on-Sea; Goldsmiths Coll., Univ. of London (BA Hons Eng. and Drama; Hon. Fellow 2012); Welsh Coll. of Music and Drama (Dip. Acting). *Plays* include: Jordan (with Anna Reynolds), 1992; Blavatsky's Tower, 1997; Gabriel, 1998; Silence, 1999; Loveplay, 2001; Dinner, 2002; A Vampire Story, 2008; Dying For It, 2008; Welcome to Thebes, 2010; Handbagged, 2013; (with Damon Albarn) wonder.land, 2015. *Screenplays* include: Tamara Drewe, 2010; Jane Eyre, 2011; Byzantium, 2013; Harlots (TV series), 2017. FRSL 2014. Hon. FRWCMD 2016. *Publications:* Dinner, 2002; Plays 1, 2006; Dying For It, 2007; Marianne Dreams, 2007; Welcome to Thebes, 2010; (jtly) Greenland, 2011; Handbagged, 2013; Plays 2, 2015; (jtly) wonder.land, 2015. *Address:* c/o St John Donald, United Agents, 12–26 Lexington Street, W1F 0LE. *E:* sdonald@unitedagents.co.uk.

**BUFORD, William Holmes;** staff writer, The New Yorker, 2006–11 (Literary and Fiction Editor, 1995–2002); *b* 6 Oct. 1954; *s* of late William H. Buford and of Helen Shiel; *m* 1991, Alicja Kobiernicka (marr. diss. 2000); *m* 2002, Jessica Green; twin *s*. *Educ:* Univ. of California, Berkeley (BA); King's College, Cambridge (MA). Editor, Granta, 1979–95; former Chm., Granta Publications Ltd. *Publications:* (as Bill Buford): Among the Thugs, 1991; (ed) The Best of Granta Travel, 1991; (ed) The Best of Granta Reportage, 1993; (ed) The Granta Book of the Family, 1995; Heat, 2006; (ed) The Best American Travel Writing 2010, 2010; (contrib.) Daniel: my French cuisine, by Daniel Boulud, 2013; Waiting for a Goal, 2014; (with W. Ford) Walton Ford: Pancha Tantra, 2015.

**BUFTON, John Andreas;** Member (UK Ind) Wales, European Parliament, 2009–14; *b* Llanidloes, 31 Aug. 1962; *s* of Cecil and Trudy Bufton; *m* 2013, Denise Robinson; one *s*. Manager, residential care home, Powys CC. Member (Ind): Rhayader Town Council, 1987–99 (Mayor, Rhayader, 1995–99); Powys UA, 1995–99. *Recreations:* Rugby, running, sports, walking, reading.

**BUHARI, Alhaji Haroun Madani;** media relations and public affairs consultant; High Commissioner for Sierra Leone in London, and Ambassador for Sierra Leone to Sweden, Denmark, Norway, Spain, Portugal, Greece, India and Tunisia, 1995–96; *b* 23 Aug. 1945; *s* of Alhaji Mohammed Buhari and Haja Fatmatta M'balu (*née* Tejan-Sie); *m* 1st, 1975, Haja Sakinatu Onikeh Adams; three *s*; 2nd, 1990, Máriam Zainab Koroma; one *s* one *d*. *Educ:* St Helena Secondary Sch., Freetown; Islamic Missions Inst. at Al-Azhar Univ., Cairo; El Nasr Boys' Coll., Cairo; Univ. of Alexandria, Egypt (BA Hons 1970); Inst. of Social Studies, Univ. of Alexandria; SW London Coll.; Internat. Inst. for Journalism, W Berlin; Diplomatic Acad., Univ. of Westminster (MA 1997). Ministry of Information and Broadcasting, Sierra Leone: Inf. Officer, 1971–78; Sen. Inf. Officer, 1978–82 (Press. Sec.), Office of Pres., 1981–82); Asst Controller/Principal Inf. Officer, 1982–90; Editor-in-Chief, Sierra Leone News Agency, 1986–87; Controller, Govt Inf. Services, 1990–91; Asst Dir of Inf., 1991–92 (Press Sec., Office of Pres., 1987–92); High Comr to Gambia and Ambassador to Senegal, Mauritania and Morocco, 1992–95. Founder Mem., Sierra Leone Assoc. of Journalists, 1971 (Chm., Interim Exec., 1992–93). Member: Sierra Leone Rent Assessment Cttee (Freetown E), 1987–93; Bd of Govs, Sierra Leone Muslim Congress Secondary Sch., 1987–93. Sec.-Gen., Sierra Leone Islamic Foundn, 1982–85; Exec. Sec. Federation of Sierra Leone Muslim Orgns, 1987. Governor: Commonwealth Foundn, 1995–96; Commonwealth Inst., 1995–96. Vice-Pres., Royal Over-Seas League, 1996–. *Publications:* articles on literary, political, social and religious issues for Sierra Leone and internat. press. *Recreations:* football, reading, travelling. *E:* HarounBuhari@hotmail.com.

**BUITER, Prof. Willem Hendrik,** CBE 2000; PhD; FBA 1998; Special Economic Adviser, Citigroup, New York City, since 2018 (Chief Economist: London, 2010–13; New York City, 2013–17); *b* 26 Sept. 1949; *s* of Harm Geert Buiter and Hendrien Buiter (*née* van Schooten); *m* 1st, 1973, Jean Archer (marr. diss. 1998); one *s* one *d*; 2nd, 1998, Prof. Anne C. Sibert. *Educ:* Cambridge Univ. (BA 1971); Yale Univ. (PhD 1975). Asst Prof., Princeton Univ., 1975–76; Lectr, LSE, 1976–77; Asst Prof., Princeton Univ., 1977–79; Prof. of Economics, Univ. of Bristol, 1980–82; Cassel Prof. of Economics, LSE, Univ. of London, 1982–85; Prof. of Econs, 1985–90, Juan T. Trippe Prof. of Internat. Econs, 1990–94, Yale Univ.; Prof. of Internat. Macroecons, and Fellow of Trinity Coll., Cambridge Univ., 1994–2000; Chief Economist, EBRD, 2000–05; Prof. of Eur. Political Economy, 2005–09, Prof. of Political Economy, 2009–11, LSE. Adjunct Sen. Res. Scholar, 2014–15, Adjunct Prof. of Econs, 2015–, Sch. of Internat. and Public Affairs, Columbia Univ., NY. Consultant: IMF, 1979–80; World Bank, 1986–; Inter-American Develt Bank, 1992–; EBRD, 1994–2000; Specialist Advr, House of Commons Select Cttee on the Treasury and CS, 1980–84; Advr, Netherlands Min. of Educn and Science, 1985–86; External Mem., Monetary Policy Cttee, Bank of England, 1997–2000; Chm., Netherlands Council of Econ. Advrs, 2005–07; Mem., Council of Economists, Conference Bd, 2015–. Adjunct Sen. Fellow, Council on Foreign Relations, New York, 2014–. Mem. Council, Royal Economic Soc., 1997–. Blogs for FT.com. Associate Editor, Econ. Jl, 1980–84. Foreign Mem., Koninklijke Nederlandse Academie van Wetenschappen, 1989. Hon. Dr Amsterdam, 2012. *Publications:* Temporary and Long Run Equilibrium, 1979; Budgetary Policy, International and Intertemporal Trade in the Global Economy, 1989; Macroeconomic Theory and Stabilization Policy, 1989; Principles of Budgetary and Financial Policy, 1990; International Macroeconomics, 1990; (jtly) Financial Markets and European Monetary Co-operation: the lessons of the 1992–93 ERM crisis, 1998; articles in learned jls. *Recreations:* science fiction and fantasy novels, tennis, poetry, music, hiking. *Address:* 60 Riverside Boulevard, Apt 1201, New York, NY 10069–0214, USA. *W:* willembuiter.com.

**BULEY, Timothy Laurence Howard;** QC 2019; *b* Epsom, 13 May 1975; *s* of Dr Anthony Buley and Dr Pamela Helen Buley. *Educ:* Lincoln Coll., Oxford (BA Hons PPE 1997); City Univ., London (CPE 1999); King's Coll. London (LLM 2001). Called to the Bar, Inner Temple, 2000. *Recreations:* walking, ski-ing, mountaineering, reading. *Address:* Landmark Chambers, 180 Fleet Street, EC4A 2HG. *E:* tbuley@landmarkchambers.co.uk.

**BULFIELD, Prof. Grahame,** CBE 2001; PhD; FRSE; FRSB; Vice-Principal, Head of College of Science and Engineering, and Professor of Animal Genetics, University of Edinburgh, 2002–08, now Emeritus Professor of Genetics and Senior Honorary Professorial Fellow; consultant on genetics and biotechnology; *b* 12 June 1941; *s* of Frederick Bulfield and Madge (*née* Jones). *Educ:* King's Sch., Macclesfield; Univ. of Leeds (BSc 1964); Univ. of Edinburgh (Dip. Animal Genetics 1965; PhD 1968). FRSE 1992; FRSB (FIBiol 1995). Fulbright Fellow and NIH Postdoctoral Fellow, Dept of Genetics, Univ. of Calif., Berkeley, 1968–70; SRC Resettlement Fellow, 1970–71, Res. Associate, 1971–76, Inst. of Animal Genetics, Univ. of Edinburgh; Lectr and Convenor of Med. Genetics, Dept of Genetics, Med. Sch. and Sch. of Biol Scis, Univ. of Leicester, 1976–81; Hd, Genetics Gp, AFRC Poultry Res. Centre, Roslin, 1981–86; Hd, Gene Expression Gp, 1986–88, and Hd of Station and Associate Dir, 1988–93, Edinburgh Res. Station of Inst. of Animal Physiology and Genetic Res., Roslin; Dir and Chief Exec., Roslin Inst., BBSRC, 1993–2002. Hon. Fellow, 1981–90, Hon. Prof., 1990–2002, Div. of Biol Scis, Univ. of Edinburgh. Member: Animal Procedures Cttee, Home Office, 1998–2006; Res. Policy Cttee, SHEFC, 2002–05; Res. and Knowledge Transfer Cttee, SFC, 2005–06; Bd, SRUC (formerly Scottish Agricl Coll.), 2007–18. Member, Enterprise Fellowship Committee: Scottish Enterprise/RSE, 2001–13; BBSRC/RSE, 2007–18 (Chm., 2010–18). Hon. FRASE 1999. Hon. DSc: Edinburgh, 2000; Abertay, 2002. *Publications:* res. papers, reviews and book chapters on biochemical and molecular genetics. *Recreations:* fell-walking, cricket, genetic genealogy. *Address:* School of Biological Sciences, University of Edinburgh, The King's Buildings, Edinburgh EH9 3FD. *T:* 07831 305602. *E:* Grahame.Bulfield@ed.ac.uk.

**BULFIELD, Peter William,** CA; Deputy Chairman, Yamaichi Bank (UK) PLC, 1991–94 (Managing Director and Chief Executive, 1988–91); *b* 14 June 1930; *s* of Wilfred Bulfield and Doris (*née* Bedford); *m* 1958, Pamela June Beckett; two *d*. *Educ:* Beaumont Coll., Old Windsor. Peat Marwick Mitchell & Co., 1947–59; J. Henry Schroder Wagg & Co., 1959–86, Dir, 1967–86; Director: Schroder Finance, 1966–73; Schroder Darling Hldgs, Sydney, 1973–80; Vice-Chm., Mitsubishi Trust & Banking Corporation (Europe) SA, 1973–84; Jt Dep. Chm., Schroder Internat., 1977–86; Dep. Chm., Crown Agents for Oversea Govts and Admin, 1982–85 (Mem., 1978–85); Director: Yamaichi Internat. PLC, 1986–87; London Italian Bank, 1989–91. Member: Overseas Projects Board, 1983–86; Overseas Promotions Cttee, BIEC, 1984–86; Export Guarantees Adv. Council, 1985–88. Mem., Finance Cttee, CAFOD, 1994–2002; Hon. Treas., W Sussex Assoc. for the Blind, 1998–99. KSG 2001. *Recreations:* sailing, music, painting. *Address:* Snow Goose Cottage, Sandy Lane, East Ashling, W Sussex PO18 9AT. *T:* and *Fax:* (01243) 575298. *Club:* Royal Thames Yacht.

**BULFORD, Anne Judith;** *see* Weyman, A. J.

**BULKELEY, Sir Richard Thomas W.;** *see* Williams-Bulkeley.

**BULL,** Baroness *cr* 2018 (Life Peer), of Aldwych in the City of Westminster; **Deborah Clare Bull,** CBE 1999; Vice President and Vice-Principal (London), King's College London, since 2018 (Assistant Principal (London), 2015–18); *b* 22 March 1963; *d* of Rev. Michael John Bull and Doreen Audrey Franklin (*née* Plumb). *Educ:* Royal Ballet Sch. Joined Royal Ballet, 1981; Principal Dancer, 1992–2001; Nutrition Teacher, Royal Ballet Sch., 1996–99; Dir, Artists' Develt Initiative, 1999–2001, first Artistic Dir, then Creative Dir of ROH2, later Creative Dir, 2002–12, Royal Opera House; Dir, Cultural Partnerships, 2012–15, Sen. Adv. Fellow for Culture, 2015–, KCL. Has danced a wide range of work, incl. leading rôles in: Swan Lake; Sleeping Beauty; Don Quixote; particularly noted for modern rôles, incl. Steptext, and Symbiont(s) (Time Out Outstanding Achievement Award); appeared in Diamonds of World Ballet Gala, Kremlin Palace, Moscow, 1996. Member: Arts Council, 1998–2004 (Mem., Dance Panel, 1996–98; Annual Lecture, 1996); AHRC, 2012–19. Governor: S Bank Centre, 1997–2003; BBC, 2003–06. Mem. Bd, Sci. Gall. Internat., 2013–; Vice Pres., Cultural Develt, British Sci. Assoc., 2015–18. Columnist, The Telegraph, 1999–2002; contributing editor, Harpers & Queen, 2000–01. Wrote and presented: *television:* Dance Ballerina Dance, 1998; Travels with my Tutu, 2000; The Dancer's Body, 2002; Saved for the Nation, 2006; Dancing for Russia, 2014; Bolshoi Unseen, 2014; *radio:* Leaving Barons Court, 1999; Breaking the Law, 2001; Law in Order, 2002; Hothouse Kids, 2009; After I Was Gorgeous, 2011; Something Understood—Steps in Time, 2011; Deborah Bull's Dance Nation, 2012; Dance for your Life, 2012; Classic FM Goes to the Ballet, 2014; regular appearances on Saturday Review, BBC Radio 4. DUniv: Derby, 1998; Sheffield, 2001; Open, 2005; Kent, 2010; Lincoln, 2017. Prix de Lausanne, 1980. *Publications:* The Vitality Plan, 1998; Dancing Away, 1998; (jtly) Faber Guide to Classical Ballets, 2004; The Everyday Dancer, 2011; articles in jls and newspapers. *Recreations:* reading, writing, dancing, piano, neurology, psychology, nutrition, people. *Address:* King's College London, Somerset House East Wing, Strand, WC2R 2LS. *W:* www.deborahbull.com; c/o Rosemary Scoular, United Agents, 12–26 Lexington Street, W1F 0LE.

**BULL, Christopher John;** bodger, spoon-maker and book dealer; Director of Corporate Services, Government Equalities Office, 2007–11; *b* 26 July 1954; *s* of George William and Kathleen Bull; *m* 1983, Alison Jane Hughes; two *d*. *Educ:* UCW, Aberystwyth (BA). CPFA 1983. With Nat. Audit Office, 1977–97; Inspector, Benefit Fraud Inspectorate, DSS, 1997–99; Dir, Benefit Fraud Inspectorate, DSS, subseq. DWP, 1999–2007. Ind. Mem., Audit Cttee, CRE, 2006–07. Mem., Assoc. of Pole-Lathe Turners and Green Woodworkers, 2018. FRSA 2000. *Recreations:* books, wood, beer.

**BULL, David Neill,** CBE 2015; consultant, mentor, blogger; Executive Director, UNICEF UK, 1999–2016; *b* 21 June 1951; *s* of Denis Albert and Doreen Lilian Bull; *m* 1978, Claire Grenger; one *d*. *Educ:* Sussex Univ. (BA Econ); Bath Univ. (MSc Develt Studies); OCM Cert. Coaching and Mentoring. Public Affairs Unit Officer, Oxfam, 1979–84; Dir, Environment Liaison Centre, Nairobi, 1984–87; Gen. Sec., World University Service (UK), 1987–90; Dir, Amnesty International (UK Sect.), 1990–99. Trustee: Refugee Council, 1987–90; Pesticides Trust, 1987–99; Mem., Exec. Cttee, ACENVO, 1994–98; Power of Nutrition, 2016–; United Purpose, 2016–. Hon LLD Bath, 2009. *Publications:* A Growing Problem: pesticides and the Third World Poor, 1982; The Poverty of Diplomacy:

Kampuchea and the outside world, 1983. *Recreations:* walking, reading, esp. science fiction, family history, photography, astronomy. *W:* www.worldtorights.org, www.twitter.com/davidnbull.

**BULL, Sir George (Jeffrey),** Kt 1998; Group Chief Executive, 1993–95, Chairman, 1995–97, Grand Metropolitan PLC; Joint Chairman, Diageo plc, 1997–98 (non-executive Director, 1998–2000); Chairman, J Sainsbury PLC, 1998–2004; *b* 16 July 1936; *s* of late Michael Herbert Perkins Bull and Hon. Noreen Madeleine Bull (*née* Hennessy), *d* of 1st Baron Windlesham, OBE; *m* 1960, Jane Fleur Thérèse, *d* of late Patrick Freeland; four *s* one *d*. *Educ:* Ampleforth Coll. Lt Coldstream Guards, 1954–57, served Germany and UK. Dorland Advertising Ltd, 1957; Twiss Browning & Hallowes wine merchants, 1958; Man. Dir, Gilbey Vintners, 1970; International Distillers & Vintners Ltd: Man. Dir, IDV UK Ltd, 1973; Man. Dir, IDV Europe Ltd, 1977; Dep. Man. Dir, 1982–84; Chief Exec., 1984–92; Chm., 1988–92; Dir, Grand Metropolitan Ltd, 1985; Chief Exec., Grand Metropolitan Drinks Sector, 1987; Chm. and Chief Exec., Grand Metropolitan Food Sector, 1992–95. Non-executive Director: United Newspapers, 1993–98; BNP Paribas Ltd, 2000–04; Maersk Co. Ltd, 2001–06. Dir, BOTB, 1990–95; founding Dir, Marketing Council, 1995–2000. Mem., Adv. Bd, Marakon Associates, 2002–06. Chm., Wine and Spirit Assoc. of GB, 1975–76; Vice-Pres., CIM, 1994 (Hon. FCIM, 1995); Member: Presidents' Cttee, CBI, 1993–96; Adv. Bd, British Amer. Chamber of Commerce, 1994–98. Dir, US Adv. Educ. Foundn, 1994–98; President: Advertising Assoc., 1996–2000; Wine and Spirit Benevolent Soc., 2000–01; Vice Pres., Mencap, 2000–18. Chm., Old Codgers Assoc., 2006–17. Confrater, Ampleforth Abbey, 2005–; Dir/Sec., Chapel Annunciation, Furneux Pelham, 2010–14. Patron, Caritas Anchor House (formerly Anchor House Project), 2010–. Hon. Fellow, Marketing Soc., 1997. Hon. Pres., Perkins Bull Collection, 2008–. Grand Master, Keepers of the Quaich, 1995–96 (Patron, 1996–2005). Freeman, City of London, 1995. Liveryman, Distillers' Co., 1995–. Chevalier, Légion d'Honneur (France), 1994; Chevalier du Tastevin, 2005. *Recreations:* golf, photography. *Address:* The Old Vicarage, Arkesden, Saffron Walden, Essex CB11 4HB. *T:* (01799) 550445. *Clubs:* Cavalry and Guards, Pilgrims; Royal Worlington and Newmarket Golf (Suffolk) (Mem. Council, 2008–11).

**BULL, Gregory;** QC 2003; a Recorder, since 2000; *b* 14 Aug. 1953; *s* of Mansel and Joyce Bull; *m* 1983, Helen Ruth Bookes Parsons (marr. diss. 2011); one *s* one *d*. *Educ:* Mardy House Church in Wales Secondary Sch.; Aberdare Boys' Grammar Sch.; Univ. of Birmingham (LLB Hons). Called to the Bar, Inner Temple, 1976; in practice, specialising in crime, fraud and common law; Asst Recorder, 1995–2000; Advocate, Public Defender Service, 2014. Leader, Wales and Chester Circuit, 2010–13 (Treas., 2007–10). Member: Bar Council, 2007–13; Criminal Bar Assoc., 2007–13. *Recreations:* Rugby Union, walking, politics, music, theatre.

**BULL, John;** *see* Bull, R. J.

**BULL, His Honour John Michael;** QC 1983; DL; a Circuit Judge, 1991–2006; a Deputy Circuit Judge, 2006–08; *b* 31 Jan. 1934; *s* of John Godfrey Bull and Eleanor Bull (*née* Nicholson); *m* 1959, Sonia Maureen, *d* of Frank Edward Woodcock; one *s* three *d*. *Educ:* Norwich Sch. (State Schol.); Corpus Christi Coll., Cambridge (Parker Exhibnr in Modern History; BA 1958; LLM 1959; MA 1963). Called to the Bar, Gray's Inn, 1960; Dep. Circuit Judge, 1972; Standing Counsel to the Board of Inland Revenue, Western Circuit, 1972–83; a Recorder, 1980–91; Resident Judge, Crown Court at Guildford, 1992–2000. Judge, Employment Appeal Tribunal, 1993–2000. Hon. Recorder of Guildford, 1998–2010. Hon. Vis. Prof., Surrey Univ., 1999–2005. DL Surrey, 1996. DUniv Surrey, 2010.

**BULL, Michelle;** *see* Harrison, Michelle.

**BULL, Nicholas James Douglas;** Chairman, Fidelity China Special Situations plc, since 2016 (Director, since 2010); Senior Independent Director, Coats Group plc, since 2015; *b* London, 17 April 1952; *s* of late Dr James William Douglas Bull, CBE, FRCP and Edith Bull (*née* Burch Schiff, then Schiff Burch); *m* 1989, Katusha Ostroumoff; one *s*. *Educ:* Eton Coll.; Univ. of Exeter (BSc Chem. 1973). ACA 1976, FCA 1981. Articled Clerk, 1973–76, Audit Sen., 1976–77, Spicer & Pegler; Corporate Finance, Morgan Grenfell & Co. Ltd, 1977–86; Hd of Corporate Finance, 1986, Chief Exec., 1987–88, Morgan Grenfell Australia, Sydney; Corporate Finance Dir, Morgan Grenfell & Co. Ltd, London, 1989–92; Regl Dir, Morgan Grenfell Asia, Singapore, 1993; Regl Dir, Deutsche Morgan Grenfell Asia, Hong Kong, 1994–95; Man. Dir, M&A, Deutsche Bank, London, 1996–99; Man. Dir and Hd of Consumer Sector M&A, Société Générale, 2000–02; Man. Dir and Hd of Global Clients for UK, ABN AMRO, 2002–08; Chm., Smith's Corporate Adv. Ltd, 2009–10. Dir, De Vere Gp Ltd, 2010–15 (Chm., 2012–15). Chm., Adv. Bd, Westhouse Securities, 2011–15. Mem. Council, Univ. of Exeter, 2009–18 (Chm., Fundraising Campaign Bd, 2007–11). Associate Gov., Greig City Acad., 2013–18. Trustee: Design Mus., 1988–93 and 2012–; Conran Foundn, 1996–; Camborne Sch. of Mines, 2014–; Creative Educn Trust. 2018–. Liveryman, Tallow Chandlers' Co., 1990– (Master, 2015–16). Chm., Thames Traditional Rowing Assoc., 2005–15. *Recreations:* rowing, propagating philanthropy. *Address:* 19 Spencer Park, SW18 2SZ. *T:* 07900 473513. *E:* nicholasbull@ymail.com. *Clubs:* Leander (Henley-on-Thames); Huntercombe Golf, Royal Mid-Surrey Golf; St Moritz Tobogganing; Vail Mountain.

**BULL, Prof. (Roger) John,** CBE 2002; Deputy Chairman, Universities Superannuation Scheme Ltd, 2006–14 (Director/Trustee, 2004–14); *b* 31 March 1940; *s* of William Leonard Bull and Margery Bull (*née* Slade); *m* 1964, Margaret Evelyn Clifton; one *s* one *d*. *Educ:* Churcher's Coll.; LSE (BSc Econ). FCCA. Research Fellow, DES/ICA, 1967–68; Principal Lectr in Accounting, Nottingham Poly., 1968–72; Head, Sch. of Accounting and Applied Econs, Leeds Poly., 1972–85; Dep. Dir (Academic), Plymouth Poly., 1986–89; Dir and Chief Exec., Poly. SW, Plymouth, 1989–92; Vice-Chancellor and Chief Exec., Univ. of Plymouth, 1992–2002. Chm., Devon and Cornwall LSC, 2002–08. Chm., Open Learning Foundn, 1994–97; Dir, HEQC, 1994–97; Hon. Treas., UUK (formerly CVCP), 1994–2002. Non-exec. Dir/Trustee, UK eUniversities Worldwide Ltd, 2001–04; Chm., Plymouth Hospitals NHS Trust, 2002–10 (non-exec. Dir, 1993–2002). Dir, Plymouth Chamber of Commerce, 1994–97. Member: Council, CNAA, 1981–87; Council for Industry and Higher Educn, 1993–2002. Chm., Dartington Coll. of Arts, 2003–08 (Gov., 1996–2003). *Publications:* Accounting in Business, 1969, 6th edn 1990; articles on accounting and educnl mgt. *Recreation:* music.

**BULL, Prof. Stephen John,** PhD; CEng; FIMMM; FInstP; FREng; Cookson Group Chair of Materials Engineering, since 2008, and Director of Expertise in Materials and Manufacturing, School of Engineering, since 2017, Newcastle University; *b* Carshalton, Surrey, 12 Aug. 1963; *s* of Ronald John and Jean Margaret Bull; *m* 1989, Catherine Ruth Le Sueur; one *s* three *d*. *Educ:* Wallington High Sch. for Boys; St Catharine's Coll., Cambridge (BA 1984; MA 1988; PhD 1988). FIMMM 1997; FInstP 2007; CEng 2012; FREng 2014. Harwell Laboratory: HSO, Coatings and Interface Technol. Gp, 1988–90; Section Manager: Advanced Physical Vapour Deposited Coatings and Coatings Design Section, 1991; PVD and Ion Assisted Coatings Section, 1991–93; PVD Coatings and Interfaces Section, 1993–96; Newcastle University: Reader in Surface Technol., 1996–2002; Prof. of Surface Engrg, 2002–07; Hd, 2005–10, Dir of Res., 2012–17, Sch. of Chemical Engrg and Advanced Materials; RAEng/Leverhulme Trust Sen. Res. Fellow, 2010–11. *Publications:* contrib. articles to learned jls and conf. proceedings. *Recreations:* music, science fiction reading and writing. *Address:* School of Engineering, Newcastle University, Bedson Building, Newcastle-upon-Tyne NE1 7RU. *T:* (0191) 208 7913. *E:* steve.bull@ncl.ac.uk.

**BULL, Sir Stephen Louis,** 5th Bt *cr* 1922, of Hammersmith; *b* 5 April 1966; *s* of Sir Simeon George Bull, 4th Bt and Annick Elizabeth Renée Geneviève Bull (*née* Bresson); *S* father, 2019, but his name does not appear on the Official Roll of the Baronetage; *m* 1994, Maria Brampton; twin *s* three *d*. *Heir: s* Dominic Simeon Bull, *b* 29 July 2005.

**BULLARD, Felicity;** *see* Lawrence, F.

**BULLARD, Gary Bruce;** Chairman, New Model Identity, since 2013; *b* Chislehurst, Kent, 3 April 1957; *s* of late Cyril Charles Bullard and of Margaret Irene Elizabeth Bullard; *m* 1983, Elaine May Sullivan. *Educ:* St Olave's and St Saviour's Grammar Sch.; Exeter Univ. (BSc Combined Hons). Gen. Manager, Global Solutions, IBM Corp., 1978–2004; Pres., BT Global Services, BT plc, 2004–08; Chief Executive Officer: Catquin, 2007–11; Logica UK, 2011–12. Non-executive Director: Chloride plc, 2006–10; Rotork plc, 2010–; Smart Cube, 2013–14; Spirent plc, 2016–. MInstD 2010. *Address:* 4 The Terrace, 140 Richmond Hill, Richmond, Surrey TW10 6RN. *T:* 07802 246270. *E:* gary.bullard@btopenworld.com. *Clubs:* Morton's, Tramp.

**BULLER;** *see* Manningham-Buller.

**BULLER;** *see* Manningham-Buller, family name of Viscount Dilhorne.

**BULLER;** *see* Yarde-Buller, family name of Baron Churston.

**BULLER, Emma Katherine;** *see* Himsworth, E. K.

**BULLIMORE, His Honour John Wallace MacGregor;** a Circuit Judge, 1991–2010; *b* 4 Dec. 1945; *s* of late James Wallace Bullimore and Phyllis Violet Emily Bullimore (*née* Brandt); *m* 1975, Rev. Christine Elizabeth Kinch; two *s* (one *d* decd). *Educ:* Queen Elizabeth Grammar School, Wakefield; Univ. of Bristol (LLB). Called to the Bar, Inner Temple, 1968; Chancellor, Diocese of Derby, 1980–, of Blackburn, 1990–, of W Yorkshire and the Dales, 2014–15. Mem., Gen. Synod of the Church of England, 1970–2010.

**BULLIVANT, Lucy Georgina;** author, critic, curator, guest lecturer and consultant; *b* London, 4 Nov. 1958; *d* of Dargan Bullivant and Patricia Bullivant. *Educ:* Leeds Univ. (BA Hons Art Hist. 1980); Royal Coll. of Art (MA Cultural Hist. 1984); London Metropolitan Univ. (PhD 2015). Consultant to: Milan Triennale, ICA, Archis, 1984–; British Council, AD/Wiley, Yorkshire Forward, FRAC Orléans, V&A, 1990–; ArchMarathon, 2014–; Design Council Cabe, 2015–; Enfield Council; Qatar Univ. Adjunct Prof., Syracuse Univ., 2013–14. Guest lecturer for Univ. of Qatar, IAAC Barcelona and other architectural colls. Mem., Scientific Cttee, Institut pour la Ville en Mouvement, PSA Peugeot Citroën, Paris, 2012–. Correspondent to Domus, Architectural Rev., Indesign, Volume. Mem., AA. Hon. FRIBA 2010. *Publications:* Kid size: the material world of childhood, 1997; (ed) Home Front: new developments in housing, 2003; (ed) 4dspace: interactive architecture, 2004; Anglo Files: UK architecture's rising generation, 2005; Responsive Environments: art, architecture and design, 2006; (ed) 4dsocial: interactive design environments, 2007; New Arcadians: emerging UK architects, 2012; Masterplanning Futures, 2012 (Book of the Year, Urban Design Group Awards, 2014), 2nd edn 2019; (with Thomas Ermacora) Recoded City: co-creating urban futures, 2015. *Recreations:* travelling, walking, running, photography, cinema. *Address:* 73B Southampton Row, WC1B 4ET. *T:* (020) 7323 4629. *E:* office@lucybullivant.net.

**BULLMORE, Prof. Edward Thomas,** PhD; FMedSci, FRCPsych, FRCP; Professor of Psychiatry, since 1999, Head, Department of Psychiatry, since 2014, and Director, Wolfson Brain Imaging Centre, since 2014, University of Cambridge; Hon. Consultant Psychiatrist, Addenbrooke's Hospital, Cambridge, since 1999; *b* 27 Sept. 1960; *s* of (John) Jeremy David Bullmore, *qv* and Pamela Audrey Bullmore (*née* Green); *m* 1992, Mary Pitt, *d* of late Arthur Pitt and of Elizabeth Pitt; three *s*. *Educ:* Westminster Sch.; Christ Church, Oxford (BA); St Bartholomew's Hosp. Med. Coll. (MB BS); PhD London 1997. MRCP 1989; MRCPsych 1992, FRCPsych 2009; FRCP 2010. Lectr in Medicine, Univ. of Hong Kong, 1987–88; SHO in Psychiatry, St George's Hosp., London, 1989–90; Registrar in Psychiatry, Bethlem Royal and Maudsley Hosps, 1990–93; Wellcome Trust Res. Trng Fellow, 1993–96; Advanced Res. Trng Fellow, 1996–99; Hon. Consultant Psychiatrist, Maudsley Hosp., London, 1996–99; Clinical Dir, MRC/Wellcome Trust Behavioural and Clin. Neurosci. Inst., Cambridge, 2005–; Fellow, Wolfson Coll., Cambridge, 2002–10; Vice-Pres., Exptl Medicine, GlaxoSmithKline, 2005–19 (Hd, Clin. Unit, Cambridge, 2005–13); Dir, R&D, Cambs and Peterborough NHS Foundn Trust, 2011–; Co-Chair, Cambridge Neuroscience, 2013–17; Chm. Cambridge Health Imaging, Cambridge Univ. Health Partners, 2015–18. NIHR Sen. Investigator, 2014–. Vis. Prof. Inst. of Psychiatry, KCL, 2000–. Mem., MRC Neurosci and Mental Health Bd, 2002–06. FMedSci 2008 (Mem. Council, 2017–; Treas., 2019–). *Publications:* Fundamentals of Brain Network Analysis, 2016; The Inflamed Mind, 2018; papers on anatomical and functional brain imaging methods and applications to psychiatry and neuroscience. *Recreations:* running, birding. *Address:* Department of Psychiatry, University of Cambridge, Herchel Smith Building for Brain and Mind Sciences, Cambridge Biomedical Campus, Cambridge CB2 0SZ. *T:* (01223) 336582.

**BULLMORE, (John) Jeremy David,** CBE 1985; Chairman, J. Walter Thompson Co. Ltd, 1976–87; Director: The Guardian Media Group (formerly The Guardian and Manchester Evening News plc), 1988–2001; WPP Group plc, 1988–2004 (Member, Advisory Board, since 2005); *b* 21 Nov. 1929; *s* of Francis Edward Bullmore and Adeline Gabrielle Bullmore (*née* Roscow); *m* 1958, Pamela Audrey Green; two *s* one *d*. *Educ:* Harrow; Christ Church, Oxford. Military service, 1949–50. Joined J. Walter Thompson Co. Ltd, 1954: Dir, 1964; Dep. Chm., 1975; Dir, J. Walter Thompson Co. (USA), 1980–87. Mem., Nat. Cttee for Electoral Reform, 1978–. Chm., Advertising Assoc., 1981–87; President: Nat. Advertising Benevolent Soc., 1999–2001; Market Res. Soc., 2004–09. Mackintosh Medal, Advertising Assoc., 2011. *Publications:* Behind the Scenes in Advertising, 1991, 3rd edn 2003; Another Bad Day at the Office?, 2001; Ask Jeremy, 2004; Apples, Insights and Mad Inventors, 2006; The Quality Quotient, 2018. *Address:* 17/20 Embankment Gardens, SW3 4LW. *T:* (020) 7351 2197.
*See also* E. T. Bullmore.

**BULLOCK, Hugh Jonathan Watson,** FRICS, FRTPI; Chairman, Gerald Eve LLP, Chartered Surveyors, since 2015; *b* Brussels, 27 Dec. 1957; *er s* of late (Edward) Anthony (Watson) Bullock and Jenifer Myrtle Bullock, *e d* of Sir (Herbert) Richmond Palmer, KCMG, CBE; *m* 1980, Gabriella Zofia Stanley, *yr d* of late Major Ivan William Stanley Moss, MC and Countess Zofia Tarnowska Moss; three *d*. *Educ:* Eton Coll.; Univ. of St Andrews; London South Bank Univ. (BSc 1st Cl. Hons 1985; Rubens Meml Prize 1985). ARICS 1986, FRICS 1992; MRTPI 1996, FRTPI 2006. Gerald Eve LLP, Chartered Surveyors: joined as grad. trainee, 1985; Partner, 1989–; Sen. Partner, 2008–15. Vis. Lectr, Univ. of Reading, 2004–15. Advr, Westminster Property Assoc., 1990–; Mem., Property

Adv. Gp, The Passage, 2012–16; Trustee: Duke of Lancaster Housing Trust, 2016–; Duke of Lancaster Jubilee Trust, 2016–. Mem. Council, Duchy of Lancaster, 2015–. Member: Mayor of London's West End Commn, 2005–06; Mayor of London's Homes for Londoners Bd, 2016–. Chair, Planning and Devlt Adv. Gp, London First, 2009–17. Member: Monitoring and Investigation Cttee, RICS, 1996–98; London Regl Council, CBI, 1997–2001; Cambridge Land Economy Adv. Bd, Univ. of Cambridge, 2013–19. Member, Board of Trustees: LAMDA, 2006–17; Imperial War Museum, 2018– (Chair, Estates Adv. Cttee, 2019–); Trustee, Patrick Leigh Fermor Soc., 2015–. Court Asst, Chartered Surveyors' Co., 2018–. (Jtly) London Planning Award for Best Private Sector Planning Orgn, 2004. *Publications:* Commercial Viability in Planning, 1993; A Positive Approach to Town and Country Planning, 2007; Economic Realities of Taxing Development, 2009; Localism and Growth, 2011; Localism and Planning, 2012. *Recreations:* theatre, walking dogs, selected history, sports, travel. *Address:* Gerald Eve LLP, 72 Welbeck Street, W1G 0AY. *T:* (020) 7333 6302. *E:* hbullock@geraldeve.com. *Clubs:* Royal Air Force, Surveyors' Association.

**BULLOCK, Jonathan Deryck;** Member for East Midlands, European Parliament, since 2017 (UK Ind, 2017–18; Ind, 2018–19; Brexit, since 2019); *b* Nottingham, 3 March 1963; *s* of Deryck Bullock and Joan Bullock; *m* 2000, Claire Williams. *Educ:* Nottingham High Sch.; Portsmouth Poly. (BA Hons Politics 1984). Res. Asst to MPs, H of C, 1984–85; Advertising Agency Exec., 1987–94; Head: External Affairs and PR, Advertising Assoc., 1994–97; Communications, British Road Fedn, 1997–2001; Dir, Policy, CILT, 2002–07. Mem., Kettering BC, 2007–15. Contested: (C) Manchester Gorton, 1992, Gedling, 2001; (UK Ind) Kettering, 2015, Northampton N, 2017. FRSA. *Recreations:* ski-ing, shooting, fishing, sailing, theatre. *Address:* (office) 21 Manor Walk, Market Harborough, Leics LE16 9BP. *T:* (01858) 432020. *E:* jonathan.bullock@europarl.europa.eu. *Club:* Royal Naval and Royal Albert Yacht.

**BULLOCK, Hon. Matthew Peter Dominic;** Master, St Edmund's College, Cambridge, 2014–19; *b* 9 Sept. 1949; *s* of Baron Bullock, FBA and Hilda Yates Bullock; *m* 1970, Anna-Lena Margareta Hansson; one *s* two *d. Educ:* Magdalen College Sch., Oxford; Peterhouse, Cambridge (BA Hist. 1970); Harvard Business Sch. (AMP 1991). CBI, 1970–74; Barclays Bank plc, 1974–98: Corporate Finance Dir, 1983–86; Regl Dir, Yorkshire, 1986–91; Dir, Risk Mgt, 1991–93; Man. Dir, BZW/Barclays Capital, 1993–98; Gp Chief Exec., Norwich and Peterborough Bldg Soc., 1999–2011. Chm., Automation Partnership Gp plc, 1999–2012. Member: Cabinet Adv. Cttee on Application of R&D, 1983–88; Econ. Policy Cttee, EEF, 1991–97; Industrial Adv. Bd, DTI, 1993–99; Financial Services Practitioner Panel, 2001–07. Chm., Building Socs Assoc., 2006–07. University of Cambridge: Chm. Adv. Bd, Centre for Business Res., 1994–2013; Mem., Audit Cttee, 2002–10; Mem. Adv. Bd, 1985–2002, Chm., Chinese Big Business Prog., 1999–2001, Judge Inst. of Mgt Studies. Non-exec. Dir, Cambridge Univ. Hosp. Trust, 2010–13 (Chm., Audit Cttee, 2011–13). Chairman: Internat. House Trust Ltd, 2011–14; Pathology Partnership (formerly Transforming Pathology Partnership), 2013–16. Dir, Cambridge Ahead Ltd, 2013–. Trustee, Cambridge Past, Present and Future, 2011–15. Governor: Imperial Coll., London, 1981–86; Leeds Univ., 1986–91. *Publications:* Academic Enterprise, Industrial Innovation and the Development of High Technology Financing in the USA, 1981. *Recreations:* walking, gardening, music, opera. *Address:* Easby House, High Street, Great Chesterford, Essex CB10 1PL. *E:* mpdbullock@gmail.com. *Club:* Oxford and Cambridge.

**BULLOCK, Rt Rev. Sarah Ruth;** *see* Shrewsbury, Area Bishop of.

**BULLOCK, Sir Stephen Michael,** Kt 2007; DL; Chair: Sutton Housing Partnership, since 2018; Housing and Finance Institute; *b* 26 June 1953; *s* of late George Bullock and Florence (*née* Gott); *m* 1992, Kristyne Margaret Hibbert. *Educ:* Sir William Turner's Sch., Redcar; Leeds Univ. (BA Hons); Goldsmiths' Coll. (PGCE). Greater London Council: Admin. Officer, 1977–79; Dep. Hd, Labour Gp Office, 1979–83; Asst Dir, Public Relns, 1983–86; Chief Officer, Greenwich CHC, 1986–90. Dir, 1993–97, Chm., 1997–2002, Univ. Hosp. Lewisham NHS Trust. London Borough of Lewisham: Councillor (Lab), 1982–98, 2001–02; Leader of Council, 1988–93; Exec. Mayor, 2002–18. Exec. Mem. for Housing, London Councils, 2010–18. Chm., ALA, 1992–93; Dep. Chm., AMA, 1992–94; Hd, Labour Gp Office, LGA, 1997–2002. Board Member: London Pension Fund Authy, 1989–98; London First, 1993–96; Independent Housing Ombudsman Ltd, 1997–2001; Mus. of London, 2011–17; Chairman: Deptford City Challenge Ltd, 1992–93; London Connects, 2004–09; Vice-Chm., Local Govt Management Bd, 1994–95 (Chm., 1992–93); Dep. Chm., LGA, 2013–17; Dir, Civic Skills Consultancy, 1994–95; Prin. Consultant, Capita Gp, 1995–97. Mem., Commn for Local Democracy, 1994–96. Trustee, Horniman Mus. and Gdns, 1999–2010. DL Lewisham, 2018. Hon. Fellow, Goldsmiths, Univ. of London, 2018. *Publications:* (contrib.) A Transatlantic Policy Exchange, 1993; (with R. Hambleton) Revitalising Local Democracy: the leadership options, 1996. *Recreations:* folk music, watching Middlesbrough FC, seeking the "Moon under Water". *Address:* Garden Flat, 9 Tyson Road, Forest Hill, SE23 3AA. *T:* (020) 8291 5030. *E:* steve.bullock53@gmail.com.

**BULLOCK, Susan Margaret,** CBE 2014; FRAM; soprano; *b* 9 Dec. 1958; *d* of late John Robert Bullock and Mair Bullock (*née* Jones); *m* 2009, Richard Berkeley-Steele. *Educ:* Cheadle Hulme Sch.; Royal Northern Coll. of Music Jun. Sch.; Royal Holloway Coll., Univ. of London (BMus Hons); Hon. Fellow, 2004); Royal Acad. of Music (LRAM; FRAM 1997); Nat. Opera Studio. Mem., Glyndebourne Fest. Opera Chorus, 1983–84; Principal Soprano, ENO, 1985–89; freelance internat. soprano, 1989–; *rôles* include: Madama Butterfly (title rôle) with ENO, Houston Grand Opera, Oper der Stadt, Bonn, New Israeli Opera, Portland Opera, USA, NYC Opera and Teatro Colon, Buenos Aires; Jenůfa (title rôle) with ENO, New Israeli Opera, Glyndebourne and Spoleto Fest., USA; Magda Sorel in The Consul with Teatro Colon, Buenos Aires and Spoleto Fest., Italy; Isolde, in Tristan and Isolde, with Opera North, Bochum Symphony, ENO, Rouen, Oper Frankfurt and Verona; Brünnhilde, in Der Ring des Nibelungen, Tokyo, Perth Fest., Aust., Budapest, Lisbon, Royal Opera, Oper Frankfurt and Vienna State Opera; Elektra (title rôle), with Oper Frankfurt, La Monnaie, Brussels, Royal Opera, Metropolitan Opera, La Scala, Milan, and Washington Opera; Marie, in Wozzeck, Royal Opera; La Fanciulla del West, Edinburgh Fest.; Makropulos Case, Frankfurt; Gloriana (title rôle), Royal Opera; Miss Wingrave, in Owen Wingrave, Aldeburgh Fest.; Mrs Lovett, in Sweeney Todd, Houston Grand Opera; Mum, in Greek, Edinburgh Fest.; Mother and Witch, in Hansel and Gretel, Opera North; Kostelnicka, in Jenufa, Grange Park Opera; Klytemnestra, in Elektra, Canadian Opera Co.; appears with all major British orchestras and also in Europe, N and S America and Australia. Frequent broadcasts; recitals at Wigmore Hall, Edinburgh Fest. and abroad with Malcolm Martineau; soloist in BBC Last Night of the Proms, 2011; has made recordings. Hon. MusD Manchester, 2014. Singers Award, Royal Philharmonic Soc., 2008. *Recreations:* playing the piano, cooking, theatre, jazz. *Address:* c/o HarrisonParrott Ltd, The Ark, 201 Talgarth Road, W6 8BJ.

**BULLOUGH, Dr Ronald,** FRS 1985; consultant in UK and USA; Chief Scientist, UK Atomic Energy Authority, 1988–93, and Director for Corporate Research, Harwell, 1990–93; *b* 6 April 1931; *s* of Ronald Bullough and Edna Bullough (*née* Morrow); *m* 1954, Ruth Corbett; four *s. Educ:* Univ. of Sheffield. BSc, PhD, DSc. FIMMM (FIM 1964); FInstP 1962. Res. Scientist, AEI Fundamental Res. Lab., Aldermaston Court, Aldermaston, 1956–63; Theoretical Physicist and Group Leader, Harwell Res. Lab., Didcot, Berks, 1963–84; Hd, Materials Develt Div., Harwell, 1984–88; Dir for Underlying Res., Harwell, 1988–90. Visiting Professor: Univ. of Illinois, USA, 1964, 1973, 1979; Univ. of Wisconsin, USA, 1978; Rensselaer Polytechnical Inst., USA, 1968; UCL, 1994–; Univ. of Liverpool, 1994–; Visiting Scientist: Nat. Bureau of Standards, USA, 1965; Oak Ridge Nat. Lab., USA, 1969, 1979; Comisión Nacional de Energía Atómica, Buenos Aires, Argentina, 1977. For. Associate, NAE (USA), 2011. Hon. Citizen of Tennessee, 1967. *Publications:* articles in learned jls such as Proc. Roy. Soc., Phil. Mag., Jl of Nucl. Materials etc., on defect properties in crystalline solids, particularly in relation to the irradiation and mechanical response of materials. *Recreations:* reading, music. *Address:* 4 Long Meadow, Manor Road, Goring-on-Thames, Reading, Berkshire RG8 9EG. *T:* (01491) 873266.

**BULMER, Derek John;** freelance consultant, hotel and catering industry; Editor, Great Britain and Ireland Michelin Guide, 1996–2010; *b* Hampstead, 24 March 1950; *s* of George Henry Bulmer and Barbara Joan Bulmer (*née* Gray); *m* 1979, Lynn Barton; one *s* one *d. Educ:* Christ Church, N Finchley; Westminster Hotel Sch. (HND). Trust Houses Forte, 1972–77; Asst Manager, White Horse Inn, Hertingfordbury, 1972–74; Dep. Manager, Randolph Hotel, Oxford, 1974–75; Personnel Manager, Brown's Hotel, Mayfair, 1975–77; Michelin Guide: Hotel and Restaurant Insp., 1977–90; Dep. Ed., GB and Ireland, 1990–96; Editor: Main Cities of Europe, 1998–2010; Eating Out in Pubs, 2005–10. Dir, Martini Consulting, 2010–. *Recreations:* wine, musical theatre, photography. *E:* derekbulmer@gmail.com.

**BULMER, (James) Esmond;** Director, H. P. Bulmer Holdings plc, 1962–2003 (Deputy Chairman, 1980; Chairman, 1982–2000); *b* 19 May 1935; *e s* of late Edward Bulmer and Margaret Rye; *m* 1st, 1959, Morella Kearton; three *s* one *d;* 2nd, 1990, Susan Elizabeth Bower (*née* Murray). *Educ:* Rugby; King's Coll., Cambridge (BA); and abroad. Commissioned Scots Guards, 1954. Dir (non-exec.), Wales and W Midlands Regional Bd, National Westminster Bank PLC, 1982–92. Chm., Hereford DHA, 1987–94. MP (C): Kidderminster, Feb. 1974–1983; Wyre Forest, 1983–87. PPS to Minister of State, Home Office, 1979–81. Mem. Council, CBI, 1998–2002. Mem. Exec. Cttee, Nat. Trust, 1977–87. *Recreations:* gardening, fishing. *Clubs:* Boodle's, Beefsteak.

**BULMER, Dr Michael George,** FRS 1997; Professor, Department of Biological Sciences, Rutgers University, 1991–95; *b* 10 May 1931; *s* of Dr Ernest and Dr Eileen Mary Bulmer; *m* 1966, Sylvia Ann House (*d* 2011). *Educ:* Rugby Sch.; Merton Coll., Oxford (MA, DPhil 1957; DSc 1985). Lectr in Med. Stats, Univ. of Manchester, 1957–59; Lectr in Biomaths, 1959–91, Fellow of Wolfson Coll., 1965–91, now Emeritus, Univ. of Oxford. *Publications:* Principles of Statistics, 1965; The Biology of Twinning in Man, 1970; The Mathematical Theory of Quantitative Genetics, 1980; Theoretical Evolutionary Ecology, 1994; Francis Galton: pioneer of heredity and biometry, 2003; articles in scientific jls on biometry and evolutionary biology. *Recreation:* walking.

**BULMER, Prof. Simon John,** PhD; Professor of European Politics, University of Sheffield, since 2007; *b* 29 June 1954; *s* of late Dawson Vivian Bulmer and Kathleen Amy Bulmer; *m* 1986, Helen Margaret Donaldson. *Educ:* Univ. of Loughborough (BA Hons Eur. Studies 1975); Univ. of Hull (MA Eur. Politics 1976); London Sch. of Economics (PhD 1982). Lecturer: in Govt, Heriot-Watt Univ., 1979–83; in Eur. Studies, UMIST, 1983–89; Sen. Lectr, then Reader, in Govt, 1989–94, Prof. of Govt, 1995–2007, Univ. of Manchester. Vis. Prof., Coll. of Europe, Bruges, 1994–99. Mem., Trng and Develt Bd, ESRC, 2005–10. FAcSS (AcSS 2001). *Publications:* The Domestic Structure of European Community Policy-Making in West Germany, 1986; (jtly) The European Council, 1987; (jtly) The Federal Republic of Germany and the European Community, 1987; (ed) The Changing Agenda of West German Public Policy, 1989; (ed jtly) The United Kingdom and EC Membership Evaluated, 1992; (ed jtly) Economic and Political Integration in Europe, 1994; (jtly) The Governance of the Single European Market, 1998; (jtly) Germany's European Diplomacy, 2000; (jtly) British Devolution and European Policy-Making, 2002; (ed jtly) The Member States of the European Union, 2005, 2nd edn 2013; (jtly) Policy Transfer in European Union Governance, 2007; (jtly) The Europeanisation of Whitehall, 2009; (ed jtly) Rethinking Germany and Europe, 2010; (jtly) Politics in the European Union, 2011, 4th edn 2015; (jtly) Germany and the European Union, 2019; contrib. numerous jl articles. *Recreations:* travel, jazz, current affairs, walking. *Address:* Department of Politics, University of Sheffield, Elmfield, Northumberland Road, Sheffield S10 2TU. *T:* (0114) 222 1706, *Fax:* (0114) 222 1717. *E:* S.Bulmer@sheffield.ac.uk.

**BULMER-THOMAS, Prof. Victor Gerald,** CMG 2007; OBE 1998; DPhil; Director, Royal Institute of International Affairs (Chatham House), 2001–06; Emeritus Professor, London University, since 1998; *b* 23 March 1948; *s* of late Ivor Bulmer-Thomas, CBE and of Margaret Joan Bulmer-Thomas; *m* 1970, Barbara Ann Swasey; two *s* one *d. Educ:* Westminster Sch.; New Coll., Oxford (MA); St Antony's Coll., Oxford (DPhil). Research Fellow, Fraser of Allander Inst., Strathclyde Univ., 1975–78; Queen Mary, subseq. Queen Mary and Westfield, College, London University: Lectr in Econs, 1978–87; Reader in Econs of Latin America, 1987–90; Prof. of Econs, 1990–98; Institute of Latin American Studies, London University: Dir, 1992–98; Sen. Res. Fellow, 1998–2001; Hon. Res. Fellow, 2001–04; Hon. Res. Fellow, Inst. for the Study of the Americas, then Inst. of Latin American Studies, 2004–; Hon. Prof., UCL, 2012–. Associate Fellow, Chatham House, 2007–. Vis. Prof., Florida Internat. Univ., Miami, 2007–10. Director: Schroders Emerging Countries Fund, 1996–2003; Deutsche Latin American Companies Trust, 2004; New India Investment Trust, 2004–16; Caribbean Foundn, 2008–10; J. P. Morgan Brazil Investment Trust, 2010–. Dir, UK-Japan 21st Century Gp, 2001–03. Editor, Jl of Latin American Studies, 1986–97. Comdr, Order of San Carlos (Colombia), 1998; Comdr, Order of Southern Cross (Brazil), 1998. *Publications:* Input-Output Analysis for Developing Countries, 1982; The Political Economy of Central America since 1920, 1987; Studies in the Economics of Central America, 1988; (ed) Britain and Latin America, 1989; (jtly) Central American Integration, 1992; (ed jtly) Mexico and the North American Free Trade Agreement: Who Will Benefit?, 1994; The Economic History of Latin America since Independence, 1994, 3rd edn 2014; (jtly) Growth and Development in Brazil: Cardoso's *real* challenge, 1995; (ed) The New Economic Model in Latin America and its Impact on Income Distribution and Poverty, 1996; (ed) Rebuilding the State: Mexico after Salinas, 1996; (ed) Thirty Years of Latin American Studies in the United Kingdom, 1997; (jtly) US-Latin American Relations: the new agenda, 1999; (ed) Regional Integration in Latin America and the Caribbean: the political economy of open regionalism, 2001; (ed jtly) The Cambridge Economic History of Latin America, 2 vols, 2006; The Economic History of the Caribbean since the Napoleonic Wars, 2012; (jtly) The Economic History of Belize: from 17th century to post-independence, 2012; Empire in Retreat: the past, present and future of the United States, 2018; From Slavery to Service: the struggle for economic independence in the Caribbean, 2019. *Recreations:* tennis, hill-walking, kayaking, music (viola), underwater photography. *Club:* Athenæum.

**BUMBRY, Grace;** opera singer and concert singer; founder, Grace Bumbry Vocal and Opera Academy; *b* St Louis, Mo, 4 Jan. 1937. *Educ:* Boston Univ.; Northwestern Univ.; Music Academy of the West (under Lotte Lehmann). Début: Paris Opera, 1960; Bayreuth

Fest., 1961; Chicago Lyric Opera, 1962; Royal Opera, Covent Gdn, London, 1963; San Francisco Opera, 1963; Vienna State Opera, 1964; Salzburg Festival, 1964; Metropolitan Opera, 1965; La Scala, 1964; has also appeared in all major opera houses in Europe, S America and USA. Has made numerous recordings. Film, Carmen, 1968. Hon. Dr of Humanities, St Louis Univ., 1968; Hon. doctorates: Rust Coll., Holly Spring, Miss; Rockhurst Coll., Kansas City; Univ. of Missouri at St Louis. Richard Wagner Medal, 1963; Kammersänger, Austria; Kennedy Center Honor, 2009. Commandeur de l'Ordre des Arts et des Lettres (France). *Recreations:* psychology, entertaining.

**BUNBURY;** *see* McClintock-Bunbury, family name of Baron Rathdonnell.

**BUNBURY, Bishop of,** since 2018; **Rt Rev. Dr Ian Alexander Coutts;** *b* Portsmouth, 1956; *s* of Philip and Queenie Coutts; *m* 1978, Anne Jane Coutts, *qv;* two *d. Educ:* Southern Grammar Sch., Portsmouth; Warwick Univ. (BA 1977); Jesus Coll., Oxford (MSc 1980); St John's Theol Coll., Nottingham (DipTh 1989); King's Coll. London and Charles Sturt Univ., Sydney (PhD 2015). Residential Social Worker, Coventry Social Services, 1977–82; Children's Soc., 1982–84; Sen. and Principal Social Worker, Birmingham Educn Dept, 1984–87; ordained deacon, 1989, priest, 1990; Asst Curate, Hamstead, Birmingham, 1989–92; Team Vicar, Warlingham, Chelsham and Farleigh, 1992–2000; Social Worker, Wandsworth Social Services, 2000–03; Sen. Social Worker, Oxfordshire CAMHS, later Ct Advr, CAFCASS, 2004–10; Adjunct Lectr, Nat. Theol Centre, Canberra and Gen. Manager, Anglicare, 2012–18. *Recreations:* jogging, swimming, flying. *Address:* Anglican Diocese of Bunbury, 7 Oakley Street, Bunbury, WA 6230, Australia. *T:* (8) 97212100. *E:* bishop@bunbury.org.au.

**BUNBURY, Sir Michael (William),** 13th Bt *cr* 1681, of Stanney Hall, Cheshire; KCVO 2005; DL; company director, landowner and farmer; Partner, 1974–97, and Chairman, 1986–93, Smith & Williamson; *b* 29 Dec. 1946; *s* of Sir John William Napier Bunbury, 12th Bt, and of Pamela, *er d* of late Thomas Alexander Sutton; *S* father, 1985; *m* 1976, Caroline Anne, *d* of late Col A. D. S. Mangnall, OBE; two *s* one *d. Educ:* Eton; Trinity College, Cambridge (MA). Buckmaster & Moore, 1968–74. Chairman: Fleming High Income Investment Trust plc, 1996–97 (Dir, 1995–97); HarbourVest Global Private Equity Ltd, 2007–; BH Global Ltd, 2013–; Director: JP Morgan Claverhouse Investment Trust plc, 1996–2015 (Chm., 2005–15); Foreign & Colonial Investment Trust plc, 1998–2012; Invesco Perpetual Select Trust plc, 2008–18. Mem. Council, Duchy of Lancaster, 1993–2005 (Dep. Chm., 1995–2000, Chm., 2000–05). Mem. Exec. Cttee, CLA, 1992–97 and 1999–2004 (Chm., Taxation Cttee, 1999–2003; Chm. Cttee, Suffolk Br., 1995–97); Pres., Suffolk Agricl Assoc., 2000–02. Trustee, Calthorpe Edgbaston Estate, 1991–2013. DL 2004, High Sheriff, 2006–07; Suffolk. *Heir: s* Henry Michael Napier Bunbury, *b* 4 March 1980. *Address:* Naunton Hall, Rendlesham, Woodbridge, Suffolk IP12 2RD. *T:* (01394) 460235. *Club:* Boodle's.

**BUNBURY, Sir Thomas (William) Richardson-,** 6th Bt *cr* 1787; Headmaster, Papplewick School, since 2004; *b* Yeovil, 4 Aug. 1965; *s* of Lt-Comdr Sir (Richard David) Michael Richardson-Bunbury, 5th Bt and Jane Louise Richardson-Bunbury; *S* father, 2017; *m* 2001, Sallie Ann Lofts; two *s* two *d. Educ:* Woodcote Hse Sch.; Millfield Sch.; Durham Univ. (BA Hons Law); Homerton Coll., Cambridge (PGCE). Solicitor, 1989–91; Papplewick School: Dir of Studies, 1996–99; Sen. Master, 1999–2000; Dep. Headmaster, 2000–03. *Recreations:* theatre, tennis, walking. *Heir: s* Harry William Richardson-Bunbury, *b* 2 Dec. 2002. *Address:* New Lodge, Papplewick School, Windsor Road, Ascot, Berks SL5 7LH. *E:* hm@papplewick.org.uk.

**BUNCE, Rev. Dr Michael John,** FSAScot; Permission to officiate, Diocese of Norfolk, 2014–16; Chaplain, Santa Margarita, Menorca, 2000–12; *b* 5 Dec. 1949; *s* of Harold Christopher and Kathleen June Bunce; *m* 1973, Frances Sutherland; one *s* one *d. Educ:* St Andrews Univ. (MTh); Westcott House and Trinity Hall, Cambridge; Greenwich Univ. (PhD). Glazing clerk, Middleton Glass Merchant, 1965–69; Personnel Labour Controller, Bird's Eye Unilever, 1969–75. Ordained deacon, 1980, priest, 1981; Curate, 1980–83, Hosp. Chaplain and Team Vicar, 1983–85, Grantham Parish Church; Rector, St Andrew's, Brechin with St Drostan's, Tarfside and St Peter's, Auchmithie (Angus), 1985–92; Provost, St Paul's Cathedral, Dundee, 1992–97. FRSA. *Recreations:* tennis, ski-ing, art, antiques. *Club:* Edinburgh Angus.

**BUNCH, Dr Christopher,** FRCP, FRCPE; Consultant Physician, Oxford Radcliffe Hospitals NHS Trust, since 1994 (Medical Director, 1994–2001; Caldicott Guardian, since 1998); *b* 25 Feb. 1947; *s* of Douglas Campbell Bunch and Barbara Bunch (*née* Hall); *m* 1977, Kathleen Josie Andrew; two *d. Educ:* King's School, Worcester; Birmingham Univ. (MB ChB 1969). FRCP 1984; FRCPE 1988. University of Oxford: Clinical Lectr in Medicine, 1975–81; Clinical Reader in Medicine, 1981–94; Professorial Fellow, Wolfson Coll., Oxford, 1981–94, Fellow Emeritus 1994–. Dir, British Assoc. of Medical Managers, 1995–2005 (Chm., 2001–04). Secondary Care Consultant Mem., Governing Body, Nene CCG, 2012–. Chm., UK Council, Caldicott Guardians, 2017–. Goulstonian Lectr, RCP, 1985. Mem. Council, RCP, 1999–2002. *Publications:* (ed) Horizons in Medicine I, 1989; contrib. various scientific and medical articles in haematology, especially control of erythropoiesis. *Recreations:* cooking (and eating) Mediterranean, Middle Eastern and SE Asian food, music, photography, computer science and programming. *Address:* 55 Sandfield Road, Headington, Oxford OX3 7RW. *T:* (office) (01865) 221343.

**BUNCLE, Thomas Archibald;** Managing Director, Yellow Railroad Ltd, since 2000; *b* 25 June 1953; *s* of Thomas Edgar Buncle and Helen Elizabeth Buncle; *m* 1979, Janet Michelle Louise Farmer; two *s. Educ:* Trinity Coll., Glenalmond; Exeter Univ. (BA Sociology and Law 1975); Sheffield Univ. (MA Criminology 1978); London Business Sch. (Sen. Exec. Prog.). Various posts, incl. Law Tutor, Sheffield Univ., and tour guide, Amer. Leadership Study Gps and Voyages Sans Frontières, 1975–77; British Tourist Authority: graduate trainee, 1978–79; Asst Internat. Advertising Manager, 1979–80; Asst Manager, Western USA, 1981–84; Manager, Norway, 1984–86; Regl Dir, SE Asia, 1986–91; Scottish Tourist Board: Internat. Mktg Dir, 1991–96; Chief Exec., 1996–2000. Dir, Edinburgh Festival Council, 1997–2000; Board Member: Scotland the Brand, 1996–2000; Cairngorm Partnership, 1997–2000; Member: Exec. Council, Scottish Council for Develt and Industry, 1998–2000; Risk Monitoring and Audit Cttee, Scottish Prison Service, 2004–14. Fellow: Tourism Soc., 2001; Tourism Mgt Inst., 2014; Member: Panel of Experts, UN World Tourism Orgn, 2010–; Sustainable Tourism Certification Alliance Africa, 2012–; Experts' Cttee, World Tourism Cities Forum, China, 2014–; Nat. Cttee, UK Tourism Consultants Network, 2015–. Hon. Prof., Heriot-Watt Univ., 2016–. *Recreations:* windsurfing, sailing, scuba diving, Rugby, hill walking, cycling, photography. *W:* www.twitter.com/TomYellowRail.

**BUNDRED, Stephen;** Chief Executive, Audit Commission, 2003–10; Director, Bundred Consulting Ltd, since 2016; *b* 12 Dec. 1952; *s* of George Bundred, CBE, JP, DL and Theresa Bundred (*née* Hynes); *m* 1976, Kathleen McVeigh; one *s. Educ:* St Catherine's Coll., Oxford (BA PPE); Birkbeck Coll., London (MSc Econs); Liverpool Poly. (CPFA). Res. Asst to Eric Varley, MP, 1973–74; Special Advr to Sec. of State for Energy, 1974–75; Hd, Res. Dept, NUM, 1975–83; Principal Technical Accountant, Hackney LBC, 1983–87; Chief Accountant, Lewisham LBC, 1987–88; Financial Sec., Birkbeck Coll., Univ. of London, 1988–90; Dep. Dir of Finance, Hackney LBC, 1990–92; Dir of Finance and Dep. Chief Exec., 1992–95, Chief Finance Officer, 1995–99, Chief Exec., 1995–2003, Camden LBC; Clerk, N London Waste Authy, 1995–2003; Exec. Dir, Improvement and Develt Agency, 2003; Chm., Monitor, Ind. Regulator of NHS Foundn Trusts, 2010–11. Strategic Advr, Deloitte LLP, 2010–15. Chm., Higher Educn Regulation Rev. Gp, 2006–08; Member: TEC Assessors Cttee, 1998–99; Rethinking Construction Local Govt Task Force, DETR, 1999–2003; Bd, HEFCE, 1999–2005 (Chm., Audit Cttee, 2002–05); London Central Learning and Skills Council, 2001–03; Putting the Frontline First Taskforce, DCLG, 2010; Bd, Office for Nuclear Regulation, 2011–15 (Chm., Audit Cttee, 2011–15); Higher Educn Commn, 2013–. Dir, Pioneer Theatres Ltd, 2016–17. Member (Lab): Islington LBC, 1975–78; GLC, 1981–86; ILEA, 1981–90. Mem. Council, 1999–2008, Dep. Pro Chancellor, 2006–08; City Univ. Freeman, City of London, 2001. FRSA. Hon. DSc City, 2006. *Publications:* (contrib.) Policing the Riots, 1982; (contrib.) Reinventing Government Again, 2004; (contrib.) Public Services Inspection in the UK, 2008; (contrib.) Opportunities in an Age of Austerity, 2009; contribs to jls. *Address:* 3 Colebrooke Row, Islington, N1 8DB. *T:* (020) 7278 7742.

**BUNDY, Prof. Alan Richard,** CBE 2012; PhD; FRS 2012; FREng; FRSE; FACM; Professor of Automated Reasoning, University of Edinburgh, since 1990 (Head of Division of Informatics, 1998–2001); *b* 18 May 1947; *s* of Stanley Alfred Bundy and Joan Margaret Bundy; *m* 1967, D. Josephine A. Maule; one *d. Educ:* Univ. of Leicester (BSc 1st Cl. Maths 1968; PhD Mathematic Logic 1971). Teaching Asst, Dept of Maths, Univ. of Leicester, 1970–71; University of Edinburgh: Res. Fellow, Metamathematics Unit, 1971–74; Department of Artificial Intelligence: Lectr, 1974–84; Reader, 1984–87; Professorial Fellow, 1987–90. Vice Pres. and Trustee, BCS, 2010–12. FAAAI 1990; FRSE 1996; FBCS 2002; FIET (FIEE 2005); FREng 2008; FACM 2015; Fellow: Soc. for Study of Artificial Intelligence and Simulation of Behaviour, 1997; Eur. Co-ordinating Cttee for Artificial Intelligence, 1999. Donald E. Walter Dist. Service Award, 2003, Res. Excellence Award, 2007, Internat. Jt Conf. on Artificial Intelligence; Herbrand Award, Internat. Conf. on Automated Deduction, 2007; Skolem Award, Internat. Conference on Automated Deduction, 2017. *Publications:* Artificial Intelligence: an introductory course, 1978; The Computer Modelling of Mathematical Reasoning, 1983, 2nd edn 1986; The Benefits and Risks of Knowledge Based Systems, 1989; Eco-logic: logic based approaches to ecological modelling, 1991; Catalogue of Artificial Intelligence Techniques, 1984, 4th edn 1996; Rippling: meta-level guidance for mathematical reasoning, 2005. *Recreation:* valley walking. *Address:* School of Informatics, University of Edinburgh, Informatics Forum, 10 Crichton Street, Edinburgh EH8 9AB.

**BUNDY, Prof. Colin James,** DPhil; Principal, Green Templeton College, Oxford, 2008–10 (Hon. Fellow, 2010); *b* 4 Oct. 1944; *s* of Guy Stanhope Bundy and Winifred Constance Bundy (*née* Tooke); *m* 1st, 1969, Carol Ann Neilson (marr. diss. 1993); one *s* one *d*; 2nd, 2001, Evelyn Jeannette Bertelsen. *Educ:* Graeme Coll., Grahamstown; Univ. of Natal (BA); Univ. of Witwatersrand (BA Hons); Merton Coll., Oxford (Rhodes Schol., 1968); MPhil 1970, DPhil 1976, Oxon. Beit Sen. Res. Scholar, St Antony's Coll., Oxford, 1971–73. Lectr and Sen. Lectr in Hist., Manchester Poly., 1973–78; Res. Fellow, Queen Elizabeth House, Oxford, 1979–80; Tutor in Hist., Dept for External Studies, Oxford Univ., 1980–84; Prof. of Hist., Univ. of Cape Town, 1985–86; Prof. of Hist., concurrently Univs of Cape Town and Western Cape, 1987–90; University of Western Cape: Prof. of Hist., 1991–95; Dir, Inst. of Histl Res., 1992–94; Actg Vice-Rector, 1994–95; Vice-Rector (Academic), 1995–97; Vice-Chancellor and Principal, Univ. of Witwatersrand, Johannesburg, 1998–2001; Dir and Principal, SOAS, 2001–06, and Dep. Vice-Chancellor, 2003–06, Univ. of London; Warden, Green Coll., Oxford, 2006–08. Chm., South African Nat. Commn for UNESCO. Mem. Council, Robben Island Mus., 1997–2001. Hon. Fellow, Kellogg Coll., Oxford, 1998. Hon. DLitt: Manchester Metropolitan, 1999; Univ. of Western Cape, 2005. *Publications:* The Rise and Fall of the South African Peasantry, 1979, 2nd edn 1988; (jtly) Hidden Struggles in Rural South Africa, 1988; (contrib.) Encyclopedia Britannica, other books, and periodicals. *Recreations:* hiking, cricket, chess, music.

**BUNEMAN, Prof. (Oscar) Peter,** MBE 2013; PhD; FRS 2009; FRSE; Professor of Database Systems, University of Edinburgh, since 2002. *Educ:* Gonville and Caius Coll., Cambridge (BA Maths 1965); Univ. of Warwick (PhD 1970). Res. Associate, then Lectr, Sch. of Artificial Intelligence, Univ. of Edinburgh, 1969–74; University of Pennsylvania: Asst Prof. of Computer Sci., Moore Sch., and Asst Prof. of Decision Scis, Wharton Sch., 1975–81; Associate Prof. of Computer Sci., 1981–89; Grad. Chm., Dept of Computer and Inf. Sci., 1981–87; Prof. of Computer Sci., 1990–2001; Adjunct Prof. of Computer Sci., 2002–; Res. Dir, Digital Curation Centre, Edinburgh, 2004–. FRSE 2004. *Publications:* (contrib.) Theoretical Aspects of Object-oriented Programming, 1994; (contrib.) Bioinformatics, 1998; (contrib.) Semantics of Databases, 1998; (jtly) Data on the Web: from relations to semi-structured data and XML, 1999; contribs to conf. proceedings and to jls incl. Internat. Jl on Digital Libraries, Jl Computer and System Scis, Theoretical Computer Sci. *Address:* Laboratory for Foundations of Computer Science, School of Informatics, University of Edinburgh, 10 Crichton Street, Edinburgh EH8 9AB.

**BUNGEY, Michael;** Chairman and Chief Executive Officer, Bates Worldwide (formerly BSB Worldwide), 1994–2003; Chief Executive Officer, Cordiant Communications Group, 1997–2003; *b* 18 Jan. 1940; *s* of William Frederick George and Irene Edith Bungey; *m* 1976, Darleen Penelope Cecilia Brooks (marr. diss.); one *s* two *d. Educ:* St Clement Danes Grammar Sch.; LSE (BSc Econ). Marketing with Nestlé, 1961–65; Associate Dir, Crawfords Advertising, 1965–68; Account Dir, S. H. Benson Advertising, 1969–71; Chm., Michael Bungey & Partners, 1972–84; Dep. Chm., Dorland Advertising, 1984; Chm., Bates Dorland Advertising Ltd, 1987–96; Chairman and Chief Executive Officer: DFS Dorland, 1987; Bates Dorland, 1988; Bates Europe, 1989; Pres. and Chief Operating Officer, BSB Worldwide, 1993–94; Chairman: Bates Americas' Reg., 1993; Bates USA, 1993; Kingstreet Media Gp, 2004–05; Honeycomb TV, 2016–. Dir, Cordiant plc (formerly Saatchi & Saatchi), 1995. *Club:* Hurlingham.

**BUNKER, Prof. Christopher Barry,** MD; FRCP; Consultant Dermatologist, University College London Hospitals NHS Foundation Trust, since 2010; *b* Aylesbury, Bucks, 22 Nov. 1956; *s* of Sqn Leader Nigel Vincent Delahuntey Bunker, MBE and Joy Bunker (*née* Bolsover); *m* 1991, Dr Anna Kurowska; two *d. Educ:* Wycliffe Coll. (Scholar.); St Catharine's Coll., Cambridge (Kitchener Schol.); BA 1978; MD 1992); Westminster Med. Sch. (MB BS 1981). MRCP 1995, FRCP 1996. Sir Jules Thorn Res. Fellow, UCL, 1988–90; Consultant Dermatologist: Charing Cross Hosp., 1992–2003; Chelsea and Westminster (formerly Westminster) Hosp., 1992–; Royal Marsden Hosp., 1997–2010. Honorary Professor: Imperial Coll. London, 2005–; UCL, 2010–. President: St John's Hosp. Dermatol Soc., 2006–07; W London Medico-Chirurgical Soc., 2007–08; Chelsea Clin. Soc., 2010–11; British Assoc. of Dermatologists, 2012–14; Dermatol. Section, RSocMed, 2015–16. Sir Walter Langdon-Down Prize, Univ. of Cambridge, 1992; Bristol Cup, British Assoc. of Dermatologists, 1998. *Publications:* Male Genital Dermatology, 2004; chapters in textbooks and contrib. over 300 pubns. *Recreations:* literature, music, opera, drama, stalking. *Address:* King Edward VII Hospital, Beaumont Street, W1G 6AA. *T:* (020) 7794 5943. *E:* c.bunker@ucl.ac.uk. *Club:* Garrick.

**BUNKER, Very Rev. Michael;** fundraising consultant, since 2006; Dean of Peterborough, 1992–2006, now Dean Emeritus; *b* 22 July 1937; *s* of Murray Bunker and Nora Bunker; *m* 1957, Mary Helena Poulten; four *s*. *Educ:* Acton Technical Coll. and Brunel Coll., Acton (ONC and HNC in Engineering); Oak Hill Theol Coll. Work Study Engr, Napiers of Acton, London, 1956–60. Ordained deacon, 1963, priest, 1964; Assistant Curate: St James' Church, Alperton, Middlesex, 1963–66; Parish Church of St Helen, Merseyside, 1966–70; Incumbent: St Matthew's Church, Muswell Hill, London, 1970–78; St James with St Matthew, Muswell Hill, 1978–92. Prebendary of St Paul's Cathedral, 1990. Chairman: Habitat for Humanity GB, 2000–02; Souster Youth Trust, 2015–. Trustee, Nat. Kidney Res. Fund, 1999–2002. *Publications:* The Church on the Hill, 1988; Peterborough Cathedral 2001–2006: from devastation to restoration, 2007. *Recreation:* reading. *Address:* 21 Black Pot Lane, Oundle, Peterborough PE8 4AT. *T:* (01832) 273032, 07887 854917. *E:* m.bunker@me.com.

**BUNTING, Martin Brian,** FCA; *b* 28 Feb. 1934; *s* of late Brian and Renee Bunting; *m* 1959, Veronica Mary Cope; two *s* one *d*. *Educ:* Rugby School. 2nd Lieut, 8th Kings Royal Irish Hussars, 1952–54. Deloitte, 1954–60; joined Courage Ltd, 1961, Man. Dir, 1972, Dep. Chm., 1974–84; Dir, Imperial Group plc, 1975–84; Chief Executive, Clifford Foods PLC, 1990–93. Non-executive Director: George Gale & Co. Ltd, 1984–2004; Longman Cartermill Ltd, 1985–90; Norcros plc, 1986–93; Shepherd Neame Ltd, 1986–2004; NAAFI, 1993–98; Hobson plc, 1994–96; Chairman: Inn Business Gp plc, 1996–97; Select Catalogues Ltd, 1996–98; Bluebird Toys plc, 1996–98 (Dir, 1991–98). Member, Monopolies and Mergers Commission, 1982–88. Chm. Trustees and Gov., Lord Wandsworth Coll., 2000–04. *Address:* The Long House, 41 High Street, Odiham, Basingstoke, Hants RG29 1LF. *T:* (01256) 703585.
*See also* Duke of Fife.

**BUNTING, Prof. Rebecca Mary;** Vice-Chancellor and Chief Executive, Buckinghamshire New University, 2015–18; *b* Lytham St Annes, 27 Sept. 1955; *d* of Henry Bunting and Roma Bunting; partner, Dr Peter Weston. *Educ:* Fleetwood Grammar Sch.; Girton Coll., Cambridge (BA 1977); Inst. of Educn, Univ. of London (MA; PGCE). ATCL 1973, LTCL 1974. Roehampton Institute of Higher Education, London, later University of Surrey, Roehampton: Sen. Lectr, 1985–87; Hd, English Educn, 1987–89; Dir, Inner London Lang. Proj., 1989–92; Principal Lectr, 1992–95; Associate Dean of Educn, 1995–98; Dean of Educn, Anglia Polytechnic Univ., 1998–2002; Pro-Rector, University Coll. Northampton, 2002–04; Pro Vice-Chancellor, 2004–07, Dep. Vice-Chancellor, 2007–15, Univ. of Portsmouth. FHEA 2004; FRSA. *Publications:* Teaching about Language in the Primary Years, 1998, 2nd edn 2001.

**BUNYAN, Dr Peter John;** Chief Scientific Adviser to Ministry of Agriculture, Fisheries and Food, 1990–95; *b* London, 13 Jan. 1936; *o s* of Charles and Jenny Bunyan; *m* 1961, June Rose Child; two *s*. *Educ:* Raynes Park County Grammar Sch.; University Coll., Durham Univ. (BSc, DSc); King's Coll., Univ. of London (PhD). FRSC; FRSB; FIFST. Research at KCL, 1960–62, at UCL, 1962–63; Ministry of Agriculture, Fisheries and Food: Sen. Scientific Officer, Infestation Control Lab., 1963–69; PSO, Pest Infestation Control Lab., 1969–73; Head of Pest Control Chemistry Dept, 1973–80; Head of Food Science Div., 1980–84; Head of Agricl Sci. Service, ADAS, 1984–87; Dir of R & D Services, ADAS, 1987–90; Dir Gen., ADAS and Regl Orgn, 1990–91. Member: AFRC, 1990–94; BBSRC, 1994–95; NERC, 1991–95; Chm., British Crop Protection Council, 1998–2002. Special Advr to Vice-Chancellor, Surrey Univ., 1996–2008. Hon. Sec., Inst. of Biol., 1996–2001. Vis. Prof., Sch. of Agriculture, De Montfort Univ., 1996–2001. Governor: Portsmouth Univ., 2010–18; Mill Chase Acad., Bordon, 2015–17. FRSA. Hon. DSc De Montfort, 2001; DUniv Surrey, 2009. *Publications:* numerous scientific papers in wide variety of scientific jls. *Recreations:* gardening, walking. *Address:* Flushings Meadow, 16A Lavant Road, Chichester, W Sussex PO19 5RG. *T:* (01243) 527542.

**BUNYARD, Sir Robert (Sidney),** Kt 1991; CBE 1986; QPM 1980; DL; Commandant, Police Staff College, Bramshill and HM Inspector of Constabulary, 1988–93; *b* 20 May 1930; *s* of Albert Percy Bunyard and Nellie Maria Bunyard; *m* 1948, Ruth Martin; two *d*. *Educ:* Queen Elizabeth Grammar Sch., Faversham; Regent Street Polytechnic Management Sch. (Dip. in Mgt Studies). BA (Hons) Open Univ. MIPD; CCMI. Metropolitan Police, 1952; Asst Chief Constable, Leics, 1972; rcds, 1977; Dep. Chief Constable, 1977, Chief Constable, 1978–87, Essex Police. Man. Editor, Police Jl, 1981–88. Member: Royal Commn on Criminal Justice, 1991–93; Parole Bd, 1994–98. Chm., Essex Reg., Royal Assoc. in Aid of Deaf People, 1994–95; Dir, Addaction, 1998–2001. Pres., Essex Youth Orch. Assoc., 2001–09; Patron, InterAct, 2006–10 (Trustee, 2003–06). DL Essex, 1997. *Publications:* Police: organization and command, 1978; Police Management Handbook, 1979; (contrib.) Police Leadership in the Twenty-first Century, 2003; contrib. Record Collector, 1999–. *Recreations:* music, opera. *Address:* Bellmans, Mounthill Avenue, Springfield, Essex CM2 6DB.

**BUONFINO, Alessandra,** PhD; Head, International Development, Mishcon de Reya LLP, since 2017; *b* Milan, 8 Aug. 1978; *d* of Paolo Buonfino and Eleonora Franceschinelli Buonfino; *m* 2009, Arlo Kristjan Brady; twin *s*. *Educ:* Liceo Scientifico Vittorio Sereni, Luino; Durham Univ. (BA Hons Anthropol. and Archaeol. 2000); Queens' Coll., Cambridge (MPhil Develt Studies 2001; PhD Internat. Relns 2004). Postdoctoral Fellow, Dept for Pol Scis and Internat. Studies, Univ. of Birmingham, 2004–05; Res. Associate, Young Foundn, 2005–07; Hd of Res., Demos, 2007–08; Prog. Leader, Young Foundn, 2008–10; Head: UK Govt Affairs, Tesco plc, 2010–11; Sector Partnerships, Cabinet Office, 2011–14; Dep. Dir, Capital Investment and Hd, GREAT Investors, DIT, 2014–17. Mem., Adv. Bd, Commonwealth Enterprise and Investment Council, 2018–. Trustee: Demos, 2018–; Water Unite, 2019–. *Publications:* (jtly) People Flow: managing migration in a new European Commonwealth, 2003; (ed with Geoff Mulgan) Porcupines in Winter: the pleasures and pains of living together in modern Britain, 2006. *Recreations:* boating, politics, travel photography, interior design and restoring old wrecks to former glory. *Address:* Mishcon de Reya LLP, Africa House, 70 Kingsway, WC2B 6AH. *E:* alessandra.buonfino@icloud.com. *Club:* Conduit.

**BURBERRY, Very Rev. Frances Sheila;** Rector, St Ninian's, Comely Bank, Edinburgh, since 2011; Dean of Edinburgh, since 2017; *b* 1960. *Educ:* Theol. Inst. of Scottish Episcopal Church. ACII 1983. Ordained deacon, 2006, priest, 2007; Curate, St Peter, Edinburgh, 2006–11; Canon, St Mary's Cathedral, 2016–. Synod Clerk, 2016–17. Chaplain, Edinburgh Univ., 2006–. *Address:* 163 Craigleith Road, Edinburgh EH4 2EB.

**BURBIDGE, David Lovell,** CBE 2016 (OBE 1998); DL; Chairman: Burbidge & Son Ltd, since 2005; Coventry City of Culture Trust, since 2015; City of Birmingham Symphony Orchestra, since 2018; *b* Coventry, 15 Oct. 1943; *s* of Harry Lovell Burbidge and Phyllis Evelyn Mary Burbidge; *m* 1965, Sandra Elizabeth Mills; two *s* one *d*. *Educ:* Shrewsbury Sch.; Keble Coll., Oxford (MA Law). Man. Dir, Burbidge & Son Ltd, 1973–2005. Non-exec. Chm., Burbidge Capital Ltd, Nairobi, 2010–16; non-executive Director: Coventry Building Soc., 1981–2005; Albany Piccadilly Trustee Cos, 2016–. Chairman: Coventry Cathedral Develt Trust, 1992–2005; Belgrade Th., Coventry, 2001–08; Central Campaign for RSC Transformation of Stratford Theatres, 2008–14; Mem. Bd, RSC, 2008–14. Founding Chm., Furniture Makers Hall, 2005. Master, Furniture Makers' Co., 2004–05. High Sheriff 1990, DL 1992, W Midlands. Hon. LLD Coventry, 2015; Hon. DLitt Warwick, 2017. *Recreations:* arts, painting, sailing, Real tennis, golf. *Address:* Cedar House, Wasperton, Warwick CV35 8EB. *T:* (01926) 624304. *E:* david.burbidge@burbidge.org.uk. *Clubs:* Garrick; Leamington Real Tennis.

**BURBIDGE, Eileen,** MBE 2015; Partner, Passion Capital, since 2011; *b* Illinois, 16 June 1971; *d* of Robert Tso and Rae C. Tso; three *s* one *d*. *Educ:* Univ. of Illinois at Urbana-Champaign (BSc Computer Sci. 1993). Product Mktg, Apple Computer, 1995–96; Mkt Develt, Sun Microsystems, 1996–99; Dir Account Mgt, Palmsource, 2002–04; Product Develt Dir, Skype, 2004–05; Products Dir, Yahoo! Europe, 2005–07; Investment Dir, Ambient Sound Investments, 2007–11; Co-Founder and Dir, White Bear Yard, 2009–. Chair, Tech City UK, 2015–. Special Envoy for FinTech, HM Treasury, 2015–; Mem., Prime Minister's Business Adv. Gp, 2015–16. *Address:* Passion Capital, 2nd Floor, White Bear Yard, 144A Clerkenwell Road, EC1R 5DF. *T:* (020) 7833 3373. *E:* eileenburbidge@yahoo.com.

**BURBIDGE, (Eleanor) Margaret, (Mrs Geoffrey Burbidge),** FRS 1964; Professor of Astronomy, 1964–90, University Professor, 1984–90, now Emeritus, and Research Professor, Department of Physics, since 1990, University of California at San Diego; *d* of late Stanley John Peachey, Lectr in Chemistry and Research Chemist, and of Marjorie Peachey; *m* 1948, Prof. Geoffrey Burbidge, FRS (*d* 2010); one *d*. *Educ:* Francis Holland Sch., London; University Coll., London (BSc); Univ. of London Observatory (PhD). Asst Director, 1948–50, Actg Director, 1950–51, Univ. of London Observatory; fellowship from IAU, held at Yerkes Observatory, Univ. of Chicago, 1951–53; Research Fellow, California Inst. of Technology, 1955–57; Shirley Farr Fellow, later Associate Prof., Yerkes Observatory, Univ. of Chicago, 1957–62; Research Astronomer, 1962–64, Dir, Center for Astrophysics and Space Scis, 1979–88, Univ. of California at San Diego; Dir, Royal Greenwich Observatory, 1972–73. Abby Rockefeller Mauzé Vis. Prof., MIT, 1968. Chief scientist, Faint Object Spectrograph team, Hubble Space Telescope, 1990–96. Member: American Acad. of Arts and Scis, 1969; US Nat. Acad. of Scis, 1978; Nat. Acad. of Scis Cttee on Science and Public Policy, 1979–81; Pres., Amer. Astronomical Soc., 1976–78; Chairwoman Bd of Dirs, Amer. Assoc. for Advancement of Science, 1983 (Pres., 1982); Mem., Amer. Philosophical Soc., 1980. Fellow University Coll., London, 1967; Hon. Fellow: Girton Coll., Cambridge, 1970; Lucy Cavendish Collegiate Soc., Cambridge, 1971. Hon. DSc: Smith Coll., Massachusetts, USA, 1963; Sussex, 1970; Bristol, 1972; Leicester, 1972; City, 1974; Michigan, 1978; Massachusetts, 1978; Williams Coll., 1979; State Univ. of NY at Stony Brook, 1984; Rensselaer Poly. Inst., 1986; Notre Dame Univ., 1986; Chicago, 1991. Catherine Wolfe Bruce Medal, Astronomical Soc. of the Pacific, 1982; Nat. Medal of Science (awarded by President of USA), 1984; Sesquicentennial Medal, Mt Holyoke Coll., 1987; Einstein Medal, World Cultural Council, 1988; Gold Medal, RAS, 2005. *Publications:* Quasi-Stellar Objects (with Geoffrey Burbidge), 1967 (also USA, 1967); contribs to learned jls (mostly USA), Handbuch der Physik, etc. *Address:* Center for Astrophysics and Space Sciences, 0424, University of California, La Jolla, CA 92093, USA. *T:* (858) 5344477.

**BURBIDGE, James Michael;** QC 2003; **His Honour Judge Burbidge;** a Circuit Judge, since 2011; Resident Judge, Worcester Crown Court, from April 2020; *b* 16 June 1957; *s* of George John Burbidge and late Margaret Elizabeth Burbidge; *m* 1998, Denise McCabe; one *d*. *Educ:* Brockley Co. Grammar Sch.; Leicester Univ. (LLB Hons). Called to the Bar, Lincoln's Inn, 1979, Bencher, 2009; specialist in criminal law; Asst Recorder, 1998–2000; Recorder, 2000–11. Hon. Recorder, City of Wolverhampton, 2018. *Recreations:* ski-ing, golf, travel, theatre. *Address:* (until April 2020) Wolverhampton Crown Court, Pipers Row, Wolverhampton WV1 3LQ; (from April 2020) Worcester Combined Court, The Shirehall, Foregate Street, Worcester WR1 1EQ.

**BURBIDGE, Margaret, (Mrs Geoffrey Burbidge);** *see* Burbidge, E. M.

**BURBIDGE, Sir Peter Dudley,** 6th Bt *cr* 1916, of Littleton Park, co. Middlesex; *b* 20 June 1942; *s* of Sir Herbert Dudley Burbidge, 5th Bt and Ruby Bly Burbidge (née Taylor); *S* father, 2001; *m* 1967, Peggy Marilyn Anderson; one *s* one *d*. *Educ:* Sir Winston Churchill Sch., Vancouver. *Heir:* *s* John Peter Burbidge [*b* 1 April 1975; *m* 2000, Jackie Davies].

**BURBIDGE, Very Rev. (John) Paul,** MA Oxon and Cantab; FSA; Dean of Norwich, 1983–95, now Emeritus; *b* 21 May 1932; *s* of late John Henry Gray Burbridge and Dorothy Vera Burbridge; *m* 1956, Olive Denise Grenfell; four *d*. *Educ:* King's Sch., Canterbury; King's Coll., Cambridge; New Coll., Oxford; Wells Theol Coll. Nat. Service Commn in RA, 1957. Jun. Curate, 1959, Sen. Curate, 1961, Eastbourne Parish Church; Vicar Choral of York Minster, 1962–66; Chamberlain, 1962–76; Canon Residentiary, 1966–76; Succentor Canonicorum, 1966; Precentor, 1969–76; Archdeacon of Richmond and Canon Residentiary of Ripon Cathedral, 1976–83; Canon Emeritus, 1998. *Recreations:* organ playing, historical research. *Address:* The Clachan Bothy, Newtonairds, Dumfries, Scotland DG2 0JL. *T:* (01387) 820403.

**BURCH, Monica;** Consultant, Addleshaw Goddard LLP, 2016–17 (Senior Partner, 2010–16); a Recorder (Civil), since 2010; *b* York, 14 Feb. 1966; *d* of Fraser Burch and Katia Burch (née Hajicristofis); *m* 1994, Paul Lister; one *s* two *d*. *Educ:* Queen's Sch., Rheindahlen; Pembroke Coll., Oxford (BA Juris.); Nottingham Law Sch. (LLM); Guildford Coll. of Law (Law Soc. Finals). Litigation Partner: Theodore Goddard, 1999–2003; Addleshaw Goddard, 2003–10. Non-executive Director: Channel 4 Corp., 2010–16; CPS, 2017–. Dir, Prime (charity), 2012–15. Chm., Mentoring Foundn, 2015–. *Recreations:* family, theatre, museums, reading, watching Channel 4.

**BURCHELL, Andrew;** Associate Hospital Manager, South West London and St George's Mental Health Trust, 2011–17; *b* 26 March 1955; *s* of Joseph Fredrick Bertram Burchell and Myrtle Miriam Burchell; *m* 1974, Susan Margaret Hewing; one *s* one *d*. *Educ:* London School of Economics and Political Science (BSc (Econ) 1976; MSc 1980). Economist, DHSS, 1976–84; Economic Advr, National Audit Office, 1984–85; Economic Advr, 1985–89, Sen. Economic Advr, 1989–90, Dept of Health; Department of Transport, later Department of the Environment, Transport and the Regions: Sen. Economic Advr, Railways, 1990–96; Director: Strategy and Analysis, 1996; Transport Strategy, 1997; Envmt Protection Strategy, 1998–2001; Department for Environment, Food and Rural Affairs: Dir, Envmt Protection Strategy, 2001; Finance Dir, 2001–05; Chief Operating Officer and Dir Gen., Service Transformation Gp, 2005–08; Business Consultant, Appeals Decision Maker, DfT, 2008–14. Ind. Mem., Sutton and Merton Community Services Bd, 2009–11. Trustee, Sutton Citizen's Advice, 2008– (Chm., Trustee Bd, 2010–16). *Publications:* articles on health economics. *Recreations:* golf, playing the guitar, spectating football, reading.

**BURCHILL, Julie;** columnist and author; *b* 3 July 1959; *d* of Thomas William Burchill and Bette Doreen Burchill (née Thomas). *Educ:* Brislington Comprehensive Sch., Bristol. Columnist: New Musical Express, 1976–80; The Face, 1980–84; Sunday Times, 1984–86; Mail on Sunday, 1986–98; The Guardian, 1998–2003; The Times, 2004–06; Sunday Telegraph, 2018–. *Publications:* The Boy Looked at Johnny, 1979; Love It or Shove It, 1985; Girls on Film, 1986; Damaged Gods, 1986; Ambition, 1989; Sex and Sensibility, 1992; No Exit, 1993; I Knew I Was Right (autobiog.), 1998; Diana, 1998; Married Alive, 1999; The

Guardian Columns 1998–2000, 2001; Burchill on Beckham, 2001; Sugar Rush, 2004; Sweet, 2007; (with Daniel Raven) Made in Brighton, 2007; (with C. Newkey-Burden) Not In My Name, 2008; Unchosen: the memoirs of a philo-Semite, 2014. *Recreations:* luncheon, philanthropy, Modern Hebrew. *Club:* Sussex Arts (Brighton).

**BURD, Michael;** Partner, since 1988, and Chair, since 2016, Lewis Silkin LLP; *b* New York City, 7 Feb. 1958; *s* of Donald and Shane Gale Burd; *m* 1984, Jacqueline Margaret Thomas; three *d. Educ:* Columbia Univ. (BA 1980); Clare Coll., Cambridge (MPhil 1982). Admitted as solicitor, 1986; Lewis Silkin LLP: articled clerk, 1984–86; Associate, 1986–88; Jt Hd of Employment and Incentives, 1994–2016. Pres., City of London Law Soc., 1995–96. Member: Cttee, London Solicitors' Litigation Assoc., 1997–; Exec. Cttee, Ius Laboris, 2007–. *Recreations:* hiking, fine food, wines. *Address:* Lewis Silkin LLP, 5 Chancery Lane, Clifford's Inn, EC4A 1BL. *T:* (020) 7074 8176, *Fax:* (020) 7864 1722. *E:* michael.burd@lewissilkin.com.

**BURDEKIN, Prof. Frederick Michael,** OBE 2008; FREng; FRS 1993; Professor of Civil and Structural Engineering, University of Manchester Institute of Science and Technology, 1977–2002, now Professor Emeritus, University of Manchester; *b* 5 Feb. 1938; *s* of Leslie and Gwendoline Burdekin; *m* 1965, Jennifer Meadley; two *s. Educ:* King's School, Chester; Trinity Hall, Cambridge (MA, PhD). MSc Manchester. FICE, FIMechE, FIStructE, FInstNDT; FREng (FEng 1987). Welding Inst., 1961–68; Associate, Sandberg, Consulting Engineers, 1968–77. Vice-Principal External Affairs, UMIST, 1983–85. Chm., Manchester Science Park Ltd, 1988–95. Mem., Engrg Council, 1990–93. President: Manchester Assoc. of Engrs, 2003–05; Welding Inst., 2004–06 (Hon. FWeldI). Lectures: John Player, IMechE, 1981, 2006; Richard Weck, Welding Inst., 1996; Finniston, Inst. of Materials, 2000; Brunel Internat., ICE, 2000. (Jtly) Ludwig Mond Prize, 1971, (jtly) James Clayton Prize, 1982, IMechE; Dist. Service Award, 1990, Brooker Medal, 1996, Welding Inst.; James Alfred Ewing Medal, ICE, 1997; Arata Prize, Internat. Inst. of Welding, 1997; Gold Medal, IStructE, 1998. *Publications:* numerous papers on fracture, fatigue and welded structures. *Recreations:* music, sport, countryside. *Address:* 27 Springbank, Bollington, Macclesfield, Cheshire SK10 5LQ.

**BURDEN,** family name of **Baron Burden.**

**BURDEN,** 4th Baron *cr* 1950, of Hazlebarrow, Derby; **Fraser William Elsworth Burden;** *b* 6 Nov. 1964; *s* of 2nd Baron Burden and of Audrey Elsworth, *d* of Maj. W. E. Sykes; *S* brother, 2000; *m* 1991, June Ellen (marr. diss. 2006), *d* of James Canham. *Heir: b* Hon. Ian Stuart Burden, *b* 24 Oct. 1967.

**BURDEN, Sir Anthony (Thomas),** Kt 2002; QPM 1995; Chief Constable, South Wales Police, 1996–2003; *b* 28 Jan. 1950; *s* of late Thomas Edward Burden and Nora Burden (*née* Dowding); *m* 1971, Beryl Myra Hill; one *s* two *d. Educ:* St Thomas Sch., Salisbury; BSc Hons. Joined Wilts Constabulary, 1969 (Detective Chief Superintendent, 1988–89); Asst Chief Constable, then Dep. Chief Constable, W Mercia Constabulary, 1989–93; Chief Constable, Gwent Constabulary, 1994–96. Member: Morris Inquiry, 2004; Rosemary Nelson Public Inquiry, 2005–11. Advr, Police Assistance Mission of EU in Albania, 2005–07. Deputy Chairman: Reliance Secure Task Mgt, 2005–11; Reliance Security Services Ltd, 2005–10. Pres., ACPO, 2000–01. Life Vice-Pres., Police Sport UK, 2004. Trustee, British Police Symphony Orch., 1994–2010. CCMI 2002. DUniv Glamorgan, 2004. SBStJ 1998. *Recreations:* walking, gardening, fly fishing. *Club:* Worcs CC.

**BURDEN, Maj.-Gen. David Leslie,** CB 1996; CVO 2009; CBE 1988; Chapter Clerk and Receiver General, Westminster Abbey, 1999–2008; *b* 14 July 1943; *s* of late Jack Leslie Burden and Elizabeth Mary Burden (*née* Attkins); *m* 1974, Susan Stuart Watson; two *d. Educ:* Portsmouth Grammar School. Commissioned RASC 1964, RAOC 1965. Served England, Berlin, W Germany, NI, Cyprus and Hong Kong; NDC, 1981; Chief, Personnel and Logistics, UN Force in Cyprus, 1981–83; CO, 1 Ordnance Bn, 1983–85; ACOS, British Forces, Hong Kong, 1985–87; RCDS, 1988; ACOS, BAOR, 1989–91; Dir-Gen., Resettlement, MoD, 1991–92; Dir-Gen., Logistic Support (Army), 1992–95; Dir Gen., Army Manning and Recruiting, 1995; Dir Gen., Army Personnel Centre, 1996–97; Mil. Sec., and Chief Exec. of Army Personnel Centre, 1997–99. Chm., Right from the Start, 2008–. Chairman: Hong Kong Locally Enlisted Personnel Trust, 2011–15; WabiSabie Ltd, 2015–; Director: Armed Forces Common Investment Fund, 2009–16; LGS Matrix, 2009–14. Governor: Sutton Valence Sch., 2008–17; Littlegarth Sch., 2017–. Trustee, Army Museums Ogilby Trust, 2006–18; Chm., Friends of Imperial War Mus., 2016–18. Freeman, City of London, 1993. *Recreations:* cricket, walking, narrowboating, travelling. *Address:* c/o Barclays Bank, 54 Highgate High Street, N6 5JD. *Clubs:* Army and Navy, MCC; Highgate Taverners (Pres., 2002–), Fadeaways.

**BURDEN, Prof. Michael John,** PhD; FAHA; Professor of Opera Studies, University of Oxford, since 2010; Fellow in Music and Pictures and Chattels Fellow, since 1995, and Dean, since 2001, New College, Oxford; *b* Adelaide, SA, 14 March 1960; *s* of Robert Michael Burden and Margaret Anne Burden (*née* Leahy). *Educ:* Pulteney Grammar Sch., Adelaide; Univ. of Adelaide (BA 1980; BA Hons 1981; MA 1987); Univ. of Edinburgh (PhD 1991); MA Oxon 1999. University of Oxford: Stipendiary Lectr in Music, New Coll., 1989–95; Lectr in Opera Studies, 1995–2000; Reader in Music, 2002–10; Chair of Bd, Faculty of Music, 2015–18. Founder and Dir, New Chamber Opera, 1990–. Mem., various cttees, Arts Council of England, 1994–2001. Mem. Council, Royal Musical Assoc., 1999–2001. Pres., British Soc. for 18th Century Studies, 2010–13. Judge, Duff Cooper Prize, 2003–08. Visitor, Ashmolean Mus., Oxford, 2008–15. Trustee: Répertoire Internat. des Sources Musicales, UK, 2007–; Gerald Coke Handel Foundn, 2015–. *Publications:* Lost Adelaide: a photographic record, 1983, repr. 2002; Garrick, Arne and the Masque of Alfred, 1994; (ed) The Purcell Companion, 1995; Purcell Remembered, 1995; (ed) Performing the Music of Henry Purcell, 1996; (ed) A Woman Scorn'd: the myth of Dido, Queen of Carthage, 1998; (ed) Purcell's Operas: the complete texts, 2001; (ed with J. Thorp) Le Ballet de la Nuit, 2010; Regina Mingotti: diva and impresario at the King's Theatre, London, 2013; London Opera Observed 1711–1844, 5 vols, 2013; (ed with J. Thorp) The Works of Monsieur Noverre Translated from the French: Noverre, his circle, and the English lettres sur la danse, 2014; *editions of music*: Benedetto Marcello, Il pianto e il riso delle quattro stagioni, 2002; Henry Purcell, The Fairy-Queen, 2009; William Walton, The Bear, 2010; Benedetto Marcello, Il Trionfo della Poesia, e della Musica nel celebrasi la morte, le esaltazione, e la inconronazione di Maria Sempore Virgine assunta in Cielo, 2016; Francesco Cavalli, Erismena, 2018; contribs to Music Rev., Early Music, Music and Letters, Royal Musical Assoc. Res. Chronicle, Studies in Music, Th. Notebook, Cambridge Companion to Th., Eighteenth-Century Music, Cambridge Companion to Eighteenth-Century Opera, Cambridge Hist. of Eighteenth-Century Music, Music in Art, Revue LISA/LISA, Jl for Eighteenth-Century Studies, Cambridge Opera Jl, Eighteenth Century Shakespeare. *Recreations:* art, architecture, reading detective fiction. *Address:* New College, Oxford OX1 3BN. *T:* (01865) 279555, 07786 061613. *E:* michael.burden@new.ox.ac.uk.

**BURDEN, Richard Haines;** MP (Lab) Birmingham Northfield, since 1992; *b* 1 Sept. 1954; *s* of late Kenneth Rodney Burden and Pauline Langan Burden (*née* Ronnan). *Educ:* Wallasey Technical Grammar Sch.; Bramhall Comprehensive Sch.; St John's Coll. of Further Educn, Manchester; York Univ. (BA Politics); Warwick Univ. (MA Indust. Relns). Pres., York Univ. Students' Union, 1976–77. Br. Organiser, 1979–81, Dist Officer, 1979–92, NALGO; whilst working for NALGO led Midlands campaign against water privatisation. Founder and Sec., Joint Action for Water Services, 1985–90. Contested (Lab) Meriden, 1987. PPS to Minister of State: MAFF, 1997–99; DSS, 1999–2001; Shadow Minister for Transport, 2013–17. Member: Trade and Industry Select Cttee, 2001–05; Internat. Develt Select Cttee, 2005–13, 2017–; Cttee on Arms Export Controls, 2005–13; Parly Advr to Sports Minister on Motor Sports, 2002–10. Secretary: All Party Parly Water Gp, 1994–97; PLP Trade and Industry Cttee, 1996–97 (Vice-Chm., 1995–96); Chm., Birmingham Gp of Labour MPs, 2001–11 (Sec., 1997–2001); Chairman: All Party Parly Gp on Electoral Reform, 1997–2011; All Party Parly Motor Gp, 1998–; Britain-Palestine All Party Parly Gp, 2001–; Jordan All Party Parly Gp, 2010–13; W Midlands Regl Select Cttee, 2009–10. Chm., Labour Campaign for Electoral Reform, 1996–98 (Vice-Chm., 1998–99). Mem., Austin Br., RBL. *Publications:* Tap Dancing: water, the environment and privatisation, 1988; contribs to Tribune, Chartist and other jls. *Recreations:* motor racing, cinema, reading, food. *Address:* House of Commons, SW1A 0AA. *T:* (020) 7219 2318, (0121) 477 7746. *W:* www.richardburden.com. *Clubs:* Austin Sports and Social, Kingshurst Labour, 750 Motor.

**BURDEN, Roger Francis,** FCIB; Director, Football Association, 2001–16 (Acting Chairman, 2010–11); *b* 3 June 1946; *s* of Henry A. Burden and Rose K. Burden, SRN; *m* 1970, Julie Hopkins; two *s. Educ:* Cheltenham Tech. High Sch. MBCS 1975; FCIB 1983. Cheltenham & Gloucester Building Society, later Cheltenham & Gloucester plc: various appts, 1969–97; Man. Dir, 1997–2003; Chm., 2003–04. Dir, Yorkshire Building Soc., 2010–13. Chm., Council of Mortgage Lenders, 2001–02. Mem. Council, FA, 1995– (Vice Pres.); Chm., Glos FA, 2002–. Hon. PhD Glos, 2003.

**BURDETT, Sir Crispin Peter,** 12th Bt *cr* 1665; Director, Verex UK, since 2006; *b* 8 Feb. 1967; *s* of Sir Savile Aylmer Burdett, 11th Bt; *S* father, 2017; *m* 1988, Julia Winifred Gresham (marr. diss.), *yr d* of John Gresham Copeland. *Educ:* Univ. of Manchester (BSc Maths 1988). Associate Dir, CMG, 1994–98; Divl Dir, Olympic Gp, 1998–2001; Dir, Stochastic Financial Modelling, 2001–; Chm., Worldlink Gp, 2001–13; Co. Sec., Aquilo plc, 2004–07. Chair, Bd of Trustees, Holborn Community Assoc., 2007–.

**BURDETT, Prof. Richard Michael,** CBE 2017; Professor of Urban Studies and Director, LSE Cities, London School of Economics and Political Science, since 2010; *b* 27 Jan. 1956; *s* of Winston Burdett and Giorgina Nathan Burdett; *m* 1986, Mika Hadidian; one *s* one *d. Educ:* Bristol Univ. (BSc Hons Architecture); Bartlett Sch. of Architecture, University Coll. London (DipArch, MSc). Director: 9H Gall., London, 1985–90; Architecture Foundn, London, 1991–95; Dir, Cities Prog., 1995–2005, Centennial Prof. in Architecture and Urbanism, 2005–10, LSE. Global Dist. Prof., NY Univ., 2010–14; Vis. Prof., Graduate Sch. of Design, Harvard Univ., 2014. Architectural Advr to Mayor of London, 2001–06; Chief Advr on Architecture and Urbanism for London 2012 Olympic Games, Olympic Delivery Authy, 2006–10; Chief Advr on Architecture, City of Genoa, 2009. Member: Mayor of London's Promote London Council, 2009–10; Mayor of London's Smart London Bd, 2013–15; Ambassador, Mayor of London's Cultural Leadership Bd, 2017–April 2020; Member: Ind. Airports Commn for UK Govt, 2012–15; Rebuild by Design, US Dept of Housing and Urban Develt, 2013–14. Architectural Adviser: Tate, 1995–2005; BBC, 2001–03; ROH, 2012; Penn Plaza, NY, 2013–16; Illuminated River Foundn, 2016; British Library, 2016–17; Gt Ormond St Hosp., 2016–17; Centre for Music, Barbican Arts Centre, LSO and GSMD, 2017–18. Dir, Internat. Architecture Exhibn, Venice Biennale, 2006; Curator, Global Cities Exhibn, Turbine Hall, Tate Modern, 2007. Mem. Council, RCA, 2006–18 (Hon. Fellow, 2019); Mem. Jury, RA Architecture Awards, 2019. Trustee: Somerset House, 2000–11; Norman Foster Foundn, 2015–Dec. 2020. Chair, Mies Crown Hall Americas Prize, 2018. *Publications:* (ed) Richard Rogers Partnership, 1994; (ed) Cities, Architecture and Society, 2006; (ed jtly) The Endless City, 2008; (ed jtly) Living in the Endless City, 2011; (ed jtly) Transforming Urban Economies, 2013; (ed jtly) The SAGE Handbook of the 21st Century City, 2017; (ed jtly) The Quito Papers and the New Urban Agenda, 2018; (ed jtly) Shaping Cities in an Urban Age, 2018. *Recreations:* cities, food, culture. *Address:* 53 Camden Square, NW1 9XE. *T:* (020) 7267 1942. *E:* r.burdett@lse.ac.uk.

**BURDETT-COUTTS, William Walter;** Artistic Director: Assembly Theatre, Edinburgh, since 1981; Riverside Studios, London, since 1993; *b* 17 Feb. 1955; *m* 1999, Fiona Jane Keaney; one *s* two *d. Educ:* Radley Coll.; Rhodes Univ., SA (BA Hons Drama 1978); Univ. of Essex (MA Drama 1980). Artistic Dir, Mayfest, Glasgow, 1981–90; Hd of Arts, Granada Television, 1989–93; Chief Executive: Assembly Film and Television, 1993–2006; Assembly Media Gp, 2000–12; Chairman: Kiss 102 and Kiss 105, 1993–97; Riverside TV Studios, 2002–; Red61, 2006–; Artistic Dir, Brighton Comedy Fest., 2002–15. *Address:* Riverside Studios, 101 Queen Caroline Street, Hammersmith, W6 9BN. *T:* (020) 8237 1000, *Fax:* (020) 8237 1001. *E:* wbc@riversidestudios.co.uk. *Club:* Soho House.

**BURDUS, (Julia) Ann, (Mrs D. L. Parker),** CBE 2003; non-executive Director, Next, 1993–2004; *b* 4 Sept. 1933; *d* of Gladstone Beaty and Julia W. C. Booth; *m* 1st, 1956, William Burdus (marr. diss. 1961); 2nd, 1981, Ian B. Robertson (*d* 1996); 3rd, 2005, David L. Parker. *Educ:* Durham Univ. (BA Psychology). Clinical psychologist, 1956–60; Res. Exec., Ogilvy, Benson & Mather, 1961–67; Res. Dir, McCann Erickson, 1971–75, Vice Chm., 1975–77; Senior Vice-Pres., McCann Internat., 1977–79; Chm., McCann & Co., 1979–81; Director: Strategic Planning and Development, Interpublic, 1981–83; Audits of Great Britain Ltd, 1983–86; AGB Research, 1986–89; Dir of Communications and Marketing, Olympia & York, Canary Wharf, 1989–92. Non-executive Director: Dawson Internat., 1992–98; Argyll Gp, later Safeway, 1993–99; Prudential plc, 1996–2003. Chairman: Advertising Assoc., 1980–81; EDC for Distributive Trades, 1983–87. Jt Dep. Chm. and Mem., Health Educn Authority, 1987–90; Member: Sen. (formerly Top) Salaries Rev. Bd, 1991–94; Adv. Council on Business and the Envmt, 1993–96; part-time Mem., CAA, 1993–97. Member: Cttee, Automobile Assoc., 1995–99; Council, Inst. of Dirs, 1995–2002. *Recreations:* dog walking, gardening.

**BURFORD, Earl of,** (known as **Charles Beauclerk**); **Charles Francis Topham de Vere Beauclerk;** *b* 22 Feb. 1965; *s* and *heir* of Duke of St Albans, *qv*; *m* 1st, 1994, Louise Anne (marr. diss. 2001), *e d* of Col Malcolm Vernon Robey; one *s*; 2nd, 2017, Sarah Bethan, *o d* of John Davenport. *Educ:* Sherborne; Hertford Coll., Oxford. Vice-Pres., Royal Stuart Soc., 1989–. Artist-in-Residence, Bestwood Lodge, Notts, 2015–. Founder, De Vere Tutors, 2018. Freeman, City of London, 1986; Liveryman, Drapers' Co., 1990. *Publications:* Visions, 1998; In Defence of Hereditary Peers, 1999; Nell Gwyn: a biography, 2005; Shakespeare's Lost Kingdom, 2010; Piano Man: a life of John Ogdon, 2014. *Heir: s* Lord Vere of Hanworth, (known as James Beauclerk), *qv. E:* c.beauclerk446@btinternet.com.

**BURG, Gisela Elisabeth,** Hon. CBE 1987 (for services to exports); Managing Director, GEB Enterprises Ltd, 1995; *b* 12 Oct. 1939; *d* of Friedrich and Gerda Schlüsselburg. *Educ:* Gymnasium Philippinum, Weilburg, Germany; Ladies Coll., Wetzlar, Germany. Polytechnic of Central London. Founded Expotus Ltd, 1968, Man. Dir, 1968–96. Vice-Pres., Fedn of British Audio, 1979–85 (Chm., 1976); Member: NEDO, 1979–84 (Mem Electronic Sector Working Party); BOTB, 1982–89. Non-exec. Dir, Royal Mint 1993–2001. CIEx 1992. The Times/Veuve Clicquot Business Woman of the Year, 1981

*Recreations:* golf, horseracing. *Address:* 82 Kensington Heights, 91–95 Campden Hill Road, W8 7BD. *T:* (020) 7727 8884. *Clubs:* Hampstead Golf; Erinvale Golf (Somerset West, S Africa); Jockey (S Africa).

**BURGE, Edmund John;** QC 2019; a Recorder, since 2018; *b* London, 1 Dec. 1966; *s* of John David Burge and M. Claire Burge (*née* Lambert); *m* 2000, Camilla Jane Cranston Smallwood; one *s* one *d. Educ:* Perse Sch.; Ipswich Sch.; Univ. of York (BA Hons PPE); BPP Law Sch., London (DipLaw). Called to the Bar, Lincoln's Inn, 1997 (Buchanan Prize); in practice as a barrister, specialising in serious fraud and commercial crime, 5 St Andrew's Hill, 1997–; Attorney Gen.'s Panel of Special Advocates, 2007–. Mem., Fitness to Practise Panel, GDC, 2013–17. Mem., Elmsted Parish Council, 2010–. *Recreations:* walking, shooting, coaxing wild flowers from a patch of scrub, supporting the village pub. *Address:* 5 St Andrew's Hill, EC4V 5BZ. *T:* (020) 7332 5400. *E:* edmundburge@5sah.co.uk.

**BURGE, Richard David Arthur;** Chief Executive, Commonwealth Enterprise and Investment Council, 2017–19; *b* 5 April 1958; *s* of Col Arthur Burge and Elsie (*née* Kimberley); *m* 1980, Karen Jayne Bush; one *s* one *d. Educ:* Adams Grammar Sch., Newport; Univ. of Durham (BSc Hons Zoology 1980). Biology Master and Asst Housemaster, King Edward's Sch., Witley, 1980–83; Commonwealth Res. Schol., Dept of Zoology, Univ. of Peradeniya, Sri Lanka, 1983–86; British Council: Asst Dir, Nigeria, 1986–90; Projects Dir, Develt and Trng, 1990–93; Hd, Africa and ME Develt, 1993–95; Dir Gen., Zoological Soc. of London, 1995–99; Chief Exec., Countryside Alliance, 1999–2003; Partner, Kimberley Burge Associates, then Dir, Kimberley Burge Ltd, later Dir, Beyond Carbon, 2003–09; Chief Exec., Wilton Park, 2009–17. Dir, Urban and Rural Catalyst Ltd, 2003–06; Dir of Strategy, African Parks Foundn, 2003–06. Dep. Chm., Rural Regeneration Unit, 2003–05; Member, Board: Countryside Agency, 2005–06; Commn for Rural Communities, 2006–09. Member: Exec. Cttee, ACEVO, 1997–2001; Council, Shropshire and W Midlands Agricl Soc., 1997–2003; Bd, Assoc. of Chief Execs, 2012–15 (Vice Chm., 2014). Non-exec. Dir, Property Merchant Gp, 2008–09; non-exec. Chair, LEBC Gp, 2019–; Dir, ESG Validation Ltd. Lay Mem. Council, Durham Univ., 2011–18 (Chm. Council, Hatfield Coll., 2012–; Chm., Ethics Cttee, 2014–); Comr, Commonwealth Scholarship Commn, 2012–18; Mem. Bd, FCO Diplomatic Acad., 2014–17. Chm., Global Health Assce Partnership, 2016–. Chm. Trustees, Get Hooked on Fishing, 2002–06; Trustee: Television Trust for the Envmt, 1996–99; Iwokrama Rainforest Project, Guyana, 2002–06; Game Conservancy Trust, 2004–08; Gunmakers' Charitable Trust, 2010–14. Internat. Expert, Internat. Congress on Game and Conservation, 2004–09. Sen. Advr on Diplomatic Engagement, City Corp. of London, 2019–. Vice Chm. Govs, Bridewell Royal Hosp., 2010–14 (Gov., 2008–14). Mem., Sussex Piscatorial Soc., 2010–. FRSA 2003. Liveryman, Gunmakers' Co., 2001–16; Liveryman, World Traders' Co., 2018–. *Recreations:* theatre, gardening, fishing, shooting, woodcut printing.

**BURGE, Prof. Ronald Edgar,** CPhys; FInstP; Wheatstone Professor of Physics, King's College, London, 1989–2000; Director, Leverhulme Trust Grant to Cavendish Laboratory, University of Cambridge, 1994–98; *b* 3 Oct. 1932; *s* of John Henry Burge and Edith Beatrice Burge (*née* Thompson); *m* 1953, Janet Mary (*née* Pitts); two *s. Educ:* Canton High Sch., Cardiff; King's Coll. London (BSc, PhD; FKC 1989); DSc London 1975. FInstP 1963. King's College London: Asst Lectr in Physics, 1954–58; Lectr in Physics, 1958–62; Reader in Biophysics, 1962–63; Prof. and Head of Dept of Physics, Queen Elizabeth Coll., Univ. of London, 1963–84; Prof. of Physics, 1984–89, Head of Dept of Physics, 1984–92, Vice Principal, 1988–92, KCL. Vis. Fellow, 1992, Life Mem., 1993, Clare Hall, Cambridge; Vis. Prof. of Physics, Cavendish Lab., Univ. of Cambridge, 1994–2012. Nanyang Prof. of Elect. Engrg, Nanyang Technol Univ., Singapore, 2000–01. Member: Swinnerton-Dyer Cttee concerning Academic Governance of Univ. of London, 1979–82; Computer Bd for Univs and Res. Councils (responsible for computer develt in univs in Scotland and, latterly, SW England), 1978–82. FRMS 1964; MRI 1988 Rodman Medal, RPS, 1993. *Publications:* papers in sci. jls on structure of proteins, membranes and bacterial cell walls, and on theory of scattering (electrons, x-rays and radar) and develts in electron microscopy and x-ray microscopy. *Recreations:* gardening, music.

**BURGEN, Sir Arnold (Stanley Vincent),** Kt 1976; FRCP; FMedSci; FRS 1964; Master of Darwin College, Cambridge, 1982–89 (Hon. Fellow, 1989); Deputy Vice-Chancellor, Cambridge University, 1985–89; *b* 20 March 1922; *s* of late Peter Burgen and Elizabeth Wolfers; *m* 1st, 1946, Judith Browne (*d* 1993); two *s* one *d*; 2nd, 1993, Dr Olga Kennard, *qv. Educ:* Christ's Coll., Finchley; student, Middlesex Hospital Med. Sch., 1939–45; MB BS 1945, MD 1950. FRCP 1969. Ho. Phys., Middlesex Hospital, 1945; Demonstrator, 1945–48, Asst Lectr, 1948–49, in Pharmacology, Middlesex Hospital Med. Sch. Prof. of Physiology, McGill Univ., Montreal, 1949–62; Dep. Dir, Univ. Clinic, Montreal Gen. Hospital, 1957–62; Sheild Prof. of Pharmacology, Univ. of Cambridge, 1962–71; Fellow of Downing Coll., Cambridge, 1962–71, Hon. Fellow 1972; Dir, Nat. Inst. for Med. Res., 1971–82. Medical Research Council: Member, 1969–71, 1973–77; Hon. Dir, Molecular Pharmacology Unit, 1967–72; Chm., Tropical Medicine Res. Bd, 1977–81; Assessor, 1985–86. Pres., Internat. Union of Pharmacology, 1972–75; Member: Council, Royal Soc., 1972–73, 1980–86 (Vice Pres., 1980–86; Foreign Sec., 1981–86); Nat. Biol. Standards Bd, 1975–78; Med. Cttee, British Council, 1973–77; Gen. Cttee, ICSU, 1982–88; Exec. Cttee, Eur. Science Foundn, 1985–90; Bureau, European Science and Technol. Assembly, 1994–; Chm., Adv. Cttee on Irradiated and Novel Foods, 1982–87. Dir, Amersham Internat., 1985–92. Sustaining Corresp., NAS/NAE/Inst. of Medicine Cttee on Human Rights. Trustee, CIBA Foundn, 1985–. Editor, European Review, 1993–2007. Pres., Academia Europaea, 1988–94. Founder FMedSci 1998. Académico Correspondiente, Royal Acad. of Spain, 1983; Mem., Deutsche Akad. der Naturforscher Leopoldina, 1984; For. Associate, US Nat. Acad. of Scis, 1985; For. Mem., Ukraine Acad. of Scis. Hon. Fellow, Wolfson Coll., Oxford, 1990. Hon. FRCP (C); Hon. Mem., Amer. Assoc. of Physicians; Academician of Finland, 1990. Hon. DSc: Leeds, 1973; McGill, 1973; Liverpool, 1989; Hon. MD: Utrecht, 1983; Zürich, 1983; DUniv Surrey, 1983. Gold Medal, British Pharmacol Soc., 1999. *Publications:* (ed with J. F. Mitchell) Gaddum's Pharmacology, 6th rev. edn, 1968; (ed with E. A. Barnard) Receptor Subunits and Complexes, 1992; (ed) Goals and Purposes of Higher Education in the 21st Century, 1996; (ed with K. Härnqvist) Growing up with Science, 1997; papers in Journals of Physiology and Pharmacology. *Address:* Keelson, 8a Hills Avenue, Cambridge CB1 7XA. *E:* asvb@cam.ac.uk.

**BURGER, Lisa Jane;** Executive Director, National Theatre, since 2014; *b* Cardiff, 28 May 1962; *d* of Peter Williams and Shirley Williams; two *d. Educ:* Univ. of Sheffield (BMus). Chartered Accountant 1986. Actg Finance Dir, Royal Opera House, 1996–97; Dir, Finance and Ops, Nat. Gall., 1997–2001; National Theatre: Finance Dir, 2001–09; Chief Operating Officer, 2009–14. Chair, Lyric Th., Hammersmith, 2018–. *Address:* National Theatre, Upper Ground, SE1 9PX. *T:* (020) 7452 3575.

**BURGESS, Hon. Anna Elizabeth;** *see* Burke, Hon. A. E.

**BURGESS, Anthony Reginald Frank, (Tony),** CVO 1983; consultant on Third World development; HM Diplomatic Service, retired; *b* 27 Jan. 1932; *s* of Beatrice Burgess; *m* 1960, Carlyn Shawyer; one *s. Educ:* Ealing Grammar Sch.; University College London (BScEcon). National Service, 1953–55; TA, 16 Airborne Div., 1955–57. Journalism, 1955–62; European Community Civil Service, 1962–65; HM Diplomatic Service, 1966–89: 1st Sec., European Economic Organisations Dept, FCO, 1966–67; 1st Sec. (Political), Dhaka, 1967–69; 1st Sec., SE Asia Dept, FCO, 1970–72; 1st Sec. (Economic), Ottawa, 1972–76; Head of Chancery and HM Consul, Bogota, 1976–79; 1st Sec., Rhodesia Dept, FCO, 1979–80; Asst Head of Information Dept, FCO, 1980–82; Dep. High Comr, Dhaka, 1982–86; Counsellor and Hd of Chancery, 1986–88, Chargé d'Affaires, 1988–89, Havana. *Publications:* (jtly) The Common Market and the Treaty of Rome Explained, 1967. *Recreations:* travel, photography, shooting. *Address:* 16 Langford Green, Champion Hill, SE5 8BX. *Club:* Brooks's.

**BURGESS, Averil,** OBE 1994; Chairman, Independent Schools Inspectorate, Independent Schools Council (formerly Accreditation Review and Consultancy Service, Independent Schools Joint Council), 1993–2000; *b* 8 July 1938; *d* of David and Dorothy Evans (*née* Owen); *m* 1959, Clifford Burgess (marr. diss. 1973). *Educ:* Ashby-de-la-Zouch Girls' Grammar Sch.; Queen Mary Coll., Univ. of London. BA Hons History. Assistant Mistress: Langleybury Secondary Modern Sch., 1959–60; Ensham Sch., 1960–62; Hatfield Sch., 1963–65; Fulham County Sch., 1965–69; Wimbledon High Sch., GPDST, 1969–74 (Head of History and Second Mistress); Headmistress, South Hampstead High School, GPDST, 1975–93. Chm., Camden and Islington FHSA, 1993–96. Chm., Policy Gp, ISJC, 1990–97; Member: Council for Accreditation of Teacher Educn, 1990–93; Nat. Commn on Educn, 1991–93. Ind. Public Appts Assessor (formerly Adv. Panel on Public Appointments), DCMS, 1997–2013; Lay Mem., Professional Conduct Cttee, Bar Council, 1996–2005; Ind. Mem., Appts Cttee, Bar Standards Bd, 2005–15. Pres., GSA, 1988–89. Governor: Central Sch. of Speech and Drama, 1981–95; Mus. of London, 1994–2000; Mem. Council, Alpha Plus Gp, 2011–18. *Recreations:* birdwatching and walking on the level along London waterways, opera, theatre, film, good meals with friends, painting watercolours, all enjoyed while sitting down. *Address:* 123 North Hill, Highgate, N6 4DP.

**BURGESS, Rev. Preb. David John,** FSA; Guild Vicar of St Lawrence Jewry Next Guildhall, The Church of the City of London Corporation (formerly Corporation of London), 1987–2008; a Chaplain to the Queen, 1987–2009; Prebendary of St Paul's Cathedral, 2002–08; *b* 4 Aug. 1939; *e s* of Albert Burgess and Mary Burgess (*née* Kelsey); *m* 1976, Dr Kathleen Louise, *d* of Philip Lindsay Costeloe; one *s* one *d. Educ:* King's School, Peterborough; Trinity Hall, Cambridge; Cuddesdon Theological Coll. FSA 1992. Orthodox Studentship, Halki, Istanbul, 1963–64. Curate, All Saints, Maidstone, 1965; Assistant Chaplain, University Coll., Oxford, 1966; Fellow, 1969; Chaplain, 1970; Domestic Bursar, 1971; Canon of St George's Chapel, Windsor, 1978–87. Hon. Fellow, Inst. of Clerks of Works, 1978; Churchill Hon. Fellow, Westminster Coll., Fulton, Miss, 1989. *Publications:* articles and reviews. *Recreations:* opera, art, cooking. *Address:* 62 Orbel Street, SW11 3NZ. *T:* (020) 7585 1572. *Club:* Athenæum.

**BURGESS, (David) Patrick (Henry),** OBE 2015 (MBE 2002); DL; Chairman, Intu Properties (formerly Liberty International, then Capital Shopping Centres Group) plc, 2008–17; *b* Cheam, 31 Oct. 1944; *s* of David Clement Burgess and Dr Ethne Nanette Moira Barnwall Burgess (*née* Ryan); *m* 1st, 1969, Kathryn Mary Ralphs (marr. diss. 1982; she later *m* Sir William Frederick Cotton, CBE); two *s* one *d*; 2nd, 1994, Margaret Ann Mosey. *Educ:* Beaumont Coll.; Gonville and Caius Coll., Cambridge (BA 1967). Admitted solicitor, 1972; Gouldens, solicitors: Partner, 1974; Hd, Corporate Dept, 1982–95; Sen. Partner, 1996–2003. Non-exec. Dir, Standard Bank London plc, 2000–15. Chairman: Thrombosis Res. Inst., 2000–; Bulldog Trust, 2009–12; trustee of various charities. Chm., Sussex, St John Ambulance, 2006–12. Chancellor: Lieutenancy of England and Wales, Order of the Holy Sepulchre, 2008–14; Most Venerable Order of Hospital of St John of Jerusalem, 2014–. Master, Feltmakers' Co., 2003–04. High Sheriff, 2013–14, DL 2014, W Sussex. GCStJ 2014 (CStJ 2009); KGCHS 2014. *Recreations:* walking, shooting, sailing, music, history, poetry, divinity, painting, opera. *Address:* Shopwyke Hall, near Chichester. *Clubs:* Boodle's, Royal Thames Yacht, Leander.

**BURGESS, Dilys Averil;** *see* Burgess, A.

**BURGESS, Geoffrey Kelsen;** Chief Executive and Clerk, Cornwall County Council, 1982–93 (Deputy Clerk, 1969–82); *b* 4 June 1935; *s* of Monty and Edith Burgess; *m* 1959, Brenda (*née* Martin); three *s. Educ:* Central Foundn Boys' Grammar Sch.; London Sch. of Econs and Pol Science (LLB). Admitted solicitor, 1959. Articled with Simon, Haynes, Barlas & Cassels, London, 1956–59; Assistant Solicitor: East Ham CBC, 1960–62; Worcs CC, 1962–63; Northumberland CC, 1963–65; Asst Clerk, Berks CC, 1965–69; Clerk: Cornwall Magistrates' Courts Cttee, 1982–93; Cornwall Sea Fisheries Cttee, 1982–93; Devon and Cornwall Police Authy, 1988–93; Secretary: Adv. Cttee on appt of Magistrates in Cornwall, 1982–93; Cornwall Probation Cttee, 1982–93. Chairman: Jeffrey Kelson Foundn, 1994–2000; Promoting Effective Parenting, 1999–2005; Cornwall Bd for Young Enterprise, 1999–2006. Humanist Rep., Cornwall Standing Adv. Council for Religious Educn, 2010–14. *Recreations:* music, walking, creative writing, discussing philosophy.

**BURGESS, Graham;** non-executive Chair, Torus Housing Group, since 2015; Chair, Blackburn with Darwen Clinical Commissioning Group, since 2015; *b* Liverpool, 1952; *s* of William and Patricia Burgess; *m* 1997, Jan; two *d. Educ:* Ellergreen High Sch.; C. F. Mott Coll. of Educn; Liverpool Poly. Social worker, Walton and Kirkdale, and Vauxhall, Liverpool CC; NALGO: Nat. Exec. Co-ordinator; Chm., NW and N Wales Reg.; full time work in Liverpool br.; sen. social worker, Garston and Speke, Liverpool CC; Blackburn with Darwen Council: Exec. Dir Regeneration and Technical, and Dep. Chief Exec., 1997–2006; Chief Exec., 2006–12; Chief Exec., Wirral MBC, 2012–14. *Recreation:* watching Everton Football Club/Team.

**BURGESS, Ven. Jean Ann;** Archdeacon of Bolton, since 2018; *b* Derby, 10 June 1962; *d* of John Bray and Ann Bray; *m* 1982, Graham Burgess; one *s* two *d. Educ:* Nottingham Univ. (MA Theology and Pastoral Studies 2003); Derby Sch. of Nursing (SEN, SRN). Intensive Care of Newborn Nurse, Derby City Hosp., 1983–87; District Nurse, Derby PCT, 1988–2001; Practise Nurse, Charnwood Surgery, Derby, 2001–03; ordained deacon, 2003, priest, 2004; Curate, St George and St Mary's, Gresley, 2003–08; Interim Minister, 2008–13, Priest-in-charge, 2013–18, St Alkmund and St Werburgh, Derby; Dean of Women's Ministry, Dio. of Derby, 2010–18; Asst Archdeacon of Derby, 2017; licensed as incumbent, St Alkmunds, 2018. *Recreations:* swimming, playing guitar, painting, walking, family and friends, travel. *E:* jeanburgess@manchester.anglican.org.

**BURGESS, Rear-Adm. John,** CB 1987; LVO 1975; CEng; Director, Rolls-Royce and Associates, 1987; *b* 13 July 1929; *s* of Albert Burgess and Winifred (*née* Evans); *m* 1952, Avis (*née* Morgan) (*d* 2015); two *d. Educ:* RN Engineering College; Advanced Engineering RN College, Greenwich; nuclear courses, RN College. HM Ships Aisne, Maidstone, Theseus, Implacable, Cumberland, Caprice; Lectr in Thermodynamics, RNEC, 1962–65; HMS Victorious; nuclear reactor design and manufacture at Rolls Royce, 1968–70; Naval Staff, Washington, DC, 1970–72; Royal Yacht Britannia, 1972–75; Head, Forward Design Group, Ship Dept, 1975–77; Naval Asst to Controller of the Navy, 1977–79; in Command, HMS Defiance, 1979–81; in Command, HMS Sultan, 1981–83; Man. Dir, HM Dockyard,

Rosyth, 1984–87. Occasional involvement with urban develt and waterfront management cttees. *Publications:* papers to professional bodies. *Recreations:* golf, sailing. *Club:* Cawsand Bay Sailing (Pres., 1999–).

BURGESS, John Edward Ramsay; His Honour Judge Burgess; a Circuit Judge, since 2002; *b* 11 March 1956; *s* of Gen. Sir Edward Arthur Burgess, KCB, OBE and Jean Angelique Leslie Burgess (*née* Henderson); *m* 1st, 1980, Juliet Davina Alford (now Bowmaker) (marr. diss. 2000); one *s* one *d*; 2nd, 2001, Cherry Anna Searle; one *d*. *Educ:* St Edward's Sch., Oxford; Exeter Univ. (LLB). Called to the Bar, Middle Temple, 1978; in practice as barrister, 1978–2002; Asst Recorder, 1995–2000; Recorder, 2000–02; Judge Advocate (pt-time), 2001–07; Resident Judge, Derby Combined Court, 2008–16. Hon. Recorder of Derby, 2009–16. *Recreations:* rowing, walking, going to the seaside. *Address:* Midland Circuit Secretariat, The Priory Courts, 33 Bull Street, Birmingham B4 6DW.

BURGESS, Sir (Joseph) Stuart, Kt 1994; CBE 1984; PhD; FRSC; Chairman, Finsbury Worldwide Pharmaceutical Trust plc, 1995–2004; *b* 20 March 1929; *s* of late Joseph and Emma Burgess (*née* Wollerton); *m* 1955, Valerie Ann Street; one *s* one *d*. *Educ:* Barnsley Holgate Grammar School; University College London (1st Class Hons BSc Chem., PhD; Fellow, 1994). Amersham International plc (formerly The Radiochemical Centre), 1953–89: Chief Exec., 1979–89; Pres., Amersham Corp. USA, 1975–77; Advr, Immuno Internat. AG, 1990–96; Chm., Immuno UK, 1992–96; Dir, 1992–2003, Chm., 1998–2003, Haemonetics Corp.; Dir, Anagen plc, 1993–96. Chairman: Oxford RHA, 1990–94; Anglia and Oxford RHA, subseq. Anglia and Oxford Reg., NHS Exec., DoH, 1994–97; Mem., NHS Policy Board, 1994–97. Dir, American Chamber of Commerce (UK), 1988–90. Member: Innovation Adv. Bd, DTI, 1988–93; ACOST Med. Res. and Health Cttee, 1991–92; Chm., CBI Res. and Manufacturing Cttee, 1990–93; Mem., CBI Nat. Manufacturing Council, 1991–92. Vice-Chm., 2000–07, Vice-Pres., 2007–16, Asthma UK (formerly Nat. Asthma Campaign). CCMI (CBIM 1986; Mem., 1996–2001, Chm., 1998–2001, Bd of Companions). *Recreations:* family, friends, music, travel. *Address:* 3 Abbotswood, Gregories Road, Beaconsfield, Bucks HP9 1HQ. *T:* (01494) 730142.

BURGESS, Keith, OBE 2004; Crown Representative, Cabinet Office, since 2014; *b* 1 Sept. 1946; *s* of Bert Burgess and Mary Burgess; *m* 1970, Patricia Mitchell; two *d*. *Educ:* Lewis Sch. for Boys, Pengam; Univ. of Bristol (BSc 1967; PhD 1971). Joined Arthur Andersen & Co., 1971: Partner, 1980–2000; Managing Partner, Andersen Consulting, UK and Ireland, 1989–97; Global Managing Partner: Practice Competency, 1994–97; Business Process Mgt & Enterprises, 1997–99; Sen. Partner, Andersen Consulting UK, 2000; Exec. Chm., QA plc, 2000–06. Chm., EMEA, BearingPoint, 2006–08. Vice-Chm., Public Services Productivity Panel, HM Treasury, 2000–06. Non-executive Director: MORI, 2003–05; DWP Digital, 2017–. Pres., Mgt Consultancies Assoc., 1994–95. Chm., Corporate Action for the Homeless, 1993–96. Patron, Univ. of Bristol Campaign for Resource, 1991–2001. Guild of Management Consultants, later Co. of Management Consultants: Mem., 1994–; Master, 1998–99; Warden, 2010–12. Hon. LLD Bristol, 2000. *Publications:* (jtly) Foundations of Business Systems, 1989, 2nd edn 1992. *Recreations:* getting out and about, relearning what I once knew and filling in the gaps in my life. *Address:* Hengrove, The Chivery, Tring, Herts HP23 6LE.

BURGESS, Margaret; Member (SNP) Cunninghame South, Scottish Parliament, 2011–16; Minister for Welfare and Housing, 2012–16; *b* Ayrshire. Manager, East Ayrshire CAB, 1987–2011; former Mem. Bd, Citizens Advice Scotland.

BURGESS, Melvin; author (children and young adults); *b* 25 April 1954; *s* of Chris Burgess and Helen Burgess; *m* 1998, Judith Ligyett; one *s* one *d*, and one step *s*. *Publications:* The Cry of the Wolf, 1990; Burning Issy, 1992; An Angel for May, 1992; The Baby and Fly Pie, 1993; Loving April, 1995; The Earth Giant, 1995; Tiger, Tiger, 1996; Junk, 1996 (Carnegie Medal, 1996; Guardian Fiction Prize, 1997); Kite, 1997; The Copper Treasure, 1998; Bloodtide, 1999 (jt winner, Lancashire County Library Children's Book of the Year, 2001); Old Bag, 1999; The Ghost Behind the Wall, 2000; The Birdman, 2000; Billy Elliot, 2001; Lady, 2001; Doing It, 2003; Robbers on the Road, 2003; Bloodsong, 2005; Sara's Face, 2006; Nicholas Dane, 2009; Kill All Enemies, 2011; The Hit, 2013; The Lost Witch, 2018. *Recreations:* walking, cooking. *Address:* c/o Andersen Press, Publicity Department, 20 Vauxhall Bridge Road, SW1V 2SA.

BURGESS, Prof. Neil, PhD; FRS 2017; FMedSci; Professor of Cognitive and Computational Neuroscience, since 2004, and Director, Institute of Cognitive Neuroscience, since 2014, University College London; Wellcome Trust Principal Research Fellow, since 2011; *b* Oakington, Cambs, 13 July 1966; *s* of Alan Burgess and Lore Burgess (*née* Freudenthal); *m* 1997, Cathryn Jane McDowell; two *s* one *d*. *Educ:* Newnham Croft Primary Sch., Cambridge; Parkside Community Coll., Cambridge; Hills Rd Sixth Form Coll., Cambridge; University Coll. London (BSc 1st Cl. Hons Maths and Physics 1987); Univ. of Manchester (PhD Theoretical Physics 1990). Royal Soc. Eur. Scientific Exchange Prog. Res. Fellow, IBM Eur. Centre of Sci. and Engrg Computation, Rome, 1990–91; University College London: Postdoctoral Res. Fellow, 1991–93, Royal Soc. Univ. Res. Fellow, 1993–2001, Dept of Anatomy; MRC Sen. Non-clinical Res. Fellow, 2001–11, Dep. Dir, 2006–12, Inst. of Cognitive Neurosci. FMedSci 2009. *Publications:* contribs to learned jls incl. Nature, Science, Neuron, Nature Neurosci., Current Biol., Nature Communications, Proc. NAS, PLoS Biol., Psychol Rev., Biol Psychiatry, Neurosci. *Address:* Institute of Cognitive Neuroscience, University College London, 17–19 Queen Square, WC1N 3AZ. *T:* (020) 7679 1164. *E:* n.burgess@ucl.ac.uk.

BURGESS, Patrick; *see* Burgess, D. P. H.

BURGESS, Prof. Sir Robert George, Kt 2010; DL; PhD; Vice-Chancellor, University of Leicester, 1999–2014; *b* 23 April 1947; *s* of George Burgess and Olive (*née* Andrews); *m* 1974, Hilary Margaret Mary Joyce. *Educ:* Univ. of Durham (Teachers' Cert. 1968; BA 1971); Univ. of Warwick (PhD 1981). University of Warwick: Lectr in Sociol., 1974–84; Sen. Lectr in Sociol., 1984–88; Chair of Dept of Sociol., 1985–88; Dir, Centre for Educnl Develt, Appraisal and Res., 1987–99; Prof. of Sociology, 1988–99; Chair, Faculty of Social Studies, 1988–91; Founding Chair, Graduate Sch., 1991–95; Sen. Pro-Vice-Chancellor, 1995–99. Founding Chair, UK Council for Graduate Educn, 1994–99. Economic and Social Research Council: Member: Res. Resources Bd, 1991–96; Council, 1996–2000; Chair, Trng Bd, 1997–2000 (Mem., 1989–93); Jt Equality Steering Gp, 2001–03. Chm., E Midlands Univs Assoc., 2001–04; Higher Education Funding Council for England: Chm., Quality Assessment Cttee, 2001–03; Member: Res. Libraries Strategy Gp, 2001–02; Quality Assurance Learning and Teaching, 2003–07; Chair: ESRC/Funding Councils Teaching and Learning Res. Prog., 2003–09; Bd, UCAS, 2005–11 (Mem. Bd, 2001–05); Res. Information Network, 2005–11; Scoping Gp, 2003–04, Steering Gp, 2004–07, Implementation Gp, 2008–, UUK/GuildHE Measuring and Recording Student Achievement (Burgess Gp); Bd, GSM London, 2015–; Mem., Sch. Teachers' Rev. Bd, 2015–. Mem., British Liby Bd, 2003–10. President: British Sociological Assoc., 1989–97; Assoc. for Teaching of Social Scis, 1991–99; Soc. for Res. into HE, 2013–. Chm., Higher Educn Acad., 2007–14 (Bd Mem., 2003–07); Trustee and Chm., Bd, NatCen Social Research, 2012–. FAcSS (AcSS 2000); Life Fellow, Bishop Grosseteste Univ., 2015. DL Leics, 2010. Hon. DLitt Staffordshire, 1998; DUniv Northampton, 2007; Hon EdD De Montfort, 2013; Hon. LLD Leicester, 2015; Hon DCL Durham. Lifetime Contribution to Midlands Business Award, 2012; E Midlands Chamber Outstanding Contribn to Business Award, 2015. *Publications:* Experiencing Comprehensive Education, 1983; In the Field, 1984; Education, Schools and Schooling, 1985; Sociology, Education and Schools, 1986; (jtly) Implementing In-Service Education, 1993; Research Methods, 1993; (with J. Wood) Reflections of the University of Leicester, 2010; ed. of 24 books; numerous contribs to social sci. jls. *Recreations:* walking, listening to music, some gardening. *Address:* Feldon House, Lower Brailes, Banbury, Oxfordshire OX15 5HS.

BURGESS, Sally Anne; classical singer, vocal teacher and opera director; *b* 9 Oct. 1953; *d* of Edna Rushton (formerly Burgess; *née* Sharman) and Douglas Burgess; *m* 1988, Neal Scott Thornton; one *s*. *Educ:* Royal College of Music (ARCM; FRCM 2011). Joined ENO 1977 (Mem., Bd, 2017–); for *ENO* rôles incl., as a soprano: Zerlina, Cherubino, Pamina, Mimi, Micaela; as a mezzo: Composer (Ariadne), Sextus (Julius Caesar), Charlotte (Werther), Carmen, Fennimore (Fennimore and Gerda), 1990; Judith (Duke Bluebeard's Castle), 1991; Octavian (Rosenkavalier), 1994; Mrs Begbick (Mahagonny), 1995; Herodias (Salome), 1996; Dulcinée (Don Quixote), 1996; Amelia (Twice Through the Heart), 1997; Baba the Turk (Rake's Progress), Polinesso (Ariodante), 2002; Mistress Quickly (Sir John in Love), 2006; *Opera North:* Amneris (Aida), Dido (Trojans), Julie (Showboat), 1989–90; Orfeo (Glück), 1990; Laura (La Gioconda), 1993; Azucena (Trovatore), 1994; Eboli (Don Carlos), 1998; Margaretha (Genoveva), 2000; Judith (Duke Bluebeard's Castle), 2005; Kabanicha (Katya Kabanova), 2007; *Royal Opera, Covent Garden:* Siebel (Faust), Maddalena (Rigoletto), 1989; *Scottish Opera:* Fricka (Die Walküre), Amneris (Aida), 1991; Mistress Quickly (Sir John in Love), 2008; Mistress Quickly (Falstaff), 2008; *New York Metropolitan:* Carmen, 1995; Queen Isabella (The Voyage), 1996; title rôle (Merry Widow), 2003; *Glyndebourne:* Smeraldina (Love for Three Oranges); Witch (Hansel), tour, 2008; *Welsh National Opera:* Ottavia (Coronation of Poppea), 1998 (also televised); Herodias (Salome), 2009; Mother Marie (The Carmelites), Kabanicha (Katya Kabanova), Munich, 1999; Fricka (Das Rheingold), 1999, (Die Walküre), 2000, Geneva; Polinesso (Ariodante), Houston, 2002; Fortunata (Satyricon), Nancy, Ghent, Antwerp, 2004; Marta/Pantalis (Mefistofele), Netherlands Opera, 2004; Amneris, Strasbourg, Wiesbaden, Lausanne and Nancy; Carmen, Munich, Oregon, Zürich, Berlin, Paris and NZ; Delilah, Nantes; Bernstein on Broadway (tour), 2007; Sally Burgess' Women (one-woman show), Lyric Th., Hammersmith, 1997; numerous concert appearances; concert tour, NZ, 2005; as opera director: Così fan Tutte, English Chamber Opera, London, 2009 and Buxton, 2010, Dubrovnik Summer Fest., 2013; Sonya's Story Thornton/Chekhov, Riverside Studios, Tête à Tête Opera Fest., 2010; Il Trovatore, Dorset Opera, 2012; also dir reduced opera prodns for GSMD: The Magic Flute, 2011, 2017, 2018, Il Coronazione di Poppea, 2012, Albert Herring, 2013, The Marriage of Figaro, 2014, Carmelites, 2015, Cunning Little Vixen, 2016, Underworld, 2017; opera scenes for RCM, 2014, 2018–19; numerous recordings, incl. Liverpool Oratorio, and jazz. Teaching: at RCM (mentoring work with singers and performance classes with chamber gps and solo instrumentalists), 2002–, privately, 2005–, and GSMD, 2011–18 re. project, The Creative Singer, 2018); annual summer masterclasses for Les Azuriales Opera Fest. Young Artists Prog., 2008–; masterclasses for: London Gates Educn Gp, Moscow, 2010, 2012, 2014; Amazwi Omzansi Africa, Durban, 2013, 2015; Les Azuriales Opera Fest., 2013; Stellenbosch and Cape Town, 2015; Sally Burgess Singers Course, London, 2015; London Song Fest., 2018; Audition Workshops, London, 2018; Singer's Workshop (with Fiona Dobie), Oxford, 2019; vocal coach for Little Green Swallow, 2014, Cunning Vixen, 2015, British Youth Opera, 2018. *Recreations:* family, cooking, walking, reading, singing jazz, theatre. *Address:* AOR Management, 6910 Roosevelt Way NE PMB 221, Seattle, WA 98115, USA. *E:* aormanagementuk@gmail.com.

BURGESS, Prof. Simon Mark, DPhil; Professor of Economics, since 1998, Director, Centre for Market and Public Organisation, 2004–15, and Director, Centre for Understanding Behaviour Change, 2010–14, University of Bristol; *b* Macclesfield, Cheshire, 11 April 1960; *s* of Norman and Jean Burgess; *m* 1982, Amy Barham; one *s* one *d*. *Educ:* Christ's Coll., Cambridge (BA Econs 1982); St Antony's Coll., Oxford (MPhil Econs; DPhil Econs 1987). University of Bristol: Lectr in Econs, 1987–93; Reader, 1993–98; Res. Dean, Faculty of Social Sci., 2000–03. *Publications:* contribs to learned jls incl. Econ. Jl, Jl Labor Econs, Jl Public Econs, Jl Applied Econometrics. *Recreations:* landscape photography, hiking. *Address:* Centre for Market and Public Organisation, University of Bristol, 2 Priory Road, Bristol BS8 1TX. *E:* simon.burgess@bristol.ac.uk.

BURGESS, Stella Anne, CBE 2016; Managing Director, DDCAP Group, since 1998; *b* Crayford, Kent, 22 March 1964; *d* of Bernard Cox and Margery Cox; *m* 1995, Martin Burgess; two *s* one *d*. *Educ:* Haberdashers' Aske's Hatcham Girls' Sch. Kleinwort Benson Ltd, 1984–98 (Dir, 1995–98). Non-exec. Dir, Gatehouse Bank, 2007–09. Practitioner Mem., Islamic Finance Experts Gp, 2013–. Chair, Islamic Finance Mkt Adv. Gp, TheCityUK, 2014–. Trustee, RFI Foundn, 2015–. Mem., Islamic Finance Adv. Bd, UEL, 2014–. Member: Adv. Bd, Ethical Finance Challenge Innovation Awards, 2016–; Nomination Cttee, Royal Award for Islamic Finance, 2018. Fellow, Inst. of Islamic Banking and Insce, 1992. *Publications:* Structuring Islamic Finance Transactions, 2005. *Recreations:* cycling, running, family, theatre, cinema, travel. *Address:* DDCAP Group, 8–10 Grosvenor Gardens, SW1W 0DH. *T:* (020) 7863 1251. *E:* s.cox@ddcap.co.uk.

BURGESS, Sir Stuart; *see* Burgess, Sir J. S.

BURGESS, Rev. Stuart John, CBE 2009; Chairman, Commission for Rural Communities, 2006–13, and Government's Rural Advocate, 2004–13 (Chairman, Countryside Agency, 2004–06); President, Methodist Conference, 1999–2000; Chairman, Anchor Hanover Housing Group (formerly Hanover Housing Association), since 2014; *b* 18 March 1940; *s* of Frederick John Burgess and Winifred May (*née* Gowan); *m* 1965, Elisabeth Maud Fowler; two *d*. *Educ:* Moseley Grammar Sch., Birmingham; Univ. of London (BD ext.); Univ. of Nottingham (MEd; MTh). Minister: Headingley Methodist Church, 1965–68; Nottingham W Circuit, and Chaplain, Univ. of Nottingham, 1968–81; Birmingham SW Circuit, and Chaplain, Univ. of Birmingham, 1981–89; Chm., York and Hull Methodist Dist, 1989–2004. Mem., Ethical Cttee, DWP, 2004–. Chm., Patient Liaison Gp, BMA, 2004–07; Mem., Lay Cttee (formerly Patient Liaison Gp), RCAnaes, 2014–. Mem. Bd, Transport Focus (formerly Passenger Focus), 2013–. Chairman: Dirs, E Wesley, 2013–; Ammerdown Centre, 2016–. Hon. Fellow, UC of York St John, 2003. Hon. MA 1989, DUniv 2006, Birmingham; Hon. DD Hull, 2001; DD Lambeth, 2003. Hon. DPh Gloucestershire, 2008. *Publications:* Seeds of Joy, 1985; Spiritual Journey of John Wesley, 1988; Stations of the Cross, 1991; Making Connections, 1998; Coming of Age: challenges and opportunities for the 21st century, 1999. *Recreations:* music, tennis. *Address:* The Wesley, 83–101 Euston Street, NW1 2EZ. *T:* 07900 608249.

BURGESS, Tony; *see* Burgess, A. R. F.

BURGH, 8th Baron *cr* 1529 (called out of abeyance, 1916); Alexander Gregory Disney Leith; *b* 16 March 1958; *er s* of 7th Baron Burgh and Anita Lorna Burgh (*née* Eldridge); *s* father, 2001; *m* 1st, 1984, Catherine Mary (marr. diss. 1999), *d* of David Parkes; two *s* one *d*; 2nd, 1999, Emma Jane, *d* of Martin Burdick; one *s* one *d*. Formerly with St James's Place

Wealth Management. Patron, Lord Thomas Burgh Retinue. *Heir: s* Hon. Alexander James Strachan Leith, *b* 11 Oct. 1986. *Address:* Leigh House, North Road, Bristol BS8 3PL. *E:* alex@alexburgh.co.uk.

**BURGHART, (Michael) Alex,** PhD; MP (C) Brentwood and Ongar, since 2017; *b* Poole, 7 Sept. 1977; *s* of Michael Burghart and Penelope Burghart (*née* Moss); *m* 2011, Hermione Eyre; two *d. Educ:* Millfield Sch.; Christ Church, Oxford (MA Hons Mod. Hist.; MSt); King's Coll. London (PhD 2007). Researcher and Tutor in Hist., KCL, 2001–08; Researcher to Tim Loughton, MP, 2008–10; Policy Advr, DFE, 2010–11; Dir, Policy, Centre for Social Justice, 2012–16; Dir, Strategy, Office of the Children's Comr, 2016; Special Advr to Prime Minister, Policy Unit, 10 Downing St, 2016–17. PPS to the Attorney Gen., 2018–. Member: Work and Pensions Select Cttee, 2017–18; Jt Cttee on Human Rights, 2017–18. *Recreations:* eating breakfast, medieval history, boxing, poetry, slow cooking. *Address:* House of Commons, SW1A 0AA. *T:* (020) 7219 1613. *E:* alex.burghart.mp@parliament.uk. *Club:* Carlton.

**BURGHLEY, Lord; Anthony John Cecil;** *b* 9 Aug. 1970; *s* and *heir* of Marquess of Exeter, *qv; m* 1996, Holly Stewart; one *d. Educ:* Eton; Oxford Univ. (MA); Univ. of Victoria (MSc).

**BURGON, Colin;** *b* 22 April 1948; *s* of Thomas and Winifred Burgon; *m* Kathryn Stainburn. *Educ:* St Michael's Coll., Leeds; Carnegie Coll., Leeds; Huddersfield Poly. Former teacher of History, Foxwood High Sch., Leeds; Policy Advr, Wakefield CC, 1987–95. Contested (Lab) Elmet, 1987, 1992. MP (Lab) Elmet, 1997–2010.

**BURGON, Richard;** MP (Lab) Leeds East, since 2015; *b* Leeds; *s* of Terry Burgon and Mary Burgon (*née* Shaw). *Educ:* Cardinal Heenan RC High Sch.; St John's Coll., Cambridge (BA Eng. Lit.). Admitted as solicitor, 2006; trade union lawyer, Thompsons Solicitors, Leeds, 2005–15. Shadow Sec. of State for Justice and Shadow Lord Chancellor, 2016–. *Address:* House of Commons, SW1A 0AA.

**BURK, Prof. Kathleen Mildred,** DPhil; Professor of Modern and Contemporary History, University College London, 1995–2011, now Emerita; *d* of Wayne Eliot Burk and Martha Ann Burk (*née* Ankney); *m* 1980, Dr Michael Jewess; one *d. Educ:* Sanger Union High Sch., California; Univ. of California, Berkeley (BA 1969); St Hugh's Coll., Oxford (MA, DPhil 1977); Dip. in Wine and Spirits, WSET, 2002. Tutorial Asst in Mod. Hist., Univ. of Dundee, 1976–77; Rhodes Res. Fellow for N America and Caribbean, St Hugh's Coll., Oxford, 1977–80; Lectr in Hist. and Politics, Imperial Coll., London, 1980–90; University College London: Lectr in Hist., 1990–93; Reader in Mod. and Contemp. Hist., 1993–95. Visiting Professor: Kyung Hee Univ., Seoul, Korea, 1986; Univ. of Trondheim, 1994; Univ. of Tübingen, 1999; Univ. of Oslo, 2004; Univ. of Oslo and Nobel Inst., 2009; Vis. Fellow, All Souls Coll., Oxford, 1998. Gresham Prof. of Rhetoric, 2003–06; Alec Cairncross Lecture, 1994; Commonwealth Fund Lecture in American Hist., 2005; Crabtree Oration, 2006; Saki Dockrill Lecture, 2018. Wine correspondent, Prospect magazine, 2002–05. Chm., Historians' Press, 1983–99; Founding Co-Editor, Contemporary European History, 1989–2001. FRHistS 1989 (Mem. Council, 1994–97; Hon. Treas., 1997–2001). Foreign Member: Royal Norwegian Soc. for Scis and Letters, 2002; Norwegian Acad. of Scis and Letters, 2009. Judge, Internat. Wine and Spirits Comp., 2005–. Henry Adams Prize, Soc. for History in the Federal Govt, 2009. *Publications:* (ed and contrib.) War and the State: the transformation of British Government 1914–1919, 1982; Long Wittenham 1800–1920, 1984; Britain, America and the Sinews of War 1914–1918, 1985; The First Privatisation: the politicians, the city and the denationalisation of steel, 1988; Morgan Grenfell 1838–1988: the biography of a merchant bank, 1989; (with Alec Cairncross) Goodbye, Great Britain: the 1976 IMF crisis, 1992; (with Manfred Pohl) The Deutsche Bank in London 1873–1998, 1998; (ed with Melvyn Stokes) The United States and the Western Alliance since 1945, 1999; Troublemaker: the life and history of A. J. P. Taylor, 2000; (ed) The British Isles since 1945, 2003; Old World, New World: the story of Britain and America, 2007; (with Michael Bywater) Is This Bottle Corked? The Secret Life of Wine, 2008; The Lion and the Eagle: the interactions of the British and American empires, 1783–1972, 2018; articles in Histl Jl, Econ. Hist. Rev., Internat. Hist. Rev., World of Fine Wine, etc. *Recreations:* collecting antiquarian history books, playing early music, wine. *Address:* The Long Barn, Townsend, Harwell, Oxon OX11 0DX. *T:* (01235) 835637. *E:* k.burk@ucl.ac.uk. *Clubs:* Athenæum, Academy, 67 Pall Mall.

**BURKE, Hon. Anna Elizabeth,** AO 2019; Member, Administrative Appeals Tribunal, since 2017; *b* Melbourne, 1 Jan. 1966; *d* of Bernard and Joan Burke; *m* 1994, Stephen Burgess; one *s* one *d. Educ:* Presentation Coll., Windsor (HSC 1983); Monash Univ. (BA Hons); Melbourne Univ. (MCom Hons). Industrial Officer: Victoria Roads Corp., 1988–93; Victoria Inst. of Technol., 1993–94; Nat. Industrial Officer, Finance Sector Union, 1994–98. MLA (ALP) Chisholm, Vic, Australia, 1998–2016; Dep. Speaker, 2008–10 and 2011–12, Speaker, 2012–13, Australian Hse of Reps. Member: Fabian Soc.; Amnesty Internat. Associate Mem., RSL Oakleigh. *Recreations:* time with family, reading. *Clubs:* Box Hill Lions, Mont Albert and Surrey Hills Rotary, Box Hill Hawks (Vic).

**BURKE, Hon. Brian Thomas;** Australian Ambassador to Republic of Ireland and to the Holy See, 1988–91; *b* 25 Feb. 1947; *s* of late Thomas Burke (Federal ALP Member for Perth, 1942–55), and Madelaine Burke; *m* 1965, Susanne May Nevill; four *s* two *d. Educ:* Brigidine Convent; Marist Brothers' Coll.; Univ. of Western Australia. FAMI. Former journalist. MLA (Lab) Balga, WA, 1973–88; Opposition Shadow Minister, 1976–81; Leader of the Opposition, 1981–83; Premier and Treasurer of WA, 1983–88. AC 1988. *Recreations:* reading, swimming. *Address:* PO Box 669, Scarborough, WA 6922, Australia.

**BURKE, Ven. Christopher Mark;** Archdeacon of Barking, since 2019; *b* E Yorks, 1965; *m* 1994, Helen Brown; two *d. Educ:* Coventry Poly. (LLB Hons Business Law 1987); Ripon Coll., Cuddesdon, Oxford (Cert. Theol. 1992); Heythrop Coll., Univ. of London (MA 2006). Ordained deacon, 1992, priest, 1993; Asst Curate, St Mary the Virgin, Nunthorpe, 1992–96; Vicar, St John the Evangelist, South Bank, Middlesbrough, 1996–2002; Rector, St Dunstan and All Saints, Stepney, 2002–10; Sheffield Cathedral: Residentiary Canon for Learning and Develt, 2010–13; Canon Precentor, 2013–19; Vice Dean, 2014–19. *Recreations:* travel, good food, fine wine, family time. *Address:* 11 Bridgefields Close, Hornchurch RM11 1GQ. *T:* (01708) 474951. *E:* a.barking@chelmsford.anglican.org. *Club:* Army and Navy.

**BURKE, David Thomas, (Tom),** CBE 1997; Founding Director, since 2003, and Chairman, since 2012, E3G; *b* 5 Jan. 1947; *s* of J. V. Burke, DSM, and Mary (*née* Bradley). *Educ:* St Boniface's, Plymouth; Liverpool Univ. (BA (Hons) Philosophy). Great George's Community Arts Project, 1969–70; Lecturer: West Cheshire Coll., 1970–71; Old Swan Technical Coll., 1971–73; Friends of the Earth: Local Groups Co-ordinator, 1973–75; Executive Director, 1975–79; Dir of Special Projects, 1979–80; Vice-Chm., 1980–81; Dir, The Green Alliance, 1982–91; Special Advr to Sec. of State for the Environment, 1991–97; Environmental Policy Adviser: BP Amoco, 1997–2001; Rio Tinto plc, 1997–2016; Advr, Central Policy Gp, Cabinet Office, 2001–03; Sen. Advr to Special Representative on Climate Change, 2006–12. Press Officer, European Environment Bureau, 1979–87; Sec., Ecological Studies Inst., 1987–92. Member: Bd of Dirs, Earth Resources Research, 1975–87; Waste Management Adv. Council, 1976–81; Packaging Council, 1978–82; Exec. Cttee, NCVO, 1984–89; UK Nat. Cttee, European Year of the Environment, 1986–88; Exec. Cttee, European Environment Bureau, 1987–91; Council, English Nature, 1999–2006; London Sustainable Develt Commn, 2002–06. Chairman: Rev. of Envmtl Governance in NI, 2006–07; China Dialogue Trust, 2016–. Contested (SDP): Brighton Kemptown, 1983; Surbiton, 1987. Vis. Fellow, Cranfield, 1991–94; Vis. Prof., Imperial Coll., 1997–; Sen. Associate, Cambridge Inst. for Sustainability Leadership, 2012–. Hon. Vis. Fellow, Manchester Business Sch., 1984; Hon. Prof., Faculty of Laws, UCL, 2003–. FRSA 1988 (Mem. Council, 1990–92); FEI 2009. Royal Humane Society Testimonials: on Vellum, 1966; on Parchment, 1968; Global 500 Laureate, UNEP, 1993. *Publications:* Europe: environment, 1981; (jtly) Pressure Groups in the Global System, 1982; (jtly) Ecology 2000, 1984; (jtly) The Green Capitalists, 1987; (jtly) Green Pages, 1988; (jtly) The Fragile City, 2014. *Recreations:* photography, birdwatching. *Address:* Studio 2, Clink Wharf Studios, Clink Street, SE1 9DG. *T:* (020) 7357 9146. *Club:* Reform.

**BURKE, Ian;** see Burke, M. I.

**BURKE, Sir James (Stanley Gilbert),** 9th Bt *cr* 1797 (Ire.), of Marble Hill, Galway; *b* 1 July 1956; *s* of Sir Thomas Stanley Burke, 8th Bt and Susanne Margaretha (*d* 1983), *e d* of Otto Salvisberg, Thun, Switzerland; *S* father, 1989; *m* 1980, Laura, *d* of Domingo Branzuela; one *s* one *d. Heir: s* Martin James Burke, *b* 22 July 1980. *Address:* Bleierstrasse 14, 8942 Oberrieden, Switzerland.

**BURKE, His Honour Jeffrey Peter;** QC 1984; a Circuit Judge, 2002–13; *b* 15 Dec. 1941; *s* of Samuel and Gertrude Burke; *m;* two *s* one *d; m* 1994, Joanna Mary Heal; one *s* one *d. Educ:* Shrewsbury Sch.; Brasenose Coll., Oxford (BA 1963). Called to the Bar, Inner Temple, 1964, Bencher, 1997. A Recorder, 1983–2002. Legal Mem., Mental Health Review Tribunal, 1994–2014; Judge, Employment Appeal Tribunal, 2000–09, 2012–13; Legal Mem., Parole Bd, 2009–. Trustee, Aplastic Anaemia Trust. *Recreations:* sport, wine, choral singing, charity triathlons, learning theory of music. *Clubs:* De Todeni (Flamstead); Economicals AFC; Flamstead Cricket.

**BURKE, Joanna Margaret,** CMG 2013; Regional Director, Wider Europe Region, British Council, since 2019; *b* 2 May 1960; *d* of James Brian Burke and Margaret Ann Burke; *m* 1987, Eliseo Mayoral-Martinez; one *s* one *d. Educ:* Beijing Langs Inst.; Tübingen Univ.; Leeds Univ. (BA Chinese and German 1982). British Council: Asst Dir, China, 1990–95; Dep. Dir, Argentina, 1995–99; Dir, Shanghai, 1999–2003; Regl Dir, Americas and Australasia, 2003–04; Dir, Japan, 2005–07; Regl Dir, China, 2007–13; Dir, Portugal, 2013–16; Dep. Regl Dir, EU Region, 2016–19. *Recreations:* Beijing history, book collecting, travel, music, gardens. *Address:* British Council, Esentepe Mahallesi, Büyükdere Cd. 100–102, 34394 Şişli, Istanbul, Turkey.

**BURKE, Kathy;** actress and director; *b* 13 June 1964. *Educ:* Anna Scher Drama Sch. *Films:* Scrubbers, Forever Young, 1983; Sacred Hearts, 1985; Sid and Nancy, 1986; Straight to Hell, Walker, Eat the Rich, 1987; Work Experience, 1989; Amongst Barbarians, 1990; Sin Bin, 1994; Hello, Hello, Hello, 1995; Nil by Mouth, 1997; Dancing at Lughnasa, Elizabeth, 1998; This Year's Love, 1999; Kevin and Perry Go Large, Love, Honour and Obey, 2000; The Martins, 2001; Once Upon a Time in the Midlands, Anita and Me, 2002; Tinker, Tailor, Soldier, Spy, 2011; Pan, 2015; Absolutely Fabulous: The Movie, 2016. *Television:* Past Caring, 1985; Two of Us, 1987; Harry Enfield's Television Programme (series), 1990; Mr Wroe's Virgins, 1993; Harry Enfield and Chums (series), 1994; Common as Muck (series), 1994–97; Life's a Bitch, 1995; After Miss Julie, 1995; The History of Tom Jones, a Foundling, 1997; Ted & Ralph, 1998; Gimme, Gimme, Gimme (series; also script editor), 1999–2001; Shooting Gallery, 1999; Harry Enfield Presents Kevin's Guide to Being a Teenager, 1999; Harry Enfield Presents Wayne and Waynetta's Guide to Wedded Bliss, 2001; dir, Horne and Corden, 2009; presenter, Kathy Burke: all woman, 2019. Writer: play, Mr Thomas; film, The End, 1998; writer and dir, TV series: Renegade TV Gets Dazed, 1998; Walking and Talking, 2012. Director: Out in the Open, 2001, Born Bad, 2003, Love Me Tonight, 2004, Hampstead Th.; Kosher Harry, Royal Court, 2002; Betty, Vaudeville, 2002; The Quare Fellow (tour), 2004; Blue/Orange, Crucible, Sheffield, 2005; The God of Hell, Donmar Warehouse, 2005; Smaller, Lyric, 2006; Once a Catholic, Tricycle, 2013; The Retreat, Park, 2017; Lady Windermere's Fan, Vaudeville Th., 2018. *Publications:* (ed) 24 Stories of Hope for Survivors of the Grenfell Tower Fire, 2018. *Address:* c/o Hatton McEwan Penford, Studio 11, B1, The Leather Market, Weston Street, SE1 3ER.

**BURKE, Hon. Sir Kerry;** see Burke, Hon. Sir T. K.

**BURKE, (Michael) Ian;** Chairman, Findel plc, since 2017; *b* 21 June 1956; *s* of Ronald and Rosemary Burke; *m* 1979, Jane McGuinness; one *s* one *d. Educ:* Imperial Coll., London (BSc Maths); London Business Sch. (MSc Business Admin). ACMA 1981. With Lever Bros, 1978–81; finance and planning, Esso UK, 1981–86; Gp Planning Manager, Gateway Corp., 1986–90; Bass plc: Commercial Dir, Bass Leisure, 1990–92; Man. Dir, Gala Clubs, 1992–95; Exec. Vice Pres. and Man. Dir, Holiday Inn Worldwide, Europe, ME and Africa, 1995–98; Chief Executive: Thistle Hotels plc, 1998–2003; Health Club Hldgs, 2003–06; Chief Exec., 2006–14, Chm., 2011–19, Rank Group plc. Dir, London Tourist Bd, 1998–2003; Bd Mem., BTA, 2000–03. *Recreations:* fell-walking, cycling. *Address:* Findel plc, Henry Street, Accrington BB5 4EE.

**BURKE, Peter;** see Burke, U. P.

**BURKE, Simon Paul,** FCA; Chairman: Light Cinema Group, since 2014; Bakkavor, since 2017; *b* 25 Aug. 1958; *s* of Vincent Paul Burke and Beryl Mary Burke (*née* Cregan). *Educ:* St Mary's Coll., Dublin. FCA 1980. Man. Dir, Virgin Retail, 1988–94; Chief Executive: Virgin Our Price, 1994–96; Virgin Entertainment Gp, 1996–99; Chairman: Hamleys plc, 1999–2003; Superquinn Ltd, 2005–10; Majestic Wine plc, 2005–10; Hobbycraft Ltd, 2010–14; Mitchells and Butlers plc, 2011 (Dep. Chm., 2010–11); Eagle Eye Solutions, 2011–14; Bathstore.com, 2012–14; Blue Diamond Gp, 2015–. Dir, W H Smith plc, 1995–96; non-exec. Dir, Co-operative Gp, 2014–. Non-exec. Mem., Exec Bd, BBC, 2011–17; Mem., BBC Bd, 2017–. Trustee, Nat. Gall., 2003–11; Chm., Nat. Gall. Co. Ltd, 2004–11. *Recreations:* 17th century Dutch art, mediaeval history, flying (private pilot), astronomy, travel. *E:* l.simonburke@gmail.com.

**BURKE, Hon. Sir (Thomas) Kerry,** Kt 1990; Member, 1998–2009, and Chairman, 2004–10, Canterbury Regional Council, Christchurch; *b* 24 March 1942; *m* 1st, 1968, Jennifer Shiel (marr. diss. 1984); two *s;* 2nd, 1984, Helen Paske (*d* 1989); one *s;* 3rd, 1997, Fahimeh Rastar; one step *s* two step *d. Educ:* Linwood High Sch.; Univ. of Canterbury (BA); Christchurch Teachers' Coll. (Dip. Teaching). General labourer, Auckland, 1965–66; factory deleg., Auckland Labourers' Union; teacher: Rangiora High Sch., 1967–72; Greymouth High Sch., 1975–78; lang. and immigration consultant, Vienna, Austria, 1991–98. Chm., Rangiora Post-Primary Teachers' Assoc., 1969–71. MP (Lab) Rangiora, NZ, 1972–75, West Coast, 1978–90; Minister of Regional Develt, and of Employment and Immigration, 1984–87; Speaker, NZ House of Reps, 1987–90. *Recreations:* ski-ing, swimming. *Address:* 44 Naseby Street, Merivale, Christchurch 8014, New Zealand.

**BURKE, Tom**; see Burke, D. T.

**BURKE, Tracey Mary**; Director General, Education and Public Services, Welsh Government, since 2017; *b* Cardiff; *d* of John F. and June M. Burke. *Educ*: Our Lady's Convent Sch.; Cardiff High Sch.; Sheffield Univ. (BA Hons Psychol. 1985); Trinity Coll., Dublin (MBA 1993). Policy Evaluator, Dept of Enterprise and Employment, Irish Govt, 1993–97; Hd of Chm.'s Office, 1997–2000, Eur. Structural Funds Dir, 2000–01, WDA; PM's Strategy Unit, Cabinet Office, 2001–02; Planning Dir, 2002–05, Exec. Dir, Strategy Develt, 2005–06, WDA; Welsh Assembly Government, later Welsh Government: Dir, Strategy and Review, Dept for Enterprise, Innovation and Networks, 2006–08; Acting Dir, Policy Strategy and Corporate Services, Economy and Transport, 2008–09; Dir, Econ. Renewal Prog., 2009–10; Actg Dir, Strategy and Ops, 2010–12; Strategy Dir, Dept for Economy, Sci. and Transport, 2012–16; Strategy Dir, Economy, Skills and Natural Resources, 2016–17. *Recreations*: spending time with my family and friends, passionate supporter of Welsh Rugby team and Cardiff City and Sunderland Football Clubs. *Address*: Welsh Government, Cathays Park, Cardiff CF10 3NQ.

**BURKE, Trevor Michael**; QC 2001; *b* 16 Oct. 1958; *s* of Michael George Burke and Philomena Burke. *Educ*: Handsworth Grammar Sch.; South Bank Univ., (BA Hons Law). Called to the Bar, Middle Temple, 1981. *Recreation*: golf. *Address*: Three Raymond Buildings, Gray's Inn, WC1R 5BH. *Club*: Brocket Hall Golf.

**BURKE, Prof. (Ulick) Peter**, FBA 1994; Professor of Cultural History, 1996–2004, now Emeritus, and Fellow of Emmanuel College, since 1979, University of Cambridge; *b* 16 Aug. 1937; *s* of John Burke and Jennie Burke (*née* Colin); *m* 1st, 1972, Susan Patricia Dell (marr. diss. 1983); 2nd, 1989, Maria Lúcia Garcia Pallares. *Educ*: St John's Coll., Oxford (Hon. Fellow, 2009); St Antony's Coll., Oxford (MA). Asst Lectr, then Lectr in History, subseq. Reader in Intellectual History, Sussex Univ., 1962–78; Reader in Cultural History, Univ. of Cambridge, 1988–96. *Publications*: The Renaissance Sense of the Past, 1969; Culture and Society in Renaissance Italy, 1972, 3rd edn 1986; Venice and Amsterdam: a study of Seventeenth Century elites, 1974, 2nd edn 1994; Popular Culture in Early Modern Europe, 1978, 2nd edn 1994; Sociology and History, 1980; Montaigne, 1981; Vico, 1985; Historical Anthropology in Early Modern Italy: essays on perception and communication, 1987; The Renaissance, 1987; The French Historical Revolution: the Annales School 1929–89, 1990; The Fabrication of Louis XIV, 1992, 2nd edn 1994; History and Social Theory, 1992; Antwerp, a Metropolis in Europe, 1993; The Art of Conversation, 1993; The Fortunes of the Courtier, 1995; Varieties of Cultural History, 1997; The European Renaissance, 1998; A Social History of Knowledge, 2000; Eyewitnessing, 2001; (jtly) A Social History of the Media, 2002; What is Cultural History?, 2004; Languages and Communities in Early Modern Europe, 2004; (with M. L. Pallares-Burke) Social Theory in the Tropics, 2008; Cultural Hybridity, 2009; A Social History of Knowledge, Vol. II: from the Encyclopédie to Wikipedia, 2011; What is the History of Knowledge?, 2016; Exiles and Expatriates in the History of Knowledge 1500–2000, 2017. *Recreation*: travel. *Address*: Emmanuel College, Cambridge CB2 3AP. *T*: (01223) 334272. *Club*: Paineras de Morumbi (São Paulo).

**BURKE-GAFFNEY, John Campion**; Director-General, The British Red Cross Society, 1985–90; *b* 27 Feb. 1932; *s* of late Dr Henry Joseph O'Donnell Burke-Gaffney, OBE and Constance May (*née* Bishop); *m* 1956, Margaret Mary Jennifer (*née* Stacpoole); two *s* two *d*. *Educ*: Douai School. Called to the Bar, Gray's Inn, 1956. Served: RAC, 1950–52; E Riding of Yorks Imperial Yeomanry (Wenlock's Horse), 1952–56. Shell-Mex and BP Ltd, 1956–75; Shell UK Ltd, 1976–77; Man. Dir, Shell and BP Zambia Ltd, 1977–81; Gp Public Affairs, Shell Internat. Petroleum Co. Ltd, 1981–85. *Address*: c/o Coutts & Co., 440 Strand, WC2R 0QS.

**BURKILL, Guy Alexander**; QC 2002; *b* 5 March 1957; *s* of Arthur and Helen Burkill; *m* 1984, Lorely Claire Owen; two *s*. *Educ*: Winchester Coll.; Corpus Christi Coll., Cambridge (MA Engrg (Electrical option) 1st Cl. Hons). Called to the Bar, Middle Temple, 1981; in practice at Patent and Intellectual Property Bar, 1981–. *Publications*: (ed jtly) Terrell on the Law of Patents, 15th edn 2000, 17th edn 2011. *Recreations*: violin (performs with London Phoenix Orchestra, Fulham Opera et al), programming, trying to mend things. *Address*: 3 New Square, Lincoln's Inn, WC2A 3RS. *T*: (020) 7405 1111, *Fax*: (020) 7405 7800. *E*: clerks@3newsquare.co.uk.

**BURLAND, James Alan**; Aura Planning and architectural consultant, since 2010; *b* 25 Sept. 1954; *s* of late James Glyn Burland and Elizabeth Beresford Thompson. *Educ*: King Henry VIII Sch., Coventry; Bath Univ. (BSc 1978; BArch 1980); Acad. of Contemporary Music, Guildford (CertHE Professional Music Perf. 2013; Cert. Performance Guitar 2014); MSt Cantab 2018. RIBA 1983. Arup Associates, 1978, 1980–86; Philip Cox Richardson and Taylor Architects, 1986–90; Arup Associates, 1990–2000, Dir and Principal, 1994–2000; private practice, 2000–10. Projects include: Stockley Park, Heathrow, 1983–2000; Eton Coll. Labs, 1984; Bedford High Sch. Sch. Labs, 1984–85; (with Philip Cox Architects, Sydney) Sydney Olympics 2000 Stadium Studies, 1985–90; City of Manchester Stadium, 1992–2000; Plantation Place, Fenchurch Street, London, 1993–2000; Johannesburg Athletics Stadium, 1993–94; new coll., Durham Univ., 1994–2000; Crystal Palace Sports Complex, 1998; BP Solar Showcase G8 Summit, Arup campus building, Birmingham, 1998; private commn, design for Body Shop, including Bath and Brighton, 1982; Burland TM projects include: Ealing Studios, 2000; Bermondsey Market, 2000; Spitalfields Refuge and Convent restoration, 2000; Falcon Wharf apartments, 2000–03; Harlequins RFC, 2002; Pinewood and Shepperton Studios, 2003; Billiardrome, 2003; Portable Olympic Stadium studies, 2003; Bristol Arena Quarter, 2005; Fieldgate St, student housing, 2006; Edward Jenner Unit, Gloucester Royal Hosp., 2008; Stirling Billiardrome, 2010; private house in Arun, 2011; domestic projects on Lake Como, 2012; student projects in Europe and UK, 2012; film studios masterplanning, UK. Bovis/Architects' Jl RA Summer Exhibn Grand Award, 1998. *Recreations*: music, art, architecture, cycling. *T*: 07968 162128. *E*: jb@burlandtm.com, jb@jamesburland.com. *W*: www.burlandtm.com. *Club*: London Road (Cyclosports).

**BURLAND, Prof. John Boscawen**, CBE 2005; FRS 1997; FREng; Professor of Soil Mechanics, Imperial College (formerly Imperial College of Science and Technology), University of London, 1980–2001, now Emeritus; *b* 4 March 1936; *s* of John Whitmore Burland and Margaret Irene Burland (*née* Palmer); *m* 1963, Gillian Margaret, *d* of J. K. Miller; two *s* one *d*. *Educ*: Parktown Boys' High Sch., Johannesburg; Univ. of the Witwatersrand (BSc Eng, MSc Eng, DSc Eng); Univ. of Cambridge (PhD). FICE, Hon. FICE 2014; FIStructE; FREng (FEng 1981). Res. Asst, Univ. of the Witwatersrand, 1961; Engineer, Ove Arup and Partners, London, 1961–63; Res. Student, Cambridge Univ., 63–66; Building Research Station: SSO and PSO, 1966–72; Head of Geotechnics Div., 1972–79; Asst Dir and Head of Materials and Structures Dept, 1979–80. Visiting Prof., Dept of Civil Engineering, Univ. of Strathclyde, 1973–82. Member: Adv. Panel to Sec. of State for Environment on Black Country Limestone, 1983–95; Italian Prime Minister's Commn for stabilising the Leaning Tower of Pisa, 1990–2001. Mem. Council, CIRIA, 1987–95 (Vice Pres., 1995–98); Official Visitor, BRE, 1990–97. Trustee, BRE Trust, 2001–13 (Chm., Res. Cttee, 2003–13). Advr, Ove Arup Foundn, 2003–. Chm., Steering Gp, Centre for Smart Infrastructure and Construction, Univ. of Cambridge, 2011–. Chm., Wheathampstead Churches Together, 1990–97. FIC 2004. Hon. Fellow: Emmanuel Coll., Cambridge, 2004; Cardiff Univ., 2005. Royal Academy of Engineering: Mem. Council, 1994–97; Public Promotion of Engrg Medal, 2006; Institution of Structural Engineers: Mem. of Council, 1979–82; Murray Buxton Silver Medal, 1977; Oscar Faber Bronze Medal, 1979; Gold Medal, 1998; named in Special Award to DoE for Underground Car Park at Palace of Westminster, 1975; Oscar Faber Diploma, 1982; Murray Buxton Diploma, 2002; Sir Arnold Walters Medal, 2006; Murray Buxton Medal, 2007; Institution of Civil Engineers: Vice Pres., 2003–05; Telford Premium, 1972, 1985, 1987; Coopers Hill War Meml Medal, 1985; Baker Medal, 1986; Kelvin Medal, for outstanding contribn to engrg, 1989; Gold Medal, 2001; Geotechnical Res. Medal, 2013; Brit. Geotechnical Soc. Prize, 1968, 1971, 1974 and 1986; Kevin Nash Gold Medal, Internat. Soc. of Soil Mechanics and Foundn Engrs, 1994; H. Bolton Seed Medal, ASCE, 1996; Gold Medal, World Fedn of Engrg Orgns, 1997; Lord Lloyd of Kilgerran Prize, Foundn for Sci. and Technol., 2002; Dickinson Meml Medal, Newcomen Soc., 2007. Hon. Mem., Japanese Geotechnical Soc., 2005; Foreign Mem., NAE, 2016. Hon. DEng: Heriot-Watt, 1994; Glasgow, 2001; Hon. DSc: Nottingham, 1998; Warwick, 2003; Herts, 2011; Hon. DSc (Eng) Witwatersrand, 2007. Commendatore: Nostro Real Ordine di Francesco 1 (Italy), 2001; Ordine della Stella di Solidarietà Italiana, 2003. *Publications*: numerous papers on soil mechanics and civil engineering. *Recreations*: sailing, golf, painting.

**BURLEIGH, Prof. Michael Christopher Bennet**, PhD; FRHistS; Research Professor, University of Buckingham, since 2011; *b* 3 April 1955; *s* of late Wing Comdr B. G. S. Bennet Burleigh and C. Burleigh; *m* 1990, Linden Mary Brownbridge. *Educ*: University Coll. London (BA 1st Cl. Hons 1977); Bedford Coll., London (PhD 1982). FRHistS 1988. Weston Jun. Res. Fellow, New Coll., Oxford, 1984–87; British Acad. Post-doctoral Fellow, QMC, 1987–88; London School of Economics and Political Science: Lectr, 1988–93; Reader in Internat. Hist., 1993–95; Dist. Res. Prof. in Modern European Hist., Cardiff Univ., 1995–2001; William R. Kenan Jr Prof. of Hist., Washington & Lee Univ., 2001–02. Raoul Wallenberg Vis. Prof. of Human Rights, Rutgers Univ., 1999–2000; Kratter Vis. Prof. of Hist., Stanford Univ., 2003; Engelsberg Vis. Prof., LSE Ideas, 2019–. Cardinal Basil Hume Meml Lectr, Heythrop Coll., 2002; Fisher Lect., Cambridge Univ., 2007; Basil Liddell Hart Meml Lect., KCL, 2010. Mem., Academic Adv. Council, Inst. für Zeitgeschichte, Munich, 2004–12. Mem., Adv. Bd, New Culture Forum, 2009–; Mem., First World War Centenary Adv. Gp, 2012–. Ed., Totalitarian Movements and Political Religions, 2000–05; Contrib. Ed., Literary Review, 2010–. Writer and presenter, Dark Enlightenment, TV prog., 2006. Award for Archival Achievement, BFI, 1991; Bronze Medal, NY Film and TV Fest., 1994; Master of his Time, Premio Nonino, 2012. *Publications*: Prussian Society and the German Order, 1984; Germany Turns Eastwards, 1988; The Racial State: Germany 1933–45, 1991 (trans. Italian, Japanese, Czech); Death and Deliverance: euthanasia in Germany, 1994 (trans. German); (ed) Confronting the Nazi Past, 1996 (trans. Hungarian); Ethics and Extermination: reflections on Nazi genocide, 1997; The Third Reich: a new history, 2000 (Samuel Johnson Prize, 2001) (trans. Dutch, Estonian, German, Italian, Finnish, French, Spanish, Czech, Hebrew, Polish, Chinese); Earthly Powers: religion and politics in Europe from the French Revolution to the Great War, 2005 (trans. German, Italian, Spanish, Dutch, French, Polish); Sacred Causes: religion and politics from the European dictators to Al-Qaeda, 2006 (trans. Dutch, German, Italian, Spanish, French, Polish); Blood and Rage: a cultural history of terrorism, 2008 (trans. Dutch, Danish, German, Italian, Spanish, French); Moral Combat: a history of World War II, 2010 (trans. Spanish, Czech); Small Wars, Far Away Places: the genesis of the modern world 1945–65, 2013 (trans. Italian, Spanish, Portuguese); The Best of Times, The Worst of Times: a history of now, 2017. *Recreations*: gardening, sea fishing. *Address*: c/o Rogers, Coleridge & White Ltd, 20 Powis Mews, W11 1JN. *Club*: Travellers.

**BURLEY, Aidan**; entrepreneur; *b* Auckland, NZ, 22 Jan. 1979; *s* of Geoff Burley and Lois Burley; *m* 2014, Jodie Jones; one *s*. *Educ*: King Edward's Sch., Edgbaston; St John's Coll., Oxford (MA). Sen. Consultant, Accenture, 2002–05; Mgt Consultant, Mouchel, 2005–08; Hd, Govt Relations, CSC, 2008–10. Mem. (C) Hammersmith and Fulham LBC, 2006–10. MP (C) Cannock Chase, 2010–15. *Recreations*: Rugby, tennis, cooking. *E*: aidanburley@gmail.com.

**BURLEY, George Elder**; Manager, Crystal Palace Football Club, 2010–11; *b* Cumnock, Ayrshire, 3 June 1956; *s* of William and Sarah Burley; *m* 1978, Jill Askew; two *s* one *d*. *Educ*: Cumnock Acad. Professional footballer: Ipswich Town, 1973–85 (winner, FA Cup, 1978, UEFA Cup, 1981); Sunderland, 1985–88; Gillingham, 1988–89; Motherwell, 1989–91 and 1993–94; (and Manager) Ayr Utd, 1991–93; Falkirk, 1993; (and Manager) Colchester Utd, 1994; 11 caps for Scotland, 1979–82; Manager: Ipswich Town, 1995–2002; Derby Co., 2003–05; Heart of Midlothian, 2005; Southampton, 2005–08; Scottish Nat. Football Coach, 2008–09. *Recreations*: golf, tennis.

**BURLEY, Helen**; see Boaden, H.

**BURLEY, Prof. Jeffery**, CBE 1991; PhD; Professor of Forestry, 1996–2002, Director, Oxford Forestry Institute, 1985–2002, Oxford University; Professorial Fellow, Green College, Oxford, 1981–2002, now Emeritus Fellow (Vice-Warden, 1997–2002; Development Fellow, 2003–07); *b* 16 Oct. 1936; *s* of Jack Burley and Eliza Burley (*née* Creese); *m* 1961, Jean Shirley (*née* Palmer); two *s*. *Educ*: Portsmouth Grammar Sch.; New College, Oxford (BA 1961); Yale (MF 1962; PhD 1965; Dist. Alumnus 2015). Lieut, Royal Signals, 1954–57. O i/c and Unesco Expert, Forest Genetics Res. Lab., ARC of Central Africa, 1965–69; Sen. Res. Officer, Commonwealth Forestry Inst., Oxford, 1969–76; Lectr, 1976–83, Head of Dept of Forestry, 1983–85, Oxford Univ. Pres., Internat. Union of Forestry Res. Orgns, 1996–2000; Chairman: Tropical Forest Resource Gp, 1994–2006; Marcus Wallenberg Prize Selection Cttee, Stockholm, 1998–2006; Commonwealth Forestry Assoc., 2002–05. Chm. Bd, C-Questor Ltd, 2005–09. Mem. Bd, Marcus Wallenberg Foundn, 2006–17. Patron, Speedwell and WellBeing Trust, 2000–. Hon. Res. Prof., Chinese Acad. of Forestry, 2001. International Fellow: Italian Acad. of Forest Sci., 1996; Royal Swedish Acad. of Agriculture and Forestry, 1998; Hon. FICFor, 2003; Hon. Fellow, Soc. of Amer. Foresters, 2003. Hon. DSc CATIE, Costa Rica, 2008. *Publications*: (ed jtly) Multipurpose tree germplasm, 1984; (ed jtly) Increasing productivity of multipurpose species, 1985; (Ed. in Chief) Elsevier Encyclopedia of Forest Sciences, 2004; many book chapters resulting from conference papers; many contribs to periodicals and learned jls on forestry, agroforestry and forest tree breeding. *Recreations*: beekeeping, gardening, piano and church organ, Wantage Male Voice Choir. *Address*: Green Templeton College, Woodstock Road, Oxford OX2 6HG. *T*: (01865) 274770.

**BURLEY, Jessica Jane**; Global Chief Executive Officer, m/SIX Communications Ltd (formerly MCHI), since 2010; *b* Lympstone, Devon, 24 Jan. 1966; *d* of Anthony Douglas Wiseman and Jean Shirley Darby (*née* Evernden); *m* 1994, Mark David Burley. *Educ*: Bristol Poly. (BA Hons Eng. Lit. and Theatre Arts); CAM Cert. Communications Studies. Nat. Accounts Supervisor, Bristol United Press, 1987–90; Sales Exec., Mirror Extra South West, Mirror Gp Newspapers, 1990; Dep. Ad Manager, NME and Melody Maker, IPC Magazines, 1990–92; Advertising Manager, This Week, Daily Express, Express Newspapers, 1992–95; Advertising Director: Company Magazine, 1995, Cosmopolitan Magazine, 1995–96, Nat. Magazine Co.; Publishing Dir, Gruner+Jahr, 1997–99; Gp

Publishing Dir, Financial Times Business, 1999–2000; Exec. Gp Publishing Dir, Future Publishing, 2000–01; Gp Publishing Dir, National Magazines Co., 2001–04; Chief Operating Officer, ACP-NatMag Co., 2004–06; Man. Dir, National Magazines Co. 2006–10. Non-executive Director: Jacques Vert plc, 2009–11; Talk Talk Telecom Gp plc, 2010; UK Mail plc, 2012–17; Quarto Publishing Gp plc, 2014–. Exec. Mem., WACL, 2008–; Mem., Eur. Professional Women's Network, 2011–. Trustee, The Mix (formerly Get Connected), 2013. *Recreations:* golf, music, art.

**BURLEY, Kay Elizabeth;** presenter, Kay Burley Show, Sky News, since 2018; *b* Wigan, 17 Dec. 1960; *d* of Frank and Kathleen McGurrin; *m* 1st, 1980, Steve Burley; 2nd, 1992, Steve Kutner; one *s*. *Educ:* Beech Hill Primary Sch., Wigan; Whitley High Sch., Wigan; Nat. Council for Trng of Journalists Coll., Preston. Reporter, Evening Post and Chronicle, Wigan, 1978–83; freelance TV and radio journalist in NW, 1984; news producer, Tyne Tees TV, 1985; reporter and presenter, TV-am, 1985–88; presenter, Sky News, 1988–2018. *Publications:* Blooming Pregnant: the real facts about having a baby (jtly), 1993; First Ladies, 2011; Betrayal, 2012. *Recreations:* sports, theatre, family, friends, animal care. *Address:* Sky News Centre, Grant Way, Isleworth TW7 5QD. *E:* Kay.Burley@BSkyB.com.

**BURLEY, Lindsay Elizabeth,** CBE 2011; FRCPE, FRCGP; mediator, since 2004; Chairman, NHS Education for Scotland, 2010–18 (non-executive Director, 2002–10); *b* Blackpool, 2 Oct. 1950; *d* of William and Elizabeth Lamont; *m* 1972, Robin Burley. *Educ:* Edinburgh Univ. (MB ChB 1973). FRCPE 1985; FRCGP 1995. Sen. Lectr, Univ. of Edinburgh, 1982–87, Hon. Sen. Lectr, 1991–2013. Consultant Physician, 1982–91, Dir of Planning and Develt, 1991–95, Lothian Health Bd; Chief Exec., Borders Health Bd, 1995–2003; Chm., Nat. Waiting Times Centre Bd for Scotland, 2003–10. Mem., SFC, 2006–13. Partner, Eskhill & Co., 2003–. Chm., Scottish Assoc. for Mental Health, 2009–15. *Recreations:* gardening, ski-ing, piano playing. *Address:* Eskhill & Co., Green House at Eskhill, 15A Inveresk Village, Musselburgh EH21 7TD. *T:* (0131) 271 4000, 07831 605858. *E:* lindsay@eskhill.com.

**BURLEY, Maj. Gen. Shaun Alex,** CB 2013; MBE 1995; Military Secretary, 2013–15; Director, Army Sport Control Board, since 2015; *b* Shipston on Stour, 4 March 1962; *s* of George Burley and Maisie Burley; *m* 1983, Jayne Young; one *s* one *d*. *Educ:* King Edward VI Sch., Stratford on Avon; RMA Sandhurst. Joined Army, 1981; CO 35 Engr Regt, 1999–2002; Dep. Asst COS Orgn, HQ Land Forces, 2004–05; Commander: 8 Force Engr Bde, 2006–07; Operational Support Gp, Land Warfare Centre, 2008–09; Dir, Advanced Comd and Staff Course, JSCSC, 2010–11; GOC Theatre Troops, 2011–13. Hon. Col, Engr and Logistic Staff Corps, 2011–15; Col Comdt, RE, 2011–. Hon. Life Vice Pres., Army Rugby Union, 2014 (Chm., 2011–14). *Recreations:* sport (Pres., Corps Rugby, 2005–), military history, music, cinema, running, family, travel. *Address:* c/o Army Sport Control Board, Mackenzie Building, Fox Lines, Aldershot, Hants GU11 2LB.

**BURLINGTON, Earl of; William Cavendish;** photographer; *b* 6 June 1969; *s* and *heir* of Duke of Devonshire, *qv; m* 2007, Laura Ann Montagu, *d* of Richard Roundell; one *s* two *d*. High Sheriff, Derbyshire, 2019–20. *Heir: s* Lord Cavendish, *qv*. *Address:* c/o Chatsworth, Bakewell, Derbyshire DE45 1PP.

**BURMAN, Roger Stephen,** CBE 1991; DL; Chairman, since 1976, and Managing Director, since 1973, Teledictor; *b* 3 April 1940; *s* of Sir Stephen France Burman, CBE and Lady (Joan Margaret) Burman; *m* 1964, Felicity Jane Crook; four *s*. *Educ:* Oundle Sch.; Univ. of Birmingham (BSc Hon.). Burman & Sons, 1961–72 (Dir, 1965–72); Teledictor, 1972–. Chairman: Nat. Exhibn Centre, 1989–2005 (Dir, 1984–2005); Performances Birmingham Ltd (formerly Symphony Hall (Birmingham) Ltd), 1991–2014; Director: Black Country Develt Corp., 1992–98; Chrysalis Radio (Midlands), 2001–04; Baugh & Weedon Ltd, 2004–08. Gen. Tax Comr, 1973–2009. Member: British Hallmarking Council, 1980–2006 (Chm., 1989–97); BOTB, 1990–94 and 1996–99; Council, ICC, 1992–2006; Pres., Birmingham Chamber of Commerce, 1984–85; Chm., Assoc. of British Chambers of Commerce, 1988–90. Guardian, 1965–2010, Chm., 2000–06, Birmingham Assay Office. University of Birmingham: Life Governor, 1983–; Pro-Chancellor, 1994–2001. Liveryman, Goldsmiths' Co., 1993–. DL 1991, High Sheriff 1999, W Midlands. Hon. LLD Birmingham, 1994. *Recreation:* golf. *Address:* Astwood Hill House, Astwood Lane, Astwood Bank, Redditch, Worcs B96 6PT. *T:* (01522) 893951.

**BURN, Adrian;** *see* Burn, B. A. F.

**BURN, Angus Maitland P.;** *see* Pelham Burn.

**BURN, (Bryan) Adrian (Falconer);** *b* 23 May 1945; *s* of Peter and Ruth Burn; *m* 1968, Jeanette Carol; one *s* three *d*. *Educ:* Abingdon Sch. FCA. Whinney Murray, 1963–72; joined Binder Hamlyn, 1972; seconded to DTI, 1975–77; Partner, 1977, Managing Partner, 1988–94, Binder Hamlyn; Partner, Arthur Andersen, 1994–99. Non-executive Chairman: Atlas Gp Hldgs, 1999–2002; Search Holdings Ltd, 2000–06; non-executive Director: Sinclair-Stevenson Ltd, 1990–92; Brent Internat. plc, 1994–99; GE Capital Bank Ltd, 1999–2009; Pinewood Shepperton Plc, 2000–11; Wolff Olins Ltd, 1999–2001; Strutt and Parker, 1999–2006; Richards Butler, 1999–2006; Smart and Cook Hldgs Ltd, 2004–07; Acertec plc, 2006–09; GE Money Home Lending Ltd, 2007–16. Mem., Financial Adjudication Panel, Second Severn Crossing, 1991–98. Trustee and Hon. Treas., NSPCC, 1999–2008; Trustee, Royal British Legion, 2009–18. Chm. Govs, Abingdon Sch., 2013–18. *Address:* 13 Woodthorpe Road, Putney, SW15 6UQ. *T:* (020) 8788 6383. *E:* email@adrianburn.com. *Club:* Roehampton.

**BURN, Colin Richard; His Honour Judge Colin Burn;** a Circuit Judge, since 2010; Senior Judge, since 2012, and President, Investigatory Powers Tribunal, since 2016, Sovereign Base Areas Court Cyprus; *b* Newcastle upon Tyne, 24 Sept. 1962; *s* of John Burn and Margaret Burn (*née* Smithson); *m* 1994, Susan, *d* of His Honour (Anthony) Nigel Fricker, *qv*; three *s* one *d*. *Educ:* Durham Johnston Sch.; University Coll. London (LLB Hons); St Catherine's Coll., Oxford (MSt). Called to the Bar, Middle Temple, 1985; pupil barrister, 1985–86; Commnd Officer, Army Legal Corps, 1986–90; Bde Legal Officer, 3 Cdo Bde, RM, 1990; in practice as a barrister, 32/30 Park Sq., Leeds, 1990–2001; Dep. Judge Advocate, 1995–2001; Asst Judge Advocate Gen., 2001–10; Recorder, 2003–10; Magistrate, Standing Civilian Court (British Forces Germany), 2004–07. Judicial Mem., Parole Bd, 2010–13. Captain, RMP (TA), 1994–95. *Recreations:* walking, food and wine, military history, playing guitar, planning and experiencing travel. *Address:* Bradford Crown Court, Exchange Square, Bradford BD1 1JA. *Club:* Victory Services.

**BURN, Sir John,** Kt 2010; MD; FRCP, FRCPE, FRCOG, FRCPCH, FMedSci; Professor of Clinical Genetics, since 1991, and Head, Institute of Human Genetics, 2005–10, University of Newcastle upon Tyne; Chairman, Newcastle upon Tyne NHS Foundation Trust, since 2017; *b* 6 Feb. 1952; *s* of Harry and Margaret Burn; *m* 1972, Linda M. Wilson; one *s* one *d*. *Educ:* Barnard Castle Grammar Sch.; Newcastle upon Tyne Univ. (BMedSci 1973; MB BS 1976; MD 1990). FRCP 1989; FRCPCH 1996; FRCOG 1998; FRCPE 2001. Professional trng in medicine and paediatrics, Royal Victoria Infirmary, Newcastle Gen. Hosp., Freeman Hosp., Newcastle, 1976–80; Sen. Registrar, Hosp. for Sick Children, Gt Ormond St, and Clinical Scientific Officer, MRC Genetics Unit, Inst. of Child Health, 1980–84; Consultant Clinical Geneticist, Royal Victoria Infirmary, Newcastle upon Tyne, 1984–91. Lead Clinician, NHS North East, 2009–13; non-exec. Dir, NHS England, 2014–18. Mem., Human Genetics Commn, 1999–2005; Chm., Innovation Cttee, UK Human Genomics Strategy Gp, 2010–12. Chm., Genetics Speciality Gp, 2008–15, Sen. Investigator, 2011–19, Nat. Inst. of Health Res.; Chm., British Soc. for Genetic Medicine (formerly Human Genetics), 2011–13. CMO, 2009–, Chm., 2015–, QuantuMDx Ltd. Pres., Eur. Soc. of Human Genetics, 2006–07. FMedSci 2000. *Publications:* over 350 peer-reviewed contribs in field of clinical genetics with particular interest in birth defects and hereditary cancers. *Recreations:* playing the drums, running, reading, golf. *Address:* Institute of Genetic Medicine, Newcastle University, Newcastle upon Tyne NE1 3BZ. *T:* (0191) 241 8794. *E:* john.burn@ncl.ac.uk.

**BURN, His Honour Lindsay Stuart;** a Circuit Judge, 2003–14; *b* 29 Aug. 1948; *m* 1975, Hon. Anne-Catherine, *d* of Baron Wilberforce, CMG, OBE, PC; one *s* two *d*. *Educ:* Newcastle upon Tyne Univ. (LLB Hons). Called to the Bar, Middle Temple, 1972; barrister, 1972–2003; Asst Recorder, 1995–99, Recorder, 1999–2003; Standing Counsel to DTI, SE Circuit, 1995–2003. *Recreations:* photography, historical novels.

**BURN, Rear Adm. Richard Hardy,** CB 1992; AFC 1969; Director General Aircraft (Navy), Ministry of Defence, 1990–92; *b* 26 May 1938; *s* of Margaret (*née* Hardy) and Douglas Burn; *m* 1967, Judith Sanderson (*née* Tigg); one *s* one *d*, and one step *s* one step *d*. *Educ:* Berkhamsted; BRNC Dartmouth; RNEC Manadon. MIMechE. HMS Broadsword 1958, fighter pilot, 890 Naval Air Sqdn, HMS Ark Royal, 1961–62; test flying work (incl. 3 years exchange, US Navy), NDC Latimer, to 1975; develt of Sea Harrier, MoD (PE), 1975–78; Ops Officer, A&AEE, 1978–79; Air Eng. Officer, RNAS Yeovilton, 1980; Asst Dir Eng. (N), MoD, 1981–84; RCDS 1985; Dir, Aircraft Maint. and Repair, MoD (N), 1986–87; Dir, Helicopter Projects, MoD (PE), and ADC, 1988–90. Chm., Thomas Heatherley Educnl Trust, 2003–09. Mem., Soc. of Experimental Test Pilots. FRAeS 1984. Commendation, US Navy, 1974; Médaille d'Honneur, Soc. d'Encouragement au Progrès, 1989. *Recreations:* golf, painting, sculpture.

**BURNAND, Aisling Maria,** MBE 2007; Director, DNA Coaching, 2013; Chief Executive, Association of Medical Research Charities, since 2014; *b* London, 22 Dec. 1964; *d* of Paul Mullen and Maureen Mullen; *m* 1997, William Burnand; two *s*. *Educ:* Coll. for Distributive Trades, London (HND Business Studies 1985). Advertising Exec., Haymarket Publishing, 1986; Press and PR Asst, British Safety Council, 1986–87; Public Relns Officer, Rhône-Poulenc Ltd, 1987–89; Internat. Media Relns Manager, Rhône-Poulenc SA, 1989–94; Business Gp Dir, Rowland Co., 1994–97; sabbatical, NY, 1997–98; Bioindustry Association: Public Affairs Dir, 1998–2001; Dep. Chief Exec., 2001–03; Chief Exec., 2003–09; Exec. Dir, Policy and Public Affairs, CRUK, 2009–11. Director: Campaign for Sci. and Engrg, 2012–16; LifeArc, 2017–. Gov., St Joan of Arc Sch., 2008–15. *Recreations:* theatre, ballet, opera, cinema, walking, family, art. *T:* 07775 516760. *E:* a.wburnand@virginmedia.com.

**BURNE, Dr Yvonne Ann,** OBE 2008; senior educational consultant; Head, City of London School for Girls, 1995–2007; *b* 29 Aug. 1947; *d* of Archibald Ford and Florence Louise Ford (*née* Knott); *m* 1968, Anthony Richard Burne; one *s* one *d*. *Educ:* Redland High Sch. for Girls, Bristol; Westfield Coll., Univ. of London (BA Hons; PhD). School teacher: Harrow Co. Grammar Sch. for Girls, 1971–74; Lowlands Sixth Form Coll., 1974–77; Hd, Mod. Langs and Careers Guidance, Northwood Coll., 1984–87; Headmistress, St Helen's Sch. for Girls, Northwood, 1987–95. Editor: Educnl Challenges Inc. (VA, USA), 1978–82; Mary Glasgow Pubns, 1983–84; Heinemann Educnl Books, 1984. Member: Hillingdon FHSA, 1990–96; Wolfson Foundn Schs Panel, 2007–. Lead Education Consultant: Thewlis Graham Associates, 2011–13; RSAcademics, 2013–. Governor: Berkhamsted Sch., 2005–16; Brighton Univ., 2006–16; Haberdashers' Aske's Boys' and Girls' Schs, 2011–; St Dunstan's Coll., 2017–. Patron, Tomorrow's Achievers, 2014– (Trustee, 2007–14); Trustee, 9/11 Project, 2010–15. Master, Educators' Co., 2009–10. FRSA 1991. JP City of London, 2007–17. *Publications:* Tomorrow's News, 1979; The Circus Comes to Town, 1979; articles and children's stories. *Recreations:* theatre, entertaining friends, walking.

**BURNELL, Dame (Susan) Jocelyn B.;** *see* Bell Burnell.

**BURNELL-NUGENT, Adm. Sir James (Michael),** KCB 2004; CBE 1999; Commander-in-Chief Fleet, and NATO Maritime Component Commander Northwood, 2005–07; Vice-Admiral of the United Kingdom, 2005–07; company director, since 2008; *b* 20 Nov. 1949; *s* of late Comdr Anthony Frank Burnell-Nugent, DSC, RN and Gian Burnell-Nugent; *m* 1973, Henrietta Mary, (DL, MA, MB, BChir), *d* of Rt Rev. R. W. Woods, KCMG, KCVO; three *s* one *d*. *Educ:* Stowe; Corpus Christi Coll., Cambridge (MA Hons; Hon. Fellow, 2006). Joined RN, 1971; BRNC Dartmouth (Queen's Gold Medal); Submarines, 1973–86; Max Horton Prize, 1974; CO HMS Olympus, 1979–80; CO HMS Conqueror, 1984–86; Comdr, 1985; Captain, 1990; Captain, F2 and CO HMS Brilliant, (Bosnia), 1992–93; Cdre, 1994; on secondment to HM Treasury, 1996; Dep. FO Surface Flotilla, 1997; CO HMS Invincible, (Gulf, Kosovo), 1997–99; Rear Adm., 1999; ACNS, MoD, 1999–2001; Mem., Admiralty Bd, 1999–2001 and 2003–07; Dep. Coalition Maritime Comdr, (Op. Enduring Freedom, Afghanistan), 2001–02; Comdr UK Maritime Forces, and Comdr Anti Submarine Warfare Striking Force, 2001–02; Second Sea Lord and C-in-C Naval Home Comd, Mem. of Admiralty Bd, and Flag ADC to the Queen, 2003–05. Founder and Dir, Orchard Leadership Ltd, 2008–; Chm., Plymouth Marine Lab., 2015– (Trustee and Dir, 2008–); Chm., Develt Council, 2009–14; Dep. Chm., 2012–15). Chm., Aerospace, Defence and Maritime (formerly Industry and Govt) Practice, Regester Larkin, 2013–16; Chm., Witt Ltd, 2016–; non-exec. Dir, QinetiQ Gp plc, 2010– (Chm., Risk and Corporate Social Responsibility and Security Cttees, 2014–). Internat. Advr, Shell Shipping, 2008–17; Senior Adviser: Evercore Partners, 2008–18; Deloitte, 2017–; Special Advr, Oil Cos Internat. Marine Forum, 2008–; Strategic Advr and Chm., Adv. Bd, Risk Internat. 2012–; Leadership Develt Advr, Newton Europe, 2012–; Advr, Dabble Towelling Ltd, 2014–; Strategic Advr, Sonardyne, 2014–. Dir, St George's House, Windsor Castle, 2014–18. Sen. Fellow, One Earth Future Foundn, 2012–. Pres., HMS Ganges Assoc., 2009–; Mem. Fundraising Cttee, Sea Cadet TS Royalist, 2013–15. Trustee, Annual Nat. Service for Seafarers, 2014– (Vice Chm., 2015–). Ambassador for RN Submarine Mus., 2012–; Gov., Stowe, 2008–. Comp. Inst. of Leadership and Mgt, 2006. Freeman, City of London, 1999. High Sheriff, Devon, 2015–16. Younger Brother, Trinity House, 2004. *Publications:* My Royal Navy Scrapbook, 2014; Brothers-in-Law in the Great War, 2016; pamphlets incl. Leadership in the Office, Keeping an Eye on the Cost of Government; numerous articles in Naval Review and RUSI Jl; contrib. to Spectator. *Recreation:* living in the country. *Address:* c/o Naval Secretary, Leach Building, Whale Island, Portsmouth, Hants PO2 8BY. *Club:* Cychod Trefdraeth.

**BURNER, (Edward) Alan;** HM Diplomatic Service, retired; Ambassador to Senegal and, concurrently, to Guinea Bissau, Cape Verde and Mali, 2000–04; *b* 26 Sept. 1944; *s* of late Douglas Keith Burner and Mary Burner; *m* 1969, Jane Georgine Du Port; one *s* two *d*. *Educ:* Uppingham Sch., Rutland; Emmanuel Coll., Cambridge (MA Hons Mod. Langs). Volunteer, Nigeria, VSO, 1966–67; joined HM Diplomatic Service, 1967: Sofia, 1970–72; Bonn, 1972–74; Bridgetown, 1974–78; N America Dept, FCO, 1979; Asst Private Sec. to Minister for Overseas Develt, 1979–82; Dep. Head of Recruitment, FCO, 1982–84; Dep. Hd of Mission, Sofia, 1984–87; on loan to ODA, 1987–90; Hd, Med. Welfare Unit, FCO,

1990–92; Commercial Counsellor, then Dep. Hd of Mission, Lagos, 1992–95; Consul-Gen., Munich, 1995–99. *Recreations:* tennis, walking. *Address:* 12 Hillside Road, Sevenoaks, Kent TN13 3XJ. *T:* (01732) 453885.

**BURNET, Catherine Emma;** Scotland Regional Chair, KPMG LLP, since 2016; *b* Belfast, 17 Nov. 1970; *d* of David Allen and Margaret Allen; *m* 1997, James Burnet; two *s. Educ:* Methodist Coll. Belfast; Univ. of St Andrews (BSc Hons). CA, ICAS, 1997. KPMG: joined, 1994; Partner, 2009–; Hd, Financial Services Scotland, 2011. Mem., Financial Services Adv. Bd, Scottish Govt, 2015–. Dep. Pres., ICAS, 2019–20. *Address:* KPMG LLP, Saltire Court, 20 Castle Terrace, Edinburgh EH1 2EG. *T:* (0131) 527 6671. *E:* catherine.burnet@kpmg.co.uk.

**BURNET, George Wardlaw,** LVO 1981; JP; Lord-Lieutenant of Midlothian, 1992–2002; *b* 26 Dec. 1927; *s* of late Sheriff John Rudolph Wardlaw Burnet, KC and Lucy Margaret Ord Burnet (*née* Wallace); *m* 1951, Jane Elena Moncrieff, *d* of late Malcolm Moncrieff Stuart, CIE, OBE; two *s* one *d. Educ:* Edinburgh Acad.; Lincoln Coll., Oxford (BA); Edinburgh Univ. (LLB). Served Black Watch (RHR) TA, retired as Captain, 1957. WS 1954; Partner, Murray Beith and Murray, 1956–90. County Councillor, Midlothian, 1967–76. Church of Scotland: Elder, 1961–; Convener, Gen. Finance Cttee, 1980–83. Secretary: Scottish Building Contract Cttee, 1962–87; RIAS, 1964–87. Chairman: Life Assoc. of Scotland, 1985–93; Caledonian Res. Foundn, 1989–99. Captain, Royal Company of Archers, Queen's Body Guard for Scotland, 2004–. Hon. FRIAS 1980. DL 1975, JP 1991, Midlothian. KStJ. *Recreations:* country pursuits, architecture, gardening. *Address:* Rose Court, Inveresk, Midlothian EH21 7TD. *T:* (0131) 665 2689. *Club:* New (Edinburgh).

**BURNETT,** family name of **Barons Burnett** and **Burnett of Maldon**.

**BURNETT,** Baron *cr* 2006 (Life Peer), of Whitchurch in the County of Devon; **John Patrick Aubone Burnett;** Consultant, Stephens & Scown, since 2005; *b* 19 Sept. 1945; *s* of late Lt-Col Aubone Burnett, OBE and Joan (*née* Bolt); *m* 1971, Elizabeth Sherwood, *d* of Sir Arthur de la Mare, KCMG, KCVO; two *s* two *d. Educ:* Ampleforth Coll., Yorks; Britannia RNC, Dartmouth; Coll. of Law, London. Served RM, 1964–70: Troop Comdr, 42 Commando RM, Borneo, 1965–66; Troop Comdr and Co. 2nd in command, 40 Commando RM, FE and ME, 1967–69. Farmer, 1976–98. Admitted Solicitor, 1975; Partner, then Sen. Partner, Burd Pearse, Okehampton, 1976–97. Mem., Law Soc. Revenue Law Cttee, 1984–96. Contested (Lib Dem) Devon West and Torridge, 1987. MP (Lib Dem) Devon West and Torridge, 1997–2005. Lib Dem spokesman on legal affairs, 1997–2002; Lib Dem Shadow Attorney Gen., 2002–05. Mem. Council, Devon Cattle Breeders' Soc., 1985–97 (winner Nat. Herd competition, 1989). *Address:* Stephens & Scown, Curzon House, Southernhay West, Exeter EX1 1RS.

**BURNETT OF MALDON,** Baron *cr* 2017 (Life Peer), of Maldon in the County of Essex; **Ian Duncan Burnett,** Kt 2008; PC 2014; Lord Chief Justice of England and Wales, since 2017; *b* 28 Feb. 1958; *yr s* of late David John Burnett and Maureen Burnett (*née* O'Brien); *m* 1991, Caroline Ruth Monks; one *s* one *d. Educ:* St John's Coll., Southsea; Pembroke Coll., Oxford (MA; Hon. Fellow, 2008). Called to the Bar, Middle Temple, 1980, Bencher, 2001; in practice as barrister, Temple Gdn Chambers, 1982–2008 (Hd of Chambers, 2003–08); Jun. Crown Counsel, Common Law, 1992–98; QC 1998; Asst Recorder, 1998–2000; Recorder, 2000–08; a Dep. High Court Judge, 2008; a Judge of the High Court of Justice, QBD, 2008–14; Presiding Judge, Western Circuit, 2011–14; a Lord Justice of Appeal, 2014–17. Dep. Chm., Security Vetting Appeals Panel, 2009–14; Vice Chm., Judicial Appts Commn, 2015–17. *Recreations:* history, music, silver, wine. *Address:* Royal Courts of Justice, Strand, WC2A 2LL.

**BURNETT, of Leys,** Baronetcy of (unclaimed); *see under* Ramsay, Sir Alexander William Burnett, 7th Bt.

**BURNETT, Prof. Alan Kenneth,** MBE 2008; MD; FRCPGlas, FRCPE, FRCP, FRCPath, FMedSci; Professor of Haematology, Cardiff University (formerly University of Wales College of Medicine), 1992–2014; Global Lead for Myeloid Diseases, CTI Life Sciences, 2014–17; *b* 27 May 1946; *s* of George Binnie Burnett and Janet Maloch Burnett (*née* Henderson); *m* 1971, Alison Forrester Liddell; two *s. Educ:* Glasgow Acad.; Univ. of Glasgow (ChB; MD Hons 1988). FRCPGlas 1984; FRCPath 1986; FRCPE 1988; FRCP 1993. Res. Fellow, Univ. of Chicago, 1975–76; Consultant Haematologist, Glasgow Royal Infirmary, 1979–92; Clin. Dir of Service, University Hosp. of Wales, 1992–2007. Visiting Professor: Univ. of Miami, 1994; Northwestern Univ., Chicago, 1999; Univ. of Kuwait, 2000. Chairman: MRC Adult Leukaemia Wkg Party, 1990–2013; Nat. Cancer Res. Network Gp for Haematol Oncology, 2002–07; Mem., Med. Advisory Panel, Leukaemia Res. Fund, 1989–93. Pres., British Soc. of Haematol., 1998–99. FMedSci 2000. Ham Wasserman Award, Amer. Soc. of Hematology, 2012. *Publications:* contrib. more than 300 papers to medical literature predominantly on treatment and biol. of leukaemia. *Recreations:* golf, DIY. *Address:* Ty Mawr, Blackwaterfoot, Isle of Arran KA27 8EU.

**BURNETT, Dr Andrew Michael,** CBE 2012; FBA 2003; FSA; Deputy Director, British Museum, 2003–13; *b* 23 May 1952; *s* of Sir John (Harrison) Burnett and of E. Margaret Burnett, *er d* of Rev. Dr E. W. Bishop; *m* 1978, Susan Jennifer Allix; two *d. Educ:* Fettes Coll., Edinburgh; Balliol Coll., Oxford (BA, MA); Inst. of Archaeology, Univ. of London (PhD). Department of Coins and Medals, British Museum: Res. Assistant, 1974–79; Asst Keeper, 1979–90; Dep. Keeper, 1990–92; Keeper, 1992–2003. Secretary: RNS, 1983–90 (Vice-Pres., 1999–2004; Hon. Vice-Pres., 2009; Pres., 2013–18; Hon. Vice-Pres., 2019–); Internat. Numismatic Commn, 1992–97 (Pres., 1997–2003). Pres., Roman Soc., 2008–12, Vice-Pres., 2012–. Trustee, Royal Armouries, 2014–; Chm., Royal Mint Mus. Trust, 2015–. Hon. Prof., Inst. of Archaeology, UCL, 2013–. Chm. Adv. Cttee, Inst. of Classical Studies, Univ. of London, 2014–18. Corresponding Member: Amer. Numismatic Soc., 1982 (Trustee, 2015–; Vice Pres., 2017); German Archaeol. Inst., 2001. Hon. Member: Internat. Numismatic Commn, 2015; Soc. Française de Numismatique, 2015; Belgian Numismatic Soc., 2017. FSA 1982. Norwegian Numismatic Soc. Medal, 1991; Silver Medal, RNS, 1993; Prix Allier de Hauteroche, Acad. des Inscriptions et Belles-Lettres, 1999; Meshorer Prize, Israel Mus., 2002; Jeton de Vermeil, Soc. Française de Numismatique, 2004; Huntington Medal, Amer. Numismatic Soc., 2008. *Publications:* Coinage in the Roman World, 1987; Interpreting the Past: Coins, 1991; Roman Provincial Coinage, Vol. 1, 1992, Vol. 2, 1999, Vol. 3, 2015; Behind the Scenes at the British Museum, 2001; Roman Coins, Money and Society in Elizabethan England: Sir Thomas Smith's 'On the Wages of the Roman Footsoldier', 2017; contrib. Numismatic Chronicle, Schweizerische Numismatisches Rundschau, Quaderni Ticinesi, Jl Roman Studies, Britannia, etc; *festschrift:* (ed. R. Bland and D. Calomino) Essays in Ancient Coinage in Honour of Andrew Burnett, 2015. *Address:* 19 Almorah Road, N1 3ER.

**BURNETT, Sir Charles (David),** 4th Bt *cr* 1913, of Selborne House, in the Borough of Croydon; *b* 18 May 1951; *er s* of Sir David Humphery Burnett, 3rd Bt, MBE, TD and Geraldine Elizabeth Mortimer, *d* of Sir Godfrey Fisher, KCMG; *S* father, 2002; *m* 1st, 1989, Victoria Joan Simpson (marr. diss. 1997); one *d*; 2nd, 1998, Kay Rosemary Naylor; one *d. Educ:* Harrow; Lincoln Coll., Oxford. *Heir: b* John Godfrey Burnett, *b* 29 March 1954.

**BURNETT, Charles John;** Ross Herald, 1988–2010, Ross Herald Extraordinary, 2011–15 (Dingwall Pursuivant, 1983); *b* 6 Nov. 1940; *s* of Charles Alexander Urquhart Burnett and Agnes Watt; *m* 1967, Aileen Elizabeth McIntyre; two *s* one *d. Educ:* Fraserburgh Academy; Gray's Sch. of Art, Aberdeen (DA); Aberdeen Coll. of Education (Teaching Cert.); MLitt Edinburgh 1992. AMA. House of Fraser, 1963–64; COI, 1964–68; Asst Dir, Letchworth Mus., 1968–71; Head of Design, Nat. Mus. of Antiquities of Scotland, 1971–85; Curator of Fine Art, Scottish United Services Mus., Edinburgh Castle, 1985–96; Chamberlain, Duff House Country Gall., Banff, 1997–2004. Heraldic Adviser: Girl Guide Assoc. in Scotland, 1978–2010; NADFAS Church Recorders, Scotland, 2000–; Chm., Banff Preservation & Heritage Soc., 2002–10. Vice-Patron, Geneal. Soc. of Queensland, 1986–2010; Vice-Pres., Soc. of Antiquaries of Scotland, 1992–95; Trustee, St Andrews Fund for Scots Heraldry, 2001–15; Pres., Heraldry Soc. of Scotland, 2003–15, now Pres. Emeritus. Pres., Internat. Congress of Geneal and Heraldic Scis, St Andrews, 2006. Trustee, Bield Retirement Housing Trust, 1992–96. Chm., Pitsligo Castle Trust, 2010–14. Hon. Pres., Moray Burial Ground Res. Gp, 2012–. Convenor, Companions of the Order of Malta, 1991–94. KStJ 1991; Librarian, Priory of Order of St John in Scotland, 1987–99. Hon. Teaching Fellow, Univ. of Dundee, 2017. Hon. Citizen, Oklahoma, 1989. Kt, Order of SS Maurice and Lazarus, 1999; Kt, Order of Francis I, 2002. *Publications:* Scotland's Heraldic Heritage, 1997; The Order of St John in Scotland, 1997; Thistle Stall Plates, 2001; Officers of Arms in Scotland 1290–2016, 2016; numerous articles on Scottish heraldry. *Recreations:* reading, visiting places of historical interest. *Address:* Seaview House, Portsoy, Banffshire AB45 2RS. *T:* (01261) 843378.

**BURNETT, Prof. Charles Stuart Freeman,** PhD; FBA 1998; Professor of the History of Islamic Influences in Europe, since 1999, and Co-director, Centre for the History of Arabic Studies in Europe, since 2012, Warburg Institute, University of London; *b* 26 Sept. 1951; *m* 1st, 1985, Mitsuru Kamachi (marr. diss. 1991); 2nd, 1995, Tamae Nakamura; two *s. Educ:* Manchester Grammar Sch.; St John's Coll., Cambridge (BA 1972; PhD 1976). LGSM 1980. Jun. Res. Fellow, St John's Coll., Cambridge, 1975–79; Sen. Res. Fellow, 1979–82, Lectr, 1985–99, Warburg Inst., Univ. of London; Leverhulme Res. Fellow, Dept of History, Univ. of Sheffield, 1982–84, 1985; Mem., Inst. for Advanced Study, Princeton, 1984–85. Dist. Vis. Prof., Univ. of Calif, Berkeley, 2003; Vis. Prof., Univ. of Munich, 2009; Dist. Visitor, Pontifical Inst. of Mediaeval Studies, Toronto, 2017. Brauer Fellow, Univ. of Chicago, 2008. Corresp. Fellow, Medieval Acad. of America. Mem., Internat. Acad. of History of Science. *Publications:* (with Masahiro Takenaka) Jesuit Plays on Japan and English Recusancy, 1995; Magic and Divination in the Middle Ages: texts and techniques in the Islamic and Christian worlds, 1996; The Introduction of Arabic Learning into England, 1997; Arabic into Latin in the Middle Ages: the translators and their intellectual and social context, 2009; Numerals and Arithmetic in the Middle Ages, 2010; several edns of Latin and Arabic texts; over 100 articles in learned jls. *Recreations:* playing music (viola, piano, viola da gamba, shakuhachi), hill walking, religious activities (Iona community, Japanese Buddhist and Shinto traditions). *Address:* Warburg Institute, Woburn Square, WC1H 0AB. *T:* (020) 7862 8920.

**BURNETT, Clare Elizabeth;** sculptor; President, Royal Society of Sculptors (formerly Royal British Society of Sculptors), since 2015; *b* Canterbury, 7 Dec. 1964; *d* of David and Stephanie Gibbons; *m* 1984, Sandy Burnett; one *s* one *d. Educ:* British Sch. at Brussels; English Sch. of Paris; Marlborough Coll.; Christ's Coll., Cambridge (BA 1986); Byam Shaw Sch. of Art (Foundn and Dip. 1994); Inst. of Educn, Univ. of London (PGCE 2004). PR Exec., Burson Marsteller PR, 1986–88; HIV/AIDS Campaign Officer, HEA, 1988–90; self-employed artist, 1994–; art teacher (pt-time), Grey Coat Hosp., 2012–17. Visiting Artist: Univ. of Leeds, 2014–17; Leeds Coll. of Art, 2017; Art Acad., 2017–. Solo exhibitions include: All Soles, Brompton Cemetery with James Colman Gall., 2001; Formes, Le Corbusier Unité d'Habitation, Marseille, 2002; Folded, Leighton House, London, 2012; Pink, William Benington Gall., London, 2015; Improvisations, Sch. of Design, Univ. of Leeds, 2016. Vice Pres., RBS, 2012–15. *Recreations:* involvement in refugee issues, cinema, exhibitions, walking in cities, technology. *E:* art@clareburnett.net. *Club:* Chelsea Arts.

**BURNETT, Sir Keith,** Kt 2013; CBE 2004; DPhil; FRS 2001; FInstP; Vice-Chancellor, University of Sheffield, 2007–18; Chair, Nuffield Foundation, since 2018 (Trustee, since 2017); *b* 30 Sept. 1953; *s* of Royston Ifor Burnett and Jean Marion Burnett; *m* 1975, Elizabeth Anne Mustoe; one *s* one *d. Educ:* Brynteg Comprehensive Sch.; Jesus Coll., Oxford (BA 1975; DPhil 1979; Hon. Fellow, 2007). FInstP 1996. Asst Prof., Univ. of Colorado, 1980–84; Fellow, Jt Inst. for Lab. Astrophysics, Colorado Univ. and Nat. Inst. of Standards and Technol., 1981–84; Lectr in Physics, Imperial Coll., London, 1984–88; Oxford University: Lectr in Physics, 1988–96; Prof., 1996–2007; Hd of Atomic and Laser Physics, 1999–2002; Chm. of Physics, 2002–05; Hd of Math., Physical and Life Scis Div., 2005–07; Fellow, St John's Coll., Oxford, 1988–2007, now Hon. Fellow. Non-exec. Dir, UKAEA, 2010–18. Member: EPSRC, 1999–2004; CCLRC, 2005–07; STFC, 2007–11; Council for Sci. and Technol., 2011–; Bd, HEFCE, 2015–18; Pres., UK Sci. Council, 2016–. Chair, UCEA, 2009–11. Fellow: APS, 1996; Optical Soc. of America, 1996; FLSW 2014. Wolfson Merit Award, Royal Soc., 2003. *Publications:* articles in learned jls, incl. Physical Review, Jl Physics B, Telegraph, Guardian, FT. *Recreations:* reading, music, Chinese. *Address:* Nuffield Foundation, 28 Bedford Square, WC1B 3JS.

**BURNETT, Richard George,** FCILT; Chief Executive, Road Haulage Association, since 2014; *b* Birkenhead, 2 March 1967; *s* of John William Michael Burnett and Barbara Dorothy Burnett; *m* 1992, Deborah Joanna Walker; three *d. Educ:* Upton by Chester Co. High Sch. Raw Material Intake Co-Ordinator, North Western Farmers, 1985–89; Transport Manager, then Depot Manager, Transport Develt Gp, 1989–97; Primary Distribution Manager, Hayes Distribution, 1997–99; Nat. Contract Manager, B&Q, 1999–2002; Contract Gen. Manager, then Business Unit Dir, Wincanton, 2002–12; Man. Dir, Samworth Bros Supply Chain, 2012–14. Chm., Motorists' Forum, 2016–. *Recreations:* running, music, sailing. *Address:* Road Haulage Association, 22 Greencoat Place, Westminster, SW1P 1PR. *T:* (office) (01733) 256 1131. *E:* r.burnett@rha.uk.net.

**BURNEY, Matthew John;** Director, Japan, British Council, since 2015; Counsellor (Culture), British Embassy, Tokyo, since 2015; *b* Manchester, 11 June 1970; *s* of late John Burney and of Mary Burney; civil partnership 2012, Liang Chuanbao, (Paul Liang). *Educ:* Montgomery High Sch., Blackpool; Blackpool Sixth Form Coll.; Junior Royal Northern Coll. of Music; Royal Northern Coll. of Music; St Anne's Coll., Oxford (BA Hons 1992). Nanzan Univ. Japanese Exchange and Teaching Prog., 1992–94; Coordinator for Internat. Relns, Aichi Shukutoku Univ., 1996–97; British Council: Liaison Officer, Nagoya Area 1997–2000; Dir, Southwest China and Cultural/Educn Consul, 2000–03; Dep. Regl Dir E Asia, London, 2003–05; Dep. Dir, 2005–07, Dir, 2007–08, Czech Republic; Dir, Ireland, 2008–11; Dir, East China and Consul (Culture/Educn), 2011–15. Ex-Officio Mem. Bd British Chamber of Commerce, Japan, 2015–; Mem. Bd, Japan British Soc., 2016–. *Recreations:* music, studying Japan and Japanese. *T:* (Japan) (3) 32358041, *Fax:* (3) 32358040 *E:* matt.burney@britishcouncil.or.jp.

**BURNEY, Sir Nigel (Dennistoun)**, 4th Bt cr 1921, of Preston House, Preston Candover, Southampton; b 6 Sept. 1959; er s of Sir Cecil Burney, 3rd Bt and Hazel Marguerite de Hamel (née Coleman); S father, 2002; m 1992, Lucy Brooks; two s two d. Educ: Eton; Trinity Coll., Cambridge. Recreations: tennis, music, ski-ing. Heir: s Max Dennistoun Burney, b 15 Sept. 1994. E: nigel@nigelburney.com. Clubs: White's, Annabel's, Queen's.

**BURNHAM**, 7th Baron cr 1903, of Hall Barn, Beaconsfield, Bucks; **Harry Frederick Alan Lawson**; Bt 1892; Investment Director, JM Finn & Co., 2016–19; b 22 Feb. 1968; s of 6th Baron Burnham and of Lady Burnham (née Hilary Margaret Hunter); S father, 2005. Educ: Summer Fields Sch., Oxford; Eton Coll. Associated Newspapers, 1988–95; Williams de Broë plc, 1996–2000; Dir, Investment Mgt, Brewin Dolphin Securities Ltd, 2000–13; CEO, Ashcourt Rowan Asset Mgt, 2013–15; Investment Dir, Towry/Tilney Asset Mgt, 2015–16. Liveryman, Gunmakers' Co. Recreations: shooting, horse and dog racing, tobogganing, oenology, golf. Heir: none. Address: Woodlands Farm, Beaconsfield, Bucks HP9 2SF. Clubs: Turf, Pratt's; St Moritz Tobogganing; Burnham Beeches Golf.

**BURNHAM, Rt Rev. Mgr Andrew**; Bishop Suffragan of Ebbsfleet, 2000–10; Provincial Episcopal Visitor, Province of Canterbury, 2000–10; Parish Priest, East Hendred Catholic Parish, 2015; b 19 March 1948; s of David Burnham and Eileen Burnham (née Franks); m 1984, Cathy Ross; one s one d. Educ: New Coll., Oxford (BA 1969, 1971; MA 1973); Westminster Coll., Oxford (CertEd 1972); St Stephen's House, Oxford. ARCO(CHM). Ordained deacon, 1983, priest, 1984; Hon. Curate, Clifton, Southwell Dio., 1983–85; Curate, Beeston, 1985–87; Vicar, Carrington, 1987–94; Vice-Principal, St Stephen's House, Oxford, 1995–2000. Assistant Bishop: Dio. of Bath and Wells, 2001–10; Dio. of Oxford, 2001–10; Dio. of Exeter, 2001–10; Dio. of Lichfield, 2001–10; Dio. of Worcester, 2008–10. Ordained RC deacon and priest, 2011; Prelate of Honour, 2011. Publications: A Manual of Anglo-Catholic Devotion, 2000, pocket edn, 2004; Heaven and Earth in Little Space: the re-enchantment of liturgy, 2010; Customary of Our Lady of Walsingham, 2012. Recreations: liturgy, music. Address: St Mary's Catholic Church, St Mary's Road, East Hendred, Wantage OX12 8LF. E: andrew.burnham@ordinariate.org.uk.

**BURNHAM, Rt Hon. Andrew (Murray)**; PC 2007; Mayor of Greater Manchester (Lab), since 2017; b Liverpool, 7 Jan. 1970; s of Kenneth Roy Burnham and Eileen Mary (née Murray); m 2000, Marie-France van Heel; one s two d. Educ: St Aelred's RC High Sch., Merseyside; Fitzwilliam Coll., Cambridge (MA Hons Eng.). Researcher to Tessa Jowell, MP, and Labour Health Team, 1994–97; Parly Officer, NHS Confedn, 1997; Advr to Football Task Force, 1997–98; Special Advr to Rt Hon. Chris Smith, MP, DCMS, 1998–2001. MP (Lab) Leigh, 2001–17. PPS to Sec. of State for Home Dept, 2003–05; Parly Under-Sec. of State, Home Office, 2005–06; Minister of State, DoH, 2006–07; Chief Sec. to HM Treasury, 2007–08; Sec. of State for Culture, Media and Sport, 2008–09, for Health, 2009–10; Shadow Sec. of State for Health, 2010, for Educn and Election Coordinator, 2010–11, for Health, 2011–15; Shadow Home Sec., 2015–16. Mem., Health Select Cttee, 2001–03. Chm., Supporters Direct, 2002–05; Pres., Rugby Football League, 2018–19. Recreations: football (Everton FC), Rugby league (Leigh RLC), cricket. Address: Greater Manchester Combined Authority, Churchgate House, 56 Oxford Street, Manchester M1 6EU.

**BURNHAM, Rev. Anthony Gerald**; Moderator, Free Churches Group (formerly Free Churches' Council), and a President, Churches Together in England, 1999–2003; b 2 March 1936; s of Selwyn and Sarah Burnham; m 1961, Valerie Florence Cleaver; one s two d. Educ: Silcoates Sch.; Manchester Univ. (BA Admin); Northern Coll., Manchester. Minister: Brownhill Congregational Church, Blackburn, 1961–66; Poulton-le-Fylde and Hambleton Congregational Churches, 1966–69; Lectr, Northern Coll., Manchester, 1969–77; Minister, SW Manchester United Reformed Churches, 1973–81; Moderator, NW Synod, URC, 1981–92; Gen. Sec., URC, 1992–2001. Chm. of Corps, Council for World Mission, 1995–99. Religious broadcasting for radio and TV. Publications: In The Quietness, 1981; Say One For Me, 1990; Jesus in Nazareth, 2017. Recreations: theatre, jazz. Address: 30 Sandhurst Road, Didsbury, Manchester M20 5LR.

**BURNHAM, Eleanor**; Member (Lib Dem) Wales North, National Assembly for Wales, March 2001–2011; b 17 April 1951; one s one d. Educ: Radbrook Coll., Shrewsbury; Yale Coll., Wrexham; Manchester Metropolitan Univ. (BSc). Worked in social services, healthcare and arts mgt; teacher; lectr in complementary therapy and complementary health practitioner. Formerly Mem., Mental Health Tribunal. National Assembly for Wales: Lib Dem spokesman for post 16 educn, 2001, for envmt, planning and transport, 2001–03, for culture, sport and Welsh lang., 2003–11, for children and young people, 2007–11; Lib Dem Shadow Minister for culture, communities and equality, 2007–11; Older Persons' Champion, 2007–11. Contested: (Lib Dem) Alyn and Deeside, 1997; (Lib Dem) Delyn, 1999, Clwyd W, 2003, Wales N, 2011, Nat. Assembly for Wales. Mem., N Wales Community Health Council. Volunteer, Robert Jones and Agnes Hunt Orthopaedic Hosp., Oswestry. JP Wrexham, 1992–2001.

**BURNLEY, Bishop Suffragan of**, since 2015; **Rt Rev. Philip John North**; Priest-in-charge, St Mark's, Burnley, since 2019; b London, 2 Dec. 1966; s of John and Christine North. Educ: Latymer Sch., Edmonton; Univ. of York (BA Hons Hist. 1988); St Stephen's House, Oxford (MA Theol. 2001). Ordained deacon, 1992, priest, 1993; Asst Curate, St Mary and St Peter, Sunderland, 1992–96; Vicar, Holy Trinity, Hartlepool, 1996–2002; Area Dean of Hartlepool, 2000–02; Priest Administrator, Shrine of Our Lady of Walsingham, 2002–08; Team Rector, Parish of Old St Pancras, 2008–15. Publications: Sacred Space, 2007. Recreations: fell walking, road cycling. Address: Dean House, 449 Padiham Road, Burnley BB12 6TE. T: (01254) 503087. E: bishop.burnley@blackburn.anglican.org.

**BURNLEY, Elizabeth, (Liz)**, CBE 2010; b 14 March 1959; d of Joan and Jack Noden; m 2000, Roger Burnley. Educ: Univ. of Nottingham (BSc Hons Psychol.; MSc Occupational Psychol.); Open Univ. (MBA 2009). Human Resources Manager: British Rail Engrg Ltd, 1982–87; RFS Engrg Ltd, 1987–93; occupational psychologist: Barnes Kavelle Ltd, 1994–98; Boots Co. plc, 1998–2001; HR Manager, Huntsman, 2001–07; Chief Guide, Girlguiding UK, 2006–11. Programme Dir, Common Purpose, 2007–10. Non-exec. Dir, NHS, 2010–13. Lay Member: Fitness to Practise Cttee, Gen. Pharmaceutical Council, 2011–19; Judicial Appts Bd Scotland, 2016–; Chair of panels, Conduct and Competence Cttee, NMC, 2013–. Trustee, RVS (formerly WRVS), 2011–15. DL S Yorks, 2011–14. Recreations: girlguiding, hill-walking, interesting textile crafts.

**BURNLEY, Roger Michael**; Chief Executive Officer and President, Asda, since 2018; b Dewsbury, June 1966; s of Michael Burnley and Barbara Burnley; m Lucy; one s one d. Educ: Heckmondwike Grammar Sch.; Univ. of Bournemouth (BSc 1st Cl. Hons Geog.). J. Sainsbury plc: Supply Chain Dir, 2006; Retail and Ops Dir; Chief Ops Officer, Asda, 2016–18. Non-exec. Dir, Huddersfield Town FC. Fundraising Bd, Cystic Fibrosis Trust. Recreations: cycling, sailing, flyfishing. Clubs: Appletreewick, Barden and Burnsall Angling.

**BURNS**, family name of **Baron Burns**.

**BURNS**, Baron cr 1998 (Life Peer), of Pitshanger in the London Borough of Ealing; **Terence Burns**, GCB 1995; Kt 1983; Chairman, Ofcom, since 2018; b 13 March 1944; s of Patrick Owen and Doris Burns; m 1969, Anne Elizabeth Powell; one s two d. Educ: Houghton-le-Spring Grammar Sch.; Univ. of Manchester (BAEcon Hons). London Business School: research posts, 1965–70; Lecturer in Economics, 1970–74; Sen. Lectr in Economics, 1974–79; Prof. of Economics, 1979; Director, LBS Centre for Economic Forecasting, 1976–79, Fellow, 1989; Chief Econ. Advr to the Treasury and Hd of Govt Econ. Service, 1980–91; Perm. Sec., HM Treasury, 1991–98. Member, HM Treasury Academic Panel, 1976–79. Chm., Financial Services and Mkts Jt Cttee, 1999; non-exec. Mem., Office for Budget Responsibility, 2011–18. Chm., Cttee of Inquiry into Hunting with Dogs, 2000. Chairman: Nat. Lottery Commn, 2000–01; Commn on Freedom of Information, 2015–. Chairman: Abbey (formerly Abbey National) plc, 2002–10; Santander UK plc, 2010–15; Channel 4 Television, 2010–16; Dep. Chm. and Chm.-designate, 2005–06, Chm., 2006–08, Marks & Spencer; non-executive Director: Legal & General Group plc, 1999–2001; Pearson plc, 1999–2010; British Land Co. plc, 2000–05; Glas Cymru Cyfyngedig, 2000–10; Banco Santander Central Hispano SA, 2004–13. Pres., NIESR, 2003–11. Pres., Soc. of Business Economists, 1999–2012 (Vice-Pres., 1985–99); Vice-Pres., REconS, 1992–. CCMI (CIMgt 1992). Bd Mem., Manchester Business Sch., 1992–98. Dir, Queens Park Rangers FC, 1996–2000. Vice-Pres., Royal Acad. of Music, 1998–2014 (former Chm. Governing Body). Trustee, Monteverdi Choir and Orch., 1998–2001 (Chm. Trustees, 2001–07); Chm., Mid-Wales Music Trust (formerly Cambrian Music Trust), 2010–. Hon. degrees: Manchester Univ.; Sunderland Univ.; Durham Univ.; Sheffield Univ.; Cardiff Univ.; Cardiff Metropolitan Univ. Publications: various articles in economic jls. Recreations: music, golf. Club: Reform.

**BURNS, Alison Sarah**; Strategic Business Consultant, Powell Communications, since 2012; b 26 April 1963; d of Roy Butler and Judith Cornwell; m 1996, Anthony John Burns; one d. Educ: Univ. of York (BA Hons 1984). Account Management: Fletcher Shelton Delaney, 1984–86; Boase Massimi Pollitt, 1986–89; Bartle Bogle Hegarty, 1989–92; Young and Rubicam, 1992–93; Global Vice Pres., Mktg, PepsiCo, 1993–96; CEO, Kendall Tarrant, 1996–98; Pres., Fallon McElligott, 1998–2003; CEO, JWT London, 2006–09; Global Client Services Dir, JWT, New York, 2009. Recreations: sport, interior design, travel, good food and wine.

**BURNS, Prof. Alistair Stanyer**, CBE 2015; MD; FRCP, FRCPsych; Professor of Old Age Psychiatry, and Hon. Consultant Psychiatrist, University of Manchester, since 1992; National Clinical Director for Dementia, since 2010; b 4 July 1958; s of Richard and Janet Burns; m 1986, Alison Wise; two d. Educ: Hutchesons' Boys' Grammar Sch., Glasgow; Univ. of Glasgow (MB ChB 1980; MD Hons 1991; DHMSA 1984; MPhil London 1990). FRCPGlas 1993; FRCPsych 1996. Registrar in Psychiatry, Maudsley Hosp., 1983–86; Institute of Psychiatry, London: res. worker/Sen. Registrar, 1986–91; Sen. Lectr, 1991–92. Publications: Alzheimer's Disease, 1992; Ageing and Dementia, 1993; Dementia, 1994, 2nd edn 2001; Rating Scales in Old Age Psychiatry, 2000; Alzheimer's Disease Explained, 2005; Severe Dementia, 2005; Geriatric Medicine for Old Age Psychiatrists, 2005; Standards of Care in Dementia, 2005; over 300 contribs to med. and scientific jls. Recreations: estate management, walking, cars, writing. Address: University of Manchester, Room 3.304, Jean McFarlane Building, Oxford Road, Manchester M13 9PL. T: (0161) 306 7942. E: Alistair.Burns@manchester.ac.uk.

**BURNS, Sir Andrew**; see Burns, Sir R. A.

**BURNS, Rear Adm. Andrew Paul**, OBE 2015; Commander, United Kingdom Maritime Strike Force and Rear Admiral Surface Ships, since 2019; b Portsmouth, 20 Nov. 1969; s of Bryan Burns and Pamela Burns; m 2000, Wendy Smart; one s. Educ: Portsmouth Grammar Sch.; Sherborne Sch.; Durham Univ. (BA Hons Geog.); King's Coll. London (MA Defence Studies). Joined RN, 1989; Commanding Officer: HMS Berkeley, 1997–99; HMS Somerset, 2008–11; HMS Bulwark, 2012–13; Comdr, Amphibious Task Gp, 2016–18. Trustee: Naval Rev., 2017–; Devon Wildlife Trust, 2018–. Vice Pres., RNRU, 2017–. Vis. Fellow, Pembroke Coll., Oxford, 2016. FRGS; FCMI. Freeman, Coachmakers' and Coach Harness Makers' Co. Younger Brother, Trinity House. Recreations: cricket, Rugby, natural history, geopolitics, art, modern history. Address: c/o Naval Secretary, Navy Command Headquarters, Whale Island, Portsmouth PO2 8BY. T: (023) 9262 5542. E: navynavsec-acnspecs@mod.uk. Club: MCC.

**BURNS, Andrew Philip**, QC 2015; a Recorder, since 2009; b Bromsgrove, 8 April 1971; s of Christopher Burns and Lynne Burns; m 1995, Ruth Farries; two s. Educ: Dover Grammar Sch. for Boys; Downing Coll., Cambridge (BA Law 1992; MA). Called to the Bar, Middle Temple, 1993, Bencher, 2018; in practice as barrister, specialising in commercial and employment law; Advocate, DIFC Courts, Dubai, 2011–. Mem., Professional Conduct Cttee, Bar Standards Bd, 2007–13. Churchwarden, St Andrew's, Oxshott, 2006–10; Dep. Chancellor, Dio. of Guildford, 2018. Publications: (with Colin Edelman, QC) The Law of Reinsurance, 2005, 2nd edn 2013; Discrimination Law, 2012; (with Sir David Bean) Injunctions, 11th edn 2012 to 13th edn 2018. Recreations: Scout leader, water sports, music, opera, Doctor Who, Scotch malt whisky. Address: Devereux Chambers, Queen Elizabeth Building, Temple, EC4Y 9BS. T: (020) 7353 7534. E: burns@devchambers.co.uk.

**BURNS, Anna Mary**; writer, since 1995 (self-employed, since 1999); b Belfast, 7 March 1962; d of James Burns and Ann Burns. Educ: Coll. of Business Studies, Belfast (night sch.); Rupert Stanley Coll. of Further Educn, Belfast (night sch.); Queen Mary Coll., Univ. of London. Chambermaid, I of M, 1978; office jun., Belfast, 1978; office worker, Youth Trng Prog., Belfast, 1979; typist: Housing Exec., Belfast, 1979–80; NI Civil Service, 1979–82; copytaker (pt-time): Belfast Telegraph, Ireland Saturday Night and Irish News, 1982–87; Daily Telegraph, Sunday Telegraph, Independent, Independent on Sunday, 1987–92. Publications: No Bones, 2001; Little Constructions, 2007; Mostly Hero (novella), 2014; Milkman, 2018 (Man Booker Prize, 2018; US Nat. Book Critics Circle Award for Fiction, 2018; Orwell Prize, 2019). Recreations: walking, swimming, yoga, spending time with my friends and family. Address: c/o David Grossman Literary Agency, 9 Lamington Street, W6 0HU. T: (020) 8741 2860. E: general@dglal.co.uk.

**BURNS, Rt Hon. Conor**; PC 2019; MP (C) Bournemouth West, since 2010; Minister of State, Department for International Trade, since 2019; b Belfast, 24 Sept. 1972; s of Thomas Burns and Kathleen Burns (née Kennedy). Educ: St Columba's Coll., St Albans; Southampton Univ. (BA Hons Modern Hist. and Politics 1994). Co. Sec., De Havilland Global Knowledge Distribution plc, 1998–2003; Regl Sales Manager, Zurich Advice Network, 2003–04; self-employed, 2004–08; Associate Dir, PLMR, 2008–10. Mem. (C) Southampton CC, 1999–2002. Contested (C) Eastleigh, 2001, 2005. PPS to Minister of State in NI Office, 2010–11, to Sec. of State for NI, 2011–12, to Financial Sec. to the Treasury, 2015–16, to Sec. of State for Business, Energy and Industrial Strategy, 2016–17, to Sec. of State for Foreign and Commonwealth Affairs, 2017–18. Member: Educn Select Cttee, 2010; Culture, Media and Sport Select Cttee, 2012–15. Mem. Exec., 1922 Cttee, 2013–15. Chm., Margaret Thatcher Centre; Trustee, Cherish Freedom Trust. Recreations: swimming, cooking, watching snooker, collecting political biography. Address: House of

Commons, SW1A 0AA. *T:* (020) 7219 2071. *E:* conor.burns.mp@parliament.uk, cb@conorburns.com. *Clubs:* Southern Parishes Conservative (Life Mem.) (Southampton); Westbourne Conservative, Kinson Conservative (Bournemouth).

**BURNS, Elizabeth Kerr,** CMG 2005; OBE 1995; President and Chief Executive, International Association for Volunteer Effort, 2001–07; *b* 6 Jan. 1939; *d* of Thomas Thomson and Morag Thomson (*née* Cunningham); *m* 1964, William Burns (*d* 2000); two *s* one *d. Educ:* Edinburgh Univ. (MA Hons; DipEd); Moray House Coll. (Cert. Chapter V). Teacher of modern langs, 1962–67; Develt Officer, SCVO, 1981–83; Dir, Volunteer Develt Scotland, 1983–2001. Active in Scottish Playgps' Assoc., 1970–81 (Nat. Chair, 1978–80; Pres., 1986–90). Mem., Govt Strategy Gps, 1994–95, 1999–2000 and 2000–01. Chair, Historic Envmt Adv. Council for Scotland, 2003–09. Board Member: Scottish Community Educn Council, 1998–2000; Learning & Teaching Scotland, 2000–02. Pres., Eur. Volunteer Centre, 1998–2000. Member: UN Dept of Public Information liaison cttee for voluntary sector, 2007–10; High-level Adv. Gp for UN Report on volunteering in the world, 2011. *Publications:* contrib. papers to specialist and res. jls in field of volunteering. *Recreations:* reading, reading, reading.

**BURNS, Gerard,** MBE 1988; Pro-Chancellor, 2001–10, and Chairman of Council, 2002–10, University of Ulster; *b* 15 Nov. 1934; *s* of Bernard and Sarah Ellen Burns; *m* 1962, Moyra Connolly; three *s* two *d. Educ:* St Mary's Christian Brothers Grammar Sch.; Queen's Univ., Belfast. Divl Inspector, Trading Standards, NI, 1954–68; Lectr in Business Studies, Armagh Coll. of Further and Higher Educn, 1968–76; Chief Exec., Fermanagh DC, 1976–96; Assembly Ombudsman for NI and Comr for Complaints, 1995–2000. Chm., Review Body on Post Primary Educn, NI, 2000–02. Dir, Irish Times Ltd, 1997–2007; Gov., Irish Times Trust Ltd, 1997–2007. Member: EOC, NI, 1979–85; Historic Bldgs Council, 1988–91; Regl Council, Nat. Trust, 1989–94; Solicitors' Disciplinary Tribunal, NI, 1989–2009; Local Govt Staff Commn, 1990–95; Standing Adv. Commn on Human Rights, 1996–2000; NI Cttee, Heritage Lottery Fund, 2009–16. Mem., NI Tourist Bd, 1992–96. Chm., Ind. Appts Commn, Irish FA, 2008–11. Dir, Fermanagh Training Ltd, 1990–2010. Chm., Soc. of Local Authority Chief Execs (NI), 1990–92. Chairman: Fermanagh Univ. Foundn, 1998–2005; Fermanagh-Univ. Partnership Bd, 2001–05. Mem., Clogher and Kilmore Diocesan Cttee for Catholic Maintained Schools, 1987–95. Trustee, Spirit of Enniskillen Trust, 1988–2002 (Vice-Pres., 2002–12); Chm., Enniskillen Civic Trust, 1988–. Patron: Marie Curie Nursing Gp, Co. Fermanagh, 1998–2007; Fermanagh Co. Museum, 1999–2016. DUniv QUB, 1996; Hon. LLD Ulster, 2009. *Recreations:* walking, swimming, the arts.

**BURNS, Sir Henry James Gerard,** Kt 2011; FRCS, FRCP, FFPH; Professor of Global Public Health, University of Strathclyde, since 2014; *b* 25 Jan. 1951; *s* of Henry Burns and Mary (*née* Boyle); *m* 1983, Agnes Capaldi; two *s* four *d. Educ:* St Aloysius Coll., Glasgow; Glasgow Univ. (MB, ChB). FRCS 1979; MPH 1990; MFPHM 1993, FFPH (FFPHM 2005); FRCP 2000. Glasgow University: Lectr in Surgery, 1975–83; Sen. Lectr, 1983–89; Dir of Public Health, Gtr Glasgow Health, then NHS, Bd, 1994–2005; CMO, Scottish Govt (formerly Exec.) Health Directorate, 2005–14. Mem., MRC, 2007–09. *Recreations:* cycling, running.

**BURNS, Ian Morgan,** CB 1990; Director-General, Policy (formerly Director of Policy), Lord Chancellor's Department, 1995–99; *b* 3 June 1939; *s* of late Donald George Burns and Margaret Brenda Burns; *m* 1965, Susan Rebecca (*née* Wheeler); two *d. Educ:* Bootham, York. LLB, LLM London. HM Forces, 1957–59. Examiner, Estate Duty Office, 1960; Asst Principal, 1965, Principal, 1969, Home Office; Principal, 1972, Asst Sec., 1974, NI Office; Asst Sec., Home Office, 1977; Under Sec., NI Office, 1979–84; Under Sec. (Finance), 1985, and Gen. Manager, Disablement Services, 1986, DHSS; Deputy Under Secretary of State: NI Office, 1987–90; Police Dept, Home Office, 1990–95. FRSA 1993. *Recreations:* travelling, theatre, garden. *Club:* Athenæum.

**BURNS, James Andrew;** Head of Americas, Clyde & Co. LLP, since 2016 (Senior Partner, 2013–16); *b* Merton, London, 5 Oct. 1967; *s* of Michael Lowrie Burns and Mary Susan Burns (*née* Miller); *m* 2009, Catherine Bly; two *s* one *d. Educ:* Beverley Boys Sch., Surrey; Kent Univ. (BA Hons Law). Admitted as solicitor, 1992. With Clyde & Co., 1989–; trainee solicitor, 1989; Partner, 1998–. Freeman, City of London, 2014. *Recreations:* all types of sport, theatre. *Address:* Clyde & Co. LLP, 101 2nd Street, San Francisco, CA 94105, USA. *E:* james.burns@clydeco.com.

**BURNS, Julian Delisle;** company director; a founder and Director, All3Media, 2003–14 (Chief Operating Officer, 2003–11); *b* 18 Sept. 1949; *s* of Benedict Delisle Burns, FRS and of Angela Hugheson (*née* Ricardo); *m* 1976, Cheryl Ann Matthews; one *s* one *d. Educ:* Betteshanger Prep. Sch., Kent; Haberdashers' Aske's Sch., Elstree. Manager, Mendel's Garage, Hampstead, 1968–71; musician, various musical groups, 1972–75; Granada Television Ltd, 1976–2004: Prodn Manager, Regl Progs, 1976–80; Manager, Prog. Services, 1980–86; Hd, Business Affairs, 1986–90; Dir, Business and Legal Affairs, 1990–94; Jt Man. Dir, 1994–96; Jt Man. Dir, Granada Production, 1996–2000; Man. Dir, Ops, Granada plc, 2000–02. Dir, Royal Exchange Theatre, Manchester, 1995–2003. Member: Adv. Cttee on Film Finance, DNH, 1996–2001; Adv. Cttee on TV Production, DCMS, 1999–2001; Bd, 2002 Commonwealth Games, 1998–2002; Bd, Liverpool FC, 1999–2007. Trustee: Camden CAB, 2013–16; Burgh Hse, 2013–; Hofesh Shechter Co., 2014–18; Sadlers Wells, 2014–17. *Recreations:* walking, reading, music, television, art, the Lake District.

**BURNS, Kevin Francis Xavier,** CMG 1984; HM Diplomatic Service, retired; *b* 18 Dec. 1930; *s* of late Frank Burns and Winifred Burns (*née* O'Neill); *m* 1st, 1963, Nan Pinto (*d* 1984); one *s* two *d*; 2nd, 1992, Elizabeth Hassell. *Educ:* Finchley Grammar Sch.; Trinity Coll., Cambridge (BA 1953). CRO, 1956–58; Asst Private Sec. to Sec. of State, 1958; 2nd Sec., 1959, 1st Sec., 1960–63, Colombo; CRO/FO, 1963–67; 1st Sec., Head of Chancery and Consul, Montevideo, 1967–70; FCO, 1970–73; Counsellor, UK Mission, Geneva, 1973–79; RCDS, 1979; Head of SE Asian Dept, FCO, 1980–83; High Comr, Ghana, and Ambassador, Togo, 1983–86; High Comr, Barbados and Eastern Caribbean States, 1986–90; Personnel Assessor, FCO, 1991–99; Harassment Investigator, FCO, 2000–06. *Address:* 11 Wentworth Hall, The Ridgeway, NW7 1RJ.

**BURNS, Linda Hamilton;** *see* Urquhart, L. H.

**BURNS, Margaret,** CBE 2003; Chair, Institute of Occupational Medicine, since 2015; *b* Glasgow, 30 Dec. 1956; *d* of Jim and Jean Burns; *m* 1985, Dr John S. Callender; two *s* one *d. Educ:* Kilsyth Acad.; Glasgow Univ. (LLB Hons 1977). Legal Adv. Officer, Scottish Consumer Council, 1981–86; Scottish Affairs Consultant, Consumers' Assoc., 1987–91; Teaching Fellow (pt-time), Law Faculty, Univ. of Aberdeen, 1988–2008. Chair: Partnership for Health and Safety in Scotland, 2005–07; NHS Health Scotland, 2007–15; Member: HSC, 1998–2007 (Chair, Rail Industry Adv. Cttee, 2001–05); Cttee on Radioactive Waste Mgt, 2007–12. Non-exec. Mem., NHS Grampian Health Bd, 2003–09. Mem., Scottish Cttee, Council on Tribunals, 1992–98. Chair: PTA, Ferryhill Primary Sch.,  1995–99; Sch. Bd, Harlaw Acad., 2004–09. Trustee, Inst. of Occupational Medicine, 2011–. *Recreations:* family, walking, reading, cooking, looking at art. *Club:* Capelrigg Climbing.

**BURNS, Richard Ronald James;** company director; Partner, Baillie Gifford & Co., 1977–2006; *b* Gourock, 5 May 1946; *s* of Ronald and Mary Burns; *m* 1st, 1974, Catriona Douglas Walker (marr. diss. 1994); two *s* one *d*; 2nd, 1994, Catherine Ogilvie Bryson; one *d. Educ:* Dundee High Sch.; Craigflower Prep. Sch.; Trinity Coll., Glenalmond; Merton Coll., Oxford (BA Mod. Hist. 1967); Univ. of Edinburgh (LLB 1969). WS 1972. Apprentice and Asst Solicitor, W. & J. Burness, 1969–73; Trainee Investment Manager, Baillie Gifford & Co., 1973–2006. Chairman: Mid Wynd International Investment Trust plc, 2012–16 (Dir, 1981–); Aberdeen Standard Equity Income (formerly Standard Life Equity Investment) Trust plc, 2014– (Dir, 2006–); JPMorgan Indian Investment Trust plc, 2015– (Dir, 2006–); Director: EP Global Opportunities Trust plc, 2003–14; Bankers Investment Trust plc, 2006–15. Trustee: Donaldson Trust, 1999–2013; Dundee Disabled Children's Assoc., 2001–; Carnegie Trust for Univs of Scotland, 2005–19; Nat. Galls of Scotland, 2007–13; Paxton Trust, 2012–; Nat. Liby of Scotland Foundn, 2014–. Mem. Court, Univ. of Dundee, 2006–14. *Recreations:* reading, foreign travel, golf. *Address:* 31 Saxe Coburg Place, Edinburgh EH3 5BP. *T:* (0131) 332 5819. *Clubs:* New (Edinburgh); Royal and Ancient Golf (St Andrews).

**BURNS, Sir (Robert) Andrew,** KCMG 1997 (CMG 1992); HM Diplomatic Service, retired; *b* 21 July 1943; *e s* of late Robert Burns, CB, CMG and Mary Burns (*née* Goodland); *m* 1973, Sarah Cadogan, JP; two *s* and one step *d. Educ:* Highgate Sch.; Trinity Coll., Cambridge. BA (Classics), MA. Entered Diplomatic Service, 1965; UK Mission to UN, NY, 1965; FO 1966; Sch. of Oriental and African Studies, 1966–67; Univ. of Delhi, 1967; served New Delhi, FCO, and UK Delegation to CSCE, 1967–76; First Secretary and Head of Chancery, Bucharest, 1976–78; Private Sec. to Perm. Under Sec. and Head of Diplomatic Service, FCO, 1979–82; Fellow, Center for Internat. Affairs, Harvard Univ., 1982–83; Counsellor (Information), Washington, and Head of British Information Services, NY, 1983–86; Head of S Asian Dept, FCO, 1986–88; Head of News Dept, FCO, 1988–90; Asst Under-Sec. of State (Asia), FCO, 1990–92; Ambassador to Israel, 1992–95; Dep. Under Sec. of State, FCO, 1995–97; Consul-Gen., Hong Kong and Macau, 1997–2000; High Comr to Canada, 2000–03. Director: J. P. Morgan Chinese Investment Trust, 2003–16; Aberdeen All Asia, later Aberdeen Japan, Investment Trust, 2008–16. Internat. Gov., BBC, 2005–06. Chm., Bar Standards Bd, 2015–17. UK Envoy for post-Holocaust Issues, 2010–15. Chairman: Exec. Cttee, Anglo-Israel Assoc., 2004–05, 2008–11; Internat. Holocaust Remembrance Alliance, 2014–15; Steering Cttee, Anglo-Israel Colloquia, 2016–; Oasis of Peace UK, 2017–. Chm., Adv. Council, British Expertise (formerly British Consultants and Construction Bureau), 2006–09; Member: British N Amer. Cttee, 2004–13; British N Amer. Res. Assoc., 2004–13. Chm. Council, Royal Holloway, Univ. of London, 2004–11 (Mem., 2003–11); Vice-Chm., 2007–08, Chm., 2008–11, Cttee of University Chairs; Chm., Trinity in the Arts and Media Assoc., 2009–14; Trustee: UK Foundn, Univ. of BC, 2004–11; Foundn for Canadian Studies, 2008–14; Mem., Bd of Govs, GSMD, 2010–19. President: Canada UK Colloquia, 2004–11; China Assoc., 2008–14; Mem., HK Soc. Cttee, 2008–11. Chairman: Hestercombe Gardens Trust, 2004–; Internat. Polar Foundn UK, 2006–18; Oasis of Peace UK, 2017–. FRSA 1997; Fellow, Portland Trust, 2004. *Publications:* Diplomacy, War and Parliamentary Democracy, 1985. *Recreations:* choral singing, theatre, Exmoor. *Address:* Walland Farm, Wheddon Cross, Minehead, Somerset TA24 7EE. *Clubs:* Garrick, Royal Automobile, Royal Over-Seas League; Hong Kong.

**BURNS, Sandra Pauline,** CB 1989; Parliamentary Counsel, 1980–91, retired; *b* 19 June 1938; *d* of John Burns and Edith Maud Burns. *Educ:* Manchester Central High Sch.; Somerville Coll., Oxford (BCL, MA). Called to the Bar, Middle Temple, 1964. *Recreation:* painting. *Address:* 9 Lark Hill, Oxford OX2 7DR.

**BURNS, Rt Hon. Sir Simon (Hugh McGuigan),** Kt 2015; PC 2011; *b* 6 Sept. 1952; *s* of late Brian Stanley Burns, MC, and Shelagh Mary Nash; *m* 1982, Emma Mary Clifford (marr. diss. 2000); one *s* one *d. Educ:* Christ the King Sch., Accra, Ghana; Stamford Sch.; Worcester Coll., Oxford (BA Hons Modern History). Political Adviser to Rt Hon. Sally Oppenheim, 1975–81; Dir, What to Buy Ltd, 1981–83; Policy Exec., Inst. of Dirs, 1983–87. MP (C) Chelmsford W, 1997–2010, Chelmsford, 1987–97 and 2010–17. PPS to Minister of State: Dept of Employment, 1989–90; Dept of Educn, 1990–92; DTI, 1992–93; PPS to Minister of Agric., Fisheries and Food, 1993–94; an Asst Govt Whip, 1994–95; a Lord Comr of HM Treasury (Govt Whip), 1995–96; Parly Under-Sec. of State, DoH, 1996–97; Opposition spokesman on: social security, 1997–98; envmt, housing and planning, 1998–99; health, 2001–05; an Opposition Whip, 2005–10; Minister of State: DoH, 2010–12; DfT, 2012–13. Mem., Health Select Cttee, 1999–2005. Treas., 1922 Cttee, 1999–2001, 2015–17 (Mem. Exec., 1999). *Recreations:* American politics, reading, swimming, travelling. *Club:* Essex.

**BURNS, Thomas;** Member (SDLP) South Antrim, Northern Ireland Assembly, 2003–11; *b* Antrim, 19 Aug. 1960; *m* Therese; three *s. Educ:* trained as electrical engr. Mem. (SDLP), Antrim and Newtownabbey (formerly Antrim) BC, 1997–. Founder Mem., Crumlin Credit Union; Dir, Antrim Dist CAB. Governor: Rathenraw Integrated Primary Sch.; St Joseph's Primary Sch.; Crumlin High Sch. Specialist interest in dyslexia and autism support gps. Contested (SDLP) S Antrim, NI Assembly, 2011. *Recreations:* supporter of recycling and environmental issues, sport (supporter of St James', Aldergrove), committed to GAA youth initiatives and campaigner for development of recreational facilities in South Antrim.

**BURNS, Rt Rev. Thomas Matthew;** *see* Menevia, Bishop of, (R.C).

**BURNS, Prof. Thomas Patrick,** CBE 2006; MD, DSc; FRCPsych; Professor of Social Psychiatry, University of Oxford, 2003–14, now Emeritus; Fellow, Kellogg College, Oxford, 2003–14, now Emeritus; *b* 20 Sept. 1946; *s* of Reginald Burns and Jane Burns (*née* Cassidy); *m* 1976, Eva Burns-Lundgren; two *d. Educ:* Churchfields Comprehensive Sch., West Bromwich; Selwyn Coll., Cambridge (MA 1968, MB BChir 1971); Guy's Hosp., London; MD Cambridge 1984; DSc London 2020. FRCPsych 1984. Consultant Psychiatrist: University Hosp., Uppsala, 1980–83; St George's Hosp., London, 1983–93; Prof. of Community Psychiatry, St George's Hosp. Med. Sch., 1984–2003. Chm. Social Psych. Section, RCPsych, 1988–92. *Publications:* Assertive Outreach in Mental Health, 2002; Community Psychiatric Mental Health Teams: a guide to current practices, 2004; Psychiatry: a very short introduction, 2006, 2nd edn 2018; Our Necessary Shadow: the nature and meaning of psychiatry, 2013; (with E. Burn-Lundgren) Psychotherapy: a very short introduction, 2015; scientific articles on mental health care, anorexia nervosa in men, etc. *Recreations:* theatre, walking, armchair socialism. *Address:* Department of Psychiatry, University of Oxford, Warneford Hospital, Oxford OX3 7JX. *T:* (01865) 226474. *E:* tom.burns@psych.ox.ac.uk. *Club:* Athenæum.

**BURNS, William Joseph,** DPhil; President, Carnegie Endowment for International Peace, since 2015; Deputy Secretary of State, United States Department of State, 2011–14; *b* 11 April 1956; *s* of William F. and Margaret C. Burns; *m* 1984, Lisa A. Carty; two *d. Educ:* La Salle Univ. (BA Hist. 1978); St John's Coll., Oxford (MPhil 1980; DPhil 1981 Internat.

Relns). Special Asst to the President and Sen. Dir for Near East and S Asian Affairs, Nat. Security Council Staff, 1986–89; Actg Dir and Principal Dep. Dir for State Dept's Policy Planning Staff, 1989–93; Minister Counselor for Pol Affairs, Moscow, 1994–95; Exec. Sec. of the State Dept and Special Asst to the Sec. of State, 1996–98; Ambassador to Jordan, 1998–2001; Asst Sec. of State for Near Eastern Affairs, 2001–05; Ambassador to Russia, 2005–08; Under Sec. for Political Affairs, US Dept of State, 2008–11. Four hon. degrees. Three Presidential Dist. Service Awards. *Publications:* Economic Aid and American Policy Toward Egypt 1955–1981, 1985; The Back Channel: a memoir of American diplomacy and the case for its renewal, 2019. *Recreation:* sports. *Address:* Carnegie Endowment for International Peace, 1779 Massachusetts Avenue NW, Washington, DC 20036–2103, USA.

**BURNSIDE, David Wilson Boyd;** Chairman, New Century Media Ltd, since 2007; *b* 24 Aug. 1951; *s* of Jack and Betty Burnside; *m* 1999, Fiona Rennie; one *d*; and one *d* by a previous marriage. *Educ:* Coleraine Academical Instn; Queen's Univ. Belfast (BA). Teacher, 1973–74; Press Officer, Vanguard Unionist Party, 1974–76; PR Dir, Inst. of Dirs, 1979–84; Public Affairs Dir, British Airways, 1984–93. Chairman: DBA Ltd, 1993–; New Century Hldgs Ltd, 1995–. MP (UU) South Antrim, 2001–05; contested (UU) same seat, 2005. Mem., (UU) South Antrim, NI Assembly, 2003–09. *Recreations:* fishing, shooting, motorcycling. *Address:* The Hill, Secon, Ballymoney, Co. Antrim BT53 6QB. *Clubs:* Carlton; Portballintrae Boat; Coleraine and District Motor.

**BURNSIDE, John,** FRSL; FRSE; writer; *b* 19 March 1955; *m* 1996, Sarah Dunsby; two *s.* Prof. in Creative Writing, Univ. of St Andrews, 2009– (Reader, 1999). FRSL 1998; FRSE 2016. *Publications: poetry:* The Hoop, 1988; Common Knowledge, 1991; Feast Days, 1992; The Myth of the Twin, 1994; Swimming in the Flood, 1995; (jtly) Penguin Modern Poets 9, 1996; A Normal Skin, 1997; The Asylum Dance, 2000 (Whitbread Poetry Award, 2000); The Light Trap, 2002; (ed with M. Riordan) Wild Reckoning (anthology), 2004; The Good Neighbour, 2005; Selected Poems, 2006; Gift Songs, 2007; The Hunt in the Forest, 2009; Black Cat Bone, 2011 (Forward Poetry Prize, 2011; T. S. Eliot Prize, 2011); All One Breath 2014; Still Life with Feeding Snake, 2017; *fiction:* The Dumb House, 1997; The Mercy Boys, 1999; Burning Elvis, 2000; The Locust Room, 2001; Living Nowhere, 2003; The Devil's Footprints, 2007; Glister, 2008; A Summer of Drowning, 2011; Something Like Happy (short stories), 2013; Ashland & Vine, 2017; Havergey, 2017; *memoirs:* A Lie About My Father: a memoir, 2006; Waking Up in Toytown, 2010; I Put a Spell on You, 2014; *non-fiction:* John Burnside on Henry Miller, 2018. *Address:* c/o Anna Webber, United Agents, 12–26 Lexington Street, W1F 0LE.

**BURNSIDE, Stella Maris,** OBE 2003; Vice Lord-Lieutenant of County Londonderry, since 2015; *b* Ballynahinch, Co. Down, 22 Aug. 1949; *d* of Robert John Leahy and Elizabeth Leahy (née Baird); *m* 1977, Samuel John Burnside, MBE, PhD; one *s* two *d. Educ:* St Mary's High Sch., Downpatrick; Belfast City Hosp. (SRN 1970; RMN 1973); Magee Coll. (Nurse Tutors Dip. 1976); Univ. of Ulster (BPhil Hons 1987). Nursing, clinical teaching and nurse tutor, 1970–80; Asst Dir, Nurse Educn, Magee Coll., 1980; Unit Gen. Manager, Foyle Community Unit, 1989; Chief Executive: Altnagelvin Hosps Trust, 1996; Regulation and Quality Improvement Authy, 2004–07. Vis. Prof., Univ. of Ulster, 2006–11. Member: BBC Broadcasting Council NI, 1994–97; NHS Health Technol. Assessment Panel, 1997–2000; Equality Commn for NI, 2008–15; Independent Monitoring Bd for NI, 2013–16. Mem. Cttee, Baby Friendly Initiative, UNICEF, 2000–04. Lay Mem., Disciplinary Cttee, Bar Council for NI, 2003–15. Mem., Soroptomist Internat., Londonderry. DL Co. Londonderry, 2002. Medal for Strengthening the Combat Community, Russian Fedn, 2006. *Recreations:* travel (incl. visiting cathedrals), exploring Antrim, Donegal and Londonderry coast, music as much as possible, family and being a grandparent. E: stellaleahy@aol.com.

**BURNSTOCK, Prof. Geoffrey,** AC 2018; FRS 1986; FAA 1971; Emeritus Professor, Department of Pharmacology and Therapeutics, University of Melbourne, 1993; Hon. Professorial Fellow, Florey Institute of of Neuroscience and Mental Health, Melbourne, since 2017; Professor of Anatomy, University of London, 1975–2004, now Professor Emeritus; Professor and President, Autonomic Neuroscience Centre, UCL Medical School (formerly Royal Free and University College Medical School), 2004–17, and Convener, Centre for Neuroscience, 1979–2017, University College London; *b* 10 May 1929; *s* of James Burnstock and Nancy Green; *m* 1957, Nomi Hirschfeld; three *d. Educ:* King's Coll., London; Melbourne Univ. BSc 1953, PhD 1957 London; DSc Melbourne 1971. National Inst. for Medical Res., Mill Hill, 1956–57; Dept of Pharmacology, Oxford Univ., 1957–59; Rockefeller Travelling Fellowship, Univ. of Ill, 1959; University of Melbourne: Sen. Lectr, 1959–62, Reader, 1962–64, Dept of Zoology; Prof. of Zoology and Chm. of Dept, 1964–75; Associate Dean (Biological Sciences), 1969–72; Head, Dept of Anatomy and Embryology, then Anatomy and Developmental Biology, UCL, 1975–97, Fellow, UCL, 1996; Prof. and Dir, Autonomic Neurosci. Inst., Royal Free Med. Sch., 1997–2004. Vis. Prof., Dept of Pharmacology, Univ. of Calif, LA, 1970; Hon. Professorial Res. Fellow, Mental Health Res. Inst. of Vic, Australia, 2006. Numerous named lectures, 1976–, including: J. Z. Young, Oxford, 1999; G. W. Harris Prize, Physiol Soc., 1998; Prof. M. Rocha e Silva Award, Caxambu, Brazil, 1999; Horace Davenport Dist., Amer. Physiol. Soc., 2001; Stevenson Meml, London, Ont, 2003. Chm., Scientific Adv. Bd, Eisai London Ltd, 1990–96. Editor-in-Chief: Autonomic Neuroscience: Basic & Clinical, 1985–2016; Purinergic Signalling, 2004–; mem. editl bd of over 20 jls. Vice-Pres., Anatomical Soc. of GB and Ireland, 1990. Member: Academia Europaea, 1992; Russian Soc. of Neuropathology, 1993; Corresp. Academician, Real Acad. Nacional de Farmacia, Spain, 2003. Hon. Member: Physiol Soc., 2003; Pharmacol Soc., 2004; Hungarian Soc. of Exptl and Clin. Pharmacol., 2006; Australian Physiol Soc., 2008. Founder FMedSci 1998. Hon. MRCP 1987, Hon. FRCP 2000; Hon. FRCS 1999. Hon. MSc Melbourne 1962; Dr *hc:* Antwerp, 2002; J. W. Goethe, Frankfurt, 2007. Silver Medal, Royal Soc. of Victoria, 1976; Special Award, NIH Conf., Bethesda, USA, 1989; Royal Gold Medal, Royal Soc., 2000; Janssen Award in Gastroenterol., 2000; Copernicus Gold Medal, Univ. Degli Studi di Ferrara, 2009; Award for Outstanding Contribn to British Neurosci., British Neurosci. Assoc., 2009; Gaddum Meml Award, British Pharmacol Soc., 2010. *Publications:* (with M. Costa) Adrenergic Neurons: their Organisation, Function and Development in the Peripheral Nervous System, 1975; (with Y. Uehara and G. R. Campbell) An Atlas of the Fine Structure of Muscle and its Innervation, 1976; (ed) Purinergic Receptors, 1981; (ed with G. Vrbová and R. O'Brien) Somatic and Autonomic Nerve-Muscle Interactions, 1983; (ed with S. G. Griffith) Nonadrenergic Innervation of Blood Vessels, 1988; (ed with S. Bloom) Peptides: a target for new drug development, 1991; series editor, The Autonomic Nervous System, vols 1–15, 1992–2003; (ed jtly) Nitric Oxide in Health and Disease, 1997; (ed jtly) Cardiovascular Biology of Purines, 1998; (ed with A. Verkhratsky) Purinergic Signalling and the Nervous System, 2012; papers on smooth muscle and autonomic nervous system, incl. purinergic signalling in health and disease in sci. jls. *Recreations:* tennis, wood sculpture. *Address:* Department of Pharmacology and Therapeutics, University of Melbourne, Parkville, Vic 3010, Australia.

**BURNTON, Rt Hon. Sir Stanley (Jeffrey),** Kt 2000; PC 2008; a Lord Justice of Appeal, 2008–12; Arbitrator, since 2012; Interception of Communications Commissioner, 2015–17; *b* 25 Oct. 1942; *s* of Harry and Fay Burnton; *m* 1971, Gwenyth Frances Castle; one *s* two *d. Educ:* Hackney Downs Grammar Sch.; St Edmund Hall, Oxford (MA; Hon. Fellow, 2008). Called to the Bar, Middle Temple, 1965, Bencher, 1991 (Treas., 2010); QC 1982; a Recorder, 1994–2000; a Judge of the High Court of Justice, QBD, 2000–08. Chm., British and Irish Legal Information Inst., 2011–17; Sen. Legal Chm., Disciplinary Tribunals, Financial Reporting Council, 2016–. Trustee: British Inst. Internat. and Comparative Law, 2011–17; Slynn Foundn, 2014– (Pres., 2015–). Vis. Prof., QMUL, 2012–. Mem. Council, University Coll. Sch., 2013–16. *Recreations:* classical music, theatre, reading, travel. *Address:* One Essex Court, Temple, EC4Y 9AR.

**BURNYEAT, Myles Fredric,** CBE 2007; FBA 1984; Senior Research Fellow in Philosophy, All Souls College, Oxford, 1996–2006, now Emeritus Fellow; *b* 1 Jan. 1939; *s* of Peter James Anthony Burnyeat and Cynthia Cherry Warburg; *m* 1st, 1971, Jane Elizabeth Buckley (marr. diss. 1982); one *s* one *d*; 2nd, 1984, Ruth Sophia Padel (marr. diss. 2000); one *d*; 3rd, 2002, Heda Segvic (*d* 2003); partner, Margaret Hilda Bent, *qv. Educ:* Bryanston Sch.; King's Coll., Cambridge (BA). Qualified as Russian Interpreter (Civil Service Commn, 2nd Class), 1959. Assistant Lecturer in Philosophy 1964, Lecturer in Philosophy 1965, University Coll. London; Cambridge University: Lectr in Classics, 1978–84; Laurence Prof. of Ancient Philosophy, 1984–96; Fellow, 1978–96, Lectr in Philosophy, 1978–84, Hon. Fellow, 2006, Robinson Coll. For. Hon. Mem., Amer. Acad. of Arts and Scis, 1992. *Publications:* The Theaetetus of Plato, 1990; A Map of Metaphysics Zeta, 2001; Aristotle's Divine Intellect, 2008; co-editor: Philosophy As It Is, 1979; Doubt and Dogmatism, 1980; Science and Speculation, 1982; The Original Sceptics, 1997; (ed) The Skeptical Tradition, 1983; Explorations in Ancient and Modern Philosophy, 2 vols, 2012; contribs to classical and philosophical jls. *Recreation:* travel. *Address:* All Souls College, Oxford OX1 4AL.

**BURR, His Honour Michael Rodney;** a Circuit Judge, 1992–2008; a Deputy Circuit Judge, 2008–16; *b* 31 Aug. 1941; *s* of Frank Edward Burr and Aileen Maud Burr; *m* 1963, Rhoda Rule; four *s* one *d. Educ:* Brecon County Grammar Sch.; King Edward VI Sch., Chelmsford; Coll. of Law. Solicitor, 1964. Asst Solicitor, Hilliard & Ward, Chelmsford, 1964–69; Sen. Partner, Peter Williams & Co., Swansea, 1972–92; Recorder, 1988. Sec., Incorp. Law Soc. of Swansea and Dist, 1980–83; Law Society: non-Council Member: Professional Purposes Cttee, 1985–86; Adjudication Cttee, 1986–89. Mem., Parole Bd, 2008–18. *Recreations:* flying, travel.

**BURR, Timothy John,** CB 2008; Comptroller and Auditor General, National Audit Office, 2008–09 (Deputy Comptroller and Auditor General, 2000–08); *b* 31 March 1950; *s* of Eric Cyril Burr and Myrtle Burr (née Waters); *m* 1975, Gillian Heather Crosse; two *s. Educ:* Dulwich Coll.; Univ. of Southampton (MA). Entered HM Treasury, 1968; Cabinet Office, 1984; Asst Sec., HM Treasury, 1985; Under-Sec., Cabinet Office, 1990; Treasury Officer of Accounts, 1993–94; Asst Auditor Gen., Nat. Audit Office, 1994–2000. Mem., S Downs Nat. Park Authy, 2017–.

**BURRELL, Sir Charles Raymond,** 10th Bt *cr* 1774, of Valentine House, Essex; *b* 27 Aug. 1962; *s* of Sir (John) Raymond Burrell, 9th Bt, and of Rowena Frances, *d* of late M. H. Pearce; *S* father, 2008; *m* 1993, Isabella Elizabeth Nancy, adopted *d* of M. L. Tree; one *s* one *d. Educ:* Millfield; Royal Agricultural Coll., Cirencester. *Heir: s* Edward Lambert Burrell, *b* 10 Oct. 1996. *Address:* Knepp Castle, West Grinstead, Horsham, W Sussex RH13 8LJ.

**BURRELL, Diana Elizabeth Jane;** composer; Artistic Director: Spitalfields Festival, 2006–09; Harwich Festival of the Arts, 2012–14; *b* 25 Oct. 1948; *d* of Bernard Burrell and Audrey (née Coleman); *m* 1971, Richard Fallas; one *s* one *d. Educ:* Norwich High Sch.; Girton Coll., Cambridge Univ. (BA Hons Music). Music teacher, Sutton High Sch., 1971–75; freelance viola player and teacher, 1978–90; pianist, Holy Trinity Ch, Mile End, 1985–2006; part-time Lectr in Composition and 20th Century Studies, Goldsmiths' Coll., London, 1989–93; Composer-in-residence, Pimlico Sch., London, 1990–91; Living Composer, Eastern Orchestral Bd, 1993–95; Composer-in-Association, City of London Sinfonia, 1994–96; Composition Prof., GSMD, 1999–2006; AHRC Creative Arts Fellow, RAM, 2006–11. Recordings of own works (Classic CD Award, 1998, for Viola Concerto and other works). Hon. FTCL 1997. *Compositions* include: The Albatross (opera), 1987; commissions: Landscape, 1988; Resurrection, 1992; Dunkelhvide Månestråler, 1996; Clarinet Concerto (for Northern Sinfonia), 1996; Symphonies of Flocks, Herds and Shoals (for BBC SO), 1997; Concerto for Violin with Singer and 3 Ensembles, 2009; The Hours, 2011; Blaze (for tenThing), 2013; Concerto for Brass and Orchestra, 2016. *Recreations:* birdwatching, walking, gardening. *Address:* c/o United Music Publishers, 71 Chedburgh Road, Bury St Edmunds, Suffolk IP29 5QU.

**BURRELL, (Francis) Gary;** QC 1996; **His Honour Judge Burrell;** a Circuit Judge, since 2009; *b* 7 Aug. 1953; *s* of Francis Ivan George Burrell and Louisa Shane Burrell; *m* 1979, Heather Young; three *s. Educ:* Belfast Boys' Model Sch.; Univ. of Exeter (LLB). Called to the Bar, Inner Temple, 1977, Bencher, 2007; Asst Recorder, 1992–96; Recorder, 1996–2009; Dep. High Court Judge, 2001–. Mem., Bar Council, 1995–2010. Pres., S Yorks Medico-Legal Soc., 1991–92; NE Circuit Rep., Personal Injury Bar Assoc., 1995–97. *Recreations:* sailing, fly fishing. *Address:* Southampton Combined Court Centre, London Road, Southampton SO15 2XQ.

**BURRELL, Mark William;** DL; Director, Pearson plc, 1977–97; *b* 9 April 1937; *s* of Sir Walter Burrell, 8th Bt, CBE, TD and Hon. Anne Judith, OBE, *o d* of 3rd Baron Denman, PC, GCMG, KCVO; *m* 1966, Margot Rosemary Pearce; two *s* one *d. Educ:* Eton; Pembroke Coll., Cambridge (BA 1st Cl. Hons Engrg). With Sir Alexander Gibb & Partners, 1959, then Vickers, 1960–61; joined Pearson plc, 1963; Whitehall Petroleum: Dir, 1964–80; Chm., 1987–88; joined Lazard Brothers, 1970; Dir, 1974; Man. Dir, 1984–86; non-exec. Dir, 1986–97; Director: BSB Holdings, 1987–99; BSkyB Group plc, 1991–94; Dir, then Chm., Royal Doulton plc, 1993–98; Chm., Millbank Financial Services Ltd, 1986–; non-executive Director: RM plc, 1997–2001; Conafex SA, 1999–2008 (Chm.); Dir, then Chm., Merlin Communications Internat., 1997–2001. Mem. Ct, Sussex Univ. Gov., Northbrook Coll., Sussex, 2004–08. High Sheriff, 2002–03, DL, 2004, W Sussex. *Recreations:* hunting, polo, tennis, golf, ski-ing. *Address:* Bakers House, Bakers Lane, Shipley, W Sussex RH13 8GJ. *Club:* White's.

**BURRELL, Michael Peter;** Judge, Court of First Instance of High Court (formerly Judge, Supreme Court), Hong Kong, 1995–2010; President, Court of Appeal, Brunei Darussalam, since 2018; *b* 18 July 1948; *s* of Peter Burrell and Gwynneth Burrell; *m* 1975, Anne Hughes; two *d*, and one step *s. Educ:* Birkenhead Sch.; Magdalene Coll., Cambridge (MA). Called to the Bar, Inner Temple, 1971; in practice on Northern Circuit, 1972–86 (Junior, 1973); Hong Kong: Perm. Magistrate, 1986–90; Dist Judge, 1991–95. Mem., Hong Kong Judicial Studies Bd, 1992–95; Chm., Hong Kong Insider Dealing Tribunal, 1996–98; Mem., HK Internat. Arbitration Centre, 2009–; Judicial Comr, Court of Appeal, Brunei Darussalam, 2013–18. Fellow, HK Inst. of Arbitrators, 2009–. Hon. Fellow, HK Inst. of Surveyors, 2004. *Recreations:* sport, reading, walking. *Address:* 2 The Lodge, Vyner Road South, Noctorum CH43 7PS. *Clubs:* Artists' (Liverpool); Royal Liverpool Golf (Hoylake); Oxton Cricket (Wirral); Old Birkonian Football (Pres., 2014–17); Hong Kong, Hong Kong Cricket (Hong Kong).

**BURRELL, Prof. Robert Geoffrey,** PhD; Professor of Intellectual Property and Information Technology, University of Oxford, since 2019; Fellow, St Peter's College, Oxford, since 2019; *b* Rochford, 15 July 1973; *s* of Richard and Barbara Burrell; *m* 2002, Dr Gita Sarda; one *s* one *d*. *Educ*: Westcliff High Sch. for Boys; King's Coll. London (LLB, LLM); Griffith Univ. (PhD 2005). Lectr in Law, KCL, 1998–2002; Sen. Lectr in Law, ANU, 2002–05; Associate Prof. of Law, Univ. of Qld, 2005–12; Professor of Law: Univ. of WA, 2012–13; Univ. of Sheffield, 2013–19. Vis. Prof., Melbourne Law Sch., 2017–. *Publications*: (with A. Coleman) Copyright Exceptions: the digital impact, 2005; (with M. Handler) Australian Trademark Law, 2010, 2nd edn 2016. *Recreations*: mixed martial arts, making bread. *Address*: St Peter's College, New Inn Hall Street, Oxford OX1 2DL. *T*: (01865) 278900. *E*: robert.burrell@law.ox.ac.uk.

**BURRIDGE, Rev. Canon Prof. Richard Alan;** Dean, 1994–2019, and Professor of Biblical Interpretation, 2008–19, King's College London; Canon Theologian and Sarum Canon, Salisbury Cathedral, since 2013; Assistant Curate, St Mary-le-Strand with St Clement Danes, since 2017; *b* 11 June 1955; *s* of Alan Burridge and Iris Joyce (*née* Coates); *m* 1st, 1979, Susan Morgan (marr. diss. 2009); two *d*; 2nd, 2014, Megan Warner. *Educ*: University Coll., Oxford (Exhibnr; BA Lit.Hum. 1st Cl. Hons, MA 1981); Univ. of Nottingham (PGCE 1978; Postgrad. DTh 1984; PhD 1989); St John's Coll., Nottingham. Classics Master and House Tutor, Sevenoaks Sch., 1978–82; ordained deacon 1985, priest 1986; Curate, St Peter and St Paul, Bromley, Kent, 1985–87; Lazenby Chaplain, Univ. of Exeter and part-time Lectr, Depts of Theol. and of Classics and Ancient Hist., 1987–94; Dir of NT Studies, Dept of Theol. and Religious Studies, KCL, 2007–14 (FKC 2002). Mem., Gen. Synod of C of E, 1994–2015. Mem., Ethical Investment Adv. Gp, C of E, 2008–17 (Dep. Chair, 2010–15). Member: Council of Mgt, St John's Coll., Nottingham, 1986–99; Council of Ref., Monarch Pubns, Tunbridge Wells, 1992–2000. Mem., Academic Bd (formerly Bd of Studies), N Thames Ministerial Trng Course, 1994–2015; Ext. Examr, SW Ministerial Trng Course, 1995–99; Commissary, Bp of the High Veld, CPSA, 1997–2009. Member: SNTS, 1995–; Soc. for Study of Theol., 1995–; Soc. of Biblical Lit., 1996–. Expert Advr (Faith Zone, Greenwich Dome), Nat. Millennium Experience Co., 1998–2000. Chaplain to Hendon Golf Club, 2004–. Trustee: Christian Evidence Soc., 1994– (Chm., 2001–17); Foundn of St Catherine, Cumberland Lodge, 1998–2008. (Jtly) Ratzinger Prize for Theology, Joseph Ratzinger Benedict XVI Foundn, 2013. *Publications*: Sex Therapy: some ethical considerations, 1985; What are the Gospels?: a comparison with Graeco-Roman biography, 1992, 3rd edn 2018; Four Gospels, One Jesus?: a symbolic reading, 1994 (also Korean edn, 2000, 2nd edn 2017), 2nd edn 2005 (also US and Australian edns, US 3rd edn 2014), Classic edn 2013; John (People's Bible Commentary), 1998, Lambeth Conference edn 2008 (also US edn, 2007); Faith Odyssey: a journey through Lent, 2000; (ed jtly) The Lectionary Commentary, 2002; Faith Odyssey: a journey through life, 2003 (also Norwegian edn, 2003); (jtly) Jesus Now and Then, 2004; Imitating Jesus: an inclusive approach to New Testament ethics, 2007; *contributor to*: A Dictionary of Biblical Interpretation, 1990; The New Dictionary of Christian Ethics and Pastoral Theology, 1995; A Handbook of Classical Rhetoric in the Hellenistic Period 330 BC–AD 400, 1997; The Gospels for all Christians: rethinking the gospel audiences, 1998; Where Shall We Find God?, 1998; The Lion Handbook to the Bible, 1999; Christology, Community and Controversy, 2000; Dictionary of New Testament Background, 2000; The Story of Christian Spirituality, 2001; Exploring and Proclaiming the Apostles' Creed, 2004; The Dictionary for Theological Interpretation of Scripture, 2005; The Written Gospel, 2005; The Person of Christ, 2005; The Oxford Handbook of Biblical Studies, 2006; The Fourfold Gospel Commentary, 2006; Tutu As I Know Him: on a personal note, 2006; The Dictionary of Biblical Criticism and Interpretation, 2007; John, Jesus and History, vol. 2, 2009; Moral Language in the New Testament, 2010; The Dictionary of Scripture and Ethics, 2011; Jesus, Matthew's Gospel and Early Christianity, 2011; Reading Acts Today, 2011; The Gospels: history and Christology: the search of Joseph Ratzinger—Benedict XVI, 2013; Death, Resurrection and Human Destiny: Christian and Muslim perspectives, 2014; Vocabulary for the Study of Religion, 2015; Jesus and Brian: exploring the historical Jesus and his times via Monty Python's Life of Brian, 2015; Four Ministries One Jesus, 2017; (contrib.) Cooperatores Veritatis: tributes to Pope Emeritus Benedict XVI on his 90th birthday, 2017; (ed jtly) Confronting Religious Violence: a counternarrative, 2018; (contrib.) New Approaches to Biblical Ethics, 2018; articles in Theology, Church Times, St John the Evangelist Mag., C of E Newspaper, THES, Wholeness, Dialogue, The Times, Sewanee Theological Review. *Recreations*: being with my family, ski-ing, golf, cycling.

**BURRILL, Timothy;** Managing Director, Cranbury Productions Ltd, since 2014; Chairman, Film Asset Developments Plc, 1987–94; *b* 8 June 1931; *yr s* of L. Peckover Burrill, OBE and Marjorie S. Burrill; *m* 1st, 1959, Philippa (marr. diss. 1966), *o d* of Maurice and Margot Hare; one *d*, 2nd, 1968, Santa (marr. diss. 1993), *e d* of John and Betty Raymond; one *s* two *d*. *Educ*: Eton Coll.; Sorbonne Univ. Served Grenadier Guards, 1949–52: commnd 1950; served 2nd Bn, 1950–52. Jun. management, Cayzer Irvine & Co., 1952–56; entered film industry, 1956; joined Brookfield Prodns, 1965; Man. Dir, Burrill Prodns, 1966–2014; Dir, World Film Services, 1967–69; first Prodn Administrator, National Film and TV Sch., 1972; Man. Dir, Allied Stars (resp. for Chariots of Fire), 1979–80; Director: Artistry Ltd, 1982–87 (resp. for Superman and Supergirl films); Pathé (formerly Chargeurs) Productions Ltd, 1994–99; Pathé Pictures, 1994–99; Little Dragon Prodns Ltd, 2016–; Consultant: National Film Develt Fund, 1980–81; Really Useful Group, 1989–90; Script Factory, 1998–; Knight Dragon, 2014–15. UK Rep., Eurimages, 1994–96. Chairman: BAFTA, 1981–83 (Vice-Chm., 1979–81); First Film Foundn, 1989–98; Producer Mem., Cinematograph Films Council, 1980–85; Member: Gen. Council, ACTT, 1975–76; Exec. Council, British Film and Television Producers Assoc., 1981–89; Exec. Council, The Producers Assoc., 1989–91; Exec. Council, Producers' Alliance for Cinema and Television, 1991–2001 (Vice-Chm., 1993–94); Sir Peter Middleton's Adv. Cttee of Film Finance, 1996–97; Dir, British Film Commn, 1998–2000. Chm., Impact Campaign, 1994–95. Governor: National Film and Television Sch., 1981–92; National Theatre, 1982–88. Films include Tess, The Fourth Protocol, The Pirates of Penzance, The Pianist, Oliver Twist, La Vie en Rose, The Ghost, Playmobil: The Movie, etc. *Recreation*: theatre. *Address*: 19 Cranbury Road, SW6 2NS. *T*: (020) 7736 8673, *Fax*: (020) 7731 3921. *E*: timothy@timothyburrill.co.uk.

**BURROUGHES, Dr Jeremy Henley,** FRS 2012; FREng, FIET, FInstP; Chief Technology Officer, Cambridge Display Technology, since 2001; *b* Aug. 1960. With Toshiba, UK and Japan, 1991–97; Cambridge Display Technology Ltd: Co-founder, 1992; Tech. Dir, 1997–2000; Product Business Unit Dir, 2000–01. Dir, Opsys Ltd, 2004–11. Fellow, Sumitomo Chemical Co. Ltd. Vis. Prof. of Physics, Imperial Coll. London. FREng 2009. *Address*: Cambridge Display Technology Ltd, Unit 12, Cardinal Park, Cardinal Way, Godmanchester, Cambs PE29 2XG.

**BURROW, John Halcrow,** CBE 1993 (OBE 1987); QPM 1998; DL; Chief Constable of Essex Police, 1988–98; *b* 1935; *s* of John and Florence Burrow; *m* 1958, Ruth (*née* Taylor); two *s* one *d*. *Educ*: Ulverston Grammar School; University College London (LLB Hons). Lieut, 3rd Kenya Bn, King's African Rifles, 1953–55. Metropolitan Police, 1958–77; Asst/ Dep. Chief Constable, Merseyside Police, 1977–88; RCDS, 1979. Pres., ACPO, 1992–93; Chairman: Technical and Res. Cttee, ACPO, 1990–92; ACPO No 5 (SE) Region Cttee, 1991–98; Shotley Training Centre Cttee, 1990–92. Chairman: St John Ambulance, Essex, 2004–10 (Co. Comdr, 1999–2004); Essex Br., SSAFA, 2001–17. DL Essex, 1998. CStJ 2004. *Recreations*: travelling, gardening. *Address*: Acorns, Church End, Shalford, Braintree, Essex CM7 5HA. *T*: (01371) 850577.

**BURROWES, David John Barrington;** Chairman, Equity Release Council, since 2017; Executive Director, Strengthening Families Manifesto, since 2017; *b* 12 June 1969; *m* 1996, Janet; four *s* two *d* (of whom one *s* one *d* are twins). *Educ*: Highgate Sch.; Univ. of Exeter (LLB 1991). Asst Solicitor, Shepherd Harris and Co., Enfield, 1995–2005 and 2017–. Mem. (C), Enfield BC, 1994–2006 (Cabinet Mem. for voluntary and community develt, 2003–04). Contested (C) Edmonton, 2001. MP (C) Enfield Southgate, 2005–17; contested (C) same seat, 2017. Parliamentary Private Secretary: to Minister for Cabinet Office and Minister for Policy, 2010; to Minister for Policy, 2010–12; to Sec. of State for Envmt, Food and Rural Affairs, 2012–14. Gov., Dame Alice Owen's Sch., 2018–. *Publications*: (jtly) Moral Basis of Conservatism, 1995; Such a Thing as Society: Maggie's children and volunteering, 2006. *Recreations*: sports, particularly football and cricket.

**BURROWES, Norma Elizabeth;** opera and concert singer; teacher of classical voice and Baroque studies, York University, Toronto; *d* of Henry and Caroline Burrowes; *m* 1st, 1969, Steuart Bedford, *qv* (marr. diss.); 2nd, 1987, Emile Belcourt (*d* 2017); one *s* one *d*. *Educ*: Sullivan Upper Sch., Holywood, Co. Down; Queen's Univ., Belfast (BA); Royal Academy of Music (FRAM 1992). Operas include: Zerlina in Don Giovanni, Glyndebourne Touring Opera (début); Blöndchen in Die Entführung aus dem Serail, Salzburg Festival, and again Blöndchen, Paris Opera, 1976 (début); Fiakermili, Royal Opera House (début), also Oscar, Despina, Nanetta, Woodbird; Entführung aus dem Serail, Ballo in Maschera, Der Rosenkavalier, Metropolitan, NY; Daughter of the Regiment, Midsummer Night's Dream, Elisir d'Amore, Canada; Così Fan Tutte, Romeo and Juliet, France; Marriage of Figaro, Germany; Gianni Schicchi, Switzerland; Marriage of Figaro, La Scala. Television operas include: Nanetta in Falstaff; Susanna in Marriage of Figaro and Lauretta in Gianni Schicchi. Has sung regularly with major opera companies, giving concerts and recitals, GB and abroad; many recordings. Hon. DMus Queen's Univ. Belfast, 1979. *Recreations*: swimming, gardening, needlework and découpage.

**BURROWS, Prof. Andrew Stephen,** DCL; FBA 2007; Professor of the Law of England, and Senior Research Fellow, All Souls College, University of Oxford, since 2010; a Deputy High Court Judge, 2007–June 2020; a Recorder, 2000–June 2020; a Justice of the Supreme Court of the United Kingdom, from June 2020; *b* 17 April 1957; *s* of William George Burrows and Dora Burrows; *m* 1982, Rachel Jane Gent; three *s* one *d*. *Educ*: Prescot Grammar Sch.; Brasenose Coll., Oxford (Schol.; Martin Wronker Prize 1978; MA; BCL; DCL 2014; Hon. Fellow, 2015); Harvard Law Sch. (LLM). Called to the Bar, Middle Temple, 1985 (Hon. Bencher, 2000); Mem., Fountain Court Chambers, Temple. Lectr in Law, Merton Coll., Oxford, 1979–80; Harkness Fellow, Harvard Law Sch., 1980–81; Lectr in Law, Univ. of Manchester, 1981–86; Fellow and CUF Lectr in Law, 1986–94, Hon. Res. Fellow, 1994–, LMH, Oxford; Prof. of English Law, UCL, 1994–99; Law Comr for England and Wales, 1994–99; Norton Rose Prof. of Commercial and Financial Law, Univ. of Oxford, 1999–2010; Fellow, 1999–2010, Hon. Fellow, 2010–, St Hugh's Coll., Oxford. Chair, Video Appeals Cttee, 2011–18. Pres., Soc. of Legal Scholars, 2015–16. Hon. QC 2003. Jt winner, Prize for Outstanding Legal Scholarship, SPTL, 1993. *Publications*: Remedies for Torts and Breach of Contract, 1987, 4th edn as Remedies for Torts, Breach of Contract, and Equitable Wrongs, 2019; (ed jtly) Clerk and Lindsell on Torts, 16th edn 1989 to 22nd edn 2018; Essays on the Law of Restitution (ed Burrows), 1991; The Law of Restitution, 1993, 3rd edn 2011; (ed jtly) Chitty on Contracts, 28th edn 1999 to 33rd edn 2018; (ed jtly) Scrutton on Charterparties, 20th edn 1996, 21st edn 2008; (jtly) Cases and Materials on the Law of Restitution, 1997, 2nd edn 2007; Understanding the Law of Obligations, 1998; (jtly) English Private Law, 2000, (Gen. Ed.) 3rd edn 2013; (ed jtly) Commercial Remedies, 2003; (ed jtly) Mapping the Law, 2006; (ed jtly) Contract Terms, 2007; A Casebook on Contract, 2007, 6th edn 2018; (ed jtly) Contract Formation and Parties, 2010; (ed jtly) Anson's Law of Contract, 29th edn, 2010, 30th edn, 2016; A Restatement of the English Law of Unjust Enrichment, 2012; (ed jtly) Judge and Jurist, 2013; A Restatement of the English Law of Contract, 2016; Thinking about Statutes, 2018; numerous articles in legal jls. *Recreations*: sport (esp. football), mountain walking. *Address*: All Souls College, Oxford OX1 4AL; (from June 2020) Supreme Court of the United Kingdom, Parliament Square, SW1P 3BD.

**BURROWS, Christopher Parker;** Director, Orbis Business Intelligence Ltd, since 2009; *b* 12 Sept. 1958; *s* of John Brian and Margaret Katherine Burrows; *m* 1st, 1988, Betty Burrows (*née* Cordi) (marr. diss. 2008); one *s* two *d*; 2nd, 2010, Claire Jane Rothwell; one *s* one *d*. *Educ*: Cleethorpes Grammar Sch.; Liverpool Univ. Entered FCO, 1980; Third Sec., East Berlin, 1982–85; Third, later Second, Sec., Bonn, 1987–89; First Sec. (External), Athens, 1993–96; First Sec., later Counsellor, Brussels, 1998–2002; Counsellor: FCO, 2002–05; New Delhi, 2005–06; FCO, 2006–09. *Recreations*: jazz piano, gardening, football. *Address*: (office) 9–11 Grosvenor Gardens, SW1W 0BD.

**BURROWS, Clive,** CEng; FREng, FIET, FIMechE, FCILT, FIRSE; Group Engineering Director, FirstGroup plc, since 2008; *b* 1 Aug. 1958; *s* of Gordon and Barbara Burrows; *m* 1999, Norma Silvia de Anda Marquez. *Educ*: Univ. of Bath (BSc Hons Electrical and Electronic Engrg). CEng 1992, FREng 2004; MIEE 1992, FIET (FIEE 2002); FIMechE 2002. Intercity Route Fleet Manager, BR, 1989–91; Depot Manager, N Pole Internat., and Project Engr, Eurostar UK, 1991–93; Man. Dir, Transportation Consultants Internat., 1993–98; Gp Rail Engrg Dir, First Gp plc, 1998–2005; Dir, Technical and Professional, DfT, 2005–08. Hon. Prof. of Railway Engrg, Univ. of Nottingham, 2011–; Advisory Prof., Beijing Jiaotong Univ., 2018–. MInstD 1999. *Publications*: contrib. learned jls. *Recreations*: keen student of all matters relating to travel, transport and technology, collector and restorer of historic vehicles and artifacts. *Address*: FirstGroup, Milford House, 1 Milford Street, Swindon SN1 1HL. *E*: Clive.Burrows@firstgroup.com.

**BURROWS, Fred,** CMG 1981; PhD; international law consultant, since 1990; *b* 10 Aug. 1925; *s* of late Charles Burrows; *m* 1955, (Jennifer) Winsome Munt; two *s*. *Educ*: Altrincham Grammar Sch.; Trinity Hall, Cambridge (MA). PhD Cantab, 1988. Served in RAF, 1944–47. Called to Bar, Gray's Inn, 1950; Asst Legal Adviser, Foreign Office, 1956–65; Legal Adviser, British Embassy, Bonn, 1965–67; returned to FO, 1967; Legal Counsellor, FCO, 1968–77; Counsellor (Legal Adviser), Office of UK Perm. Rep. to European Communities, 1977–80; Legal Counsellor, FCO, 1980–85; Law Officer (Special Duties), then (International Law), Hong Kong, 1985–90. JP Hong Kong, 1986–90. *Publications*: Free Movement in European Community Law, 1985. *Recreations*: sailing, trombone. *Address*: c/o Foreign and Commonwealth Office, SW1A 2AH.

**BURROWS, (George) Richard (William);** Chairman, British American Tobacco plc, since 2009; *b* 16 Jan. 1946; *m* 1970, Sherril Dix; one *s* three *d*. *Educ*: Wesley College, Dublin; Rathmines College of Commerce. FICA. Articled Stokes Bros & Pim, 1963–70; Asst to Man. Dir, Edward Dillon & Co., 1970; Man. Dir, Old Bushmills Distillery Co., 1972; Gen. Manager, Irish Distillers, 1976; Man. Dir, 1978, Chief Exec., 1991–2000, Chm., 1991–2007, Irish Distillers Group; Dir Gen., 2000–05, Bd Dir, 2004–08, Pernod Ricard. Non-executive Director: Rentokil Initial plc, 2008– (Sen. Ind. Dir, 2017–);

Carlsberg, 2009–; VoiceSage Global Hldgs Ltd, 2011–15. Gov., Bank of Ireland, 2005–09. *Recreation:* sailing. *Address:* British American Tobacco plc, Globe House, 4 Temple Place, WC2R 2PG.

**BURROWS, Prof. John Philip,** FRS 2016; Professor of Physics of the Ocean and Atmosphere, University of Bremen, since 1992; *b* Liverpool, 16 Aug. 1954; *s* of William Frederick Burrows and Kathleen Mary Burrows; *m* 1990, Brigitte Holtkotte; one *s. Educ:* Our Lady's and St Joseph's RC Prim. Sch., Prescot; West Park Grammar Sch., St Helens; Trinity Coll., Cambridge (BA Hons 1975; PhD 1978). Royal Soc. Gassiot Cttee Res. Student, 1975–78; Res. Scientist, Harvard-Smithsonian Center for Astrophysics, Cambridge, Mass, 1978–79; HSO, Envmtl and Med. Scis Div., AERE Harwell, 1979–81; Res. Scientist, 1981–85, Res. Gp Leader, 1985–92, Atmospheric Chem. Dept, Max Planck Institut für Chemie; on secondment from Univ. of Bremen as Sci. Dir, Centre for Ecol. and Hydrol., NERC, 2008–10 (Hon. Fellow, 2010–16). Guest Scientist: Physical Chem. Lab., Univ. of Oxford, 1979–81; Lab. of the Atmospheres, NASA GSFC, 1992–; Guest Scientist, 1992–, Adjunct Prof., 2006–, Univ. of Maryland. Member: EU Copernicus (formerly GMES) Wkg Gp 4, 2006; Cttee on Earth Observation Satellites Carbon Task Force, 2010. Lectures: Dist. Guest, Envmtl Chem. Gp, RSC, 2004; Noble, Univ. of Toronto, 2007; Harold S. Johnston, Univ. of Calif, Berkeley, 2008; Eur. Geoscis Union, 2014. FAAAS 2003; Fellow: Amer. Geophysical Union, 2004; IUGG, 2015 (Silver Medal, 2015); Mem., Internat. Acad. of Aeronautics, 2008. William Nordberg Medal, COSPAR, 2006; Haagen Smit Prize, Atmospheric Envmt, 2012; Vilhelm Bjerknes Medal, 2013, Alfred Wegener Medal, 2016, Eur. Geoscis Union. *Publications:* (jtly) The Nitrate Radical: physics, chemistry and the atmosphere, 1991; (jtly) Halogen Oxides: radical sources and reservoirs in the laboratory and in the atmosphere, 1995; (ed jtly) Sounding the Troposphere from Space: a new era for atmospheric chemistry, 2004; (contrib.) SCIAMACHY: exploring the changing Earth's atmosphere, 2011; (contrib.) Chemie über den Wolken: und darunter, 2011; (ed jtly) The Remote Sensing of Tropospheric Composition from Space, 2011; (contrib.) Climate and Weather of the Sun-Earth System: highlights from a priority program, 2013. *Recreations:* working holidays, cycling, sport in moderation, music, theatre. *Address:* Institute of Environmental Physics/Institute of Remote Sensing, University of Bremen - FB1, Postfach 330440, 28334 Bremen, Germany. *T:* (421) 21862100, 1736241781, *Fax:* (421) 21862070. *E:* burrows@iup.physik.uni-bremen.de.

**BURROWS, Prof. Malcolm,** FRS 1985; Professor of Zoology, University of Cambridge, 1996–2010, now Emeritus; Fellow of Wolfson College, Cambridge, 1991–2010, now Emeritus; *b* 28 May 1943; *s* of William Roy Burrows and Jean Jones Burrows; *m* 1966, Christine Joan Ellis; one *s* one *d. Educ:* Cambridge Univ. (MA; ScD 1983); St Andrews Univ. (PhD 1967). Reader in Neurobiology, 1983–86, Prof. of Neurosci., 1986–96, Univ. of Cambridge. Vis. Prof., Konstanz Univ., 1987; Cornelius Wiersma Vis. Prof., CIT, 1991; Distinguished Vis. Prof., Univ. of California, Davis, 1992. Pres., Internat. Soc. for Neuroethology, 1998–2001. MAE 1992. Mem., Bayerische Akad. der Wissenschaften, 1996. Scientific Medal, 1980, Frink Medal, 2005, Zoological Soc.; Alexander von Humboldt award, 1993. *Publications:* The Neurobiology of an Insect Brain, 1996; 200 res. articles.

**BURROWS, Margaret Ann;** *see* Buck, M. A.

**BURROWS, Rt Rev. Michael Andrew James;** *see* Cashel, Ferns and Ossory, Bishop of.

**BURROWS, Michael Peter;** QC 2008; a Recorder, since 2000; *b* Birmingham, 26 June 1957; *s* of Peter and Margaret Burrows; *m* 1990, Gail Burbridge; three *d. Educ:* Tudor Grange Grammar Sch., Solihull; Solihull Sixth Form Coll.; Queens' Coll., Cambridge (BA 1978). Called to the Bar, Inner Temple, 1979; in practice at the Bar, specialising in criminal law, 1979–; Asst Recorder, 1997–2000. *Recreations:* walking in the Lake District, holidays in Scotland, theatre and music. *Address:* 5 Fountain Court, Steelhouse Lane, Birmingham B4 6DR.

**BURROWS, Richard;** *see* Burrows, G. R. W.

**BURSELL, His Honour Rev. Canon Rupert David Hingston;** QC 1986; a Senior Circuit Judge, 2003–08 (a Circuit Judge, 1988–2008); a Deputy High Court Judge, 2009–11; *b* 10 Nov. 1942; *s* of Henry and Cicely Mary Bursell; *m* 1967, Joanna Ruth Gibb; two *s* one *d. Educ:* St John's School, Leatherhead; Univ. of Exeter (LLB); St Edmund Hall, Oxford (MA, DPhil). Called to the Bar, Lincoln's Inn, 1968; Sir Thomas More Bursary and Hubert Greenland Studentship, Lincoln's Inn, 1969; a Recorder, 1985–88; an Official Referee, 1992–98; a nominated Judge of the Technology and Construction Court, 1998–2008; Designated Civil Judge, 1999–2008. Chancellor, Vicar-General and Official Principal, Diocese of Durham, 1989–2017; Chancellor, Dio. of Bath and Wells, 1992–93; Chancellor, VG and Official Principal, Dio. of St Albans, 1992–2002; Dep. Chancellor, Dio. of York, 1994–2007; Chancellor, VG and Official Principal, Dio. of Oxford, 2002–13, now Chancellor Emeritus. Member: Legal Adv. Commn, Gen. Synod, 1990– (Chm., 2007–); Provincial Panels for Canterbury and York, Clergy Discipline Measure, 2006–. Deacon, 1968; Priest, 1969; Hon. Curate: St Marylebone, 1968–69; St Mary the Virgin, Almondsbury, 1969–71; St Francis, Bedminster, 1971–83; Christ Church, and St Stephen, Bristol, 1983–88; St Andrew, Cheddar, 1993–2011; Gen. Licence to officiate, Oxford dio., 2011–; permission to officiate, Bath & Wells dio., 2011–14. Hon. Canon: St Albans Cathedral, 1996–2002; Cathedral Ch of Christ, Oxford, 2011–. Archbp of Canterbury's visitation commissary to Dio. of Chichester, 2012–13. Hon. Chaplain, 3rd (Vol.) Military Intelligence Bn, 1996–2001. Canterbury Cross for Services to C of E, 2019. *Publications:* (contrib.) Atkin's Court Forms, 1972, 2nd edn 1985; (contrib.) Halsbury's Laws of England, 1975, 2011; (jtly) Crown Court Practice, 1978; (contrib.) Principles of Dermatitis Litigation, 1985; Liturgy, Order and the Law, 1996; articles in legal jls. *Recreations:* Church music, military history, archaeology of Greece, Turkey and Holy Land. *Address:* Pear Tree Cottage, Hatchet Leys Lane, Thornborough, Bucks MK18 2BU. *Club:* MCC.

**BURSLEM, Dame Alexandra Vivien, (Dame Sandra),** DBE 2004 (OBE 1993); DL; Vice-Chancellor, Manchester Metropolitan University, 1997–2005; *b* Shanghai, China, 6 May 1940; *d* of Stanley Morris Thornley, CA and Myrra Thornley (*née* Kimberley); *m* 1st, 1960 (marr. diss. 1971); two *s*; 2nd, 1977, Richard Waywell Burslem, MD, FRCOG (*d* 2001); one *d. Educ:* Arnold High Sch. for Girls, Blackpool; Manchester Univ. (BA 1st Cl. Hons Politics and Modern Hist. 1971); Manchester Business Sch. (DipBA 1986). Manchester Polytechnic, later Manchester Metropolitan University: Lectr, 1973, Sen. Lectr, 1975–80 and Principal Lectr, 1980–82, Dept of Social Sci., 1973–82; Hd, Dept of Applied Community Studies, 1982–86; Dean, Faculty of Community Studies and Educn, 1986–88; Academic Dir, 1988–92; Dep. Vice-Chancellor, 1992–97. Vice-Chm., Manchester FPC, 1974–89. Chm., BBC Regl Adv. Council, 1983–92. A Civil Service Comr, 2005–10. Member: Council, FEFC, 2000–01; Nat. Learning and Skills Council, 2000–06 (Dep. Chm., 2004–06); Gen. Teaching Council, 2000–02; Council, ACU, 2001–05; HEFCW, 2008–; Bd, Ofqual, 2010–13 (Dep. Chm., 2010–). Chairman: British Council Education-UK Partnership, 2005–11; Educn Honours Cttee, 2005–11. Mem. Bd, Anchor Trust, 1995–97; Chm., Manchester and Cheshire Anchor Trust, 1995–97; Trustee: HE Policy Inst., 2015–; Manchester Internat. Soc., 2015– (Chair, 2015–). Member: Board: RNCM, 2006–14; Cumbria Univ., 2008–11. Gov., Eccles Coll., 1996–98; Feoffee,

Chetham's Sch. of Music, 2001– (Chm., Sch. Govs, 2005–). Mem., Manchester Literary and Philosophical Soc., 1988–. FRSA 1989. JP Inner Manchester, 1981; DL 2004, High Sheriff 2006–07, Greater Manchester. Hon. RNCM 2004. Hon. Fellow, St Martin's UC, 2007. Hon. LLD Manchester, 2001; Hon. DLitt: UMIST, 2004; Salford, 2005; Manchester Metropolitan, 2006; Hon. DEd Leeds Metropolitan, 2006. *Recreations:* opera, theatre, reading, travel. *Address:* 17 Bexton Lane, Knutsford, Cheshire WA16 9BW. *T:* (01565) 631200.

**BURSTEIN, Joan,** CBE 2006; Hon. Chairman, Browns fashion stores, since 2015 (Owner, 1970–2015); *b* 21 Feb. 1926; *d* of Ashley Jotner and Mary Jotner; *m* 1946, Sidney Burstein (*d* 2010); one *s* one *d. Educ:* Henrietta Barnett Sch. Owner: Neatawear fashion stores, 1955–67; Feathers boutique, High St Kensington, 1968–70. Hon. Dr Univ. of the Arts, 2007. V&A Award for Outstanding Achievement in Fashion, 2000. *Recreations:* theatre, gardening, travel. *Address:* Browns, 23–27 South Molton Street, W1K 5RD. *T:* (020) 7514 0000, *Fax:* (020) 7408 1281.

**BURSTOW, Rt Hon. Paul (Kenneth);** PC 2012; Chair: Tavistock and Portman NHS Foundation Trust, since 2015; Social Care Institute for Excellence, since 2017; Professor of Health and Social Care, City, University of London (formerly City University London), 2015–16, now Hon. Professor; Professor of Mental Health Policy (part-time), University of Birmingham, 2016–19; *b* 13 May 1962; *s* of Brian Seymour Burstow and Sheila Burstow; *m* 1995, Mary Everdell Kemm; one *s* two *d. Educ:* Poly. of South Bank (BA Hons Business Studies). Buying asst, Allied Shoe Repairs, 1985–86; print sales, Kallkwik Printers, 1986–87; research asst (part time), London Borough of Hounslow, 1987–89; Association of Social Democrat, then Liberal Democrat Councillors: Organising Sec. (part time), 1987–89; Councillors Officer, 1989–92; Campaigns Officer, 1992–96; Actg Political Sec., 1996–97. Council, London Borough of Sutton: Mem., 1986–2002; Chm., Envmtl Service Cttee, 1988–91 and 1993–96; Dep. Leader, 1994–97. Contested (Lib Dem) Sutton and Cheam, 1992. MP (Lib Dem) Sutton and Cheam, 1997–2015; contested (Lib Dem) same seat, 2015. Lib Dem Local Govt Team Leader, 1997–99; Lib Dem spokesman on: older people, 1999–2003; health, 2003–05; Lib Dem Chief Whip, 2006–10; Minister of State, DoH, 2010–12. Member: Select Cttee on Health, 2003–04, 2005–06; Modernisation Select Cttee, 2006–08; Finance and Service Cttee, 2006–10; Public Accounts Cttee, 2008–10; Chair, Jt Select Cttee on Draft Care and Support Bill, 2012–13. Chair, Nat. Adv. Bd, Transform Ageing, Design Council, 2017–19; Ind. Chair, Herts and W Essex Sustainability and Transformation Partnership, 2018–. Pres. Teleservices Assoc., 2017–. FRSA 2015. *Recreations:* cycling, walking, cooking, gym work.

**BURT OF SOLIHULL,** Baroness *cr* 2015 (Life Peer), of Solihull in the County of West Midlands; **Lorely Jane Burt;** *b* 10 Sept. 1954; *d* of Raymond Claude Baker and Hazel June Baker (*née* Abbiss); *m* 1992, Richard George Burt; one *d*, and one step *s. Educ:* University Coll., Swansea (BSc Hons Econ.); Open Univ. (MBA). Asst Gov., HM Prison Service; personnel and trng mgt and consultancy; Man. Dir, trng co.; Director: mktg co.; financial services co.; business consultant. MP (Lib Dem) Solihull, 2005–15; contested (Lib Dem) same seat, 2015. PPS to Chief Sec. to the Treasury, 2013–15; an Asst Govt Whip, 2014–15. Govt Champion for Women in Enterprise, 2014–15. Lib Dem spokesperson for NI, 2015, for business, innovation and skills, 2015–16, for equalities, 2016–. Mem. (Lib Dem) Dudley MBC, 1998–2003. *Recreations:* keeping fit, socialising with friends, painting, cooking. *Address:* House of Lords, SW1A 0PW.

**BURT, Prof. Alastair David,** MD; FRCPath, FRCP, FRCPA, FAcadMed, FAHMS; FRSB; Executive Dean of Medicine, Faculty of Health and Medical Sciences (formerly Faculty of Health Sciences), University of Adelaide, 2014–19; *b* Dunfermline, 9 March 1957; *s* of George Hoggan Burt and Iris Helen Forrest Burt; *m* 1980, Alison Carol Tweedlie; one *s* one *d. Educ:* Hawkhill Prim. Sch., Dundee; Hummersknott Grammar Sch., Darlington; Eastwood High Sch., Newton Mearns; Univ. of Glasgow (BSc 1st Cl. Hons 1979; MB ChB with Commendation 1981; MD Hons and Bellahouston Medal 1991). MRCPath 1988, FRCPath 1997; FRSB (FIBiol 1996); FRCP 2009; FRCPA 2014; FAcadMed 2015; FAHMS 2015. Jun. House Officer in Medicine and Surgery, Western Infirmary, Glasgow and Glasgow Royal Infirmary, 1981–82; Registrar, then Sen. Registrar in Pathol., Western Infirmary, Glasgow, 1982–89; Peel Trust Travelling Res. Officer, Free Univ. of Brussels, 1985–86; Newcastle University: Sen. Lectr in Pathol., 1989–95; Personal Prof. in Hepatopathol., 1995–98; Prof. of Pathol., 1998–2012; Hd, Sch. of Clin. and Lab. Scis, 2002–05; Dean, Clin. Medicine, 2005–12; Dean of Medicine, Univ. of Adelaide, 2013–14. Hon. Clin. Histopathologist, 1989–2012, Head of Service, Cellular Pathol., 2000–05, Newcastle upon Tyne Hosps NHS Foundn Trust. Hon. Treas. and Trustee, Pathological Soc., 2002–12. Editor-in-Chief: Liver, 1998–2002; Histopathol., 2012–; Member, Editorial Board: Clinical Sciences, 2002–; Medical Electron Microscopy, 2002–; Jl of Pathology, 2004–; Hepatology, 2006–11; World Jl of Gastroenterology, 2007–; World Jl of Hepatology, 2009–. *Publications:* (ed jtly) Pathology of the Liver, 3rd edn, 1994 to 7th edn, 2017; (Ed.-in-Chief) MacSween's Pathology of the Liver, 5th edn, 2006, 6th edn, 2011; (ed jtly) Muir's Textbook of Pathology, 14th edn, 2007; articles in scientific jls on mechanisms and patterns of liver injury, incl. fatty liver disease, fibrosis and autoimmune disease. *Recreations:* chamber music, walking, Asian cookery, foreign travel. *Club:* Athenæum.

**BURT, Rt Hon. Alistair (James Hendrie);** PC 2013; MP for North East Bedfordshire, since 2001 (C, 2001–19; Ind, since 2019); *b* 25 May 1955; *s* of James Hendrie Burt, med. practitioner and late Mina Christie Robertson; *m* 1983, Eve Alexandra Twite; one *s* one *d. Educ:* Bury Grammar Sch.; St John's Coll., Oxford (BA Hons Jurisprudence 1977). Pres., OU Law Soc., Michaelmas term, 1976. Articled Slater Heelis & Co., Manchester, 1978–80; solicitor, Watts, Vallance & Vallance, 1980–92; Consultant, Teeman, Levine and Co. (Solicitors), Leeds, 1992. Councillor, Archway Ward, London Bor. of Haringey, 1982–84. MP (C) Bury North, 1983–97; contested (C) same seat, 1997. Parliamentary Private Secretary: to Sec. of State for the Environment, 1985–86; to Sec. of State for Educn and Science, 1986–89; to Chancellor of Duchy of Lancaster and Chm. of Cons. Party, 1989–90; Parly Under-Sec. of State, DSS, 1992–95; Minister of State (Minister for Disabled People), DSS, 1995–97; Opposition frontbench spokesman on Higher and Further Educn, 2001–02; PPS to Leader of the Opposition, 2002–05; Shadow Minister for Communities and Regeneration, 2005–08; Dep. Chm., Cons. Party, 2007–10; Asst Opposition Chief Whip, 2008–10; Parly Under-Sec. of State, FCO, 2010–13; Minister of State: DoH, 2015–16; FCO and DFID, 2017–19. Vice-Chm., 1985–88, Vice Pres., 2003, Tory Reform Gp. Secretary: NW Cons. MPs Group, 1984–88; Parly Christian Fellowship, 1984–97 (Chm., 2003–06). Consultant, Whitehead Mann plc, 1997–2001. Chm., Enterprise Forum, 1998–2002. *Recreations:* reading left-wing publications, sport, modern art, marathon running, gardening. *Address:* c/o House of Commons, SW1A 0AA. *W:* www.alistair-burt.co.uk.

**BURT, Charles Anthony J.;** *see* Johnstone-Burt.

**BURT, Hon. E. David G.;** MP (Progressive Labour Party) Pembroke West Central, since 2012; Premier of Bermuda, since 2017; *b* Paget, Bermuda; *s* of Gerald Burt and Merlin Burt; *m* 2012, Kristin; one *s* one *d. Educ:* George Washington Univ., Washington DC (BBA

**BURT, Katherine Victoria**; Executive Director, Marketing and Fundraising, Leonard Cheshire Disability, since 2017; b Roydon, Essex, 7 Nov. 1965; d of Jeremy Burt and Victoria Burt (née Masefield). Educ: Haileybury Coll.; Corpus Christi Coll., Cambridge (BA Hons 1987; MA 1990). Commercial Dir, ReActions Ltd, 1987–91; USA Today, 1992–94; Commercial Dir, BBC Worldwide, 1994–98; Head: Fundraising, Variety Club, 1998–2002; Commercial Develt, Prince's Trust, 2002–09; Vice Pres., Global Develt, Right to Play, 2009–12; CEO, British Rowing, 2012–14; Chief Operating Officer, Greenhouse, 2014–16; Dir of Develt, Police Now, 2016–17. Trustee, Swan Foundn, 2016–. Recreations: diving, swimming.

**BURT, Nicolette**; see Zeeman, N.

**BURT, Prof. Timothy Peter**, PhD, DSc; Master of Hatfield College and Professor of Geography, Durham University, 1996–2017, now Emeritus Professor; b Mells, Som, 23 Dec. 1951; s of Donald Sydney Burt and Evelean Gertrude Burt (née Twynham); m 1973, Elizabeth Anne Sapsford; one s one d. Educ: Sexey's Sch., Bruton, Som; St John's Coll., Cambridge (BA Geog. 1st cl. 1973); Carleton Univ., Ottawa (MA 1974); Bristol Univ. (PhD 1978; DSc 1999). Sen. Lectr, Huddersfield Poly., 1977–84; Lectr in Geog., Oxford Univ. and Fellow, Keble Coll., Oxford, 1984–96. Visiting Professor: Oregon State Univ., 2010; Univ. of Bristol, 2017–; Collaborating Res. Scholar, Keble Coll., Oxford, 2017–. Field Studies Council: Trustee, 1982–; Chm., 1996–2014; Pres., 2014–. Fellow: Amer. Geophysical Union, 2012; British Soc. for Geomorphol., 2014. Hon. Fellow, Hatfield Coll., Durham, 2017. David Linton Medal, British Soc. for Geomorphol., 2017. Publications: Catchment Experiments in Fluvial Geomorphology, 1984; Hydrological Forecasting, 1985; Computer Simulation in Physical Geography, 1987; Process Studies in Hillslope Hydrology, 1990; Nitrate, 1993; Buffer Zones, 1997; (ed) History of the Study of Landforms, vol. 4, 2008; Sediment Cascades, 2010; (ed with H. M. Evans) The Collegiate Way: university education in a collegiate context, 2016; numerous contribs scientific papers and book chapters. Recreations: walking, sport, music, grandchildren, Field Studies Council. Address: Little Orchard, Lower Town, Sampford Peverell, Devon EX16 7EG. T: (01884) 821311. E: t.p.burt@durham.ac.uk, tim.burt@bristol.ac.uk.

**BURTENSHAW, Alistair John**; Director, Watts Gallery Trust, since 2017 (Trustee, since 2017); b Westminster, 11 Nov. 1969; s of George Neville Burtenshaw and Christine Mary Burtenshaw (née Menzies); m 1998, Francisca Beloso-Garcia; one d. Educ: Hove Park Upper Sch.; Univ. of Hertfordshire (BA Hons Business Studies 1993). Dip. CIM 1994, MCIM; Dip. Mkt Res. Soc. 1993, AMRS. Sales exec., Centaur Communications plc, 1994–96; Reed Exhibitions Ltd: Sales Exec., 1996–98, Sales Manager, 1998–2000, Internat. Direct Mktg Fair; Exhibn Manager, 2000–01, Exhibn Dir, 2001–05, Gp Exhibn Dir, 2005–12, London Book Fair; Director: Books and Publishing Worldwide, 2011–12; Publishing Connections Ltd, 2012–17. Dir, Charleston Trust, 2013–17. Chairman: Trustees, Booktrust, 2012–13 (Trustee, 2006–08; Dep. Chair, 2008–12); Trustees, Arvon Foundn, 2014–17. Pres. of Honour, Paris Cook Book Fair, 2013. Trustee, Book Trade Benevolent Soc., 2002–08. Member: Exec. Cttee, English Pen, 2002–04; The Book Soc. (formerly Soc. of Bookmen), 2005–. FRSA 2012. Recreations: family, reading, current affairs, international relations, opera, running, ski-ing, encouraging literacy, the arts, foreign travel, Spanish and Italian languages. Address: Watts Gallery Trust, Down Lane, Compton, Guildford, Surrey GU3 1DQ. Club: Academicians' Room.
See also Dr H. J. Caldwell.

**BURTON, 4th Baron cr 1897; Evan Michael Ronald Baillie**; b 19 March 1949; s of 3rd Baron Burton and Elizabeth Ursula Forster Baillie (née Wise); S father, 2013; m 1st, 1970, Lucinda Anne Law (marr. diss. 1984); two s one d; 2nd, 1998, June Gordon. Educ: Harrow; RAC Cirencester. Heir: s Hon. James Evan Baillie [b 3 Dec. 1975; m 2011, Katie Elizabeth Wright; two s].

**BURTON, Air Vice-Marshal Andrew John**, OBE 1991 (MBE 1986), FCIS, Chartered FCIPD; Bursar and Clerk to the Governors, 2003–16, Capital Project Manager, 2017–18, Sevenoaks School; b 11 Nov. 1950; s of Walter Joseph Burton and Phyllis Jane Burton (née Flear); m 1977, Sheila Hanson; two s. Educ: Llanelli Boys' Grammar Sch.; Univ. of Wales Inst. of Sci. and Technol. (BScEcon 1972). FCIS 1993 (ACIS 1982); Chartered FCIPD 2003 (FCIPD 2000). Commnd RAF, 1972; Sqn Leader, 1980; Wing Comdr, 1986; Defence Staff, British Embassy, Washington, 1988–90; Gp Capt., 1991; Station Comdr, RAF Uxbridge, 1994–95; Air Cdre, 1996; Dir of Personnel (RAF), 1995–98; Air Vice-Marshal, 1998; AOA and AOC Directly Administered Units, HQ Strike Comd, 1998–2001, PTC, 2001–03. Recreations: golf, sport, theatre. Club: Royal Air Force.

**BURTON, Anthony Charles**, CBE 2012; solicitor; a Senior Partner, Simons Muirhead and Burton, since 1976; a Recorder, since 1999; b Folkestone, 12 July 1947; s of late Dr Peter John Charles Burton and Violet Marie Aurelie Burton (née Branson); m 1996, Leonie Mellinger; one s two d. Educ: Beaumont Coll.; Coll. of Law, London. Admitted solicitor, 1972. Mem. Council, Justice, 1990–. Chm., Royal Court Th., 2005–. Recreations: theatre, reading, family, cricket, Rugby. Address: 41a Montague Road, Richmond, Surrey TW10 6QJ. T: (020) 3206 2713, Fax: (020) 3206 2800. E: anthony.burton@smab.co.uk. Clubs: Groucho, Chelsea Arts.

**BURTON, (Anthony) David**, CBE 1992; business consultant, 1998–2019; b 2 April 1937; s of Leslie Mitchell Burton and Marion Burton (née Marsh); m 1964, Valerie (née Swire); one s one d. Educ: Arnold Sch., Blackpool. FCIB; FCT. Bank of America National Trust and Savings Assoc., 1966–72; S. G. Warburg & Co. Ltd, 1972–92 (Dir, 1977–92). Dir, LIFFE, 1981–94 (Chm., 1988–92). Chairman: Marshalls Finance Ltd, 1989–98; The 181 Fund Ltd (formerly Ludgate 181 plc, then Ludgate 181 (Jersey) Ltd), 1999–2019; Ashley House plc, 2004–07; Ashley House Medical Properties plc (formerly Ashley House Properties Ltd), 2004–07; Ludgate Investments Ltd, 2004–10; Beechwood House Finance Ltd, 2004–11; Dir, Car Crash Line Gp plc, 2003–05. Publications: Antique Sealed Bottles 1640–1900 and the families who owned them, 2015. Recreations: antique glass, German pottery, music, opera, historical and genealogical research.

**BURTON, Anthony George Graham**; author and broadcaster, since 1968; b 24 Dec. 1934; s of Donald Graham Burton and Irene Burton; m 1959, Pip Sharman; two s one d. Educ: King James's Grammar Sch., Knaresborough; Leeds Univ. National Service, RAF, 1955–57. Research chemist, 1958–60; publishing, 1960–68. Has written and presented TV progs for all major channels. Founding Mem. and former Chm., Stroudwater Textile Trust. Publications: A Programmed Guide to Office Warfare, 1969; The Jones Report, 1970; The Canal Builders, 1972, 5th edn 2015; Canals in Colour, 1974; Remains of a Revolution, 1975, 2nd edn 2001; Josiah Wedgwood, 1976; (jtly) Canal, 1976; The Miners, 1976; Back Door Britain, 1977; Industrial Archaeological Sites of Britain, 1977; (jtly) The Green Bag Travellers, 1978; The Past At Work, 1980; The Rainhill Story, 1980; The Past Afloat, 1982; The Changing River, 1982; The Shell Book of Curious Britain, 1982; The National Trust Guide to Our Industrial Past, 1983; The Waterways of Britain, 1983; The Rise and Fall of King Cotton, 1984; (ed jtly) Canals: a new look, 1984; Walking the Line, 1985; Wilderness Britain, 1985; (jtly) Britain's Light Railways, 1985; The Shell Book of Undiscovered Britain and Ireland, 1986; (jtly) Landscape Detective, 1986; Britain Revisited, 1986; Opening Time, 1987; Steaming Through Britain, 1987; Walking Through History, 1988; Walk the South Downs, 1988; The Great Days of the Canals, 1989; Cityscapes, 1990; Astonishing Britain, 1990; Slow Roads, 1991; The Railway Builders, 1992; Canal Mania, 1993; (jtly) The Grand Union Canal Walk, 1993; The Railway Empire, 1994; The Rise and Fall of British Shipbuilding, 1994; The Cotswold Way, 1995, new edn 2007; The Dales Way, 1995; The West Highland Way, 1996; The Southern Upland Way, 1997; William Cobbett: Englishman, 1997; The Caledonian Canal, 1998; The Wye Valley Walk, 1998; Best Foot Forward, 1998; The Cumbria Way, 1999; The Wessex Ridgeway, 1999; Thomas Telford, 1999; Weekend Walks Dartmoor and Exmoor, 2000; Weekend Walks the Yorkshire Dales, 2000; Traction Engines, 2000; Richard Trevithick, 2000; Weekend Walks The Peak District, 2001; The Orient Express, 2001; The Anatomy of Canals: the early years, 2001; The Daily Telegraph Guide to Britain's Working Past, 2002; Hadrian's Wall Path, 2003; The Daily Telegraph Guide to Britain's Maritime Past, 2003; The Anatomy of Canals: decline and renewal, 2003; On the Rails, 2004; The Ridgeway, 2005; Tracing your Shipbuilding Ancestors, 2010; Canal 250, 2011; (with Rob Scott) Crafted in Britain: the survival of Britain's traditional industries, 2017; The Canal Pioneers: canal construction from 2,500 BC to the early 20th century, 2017; The Locomotive Pioneers: early steam locomotive development 1801–1851, 2017; History's Most Dangerous Jobs: The Navvies, 2012; The Miners, 2013; Life on the Farm, 2013; Life in the Mine, 2013; Life in the Mill, 2013; Life on the Railway, 2013; Life on the Canal, 2013; Matthew Boulton, 2013; Mary Rose Museum, 2014; novels: The Reluctant Musketeer, 1973; The Master Idol, 1975; The Navigators, 1976; A Place to Stand, 1977. Recreation: travelling Britain in search of steam engines and good beer. E: anthonyggburton@btinternet.com.

**BURTON, Anthony James Harris**, CBE 2012; freelance planning, environment, community and design consultant, since 2012; b Hobart, 14 Feb. 1964; s of Jim and Dawn Burton. Educ: Dulwich Coll.; St John's Coll., Cambridge (BA Geog. 1986); Bartlett Sch. of Architecture, University Coll. London (MPhil Town Planning). Campaign to Protect Rural England: Planning Officer, 1988–90; Sen. Planner, 1990–93; Asst Dir (Policy), 1993–2000; Dep. Dir, 2000–01; Dir, Strategy and Ext. Affairs, NT, 2001–09; Dir, Civic Soc. Initiative, 2009–10; Founder and Chief Exec., Civic Voice, 2010–12; Dir, Policy and Communications, Design Council, 2012. Exec. Chm., Sustainable Homes, 2013–17. Mem., Lord Roger's Urban Task Force, 1998–2000, 2005. Vice Chairman: UK Bd, Big Lottery Fund, then Nat. Lottery Community Fund, 2012– (Chm., Audit and Risk Cttee, 2013–); HS2 Ind. Design Panel, 2015–. Vice Chm., Friends of the Earth, 2016–19. Chairman: Wildlife and Countryside Link, 2000–03; Wandle Valley Forum, 2015–; Dir, Greenspace Information for Gtr London, 2018–. Founder Trustee, Heritage Alliance, 2002–06; Trustee: TCV, 2014–; mySociety, 2016–; CPRE London, 2018–. Convener, Neighbourhood Planners.London, 2017–. Hon. FRIBA 2000. Recreation: orienteering. Address: Mitcham, London. E: tony@tonyburton.org.uk.

**BURTON, Rt Rev. Anthony John**; Rector, Church of the Incarnation, Dallas, Texas, since 2008; b 11 Aug. 1959; s of Peter and Rachel Burton; m 1989, Anna Kristine Erickson; one s one d. Educ: Trinity Coll., Toronto Univ. (BA (Hons) 1982); King's Coll., Dalhousie Univ.; Wycliffe Hall, Oxford (BA, MA). Ordained deacon, 1987, priest, 1988; Curate, St John the Baptist, N Sydney, Nova Scotia, 1987–88; Rector, Trinity Church, Sydney Mines, 1988–91; Rector and Canon Residentiary, Cathedral Church of St Alban the Martyr, Saskatchewan, 1991–93; Dean of Saskatchewan, 1991–94; Bishop of Saskatchewan, 1993–2008. Anglican-Roman Catholic Bps' Dialogue, Canada, 1994–97, 2000–02, Co-Chm., 2007–08. Chancellor, James Settee Coll., 1995–2008. Member, Board: Scholarly Engagement with Anglican Doctrine, USA, 2003–04; Living Ch Foundn, 2010–13. Chair, Council of the North, 2004–07; Chairman: Bd, Elliott Hse of Studies, 2010–; Bd of Visitors, Ralston Coll., Savannah, Ga, 2013–; Vice Chm., Bd, Incarnation House, 2016–; Mem. Bd of Trustees, Anglican Digest, 2016–. Vice-Chm., Prayer Book Soc. of Canada, 1999–2008. Episcopal Visitor, S American Missionary Soc., Canada, 2002–08. Hon. DD King's Coll., Halifax, 1994. Publications: (contrib.) Anglican Essentials: reclaiming faith in the Anglican Church of Canada, 1995; contrib. to Machray Rev., Liturgy Canada, Anglican Digest, Living Ch. Recreations: walking, fighting ignominiously in last ditches. Address: Church of the Incarnation, 3966 McKinney Avenue, Dallas, TX 75204, USA.

**BURTON, Prof. (Anthony) Michael**, PhD; FBA 2017; FRSE; Professor of Psychology, University of York, since 2015; b Harrogate, 21 Jan. 1959; s of Peter Burton and Marie Burton (née Twist); m 2006, Helen Long; one step d. Educ: Lancaster Royal Grammar Sch.; Univ. of Nottingham (BSc Jt Hons Maths and Psychol. 1980; PhD Psychol. 1983). Lecturer: Univ. of Nottingham, 1983–92; Univ. of Stirling, 1992–94; Professor of Psychology: Univ. of Glasgow, 1994–2011; Univ. of Aberdeen, 2011–15. Panellist, REF 2014. Pres., Exptl Psychol. Soc., 2016–17. FRSE 2006. Cognitive Award, BPsS, 2000, 2017. Publications: (with N. Shadbolt) Pop-11 Programming for Artificial Intelligence, 1987; (with V. Bruce) Processing Images of Faces, 1992; contrib. articles to scientific jls. Recreations: fishing, Scottish hills, English concertinas. Address: Department of Psychology, University of York, Heslington, York YO10 5DD. T: (01904) 323140. E: mike.burton@york.ac.uk.

**BURTON, Anthony Philip**; Senior Research Fellow in Museology and Museum History, Research Department, Victoria and Albert Museum, 1997–2002; Chairman of Trustees, Charles Dickens Museum, London, 2003–05; b 25 Oct. 1942; s of late Frank Burton and Lottie Burton (née Lax); m 1985, Carol Deborah Baker. Educ: King's Sch., Macclesfield; Wadham Coll., Oxford (BLitt, MA). Res. Asst, Dept of English, Birkbeck Coll., Univ. of London, 1965–68; Victoria and Albert Museum: Asst Keeper, Nat. Art Libry, 1968–79; Asst Keeper, Directorate, 1979–81; Hd, Bethnal Green Mus. of Childhood, 1981–97. Trustee: Hoxton Hall, 2007–13; St Martin's Low Marple Heritage Trust, 2014–; Elizabeth Gaskell's House, Manchester, 2015–18. Publications: (with S. Haskins) European Art in the Victoria and Albert Museum, 1983; Children's Pleasures: books, toys and games from the Bethnal Green Museum of Childhood, 1996; Vision & Accident: the story of the Victoria and Albert Museum, 1999; (with E. Bonython) The Great Exhibitor: the life and work of Henry Cole, 2003; articles on liby and mus. subjects. Recreations: cultural pursuits, reading crime fiction. Address: 20 Lockside, Marple, Stockport SK6 6BN. T: (0161) 258 9077, 07847 144901.

**BURTON, Caroline Oldcorn**; see Reid, C. O.

**BURTON, David**; see Burton, A. D.

**BURTON, David Harold**; Managing Director, West Anglia Great Northern Railway, 1996–99; b 28 Jan. 1947; s of George and Helen Burton; m (marr. diss.); one s; m 2006, Julia Ramsay; one step s two step d. Educ: Bridlington Sch.; Leeds Univ. (BA (Hons) Geography). British Rail: Network Man., S Central Network SE, 1986; Dep. Gen. Man., Southern Region, 1988; Gen. Man., Anglia Region, 1989–91; Gp Dir North, Network SouthEast, 1991–92; Director: Express Parcels, BR Parcels, 1992–93; Restructuring, Network SouthEast, 1993–94; Dir, Product Quality, and Dep. Man. Dir (S & E), BRB,

1994–96. Transport mgt consultant, 1999–2005. Mem. Bd, Passenger Focus, 2005–12. Non-exec. Dir, Norfolk, Suffolk and Cambs Strategic HA, 2002–06; Gov., Papworth Hosp. Foundn Trust, 2004–06. *Recreations:* spectator sport, golf, reading.

**BURTON, Lt-Gen. Sir Edmund Fortescue Gerard,** KBE 1999 (OBE); DL; FIET, FBCS; Chairman, Philip Barker Charity, since 1997; *b* 20 Oct. 1943. *Educ:* Trinity Hall, Cambridge (BA 1968; MA 1972); RMA Sandhurst. Commissioned RA, 1963; Brig., 1987; Mil. Attaché, Washington, 1989–91; Maj.-Gen., 1991; Comdt, RMCS, 1991–94; ACDS, Operational Requirements (Land), 1994–97; DCDS (Systems), 1997–99; retd 2000. Vis. Prof., Cranfield Univ., 2000–. Jt Chm., Telecommunications Ind. Security Adv. Council, 2004–11. Exec. Chm., Police Information Technol. Orgn, 2001–03. Pres., Trustworthy Software Initiative, 2013–16. Chm. Council, Chester Cathedral, 2008–14. Hon. Col, OTC (Cambridge), 1996–2003; Col Comdt, RA, 1998–2004; Hon. Regtl Col, 26 Regt RA, 1999–2006. Hon. DSc: Cranfield, 2009; Chester, 2017. DL Cheshire, 2013–15.

**BURTON, Frances Rosemary;** an Upper Tribunal Judge (Administrative Appeals Chamber), 2009–11; Co-Director, International Centre for Family Law, Policy and Practice, since 2013; *b* Bury St Edmunds, 19 June 1941; *d* of late Major Richard Francis Heveningham Pughe, DFC, ERD and Pamela Margaret Pughe (*née* Coates); *m* 1st, 1963, Robert Scott Alexander (Baron Alexander of Weedon, QC) (marr. diss. 1973; he *d* 2005); two *s* one *d*; 2nd, 1975, David Michael Burton (*d* 2000); two *d*. *Educ:* St Anne's Coll., Oxford; Univ. of London (LLB); Univ. of Leicester (LLM); Open Univ. (MA); Liverpool John Moores Univ. (PhD). Called to the Bar, Middle Temple, 1970 (Harmsworth Major Entrance Exhibnr); in practice as a barrister, 1972–75, 1989–2012; mediator, 2000–; Family Arbitrator, MCIArb, 2013–. Vis. Lectr, City of London Poly., 1989–93; Vis. Lectr, 1989–93, Sen. Lectr in Law, 1993–2001, London Guildhall Univ.; Lectr, Coll. of Law, London and Birmingham, 2001–02; Principal Lectr, UWE, 2002–08; Dir, BVC Open Learning, 2002–08; Vis. Lectr, 2009, Research Fellow, 2010–13, London Metropolitan Univ.; Associate Lectr, 2012–15, Sen. Lectr in Law, 2015–17, Bucks New Univ.; Vis. Lectr, Middlesex Univ., 2013–15; Vis. Lectr, 2014–15, Sen. Lectr in Law, 2017–18, Aston Univ.; Sen. Lectr in Law, Buckingham Univ., 2018–. BVC Course Dir, 1992–93, Consultant, Mem. and Hon. Sec., Academic Adv. Bd, 1993–2000, BPP Law Sch. Co-Dir, Centre for Family Law and Practice, London Metropolitan Univ., 2009–13. Lawyer Chm., Residential Property Tribunal Service, 1996–2011; Chm., Transport Tribunal, 2002–09. Co-Dir, Internat. Centre for Family Law, Policy and Practice, 2013–. *Publications:* Family Law for Law Society Final Examination, 1988, 2nd edn 1990; Bar Final General Paper II Textbook, 1990; (jtly) Criminal Procedure, 1993, 3rd edn 1996; Family Law, 1996; Guide to the Family Law Act 1996, 1996; Teaching Family Law, 1999; Family Law Textbook, 2003; Family Law, 2012, 2nd edn 2015; Core Statutes in Family Law, 14th edn 2019. *Recreations:* opera, history, archaeology. *Address:* 10 Old Square, Lincoln's Inn, WC2A 3SU. *T:* 07775 655088. *E:* frb@frburton.com. *Club:* Oxford and Cambridge.

**BURTON, Dr Frank Patrick;** QC 1998; a Recorder, since 1999; a Deputy High Court Judge, since 2010; *b* 19 June 1950; *s* of late Ronald Burton and Ita Burton; *m* 1983, Caroline Oldcorn Reid, *qv*; two *s* one *d*. *Educ:* Salesian Coll., Farnborough; Univ. of Kent at Canterbury (BA 1st Cl. Hons 1971); London School of Economics and Political Science (PhD 1974). Lecturer in Social Science: Brunel Univ., 1976–79; City Univ., 1979–82; called to the Bar, Gray's Inn, 1982, Bencher, 2004; in practice at the Bar, 1982–. Chairman: Law Reform Cttee, Bar Council, 2003–05; Personal Injury Bar Assoc., 2004–06 (Vice Chm., 2002–04). Motor Insurers' Bureau Arbitrator, 2001–. *Publications:* Medical Negligence Case Law, 1990, 2nd edn 1995; Personal Injury Limitation Law, 1994, 3rd edn 2013. *Recreations:* sport, reading, Suffolk, bee keeping. *Address:* 12 King's Bench Walk, Temple, EC4Y 7EL.

**BURTON, Prof. Graham James,** MD, DSc; FMedSci; Mary Marshall and Arthur Walton Professor of the Physiology of Reproduction, since 2013, Director, Centre for Trophoblast Research, since 2007, and Chair of Strategic Research Initiative in Reproduction, since 2018, University of Cambridge; Fellow, St John's College, Cambridge, since 1982; *b* Cambridge, 27 Jan. 1953; *s* of William and Pamela Burton; *m* 1979, Hilary Jordison; one *s* four *d*. *Educ:* Colchester Royal Grammar Sch.; Christ's Coll., Cambridge (BA Med. Sci. 1974; MD 1984); Magdalen Coll., Oxford (BM BCh 1977; DSc 2005). University of Cambridge: Lectr, 1982–2001; Reader in Human Reproduction, 2001–04; Prof. of Reproductive Biol., 2004–13. Eur. Ed., Placenta, 2008–15; Associate Ed., Human Reproduction Update, 2015–. FMedSci 2011. *Publications:* Comparative Placentation, 2008; The Human Placenta and Developmental Programming, 2010; Pathology of the Human Placenta, 6th edn 2012; contrib. book chapters; contrib. papers to scientific jls. *Recreations:* walking, family. *Address:* Department of Physiology, Development and Neuroscience, University of Cambridge, Downing Street, Cambridge CB2 3EG. *T:* (01223) 333856, *Fax:* (01223) 333840. *E:* gjb2@cam.ac.uk.

**BURTON, Sir Graham (Stuart),** KCMG 1999 (CMG 1987); HM Diplomatic Service, retired; High Commissioner, Nigeria, also concurrently Ambassador (non-resident) to the Republic of Benin, 1997–2001; *b* 8 April 1941; *s* of late Cyril Stanley Richard Burton and of Jessie Blythe Burton; *m* 1965, Julia Margaret Lappin; one *s* one *d*. *Educ:* Sir William Borlase's Sch., Marlow. Foreign Office, 1961; Abu Dhabi, 1964; Middle East Centre for Arabic Studies, 1967; Kuwait, 1969; FCO, 1972; Tunis, 1975; UK Mission to United Nations, 1978; Counsellor, Tripoli, 1981; Head, Security Co-ordination Dept, FCO, 1984; Consul General, San Francisco, 1987; Ambassador: UAE, 1990; Indonesia, 1994. Director: Magadi Soda Co., Kenya, 2001–08; Gulf of Guinea Energy, 2006–09; Advr, Control Risks Gp, 2001–12. Dir, W African Business Assoc., 2003–11. Trustee: Royal Commonwealth Soc. for the Blind, 2005–09 (Vice Pres., 2012–); Chalker Foundn, 2006–. *Recreations:* golf, watching cricket, baseball and most other sports; opera. *Clubs:* MCC; Wildcat Run Golf and Country (Estero).

**BURTON, Humphrey McGuire,** CBE 2000; writer and broadcaster; *b* 25 March 1931; *s* of Harry (Philip) and Kathleen Burton; *m* 1st, 1957, Gretel (*née* Davis); one *s* one *d*; 2nd, 1970, Christina (*née* Hellstedt); one *s* one *d*. *Educ:* Long Dene Sch., Chiddingstone; Judd Sch., Tonbridge; Fitzwilliam House, Cambridge (BA; Hon. Fellow, Fitzwilliam Coll., 1997; MA 2008). BBC Radio, 1955–58; BBC TV, 1958–67: Editor, Monitor, 1962; Exec. Producer, Music Programmes, 1963; Head of Music and Arts Programmes, 1965–67, productions inc. Workshop, Master Class, In Rehearsal, Britten at 50, Conversations with Glenn Gould; London Weekend TV: Head of Drama, Arts and Music, 1967–69; Editor/Introducer, Aquarius, 1970–75, programmes incl. Mahler Festival, Verdi Requiem, Trouble in Tahiti, The Great Gondola Race, Anatomy of a Record, etc.; Head of Music and Arts, BBC TV, 1975–81; Presenter: Omnibus, 1976–78, 1984–85 (Producer, West Side Story documentary, 1985; RAI Prize, Prix Italia, BAFTA Robert Flaherty Best Documentary Award, 1985); In Performance, 1978–82; Young Musician of the Year, biennially 1978–94; Producer/Director: TV Proms with Giulini and Solti, 1981, and with others, 1982–95; Walton 80th Birthday Concert (Previn); Verdi Requiem (Abbado), and Call me Kiri (Te Kanawa), 1982; Candide, Scottish Opera, Glasgow, 1988 and Barbican (conducted by Leonard Bernstein), 1989; Covent Garden opera relays, incl. Die Fledermaus (Joan Sutherland farewell), 1990; Artistic Dir, 1988–90, Artistic Advr, 1990–93, Barbican Centre. Other productions include: 5 Glyndebourne operas, adapted and produced, Southern TV, 1972–74; The Beach at Falesa, World Première, Harlech TV, 1974; Channel 4 operas include: Eugene Onegin, 1994; Ermione, 1995; Lulu, 1996; The Damnation of Faust, Manon Lescaut, 1997; Rodelinda, Hansel and Gretel, 1998; Pelléas et Mélisande, Flight, 1999; BBC2 opera, Falstaff, 1999; BBC4 drama, Vincent in Brixton, 2002; UN Day Concert with Pablo Casals, 1971, and subseq. UN days, 1972–92; Berlioz' Requiem, at Les Invalides, 1975, The Return of Ulysses, at Aix-en-Provence, 2002, French TV; many free-lance prodns in Austria, Czechoslovakia, Germany, Hungary, Italy, Israel, Poland, Russia and USA, including: Mahler, Brahms, Schumann and Beethoven Cycles with Bernstein and Vienna Philharmonic; concerts with von Karajan and Berlin and Vienna Philharmonic, Giulini and LA Philharmonic, Mehta and NY Philharmonic, Maazel and Bayerisches Rundfunk Orch., Solti and Chicago SO; world première, Epitaph, by Charles Mingus, NY, 1989; Director: Boris Godunov, Kirov, 1990; War and Peace, Kirov, 1991; Mozart Requiem, Vienna Bicentennial 1991; Producer: Leonard Bernstein's 70th Birthday Gala Season, Tanglewood, 1988; Bernstein Meml Concert, Carnegie Hall, 1990; Guest Dir, 1983 Hollywood Bowl Summer Music Fest.; conducting début, Verdi Requiem, Philharmonia Orch., RAH, 2001 (raised £75,000 for Prostate Research); host, Matinées Musicales, Aldeburgh cinema, 2004–; devised and conducted Schubert season, Snape Maltings and Jubilee Hall, Aldeburgh, 2011; video curator, Aldeburgh Fest., 2013–; *radio:* writer/presenter of series, incl. Life of Leonard Bernstein, Menuhin-Master Musician, William Walton: the romantic loner, Classic FM, Artist in Focus, etc., BBC. Columnist: Classic FM Magazine, 1995–98; BBC Music Magazine, 1998–99. Cruise ship lectr, 2000–. Chairman: EBU Music Experts Gp, 1976–82; EBU TV Music Working Party, 1982–86; Mem., New Music Sub-Cttee, Arts Council, 1981–83; Advr, Manchester Olympic Fest., 1990; Administrator, Royal Philharmonic Soc.'s Music Awards, 1989–91. Hon. Professorial Fellow, University Coll., Cardiff, 1983–87. Hon. FCSD 1990. Desmond Davis Award, SFTA, 1966; Royal TV Soc. Silver Medal, 1971; Emmy, 1971 for 'Beethoven's Birthday' (CBS TV); Peabody Award, 1972; SFTA Best Specialised Series, 1974; Christopher Award, 1979; Emmy, 1988, for 'Celebrating Gershwin' (PBS/BBC TV). Chevalier de l'Ordre des Arts et des Lettres, 1975. *Publications:* Leonard Bernstein, 1994 (trans. German, Chinese and Japanese; ASCAP book award, 1995), repr. 2017; Menuhin: a life, 2000 (trans. German); (jtly) William Walton: the romantic loner, 2002. *Recreations:* music-making, travel. *Address:* 13 Linden Road, Aldeburgh, Suffolk IP15 5JQ.

**BURTON, Ian Richard;** Founder and Senior Partner, BCL Solicitors LLP (formerly BCL Burton Copeland), London, since 1991; *b* Manchester, 25 March 1947; *s* of Jack Burton and Faie Glaisher; *m* 1973, Sarah Ruth Ashbrook; one *s* one *d*. *Educ:* Whittingehame Coll., Brighton. Admitted solicitor, 1971; Partner: Nigel Copeland Glickman, 1971–75; Gardner Burton, 1975–82; Founder and Sen. Partner, Burton Copeland, Manchester, 1982–2001. *Recreations:* family, opera, contemporary art. *Address:* BCL Solicitors LLP, 51 Lincoln's Inn Fields, WC2A 3LZ. *T:* (020) 7430 2277, *Fax:* (020) 7430 1101. *E:* ianburton@bcl.com. *Club:* Royal Automobile.

**BURTON, Iris Grace, (Mrs Joe Lucas);** Editor-in-Chief: Woman's Realm, 1991–99; Woman's Weekly, 1992–99; Eva, 1994–97; Chat, 1997–99; *d* of late Arthur Burton and Alice Burton; *m* 2012, Joe Lucas; one *s* one *d*. *Educ:* Roan Girls' Grammar Sch., Greenwich; City of London Coll. Local newspaper, SE London Mercury, until 1966; Writer, then Features Editor, Woman's Own, 1966–78; Asst Editor, TV Times, 1978–80; Editor, Woman's Own, 1980–86; Editor-in-Chief: Prima magazine, 1986–87; Best magazine, 1987–88; Editorial Dir, G+J of the UK publications, 1988–91; Launch Ed., Now mag., 1996. Mem., Press Complaints Commn, 1993–99. *Address:* 13 Wheathill Road, SE20 7XQ.

**BURTON, Jane;** Chief Executive Officer, Girls' Learning Trust (formerly Executive Head, Nonsuch and Wallington Education Trust), since 2015; *b* London, 25 Aug. 1965; *d* of Victor Shore and Jean Kritz; *m* 2002, Christopher Burton; one *s*. *Educ:* Marshalls Park Sch.; Univ. of Salford (BSc Econs 1986); Univ. of Kingston (PGCE 2000). Commercial mgt, Marks and Spencer plc and Stirling Gp plc, 1986–99; teacher, Wilsons Sch., 2000–10 (Asst Hd); Dep. Hd, Nonsuch High Sch. for Girls, 2010–12; Headteacher, Wallington High Sch. for Girls, 2012–15. *Recreations:* family, reading. *Address:* Girls' Learning Trust, Ewell Road, Cheam, Sutton, Surrey SM3 8AB.

**BURTON, Prof. John Lloyd,** MD; FRCP; Professor of Dermatology, University of Bristol, 1992–98; *b* 29 Aug. 1938; *s* of Lloyd Burton and Dorothy Mary Burton; *m* 1964, Patricia Anne Crankshaw, DRCOG, FRCPath; one *s* two *d*. *Educ:* Heanor Grammar Sch., Derbys; Manchester Univ. (BSc; MD 1971). FRCP 1978. Trng posts in hosps in Manchester, London, Edinburgh and Newcastle upon Tyne, 1964–73; Consultant Dermatologist, Bristol Royal Infirmary, 1973–98. Numerous guest lectures, including: Dowling Oration, 1980, Deville, 1995, RSM; Parkes-Weber, RCP, 1988; Long-Fox, Bristol Univ., 1994. Advr in Dermatol. to CMO, DoH, 1988–94. Examr, RCP, 1987–92. Chm., Dermatol. Cttee, RCP, 1993–95; President: Dermatol. Sect., RSocMed, 1994–95; Brit. Assoc. Dermatologists, 1995–96. Editor, Brit. Jl Dermatol., 1981–85. *Publications:* Aids to Postgraduate Medicine, 1970, 6th edn 1994; Aids to Undergraduate Medicine, 1973, 6th edn 1997; Essentials of Dermatology, 1979, 3rd edn 1990; (ed jtly) Textbook of Dermatology (4 Vols), 4th edn 1986 to 6th edn 1998; 600 Miseries: the 17th century womb, 2005; Why Man Made Gods and Dogs: the evolution of religion, 2010; Birds of the Franschhoek Valley: a guide for the novice, 2012; numerous chapters and scientific papers. *Recreations:* painting, book-binding. *Address:* Eastfield House, East Street, North Perrott, Somerset TA18 7SW. *T:* (01460) 75156.

**BURTON, John Malcolm;** QC 2010; Advocate, Public Defender Service, since 2014; *b* Blackpool, 29 July 1957; *s* of Malcolm Burton and Ruby Burton; *m* 1st, 1986, Karen Falkingham (*d* 1992); two *s*; 2nd, 2006, Katherine Lissanevitch; one *d*. *Educ:* Culcheth High Sch.; Queen Mary Coll., London (LLB Hons 1978). Called to the Bar, Inner Temple, 1979; in practice as a barrister, 1979–, specialising in serious crime, fraud, terrorism and murder. *Publications:* The Myth of Sparta, 2013; The Return of the Spartans, 2013; Parricide, 2013; The Silk Brief, 2013; The Silk Head, 2014; The Trial of Admiral Byng, 2014; The Silk Returns, 2015; articles in law jls and Index on Censorship. *Recreations:* reading, drawing, painting, writing, ski-ing, travel. *Address:* Public Defender Service Advocacy Unit, 102 Petty France, SW1H 9AJ.

**BURTON, John Michael,** MBE 2013; RIBA; Partner, Purcell LLP (formerly Purcell Miller Tritton), Architects, since 2014 (Principal Partner, 1978–2014); Surveyor to the Fabric, Canterbury Cathedral, 1990–2014; Surveyor of the Fabric of Westminster Abbey, 1999–2012; *b* 21 May 1945; *s* of Gerald Victor Burton and Kathleen Blodwen (*née* Harper); *m* 1971, Sally Bason; one *s* one *d*. *Educ:* Duston Secondary Mod. Sch., Northampton; Northampton Coll. of Further Educn; Oxford Sch. of Architecture (DipArch). RIBA 1972; IHBC 1998; AABC 1999. Asst to Surveyor to Ely Cathedral, 1971–73; Parish Architect to numerous churches in E Anglia incl. Long Melford and Thaxted, 1973–; Commissioned Architect to English Heritage, 1983–2002; Architect to NT, Melford Hall, Lavenham Guildhall and Flatford Mill, 1973–96; work on restoration of Colchester Castle, 1984–90; Architect, American Ambassador's Residence, London, 1998–2003; Conservation Advr to Crown Urban Estate, 2003–. Chm., Cathedral Architects' Assoc., 1997–99. Member: Cathedrals Fabric Commn for England, 1996–2006; Redundant Churches Cttee, Church Comrs, 1999–2002; Places of Worship Panel, 2000–03, Historic Built Envmt Adv. Cttee,

2000–03, English Heritage; Chm., Redundant Churches Uses Cttee, Chelmsford, 1990–99. Mem., DAC for Chelmsford, 1977–, St Edmundsbury and Ipswich, 1986–98. Mem. Council, Nat. Trust, 2007–. Vice Chm., Georgian Gp, 2014– (Chm., Awards Cttee, 2014). Dir, Mercury Theatre, Colchester, 1999–2003. Mem., Colchester Trinity Rotary Club; Pres., Surveyors' Club, 2012–13. Stone Awards Judge, Stone Fedn of GB, 1995 and 1997 (Chm. of Judges, 1999–). Freeman, City of London, 1996; Master, Masons' Co., 2013–14 (Liveryman, 1996–2005; Court Asst, 2005–); Liveryman, Carpenters' Co., 2007–. *Recreations:* cycling, ski-ing, woodwork. *Address:* Purcell LLP, 25 Bermondsey Square, Tower Bridge Road, SE1 3UN. *T:* (020) 7397 7171. *E:* john.burton@purcelluk.com.

**BURTON, Hon. Mark;** *see* Burton, Hon. R. M.

**BURTON, Rt Rev. Dr Mark Gregory;** barrister, since 2018; Dean of Melbourne, 2008–12; *b* Sydney, 18 May 1956; *s* of late Kenneth Burton and Patricia Burton; *m* 1st, 1975, Annette Gill (marr. diss. 2013); three *d*; 2nd, 2014, Rena Sofroniou. *Educ:* Ridley Coll., Melbourne (BTh 1988); Australian Coll. of Theology (ThD 2001); Univ. of Melbourne Law Sch. (JD 2015); Leo Cussen Centre for Law, Melbourne (Graduate Dip. Legal Practice 2016). Tutor, Ridley Coll., Melbourne, 1989–97; ordained deacon, 1990, priest, 1990; Asst Curate, Werribee, 1990–91; Priest-in-charge, St James', Glen Iris, 1991–97; Examining Chaplain, Dio. of Melbourne, 1996–2000; Chaplain to Archbishop of Melbourne, and Dir of Ordinands, 1997–2000; Archbishop's Chaplain and Aide, 2000; Chaplain: RAN, 2001; HMAS Cerberus Westernport, 2002; HMAS Melbourne, 2003; HMAS Kanimbla/HMAS Adelaide, 2004–05; HMAS Creswell, 2006; Asst Bishop, Dio. of Perth, WA, 2006–09. Called to the Bar, NSW, 2018. Mem., NSW Bar Assoc. Mem. Bd, Slavery Links Inc. (Vic). Australian Service Medal, 1983; Australian Active Service Medal, 2003; Iraq Campaign Medal, 2003; Humanitarian Overseas Service Medal, 2004; Australian Defence Medal, 2005; Australian Operational Service Medal, 2014. OStJ 2012; KSJ 2013. *Recreations:* sailing, scuba diving, motorcycling, archery. *Address:* 6th Floor, St James Hall Chambers, 169 Phillip Street, Sydney, NSW 2000, Australia.

**BURTON, Michael;** *see* Burton, A. M.

**BURTON, Hon. Sir Michael (John),** GBE 2019; Kt 1998; QC 1984; FCIArb; a Judge of the High Court of Justice, Queen's Bench Division, 1998–2016; Judge of the Commercial Court of Abu Dhabi, since 2016; President, Investigatory Powers Tribunal, 2013–18 (Vice President, 2000–13); *b* 12 Nov. 1946; *s* of late Henry Burton, QC, and Hilda Burton; *m* 1972, Corinne Ruth (*d* 1992), *d* of late Dr Jack Cowan, MC, and Dorothy Cowan; four *d*. *Educ:* Eton Coll. (KS, Captain of the School; Fellow, 2005–16); Balliol Coll., Oxford (MA). FCIArb 2016. President, Balliol JCR, 1967; First President, Oxford Univ. SRC, 1968. Called to Bar, Gray's Inn, 1970, Bencher, 1993 (Vice-Treas., 2011; Treas., 2012); Law Lectr, Balliol Coll., Oxford, 1972–74; Head of Littleton Chambers, 1991–98; a Recorder, 1989–98; Judge, Employment Appeal Tribunal, 1999–2016 (Pres. 2002–05); Pres., Interception of Communications Tribunal, 2000. Chairman: Central Arbitration Cttee, 2000–17; Conduct and Appeal Cttee, RICS, 2017–. Chm., High Court Judges Assoc., 2010–11. Contested: (Lab) RBK&C (local elections), 1971; (Lab) Stratford upon Avon, Feb. 1974; (SDP) Putney, GLC, 1981. Hon. Fellow, Goldsmiths Coll., London, 1998. *Publications:* (contrib.) Bullen & Leake & Jacob's Precedents of Pleadings, 13th edn 1990; (ed) Civil Appeals, 2002, 2nd edn 2013. *Recreations:* amateur theatricals, lyric writing, singing, grandchildren. *Address:* Littleton Chambers, Temple, EC4Y 7HR.

**BURTON, Sir Michael (St Edmund),** KCVO 1992 (CVO 1979); CMG 1987; HM Diplomatic Service, retired; independent consultant and lecturer; *b* 18 Oct. 1937; *s* of late Brig. G. W. S. Burton, DSO (and two Bars), and Barbara Burton (*née* Kemmis Betty); *m* 1967, Henrietta Jindra Hones; one *s* one *d* (and one *d* decd). *Educ:* Bedford Sch.; Magdalen Coll., Oxford (William Doncaster Scholar; BA Hons; MA). 2nd Lt, Rifle Brigade, 1955–57. Foreign Office, 1960; lang. trng, Middle East Centre for Arabic Studies, Lebanon, 1960–62; Asst Political Agent, Dubai, Trucial States, 1962–64; Private Sec. to Minister of State, FO, 1964–67; Second (later First) Sec. (Information), Khartoum, 1967–69; First Sec. (Inf.), Paris, 1969–72; Asst, Science and Technology Dept, FCO, 1972–75; First Sec. and Head of Chancery, Amman, 1975–77; Counsellor, Kuwait, 1977–79; Head of Maritime, Aviation and Environment Dept, FCO, 1979–81; Head of S Asian Dept, FCO, 1981–84; on secondment to BP as Head of Policy Rev. Unit, 1984–85; Berlin: Minister, 1985–92; Dep. Comdt, BMG, 1985–90; Head of Embassy Office, 1990–92; Asst Under-Sec. of State (ME and N Africa), FCO, 1993; Ambassador to Czech Republic, 1994–97. Chairman: Eur.-Atlantic Gp, 2001–02 (Pres., 2002–05); British Czech and Slovak Assoc., 2001–14 (Pres., 2014–); Clovelly Lectures, 2011–; Mem. Council, RSAA, 2001–06, 2007–13. Pres., Arts Soc. Kensington & Chelsea (formerly RBK&C DFAS), 2015–. Hon. Pres., Hinduja Foundn, 2003–. Order of Merit, Berlin, 1992. *Recreations:* tennis, travel, wine. *Address:* 6 Napier Court, Ranelagh Gardens, SW6 3UT. *Clubs:* Oxford and Cambridge, Hurlingham (Chm., 2004–07), Pilgrims; Vincent's (Oxford).

**BURTON, Neil Henry,** FSA; Director, Architectural History Practice, since 2001; *b* 23 June 1947; *s* of Angus Robert Burton and Joan Burton (*née* Grant); *m* 1st, 1975, Anna Southall (marr. diss. 1978); 2nd, 1989, Susie Barson (marr. diss. 2014); one *s* one *d*; 3rd, 2016, Caroline Dakers. *Educ:* Christ's Hosp. Sch., Horsham; Pembroke Coll., Oxford (BA Hons Modern Hist.); Edinburgh Univ. (Dip. Hist. of Art). Historian, Historic Bldgs Div., GLC, 1973–88; Inspector of Historic Bldgs, English Heritage, 1988–94; Sec., Georgian Gp, 1994–2001. Dir, Architects Accredited in Building Conservation, 2000–06, 2016–; Jt Dir, Attingham Study Week, 2003–07. Trustee, Historic Chapels Trust, 1995–. IHBC 1998; FSA 1998. *Publications:* Historic Houses Handbook, 1981, 3rd edn 1984; Life in the Georgian City, 1990; Behind the Facade: London town house plans 1660–1840, 2006; contrib. articles to Architectural Rev., Country Life, etc. *Recreation:* walking. *Address:* 8 Gower Mews Mansions, WC1E 6HR. *T:* and *Fax:* (020) 7636 9935. *E:* neil.burton@architecturalhistory.co.uk.

**BURTON, Hon. (Richard) Mark;** MP (Lab) Taupo, 1996–2008 (Tongariro, 1993–96); Deputy Leader of the House, 1999–2008, and Minister of Justice and of Local Government, 2005–08, New Zealand; Minister in Charge of Treaty of Waitangi Negotiations and Responsible for the Law Commission, 2005–08; *b* 16 Jan. 1956; *m* 1977, Carol Botherway; two *s* one *d*. *Educ:* Waikato Univ. (Cert. Contg Educn); Massey Univ. (Cert. Social Service Supervision); NZ Council of Recreation and Sport (Dip.). Residential Social Worker, Dept of Social Welfare, 1976–78; Community Recreation Advr, Palmerston North City Corp., 1978–82; Community Educn Organiser, Central Plateau Rural Educn Activities Prog., 1982–93. Lab. Party spokesman for adult and community educn, 1994–99; Sen. Labour Party Whip, 1996–99; Minister: of Internal Affairs and of Veterans' Affairs, 1999–2002; of State Owned Enterprises, 1999–2004; of Defence and of Tourism, 1999–2005. Various posts with NZ Assoc. for Community and Contg Educn, 1983–93; Member: Bd of Studies, Contg Educn, Waikato Univ., 1985–86; Bd, NZ Career Develt and Transition Educn Service, 1990–92. NZ Medal, 1990. *Address:* c/o Parliament Buildings, Wellington, New Zealand.

**BURTON, Tim;** film director and producer; *b* Burbank, Calif, 25 Aug. 1958; *s* of late Bill Burton and of Jean Burton; *m* 1989, Lena Gieseke; one *s* one *d* with Helena Bonham Carter, *qv*. *Educ:* Calif Inst. of the Arts. Formerly apprentice animator, Walt Disney Studios (projects incl. The Fox and the Hound, 1981; The Black Cauldron, 1985). Animator and dir, Vincent (short film), 1982; *films include: director:* Hansel and Gretel (TV), 1982; Aladdin (TV), 1984; Frankenweenie (short), 1984; Pee-wee's Big Adventure, 1985; Beetlejuice, 1988; Batman, 1989; Sleepy Hollow, 2000; Planet of the Apes, 2001; Big Fish, 2004; Charlie and the Chocolate Factory, 2005; Sweeney Todd: The Demon Barber of Fleet Street, 2008; Dark Shadows, 2012; Miss Peregrine's Home for Peculiar Children, 2016; *director and producer:* Edward Scissorhands, 1991; Batman Returns, 1992; Ed Wood, 1994; Mars Attacks!, 1997; Corpse Bride, 2005; Alice in Wonderland, 2010; Frankenweenie, 2012; Big Eyes, 2014; Dumbo, 2019; *producer:* The Nightmare Before Christmas, 1993; Cabin Boy, 1994; Batman Forever, 1996; James and the Giant Peach, 1996; Nine, 2009; Abraham Lincoln: Vampire Hunter, 2012. Chm. Jury, Cannes Film Fest., 2010. Fellow, BFI, 2012. Chevalier des Arts et des Lettres (France), 2010. *Publications:* My Art and Films, 1993; The Melancholy Death of Oyster Boy and Other Stories, 1997. *Address:* c/o William Morris Endeavor Entertainment, 9601 Wilshire Boulevard, Beverly Hills, CA 90210, USA.

**BURTON-CHADWICK, Sir Joshua (Kenneth),** 3rd Bt *cr* 1935, of Bidston; Brand Partner/Network Distribution, Jeunesse Global, since 2015; *b* 1 Feb. 1954; *s* of Sir Robert Burton-Chadwick, (Sir Peter), 2nd Bt, and of Beryl Joan, *d* of Stanley Frederick J. Brailsford; *S* father, 1983. Founder, Internat. Acad. of Human Relns, 1986–2005; Workshop Facilitator. *Heir:* none.

**BURTON-JONES, Rt Rev. Simon David;** *see* Tonbridge, Bishop Suffragan of.

**BURTON-PAGE, Piers John;** writer, lecturer, critic and broadcaster; *b* 25 July 1947; *s* of John Garrard Burton-Page and Audrey Ruth Burton-Page (*née* Marley); *m* 1976, Patricia Margaret Cornish; two *s*. *Educ:* Harrow Sch.; Wadham Coll., Oxford (MA); Univ. of Sussex (MA in Russian Studies). Joined BBC, 1971: studio manager, 1971–75; announcer and newsreader, Radio 4, 1975–77; Producer, Gramophone Dept, 1977–83; External Services Music Organiser, 1983–85; Radio 3: Presentation Editor, 1985–90; presenter/producer, 1990–97; Exec. Producer, 1998–2002. Acting Editor, Opera, 1997. (Jtly) Ohio State Award, for series The Elements of Music, 1984. *Publications:* Philharmonic Concerto: the life and music of Sir Malcolm Arnold, 1994; The Allegri at 50: a quartet in 5 movements, 2004; contrib. articles and reviews on musical and other subjects. *Recreations:* playing the cello, cricket, theatre, travel, languages, cosmology, the open air. *Club:* Bushmen.

**BURTON-RACE, John William;** *b* 1 May 1957; *s* of Keith Burton and Shirley Burton, later Race; *m* (marr. diss. 2008); one *s* one *d*; *m* 2010, Suzi Ward; one *s*. *Educ:* St Mary's Coll., Bitterne; American Sch., Bangkok. Apprentice, Wessex Hotel, Winchester, 1973–75; Commis, Quaglino's Hotel Meurice, London, 1975–76; First Commis, Chewton Glen Hotel, 1976–78; Chef, Olivers, Midhurst, 1978–79; Chef tournant, La Sorbonne, Oxford, 1979–82; Pvte Chef, MacKenzie-Hill Property Develt Internat., 1982–83; Sous Chef, Les Quat' Saisons, Oxford, 1983–84; Head Chef and Manager, Le Petit Blanc, Oxford, 1984–86 (1 Michelin star, 1984–86); Chef-Proprietor, L'Ortolan, Berks, 1986–2000 (1 Michelin star, 1987–90, 2 Michelin stars, 1991–96, 1999); 1st Cl. and Concorde, BA, 1994, 1995, 1996; Chef, John Burton-Race at Landmark Hotel, London, 2000–02 (2 Michelin stars, 2001); in France, 2002–03; Co-owner, 2004, and Chef, The New Angel, Dartmouth, 2004–10 (1 Michelin star, 2005–10); opened New Angel Cookery Sch., 2005; co-owner, New Angel Rooms, 2005; consultant, YTL Gp, Malaysia, 2010; Consultant Exec. Chef, Sanctum on the Green, Berks, 2010–11; Guest Chef, My Dining Room, Fulham, 2011; Chef Patron, New Angel, Notting Hill, 2014–15. Brand Ambassador and Exec. Develt Chef, Kerrygold and Pilgrim's Choice, Adam's Foods, 2011–. Television series include: Master Chefs of Europe, 1988; Great British Chefs, 1989; Great European Chefs, 1990; French Leave, 2003; Return of the Chef, 2005; Britain's Best Dish, 2007–11; Best Dish: The Chefs, 2011, 2012; Put Your Menu Where Your Mouth Is, 2013. Many gastronomic awards, incl. Chef of the Year, Caterer and Hotelkeeper Awards, 1996. *Publications:* Recipes from an English Master Chef, 1994; French Leave, 2003; French Leave: a wonderful year of escape and discovery, 2004; Coming Home, 2005; First Crack Your Egg, 2007; Flavour First, 2008; (jtly) Cooking for Beginners, 2008. *Recreations:* Porsche cars, fishing, antiques, horse riding.

**BURY, Viscount; Augustus Sergei Darius Keppel;** *b* 8 Feb. 2003; *s* and *heir* of Earl of Albemarle, *qv*.

**BURY, (Anne) Carolyn;** *see* Hayman, Anne C.

**BURY, Lindsay Claude Neils;** Chairman, Electric & General Investment Trust (formerly Henderson Electric & Investment Trust), 2001–12 (Director, 1995–2012); *b* 13 Feb. 1939; *s* of Frank James Lindsay Bury and Diana Mary Lewis; *m* 1968, Sarah Ann Ingall; one *s* one *d*. *Educ:* Eton; Trinity College, Cambridge (BA History). J. Henry Schroder Wagg, 1960–66; Singer & Friedlander, 1966–73; Dunbar & Co., 1973–83. Director: ACT (formerly Apricot Computers), 1968–95 (Chm., 1972–89); Portals Holdings, 1973–95; Christie Group, 1989–94; Roxboro Gp, 1993–2001; Sage Gp, 1995–2006; Chairman: Unicorn Internat., 1995–97; S Staffs Gp (formerly S Staffs Waterworks Co.), 1992–2004 (Dir, 1981–2004); Bango plc, 2000–11; Service Power Technologies plc, 2007–17 (non-exec. Dir, 1997–2007). Trustee, City of Birmingham Touring Opera, 1989–92. Chm. of Govs, Moor Park Sch., 1982–90; Trustee: Millichope Foundn, 1984–; Brazilian Atlantic Rainforest Trust, 2004– (Chm., 2013–); Vice Pres., Fauna and Flora Internat., 2016– (Chm., 1994–2002; Pres., 2002–12; Chm., Global Canopy Prog., 2008–). High Sheriff, Shropshire, 1998. *Publications:* A Shaky Start and a Lot of Luck: a memoir, 2019. *Recreations:* music, wildlife. *Address:* The Old Rectory, Tugford, Craven Arms, Shropshire SY7 9HS. *T:* (01584) 841234; Ruantallain Lodge, Island of Jura, Scotland. *Clubs:* Turf, Pratt's, MCC.

**BURY, Very Rev. Nicholas Ayles Stillingfleet;** Dean of Gloucester, 1997–2010; *b* 8 Jan. 1943; *s* of Major John J. S. Bury, MC, RA and Joan A. M. Bury; *m* 1973, Jennifer Anne Newbold; two *s* one *d*. *Educ:* King's Sch., Canterbury; Queens' Coll., Cambridge (MA 1969); MA Oxon 1971; DipEd Oxon; Cuddesdon Theol Coll. Ordained deacon, 1968, priest, 1969; Asst Curate, Our Lady & St Nicholas, Liverpool, 1968–71; Chaplain, Christ Church, Oxford, 1971–75; Vicar: St Mary's, Shephall, Stevenage, Herts, 1975–84; St Peter in Thanet, Broadstairs, 1984–97. Hon. Fellow, Univ. of Gloucester, 2003. *Recreations:* golf, water-colour painting. *Address:* 122 The Homend, Ledbury, Herefordshire HR8 1BZ. *E:* n.bury95@btinternet.com.

**BUSBY, George Benedict Joseph Pascal,** CMG 2015; OBE 1996; HM Diplomatic Service, retired; Counsellor, Dubai, 2014–15; *b* 18 April 1960; *s* of Christopher Raymond Busby and Anne Margaret Busby; *m* 1988, Helen Frances Hurll; one *s* three *d*. *Educ:* Sch. of Slavonic Studies, London Univ. (BA Hons); St Antony's Coll., Oxford (Diploma). Joined Diplomatic Service, 1987; Second Sec., FCO, 1987; Second, then First Sec., Bonn, 1989–91; First Secretary: FCO, 1991–92; Belgrade, 1992–96; First Sec., then Counsellor, FCO, 1996–2000; Counsellor: Vienna, 2000–04; FCO, 2004–11; Islamabad, 2011–14.

**BUSBY, Prof. Stephen John Williams,** DPhil; FRS 2005; Professor of Biochemistry, University of Birmingham, since 1995; *b* 5 March 1951; *s* of Peter Busby and Joan Busby (*née* Williams); *m* 1980, (Elizabeth) Jane Cooper; two *s* one *d*. *Educ:* Moseley Hall Co. Grammar Sch., Cheadle; Sidney Sussex Coll., Cambridge (BA 1972); Merton and St John's

Colls, Oxford (DPhil 1975). Postdoctoral scientist, 1975–78, on Scientific Staff, 1979–83, Inst Pasteur, Paris; University of Birmingham: Lectr, 1983–88; Sen. Lectr, 1988–90; Reader, 1990–95; Dean of Sci., then Dean of Life and Health Sci., 2000–04; Hd, Sch. of Biocsis, 2012–16. Vis. Scientist, NIH, Bethesda, USA, 1979–80. Chair, Biochem. Soc., 2014–16. *Publications:* contrib. numerous res. papers to learned jls. *Recreations:* family, travel, food, walking, doing nothing! *Address:* School of Biosciences, University of Birmingham, Edgbaston, Birmingham B15 2TT. *T:* (0121) 414 5439. *E:* s.j.w.busby@bham.ac.uk.

**BUSCH, Lisa Virginia;** QC 2016; *b* Buffalo, NY, 16 May 1969; *d* of Douglas Raymond Busch and Janice Evelyn Busch (*née* Wilson); partner, 2004, David Bowen. *Educ:* Fort Street High Sch.; Hollywood Sen. High Sch.; Univ. of Western Australia (BA Hons 1, LLB); Balliol Coll., Oxford (BPhil 1997; MSt 1998). Res. Asst, Law Commn for England and Wales, 1998–99; called to the Bar, Inner Temple, 2000; in practice as a barrister, specialising in public law, local govt, planning and envmtl law, 2000–. Vis. Lectr in Envmtl Law, KCL, 2007–08. *Recreations:* visiting Greece and learning Greek, reading, walking, swimming. *Address:* Cornerstone Barristers, 2–3 Gray's Inn Square, WC1R 5JH.

**BUSCOMBE,** family name of **Baroness Buscombe**.

**BUSCOMBE,** Baroness *cr* 1998 (Life Peer), of Goring in the co. of Oxfordshire; **Peta Jane Buscombe;** *b* 12 March 1954; *m* 1980, Philip John Buscombe; twin *s* one *d. Educ:* Hinchley Wood Sch.; Rosebery Grammar Sch., Epsom; Inns of Ct Sch. of Law. Called to the Bar, Inner Temple, 1977. Legal Advr, Dairy Trade Fedn, 1979–80; lawyer, Barclays Bank International, NY, then Hd Office Lawyer and Inspector, Barclays Bank plc, UK, 1980–84; Asst Sec., Inst. of Practitioners in Advertising, 1984–87. Mem. (C) S Oxfordshire DC, 1995–99. Opposition front bench spokesman, H of L, on trade and industry, social security and legal affairs, 1999–2001, on home and legal affairs, 2001–06; Shadow Minister for Cabinet Office affairs, 2000, for culture, media and sport, 2002–05, for Educn and Skills, 2005–06; a Baroness in Waiting (Govt Whip), 2016–18; Parly Under-Sec. of State, DWP, 2017–19. Cons. spokesman for MoJ, for Business, Energy and Industrial Strategy, and for Culture, Media and Sport, H of L, 2016–17. Vice Chm., All Party Gp for Mgt Consultants, 2001–09; Member: British-American All Party Gp, 1998–; All Party Gp for Corporate Social Responsibility, 2001–, for Intellectual Property, 2004–, for Corporate Governance, 2004–; H of L Select Cttee on Inquiries Act 2005, 2012–14; Mem., Jt Cttee on Human Rights, 2014–16; Vice Pres., All Party Parly Gp for Sexual Equality, 2004–08. Mem., UK Delegn to Parly Assembly, Council of Europe, 2013–15. Vice Chm. resp. for Develt, Cons. Party, 1997–99; Founder, Cons. Network and Cons. Cultural Unit; President: Slough Cons. Assoc., 1997–2001; S Oxfordshire Cons. Patrons, 2008–11; S Oxfordshire Cons. Assoc., 2015– (Vice Chm., 1995–98). Contested (C) Slough, 1997. Mem. Adv. Bd, Gow and Partners, 2003–05. Chief Exec. and Dir-Gen., Advertising Assoc., 2007–09; Dir, Advertising Standards Bd of Finance, 2007–09; Chm., Press Complaints Commn, 2009–11. Non-executive Director: Affinity Water plc (formerly Three Valleys plc, later Veolia Water Central plc), 2006–15; Local World Ltd, 2013–15. Chm., Goring and Streatley Amenity Assoc., 1995–98; Mem., Assoc. of Rural Businesses in Oxfordshire, 1994–2002. Vice Pres., Debating Soc., 2005–. Vice Chair, Globe UK, 2007–10; Member: RSA Risk Commn, 2006–10; Council for Child Internet Safety, 2008–; Jt Cttee, Nat. Security Strategy, 2015–17; Trustee, Index on Censorship, 2015–17. Chm., Adv. Bd, Samaritans, 2011–17. Trustee and Gov., Langley Hall Primary Acad., 2015–17. Patron: Foundn for Internat. Commercial Arbitration and Alternative Dispute Resolution, 1999–2010; Inns of Ct Sch. of Law Cons. Assoc.; PALS, 2000–15; Westminster Media Forum, 2002–; Robert Bowman Gall. Trust, 2004–08; Westminster eForum, 2005–; Westminster Educn Forum, 2005–; Founder Patron, Inst. of Paralegals, 2005–09; Vice Patron, Abbeyfield House Appeal, 1998–2002; Ambassador, Guide Assoc., 2002–. Vice Pres., Henley Soc.; Mem., Chiltern Soc. FRSA 2004–11. *Recreations:* theatre, opera, shooting, riding, fishing. *Address:* House of Lords, SW1A 0PW.

**BUSE, Diana Anjoli;** *see* Garnham, D. A.

**BUSH, Prof. Andrew,** MD; FRCP, FRCPCH; Professor of Paediatrics, and Head, Paediatrics Section, Imperial College London, since 2013 (Professor of Paediatric Respirology, 2002–13); Consultant Paediatric Chest Physician, Royal Brompton and Harefield Foundation Trust, since 1991; *b* London, 24 April 1954; *s* of Geoffrey Bush and Julie Kathleen Bush; *m* 1975, Susan Joan Crucefix; three *s* one *d. Educ:* University College Sch., London; Corpus Christi Coll., Cambridge (BA 1st Cl. Hons 1975; MD 1987); University College Hosp., London (MB BS Hons Surgery 1978). MRCP 1980, FRCP 1996; MRCPCH 1996, FRCPCH 1997. House Physician, Stafford Gen. Infirmary, 1978–79; House Surgeon, UCH, 1979; Med. SHO, Taunton Hosp., 1979–80, Brompton Hosp., 1981; Renal Registrar, St Mary's Hosp., 1981–82; Registrar, St Charles' Hosp., 1982–83; Res. Fellow, Brompton Hosp., 1983–88; SHO, Neonatal Paediatrics, UCH, 1988; Paediatric Registrar, Hillingdon Hosp., 1988–89, Brompton Hosp., 1989–90; Sen. Paediatric Registrar, RPMS Hammersmith Hosp., 1990–91; Consultant Paediatric Chest Physician, Royal Brompton Hosp., 1991–; Academic Dir of Paediatrics, Nat. Heart and Lung Inst., Imperial Coll. London, 1999–. FHEA 2007; FERS 2014; Fellow, Asian Pacific Soc. of Respirology, 2017; Amer. Thoracic Soc. Fellowship, 2018. *Publications:* (ed jtly) Growing up with Lung Disease: the lung in transition to adult life (monograph), 2002; Progress in Respiratory Research, vol. 34, Cystic Fibrosis in the 21st Century, 2005; Kendig's Disorders of the Respiratory Tract in Children, 7th edn 2006, 8th edn as Kendig's and Chernick's Disorders of the Respiratory Tract in Children (ed jtly), 2012; Cystic Fibrosis, 3rd edn 2007 to 4th edn 2016; Paediatric Respiratory Disease: airways and infection, 2010; Paediatric Respiratory Disease: parenchymal diseases, 2010; co-author of papers, chapters and articles. *Recreations:* reading, listening to music, walking, ball games, the evasion of domestic responsibilities. *Address:* Department of Paediatric Respiratory Medicine, Royal Brompton and Harefield NHS Foundation Trust, Sydney Street, SW3 6NP. *T:* (020) 7351 8232, *Fax:* (020) 7351 8377. *E:* a.bush@imperial.ac.uk.

**BUSH, Charles Martin Peter,** MA; Headmaster, Oundle School, 2005–15; *b* 28 June 1952; *s* of late Dr John Peter Bush and Edith Mary (*née* Farnsworth); *m* 1977, Rosalind Mary Nevin; three *s. Educ:* Melbourne C of E Grammar Sch.; Univ. of Melbourne; Trinity Coll., Oxford (MA). Aylesbury Grammar Sch., 1975–78, Hd of Pure Maths, 1977–78; Hd of Maths, Abingdon Sch., 1978–82; Marlborough College, 1982–93: Hd of Maths, 1982–89; Housemaster, B1 House, 1988–93; Headmaster, Eastbourne Coll., 1993–2005. *Publications:* (co-author in SMP Team) Revised Advanced Mathematics (Book 1), 1988. *Recreations:* golf, cricket, mathematics, fell walking. *Address:* 8 Conway House, 6 Ormonde Gate, SW3 4EU. *Clubs:* MCC; Melbourne Cricket.

**BUSH, Geoffrey Hubert,** CB 1998; DL; Deputy Chairman, Board of Inland Revenue, 1998–99, retired; *b* 5 April 1942; *s* of late Sidney Arthur Bush and Dorothy Elizabeth Bush; *m* 1965, Sylvia Mary Squibb; one *s* one *d. Educ:* Cotham Grammar Sch., Bristol. Tax Officer, 1959; Inspector of Taxes, 1968; Dist Inspector of Taxes, 1973; Principal Inspector of Taxes, 1981; Board of Inland Revenue: Under Sec., 1988–94; Dir Gen., 1994–98. Adviser: Office of Govt Commerce, 2000–08; Bank of England, 2003–08; DFE, 2006–10; BIS, 2011–13; Mem. Bd, CAFCASS, 2012–15. Trustee: Devon Co. Agricl Assoc., 2001– (Hon. Life Vice Pres., 2018); Exeter Univ. Foundn, 2006–15; Hospiscare Exeter, 2012–; WESC Foundn, 2012–15 (Vice Chm., 2014–15). Samaritan, 2018–. Chm. Council, 2008–17, Lay Canon, 2015–, Exeter Cathedral. DL Devon, 2008. CStJ 2007 (Chm. Council, Devon, 2001–08). *Recreations:* travel, golf. *Address:* (home) Exmouth, Devon. *Club:* Exeter Golf and Country (Devon) (Vice Chm., 2007–09; Chm., 2009–12).

**BUSH, George Walker;** President of the United States of America, 2001–09; *b* 6 July 1946; *e s* of late George Herbert Walker Bush, Hon. GCB, former President of USA, and Barbara Bush; *m* 1977, Laura Welch; twin *d. Educ:* Phillips Acad., Andover; Yale Univ. (BA History 1968); Harvard Business Sch. (MBA 1975). F-102 Pilot, Texas Air Nat. Guard. Founded Bush Exploration, 1975; merged with Spectrum 7 Energy Corp., 1984 (Pres.), subseq. Harken Energy Corp., 1986 (Consultant); advr and speechwriter to father during Presidential campaign, 1986–88; Governor of Texas, 1995–2000. Republican. Part-owner, Texas Rangers baseball team, 1989–98. *Publications:* A Charge to Keep, 1999; Decision Points, 2010; 41: a portrait of my father, 2014; Portraits of Courage: a commander in chief's tribute to America's warriors, 2017.

**BUSH, Dr Harry John,** CB 2000; independent regulatory consultant and advisor, since 2011; *b* 26 Aug. 1953; *s* of Harold Leslie Bush and Bridget Bush (*née* Gorman). *Educ:* Quintin Grammar Sch.; Quintin Kynaston Sch.; Merton Coll., Oxford (BA Mod. Hist. and Econs 1974); DPhil Oxon 1980. Nuffield College, Oxford: Student, 1974–77; Prize Res. Fellow, 1977–79; Jun. Dean, 1978–79; HM Treasury, 1979–2003: Private Sec. to Minister of State, 1981–82; Principal, 1982; Dep. Press Sec., 1987–89; Asst Sec., 1989; Head of Privatisation, 1993–97; Dep. Dir, then Dir, and Hd of Enterprise and Growth Unit, 1997–2003; Gp Dir, Econ. Regulation, CAA, 2003–10. Chm., OECD Privatisation Network, 1996–98; Dir, EIB, 2002–03; Member: Performance Review Commn, Eurocontrol, 2005–09; Commn for Integrated Transport, 2007–10. Non-executive Director: University Coll. Hosps NHS Trust, 2012– (Vice-Chm., 2013–); Airline Group Ltd, 2014–; NATS Hldgs Ltd, 2014–. FRAeS 2007. *Recreations:* political biography, travel, food, wine, moderate exercise.

**BUSH, Janet Elizabeth;** Senior Editor, McKinsey Global Institute, since 2006; *b* Lytham St Annes, 2 June 1960; *d* of Arthur and Mary Bush; partner, Nick de Cent; one *d. Educ:* Berkhamsted Sch. for Girls; Somerville Coll., Oxford (BA Eng. Lang. and Lit., MA); Centre for Journalism Studies, Cardiff (Reuters schol., postgrad. degree in journalism). Frankfurt Correspondent, 1983–84, Econs writer, 1984–86, Reuters; Dep. Econs Correspondent, 1986–87, NY Correspondent, 1987–90, Financial Times; Presenter, economic documentaries, Money Prog., BBC, 1990–92; Econs Correspondent, 1992–96, Economics Editor, 1997–99, The Times; Director: New Europe, 1999–2003; The No Campaign, 2000–03; Advocacy International Ltd, 2004–05. Harold Wincott Young Financial Journalist of the Year, 1987. *Publications:* (ed) The Real World Economic Outlook, 2003; Consumer Empowerment and Competitiveness, 2004. *Recreations:* dancing, seeing the world, staying alive. *Address:* 44 St David's Hill, Exeter EX4 4DT. *T:* 07970 909495. *E:* janet@janet-bush.com.

**BUSH, John Barnard,** CVO 2012; OBE 2004; JP; farmer; Lord-Lieutenant of Wiltshire, 2004–12; *b* 5 Feb. 1937; *s* of Barnard Bush and Elizabeth (*née* Weeks); *m* 1961, Pamela Bagwell; one *s* one *d. Educ:* Monkton Combe Sch.; Balliol Coll., Oxford (MA). Chairman: WMF Ltd, 1995–99; Countrywide Farmers plc, 1999–2004. Member: Agricl Land Tribunal, 1975–85; Dairy Produce Quota Tribunal, 1984–86. Mem. Council, RASE, 1980–92. Co. Chm., Wilts Br., NFU, 1977–78. Chm., Bristol Avon Flood Defences Cttee, 1981–2000. Chm., Wilts Magistrates' Courts Cttee, 2001–05. Patron: Wilts and Swindon Community Foundn, 2004–; Prospect Hospice, Swindon, 2004–; Mediation Plus (N Wilts), 2004–; Carers Support W Wilts, 2004–; Wilts Ind. Living Centre, 2004–; Anglo-Polish Soc., 2004–12; Relate, N Wilts, 2004–; Wilts Br., Royal Soc. St George, 2004–12; Wilts Archaeol and Natural Hist. Soc., 2010–; Vice-Patron, Friends of Erlestoke Prison, 2012–. President: Wilts Council, Order of St John, 2004–12; ABF Wilts, 2004–12; CPRE, Wilts, 2004–12; Salisbury Br., ESU, 2004–12. Chm., Wilts Historic Bldgs Trust, 2017–. JP NW Wilts, 1980; High Sheriff, 1997–98, DL 1998, Wilts. Gov., Lackham Coll., 1986–98. KStJ 2010 (CStJ 2005). *Address:* Fullingbridge Farm, Heywood, Westbury, Wilts BA13 4NB. *T:* and *Fax:* (01373) 824609. *E:* johnbush@btconnect.com. *Club:* Farmers.

**BUSH, Neil Richard;** HM Diplomatic Service; Ambassador, and Head of UK Delegation to the Organisation for Security and Co-operation in Europe, Vienna, since 2019; *b* Kendal, 15 July 1980; *s* of Basil John Bush and Ingrid Sheila Bush; *m* 2018, Veeral Dattani. *Educ:* Lincoln Coll., Oxford (BA Hons PPE); Columbia Univ., NY and London Sch. of Econs and Political Sci. (MPA 2008). Economist, Bank of England, 2001–03; Strategy and Prog. Officer, World Bank Gp, Washington DC, 2003–05; Sen. Consultant, 2008–09, Sen. Exec. and Man. Consultant, 2009–11, London Economic Internat.; Dep. Dir and Hd Energy Economist, DECC, 2011–15; Hd, Arabian Peninsula (and Iran) Dept, FCO, 2015–19. *Address:* UK Delegation to the Organisation for Security and Co-operation in Europe, Jauresgasse 12, 1030 Vienna, Austria. *T:* (1) 7131575. *E:* neil.bush@fco.gov.uk.

**BUSH, Very Rev. Roger Charles;** Dean of Truro, since 2012; *b* 22 Nov. 1956; *s* of Harvey John Bush and Edith May Rose Bush (*née* Spurgeon); *m* 1984, Lois Mary (*née* Nichols); one *s* one *d. Educ:* King's Coll., London (BA Hons 1978); Univ. of Leeds (BA 1985). Ordained deacon, 1986, priest, 1987; Curate, Newbold with Dunstan, Chesterfield, 1986–90; Team Vicar, Parish of the Resurrection, Leicester, 1990–94; Rector, Redruth with Lanner and Treleigh, Cornwall, 1994–2004; RD, Carnmarth North, 1996–2003; Hon. Canon, 2003–04, Residentiary Canon, 2004–06, Truro Cathedral; Archdeacon of Cornwall, 2006–12. *Recreations:* reading history, theology and fiction, music - anything classical (sings tenor in St Mary's Singers, Truro), walking, collecting maps, watching Humphrey Bogart films. *Address:* Westwood House, Tremorvah Crescent, Truro TR1 1NL. *T:* (01872) 225630, (office) (01872) 276782. *E:* dean@trurocathedral.org.uk.

**BUSH, Prof. Ronald Lee,** PhD; Drue Heinz Professor of American Literature, University of Oxford, 1997–2013, now Emeritus; Fellow, St John's College, Oxford, 1997–2013, now Emeritus Research Fellow; Senior Research Fellow, Institute for English Studies, University of London, since 2013; *b* 16 June 1946; *s* of Raymond J. Bush and Esther S. Bush; *m* 1969, Marilyn Wolin; one *s. Educ:* Univ. of Pennsylvania (BA 1968); Pembroke Coll., Cambridge (BA 1970); Princeton Univ. (PhD 1974). Asst Prof., later Associate Prof. of English, Harvard Univ., 1974–82; Associate Prof., later Prof. of Literature, CIT, 1982–97. NEH Fellow, 1977–78, 1992–93; Vis. Fellow, Exeter Coll., Oxford, 1994–95; Fellow, Amer. Civilization Prog., Harvard, 2004; Hurst Dist. Vis. Prof., Washington Univ., St Louis, 2013; Vis. Scholar, Amer. Acad. in Rome, 2014–15. *Publications:* The Genesis of Ezra Pound's Cantos, 1976; T. S. Eliot: a study of character and style, 1984; (ed) T. S. Eliot: the modernist in history, 1991; (ed) Prehistories of the Future: the primitivist project and the culture of modernism, 1995; American Voice/American Voices, 1999; (ed) Claiming the Stones/Naming the Bones: cultural property and the negotiation of national and ethnic identity, 2002. *Recreation:* tennis. *Address:* St John's College, Oxford OX1 3JP. *T:* (01865) 277300.

**BUSH, William;** Director of Public Policy and Communications, The Premier League (formerly Football Association Premier League), since 2005; *b* 2 Oct. 1951; *s* of Douglas Stewart Murray Bush and Dorothy Yvonne Anna Bush; *m* 1973, Susan Holmes (marr. diss.); one *s. Educ:* Bedford Coll. (BA); London Sch. of Econs (MSc Econ). Head: Leader's Office,

**BUSHELL**, (Rosalind) Morag; *see* Ellis, Rosalind M.

**BUSHILL-MATTHEWS, Philip Rodway**; Member (C) West Midlands, European Parliament, 1999–2009; *b* 15 Jan. 1943; *s* of William Bushill-Matthews, MBE and Phyllis Bushill-Matthews, OBE; *m* 1967, Angela Loveday Bingham; one *s* two *d. Educ*: Malvern Coll.; University Coll., Oxford (MA); Harvard Business Sch. (AMP 1987); Univ. of Leicester (BA 1st cl. Hons Archaeol 2015). Joined Birds Eye Foods Ltd, 1965; seconded to Thomas Lipton Inc., USA, 1976; Nat. Accounts Dir, Birds Eye Sales Ltd, 1977–80; Man. Dir, Iglo industrias de gelados, Lisbon, 1980–81; Sales Dir, then Sales and Distribution Dir, Birds Eye Wall's Ltd, 1981–88; Managing Director: Craigmillar Ltd, 1988–91 (also Dir, Van den Bergh & Jurgens Ltd); Red Mill Snack Foods Ltd, 1991–99; Red Mill Co., BV, Netherlands, 1993–99. Leader, Cons. MEPs, 2008 (Dep. Leader, 2007–08). Non-exec. Dir, Coventry and Warwickshire NHS Partnership Trust, 2011–14 (Vice-Chm., 2012–14). FInstD 1994. *Publications*: The Gravy Train, 2003; Who Rules Britannia?, 2005; The Eras of La Gomera, 2018. *Recreations*: bridge, the theatre, archaeology, enjoying the countryside. *E*: bushillm@outlook.com.

**BUSK, Glennis**; *see* Haworth, S. G.

**BUSK, Maj.-Gen. Leslie Francis Harry**, CB 1990; Director General, British Heart Foundation, 1990–2003; *b* 12 Sept. 1937; *s* of late Lt-Col Charles William Francis Busk and Alice (*née* van Bergen); *m* 1st, 1960, Jennifer Helen Ring (*d* 1992); three *s*; 2nd, 1993, Sheila Glennis McElwain (*see* S. G. Haworth). *Educ*: Wellington Coll.; RMA, Sandhurst; RMCS, Shrivenham (BSc (Eng) London Univ.). Commnd RE, 1957; served in UK, NI, BAOR, India and Singapore; Defence Services Staff Coll., India, 1969; OC 25 Field Sqn, 1971–73; Instr, Staff Coll., Camberley, 1975–77; CO 35 Engr Regt, 1977–79; C of S 2nd Armoured Div., 1979–81; Bde Comd 11 Engr Bde, 1981–83; RCDS, 1984; DMO, MoD, 1985–86; Army Pilots Course, 1986–87; Dir, AAC, 1987–89, retd. Hon. Col, RE Volunteers (Sponsored Units), 1986–91; Col Comdt, RE, 1990–95. Chairman: AMRC, 1991–95, 1999–2002; Eur. Heart Network, 1998–2002. DUniv Glasgow, 2003. *Recreations*: golf, tennis. *Address*: Bushwood, Witheridge Hill Bottom, Highmoor, Henley on Thames, Oxon RG9 5PE. *Club*: Boodle's.

**BUSQUIN, Philippe**; Member (Soc.), European Parliament, 2004–09; *b* 6 Jan. 1941; *m. Educ*: Univ. Libre de Bruxelles (Licence in Phys. Scis 1962; Cand. in Philosophy 1971; post-grad. in Envmt 1976). Asst in Physics, Faculty of Medicine, Univ. Libre de Bruxelles, 1962–77; Prof., Teachers' Coll., Nivelles, 1962–77; Pres., Bd of Dirs, IRE, 1978–80. Deputy: Province of Hainaut, 1977–78; Chamber of Reps, Belgium, 1978–95; Senator, Belgium, 1995–99; Minister of Educn, 1980; Minister for the Interior, 1981; Walloon Minister for Budget and for Energy, 1982–85; Walloon Minister for Economy, 1988; Minister of Social Affairs, 1988–92; Hon. Minister, 1992. Mem., EC, 1999–2004. Mayor of Seneffe, 1995–99. Mem., Community Exec., 1980–81. Pres., Socialist Party, Belgium, 1992–99; Vice-President: Internat. Socialists, 1992–99; European Socialist Party, 1995–97. Chm., Nat. Geographic Inst., Belgium, 2004–.

**BUSSELL, Dame Darcey (Andrea)**, DBE 2018 (CBE 2006; OBE 1995); Principal Ballerina, 1989–2006, Principal Guest Artist, 2006–07, Royal Ballet; *b* 27 April 1969; *d* of Philip Michael Bussell and Andrea Pemberton (*née* Williams); *m* 1997, Angus Forbes; two *d. Educ*: Arts Educnl Sch.; Royal Ballet Sch. Joined Sadler's Wells Royal Ballet (later Birmingham Royal Ballet), 1987; joined Royal Ballet, 1988: soloist, 1988; first soloist, 1989. *Leading rôles in*: Giselle; Swan Lake; Sleeping Beauty; La Bayadère (also with Kirov and Australian Ballet, 1998); Laurentia pas de six; Song of the Earth; Requiem; Galanteries; Spirit of Fugue; Pursuit; first Royal Ballet perf. of Balanchine's Rubies; Cinderella; Enigma Variations; Nutcracker; MacMillan's Elite Syncopations; Raymonda; Monotones; Symphony in C; first Royal Ballet perf. of Balanchine's Stravinsky Violin Concerto; Agon; Bloodlines; Les Biches; Tchaikovsky pas de deux; Beyond Bach; first perf. of William Forsythe's In the middle, somewhat elevated; Romeo and Juliet; Gong; Sylvia; The Four Temperaments; Kiss; Theme and Variations; *rôles created*: Princess Rose in Prince of the Pagodas, Royal Opera House, 1989; pas de deux (Farewell to Dreams) for HM Queen Mother's 90th Birthday Tribute, Palladium and Royal Opera House, 1990; Masha in Winter Dreams, 1991; Mr Worldly Wise, 1995; Dances With Death, 1996; Pavane pour une infante défunte, 1996; Amores, 1997; Towards Poetry, 1999; Lento, 1999; There Where She Loves, 2000; Dance Variations, 2000; Tryst, 2002; Tryst à Grande Vitesse, 2005. Touring song and dance show, Viva La Diva, 2007–08. Pres., Royal Acad. of Dance, 2012–; Mem. Bd, Margot Fonteyn Foundn. Pres., Fundraising Appeal, Birmingham Royal Ballet. Internat. Patron, Sydney Dance Co., 2012–; Patron: Internat. Dance Teachers Association; Ceccetti UK; Ceccetti Australia; Dance Teachers' Benevolent Fund UK; Du Boisson Dance Foundn; New English Ballet Th.; Sight for All; Borne; Henry Spink Foundn; Re:Bourne; Ambassador, Giving Prog., NZ Sch. of Dance. Judge, Strictly Come Dancing, 2012–18; TV Presenter: live cinema relays for Royal Ballet, 2013–; Darcey Bussell: looking for Margot, 2016. Founder, Diverse Dance Mix, 2015. Hon. DLitt Oxford, 2009; Hon. Dr of Univ Royal Conservatoire, Glasgow, 2017. Prix de Lausanne, 1986; Variety Club of GB Award for most promising newcomer, 1990; Dancer of Year Award, Dance and Dancers Mag., 1990; Evening Standard Award for dance, 1990. *Publications*: The Young Dancer, 1994; (with Judith Mackrell) Life in Dance (autobiog.), 1998; Pilates For Life, 2005; Dance Body Workout, 2007; Darcey Bussell: A Life in Pictures, 2012; Darcey Bussell: evolved, 2018; *for children*: Magic Ballerina (series), 2007. *Recreations*: art and painting, reading, swimming. *Address*: c/o TCB Group, 24 Kimberley Court, Kimberley Road, Queens Park, NW6 7SL.

**BUSSON, André-Arpad Pascal Cyril, (Arpad Busson)**; Chairman, LumX Group (formerly Gottex Group), since 2014 (Founder and Chairman, EIM, 1992–2014); *b* Boulogne-Billancourt, 27 Jan. 1963; *s* of Pascal Cyril Busson and Florence Harcourt-Smith; two *s. Educ*: Institut Le Rosey. Founder and Chm., Absolute Return for Kids (ARK), 2002–09. *Recreations*: ski-ing, shooting. *Address*: LumX Group Ltd, 6th Floor, 54 Jermyn Street, SW1Y 6LX. *Clubs*: White's, Travellers; Corviglia Ski; MBC.

**BUSTANI, José Mauricio**; Ambassador of Brazil to France, 2008–15, and to Monaco, 2011–15; *b* 5 June 1945; *s* of Mauricio José Bustani and Guajá de Figueiredo Bustani; *m* 1971, Janine-Monique Lazaro; two *s* one *d. Educ*: Pontifícia Universidade Católica, Rio de Janeiro (LLB 1967); Brazilian Diplomatic Acad., Rio Branco Inst. Joined Brazilian Foreign Service, 1965; postings include: Moscow, 1970–73; Vienna, 1973–77; UN, NY, 1977–84; Montevideo, 1984–87; Montreal, 1987–92; Dir-Gen., Dept for Internat. Orgns, 1993–97; has held rank of Ambassador, 1995–; Dir-Gen., Orgn for Prohibition of Chem. Weapons, 1997–2002; Ambassador to the Court of St James's, 2003–08. Delegate to international negotiations including: 3rd UN Conf. on Law of the Sea, 1974–82; UN Gen. Assembly, 1977–83, 1993–96; 1st and 2nd Special Sessions of UN Gen. Assembly (Disarmament Affairs), 1978 and 1982; Montreal Protocol on Substances that Deplete the Ozone Layer (Leader), 1989–92; Multilateral Fund for Implementation of Montreal Protocol, 1990–91; 13th and 15th Sessions of Prep. Commn for Orgn for Prohibition of Chem. Weapons (Leader), 1996–97. *Recreation*: classical music.

**BUTCHER, Anthony John**; QC 1977; a Recorder, 1985–97; *b* 6 April 1934; *s* of late F. W. Butcher and O. M. Butcher (*née* Ansell); *m* 1959, Maureen Workman (*d* 1982); one *s* two *d. Educ*: Cranleigh Sch.; Sidney Sussex Coll., Cambridge (MA, LLB). Called to the Bar, Gray's Inn, 1957, Bencher, 1986; in practice at English Bar, 1957–97. Mem., Bar Council, 1989–91, and 1993–97; Chm., Official Referees Bar Assoc., 1986–92. *Recreations*: enjoying the arts and acquiring useless information. *Address*: Anthony Cottage, Polecat Valley, Hindhead, Surrey GU26 6BE. *T*: (01428) 609053. *Clubs*: Garrick, Beefsteak.
*See also* Hon. Sir C. J. Butcher.

**BUTCHER, Hon. Sir Christopher (John)**, Kt 2018; Hon. Mr Justice Butcher; a Judge of the High Court, Queen's Bench Division, since 2018; *b* 14 Aug. 1962; *o s* of Anthony John Butcher, *qv*; *m* 1992, Fiona, *y d* of late Prof. Maxwell Gaskin, DFC; one *s* one *d. Educ*: Charterhouse (Sen. Schol.); Magdalen Coll., Oxford (Demy; Gibbs Prize in Mod. Hist. 1982; BA 1st Cl. Hons Mod. Hist.; MA); City Univ. (Dip. Law); King's Coll., London (Dip. EC Law; PhD 2019). Fellow, All Souls Coll., Oxford, 1983–98, 2005–07 (Jun. Dean, 1988–90 and 1992–98); Eldon Law Schol., Univ. of Oxford, 1987; called to the Bar, Gray's Inn, 1986 (Bacon Schol., Atkin Schol.; Bencher, 2005); QC 2001; a Recorder, 2009–18; a Dep. High Court Judge, 2013–18. Gov., Berkhamsted Collegiate Sch., 1995–2009. FRSA 2002. *Publications*: contrib. to various legal pubns. *Recreations*: history, literature, travel, the arts. *Address*: Royal Courts of Justice, Rolls Building, Fetter Lane, EC4A 1NL.

**BUTCHER, Peter Roderick**; HM Diplomatic Service; Ambassador to Turkmenistan, 2005–10; *b* 6 Aug. 1947. *Educ*: Univ. of Bath. Entered FCO, 1974; Second Sec., Peru, 1979–83; Madrid, 1983; Second Sec., Bombay, 1983–87; First Sec., FCO, 1987–90; Dep. High Comr, Lesotho, 1990–93; St Vincent and the Grenadines, 1994; First Sec., FCO, 1994–96; Dep. Gov., Port Stanley, 1996; on secondment to DFID, 1997–99; Dep. Hd of Mission, Mozambique, 2000–03.

**BUTCHERS, Ven. Dr Mark Andrew**; Archdeacon of Barnstaple, since 2015; *b* 1959. *Educ*: Trinity Coll., Cambridge (BA 1981); Chichester Theol Coll. (BTh 1987); King's Coll. London (MTh 1990; PhD 2006). Ordained deacon, 1987, priest, 1988; Curate: St Luke, Chelsea, 1987–90; St Peter and St Paul, Mitcham, 1990–93; Rector, St Peter, North Tawton, Bondleigh and Sampford Courtenay with Honeychurch, 1993–99; Chaplain and Fellow, Keble Coll., Oxford, 1999–2005; Curate, 2005–07, Priest-in-charge, 2007–10, Vicar, 2010–15, St Peter, Wolvercote, Oxford; Area Dean, Oxford, 2012–15. *Address*: Stage Cross, Sanders Lane, Bishops Tawton, Barnstaple EX32 0BE.

**BUTE**, 7th Marquess of, *cr* 1796; **John Colum Crichton-Stuart, (John C. Bute)**; Viscount Ayr, 1622; Br (NS), 1627; Earl of Dumfries, Lord Crichton of Sanquhar and Cumnock, 1633; Earl of Bute, Viscount Kingarth, Lord Mountstuart, Cumrae and Inchmarnock, 1703; Baron Mountstuart, 1761, Baron Cardiff, 1776; Earl of Windsor, Viscount Mountjoy, 1796; Hereditary Sheriff of Bute; Hereditary Keeper of Rothesay Castle; *b* 26 April 1958; *s* of 6th Marquess of Bute, KBE and of his 1st wife, Nicola (*née* Weld-Forester); S father, 1993; *m* 1st, 1984, Carolyn E. R. M. (marr. diss. 1993), *d* of late Bryson Waddell; one *s* two *d*; 2nd, 1999, Serena Solitaire Wendell; one *d*. Motor racing career (as Johnny Dumfries), 1980–92: British Formula Three Champion, 1984; FIA European Formula Three Championship runner-up, 1984 (15 wins); Formula One Ferrari test driver, 1985; JPS Team Lotus Formula One Driver, FIA Formula One World Championship, 1986; FIA World Sports Prototype Championship: 1 win, 1987; Team Silk Cut Jaguar Driver, 1988 (Jt Winner, 24 hr Le Mans sports car race, estd new outright lap record); Team Toyota GB Driver, 1989, 1990; test driver for Benetton Formula One and other Sports Prototype teams, 1990–92. *Heir*: *s* Earl of Dumfries, *qv*.

**BUTLER**, family name of **Earl of Carrick**, **Viscount Mountgarret**, and **Barons Butler of Brockwell** and **Dunboyne**.

**BUTLER OF BROCKWELL**, Baron *cr* 1998 (Life Peer), of Herne Hill in the London Borough of Lambeth; **Frederick Edward Robin Butler**, KG 2003; GCB 1992 (KCB 1988); CVO 1986; PC 2004; Master, University College, Oxford, 1998–2008; Secretary of the Cabinet and Head of the Home Civil Service, 1988–98; *b* 3 Jan. 1938; *s* of late Bernard and Nora Butler; *m* 1962, Gillian Lois Galley; one *s* two *d. Educ*: Harrow Sch.; University Coll., Oxford (BA Lit. Hum., 1961). Joined HM Treasury, 1961; Private Sec. to Financial Sec. to Treasury, 1964–65; Sec., Budget Cttee, 1965–69; seconded to Cabinet Office as Mem., Central Policy Rev. Staff, 1971–72; Private Secretary: to Rt Hon. Edward Heath, 1972–74; to Rt Hon. Harold Wilson, 1974–75; returned to HM Treasury as Asst Sec. i/c Gen. Expenditure Intell. Div., 1975; Under Sec., Gen. Expenditure Policy Gp, 1977–80; Prin. Establishments Officer, 1980–82; Principal Private Sec. to Prime Minister, 1982–85; Second Perm. Sec., Public Expenditure, HM Treasury, 1985–87. Mem., Royal Commn on H of L reform, 1999; Chm., Review of Intelligence on Weapons of Mass Destruction, 2004. Non-executive Director: HSBC Hldgs, 1998–2008; ICI plc, 1998–2008. Ind. Chm., Kings Health Partners, 2009–14. Gov., Harrow Sch., 1975–91 (Chm. of Govs, 1988–91); Chm. Govs, Dulwich Coll., 1997–2003. *Recreation*: competitive games. *Address*: House of Lords, SW1A 0PW. *Clubs*: Athenæum, Brooks's, Beefsteak, Royal Anglo-Belgian, MCC, Oxford and Cambridge.
*See also* Hon. A. Butler.

**BUTLER, Alison Sarah**; *see* Burns, A. S.

**BUTLER, Hon. Andrew**; QC 2018; *b* London, 29 June 1968; *s* of Baron Butler of Brockwell, *qv*; *m* 1998, Catriona MacLaren; one *s* one *d. Educ*: Harrow Sch.; University Coll., Oxford (BA Lit.Hum.). MCIArb 2015. Called to the Bar, Middle Temple, 1993; in practice as a barrister, specialising in property and commercial work, Francis Taylor Bldg, subseq. Tanfield Chambers, 1995–. Chm., Abbeyfield Dulwich Soc., 2017–. Gov., Harrow Sch., 2015–; Pres., Old Harrovian Assoc. FC, 2013–. Freeman, Drapers' Co. *Recreations*: Rugby Union (Mem., London Soc. of Rugby Union Referees), cricket, golf. *Address*: Tanfield Chambers, 2–5 Warwick Court, WC1R 5DJ. *T*: (020) 7421 5300. *E*: andrewbutler@tanfieldchambers.co.uk. *Club*: Garrick.

**BUTLER, Arthur William**; ERD 1964; consultant on parliamentary relations; Secretary, Parliamentary & Scientific Committee, 1979–95, Hon. Life Member 1996, Life Member 2018; *b* 20 Jan. 1929; *s* of late F. Butler and E. Butler; *m* 1958, Evelyn Mary Luetchford; one *d. Educ*: Wanstead High Sch.; LSE (BSc (Econ)). Universities' Prize Essayist, RAS, 1950. Nat. Service, India Cadet Co., Queen's Royal Regt, RAOC, 1946–48, 2nd Lt; Lt, AER, RAOC, 1953, Capt., 1957–64. Trainee, Kemsley Newspapers Graduate Trng Course, Middlesbrough Evening Gazette, 1951–55; Political Correspondent, News Chronicle, 1956–60; Political Ed., Reynolds News, 1960–62; Political Correspondent, Daily Express, 1963–69; Political Ed., Daily Sketch, 1969–71; Man. Dir, Partnerplan Public Affairs, 1971–74; Dir, Public Affairs Div., John Addey Associates, 1974–77; Vice-Chm., Charles Barker Watney & Powell, 1988–89 (Jt Man. Dir, 1978–87). Dir, CSM Parly Consultants Ltd, 1995–2012. Secretary: Roads Campaign Council, 1974–86; All-Party Roads Study Gp, 1974–86; Founder Secretary: Parly All-Party Motor Industry Gp,

1978–90; Parly IT Cttee, 1981–84; Associate Parly Gp on Meningitis, 1999–2001. Consultant on Parly Relns, McAvoy Wreford Bayley, 1989–92; GCI London, 1992–93. Media Advr, Archer Inquiry into NHS contaminated blood, 2007–09. Patron, Art Fund, 2014–. Jt Managing Editor, Science in Parliament, 1989–98; Editor, Free Romanian (English edn), 1985–95. Freeman, City of London, 1976; Liveryman, Co. of Tobacco Pipe Makers, 1977. Governor, Shelley Sch., Kennington, 1999–2003. *Publications:* (with Alfred Morris, MP) No Feet to Drag, 1972; (with C. Powell) The First Forty Years: a history of the Parliamentary & Scientific Committee, 1980; (with D. Smith) Lobbying in the British Parliament, 1986; People, Politics and Pressure Groups, 2010; Jinx of Fleet Street, 2012; Memoirs of a Jazz-Age Babe, 2013; Cmdr of the Fifth Estate, 2016; articles in newspapers and various pubns. *Recreations:* travel, collecting books and militaria, gardening. *Address:* 30 Chester Way, Kennington, SE11 4UR. *T:* (020) 7587 5170.

**BUTLER, Mrs Audrey Maude Beman,** MA; Headmistress, Queenswood (GSA), Hatfield, Herts, 1981–96; *b* 31 May 1936; *d* of Robert Beman Minchin and Vivien Florence Fraser Scott; *m* 1959, Anthony Michael Butler (marr. diss. 1981); two *d*. *Educ:* Queenswood, Hatfield; St Andrews Univ., Scotland (1st Cl. MA Hons, Geography and Polit. Economy; Scottish Univs Medal, RSGS, 1957–58; Double Blue (tennis, hockey)). Asst Geography Teacher, Queenswood, 1958–59; part-time teacher, Raines Foundn Sch. for Girls, Stepney, 1959–61; Head of Geography, S Michael's, Burton Park, 1970–73, VI Form Tutor/Geography asst, 1974–78; first House Mistress of Manor House, Lancing Coll., 1978–81. Chm., Boarding Schs Assoc., 1989–91 (Hon. Life Mem., 1996); Mem. Exec. Cttee, GSA, 1987–90 (Hon. Life Mem., GSA, 1996). Governor: Duncombe Sch., 1982–97; Tockington Manor Sch., 1984–97 (Chm., 1995–97); Aldenham Sch., 1987–2001; Maltman's Green Sch., 1988–98; St Mary's, Ascot, 1995–2002; St Leonard's, Mayfield, 1999–2004. Trustee, Bloxham Project, 1999–2003 (Vice-Chm., 1992–99). Dir, British Tennis Foundn, 1997–2007. Vice-Pres., Herts LTA, 1986–2018. Freeman, City of London, 1997. *Recreations:* golf (Sussex County Colours, 1970), travel, music. *Address:* Chandlers Cottage, Lodsworth Common, Petworth, W Sussex GU28 9DT. *T:* (01798) 861845.

**BUTLER, Basil Richard Ryland,** CBE 1997 (OBE 1976); FREng; FIMMM; Chairman, KS Biomedix plc, 1995–2001; Director, Murphy Oil Corp., Arkansas, 1991–2002; Managing Director, British Petroleum Co. plc, 1986–91; *b* 1 March 1930; *s* of Hugh Montagu Butler and Annie Isabel (*née* Wiltshire); *m* 1954, Lilian Joyce Haswell; one *s* two *d*. *Educ:* Denstone Coll., Staffs; St John's Coll., Cambridge (MA). Nat. Service, 2nd Lieut, 5th Royal Inniskilling Dragoon Guards, 1948–49. Reservoir Engr, Trinidad Leaseholds Ltd, 1954; Petroleum Engr to Chief Petroleum Engr and Supt Prodn Planning Div., Kuwait Oil Co., 1958–68; transf. to BP, Operations Man., Colombia, 1968; Ops Man., BP Alaska Inc., Anchorage, 1970; seconded to Kuwait Oil Co. as Gen. Man. Ops, 1972; Manager: Ninian Develts, BP Petroleum Development Co. Ltd, London, 1975; Sullom Voe Terminal, Shetland Is, 1976; BP Petroleum Development Ltd: Gen. Man., Exploration and Prodn, Aberdeen, 1978; Chief Exec., London, 1980; Dir, BP Internat. Ltd; Chm., BP Exploration Co. Ltd, 1986–89 (Man. Dir and Chief Exec., 1986); Dir, BP Solar Internat., 1991–98 (Chm., 1991–95). Chairman: Devonport Management, 1992–94; Brown and Root Ltd, 1993–98 (Dir, 1991–98). Chm., Eur. Council of Applied Scis and Engrg, 1992–97. Mem., Cttee for ME Trade, 1985–93. Pres., Inst. of Petroleum, 1990–92; Mem. Council, Royal Acad. of Engrg, 1994–2002 (Hon. Sec. for Internat. Affairs, 1995–98; Sen. Vice Pres., 1996–99). FInstPet 1965; Hon. FIChemE 1991. Liveryman, Shipwrights' Co., 1988. Cdre, Royal Western Yacht Club, 2004–08. *Recreations:* sailing, music. *Address:* Royal Academy of Engineering, SW1Y 5DG.

**BUTLER, Brian;** Managing Director, Lines2take Ltd, since 2010; *b* 3 May 1949; *s* of Joseph and Alice Eileen Butler; *m* 1978, Margaret Ruth Anne Macdonald (marr. diss. 1990). *Educ:* Hunslet Carr Primary Sch., Leeds; Cockburn High Sch., Leeds; Univ. of Birmingham (BA). Journalist, Westminster Press, 1971–75; Central Office of Information: Information Officer, Newcastle upon Tyne, 1975–79; Sen. Information Officer, Birmingham, 1979–86; Sen. Information Officer, then Grade 7, DoH, 1986–88; Media and Govt Relns Manager, Lloyds Bank, 1988–94; Co-ordinator, Deregulation Task Forces, DTI, 1993–94; Head of Information Services, Benefits Agency, 1994–96; Head of News, 1996–98, Dir of Communication, 1998–2002, Home Office; Dir, Counter-Terrorism Communications, Cabinet Office, 2002–03; Dir of Communications, BMA, 2003–10. Pres., Westminster Players, 2001–05. Chm., The Spokesmen Gp, 2006–15. Theatre Critic, Gscene mag., 2017–. FRSA 2000. *Publications:* (ed jtly and contrib.) Oxford Dictionary of Finance, 1993; (ed jtly and contrib.) Oxford Dictionary of Finance and Banking, 1997. *Recreations:* acting, writing, singing, directing, the USA, the works of Stephen Sondheim, film script writing. *E:* brianbbutler2014@gmail.com. *Club:* Meanwood Working Men's (Leeds) (Life Mem.).

**BUTLER, (Christopher) David,** CB 1995; Director, Department for National Savings, 1991–95 (Deputy Director, 1989–91); *b* 27 May 1942; *s* of Major B. D. Butler, MC (killed in action, 1944) and H. W. Butler (*née* Briggs); *m* 1967, Helen Christine, *d* of J. J. Cornwell and G. Cornwell (*née* Veysey); two *d*. *Educ:* Christ's Hospital; Jesus College, Oxford (BA); St Mary's Twickenham (TESOL Cert. 2006). Joined HM Treasury, 1964; Asst Private Sec. to Chancellor of Exchequer, 1967–69; Sec., Cttee to Review Nat. Savings (Page Cttee), 1970–72; Head of public expenditure divs, HM Treasury, 1978–82; Head of corporate planning div., Central Computer and Telecoms Agency, 1982–85; HM Treasury: Under-Sec., 1985–89; Head of running costs, manpower and superannuation group, 1985–86; Principal Estabt and Finance Officer, 1987–89. Chief Exec., The Princess Royal Trust for Carers, 1996–99; Res. Manager, 1999–2001, Claims Process Manager, 2001–05, Internat. Commn on Holocaust Era Insurance Claims. Governor, Sadler's Wells Foundn, 1989–94; Dir, Sadler's Wells Trust Ltd, 1989–95; Trustee, Royal Ballet Benevolent Fund, 2008–17; Mem., Finance and Gen. Purposes Cttee, Birkbeck Coll., London, 2009–12. Sec., Wimbledon Soc., 2006–14. (Pt-time) Teacher of English as foreign lang., 2005–12. *Recreations:* ballet, opera, reading, family interests. *Club:* Civil Service (Chm., 1994–96).

**BUTLER, Christopher John;** Owner, Butler Kelly, since 2015; *b* 12 Aug. 1950; *s* of late Dr John Lynn Butler and Eileen Patricia Butler; *m* 1989, Jacqueline Clair, *d* of Mr and Mrs R. O. F. Harper, Glos; one *s*. *Educ:* Emmanuel Coll., Cambridge (MA). Market Research Consultant, 1975–77; Cons. Res. Dept, 1977–80; Political Office, 10 Downing Street, 1980–83; Special Advr, Sec. of State for Wales, 1983–85; Market Res. Consultant, 1985–86; Special Advr, Minister for the Arts, and of the Civil Service, 1986–87; Consultant in Public Policy, Public Policy Unit, 1992–95; Dir, Grandfield Public Affairs, 1995–97. MP (C) Warrington South, 1987–92; contested (C): Warrington South, 1992; Wales, Eur. Parlt, 1999; S Wales E, Welsh Assembly, 2016. Mem., Select Cttee on Employment, 1990–92. Vice Chm., All Party Leasehold Reform Gp, 1989–92; Secretary: All Party Drugs Misuse Cttee, 1989–92; All Party Penal Affairs Cttee, 1990–92. Mem., Exec. Cttee, CPA, 1991–92. Dir, Butler Kelly Ltd, 1998–2015. *Recreations:* writing, deltiology, book collecting. *Address:* Longwall House, Seven Mile Lane, Borough Green, Kent TN15 8QY.

**BUTLER, Cortina Maxine Ann Cotterell;** Director, Literature, British Council, since 2013; *b* London, 21 April 1958; *d* of Reg Butler and Rosemary Young Butler; one *d*. *Educ:* Berkhamsted Sch. for Girls; Somerville Coll., Oxford (MA Psychol. and Philosophy 1980). Reader's Digest Association Ltd: Asst Ed., 1981–85; Project Ed., 1985–87; Sen. Ed., Conran Octopus, 1987–90; Publisher, Charles Letts, 1990–93; London Office Manager, Dumont Buchverlag, 1993–94; Reader's Digest Association Ltd: Series Ed., 1994–96; Editl Dir, Books, 1996–2005; Reader's Digest Association Inc.: Internat. Ed., 2005–07; Vice Pres. Global Ed.-in-Chief, Books and Home Entertainment, 2007–11; Man. Dir, BookBrunch, 2012–13. Non-exec. Dir, DACS, 2013–; Trustee, Art360 Foundn (formerly DACS Foundn), 2015–. Gov., Dallington Sch., 2008–. *Publications:* (with R. Anness) Cupcakes for Kids, 2014. *Recreations:* reading, country walking, theatre, opera, art exhibitions. *Address:* British Council, 10 Spring Gardens, SW1A 2BN. *T:* (020) 7389 4385. *E:* cortina.butler@britishcouncil.org.

**BUTLER, Creon Adrian John Cotterell;** HM Diplomatic Service; Director, National Security Secretariat, Cabinet Office, since 2016; *b* 1960; *m* 1991, Wendy Joanne Niffikeer; one *s* one *d*. *Educ:* LSE (BSc, MSc). Bank of England, 1984–99: posts incl. Hd, Monetary Instruments and Markets Div.; Foreign and Commonwealth Office: Chief Economist, 1999–2006; Dir, Econ. Policy, 2004–06; Minister and Dep. High Comr, New Delhi, 2006–09; Sen. Advr, Internat. and Finance Directorate, subseq. Internat. and EU Gp, HM Treasury, 2009–12; Dir, Eur. and Global Issues Secretariat, Cabinet Office, 2012–16. *Address:* National Security Secretariat, Cabinet Office, 70 Whitehall, SW1A 2AS.

**BUTLER, David;** *see* Butler, C. D.

**BUTLER, David;** Director, Butler Lasher Ltd, 2013–16; *b* 1 Feb. 1936; *s* of James Charles Butler and Ethel Violet (*née* Newell); *m* 1st, 1956, Catherine Anita Harry (marr. diss. 1974); one *s* two *d*; 2nd, 1975, Frances Mary McMahon; one *d*. *Educ:* Mill Hill Sch.; Keble Coll., Oxford (BA Lit. Hum.). Management Trainee, Herts CC, 1960–64; Computer Manager, NW Metropolitan Hosp. Bd, 1964–65; Management Consultant, Urwick Gp, 1965–72; Dir, Diebold Europe, 1972–76; Chm., Butler Cox plc and Butler Cox Foundn, 1977–92; Sen. Advr, Computer Scis Corp., 1994–2004; Chief Executive Officer: Triple IC Ltd, 2007–13; Butler Basford and Lord Ltd, 2012–13. Dir, Istel, 1983–92; Investment Advr, United Bank of Kuwait, 1985–92. Chairman: Executive Learning Alliance Ltd, 2003–05; Global Business Partnership Alliance, 2006. Mem., Fraud Trials Cttee, 1984–85; Vice Pres., BCS, 1981–83. *Publications:* The Convergence of Technologies, 1977; Britain and the Information Society, 1981; A Director's Guide to Information Technology, 1982; Trends in Information Technology, 1984; Information Technology and Realpolitik, 1986; The Men who Mastered Time (novel), 1986; Senior Management IT Education, 1987; Measuring Progress in IT, 1995; The Outsource Revolution, 2010; IT Outsourcing: the end of business as usual?, 2010; Lord of the Lightning (novel), 2011; numerous press articles. *Recreations:* cricket, Rugby, ancient history. *Address:* 12 Laurel Road, SW13 0EE. *T:* (020) 8876 1810.

**BUTLER, Sir David (Edgeworth),** Kt 2011; CBE 1991; FBA 1994; Fellow of Nuffield College, Oxford, 1954–92, now Emeritus; *b* 17 Oct. 1924; *yr s* of late Professor Harold Edgeworth Butler and Margaret, *d* of Prof. A. F. Pollard; *m* 1962, Marilyn Speers Evans (Prof. Marilyn Speers Butler, FBA) (*d* 2014); two *s* (and one *s* decd). *Educ:* St Paul's; New Coll., Oxford (MA, DPhil). J. E. Procter Visiting Fellow, Princeton Univ., 1947–48; Student, Nuffield Coll., 1949–51; Research Fellow, 1951–54; Dean and Senior Tutor, 1956–64. Served as Personal Assistant to HM Ambassador in Washington, 1955–56. Co-editor, Electoral Studies, 1982–92. Chm., Hansard Soc., 1993–2001. DUniv Paris, 1978; Hon. DSSc QUB, 1985; Dr *hc* Essex, 1993; Hon. Dr: Plymouth, 1994; Teesside, 1999. OAM 2002. *Publications:* The British General Election of 1951, 1952; The Electoral System in Britain 1918–51, 1953; The British General Election of 1955, 1955; The Study of Political Behaviour, 1958; (ed) Elections Abroad, 1959; (with R. Rose) The British General Election of 1959, 1960; (with J. Freeman) British Political Facts, 1900–1960, 1963; (with A. King) The British General Election of 1964, 1965; The British General Election of 1966, 1966; (with D. Stokes) Political Change in Britain, 1969; (with M. Pinto-Duschinsky) The British General Election of 1970, 1971; The Canberra Model, 1973; (with D. Kavanagh) The British General Election of February 1974, 1974; (with D. Kavanagh) The British General Election of October 1974, 1975; (with U. Kitzinger) The 1975 Referendum, 1976; (ed) Coalitions in British Politics, 1978; (ed with A. H. Halsey) Policy and Politics, 1978; (with A. Ranney), Referendums, 1978; (with A. Sloman) British Political Facts 1900–79, 1980; (with D. Kavanagh) The British General Election of 1979, 1980; (with D. Marquand) European Elections and British Politics, 1981; (with A. Ranney) Democracy at the Polls, 1981; (with V. Bogdanor) Democracy and Elections, 1983; Governing without a Majority, 1983; (with D. Kavanagh) The British General Election of 1983, 1984; A Compendium of Indian Elections, 1984; (with P. Jowett) Party Strategies in Britain, 1985; (with G. Butler) British Political Facts 1900–85, 1986; (with D. Kavanagh) The British General Election of 1987, 1988; British Elections since 1945, 1989; (with P. Roy) India Decides, 1989, 3rd edn as India Decides 1952–1991, 1995; (with A. Low) Sovereigns and Surrogates, 1991; (with B. Cain) Congressional Redistricting, 1991; (with D. Kavanagh) The British General Election 1992, 1992; (with A. Ranney) Electioneering, 1992; Failure in British Government, 1994; (with G. Butler) British Political Facts 1900–94, 1994; (with D. Kavanagh) The British General Election of 1997, 1997; (with M. Westlake) British Politics and European Elections 1994, 1999; (jtly) Law and Politics, 1999; (with G. Butler) British Political Facts 1900–2000, 2000; (with D. Kavanagh) The British General Election of 2001, 2001; (with M. Westlake) British Politics and European Elections 2004, 2005; (with D. Kavanagh) The British General Election of 2005, 2005. *Address:* Nuffield College, Oxford OX1 1NF. *T:* (01865) 278500.

**BUTLER, Dawn;** MP (Lab) Brent Central, since 2015; *b* 3 Nov. 1969; *d* of Milo and Ambrozene Butler. *Educ:* Tom Hood Sch.; Waltham Forest Coll. Associate CIPD 1993. Systems analyst, Johnson Matthey, 1989–92; Exec. Officer, Employment Service, 1993–97; Union Officer and Race Audit Co-ordinator, GMB, 1997–2005. Voluntary work, incl. at African Caribbean Centre; mentor; fund-raising co-ordinator. MP (Lab) Brent South, 2005–10; contested (Lab) Brent Central, 2010. PPS to Minister of State, Dept of Health, 2005–06; an Asst Govt Whip, 2008–10; Minister for Young Citizens and Youth Engagement, Cabinet Office, 2009–10; Shadow Minister for Diverse Communities, 2016–17; Shadow Sec. of State for Women and Equalities, 2017–. Chm., All Party Parly Gp on Youth Affairs, 2006–10; Member, All Party Parliamentary Group: on Governance and Inclusive Leadership; on Jamaica; on Road Passenger Transport (Co-Chm.); Chair, Women's PLP; Vice Chair: Parly Renewable and Sustainable Energy Gp; Lab. Friends of Palestine; London Lab. MPs; official spokesperson, Lab. delegn on gender and equalities, Council of Europe. Trng and develt executive, 2010–15; bespoke trng designer and developer, 2010–15. Political commentator, leadership mentor, and consultant on diversity and policy. Founder: Bernie's List, 2008–; Labour Friends of the Caribbean, 2009–. Patron: W Indian Self Effort, Brent; Mathematics, Brent; Black Women's Mental Health Project, Brent; Hindu Forum Britain; City Mission Community Project; Sister Circle; Sickle Cell Soc.; Betterdays Cancer Care; London Young Labour. Associate Mem., Westminster Abbey Inst. *Recreations:* salsa, mentoring. *Address:* House of Commons, SW1A 0AA. *E:* dawn@dawnbutler.org.uk.

**BUTLER, Eamonn Francis,** PhD; Director, Adam Smith Institute, since 1978; *b* 1952; *s* of Richard Henry Bland Butler and Janet Provan Butler; *m* 1986, Christine Anna Pieroni; two *s*. *Educ:* Univ. of Aberdeen; Univ. of St Andrews (MA 1973, MA Hons 1974; PhD

1978). Research Associate, US House of Representatives, 1976–77; Asst Prof. of Philosophy, Hillsdale Coll., Michigan, 1977–78. Editor, The Broker, 1979–87. Sec., Mont Pelerin Soc., 2012–. Hon. DLitt Heriot-Watt, 2012. *Publications:* Hayek: his contribution to the social and economic thought of our time, 1983; Milton Friedman: a guide to his economic thought, 1985; Ludwig von Mises: fountainhead of the modern microeconomics revolution, 1989; Adam Smith: a primer, 2007; The Best Book on the Market, 2008; The Rotten State of Britain, 2009; The Alternative Manifesto, 2010; Austrian Economics: a primer, 2010; Ludwig von Mises: a primer, 2010; Milton Friedman: a guide to the work and influence of the free-market, libertarian economist, 2011; Public Choice: a primer, 2012; The Condensed Wealth of Nations, 2012; Friedrich Hayek: the ideas and influence of the libertarian economist, 2012; Foundations of a Free Society, 2013; The Economics of Success, 2014; Classical Liberalism: a primer, 2015; Magna Carta: a primer, 2015; Ayn Rand: a primer, 2018; Capitalism: a primer, 2018; (with R. L. Schuettinger) Forty Centuries of Wage and Price Controls, 1979; with M. Pirie: Test Your IQ, 1983; Boost Your IQ, 1990; The Sherlock Holmes IQ Book, 1995; IQ Puzzlers, 1995; contrib. articles to various newspapers and jls. *Recreations:* archaeology, antiquarian books and prints. *Address:* The Adam Smith Institute, 23 Great Smith Street, SW1P 3DJ. *E:* eamonn.butler@adamsmith.org.

BUTLER, Edward Thomas; broadcaster, journalist and writer; *b* Newport, S Wales, 8 May 1957; *s* of Kenneth Butler and Margaret Butler; *m* 2009, Susan Roberts; three *s* three *d*. *Educ:* Monmouth Sch.; Fitzwilliam Coll., Cambridge (BA 1979). Rugby player, 1980–84 (Captain, Wales Rugby, 1983); writer and commentator, BBC, 1984, Sports Dept, 1985–; Rugby correspondent, Observer, 1991–2016. *Publications:* The Tangled Mane, 2001; The Greatest Welsh XV, 2011; The Head of Gonzo Davies, 2014; Gonzo Davies, Caught in Possession, 2015; The Asparagus Thieves, 2017. *Recreation:* mountain walking. *Address:* Great Llyfos Farm, Cross Ash, Monmouthshire NP7 8PT. *E:* edbutler100@btinternet.com.

BUTLER, Elizabeth Jane, (Mrs Ian Jones); Chairman, Lewisham and Greenwich NHS Trust (formerly Lewisham Healthcare NHS Trust), 2010–17; *b* Southsea, Hants, 1 June 1961; *d* of Derek and Kathleen Butler; *m* 1988, Ian Jones; two *s* one *d*. *Educ:* Univ. of Exeter (BSc Hons Maths 1982). ACA 1986, FCA 2009. Audit Sen., Dearden Farrow, 1982–86; Manager, Price Waterhouse, 1986–92. Non-exec. Dir, 1995–2000, Chm., 2000–05, Queen Mary's Sidcup NHS Trust; Chm., Bromley PCT, 2005–10. Chair, Audit Committee: RCN, 2004–12; Electoral Commn, 2008–14; RCVS, 2012–; Member: Audit Cttee, Local Govt Boundary Commn for England, 2010–16; Audit and Risk Cttee, GMC, 2013–; Regulatory Cttee, Homes and Communities Agency, 2017–18; Lay Mem., Governance, Risk and Assurance Cttee, Bar Standards Bd, 2018–; Mem. Bd and Chair, Audit and Risk Cttee, Regulator of Social Housing, 2018–. Mem., Gp Bd, Hyde Housing Assoc., 1998–2012. Trustee and Treasurer: Dee Beechinor Trust, 2002–14; Nakesido Educn and Welfare Trust, 2017–; Trustee and Chair, Audit and Risk Cttee, RBL, 2018–. Treas., 5th Beckenham S Scout Gp, 2002–. Chair of Govs, St Mary's RC Primary Sch., Beckenham, 2005–16. Mem., Univ. of Exeter Alumnae. *Recreations:* family, travel. *E:* lizbutler42@outlook.com.

BUTLER, Georgina Susan; HM Diplomatic Service, retired; Ambassador to Costa Rica and Nicaragua, 2002–06; *b* 30 Nov. 1945; *d* of Alfred Norman Butler, LDS RCS and Joan Mary Butler (*née* Harrington); *m* 1st, 1970, Stephen John Leadbetter Wright (marr. diss. 2000); one *s* one *d*; 2nd, 2003 (marr. diss. 2009). *Educ:* University Coll. London (LLB 1968; Fellow 2003). British Embassy, Paris, 1969–70; Southern European Dept, FCO, 1971–75; UN Secretariat, NY, 1975–77; Directorate Gen. Develt, EC, Brussels, 1982–84; Deputy Head: Information Dept, FCO, 1985–87; Latin American Dept, FCO, 1999–2001. British Consul, Tangier, 2007–09. Election Observer: Nicaragua, 2006; Venezuela, 2006; Azerbaijan, 2008; Algeria, 2012. Clerk, Fletchers' Co., 2010–12. Chair: Foreign Affairs and Defence Gp, Cons. Policy Forum, 2012–14; S Richmond Ward, Cons. Party, 2015–16; Richmond Park and N Kingston Cons. Party Assoc., 2017–. Trustee, Anglo-Central American Soc., 2014–16 (Chair, 2015–16). Chair, Denys Holland Scholarship Fund, UCL, 2010–18; Elder, Crabtree Foundn, UCL, 2017– (Pres., 2015–16). Contested (C) SW and Gibraltar Reg., EP, 2014. *Recreations:* travel, riding, watersports. *Address:* 49 Sheen Road, Richmond, Surrey TW9 1AJ.

BUTLER, Sir James; *see* Butler, Sir P. J.

BUTLER, (James) Pearse; Chairman, Blackpool Teaching Hospitals NHS Foundation Trust, since 2018; *b* 27 Jan. 1957; *s* of James and Nancy Butler; *m* 1979, Deborah Veronica Downing (*d* 2013); one *s* one *d*. *Educ:* St Mary's Coll., Crosby; Keble Coll., Oxford (BA). Community Worker, Liverpool CVS, 1979–80; Hosp. Admin, S Birmingham HA, 1980–83; Dep. Adminr, then Adminr, Bolton Gen. Hosp., 1983–85; Mgt Consultant, HAY-MSL Mgt Consultants, 1985–86; Gen. Manager, Obst. and Gyn. Service, Liverpool HA, 1986–88; Dist Gen. Manager, Chester HA, 1988–89; Chief Executive: Royal Liverpool Children's NHS Trust, 1990–93; Wirral HA, 1993–97; Wigan and Leigh NHS Trust, 1997–99; Royal Liverpool and Broadgreen Univ. Hosps NHS Trust, 1999–2002; Cumbria and Lancashire Strategic HA, 2002–06; Interim Chief Exec., E of England Strategic HA, 2006; Dir of Clinical Engagement, Computer Scis Corp., 2007–14; Chm., Univ. Hosps of Morecambe Bay NHS Foundn Trust, 2014–18. *Recreations:* family, Everton FC, golf. *Address:* Blackpool Teaching Hospitals Foundation Trust, Blackpool Victoria Hospital, Whinney Heys Road, Blackpool FY3 8NR. *Clubs:* West Lancashire Golf, Campion Lawn Tennis.

BUTLER, James Walter, MBE 2009; RA 1972 (ARA 1964); RWA; FRSS; *b* 25 July 1931; *m* (marr. diss.); one *d*; *m* 1975, Angela, *d* of Col Roger Berry, Johannesburg, South Africa; four *d*. *Educ:* Maidstone Grammar Sch.; Maidstone Coll. of Art; St Martin's Sch. of Art; Royal Coll. of Art. National Diploma in Sculpture, 1950. Nat. Service, Royal Signals, 1951–53. Worked as Architectural Carver, 1950–53, 1955–60. Tutor, Sculpture and Drawing, City and Guilds of London Art School, 1960–75. Major commissions include: *portrait statues:* Pres. Kenyatta, Nairobi, 1973; Sir John Moore, Sir John Moore Barracks, Winchester, 1987; John Wilkes, New Fetter Lane, 1988, Wilkes Univ., USA, 1995; Thomas Cook, Leicester, 1994; Billy Wright, 1996, Stan Cullis, 2003, Molineux Stadium, Wolverhampton; James Brindley, Coventry Canal Basin, 1998; Duncan Edwards, Dudley, 1999; Jack Walker, Blackburn Rovers FC, 2001; Isambard Kingdom Brunel, for Felix Dennis, 2009; HM Queen Elizabeth II, Runnymede, 2015; Sir Jack Hayward, Wolverhampton Wanderers, 2018; *portrait busts:* Sir Nicholas Bacon, St Albans Sch., 1994; Sir Frank Whittle, 1995, R. J. Mitchell, 2001, Roy Chadwick, 2003, RAF Club; Robert Beldam, Corpus Christi Coll., Cambridge, 2000; Queen Mother, Butchers' Co., Butchers' Hall, London, 2008; Prof. Michael Farthing, St George's, Univ. of London, 2009; Dr Thomas (Tommy) Flowers, MBE, Adastral Park, BT, 2013; *memorial statues:* Richard III, Leicester, 1980; Field Marshal Earl Alexander of Tunis, Wellington Barracks, London, 1985; Reg Harris, Manchester, 1994; *other:* Monument to Freedom Fighters of Zambia, Lusaka, 1974; The Burton Cooper, Burton-on-Trent, 1977; Dolphin Fountain, Dolphin Square, London, 1988; Skipping girl, Harrow, 1988; The Leicester Seamstress, Leicester, 1990; James Henry Greathead, Cornhill, 1994; The Stratford Jester, Stratford-upon-Avon, 1995; D-day Memorial for Green Howards, Crépon, Normandy, 1996; Seagull Sculpture, Anchorpoint, Singapore, 1997; Memorial to Fleet Air Arm, Victoria Embankment Gdns,

London, 2000; Great Seal of the Realm, 2001; 50p piece commemorating 50th anniv. of first sub 4 min. mile, 2004; crown piece commemorating 200th anniv. of death of Lord Nelson, 2005; Memorial to Men of 167th Alabama Inf. Regt, Rainbow Div., Fère-en-Tardenois, 2011, and Montgomery, Ala. Silver Medal, RBS, 1988. *Recreation:* interested in astronomy. *Address:* Valley Farm, Radway, Warwick CV35 0UJ. *T:* (01926) 641938. *Club:* Arts.

BUTLER, John Michael, CPFA, FCCA, FIRRV; consultant, 2005–17; Director of Finance and Information Technology, East Riding of Yorkshire Council, 1995–2005; *b* 12 Sept. 1943; *s* of late Reginald Butler and Kathleen (*née* Garside); *m* 1964, Daphne Ann Head (*d* 1999); two *s*. *Educ:* Beckenham and Penge Boys' Grammar Sch. CPFA 1966; FIRRV (IRRV 1974); FCCA 1980. Audit Asst, Beckenham BC, 1960–61; Accountancy Assistant: Dorking UDC, 1961–63; Caterham UDC, 1963–64; Sen. Accountant, Dorking UDC, 1964–66; Asst Treas., Esher UDC, 1966–70; Asst Borough Treas., Greenwich LBC, 1970–74; Chief Finance Officer, Lambeth LBC, 1974–79; City Treas., Swansea CC, 1979–95. National President: IRRV, 1989–90 (Mem. Council, 1980–94); Soc. of Dist Council Treasurers, 1992–93 (Mem. Cttee, 1981–2005); CIPFA, 2007–08 (Mem. Council, 1994–2009). Treasurer: Welsh Orienteering Assoc., 2006–12; Welsh Soc. of Hull and E Yorks, 2007–; Age Concern E Yorks, then Age UK East Riding, 2007–; Humber Bridge Bd, 2011–17; Humberside and Lincs Orienteers, 2011–; Yorks and Humberside Orienteering Assoc., 2014–. FCMI (FBIM 1969). *Recreation:* orienteering. *Address:* 118 Woodhall Way, Beverley HU17 7DA. *T:* (01482) 870312. *E:* john@the-butlers.co.uk. *Clubs:* Humberside and Lincs Orienteers, Swansea Bay Orienteering.

BUTLER, Prof. Martin Howard, PhD; FBA 2013; Professor of English Renaissance Drama, University of Leeds, since 1998; *b* Peterborough, 31 May 1956; *s* of Roy Alec Butler and Mavis Eileen Butler (*née* Church); *m* 1977, Jane-Amanda Barsby; one *s* one *d*. *Educ:* Deacon's Sch., Peterborough; Trinity Hall, Cambridge (BA 1977; MA 1981; PhD 1981). British Acad. Res. Fellow, 1980–81; Res. Fellow, Trinity Hall, Cambridge, 1981–84; University of Leeds: Lectr, 1984–92; Sen. Lectr, 1992–95; Reader, 1995–98. Fellow, Woodrow Wilson Center, Washington, 1990–91; Leverhulme Res. Fellow, 1994–95. Chatterton Lectr, British Acad., 1995. Contributing Ed., Oxford DNB, 1998; Gen. Ed., The Cambridge Edition of the Works of Ben Jonson Online, 2014. *Publications:* Theatre and Crisis 1632–1642, 1984; Ben Jonson's Volpone, 1987; (ed) The Selected Plays of Ben Jonson, vol. 2, 1989; (ed) Re-Presenting Ben Jonson: text, history, performance, 1999; (ed) W. Shakespeare, Cymbeline, 2004; (ed) W. Shakespeare, The Tempest, 2007; The Stuart Court Masque and Political Culture, 2008; (ed jtly) The Cambridge Edition of the Works of Ben Jonson, 7 vols, 2012. *Recreations:* flute, piano, opera, fell-walking. *Address:* School of English, University of Leeds, Leeds LS2 9JT. *T:* (0113) 343 4766. *E:* m.h.butler@leeds.ac.uk.

BUTLER, Megan Veronica; Executive Director of Supervision - Investment, Wholesale and Specialists Division, Financial Conduct Authority, since 2015; *b* London, 23 June 1964; *d* of Dr William Butler and Dr Anne Butler (*née* Stow); *m* 1989, Christopher William Hames, *qv*; one *s* one *d*. *Educ:* Withington Girls' Sch., Manchester; Sheffield Univ. (LLB Law). Called to the Bar, Inner Temple, 1987; in practice as barrister specialising in Chancery Law, 1987–89; London Stock Exchange, 1989–2000: legal advr; Exec. Asst to CEO and Chm.; Hd, Capital Mkts; Dep. Hd of Listing; joined Financial Services Authority, 2000: Chief Legal Counsel of Mkts; Head: of Enforcement Law and Policy; of Investment Bank Supervision, 2008–11; Dir, Internat. Banks Div., 2011–12; joined Prudential Regulation Authy, Bank of England, 2012; Exec. Dir Internat. Banks, Prudential Regulation Authority, Bank of England, 2014–15. *Recreations:* running, travelling, cooking. *Address:* Financial Conduct Authority, 12 Endeavour Square, E20 1JN. *E:* megan.butler@fca.org.uk.

BUTLER, Michael Howard, OBE, FCA; Finance Director, British Coal (formerly National Coal Board), 1985–93, Member of the Board, 1986–93; *b* 13 Feb. 1936; *s* of Howard Butler and Constance Gertrude Butler; *m* 1961, Christine Elizabeth Killer; two *s* one *d*. *Educ:* Nottingham High School. Articled pupil, H. G. Ellis Kennewell & Co., Nottingham, 1952–58; Stewarts & Lloyds Gp, 1960–62; National Coal Board: various posts, NCB HQ, W Midlands Div. and NE Area, 1962–68; Chief Accountant, Coal Products Div., 1968; Dep. Treas., NCB HQ, 1970; Treas. and Dep. Dir Gen. of Finance, 1978; Dir Gen. of Finance, 1981; Chm., British Fuels Co., 1992–93. Director: British Coal Enterprises, 1988–96; Edinburgh Fund Managers, 1993–95; Chairman: CIN Management Ltd, 1993–96; British Investment Trust, 1993–97. Trustee, Mineworkers Pension Fund (formerly British Coal Pension Funds), 1981–2000 (Chm., 1995–2000). *Recreations:* gardening, listening to music, playing tennis. *Address:* Banstead Down, Chorleywood Road, Rickmansworth, Herts WD3 4EH. *T:* (01923) 778001.

BUTLER, Nicholas Jones; Visiting Professor and founding Chairman, The Policy Institute, King's College London, since 2010; *b* Amersham, Bucks, 22 Nov. 1954; *s* of Frank Butler and Jessie Butler (*née* Ridge); *m* 1987, Dr Rosaleen Hughes; one *d* (and one *s* decd). *Educ:* Blackpool Grammar Sch.; Trinity Coll., Cambridge (BA Hons 1977). Economic posts with BP, 1977–92; Hd of Internat. Govt Affairs, BP Exploration, 1992–95; Gp Policy Advr, 1995–2002, Gp Vice Pres. for Strategy and Policy Develt, 2002–07, BP; Chm., Cambridge Centre for Energy Studies, 2007–09; Sen. Policy Advr to Prime Minister, 2009–10. Mem., Adv. Bd, Centre for Eur. Reform, 1995– (Chm., 1995–2008); Advr, Cavendish Lab., Univ. of Cambridge, 2009–; Member: President's Internat. Adv. Bd, Yale Univ., 2006–13; Strategic Adv. Bd, Statoil, 2015–; Expert Adv. Panel, Faraday Inst., 2018–. Dir, Cambridge Econometrics, 2010–18; Chair, Ridgeway Information Ltd, 2017–. Vice President: Hay Fest., 2005–; Fabian Soc., 2013– (Hon. Treas., 1982–2013; Chm., 1987). Trustee, Asia Hse, 2009–. Editor, FT energy blog, 2012–. *Publications:* The IMF, Time for Reform, 1982; (ed) The Economic Consequences of Mrs Thatcher, by Baron Kaldor, 1983; The International Grain Market, 1985; (with R. Lambert) European Universities: renaissance or decay, 2006; (contrib.) Trinity: a portrait, 2011. *Recreations:* reading, music. *Address:* King's College, Strand, WC2R 2LS. *E:* Nick.Butler@kcl.ac.uk. *Club:* Athenæum (Member: Gen. Cttee, 2016–; Exec. Cttee, 2017–).

BUTLER, Norman John Terence, (Terry), CBE 1993; Adviser in Public Services and Social Care, 2005–16; Director of Social Services, Hampshire, 1988–2005; *b* 18 Feb. 1946; *s* of Arthur Reginald Butler and Lucy Mary Butler; *m*; one *s* two *d*. *Educ:* Peveril Bilateral Sch., Nottingham; Trent Polytechnic, Nottingham (Cert. in Social Work); Nat. Inst. of Social Work, London; Brunel Univ. (MA Public and Social Admin). Mental Welfare Officer, Nottingham, 1965–71; Sen. Social Worker, Nottingham, 1971–73; Area Man., Haringey, 1974–81; Asst Dir of Social Services, Royal Bor. of Kingston upon Thames, 1981–83; Dep. Dir of Social Services, E Sussex, 1983–88. Non-exec. Dir, NHS S of England (formerly NHS S Central Strategic HA), 2006–13. Member: Firth Cttee, examining public expenditure on residential care, 1987; Algebra Gp, 1992–93; Inf. Tribunal (formerly Data Protection Tribunals Bd), 1996–2010; Standing Gp for Service Delivery and Orgn, NHS R & D Directorate, 1997–99; Co-Leader, Community Care Support Force, providing practical support to local and health authorities in implementation of NHS and Community Care Act, 1992–93; Mem. Adv. Bd for Restricted Patients, 1995–2001; Advr, Clinical Speciality (Social Care), to Nat. Patient Safety Agency, 2003–07; Ind. Member: Gen. Social Care Council, 2005–12; Nat. Clinical Audit Adv. Gp, 2008–11. Patron,

Relatives and Residents Assoc., 2007–12 (Vice-Pres., 1995–2007). Trustee, Emmaus, Hants, 2015– (Chm., 2017–). Hon. Treas., 1997–2003, Co.-Chm., Mental Health Cttee, 2003–05, Assoc. of Dirs of Social Services. *Publications:* (with M. Henwood and K. Pollard) Slaying the Demon: the dementia challenge, 2015; articles in various jls, incl. Social Work Today, Insight and Community Care. *Recreations:* travel, tennis, golf, Notts County supporter, painting. *Address:* Edgar House, 17 Lansdowne Avenue, St Cross, Winchester, Hants SO23 9TU.

BUTLER, Patricia Josephine; *see* Ferguson, P. J.

BUTLER, Rt Rev. Paul Roger; *see* Durham, Bishop of.

BUTLER, Pearse; *see* Butler, J. P.

BUTLER, Sir (Percy) James, Kt 2001; CBE 1981; DL; FCA; Deputy Chairman, Camelot PLC, 1995–2002 (Director, 1994–2002); farmer, since 1974; *b* 15 March 1929; *s* of late Percy Ernest Butler and Phyllis Mary Butler (*née* Bartholomew); *m* 1954, Margaret Prudence Copland (*d* 2018); one *s* two *d*. *Educ:* Marlborough Coll.; Clare Coll., Cambridge (MA). Joined Peat, Marwick, Mitchell & Co. (later KPMG Peat Marwick), 1952; qualified, 1955; Partner, 1965; Gen. Partner, 1971; Managing Partner, London Reg., 1981–85; Dep. Sen. Partner, 1985–86; Sen. Partner, 1986–93; Mem. of KPMG Exec. Cttee and Council, 1987–93; Chm., KPMG Internat., 1991–93. Director: Mersey Docks and Harbour Co., 1972–90 (Dep. Chm., 1987–90); Tompkins PLC, 1994–95; Wadworth and Co. Ltd, 1994–2016; Nicholson, Graham & Jones, 1994–2004; Chairman: European Passenger Services Ltd, 1994–96; Union Railways, 1995–96. Mem. (part time), BRB, 1994–95. Business Advr to Treasury and CS Cttee, 1980–82; Member: Cttee on review of Railway Finance, 1982; Cadbury Cttee on Financial Aspects of Corporate Governance, 1990–95. Member: Council, Business in the Community, 1988–90; ICAEW Council, 1992–94; Council, CBIs, 1989–94; Governing Body, City Res. Project, 1991–95; Adv. Council, Prince's Youth Business Trust, 1993–2001; Council, SCF, 1994–2000 (Chm., SCF Private Appeal, 1994–2000). Treasurer, Pilgrims Soc., 1982–97; Trustee, Royal Opera House Trust, 1991–99 (Chm., 1993–95; Vice Chm., 1995–99); Dir, Royal Opera House, 1994–98; Trustee: Winchester Cathedral Trust, 1991– (Chm., Cathedral Appeal, 1991–94); RA, 1997–2005 (Mem., Mgt Cttee, 1997–2009; Mem., Audit Cttee, 1994–2010 (Chm., 1996–2006); Trustee Emeritus, 2009–); Brendoncare Foundn Develt Trust, 1998–2005 (Chm., Brendoncare Foundn Appeal, 1998–2005); Chm. Trustees, Music at Winchester, 1999–2009; Chm., Lord Mayor's Appeal, 2002–03. Mem., Marlborough Coll. Council, 1975–2001 (Chm., 1992–2001). Liveryman: Worshipful Co. of Cutlers, 1965– (Mem. Court, 1985–; Master, 1995–96); Worshipful Co. of Chartered Accountants in England and Wales, 1977–2013. DL Hants, 1994. *Recreations:* bridge, opera, farming. *Club:* Boodle's.

BUTLER, Peter; Chief Executive, Flying Scotsman plc, 2001–09; *b* 10 June 1951; *s* of late Kenneth Jonathan Butler and Barbara Butler; *m* 1973, Peggy Mary, *d* of Richard Nott; three *d*. *Educ:* Adams Grammar Sch., Newport, Shropshire; St Edmund Hall, Oxford (MA English Lit.; PGCE 1974). Admitted Solicitor, 1978; Solicitor, Thames Valley Police, 1978–80; Partner, 1981–92, Consultant, 1992–2000, Linnells, solicitors, Oxford. Nat. Chm., Trainee Solicitors, England and Wales, 1976. Mem. (C) Oxfordshire CC, 1985–89. MP (C) Milton Keynes North East, 1992–97; contested (C) same seat, 1997. PPS to Minister of State, DoH, 1994–95, to Chancellor of Exchequer, 1995–97. Mem., Home Affairs Select Cttee, 1992. Contested (C) W Midlands, Eur. Parlt, 2004. Former non-executive Director: Continental Trustees Ltd; Milton Keynes Chamber of Commerce; Milton Keynes City Orch., 2006; Milton Keynes Theatre and Gall. Co., 2007. Sch. Gov., 1985–92. Pres., Olney Archaeol Soc.; Prog. Sec., N Bucks DFAS. *Recreations:* music, three energetic daughters, one grandson (*b* 2014), seeking organised exercise after near-fatal stroke in 2002, Austin 7. *Address:* Castle Farm, Lavendon, Olney, Bucks MK46 4JG. *T:* (01234) 240046. *Club:* Vintage Sports Car.

BUTLER, Prof. Peter Anthony, PhD; FRS 2019; Professor of Physics, since 1999 and Senior Research Fellow, since 2015, University of Liverpool; *b* Sittingbourne, Kent, 22 Nov. 1949; *s* of late Eric James Butler and Anne Rose Butler; *m* 2004, Miriam Afrakoma Edwin; two *s* two *d*. *Educ:* Borden Grammar Sch.; King's Coll. London (BSc Hons 1st Cl.); Univ. of Liverpool (PhD 1974). CPhys 1978; FInstP 1992. SRC/NATO Fellow, Lawrence Berkeley Lab., Calif, 1974–76; Res. Staff Mem., MIT, 1976–77; University of Liverpool: SRC Advanced Fellow, Dept of Physics, 1978–83; Lectr, 1983–89; Sen. Lectr, 1989–93; Reader in Physics, 1993–99. Marie Curie Fellow and Sen. Researcher, Univ. of Jyväskylä, 1999–2000; Hd, ISOLDE Gp, CERN, Switzerland, 2002–05. Hon. DPhil Jyväskylä, 2019. Rutherford Medal and Prize, Inst. of Physics, 2012. *Publications:* articles in Annual Rev. of of Nuclear Particle Sci., Rev. of Mod. Physics, Jl of Physics G. *Recreations:* leisure windsurfing, pursuing studies of atomic nuclei. *Address:* Oliver Lodge Laboratory, Department of Physics, University of Liverpool, Oxford Street, Liverpool L69 7ZE. *T:* (0151) 794 3377, 07973 247750. *E:* peter.butler@liverpool.ac.uk.

BUTLER, His Honour Philip Andrew; a Circuit Judge, 2009–17; *b* Manchester, 13 April 1957; *s* of Bernard Hannan Butler and Dorothy Eileen Butler (*née* McCann); *m* 1993, Alison Laura Hayden; one *s* one *d*. *Educ:* St Peter's Grammar Sch., Manchester; Manchester Univ. (LLB 1st Cl. Hons 1978; LLM 1980); Inns of Court Sch. of Law. Called to the Bar, Middle Temple, 1979; in practice as barrister, Northern Circuit, 1979–2009; Asst Recorder, 1998–2000; Recorder, 2000–09; Designated Civil Judge, Cumbria and Lancs, 2011–17. Legal Assessor, GMC, 2002–07; Legal Chm., Fitness to Practise Cttee, Council for Registration of Forensic Practitioners, 2004–08. Mem., 1000 Club, Shakespeare's Globe Th. KCSHS 2012 (KCHS 2006; KHS 1999). *Recreations:* mediaeval history and architecture, reading (detective fiction), theatre, travel, family outings.

BUTLER, Sir (Reginald) Richard (Michael), 4th Bt *cr* 1922, of Old Park, Devizes; *b* 3 Oct. 1953; *e s* of Sir (Reginald) Michael (Thomas) Butler, 3rd Bt, QC (Ont) and of Marja McLean; *S* father, 2012; *m* 1st, 1982, Dale Karen Piner (marr. diss. 1998); three *s*; 2nd, 1999, Penelope Joy Lipsack. *Heir: e s* Reginald Paul Butler, *b* 26 June 1988. *Address:* 935 Richmond Road, Victoria, BC V8S 3Z4, Canada.

BUTLER, Sir Richard (Pierce), 13th Bt *cr* 1628 (Ire.), of Cloughgrenan, Co. Carlow; *b* 22 July 1940; *s* of Col Sir Thomas Pierce Butler, 12th Bt, CVO, DSO, OBE and Rosemary Liège Woodgate Davidson-Houston (*d* 1997). *S* father, 1994; *m* 1965, Diana, *yr d* of Col S. J. Borg; three *s* one *d*. *Educ:* Eton; NY Univ. MBA. FCA 1963. Partner, Charles Wakeling & Co., 1964–66; Director: The First Boston Corp. (NY), 1967–78; PaineWebber Inc. (NY), 1978–88 (Management Council, 1985–88); PaineWebber International Bank, 1986–89; Emesco Industrial Equity Co. SA, 1987–2005; The Transportation Gp Ltd, 1989–94; RP&C Internat. (formerly Rauscher Pierce & Clark) Inc., 1992–2000. Mem. Council, Pestalozzi Children's Village Trust, 1983–2009 (Chm., 1985–94); Founder, PestalozziWorld (Pestalozzi Overseas Children's Trust), 1995. *Heir: s* Thomas Pierce [*b* 9 Oct. 1966; *m* 1993, Lucinda Pamela Murphy; two *s* two *d*]. *Address:* Ballin Temple, Co. Carlow.

BUTLER, Robbie; Member (UU) Lagan Valley, Northern Ireland Assembly, since 2016; *b* Lisburn, 16 April 1972; *s* of Robert Butler and Marilyn Butler; *m* 1996, Belinda; one *s* one *d*. *Educ:* Lisnagarvey High Sch. BA (Hons) Mgt Practice. Butcher, 1988–96; Auxiliary Officer, 1996–2000, Fire Officer, 2000–16, NI Fire and Rescue Service. Mem., Lisburn and Castlereagh CC, 2014–16. Contested (UU) Lagan Valley, 2017. *Recreations:* football, reading. *Address:* 59 Bridge Street, Lisburn BT28 1XZ. *T:* (028) 9244 9898. *E:* robbie.butler@mla.niassembly.gov.uk.

BUTLER, Robin Elliott; Managing Director, Urban&Civic plc, since 2009; *b* Plymouth, 9 June 1959; *s* of Elliott Ian and Joan Butler; *m* 1998, Jane Carolyn Giles; one *s* two *d*. *Educ:* Fitzwilliam Coll., Cambridge (BA 1981; MA). MRICS 1984. Founder Dir, Chelsfield PLC, 1986–2004; CEO, Lendlease Europe, 2005–09. Dir, Nat. Retail Planning Forum, 1999–2016. Chm., New Heritage Regeneration, 2008–. Gov., RAM, 2015–. Chm., Cowdray Park Polo Club, 2007–14; Vice Chm., Hurlingham Polo Assoc., 2008–12. Hon. FRAM 2018. *Recreations:* dressage, guitar playing, ski-ing, viticulture. *Address:* Urban&Civic plc, 50 New Bond Street, W1S 1BJ. *T:* (020) 7509 5555.

BUTLER, Rosemary Jane; Director of Statistics, Department of Health, 1991–98; *b* 15 July 1946; *d* of Samuel Laight Medlar and Rosemary Peggy Medlar; *m* 1971, Anthony David Butler. *Educ:* Maynard School, Exeter; LSE (BSc Econ). Central Statistical Office, 1967–73; Unit for Manpower Studies, 1973–77; Dept of Employment, 1977–80; Statistician and Chief Statistician, MoD, 1980–85; Chief Statistician, HM Treasury, 1985–89; Asst Sec., DSS, 1989–91. FRSA 1993. *Recreations:* theatre, music, birdwatching.

BUTLER, Dame Rosemary (Janet Mair), DBE 2014; Member (Lab) Newport West, 1999–2016, and Presiding Officer, 2011–16, National Assembly for Wales; *b* 21 Jan. 1943; *d* of late Godfrey McGrath and Gwyneth Jones. *Educ:* St Julian's High Sch., Newport. Qualified chiropodist, 1962; in practice, 1962–75. Dir, Tourism S and W Wales, 1993–99. Mem. (Lab) Newport BC, subseq. CBC, 1973–99 (Chm., Leisure Services, 1983–97); Mayor of Newport, 1989–90. National Assembly for Wales: Sec. for Educn and Children, 1999–2000; Chm., Culture, Sport and Welsh Lang. Cttee, 2004–07; Dep. Presiding Officer, 2007–11. Founder and Chair: Newport Internat. Comp. for Young Pianists, 1979–; Newport-Kutaisi (Republic of Georgia) Twinning Assoc., 1989–99. Hon. Fellow: Univ. of S Wales (formerly Univ. of Wales, Newport), 2012; Cardiff Metropolitan Univ., 2012. Hon. Dr S Wales, 2013. Hon. Citizen, Kutaisi, Republic of Georgia, 1997. *Recreations:* museums, galleries, the arts, foreign travel.

BUTLER, Air Vice Marshal Stuart Denham; Training and Operational Requirements Director, BAE Systems Air, since 2009; *b* 15 Jan. 1956; *s* of Ralph and Melody Butler; *m* Linda Dorothy Ritchie (marr. diss. 2012); two *d*; *m* 2016, Jane Livingstone Russell (*née* Hoare). *Educ:* Lafford Sch., Billinghay, Lincs. Joined RAF, 1974; Nimrod pilot, 1979–84; Jet Provost flying instructor; Nimrod Sqdn Comdr; Stn Comdr, Kinloss; Dep. Dir, Underwater Battlespace, MoD; AO, Intelligence, Surveillance, Target Acquisition and Reconnaissance, HQ Strike Comd; Dir, Equipt Capability (ISTAR), MoD, 2005–06; Capability Manager (Inf. Superiority), 2006–08, and Air Mem. for Equipment Capability, 2007–08, MoD. *Recreations:* fanatical golfer, DIY. *Address:* 3 Silverdale Avenue, Oxshott, Leatherhead, Surrey KT22 0JX. *T:* (01372) 843130. *E:* pilotstu@btinternet.com. *Clubs:* Royal Air Force; South Kyme Golf (Lincs), Bramley Golf.

BUTLER, Terry; *see* Butler, N. J. T.

BUTLER, Rt Rev. Thomas Frederick; Bishop of Southwark, 1998–2010; an Honorary Assistant Bishop, Diocese of Leeds (formerly West Yorkshire and the Dales), since 2014; *b* 5 March 1940; *s* of Thomas John Butler and Elsie Butler (*née* Bainbridge); *m* 1964, Barbara Joan Clark; one *s* one *d*. *Educ:* Univ. of Leeds (BSc 1st Cl. Hons, MSc, PhD). CEng. College of the Resurrection, Mirfield, 1962–64; Curate: St Augustine's, Wisbech, 1964–66; St Saviour's, Folkestone, 1966–68; Lecturer and Chaplain, Univ. of Zambia, 1968–73; Acting Dean of Holy Cross Cathedral, Lusaka, Zambia, 1973; Chaplain to Univ. of Kent at Canterbury, 1973–80; Archdeacon of Northolt, 1980–85; Area Bishop of Willesden, 1985–91; Bishop of Leicester, 1991–98; Asst Bishop, Dio. of Wakefield, 2010–14; Acting Area Bishop of Bradford, 2014. Chairman: Bd of Mission, Gen. Synod of C of E, 1995–2001; C of E Bd for Social Responsibility, 2001–02; Vice-Chm., Council for Mission and Public Affairs, 2002–. Six Preacher, Canterbury Cathedral, 1979–84. Took seat in H of L, 2007. FKC 2008. Hon. LLD: Leicester, 1995; De Montfort, 1998; Hon. DSc Loughborough, 1997; Hon. DD Kent, 2005; Hon. DLit South Bank, 2005. *Publications:* (with B. J. Butler) Just Mission, 1993; (with B. J. Butler) Just Spirituality in a World of Faiths, 1996; Religion and Public Life, 2011. *Recreations:* reading, mountain walking.

BUTLER, Prof. William Elliott; John Edward Fowler Distinguished Professor of Law (formerly of Law and International Affairs), Pennsylvania State University, since 2005; Professorial Research Associate, School of Oriental and African Studies, University of London, since 2006; Professor of Comparative Law in the University of London, 1976–2005, now Emeritus; Director, Vinogradoff Institute (formerly Centre for the Study of Socialist Legal Systems), University College London, later at Pennsylvania State University, since 1982; *b* 20 Oct. 1939; *s* of late William Elliott Butler and Maxine Swan Elmberg; *m* 1st, 1961, Darlene Mae Johnson (*d* 1989); two *s*; 2nd, 1991, Maryann Elizabeth Gashi. *Educ:* The American Univ. (BA); Harvard Law School (JD); Acad. Law Sch., Russian Acad. of Scis (LLM); The Johns Hopkins Univ. (MA, PhD); London Univ. (LLD). FSA 1989. Res. Asst, Washington Centre of Foreign Policy Res., Sch. of Advanced Internat. Studies, The Johns Hopkins Univ., 1966–68; Res. Associate in Law, and Associate, Russian Res. Centre, Harvard Univ., 1968–70; University of London: Reader in Comparative Law, 1970–76; Mem. Council, SSEES, 1973–93 (Vice-Chm., 1983–88); Dean of Faculty of Laws, UCL, 1977–79; Vice Dean, 1986–88, Dean, 1988–90, Faculty of Laws, London Univ.; Mem., Cttee of Management, Inst. of Advanced Legal Studies, 1985–88. M. M. Speransky Prof. of Internat. and Comparative Law, 1993–2004, Dean, Faculty of Law, 1993–98, Moscow Higher Sch. of Social and Econ. Scis. Visiting Scholar: Faculty of Law, Moscow State Univ., 1972, 1980; Inst. of State and Law, USSR Acad. of Scis, 1976, 1981, 1983, 1984, 1988; Mongolian State Univ., 1979; Harvard Law Sch., 1982; Visiting Professor: NY Univ. Law Sch., 1978; Ritsumeikan Univ., 1985; Harvard Law Sch., 1986–87; Washington and Lee Univ. Law Sch., 2005; Lectr, Hague Acad. of Internat. Law, 1985; Professorial Lectr in Internat. Law, Sch. of Adv. Internat. Studies, Johns Hopkins Univ., 2009. Associate, Internat. Acad. of Comparative Law, 1982–; Member, Bar: Dist of Columbia; US Supreme Court; Union of Jurists, 1990; Member: Russian Ct of Internat. Commercial Arbitration, 1995–; Kazakhstan Ct of Internat. Commercial Arbitration, 2012–. Chm., Civil Rights in Russia Adv. Panel, Univ. of London, 1983–87; Co-ordinator, UCL-USSR Acad. of Sciences Protocol on Co-operation, 1981–2005; Special Counsel, Commn on Econ. Reform, USSR Council of Ministers, 1989–91; Of Counsel, Clifford Chance, London, Moscow and Almaty, 1992–94; Partner: White & Case, 1994–96; PricewaterhouseCoopers, 1997–2001; Sen. Partner, Phoenix Law Associates, Moscow, 2002–12. Member: EC Joint Task Force on Law Reform in CIS, 1992–93; Working Gp on Commercial Law, Govt of Russian Fedn, 1992; Advr, State Property Fund, Rep. of Kyrgyzstan, 1992; Advr on Corporate Law Reform, Russian Min. of Econ. Develt and Trade, 2004–; Consultant, World Bank, 1992–. Mem., Secretariat, Internat. Assoc. of Mongolists (Ulan Bator), 1997; Hon. Member: All-Union Soc. of Bibliophiles, USSR, 1989; Soviet Assoc. of Maritime Law, 1990. Mem., Court of Governors, City of London Polytechnic, 1985–89. Sec., The Bookplate Soc., 1978–86 (Foreign Sec., 1988–94); Exec. Sec., Féd. Internat. des Sociétés d'Amateurs d'Ex-Libris, 1986–2016 (Vice-Pres., 1984–86);

Exec. Comr, Russian Assoc. of Maritime Law, 2008–; Chm., Fellowship of Amer. Bibliophile Socs, 2019–. Academician: Internat. Acad. of the Book and Art of the Book, Russia, 1992; Russian Acad. of Natural Scis (Russian Encyclopedia Section), 1992; Nat. Acad. of Scis of Ukraine, 1992; Russian Acad. of Legal Scis, 1999; Nat. Acad. of Legal Scis of Ukraine, 2013. George F. Kennan Fellow, Kennan Inst., Woodrow Wilson Center, 2019. Mem., Amer. Law Inst., 2009. Trustee, Hakluyt Soc., 2004–. Editor, Year Book on Socialist Legal Systems, 1985–90; Co-editor: The Bookplate Jl, 1989–91 (Editor, 1983–86); Jl of Comparative Law, 2008– (Mem., Editl Bd, 2006–); Editor: Bookplate Internat., 1994–; Sudebnik, 1996–2009; Russian Law: Theory and Practice, 2004–09; E European and Russian Yearbook of Internat. and Comparative Law, 2007–16; Jus Gentium: Jl of Internat.-Legal Hist., 2016–; Mem., editorial bds of learned jls, incl. Marine Policy, 1988–2004, European Business Law Rev., 1990–2004, Internat. Law, 2002–; Mem., Acad. Bd, Pravo Ukrainy (Law of Ukraine), 2011–; Member, Senior Editorial Board: Law of Ukraine (Kyiv), 2011– (Editor, 2014–); Comparative Legal Studies (Kyiv), 2011; Kutafin Univ. Law Rev. (Moscow), 2014–; editor of looseleaf services and microfiche projects. FRSA 1986. Hon. LLD: Kyiv Univ. of Law, 2012; Acad. Internat. Ind. Ecological-Politological Univ., Moscow, 2016; Hon. JD Uppsala, 2018. *Publications*: more than 800 books, articles, translations, and reviews, including: The Soviet Union and the Law of the Sea, 1971; Russian Law, 1977; (with others) The Soviet Legal System, 3rd and 4th edns, 1977–84; A Source Book on Socialist International Organizations, 1978; Northeast Arctic Passage, 1978; International Law in Comparative Perspective, 1980; Basic Documents on Soviet Legal System, 1983, 3rd edn 1992; Chinese Soviet Republic 1931–1934, 1983; Soviet Law, 1983, 2nd edn 1988; Comparative Law and Legal System, 1985; The Law of the Sea and International Shipping, 1985; The Golden Era of American Bookplate Design, 1986; Justice and Comparative Law, 1987; International Law and the International System, 1987; The Non-Use of Force and International Law, 1989; Perestroika and International Law, 1990; The History of International Law in Russia 1647–1917, 1990; (with D. J. Butler) Modern British Bookplates, 1990; Sherlockian Bookplates, 1992; The Butler Commentaries: USSR Law on Ownership, 1991; USSR Fundamental Principles on Investment Activity, 1991; Foreign Investment Legislation in the Republic of the Former Soviet Union, 1993; (with M. E. Gashi-Butler) Doing Business in Russia, 1994; Russian-English Legal Dictionary, 1995, 2nd edn 2001; Russian Law, 1999, 3rd edn 2009; Tadzhikistan Legal Texts, 1999; Uzbekistan Legal Texts, 1999; American Bookplates, 2000; The Law of Treaties in Russia and Other Countries of the Commonwealth of Independent States, 2002; Russian Company and Commercial Law, 2003; Civil Code of the Russian Federation, 2003; Russian Foreign Relations and Investment Law, 2006; Russian Legal Biography, 2007; Russia and the Law of Nations in Historical Perspective, 2009; Peter Stephen Du Ponceau: legal bibliophile, 2010; Russian Criminal Law and Procedure, 2011; The Russian Legal Practitioner, 2011; Russian Law and Legal Institutions, 2014, 2nd edn 2018; Russian Inheritance Law, 2014; Russian Family Law, 2015; International and Comparative Law: a personal bibliography, 2015; *translations of:* G. I. Tunkin, Theory of International Law, 1974, 2nd edn 2003; A. Kuznetsov, The Journey, 1984; Kazakhstan Civil Code, 1995, 2008; Uzbekistan Civil Code, 1998, 2007; Russian Civil Legislation, 1999; Foreign Investment Law in the Commonwealth of Independent States, 2002; A. Saidov, Comparative Law, 2003; A. A. Kovalev, Contemporary Issues of the Law of the Sea, 2004; A. N. Vylegzhain and V. K. Zilanov, Spitzbergen, 2007; V. Kuznetsov and B. Tuzmukhamedov, International Law: a Russian introduction, 2009; A. L. Kolodkin, *et al*, The World Ocean: international legal regime, 2010; Ukrainian Legal System (5 vols), 2013; Ukrainian Legal Doctrine (6 vols), 2016–18; O. V. Kresin, Comparative Legal Studies, 1750–1835 (2 vols), 2019; *festschrift*: The Best in the West: liber amicorum for Professor William Butler, ed N. Erpyleva and M. E. Gashi-Butler, 2014. *Recreations:* book collecting, bookplate collecting. *Address:* 155 Mount Rock Road, Newville, PA 17241–8916, USA. *T:* (717) 7767359. *Clubs:* Cosmos (Washington, DC); Grolier (New York); National Union of Bibliophiles (Moscow).

**BUTLER, William Gerard;** Chairman, Cordia (Services) LLP, 2012; *b* 30 March 1956; *s* of William Muir Butler and Mary Butler (*née* Watters); *m* 1988, Patricia Josephine Ferguson, *qv. Educ:* St Mungo's Acad., Glasgow; Univ. of Stirling (BA Hons); Notre Dame Coll. of Educn (PGCE 1980). Teacher of English: Greenock High Sch., 1980–83; Port Glasgow High Sch., 1983–84; Castlehead High Sch., 1984–85; John Street Secondary Sch., 1985–86; Stonelaw High Sch., 1986–2000. Member (Lab) Glasgow CC, 1987–2001, 2012– (Convener: Property Services, 1995–98, Policy Formulation, 1998–99; Health and Social Care Policy Develt Cttee, 2012; Vice-Convener, Policy and Resources, 1998–2000). Sec., Glasgow City Labour Gp, 1998–2000. Mem. (Lab) Glasgow Anniesland, Scottish Parlt, Nov. 2000–2011; contested (Lab) same seat, 2011. *Recreations:* reading, theatre, film, visiting Italy, following Partick Thistle FC.

**BUTLER, William Gibson;** third sector leadership and management professional (consultancy and interim management), since 2010; *b* 11 May 1953; *s* of late William Gibson Butler and Anna Elizabeth Butler; *m* 1975, Jennifer Anne (*née* Dickson); two *d*. *Educ:* Ulster Poly. (CQSW 1975); Open Univ. (BA 1984; MBA 1993). Sen. Social Worker (community work), Eastern Health and Social Services Bd, 1979–86; Principal Community Services Develt Officer, Milton Keynes Develt Corp., 1986–92; Regl Dir, 1992–98, Ops Dir, 1998–2001, Nat. Schizophrenia Fellowship; Chief Exec., Arthritis Care, 2001–04; Chief Operating Officer, Addaction, 2005–10. Chm., Substance Misuse Skills Consortium, 2010–12. Trustee: Denbigh Alliance MAT; Directory of Social Change; The Pavement; Shenley Leisure Centre Trust; Community Action Beds. FRSA. *Recreation:* going to meetings. *E:* william.butler@ellisgibson.co.uk.

**BUTLER-ADAMS, William David,** OBE 2015; CEng, FIMechE; FRGS, FCGI; Managing Director, Brompton Bicycle Ltd, since 2008; *b* London, 11 May 1974; *s* of David Bernard Butler-Adams and Rosalie Annette Butler-Adams; *m* 2004, Sarah Georgina MacIntyre; three *d*. *Educ:* Aysgarth Sch., N Yorks; Rugby Sch.; Univ. of Newcastle upon Tyne (MEng and Spanish (1st cl.) 1997). MIMechE 1993, FIMechE 2014; CEng 2001. Proj. Manager, ICI, 1997–2000; Plant Manager, Dupont, 2000–02; Brompton Bicycle Ltd: Proj. Manager, 2002–05; Engrg Dir, 2005–08. Mem., UK Commn for Employment and Skills, 2013–16. Trustee, Educn and Employers Taskforce, 2010–; Mem. Bd, London Regl Council, EEF. FRGS 2013. Liveryman, Vintners' Co., 2010. *Recreations:* flying (Private Pilot Licence), ski-ing, climbing, wine, gardening, the environment; led nine-week expedition up Amazon, 1995 (filmed for documentary by Channel 4) and expedition to summit of Aconcagua (raised over £130,000 for charity), 2000; travelled extensively through South America, Europe, Africa and Asia. *Address:* Brompton Bicycle Ltd, Unit 1, Ockham Drive, Greenford UB6 0FD.

**BUTLER-BOWDON, Humphrey Anthony Erdeswick, (Humphrey Ocean),** RA 2004; painter; *b* 22 June 1951; *s* of late Capt. Maurice Erdeswick Butler-Bowdon, OBE, RN, and Anne (*née* Darlington); *m* 1982, Miranda Argyle; two *d*. *Educ:* Ampleforth; Tunbridge Wells Art Sch.; Brighton Coll. of Art; Canterbury Coll. of Art. Bass player, Kilburn and the Highroads, 1971–73. Prof. of Perspective, Royal Acad. Schs, 2012–. Mem., Artistic Records Cttee, Imperial War Mus., 1985–98. Work includes: The First of England, Nat. Maritime Mus., 1999; *portrait commissions* for National Portrait Gallery: Randy Lerner; Tony Benn; William Whitelaw; A. J. Ayer; Philip Larkin; Paul McCartney; one-man *exhibitions:* Nat. Portrait Gall., 1984; Ferens Art Gall., Hull, 1986; Double-Portrait, Tate Gall., Liverpool, 1992; urbasuburba, Whitworth Art Gall., Manchester, 1997; The Painter's Eye, Nat. Portrait Gall., 1999; how's my driving, Dulwich Picture Gall., 2003; Perfectly Ordinary, Sidney Cooper Gall., Canterbury Christ Church Univ., 2009; Here and There, Jesus Coll., Cambridge, 2011; A handbook of modern life, Nat. Portrait Gall., 2012–13; I've No Idea Either, Sims Reed Gall., London, 2018; Birds, Cars and Chairs, Royal Acad. of Arts, 2019; Horsham Are You Receiving Me?, Horsham Mus. and Art Gall., 2019; *group exhibitions* include: Das Automobil in der Kunst, Haus der Kunst, Munich, 1986; Royal Treasures, Queen's Gall., Buckingham Palace, 2002; Works Printed by Maurice Payne, Pace Prints, NY, 2011; Ship to Shore, John Hansard Gall., Univ. Southampton, 2014; Art Everywhere, Art Fund, 2013; books + papers, 2015, Wären Fluss und Meere Tinte, 2017, Christine König Galerie, Vienna; Towards Night, Towner Gall., Eastbourne, 2016; From Life, Royal Acad. of Arts, 2017; *work in collections:* Ferens Art Gall., Hull; Imperial War Mus.; Christ Church, Oxford; Nat. Maritime Mus.; NPG; Royal Liby, Windsor Castle; Royal Opera House, Covent Gdn; Scottish NPG; Southwark Collection; Wellcome Trust; Wolverhampton Art Gall.; British Council; Whitworth Art Gall., Manchester; Goldsmiths Coll., Univ. of London; Port Authy, Bruges-Zeebrugge; V&A; Pallant Hse Gall., Chichester; Fitzwilliam Mus., Cambridge. Writer and presenter, The Essay, BBC Radio 3, 2016. Trustee, Royal Drawing Sch., 2016–. Hon. Fellow, Univ. for the Creative Arts (formerly Kent Inst. of Art and Design), 2002. Hon. Dr: Canterbury Christ Ch, 2012; Kent, 2015. Imperial Tobacco Portrait Award, 1982; Wellcome Trust Sci-Art Award, 1998. *Publications:* The Ocean View, 1982; (with S. Nugent) Big Mouth: the Amazon speaks, 1990; Zeebrugge, 2001; A handbook of modern life, 2012; Humphrey Ocean: a collection, 2017. *Recreation:* carrying binoculars. *Address:* 22 Marmora Road, SE22 0RX. *T:* (020) 8693 8387, *T:* (studio) (020) 8761 7400. *W:* www.humphreyocean.com.

**BUTLER-SLOSS,** family name of **Baroness Butler-Sloss**.

**BUTLER-SLOSS, Baroness** *cr* 2006 (Life Peer), of Marsh Green in the County of Devon; **Ann Elizabeth Oldfield Butler-Sloss,** GBE 2005 (DBE 1979); PC 1988; President of the Family Division, 1999–2005; *b* 10 Aug. 1933; *d* of Sir Cecil Havers, QC and Enid Snelling; *m* 1958, Joseph William Alexander Butler-Sloss, *qv*; one *s* one *d* (and one *s* decd). *Educ:* Wycombe Abbey Sch. Called to Bar, Inner Temple, Feb. 1955, Bencher, 1979, Treasurer, 1998; practice at Bar, 1955–70; Registrar, Principal Registry of Probate, later Family, Division, 1970–79; a Judge of the High Court, Family Div., 1979–88; a Lord Justice of Appeal, 1988–99. Chairman: Cleveland Child Abuse Inquiry, 1987–88; Security Commn, 1993–2005; Adv. Council, St Paul's Cathedral, 2001–09; Commn on Appointment of Archbishop of Canterbury, 2002. Contested (C), Lambeth, Vauxhall, 1959. Mem., Judicial Studies Bd, 1985–89; Pres., Commonwealth and England Bar Assoc., 2000–07. Pres., Honiton Agricultural Show, 1985–86; Chancellor, Univ. of West of England, 1993–2010; Visitor, St Hilda's Coll., Oxford, 2000–. Gov., Merchant Taylors' Sch., Moor Park, 2006–13. Gov., Coram, 2005; Pres., Grandparents' Assoc., 2008. Freedom, City of London; Hon. Mem., Merchant Taylors' Co. Hon. Mem., American Law Inst., 1990. Hon. Fellow: St Hilda's Coll., Oxford, 1988; Sarum Coll., 2004; Fellow, KCL, 1991. FRSocMed 1992, Hon. FRSocMed 1997; Hon. FRCP 1992; Hon. FRCPsych 1993; Hon. FRCPCH 1996 (Hon. Mem., BPA, 1988). Hon. LLD: Hull, 1988; Keele, Bristol, 1991; Exeter, Brunel, 1992; Manchester, 1995; Cantab, Greenwich, 2000; Liverpool, E Anglia, 2001; London, Ulster, 2004; Buckingham, 2006; Hon. DLitt Loughborough, 1992; DUniv: Central England, 1994; Bath, 2004; Open, 2005; UWE, 2009; Wolverhampton, 2010. *Publications:* Joint Editor: Phipson on Evidence (10th edn); Corpe on Road Haulage (2nd edn); a former Editor, Supreme Court Practice, 1976 and 1979. *Clubs:* Lansdowne, Royal Society of Medicine.

**BUTLER-SLOSS, Joseph William Alexander;** Chairman, 1992 Delimitation Commission, Botswana, 1992–93; *b* 16 Nov. 1926; 2nd and *o* surv. *s* of late Francis Alexander Sloss and Alice Mary Frances Violet Sloss (*née* Patchell); *m* 1958, Ann Elizabeth Oldfield Havers (*see* Baroness Butler-Sloss); one *s* one *d* (and one *s* decd). *Educ:* Bangor Grammar Sch., Co. Down; Hertford Coll., Oxford. Ordinary Seaman, RN, 1944; Midshipman 1945, Sub-Lieut 1946, RNVR. MA (Jurisprudence) Hertford Coll., Oxford, 1951. Called to Bar, Gray's Inn, 1952; joined Western Circuit, 1954; joined Inner Temple; a Recorder, 1972–84; a Judge of High Court, Kenya, 1984–90. Joint Master, East Devon Foxhounds, 1970–76. Hon. Editor, The Irish Genealogist, 1993–2001. *Recreations:* racing, the violin. *Address:* Higher Marsh Farm, Marsh Green, Rockbeare, Exeter EX5 2EX. *Club:* Carlton.

**BUTLER-WHEELHOUSE, Keith Oliver;** Chief Executive, Smiths Group (formerly Smiths Industries), 1996–2008; *b* 29 March 1946; *s* of late Kenneth Butler-Wheelhouse and May (*née* Page); *m* 1973, Pamela Anne Bosworth Smith; two *s*. *Educ:* Queen Mary's, Walsall; Grey Sch. and Technicon, Port Elizabeth; Witwatersrand Univ. (BCom); Cape Town Univ. Grad. Sch. Mfg, Product Develt, Finance and Mktg Depts, Ford Motor Co., 1965–85; General Motors, 1985–86, led mgt buy-out of GMSA to form Delta, 1987–92; Pres., Saab Automobile, Sweden, 1992–96. Non-executive Director: Atlas Copco, 1993–96; J. Sainsbury plc, 1999–2004; Plastics Capital plc, 2011–. Chairman: Niu Solutions, 2009–11; Chamberlin, 2012–. Citizen of Year, Port Elizabeth, 1987. *Recreations:* golf, tennis, surfing. *Clubs:* Moor Park Golf, Royal and Ancient, Sunningdale Golf, Queen's Tennis; Humewood Golf, St Francis Golf, Fancourt Golf, Johannesburg Country (S Africa).

**BUTLIN, Martin Richard Fletcher,** CBE 1990; FBA 1984; Keeper of Historic British Collection, Tate Gallery, 1967–89; *b* 7 June 1929; *s* of late Kenneth Rupert Butlin and Helen Mary (*née* Fletcher), MBE, JP; *m* 1969, Frances Caroline Chodzko. *Educ:* Rendcomb Coll.; Trinity Coll., Cambridge (MA); Courtauld Inst. of Art, London Univ. (BA). DLit London 1984. Asst Keeper, Tate Gall., 1955–67. *Publications:* A Catalogue of the Works of William Blake in the Tate Gallery, 1957, 3rd edn 1990; Samuel Palmer's Sketchbook of 1824, 1962, 2nd edn as Samuel Palmer: the sketchbook of 1824, 2005; Turner Watercolours, 1962; (with Sir John Rothenstein) Turner, 1964; (with Mary Chamot and Dennis Farr) Tate Gallery Catalogues: The Modern British Paintings, Drawings and Sculpture, 1964; The Later Works of J. M. W. Turner, 1965; William Blake, 1966; The Blake-Varley Sketchbook of 1819, 1969; (with E. Joll) The Paintings of J. M. W. Turner, 1977, 2nd edn 1984 (jtly, Mitchell Prize for the History of Art, 1978); The Paintings and Drawings of William Blake, 1981; Aspects of British Painting 1550–1800, from the Collection of the Sarah Campbell Blaffer Foundation, 1988; (with Mollie Luther and Ian Warrell) Turner at Petworth, 1989; (with Ted Gott and Irena Zdanowicz) William Blake in the Collection of the National Gallery of Victoria, 1989; (ed with E. Joll and L. Herrmann) The Oxford Companion to J. M. W. Turner, 2001; (with Morton D. Paley) William Blake's Watercolour Inventions in illustration of The Grave by Robert Blair, 2009; selected paintings and prepared catalogues for following exhibitions: (with Andrew Wilton and John Gage) Turner 1775–1851, 1974; William Blake, 1978; (with Gert Schiff) William Blake, Tokyo, 1990; (jtly) William Blake in Sussex: visions of Albion, Petworth, 2018; articles and reviews in Burlington Mag., Connoisseur, Master Drawings, Blake Qly, Blake Studies, Turner Studies. *Recreations:* music, travel. *Address:* 74c Eccleston Square, SW1V 1PJ.

**BUTLIN, Prof. Robin Alan,** OBE 2004; DLitt; Professor of Historical Geography, University of Leeds, 2000–03, now Emeritus Professor of Geography (Leverhulme Emeritus Research Fellow, 2003–05; Visiting Research Fellow, School of Geography, since 2009); *b* 31 May 1938; *s* of late Rowland Henry Butlin and Mona Butlin; *m* 1961, Norma Coroneo; two *s* one *d*. *Educ:* Liverpool Univ. (BA, MA); DLitt Loughborough, 1987. Demonstrator, University Coll. of N Staffordshire, 1961–62; Lectr in Geography, UC Dublin, 1962–71; Queen Mary College, University of London: Lectr in Geography, 1971; Sen. Lectr, 1975; Reader in Historical Geography, 1977–79; Loughborough University: Prof. of Geography, 1979–95; Hd of Dept, 1979–91; Dean, Sch. of Human and Environmental Studies, 1983–86; Principal, and Prof. of Historical Geography, UC of Ripon and York St John, 1995–98. Vis. Associate Prof. of Geography, Univ. of Nebraska, 1969–70; Vis. Professorial Fellow and Leverhulme Res. Fellow, Wolfson Coll., Cambridge, 1986–87; Vis. Prof., Leeds Univ., 1998–2000. Gov., St Peter's Sch., York, 2002–10. FRGS 1972 (Vice-Pres., RGS/IBG, 1995–98); CGeog 2002. Victoria Medal, RGS, 1999. *Publications:* (ed with A. R. H. Baker) Studies of Field Systems in the British Isles, 1973; (ed) The Development of the Irish Town, 1977; (ed with R. A. Dodgshon) An Historical Geography of England and Wales, 1978, 2nd edn 1990; (ed with H. S. A. Fox) Change in the Countryside: essays on rural England 1500–1900, 1979; The Transformation of Rural England c. 1580–1800, 1982; Historical Geography: through the gates of space and time, 1993; (ed jtly) Geography and Imperialism 1820–1940, 1995; (ed with N. Roberts) Ecological Relations in Historical Times, 1995; (ed with R. A. Dodgshon) Historical Geography of Europe, 1999; (ed with I. S. Black) Place, Culture and Identity, 2001; (ed) Historical Atlas of North Yorkshire, 2003; Geographies of Empire: European empires and colonies *c* 1880–1960, 2009; The Historical Geography Research Group: a history, 2013; The Origins and Development of Geography at the University of Leeds *c* 1874–2014, 2015. *Recreations:* music, walking, reading, collecting wood engravings. *Address:* 15 Lawnway, Stockton Lane, York YO31 1JD. *T:* (01904) 416544.

**BUTROS, Prof. Albert Jamil;** Istiqlal Order First Class, Jordan, 1987; Professor of English, University of Jordan, 1967–79 and 1985–2004, now Emeritus; *b* 25 March 1934; *s* of Jamil Issa and Virginie Antoine (Albina); *m* 1962, Ida Maria Albina (*d* 2018); four *d*. *Educ:* Univ. of London (BA Hons English 1958); Univ. of Exeter (BA *ad eundem* 1958); Columbia Univ. (PhD English 1963). Teacher, Amman, 1950–55; Instructor in English, Teacher's Coll., Amman, 1958–60; Lectr, Hunter Coll., City Univ., NY, 1961; Instructor, Miami Univ. Oxford, Ohio, 1962–63; University of Jordan: Asst Prof., English, 1963–65; Associate Prof., 1965–67; Acting Chm., Dept of English, 1964–67; Chm., Dept of English, 1967–73, 1974–76; Dean, Research and Graduate Studies, 1973–76; Ambassador to UK, 1987–91, and (non-res.) to Ireland, 1988–91, and to Iceland, 1990–91. Special Advr to HRH Crown Prince Hassan of Jordan, 1984–85. Dir Gen./Pres., Royal Sci. Soc., Amman, 1976–84. Vis. Prof., Ohio Wesleyan Univ., 1971–72; Sen. Res. Fellow, Internat. Develt Res. Centre, Canada, 1983–84. Rapporteur, Cttee on Jordan Incentive State Prize in Translation, 2001; Member: Cttee on Selection for Shoman Foundn Prize for Young Arab Scholars in Humanities and Social Scis, 2002; Cttee on Selection of Outstanding Researchers in Jordan, 2004. Member: World Affairs Council, Amman, 1978–91; Arab Thought Forum, 1981–95. Gov., Internat. Develt Res. Centre, Canada, 1986–98; Mem., Bd of Trustees, Philadelphia Univ., Amman, 1995–2009. Mem., Adv. Bd, Jordanian Jl of Modern Langs and Lit., 2006–. Fellow, World Acad. of Art and Sci., 1986. KStJ 1991. Order of Merit, Italy, 1983. *Publications:* Tales of the Caliphs, 1965; Leaders of Arab Thought, 1969; The Translatability of Chaucer into Arabic: a test case, 1997; The English Language and Non-Native Writers of Fiction, 2004; (in Arabic) Geoffrey Chaucer: introduction and selected translations, 2009; translations include: (in English) Suleiman Mousa's T. E. Lawrence: an Arab view, 1966; (in Arabic) Glanville Downey's Antioch in the Age of Theodosius the Great, 1968; articles. *Recreations:* reading, writing, translation, art, world affairs, application of science and technology to development. *Address:* PO Box 309, Amman 11941, Jordan.

**BUTT, Amanda Jane;** *see* Finlay, A. J.

**BUTT, Geoffrey Frank;** Principal Assistant Solicitor, Inland Revenue, 1993–96; *b* 5 May 1943; *s* of late Frank Thomas Woodman Butt and Dorothy Rosamond Butt; *m* 1972, Lee Anne Davey; two *s* one *d*. *Educ:* Royal Masonic Sch., Bushey; Univ. of Reading (BA). Solicitor 1970. Joined Solicitor's Office, HM Customs and Excise as Legal Asst, 1971; Sen. Legal Asst, 1974; Asst Solicitor, 1982; Prin. Asst Solicitor, 1986–93. *Recreations:* family life, classical music, literature and art, gardening. *Address:* 14 Richmond Close, Wellswood, Torquay, Devon TQ1 2PW.

**BUTT, Prof. John Anthony,** OBE 2013; PhD; FBA 2006; FRSE; Gardiner Professor of Music, University of Glasgow, since 2001; *b* 17 Nov. 1960; *s* of late Wilfred Roger Butt and of Patricia Doreen Butt; *m* 1989, Sally Ann Cantlay; three *s* two *d*. *Educ:* Solihull Sch.; King's Coll., Cambridge (BA 1982; MPhil 1984; PhD 1987). FRCO(CHM); ADCM. Temp. Lectr, Univ. of Aberdeen, 1986–87; Res. Fellow, Magdalene Coll., Cambridge, 1987–89; Prof. of Music and Univ. Organist, Univ. of Calif. Berkeley, 1989–97; Lectr in Music and Fellow, King's Coll., Univ. of Cambridge, 1997–2001. A Principal Artist, Orch. of Age of Enlightenment, 2015–. Conductor of several recordings with Dunedin Consort, including: Bach, St John Passion and Brandenburg Concertos, 2013; Mozart Requiem, 2014 (Gramophone Classical Music Award for Choral Music, 2014). Mem., AHRC, 2010–14. FRSE 2003. *Publications:* Bach Interpretation, 1990; Bach Mass in B Minor, 1991; Music Education and the Art of Performance in the German Baroque, 1994; (ed) Cambridge Companion to Bach, 1997; Playing with History, 2002; (ed) Cambridge History of 17th Century Music, 2005; Bach's Dialogue with Modernity: perspectives on the passions, 2010. *Recreations:* reading, hill-walking. *Address:* Upper Culverden, 2 West Lennox Drive, Helensburgh G84 9AD. *T:* (01436) 673942.

**BUTT, Loren Oliver Wallington;** independent consulting engineer, since 1987; *b* London, 24 March 1936; *s* of Roderick Butt and Cynthia Butt (*née* Cooper-Smith); *m* 1959, Jennifer Margaret Perham; two *s*. *Educ:* Clifton Coll., Bristol; University Coll. London (BSc Eng 1959). CEng, MIMechE 1967. Associate, D. W. Thomson & Co., Vancouver, BC, 1967; Exec. Engr, G. N. Haden and Sons Ltd, 1968–70; Design Engr, 1970–72, Associate, 1972–80, Foster Associates; Dir, Foster Associates Ltd, 1980–87. Hon. FRIBA 2009. *Recreations:* architectural and engineering history, walking, playing guitar, playing petanque. *Address:* 22 Croft Road, Wallingford, Oxon OX10 0HT. *T:* (01491) 200316. *E:* loren.butt@virginmedia.com.

**BUTT, Michael Acton,** OBE 2011; Chairman, AXIS Capital Holdings Ltd, Bermuda, since 2002; *b* Thruxton, 25 May 1942; *s* of Leslie Acton Kingsford Butt and Mina Gascoigne Butt; *m* 1st, 1964, Diana Lorraine Brook; two *s*; 2nd, 1986, Zoé Benson. *Educ:* Rugby; Magdalen Coll., Oxford (BA History); INSEAD, France (MBA 1967). Bland Welch Gp, 1964; Dir, Bland Payne Holdings, 1970; Chm., Sedgwick Ltd, 1983–87; Dep. Chm., Sedgwick Gp plc, 1985–87; Chm. and Chief Exec., Eagle Star Hldgs, 1987–91; Dir, BAT, 1987–91; Pres. and CEO, Mid Ocean Ltd, 1993–98; Dir, XL Capital Ltd, 1998–2002. Director: Marceau Investissements, Paris, 1987–94; Phoenix International (Bermuda), 1992–97; INA, 1994–97; Bank of N. T. Butterfield & Son Ltd, 1996–2002. Board Mem., Internat. Adv. Council, INSEAD, 1982–2010. Vice Chm., 2001–07, Dir, 2008–13, Assoc. of Bermuda Internat. Cos; Chm., Assoc. of Bermuda Insurers and Reinsurers, 2008–09. Mem., Bd of Trustees, Bermuda Biological Station for Res., 1996–2007 (Trustee Emeritus, 2006); Founding Mem., Bermuda Foundn for Insurance Studies, 1996 (Mem., Steering Cttee; Adv. Trustee, 2000). Bermuda Insurance Inst. Lifetime Award, 2008; Insurance Day Lifetime Achievement Award, 2015; Insurance Hall of Fame Laureate, 2019. *Recreations:* travel, tennis, opera, reading, family, the European movement. *Address:* Leamington House, 50 Harrington Sound Road, Hamilton Parish CR 04, Bermuda. *T:* (441) 2931378, *Fax:* (441) 2938511. *Clubs:* Royal Bermuda Yacht, Mid Ocean, Coral Beach (Bermuda).

**BUTT, Richard Bevan;** Chief Executive, Rural Development Commission, 1989–98; *b* 27 Feb. 1943; *s* of late Roger William Bevan and Jean Mary (*née* Carter); *m* 1975, Amanda Jane Finlay, *qv*; two *s*. *Educ:* Magdalen Coll., Oxford (BA Hist.); Lancaster Univ. (MA Regional Econs). Asst Principal, Min. of Housing, 1965–68; Sen. Res. Associate, Birmingham Univ., 1969–72; Consultant, 1972; HM Treasury: Principal, 1973–78; Asst Sec., 1978–86; seconded as Financial Counsellor, UK Perm. Repn to EC, 1981–84; Head of Conservation, English Heritage, 1986–89. Specialist Advr to Agriculture Select Cttee, 1998–99. Trustee: Action for Market Towns, 1998–2003; Churches Conservation Trust, 1999–2008 (Dep. Chm., 2006–08); TCPA, 2004–08 (Mem., Policy Council, 1998–2008). *Recreations:* ceramics, architecture, gardening, travel. *Address:* 35 Gloucester Circus, SE10 8RY.

**BUTT, Simon John;** HM Diplomatic Service, retired; Ambassador to Lithuania, 2008–11; *b* 5 April 1958; *s* of William Hedley Butt and Joan Marion Newton Butt. *Educ:* New Coll., Oxford (BA 1st Cl. Hons PPE 1979; MA). Entered FCO, 1979; E Europe and Soviet Dept, FCO, 1979–80; lang. trng, 1980–82; Third Sec., Moscow, 1982–84; Second Secretary: Rangoon, 1984–86; Soviet Dept, FCO, 1986–88; ministerial speechwriter, 1988–90; First Sec., UK Perm. Representation to EC, 1990–94; Dep. Hd, Eastern Dept, FCO, 1994–97; Counsellor and Dep. Hd of Mission, Kiev, 1997–2000; Hd, Eastern Dept, FCO, 2001–04; Dep. High Comr, Islamabad, Pakistan, 2005–08. *Recreations:* travel, the company of friends, history, including a harmless obsession with Napoleon on St Helena. *E:* sjbutt295@yahoo.co.uk.

**BUTTER, His Honour Neil (McLaren),** CBE 2001; QC 1976; a Circuit Judge, 1982–2001; a Judge of Central London County Court, 1994–2001; Designated Civil Judge, London County Court Group, 1998–2001; Senior Circuit Judge, 1998–2001; *b* 10 May 1933; *y s* of late Andrew Butter, MA, MD and late Ena Butter, MB, ChB; *m* 1974, Claire Marianne Miskin, LLM (*d* 2011). *Educ:* The Leys Sch.; Queens' Coll., Cambridge (MA). Called to Bar, Inner Temple, 1955, Bencher, 1994; an Asst and Dep. Recorder of Bournemouth, 1971; Recorder of the Crown Court, 1972–82; a Judge of Bow County Court, 1986–94; occasional Judge of Employment Appeal Tribunal, 1995–98. Member: Senate of the Inns of Court and the Bar, 1976–79; County Court Rule Cttee, 1993–99; Clinical Disputes Forum, 1997–2001; Chm., Court Mediation Scheme Cttee, 1996–2001. Inspector, for Dept of Trade, Ozalid Gp Hldgs Ltd, 1977–79. A Legal Assessor to GMC and GDC, 1979–82; Mem., Mental Health Review Tribunal, 1983–92. Chm., London County Court Assoc. of Circuit Judges, 1998–2001. Trustee, Kingdon-Ward Speech Therapy Trust, 1980–87. *Publications: collections of short stories:* Doctor George, 2007; Burning Desire, 2010; Below the Window, 2014. *Recreations:* dining out with friends, browsing through Who's Who. *Club:* Royal Over-Seas League.

**BUTTER, Peter Joseph Michael,** CB 1992; Deputy Managing Director, Property Services Agency, Building Management, Department of the Environment, 1992, retired; *b* 9 Dec. 1932; *s* of Joseph Butter and Kathleen (*née* Woodward); *m* 1956, Pamela Frances Roberts; three *s*. *Educ:* Brighton, Hove and Sussex Grammar School. Served Royal Signals, 1951–53. BR, 1953–67; Principal, Min. of Transport, 1967–73; Private Sec. to Minister of Transport, 1973; joined PSA, 1974: Hd, Defence Secretariat (Navy), 1974–79; Asst Dir, Estate Surveying Services, 1979–84; Dir, SE Region, 1984–88; Dir, Home Regional Services, 1988–90; Dir of Ops, PSA, Bldg Management, DoE, 1990–91. Chm., Sussex Cricket League, 2010 (Sec., 1999–2007; Vice Pres., 2008–). *Recreations:* cricket administration, listening to music, exploring Britain. *Address:* 6 Scarletts Close, Uckfield, E Sussex TN22 2BA. *Club:* Sussex CC.

**BUTTERFIELD, Hon. Sir (Alexander) Neil (Logie),** Kt 1995; a Judge of the High Court of Justice, Queen's Bench Division, 1995–2012. *Educ:* Sidney Sussex Coll., Cambridge (BA 1964). Called to the Bar, Inner Temple, 1965; a Recorder, 1978–95; QC 1985. Leader, 1992–95, Presiding Judge, 1997–2000, Western Circuit. Member: Parole Bd, 2003–15 (Vice Chm., 2005–15); Bd, Ind. Parly Standards Authy, 2013–16. Trustee, RC Dio. of Plymouth, 2014–. KSG 2017. *Address:* c/o Royal Courts of Justice, Strand, WC2A 2LL. *Club:* Athenæum.

**BUTTERFIELD, Ven. David John;** Archdeacon for Generous Giving and Stewardship, and Residentiary Canon, York Minster, 2014–17, now Archdeacon Emeritus; *b* 1 Jan. 1952; *s* of John Alfred Butterfield and Agnes Butterfield (*née* Winn); *m* 1977, Irene Mary Abel; two *s*. *Educ:* Belle Vue Boys' Grammar Sch., Bradford; Royal Holloway Coll., London Univ. (BMus 1973); Nottingham Univ. (DipTh 1975); St John's Theol Coll., Nottingham. Ordained deacon, 1977; priest, 1978; Curate, Christ Church, Southport, 1977–81; Minister, St Thomas, Aldridge, 1981–91; Vicar, St Michael's, Lilleshall, St John's, Muxton, and St Mary's, Sheriffhales, 1991–2007; Rural Dean, Edgmond and Shifnal, 1997–2006; Archdeacon of East Riding, 2007–14. Mem., Crown Appts Commn, 2003. Mem., Gen. Synod, C of E, 1990–2005 (Chair, House of Clergy, Dio. of Lichfield, 2003–06). *Publications:* Getting Going, 1987. *Recreations:* piano, organ, walking, swimming, reading, making marmalade. *Address:* 18 Kirkby Drive, Ripon HG4 2DP. *T:* (01765) 609394.

**BUTTERFIELD, Jeremy Nicholas,** PhD; FBA 1996; Senior Research Fellow, Trinity College, Cambridge, since 2006; *b* 23 Dec. 1954; *s* of Baron Butterfield, OBE, DM, FRCP and Isabel-Ann Foster Butterfield (*née* Kennedy); *m* 1st, 1978, Sally Damon Snell (marr. diss. 2007); one *s* one *d*; 2nd, 2008, Mari Hirano. *Educ:* Trinity Coll., Cambridge (BA 1976; PhD 1984). Cambridge University: Asst Lectr in Philosophy, 1981–85; Lectr, 1985–97; Reader in Philosophy, 1997; Fellow of Jesus Coll., 1981–97; Sen. Res. Fellow, All Souls Coll., Oxford, 1998–2006. Visiting Professor: Princeton Univ., 1989, 2004; Univ. of Pittsburgh, 2008; Univ. of Sydney, 2009. *Publications:* edited: Language, Mind and Logic, 1986; (with G. Belot and M. Hogarth) Spacetime, 1996; (with C. Pagonis) From Physics to Philosophy, 1999; The Arguments of Time, 1999; (with T. Placek) Non-Locality and Modality, 2002; (with H. Halvorson) Quantum Entanglements: selected papers of Rob Clifton, 2004; (with J. Earman) The Handbook of Philosophy of Physics, 2 vols, 2006; (with M. Ozawa *et al*) Reality and Measurement in Algebraic Quantum Theory, 2018; articles in learned jls. *Recreation:* the Muppets. *Address:* Trinity College, Cambridge CB2 1TQ. *T:* (01223) 338400.

**BUTTERFIELD, John Arthur;** QC 2014; a Recorder, since 2009; *b* Keighley, W Yorks, 27 Feb. 1972; *s* of James and Muriel Butterfield; *m* 2001, Elizabeth Dolan; one *s* two *d*. *Educ:* Beckfoot Grammar Sch.; Univ. of Liverpool (LLB 1st Cl. Hons; Pres., Legal Soc., 1992–93); Inns of Court Sch. of Law. Called to the Bar, Lincoln's Inn, 1995; in practice as barrister, specialising in crime, 1995–. *Recreations:* songwriting, recording in home music studio, cinema. *Address:* 5 Fountain Court, Steelhouse Lane, Birmingham B4 6DR. *T:* 0845 210 5555, *Fax:* (0121) 606 1501. *E:* jab@no5.com.

**BUTTERFIELD, Leslie Paul**, CBE 2007; brand strategy and communications consultant; Partner, Butterfield Harris, since 2015; Chairman, Join the Dots Research Ltd, since 2017; *b* Reading, 31 Aug. 1952; *s* of Leslie John and Ruth Butterfield; *m* 1988, Judy Tombleson (marr. diss.); partner, Penny Harris; one *s* one *d*. *Educ:* North East London Poly. (BA 1st Cl. Hons Business Studies 1974); Lancaster Univ. (MA Mktg Educn (Dist.) 1975); Babson Coll., Boston, Mass (short MBA prog. 2012). Account Planner, BMP/DDB, 1975–80; Planning Dir, AMV/BBDO, 1980–87; Planning Dir and Chm., Butterfield Day Devito Hockney, subseq. Partners BDDH, 1987–2001; CEO, Butterfield 8, 2001–03; Partner, Ingram, 2003–07; CEO, ButterfieldPartners, 2007–08; Global Chief Strategy Officer, Interbrand Gp, 2008–15. Dir, Mindful Chef Ltd, 2015–. *Publications:* Excellence in Advertising, 1997, 2nd edn 1999; Understanding the Financial Value of Brands, 1998; Advalue: twenty ways advertising works for business, 2003; Enduring Passion: the story of the Mercedes-Benz brand, 2005. *Recreations:* my children Alexa and Cerian, cars, ski-ing, railway archaeology, music, travel, cocktails. *Address:* The Shire Barn, Foxhill Farm, Fosse Way, Bourton-on-the-Water, Glos GL54 3BL. *T:* (01451) 821675, (mobile) 07885 678581.

**BUTTERFIELD, Hon. Sir Neil;** *see* Butterfield, Hon. Sir A. N. L.

**BUTTERFIELD, Stewart David;** Managing Director, Broadcasting, Granada plc (formerly Granada UK Broadcasting), 1997–2002; *b* 10 Sept. 1947; *s* of Bernard and Moray Butterfield. *Educ:* Mount St Mary's Coll., Spinkhill, Derbys; London Sch. of Econs (BSc Econ). McCann-Erickson, 1973–91, European Media Dir, 1989–91; Dir of Advertising Sales and Mktg, Channel Four, 1991–97. Trustee, VSO, 2002–08.

**BUTTERFIELD, Venetia;** Publisher, Penguin General, and Publishing Director, Viking, since 2005, Portfolio, since 2010, and Penguin Life, since 2016, Penguin Random House UK; *b* Northampton, 9 May 1970; *d* of William Butterfield and Verity Butterfield; *m* 2002, Christopher Lockwood; three *s*. *Educ:* Tudor Hall Sch.; Newcastle Univ. (BA English, Hist., Film). HarperCollins: grad. trainee, 1992–94; Mktg Exec., 1994, Mktg Manager for Secondary Educn, 1995–97, Hd of Mktg, 1997–99, Collins Educnl; Mktg Manager, 1999–2001; Mktg Dir, 2001–03; Paperback Publisher, 2003–05. Gov., Southbank Centre, 2016–. Vice Chairman, Governors: West London Free Sch., 2013–17; Earls Court Free Sch., 2013–17. *Recreations:* reading, theatre, family, cooking, art, eating with friends. *Address:* Penguin Random House, 80 Strand, WC2R 0RL. *T:* (020) 7010 3000. *E:* vbutterfield@penguinrandomhouse.co.uk.

**BUTTERFILL, Sir John (Valentine)**, Kt 2004; *b* 14 Feb. 1941; *s* of George Thomas Butterfill and Elsie Amelia (*née* Watts); *m* 1965, Pamela Ross-Symons; one *s* three *d*. *Educ:* Caterham Sch.; Coll. of Estate Management. FRICS 1974. Valuer, Jones, Lang, Wootton, 1961–64; Sen. Exec., Hammerson Gp, 1964–69; Dir, Audley Properties Ltd (Bovis Gp), 1969–71; Man. Dir, St Paul's Securities Gp, 1971–76; Sen. Partner, Curchod & Co., 1977–91, Consultant, 1992–. Chm., Conservation Investments, 1978–2002; Director: Micro Business Systems, 1977–79; John Lelliott Developments, 1984–88; ISLEF Building and Construction, 1984–91; Pavilion Services Gp, 1992–94; Delphi Gp, 1996–99. Pres., European Property Associates, 1979–2003. MP (C) Bournemouth West, 1983–2010. Parliamentary Private Secretary: to Sec. of State for Energy, 1988–89; to Sec. of State for Transport, 1989–90; to Minister of State for NI, 1991–92. Member: Trade and Industry Select Cttee, 1992–2001; Select Cttee on Unopposed Bills, 1995–2010. Vice-Chairman: Backbench Tourism Cttee, 1986–88; Backbench Finance Cttee, 1992–2000; Sec., Backbench Trade and Industry Cttee, 1987–88, and 1991; Chm., Backbench European Affairs Cttee, 1995–97. Member: Parly Ct of Referees, 1995–2010; Speaker's Panel of Chairmen, 1996–2010. Chm., All Party Parly Gp on Occupational Pensions, 1992–2010; Vice-Chairman: All Party Parly Gp on Bldg Socs and Financial Mutual Instns, 1997–2010 (Sec., 1996); All Party Parly Gp on ELT, 2008–10; Jt Sec., All Party Parly Gp on Insurance and Financial Services, 1997–2010. Chm., Parly Members' Fund, 1997–2002; Trustee, 1997–2010, Chm. of Trustees, 2001–10, Parly Contributory Pension Fund. 1922 Committee: Sec., 1996–97; Vice Chm., 1997–2001, 2005–06; Treas., 2001–05. Vice Pres., Cons. Gp for Europe, 1992–95 (Chm., 1989–92); Vice-Chm., Parly Gp, Cons. Friends of Israel, 1995–2010. Mem., Council of Management, PDSA, 1990–; Chm. of Trustees, PDSA Pension Fund, 2002–07. *Publications:* occasional contribs to property, insurance and financial publications. *Recreations:* ski-ing, tennis, bridge, music.

**BUTTERWORTH, Anthony;** *see* Butterworth, C. A.

**BUTTERWORTH, Anthony Edward**, PhD; FRS 1994; MRC External Scientific Staff, 1979–95, retired; *b* 8 July 1945; *s* of late Edward Alexander Butterworth and Sylvia (*née* Hardy); *m* 1st, 1972, Margot Lois Hudson (marr. diss. 1999); one *s* one *d*; 2nd, 2001, Elizabeth Lucy Corbett; one *s* one *d*. *Educ:* Harrow Sch.; Trinity Hall, Cambridge (BA, MB, BChir); St Mary's Hosp. Med. Sch., London; Clare Coll., Cambridge (PhD). Wellcome Trust Research Fellow: Nairobi, Kenya, 1973–77; Harvard Med. Sch., Boston, 1977–79; University of Cambridge: Associate Lectr, 1980–89; Hon. Reader, 1989–93; Hon. Prof. of Med. Parasitology, 1993–95. Hon. Professor: LSHTM, 2001–14; Coll. of Medicine, Univ. of Malawi, 2009–13. Hon. Scientific Dir, Biomedical Res. and Trng Inst., Harare, 2001–06. Frederick Murgatroyd Prize, RCP, 1979; Bernhard Nocht Medal, 1987; King Faisal Internat. Prize in Medicine, 1990; Chalmers Medal, RSTM&H, 1990. *Publications:* papers and book chapters on immunology and parasitology.

**BUTTERWORTH, Prof. Brian Lewis**, PhD; FBA 2002; CPsychol, FBPsS; Professor of Cognitive Neuropsychology, University College London, 1992–2009, now Emeritus; *b* 3 Jan. 1944; *s* of Henry Lewis Butterworth and Cicely Rebecca (*née* Haringman); partner, Diana Margaret Laurillard; two *d*. *Educ:* Quintin Sch., London; Merton Coll., Oxford (BA); Univ. of Sussex (MA); PhD London 1972. CPsychol 1990; FBPsS 1990. Jun. Res. Fellow, MRC Speech and Communication Unit, Edinburgh, 1971–72; Lectr in Psychol., Dept of Exptl Psychol., Univ. of Cambridge, 1972–80; Lectr in Psychol., 1980–86, Reader, 1986–92, Dept of Psychol., UCL. Hon. and pt-time posts at Univ. of Tennessee, MIT, Univ. of Padova, Univ. of Trieste, Max Planck Inst. for Psycholinguistics, Nijmegen; Sen. Vis. Res. Fellow, 2000–03, Professorial Fellow, 2003–, Melbourne Univ.; Hon. Prof., Dalian Univ., China, 2007–09; Res. Consultant, Ospedale San Camillo, Venice, 2011–; Univ. Chair Prof., Nat. Cheng Chi Univ., Taiwan, 2013–. Chair, Centre for Educnl Neurosci., UCL, Inst. of Educn and Birkbeck, Univ. of London, 2008–09. Ed.-in-Chief, Linguistics, 1978–83; Co-founding Ed., Lang. and Cognitive Processes, 1983–; Founding Ed., Mathematical Cognition, 1983–2000. Co-ordinator, Mathematics and the Brain, 1999–2003, Numeracy and Brain Develt, 2004–08, Eur. Network. (Jtly) Babble to Babel (installation in Millennium Dome), 2000; (jtly) The Brain Unravelled (exhibn, Slade Res. Centre, UCL), 2009; (jtly) The Origins of Numerical Abilities, Discussion and Satellite meetings, Royal Society, 2017. *Publications:* (ed) Language Production, Vol. 1 1980, Vol. 2 1983; (ed jtly) Explanations for Language Universals, 1983; The Mathematical Brain, 1999; (ed) Mathematical Cognition, 2000; Dyscalculia Screener, 2003 (British Educn & Teaching with Technology Award for educnl software, 2004); (with Dorian Yeo) Dyscalculia Guidance, 2004; (ed jtly) Educational Neuroscience, 2013; Dyscalculia: from science to education, 2019; contrib. numerous acad. papers on speech production, aphasia, gestures, dyslexia, mathematical cognition and dyscalculia. *Recreations:* family holidays, rock art, archaeology and anthropology of numbers. *Address:* Institute of Cognitive Neuroscience, University College London, 17 Queen Square, WC1N 3AZ. *T:* (020) 7679 1150, *Fax:* (020) 7813 2835. *E:* b.butterworth@ucl.ac.uk.

**BUTTERWORTH, Prof. (Charles) Anthony**, CBE 1996; PhD; FRCN; FMedSci; Joint Director, Centre for Clinical and Academic Workforce Innovation, University of Lincoln, 2005–08, now Emeritus Professor of Health Care Workforce Innovation; Chair, Foundation of Nursing Studies, since 2011; *b* 14 March 1947; *s* of Norman Butterworth and Anne Alison Butterworth; *m* 1971, Jacqueline; one *s* one *d*. *Educ:* Univ. of Aston, Birmingham (MSc; PhD 1986); Storthes Hall Hosp., Huddersfield (RMN); Manchester Royal Infirmary (RGN); Univ. of Manchester (RNT). Clinical nurse, Yorks and Gtr Manchester, 1968–75; Lectr, then Sen. Lectr, 1975–80, Principal Lectr and Hd of Nursing, 1980–86, Manchester Poly.; University of Manchester: Prof. of Community Nursing, Queen's Nursing Inst., 1987–2001; Pro-Vice-Chancellor, 1999–2001; Vis. Prof., 2001–; Chief Exec., Trent NHS Workforce Develt Confedn, 2001–05; Dir, Res. Unit, Univ. of Lincoln, 2005–09; Chair: Acad. of Nursing, Midwifery and Health Visiting Res., 2007–11; NHS Inst. for Innovation and Improvement, 2011–13 (non-exec. Dir, 2005–11). FRCN 1996; Founder FMedSci 1998; FQNI 2008. Hon. FRCPsych 1999. FRSA 1996. Trustee: Dementia UK, 2008–; RCN Foundn, 2010– (Vice-Chair, 2010–). *Publications:* Community Psychiatric Nursing, 1980; Caring for the Mentally Ill in the Community, 1981; Clinical Supervision and Mentorship in Nursing, 1992, 2nd edn 1999. *Recreations:* gardening, football, walking. *E:* tbutterworth@lincoln.ac.uk.

**BUTTERWORTH, Nicholas John;** writer and illustrator of children's books, since 1980; *b* 24 May 1946; *s* of George and Nancy Butterworth; *m* 1975, Annette Fancourt; one *s* one *d*. *Educ:* Royal Liberty Grammar Sch., Romford. Left sch., aged 16; compositor and typographic designer, Printing Dept, NCH, Harpenden, 1962–65; graphic designer: Frank Overton Associates, 1965–67; with Crosby Fletcher Forbes, for Cunard Line, Southampton, then freelance, 1967–68; formed Baxter Butterworth Cope, 1968; worked in various graphic partnerships, 1968–80, incl. partnership with Mick Inkpen in graphics, illustration and writing; started writing for children, 1981 and went solo, 1988. Founding Partner, Snapper Prodns Ltd, 2008–; Dir, Q Pootle 5 Ltd, 2011–; Exec. Prod. and Prodn Designer, Q Pootle 5 (children's animated TV series, 52 episodes; Christmas special, Pootle All the Way!), 2011–. Presenter, Rub-a-dub-tub (children's prog.), TV AM, 1982–83. *Publications:* books include: B B Blacksheep and Company, 1981; (with Mick Inkpen) The Nativity Play, 1985; (with Mick Inkpen) Just Like Jasper, 1989; One Snowy Night, 1989; Amanda's Butterfly, 1991; After the Storm, 1992; (with Mick Inkpen) Jasper's Beanstalk, 1992; Making Faces, 1993; The Rescue Party, 1993; The Secret Path, 1994; All Together Now, 1995; A Year in Percy's Park, 1995; (illus.) Jake, 1995; The Hedgehog's Balloon, 1996; The Treasure Hunt, 1996; THUD!, 1997; Four Feathers in Percy's Park, 1998; Jingle Bells, 1998; Percy's Bumpy Ride, 1999; Q Pootle 5, 2000; Everyone's Friend Percy, 2001; Albert Le Blanc, 2002; Q Pootle 5 In Space!, 2003; The Whisperer, 2004; Tiger!, 2006; Tiger in the Snow, 2006; Albert Le Blanc to the Rescue, 2007; Trixie the Witch's Cat, 2009; One Springy Day, 2019. *Recreations:* ski-ing, squash, tennis, pottering in the shed, gardening, woodworking, travel, music – listening – and playing piano badly! *Address:* Snapper Productions Ltd, 1 Belmont House, 23 New Street, Henley-on-Thames, Oxon RG9 2BP.

**BUTTLE, Eileen**, CBE 1995; PhD; FRSB; Member, Scientific Committee, European Environment Agency, 1994–2002; *b* 19 Oct. 1937; *d* of late George Ernest Linford and Mary Stewart Linford; *m* 1970, Hugh Langley Buttle. *Educ:* Harrow Weald County Grammar Sch.; Univ. of Southampton (BSc (Hons); PhD). FRSB (FIBiol 1990). Post-doctoral Res. Fellow, Univ. of Southampton, 1963–65; Research Scientist: Nat. Inst. of Res. in Dairying, 1965–71; Cattle Breeding Centre, MAFF, 1971–76; Policy Administrator, MAFF, 1976–89; Sec., NERC, 1989–94; Dir, World Humanity Action Trust, 1994–97. Dir, Shell Transport and Trading Co. plc, 1998–2005. Trustee: Buckland Foundn, 1994–2002; Horniman Mus. of Gdns, 1994–98; Onyx Envmtl Trust, 1997–2002; Earthwatch Europe, 1997–2003. Mem., 1999–2006, Dep. Chm., 2002–06, Council, ICSTM; Gov., Macaulay Inst., 2001–05. *Recreations:* golf, fly fishing. *Club:* Farmers.

**BUTTON, Jenson Alexander Lyons**, MBE 2010; Formula 1 racing driver, 2000–16; *b* Frome, 19 Jan. 1980; *s* of late John Button and of Simone Lyons; *m* 2014, Jessica Michibata (marr. diss. 2017). *Educ:* Frome Community Coll. Kart racing: winner: British Super Prix, 1989; British Cadet Championship, 1991; British Open Kart series, 1992, 1993; Eur. Super A Championship, 1997; Ayrton Senna Meml Cup, 1997; car racing: winner, British Formula Ford Championship (with Haywood Racing), 1998; Formula 3, with Promatecme team, 1999; Formula One Grand Prix début, 2000; Williams team, 2000; Benetton team, 2001; Renault team, 2002; BAR team, 2003–05; Honda Racing team, 2006–08; Brawn team, 2009 (World Champion); McLaren Honda (formerly Vodafone McLaren Mercedes, later McLaren Mercedes), 2010–16; Grand Prix winner: Hungarian, 2006; Australian, Malaysian, Bahrain, Spanish, Monaco, Turkish, 2009; Australian, Chinese, 2010; Canadian, Hungarian, Japanese, 2011; Australian, Belgian, Brazilian, 2012; with Team Kunimitsu, Super GT Japan Series, 2018 (Championship winner), 2019; competed in 2018 Le Mans 24 Hrs Race (for SMP Racing). Mem., Sky Sports F1 commentary team, 2019. McLaren Autosport Young Driver Award, 1998. *Publications:* My Championship Year, 2009; Life to the Limit, 2017. *Address:* Jenson Button Ltd, PO Box 454, Bicester, Oxon OX26 9LB.

**BUTTRESS, Donald Reeve**, LVO 1997; OBE 2008; FSA; architect; Partner, Buttress Fuller Alsop Williams, Manchester, 1974–2007; Surveyor of the Fabric of Westminster Abbey, 1988–99, now Surveyor Emeritus; *b* 27 April 1932; *s* of Edward Crossley Buttress and Evelyn Edna Reeve-Whaley; *m* 1956, Elsa Mary Bardsley; two *s* three *d*. *Educ:* Stockport Sch.; Univ. of Manchester (MA, DipArch). ARIBA. Flying Officer, RAF, 1958–61. Lectr, Manchester Univ., 1964–78; Vis. Prof. and Fulbright Travelling Scholar, Univ. of Florida, 1967–68. Architect to: Bangor and Sheffield Cathedrals, 1978–88; Leeds (RC) Cathedral, 1983–95; Llandaff Cathedral, 1986–97; Surveyor to the Fabric, Chichester Cathedral, 1984–2007. Principal works: Stockport SS Community Centre, 1973; extn, St Matthew, Hayfield, 1978; St George's Chapel, Sheffield Cathedral, 1981; rebldg, St Matthew, Westminster, 1982; repair of spire, All Souls, Halifax, 1984; repair of nave, choir, North and South transepts and West front, Chichester Cath., 1985–2003; reconstruction, Tonbridge Sch. Chapel, 1992–95; restoration of West front and Henry VII Chapel, Westminster Abbey, 1989–95; design of national Memorial to King George VI and Queen Elizabeth, the Queen Mother, 2009. Member: Cathedrals and Churches Adv. Cttee (formerly Churches Sub-Cttee, English Heritage), 1988–94; Council for the Care of Churches, 1976–86, 1991–96; Council, Royal Archaeological Inst., 1991–94; Chester DAC, 1970–88; St Albans DAC, 1998–2010. President: Ecclesiol Soc., 1995–2010, now Pres. Emeritus (Vice Pres., 1992–95); Surveyors' Club, 1999–04; ASCHB, 2006–07; Baconian Club, 2006–07. Gov., Sutton's Hosp. in Charterhouse, 2001–12. Master, Art Workers' Guild, 2000 (Brother, 1989). Mem., Editl Bd, Church Building magazine, 1982–. DLitt Lambeth, 2001. *Publications:* Manchester Buildings, 1967; Gawthorpe Hall (NT guide), 1971; articles in learned jls. *Recreations:* ecclesiology, 18th Century furniture, stained glass, heraldry. *Address:* The Old Vicarage, Church Lane, Bishop's Castle, Shropshire SY9 5AF. *T:* (01588) 630509. *Club:* Royal Air Force.

BUXTON; *see* Noel-Buxton, family name of Baron Noel-Buxton.

BUXTON, Andrew Robert Fowell, CMG 2003; *b* 5 April 1939; *m* 1965, Jane Margery Grant (*d* 2015); two *d*. *Educ:* Winchester Coll.; Pembroke Coll., Oxford. Joined Barclays Bank, 1963; Man. Dir., 1988–92; Chief Exec., 1992–93; Chm., 1993–99. Director: Capitaland Ltd, Singapore, 2003–07; Development Bank of Singapore, 2006–11. Mem. Court, Bank of England, 1997–2001. Pres., British Bankers' Assoc., 1997–2002. *Club:* Royal Automobile.

BUXTON, Sir Crispin Charles Gerard, 8th Bt *cr* 1840, of Belfield, Dorset; *b* 29 March 1958; *s* of Gerard St John Roden Buxton and Judith Averil Buxton (*née* Campbell); *S* uncle 2014; *m* 2006, Diana Nafula; one *s* [Milo Akizacare Crispin Buxton, *b* 28 Dec. 2005].

BUXTON, David Colleton; Chief Executive, Action on Disability, since 2017; *b* Chiswick, 10 Sept. 1964; *s* of Robert Buxton and Helen Buxton; *m* 2000, Bronwynne Pringle; one *s*. *Educ:* Thames Valley Univ. (HNC Engrg Services); South Bank Univ. (HNC Building Studies; DipM; CertM); Open Univ. (MBA). Asst Dir and Dir of Fundraising and Mktg, Breakthrough Deaf-Hearing Integration, 1996–2001; Sen. Strategic Commng Manager for Disabilities and HIV/AIDS, Hammersmith and Fulham LBC, 2001–06; Regl Ops Manager, Adult Services, Scope, 2006–11; CEO, 2011–14, Dir of Campaigns and Comms, 2015–17, British Deaf Assoc. Member (Lib Dem): Southwark LBC, 1990–94; Epsom and Ewell BC, 2007–11. Contested (Lib Dem): Lewisham E, 1997, 2001; Lewisham and Greenwich, London Assembly, GLA, 2000. Co-Founder, Liberal Democrats Disability Assoc., 1991–; Co-op. Trustee, Greater London Action on Disability, 1994–96; Trustee: UK Council on Deafness, 1997–2000; Christian Deaf Link UK, 2002–08 (Chm., 2005–08); Hon. Treas., BDA, 2003–08. Chm., Pumphouse Educnl and Mus. Trust, Rotherhithe, 1991–96. Vice Chm., Peckham Park Primary Sch., 1993–96. Editor, Go!, Sign mag., 1989–2010. *Recreations:* specialist stamp collection (Tristan Da Cunha), politics and law reading, golf, historical visits. *Address:* 4 Norris Close, Epsom, Surrey KT19 8BF. *E:* buxtondc@aol.com.

BUXTON, Rt Hon. Sir Richard (Joseph), Kt 1994; PC 1997; a Lord Justice of Appeal, 1997–2008; *b* 13 July 1938; *o s* of late Bernard Buxton, DSO, chartered mechanical engineer, and Sybil (*née* Hurley), formerly of Burton-upon-Trent; *m* 1987, Mary Tyerman, JP, *y d* of late Donald Tyerman, CBE and Margaret Tyerman. *Educ:* Brighton Coll. (Schol.); Exeter Coll., Oxford (Schol.; First Cl. Final Hon. Sch. of Jurisprudence 1961, First Cl. BCL 1962; Vinerian Schol. 1962; MA; Hon. Fellow, 1998). FCIArb 1992. Lectr, Christ Church, 1962–63; Lectr 1963–64, Fellow and Tutor 1964–73, Sub-Rector 1966–71, Exeter Coll., Oxford. Called to the Bar, Inner Temple, 1969; Bencher, 1992; in practice, 1972–88; QC 1983; a Recorder, 1987–93; a Law Comr, 1989–93; a Judge of the High Court, QBD, 1994–97; a Judge, Restrictive Practices Court, 1994–97. Second Lieut RAOC, 1957–58. Councillor, Oxford CC, 1966–69. Chm. of Governors, Penton I and JM Sch., London N1, 1986–91. Hon. LLD Nottingham, 2000. Médaille de la Ville de Paris (échelon argent), 1999. *Publications:* Local Government, 1970, 2nd edn 1973; articles in legal periodicals. *Recreation:* baseball. *Address:* c/o Royal Courts of Justice, Strand, WC2A 2LL.

BUXTON, Richard Moberly; Founding Partner, Richard Buxton Environmental Planning & Public Law, solicitors, since 1990; *b* Butleigh, Somerset, 30 June 1953; *s* of Robert James Buxton and Lilla Mary Alyson Buxton (*née* Pumphrey); *m* 1979, Julia Grace Elcock; two *s* one *d*. *Educ:* Harrow Sch.; Trinity Coll., Cambridge (BA 1974); Sch. of Forestry, Yale Univ. (MES 1986). Trained as solicitor, Farrer & Co., 1976–78; admitted solicitor, 1978; Sinclair Roche & Temperley, solicitors, 1978–81; Japan Line, Tokyo, 1981–84; DPA Gp, consultants, Halifax, NS, 1986–89; Mills & Reeve, solicitors, Cambridge, 1989–90. *Recreations:* sea-kayaking, hill walking, exercising labrador. *Address:* 40 Clarendon Street, Cambridge CB1 1JX. *T:* (01223) 328933. *E:* richard@richardbuxton.co.uk.

BUXTON, Richard William; Director, Europa-Institut, Reutlingen, 2013–18; *b* 11 Oct. 1956; *s* of Rev. William, (Paddy), and Pamela Buxton; *m* 1993, Christiane Regine Topf; two *s*. *Educ:* Downing Coll., Cambridge (MA); Univ. of Westminster (MBA); Open Univ. (MSc Psychology). Coopers & Lybrand, 1989–91; Asst Dir (Housing and Social Services), Bexley BC, 1991–93; Dir, Local Govt Consultancy, Capita plc, 1993–95; Dir of Housing, City of Westminster, 1995–98; Dir of Ops, Legal Services Commn, 1998–2001; Chief Exec., Nat. Lottery Charities Bd, then Community Fund, 2001–04; Hd, Econ. Develt, City of Reutlingen, Germany, 2005–06; Business Redesign Dir, Essex CC, 2006–08; Prog. Dir, leading merger of Age Concern and Help the Aged, 2008–09; Interim Chief Exec., 4ps, then Local Partnerships, 2009; Interim Ops Dir, Refugee Council, 2010–11; Partnership Prog. Manager, Darlington, Hartlepool and Redcar, and Cleveland Bor. Councils, 2012. Mem., ESRC Res. Grants Bd, 2002. Associate Lectr, Open Univ., 2005–. Trustee, Langley House Trust, 1996–2003. FRSA 2007. *Recreations:* running, learning Italian. *Address:* Via Nino Bixio 8, 97016 Pozzallo, Italy.

BUZAN, Prof. Barry, PhD; FBA 1998; Montague Burton Professor of International Relations, London School of Economics, 2008–11, now Professor Emeritus; *b* 28 April 1946; *s* of Gordon Frank Buzan and Jean May Buzan (*née* Burn); *m* 1973, Deborah Skinner. *Educ:* Univ. of British Columbia (BA Hons 1968); London Sch. of Econs (PhD 1973). Res. Fellow, Inst. of Internat. Relns, Univ. of BC, 1973–75; University of Warwick: Lectr, 1976–83, Sen. Lectr, 1983–88, Reader, 1988–90, Dept of Internat. Studies; Prof., Dept of Politics and Internat. Studies, 1990–95; Res. Prof. of Internat. Studies, Univ. of Westminster, 1995–2002; Prof. of Internat. Relns, LSE, 2002–08. Vis. Prof., Internat. Univ. of Japan, 1993; Olof Palme Vis. Prof., Sweden, 1997–98; Hon. Prof., Univ. of Copenhagen, 2002–. Dir, project on European security, Copenhagen Peace Res. Inst., 1988–2002. Chm., British Internat. Studies Assoc., 1988–90; Internat. Vice-Pres., Internat. Studies Assoc., 1993–94. Ed., European Jl of Internat. Relns, 2004–07 (Member: Internat. Adv. Bd, 1994–99; Editl Cttee, 2008–). AcSS 2001. Francis Deak Prize, Amer. Jl of Internat. Law, 1982; British Internat. Studies Assoc. Dist. Contribn Prize, 2016. *Publications:* Seabed Politics, 1976; (ed with R. J. Barry Jones) Change and the Study of International Relations: the evaded dimension, 1981; People, States and Fear: the national security problem in international relations, 1983, 2nd edn as An Agenda for International Security Studies in the Post-Cold War Era, 1991, 2007; (jtly) South Asian Insecurity and the Great Powers, 1986; An Introduction to Strategic Studies: military technology and international relations, 1987; (ed) The International Politics of Deterrence, 1987; (jtly) The European Security Order Recast: scenarios for the post-cold war era, 1990; (jtly) The Logic of Anarchy: neorealism to structural realism, 1993; (jtly) Identity, Migration and the New Security Agenda in Europe, 1993; (with T. Buzan) The Mind Map Book, 1993; (jtly) Security: a new framework for analysis, 1998; (with G. Segal) Anticipating the Future: twenty millennia of human progress, 1998; (with E. Herring) The Arms Dynamic in World Politics, 1998; (with R. Little) International Systems in World History: remaking the study of international relations, 2000; (with Ole Wæver) Regions and Powers, 2003; From International to World Society?, 2004; The United States and the Great Powers: world politics in the twenty-first century, 2004; (with L. Hansen) The Evolution of International Security Studies, 2009; (ed) International Society and the Middle East, 2009; (ed) Non-Western International Relations Theory: perspectives on and beyond Asia, 2010; An Introduction to the English School of International Relations, 2014; (ed) Contesting International Society in East Asia, 2014; (with G. Lawson) The Global Transformation: history, modernity and the making of international relations, 2015 (Francesco Guicciardini Prize for Best Book in Histl Internat. Relns, Internat. Studies Assoc., 2017); (with L. Schouenborg) Global International Society: a new framework for analysis, 2018; (with A. Acharya) The Making of Global International Relations: origins and evolution of IR at its centenary, 2019. *Recreations:* chess, travel, gardening. *Address:* Garden Flat, 17 Lambolle Road, NW3 4HS.

BUZEK, Jerzy Karol; Member (European People's Party Group), European Parliament, since 2004 (President, 2009–12); *b* 3 July 1940; *s* of Paweł Buzek and Bronisława Szczuka; *m* 1974, Ludgarda; one *d*. *Educ:* Silesian Poly.; Dr Tech. Scis, Polish Acad. of Scis. Chemical Engineering Institute, Polish Academy of Sciences: scientific res.; Dir for Scientific Affairs, 1963–97; Lecturer: Silesian Technical Univ., 1975–80; Technical Univ., Opole, 1993–97; Researcher and Pro-Rector, 2002, Vice Rector, 2002–04, Polonia Univ., Częstochowa. Prime Minister of Poland, 1997–2001. Chm., Cttee of European Integration, 1998; Vice Pres., European Energy Forum, 2004–. Led High Level Reflection Gp of Energy Community, 2013–14; EP Rapporteur, EU Internal Energy Market, Eur. Strategic Energy Tech. Plan and 7th EU Framework Prog. for Res.; Chm., Cttee on Industry, Res. and Energy, EP, 2014–. Mem., Solidarity, 1980–97: Chm., 1st, 4th, 5th and 6th Nat. Congress; Chm., Econ. Sub-Cttee, Election Cttee. Dr *hc:* Seoul, 1999; Dortmund, 2000; Isparta 2006; numerous Polish univs. Golden Cross of Commitment (Poland), 1989; Order of White Eagle (Poland), 2012. *Publications:* books, patents, numerous sci. articles, papers and speeches. *Recreations:* poetry, theatre, horse riding, tennis, sailing, canoeing. *Address:* European Parliament, Bâtiment Paul-Henri Spaak, 08B046, 60 rue Wiertz, 1047 Brussels, Belgium. *E:* jerzy.buzek@europarl.europa.eu.

BUZZARD, Sir Anthony (Farquhar), 3rd Bt *cr* 1929; Lecturer in Theology, Atlanta Bible (formerly Oregon Bible) College, since 1982 (part-time, since 2012); *b* 28 June 1935; *s* of Rear-Adm. Sir Anthony Wass Buzzard, 2nd Bt, CB, DSO, OBE, and Margaret Elfreda (*d* 1989), *d* of Sir Arthur Knapp, KCIE, CSI, CBE; *S* father, 1972; *m* 1970, Barbara Jean Arnold, Mendon, Michigan, USA; three *d*. *Educ:* Charterhouse; Christ Church, Oxford (MA 1960); MA Th Bethany Theol Seminary, 1990. ARCM. Peripatetic Music Teacher for Surrey County Council, 1966–68; Lectr in French and Hebrew, Ambassador Coll., Bricket Wood, Herts, 1969–74; teacher of mod. langs, American Sch. in London, 1974–81. Founded Restoration Fellowship, 1981. Hon. PhD Theol. Paul Bible Seminary, LA, 2009. *Publications:* Who is Jesus?: a plea for a return to Jesus as Messiah, 1980; What Happens when we Die?, 1986; The Coming Kingdom of the Messiah: a Solution to the Riddle of the New Testament, 1988; The Doctrine of the Trinity: Christianity's Self-Inflicted Wound, 1994; Our Fathers who Aren't in Heaven: the forgotten Christianity of Jesus the Jew, 1995; The Law, the Sabbath and New Covenant Christianity, 2005; The Amazing Aims and Claims of Jesus: what you didn't learn in Church, 2006; Jesus was Not a Trinitarian: a call for a return to the creed of Jesus, 2007; One God, the Father, One Man Messiah: translation of the New Testament with commentary, 2015; articles on eschatology and Christology in various jls. *Recreations:* oboe, classical music (Founder, Peachtree Chamber Ensemble, 2015). *Heir:* *b* Timothy Macdonnell Buzzard [*b* 28 Jan. 1939; *m* 1970, Jennifer Mary, *d* of late Peter Patching; one *s* one *d*]. *Address:* (home) 175 West Lake Drive, Fayetteville, GA 30214, USA. *T:* (770) 9641571; (office) PO Box 2950, McDonough, GA 30253, USA. *T:* (404) 3620052.

BYAM SHAW, Jane Elizabeth; *see* Scott, J. E.

BYAM SHAW, Justin David Elliott; Chairman and part owner, Independent and Evening Standard, since 2012; Founder and Trustee, The Felix Project, since 2016; *b* Sussex, 2 April 1960; *s* of Nicholas Glencairn Byam Shaw, *qv* and Joan Mary Patricia Elliott; *m* 1981, Jane Elizabeth Scott, *qv*; one *s* (and one *s* decd). *Educ:* Westminster Sch.; Christ Church, Oxford (BA Classics 1982; MA). Graduate trainee, Ogilvy & Mather, 1982–84; British Telecom, 1984–87; Founder and Chm., Legion Gp, 1987–94. *Recreations:* gardening, poetry, cricket, Eton Fives. *T:* 07973 313833. *E:* justin@thefelixproject.org.
*See also* M. J. Byam Shaw.

BYAM SHAW, Matthew James; theatre producer; Co-Founder and Director, Playful Productions, since 2010; *b* Sussex, 8 April 1963; *s* of Nicholas Glencairn Byam Shaw, *qv*; partner, Melanie Thaw, *d* of Sheila Hancock, *qv*; two *s* one *d*. *Educ:* Cumnor House Sch., Danehill; Westminster Sch.; Bristol Univ. (BA Drama); RADA. Actor, 1987–98; producer, 2000–; West End productions include: In Flame, 2000; Humble Boy, 2002; Pretending To Be Me, 2003; Don Carlos, 2005; The Anniversary, 2005; A Voyage Round My Father, 2006; See How They Run, 2006; Frost/Nixon, 2006, transf. NY, 2007; Mary Stuart, 2006, transf. NY, 2009; Boeing-Boeing, 2007, transf. NY, 2008; Whipping It Up, 2007; A Midsummer Night's Dream, Roundhouse, 2007; Spring Awakening; Legally Blonde, 2010; Krapp's Last Tape, 2010; Flare Path, 2011; The King's Speech, 2012; Hay Fever, 2012; The Audience, 2013 and 2015, NY 2015; The Weir, 2014; American Buffalo, 2015; No Man's Land, 2016; Don Juan in Soho, 2017; The Goat, or Who is Sylvia?, 2017; Quiz, 2018; The Moderate Soprano, 2018; Chichester Festival Theatre: Enron, 2009, transf. Royal Court, 2009, Noel Coward, 2010, NY, 2010; Yes, Prime Minister, 2010, transf. Gielgud, 2010; Sweeney Todd, 2011, transf. Adelphi, 2012; South Downs, The Browning Version, 2011, transf. Harold Pinter, 2012; other productions include: Red, NY, 2010; Wolf Hall, Bring up the Bodies, Swan Th., Stratford, 2014, transf. Aldwych, 2014, NY 2015; Hangmen, Royal Court, 2015, transf. Wyndham's, 2015; Shrek The Musical, UK and Ire. tour, 2018; Imperium, Swan Th., Stratford, 2018, transf. Gielgud, 2018; films include: Frost/Nixon, 2009; exec. prod., TV series, The Crown, 2016–. Trustee: Bush Th., 1998–; Crucible Th., 2001–; Mem. Council, RADA, 2013–. *Address:* Playful Productions, 41–44 Great Queen Street, WC2B 5AD. *T:* (020) 7811 4600. *E:* annie@playfuluk.com.

BYAM SHAW, Nicholas Glencairn; Deputy Chairman, Macmillan Ltd, 1998–99 (Chairman, 1990–97); *b* 28 March 1934; *s* of Lieut. Comdr David Byam Shaw, RN, OBE (killed in action, 19 Dec. 1941) and Clarita Pamela Clarke; *m* 1st, 1956, Joan Elliott; two *s* one *d*; 2nd, 1974, Suzanne Filer (*née* Rastello); 3rd, 1987, Constance Wilson (*née* Clarke). *Educ:* Royal Naval Coll., Dartmouth. Commnd RN, 1955 (Lieut). Joined William Collins Sons & Co. Ltd, Glasgow, as salesman, 1956; Sales Manager, 1960; Macmillan and Co., subseq. Macmillan Publishers Ltd: Sales Manager, 1964; Sales Dir, 1965; Dep. Man. Dir, 1967; Man. Dir, 1969–90. Director: St Martins Press, 1980–99 (Dep. Chm., 1997–99); Pan Books, 1983–99 (Chm., 1986–99); Gruppe Georg von Holtzbrinck, Stuttgart, 1996–99. *Recreations:* gardening, travel. *Address:* 9 Kensington Park Gardens, W11 3HB. *T:* (020) 7221 4547.
*See also* J. D. E. Byam Shaw, M. J. Byam Shaw.

BYATT, Antonia; *see* Byatt, H. A.

**BYATT, Dame Antonia (Susan), (Dame Antonia Duffy),** DBE 1999 (CBE 1990); FRSL 1983; writer; *b* 24 Aug. 1936; *d* of His Honour John Frederick Drabble, QC and late Kathleen Marie Bloor; *m* 1st, 1959, Ian Charles Rayner Byatt (*see* Sir I. C. R. Byatt) (marr. diss. 1969); one *d* (one *s* decd); 2nd, 1969, Peter John Duffy; two *d*. *Educ:* Sheffield High Sch.; The Mount Sch., York; Newnham Coll., Cambridge (BA Hons; Hon. Fellow 1999); Bryn Mawr Coll., Pa, USA; Somerville Coll., Oxford (Hon. Fellow). Extra-Mural Lectr, Univ. of London, 1962–71; Lectr in Literature, Central Sch. of Art and Design, 1965–69; Lectr in English, 1972–81, Sen. Lectr, 1981–83, UCL (Hon. Fellow, 2004). Associate of Newnham Coll., Cambridge, 1977–82. Member: Social Effects of Television Adv. Gp, BBC, 1974–77; Bd of Communications and Cultural Studies, CNAA, 1978–84; Bd of Creative and Performing Arts, CNAA, 1985–87; Kingman Cttee on English Language, 1987–88; Management Cttee, Soc. of Authors, 1984–88 (Dep. Chm., 1986; Chm., 1986–88); Bd, British Council, 1993–98 (Mem., Literature Adv. Panel, 1990–98). Mem. Cttee, London Liby, 1989–92. Broadcaster, reviewer; judge of literary prizes (Hawthornden, Booker, David Higham, Betty Trask). Fellow, Sunday Times Oxford Lit. Fest., 2010. FRSL. Hon. Fellow: London Inst., 2000; RA, 2009; Hon. FBA 2017. Hon. DLitt: Bradford, 1987; Durham, 1991; Nottingham, 1992; Liverpool, 1993; Portsmouth, 1994; London, 1995; Sheffield, 2000; Kent, 2004; Oxford, 2007; Winchester, 2007; St Andrews, 2012; Hon. LittD Cambridge, 1999; DUniv York, 1991; Hon. Dr Leiden, 2010. Premio Malaparte, Capri, 1995; Shakespeare Prize, Hamburg, 2002; Erasmus Prize, Netherlands, 2016; Pak Kyongni Prize, South Korea, 2017; Hans Christian Andersen Literature Award, 2018; Charleston-Bede Award, 2018. Chevalier de l'Ordre des Arts et des Lettres (France), 2003. *Publications:* Shadow of the Sun, 1964; Degrees of Freedom, 1965 (reprinted as Degrees of Freedom: the early novels of Iris Murdoch, 1994); The Game, 1967; Wordsworth and Coleridge in their Time, 1970 (reprinted as Unruly Times: Wordsworth and Coleridge in their Time, 1989); Iris Murdoch, 1976; The Virgin in the Garden, 1978; (ed) George Eliot, The Mill on the Floss, 1979; Still Life, 1985 (PEN/ Macmillan Silver Pen of Fiction, 1986); Sugar and Other Stories, 1987; (ed) George Eliot: selected essays, 1989; Possession: a romance, 1990 (Booker Prize, 1990; Irish Times/Aer Lingus Internat. Fiction Prize, 1990; Eurasian section of Best Book in Commonwealth Prize, 1991) (filmed 2002); (ed) Robert Browning's Dramatic Monologues, 1990; Passions of the Mind (essays), 1991; Angels and Insects (novellae), 1992 (filmed, 1996); The Matisse Stories (short stories), 1993; The Djinn in the Nightingale's Eye: five fairy stories, 1994 (Mythopoeic Fantasy Award for Adult Lit., 1998); (jtly) Imagining Characters, 1995; (ed jtly) New Writing 4, 1995; Babel Tower, 1996; (ed jtly) New Writing 6, 1997; (ed) The Oxford Book of English Short Stories, 1998; Elementals: stories of fire and ice (short stories), 1998; The Biographer's Tale, 2000; On Histories and Stories (essays), 2000; Portraits in Fiction, 2001; (jtly) The Bird Hand Book, 2001; A Whistling Woman (novel), 2002; Little Black Book of Stories, 2003; (ed jtly) Memory: an anthology, 2008; The Children's Book (novel), 2009 (Blue Metropolis Internat. Literary Grand Prix, Montreal, 2009; James Tait Black Meml Prize, 2010); The Shadow of the Sun, 2009; Ragnarok: the end of the gods, 2011; Peacock & Vine, 2016. *Address:* c/o Rogers, Coleridge & White Ltd, 20 Powis Mews, W11 1JN.
*See also* H. A. Byatt.

**BYATT, Deirdre Anne, (Lady Byatt);** *see* Kelly, D. A.

**BYATT, (Helen) Antonia;** Director, English PEN, since 2018 (Interim Director, 2017–18); *b* 13 April 1960; *d* of Sir Ian Charles Rayner Byatt, *qv* and Dame Antonia Susan Byatt, *qv*; partner, Sampson Patrick Lincoln Collyns; one *s* two *d*. *Educ:* Mayfield Comprehensive Sch.; Putney High Sch.; Selwyn Coll., Cambridge (BA Hons). Gen. Sec., Fawcett Soc., 1987–88; Literature Officer, Arts Council of England, 1988–93; Hd of Literature, South Bank Centre, 1993–2000; Dir, The Women's Liby, London Metropolitan Univ., 2000–07; Dir, Literature and SE, Arts Council England, 2007–15; Dir, Cheltenham Literature Festival, 2016–17. Mem., Children's Laureate Cttee, 2001. Member of Board: Bishopsgate Inst., 2004; New Buckinghamshire Univ., 2009. Gov., Dog Kennel Hill Primary Sch., 2004–10. Hon. FBA 2017. *Publications:* (ed) The Chatto Book of Love Stories, 1993. *Recreations:* my family, swimming, walking.

**BYATT, Sir Ian (Charles Rayner),** Kt 2000; Chairman, Water Industry Commission for Scotland, 2005–11; Senior Associate, Frontier Economics, since 2001; Director General of Water Services, 1989–2000; *b* 11 March 1932; *s* of Charles Rayner Byatt and Enid Marjorie Annie Byatt (*née* Howat); *m* 1st, 1959, A. S. Byatt (*see* Dame A. S. Byatt) (marr. diss. 1969); one *d* (one *s* decd); 2nd, 1997, Prof. Deirdre Anne Kelly, *qv*; two step *s*. *Educ:* Kirkham Grammar Sch.; Oxford University; Harvard Univ. Commonwealth Fund Fellow, Harvard, 1957–58; Lectr in Economics, Durham Univ., 1958–62; Economic Consultant, HM Treasury, 1962–64; Lectr in Economics, LSE, 1964–67; Sen. Economic Adviser, Dept of Educn and Science, 1967–69; Dir of Econs and Stats, Min. of Housing and Local Govt, 1969–70; Dir Economics, DoE, 1970–72; Under Sec., 1972–78, Dep. Chief Econ. Advr, 1978–89, HM Treasury. Chm., Economic Policy Cttee of the European Communities, 1982–85 (Mem., 1978–89); Member: Central Council of Educn (England), 1965–66; Economics Cttee, CNAA, 1968–70; Urban Motorways Cttee, 1970; Cttee on Water Services: Econ. and Financial Objectives, 1970–73; ESRC, 1983–89; Public Services Productivity Panel, HM Treasury, 2000–02; Chief Sec.'s Adv. Panel on Better Public Services, 2002–06; Adv. Panel, Water Industry Comr for Scotland, 2002–04; Panel of Experts on Water Reforms in NI, 2003–06. Chm., Taskforce to Review Local Govt Procurement in England, 2000–01. Chm., Adv. Cttee to HM Treasury on Accounting for Econ. Costs and Changing Prices, 1986; Member: Bd, Public Finance Foundn, 1984–89; Bd of Mgt, Internat. Inst. of Public Finance, 1987–90, 2000–06; Council of Mgt, NIESR, 1996–2002; Council, Regulatory Policy Inst., 2001–07; non-exec. Mem., Public Interest Cttee, RSM (formerly Baker Tilly) UK Audit LLP, 2014–. Member: Council, REconS, 1983–92 (Mem. Exec. Cttee, 1987–89); Governing Body, Birkbeck Coll., 1997–2005 (Chm., F and GP Cttee, 2001–05; Fellow, 2005); Bd of Advisors, St Edmund Hall, 1998–2003; Internat. Adv. Cttee, Public Utilities Res. Centre, Univ. of Florida, 2001–; Bd, Acad. of Youth, 2001–05; Mem., Council, 2003–, Chm., Finance Cttee, Chapter, 2012–14, Birmingham Cathedral; Chm. Trustees, David Hume Inst., 2008–11. Hon. Prof., Birmingham Univ., 2003–. President: Econs and Business Educn Assoc., 1998–2001; Human City Inst., 1999–2002; Vice-Pres., Strategic Planning Soc., 1993–; Co-Sec.-Gen., Foundn for Internat. Studies in Social Security, 2000–02. Treas., 1988–2002, Patron, 2006–, Holy Cross Centre Trust. Chm., Friends of Birmingham Cathedral, 1999–2015. FCIWEM 1995; FCIPS 2005. CCMI (CIMgt 1993). Hon. Fellow, St Edmund Hall, 2007. DUniv: Brunel, 1994; Central England, 2000; Hon. DSc: Aston, 2005; Birmingham, 2007. *Publications:* The British Electrical Industry 1875–1914, 1979; Delivering Better Services for Citizens, 2001; (with Sir Michael Lyons) Role of External Review in Improving Performance, 2001; articles on economics in books and learned jls; official reports. *Recreations:* painting, family life. *Address:* Frontier Economics, 71 High Holborn, WC1V 6DA. *T:* (020) 7031 7000; 34 Frederick Road, Birmingham B15 1JN. *T:* (0121) 689 7946; 17 Thanet Street, WC1H 9QL. *T:* (020) 7388 3888. *E:* ianbyatt@blueyonder.co.uk. *Club:* Oxford and Cambridge.
*See also* H. A. Byatt.

**BYATT, Ronald Archer Campbell, (Robin),** CMG 1980; HM Diplomatic Service, retired; High Commissioner in New Zealand and concurrently to Western Samoa, and Governor (non-resident), Pitcairn Islands, 1987–90; *b* 14 Nov. 1930; *s* of late Sir Horace Byatt, GCMG and late Olga Margaret Campbell, MBE; *m* 1954, Ann Brereton Sharpe, *d* of C. B. Sharpe; one *s* one *d*. *Educ:* Gordonstoun; New Coll., Oxford; King's Coll., Cambridge. Served in RNVR, 1949–50. Colonial Admin. Service, Nyasaland, 1955–58; joined HM Foreign (now Diplomatic) Service, 1959; FO, 1959; Havana, 1961; FO, 1963; UK Mission to UN, NY, 1966; Kampala, 1970; Head of Rhodesia Dept, FCO, 1972–75; Vis. Fellow, Glasgow Univ., 1975–76; Counsellor and Head of Chancery, UK Mission to UN, NY, 1977–79; Asst Under Sec. of State, FCO, 1979–80; High Comr in Zimbabwe, 1980–83; Mem., Directing Staff, RCDS, 1983–84; Ambassador to Morocco, 1985–87. CSSB Panel Chm., 1992–95. Founder Mem., UK Antarctic Heritage Trust, 1992–2001; Mem., HGTAC, 1993–98 (Chm., Envmt Sub-Cttee, 1993–98). Trustee, Beit Trust, 1987–2011. Alaouite Order, 1st cl. (Morocco), 1987. *Recreations:* sailing, gardening, watching and painting birds. *Address:* Drim-na-Vullin, Lochgilphead, Argyll PA31 8LE. *Club:* Oxford and Cambridge.

**BYCROFT, Prof. Barrie (Walsham),** PhD; CChem, FRSC; Professor of Pharmaceutical Chemistry, University of Nottingham, 1979–2003, Emeritus Professor, 2004 (Head, Department of Pharmaceutical Sciences and School of Pharmacy, 1985–89 and 1995–2000); *b* 26 Jan. 1939; *s* of Henry Thomas Bycroft and Cissie Bycroft; *m* 1962, Jean Skinner (separated); one *s* one *d*. *Educ:* Univ. of Nottingham (BSc Chem.; PhD 1963). CChem 1982; FRSC 1982. NATO Fellow, Univ. of Zurich, 1963–65; University of Nottingham: Lectr, then Reader, Dept of Chemistry, 1965–79; Pro-Vice Chancellor (Research), 1990–94; Dean, Grad. Sch., 1994–96. Vis. Prof., Med. Sch., Federal Univ., Rio de Janeiro, 1973. Mem., Food Adv. Cttee, MAFF, 1988–92. Non-exec. Mem., Nottingham HA, 1990–94. Biotechnology and Biological Sciences Research Council: Mem., Sci. and Engrg Bd, 1993–96; Chm., Postgrad. Trng Award Panel, 1994–2000. Vice-Chm., UK Council for Grad. Educn, 1993–96. Hon. MRPharmS 1990. *Publications:* numerous contribs to learned jls. *Recreations:* tennis, golf, good food and wine, travel. *Address:* 14 The Cloisters, Beeston, Nottingham NG9 2FR. *T:* (0115) 925 9415.

**BYE, Christopher Harwood;** freelance writer and music critic; Editor, Yorkshire Evening Post, 1987–98; Director, Yorkshire Post Newspapers Ltd, 1987–98; *b* 6 Feb. 1952; *s* of John Harwood Bye and Joan Alice (*née* Cushing). *Educ:* Tadcaster Grammar Sch.; Univ. of Leeds (Cert. Creative Writing 2008). News Editor, Yorkshire Post, 1980–82; Editor, Yorkshire Post Colour Magazine, 1981–83; Dep. Editor, Yorkshire Post, 1982–87. Contributor: British Music Soc.; The Dalesman mag. Member: Soc. of Editors; British Music Soc. British Press award for investigative journalism, 1986. *Recreations:* classical music, antiques, wine, food, travel, walking, sport.

**BYE, Ruby;** *see* Wax, R.

**BYERS, His Honour the Hon. Charles William;** a Circuit Judge, 1999–2014; *b* 24 March 1949; *o s* of Baron Byers, PC, OBE and Joan Elizabeth Byers (*née* Oliver); *m* 1972, Suzan Mary Stone (marr. diss. 1995); two *s*; *m* 2002, Mary Louise Elizabeth Ilett. *Educ:* Westminster Sch.; Christ Church, Oxford. Called to the Bar, Gray's Inn, 1973; Recorder, 1993–99; Resident Judge, Woolwich Crown Court, 2007–12. Dep. Chm., Gray's Inn Continuing Education Cttee, 1997–98; Mem., Adv. Panel, Coll. of Law, 1996. Gov., Hurstpierpoint Coll., 1993–2003. *Recreations:* gardening, agriculture, sport, aquatics, acquiring practical skills. *Club:* National Liberal.

**BYERS, Philippa Tansy Kemp;** *see* Saunders, P. T. K.

**BYERS, Rt Hon. Stephen (John);** PC 1998; *b* Wolverhampton, 13 April 1953; *s* of late Robert Byers. *Educ:* Chester City Grammar Sch.; Chester Coll. of Further Educn; Liverpool Polytechnic (LLB). Sen. Lectr in Law, Newcastle Polytechnic, 1977–92. Mem. (Lab) North Tyneside MBC, 1980–92 (Dep. Leader, 1985–92; Chm. Educn Cttee, 1982–85). Contested (Lab) Hexham, 1983. MP (Lab) Wallsend, 1992–97, North Tyneside, 1997–2010. An Opposition Whip, 1994–95; frontbench spokesman on educn and employment, 1995–97; Minister of State, DfEE, 1997–98; Chief Sec. to HM Treasury, 1998; Sec. of State for Trade and Industry, 1998–2001; Sec. of State for Transport, Local Govt and the Regions, 2001–02. Mem., Select Cttee on Home Affairs, 1994. Chm., PLP Home Affairs Cttee, 1992–94. Leader, Council of Local Educn Authorities, 1990–92; Chairman: Nat. Employers' Orgn for Teachers, 1990–92; Educn Cttee, AMA, 1990–92; Mem., BTEC, 1985–89. FRSA 1991.

**BYFORD,** family name of **Baroness Byford**.

**BYFORD, Baroness** *cr* 1996 (Life Peer), of Rothley in the county of Leicestershire; **Hazel Byford,** DBE 1994; DL; *b* 14 Jan. 1941; *d* of Sir Cyril Osborne, MP and Lady Osborne; *m* 1962, C. Barrie Byford, CBE (*d* 2013); one *d* (one *s* decd). *Educ:* St Leonard's Sch., St Andrews; Moulton Agricl Coll., Northampton. WRVS Leics, 1961–93, County Organiser, 1972–76. House of Lords: an Opposition Whip, 1997–98; Opposition spokesman: on agriculture and rural affairs, 1998–2001; on envmt, 1998–2003; on food, farming and rural affairs, 2001–07. Chm., Nat. Cttee, Conservative Women, 1990–93; Vice Pres., 1993–96, Pres., 1996–97, Nat. Union of Cons. and Unionist Assocs. Member: Transport Users' Consultative Cttee, 1989–94; Rail Users' Consultative Cttee, 1994–95. President: Nat. Farm Attractions Network, 2002–09; Concordia, 2004–09; Guild of Agricl Journalists, 2004–07; Young Leics (formerly Leics Clubs for Young People), 2005–; LEAF, 2006–16; Royal Assoc. of British Dairy Farmers, 2007–10; Royal Smithfield Club, 2010; RASE, 2016–17 (Associate Mem., 2003); Suffolk Agricl Assoc., 2018–19. Patron: Village Retail Services Assoc., 1998–2004; Inst. of Agricl Secs and Admnrs, 2000; Rural Stress Inf. Network, 2001–06; Women's Food and Farming Union, 2007–15. Mem., Ct, Univ. of Leicester, 2002–08; Pres., St Leonard's Sch., St Andrews, 2003–14. Hon. Canon, Leicester Cathedral, 2010–. DL Leics, 2010. Master, Farmers' Co., 2013–14. *Recreations:* golf, bridge, reading. *Club:* Farmers.

**BYFORD, Mark Julian;** author; Deputy Director-General, BBC, and Head of BBC Journalism, 2004–11; *b* 13 June 1958; *s* of Sir Lawrence Byford, CBE, QPM; *m* 1980, Hilary Bleiker; two *s* three *d*. *Educ:* Lincoln Sch.; Univ. of Leeds (LLB 1979). BBC Television: Look North, Leeds, 1979–82; producer, South Today and Inquiry, Southampton, 1982–87; editor, Points West, Bristol, 1987–88; Home Editor, BBC News and Current Affairs, 1988–89; Head of Centre, Leeds, 1989–90; Asst Controller, 1991, Controller, 1991–94, Dep. Man. Dir, 1995–96, Dir, 1996–98, BBC Regl Broadcasting; Director: BBC World Service, 1998–2001; BBC World Service and Global News, 2002–04. Director: BARB, 1993–96; Radio Joint Audience Research Ltd, 1993–96. Trustee: BBC Children in Need Appeal, 1993–96; RNLI, 2011–; Winchester Th. Royal, 2018–; Winchester Hospice Fundraising Charity, 2018–. Gov., Univ. of Winchester, 2014–. Fellow, Radio Acad., 2000. Lay Canon and Mem., Chapter, Winchester Cath., 2017–. DUniv Winchester, 2006; Hon. LLD Leeds, 2008; Hon. DLitt Lincoln, 2010. *Publications:* A Name On A Wall, 2013; The Annunciation: a pilgrim's quest, 2018. *Recreations:* family, rock music, football, cricket, travel, the seaside, cathedrals, fell-walking, swimming. *Address:* Bolberry House, 1 Clifton Hill, Winchester, Hants SO22 5BL.

**BYLES, Daniel Alan**, FRGS; Vice President, Corporate Development, Living PlanIT, since 2015; *b* Hastings, 24 June 1974; *s* of Alan Byles and Janice Byles (now Meek); *m* 2007, Prashanthi Reddy. *Educ:* Warwick Sch.; Univ. of Leeds (BA Jt Hons Econs and Mgt Studies 1996); Nottingham Trent Univ. (MA Creative Writing 2007). Served Army, 1996–2005; Royal Army Medical Corps: Dressing Station Comdr, 19 Airmobile Field Ambulance, 1997–99; Regtl Signals Officer, 24 Armd Field Ambulance, 2000; Adjt, 2000–01, Ops Officer, 2002, 3 Close Support Medical Regt; SO2 Medical Manning, Defence Med. Service Dept, MoD, 2002–04; SO2 Med. Ops and Plans, HQ Multinat. Task Force (N), Banja Luka, Bosnia, 2004–05. MP (C) N Warwickshire, 2010–15. Member, Select Committee: on Energy and Climate Change, 2010–15; on Sci. and Technol., 2014–15; Chairman: All-Party Envmt Gp, 2012–15; All-Party Parly Gp for Unconventional Oil and Gas, 2013–15; All-Party Parly Gp for Smart Cities, 2014–15. Chm., SmarterUK, 2015–. *Recreations:* writing, reading, sub-aqua, expeditions, sailing.

**BYLES, Timothy John**, CBE 2006; Chairman: Cornerstone Ltd, since 2018 (Chief Executive, 2011–18); BDTP Ltd, since 2018; *b* 7 Dec. 1958; *s* of Charles Humphrey Gilbert Byles and Pamela Beatrice Byles; *m* 1985, Shirley Elizabeth Rowland; three *s. Educ:* Univ. of Kent (BA Hons); Mid Kent Coll. of Further Educn (DMS London). British Gas, 1980–84: mgt trainee; Marketing Dept; Corporate Planning; English Tourist Board, 1984–88: Manager, Mgt Services, 1984–85; Asst Dir of Develt, 1985–88; Dir of Economic Develt, Kent CC, 1988–96; Chief Executive: Norfolk CC, 1996–2006; Partnerships for Schools, 2006–11. *Recreations:* music, swimming, church.

**BYNG**, family name of **Earl of Strafford**, and of **Viscount Torrington**.

**BYNG, Hon. James Edmund**; Publisher, since 1994, and Managing Director, since 2006, Canongate Books Ltd; *b* 27 June 1969; *s* of 8th Earl of Strafford; *m* 1st, 1994, Whitney Osborn McVeigh (marr. diss. 2004); one *s* one *d*; 2nd, 2005, Elizabeth Sheinkman; one *s* one *d. Educ:* Winchester Coll.; Edinburgh Univ. (BA). FRSA. *Recreations:* cooking, deejaying, reading, tennis. *Address:* Canongate Books Ltd, 14 High Street, Edinburgh EH1 1TE. *T:* (0131) 524 9345, *Fax:* (0131) 557 5211. *E:* jamie@canongate.co.uk. *Clubs:* Black's, Groucho, Union.
See also Earl of Strafford.

**BYNUM, Prof. William Frederick**, MD; PhD; FRCP, FRCPE; Professor of History of Medicine, University College London, 1992–2003, now Professor Emeritus; *b* 20 May 1943; *s* of Raymond Tapley Bynum and Mary Catherine Adamson Bynum; *m* 1st, 1966, Annetta Boyett (marr. diss.); one *s*; 2nd, 2000, Dr Helen Joy Power. *Educ:* Swarthmore Coll. (BA 1964); Yale Univ. (MD 1969); King's Coll., Cambridge (PhD 1974). FRCP 1996; FRCPE 2000. Lectr, 1973–85, Reader, 1985–92, UCL; Hd, Jt Wellcome Inst./UCL Unit for Hist. of Medicine, 1973–96. Visiting Professor: Univ. of Minnesota, 1975; Union Coll., 1977; Johns Hopkins Univ., 1990, 1996. Co-Ed., Medical Hist., 1980–2002. *Publications:* Dictionary of the History of Science, 1981 (trans. Italian, Spanish and Chinese); Science and the Practice of Medicine in the Nineteenth Century, 1994 (trans. Chinese); Companion Encyclopedia of the History of Medicine, 2 vols, 1993; The Beast in the Mosquito: the correspondence of Ronald Ross and Patrick Manson, 1998; (ed with Roy Porter) Oxford Dictionary of Scientific Quotations, 2005; (ed with Helen Bynum) Dictionary of Medical Biography, 5 vols, 2007; The History of Medicine: a very short introduction, 2008 (trans. 4 langs); (ed) Charles Darwin, On the Origin of Species, 2009; (ed with Linda Kalof) A Cultural History of the Human Body, 6 vols, 2010; (ed with Helen Bynum) Great Discoveries in Medicine, 2011 (trans. 4 langs); A Little History of Science (trans. 17 langs), 2012; (with Helen Bynum) Remarkable Plants that Shape our World (trans. 3 langs), 2014; (with Helen Bynum) Botanical Sketchbooks, 2017. *Recreations:* theatre, gardening, duck-keeping. *Address:* The Courtyard, London Road, Shadingfield, Suffolk NR34 8DF. *T:* (01502) 575410. *Club:* MCC.

**BYRAM-WIGFIELD, Timothy**, FRCO; Director of Music, All Saints, Margaret Street, London, 2013–18; *b* 15 Sept. 1963; *s* of David and Morwen Byram-Wigfield. *Educ:* Oundle Sch. (Music Schol.); Royal Coll. of Music; Christ Church, Oxford (Organ Schol.; BA Hons). FRCO 1986. Chorister, King's Coll., Cambridge, 1972–76; Sub-organist, Winchester Cathedral, 1985–91; Master of the Music, St Mary's Episcopal Cathedral, Edinburgh, 1991–99; Director of Music: Jesus Coll., Cambridge, 1999–2003; St George's Chapel, Windsor, 2004–13. Has made numerous recordings. *Recreations:* cooking, gardening, keep fit (swimming, gym, running), reading.

**BYRNE, Colin**; Chief Executive Officer, Weber Shandwick, UK and Europe, the Middle East and Africa (formerly UK and Europe), 2008–18; *b* 25 Feb. 1957; *s* of late Anthony Byrne and of Catherine Byrne; *m*; four *s* one *d. Educ:* Kingston Polytech. (BA Hons English). Press Officer, Automobile Assoc., 1981–83; Press and Campaigns Office, NUS, 1983–86; Press Officer, 1986–88, Chief Press Officer, 1988–92, Labour Party; Communications Dir, Prince of Wales Business Leaders Forum, 1992–95; PR Manager, NFU, 1995; Associate Public Affairs Dir, 1995–96, Dir, 1996–97, Shandwick Consultants; Man. Dir, Public Affairs, Shandwick, 1997–2000; Jt CEO, 2001–03, CEO, 2003–08, Weber Shandwick UK and Ireland. *Recreations:* art, music, cooking, literature.

**BYRNE, Colin David**; Assistant Commissioner, Boundary Commission for England, 2011–13 and 2016–18; *b* 11 June 1957; *s* of Liam and Theresa Byrne; *m* 1986, Dr Mary Morrison; four *d. Educ:* Univ. of Edinburgh (BSc Hons Envmtl Chem.); Univ. of Pennsylvania. SO, MAFF, 1979–85; Department of the Environment, 1985–91: SSO, 1985–87; Nat. Expert, EC, 1988–91; Grade 6, DETR, 1991–97; Hd of Div., HSE, 1997–2000; Dir for Hampshire and IoW, Govt Office for South East, 2000–06; Dir, Town and Country Planning, 2006–07, Home Information Pack Implementation, 2007, DCLG; Regl Dir, Govt Office for SE, 2008–11. Dir, Retirement Lease Housing Assoc., 2014–. Gov., Guildford Coll. Gp, 2012–. Trustee, Guildford CAB, 2013–. *Recreations:* walking, gardening, opera.

**BYRNE, David**; Senior Counsel, 1985; *b* 26 April 1947; *m* 1972, Geraldine Fortune; two *s* one *d. Educ:* University Coll. Dublin (BA; Hon. LLD). FCIArb 1998. Called to the Bar, King's Inns, Dublin, 1970; called to Inner Bar, 1985; Attorney General, Ireland, 1997–99; Mem., EC, 1999–2004. Special Envoy, WHO, 2004–05. Chm., Nat. Treasury Mgt Agency Adv. Cttee, 2008–12. Adjunct Prof. of Law, UCD, 2005–06. Chancellor, Dublin City Univ., 2006–11, now Emeritus. Non-exec. Dir, Kingspan Gp, 2005–14; Sen. Ind. Dir and Dep. Chm., DCC plc, 2009–16. Chm., Nat. Concert Hall, Dublin, 2006–11. Chair, Eur. Alliance for Personalised Medicine, Brussels, 2012–. Mem. Council, RCPI, 2013–. Hon. FRCPI 2000; Hon. FRCP. *Address:* (office) Park Lodge Mews, 36A Booterstown Avenue, Blackrock, Co. Dublin, Ireland.

**BYRNE, Dorothy**; Head of News and Current Affairs, Channel 4 Television, since 2004; *d* of Charles and Agnes Byrne; one *d. Educ:* Manchester Univ. (BA Hons Philosophy); Sheffield Univ. (Dip. Business). Producer, World in Action, 1987–94; Ed., The Big Story, 1996–98; Commng Ed., Current Affairs, Channel 4 TV, 1998–2003. Visiting Professor: Sch. of Journalism, Lincoln Univ., 2005–16; De Montfort Univ., 2016–. Hon. LittD Sheffield, 2018. *Recreation:* being angry. *Address:* Channel 4 Television, 124 Horseferry Road, SW1P 2TX. *T:* (020) 7306 8664, *Fax:* (020) 7306 8359. *E:* dbyrne@channel4.co.uk.

**BYRNE, Prof. Edward**, AC 2014 (AO 2006); MD, DSc; FRACP, FRCPE, FRCP, FMedSci; FAAN; FTSE; President and Principal, King's College London, since 2014; *b* 15 Feb. 1952; *s* of Henry Byrne and Marion Byrne (*née* Davis); *m* 1975, Melissa Elisabeth Youl; three *s* one *d. Educ:* Univ. of Tasmania (MB BS 1st Cl. Hons 1974; MD 1982); Univ. of Melbourne (DSc 1995); Univ. of Queensland (MBA 2005). FRACP 1980; FAAN 1997; FRCPE 1998; FRCP 2008; FTSE 2012. Hd of Neurol., St Vincent's Hosp., Melbourne, 1983–2000; University of Melbourne: Prof. of Neurol., 1992–2000; Prof. of Exptl Neurol. and Dir, Centre for Neurosci., 2000–03; Dean, Faculty of Medicine, Nursing and Health Scis, Monash Univ., 2003–07; Exec. Dean, Faculty of Biomed. Scis, Hd, Royal Free and University Coll. Med. Sch., later UCL Med. Sch., and Vice Provost, Health, UCL, 2007–09; Vice-Chancellor and Pres., Monash Univ., 2009–14. FMedSci 2019. Hon. FAHMS, 2017. Hon. MD Adelaide, 2014; Hon. DSc: Warwick, 2014; Western, 2014; Hon. LLD: Monash, 2017; Sydney, 2019. Hon. Citizen, Jiangsu Province, China, 2014. Ed., Internal Medicine Jl, 1999–2005. *Publications:* poetry: Poems from the City: a London interlude, 2010; Transit Lounge, 2013; Soul Poems, 2014; From Two Worlds, 2016; over 200 articles on neuromuscular and metabolic disorders. *Address:* King's College London, Strand, WC2R 2LS. *Clubs:* Athenæum; Melbourne.

**BYRNE, Garrett Thomas; His Honour Judge Byrne**; a Circuit Judge, since 2019; *b* Wicklow, 8 Jan. 1962; *s* of Garrett Byrne and Elizabeth Wall; *m* 2013, Berenice Jane D'Arcy; one *s* one *d. Educ:* Wimbledon Coll.; Univ. of Bristol (LLB Hons); Univ. of London (LLM Internat. Envmtl Law). Called to the Bar, Gray's Inn, 1986; in private practice as barrister, 1987–2012; a Recorder, 2007–19; Sen. Crown Counsel, DPP's Office, Bermuda, 2012–16; Chief Enforcement Officer, Bermuda Monetary Authy, 2016–19. Chm., Fulham Legal Advice Centre, 2002–12. *Recreations:* photography, piano, theatre, walking, scuba-diving.

**BYRNE, Rev. Canon Dr Georgina Ann**; Residentiary Canon, Worcester Cathedral, since 2009; a Chaplain to the Queen, since 2017; *b* Wolverhampton, 18 March 1972; *d* of Michael Byrne and Sheila Byrne; *m* 2004, Timothy Clarke; one *s. Educ:* Colton Hills Sch., Wolverhampton; Trinity Coll., Oxford (BA Theol. 1992); Corpus Christi Coll., Cambridge (MPhil Ecclesiastical Hist. 1998); King's Coll. London (PhD Hist. 2007). Ordained deacon, 1997, priest, 1998; Asst Curate, All Saints, West Bromwich, 1997–2001; Chaplain to Bishop of Kensington, 2001–04; Team Vicar, Halas Team, 2004–09; Diocesan Dir of Ordinands, Dio. of Worcester, 2009–15. *Publications:* Modern Spiritualism and the Church of England, 1850–1939, 2010; (ed jtly) Life After Tragedy, 2017. *Recreations:* creative writing, distance running, dressmaking, opera. *Address:* 15b College Green, Worcester WR1 2LH. *T:* (01905) 732938. *E:* georginabyrne@worcestercathedral.org.uk.

**BYRNE, John Anthony**; international freelance teacher, lecturer, writer, examiner, 1979–97 and since 2005; Founding Director of Ballet and Dance, Sydney Church of England Co-educational Grammar School (Redlands), 1997–2005; *b* Sydney, Australia, 14 Dec. 1945; *s* of late Reginald Thomas Byrne and Mary Ida (*née* Sinclair). *Educ:* Scully-Borovansky Ballet Sch. and Australian Acad. of Ballet, Sydney; Univ. of Sydney (BA); Polytechnic of Central London (Dip. Arts Admin 1977); Royal Acad. of Dancing (ARAD; Dip. PDTC 1979). Professional dancer with various companies in ballet, opera-ballet and musicals, Australia, NZ, Germany, UK and Hong Kong, 1970–76; teaching classical ballet in Australia, 1979–90; Royal Academy of Dance (formerly Dancing): Internat. Vocational Examr, 1987–2015; Tutor, Sydney and London HQ, 1990–91; Artistic Dir and Chm., Bd of Examrs, London, 1991–93. Estab. Classical Dance Australia (Dir, 2015–). FRAD 2002. *Publications:* (jtly) Body Basics, 1992; Advanced Classical syllabus for boys, 1992; for Classical Dance Australia: Preparatory Syllabus, 2015; Vocational Level 1 Syllabus in Classical Ballet, 2018; choreographic and syllabus contribs to Higher Grades and Vocational Syllabi of Royal Acad. of Dance; contrib. articles on dance criticism, etc to Dance Australia Mag., 1981–90. *Recreations:* walking, reading, gardening, playing the piano (studies in Pianoforte, Australian Music Exams Bd, 2009–).

**BYRNE, Rev. Canon John Victor**; Chaplain to the Queen, 2003–17; *b* 14 Nov. 1947; *s* of Frederick Albert Victor Byrne and Joan Blumer Byrne (*née* Robin); *m* 1970, Gillian Waveney Bannard-Smith; one *s* two *d. Educ:* John Lyon Sch., Harrow; St John's Coll., Nottingham (LTh 1973). FCA 1979. Chartered Accountant, Nevill, Hovey, Gardner & Co., London, 1965–70; ordained deacon, 1973, priest, 1974; Curate: St Mark's, Gillingham, 1973–76; St Luke's, Cranham Park, 1976–80; Vicar: St Mary's, Balderstone, Rochdale, 1980–87; St Jude's, Southsea, 1987–2006; All Saints, Branksome Park, 2006–12; Priest-in-charge, St Peter's, Southsea, 1995–2003. Hon. Canon, Portsmouth Cathedral, 1997–2006, now Canon Emeritus; Rural Dean of Portsmouth, 2001–06. Portsmouth Diocesan Stewardship Advr, 1994–97; Archbishops' Pastoral Advr, 1999–2010. *Recreations:* photography, reading, walking, arts, music. *Address:* 4 St Georges Terrace, Southwick Road, Denmead PO7 6FR.

**BYRNE, Lavinia**; writer; *b* 10 March 1947; *d* of Basil James Byrne and (Edith Marion) Josephe Byrne. *Educ:* St Mary's Convent, Shaftesbury; Queen Mary College, London (BA Modern Langs); Hughes Hall, Cambridge (PGCE). Entered Inst. of Blessed Virgin Mary, 1964, resigned 2000; Tutor, Westcott House, Cambridge, 1997–2003. Associate Sec., CCBI, 1990–95. Co-Editor, The Way, 1985–90; internet columnist, The Tablet, 1999–2006; reporter, The Wells Jl, 2002–04. Hon. DD Birmingham, 1997. *Publications:* Women Before God, 1988; Sharing the Vision, 1989; (ed) The Hidden Tradition, 1990; (ed) The Hidden Journey, 1992; (ed) The Hidden Voice, 1994; Woman at the Altar, 1995; A Time to Receive, 1997; (ed) The Daily Service, 1997; The Dome of Heaven, 1999; The Journey is My Home, 2000; (ed) Pause for Thought, 2002; (ed) More Pause for Thought, 2004; Original Prayer: themes from the Christian tradition, 2008. *Recreations:* computers, cookery, travel. *Address:* Garden Flat, 6 Cleveland Place West, Bath BA1 5DG.

**BYRNE, Rt Hon. Liam (Dominic)**; PC 2008; MP (Lab) Birmingham, Hodge Hill, since July 2004; *b* 2 Oct. 1970; *s* of Dermot and Ruth Byrne; *m* 1998, Sarah; two *s* one *d. Educ:* Manchester Univ. (BA Hons); Harvard Business Sch. (Fulbright Schol.; MBA). Leader, Manchester Univ. Students' Union, 1992–93; Sen. Business Analyst, Strategic Services, Andersen Consulting, 1993–96; Advr on Reinventing Govt, then Dir, Business Liaison, Office of the Leader of the Labour Party, 1996–97; Exec., N. M. Rothschild & Sons Ltd, 1997–99; Co-Founder, EGS Gp Ltd, 2000–04. Associate Fellow, Social Market Foundn, 2001–05. Parly Under-Sec. of State, DoH, 2005–06; Minister of State, Home Office, 2006–08; Minister for the W Midlands, 2007–08; Chancellor of the Duchy of Lancaster and Minister for the Cabinet Office, 2008–09; Chief Sec. to the Treasury, 2009–10; Shadow Chief Sec. to the Treasury, 2010; Shadow Minister for the Cabinet Office, 2010–11; Shadow Sec. of State for Work and Pensions, 2011–13; Shadow Minister for: Univs, Sci. and Skills, 2013–15; Digital Economy, 2017–. *Publications:* Local Government Transformed, 1996; Information Age Government, 1998; Cities of Enterprise: new strategies for full employment, 2002; Britain in 2020, 2003; Reinventing Government Again, 2004; Turning to Face the East; how Britain can prosper in the Asian century, 2013; Dragons: ten entrepreneurs who built Britain, 2016; contribs to Parly Affairs and Progress mag. *Recreation:* spending time with family. *Address:* House of Commons, SW1A 0AA. *T:* (020) 7219 3000.

**BYRNE, His Honour Michael David;** a Circuit Judge, 2002–15; *b* 7 Dec. 1945; *s* of Gerard Robert Byrne and Margaret Doreen Byrne; *m* 1985, Felicity Jane Davies. *Educ:* St Edward's Coll., Liverpool; Liverpool Univ. (BA, LLB). Called to the Bar, Gray's Inn, 1971; in practice on Northern Circuit, 1971–2002; Asst Recorder, 1989–92; Recorder, 1992–2002. Mem., Lancs and Cumbria Courts Bd, 2007–11. Chm., Managers Adv. Cttee, Ashworth Special Hosp., 1989–98 (non-exec. Dir, 1996–97); Vice-Chm., Ashworth SHA 1997–98. Legal Mem., Restricted Patients Panel, Mental Health Review Tribunal, 2006–15. Gov., St Edward's Coll., Liverpool, 1993–2005 (Chm. Govs, 1995–2004). Member: Broughton Soc.; Thomas Soc. FRSA 2006. KHS 2006 (Lieut, 2017); KCHS 2012. *Publications:* A Tour Around the Tuscan Renaissance, 2015. *Recreations:* music, literature, theatre, travel. *Club:* Athenæum (Liverpool).

**BYRNE, Richard John Thomas;** Regional Employment Judge, South East, since 2015 (East Anglia, 2012–15); *b* Dorking, Surrey, 19 Jan. 1955; *s* of Thomas John and Hilda Margaret Byrne; *m* 1984, Katharine Helen Wilson; one *s*. *Educ:* St Mary's Coll., Southampton; Coll. of Law, Guildford. FRGS 1990. Admitted Solicitor, 1978; Assistant Solicitor: Paris Smith & Randall, Southampton, 1978–80; Warner Goodman & Streat, Southampton, 1980; Reeves and Haynes, Oxford, 1981–82; Asst Solicitor, 1983–85, Partner, Commercial Litigation, 1985–2003, Lester Aldridge, Bournemouth; Fee-paid Chm., Industrial Tribunals, Southampton, 1994–2003; Salaried Chm., Industrial Tribunals, subseq. Employment Judge, Reading, 2003–12. Pres., Council of Employment Judges, 2009–10. Former Hon. Sec., RGS; Sec. and Treas., Geographical Club, 2006–12. Mem., James Caird Soc. *Recreations:* travel, cycling, playing golf (badly), theatre, absorbing the history of polar exploration, watching motor racing and looking at classic cars. *Address:* Employment Tribunals, Radius House, 51 Clarendon Road, Watford, Herts WD17 1HU. *T:* (01923) 281750, *Fax:* (01923) 281781. *E:* gtored@icloud.com. *Clubs:* Geographical; Goodwood Road Racing.

**BYRNE, Rt Rev. Robert John;** *see* Hexham and Newcastle, Bishop of, (R.C).

**BYRNE, Rosemary;** Member for Scotland South, Scottish Parliament, 2003–07 (Scot Socialist, 2003–06, Solidarity, 2006–07); Co-Convenor, Solidarity (Scotland), 2006. A principal teacher, Ardrossan Acad. Sec., Irvine and N Ayrshire Trades Union Council. Scot Socialist spokesman for educn and young people, Scottish Parlt, 2003–07. Contested (Scot Socialist) Cunninghame South, 2001.

**BYRNE, Simon,** QPM 2016; Chief Constable, Police Service of Northern Ireland, since 2019; *b* Epsom, Surrey, 29 April 1963; *s* of Thomas Byrne and Nola Byrne; *m* 1990, Susan Elaine Kerfoot; two *c* (and one *d* decd). *Educ:* Neston Co. Comp. Sch.; Univ. of Manchester (MA Dist. Police Mgt). Joined Metropolitan Police Service, 1982; Merseyside Police, 1985–2002; BCU Comdr, Knowsley, 2002–06; Asst Chief Constable, Merseyside Police, 2006–09; Dep. Chief Constable, Greater Manchester Police, 2009–11; Asst Comr, Metropolitan Police Service, 2011–14; Chief Constable, Cheshire Police Service, 2014–17. Member: Criminal Rules Procedure Cttee, 2016–; Sentencing Council, 2016–. Police Long Service and Good Conduct Medal, 2005. *Recreations:* cycling, tennis, ski-ing, building model railways. *Address:* Police Service of Northern Ireland, Brooklyn, 65 Knock Road, Belfast BT5 6LE.

**BYRNE, Terence Niall;** HM Diplomatic Service, retired; Clerk Adviser, House of Commons European Scrutiny Committee, 2002–17; *b* 28 April 1942; *e s* of late Denis Patrick Byrne and Kathleen Byrne (*née* Carley); *m* 1st, 1966, Andrea Dennison (marr. diss. 1977); one *s* one *d*; 2nd, 1981, Susan Haddow Neill; two *d*. *Educ:* Finchley Catholic Grammar Sch.; Open Univ. (BA Hons). Min. of Housing and Local Govt, 1964–68; Prime Minister's Office, 1968–70; MAFF, 1971–78 (Private Sec. to Parly Sec., MAFF, 1974–75); First Sec. (Agriculture), The Hague, 1978–82; Commonwealth Co-ordination Dept, FCO, 1982–84; Asst Head, UN Dept, FCO, 1984–85; Head of Chancery and Consul, Quito, 1986–89; Counsellor and Dep. High Comr, Lusaka, 1990–93; Dir of Trade Promotion, Canberra, 1993–94; Dep. High Comr, Kuala Lumpur, 1994–98; Consul-Gen. and Dir of Trade Promotion, Auckland, 1999–2002. *Recreations:* gardening, history, cinema.

**BYRNE, Terrance Dennis,** CB 2003; a Commissioner, 1999–2004, and Director General, Law Enforcement, 2002–04, HM Customs and Excise; *b* 26 Nov. 1944; *s* of Thomas Edward Byrne and Sybil Elizabeth Byrne; *m* 1966, Pamela Ashley; one *s* one *d*. *Educ:* Downham Market Grammar Sch., Norfolk. Joined Civil Service, 1962; HM Customs and Excise, 1964–2004: specialist investigator, 1971–84; Mgt Consultant, 1984–88; Dep. Chief Investigation Officer, 1988–91; Head, Customs Enforcement Policy, 1991–99; Dir, Fraud and Intelligence, then Law Enforcement, 1999–2000. *Recreations:* horticulture, sport (mainly golf), reading.

**BYRNE, Timothy Russell,** FCA; Director, Ginger Recruitment Services Ltd, since 2014; Chief Finance Officer, Nerudia Ltd, since 2015; *b* 16 March 1959; *s* of late Russell Vincent Byrne and of Barbara Ann Byrne; three *d*; *m* 2015, Angela Thomas; one step *s* one step *d*. *Educ:* Stanney High Sch. FCA 1994. With Lowndes McLintock, 1980–84; Accountancy Tuition Centre, 1984–85; Granada TV Div., 1985–92; Airtours plc, subseq. Mytravel Group, 1993–2002: Group Financial Controller, 1993–97; Group Finance Dir, 1997–99; Group Chief Exec., 1999–2002; Partner, Management Alliance LLP, 2004–14; Chairman: Everything4Travel (formerly E-Travel Money) Ltd, 2004–14; Andrew Sumners Associates Ltd, 2005–11; Chief Financial Officer, CN Creative Ltd, 2011–12; Chief Finance Officer, Nicoventures Trading, 2012–15. *Recreations:* country pursuits, Prince's Trust Mentor. *T:* 07785 234293.

**BYROM, Peter Craig,** OBE 1987; self-employed textile consultant, 1985–2010; *b* 4 Dec. 1927; *s* of Robert Hunter Byrom, Master Cotton Spinner and Winifred Agnes Byrom (*née* Goodwin); *m* 1st, 1952, Norma Frances Mawdesley Harris (marr. diss. 1984); three *s* three *d*; 2nd, 1984, Gillian Elizabeth Hoyte. *Educ:* Virginia Episcopal Sch., Lynchburg, USA; St Edward's Sch., Oxford; Univ. of Liverpool, Sch. of Architecture; Salford Royal Tech. Coll.; Admin. Staff Coll., Henley; Open Univ. (BA). CText; FTI 1986. RNVR, 1945–48. Asst Gen. Manager, Robert Byrom (Stalybridge), cotton spinners, 1951–59; Merchandising Manager, British Nylon Spinners, 1959–64; Marketing Manager and Adv. and Promotions Manager, ICI Fibres, 1964–71; Dir, Deryck Healey Internat., 1972–74; Man. Dir, Dartington Hall Tweeds, 1975–85. Non-exec. Dir, Parry Murray & Co. Ltd, 1992–2010. Lay Inspector of Schs, OFSTED, 1993–98. Consultant to: ODA, Nepal, 1980; Intermediate Tech. Gp, India, 1986; Chm., British Colour Council, 1971–73; Mem., Textile and Fashion Bd, CNAA, 1974–77; Chm. Council, RCA, 1981–86 (Mem., 1973–86; Sen. Fellow, 1983); Mem. Council, Textile Inst., 1986–96 (Service Medal, 1992); External Assessor, Manchester Metropolitan Univ., 1992–95. Governor: Dartington Coll. of Arts, 1979–89; Loughborough Coll. of Art and Design, 1993–98 (Vice-Chm., Govs, 1996–98). FRSA 1970 (Mem. Council, 1987–93; Mem. Design Bd, 1986–91; Chm., Textiles, Young Designers into Industry, 1985–90). Hon. Treasurer: Woodland PCC, 1995–2011; Priory Residents' Assoc., 2011–17; Mem., Financial Monitoring Gp, The Priory, Abbotskerswell, 2014–. *Publications:* Textiles: product design and marketing, 1987; (foreword) Fancy Yarns: their manufacture and application, 2002; contrib. to Young Designers into the Textile Industry. *Recreations:* walking, swimming, theatre, music, books. *Address:* 29 The Priory, Abbotskerswell, Newton Abbot, Devon TQ12 5PP. *T:* (01626) 335359.

*See also* Rt Rev. M. J. Rylands.

**BYRON,** family name of **Baron Byron**.

**BYRON,** 13th Baron *cr* 1643, of Rochdale, Co. Lancaster; **Robert James Byron;** Partner, Holman Fenwick & Willan, 1984, then Consultant; *b* 5 April 1950; *o* surv. *s* of 12th Baron Byron, DSO and Dorigen Margaret (*d* 1985), *o d* of Percival Kennedy Esdaile; *S* father, 1989; *m* 1979, Robyn Margaret, *o d* of John McLean, Hamilton, NZ; one *s* three *d*. *Educ:* Wellington Coll.; Trinity Coll., Cambridge (MA). Called to the Bar, Inner Temple, 1974; admitted solicitor, 1978. *Heir: s* Hon. Charles Richard Gordon Byron, *b* 28 July 1990.

**BYRON, Rt Hon. Sir (Charles Michael) Dennis,** Kt 2000; PC 2005; President, Caribbean Court of Justice, 2011–18; *b* 4 July 1943; *s* of late Vincent Fitzgerald Byron, MBE and Pearl Eulalie Byron (*née* O'Loughlin); *m* 1st, 1966, Monika Botfeldt (marr. diss.); four *s*; 2nd, 2006, Norma Theobalds-Willie. *Educ:* Fitzwilliam Coll., Cambridge (MA, LLB 1966). Called to the Bar, Inner Temple, 1965, Bencher, 2003; barrister-at-law, W Indies (Leeward Is), 1966–82; Eastern Caribbean Supreme Court: High Ct Judge, 1982–90; Justice of Appeal, 1990–96; Actg Chief Justice, 1996–99; Chief Justice, 1999–2008 (on leave of absence, 2004–08); Judge, 2004–11, Pres., 2007–11, Internat. Criminal Tribunal for Rwanda. Pres., Commonwealth Judicial Educn Inst., 1999. *Recreations:* tennis, golf, reading.

**BYRON, Prof. Tanya,** PsyD; consultant clinical psychologist, broadcaster, journalist, author and government adviser; Consultant in Child and Adolescent Mental Health, NHS and independent sectors, since 2002; *b* Barnet, 6 April 1967; *d* of John and Elfie Sichel; *m* 1990, Bruce Byron; one *s* one *d*. *Educ:* North London Collegiate Sch. for Girls; Univ. of York (BSc Hons Psychol. 1989); University Coll. London (MSc Clin. Psychol. 1992); Univ. of Surrey (PsyD 1995). Clinical Psychologist, UCH and Middlesex Hosp., 1992–96; Consultant Clinical Psychologist, Herts PCT Adolescent Unit, 1996–2002; Consultant in Child and Adolescent Mental Health, Herts Partnership NHS Trust, 1998–2002. BBC TV: Expert Presenter, series incl. Little Angels, 2003–05, House of Tiny Tearaways, 2005–07, Am I Normal?, 2008; Horizon, 2015; Weight for Love, 2016; Child of Our Time, 2016; co-writer (with Jennifer Saunders), The Life and Times of Vivienne Vyle, 2007. Columnist: The Times (weekly), 2005–; Good Housekeeping mag., 2009–18. Led ind. govt review on Children and New Technol. (Byron Review), 2007–08. Prof. in the Public Understanding of Sci. and Chancellor, Edge Hill Univ., 2008–18; Guest Prof., Shandong Normal Univ., China, 2011. Patron, Relate; Ambassador, Place2Be, 2010–; Trustee, NSPCC, 2017–. FRSA. DUniv: York, 2009; Open, 2010. *Publications:* Little Angels (jtly), 2005; The House of Tiny Tearaways, 2005; Your Child Your Way, 2007; Your Toddler Month By Month, 2008; The Skeleton Cupboard (autobiog.), 2014. *Recreations:* cinema, theatre, creative arts, creative writing, walking, piano, dancing, having a laugh en famille. *Address:* c/o Sophie Laurimore, The Soho Agency, 2nd Floor, 16–17 Wardour Mews, W1F 8AT. *T:* (020) 7471 7900. *E:* sophie@thesohoagency.co.uk. *W:* www.professortanyabyron.com.

**BYRT, His Honour (Henry) John;** QC 1976; a Circuit Judge, 1983–99; *b* 5 March 1929; *s* of Dorothy Muriel Byrt and Albert Henry Byrt, CBE; *m* 1957, Eve Hermione Bartlett; one *s* two *d*. *Educ:* Charterhouse; Merton Coll., Oxford (BA, MA). Called to the Bar, Middle Temple, 1953; called within the Bar, 1976; a Recorder of the Crown Court, 1976–83. First Pres., Social Security Appeal Tribunals and Medical Appeal Tribunals, 1983–90: Dep. Chm., Employment Appeal Tribunal, 1992–99. Judge, Mayors and City of London Court, 1990–99 (Sen. Judge, 1994–99). Working Men's College, London: teacher, 1952–87; Vice-Principal, 1978–82; Principal, 1982–87; Mem. Council, Queen's Coll., London, 1982–99. Trustee, Cotswold Community Trust, 2003–11. Patron, Jedidiah Foundn, 2005–. Freeman, City of London, 1999. *Recreations:* building, gardening, travel, music. *Address:* 46 Skyline House, Dickens Yard, Longfield Avenue, Ealing, W5 2BJ. *T:* (020) 3665 7791. *Clubs:* Guildhall Alderman's, Leander.

# C

**CABLE, Dr the Rt Hon. Sir (John) Vincent,** Kt 2015; PC 2010; MP (Lib Dem) Twickenham, since 2017; *b* 9 May 1943; *s* of John Leonard Cable and Edith Cable; *m* 1st, 1968, Olympia Rebelo (*d* 2001); two *s* one *d*; 2nd, 2004, Rachel Wenban Smith. *Educ:* Fitzwilliam Coll., Cambridge (BA Hons; Pres., Cambridge Union); Glasgow Univ. (PhD). Finance Officer, Kenya Treasury, 1966–68; Lectr in Econs, Univ. of Glasgow, 1968–74; First Sec., FCO, 1974–76; Dep. Dir, ODI, 1976–83; Special Advr (Dir), Econs, Commonwealth Secretariat, 1983–90; Gp Planning Dept, Shell, 1990–93; Hd of Economic Prog., Chatham House, 1993–95; Chief Economist, Shell, 1995–97. Advr to Chm., World Commn on Envmt and Develt, UN, 1975–77; Special Advr to Sec. of State for Trade, 1979. Mem (Lab), Glasgow CC, 1971–74. Contested: (Lab) Glasgow, Hillhead, 1970; (SDP/L Alliance) York, 1983, 1987; (Lib Dem) Twickenham, 1992. MP (Lib Dem) Twickenham, 1997–2015; contested (Lib Dem) same seat, 2015. Lib Dem spokesman on Trade and Industry, 1999–2003, on the economy, 2003–10; Dep. Leader, 2006–10, Acting Leader, 2007, Leader, 2017–19, Lib Dems; Sec. of State for Business, Innovation and Skills, 2010–15. Mem., Treasury Select Cttee, 1998–99. Chm., HCT Gp, 2016–; Former Vis. Fellow, Nuffield Coll., Oxford; Vis. Prof., LSE, Nottingham Univ., Sheffield Univ., St Mary's Univ., Twickenham, 2016–. *Publications:* Protectionism and Industrial Decline, 1983; (with B. Persaud) Foreign Investment and Development, 1985; Global Super Highways, 1994; The New Giants: China and India, 1994; The World's New Fissures, 1994; Globalisation and Global Governance, 2000; Public Services: reform with a purpose, 2005; Multiple Identities, 2005; The Storm, 2009; Free Radical (memoir), 2009; Tackling the Fiscal Crisis, 2009; After the Storm, 2015; Open Arms (novel), 2017. *Recreations:* walking, cycling, dancing. *Address:* 102 Whitton Road, Twickenham TW1 1BS. *T:* (020) 8892 3212; House of Commons, SW1A 0AA.

See also S. C. W. Kenny.

**CABLE, Margaret Ann, (Mrs J. R. W. Fletcher),** FRCM; Professor of Singing, Royal College of Music, 1964–2006; *b* 3 June 1942; *d* of Sidney Frank Cable and Gladys Alfreda Cable (*née* Roberts); *m* 1967, John Richard William Fletcher; one *s* one *d*. *Educ:* Sawston Village Coll., Cambs; Royal Coll. of Music (Foundn Schol. and Exhibnr). FRCM 1985. Concert singer, 1963–2000; sang at major festivals incl. Lucerne, Edinburgh, Utrecht, Aldeburgh, Three Choirs and Henry Wood Promenade Concerts; roles at Kent Opera, 1974–80, include: Dorabella, in Così fan tutte; Marcellina, in Le nozze di Figaro; Mrs Grose, in The Turn of the Screw. Has made numerous recordings. Gov., Royal Soc. of Musicians, 2011–. Warden, Solo Performers' Section, ISM, 1985–86. *Recreations:* walking, theatre. *Address:* 79 Haven Lane, Ealing, W5 2HZ. *T:* (020) 3605 6455.

**CABLE, Rt Hon. Sir Vincent;** *see* Cable, Rt Hon. Sir J. V.

**CABLE-ALEXANDER, Lt-Col Sir Patrick (Desmond William),** 8th Bt *cr* 1809, of the City of Dublin; Chief Executive (formerly Chief Executive (Administration)), Institute of Optometry, 1999–2006 and 2007–08; *b* 19 April 1936; *s* of Sir Desmond William Lionel Cable-Alexander, 7th Bt and of Mary Jane, *d* of James O'Brien, Enniskillen; S father, 1988, but his name does not appear on the Official Roll of the Baronetage; *m* 1st, 1961, Diana Frances Rogers (marr. diss. 1976); two *d*; 2nd, 1976, Jane Mary Weekes (*née* Lewis); one *s*. *Educ:* Downside School; RMA Sandhurst; Army Staff Coll., 1966–67; National Defence Coll., 1975–76. Commnd 3rd Carabiniers (POWDG), 1956; Lt-Col Royal Scots Dragoon Guards, 1976; comd Duke of Lancaster's Own Yeomanry, 1978–80; Chief of Staff, HQ North West District, 1980–83; retd, 1984. Sec. to the Council and Bursar, Lancing Coll., 1984–98. Trustee, Friends of Sussex Hospices, 2013–17 (Chm., W Sussex Fundraising Cttee, 2014–17). *Recreations:* art, cooking, theatre, fly fishing, city breaks. *Heir: s* Fergus William Antony Cable-Alexander [*b* 19 June 1981; *m* 2011, Claire Whiteside; three *s*]. *Address:* The Dovecote, Letcombe Regis, Wantage, Oxon OX12 9RQ.

**CABORN, Rt Hon. Richard (George);** PC 1999; *b* 6 Oct. 1943; *s* of late George and of Mary Caborn; *m* 1966, Margaret Caborn; one *s* one *d*. *Educ:* Hurlfield Comprehensive Sch.; Granville Coll. of Further Educn; Sheffield Polytechnic. Engrg apprentice, 1959–64; Convenor of Shop Stewards, Firth Brown Ltd, 1967–79. Mem. (Lab) Sheffield, European Parlt, 1979–84. MP (Lab) Sheffield, Central, 1983–2010. Minister of State: (Minister for the Regions, Regeneration and Planning), DETR, 1997–99; (Minister for Trade) DTI, 1999–2001; (Minister for Sport), 2001–07, (Minister for Tourism), 2003–05, DCMS; PM's Ambassador for the World Cup 2018, 2007–09. Chm., Select Cttee on Trade and Industry, 1992–95. President: ABA of England, 2008–; YHA, 2008–; UK Sch. Games, 2008–; Trustee, Football Foundn 2008–. Non-exec. Dir, Nuclear Mgt Partners, 2007–11. Consultant: AMEC, 2007–10; Fitness Industry Assoc., 2008–10; Strategic Advr to Advanced Manufg Res. Centre, Univ. of Sheffield, 2010–; Adviser: Nat. Centre for Sport and Exercise Medicine, 2012–; Quest, 2012–; Advr on business, trade and industry to Leader, Sheffield CC, 2015–. Chair: Sheffield City Trust, 1991–97; Olympic Legacy Park, Sheffield, 2015–. Hon. Fellow: Faculty of Sport and Exercise Medicine, 2007; C&G, 2015. Hon. Dr Sport Sci. Leeds Metropolitan, 2007; Hon Dr Sheffield Hallam, 2012; Hon. DLitt Sheffield, 2013. *Recreations:* golf, running. *Address:* 29 Quarry Vale Road, Sheffield S12 3EB. *T:* (0114) 239 3802. *Clubs:* Carlton Working Men's, Trades and Labour (Pres., 1981–) (Sheffield).

**CABRERA, Pablo;** Director, Diplomatic Academy, Ministry of Foreign Affairs Chile, 2010–14; *b* Santiago, 18 Jan. 1948; *m* 1973, Cecilia Pérez Waulker; two *s* one *d*. *Educ:* Catholic Univ. of Chile (Lic. Juridical and Social Scis). Lawyer; entered Foreign Service, Chile, 1970: Consul, 1974, Second Sec., 1975–76, La Paz; Second Sec., Carácas, 1977–78; Consul Gen., Toronto, 1981–82; Chargé d'Affaires, Bucharest, 1983–85; Counsellor and Minister Counsellor, London, 1987–91; Minister Counsellor, Madrid, concurrent with Greece, 1991–93; Dep. Head, 1993, Head, 1994, Special Policy Dept, Min. of Foreign Affairs, Santiago; Under-Sec. of State for Navy, MoD, Santiago, 1995–99; Ambassador of Chile: to UK and Ireland, 1999–2000; to Russian Fedn, 2000–04, and concurrently to the Ukraine, 2001–04; to China, 2004–06; Ambassador to the Holy See, 2006–10. Formerly Head, Chilean Delegns to internat. confs. Vis. Prof., Nat. Acad. for Political and Strategic Studies, 1993. Mem., Internat. Law Soc. of Chile, 1963–. Mem., Christian Democratic Party, 1963–. Official, 1980, and Great Cross, 1995, Order of Rio Branco (Brazil); Great Cross, Order of Civil Merit (Spain), 1996; Comdr First Cl., Polar Star Royal Order (Sweden), 1996. *Recreations:* golf, tennis, football. *Club:* Los Leones Golf (Santiago).

**CACKETTE, Paul Henry;** Interim Director, Legal Services, Scottish Government, since 2018; *b* Edinburgh, 26 March 1960; *s* of George and Erica Cackette; *m* 1987, Helen Elizabeth Thomson; one *s* two *d*. *Educ:* Univ. of Edinburgh (LLB Hons 1982); Univ. of Glasgow (DipLP 1983). Trainee solicitor, Edinburgh DC, 1983–85; Solicitor, Kirkcaldy DC, 1985–88; Govt Legal Service, 1988–; Divl Solicitor (Rural Affairs), 2000–03; Hd, Civil Justice and Internat. Div., Justice Directorate, Scottish Govt, 2003–08; Legal Sec. to Lord Advocate, 2008–09; Dep. Solicitor, 2009–16, Chief Planning Reporter, 2016–18, Scottish Govt. *Recreations:* athletics, literature. *Address:* Legal Directorate, Scottish Government, Victoria Quay, Edinburgh EH6 6QQ. *T:* (0131) 244 0531. *E:* paul.cackette@gov.scot.

**CADBURY, Sir (Nicholas) Dominic,** Kt 1997; Chairman: The Wellcome Trust, 2000–06 (a Governor, 1999–2006); Cadbury Schweppes plc, 1993–2000 (Chief Executive, 1984–93); *b* 12 May 1940; *s* of late Laurence John Cadbury, OBE and Joyce Cadbury, OBE; *m* 1972, Cecilia Sarah Symes; three *d*. *Educ:* Eton Coll.; Trinity Coll., Cambridge; Stanford Univ. (MBA). Chairman: Economist Gp, 1994–2003 (Dir, 1990–2003); Transense Technologies plc, 2000–03; Dep. Chm., Guinness PLC, 1994–97; Jt Dep. Chm., EMI Gp plc, 1999–2004 (Bd Mem., 1998–2004). Non-executive Director: Misys plc, 2000–09 (Chm., 2005–09); New Star Asset Mgt, 2005–07; Cotswold Distillery, 2018–. Mem., President's Cttee, 1989–94 and 1998–2000, Chm., Educn and Trng Affairs Cttee, 1993–97, CBI; Dep. Chm., Qualifications and Curriculum Authority, 1997–2000; Sen. Advr, FSA, 2010–13; Member: Royal Mint Adv. Cttee, 1986–94; Stanford Adv. Council, 1989–95; Food Assoc., 1989–2000; NACETT, 1993–95; Marketing Council, 1997–2000; Council of Mgt, NIESR, 1998–2000. Pres., Food and Drink Fedn, 1998–99. Chancellor, Univ. of Birmingham, 2002–13. Pres., Edgbaston High Sch. for Girls, Birmingham, 2015– (Vice-Pres., 1987–2015); Gov., Tudor Hall Sch., 1993–96. Trustee, Heart of England Community Foundn, 2015–. Fellow, Eton Coll., 1996–2010. CCMI (CBIM 1984); FCIM (Pres., 1996–97). *Recreations:* golf, shooting.

**CADBURY, Nigel Robin;** Independent Adjudicator (Prisons), since 2004; District Judge (Magistrates' Courts), West Mercia, 2011–19; *b* 6 July 1956; *s* of late Robin Norman Cadbury, JP, and of Rosemary Jayne Cadbury, MBE; *m* 1982, Julie Ann Dean; two *s* one *d*. *Educ:* Rugby Sch.; Kent Univ. (BA Law 1978). Called to the Bar, Middle Temple, 1979; in practice at the Bar, 1979–97; Mem., Midland and Oxford Circuit, 1979–97; Stipendiary Magistrate, Leeds, 1997–2000; District Judge (Magistrates' Courts): Birmingham, 2000–05; Solihull and Sutton Coldfield, 2005–11. Mem., Criminal Bar Assoc., 1990–97. Trustee: Edward Cadbury Charitable Trust, 1991–; Bourneville Village Trust, 2011–. *Recreations:* golf, ski-ing, gardening. *Clubs:* Blackwell Golf, Royal Cinque Ports Deal Golf, St Enedoc Golf.

**CADBURY, Roger Victor John,** CBE 2016; Trustee, Bourneville Village Trust, since 1993 (Chairman, 1996–2013); *b* Birmingham, 21 Dec. 1937; *s* of Christopher Cadbury and Honor Cadbury; *m* 1st, 1962, Terry Argent (*d* 2009); one *s* two *d* (and one *d* decd); 2nd, 2010, Lesley Birkett (*née* Wyness). *Educ:* Leighton Park Sch., Reading; King's Coll., Cambridge (BA 1961; MA 1965). National Service, 2nd Lieut Worcestershire Regt, 1956–58. Beechams, 1961–63; General Foods Ltd, UK and Ire., 1963–90: Dep. Man. Dir, 1984–87; Man. Dir, 1987–90; Chief Exec., Whitworth Hldgs, 1990–93; Exec. Chm., Premier Brands, 1993–96. Chm., Soil Association Certification Ltd, 1993–99; non-executive Director: Archant Ltd, 1993–99; NFU Mutual, 1998–2004; NHS Warwickshire Primary Care Trust, 2006–11. Trustee, Soil Assoc., 1998–2004; Mem. Council, Nat. Trust, 2001–04. Gov., Fircroft Coll., 1980–2009; Chairman: Age Concern Warwickshire, 1993–99; Croft Trust for Adult Educn, 1995–2006; Warwickshire Wildlife Trust, 2000–09; Warwick Independent Foundn, 2004–07. *Recreations:* ornithology, music (singing), art, walking, travelling. *Club:* Sloane.

**CADBURY, Ruth;** MP (Lab) Brentford and Isleworth, since 2015; *m* Nick; two *s*. *Educ:* Mount Sch., York; Bourneville FE Coll.; Univ. of Salford (BSc Hons 1981). Community develt worker, Covent Garden Community Assoc., 1983–89; Planning Advr, Planning Aid for London, 1989–96; Policy Planner, Richmond upon Thames LBC, 1996–2001; freelance consultant, 2006–14. Mem. (Lab), Hounslow LBC, 1986–94 and 1998–2015 (Dep. Leader, 2010–12; Cabinet Mem., 2010–13). Trustee, Barrow Cadbury Trust, 1984–2015 (Chair, 2007–13). *Address:* House of Commons, SW1A 0AA.

**CADDICK, Prof. Stephen,** PhD; Director of Innovations, Wellcome Trust, since 2015; Professor of Chemistry, University College London, since 2015; *b* Surrey, 1963; *s* of Raymond Caddick and Elizabeth Caddick; *m* 1989, Pauline Mary Tuck; one *s* one *d*. *Educ:* Paisley Coll. (BSc Chem. 1984); Cambridgeshire Coll. of Arts and Technol. (Graduate RSC 1986); Univ. of Southampton (PhD 1989). Res. Fellow, Imperial Coll. London, 1989–91; Lectr in Chem., Birkbeck Coll., Univ. of London, 1991–93; Lectr, 1993–97, Sen. Lectr, 1997–2002, Prof. of Chem., 2003, Univ. of Sussex; Charles Vernon Prof. of Organic Chem. and Chemical Biol., 2003–15, Hd, Dept of Chem., 2008–10, Vice-Provost, 2010–15, UCL. *Publications:* over 150 articles in jls in synthetic organic chem. and chemical biol., particular interests in free radical methods and chemical modification of proteins and antibodies for development of therapeutics. *Recreation:* running. *Address:* Wellcome Trust, Gibbs Building, 215 Euston Road, NW1 2BE.

**CADELL of Grange, William Archibald,** RIBA; FRIAS; *b* 9 March 1933; *s* of late Col Henry Moubray Cadell of Grange, OBE, RE and Christina Rose Cadell (*née* Nimmo); *m* 1960, Mary-Jean Carmichael; three *s*. *Educ:* Merchiston Castle Sch.; Trinity Coll., Cambridge (BA 1956; MA); Regent St Poly., London (DipArch). RIBA 1961. Founded William A. Cadell Architects, 1968, retired, 1995; manager, Grange Estate, 1971–2000. Chm., Drum Housing Develt, 1991–2009. Comr, Royal Fine Art Commn for Scotland, 1992–2000; Trustee, Architectural Heritage Fund, 1997–2010. DL 1982–2000, Vice Lord-Lieutenant, 2000–01, West Lothian. *Recreations:* gardening, forestry, the Arts. *Address:* Swordie Mains, Linlithgow, West Lothian EH49 7RQ. *T:* (01506) 842946.

**CADMAN,** family name of **Baron Cadman**.

**CADMAN,** 3rd Baron cr 1937, of Silverdale; **John Anthony Cadman;** farmer, 1964–85; restaurateur, 1986–94; b 3 July 1938; s of 2nd Baron Cadman and Marjorie Elizabeth Bunnis; S father, 1966; m 1975, Janet Hayes; two s. Educ: Harrow; Selwyn Coll., Cambridge; Royal Agricultural Coll., Cirencester. H of L, 1993–99. Mem., Select Cttee, Channel Tunnel Rail Link Bill, H of L, 1996. Heir: s Hon. Nicholas Anthony James Cadman, b 18 Nov. 1977. Address: 4 Drovers Way, Potterspury, Towcester, Northants NN12 7QH. T: (01908) 990744. E: lord.cadman@gmail.com.

**CADMAN, Deborah Ann,** OBE 2006; Chief Executive, West Midlands Combined Authority, since 2017; b Birmingham, 11 Feb. 1963; d of Ronald and Pamela Cadman; m 2001, Geoffrey John Rivers; one s one d. Educ: Sir Wilfrid Martineau Sch., Birmingham; Loughborough Univ. (BSc Hons); Birmingham Univ. (MSocSc Urban and Regl Econs); Teesside Univ. (MA Mgt Practice). London Borough of Newham, 1984–87; community devel't voluntary orgn, Birmingham, 1987–89; econ. devel't officer, Birmingham CC, 1989–96; Hd of Policy, Redcar and Cleveland BC, 1996–98; Special Advr, DETR, 1998–99; Audit Commn, 1999–2001; Chief Executive: St Edmundsbury BC, 2001–08; East of England Develt Agency, 2008–12; Suffolk CC, 2012–17. Vis. Fellow, Sch. of Business, Leadership and Enterprise, 2011–, Mem. Bd, 2011–, Univ. Campus Suffolk, then Univ. of Suffolk; Mem. Bd, Univ. of Birmingham. Chm., Birmingham Univ. Policy Commn, 2011. Member: Bd, New Local Govt Network, 2013–; Social Integration Commn, 2014–. Trustee: Suffolk Foundn; Joseph Rowntree Foundn/Joseph Rowntree Housing Trust, 2016–. FRSA. Recreations: theatre, ceramics, boxing. Address: West Midlands Combined Authority, 16 Summer Lane, Birmingham, W Mids B19 3SD.

**CADMAN, Mark Robert;** Executive Vice President and Managing Director, BBDO North America, since 2013; b Farnborough, 30 Dec. 1963; s of Colin and Jan Cadman; m 1998, Ayesha; two d. Educ: King's Sch., Canterbury; Queen Mary Coll., Univ. of London (LLB Hons). Managing Director: Lowe London, 2002–04; J. Walter Thomson, 2005; CEO, Euro RSCG London, 2006–08; Chief Exec., Publicis Seattle, 2010–13. Recreations: tennis, golf, running. Club: Harbour.

**CADOGAN,** family name of **Earl Cadogan**.

**CADOGAN,** 8th Earl cr 1800; **Charles Gerald John Cadogan,** KBE 2012; DL; Baron Cadogan 1718; Viscount Chelsea 1800; Baron Oakley 1831; b 24 March 1937; o s of 7th Earl Cadogan, MC and his 1st wife, Hon. Primrose Lilian Yarde-Buller (d 1970), yr d of 3rd Baron Churston; S father, 1997; m 1st, 1963, Lady Philippa Wallop (d 1984), d of 9th Earl of Portsmouth; two s one d; 2nd, 1989, Jennifer Jane Greig Rae (marr. diss. 1994), d of J. E. K. Rae and Mrs S. Z. de Ferranti; 3rd, 1994, Dorothy Ann Shipsey, MVO, yr d of late Dr W. E. Shipsey. Educ: Eton. Chairman: London Playing Fields Foundn, 2001–; Life Fellow, Coll. of Advocates, St Paul's Cath., 2012; Mem., Ct of Patrons, RCS, 2012–. Freeman, City of London, 1979; Liveryman, Hon. Co. of Air Pilots (formerly GAPAN); Hon. Freeman: Apothecaries' Soc., 2012–; Royal Bor. of Kensington and Chelsea, 2015. DL Greater London, 1996. Heir: s Viscount Chelsea, qv. Clubs: White's, Royal Automobile.

**CADOGAN, Prof. Sir John (Ivan George),** Kt 1991; CBE 1985; PhD, DSc London; FRS 1976; FRSE, FLSW; CChem, FRSC; first Director General, Research Councils, 1994–98; first President, Learned Society of Wales, 2010–14; b Pembrey, Carmarthenshire, 8 Oct. 1930; er s of late Alfred Cadogan and Dilys Cadogan, MBE; m 1st, 1955, Margaret Jeanne (née Evans) (d 1992); one s (one d decd); 2nd, 1997, Elizabeth Purnell (d 2017); one step s one step d. Educ: Grammar Sch., Swansea; King's Coll., London (State Scholar, 1948; 1st cl. Hons Chem. 1951; Pres., Chem. Soc., 1951–52; soccer colours, 1952). King's Scout. Research at KCL, 1951–54. Civil Service Research Fellow, 1954–56; Lectr in Chemistry, King's Coll., London, 1956–63; Purdie Prof. of Chemistry and Head of Dept, St Salvator's Coll., Univ. of St Andrews, 1963–69; Forbes Prof. of Organic Chemistry, Edinburgh Univ., 1969–79; Chief Scientist, BP Res. Centre, 1979–81; Dir of Res., BP, 1981–92. Chm., BP Vencap, 1988–92; Director: BP Gas International, 1983–87; BP Ventures, 1981–90 (Chief Exec., 1988–90); BP Chemicals, 1983–92; BP Venezuela, 1985–92; BP Solar International, 1988–92 (Chm., 1988–90); Chairman: Kaldair Internat., 1988–90; DNA Res. Innovations Ltd, 1999–2004, acquired by Invitrogen Corp.; Dir, Fusion Antibodies Ltd, 2001–17 (Chm., 2005–10). Advr to EC Comr for Sci., R&D, 1993–94. Mem., Royal Commn on Criminal Justice, 1991–93. Chairman: Defence Sci. Adv. Council, 1985–91; Nuclear Weapons Safety Cttee, 1992–98; Nuclear Powered Warships Safety Cttee, 1992–98; Defence Nuclear Safety Cttee, 1998–2000. Member: Chemistry Cttee, SRC, 1967–71 (Chm. 1972–75); Council, SERC, 1981–85 (Chm., Science Bd, 1981–85); Mem., Science Bd, SRC, 1972–75); ACORD, Dept of Energy, 1987–89; HEFCW, 1992–95 (Chm., Res. Gp, 1992–94); HEFCE, 1994–98; Hong Kong Technol. Review Bd, 1992–95; Commn on New Policy, Irish Council for Sci. and Technol., 2002–03; Sci. Policy Advr, Sci. Foundn Ireland, 2000–05. Member: Council, Chem. Soc., 1966–69, 1973–76; Council, RIC, 1979–80; Chem. Soc.-RIC Unification Cttee, 1975–80; Council, RSC, 1980–85, 1989–92 (Pres. RSC, 1982–84); Council of Management, Macaulay Inst. for Soil Res., Aberdeen, 1969–79; Council, St George's Sch. for Girls, 1974–79; Council, RSE, 1975–80 (Vice-Pres., 1978–80); Council, Royal Soc., 1989–91, 1993–95 (Mem., Royal Soc. Sci. Inquiry, 1990–92); COPUS, 1994–97; Conseil d'Admin, Fondation de la Maison de la Chemie, 1994–2012; Vice-Pres., Royal Instn, 1986–87 (Mem. Council, 1984–87). Chm., Develt Bd, Cardiff Univ. Sch. of Medicine, 2008–; Member: Bd of Trustees, Royal Observatory Trust, Edinburgh, 1979–86; Adv. Bd, RCDS, 1989–2001; Adv. Bd, Eur. Business Management Sch., UC Swansea, 1990–95; Adv. Council, RMCS, 1992–2002; Res. Cttee, Univ. of Newcastle upon Tyne, 1992–94; Ind. Adv. Cttee, Univ. of Durham, 1992–94; Trustee: Overseas Students Trust, UC Swansea, 1989–2000; RSE Scotland Foundn, 1998–2001. Governor: Jt Res. Centre, EC, 1994–2000; Salters' Inst. of Industrial Chem., 1999–2015. Pres., Chem. Sect., BAAS, 1981. Chemistry Advr, Carnegie Trust Univ. of Scotland, 1985–. Pres., Techniquest, 1997–99. Professorial Fellow, Univ. Coll. of Swansea, Univ. of Wales, then Univ. of Wales, Swansea, later Swansea Univ., 1979–2009; Vis. Prof. of Chemistry, Imperial Coll., London Univ., 1979–2002. Fellow: KCL, 1976 (Mem. Council, 1980–94; Vice-Chm., 1990–94); UC Swansea, 1992; Cardiff Univ., 1998; Swansea Inst. of Higher Educn, 2004; FIC 1992. Hon. FREng (Hon. FEng 1992); Hon. FRSC 1999. Lectures: Tilden, Chem. Soc., 1971; first RSE Schs Christmas, 1980; David Martin Royal Soc. BAYS, 1981; Humphry Davy, Royal Instn, 1982; Holroyd Meml, Soc. Chem. Ind., 1984; Salters' Co., Royal Instn, 1984; Philips, Royal Soc., 1985; Pedler, RSC, 1986; Dalton, RSC, 1995; BGS Dist., 1995; Irvine Meml, St Andrews, 1995; Salters' Millennium, 2000; William Menelaus Meml, 2013. Freeman, City of London; Liveryman, Salters' Co., 1993. Hon. DSc: St Andrews, 1983; Wales, 1984; Edinburgh, 1986; Aberdeen, 1991; Durham, 1992; Leicester, 1992; London, 1992; Sunderland, 1994; Cranfield, 1995; Glamorgan, 1996; Nottingham, 1999; Nottingham Trent, 1999; DUniv Stirling, 1984; Hon. Dr l'Université Aix-Marseille, 1984. Samuel Smiles Prize, KCL, 1950; Millar Thomson Medallist, KCL, 1951; Meldola Medallist, Soc. of Maccabaeans and Royal Inst. of Chemistry, 1959; Corday-Morgan Medallist, Chem. Soc., 1965; SCI Medal, 2001; Lord Lewis Prize, RSC, 2010; Royal Medal, RSE, 2013; Menelaus Medal, Learned Soc. of Wales and S Wales Inst. of Engrs Educnl Trust, 2014. Publications: Principles of Free Radical Chemistry, 1971; Organophosphorus Reagents in Organic Synthesis, 1979; about 330 scientific papers, mainly in Jl RSC, and patents; contrib. policy papers to www.learnedsocietywales.org.uk. Recreations: being in France, music, thinking about gardening, thinking, supporting Rugby football (Vice-Pres., Crawshay's Welsh RFC, London Welsh RFC; Patron, Swansea RFCC). Address: Learned Society of Wales, The University Registry, King Edward VII Avenue, Cathays Park, Cardiff CF10 3NS. T: (029) 2037 6951. Clubs: Athenæum; Cardiff and County; Bristol Channel Yacht.

**CADWALLADER, James Richard,** CMG 2007; Counsellor, Foreign and Commonwealth Office, 2001–08; b 1953; s of George Cadwallader and Kathleen Cadwallader; m 1975, Deborah Jane; two s one d. Educ: Ludlow Grammar Sch.; Keble Coll., Oxford (BA Engrg Sci., MA). FIET. Royal Corps of Signals, 1973–82; joined FCO, 1982. Recreations: hill walking, golf, technology and people. E: j.cadwallader@btinternet.com. Club: Victory Services.

**CAFFARI, Denise, (Dee),** MBE 2007; professional sailor; Managing Director, Dee Caffari Ltd, since 2006; b 23 Jan. 1973; d of late Peter Caffari and Barbara Caffari; partner, Harry Spedding. Educ: St Clement Danes Sch., Chorleywood; Leeds Metropolitan Univ. (BA Hons Sport Sci. 1994; PGCE Sec. Educn 1995). PE teacher, secondary sch.; Manager, Sports Coll. First woman to sail single-handed non-stop around the world in both directions (west around the world against the prevailing winds and currents, 2005–06 and eastwards, 2008–09); monohull speed record, Round Britain and Ireland Race, 2009; first woman to sail non-stop around the world three times on completion of the Barcelona World Race, 2011; skipper, Turn the Tide on Plastic, Volvo Ocean Race, 2017–18. Mem., Ops Cttee, RNLI, 2015–. Mem., Inst. of Navigation. Hon. Comdr, RNR, 2011. Hon. Dr Sport Sci. Leeds Metropolitan, 2006. Patron: St Mary's Jun. Sailing Club, 2007–; Gosport and Fareham Inshore Rescue Service, 2011–15. Ambassador for tri-service initiative, Toe in the Water. Contrib., Yachting World, 2016–. Publications: Against the Flow, 2007. Recreations: outdoor activities, fitness, travel, reading, theatre. Address: Dee Caffari Ltd, 4 Talisman Business Centre, Duncan Road, Park Gate, Southampton, Hants SO31 7GA. Club: Royal Southampton Yacht.

**CAGE, Nicolas;** actor, director and producer; b 7 Jan. 1964; né Nicholas Kim Coppola; s of Prof. August Coppola and Joy Vogelsang; one s by Kristina Fulton; m 1st, 1995, Patricia Arquette (marr. diss. 2001); 2nd, 2002, Lisa Marie Presley (marr. diss. 2004); 3rd, 2004, Alice Kim (marr. diss. 2016); one s. Educ: Beverly Hills High Sch. Co-owner, Saturn Films, prodn co. Films include: Valley Girl, Rumble Fish, 1983; The Cotton Club, Racing with the Moon, Birdy, 1984; Peggy Sue Got Married, 1986; Raising Arizona, Moonstruck, 1987; Vampire's Kiss, 1989; Wild at Heart, 1990; Honeymoon in Vegas, 1992; It Could Happen to You, 1994; Leaving Las Vegas, 1995 (Golden Globe and Acad. Awards for Best Actor, 1996); The Rock, 1996; Con Air, Face/Off, 1997; City of Angels, Snake Eyes, 1998; 8mm, 1999; Bringing Out the Dead, Gone in 60 Seconds, The Family Man, 2000; Captain Corelli's Mandolin, 2001; (also dir and prod.) Sonny, Windtalkers, Adaptation, 2002; Matchstick Men, 2003; National Treasure, 2004; (also prod.) Lord of War, 2005; The Weather Man, World Trade Center, The Wicker Man, 2006; Ghost Rider, Next, 2007; National Treasure: Book of Secrets, Bangkok Dangerous, 2008; Kick-Ass, Bad Lieutenant, The Sorcerer's Apprentice, 2010; Trespass, Justice, 2011; The Frozen Ground, 2013; Joe, Tokarev, 2014; Dying of the Light, 2015; The Runner, Pay the Ghost, 2015; The Trust, Dog Eat Dog, Snowden, 2016; Arsenal, 2017; Mom and Dad, Mandy, 2018; producer: Shadow of the Vampire, 2000; The Life of David Gale, 2003; The Dresden Files (TV series), 2007. Address: c/o Creative Artists Agency, 2000 Avenue of the Stars, Los Angeles, CA 90067, USA; Saturn Films, Suite 911, 9000 Sunset Boulevard, Los Angeles, CA 90069, USA.

**CAHILL, Frances Rebecca;** see Gibb, F. R.

**CAHILL, Jeremy;** see Cahill, P. J.

**CAHILL, Kevin James Patrick,** CBE 2007; Chief Executive, Comic Relief, 1997–2016, now Hon. Life President (Deputy Director, 1993–97); b 4 March 1952; s of James and Jean Cahill; m 1975, Shân Jones (marr. diss. 1982); one s one d; partner, Becky Webb; one s. Educ: Manchester Univ. (BA Hons English and Drama); PGCE Liberal Studies; RSA Dip. TEFL. Head of Educn, Nat. Theatre, later Royal Nat. Theatre, 1982–91; Dir of Educn, 1991–92, of Communications, 1992–93, Comic Relief. Founder, Sport Relief, 2002. Patron, Nxt Theatre Co., 1999. Chm., Gate Theatre, 1988–2008. Member: Council, Drama Centre, 1989–92; Bd, Young Vic Theatre, 1993–2001; Adv. Cttee, Active Community Unit, 2000–03. Chair, Trinity Coll. London, 1998–2002. Trustee: Internat. Broadcasting Trust, 1993–2002; Harlequins Foundn, 2017–; Pres. Bd, Comic Relief USA (formerly Charity Projects Entertainment Fund, then America Gives Back), 2007–18 (Trustee, 2018–); Mem. Bd, Malaria No More UK, 2008–12. Chancellor, Nottingham Trent Univ., 2014–17. Chair, Zero 30 Media, 2016–; Founder Dir, Ramifications Ltd, 2016–. Hon. DLitt Nottingham Trent, 2008. Recreations: football (Manchester United supporter), France, food. Clubs: Groucho, Soho House.

**CAHILL, (Paul) Jeremy,** QC 2002; b 28 Jan. 1952; s of late Timothy Cahill and Mary (née O'Mahony); two d; m 2011, Bettina Lugge. Educ: Ratcliffe Coll., Leicester; Liverpool Univ. (LLB). Called to the Bar, Middle Temple, 1975 (Blackstone Schol.); in practice, 1976–2018, specialising in planning and environmental law. Recreations: conversation, theatre, golf, West Cork, wine, travel, music, reading. Clubs: Royal Automobile; Copt Heath Golf.

**CAHILL, Sally Elizabeth Mary,** QC 2003; **Her Honour Judge Cahill;** a Circuit Judge, since 2004; b 12 Nov. 1955; m 1981, Patrick Cahill (d 2003); two s one d. Educ: Harrogate Ladies' Coll.; Leeds Univ. (LLB (Hons)). Called to the Bar, Gray's Inn, 1978; an Asst Recorder, 1997–2000; a Recorder, 2000–04. Chm. Leeds Reg., Family Law Bar Assoc., 1994–2004. Special Trustee, Leeds NHS Trust, 2001–09. Gov., Richmond House Sch., 1994–2004. Recreations: sailing, ski-ing, golf. Address: Leeds Combined Court Centre, 1 Oxford Row, Leeds LS1 3BG.

**CAHILL, Teresa Mary;** opera and concert singer; b 30 July 1944; d of Florence and Henry Cahill; m 1st, 1971, John Anthony Kiernander (marr. diss. 1978); 2nd, 2005, Robert Louis Alfred Saxton, qv. Educ: Notre Dame High Sch., Southwark; Guildhall School of Music and Drama; London Opera Centre (LRAM Singing, AGSM Piano). Glyndebourne début, 1969; Covent Garden début, 1970; La Scala Milan, 1976, Philadelphia Opera, 1981, specialising in Mozart, Strauss and Elgar; concerts: all London orchestras; Boston Symphony Orch., Chicago Symphony Orch., Rotterdam Philharmonic Orch., West Deutscher Rundfunk, Warsaw Philharmonic, RAI Turin, Frankfurt Radio Orch.; Promenade concerts; Festivals: Vienna, 1983; Berlin, 1987; Bath, 2000; BBC radio and TV; recordings, incl. Mozart, Strauss, Elgar and Mahler, for all major companies; master classes: Dartington Fest., 1984, 1986; Oxford Univ., 1995–; s'Hertogenbosch Vocal Concours, 1998 (Mem. Internat. Jury), 2000; Peabody Inst., Baltimore, 1999; Bowdoin Coll., Maine, 2004; recitals and concerts throughout Europe, USA, Far East. Prof., Trinity Coll. of Music, 1992–. Artistic Advr, Nat. Mozart Competition, 1994–2002. Mem. Jury, Kathleen Ferrier Comp., 1988; Adjudicator, 1988–, Music Advr, 2000–, Live Music Now; Adjudicator: Young

Concert Artists' Trust, 1989–; annual music comp., Royal Over-Seas League, 1985–89, 1992, 1995, 2000; Joaninha Trust. Trustee, Mus. of Music History. Gov., Royal Soc. of Musicians, 2000–. Silver Medal, 1966, Sir Charles Santley Meml Gift, 2017, Worshipful Co. of Musicians; John Christie Award 1970; Elgar Medal, 2017. Work archived at BL. *Recreations:* cinema, theatre, travel, reading, collecting things, sales from car boots to Sotheby's, photography. *Address:* 65 Leyland Road, SE12 8DW. *W:* www.teresacahill.net. *Club:* Royal Over-Seas League (Hon. Life Mem.).

**CAHN, Sir Albert Jonas,** 2nd Bt *cr* 1934; marital, sexual and hypno therapist; *b* 27 June 1924; *s* of Sir Julien Cahn, 1st Bt, and Phyllis Muriel, *d* of A. Wolfe, Bournemouth; *S* father, 1944; *m* 1948, Malka (*d* 2001), *d* of late R. Bluestone; two *s* two *d*. *Educ:* Headmaster's House, Harrow. Dir, Elm Therapy Centre, New Malden, 1983–93. *Recreations:* cricket, horse riding, photography. *Heir: s* Julien Michael Cahn [*b* 15 Jan. 1951; *m* 1987, Marilynne Janelle, *d* of Frank Owen Blyth; one *s* one *d*].

**CAHN, Sir Andrew (Thomas),** KCMG 2009 (CMG 2001); Chairman, WWF (UK), since 2014 (Member of Board, since 2014; Chairman, Audit Committee, WWF International, since 2015); Chief Executive, UK Trade and Investment, 2006–11; *b* 1 April 1951; *s* of Prof. Robert Wolfgang Cahn, FRS and of Pat (*née* Hanson); *m* 1976, Virginia Zachry Beardshaw, *qv*; two *s* one *d*. *Educ:* Bedales Sch.; Trinity Coll., Cambridge (BA 1st Cl. Hons). MAFF, 1973–77; FCO, 1977–78; Private Sec. to Perm. Sec., MAFF, 1978–79; 1st Sec., Office of UK Perm. Repn to EC, FCO, 1982–84, Cabinet of Vice Pres., CEC, 1984–88; Asst Sec., MAFF, 1988–92; Principal Private Secretary to: Chancellor of Duchy of Lancaster, 1992–94; Minister of Agriculture, 1994–95; Dep. Head, European Secretariat, Cabinet Office, 1995–97; Chef de Cabinet to Rt Hon. Neil Kinnock, EC, Brussels, 1997–2000; Dir, Govt and Industry Affairs, British Airways plc, 2000–06; Acting Perm. Sec., BERR, March–May 2009; Mem., Capability Rev. of HM Treasury, 2008–09. Non-executive Director: Cadbury Ltd, 1990–92; Deutsche BA, 2002–04; Nomura Internat. plc, 2012–18 (Vice-Chm., 2011–12; Sen. Ind. Dir, 2017–18); Huawei Technologies (UK), 2015– (Chm. Audit and Risk Cttee, 2015–; Chm. UK Adv. Bd, 2011–14). Member, Board: Internat. Financial Services Ltd, 2006–08; City (UK), 2011–15 (Chm., Internat. Trade and Investment Gp, 2013–15); General Dynamics (UK), 2012–19; Financial Services, Trade and Investment Board, 2013–15; Start Up Loans Co., 2013–14. Member: Governing Bd, 2008–, Exec. Cttee, 2009–, Inst. for Govt; Adv. Council, Univ. of the Arts, London, 2012–17; Assoc. Mem., BUPA, 2012–. Member: Adv. Council to the Duke of York, 2006–11; Adv. Cttee, British Amer. Business Council, 2007–11; Internat. Bd, SOAS, 2010–11; Franchise Bd, 2011–19, Risk Cttee, 2017–18, Lloyd's of London; Internat. Regulatory Strategy Gp, Corp. of London, 2011–17; Internat. Adv. Bd, Asia House, 2011–16; Bd, Japan Soc., 2011–; Adv. Bd, Business for a New Europe, 2011–16; Adv. Bd, AirCargoLogic, 2018–19. Sen. Responsible Officer, UK Participation in Shanghai Expo 2010, 2010. Governor: Bedales Sch., 1993–98; Ditchley Foundn, 2016–; Chair of Govs, Birkbeck, Univ. of London, 2019–. Trustee: Gatsby Charitable Foundn, 1996–; Royal Botanic Gardens, Kew, 2002–08 (Chm., Audit Cttee, 2004–08); Arvon Foundn, 2011–17. FRSA 1979. *Recreations:* family, reading, long distance walks, golf, cold water swimming. *Address:* c/o WWF (UK), Living Planet Centre, Rufford House, Woking GU21 4LL. *E:* andrew@cahn.co. *Clubs:* Royal Automobile; Highgate Golf; St Cyr (Poitiers).

**CAHN, Virginia Zachry;** *see* Beardshaw, V. Z.

**CAIE, Andrew John Forbes;** HM Diplomatic Service, retired; Managing Director, Ethos Consulting (Brunei) Sdn Bhd, since 2014; *b* 25 July 1947; *s* of Norman Forbes Caie and Joan Margaret Caie (*née* Wise); *m* 1976, Kathie-Anne Williams; one *s* one *d*. *Educ:* St Dunstan's Coll., Catford; Sidney Sussex Coll., Cambridge (MA). Joined FCO, 1969; Manila, 1976–80; FCO, 1980–84; Dep. Head of Mission, Bogotá, 1984–88; FCO, 1988–93; Dep. High Comr, Islamabad, 1993–96; FCO Resident Chair, CSSB, 1996–97; FCO, 1997–98; Ambassador to Guatemala, 1998–2001; High Comr, Brunei, 2002–05. Exec. Sen. Advr, SE Asia, CfBT Educn Trust, 2006–08; Executive Director: CfBT Educn Malaysia, 2007–08; Study Tracks Gp Sdn Bhd Malaysia, 2009–11; Dir, HR Develt and Assessment, L,S&A Sdn Bhd, Brunei Darussalam, 2010–14; Sen. Advr, then Consultant (SE Asia), QinetiQ Ltd UK, 2011–19. *E:* andrewjfcaie@gmail.com.

**CAIE, Prof. Graham Douglas,** CBE 2015; PhD; FRSE; FEA; Professor of English Language, 1990–2012, and Clerk of Senate and Vice-Principal, 2008–12, University of Glasgow, now Professor Emeritus and Professorial Research Fellow, since 2012; *b* Aberdeen, 3 Feb. 1945; *s* of William and Adeline Caie; *m* 1972, Ann Pringle Abbott; one *s* one *d*. *Educ:* Aberdeen Grammar Sch.; Aberdeen Univ. (MA Hons English); McMaster Univ. (MA, PhD 1973). Amanuensis and Lektor, English Dept, 1972–90, Chm., Medieval Centre, 1984–88, Univ. of Copenhagen; University of Glasgow: Hd, Dept of English Lang., 1992–96; Hd of Sch., 1994–98; Associate Dean (Res.), Arts Faculty, 2005–08. Vis. Associate Fellow, Clare Hall, Cambridge, 1976–77; Visiting Professor: McMaster Univ., 1985–86; Univ. of Guelph, 1989–90. Lead Assessor, Teaching Quality Assessment (Scotland), 1996–98. Member, Panel: RAE (English) 2001 and 2008; AHRC, 2005–08. Dep. Chm., Bd of Trustees, 1998–2014, Mem. Governance Cttee, 2012–14, Nat. Liby of Scotland. Chairman: Christie's Jt Educn Bd, 2002–12; Jt Liaison Bd, Glasgow Sch. of Art and Glasgow Univ., 2008–12, Scottish Agric. Coll. and Glasgow Univ., 2008–12. Senate Assessor, Court, Univ. of Glasgow, 1998–2003; Mem. Court, Queen Margaret Univ., 2014– (Chm., Audit and Risk Cttee, 2018–); Mem. Bd, All European Acads, 2014– (Vice Pres., 2018–). Chairman: Swedish Res. Council Linnaeus Res. Grants, 2007–08; Evaluation Panel, English Studies in Denmark, 1998–99; Assessment of Res. in Mod. Langs, Univs of Helsinki, Oulu and Tampere, (periodically) 2000–10. Vice-President: Scottish Text Soc., 1998–; (Humanities and Social Scis) RSE, 2010–14 (Mem., Internat. Cttee, 2008–16, Develt Cttee, 2018–); Mem. Council, Dictionary of Older Scottish Tongue, 1990–2000. Member: Erasmus Consultative Gp, British Council, 2011–15; Bd, Glasgow Student Villages, 2008–12; Univ. of Glasgow Trust, 2008–12; Faculty of Advocates Abbotsford Collection Trust, 2011–; British Council Adv. Cttee for Scotland, 2015–. Observer, Lloyds TSB Foundn for Scotland, 2015–. Hon. Sec., Eur. Soc. for Study of English, 1998–2002. Founding FEA 2000; FRSE 2004; Fellow, Japan Soc. of Medieval English, 2012. FRSA 1997. Hon. Fellow, Glasgow Univ. Liby, 2012. *Publications:* The Judgement Day Theme in Old English Poetry, 1976; Bibliography of Junius XI Manuscript, 1979; (ed jtly) A Literary Miscellany, 1988; The Old English "Judgement Day II": a critical edition, 2000; (ed jtly) The European Sun, 2001; (ed jtly) The Power of Words, 2007; (ed jtly) Medieval Texts in Context, 2008; (ed jtly) Transitional States: change, tradition and memory in medieval literature and culture; contrib. articles on medieval lang., lit., manuscript studies. *Recreations:* reading, travel. *Address:* 12B Upper Glenburn Road, Bearsden, Glasgow G61 4BW.

**CAIGER-SMITH, Frances Mary;** *see* Morris, F. M.

**CAILLARD, Air Vice-Marshal (Hugh) Anthony,** CB 1981; retired 1982; Director General, Britain-Australia Society, and Hon. Secretary, Cook Society, 1982–89; *b* 16 April 1927; *s* of late Col Felix Caillard, MC and Bar (mentioned in despatches), and Mrs Monica Y. Caillard; *m* 1957, Margaret-Ann Crawford, Holbrook, NSW, Australia; four *s*. *Educ:* Downside; Oriel Coll., Oxford. Joined RAF 1945; flying trng, 1946; Cranwell, 1947–49; served, 1949–65: 13 Sqdn, Egypt; ADC to C-in-C MEAF, and to AOC-in-C Tech. Trng Comd; 101 Sqdn, Binbrook; RAAF No 2 Sqdn; 49 Sqdn (Sqdn Ldr) and 90 Sqdn; RN Staff Coll.; HQ Bomber Comd (Wg Comdr); OC 39 Sqdn, Malta, 1965–67; Jt Services Staff Coll., 1967; Planning Staffs, MoD, 1967–70; Asst Air Attaché, Washington (Gp Captain), 1970–73; OC Marham, 1974–75; Def. Intell. Staff (Air Cdre), 1975–79; Dep. Chief of Staff, Ops and Intelligence, HQ Allied Air Forces, Central Europe, 1979–82. Specialist Air Advr, H of C Defence Cttee, 1985–92. Chairman: Ex Forces Fellowship Centre, 1987–93; Ex Services Mental Welfare Soc., 1990–93; Member: Grants and Appeals Cttee, RAF Benevolent Fund, 1987–93; Britain-Australia Bicentennial Cttee, 1984–88; Council, British Atlantic Cttee, 1988–92; Lord Mayor of Sydney's Sister City Cttee, 1994–2011; Trustee, Australian Arts Foundn, 1985–89. *Address:* 58 Hilltop Road, Clareville, NSW 2107, Australia. *Club:* Royal Air Force.

**CAIN;** *see* Nall-Cain, family name of Baron Brocket.

**CAIN, James Crookall,** FCA; Speaker, House of Keys, Isle of Man, 1991–96; Deputy President of Tynwald, 1992–96; *b* Douglas, IOM, 19 March 1927; *s* of James Mylchreest Cain, OBE, JP, formerly MHK and Jean (*née* Crookall); *m* 1959, Muriel Duckworth; two *d*. *Educ:* King William's Coll., IOM. Nat. Service, 1945–48, SSC, E Lancs, 1946. Qualified as Chartered Accountant with W. H. Walker & Co. (Liverpool), 1953; returned to Douglas office, 1954; Partner, 1959–71; Pannell Kerr Forster, 1971–86: Sen. IOM Partner, 1974; retd 1986. Mem., House of Keys, 1986–96; Member: Treasury, 1986–88; Dept of Highways Posts & Properties, 1989; Minister for Health and Social Security, 1989–91. Pres., Hospice Care, 1990 (Chm., 1983–89). *Recreations:* walking, reading. *Address:* Maughold, Alexander Drive, Douglas, Isle of Man IM2 3QX. *T:* (01624) 675068.

**CAIN, Hon. John;** MLA (Lab) for Bundoora, 1976–92; Premier of Victoria, 1982–90; Professorial Associate, School of Social and Political Science (formerly Department of Political Science), University of Melbourne, since 1991; *b* 26 April 1931; *s* of late Hon. John Cain; *m* 1955, Nancye Williams; two *s* one *d*. *Educ:* Melbourne Univ. (LLB). Practised as barrister and solicitor. Mem., Law Reform Commn, 1975–77. Pres., Law Inst. of Victoria, 1972–73 (Treasurer, 1969–70; Chm. of Council, 1971–72); Mem. Exec., Law Council of Australia, 1973–76. Vice-Chm., Vic Br., Australian Labor Party, 1973–75; Mem., Parly Labor Exec., 1977–90; Leader, State Labor Party, 1981–90; Leader of Opposition, 1981–82; Minister: for Fed. Affairs, 1982; for Women's Affairs, 1982–90; Attorney-General of Vic, 1982–83. Commonwealth Observer, S African elecns, Apr. 1994. Member: Academic Adv. Bd, Faculty of Business and Law, Deakin Univ., 2004–12; Liby Bd of Victoria, 2005–12 (Pres., 2006–12). Chm., Learning Adv. Bd, Hume Global Village, 2004–14. Trustee, LUCRF Community Partnership Trust, 2010–. Trustee, Melbourne Cricket Ground, 1982–98, 1999–2013; Member: Nat. Tennis Centre (Flinders Park), 1990–94; Melbourne and Olympic Parks Trust, 2005–13. Pres., Grad. Union, Melbourne Univ., 2005–11. *Publications:* John Cain's Years: power, parties and politics, 1994; On with the Show, 1998; (with John Hewitt) Off Course: from public place to marketplace at Melbourne University, 2004. *Address:* 9 Magnolia Road, Ivanhoe, Vic 3079, Australia.

**CAIN, Steven Anthony;** Chief Executive Officer, Coles, since 2018; *b* 30 Sept. 1964; *s* of Peter and Patricia Cain; *m* 1993; two *s* one *d*. *Educ:* Imperial Coll., London (MEng Chem. Engrg); Harvard; London Business Sch. Consultant, Bain & Co., 1987–89; Gp Develt Manager, Kingfisher plc, 1989–92; Asda plc: Mktg Controller, 1992–94; Grocery Trading Dir, 1994–95; Store Develt Dir, 1995–97; Mktg Dir, 1997–99; Chief Exec., Carlton Communications, 1999–2000; Co-Founder and Dir, GoinGreen, 2002–12; Gp Man. Dir, Coles Myer Ltd, 2003–05; Dir, Pacific Equity Partners, 2005–11; CEO Supermarkets, Metcash Ltd, 2015–18. Non-executive Director: Godfreys, 2006–; ARW, 2007–; Borders (Australia), 2008. Mem., Young Global Leaders, World Econ. Forum, 2005. *Recreations:* golf, tennis, soccer. *Clubs:* Groucho; National Golf, Kooyong Tennis.

**CAIN, His Honour Thomas William,** CBE 2003; QC 1989; HM First Deemster and Clerk of the Rolls, Isle of Man, 1998–2003; *b* 1 June 1935; *s* of late James Arthur Cain and Mary Edith Cunningham Cain (*née* Lamb); *m* 1961, Felicity Jane, *d* of late Rev. Arthur Stephen Gregory; two *s* one *d*. *Educ:* King's College Choir Sch., Cambridge; Marlborough Coll.; Worcester Coll., Oxford (BA 1958, MA 1961). National Service, 2nd Lieut RAC, 1953–55. Called to the Bar, Gray's Inn, 1959; Advocate, Manx Bar, 1961. Attorney-General, Isle of Man, 1980–93; Second Deemster, 1993–98. Pres., I of M Law Soc., 1985–89. Convener, first meeting of Law Officers, Small Commonwealth Jurisdictions, I of M, 1983. Hon. Fellow, Soc. for Advanced Legal Studies, 2000. Tynwald Medal of Honour, I of M, 2011; Reih Bleeaney Vanannan, Culture Vannin, 2015. *Recreations:* sailing, Manx Wildlife Trust (Chm., 1973–2010; Christopher Cadbury Medal, 2010). *Address:* Ivie Cottage, Kirk Michael, Isle of Man IM6 1AU. *T:* (01624) 878266.

**CAINE, Baron** *cr* 2016 (Life Peer), of Temple Newsam in the City of Leeds; **Jonathan Michael Caine;** Special Adviser to the Secretary of State for Northern Ireland, since 2010; *b* Leeds, 1966. *Educ:* Templenewsam Halton Primary Sch., Leeds; Halton Middle Sch., Leeds; Temple Moor High Sch., Leeds; Univ. of Leicester (Hist.). Cons. Res. Dept, 1987–88; NI Desk, Cons. HQ, 1988–91; Special Advr to Sec. of State for NI, 1991–95; Dir, Communication Gp plc, 1995–97; Asst Dir, Cons. Res. Dept, 1998–2007; Dir, Bell Pottinger Public Affairs, 2007–09. *Recreations:* British and Irish history, cricket, Rugby League and Union; season ticket holder of Leeds Rhinos Rugby League Club. *Address:* House of Lords, SW1A 0PW.

**CAINE, Sir Michael,** Kt 2000; CBE 1992; actor; *b* Old Kent Road, London, 14 March 1933; (Maurice Joseph Micklewhite); *s* of late Maurice and of Ellen Frances Marie Micklewhite; *m* 1st, 1955, Patricia Haines (marr. diss.); one *d*; 2nd, 1973, Shakira Baksh; one *d*. *Educ:* Wilson's Grammar Sch., Peckham. Began acting in youth club drama gp. Served in Army, Berlin and Korea, 1951–53. Asst Stage Manager, Westminster Rep., Horsham, Sx, 1953; actor, Lowestoft Rep., 1953–55; Theatre Workshop, London, 1955; numerous TV appearances (over 100 plays), 1957–63; *play:* Next Time I'll Sing for You, Arts, 1963; *films:* A Hill in Korea, 1956; How to Murder a Rich Uncle, 1958; Zulu, 1964; The Ipcress File, 1965; Alfie, The Wrong Box, Gambit, 1966; Hurry Sundown, Woman Times Seven, Deadfall, 1967; The Magus, Battle of Britain, Play Dirty, 1968; The Italian Job, 1969; Too Late the Hero, 1970; The Last Valley, Get Carter, 1971; Zee & Co., Kidnapped, Pulp, 1972; Sleuth, 1973; The Black Windmill, Marseilles Contract, The Wilby Conspiracy, 1974; Fat Chance, The Romantic Englishwoman, The Man who would be King, Harry and Walter Go to New York, 1975; The Eagle has Landed, A Bridge Too Far, Silver Bears, 1976; The Swarm, 1977; California Suite, 1978; Ashanti, Beyond the Poseidon Adventure, The Island, Dressed to Kill, 1979; Escape to Victory, 1980; Death Trap, 1981; Jigsaw Man, Educating Rita, The Honorary Consul, 1982; Blame it on Rio, 1984; Water, The Holcroft Covenant, 1985; Hannah and Her Sisters (Academy Award), Half Moon Street, Mona Lisa, 1986; The Fourth Protocol, The Whistle Blower, Surrender, Jaws The Revenge, 1987; Without a Clue, Dirty Rotten Scoundrels, 1989; A Shock to the System, Bullseye, Mr Destiny, 1990; Noises Off, Blue Ice, The Muppet Christmas Carol, 1992; On Deadly Ground, 1993; Bullet to Beijing, 1994; Mandela and de Klerk, 1996; Blood & Wine, Curtain Call, Shadowrun, 1997; The Debtors, 1998; Little Voice, 1999; The Cider House Rules (Academy Award), Quills, Last Orders, Quick Sands, 2000; Miss Congeniality, Shiner, 2001; Last Orders, The Quiet American, Austin Powers in Goldmember, 2002; The Actors, Secondhand Lions, The Statement, 2003; Around the

Bend, Batman Begins, Bewitched, 2005; The Weather Man, Children of Men, The Prestige, 2006; Sleuth, 2007; The Dark Knight, Flawless, 2008; Is Anybody There?, Harry Brown, 2009; Inception, 2010; Journey 2: Mysterious Island, 2011; The Dark Knight Rises, 2012; Now You See Me, 2013; Mr Morgan's Last Love, Interstellar, 2014; Kingsman: the Secret Service, The Last Witch Hunter, Youth (Best Actor, Eur. Film Awards), 2015; Now You See Me 2, 2016; Going in Style, 2017; Dear Dictator, King of Thieves, 2018; *films for TV:* Jack The Ripper, 1988; Jekyll and Hyde, 1989; World War II: When Lions Roared, 1994. Fellow, BAFTA, 2000. Comdr, Ordre des Arts et des Lettres (France), 2011; Honorary Award, European Film Awards, 2015. *Publications:* Not Many People Know That, 1985; Not Many People Know This Either, 1986; Moving Picture Show, 1988; Acting in Film, 1990; What's It All About (autobiog.), 1992; The Elephant to Hollywood: the autobiography, 2010; Blowing the Bloody Doors Off: and other lessons in life, 2018. *Recreations:* cinema, theatre, travel, gardening, cooking. *Address:* 42 M&P Ltd, First Floor, 8 Flitcroft Street, WC2H 8DL.

**CAINES, Dr Eric**, CB 1993; independent researcher, since 2011; *b* 27 Feb. 1936; *s* of Ernest and Doris Caines; *m* 1st, 1958 (marr. diss. 1984); three *s*; 2nd, 1984, Karen Higgs; two *s*. *Educ:* Rothwell Grammar School, Wakefield; Leeds Univ. (LLB Hons); Oxford Univ. (MA, MSt; DPhil 2011); Dip. Hist. Art, London Univ., 1984; King's Coll. London (MRes 2014). Short Service Commission, RAEC, 1958–61. NCB, 1961–65; BBC, 1965–66; as Principal, Min. of Health, Management Side Sec., General Whitley Council, 1966–70; Sec., NHS Reorganisation Management Arrangements Study, 1970–73; Assistant Sec., DHSS, 1973–77; IMF/World Bank, Washington, 1977–79; Under Sec., DHSS, 1979, Dir, Regl Organisation, 1981–84; Dir, Personnel and Finance, Prison Dept, Home Office, 1984–87; Dir, Operational Strategy, DHSS, then DSS, 1987–90; Dir of Personnel, NHS, DoH, 1990–93; Prof. of Health Service Mgt, Nottingham Univ., 1993–96. Mem., Sheehy Inquiry into Police Responsibilities and Rewards. Director: Trebor Ltd, 1985–90; Premier Prisons, 1994–98. *Publications:* Heath and Thatcher in Opposition, 2017; articles on public sector mgt for nat. newspapers and jls, 1993–97. *Recreation:* family and history. *Club:* Athenæum.

**CAINES, Sir John**, KCB 1991 (CB 1983); Permanent Secretary, Department for Education (formerly of Education and Science), 1989–93; *b* 13 Jan. 1933; *s* of late John Swinburne Caines and Ethel May Stenlake; *m* 1963, Mary Large (*d* 2008); one *s* two *d*. *Educ:* Sherborne Prep. Sch.; Westminster Sch.; Christ Church, Oxford (MA). Asst Principal, Min. of Supply, 1957; Asst Private Sec., Min. of Aviation, 1960–61; Principal, Min. of Aviation, 1961–64; Civil Air Attaché in Middle East, 1964–66; Manchester Business Sch., 1967; Asst Sec., BoT, 1968; Sec., Commn on Third London Airport, 1968–71; Asst Sec., DTI, 1971–72; Principal Private Sec. to Sec. of State for Trade and Industry, 1972–74; Under-Sec., Dept of Trade, 1974–77; Sec., 1977–80, Mem. and Dep. Chief Exec., 1979–80, NEB; Dep. Sec., Dept of Trade, and Chief Exec., BOTB, 1980–82; Dep. Sec., Central Policy Review Staff, Cabinet Office, 1983; Dep. Sec., DTI, 1983–87; Permanent Sec., ODA, FCO, 1987–89. Director: Investors Compensation Scheme, 1993–2001 (Dep. Chm., 1997–2001); Norsk Hydro (UK) Ltd, 1994–2000; Medical Defence Union, 1998–2004; Chm., European Capital, 1995–2000. Mem., Gibraltar Financial Services Commn, 1995–2002. Ind. Reviewer for ASA, 1999–2009. Member of Council: Southampton Univ., 1993–2000; Open Univ., 1993–2001 (Chm., Audit Cttee, 1993–2001). Chm., Dr Busby's Trustees, Westminster Sch., 2002–12. DUniv Open, 1993. *Address:* Flat A32 Parliament View Apartments, 1 Albert Embankment, SE1 7XH.

**CAINES, Michael Andrew**, MBE 2006; Chef-Patron, Lympstone Manor, since 2017; *b* Exeter, 3 Jan. 1969; *s* of Peter and Mary Caines; one *s* two *d*. *Educ:* Exeter Catering Coll. (Student of Year 1987). Chef: Grosvenor Hse Hotel, Park Lane, 1987–89; Le Manoir aux Quat'Saisons, 1989–92; work in France, 1992–94; Head Chef: Gidleigh Park, 1994–2016; Bath Priory, 2009–12; founded Michael Caines Restaurants, 2000; opened Michael Caines at Royal Clarence, Exeter, 2000; at Bristol Marriott Royal Hotel, 2003; The Coach Hse, Barnstaple, 2015; Pearls (pop up), Dubai, 2015. Dir and Operational Partner, Andrew Brownsword Hotels Ltd (ABode Hotels), 2003–16. Hon. LLD St Loyes Sch. of Health Scis, 2004. Chef of Year, Independent, 1994; 2nd Michelin Star for Gidleigh Park, 1999; Chef of Year, Cateys Awards, 2002; AA Chefs Chef of Year, 2007.

**CAIO, Francesco**; Chief Executive, Poste Italiane, 2014–17; *b* 23 Aug. 1957; *m* 1986, Meryl Wakefield; two *s*. *Educ:* Politecnico of Milan (Master Computer Sci. 1980); Insead, France (Luca Braito Schol.; MBNA 1985). Product Manager, Telecom Systems, Olivetti SpA, 1982–84; McKinsey & Co., London, 1986–91; Olivetti SpA, 1991; founder and CEO, Omnitel Pronto Italia SpA, 1993–96; CEO, Olivetti SpA, Ivrea, 1996; CEO, Merloni Elettrodomestici SpA, 1997–2000; founder and CEO, Netscalibur Co., 2000–03; CEO, Cable and Wireless plc, 2003–06; Vice-Chm., Europe, 2006–08, Chm., European Adv. Bd, 2007–08, Lehman Brothers; Vice-Chm., Investment Banking, Europe, Nomura, 2008–11; Chief Exec., Avio Gp, SpA, 2011–13; Chm., Saipem SpA, 2018–. Non-executive Director: Invensys plc, 2009–13; Indesit Co. SpA, 2010–13; Il Sole 24 Ore SpA, 2010–11. *Recreations:* photography, Inter Milan FC, family.

**CAIRD, Prof. George**, FRAM; oboist, since 1970; Interim Principal, Royal Welsh College of Music and Drama, 2017–18; freelance oboist, conductor, teacher and adjudicator, since 2018; *b* 30 Aug. 1950; *s* of late Rev. Dr George Bradford Caird, FBA, and Viola Mary Caird (*née* Newport); *m* 1st, 1974, Sarah Dorothy Verney (marr. diss. 1999); three *s* one *d*; 2nd, 2001, Jane Amanda Salmon; one *d*. *Educ:* Magdalen Coll. Sch., Oxford; Royal Acad. of Music (LRAM 1972; FRAM 1989); Peterhouse, Cambridge (MA). ARCM 1972; FRCM 1999. Hd, Woodwind and Orchestral Studies, RAM, 1987–93; Prof. and Principal, Birmingham Conservatoire, 1993–2010, now Emeritus Prof., Birmingham Sch. of Acting, 2006–08, UCE, later Birmingham City Univ.; Artistic Dir, Classical Music, Codarts Rotterdam, 2011–16. Orchestral musician, notably with Acad. of St Martin-in-the-Fields, 1983–93; chamber musician, notably with Albion Ensemble, Caird Oboe Quartet. Has made recordings. Sec., Fedn of British Conservatoires, 1998–2003; Sec.-Gen., Assoc. of Eur. Conservatoires, 2004–10. Chairman: Music Educn Council, 2001–04; Nat. Assoc. of Youth Orchestras, 2005–10. Mem. Regl Cttee, Arts Council W Midlands, 2002–04. President: ISM, 2004–05; Barbirolli Internat. Oboe Fest. and Competition, 2008–; Bromsgrove Internat. Music Competition, 2017–; Chm., ARD Internat. Munich Flute Competition, 2010, Wind Quintet Competition, 2014; Music Advr, Wingate Foundn, 2010–11; Chm., Music Panel, Sir James Caird Travelling Scholarship Trust, 2012–. Second Vice-Pres., Internat. Double Reed Soc., 2006–09 (Dir, Conference, Birmingham, 2009). Trustee: Symphony Hall Birmingham, 1998–2011; G. B. Caird Meml Trust, 2002–; Youth Music, 2004–11; Countess of Munster Musical Trust, 2007–; Nat. Children's Orchestras of GB, 2017–; Chm., Schubert Ensemble Trust, 2015–. Bd Mem., Culture W Midlands (formerly W Midlands Life), 2003–09. Director: New Generation Arts Fest., Birmingham, 2005–10; Boulez in Birmingham Fest., 2008; Internat. Double Reed Soc. Conf., 2009; Patron, Tunbridge Wells Internat. Music Competition, 2010–. President: Royal Acad. Music Club, 2007–08; Royal Birmingham Conservatoire Assoc. (formerly Birmingham Conservatoire Assoc.), 2009–. FRSA 1994. FRCM 1999; FRNCM 2004; Hon. FLCM 1999; Hon. FRBC (Hon. FBC 2010). President's Medal, RWCMD, 2018. *Publications:* contrib. articles to music and music educn jls. *Recreations:* reading, theatre, languages, travel, fell-walking, seven grandchildren. *Address:* Huggins Cottage, Old Road, Shotover Hill, Headington, Oxford OX3 8SZ. *W:* www.georgecaird.co.uk.
*See also* J. N. Caird.

**CAIRD, John Newport**; director, writer and producer of plays, opera and musical theatre; Hon. Associate Director, Royal Shakespeare Company, since 1990; Principal Guest Director, Royal Dramatic Theatre, Stockholm, since 2009; *b* 22 Sept. 1948; *s* of late Rev. George Bradford Caird, DPhil, DD, FBA and Viola Mary Newport, MA; *m* 1st, 1972, Helen Frances Brammer (marr. diss. 1982); 2nd, 1982, Ann Dorszynski (marr. diss. 1990); two *s* one *d*; 3rd, 1990, Frances Ruffelle (marr. diss. 1997); one *s* one *d*; 4th, 1998, Maoko Imai; one *s* two *d*. *Educ:* Selwyn House Sch., Montreal; Magdalen Coll. Sch., Oxford; Bristol Old Vic Theatre Sch. Associate Dir, Contact Theatre, Manchester, 1974–76; directed, Contact: Games, After Liverpool, Krapp's Last Tape, Look Back in Anger, Downright Hooligan, Twelfth Night; Jt founder and Dir, Circle of Muses, touring music theatre troupe, 1976; Director: Regina v. Stephens, Avon Touring Th. Co.; Last Resort, Sidewalk Th. Co., 1976; Resident Dir, 1977–82, Associate Dir, 1983–90, RSC; directed, RSC: Dance of Death, 1977; Savage Amusement, Look Out, Here Comes Trouble, (co-dir, with Howard Davies) The Adventures of Awful Knawful, 1978; Caucasian Chalk Circle, 1979; (co-dir, with Trevor Nunn) Nicholas Nickleby, London, New York and Los Angeles, 1980, 1982, 1986 (SWET Award, 1980, Tony Award, 1982, for Best Dir; televised, 1981, Emmy Award, 1983); Naked Robots, Twin Rivals, 1981; Our Friends in the North, 1982; Peter Pan (adapted and co-dir with Trevor Nunn), 1982–84; Twelfth Night, Romeo and Juliet, 1983; The Merchant of Venice, Red Star, 1984; Philistines, 1985; Les Misérables (adapted and co-dir with Trevor Nunn), London, 1985 and worldwide, 1985– (Tony Award for Best Dir, 1987); Every Man in his Humour, Misalliance, 1986; A Question of Geography, The New Inn, 1987; As You Like It, A Midsummer Night's Dream, 1989; Columbus and the Discovery of Japan, Antony and Cleopatra, 1992; directed, RNT: Trelawny of the 'Wells', 1993; The Seagull, 1994; Stanley, 1996, NY, 1997 (Outer Critics Circle Award for Best Dir); Peter Pan, 1997; Money, Candide (a new version with music by Leonard Bernstein), 1999 (Olivier Award, 2000); Hamlet, 2000 (world tour, 2001), Tokyo, 2017; Humble Boy, 2001, transf. Gielgud, 2002, NY, 2003, UK tour, 2003; Chain Play, 2001. Director: Song and Dance, London, 1982; As You Like It, Stockholm, 1984 (also for TV, 1985); Zaïde by Mozart, Battignano, 1991; Life Sentences, NY, 1993; The Millionairess (UK tour), 1995; Murder in the Red Barn, Tiller-Clowes Marionettes, Theatre Mus., 1999; Midsummer Night's Dream, 2000, Twelfth Night, 2002, Stockholm; What the Night is For, 2002, Rattle of a Simple Man, 2004, Comedy Th.; Becket, Th. Royal, Haymarket, The Screams of Kitty Genovese, NY, 2004; Macbeth, Almeida, 2005; Don Carlos, WNO, 2005; The Beggar's Opera, Tokyo and Osaka, 2006–08 (televised 2006); Dödsdansen, Stockholm, 2007 (televised 2007); A Midsummer Night's Dream, Tokyo, 2007, 2009; Don Carlos, Canadian Opera Co., Toronto, 2007; Aida, WNO, 2008; Private Lives, Tokyo, 2008; Merry Wives of Windsor, Stockholm, 2009; Tosca, Houston Grand Opera, 2010, 2015, LA Opera, 2013, 2017, Chicago Lyric Opera, 2015; Candide, Tokyo, 2010; The Tempest (Stormen), Stockholm, 2010; Romeo and Juliet, Stockholm, 2011; Don Giovanni, WNO, 2011; Don Carlos, La Bohème, Houston Grand Opera, 2012, 2018; La Bohème, Canadian Opera Co., 2013, 2019, San Francisco Opera, 2014, 2017; Parsifal, Chicago Lyric Opera, 2013; Gertrud, Stockholm, 2014; Twelfth Night, Tokyo, 2015; McQueen, St James Th., transf. Haymarket Th., 2015; Love's Labour's Lost, Stratford Fest. Th., Canada, 2015 (televised, 2016). Devised and directed: Intimate Letters (a series of concerts for actors and string quartet); At Home in the World (charity concert), Sendai and Tokyo, 2014, NY and Washington DC, 2015, Kampala, 2016; Alcina, St John's Smith Sq. (concert), 2019; staged: WWF Religion and Interfaith Ceremony, Assisi, 1986; WWF Sacred Gifts for a Living Planet Ceremony, Bakhtapur, Nepal, 2000; wrote and directed: The Kingdom of the Spirit, London, 1986; Siegfried & Roy at the Mirage, Las Vegas, 1989; Children of Eden, a musical drama (with music and lyrics by Stephen Schwartz), London, 1991, and worldwide, 1991–; The Beggar's Opera (a new version with music by Ilona Sekacz), RSC and worldwide, 1992–; Jane Eyre, a musical drama (music by Paul Gordon), Canada and USA, 1995–, Tokyo, 2009, 2012; Daddy Long Legs, a musical romance (music by Paul Gordon), 2004, Ventura, Palo Alto, Cincinnati and N American tour, 2009–12 (LA Ovation Award, 2011), Tokyo, 2012, 2014, transf. St James Th., 2012, Davenport Th., NY, 2015 (Drama Desk Award, 2016); Twin Spirits, Royal Opera Hse Gala, 2005, New Victory Th., NY, Windsor Castle, Salisbury Cath., Cortona Fest., and worldwide (televised 2008); Kinshu (with Kiyomi Fujii), Tokyo, 2007 (Japan Maj. Theatres Award, 2008), 2009; Brief Encounter, opera (with music by André Previn), 2007 (première), Houston Grand Opera, 2009); Little Miss Scrooge (with Paul Gordon and Sam Caird), Ventura, 2012; Knight's Tale, musical (music and lyrics by Paul Gordon), Imperial Th., Tokyo, 2018; The Phoenix, opera (music by Tarik O'Regan), Houston Grand Opera, 2019; adapted and dir., Henry IV (BBC TV), 1995. Produced: (with Holly Kendrick) Fortnight of New Writing and Directing, Caird Co., Highgate, 2001; Observe the Sons of Ulster Marching Towards the Somme, Playing Soldiers, Pleasance Th., 2002; Disintegration, Arcola Th., 2002; New British Plays, Jerwood Space, 2002; Northern Lights, Soho Th., 2002; Robin Hood, NT, 2002; Five Corners, Jerwood Centre, 2003; Theatre Café, Arcola Th., 2004; Arab-Israeli Cookbook, Gate Th., 2004; Cancer Time, Theatre 503, New Directions, Th. Royal, Haymarket, 2004. Recordings: Beggar's Opera; Children of Eden; Les Misérables; Jane Eyre; Candide; Daddy Long Legs; Brief Encounter. Trustee: G. B. Caird Meml Trust, 1990–; Friends of Highgate Cemetery Trust Ltd, 1999–2014; Angus Lindsay Trust, 2000–; Mustardseed Trust (formerly Georgeville Trust), 2001–. Internat. Advr, Ashinaga Ikueikai, 2012–. Companion, Liverpool Inst. for Performing Arts, 2017. Hon. FRWCMD; Hon. FRAM, 2019. Hon. Fellow, Mansfield Coll., Oxford, 2000. Hon. DLitt UEA, 2006. *Publications:* (with Trevor Nunn) Peter Pan, by J. M. Barrie (new versions), 1993, 1998; (with Stephen Schwartz) Children of Eden, 1996; The Beggar's Opera (new version, with Ilona Sekacz), 1999; Candide (new version, with music by Leonard Bernstein), 2003; (with Paul Gordon) Jane Eyre, 2003; Theatre Craft: a director's practical companion from A–Z, 2010; (with André Previn) Brief Encounter, 2011; (with Paul Gordon) Daddy Long Legs, 2016. *Recreations:* music, birds, mountains. *Address:* Church House, 10 South Grove, Highgate, N6 6BS.
*See also* G. Caird.

**CAIRNCROSS, Dame Frances (Anne), (Dame Frances McRae)**, DBE 2015 (CBE 2004); Rector, Exeter College, University of Oxford, 2004–14; Chairman, Economic and Social Research Council, 2001–07; Interim Director, National Institute for Economic and Social Research, 2015–16; *b* 30 Aug. 1944; *d* of Sir Alexander Kirkland Cairncross, KCMG, FBA and late Mary Frances (*née* Glynn); *m* 1971, Hamish McRae, *qv*; two *d*. *Educ:* Laurel Bank Sch., Glasgow; St Anne's Coll., Oxford (MA History; Hon. Fellow 1993); Brown Univ., Rhode Island (MAEcon). On Staff of: The Times, 1967–69; The Banker, 1969; The Observer, 1970–73; Economics Correspondent, 1973–81, Women's Page Editor, 1981–84, The Guardian; The Economist: Britain Ed., 1984–89; Envmt Ed., 1989–94; Media Ed., 1994–97; Public Policy Ed., 1997–98; Mgt Ed., 1999–2004. Member: SSRC Economics Cttee, 1972–76; Newspaper Panel, Monopolies Commn, 1973–80; Council, Royal Economic Soc., 1980–85; Council, PSI, 1987–90; Cttee of Inquiry into Proposals to Amend the Shops Act, 1983–84; Inquiry into British Housing, 1984–85; School Teachers

Review Body, 1991–94; Council, Inst. for Fiscal Studies, 1995–2001, 2007– (Chm. Exec. Cttee, 2008–15); Scottish Council of Econ. Advrs, 2007–11; Adv. Bd, Foundn for Effective Governance, Ukraine, 2007–13. Chair, Rev. of Sustainability Future of High Quality Journalism in UK, 2018–19 (report, 2019). Director: Prolific Gp plc, 1988–89; Alliance & Leicester Gp plc (formerly Alliance & Leicester Building Soc.), 1990–2004; Stramongate Ltd, 2005–11. Pres., BAAS, 2005–06 (Hon. Fellow, 2006). Gov., NIESR, 1995–2001. Vis. Fellow, Nuffield Coll., Oxford, 2001–04; Woodrow Wilson Vis. Fellow, 2015–. Hon. Treas., Nat. Council for One Parent Families, 1980–83; Trustee: Kennedy Memorial Trust, 1974–90; Natural History Mus., 2016– (Chm., Develt Trust, 2015–16). Chm. Court, Heriot-Watt Univ., 2015–. High Sheriff, Greater London, 2004–05. Founding Fellow, Inst. of Contemporary Scotland, 2000; FRSE 2003; FAcSS 2016. Hon. Fellow: St Peter's Coll., Oxford, 2003; Cardiff Univ., 2004. Hon. Life FRSA, 2006. Hon. DLitt: Glasgow, 2001; Loughborough, 2003; Hon. DSc: Birmingham, 2002; City, 2003; Bristol, 2004; TCD, 2005; Hon. DPhil London Metropolitan, 2004; Hon. DBA Kingston, 2005; DUniv York, 2011; Hon. DLitt Aberdeen, 2016. European Women of Achievement Award, 2002 (Awards Pres., 2007–09); President's Medal, British Acad., 2018. *Publications:* Capital City (with Hamish McRae), 1971; The Second Great Crash (with Hamish McRae), 1973; The Guardian Guide to the Economy, 1981; Changing Perceptions of Economic Policy, 1981; The Second Guardian Guide to the Economy, 1983; Guide to the Economy, 1987; Costing the Earth, 1991; Green, Inc., 1995; The Death of Distance, 1997; The Company of the Future, 2002. *Recreation:* home life. *Address:* 6 Canonbury Lane, N1 2AP.

**CAIRNES, (Simon) Paul (Steven);** QC 2016; *b* Ballabeg, I of M, 19 Dec. 1957; *s* of Edward Michael Hornby Cairnes and Audrey Mary Cairnes (née Stevens); *m* 2004, Patricia Alison Glenn (*d* 2012); three *d*. *Educ:* University Coll. of Wales, Aberystwyth (LLB 1979); Univ. of Bristol (LLM 2010). Called to the Bar, Gray's Inn, 1980; in practice as a barrister, specialising in planning and envmtl law, 1980–. Mem., Planning and Envmt Bar Assoc. *Recreations:* sailing, ski-ing, Rugby. *Address:* No5 Chambers, Greenwood House, 4–7 Salisbury Court, EC4Y 8AA. *T:* 0845 210 5555. *E:* psc@no5.com. *Clubs:* Lansdowne; Blandford Rugby Football.

**CAIRNS,** family name of **Earl Cairns**.

**CAIRNS, 6th Earl** *cr* 1878; **Simon Dallas Cairns,** CVO 2000; CBE 1992; Baron Cairns 1867; Viscount Garmoyle 1878; Founding Chair, Africa's Voices Foundation, since 2014; *b* 27 May 1939; *er s* of 5th Earl Cairns, GCVO, CB and Barbara Jeanne Harrisson, *y d* of Sydney H. Burgess; *S* father, 1989; *m* 1964, Amanda Mary, *d* of late Major E. F. Heathcoat Amory, and Mrs Roderick Heathcoat Amory; three *s*. *Educ:* Eton; Trinity Coll., Cambridge. Man. Dir, 1981–84, a Vice-Chm., 1984–86, Mercury Securities plc; S. G. Warburg & Co.: Man. Dir, 1979–85; Dir, 1985–95; a Vice-Chm., 1985–87; Jt Chm., 1987–91; Chief Exec. and Dep. Chm., 1991–95; Chairman: Commonwealth Develt Corp., subseq. CDC Gp plc, 1995–2004, subseq. Actis, 2004–05; BAT Industries, 1996–98 (Dir, 1990–98); Allied Zurich, 1998–2000; Vice-Chairman: Zurich Financial Services, 1998–2000; Zurich Allied AG, 1998–2000; Dep. Chm., 2004–07, Chm., 2007–10, Zain Africa (formerly Celtel Internat.) BV; Dir, Fresnillo plc, 2008–14. Receiver-General, Duchy of Cornwall, 1990–2000. Mem., City Capital Markets Cttee, 1989–94. Chairman: VSO, 1981–92; ODI, 1995–2002; Commonwealth Business Council, 1997–2002 (Chm. Emeritus, 2003); Look Ahead Housing and Care, 2003–05. Curator, Oxford Univ. Chest, 1995–2000. Trustee, The Diana Princess of Wales Meml Fund, 1998–2006; Dir, M. Ibrahim Foundn, 2007–16; Chm., Charities Aid Foundn, 2003–10. *Heir: s* Viscount Garmoyle, *qv*. *Address:* 39 Arundel Gardens, W11 2LW. *Club:* Turf.

**CAIRNS, (Agnes Lawrie Addie) Shonaig;** *see* Macpherson, A. L. A. S.

**CAIRNS, Rt Hon. Alun (Hugh);** PC 2016; MP (C) Vale of Glamorgan, since 2010; Secretary of State for Wales, since 2016; *b* 30 July 1970; *s* of Hewitt and Margaret Cairns; *m* 1996, Emma Elizabeth Turner; one *s*. *Educ:* Ysgol Gyfun Ddwyieithog Ystalyfera; MBA Wales 2001. Joined Lloyds Bank Gp, 1989; Business Develt Consultant, 1992–98; Field Manager, 1998–99, Lloyds TSB (formerly Lloyds Bank). Mem. (C) S Wales W, Nat. Assembly for Wales, 1999–2011; econ. spokesman, 1997–2007; educn spokesman, 2007–08. Parly Under-Sec. of State, Wales, 2014–16; a Lord Comr of HM Treasury (Govt Whip), 2014–16. Contested (C): Gower, 1997; Vale of Glamorgan, 2005. Joined Conservative Party, 1987. *Address:* House of Commons, SW1A 0AA.

**CAIRNS, Andrew Ruaraidh A.;** *see* Adams-Cairns.

**CAIRNS, David Adam;** writer; Music Critic, Sunday Times, 1985–92; *b* 8 June 1926; *s* of Sir Hugh William Bell Cairns, KBE, FRCS and Barbara Forster Cairns, *d* of A. L. Smith, sometime Master of Balliol; *m* 1959, Rosemary, *d* of Aubrey and Hilary Goodwin; three *s*. *Educ:* Trinity Coll., Oxford (1st Cl. Mod. History). Nat. Service, Intell. Corps, 1949–50. Co-Founder, Chelsea Opera Gp, 1950; Jane Eliza Procter Fellow, Princeton, 1950–51; Liby Clerk, H of C, 1951–53; TES, 1955–58; Music Critic, Evening Standard, and Spectator, 1958–62; Arts Editor, Spectator, 1961–62; Asst Music Critic, Financial Times, 1962–67; Music Critic, New Statesman, 1967–70; Classical Programme Co-ordinator, Philips Records, 1968–73; freelance music critic, 1973–85; founder and conductor, Thorington Players, 1983. Dist. Vis. Prof., Univ. of California, Davis, 1985; Vis. Scholar, Getty Center for History of Art and Humanities, 1992; Vis. Res. Fellow, Merton Coll., Oxford, 1993. FRSL 2001. Hon. RAM 2000. Hon. DLitt Southampton, 2001. CBE 1997; Commandeur de l'Ordre des Arts et des Lettres, 2013 (Chevalier, 1975; Officier, 1991). *Publications:* The Memoirs of Hector Berlioz (ed and trans.), 1969, 5th edn 2002; Responses: musical essays and reviews, 1973; Berlioz, vol. 1, The Making of an Artist 1803–1832, 1989, rev. edn 1999 (Yorkshire Post Prize; Royal Phil. Soc. Award; Derek Allen Meml Prize, British Acad.; ASCAP Deems Taylor Award, 2001), vol. 2, Servitude and Greatness 1832–1869, 1999 (Whitbread Award for Biography, 1999; Royal Phil. Soc. Award, 1999; Samuel Johnson Non-fiction Prize, 2000; Prix de l'Académie Charles Croz, 2003); Mozart and His Operas, 2006; (jtly) English National Opera Guides: The Magic Flute, 1980; Falstaff, 1982. *Recreations:* conducting, Shakespeare, Jane Austen, France and the French, cricket. *Address:* 49 Amerland Road, SW18 1QA. *T:* (020) 8870 4931.

**CAIRNS, David Seldon;** HM Diplomatic Service; Ambassador to Sweden and Director, Nordic Baltic Region, 2015–19; *b* Suffern, NY, 17 April 1969; *s* of Dr Robert Lacock Cairns and Vivienne Cairns; *m* 1996, Sharon Anouk Aberhard; one *s* one *d*. *Educ:* Oundle Sch.; Pembroke Coll., Oxford (MA Oriental Studies 1992). With Nomura Internat., 1992–93; entered FCO, 1993; Desk Officer, Security Policy Dept, FCO, 1993–95; Second Sec., Commercial, Tokyo, 1995–99; Hd, Public Diplomacy, Europe Comd, FCO, 1999–2000; Private Sec. to Ministers for Africa and N Americas, FCO, 2000–02; Hd, WTO Section, Geneva, 2002–06; Dir, Trade and Investment, Tokyo, 2006–10; Dir, Estates and Security, Corporate Services, FCO, 2010–15. Vice-Chm., Japan Soc., 2010–15. Mem., Coton Parish Council, 2010–15. *Recreations:* sport (almost all of them), travel (almost everywhere). *Address:* The Tower House, 5 St Catharine's Hall, Coton, Cambridge CB23 7GU. *T:* (01954) 212481. *E:* David.Cairns@fco.gov.uk. *Club:* Oxford and Cambridge.

**CAIRNS, Prof. Douglas Laidlaw,** PhD; FBA 2018; FRSE; Professor of Classics, University of Edinburgh, since 2004; *b* Glasgow, 10 Jan. 1961; *s* of James Cairns and Mary Cairns; *m* 1986, Nicolette Margaret Davies (*d* 1996); one *s*. *Educ:* Eastbank Acad., Glasgow; Univ. of Glasgow (MA 1983; PhD 1987). Lectr in Greek, Univ. of St Andrews, 1986; Post-doctoral Fellow, Georg-August Universität, Göttingen, 1987–88; Lectr in Classics, Univ. of Otago, 1988–92; Lectr, then Sen. Lectr in Classics, Univ. of Leeds, 1992–99; Lectr, then Sen. Lectr in Classics, Univ. of Glasgow, 1999–2004. Vis. Prof., Kyoto Univ., 2008; George R. Langford Family Dist. Scholar Chair, Florida State Univ., 2012. Mercator Fellow, Johannes Gutenberg Univ., Mainz, 2018–19. MAE 2013; FRSE 2018. Anneliese Maier Prize, Alexander von Humboldt Foundn, 2018. *Publications:* Aidōs: the psychology and ethics of honour and shame in ancient Greek literature, 1993; Bacchylides: five epinician odes, 2010; Sophocles: Antigone, 2016. *Recreations:* music, travel, cinema, food and wine. *Address:* Department of Classics, University of Edinburgh, Edinburgh EH8 9AG. *T:* (0131) 651 1647. *E:* douglas.cairns@ed.ac.uk.

**CAIRNS, Very Rev. John Ballantyne,** KCVO 2013; a Chaplain to the Queen, 1997–2013, an Extra Chaplain, since 2013; Dean: Chapel Royal in Scotland, 2005–13; Order of St John Scotland, since 2011; *b* 15 March 1942; *s* of William Cairns and Isobel Margaret (née Thom); *m* 1968, Elizabeth Emma Bradley; three *s*. *Educ:* Sutton Valence Sch., Kent; Bristol Univ. (LLB); Edinburgh Univ. (LTh). Messrs Richards, Butler & Co., Solicitors, 1964–68; E Lothian CC, 1968–69; Asst Minister, St Giles, Elgin, 1973–75; ordained, 1974; Minister: Langholm, Ewes and Westerkirk, 1975–85, also linked with Canonbie, 1981–85; Riverside, Dumbarton, 1985–2001; Aberlady and Gullane, 2001–09; Locum Minister: St Columba's Church, London, 2010–12; St Mary's Church, Haddington, 2017–. Moderator, Presbytery of Dumbarton, 1993–94. General Assembly of the Church of Scotland: Convener: Cttee on Maintenance of the Ministry and Bd of Ministry and Mission, 1984–88; Cttee on Chaplains to HM Forces, 1993–98; Chm., Judicial Commn, 1993–98; Chaplain to the Moderator, 1995–96; Moderator, 1999–2000; Chaplain to Lord High Comr (HRH the Duke of York), 2007. Gen. Trustee, Church of Scotland, 1996–2017. Chaplain, Queen's Body Guard for Scotland, Royal Co. of Archers, 2007–. Pres., Friends of St Andrew's, Jerusalem, 2005–11; Dunbar Choral Soc., 2018–. Chm. Govs, Compass Sch., Haddington, 2008–15. Hon. DD Aberdeen, 2003; Hon. LLD Bristol, 2004. KStJ 2018. *Publications:* Keeping Fit for Ministry, 1988; articles in various theol jls. *Recreations:* golf, gardening, Robert Burns. *Address:* Bell House, Roxburghe Park, Dunbar, East Lothian EH42 1LR. *T:* (01368) 862501. *Club:* New (Edinburgh).

**CAIRNS, Patricia Rose Marie R.;** *see* Roberts Cairns.

**CAIRNS, Richard James;** Head Master, Brighton College, since 2006; *b* Nairobi, 2 July 1966; *s* of Brian and Christina Cairns. *Educ:* Oratory Sch., Reading; Lady Margaret Hall, Oxford (BA 1st cl. Hons Mod. Hist.; MA). Asst Master, Oratory Sch., Reading, 1989–91; Asst Master, 1991–92, Hd of Hist., 1992–99, Daniel Stewart's and Melville Coll., Edinburgh; Usher, Magdalen College Sch., Oxford, 1999–2005. Dir, Brighton College International Schools Ltd, 2008–. Governor: King's College Sch., Wimbledon, 2009–16; Kingsford Community Sch., Beckton, 2009–; London Acad. of Excellence, 2012–; Brighton Coll. Abu Dhabi, 2012–; Brighton Coll. Al Ain, 2013–; Brighton Coll. Bangkok, 2016–. FRSA. *Recreations:* medieval history, cinema, African wildlife, politics. *Address:* Headmaster's House, Brighton College, Eastern Road, Brighton BN2 0AL. *T:* (01273) 704339. *E:* headmaster@brightoncollege.net. *Club:* Lansdowne.

**CAIRNS, Robert;** Chairman, East of Scotland Water, 1998–2002; *b* 16 July 1947; *s* of William and Mary Cairns; *m* 1st, 1972, Pauline Reidy (marr. diss. 1995); two *s*; 2nd, 2003, Jean Margaret Smith (née Dow). *Educ:* Morgan Acad., Dundee; Univ. of Edinburgh (MA Hons); Moray House Coll. (DipEd). Asst Ed., Scottish Nat. Dictionary, 1969–74; teacher, James Gillespie's High Sch., 1975–96. Mem. (Lab), Edinburgh CC, 1974–2007 (Convener, Planning Cttee, 1986; Exec. Mem. for Envmt and Streets, 2003–07). Contested (Lab) N Edinburgh, Nov. 1973, Feb. 1974. *Recreations:* walking, photography, genealogy. *Address:* Eastergate Cottage, Harrietfield, Logiealmond, Perthshire PH1 3TD.

**CAITHNESS, 20th Earl of,** *cr* 1455; **Malcolm Ian Sinclair,** PC 1990; FRICS; Lord Berriedale, 1455; Bt 1631; consultant and trustee to various companies and trusts, since 1994; Chief Executive, Clan Sinclair Trust, since 1999; *b* 3 Nov. 1948; *s* of 19th Earl of Caithness, CVO, CBE, DSO, DL, JP; *S* father, 1965; *m* 1st, 1975, Diana Caroline (*d* 1994), *d* of Major Richard Coke, DSO, MC, DL; one *s* one *d*; 2nd, 2004, Leila Jenkins (marr. diss. 2007); 3rd, 2015, Diana Penelope Wilson. *Educ:* Marlborough; Royal Agricl Coll., Cirencester. Savills, land and estate agents, 1972–78; Brown and Mumford, 1978–80; property developer and other small businesses, 1980–84. A Lord in Waiting (Govt Whip), 1984–85; parly spokesman on health and social security, 1984–85, on Scotland, 1984–86; Parly Under-Sec. of State, Dept of Transport, 1985–86; Minister of State: Home Office, 1986–88; DoE, 1988–89; Paymaster Gen. and Minister of State, HM Treasury, 1989–90; Minister of State: FCO, 1990–92; Dept of Transport, 1992–94; elected Mem., H of L, 1999. Dir, 1995–98, Consultant, 1998–2006, Victoria Soames, Residential Property Consultants; Consultant, Rickett-Tinne, 2006–. Trustee, 1996–2016, Vice Patron, 2017–, Queen Elizabeth Castle of Mey Trust. *Heir: s* Lord Berriedale, *qv*. *Address:* c/o House of Lords, SW1A 0PW.

**CALATRAVA-VALLS, Dr Santiago;** architect; *b* Valencia, 28 July 1951; *m* 1976, Robertina Calatrava-Maragoni; three *s*. *Educ:* art sch., Valencia; Escuela Técnica Superior de Arquitectura de Valencia; Swiss Fed. Inst. of Technol., Zürich (studies in civil engrg; Dr Tech. Sci.). Asst. Inst. for Bldg Statics and Construction and for Aerodynamics and Light Weight Constructions, Zürich, 1979–81; Founder: architectural and civil engrg practice, Zürich, 1981; architectural practice, Paris, 1989, and Valencia, 1991. Major projects include: Stadelhofen Rly Stn, Zürich, 1983–90; Lucerne Stn Hall, 1983–89; BCE Place, Toronto, 1987–92; Alamillo Bridge and La Cartuja Viaduct, Seville, 1987–92; Lusitania Bridge, Merida, 1988–91; Montjuic Communication Tower, Barcelona, 1989–92; Lyon Airport Rly Stn, 1989–94; Campo Volantin Footbridge, Bilbao, 1990–97; Alameda Bridge and underground stn, Valencia, 1991–95; Kuwait Pavilion, Expo '92, Seville, 1991–92; Auditorio de Tenerife, 1991–2003; Oriente Rly Stn, Lisbon, 1993–98; Sondica Airport, Bilbao, 2000; Milwaukee Art Mus. expansion, 2001; Olympic Sports Complex, Athens, 2004; Zürich Univ. Law Faculty, 2004; Turning Torso Tower, Malmö, 2005; Petah-Tikva Footbridge, Tel Aviv, 2006; Reggio Emilia Ponti, 2007; Puente de L'Assut d'Or, Valencia, 2008; Quarto Ponte sul Canal Grande, Venice, 2008; Palau de las Arts, Valencia, 2008; Light Rail Train Bridge, Jerusalem, 2008; Liège Guillemins TGV Railway Station, 2009; Samuel Beckett Bridge, Dublin, 2009; New York City Ballet, 2010; World Trade Center Transportation Hub, NY, 2016; Ponte Sul Crati, Cosenza, 2018. Exhibitions of work include: Mus. of Architecture, Basel, 1987; Design Mus., Zürich, 1991; Mus. of Modern Art, NY, 1993; retrospective, RIBA, London, 1992; Deutsches Mus., Munich, 1993; Valencia, Lübeck and Copenhagen, 1993; Florence, 2000. Member: Union of Swiss Architects, 1987; Internat. Acad. of Architecture, 1987; European Acad., 1992. Hon. FRIBA 1993. Hon. Mem., Union of German Architects, 1989. Hon. doctorates include Dr *hc*: Valencia, 1993; Seville, 1994. Numerous international prizes and awards including: Internat. Assoc. for Bridge and Structural Engrg Award, 1988; Gold Medal, IStructE, 1992. *Address:* Parkring 11, 8002 Zürich, Switzerland. *T:* (1) 204500, *Fax:* (1) 2045001.

**CALCRAFT, Helen Victoria;** Founding Partner, Lucky Generals, since 2013; *b* St Albans, 18 Nov. 1966; *d* of Prof. Patrick Karl O'Brien, *qv*; two *d*. *Educ:* Lord William's Sch., Thame; Royal Holloway Coll., Univ. of London (BA Drama and Theatre Studies); London Business Sch. (MBA with Dist.). New Business Dir then Bd Dir, AMV-BBDO, 1989–99; Co-founder, Man. Dir, 1999–2007, CEO, 2007–09, MCBD; Chm., Dare, 2010–12. Trustee, CRUK, 2010–16. Mem., WACL, 2000– (Pres., 2006); Founder Mem., Steering Cttee, timeTo. *Address:* Lucky Generals, 160 Exmouth House, 3–11 Pine Street, EC1R 0JH. *T:* (020) 3371 6360. *E:* Helen.calcraft@luckygenerals.com. *Club:* Thirty.

**CALDAS, Prof. Carlos Manuel Simao da Silva,** MD; FRCP, FRCPath, FACP, FMedSci; Professor of Cancer Medicine (formerly Clinical Oncology), University of Cambridge, since 2002; Hon. Consultant, Addenbrooke's Hospital, Cambridge, since 1996, Director, Cambridge Breast Cancer Research Unit, since 2008; *b* 27 June 1960; *s* of Carlos da Silva Caldas and Isilda de Jesus Catarino Simão; *m* 1988, Maria Isabel Rebelo de Andrade e Sousa; one *s* one *d*. *Educ:* Univ. of Lisbon (MD 1984). FACP 1999; FRCP 2002; FRCPath 2008. Jun. House Officer, 1985–86, SHO, 1986–88, Santa Maria Univ. Hosp., Lisbon; Resident in Internal Medicine, Univ. of Texas Southwestern Med. Center, Dallas, 1988–91; Fellow in Med. Oncology, Johns Hopkins Univ. and Med. Instns, Baltimore, 1991–94; Sen. Res. Fellow, Chester Beatty Lab., Inst. of Cancer Res., London, 1994–96. FMedSci 2004; Fellow, Eur. Acad. of Cancer Scis, 2010. Dr *hc* Porto, 2014. Officer, Order of St James of the Sword (Portugal), 2009. *Publications:* articles in New England Jl of Medicine, Nature, Nature Genetics, Cell, Cancer Res., Oncogene, Science Translational Medicine, EMBO Molecular Medicine. *Recreations:* supporter of Benfica (the team of Eusebio), lover of Santa Cruz beach, Portugal. *Address:* Functional Breast Cancer Genomics Laboratory, Cancer Research UK Cambridge Research Institute and Department of Oncology, University of Cambridge, Li Ka Shing Centre, Robinson Way, Cambridge CB2 0RE. *T:* (01223) 769648, *Fax:* (01223) 769510. *E:* cc234@cam.ac.uk.

**CALDECOTE,** 3rd Viscount *cr* 1939, of Bristol, co. Gloucester; **Piers James Hampden Inskip;** *b* 20 May 1947; *o s* of 2nd Viscount Caldecote, KBE, DSC and Jean Hamilla, *d* of Rear-Adm. H. D. Hamilton; *S* father, 1999; *m* 1st, 1970, Susan Bridget (*née* Mellen); 2nd, 1984, Kristine Elizabeth, *d* of Harvey Holbrooke-Jackson; one *s*. *Educ:* Eton; Magdalene Coll., Cambridge. Gp Exec., Carlton Communications, 1989–2004. *Heir: s* Hon. Thomas James Inskip, *b* 22 March 1985. *Address:* 18 Langside Avenue, SW15 5QT.

**CALDECOTT, Andrew Hilary;** QC 1994; *b* 22 June 1952; *s* of Andrew Caldecott, CBE and Zita (*née* Belloc); *m* 1977, Rosamond Ashton Shuttleworth; two *s* two *d*. *Educ:* Eton Coll.; New Coll., Oxford (BA Hons Mod. Hist.). Called to the Bar, Inner Temple, 1975, Bencher, 2004. Specialist Advr to Jt Parly Select Cttee on Defamation Bill, 2011. Play: Higher than Babel, Bridewell Theatre, 1999. *Publications:* novels: Rotherweird, 2017; Wyntertide, 2018; Lost Acre, 2019. *Address:* 5 Raymond Buildings, WC1R 5AH.

**CALDECOTT, Benjamin,** FRAS, FRGS; Director, Oxford Sustainable Finance Programme, since 2013, Senior Research Fellow, since 2019 and Associate Professor, since 2019, Smith School of Enterprise and the Environment, University of Oxford (Visiting Fellow, 2012–13); *b* London, 30 June 1985; *s* of Dr Julian Caldecott and Hong Caldecott (*née* Tan). *Educ:* Sch. of Oriental and African Studies, Univ. of London (BSc Hons Econs); Selwyn Coll., Cambridge (MPhil Chinese Studies and Econs); Brasenose Coll., Oxford (DPhil Econ. Geog.). FRAS 2005; FRGS 2006. Res. Dir, Envmt and Energy, Policy Exchange, 2008–09; Hd of Policy, Climate Change Capital Gp Ltd, 2009–13; Dep. Dir (on secondment), Strategy Directorate, DECC, 2010–11; Hd of Govt Adv., Bloomberg New Energy Finance, 2013–14; Policy Associate, (on secondment), Strategy Directorate, DEFRA, 2018–. Member, Senior Common Room: Brasenose Coll., Oxford, 2012–14; Oriel Coll., Oxford, 2014–. Visiting Scholar: Peking Univ., 2007; Stanford Univ., 2016–; Visiting Researcher: Internat. Inst. of Green Finance, Central Univ. of Finance and Economics, 2018–; Alan Turing Inst., 2019–; Visiting Fellow: Univ. of Sydney, 2015; Univ. of Melbourne, 2016; non-resident Fellow, Payne Inst. for Earth Resources, Colorado Sch. of Mines, 2018–. Sherpa, Green Investment Bank Commn, 2010; Internat. Visitor, Leadership Prog., US Dept of State, 2011; Academic Visitor, Bank of England, 2015–. Co-Founder and Mem. Bd, Cons. Envmt Network, 2008–. Chair, Energy and Envmt, and Sen. Associate Fellow, Bright Blue, 2014–19. Member: Socially Responsible Investment Review Cttee, Univ. of Oxford, 2014–; Bd, Commonwealth Climate and Law Initiative, 2015–; City of London Green Finance Initiative, 2016– (Chair, Wkg Gp on Data, Disclosure and Risk, 2017–); Academic Adv. Gp, One Bank Res. Steering Cttee, Bank of England, 2016–; UK Green Finance Taskforce, 2017–18 (Chair, Disclosure Workstream, 2017–18); Expert Adv. Gp, Centre for Global Disaster Protection, 2018–; Adv. Bd, UK Green Finance Inst., 2018–; Advr, One Planet Sovereign Wealth Fund Wkg Gp, 2018–. Trustee, Green Alliance, 2010–. Founder and Co-Chair, Global Res. Alliance for Sustainable Finance and Investment, 2017–. Advr, Prince of Wales's Charitable Foundn (formerly Prince's Charities' Internat. Sustainability Unit), 2014–17; Expert Panel, Prince of Wales's Accounting for Sustainability Project, 2016–. Associate Editor, Jl of Sustainable Finance and Investment, 2015–. Sir Peter Holmes Meml Award, RSAA, 2005. *Recreations:* travelling, entertaining, gardening, walking, scuba diving, opera, historical fiction, watching tennis, fine wine, good food, good company. *Address:* Smith School of Enterprise and the Environment, University of Oxford, South Parks Road, Oxford OX1 3QY. *E:* ben.caldecott@smithschool.ox.ac.uk. *Clubs:* Travellers (Mem., Election Cttee, 2008–14), 5 Hertford Street.

**CALDER, Prof. Andrew Alexander,** MBE 2018; MD; FRCSE, FRCPGlas, FRCPE, FRCOG; Professor of Obstetrics and Gynaecology, 1987–2009, now Emeritus, and Assistant Principal for Reproductive Health, 2009–15, University of Edinburgh; Hon. Consultant Obstetrician and Gynaecologist, 1987–2009, and Scientific Director, Jennifer Brown Research Laboratory, 2004–12, Queen's Medical Research Institute, Royal Infirmary of Edinburgh; *b* 17 Jan. 1945; *s* of Rev. Alastair Scott Calder and Aileen Calder (*née* Alexander); *m* 1972, Valerie Anne Dugard; one *s* two *d*. *Educ:* Glasgow Acad.; Glasgow Univ. Med. Sch. (MB ChB 1968; MD 1978). FRCOG 1984; FRCPGlas 1987; FRCPE 1993; FRCSE 1994. Res. Fellow, Nuffield Dept of Obstetrics and Gynaecology, Univ. of Oxford, 1972–75; Lectr, then Sen. Lectr in Obstetrics and Gynaecology, Univ. of Glasgow, 1975–86; University of Edinburgh: Vice Dean of Medicine, 1998–2003; Hd, Div. of Reproductive and Develtl Scis, 1999–2009; Dir of Quality Assce, Coll. of Medicine and Vet. Medicine, 2003–09; Scientific Dir, Tommy's Centre for Maternal and Fetal Health, Queen's Med. Res. Inst., Royal Infirmary of Edinburgh, 2007–09. Chm., Acad. of Royal Colls and Faculties in Scotland, 2001–04. British Exchange Prof., UCLA, 1992; Vis. Prof., Univ. of Pretoria, 2005; Hon. Prof., Sch. of Medicine, Univ. of St Andrews, 2012–17. Chairman: Tenovus Scotland, 2011–19; Scotland's Churches Trust, 2015–19. Hon. FCOG(SA) 2005. *Publications:* (with W. Dunlop) High Risk Pregnancy, 1992; (with J. O. Drife) Prostaglandins and the Uterus, 1992; (jtly) Munro Kerr's Operative Obstetrics, 11th (centenary) edn 2007, 12th edn, 2013; numerous scientific papers in Lancet, British Jl of Obstetrics and Gynaecology, Human Reproduction, etc. *Recreations:* music (especially organ), golf, curling, medical history. *Address:* Simpson Centre for Reproductive Health, Royal Infirmary, 51 Little France Crescent, Edinburgh EH16 4SA. *T:* (0131) 242 2694. *E:* a.a.calder@ed.ac.uk. *Clubs:* New (Edinburgh); Honourable Company of Edinburgh Golfers (Muirfield).

**CALDER, Elisabeth Nicole,** CBE 2018; Director, Full Circle Editions, since 2009; *b* 20 Jan. 1938; *d* of Florence Mary Baber and Ivor George Baber; *m* 1st, 1958, Richard Henry Calder (marr. diss. 1972); one *d* one *s*; 2nd, 2000, Louis Baum. *Educ:* Broadfields, Edgware; Palmerston North Girls' High Sch., NZ; Canterbury Univ., NZ (BA 1958). Reader, Metro-Goldwyn-Mayer story dept, 1969–70; Publicity Manager, Victor Gollancz, 1971–74; Editorial Director: Victor Gollancz, 1975–78; Jonathan Cape, 1979–86; Publisher (formerly Publishing Dir), Bloomsbury Publishing, 1986–2009. Chair, Royal Ct Th., 2000–03. Mem. Bd, Folio Prize, 2013–. Founder Dir, Groucho Club, 1985–95; Co-founder and Pres., Internat. Fest. of Literature, Parati, Brazil, 2003; Founder Dir, Flipside Fest., 2013–; Trustee, Wonderful Beast Th. Co., 2012–16. Hon. FRSL 2018 (Benson Medal, 2018). DUniv University Campus Suffolk, 2012; Hon. DLitt Canterbury, NZ, 2019. Order of Merit for Culture (Brazil), 2004; Nat. Order of the Southern Cross, 2004. *Recreations:* reading, theatre, music – esp. Brazilian, thinking about gardening, junking.

**CALDER, Dr Ian Maddison,** TD 1973; FRCPath; FFOM; Medical Director, Medico-Legal Centre, London, 2005–15; Prosector and Demonstrator in Morphology and Applied Anatomy, University of Cambridge, since 2017; *s* of late Walter James Calder, MIMechE, and Alice (*née* Maddison); *m* 1964, Dorothy Joan Hubbard, MBE, RGN; one *s* one *d*. *Educ:* Norwich Sch.; Univ. of St Andrews (MB ChB 1962; State Scholar); Univ. of Dundee (MD 1977; DSc 1992). MRCPath 1981, FRCPath 1996; FFOM 1990; FCPath (HK) 1993; MRCP 1996. Served RA, 1955 (2nd Lieut); Hon. Col, 254 Field Ambulance, RAMC (V), 1991; Mem., E Anglia TAVRA Cttee, 1990. Lectr in Forensic Medicine, St George's Hosp. Med. Sch., Univ. of London, 1972–76; Lectr, London Hosp. Med. Coll., 1976–81, then Hon. Lectr; Lectr in Forensic Science, Anglia Ruskin Univ., Cambridge, 2005–16. Visiting Fellow: St Edmund's Coll., Cambridge, 1978; Wellcome Inst. of Comparative Neurology, Univ. of Cambridge, 1978–; Travelling Scholar, UCLA, 1976; Advr to Nat. Undersea Res. Centre, Univ. of N Carolina. Ext. Examr, Univ. of Hong Kong, 1985–90; Advr to Labour Dept, Hong Kong, 1991–94; Consultant advr on occupational medicine, MoD, 1994–2000; Advr to E and N Herts NHS Trust, 2000–04. Member: MoD Ethical Cttee, 1983–2016; DoH Dangerous Pathogens Working Party; E Anglia MoD Pension Adv. Cttee for Veterans; Council, Order of St John, Cambs. Mem., Physicians for Human Rights. *Publications:* chapters in textbooks of pathology and occupational medicine; papers on diving and hyperbaric medicine research. *Recreations:* sailing, boat-building, antique furniture and cabinet making, rowing, church music, industrial archaeology. *Address:* Thorpe, Huntingdon Road, Girton, Cambridge CB3 0LG. *T:* (01223) 277220. *Club:* Athenæum.

**CALDER, Julian Richard;** Director of Statistical Support Services (formerly Survey and Statistical Services) Group, Office for National Statistics, 1996–2000; *b* 6 Dec. 1941; *s* of Donald Alexander and Ivy O'Nora Calder; *m* 1965, Avril Tucker; two *s*. *Educ:* Dulwich College; Brasenose College, Oxford; Birkbeck College, London. Statistician, 1973, Chief Statistician, 1978, Central Statistical Office; Chief Statistician, 1981, Dir of Stats, 1985–94, Board of Inland Revenue; Hd of Div., Govt Statistical Service and Gen. Div., Central Statistical Office, 1994–96. *Recreations:* cycling, listening to music.

**CALDER, Prof. Muffy,** OBE 2011; PhD; FRSE; FREng, FIEE, FBCS; Professor of Computer Science, since 1998, and Vice Principal and Head, College of Science and Engineering, since 2014, University of Glasgow; *b* Shawinigan, Québec, 21 May 1958; *d* of Carmen van Thomas and Lois van Thomas (*née* Hallen); *m* 1998, David Calder. *Educ:* Univ. of Stirling (BSc); Univ. of St Andrews (PhD 1987). FRSE 2000; FIEE 2002; FBCS 2002; FREng 2013. British Ship Res. Assoc., 1977; with Burroughs Computers; Dept of Computer Sci., Univ. of Edinburgh, 1983–84; Dept of Computing Sci. and Maths, Univ. of Stirling, 1984–87; University of Glasgow, 1988–: Hd, Computing Sci., 2004–07; Dean of Res., Coll. of Sci. and Engrg, 2010–12; Chief Scientific Advr for Scotland, 2012–14. BT Res. Fellow, BT Labs, Martlesham, 1992–; Vis. Scientist, Systems Res. Center, Digital Equipt Corp., Calif, 1994. Chair, UK Computing Res. Cttee, 2009–11; Mem., UKRI-EPSRC (formerly EPSRC), 2015–. *Publications:* contribs to scientific jls. *Recreations:* running, string quartet (violin). *Address:* School of Computing Science, Sir Alwyn Williams Building, Lilybank Gardens, University of Glasgow, Glasgow G12 8RZ. *E:* muffy.calder@glasgow.ac.uk. *Club:* Westerlands Cross Country.

**CALDER, Simon Peter Ritchie;** Travel Correspondent, The Independent, since 1994; *b* Crawley, 25 Dec. 1955; *s* of late Nigel David Ritchie Calder; *m* 1997, Charlotte Hindle; two *d*. *Educ:* Univ. of Warwick (BSc Maths). Studio Manager, BBC Radio, 1979–94; presenter, BBC TV, 1996–. *Publications:* No Frills: the truth behind the low-cost revolution in the skies, 2002, 3rd edn 2006. *Recreations:* cycling, walking, hitch-hiking. *Address:* The Independent, Northcliffe House, 2 Derry Street, W8 5HF. *W:* www.simoncalder.com, www.twitter.com/SimonCalder.

**CALDERWOOD, (Andrew) Bruce;** Director of Mental Health and Disability, Department of Health, 2009–13; *b* 14 March 1954; *s* of Bob and Betty Calderwood; *m* 1989, Vivienne Bennett; two *s* one *d*. *Educ:* York Univ. (BA Hons Philosophy and English). Chocolate packer, Rowntrees, 1978–79; computer programmer, CCTA, 1979–81; Policy Advr, DHSS, 1981–92; Policy Manager, DSS, 1993–95; Advr, Premier's Dept, Victoria, 1995–96; Business Architect, DSS, 1997–2002; Dir, Older People, 2003–04, Dir, Disability and Carers Directorate, 2004–09, Dir, Office for Disability Issues, 2005–09, DWP. Mem., Social Security Adv. Cttee, 2016–. Chair, Avenues SE. *Recreations:* my allotment, hill walking, cooking, malt whisky, reading, films.

**CALDERWOOD, Catherine Jane,** FRCOG; Consultant Obstetrician and Gynaecologist, NHS Lothian, since 2006; Chief Medical Officer, Scottish Government, since 2015 (Deputy Chief Medical Officer, 2014–15); *b* Belfast, 26 Dec. 1968; *d* of James and Lesley Calderwood; one *s* two *d*. *Educ:* Methodist Coll., Belfast; Newnham Coll., Cambridge (BA 1990); Glasgow Univ. (MB ChB 1993). FRCOG 2015. Trainee in Obstetrics and Gynaecology, SE Scotland, 2001–06; trainee in maternal medicine, St Thomas' Hosp., 2003–04; SMO, Scottish Govt, 2010–14; Nat. Clin. Dir, Maternity and Women's Health, NHS England, 2013–15. Hon. FRCPE 2012. *Recreations:* laughter, family, friends, golf, running, climbing hills. *Address:* Scottish Government Health Department, St Andrews House, Regent Road, Edinburgh EH1 3DG. *E:* cmo@gov.scot.

**CALDICOTT, Dame Fiona,** DBE 1996; FRCP, FRCPsych; Principal, Somerville College, Oxford, 1996–2010; a Pro-Vice-Chancellor, Oxford University, 2001–10 (Pro-Vice-Chancellor (Personnel and Equal Opportunities), 2005–09); National Data Guardian for Health and Social Care, since 2014; *b* 12 Jan. 1941; *d* of Joseph Maurice Soesan and Elizabeth Jane (*née* Ransley); *m* 1965, Robert Gordon Woodruff Caldicott; one *d* (one *s* decd). *Educ:* City of London Sch. for Girls; St Hilda's Coll., Oxford (MA, BM, BCh; Hon. Fellow 1996). DPM; FRCPsych 1985; FRCP 1995; FRCPI 1996; FRCGP 1996. House Surgeon and Physician, Coventry Hosps, 1966–67; General Practice, Family Planning and Child Welfare, 1968–70; training in Psychiatry, Walsgrave Hosp., Coventry and Central Hosp., Warwick, 1970–74; Sen. Registrar in Psychiatry, W Midlands Regl Trng Scheme, 1977–79; Consultant Psychiatrist, Univ. of Warwick, 1979–85; Consultant Psychotherapist, Uffculme Clinic, Birmingham, 1979–96; Sen. Clinical Lectr in Psychotherapy, Univ. of Birmingham, 1982–96; Unit General Manager, Mental Health, Central Birmingham, 1989–91; Clin. Dir, Adult Psychiatric and Psychotherapy Service, Mental Health Unit, S Birmingham, 1991–94; Med. Dir, S Birmingham Mental Health NHS Trust, 1994–96

(Hon. Consultant Psychiatrist, 1996–2012). Non-executive Director: Coventry Building Soc., 1997–2001; Oxford Univ. Hosps (formerly Oxford Radcliffe Hosps) NHS Foundn Trust, 2002–19 (Chm., 2009–19). Chairman: Cttee to Review Patient-Identifiable Information, reported 1997; Cttee to Review Confidentiality and Sharing of Health and Social Care Information, 2012–13; Nat. Information Governance Bd, 2011–13; Rev. of Data Security and Consent/Opt Outs for Sec. of State for Health, 2015–16; Mem., Sec. of State's Standing Adv. Cttee, on Med. Workforce (formerly Manpower) Planning, 1991–2000. Mem., Broadcasting Standards Commn (formerly Council), 1996–2001. Pres., Section for Psychiatry, 1995–99 (Sec., 1991–95), Sec., European Bd of Psychiatry, 1992–96, Union of European Med. Specialists; Member: Council: BMA, 1996–2000 (Chm., Bd of Med. Educn, 1996–2000); RSocMed, 1996–99; Acad. Med. Sci., 1998–2001; GMC, 1999–2003; UN Univ., 2011–16; Mem., Hebdomadal Council, 1998–2000, Council, 2000–09, Oxford Univ.; Lay Mem. Council, Warwick Univ., 2011–16. Sub-Dean 1987–90, Dean 1990–93, Pres., 1993–96, RCPsych; Chm., Acad. of Med. Royal Colls, 1995–96. Pres., British Assoc. of Counselling, 2000–06. Consultant Advr to Commissioning Bd for High Security Psychiatric Care, 1996–2000. Chm., Ind. Inquiry Panel into Umar Farouk Mutallab's time at UCL, 2009–10. Trustee: Zito Trust, 1994–2009; Bethlem Art and History Collections Trust, 1995–99; Nuffield Trust, 1998–2008. Patron: Oxford Healthy Living Centre, 1996–2005; Family Nurturing Network, Oxford, 1997–2009; Hon. Pres., Guild of Health Writers, 1996–99. Founder FMedSci 1998; Fellow, Acad. of Medicine, Singapore, 1994; Mem., Czech Psychiatric Soc., 1994. Hon. DSc Warwick, 1997; Hon. MD Birmingham, 1997. Chevalier du Tastevin, 1991. Lifetime Achievement Award, First Women, 2017. *Publications:* contrib. Discussing Doctors' Careers (ed Isobel Allen), 1988; papers in Bull. RCPsych, Current Opinion in Psychiatry, Postgraduate Psychiatry. *Recreations:* family, friends, reading, wine. *Address:* 27 High Street, Warwick CV34 4AX. *Club:* Royal Society of Medicine.

**CALDICOTT, Gillian Anne;** Director, British Council, Sri Lanka, since 2017; *b* 14 July 1954; *d* of Ronald Frederick Caldicott and Grace Anne Caldicott; partner, Jan Alexander Kingsley; one *s. Educ:* University Coll., Cardiff (BA Lit. and Lang. 1975); Dip. Teaching English to Adults; Nottingham Trent Univ. (Cert. Teaching in Further Educn); Univ. of Reading (MA Applied Linguistics 1985); Open Univ. (MBA 1992). Teaching posts in UK, Spain and Syria, 1976–86; British Council: Dep. Teaching Centre Manager, Thessaloniki, Greece, 1986–89; Teaching Centre Manager, Kuwait, 1989–90; Product Develt Manager, Central Mgt of Direct Teaching, 1990–93; Hd, Press and PR, 1993–95; Dir, Milan, 1995–98; Dep. Dir and Dir, English Lang. Services, Hong Kong, 1998–2002; Dep. Dir, Egypt, 2002–04; Project Manager, Regionalisation, 2004–05; Regl Dir (Europe and Latin America), English and Exams, 2005–07; Dir, Business Develt (English), 2007–08; Dir, Portugal, 2008–13; Dir, Operations, India, 2013–17. *Recreations:* scuba diving, archaeology, literature, travelling, wildlife photography. *Address:* British Council, 49 Alfred House, Gardens, Colombo 00300, Sri Lanka.

**CALDWELL, Dr Darwin Gordon,** FREng; Research Director, since 2006, and Deputy Director, since 2016, Italian Institute of Technology; *b* Ballymena, NI, 2 Feb. 1964; *s* of John Gordon Caldwell and Norah Scott Caldwell (*née* Kennedy); partner, Sandra Skeels; two *s* one *d. Educ:* Ballymena Acad.; Univ. of Hull (BSc 1986; PhD 1990); Univ. of Salford (MSc). FREng 2015. University of Salford: Lectr, 1989–96; Sen. Lectr, 1996–97; Reader, 1997–98; Prof. of Advanced Robotics, 1998–2006. Hon. Professor: Univ. of Bangor, 2006–; Univ. of Manchester, 2007–16; Univ. of Sheffield, 2007–16; KCL, 2008–; Tianjin Univ., China, 2011–. *Publications:* Advanced Robotics and Intelligent Machines, 1995; (ed) Robotics and Automation in the Food Industry: current and future technologies, 2012; contribs to learned jls on robotics and automation. *Recreations:* sport, reading, cinema, family. *Address:* Italian Institute of Technology, Via Morego 30, Genoa 16163, Italy. *T:* (010) 71781407, 427. *E:* Darwin.Caldwell@iit.it.

**CALDWELL, Dr David Hepburn;** Keeper, Department of Scotland and Europe, 2004–12, and Department of Archaeology, 2011–12, National Museums Scotland; *b* 15 Dec. 1951; *s* of Alexander Caldwell and Dorothy (*née* Hepburn); *m* 1975, Margaret McGovern; one *s* two *d. Educ:* Ardrossan Acad.; Edinburgh Univ. (MA; PhD 1982). Curator, Nat. Mus. of Antiquities of Scotland, 1973–85; Asst Keeper, Scottish Medieval Collections, 1985–2001, Keeper, Hist. and Applied Art Dept, 2001–04, Nat. Mus of Scotland. Chair, Fife Cultural Trust, 2017–. Pres., Soc. of Antiquaries of Scotland, 2014–; Vice-Pres., Soc. for Post Medieval Archaeology, 2014–17 (Pres., 2011–14). *Publications:* The Scottish Armoury, 1979; Scottish Weapons and Fortifications, 1981; Scotland's Wars and Warriors, 1999; An Historical Guide to Islay, Jura and Colonsay, 2001; Islay: the land of the Lordship, 2008; The Lewis Chessmen Unmasked, 2010; The Lewis Chessmen: new perspectives, 2014. *Recreations:* travel, table tennis, sewing.

**CALDWELL, Sir Edward (George),** KCB 2002 (CB 1990); Parliamentary Counsel, Law Commission, 2002–06; *b* 21 Aug. 1941; *s* of Arthur Francis Caldwell and Olive Caldwell (*née* Riddle); *m* 1st, 1965, Bronwen Crockett (marr. diss.); two *d*; 2nd, 1992, Dr Helen Janet Beynon (*see* H. J. Caldwell); two step *d. Educ:* St Andrew's, Singapore; Clifton College; Worcester College, Oxford. Law Commission, 1967–69, 1975–77, 1986–88; joined Office of Parly Counsel, 1969: Parly Counsel, 1981–99; First Parly Counsel, 1999–2002. Hon. QC 2002; Hon. Bencher, Inner Temple, 2005. Patron, Human Rights Lawyers' Assoc. Mem. Cttee, Clarity. *Address:* The Old School, School Lane, Chilson, Chipping Norton, Oxon OX7 3HT.

**CALDWELL, Dr Helen Janet, (Lady Caldwell),** CB 2007; Parliamentary Counsel, 2002–08; *b* 13 Sept. 1952; *d* of George Neville Burtenshaw and Margaret Deforel Burtenshaw (*née* Rose); *m* 1st, 1975, Gareth Wyn Beynon (marr. diss.); two *d*; 2nd, 1992, Sir Edward George Caldwell, *qv*; two step *d. Educ:* Dunottar Sch., Reigate; Reigate Co. Sch. for Girls; Girton Coll., Cambridge (Exhibnr; MA); Wolfson Coll., Oxford (DPhil). Called to the Bar, Lincoln's Inn, 1975 (Hardwick Schol.); Lectr in Law, Univ. of Reading, 1979–87; joined Parliamentary Counsel Office, 1987; at Law Commn, 1996–99; Head of Drafting Team: Tax Law Rewrite Project, 1999–2001; Law Commn, 2001–02. *Publications:* contrib. articles to Law Qly Rev., Modern Law Rev., Criminal Law Rev., etc.
*See also* A. J. Burtenshaw.

**CALDWELL, Prof. John,** PhD, DSc; CBiol, FRSB; Chairman, Health Education Thames Valley, 2014–16; *b* 4 April 1947; *s* of Reginald and Marian Caldwell; *m* 1969, Jill Gregory; two *s. Educ:* Chelsea Coll., Univ. of London (BPharm 1969); St Mary's Hosp. Med. Sch. (PhD Biochem. 1972); DSc Pharmacol. London, 1987. CBiol, FRSB (FIBiol 1992). St Mary's Hospital Medical School: Lecturer: in Biochem., 1972–74; in Biochem. Pharmacol., 1974–78; Sen. Lectr, 1978–82; Reader in Drug Metabolism, 1982–88; Prof. of Biochem. Toxicol., 1988–2002; Hd, Dept of Pharmacol. and Toxicol., 1992–97; Dean, ICSM at St Mary's, 1995–97; Hd, Div. of Biomed. Scis, 1997–2002, Hd, Undergrad. Medicine, 2000–02, Imperial Coll. London; Dean, Faculty of Medicine, 2002–08, Pro-Vice-Chancellor, 2007–12, Exec. Pro-Vice-Chancellor, Faculty of Health and Life Scis, 2008–10, Univ. of Liverpool. Fondation Herbette Vis. Prof., Univ. of Lausanne, 1986; Sterling-Winthrop Dist. Prof., Univ. of Michigan Med. Center, 1995. Dir and Co-founder, Amedis Pharmaceuticals Ltd, 2000–02; Chairman: MorEx Develt Partners LLP, 2008–; Drouzin Therapies Ltd, 2014–; non-executive Director: Eden Biopharma Gp Ltd, 2004–10; ULive plc, 2008–12. Chm., Mid-Staffs NHS Foundn Trust, 2012–14; Dir, Liverpool Sci. Park, 2008–11. Non-executive Director: St Mary's Hosp. NHS Trust, 1995–98; Cheshire and Merseyside Strategic HA, 2003–06; NW Strategic HA, 2006–11. Chm., Scientific Cttee, NW Cancer Res., Fund, 2003–09. Pres., Internat. Soc. for Study of Xenobiotics, 1994–95 (Hon. Mem., 2001). Hon. MRCP 1998; Hon. Mem., Canadian Soc. for Pharmaceutical Scis, 2002. Founder and Ed., Chirality, 1989– (Best New Jl in Sci., Technol. and Medicine Award, Assoc. Amer. Publishers, 1991). *Publications:* (ed) Amphetamines and Related Stimulants: chemical, biological, clinical and sociological aspects, 1980; *edited jointly:* Metabolic Basis of Detoxication, 1982; Sulfate Metabolism and Sulfate Conjugation, 1982; Biological Basis of Detoxication, 1983; Foreign Compound Metabolism, 1984; Microsomes and Drug Oxidations, 1985; Xenobiotic Conjugation Chemistry, 1986; Metabolism of Xenobiotics, 1988; Intermediary Xenobiotic Metabolism in Animals, 1989; Biochemistry and Redox Reactions, 1994; Organic Stereochemistry: guiding principles and biomedicinal relevance, 2014; contribs on drug metabolism. *Recreations:* weekends in good hotels, Venice, theatre. *E:* john@drouzin.co.uk. *Club:* Athenæum.

**CALDWELL, Prof. John Anthony,** DPhil; Titular Professor of Music, University of Oxford, 1999–2005; Senior Research Fellow, Jesus College, Oxford, 1999–2005, now Emeritus Fellow; *b* 6 July 1938; *s* of George Wilfrid Caldwell and Susannah Marion Caldwell (*née* Haywood); *m* 1967, Janet Susan Kellar; one *s* one *d. Educ:* Birkenhead Sch.; Keble Coll., Oxford (BA 1960; BMus 1961; MA 1964; DPhil 1965). FRCO 1957. Asst Lectr in Music, Bristol Univ., 1963–66; Oxford University: Lectr in Music, 1966–96, Reader in Music, 1996–99; Keble College: Lectr in Music, 1966–67; Res. Fellow, 1967–75; Official Fellow, 1975–92; Emeritus Fellow, 2012; Lecturer in Music: Balliol Coll., 1966–2005; Jesus Coll., 1970–2005; Lincoln Coll., 1972–2005. General Editor: Corpus of Early Keyboard Music, 1982–; Early English Church Music, 1995–2007; Co-editor, Plainsong and Medieval Music, 1992–96; Mem., Editl Bd and Trustee, Music and Letters, 1995– (Chm., 2005–16). Organist: St Luke's, Tranmere, Birkenhead, 1955–57; St Giles', Oxford (also Choirmaster), 1966–67; SS Philip and James, Oxford, 1968–77; SS Gregory and Augustine, Oxford, 1995–. MAE 2012. Hon. Fellow, Acad. St Cecilia, 2007. *Compositions:* Divertimento for orch., 1999; dramatic trilogy Paschale Mysterium (opera): Good Friday, prod 1998; The Word, prod 2001; Pascha Nostrum, prod 2002; The Story of Orpheus (opera), prod 2004; La Corona for soprano, chorus and strings, 2005; Seven Words from the Cross, 2008; songs, motets, organ and chamber music. RCO Medal, 2016. *Publications:* (ed) Early Tudor Organ Music I, 1966; English Keyboard Music before the Nineteenth Century, 1973; Medieval Music, 1978, rev. trans. as La música medieval, 1984; Editing Early Music, 1985, 2nd edn 1996; The Oxford History of English Music, Vol. i 1991, Vol. ii 1999; (ed) Tudor Keyboard Music, 1995; (ed) The Mulliner Book, 2011. *Recreation:* visiting churches and archaeological sites. *Address:* Jesus College, Oxford OX1 3DW. *T:* (home) (01865) 310956.

**CALDWELL, Prof. John Bernard,** OBE 1979; PhD; FREng, FRINA; Emeritus Professor of Naval Architecture, University of Newcastle upon Tyne, since 1991; *b* 26 Sept. 1936; *s* of John Revie Caldwell and Doris (*née* Bolland); *m* 1955, Jean Muriel Frances Duddridge; two *s. Educ:* Bootham Sch., York; Liverpool Univ. (BEng); Bristol Univ. (PhD). CEng; FRINA 1963; FREng (FEng 1976). Res. Fellow, Civil Engrg, Bristol Univ., 1953; Sen. Scientific Officer 1955, Principal Sci. Off. 1958, Royal Naval Scientific Service; Asst Prof. of Applied Mechanics, RNC Greenwich, 1960–66; Newcastle upon Tyne University: Prof. of Naval Architecture, 1966–91; Hd of Dept of Naval Architecture, 1966–83; Hd, Sch. of Marine Technol., 1975–80, 1986–88; Dean of Faculty of Engrg, 1983–86. Director: Nat. Maritime Inst. Ltd, 1983–85; Marine Design Consultants Ltd, 1985–89; Newcastle Technology Centre, 1985–90; Northern Engrg Centre, 1989–92. Vis. Prof. of Naval Arch., MIT, 1962–63. President: N-E Coast Instn of Engrs and Shipbuilders, 1976–78; RINA, 1984–87 (Vice-Pres., 1977–84). Mem., Engineering Council, 1988–94 (Chm., Bd for Engrs' Registration, 1990–92). FRSA 1982. Hon. DSc Gdansk Tech. Univ., 1985. Froude Medal, RINA, 1984; David W. Taylor Medal, SNAME, 1987. *Publications:* numerous papers on research and educn in naval arch. *Address:* Barkbooth, Winster, Windermere, Cumbria LA23 3NZ. *T:* (01539) 568222.

**CALDWELL, Marion Allan,** QC (Scot.) 2000; *d* of late Henry Caldwell and of Elizabeth Caldwell; *m* 2016, Dr Howard John Manning. *Educ:* Eastbank Acad., Glasgow; Aberdeen Univ. (LLB Hons); European Univ. Inst., Florence; Glasgow Univ. (DipLP). Journalist, 1970–77; trainee Solicitor, 1983–84; Solicitor, 1984–85; admitted to Faculty of Advocates, 1986; called to the Bar, Inner Temple, 1991; Standing Jun. Counsel to Accountant of Court and Accountant in Bankruptcy, Scotland, 1991–2000. Legal Chm., 2001–13, Pres., 2013–; Pensions Appeal Tribunals for Scotland; Dep. Judge, Upper Tribunal, 2014–. *Recreations:* swimming, ski-ing, walking, social tennis, reading. *Address:* Advocates Library, Parliament House, Edinburgh EH1 1RF. *T:* (0131) 226 5071.

**CALDWELL, Sandra Mary,** CB 2008; JP; Director, Field Operations, 2004–09, and Deputy Chief Executive, 2008–09, Health and Safety Executive; *b* 20 June 1948; *m. Educ:* Imperial Coll., Univ. of London (BSc, MSc; dip. occupational health and safety). Joined HSE, 1976; Regl Dir, London and SE, HSC and Chief Inspector of Construction, HSE, 1998–99; Director: Health, then Health and Safety, 2000–03; Policy, 2003–04. Trustee: Victim Support, 2009–15; St Albans CAB, 2009–. JP W Herts, 2003.

**CALEDON, 7th Earl of,** *cr* 1800; **Nicholas James Alexander,** KCVO 2015; Baron Caledon, 1790; Viscount Caledon, 1797; Lord Lieutenant of County Armagh, since 1989; *b* 6 May 1955; *s* of 6th Earl of Caledon, and Baroness Anne (*d* 1963), *d* of late Baron Nicolai de Graevenitz; *S* father, 1980; *m* 1st, 1979, Wendy (marr. diss. 1985), *d* of Spiro Coumantaros and Mrs Suzanne Dayton; 2nd, 1989, Henrietta (marr. diss. 2000), *d* of John Newman, Compton Chamberlayne, Wilts; one *s* one *d*; *m* 2008, Mrs Amanda Cayzer (*née* Squire). *Educ:* Sandroyd School; Gordonstoun School (Round-Square House). *Recreations:* ski-ing, tennis, swimming, photography, travel. *Heir: s* Viscount Alexander, *qv. Address:* Caledon Castle, Caledon, Co. Tyrone, Northern Ireland BT68 4TU. *T:* (028) 3756 8695.

**CALEDONIA, Bishop of,** since 2018; **Rt Rev. David Thomas James Lehmann;** *b* Toronto, 19 Nov. 1969; *s* of Bruce Paton Lehmann and Isabel Lehmann (*née* McGee). *Educ:* Camrose Lutheran Coll. (BA 1990); Wycliffe Coll., Univ. of Toronto (MDiv 1994). RESO (C): Phase 1 and 2, Canadian Forces Base Esquimalt/NOTC, Victoria, 1992; Phase 3, Canadian Forces Base Stadacona, Halifax, 1994; Incumbent, Deh Cho Parish, Fort Simpson, 1994–2000; CO, 2860 RCACC, Fort Simpson, 1996–99; Rector: Cold Lake Parish, Cold Lake, 2000–05; St George's Anglican Church, Fort Saskatchewan, 2005–12; St John's Anglican Church, Fort Smith, 2012–17. Theol Advr, HMCS York, Toronto, 1993–94. Chaplain: Cold Lake Regl Hosp., 2003–05; Fort Saskatchewan Fire Dept; Royal Canadian Mounted Police, Fort Smith, 2012–17; 15 Field Ambulance, Edmonton, 2014–16; Royal Canadian Legions, Ashmont, Fort Saskatchewan and Fort Smith. Mem., Order of St John of Jerusalem (Chaplain, Edmonton Commandery). DD Wycliffe Coll., Univ. of Toronto, 2018. *Recreations:* sailing, cooking, hiking, kayaking. *Address:* #201–4716 Lazelle Avenue, Terrace, BC V8G 1T2, Canada. *T:* (250) 6356016. *E:* bishopdavid@telus.net.

**CALEGARI, Prof. Danny Cornelius**, PhD; Professor of Mathematics, University of Chicago, since 2012; *b* Melbourne, Australia, 24 May 1972; *s* of Giacomo Peter Calegari and Cornelia Calegari (*née* Van-Veldhuisen); *m* 1995, Therese Elizabeth Walsh; one *s* two *d*. *Educ:* Univ. of Melbourne (BA Hons 1994); Univ. of Calif, Berkeley (PhD Maths 2000). Benjamin Peirce Asst Prof., Harvard Univ., 2000–02; California Institute of Technology: Asst Prof., 2002; Associate Prof., 2003–06; Prof., 2006–07; Richard Merkin Prof., 2007–12; Prof. of Pure Maths, Univ. of Cambridge, 2011–12. Namboodiri Lectr, Univ. of Chicago, 2012. Clay Res. Award, Clay Maths Inst., 2009. *Publications:* Foliations and the Geometry of 3-Manifolds, 2007; SCL, 2009. *Recreations:* jogging, walking, used books, spanking. *Address: c/o* Department of Mathematics, 5734 S University Avenue, Chicago, IL 60637, USA. *E:* dannyc@math.uchicago.edu.

**CALGARY, Archbishop of**, and Metropolitan of the Ecclesiastical Province of Rupert's Land; since 2015; **Most Rev. Gregory Keith Kerr-Wilson**; Bishop of Calgary, since 2012; *b* St Boniface, Manitoba, 12 April 1962; *s* of Keith Kerr-Wilson and Mary Magdalene Kerr-Wilson; *m* 1986, Victoria Anne Evans; one *s* two *d*. *Educ:* Univ. of British Columbia (BASc 1985); Nashotah House, Wisconsin (MDiv *cum laude* 1989). Ordained deacon, 1989, priest, 1990; Asst Curate, St Paul's, Bloor St, Toronto, 1989–91; Incumbent, Church of the Holy Family, Brampton, 1991–98; Rector, All Saints' Cathedral and Dean, Dio. of Edmonton, 1998–2006; Bishop of Qu'Appelle, 2006–12. *Recreations:* reading, music, hiking, cooking. *Address:* Anglican Diocese of Calgary, #180, 1209–59 Avenue SE, Calgary, AB T2H 2P6, Canada. *T:* (403) 243 3673, *Fax:* (403) 243 2182. *E:* bishop@calgary.anglican.ca.

**CALHOUN, Prof. Craig Jackson**, DPhil; FBA 2015; FAcSS; University Professor of Social Sciences, Arizona State University, since 2018; Centennial Professor, London School of Economics and Political Science, since 2016 (Director and Professor, 2012–16); *b* Illinois, 16 June 1952; *m* 1980, Pamela DeLargy; one *s* one *d*. *Educ:* Univ. of Southern Calif (BA Anthropol. 1972); Columbia Univ. (MA Anthropol. 1974); Manchester Univ. (MA Social Anthropol. 1975); St Antony's Coll., Oxford (DPhil Mod. Social and Econ. Hist./Sociol. 1980). Univ. of North Carolina, Chapel Hill, 1977–96, Prof. of Sociol. and History, 1989–96; Prof., New York Univ., 1996–2012, Univ. Prof., 2004–12; Prof. of Sociol., Columbia Univ. 2006–07. Pres., 2016–18, Sen. Advr, 2018–, Berggruen Inst. Vis. Lectr, Univ. of Oslo, 1991; Prof. (pt-time), Humboldt Univ., 2010–15; Hon. Prof., Maison des Scis de l'Homme, 2011–. FAAAS 2000; FRSA 2012; FAcSS 2014; Fellow, APS, 2012. Hon. LLD: La Trobe, 2005; Erasmus, 2013. Sigillum Magnum, Univ. of Bologna, 2019. *Publications:* (ed jtly) The Anthropological Study of Education, 1976; The Question of Class Struggle, 1982; (jtly) Sociology, 1989; (ed) Habermas and the Public Sphere, 1992; (ed jtly) Bourdieu: critical perspectives, 1993; Neither Gods Nor Emperors, 1994; (ed) Social Theory and the Politics of Identity, 1994; Critical Social Theory: culture, history and the challenge of difference, 1995; Nationalism, 1997; (ed jtly) Hannah Arendt and the Meaning of Politics, 1997; (ed) Dictionary of Social Sciences, 2002; (ed jtly) The Classical Social Theory Reader, 2002, 4th edn 2019; (ed jtly) The Contemporary Social Theory Reader, 2002, 4th edn 2019; (ed jtly) Understanding September 11, 2002; (ed jtly) The Sage Handbook of Sociology, 2005; (ed jtly) Lessons of Empire?, 2006; (ed) Sociology in America: a history, 2007; (ed jtly) Practicing Culture, 2007; Nations Matter: citizenship, solidarity and the cosmopolitan dream, 2007; (ed jtly) Varieties of Secularism, 2010; (ed) Robert K. Merton: sociology of science, sociology as science, 2010; (ed jtly) Knowledge Matters, 2011; (ed jtly) Business as Usual: the roots of the global financial crisis, 2011; (ed jtly) The Deepening Crisis: governance challenges after neoliberalism, 2011; (ed jtly) Aftermath: a new global economic order?, 2011; (ed jtly) Rethinking Secularism, 2011; The Roots of Radicalism: tradition, the public sphere and early 19th century social movements, 2012; (ed jtly) Habermas and Religion, 2013; (jtly) Does Capitalism Have a Future?, 2013. *Recreations:* music, reading. *Address:* Coor Hall, Arizona State University, Tempe, AZ 85287–3902, USA. *T:* (480) 7277717. *E:* craig.calhoun@asu.edu.

**CALIGARI, Prof. Peter Douglas Savaria**, PhD, DSc; CBiol, FRSB; Titular Professor, Instituto de Ciencias Biológicas (formerly Biología Vegetal y Biotecnología), 2002–15, Académico de Excelencia, 2015, Universidad de Talca, Chile (Director, 2004–09); Professor of Agricultural Botany, University of Reading, 1986–2006 (on leave of absence, 2002–06) (Head of Department, 1987–98); Science Strategy Executive Director, Verdant Bioscience, since 2014; *b* 10 Nov. 1949; *s* of late Kenneth Vane Savaria Caligari, DFM, RAF, and of Mary Annetta (*née* Rock); *m* 1st, 1973 (marr. diss. 2004); two *d*; 2nd, 2007, Andrea Veronica Moreno Gonzalez; two step *d*. *Educ:* Hereford Cathedral Sch.; Univ. of Birmingham (BSc Biol Sci., 1971; PhD Genetics, 1974; DSc Genetics, 1989). CBiol 1997; FRSB (FIBiol 1997). Res. Asst, 1971–74, Res. Fellow, 1974–81, Dept of Genetics, Univ. of Birmingham; SSO, 1981–84, PSO, 1984–86, Scottish Crop Res. Inst. Managing Director: BioHybrids International Ltd, 1996–; BioMarkers Ltd, 1997–2003. Director: Genberries Ltd, 2008–16; Ghana Sumatra Ltd, 2008–12 (Chm., 2008–12); Sumatra Bioscience Pte Ltd, 2008–12; Sustainable Plant Nutrition Ltd, 2011–14; BioHybrids Technologies Limitada (Chile), 2011–; BioHybrids Genetics Ltd, 2011–15; BioProperties Private Ltd, 2012–13; Ardent Bioscience Private Ltd, 2012–13; BioSing Private Ltd (Singapore), 2013–; Verdant Bioscience Private Ltd (Singapore), 2013–; PT Timbang Deli Indonesia, 2014–17; Chm., NG-Seeds SA (Chile), 2013–. Coordinator, Internat. Relns and Postgrad. Studies, Centro de Genómica Nutricional Agroacuícola, Temuco, Chile, 2014–. Member: Exec. Cttee, XVIIth Internat. Congress of Genetics, 1991–93; Governing Body, Plant Science Research Ltd, 1991–94; Governing Council, John Innes Centre, 1994–99; European Council, Volcani Centre, 1999–2002; Bd, Internat. Lupin Assoc., 1999–; Comité de Expertos, Beca Presidente de la República, Chile, 2006–07; Academia Chilena de Ciencias Agronómicas, 2003–; Internat. Soc. for Horticultural Sci., 2014–; Chm., Sci. Prog., Triennial EUCARPIA Congress, 1999–2001. Vice Pres., Inst. of Biology, 1999–2002 (Chm., Sci. Policy Bd, 1999–2002). FRSA 1990. Editor, Heredity, 1987–90 (Jun. Editor, 1985–87). *Publications:* (contrib.) The Potato Crop, 1991; (contrib.) Applications of Synthetic Seeds to Crop Improvement, 1992; (jtly) Selection Methods in Plant Breeding, 1995, 2nd edn 2008; (ed jtly) Compositae: biology and utilization, 1996; (contrib.) Lupins: production and utilization, 1998; (ed jtly) Cashew and Coconuts: trees for life, 1998; (jtly) Introduction to Plant Breeding, 2008; (jtly) Plant Breeding, 2014; (ed jtly) Genetic Improvement of Tropical Crops, 2017; scientific papers and reports on genetics, plant breeding and biotechnology (*c* 450 papers, *c* 80 reports). *Address:* Loteo San Agustin, 5 Poniente #244, Talca, Chile. *E:* peter.caligari@verdantbioscience.com.

**CALLADINE, Prof. Christopher Reuben**, ScD; FRS 1984; FREng; Professor of Structural Mechanics, University of Cambridge, 1986–2002, now Emeritus; Fellow of Peterhouse, 1960–2002, now Emeritus; *b* 19 Jan. 1935; *s* of Reuben and Mabel Calladine (*née* Boam); *m* 1964, Mary R. H. Webb; two *s* one *d*. *Educ:* Nottingham High Sch.; Peterhouse, Cambridge; Massachusetts Inst. of Technology. Development engineer, English Electric Co., 1958; Demonstrator in Engrg, Univ. of Cambridge, 1960, Lectr, 1963; Reader, 1978. Vis. Research Associate, Brown Univ., 1963; Vis. Prof., Stanford Univ., 1969–70. Mem. Council, Royal Soc., 2000–02. Trustee, EMF Biol. Res. Trust, 2005–19 (Chm., 2007–19). FREng (FEng 1994). Hon. DEng Univ. of Technol., Malaysia, 2002. James Alfred Ewing Medal, ICE, 1998. *Publications:* Engineering Plasticity, 1969; Theory of Shell Structures, 1983; (with H. R. Drew) Understanding DNA, 1992, 3rd edn 2004; papers in engrg and biological jls. *Recreations:* music, architecture, mending toys. *Address:* 25 Almoners Avenue, Cambridge CB1 8NZ. *T:* (01223) 246742.

**CALLAGHAN, Rev. Brendan Alphonsus**, SJ; Catholic Chaplain, universities in Manchester, since 2017; *b* 29 July 1948; *s* of Dr Kathleen Callaghan (*née* Kavanagh) and Dr Alphonsus Callaghan. *Educ:* Stonyhurst; Heythrop, Oxon; Campion Hall, Oxford (MA 1977); Univ. of Glasgow (MPhil 1976); Heythrop Coll., Univ. of London (MTh 1979). Joined Society of Jesus, 1967; Clinical Psychologist, Glasgow, 1974–76; Middx Hosp., 1976–79; ordained priest, 1978; curate, St Aloysius, Glasgow, 1979–80; Heythrop College, University of London: Lectr, 1980–2007, Sen. Lectr, 2007–08, in Psychol.; Principal, 1985–97; Acting Principal, 1998–99; Dir, Academic Standards Cttee, 2005–08; Dir of Academic Develt, 2007–08; Fellow, 2009; Lectr in Psychol., Allen Hall, Chelsea, 1981–87. Superior: Brixton Jesuit Community, 1993–94; Merrivale Jesuit Community, KwaZulu-Natal, 1998; Wimbledon Jesuit Community, 1998–2005; Clapham Jesuit Community, 2007–08; Master of Campion Hall, Oxford, 2008–13; Dir of Novices, North-Western European Provinces of Soc. of Jesus, 2014–16. Formation Asst to British Jesuit Provincial, 2001–07. University of London: Chm., Bd of Examrs, Theol and Religious Studies, 1987–89; Schools Examn Bd, 1987–97; Collegiate Council and Senate, 1989–94; Council, 1994–97; Institute of Medical Ethics: Hon. Asst/Associate Dir, 1976–89; Governing Body, 1989–2002; Gen. Sec., 1999–2002. Visiting Lecturer: St Joseph's Theol Inst., KwaZulu-Natal, 1987 and 1997–98; (in Med. Ethics), Imperial Coll., London, 1990–; KCL, 1991–94; Vis. Prof., Fordham Univ., NY, 1990; Vis. Scholar, Weston Sch. of Theol., Cambridge, Mass, 1992. Member: Conf. of Seminary Rectors, 1987–97; Cttee of Catholic Principals, 1985–97; Ethics Cttee, St Thomas' Hosp., 1990–2002; Higher Educn Cttee, RC Bps Conf. of England and Wales, 1986–97; Academic Bd, 1982–97, Governing Body, 1982–97 and 2012–19, Heythrop Coll.; Academic Adv. Cttee, Jews' Coll., 1993–97. Chm. Govs, Digby Stuart Coll., 1998–2002, Mem. Council, 1998–2002, Univ. of Surrey Roehampton (formerly Roehampton Inst.); Member, Advisory Boards: Campion Hall, Oxford, 1985–95; Syon House, Angmering, 1985–97; Centre for the Study of Communication and Culture (Chm.), 1990–; Inst. of St Anselm, Westgate (Chm.), 1991–98. Vice Pres., Catholic Students Trust Appeal. Consultant Psychologist to Marriage Care (formerly Catholic Marriage Adv. Council), 1981–, and to religious congregations and orders. Hon. FCP 1996. Broadcaster, BBC and World Service radio, Channel Four. Member, Editorial Board: Law and Justice, 1986–; Jl of Contemp. Religion, 1994–97; Mental Health, Religion and Culture, 1997–. *Publications:* Life Before Birth (with K. Boyd and E. Shotter), 1986; articles, reviews and verse in Br. Jl Psych., Jl Med. Ethics, Heythrop Jl, The Way and magazines. *Recreations:* photography, long distance walking, poetry. *Address:* Holy Name Jesuit Community, 335–337 Oxford Road, Manchester M13 9PG. *T:* 07946 485422.

**CALLAGHAN, Prof. Terence Vincent**, CMG 2018; PhD, DSc; Professor of Arctic Ecology, University of Sheffield, since 1993; Professor of Botany, Tomsk State University, since 2010; *b* Stockport, 11 March 1945; *s* of John Callaghan and Edith Callaghan; two *s* one *d*. *Educ:* Burnage Grammar Sch., Manchester; Univ. of Manchester (BSc Hons 1967); Univ. of Birmingham (PhD 1972); Univ. of York; Univ. of Manchester (DSc 1993). Research Fellow: Univ. of York, 1972–74; Univ. of Manchester, 1974–75; Scientific Officer to Sen. Principal Scientific Officer, Inst. of Terrestrial Ecol., 1975–92; Prof. of Arctic Ecol., Univ. of Manchester, 1992–93. Mem., Royal Swedish Acad. of Scis, 2002. Hon. PhD: Lund, 1991; Oulu, 2002; Tomsk, 2012. Vega Medal, Swedish Soc. for Anthropol. and Geog., 2011; Polar Medal, 2013; Internat. Actic Scientific Cttee Medal, 2017. *Publications:* 430 scientific publications. *Recreations:* landscaping, conservation. *Address:* Rose Grove, Woodseats Lane, Charlesworth, High Peak, Derbys SK13 5DT. *T:* 07770 542123. *E:* terry_callaghan@btinternet.com.

**CALLAGHAN, Sir William (Henry)**, Kt 2007; Chair, Marine Management Organisation, 2011–18; *b* 19 May 1948; *s* of Henry William Callaghan and Constance Callaghan; *m* 1st, 1977, Frances Sproat (marr. diss. 1981); 2nd, 2001, Pauline Ortiz (*d* 2002); one *s*; 3rd, 2007, Dr Josephine Glover (marr. diss. 2013); 2018, Christine Laugharne. *Educ:* St John's Coll., Oxford (BA PPE); Univ. of Kent at Canterbury (MA Econs). Trades Union Congress: Asst, 1971–74, Asst Sec., 1974–77, Head, 1978–93, Econ. Dept; Head, Econ. and Social Affairs, and Chief Economist, 1994–99; Chairman: HSC, 1999–2007; Legal Services Commn, 2008–13. Member: Low Pay Commn, 1997–2000; Res. Priorities Bd, ESRC, 1994–99; Ind. Mem., Rev. of HE Finance and Pay Data for Univ. Employers and Trade Unions, 2007–08; Chair, Rev. of Regulatory Framework for Animal Pathogens, 2007. Member Board: BITC, 1991–99; Basic Skills Agency, 1996–99; DTI Innovation Gp, 2002–04; DTI Fair Markets Bd, 2004–07. Chair: British Occupational Health Res. Foundn, 2007–; Nat. Examination Bd for Occupational Safety and Health, 2011–18. JP Surrey, 2005–18. Vis. Fellow, Nuffield Coll., Oxford, 1999–2007. *Publications:* numerous TUC pubns on econ. and social affairs. *Recreations:* sailing, cycling, walking, listening to music.

**CALLAN, Hilary Margaret West**; Director, Royal Anthropological Institute of Great Britain and Ireland, 2000–10, now Director Emerita; *b* 27 Oct. 1942; *d* of late John Sydney Flashman and Marion Louise Flashman (*née* Thornton) (Silver Laurel Leaf Emblem and King's Commendation for Brave Conduct in Civil Defence, 1941); *m* 1965, Ivan Roy Callan (marr. diss. 1987); one *d*. *Educ:* Marsden Sch., NZ; St Paul's Girls' Sch.; Somerville Coll., Oxford (MA, MLitt, Dip. Social Anthropol.). Sen. Res. Associate, Birmingham Univ., 1968–70; Asst Prof., American Univ. of Beirut, Lebanon, 1971–75; Lecturer: Univ. of Kent at Canterbury, 1977–80; Trent Univ., Canada, 1981–84 (Harry Frank Guggenheim Res. Award, 1982–84); Oxford Poly., 1987–88; Brunel Univ., 1988–89; Asst Dir, UKCOSA: Council for Internat. Educn, 1989–93; Exec. Dir, Eur. Assoc. for Internat. Educn, 1993–2000 (Hon. Life Mem., 2000). Mem. Bd of Trustees, Gemini Action Internat., 2005–12; Trustee, Mass Observation Archive, 2012–19. Mem., Common Room, St Cross Coll., Oxford, 2010–. Contested (SDP/Lib Alliance) Scarborough, 1987. Patron's Medal, Royal Anthropol Inst., 2011. Ed.-in-Chief, Wiley-Blackwell Internat. Encyclopedia of Anthropology, 2010–. *Publications:* Ethology and Society: towards an anthropological view, 1970; (ed jtly) The Incorporated Wife, 1984; (ed) International Education: towards a critical perspective, 2000; (contrib.) Engagements with Learning and Teaching in Higher Education: a view from anthropology, 2006; (contrib.) Identity and Networks, 2007; (contrib.) Professional Identities, 2007; (ed jtly) Early Human Kinship: from sex to social reproduction, 2008; (contrib.) Pathways to Anthropology, 2010; (ed jtly) Introductory Readings in Anthropology, 2012; (ed jtly and contrib.) Human Origins: contributions from social anthropology, 2017; (Ed.-in-Chief) International Encyclopedia of Anthropology, 2018; numerous articles in books and jls in anthropology and internat. educn. *Recreations:* reading, music, family and friends. *Address: c/o* St Cross College, St Giles, Oxford OX1 3LZ.

**CALLAN, Sir Ivan**, KCVO 1998; CMG 1990; HM Diplomatic Service, retired; Ambassador to Oman, 1999–2002; *b* 6 April 1942; *s* of Roy Ivan Callan and (Gladys) May Callan (*née* Coombe); *m* 1st, 1965, Hilary Flashman; one *d*; 2nd, 1987, Mary Catherine Helena Williams; two step *s* one step *d*. *Educ:* Reading Sch.; University Coll., Oxford. BA, Dip. Soc. Anthrop., BLitt, MA. Entered FCO, 1969; Middle East Centre for Arab Studies, 1970–71; Second, later First Sec., Beirut, 1971–75; FCO, 1975–80; First Sec. and Head of Chancery, Ottawa, 1980–83; Counsellor, Hd of Chancery and Consul-General, Baghdad,

1983–87; Consul-General, Jerusalem, 1987–90; Counsellor, FCO, 1991–94; High Comr, Brunei, 1994–98. Gt Commander, Orthodox Knights of the Holy Sepulchre, 1988. *Recreations:* fine arts, painting, craftsmanship, fly fishing. *Clubs:* Reform, Royal Over-Seas League; Kildorrery Gun; Kildorrery Trout Anglers.

**CALLANAN,** family name of **Baron Callanan**.

**CALLANAN, Baron** *cr* 2014 (Life Peer), of Low Fell in the County of Tyne and Wear; **Martin John Callanan;** Minister of State, Department for Exiting the European Union, since 2017; *b* 8 Aug. 1961; *s* of John and Ada Callanan; *m* 1997, Jayne Burton; one *s. Educ:* Newcastle Poly. (BSc Electrical and Electronic Engrg). Project Engr, Scottish & Newcastle Breweries, 1986–99. MEP (C) NE Reg., England, 1999–2014; contested (C) same seat, 2014. European Parliament: Leader, UK Conservatives, 2010–14; Chm., Eur. Conservatives and Reformists Gp, 2011–14. Parly Under-Sec. of State, DfT, 2017. *Recreations:* squash, football.

**CALLANDER, Lt Col Richard,** LVO 2019; OBE 2008; TD 1986; landowner, farmer; Secretary, Queen's Body Guard for Scotland, Royal Company of Archers, 2007–19; Vice Lord-Lieutenant of Midlothian, since 2014; *b* London, 2 April 1950; *s* of Major John David Callander, MC and Mary Callander (*née* Crompton-Roberts); *m* 1973, Lady Mary Douglas, *d* of 22nd Earl of Morton; one *s* two *d. Educ:* Eton; Royal Agricultural Coll., Cirencester. FRICS. Chartered Surveyor in private practice, 1968–91; Hd Factor, NT for Scotland, 1991–95. QOY, 1972–2012; CO, City of Edinburgh Univs OTC, 1992–94; Full-Time Reserve Service: operational tour, Bosnia and Herzegovina, 1996; staff appt, MoD, London, 2000; Project Dir, Armed Forces Meml, 2001–08. Chm., Scottish Veterans' Garden City Assoc., 2011–. DL Midlothian, 2011. *Recreations:* longbow archery, gardening, country sports, travelling, ski-ing. *Address:* Saughland House, Pathhead, Midlothian EH37 5XP. *Club:* New (Edinburgh).

**CALLAWAY, Anthony Leonard;** a District Judge (Magistrates' Courts), since 2002; *b* 13 Oct. 1953; *s* of Leonard Cecil Callaway, CEng, MICE and Daphne Noreen Callaway (*née* Ibbett); *m* 2000, Heather Jean Foot, FIDM; one step *s* one step *d. Educ:* St Lawrence Coll.; KCL (BA Hons Pol Sci.; MA War Studies; MSc with Dist. War and Psychiatric Medicine; MPhil Psychiatric Medicine Res.). Called to the Bar, Middle Temple, 1978; in practice, S Eastern Circuit, 1978–2002; Actg Dep. Dist Judge, formerly Metropolitan Stipendiary Magistrate, 1997–2002; Designated Dist Judge, Croydon Magistrates' Court, 2007–09. Member: IISS, 2003–; RIIA, 2011–. *Recreations:* sailing, ski-ing, reading (military history), motoring. *Address:* Steeples, Mill Lane, Steep, Hants GU32 2DJ. *Clubs:* Royal Automobile, Royal Thames Yacht, Bar Yacht; Royal Solent Yacht (Yarmouth).

**CALLBECK, Hon. Catherine Sophia,** CM 2015; OPEI 2017; Senator, Senate of Canada, 1997–2014; with Callbeck's Ltd, family business, 1968–74, 1978–88 and since 1996; *b* 25 July 1939; *d* of Ralph Callbeck and Ruth Callbeck (*née* Campbell), Central Bedeque, PEI. *Educ:* Mt Allison Univ. (BComm 1960); Dalhousie Univ. (BEd 1963); Syracuse Univ. Prince Edward Island: MLA (L) Fourth Dist, 1974–78; Minister of Health and Social Services, Minister responsible for Disabled and Minister responsible for Non-Status Indians, 1974–78; MP (L) Malpeque, 1988–93; Official Opposition Critic for Consumer and Corporate Affairs, Energy, Mines and Resources and Financial Instns, 1988–93; former Associate Critic for Privatization and Regulatory Affairs; MLA (L) First Dist of Queens, and Premier of PEI, 1993–96; Member, Senate Standing Committees: on Internal Economy, Budgets and Admin; on Social Affairs, Sci. and Technol.; on Banking, Trade and Commerce; on Transport and Communications; on Nat. Finance; on Agriculture and Forestry; Vice-Chm., Task Force on Women Entrepreneurs, 2002–03. Former Mem., Higher Educn Commn, Maritime Provinces. Leader, Liberal Party of PEI, 1993–96; Vice-Chm., Nat. Liberal Caucus, 2005–07. Member: Nat. Adv. Council of Family Resource Progs Canada; Child Alliance Adv. Cttee, PEI, 1998–. Former Vice-Pres., Canada-Cuba Interparly Gp. Chancellor, Univ. of PEI, 2018–. Hon. Mem. Bd, Glaucoma Res. Soc. of Canada, 1998–. Paul Harris Fellow, Rotary, 2014. Hon. LLD Mt Allison, 1996; Hon. DLaws Prince Edward Island, 2015. *Address:* Box 3947, Central Bedeque, PE C0B 1G0, Canada. *T:* (902) 8872988. *E:* catherine.callbeck@bellaliant.net.

**CALLENDER, Margaret;** *see* Burns, M.

**CALLER, Maxwell Marshall,** CBE 2005; independent consultant, local government; Chair, Local Government Boundary Commission for England, 2010–15 (Chair, Boundary Committee for England, 2007–10); Intervention Commissioner, London Borough of Tower Hamlets, 2014–17; *b* 9 Feb. 1951; *s* of Abraham Leon Caller and Cynthia Rachel Caller; *m* 1972, Linda Ann Wohlberg; three *s* one *d. Educ:* Newport High Sch.; University Coll. London (BSc Hons Engrg). CEng, MICE; CDipAF. GLC, 1972–74; Thames Water Authority, 1974–75; London Boroughs of: Hammersmith, 1975–78; Newham, 1978–81; Merton, 1981–85 (Asst Dir of Development); Barnet: Controller of Engrg Services, 1985–87; Dir of Technical Services, 1987–89; Chief Exec., 1989–2000; Man. Dir, subseq. Chief Exec., London Bor. of Hackney, 2000–04; Interim Chief Exec., London Bor. of Haringey, 2005–06. Mem., Electoral Commn, 2007–14; Interim Chair, Local Govt Boundary Commn for Wales, 2011–12. Technical Advr, N London Waste Authy, 1985–87; Adviser, Highways Cttee 1987–89, Public Works Cttee 1990–97, AMA. Lead Inspector, Best Value Inspection, Northants CC, 2018. Founder Mem., 1990, and Vice Chm., Steering Cttee, 1990–2000, Barnet Crime Reduction Partnership; Director: Enfield Enterprise Agency, 1994–99; N London TEC, 1995–2000; Prospects Careers Services Ltd, 1999–2000; The Learning Trust, 2002–04; Bernie Grant Centre Ltd, 2005–06; Chm., Barfield Group Ltd, 1995–98. Trustee, Barnet War Memorials Initiative, 1994–2000. Mem., Adv. Council, Norwood, 2006–. Freeman, City of London, 1991. DUniv Middlesex, 2000. *Recreation:* watching Welsh Rugby Union.

**CALLICOTT, Richard Kenneth,** OBE 2012; Founder, 2004, and Chief Executive Officer, since 2013, Reddenhill Consulting (Managing Director, 2004–13); *b* 18 Sept. 1946; *s* of Ernest Victor Callicott and Joan Alfreda Callicott (*née* Furley); *m* 1st, 1972, Diane Lesley Kidd (marr. diss. 1984); two *s*; 2nd, 1985, Jacqueline Steele (marr. diss. 1995); one *s*; 3rd, 2003, Maroline Lasebikan. *Educ:* Colston's Sch., Bristol; City of Birmingham Coll. of Educn (Cert Ed); Univ. of Birmingham (BPhil Ed). Teacher, jun. schs, Smethwick and Warley, 1968–74; Warden, Churchbridge Teachers' Centre, 1974–80; Community Educn and Recreation Officer, Birmingham CC, 1980–83; Vice Principal, Central Inst., Birmingham, 1983–85; Area Manager, Recreation and Community, Birmingham CC, 1985; Co-ordinator, Birmingham's Olympic Bid, 1985–86; Develt Manager, Sport and Leisure, Birmingham CC, 1988–89; Dir of Sport, NEC Gp, 1989–99, and Hd of Sport, City of Birmingham, 1996–99; Chief Exec., UKSport, 1999–2004. Director: Saga Radio, 2001–08; SBM (Sports) Ltd, 2007–. Director: British Paralympic Assoc., 2005–17; Active Black Country, 2016–; Member: Leisure Infrastructure Adv. Gp, UK Trade & Investment, 2003–; Nat. Olympic Cttee, 2006–; Ethics Panel, Internat. Volleyball Fedn, 2016–. President: British Volleyball Fedn, 2005–14 and 2015–; Commonwealth Volleyball Fedns, 2010–; World ParaVolley Judicial Commn, 2015–. Trustee: World Professional Billiards and Snooker Assoc. Benevolent Fund, 2008–12; Youth Charter for Sport, 2015–17; Sporting Equals, 2016–17. Hon. Pres., Volleyball England, 2014–; Hon. Vice Pres., GB Wheelchair Basketball Assoc., 2012. *Recreations:* golf, cycling, reading, gardening, theatre, insatiable appetite for sport. *Address:* Reddenhill Consulting, Stourbridge Road, Wombourne, S Staffs WV4 5NF.

**CALLIL, Dame Carmen (Thérèse),** DBE 2017; Founder, 1972, and Chairman, 1972–95, Virago Press; writer; critic; *b* 15 July 1938; *d* of Frederick Alfred Louis Callil and Lorraine Clare Allen. *Educ:* Star of the Sea Convent, Gardenvale, Melbourne; Loreto Convent, Mandeville Hall, Melbourne; Melbourne Univ. (BA). Buyer's Asst, Marks & Spencer, 1963–65; Editorial Assistant: Hutchinson Publishing Co., 1965–66; B. T. Batsford, 1966–67; Publicity Manager, Panther Books, later also of Granada Publishing, 1967–70; André Deutsch, 1971–72; publicity for Ink newspaper, 1972; founded Carmen Callil Ltd, book publicity co., 1972; founded Virago Press, 1972, incorp. as co., 1973, Man. Dir, 1972–82. Man. Dir, Chatto & Windus: The Hogarth Press, 1983–93; Publisher-at-Large, Random House UK, 1993–94; Ed.-at-Large, Knopf, NY, 1993–94. Mem. Bd, Channel 4, 1985–91. FRSA. Hon. LittD: Sheffield, 1994; Oxford Brookes, 1995; DUniv: York, 1995; Open, 1997. *Publications:* (ed with Craig Raine) New Writing 7, 1998; (with Colm Tóibín) The Modern Library: the 200 best novels in English since 1950, 1999; Bad Faith: a forgotten history of family and fatherland, 2006. *Recreations:* friends, reading, animals, television, sport, politics, films, gardening, France.

**CALLINAN, Hon. Ian David Francis,** AC 2003; Judge (*ad hoc*), International Court of Justice, 2014–15; Judge of the High Court of Australia, 1998–2007; *b* 1 Sept. 1937; *s* of William Peter Callinan and Lilian Rose Callinan; *m* 1960, Wendy Mary Ruth Hamon; one *s* one *d. Educ:* Univ. of Queensland (LLB). Admitted solicitor, 1960, called to the Bar, 1965, Qld; QC (Aust.) 1978. Hon. Dir, Barr Chambers Ltd, 1974–91. Chm., Qld Barrister Bd, 1987–88; Hon. President: Qld Bar Assoc., 1984–87; Australian Bar Assoc., 1984–85. Vis. Prof. of Law, Newcastle Univ., 1993; Adjunct Prof. of Law, Univ. of Queensland, 2009–. Chm., Australian Defence Force Acad., 2000–04. Chm., Qld Totalizator Agency Bd, 1985–90; Director: QCT Ltd, 1988–97; Santos Ltd, 1996–97; ABC, 1997. Chm. Trustees, Qld Art Gallery, 1997–98; Dir, Nat. Gall. of Australia, 2007–. Hon. Fellow, Inst. of Arbitrators and Mediators Australia, 2008. Hon. DLaws: Queensland, 2010; James Cook, 2012. *Publications:* plays: Brazilian Blue, 1995; The Cellophane Ceiling, 1996; The Acquisition, 2000; A Hero's Funeral; *novels:* The Lawyer and the Libertine, 1997; The Coroner's Conscience, 1999; The Missing Masterpiece, 2001; Appointment at Amalfi, 2003; After the Monsoon, 2005; The Russian Master, 2009; Betrayals, 2011; Dislocation, 2012; The Only Case, 2014; Belvedere Woman, 2016; contrib. short stories to various anthologies. *Recreations:* history of Australian art, reading, tennis, cricket, Rugby. *Address:* Level 11, Inns of Court, 107 North Quay, Brisbane, Qld 4000, Australia. *Clubs:* Queensland, Tattersall's (Brisbane).

**CALLMAN, His Honour Sir Clive (Vernon),** Kt 2012; a Circuit Judge, 1973–2000, assigned to South-Eastern Circuit; a Deputy Circuit Judge, 2000–02; a Deputy High Court Judge, 1976–2000; *b* 21 June 1927; *o s* of Felix Callman, DMD, LDS, RCS and Edith Callman, Walton-on-Thames, Surrey; *m* 1967, Judith Helen Hines, BA, DipSocStuds (Adelaide), *o d* of Gus Hines, OBE, JP, and Hilde Hines, St George's, Adelaide, S Aust.; one *s* one *d. Educ:* Ottershaw Coll.; St George's Coll., Weybridge; LSE, Univ. of London (BSc(Econ), Commercial Law); Univ. of Notre Dame (Mediator Dip. 2000). Called to the Bar, Middle Temple, 1951; Blackstone Pupillage Prizeman, 1951; practised as Barrister, London and Norwich, 1952–73 (Head of London chambers, 1963), South-Eastern Circuit; Hon. Mem., Central Criminal Court Bar Mess; Dep. Circuit Judge in Civil and Criminal Jurisdiction, 1971–73; Mediator, Ct of Appeal, 2004–. Legal Assessor: GMC, 2000–04; GDC, 2000–04. Dir, Woburn Press, Publishers, 1971–73; dir of finance cos, 1961–73; non-executive Director: Frank Cass & Co. Ltd, 2000–03; Vallentine Mitchell & Co. Ltd, 2000–15. University of London: Fac. Mem., Standing Cttee of Convocation, 1954–79; Senator, 1978–94; Mem. Careers Adv. Bd, 1979–92; Mem., Commerce Degree Bureau Cttee, 1980; Mem., Adv. Cttee for Magistrates' Courses, 1979; Mem., Univ. Governing Council, 1994–2001; Vice-Pres., Graduates' Soc.; Governor: Birkbeck Coll., 1982–2000 (Fellow, 2000); LSE, 1990–2008 (Gov. Emeritus, 2008); Hebrew Univ. of Jerusalem, 1992–; Mem. Court, City Univ., 1991–2001. Mem. Exec. Cttee, Soc. of Labour Lawyers, 1958; Chm., St Marylebone Constituency Labour Party, 1960–62. Mem. Council, Anglo-Jewish Assoc., 1956–; Trustee, Jewish Studies Foundn, 2004–14. Editor, Clare Market Review, 1947; Member Editorial Board: Professional Negligence, 1985–95; Jl of Child Law, 1989–95; Child and Family Law Qly, 1995–2002. *Recreations:* reading, travelling, the arts. *Address:* 11 Constable Close, NW11 6UA. *T:* (020) 8458 3010. *Clubs:* Garrick, Bar Yacht.

**CALLOW, Maj. Gen. Christopher George,** CB 2001; OBE 1984; Chief Executive, Defence Secondary Care Agency, 1998–2000; *b* 12 July 1941; *s* of George Alexander Callow and Barbara Callow (*née* Tannahill); *m* 1967, Elizabeth Anne Macmillan Hynd; one *s* two *d. Educ:* Duke of York Sch., Nairobi; Univ. of Edinburgh (MB ChB 1966). DPhysMed 1971; MSc London 1984. MFCM 1987, FFPH (DPPHM 1996). RMO, 1st Bn, Green Howards, 1968–69; Army Staff Coll., 1976; Dep. Asst Dir Gen. AMS, MoD, 1977–79; CO, Armd Field Amb., 1979–83; Col, Med. Ops & Plans, MoD, 1985–88; Comdr Med., 1 Armd Div., 1988–90; Chief, Med. Plans & Policy, SHAPE, 1990–93; Comdr Med., BAOR, subseq. UKSC (Germany), 1993–96; Dir Gen., Defence Med. Trng, 1996–99. QHP 1995–2000. Consultant in Army Occupnl and Public Health Medicine, 1987–2000. Hon. Col, Yorks (N & W) ACF, 2005–11. OStJ 1995. *Publications:* articles on noise-induced hearing loss. *Recreations:* golf, music, travel, computing.

**CALLOW, Prof. James Arthur,** PhD; Mason Professor of Botany, University of Birmingham, 1983–2012, now Emeritus; *b* 17 Jan. 1945; *s* of James and Olive Callow; *m* 1968, Dr Maureen Elizabeth Wood; one *s. Educ:* Barrow-in-Furness Grammar Sch. for Boys; Univ. of Sheffield (BSc 1st cl. Hons Botany 1966; PhD 1969). Lectr in Botany, Univ. of Leeds, 1969–83. *Publications:* numerous, including books, professional academic jl articles. *Recreations:* golf, gardening, antiques, photography, travel. *Address:* School of Biosciences, University of Birmingham, Birmingham B15 2TT. *T:* (0121) 414 5559.

**CALLOW, Simon Phillip Hugh,** CBE 1999; actor, director, writer; *b* 15 June 1949; *s* of late Neil Callow and Yvonne Mary Callow; *m* 2016, Sebastian Fox. *Educ:* London Oratory Grammar Sch.; Queen's Univ. Belfast; Drama Centre. London productions include: Schippel, 1975; A Mad World My Masters, 1977; Arturo Ui, Mary Barnes, 1978; As You Like It, Amadeus, NT, 1979; The Beastly Beatitudes of Balthazar B, Total Eclipse, Restoration, 1981; The Relapse, 1983; On the Spot, 1984; Kiss of the Spider Woman, 1985; Faust I and II, Lyric, Hammersmith, 1988; Single Spies (double bill: A Question of Attribution (also dir); An Englishman Abroad), NT, 1988, Queen's, 1989; The Destiny of Me (also dir), Leicester Haymarket, 1994; The Alchemist, RNT, 1996; The Importance of Being Oscar, Savoy, 1997; In Defence of Fairies, Criterion, 1997; Chimes at Midnight, Chichester, 1998; The Mystery of Charles Dickens, Comedy, transf. Albery, 2000; Chicago, Albery, NY, Australia, 2002; Through the Leaves, Southwark, transf. Duchess, 2003; The Holy Terror, Duke of York's, 2004; The Woman in White, Palace, 2005; Aladdin, Richmond, 2005; Present Laughter, tour, 2006; Merry Wives: the Musical, RSC, 2006; Equus, tour, 2008; There Love Reigns, Stratford Ontario, 2008; A Festival Dickens, Edinburgh, 2008; Waiting for Godot, tour and Th. Royal Haymarket, 2009; Dr Marigold and Mr Chops, Riverside Studios, 2009, transf. Duke of York's, 2010, and UK tour; Shakespeare - the man from Stratford, UK tour, 2010, (as Being Shakespeare) Trafalgar Studios, 2011, transf. Brooklyn Acad. of Music, Broadway Th. Chicago, 2012, Harold Pinter, 2014; Twelfth Night, NT, 2011; Tuesdays at Tescos, Edinburgh, 2011, NY, 2015; A Christmas Carol, Arts Th., 2011, 2012, 2016 and 2018; The Mystery of Charles Dickens, Playhouse, 2012; The Man Jesus, Lyric, Belfast, 2013, UK tour, 2014; Inside Wagner's Head, Linbury Studio Th., 2013; Chin-Chin, tour, 2013; Juvenalia, Assembly Hall, Edinburgh, 2014; A Song at Twilight, Th. Royal Bath, and UK tour, 2019; *directed*: Loving Reno, Bush, 1984; The Passport, 1985, Nicolson Fights, Croydon, 1986, Offstage; Amadeus, Theatr Clwyd, 1986; The Infernal Machine, 1986; Così fan Tutte, Switzerland, 1987; Jacques and his Master, LA, 1987; Shirley Valentine, Vaudeville, 1988, NY, 1989; Die Fledermaus, Theatre Royal, Glasgow, 1988, 1989; Stevie Wants to Play the Blues, LA Theater Center, 1990; Carmen Jones, Old Vic, 1991; Ballad of the Sad Café (film), 1991; Shades, 1992; My Fair Lady, 1992; Les Enfants du Paradis, Barbican, 1996; Stephen Oliver Trilogy, 1996; Calisto, NY, 1996; Il Turco in Italia, Broomhill Opera, 1997; HRH, Playhouse, 1997; The Consul, Holland Park, 1999; The Pajama Game, Victoria Palace, 1999; Jus' Like That!, Garrick, 2003; Le Roi Malgré Lui, Grange Park, 2003; The Magic Flute, Opera Holland Park, 2008; A Christmas Carol (opera), Houston Grand Opera (world premiere), 2014; The Philanthropist, Trafalgar Studios, 2017. *Films*: Amadeus, 1983; A Room with a View, The Good Father, 1986; Maurice, 1987; Manifesto, 1988; Mr & Mrs Bridge, Postcards from the Edge, Crucifer of Blood, 1991; Soft Top, Hard Shoulder, Don't Look Away (also dir), 1993; Four Weddings and a Funeral, 1994; Jefferson in Paris, 1995; Ace Ventura: when Nature calls, James and the Giant Peach, 1996; The Scarlet Tunic, 1998; Bedrooms and Hallways, Shakespeare in Love, 1999; Thunderpants, No Man's Land, George and the Dragon, 2002; Angels in America, Bright Young Things, 2003; Merci Docteur Rey, Phantom of the Opera, 2004; Bob the Butler, Ragtale, 2005; Surveillance, 2006; Chemical Wedding, 2008; No Ordinary Trifle, Acts of Godfrey, 2010; Golden Years, 2016; The Viceroy's House, Mindhorn, Hampstead, Victoria and Abdul, The Man Who Invented Christmas, 2017; Blue Iguana, 2018. *Television series*: Chance in a Million, 1983, 1985–86; David Copperfield, 1986; Outlander, 2015–16; The Rebel, 2016, 2018; *other television includes*: Cariani and the Courtesans, 1987; Charles Laughton (documentary), 1987; Old Flames, 1989; Revolutionary Witness, 1989; Femme Fatale, 1993; The Purcell Film, 1995; An Audience with Charles Dickens, 1996; The Woman in White, 1997; A Christmas Dickens, 1997; The Mystery of Charles Dickens, 2002; Galileo's Daughter, 2003; Marple: The Body in the Library, 2004; Dr Who, Rome, 2005; Midsomer Murders, 2006, 2017; Roman Mysteries, 2007; Lewis, 2009; (and writer) Orson Welles Over Europe (documentary), 2009; Space Age, 2014; A Christmas Carol, 2018; The Dead Room, 2018. *Publications*: Being an Actor, 1984, rev. edn 2004, trans. French as Dans la Peau d'un Acteur, 2006; A Difficult Actor: Charles Laughton, 1987; trans. Jacques et son Maître, by Kundera, 1986; Acting in Restoration Comedy, 1990; Shooting the Actor, 1990, rev. edn 2004; Orson Welles: The Road to Xanadu, 1995; Snowdon on Stage: with a personal view of the British theatre 1954–1996, 1997; The National, 1997; Love is Where it Falls, 1999; Shakespeare On Love, 2000; Oscar Wilde and his Circle, 2000; The Night of the Hunter, 2001; Dickens' Christmas, 2003; Actors on Shakespeare series: Henry IV Part One, 2002; Henry IV Part Two, 2003; Orson Welles: Hello Americans, 2006; Classical Destinations, 1, 2007, 2, 2008; My Life in Pieces (autobiog.), 2010; Charles Dickens and the Great Theatre of the World, 2012; Orson Welles: One-Man Band, 2015; Being Wagner: The Triumph of Will, 2017; London's Great Theatres. *Address*: c/o MGR Weston Kay, 55 Loudoun Road, NW8 0DL.

**CALLOWAY, Carol Elspeth Goodeve;** *see* Brayne, C. E. G.

**CALLUM, Ian Stuart,** CBE 2019; RDI 2007; FRSE; Director of Design, Jaguar Cars, since 1999; *b* 30 July 1954; *s* of late Stuart Callum and Sheila Callum; *m* 1977, Lesley Anne Watson; two *s*. *Educ*: Glasgow Sch. of Art (BA Product Design 1977); Royal Coll. of Art (MA Automotive Design 1979). Designer, Ford Motor Co., 1979–90, Manager, Ghia design studio, Turin, 1988–90; Manager, TWR Design, 1990–99. FRSE 2018. Hon. FRIBA 2016. Hon. DHL Acad. of Art, San Francisco, 2000; Hon. DDes De Montfort, 2002; Hon. DArts: Abertay, 2006; Coventry, 2016; DUniv: Birmingham City, 2012; Glasgow, 2012. Jim Clark Meml Award, Assoc. of Scottish Motoring Writers, 1995, 2006; Minerva Medal, CSD, 2014. *Recreations*: painting, designing, building hot rods, cycling. *T*: (024) 7656 4200, *Fax*: (024) 7620 6177. *E*: icallum@jaguar.com.

**CALLWAY, Eric Willi;** HM Diplomatic Service, retired; Consul General, Frankfurt, 1997–2001; *b* 30 Jan. 1942; *s* of Edward and Auguste Callway; *m* 1st, 1965, Gudrun Viktoria Granström (*d* 2001); two *s*; 2nd, 2008, Barbara Anne Kleiner. Joined HM Foreign, later Diplomatic, Service, 1960: FO, 1960–61; CRO, 1961–63; New Delhi, 1963–66; Georgetown, Guyana, 1966–70; Second Sec., FCO, 1970–72; RAF Staff Coll., Bracknell, 1972; UK Mission, Geneva, 1973–77; First Secretary: FCO, 1977–79; on loan to MoD, 1979–80; FCO, 1980–81; (Commercial), E Berlin, 1981–84; (Labour), 1984–86, then (Commercial), Stockholm, 1986–88; on loan to ODA, 1988; FCO, 1989–94; Counsellor, and Dep. High Comr, Karachi, 1994–97. Vice Chm., Pakistan Soc., 2001–04. *Address*: 76 York Mansions, Prince of Wales Drive, SW11 4BW. *T*: (020) 7720 3994. *E*: ericcallway@gmail.com. *Clubs*: Hurlingham, Royal Over-Seas League.

**CALMAN, Sir Kenneth (Charles),** KCB 1996; DL; MD; FRCP, FRCS; FRSE; Chairman: National Trust for Scotland, 2010–15; National Library of Scotland, since 2016; Chancellor, University of Glasgow, since 2006; Deputy Chairman, British Library, 2011–15; *b* 25 Dec. 1941; *s* of Arthur McIntosh Calman and Grace Douglas Don; *m* 1967, Ann Wilkie; one *s* two *d*. *Educ*: Allan Glen's Sch., Glasgow; Univ. of Glasgow (BSc, MD, PhD). FRCSGlas 1971; FRCP 1985, FRCPE 1989; FRCGP 1989; FFPH (FFCM 1989); FRSE 1979. Hall Fellow in Surgery, Western Infirmary, Glasgow, 1968; Lectr in Surgery, Univ. of Glasgow, 1969; MRC Clinical Res. Fellow, Inst. of Cancer Res., London, 1972; University of Glasgow: Prof. of Clinical Oncology, 1974; Dean of Postgrad. Medicine and Prof. of Postgrad. Med. Educn, 1984–88; Chief Medical Officer: Scottish Office Home and Health Dept, 1989–91; DES, later DFE, then DFEE, based at DoH, 1991–98; Vice-Chancellor and Warden, Univ. of Durham, 1998–2007. Chm., Nat. Cancer Res. Inst., 2008–11. Mem., Statistics Commn, 2000–08; Chm., Commn on Scottish Devolution, 2008–09. Pres., BMA, 2008–09. Lectures include: Honeyman Gillespie, Edinburgh Royal Infirmary, first annual Douglas, Liverpool Univ., Neil Wates Meml, RSocMed, Stanley Melville Meml, ICE, Wade, Keele Univ., 1993; Sir William Weipers Meml, Glasgow Univ., 1994; Frank Lowe, Liverpool Univ., 1995; Calman Muir Meml, RCPE, Brough, Paisley Univ., 1996; Dow Meml, Dundee Univ., 1997; Harben, RIPHH, 1998; Finlayson, RCPSGlas, Meriel, Academic Vet. Soc., first Hastings, Oxford, 1999; Henry Cohen, Hebrew Univ., Jerusalem, 2000. DL Durham, 2000–07; Glasgow, 2009. Hon. FRCR 1990; Hon. FRCSE 1991; Hon. FRCPath 1992; Hon. FFPM 1992; Hon. FFOM 1993; Hon. FRCS 1995; Hon. FRCOG 1996; Hon. FRCSI 1997; Hon. FRSocMed 1997; Founder FMedSci 1998; Hon. FRCOphth 1999; Hon. Fellow, Inst. of Cancer Res., 1999; Hon. FRIAS 2015. DUniv: Stirling, 1992; Open, 1996; Paisley, 1997; Hon. DSc: Strathclyde, 1993; Westminster, 1995; Glasgow Caledonian, 1995; Glasgow, 1996; Brighton, 2000; Hon. MD: Nottingham, 1994; Newcastle, 1995; Birmingham, 1996; Hon. LLD Aberdeen, 2005. Medals include: Sir Thomas and Lady Dixon, Belfast, 1994; Francis Bissett Hawkins, RCP, 1995; Crookshanks, RCR, 1995; Alexander Hutchison, RSocMed, 1995; Gold, Macmillan Cancer Relief, 1996; Heberden (also Orator), British Soc. of Rheumatol., 1996; Silver, RCSI, 1997; Allwyn Smith, FPHM, 1998; Bradlaw, RCS Dental Faculty, 1999; Thomas Graham, Royal Philosophical Soc., Glasgow, 1999. *Publications*: Basic Skills for Clinical Housemen, 1971, 2nd edn 1983; Basic Principles of Cancer Chemotherapy, 1982; Invasion, 1984; Healthy Respect, 1987, 2nd edn 1994; The Potential for Health, 1998; Risk Communication and the Public Health, 1999, 2nd edn 2009; Storytelling, Humour and Learning in Medicine, 2001; Medical Education: past, present and future, 2006; A Doctor's Line, 2014; Afterthoughts, 2017. *Recreations*: gardening, golf, collecting cartoons, Scottish literature. *Address*: University of Glasgow, Glasgow G12 8QQ.

**CALNE, Sir Roy (Yorke),** Kt 1986; MA, MS; FRCS; FRS 1974; Professor of Surgery, University of Cambridge, 1965–98, now Emeritus; Fellow of Trinity Hall, Cambridge, 1965–98, now Emeritus; Visiting Professor, National University of Singapore, since 1998 (Yeoh Ghim Seng Professor of Surgery, 1998–2006); *b* 30 Dec. 1930; *s* of Joseph Robert and Eileen Calne; *m* 1956, Patricia Doreen Whelan; two *s* four *d*. *Educ*: Lancing Coll.; Guy's Hosp. Med. Sch. MB, BS London with Hons (Distinction in Medicine), 1953. House Appts, Guy's Hosp., 1953–54; RAMC, 1954–56 (RMO to KEO 2nd Gurkhas); Deptl Anatomy Demonstrator, Oxford Univ., 1957–58; SHO Nuffield Orthopædic Centre, Oxford, 1958; Surg. Registrar, Royal Free Hosp., 1958–60; Harkness Fellow in Surgery, Peter Bent Brigham Hosp., Harvard Med. Sch., 1960–61; Lectr in Surgery, St Mary's Hosp., London, 1961–62; Sen. Lectr and Cons. Surg., Westminster Hosp., 1962–65; Hon. Consulting Surgeon, Addenbrooke's Hosp., Cambridge, 1965–98. Royal Coll. of Surgeons: Hallet Prize, 1957; Jacksonian Prize, 1961; Hunterian Prof., 1962; Cecil Joll Prize, 1966; Mem. Ct of Examiners, 1970–76; Mem. Council, 1981–90; Vice-Pres., 1986–89; Hunterian Orator, 1989. Founder FMedSci 1998. Fellow Assoc. of Surgeons of GB; Mem. Surgical Research Soc.; Pres., European Soc. for Organ Transplantation, 1983–84; Corresp. Fellow, Amer. Surgical Assoc., 1972, Hon. Fellow 1981; Hon. FRCP 1989; Hon. FRCS Thailand, 1992; Hon. FRCSE 1993. Hon. MD: Oslo, 1986; Athens, 1990; Hanover, 1991; QUB, 1994; Karachi, 1994; Hon. DSc Edinburgh, 2001. Prix de la Société Internationale de Chirurgie, 1969; Faltin Medal, Finnish Surgical Soc., 1977; Lister Medal, 1984; Fothergill Gold Medal, Med. Soc. of London, 1989; Cameron Prize, Edinburgh Univ., 1990; Ellison-Cliffe Medal, 1990; Ernst Jung Preis, 1992; Medawar Prize, Transplantation Soc., 1992; Medal of Helsinki Univ., 1993; Gold Medal, Catalan Transplantation Soc., 1996; King Faisal Internat. Prize for Medicine, 2001; Prince Mahidal Internat. Award for Medicine, 2002; Hamdan Award for Med. Res. Excellence, Dubai, 2008; Maharshi Sushruta Prize, Ahmedabad, 2009; ASTS-Roche Pioneer Award, Amer. Soc. of Transplant Surgeons, 2009; (jtly) Lasker~DeBakey Clinical Medical Res. Award, Lasker Foundn, 2012. Grand Officer, Order of Merit (Republic of Italy), 2000; Encomienda con Placa, Orden Civil de Sanidad (Spain) 2008. *Publications*: Renal Transplantations, 1963, 2nd edn 1967; (with H. Ellis) Lecture Notes in Surgery, 1965, 12th edn 2010; A Gift of Life, 1970; (ed and contrib.) Clinical Organ Transplantation, 1971; (ed and contrib.) Immunological Aspects of Transplantation Surgery, 1973; (ed and contrib.) Liver Transplantation, 1983; (ed and contrib.) Transplantation Immunology, 1984; Surgical Anatomy of the Abdomen in the Living Subject, 1988; (ed) Operative Surgery, 1992; Too Many People, 1994; Art Surgery and Transplantation, 1996; The Ultimate Gift, 1998; (ed jtly) Scepticism: hero and villain, 2013; The Ratchet of Science: curiosity killed the cat, 2014; contrib. to Current Gene Therapy; papers on tissue transplantation and general surgery; sections in several surgical text-books. *Recreations*: tennis, squash, painting, sculpture (art exhibitions at Barbican, Rotterdam, Basle, 1991; New Orleans, 1992; Toronto, Cambridge, Edinburgh, 1993; Rio de Janeiro, Kyoto, 1994; Karachi, 1998; Shalini Ganendra Fine Art, Malaysia, 1998, 2003, 2008, 2011; Trinity Hall, Cambridge, 2001; Churchill Coll., Cambridge, 2003; London, 2011). *Address*: 22 Barrow Road, Cambridge CB2 8AS. *T*: (01223) 359831.

**CALOW, Prof. Peter,** OBE 2000; PhD, DSc; CBiol, FRSB; FLS; Professor of Zoology, University of Sheffield, 1984–2004, now Emeritus; Adjunct Professor, University of Roskilde, Denmark, since 2004; Professor, Humphrey School of Public Affairs, since 2015, and Fellow, Institute on Environment, since 2017, University of Minnesota; *b* 23 May 1947; *s* of late Harry Calow and Norah K. Calow; *m* 1st, 1971, Lesley Jane Chapman (marr. diss. 1991); one *s* one *d*; 2nd, 2010, Valery E. Forbes. *Educ*: William Rhodes Sch., Chesterfield; Univ. of Leeds (BSc; PhD 1972; DSc 1984). CBiol, FRSB (FIBiol 1985); FLS 1987. Lectr, then Reader, Univ. of Glasgow, 1972–84; Warden, Wolfson Hall of Residence, 1975–84. Res. Prof., Univ. of Nebraska-Lincoln, 2011–15. Dir, Envmt Assessment Inst., Denmark, 2004–06. Founding Editor (with J. Grace), Functional Ecology, 1986–98; Editor, Integrated Environmental Management, 1991–95. Chairman: UK Govt Adv. Cttee on Hazardous Substances, 1991–2000; Jt Govt/Business Task Force on Application of Risk Benefit Analysis to Chemical Controls, 1993–95; Member: NE Regl Envmtl Adv. Cttee, Envmt Agency, 1996–2000; Adv. Cttee on Pesticides, 1997–2002 (Chm., Envmtl Panel, 1999–2002); Expert Panel, Res. Inst. for Fragrance Materials, 1999–2016; External Sci. Adv. Panel, European Chemical Industry Long-range Res. Initiative, 1999–2004 (Chm., 2003–04); Scientific Cttee on Toxicity, Ecotoxicity and Envmt, EC, 2000–04; Scientific Cttee, European Centre for Ecotoxicology and Toxicology of Chemicals, 2001–11; Scientific Cttee on Health and Envmtl Risks, EU, 2004–11 (Vice-Chm. (Envmt), 2009–11); UK Chemicals Stakeholder Forum, DEFRA, 2010. Vice-Pres., European Soc. of Evolutionary Biol., 1988–89; Pres., Soc. of Envmtl Toxicol. and Chemistry (UK), 1990–91, (Europe) 1991–92. Mem., Bd of Trustees, Health and Envmtl Scis Inst., 1996–2002; Member Council: Freshwater Biol Assoc., 1988–92 and 1995–99; Univ. of Buckingham, 1997–2002 (Chm., Acad. Adv. Council, 1999–2002). FRSA 1992–2014. *Publications*: Biological Machines, 1976; Life Cycles, 1979; Invertebrate Biology, 1981; Evolutionary Principles, 1983; (with R. Sibly) Physiological Ecology of Animals, 1986; (with R. S. K. Barnes and P. J. W. Olive) The Invertebrates: a new synthesis, 1988, 3rd edn 2001; (ed) Handbook of Ecotoxicology, vol. 1 1993, vol. 2 1994; Controlling Environmental Risks from Chemicals, 1997; Handbook of Environmental Risk Assessment and Management, 1998; (Ed.-in-Chief) The Encyclopedia of Ecology & Environmental Management, 1998; numerous contribs to learned jls. *Recreations*: reading, writing, running. *Address*: Science, Technology and Environmental Policy Area, Humphrey School of Public Affairs, 301 19th Avenue South, Minneapolis, MN 55455, USA.

**CALTHORPE;** *see* Anstruther-Gough-Calthorpe.

**CALVER, Rev. Canon Gillian Margaret;** Chaplain to the Queen, 2008–17; permission to officiate, Diocese of Canterbury, since 2012; *b* Dulwich, 12 Jan. 1947; *d* of Eric Burnett and Hilda Burnett; *m* 1971 (marr. diss. 1999); one *s* two *d*. *Educ*: Queen Elizabeth Coll., London (BSc Hons 1968); Canterbury Sch. of Ministry; Univ. of Kent (Cert. in Counselling Studies 2001). VSO, Zambia, 1968–69; Lectr in Nutrition, Thanet Technical Coll., Broadstairs, 1969–71; Science Teacher, Channel High Sch., Folkestone, 1971–74, 1986–89; child rearing, 1974–81; Sci. Teacher and Year Hd, Pent Valley Sch., Folkestone, 1989–95; ordained deacon, 1992, priest, 1994; Priest-in-charge, Alkham Capel and Hougham, and Chaplain, Dover Coll., 1995–2002; Rector, All Saints, Staplehurst, 2002–11; Area Dean of Weald, 2006–10. Hon. Canon, Canterbury Cathedral, 2008–11, now Canon Emeritus. *Recreations:* walking, foreign travel, cooking and sharing meals with family and friends. *Address:* 6 Grand Court, Grand Parade, Littlestone, Kent TN28 8NT. *E:* gill.calver@btinternet.com.

**CALVER, Marie-Eleni Eliza;** *see* Demetriou, M.-E. E.

**CALVER, Neil Richard;** QC 2006; a Recorder, since 2009; *b* 4 Sept. 1963; *s* of Richard George and Joyce Elizabeth Calver; *m* 2009, Marie-Eleni Eliza Demetriou, *qv*; one *s* one *d*, and one *d* by a previous marriage. *Educ:* York Rd Co. Primary Sch., Kent; Dartford Grammar Sch.; Christ's Coll., Cambridge (BA 1st Cl. Hons Law 1986). Called to the Bar, Gray's Inn, 1987; in practice, 1987–, specialising in commercial and European law. *Recreations:* my children, Charlton Athletic FC, occasional climbing of mountains, opera. *Address:* Brick Court Chambers, 7–8 Essex Street, WC2R 3LD. *T:* (020) 7520 7895, *Fax:* (020) 7520 4137. *E:* calver@brickcourt.co.uk. *Clubs:* Ivy, Ten Trinity Square.

**CALVERLEY,** 3rd Baron *cr* 1945; **Charles Rodney Muff;** *b* 2 Oct. 1946; *s* of 2nd Baron Calverley and of Mary, *d* of Arthur Farrar, Halifax; *S* father, 1971; *m* 1972, Barbara Ann (marr. diss. 2000), *d* of Jonathan Brown, Kelbrook, near Colne; two *s*; *m* 2008, Jenifer, *d* of late Leslie Green, Brighouse, W Yorks. *Educ:* Fulneck School for Boys. Police Officer, City of Bradford Police, 1963–74, W Yorks Police, 1974–97 (RUC secondment, 1979–80). *Heir:* s Hon. Jonathan Edward Brown (surname changed from Muff by Deed Poll), *b* 16 April 1975. *Address:* 24 Dilkera Place, Quinns Rocks, Perth, WA 6030, Australia. *T:* (8) 64013298.

**CALVERLEY, Prof. Peter Martin Anthony,** DSc; FRCP, FRCPE, FMedSci, FERS; Professor of Medicine (Pulmonary Rehabilitation), University of Liverpool, 1995–2010, now Emeritus; *b* 27 Nov. 1949; *s* of Peter Calverley and Jennifer (*née* Taylor); *m* 1973, Margaret Tatam; four *s*. *Educ:* Univ. of Edinburgh (MB ChB; DSc 2012). FRCP 1990; FRCPE 1990. Jun. physician posts in Edinburgh and Leicester, 1973–76; MRC Clinical Fellow, 1976–79, Sen. Registrar, 1979–85, Dept of Medicine, Royal Infirmary, Edinburgh; Consultant Physician, Aintree NHS Trust, Liverpool (later Aintree Univ. Hosps NHS Foundn Trust), 1988–95 (Hon. Consultant Physician, 1995–). Chm., Respiratory Disorders Specialty Gp, NIHR, 2009–15. Travelling Fellow, Meakin-Christie Labs, McGill Univ., Montreal, 1982–83. Pres., British Thoracic Soc., 2005. FMedSci 2011; FERS 2014. *Publications:* (ed jtly) Chronic Obstructive Pulmonary Disease, 1994; papers on pathophysiology and treatment of chronic obstructive pulmonary disease and sleep-related breathing disorders. *Recreations:* sailing, ski-ing, travel, family. *Address:* University Hospital Aintree, Aintree University Hospitals NHS Foundation Trust, Longmoor Lane, Liverpool L9 7AL. *T:* (0151) 529 5886. *Club:* Artists (Liverpool).

**CALVERT, Prof. (Alan) Hilary,** MD; FRCP, FMedSci; Director, Cancer Drug Discovery and Development, UCL Cancer Institute, 2009–14, Head, Department of Oncology, 2010–14, and Professor of Cancer Therapeutics, 2011–14, now Professor Emeritus, University College London; *b* 18 Feb. 1947; *s* of Norman Geoffrey Calvert and Mary Christine Calvert (*née* Whitehead); *m* 1969, Drusilla Dean; three *d*. *Educ:* Birkenhead Sch.; Peterhouse, Cambridge (BA Med. Sci. and Maths 1969; MB BChir 1972; MD 1981); University Coll. Hosp., London (Clinical Studies); Chelsea Coll., London (MSc Biochem. 1978). MRCP 1975, FRCP 1988; Accreditation Med. Oncol., RCP 1987. Clinical Res. Fellow, Royal Marsden Hosp., 1975–77; Institute of Cancer Research, London: Lectr in Clinical Pharmacol., 1977–80; Sen. Lectr, 1980–85; Reader, 1985–89; University of Newcastle upon Tyne: Prof. of Med. Oncol., 1989–2009, now Prof. Emeritus; Dir, Cancer Res. Unit, 1989–2003; Clinical Dir, subseq. Dir of Clinical and Translational Res., Northern Inst. for Cancer Res., 2003–09 (drug, PARP Inhibitor (rucaparib) developed in Newcastle, licensed in USA, 2016, EU 2018). Hon. Consultant: in Medicine, Royal Marsden Hosp., 1980–89; in Med. Oncol., Northern Centre for Cancer Treatment, Newcastle upon Tyne, 1989–2009; UCLH, 2009–14, 2016–. Vis. Prof., Dept of Maths and Statistics, Newcastle Univ., 2010–13. Fitzpatrick Lect., RCP, 2013; Targeted Anticancer Therapies Hon. Award Lect., 2015. Mem., Gene Therapy Adv. Cttee, 2006–12; Chm., New Agents Cttee, CRUK, 2009–13; Mem., Internat. Scientific Adv. Bd, Associazione Italiana per la Ricerca sul Cancro, 2012–16. FMedSci 2002. Pfizer Award for Innovative Sci., 2005; Lifetime Achievement Award: British Oncol Assoc., 2009; Eur. Soc. of Med. Oncol., 2010; (jtly) Translational Res. Prize, CRUK, 2010. *Publications:* (ed jtly) Handbook of Anticancer Drug Development, 2003; contrib. to Jl Clin. Oncol. on carboplatin dosage, the Calvert Formula; contribs on cancer research, esp. cancer therapy, incl. develt of platinum drugs, antifolates and inhibitors of poly (ADP-ribose) polymerase; also contribs on application of mathematical methods to cancer treatment. *Recreations:* classical music, opera, hi-fi circuit design and development, olive oil production, computer programming of MACREX indexing software (with Drusilla). *Address:* UCL Cancer Institute, Paul O'Gorman Building, 72 Huntley Street, WC1E 6BT. *E:* hilary.calvert@cancer.ucl.ac.uk.

**CALVERT, Denis;** *see* Calvert, L. V. D.

**CALVERT, Hilary;** *see* Calvert, A. H.

**CALVERT, John Raymond;** Chairman, Worcestershire Partnership Mental Health NHS Trust, 1999–2007; *b* 14 June 1937; *s* of Matthew and Eva Mary Calvert; *m* 1962, Elspeth Sarah Naish; one *s* one *d*. *Educ:* Bootham, York; Manchester Univ. (BA Econs). FIPD (FIPM 1986). Cadbury Schweppes Ltd, 1961–70; Delta Metals Ltd, 1970–73; Pilkington Bros Ltd, 1973–84; Personnel Dir, Triplex Safety Glass Ltd, 1973–80; Dir, Chance Bros Ltd, 1973–80; Gp Employee Relations Manager, 1980–84; Dir, Industrial Relations, ITCA, 1984–88; Gp Personnel Dir, Yorkshire Tyne Tees TV Hldgs plc, 1988–93; Man. Dir, 1993–97, Dep. Chm., 1996–97, Tyne Tees TV. Director: Northern Sinfonia, 1993–; Newcastle Initiative, 1994–. Council Member: Industrial Soc., 1994–; NE Chamber of Commerce, 1995–. Chm., Newcastle Educn Business Partnership, 1995–. Trustee, Cleveland Community Foundn, 1995–. Gov., Newcastle Coll., 1994–. Chm., Feckenham Community Shop, 2009–13. FRSA 1989. *Recreations:* church organist and choirmaster, fell walking, tennis. *Address:* Strands, Droitwich Road, Feckenham, near Redditch, Worcs B96 6RT. *T:* (01527) 821607.

**CALVERT, Jonathan Richard;** Insight Editor, The Sunday Times, since 2005; *b* Pontefract; *s* of Derek Calvert and Rita Calvert; one *s* one *d*. *Educ:* Univ. of Leeds (BA Hons English and Hist.). Reporter, Western Mail, 1990–93; Insight Reporter, The Sunday Times, 1993–95; Investigations Ed., The Observer, 1995–99; Asst Ed. Investigations, Express Newspapers, 1999–2001; Investigative Reporter, The Sunday Times, 2001–. *Publications:* The Ugly Game: the Qatari plot to buy the World Cup (with Heidi Blake), 2015. *Recreations:* running, cycling, reading, cooking. *Address:* West London. *T:* (office) (020) 7782 5035. *E:* jonathan.calvert@sunday-times.co.uk.

**CALVERT, Kate;** musician, lyricist and author; *b* Lewisham, London, 22 Dec. 1985. *Educ:* BRIT Sch. for Performing Arts and Technol.; Goldsmiths, Univ. of London (Eng. Lit.). Albums: Everybody Down, 2014; Let Them Eat Chaos, 2016; The Book of Traps and Lessons, 2019. FRSL 2015. *Publications:* as Kate Tempest: Brand New Ancients, 2013 (Ted Hughes Award, 2013); Wasted (play), 2013; Hold Your Own, 2014; Hopelessly Devoted (play), 2014; The Bricks That Built The Houses, 2016; Running Upon the Wires, 2018.

**CALVERT, Lorne Albert;** Principal, St Andrew's College, University of Saskatchewan, 2009–18; *b* Moose Jaw, Sask, 24 Dec. 1952; *s* of Albert Calvert and Beulah Awilda (*née* Phillips); *m* 1975, Betty Anne Sluzalo; one *s* one *d*. *Educ:* Univ. of Regina (BA 1973); Univ. of Saskatchewan (BD 1976). Ordained minister, United Ch of Canada, 1976; Minister: Gravelbourg United Ch, 1976–79; Zion United Ch, Moose Jaw, 1979–86. MLA (NDP) Moose Jaw South, 1986–91, Moose Jaw Wakamow, 1991–2001, Saskatoon Riversdale, 2001–09; Associate Minister of Health, and Minister resp. for Wakamow Valley Authy, 1992–95; Minister resp. for SaskPower and SaskEnergy, 1992–93; Minister: of Health, 1995; of Social Services, 1995–98 (also resp. for Seniors and Public Service Commn); Minister resp. for Disabilities Issues, 1997–98; Premier, and Pres., Exec. Council, 2001–07; Leader of the Opposition, 2007–09. Dep. Chm., Crown Corporations Cttee, 1991–92; Mem., Standing Cttee on the Envmt, 1991–92. Leader, NDP, 2001–09.

**CALVERT, (Louis Victor) Denis,** CB 1985; Comptroller and Auditor General for Northern Ireland, 1980–89, retired; *b* 20 April 1924; *s* of Louis Victor Calvert, Belfast and Gertrude Cherry Hobson, Belfast; *m* 1949, Vivien Millicent Lawson; two *s* one *d*. *Educ:* Belfast Royal Academy; Queen's Univ., Belfast (BScEcon); Admin. Staff Coll., Henley-on-Thames. Served with RAF, 1943–47, navigator (F/O). Northern Ireland Civil Service, 1947–80: Min. of Agriculture, 1947–56; Dep. Principal 1951; Principal, Min. of Finance, 1956–63; Min. of Health and Local Govt, 1963–65; Asst Sec. 1964; Min. of Development, 1965–73; Sen. Asst Sec. 1970; Dep. Sec. 1971; Min. of Housing, Local Govt and Planning, 1973–76; DoE for NI, 1976–80. Mem. Bd, Internat. Fund for Ireland, 1989–92. *Recreations:* gardening, reading, TV.

**CALVERT, Margaret Vivienne,** OBE 2016; RDI 2011; (independent) graphic designer and typographer, since 2001; *b* Durban, SA, 12 May 1936; *d* of Stanley Gordon Calvert and Jessie Margaret Calvert (*née* Tassie). *Educ:* Hatfield Primary Sch., Pretoria; Pretoria High Sch. for Girls; St Paul's Sch. for Girls, London; Chelsea Sch. of Art. Asst Designer to Jock Kinneir, 1957–66; Partner, Kinneir Calvert & Associates, 1966–72; Dir, Kinneir Calvert Tuhill, 1972–79; Hd, Graphic Design, RCA, 1987–91 (Sen. Fellow, 2001). Pt-time Lectr in Graphic Design and Typography, RCA, 1966–2001. Speaker, Design Indaba, Cape Town, 2016. Mem., Alliance Graphique Internat., 1977–. Hon. Fellow, Univ. of Arts, London, 2004. Hon. DLitt Brighton, 2006; Hon. Dr RCA, 2016. Pres.'s Award, D&AD, 2015; Sir Misha Black Medal for Dist. Services to Design Educn, Coll. of Medallists, RCA, 2016; Lifetime Achievements Medal, British Land Celebration of Design Awards, 2017; Churchill Award for Art, Churchill Retirement Living, 2017. *Publications:* (contrib.) AGI: graphic design since 1950, 2007; (contrib.) D&AD Annual, 2016. *Recreations:* cinema, reading, walking, table-tennis.

**CALVERT, Rev. Canon Peter Noel;** House for Duty Team Vicar, Cartmel Peninsula Team Ministry, 2012–15; Chaplain to the Queen, 1998–2011; *b* 20 Dec. 1941; *s* of Harry and Beatrice Annie Calvert; *m* 1980, Stella Christine Horrocks; two *s* one *d*. *Educ:* Queen Elizabeth GS, Wakefield; Arnold Sch., Blackpool; Christ's Coll., Cambridge (BA 1963; MA 1967). Ordained deacon, 1966, priest, 1967; Curate, Brighouse, 1966–71; Vicar, Heptonstall, 1971–82; Vicar of Todmorden, W Yorks, 1982–2007; Priest-in-charge, Cross Stone, 1983–93; Rural Dean, Calder Valley, 1984–2006; House for Duty Priest-in-charge, Leven Valley Benefice, 2007–11; Hon. Canon, Wakefield Cathedral, 1992–2007, now Canon Emeritus. *Recreations:* photography, philately, walking, interest in transport. *Address:* 26 Stonemere Avenue, Todmorden OL14 5RW. *T:* (01706) 817166.

**CALVERT-SMITH, Sir David,** Kt 2002; Member, Parole Board of England and Wales, since 2017 (Chairman, 2012–16); *b* 6 April 1945; *s* of late Arthur and Stella Calvert-Smith; *m* 1971, Marianthe Phoca; one *s* one *d*. *Educ:* Eton; King's Coll., Cambridge (MA). Called to the Bar, Middle Temple, 1969, Bencher, 1994; a Recorder, 1986–98; Jun. Treasury Counsel, 1986; Sen. Treasury Counsel, 1991; First Sen. Treasury Counsel, 1995; QC 1997; Dir of Public Prosecutions, 1998–2003; a Judge of the High Court of Justice, QBD, 2004–12; a Presiding Judge, SE Circuit, 2006–10; a Judge, Courts of Appeal, Jersey and Guernsey, 2012–17. Mem., CRE, 2004–06. Vice-Chm., 1997–98, Chm., 1998, Criminal Bar Assoc.; Mem., Criminal Cttee, Judicial Studies Bd, 1997–98. *Recreations:* music, sports. *Address:* QEB Hollis Whiteman, 1–2 Laurence Pountney Hill, EC4R 0EU.

**CALVET, Jacques;** President, Peugeot SA, 1984–97; Referendary Councillor, Cour des Comptes (Audit Office), since 1963; *b* 19 Sept. 1931; *s* of Prof. Louis Calvet and Yvonne Calvet (*née* Olmières); *m* 1956, Françoise Rondot; two *s* one *d*. *Educ:* Lycée Janson-de-Sailly; Law Faculty, Paris (Licencié en droit); Dipl. Inst. d'Etudes Politiques; Dipl. d'Etudes Supérieures d'Economie Politique et des Sciences Economiques). Trainee, l'Ecole Nationale d'Administration, 1955–57; Audit Office, 1957–59; Office of Sec. of State for Finance, 1959–62, of Minister of Finance, 1962–66; Dep. Dir, 1964, Head of Dept, 1967, Central Finance Admin; Head of Finance Dept, Paris Préfecture, 1967–69; Asst Dir, later Dir, Office of Minister of Economy and Finance, 1969–74; Dir in Ministry of Finance, 1973; Asst Dir Gen., 1974, Dir Gen., 1976, Pres., 1979–82, Banque Nationale de Paris; Vice-Prés. du Conseil d'Administration, 1984, Prés., 1990, Automobiles Peugeot; Président du Conseil d'Administration: Automobiles Citroën, 1983–97; Publicité Française, 1991–97. Vice Prés., Conseil de surveillance, Galeries Lafayette; Prés., Comité de surveillance, Bazar de l'hôtel de Ville; Administrateur, Société Foncière Lyonnaise. Consulting Advr, Banque de France. Commandeur, Légion d'Honneur, 1996; Officier: Ordre Nat. du Mérite, 1970; Ordre Nat. du Mérite Agricole, 1970; Chevalier des Palmes académiques, 1964; Grande Ufficiale, Ordine al Merito della Repubblica Italiana, 1995. *Address:* 31 avenue Victor Hugo, 75116 Paris, France.

**CALVIN, Michael;** author, broadcaster, columnist, owner, Integr8Communications, since 2007; *b* 3 Aug. 1957; *s* of Charles Calvin and Margaret Calvin (*née* Platts); *m* 1977, Lynn Goss; three *s* one *d*. *Educ:* Watford Grammar Sch. Reporter: Watford Observer, 1975–77; Hayters Sports Agency, 1977–79; writer and broadcaster, Thames TV, 1983–84; Chief Sports Writer, Westminster Press, 1979–83; Feature Writer, 1984–86, Chief Sports Writer, 1986–96, Daily Telegraph; Sen. Sports Writer, The Times, 1997–98; Chief Sports Feature Writer, Mail on Sunday, 1998–2002; Dep. Dir, English Inst. of Sport, 2002–07; Chief Sports Writer, Sunday Mirror, 2008–11; columnist, Independent on Sunday, 2011–16. Segrave Trophy for Outstanding Achievement, 1990; Sports Journalist of the Year, English Sports Council, 1992; Sports Reporter of the Year, British Press Awards, 1992, 1999; Award for Services to Yachting Journalism, RYA, 1993; led winning team for coverage of disabled sport, British Sports Assoc. for Disabled, 1994, 1995, 1996. *Publications:* Captaincy, 1977; Only Wind and Water, 1998; Family: life, death and football, 2010; Life's a Pitch, 2012; The Nowhere Men, 2013 (The Times Sports Book of the Year, 2014); (with G. Thomas) Proud, 2014 (Cross Sports Book of Year, 2015); Living on the Volcano: the secrets of surviving as a football manager, 2015; (with J. Barton) No Nonsense, 2016 (Best Autobiog., British Sports Book Awards, 2017); No Hunger in Paradise, 2017; State of Play, 2018; (with T. Bjorn) Mind Game, 2019. *Recreation:* long distance sailing. *Clubs:* Royal Ocean Racing; Cape Horners.

**CALVOCORESSI, Richard Edward Ion,** CBE 2008; Director and Chief Curator, Gagosian Gallery, London, since 2015; *b* 5 May 1951; *s* of late Ion Melville Calvocoressi and of Katherine (*née* Kennedy); *m* 1976, Francesca Temple Roberts; one *s* two *d*. *Educ:* Eton; Brooke House, Market Harborough; Magdalen Coll., Oxford (Exhibnr; BA (Hons)

English Lang. and Lit.); Courtauld Inst. of Art (MA Hist. of Art, 19th and 20th centuries). Research Assistant: Scottish Nat. Gall. of Modern Art, Edinburgh, 1977–79; Modern Collection, Tate Gall., 1979–82; Asst Keeper, Tate Gall., 1982–87; Keeper, then Dir, Scottish Nat. Gall. of Modern Art, 1987–2007; Dir, Henry Moore Foundn, 2007–15. Art Advr, Chelmsford Mus., 1980–86; Member: Cttee, British Council, Scotland, 1989–98; Visual Arts Adv. Cttee, British Council, 1991–2006 (Chm., 1999–2006); Visual Arts Cttee, Scottish Arts Council, 1993–95; Reviewing Cttee on Export of Works of Art, 2012–. Dir, Grimsthorpe and Drummond Castle Trust, 1993–. Governor, Glasgow Sch. of Art, 1988–91; Expert Mem., Comité Magritte, 2001–; Mem., Francis Bacon catalogue raisonné Cttee, 2006–16. Trustee: Edward James Foundn, 2007–10; Art Fund, 2008–18; Artist Rooms Foundn, 2018–; Foundation Foundn, 2018–. *Publications:* Magritte, 1979, rev. edn 1984; Lee Miller: portraits from a life, 2002; Lucian Freud on Paper, 2008; numerous exhibn catalogues, reviews and articles with emphasis on modern European artists and modern British artists. *Address:* 20 Warriston Crescent, Edinburgh EH3 5LB.

**CAMA, Most Rev. Fereimi;** see Polynesia, Bishop of.

**CAMBRIDGE, Archdeacon of;** see Hughes, Ven. A. J.

**CAMDEN, 6th Marquess** cr 1812; **David George Edward Henry Pratt;** Baron Camden, 1765; Earl Camden, Viscount Bayham, 1786; Earl of Brecknock, 1812; b 13 Aug. 1930; o s of 5th Marquess Camden and Marjorie, Countess of Brecknock, DBE (d 1989); S father, 1983; m 1961, Virginia Ann (marr. diss. 1984), o d of late F. H. H. Finlaison, Arklow Cottage, Windsor, Berks; one s one d (and one s decd). *Educ:* Eton. Late Lieutenant, Scots Guards. Dir, Clive Discount Co. Ltd, 1958–69. *Heir:* s Earl of Brecknock, qv. *Address:* Wherwell House, Andover, Hants SP11 7JP. *T:* (01264) 860020.

**CAMDESSUS, Michel Jean,** Hon. CBE 2007; Managing Director, International Monetary Fund, 1987–2000; b 1 May 1933; s of Alfred Camdessus and Madeleine Camdessus (née Cassembon); m 1957, Brigitte d'Arcy; two s four d. *Educ:* Inst. of Political Studies, Paris; Diploma, Nat. Sch. of Administration. Administrateur Civil, French Treasury, 1960; Financial Attaché, Permt French Delegn to European Communities, 1966–68; Asst Dir, Treasury, 1971, Dep. Dir, 1974, Dir, 1982; Dep. Governor, Bank of France, Aug. 1984, Governor, Nov. 1984. Chm., Paris Club, 1978–84. Grand Officier de la Légion d'Honneur; Chevalier de l'Ordre National du Mérite; Croix de la valeur militaire. *Address:* 29 rue de Valois, 75001 Paris, France.

**CAMERON,** family name of **Barons Cameron of Dillington** and **Cameron of Lochbroom.**

**CAMERON OF DILLINGTON,** Baron cr 2004 (Life Peer), of Dillington in the County of Somerset; **Ewen James Hanning Cameron,** Kt 2003; DL; FRICS; Owner and Manager, Dillington Estate, Somerset, since 1971; b 24 Nov. 1949; s of Maj. Allan John Cameron and Elizabeth Cameron (née Vaughan-Lee); m 1975, Caroline Anne Ripley; three s one d. *Educ:* Harrow Sch.; Christ Church, Oxford (MA). FRICS 1992; FRAgS 1995. Founding Chm., Orchard Media Ltd, 1989–99; Chairman: Lets Go Travel Ltd, 1998–2006; Airports Direct Travel Ltd, 2006–. Mem., Minister of Agriculture's CAP rev. gp, 1995; Govt's Rural Advocate, 2000–04. Jt Chm., All Party Parly Gp for Agric., Food and Develt, 2009–; Chm., Strategy Adv. Bd, Global Food Security Prog., 2011–. Dir, Village Retail Services Assoc. for Village Shops, 1992–2000. Nat. Pres., CLA, 1995–97. Mem., UK Round Table for Sustainable Develt, 1997–2000. Chairman: Countryside Agency, 1999–2004; Charities' Property Assoc., 2005–; Centre for Ecol. and Hydrol., 2015–; Dir, Lawes Agricl Trust (Rothamsted), 2005–; Pres., British Guild of Agricl Journalists (formerly Agricl Guild of Journalists), 2010–15. Pres., Somerset Young Farmers, 1990–91; Mem., Mgt Bd, Nat. Fedn of Young Farmers, 1998–2000. Chm., Somerset Strategic Partnership, 2004–10. Dir, Royal Bath and West Soc., 2005–15 (Pres., 2006–07). Crossbencher, H of L. FRSA 1996. High Sheriff, 1986–87, DL 1989, Somerset. Hon. Fellow, RAU, 2013. Hon. LLD Exeter, 2004. *Recreations:* golf, shooting, windsurfing. *Address:* Clouds, Rock, Cornwall PL27 6LD.

**CAMERON OF LOCHBROOM,** Baron cr 1984 (Life Peer), of Lochbroom in the District of Ross and Cromarty; **Kenneth John Cameron;** PC 1984; a Senator of the College of Justice in Scotland, 1989–2003; b 11 June 1931; s of Hon. Lord Cameron, KT, DSC; m 1964, Jean Pamela Murray; two d. *Educ:* The Edinburgh Academy; Corpus Christi Coll., Oxford (MA 1955; Hon. Fellow, 1989); Edinburgh Univ. (LLB). Served RN, 1950–52; commissioned RNVR, 1951 (Lt). Admitted Faculty of Advocates, 1958; QC (Scot.) 1972; Standing Junior to Dept of Transport, 1964–71; to DoE, 1971–72; Chairman of Industrial Tribunals in Scotland, 1966–81; Advocate Depute, 1981–84; Lord Advocate, 1984–89. Chm. of Pensions Appeal Tribunal (Scotland), 1975, Pres. 1976–84. Mem., H of L, 1984–2016. Chairman: Cttee for Investigation in Scotland of Agricultural Marketing Schemes, 1980–84; Scottish Civic Trust, 1989–95; Edinburgh New Town Conservation Cttee, 1991–94; Royal Fine Art Commn for Scotland, 1995–2005. Pres., Scottish Council for Voluntary Orgns, 1989–2001. Hon. Bencher, Lincoln's Inn, 1984. FRSE 1990. Hon. FRIAS 1994. *Recreations:* fishing, music. *Address:* Stoneyhill House, Musselburgh EH21 6RP. *T:* (0131) 665 1081. *Club:* New (Edinburgh).

**CAMERON, Alan John,** AO 2011 (AM 1997); Chairman and Director, Property Exchange Australia Ltd (formerly National e-Conveyancing Development Ltd), since 2010; b 9 Feb. 1948; s of John and Norma Cameron; m 1971, Susan Patricia Sanders; two s. *Educ:* Sydney Univ. (BA, LLB, LLM). Principal Solicitor, NSW Aboriginal Legal Service, 1973–75; Lectr in Law, Univ. of N Sumatra, 1975–77; Dawson Waldron, Solicitors, later Blake Dawson Waldron: Partner, 1979–91; Man. Partner, 1982–85, 1989–91; Commonwealth Ombudsman (Australia), 1991–92; Chairman: Australian Securities & Investments Commn, 1993–2000; NSW Growth Centres Commn, 2005–08; ASX Compliance Pty Ltd (formerly ASX Market Supervision Pty Ltd), 2008–17; Hastings Funds Mgt Ltd, 2009–16; ASX Corporate Governance Council, 2011–17; Chm. and Dir, Reliance Rail Gp, 2007–10; Dir, Sydney Inst. of Marine Sci., 2015–. Mem., Judicial Commn of NSW, 2001–09; Chm., NSW Law Reform Commn, 2015–18. Dir, Westpac Funds Management Ltd, 2006–10. Dep. Chancellor, Univ. of Sydney, 2007–14. *Recreations:* tennis, walking, reading. *Address:* 32 Hart Street, Balmain, NSW 2041, Australia.

**CAMERON, Alexander,** CBE 2008; Chairman, Parole Board for Scotland, 2006–13; Panel Member, Independent Jersey Care Inquiry, since 2014; b 29 April 1950; s of Æneas and Ruby Cameron; m 1975, Linda J. T. Dobbie; two s. *Educ:* Duncanrig Sen. Secondary Sch.; Univ. of Strathclyde (BA); Univ. of Aberdeen (Cert. Applied Social Studies; CQSW 1973). Social worker, Clackmannan Co., 1973–75; Principal Officer, 1975–81, Asst Dir of Social Work, 1981–87, Central Reg.; Dir of Social Work, Borders Reg., 1987–95; Exec. Dir of Social Work, S Lanarks, 1995–2006. Vis. Prof., Strathclyde Univ., 1997–. Chair: Inst. for Res. and Innovation in Social Services (formerly Scottish Inst. for Excellence in Social Work Educn), 2003–; Scottish Inst. for Residential Child Care, 1996–2007. Nonexec. Dir, State Hosps Bd for Scotland, 2005–13. Chm., Exec. Governance Gp, Centre for Youth and Criminal Justice, Univ. of Strathclyde, 2013–; Mem. Bd, SACRO, 2013– (Chm., 2014–). Dir, Care Visions, 2006–. Chm., Scottish Assoc. for Study of Offending, 2016–. Trustee, Lloyds TSB Foundn for Scotland, 2009–16; Chairman: Fred Edwards Trust, 2010–16; Capability Scotland, 2018– (Mem. Bd, 2012). Chair, Gattonside Village Hall SCIO; Vice Chair, Gattonside Community Trust SCIO. Pres., Assoc. of Dirs of Social Work, 1996–97. Fellow, British Amer. Project, 1988. *Recreations:* reading, architecture and design, cooking, dining out, travel, especially to USA. *T:* 07792 229964. *E:* cameronsathome@btinternet.com.

**CAMERON, Alexander Allan;** QC 2003; b 27 Aug. 1963; s of late Ian Donald Cameron and of Mary Fleur Cameron; m 1990, Sarah Louise Fearnley-Whittingstall; one s one d. *Educ:* Eton Coll.; Bristol Univ. (LLB Hons). Called to the Bar, Inner Temple, 1986; in practice, specialising in law of crime, esp. commercial crime. *Recreations:* various. *Address:* 3 Raymond Buildings, Gray's Inn, WC1R 5BH. *T:* (020) 7400 6400. *E:* clerks@3rblaw.com. *Clubs:* White's, Queen's, MCC.

See also Rt Hon. D. W. D. Cameron.

**CAMERON, Prof. Alexander John,** DPhil; Vice-Chancellor and Chief Executive, Aston University, since 2016; b Sydney, Australia, 5 Feb. 1963; s of Peter John Cameron and Margaret Jennifer Cameron; m 1987, Elizabeth Jane Kellaway; one s one d. *Educ:* Knox Grammar Sch., Wahroonga, Australia; Univ. of Sydney (BSc 1983; BE Hons 1985); University Coll., Oxford (DPhil Robotics 1989); Poly. Inst. of New York Univ. (MSc Mgt of Technol. 1993); Harvard Business Sch. (AMP 2015). Sen. Mem., Res. Staff, Philips, NY, 1989–93; Prog. Dir, Australian Grad. Sch. of Engrg Innovation, 1993–96; Nat. Gen. Manager, Telstra, 1996–2000; Dir, Technol., CoMindico, 2000–01; Telstra Account Dir, Alcatel Australia, 2001–02; Nat. Manager, Product Mgt, Sun Microsystems, 2002–03; Dep. Vice Chancellor, Resources and Infrastructure, Univ. of NSW, 2003–06; Dean, UNSW Business Sch., Univ. of NSW, 2006–12; Dep. Vice Chancellor (Educn), Univ. of WA, 2013–16. Dir, Innovation Birmingham Ltd, 2016–. Mem. Gen. Council, Chamber of Commerce and Industry of WA, 2013–16. Pres., Australian Business Deans' Council, 2011–12. *Recreations:* cycling, golf, walking. *Address:* Aston University, Birmingham B4 7ET. *T:* (0121) 204 4884. *E:* alec.cameron@aston.ac.uk. *Clubs:* Vincent's (Oxford); Australian (Sydney).

**CAMERON, Rt Rev. Andrew Bruce;** Bishop of Aberdeen and Orkney, 1992–2006 and Primus of the Episcopal Church in Scotland, 2000–06; b 2 May 1941; s of Andrew and Helen Cameron; m 1974, Elaine Gingles; two s. *Educ:* Eastwood Secondary Sch., Glasgow; Edinburgh Theol Coll.; Edinburgh Univ. (Cert. in Past. Studies); Urban Theology Unit, Sheffield (Dip. in Theology and Mission). Ordained deacon 1964, priest 1965; Assistant Curate: St Michael and All Angels, Helensburgh, 1964–67; Holy Cross, Edinburgh, 1967–70; Diocesan and Provincial Youth Chaplain and Chaplain, St Mary's Cathedral, Edinburgh, 1970–75; Rector, St Mary's, Dalmahoy and Anglican Chaplain, Heriot-Watt Univ., 1975–82; Churches Develt Officer in Livingston Ecumenical Parish, 1982–88; Rector, St John's, Perth and Convenor of Provincial Mission Bd, 1988–92. Resident Scholar, Bruton Parish Church, Williamsburg, Va, 2006–07. Interim Warden, Scottish Churches House, 2008. *Recreations:* swimming, walking, gardening, singing, listening to music, theatre, reading. *Address:* 21/1 Barossa Place, Perth PH1 5HH. *T:* (01738) 441172. *E:* bruce2541@gmail.com.

See also Rt Rev. D. M. Cameron.

**CAMERON, Dame Averil (Millicent),** DBE 2006 (CBE 1999); MA, PhD, DLitt; FBA 1981; FSA 1982; historian; Warden, Keble College, Oxford, 1994–2010; Professor of Late Antique and Byzantine History, 1998–2010, Pro-Vice-Chancellor, 2001–10, Chair, Oxford Centre for Byzantine Research, since 2010, University of Oxford; b 8 Feb. 1940; d of T. R. Sutton, Leek, Staffs; m 1962, Prof. Alan Douglas Edward Cameron, FBA (marr. diss. 1980; he d 2017); one s one d. *Educ:* Westwood Hall Girls' High Sch., Leek, Staffs; Somerville Coll., Oxford (Passmore Edwards Schol. 1960; Rosa Hovey Schol. 1962; MA); Univ. of Glasgow; University Coll. London (PhD; FKC 1987); Univ. of Oxford (DLitt 2008). King's College London: Asst Lectr, 1965; Lectr, 1968; Reader in Ancient History, 1970; Prof. of Ancient History, 1978–89; Head of Dept of Classics, 1984–89; Prof. of Late Antique and Byzantine Studies, and Dir, Centre for Hellenic Studies, 1989–94. Visiting Professor: Columbia Univ., 1967–68; Collège de France, 1987; Sather Prof., Univ. of Calif. at Berkeley, 1985–86; Vis. Member, Inst. of Advanced Study, Princeton, 1977–78; Summer Fellow, Dumbarton Oaks Center for Byzantine Studies, 1981; British Acad. Wolfson Res. Reader in Hist., 1990–92. Chm., British Nat. Byzantine Cttee, 1983–89; President: Roman Soc., 1995–98 (Vice-Pres., 1983–95, 1999–); Council for British Res. in the Levant, 2004–; Ecclesiastical History Soc., 2005–06; Fédn Internat. des Assocs d'Etudes Classiques, 2009–14 (Vice-Pres., 2005–09); Soc. for Promotion of Byzantine Studies, 2017–. Mem., British Acad. Council, 1983–86. Chm., Cathedrals Fabric Commn for England, 1999–2005 (Vice-Chm., 1999). Editor, Jl of Roman Studies, 1985–90. Corresp. mem., Akad. der Wiss. zu Göttingen, phil.-hist. Klasse, 2006; Corresp. Fellow, Centre for Byzantine Res., Aristotelian Univ., Thessaloniki, 2014; Fellow, Medieval Acad. of America, 2017. Hon. DLitt: Warwick, 1996; St Andrews, 1997; QUB, 2000; Aberdeen, 2003; London, 2005; DTheol Lund, 2001. *Publications:* Procopius, 1967; Agathias, 1970; Corippus: In laudem Iustini minoris, 1976; Change and Continuity in Sixth-Century Byzantium, 1981; (ed jtly) Images of Women in Antiquity, 1983, 2nd edn 1993; (ed jtly) Constantinople in the Eighth Century: the Parastaseis Syntomoi Chronikai, 1984; Procopius and the Sixth Century, 1985; (ed) History as Text: the writing of ancient history, 1989; Christianity and the Rhetoric of Empire, 1991; (ed jtly) The Byzantine and Early Islamic Near East, vol. I: Problems in the Literary Source Material, 1992, vol. II: Land Use and Settlement Patterns, 1994, vol. III: States, Resources and Armies, 1995; The Later Roman Empire, 1993; The Mediterranean World in Late Antiquity, AD 395–600, 1993, AD 395–700, 2nd edn 2011; Changing Cultures in Early Byzantium, 1996; (ed with P. D. Garnsey) Cambridge Ancient History, vol. XIII, 1998; (ed with S. G. Hall) Eusebius, Life of Constantine, 1999; (ed jtly) Cambridge Ancient History, vol. XIV, 2001; (ed) Fifty Years of Prosopography, 2003; (ed jtly) Cambridge Ancient History, vol. XII, 2005; The Byzantines, 2006; (ed with R. Hoyland) Doctrine and Debate in the East Christian World, 300–1500, 2011; (ed) Late Antiquity on the Eve of Islam, 2013; Byzantine Matters, 2014; Dialoguing in Late Antiquity, 2014; Arguing it Out, 2016; (ed with Niels Gaul) Dialogues and Debates from Late Antiquity to Late Byzantium, 2017; Byzantine Christianity, 2017; numerous articles in learned jls. *Address:* Keble College, Oxford OX1 3PG.

**CAMERON, Her Honour Barbara Alexander;** a Circuit Judge, 2007–19; b Totteridge, 3 June 1950; d of Thomas and Paula Alexander Cameron; m 1983; two d. *Educ:* Queen's Coll., Harley St; Lucy Cavendish Coll., Cambridge (BA Hons Law 1980). Dental nurse; ran dental practices in Herts and Harley St, 1967–77. Called to the Bar, Lincoln's Inn, 1979; Mem., Inner Temple, 1983. Lectr in Law, City of London Poly., 1980–82; barrister, Henderson Chambers, Temple, 1982–2007; Recorder, 1999–2007; Dep. Dist Judge, 1999–2007. Family and Divorce Mediator, 1998–2007. Legal Assessor: to NMC, 1993–2007; to GDC, GMC and Gen. Chiropractic Council, 2004–07. Member: Appeals Cttee, Legal Services Commn, 1993–2007; Bar Disciplinary Tribunal, 1997–2007. Member: Family Law Bar Assoc., 1983–2017; Professional Negligence Bar Assoc., 1990–2008 (Mem., Exec. Cttee, 1993–95); Personal Injuries Bar Assoc., 1995–2008; Assoc. of Women Lawyers, 2003–08; Assoc. of Regulatory and Disciplinary Lawyers, 2004–08. Panel Mem., Barristers' Complaints Adv. Service, 1997–2007. *Recreations:* family and country life, opera, cooking, walking.

**CAMERON, Clare**; Director, Defence Innovation, Ministry of Defence, since 2019; *b* London, 5 Sept. 1980; *d of* Giles Caldin and Rachel Caldin; *m* 2013, Brig. Peter Cameron, OBE; one *s*, and one step *s* one step *d*. *Educ*: Cheltenham Ladies' Coll.; Durham Univ. (BA Hist.). Ministry of Defence, 2003–: Policy Advr on Nat. Security, Cabinet Office, 2009–11; Policy for Mil. Ops, MoD, 2013–15; Dep. Dir, Defence, Cabinet Office, 2016–18. Trustee, Tiyeni Fund, 2006–. *Recreations*: walking, art, history, travelling, family. *Address*: Ministry of Defence, Main Building, Whitehall, SW1A 2HB.

**CAMERON, Rt Hon. David William Donald**; PC 2005; *b* 9 Oct. 1966; *s of late* Ian Donald Cameron and of Mary Fleur Cameron; *m* 1996, Samantha Gwendoline, *e d of* Sir Reginald Sheffield, Bt, *qv*; one *s* two *d* (and one *s* decd). *Educ*: Eton Coll.; Brasenose Coll., Oxford (BA 1st Cl. Hons PPE; Hon. Fellow, 2006). Cons. Res. Dept, 1988–92; Special Adviser: HM Treasury, 1992–93; Home Office, 1993–94; Hd, Corporate Affairs, Carlton Communications plc, 1994–2001. MP (C) Witney, 2001–Sept. 2016. Shadow Sec. of State for Educn and Skills, 2005; Leader of the Opposition, 2005–10; Prime Minister and First Lord of the Treasury, 2010–16. Mem., Select Cttee on Home Affairs, 2001–05. Dep. Chm., Cons. Party, 2003–04. Pres., Alzheimer's Res. UK, 2017–; Chm. Patrons, Nat. Citizen Service, 2016–. *Publications*: (with Dylan Jones) Cameron on Cameron: conversations with Dylan Jones, 2008; For the Record (autobiog.), 2019. *Recreations*: tennis, cooking.

See also A. A. Cameron.

**CAMERON, Rt Rev. Donald;** *see* Cameron, Rt Rev. E. D.

**CAMERON, Donald Allan**, MBE 2014; RDI 2004; FRAeS; Managing Director, Cameron Balloons Ltd, since 1970; *b* 16 July 1939; *s of late* David Stuart Cameron and Madge Kaye Cameron; *m* 1st, 1969, Dorothy Anne Golding (marr. diss. 1980); one *s* one *d*; 2nd, 1980, Margaret Louise Tobin; six *s* one *d*. *Educ*: Allan Glen's Sch.; Glasgow Univ. (BSc); Cornell Univ. (MS). FRAeS 2010. Chm., Bristol Balloon Fiestas Ltd, 1992–. British Delegate to FAI (Ballooning), 1987–2002 and 2010–16. Mem. Bd, Children's Hospice SW, 2003–08. Mem., Bath Royal Literary and Scientific Instn, 2002– (Convenor, 2004–; Trustee, 2006–15). Treas., 2011–14, Chm., 2014–16, N Somerset Conservative Assoc. Pres., Airship Assoc., 2016–. Hon. Pres., 2494 Sqdn ATC, 2003–10. Hon. Pres., City of Bristol Pipes & Drums, 2001–. Patron, IMechE, 2003–. Mem., Portishead (formerly Portishead and North Weston) Town Council, 2007– (Chm., 2014–15). Hon. Freeman, City of Bristol, 2007. Hon. MA Bristol, 1980; Hon. DEng: Glasgow, 2000; Bristol, 2017; Hon. DBA UWE, 2001. *Publications*: Ballooning Handbook, 1981; Purpose of Life, 2001. *Recreations*: ballooning, sailing, natural history. *Address*: c/o Cameron Balloons Ltd, St John Street, Bristol BS3 4NH. *T*: (0117) 963 7216, *Fax*: (0117) 966 1168. *E*: dcameron@cameronballoons.co.uk. *Clubs*: Royal Aero (Mem. Council, 1990–), British Balloon and Airship (Mem. Cttee, 1972–2016; Pres., 2015–).

**CAMERON, Donald Andrew John;** Member (C) Highlands and Islands, Scottish Parliament, since 2016; *b* London, 26 Nov. 1976; *s of* Donald Angus Cameron of Lochiel, *qv*; *m* 2009, Sarah Elizabeth Maclay; three *s* one *d*. *Educ*: Harrow Sch.; Oriel Coll., Oxford (BA Hons Mod. Hist.); City Univ. (DipLaw; BVC). Called to the Bar, Middle Temple, 2002; admitted to Faculty of Advocates, 2005; Standing Jun. Counsel to Scottish Govt, 2009–16. *Recreations*: hill-walking, theatre, travel. *Address*: Scottish Parliament, Edinburgh EH99 1SP. *T*: (0131) 348 6989. *E*: donald.cameron.msp@parliament.scot. *Club*: New (Edinburgh).

**CAMERON of Lochiel, Donald Angus**, CVO 2018; 27th Chief of the Clan Cameron; Lord-Lieutenant of Inverness, since 2002; *b* 2 Aug. 1946; *s of* Col Sir Donald Hamish Cameron of Lochiel, KT, CVO, TD, 26th Chief of the Clan Cameron and Margaret (*née* Gathorne-Hardy); *S* father as 27th Chief, 2004; *m* 1974, Lady Cecil Kerr, OBE, *d of* 12th Marquess of Lothian, KCVO; one *s* three *d*. *Educ*: Harrow; Christ Church, Oxford (MA). FCA. Dir, J. Henry Schroder Wagg, subseq. J. Henry Schroder & Co., 1984–99. 2nd Lieutenant, Queen's Own Cameron Highlanders (TA), 1966–68. Pres., Highland Soc. of London, 1994–97. JP Highland, 2002–07. *Address*: Achnacarry, Spean Bridge, Invernessshire PH34 4EJ. *T*: (01397) 712708.

See also D. A. J. Cameron.

**CAMERON, Donald William;** President, Maritime Steel and Foundries Ltd, 2002; *b* 20 May 1946; *m* 1969, Rosemary Simpson; one *s* two *d*. *Educ*: East Pictou Rural High Sch.; Nova Scotia Agricl Coll.; McGill Univ. (BSc). Dairy farmer; MLA (PC) Pictou East, 1974–93; Minister of: Recreation, 1978–79; Fisheries, 1978–80; Industry, Trade and Technology, 1988–91; Leader, Nova Scotia Progressive Cons. Party, 1991; Premier of Nova Scotia, 1991–93; Canadian Consul Gen. to New England, 1993–97. *Recreations*: skiing, boating, hockey, tennis. *Address*: RR #1, New Glasgow, NS B2H 5C4, Canada.

**CAMERON, Rt Rev. Douglas Maclean;** Bishop of Argyll and The Isles, 1993–2003; *b* 23 March 1935; *s of* Andrew McIntyre Cameron and Helen Adam McKechnie; *m* 1969, Anne Patricia Purnell; two *d*. *Educ*: Eastwood Grammar Sch., Clarkston, Glasgow; Theol Coll., Edinburgh; Univ. of the South, Sewanee, Tennessee, USA. Bank of Scotland, 1951–59; RAF, 1953–55. Ordained: deacon, 1962; priest, 1963; curate, Christ Church, Falkirk, 1962–65; Anglican Church in Papua New Guinea: Mission Priest, 1966–67; priest in charge, Movi, 1967–72; Rector, St Francis, Goroka, 1972–74; Archdeacon of New Guinea Mainland, 1972–74; Priest in charge, St Fillan's, Edinburgh, 1974, Rector, 1978–88; Rector: St Hilda's, Edinburgh, 1977–88; St Mary's, Dalkeith and St Leonard's, Lasswade, 1988–93; Canon, St Mary's Cathedral, Edinburgh and Synod Clerk, 1990–91; Dean of Edinburgh, 1991–92. *Recreations*: walking, travelling, cooking, grandchildren. *Address*: 23 Craigs Way, Rumford, Falkirk FK2 0EU. *T*: (01324) 714137.

See also Rt Rev. A. B. Cameron.

**CAMERON, Elizabeth;** Member, Glasgow City Council, 1992–2017; Lord Provost and Lord-Lieutenant of Glasgow, 2003–07; *o d of* John and Elizabeth Gregory; *m* Duncan Cameron; one step *d*. *Educ*: Glasgow Univ. (MA Hons English Lang. and Lit.). Lectr, Further and Adult Educn. Glasgow City Council: Deputy Convener: Women's Cttee, 1993–95; Arts and Culture, 1995–98; Convener, Culture and Leisure Services, 1998–2003. Vice Chm., Glasgow City Mktg Bureau, 2007–; Chm., Culture and Sport Glasgow. Member: Scottish Arts Council, 2002–06; Bd of Trustees, Nat. Galls of Scotland, 2002–06; Board: Scottish Ensemble (Chm.); Arches Th.; Glasgow Film Th. (Chm., 2008–); Scottish Internat. Piano Comp. (Chm., 2009–); Nat. Youth Choir Scotland; Royal Scottish Nat. Orch. Chorus Trust; Pres., Culture Commn Confedn of Cities of Atlantic Arc; Vice Chm., Les Rencontres Assoc. of European Cultural Cities. Patron, Glasgow Celtic Soc. Vis. Prof., Glasgow Caledonian Univ., 2007–. DUniv: Glasgow, 2006; Caledonian, 2006; Strathclyde, 2006. Officier, Ordre des Arts et des Lettres (France). *Recreations*: music, choral singing, languages (French and Italian), reading, theatre.

**CAMERON, Rt Rev. (Ewen) Donald;** Assistant Bishop, Diocese of Sydney, 1975–93; *b* 7 Nov. 1926; *s of* Ewen Cameron, Balranald, NSW, and Dulce M. Cameron, Sydney, NSW; *m* 1952, Joan R. (*d* 2015), *d of* T. Wilkins, Mosman, NSW; one *s* two *d*. *Educ*: Sydney C of E Grammar Sch., N Sydney; Moore Theological Coll., Sydney. CA; BD (London); ThSchol (Aust. Coll. of Theol.). Public Accountancy, 1945–57. Lectr, Moore Theological Coll., 1960–63; Rector, St Stephen's, Bellevue Hill, 1963–65; Federal Secretary, CMS of Aust., 1965–72; Archdeacon of Cumberland with Sydney, 1972–75; Bishop of North Sydney, 1983–90; Registrar, dio. of Sydney, 1990–93. Mem., ARCIC, 1983–90. *Address*: Unit 322, Rohini Village, 51 Rohini Street, Turramurra, NSW 2074, Australia. *T*: (2) 04499957.

**CAMERON, Francis (Ernest)**, MA, DipEth (Oxon); FRCO(CHM), ARAM; independent scholar; Choirmaster and Organist, City Church of St Michael at the North Gate, Oxford, 1988–94; *b* London, 5 Dec. 1927; *er s of* Ernest and Doris Cameron; *m* 1952, Barbara Minns; three *d*. *Educ*: Mercers' Sch.; Caerphilly Boys' Grammar Sch.; Royal Acad. of Music; University Coll., Oxford; Univ. of Sydney. Henry Richards Prizewinner, RAM, 1946. Organist, St Peter's, Fulham, 1943; Pianist, Canadian Legion, 1944; Organist, St Luke's, Holloway, 1945; Sub-organist, St Peter's, Eaton Square, 1945; Organist, St Jamesthe-Less, Westminster, 1946; commissioned RASC, 1948; Organ Scholar, University Coll., Oxford, 1950; Organist: St Anne's, Highgate, 1952; St Barnabas', Pimlico, 1953; St Mark's, Marylebone Road, 1957–58; Choirmaster, St Aloysius, Somers Town, 1959; Master of Music, Westminster Cathedral, 1959; Visiting Organist, Church of St Thomas of Canterbury, Rainham, Kent, 1961; Organist and Choirmaster, Church of Our Lady of the Assumption and St Gregory, Warwick Street, W1, 1962–68. Travel for UNESCO, 1952–55; Dep. Dir of Music, LCC (subsequently GLC), 1954–68; Asst-Dir of Music, Emanuel Sch., 1954; Music Master, Central Foundation Boys' Grammar Sch., 1956; Prof. of Organ and Composition, RAM, 1959–68; *locum tenens* Dir of Music, St Felix Sch., Southwold, 1963 and 1964; Asst Dir, 1968, Chm. of Musicology, 1974–79, NSW State Conservatorium of Music; Organist, Church of St Mary the Virgin, Iffley, 1980–88; Sen. Lectr, Musical Studies, Oxford Poly., 1982–86; Demonstrator: Oxford Univ. Computing Services, 1988–96; computing, Univ. of Oxford Dept for Continuing Educn, 1994–96, 2000–04; computer programming tutor, Oxford Centre for Adult Learning, 1992–96. Inaugural Conductor, Witan Operatic Soc., 1957–58; Conductor: "I Cantici", 1961–65; Francis Cameron Chorale, 1965–68; Singers of David, 1973–76; British Adjudicator, Fedn of Canadian Music Festivals, 1965; Examr Associated Bd of Royal Schools of Music, 1965–68; Dep. Chm., NSW Adv. Bd, Aust. Music Exams Bd, 1969–74. Field Officer, Deep Creek Aboriginal Monuments res. and recording prog., 1973; Mem., Lancefield Archaeol Expedn, 1975. President: "Open Score", 1946–68; Musicol Soc. of Aust., 1971–75 (jt leader, ethnomusicol expedn to New Hebrides, 1971–72); Sydney Univ. Anthropol Soc., 1974–75; Phoenix Photographic Circle, 1977–79; Conservatorium Professional Staff Assoc., 1978–79; Vice-Pres., Aust. Chapter, ISCM, 1970–77; Ed., INFO, European Seminar in Ethnomusicology, 1986–90. Beethoven Commemorative Medal, Fed. Repub. of Germany, 1970. *Publications*: editor (with John Steele) Musica Britannica vol. xiv (The Keyboard Music of John Bull, part I), 1960; Old Palace Yard, 1963; Eight dances from Benjamin Cosyn's Second Virginal Book, 1964; I Sing of a Maiden, 1966; John Bull, ausgewählte Werke, 1967; I Believe, 1969; incidental music for film The Voyage of the New Endeavour, 1970; songs and incidental music for Congreve's Love for Love, 1972; Alleluia, 1990; contributor to: Church Music; Composer; The Conductor; Liturgy; Musical Times; Australian Jl of Music Education; Studies in Music; Music in Tertiary Educn; Con Brio; Musicology IV; Aust. Nat. Hist.; Nation Review; Quanta; ICTM (UK) Bulletin; Eur. Studies in Ethnomusicol.; Pagan Dawn; Pagan Times; Pentacle; Druids Voice; The Cauldron. *Address*: 12 Norreys Avenue, Oxford OX1 4SS. *T*: (01865) 240058.

**CAMERON, Rt Rev. Gregory Kenneth;** *see* St Asaph, Bishop of.

**CAMERON, Sir (Hugh) Roy (Graham)**, Kt 1999; QPM 1994; HM Chief Inspector of Constabulary, Scotland, 2002–04; *b* 14 April 1947; *s of* Angus and May Cameron; *m* 1969, Margaret Scott; two *s*. *Educ*: Bearsden Acad.; Univ. of Strathclyde (BA 1976; MPhil 1992). Cadet, Dunbartonshire Constabulary, 1964–66; Constable, 1966, Asst Chief Constable, 1990–94, Strathclyde Police; Chief Constable: Dumfries and Galloway Constabulary, 1994–96; Lothian and Borders Police, 1996–2002. DL East Lothian, 2004–08. *Recreations*: golf, music, cinema, reading.

**CAMERON, Prof. Iain Thomas**, MD; Professor of Obstetrics and Gynaecology, 1999–2018, now Emeritus, and Dean, Faculty of Medicine, 2010–18, University of Southampton (Head, School of Medicine, 2004–10); *b* 21 Feb. 1956; *s of late* James David Cameron and Stella (*née* Turner); *m* 1st, 1983 (marr. diss.); two *d*; 2nd, 1992, Heidi Wade; one *s* one *d*. *Educ*: Hutton Grammar Sch.; Univ. of Edinburgh (BSc Med. Sci. 1977; MB ChB 1980; MD 1988); MA Cantab 1992. MRCOG 1986, FRCOG 1999; MRACOG 1987; ILTM 2002; FRCPEd 2011; FRSB (FSB 2011). House Officer and Sen. House Officer, Western Infirmary, Glasgow, Royal Infirmary, Edinburgh and Simpson Meml Maternity Pavilion, Edinburgh, 1980–82; University of Edinburgh: Research Fellow, Dept of Obstetrics and Gynaecology, 1982–84; Lectr and Registrar, 1984–86; Monash University: Clinical Res. Fellow, 1986–88; Lectr, 1987–88; Sen. Registrar, Royal Women's Hosp., Melbourne, 1988–89; University of Cambridge: Lectr, 1989–92; Sen. Registrar, 1989–91; Consultant, 1991–92; Regius Prof. of Obstetrics and Gynaecology, Glasgow Univ., 1993–99; Mem., HFEA, 2001–06. Chm., Blair Bell Res. Soc., 1999–2002, Chm., Meetings Cttee, and Convenor, Postgrad. Meetings, 2000–03, Chm., Jt Wellbeing of Women Res. Adv. Cttee, 2004–08, Mem., Academic Cttee, 2006–15, RCOG. Specialist Advr, Menorrhagia, NICE, 2000; Member: Pharmaceuticals Panel, 2001–04, Expert Adv. Network, 2004–10, Dean for Trng's Adv. Panel, 2010–13, NIHR Health Technol. Assessment Prog.; Scientific and Ethical Rev. Gp, Special Prog. in Human Reproduction, WHO, 2003–14; MRC Coll. of Experts, 2005–09; Exec. Cttee, Med. Schs Council (formerly Council of Hds of Med. Schs), 2006–16 (Dep. Chm., 2012–13; Chm., 2013–16), UK Clin. Res. Collaboration; UK Res. Integrity Office Adv. Bd, 2009–13; Sub-panel, Clin. Medicine, REF 2014, 2011–14; Wessex Acad. Health Sci. Network Bd, 2012–18; NIHR Adv. Bd, 2013–16; Health Educn England Medical Adv. Gp, 2013–16; Centre for Workforce Wellbeing, Health Educn England Wessex, 2018–; NICE Guideline Chair, 2017–. Non-executive Director: University Hosp. Southampton NHS Foundn Trust, 2011–17; Med. and Dental Defence Union of Scotland, 2017–. Mem. Bd of Trustees, Wessex Med. Res., 2008–18. Ed.-in-Chief, Reproductive Medicine Rev., 1999–2002. FHEA 2007; Hon. FAcadMed 2016. *Publications*: articles and other contribs on menstrual disorders, endometrium, and reproductive medicine. *Recreation*: solo piping. *Club*: Athenæum.

**CAMERON, Ian Alexander;** Sheriff of Grampian, Highland and Islands at Elgin, 2001–08; *b* 5 Nov. 1938; *s of late* James Cameron and Isabella Cameron; *m* 1968, Dr Margaret Anne Innes; one *s*. *Educ*: Elgin Acad.; Edinburgh Univ. (MA); Aberdeen Univ. (LLB with dist.). Qualified as solicitor, 1961; Partner, Stewart & McIsaac, Solicitors, Elgin, 1962–87; Sheriff: of Lothian and Borders at Edinburgh, 1987–93; of Grampian, Highland and Is at Wick, Dornoch and Stornoway, 1993–2001. *Recreations*: travel, railway history. *Address*: Braemoray, Elgin, Moray IV30 4NJ. *T*: (01343) 542731; 19/4 Damside, Dean Village, Edinburgh EH4 3BB.

**CAMERON, Prof. Ian Rennell**, CBE 1999; DM; FRCP, FMedSci; FLSW; Vice-Chancellor, University of Wales College of Medicine, 1994–2001; Chairman, Enfis Ltd, 2001–07; *b* 20 May 1936; *s of* James and Frances Mary Cameron; *m* 1st, 1964, Jayne Bustard (marr. diss.); one *s* one *d*; 2nd, 1980, Jennifer (*d* 2014), *d of* Stewart and Josephine Cowin.

*Educ:* Westminster Sch.; Corpus Christi Coll., Oxford (BA 1958 1st Cl. Hons Animal Physiol.; MA 1961; DM 1969; Hon. Fellow, 2000); St Thomas's Hosp. Med. Sch. (BM BCh 1961). FRCP 1976. Jun. med. appts, St Thomas's Hosp., 1961–64; Res. Asst, Dept of Physiol., UCL, 1966–68; Lectr 1967, Sen. Lectr 1969, Reader 1975, St Thomas's Hosp. Med. Sch.; Prof. of Medicine, UMDS of Guy's and St Thomas' Hosps, 1979–94 (Dean, St Thomas', 1986–89; Principal, UMDS, 1989–92, Hon. Fellow, 1997); Hon. Consultant Physician, St Thomas' Hosp., 1970–94. NIH Postdoctoral Fellowship at Cedars-Sinai Med. Center, LA, and Asst Prof., Dept of Physiol., UCLA, 1968–69. Mem., Medway HA, 1981–86; non-exec. Dir, Bro Taf HA, 1996–99; Dir, R&D, SE Thames RHA, 1993–94. Examiner, Univ. of London Final MB, 1980–94; Mem. Senate, Univ. of London, 1989–92. Member: Med. Res. Soc., 1966–; Physiol Soc., 1974–; Assoc. of Physicians of GB and Ire., 1979–; Council, RCP, 1992–95; GMC, 1994–2001 (Treas., 1997–2001); Univs UK (formerly CVCP), 1994–2001; Commn for Health Improvement, 1999–2004. Chm., UK Centre for Advancement of Inter-professional Educn, 1998–99. Mem. Council, KCL, 1993–99. Hon. FKC 1998; Hon. Fellow, Cardiff Univ., 2002; Founder FMedSci 1998; FLSW 2014. Hon. LLD Wales, 2001; Hon. DSc Glamorgan, 2001; Hon. PhD: Kobe Gakuin Univ., Tokyo Women's Medical Univ., 2001. *Publications:* Respiratory Disorders (with N. T. Bateman), 1983; papers in various med. and physiol jls. *Recreation:* collecting (and selling) paintings. *Club:* Athenæum.

**CAMERON, Ivor Gill S.;** *see* Smith-Cameron.

**CAMERON, James;** *see* Cameron, J. J. O'G.

**CAMERON, John Alastair;** *see* Abernethy, Rt Hon. Lord.

**CAMERON, John Bell,** CBE 1982; Chairman, World Meats Group, International Federation of Agricultural Producers, since 1984; Director, Argent Energy, since 2010; *b* 14 June 1939; *s* of John and Margaret Cameron; *m* 1964, Margaret (*née* Clapperton). *Educ:* Dollar Academy. AIAgrE; FRAgS. Studied agriculture in various countries, Scandinavia, S America and Europe, 1956–61; farmed in Scotland, 1961–64. National Farmers' Union of Scotland: Mem. National Council, 1964; Vice-Pres., 1976; Pres., 1979–84 (first long-term Pres.). Mem., Agricultural Praesidium of EEC, 1979–89; Chairman: EEC Adv. Cttee for Sheep Meat, 1982–89; UK Sheep Consultative Cttee, 1986–87; Scottish Beef Council, 1997–2000; Standards Cttee, Quality Meat Scotland, 2005–. President: British Hereford Cattle Soc., 2003–05; Scottish Beef Cattle Assoc., 2005–; Scottish Nat. Sheep Assoc., 2005–; Vice-Pres., Nat. Sheep Assoc., 2015–. Chm., BR (Scotland) and Scottish Mem., BRB, 1988–93; Dir, SW Trains and Island Line, 1996–2007. Chm. Governors, Dollar Acad., 1984–2014. Hon. DTech Napier, 1998; Hon. DLaws St Andrews, 2017. Winner: George Headley Award to the UK Sheep Industry, 1986; Sir William Young Award to the Scottish Livestock Industry, 1986; NFU Scotland Ambassador Award, 2013; Achievement Award, Scottish Farming Inst., 2015. *Recreations:* flying, shooting, travelling. *Address:* Balbuthie Farm, By Leven, Fife, Scotland KY9 1EX. *T:* (01333) 730210.

**CAMERON, Prof. John Robinson;** Regius Professor of Logic, University of Aberdeen, 1979–2001; *b* 24 June 1936; *s* of Rev. George Gordon Cameron and Mary Levering (*née* Robinson); *m* 1st, 1959, Mary Elizabeth Ranson (*d* 1984); one *s* two *d*; 2nd, 1987, Barbara Elizabeth Blair. *Educ:* Dundee High Sch.; Univ. of St Andrews (MA 1st Cl. Hons Maths, BPhil Philosophy); Univ. of Calif, Berkeley; Cornell Univ. Harkness Fellow, Berkeley and Cornell, USA, 1959–61; University of Dundee (formerly Queen's College): Asst in Phil., 1962–63; Lectr in Phil., 1963–73; Sen. Lectr in Phil., 1973–78. FRSA 2002. *Publications:* articles in phil jls. *Recreation:* bricolage. *Address:* 44 Ashgrove Road West, Aberdeen AB16 5EE. *T:* (01224) 486700.

**CAMERON, (Jonathan) James (O'Grady);** international lawyer, policy adviser and entrepreneur; Chairman, Overseas Development Institute, since 2012; *b* 28 Oct. 1961; *s* of late John O'Grady Cameron and Valerie Cameron (*née* Bromley); *m* 1988, Juliet Mary May (*see* Hon. Dame J. M. May); three *d*. *Educ:* Windlesham House Sch., Sussex; Stowe Sch., Bucks; Univ. of Western Australia; University Coll. London (LLB); Queens' Coll., Cambridge (LLM 1st Cl.). Called to the Bar, Inner Temple, 1987; Res. Associate, Centre for Internat. Law, Cambridge, 1986–87; Dir of Studies in Law, Clare Hall, Cambridge, 1986–89; Lecturer in Law: KCL, 1989–92; SOAS, 1992–98; Prof., Coll. of Europe, Bruges, 1994–2002; Counsel, Baker & McKenzie, 1997–2003. Founder Director: Centre for Internat. Envmtl Law, 1989–99; Foundn for Internat. Envmtl Law and Develt (negotiated UN framework for Convention on Climate Change, 1992 and Kyoto Protocol, 1997 on behalf of Alliance of Small Island States); Founder, 2004, Chm., 2012–15, Climate Change Capital, specialist investment gp (Vice-Chm., 2003–12). Visiting Professor: Australian Centre for Envmtl Law, Univ. of Sydney, 1996; Yale Center for Envmtl Law & Policy, 2005– (Exec. Fellow, 2015–). Sen. Advr, SystemIQ, 2016–; Chairman: Carbon Disclosure Project, 2002–15; Chinadialogue, 2009–15; Agrica, 2013–19; Green Running/VERV, 2016–; ET Index, 2016–; Treas., Renewable Energy and Energy Efficiency Partnership, 2004–10; Member, Advisory Board: Centre Forum, 2007–; Policy Exchange, 2009; Member: World Econ. Forum Global Agenda Council on Climate Change, 2008–13; Adv. Develt Bd, Oxfam, 2009–11; Prime Minister's Business Adv. Gp, 2010–12; Adv. Council, Infrastructure UK, HM Treasury, 2013–; London Sustainable Develt Commn, 2015–; Senior Adviser: Presidency of COP22 (Morocco), 2016–17; Presidency of COP23 (Fiji), climate negotiations, 2017–18. Trustee: Climate Gp, 2006–11; UK Green Building Council, 2010–17. Mem., GE Ecomagination Adv. Bd, 2006–17. Chm., ODI, 2012–. FRSA. *Publications:* (with M. Sheridan) EC Legal Systems: an introductory guide, 1992; (with M. Sheridan) EFTA Legal Systems, 1993; (with D. Gerardin) Trade and Environment: the search for balance, 1994; (with T. O'Riordan) Interpreting the Precautionary Principle, 1994; Improving Compliance with International Environmental Law, 1995; (with K. Campbell) Dispute Resolution in the WTO, 1998; (jtly) Trade and Environment: law and policy introduction, cases and materials, 2000; (jtly) Re-Interpreting the Precautionary Principle, 2001; articles in legal jls. *Recreations:* sport, music, journeys, clothes, conversation, family. *Clubs:* Conduit, h; Berkshire Golf.

**CAMERON, Hon. Dame Juliet Mary;** *see* May, Hon. Dame J. M.

**CAMERON, Lewis;** Sheriff of South Strathclyde, Dumfries and Galloway at Hamilton, 1994–2002; part-time Sheriff, 2002–05; *b* 12 Aug. 1935; *s* of James Aloysius Cameron and Marie Isobel McKenzie; *m* 1962, Sheila Colette Gallacher; two *s* two *d*. *Educ:* Blairs Coll., Aberdeen; St Sulpice, Paris; Glasgow Univ. (MA, LLB). Admitted Solicitor, 1962. RAF (Nat. Service), 1954–56. Chm., Social Security Appeal Tribunals, 1983–88; Mem., Legal Aid Central Cttee, 1970–80; Legal Aid Sec., Airdrie, 1978–87; Dean, Airdrie Soc. of Solicitors, 1984–85; Tutor, Strathclyde Univ., 1981–88; Sheriff of S Strathclyde, Dumfries and Galloway at Dumfries, 1988–94. Treas., Monklands Victim Support Scheme, 1983–88; Chairman: Dumfries and Galloway Family Conciliation Service, 1988–92; Dumfries and Galloway Scottish Assoc. for Study of Delinquency, 1989–92. Mem., Scotland Cttee, Nat. Children's Homes, 1991–94; Chm., Phew (Parental Help Evenings/Weekends, Mentally Handicapped), 1994–2000. Trustee, Oscar Marzaroli Trust, 1990–93. *Publications:* occasional articles and journalism. *Recreations:* cinema, theatre, tennis, travel. *Club:* Glasgow Art.

**CAMERON, Dr Lisa;** MP (SNP) East Kilbride, Strathaven and Lesmahagow, since 2015; *b* Glasgow, 8 April 1972; *d* of Campbell McCulloch and Sandra Cameron; *m* 2009, Mark Horsham; two *d*. *Educ:* Univ. of Strathclyde (BA Hons); Univ. of Stirling (MSc Psychol. and Health); Univ. of Glasgow (DClinPsy). NHS Greater Glasgow, 1999–2001; Clin. Psychologist, NHS Lanarks, 2001–04; Consultant Clin. Psychologist, NHS Greater Glasgow, 2004–06; Consultant Forensic and Clin. Psychologist, NHS Greater Glasgow and Clyde, 2006–15. Accredited Risk Assessor, Risk Mgt Authy Scotland, 2012–15. *Recreations:* gym, swimming, travel. *Address:* House of Commons, Room 510, 1 Parliament Street, Westminster, SW1A 0AA. *E:* lisa.cameron.mp@parliament.uk. *Club:* Rotary (Lanark).

**CAMERON, Neil St Clair;** QC 2009; a Recorder, since 2002; a Deputy High Court Judge, since 2013; *b* Cuckfield, Sussex, 11 July 1959; *s* of Donald Cameron and Jill Cameron; *m* 1987, Phoebe, *d* of late (Cecil) James (Olaf) Moorhouse and of Elizabeth Moorhouse; one *s* two *d*. *Educ:* Eton Coll.; Durham Univ. (BA Hons; Pres., Durham Union Soc.). Short Service Ltd Commn, 14th/20th King's Hussars, 2nd Lieut, 1978. Called to the Bar, Gray's Inn, 1982, Bencher, 2015; barrister specialising in town and country planning; Jt Hd, Landmark Chambers, 2015–18. Mem. (C), Lambeth LBC, 1986–90. Contested (C) Worsley, 1992. *Recreations:* ski-ing, country. *Address:* Landmark Chambers, 180 Fleet Street, EC4A 2HG. *Clubs:* Athenæum, Cavalry and Guards; Southampton Football.

**CAMERON, Pamela;** Member (DemU) South Antrim, Northern Ireland Assembly, since 2011; *b* Belfast, 30 Dec. 1971. *Educ:* Glengormley High Sch. Mem. (DemU), Antrim BC, 2005–13 (Mayor, 2010–11). *Address:* Northern Ireland Assembly, Parliament Buildings, Stormont, Belfast BT4 3XX. *T:* (028) 9034 2234. *E:* pam.cameron@mla.niassembly.gov.uk.

**CAMERON, Sir Roy;** *see* Cameron, Sir H. R. G.

**CAMERON, Sheila Morag Clark, (Mrs G. C. Ryan),** CBE 2004; QC 1983; Dean, Arches Court of Canterbury and Auditor, Chancery Court of York, 2001–09; *b* 22 March 1934; *d* of Sir James Clark Cameron, CBE, TD, and Lady (Irene M.) Cameron; *m* 1960, Gerard Charles Ryan, *qv*; two *s*. *Educ:* Commonweal Lodge Sch., Purley; St Hugh's Coll., Oxford (MA); Cardiff Univ. (LLM Canon Law 2008). Called to the Bar, Middle Temple, 1957, Harmsworth Law Scholar, 1958, Bencher, 1988; Part-time Lectr in Law, Southampton Univ., 1960–64; part-time Tutor, Council of Legal Educn, 1966–71; a Recorder, 1985–99. Mem., Bar Council, 1967–70. Comr, Boundary Commn for England, 1989–96 (Asst Comr, 1981–89). Official Principal, Archdeaconry of Hampstead, 1968–86; Chancellor: Dio. of Chelmsford, 1969–2001; Dio. of London, 1992–2001; Vicar-Gen., Province of Canterbury, 1983–2005. Chairman: Archbishops' Group on the Episcopate, 1986–90; Ecclesiastical Judges Assoc., 1997–2004; Member: Legal Adv. Commn, Gen. Synod of C of E, 1975–2015; Gen. Synod Marriage Commn, 1975–78; Council on Tribunals, 1986–90. Pres., Ecclesiastical Law Soc., 2010–19. Mem. Council, Wycombe Abbey Sch., 1972–86. DCL Lambeth, 2002. *Address:* Bayleaves, Bepton, Midhurst, W Sussex GU29 9RB.

**CAMERON, Susan Ruth;** Headmistress, North Foreland Lodge, 1996–2002; *b* Edinburgh; *e d* of late James Norval Cameron and Ruth Scott Doig (*née* Nicolson). *Educ:* Wycombe Abbey Sch.; Westfield Coll., London (Exhibnr; BA Hons; Pres., Students' Union). VSO, Oguta, Eastern Nigeria; Housemistress, Godstowe Sch., High Wycombe; teacher, Housemistress, then Dep. Head, Woodford House, Hawkes Bay, NZ; Housemistress: Queenswood Sch., 1977–78; Sherborne Sch. for Girls, 1978–84; Headmistress: Cobham Hall, 1985–89; Downe House, 1989–96. Governor: Queen Margaret's Sch., York, 1986–95; Farlington Sch., Horsham, 1987–95; Repton Sch., 1995–2002; Gordonstoun Schs, 2000–02; Maynard Sch., Exeter, 2003–08; Bearwood Coll., 2004–; Marchant-Holliday Sch., 2005–16. Vice-Pres., Seniors' Assoc., Wycombe Abbey Sch., 2004–16 (Pres., 1996–2004); Mem. Cttee, Sherborne Literary Soc. Fest., 2016–. *Recreations:* music, sport (mostly non-active now), travel, language, creative thinking, scribbling. *Address:* 5 Minterne House, Minterne Magna, Dorchester, Dorset DT2 7AX. *T:* (01300) 341616.

**CAMERON, Thomas Anthony, (Tony),** CB 2007; Chief Executive, Scottish Prison Service, and Chairman, Scottish Prisons Board, 1999–2007; *b* 3 Feb. 1947; *o s* of late Thomas Alexander and Olive Cameron; *m* 1970, Elizabeth Christine Sutherland; two *s*. *Educ:* Stranraer High Sch. Dept of Agric. and Fisheries for Scotland, Scottish Office, 1966–72; Private Secretary: to Dep. Under Sec. of State, 1972; to Perm. Under Sec. of State, 1973–74; Department of Agriculture and Fisheries for Scotland: HEO(D), 1974–77; Principal, 1977–82; Asst Sec., 1982–87; Scottish Office Finance Div., 1987–92; Under Sec., 1992; Head of Food and Agric., Scottish Office, 1992–99. Mem., Duke of Edinburgh's Sixth Commonwealth Study Conf., Australia, 1986. Pres., Internat. Corrections and Prisons Assoc., 2003–11. Trustee: Turning Point Scotland, 2007–16; Scottish Wildlife Trust, 2014–17. *Recreations:* reading, walking. *Address:* 18 St Ninians Terrace, Edinburgh EH10 5NL.

**CAMERON-RAMSAY-FAIRFAX-LUCY;** *see* Fairfax-Lucy.

**CAMLEY, Mark;** Executive Director, Park Operations and Venues, London Legacy Development Corporation, since 2013 (Director, Park Operations, 2012–13); *b* 11 June 1964; *s* of Martin and Frances Camley; *m* 2002, Camilla Rosier; two *d*. *Educ:* Lornshill Acad., Alloa; Univ. of Edinburgh (MA). Exec. Officer, Cabinet Office, 1986–88; Asst Statistician, CSO, 1988–90; Lord Chancellor's Department: Statistician, 1990–97; Hd, Estates Policy, 1997–98; Private Sec. to Perm. Sec., 1998–99; Dir, Crown Court, 1999–2001; Customer Service Dir, 2001–03; Dir, Supreme Court, 2003–05; Chief Exec., Royal Parks, 2005–12. Dir, London Stadium 185 Ltd, 2019–. Chairman of Governors: Norwood Sch., 2005–07; Royal Docks Sch., 2007–12. Hon. Crown Estate Paving Comr, 2005–12. Member: Places Bd, Poplar Housing and Regeneration Community Assoc., 2009–14; Social Enterprise Cttee, Bromley-by-Bow Centre, 2009–12 (Dir, 2011–14); Dir, Royal Docks Co-op. Learning Partnership, 2010–12; Trustee, GreenSpaces, 2012–13. Mem. Council, London Garden Soc., 2011–; Chm., Parks Alliance, 2013–16; Dir, World Urban Parks, 2016–. *Publications:* contributor: Economic Trends, 1986; Social Trends and Regional Trends, 1988; Judicial Statistics, annually 1990–97; contribs to New Law Jl. *Recreations:* sport, nature, culture, art. *Address:* London Legacy Development Corporation, Level 10, 1 Stratford Place, Montfichet Road, E20 1EJ. *T:* (020) 3288 1857. *E:* markcamley@londonlegacy.co.uk.

**CAMM, Prof. A(lan) John,** MD; FRCP, FRCPGlas, FRCPE, FMedSci; FACC, FAHA, FESC; QHP; Professor of Cardiology, Imperial College London, since 2012; St George's, University of London (formerly St George's Hospital Medical School): Prudential Professor of Clinical Cardiology (British Heart Foundation), 1986–2012, now Emeritus; Chairman: Department of Medicine, 1991–94; Department of Cardiological Sciences, 1986–2002; Division of Cardiac and Vascular Sciences, 2002–10; *b* 11 Jan. 1947; *s* of John Donald and Joan Camm; *m* 1987, Joy-Maria Frappell (LVO 2015); one *s* one *d*. *Educ:* Guy's Hosp. Med. Sch., London Univ. (BSc 1968; MB BS 1971; MD 1981). LRCP, MRCS 1971; FACC 1981; FRCP 1984; FESC 1988; FRCPE 2003; FRCPGlas (*ad eundem*) 2011. Guy's Hospital: House Surgeon, 1971; House Physician, 1971–72; Jun. Registrar, 1972; Jun. Lectr in Medicine, 1972–73; Registrar in Cardiology, 1973–74; Clin. Fellow in Cardiology,

Univ. of Vermont, USA, 1974–75; St Bartholomew's Hospital: British Heart Foundn Res. Registrar, 1975–76, Sen. Registrar 1977–79; Wellcome Sen. Lectr and Hon. Consultant Cardiologist, 1979–83; Sir Ronald Bodley Scott Prof. of Cardiovascular Medicine, 1983–86. Convener of Medicine, London Univ., 1994–. Editor in Chief: Europace Jl, 2007–; Clinical Cardiology Jl, 2011–. Dir, Eur. Soc. of Cardiol. Res. Foundn, 2008. Member, Council: RCP, 1994–97; British Cardiac Soc., 1997–98 (Pres. elect, 1996–97, Pres., 2001–03); Eur. Heart Rhythm Assoc., 2007– (Pres., 2017–); Pres., Arrhythmia Alliance, 2005–. QHP 1992–. FCGC 1997; FAHA 2000; FMedSci 2005; FHRS 2006. Trustee: N American Soc. of Pacing and Electrophysiology, 1998–2001 (Dist. Teacher, 2001); Amer. Coll. of Cardiology, 2007–12; Drug Safety Res. Unit, 2009–; Founder Trustee, Atrial Fibrillation Assoc., 2008–. Hon. Internat. Mem., Japanese Circulation Soc., 2006; Hon. Fellow, Hong Kong Coll. of Cardiology, 2006. Freeman, City of London, 1984. Gold Medal, European Soc. of Cardiology, 2006; Berzelius Medal, Swedish Soc. of Cardiology, 2006; Cardiostim Medal, Cardiostim, 2006; Mackenzie Medal, British Cardiovascular Soc., 2008; Libin Prize for Cardiovascular Res. Excellence, Calgary Heart Inst., 2011; Maseri-Fiorio Prize, Amer. Coll. of Cardiol., 2014. CStJ 1990. *Publications:* First Aid, Step by Step, 1978; Pacing for Tachycardia Control, 1983; Heart Disease in the Elderly, 1984, 2nd edn 1994; Clinical Electrophysiology of the Heart, 1987; Heart Disease in Old Age, 1988, 2nd edn 1996; Clinical Aspects of Cardiac Arrhythmias, 1988; Diseases of the Heart, 1989, 2nd edn 1996; Geriatric Cardiology, 1994; Non-pharmacological Management of Atrial Fibrillation, 1997; Heart Rate Variability, 1998; Evidence Based Cardiology, 1998, 3rd edn 2010; Atrial Fibrillation, 2000, Hungarian edn 2002; Drug-induced Long QT Syndrome, 2002; Cardiovascular Risk Associated with Schizophrenia and its Treatment, 2003; ABC of Clinical Electrocardiology, 2003, 2nd edn 2008; Acquired Long QT Syndrome, 2004; Clinical Electrophysiological Disorders of the Heart, 2004, 2nd edn 2011; Dynamic Electrocardiography, 2004; European Society of Cardiology Textbook, 2005, 2nd edn 2009; Heart Rate Slowing by Inhibition of the If Current, 2006; Comprehensive Electrocardiology, 2nd edn, 2011; Clinical Cardiology, 2013, 2nd edn 2016; Clinical Guide to Cardiology, 2016; approx. 1,400 papers in major jls and over 300 chapters in med. textbooks. *Recreations:* collector of prints, watercolours and other antiques, model railway enthusiast. *Address:* St George's, University of London, Cranmer Terrace, Tooting, SW17 0RE. *Clubs:* Oriental, Royal Society of Medicine.

**CAMM, Gillian Elizabeth;** DL; NHS Regional Appointments Commissioner for South West, 2001–03; *b* 31 Dec. 1959; *d* of Sir Robert Shields; *m* 1987, Ian Sutcliffe Camm; one *s* one *d*. *Educ:* Birkenhead High Sch. for Girls; Univ. of Liverpool (BSc Hons Psychol.). Personnel Officer, Perkins Diesel Engines, 1981–84; Personnel Manager, Internat. Computers Ltd, 1984–87; Partner, Hay Mgt Consultants, 1987–94; Gen. Manager, Human Resources, 1994–97, Business Transformation Dir, 1997–2001, Clerical Medical Investments Gp. Non-executive Director: Supervisory Bd, Immigration and Nationality Directorate, Home Office, 2002; Rok plc, 2002– (Sen. Ind. Dir, 2006–10); Wessex Water, 2011– (Sen. Ind. Dir, 2011–); Capsticks, 2012–14. Mem., GMC, 2003. Chairman: Bd of Govs, UWE, 2009–16; Council, Wycliffe Coll., 2009– (Chm. Govs, 2014); Bd, Leadership Foundn for Higher Educn, 2015–. Vice-Pres., Quartet Community Foundn (formerly Gtr Bristol Foundn), 2010–; Mem. Council, St Monica Trust, 2003–12. Mem., Merchant Venturers, 2004– (Jun. Warden, 2018–). Mem., Hon. Glos Soc., 2009–. DL Glos 2010. *Recreation:* reading. *E:* gillian.camm1@gmail.com.

**CAMMEGH, John Stephen;** QC 2019; *b* Swindon, 5 March 1963; *s* of Bill Cammegh and Barbara Cammegh. *Educ:* Norton Knatchbull Sch. for Boys; University Coll. London (LLB 1985); Coll. of Legal Educn. Called to the Bar, Inner Temple, 1987; in practice as a barrister specialising in serious and complex, internat. and commercial crime, Goldsmith Bldg, 1988–92, 4 Brick Ct, 1992–2000, 9 Bedford Row, 2000–19, The 36 Gp, 2019–. *Publications:* articles on internat. crime issues in The Economist, New York Times, Internat. Herald Tribune. *Recreations:* wildlife conservation, Tour de France, mid-century furniture, Apollo missions, Peter Cook, Deezer, watching television, Dolly the dog. *Address:* The 36 Group, 4 Field Court, WC1R 5EF. *T:* (020) 7421 8000. *E:* jcammegh@36crime.co.uk. *Clubs:* Reform; Rapha Cycling.

**CAMMERMAN, Gideon Saul;** QC 2017; *b* Reading, 1972; *s* of Philip Cammerman and Sheila Cammerman (née Raviv); *m* 2000, Dr Stephanie Styles; two *s* one *d*. *Educ:* Leeds Grammar Sch.; Fitzwilliam Coll., Cambridge (BA Hons 1994). Called to the Bar, Middle Temple, 1996; in practice as a barrister, specialising in fraud and regulatory law, 1996–. *Recreations:* Rugby, music. *Address:* 187 Fleet Street, EC4A 2AT. *T:* (020) 7430 7430. *E:* gideoncammerman@187fleetstreet.com.

**CAMOYS,** 7th Baron *cr* 1264 (called out of abeyance, 1839); **Ralph Thomas Campion George Sherman Stonor,** GCVO 1998; PC 1997; DL; Lord Chamberlain of HM Household and Chancellor of Royal Victorian Order, 1998–2000; a Permanent Lord in Waiting to the Queen, since 2000; *b* 16 April 1940; *s* of 6th Baron Camoys and Mary Jeanne (*d* 1987), *d* of late Captain Herbert Marmaduke Joseph Stourton, OBE; *S* father, 1976; *m* 1966, Elisabeth Mary Hyde, *d* of Sir William Stephen Hyde Parker, 11th Bt; one *s* three *d*. *Educ:* Eton Coll.; Balliol Coll., Oxford (MA). Chm., Jacksons of Piccadilly, 1968–85; Gen. Manager and Director, National Provincial and Rothschild (London) Ltd, 1968; Man. Director, Rothschild Intercontinental Bank Ltd, 1969; Chief Exec. Officer and Man. Dir, 1975–77, Chm., 1977–78, Amex Bank Ltd; Man. Dir, 1978–84, Exec. Vice-Chm., 1984–86, Barclays Merchant Bank; Chief Exec., 1986–88, Dep. Chm., 1987–98, Barclays de Zoete Wedd (BZW); Dep. Chm., Sotheby's, 1993–97. Director: Barclays Bank Internat. Ltd, 1980–84; Barclays Bank PLC, 1984–94; Mercantile Credit Co. Ltd, 1980–84; National Provident Instn, 1982–93; Administrative Staff Coll., 1989–2000; 3i Group, 1991–2002; Perpetual, 1994–2000. A Lord in Waiting, 1992–97. Member: House of Lords EEC Select Cttee, 1979–81; Historic Bldgs and Monuments Commn for England, 1985–87; Royal Commn on Historical MSS, 1987–94. Pres., Mail Users' Assoc., 1977–84. Consultor, Extraordinary Section of Administration of Patrimony of Holy See, 1991–2006. Chm., Tablet Trust, 2009–17. Mem. Court of Assistants, Fishmongers' Co., 1980– (Prime Warden, 1992–93). Hon. Fellow, St Edmund's Coll., Cambridge, 2016. DL Oxfordshire, 1993. Hon. DLitt Sheffield, 2001. Order of Gorkha Dakshina Bahu, 1st class (Nepal), 1981. GCSG 2006. *Recreations:* the arts, family. *Heir: s* Hon. (Ralph) William (Robert Thomas) Stonor [*b* 10 Sept. 1974; *m* 2004, Lady Ailsa Mackay, *d* of Earl of Inchcape, *qv*; two *s* one *d*]. *Address:* Wool House, Stonor Park, Henley-on-Thames, Oxon RG9 6HF. *Clubs:* Boodle's; Leander (Henley-on-Thames).

See also Earl of Stair.

**CAMP, Anthony John,** MBE 1999; Director, Society of Genealogists, 1979–97; *b* 27 Nov. 1937; *s* of late Henry Victor Camp and Alice Emma Camp (née Doidge); *m* 1976, Deborah Mary (marr. diss. 1978), *d* of D. J. Jeavons; one *s*. *Educ:* Alleyne's Sch., Stevenage; University College London (BA Hons). Society of Genealogists: Res. Assistant, 1957; Librarian, 1959; Dir of Res., 1962; Hon. Fellow, 1982. Association of Genealogists and Researchers in Archives (formerly Association of Genealogists and Record Agents): Mem. Council, 1968–75; Chm., 1973–75; Vice-Pres., 1980–2011; Fellow, 2011; Member, Council: British Record Soc., 1967–71, 1983–2005; British Records Assoc. (Record Preservation Sect.), 1980–83, 1985–88; English Genealogical Congress, 1975–90 (Pres., 1991–92); Friends of Public Record Office, 1988–94; Marc Fitch Fund, 1991–2003; Fedn of Family History Socs, 1992–98 (Pres., 1998–2000); Pres., Herts Family and Population Hist. Soc., 1982–2020. Lecturer: yearly Nat. Geneal. Soc. Confs, USA, 1981–2006; Australasian Congress, Canberra, 1986; Sesquicentennial Conf., Auckland, 1990; First Irish Genealogical Congress, 1991. Fellow, Utah Geneal. Assoc., 1989. Freeman, City of London, 1984. Award of Merit, Nat. Geneal. Soc., USA, 1984. *Publications:* (with P. Spufford) Genealogists Handbook, 1961; Wills and their Whereabouts, 1963; Tracing Your Ancestors, 1964; Index to Wills proved in the Prerogative Court of Canterbury 1750–1800, 6 vols, 1976–92; Everyone has Roots, 1978; (contrib.) My Ancestor series, 1987–; (contrib.) The Records of the Nation, 1990; Royal Mistresses and Bastards: fact and fiction 1714–1936, 2007; On the City's Edge: a history of Fann Street, London, 2016; articles to Family Tree and other jls. *Recreation:* genealogy. *Address:* 19 Tudor Rose Court, 35 Fann Street, EC2Y 8DY. *T:* (020) 7374 6836.

**CAMP, Jeffery Bruce,** RA 1984 (ARA 1974); artist; Lecturer, Slade School of Fine Art, 1963–88; *b* 1923. *Educ:* Edinburgh Coll. of Art. DA (Edin.). One-man exhibitions include: Galerie de Seine, 1958; Beaux Arts Gallery, 1959, 1961, 1963; New Art Centre, 1968; S London Art Gall., 1973 (retrospective); Serpentine Gall., 1978; Bradford City Art Gallery, 1979; Browse & Darby, 1984, 1993, 1997, 2001; Aldeburgh Fest., 1986; Nigel Greenwood Gall., 1986, 1990, 1993; Royal Acad., 1988 (retrospective); Flowers East, 1999; Art Space Gall., 2002, 2005, 2007, 2010, 2012; Jerwood Gall., Hastings, 2013; other exhibitions include: Hayward Annual, 1974, 1982, 1985; Serpentine Gall., 1974, 1987; Narrative Painting, ICA and Arts Council tour, 1979; British Council touring exhibns to China and Edinburgh, 1982, to India, 1985, to Kuala Lumpur, 1988; Chantrey Bicentenary, Tate Gall., 1981; The Hardwon Image, Tate Gall., 1984; group exhibn, Twining Gall., NY, 1985; Peter Moores exhibn, Liverpool, 1986; Athena Art Awards, 1987; represented in public collections including Arts Council, British Council, Tate Gall. and Royal Acad. *Publications:* Draw, 1981; Paint, 1996; Almanac, 2010. *Address:* 27 Stirling Road, SW9 9EF; c/o Art Space Gallery, Michael Richardson Contemporary Art, 84 St Peter's Street, N1 8JS.

**CAMP, Robert Michael;** Director, Strategic Innovation, Stephens Scown LLP, since 2019 (Managing Partner, 2010–19); *b* Barnsley, 12 Feb. 1961; *s* of Graham Camp and Patricia Camp; *m* 1988, Elizabeth Hall; one *s* two *d*. *Educ:* Trent Poly. (BA Hons Legal Studies 1983); Guildford Coll. of Law (Solicitors Finals 1984); Harvard Law Sch. (Leadership in Law Firms Exec. Educn Course). Admitted solicitor, 1986; solicitor: Berwin Leighton, London, 1986–88; Simmons and Simmons, London and Hong Kong, 1988–90; Minter Ellison, Sydney, 1990–91; Solicitor, 1992–, Partner and Mem. Bd, 1994–, Stephens Scown LLP, Exeter. Mem. Regl Cttee, SW Reg., CBI, 2011–17; Mem. Bd, Cornwall and Scilly Isles LEP, 2018–. Non-exec. Dir, Vickery Holman Ltd, 2019–. Trustee and Member, Board: Tearfund, 1997–2017; New Wine Trust, 2019–. Dir, Exeter Fest. of Food and Drink, 2012–. *Recreations:* cycling, tennis, keen bass singer in workplace choir (aka The Rolling Scowns), active member of Exeter Network Church. *Address:* Stephens Scown LLP, Curzon House, Southernhay West, Exeter EX1 1RS. *T:* (01392) 210700. *E:* r.camp@stephens-scown.co.uk.

**CAMPANALE, Mark Adrian;** Founder and Executive Director, Carbon Tracker Initiative, since 2009; Founder, Planet Tracker Initiative, since 2017; *b* Carshalton, Surrey, 2 Dec. 1963; *s* of Mario and Barbara Campanale; *m* 1993, Charlotta Martin; two *s* one *d*. *Educ:* Teddington Sch.; Kingston Coll. of Further Educn; Univ. of York (BA Politics and Econ. Hist. 1985); Wye Coll., Univ. of London (MSc Agricl Econs 1987). Investment Analyst, Jupiter Asset Mgt, 1989–94; Sen. Investment Analyst, NPI Asset Mgt, 1994–99; Hd, Socially Responsible Investing Business Develt, Henderson Global Investors, 1999–2008; Sen. Advr, Consilium Capital, 2014–. Dir, UK Sustainable and Responsible Investment Forum, 1990–2006. Member: Wkg Gp on capital mkts, World Business Council for Sustainable Develt, Earth Summit, 1992; Steering Cttee, Financial Sector Initiative, UNEP, 1999–2003; Adv. Council, ImpactBase.org, 2009–. Mem., Adv. Bd, Conservation and Mkts Initiative, Gordon and Betty Moore Foundn, 2017–. Hon. Treas., Rainforest Foundn, UK, 2010–. Hon. Fellow, Tribe Impact Capital, 2016–. *Recreations:* walking, cinema, theatre, folk music, cooking. *E:* mark@campanale.co.uk. *Club:* Conduit.

**CAMPBELL;** see Methuen-Campbell, family name of Baron Methuen.

**CAMPBELL,** family name of **Duke of Argyll,** of **Earl Cawdor,** and of **Barons Colgrain** and **Stratheden**.

**CAMPBELL OF LOUGHBOROUGH,** Baroness *cr* 2008 (Life Peer), of Loughborough in the County of Leicestershire; **Susan Catherine Campbell,** CBE 2003 (MBE 1991); Director of Women's Football, Football Association, since 2018 (Head of Women's Football, 2016–17); *b* 10 Oct. 1948. *Educ:* Long Eaton Grammar Sch.; Bedford Coll. of Physical Educn; Univ. of Leicester (Adv. DipEd; MEd). Teacher of Physical Educn, Whalley Range High Sch., Manchester, 1970–72; Dep. Dir of Physical Educn, Univ. of Leicester, 1972–76; Lectr, Dept of Physical Educn and Sports Sci., Univ. of Loughborough, 1976–80; Regl Officer, E Midlands, Sports Council, 1980–84; Dep. Chief Exec., 1984, Chief Exec., 1985–95, Nat. Coaching Foundn; Chief Exec., Youth Sport Trust, 1995–2005. Chairman: UK Sport, 2003–13; Youth Sport Trust, 2005–17. Advr (non-political), DCMS and DFES, 2000–03.

**CAMPBELL OF PITTENWEEM,** Baron *cr* 2015 (Life Peer), of Pittenweem in the County of Fife; **(Walter) Menzies Campbell,** CH 2013; Kt 2004; CBE 1987; PC 1999; QC (Scot.) 1982; Leader, Liberal Democrats, 2006–07 (Deputy Leader, 2003–06); *b* 22 May 1941; *s* of George Alexander Campbell and Elizabeth Jean Adam Phillips; *m* 1970, Elspeth Mary Urquhart or Grant-Suttie, *d* of Maj.-Gen. R. E. Urquhart, CB, DSO. *Educ:* Hillhead High School, Glasgow; Glasgow Univ. (MA 1962, LLB 1965; President of the Union, 1964–65); Stanford Univ., Calif. Advocate, Scottish Bar, 1968; Advocate Depute, 1977–80; Standing Jun. Counsel to the Army, 1980–82. Member: Clayson Cttee on licensing reform, 1971; Legal Aid Central Cttee, 1983–87; Scottish Legal Aid Bd, 1987; Broadcasting Council for Scotland, 1984–87. Part-time Chairman: VAT Tribunal, 1984–87; Medical Appeal Tribunal, 1985–87. Chm., Scottish Liberal Party, 1975–77; contested (L): Greenock and Port Glasgow, Feb. 1974 and Oct. 1974; E Fife, 1979; NE Fife, 1983. MP NE Fife, 1987–2015 (L 1987–88, Lib Dem, 1988–2015). Lib. spokesman on arts, broadcasting and sport, 1987–88; Lib Dem spokesman on arts, broadcasting and sport, 1988, on sport and defence, 1988–94, on foreign affairs and defence, 1994–97, chief spokesman on foreign affairs, 1997–2006, on Europe, 1997–2001, on defence, 1997–2001; Mem., Jt Cabinet Cttee on Constitutional Reform, 1997–2001. Member: Select Cttee on Members Interests, 1987–90; Select Cttee on Trade and Industry, 1990–92; Defence Select Cttee, 1992–99; Intelligence and Security Cttee, 2008–15; Foreign Affairs Cttee, 2008–15. Member: UK Delegn to N Atlantic Assembly, 1989–2015 (Leader, 2010–15); UK Delegn to Parly Assembly, OSCE, 1992–97 and 1999–2006. Mem. Bd, British Council, 1998–2002; Gov., Ditchley Foundn, 1999–; Chancellor, Univ. of St Andrews, 2006–. Chm., Royal Lyceum Theatre Co., Edinburgh, 1984–87. Member: UK Sports Council, 1965–68; Scottish Sports Council, 1971–81. Governor, Scottish Sports Aid Foundn, 1981–90; Trustee: Scottish Internat. Educn Trust, 1984–2012; London Marathon, 1997–2000; Mem., London 2012 Olympic Bd, 2010–12. AAA 220 Yards Champion, 1964 and 1967; UK 100 Metres Record Holder, 1967–74; competed at Olympic Games, 1964 and Commonwealth Games,

1966; Captain, UK Athletics Team, 1965 and 1966. *Publications:* Menzies Campbell: my autobiography, 2008. *Recreations:* all sports, reading, music, theatre. *Clubs:* Reform, National Liberal.
See also Sir J. Grant-Suttie, Bt.

**CAMPBELL OF SURBITON**, Baroness *cr* 2007 (Life Peer), of Surbiton in the London Borough of Kingston upon Thames; **Jane Susan Campbell**, DBE 2006 (MBE 2000); Member, House of Lords Appointments Commission, 2008–14; *b* 19 April 1959; *d* of Ronald James Campbell and Jessie Mary Campbell; *m* Roger Symes. *Educ:* Hatfield Poly. (BA Hons Humanities (Hist. Major) 1979); Sussex Univ. (MA Political Hist. 1982). Admin. Officer to REMAP, RADAR, 1983–84; Equal Opportunities Liaison Officer, GLC, 1984–86; Disability Training Develt Officer, London Boroughs Jt Disability Cttee, 1986–87; Prin. Disability Advr, Hounslow Council, 1987–88; Dir of Training, London Boroughs Disability Resource Team, 1988–94; freelance consultant, 1994–96; Co-Dir, Nat. Centre for Independent Living, 1996–2001; Exec. Chair, Social Care Inst. for Excellence, 2001–05. Comr, Disability Rights Commn, 2000–07. Chair: British Council of Disabled People, 1991–95; Right to Control Adv. Gp (formerly Right to Control Individual Budgets Wkg Gp), 2008–12, Independent Living Scrutiny Gp, 2009–11, Office for Disability Issues, DWP; Member: Commn for Equality and Human Rights, 2006–09; Standing Commn on Carers, DoH, 2008–09. Mem., H of L Jt Cttee on Human Rights, 2010–12. Voluntary Sector Rep., Kingston LA Social Services Cttee, 1990–96; Trustee, Disability Awareness in Action, 1991–2003; Gov., NISW, 1995–2001; Patron: Nat. Disability Arts Collection and Archive, 2013–; Just Fair, 2014–; River Thames Boat Project, 2016–. Hon. LLD Bristol, 2002; DUniv: Sheffield Hallam, 2002; Birmingham, 2009. Lifetime Achievement Award, Liberty Human Rights Awards, 2012. Mem., Editl Bd, British Jl of Social Work, 2007–11. *Publications:* Good Guide to Disability Training, 1990; (with Mike Oliver) Disability Politics, 1996; (jtly) Direct Routes to Independence, 1999; (jtly) Disabled People and the Right to Life, 2008. *Recreations:* gardening, theatre, travel. *Address:* House of Lords, SW1A 0PW.

**CAMPBELL, Aileen Elizabeth**; Member (SNP) Clydesdale, Scottish Parliament, since 2011 (Scotland South, 2007–11); Cabinet Secretary for Communities and Local Government, since 2018; *b* 18 May 1980; *d* of Peter Campbell and Ann Campbell (*née* Webster); *m* 2009, Fraser White; two *s. Educ:* Collace Primary Sch.; Perth Acad.; Univ. of Glasgow (MA Hons Econ. and Soc. Hist. with Pols). Editor, Keystone (construction mag.), 2004–05; Editl Asst, Scottish Standard, 2005; Parly Asst to Nicola Sturgeon, MSP, 2005–06; Parly Researcher to Shona Robison, MSP, and Stewart Hosie, MP, 2006–07. Minister for Local Govt and Planning, 2011, for Children and Young People, 2011–16, for Public Health and Sport, 2016–18, Scottish Parlt. *Recreations:* music, cinema, reading, football (St Johnstone FC). *Address:* Kirkton Chambers, 12 Kirkton Street, Carluke ML8 4AB. *T:* (01555) 750249. *E:* aileen.campbell.msp@parliament.scot.

**CAMPBELL, Rt Hon. Sir Alan**, Kt 2019; PC 2014; MP (Lab) Tynemouth, since 1997; *b* 8 July 1957; *s* of Albert Campbell and Marian Campbell (*née* Hewitt); *m* 1991, Jayne Lamont; one *s* one *d. Educ:* Univ. of Lancaster (BA Hons); Univ. of Leeds (PGCE); Newcastle Poly. (MA). Teacher: Whitley Bay High Sch., 1980–89; Hirst High Sch., Ashington, 1989–97. An Asst Govt Whip, 2005–06; a Lord Comr of HM Treasury (Govt Whip), 2006–08; Parly Under-Sec. of State, Home Office, 2008–10; Dep. Opposition Chief Whip, 2010–. *Address:* House of Commons, SW1A 0AA; (office) 99 Howard Street, North Shields NE30 1NA.

**CAMPBELL, Alan Dermont**; Managing Partner, Dundas & Wilson CS LLP, 2006–12; *b* 17 Sept. 1960; *s* of late Dermont Campbell and Doreen Catherine Campbell (*née* McCreath, later Morton); *m* 1986, Jane Porteous; two *d. Educ:* Fettes Coll.; Edinburgh Univ. (LLB Hons; DipLP). Joined Dundas & Wilson, Solicitors, 1984, Partner, 1992. Chm., Infrastructure Managers Ltd, 2016–. *Recreations:* golf, ski-ing, walking, cooking. *Clubs:* Golf House (Elie); Gullane Golf.

**CAMPBELL, Alan Grant**, CBE 2002; Member, Accounts Commission for Scotland, 2011–18; Chief Executive, Aberdeenshire Council, 1995–2008; *b* 4 Dec. 1946; *s* of late Archie and Catherine Campbell; *m* 1974, Susan Marion Black; one *s* two *d. Educ:* Aberdeen GS; Aberdeen Univ. (LLB 1968). Admitted Solicitor, Scotland, 1970; legal appts, Aberdeen CC, 1968–75; Grampian Regional Council: Asst Dir, 1975–79, Depute Dir, 1979–84, Dir, 1984–91, of Law and Admin; Chief Exec., 1991–95. Chm., SOLACE (Scotland), 1997–99. Chm., Inquiry into Future Fisheries Mgt for Scottish Govt, 2009–10; Mem., Cttee of Inquiry into professional conditions of service for teachers, 2000. Pres., Deeside Thistle Cycling Club, 2014– (Chm., 1979–2010); Chm., Exec. Cttee, Aberdeen GS Former Pupils' Club, 2015–. Hon. LLD Aberdeen, 2005. *Recreations:* competitive cycling and following the Tour de France, gardening, photography, the enjoyment of wine. *Address:* 72 Hamilton Place, Aberdeen AB15 5BA.

**CAMPBELL, Alastair John**; freelance speaker, consultant and writer; *b* 25 May 1957; *s* of late Donald Campbell and of Elizabeth (*née* Caldwell); partner, Fiona Millar, *qv;* two *s* one *d. Educ:* City of Leicester Boys Sch.; Gonville and Caius Coll., Cambridge (MA). Trainee reporter, Tavistock Times and Sunday Independent, 1980–82; freelance reporter, London, 1982–83; reporter, Daily Mirror, 1982–85; news editor, Sunday Today, 1985–86; reporter, Daily Mirror, 1986; Sunday Mirror: Political Corresp., 1986–87; Political Editor, 1987–89; Columnist, 1989–91; Daily Mirror: Political Editor, 1989–93; Columnist, 1991–93; Asst Editor and Columnist, Today, 1993–95; Press Sec. to Leader of Opposition, 1994–97; Prime Minister's official spokesman, 1997–2001; Dir of Communications and Strategy, Prime Minister's Office, 2001–03; Strategy and Commns Consultant, British and Irish Lions Tour to NZ, 2005; Dir, Election Communications, Labour Party, 2005; Advr to Labour Party, General Election, 2010, 2015; Member, Advisory Board: Portland, 2011–; Univ. Coll. of Football Business, Burnley, 2011–; Strategic Adviser: Albanian Socialist Party, 2011–; Albanian govt, 2013–; Chief Interviewer, GQ mag., UK, 2014–. Humanitas Vis. Prof. of Media, Cambridge Univ., 2013. Chm., Fundraising, Leukaemia and Lymphoma Res. (formerly Leukaemia Res. Fund), 2004–; Ambassador: Time to Change campaign, 2008–; Alcohol Concern, 2013–; Rethink, 2016–. Patron, Maytree Suicide Sanctuary, 2015–. Hon. Life Mem., Law Soc., UCD, 2014. Freelance writer, The Times and elsewhere, 2003–; columnist, Internat. Business Times, 2016–; Ed.-at-Large, New European, 2017–. Hon. FRCPsych 2017. Mind Champion of the Year, 2009. *Publications:* The Blair Years, 2007; (with Bill Hagerty) The Alastair Campbell Diaries: Volume One: prelude to power 1994–1997, 2010, Volume Two: power and the people 1997–99, 2011, Volume Three: power and responsibility 1999–2001, 2011, Volume Four: the burden of power 2001–03, 2012; Volume Five: outside inside, 2016; Volume Six: from Blair to Brown 2005–07, 2017; Volume Seven: from crash to defeat 2007–10, 2018; Volume Eight: on the slide to Cameron 2010–15, 2020; The Happy Depressive, 2012; The Irish Diaries, 2013; Winners and How They Succeed, 2015; *novels:* All in the Mind, 2008; Maya, 2010; My Name is…, 2013; (with P. Fletcher) Saturday Bloody Saturday, 2016. *Recreations:* running, triathlon, bagpipes, Burnley Football Club.

**CAMPBELL, Alastair Peter;** *see* Bracadale, Rt Hon. Lord.

**CAMPBELL, Prof. Alastair Vincent;** Chen Su Lan Centennial Professor of Medical Ethics and Director, Centre for Biomedical Ethics, 2006–16, now Director Emeritus, and Visiting Professor in Medical Ethics, since 2016, National University of Singapore; *b* 16 April 1938; *s* of William Lee Campbell and Jean Graham Dow; *m* 1st, 1959, Paula Barker (marr. diss.); one *s* four *d;* 2nd, 1979, Sally Barbara Forbes; two *s. Educ:* Hamilton Acad.; Univ. of Edinburgh (MA, BD); San Francisco Theol Seminary (ThD). Ordained Minister, Church of Scotland, 1963. Associate Chaplain, Univ. of Edinburgh, 1964–69; Lectr in Ethics, RCN, Scotland, 1966–72; University of Edinburgh: Lectr and Sen. Lectr, Dept of Christian Ethics and Practical Theology, 1969–90; Head of Dept, 1987–90; Associate Dean, Faculty of Divinity, 1978–81; Prof. of Biomedical Ethics, Otago Med. Sch., and Dir, Bioethics Res. Centre, Dunedin, Univ. of Otago, NZ, 1990–96; Prof. of Ethics in Medicine, Univ. of Bristol, 1996–2003, now Emeritus. Fellow: Hastings Center, NY, 2002; Ethox Centre, Univ. of Oxford, 2012. Foundn Editor, Jl of Medical Ethics, 1975–80. FRSE, 2017. Milligan Soc. Medallion, 1980; H. K. Beecher Award, Hastings Center, NY, 1999. Public Service Medal (Singapore), 2018. *Publications:* Moral Dilemmas in Medicine, 1972; Medicine, Health and Justice, 1978; Rediscovering Pastoral Care, 1981; (with R. Higgs) In That Case, 1982; Moderated Love, 1984; Paid to Care?, 1985; The Gospel of Anger, 1986; The Dictionary of Pastoral Care, 1987; (with G. R. Gillett and D. G. Jones) Practical Medical Ethics, 1992, 4th edn, as Medical Ethics, 2005; Health as Liberation, 1995; The Body in Bioethics, 2009; Bioethics: the basics, 2013, 2nd edn 2017; articles in learned jls. *Recreations:* music, cross country ski-ing, hill walking. *Address:* 2 Ravelston Dykes Lane, Edinburgh EH4 3NY.

**CAMPBELL, Hon. Alexander Bradshaw**, OC 2013; OPEI 2013; PC (Canada) 1967; Premier of Prince Edward Island, 1966–78; Judge, Supreme Court of Prince Edward Island, 1978–94; *b* 1 Dec. 1933; *s* of Dr Thane A. Campbell and late Cecilia B. Campbell; *m* 1961, Marilyn Gilmour; two *s* one *d. Educ:* Dalhousie Univ. (BA, LLB). Called to Bar of Prince Edward Island, 1959; practised law with Campbell & Campbell, Summerside, PEI, 1959–66; QC (PEI) 1966. MLA, Prince Edward Island, 1965–78; Leader of Liberal Party, Dec. 1966–78; served (while Premier) as Attorney-Gen., 1966–69, Minister of Development, 1969–72, Minister of Agriculture, 1972–74, and Minister of Justice, 1974–78. Dir, Inst. of Man and Resources, 1976–80. Pres., Summerside YMCA, 1981–91; Founder Pres., Summerside Area Historical Soc., 1983; Founder Chm., PEI Council, Duke of Edinburgh Awards (Canada), 1984. Mem., Wyatt Foundn, 1993–2006. Mem., Heedless Hoarsemen Men's Chorus, Largo, Fla, 1996– (Manager, 2004–09). Chm., PEI Day Cttee, Fla, 2000–. Elder of Trinity United Church, Summerside. Sigma Chi Fraternity. Hon. LLD: McGill 1967; PEI, 1978. *Recreations:* golf, boating, gardening. *Address:* Stanley Bridge, Kensington, RR #6, PE C0B 1M0, Canada. *T:* (902) 8862081. *Club:* Y's Men's (Summerside).

**CAMPBELL, Sir Alexander Thomas C.;** *see* Cockburn-Campbell.

**CAMPBELL, Alexis Anne;** QC 2017; a Recorder, since 2010; *b* Herts, 23 March 1967; *d* of John Campbell and Gillian Campbell; *m* 1998, Rosario Castagna; two *s. Educ:* Ashlyns Sch., Berkhamsted; Univ. of Leeds (LLB); Council of Legal Educn. Called to the Bar, Inner Temple, 1990; in practice as a barrister, specialising in matrimonial finance, 1990–. Fellow, Internat. Acad. of Family Lawyers (formerly Internat. Acad. of Matrimonial Lawyers), 2010. *Recreations:* family, reading, ballet, sailing, walking, making wine and drinking it. *Address:* 29 Bedford Row, WC1R 4HE. *T:* (020) 7404 1044. *E:* acampbell@29br.co.uk.

**CAMPBELL, His Honour Andrew Bruce;** a Circuit Judge, 2004–18; *b* 20 Feb. 1949; *s* of Keith Bruce Campbell and Betty Joan Campbell; *m* 1977, Felicity Jane (*née* Owen); two *d. Educ:* Harrow Sch.; Brasenose Coll., Oxford (MA Jurisprudence). Called to the Bar, Inner Temple, 1972; Asst Recorder, 1998–2000, Recorder, 2000–04. *Recreations:* long distance walking, theatre.

**CAMPBELL, Andrew Neville;** QC 1994; a Recorder, 1989–2014; *b* 17 June 1949; *s* of Archibald Campbell, CMG and of Peggie Campbell (*née* Hussey); *m* 1980, Rebecca Thornton; two *s* one *d. Educ:* Berkhamsted Sch.; New Coll., Oxford (BA Hons Jurisprudence). Called to the Bar, Middle Temple, 1972, Bencher, 2005. *Recreations:* fishing, shooting, cricket, squash, ski-ing, walking. *Clubs:* Vincent's (Oxford); Harrogate Cricket (Pres.).

**CAMPBELL, Andrew Simon**, CB 2013; Consultant, Local Government Association, since 2017 (Associate Director, 2015–17); *b* 30 Sept. 1957; *s* of Brian Andrew Humphrey Campbell and Rita Audrey Campbell; *m* 1982, Jacqueline Fraser Craik; two *s* one *d. Educ:* St Andrews Univ. (MA); University Coll. London (MPhil). Joined Dept of Transport, 1983; DoE, 1988–96; seconded to EC, Brussels, 1990–93; Sec., Econ. and Domestic Secretariat, Cabinet Office, 1996–98; Area Dir, Kent, Govt Office for SE, 1998–2001; Private Secretary to Secretary of State: for Transport, Local Govt and the Regions, 2001–02; for Transport and Sec. of State for Scotland, 2002–03; Dir, Regl Co-ordination Unit, ODPM, subseq. DCLG, 2003–06; Dir, Local Strategic Partnerships and Performance, later Local Govt Policy and Performance, DCLG, 2006–11; Dir, Strategy and Progs, later Strategy and Performance, DCLG, 2011–13; Acting Director General: for Local Govt and Regeneration, 2010; for Neighbourhoods, 2011–12; Exec. Dir for Civil Service Reform, Cabinet Office (on secondment), 2012; Dir Gen., Finance and Corp. Services, DCLG, 2013–15. *Recreations:* tennis, golf, football, reading novels, listening to nearly all types of music. *Clubs:* Southampton FC; West Surrey Golf.

**CAMPBELL, Angus;** *see* Campbell, I. A.

**CAMPBELL, Anne;** Chairman, Parkside Federation Academies, Cambridge, 2013–18; *b* 6 April 1940; *d* of late Frank Lucas and Susan (*née* Chadwick); *m* 1963, Archibald MacRobert Campbell; one *s* two *d. Educ:* Newnham Coll., Cambridge (Maths Tripos Pt II, 1962; MA 1965). CStat (FSS 1985). Sen. Lectr in Statistics, Cambs Coll. of Arts and Technol., 1970–83; Head of Stats and Data Processing, Nat. Inst. of Agricl Botany, Cambridge, 1983–92. MP (Lab) Cambridge, 1992–2005; contested (Lab) same seat, 2005. PPS to Minister for E-commerce and Small Businesses, 1999–2001, to Sec. of State for Trade and Industry, 2001–03. Mem., Cambs CC, 1985–89. Chm., Cambs and Peterborough NHS Foundn Trust, 2005–12. Nat. Leader of Governance, 2016–. FRSA 1992. *Publications:* Calculation for Commercial Students, 1972. *Recreations:* tennis, ski-ing, gardening, mountain walking. *Address:* 20 St Barnabas Road, Cambridge CB1 2BY.

**CAMPBELL, Rt Hon. Sir Anthony;** *see* Campbell, Rt Hon. Sir W. A.

**CAMPBELL, Prof. Anthony Keith**, PhD; Professor, School of Pharmacy and Pharmaceutical Sciences (formerly Welsh School of Pharmacy), Cardiff University, 2010–14, Honorary Professor, since 2014; *b* 30 April 1945; *s* of Harold Keith Campbell and Jennet Mary Seth Campbell; *m* 1985, Dr Stephanie Beatrix Matthews; one *s* two *d,* and two *s* by previous marriage. *Educ:* City of London Sch.; Pembroke Coll., Cambridge (Exhibnr; Foundn Schol.; MA 1st cl. Natural Sci. 1967; PhD 1971). Lectr, 1970–78, Sen. Lectr, 1978–83, Welsh Nat. Sch. of Medicine; Reader, 1983–91, Prof. in Med. Biochem., 1991–2010, Univ. of Wales Coll. of Medicine, later Cardiff University. Founder, 1993, and Dir, Cardiff, 1993–2000, Pembs 2000–, Darwin Centre. Founder and Ed.-in-Chief, Young Darwinian (internat. schs jl), 2017–. Mem. Council, Linnean Soc., 2012–15.

Founder, Internat. Soc. for Bioluminescence and Chemiluminescence, 1994; Foreign Mem., Royal Soc. of Scis, Uppsala, 2001. FLS 1995; FLSW 2013. Inspire Wales Award for Sci. and Technol., 2011. *Publications*: Intracellular Calcium: its universal role as regulator, 1983; Chemiluminescence: principles and applications in biology and medicine, 1988; Rubicon: the fifth dimension of biology, 1994; (with S. B. Matthews) Lactose Intolerance and the MATHS Syndrome, 2001; Tony's Lactose-free Cookbook: the science of lactose intolerance and how to live without lactose, 2005; Hands on Darwin: Charles Darwin in the 21st century, 2011; Intracellular Calcium, 2015; (ed) The Story of the Pryce Family, 2015; Fundamentals of Intracellular Calcium, 2017; 7 patents; contrib. numerous scientific pubns, and papers to Nature, Proc. of NAS, Lancet, Postgrad. Med. Jl, Jl of Molecular Biol. *Recreations*: music (singing/conducting), bridge (Chm., Penarth Bridge Club; plays for E Wales), cooking, natural history. *Address*: School of Pharmacy and Pharmaceutical Sciences, Cardiff University, Redwood Building, King Edward VII Drive, Cardiff CF10 3NB. *E*: campbellak@cf.ac.uk, tony@theyoungdarwinian.com.

**CAMPBELL, Arthur McLure**, CBE 1990; Principal Clerk of Session and Justiciary, Scotland, 1982–89, retired; *b* 15 Aug. 1932; *s* of late Hector Brownlie Campbell, MBE (Mil.), AIPA and Catherine Smylie (*née* Renwick). *Educ*: Queen's Park Sch., Glasgow; Open Univ. (BA Hons 2001; BSc Hons 2008; MA (Dist.) 2012). Deptl Legal Qual., Scottish Court Service, 1956. National Service, FAA, 1950–52. Admiralty Supplies Directorate, 1953–54; entered Scottish Court Service, 1954; Sheriff Clerk Depute, Kilmarnock, 1957–60; Sheriff Clerk of Orkney, 1961–65; seconded HM Treasury (O & M), 1965–69; Principal Sheriff Clerk Depute, Glasgow, 1969; Sheriff Clerk, Airdrie, 1969–72; Principal, Scottish Court Service Staff Trng Centre, 1973–74; Asst Sheriff Clerk of Glasgow and Strathkelvin, 1974–81. Clerk of Cttees, H of L (temp.), 1991. Secretary: Lord Chancellor's Cttee on Re-sealing of Probates and Confirmations, 1967–68; Scottish Office Cttee on Money Transfer Services, 1968–69; Chm., Simplified Divorce (Scotland) Implementation Gp, 1981–82 (Scottish Consumer Council's Consumer Champion Award, 1983); Mem., Review Body on Use of Judicial Time in Superior Courts in Scotland, 1985–86. Chm., Sheriff Clerks' Assoc., 1971–72. *Recreation*: opsimathy. *Address*: 1 West Hill, Lord Street West, Southport PR8 2BJ; Carrer Mestre Nicolau 8, 07181 Palma Nova-Calvia, Mallorca. *Clubs*: National Liberal, Civil Service.

**CAMPBELL, Rt Hon. Avril Phaedra;** *see* Campbell, Rt Hon. Kim.

**CAMPBELL, Bridget;** Director, Environment and Forestry, Scottish Government, since 2015; *b* 9 March 1959; *d* of Allan Walter Campbell and Margaret Campbell (*née* Brettell). *Educ*: St Anne's Coll., Oxford (BA Hons Lit. Hum.). Various posts in Depts of Envmt and Transport, dealing with housing, local govt and internat. envmtl policy, 1982–96; Cycle Internat. course, l'Ecole Nat. d'Admin, Paris, 1989–90; Head, Housing Policy and Home Ownership Div., DoE, 1996–98; Scottish Executive: Head: Envmt Protection Unit, 1998–99; Cabinet Secretariat, 2000–01; Dir, Public Service Delivery, 2002–03; Hd, Police and Community Safety Gp, Scottish Exec., later Scottish Govt, Justice Dept, then Dir, Police and Community Safety, Scottish Govt, 2005–09; Scottish Government: Dir, Criminal Justice, then Justice, 2009–14; Dir, Readiness, 2014. *Address*: Scottish Government, St Andrew's House, Edinburgh EH1 3DG. *T*: (0131) 244 4891. *E*: bridget.campbell@scotland.gsi.gov.uk.

**CAMPBELL, Bruce;** *see* Campbell, W. B.

**CAMPBELL, Prof. Bruce Mortimer Stanley**, PhD; FBA 2009; FRHistS; Professor of Medieval Economic History, Department of Economic and Social History, 1995–2003, School of Geography, Archaeology and Palaeoecology, 2003–14, Queen's University Belfast, now Emeritus Professor; *b* Rickmansworth, 11 June 1949; *s* of Reginald Arthur Mortimer and Mary Campbell. *Educ*: Liverpool Univ. (BA 1st Cl. 1970); Darwin Coll., Cambridge (PhD 1975). FRHistS 2001. Lectr in Geog., 1973–89, Reader in Econ. Hist., 1992–95, QUB (on secondment to Dept of Econ. and Social Hist., 1989–2003). Fellow, Wissenschaftskolleg zu Berlin, 2010–11. Ellen McArthur Lectr, Cambridge Univ., 2013. MRIA 1997. FAcSS (AcSS 2003); MAE 2013. *Publications*: (ed with M. Overton) Land, Labour and Livestock: historical studies in European agricultural productivity, 1991; (ed) Before the Black Death: studies in the 'crisis' of the early fourteenth century, 1991; (jtly) A Medieval Capital and its Grain Supply: agrarian production and its distribution in the London region *c.* 1300, 1993; (ed with R. H. Britnell) A Commercialising Economy: England 1086–*c.* 1300, 1995; English Seigniorial Agriculture 1250–1450, 2000; (with K. Bartley) England on the Eve of the Black Death: an atlas of lay lordship, land and wealth, 1300–49, 2006; The Medieval Antecedents of English Agricultural Progress, 2007; Field Systems and Farming Systems in Late Medieval England, 2008; Land and People in Late Medieval England, 2009; (jtly) British Economic Growth 1270–1870, 2015; The Great Transition: climate, disease and society in the late-medieval world, 2016 (Gyorgy Ranki Biennial Prize, Econ. Hist. Assoc., 2017); contrib. chapters to books and articles to Agricl Hist. Rev., Continuity and Change, Econ. Hist. Rev., Explorations in Econ. Hist., Jl Econ. Hist. (Arthur H. Cole Prize, Econ. Hist. Assoc. 1984), Jl Histl Geog., Past and Present, Trans IBG, Trans Geographical Inf. System. *Recreations*: attending live performances of classical music and opera, looking at architecture of all periods, Newfoundland dogs. *Address*: School of Geography, Archaeology and Palaeoecology, Queen's University Belfast, Belfast BT7 1NN. *Fax*: (028) 9097 3212. *E*: b.m.campbell@qub.ac.uk.

**CAMPBELL, Camilla Anne MacNeill;** Joint Founder and Director, Noho Film and Television, since 2012; *b* Rinteln, W Germany, 1 Dec. 1971; *d* of Alasdair Campbell and Carol Campbell; *m* 2005, Julian Kingsland; two *s*. *Educ*: Roedean Sch.; Newnham Coll., Cambridge (BA Hons Classics 1993). Editorial Assistant: AP Watt, 1994–96; Whitehall Films, 1996–99; Development Executive: Granada Television, 1999–2001; Tiger Aspect Prodns, 2001–04; Channel 4, 2004–09; Head of Drama, Channel 4, 2009–11. *Recreation*: sons Hal and Brock. *Address*: Noho Film and Television, Third Floor, 59 Charlotte Street, W1T 4PE.

**CAMPBELL, Cheryl Anne;** actress. *Educ*: London Acad. of Music and Dramatic Art (Rodney Millington Award). Acted at Glasgow Citizens Theatr, Watford Rep., Birmingham Rep., King's Head, National Theatre and Theatre Clwyd; Blanche Dubois in A Streetcar Named Desire (Best Actress, Regl Theatre Awards); Nora in A Doll's House (SWET Award, 1983, for best actress of 1982 in a revival), RSC; title rôle in Miss Julie, Lyric, Hammersmith, and Duke of York's, 1983; title rôle in Daughter-in-Law, Hampstead, 1985; The Sneeze, Aldwych, 1988; Betrayal, Almeida, 1991; The Changeling, RSC, 1992; Misha's Party, Macbeth, RSC, 1993; The Strip, Royal Court, 1995; Some Sunny Day, Hampstead, 1996; The Last Yankee, Mercury Th., Colchester, 1996; The Seagull, Donmar, 1997; What the Butler Saw, Sheffield Crucible, 1997; Passion Play, Donmar, 2000; Noises Off, Piccadilly and tour, 2003. *Television* serials and series include: Pennies from Heaven, 1978; Testament of Youth (Best Actress Award, BAFTA, and British Broadcasting Press Guild Award, 1979); Malice Aforethought; Centrepoint; The Secret Agent, 1992; The Way We Live Now, 2001; William and Mary, 2003, 2004, 2005; Fantabulosa, 2006; Spooks, 2006; Peep Show, 2007; Poirot, 2008; Casualty, 2011; Breathless, 2013; Call the Midwife, 2012–14; Doctor Foster, 2015. *Films* include: Chariots of Fire, 1981; Greystoke, 1983; The Shooting Party, 1985. *Address*: c/o AHA Talent Ltd, 2 Percy Street, W1T 1DD. *T*: (020) 7250 1760.

**CAMPBELL, Christopher James**, CBE 1993; Chairman, British Shipbuilders, 1989–2002; *b* 2 Jan. 1936; *s* of David Heggie Campbell and Nettie Phyllis (*née* Burgess). *Educ*: Epsom College. FCA. Served RAPC, 1959–61. Debenhams and subsidiaries, 1966–86, incl. Man. Dir, Hardy Amies, 1978–79; former Director: Debenhams dept stores; Harvey Nichols; Lotus; Debenhams Finance; Debenhams (M & S). Mem., and chief negotiator, 1986–88, non-exec. Mem., 1988–91, National Bus Co.; Finance Dir, Nat. Rivers Authy Adv. Cttee, 1988–89; Director: Harrods Bank Ltd, 1991–2000; Crown Timber plc, 1996–2000; Riverside Mental Health NHS Trust, 1993–96; Mem., BRB, 1994–97 (Vice-Chm., 1994–96). Mem. Council, Specialist Schs and Academies Trust (formerly Technology Colls, then Specialist Schs, Trust), 2001–07. Gov., United World Coll. of the Atlantic, 1993–2002. Trustee: Cobbe collection of ancient keyboard instruments, 1998–2007; British Youth Opera, 2003–10. Chm., Lucy Crowe Fan Club, 2006–. Captain Paymaster, HAC Inf. Bn, 1960–63. *Recreations*: politics, opera, entertaining, visual arts. *Address*: 19 Morpeth Mansions, Morpeth Terrace, SW1P 1ER. *T*: (020) 7630 7527. *Club*: Garrick.

**CAMPBELL, Christopher John;** HM Diplomatic Service; Ambassador to the Dominican Republic, 2015–Aug. 2020; *b* London, 12 April 1963; *s* of John and Kathleen Campbell; *m* 1989, Sharon Isabel Hale (*see* S. I. Campbell). *Educ*: Wimbledon Coll.; Open Univ. (Professional Cert. and Dip. Mgt). Entered FCO, 1982; N America Dept, FCO, 1982–84; Sec. of State's Office, FCO, 1984–85; Accountant, Khartoum, 1985–88; Third Secretary: (Immigration), Dhaka, 1988–92; (Mgt), Jakarta, 1992–96; Desk Officer, Polar Regns Section, FCO, 1996–98; Second Secretary: (Commercial), Caracas, 1999–2003; Ext. Relns Policy, UK Delegn NATO, Brussels, 2003–07; Strategy Manager, Internat. Mil. Capacity Bldg, 2008–09; Hd of Peacekeeping, 2009–11, Conflict Gp, FCO; non-resident Ambassador to Nicaragua, 2011–15. *Recreations*: playing golf and tennis, scuba diving, watching Rugby, cooking. *Address*: c/o Foreign and Commonwealth Office, King Charles Street, SW1A 2AH. *E*: chris.campbell@fco.gov.uk.

**CAMPBELL, Colin Donald Norman;** Master of the Senior Court Costs Office (formerly Supreme Court Taxing, later Costs, Office), 1996–2015; Consultant, Kain Knight, since 2015; *b* 26 Nov. 1952; *s* of late Maj. Gregory Campbell, TD and Myra Campbell (*née* Robertson); *m* 1985, Jacqueline Merete Mollett; one *s* one *d*. *Educ*: Oundle; Univ. of London (BA). Admitted as solicitor, 1983; Partner, Brown Cooper Solicitors and Privy Council Agents, 1987–96; Dep. Taxing Master, 1993–96; Dep. Dist Judge, Midland Circuit, 2001–. *Recreations*: Rugby Union, ski-ing, fly-fishing. *Address*: The Old Vicarage, Syleham, near Eye, Suffolk IP21 4LN. *T*: (01379) 668306. *Club*: MCC.

**CAMPBELL, Colin Douglas**, FRSB; FRSE; Chief Executive, James Hutton Institute, since 2016; *b* Gibraltar, 24 June 1961; *s* of James and Andrée Campbell; *m* 1982, Mary-Anne Gillen; two *s* one *d*. *Educ*: Ardrossan Acad.; Univ. of Strathclyde (BSc; PhD 1987). FRSB 2015. Res. Scientist, Hill Farming Res. Orgn, Edinburgh, 1986–87; Macaulay Land Use Research Institute: Research Scientist: Edinburgh, 1987–94; Aberdeen, 1994–2002; Hd, Soils Gp, Aberdeen, 2008–11; Dir, Sci. Excellence, James Hutton Inst., Dundee and Aberdeen, 2011–16. Vis. Prof., Dept of Soil Sci., Swedish Agricl Univ., Uppsala, 2009–13. MInstD 2015; ARAgS 2017. FRSE 2018. *Publications*: contrib. scientific papers on soil microbiol., soil plant interactions, land use, agric. and ecosystem health to learned jls and books. *Recreations*: ski-ing, hill walking, tennis, golf, travel. *Address*: James Hutton Institute, Craigiebuckler, Aberdeen AB15 8QH. *T*: 0344 928 5428.

**CAMPBELL, Colin MacIver;** Member (SNP) Scotland West, Scottish Parliament, 1999–2003; *b* 31 Aug. 1938; *s* of Archibald James Campbell, MB ChB, DPH, and Christina Ellen Campbell (*née* MacIver); *m* 1963, Evelyn Jean Marcella George; three *s* (and one *s* decd). *Educ*: Paisley Grammar Sch.; Glasgow Univ. (MA Hons); Jordanhill Coll. of Educn. Teacher: Hillhead High Sch., 1961–63; Paisley GS, 1963–67; Principal Teacher, Greenock Acad., 1967–73; Depute Head, Merksworth High Sch., 1973–77; Head, Westwood Secondary Sch., 1977–89; Tutor, Sen. Studies Inst., Strathclyde Univ., 1995–98. Mem., Renfrewshire Council, 1995–99. Nat. Sec., SNP, 1997–99 (Defence Spokesperson, 1995–2003). Chair, Kilbarchan Pipe Band, 2006–11. Mem., Lowland Reserve Forces and Cadets Assoc., 1999–2004. *Publications*: (jtly) Can't Shoot a Man with a Cold: Lt E. Alan Mackintosh, MC, 1893–1917, Poet of the Highland Division, 2004; Engine of Destruction: the 51st (Highland) Division in the Great War, 2013; The 51st (Highland) Division in the Great War: engine of destruction, 2018. *Recreation*: military history of the Great War. *Address*: Braeside, Shuttle Street, Kilbarchan, Renfrewshire PA10 2PR.

**CAMPBELL, Colin Malcolm;** *see* Malcolm, Rt Hon. Lord.

**CAMPBELL, Sir Colin (Murray)**, Kt 1994; DL; Vice-Chancellor, University of Nottingham, 1988–2008; Professor Emeritus, Queen's University, Belfast; First Commissioner for Judicial Appointments, 2001–06; *b* 26 Dec. 1944; *s* of late Donald Campbell and Isobel Campbell; divorced; one *s* one *d*. *Educ*: Robert Gordon's Coll., Aberdeen; Univ. of Aberdeen (LLB 1st Cl. Hons). Lecturer: Faculty of Law, Univ. of Dundee, 1967–69; Dept of Public Law, Univ. of Edinburgh, 1969–73; Prof. of Jurisprudence, 1974–88, Dean of Faculty of Law, 1977–80, Pro-Vice-Chancellor, 1983–87, QUB. Member: Council, Soc. for Computers and Law, 1973–88; Standing Adv. Commn on Human Rights, 1977–80; Legal Aid Adv. Cttee, NI, 1978–82; Mental Health Legislation Rev. Cttee, NI, 1978–82; UGC, 1987–88; Nottingham Develt Enterprise, 1988–91; UFC Scottish Cttee, 1989–93; HEFCE, 1992–97; Inquiry into Police Responsibilities and Rewards, 1992–93; Trent RHA, 1992–96. Chairman: QUBIS Ltd, 1983–88; Zeton Ltd, 1990; Ind. Adv. Gp on Consumers Protection in NI, 1984; NI Economic Council, 1987–94 (Mem., 1985–94); Lace Market Develt Co., 1989–97; Human Fertilisation and Embryology Authy, 1990–94; Med. Workforce Standing Adv. Cttee, 1991–2001; Food Adv. Cttee, 1994–2001; Human Genetics Adv. Commn, 1996–99. Non-exec. Dir, Swiss Re GB, 1999–2005. DL Notts, 1996. *Publications*: (ed jtly) Law and Society, 1979; (ed) Do We Need a Bill of Rights?, 1980; (ed) Data Processing and the Law, 1984; numerous articles in books and jls. *Recreations*: sport, walking, music, reading.

**CAMPBELL, Darren Andrew**, MBE 2005; international athlete; Ambassador, Sky Sports Living for Sport; *b* 12 Sept. 1973; *s* of Marva Campbell; *m* 2004, Clair Jacobs; two *s* one *d*. Athletic achievements include: Gold medals, 100m, 200m and 4 x 100m relay, Eur. Jun. Championships, 1991; Gold medal, 4 x 100m relay, Silver medals, 100m and 200m, World Jun. Championships, 1992; winner, 100m, National Championships, 1998; European Championships: Gold medals, 100m and 4 x 100m relay, 1998; Gold medal, 4 x 100m relay, 2002; World Championships: Bronze medal, 4 x 100m relay, 1997; Silver medal, 4 x 100m relay, 1999; Silver medal, 4 x 100m relay and Bronze medal, 100m, 2003; Commonwealth Games: Gold medal, 4 x 100m relay, Malaysia, 1998; Bronze medal, 200m, Gold medal, 4 x 100m relay, Manchester, 2002; Olympic Games: Silver medal, 200m, Sydney, 2000; Gold medal, 4 x 100m relay, Athens, 2004. Dir, Pro Athlete Supplementation Ltd, 2009–. *Recreation*: football. *Address*: c/o Nuff Respect, No 1 Constable's Boatyard, 15 Thames Street, Hampton, Middx TW12 2EW. *Club*: Sale Harriers.

**CAMPBELL, David;** Director, Sports and Entertainment (UK) Ltd, since 2012; Chief Executive, Ivy Collection, since 2018; Chairman, Bill's Restaurants, since 2018; *b* 4 Sept. 1959; *s* of Archibald and Jean Campbell; *m* 1995, Tracey; three *s* (incl. twin *s*) one *d*. *Educ*: Kelvinside Acad., Glasgow; Reed's Sch., Cobham; Washington Univ., St Louis (MBA, AB Media). Mktg, General Mills, 1981–92; Mktg Manager, Pepsi-Cola, 1982–86; various posts, Virgin Gp, 1986–90; Chief Executive Officer: Virgin TV (Europe), 1990–92; Virgin Radio, 1992–96; Virgin Media, 1997; Ginger Media Gp, 1997–2000; Vice Chm., Ministry of Sound, 2001–02; CEO, Visit London, 2003–05; CEO, AEG Europe and The O2, 2005–11; Main Bd Dir, Formula One (Delta Topco), 2011–12; Chief Exec., Wagamama, 2013–17. *Recreations:* music, travel, family. *E:* david.campbell@sportsnet.com. *Club:* Soho House.

**CAMPBELL, David Ian;** HM Diplomatic Service; High Commissioner to Brunei, 2013–17; *b* 9 July 1958; *s* of Ian Flett Campbell and Irene Joyce Campbell (*née* Cook). *Educ:* St Nicholas Grammar Sch., Northwood; Univ. of Bristol (LLB Hons 1980). Joined FCO, 1981; served: Budapest, 1984–85; Georgetown, 1985–87; FCO, 1987–89; First Sec., UK Mission to UN, Geneva, 1989–93; Dep. Hd of Mission, Belgrade, 1994; Dep. Hd, then Hd, Human Rights Policy Dept, FCO, 1995–99; Dep. Hd of Mission, Manila, 2000–03; Deputy High Commissioner: Singapore, 2003–07; Canberra, 2008; Dir, British Trade and Cultural Office, Taiwan, 2009–13. *Recreations:* books, theatre, travel.

**CAMPBELL, David Ross,** CBE 2000; Chairman, NHS National Services Scotland, 2004–08; *b* 27 Sept. 1943; *s* of William Pancost Clyde Campbell and Davidina (*née* Ross); *m* 1968, Moira Bagley Donald. *Educ:* Whitehill Sch.; James Watt Meml Coll. Radio Officer, MN, 1961–67; Sales Exec., Remington Rand, 1967–69; various posts, Glasgow Herald & Evening Times, 1969–75; Man. Dir, Scottish & Universal Newspapers, 1975–79; Exec. Dir, Scottish & Universal Investments, 1978–83; Dir, Clyde Cablevision Hldgs Ltd, 1983–87; Chm. and Chief Exec., West Independent Newspapers Ltd, 1984–94. Chairman: Saltire Hldgs Ltd, 1990–93; Clansman Leisure Ltd, 1990–93; Dep. Chm., Enterprise Ayrshire, 1991–2000. Scotland Bd Mem., New Opportunities Fund, 1998–2004, Big Lottery Fund, 2004–06; Chm., Health Educn Bd for Scotland, 1995–2001. Dir, Wise Gp, 2009–. Public Mem., Network Rail, 2009–15. Member: PPITB, 1976–78; Press Council, 1988–90. Pres., Glasgow Chamber of Commerce, 1988–90. Also holds various other public and private sector chm. and dir positions. FInstD 1980. Scottish Free Enterprise Award, Aims of Industry, 1990. *Recreations:* golf, theatre, travel, reading. *Address:* Summerlea, Summerlea Road, Seamill, W Kilbride KA23 9HP.

**CAMPBELL, Diane Eva; Her Honour Judge Diane Campbell;** a Circuit Judge, since 2018; *b* Belfast, 31 May 1973; *d* of James Campbell and Eva Campbell; *m* 2004; one *s* two *d*. *Educ:* Sullivan Upper Sch., Holywood; Durham Univ. (LLB 1994); Inns of Court Sch. of Law (BVC 1995). Called to the Bar, Gray's Inn, 1995; in practice as a barrister, York Chambers, subseq. Dere Street Barristers, 1995–2018; a Recorder, 2016–18. *Recreations:* spending time with my husband and three children, going to the theatre.

**CAMPBELL, Douglas James;** QC 2016; a Recorder, since 2010; *b* Bridge of Allan, Scotland, 15 Nov. 1966; *s* of Alastair Dick Campbell and Mary Morrison Campbell; *m* 1993, Dr the Hon. Madeleine Langley Higgins, *d* of Baron Higgins, *qv* and Dame Rosalyn Higgins, *qv*; one *s*. *Educ:* Dollar Acad.; Hertford Coll., Oxford (BA 1st Cl. Hons Chem. with distinction in Quantum Chem. 1988); City Univ. (DipLaw with distinction 1991). Called to the Bar, Inner Temple, 1993; Attorney-Gen.'s Panel of Jun. Counsel to Crown, 2010–15; a Dep. High Court Judge, 2015–. Pegasus Scholar, Melbourne, 1996. Gov., Contemporary Dance Trust, 2008–16. *Publications:* (jtly) Terrell on the Law of Patents, 16th edn 2006 to 18th edn 2016. *Address:* 3 New Square, Lincoln's Inn, WC2A 3RS. *T:* (020) 7405 1111, *Fax:* (020) 7405 7800. *E:* clerks@3newsquare.co.uk. *Clubs:* Vincent's (Oxford); Achilles.

**CAMPBELL, Duncan;** Director of Communications, Scottish Natural Heritage, 1992–95; *b* 23 Sept. 1935; *s* of late Duncan Campbell, sometime Manager, Chartered Bank of India and Australasia, and Mary Beryl Campbell; *m* 1959, Morny Key (*d* 2012); two *s*. *Educ:* Merchiston Castle Sch., Edinburgh; Edinburgh Univ.; Newcastle upon Tyne Univ. Nat. service, RHA, 1954–56. Forestry Commission: Forest Manager, 1960–73; Landscape Architect, 1973–80; Head of Design and Recreation Br., 1980–85; Head of Environment Br., 1985–88; Dir, Countryside Commission for Scotland, 1988–92. Director: Edinburgh & Lothians Greenspace Trust Ltd, 1997–2007; Colinton Community Conservation Trust Ltd, 2000–; Mavisbank Trust Ltd, 2002–; Chm., Colinton Amenity Assoc., 2002–05. Member Council: Scottish Council for Nat. Parks, 1997–2007; Edinburgh Civic Trust, 2003–12, 2013–17; Assoc. for Protection of Rural Scotland, 2015– (Chm., Green Belt Alliance, 2016–; Mem., Exec. Cttee, 2017–). Civic Champion, Scottish Civic Trust, 2013. *Publications:* articles in Landscape Design, Jl of RASE, Landscape Design Trust. *Recreations:* landscape appreciation, fishing. *Address:* 62 Bonaly Wester, Edinburgh EH13 0RQ.

**CAMPBELL, Prof. Eleanor Elizabeth Bryce,** PhD; FRS 2010; FRSE; FRSC, FInstP; Professor of Chemistry, Edinburgh University, since 2013 (Professor of Physical Chemistry, 2007–13); *b* Rothesay, Isle of Bute, 13 April 1960; *d* of William and Isobel Cowan; *m* 1st, 1984, Iain Campbell (marr. diss. 1991); 2nd, 2003, Prof. Mats Jonson. *Educ:* Rothesay Acad.; Edinburgh Univ. (BSc; PhD 1985); Freiburg Univ. (Dr rer. nat. habil. 1991). FRSC 2008; FInstP 2008. Asst Prof., Freiburg Univ., 1988–93; Dept Hd, Max Born Inst., Berlin, 1993–98; Prof. of Atomic and Molecular Physics, Gothenburg Univ., 1998–2007. FRSE 2004. *Publications:* Fullerene Collision Reactions, 2003. *Address:* School of Chemistry, Edinburgh University, Edinburgh EH9 3FJ. *T:* (0131) 650 4729. *E:* eleanor.campbell@ed.ac.uk.

**CAMPBELL, Francis Martin;** Vice Chancellor, University of Notre Dame Australia, from Jan. 2020; *b* 20 April 1970; *s* of Daniel Joseph Campbell and Brigid Mary Campbell (*née* Cosgrove). *Educ:* Queen's Univ., Belfast (BA 1992); Katholieke Universiteit, Leuven (MA 1995); Univ. of Pennsylvania (MA). Joined HM Diplomatic Service, 1997; FCO, 1997; EC Delegn to the UN, NY, 1997–98; FCO, 1998–99; Policy Advr, 1999–2001, Private Sec., 2001–03, to the Prime Minister; First Sec. (External), Rome, 2003–05; Sen. Dir of Policy, Amnesty Internat., 2005; Ambassador to the Holy See, 2005–11; Dep. High Comr and Dir, Trade and Investment, Pakistan, 2011–13; Hd, Policy Unit, FCO, 2013–14; Vice Chancellor, St Mary's Univ., Twickenham, 2014–20. Trustee: St Elizabeth's Primary Sch., Richmond; Forward Thinking; St Joseph's Hospice, Hackney. Hon. Fellow, St Edmund's Coll., Cambridge, 2014. DUniv QUB, 2009; Hon. PhD: Catholic Univ. of Steubenville, 2010; Fordham, NY, 2010; Inst. of Business and Technol., Pakistan, 2013; St Francis, Penn, 2019; Hon. DLitt Misericordia, Dallas, 2017. President's Medal, Catholic Univ. of America, 2009. *Publications:* (contrib.) Federalism Doomed, 2001. *Recreations:* reading, walking, swimming.

**CAMPBELL, Gordon Muir,** OC 2018; OBC 2011; High Commissioner for Canada in the United Kingdom, 2011–16; *b* 12 Jan. 1948; *s* of Charles Gordon Campbell and Margaret Janet Campbell (*née* Muir); *m* 1970, Nancy Jean Chipperfield (marr. diss. 2016); two *s*. *Educ:* Dartmouth Coll., New Hampshire; Simon Fraser Univ. (MBA). Secondary sch. teacher, and basketball and track coach, Yola, Nigeria, with Can. Univ. Students Overseas orgn, 1970–72; asst to Mayor of Vancouver, 1972–76; Marathon Realty, 1976–81 (Gen. Manager); Founder, Citycore Develt Corp., 1981. Mem., Vancouver CC, 1984–86, Mayor, 1986–93. MLA (L) Vancouver-Quilchene, 1994–96, Vancouver-Point Grey, 1996–2011; Premier, British Columbia, Canada, 2001–11. Leader, Liberal Party of BC, 1993–2011. *Publications:* (for children) Tuaq: The Only One, 1995.

**CAMPBELL, Prof. Gordon Roy,** DPhil, DLitt; FBA 2011; Fellow in Renaissance Studies, University of Leicester, since 2010 (Professor of Renaissance Studies, 1994–2010); *b* Carshalton, Surrey, 29 Nov. 1944; *s* of Clifford Earl Campbell and Diamond Davina Campbell (*née* Lecky); *m* 1966, Mary Elisabeth Freeland; two *s* one *d*. *Educ:* state schs in Canada; Univ. of Waterloo (BA 1967); Queen's Univ., Canada (MA 1969); Univ. of York (DPhil 1973; DLitt 1998). Lectr in English, Univ. of Aarhus, 1973–74; Lectr in English Lit., Univ. of Liverpool, 1974–79; University of Leicester: Lectr in English, 1979–87; Reader in Renaissance Lit., 1987–94; Public Orator, 2004–16; Chm., 1993–95, Pres., 1995–97, English Assoc.; Chm., Soc. for Renaissance Studies, 1998–2001. Founder Chairman: UK-Saudi Interest Gp, 2002–10; British Univs Iraq Consortium, 2004–06. Patron, Milton's Cottage Trust, 2005–. Founder Ed., Renaissance Studies, 1987–96; Ed., The Year's Work in English Studies, 1991–93; Series Ed., Essays and Studies, 1996–2001; Gen. Ed., Review of English Studies, 1997–2009; Jt Gen. Ed., The Complete Works of John Milton, 13 vols, 2008–; Mem., ten editl bds. FRHistS 1988; FRGS 1998; FRAS 2006; FSA 2008; FLS 2012. Hon. FEA 2015. Dr *hc* Bucharest, 1999; Hon. DLitt Leicester, 2017. *Publications:* (ed) John Milton: the complete poems, 1980; (ed) The Renaissance 1550–1660, 1989; (ed) John Milton, Complete English Poems, Of Education, Areopagitica, 1990; (ed) Ben Jonson: The Alchemist and other plays, 1995; (ed) John Milton: selected poems, 1996; (ed) Milton: a biography, by W. R. Parker, 2 vols, 1996; (ed) Andrew Marvell: selected poems, 1997; A Milton Chronology, 1997; The Oxford Dictionary of the Renaissance, 2003; Renaissance Art and Architecture, 2004; (ed and contrib.) Grove Encyclopedia of Decorative Arts, 2 vols, 2006; (jtly) Milton and the Manuscript of 'De Doctrina Christiana', 2007; John Milton, 2007; (ed) Grove Encyclopedia of Classical Art and Architecture, 2 vols, 2007; (jtly) John Milton: life, work and thought, 2008; (ed) John Milton, Paradise Lost and Paradise Regained, 2009; (ed) Grove Encyclopedia of Northern Renaissance Art, 3 vols, 2009; Bible: the story of the King James Version 1611–2011, 2010; (ed) The Holy Bible: quatercentenary edition, 2010; The Hermit in the Garden: from Imperial Rome to ornamental gnome, 2013; A Short History of Gardens, 2016; (ed) The Oxford Illustrated History of the Renaissance, 2019. *Recreation:* travel. *Address:* School of Arts, University of Leicester LE1 7RH. *E:* leb@le.ac.uk.

**CAMPBELL, Gregory Lloyd;** MP (DemU) Londonderry East, since 2001; *b* 15 Feb. 1953; *m* Frances; one *s* three *d*. *Educ:* Ebrington Primary Sch.; Londonderry Tech. Coll.; Magee Coll. Civil Servant, 1972–82 and 1986–94; businessman, 1994–. Mem. (DemU) Londonderry CC, 1981–2011. Mem. (DemU), NI Assembly, 1982–86; Mem., NI Forum for Political Dialogue, 1996–98. Mem. (DemU) E Londonderry, NI Assembly, 1998–2016. Minister for Regl Develt, 2000–01, for Culture, Arts and Leisure, 2008–09, NI. Contested (DemU): Foyle, 1992; E Londonderry, 1997. *Publications:* Discrimination: the truth, 1987; Discrimination: where now?, 1993; Ulster's Verdict on the Joint Declaration, 1994; Working Toward 2000, 1998. *Recreations:* soccer, music, reading. *Address:* (office) 25 Bushmills Road, Coleraine, Co. Londonderry, Northern Ireland BT52 2BP; 6–8 Catherine Street, Limavady BT49 9DB.

**CAMPBELL, Guy McGregor;** General Manager (Atlantic), China Navigation Co. Pte Ltd, since 2013; Chairman, Baltic Exchange, 2014–16; *b* Walthamstow, 17 July 1966; *s* of late Peter Campbell and of Monica Campbell; *m* 1991, Virginia Julie Scott; two *s* one *d*. *Educ:* Herne Bay Secondary Sch. FICS 2004; MCIArb 2014. Shipbroker, JE Hyde & Co., 1990–97; chartering manager, 1997–2000, Dir, 2000–07, Ocean Freight, Koch Carbon LLC; Man. Dir, Dry Cargo Chartering, H. Clarksons & Co., 2007–13. Chm., Freight Mkt Users Inf. Gp, 2005, Bd Dir, 2009–16, Baltic Exchange. *Recreations:* rowing (winner, Thames Challenge Cup, Henley Royal Regatta, 1992), cycling. *Address:* Swire Bulk, China Navigation Co. Pte Ltd, Swire House, 59 Buckingham Gate, SW1E 6AJ. *T:* (020) 7963 9485.

**CAMPBELL, Hugh Hall;** QC (Scot.) 1983; FCIArb; *b* 18 Feb. 1944; *s* of William Wright Campbell and Marianne Doris Stuart Hutchison or Campbell; *m* 1969, Eleanor Jane Hare; three *s*. *Educ:* Glasgow Acad.; Trinity Coll., Glenalmond (Alexander Cross Scholar); Exeter Coll., Oxford (Open Scholar in Classics; BA Hons, MA); Edinburgh Univ. (LLB Hons). FCIArb 1986. Called to the Scottish Bar, 1969; Standing Jun. Counsel to Admiralty, 1976. Hon. Citizen, Antigua and Barbuda, 2010. *Recreations:* carnival, wine, music. *Address:* 12 Ainslie Place, Edinburgh EH3 6AS. *T:* (0131) 225 2067. *Club:* Hon. Company of Edinburgh Golfers.

**CAMPBELL, (Ian) Angus;** farmer, since 1980; Lord-Lieutenant for Dorset, since 2014; *b* London, 4 Sept. 1949; *s* of late Lt Col Duncan Lorne Campbell, MBE, MC and Christine Marion Campbell (*née* Phillipps); *m* 1977, Carola Claire Schulte; two *d*. *Educ:* Shebbear Coll., N Devon; Poole Tech. Coll.; RMA, Sandhurst; Army Sch. of Flying. Herd Tester, Auckland Herd Improvement Assoc., NZ, 1970–72. Served AAC, Officer and helicopter pilot, 658 Sqdn, 1975–79: W Germany; Aviation Flight, UN Peacekeeping Force in Cyprus; emergency tours, S Armagh and Belfast (AAC Commendation); Suffield Battle Gp Trng, Canada; Second i/c, 16 Flight AAC, Cyprus; TA 662 Sqdn AAC, 1979–81. Mem. (C) Dorset CC, 1989–93 and 2001–13 (Vice Chm., Educn Cttee, 1992–93; Dep. Leader, with portfolio resp. for Educn, then Roads, Transport and Regl Strategy, 2002–06; Leader, 2006–13); Mem. (C) N Dorset DC, 1999–2011 (Leader, 1999–2003). Chm., Strategic Leaders Bd for SW and SW Councils, 2008–13. Chm., Dorset Olympic Bd (sailing events), 2006–12. Chm., 1998–2001 and 2002–03, Pres., 2004–13, N Dorset Cons. Assoc. Chm., Lord Chancellor's Adv. Cttee on JPs for Dorset/Custos Rotolorum, 2014–. President: Dorset Co. Priory Gp of St John, 2014–; Dorset Br., Army Benevolent Fund, 2014–; Dorset SSAFA, 2014–; Dorset Army Cadet League, 2014–; Dorset Historic Chs Trust, 2014–; Dorset Youth Assoc., 2014–; Jt Pres., Somerset and Dorset Marine Soc. and Sea Cadets, 2014–; Patron: Dorset Child and Family Counselling Trust, 2014–; Dorset Community Action, 2014–; Dorset Community Foundn, 2014–; Dorset Co. Arts in Hosp., 2014–; Somerset and Dorset Air Ambulance, 2014–; Friends of Salisbury Cath., 2014–; Dorset SafeWise, 2014–; Wessex Br., Western Front Assoc., 2014–. *Recreations:* game shooting, fly-fishing, writing. *Address:* Lieutenancy Office, County Hall, Colliton Park, Dorchester, Dorset DT1 1XJ; Preston Hill Farm, Iwerne Minster, Blandford, Dorset DT11 8NL. *T:* (01747) 811219. *E:* prestonhil@aol.com.

**CAMPBELL, His Honour Ian Burns,** CMG 2003; a Circuit Judge, 1984–2003; Deputy High Representative for Legal Affairs, and Head, Legal Affairs Department, Office of High Representative, Sarajevo, 2000–03 (on secondment from Lord Chancellor's Department); *b* 7 July 1938; *s* of late James Campbell and Laura Campbell; *m* 1967, Mary Elisabeth Poole, BArch, MCD Liverpool; two *s* one *d*. *Educ:* Tiffin Boys' Sch.; Cambridge Univ. (MA, LLM, PhD); Diplôme d'Etudes Supérieures de Droit Comparé, Strasbourg, 1964. Called to the Bar, Middle Temple, 1966. French Govt Scholar, Univ. of Paris, 1961–62; Asst Lectr in Law, Liverpool Univ., 1962–64, Lectr 1964–69; a Recorder, 1981–84; Liaison Judge, N and S Sefton Benches, 1988–2000; seconded to Legal Dept, Office of High Rep., Sarajevo, 1999–2000. Mem., Franco-British Judicial Co-operation Cttee, 1996–2000. Hon. Mem.,

Albanian Nat. Judicial Conf., 1999–2000. A Dep. Chm. Adv. Bd, CARDS Regl Project 2003, for establt of an indep., reliable and functioning judiciary in Western Balkans, 2006–07. Hon. Vis. Prof., Sch. of Law, Liverpool Univ., 1995–2006, 2009–12, 2014–. Chm., Adv. Bd, Liverpool Univ. Law Sch., 2008–13. Member, Editorial Board: Liverpool Law Review, 1996–2005; Judicial Studies Bd Jl, 1996–2000. Hon. LLD Liverpool, 2005. *Publications*: (contrib.) Legal Visions of the New Europe, 1993; contrib. legal jls. *Recreations*: journeying, Gaelic studies.

**CAMPBELL, Ian H.;** *see* Hay-Campbell.

**CAMPBELL, Sir Ian (Tofts),** Kt 1988; CBE 1984; VRD 1961; JP; Director, Conservative Board of Finance, 1978–90; Director of Finance and Administration, Scottish Conservative Party, 1988–90; *b* 3 Feb. 1923; *o s* of John Walter Campbell and Mary Hardie Campbell (*née* Scott); *m* 1961, Marion Kirkhope Paterson (*née* Shiel) (*d* 2010); one *d*. *Educ*: Daniel Stewart's College, Edinburgh. FInstD 1964. RN 1942–46, RNR 1946–65 (Comdr). Man. Dir, MacGregor Wallcoverings, 1966–78. Chm., Select Assured Properties, Glasgow, 1989–96; Dep. Chm., Heath (Scotland) Ltd, 1988–95 (Dir, 1987–96; consultant, 1996–2000); Director: Travel System, 1987–89; Hermiston Securities, 1990–. Mem., Transport Users' Cons. Cttee for Scotland, 1981–87. Councillor, City of Edinburgh District Council, 1984–88. JP Edinburgh, 1987. Freeman, City of Glasgow, 1992. OStJ 1987. KLJ 1984. *Recreations*: golf, water colour painting, vintage cars. *Address*: Merleton, 10 Boswall Road, Edinburgh EH5 3RH. *T*: (0131) 552 4825. *Club*: New (Edinburgh).

**CAMPBELL, James Alastair G.;** *see* Graham-Campbell.

**CAMPBELL, Sir James (Alexander Moffat Bain),** 9th Bt *cr* 1667, of Aberuchill, Perthshire; farmer; property owner; *b* 23 Sept. 1956; *er s* of Sir Colin Campbell, 8th Bt and of Mary Campbell (*née* Bain); *S* father, 1997; *m* 1993, Carola Jane Denman; one *s* two *d*. *Educ*: Stowe. Scots Guards (Capt.), 1975–83. Motorcycle despatch rider, 1984; insurance broker: Bain Dawes Ltd, Bain Clarkson plc, Bain Hogg plc, Aon Corp., 1984–97; R. K. Harrison Ltd, 1997–2001; indep. insurance consultant, 2001–07; insurance broker, Lycetts Insurance Brokers, 2007–16. *Recreations*: shooting, trees, gardening. *Heir*: *s* Colin George Denman Bain Campbell, *b* 1 Oct. 1999. *Address*: Kilbryde Castle, Dunblane, Perthshire FK15 9NF. *T*: (01786) 824897.

**CAMPBELL, James MacRae,** CBE 2012; Director (formerly Head) of Energy Development (formerly Licensing and Consents, later Energy Resources and Development) Unit, Energy Markets and Infrastructure (formerly Energy) Group, Department of Energy and Climate Change (formerly Department of Trade and Industry, then Department for Business, Enterprise and Regulatory Reform), 2003–12; *b* 17 June 1952; *s* of late Alistair Campbell and Flora MacKay Campbell (*née* MacRae); *m* 1975, Catherine Russell (marr. diss. 2018); one *s* one *d*. *Educ*: Strathclyde Univ. (BSc Hons (Physics) 1974). MInstP 1975; CPhys 1987. Res. Scientist, NEL, 1974–79; Offshore Supplies Office: Res. and Develt Assessor, 1979–82; Industrial Liaison, 1982–91; Asst Dir, and Hd UK Continental Shelf Develts, 1991–94; Asst Dir, Oil and Gas Projects and Supplies Office, 1994–96; Director: Industry and Downstream Exports, British Trade Internat., 1996–2000; Oil and Gas Envmt and Decommissioning, DTI, 2000–02. Mem. Bd, Aberdeen Foyer, 2012–15. Hon. FEI 2010. FRSA 2000. *Recreations*: hill walking, reading, running, cinema, photography.

**CAMPBELL, Jim;** *see* Campbell, R. J.

**CAMPBELL, Prof. John Joseph,** DPhil; Willis S. and Marion Slusser Professor of Philosophy, University of California at Berkeley, since 2004; *b* 2 Nov. 1956; *s* of Roderick Campbell and Catriona (*née* MacKinnon); *m* 1st, 1978, Patricia Carrol (marr. diss. 1986); 2nd, 2002, Allison Harvey (marr. diss. 2007). *Educ*: Univ. of Stirling (BA); Univ. of Calgary (MA); Wolfson Coll., Oxford (BPhil, DPhil 1986). University of Oxford: Res. Lectr, Christ Church, 1983–86; Fellow and Tutor in Philosophy, New Coll., 1986–2001; British Acad. Res. Reader, 1995–97; Reader in Philosophy, 1997–2001; Wilde Prof. of Mental Philosophy, 2001–04; Fellow, Corpus Christi Coll., 2001–04. Visiting posts at: UCLA, 1988; Univ. of Cambridge, 1990–91; ANU, 1991–92; Cornell Univ., 1998. Guggenheim Fellow, 2011. Jean Nicod Prize, 2017. *Publications*: Past, Space and Self, 1994; Reference and Consciousness, 2002; (with Quassim Cassam) Berkeley's Puzzle, 2014. *Recreations*: gardening, country pubs. *Address*: University of California, Department of Philosophy, Berkeley, CA 94720–2390, USA.

**CAMPBELL, Sir John Park,** Kt 2017; OBE 2000; Chairman, Glenrath Farms Ltd, since 1957; *b* Gourock, 1 April 1934; *s* of Keith Campbell and Joan Campbell (*née* Park); *m* 1957, Catherine Kent; three *s* one *d*. *Educ*: Strathallan Sch. Farmer. Mem., Tweeddale DC, 1975–93 (Chm.). Hon. Fellow, SRUC, Scotland's Rural Coll., 2016. UK Poultry Person of the Year, British Poultry Council/ForFarmers, 2016. *Address*: Glenfyne, Stobo, Peebles EH45 8NP. *Club*: Farmers.

**CAMPBELL, His Honour (John) Quentin;** a Circuit Judge, 1996–2008; *b* 5 March 1939; *s* of late John McKnight Campbell, OBE, MC, and late Katharine Margaret Campbell; *m* 1st, Penelope Jane Redman (marr. diss. 1976); three *s* one *d*; 2nd, 1977, Ann Rosemary Beeching (Her Honour Ann Campbell, DL); one *s* one *d*. *Educ*: Loretto Sch., Musselburgh, Scotland; Wadham Coll., Oxford (MA). Admitted as solicitor, 1965; private practice, Linnell & Murphy, Oxford (Partner, 1968–80); Metropolitan Stipendiary Magistrate, 1981–96; Asst Recorder, 1983–89; a Recorder, 1989–96. A Pres., Mental Health Review Tribunals, 1996–2008; Mem., Parole Bd, 2000–07. Mem., Student Appeal Panel, Univ. of Oxford, 2009–. Chairman, Bd of Governors, Bessels Leigh Sch., near Oxford, 1979–96. *Recreations*: opera, music, travel. *Clubs*: Travellers; Frewen (Oxford).

**CAMPBELL, Juliet Jeanne d'Auvergne,** CMG 1988; HM Diplomatic Service, retired; Mistress of Girton College, Cambridge, 1992–98, now Life Fellow; *b* 23 May 1935; *d* of Maj.-Gen. Wilfred d'Auvergne Collings, CB, CBE and of Nancy Draper Bishop; *m* 1983, Prof. Alexander Elmslie Campbell (*d* 2002). *Educ*: a variety of schools; Lady Margaret Hall, Oxford (BA; Hon. Fellow, 1992). Joined Foreign Office 1957; delegation negotiating for British entry to EEC, 1961–63; FO, 1963–64; Second, later First Secretary, Bangkok, 1964–66; News Dept, FO, 1967–70; Head of Chancery, The Hague, 1970–74; European Integration Dept, FCO, 1974–77; Counsellor (Inf.), Paris, 1977–80; RCDS, 1981; Counsellor, Jakarta, 1982–83; Head of Training Dept, FCO, 1984–87; Ambassador to Luxembourg, 1988–91. Member: Cambridge Univ. Council of Senate (later Council), 1993–97; Wilton Park Academic Council, 1993–2000. Dep. Vice-Chancellor, Cambridge Univ., 1993–98. Mem. Council, RSAA, 2008–14. Trustee: Changing Faces, 1992–2006; Cambridge European Trust, 1994–98; Kurt Hahn Trust, 1995–98; Cambridge Overseas Trust, 1995–98; Henry Fellowships, 1997–2005. Governor: Queen's Coll., Harley St, 1992–2002; Marlborough Coll., 1999–2007. *Publications*: (with W. d'A. Collings) One Small Island and Two World Wars: the life and times of Maj. Gen. Wilfred d'A. Collings, CB, CBE, 2016. *Address*: 3 Belbroughton Road, Oxford OX2 6UZ. *Club*: Oxford and Cambridge.

**CAMPBELL, Air Vice-Marshal Kenneth Archibald,** CB 1989; consulting engineer; Air Officer Maintenance, RAF Support Command, 1987–89; *b* 3 May 1936; *s* of John McLean and Christina Campbell; *m* 1959, Isobel Love Millar (*d* 2005); two *d*. *Educ*: George Heriot's Sch.; Glasgow Univ. (BSc); College of Aeronautics, Cranfield (MSc). Various engrg appts, RAF, 1959–90; Air Officer, Wales, 1977–79; Dir, Engrg Policy (RAF), 1981–83; AO, Engrg and Supply, RAF Germany, 1983–85; DG Personal Services (RAF), 1985–87. *Recreation*: golf.

**CAMPBELL, Kenneth Ewen;** Director, Jazz Cat, since 2015; *b* 20 Nov. 1967; *s* of Ewen and Christine Campbell; *m* 2012, Helen Jane Beckett. *Educ*: Caol Primary Sch., Caol; Lochaber High Sch., Fort William; Univ. of Aberdeen (MA Hons Politics and Econs). Trainee manager, Marks & Spencer, Perth, 1989–90; journalist: Press and Jl, Aberdeen, 1990–92; Evening News, Edinburgh, 1992–94; Chief Sub-Ed., Daily Mail, Glasgow, 1994–97; Night Ed., Daily Express, Glasgow, 1997–99; Deputy Editor: Metro, London, 1999–2000; Daily Mail, Glasgow, 2000–01; Ed., Metro (UK), London, 2001–14; Dir, Campbell Brown PR, 2014–15. Freeman, Co. of Stationers and Newspaper Makers, 2007. *Recreations*: motor racing, whisky, photography. *E*: kennyc@hotmail.co.uk.

**CAMPBELL, Rt Hon. Kim;** PC (Canada) 1989; CC 2008; OBC 2012; QC (BC) 1990; international speaker and consultant, since 2007; Founding Principal, Peter Lougheed Leadership College, University of Alberta, since 2014; *b* 10 March 1947; *m* 1997, Hershey Felder. *Educ*: Univ. of British Columbia (BA 1969; LLB 1983); LSE (Hon. Fellow, 1994). Called to the Bar of BC, 1984, Ont, 1990. Lectr in Pol Sci., Univ. of BC, 1975–78; Lectr in Pol Sci. and Hist., Vancouver Community Coll., 1978–81; Articled student, 1983–84, Associate, Gen. Litigation, 1984–85, Ladner Downs Vancouver; Exec. Dir, Office of Premier of BC, 1985–86; MLA Vancouver Point Grey, 1986–88; MP (PC) Vancouver Centre, 1988–93; Minister of State, Indian Affairs and Northern Develt, 1989–90; Minister of Justice and Attorney Gen., 1990–93; Minister of Nat. Defence and Minister of Veterans' Affairs, 1993; Prime Minister of Canada, 1993; Canadian Consul-Gen., LA, 1996–2000. Club of Madrid: Founding Mem., 2001; Interim Pres., 2002–03; Vice Pres., 2003–04; Sec. Gen., 2004–06; Mem. Bd, 2007–11. Lectr, John F. Kennedy Sch. of Govt, Harvard Univ., 2003–04 (Vis. Prof. of Practice, 2001–04). Chair Emerita, Council of Women World Leaders, 2003 (Chair, 1999–2003); Pres., Internat. Women's Forum, 2003–05; Chair, Internat. Steering Cttee, World Movt for Democracy, 2008–15. Founding Principal, Peter Lougheed Leadership Coll., Univ. of Alberta, 2014–18. Trustee, Vancouver School Bd, 1980–84; Founding Trustee, Internat. Centre for Study of Radicalisation and Political Violence, KCL, 2008–. Hon. LLD: Law Soc. of Upper Canada, 1991; Brock Univ., 1998; UBC, 2000; Mt Holyoke Coll., 2004; Chatham Coll., 2005; Alberta, 2010; Trent, 2011; Simon Fraser, 2014; Hon. DPS Northeastern, 1999; Hon. LHD Arizona State, 2005. *Publications*: Time and Chance: the political memoirs of Canada's first woman prime minister, 1996, 4th edn 2017. *W*: www.kimcampbell.com, www.bitesizechunks.org.

**CAMPBELL, Sir Lachlan (Philip Kemeys),** 6th Bt *cr* 1815; book illustrator and author, since 2007; *b* 9 Oct. 1958; *e s* of Col Sir Guy Campbell, 5th Bt, OBE, MC and Lizbeth Webb, *d* of late Frederick Holton; *S* father, 1993; *m* 1986, Harriet Jane Sarah, *o d* of F. E. J. Girling; two *s* one *d*. *Educ*: Temple Grove; Eton; RMA Sandhurst. The Royal Greenjackets; served NI. *Recreations*: golf, Rugby, cricket, painting, drawing. *Heir*: *s* Archibald Edward FitzGerald Campbell, *b* 13 June 1990. *Address*: The Dairy House, Hanford, Blandford Forum, Dorset DT11 8HH. *Clubs*: Royal Greenjackets, MCC; Rushmore Golf; Eton Rambler Cricket.

**CAMPBELL, Sir Louis (Auchinbreck),** 16th Bt *cr* 1628 (NS), of Auchinbreck; *b* 17 Jan. 1953; *o s* of Sir Robin Auchinbreck Campbell, 15th Bt and Rosemary, (Sally), Campbell (*née* Dean); *S* father, 2016; *m* 1976, Fiona Mary St Clair, *d* of Gordon King; two *d*. *Address*: 145B Wrekin Road, Fairhall, RD2 Blenheim 7272, New Zealand.

**CAMPBELL, Very Rev. Canon Margaret Ruth;** Provost, St John the Divine Cathedral, Oban with St James, Ardbrecknish, and Canon of the Cathedral of the Isles, Cumbrae, since 2018; *b* Farnborough, Kent, 1962; *d* of Frederick Street and Joan Street; *m* 1989, James Campbell; two *s*. *Educ*: Trinity Theol Coll., Bristol (BA 2002). Ordained deacon, 2002, priest, 2003; Curate, St John's, Yeovil, 2002–06; Team Vicar, E Gp Wellington, 2006–11; Rector, Benefice of Backwell with Chelvey and Brockley, 2011–18; Asst Rural Dean, 2012–17, Rural Dean, 2017–18, Portishead. *E*: provostoban@argyll.anglican.org.

**CAMPBELL, Mark;** Special Counsel, Finance Practice, Clifford Chance LLP, since 2017; *b* Liverpool, 23 June 1960; *s* of George and Thelma Campbell; *m* 1994, Susan Gaye Carter; four *s* three *d*. *Educ*: St Wilfrid's High Sch., Litherland; Oriel Coll., Oxford (MA Juris. 1978); Coll. of Law, Guildford. Admitted solicitor, 1984; with Clifford Chance LLP, 1982–: Partner, 1991–2017; Managing Partner, London Finance Practice, 1998–2002; Hd, Global Finance Practice, 2002–14; Mem., Mgt Cttee, 2002–14; Mem., Mgt Cttee, 2002–14. Mem., Finance Law Cttee, City of London Solicitors' Co., 1996–2011. Member: Bd, Tower Hamlets Educn Business Partnership, 2011– (Chm., 2015–); MLF Adv. Bd, Univ. of Oxford, 2011–17; MCL Practitioners Adv. Bd, Univ. of Cambridge, 2012–. Chm. Govs, Shapla Sch., 2008–. *Publications*: (jtly) Syndicated Lending: documentation and practice, 1993, 6th edn 2013. *Recreations*: music, novels, football, tennis. *Address*: c/o Clifford Chance LLP, Canary Wharf, E14 5JJ.

**CAMPBELL, Melfort Andrew,** OBE 2003; Chairman, Imes Group Ltd, since 2009 (Founder and Chief Executive Officer, 1997–2009); *b* Budleigh Salterton, 6 June 1956; *s* of late Lt Col Robert Campbell and of Norma Campbell; *m* 1983, Hon. Lucy Jane, *d* of Baron Nickson, *qv*; three *d*. *Educ*: Ampleforth Coll. Founder and Owner, Water Weights Ltd, 1984–2018. Chairman: CBI Scotland, 2007–09; Tax Reform Commn, 2005–06; Mem. Bd, Scottish Enterprise, 2013–; Co Chair, Innovation Scotland Forum, 2014–17. Director: Dreamstore, 2005–; Oil and Gas Technol. Centre, 2017–. Vis. Prof., Univ. of Strathclyde, 2013–. Chm., Bd of Govs, Robert Gordon Univ., 2008–10. Hon. Col, Scottish and Northern Irish Yeomanry, 2014–. FRSA. Hon. DBA Robert Gordon, 2006. *Recreations*: fishing, travel, family, classic cars. *Address*: (office) Old School, Maryculter, Aberdeen AB12 5GN. *T*: (01224) 533533. *Club*: MCC.

**CAMPBELL, Rt Rev. Michael Gregory,** OSA; Bishop of Lancaster, (RC), 2009–18, now Bishop Emeritus; *b* Larne, NI, 2 Oct. 1941. *Educ*: Campion House, Osterley; University Coll. Dublin (BA Semitic Langs); Gregorian Univ., Rome; King's Coll. London (MA Biblical Studies). Entered Augustinian Order, Clare Priory, 1962; ordained priest, 1971; Teacher/Chaplain, Christ the King Sch., Southport; Parish Curate, St John Stone's, 1972–75; Prior of the Community, St Monica's, Hoxton, 1972–85; Teacher/Chaplain, Bishop Challoner Girls' Sch., London, 1972–85; Lectr, St Augustine's Major Seminary, Jos, Nigeria, 1985–89; Episcopal Vicar, Dio. of Lancaster, 1990–99; Prior and Parish Priest, St Augustine's, Hammersmith. Mem. Editl Cttee, Internat. Commn on English in the Liturgy.

**CAMPBELL, Natasha Pui-Wai;** *see* Wong, N. P.-W.

**CAMPBELL, Niall Gordon;** Under Secretary, Civil and Criminal Law Group, Scottish Executive Justice (formerly Scottish Office Home) Department, 1997–2001; *b* 9 Nov. 1941; *s* of Ian M. Campbell and Jean G. Sanderson; *m* 1975, Alison Margaret Rigg; three *s*. *Educ*: Edinburgh Academy; Merton College, Oxford (BA). Entered Scottish Office, 1964; Asst Sec., 1978; posts in Scottish Educn and Scottish Develt Depts; Under Sec., Social Work Services Gp, SHHD, then Scottish Office Home Dept, 1989–97. Mem., Parole Bd for

Scotland, 2003–09. Chairman: Scottish Assoc. for Study of Offending, 2001–06; SACRO, 2002–07. Mem. Council, 2006–11, Treas., 2008–11, British Trust for Ornithol. *Address:* 15 Warriston Crescent, Edinburgh EH3 5LA. *T:* (0131) 556 2895.

**CAMPBELL, Nicholas Charles Wilson;** QC 2000; *b* 8 May 1954; *s* of late Wilson Campbell and Pearl Campbell (*née* Ackrill); *m* 1987, Hon. Nicole Montagu. *Educ:* King's Sch., Canterbury; Trinity Coll., Cambridge (BA). Called to the Bar, Inner Temple, 1978; a Recorder, 2000–14. *Address:* KBW Chambers, The Engine House, 1 Foundry Square, The Round Foundry, Leeds LS11 5DL.

**CAMPBELL, Oliver Edward Wilhelm;** QC 2014; *b* Edinburgh, 20 July 1970; *s* of Edward Campbell and Ellen Campbell; *m* 2006, Annabel Walker; two *d*. *Educ:* Edinburgh Acad.; St Hugh's Coll., Oxford (BA 1991). Called to the Bar, Middle Temple, 1992; in practice as a barrister, specialising in commercial and regulatory law, Henderson Chambers, 1992–. Mem., Examinations Bd, Bar Standards Bd, 2011–; Chief Examr, Civil Litigation, Bar Professional Trng Course, 2015–. Trustee, Lambeth Law Centre, 2010–, Pres., Oxford Union, 1990. *Recreations:* cricket, football. *Address:* Henderson Chambers, 2 Harcourt Buildings, Temple, EC4Y 9DB. *T:* (020) 7583 9020. *Club:* MCC.

**CAMPBELL, Sir Philip (Henry Montgomery),** Kt 2015; PhD; Editor-in-Chief, Springer Nature, since 2018 (Chief Editorial Adviser, 2016–18; Editor-in-Chief, Nature Publications, 1995–2018); *b* 19 April 1951; *s* of late Hugh and Mary Montgomery Campbell; *m* 1st, 1980, Judie Yelton (*d* 1992); two *s*; 2nd, 2014, Charis Mary Thompson. *Educ:* Shrewsbury Sch.; Bristol Univ. (BSc Aeronautical Engrg 1972); Queen Mary Coll., Univ. of London (MSc Astrophysics 1974; Hon. Fellow 2009); Leicester Univ. (PhD Ionospheric Physics 1978). FRAS 1979; FInstP 1995. Res., Leicester Univ., 1977–79; Asst Editor, 1979–82, Physical Scis Editor, 1982–88, Ed.-in-Chief, 1995–2018, Nature; Founding Editor, Physics World, 1988–95. Broadcasts on BBC. Trustee: Cancer Res. UK, 2003–12; MQ: transforming mental health, 2012– (Chm., 2015–). Associate, Clare Hall, Cambridge, 2008–13 (Hon. Fellow, 2016). Hon. Prof., Peking Union Med. Coll., 2009. Hon. DSc: Leicester, 1999; Bristol, 2008. *Publications:* papers and articles in learned jls, magazines and newspapers. *Recreations:* music, art galleries. *Address:* Nature, 4 Crinan Street, N1 9XW. *T:* (020) 7833 4000.

**CAMPBELL, Quentin;** *see* Campbell, His Honour J. Q.

**CAMPBELL, Rhona Lynn; Her Honour Judge Rhona Campbell;** a Circuit Judge, since 2019; *b* Glasgow, 11 April 1971; *d* of Colin George Campbell and Irene Robertson Campbell; *m* 1999, Anthony John Potter (His Honour Judge Anthony Potter); two *s*. *Educ:* High Sch. of Glasgow; Durham Univ. (BA Hons Law). Called to the Bar, Inner Temple, 1993; a Recorder, 2009–19; a Judge, First-tier Tribunal (Social Entitlement), 2011–19. *Address:* Wolverhampton Combined Court Centre, Pipers Row, Wolverhampton WV1 3LQ.

**CAMPBELL, Prof. Robert James, (Jim);** Professor of Education, University of Warwick, 1992–2007, now Emeritus; *b* 19 Dec. 1938; *s* of William Campbell and Elsie Campbell (*née* O'Connor); *m* 1st, 1964, Jennifer Rhodes (marr. diss. 1970); 2nd, 1972, Sarah Miranda Frankland (marr. diss. 2006); two *d*; 3rd, 2007, Wendy Robinson. *Educ:* Hull Univ. (BA Upper 2nd Cl. Classics 1959; PGCE 1960); Bradford Univ. (MSc Educnl Res. 1971). Teacher: Westgate Primary Sch., Newcastle upon Tyne, 1959; Nettleswell Comprehensive Sch., Harlow, 1960–62; Mkt Res. Officer, Mkt Res. Associates, London, 1962–63; Teacher, Latton Bush Comprehensive Sch., Harlow, 1963–64; Lectr, W Suffolk Coll. of Further Educn, Bury St Edmunds, 1964–67; Res. Student, Univ. of Bradford, 1967–68; Res. Officer, Curriculum Res. Unit, Inst. of Educn, Univ. of London, 1968–70; Lectr, Coventry Coll. of Educn, 1970–78; University of Warwick: Lectr, 1978–86; Sen. Lectr, 1986–89; Reader, 1989–92; Dir, Inst. of Educn, 1996–2001; Dir of Res., Nat. Acad. for Gifted and Talented Youth, Univ. of Warwick, 2004–07. Vis. Prof., Univ. of Plymouth, 2009–11. FRSA 1998. Phi Delta Kappa, 1974. *Publications:* Developing the Primary School Curriculum, 1985; Humanities in the Primary School, 1989; Breadth and Balance in the Primary School Curriculum, 1991; Primary Teachers at Work, 1994; Secondary Teachers at Work, 1994; The Meaning of Infant Teachers' Work, 1994; Curriculum Reform at Key Stage 1: teacher commitment and policy failure, 1994; Assessing Teacher Effectiveness, 2004; Effective Teaching in Gifted Education, 2010; Families, Education and Giftedness, 2012; contrib. numerous articles to jls. *Recreations:* wine, whisky, jazz. *Address:* Centre for Education Studies, University of Warwick, Coventry CV4 7AL. *T:* (024) 7652 3850.

**CAMPBELL, Sir Roderick (Duncan Hamilton),** 9th Bt *cr* 1831, of Barcaldine and Glenure, Argyllshire; Managing Partner, Barcaldine holdings, since 2003; *b* 24 Feb. 1961; *s* of Sir Niall Campbell, 8th Bt and Norma Joyce Campbell (*née* Wiggin); *S* father, 2003; *m* 1989, Jean Caroline (*née* Bicknell); three *d*. *Educ:* Chiswick. Vardon plc, 1988–99; Nat. Trust for Scotland, 1999–2004; Historic Scotland, 2013. *Recreations:* talking to my wife, household maintenance, following sport, family history. *Heir: b* Angus Charles Dundas Campbell, *b* 27 Oct. 1967. *Address:* 47/1 East London Street, Edinburgh EH7 4BW; Lossit, Benderloch, Oban PA37 1QS. *E:* rdhcampbell@btconnect.com. *Clubs:* West Bromwich Albion; Argyllshire Gathering.

**CAMPBELL, Ronald, (Ronnie);** MP (Lab) Blyth Valley, since 1987; *b* 14 Aug. 1943; *m* 1967, Deirdre (*née* McHale); five *s* one *d*. *Educ:* Ridley High Sch., Blyth. Miner, 1958–86. Member: Blyth Borough Council, 1969–74; Blyth Valley Council, 1974–88 (Chm., Environmental Health Cttee; Vice-Chm., Housing Cttee). Mem., NUM. *Address:* 82 Middleton Street, Blyth, Northumberland NE24 2LX; House of Commons, SW1A 0AA.

**CAMPBELL, Sarah Jane; Her Honour Judge Sarah Campbell;** a Circuit Judge, since 2018; *b* London, 1 Oct. 1973; *m* Anthony John Richards; two *s* one *d*. *Educ:* Newstead Wood Sch. for Girls; Pembroke Coll., Cambridge (BA 1995). Called to the Bar, Inner Temple, 1997; a Recorder, 2012–18. *Recreations:* walking, cycling, tennis. *Address:* Reading Crown Court, Old Shire Hall, The Forbury, Reading RG1 3EH. *T:* 07785 916016. *E:* hhj.sarah.campbell@ejudiciary.net.

**CAMPBELL, Sharon Isabel;** HM Diplomatic Service; non-resident Ambassador to Haiti, 2015–Aug. 2020; *b* 12 Feb. 1962; *née* Hale; *m* 1989, Christopher John Campbell, *qv*. Entered FCO, 1983; Trade Relns and Exports Dept, 1983–84, Minister of State's Office, 1984–85, FCO; Third Sec., Warsaw, 1985; Desk Officer, Finance Dept, FCO, 1986–88; Third Sec. (Mgt), Dhaka, 1988–92; Vice Consul, Jakarta, 1992–95; Asst Private Sec. to Minister of State, FCO, 1996–99; Sen. Mgt Officer and Consul, Cararcas, 2000–03; Deputy Head: Jt Mgt Office, Brussels, 2003–07; Consular Resources Gp, FCO, 2008–11; Ambassador to Costa Rica, 2011–15. *Address:* c/o Foreign and Commonwealth Office, King Charles Street, SW1A 2AH.

**CAMPBELL, Sir Simon (Fraser),** Kt 2015; CBE 2006; PhD; FRS 1999; FRSC; FMedSci; Senior Vice-President, Worldwide Discovery and Medicinals R&D Europe, Pfizer Central Research, 1996–98; Director and Board Member, Pfizer Ltd, 1996–98, retired; *b* 27 March 1941; *s* of William Fraser Campbell and Ellen Mary Campbell; *m* 1966, Jill Lewis; two *s*. *Educ:* Birmingham Univ. (BSc 1st Cl. Hons 1962; PhD 1965). FRSC 1985. Postdoctoral Fellow: Univ. Tecnica Santa Maria, Valparaiso, 1966–67; Stanford Univ., Calif, 1968–70; Vis. Prof., Univ. do São Paulo, 1970–72; joined Pfizer Central Research, Sandwich, 1972: staff chemist, 1972–78; Manager, 1978–83, Dir, 1983–92, Discovery Chemistry; Gp Dir, 1992–93, Vice-Pres., 1993–96, Medicinals Discovery. Visiting Professor: Birkbeck Coll., Univ. of London, 1987–90; Univ. of Leeds, 1996–99. Chm., WHO Expert Scientific Adv. Cttee for Malaria, 1999–2003; Member: BP Technology Council, 1999–2004; Expert Scientific Adv. Cttee, Medicines for Malaria Venture, 2009–; Council, Royal Soc., 2011–13. Pres., RSC, 2004–06 (Chm., Strategy Cttee, 2001–02). FMedSci 2003. Jt-Ed., Current Opinion in Drug Discovery and Develt, 1998–2004. Member: Acad. Adv. Bd, Dept of Chem., Bristol Univ., 1998–2001; Council, Univ. of Kent, 1999–2007. Award for Medicinal Chem., RSC, 1989; E. B. Hershberg Award, ACS, 1997; Achievement Award, Industrial Res. Inst. (US), 1997; Individual Achievement Award, CIA, 2006; Galen Medal, Soc. of Apothecaries, 2007; Sir James Black Award for Contribns to Drug Discovery, British Pharmacol Soc., 2012. *Publications:* contribs to learned jls; patents. *Recreations:* gardening, travel, wine, active sports player.

**CAMPBELL, Dr Thomas Patrick,** FSA; Director and Chief Executive Officer, Fine Arts Museums of San Francisco, since 2018; *b* Singapore, 12 July 1962; *m* Phoebe Anne; one *s* one *d*. *Educ:* New Coll., Oxford (BA 1984); Dip. Christie's Fine and Decorative Arts Course, 1985; Courtauld Inst. of Art, Univ. of London (MA 1984; PhD 1999). Creator, Franses Tapestry Archive, 1987–94; Metropolitan Museum of Art: Supervising Curator, Antonio Ratti Textile Center, 1995–2008, Asst Curator, 1995–97, Associate Curator, 1997–2003, Curator, 2003–08, Dept of Eur. Sculpture and Decorative Arts; Dir and CEO, 2009–17. Getty Rothschild Fellow, 2017–18. *Publications:* Tapestry in the Renaissance: art and magnificence, 2002; The Art of Majesty: Henry VIII's tapestry collection, 2007; Tapestry in the Baroque: threads of splendor, 2008.

**CAMPBELL, Rt Hon. Sir (William) Anthony,** Kt 1988; PC 1999; a Lord Justice of Appeal, Supreme Court of Northern Ireland, 1998–2008; a Judge of the Court of Appeal, Cayman Islands, 2010–14; *b* 30 Oct. 1936; *s* of late H. E. Campbell and of Marion Wheeler; *m* 1960, Gail, *e d* of F. M. McKibbin; three *d*. *Educ:* Campbell Coll., Belfast; Queens' Coll., Cambridge. Called to the Bar, Gray's Inn, 1960, Hon. Bencher, 1995; called to the Bar of NI, 1960 (Bencher, 1983; Chm., Exec. Council, 1985–87). Jun. Counsel to Attorney-Gen. for NI, 1971–74; QC (NI) 1974; Senior Crown Counsel in NI, 1984–88; Judge of the High Ct of Justice, NI, 1988–98. Chairman: Council of Legal Educn in NI, 1994–2008; Judicial Studies Bd, NI, 1995–2008. Governor, Campbell Coll., 1976–98 (Chm., 1984–86). Hon. Fellow, Amer. Bar Foundn, 1997. *Recreations:* sailing, hill walking. *Clubs:* New (Edinburgh); Royal Ulster Yacht.

**CAMPBELL, Prof. (William) Bruce,** FRCP, FRCS; Consultant in Vascular and General Surgery, Royal Devon and Exeter Hospital, 1986–2015, now Hon. Vascular Consultant; Consultant Vascular Surgeon, Exeter Medical, since 2015; Chairman, Interventional Procedures Advisory Committee, 2002–15, and Medical Technologies Advisory Committee, 2009–15, National Institute for Health and Care (formerly Clinical) Excellence; *b* London, 3 Dec. 1950; *s* of Dr William Campbell and Jill Campbell; *m* 2008 (marr. diss. 2016); one *s* one *d* from former marriage. *Educ:* Sherborne Sch.; Medical Coll. of St Bartholomew's Hosp., Univ. of London (MB BS Hons 1974; MS 1984). FRCS 1978; FRCP 1996. Registrar, 1979–81, Res. Fellow, 1981–83, Bristol Royal Infirmary; Clin. Lectr in Surgery, Univ. of Oxford, 1983–86. Chm., Therapeutic Procedures Panel, NIHR Health Technol. Assessment Prog., 2000–08. Hon. Professor: Univ. of Exeter, 2000–; Peninsula Med. Sch., Univs of Exeter and Plymouth, 2003–. Non-exec. Dir, Medicines and Healthcare Regulatory Agency, 2015–. Hon. Sec., Vascular Soc. of GB and Ireland, 1998–2002. *Publications:* Complications in Arterial Surgery, 1996; Understanding Varicose Veins, 2000; contrib. surgical and med. jls. *Recreations:* gardening, enjoying my home, writing, military history. *Address:* 13 Wonford Road, Exeter EX2 4LH.

**CAMPBELL BANNERMAN, David;** Member for Eastern, European Parliament, 2009–19 (UK Ind, 2009–11, C, 2011–19); *b* Bombay, 28 May 1960; *s* of Henry Campbell Bannerman and Elizabeth Monica Scott Bannerman. *Educ:* Univ. of Edinburgh (MA Hons Econs and Politics); Wharton Business Sch., Univ. of Pennsylvania (Exchange Schol.). Exec. Dir, Vantagepoint Communications, 1987–; Special Advr to Sec. of State for NI, 1996–97; Communications Dir, Assoc. of Train Operating Cos, 1997–99; Hd of Communications, United News and Media, 2000; Public Affairs Dir, Chm., 2005–06, Dep. Leader and Hd of Policy, 2006–10, UKIP. Contested (UK Ind) S Suffolk, 2010. FInstD. *Recreations:* film screenplay writing, heritage associations, country walks. *Address:* 19 Allison Road, W3 6JF. *E:* dcbdcbuk@yahoo.co.uk.

**CAMPBELL DAVIS, Trevor Fraser;** Chief Executive, Oxford Radcliffe Hospitals NHS Trust, 2003–09; Lead, World Economic Forum, Department of Health, 2009–11; *b* 16 July 1950; *o s* of Rev. Thomas Campbell Davis and Elizabeth Mary Evelyn, (Maeve), Davis (*née* Fraser); *m* 1978, Anne Eperon; partner, 1991, Dr Gwenda Elizabeth Porter; one *d*. *Educ:* Methodist Coll., Belfast; UMIST (BSc 1971). Accountant, Coopers and Lybrand, 1971–76; Financial Controller, Howard & Wyndham Gp, 1976–77; Financial Dir, W. H. Allen & Co. Ltd, 1977–80; Dir of Finance and Admin, McGraw-Hill Book Co. (UK) Ltd, 1980–84; Man. Dir, McGraw-Hill Internat. Trng Systems Ltd, 1984–87; Trustee, McGraw-Hill UK Pensions Schemes, 1980–87; Man. Dir, 1987–98, Chm., 1998, European Communications Gp Ltd. Director: The Not So Silly Trng Co. Ltd, 1992–; Training Media and Copyright Assoc., 1992–2001; Future Health Network Ltd, 2002–. Chairman: Parkside NHS Trust, 1992–98; St Mary's Hosp. NHS Trust, Paddington, 1998–2000; Chief Exec., Whittington Hosp. NHS Trust, 2000–03. Member: London NHS Communications Gp, 1994–96; London Ambulance Service Communications Task Force, 1995–96; Consultant Workforce Review Gp, London, 2001–02; DoH Day Surgery Review Gp, 2001–02; Dr Foster Ethics Cttee, 2001–; Council, UCL Clin. Res. Network, 2001–03; Steering Gp, HFEA, 2002–03. Treasurer: MCB Assoc. in London, 1990– (Pres., 2002–04); Assoc. of UK Univ. Hosps, 2004–. Trustee, NHS Confedn, 2001 (Vice-Chm., 2001–03; Chm., Acute Services Policy Adv. Cttee, 1998–2000, 2001). Special Trustee, St Mary's Hosp., Paddington, 1998–2000. Chm., British Amateur Radio Teledata Gp, 1978–83. Member Court: Middx Univ., 2000–03; Oxford Brookes Univ., 2004. AIEE 1975; FInstD 1980; FIAA 1983; FCIM 1985; FRSA 1998. *Publications:* articles in jls on leadership, change mgt and communications. *Recreations:* helping organisations to change, opera, alpine sports, scuba diving, managing collections. *Club:* Downhill Only (Wengen).

**CAMPBELL-GRAY,** family name of **Lord Gray**.

**CAMPBELL-JOHNSTON, Very Rev. Michael Alexander Ninian,** SJ; *b* 27 Sept. 1931; *s* of Ninian Campbell-Johnston and Marguerite Antoinette Shakespear. *Educ:* Beaumont College; Séminaire Les Fontaines, France (Lic. Phil); LSE (BSc Econs, DipEd); Col. Max. Christi Regis, Mexico (STL). Dir, Guyana Inst. for Social Research and Action, 1967–75; Dir, Social Secretariat, Jesuit Generalate, Rome, 1975–84; Regional Co-ordinator, Jesuit Refugee Service for Mexico and Central America, El Salvador, 1984–87; Provincial, British Province, SJ, 1987–93; Dir, Servicio Jesuita para el Desarrollo, San Salvador, 1994–2002; Parish Priest, St Francis of Assisi, Barbados, 2002–10. Editor: Gisra; Promotio Justitiae. *Recreations:* reading, motorbike riding. *Address:* 757 Christchurch Road, Boscombe, Bournemouth BH7 6AN. *E:* mancjsj@gmail.com.

**CAMPBELL-JOHNSTON, Rachel**, PhD; Chief Art Critic, The Times, since 2002; *b* 4 Oct. 1963; *d* of Christopher Campbell-Johnston and Mary Campbell-Johnston (*née* Symington); *m* 2007, William Nickerson (marr. diss. 2014); one adopted *d*. *Educ:* Convent of the Sacred Heart, Woldingham; Univ. of Edinburgh (MA 1st Cl. Hons Eng. Lit.; PhD Eng. Lit. 1991). The Times: Dep. Lit. Editor, 1995–97; Obituary Writer, 1997–99; Leader Writer, 1999–2002; Poetry Critic, 1998–. FRSA. *Publications:* Mysterious Wisdom: the life and work of Samuel Palmer, 2011; The Child's Elephant, 2013. *Recreations:* wildlife, wandering about, leaning on the Aga. *Address:* The Times, 1 London Bridge Street, SE1 9GF. *T:* (020) 7782 5000. *E:* rachel.johnston@thetimes.co.uk.

**CAMPBELL-ORDE, Sir John Simon Arthur**; *see* Orde, Sir J. S. A. C.

**CAMPBELL-PRESTON, Dame Frances (Olivia)**, DCVO 1990 (CVO 1977); Woman of the Bedchamber to HM Queen Elizabeth the Queen Mother, 1965–2002; *b* 2 Sept. 1918; *d* of Lt-Col Arthur Grenfell and Hilda Margaret Grenfell (*née* Lyttelton); *m* 1938, Lt-Col George Patrick Campbell-Preston (*d* 1960), The Black Watch; two *s* two *d*. *Educ:* St Paul's Girls' Sch. WRNS, 1941–43. Mem., Argyll CC, 1960–64; Chm., Children's Panel, Argyle and Argyll and Bute, 1970–80. *Publications:* The Rich Spoils of Time (autobiog.) (with Hugo Vickers), 2006; Grandmother's Steps (reminiscences), 2010. *Address:* 93 Whitelands House, Cheltenham Terrace, SW3 4RA.
See also R. G. Campbell-Preston.

**CAMPBELL-PRESTON, Robert Grenfell**; Vice Lord-Lieutenant for Argyll and Bute, 2011–15; *b* 8 Jan. 1948; *s* of late Lt-Col George Patrick Campbell-Preston and of Dame Frances (Olivia) Campbell-Preston, *qv*; *m* 1971, Rosalind Mary; one *s* one *d* (and one *d* decd). *Educ:* Eton Coll. Owner and Chm., Inverawe Smokehouses, Taynuilt. Trustee: Argyll and Bute Trust; St Conan's Kirk; Dunstaffnage Estate; Laura Campbell-Preston Charitable Trust. *Recreations:* golfing, gardening, walking, farming. *Address:* Inverawe House, Taynuilt, Argyll PA35 1HU. *T:* (01866) 822542, (office) (01866) 822777. *E:* robertcp@inverawe.co.uk.

**CAMPBELL-SAVOURS**, family name of **Baron Campbell-Savours**.

**CAMPBELL-SAVOURS, Baron** *cr* 2001 (Life Peer), of Allerdale in the County of Cumbria; **Dale Norman Campbell-Savours**; *b* 23 Aug. 1943; *s* of late John Lawrence and of Cynthia Lorraine Campbell-Savours; *m* 1970, Gudrun Kristin Runolfsdottir; two *s* (and one *s* decd). *Educ:* Keswick Sch.; Sorbonne, Paris. Technical and Export agent, 1964–69; Dir. manufacturing co., 1969–77. Member, Ramsbottom UDC, 1972–73. Mem., UNISON (formerly COHSE), 1970–. Contested (Lab): Darwen Division of Lancashire, Feb. 1974, Oct. 1974; Workington, Nov. 1976. MP (Lab) Workington, 1979–2001. Opposition front bench spokesman on overseas develt, 1990–92, on agric., 1992–94. Member: Public Accounts Cttee, 1979–90; Select Committees: on Members Interests, 1983–91; on Procedure, 1984–90; on Agric., 1994–97; Intelligence and Security Cttee, 1997–2001; Standards and Privileges Cttee, 1996–2001. *Publications:* The Case for the Supplementary Vote (pamphlet), 1990; research into case for the University of the Lakes, 1996. *Address:* House of Lords, SW1A 0PW.

**CAMPBELL-TIECH, Andrew**; QC 2003; a Recorder, since 2000; *b* 5 Aug. 1955; *s* of Dr Paul Campbell-Tiech and Maureen (*née* Windsor, *m* 1973, 3rd Baron Ponsonby of Shulbrede); *m* 1992, Sarah Rosemary Ann Lewis; one *d*. *Educ:* Highgate Sch.; College of Law. Called to the Bar, Inner Temple, 1978. *Recreations:* piano, violin, paying bills. *Address:* Drystone Chambers, 35 Bedford Row, WC1R 4JH. *T:* (020) 7404 1881, *Fax:* (020) 7404 1991.

**CAMPBELL-WHITE, Martin Andrew**, MBE 2014; Joint Chief Executive, Askonas Holt Ltd, 1999–2013, now Consultant; *b* 11 July 1943; *s* of late John Vernon Campbell-White and Hilda Doris (*née* Ash); *m* 1969, Dr Margaret Mary Miles; three *s*. *Educ:* Dean Close Sch., Cheltenham; St John's Coll., Oxford; Univ. of Strasbourg. Thomas Skinner & Co. Ltd (Publishers), 1964–66; Ibbs & Tillett Ltd (Concert Agents), 1966–72, Dir, 1969–72; Harold Holt Ltd (Concert Agents), subseq. Askonas Holt Ltd, 1972–: Dir, 1973–2013; Dep. Chm., 1989–92; Chief Exec., 1992–99. Consultant, Opera Comique, Paris, 2014–. Chm., Brit. Assoc. of Concert Agents, 1978–81. Council Mem., London Sinfonietta, 1973–86; Dir, Chamber Orchestra of Europe, 1983–93; Mem. Bd, Première Ensemble, 1991–98. Asst Dir, Fest. of German Arts, 1987; Founding Dir, Japan Fest. 1991, 1991. Trustee: Abbado Trust for Young Musicians, 1987–2006; Salzburg Fest. Trust, 1996–2000; Cape Town Opera, 2015–; Exec. Trustee, Help Musicians UK (formerly Musicians Benevolent Fund), 2006–17; Chm. Trustees, Mahler Foundn, 2017–. Mem. Bd, Riverside Studios, 1988–2014. FRSA 1980. Hon. Mem., Royal Philharmonic Soc., 2014. Hon. DArts City, 2010. Sebetia Ter Prize for Culture, Naples, 2019. *Recreations:* golf, watching cricket, classical music, travel, bird watching. *Address:* c/o Askonas Holt Ltd, 15 Fetter Lane, EC4A 1BW. *T:* (020) 7400 1700, *Fax:* (020) 7400 1799. *Club:* MCC.

**CAMPDEN, Viscount; Henry Robert Anthony Noel**; *b* 1 July 1977; *s* and *heir* of Earl of Gainsborough, *qv*; *m* 2005, Zara, *yr d* of Geoffrey van Cutsem; two *s* one *d*. *Heir:* *s* Hon. Edward Noel, *b* 30 April 2007. *Address:* Exton Park, Oakham, Rutland LE15 8AN.

**CAMPION, Charles Robert**; restaurant critic, since 1992; food writer and broadcaster, since 1994; *b* Leamington Spa, 17 Oct. 1951; *s* of Geoffrey Campion and Meriel Campion; *m* 1986, Sylvia Murray; one *s* one *d*. *Educ:* Blundell's Sch., Tiverton; Watford Art Sch. Advertising copy writer, 1970–88; hotel proprietor and chef, Cold Springs House, Buxton, 1988–92. Glenfiddich Restaurant Writer of the Year, 1997. *Publications:* (with Theodore Kyriakou) The Livebait Cookbook, 1998; (with Theodore Kyriakou) Real Greek Food, 2000; (with Theodore Kyriakou) The Real Greek at Home, 2004; Fifty Recipes to Stake Your Life On, 2004; Food from Fire, 2006; Charles Campion's London Restaurant Guide, 2009; Eat Up!, 2010. *Recreations:* cider making, fly fishing, pickles and preserves, bread making. *T:* 07721 340071. *E:* charles@charlescampion.com. *Club:* Worcester Rugby Football.

**CAMPION, Peter James**, DPhil; FInstP; physicist; *b* 7 April 1926; *s* of Frank Wallace Campion and Gertrude Alice (*née* Lambert); *m* 1st, 1950, Beryl Grace Stanton (*d* 1995), *e d* of John and Grace Stanton; one *s* one *d* (and one *s* decd); 2nd, 1997, Rev. Patricia Adele Houseman (*née* O'Brien); three step *d*. *Educ:* Westcliff High Sch., Essex; Exeter Coll., Oxford (MA, DPhil). FInstP 1964. RNVR, 1943. Nuffield Res. Fellow, Oxford, 1954; Chalk River Proj., Atomic Energy of Canada Ltd, 1955; National Physical Lab., Teddington, 1960–86: Supt, Div. of Radiation Science, 1964; Supt, Div. of Mech. and Optical Metrology, 1974; Dep. Dir, 1976. Mem., Comité Consultatif pour les Etalons de Mesure des Rayonnements Ionisants, 1963–79; Chm., Sect. II, reconstituted Comité Consultatif, Mesure des radionucléides, 1970–79; Mem., NACCB, 1984–86; consultative projects for World Bank, UN and Commonwealth Sci. Council, 1986–92. Editor, Internat. Jl of Applied Radiation and Isotopes, 1968–71. *Publications:* A Code of Practice for the Detailed Statement of Accuracy (with A. Williams and J. E. Burns), 1973; A Campion Saga, 2000; Some Campion Wives, 2003; technical and rev. papers in learned jls on neutron capture gamma rays, measurement of radioactivity, and on metrology generally. *Recreations:* watercolour painting, genealogy.

**CAMPLING, Very Rev. Christopher Russell**; Dean of Ripon, 1984–95; *b* 4 July 1925; *s* of Canon William Charles Campling; *m* 1953, Juliet Marian Hughes; one *s* two *d*. *Educ:* Lancing Coll.; St Edmund Hall, Oxford (MA; Hons Theol. cl. 2); Cuddesdon Theol Coll. RNVR, 1943–47. Ordained deacon 1951, priest 1952; Curate of Basingstoke, 1951–55; Minor Canon of Ely Cathedral and Chaplain of King's School, Ely, 1955–60; Chaplain of Lancing Coll., 1960–67; Vicar of Pershore with Pinvin and Wick and Birlingham, 1968–76; RD of Pershore, 1970–76; Archdeacon of Dudley and Director of Religious Education, Diocese of Worcester, 1976–84. Mem., General Synod of Church of England, 1970–92; Chm., House of Clergy, Diocese of Worcester, 1981–84; Chm., Council for the Care of Churches, 1988–94. Lectr, Leeds Parish Church, 1988–. *Publications:* The Way, The Truth and The Life: Vol. 1, The Love of God in Action, 1964; Vol. 2, The People of God in Action, 1964; Vol. 3, The Word of God in Action, 1965; Vol. 4, God's Plan in Action, 1965; also two teachers' volumes; Words of Worship, 1969; The Fourth Lesson, Vol. 1 1973, Vol. 2 1974; The Food of Love, 1997; I Was Glad (memoirs), 2005; Sonnets of Faith, 2010; Christian Breadcrumbs, 2017. *Recreations:* music, drama, golf. *Address:* Pebble Ridge, Aglaia Road, Worthing, West Sussex BN11 5SW. *Club:* Naval.

**CAMPOS, Prof. Christophe Lucien**, OBE 1994; writer and book reviewer; Director, British Institute in Paris, 1978–2003; *b* 27 April 1938; *s* of Lucien Antoine Campos and Margaret Lilian (*née* Dunn); *m* 1977, Lucy Elizabeth Mitchell; one *s* two *d*; two *d* by former marriage. *Educ:* Lycée Lamoricière, Oran; Lycée Français de Londres; Lycée Henri IV, Paris; Gonville and Caius Coll., Cambridge. LèsL (Paris), PhD (Cantab). Lector in French, Gonville and Caius Coll., 1959; Lecturer in French: Univ. of Maryland, 1963; Univ. of Sussex, 1974; Lectr in English, Univ. i Oslo, 1969; Prof. of French, University Coll., Dublin, 1974. Gen. Editor, Franco-British Studies, 1988–2004; author and webmaster, http://fleurusalgerie.fr, 2012–. Chevalier de l'Ordre des Arts et des Lettres (France), 1988. *Publications:* The View of France, 1964; L'Enseignement de la civilisation française, 1988; Stéréotypes et prototypes nationaux en Europe, 2007; Fleurus en Oranie 1848–1962, 2016 (Algérianiste Prize, 2017); contribs to Th. Qly, TLS, Univs Qly, Franco-British Studies, History of Sport, Bulletin d'histoire et d'archéologie du Ried nord. *Recreations:* bees, football, gastronomy, environment. *Address:* 6 La Hocherie, 86230 Sossay, France.

**CAMPRUBI, Catherine Jane**; *see* Royle, C. J.

**CAMPSIE, Nicholas James**; Chairman, Madison Foundation, since 2018; *b* Oxford, 13 Feb. 1975; *s* of Raymond Campsie and Julie Campsie. *Educ:* Island Sch., Hong Kong; Exeter Coll., Oxford (BA 1st Cl. PPE; George Webb Jun. Prize (Econs); Fitzgerald Prize (Politics)). Transaction Exec., Principal Finance Gp, Nomura Internat., 1998–2004; Global Hd, Illiquid Investments, Eton Park Capital Mgt, 2004–17. Non-exec. Dir, MoJ, 2018–. Chm., Down Syndrome Educn Internat., 2013–; Dep. Chm., Chickensheed Th. Trust, 2016–. *E:* nick@madisonfoundation.co.uk.

**CAMRE, Prof. Henning Niels Juel**; Knight, Order of the Dannebrog, 2005; Professor, Norwegian Film School, Inland Norway University of Applied Sciences, since 2016; *b* 15 Nov. 1938; *s* of Sigfred N. J. Camre and Carna (*née* Petersen); *m* 1st, 1967, Merete Friis (marr. diss.); one *d*; 2nd, 1978, Janne Giese (marr. diss.); one *d* and one adopted *d*; 3rd, 2005, Regitze Oppenhejm. *Educ:* Univ. of Copenhagen; Nat. Film Sch. of Denmark (Dip. in Cinematography). Dir of Photography (feature and documentary film), 1968–88; Director: Nat. Film Sch. of Denmark, 1975–92; Nat. Film and TV Sch., UK, 1992–98; Chief Exec., Danish Film Inst., 1998–2007; Founding Pres., 2006, Exec. Dir, 2007–17, Eur. Think Tank on Film and Film Policy. Adjunct Prof., Copenhagen Business Sch., 2005; Prof., Lillehammer UC, Norway, 2015–16. Chairman: Nordic Film Council, 1979–89; Danish State Film Studio, 1989–92; European Film Coll., 2014–; Centre International de Liaison des Ecoles de Cinéma et de Télévision: Mem., Exec. Council, 1980–86; Chm., Programme for Developing Countries, 1982–2002; Vice-Pres., 1986–2002; Hon. Mem., 2002. Chairman: Cultural Area, Danish Nat. UNESCO Commn, 1999–2010; Screen Inst. Beirut, 2009–; Member, Board: Norwegian Film Inst., 2009–12; Greek Film Centre, 2011–14. Chevalier de l'Ordre des Arts et des Lettres (France), 1990; Gloria Artis Medal (Poland), 2005. *Publications:* Bridging the Gap, 1982; Film and Television Training in Indonesia, 1985; Asia-Pacific Film and Television Schools, 1991. *Recreation:* cycling. *Address:* Callisensvej 25, 2900 Hellerup, Denmark. *E:* henning.camre@filmthinktank.org, hcamre@gmail.com, hcamre@screeninstitutebeirut.org, henning.camre@inn.no.

**CAMROSE, 5th Viscount** *cr* 1941, of Hackwood Park, Southampton; **Jonathan William Berry**; Bt 1921; Baron 1929; Founder and Director, Camrose Management Ltd, since 2015; *b* London, 26 Feb. 1970; *s* of 4th Viscount Camrose and of Marina Beatrice Berry (*née* Sulzberger); *S* father, 2016; *m* 1996, Aurélie Molin; two *s* two *d*. *Educ:* Durham Univ. (BA Jt Hons French and German 1993); Carnegie Mellon Univ., Pittsburgh (MBA). Hd of Change Mgt, BP, 2008–09; Founder, Camrose Communications Ltd, 2010. MInstD. *Recreations:* sailing, jazz guitar player, golf, country sports. *Heir:* *s* Hon. Hugo William Berry, *b* 25 Feb. 2000. *Address:* 17 Barclay Road, SW6 1EJ. *T:* 07770 823489. *E:* jonathan.berry@camrosepartners.com. *Clubs:* White's, Royal Automobile.

**CANADA, Primate of the Anglican Church of**, since 2019; **Most Rev. Linda Carol Nicholls**; *b* Calgary, Alberta, 25 Oct. 1954; *d* of Gerald J. Nicholls and Carol G. Nicholls (*née* Neumann). *Educ:* Sir John A. Macdonald Collegiate, Scarborough; Royal Conservatory of Music (Associate Dip. Piano Perf. 1974); Univ. of Toronto (BMus 1976; BEd 1977); Wycliffe Coll., Univ. of Toronto (MDiv 1986; DMin 2002); Toronto Sch. of Theology (Cert. in Spiritual Direction, Jubilee Prog. 1996). Music and Maths Teacher, Woodstock Internat. Christian Sch., Mussoorie, India, 1977–82; ordained deacon, 1985, priest, 1986; Asst Curate, St Paul's L'Amoreaux, Scarborough, 1985–87; Incumbent: Parish of Georgina, St James', Sutton and St George, Sibbald Point, 1987–91; Holy Trinity, Thornhill, 1991–2005; Co-ordinator for Dialogue (Ethics, Interfaith Relations & Congregational Develt), Faith, Worship and Ministry Dept, Anglican Church of Canada, 2005–08; Mem., ARCIC III, 2011–; Co-Chm., Anglican-RC Dialogue in Canada, 2012–; Suffragan Bishop of Toronto (Area Bishop of Trent-Durham), 2008–16; Coadjutor Bishop, Dio. of Huron, Canada, 2016; Bishop of Huron, 2016–19. Mem., Tapestry Chamber Choir, 2002–16. Hon. DD: Wycliffe Coll., Univ. of Toronto, 2008; Huron Univ. Coll., 2016. *Recreations:* wilderness canoeing, choral singing. *Address:* Anglican Church of Canada, 80 Hayden Street, Toronto, ON M4Y 3G2, Canada. *T:* (416) 9249192. *Club:* Newmarket (Ontario).

**CANAVAN, Dennis Andrew**; Member (Ind) Falkirk West, Scottish Parliament, 1999–2007; *b* 8 Aug. 1942; *s* of late Thomas and Agnes Canavan; one *s* (and three *s* one *d* decd). *Educ:* St Bride's Primary Sch., Cowdenbeath; St Columba's High Sch., Cowdenbeath; Edinburgh Univ. (BSc Hons, DipEd). Head of Maths Dept, St Modan's High Sch., Stirling, 1970–74; Asst Head, Holy Rood High Sch., Edinburgh, 1974. District Councillor, 1973–74; Leader of Labour Gp, Stirling District Council, 1974; Member: Stirling Dist Educn Sub-cttee, 1973–74; Stirlingshire Youth Employment Adv. Cttee, 1972–74. Sec., W Stirlingshire Constituency Labour Party, 1972–74; Labour Party Agent, Feb. 1974; Treasurer, Scottish Party Lab. Gp, 1976–79, Vice-Chm., 1979–80, Chm., 1980–81. MP (Lab 1974–99, Ind. 1999–2000) W Stirlingshire, Oct. 1974–1983, Falkirk W, 1983–2000. Member: H of C Select Cttee on For. Affairs, 1982–97, on Internat. Develt, 1997–99; Chair: PLP NI Cttee, 1989–97; Parly Br., EIS, 1983–2000; Vice-Chm., All-Party Hospice Gp, 1992–2000; Founder and Convener, All-Party Parly Scottish Sports Gp,

1987–99; Mem., British-Irish Inter-Parly Body, 1992–2000. Scottish Parliament: Mem., European and External Relns Cttee, 1999–2007; Founder and Convener, Sports Gp, 1999–2007. Columnist, The Herald, 1999–2000. Ramblers Scotland: Pres., 2007–09; Convener, 2009–12; Vice-Pres., 2012–. Chm., YesScotland, 2012–14. Mem., Ind. Rev. Panel set up by Scottish Govt to inquire into policing during 1984–85 Miners' Strike in Scotland and impact on mining communities, 2018–. Mem., Bd of Trustees, Nat. Mining Mus. of Scotland (formerly Scottish Mining Mus.), 2007–. Chm., Parent Council, St Mary's Sch., Bannockburn, 2009–14; Chair, Falkirk Football Community Foundn, 2010–16. Hon. Pres., Rivers Forth and Teith Anglers Assoc., 2008–. Patron: William Simpson's Home, Plean, 2007–14; Falkirk and Dist Assoc. for Mental Health, 2008–; Driving Force, Bonnybridge, 2009–; Falkirk Forum, Crossroads Caring Scotland, 2010–15; Wiston Lodge Charity, 2012–. Mem., Panel of Judges, Dennis Canavan Scholarship, 2008–. DUniv Stirling, 2008; LLD Strathclyde, 2008. *Publications*: Let the People Decide (autobiog.), 2009; contribs to various jls on educn and politics. *Recreations*: hill walking, swimming, reading, football (Scottish Univs football internationalist, 1966–67 and 1967–68; Hon. Pres., Milton Amateurs FC), cycling. *Address*: Ardsonas, Sauchieburn, Bannockburn, Stirlingshire FK7 9PZ. *T*: (01786) 812581. *E*: canavan897@btinternet.com.

**CANAVAN, Sheelagh Mary, (Sandy); Her Honour Judge Canavan;** a Circuit Judge, since 2014; *b* London, 8 Aug. 1964; *d* of Brendan and Margaret Canavan; *m* 2006, Kalai Sivanadian. *Educ*: Our Lady's Convent High Sch., Hackney; King's Coll. London (LLB Hons); Inns of Court Sch. of Law. Called to the Bar, Lincoln's Inn, 1987; in practice as barrister, specialising in criminal law, 1987–2014; a Recorder, 2010–14. *Recreations*: gardening, theatre, jam making, travelling, school governor (primary), singing in a choir, retail therapy. *Address*: Snaresbrook Crown Court, 75 Hollybush Hill, E11 1QW. *T*: (020) 8530 0000.

**CANAVAN, Vincent Joseph;** Sheriff of North Strathclyde at Greenock, 2001–11; *b* 13 Dec. 1946; *s* of James Canavan and Catherine Ludivine Brogan; *m* 1973, Mary Allison; three *s* three *d*. *Educ*: St Aloysius Coll., Glasgow; Univ. of Glasgow (LLB Hons 1968). Qualified as Solicitor, 1970; Advocate, 1980. Sheriff of S Strathclyde, Dumfries and Galloway at Hamilton, 1987–2001. Member: Victim Support (Scotland) Hamilton Court Project Working Party, 1990–94; Strathclyde Regl Council Cons. Cttee on Social Work in criminal justice system, 1991–96; Council, Sheriffs' Assoc., 1997–2000; Working Party on law of foreshore, 2000. Chm., Lanarks Br., Scottish Assoc. for Study of Delinquency, 1992–95 (Vice-Chm., 1991–92). *Recreations*: reading history, Italian cuisine, visiting art exhibitions. *Club*: Glasgow Art.

**CANBERRA AND GOULBURN, Archbishop of, (RC),** since 2013; **Most Rev. Christopher Charles Prowse;** *b* Melbourne, 14 Nov. 1953; *s* of Francis Joseph Prowse and Marian Lois Prowse (*née* Atkinson). *Educ*: Monash Univ. (BA 1978); Melbourne Coll. of Divinity (BTh 1979); Gregorian Univ., Rome (STL 1987); Lateran Univ., Rome (STD 1995). Vicar General, Archdiocese of Melbourne, 2001–03; Auxiliary Bishop of Melbourne, 2003–09; Bishop of Sale, 2009–13. Mem., Pontifical Council for Interreligious Dialogue, Vatican, 2009–; Chairman: Australian Catholic Bishops Commn for Ecumenism and Inter-religious Relations, 2012–18; Australian Catholic Bishops Commn for Evangelisation, Laity and Ministry, 2018–; Mem., Internat. Anglican RC Commn for Unity and Mission, 2014–; Consultor, Commn for religious relations with the Jews, 2014–. Apostolic Adminr, Dio. of Wagga Wagga, 2016–. *Recreations*: walking, bicycle riding, swimming. *Address*: GPO Box 89, Canberra, ACT 2601, Australia. *T*: (2) 62399811. *E*: archbishop@cg.org.au.

**CANBERRA AND GOULBURN, Bishop of,** since 2019; **Rt Rev. Dr Mark Graham Short;** *b* Marrickville, NSW, 20 Dec. 1966; *s* of Graham and Iolanthe Short; *m* 1991, Monica Ann Willcocks; two *s*. *Educ*: Univ. of NSW (BCom Hons 1990); Moore Theol Coll. (BTh Hons 1996); Univ. of Durham (PhD 2004). Cadet journalist, then journalist, Sydney Morning Herald, 1985–89; Graduate Economist, Commonwealth Dept of Industrial Relns, 1991–93. Ordained priest, 1997; Rector, Turvey Park, 2002–11; Archdeacon of Wagga Wagga, 2009–11; Nat. Dir, Bush Church Aid Soc., 2011–19. *Recreations*: bush walking, trains, reading. *Address*: c/o GPO Box 1981, Canberra, ACT 2601, Australia. *T*: (2) 62323612. *E*: mark.short@anglicancg.org.au.

**CANDELAS, Prof. Philip,** DPhil; FRS 2010; Rouse Ball Professor of Mathematics, University of Oxford, and Fellow of Wadham College, Oxford, since 1999; *b* 24 Oct. 1951; *m* Xenia de la Ossa. *Educ*: Christ's Coll., Cambridge (BA 1973); Wadham Coll., Oxford (DPhil 1978). Jun. Res. Fellow, Balliol Coll., Oxford, 1975–76; Res. Asst, 1976–77, Asst Prof., 1977–82, Associate Prof., 1982–89, Prof., 1989–99, Dept of Physics, Univ. of Texas, Austin. *Publications*: papers in learned jls. *Address*: Wadham College, Oxford OX1 3PN.

**CANDY, Lorraine Ann;** Luxury Content Editor, and Editor-in-Chief, Style magazine, Sunday Times, since 2017; *b* 8 July 1968; *d* of A. R. Butler and V. S. Butler; *m* 2000, C. James Candy; one *s* three *d*. *Educ*: Liskeard Comprehensive Sch., Cornwall. Feature writer, Daily Mirror, 1990–93; Woman's Editor: Sun, 1993; Today, 1993–95; Associate Ed., Marie Claire mag., 1995–97; Dep. Ed., Times Saturday Mag., 1997–98; Ed., B mag., 1998–99; Features Ed., The Times, 1999–2000; Editor: Cosmopolitan, 2000–04; Elle, 2004–17. *Recreations*: riding, shopping. *Address*: Sunday Times, News Building, 1 London Bridge Street, SE1 9GF.

**CANDY, Stuart Graham C.;** *see* Cull-Candy.

**CANE, Very Rev. Dr Anthony William Nicholas Strephon;** Dean of Portsmouth, since 2019; *b* Cape Town, 25 Aug. 1961; *s* of James and Brenda Cane; *m* 1986, Clare Shuttleworth; two *s* one *d*. *Educ*: Diocesan Coll., Cape Town; Univ. of Cape Town (BA 1981); Univ. of Birmingham (MPhil 1993; PhD 2003); Westcott House Theol Coll. Care Worker, Elizabeth House Assoc., 1983–84; Church Community Worker, Chelsea Methodist Church, 1984–87; ordained deacon, 1990, priest, 1991; Curate, All Saints, Kings Heath, 1990–93; Sen. Chaplain, Univ. of Brighton, 1993–99; Diocesan Advr and Priest-incharge, St Luke's, Torquay, 1999–2001; Diocesan Advr for Educn and Trng of Adults, Dio. of Chichester, 2001–07; Chancellor and Canon Librarian, Chichester Cathedral, 2007–19. *Publications*: The Place of Judas Iscariot in Christology, 2005; contribs to learned jls incl. New Blackfriars, Theology, Crucible, Expository Times, Religion and Theology. *Recreations*: downland walking, lifelong learning, observing wildlife, literary worlds, the silver screen, travelling east. *Address*: The Deanery, 13 Pembroke Road, Portsmouth PO1 2NS. *T*: (023) 9282 4400. *E*: anthonycane@live.co.uk. *Clubs*: Royal Naval, Royal Albert Yacht.

**CANE, (Barbara) Jane;** *see* Stapleton, B. J.

**CANHAM, Paul George,** LVO 1991; JP; Official Secretary to Governor-General of New Zealand, 1985–90; *b* 25 Oct. 1933; *s* of George Ernest Canham and Ella Mary (*née* Mackenzie); *m* 1964, Diane Alderton; one *s* one *d*. *Educ*: Timaru Boys' High Sch.; Victoria Univ. of Wellington (BA, MA Hons History). Teacher: Pomfret Sch., Conn., 1957; Matamata Coll., NZ, 1960; Hauraki Plains Coll., 1967; Heretaunga Coll., 1969; Dep. Prin., Hutt Valley High Sch., 1973; Prin., Wanganui High Sch., 1979. Dist Manager, Baucau, Timor Leste, UN Population Fund Nat. Census, 2004. JP Hawkes Bay, 1991. *Publications*: The Return (novel), 1999; Ben and the Stag, 2012; The Final Redemption, 2013; No Way Back, 2014. *Recreation*: bridge. *Address*: 10 Waimea Way, Poraiti, Napier 4112, New Zealand. *T*: (6) 8438877. *E*: panddcanham@gmail.com.

**CANN, Anthony;** *see* Cann, J. W. A.

**CANN, Charles Richard,** CB 1996; Deputy Secretary, Ministry of Agriculture, Fisheries and Food, 1991–96; *b* 3 Feb. 1937; *s* of late Charles Alfred Cann and Grace Elizabeth Cann; *m* 1979, Denise Ann Margaret Love; two *s*. *Educ*: Merchant Taylors' Sch., Northwood, Middx; St John's Coll., Cambridge (MA). Asst Principal, MAFF, 1960, Principal 1965; Cabinet Office, 1969–71; Asst Sec., MAFF, 1971; Under Sec., 1981; Fisheries Sec., MAFF, 1987–91. Mem. Policy Cttee, CPRE, 1996–2002.

**CANN, (John William) Anthony;** Partner, 1978–2006, Senior Partner, 2001–06, Linklaters; *b* 21 July 1947; *s* of late Dr John Cann and Enid Grace Cann (*née* Long); *m* 1973, Anne Clausen; two *s* one *d*. *Educ*: Shrewsbury Sch.; Southampton Univ. (LLB Law 1969); Coll. of Law/Law Soc. (Hons). With Linklaters, 1970–2006: articled clerk, 1970–72; Associate Solicitor, 1972–78; NY Office, 1975–82; Hd of Corporate Dept, 1995–2000. Director: Connect Gp (formerly Smiths News PLC), 2006–16; Panmure Gordon & Co. plc, 2007–16; Social Investment Business (formerly Futurebuilders England Fund Management) Ltd, 2008–14. Chm., Changing Faces, 2007–09; Trustee, Social Investment Business Foundn (formerly Adventure Capital Fund), 2006–16. Gov., 2007–11, Dir, 2018–, Haberdashers' Aske's Fedn; Gov., Haberdashers' Adams' Fedn, 2011– (Chm., 2013–). Liveryman, Haberdashers' Co., 2012 (Ct of Assts, 2013). *Publications*: Mergers and Acquisitions Handbook Part D, 1986; European Mergers and Acquisitions (United Kingdom), 1991. *Recreations*: photography, travel, ski-ing, sailing. *Address*: Langrick, 13 Murray Road, SW19 4PD. *T*: (020) 8946 6731. *E*: anthony.cann@yahoo.com. *Clubs*: Athenæum, MCC.

**CANN, Mark James Alexander;** Chief Executive Officer, British Forces Foundation, since 2000; *b* Holywood, 28 Nov. 1965; *s* of late John and Penny Cann; *m* 1999, Emma Francis; two *s* one *d*. *Educ*: Repton Sch.; Loughborough Univ. (BA Hons Pols and Econ. Hist.); RMA Sandhurst. Served Army, 17th/21st Lancers, Queen's Royal Lancers, 1988–99, Royal Yeomanry, 2000–02. Dir, CU2 Ltd, 1999–. Chairman: First Defence, 2011–16; ChariAdmin Ltd, 2015–. Director: Armed Forces Charities Adv. Co., 2009–16; Global Forces Entertainment, 2014–; Adminr, Erach and Roshan Sadri Foundn, 2007–; Trustee, Wilts Bobby Van Trust, 2009–. Trustee, UK Armed Forces Polo Assoc. (formerly Combined Services Polo Assoc.), 2012– (Dir, 1997–2012); Mem. Council, Hurlingham Polo Assoc., 1997–. *Recreations*: all sport (especially polo, ski-ing and tennis), enthusiastic but awful golfer, supporting Arsenal, collecting first edition political autobiographies, early 20th century novels and portrait photographs. *Address*: British Forces Foundation, 10A High Street, Pewsey, Wilts SN9 5AQ. *T*: (01672) 564911, *Fax*: (01672) 562101. *E*: info@bff.org.uk. *Clubs*: Cavalry and Guards, Royal Automobile.

**CANN, Paul Lewis;** Chief Executive, Age UK Oxfordshire (formerly Age Concern Oxfordshire), 2009–16; *b* 29 Aug. 1953; *s* of John Samuel Jones Cann and Eileen Dorothy Jean (*née* Daymond John); *m* 1981, Phillippa Terese Cooke; one *s* one *d*. *Educ*: Tiffin Sch.; King's Coll., Cambridge (BA Hons 1975; MA 1979); Westminster Coll., Oxford (Cert Ed 1976). Schoolmaster: Christchurch Cathedral Sch., 1976–78; Abingdon Sch., 1978–81; Civil Service, 1981–88: Asst Private Secretary to: Lord Privy Seal, 1982–83; Minister for Arts, 1983–84; Principal, Cabinet Office, 1985–88; Sen. Consultant, Hay Mgt Consultants, 1988–90; Hd of Personnel, Newspaper Publishing plc, 1990–92; Exec. Dir, British Dyslexia Assoc., 1992–97; Chief Exec., Nat. Autistic Soc., 1997–2000; Dir, Policy, Res. and Internat. Dept, Help the Aged, 2000–09. Chm., Social Inclusion Adv. Gp, 2010–12; Mem. Bd, Nat. Develt Team for Inclusion, 2015–. Vis. Fellow, Inst. of Ageing, Oxford Univ., 2004–07; Associate Fellow, Internat. Longevity Centre, 2009–; Gary Andrews Vis. Fellow, Australian Assoc. of Gerontol., 2016. Founder Mem. and Mem., Mgt Gp, Campaign to End Loneliness, 2011–. Trustee: Contact a Family, 2001–06; Oxford Lieder, 2006–; Age and Employment Network, 2006–09. Corporate Mem., Inst. Personnel and Develt, 1986. Medal for outstanding contrib to older people, British Geriatrics Soc., 2008. *Publications*: (ed jtly) Unequal Ageing, 2009. *Recreations*: singing, drinking wine, enjoying Hook Norton. *Address*: 7 Bell Hill, Hook Norton, Oxon OX15 5NG. *T*: (01608) 737282.

**CANNADINE, Prof. Sir David (Nicholas),** Kt 2009; DPhil, LittD; FR HistS; FBA 1999; FSA; FR SL; Dodge Professor of History, Princeton University, since 2011 (Whitney J. Oates Senior Research Scholar, Humanities Council, 2008–11); Editor, Oxford Dictionary of National Biography, since 2014; President, British Academy, since 2017; *b* 7 Sept. 1950; *s* of Sydney Douglas Cannadine and Dorothy Mary Cannadine (*née* Hughes); *m* 1982, Linda Jane Colley, *qv*; one *d* decd. *Educ*: King Edward's Five Ways Sch., Birmingham; Clare Coll., Cambridge (schol.; BA 1st cl. Hons 1972; MA 1975; LittD 1993; Hon. Fellow, 2012); Princeton Univ. (Jane Eliza Procter Vis. Fellow); St John's Coll., Oxford (Sen. Schol.; DPhil 1975; Hon. Fellow, 2015). FR HistS 1981; FSA 2005. Cambridge University: Res. Fellow, St John's Coll., 1975–77; Asst Lectr, 1976–80, Lectr, 1980–88, in Hist.; Christ's College: Fellow, 1977–88 (Hon. Fellow, 2005); Dir of Studies in Hist., 1977–83; Tutor, 1979–81; Prof. of History, 1988–92, Moore Collegiate Prof. of History, 1992–98, Columbia Univ.; Prof. of History and Dir, 1998–2003, Queen Elizabeth the Queen Mother Prof. of British History, 2003–08, Hon. Fellow, 2005, Inst. of Historical Res., Sch. of Advanced Study, Univ. of London. Dist. Sen. Fellow, Sch. of Advanced Study, 2008, Hon. Prof., 2008, Univ. of London. Vis. Mem., 1980–81, Dir's Visitor, 2011, Inst. for Advanced Study, Princeton; Visiting Professor: Birkbeck Coll., London Univ., 1995–97; Univ. of Oxford, 2014–; Vis. Scholar, Pembroke Coll., Cambridge, 1997; Visiting Fellow: Whitney Humanities Center, Yale Univ., 1995–98; Humanities Council, Princeton Univ., 2003–05; ANU, 2005; Nat. Humanities Center, N Carolina, 2006; Adjunct Prof., ANU, 2006–; Fletcher Jones Foundn Dist. Fellow, Huntington Liby, 2010; Vis. Prof., Stern Business Sch., New York Univ., 2013–14; Vis. Fellow, Swedish Collegium for Advanced Study, Uppsala, 2017–18. Lectures: Motitz, Kalamazoo, 1992; Leonard Hastings Schoff, Columbia Univ., 1993; Hayes Robinson, RHC, 1994; Raleigh, British Acad., 1997; Charles Edmonson, Baylor Univ., 1997; George Orwell Meml, Sheffield Univ., 1997; Curtis, Univ. of Central Lancs, 1998; Earl, Keele, 1999; Beall-Russell, Baylor Univ., 1999; Esmée Fairbairn, Lancaster Univ., 1999; London Liby, 2001; Carnochan, Stanford Univ., 2001; Throckmorton, Lewis and Clark Coll., 2001; Burrows, Univ. of Essex, 2002; Rothschild Archive, 2002; Linbury Nat. Gall., 2002; Golden Jubilee, Univ. of Newcastle, 2002; Dickinson, Newcomen Soc., 2003; T. S. Eliot, Washington Univ., St Louis, 2003; Roy Jenkins Meml, RSL, 2004; Thorpe, Princeton Univ., 2004; PSCP, Getty Res. Inst., 2006; Ramsay Murray, Selwyn Coll., Cambridge, 2006; History of Parlt, 2006; University, Carnegie-Mellon, 2006; George Macaulay Trevelyan, Cambridge Univ., 2007; John Hayes Meml, NPG, 2007; Eaton, Boston Athenaeum 2008; Fulbright, BL, 2009; Linbury, Dulwich Picture Gall., 2010; Eugene Meyer, Bard Coll., 2011; Crosby Kemper, Westminster Coll., Fulton, Mo, 2012; Jon Sigurdsson, Univ. of Iceland, 2012; Gladstone, Gladstone's Liby, 2012; Haaga, Huntington Liby, San Marino, Calif, 2012; Creighton, Univ. of Toronto, 2013; Fred Freeman, Univ. of Liverpool, 2013; Robb, Univ. of Auckland, 2015; Wolfson Anniversary, Univ. of Glasgow, 2015; Exeter Coll., Oxford, 2016; Humanities, Clemson Univ., 2016; Oxford DNB/OUP Centenary, Univ. of

Oxford, 2017; Athenaeum, 2019. Fellow: Berkeley Coll., Yale Univ., 1985–; ACLS, 1990–91; J. P. Morgan Liby, NY, 1992–98. Regular broadcaster on wireless and television; presenter: A Point of View, BBC Radio 4, 2005–; Churchill's Other Lives, 2011, Prime Minister's Props, 2016–18, BBC Radio 4. Member: Eastern Regl Cttee, Nat. Trust, 2001–10; Cttee of Mgt, Centre for Res. in the Arts, Social Scis and Humanities, Univ. of Cambridge, 2001–03; Archives Task Force, 2002–04; Royal Mint Adv. Cttee, 2004–14; Rev. of 30 Year Rule, 2007–09; Adv. Cttee, Center for Hist. of Collecting in America, Frick Collection, NY, 2009–; Bank Note Character Adv. Cttee, Bank of England, 2015–; Historical Consultant, Cabinet War Rooms, 2002–04; Historical Advr, Ian Fleming Centenary Exhibn, Imperial War Mus., 2007–08; Comr, English Heritage, 2001–09 (Chm., Blue Plaques Panel, 2006–13). Vice-President: British Records Soc., 1998–; RHistS, 1998–2002; Victorian Soc., 2009–; Worcs Histl Soc., 2011– (Pres., 1999–2010). Mem. Adv. Council, PRO, then Nat. Archives, 1999–2004; London University: Member Advisory Council: Warburg Inst. (formerly Adv. Bd), 1998–2003; Inst. of US Studies, 1999–2003; Inst. of English Studies, 2000–03; Inst. of Latin Amer. Studies, 2000–03; Inst. for Study of the Americas, 2004–08. Trustee: Kennedy Meml Trust, 2000–10 (Vice-Chm., 2005–10); Nat. Portrait Gall., 2000–12 (Vice-Chm., 2003–05; Chm., 2005–12; Trustee, Portrait Trust, 2012–17); British Empire and Commonwealth Mus., 2003–13; Rothschild Archive Trust, 2005–19; Wolfson Foundn, 2010– (Chm., Arts Panel, 2010–; Chm. Judges, Wolfson Hist. Prize, 2015–); Gladstone Library, 2011–; Gordon Brown Archives Trust, 2011–; Liby of Birmingham Trust, 2011–16; RA Trust, 2013–19; Historic Royal Palaces, 2015–19 (Vice Chm., 2016–19; Hon. Ambassador, 2019–); Vice Chm., Fabric Cttee, Westminster Abbey, 2010–; Dir, Royal Oak Foundn, NY, 2011–. President: Friends of Imperial War Mus., 2012–18; Friends of Humanities Res. Centre, ANU, 2016–; Chm., Churchill 2015, 2013–15; Mem. Adv. Bd, Nat. Churchill Library Center, Washington, DC, 2017–. Patron: Attingham Trust, 2006–; Friends of Birmingham Archives and Heritage, 2009–. Gov., Ipswich Sch., 1982–88. General Editor: Studies in Modern Hist., 1979–2002; Penguin Hist. of Britain, 1989–; Penguin Hist. of Europe, 1991–; Historical Res., 1998–2003; Reviews in History, 1998–2003; History Compass, 2000–03; Member, Editorial Board: Urban Hist. Yearbook, 1979–83; Past and Present, 1983– (Vice Chm., 2000–18); Midland Hist., 1985–88; Twentieth Century British Hist., 1990–2007; Rural Hist., 1995–; Prospect, 1995–2016; Library Hist., 1998–; England's Landscape, 2000–06; History of Parliament, 2004–16. MAE 2010; Internat. Hon. Mem., Amer. Acad. of Arts and Scis, 2018. FRSA 1998; FRSL 1999; Fellow, APS, 2019. Hon. FHA 2011 (Hon. Vice Pres., 2013); Hon. Churchill Fellow, Westminster Coll., Fulton, Mo, 2012. Hon. DLitt: UEA, 2001; South Bank, 2001; Birmingham, 2002; Worcester, 2011; London, 2017; Leicester, 2019; DUniv Open, 2016. T. S. Ashton Prize, Econ. Hist. Soc., 1977; Silver Jubilee Prize, Agricl Hist. Soc., 1977; Dean's Dist. Award in the Humanities, Columbia Univ., 1996; Dickinson Medal, Newcomen Soc., 2003; Tercentenary Medal, Soc. of Antiquaries, 2008; Minerva Medal, Royal Philosophical Soc. of Glasgow, 2012; Norton Medlicott Medal, Histl Assoc., 2013; Blenheim Award, Internat. Churchill Soc., 2016. *Publications*: Lords and Landlords: the aristocracy and the towns 1774–1967, 1980; (ed and contrib.) Patricians, Power and Politics in Nineteenth-Century Towns, 1982; (ed jtly and contrib.) H. J. Dyos, Exploring the Urban Past, 1982; (ed jtly and contrib.) Rituals of Royalty: power and ceremonial in traditional societies, 1987; The Pleasures of the Past, 1989; (ed and contrib.) Winston Churchill's Famous Speeches, 1989; (ed jtly and contrib.) The First Modern Society: essays in English history in honour of Lawrence Stone, 1989; The Decline and Fall of the British Aristocracy (Lionel Trilling Prize), 1990; G. M. Trevelyan: a life in history, 1992; Aspects of Aristocracy: grandeur and decline in modern Britain, 1994; (ed jtly and contrib.) History and Biography: essays in honour of Derek Beales, 1996; Class in Britain, 1998; History in Our Time, 1998; Ornamentalism: how the British saw their Empire, 2001; In Churchill's Shadow: confronting the past in modern Britain, 2002; (ed and contrib.) What is History Now?, 2002; (ed and contrib.) History and the Media, 2004; (ed and contrib.) Admiral Lord Nelson: his context and legacy, 2005; (ed and contrib.) Trafalgar in History: a battle and its afterlife, 2006; Mellon: an American life, 2006; The National Portrait Gallery: a brief outline history, 2007; (ed and contrib.) Empire, the Sea and Global History: Britain's maritime world 1763–1833, 2007; (ed jtly and contrib.) History and Philanthropy: past, present, future, 2008; Making History Now and Then: discoveries, controversies and explorations, 2008; (jtly) Review of the 30 Year Rule, 2009; (jtly) The Right Kind of History, 2011; The Undivided Past: humanity beyond our differences, 2013; George V: the unexpected king, 2014; Heroic Chancellor: Winston Churchill and the University of Bristol, 1929–1965, 2015; Margaret Thatcher: a life and legacy, 2017; Victorious Century: the United Kingdom 1800–1906, 2017; (ed and contrib.) Churchill: the statesman as artist, 2018; (ed jtly and contrib.) The Country House: past, present and future, 2018; Why Collect?: a report on museum collecting today, 2018; (ed and contrib.) Westminster Abbey: a church in history, 2019; numerous contribs to other books and learned jls. *Recreations*: life, laughter. *Address*: Department of History, Dickinson Hall, Princeton University, NJ 08544, USA. *E*: david.cannadine@sas.ac.uk; British Academy, 10–11 Carlton House Terrace, SW1Y 5AH. *Clubs*: Athenæum, Brooks's; Norfolk (Norwich); Century (NY).

**CANNAN, (John) David (Qualtrough);** Speaker, House of Keys, Isle of Man, 2000–01; MHK (Ind) Michael, 1982–2011; *b* 24 Aug. 1936; *s* of Rev. Canon Charles Alfred Cannan and Mary Eleanor Cannan (*née* Qualtrough); *m* 1966, Patricia Mary, *d* of Bernard and Jean Roberts, Taranaki, NZ; three *s* one *d*. *Educ*: King William's Coll., IOM. Martin's Bank, IOM, 1953–54; Nat. Service, RA, 1954–56; tea and rubber industries, Ceylon, 1956–61, Malaya, 1961–67; business interests, Berks, 1967–79. Mem. (C), Bradfield DC, 1970–74; returned to IOM, 1980; Minister for Treasury, 1986–89; Chm., Financial Supervision Commn, 1987–89; Vice-Chm., Public Accounts Commn, 1997–2000. *Recreations*: gardening, bee-keeping, Manx history. *Address*: White Gables, Curragh Road, Ballaugh, Isle of Man IM7 5BG. *T:* and *Fax*: (01624) 897926. *E*: whitegables@manx.net.

**CANNELL, Prof. Robert Quirk;** Director, Virginia Agricultural Experiment Station and Associate Dean for Research, Virginia Polytechnic Institute and State University, 1994–99, now Emeritus; *b* 20 March 1937; *s* of William Watterson Cannell and Norah Isabel Corjeag; *m* 1962, Edwina Anne Thornborough; two *s*. *Educ*: King's Coll., Newcastle upon Tyne; Univ. of Durham (BSc, PhD). FRSB (FIBiol 1986). Shell Chemical Co., London, 1959; School of Agriculture, Univ. of Newcastle upon Tyne, 1961; Dept of Agronomy and Plant Genetics, Univ. of Minnesota, 1968–69; Letcombe Lab., AFRC, Oxon, 1970; Dir, Welsh Plant Breeding Station, Aberystwyth, 1984–87; Head of Crop and Soil Envmtl Scis Dept, Virginia Polytech. Inst. and State Univ., 1987–94. *Publications*: papers in agricultural science jls. *Address*: Berk, Peel Road, Kirk Michael, Isle of Man IM6 1AP. *T*: (01624) 878039. *E*: robertcannell@manx.net.

**CANNELL, Sheila Elizabeth;** Director, Library Services, 2003–12, and Deputy Head, Information Services, 2007–12, University of Edinburgh; *b* 2 Oct. 1951; *d* of late Prof. Ernest and Sadie Best; *m* 1981, Peter Malcolm Cannell; one *s*. *Educ*: Univ. of Edinburgh (MA Hons); Univ. of Sheffield (MA Librarianship). Asst Librarian, Univ. of Glasgow, 1975–85; Medical Librarian, 1985–98, Dep. Librarian, 1998–2003, Univ. of Edinburgh. Project Dir, Enhancing Res. Infrastructure in Scotland, 2009–12. Member: Mgt Cttee, Scottish Liby and Inf. Council, 1994–97 and 2004–09; Res. Libraries UK (formerly Consortium of Univ. and Res. Libraries Bd), 2007–12 (Treas., 2009–12); Steering Gp, Scottish Higher Educn Digital Liby, 2007–12; Steering Gp, Designing Libraries, 2008–11; Council, Edinburgh City of Literature, 2013–; Chair: Wkg Gp on Space, SCONUL, 2006–11; Scottish Confedn of Univ. and Res. Libraries, 2007–09; Jt Chm., Bd, Scottish Digital Liby Consortium, 1999–2012. Director: My Edinburgh Life Ltd, 2014–; Scotland in Union, 2015–. Researcher, Scottish Love in Action, 2013– (Trustee, 2016–). Trustee, Edinburgh City of Literature, 2005–13. FRSA 2007. *Publications*: (contrib.) How to do it, 2nd edn 1985; (ed) World Book Day 2004: celebration of the book by members of the University of Edinburgh, 2004; (contrib.) University libraries and space in the digital world, 2013; contribs to Jl of Librarianship, Library Assoc. Record, Health Libraries Rev., Program, Univ. of Edinburgh Jl, Alexandria. *Recreations*: gardening, music, family life. *E*: sheila.cannell@googlemail.com.

**CANNING,** family name of **Baron Garvagh**.

**CANNING, Hugh Donaldson;** Music Critic, The Sunday Times, since 1989; *b* 28 May 1954; *s* of David Donaldson Canning and Olga Mary Canning (*née* Simms). *Educ*: Oakham Sch.; Pembroke Coll., Oxford (BA). Freelance music critic, 1979–87; Music Critic: London Daily News, 1987; The Guardian, 1987–89; Opera Critic, The Listener. Critic of Year Award, Brit. Press Awards, 1994. *Recreations*: music, theatre, tennis, food, gossip. *Address*: c/o The Sunday Times, 1 London Bridge Street, SE1 9GF.

**CANNING, Iain;** film producer; Co-Founder, Producer and Joint Managing Director, See-Saw Films Ltd, since 2008; *b* Bristol, 23 July 1979; *s* of John Canning and Alexis King (*née* Wilson). *Educ*: Univ. of Cardiff (BA Journalism, Film and Broadcasting). Develt and Logistics Co-ordinator, South West Film Commn, 1999–2000; Renaissance Films: Develt and Mktg Manager, 2000–01; Develt and Acquisitions Exec., 2001–03; Hd, Develt, Acquisitions and Prodn, 2003–05; Hd, Sales and Acquisitions, Becker International and Dendy Films, 2005–08. *Address*: See-Saw Films Ltd, 3rd Floor, 45 Folgate Street, E1 6GL. *T*: (020) 3301 6268. *E*: info@see-saw-films.com.

**CANNING, Mark,** CMG 2009; HM Diplomatic Service, retired; corporate adviser; Ambassador to Indonesia (and concurrently to Association of South East Nations and to East Timor), 2011–14; *b* 15 Dec. 1954; *s* of late John Canning, OBE and of Paula Canning; *m* 2004, Cecilia Kenny; one *d*. *Educ*: Downside Sch.; University Coll. London (BA (Hons)); MBA 2003. First Sec., FCO, 1988–93; First Sec. (Commercial), Jakarta, 1993–97; First Sec., FCO, 1997–2001; Counsellor, FCO, 2001; Dep. High Comr, Kuala Lumpur, 2002–06; Ambassador to Burma/Myanmar, 2006–09; Ambassador to Zimbabwe, 2009–11. *Recreations*: cooking, reading, hiking, fishing. *Address*: 50 Belgrave Square North, Rathmines, Dublin 6, Ireland. *E*: markcanning@aldwickpartners.com.

**CANNON, Jane Elizabeth,** MBE 2003; Director, Transition, Cannon Electronics and Automation Ltd, since 2017; *b* UK, 15 Nov. 1964; *d* of Edgar David Cannon and Barbara Mary Cannon; *m* 2000, Ian Gould; twin *d*. *Educ*: Herts and Essex High Sch.; University Coll. London (BSc Engrg); Open Univ. (MBA Technol. Mgt). FIET 2003. Tech. Dir, Cannon Electronics and Automation Ltd, 1988–99; Hd, BT Internat., BT plc, 1999–2004; Gp Dir, Strategy and Planning, 2004–06, Man. Dir, Security Solutions, 2006–08, QinetiQ; Gp Man. Dir, UK Inf. Systems and Global Services, Lockheed Martin, 2008–10; Partner, Advisory, Ernst & Young, 2010–13; Exec. in Residence, Amadeus Capital Partners Ltd, 2013–15; Dir, Security Industry Engagement, Home Office, 2015–17. CEO, SCARS Campaign, 2019–. Fellow, UCL, 2009. Col, Engr and Logistics Staff Corps, 2015–. *Recreations*: mental health campaigning, horse riding. *Address*: Cambridge. *T*: 07860 810485. *E*: gould.cannon@btinternet.com.

**CANNON, Mark Rennison Norris;** QC 2008; *b* 9 June 1961; *s* of late Brian Norris Cannon and Ann Buckham Cannon (*née* Williams). *Educ*: St Dunstan's Coll., London; Lincoln Coll., Oxford (BA Mod. Hist. 1983); Robinson Coll., Cambridge (Pt 1B Law Tripos 1984). Called to the Bar: Middle Temple, 1985, Bencher, 2012; NI, 2014; in practice as a barrister, 1986–. *Publications*: (ed) Jackson & Powell on Professional Liability, 3rd edn 1992 to 8th edn 2016; (with B. McGurk) Professional Indemnity Insurance, 2010, 2nd edn 2016. *Recreations*: ski-ing, history, wine, Italy. *Address*: 95 Portland Road, W11 4LN; Brinshope House, Wigmore, Leominster, Herefordshire HR6 9UR; 4 New Square, Lincoln's Inn, WC2A 3RJ. *Clubs*: Buck's, Oxford and Cambridge.

**CANNON, Nicholas,** OBE 2002; HM Diplomatic Service; Ambassador to Republic of Albania, 2012–16; *b* 29 May 1958; *m* 1982, Alice Cheung; two *s*. Entered FCO, 1988; Desk Officer, Econ. Relns Dept, 1988, Hong Kong Dept, 1989, FCO; Third, later Second Sec., Paris, 1990–92; Desk Officer, EC Dept (Ext.), FCO, 1992–93; Turkish lang. trng, 1993–94; Second Sec. (Pol/Commercial), Nicosia, 1994–97; Hd, Gibraltar Sect., Southern Eur. Dept, FCO, 1997–2000; First Sec. and Hd, Pol Sect., Islamabad, 2000–02; Asst Private Sec., Prime Minister's Office (on secondment), 2003–04; Iraq Directorate, FCO, 2004; Dep. Hd, Africa Dept (Southern), FCO, 2004–07; Ambassador, then High Comr, Republic of Rwanda, 2008–11. *Address*: c/o Foreign and Commonwealth Office, King Charles Street, SW1A 2AH.

**CANNON, Prof. Paul Stephen,** OBE 2014; PhD; FREng; FIET; Professor of Radio Science and Systems, University of Birmingham, since 2013; *b* Enfield, Middx, 28 Oct. 1953; *s* of late John James Peter Cannon and Betty Cannon (*née* Carter); *m* 1976, Vivian Avis Goodwin; one *s* one *d*. *Educ*: Edmonton County Grammar Sch.; Univ. of Southampton (BSc 1975; MSc 1976; PhD 1981). FREng 2003. Res. Asst, Space Radio Physics Gp, Southampton Univ., 1978–79; Sen. Communications Engr, Marconi Space Systems, 1979–81; HSO, 1981–83, SSO, 1983–86, PSO, 1986–89, Royal Aerospace (formerly Aircraft) Establishment; Vis. Scientist, Center for Atmospheric Res., Univ. of Mass, Lowell, 1989–90; Fellow, DERA, 1993–2002; Qinetiq: Tech. Dir, Communications Dept, 2000–04; Sen. Fellow, 2002–13; Chief Scientist, Communications Div., 2004–08; Univ. Partnership Dir, 2004–05; Dir, Poynting Inst., Univ. of Birmingham, 2011–13. Prof. of Communications and Atmospheric Scis (pt-time), Univ. of Bath, 1998–2011. Member: DSAC, 2014–17; Strategy Wkg Gp, ICSU, 2017–18. Pres., URSI, 2014–17 (Mem. Bd, 2017–Sept. 2020; Fellow). Editor, Radio Sci. Jl, 2009–14. *Publications*: articles in learned jls. *Recreations*: photography, travelling, American presidential history. *Address*: School of Engineering, University of Birmingham, Edgbaston, Birmingham B15 2TT. *T*: (0121) 414 4323, 07990 564772. *E*: p.cannon@bham.ac.uk.

**CANNON, Richard,** RIBA, FRIAS; RSA 2007; Consultant, Elder & Cannon Architects, since 2009 (Partner, 1980–2006; Director, 2006–09); *b* 18 Nov. 1943; *s* of Richard Cannon and Clara Cannon (*née* Benassi); *m* 1971, Angela Boyle; two *s* one *d*. *Educ*: Duncan of Jordanstone Coll. of Art. RIBA 1974; FRIAS 1986. Work on schs prog., Lanark Co. Architects, 1970–80. Major projects include: Ingram Sq. Develt, Glasgow, 1991 (Civic Trust Scotland Award); St Aloysius Jun. Sch., Glasgow, 1999 (RIBA and Glasgow Inst. of Archts Awards); Homes for the Future, Glasgow, 2000 (awards from RIBA, Glasgow Inst. of Archts, Civic Trust, Saltire Soc.; Regeneration of Scotland Supreme Award); Clavius Maths, Science and Technology Building, 2004 (Best Scottish Building Award, RIAS; awards from RIBA and Glasgow Inst. of Archts); Castlemilk Stables Block, Glasgow, 2008 (Best Scottish Building Award, RIAS). Gold Medal for Architecture, Royal Scottish Acad., 1991; (jtly) Lifetime Achievement Award for Architecture, Scottish Design Awards, 2010.

*Publications:* contribs to numerous architectural jls and books. *Recreation:* travel in Italy. *Address:* Elder & Cannon, 40 Berkeley Street, Glasgow G3 7DW. *T:* (0141) 204 1833, *Fax:* (0141) 204 1844. *E:* d.cannon@elder-cannon.co.uk.

**CANNON, Richard Walter,** CEng, FIET; Joint Managing Director, 1977–83, Managing Director, 1980–83, Cable and Wireless plc; retired; *b* 7 Dec. 1923; *s* of Richard William Cannon and Lily Harriet Cannon (*née* Fewins); *m* 1949, Dorothy (formerly Jarvis); two *d. Educ:* Eltham Coll. Joined Cable and Wireless Ltd, 1941; Exec. Dir, 1973. Director: Batelco (Bahrain), 1981–90; Teletswana (Botswana), 1984–86. *Publications:* several telecommunications papers for IEE and IERE.

**CANNON, Stephen Robert,** MBE 2016; FRCS; Honorary Consultant Orthopaedic Surgeon, Royal National Orthopaedic Hospital, Stanmore, since 1988; Vice President, Royal College of Surgeons of England, 2014–17; *b* Sheffield, 8 Feb. 1950; *s* of Arthur Cannon and Adeline Cannon; *m* 1975, Doreen Catherine Clancy; one *s* two *d. Educ:* Firth Park Grammar Sch., Sheffield; Trinity Coll., Cambridge (BA 1971; MB BChir 1974); Middlesex Hosp. Med. Sch.; Univ. of Liverpool (MChOrth 1985). FRCS 1979. Sen. Orthopaedic Registrar, Middx Hosp., 1983–88; Consultant Orthopaedic Surgeon, Edgware Gen. Hosp., 1988–96. Orthopaedic Advr to FA, 1991–2005. President: British Orthopaedic Assoc., 2008–09; Eur. Fedn of Nat. Assocs of Orthopaedics and Traumatol., 2014–15. Mem. Council, RCS, 2008–17. Chm., Skeletal Cancer Action Trust, 2002–; Trustee, Newman Foundn, 2012–. *Publications:* (contrib.) Oxford Textbook of Oncology, 1995, 2nd edn 2002; (contrib.) Oxford Textbook of Orthopaedics and Traumatology, 2002; (section ed) European Surgical Orthopaedics and Traumatology, 2014; contrib. chapters on orthopaedic oncol. in many textbooks; over 120 articles on knee pathol. and orthopaedic oncol. *Recreations:* golf, tennis, National Hunt racing, theatre. *Address:* St Giles Lodge, Amersham Road, Chalfont St Giles, Bucks HP8 4RZ. *T:* (01494) 872440. *E:* cannon.frcs@gmail.com.

**CANNON, Prof. Thomas;** Professor of Strategic Development, and Special Adviser to the Vice Chancellor, University of Liverpool, 2009–15, now Professor Emeritus; Mercers' School Memorial Professor of Commerce, Gresham College, 1996–2000, now Emeritus; *b* 20 Nov. 1945; *s* of Albert and Bridget Cannon; *m* 1971, Frances Cannon (*née* Constable); one *s* one *d. Educ:* St Francis Xavier's Grammar Sch., Liverpool; Borough Polytechnic. BSc (Hons) Sociology (London Univ. external degree). Res. Associate, Warwick Univ., 1969–71; Lectr, Middlesex Poly., 1971–72; Products Man., Imperial Gp, 1972–74; Lectr, Durham Univ., 1975–81; Prof., Univ. of Stirling, 1981–89; Dir, 1989–92, Vis. Prof., 1992–95, Manchester Business Sch.; Associate Rector, Hajioannion Univ., Cyprus, 1993–94. Visiting Professor: Kingston Univ., 1993–; Bradford Univ., 1997–2004; Middlesex Univ., 1997–. Chief Exec., MDE Services, 1982; Director: Stirling Gp, 1993–99; HIT Ltd, 2006–09; Thoroughbred Industries MBA, Univ. of Liverpool, 2015–16; Chief Executive: Mgt Charter Initiative, 1995–2001; Respect London Ltd, 2001–06; Ideopolis Internat. Ltd, 2004–17. Member: ESRC; Industry, Environment and Economy R&D Gp, 1990–92; Jt Cttee, ESRC/SERC, 1990–94; Business Links Gp, 1993–94; Chairman: Jt Working Party, Scottish Examinations Bd, 1988–90; Rail Users Consultative Cttee for NW, 1996–97; Dep. Chm., Management Develt to the Millennium, Inst. of Management, 1992–95. Member: Quality Standard Cttee, NCVO, 1997–99; BBC Educn Council, 1998–2000. Trustee: CAPITB Trust, 2000–14; ITB Pension Trust, 2004–08. FCGI; FRSA. Hon. Dr, Vietnam Nat. Univ. Man. Editor, New Academy Rev., 2001–04. *Publications:* Advertising Research, 1972; Distribution Research, 1973; Advertising: the economic implications, 1974; Basic Marketing, 1976, 6th edn 1998; How to Win Profitable Business, 1983; How to Win Business Overseas, 1984; Enterprise, 1991; The World of Business, 1991; Women as Entrepreneurs, 1992; Corporate Responsibility, 1993; (ed jtly) The Times Good University Guide, 1994; How to Get Ahead in Business, 1994; The Guinness Book of Business Records, 1996; Welcome to the Revolution, 1998; The Good Sales Manager's Guide; The Ultimate Book of Business Breakthroughs, 2000; Football Finance After the Revolution, 2005; Corporate Responsibility: new issues and challenges, 2015; papers in learned jls. *Recreations:* soccer, supporting Everton FC, walking, writing, travel, horse racing, my grandchildren. *Address:* 13 Old Broadway, Manchester M20 3DH. *T:* (0161) 434 2989.

**CANNON-BROOKES, Peter,** PhD; FMA, FIIC; international museum consultant; *b* 23 Aug. 1938; *s* of late Victor Montgomery Cannon Brookes and Nancy Margaret (*née* Markham Carter); *m* 1966, Caroline Aylmer, *d* of John Aylmer Christie-Miller; one *s* one *d. Educ:* Bryanston; Trinity Hall, Cambridge (MA); Courtauld Inst. of Art, Univ. of London (PhD). FMA 1975. Gooden and Fox Ltd, London, 1963–64; Keeper, Dept of Art, City Museums and Art Gall., Birmingham, 1965–78; Sessional Teacher in History of Art, Courtauld Inst. of Art, London, 1966–68; Keeper of Dept of Art, Nat. Mus. of Wales, Cardiff, 1978–86; Mus. Services Dir, STIPPLE Database Services, 1986–90. Internat. Council of Museums: Mem. Exec. Bd, UK Cttee, 1973–81; Pres., Internat. Art Exhibns Cttee, 1977–79 (Dir, 1974–80; Sec., 1975–77); Dir, Conservation Cttee, 1975–81 (Vice Pres., 1978–81). Member: Town Twinning Cttee, Birmingham Internat. Council, 1968–83; Birm. Diocesan Synod, 2000–06; Birm. DAC for Care of Churches, 1972–78; Edgbaston Deanery Synod, 1970–78 (Lay Jt Chm., 1975–78); Abingdon Deanery Synod, 2000–06, 2009–; Oxford Dio. Synod, 2003–06; Oxford Dio. Bd of Educn, 2004–06. Member: Society of Authors, 1972–; Chartered Inst. Journalists, 1972–; Art and Design Adv. Panel, Welsh Jt Educn Cttee, 1978–86; Welsh Arts Council, 1979–84 (Member: Art Cttee, 1978–84; Craft Cttee, 1983–87); Projects and Orgns Cttee, Crafts Council, 1985–87. President: Welsh Fedn of Museums and Art Galleries, 1980–82; S Wales Art Soc., 1980–87. Trustee: Welsh Sculpture Trust, 1981–94; Bosnia-Herzegovina Heritage Rescue, 1992–99; Consultant Curator, Tabley House Collection, Manchester Univ., 1988–. Jt Editor, Museum Management and Curatorship, 1981–2003 (Founder Editor, 2003–). Freeman 1969, Liveryman 1974, Worshipful Co. of Goldsmiths. FRSA. JP Birmingham, 1973–78, Cardiff, 1978–82. Prize, Masaryk Acad. of Arts, Prague, 1998. *Publications:* (with H. D. Molesworth) European Sculpture, 1964; (with C. A. Cannon-Brookes) Baroque Churches, 1969; Omar Ramsden, 1973; Lombard Painting, 1974; After Gulbenkian, 1976; The Cornbury Park Bellini, 1977; Michael Ayrton, 1978; Emile Antoine Bourdelle, 1983; Ivor Roberts-Jones, 1983; Czech Sculpture 1800–1938, 1983; Paintings from Tabley, 1989; The Painted Word, 1991; William Redgrave, 1998; The Godolphin Arabian, 2004; Pantaloon, 2011; contrib. Apollo, Art Bull., Arte Veneta, Burlington Mag., Connoisseur, Internat. Jl of Museum Management and Curatorship, and Museums Jl. *Recreations:* photography, growing vegetables, cooking. *Address:* Thrupp Farm, Abingdon, Oxon OX14 3NE. *T:* (01235) 520595. *E:* cannonbrookesassociates@gmail.com. *Club:* Athenæum.

**CANTER, Prof. David Victor,** PhD; Professor of Psychology and Director, International Research Centre for Investigative Psychology (formerly International Centre for Investigative Psychology), University of Huddersfield, since 2009; *b* 5 Jan. 1944; *s* of late Hyman Victor Canter and Coralie Lilian Canter (*née* Hyam); *m* 1967, Sandra Lorraine Smith; one *s* two *d. Educ:* Liverpool Collegiate Grammar Sch.; Liverpool Univ. (BA Hons 1964; PhD 1969); Univ. of Huddersfield (MA 2015). Research Associate, Liverpool Univ., 1964–65; Strathclyde University: Res. Associate, 1966; Res. Fellow, Building Performance Res. Unit, 1967–70; Lectr, 1971–72; University of Surrey: Lectr, 1972–78; Reader, 1978–83; Prof. of Applied Psychology, 1983–87; Prof. of Psychology, 1987–94; Hd of Dept of Psychology, 1987–91; University of Liverpool: Prof. of Psychology, 1994–2009, now Emeritus; Dir, Centre for Investigative Psychology, 1996–2009. Managing Editor: Jl of Envmtl Psychology, 1981–2001; Jl of Investigative Psychology and Offender Profiling, 2004–15; Ed., Jl of Contemporary Social Sci. (formerly Jl of 21st Century Soc.), 2010–. Writer and presenter, TV documentary series Mapping Murder, 2002. CPsychol 1988; FAPA; FRSocMed 2009; FHEA 2012; FAcSS. Mem., Forensic Sci. Soc. Hon. Mem., Japanese Inst. of Architects, 1971. Hon. FBPsS 2008. Hon. Fellow, Psychol Soc. of S Africa, 1998. Freedom, City of Quito, 1983. Life Time Achievement Award, Alliant Univ., Calif, 2011. *Publications:* Architectural Psychology, 1970; Psychology for Architects, 1974; (ed jtly) Psychology and the Built Environment, 1974; Environmental Interaction, 1975; (with P. Stringer) Psychology of Place, 1977; (ed jtly) Designing for Therapeutic Environments, 1979; (ed jtly) Fires and Human Behaviour, 1980, 2nd edn 1990; (ed jtly) Psychology in Practice, 1982; (ed) Facet Theory, 1985; (ed jtly) The Research Interview, 1985; (ed jtly) Environmental Perspectives, 1988; (ed jtly) Environmental Policy, Assessment and Communication, 1988; (ed jtly) New Directions in Environmental Participation, 1988; (ed jtly) Environmental Social Psychology, 1988; (with M. Comber and D. Uzzell) Football in its Place, 1989; (ed jtly) Empirical Approaches to Social Representations, 1992; Criminal Shadows: inside the mind of the serial killer (Golden Dagger Award, Anthony Award), 1994; (jtly) The Faces of Homelessness, 1995; Psychology in Action, 1996; (ed jtly) Criminal Detection and the Psychology of Crime, 1997; (ed jtly) Profiling in Policy and Practice, 1999; Interviewing and Deception, 1999; The Social Psychology of Crime, 2000; Profiling Property Crimes, 2000; Mapping Murder, 2003; (with G. Fairbairn) Becoming an Author, 2006; (with D. Youngs) Geographical Offender Profiling, vols 1 and 2, 2008; (with R. Zukauskiene) Psychology and Law, 2008; Criminal Psychology, 2008, 2nd edn 2017; The Faces of Terrorism, 2009; (jtly) Safer Sex in the City, 2009; (with D. Youngs) Investigative Psychology: offender profiling and the analysis of criminal action, 2009; Forensic Psychology: a very short introduction, 2010; Forensic Psychology for Dummies, 2012; (ed jtly) Biologising the Social Sciences, 2014; Social Science Perspectives on Climate Change, 2015; Criminal Psychology, 2017; contribs to learned jls, newspapers, radio, TV. *Recreations:* clarinet, musical composition, horticulture. *Address:* Rupert Crew Ltd, 6 Windsor Road, N3 3SS. *T:* (020) 8346 3000.

**CANTERBURY, Archbishop of,** since 2013; **Most Rev. and Rt Hon. Justin Portal Welby;** PC 2013; *b* 6 Jan. 1956; *m* 1979, Caroline Eaton; two *s* three *d* (and one *d* decd). *Educ:* Eton Coll.; Trinity Coll., Cambridge (BA 1978; Hon. Fellow 2015); St John's Coll., Durham (BA 1991). Manager, Project Finance, Société Nationale Elf Aquitaine, Paris, 1978–83; Treas., Elf UK, 1983–84; Gp Treas., Enterprise Oil plc, 1984–89; ordained deacon, 1992, priest, 1993; Curate, All Saints, Chilvers Coton, Nuneaton, with St Mary the Virgin, Astley, 1992–95; Rector: St James, Southam, 1995–2002; St Michael and All Angels, Ufton, 1996–2002; Coventry Cathedral: Co-Dir of Internat. Ministry and Canon Residentiary, 2002–05; Sub-Dean and Canon for Reconciliation Ministry, 2005–07; Dean of Liverpool, 2007–11; Bishop of Durham, 2011–13. Non-exec. Dir, S Warwicks Gen. Hosps NHS Trust, 1998–2000 (Chm., 2000–02). Mem., Cttee of Reference, F&C Stewardship Funds, 2006–13 (Chm., 2010–13). Mem., ACT, 1983. *Publications:* Can Companies Sin?, 1992; (contrib.) The Role of Large Enterprises in Democracy and Society, 2010; (contrib.) Just Reconciliation: the practice and morality of making peace, 2011; Dethroning Mammon: making money serve grace, 2016; Reimagining Britain: foundations for hope, 2018; numerous articles on treasury mgt, finance and ethics, and reconciliation. *Recreations:* anything French, sailing. *Address:* Lambeth Palace, SE1 7JU.

**CANTERBURY, Dean of;** *see* Willis, Very Rev. R. A.

**CANTLAY, Michael Brian,** OBE 2015; Chair: Scottish Funding Council, since 2017; Scottish Natural Heritage, since 2017; William Glen & Son, since 1982; William Glen Ltd, since 1993; *b* Galashiels, 2 Feb. 1964; *s* of Alan and Daphne Cantlay; *m* 1997, Linda McCombe; one *s* one *d. Educ:* McLaren High Sch., Callander; Strathclyde Univ. (BA 1985; MBA 1989). Pres., William Glen & Son, San Francisco, 1995–; Chair, William Glen & Son Canada Ltd (formerly Cairngorm Scottish Imports), Toronto, 1997–. Chm., Highlands & Islands Airports Ltd, 2016–17 (Mem., Audit Cttee, 1999–2005; non-exec. Dir, 2009–14); Non-executive Director: Airport Mgt Services Ltd, 2009–14; Dundee Airport Ltd, 2009–14. Chair: Forth Valley Enterprise, 1995–2001; VisitScotland, 2010–16 (Dep. Chair, 2001–05); Mem. Adv. Bd, Scottish Enterprise, 2000–02. Mem. Bd, VisitBritain, 2010–16. Convenor, Loch Lomond and The Trossachs Nat. Park Authy, 2006–11. Chair, Forth Valley Coll., 2005–09. Mem., Callander and Dist Round Table. DUniv Stirling, 2003. *Recreations:* golf, hill running, percussion. *Address:* Callandrade, Callander, Perthshire FK17 8HW. *T:* (01877) 339999. *E:* mike@williamglen.co.uk. *Clubs:* Dun Whinny Golf, Callander Golf.

**CANTLE, Edward Francis,** CBE 2004; DL; Director, iCoCo Foundation CIC, since 2012; *b* 12 Feb. 1950; *s* of John Victor Cantle and Isabel Ruth Cantle; *m* 1974, Heather Ann Welburn; two *d. Educ:* Shooters Hill Grammar Sch., London; Portsmouth Poly. (BSc Hons); Dip. Housing 1978. FCIH 1986 (Hon. Life Mem., 2005). Housing Advr, 1972–73, Area Improvement Officer, 1973–74, Manchester CC; Asst Chief Housing Officer, 1974–80, Chief Housing Officer, 1980–83, City of Wakefield; Under Sec., AMA, 1983–88; Dir of Housing, Leicester City, 1988–90; Chief Exec., City of Nottingham, 1990–2001. Prof., Inst. of Community Cohesion, Coventry Univ., 2005–12. Associate Dir, Improvement and Develt Agency, subseq. Local Govt Improvement and Develt, 2001–11; Chairman: DETR Local Govt Construction Task Force, 1999–2002; Community Cohesion Ind. Review Team, 2001–04 (reported on racial disturbances in northern towns and cities, 2001; final report, 2006); Integration of New and Renewable Energy in Buildings, Faraday Partnership, 2004–07. Mem. Bd, EA, 2000–08 (Dep. Chm., 2005–08). Chm., Queen's Medical Centre, Nottingham Univ. Hosp. NHS Trust, 2001–06. Chm., Nottingham and Notts Co. Sports Partnership, 2006–12. Chairman: Sustainability First (charity), 1999–2018; Nottingham Castle Trust, 2012–; Cohesion and Integration Network (charity), 2018–. Vis. Prof., Business Sch., Nottingham Trent Univ., 2003–; Hon. Prof., Nottingham Univ., 2011–. DL Notts, 2004. Hon. LLD: Portsmouth, 2006; Nottingham, 2018; DUniv Oxford Brookes, 2006. *Publications:* Community Cohesion: a new framework for race and diversity, 2005, 2nd edn 2008; Interculturalism: the new era of cohesion and diversity, 2012; contrib. AMA studies, incl. Defects in Housing series; contrib. various chapters in academic books; numerous contribs to academic jls and specialist press. *Recreations:* sports, including walking, tennis and golf. *W:* www.tedcantle.co.uk.

**CANTOR, Anthony John James;** HM Diplomatic Service, retired; Ambassador to Armenia, 2006–08; *b* 1 Feb. 1946; *s* of late John Stanley Frank Cantor and Olive Mary Cantor (*née* McCartney); *m* 1968, Patricia Elizabeth Naughton; one *s* two *d. Educ:* Bournemouth Grammar Sch. Joined Diplomatic Service, 1965; FCO, 1965–68; Rangoon, 1968–71; Japanese lang. trng, Sheffield Univ., 1971–72, Tokyo, 1972–73; Third, then Second, Sec., Tokyo, 1973–76; Accra, 1977–80; Aid Policy Dept, 1980–82, W Indian and Atlantic Dept, 1982–83, FCO; Consul (Commercial), Osaka, 1983–89; Dep. Hd of Mission, Hanoi, 1990–92; Dep. Dir, Invest UK, 1992–94; First Sec., Tokyo, 1994–95; Dep. Consul-Gen., Osaka, 1995–98; EU Dept (Bilateral), FCO, 1999–2000; Dep. Comr-

Gen., UK Pavilion, Hanover, 2000; Public Diplomacy Dept, FCO, 2000–01; Ambassador to Paraguay, 2001–05. Meetings Sec., Britain-Burma Soc. *Recreations:* travel, languages, World War II in Asia. *Club:* Kobe (Japan).

**CANTOR, Prof. Brian,** CBE 2013; PhD; FREng; FIMMM; FInstP; Vice-Chancellor, University of Bradford, 2013–19; *b* 11 Jan. 1948; *s* of Oliver Horace Cantor and Gertrude Mary Cantor (*née* Thompson); *m* 1st, 1967, Margaret Elaine Pretty (marr. diss. 1979); two *s*; 2nd, 1981, Anne Catherine Sharry (*d* 1993); 3rd, 2016, Gill Partridge. *Educ:* Manchester Grammar Sch.; Christ's Coll., Cambridge (BA, MA, PhD 1972). CEng 1979, FREng (FEng 1998); FIMMM (FIM 1989); FRMS 1993–2003; FInstP 1999. Res. Fellow, Sch. of Engrg, Sussex Univ., 1972–81; Oxford University: Lectr, 1981–91, Reader in Materials Processing, 1991–95, Head, 1995–2000, Dept of Materials; Cookson Prof. of Materials, 1995–2002; Head, Div. of Math. and Physical Scis, 2000–02; Sen. Res. Fellow, Jesus Coll., 1987–95; Fellow, St Catherine's Coll., 1995–2002; Founder and Dir, Oxford Centre for Advanced Materials and Composites, 1990–95; Founder and Academic Dir, Begbroke Sci. Park, 1998–2002; Vice-Chancellor, Univ. of York, 2002–13. Visiting Fellow: Northeastern Univ., 1977; Washington State Univ., 1988; British Council Vis. Fellow, Banaras Hindu Univ., 1980; Industrial Fellow, GE Corporate Labs, Schenectady, NY, 1982. Chm. Bd, Amaethon, 2003–06; Dep. Chm. Bd, Yorkshire Innovation (formerly Yorkshire Science), 2005–10; Member, Board: Isis Innovation, 2000–02; White Rose, 2002–13 (Chm., 2007–11); Worldwide University Network, 2002–13; Yorkshire Univs, 2002– (Dep. Chm., 2011–13); Nat. Sci. Learning Centre, 2003–13 (Chm., 2003–04); York Economic Partnership, 2008–13; Leeds City Region LEP, 2011–13; Bradford Economic Partnership (formerly Producer City Bd), 2013–; Science Museum Gp, 2016–; Chm. Bd, People and Innovation Bradford, 2013–. Mem., Marshall Aid Commemoration Commn, 2016–. Dir, Univ. of York Pensions Trust Fund Ltd, 2002–13 (Chm., 2002–10); Chm., UUK/UCEA Employers Pension Forum, 2010–13. Consultant: Alcan Internat., Banbury Labs, Oxon, 1986–94; Rolls-Royce, 1996–2015. Mem., World Technol. Network, 2000–; Founder and Chm., World Technol. Univs Congress and Network, 2016–. Mem. Council, RAEng, 2009–13 (Vice Pres., 2010–13). Member, Board: Without Walls, 2003–13; UK Coll. of Business and Computing, 2015–17. Hon. Professor: Zhejiang Univ.; Nanjing Univ.; Northeastern Univ., Shenyang, 1996; Nat. Materials Inst., Chinese Acad. of Scis, 2000; India Inst. of Sci., Bangalore, 2013. CCMI 2008. Rosenhain Medal, 1993, Platinum Medal, 2002, IMMM; Lifetime Achievement Award, York Press, 2011. Editl Advr, Inst. of Physics Press, 1983–2006; Jt Ed., Progress in Materials Science, 1988–. *Publications:* (ed) Rapidly Quenched Metals III, 1978; (ed with P. B. Hirsch) Tribute to J. W. Christian, 1992; (jtly) Stability of Microstructure in Metallic Systems, 1997; (ed jtly) Aerospace Materials, 2001; (ed jtly) Solidification and Casting, 2003; (ed jtly) Metal and Ceramic Matrix Composites, 2004; Novel Nanocrystalline Alloys & Magnetic Nanomaterials, 2005. *Recreations:* mountain walking, playing the guitar, collecting modern art.

**CANTOR, Deborah;** *see* Klein, D.

**CANTRELL, Prof. Doreen Ann,** CBE 2014; FRS 2011; FRSE; FMedSci; Professor of Cellular Immunology, University of Dundee (Head, College of Life Sciences and Vice Principal, 2011); Wellcome Trust Principal Research Fellow, since 2012. Formerly Project Leader, Lymphocyte Activation Lab., ICRF. Mem., MRC, 2014–18. FMedSci 2000; FRSE 2005. *Publications:* contribs to scientific jls incl. Nature Immunol., Molecular Cell Biol., Jl Immunol., Biochem. Jl, Blood, Eur. Jl Immunol. *Address:* School of Life Sciences, University of Dundee, Dow Street, Dundee DD1 5EH.

**CANTRILL, Eilís Veronica;** *see* Ferran, E. V.

**CANTY, Brian George John,** CBE 1993 (OBE 1988); HM Diplomatic Service, retired; Governor of Anguilla, 1989–92; *b* 23 Oct. 1931; *s* of George Robert Canty and Phœbe Charlotte Canty (*née* Cobb); *m* 1954, Maureen Kathleen Kenny; one *s* one *d*. *Educ:* South West Essex Technical College; external student, London University (Social Studies); RAF Staff College (psc 1970). RN 1950; Air Ministry, 1957; Financial Adviser's Office, Cyprus, 1960; MoD (Air), 1963; FCO, 1971; served Oslo, 1973, Kingston, 1977, Vienna, 1979; FCO, 1984; Dep. Governor, Bermuda, 1986. Director: A. S. Trust Ltd, 1993–2006; St Helena Transhipment Services Ltd, 2002–06. JP Bermuda, 1986. *Publications:* (as Byron Casey) The Holy Loch Affair, 2006; The Lives of Brian (autobiog.), 2011. *Recreations:* travel, writing.

**CAPALDI, Nicholas;** Chief Executive, Arts Council of Wales, since 2008; *b* Lichfield, 25 July 1961; *s* of Nicholas and Norma Capaldi; *m* 1989, Lucy Marsh; one *s* one *d*. *Educ:* Chetham's Music Sch., Manchester (ARCM 1978); Royal Coll. of Music, London (Dip. RCM); City Univ., London (Dip. Arts Policy and Mgt). LRAM 1979. Performing pianist, 1982–88; South West Arts: Music Officer, 1988–89; Dir of Performing Arts, 1989–97; Chief Exec., 1997–2001; Chief Exec., Arts Council England SW, 2001–08. Chair, Arts 2000, 1999–2001; Member: Bd, Bristol Cultural Develt Partnership, 1996–2008; Bd, Culture SW, 2004–08. Hon. DA City, London, 2016. *Recreations:* reading, travel, watching sport (especially Rugby and cricket), blurring lines between work and leisure by taking every opportunity to enjoy arts. *Address:* Arts Council of Wales, Bute Place, Cardiff CF10 5AL. *T:* (029) 2044 1358, *Fax:* (029) 2044 1400. *E:* nick.capaldi@arts.wales.

**CAPE TOWN, Archbishop of,** and Metropolitan of Southern Africa, since 2008; **Most Rev. Dr Thabo Cecil Makgoba;** *b* S Africa, 15 Dec. 1960; *s* of Masilo and Kedibome Makgoba; *m* 1991, Lungi Manona; one *s* one *d*. *Educ:* St Paul's Coll., Grahamstown (DipTh 1989); Univ. of Witwatersrand (MEd 1993); Univ. of Cape Town (PhD 2009). Asst Priest, St Mary's Cathedral, Johannesburg, 1990–99; Priest-in-charge, St Albans Parish, 1993–99; Lectr, 1993–96, Chaplain, 1994–98, Univ. of Witwatersrand; Dean, Knockando Residence and Sen. Lectr, Witwatersrand Coll. of Educn, 1996–98; Rector and Archdeacon, Sophiatown, 1998–2002; Suffragan Bishop of Grahamstown, 2002–04; Bishop of Grahamstown, 2004–08. Mem., Design Gp, Lambeth Conf., 2008. Patron, Western Cape Religious Forum, 2010–. Chancellor, Univ. of Western Cape, 2012–. Involved with NGOs incl. Hope Africa, Anglican Aids Trust, Tshwaranang, Trevor Huddleston Meml Centre, 1999–; Patron: Africa for Haiti Campaign; Equal Educn and Social Justice Coalition. Patron to several children's homes and orphanages. Visitor to several church schs. Hon. DD Gen. Theol Seminary, Episcopal Ch in NY, 2009. KStJ 2018. Cross of St Augustine, 2008. *Publications:* Connectedness, 2005; Workplace Spirituality in a South African Mining Context, 2012; Faith and Courage: praying with Mandela, 2019; contrib. Jl of Anglican Studies. *Recreations:* reading theology, walking, writing, promoting leadership development. *Address:* 20 Bishopscourt Drive, Cape Town, 7708, South Africa. *E:* archpa@anglicanchurchsa.org.za.

**CAPECCHI, Prof. Mario Renato,** PhD; Professor of Human Genetics, since 1989, and Distinguished Professor of Human Genetics and Biology, since 1993, University of Utah School of Medicine; Investigator, Howard Hughes Medical Institute, since 1988; *b* Verona, Italy, 6 Oct. 1937; *s* of Luciano Capecchi and Lucy Ramberg; *m* Laurie Fraser; one *d*. *Educ:* George Sch., Philadelphia; Antioch Coll., Yellow Springs, Ohio (BS Chem. and Physics 1961); Harvard Univ. (PhD Biophysics 1967). Jun. Fellow, Soc. of Fellows, Harvard Univ., 1967–69; Asst Prof., 1969–71, Associate Prof., 1971–73, Harvard Med. Sch.; University of Utah: Prof. of Biol., 1973–; Adjunct Prof. of Oncol Scis, 1982–, Co-Chm., Dept of Human Genetics, 2002–08, Sch. of Medicine. Member: NAS, 1991; Eur. Acad. Scis, 2002. Albert Lasker Award, Lasker Foundn, 2001; Nat. Medal of Sci., USA, 2001; Wolf Prize in Medicine, Wolf Foundn, 2002/03; (jtly) Nobel Prize in Physiol. and Medicine, 2007. *Publications:* contributor: Regulation of Nucleic Acid and Protein Synthesis, 1967; RNA Phages, 1975; Mutations and tRNA Nonsense Suppressors, 1978; (and ed) Molecular Genetics of Early Drosophila and Mouse Development, 1989; Accomplishments in Cancer Research 1994, 1995; Molecular and Cellular Approaches to Neural Development, 1997; Engineering the Human Germline, 2000; contribs to learned jls. *Address:* University of Utah, 15 North 2030 East, Room 5440, Salt Lake City, UT 84112–5331, USA.

**CAPEL, Luke Thomas I.;** *see* Irvine-Capel.

**CAPELL,** family name of **Earl of Essex**.

**CAPELLA, Josephine Marie;** *see* Durning, J. M.

**CAPELLAS, Michael D.;** Founder and Chief Executive Officer, Capellas Partners LLC, since 2012; *m* Marie; two *c*. *Educ:* Kent State Univ. (BBA 1976). CPA. Systems analyst and manufg posts, Republic Steel Corp., 1976–81; Schlumberger Ltd, 1981–96: posts included Dir for Inf. Systems; Controller and Treas., Asia Pacific; Chief Financial Officer, Dowell Schlumberger Inc.; Ops Manager, Fairchild Semiconductor Unit; Founder, and Man. Partner, Benchmarking Partners, 1996; Dir of Supply Chain Mgt, SAP America, 1996–97; Sen. Vice-Pres. and Gen. Manager, Oracle Corp., 1997–98; Chief Inf. Officer, 1998–99, Chief Operating Officer, 1999, CEO, 1999–2002, Compaq Computer Corp.; Pres., Hewlett-Packard Co., 2002; CEO, 2002–06, Chm., 2002–04, and Pres., 2004–06, WorldCom, later MCI; Chm. and CEO, First Data, Colorado, 2007–10; CEO, 2010–11, Chm., 2011–12, VCE. Chm., Flex Ltd, 2017– (non-exec. Dir, 2014–); Dir, Cisco Systems Inc., 2006–; Senior Advisor: Silver Lake Partners, 2006; Kohlberg Kravis Roberts & Co., 2010; Mem. Adv. Bd, Kony Inc., 2015–; Dir, Mulesoft, 2015–18.

**CAPELLO, Fabio;** Head Coach, Jiangsu Suning Football Club, Nanjing, 2017–18; *b* San Canzian d'Isonzo, Italy, 18 June 1946; *s* of Guerrino and Evelina Capello; *m* Laura; two *c*. Footballer: SPAL, 1964–67 (youth team, 1963–64); Roma, 1967–70; Juventus, 1970–76; AC Milan, 1976–80; Italian Nat. Team, 1972–76 (32 appearances); football pundit, Italian TV; caretaker Manager, AC Milan, 1986–87; coach, Atalanta Bergamasca Calcio, 1987–89; Manager: AC Milan, 1991–96 (winner, UEFA Champions League, 1994); Real Madrid, 1996–97; AC Milan, 1997–98; Roma, 1999–2004; Juventus, 2004–06; Real Madrid, 2006–07; England Football Team, 2008–12; Russian Nat. Football Team, 2012–15. Sports Personality of Year Coach Award, BBC, 2009.

**CAPES, Mark Andrew;** HM Diplomatic Service, retired; Governor, St Helena, Ascension Island and Tristan da Cunha, 2011–16; *b* England, 1954; *m* 1980, Tamara Rossmanith; two *d*. Entered FCO, 1971; UK Repn, Brussels, 1974; Lisbon, 1975–79; Zagreb, 1978–80; Amman 1980; Commercial Attaché, Lagos, 1982–85; Third Sec. (Pol), Vienna, 1986–89; Second Sec. (Pol), FCO, 1989–91; Dep. Chief Sec., Providenciales, Turks and Caicos Is, 1991–94; First Secretary: (Econ. and Trade Policy), Wellington, 1994–99; Dep. Hd, Parly Relns and Devolution Dept, FCO, 1999; Deputy Governor: Anguilla, 2002–06; Bermuda, 2006–09; CEO, Turks and Caicos Is Interim Govt, 2009–11. *Recreations:* spending time with my family, relaxing in Croatia. *E:* zagorje2016@outlook.com.

**CAPEWELL, Lt Gen. Sir David (Andrew),** KCB 2014; OBE 2002; Chief of Joint Operations, 2011–14; *b* Huddersfield, 21 Aug. 1959; *s* of late Dennis Capewell and Greta Capewell (*née* Rhodes); *m* 1981, Deborah Joy Snookes; two *d*. *Educ:* Holme Valley Grammar Sch.; Canadian Forces Command and Staff Coll. Joined RM, 1979; COS 3 Cdo Bde, 1998–2000; CO 40 Cdo RM, 2000–02; COS UK Jt Force HQ, 2002–04; HCSC 2004; UK CDS Liaison Officer to US Chm. of Jt Chiefs, 2005; ACOS J3 PJHQ, 2005–07; Comdr, 3 Cdo Bde, 2007–08; Dep. Comdr, NATO RRC (Italy), 2008–10; ACDS (Ops), MoD, 2010–11. Pres., RM Rugby League Assoc., 2007–08. RN Hudson Vis. Fellow, Univ. of Oxford, 2015. *Publications:* UK Approach to Amphibious Operations, 1997. *Recreations:* hill-walking, military history, kite surfing.

**CAPEWELL, Vasanti Emily Indrani;** *see* Selvaratnam, V. E. I.

**CAPLAN, Prof. (Ann) Patricia (Bailey),** PhD; FRAI; Professor of Social Anthropology, Goldsmiths College, University of London, 1989–2003, now Emeritus; *b* 13 March 1942; *d* of Sylvester Launcelot Bailey and Marjorie Bailey (*née* Parr); *m* 1967, Prof. Lionel Caplan; one *s* one *d*. *Educ:* Sch. of Oriental and African Studies, Univ. of London (BA Hons African Studies 1963; MA Social Anthropology 1965; PhD 1968). Tutor: Birkbeck Coll., Univ. of London, 1964–65 and 1968–69; Open Univ., 1970–71 and 1974–75; Postdoctoral Fellow, SOAS, 1968–70 and 1974–76; Lectr, then Sen. Lectr, in Anthropology, Goldsmiths Coll., Univ. of London, 1977–89; Dir, Inst. of Commonwealth Studies, Univ. of London, 1998–2000. Chair, Assoc. of Social Anthropologists, 1997–2001. Trustee and Mem. Bd, Action Aid, 2006–09. *Publications:* Priests and Cobblers: social change in a Hindu village in Western Nepal, 1972; Choice and Constraint in a Swahili Community: property, hierarchy and cognatic descent on the East African Coast, 1975; (ed with J. Bujra) Women United, Women Divided: cross cultural perspectives on female solidarity, 1978; Class and Gender in India: women and their organisations in a South Indian city, 1985; (ed) The Cultural Construction of Sexuality, 1987; (ed with F. le Guennec-Coppens) Les Swahili entre Afrique et Arabie, 1992; (ed jtly) Gendered Fields: women, men and ethnography 1993; (ed) Understanding Disputes: the politics of law, 1995; African Voices, African Lives: personal narratives from a Swahili village, 1997; (ed) Food, Health and Identity: approaches from the social sciences, 1997; (ed) Risk Revisited, 2000; (ed) The Ethics of Anthropology, 2003; (ed jtly) Swahili Modernities, 2004; Mikidedi: individual biography and national history in Tanzania, 2016; numerous articles in learned jls. *Recreations:* swimming, walking, classical music, gardening. *Address:* Department of Anthropology, Goldsmiths, University of London, SE14 6NW. *T:* (020) 7919 7800, *Fax:* (020) 7919 7813. *E:* p.caplan@gold.ac.uk.

**CAPLAN, Jonathan Michael;** QC 1991; a Recorder, since 1995; *b* 11 Jan. 1951; *s* of Dr Malcolm Denis Caplan and late Jean Hilary Caplan, JP; *m* 1993, Selena Lennard (*née* Peskin); one *s*, and one step *s* one step *d*. *Educ:* St Paul's Sch.; Downing Coll., Cambridge (MA). MCIArb. Called to Bar, Gray's Inn, 1973, Bencher, 2000 (Master of Finance, 2018; Chm., Mgt Cttee, 2019). Asst Recorder, 1989–95. Mem., General Council of Bar, 1986–90; Chairman: Bar Council Report on Televising the Courts, 1989; Public Affairs Cttee, Bar Council, 1991–92. Mem., Broadcast and Publishing Standards Tribunal, Dubai, 2003–. Member: BBC Ind. Rev. Panel on documentaries, 1997; Develt Bd, Royal Court Theatre, 1997–2006. Chairman: BAFTA Management Ltd, 2003–17; BAFTA Hong Kong Adv. Bd, 2013–. Patron, Wiener Liby, 2006–. Mem. Editl Bd, Jl of Criminal Law, 1988–2005. *Publications:* The Confait Confessions, 1977; (contrib.) Disabling Professions, 1978. *Recreations:* writing, tennis, collecting historical newspapers and manuscripts, Khmer and Thai sculpture, cinema, ballet, books, flat horseracing, ufology. *Address:* 5 Paper Buildings, Temple, EC4Y 7HB. *T:* (020) 7583 6117. *Clubs:* Queen's, Alfred's.

**CAPLAN, Michael Geoffrey;** QC 2002; solicitor; Partner, Kingsley Napley LLP, 1982–2016, now Consultant; a Recorder, since 2000; a Deputy High Court Judge, since 2010; *b* 3 May 1953; *s* of late Alf and Hetty Caplan; *m* 1977, Jane Freedman; one *s* one *d*.

*Educ:* Henry Thornton Sch., Clapham; King's Coll., London (LLB Hons, AKC 1974). Qualified solicitor, 1977. An Asst Recorder, 1994–2000. Chm., Solicitors' Assoc. of Higher Court Advocates, 2001–03. A Chm., Police Appeals Tribunal, 2003–. Mem., Sentencing Council, 2013–16. Mem., Law Soc., 1977–. *Recreations:* reading, writing, sport. *Address:* Kingsley Napley LLP, Knights Quarter, 14 St John's Lane, EC1M 4AJ. *T:* (020) 7814 1200.

**CAPLAN, Patricia;** *see* Caplan, A. P. B.

**CAPLAN, Prof. Richard Dana,** PhD; Professor of International Relations, since 2006 and Director, Centre for International Studies, since 2009, University of Oxford; Fellow, Linacre College, Oxford, since 2003; *b* Waterbury, Conn, 31 May 1957; *s* of Leonard Caplan and Hilary Caplan; *m* 2001, Luisa Calè; one *s. Educ:* McGill Univ. (BA Hons 1980); King's Coll., Cambridge (MPhil 1996); Univ. of London (PhD 2000). Editor, World Policy Jl, 1986–92; Dep. Dir, Inst. for War and Peace Reporting, 1992–94; Research Fellow: Jesus Coll., Oxford, 1998–2001; Centre for Internat. Studies, Oxford, 2001–03; Lectr in Internat. Relns, Univ. of Reading, 2001–03; Univ. Lectr in Internat. Relns, Univ. of Oxford, 2003–06. Mem., Global Agenda Council on Fragile States, World Economic Forum, 2009–11. Res. Associate, IISS, 1999–2001. Specialist Advr, Select Cttee on Foreign Affairs, 1999–2001. Visiting Professor: Univ. of Konstanz, 2010; Princeton Univ., 2010; SciencesPo, Paris, 2018; Vis. Sen. Res. Fellow, Eur. Univ. Inst., 2007–08. *Publications:* (ed jtly) State of the Union: the Clinton Administration and the nation in profile, 1994; (ed jtly) Europe's New Nationalism: states and minorities in conflict, 1996; A New Trusteeship?: the international administration of war-torn territories, 2002; International Governance of War-torn Territories: rule and reconstruction, 2005; Europe and the Recognition of New States in Yugoslavia, 2005; (ed) Exit Strategies and State Building, 2012; Measuring Peace: principles, practices and politics, 2019. *Recreations:* walking, cooking, film. *Address:* Department of Politics and International Relations, Manor Road, Oxford OX1 3UQ. *T:* (01865) 288563, *Fax:* (01865) 278725.

**CAPLEN, Andrew Howard Arthur;** President, Law Society of England and Wales, 2014–15; *b* Awbridge, Hants, 3 July 1958; *s* of Frederick Gordon Caplen and Beryl Maud Caplen (*née* Scurlock); *m* 1995, Rev. Lindsay Andrea Shaw. *Educ:* Barton Peveril Grammar Sch. and Sixth Form Coll., Eastleigh; Univ. of Hull (LLB Hons); Coll. of Law, Guildford. Admitted Solicitor, 1982; NP 1988. Solicitor, Abels, Southampton, 1982–2012. Dep. Vice Pres., 2012–13, Vice Pres., 2013–14, Law Soc. of England and Wales. Chair, Spurgeons' Children's Charity, 2017–. *Publications:* (jtly) Speaking Up: defending and delivering access to justice today, 2015. *Recreations:* long-distance trail walker, Southampton Football Club supporter, committed Christian, married to a Baptist Minister. *Address:* 41 Severn Road, Portishead, Bristol BS20 6NG.

**CAPLIN, Anthony Lindsay;** Chairman, North West London Hospitals NHS Trust, 2008–13; *b* Southport, 13 April 1951; *s* of Maxwell and Vera Caplin; *m* 1985, Angie Littlechild; two *d. Educ:* Merchant Taylors' Sch., Liverpool. Former Chairman: Panmure Gordon plc; Durlacher plc; Alternative Networks plc; Dep. Chm., Strand Partners. Comr, Public Works Loan Bd, 2004–14 (Chm., 2013–14). Non-exec. Dir, MRC, 2009–14 (Chm., Audit Cttee, 2009–14). *Recreation:* politics. *T:* 07774 611611.

**CAPLIN, Carol Ann;** *see* Homden, C. A.

**CAPLIN, Ivor Keith;** Founder, owner and Managing Director, Ivor Caplin Consultancy Ltd, since 2005; Head of Public Affairs, English UK, 2014–15; *b* 8 Nov. 1958; *s* of late Leonard Caplin and of Alma Caplin (*née* Silver); two *s* one *d. Educ:* King Edward's Sch., Witley; Brighton Coll. of Technol. (Nat. Cert. Business Studies 1979). Joined Legal & General Assurance Society, 1978: various mgt posts, 1989–94; Quality Manager, Sales Div., 1994–97. Nat. Sec., ASTMS, 1983–88. Hove Borough Council: Mem. (Lab), 1991–97; Leader, 1995–97; Mem., Brighton and Hove UA, 1996–98. MP (Lab) Hove, 1997–2005. PPS to Leader of H of C, 1998–2001; an Asst Govt Whip, 2001–03; Parly Under-Sec. of State, MoD, 2003–05. Chm., All Party Parly Gp on English Lang. Teaching, 1997–2000; Treas., All Party Animal Welfare Gp, 1997–2001; Sec., Parly Lab. Local Govt Gp, 1997–99; Officer, All Party Football Gp, 1998–2001. Chief Exec., Mayfair Capital Management Gp, 2009–11. Dir, Both Sides Ltd, 2015–16. Dir, prog. of events, 250th celebrations of 1st Jewish citizen of Brighton, 2015–16. Chm., Adv. Bd, Terrence Higgins Trust, 2017–. Vice-Chm., Lab. Friends of Israel, 1997–2005; Chair, SE reg., Jewish Labour Movt, 2016– (UK Chair, 2018–19). Trustee: Old Market Trust, Brunswick, Hove, 1997–2003; Concordia UK, 2018–. *Recreations:* supporter Brighton and Hove Albion FC and Sussex CCC, music, reading, film, theatre, cooking, playing golf. *Address:* 2–4 Packhorse Road, Gerrards Cross, Bucks SL9 7QE. *E:* ivorcaplin@outlook.com.

**CAPLIN, Maj. Gen. Nicholas John,** CB 2012; FRAeS; Chief Executive, Blind Veterans UK, since 2014; *b* England, 4 Dec. 1958; *s* of John and Daphne Caplin; *m* 1983, Isobel McIntosh; one *s* one *d. Educ:* Broadstone Primary Sch.; Poole Grammar Sch.; Univ. of Surrey (BSc Hons Econ); RMA, Sandhurst; Army Staff Coll. CGIA. Commnd AAC, 1980; Infantry Attachment, 1 RGJ, 1981; Army Pilot Trng, 1981–82; Flight Comdr, 1982–85; Adjt, 1985–87; Ind. Flight Comdr, 1988 (Maj.); Army Staff Coll., 1989–90; MoD, 1991–93; Sqdn Comdr (incl. Bosnia), 1993–95; Directing Staff, Army Staff Coll., 1995–97 (Lt Col); CO, 3 Regt, AAC, 1997–2000; Private Office, 2000–01; Comdt, Sch. of Army Aviation, 2001–02 (Col); Dep. Comdr, Jt Helicopter Comd, 2003–05 (Brig.); Comdr, Collective Trng Gp, 2006–07; Kosovo Protection Corps Co-ordinator, 2008–09; GOC UK Support Comd, 2009–12; GOC British Forces Germany, 2012; Sen. Directing Staff (Army), RCDS, 2012–13. Advr, Coode Associates, 2013–. Dir, COBSEO, 2013–17. Trustee, Action against Age-related Macular Degeneration, 2016–. FRAeS 2004. *Recreations:* classical music (especially organ and piano), sailing (dinghy and offshore), enjoying the family and the Hebrides, President of Crossed Swords Pipe Band 2009–12. *Address:* c/o AAC Regimental Office, HQ Director Army Air Corps, Middle Wallop, Stockbridge, Hants SO20 8DY. *Clubs:* Naval and Military; British Kiel Yacht (Cdre, 2009–12).

**CAPON, Very Rev. Gerwyn Huw;** Vicar, Cathedral of St Peter and St Paul, Llandaff, and Dean of Llandaff, since 2014; *b* 9 April 1965. *Educ:* Liverpool John Moores Univ. (BSc Hons 1992); St Stephen House, Oxford. Chartered Surveyor, 1994; ordained deacon, 2003, priest, 2004; Curate, St Mary, West Derby, Liverpool, 2003–07; Chaplain to the Archbishop of Wales and Dir of Ordinands, 2007–09; Priest-in-charge, Holy Trinity, Bolton-le-Sands, 2009–12; Bishop's Domestic Chaplain, Dio. of Llandaff, 2012–14. *Address:* The Deanery, The Cathedral Green, Cardiff CF5 2YF. *T:* (029) 2056 1545. *E:* thedean@llandaffcathedral.org.uk.

**CAPP, Prof. Bernard Stuart,** DPhil; FBA 2005; FRHistS; Professor of History, University of Warwick, 1994–2010, now Emeritus; *b* 19 Nov. 1943; *s* of Walter Henry Capp and Marjorie Highwood Capp (*née* Coast); *m* 1966, Elizabeth Seal (marr. diss. 1980); one *s* one *d. Educ:* City of Leicester Boys' Sch.; Pembroke Coll., Oxford (Open Exhibnr 1962; BA 1st Cl. Hons Hist. 1965; Bryce Res. Student; MA; DPhil 1970). FRHistS 1975. University of Warwick: Asst Lectr in Hist., 1968–70; Lectr, 1970–80; Sen. Lectr, 1980–90; Reader, 1990–94; Chair, Hist. Dept, 1992–95. *Publications:* The Fifth Monarchy Men, 1972, reissued 2008; Astrology and the Popular Press: English almanacs 1500–1800, 1979, reissued 2008; Cromwell's Navy: the Fleet and the English Revolution 1648–60, 1989; The World of John Taylor, the Water Poet, 1578–1653, 1994; When Gossips Meet: women, family and neighbourhood in early modern England, 2003; England's Culture Wars: Puritan reformation and its enemies in the Interregnum, 1649–1660, 2012; The Ties that Bind: siblings, family and society in early modern England, 2018; (contrib. and Associate Ed.) Oxford DNB, 2004; contribs to many ed collections; contrib. to Past and Present, Historical Jl, Seventeenth Century, English Historical Rev., Jl of Religious History. *Address:* Department of History, University of Warwick, Coventry CV4 7AL. *T:* (024) 7652 3410, *Fax:* (024) 7652 3437. *E:* b.s.capp@warwick.ac.uk.

**CAPPE, Melvin Samuel,** OC 2009; Professor, Munk School of Global Affairs and Public Policy (formerly School of Public Policy and Governance), University of Toronto, since 2009; *b* 3 Dec. 1948; *s* of Dave and Patty Cappe; *m* 1971, Marni Pliskin; one *s* one *d. Educ:* Univ. of Toronto (BA); Univ. of Western Ontario (MA). Sen. official, Treasury Bd, Dept of Finance, and Consumer & Corporate Affairs, Canada, 1975–86; Asst Dep. Minister, Consumer & Corporate Affairs, 1986–90; Dep. Sec., Treasury Bd, 1990–94; Deputy Minister: of Envmt, 1994–96; of Human Resources Develt, 1996–99; Clerk of Privy Council, Sec. to Cabinet and Hd, Public Service of Canada, 1999–2002; High Comr of Canada in UK, 2002–06; Pres. and CEO, Inst. for Res. on Public Policy, Montreal, 2006–11. Comr, Canada's Ecofiscal Commn, 2015–. Vice Chm., Canadian Partnership Against Cancer, 2009–15; Mem. Bd, Canadian Consortium for Stem Cell Res., 2012–; Chm., Health Res. Foundn, 2014–; Chair, Bd of Dirs, Canadian Blood Services, 2018–. Hon. LLD: Univ. of Western Ontario, 2006; Toronto, 2008. Queen's Golden Jubilee Medal, 2002; Queen's Diamond Jubilee Medal, 2012. *Recreations:* hiking, travel, family. *E:* mel.cappe@utoronto.ca.

**CAPPER, Lynne;** *see* Sedgmore, L.

**CAPPS, Maj. Gen. Duncan Francis,** CBE 2014; General Officer Commanding Regional Command, 2017–Feb. 2020; *b* Slough, 21 Dec. 1966; *s* of Derek Francis and Doreen Margaret Capps; *m* 2000, Robyn Vanessa Maclaine; two *d. Educ:* Charters Comprehensive Sch., Sunningdale; Cranfield Univ. (MA 1999). Joined Army, 1985; CO, 7 Regt RLC, 2006–08; Comdr, 104 Logistics Bde, 2011–13; ACOS, PJHQ, 2013–15; rcds, 2015–16; Hd, Defence Supply Chain Ops and Movements, 2016–17. *Recreation:* marathon kayaking. *Address:* HQ Regional Command, Montgomery House, Queens Avenue, Aldershot, Hants GU11 2JN. *T:* (01252) 347837. *E:* duncan.capps948@mod.gov.uk.

**CAPRON, (George) Christopher;** independent television producer; Director, Capron Productions, 1987–99; *b* 17 Dec. 1935; *s* of late Lt-Col George Capron and Hon. Mrs (Edith) Christian Capron (*née* Hepburne-Scott); *m* 1958, Edna Naomi Goldrei; one *s* one *d. Educ:* Wellington Coll.; Trinity Hall, Cambridge (MA). Served Army, 12th Royal Lancers (Prince of Wales's), 1954–56. British Broadcasting Corporation: radio producer, 1963–67; television producer, 1967–76; Editor, Tonight, 1976–77; Editor, Panorama, 1977–79; Asst Head, 1979–81, Head, 1981–85, TV Current Affairs Programmes; Head of Parly Broadcasting, 1985–87. FRTS 1996. *Recreations:* golf, walking, watching cricket. *Address:* Old Rectory, Church Lane, Stoke Doyle, Peterborough PE8 5TH. *Club:* MCC.

**CAPSTICK, Charles William,** CB 1992; CMG 1972; Deputy Secretary, Food Safety Directorate, Ministry of Agriculture, Fisheries and Food, 1989–94; *b* 18 Dec. 1934; *s* of late William Capstick and Janet Frankland; *m* 1962, Joyce Alma Dodsworth; two *s. Educ:* King's Coll., Univ. of Durham (BSc (Hons)); Univ. of Kentucky, USA (MS). Ministry of Agriculture, Fisheries and Food: Asst Agricl Economist, 1961; Principal Agricl Economist, 1963; Senior Principal Agricl Economist, 1968; Sen. Econ. Advr and Head, Milk and Milk Products Div., 1976; Under Sec., 1977, Dir of Econs and Statistics, 1977. Chm., Salix Estates Ltd, 2002–. Pres., Agricultural Economics Soc., 1983. Pres., Old Clitheronians Assoc., 2001. *Recreations:* gardening, golf. *Address:* 6 The Hazels, Wilpshire, Blackburn, Lancs BB1 9HZ.

**CAPSTICK, Martin Harold;** Managing Director, North London Waste Authority, since 2017; *b* Keighley, 19 Sept. 1965; *s* of John Harold Capstick and Marjorie Capstick (*née* Mitchell); *m* 1989, Wendy Bristow; one *s* one *d. Educ:* Ermysted's Grammar Sch., Skipton; Univ. of Exeter (BA Hons Modern Langs (French and German)). Joined Dept of Transport, 1988: Private Sec. to Minister for Roads and Traffic, 1990–92; Team Leader: Public Transport London, 1992–95; Railways Directorate, 1995; Econ. and Domestic Secretariat, Cabinet Office, 1995–98; Water Supply and Regulation, 1998–2000, Private Sec. to Perm. Sec., 2000–02, DETR; Hd, Europe Wildlife Div., DEFRA, 2002–04; Department for Transport: Hd, Aviation Envmtl Div., 2005–09; Dir, Strategic Roads and Nat. Networks, 2009–10; Dir, High Speed Rail, Smart Ticketing and Safe Transport of Dangerous Goods, 2011–13; Dir, High Speed Rail Policy, Funding and Legislation, 2013–15; Dir, Northern Transport Strategy, subseq. Regl Transport Strategies, 2015–17. Gov., All Saints Sch., Didcot, 2004–13. *Recreations:* walking, running, cycling. *Address:* North London Waste Authority, 1b Berol House, 25 Ashley Road, Tottenham Hale, N17 9LJ. *E:* martin.capstick@nlwa.gov.uk.

**CARAMITZOS-TZIRAS, Dimitris;** Ambassador of Greece to the Court of St James's, since 2016; *b* Athens, 7 Sept. 1958; *m* 1990, Margarita Mavromichalis; two *d. Educ:* Univ. of Athens (LLM); Univ. of Thessaloniki (Dip. Internat. Law). Joined Greek Diplomatic Service, 1983; assigned to Depts of Council of Europe, UN and EU (Internal Mkt and Eurozone), Min. of Foreign Affairs; Alternate Rep. to ICAO, Montreal, 1989–91; Consul, Cape Town, 1991–94; First Counsellor, Political Affairs, Sofia, 1994–98; Athens 2004 Olympic Games Organizing Committee: Gen. Manager in charge of Personnel and Volunteers, 2002; Mem., Games Operation Cttee and Ops Centre in charge of Personnel and Volunteers for Athens 2004 Olympic Games and Athens 2004 Paralympic Games (on secondment), 2002–14; Coordinator for Anti-Terrorism and Hd, Crisis Mgt Unit, Min. of Foreign Affairs, 2004–05; Consul Gen. responsible for Western US States, LA, 2005–09; Dep. Perm. Rep. of Greece to UN, NY, 2009–13; Hd, Office of 2014 Hellenic Presidency of the Council of the EU, 2013–14; Dir Gen. in charge of EU Affairs, Min. of Foreign Affairs, 2014–16. *Address:* Embassy of Greece, 1A Holland Park, W11 3TP.

**CARBERRY, Caroline Rosemary;** QC 2017; a Recorder, since 2018; *b* Co. Armagh, NI, 28 Sept. 1971; *d* of Michael Carberry and Marie Carberry; *m* 2006, Jonathan Barnaby Larson Oliver, *qv*; one *s* two *d. Educ:* LLB Hons. Called to the Bar, Gray's Inn, 1995; a Tribunal Judge, 2014–. *Recreations:* standing on the sidelines supporting my children, researching holidays and occasionally taking them, acquiring books I'll never get round to reading, keeping up with friends and family. *Address:* Furnival Chambers, 32 Furnival Street, EC4A 1JQ.

**CARBERRY, Kay,** CBE 2007; Assistant General Secretary, Trades Union Congress, 2003–16; *b* 19 Oct. 1950; *d* of Sean and Sheila Carberry; one *s* by Peter Ashby. *Educ:* Royal Naval Sch., Malta; Sussex Univ. (BA Hons English); QTS. Secondary sch. teacher, 1972–75; Researcher, NUT, 1975–78; Trades Union Congress: Policy Officer, 1978–84; Sen. Policy Officer, 1984–88; Head, Equal Rights Dept, 1988–2003. Member: Women's Nat. Commn, 1987–92; EOC, 1999–2007; Equality and Human Rights Commn (formerly Commn for Equality and Human Rights), 2006–12; Low Pay Commn, 2012–. Member:

Nat. Adv. Body for Public Sector Higher Educn, 1984–87; Adv. Cttee for Women's Employment, Dept of Employment, 1987–90; Race Relations Employment Adv. Gp, Dept of Employment, then DfEE, 1990–96; Ministerial Adv. Cttee on Work-Life Balance Employment, DfEE, 2000–02; Ministerial Adv. Gp on Age, DTI, 2001–03; Work and Parents Taskforce, DTI, 2001; Steering Gp on Illegal Working, Home Office, 2003–06; Pensions Adv. Gp, DWP, 2003–04; Women and Work Commn, DTI, 2004–06. Dir, TU Mgt Services Ltd, 2013–. Member: Civil Justice Council, 2016–; Bd, TfL, 2016–. Gov., Pensions Policy Inst., 2009–18. Trustee: Gingerbread (formerly NCOPF), 1990–2010; People's History Mus., 2003–; Work Foundn, 2005–10. Mem., Franco-British Council, 2004–09. Hon. Fellow, St Hugh's Coll., Oxford, 2016.

**CARBERY,** 12th Baron cr 1715 (Ire.); **Michael Peter Evans-Freke;** Bt 1768; b 11 Oct. 1942; e s of 11th Baron Carbery and Joyzelle Mary (née Binnie); S father, 2012; m 1st, 1967, Claudia Janet Elizabeth Gurney (marr. diss. 2007); one s three d; 2nd, 2008, Dr Wei Li Qiu; one s. Educ: Downside; Christ Church, Oxford (MA 1969); Strathclyde Univ. (MBA); King's Coll. London (PGCE). Heir: s Hon. Dominic Ralfe Cecil Evans-Freke [b 29 June 1969; m 2003, Marina Whetherly; two s one d].

**CARBONE, Charlotte Helen;** see Watts, C. H.

**CARDELLI, Luca,** PhD; FRS 2005; Royal Society Research Professor, University of Oxford, since 2013 (part-time, 2013–18). Educ: Univ. of Pisa; Univ. of Edinburgh (PhD 1982). Mem. of technical staff, AT&T Bell Labs, Murray Hill, 1982–85; mem. of res. staff, Digital Equipment Corp., Systems Res. Center, Palo Alto, 1985–97; Microsoft Research Ltd: Researcher, 1997–2000; Asst Dir, 2000–06; Principal Researcher, 2006–18. Publications: (with Martin Abadi) A Theory of Objects, 1996.

**CARDEN, (Sir) Christopher Robert,** (5th Bt cr 1887, of Molesey, Surrey; but does not use the title); small organic farmer/prepper, since 2010; conservationist; Forestry and Rural Development Consultant, Santa Cruz, Bolivia, 1991–2012; b 24 Nov. 1946; o s of Sir Henry Carden, 4th Bt, OBE and of his 1st wife, Jane St Clare Daniell; S father, 1993, but his name does not appear on the Official Roll of the Baronetage; m 1st, 1972, Sainimere Rokotuibau (marr. diss. 1979), Suva, Fiji; 2nd, 1981, Clarita Eriksen (marr. diss. 1996), Manila, Philippines. Educ: Eton; Univ. of Aberdeen (BSc Forestry, 1970). Guide, internat. Raëlian Movement; Forester, Govt of Papua New Guinea, 1970–74; Manager, Mgt Services Div., Fiji Pine Commn, 1976–79; Sen. Partner, CR Forestry Services, UK, 1980–81; Forest Planning and Trng Manager, Usutu Pulp Co. Ltd, Swaziland, 1982–86; Forestry Lectr, Coll. of Higher Educn, Solomon Islands, 1987–88; Internat. Forestry Consultant, 1989–90. Address: Quinta Sobrevivir, Candelaria, Buenavista, Prov. Ichilo, Santa Cruz, Bolivia.

**CARDEN, Daniel Joseph;** MP (Lab) Liverpool Walton, since 2017; b Liverpool, 28 Oct. 1986; s of Mike Carden and Mary Collings. Educ: London Sch. of Econs and Pol Sci. (BSc Internat. Relns). Aide to Gen. Sec., Unite, 2012. Shadow Minister for Internat. Develt, 2018–. Address: House of Commons, SW1A 0AA.

**CARDEN, Sir John (Craven),** 8th Bt cr 1787, of Templemore, Tipperary; b 17 Nov. 1953; s of Derrick Charles Carden, CMG and Elizabeth Anne, d of late Capt. Alfred Spalding Russell, DSO, RN; S cousin, 2008; m 1983, Celia Jane Cameron, d of late Angus Cameron Howitt; one s. Educ: Winchester Coll.; Sch. of Oriental and African Studies, London Univ.; Portsmouth Poly. (BA Arch.); Dept of Psychol., Univ. of Surrey. Sch. of Arch., Portsmouth Poly., 1980–82; Carden Publishing Services, 1982–88; Carden Publications Ltd, 1988–92; Fernhurst Books, 1995–98; John Wiley & Sons Ltd, 1999–2001; Tesco Stores Ltd, 2002–16. Recreations: music of the romantic era, having my head in a book. Heir: s Patrick John Cameron Carden, b 7 March 1988. Address: 154 St Pancras, Chichester, W Sussex PO19 7SH. T: (01243) 784943.

**CARDEN, Kathryn Ann;** see Bishop, K. A.

**CARDEN, Richard John Derek,** CB 1998; Directorate-General for Trade, European Commission (on secondment), 2003–05; b 12 June 1943; s of late John and Hilda Carden; m 1971, Pamela Haughton; one s one d. Educ: Merchant Taylors' Sch., Northwood; St John's Coll., Oxford (Craven Scholar, 1964; Derby Scholar, 1966; MA Lit. Hum. 1969; DPhil 1970); Freie Universität, Berlin. Research for Egypt Exploration Soc., 1969–70; entered Civil Service, MAFF, 1970; HM Treasury, 1977–79; MAFF, 1979–93 and 1994–2000: Chief Regional Officer, Midlands and Western Region, 1983–86; Under Sec., European Community and Ext. Trade Policy, 1987–91; Fisheries Sec., 1991–93; Dep. Hd, Eur. Secretariat, Cabinet Office, 1993–94; Dep. Sec., Food Safety Directorate, 1994–96; Hd, Food Safety and Envmt Directorate, 1996–2000; actg Perm. Sec., Feb.–May 2000; Dir-Gen., Trade Policy, subseq. Europe and World Trade, DTI, 2000–03. Dir (non-exec.), Golden Wonder Ltd, 1985–86; Associate, Mega Ace Consultancy (Mumbai and London), 2005–07; Mem. Bd, Centre for Business and Strategic Affairs (Mumbai), 2013–17. Vis. Fellow, Internat. Relations Dept, LSE, 2003–05. Member, Council: RSPB, 2003–08; World Pheasant Assoc., 2008– (Chm., 2011–13); Anglo-Hellenic League, 2010– (Adminr, Runciman Book Award, 2015–); Mem., Bd of Advrs, Holkham Nat. Nature Reserve, 2012–. Fellow, St George's House, Windsor Castle, 2008–. Publications: The Papyrus Fragments of Sophocles, 1974; (contrib.) The Oxyrhynchus Papyri, vol. LIV, 1987; (contrib.) The New Economic Diplomacy, 2003; Quite Close to Europe, 2019; articles on Greek literature. Address: Rectory House, Brandon Road, Hilborough, Thetford, Norfolk IP26 5BW. E: rcarden2@btinternet.com. Club: Travellers.

**CARDEW, Anthony John,** consultant; Founder and Chairman, Cardew Group (formerly Cardew & Co. Ltd), since 1991; b 8 Sept. 1949; s of late Dr Martin Philip Cardew and Anne Elizabeth Cardew (née Foster); m 1971, Janice Frances Smallwood; one s one d. Educ: Thornegate; army schools in Kuala Lumpur and Hong Kong; Bishop Wordsworth's Sch.; Marlborough Coll. Journalist, regl newspapers, 1967–70; news reporter, United Press Internat., 1970–71; Financial Corresp., Reuters Economic Services, 1971–74; developed financial communication, investor relns, M&A and crisis mgt, Charles Barker City, 1974–83; Dir, 1976–83; Hd, Financial Public Relns, 1979–83; Dep. Chm., 1983–85; Chm., 1985–91, Grandfield Rork Collins Financial. Ind. Dir, Western Power Distribution, 2017–. Trustee, Awareness Foundn, 2009–12. Recreations: book collecting, walking, grandchildren, theatre. Club: Athenæum.

**CARDIFF, Archbishop of, (RC),** since 2011; **Most Rev. George Stack;** b 9 May 1946; s of Gerald Stack and Elizabeth (née McKenzie). Educ: St Aloysius Coll., Highgate; St Edmund's Coll., Ware; St Mary's Coll., Strawberry Hill. BEd (Hons). Ordained priest, 1972; Curate, St Joseph's, Hanwell 1972–75; Diocesan Catechetical Office, 1975–77; Curate, St Paul's, Wood Green, 1977–83; Parish Priest, Our Lady Help of Christians, Kentish Town, 1983–90; VG, Archdiocese of Westminster, 1990–93; Administrator, Westminster Cathedral, 1993–2001; Auxiliary Bishop of Westminster (RC), and Titular Bp of Gemellae in Numidia, 2001–11. Hon. Canon Emeritus, St Paul's Cathedral, 2001. Prelate of Honour to HH The Pope, 1993; KCHS 2003. Address: Archbishop's House, 41–43 Cathedral Road, Cardiff CF11 9HD. T: (029) 2022 0411.

**CARDIGAN, Earl of; David Michael James Brudenell-Bruce;** Manager, since 1974, owner, and 31st Hereditary Warden, since 1987, Savernake Forest; b 12 Nov. 1952; s and heir of 8th Marquess of Ailesbury, qv; m 2011, Joanne Powell, Flagstaff, Arizona; one d, and one s one d from a previous marriage. Educ: Eton; Rannoch; Royal Agricultural Coll., Cirencester. Sec., Marlborough Conservatives, 1985–; Mem. Exec., Devizes Constituency Cons. Assoc., 1988–. Heir: s Viscount Savernake, qv. Address: Savernake Lodge, Savernake Forest, Marlborough, Wilts SN8 3HP.

**CARDIN, Pierre;** Commandeur de la Légion d'Honneur, 1997; couturier; b 2 July 1922. Designer: Paquin, Paris, 1945–46; Dior, Paris, 1946–50; founded own fashion house, 1950. Founder and Dir, Théâtre des Ambassadeurs, now Espace Pierre Cardin complex, 1970–; Chm., Maxim's Restaurant, 1981–. Founder, Chateau Lacoste Fest., Provence, 2001. Designed costumes for films, including: Cocteau's La Belle et la Bête, 1946; The Yellow Rolls Royce, 1965. Retrospective exhibition, V&A, 1990. Dé d'Or, 1977, 1979, 1982; Fashion Oscar, 1985; prize of Foundn for Advancement of Garment and Apparel Res., Japan, 1988. Grand Officer, Order of Merit (Italy), 1988. Address: (office) 27 avenue Marigny, 75008 Paris, France; 59 rue du Faubourg Saint-Honoré, 75008 Paris, France.

**CARDOSO E CUNHA, António José Baptista;** Commissioner General, EXPO '98, 1993–98; Chairman: PARQUE EXPO '98 SA, 1993–98; TAP Air Portugal, 2003–05; b 28 Jan. 1934; s of Arnaldo and Maria Beatriz Cardoso e Cunha; m 1958, Dea Cardoso e Cunha; four s. Educ: Instituto Superior Técnico; Lisbon Univ. MSc Chem. Engrg. Professional engineer, Lisbon, 1957–65; Man. Dir/Chief Exec. Officer of private cos, Sa da Bandeira, Angola, 1965–77; in business, director of private cos, Lisbon, 1977–78 and 1982–85. Mem. Portuguese Parlt, 1979–83 and 1985–89; Mem. Portuguese Government: Sec. of State for Foreign Trade, 1978, for Industry, 1979; Minister for Agriculture/Fisheries, 1980–82; Mem., European Commn, 1986–92. Medalha de Honra, Lisbon, 2003. Grã-Cruz: Ordem Infant D. Henrique (Portugal), 1993; Ordem de Cristo (Portugal), 1999; Grand Croix, Leopold II (Belgium), 1980; Gran Cruz, Merito Agricola (Spain), 1981.

**CARDOZO, Prof. Linda Dolores,** OBE 2014; MD; FRCOG; Professor of Urogynaecology, King's College London School of Medicine (formerly Guy's, King's and St Thomas' School of Medicine, King's College London), since 1994; Consultant Obstetrician and Gynaecologist, King's College Hospital, since 1985; b 15 Sept. 1950; d of Felix Cardozo and Olga Cardozo (née Watts); m 1974, Stuart Hutcheson; one s two d. Educ: Liverpool Univ. Med. Sch. (MB ChB 1974; MD 1979). MRCOG 1980, FRCOG 1991. Hse Officer, Liverpool, 1974–75; SHO, Mill Rd Maternity Hosp., Liverpool, 1975–76; Clin. Res. Fellow in Urodynamics, St George's Hosp., London, 1976–78; Registrar, 1979–81, Sen. Registrar, 1981–84, Obstetrics and Gynaecol., KCH. Co-Dir, Internat. Consultation on Incontinence, 2001, 2004, 2008, 2012, 2016. Chairman: Continence Foundn UK, 1998–2006; British Menopause Soc., 2001–03; founder Chm., British Soc. of Urogynaecology, 2001–06; President: Assoc. of Chartered Physiotherapists in Women's Health, 1995–2009; Internat. Urogynaecol Assoc., 1998–2000; Sect. of Obstetrics and Gynaecol., RSocMed, 2001–02; Eur. Urogynaecol Assoc., 2011–15; Mem. Exec., 2001–06, and Chm. Educn Cttee, 2001–07, Internat. Continence Soc.; Internat. Fellows Rep., RCOG, 2010–16. Dr hc Athens, 2016. Lifetime Achievement Award: Internat. Urogynaecol Assoc., 2013; Internat. Continence Soc., 2017. Publications: 25 books incl. Update on drugs and the lower urinary tract, 1988; (jtly) Basic Urogynaecology, 1993 (trans. Italian, 1994, Polish, 1995); Urogynaecology: the King's approach, 1997; (jtly) Understanding Female Urinary Incontinence, 1999, 2nd edn 2002; (jtly) Family Doctor Guide to Urinary Incontinence in Women, 1999; (jtly) Urinary Incontinence in Primary Care, 2000; Gynaecological Urology, 2000; (jtly) The Effective Management of Detrusor Instability, 2001; (wit D. Staskin) Textbook of Female Urology and Urogynaecology, 2001, 4th edn 2016; (ed jtly) Incontinence, 2nd edn 2002 to 5th edn 2013; Incontinence in Women, 2002; (jtly) Female Urinary Incontinence, 2004; (ed jtly) Incontinence, 2005; (ed jtly) Clinical Manual of Incontinence in women, 2005; (ed jtly) The Effective Management of Stress Urinary Incontinence, 2006; (jtly) Obstetrics and Gynaecology: an evidence based text, 2nd edn 2010; contrib. over 650 papers and articles in peer review jls and over 130 book chapters relating to lower urinary tract problems in women, incl. urinary incontinence, prolapse and reconstructive surgery. Address: King's College Hospital, Denmark Hill, SE5 9RS. T: (020) 3299 3449, Fax: (020) 7346 3449; 8 Devonshire Place, W1G 6HP. T: (020) 7935 2357, Fax: (020) 7224 2797. E: linda@lindacardozo.co.uk. Club: Royal Society of Medicine.

**CARDOZO, Lydia Helena L.;** see Lopes Cardozo Kindersley.

**CARDROSS, Lord; Henry Thomas Alexander Erskine;** glass designer; joint Partner, Cardross Glass, 2006–18; b 31 May 1960; s and heir of 17th Earl of Buchan, qv; m 1987, Charlotte (d 2013), d of Hon. Matthew Beaumont and Mrs Alexander Maitland; two s. Educ: Central St Martin's Sch. of Art.

**CARDWELL, Prof. David Anthony,** PhD; FInstP, FIET, FREng; Professor of Superconducting Engineering, since 2003, and Pro Vice Chancellor, Strategy and Planning, since 2018, University of Cambridge; Fellow, Fitzwilliam College, Cambridge, since 1993; b Matlock, Derbys, 18 Nov. 1960; s of William and Margaret Annie Cardwell; m 1982, Sharon Redfern; two s. Educ: Aldercar Comprehensive Sch.; SE Derbys Coll.; Univ. of Warwick (BSc Physics 1983; PhD Physics 1987); Univ. of Cambridge (MA Engrg 1995; ScD Engrg 2014). CPhys, FInstP 2006; CEng, FIET 2010; FREng 2012. Associate Lectr (pt-time), Open Univ., 1986–99; Principal Scientist, Plessey Res. (Caswell) Ltd, 1986–90; Sen. Principal Scientist, GEC-Marconi Materials Technol. Ltd, 1990–92; University of Cambridge: Asst Dir of Res., 1992–96; Lectr, 1996–99; Reader in Superconducting Materials, 1999–2003; Hd, Dept of Engrg, 2014–18. Hon. DSc Warwick, 2015. Publications: Handbook of Superconducting Materials, 2002, 2nd edn 2017; contribs to scientific and tech. jls. Recreations: football. Address: The Old Schools, University of Cambridge, Trinity Lane, Cambridge CB2 1TN. T: (01223) 765695, Fax: (01223) 765693. E: dc135@cam.ac.uk.

**CARDY, Prof. John Lawrence,** PhD; FRS 1991; Professor of Physics, University of Oxford, 1996–2014; Senior Research Fellow, All Souls College, Oxford, 1993–2014, now Emeritus Fellow; Research Physicist, University of California, Berkeley, since 2017; b 19 March 1947; s of late George Laurence Cardy and Sarah Cardy; m 1985, Mary Ann Gilreath. Educ: Downing Coll., Cambridge (BA 1968; PhD 1971; Hon. Fellow, 2013). Research Associate, European Orgn for Nuclear Res., Geneva, 1971–73; Daresbury Lab., 1973–74; Res. Associate, 1974–76, Prof. of Physics, 1977–93, Univ. of California, Santa Barbara; Fellow: European Orgn for Nuclear Res., 1976–77; Alfred P. Sloan Foundn, 1978; Guggenheim Foundn, 1986. Vis. Prof., Univ. of Calif, Berkeley, 2015–16. Paul Dirac Medal, Inst. of Physics, 2000; Lars Onsager Prize, APS, 2004; Boltzmann Medal, IUPAP, 2010; Dirac Medal, Abdus Salam Internat. Centre for Theoretical Physics, 2012. Publications: Finite-Size Scaling, 1988; Scaling and Renormalization in Statistical Physics, 1996; Non-Equilibrium Statistical Mechanics and Turbulence, 2008; contrib. to learned jls. Recreations: mountaineering, painting. Address: 1109 Glengarry Drive, Walnut Creek, CA 94596, USA.

**CARDY, Peter John Stubbings;** Counsel of Experience mentoring non-profit Chief Executive Officers, since 2015; Secretary, Marine Business Network (Gosport Marine Scene), 2013–17; *b* 4 April 1947; *s of* Gordon Douglas Stubbings and Eva Stubbings (*née* Walker), assumed name of Cardy, 1987; *m* 1987, Christine Mary Cardy (marr. diss. 2011). *Educ:* University Coll., Durham (BA 1968); Cranfield Inst. of Technol. (MSc 1983). Adult Educn Principal, Cromwell Community Coll., Cambs, 1968–71; Dist Sec., WEA N of Scotland, 1971–77; Dep. Dir, Volunteer Centre, UK, 1977–87; Dir, Motor Neurone Disease Assoc., 1987–94; Chief Executive: Multiple Sclerosis Soc. of GB and NI, 1994–2001; Macmillan Cancer Relief, then Macmillan Cancer Support, 2001–07 (Vice Pres., 2007–); Maritime and Coastguard Agency, 2007–10; Chief Executive Officer: Aquaterra, 2010–11; Sail Training Internat., 2012–13. Speaker on non-profit, nautical and public affairs, 2010–. Chm., Nat. Assoc. of Volunteer Bureaux, 1988–91; Member: Charities Effectiveness Rev. Trust, 1990–93; HTA Pharmaceuticals Panel, 2002–04; Taskforce on Medicines Partnership, 2003–05; NHS Modernisation Bd, 2004; Bd, NCRI, 2003–06 (Chm., Lung Cancer Strategic Planning Gp); Sec.-Gen., Internat. Alliance of MND/ALS Assocs, 1991–94; Chairman: Neurological Alliance, 1998–2001; OST Foresight Healthcare Panel, 1999–2000; Brain and Spine Foundn, 2005–08; Disability Benefits Consortium, 2006; The Health Hotel, 2006; Comr, Medicines Commn, 1998–2003. Mem., Kilfinan Gp, 2016–. Non-executive Director: Northampton NHS Community Health Trust, 1993–97; Commonwealth Navigation Ltd, 2013–15. Reviewer and author of report, Rev. of UK Powerboat Racing, 2015. Patron, The Cancer Resource Centre, 2007–12. Vis. Fellow, Cass Business Sch., City Univ., 2006–09. Dep. Chm., Southampton Solent Univ., 2011–15 (Gov., 2015–17). Writer, Agony, column for Third Sector mgt jl, 2014–. Companion, Nautical Inst., 2009–. Mem., Master Mariners' Co., 2010–. Mem., RYA, 2010– (Mem., 2010–15, Chm., 2016–, Govt Affairs Cttee). Charcot Medal, Assoc. British Neurologists and MS Soc., 2001. *Publications:* numerous articles in voluntary sector, medical and nautical jls. *Recreations:* offshore sailing, conversation, travel, writing.

**CAREW, 7th Baron** (UK) *cr* 1838; **Patrick Thomas Conolly-Carew;** Baron Carew (Ire.) 1834; *b* 6 March 1938; *er s of* 6th Baron Carew, CBE and Lady Sylvia Maitland (*d* 1991), *o d of* 15th Earl of Lauderdale; *S father*, 1994; *m* 1962, Celia Mary, *d of* Col Hon. (Charles) Guy Cubitt, CBE, DSO, TD; *one s three d*. *Educ:* Harrow Sch.; RMA Sandhurst. RHG (The Blues), 1958–65 (Captain); served UK, Cyprus, Germany. Member, Irish Three Day Event Team: European Championships, 1959, 1962, 1967; World Championships, 1966; Olympics, Mexico 1968, Munich 1972, Montreal 1976. President: Equestrian Fedn of Ireland, 1979–84; Irish Horse Trials Soc., 1998–; Ground Jury, 3 Day Event, Olympic Games, 1992, 1996. Mem. Bureau, Fédération Equestre Internationale, 1989–97 (Hon. Mem., 1997; Chm., 3 Day Event Cttee, 1989–97). Trustee and Mem. Council, World Horse Welfare (formerly Internat. League for Protection of Horses), 2004–12. Dir, Castletown Foundn, 1995–. Gold Medal for Three Day Eventing, FEI, 1991; Badge of Honour, Equestrian Fedn of Ire., 1995. *Recreations:* all equestrian sports, cricket, shooting, bridge. *Heir: s* Hon. William Patrick Conolly-Carew [*b* 27 March 1973; *m* 2000, Jane Anne, *d of* Joseph Cunningham, Dublin; *one s three d*]. *Address:* The Garden House, Donadea, Naas, Co. Kildare, Ireland. *T:* (45) 868204, *Fax:* (45) 861105. *E:* carewcelia@hotmail.com. *Club:* Kildare Street and University (Dublin).

*See also* Hon. G. E. I. Maitland-Carew.

**CAREW, Hon. Gerald Edward Ian M.;** *see* Maitland-Carew.

**CAREW, Sir Rivers (Verain),** 11th Bt *cr* 1661; journalist; *b* 17 Oct. 1935; *s of* Sir Thomas Palk Carew, 10th Bt, and Phyllis Evelyn (*d* 1976), *oc of* Neville Mayman; *S father*, 1976; *m* 1st, 1968, Susan Babington (marr. diss. 1991), *yr d of* late H. B. Hill, London; *one s three d* (and *one s decd*); 2nd, 1992, Siobhán (marr. diss. 2003), 2nd *d of* late C. MacCárthaigh, Cork. *Educ:* St Columba's Coll., Rathfarnham, Co. Dublin; Trinity Coll., Dublin. MA, BAgr (Hort.). Asst Editor, Ireland of the Welcomes (Irish Tourist Bd magazine), 1964–67; Joint Editor, The Dublin Magazine, 1964–69; Irish Television, 1967–87; BBC World Service, 1987–93. *Publications:* (with Timothy Brownlow) Figures out of Mist (verse); Footprints in the Sand: the story of the Carews of Devon 1086–1945, 2018. *Recreations:* reading, music, reflection. *Heir: s* Gerald de Redvers Carew, *b* 24 May 1975. *Address:* Cherry Bounds, 37 Hicks Lane, Girton, Cambridge CB3 0JS.

**CAREW POLE, Sir (John) Richard (Walter Reginald),** 13th Bt *cr* 1628, of Shute House, Devonshire; OBE 2000; DL; farmer and chartered surveyor; *b* 2 Dec. 1938; *s of* Sir John Gawen Carew Pole, 12th Bt, DSO, TD and Cynthia Mary (*d* 1977), OBE, *o d of* Walter Burns; *S father*, 1993; *m* 1st, 1966, Hon. Victoria Marion Ann Lever (marr. diss. 1974), *d of* 3rd Viscount Leverhulme, KG, TD; 2nd, 1974, Mary Dawnay (*see* Dame Mary Carew Pole); *two s*. *Educ:* Eton Coll.; Royal Agricultural Coll., Cirencester. MRICS (ARICS 1967). Lieut, Coldstream Guards, 1958–63. Asst Surveyor, Laws & Fiennes, Chartered Surveyors, 1967–72. Director: South West Venture Capital, 1985–87; Eden Project Ltd, 1999–2001; Mem. Regional Bd, West of England, subseq. Portman, Bldg Soc., 1989–91. Chm., Devon and Cornwall Police Authority, 1985–87 (Mem., 1973–89); Member: SW Area Electricity Bd, 1981–90; NT Cttee for Devon and Cornwall, 1979–83. President: Surf Life Saving Assoc. of GB, 1976–86; Royal Cornwall Agricultural Show, 1981; RHS, 2001–06 (Mem. Council, 1999–2006); Trustee: Nat. Heritage Meml Fund, 1991–2000; Countryside Commission, 1991–96; Tate Gall., 1993–2003. Chm., Steering Cttee, Combined Univs in Cornwall, 2000–03. Governor: Seale Hayne Agric. Coll., 1979–89; Plymouth Coll., 1985–96; Mem. Bd, Theatre Royal, Plymouth, 1985–97. Trustee: Eden Trust, 1996–2007; Trusthouse Charitable Foundn, 1999–2009 (Chm., 2002–09); Pilgrim Trust, 2000–08; Royal Acad. of Arts Trust, 2007–. County Councillor, Cornwall, 1973–93 (Chairman: Planning Cttee, 1980–84; Finance Cttee, 1985–89; Property Cttee, 1989–93); High Sheriff of Cornwall, 1979; DL Cornwall, 1988. Liveryman, Fishmongers' Co., 1960 (Mem. Court of Assistants, 1993–; Prime Warden, 2006). *Recreations:* gardening, daydreaming, contemporary art. *Heir: s* Tremayne John Carew Pole [*b* 22 Feb. 1974; *m* 2010, Charlotte Watkins; *one s one d*]. *Address:* Clift Barn, Antony, Torpoint, Cornwall PL11 3AA. *T:* (01752) 814914.

**CAREW POLE, Dame Mary, (Lady Carew Pole),** DCVO 2018 (CVO 2003); Senior Lady in Waiting to the Princess Royal, since 1970; *b* London, 15 April 1936; *d of* late Lt Col Ronald Dawnay and Lady Elizabeth Dawnay; *m* 1974, Sir (John) Richard (Walter Reginald) Carew Pole, Bt, *qv*; *two s*. *Educ:* St Mary's, Wantage; Wandsworth Coll. (Teaching Dip.). PA to Aiden Crawley, MP, 1962–66. JP SE Cornwall, 1976–96. *Recreations:* travelling, gardening, reading, Pilot's Licence in 1960s. *Address:* Clift Barn, Antony, Torpoint, Cornwall PL11 3AA. *T:* (01752) 814914. *E:* mary@antonyestate.com.

**CAREY,** family name of **Baron Carey of Clifton.**

**CAREY OF CLIFTON,** Baron *cr* 2002 (Life Peer), of Clifton in the City and County of Bristol; **Rt Rev. and Rt Hon. George Leonard Carey;** Royal Victorian Chain, 2002; PC 1991; Archbishop of Canterbury, 1991–2002; Chancellor, London School of Theology, 2005–14; *b* 13 Nov. 1935; *s of* George and Ruby Carey; *m* 1960, Eileen Harmsworth Hood, Dagenham, Essex; *two s two d*. *Educ:* Bifrons Secondary Modern Sch., Barking; London College of Divinity; King's College, London. BD Hons, MTh; PhD London. National Service, RAF Wireless Operator, 1954–56. Deacon, 1962; Curate, St Mary's, Islington, 1962–66; Lecturer: Oak Hill Coll., Southgate, 1966–70; St John's Coll., Nottingham, 1970–75; Vicar, St Nicholas' Church, Durham, 1975–82; Principal, Trinity Coll., Stoke Hill, Bristol, 1982–87; Hon. Canon, Bristol Cathedral, 1983–87; Bishop of Bath and Wells, 1987–91; Hon. Asst Bp, Swansea and Brecon, 2004–11. Co-Founder and Chm., World Faiths Develt Dialogue. Chancellor, Univ. of Glos, 2003–10. Freeman: City of Wells, 1990; City of Canterbury, 1992; City of London, 1997. FKC 1994; Fellow, Canterbury Christ Church UC, 1999. Hon. doctorates from UK and USA univs. *Publications:* I Believe in Man, 1975; God Incarnate, 1976; (jtly) The Great Acquittal, 1980; The Church in the Market Place, 1984; The Meeting of the Waters, 1985; The Gate of Glory, 1986, 2nd edn 1992; The Message of the Bible, 1988; The Great God Robbery, 1989; I Believe, 1991; (jtly) Planting New Churches, 1991; Sharing a Vision, 1993; Spiritual Journey, 1994; My Journey, Your Journey, 1996; Canterbury Letters to the Future, 1998; Jesus 2000, 1999; Know the Truth (autobiog.), 2004; (jtly) We Don't Do God: the marginalization of public faith, 2012; contributor to numerous jls. *Recreations:* reading, writing, walking. *Address:* House of Lords, SW1A 0PW.

**CAREY, Charles John,** CMG 1993; Member, European Communities' Court of Auditors, 1983–92; *b* 11 Nov. 1933; *s of* Richard Mein Carey and Celia Herbert Amy (*née* Conway); *m* 1990, Elizabeth Dale (*née* Slade). *Educ:* Rugby; Balliol Coll., Oxford. Nat. Service, Russian interpreter, 1951–53. HM Treasury: Asst Principal, 1957; Principal, 1962; Asst Sec., 1971; seconded to HM Diplomatic Service as Counsellor (Econs and Finance), Office of UK Perm. Rep. to EEC, Brussels, 1974–77; Under Sec., HM Treasury, 1978–83. Chm., EC Conciliation Body for clearance of European Agricl Guidance and Guarantee Fund accounts, 1994–2001. Mem., CIPFA, 1988. Grand Croix de l'ordre de Merite (Luxembourg), 1992. *Publications:* (contrib.) Encyclopaedia of the European Union, 1998; articles on audit and financial mgt of EC funds in jls in UK, France and Netherlands. *Recreations:* Russian history and culture, Trollope novels. *Club:* Oxford and Cambridge.

**CAREY, Prof. Christopher,** PhD; FBA 2012; Professor of Greek, University College London, 2003–16, now Emeritus (Head of Department of Greek and Latin, 2004–09; Vice-Dean, Faculty of Arts and Humanities, 2005–06); *b* 14 Sept. 1950; *s of* Christopher and Alice Carey; *m* 1969, Pauline Hemmings; *two s one d*. *Educ:* Alsop High Sch., Liverpool; Jesus Coll., Cambridge (BA 1972, MA; PhD 1976). Res. Fellow, Jesus Coll., Cambridge, 1974–77; Lectr in Greek, St Andrews Univ., 1977–91; Prof. of Classics, RHUL (formerly RHBNC, Univ. of London), 1991–2003 (Dean of Arts, 1998–2000; acting Vice-Principal, 2001); Acting Dir, Inst. of Classical Studies, London Univ., 2003–04, 2015. Visiting Professor: Univ. of Minn, 1987–88; Carleton Coll., Minn, 1988; British Acad./Leverhulme Sen. Res. Fellow, 1996–97, 2009–10. Arts and Humanities Research Board (later Council): Mem., 1998–2002, Chm., 2002–06, Postgrad. Panel (Classics); Member: Postgrad. Cttee, 2002–06; Bd of Mgt, 2002–04; Strategic Adv. Gp, 2004–06; Nominations Cttee, 2005–07; Mem. Council, Fédération Internat. des Assocs d'Etudes classiques, 2014–19. Chairman: Classics, Ancient History, Byzantine and Modern Greek Panel, 2001 RAE; Classical Assoc. Jls Bd, 2009–15; Section H1 (Classical Antiquity), British Acad., 2015–18. Pres., Soc. for Promotion of Hellenic Studies, 2011–14. Hon. Prof., Univ. of Peloponnese, Kalamata, 2017. Hon. PhD Athens, 2005. *Publications:* A Commentary on Five Odes of Pindar, 1981; (with R. A. Reid) Demosthenes: Selected Private Speeches, 1985; Lysias: Selected Speeches, 1989; Apollodoros Against Neaira: [Demosthenes] 59, 1992; Trials from Classical Athens, 1997, 2nd edn 2011; The Speeches of Aeschines, 2000; Democracy in Classical Athens, 2000, 2nd edn 2017; Lysiae orationes cum fragmentis, 2007; (ed jtly) Reading the Victory Ode, 2012; (ed jtly) Receiving the Komos, 2012; (ed jtly) Marathon: 2,500 years, 2013; (ed jtly) Eros in Ancient Greece, 2013; (ed jtly) Iambus and Elegy: new approaches, 2016; Thermopylae, 2019; (ed jtly) Use and Abuse of Law in the Athenian Courts, 2019; (ed jtly) Greek Epigram from the Hellenistic to the Early Byzantine Era, 2019; articles on Greek lyric, epic, drama, oratory and law. *Address:* Department of Greek and Latin, University College London, Gower Street, WC1E 6BT. *T:* (020) 7679 7522.

**CAREY, Sir de Vic (Graham),** Kt 2002; Bailiff of Guernsey, 1999–2005; a Judge of the Court of Appeal, Guernsey, 2005–12; Commissioner, Royal Court of Jersey, 2006–10 (Judge of the Court of Appeal, 1999–2005); *b* 15 June 1940; *s of* Victor Michael de Vic Carey and Jean Burnett (*née* Bullen); *m* 1968, Bridget Lindsay Smith; *two s two d*. *Educ:* Cheam Sch.; Bryanston Sch.; Trinity Hall, Cambridge (BA 1962; MA 1967); Univ. of Caen (Cert. des études juridiques françaises et normandes 1965). Admitted Solicitor, 1965; Advocate, Royal Court of Guernsey, 1966; QC (Guernsey) 1989. People's Dep., States of Guernsey, 1976; Solicitor-Gen. for Guernsey, 1977–82; Attorney-Gen., 1982–92; Receiver-Gen., 1985–92; Dep. Bailiff, 1992–99. Mem., Gen. Synod of C of E, 1982–98; Chm., House of Laity, Winchester Dio. Synod, 1993–97. Consultant to Archbishop of Canterbury's Commn on relationship of the CI to the wider C of E, 2018. *Address:* Les Padins, St Saviours, Guernsey GY7 9JJ. *T:* (01481) 264587.

**CAREY, Godfrey Mohun Cecil;** QC 1991; a Recorder of the Crown Court, 1986–2013; *b* 31 Oct. 1941; *s of* Dr Godfrey Fraser Carey, LVO and Prudence Loveday (*née* Webb); *m* 1st, 1965, Caroline Jane Riggall (marr. diss. 1975); *one s one d* (and *one s decd*); 2nd, 1978, Dorothy May Sturgeon (marr. diss. 1983); *one d*. *Educ:* Highfield, Liphook; Eton. Legal Advr, Small Engine Div., Rolls Royce Ltd, 1964–70. Called to the Bar, Inner Temple, 1969, Bencher, 2000; in practice at the Bar, 1971–2009. Legal Mem., Mental Health Review Tribunals, 2000–12. Fellow, NSPCC Full Stop Campaign, 2000–09. Trustee, Citizens Advice, 2015–18. Church Recorder, Arts Soc., 2017–. *Recreations:* music, the history of muffins. *Address:* 5 Paper Buildings, EC4Y 7HB. *T:* (020) 7583 6117. *Club:* Boodle's.

**CAREY, His Honour Jeremy Reynolds;** DL; a Circuit Judge, 2004–18; Resident Judge, Maidstone Crown Court, 2010–18; a Deputy High Court Judge, 2013–18; *b* 15 Jan. 1950; *s of* late Edward Carey and Dr Audrey Carey (*née* Coghlan); *m* 1972, Alysoun Marshall; *one s two d*. *Educ:* King's Sch., Canterbury; Selwyn Coll., Cambridge (BA 1973). Called to the Bar, Inner Temple, 1974, Bencher, 2015; Asst Recorder, 1998–2000, Recorder, 2000–04; Liaison Judge for Kent Magistracy, 2005–10. Hon. Recorder, Maidstone, 2006–. Lay Assessor to GMC, 2000–04. Mem., Disciplinary Cttee, Bar Council, 2001–04. Member: Inst. of Arbitrators, 2000–04; Parole Bd, 2010–15. DL Kent, 2013. *Publications:* (sub-ed) Butterworth's Law of Limitation, 2003. *Recreations:* walking, golf, cricket, wine-tasting. *Clubs:* Boodle's; Royal St George's Golf (Sandwich), Rye Golf, Band of Brothers Cricket; Lucifer Golfing Society.

**CAREY, Prof. John,** FBA 1996; FRSL 1982; Merton Professor of English Literature, Oxford University, 1976–2001; Fellow of Merton College, Oxford, 1976–2001, now Emeritus; *b* 5 April 1934; *s of* Charles William Carey and Winifred Ethel Carey (*née* Cook); *m* 1960, Gillian Mary Florence Booth; *two s*. *Educ:* Richmond and East Sheen County Grammar Sch.; St John's Coll., Oxford (MA, DPhil; Hon. Fellow, 1991). 2nd Lieut, East Surrey Regt, 1953–54; Harmsworth Sen. Scholar, Merton Coll., Oxford, 1957–58; Lectr, Christ Church, Oxford, 1958–59; Andrew Bradley Jun. Research Fellow, Balliol, Oxford, 1959–60; Tutorial Fellow: Keble Coll., Oxford, 1960–64; St John's Coll., Oxford, 1964–75. Principal book reviewer, Sunday Times, 1977–. Chairman: Booker Prize Judges, 1982, 2003; Man Booker Internat. Prize Judges, 2005; W. H. Smith Prize Judge, 1990–2004; Irish Times Lit. Prize Judge, 1993. Mem. Council, RSL, 1989–95. Hon.

Fellow, Balliol Coll., Oxford, 1992. Honored Scholar, Milton Soc. of America, 2013. *Publications:* The Poems of John Milton (ed with Alastair Fowler), 1968, 2nd edn 1997; Milton, 1969; (ed) Andrew Marvell, 1969; (ed) The Private Memoirs and Confessions of a Justified Sinner, by James Hogg, 1969, 2nd edn 1981; The Violent Effigy: a study of Dickens' imagination, 1973, 2nd edn 1991; (trans.) Milton, Christian Doctrine, 1973; Thackeray: Prodigal Genius, 1977; John Donne: Life, Mind and Art, 1981, 2nd edn 1990; (ed) William Golding—the Man and his Books: a tribute on his 75th birthday, 1986; Original Copy: selected journalism and reviews, 1987; (ed) The Faber Book of Reportage, 1987; (ed) Donne, 1990; The Intellectuals and the Masses, 1992; (ed) Saki, Short Stories, 1994; (ed) The Faber Book of Science, 1995; (ed) The Faber Book of Utopias, 1999; Pure Pleasure, 2000; What Good Are the Arts?, 2005; William Golding, the Man Who Wrote Lord of the Flies: a life, 2009 (James Tait Black Meml Prize, 2010); The Unexpected Professor: an Oxford life in books, 2014; The Essential Paradise Lost, 2017; articles in Rev. of English Studies, Mod. Lang. Rev., etc. *Recreations:* swimming, gardening, bee-keeping. *Address:* Brasenose Cottage, Lyneham, Oxon OX7 6QL; 57 Stapleton Road, Headington, Oxford OX3 7LX. *T:* (01865) 764304.

**CAREY, Dr Nicholas Anthony Dermot**; Chairman, Alzheimer's Society, 2001–07; *b* 4 May 1939; *s* of Eustace Dermot Carey and Audrey Mabel Carey (*née* Grenfell); *m* 1964, Helen Margaret Askey; two *s*. *Educ:* Shrewsbury Sch.; Trinity Coll., Dublin (BA, MA); King's Coll., Cambridge (PhD). ICI, 1968–93: Gen. Manager, Chlorine and derivatives, 1980–87; Man. Dir, Petrochemicals and Plastics, 1987–92; Planning Manager, Millbank, 1992–93; Dir Gen., City and Guilds of London Inst., 1993–2001. Chm., Llandudno Dwellings Co., 1998–2015. Governor, Reaseheath Coll., 2001–13. Liveryman: Vintners' Co., 1960–; Tallow Chandlers' Co., 1995–; Guild of Educators, 2001– (Master, 2004–05; Treas., 2008–14). *Recreations:* opera, travel. *E:* nadcarey@aol.com. *Club:* Athenæum.

**CAREY, Peter Philip**, AO 2012; FRSL; writer; *b* 7 May 1943; *s* of Percival Stanley Carey and Helen Jean Carey; *m* 1st, 1964, Leigh Weetman; 2nd, 1985, Alison Margaret Summers; two *s*; 3rd, 2007, Frances Rachel Coady, *qv*. *Educ:* Geelong Grammar Sch., Vic, Aust. Member: Amer. Acad. Arts and Scis, 2003; AAAL, 2016. FRSL 1988. Hon. Fellow, Australian Acad. Humanities 2001. Hon. DLitt: Queensland, 1989; Monash, 2000; Sydney, 2015; Hon. DFA New School Univ., NY, 1998. *Publications:* Fat Man in History, 1980; Bliss, 1981; Illywhacker, 1985; Oscar and Lucinda, 1988 (Booker Prize, 1988; filmed, 1998); The Tax Inspector, 1991; The Unusual Life of Tristan Smith, 1994; Collected Stories, 1995; The Big Bazoohley, 1995; Jack Maggs, 1997; True History of the Kelly Gang, 2000 (Commonwealth Writers' Prize, Booker Prize, 2001); 30 Days in Sydney, 2001; My Life as a Fake, 2003; Wrong About Japan, 2004; Theft: a love story, 2006; His Illegal Self, 2008; Parrot and Olivier in America, 2010; The Chemistry of Tears, 2012; Amnesia, 2014; A Long Way From Home, 2018. *Recreation:* sleeping. *Address:* c/o Rogers, Coleridge & White, Powis Mews, W11 1JN.

**CAREY-ELMS, Marsha Marilyn;** *see* Elms, M. M.

**CAREY EVANS, David Lloyd**, OBE 1984; JP; DL; farmer; *b* 14 Aug. 1925; *s* of Sir Thomas Carey Evans, MC, FRCS and Lady Olwen Carey Evans, DBE; *m* 1959, Annwen Williams; three *s* one *d*. *Educ:* Rottingdean Sch.; Oundle Sch.; Univ. of Wales, Bangor. BSc (Agric.) 1950. Sub-Lieut, RNVR, 1943–46; farming, 1947–; Chm., Welsh Council, NFU, 1976–79; Welsh Representative and Chm., Welsh Panel, CCAHC, 1974; Chm., WAOS. JP Portmadoc, Gwynedd, 1969. DL Gwynedd 1988. *Address:* Eisteddfa, Pentrefelin, Criccieth, Gwynedd LL52 0PT. *T:* (01766) 522104.

**CAREY-HUGHES, Richard John**; QC 2000; a Recorder, since 2000; *b* 18 Dec. 1948; *s* of John Carey-Hughes and Esme (*née* Klein); *m* 1st, 1972, Elizabeth Blackwood (marr. diss. 1976); one *d*; 2nd, 1987, Sophia Bayne-Powell (marr. diss. 1998); one *s* two *d*. *Educ:* Rugby Sch. Airline pilot with BOAC, then British Airways, 1969–76; called to the Bar, Gray's Inn, 1977, Bencher, 2007; specialist in crime cases. Member, Committee: Criminal Bar Assoc., 1991–98 (Hon. Sec., 1996–98); S Eastern Circuit, 1998–2001. *Recreations:* gardening, cycling, cinema. *Address:* Church Court Chambers, 2nd Floor, Goldsmith Building, Temple, EC4Y 7BL. *Club:* Chelsea Arts.

**CARFRAE, Tristram George Allen**, RDI 2006; FREng; FTSE; FIStructE; Deputy Chair, Arup Group Ltd, since 2014 (Director, since 2005); *b* 1 April 1959; *s* of Lt Col Charles Cecil Allen Carfrae and June Beatrice de Warrenne Carfrae; *m* 1987, Jane Irving Burrows; one *s* one *d*. *Educ:* Dartington Primary Sch., Devon; King Edward VI Comprehensive Sch., Totnes; Clare Coll., Cambridge (BA Mech. Scis Tripos 1981). MIStructE 1989; MIE(Aust) 1992, FIE(Aust) 2010; FTSE 2004; FREng 2011; FIStructE 2018. Structural engr with Arup, in London and Sydney, 1981–; involved in design of: Lloyds of London, 1986; Schlumberger Res. Centre, Cambridge, 1984; Sydney Football Stadium, 1988; San Nicola Stadium, Bari, 1990; Pavilion of the Future, Seville, 1992; Brisbane Convention Exhibn Centre, 1994; Sydney Olympic Velodrome, Tennis Centre and Sports Halls, 2000; Aurora Place, Sydney, 2000; City of Manchester Stadium, 2002; Khalifa Olympic Stadium, Doha, 2005; Northern Stand, Melbourne Cricket Ground, 2006; Beijing Olympic Aquatic Centre, 2008; 1 Shelley Street, Sydney, 2009; Kurilpa Bridge, Brisbane, 2009; Helix Bridge, Singapore, 2009; AAMI Park Stadium, Melbourne, 2010; 111 Eagle Street, Brisbane, 2012; Sagrada Familia, 2013–; Singapore Sports Hub, 2014; Kuwait Internat. Airport, 2018. Chair: Arup Design and Tech. Exec., 2004–07; Arup Bldgs Exec., 2007–14; Arup Univ. Council, 2009–18; Arup People Council, 2017–19. Trustee, Powerhouse Mus. Trust, 2009–11. Arup Fellow, 2002–. FRSA. Master, Faculty of RDIs, 2017. Australian Professional Engr of Year, Instn of Engrs, Australia, 2001; Milne Medal, British Gp, IABSE, 2006; MacRobert Award, RAEng, 2009; Gold Medal, Instn of Structural Engrs, 2014; Internat. Award of Merit, IABSE, 2018. *Publications:* contribs to Australian Jl Structural Engrg, The Structural Engr. *Recreations:* sailing, travelling, eating and drinking. *Address:* (office) 13 Fitzroy Street, W1T 4BQ. *E:* tristram.carfrae@arup.com.

**CARINE, Rear-Adm. James;** Chief of Staff to Commander-in-Chief Naval Home Command, 1989–91; Registrar, Arab Horse Society, 1992–2000; *b* 14 Sept. 1934; *s* of Amos Carine and Kathleen Prudence Carine (*née* Kelly); *m* 1961, (Carolyn) Sally Taylor; three *s* one *d* (and two *s* decd). *Educ:* Victoria Road Sch., Castletown, IoM; King William's Coll., IoM. FCIS 1971. Joined Royal Navy 1951; Captain 1980; Sec., Second Sea Lord, 1979–82; SACLANT HQ, Norfolk, Va, 1982–85; Naval Home Staff, 1985–88; Commodore in Comd, HMS Drake, 1988–89. Pres., RN Assoc. (IOM), 1992–2000. Member: London Campaign Cttee for Multiple Sclerosis, 1993–95; Cttee, Ex-Services Mental Welfare Soc., 1997–2003; Copyright Tribunal, 1999–2009. Chairman: Age Concern Swindon, 2000–05; Wilts NHS Ambulance Service, 2002–06; Royal United Hosp. Bath NHS Trust, 2006–10. Dir, United Services Trust, 1995–2005. Governor, St Antony's-Leweston Sch., 1996–2003. Chartered Secretaries' & Administrators' Co.: Liveryman, 1988; Mem., Court of Assistants, 1989; Jun. Warden, 1995–96; Sen. Warden, 1996–97; Master, 1997–98. KSG 1983. *Publications:* Odyssey of a Castletown Boy, 2012. *Recreation:* horse racing. *Address:* 5 Little Sands, Yatton Keynell, Chippenham, Wilts SN14 7BA.

**CARINGTON,** family name of **Baron Carrington.**

**CARLAW, (David) Jackson**, CBE 2019; Member (C) Eastwood, Scottish Parliament, since 2016 (Scotland West, 2007–16); *b* 12 April 1959; *s* of Ian Alexander Carlaw and Maureen Patricia Carlaw; *m* 1987, Wynne Stewart Martin; two *s*. *Educ:* Glasgow Acad. Man. Dir, Wylies Ltd, 1987–2000; Chm., First Ford (trading name of Eleander Ltd), 2000–02. Nat. Chm., Scottish Young Conservatives, 1984–86; Chm., Eastwood Conservatives, 1988–92; Scottish Conservative and Unionist Party: Vice Chm., 1992–97; Dep. Chm., 1997–98, 2005–06; Mem. Scottish Conservative Exec., 2003–07. Scottish Government: Shadow Minister for Public Health, 2007–10, for Transport, Infrastructure and Climate Change, 2010–11, for Health, 2011–16; Shadow Cabinet Sec. for Culture, Tourism and Ext. Affairs, 2016–. Convenor: Forth Crossing Bill Cttee, Scottish Parlt, 2009–10; Cross-Party Gp, Building Bridges with Israel, 2016–. Member: Public Petitions Cttee, 2012–16; Commn on Parly Reform, 2016–; Culture, Tourism and Ext. Affairs Cttee, 2016–18; Scottish Parly Corporate Body, 2016–. Dep. Leader, Scottish Cons. and Unionist Party, 2011– (Interim Leader, 2018–19). Trustee, Glasgow Educnl and Marshall Trust, 2000–14. Gov., Hutchesons' Grammar Sch., 2000–03. *Recreations:* theatre, film, reading, travel, family life. *Address:* Scottish Parliament, Edinburgh EH99 1SP. *T:* (0131) 348 6800. *E:* Jackson.Carlaw.msp@parliament.scot.

**CARLETON, Air Vice-Marshal Geoffrey Wellesley**, CB 1997; Director, Royal Air Force Legal Services, Ministry of Defence, 1992–97; Head of RAF Prosecuting Authority, 1997, retired; *b* 22 Sept. 1935; *s* of Gp Capt. Cyril Wellesley Carleton and Frances Beatrice (*née* Hensman); *m* 1985, Dianne Margaret Creswick; one *s*. *Educ:* Sherborne Sch. Admitted solicitor, 1959; commnd RAF, 1959, Pilot Officer, 1959–61; Asst Solicitor, Herbert Smith & Co., 1961–65; re-joined RAF, 1965 as Flt Lieut; Legal Officer, HQ MEAF, Aden, HQ NEAF, Cyprus, HQ FEAF, Singapore, HQ RAF, Germany, 1965–78; Deputy Director of Legal Services: HQ RAF, Germany, 1978–82 and 1985–88; MoD, 1988–92. Non-exec. Dir, Poole Hospital NHS Trust, 1998–2006; Gov., Poole Hospital NHS Foundn Trust, 2009– (Vice Chm., 2014–). *Publications:* articles in professional and service jls and pubns. *Recreations:* sailing, ski-ing, equitation, opera. *Address:* c/o National Westminster Bank, 5 Old Christchurch Road, Bournemouth BH1 1DU. *Clubs:* Royal Air Force, Royal Ocean Racing.

**CARLETON-SMITH, Gen. Sir Mark (Alexander Popham)**, KCB 2019; CBE 2009 (OBE 2003; MBE 1999); Chief of the General Staff, since 2018; Aide-de-Camp General to the Queen, since 2018; *b* Bielefeld, W Germany, 9 Feb. 1964; *s* of Maj.-Gen. Sir Michael (Edward) Carleton-Smith, *qv*; *m* 1991, Catherine Mary Nalder; one *s* one *d*. *Educ:* Eton Coll.; Durham Univ. (BA Hons Hist. and Politics); RMA, Sandhurst. Commnd Irish Guards, 1986; psc 1996; COS, 19 Mechanized Bde, 1999–2001; MA to C-in-C Land Forces, 2001–02; CO 22 SAS Regt, 2002–05; Dep. Dir, Policy Planning, MoD, 2005–06; Commander: 16 Air Assault Bde, 2006–08; Helmand Task Force, and British Forces, Afghanistan, 2008; Dir, Army Resources and Plans, MoD, 2008–11; Dir, Special Forces, MoD, 2012–15; Dir Strategy, Army HQ, 2015–16; Dep. Chief of Defence Staff (Military Strategy and Operations), MoD, 2016–18. Regtl Lt Col, Irish Guards, 2012–; Hon. Col, Oxford Univ. OTC, 2017–. Trustee, Gerry Holdsworth Charitable Trust, 2011– (Chm.). *Recreations:* travel, hill-walking, history, riding, ski-ing. *Address:* Regimental Headquarters, Irish Guards, Wellington Barracks, Birdcage Walk, SW1E 6HQ. *Clubs:* Pratt's, Pilgrims', Chelsea Arts, Pitt, Cavalry and Guards, Army and Navy.

**CARLETON-SMITH, Maj.-Gen. Sir Michael (Edward)**, Kt 1998; CBE 1980 (MBE 1966); *b* 5 May 1931; *s* of late Lt-Col D. L. G. Carleton-Smith and Mrs B. L. C. Carleton-Smith (*née* Popham); *m* 1st, 1963, Helga Katja Stoss (*d* 1993); three *s*; 2nd, 2011, Lady Francis, (Penny), *widow* of Sir Richard Francis, KCMG; two step *s*. *Educ:* Cheltenham Coll. Jun. Sch.; Radley Coll.; RMA, Sandhurst. Graduate: Army Staff Coll.; JSSC; NDC; RCDS. Commissioned into The Rifle Brigade, 1951; Rifle Bde, Germany, 1951–53; active service: Kenya, 1954–55; Weapon Trng Officer, Eaton Hall OCS, 1956; Malaya, 1957; Exchange PPCLI, Canada, 1958–60; GSO2 General Staff, HQ1(BR) Corps, 1962–63; Rifle Brigade: Cyprus, Hong Kong, active service, Borneo, 1964–66; Sch. of Infantry Staff, 1967–68; Comd Rifle Depot, 1970–72; Directing Staff NDC, 1972–74; Col General Staff, HQ BAOR, 1974–77; Commander Gurkha Field Force, Hong Kong, 1977–79; Dep. Director Army Staff Duties, MoD, 1981; Defence Advr and Head of British Defence Liaison Staff, Canberra, Australia, also Mil. Advr, Canberra, and Wellington, NZ, and Defence Advr, PNG, 1982–85, retd. Dir-Gen., Marie Curie Meml Foundn, then Marie Curie Cancer Care, 1985–96 (Vice-Pres., 2010–); Chm., Marie Curie Trading Co., 1990–95. Chm., Leicester Royal Infirmary NHS Trust, 1998–2000. Vice-Chm., Nat. Council for Hospice and Specialist Palliative Care Services, 1992–96. Chairman: Suzy Lamplugh Trust, 2000–01; Progressive Supra Nuclear Palsy Assoc. (Europe), 2001–07; Patron, Integrated Neurological Services, 2009–. Gov., Royal Star and Garter Home, 1998–2002. Trustee, Britain Australia Soc., 1999–2003. DL Leics, 1992–2011. *Recreations:* travel, current affairs, history. *Address:* Cambridge Villa, Jocelyn Road, Richmond, Surrey TW9 2TJ. *E:* mike@carleton-smith.com.
*See also* Gen. Sir M. A. P. Carleton-Smith.

**CARLIER, Maj.-Gen. Anthony Neil**, CB 1992; OBE 1982; Director, Haig Homes, 1992–2002; *b* 11 Jan. 1937; *s* of Geoffrey Anthony George and Sylvia Maude Carlier; *m* 1974, Daphne Kathleen Humphreys; one *s* one *d*. *Educ:* Highgate Sch.; RMA Sandhurst; RMCS. BSc(Eng) London. Troop Comdr, Cyprus, 1962–64; GSO3, 19 Inf. Bde, Borneo, 1965–66; Instructor, RMA Sandhurst, 1967–70; Staff Course: RMCS Shrivenham, 1971; BRNC Greenwich, 1972; GSO2, Staff of Flag Officer, Carriers and Amphibious Ships, 1973–74; Sqn Comdr, 1975–76; Regtl Comdr, 1977–80; Mil. Asst to Army Bd Mem., 1980–83; Engr Gp Comdr, 1983–85; rcds, 1986; Comdr British Forces, Falkland Is, 1987–88; Chief, Jt Services Liaison Organisation, Bonn, 1989–90; Team Leader, QMG's Logistic Support Review, 1991–92. Col Comdt, RE, 1993–2000. President: Officers' Christian Union, 1992–97; Mission to Mil. Garrisons, 1992–2017; Chm., UK Appeal Cttee for Christ Church Cathedral, Falkland Is, 1989–2000. Trustee: Cornelius Trust, 1992–2002; Royal Engineer Yacht Club, 1992–2013; Leadership and Ethics Centre, Ballycastle, Co. Antrim, 2001–15. Gov., Monkton Combe Sch., 1996–2004; Chm., Clare Park Private Retirement Residences, 2007–16. *Recreations:* offshore sailing, fishing, gardening, DIY. *Clubs:* Royal Engineer Yacht; International Association of Cape Horners (Faversham).
*See also* Master of Polwarth.

**CARLILE,** family name of **Baron Carlile of Berriew.**

**CARLILE OF BERRIEW,** Baron *cr* 1999 (Life Peer), of Berriew in the County of Powys; **Alexander Charles Carlile,** CBE 2012; QC 1984; a Recorder, 1986–2014; a Deputy High Court Judge, 1998–2014; *b* 12 Feb. 1948; *m* 1st, Frances (marr. diss. 2007), *d* of Michael and Elizabeth Soley; three *d*; 2nd, Alison Frances Josephine Levitt, *qv*; two step *d*. *Educ:* Epsom Coll.; King's Coll., London (LLB; AKC; FKC 2003). Called to the Bar, Gray's Inn, 1970, Bencher, 1992. Hon. Recorder, 1995–2009, Dep. Chief Steward, 2009–, City of Hereford. Contested (L) Flint E, Feb. 1974, 1979. MP (L) 1983–88, (Lib Dem) 1988–97, Montgomery. Chm., Welsh Liberal Party, 1980–82; Leader, Welsh Lib Dems, 1992–97. Chm., Welsh Assembly Review on Safety of Children in the NHS, 2000–02; Ind. Reviewer of Terrorism Legislation, 2002–11. Non-executive Director: Wynnstay Group (formerly Wynnstay & Clwyd Farmers) plc, 1998–2015; SC Strategy Ltd, 2012–. Member: Adv. Council on Public Records, 1989–95; GMC, 1989–99; Bar Council, 2012–14; Commn on Freedom of Information, 2015–16. Chairman: Competition Appeals Tribunal, 2005–13; Lloyd's Enforcement Bd, 2011–; Chartered Security Professionals Registration Authy, 2011–; London Policing Ethics Panel, 2014–16; Addaction, 2017–; Commonwealth Human Rights Initiative UK, 2018–. Pres., Howard League for Penal Reform, 2006–11. Director and Trustee: Nuffield Trust, 1997–2007; White Ensign Assoc. Ltd, 2002– (Vice-Chm., 2018–); Trustee, Royal Med. Foundn of Epsom Coll., 2003– (Pres., 2017–); Patron, Soc. for Radiol Protection, 2017–. Fellow, Industry and Parlt Trust, 1985. Hon. Prof. of Law, Univ. of Swansea, 2018–. *Recreations:* theatre, reading, Burnley FC, food. *Address:* House of Lords, SW1A 0PW.

**CARLILE OF BERRIEW, Lady;** *see* Levitt, A. F. J.

**CARLILE, Trevor Mansfield;** Director, Strategy, Health and Safety Executive, since 2010; *b* Portland, Dorset, 23 April 1961; *s* of Owen Carlile and Yvonne Carlile; *m* 1985, Maureen Hutchings; two *s* one *d*. *Educ:* Royal Hospital Sch., Ipswich; Open Univ. (BSc 1st Cl. Hons, MBA). Royal Military Police, 1978–86; Scenes of Crime Officer, Kent Police, 1987–98; Scientific Support Officer, 1998–2000, Hd, Forensic Services, Major Crime Scenes, 2000–04, Metropolitan Police Service; Hd, Cross Govt Identity Strategy, Home Office, 2004–07; Dir, Services Delivery, Criminal Records Bureau, 2007–10. *Recreations:* Rugby, golf, running, gym, reading. *Address:* 4 Roseleigh Road, Sittingbourne, Kent ME10 1RP. *T:* 07814 711544, (01795) 474970. *Club:* Sittingbourne Rugby.

**CARLING, Philip George;** Chairman, Sports Council Wales, 2004–10; Partner, Equus International, since 2010; *b* Carshalton, 25 Nov. 1946; *s* of late George Carling and Alice Carling; *m* 2009, Janet Powell; one step *s* one step *d*, and two *s* two *d* by a previous marriage. *Educ:* Kingston Grammar Sch.; St Catharine's Coll., Cambridge (BA 1969; MA 1972). Schoolmaster, Dulwich Coll., 1971–73; Man. Dir, Lambton Squash Hldgs, 1973–78; Chief Executive: Nottinghamshire CCC, 1978–83; Glamorgan CCC, 1983–90; Chm., Carling Associates, 1990–2004. UK Sport: Mem. Bd, 2004–10; Chm., Remuneration Cttee, 2005–; Member: Audit Cttee, 2006–; Major Events Panel, 2006–. Chair, Nat. Anti-Doping Proj. Bd, 2008–09; Vice Chair, UK Anti-Doping, 2009–16. Member: TCCB, 1983–90; UK Sports Cabinet, 2004–10; London 2012 Olympic Legacy Bd, 2009–10. *Recreations:* golf, folk music, cinema, watching cricket and Association Football (cricket and hockey blue, Cambridge). *T:* 07802 200122. *E:* carlingphil@gmail.com. *Club:* Southerndown Golf.

**CARLING, William David Charles,** OBE 1991; Rugby football commentator, ITV, since 1997; Leadership Mentor, England Rugby, since 2018; *b* 12 Dec. 1965; *s* of Pamela and Bill Carling; *m* 1999, Lisa Cooke; two *c*. *Educ:* Sedbergh School; Durham Univ. (BA Psych.). Played for Harlequins, 1987–97 and 1999–2000; international career, 1988–97: 1st cap for England, 1988; 72 caps, 59 as Captain; Captain of England, 1988–96 (centre three-quarter); captained: three Grand Slam sides, 1991, 1992, 1995; World Cup final, 1991; Barbarians, in Hong Kong 7's, 1991; England tour, South Africa, 1994; World Cup, South Africa, 1995; Mem., British Lions, NZ tour, 1993. *Publications:* Captain's Diary, 1991; Rugby Skills, 1994; (with R. Heller) The Way to Win, 1995; (with P. Ackford) Will Carling: my autobiography, 1998. *Recreations:* theatre, sketching, golf. *Address:* WCM, 19–20 Bourne Court, Southend Road, Woodford Green, Essex IG8 8HD. *Clubs:* Special Forces, Groucho; Harlequins, Harbour.

**CARLISLE, 13th Earl of,** *cr* 1661; **George William Beaumont Howard;** Viscount Howard of Morpeth, Baron Dacre of Gillesland 1661; Lord Ruthven of Freeland 1651; *b* 15 Feb. 1949; *s* of 12th Earl of Carlisle, MC, and Hon. Ela Hilda Aline Beaumont, *o d* of 2nd Viscount Allendale, KG, CB, CBE, MC; *S* father, 1994. *Educ:* Eton Coll.; Balliol Coll., Oxford; Army Staff Coll., Camberley. 9th/12th Royal Lancers, 1967–87; Lieut 1970, Captain 1974, Major 1981. Lectr, Estonian Nat. Defence and Public Service Acad., 1995–96. Sec., British-Estonian All-Party Parly Gp, 1997–99. Contested: (L/Alliance) Easington, 1987; (Lib Dem): Northumbria, European parly elecn, 1989; Leeds West, 1992. Order of Marjamac, 1st class, 1998. *Recreations:* reading, travel, learning Estonian. *Heir: b* Hon. Philip Charles Wentworth Howard [*b* 25 March 1963; *m* 1992, Elizabeth Harrison (*née* Moore); one *s* one *d*]. *Clubs:* Beefsteak, Pratt's.

**CARLISLE, Bishop of,** since 2009; **Rt Rev. James William Scobie Newcome;** DL; Clerk of the Closet to the Queen, since 2014; *b* 24 July 1953; *s* of John Newcome and Jane Newcome (*née* Scobie); *m* 1977, Alison Margaret (*née* Clarke); two *s* two *d*. *Educ:* Marlborough Coll.; Trinity Coll., Oxford (BA Mod. Hist. 1974, MA 1978); Selwyn Coll., Cambridge (BA Theol. 1977, MA 1981); Ridley Hall, Cambridge. Ordained deacon, 1978, priest, 1979; Asst Curate, All Saints, Leavesden, 1978–82; Minister, Bar Hill LEP, 1982–94; Tutor in Pastoral Studies, Ethics and Integrating Theology, Ridley Hall, Cambridge, 1983–88; RD, N Stowe, 1993–94; Residentiary Canon, Chester Cathedral, 1994–2002; Diocesan Dir of Ordinands, 1994–2000, of Ministry, 1996–2002, dio. Chester; Bishop Suffragan of Penrith, 2002–09. Entered H of L, 2013. Lead Bishop: on Health, 2010–; for URC, 2012–; Jt Chair, Rose Castle Foundn, Nat. Stewardship Cttee, 2011–17. Nat. Chaplain, RBL, 2016–. Mem., Soc. for Study of Christian Ethics, 1985–. Pres., St John's Coll., Durham, 2012 (Hon. Fellow). DL Cumbria, 2013. Mem., H of L Select Cttee on Long Term Sustainability of NHS, 2017. FRSA. *Publications:* (contrib.) Setting the Church of England Free, 2003; At the End of the Day, 2014; book reviews for Anvil. *Recreations:* film, contemporary novels, cross-country running, furniture restoration. *Address:* Bishop's House, Ambleside Road, Keswick, Cumbria CA12 4DD. *T:* (01768) 773430. *E:* bishop.carlisle@carlislediocese.org.uk. *Club:* Athenæum.

**CARLISLE, Dean of;** *see* Boyling, Very Rev. M. C.

**CARLISLE, Archdeacon of;** *see* Townend, Ven. L. S.

**CARLISLE, Hugh Bernard Harwood,** QC 1978; *b* 14 March 1937; *s* of late W. H. Carlisle, FRCS (Ed), FRCOG, and Joyce Carlisle; *m* 1964, Veronica Marjorie, *d* of late George Arthur Worth, MBE; one *s* one *d*. *Educ:* Oundle Sch.; Downing Coll., Cambridge. Nat. Service, 2nd Lt, RA. Called to the Bar, Middle Temple, 1961, Bencher, 1985. Jun. Treasury Counsel for Personal Injuries Cases, 1975–78; a Recorder, 1983–2002; a Deputy High Court Judge, 1984–2002; Hd of Chambers, 1988–2000. Dept of Trade Inspector: Bryanston Finance Ltd, 1978–87; Milbury plc, 1985–87. Pres., Transport Tribunal, 1997–2009; a Judge of Upper Tribunal, 2009–12. Member: Criminal Injuries Compensation Bd, 1982–2000; Bar Council, 1989–92 (Chm., Professional Conduct Cttee, 1991–92). *Recreations:* fly fishing, woodworking, croquet. *Address:* Temple Garden Chambers, 1 Harcourt Buildings, Temple, EC4Y 9DA. *T:* (020) 7583 1315. *Clubs:* Garrick, Hurlingham (Chm., 1982–85).

**CARLISLE, Sir James (Beethoven),** GCMG 1993; KGN 1998; Governor-General of Antigua and Barbuda, 1993–2007; *b* 5 Aug. 1937; *s* of late James Carlisle and of Jestina Jones; *m* 1st, 1963, Umilta Mercer (marr. diss. 1973); one *s* one *d*; 2nd, 1973, Anne Jenkins (marr. diss. 1984); one *d*; 3rd, 1984, Nalda Amelia Meade; one *s* one *d*. *Educ:* Univ. of Dundee (BDS). Dental surgeon, 1972–93. Chief Scout of Antigua and Barbuda. Chm., Nat. Parks Authority, 1986–90. Member: BDA; Amer. Acad. of Laser Dentistry; Internat. Assoc. of Laser Dentistry. FICD. Hon. FDSRCSE 1995. Hon. LLD Andrews Univ., USA, 1995. Kt Grand Cross, Order of Queen of Sheba (Ethiopia), 1995. KStJ 2001. *Recreations:* gardening, music, reading. *Address:* PO Box W1644, St John's, Antigua, West Indies.

**CARLISLE, Sir (John) Michael,** Kt 1985; DL; CEng, FIMechE, FIMarEST; Chairman, Trent Regional Health Authority, 1982–94; *b* 16 Dec. 1929; *s* of John Hugh Carlisle and Lilian Amy (*née* Smith); *m* 1957, Mary Scott Young; one *s* one *d*. *Educ:* King Edward VII Sch., Sheffield; Sheffield Univ. (BEng). Served Royal Navy (Lieut), 1952–54. Production Engr, Lockwood & Carlisle Ltd, 1954–57, Man. Dir, 1958–70, Chm. and Man. Dir, 1970–81; Dir of several overseas subsid. cos; Director: Eric Woodward (Electrical) Ltd, 1965–85; Diesel Marine Internat., 1981–89; Torday & Carlisle, 1981–94. Chairman: N Sheffield Univ. HMC, 1971–74; Sheffield AHA(T), 1974–82; Community Health Sheffield NHS Trust, 1994–99; Scarborough and NE Yorks Healthcare NHS Trust, 2007–12; Healthwatch N Yorks, 2014–16; Member: Sheffield HMC, 1969–71; Bd of Governors, United Sheffield Hosps, 1972–74; MRC, 1991–95; NHS Policy Bd, 1993–94; Scarborough, Whitby and Ryedale Patient and Public Involvement Forum, 2003–07. Member Council: Sheffield Chamber of Commerce, 1967–78; Production Engrg Res. Assoc., 1968–73; Chm., Sheffield Productivity Assoc., 1970; Pres., Sheffield Jun. Chamber of Commerce, 1967–68; non-executive Director: Fenchurch Midlands Ltd, 1986–94; Norhomes plc, 1989–97; Welpac plc, 1991–95; Residences at York plc, 1992–97; York Science Park Ltd, 1992–; York Science Park (Innovation) Centre Ltd, 1992–2001; Headrow Northern plc, 1992–97; Headrow Western plc, 1993–97; Xceleron (formerly CBAMS) Ltd, 1997–2005; SE Sheffield Primary Care Gp, 1999–2001. Chm., Sheffield Macmillan Horizons Appeal, 1999–2002; Trustee, Age Concern (Scarborough and Dist.), 2004–09. Governor: Sheffield City Polytechnic, 1979–82 (Hon. Fellow, 1977); Sheffield High Sch., 1977–87; Member: Sheffield Univ. Court, 1968–2005; Sheffield Univ. Careers Adv. Bd, 1974–82; Nottingham Univ. Court, 1982–94; Court, York Univ., 1991– (Mem. Council, 1991–2006); Pro-Chancellor, 1996–2006; Vice-Chm., 2001–06); Bd, Hull-York Med. Sch., 2002–07 (Chm., Fitness to Practise Cttee, 2006–13). CCMI. Freeman, City of London, 1989; Freeman, Co. of Cutlers in Hallamshire. DL S Yorks, 1996. Hon. LLD: Sheffield, 1988; Nottingham, 1992; DUniv York, 1998. *Recreations:* golf, oil and water colour painting, genealogy, Scottish dancing, bowling. *Address:* 15 Castle Court, Helmsley, N Yorks YO62 5AZ. *T:* (01439) 771579. *Clubs:* Royal Society of Medicine; Kirkbymoorside Golf.

**CARLISLE, Judith Margaret;** Head, Bishop Strachan School, Toronto, since 2017; *b* Leics, 15 Jan. 1959; *d* of Anthony and Joan Carlisle; *m* 1996, David Gough. *Educ:* Convent of the Nativity, Sittingbourne; Univ. of Bristol (BA Hons Drama and English 1979); Drama Studio, London (Dip. Acting 1981); Goldsmiths Coll., Univ. of London (PGCE 1986); Nat. Coll. of Sch. Leadership (NPQH 2004). Actor, Theatre in Education, 1981–85; Teacher of Drama and Media Studies, Trinity Sch., Leamington Spa, 1986–89; Hd of Drama Dept, 1990–94, Academic Team Leader, 1994–98, Whitley Abbey Sch., Coventry; Dep. Head, King Edward VII Sch., King's Lynn, 1998–2004; Headteacher, Dover GS for Girls, 2004–10; Head, Oxford High Sch., 2011–17. *Recreations:* trekking, cycling, cross-country ski-ing, theatre, gardening, owl and hare watching in N Norfolk. *Address:* Bishop Strachan School, 298 Lonsdale Road, Toronto, ON M4V 1X2, Canada. *Clubs:* Lansdowne; Verity (Toronto).

**CARLISLE, Sir Kenneth (Melville),** Kt 1994; *b* 25 March 1941; *s* of late Kenneth Ralph Malcolm Carlisle, TD and of Hon. Elizabeth Mary McLaren, *d* of 2nd Baron Aberconway; *m* 1986, Carla, *d* of A. W. Heffner, Md, USA; one *s*. *Educ:* Harrow; Magdalen Coll., Oxford (BA History). Called to Bar, Inner Temple, 1965. Brooke Bond Liebig, 1966–74; farming in Suffolk, 1974–. MP (C) Lincoln, 1979–97. PPS to: Minister of State for Energy, 1981–83; Minister of State for Home Office, 1983–84; Sec. of State for NI, 1984–85; Home Secretary, 1985–87; an Asst Govt Whip, 1987–88; a Lord Comr of HM Treasury, 1988–90; Parly Under-Sec. of State, MoD, 1990–92, Dept of Transport, 1992–93. Mem., Public Accts Cttee, 1994–97. Member Council: RSPB, 1985–87; RHS, 1996–2006; Suffolk Wildlife Trust, 2007–14. Trustee, World Land Trust, 2009–17. *Recreations:* botany, gardening, history. *Address:* Wyken Hall, Stanton, Bury St Edmunds, Suffolk IP31 2DW. *T:* (01359) 250240.

**CARLISLE, Sir Michael;** *see* Carlisle, Sir J. M.

**CARLOS, Vanessa;** Founder and owner, Carlos/Ishikawa Gallery, since 2011; Founder, Condo, since 2016; *b* São Paulo, Brazil, 1982. *Educ:* St Paul's Sch., Brazil; Central St Martins (Art Foundn); St Anne's Coll., Oxford (BA Fine Art 2005). Asst Dir, The Approach, 2005–11; Dir, Wallis Gall., 2007–09. Mem. Bd, ICA, 2016–. *E:* gallery@carlosishikawa.com.

**CARLOW, Viscount; Charles George Yuill Seymour Dawson-Damer;** *b* 6 Oct. 1965; *s* and *heir* of 7th Earl of Portarlington, *qv*; *m* 2002, Clare, *y d* of Rodney Garside; one *s* three *d*. *Educ:* Eton College; Univ. of Edinburgh (MA Hons 1988). A Page of Honour to the Queen, 1979–80. *Heir: s* Hon. Henry, (Harry), Charles Yuill Seymour Dawson-Damer, *b* 13 Nov. 2009. *Address:* 7 Cambridge Avenue, Vaucluse, Sydney, NSW 2030, Australia. *Clubs:* Australian, Royal Sydney Golf (Sydney).

**CARLOWAY, Rt Hon. Lord; Colin John MacLean Sutherland;** PC 2008; a Senator of the College of Justice in Scotland, since 2000; Lord Justice General of Scotland and Lord President of the Court of Session, since 2016; *b* 20 May 1954; *s* of Rex Alexander Cruickshank Sutherland and Mary Macaulay or Sutherland; *m* 1988, Jane Alexander Turnbull; two *s*. *Educ:* Hurst Grange Prep. Sch., Stirling; Edinburgh Acad.; Edinburgh Univ. (LLB Hons). Advocate, 1977; Advocate Depute, 1986–89; QC (Scot.) 1990. Lord Justice Clerk and Pres., Second Div., Court of Session, 2012–16. Treas., Faculty of Advocates, 1994–2000. *Address:* Supreme Courts, Parliament House, Edinburgh EH1 1RQ. *T:* (0131) 240 6883. *Club:* Scottish Arts (Edinburgh).

**CARLTON, Viscount; Reed Montagu Stuart Wortley;** *b* 5 Feb. 1980; *s* and *heir* of Earl of Wharncliffe, *qv*; *m* 2001, Kim Smith; two *s* one *d*.

**CARLTON, Damian W.;** *see* Woodward-Carlton.

**CARLTON, Prof. John Stephen,** FREng; CEng, CMarEng, FIMechE, FRINA, FIMarEST; Professor of Marine Engineering, and Director, Marine Courses, City, University of London (formerly City University London), since 2010; President, Institute of Marine Engineering, Science and Technology, 2011–12; *b* 26 Nov. 1946; *s* of Cecil Leonard Carlton and Florence Emily Carlton; *m* 1st, 1975, Jeanette Barham (marr. diss. 2005); one *d* (one *s* decd); 2nd, 2007, Janet Rosemary Gooding; two step *d*. *Educ:* Winchelsea Sch.; Pernovena Sch.; Cannock House Sch.; Bromley Tech. Coll. (IMechE Pts I, II, III); Open Univ. (BA). CEng 1973; FREng 2011. Served RN Scientific Service, 1965–70. Design and Res. engr, Stone Manganese Marine, 1970–75; Lloyd's Register: Tech. Investigation, 1975–84; Deputy Head: Advanced Engrg, 1984–87; Performance Technol., 1987–90; Principal Surveyor and Hd, Propulsion, Performance and Envmtl Engrg, 1990–92; Sen. Principal Surveyor and Hd, Tech. Investigation, 1992–2003; Global Hd, Marine Technol., 2003–10. Dir, Carlton and Associates Ltd, Marine Propulsion Consultants, 2010–. Dir, Thermo-Fluids Res. Centre, City, Univ. of London (formerly

City Univ. London), 2014–17. Chairman: internat. res. gps on ship propulsion, propeller backing stresses, 1992–96, cavitation phenomenology I, 1997–2000, and II, 2000–04, cavitation erosion, 2004–07, multi-hull ship performance, 2007–10; RAEng Wkg Gp on Future Ship Powering Options, 2009–13. Mem., Athens Inst. for Educn and Res., 2016–. Mem., Master Mariners' Co. (Member: Tech. Cttee, 2014–; Educn Cttee, 2014–). Hon. DSc City, 2006. Stanley Gray Award, 1990 and 1998, Denny Gold Medal, 1998 and 2008, Inst. of Marine Engrg, Sci. and Technol.; Marine Propulsion Lifetime Achievement Award, 2015; Amity Global Academic Excellence Award, 2019. *Publications:* Marine Propellers and Propulsion, 1994, 3rd edn 2012; (contrib.) Maritime Engineering Reference Book, 2008; Ship Noise and Vibration, 2015; (Ed.-in-Chief) Encyclopaedia of Marine and Offshore Engineering, 2017; contrib. 137 technical papers and articles. *Recreations:* sailing, railway history and steam locomotives, bird watching and animal behaviour, watercolour and pastel painting and drawing, music, literature and poetry, theatre. *Address:* School of Mathematics, Computer Science and Engineering, City, University of London, Northampton Square, EC1V 0HB. *Club:* Royal Over-Seas League.

**CARLYLE, Joan Hildred**; soprano; *b* 6 April 1931; *d* of late Edgar James and Margaret Mary Carlyle; *m*; two d. *Educ:* Howell's Sch., Denbigh, N Wales. Became Principal Lyric Soprano, Royal Opera House, Covent Garden, 1955; Oscar in Ballo in Maschera, 1957–58 season; Sophie in Rosenkavalier, 1958–59; Micaela in Carmen, 1958–59; Nedda in Pagliacci (new Zeffirelli production), Dec. 1959; Mimi in La Bohème, Dec. 1960; Titania in Gielgud production of Britten's Midsummer Night's Dream, London première, Dec. 1961; Pamina in Klemperer production of The Magic Flute, 1962; Countess in Figaro, 1963; Zdenko in Hartman production of Arabella, 1964; Sœur Angelica (new production), 1965; Desdemona in Otello, 1965, 1967; Sophie in Rosenkavalier (new production), 1966; Pamina in Magic Flute (new production), 1966; Arabella in Arabella, 1967; Marschallin in Rosenkavalier, 1968; Jenifer, Midsummer Marriage (new prod.), 1969; Donna Anna, 1970; Reiza, Oberon, 1970; Adrianna Lecouvreur, 1970; Rusalka, for BBC, 1969; Elizabeth in Don Carlos, 1975. Roles sung abroad include: Oscar, Nedda, Mimi, Pamina, Zdenko, Micaela, Desdemona, Donna Anna, Arabella, Elizabeth. Has sung in Buenos Aires, Belgium, Holland, France, Monaco, Naples, Milan, Berlin, Cape Town, Munich. Has made numerous recordings; appeared BBC, TV (in film). Teaches at home and gives masterclasses. *Recreations:* gardening, cooking, interior decorating, countryside preservation. *Address:* Laundry Cottage, Hanmer, N Wales SY13 3DQ. *E:* joancarlyle6@gmail.com. *W:* www.joancarlyle.co.uk.

**CARLYLE, Robert**, OBE 1990; actor; *b* Glasgow, 14 April 1961; *s* of late Joseph Carlyle and of Elizabeth Carlyle; *m* 1997, Anastasia Shirley; two s one d. *Educ:* North Kelvinside Secondary Sch.; RSAMD. Founder, Rain Dog Theatre Co., 1990; dir of prodns incl. Wasted, One Flew Over the Cuckoo's Nest, Conquest of the South Pole, Macbeth. *Theatre includes:* Twelfth Night; Dead Dad Dog; Nae Problem; City; No Mean City; Cuttin' a Rug; Othello. *Television includes:* The Part of Valour, 1981; Hamish Macbeth, 1995; Cracker, 1993, 1997, 1999–2001; Safe, 1993; The Advocates; Arena; Byrne on Byrne; Taggart; Looking After Jo Jo, 1998; Hitler: the rise of evil, 2003; Gunpowder, Treason and Plot, 2004; Class of '76, 2005; The Last Enemy, 2008; The Unloved, Zig Zag Love, 2009; Stargate Universe (series), 2009–11; Once Upon a Time, 2011–18. *Films include:* Riff Raff, 1990; Silent Scream, 1990; Being Human, 1993; Priest, 1994; Go Now, 1995; Trainspotting, 1996; Carla's Song, 1996; Face, 1997; The Full Monty, 1997 (Best Actor, BAFTA, 1998); Ravenous, 1999; Plunkett & Macleane, 1999; The World is Not Enough, 1999; Angela's Ashes, 2000; The Beach, 2000; There's Only One Jimmy Grimble, 2000; To End All Wars, 2000; The 51st State, 2001; Once Upon a Time in the Midlands, 2002; Black and White, 2004; The Mighty Celt, Marilyn Hotchkiss' Ballroom Dancing and Charm School, 2005; Eragon, 2006; Flood, 2007; 28 Weeks Later, 2007; Summer, Stone of Destiny, 2008; I Know You Know, 2010; The Tournament, 2010; The Legend of Barney Thomson (also dir), 2015; T2: Trainspotting, 2017. Best Actor: Evening Standard Film Awards, 1998; Film Critics' Circle Awards, 1998; Bowmore Whisky/Scottish Screen Awards, 2001; Michael Elliott Awards, 2001; David Puttnam Patrons Award. *Address:* c/o Hamilton Hodell, 20 Golden Square, W1F 9JL.

**CARMICHAEL, Hon. Lady; Ailsa Jane Carmichael;** a Senator of the College of Justice in Scotland, since 2016; *b* Paisley, 28 Nov. 1969; *d* of Ian Henry Buist Carmichael and Jean Cowie Carmichael (*née* Davidson); *m* 1997, Paul Barnaby (marr. diss. 2008); one s one d; *m* 2010, Pino Di Emidio; one d. *Educ:* Univ. of Glasgow (LLB Hons, DipLP). Admitted as Advocate, 1993; Standing Jun. Counsel to Home Dept in Scotland, 2000–08; QC (Scot.) 2008; Mem., Mental Health Tribunal Scotland, 2005–; pt-time Sheriff, 2007–; a Dep. Judge, Upper Tribunal (Admin. Appeals Chamber), 2014–. *Publications:* (with D. Auchie) The Scottish Mental Health Tribunal: practice and procedure, 2010. *Recreations:* music, cinema, literature, cooking, travel. *Address:* Court of Session, Parliament House, Edinburgh EH1 1RQ.

**CARMICHAEL, Ailsa Jane;** see Carmichael, Hon. Lady.

**CARMICHAEL, Rt Hon. Alexander Morrison, (Rt Hon. Alistair);** PC 2010; MP (Lib Dem) Orkney and Shetland, since 2001; *b* 15 July 1965; *s* of Alexander C. Carmichael and Mina Neil McKay or Carmichael; *m* 1987, Kathryn Jane Eastham; two s. *Educ:* Port Ellen Primary Sch.; Islay High Sch.; Aberdeen Univ. (LLB 1992; DipLP 1993). Hotel Manager, Glasgow and Orkney, 1984–89; Procurator Fiscal Depute, Crown Office, Edinburgh and Aberdeen, 1993–96; solicitor in private practice, Aberdeen and Macduff, 1996–2001. Comptroller of HM Household (Dep. Chief Whip), 2010–13; Sec. of State for Scotland, 2013–15. *Recreations:* music, theatre. *Address:* House of Commons, SW1A 0AA. *T:* (020) 7219 8181; The Old Manse, Evie, Orkney KW17 2PH. *T:* (01856) 751343.

**CARMICHAEL, Sir David Peter William G. C.;** see Gibson-Craig-Carmichael.

**CARMICHAEL, (Katharine) Jane, (Mrs A. Craxton);** Director of Collections, National Museums Scotland, 2003–15; *b* 12 March 1952; *d* of Donald and Margaret Carmichael; *m* 1989, Adrian Craxton; two d, and one step s two step d. *Educ:* St Leonard's, St Andrews; Edinburgh Univ. (MA Modern Hist.). Imperial War Museum, 1974–2003: Keeper, Photographic Archive, 1982–95; Dir of Collections, 1995–2003. Mem., Peer Rev. Coll., AHRC, 2003–13; Scottish Observer, MLA, 2005–11. Served various cttees of Nat. Museums Dirs Conf., 1995–2003. Trustee, Collections Trust, 2008–13; Gov., Patrick-Allan Fraser of Hospitalfield Trust, 2015–. FRSA 2000; FSAScot 2011. *Publications:* First World War Photographers, 1989; contrib. various jl articles. *Recreations:* the family, country walking, going to the ballet. *Address:* 7 Otterburn Park, Edinburgh EH14 1JX.

**CARMICHAEL, Keith Stanley,** CBE 1981; FCA, FRICS; chartered accountant, 1969–81 and 1990–2018; *b* 5 Oct. 1929; *s* of Stanley and Ruby Dorothy Carmichael; *m* 1958, Cynthia Mary (*née* Jones) (*d* 2019); one s. *Educ:* Charlton House Sch.; Bristol Grammar Sch.; qualified as Chartered Accountant, 1951; FTII 1961, FCA 1961. FRICS 2010. Partner, Wilson Bigg & Co., 1957–69; Man. Partner, Longcrofts, 1981–90. Director: H. Foulks Lynch & Co. Ltd, 1967–69; Radio Rentals Ltd, 1967–69. Member: Monopolies and Mergers Commn, 1983–92; Soc. of Trust and Estate Practitioners, 1996–. Founder Mem., Soc. of Share and Business Valuers, 1995–. Lloyd's Underwriter, 1976–90. Pres., Hertsmere Cons. Assoc., 1982–2012. Chm. Bd of Governors, Royal Masonic Sch. for Girls (formerly Rickmansworth Masonic Sch.), 1984–2010, Pres., 2010– (Trustee, RMIG Endowment Trust, 1984–2013). Freeman, City of London, 1960. FInstD. Mem., Editl Bd, Simon's Taxes, 1970–82. CStJ 2001. *Publications:* Spicer and Pegler's Income Tax (ed), 1965; Corporation Tax, 1966; Capital Gains Tax, 1968; Ranking Spicer and Pegler's Executorship Law and Accounts (ed), 1969, 1987; (with P. Wolstenholme) Taxation of Lloyd's Underwriters, 1980, 4th edn 1993. *Recreations:* gardening, reading, golf. *Address:* 117 Newberries Avenue, Radlett, Herts WD7 7EN. *T:* (01923) 855098. *Clubs:* Carlton (Dep. Chm., 1989–95; Trustee, 1999–), MCC, Lord's Taverners.

**CARMICHAEL, (William) Neil;** Senior Adviser, PLMR, since 2017; Chief Education Consultant, Christine Lee & Co. (solicitors), since 2017; *b* Northumberland, 15 April 1961; *m* 1995, Laurence Jagodzinski; one s two d. *Educ:* St Peter's Sch., York; Nottingham Univ. (BA Politics 1982). Farmer, 1982–2001; land mgt, 2001–; Business Consultant, 2001–10. Vis. Lectr in British Political Hist. and Rural Econs in Europe, Sunderland and De Montfort Univs, 1996–99; Hon. Professor: of Politics and Educn, Univ. of Nottingham, 2018–; UCL Inst. of Educn, 2019–. Mem. (C) Northumberland CC, 1989–93. Contested (C): Leeds E, 1992; Stroud, 2001, 2005. MP (C) Stroud, 2010–17; contested (C) same seat, 2017. Member: Educn Select Cttee, 2010–17 (Chm., 2015–17); Envmtl Select Cttee, 2010–15. Chair: All-Party Parly Gp for Educn Leadership and Governance, 2011–17; All-Party Parly Gp for Vascular Disease, 2012–17; Sec., All-Party Health Gp, 2010–17. Chair, Cons. Europe Gp, 2014–17. Dir, Modern Europe, 2013– (Chair, 2017–). Sen. non-exec. Advr for Educn, Wild Search, 2013–; Member, Advisory Board: D Gp, 2017–; Finito, 2017–; Mem., Steering Gp, Centre for Teacher and Early Years Educn, UCL Inst. of Educn, 2019. Chair, Pearson Commn on Sustainable Learning for Work, Life and Changing Economy, 2018–. Non-exec. Chair, Assoc. of Dental Gps, 2019–. Mem. Bd, FN Strategy Commn, Funing Hldgs (Beijing) Corp., 2019–. Chm., Northumbria Daybreak, 1992–99. Trustee: Sir Heinz Koeppler Trust, 2017–; Sir Edward Heath Charitable Foundn, 2018–. Chm. Schs Govs, Marling Sch., 2008–09; Governor: Kirkley Hall Coll. of Agric., 1989–93; Stroud Coll., 2001–10 (Vice-Chm., 2007–08). *Address:* Dunshiel, Elsdon, Otterburn, Northumberland NE19 1AQ.

**CARNAC, Sir Jonathan James R.;** see Rivett-Carnac.

**CARNALL, Dame Ruth,** DBE 2011 (CBE 2004); Managing Partner, Carnall Farrar, consultancy, since 2014; *b* 26 July 1956; *d* of Alan and Joan Taylor; *m* 1988, Colin Carnall; two s. *Educ:* Henley Coll. of Mgt (MBA). ACMA 1980; CPFA (IPFA 1984); IHSM 1988. Various posts in finance, St Thomas' Hosp., 1977–87; Dir of Finance, Hastings HA, 1987–89; Unit Gen. Manager, Hastings Acute Hosps, 1989–90; Dist Gen. Manager, then Chief Exec., Hastings and Rother HA, then NHS Trust, 1990–92; Dir of Perf. Mgt, 1992–93, Actg Regl Gen. Manager, 1993–94, SE Thames RHA; Chief Exec., W Kent HA, 1994–2000; Department of Health: Regl Dir, SE, NHS Exec., 2000–02; Regl Dir of Health and Social Care (S), 2002; Dir, Change Mgt Prog., 2003–04; freelance consultant to Govt depts and NHS, 2004–06; Interim Chief Exec., 2006–07, Chief Exec., 2007–13, Strategic Health Authy for London (NHS London). Chm., Northern, Eastern and Western Devon Success Regime, 2015–. Vice Chm., King's Fund, 2015–. Non-executive Director: Care UK plc, 2004–06; SIDRA Qatar, 2015–. Mem. Council, Imperial Coll. London, 2014–. *Recreations:* family, cooking, sport. *Address:* Eversleigh, London Road, Westerham, Kent TN16 1DP. *T:* (01959) 561211, *Fax:* (01959) 563999.

**CARNARVON,** 8th Earl of, *cr* 1793; **George Reginald Oliver Molyneux Herbert;** Baron Porchester 1780; sole trader, Porchester Farms, since 2002; Partner, Highclere Enterprises LLP, since 2002; *b* 10 Nov. 1956; *er s* of 7th Earl of Carnarvon, KCVO, KBE; *S* father, 2001; *m* 1st, 1989, Jayne (marr. diss. 1997), *d* of K. A. Wilby, Cheshire; one s one d; 2nd, 1999, Fiona, *e d* of late R. Aitken; one s. *Educ:* St John's Coll., Oxford (BA). A Page of Honour to the Queen, 1969–73. Set up Highclere Castle commercial business, 1988. Founder shareholder, Telecom Express, 1992–97; Founder and Dir, Digital People, 1995–98. Chm., N Wessex Downs LEADER Local Action Gp, 2013–. Chm., Corn Exchange Trust Arts Centre, Newbury, 2007–12; Regl Chm., Thames and Chilterns Area, 2009–. Mem. Bd, 2016–, HHA; Patron: Greenham Common Trust, Newbury, 1997–; Little Stars Children's Charity, 2006–; Langa Langa Scholarship Fund, Kenya, 2009–. Pres., Southern Counties Show, 2011. *Heir: s* Lord Porchester, *qv. Address:* The Field House, Highclere Park, Newbury RG20 9RN. *Club:* White's.

**CARNE, Mark Milford Power,** CBE 2018; FREng; Chief Executive, Network Rail, 2014–18; *b* Helensburgh, 25 Feb. 1959; *s* of Oliver Carne and Sally Carne; *m* 1981, Heather Wilson; one s two d. *Educ:* Univ. of Exeter (BSc Hons 1980). FIMechE 2002; FICE 2017; FREng 2018. Res. Engr, Welding Inst., 1980–84; Shell Exploration and Production: Pipeline Engr, 1984–86; Econs Engr, 1986–88, Safety Manager, 1988–90, Shell UK; Process Engr, Shell Internat., The Hague, 1990–92; Chief Engr, Petroleum Develt, Oman, 1992–96; Shell UK: Chief Engr, 1996–98; Gen. Manager, Central North Sea, 1998–2000, Northern North Sea, 2000–02; Asset Dir, 2002–03; Man. Dir, Brunei Shell Petroleum, 2003–05; Exec. Vice Pres., Europe and Central Asia, BG Gp, 2005–09; Exec. Vice Pres., Middle East and N Africa, Shell, 2010–12. Gov., Falmouth Univ., 2012–. *Recreations:* sailing, clocks and antiques, gardening.

**CARNE, Dr Stuart John,** CBE 1986 (OBE 1977); FRCGP; Senior Partner, Grove Health Centre, 1967–91; *b* 19 June 1926; *s* of late Bernard Carne and Millicent Carne; *m* 1951, Yolande (*née* Cooper) (*d* 2019); two s two d. *Educ:* Willesden County Grammar Sch.; Middlesex Hosp. Med. Sch. MB BS; MRCS; LRCP; DCH. House Surgeon, Middlesex Hosp., 1950–51; House Physician, House Surgeon and Casualty Officer, Queen Elizabeth Hosp. for Children, 1951–52; Flight Lieut, Med. Branch, RAF, 1952–54; general practice in London, 1954–99; Sen. Tutor in General Practice, RPMS, 1970–91. DHSS appointments: Chm., Standing Med. Adv. Cttee, 1982–86 (Mem., 1974–86); Member: Central Health Services Council, 1976–79; Children's Cttee, 1978–81; Personal Social Services Council, 1976–80; Chm., Jt Cttee on Contraception, 1983–86 (Mem., 1975–86). Hon. Civil Consultant in Gen. Practice to RAF, 1974–. Royal College of General Practitioners: Mem. Council, 1961–91; Hon. Treasurer, 1964–81; Pres., 1988–91; Royal Society of Medicine: President: Section of General Practice, 1973–74; United Services Sect., 1985–87; Mem. Council, World Orgn of Nat. Colls and Acads of Gen. Practice and Family Medicine, 1970–80 (Pres., 1976–78); Hon. Treas., ASME, 1972–75; Mem. Exec. Council, British Diabetic Assoc., 1981–87. Examr in medicine, Soc. of Apothecaries, 1980–88. Chm., St Mary Abbots Court Ltd, 1981–2004. Hon. MO, 1959–89, Vice-Pres., 1989–96, Queens Park Rangers FC. Hon. Fellow, Royal NZ Coll. of GPs, 1989; Hon. FRCPCH 1996; Hon. Mem., BPA, 1982. *Publications:* Paediatric Care, 1976; (jtly) DHSS Handbook on Contraceptive Practice, 3rd edn 1984, 4th edn 1988; numerous articles in Lancet, BMJ and other jls. *Recreations:* music, theatre, philately. *Address:* 5 St Mary Abbots Court, Warwick Gardens, W14 8RA. *T:* (020) 7602 1970.

**CARNEGIE,** family name of **Duke of Fife.**

**CARNEGIE, Sir Roderick (Howard),** AC 2003; Kt 1978; FTS; Executive Chairman, Pacific Edge Holdings Pty Ltd, 1997; *b* 27 Nov. 1932; *s* of late Douglas H. Carnegie and Margaret F. Carnegie, AO; *m* 1959, Carmen (*d* 2008), *d* of W. J. T. Clarke; three s. *Educ:* Geelong Church of England Grammar Sch.; Trinity Coll., Univ. of Melbourne (BSc 1954;

Hon. Fellow, 1981); New Coll., Oxford Univ. (MA; Dip. Agricl Econs 1957); Harvard Business Sch., Boston (MBA 1959). FTSE (FTS 1985). McKinsey & Co., New York, 1958–70: Principal, 1964–68, Director, 1967–70; Exec. Dir, 1970–72, Man. Dir and Chief Exec., 1972–74, Chm. and Chief Exec., 1974–86, CRA Ltd; Chairman: Hudson Conway Ltd, 1987–2000; GIO Australia Hldgs Ltd, 1992–94; Newcrest Mining Ltd, 1993–98; Adacel Technologies Ltd, 1997–2003; World Competitive Practices Pty Ltd, 1997–2001; Director: ANZ Banking Gp, 1986–90; ANZ Executors & Trustee Co., 1990–92; John Fairfax Holdings, 1992–2004; Lexmark Internat. Inc., USA, 1994–98; Lexmark Internat. Gp Inc., 1994–98; AUSI Ltd, 1994–2002. Member: Internat. Council, J P Morgan & Co., 1986–95; Asia-Pacific Bd, IBM Corp., 1988–89; Internat. Adv. Bd, Internat. Finance Corp., 1991–92; Internat. Adv. Bd, World Bank, 1991–94. Director: Aust. Mining Industry Council, 1974 (a Sen. Vice-Pres., 1985); Macfarlane Burnet Centre for Med. Res., 1997–2000; Member: General Motors Aust. Adv. Council, 1979–2003; Aust.-China Council, 1979–82; Bd, CSIRO, 1986–91; Gp of Thirty, 1985–2001; Chm., Consultative Cttee on Relations with Japan, 1984–87; Chm., WA Energy Rev. Bd, 1992–93; President: German-Aust. Chamber of Industry and Commerce, 1985; Business Council of Aust., 1987–88; Consultant, Aust. Wool Corp., 1989–90; Patron, Australian Centre for Blood Diseases. Chm., Adv. Bd, Salvation Army, 1991–96 (Mem., 1990–91). Hon. DSc Newcastle, 1985; Hon. LLD Monash, 2011. Centenary Medal, Australia, 2003. Comdr's Cross, Order of Merit (Germany), 1991. *Recreation:* reading. *Address:* PO Box 7458, Melbourne, Vic 3004, Australia. *Clubs:* Melbourne (Vic); Australian (Vic and NSW); Harvard (New York).

**CARNEGIE-BROWN, Bruce Neil;** DL; Chairman, Lloyd's, since 2017; *b* Freetown, Sierra Leone, 27 Dec. 1959; *s* of Neil Colin Carnegie-Brown and June Carola Carnegie-Brown (*née* Tate); *m* 1986, Jane Spaven; three *s* one *d*. *Educ:* Cheltenham Coll.; Exeter Coll., Oxford (Stapeldon Schol.; MA). Bank of America, 1981–85; J. P. Morgan, 1985–2003: Sen. Credit Officer (EMEA), 1995–97, CEO, J. P. Morgan Securities (Asia) Ltd, 1997–2000; Hd, Debt Capital Mkts (Europe and Asia), 2000–03; CEO, Marsh Ltd, 2003–06; Managing Partner, 3i Gp plc, 2007–09. Chairman: Aon UK Ltd, 2012–15; Moneysupermarket.com Group plc, 2014–19 (non-exec. Dir, 2010–19); non-executive Director: Close Brothers Gp plc, 2006–14; Jelf Gp plc, 2008–10; Catlin Gp Ltd, 2010–14; Santander UK plc, 2012–; JLT Gp plc, 2016–17; Vice Chm. and Lead Ind. Dir, Banco Santander SA, 2015–. Chm., IFS Sch. of Finance, 2010–11. Pres., Chartered Mgt Inst., 2017–. Trustee: Shakespeare's Globe Trust, 2007–16; Historic Royal Palaces Trust, 2014–. Mem., Finance Cttee, MCC, 2019–. Freeman, City of London, 1989. DL Greater London, 2015. FCIB 2004. *Recreations:* theatre, golf, ski-ing, tennis. *Address:* Lloyd's, One Lime Street, EC3M 7HA. *Clubs:* Brooks's, MCC; Roehampton; Walton Heath Golf.

**CARNEGY,** family name of **Earl of Northesk**.

**CARNELLEY, Ven. Desmond;** Archdeacon of Doncaster, 1985–94, now Archdeacon Emeritus; *b* 28 Nov. 1929; *m* 1st, 1954, Dorothy Frith (*d* 1986); three *s* one *d*; 2nd, 1988, Marjorie Freeman. *Educ:* St John's Coll., York; St Luke's Coll., Exeter; William Temple Coll., Rugby; Ripon Hall, Oxford; BA (Open Univ.); Univ. of Wales, Cardiff (LLM Canon Law, 2002); Cert. Ed. (Leeds); Cert. Rel. Ed. (Exon). Curate of Aston, 1960–63; Priest-in-charge, St Paul, Ecclesfield, 1963–67; Vicar of Balby, Doncaster, 1967–72; Priest-in-charge, Mosborough, 1973; Vicar of Mosborough, 1974–85; RD of Attercliffe, 1979–84; acting Dir of Educn, dio. of Sheffield, 1991–92. *Recreations:* reading, theatre, walking, gardening. *Address:* 11 Fairways, Wickersley, Rotherham S66 1AE. *T:* (01709) 544927.

**CARNEY, Mark Joseph,** OC 2014; Governor, Bank of England, since 2013; *b* Fort Smith, NWT, 16 March 1965; *s* of Robert and Verlie Carney; *m* 1995, Diana, *d* of Christopher Fox; four *d*. *Educ:* Harvard Univ. (BA Econs 1988); St Peter's Coll., Oxford (MPhil Econs 1993); Nuffield Coll., Oxford (DPhil Econs 1995). With Goldman Sachs, London, Tokyo, NY and Toronto, 1990–2003; Dep. Gov., Bank of Canada, 2003–04; Sen. Associate Dep. Minister of Finance, Canada, 2004–08; Gov., Bank of Canada, 2008–13; Bank of England: Chairman: Monetary Policy Cttee, 2013–; Financial Policy Cttee, 2013–. Chm. Bd, Prudential Regulation Authy, 2013–. Chairman: Cttee on Global Financial Systems, Bank for Internat. Settlements, 2010–12; Financial Stability Bd, 2011–17. Member: Gp of Thirty; Foundn Bd, WEF. Hon. LLD Manitoba, 2013. *Address:* Bank of England, Threadneedle Street, EC2R 8AH.

**CARNEY, Michael;** Secretary, Water Services Association (formerly Water Authorities Association), 1987–92; *b* 19 Oct. 1937; *s* of Bernard Patrick Carney and Gwyneth (*née* Ellis); *m* 1963, Mary Patricia (*née* Davies) (marr. diss. 2000); two *s* one *d*. *Educ:* University College of North Wales, Bangor (BA). Administrative Officer, NCB, 1962–65; Staff Officer to Dep. Chm., NCB, 1965–68; Electricity Council: Administrative Officer, 1968–71; Asst Sec. (Establishments), 1971–74; Sec., S Western Region, CEGB, 1974–80, Personnel Man., Midlands Region, 1980–82; Personnel Dir, Oxfam, 1982–87. *Publications:* Britain in Pictures: a history and bibliography, 1995; Stoker: the life of Hilda Matheson, OBE, 1888–1940, 1999. *Recreations:* reading, book collecting, music, theatre. *Address:* 8 Juniper Road, Shrewsbury, Shropshire SY1 2BN. *E:* birmbot@gmail.com.

**CARNLEY, Most Rev. Peter Frederick,** AC 2007 (AO 1998); PhD; Archbishop of Perth and Metropolitan of Western Australia, 1981–2005; Primate of Australia, 2000–05; *b* 17 Oct. 1937; *s* of Frederick Carnley and Gweyennetth Lilian Carnley (*née* Read); *m* 1966, Carol Ann Dunstan; one *s* one *d*. *Educ:* St John's Coll., Morpeth, NSW; Australian Coll. of Theol. (ThL 1st Cl., 1962); Univ. of Melbourne (BA, 1st Cl. Hons, 1966); Univ. of Cambridge (PhD 1969). Deacon 1962, priest 1964, Bath; Licence to Officiate, dio. Melbourne, 1963–65; Asst Curate of Parkes, 1966; Licence to Officiate, dio. Ely, 1966–69; Chaplain, Mitchell Coll. of Advanced Education, Bath, 1970–72; Research Fellow, St John's Coll., Cambridge, 1971–72 (Hon. Fellow, 2000); Warden, St John's College, St Lucia, Queensland, 1973–81; Residentiary Canon, St John's Cathedral, Brisbane, 1975–81; Examining Chaplain to Archbishop of Brisbane, 1975–81. Adjunct Prof. of Theol., Murdoch Univ., 2004–; Vis. Prof. of Systematic Theol., Gen. Theol Seminary, NY, 2010–13. Co-Chm., ARCIC, 2003–09. Hon. Fellow: Trinity Coll., Univ. of Melbourne, 2000; Emmanuel Coll., Cambridge, 2006. DD *hc* Gen. Theological Seminary, NY, 1984; Hon. DLitt: Newcastle, 2000; W Australia, 2000; Queensland, 2002; DUniv Charles Sturt, 2001; Hon. Dr Sacred Theol. Melbourne Coll. of Divinity, 2004; DD Lambeth, 2012. ChStJ 1982 (Sub Prelate, 1991). *Publications:* The Structure of Resurrection Belief, 1987; The Yellow Wallpaper and Other Sermons, 2001; 'Friendship' in Faithfulness in Fellowship: reflections on homosexuality and the church, 2001; Reflections in Glass: trends and tensions in the Anglican church of Australia, 2004; A Kind of Retirement: more sermons from Archbishop Peter Carnley, 2016; (contrib.) New Perspectives in Ecumenism, 2019; Resurrection in Retrospect, 2 vols, A Critical Examination of the Theology of N. T. Wright, The Reconstruction of Resurrection Belief, 2019. *Recreations:* gardening, swimming. *Address:* Unit 3, 5 Irwin Street, East Fremantle, WA 6158, Australia. *Clubs:* Weld (Perth); St John's (Brisbane).

**CARNOCK,** 5th Baron *cr* 1916, of Carnock; **Adam Nicolson,** FRSL, FSAScot, FSA; Bt (NS) of that Ilk and Lasswade 1629, of Carnock 1637; author; *b* Bransgore, Hants, 12 Sept. 1957; *o s* of Nigel Nicolson, OBE, author, and Philippa Janet, *d* of Sir (Eustace) Gervais Tennyson-d'Eyncourt, 2nd Bt; *S* cousin, 2008; *m* 1st, 1982, Olivia Mary Rokeby Fane (marr. diss. 1992); three *s*; 2nd, 1992, Sarah Clare Raven; two *d*. *Educ:* Eton Coll.; Magdalene Coll., Cambridge (BA 1979; MA 1983). FRSL 2005; FSAScot 2006; FSA 2010. Journalist, Sunday Times, 1985–95; Columnist: Sunday Telegraph, 1995–2000; Daily Telegraph, 2000–06; Presenter: Atlantic Britain (series), C4, 2004; Sissinghurst (series), BBC TV, 2009; When God Spoke English, BBC TV, 2011; The Century that Wrote Itself, BBC TV, 2012; Britain's Whale Hunters, BBC TV, 2014; The Last Seabird Summer?, BBC TV, 2016. Director: Toucan Books, 1986–; Sarah Raven's Cutting Garden, 1996–. *Publications:* The National Trust Book of Long Walks, 1981; Long Walks in France, 1983; Frontiers (Somerset Maugham Award), 1985; (with Nigel Nicolson) Two Roads to Dodge City, 1986; Wetland (PBFA Topography Prize), 1987; Prospects of England, 1990; Restoration: the rebuilding of Windsor Castle, 1997; Regeneration: the story of the Dome, 1999; Perch Hill: a new life, 2000; Mrs Kipling, 2001; Sea Room, 2001; Power and Glory (W. H. Heinemann Prize; US edn as God's Secretaries), 2003; Seamanship, 2004; Men of Honour (US edn as Seize the Fire), 2005; Earls of Paradise (US edn as Quarrel with the King), 2008, rev. edn as Arcadia: the dream of perfection in Renaissance England, 2009; Sissinghurst: an unfinished history, 2008 (Ondaatje Prize, 2009); (with Sir Eric Anderson) About Eton, 2010; The Smell of Summer Grass, 2011; The Gentry, 2011; The Mighty Dead, 2014 (US edn as Why Homer Matters, 2015); The Seabird's Cry, 2017 (Wainwright Golden Beer Book Prize, Richard Jefferies Soc. Prize, 2018); The Making of Poetry: Coleridge, the Wordsworths and their year of marvels, 2019. *Recreations:* walking, sailing. *Heir: s* Hon. Thomas Nicolson, *b* 5 March 1984. *Address:* Perch Hill Farm, Brightling, Robertsbridge, E Sussex TN32 5HP. *E:* adam@shiantisles.net.

*See also J. Nicolson.*

**CARNWATH OF NOTTING HILL, Rt Hon. Lord;** Robert John Anderson Carnwath, Kt 1994; CVO 1995; PC 2002; a Justice of the Supreme Court of the United Kingdom, since 2012; *b* 15 March 1945; *s* of Sir Andrew Carnwath, KCVO; *m* 1974, Bambina D'Adda. *Educ:* Eton; Trinity Coll., Cambridge (MA, LLB; Hon. Fellow 2013). Called to the Bar, Middle Temple, 1968, Bencher 1991; QC 1985. Junior Counsel to Inland Revenue, 1980–85; Attorney Gen. to the Prince of Wales, 1988–94; a Judge of the High Court, Chancery Div., 1994–2002; a Lord Justice of Appeal, 2002–12; Chm., Law Commn, 1999–2002; Sen. Pres. of Tribunals, 2004–12. Jt Founder and Sec. Gen., EU Forum of Judges for Envmt, 2004–05; Mem., UNEP Internat. Adv. Cttee on Envmtl Justice, 2012–. Chairman: Shepherds Bush Housing Assoc., 1988–93; Administrative Law Bar Assoc., 1993–94; Tabernacle Trust, 1996–99. Pres., UK Envmtl Law Assoc., 2006–. Governor, RAM, 1989–2002 (Hon. Fellow 1994). Trustee, 1996–2009, Chm., 2001–09, Britten-Pears Foundn. *Publications:* Knight's Guide to Homeless Persons Act, 1977; (with Rt Hon. Sir Frederick Corfield) Compulsory Acquisition and Compensation, 1978; Enforcing Planning Control (report commnd for DoE), 1989; various legal texts and reports on envmtl and local govt law. *Recreations:* viola, singing (Bach Choir), tennis, golf, etc. *Address:* Supreme Court of the United Kingdom, Parliament Square, SW1P 3BD.

*See also F. A. A. Carnwath.*

**CARNWATH, Dame Alison (Jane),** DBE 2014; Senior Advisor, Evercore Partners, since 2010; Chairman, Land Securities plc, 2008–18 (non-executive Director, 2004–08); *b* 18 Jan. 1953; *d* of late Kenneth and Lois Tresise; partner, Peter Thomson. *Educ:* Howell's Sch., Denbigh; Univ. of Reading (BA Econ/German 1975). ACA 1979. Peat Marwick Mitchell, later KPMG, 1975–79; J. Henry Schroder Wagg, 1983–93; Phoenix Partnership, 1993–97; Donaldson Lufkin Jenrette, 1997–2000. Non-executive Director: Man Group plc, 2001–13; Paccar Inc., 2005–; Barclays plc, 2010–12; BP plc, 2018–; Ind. Dir, Zurich Insce Gp, 2011–; Mem. Supervisory Bd, BASF SE, 2014–; Chm., Strategic Adv. Bd, Livingbridge (formerly Isis) Private Equity, 2016– (Chm., Mgt Bd, 2005–15). Mem. Adv. Council, St George's Society of New York, 2013–. Trustee, BL, 2013–16. Hon. DLaws: Reading, 2010; Exeter, 2015. *Recreations:* food, ski-ing, music. *Address:* Evercore Partners, 15 Stanhope Gate, W1K 1LN.

**CARNWATH, Francis Anthony Armstrong,** CBE 1997; Director, Greenwich Foundation for the Royal Naval College, 1997–2002; *b* 26 May 1940; *s* of Sir Andrew Hunter Carnwath, KCVO, DL and Kathleen Marianne (*née* Armstrong); *m* 1975, Penelope Clare Rose (separated); one *s* one *d* (and one *d* decd). *Educ:* Eton (Oppidan Schol.); Cambridge (BA Econs). With Baring Brothers & Co., 1962–89: postings to S Africa, 1965–66, USA, 1969, France, 1972–73; Chief Exec. and Dir, Pertanian Baring Sanwa Multinational, Malaysia, 1977–79; Dir, 1979–89; Chm., Ravensbourne Registration Services Ltd, 1981–89. Dep. Dir, Tate Gall., 1990–94; Actg Dir, 1995, Advr, 1996–97, Nat. Heritage Meml Fund/Heritage Lottery Fund. English Heritage: Mem., London Adv. Cttee, 1990–99; Chm., Commemorative Plaques Panel, 1995–2002. Trustee and later Dep. Chm., Shelter, 1968–76; Treas., VSO, 1979–84. Chairman: Musgrave Kinley Outsider Trust, 1999–2011; Spitalfields Historic Buildings Trust, 1984–2000; Thames 21, 2003–17; Architectural Panel, NT, 2004–12; Trustee: Phillimore Estates, 1983– (Chm., 1992–); Whitechapel Art Gall., 1994–2000 (Dep. Chm., 1996–2000); Royal Armouries, 2000–07; Spitalfields Fest., 2003–10; Yorkshire Sculpture Park, 2003–12 (Chm., 2004–12). Musicians' Co.: Master, 1995–96; Treas., 1993–97; Chm., various cttees, 1993–2008. Hon. FTCL 2002; Hon. RCM 2003. *Recreations:* music, the arts, walking. *Address:* 31 Crag Path, Aldeburgh, Suffolk IP15 5BS. *Clubs:* Garrick, Beefsteak.

*See also Rt Hon. Lord Carnwath of Notting Hill.*

**CARNWATH, Robert John Anderson;** see Carnwath of Notting Hill, Rt Hon. Lord.

**CAROE, Oliver Bragg,** RIBA; Director, Caroe Architecture Ltd, since 2009; Associate, Cambridge Architectural Research Ltd, since 2009; Cathedral Architect, Ripon Cathedral, since 2010; Surveyor to the Fabric, St Paul's Cathedral, since 2012; Surveyor to King's College Chapel, Cambridge, since 2018; *b* London, 24 Aug. 1968; *s* of Martin Caroe and Mary Caroe (*née* Roskill); *m* 1998, Carole Mills; two *d*. *Educ:* Winchester Coll.; Trinity Coll., Cambridge (BA; DipArch). RIBA 1995; AABC 2008. Tim Ronalds Architects, 1994–98; Caroe & Partners, 1998–2003 (Associate, 2001–03); Purcell, Miller, Tritton, 2003–09 (Partner, 2006–09). Member: Church Bldg Council, 2000–14; Design and Conservation Panel, Cambridge City Council, 2002–14; Founder Mem., Shrinking the Footprint Steering Gp, 2002–14. Brother, Art Workers' Guild. *Recreations:* sculling, cycling, sailing, advisor to WinColl Works Committee. *Address:* Caroe Architecture Ltd, Office 5, Unit 8, 23–25 Gwydir Street, Cambridge CB1 2LG. *E:* info@caroe.biz. *Club:* Surveyors.

**CAROL, Sister;** *see* Griese, Sister Carol.

**CAROLIN, Prof. Peter Burns,** CBE 2000; ARIBA; Professor and Head of Department of Architecture, University of Cambridge, 1989–2000, now Professor Emeritus, and Fellow of Corpus Christi College, since 1989; *b* 11 Sept. 1936; *s* of late Joseph Sinclair Carolin and Jean Bell Carolin (*née* Burns); *m* 1964, Anne-Birgit Warning; three *d*. *Educ:* Radley Coll.; Corpus Christi Coll., Cambridge (MA); University Coll. London (MA Architecture). Served RNR, Lieut, 1955–61. Asst to John Voelcker, 1960–63; Architect: with Colin St John Wilson, 1965–70 (Biochemistry Laboratory, Babraham); with Sir John Burnet, Tait and Partners, 1970–71; Associate, 1971–73, and Partner, 1973–80, Colin St John Wilson and Partners (British Library, and Dunbar Cooperage housing, Haringey); Partner, Cambridge Design, 1980–81; Technical Ed., 1981–84, Editor, 1984–89, Architects' Jl.

Syndic, Fitzwilliam Mus., Cambridge, 1990–2001; Chairman: Cambridge Futures, 1997–2001; Fitzwilliam Mus. Enterprises, 1998–2001. Chm., Cambridge Design and Conservation Panel, 2006–10; Co-dir, 2030 Vision, Cambridge sub-region, 2011–13. Co-founder, Facilities Newsletter, 1983; Chm. Editl Bd, and Editor, arq (Architectural Res. Qly), 1995–2004. (Jtly) Magazine of Year Award, 1985; (jtly) Award for Innovation in Local Planning, RTPI, 2000; (jtly) Award for Learned Jls, ALPSP/Charlesworth, 2002. *Publications:* articles in professional jls. *Address:* Orchard End, 15E Grange Road, Cambridge CB3 9AS. *T:* (01223) 352723.

**CARON, Leslie (Claire Margaret);** film and stage actress; *b* 1 July 1931; *d* of Claude Caron and Margaret Caron (*née* Petit); *m* 1st, 1951, George Hormel (marr. diss.); 2nd, 1956, Peter Reginald Frederick Hall (marr. diss. 1965); one *s* one *d*; 3rd, 1969, Michael Laughlin (marr. diss.). *Educ:* Convent of the Assumption, Paris. With Ballet des Champs Elysées, 1947–50, Ballet de Paris, 1954. *Films:* American in Paris, 1950; The Man With a Cloak, 1951; Lili, Story of Three Loves, 1953; Glory Alley, The Glass Slipper, 1954; Daddy Long Legs, 1955; Gaby, 1956; Gigi, The Doctor's Dilemma, 1958; The Man Who Understood Women, 1959; The Subterraneans, Austerlitz, 1960; Fanny, 1961; The L-Shaped Room, 1962; Guns of Darkness, 1963; Father Goose, A Very Special Favour, 1964; Les Quatres Vérités, Is Paris Burning?, 1965; Promise Her Anything, 1966; Head of the Family, 1968; Madron, 1970; Chandler, 1971; QB VII; Valentino, Sérail, 1975; L'homme qui aimait les femmes, 1976; Goldengirl, 1978; Tous Vedettes, 1979; The Contract, 1980; Impératif, 1981; The Unapproachable, 1982; La Diagonale du Fou, 1983; Le Génie du Faux, 1984; Le Train de Lenine, 1987; Courage Mountain, Guerriers et Captives, 1988; Master of the Game; Damage, 1992; Funny Bones, Let it be Me, 1994; The Ring, 1995; The Reef, 1996; The Last of the Blonde Bombshells, 1999; Chocolat, 2001; Crime on the Orient Express, 2001; Le Divorce, 2003. *Plays:* Orvet, Paris, 1955; La Sauvage (TV), England; Gigi, (title rôle), New Th., 1956; 13 rue de l'Amour, USA and Australia; Ondine (title rôle), RSC, Aldwych, 1961; Carola (TV), USA; The Rehearsal, UK tour, 1983; On Your Toes, US tour, 1984; One for the Tango, USA tour, 1985; L'Inaccessible, Paris, 1985; George Sand, Greenwich Fest., 1995; Nocturne for Lovers, Chichester, 1997; A Little Night Music, Théâtre du Châtelet, 2010. *Musical:* Grand Hotel, Berlin, 1991. *Television:* Tales of the Unexpected, 1982; Law & Order: Special Victims Unit, 2006; The Durrells, 2016. *Publications:* Vengeance (short stories), 1982; Thank Heaven (autobiog.), 2009. *Recreation:* collecting antiques. *Address:* c/o Dalzell & Beresford, Paddock Suite, The Courtyard, 55 Charterhouse Street, EC1M 6HA.

**CARPANINI, Prof. David Lawrence,** RE 1982 (ARE 1979); RWA 1983 (ARWA 1977); RBA 1976; NEAC 1983; RCA 1992; painter and etcher; Professor of Art, University of Wolverhampton School of Education, 1992–2000, retired; *b* Abergwynfi, W Glam, 22 Oct. 1946; *o s* of Lorenzo and Gwenllian Carpanini; *m* 1972, Jane Allen, RWS, RBA, RWA; one *s*. *Educ:* Glanafan Grammar Sch., Port Talbot; Glos Coll. of Art & Design, Cheltenham (DipAD 1968); Royal Coll. of Art (MA 1971); Univ. of Reading (ATC 1972). Dir, Bankside Gall. Ltd, 1995–2003. Royal Society of British Artists: Hon. Treas., 1979–82; Vice-Pres., 1982–8; Mem. Council, 1993–95; Mem. Council, RWA, 1987–90; PRE, 1995–2003. Has exhibited at: RA, RBA, RWA, NEAC, Bankside Gall., Piccadilly Gall., Attic Gall., Agnews, Albany Gall., New Acad. Gall., Tegfryn; numerous one-man exhibitions, 1972–, including: Welsh Arts Council Gall., 1980; Warwick Arts Fest., 1986; Mostyn Gall., 1988; Rhondda Heritage Park, 1989, 1994; Walsall Mus., 1989; Swansea Arts Fest., 1994; Attic Gall., 1998, 2002, 2005, 2008, 2011, 2014, 2016, 2017, 2018; St David's Hall, Cardiff, 1999, 2009; Taliesin Gall., 2000; Oriel Plas Glyn-y-Weddw, Rhondda Heritage Park Gall., Pontardawe Arts Centre, 2010; Leamington Spa Mus. and Art Gall., 2014; Fosse Gall., 2018, 2020. Work in collections, including: Nat. Mus. of Wales; Contemporary Art Soc. for Wales: Nat. Liby of Wales; Newport Mus. and Art Gall.; Govt Art Collection, DoE; Fitzwilliam Mus., Cambridge; BNOC; Univs of Bangor, Bristol, Glamorgan, Swansea; Ashmolean Mus., Oxford; Leamington Spa Art Gall.; Cyfartha Castle Mus. and Art Gall.; Merthyr; Williamson Mus. and Art Gall.; Oriel Ynys Môn, Anglesey; Police Trng Centre of Wales; Rank Xerox; Glynn Vivian Art Gall., Swansea; Union of Russian Bibliophiles, Moscow. Gov., Fedn of British Artists, 1982–86. De Lazlo Medal, RBA, 1980; Agnews Drawing Prize, NEAC, 1992; Catto Gall. Award, 1993, First Prize, Daler Rowney Award, 1995; Painter-Stainers' Co. Drawing Prize, 2012, RWS Open. Hon. RWS 1996; Hon. RBSA 2002. *Publications:* Vehicles of Pictorial Expression, 1982; numerous articles and illustrations for instructional books and art periodicals. *Recreation:* opera. *Address:* 6 Old Forge Close, Bledington, Chipping Norton, Oxon OX7 6XW. *T:* (01608) 659264.

**CARPENTER,** see Boyd-Carpenter.

**CARPENTER, Prof. Barry,** CBE 2016 (OBE 2001); international educational consultant; Professor of Mental Health in Education, Oxford Brookes University, since 2017; *b* Cradley Heath, 10 April 1955; *s* of Gerald Carpenter and Betty Carpenter (*née* Lawrence); *m* 1978, Susan Cookson; one *s* two *d* (and one *d* decd). *Educ:* Rowley Regis Grammar Sch.; Westminster Coll., Oxford (Cert Ed 1976); Univ. of London (Dip. Learning Difficulties 1982); Univ. of Nottingham (MPhil 1987); Anglia Ruskin Univ. (PhD 2007). Teacher: Millfield Sch., 1976–78; Pens Meadow Sch., Dudley, 1978–80; Headteacher, Blythe Sch., Warwicks, 1982–87; Inspector of Schs, Solihull, 1987–92; Dir, Centre for Special Educn, Westminster Coll., Oxford, 1992–97; Chief Exec. and Principal, Sunfield Sch., 1997–2008; Acad. Dir, Specialist Schs and Acads Trust, 2009–12. Hon. Professor: Univ. of Worcester, 1998–; Univ. of Limerick, 2010–; Univ. of Hamburg, 2012–; Flinders Univ., Australia, 2013–; Univ. of Nottingham; Vis. Fellow, Univ. of Oxford, 2008–09. Dir, Children with Complex Learning Difficulties and Disabilities Res. Project, 2009–12. FRSA. *Publications:* Enabling Access, 1997, 2nd edn 2001; Families in Context, 1997; (jtly) Educating Children with Fetal Alcohol Spectrum Disorders, 2012; (jtly) Fetal Alcohol Spectrum Disorders: interdisciplinary perspectives, 2013; Educating Learners with Complex Learning Difficulties and Disabilities, 2015; Girls and Autism: educational, family and personal perspectives, 2019. *Recreations:* music, singing, theatre, drama, athletics, family. *W:* www.barrycarpentereducation.com. *Club:* Naval and Military.

**CARPENTER, Prof. Gary Malcolm;** composer; Professor of Composition: Royal Northern College of Music, since 2001; Royal Academy of Music, since 2003; *b* Hackney, London, 13 Jan. 1951; *s* of Albert Carpenter and Dorothy Carpenter (*née* Stock); one *s* one *d*. *Educ:* Henry Maynard Jun. Sch., Walthamstow; Sir George Monoux Grammar Sch., Walthamstow; Royal Coll. of Music, London (ARCM 1972). LRAM 1969. Kapellmeister and pianist, Vereinigte Städtische Bühnen, Krefeld/Mönchengladbach, 1974–76; composer-in-residence and pianist, Nederlands Dans Theater, 1976–79; Hd, Music, London Contemporary Dance Sch., 1982–86; composer-in-residence, City of Wakefield, 1987–88; Hd, Music, Liverpool Inst. for Performing Arts, 1994–95. Associate Music Dir, The Wicker Man (film), 1973. Resident musician, King's Head Th. Club, Islington, 1973–74; Musical Associate, Extemporary Dance Th., 1983–85; Co-Dir, The Dance Band, 1985–86. Part-time teacher: Jun. Dept, RCM, 1982–84; GSMD, 1990–94; Welsh Coll. of Music and Drama, 1991–92; Lectr, Bretton Hall Coll. of Higher Educn, 1988–90; examiner: Univ. of Kent, 1984–86; Manchester Metropolitan Univ., 1996–99; Lectr (pt-time), Liverpool Hope University Coll., 1997–99. Vis. Lectr, 2001–03, Teaching Fellow, 2004–05, Liverpool Inst. for Performing Arts; Composition Tutor, Nat. Youth Orch., 2001–08; Composer in Association, Royal Liverpool Philharmonic Orch., 2018–. Dir, BASCA, 2015– (Chm., Classical Cttee, 2015–). Member: RAM Club; Old Monovians Assoc.; Royal Soc. Musicians. *Compositions include:* Concerto for Orchestra, The Continuing Story (ballet/orch.), 1977; Chorinho Cariñoso (alto sax and piano), Da Capo (6 players), Die Flimmerkiste (11 players), 1985; Goodnight Mister Tom (musical), 1992; Bermuda Suite and Dolphin (quintet), CHI (brass band), Love's Eternity (song cycle), Sonata for Alto Sax and Piano, Sonata for clarinet and Piano, Theatre Fountain (concert band), 1993; Antiques and Curios (wind), Flying God Suite (concert band), Missa Beata Virgine (2 a capella choirs), 1994; Pantomime (13 winds), 1995; The Lamplighter (children's choir), 1996; Sunderland Lasses and Wearmouth Lads (wind band), 1997; SATIE - Variations for Orchestra, 1998; Creepy Crawlies (piano solo), Podgy Tourers (piano solo), 2002; Secret Love Songs (trombone quartet), Time Line (17 trombones), 2003; Dioscuri (2 cellos), Doubles (concerto for oboe, clarinet and wind band), Fred and Ginger (orch.), Go-Slow (guitar quartet), Sonatinas (concerto for alto sax and orch.), Sonatinas (alto sax and piano), Songs of Sadness and Piety, 2010; Bassoon Concerto (bassoon and orch.), Horn Concerto (horn and orch.), 2011; blue (solo flute), 2012; The Food of Love, SET (concerto for tenor saxophone and orch.), Two Hart Crane Songs, 2014; Dadaville, 2015; The North (sax quartet), 2014; Willie Stock (orch.), 2016; Fischietto è Morto (trombone and strings), 2017; Johnny Spielt Aus (sax and piano), 2017; Latchford Locks (wind orch.), 2018; Ghost Songs (youth choir and orch.), 2018; Mondrian (concerto for harpsichord and 6 players), (sax quartet), 2014; Mem., ISM, 2016. FRNCM 2016; FRSA 2016. Hon. RAM 2013. *Publications:* (contrib.) The Quest for 'The Wicker Man', 2006. *Recreations:* travel, cinema, walking, food, hang gliding, theatre, art. *Address:* c/o Royal Academy of Music, Marylebone Road, NW1 5HT. *E:* yrag@garycarpenter.net.

**CARPENTER, Leslie Arthur;** Chief Executive, 1982–86, Chairman, 1985–87, Reed International PLC; *b* 26 June 1927; *s* of William and Rose Carpenter; *m* 1st, 1952; one *d*; 2nd, 1989, (Elizabeth) Louise Botting, *qv. Educ:* Hackney Techn. Coll. Director: Country Life, 1965; George Newnes, 1966; Odhams Press Ltd (Managing), 1968; International Publishing Corp., 1972; Reed International Ltd, 1974; IPC (America) Inc., 1975; Chairman: Reed Hldgs Inc. (formerly Reed Publishing Hldgs Inc.), 1977; Reed Publishing Hldgs Ltd, 1981; Chm. and Chief Exec., IPC Ltd, 1974; Chief Exec., Publishing and Printing, Reed International Ltd, 1979. Dir, Watmoughs (Hldgs) plc, 1988–98. *Recreations:* racing, gardening. *Address:* Gable House, 75 High Street, Broadway, Worcs WR12 7AL.

**CARPENTER, Louise, (Mrs L. A. Carpenter);** see Botting, E. L.

**CARPENTER, Prof. Lucy Jane,** PhD; FRS 2019; FRSC; Professor of Atmospheric Chemistry, since 2009 and Director, Research, Department of Chemistry, since 2016, University of York; *b* Salisbury, 21 Oct. 1969; *d* of Brinley Carpenter and Patricia Carpenter; *m* 1999, Prof. Alastair Charles Lewis, *qv*; one *s* one *d*. *Educ:* Westwood St Thomas's Sch., Salisbury; Univ. of Bristol (BSc Hons Chem. 1991); Univ. of East Anglia (PhD Chem. 1996). FRSC 2017. University of York: Lectr, 2000–06; Sen. Lectr, 2006–09; Hd, Physical and Atmospheric Chem., 2012–16. Chair, Global Atmospheric Watch Scientific Adv. Gp on Reactive Gases, WMO, 2018–; Mem., WMO/UNEP Scientific Adv. Panel for ozone depletion, 2010, 2014, 2018. Philip Leverhulme Prize, 2006; Rosalind Franklin Award, Royal Soc., 2015; Tilden Prize, RSC, 2017; Wolfson Res. Merit Award, Royal Soc., 2018. *Recreations:* cycling, running, duathlon (competed in ITU World Duathlon Championships as Lucy Lewis). *Address:* Wolfson Atmospheric Chemistry Laboratories, Department of Chemistry, University of York, York YO10 5DD. *E:* lucy.carpenter@york.ac.uk. *Club:* Clifton Cycling.

**CARPENTER, Michael Alan;** Chief Executive Officer, Ally Financial Inc. (formerly GMAC Financial Services), 2009–15; *b* 24 March 1947; *s* of Walter and Kathleen Carpenter; *m* 1975, Mary A. Aughton; one *s* one *d*. *Educ:* Univ. of Nottingham (BSc 1968); Harvard Business Sch. (MBA 1973). Business analyst, Mond Div., ICI, Runcorn, 1968–71; Consultant, 1973–78, Vice-Pres., 1978–83, Boston Consulting Gp; joined General Electric Co., 1983: Vice-Pres., Corporate Business Develt and Planning, 1983–86; Exec. Vice-Pres., GE Capital Corp., 1986–89; Chm., Pres. and CEO, Kidder, Peabody Gp Inc., 1989–94; Chm. and CEO, Travelers Life and Annuity Co., and Vice-Chm., Travelers Gp, Inc., 1995–98; CEO, Global Corporate Investment Bank, and Chm. and CEO, Salomon Smith Barney, 1998–2002; Chm. and CEO, Citigroup Alternative Investments, 2002–06; Chm., Southgate Alternative Investments, 2006–09. Hon. LLD Nottingham, 2003. *Address:* Southgate Holdings, Suite 310, 1601 Washington Avenue, Miami Beach, FL 33139, USA.

**CARPENTER, Michael Charles Lancaster,** CB 2014; Speaker's Counsel, House of Commons, 2008–16; *b* Bristol, 16 March 1949; *s* of Charles Frederick Lancaster and Margaret Florence Carpenter (*née* Richmond); *m* 1970, Susan Valerie Robinson; one *s* three *d*. *Educ:* Hampton Grammar Sch.; Keble Coll., Oxford BA Juris. 1970; MA 1982). Called to the Bar, Inner Temple, 1971; EC Commission: Adminr, Restrictive Practices and Monopolies, Directorate-Gen. for Competition, 1973–80; Prin. Adminr, Legal Service, 1980–81; Hd, Private and Internat. Law Div., Lord Chancellor's Dept, 1985–88; Dep. Legal Sec. to Law Officers, 1989–92; Hd, Cabinet Office and Central Adv. Div., Treasury Solicitor's Dept, 1993–2000; Counsel for Eur. Legislation, H of C, 2000–08. *Publications:* (with J. A. L. Sterling) Copyright Law in the United Kingdom, 1986; (contrib.) Civil Jurisdiction and Judgements in Europe, 1992. *Recreations:* ancient and modern history, making things work. *Address:* Oaks Hill, Oakshade Road, Oxshott, Surrey KT22 0JU.

**CARPENTER, Michael Stephen Evans;** charity consultant, since 2003; Legal Commissioner, Charity Commission, 1998–2002; *b* 7 Oct. 1942; *s* of Ernest Henry Carpenter and Eugenie Carpenter (*née* Evans); *m* 1968, Gabriel Marie Lucie Brain; one *s* one *d*. *Educ:* Eastbourne Coll.; Bristol Univ. (LLB). Admitted Solicitor, 1967; Slaughter and May, 1967–94 (Partner, 1974–94); Withers, 1994–97 (Partner, 1994–96), Consultant, 1997). Sec., Garfield Weston Foundn, 1997. Dep. Chm., Charity Trustee Network, 2005–10; Trustee, Carpenter Charitable Trust, 1981–. *Recreations:* hill-walking, golf, Scottish islands, the church.

**CARR, Andrew Jonathan,** FRCS, FMedSci; Nuffield Professor of Orthopaedic Surgery and Head, Nuffield Department of Orthopaedics, Rheumatology and Musculoskeletal Science, University of Oxford, since 2001; Fellow, Worcester College, Oxford, since 2001; *b* 18 June 1958; *s* of John Malcolm Carr and Patricia (*née* Hodgson); *m* 1985, Clare Robertson; one *s* three *d*. *Educ:* Bradford Grammar Sch.; Bristol Univ. (MB ChB 1982; ChM 1989). FRCS 1986; FMedSci 2009. House surgeon and physician, 1982–83, anatomy demonstrator, 1983–84, Bristol Univ.; Surgical Lectr, Sheffield Univ., 1984–85; Metabolic Medicine Res. Fellow, Univ. of Oxford, 1985–87; Orthopaedic Registrar and Sen. Registrar, Nuffield Orthopaedic Centre and John Radcliffe Hosp., Oxford, 1988–92; Consultant Orthopaedic Surgeon, Nuffield Orthopaedic Centre, Oxford, 1993–2001. Research Fellow: Seattle, 1992; Melbourne, 1992; Hunterian Prof., RCS, 2000; Visiting Professor: Chinese Univ. of Hong Kong, 2004; Nat. Univ. of Singapore, 2015. Trustee: Arthritis Res. Campaign, 2004–11; Jean Shanks Foundn, 2006–. Assoc. Ed., Jl of Bone and Joint Surgery, 2003–08. Robert Jones Gold Medallist and British Orthopaedic Assoc. Prize Winner, 2000. *Publications:* (jtly) Outcomes in Orthopaedic Surgery, 1993; (jtly) Outcomes in Trauma, 1995; (jtly) Assessment Methodology in Orthopaedic Surgery, 1997; (jtly)

Orthopaedics in Primary Care, 1999; (jtly) Classification in Trauma, 1999; (jtly) Oxford Textbook of Orthopaedic Surgery, 2001; contrib. to learned jls etc. on shoulder surgery, genetics and osteoarthritis, patient-reported outcomes of surgery, tissue engrg. *Recreations*: rowing, Real tennis, hill walking, cooking. *Address*: Nuffield Department of Orthopaedics, Rheumatology and Musculoskeletal Sciences, Nuffield Orthopaedic Centre NHS Trust, Oxford OX3 7LD; Worcester College, Oxford OX1 2HB. *Club*: Leander (Henley-on-Thames).

**CARR, Annabel;** *see* Carr, E. A.

**CARR, Anthony Paul;** a District Judge (Magistrates' Courts), since 2003; *b* 30 March 1952; *s* of Alexander and June Carr; *m* 1983, Hilary (*née* Taylor); one *s* one *d*. *Educ*: Stockport Grammar Sch.; Selwyn Coll., Cambridge (BA 1974, MA 1975). Called to the Bar, Middle Temple, 1976; Dep. Clerk to Peterborough Justices, 1983–87; Clerk to SW Essex Justices, 1987–2000; Dir, Legal Services, and Clerk to Essex Justices, 2000–03. Mem., Family Procedure Rule Cttee, 2008–18. Trustee: Ephraim Hallam Charity, 2014–; Stopfordian Trust, 2017–. Gov., Stockport GS, 2014–. *Publications*: Criminal Procedure in Magistrates' Courts, 1982; (jtly) The Children Act in Practice, 4th edn 2008; (ed) Stone's Justices Manual, 127th edn 1995 to 150th edn 2018; (ed) Clarke Hall and Morrison on Children, 10th edn 2004. *Recreations*: reading, railways, ancient Greek. *Address*: Manchester Civil Justice Centre, 1 Bridge Street West, Manchester, Lancs M60 9DJ. *T*: (0161) 240 5000.

**CARR, Prof. Antony Michael,** DPhil; FMedSci; Professor of Molecular Genetics, and Director, Genome Damage and Stability Centre, since 2001, University of Sussex; *b* Dunfermline, 2 May 1960; *s* of Michael and Olga Carr; *m* 1991, Johanne Milne Murray; one *s* one *d*. *Educ*: Helston Comprehensive Sch.; Univ. of E Anglia (BSc Biol. 1981); Univ. of Sussex (DPhil Biochem. 1987). Postdoctoral Fellow, Univ. of Sussex, 1988–89; Mem., Scientific Staff, MRC Cell Mutation Unit, 1989–2001. Editor: Genes and Genetic Systems, 2002–; Molecular and Cellular Biol., 2007–. Mem., EMBO, 2007. FMedSci 2014. Flemming Award, Soc. of Gen. Microbiol., 1996. *Publications*: contributor: Molecular Biology for Oncologists, 1993; Hormonal Carcinogenesis II, 1996; (with J. M. Murray) Microbial Genome Methods, 1996; (with D. J. F. Griffiths) DNA Damage and Repair, 1998; (jtly) DNA Replication and Human Diseases, 2006; contribs to learned jls incl. Microbiol., Microbiol. Today, MRC News, Jl Molecular Biol., DNA Repair, Science, Biochemie, Gene, EMBO Jl, Jl Virol., Molecular and Cell Biol. *Recreations*: dinghy sailing, reading literature, walking. *Address*: Genome Damage and Stability Centre, School of Life Sciences, University of Sussex, Falmer, Brighton BN1 9RQ. *T*: (01273) 678122, *Fax*: (01273) 678123. *E*: a.m.carr@sussex.ac.uk.

**CARR, Bennet,** FRGS; Headmaster, King Edward VI School, Stratford-Upon-Avon, since 2010; *b* Bucks, 7 Dec. 1970; *s* of Francis David and Janet Mary Carr; *m* 2002, Beverley Olga Crass; two *d* (and one *d* decd). *Educ*: Queen Mary Coll., Univ. of London (BA Hons Geog. 1992); Inst. of Educn, Univ. of London (PGCE 1993); Nat. Coll. of Sch. Leadership (NPQH 2009). Teacher, 1993–97, Asst Headmaster, 1997–2002, Bishop's Stortford High Sch.; on sabbatical, travelling, 2000–01; Dep. Headmaster, St Olave's Grammar Sch., 2002–10. Member, Council: Shakespeare Birthplace Trust, 2010–; Hampton Lucy Educnl Trust (formerly Hampton Lucy Grammar Sch. Foundn), 2010–. FRGS 2010. *Recreations*: Rugby (retired), running, theatre, travel, biographies, family. *Address*: The Old Vicarage, King Edward VI School, Church Street, Stratford-Upon-Avon, Warks CV37 6HB. *T*: (01789) 293351, *Fax*: (01789) 293564. *E*: headspa@kes.net.

**CARR, Bruce Conrad;** QC 2009; a Recorder, since 1998; *b* Cambridge, 21 June 1960; *s* of William Ian Carr and Kathleen Ann Carr; *m* 2005, Tamara Nikolic; two *s*. *Educ*: London Sch. of Econs (BSc Econ.). Called to the Bar, Inner Temple, 1986. *Recreation*: all things Croatian. *Address*: Devereux Chambers, Queen Elizabeth Building, Temple, EC4Y 9BS. *T*: (020) 7353 7534. *E*: carr@devchambers.co.uk. *Club*: Leeds United Supporters.

**CARR, (Elizabeth) Annabel;** QC 1997; **Her Honour Judge Annabel Carr;** a Circuit Judge, since 2001; Designated Family Judge for South Yorkshire, since 2008; *b* 14 Nov. 1954; *d* of William John Denys Carr and Norah Betty Carr; one *s* one *d*. *Educ*: Queenswood Sch., Hatfield; Sheffield Univ. (LLB Hons 1975). Called to the Bar, Gray's Inn, 1976; in practice at the Bar, 1977–2001; Recorder, 1995–2001. *Recreations*: travelling, family, theatre. *Address*: Sheffield Combined Court Centre, 50 West Bar, Sheffield S3 8PH.

**CARR, His Honour Maurice Chapman;** a Circuit Judge, 1986–2005; *b* 14 Aug. 1937; *s* of John and Elizabeth Carr; *m* 1959, Caryl Olson (*d* 2013); one *s* one *d*. *Educ*: Hookergate Grammar Sch.; LSE (State Scholar; LLB); Harvard Univ. (Fulbright Scholar; Westengard Fellow; LLM). Lectr in Law, 1960–62, Asst Prof. of Law, 1963–64, Univ. of British Columbia; Lecturer in Law: UCW, 1964–65; Univ. of Newcastle upon Tyne, 1965–69. Called to the Bar, Middle Temple, 1966; Designated Family Judge, 1990–2005. *Recreations*: walking, music.

**CARR, Michael;** teacher; *b* 31 Jan. 1946; *s* of James and Sheila Mary Carr; *m* 1st (wife *d* 1979); one *s*; 2nd, 1980, Georgina Clare; four *s* two *d*. *Educ*: St Joseph's Coll., Blackpool; Catholic Coll., Preston; Margaret McMillan Coll. of Educn, Bradford (CertEd); Bradford and Ilkley Community Coll. (DPSE). Engrg apprentice, 1962–63; Local Govt Officer, 1964–68; partner in family retail newsagency, 1968–70; Teacher of Geography: Brookside Sec. Sch., Middlesbrough, 1973–74; Stainsby Sch., Middlesbrough, 1974–75; Head of Geog., St Thomas Aquinas RC High Sch., Darwen, Lancs, 1975–82; Head of Gen. Studies, Blackthorn County Sec. Sch. and Blackthorn Wing of Fearns CS Sch., Bacup, 1982–87; Mem., Lancs Educn Cttee Sch. Support Team (Disruptive Behaviour), 1988–91. Mem., Sabden Parish Council, 1976–78, 1979–83; Mem. (C 1978–81, SDP 1981–83), Ribble Valley BC, 1979–83. Joined SDP, 1981; contested (SDP/Lib Alliance) Ribble Valley, 1983, 1987; MP (Lib Dem) Ribble Valley, March 1991–1992; contested (Lib Dem) Ribble Valley, 1992, 1997, 2001. Mem., NAS/UWT (Dist Sec., Rossendale Assoc., 1983–87; Press Officer, Lancs Fedn, 1983–87, 1988–90). *Recreations*: hill walking, cooking, music.

**CARR, Michael Douglas,** OBE 2017; Chief Science Officer, BT, 2007–09; *b* Bletchley, 14 Sept. 1955; *s* of John Joseph Carr and Pamela Mary Carr; *m* 1981, Caroline Jane Daniels; two *d*. *Educ*: Plymouth Poly. (BScEng Hons Communication Engrg 1980). CEng, FIET 2004; FREng 2008. Joined BT as Technician Apprentice Field Engr, 1972; Researcher, Picture Compression, 1980–84, Hd, Video Conference Res. Gp, 1984–89, Gen. Manager, Video Res., 1989–94, BT Labs; Principal Advr, Multimedia, 1994–96; Hd, ICT Strategy Unit, 1996–99; Vice-Pres., Technology and Venturing USA, 1999–2001; Dir, Res. and Venturing, 2001–07. Chm., Astigan Ltd, 2014–. Non-executive Director: Ordnance Survey, 2009–; Ploughshare Innovations Ltd, 2016–. Member: Bd, EPSRC, 2008–11; Bd, Innovate UK (formerly Technology Strategy Bd), 2011–16; Enterprise Cttee, RAEng, 2015–. Trustee, IET, 2019–Oct. 2020 (Vice-Pres., 2010–13; Dep. Pres., 2016–18; Pres., 2018–19). Hon. DTech Plymouth, 2009. *Publications*: articles in jls on video comparison and video transmission. *Recreations*: woodworking, gardening, playing the piano. *E*: mike.d.carr@btinternet.com.

**CARR, Neena;** *see* Modi, N.

**CARR, Peter; His Honour Judge Peter Carr;** a Circuit Judge, since 2007; *b* Hamburg, 14 Nov. 1954; *s* of Derek and Anneliese Carr; *m* 1997, Julie Ann Campbell; one *d*. *Educ*: Dr Challoner's Grammar Sch., Amersham; Birmingham Univ. (LLB). Called to the Bar, Inner Temple, 1976; Recorder, 2001–07. *Recreations*: golf, bridge, cooking. *Address*: Birmingham Crown Court, 1 Newton Street, Birmingham B4 7NA. *T*: (0121) 681 3300. *Clubs*: Edgbaston Golf, Warwickshire County Cricket.

**CARR, Reginald Philip;** Director, University Library Services, and Bodley's Librarian, University of Oxford, 1997–2006, now Bodley's Librarian Emeritus; Fellow, Balliol College, Oxford, 1997–2006; *b* 20 Feb. 1946; *s* of Philip Henry Carr and Ida Bayley Carr (*née* Wood); *m* 1968, Elizabeth Whittaker; one *s* three *d*. *Educ*: Manchester Grammar Sch.; Univ. of Leeds (BA 1968); Univ. of Manchester (MA 1971); MA Cantab 1983; MA Oxon 1997. English lang. teaching asst, Lycée Fontenelle, Rouen, 1966–67; Asst Librarian, John Rylands Univ. Liby, Manchester, 1970–72; Librarian-in-Charge, Sch. of Educn Liby, Univ. of Manchester, 1972–76; Sub-Librarian, Univ. of Surrey, 1976–78; Deputy Librarian: Univ. of Aston, 1978–80; Univ. of Cambridge, 1980–86; University of Leeds: Univ. Librarian and Keeper, Brotherton Collection, 1986–96; Dean, Information Strategy, 1996. Mem., Jt Information Systems Cttee, 1997–2005. Chairman: Standing Conference of Nat. and Univ. Libraries, 1994–96; Res. Libraries Gp Inc., 1999–2003. Hon. Sec., Consortium of Univ. Res. Libraries, 1991–97; Trustee, Chawton House Library, 2006–12. Hon. DLitt Leicester, 2000. Hon. Citizen, Toyota City, 1998. Book Ed., Testimony mag., 2007–. *Publications*: Anarchism in France: the case of Octave Mirbeau, 1977; (jtly) Spirit in the New Testament, 1985; The Mandrake Press, 1985; (jtly) An Introduction to University Library Administration, 1987; (ed) For the Study and Defence of the Holy Scripture, vol. 1, 1987, vol. 2, 2015; The Academic Research Library in a Decade of Change, 2007; Micah Study Guide, 2010; (ed) The Pen of a Ready Writer, 2010; (ed) Testimony Handbook of Bible Principles, 2010; A Goodly Heritage, 2012; (ed) Treasure New and Old, 2018; contribs to professional and learned jls. *Recreations*: Bible study, book collecting, writing, editing and publishing. *Address*: c/o The Bodleian Library, Broad Street, Oxford OX1 3BG.

**CARR, Prof. the Hon. Robert John;** Senator (ALP) for New South Wales, 2012–13; Federal Minister for Foreign Affairs, 2012–13; Professor of International Relations and Director, Australia-China Relations Institute, University of Technology, Sydney, since 2014; *b* 28 Sept. 1947; *s* of Edward and Phyllis Carr; *m* 1973, Helena. *Educ*: Univ. of NSW (BA Hons). Journalist, ABC Current Affairs Radio, 1969–72; Educn Officer, Labor Council, NSW, 1972–78; journalist, The Bulletin, 1978–83. Government of New South Wales: MP (ALP) Maroubra, 1983–2005; Minister: for Planning and Envmt, 1984–88; for Consumer Affairs, 1986; for Heritage, 1986–88; Leader of the Opposition, 1988–95; Minister: for Ethnic Affairs, 1995–99; for the Arts, 1995–2005; for Citizenship, 1999–2005; Premier of NSW, 1995–2005. Mem., Internat. Climate Change Taskforce, 2004. World Conservation Union Internat. Parks Award, 1998; Fulbright Dist. Fellow Award, 1999. *Publications*: Thoughtlines: reflections of a public man, 2002; What Australia Means to Me, 2003; My Reading Life: adventures in the world of books, 2008; Diary of a Foreign Minister, 2014.

**CARR, Rodney Paul,** CBE 2010 (OBE 2005); yachtsman; Chairman, UK Sport, 2013–17 (Member of Board, 2005–17); *b* 10 March 1950; *s* of Capt. George Paul Carr and Alma Carr (*née* Walker); *m* 1971, Lynne Alison Ashwell; one *s* one *d*. *Educ*: Carlton le Willows Grammar Sch., Nottingham; Univ. of Birmingham (BSc Geology 1972). Chief Sailing Instructor, London Bor. of Haringey, 1972–75; Instructor, 1975–79, Chief Instructor, 1979–81, Nat. Sailing Centre, Cowes, IoW; Mem., winning British Admiral's Cup team, 1981; joined RYA, 1984; Coach, GB Olympic Team: Los Angeles, 1984; Seoul, 1988; Barcelona, 1992; Overall GB Team Manager, Atlanta Olympic Games, 1996; Racing Manager and Performance Dir, RYA, 1997–2000; Dep. Chef de Mission, GB Olympic Team, Sydney, 2000; Chief Exec., RYA, 2000–10. Field of Play Manager, Weymouth Sailing, London Olympics, 2012. Member, Board: Weymouth and Portland Nat. Sailing Acad., 2008– (Chm., 2018–); Outward Bound Trust, 2011–15. Trustee: John Merricks Sailing Trust, 1997–; 1851 Marine Trust, 2015–. Younger Brethren, Trinity House, 2006–. Hon. MBA Southampton Inst., 2002. *Recreations*: played county level U19 Rugby for Nottinghamshire, keen interest in most sports, current affairs, music, long distance walking, sailing (cruising and radio sailing), rowing. *Address*: Riverfield, Lumley Road, Emsworth, Hants PO10 8AA. *T*: (01243) 370204. *E*: rod@coachone.co.uk. *Clubs*: Royal Thames Yacht, Royal Yachting Assoc.; Hayling Island Sailing (Trustee, 2018–), Emsworth Slipper Sailing.

**CARR, Sir Roger (Martyn),** Kt 2011; Chairman, BAE SYSTEMS, since 2014; *b* 22 Dec. 1946; *s* of John and Kathleen Carr; *m* 1973, Stephanie Elizabeth; one *d*. *Educ*: Nottingham High Sch.; Nottingham Poly. Dir, Williams Hldgs plc, 1988–2000; Chief Exec., Williams plc, 1994–2000; Chm., Chubb plc, 2000–02. Dir, 1994–99, Chm., 1999–2000, Thames Water plc. Chm., Mitchells & Butlers, 2003–08; Sen. non-exec. Dir, 2000–03, Dep. Chm., 2003–08, Chm., 2008–10, Cadbury plc; Sen. non-exec. Dir, Six Continents (formerly Bass) plc, 1996–2003; non-exec. Dir, 2000–14, Chm., 2004–14, Centrica. Dep. Chm., Bank of England, 2011–14 (non-exec. Dir, 2007–14). Pres., CBI, 2011–13 (Mem., Council, 2001–04). Sen. Advr, Kohlberg, Kravis & Roberts & Co. Ltd, 2000–. Member: Industrial Adv. Bd, 2001–04; Prime Minister's Business Adv. Gp, 2011–15; Co-Chair, Prime Minister's Industrial, Infrastructure and Manufg Business Sector Council, 2019–. Vis. Fellow, Oxford Univ., 2008–. Vice Chm., BBC Trust, 2015–17. Chair, English Nat. Ballet, 2018–. Trustee, Bletchley Park, 2018–. Hon. DBus Nottingham Trent, 2018. CCMI (CIMgt 1997); FRSA 1996; FCIS 2013. *Recreations*: theatre, opera, golf. *Address*: BAE SYSTEMS, Stirling Square, 6 Carlton Gardens, SW1Y 5AD. *Clubs*: Brooks's; China (Hong Kong).

**CARR, Simon Andrew; His Honour Judge Simon Carr;** a Circuit Judge, since 2009; *b* Stafford, 9 Aug. 1961; *s* of Brian and Pamela Carr; *m* 1990, Stephanie Farrimond. *Educ*: Perse Sch., Cambridge; Southampton Univ. (LLB). Called to the Bar, Inner Temple, 1984; Recorder, 2003–09. Trustee, Cornwall Air Ambulance. *Recreations*: sub-aqua diving, travel, animal conservation, beekeeping, ECB accredited umpire. *Club*: Anglesey Aquanauts.

**CARR, Rt Hon. Dame Sue (Lascelles), (Rt Hon. Dame Sue Birch),** DBE 2013; PC 2019; **Rt Hon. Lady Justice Carr;** a Lady Justice of Appeal, since 2019; *b* 1 Sept. 1964; *d* of Richard Carr and Edda Harvey (*née* Armbrust); *m* 1993, Alexander Birch; two *s* one *d*. *Educ*: Trinity Coll., Cambridge (MA Law and Mod. Langs). Called to the Bar, Inner Temple, 1987, Bencher, 2006; QC 2003; a Recorder, 2009–13; Hd of Chambers, 2012–13; a Judge of the High Ct of Justice, QBD, 2013–19; Presiding Judge, Midland Circuit, 2016–19. Complaints Comr to Internat. Criminal Court, The Hague, 2011–13. Chm., Complaints Cttee, 2008–10; Mem., Bar Standards Bd, 2008–10. Mem., Investigatory Powers Tribunal, 2014–16. Gov., Wycombe Abbey Sch., 2007–. *Publications*: (ed) Professional Liability Precedents, 2000. *Recreations*: theatre, ski-ing, tennis. *Address*: Royal Courts of Justice, Strand, WC2A 2LL.

**CARR, Prof. Wilfred;** Professor, School of Education, University of Sheffield, 1994–2009, now Emeritus; *b* 18 March 1943; *s* of Wilfred and Leah Carr; *m* 1976, Marisse Evans; three *d*. *Educ*: Xaverian Coll., Manchester; Shenstone Coll. of Educn, Worcs (DipEd); Warwick Univ. (BA, MA). History teacher, Oldbury Tech. Sch., Warley, Worcs, 1966–70; Lectr,

Sch. of Educn, UCNW, 1974–88; University of Sheffield: Sen. Lectr, Dept of Educnl Studies, 1988–90, Reader 1990–94; Dean, Faculty of Educnl Studies, 1992–94; Head, Dept of Educnl Studies, then Sch. of Educn, 1996–2002 and 2005–06; Dean, Fac. of Soc. Scis, 2003–05. Honorary Professor: Faculty of Educn and Soc. Work, Univ. of Sydney, 2006–; Sch. of Educn, Charles Sturt Univ., NSW, 2008–. Ed., Pedagogy, Culture and Society, 1993–2009. Chm., Philosophy of Educn Soc. of GB, 1996–99, Hon. Vice-Pres., 1999–. *Publications*: (with S. Kemmis) Becoming Critical: education knowledge and action research, 1986 (trans. Spanish 1988); For Education: towards critical educational inquiry, 1995 (trans. Spanish 1996, Chinese 1997); (with A. Hartnett) Education and the Struggle for Democracy: the politics of educational ideas, 1996; (ed) The RoutledgeFalmer Reader in Philosophy of Education, 2005. *Recreations*: cookery, reading, walking. *Address*: School of Education, Department of Educational Studies, University of Sheffield, 388 Glossop Road, Sheffield S10 2JA. *T*: (0114) 222 8085. *E*: w.carr@sheffield.ac.uk.

**CARR-SMITH, Maj.-Gen. Stephen Robert;** speaker on cruise ships, since 2007; Chairman, Moving Office Ltd, since 2009; *b* 3 Dec. 1941; *s* of Charles Carr-Smith and Elizabeth Carr-Smith (*née* Marsh); *m* 1967, Nicole Bould; two *s* one *d. Educ*: Welbeck College; RMA; RMCS; BA Open Univ., 1992. Commissioned Royal Signals, 1962; served in UK, Germany, Aden and Belgium; Mil. Secretariat, 1973–74, Operational Requirements, 1978–79, MoD; CO, 1st Armoured Div. HQ and Signal Regt, 1979–82; Instructor, Army Staff Coll., 1982–84; Comdt, Army Apprentices Coll., Harrogate, 1984–86; Col MGO Secretariat, MoD, 1986–88; Chief CIS Policy Branch, SHAPE, Mons, 1988–91; Dep. Dir Gen., NATO CIS Agency, Brussels, 1992–95; Dir of Special Projects, Defence Systems Ltd, 1995–98; Sen. Mil. Advr, CORDA, BAe and SEMA, 1995–99. Ombudsman for Estate Agents, 1999–2006; Chm., Applied Systems International plc, 1999–2001. Non-exec. Dir, Council for National Land and Property Information Service, later Land Data, 2006–10; Chm., Nat. Assembly for Property Search Standards, 2007–08. Chm., Cancer Res. UK, Winchester, 2007–13. Hon. Col, FANY, Princess Royal's Volunteer Corps, 1996–2006 (Vice Pres., 2006–); Col Comdt, RCS, 1996–2002. Pres., Stragglers of Asia CC, 2003–13. *Recreations*: cricket, golf, bridge, military history. *Address*: c/o Cox's & King's, PO Box 1190, 7 Pall Mall, SW1Y 5NA.

**CARRAGHER, Anna;** Controller, BBC Northern Ireland, 2000–06; Electoral Commissioner for Northern Ireland, 2012–Oct. 2020; *b* 9 July 1948; *d* of Thomas Carragher and Eileen Carragher; *m* 1974, Alain Le Garsmeur; two *s* one *d. Educ*: St Dominic's High Sch., Belfast; Queen's Univ., Belfast (BA Hons). BBC Radio: studio manager, 1970–73; Producer, Today prog., 1973–81; BBC Television: Producer: Television News progs, 1981–85; Question Time, 1985–89; Any Questions, 1989–92; Editor: Election Call, 1992; European progs, 1992–95; Hd of Programmes, BBC NI, 1995–2000. Dir, NI Film Commn, 1995–2003. Member: Radio Acad., 2000–02; Bd, BITC NI, 2001–06; Bd, Radio Jt Audience Res. Bd Ltd, 2002–06; Human Fertilisation and Embryology Authy, 2006–12; Bd, Arts Council of NI, 2012–; Comr, Equality Commn, NI, 2009–15; NI Trustee, NHMF and NLHF (formerly HLF), 2016–. Chm., Grand Opera House Trust, Belfast, 2006–11. Mem. Council, Wildfowl and Wetlands Trust, 2009–18. *Recreations*: hill-walking, opera, reading, bird-watching, theatre. *Address*: 24 College Park Avenue, Belfast BT7 1LR.

**CARRAHER, Terezinha;** *see* Nunes, T.

**CARRELL, Rt Rev. Peter Ruane;** *see* Christchurch, Bishop of.

**CARRELL, Prof. Robin Wayne;** FRS 2002; FRSNZ 1980; FRCP; Professor of Haematology, University of Cambridge, 1986–2003; Fellow of Trinity College, Cambridge, since 1987; *b* 5 April 1936; *s* of Ruane George Carrell and Constance Gwendoline Carrell (*née* Rowe); *m* 1962, Susan Wyatt Rogers; two *s* two *d. Educ*: Christchurch Boys' High School, NZ; Univ. of Otago (MB ChB 1959); Univ. of Canterbury (BSc 1965); Univ. of Cambridge (MA, PhD 1968, ScD 2002). FRACP 1973; FRCPath 1976; MRCP 1985, FRCP 1990. Mem., MRC Abnormal Haemoglobin Unit, Cambridge, 1965–68; Dir, Clinical Biochemistry, Christchurch Hosp., NZ, 1968–75; Lectr and Consultant in Clinical Biochem., Addenbrooke's Hosp. and Univ. of Cambridge, 1976–78; Prof. of Clinical Biochem., Christchurch Sch. of Clinical Medicine, Univ. of Otago, 1978–86. Founder Dir, Canterbury Scientific Ltd, NZ, 1985–2012. Pres., British Soc. of Thrombosis and Haemostasis, 1999. Mem., Spongiform Encephalopathy Adv. Cttee, 2001–04. Member: Gen. Bd, Univ. of Cambridge, 1989–92; Court, Imperial Coll., London, 1997–2006. Commonwealth Fellow, St John's Coll. and Vis. Scientist, MRC Lab. of Molecular Biol., 1985. Founder FMedSci 1998. Hon. FRCPA 2005. Hon. Fellow, Darwin Coll., Cambridge, 2016. Pharmacia Prize for biochem. res., NZ, 1984; Hector Medal, Royal Soc., NZ, 1986; Altiora Peto Award, Christchurch Boys' High School, NZ, 2013. *Publications*: articles in sci. jls defining the SERPIN family of proteins that control key functions of cells and blood. *Recreations*: topiary, archaeology, ski-ing. *Address*: 19 Madingley Road, Cambridge CB3 0EG. *T*: (01223) 312970. *Club*: Athenæum.

**CARRERAS, José;** tenor; *b* 5 Dec. 1946; *s* of José and Antonia Carreras; *m* (marr. diss. 1992); one *s* one *d*; *m* 2006, Jutta Jäger. Opera début as Gennaro in Lucrezia Borgia, Barcelona, 1970; US début in Madama Butterfly, NY City Opera, 1972; Tosca, NY Met, 1974; Covent Garden début in La Traviata, 1974; Un Ballo In Maschera, La Scala, 1975; after break owing to illness, concerts in Barcelona, 1988, Covent Gdn, 1989; Music Dir, Barcelona Olympics, 1992; first UK perf., Stiffelio, Covent Gdn, 1993; has appeared at all major opera houses and festivals in Europe, USA and S America; has made many recordings. *Films*: Don Carlos, 1986; West Side Story (TV), 1985. Pres., José Carreras Internat. Leukaemia Foundn, 1988–. RAM 1990. Personality of the Year, Classical Music Awards, 1994; Lifetime Achievement in Music Award, Classical Brits, 2009. *Address*: c/o FIJC, Muntaner 383, 2°, 08021 Barcelona, Spain.

**CARRICK, 11th Earl of,** *cr* 1748; **Arion Thomas Piers Hamilton Butler;** Viscount Ikerrin 1629; Baron Butler (UK) 1912; *b* 1 Sept. 1975; *s* of 10th Earl of Carrick and of Philippa Janice Victoria (*née* Craxton); *S* father, 2008; *m* 2006, Yoko Shibao; two *d. Heir: b* Hon. Piers Edmund Theobald Lismalyn Butler, *b* 27 Feb. 1979.

**CARRICK, Mervyn;** *see* Carrick, W. M.

**CARRICK, Sir Roger (John),** KCMG 1995 (CMG 1983); LVO 1972; FRGS; HM Diplomatic Service, retired; author, lecturer; Chairman, Lime Finance, since 2010; *b* 13 Oct. 1937; *s* of John H. and Florence M. Carrick; *m* 1962, Hilary Elizabeth Blinman; two *s. Educ*: Isleworth Grammar Sch.; Jt Services Sch. for Linguists; Sch. of Slavonic and East European Studies, London Univ. FRGS 2016. Served RN, 1956–58. Joined HM Foreign (subseq. Diplomatic) Service, 1956; SSEES, 1961; Sofia, 1962; FO, 1965; Paris, 1967; Singapore, 1971; FCO, 1973; Counsellor and Dep. Head, Personnel Ops Dept, FCO, 1976; Vis. Fellow, Inst. of Internat. Studies, Univ. of Calif, Berkeley, 1977–78; Counsellor, Washington, 1978–82; Hd, Overseas Estate Dept, FCO, 1982–85; Consul-Gen., Chicago, 1985–88; Asst Under-Sec. of State (Economic), FCO, 1988–90; Ambassador, Republic of Indonesia, 1990–94; High Comr, Australia, 1994–97. Dep. Chm., 1999–2006, Mem., Adv. Gp, 2010–15, The D Gp; Chairman: CMB Ltd, 2001–03; Strategy Internat. Ltd, 2007–10 (non-exec. Dir, 2001–06). Churchill Fellow (Life), Westminster Coll., Fulton, Missouri, 1987. Member: Britain-Australia Soc., 1998– (Life Mem.; Dep. Chm., 1999; Chm., 1999–2001; Vice-Pres., 2002–; Mem., 2001–09, Chm., 2007–09, Educn Trust; Pres., W Country Branch, 2003–14); Anglo-Indonesian Soc.; Mem., Cook Soc., 1997 (Chm., 2002; Hon. Mem., 2013–). Mem., Bd of Trustees, Chevening Estate, 1998–2003. Jt Founder, WADE. Freeman, City of London, 2002. *Publications*: East-West Technology Transfer in Perspective, 1978; Rolleround Oz, 1998; (contrib.) Symphony of Australia, 2010; Diplomatic Anecdotage, 2012; (contrib.) The Foreign Office, Commerce and British Foreign Policy in the Twentieth Century, 2017; contrib. to London Papers in Australian Studies (No. 17 on Gov. Arthur Phillip); articles in jls; chapters in bks. *Recreations*: travel, lecturing, dabbling in carpentry, reading, writing, enjoying music, recalling sailing, avoiding gardening, acknowledging three grandchildren and three great-grandchildren. *Address*: Windrose, Wootton Courtenay, Minehead, Somerset TA24 8RE. *Club*: Royal Over-Seas League (Mem., Central Council, 2009–; Vice-Chm., 2011–; Hon. Mem., 2012–; Chm., Bldgs Sub-Cttee, 2012–15; Acting Chm., 2015–16).

**CARRICK, (William) Mervyn;** Member (DemU) Upper Bann, Northern Ireland Assembly, 1998–2003; *b* 13 Feb. 1946; *s* of late William and of Margaret Carrick; *m* 1969, Ruth Cardwell; three *s* one *d. Educ*: Portadown Technical Coll. Accountant, 1961–. Mem., NI Forum for Political Dialogue, 1996–98. Mem. (DemU), Craigavon BC, 1990–2001 (Dep. Mayor, 1997–98, Mayor, 1998–99). *Recreation*: gardening. *Address*: 72 Dungannon Road, Portadown, Co. Armagh BT62 1LQ. *T*: (028) 3833 6392.

**CARRIE, Anne Marie;** Chief Operating Officer, Cambian, since 2016 (Chief Executive, Children's Services, Cambian Group plc, 2015–16); *b* Glasgow, 25 Aug. 1955; *d* of Angus Wilson and Agnes Wilson (*née* Thomson); *m* 1983, Scott Carrie; one *d. Educ*: Lochend Secondary Sch., Easterhouse, Glasgow; Royal Scottish Acad. of Music and Drama (Dip. Speech and Drama); Jordanhill Coll. (Secondary Teaching Cert. (merit)). Asst Principal Teacher, Deans Community High Sch., 1979–85; Hd, Guidance and Counselling, Telford Coll., 1985–88; Lothian Region: Regl TVEI Manager, 1988–93; Asst Dir, Secondary Schs 1993–95; Hd, Educn, E Lothian Council, 1995–2001; Exec. Dir, Educn, N Tyneside Council, 2001–03; Regl Dir, Office of the Dep. Prime Minister, 2003–06; Dep. Chief Exec., Royal Bor. of Kensington and Chelsea, 2006–11; Chief Executive: Barnardo's, 2011–13; Kensington and Chelsea Educn Ltd, 2013–15. Non-executive Director: Scottish Seabird Centre, 1998–2001; Health Educn Bd for Scotland, 1998–2001. Chm., Nat. Educn Cttee, Assoc. of Dirs of Children's Services, 2009–10. Comr, Social Mobility and Child Poverty Commn, 2012–. Gov. and Trustee, Chelsea Acad., 2010–17; Gov., Basildon and Thurrock Univ. Hosp. Trust; Chair of Govs, Holland Park Sch.; Mem. Bd, Nat. Virtual Coll., 2010–. FRSA; FInstD 2007. *Recreations*: theatre, walking, cycling, fire walking, singing.

**CARRIER, Dr John Woolfe;** Senior Lecturer in Social Policy, 1974–2005, and Dean of Graduate Studies, 2002–05, London School of Economics and Political Science; *b* 26 Sept. 1938; *s* of Louis Carrier and Rachel Carrier; *m* 1964, Sarah Margaret Dawes; two *s* two *d. Educ*: Regent's Park Central Sch.; Chiswick Poly.; London Sch. of Econs (BSc (Soc) 1965; MPhil 1969; PhD 1983); Univ. of Westminster (LLB Hons 1994). Principal Lectr, Goldsmiths' Coll., Univ. of London, 1967–74. Lectures: William Marsden, Royal Free Hosp., 1996; Richard Titmuss Meml, Hebrew Univ. of Jerusalem, 1997. Vis. Prof., Univ. of Greenwich, 2006–07. Mem. (Lab) Camden BC, 1971–78. Mem. and Vice-Chm., Hampstead HA, 1982–91; Vice-Chm., 1991–97, Chm., 1997–2001, Royal Free Hampstead NHS Hosp. Trust; Chm., Camden PCT, 2001–13; Chair, N Middx Univ. Hosp. NHS Trust, 2013–17. Vice-Chm. and Trustee, Centre for Advancement of Inter-professional Educn, 1990–99; Chair, Cttees in Obstetrics and Gynaecol., Public Health Medicine, and Surgery, London Deanery, 2010–15. Lay Adviser: Faculty of Public Health, 2015–; Health Educn England, 2017–. Trustee: William Ellis and Birkbeck Schs Trust, 1996– (Chm. Trustees, 2005–); British Cardiovascular Soc., 2009–; Mem. Council, Royal Free Hosp. Med. Sch., 1988–98; Trustee, RNTNEH, 1997–99; Special Trustee, Royal Free Hosp., 1999–2008; Mem., London NE Sub-Cttee, Adv. Cttee on Clinical Excellence Awards, 2003– (Chm., 2008–); Mem., 2005–11 (Chm., Educn and Trng Cttee, 2007–11), Special Advr on Legal Educn, 2012–13, Bar Standards Bd. Chairman: Camden Victim Support Scheme, 1978–83; Highgate Cemetery Trust, 1983–97; NE London and City Cluster of PCTs, 2012–13. Gov., Tavistock and Portman NHS Foundn Trust, 2017–. Trustee, Hackney Youth Orch. Trust, 2002–09. Governor: Gospel Oak Primary Sch., 1972–80 (Chm., 1977–80); Brookfield Primary Sch., 1974–89 (Chm., 1981–87); William Ellis Sch., 1971–96 (Chm., 1987–96); Trustee, NE Thames Foundn Sch., 2012–. JP Highbury, 1983–90. Hon. FRSocMed 1999; Hon. FRCP 2010. Hon. Bencher, Lincoln's Inn, 2011; Mem., Lincoln's Inn Scholarship Cttee, 2013– (Chm., 2013–19). Jt Ed., Internat. Jl of Law, Crime and Justice (formerly Internat. Jl Sociol. of Law), 1993–; Member, Editorial Board: Jl Social Policy, 1975–81; Ethnic and Racial Studies, 1990–96. *Publications*: with Ian Kendall: Medical Negligence: complaints and compensation, 1990; (ed) Socialism and the NHS, 1990; Interprofessional Issues in Community and Primary Health Care, 1995; Health and the National Health Service, 1998, 2nd edn 2016; (ed jtly) Asylum in the Community, 1996; contrib. articles to learned jls. *Recreations*: running, tennis, walking, films, art galleries. *Address*: 37 Dartmouth Park Road, NW5 1SU. *T*: (020) 7267 1376.

**CARRINGTON,** family name of **Baron Carrington of Fulham.**

**CARRINGTON, 7th Baron** (Ireland) *cr* 1796, (Great Britain) *cr* 1797; **Rupert Francis John Carington;** DL; Chairman, Carington Estates Ltd, since 2004; *b* London, 2 Dec. 1948; *s* of 6th Baron Carrington and Iona (*née* McLean); *S* father, 2018; *m* 1989, Daniela Diotallevi; one *s* two *d. Educ*: Eton Coll.; Univ. of Bristol (BSc). With Morgan Grenfell & Co. Ltd, 1969–86; Chm., Schroder Asia Pacific Fund plc, 1995–2016. Chm., Sete Technical Services SA, 2002–; Dir, Alger Associates Inc., 2012–. Elected Mem., H of L, 2018–. Gov., RSC, 2017–. DL Bucks, 2005. *Recreations*: theatre, opera, gardening, walking. *Heir: s* Hon. Robert Peter Flavio Carington, *b* 7 Dec. 1990. *Address*: Manor House, Bledlow, Bucks HP27 9PD. *T*: (01844) 274461. *E*: lordcarrington@carington.co.uk. *Clubs*: White's, Pratt's.

**CARRINGTON OF FULHAM, Baron** *cr* 2013 (Life Peer), of Fulham in the London Borough of Hammersmith and Fulham; **Matthew Hadrian Marshall Carrington;** Director, 2007–17, and Chairman, 2015–17, Gatehouse Bank PLC (Deputy Chairman, 2008–15); Director, Aston Martin Global Holdings plc, since 2018; *b* 19 Oct. 1947; *s* of late Walter Carrington and Dilys Carrington; *m* 1st, 1975, Mary Lou Darrow (*d* 2008); one *d*; 2nd, 2011, Margaret Ann Milward. *Educ*: London Lycée; Imperial Coll. of Science and Technol., London (BSc Physics); London Business Sch. (MSc). Prodn Foreman, GKN Ltd, 1969–72; banker: with The First National Bank of Chicago, 1974–78; with Saudi Internat. Bank, 1978–87; Chm., Outdoor Advertising Assoc., 1998–2002. MP (C) Fulham, 1987–97; contested () Hammersmith and Fulham, 1997, 2001. PPS to Rt Hon. John Patten, MP, 1990–94; an Asst Govt Whip, 1996–97. Mem., Treasury and Civil Service Select Cttee, 1994–96; Chm., Treasury Select Cttee, 1996. London Regl Chm., 2005–08, Chm., London NW Area, 2008–10, Cons. Party. Chief Exec., Retail Motor Industry Fedn, 2002–06. Dir, Arab British Chamber of Commerce, 2011–. *Recreations*: cooking, political history. *Address*: 34 Ladbroke Square, W11 3NB.

**CARRINGTON, Michael;** Director, Entertainment and Specialist Networks, ABC, since 2018 (Head, Children's and Education, 2016–18); *b* Camden, Australia, 5 May 1961; *s* of Hubert Plicha-Carrington and Elaine (*née* Marshall); *m* 2006, S. Palluel. *Educ:* Parkes High Sch., Parkes, NSW; Ashridge Business Sch. (Strategy, 2007); Saïd Business Sch., Oxford Univ. (High Perf. Leadership Prog. 2009); London Business Sch. (Corporate Finance, 2010). Radio presenter, 2PK, Australia, 1979–82; RAN, 1982–86; Prodn Manager, Channel 10, Australia, 1986–89; Acquisitions Asst, BBC, 1990–91; Acquisitions Exec., Discovery Channel Europe, 1991–93; Producer, BBC, 1993–99; Hd, Television and New Media, LEGO Media, 1999–2004; Hd, Animation and Acquisitions, 2004–06, Controller, CBeebies, 2006–10, BBC; Chief Content Officer, Turner Broadcasting, 2010–13; Vice Pres. Creative, HIT Entertainment, 2013–14; CEO, Zodiak Kids Studios, 2014–16. Member: BAFTA; RTS; Aust. Acad. of Cinema and TV Arts Awards. *Address:* ABC-TV, GPO Box 9994, Sydney, NSW 2001, Australia. *T:* (61) 88834441. *Clubs:* Century, Ivy.

**CARRINGTON, Sir Nigel (Martyn),** Kt 2019; Vice-Chancellor (formerly Rector), University of the Arts London, since 2008; *b* Amersham, 1 May 1956; *s* of Ron and Vera Carrington; *m* 1988, Elisabeth Buchanan; one *s* two *d*. *Educ:* St John's Coll., Oxford (MA Hons Juris.; Hon. Fellow 2018); Courtauld Inst. of Art, Univ. of London (Grad. Dip. Hist. of Art). Solicitor and Partner, Baker & McKenzie, 1979–2000; Man. Partner, London, 1994–98; Chm., Eur. Regl Council, 1998–2000; Man. Dir, McLaren Gp Ltd, 2000–05 (Dep. Chm., 2005–07). Non-executive Director: University Coll. London Hosps NHS Foundn Trust, 2005–08; Hornby plc, 2007–14. Chm., Advance HE, 2018–. Dir, Creative Industries Fedn, 2014–; Trustee/Dir, Universities UK, 2015–. Trustee: Crisis, 2005–11 (Treas., 2005–08); English Concert, 2005–17 (Chm., 2006–12); Independent Opera, 2006–10; Cass Sculpture Foundn, 2015–; Burgh House and Hampstead Mus., 2017– (Chm., 2017–). Chm., Jeans for Genes, 2006–08. Chm., Henry Moore Foundn, 2014–. Governor: N London Collegiate Sch., 2008–15; Internat. Students House, 2009–17. *Publications:* Acquiring Companies and Businesses in Europe, 1994. *Recreations:* chamber music, swimming, ski-ing, walking in the mountains. *Address:* University of the Arts London, 272 High Holborn, WC1V 7EY. *T:* (020) 7514 6002, *Fax:* (020) 7514 6236. *E:* n.carrington@arts.ac.uk. *Clubs:* Chelsea Arts, Royal Automobile.

**CARRINGTON, Ruth;** *see* James, M. L.

**CARROLL, Cynthia;** Chair, Vedanta Resources Holdings Ltd, 2015–17; *b* Philadelphia, 13 Nov. 1956; *m* 1988, David Carroll; one *s* three *d*. *Educ:* Skidmore Coll., NY (BS Geol.); Univ. of Kansas (MS Geol.); Harvard Univ. (MBA). FREng 2012. Petroleum geologist, Amoco, 1981–87; Business Develt Gp, Rolled Products Div., Alcan Inc., 1989–91; Vice-Pres./Gen. Manager, Alcan Foil Products, 1991–96; Man. Dir, Aughinish Alumina Ltd, 1996–98; Pres., Bauxite, Alumina & Speciality Chemicals, 1998–2001, Pres. and CEO, Primary Metal Gp, 2002–06, Alcan Inc.; Chief Exec., Anglo American plc, 2007–13. Non-executive Director: BP plc, 2007–17; Hitachi Ltd, 2013–. *Recreations:* ski-ing, swimming, tennis, sailing, golf, horseback riding, sewing, family.

**CARROLL, Eileen Philomena, (Mrs E. P. Carroll-Mackie);** Principal Mediator and Co-Founder, Centre for Effective Dispute Resolution, since 1996; *b* 5 Dec. 1953; *d* of late Matthew Francis Carroll and of Mary Philomena Carroll; *m* 1st, Richard Peers-Jones (marr. diss.); one *d*; 2nd, 2001, Karl Joseph Mackie, *qv*. *Educ:* Holy Cross, Gerrards Cross; Univ. of Kent, Canterbury (LLB Hons (Law) 1979). Analyst, British Sulphur Corp., London, 1972–74; admitted as solicitor, 1981; Lawyer/Partner, then Internat. Strategy Partner, Turner Kenneth Brown, 1981–94; Vis. Partner, Thelen Reid Priest, San Francisco, 1988 and 1994; involved in foundn of CEDR, 1990 (Mem., Bd of Trustees, 1990–96); accredited CEDR mediator, 1993. Mem., Litigation Cttee, London Solicitors, 1987–90. Adv. Mem., Conflict Analysis Res. Centre, Univ. of Kent at Canterbury, 2006–; Member: Forum UK, 2006–/; Follett Gp, 2006–; Mem. Council, Distinguished Advisors, Straus Inst. for Dispute Resolution, 2007–. Gov., Surbiton High Sch., 2004–. Exec. Coach, Henley Bus. Sch., 2008. Hon. QC 2013. Prize for Excellence in Dispute Resolution, Center for Public Resources Inst. for Dispute Resolution, NY, 1997; European Women of Achievement Award, EUW, 2005. *Publications:* (with Dr Karl Mackie) International Mediation: the art of business diplomacy, 2000, 2nd edn 2006, 3rd edn as International Mediation: breaking business deadlock, 2016. *Recreations:* spending time with family, ski-ing, photography, travel, the outdoor life. *Address:* Centre for Effective Dispute Resolution, International Dispute Resolution Centre, 70 Fleet Street, EC4Y 1EU.

**CARROLL, Most Rev. Francis Patrick;** Archbishop of Canberra and Goulburn, (RC), 1983–2006; *b* 9 Sept. 1930; *s* of P. Carroll. *Educ:* Devlin Subsidised Sch., St Brendan's Sch., Ganmain; De La Salle Coll., Marrickville; St Columba's Coll., Springwood; St Patrick's Coll., Manly; Pontifical Urban Univ. De Propaganda Fide. Ordained priest, 1954; Asst Priest, Griffith, NSW, 1955–59; Asst Inspector of Catholic Schs, dio. of Wagga, 1957–61; Asst Priest, Albury, 1959–61; Bishop's Sec., Diocesan Chancellor, Diocesan Dir of Catholic Educn, 1965–67; consecrated Co-Adjutor Bishop, 1967; Bishop of Wagga Wagga, 1968–83. Chm., Nat. Catholic Educn Commn, 1974–78; Mem., Internat. Catechetical Council, Rome, 1974–79; Pres., Australian Catholic Bishops' Conf., 2000–06. Hon. DLitt Charles Sturt Univ., NSW, 1994; DUniv Australian Catholic Univ., 2006. *Publications:* The Development of Episcopal Conferences, 1965. *Address:* PO Box 2396, Wagga Wagga, NSW 2650, Australia.

**CARROLL, Prof. John Edward,** FREng; Professor of Engineering, University of Cambridge, 1983–2001; Fellow of Queens' College, Cambridge, since 1967; *b* 15 Feb. 1934; *s* of Sydney Wentworth Carroll and May Doris Carroll; *m* 1958, Vera Mary Jordan; three *s*. *Educ:* Oundle Sch.; Queens' Coll., Cambridge (Wrangler; Foundn Schol., 1957). BA 1957; PhD 1961; ScD 1982. FIET; FREng (FEng 1985). Microwave Div., Services Electronic Res. Lab., 1961–67; Cambridge University: Lectr, 1967–76; Reader, 1976–83; Dep. Hd of Engrg Dept, 1986–90; Head of Electrical Div., 1992–99; Chm. Council, Sch. of Technol., 1996–99. Vis. Prof., Queensland Univ., 1982. Editor, IEE Jl of Solid State and Electron Devices, 1976–82. *Publications:* Hot Electron Microwave Generators, 1970; Physical Models of Semiconductor Devices, 1974; Solid State Devices (Inst. of Phys. vol. 57), 1980; Rate Equations in Semiconductor Electronics, 1986; Distributed Feedback Semiconductor Lasers, 1998; contribs on microwaves, semiconductor devices, optical systems and Maxwellian polarization entanglement to learned jls and arXiv. *Recreations:* principal carer for spouse, cooking, understanding Maxwell's equations, watching videos, piano playing, DIY. *Address:* Queens' College, Silver Street, Cambridge CB3 9ET. *T:* (01223) 332829. *E:* jec1000@cam.ac.uk.

**CARROLL, Jonathan Neil; His Honour Judge Jonathan Carroll;** a Circuit Judge, since 2015; *b* Prescot, Lancs, 3 Nov. 1967; *s* of John Carroll and Joan Carroll; *m* 1996, Melanie Welford; one *s* one *d*. *Educ:* St Edward's Coll., Liverpool; King's Coll., London (BA Hons Hist. 1990; AKC; MA War in the Modern World 2011); Coll. of Law (DipLaw 1993). Project Officer, British Aerospace, 1990–92; called to the Bar, Gray's Inn, 1994; barrister, 1994–2010; a Dep. Judge Advocate, 2006–15; a Recorder, 2008–15; Internat. Criminal Judge, EU Rule of Law Mission, Kosovo, 2010–14. Chair, Bar Tribunal and Adjudication Service, 2019–. Commnd officer, Royal Mercian and Lancastrian Yeo., TA, 1990–2000. *Recreations:* shooting, fishing, running, Rugby, gardening. *Address:* Crown Court, Old Elvet, Durham DH1 3HW. *T:* (0191) 386 6714.

**CARROLL, Mark Steven;** Executive Director, Place and Public Health, Essex County Council, since 2017; *b* 17 June 1962; *s* of late Albert Carroll and of Anne Carroll; *m* 1998, Randhirajpall Kaur Bilan; one *s* two *d*. *Educ:* Leicester Poly. (BA Hons Public Admin 1984); Univ. of Nottingham (MA Soc. Work 1988). Social worker, 1988–90; charity director, 1990–94; mgt consultant, 1994–2002; Home Office: Advr to Permanent Sec., 2002–03; Dir, Race and Cohesion, 2003–06; Department for Communities and Local Government: Dir, Race, Cohesion and Preventing Extremism, 2006–07; short-term projects, 2008–09; Dir, Housing Mgt and Support, 2009–10; Dir, Strategy and Progs, 2010–11; Dir, Big Society and Decentralisation, 2011–13; Dir of Housing, Essex CC, 2014–15; Dir, Gtr Essex Devolution Prog., 2015–17. *Club:* Nottingham Forest Football.

**CARROLL, His Honour Michael John;** a Circuit Judge, 1996–2016; a Deputy Circuit Judge, since 2016; *b* 26 Dec. 1948; *s* of late Matthew and Gladys Carroll; *m* 1974, Stella Reilly; two *s* two *d* (and one *d* decd). *Educ:* Shebbear Coll., N Devon; City of London Business Sch. (BA Hons); Inns of Court Sch. of Law. Called to the Bar, Gray's Inn, 1973. Factory worker, 1964; shop asst, 1967; fast food chef, 1968; public service vehicle conductor, 1968–72, and driver, 1973; part-time PO counter clerk, 1968–73. In practice at the Bar, 1973–96; Asst Recorder, 1990–94; Recorder, 1994–96. Chairman: Abbeyfield Addiscombe Soc., 2002–07; Croydon Charitable Foundn, 2007–. *Recreations:* reading, antiques, football. *Address:* 2 Dr Johnson Building, Temple, EC4Y 7AY.

**CARROLL, Nancy, (Mrs Jonathan Stone-Fewings);** actress; *b* London, 29 Sept. 1973; *d* of Kenneth Carroll and Susie Carroll (*née* Cosgrove, now Perring), and step *d* of Ian Perring; *m* 2003, Jonathan Stone-Fewings; one *s* one *d*. *Educ:* Alleyn's Sch., Dulwich; Instituti di Lorenzo di Medici, Florence; Univ. of Leeds (BA Hons Fine Art); London Acad. of Music and Dramatic Art. *Theatre:* Hamlet, Bristol Old Vic; Royal Shakespeare Company: Winter's Tale, 1998; The Lion, the Witch and the Wardrobe, 1998; Henry IV, Pts 1 and 2, 2000; As You Like It, 2000; Twelfth Night, 2009; National Theatre: The Talking Cure, 2002; The False Servant, 2004; The Voysey Inheritance, 2006; The Man of Mode, 2007; The Enchantment, 2007; After the Dance, 2010 (Natasha Richardson Award, Evening Standard, 2010; Best Actress, Olivier Awards, 2011); Almeida Theatre: Waste, 2008; House of Games, 2010; Midsummer Night's Dream, Sheffield Crucible, 2003; Still Life/ Astonished Heart, Liverpool Playhouse, 2004; Mammals, Bush Th., 2005; You Never Can Tell, Garrick Th. and tour, 2005; See How They Run, Duchess, 2006; Arcadia, Duke of York Th., 2009; The Recruiting Officer, Donmar, 2012; The Magistrate, Olivier Th., 2012; The Duck House, Vaudeville, 2013; Closer, Donmar, 2015; The Moderate Soprano, Hampstead Th., 2015, Duke of York Th., 2019; Woyzeck, The Old Vic, 2017; Young Marx, Bridge Th., 2017; The Deep Blue Sea, Minerva Th., Chichester, 2019; *films:* Iris, 2002; *television:* The Gathering Storm, 2002; Cambridge Spies, 2003; In Search of Shakespeare, 2003; Midsomer Murders; The Bill; Dalziel and Pascoe; Words of the Titanic, 2012; Father Brown, 2013–; The Suspicions of Mr Whicher, 2014; Call the Midwife; Will; The Crown; Queens of Mystery; Agatha Raisin; *radio* incl. Villette, Fatal Loins, Words and Music, Fine Days in May, The Family Project, By Grand Central Station I Sat Down and Wept, Look Back in Anger, Publish and Be Damn'd. *Publications:* (contrib.) Players of Shakespeare. *Recreations:* painter, juggling. *Address:* c/o United Agents, 12–26 Lexington Street, W1F 0LE. *T:* (020) 3214 0800.

**CARROLL, Rt Rev. Mgr Philip;** Parish Priest, St Paul's, Alnwick, 2011–15; *b* 30 Nov. 1946; *s* of Joseph Carroll and Jean Carroll (*née* Graham). *Educ:* Venerable English College, Rome (PhL, STL). Ordained 1971; Assistant Priest, Our Blessed Lady Immaculate, Washington, 1972–78; Hexham and Newcastle Diocesan Religious Educn Service, 1979–88; Asst Gen. Sec., 1988–91, Gen. Sec., 1992–96, Catholic Bishops' Conf.; Parish Priest, St Bede's Ch, Washington, 1996–2006; VG, then Episcopal Vicar, RC Dio. Hexham and Newcastle, 2001–06; Spiritual Dir, Venerable English Coll., Rome, 2006–11. *Recreations:* watching sport, Italian, reading. *Address:* St Andrew's R C Church, Worswick Street, Newcastle upon Tyne NE1 6UW.

**CARROLL, Terence Patrick, (Terry);** author, sports journalist, consultant and non-executive director, since 2009; *b* 24 Nov. 1948; *s* of George Daniel Carroll and Betty Doreen Carroll (*née* Holmes); *m* 1st, 1971, Louise Mary (*née* Smith) (marr. diss. 1984); one *s*; 2nd, 1984, Penelope Julia, (Penny) (*née* Berry) (marr. diss. 1994); 3rd, 1994, Heather Carmen (*née* Summers). *Educ:* Gillingham Grammar Sch.; Univ. of Bradford (BSc Business Studies). FCA 1980; FCT 1990 (MCT 1985); FCIB (FCBSI 1986). Auditor and Computer Auditor, Armitage & Norton, 1970–76; Management Accountant, Bradford & Bingley Building Soc., 1976–80; Exec. and Mem. Stock Exchange, Sheppards & Chase, 1980–82; Treasurer, Halifax Building Soc., 1982–85; National & Provincial Building Society: Gen. Manager Finance, 1985–86; Acting Chief Exec., 1986–87; Finance Dir, 1987–90; Treasury Dir, 1990–91; Finance Dir, United Leeds Teaching Hosps NHS Trust, 1991–94; Managing Director: Hollins Consulting, later How To Be Your Best Ltd, 1994–2006; Portland Internat. HR Consultants Ltd, 1996–97; Gp Finance Dir, Eatonfield Gp plc, 2006–07; Hd of Corporate Finance, Broadhead Peel Rhodes, 2008–09. Chief Exec., Hadrian's Wall Heritage Ltd, 2006. Chairman: Bradford Breakthrough Ltd, 1989–91; Central Yorks Inst. of Mgt, 1996–98. Chair, Bradford Univ. Alumni Assoc., 2017–. Chm., Ilkley Probus, 2018–19. Coach and Consultant, Performance Alchemist, 2009–. *Publications:* The Role of the Finance Director, 1997, 3rd edn 2002; Moving Up, 1998; Understanding Swaps in a Day, 1999, new edn 2012; NLP for Traders, 2000, new edn 2012; The Risk Factor, 2001, new edn 2013; Be Your Best with NLP, 2001, new edn 2012; (contrib.) QFinance, 2009, new edn 2012. *Recreations:* golf, bridge, share trading. *Address:* 18 Skipton Road, Ilkley LS29 9EJ. *Clubs:* Ilkley Golf, Ilkley Rugby.

**CARROLL-MACKIE, Eileen Philomena;** *see* Carroll, E. P.

**CARRUTHERS, Sir Ian James,** Kt 2003; OBE 1997; Chairman, Portsmouth Hospitals NHS Trust, 2014–17; *m*; one *s* one *d*. Dist Gen. Manager, W Dorset HA, 1987; Chief Executive: S and W RHA, until 1996; Dorset HA, then Dorset and Som Strategic HA, 1996–2006; Hants and IoW Strategic HA, 2005–06; on secondment as Transitional Dir, NHS Inst. for Innovation and Improvement, DoH, 2004–05; Actg Dir of Commissioning, then Actg Chief Exec. of NHS, DoH, 2006; Chief Exec., SW Strategic Health Authy (NHS SW), later NHS S of England, 2006–13. Chm., Healthcare UK, 2013–15. Mem., NHS Modernisation Bd, then Nat. Leadership Network. Chancellor, UWE, 2011–.

**CARRUTHERS-WATT, Miranda Lucy Mary, (Mrs P. Vercoe);** Monitoring Officer, Salford City Council, since 2015; *b* 1 Sept. 1961; *d* of late Calverley Vernon Carruthers-Watt and Pauline Mary Carruthers-Watt; *m* 1988, Philip Vercoe; two *s* (one *d* decd). *Educ:* Burnley High Sch. for Girls; Lancaster Univ. (LLB Hons Law 1983); Coll. of Law, Chester; Univ. of Hull (MBA 1998); Law Soc. Dip. in Local Govt Law 1991. Admitted Solicitor, 1987; private practice and local govt, 1986–97; Asst Dir, Rights, Advice and Entitlements, Blackburn with Darwen BC, 1997–2005; Dir, NW Centre of Excellence, 2005–07; Chief Exec., Office of Police and Crime Comr for Lancs (formerly Lancs Police Authy), 2007–14. FCMI 2009; CMgr 2012. *Recreations:* family, wine, walking, Cubs.

**CARSBERG, Sir Bryan (Victor),** Kt 1989; Director General of Telecommunications, 1984–92; *b* 3 Jan. 1939; *s* of Alfred Victor Carsberg and Maryllia (*née* Collins); *m* 1960, Margaret Linda Graham; two *d*. *Educ:* Berkhamsted Sch.; London Sch. of Econs and Pol

Science (MScEcon; Hon. Fellow, 1990). Chartered Accountant, 1960. Sole practice, chartered accountant, 1962–64; Lectr in Accounting, LSE, 1964–68; Vis. Lectr, Grad. Sch. of Business, Univ. of Chicago, 1968–69; Prof. of Accounting, Univ. of Manchester, 1969–81 (Dean, Faculty of Econ. and Social Studies, 1977–78); Arthur Andersen Prof. of Accounting, LSE, 1981–87; Dir of Res., ICA, 1981–87; Dir Gen. of Fair Trading, 1992–95; Sec.-Gen., Internat. Accounting Standards Cttee, 1995–2001. Visiting Professor: of Business Admin, Univ. of Calif, Berkeley, 1974; of Accounting, LSE, 1988–89. Asst Dir of Res. and Technical Activities, Financial Accounting Standards Bd, USA, 1978–81; Mem., Accounting Standards Bd, 1990–94 (Vice-Chm., 1990–92); Chm., Pensions Compensation Bd, 2001–05. Mem. Council, ICA, 1975–79; Mem. Bd, Radiocommunications Agency, 1990–92. Director: Economists Adv. Gp, 1976–84; Economist Bookshop, 1981–91; Philip Allan (Publishers), 1981–92, 1995–2006; Cable & Wireless Communications, 1997–2000; RM plc, 2002–12; Novae Gp plc (formerly SVB Hldgs plc), 2003–15; Inmarsat plc, 2005–; Actual Experience plc, 2014–; Chm., MLL Telecom Ltd, 1999–2002; Advr on telecoms, KPMG, 2001–06; Mem., Equality of Access Bd, BT Gp plc, 2005–13. Member, Council: Univ. of Surrey, 1990–92; Loughborough Univ., 1999–2011 (Chm., 2001–11). Mem., Royal Swedish Acad. of Engrg Scis, 1994. Hon. FIA 2006; Hon. RICS 2010 (Mem., Governing Council, 2010–13). Hon. MA Econ Manchester, 1973; Hon. ScD UEA, 1992; Hon. DLitt Loughborough, 1994; DUniv Essex, 1995; Hon. LLD Bath, 1996; Hon. DBA Nottingham Trent, 2008. Chartered Accountants Founding Societies Centenary Award, 1988; Sempier Award, IFAC, 2002. *Publications:* An Introduction to Mathematical Programming for Accountants, 1969; (with H. C. Edey) Modern Financial Management, 1969; Analysis for Investment Decisions, 1974; (with E. V. Morgan and M. Parkin) Indexation and Inflation, 1975; Economics of Business Decisions, 1975; (with A. Hope) Investment Decisions under Inflation, 1976; (with A. Hope) Current Issues in Accountancy, 1977, 2nd edn 1984; (with J. Arnold and R. Scapens) Topics in Management Accounting, 1980; (with S. Lumby) The Evaluation of Financial Performance in the Water Industry, 1983; (with M. Page) Current Cost Accounting, 1984; (with M. Page *et al*) Small Company Financial Reporting, 1985. *Recreations:* gardening, theatre, music, opera. *E:* bryan.carsberg@ntlworld.com.

**CARSON, Ciaran Gerard;** Director, Seamus Heaney Centre for Poetry, Queen's University Belfast, 2003–16; *b* 9 Oct. 1948; *s* of William and Mary Carson; *m* 1982, Deirdre Shannon; two *s* one *d*. *Educ:* QUB (BA Hons). Traditional Arts Officer, 1976–94, Literature Officer, 1994–98, Arts Council of NI; freelance writer, 1998–2003. FRSL 2014. *Publications: poetry:* The New Estate, 1976; The Irish for No, 1987; Belfast Confetti, 1989; First Language, 1993; Opera Et Cetera, 1996; The Twelfth of Never, 1998; The Alexandrine Plan, 1998; Breaking News, 2003; *prose:* The Pocket Guide to Irish Traditional Music, 1986; Last Night's Fun, 1996; The Star Factory, 1997; Fishing for Amber, 1999; Shamrock Tea, 2001; *translation:* The Inferno of Dante Alighieri: a new translation, 2002. *Recreation:* playing Irish traditional music. *E:* ciaran.carson@ntlworld.com.

**CARSON, Hugh Christopher Kingsford;** Headmaster, Malvern College, 1997–2006; *b* 29 Dec. 1945; *s* of late Lt-Col James Kingsford Carson and Elsie Adeline Carson (*née* Cockersell); *m* 1972, Penelope Susan Elizabeth Hollingbury, PhD. *Educ:* Tonbridge Sch.; RMA, Sandhurst; Royal Holloway Coll., London Univ. (BA Mod. Hist., Hist. of Econs and Politics, 1979); Reading Univ. (PGCE). Commnd RTR, 1967–76. Asst Master, then Housemaster, Epsom Coll., 1980–90; Headmaster, Denstone Coll., 1990–96. Chm., Ecton Mine Educnl Trust, 2011–. Master, Skinners' Co., 2010–11. Hon. Col 39 Signal Regt (Vol.), 2011–15. *Recreations:* photography, historical research, hill-walking, music. *Address:* Broadview, Old Road, Elham, Canterbury, Kent CT4 6UH.

**CARSON, Joan;** *see* Carson, M. J.

**CARSON, John,** CBE 1981; draper; Member (OUP) for Belfast North, Northern Ireland Assembly, 1982–86; *b* 1934. Member, Belfast District Council, (formerly Belfast Corporation), 1971–97; Official Unionist Councillor for Duncairn; Lord Mayor of Belfast, 1980–81, 1985–86. MP (UU) Belfast North, Feb. 1974–1979. Dir, Laganside Corp., 1989; non-exec. Dir, Royal Gp of Hosps & Dental Hosp. HSS Trust, 1992–. Vice-Chm., NI Youth Council, 1985. Mem., Adv. Bd, Salvation Army. High Sheriff, Belfast, 1978. *Address:* 75 Donaghadee Road, Millisle, Co. Down, N Ireland BT22 2BZ.

**CARSON, (Margaret) Joan;** Member (UU) Fermanagh and South Tyrone, Northern Ireland Assembly, 1998–2003; *b* 29 Jan. 1935; *d* of Charles Patterson and Gladys Patterson (*née* Irvine); *m* 1957, James Carson; two *s* one *d*. *Educ:* Stranmillis Coll., Belfast. Teacher: Enniskillen Model Primary Sch., 1956–62; Granville Primary Sch., 1972–79; Dungannon Primary Sch., 1979–82; Principal, Tamnamore Primary Sch., 1982–88. Mem. (UU), Dungannon DC, 1997–2001. Constituency Sec., Fermanagh and S Tyrone, 1990–, Deleg. to Exec. Cttee, UUP (former Party Officer). *Recreations:* ornithology, painting, reading. *Address:* Drumgold House, 115 Moy Road, Dungannon, Co. Tyrone BT71 7DX. *T:* (028) 8778 4285.

**CARSON, Neil Andrew Patrick,** OBE 2016; Chief Executive Officer, Johnson Matthey plc, 2004–14; Chairman, Oxford Instruments plc, since 2018; *b* 15 April 1957; *s* of Patrick Carson and Sheila Margaret Rose; *m* 1988, Helen Barbara Huppler; two *s* one *d*. *Educ:* Emanuel Sch., Wandsworth; Coventry Univ. (BSc Combined Engrg). Joined Johnson Matthey plc, 1980: various sales and mktg roles, 1980–88; Mktg Dir, USA, 1988–90, Gen. Manager, London, 1990–93, Precious Metals Mktg; Sales and Mktg Dir, 1993–96, Man. Dir, 1996–97, Catalytic Systems Div., Europe; Dir, Catalysts Systems Div., 1997–99; Executive Director: Catalysts Div., 1999–2003; Catalysts and Precious Metals Div., 2003–04. Senior Independent Director: Pay Point plc, 2014–17 (Chm., Remuneration Cttee); AMEC Foster Wheeler (formerly AMEC) plc, 2015–17 (non-exec. Dir, 2012–15); Dep. Chm., TI Fluid Systems, 2017– (Chm., Remuneration Cttee); Chm., TT Electronics 2015–. Lt Chm., Chemistry Growth Partnership, 2013–16. Hon. Pres., SCI, 2015–. Hon. DBA Anglia Ruskin, 2010. *Recreations:* watching Rugby, ski-ing, family.

**CARSON, William Hunter Fisher,** OBE 1983; jockey, retired 1997; racing pundit, BBC, 1997–2012; *b* 16 Nov. 1942; *s* of Thomas Whelan Carson and Mary Hay; *m* 1963, Carole Jane Sutton (marr. diss. 1979); three *s*; *m* 1982, Elaine Williams. *Educ:* Riverside, Stirling, Scotland. Apprenticed to Captain G. Armstrong, 1957; 1st winner, Pinkers Pond, Catterick, 1962; trans. to Fred Armstrong, 1963–66; First Jockey to Lord Derby, 1967; first classic win, High Top, 1972; Champion Jockey, 1972, 1973, 1978, 1980 and 1983; became First Jockey to W. R. Hern, 1977; also appointed Royal Jockey, riding Dunfermline to the Jubilee Oaks and St Leger wins in the colours of HM the Queen; won the 200th Derby on Troy, trained by W. R. Hern, 1979; the same combination won the 1980 Derby, with Henbit, and the 1980 Oaks, with Bireme; also won King George VI and Queen Elizabeth Stakes, on Troy, 1979, on Ela-Mana-Mou, 1980, on Petoski, 1985, on Nashwan, 1989; 1983 Oaks and St Leger, with Sun Princess; Ascot Gold Cup, on Little Wolf, 1983; St Leger, on Minster Son, 1988 (only jockey ever to breed and ride a Classic winner); Derby, on Nashwan, 1989; 1,000 Guineas, Oaks and Irish Derby, on Salsabil, 1990; 1,000 Guineas and Oaks, on Shadayid, 1991; Derby, on Erhaab, 1994. During the 1989 season rode 100th Group One winner in England; by 1997 had ridden 3,828 winners including 18 Classics. DUniv Stirling, 1998; Hon. DSc Chester, 2010. *Address:* Minster House, Barnsley, Cirencester, Glos GL7 5DZ.

**CARSS-FRISK, Monica Gunnel Constance;** QC 2001. *Educ:* University Coll. London (LLB); University Coll., Oxford (BCL). Called to the Bar, Gray's Inn, 1985, Bencher, 2004; in practice at the Bar, 1986–; Jt Hd, Blackstone Chambers, 2012–. Part-time tutor in law, UCL, 1984–87. Mem., HM Treasury Solicitor's Supplementary Common Law Panel, 1997–99; Jun. Counsel to the Crown (A Panel), 1999–2001. *Publications:* contributor: Human Rights Law and Practice, 1999; European Employment Law in the UK, 2001; Halsbury's Laws of England. *Recreation:* literature. *Address:* Blackstone Chambers, Blackstone House, Temple, EC4Y 9BW.

**CARSTEN, Prof. Janet,** PhD; FBA 2011; FRSE; Professor of Social and Cultural Anthropology, University of Edinburgh; *m* 1994, Prof. Jonathan Robert Spencer, *qv*; one *d*. *Educ:* London Sch. of Econs and Pol Sci. (PhD). Res. Fellow, Univ. of Cambridge; Lectr, Univ. of Manchester. Leverhulme Maj. Res. Fellow, 2007–10; ERC Advanced Grant, 2017–. FRSE 2006. *Publications:* (ed with S. Hugh-Jones) About the House: Lévi-Strauss and beyond, 1995; The Heat of the Hearth: the process of kinship in a Malay fishing community, 1997; (ed) Cultures of Relatedness: new approaches to the study of kinship, 2000; After Kinship, 2004; (ed) Ghosts of Memory: essays on remembrance and relatedness, 2007; (ed) Blood Will Out: essays on liquid transfers and flows, 2013; contribs to jls incl. Jl RAI, Annual Rev. Anthropol., Amer. Ethnologist, Anthropol Qly. *Address:* School of Social and Political Science, University of Edinburgh, 5.24 Chrystal Macmillan Building, 15a George Square, Edinburgh EH8 9LD.

**CARSTEN, Prof. Oliver Michael John,** PhD; Professor of Transport Safety, Institute for Transport Studies, University of Leeds, since 2003; *b* 9 Aug. 1948; *s* of Francis and Ruth Carsten; *m* 1987, Svetlana; one *s* one *d*. *Educ:* Merton Coll., Oxford (BA Modern Hist. 1969); Univ. of Michigan (MA Hist. 1973; PhD Hist. 1981). University of Michigan Transportation Research Institute: Res. Asst, 1977–79; Res. Associate, 1979–85; Asst Res. Scientist, 1985–87; Institute for Transport Studies, University of Leeds: Res. Fellow, 1987–89; Sen. Res. Fellow, 1993–2003. Visiting Professor: Helsinki Univ. of Technol., 1999; Univ. of Valenciennes, 2012–13. Chm., Road Behaviour Wkg Party, Parly Adv. Council for Transport Safety, 1993–. Ed.-in-Chief, Cognition, Technol. & Work, 2014–. *Publications:* contribs to learned jls and books. *Recreations:* walking, cycling, travel. *Fax:* (office) (0113) 343 5334. *E:* o.m.j.carsten@its.leeds.ac.uk.

**CARSTENSEN, Laura Martine;** non-executive Chairman, Park Group plc, since 2016 (non-executive Director, since 2013; Chairman, Audit Committee, since 2013); *b* Stockport, 11 Nov. 1960; *d* of Gordon McRoberts and Pauline McRoberts; *m* 1995, Peter Andreas Günter Frithjof Carstensen; five *s* one *d*. *Educ:* Withington Girls Sch., Manchester; St Hilda's Coll., Oxford (BA Hons 1st Cl. Eng. Lang. and Lit. 1982; MA). Admitted Solicitor, 1985. Partner, Slaughter and May, 1994–2004. Mem., 2005–14, Dep. Chm., 2010–11, Competition Commn; Comr, Equality and Human Rights Commn, 2013–17. Mem., Business Oversight Bd, Law Soc., 2012–14. Mem., Co-operation and Competition Panel, NHS Funded Services, 2009–14; non-executive Director: Countess of Chester Hosp. NHS Foundn Trust, 2011–13; NHS Improvement, 2016–18. Non-executive Director: Co-operative Bank plc, 2014–18 (Chm., Values and Ethics, 2014–18); AJ Bell, 2018–. Chm. Council, Women's Liby, 2010–12; Gov., London Metropolitan Univ., 2010–12. Trustee, Nat. Mus Liverpool, 2011–. *Recreations:* gardening, theatre, detective fiction. *E:* laura@carstensen.co.uk.

**CARSWELL,** family name of **Baron Carswell**.

**CARSWELL,** Baron *cr* 2004 (Life Peer), of Killeen in the county of Down; **Robert Douglas Carswell,** Kt 1988; PC 1993; a Lord of Appeal in Ordinary, 2004–09; *b* 28 June 1934; *er s* of late Alan E. Carswell and Nance E. Carswell; *m* 1961, Romayne Winifred Ferris (*see* R. W. Carswell); two *d*. *Educ:* Royal Belfast Academical Instn; Pembroke Coll., Oxford (Schol.; 1st Cl. Honour Mods, 1st Cl. Jurisprudence, MA; Hon. Fellow, 1984); Univ. of Chicago Law Sch. (JD). Called to Bar of N Ireland, 1957 (Bencher, 1979), and to English Bar, Gray's Inn, 1972 (Hon. Bencher, 1993); Counsel to Attorney-General for N Ireland, 1970–71; QC (NI), 1971; Sen. Crown Counsel in NI, 1979–84; Judge of High Court of Justice, NI, 1984–93; Lord Justice of Appeal, Supreme Court of Judicature, NI, 1993–97; Lord Chief Justice of NI, 1997–2004. Chancellor, Dios of Armagh and of Down and Dromore, 1990–97. Chairman: Council of Law Reporting for NI, 1987–97; Law Reform Adv. Cttee for NI, 1989–97. Pres., NI Scout Council, 1993–2014. Pres., Royal Belfast Academical Instn, 2004– (Gov., 1967–2004); Chm. Bd of Govs, 1986–97); Pro-Chancellor and Chm. Council, Univ. of Ulster, 1984–94. Hon. Bencher, King's Inns, Dublin, 1997. Hon. DLitt Ulster, 1994. *Publications:* Trustee Acts (Northern Ireland), 1964; articles in legal periodicals. *Recreation:* golf. *Address:* House of Lords, SW1A 0PW. *Club:* Ulster Reform (Belfast).

**CARSWELL, Lady, (Romayne Winifred Carswell),** CVO 2010; OBE 1988; Lord-Lieutenant, County Borough of Belfast, 2000–09; *d* of late James Ferris, JP and Eileen Ferris, JP, of Greyabbey, Co. Down; *m* 1961, Robert Douglas Carswell (*see* Baron Carswell); two *d*. *Educ:* Victoria Coll., Belfast; Queen's Univ., Belfast (BA, LLB). Asst Principal, NICS, 1959–61; Mem., 1977–83, Dep. Chm., 1983–94, Police Complaints Bd for NI, subseq. Ind. Commn for Police Complaints; Member: Standing Adv. Commn on Human Rights, 1984–86; Industrial Tribunals, 1987–97. Mem., Bd of Govs, Victoria Coll., Belfast, 1979–99 (Dep. Chm., 1995–99). President: Friends of Ulster Mus., 1996–2011; Ulster Soc. for the Protection of the Countryside, 2009–15; Trustee: Ulster Histl Foundn, 1991–2004 (Dep. Chm., 1997–2000); Winston Churchill Meml Trust, 2002–09. Pres., RFCA for NI, 2005–09; Hon. Captain, RNR, 2005–13; Vice-Pres., Belfast Br., RN Assoc., 2010–. DL Belfast, 1997; JP 2000. DStJ 2010 (CStJ 2000). *Recreations:* heritage, conservation. *Address:* c/o Lord Carswell, House of Lords, SW1A 0PW.

**CARSWELL, (John) Douglas (Wilson);** *b* 3 May 1971; *s* of John Wilson Carswell, OBE, FRCS and Margaret Carswell (*née* Clark); *m* 2008, Clementine Bailey; one *d*. *Educ:* Charterhouse; Univ. of E Anglia (BA Hons 1993); King's Coll. London (MA). Corporate Develt Manager, Orbit Television, Rome, 1997–99; Chief Project Officer, Invesco Continental Europe, 1999–2003. Mem., Cons. Party Policy Unit, 2004–05. MP (C) Harwich, 2005–10, Clacton, 2010–Aug. 2014; MP for Clacton, Oct. 2014–2017 (UK Ind, Oct. 2014–2017, Ind, 2017). Member: Commons Select Cttee on Educn, 2006–10; Public Accounts Cttee, 2009–10. Founder, www.direct-democracy.co.uk, 2006–09; Dir, disruptive, 2017–. *Publications:* (jtly) Direct Democracy: an agenda for a new model party, 2005; (with Daniel Hannan) The Plan: 12 months to renew Britain, 2008; The End of Politics and the birth of iDemocracy, 2012; Rebel: how to overthrow the emerging oligarchy, 2017; pamphlets. *Recreations:* blogs each day at www.TalkCarswell.com, keen swimmer, occasional rider, passionate gardener.

**CARTER;** *see* Bonham-Carter and Bonham Carter.

**CARTER,** family name of **Barons Carter of Barnes** and **Carter of Coles**.

**CARTER OF BARNES,** Baron *cr* 2008 (Life Peer), of Barnes in the London Borough of Richmond upon Thames; **Stephen Andrew Carter,** CBE 2007; Group Chief Executive, Informa, since 2014 (non executive Director, 2010–13); *b* 12 Feb. 1964; *s* of Robert and Margaret Carter; *m* 1992, Anna Gorman; one *s* one *d*. *Educ:* Aberdeen Univ. (BA Hons

Law); Harvard Business Sch. (AMP 1997). Man. Dir and Chief Exec., J. W. Thompson, 1992–2000; Chief Operating Officer and Man. Dir, ntl, UK and Ireland, 2000–02; CEO, OFCOM, 2003–06; Gp Chief Exec., Brunswick Gp LLP, 2007–08; Chief of Strategy and Principal Advr to the Prime Minister, 2008; Parly Under Sec. of State, BIS (formerly BERR) and DCMS, 2008–09; Pres. and Man. Dir, EMEA, and Chief Marketing and Communications Officer, Alcatel-Lucent, 2010–13. Non-executive Director: Travis Perkins plc, 2006–08; Royal Mail Hldgs plc, 2007–08; United Utilities plc, 2014–. Non-exec. Dir, BEIS, 2017–. Trustee, RSC, 2007–. Gov., Ashridge Business Mgt Sch., 2005–14 (Chm., 2007–14). Vice Pres., UNICEF, 2005–14; Hon. Fellow, UNICEF UK, 2004. Hon. LLD Aberdeen, 2010. *Address*: House of Lords, SW1A 0PW.

**CARTER OF COLES**, Baron *cr* 2004 (Life Peer), of Westmill in the County of Hertfordshire; **Patrick Robert Carter**; Chairman, NHS Procurement and Efficiency Board, since 2014; *b* 9 Feb. 1946; *s* of Robert Carter and Ann Carter (*née* Richards); *m* 1969, Julia Bourne; two *d*. *Educ*: Brentwood Sch.; Hatfield Coll., Univ. of Durham. Hambros Bank, 1967–70; Whitecross Equipment Ltd, 1970–75; Dir, MAI plc, 1975–85; founder and Dir, Westminster Health Care plc, 1985–99. Review Chairman: Commonwealth Games, 2001; Nat. Stadium, 2002; Payroll Services, 2003; Criminal Records, 2003; Offender Services, 2004; Legal Aid, 2005–06; Pathology, 2005–08; Efficient Use of Property Across Public Sector, 2008–09. Chm., Sport England, 2002–06. *Recreations*: reading, opera, walking, ski-ing, gardening. *Address*: House of Lords, SW1A 0PW.

**CARTER, Andrew**, CMG 1995; HM Diplomatic Service, retired; Warden, St George's House, Windsor Castle, 2003–08; *b* 4 Dec. 1943; *s* of Eric and Margaret Carter; *m* 1st, 1973, Anne Caroline Morgan (marr. diss. 1986); one *d*; 2nd, 1988, Catherine Mary Tyler (marr. diss. 2003); one *s* one *d*; 3rd, 2009, Lynn Marie Marcell Collins. *Educ*: Latymer Upper Sch., Hammersmith; Royal Coll. of Music; Jesus Coll., Cambridge (Scholar 1962; MA). FRCO; LRAM; ARCM. Asst Master, Marlborough Coll., 1965–70. Joined HM Diplomatic Service, 1971; Warsaw, 1972; Geneva, 1975; Bonn, 1975; FCO, 1978; Brussels, 1986; Dep. Gov., Gibraltar, 1990–95; Minister, Moscow, 1995–97; UK Perm. Rep. to Council of Europe, Strasbourg, 1997–2003. *Recreation*: music.

**CARTER, Sir Andrew Nicholas**, Kt 2014; OBE 2003; Chief Executive Officer, South Farnham Educational Trust, since 2016 (Head Teacher, South Farnham School, 1988–2016); *b* Oswestry, Shropshire, 19 July 1949; *s* of Norman Carter and Alice Carter; *m* 1978, Mary Daniel; one *s* two *d*. *Educ*: Bishop Otter Coll.; Univ. of Sussex (BEd 1977). Teacher, Kempshott Prim. Sch., Basingstoke, 1971–78; Dep. Head, Mayfield Jun. Sch., Farnborough, 1978–83; Head Teacher, Greenfields Jun. Sch., Hartley Wintney, 1983–88. Nat. Sch. Leader, 2009. Ambassador, Investors in People UK, 2004–; Trustee, Helen Arkell Dyslexia Centre, 2010–. *Recreations*: theatre, gardening, antiques, football, reading, shed making. *Address*: South Farnham School, Menin Way, Farnham GU9 8DY. *T*: (01252) 716155.

**CARTER, Dr Brandon**, FRS 1981; Directeur de Recherche (Centre National de la Recherche Scientifique), Observatoire de Paris-Meudon, 1986–2009, now Emeritus; *b* Sydney, Australia, 26 May 1942; *s* of Harold Burnell Carter and Mary (*née* Brandon Jones); *m* 1969, Lucette Defrise; three *d*. *Educ*: George Watson's Coll., Edinburgh; Univ. of St Andrews; Pembroke Coll., Cambridge (MA, PhD 1968, DSc 1976). Res. Student, Dept of Applied Maths and Theoretical Physics, Cambridge, 1964–67; Res. Fellow, Pembroke Coll., Cambridge, 1967–68; Staff Mem., Inst. of Astronomy, Cambridge, 1968–73; Univ. Asst Lectr, 1973–74, Univ. Lectr, 1974–75, Dept of Applied Maths and Theoretical Physics, Cambridge; Maître de Recherche, co-responsable Groupe d'Astrophysique Relativiste (CNRS), Paris-Meudon, 1975–86. *Recreation*: wilderness. *Address*: 19 rue de la Borne au Diable, 92310 Sèvres, France. *T*: (1) 45344677.

**CARTER, Carolyn Jayne**; *see* Davidson, C. J.

**CARTER, Sir Charles**; *see* Carter, Sir E. C.

**CARTER, David**; *see* Carter, Ronald D.

**CARTER, Dr David**, CVO 1995; HM Diplomatic Service, retired; High Commissioner, Bangladesh, 2000–04; *b* 4 May 1945; *s* of John Carter and Kathleen Carter (*née* Oke); *m* 1968, Susan Victoria Wright; one *s* one *d*. *Educ*: Zambia; Univ. of Wales (BA Jt Hons); Univ. of Durham (PhD 1978). Joined HM Diplomatic Service, 1970; FCO, 1970–71; Accra, 1971–75; FCO, 1975–80; Hd of Chancery, Manila, 1980–83; 1st Sec., S Africa Desk, later Dep. Hd, SE Asia Dept, FCO, 1983–86; Dep. High Comr and Counsellor, Lusaka, 1986–90; Counsellor and Overseas Inspector, FCO, 1990–92; Counsellor and Dep. Hd of Mission, Cape Town/Pretoria, 1992–96; Minister and Dep. Head of Mission, New Delhi, 1996–99. Dep. Dir, Centre for Security and Diplomacy, Birmingham Univ., 2005–06. Bursar, Lucy Cavendish Coll., Cambridge, 2006–10. Advr, Advocates for Internat. Develt, 2010–11. Mem., Royal Soc. for Asian Affairs, 2012–16. *Publications*: contrib. jls on Southern Africa. *Recreations*: distant travel, music, reading, walking, manual labour. *E*: dcarter@carter42.com. *Club*: Royal Over-Seas League.

**CARTER, Sir David (Anthony)**, Kt 2013; Executive Director of System Leadership, Ambition Institute, since 2019; *b* S Wales, 29 Nov. 1959. *Educ*: Llanederyn High Sch., Cardiff; Cardiff High Sch.; Royal Holloway Coll., Univ. of London (BMus 1982); Inst. of Educn, Univ. of London (MA Music Educn); Univ. of Hull (MBA (Dist.) Internat. Educnl Leadership). Teacher: Geoffrey Chaucer Sch., Canterbury, 1983–85; Bulmershe Sch., Reading, 1985–90; Music Advr, Dorset LEA, 1990–94; Teacher, Twynham Sch, Christchurch, 1994–97; Headteacher, Cirencester Deer Park, 1997–2003; Principal, John Cabot Acad. (formerly Technol. Coll.), 2004–08; Exec. Principal, Cabot Learning Fedn, 2008–14; Regl Schools Comr for SW England, 2014–16; Nat. Schools Comr, 2016–18. Hon. LLD Bristol, 2014.

**CARTER, Sir David (Craig)**, Kt 1996; MD; FRCSE, FMedSci, FRSE; Chief Medical Officer, Scottish Executive (formerly Scottish Office) Department of Health, 1996–2000; *b* 1 Sept. 1940; *s* of Horace Ramsay Carter and Mary Florence Carter (*née* Lister); *m* 1967, Ilske Ursula Luth; two *s*. *Educ*: Cockermouth Grammar Sch.; St Andrews Univ. (MB ChB, MD). FRCSE 1967; FRCSGlas 1980; FRCPE 1993; FRCS 1995; FFPH (FFPHM 1998). FRSE 1995. British Empire Cancer Campaign Fellow, 1967; Lecturer in Surgery: Edinburgh Univ., 1969; Makerere Univ., Uganda, 1972; Wellcome Trust Sen. Lectr, Edinburgh Univ., 1974, seconded for 12 months to Center for Ulcer Res. and Educn, LA, 1976; Sen. Lectr in Surgery, Edinburgh Univ., 1974–79; St Mungo Prof. of Surgery, Glasgow Univ., 1979–88; Regius Prof. of Clinical Surgery, Edin. Univ., 1988–96. Hon. Consultant Surgeon, Royal Infirmary, Edin., 1988–96; Hon. Consultant Surgeon and Chm., Scottish Liver Transplantation Unit, 1992–96; Surgeon to the Queen in Scotland, 1993–97. External Examiner at univs incl. London, Oxford, Leeds, Dundee, Newcastle, Hong Kong, Nairobi, Penang and Kuwait. Chairman: Scottish Foundn for Surgery in Nepal, 1988–2010; Scottish Council for Postgrad. Med. Educn, 1990–96; Scientific Adv. Cttee, CRC, 2000–02; BMA Bd of Science, 2002–05; Queen's Nursing Inst., Scotland, 2002–10; Scottish Stem Cell Network, 2003–05; Bd for Academic Med., Scotland, 2005–16; Managed Service Network for Neurosurgery in Scotland, 2009–13; Mem. Council, WMA, 2002–05; Dir, Scottish Cancer Foundn, 2000–10; Member: Jt Med. Adv. Cttee, HEFC, 1993–96; Scientific Exec. Bd, Cancer Res. UK, 2002–04. President: Internat. Hepatobiliary-Pancreatic Assoc., 1988–89; Surgical Res. Soc., 1996–97; Assoc. of Surgeons of GB and Ire., 1996–97; BMA, 2001–02; Vice-Pres., RSE, 2000–03. Member: Council, RCSE, 1980–90; James IV Assoc. of Surgeons, 1981–; Internat. Surgical Gp, 1984–2005. Mem., Broadcasting Council, BBC Scotland, 1989–94. Non-exec. Dir, Lothian Health Bd, 1994–96. Company Sec., British Jl of Surgery Soc., 1991–95; Co-Editor, British Journal of Surgery, 1986–91; General Editor, Operative Surgery, 1983–96. Mem. Court, St Andrews Univ., 1997–2000; Vice-Principal, Edinburgh Univ., 2000–02; Governor: Beatson Inst. for Cancer Res., 1997–2000; The Health Foundn (formerly PPP Healthcare Med. Trust), 2001–08 (Chm., 2002–08). Trustee, CRUK, 2004–07 (Chm. Council, Res. Strategy Gp, 2004–07; Vice Chm. Council, 2005–07). Mem., Amer. Surgical Assoc., 1997; Founder FMedSci 1998. Hon. FACS 1996; Hon. FRCSI 1996; Hon. FRACS 1998; Hon. FRCGP 1999; Hon. FRCPGlas 2003; Hon. FRCP 2005; Hon. Fellow: Deutsche Ges. für Chirurgie, 1994; Coll. of Surgeons of Hong Kong, 2003; Hon. Mem., Soc. of Surgeons of Nepal, 1994; For. Associate Mem., Inst. of Medicine, USA, 1998. Hon. DSc: St Andrews, 1997; Queen Margaret Coll., 1997; Aberdeen, 2000; Hull, 2010; Inst. of Cancer Res., London, 2011; Hon. LLD Dundee, 1997; Hon. MD Edinburgh, 2005. William Leslie Prize in Surgery, Univ. of Edinburgh, 1968; Moynihan Prize in Surgery, Assoc. of Surgeons of GB and Ire., 1973; Gold Medal, RCSE, 2000; G. B. Ong Medal, Hong Kong Univ., 2005; Gold Medal, BMA, 2006; Gold Medal, RSE, 2007. Gorkha Dakshin Bahu (Nepal), 1999. *Publications*: Peptic Ulcer, 1983; Principles and Practice of Surgery, 1985; Pancreatitis, 1988; Surgery of the Pancreas, 1993, 2nd edn 1997; numerous contribs to surgical and gastroenterological jls. *Recreations*: music, gardening, philately. *Address*: 19 Buckingham Terrace, Edinburgh EH4 3AD. *T*: (0131) 332 5554. *Club*: New (Edinburgh).

**CARTER, Rt Hon. David (Cunningham)**; MP (Nat.) New Zealand, since 1999 (Selwyn, 1994–96; Banks Peninsula, 1996–99); Speaker, House of Representatives, New Zealand, 2013–17; *b* Christchurch, NZ, 3 April 1952; *s* of Maurice Rhodes Carter and Pauline Merle Carter; *m* 1991, Heather Robyn Guest; one *s* three *d*. *Educ*: Loreto Coll. Christchurch; St Bede's Coll., Christchurch; Lincoln Univ. (BAgrSc). Former farmer and business proprietor. Jun. Govt Whip, 1996–98; Associate Minister, for Food Fibre, Biosecurity and Border Control, for Revenue, and for Educn, 1998–99; Minister: for Sen. Citizens, 1998–99; for Biosecurity, 2008–11; of Agriculture and of Forestry, 2008–11; for Econ. Develt, 2011; of Local Govt, 2012–13; for Primary Industries, 2011–13. Pres., Simmental Cattle Breeders Soc. of NZ, 1989–93. *Recreations*: farming (sheep and beef), aviation, fitness. *Address*: Parliament House, Parliament Buildings, Wellington 6160, New Zealand. *T*: 48176874. *E*: David.Carter@parliament.govt.nz.

**CARTER, Sir (Edward) Charles**, KCMG 2016; President: Carter Marketing, since 1997; Carter Broadcasting, Island FM, since 2001; *b* Nassau, Bahamas, 13 April 1943; *s* of Harcourt and Mary Carter; *m* 1964, Muriell; two *c*. *Educ*: New York Univ. (Business Admin 1963); Ryerson Univ., Toronto (Cert. Broadcast Mgt 1970; Cert. TV Prodn 1979); Univ. of Manchester (Cert. Public Admin 1975). Broadcast Corp. of Bahamas, 1964–79 (Gen. Manager, 1977–79); Advertising and PR, Restaurants Bahamas Ltd, 1979–82; Chairman: Broadcasting Corp. of Bahamas, 1982–87; Bahamas Electricity Corp., 1987–89. MP for Holy Cross, Bahamas, 1982–92; Minister of Foreign Affairs, 1989–91, of Health, 1991–92; Opposition Leader of Senate, 1992–97. *Recreations*: reading, tennis, swimming. *Address*: Island FM, #76 Dowdeswell Street, Nassau, Bahamas. *T*: 3228826. *E*: ccarter@cartermktg.com. *Club*: Rotary (W Nassau).

**CARTER, (Edward) Graydon**; Founder and Editor, Air Mail, since 2019; *b* 14 July 1949; *s* of E. P. Carter and Margaret Ellen Carter; *m* 1st, 1982, Cynthia Williamson (marr. diss. 2003); three *s* one *d*; 2nd, 2005, Anna Scott, *d* of Sir Kenneth Bertram Adam Scott, KCVO, CMG; one *d*. *Educ*: Carleton Univ. (incomplete); Univ. of Ottawa (incomplete). Editor, The Canadian Review, 1973–77; Writer, Time, 1978–83; Writer, Life, 1983–86; Founder and Editor, Spy, 1986–91; Editor, New York Observer, 1991–92; Editor in Chief, Vanity Fair, 1992–2017. Hon. Editor, Harvard Lampoon, 1989. Documentary producer: 9/11, 2002; The Kid Stays in the Picture, 2002; Chicago 10, Surfwise, 2007; Public Speaking, 2010; His Way, 2011. Theatrical producer, I'll Eat You Last: a chat with Sue Mengers, 2013. *Publications*: (ed) Vanity Fair's Hollywood, 2000; (ed) Vanity Fair's Oscar Nights, 2004; What We've Lost, 2004; (ed) Vanity Fair Portraits, 2008; (ed) Vanity Fair's Tales of Hollywood, 2008; (ed) Vanity Fair's Proust Questionnaire, 2009; (ed) The Great Hangover, 2010. *Recreation*: fly fishing. *Clubs*: Brook (New York); Washington (Washington, Connecticut); Mill Reef (Antigua).

**CARTER, Elizabeth Angela**; *see* Shaw, E. A.

**CARTER, Elizabeth Mary**; Consultant Editor, Good Food Guide, since 2006; *b* Stockport, 1 July 1960; *d* of James Wilfrid Carter and Betty Carter; *m* 1989, Neil Shilling; one *s* one *d*. *Educ*: Manchester Sch. of Art (BA Hons Graphic Design). Inspector, Egon Ronay's Guides, 1986–90; Ed., AA Restaurant Guide, 1995–2000; Ed.-in-Chief, Les Routiers UK and Ireland Guide, 2001–03. *Publications*: Majorcan Food and Cookery, 1989. *Recreations*: restaurants, cooking, family, cinema, reading, working out, walking. *Address*: Waitrose Good Food Guide, Waite House, Southern Industrial Estate, Bracknell, Berks RG12 8YA. *E*: elizabeth.carter@thegoodfoodguide.co.uk.

**CARTER, Maj. Gen. Sir Evelyn John W.**; *see* Webb-Carter.

**CARTER, His Honour Frederick Brian**; QC 1980; *a* Circuit Judge, 1985–2001; *b* 11 May 1933; *s* of late Arthur and Minnie Carter; *m* 1960, Elizabeth Hughes, JP, *d* of late W. B. Hughes and Mrs B. M. Hughes; one *s* three *d* (and one *s* decd). *Educ*: Stretford Grammar Sch.; King's Coll., London (LLB). Called to Bar, Gray's Inn, 1955, practised Northern Circuit, 1957–85; Prosecuting Counsel for Inland Revenue, Northern Circuit, 1973–80; a Recorder, 1978–85. Acting Deemster, 2001–03. *Recreations*: golf, travel. *Address*: Lowcross, Combs, High Peak, Derbys SK23 9UX. *Club*: Big Four (Manchester).

**CARTER, George**; *see* Carter, W. G. K.

**CARTER, Rev. Graham**; *see* Carter, Rev. R. G.

**CARTER, Graydon**; *see* Carter, E. G.

**CARTER, Harold Mark**, CB 2015; Legal Director, Cabinet Office, since 2016; *b* Haslemere, 21 Sept. 1958; *s* of Denis Mark and Ursula Mary Carter; *m* 1989, Hilary Jane Pharaoh; one *d*. *Educ*: Reading Univ. (LLB Hons). Legal Advr's Br., Home Office, 1989–2006; FCO, 2006–09; Dep. Legal Advr, Home Office, 2009–16. Bencher, Gray's Inn, 2014. *Recreations*: chess, music, running.
*[Created a Baron (Life Peer), 2019 but title not gazetted at time of going to press.]*

**CARTER, Imelda Mary Philomena Bernadette**; *see* Staunton, I. M. P. B.

**CARTER, James Earl, Jr, (Jimmy)**; President of the United States of America, 1977–81; *b* Plains, Georgia, USA, 1 Oct. 1924; *s* of late James Earl Carter and Lillian (*née* Gordy); *m* 1946, Rosalynn Smith; three *s* one *d*. *Educ*: Plains High Sch.; Georgia Southwestern Coll.; Georgia Inst. of Technology; US Naval Acad. (BS); Union Coll., Schenectady, NY (post grad.). Served in US Navy submarines and battleships, 1946–53; Ensign (commissioned, 1947); Lieut (JG) 1950, (SG) 1952; retd from US Navy, 1953. Became farmer and warehouseman, 1953, farming peanuts at Plains, Georgia, until 1977. Member: Sumter Co. (Ga) School Bd, 1955–62 (Chm. 1960–62); Americus and Sumter Co. Hosp. Authority, 1956–70; Sumter Co. (Ga) Library Bd, 1961; President: Plains Develt Corp., 1963; Georgia Planning Assoc., 1968; Chm., W Central Georgia Area Planning and Develt Commn, 1964; Dir, Georgia Crop Improvement Assoc., 1957–63 (Pres., 1961). State Chm., March of Dimes, 1968–70; Dist Governor, Lions Club, 1968–69. State Senator (Democrat), Georgia, 1963–67; Governor of Georgia, 1971–75. Chm., Congressional Campaign Cttee, Democratic Nat. Cttee, 1974; Democratic Candidate for the Presidency of the USA, 1976. Founder, Carter Center, Emory Univ., 1982. Mem., Bd of Dirs, Habitat for Humanity, 1984–87; Chairman, Board of Trustees: Carter Center, Inc., 1986–2005; Carter-Menil Human Rights Foundn, 1986–; Global 2000 Inc., 1986–; Chairman: Council of Freely-Elected Heads of Government, 1986–; Council of Internat. Negotiation Network, 1991–. Distinguished Prof., Emory Univ., 1982–. Baptist. Hon. LLD: Morehouse Coll., and Morris Brown Coll., 1972; Notre Dame, 1977; Emory Univ., 1979; Kwansei Gakuim Univ., Japan, and Georgia Southwestern Coll., 1981; New York Law Sch., and Bates Coll., 1985; Centre Coll., and Creighton Univ., 1987; Hon. DE Georgia Inst. Tech., 1979; Hon. PhD: Weizmann Inst. of Science, 1980; Tel Aviv Univ., 1983; Haifa Univ., 1987; Hon. DHL Central; Connecticut State Univ., 1985. Awards include: Gold Medal, Internat. Inst. for Human Rights, 1979; Internat. Mediation Medal, American Arbitration Assoc., 1979; Harry S. Truman Public Service Award, 1981; Ansel Adams Conservation Award, Wilderness Soc., 1982; Distinguished Service Award, Southern Baptist Convention, 1982; Human Rights Award, Internat. League for Human Rights, 1983; Albert Schweitzer Prize for Humanitarianism, 1987; Jefferson Award, Amer. Inst. of Public Service, 1990; Nobel Peace Prize, 2002. *Publications:* Why Not the Best?, 1975; A Government as Good as its People, 1977; Keeping Faith: memoirs of a President, 1982; Negotiation: the alternative to hostility, 1984; The Blood of Abraham, 1985; (with Rosalynn Carter) Everything to Gain: making the most of the rest of your life, 1987; An Outdoor Journal, 1988; Turning Point: a candidate, a state and a nation come of age, 1992; Talking Peace: a vision for the next generation, 1993; Always a Reckoning (poetry), 1995; Living Faith, 1996; Sources of Strength, 1997; The Virtues of Ageing, 1998; An Hour Before Daylight: memoirs of a rural boyhood, 2001; Christmas in Plains, 2001; The Hornet's Nest (novel), 2003; Sharing Good Times, 2004; Our Endangered Values: America's moral crisis, 2005; Palestine: peace not apartheid, 2006; Beyond the White House: waging peace, fighting disease, building hope, 2007; A Remarkable Mother, 2008; We Can Have Peace in the Holy Land, 2009; White House Diary, 2010; Through the Year with Jimmy Carter, 2011; (ed) NIV Lessons from the Life Bible, 2012; A Call to Action: women, religion, violence and power, 2014. *Address:* (office) The Carter Center, One Copenhill, 453 Freedom Parkway, Atlanta, GA 30307, USA.

**CARTER, John,** RA 2007; sculptor; *b* Hampton Hill, Middx, 3 March 1942; *s* of E. Gordon Carter and Mercia Carter (*née* Edmonds); *m* 1986, Belinda Cadbury. *Educ:* Halliford Sch.; Twickenham Sch. of Art; Kingston Sch. of Art; British Sch. at Rome. Leverhulme Travelling Scholar, 1963. Part time lectr in various art schs, 1965–99, Chelsea Coll. of Art and Design, 1980–99. *Solo exhibitions include:* in London: Redfern Gall., 1968, 1971, 1974, 1977, 2010, 2013; Nicola Jacobs Gall., 1980, 1983, 1987, 1990; Warwick Arts Trust (retrospective), 1983; Knoedler Gall., 1991; Francis Graham Dixon Gall., 1996; Blue Gall., 2004; Between Dimensions, Tennant Gall., Royal Acad. of Arts, 2013–14; Galerie Leonhard, Graz, 2014, 2016; Galerie Wagner, Le Touquet Paris Plage, 2016; MOMA Machynlleth, Wales, 2016; in Germany: Galerie Hoffmann, Friedberg, 1990, 2008, 2014–15; Galerie Wack, Kaiserslautern, 1991, 2002, 2007, 2012, 2015; Mus. Moderner Kunst Landkreis Cuxhaven, Otterndorf, 1994; Gudrun Spielvogel, Munich, 1995, 1999, 2008, 2013; Galerie St Johann, Saarbrücken, 1998, 2009; in Switzerland: Galerie La Vitrine, Fribourg, 2017; Atelier-Editions Fanal, Basle, 2017; also in Austria, Belgium, Netherlands, Sweden, Japan, USA; *group exhibitions include:* Whitechapel Art Gall., 1966; Hayward Gall., London, 1974; British Art Show, 1979, 1984; British Council Collection, Serpentine Gall., London, 1980; Hayward Gall., London, 1981; Galerie Hoffmann, 1986; Wilhelm Hack Mus., Ludwigshafen, 1986; Musée André Malraux, Le Havre, 1988; Galerie New Space, Fulda, 1988; Musée des Beaux-Art, Mons, 1994; Pfalzgalerie Kaiserslautern, 1994; Magyar Képzőművészeti Foiskola, Budapest, 1996; Mondriaanhuis, Amersfoort, 2000; Musée Matisse, Le Cateau-Cambresis, 2003; Summer Exhibn, RA, London, 2007–; Southampton City Art Gall., 2008; Musées de Monbéliard, 2009; Musées de Sens, 2010; Musées de Chateauroux, France, 2016; Longside Gall., Yorkshire Sculpture Park, 2017; work in many public and corporate collections. Hon. Dr Art and Design Kingston, 2016. Arts Council of GB Award, 1977, 1979; Prize, Tolly Cobbold Eastern Arts 3rd Nat. Exhibn, 1981. Peter Stuyvesant Foundn Travel Bursary to the USA, 1966. *Publications:* occasional articles for German gallery publications; *relevant publication:* (monograph) John Carter, by Chris Yetton, 2010. *Recreation:* hill walking in Wales. *Address:* c/o Redfern Gallery, 20 Cork Street, W1S 3HL. *T:* (020) 7734 1732, *Fax:* (020) 7494 2908. *E:* art@redfern-gallery.com; 71a Westbourne Park Road, W2 5QH. *E:* west2studios@waitrose.com. *Clubs:* Chelsea Arts, Arts.

**CARTER, Sir John (Gordon Thomas),** Kt 1998; FIA; Chief Executive, Commercial Union plc, 1994–98; *b* 28 Dec. 1937; *s* of Gordon Percival Carter and Mary Ann Carter (*née* Edgington); *m* 1961, Margaret Elizabeth Dobson; three *s. Educ:* City of Oxford High Sch.; Jesus Coll., Oxford (Lawrence Exhibnr; MA Maths; Hon. Fellow, 1998). FIA 1966. Nat. Service, MEAF, 1956–58. Joined Commercial Union, 1961: Life Manager, 1978–80; Dep. Gen. Manager, 1981–82; Gen. Manager, 1983–86; Dir, 1987–98. Director: Trade Indemnity plc, 1991–95; Credito Italiano Bank, 1994–99; NHBC, 1998–2011 (Chm., 2002–11); Canary Wharf Gp plc, 1999–2004; Mem., UK Bd Cttee, CGU plc, 1998–2000; Chm., Travelers Insce (formerly St Paul Travelers Insce) Co., 2007–; Dep. Chm., Travelers Syndicate Mgt, 2011–. Mem., Council for Industry and Higher Educn, 1993–98. Chairman: Mgt Cttee, Motor Insurers Bureau, 1985–90; Loss Prevention Council, 1991–94; Assoc. of British Insurers, 1995–97; Policyholders Protection Bd, 2000–01. Adviser: HSBC Investment Bank, 1998–2001; Munich Reinsurance Co. Ltd, 1998–2002 and 2004–11. Curator, Univ. Chest, 1998–2000, Mem. Investment Cttee, 2000–07, Oxford Univ.; Gov., London Guildhall Univ., 1998–2002 (Chm. Govs, 1999–2002); Chairman: London Metropolitan Univ., 2002–06; Cttee of Univ. Chairmen, 2004–06. *Recreations:* golf, ski-ing, hill walking, opera, theatre. *Address:* 42 Wolsey Road, Moor Park, Northwood, Middx HA6 2EN. *Club:* Moor Park Golf.

**CARTER, Prof. (John) Timothy,** PhD; FRCP, FFOM; Professor, Norwegian Centre for Maritime Medicine, University of Bergen, 2010–14, now Emeritus; *b* 12 Feb. 1944; *s* of Reginald John Carter and Linda Mary (*née* Briggs); one *s* two *d. Educ:* Dulwich Coll.; Corpus Christi Coll., Cambridge (MB, MA); University Coll. Hosp., London; Birmingham Univ. (PhD 2005). FFOM 1984; FRCP 1987. London Sch. of Hygiene, 1972–74 (MSc). MO, British Petroleum, 1974–78; SMO, BP Chemicals, 1978–83; Health and Safety Executive: Dir of Med. Services, 1983–92, and of Health Policy, 1989–92; Dir of Field Ops Div., 1992–96; Med. Advr, 1996–97; Chief Med. Advr, Maritime and Coastguard Agency (formerly DETR, then DTLR, later DfT), 1999–2014. Member: MRC, 1983–96; Bd, Faculty of Occupnl Medicine, 1982–88 (Vice Dean, 1996–98); Hon. Sec., Occupnl Medicine Section, RSM, 1979–83; President: British Occupnl Hygiene Soc., 1987–88; Internat. Maritime Health Assoc., 2005–07. *Publications:* Merchant Seamen's Health 1860–1960: medicine, technology, shipowners and the state, 2014; articles and books on transport safety and investigation and control of occupnl health hazards and med. history. *Recreations:* history—natural, medical and local.

**CARTER, Prof. Joy,** CBE 2018; PhD; DL; Vice Chancellor, University of Winchester, since 2006; *b* 26 Dec. 1955; *d* of Douglas and Joyce; *m* Dr Martin Carter; four *s. Educ:* Univ. of Durham (BSc 1977); Univ. of Lancaster (PhD 1980). CGeol; FGS. Reader in Geochem., Univ. of Reading; Dean of Sci., Univ. of Derby; Pro-Vice-Chancellor (Academic), Univ. of Glamorgan. DL Hants, 2013–. *Publications:* (with T. Jickells) Biogeochemistry of Intertidal Sediments, 1997; (with A. Parker) Environmental Interactions of Clay Minerals, 1998; (with A. Stewart) Thematic Set on Environmental Geochemistry and Health, 2000; over 100 academic papers. *Recreations:* sports, antiques, her dog! *Address:* University of Winchester, Winchester, Hants SO22 4NR. *T:* (01962) 827222. *E:* joy.carter@winchester.ac.uk.

**CARTER, Matthew,** RDI 1981; Principal, Carter & Cone Type Inc., Cambridge, Mass, since 1992; *b* London, 1 Oct. 1937; *s* of late Harry Graham Carter, OBE and Ella Mary Carter (*née* Garratt). Punch Cutter, Netherlands, 1956; freelance designer of lettering and type, London, 1957–63; typographical advr, Crosfield Electronics, 1963–65; type designer: Mergenthaler Linotype, NY, 1965–71; Linotype Cos, London, 1971–81; Co-founder, Sen. Vice Pres. and Dir, Bitstream Inc., 1981–92. Typographical Advr, HMSO, 1980–84; Consultant, Printer Planning Div., IBM, 1980–81. Typefaces designed include: Snell Roundhand, 1966; Olympian, 1970; Galliard, 1978; Bell Centennial, 1978; Bitstream Charter, 1987; Mantinia, 1993; Verdana, and Georgia, 1996; Miller, 1997; Yale, 2004; refinements to Franklin Gothic (for MOMA, NY), 2004. Seven typefaces acquired by MOMA, NY for Architecture and Design collection, 2011. Hon. DFA Art Inst. of Boston, 1992. Middleton Award, Amer. Center for Design, 1995; Chrysler Award for Innovation in Design, 1996; Amer. Inst. of Graphic Arts Medal, 1996; Vadim Award, Moscow Acad. of Graphic Design, 1998; Special Commendation, Prince Philip Designers Prize, CSD, 2004; MacArthur Fellow, 2010; Lifetime Achievement Award, Smithsonian Cooper-Hewitt Nat. Design Mus., 2011. *Address:* 36–A Rice Street, Cambridge, MA 02140, USA.

**CARTER, Matthew John;** Founder and Director, Message House, since 2013; *b* 22 March 1972; *s* of John Carter and Jill Tasker; *m* 1997, Erica Moffitt; three *s. Educ:* Univ. of Sheffield (BA Hons (Social and Pol Studies) 1993); Univ. of York (MA (Pol Philos.) 1994, DPhil (Politics) 1999). Tutor in Politics, Univ. of York, 1994–98; Labour Party: Regl Organiser, N and Yorks, 1998–99; Regl Dir, SW, 1999–2001; Asst Gen. Sec. (Policy and Pol Develt), 2001–03; Gen. Sec., 2004–05; Man. Dir, Penn, Schoen & Berland Associates Inc., 2006–10; Chm., Penn, Schoen & Berland Associates EMEA, 2010–13; Chief Exec., Burson-Marsteller, UK, 2010–13. Member, Board of Trustees: Tamasha Th. Co., 2007–11 (Vice Chm., 2009–11); John Smith Centre for Public Service, 2016–. Mem. Bd, People United, 2013–15. *Publications:* The People's Party: the history of the Labour Party (with A. W. Wright), 1997; T. H. Green and the Development of Ethical Socialism, 2003. *Recreations:* enjoys hill walking in the Lake District, running, supporting Grimsby Town FC.

**CARTER, Gen. Sir Nicholas (Patrick),** GCB 2019 (KCB 2014); CBE 2003 (OBE 2001; MBE 1996); DSO 2011; Chief of the Defence Staff, since 2018; Aide-de-Camp General to the Queen, since 2014; *b* Nairobi, 11 Feb. 1959; *s* of late Gerald and Elspeth Carter; *m* 1984, Louise Anne Ewart; three *s* one *d. Educ:* Winchester Coll.; RMA Sandhurst. Commnd RGJ, 1978; Regtl duty, NI, Cyprus, Germany and GB, 1978–90; Staff Coll., 1991; Co. Comd, 3 RGJ, 1992–93; Mil. Asst CGS, 1994–95; DS Staff Coll., 1996–98; CO, 2 RGJ, 1998–2000; Comdr, 20 Armd Bde, 2004–05; Dir, Army Resources and Plans, 2006–08; GOC 6th (UK) Div., 2009; Comdr, Regl Comd S, ISAF, Afghanistan, 2009–10; Dir Gen. Land Warfare, 2011; Comdr Field Army, 2012; Army 2020 Team Leader, 2012; Dep. Comdr ISAF, Afghanistan and UK Nat. Contingent Comdr, Afghanistan, 2012–13; Comdr Land Forces, 2013–14; Chief of the Gen. Staff, 2014–18. Regtl Col, London Rifles, 2007–09; Dep. Col Comdt, AGC, 2011–14; Col Comdt, The Rifles, 2013–19. Col, Mil. Ops Gp (Vol.), 2011–. QCVS 1998 and 2004. Comdr, Legion of Merit (USA), 2018. *Recreations:* golf, cricket, field sports, cycling. *Clubs:* Boodle's, Grillions; Berkshire Golf, St Enodoc Golf, Seniors Golf.

**CARTER, Nigel,** OBE 2012; Chief Executive, Oral Health Foundation (formerly British and International Dental Health Foundation), since 1997; *b* Wolverhampton, 7 Aug. 1952; *s* of Wilfrid and Vera Carter. *Educ:* John Port Sch., Etwall, Derbys; Birmingham Univ. (BDS 1975); Edinburgh Univ. (LDS 1975). General Dental Practice, Birmingham, 1975–97; Man. Dir, India Hse Trng and Recruitment, 1983–2001. Mem. Bd, Platform for Better Oral Health in Europe, 2013– (Chm., 2017–). Chm., British Dental Health Foundn, 1987–89 (Trustee, 1978–97); Trustee, 2003–, Treas., 2005–18, Chair, 2019–, RSPH (formerly RSH). *Recreations:* music, opera, books, travel. *Address:* Oral Health Foundation, Smile House, 2 East Union Street, Rugby CV22 6AJ. *T:* (01788) 546365. *E:* nigel@dentalhealth.org.

**CARTER, Peter;** QC 1995; *b* 8 Aug. 1952. *Educ:* University Coll. London (LLB 1973). Called to the Bar, Gray's Inn, 1974, Bencher, 2002. *Publications:* (jtly) Offences of Violence, 1991, supplement 1994. *Recreations:* poetry, cricket, walking. *Address:* Doughty Street Chambers, 54 Doughty Street, WC1N 2LS. *T:* (020) 7404 1313.

**CARTER, Dr Peter John,** OBE 2006; independent management consultant, since 2015; Chief Executive and General Secretary, Royal College of Nursing, 2007–15; *s* of Reginald and Mary Carter; *m* Lilian Yap; two *d. Educ:* Univ. of Birmingham (MBA 1992; PhD 1998). MCIPD 1986. Psychiatric nurse trng, Hill End Hosp., St Albans, 1971; gen. nurse trng, St Albans City Hosp. and Inst. of Urology, London, 1976; clinical and managerial posts in Herts and Bedfordshire; Chief Exec., Brent, Kensington, Chelsea and Westminster Mental Health Trust, then Central and NW London Mental Health NHS Trust, 1995–2007. Interim Chm., Medway Maritime NHS Foundn Trust, 2016–17. Visiting Professor: KCL, 2009–; Anglia Ruskin Univ., 2009–. Mem., Commn on the Future of Nursing and Midwifery, 2009–. Hon. Col 203 Field Hosp. (V), 2011–18. Hon. FRCGP 2013. President's Medal, RCPsych, 2011. *Recreations:* Rugby, cricket, scuba diving, cycling, music, literature.

**CARTER, Rev. (Ralph) Graham;** Chair, Darlington District of the Methodist Church, 1997–2008; President, Methodist Conference, 2006–07; *b* 11 July 1943; *s* of Thomas Wilfrid Carter and Eva Carter (*née* Williams); *m* 1967, Rosamond Catherine Shaw; one *s* one *d. Educ:* Bede Grammar Sch., Sunderland; Queens' Coll., Cambridge (MA); Hartley Victoria Coll., Manchester. Ordained Minister, 1970; served in: Newcastle-upon-Tyne, 1967–71; Cramlington, Northumberland, 1971–74; Birkenhead, 1974–81; Liverpool, 1981–92; Durham, 1992–97. Religious producer, BBC Radio Merseyside, 1987–92. Chm., Trustees, Epworth Old Rectory, 2008–18. *Recreations:* bird-watching, walking, model railways, supporting Sunderland FC and Durham CCC, listening to music, enjoying grandparenting, gardening.

**CARTER, Raymond John,** CBE 1991; Executive, 1980–2003, Director, 1983–2003, Marathon Oil Co.; *b* 17 Sept. 1935; *s* of late John Carter and Nellie Carter (*née* Woodcock); *m* 1959, Jeanette Hills; one *s* two *d. Educ:* Mortlake Co. Secondary Sch.; Reading Technical Coll.; Staffordshire Coll. of Technology. National Service, Army, 1953–55. Sperry Gyroscope Co.: Technical Asst, Research and Development Computer Studies, 1956–65. Electrical Engineer, Central Electricity Generating Bd, 1965–70, Mem., CEGB Management, 1979–80. Mem., Gen. Adv. Council, BBC, 1974–76. Mem., Interim Adv. Cttee (Teachers' Pay and Conditions), DES, 1987–91; Dep. Chm., School Teachers' Review Body, 1991–93. Mem. Easthampstead RDC, 1963–68. Contested: Wokingham, Gen. Elecn, 1966; Warwick and Leamington, By-elecn, March 1968; MP (Lab) Birmingham, Northfield, 1970–79; Parly Under-Sec. of State, Northern Ireland Office, 1976–79. Member: Public Accounts Cttee, 1973–74; Parly Science and Technology Cttee, 1974–76; author of Congenital Disabilities (Civil Liability) Act, 1976. Delegate: Council of Europe, 1974–76; WEU, 1974–76. Trustee, BM (Nat. Hist.), 1986–96; Patron, Guild of Handicraft Trust, 1991–. Mem., Develt Cttee, Arvon Foundn, 1991–2001. Gov., Wexham and Heatherwood Hosp. NHS Trust, 2011–14. Co-cataloguer and exhibitor, works of Sir John Betjeman, 1983. *Recreations:* walking, reading, writing. *Address:* 1 Lynwood Chase, Warfield Road, Bracknell, Berkshire RG12 2JT. *T:* (01344) 420237.

**CARTER, Prof. Richard Lawrance,** CBE 1997; DM, DSc; Professorial Fellow, University of Surrey, 1994–2003; *b* 5 Sept. 1934; *o s* of Thomas Lawrance Carter and Rhoda Edith Carter (*née* Horton). *Educ:* St Lawrence Coll., Ramsgate; Corpus Christi Coll., Oxford (MA 1960; DM 1966); UCH, London (DSc 1978). FRCPath 1978; FRCP 2002. Med. posts, Radcliffe Infirmary, Oxford; UCH; Reader in Pathology, Inst. of Cancer Research, and Consultant Histopathologist, Royal Marsden Hosp., Sutton, 1985–99. Consultant, Thames Cancer Registry, 1990–2004. Ombudsman, Lancet, 1998–2004. Former chm. or mem. of govt adv. cttees and wkg parties, DoH, DoE, MAFF, MoD; former examr, RCPath, RCS, RCSI; Fellow or Mem., RSocMed, UK Children's Cancer Study Gp. *Publications:* author, jt author or editor of books and papers on lab. and experimental aspects of human cancers, mainly of the head and neck, tumours in children, and human carcinogenesis. *Recreations:* gardening, birds, books, music. *Address:* Pine Cottage, The Street, Hascombe, Surrey GU8 4JN.

**CARTER, (Ronald) David,** CBE 1980; RDI 1975; Founder, DCA Design International Ltd, 1975 (Chairman, 1975–95; Director, 1995–99); Professor of Industrial Design Engineering, Royal College of Art, and Imperial College of Science, Technology and Medicine, 1991–95; *b* 30 Dec. 1927; *s* of H. Miles Carter and Margaret Carter; *m* 1953, Theo (Marjorie Elizabeth), *d* of Rev. L. T. Towers; two *s* two *d. Educ:* Wyggeston Sch., Leicester; Central Sch. of Art and Design, London. Served RN, 1946–48. Appts in industry, 1951–60; Principal, David Carter Associates, 1960–75. Visiting Lectr, Birmingham Coll. of Art and Design, 1960–65. Examr, RCA, 1976–79 and 1987–90. Mem., Design Council, 1972–84 (Dep. Chm., 1975–84; Chm., Report on Industrial Design Educn in UK, 1977). Pres., Soc. of Industrial Artists and Designers, 1974–75; Chm., DATEC, 1977–82; Royal Fine Arts Comr, 1986–98. Vice-Chm., Design Mus. (formerly Conran Foundn), 1992– (Chm., 1986–92), Trustee, 1981–95); Moderator, Hong Kong Polytechnic, 1981–86; Mem., Prince of Wales Award for Indust. Innovation, 1981–85. Governor, London Inst., 1988–91. Design Awards, 1961, 1969, 1983; Duke of Edinburgh Prize for Elegant Design, 1967. FCSD (FSIA 1967); Sen. FRCA 1995. FRSA 1975. Hon. DDes: De Montfort, 1993; UCE, 2000. *Recreations:* dry stone walls, boats, County Cork. *Club:* Reform.

**CARTER, Sir Ronald (Powell),** ONZ 2014; KNZM 1998; consulting engineer, 2002–16; *b* Auckland, NZ, 1935; *s* of Eric Powell Carter and Sybil Muriel Carter (*née* Townsend); *m* 1960, Dianne Lewell Oxspring; two *s* one *d. Educ:* Auckland Grammar Sch.; Univ. of Auckland (BE 1956; ME 1958). Beca Carter Hollings and Ferner: Founding Partner, 1968; Mem. Bd, 1968–2002; CEO and Chm., 1986–97. Director: Electricity Corp. of NZ, 1992–99; Air New Zealand, 1998–2007; Rural Equities Ltd, 2004–16. Chm., CAA NZ, 1992–98. Mem., Royal Commn of Inquiry into Canterbury Earthquake, 2011–12. Pres., Instn of Professional Engrs NZ, 1999. Chair, Selection Panel, Sir Peter Blake Leadership Awards, 2003–13 (Trustee, 2003–09). Hon. DEng Auckland, 2001; Hon. Dr Auckland Univ. Technol., 2013. *Recreations:* sailing, Rugby, developing a seaside garden, watching grandchildren activities. *Clubs:* Northern; Royal New Zealand Yacht Squadron.

**CARTER, Sebastian;** *see* Carter, T. S.

**CARTER, Thomas Henry;** HM Diplomatic Service; Ambassador (non-resident) to Honduras, 2017–19; *b* Norwich, 22 Nov. 1953; *s* of Claude and Anne Carter; *m* 1997, Carolyn Jayne Davidson, *qv;* two *s. Educ:* Norwich Sch.; Univ. of Kent (BA Hons French and German); Ecole Nat. d'Admin, Paris (Cycle Etranger); Open Univ. (MBA 2010). Entered FCO, 1976; Third Sec., Paris, 1979–82; Third, later Second Sec., Bogotá, 1983–86; UK Mission to UN, NY, 1986; FCO, 1987–90; First Secretary: Paris, 1990; Bonn, 1990–95; FCO, 1995–99; Hd, Political Section, Bangkok, 1999–2003; Jt Dep. Hd of Mission, Bratislava, 2004–08; Jt High Comr to Zambia, 2008–12; FCO, 2012–15; Ambassador to Guatemala, 2015–17. *Recreations:* sailing, ski-ing, cycling, running, hiking up volcanoes. *Address:* c/o Foreign and Commonwealth Office, King Charles Street, SW1A 2AH.

**CARTER, (Thomas) Sebastian;** designer and printer; Partner, since 1971, and owner, since 1991, Rampant Lions Press; *b* 20 Feb. 1941; *s* of late William Nicholas Carter, OBE and Barbara Ruth Carter (*née* Digby); *m* 1966, Penelope Ann Bowes Kerr; one *s* one *d. Educ:* Christ's Hosp.; King's Coll., Cambridge (MA). Designer: John Murray, 1962–63; The Trianon Press, Paris, 1963–65; Ruari McLean Associates, 1965–66; joined Rampant Lions Press, 1966. Mem., Internat. Acad. of the Book and Art of the Book, Russia, 1995. Ed., Parenthesis (jl of Fine Press Bk Assoc.), 2006–. Francis Minns Meml Prize (for Shades by David Piper), NBL 1971; Laureate Award, Amer. Printing History Assoc., 2013. *Publications:* The Book Becomes, 1986; Twentieth Century Type Designers, 1987, 2nd edn 1995; The Rampant Lions Press: a narrative catalogue, 2013; (jtly) The History of the Monotype Corporation, 2014; (jtly) Cambridge History of the Book in Britain, vol. 7, 2019; contributor: Matrix, 1983–; Oxford Companion to the Book, 2010. *Recreations:* gardening, food, listening to music. *Address:* 14 Magrath Avenue, Cambridge CB4 3AH. *T:* (01223) 363669.

**CARTER, Timothy;** *see* Carter, J. T.

**CARTER, Prof. Timothy,** PhD; David G. Frey Distinguished Professor of Music, University of North Carolina, since 2001; *b* 3 July 1954; *s* of Thomas Carter and Thais (*née* Epifantseff); *m* 1995, Annegret Fauser. *Educ:* Univ. of Durham (BA); Univ. of Birmingham (PhD 1980). Lectr in Music, Univ. of Lancaster, 1980–87; Lectr, 1987–92, Reader, 1992–95, Prof. of Music, 1995–2001, RHBNC, Univ. of London. Fellow, Harvard Center for Italian Renaissance Studies, Villa I Tatti, Florence, 1984–85. Ed., Music & Letters, 1992–99. Has made broadcasts. *Publications:* W. A. Mozart: Le Nozze di Figaro, 1987; Jacopo Peri (1561–1633): his life and works, 1989; Music in Late Renaissance and Early Baroque Italy, 1992; Monteverdi's Musical Theatre, 2002; Oklahoma!: the making of an American musical, 2007; Orpheus in the Marketplace: Jacopo Peri and the economy of Late Renaissance Florence (I Tatti Studies in Italian Renaissance History), 2013; Understanding Italian Opera, 2015; articles and essays in Jl Royal Musical Assoc., Early Music Hist., Jl Amer. Musicological Soc. *Address:* Music Department, University of North Carolina, Chapel Hill, NC 27599–3320, USA.

**CARTER, (William) George (Key),** CBE 1994; DL; FCA; Chairman, Black Country Development Corporation, 1994–98; *b* 29 Jan. 1934; *s* of late William Tom Carter, OBE, JP and Georgina Margaret Carter (*née* Key); *m* 1965, Anne Rosalie Mary Flanagan; one *s* one *d. Educ:* Warwick School. FCA 1957. Articled with Loarridge Beaven & Co., 1951–56; joined Price Waterhouse, 1956; Nat. Service, 2nd Lieut, 16/5th Queen's Royal Lancers, 1958–60; returned to Price Waterhouse, 1960. Manager, 1963–66; Partner, London, 1966–82; Dir of Finance, 1966–70; Sen. Partner, W Midlands, 1982–94. Dir, W Midlands Develt Agency, 1989–95 (Chm., 1991–95); Mem., NW Worcs HA, 1994–96. Mem., Pharmacists Rev. Panel, 1981–97. Member: CBI W Midlands Regl Council, 1988–98; DTI Industry '96 Steering Gp, 1993–97. Pres., Birmingham Chamber of Industry and Commerce, 1993–94; Vice-Chm., Birmingham Mkting Partnership, 1993–95; Non-executive Director: Birmingham Econ. Develt Partnership, 1991–95; Birmingham Children's Hosp. NHS Trust, 1996–2003. Institute of Chartered Accountants: Member: Insce Industry Cttee (Chm., 1974–80); Parly and Law Cttee, 1978–83; Co-Chm., Auditors and Actuaries Cttee, 1975–80; Courses Cttee 1978–81. Member: Birmingham Univ. Business Sch. Adv. Bd, 1989–99; Council, Aston Univ., 1995–98. Pres., ESU, Worcs, 1998–2003. Gov. and Feoffee, Old Swinford Hosp. Sch., 1986–2000. FRSA 1993. DL W Midlands, 1996; High Sheriff, W Midlands, 1998–99. CStJ 1998 (Chm., Council, W Midlands, 1994–2001; Mem., Chapter Gen., 1996–99; Mem., Priory of England Chapter, 1999–2002). *Publications:* (jtly) Institute of Chartered Accountants Guide to Investigations, 1978. *Recreation:* trying to keep up with the digital world. *Address:* The Old Rectory, Elmley Lovett, Droitwich, Worcs WR9 0PS. *T:* (01299) 851459. *E:* wgkcarter@btinternet.com. *Club:* Cavalry and Guards.

**CARTER-MANNING, Jeremy James;** QC 1993; a Recorder, since 1993; *b* 25 Dec. 1947; *s* of Landon and Nancie Carter-Manning; *m* 1970, Bridget Mary Simpson; one *s* one *d. Educ:* St Paul's Sch. Solicitor, 1971; called to the Bar, Middle Temple, 1975, Bencher, 2002. Mem., Mental Health Rev. Tribunal, 1998–2003. Dir, Council for Registration of Forensic Practitioners, 1999–2006. *Recreations:* golf, food and wine. *Address:* Furnival Chambers, 30–32 Furnival Street, EC4A 1JQ. *T:* (020) 7405 3232. *Clubs:* Ivy; Southampton Football.

**CARTER-STEPHENSON, George Anthony;** QC 1998; *b* 10 July 1952; *s* of Raymond M. Stephenson and Brenda S. Stephenson; *m* 1974, Christine Maria; one *s* one *d. Educ:* Leeds Univ. (LLB Hons). Called to the Bar, Inner Temple, 1975; in practice at the Bar, 1975–. Jt Head of Chambers, 2009–. *Recreations:* motorcycling, theatre, cinema, music. *Address:* 25 Bedford Row, WC1R 4HD. *T:* (020) 7067 1500.

**CARTLEDGE, Sir Bryan (George),** KCMG 1985 (CMG 1980); Principal of Linacre College, Oxford, 1988–96 (Hon. Fellow, 1996); *b* 10 June 1931; *s* of Eric Montague George Cartledge and Phyllis (*née* Shaw); *m* 1st, 1960, Ruth Hylton Gass (marr. diss. 1994; she *d* 1998), *d* of John Gass; one *s* one *d;* 2nd, 1994, Dr Freda Gladys Newcombe (*d* 2001); 3rd, 2005, Helen Manolatos (*née* Mostra). *Educ:* Hurstpierpoint; St John's Coll., Cambridge (Hon. Fellow, 1985). Queen's Royal Regt, 1950–51. Commonwealth Fund Fellow, Stanford Univ., 1956–57; Research Fellow, St Antony's Coll., Oxford, 1958–59 (Hon. Fellow, 1987). Entered HM Foreign (subseq. Diplomatic) Service, 1960; served in FO, 1960–61; Stockholm, 1961–63; Moscow, 1963–66; DSAO, 1966–68; Tehran, 1968–70; Harvard Univ., 1971–72; Counsellor, Moscow, 1972–75; Head of E European and Soviet Dept, FCO, 1975–77; Private Sec. (Overseas Affairs) to Prime Minister, 1977–79; Ambassador to Hungary, 1980–83; Asst Under-Sec. of State, FCO, 1983–84; Dep. Sec. of the Cabinet, 1984–85; Ambassador to the Soviet Union, 1985–88. Lánchíd Prize (Hungary), 2013; Gabor Bethlen Award (Hungary), 2015. *Publications:* (ed) Monitoring the Environment, 1992; (ed) Energy and the Environment, 1993; (ed) Health and the Environment, 1994; (ed) Population and the Environment, 1995; (ed) Transport and the Environment, 1996; (ed) Mind, Brain and Environment, 1997; The Will to Survive: a history of Hungary, 2006; Makers of the Modern World: Károlyi and Bethlen: Hungary, 2009. *Clubs:* Hurlingham, Oxford and Cambridge.

**CARTLEDGE, Prof. Paul Anthony,** DPhil, PhD; FSA; A. G. Leventis Professor of Greek Culture, University of Cambridge, 2008–14, now Emeritus; Fellow, since 1981, and A. G. Leventis Senior Research Fellow, since 2014, Clare College, Cambridge (President, 2011–14); *b* 24 March 1947; *s* of Marcus Raymond and Margaret Christobel Cartledge; *m* 1976, Judith Portrait; one *d. Educ:* St Paul's Sch.; New Coll., Oxford (MA; DPhil 1975); MA TCD 1978; PhD Cantab 1979. FSA 1980. Craven Fellow, Oxford Univ., 1969–70; Harold Salvesen Jun. Fellow, University Coll., Oxford, 1970–72; Lecturer: in Classics, NUU, 1972–73; TCD, 1973–78; in Classical Civilization, Univ. of Warwick, 1978–79; University of Cambridge: Lectr in Classics, 1979–93; Reader in Greek History, 1993–99; Prof. of Greek History, 1999–2008; Chm., Faculty Bd of Classics, 2001–02; actg Master, Clare Coll., Cambridge, Lent term, 2012. Visiting Professor: Centre Louis Gernet, Paris, 1990; Sorbonne, Univ. de Paris VII, 1998–99; Ecole des Hautes Etudes en Sciences Sociales, Paris, 2007–08; Hellenic Parlt Global Dist. Prof., New York Univ., 2006–11. Lectures: Lansdowne, Univ. of Victoria, BC, 1989, 1993; Crayenborgh Res. Seminar, Univ. of Leiden, 1999; T. B. L. Webster Meml, Stanford Univ., 1999; M. I. Finley Meml, Syracuse Univ., 2008; M. Ostwald Meml, Tel Aviv Univ., 2016; G. F. Else Meml, Ann Arbor, 2016; M. E. White Meml, Univ. of Toronto, 2017. Syndic, 2002–16, Hon. Keeper, Dept of Antiquities, 2016–, Fitzwilliam Mus. Gov.; St Paul's Schs, 1991–2007. FRSA 2007. Hon. Dr: Thessaly, 2011; Warwick, 2017. Hon. Citizen, Sparta, Greece, 2004. Gold Cross, Order of Honour (Greece), 2002. *Publications:* Sparta and Lakonia: a regional history 1300–362 BC, 1979, 2nd edn 2002; Agesilaos and the Crisis of Sparta, 1987; (with A. Spawforth) Hellenistic and Roman Sparta: a tale of two cities, 1989, rev. edn 2002; Aristophanes and his Theatre of the Absurd, 1990, rev. edn 1999; (ed jtly) Nomos: essays in Athenian law, politics and society, 1990; (ed and trans.) Religion in the Ancient Greek City, 1992; The Greeks: a portrait of self and others, 1993, 2nd edn 2002; (ed jtly) Hellenistic Constructs: essays in culture, history and historiography, 1997; (ed jtly) The Cambridge Illustrated History of Ancient Greece, 1997, 2nd edn 2002; (with R. Waterfield) Xenophon: Hiero the Tyrant and other treatises, 1997, rev. edn 2005; (ed jtly) Kosmos: essays in order, conflict and community in classical Athens, 1998; Democritus and Atomistic Politics, 1998; The Greeks: crucible of civilization, 2001; Spartan Reflections, 2001; (ed jtly) Money, Labour and Land: approaches to the economies of ancient Greece, 2001; The Spartans: an epic history, 2002, 2nd edn 2003; Alexander the Great: the hunt for a new past, 2004; Thermopylae: the battle that changed the world, 2006; Eine Trilogie über die Demokratie, 2008; Ancient Greek Political Thought in Practice, 2009; Ancient Greece: a history in eleven cities, 2009; Forever Young: why Cambridge has a Professor of Greek Culture, 2009; (ed jtly) Responses to Oliver Stone's Alexander: film, history and cultural studies, 2010; (ed jtly) The Cambridge World History of Slavery, vol. I, 2011; Ancient Greece: a very short introduction, 2011; After Thermopylae: the oath of Plataea and the end of the Graeco-Persian Wars, 2013; (with T. Holland) Herodotus: the

Histories, 2013; Democracy: a life, 2016, rev. edn 2018. *Recreations:* ballet, opera, theatre. *Address:* Clare College, Cambridge CB2 1TL. *T:* (01223) 335163, *Fax:* (01223) 333219. *Club:* Athenæum.

**CARTLIDGE, James Roger;** MP (C) South Suffolk, since 2015; *m* Emily, *d* of Sir (James) Gerald (Douglas) Howarth, *qv*; four *c* (incl. twins). *Educ:* Univ. of Manchester. Researcher for Cons. Party; leader writer, Daily Telegraph; Founder, Share to Buy Ltd, 2004. Mem. (C) Babergh DC, 2013–15. Contested (C) Lewisham Deptford, 2005. *Address:* House of Commons, SW1A 0AA.

**CARTMELL, Simon Christopher,** OBE 2016; Chairman, Ieso Digital Health Ltd, since 2015; *b* Worcs, Jan. 1960; *s* of Leo Cartmell and Vera Cartmell; *m* 1991, Bethan Nicholas; two *s*. *Educ:* Univ. of Manchester (BSc Hons Med. Microbiol. 1981); Univ. of London (MSc Business and Econs 1992). Glaxo, subseq. Glaxo Wellcome plc: marketing/sales, 1981–91; Dir, Global Supply Chain, 1991–95; Global Commercial Dir, Anti Infectives, 1995–98; Chief Operating Officer, Vanguard Medica plc, 1997–99; CEO, Celltech Pharma, Celltech plc, 1999–2001; CEO, ApaTech Ltd, 2003–10; Operating Partner, Imperial Innovations plc, then IP Gp plc, 2015–19. Chm., OssDsign AB, 2016–; non-executive Director: ReNeuron plc, 2011–; Route 2 Advrs Ltd, 2012–; Route 2 Property Ltd, 2016–; Oviva AG, 2019–. Gov., Haberdashers' Aske's Elstree Schs, 2008– (Chair, Govs, 2017–). Freeman, City of London, 2012; Liveryman, Haberdashers' Co., 2014 (Asst, 2016). Dir, Teddington RFC Ltd, 2014–. *Recreations:* ski-ing, travel, wine, Rugby, gardening, cars. *Club:* 67 Pall Mall.

**CARTTISS, Michael Reginald Harry;** Regional Volunteer Organiser, SOS Children's Villages UK, 1999–2005; volunteer charity worker with SOS Children's Villages Nigeria, since 2004; *b* Norwich, 11 March 1938; *s* of Reginald Carttiss and Doris Culling. *Educ:* Filby County Primary Sch.; Great Yarmouth Tech. High Sch.; Goldsmiths' Coll., London Univ. (DipEd); LSE (part time, 1961–64). Nat. Service, RAF, 1956–58. Teacher: Orpington, Kent, and Waltham Cross, Herts, 1961–64; Oriel Grammar Sch., 1964–69; Cons. Party Agent, Gt Yarmouth, 1969–82. Norfolk County Council: Mem., 1966–87, 2001–17 (Vice Chm., then Dep. Leader, Cons. Gp, 2010–15); Vice-Chm., 2006–07; Chm., 2007–08; Vice-Chm., 1972, Chm., 1982–84, Educn Cttee; Mem., Gt Yarmouth BC, 1973–82 (Leader, 1980–82). MP (C) Great Yarmouth, 1983–97; contested (C) same seat, 1997. Chm., Norfolk Museums Service, 1981–85; Comr, Gt Yarmouth Port and Haven Commn, 1982–86. Mem., E Anglian RHA, 1981–85; Chairman: Gt Yarmouth and Waveney CHC, 2001–03; Norfolk Health Scrutiny Cttee, 2005–07; Norfolk Health Overview and Scrutiny Cttee, 2009–17. *Recreations:* reading, writing, talking, walking, theatre. *Address:* Melrose, Main Road, Filby, Great Yarmouth, Norfolk NR29 3HN.

**CARTWRIGHT, John Cameron;** JP; Deputy Chairman, Police Complaints Authority, 1993–99 (Member, 1992–99); *b* 29 Nov. 1933; *s* of Aubrey John Randolph Cartwright and Ivy Adeline Billie Cartwright; *m* 1959, Iris June Tant (*d* 2014); one *s* one *d*. *Educ:* Woking County Grammar School. Exec. Officer, Home Civil Service, 1952–55; Labour Party Agent, 1955–67; Political Sec., RACS Ltd, 1967–72; Director, RACS Ltd, 1972–74. Leader, Greenwich Borough Council, 1971–74. Mem., Labour Party Nat. Exec. Cttee, 1971–75 and 1976–78. MP Greenwich, Woolwich East, Oct. 1974–1983, Woolwich, 1983–92 (Lab, 1974–81; SDP, 1981–90; Soc. Dem., 1990–92); contested (Soc. Dem.) Woolwich, 1992. PPS to Sec. of State for Education and Science, 1976–77; Chm., Parly Labour Party Defence Group, 1979–81; Mem., Select Cttee on Defence, 1979–82 and 1986–92; SDP party spokesman on environment, 1981–87, on defence and foreign affairs, 1983–87; SDP/Liberal Alliance spokesman on defence, 1987; SDP Parly Whip, 1983–92; Vice Pres., SDP, 1987–88, Pres., 1988–91. Jt Chm., Council for Advancement of Arab British Understanding, 1983–87; Vice-Chm., GB-USSR Assoc., 1983–91. Mem., Calcutt Cttee on Privacy and Related Matters, 1989–90. Non-executive Director: Lambeth, Southwark and Lewisham HA, 1995–2000; Maidstone and Tunbridge Wells NHS Trust, 2000–03. Vice-Pres., Assoc. of Metropolitan Authorities, 1974–. Trustee, Nat. Maritime Museum, 1976–83. Co. Sec., Maidstone Christian Care, 2002–10. JP Inner London, 1970. *Publications:* (jtly) Cruise, Pershing and SS20, 1985. *Recreations:* do-it-yourself, listening to jazz, supporting Lincoln City FC. *Address:* 64 Squires Way, Dartford, Kent DA2 7NW. *T:* (01322) 316152.

**CARTWRIGHT, Prof. Nancy Lynn Delaney, (Lady Hampshire),** PhD; FBA 1996; FAcSS; Professor of Philosophy, Durham University, since 2012; Professor of Philosophy, University of California at San Diego, since 1997; *b* 24 June 1944; *m* 1985, Sir Stuart Hampshire, FBA (*d* 2004); two *d*. *Educ:* Pittsburgh Univ. (BS Maths 1966); Univ. of Illinois (PhD 1971). Asst Professor of Philosophy, Univ. of Maryland, 1971–73; Stanford University: Asst Prof., 1973–77; Associate Prof., 1977–83; Prof. of Philosophy, 1983–91; Prof. of Philosophy, Logic and Scientific Method, LSE, 1991–2012. Vis. Lectr, Cambridge Univ., 1974; Visiting Professor: UCLA, 1976; Princeton Univ., 1978; Pittsburgh Univ., 1984; Oslo Univ., 1993, 1994; Univ. of Calif, San Diego, 1995; Old Dominion Fellow, Princeton Univ., 1996. Assoc. Mem., Nuffield Coll., Oxford, 2001–05. President: Hist. of Sci., BAAS, 2001–02; Phil. of Sci. Assoc.; Past Pres., APA (Pacific Div.). Fellow, Amer. Phil Soc.; MacArthur Fellow, MacArthur Foundn, 1993; FAcSS 2016. Mem., Acad. Leopoldina, 1999; Hon. For. Mem., Amer. Acad. of Arts and Sci., 2001. Hon. DLitt St Andrews, 2013; Hon. DHL Southern Methodist, 2012. *Publications:* How the Laws of Physics Lie, 1983; Nature's Capacities and their Measurement, 1989; (jtly) Otto Neurath: philosophy between science and politics, 1995; The Dappled World: a study of the boundaries of science, 1999; Measuring Causes: invariance, modularity and the Causal Markov Condition (monograph), 2000; Hunting Causes and Using Them: approaches to philosophy and economics, 2007; Causal Powers: What are they? Why do we need them? What can and cannot be done with them?, 2007; (with J. Hardie) Evidence Based Policy: a practical guide to doing it better, 2012; Evidence: for policy and wheresoever rigor is a must, 2013; (jtly) Improving Child Safety: deliberation, judgement and empirical research, 2017. *Address:* Department of Philosophy, Durham University, 50 Old Elvet, Durham DH1 3HN. *T:* (0191) 334 6049.

**CARTWRIGHT, Nicolas Frederick; His Honour Judge Cartwright;** a Circuit Judge, since 2015; *b* Wolverhampton, 22 March 1963; *s* of Geoffrey Edward and Christa Cartwright; *m* 1991, Penelope Martyn-Smith; one *s* one *d*. *Educ:* Malvern Coll.; King Edward's Sch., Birmingham; Univ. of Liverpool (LLB Hons). Called to the Bar, Middle Temple, 1986; in practice as barrister, 1989–2015; a Dep. Dist Judge (Magistrates' Courts), 2005–15; a Recorder, 2009–15. *Recreation:* keen cyclist. *Address:* Worcester Crown Court, The Shirehall, Worcester WR1 1EQ.

**CARTWRIGHT, Lt-Col Robert Guy,** LVO 2005; Secretary, Central Chancery of Orders of Knighthood, 1999–2005, and Assistant Comptroller, 1999–2004, Lord Chamberlain's Office; Extra Equerry to the Queen, since 2000; *b* 6 Aug. 1950; *s* of late Major Robin Vivian Cartwright and Lovedy Elizabeth Cartwright (*née* Leigh-Pemberton); *m* 1972, Caroline, *d* of late Gilbert Stephenson and Eleanor Stephenson; two *s*. *Educ:* Wellington Coll.; RMA Sandhurst; RMCS Shrivenham; RN Staff Coll. Commissioned Grenadier Guards, 1970; CO, 1st Bn Grenadier Guards, 1990–92; Directing Staff, RN Staff Coll., 1993–94; MoD, 1995–96; retired, 1996. Bursar, Ibstock Place Sch., Roehampton, 2005–16. *Recreations:* running, reading, wine. *Address:* 151 Wakehurst Road, SW11 6BW.

**CARTWRIGHT, Hon. Dame Silvia (Rose),** PCNZM 2001; DBE 1989; QSO 2006; Governor-General of New Zealand, 2001–06; Trial Chamber Judge, Extraordinary Chambers in the Courts of Cambodia, 2006–14; *b* 7 Nov. 1943; *d* of Monteith Poulter and Eileen Jane Poulter, both of Dunedin, NZ; *m* 1969, Peter John Cartwright. *Educ:* Univ. of Otago, NZ (LLB). Partner, Harkness Henry & Co., Barristers and Solicitors, Hamilton, NZ, 1971–81; Dist Court and Family Court Judge, 1981–89; Chief Dist Court Judge, 1989–93; Judge of the High Court, NZ, 1993–2001. Mem., Commn for the Future, 1975–80; conducted Inquiry into: Soc. Sci. Funding in NZ, 1986–87; Treatment of Cervical Cancer at Nat. Women's Hosp., Auckland, NZ, 1987–88. Mem. Cttee, UN Human Rights Convention to eliminate discrimination against women, 1992–2000; Chair, NZ Commission to UNESCO, 2006–08; Advr, UN Human Rights Council Investigation on Sri Lanka, 2014–. Hon. LLD: Otago, 1993; Waikato, 1994; Canterbury, 2004; Ewha, Seoul, 2006.

**CARTWRIGHT, Hon. Dame Sonia Rosemary Susan;** *see* Proudman, Hon. Dame S. R. S.

**CARTWRIGHT, Stacey Lee;** Deputy Chairman, Harvey Nichols Group Ltd, 2017–18 (Chief Executive Officer, 2014–17); *b* Stourbridge, 18 Nov. 1963; *d* of John and Eirwen Gainham; two *s* one *d*. *Educ:* London Sch. of Econs and Pol Sci. (BSc Econ). ACA 1988. With PricewaterhouseCoopers, 1985–88; Granada Gp plc: Hd Office Accountant, 1988–89; Gp Accounting Manager, 1989–91; Gp Financial Controller, 1991–94; Finance Dir, Spring Grove Services, 1994–96; Dir, Corporate Develt, 1996–98; Commercial Dir, Granada Media, 1998–99; Chief Financial Officer, Egg plc, 1999–2003; Exec. Vice Pres. and Chief Financial Officer, Burberry Group plc, 2004–13. Sen. Ind. Dir, FA, 2018–; non-executive Director: GlaxoSmithKline plc, 2011–16; Savills, 2018–. *Recreations:* cycling, tennis, travelling, eating out.

**CARTY, Hilary;** consultant, leadership, organisation development, cultural services and change, since 2011; Director, Clore Leadership Programme, since 2017; *b* 26 May 1962; *d* of Solomon Carty and Catherine (*née* Bailey). *Educ:* Leicester Poly. (BA Hons Performing Arts, 1983); Cultural Trng Centre, Jamaica (Cert. in Dance Educn, 1984); Univ. of Westminster (MBA 1994). Advanced Cert. in Coaching and Mentoring, CIPD, 2009; Cert. in Orgn Develt, Nat. Trng Labs Inst. of Applied Scis, Oxford, 2011. Community Arts Officer, Leics Expressive Arts, 1985; Community Arts Develt Officer, The Cave, Birmingham, 1985; Arts Officer (Dance and Mime), E Midlands Arts, 1986–90; Gen. Manager, Adzido Pan African Dance Ensemble, 1990–94; Dir of Dance, Arts Council, 1994–2003; Arts Council England: Dir, Performing Arts, 2003–06; on secondment as Dir, Culture and Educn, London 2012, 2004–06; Dir, London (Arts), 2006; Dir, Cultural Leadership Prog., 2006–11. Vis. Prof., Kufstein Tirol Univ. of Applied Scis, 2012, 2017. Fellow, Goldsmiths, Univ. of London, 2012. Hon. DA De Montfort, 2001; DUniv Middx, 2009; Hon. DLitt Westminster, 2014. *Publications:* Folk Dances of Jamaica, 1988. *Recreations:* theatre, dance, sports, walking.

**CARUANA, Hon. Sir Peter (Richard),** KCMG 2013; QC (Gibraltar) 1998; MP (GSD) Gibraltar, 1991–2015; Leader of the Opposition, Gibraltar, 2011–13; *b* 15 Oct. 1956; *s* of John Joseph Caruana and Maria Teresa Caruana (*née* Vasquez); *m* 1982, Cristina Maria Triay; three *s* three *d* (and one *s* decd). *Educ:* Ratcliffe Coll., Leicester; Queen Mary Coll., London Univ. (Hon. Fellow, 1997); Council of Legal Educn, London. Called to the Bar, Inner Temple, 1979, Overseas Bencher, 2011; with law firm Triay & Triay, Gibraltar, 1979–95, Partner specialising in commercial and shipping law, 1990–95. Joined GSD, 1990, Leader, 1991–2013; Leader of the Opposition, Gibraltar, 1992–96; Chief Minister of Gibraltar, 1996–2011. *Recreation:* golf. *Address:* 10/3 Irish Town, Gibraltar.

**CARUS, Roderick;** QC 1990; a Recorder, 1990–2016; *b* 4 June 1944; *s* of Anthony and Kathleen Carus; *m* 1972, Hilary Mary (*née* Jones); two *s* two *d*. *Educ:* Wirral GS, Merseyside; University Coll., Oxford (BA Law); Manchester Business Sch. (Postgrad. Diploma in Advanced Business Studies). Called to the Bar, Gray's Inn, 1971. Merchant bank, investments, 1966–70. Asst Recorder, 1987–90. *Recreations:* chess, crosswords, fishing, gardening, sailing. *Address:* Pant Farm, Bwlchtocyn, Pwllheli, Gwynedd LL53 7BY.

**CARUSO, Adam,** RA 2018; Partner, Caruso St John Architects, since 1990; *b* 8 Feb. 1962; *s* of Irving and Naomi Caruso; *m* 1996, Helen Thomas; one *s*. *Educ:* McGill Univ., Montreal (BSc Arch 1984; BArch 1986). ARB 1990; RIBA 1991. Architectural asst, Florian Beigel, 1986–87; Architect, Arup Associates, 1987–90. Projects include: New Art Gall. and Public Sq., Walsall, 1996; Gagosian Galls, phases 1 and 2, 1999–2001, phase 3, 2004; Barbican concert hall refurbishment, 2001; Stortorget, Kalmar, Sweden, 2003; Bethnal Green Mus. of Childhood, phase 1, 2003, phase 2, 2006; Brick House, London, 2005; Hallfield Sch., London, 2005; West Range Project, Downing Coll., Cambridge, 2006; Tate Britain Masterplan, 2006; Nottingham Contemporary, 2009; Chiswick Café, London, 2009; Newport Street Gall., Vauxhall, 2015 (RIBA Stirling Prize, 2016). Taught, Univ. of North London, 1990–98; Professor: Univ. of Bath, 2002–04; ETH Zurich, Switzerland, 2011– (Guest Prof., 2007–09). Guest Prof., Acad. of Architecture, Mendrisio, Switzerland, 1999–2001; Design Critic, Graduate Sch. of Design, Harvard Univ., 2005; Vis. Prof., Cities Prog., LSE, 2006–08. *Publications:* contributor to: New Art Gallery Walsall, 2002; Caruso St John Architects: knitting, weaving, wrapping, pressing, 2002; As Built: Caruso St John Architects, 2005; Almost Everything, 2008; Feeling of Things, 2008. *Address:* Caruso St John Architects, 1 Coate Street, E2 9AG. *T:* (020) 7613 3161, *Fax:* (020) 7729 6188. *E:* acaruso@carusostjohn.com.

**CARVEL, John Douglas;** journalist, The Guardian, 1973–2009; *b* 26 May 1947; *s* of late Robert Burns Carvel and Florence Annie Carvel (*née* Wilson); marr. diss.; two *s*; partner, Alison Hargreaves. *Educ:* Merchant Taylors' Sch., Northwood; Exeter Coll., Oxford (BA Hons PPE). Reporter, Newcastle Jl, 1969–72; The Guardian: Business Reporter, 1973–75; News Ed., Financial Guardian, 1975–76; Industrial Corresp., 1976–79; Dep. Features Ed., 1979–81; Local Govt Corresp., 1981–85; Political Corresp., 1985–89; Associate Ed., 1989–2009; Home Affairs Ed., 1989–92; Eur. Affairs Ed., 1992–95; Educn Ed., 1995–2000; Social Affairs Ed., 2000–09. Core Mem., NHS Nat. Leadership Council, 2009–11; Member: Quality Inf. Cttee, 2010–13, Inf. Governance Review, 2012–13, DoH; Healthwatch England Nat. Cttee, 2012–17 (Sen. Ind. Mem., 2014–17; Chair, Audit and Risk, 2016–17); Nat. Inf. Governance Cttee, 2013–15 (Dep. Chm., 2014–15); Ind. Inf. Governance Oversight Panel, 2013–15; Panel of Nat. Data Guardian for Health and Care, 2015–. Non-exec. Dir, Dorset HealthCare Univ. NHS Foundn Trust, 2017–. Commendation, British Press Awards, 1984 and 1990; Local Govt Journalist of Year, Local Govt Inf. Services, 1985; Legal Affairs Journalist of Year, Bar Council, 1991; Freedom of Information Award, Campaign for Freedom of Inf., 1995; Medical Journalist of the Year, BMA, 2004. *Publications:* Citizen Ken, 1984, 2nd edn 1986; An Account of the Guardian Case, in Openness and Transparency in the EU, ed V. Deckmyn and I. Thomson, 1998; Turn Again Livingstone, 1999. *Recreations:* golf, gardening. *Address:* 53 Charrington Street, NW1 1RD; The Shutters, Buckhorn Weston, Gillingham, Dorset SP8 5HF.

**CARVER, James Bruce;** Member for West Midlands, European Parliament, 2014–19 (UK Ind, 2014–18; Ind, 2018–19); *b* Farnborough, Kent, 15 Aug. 1969; *s* of late Joseph Carver and Judith Carver (*née* Dale); *m* 1st, 1998, Carmen Harding (*d* 2009); 2nd, 2014, Anne

Silcock (*née* Fanning). *Educ:* St John Rigby RC Comprehensive Sch., W Wickham; Orpington Coll. of Further Educn. Solicitors' clerk, Clemence, Turner & Henry, 1987–88; Post Office HQ (PR dept), 1988–89; Solicitors' clerk, Speechly Bircham, 1989–91; Proprietor, James Carver Umbrellas, 1991–. Member: UCW, 1988–89; UKIP, 1996–2018; Chm., Orpington UKIP, 1996–99. Contested (UK Ind): Orpington, 1997; Cheltenham, 2001; Preseli Pembrokeshire, 2005; Stourbridge, 2015; London, EP, 1999. Mem., European Parliamentarians with Africa, 2015–17. Mem., London Scottish Regtl Assoc., 1992. *Recreations:* my Jack Russell terrier, running, military history, Rugby Union, metal detecting. *E:* jamesbcarver@hotmail.com. *Club:* Royal Scots.

**CARVER, Margaret Adela Miriam;** Chairman, Racecourse Association, since 2015; Deputy Chair, Ofcom, since 2018; *b* Sutton-upon-Hull, 10 July 1964; *d* of Dr Ivan Hall and Elisabeth Hall; *m* 1992, William Carver; two *d. Educ:* Beverley High Sch.; St Edmund Hall, Oxford (MA Biochem. 1986). ARCM 1987. Investment banker (Banking, Equities, Corporate Finance), S. G. Warburg, 1987–91; Gp Corporate Affairs, MAI plc, 1991–95; Man. Dir, Channel Four Racing and Global Broadcasting, 1995–97; Man. Dir, Carver Care Gp, 2006–17. Chairman: ITN, 2009–14 (Dir, 2008–18); RaceTech Ltd, 2013–15; BBFC, 2016–19 (non-exec. Dir, 2009–19; Vice Chm., 2015–16); non-executive Director: Avenir Havas Media SA, 1991–93; SIS Hldgs Ltd (formerly Satellite Information Services Ltd), 1998–2008; SDN Ltd, 2000–05; Link Licensing Ltd, 2001; Sporting Index plc, 2001–03; Channel 5 Television, 2005; RDF Media plc, 2005–09; British Waterways, 2007–11; Eden Project, 2010–13; Services Sound and Vision Corp., 2013–18; Horse Racing Betting Levy Bd, 2015–19; British Horseracing Authy, 2019–. Mem., Adv. Council, Rehearsal Orch., 1997–. Trustee, One Voice Europe charity, 2006–13; Chm., Licoricia of Winchester Statue Appeal, 2017–. *Recreations:* music, flute playing, dance, art, architecture, the environment, athletics, horse racing. *Address:* c/o Racecourse Association, Winkfield Road, Ascot, Berks SL5 7HX.

**CARVER, Prof. Martin Oswald Hugh;** Professor of Archaeology, University of York, 1986–2008, now Emeritus; *b* 8 July 1941; *s* of John Hobart Carver and Jocelyn Louisa Grace Tweedie; *m* 1st, 1963, Carolyn Rose Haigh (marr. diss. 1978); one *s* one *d*; 2nd, 1981, Madeleine Rose Hummler; three *s* one *d. Educ:* Ladycross Sch., Seaford; Wellington Coll., Crowthorne; RMA, Sandhurst; Royal Military Coll., Shrivenham (BSc London); Univ. of Durham (Dip. Archaeol). Commnd RTR, 1961; Adjt, 4th RTR, 1969; retd in rank of Captain, 1972. Freelance archaeologist, researching and digging in England, Scotland, France and Italy, 1973–86; Founder Dir, Birmingham Univ. Field Archaeol. Unit, 1978–86; Dir, Centre for Medieval Studies, Univ. of York, 2001–02. Excavation campaigns: Durham, 1974; Shrewsbury, 1975; Stafford, 1975–83; Worcester, 1979–81; Casteseprio, Italy, 1980–82; Sutton Hoo, 1983–91; Achir, Algeria, 1992–93; Portmahomack, Scotland, 1994–2007; Castronovo, Sicily, 2014–. Lectures: Dalrymple, Glasgow, 1990; Univ. of New Mexico, 2003; RSAI, 2004; Merchant Adventurers Public Sci., York, 2005; Harvard Univ., 2006; Russian Acad. of Scis, 2007; Groam House, 2007; Medieval Europe, Paris, 2007; J. M. Kemble, Dublin, 2008; Jarrow, 2008; Internat. Soc. of Anglo-Saxonists, Helsinki 2001, Newfoundland 2009; Haskins, Boston, 2009; Rhind, Edinburgh, 2010; NRA, Dublin, 2011; World Heritage, Osaka, 2012; Pirenne, 2013; Midwest Archaeol. Congress, Ill, 2014; King Saud Univ., Riyadh, 2015; Frankfurt Univ., 2015; Edinburgh Book Fest., 2016; Tamworth Literary Fest., 2018; York Festival of Ideas, 2018; University of Venice Ca' Foscari, 2018. Ed., Antiquity, 2003–12. Presenter/writer: BBC 2 progs on Sutton Hoo, 1985–88; BBC Radio 3 progs on Anglo-Saxon Women, 2012. Director: W Midlands Rescue Archaeol. Cttee, 1975–78; Tarbat Discovery Prog., 1994–. Sec., Inst. Field Archaeologists, 1983–88; Chm., Field Archaeol. Specialists (FAS Heritage), 1998–; Vice-Pres., Soc. for Medieval Archaeology, 2010–. Dir, Sutton Hoo Res. Trust, 1983–. Corresp. Mem., Deutsches Archaeologisches Institut, 2002. FSA 1981 (Vice Pres., 2001–06); FSAScot 1994, Hon. FSAScot 2011. Open Prize, BAAS, 2004; Best Project, British Archaeol Awards, 2010; European Heritage Prize, European Assoc. of Archaeologists, 2015; European Res. Council Advanced Grant for Sicily in Transition, 2016. *Publications:* (ed) Medieval Worcester, 1980; (ed) Two Town Houses in Medieval Shrewsbury, 1983; Underneath English Towns, 1987; (ed) Prehistory in Lowland Shropshire, 1991; (ed) The Age of Sutton Hoo, 1992; (ed) In Search of Cult, 1993; Arguments in Stone, 1993; Sutton Hoo: burial ground of Kings?, 1998; Surviving in Symbols: a visit to the Pictish nation, 1999; (ed) The Cross Goes North, 2003; Archaeological Value and Evaluation, 2003; Sutton Hoo: a seventh century princely burial ground and its context, 2005; Portmahomack: monastery of the Picts, 2008, 2nd edn 2016; (with C. Hills and J. Scheschkewitz) Wasperton: a Roman, British and Anglo-Saxon community in central England, 2009; Archaeological Investigation, 2009; The Birth of a Borough, 2010; (ed jtly) Signals of Belief in Early England, 2010; Making Archaeology Happen, 2011; (ed with Jan Klapste) The Archaeology of Medieval Europe, Twelfth to Sixteenth Century, 2011; (ed jtly) Field Archaeology from Around the World: ideas and approaches, 2015; (jtly) Portmahomack on Tarbat Ness: changing ideologies in North-East Scotland, sixth to sixteenth century, 2016; The Sutton Hoo Story: encounters with Early England, 2017; Formative Britain: an archaeology of Britain, fifth to eleventh century AD, 2019; numerous contribs to archaeol jls and magazines. *Recreation:* playing the flute. *Address:* Ella House, Ellerton, York YO42 4PB. *E:* martin.carver@york.ac.uk. *W:* martincarver.com.

**CARVILL, Patrick,** CB 1994; Permanent Secretary, Department of Finance and Personnel, Northern Ireland, 1998–2003; *b* 13 Oct. 1943; *s* of Bernard and Susan Carvill; *m* 1965, Vera Abbott; two *s. Educ:* St Mary's Christian Brothers Grammar School, Belfast; Queen's Univ., Belfast (BA Hons). Min. of Fuel and Power, Westminster, 1965; Min. of Development, Stormont, 1967; Min. of Community Relations, 1969; Asst Sec., Dept of Educn, 1975–83; Under-Secretary: Dept of Finance and Personnel, 1983–88; Dept of Econ. Develt, 1988–89; Dept of Finance and Personnel, 1989–90; Perm. Sec., Dept of Educn for NI, 1990–98. Comr, S Eastern Educn and Libraries Bd, NI, 2006–15; Mem. Bd, NI Libraries Authy, 2009–14. Chm., NI Clinical Excellence Awards Cttee, until 2014. Trustee, Nat. Museums of NI, 2009–13. *Recreations:* reading, hill-walking, diving.

**CARWARDINE, Mark;** freelance zoologist and environmentalist, since 1986; *b* Luton, 9 March 1959; *s* of David and Betty Carwardine; partner, Debra Taylor. *Educ:* Queen Mary's Coll., Basingstoke; Bedford Coll., London Univ. (BSc Hons Zool. 1979). Conservation Officer, WWF, UK, 1979–86. Consultant, World Conservation Union, Switzerland, 1986–90. Co-founder, wildlife tour cos, Discover the World, Wild Oceans and Ocean Wanderers. Presenter: radio progs incl. Nature, BBC Radio 4, 1997–2003; TV series incl. (with Stephen Fry) Last Chance to See, 2009–10, Museum of Life, 2010; columnist, BBC Wildlife mag., 2004– (Mem., Adv. Bd); Science Writer, UNEP, Kenya. Editl Advr, Good Book Guide; Contributing Ed., Wanderlust mag. Chair, BBC Wildlife Photographer of Year competition, 2005–11. Sen. Consultant, Whale and Dolphin Conservation; Vice-President: Wildfowl & Wetlands Trust; Avon Wildlife Trust; Vice-Pres. and Conservation Advr, David Shepherd Wildlife Foundn; Mem. Council, World Land Trust. Patron: ORCA; Save the Rhino. *Publications:* over 50 books, including: (with J. Craven) Wildlife in the News, 1990; (with D. Adams) Last Chance to See, 1990, 3rd edn 2009; Whales, Dolphins and Porpoises, 1995, 2nd edn 2000; Animal Records, 1995, 4th edn 2013; The Shark Watcher's Handbook, 2002; Shark, 2004; Last Chance to See: following in Douglas Adams' footsteps, 2009; Mark Carwardine's Ultimate Wildlife Experiences, 2011; Mark Carwardine's Guide to Whale Watching in Britain and Europe, 2nd edn 2016; Mark Carwardine's Guide to Whale Watching in North America, 2017. *Recreations:* family and friends, swimming, photography, Rugby, comedy, reading, astronomy, polar exploration, scuba diving, sleeping in own bed (i.e. not travelling). *Address:* c/o Rachel Ashton, 5 Chesterfield Road, Bristol BS6 5DN. *T:* (0117) 904 8934. *E:* rachel@markcarwardine.com.

**CARWARDINE, Prof. Richard John,** CMG 2019; DPhil; FBA 2006; FRHistS, FLSW; President, Corpus Christi College, Oxford, 2010–16; *b* 12 Jan. 1947; *s* of John Francis Carwardine and Beryl Carwardine (*née* Jones); *m* 1975, Dr Linda Margaret Kirk. *Educ:* Monmouth Sch.; Corpus Christi Coll., Oxford (BA 1968, MA 1972; Hon. Fellow, 2016); Queen's Coll., Oxford (Ochs-Oakes Sen. Schol.; DPhil 1976; Hon. Fellow 2010). FRHistS 1983. University of Sheffield: Lectr in American Hist., 1971–90; Sen. Lectr, 1990–94; Reader in Hist., 1994; Prof. of Hist., 1994–2002; Dean, Faculty of Arts, 1999–2001; University of Oxford: Rhodes Prof. of Amer. Hist. and Fellow, St Catherine's Coll., 2002–09; Pro Vice Chancellor, 2012–16. Vis. Asst Prof., Syracuse Univ., 1974–75; Fulbright-ACLS Res. Fellow, Univ. of NC, Chapel Hill, 1989; Stewart Fellow in Religion, Princeton Univ., 2011; Vis. Fellow, Henry E. Huntington Liby, 2014, 2018. Lectures: Birkbeck, Trinity Coll., Cambridge, 2004; Stenton, Univ. of Reading, 2004; Harry Allen, Univ. of London, 2006; Burns, Univ. of Richmond, 2008; Ramsey Murray, Selwyn Coll., Cambridge, 2010; Watson, Sulgrave Manor and BL, 2013; Roger Anstey, Univ. of Kent, 2015; Dist. Lectr, Orgn of American Historians, 2006–. Mem., Adv. Bd, Lincoln Studies Center, Knox Coll., Ill, 2009–. Editl advr, BBC Hist., 2000–; Member, Editorial Board: Jl Amer. Studies, 1984–88; Jl Ecclesiastical Hist., 1991–; Amer. Nineteenth Century Hist., 2000–18. Founding Mem. Council for the Defence of British Univs., 2012. Trustee, Monmouth Sch. Charitable Trust, 2013–. Elected Laureate, Lincoln Acad. of Illinois, 2009. Founding FLSW 2010. Mem., Pilgrims' Soc. of GB, 2009–. Governor: Wakefield GS Foundn, 1988–95; Manchester Grammar Sch., 2010–16; Monmouth Sch., 2017–. Freeman, Haberdashers' Co., 2011. Hon. Fellow, St Catherine's Coll., Oxford, 2009. Hon. DLitt Sheffield, 2015; Washington and Jefferson Coll., 2018. Arthur Miller Amer. Studies Prize, British Assoc. for American Studies/UEA, 1997. *Publications:* Transatlantic Revivalism: popular evangelicalism in Britain and America 1790–1865, 1978; Evangelicals and Politics in Antebellum America, 1993; Lincoln, 2003 (Lincoln Prize, 2004); Lincoln: a life of purpose and power, 2006; The Global Lincoln, 2011; Lincoln's Sense of Humor, 2017 (Abraham Lincoln Inst. Book Prize, 2018); contrib. numerous articles and essays to learned jls, incl. Jl Amer. Hist., Jl Amer. Studies, Church Hist., Jl Ecclesiastical Hist. *Recreations:* acting, theatre-going. *E:* richard.carwardine@ccc.ox.ac.uk.

**CARWOOD, Andrew;** tenor; conductor; Director of Music, St Paul's Cathedral, since 2007; Artistic Director, The Cardinall's Musick, since 1989; *b* 30 April 1965; *s* of Thomas George Carwood and Daisy Ninnes. *Educ:* John Lyon Sch., Harrow; St John's Coll., Cambridge. Lay Clerk: Christ Ch, Oxford, 1987–90; Westminster Cathedral, 1990–95; Dir of Music, Brompton Oratory, 1995–2000. Director: Edington Fest., 1992–97; Edington Schola Cantorum, 1998–2010; Jt Prin. Guest Conductor, BBC Singers, 2007–10. Has made numerous recordings as singer and as conductor. FRSCM 2016 (ARSCM 2005). Hon. Fellow Royal Acad. of St Cecilia, 2003. *Recreations:* theatre, British comedy. *E:* directorofmusic@stpaulscathedral.org.uk.

**CARY,** family name of **Viscount Falkland.**

**CARY, Anthony Joyce,** CMG 1997; HM Diplomatic Service, retired; High Commissioner to Canada, 2007–10; *b* 1 July 1951; *s* of Sir Michael Cary, GCB and Isabel Cary; *m* 1975, Clare Elworthy; three *s* one *d. Educ:* Eton; Trinity Coll., Oxford (MA English); Stanford Business Sch. (MBA). Joined FCO, 1973: BMG Berlin, 1974–77; Policy Planning Staff, FCO, 1977–80; Harkness Fellow, Stanford Business Sch., 1980–82; EC Dept, FCO, 1982–84; Private Sec. to Minister of State, FCO, 1984–86; Head of Chancery, Kuala Lumpur, 1986–88; on loan to Cabinet of Sir Leon Brittan, EC, Brussels, 1989–92; Head of EU Dept (Internal), FCO, 1993–96; Counsellor, Washington, 1997–99; on loan as Chef de Cabinet to Rt Hon. Christopher Patten, Mem. of EC, 1999–2003; Ambassador, Sweden, 2003–06. Exec. Dir, Queen's-Blyth Worldwide, 2011–13. UK Commonwealth Scholarship Comr, 2011–18. Mem. Jury, Cundill Hist. Prize, 2011, 2013, 2015. Hon. Pres., Canada-UK Council (formerly Canada-UK Colloquia), 2011– (Chm.). *Address:* The Old Vicarage, 97A Knatchbull Road, SE5 9QU.

**CARY, Dr Nathaniel Roger Blair,** FRCPath; Consultant Forensic Pathologist, Home Office Registered, since 1992; Founder Member, Forensic Pathology Services, since 2001; *b* 13 Nov. 1957; 2nd *s* of Sir Roger Hugh Cary, 2nd Bt; *m* 1st, 1978, Tesney Diane Vera Partington (marr. diss. 1994); two *s* one *d*; 2nd, 1994, Sally Ann Taylor; one *d. Educ:* St Paul's Sch., London (Foundn Schol.); Trinity Coll., Oxford (Open Schol.; MA 1982); Charing Cross Hosp. Med. Sch. (MB BS 1981; MD 1992). DMJ 1992; FRCPath 1997. Hse physician and hse surgeon, 1981–82, trainee pathologist, 1982–85, Charing Cross Hosp.; Charing Cross Trustees Res. Fellow, 1985–86; Lectr in Histopathol., Charing Cross and Westminster Med. Sch., 1986–89; Consultant Cardiac Histopathologist, Papworth Hosp., Cambs, 1989–98; Sen. Lectr in Forensic Medicine, 1998–2001, Dir, Guy's Campus, 1999–2001, GKT. Chm., Specialty Adv. Cttee on Forensic Pathol., RCPath, 2014–. Pres., British Assoc. in Forensic Med., 2010–12. *Publications:* contrib. chapters in books on pathology, and papers to med. scientific literature, mainly relating to heart pathol., incl. transplantation. *Recreations:* walking (uphill), ski-ing (downhill). *Address:* Forensic Pathology Services, Unit 12, The Quadrangle, Grove Technology Park, Wantage, Oxon OX12 9FA. *T:* (01235) 773332. *Club:* Royal Society of Medicine.

**CARY, Sir Nicolas (Robert Hugh),** 3rd Bt *cr* 1955, of Withington, co. Lancaster; FCIHT; Founder and Director, Waysphere Transport Intelligence, since 2017; *b* 17 April 1955; *er s* of Sir Roger Hugh Cary, 2nd Bt, and Ann Helen Katharine, *e d* of Hugh Blair Brenan, OBE; *S* father, 2011, but his name does not appear on the Official Roll of the Baronetage; *m* 1st, 1979, Pauline Jean (marr. diss. 1991), *d* of Dr Thomas Ian Boyd; three *s*; 2nd, 1994, Lesley Anne Gilham, one *s* one *d. Educ:* St Paul's Sch.; University Coll. London (BA). Technical Partner, Cary Digital LLP, 2008–14; Central Office of Information, 2008–12; Cabinet Office, 2012–14; Hd of Digital Transformation, 2014–16, Hd of Data Policy, 2016–17, DfT. FRSA. *Recreations:* walking, cooking, creative writing. *Heir: s* Alexander Robert Cary, *b* 27 Nov. 1981. *Address:* Westgate, 7 Lansdowne Road, Chesham, Bucks HP5 2BA.

**CASADEI, Prof. Barbara,** MD; DPhil; FRCP, FMedSci, FESC; British Heart Foundation Professor of Cardiovascular Medicine, University of Oxford, since 2013; Fellow, Wolfson College, Oxford, since 2013; Hon. Consultant Cardiologist, John Radcliffe Hospital, Oxford, since 1995; *b* Italy, 6 Nov. 1959; *d* of Urbano Casadei and Adriana Gori; *m*; one *d. Educ:* Univ. of Pavia, Italy (MD 1984); Pembroke Coll., Oxford (DPhil 1995). FRCP 2001. Joan and Richard Doll Fellow, Green Coll., Oxford, 1991–94; Sen. Fellow, BHF, 2001–12; Reader, 2002–06, Prof. of Cardiovascular Medicine, 2006–12, Univ. of Oxford. Pres., Eur. Soc. of Cardiol., 2018– (Vice Pres. for Scientific Affairs and Res., 2014–16). FESC 1997; FMedSci 2013; FAHA 2018. *Recreations:* Baroque music, snorkelling. *Address:* Division of Cardiovascular Medicine, Radcliffe Department of Medicine, L6, West Wing, John Radcliffe Hospital, Oxford OX3 9DU. *T:* (01865) 234664. *E:* barbara.casadei@cardiov.ox.ac.uk.

**CASALE, Roger Mark;** Founder and Chief Executive Officer, New Europeans, since 2013; *m* 1997, Fernanda Miucci; two *d*. *Educ:* King's Coll. Sch., Wimbledon; Hurstpierpoint Coll., Sussex (Scholar); Brasenose Coll., Oxford (BA Hons); Bologna Centre, Johns Hopkins Univ. (MA). Head, trng inst., Germany, 1986–92; Univ. teacher, LSE and Greenwich Univ., 1994–97. MP (Lab) Wimbledon, 1997–2005; contested (Lab) same seat, 2005. PPS, FCO, 2002–05. Mem., Select Cttee on Eur. Legislation, 1997–2002; Chm., All Party British-Italian Gp, 1998–2005; Hon. Sec., PLP Foreign Affairs Cttee, 1999–2002. Sen. Political Advr, Finmeccanica, 2005–14. Vice-Pres., Europe's People's Forum (Belgium), 2016–. Chm., The Portofino Dialogues, 2004–08. Hon. Pres., London and SE Direct Aid to Kosovo, 1998–2005. Governor, Wimbledon Sch. of Art, 1999–2004. Comdr, Order of Merit (Italy), 2011. Future of Britain Award, FT, 2017; People's Choice Award, Sheila McKechnie Foundn, 2017. *Recreations:* Italy, European history, opera, art.

**CASALE, Dr Silvia Suzen Giovanna,** CMG 2010; independent consultant in criminal justice and human rights, since 1984; *b* Amersham, 15 Feb. 1945; *d* of Tanga Casale and Ida Narduzzo; *m* 1974, Jerrold Katzman; one *d*. *Educ:* Haberdashers' Aske's Sch., Middx; St Hilda's Coll., Oxford (MA Mod. Langs); Univ. of Pennsylvania (MA Internat. Relns); Yale Univ. (MPhil Pol Sci.; PhD Criminol. 1978). Project Res. Dir, Vera Inst. of Justice, NY, 1977–80; Project Dir, Vera Inst. of Justice, London, 1980–83. Mem., Parole Bd England and Wales, 1987–90. UK Mem., Cttee for Prevention of Torture, Council of Europe, 1997–2009 (Pres., 2000–07); Chair: UN Subcttee on Prevention of Torture, 2007–09; Advr to Eur. Nat. Preventive Mechanism Proj., Council of Europe, 2009–12; Mem., Internat. Contact Gp for peace initiative in Basque Country, 2010–; Chair, Nat. Preventive Mechanisms Observatory, 2016–. Sentence Rev. Comr (NI), 1998–2012; Leader, Ind. Rev. of IPCC investigation into death of Sean Rigg, 2012–13 (report, 2013): Member: Daniel Morgan Ind. Panel, 2013–; Hillsborough Article 2 Reference Gp., 2013–. Trustee: Prison Advice and Care Trust, 1993–2012; Prison Reform Trust, 1994–2013; Patron, Unlock. Hon. LLD Glasgow, 2013. *Publications:* Fines in Europe, 1981; The Fine Process: the use of fines as a criminal sanction in English Magistrates' Courts, 1983; Minimum Standards for Prison Establishments, 1984; Female Remands in Custody, 1988; Minimum Standards in Prisons: a programme of change, 1989; Women Inside: the experience of women remand prisoners, 1989; Regimes for Remand Prisoners, 1990; London Prisons Community Links: a feasibility study, 1991; (ed with E. Stockdale) Criminal Justice Under Stress, 1992; (ed) HIV and Custody, 1995; contrib. articles to law and internat. jls. *Recreations:* learning languages, gardening, brass rubbing, tea with friends.

**CASE, Anthea Fiendley, (Mrs D. C. Case),** CBE 2003; Principal Adviser, Arcadia, since 2006; *b* 7 Feb. 1945; *d* of late Thomas Fiendley Stones and Bess Stones (*née* Mackie); *m* 1967, David Charles Case; one *d* (and one *d* decd). *Educ:* Christ's Hospital, Hertford; St Anne's Coll., Oxford (BA). HM Treasury: Asst Principal, 1966–70; Private Sec. to Financial Sec., 1970–71; Principal, 1971–79; Asst Sec., 1980–88; Under Sec., 1988–95 (with Fiscal Policy Gp, 1993–95); Asst Dir, Budget & Public Finances Directorate, 1995; Dir, Nat. Heritage Meml Fund (Heritage Lottery Fund), 1995–2003. Chm., Heritage Link, 2003–09. Member: Bd, Living Place (Regl Cultural Consortium), 2003–09; East of England Regl Assembly, 2003–07; NT East of England Regl Adv. Bd (formerly NT East of England Regl Cttee), 2003–15 (Chm., 2009–15); Comr, CABE, 2004–11. Trustee: Lakeland Arts Trust, 2003–; Norwich Heritage and Econ. Regeneration Trust, 2005–17 (Chm., 2015–17); Inst. for Philanthropy, 2007–14; Wende Mus. of the Cold War, LA, 2010–; Norfolk and Norwich Fest. Trust, 2011–. Chm., Coalition for Efficiency, 2010–12. *Address:* Arcadia, 6th Floor, 5 Young Street, W8 5EH. *T:* (020) 7361 4900.

**CASE, Christopher John;** Assistant Fire Chief, Chatham-Kent Fire and Emergency Services, Ontario, since 2016; *b* St Helens, Lancs, 2 Feb. 1970; *s* of David John and Catherine Case; *m* 2001, Michele Amanda; one *s* three *d*. *Educ:* Cowley High Sch.; Univ. of Bedfordshire (MSc Mgt). Merseyside Fire and Rescue Service: Gp Manager, Threat Response, 2005–09; Community Protection Manager, 2009–11; St Helens Dist Manager, 2011–12; Gp Manager, St Helens Dist, 2011–15; Hd of Logistics and Engrg, 2015–16. Director: Blackpowder Ltd, 2002–; Royal Armouries Trading and Enterprise, 2010–16. Vis. Fellow, Glasgow Univ., 2010. Vice Pres., IExpE, 2010. Trustee, Royal Armouries, 2008–16. CLJ 2012. *Recreations:* holidays, reading, pyrotechnics and explosives research. *Address:* Chatham-Kent Fire and Emergency Services, 5 Second Street, Chatham, ON N7M 5X2, Canada.

**CASE, Her Honour Janet Ruth;** a Circuit Judge, 2001–13; *b* 29 June 1943; *d* of James and Cathleen Simpson; *m* 1965, Jeremy David Michael Case (marr. diss. 1982); one *s* one *d*. *Educ:* Univ. of Durham (LLB 1965). Called to the Bar, Inner Temple, 1975; barrister, Wales and Chester Circuit, 1975–2001; Chm., Med. Appeals Tribunals, 1988–96; an Asst Recorder, 1992–95; a Recorder, 1995–2001; Designated Family Judge for Newport, S Wales, 2001–05. Chm., Mental Health Review Tribunals, 2006–13. Treas., UK Assoc. of Women Judges, 2007–12. *Recreations:* gardening, opera, travel. *Address:* Croeswylan, Morda Road, Oswestry, Shropshire SY11 2AL. *Club:* Lansdowne.

**CASE, Richard Ian,** CBE 2002; DL; FREng, FRAeS; Chairman, WFEL (formerly William Fairey Engineering Ltd), 2007–12; consultant to aerospace industry, 2005–12; *b* 14 June 1945; *m* 1975, Denise Margaret Mills; one *s* one *d*. *Educ:* Cranfield Inst. of Technology (MSc Aircraft Propulsion). FRAeS 1985; FREng (FEng 1993). Technical Manager, Arab British Helicopters, Egypt, 1978–82; Westland Helicopters Ltd: Chief Designer, 1982–85; Engrg Dir, 1985–88; EH101 Project Dir and Engrg Dir, 1988–92; Man. Dir, 1992–95; Chief Exec., GKN Westland Helicopters Ltd, 1995–2001; Man. Dir, AgustaWestland, 2001–05; Chm., Westland Helicopters, 2001–04. Non-exec. Dir, FKI plc, 2007–08. DL Somerset, 2005. RAeS Gold Medal, 1998. Cavaliere dell 'Ordine al Merito (Italy), 1995. *Recreations:* golf, opera.

**CASE, Dr Simon,** CVO 2017; Private Secretary to the Duke of Cambridge, since 2018; *b* Bristol, 27 Dec. 1978; *s* of Francis Gordon and Kaye Case; *m* 2007, Elizabeth Mary Kate Kistruck; three *d*. *Educ:* Bristol Grammar Sch.; Trinity Coll., Cambridge (BA 2002); Queen Mary, Univ. of London (PhD 2007). Policy Advr, MoD, 2006–07; Sen. Policy Advr, Cabinet Office, 2007–09; Deputy Director: Nat. Security Secretariat, Cabinet Office, 2010; NI Office, 2010–12; Hd, Olympics Secretariat, Cabinet Office, 2012; Private Sec., 2012–13, Dep. Principal Private Sec., 2014, to the Prime Minister; Exec. Dir, Implementation Unit, Cabinet Office, 2014–15; Dir, Strategic Policy, GCHQ, 2015–16; Principal Private Sec. to the Prime Minister, 2016–17; Dir Gen. for UK-EU Partnership, UK Repn to the EU, 2017–18. Vis. Prof., KCL, 2018– (Vis. Fellow, 2015). Mem., Strand Gp, 2015–. *Recreations:* cycling, rowing, running, swimming, amateur historian. *Address:* Kensington Palace, Kensington Gardens, W8 4PX. *Clubs:* Garrick, Hawks's.

**CASE, Stephen M.;** Chairman and Chief Executive Officer, Revolution LLC, since 2005; *b* Honolulu, 21 Aug. 1958; *s* of Dan and Carol Case; *m* 1st, 1985, Joanne (marr. diss.); three *d*; 2nd, Jean; two *c*. *Educ:* Punahou Sch., Honolulu; Williams Coll., Mass. (BA Pol Sci. 1980). Marketing Dept, Procter & Gamble, 1980–82; Manager, new pizza develt, Pizza Hut Div., PepsiCo, 1982–83; joined Control Video Corp., 1983, as mktg asst; co. renamed Quantum Computer Services, 1985, and became America Online, (AOL), 1991; CEO, 1991–2001, and Chm., 1995–2001, when merged with Time Warner; Chm., Time Warner Inc., 2001–03; Chm., Exclusive Resorts, 2004–07. Founder and Chm., Case Foundation, 1997–. *Address:* Case Foundation, Seventh Floor, 1717 Rhode Island Avenue NW, Washington, DC 20036, USA.

**CASEBOURNE, Michael Victor,** CEng, FICE, FASCE; private consultant; Project Director, Crossrail C610, Alstom TSO Costain Joint Venture, 2012–14; *b* 7 Oct. 1945; *s* of Eric Thomas Casebourne and Marjorie May Casebourne (*née* Chapman); *m* 1972, Margaret Dunlop (*d* 2002); one *s* one *d*. *Educ:* Harrow Co. Grammar Sch.; Nottingham Univ. (BSc). CEng 1967; FICE 1984. With Costain Civil Engrg, 1967–73; Trafalgar House Construction, 1973–90 (Dir, 1984–90); Managing Director: Wimpey Engrg & Construction UK, 1990–96; GT Railway Maintenance, 1996–99; Dir, Railtrack, 2001–02; Project Director: Nottingham Tram, 2003–04; ACTJV (Alstom and Carillion) Channel Tunnel Rail Link, 2004–06; Project Dir, BBCJV (Balfour Beatty Carillion) London Overground E London Line, 2006–12. Chief Exec. and Sec., ICE, 1999–2001. FASCE. *Recreations:* sailing, motor boating.

**CASEBY, Richard David;** Director, Caseman Communications, since 2019; *b* St Annes-on-Sea, 30 July 1960; *s* of late Donald Brown Caseby and Joan Caseby; *m* 1986, Joanna Winter; one *s* two *d*. *Educ:* King Edward VII Sch., Lytham St Annes; Durham Univ. (BA Hons Eng. Lang. and Lit.). Trainee reporter, Westmorland Gazette, 1983–84; reporter: Oxford Mail and Times, 1985–86; Daily Mail, 1986–89; Sunday Times: reporter, 1989; Asst News Ed., 1990; Dep. Focus Ed., 1991; Dep. Foreign Ed., 1992–94; Focus Ed., 1994–96; Man. Ed. (News), 1996–98; Man. Ed., 1998–2011; non-exec. Dir, Times Newspapers Hldgs Ltd, 1998–2010; Man. Ed., The Sun, 2011–13; Dir of Communications, DWP, 2014–18; Dir, Strategic Communications, Internat. Projects, PM's Office and Cabinet Office, 2016–18; Partner, Consulum, 2018–19. Co-Founder, Sunday Times Best Companies to Work For, 2000. *Publications:* The Opium Eating Editor: Thomas de Quincey, 1985. *Recreations:* cycling, sea swimming, walking the dogs, 20th century art.

**CASELLI, Prof. Francesco,** PhD; FBA 2010; Norman Sosnow Chair in Economics, London School of Economics and Political Science, since 2012 (Professor of Economics, 2004–12); *b* Trieste, 14 Oct. 1966; *s* of Giovanni Caselli and Maria Teresa Marozzi; *m* 2003, Silvana Tenreyro; two *s*. *Educ:* Univ. of Bologna (Laurea 1991); Harvard Univ. (PhD 1997). Asst Prof. of Econs, Univ. of Chicago, 1997–2000; Associate Prof. of Econs, Harvard Univ., 2000–04. Man. Ed., Rev. of Econ. Studies, 2010–14. *Publications:* contrib. articles to jls incl. Amer. Econ. Rev., Jl Political Econ., Qly Jl Econs.

**CASELLI, Silvana;** see Tenreyro, S.

**CASELY-HAYFORD, Augustus,** OBE 2018; PhD; broadcaster and art historian; Director, National Museum of African Art, Smithsonian, since 2018; *b* London, 25 May 1964; *s* of Victor and Ransolina Casely-Hayford; partner, Sarah Wason; one *d*. *Educ:* Sch. of Oriental and African Studies, Univ. of London (PhD African Hist. 1992). Freelance lectr and arts mgt consultant, 1992–2003; Director: Africa 05, British Mus., 2003–05; Inst. of Internat. Visual Arts, 2006; Exec. Dir, Arts Strategy, Arts Council England, 2007. Presenter, TV programmes: State of the Art, 2009; Lost Kingdoms of Africa, 2009; History of British Art, 2009; Where Is Modern Art Now?, 2009; The Miracle of British Art, 2010; Lost Kingdoms of Africa (series), 2011, 2012; Tate Britain's Great British Walks (series), 2017; Panellist, Big Art Project, 2009. Mem. Council, Tate Britain, 2007–; Exec. Dir, Zamyn, 2008–10; Trustee, NPG, 2008–18. *Publications:* (contrib.) Peoples and Empire in Africa, 1992; (contrib.) Tam Tam to Internet, 1998; (contrib.) Cultural Politics in a Global Age, 2008; The Lost Kingdoms of Africa, 2012; (with J. Topp Fargion) West Africa: word, symbol, song, 2015; catalogues for Mah Rana and Magdalene Odundo; contribs to History Workshop Jl, Jl of Museum Ethnography, Crafts, Internat. Jl of Art and Design Educn, London Mag. *Recreations:* watercolours, photography. *E:* augustus@runbox.com.

**CASELY-HAYFORD, Margaret Henrietta Augusta, (Mrs G. T. Quarme),** CBE 2018; Chair, Shakespeare's Globe, since 2018; *b* London; *d* of Victor Ward and Ransolina Casely-Hayford; *m* 1986, Giles Thomas Quarme, *qv*; one *d*. *Educ:* Somerville Coll., Oxford (BA Hons Juris. 1982). Called to the Bar, Gray's Inn, 1983; in practice as barrister, 1984–86; admitted as solicitor, 1987; solicitor, 1987–94 and 1996–2006, Partner, 1998–2006, Denton Wilde Sapte; solicitor, Berwin Leighton Paisner, 1994–95; Gen. Counsel, Dir of Legal Services and Co. Sec., John Lewis Partnership plc, 2006–14. Non-executive Director: British Retail Consortium, 2010–14; NHS England, 2012–16; Co-operative Gp, 2016–. Chair, ActionAid UK, 2014–18. Mem., Tailored Rev. Challenge Panel, British Council, 2018. Special Trustee, Gt Ormond St Hosp. Charity, 2000–07; Trustee: Geffrye Mus., 2007; Radcliffe Trust, 2016–. Chair, Diversity and Inclusivity Rev., CILIP Carnegie Greenaway Bk Awards, 2017–18. Chancellor, Coventry Univ., 2017–. Freeman, City of London, 1998. *Publications:* Practical Planning: permission and the application, 1995; (contrib.) Sustaining Architecture, 2001; contribs to jls incl. Estates Gazette, Bldg Design, Planning, Leisure and Hospitality Business. *Recreations:* the perpetual combat with nature that is gardening, friends, film, theatre, opera, family, an unequal struggle with the 'cello continues.

See also A. Casely-Hayford.

**CASEMENT, David John;** QC 2008; a Recorder, since 2005; Deputy High Court Judge, Queen's Bench Division and Chancery Division, since 2013; *b* Belfast, 19 Nov. 1969; *s* of late John Casement and of Helena Casement; *m* 1994, Ruth Ann Hadden; two *d*. *Educ:* Methodist Coll., Belfast; St Hugh's Coll., Oxford (MA). Called to the Bar: Middle Temple, 1992 (Astbury Schol.); Ireland, 1996; NI, 2007; in practice as barrister specialising in chancery and commercial litigation. Accredited Mediator 2007. Chairperson's List, Sport Resolutions, 2010–; Legal Chairperson: Nat. Anti-Doping Panel, 2011–; Judicial Panel, FA, 2015–. Chm., Northern Circuit Commercial Bar Assoc., 2013–14; Jt Chm., British Irish Commercial Bar Assoc., 2013–16. Pres., Oxford Univ. Law Soc., 1990. Exec. Bd, Anglo-Irish Encounter, 2000–06. *Address:* Kings Chambers, 36 Young Street, Manchester M3 3FT. *T:* (0161) 832 9082; Serle Court, 6 New Square, Lincoln's Inn, WC2A 3QS. *T:* (020) 7242 6105.

**CASEY, Aidan Patrick;** QC 2016; *b* Hayes, Hillingdon, 14 Feb. 1969; *s* of Desmond Casey and Susan Casey; *m* 1992, Anne Serdan; one *d*. *Educ:* St Edmund's Coll., Herts; King's Coll. London (LLB Hons 1991). Called to the Bar, Gray's Inn, 1992; in practice as barrister, specialising in commercial/chancery and civil fraud, 1992–, 3 Hare Court, 1993–. Non-exec. Dir, mporium Gp plc, 2016–. *Recreations:* family, squash, fishing, paddle board, ornithology, wine. *Address:* 3 Hare Court, Temple, EC4Y 7BJ. *T:* (020) 7415 7800, *Fax:* (020) 7415 7811. *E:* clerks@3harecourt.com. *Club:* 67 Pall Mall.

**CASEY, Aprampar Apar Jot Kaur, (Joti);** see Bopa Rai, A. A. J. K.

**CASEY, Ben;** see Casey, R. B.

**CASEY, Derek Grant**; international consultant; Chairman, World Leisure Organisation, 2004–13, now Emeritus (Executive Member, 2002–13); *b* 19 Feb. 1950; *s* of Andrew Casey and Jean Grant. *Educ*: St Aloysius' Coll., Glasgow; Univ. of Glasgow (MA Hons). Dir of Ops, Scottish Sports Council, 1979–88; GB Sports Council: Dir of Nat. Services, 1988–93; Chief Exec., 1993–96; Chief Exec., English Sports Council, subseq. Sport England, 1997–2001. Chairman: Cttee for Development of Sport, Council of Europe, 1993–95; UK Youth, 2003–10. Bid Dir for Glasgow, 2014 Commonwealth Games, 2006–07; Interim Chief Exec., Glasgow 2014 Commonwealth Games, 2007–08. Pres., Youth Scotland, 2012–. Sen. Fellow, Amer. Leisure Acad., 2008. Hon. Res. Fellow, Univ. of Stirling, 2003–. Hon. DSc Southampton, 1996; DUniv Strathclyde, 2009; DUniv Stirling, 2010. *Publications*: contribs on sport, recreation and physical activity, to jls and periodicals. *Recreations*: walking, theatre, American literature. *Address*: 42/5 Barnton Park Avenue, Edinburgh EH4 6EY.

**CASEY, Gavin Frank**, FCA; Chief Executive, London Stock Exchange, 1996–2000; Chairman: EDM Group Ltd, 2004–11; VSA Capital Group plc, 2012–15; *b* 18 Oct. 1946; *s* of Frank Frederick Casey and Diana Casey; *m* 1970, Lesley Riding; two *s* one *d*. Chartered Accountant, 1970; Harmood Banner & Co., 1965–70; Coopers & Lybrand, 1970–71; County Bank, later County NatWest, 1972–89; Smith New Court, later Merrill Lynch International, 1989–96; Dep. Chm., Corporate Finance Adv. Bd, PricewaterhouseCoopers, 2001–05. Chairman: Tragus Hldgs Ltd, 2002–05; Integrated Dental Hldgs Ltd, 2006–08; Director: Lawrence plc, 2002–07; VTB Bank Europe plc (formerly Moscow Narodny Bank Ltd), 2005–07; Baronsmead AiM VCT plc, 2006–08; Sen. Advr, Gardant Communications Ltd (formerly The Policy Partnership), 2005–09. Chm. of Treasurers, USPG, 1991–96. *Recreations*: theatre, horse racing. *Clubs*: Turf, City of London.

**CASEY, Dame Louise**, DBE 2016; CB 2008; Chair, Institute of Global Homelessness, De Paul University, Chicago, since 2017; *b* Redruth, 29 March 1965; *d* of late Martin and Peggy Casey. *Educ*: Oaklands RC Comprehensive Sch., Portsmouth; Goldsmiths' Coll., Univ. of London (BA Hons Hist.). Co-ordinator, St Mungo Assoc., 1988–90; Dir, Homeless Network, 1990–92; Dep. Dir, Shelter, 1992–99; Govt Homelessness Czar, 1999–2003; Nat. Dir, Anti-Social Behaviour Policy, 2003–05; Govt Co-ordinator, Respect, 2005–07; Hd, Cabinet Office review, Engaging Communities in Fight Against Crime, 2008; Dir Gen., Neighbourhood Crime and Justice Gp, Home Office, 2008–10; Comr for Victims and Witnesses, 2010–11; Dir Gen., Troubled Families Team, DCLG, 2011–15; Leader: Inspection of Rotherham MBC and child sexual exploitation, 2015; Review on Integration in UK, 2015–17 (report, The Casey Review, 2016). *Recreations*: reading novels, socialising.

**CASEY, Nigel Philip**, CMG 2017; MVO 1995; HM Diplomatic Service; High Commissioner to South Africa, since 2017; *b* Leamington Spa, 29 May 1969; *s* of late Michael Casey and of Josephine Casey; *m* 2002, Clare Crocker; one *s* one *d*. *Educ*: Blundell's Sch.; Balliol Coll., Oxford (BA Hons Mod. Hist.). Joined FCO, 1991; Vice-Consul, Johannesburg, 1993–95; Private Sec. to Ambassador, Washington, DC, 1996–98; Head: Nuclear and Missile Defence Section, Security Policy Dept, 1999–2000; G8 and OECD Section, Econ. Policy Dept, 2001; Moscow, 2003–06; Hd, Iraq Policy Unit, 2006–07; Political Counsellor, 2007–09, Dep. High Comr, 2007–11, New Delhi; Ambassador to Bosnia and Herzegovina, 2011–14; Private Sec. to the Prime Minister for Foreign Policy, 2014–16; High Comr (non-resident) to Lesotho and Swaziland, 2017–19. *Recreations*: tennis, squash, golf, theatre, cinema. *Address*: c/o Foreign and Commonwealth Office, King Charles Street, SW1A 2AH.

**CASEY, Prof. Robert Bernard, (Ben)**; Co-Founder and Executive Creative Director, Chase Creative Consultants Ltd, since 1986; Professor (part-time) of Visual Communication, University of Central Lancashire, since 1999; *b* 19 Oct. 1949; *s* of Thomas and Marie Casey; partner, Fiona Candy. *Educ*: Blackpool Coll. of Art. MCSD 1978. Typographer, Horniblow Cox-Freeman, London, 1969–72; Berkoff Associates, London, 1972–73; Designer: Conways, London, 1973–74; G&H, Manchester, 1974–77; Lecturer: Carlisle Coll. of Art, and Blackburn Coll. of Art, 1977–78; Harris Coll., Preston, 1978–83; Hd, Dept of Design, Lancs Poly., 1983–85; Sen. Lectr, Sch. of Communication Arts, London, 1985–86. Designer, Preston North End's Deepdale Stadium, 1995. Mem., Design Skills Panel, Design Council, 2005–09. External Moderator: Staffs Univ., 1989–92; Manchester Metropolitan Univ., 1990–93 and 2002–05; Bretton Hall Coll., 1998–2001; Univ. of Northumbria, 2006–09; Falmouth Univ., 2013–16; Blackpool and Fylde Coll., 2013–14. Design and Art Directors Association: Chm., Educn Gp, 1991–95; Mem., Exec. Cttee, 1991–95; Chm., D&AD North, 2006–10. *Publications*: How a Graphic Design Consultancy Thinks it Thinks, 1993; The Wood That Doesn't Look Like An Elephant, 2016. *Recreation*: watching Preston North End. *Address*: Woodbine Cottage, Dilworth Bottoms, Longridge, Preston PR3 2ZP. *E*: ben.casey@thechase.co.uk.

**CASH, Sir Andrew (John)**, Kt 2009; OBE 2001; Chief Executive, Sheffield Teaching Hospitals NHS Foundation Trust, 2004–18; *b* 14 Oct. 1955; *m* 1986, Debora; one *s* one *d*. Joined NHS as grad. mgt trainee; Chief Executive: Northern General Hosp. NHS Trust; Sheffield Teaching Hosps NHS Trust, 2001–04; Dir Gen., Provider Develt, DoH (on secondment), 2006–07. Co-Chair, DoH/MoD Partnership Bd; Chair, NHS Pay Policy Bd, 2011–; Dep. Chair, NHS Confederation, 2014–. Non-exec. Dir, Medilink. Vis. Prof. in Leadership Develt, Univs of York and Sheffield.

**CASH, Prof. John David**, CBE 1998; PhD; FRCPE, FRCPath; National Medical and Scientific Director, Scottish National Blood Transfusion Service, 1988–98; *b* 3 April 1936; *s* of John Henry Cash and May Annie Cash (*née* Taylor); *m* 1962, Angela Mary Thomson; one *s* one *d*. *Educ*: Ashville College, Harrogate; Edinburgh Univ. (BSc 1959, MB ChB 1961, PhD 1967). FRCPE 1970; FRCPath 1986; FRCPGlas 1994; FRCSE 1995; FRCP 1997. Regional Transfusion Centre Dir, Edinburgh and SE Scotland, 1974–79; Nat. Med. Dir, Scottish Nat. Blood Transfusion Service, 1979–88. Pres., RCPE, 1994–97 (Vice-Pres., 1992–94); Pres., British Blood Transfusion Soc., 1997–99. Chm., Govt Inquiry into Nat. Blood Authy, 1997–98; Member: Nat. Biol Standards Bd, 1997–2003; Internat. Review Panel, Irish Blood Transfusion Service, 2002. Hon. Prof., Edinburgh Univ., 1986. Governor, Fettes Coll., Edinburgh, 1988–2002. *Publications*: Progress in Transfusion Medicine, 1988. *Recreations*: fishing, gardening. *Address*: 1 Otterburn Park, Edinburgh EH14 1JX.

**CASH, Sir William (Nigel Paul)**, Kt 2014; MP (C) Stone, since 1997 (Stafford, 1984–97); *b* 10 May 1940; *s* of Paul Trevor Cash, MC (killed in action Normandy, July 13, 1944) and Moyra Roberts (*née* Morrison); *m* 1965, Bridget Mary Lee; two *s* one *d*. *Educ*: Stonyhurst Coll.; Lincoln Coll., Oxford (MA History). Qualified as Solicitor, 1967; William Cash & Co. (constitutional and administrative lawyer), 1979–. Shadow Attorney-General, 2001–03; Shadow Sec. of State for Constitutional Affairs, 2003. Chm., European Scrutiny Cttee (formerly Select Cttee on European Legislation), 2010– (Mem., 1985–); Chairman: Cons. Backbench Cttee on European Affairs, 1989–91; All Party Cttee on Uganda (formerly on E Africa), 1988–, on Kenya, 2007–; All Party Gp, Jubilee 2000, 1997–2003; All Party Cttee, Malaysia, 2006–; All Party Cttee, Sanitation and Water, 2007–; Jt Chm., All Party Jazz Gp, 1991–2000; Mem., Jt Cttee on Privileges, 2012–15. Founder, and Chm., European Foundn, 1993–. Vice Pres., Cons. Small Business Bureau, 1986–2000. KStJ 1998. *Publications*: Against a Federal Europe—The Battle for Britain, 1991; Europe: the crunch, 1992; John Bright—Statesman, Orator, Agitator, 2011; (jtly) From Brussels with Love, 2016. *Recreations*: history, cricket, jazz. *Address*: The Tithe Barn, Upton Cressett, near Bridgnorth, Shropshire WV16 6UH. *T*: (01746) 714307. *E*: bcash@me.com. *Clubs*: Garrick, Carlton; Vincent's (Oxford).

**CASHEL, FERNS AND OSSORY, Bishop of**, since 2006; **Rt Rev. Michael Andrew James Burrows**; *m* Claire; three *s* one *d*. *Educ*: Wesley Coll., Dublin; Trinity Coll. Dublin (MLitt). Ordained, 1987; Curate, Douglas Union with Frankfield, Cork; Dean of Residence, TCD, and Minor Canon, St Patrick's Cathedral, Dublin, 1991–94; Incumbent, Bandon Union, 1994–2002; Canon, Cork and Cloyne Cathedrals, 1996; Dean of Cork and Incumbent, St Fin Barre's Union, 2002–06. Chair of Govs, Anglican Centre in Rome, 2018–. *Address*: Diocesan Office, Palace Coach House, Church Lane, Kilkenny, Co. Kilkenny, Republic of Ireland.

**CASHMAN, Baron** *cr* 2014 (Life Peer), of Limehouse in the London Borough of Tower Hamlets; **Michael Maurice Cashman**, CBE 2013; Member (Lab) West Midlands Region, European Parliament, 1999–2014; *b* 17 Dec. 1950; *s* of John Cashman and Mary Cashman (*née* Clayton); civil partnership 2006, Paul Cottingham (*d* 2014). *Educ*: St Mary's and St Joseph's Primary Sch.; Cardinal Griffin Secondary Modern Sch., London; Gladys Dare's Sch., Surrey; Borlands Tutorial, London. Actor, director and playwright, 1963–99; work includes: *actor*: *stage*: Oliver, Albery, 1963; Bent, RNT, 1990, transf. Garrick; Noises Off, Mobil Touring Theatre, nat. tour, 1995; Merchant of Venice, and Gypsy, W Yorks Playhouse, 1996; The Tempest, internat. tour, 1997; *television*: Eastenders, 1986–89; *director*: Kiss of the Spiderwoman, New Victoria Th., Newcastle-under-Lyme, 1998; *playwright*: Before your very Eyes; Bricks 'n' Mortar. Mem. Council and Hon. Treas., Equity, 1994–98; Mem., Labour Party NEC, 1998–2000 and 2001–12. Labour Party Lesbian Gay Bisexual and Transgender Global Envoy, 2014–16. Founding Chm., Stonewall Gp, 1988–96. Patron: Terrence Higgins Trust; Omnibus Th., Clapham; FFLAG; IPAT; Peter Tatchell Foundn; Above the Stag Th., Vauxhall; Trustee, Actors Centre; Founder and Trustee, Paul Cottingham Trust. FRSA 1996. Hon. Dr Staffordshire, 2007. Special Service Award, Amer. Assoc. Physicians for Human Rights and Gay Med. Assoc., 1988; MEP of the Year Award, Justice and Human Rights, 2007, Culture and Educn, 2012, The House Mag.; Lifetime Achievement Award, European Diversity Awards, 2012; Outstanding Achievement Award, PinkNews, 2014; Stonewall Politician of Year, 2014. *Publications*: One of Them (memoir), 2020. *Recreations*: travel, writing, photography, theatre. *Address*: House of Lords, SW1A 0PW.

**CASHMORE, Prof. Roger John**, CMG 2004; DPhil; FRS 1998; FInstP; Principal, Brasenose College, Oxford, 2002–11 (Hon. Fellow, 2011); Chairman, United Kingdom Atomic Energy Authority, 2010–18; *b* 22 Aug. 1944; *e s* of C. J. C. and E. M. Cashmore; *m* 1971, Elizabeth Ann, *d* of Rev. S. J. C. Lindsay; one *s*. *Educ*: Dudley Grammar Sch.; St John's Coll., Cambridge (schol.; BA 1965; MA); Balliol Coll., Oxford (DPhil 1969). FInstP 1985. Weir Jun. Res. Fellow, University Coll., Oxford, 1967–69; 1851 Res. Fellow, 1968; Res. Associate, Stanford Linear Accelerator Centre, Calif, 1969–74; Oxford University: Res. Officer, 1974–79; Lectr, Christ Church, 1976–78; Fellow, Balliol Coll., 1979–2002 (Emeritus Fellow, 2003); Sen. Res. Fellow, Merton Coll., 1977–79; Tutor, Balliol Coll., and Univ. Lectr in Physics, 1979–90; Reader in Experimental Physics, 1990–91; Prof. of Experimental Physics, 1991–2003; Chm. of Physics, 1996–98; Res. Dir for Collider Progs, 1999–2003; Dep. Dir Gen., 2002–03, CERN. SERC Sen. Res. Fellow, 1982–87; Vis. Prof., Vrije Univ., Brussels, 1982; Guest Scientist, Fermilab, Chicago, 1986. Chairman: Sci. Cttee, Nat. Lab. of San Grasso, Italy, 2004–10; Nuclear Res. Adv. Council, 2005–14; Internat. Policy Bd, Shota Rustaveli Nat. Sci. Foundn, Georgia, 2014–; Member: Sci. Adv. Cttee, Nat. Inst. for Nuclear Physics and High Energy Physics, Amsterdam, 2005–11; policy and prog. cttees, CERN, Deutsches Elektronen–Synchrotron, Hamburg, and SERC. Abdus Salam Meml Lect., Islamabad, 2001. Gov., Ludlow Coll., 1995–98. Trustee, Tanner Foundn, 2002–11. MAE 1992. FRSA 1996; Fellow, Eur. Phys. Soc., 2010. Hon. Doctor Jt Inst. for Nuclear Res., Dubna, 2004. C. V. Boys Prize, Inst. of Physics, 1983; Humboldt Res. Award, Alexander Von Humboldt Stiftung, 1995. *Publications*: contrib. Nuclear Physics, Physics Letters, Phys. Rev., Phys. Rev. Letters. *Recreations*: sports, wine.

**CASKEN, Prof. John**, DMus; composer; Professor of Music, University of Manchester, 1992–2008, now Emeritus; *b* 15 July 1949. *Educ*: Birmingham Univ. (BMus, MA); DMus Durham, 1992. FRNCM 1996. Polish Govt Scholarship, Warsaw, 1971–72. Lectr, Birmingham Univ., 1973–79; Res. Fellow, Huddersfield Poly., 1980–81; Lectr, Durham Univ., 1981–92. Composer in Association, Northern Sinfonia, 1990–2000; Rockefeller Foundn Residency (Bellagio), 1992. Northern Electric Performing Arts Award, 1990. Hon. DCL Univ. of King's Coll., Halifax, Nova Scotia, 2011; Hon. DMus Birmingham, 2011. *Compositions include*: *orchestral*: Tableaux des Trois Ages, 1977; Masque, 1982; Orion over Farne, 1984; Maharal Dreaming, 1989; Cello Concerto, 1991; Still Mine (baritone and orch.), 1992 (Prix de Composition Musicale, Prince Pierre de Monaco, 1993); Darting the Skiff, 1993; Violin Concerto, 1995; Sortilège, 1996; Distant Variations (saxophone quartet and wind orch.), 1997; Symphony (Broken Consort), 2004; Rest-ringing (string quartet and orch.), 2005; Farness - three poems of Carol Ann Duffy (soprano, solo viola and chamber orch.), 2006; Concerto for Orchestra, 2007; That Subtle Knot (double concerto for violin and viola), 2013; Apollinaire's Bird (oboe concerto), 2014; *ensemble and instrumental*: Amarantos, 1978; Firewhirl (soprano and ensemble), 1980; String Quartet No 1, 1982; Vaganza, 1985; Salamandra, 1986; Piano Quartet, 1990; String Quartet No 2, 1994; Infanta Marina, 1994; Après un silence, 1998; The Haunting Bough (solo piano), 1999; Nearly Distant (saxophone quartet), 2000; Piano Trio, 2002; Blue Medusa (bassoon and piano), 2003; Amethyst Deceiver (solo oboe), 2009; Inevitable Rifts (string quintet), 2009; Winter Reels (mixed ensemble), 2011; Stolen Airs (cello and piano), 2015; Serpents of Wisdom (horn and piano), 2016; Misted Land (clarinet quintet), 2017; *vocal and choral*: Ia Orana Gauguin, 1978; To Fields We Do Not Know, 1984; Three Choral Pieces, 1990–93; Sharp Thorne, 1992; To the Lovers' Well, 2001; The Dream of the Rood, 2008 (BASCA Award, 2010); Deadly Pleasures (melodrama), 2009; Magnificat and Nunc Dimittis, 2012; Kokoschka's Doll (melodrama), 2016; *opera*: Golem, 1988 (first Britten Award, 1990; Gramophone Award for best contemp. recording, 1991); God's Liar, 2000; *electronic*: A Belle Pavine, 1980; Piper's Linn, 1984; Soul Catcher, 1988, rev. 2004.

**CASLEY, Henry Roberts**; non-executive Director, Scottish and Southern Energy plc, 1998–2005; *s* of Benjamin Rowe Casley and May Casley; *m* 1960, Sheila Laity (*d* 2019); one *s* one *d*. MCIM. Eastern Electricity: Energy Mkting Manager, 1975–78; Supplies Manager, 1978–82; Mkting Dir, 1982–86; Southern Electric plc: Dep. Chm., 1986–89; Man. Dir, 1989–93; Chief Exec., 1993–96; non-exec. Dir, 1996–98. *Recreations*: sport, gardening.

**CASPI, Prof. Avshalom**, PhD; FBA 2006; Edward M. Arnett Professor of Psychology and Neuroscience, Duke University, since 2008; Professor of Personality Development, Institute of Psychiatry, Psychology and Neuroscience (formerly Institute of Psychiatry), King's College London, since 1997; *b* Jerusalem, 5 May 1960; *m* 1990, Prof. Terrie Edith Moffitt, qv. *Educ*: Univ. of Calif, Santa Cruz (BA 1981); Cornell Univ. (MA 1983; PhD 1986). Asst Prof. of Psychol., Harvard Univ., 1986–89; Asst Prof., 1989–91, Associate Prof.,

1991–95, Prof. of Psychol., 1995–2007, Univ. of Wisconsin; Prof., Dept of Psychol. and Neurosci., Duke Univ., 2007–08. Mem. Council, Internat. Soc. for Study of Behavioural Devlt, 2000–06. FMedSci 2002. *Publications:* (jtly) Persons in Context; (jtly) Sex Differences in Antisocial Behaviour, 2001; (jtly) Paths to Successful Development, 2002; (jtly) Causes of Conduct Disorder and Juvenile Delinquency, 2003; articles in learned jls. *Address:* Department of Psychology and Neuroscience, Duke University, Grey House, 2020 Main Street, Durham, NC 27708, USA; Social Genetic and Developmental Psychiatry Research Centre, Institute of Psychiatry, Psychology and Neuroscience, King's College London, De Crespigny Park, SE5 8AF.

**CASS, Sir Geoffrey (Arthur),** Kt 1992; MA; Chairman: Royal Shakespeare Company, 1985–2000; Royal Theatrical Support (formerly Royal Shakespeare Theatre) Trust, since 1983; President, The Tennis Foundation (formerly British Tennis Foundation), since 2007 (Chairman, 2003–07); President, and Chairman of the Council, Lawn Tennis Association, 1997–99; Chief Executive, Cambridge University Press, 1972–92; Fellow of Clare Hall, Cambridge, since 1979; *b* 11 Aug. 1932; *oc* of late Arthur Cass and Jessie Cass (*née* Simpson), Darlington and Oxford; *m* 1957, Olwen Mary, MBE, JP, DL, *oc* of late William Leslie Richards and Edith Louisa Richards, Llanelli and Brecon; four *d. Educ:* Queen Elizabeth Grammar Sch., Darlington (Head of Sch.); Jesus Coll., Nuffield Coll., and Dept of Social and Admin. Studies, Oxford Univ. (BA 1954; MA 1958; Hon. Fellow, Jesus Coll., 1998); MA Cantab, 1972. FInstD 1968; FIWM, FIIM 1979; CCMI (CBIM 1980). Commnd RAFVR, fighter control, 1954; served RAF, 1958–60: Air Min. Directorate of Work Study; Pilot Officer, 1958; Flying Officer, 1960. Consultant: PA Management Consultants Ltd, 1960–65; British Communications Corp., and Controls and Communications Ltd, 1965; Dir, Controls and Communications Ltd, 1966–69; Managing Director, George Allen and Unwin Ltd, 1967–71; Cambridge University Press: Sec., Press Syndicate, 1974–92; Univ. Printer, 1982–83, 1991–92; Consultant, 1992–; Director: Weidenfeld (Publishers) Ltd, 1972–74; Chicago Univ. Press (UK), 1971–86; Mem., Jesus Coll., Cambridge, 1972–. Member: Univ. of Cambridge Cttee of Management of Fenner's (and Exec. Cttee), 1976–; Univ. of Cambridge Careers Service Syndicate (formerly Appts Bd), 1977–2002 (Exec. Cttee, 1982–2002); Governing Syndicate, Fitzwilliam Mus., Cambridge, 1977–78; Chm., Univ. of Cambridge Sports Centre Appeal, 2001–05; Chm. Governors, Perse Sch. for Girls, Cambridge, 1978–88 (Governor, 1977–98); Trustee, Univ. of Cambridge Foundn, 1998–13 (Chm., Audit Cttee, 2006–13); Chm., Univ. of Cambridge ADC Theatre Appeal, 2000–07. Founder Mem. Council, Royal Shakespeare Theatre Trust, 1967–; Gov., 1975–; Dep. Pres. of Govs, 2000–11, RSC (Mem., Council, 1975–2000; Mem., 1976–2000, Chm. 1982–2000, Exec. Cttee, Council); Trustee and Guardian, Shakespeare Birthplace Trust, 1982– (Life Trustee, 1994; Chm., Audit Cttee, 2008–); Founder Mem., Inigo Productions, 1996. Director: Newcastle Theatre Royal Trust, 1984–89; American Friends of the Royal Shakespeare Theatre, 1985–2000; Method & Madness (formerly Cambridge Theatre Co.), 1986–95; Cambridge Arts Th., 1997–98; Theatres Trust, 1991–2000; Marc Sinden Productions, 2001–02; The All England LTC (Wimbledon) Ltd, 1997–2000; The All England Lawn Tennis Ground PLC, 1997–2000. Pres., Macmillan Cancer Support, Cambridgeshire (formerly Macmillan Cancer Relief Cambs and Peterborough Project), 1998–. Cambridgeshire LTA: Mem. Exec., 1974–84; Chm., F and GP Cttee 1982–84; Captain 1974–78; Pres., 1980–82; Hon. Life Vice-Pres., 1982–; The Lawn Tennis Association of GB: Dep. Pres., 1994–96; Member: Council, 1976–; Management Bd, 1985–90, 1993–2000; Nat. Trng and Internat. Match Cttee (Davis Cup, Fedn Cup, Wightman Cup, etc), 1982–90, 1992–93 (Chm., 1985–90); Internat. Events Cttee, 1991–93; Chm., Nat. Ranking Cttee, 1990–99; Wimbledon Championships: Member: Cttee of Management, 1990–2002; Jt Finance Bd, 1989–93; Jt Finance Cttee, 1993–2002 (Chm., 1997–99); British Jun. Championships Cttee of Management, 1983–90 (Chm., 1985–90); Nat. Championships Cttee of Management, 1988–89; Rules and Internat. Cttee, 1980–81; Re-orgn Wkg Party, 1984–85; Chm., Reconstruction Wkg Gp, 1994–99. Tennis singles champion: Durham County, 1951; Cambridgeshire, 1976; Oxford University: tennis Blue, 1953, 1954, 1955 (Sec., 1955); badminton, 1951, 1952 (Captain, 1952); Pres., Cambridge Univ. Lawn Tennis Club, 2007– (Chm., 1977–2007; Hon. Cambridge tennis Blue, 1980); Chm., Cambridge Univ. Cricket and Athletic Club, 2003–; played in Wimbledon Championships, 1954, 1955, 1956, 1959; played in inter-county lawn tennis championships for Durham County, then for Cambridgeshire, 1952–82; represented RAF, 1958–59; Brit. Veterans (over 45) singles champion, Wimbledon, 1978; Mem., Brit. Veterans' Internat. Dubler Cup Team, Barcelona, 1978, Milano Marittima, 1979 (Captain). Patron: Cambridge Rowing Trust, 2001–; Theatre Royal Bury St Edmunds Restoration Appeal Cttee, 2001–08. FRSA 1991. Chevalier, Ordre des Arts et des Lettres (France), 1982. *Recreations:* lawn tennis, theatre. *Address:* Middlefield, Huntingdon Road, Girton, Cambridge CB3 0LH. *Clubs:* Garrick, Institute of Directors, All England Lawn Tennis and Croquet (Hon.), Queen's (Hon.), International Lawn Tennis of GB, The 45 (Hon.), Veterans' Lawn Tennis of GB; Hawks (Hon.) (Cambridge); Cambridge University Lawn Tennis; West Hants Lawn Tennis (Hon.).

**CASS, Hilary Dawn,** OBE 2015; FRCP, FRCPCH; Paediatric Neurodisability Consultant, Evelina London Children's Hospital, Guy's and St Thomas' NHS Foundation Trust, 2009–18, now Honorary Consultant; President, Royal College of Paediatrics and Child Health, 2012–15; *b* London, 19 Feb. 1958; *d* of Ralph and Mildred Cass. *Educ:* City of London Sch. for Girls; Royal Free Hosp. Sch. of Medicine (BSc 1979; MB BS 1982). FRCPCH 1992; FRCP 2004. House Physician, Royal Free Hosp., 1982–83; House Surgeon, Northwick Park Hosp., 1983; SHO, Hammersmith Hosp., 1983–84; Whittington Hospital: SHO Gen. Medicine, 1984–85; SHO Gen. Paediatrics, 1985; SHO Obstetrics and Gynaecology, 1985–86; SHO Neonatal Paediatrics, 1986–87; SHO, Harper House Children's Services, UCH, 1986; SHO, Queen Elizabeth Children's Hosp., 1987–88; Community Med. Officer and Hon. Registrar Paediatrics, Islington HA, 1988–89; Rotational Registrar Paediatrics, Newham Gen. Hosp. and London Hosp., 1989–90; Sen. Registrar in Paediatric Disability, UCH, 1990–92; Consultant in Paediatric Disability, Harper House Children's Services, 1992–98; Hon. Consultant, Camden and Islington Community Trust, 1992–2001; Great Ormond Street Hospital: Paediatric Neurodisability Consultant, 1994–2009; Dir, Med. Educn, 1998–2008; Dep. Med. Dir, 2003–08; Hd, London Sch. of Paediatrics, 2007–09. Hon. Sen. Lect, Inst. of Child Health, UCL, 1996–2009. Chair: Together for Short Lives, 2017–; British Acad. of Childhood Disability, 2017–. FHEA 2008. Hon. FRCPE 2013; Hon. FRCGP 2016. *Publications:* The NHS Experience; ed the 'Snakes and Ladders' guide for patients and professionals, 2006; contribs to scientific jls. *Recreations:* theatre, books, music.

**CASS, Richard Martin;** architect and landscape architect; Built Environment Expert, Design Council, since 2012; Chairman and Trustee, Cass Foundation, since 2013; Director, CPL Management Ltd, since 2013; *b* Princes Risborough, 25 May 1946; *s* of Edward and Hazel Cass; *m* 1977, Judith Claire Snaith; two *s. Educ:* High Wycombe Royal Grammar Sch.; Univ. of Sheffield (BArch; MA). RIBA 1972–2014. Architect: Sheffield CC, 1968–70; Ryder and Yates (Architects & Engrs), 1970–72; Architect and Landscape Architect, Brian Clouston and Partners, 1972–81; Project Manager, Merseyside Devlt Corp., 1981–83; Founding Partner, Cass Associates, 1983–2013. Projects include: Silkworth Park, Sunderland, 1978 (Community Architecture Award); Liverpool Internat. Garden Fest., 1984 (Civic Trust Award); Duisburg Nord Landpark, 1990; Buckshaw Village, Lancs, 1994–2013 (Planning Achievement Award, RTPI, 2000); Birkenhead Bus Station, 1997 (RIBA, Civic Trust and Structural Steel Awards). Mem., London 2012 Olympic Park Design Rev. Panel, 2007–12; Mem., CABE, 2008–11. Trustee: Heritage Works Bldg Preservation Trust, 2007–; Jewel on the Hill Building Preservation Trust, 2012–18. MLI 1975–2014. *Recreations:* music, theatre, opera, art, travel, gardening, sailing, hill walking, reading. *Address:* Osborne House West, Fulwood Park, Liverpool L17 5AD. *T:* 07711 570955. *E:* richard.m.cass@btinternet.com.

**CASS, Wilfred,** CBE 2006; Co-Founder, Cass Sculpture Foundation, 1992; *b* Berlin, 11 Nov. 1924; *s* of Hans and Edith Cassirer; *m* 1983, Jeannette Futter; one *s* one *d. Educ:* Regent St Poly., London (HND Communication Technol. 1951). With Pye Ltd, Cambridge, 1951–57; Joint Founder (with brother, Eric): and Dep. Chm., Cass Electronics Ltd, 1955–85; Cass McLaren Ltd (Consultancy), 1959; Founder, and Man. Dir, 1965–71, non-exec. Dir, 1971–75, Gunson Sortex Ltd (Queen's Awards to Industry for export achievement and for tech. innovation, 1968); Managing Director: Hadfield Paints Ltd, 1972–75; Buck & Hickman Ltd, 1974–75; Chm. and Man. Dir, Reeves and Sons Ltd, subseq. Reeves Dryad Ltd, 1971–76; set up: Cass Arts & Crafts Ltd, 1976, sold 1985; Image Bank UK, 1979, sold 2001; Chm. and Chief Exec., Moss Bros plc, 1987–91. UK Founder and Chm., Kennedy Foundn, 1976–93. Hon. FRCA 1995. DUniv Open, 2008. *Recreations:* films, reading, photography, travel, art. *Address:* Cass Sculpture Foundation, Goodwood, Chichester, W Sussex PO18 0QP. *T:* (01243) 538449. *E:* wilfred@sculpture.org.uk. *Club:* Kennels (Goodwood).

**CASSAM, Prof. Quassim,** DPhil; Professor of Philosophy, University of Warwick, since 2009 (Head, Department of Philosophy, 2010–12); *b* 31 Jan. 1961; *s* of Amir and Sultan Cassam; *m* 2010, Dr Deborah Ghate. *Educ:* Keble Coll., Oxford (BA 1st Cl. Hons PPE; BPhil Philosophy; DPhil Philosophy 1985). Fellow and Lectr in Philosophy, Oriel Coll., Oxford, 1985–86; Fellow and Tutor in Philosophy, Wadham Coll., Oxford, 1986–2004; Prof. of Philosophy, UCL, 2005–06; Knightbridge Prof. of Philosophy, Univ. of Cambridge, 2007–08; Fellow, King's Coll., Cambridge, 2007–08. Vis. Associate Prof., Univ. of Calif, Berkeley, 1993; John Evans Dist. Vis. Prof., Northwestern Univ., 2004. Sen. Res. Fellow, Mind, 2012–13; Leadership Fellow, AHRC, 2016–17. Bechtel Lectr, Harvard Univ., 2000; Lipkind Lectr, Univ. of Chicago, 2010; Jamie Greenberg Meml Lecture, Vassar Coll., NY, 2015; Alamshah Dist. Speaker, California State Univ., Fullerton, 2016. Pres., Aristotelian Soc., 2010–11. *Publications:* Self and World, 1997; The Possibility of Knowledge, 2007; (with J. Campbell) Berkeley's Puzzle; what does experience teach us?, 2014; Self-knowledge for Humans, 2014; Vices of the Mind: from the intellectual to the political, 2019; Conspiracy Theories, 2019. *Recreations:* Arsenal FC, cricket, audiobooks, history. *Address:* Department of Philosophy, University of Warwick, Coventry CV4 7AL.

**CASSANI, Barbara Ann,** Hon. CBE 2007; Chairman; Jurys Inns, Dublin, 2008–10; *b* 22 July 1960; *d* of James and Noreen Cassani; *m* 1985, Guy Davis; one *s* one *d. Educ:* Mount Holyoke Coll., USA (BA Hons *magna cum laude* Internat. Relns); Woodrow Wilson Sch. of Public and Internat. Affairs, Princeton Univ. (MPA). Mgt Consultant, Coopers & Lybrand, in Washington and London, 1984–87; various mgt roles with British Airways in UK and USA, 1987–97; CEO, Go Fly Ltd, 1997–2002; Chm., 2003–04, Vice-Chm., 2004–05, London 2012 Olympic Bid. *Publications:* (with K. Kemp) Go: an airline adventure, 2003. *Recreations:* reading, horse-riding, travel. *E:* bacassani@aol.com.

**CASSEL,** family name of **Baroness Mallalieu.**

**CASSEL, Sir Timothy (Felix Harold),** 4th Bt *cr* 1920; QC 1988; *b* 30 April 1942; *s* of Sir Harold Cassel, 3rd Bt, TD, QC; *S* father, 2001; *m* 1st, 1971, Jenifer Puckle (marr. diss. 1976); one *s* one *d*; 2nd, 1979, Ann Mallalieu (marr. diss. 2007) (*see* Baroness Mallalieu); two *d. Educ:* Eton College. Called to the Bar, Lincoln's Inn, 1965, Bencher, 1994; Jun. Prosecuting Counsel at Central Criminal Court, 1978, Sen. Prosecuting Counsel, 1986–88; Asst Boundaries Comr, 1979–85. *Heir: s* Alexander James Felix Cassel, *b* 25 May 1974. *Address:* West Wing, Kirtlington Park, Oxon OX5 3JN. *Clubs:* Garrick, Turf.

**CASSEN, Prof. Robert Harvey,** OBE 2008; Visiting Professor, Department of Social Policy, London School of Economics and Political Science, since 1997; Professor of the Economics of Development, Queen Elizabeth House, International Development Centre, University of Oxford, 1986–97, and Professorial Fellow, St Antony's College, 1986–97, now Emeritus; *b* 24 March 1935; *s* of John and Liliane Cassen; *m* 1988, Sun Shuyun. *Educ:* Bedford School; New Coll., Oxford (BA LitHum, MA); Univ. of California, Berkeley; Harvard (PhD Econ). Dept of Economics, LSE, 1961–69; Sen. Economist, ODM, 1966–67; First Sec. (Econ.), New Delhi, 1967–68; Sen. Economist, World Bank, Washington, 1969–72 and 1980–81; Fellow, Inst. of Devlt Studies, Sussex Univ., 1972–86; Sen. Res. Fellow, Centre for Population Studies, LSHTM, 1976–77; Dir, Queen Elizabeth House, Internat. Devlt Centre, Oxford Univ., 1986–93. Special Adviser, H of C Select Cttee on Overseas Devlt, 1973–74; Secretariat, Brandt Commn, 1978–79 and 1981–82; Mem., Bd of Trustees, Population Council, NY, 1978–87; UK Mem., UN Cttee for Devlt Planning, 1982–84. Launched www.golden-age-music.com, 2018. *Publications:* India: population, economy, society, 1978; (ed and contrib.) Planning for Growing Populations, 1979; (ed and contrib.) World Development Report, 1981; (ed and contrib.) Rich Country Interests and Third World Development, 1982; (ed) Soviet Interests in the Third World, 1985; Does Aid Work? (report), 1986, 2nd edn 1994; (ed) Poverty in India, 1992; (ed and contrib.) Population and Development: old debates, new conclusions, 1994; (ed) India: the future of economic reform, 1995; (ed and contrib.) 21st Century India: population, economy, human development and the environment, 2004; Tackling Low Educational Achievement (report), 2007; (jtly) Making a Difference in Education: what the evidence says, 2015; contribs to learned jls. *Recreations:* music, walking. *Address:* Centre for Analysis of Social Exclusion, London School of Economics and Political Science, Houghton Street, WC2A 2AE. *T:* (020) 7955 6679.

**CASSERLEY, Dominic James Andrew;** Senior Advisor, Warburg Pincus LLC, since 2017; President, Willis Towers Watson, 2016 (Chief Executive, Willis Group, 2013–15); *b* Gosport, 23 Dec. 1957; *s* of Christopher and Pamela Casperley; *m* 1986, Nancy Broadbent; two *s* one *d. Educ:* University Coll. Sch., London; Jesus Coll., Cambridge (BA Hons Hist. 1979). Pres., Cambridge Union Soc., 1979. Exec., Investment Mgt, then Mergers & Acquisitions, Morgan Grenfell & Co., 1979–83; McKinsey & Co.: Associate, 1983–87; Principal, 1988–93; Dir, 1993–2013; Leader: Gtr China Practice, 1994–99; Eur. Banking and Securities Practice, 1999–2003; Man. Partner, UK and Ire., 2003–10; Global Hd, Corporate and Investment Banking, 2010–13. David Rockefeller Fellow, NY, 1991–92. Mem., US Presidential Taskforce on Mkt Mechanisms, 1987. Member: Bd, Manhattan Th. Club, 1991–94; Bd, Donmar Th., London, 2003–11; Bd, Asia House, 2009–13; Mem. Bd and Treas., Perelman Center for Performing Arts, NY, 2016–; Chairman: Action on Addiction, 2007–11; Charities Aid Foundn, 2010–18; Trustee, National Th., 2011–16. Mem. Council, Univ. of Cambridge, 2011–13. *Publications:* Facing up to the Risks: how financial institutions can survive and prosper, 1993, 4th edn 1997; (with G. Gibb) Banking in Asia, the End of Entitlement, 1999. *Recreations:* tennis, travelling. *Clubs:* Reform, MCC, Queen's; University; Links (NY); Field, Round Hill (Greenwich, CT).

**CASSIDI, Adm. Sir (Arthur) Desmond,** GCB 1983 (KCB 1978); President, Royal Naval Association, 1987–96; Deputy Grand President, British Commonwealth Ex-Services League, 1986–96; *b* 26 Jan. 1925; *s* of late Comdr Robert A. Cassidi, RN and late Clare F. (*née* Alexander); *m* 1st, 1950, Dorothy Sheelagh Marie (*née* Scott) (*d* 1974); one *s* two *d*; 2nd, 1982, Dr Deborah Marion Pollock (*née* Bliss), FRCS. *Educ*: RNC Dartmouth. Qual. Pilot, 1946; CO, 820 Sqdn (Gannet aircraft), 1955; 1st Lieut HMS Protector, 1955–56; psc 1957; CO, HMS Whitby, 1959–61; Fleet Ops Officer Home Fleet, 1962–64; Asst Dir Naval Plans, 1964–67; Captain (D) Portland and CO HMS Undaunted, 1967–68; idc 1969; Dir of Naval Plans, 1970–72; CO, HMS Ark Royal, 1972–73; Flag Officer Carriers and Amphibious Ships, 1974–75; Dir-Gen., Naval Manpower and Training, 1975–77; Flag Officer, Naval Air Command, 1978–79; Chief of Naval Personnel and Second Sea Lord, 1979–82; C-in-C Naval Home Comd, 1982–85; Flag ADC to the Queen, 1982–85. Mem. Adv. Council, Science Museum, 1979–84, Trustee, 1984–92; Pres., FAA Museum, 1985–95. FRSA 1986. *Recreation*: country pursuits.

**CASSIDY, Bryan Michael Deece;** Founder, Cassidy and Associates International, EU Consultants, 1999; Member, European Economic and Social Committee, 2002–14 (Chairman, Single Market Observatory, 2004–06; Co-Chairman, EU/Turkey Joint Consultative Committee, 2006–08; President, Single Market Production and Consumption section, 2008–14); *s* of late William Francis Deece Cassidy and Kathleen Selina Patricia Cassidy (*née* Geraghty); *m* 1960, Gillian Mary Isobel Bohane; one *s* two *d*. *Educ*: Ratcliffe College; Sidney Sussex College, Cambridge (MA Law). Commissioned RA, 1955–57 (Malta and Libya); HAC, 1957–62. With Ever Ready, Beecham's and IPC Business Press (Dir, European associates). Mem. Council, CBI, 1981–84. Dir Gen., of a trade assoc., 1981–84. Contested (C) Wandsworth Central, 1966; Mem. GLC (Hendon North), 1977–86 (opposition spokesman on industry and employment, 1983–84). MEP (C), Dorset E and Hampshire W, 1984–94, Dorset and E Devon, 1994–99; contested (C) SW Reg., 1999. Assignments for BESO in Estonia, 2000, Mongolia, 2002. Dir of Studies, Hawksmere Brussels Briefings, 2001–04. Vis. Woodrow Wilson Fellow, American Univs, 2000, 2004. Mem., Adv. Bd, European Performance Inst., Brussels, 1999–2002. *Publications*: Hawksmere European Lobbying Guide, 2000; regular contribs to Industry Europe. *Recreations*: history, theatre, spending time at home in Dorset. *Address*: 11 Esmond Court, Thackeray Street, W8 5HB. *T*: (020) 7937 3558. *E*: bmdcassidy@aol.com.

**CASSIDY, His Eminence Cardinal Edward;** *see* Cassidy, His Eminence Cardinal I. E.

**CASSIDY, Elizabeth Grace;** Royal Navy Resources Director (formerly Command Secretary, Navy), 2007–13; *b* 6 July 1951; *er d* of late William Charles Cassidy and Mildred Joan Cassidy (*née* Ross); *m* 1984, Edward Roy Dolby. *Educ*: Girls' Grammar Sch., Prescot, Lancs; Girton Coll., Cambridge (MA); Wye Coll., Univ. of London (MSc). Ministry of Defence: Admin. Trainee, 1978; Private Sec. to Chief of Defence Procurement, 1983; Principal, 1984; Private Sec. to CAS, 1990–93; Asst Sec., Hd, IT Business Systems, then IT Strategy, 1993–95; Advr to Jt Services Comd and Staff Coll. Project, 1995–97; Dir, Finance Policy, 1997–99; Command Sec. to Second Sea Lord and C-in-C Naval Home Command, and Asst Under-Sec. of State (Naval Personnel), 1999–2001; Review of Business Continuity for MoD HQ post-9/11, 2001–02; Comd Sec. to Adjt Gen., 2002–06. Mem., Admiralty and Navy Bds, 2012–13. Dir, Regular Forces Employment Assoc. Ltd, 2006– (Chm., 2018–). Mem., Royal Patriotic Fund Corp., 2003–06. Chm. Adv. Panel, Greenwich Hosp., 1999–2001 and 2007–13; Comr, Royal Hosp. Chelsea, 2002–06. Trustee, Marine Soc. and Sea Cadets, 2014– (Dep. Chm., 2018–). *Recreations*: music, reading, travel, sailing. *Address*: c/o HSBC, 9 Rose Lane, Canterbury, Kent CT1 2JP.

**CASSIDY, Rt Rev. George Henry;** Bishop of Southwell and Nottingham (formerly Bishop of Southwell), 1999–2009; an Assistant Bishop, Diocese of Bath and Wells and Diocese of Bristol, since 2009; *b* 17 Oct. 1942; *s* of Joseph Abram Cassidy and Ethel McDonald; *m* 1966, Jane Barling Stevens; two *d*. *Educ*: Belfast High School; Queen's Univ., Belfast (BSc 1965; Cert. Bib. Studies 1968); University Coll. London (MPhil 1967); Oak Hill Theological College. MRTPI 1969. Civil Servant: N Ireland, 1967–68; Govt of Kenya, 1968–70. Curate, Christ Church, Clifton, Bristol, 1972–75; Vicar: St Edyth, Sea Mills, Bristol, 1975–82; St Paul's, Portman Square, W1, 1982–87; Archdeacon of London and Canon Residentiary, St Paul's Cathedral, 1987–99; Sub-Dean, Order of the British Empire, 1996–99. Mem., Cathedrals Fabric Commn for England, 2001–05; Chm., Churches Legislation Adv. (formerly Main) Cttee, 2005–09. Freeman: City of London, 1988; Tylers' & Bricklayers' Co., 1988; Hon. Liveryman, Founders' Co., 1994. Hon. DLitt Heriot-Watt, 2005. Entered House of Lords, 2004. *Recreations*: Rugby football, art, chamber music, walking in the Quantocks. *Address*: Darch House, 17 St Andrews Road, Stogursey, Bridgwater, Som TA5 1TE. *Clubs*: National (Pres., 2010–), Nobody's Friends.

**CASSIDY, His Eminence Cardinal Idris Edward,** AC 1990; President, Pontifical Council for Promoting Christian Unity, and Commission for Religious Relations with the Jews, 1989–2001; *b* 5 July 1924; *s* of Harold George Cassidy and Dorothy May Phillips. *Educ*: Parramatta High Sch.; St Columba Seminary, Springwood; St Patrick's Coll., Manly; Lateran Univ., Rome (DCnL 1955); Diploma of Pontifical Eccl. Acad., Rome, 1955. Ordained priest, 1949; Asst Priest, Parish of Yenda, NSW, Australia, 1950–52; Secretary, Apostolic Nunciature, India, 1955–62 and Ireland, 1962–67; El Salvador, 1967–69; Counsellor, Apostolic Nunciature, Argentina, 1969–70; ordained Archbishop, Rome, 1970; Apostolic Pro-Nuncio: to Republic of China, 1970–79; to Bangladesh, 1973–79; to Lesotho, 1979–84, and Apostolic Delegate to Southern Africa; to the Netherlands, 1984–88; Substitute of Vatican Secretariat of State, 1988–89. Cardinal, 1991. Orders from El Salvador, China, Netherlands, Italy, France, Sweden and Germany. *Recreations*: tennis, golf. *Address*: 16 Coachwood Drive, Warabrook, NSW 2304, Australia.

**CASSIDY, Michael John,** CBE 2004; Chairman: Board of Governors, Museum of London, 2005–13; Homerton University Hospital Foundation Trust, 2006–13; Ebbsfleet Development Corporation, since 2014; *b* 14 Jan. 1947; *s* of Frank and Vera Cassidy; *m* 1st, 1974, Amanda (marr. diss. 1988); one *s* two *d*; 2nd, 1997, Amelia Simpson; two *d*. *Educ*: Downing Coll., Cambridge (BA); MBA (with distinction), City Univ. Business Sch., 1985. Qualified Solicitor, 1971; Partner: Maxwell Batley, 1971–2002 (Sen. Partner, 1991–2002); D. J. Freeman, 2002–03; Hammonds, 2003–04. Director: British Land Plc, 1996–2007; UBS Investment Bank (formerly UBS Warburg, then UBS Ltd), 2000–15; Crossrail Ltd, 2008–18; Haymarket Risk Mgt Ltd, 2012–14; Chairman: Askonas Holt Ltd, 2002–; Hemingway Properties Ltd, 2003–06; Gruppo Norman, 2004–05; Trikona Trinity Capital plc (formerly Trinity Property Co.), 2005–09; Bulgarian Land Development plc, 2005–07; non-executive Director: P2P Global Investments plc, 2014–; HB Reavis Ltd, 2015–. Corporation of London: Mem., Common Council, 1980–; Chairman: Planning Cttee, 1986–89; Policy and Resources Cttee, 1992–97; Property Investment Bd, 2012–15; Chm., Barbican Arts Centre, 2000–03. Pres., London Chamber of Commerce and Industry, 2005–07 (Dep. Pres., 2004–05). Mem. Bd, London Pension Fund Authy, 2007–13. Liveryman, Solicitors' Co. (Master, 2001–02). Hon. Fellow, London Business Sch., 1995; Hon. FRIBA 1995. Hon. LLD South Bank, 1995; Hon. DCL City, 1996. *Publications*: articles on City matters and pension fund investment. *Recreation*: Barbican concerts. *Address*: 202 Cromwell Tower, Barbican, EC2Y 8DD. *T*: (020) 7628 5687.

**CASSIDY, Seamus John;** television producer; Director, Happy Endings television production company, since 2001; *b* 20 Nov. 1958; *s* of late Michael Cassidy and of Patricia Cassidy. *Educ*: St Columb's Coll., Derry; Queen's Univ., Belfast (LLB Hons). Researcher, 1982–84; Asst Ed., 1984–87; Sen. Commissioning Ed., Comedy and Entertainment, Channel 4 TV, 1987–97; Sen. Producer, Comedy and Entertainment, Planet 24, 1997–99; Producer, The Panel, Saturday Night with Miriam, Podge and Rodge, Smoke and Mirrors, Buried Alive, all RTE, 2003–09; Executive Producer: The History of the Future, BBC4, 2009; Things That Went Boom in the Bust, RTE, 2009; The Panel, RTE, 2009–11; Dirty Old Towns?, RTE, 2011–12. *Address*: Happy Endings Productions, 3 Carysfort Avenue, Blackrock, Co. Dublin, Eire.

**CASSIDY, Dr Sheila Anne;** lecturer and psychotherapist; Specialist in Psychosocial Oncology, Plymouth Oncology Centre, 1993–2002; *b* 18 Aug. 1937; *d* of late Air Vice-Marshal John Reginald Cassidy and Barbara Margaret Cassidy. *Educ*: Univ. of Sydney; Somerville Coll., Oxford (BM BCh 1963; MA). Worked in Oxford and Leicester to 1971; went to Chile to work, 1971; arrested for treating wounded revolutionary, 1975; tortured and imprisoned 2 months, released Dec. 1975; lectured on human rights; in monastic religious order, 1978–80; returned to medicine, 1980; Medical Dir, St Luke's Hospice, Plymouth, 1982–93; Palliative Care Physician, Plymouth Gen. Hosp., 1993; lecturer in UK and overseas, preacher, writer, broadcaster. Freedom, City of Plymouth, 1998. Hon. DSc Exeter, 1991; Hon. DLitt CNAA, 1992; Hon. DM Plymouth, 2001. Valiant for Truth Media Award, 1977. *Publications*: Audacity to Believe, 1977; Prayer for Pilgrims, 1979; Sharing the Darkness, 1988; Good Friday People, 1991 (Collins Religious Book Award Special Prize, 1991); Light from the Dark Valley, 1994; The Loneliest Journey, 1995; Made for Laughter, 2006; Confessions of a Lapsed Catholic, 2010; Lent is for Loving, 2012. *Recreations*: writing, sewing, creative pursuits, reading, TV, walking her two Chows.

**CASSIDY, Stuart;** ballet dancer, ballet teacher and Pilates instructor; Founder Member and Principal, since 1999, and Assistant Director, since 2010, K. Ballet Co.; *b* 26 Sept. 1968; *s* of John and Jacqueline Cassidy; *m* 1993, Nicola Searchfield; two *s*. *Educ*: Royal Ballet Sch. (Hons 1987); RAD PDTDip (Dist.) 2003; Dreas Reyneke Pilates Instructor Course, 2004. Principal, Royal Ballet Co., 1991–99. *Principal rôles with Royal Ballet Company include*: Romeo and Mercutio, in Romeo and Juliet, Albrecht in Giselle, Siegfried in Swan Lake, Solor in La Bayadère, Jean de Brienne in Raymonda, Daphnis in Daphnis and Chloë, Florimund in Sleeping Beauty, Prince in Prince of the Pagodas, Prince in Nutcracker, Prince in Cinderella, Colas in La Fille Mal Gardée, Lescaut in Manon, Basilio in Don Quixote; Thaïs Pas de Deux, Tchaikovsky Pas de Deux. Nora Roche Award, 1986; Prix de Lausanne Prof. Prize, 1987. *Recreations*: golf, gardening, antiques, cars.

**CASSON, Prof. Andrew John,** FRS 1998; Philip Schuyler Beebe Professor of Mathematics, Yale University, since 2011 (Professor of Mathematics, 2000–11). *Educ*: Trinity Coll., Cambridge (BA 1965). Res. Fellow, 1967–71, Lectr in Maths, 1971–81, Trinity Coll., Cambridge; Professor of Mathematics: Univ. of Texas, Austin, 1981–86; Univ. of Calif, Berkeley, 1986–99; Chair, Dept of Maths, Yale Univ., 2004–07. *Publications*: (with S. A. Bleiler) Automorphisms of Surfaces after Nielsen and Thurston, 1988. *Address*: Department of Mathematics, Yale University, New Haven, CT 06520, USA.

**CASSON, Dinah Victoria, (Lady Moses),** CBE 2018; RDI 2006; FCSD; Co-founder and Director, Casson Mann Ltd, 1983–2017; *b* 8 Oct. 1946; *d* of Sir Hugh Maxwell Casson, CH, KCVO, RA, RDI and late Margaret MacDonald Casson; *m* 1992, Alan George Moses (*see* Rt Hon. Sir A. G. Moses); one *s* one *d* from previous marriage. *Educ*: Ravensbourne Coll. of Art (BA 1st Cl. Hons). Jun. designer, Conran Design Gp, 1968–70; freelance design practice, 1970–83. Casson Mann design practice has worked on interior, architectural, product develt, th. and mus. projects in USA, Italy, Russia and UK; major projects include: Grangelato ice cream shop, London, 1984; CSD HQ, London, 1988; The Garden, 1996, Wellcome Wing, 2000, Atmosphere, 2010, Science Mus.; British Galls, 2001, Portrait Miniatures, 2005, Hollywood Costume, 2012–13, V&A Mus.; Churchill Mus., 2005, Camouflage, 2007, For Your Eyes Only, 2008, Extraordinary Heroes, 2010, Imperial War Mus.; Beningbrough Hall, NPG/NT, 2006; Museo Santa Caterina, Treviso, 2007; Time Galls, Royal Observatory, Greenwich, 2007; Topolski Memoir, Waterloo, 2008; Museolobby, Stanislavsky Factory, Moscow, 2008; Great North Mus., Newcastle, 2009; Beaney Inst., Canterbury, 2012. Teacher (pt-time), Kingston Poly. and RCA, 1974–94; Dir of Architecture and Interior Design, RCA, 1993–95. External Examiner: Chelsea Sch. of Art, 1985–92; Manchester Poly., 1989–91; Plymouth Sch. of Architecture, 1990–93; Newcastle Sch. of Architecture, 1994–98; Middx Univ., 1994–97; Bournemouth Univ., 1994–96; N London, 1995–99; Glasgow Sch. of Art, 1999–2003; Cardiff Sch. of Art, 2004–. Member: Design Council, 1978–82; Exec., D&AD, 2006–09; Royal Stamp Adv. Cttee, 2013–; Koestler Arts Steering Gp, 2018–. Governor: Middx Poly., 1990–94; Sevenoaks Sch., 2005–09. Trustee: Creative Educn Trust, 2010–16; Charleston Trust, 2011–17; Towner Gall., Eastbourne, 2014–; Supreme Court UK Arts Trust, 2016–. Master, Faculty of RDI, 2011–14. FRCA 1995, Hon. FRCA 2018; Hon. FRIBA 2018. Hon. DDes UC for Creative Arts, Farnham, 2003. *Publications*: (contrib.) Creating the British Galleries at the V&A, ed C. Wilk and N. Humphrey, 2004; (contrib.) Mood Indigo, vol. 2: future interiors, 2019; contrib. Blueprint, Architects' Jl, Designers' Jl, Building Design, Eye. *Address*: Flat 1, 17–18 Clere Street, EC2A 4LJ. *T*: (020) 7490 3187. *E*: dinahvcasson@gmail.com.

**CASSON, John David,** CMG 2014; HM Diplomatic Service; Ambassador to Egypt, 2014–18; *b* Birmingham, 4 June 1971; *s* of Rev. David and Helen Casson; *m* 2000, Kathryn Rachel Clarke. *Educ*: Ashcroft High Sch., Luton; Tiffin Sch., Kingston-upon-Thames; Richmond upon Thames Coll.; Queens' Coll., Cambridge (BA Hons Hist. 1993; MA); Christ's Coll., Cambridge (DipTh 1994). Parly Res. Asst, 1994–95; Res. Asst, Faculty of Divinity, Univ. of Cambridge, 1996–98; joined FCO, 1998; Desk Officer, EU Dept, 1998–99; Second Sec., UK Repn to EU, Brussels, 1999–2000; Private Sec. to Ambassador to USA, 2000–02; First Sec. (Pol), Washington, 2002–05; Sen. Policy Advr, HM Treasury, 2005–07; Arabic lang. trng, 2007–08; Dep. Hd of Mission, Amman, 2007–09; Hd, Near East and N Africa Dept, FCO, 2009–10; (on secondment) Private Sec. to Prime Minister, 10 Downing St, 2010–14. *Publications*: contrib. articles to jls on religion and politics in Kenyan history. *Recreations*: baseball, the outdoors, poems, seeking God. *Address*: c/o Foreign and Commonwealth Office, King Charles Street, SW1A 2AH.

**CASSON, Prof. Mark Christopher,** FBA 2017; Professor of Economics, since 1981, and Director, Centre for Institutions and Economic History, since 2015, University of Reading; *b* 17 Dec. 1945; *s* of Stanley Christopher Casson and Dorothy Nowell Barlow; *m* 1975, Janet Penelope Close; one *d*. *Educ*: Manchester Grammar Sch.; Univ. of Bristol (BA 1st cl. hons 1966). Churchill Coll., Cambridge (graduate student). University of Reading: Lecturer in Economics, 1969; Reader, 1977; Head, Dept of Econs, 1987–94. Visiting Professor: of Internat. Business, Univ. of Leeds, 1995–; of Mgt, Queen Mary, Univ. of London, 2004–; of Mgt, Univ. of York, 2010–13. Mem. Council, REconS, 1985–90. Vice-Pres., 2006–07, Pres., 2007–08, Assoc. of Business Historians. Chm., Business Enterprise Heritage Trust, 2000–. Fellow, Acad. of Internat. Business, 1993; FRSA 1996. Freeman, City of London, 2013. *Publications*: Introduction to Mathematical Economics, 1973; (jtly) The Future of the Multinational Enterprise, 1976; Alternatives to the

Multinational Enterprise, 1979; Youth Unemployment, 1979; Unemployment: a disequilibrium approach, 1981; The Entrepreneur: an economic theory, 1982; Economics of Unemployment: an historical perspective, 1983; (ed) The Growth of International Business, 1983; (jtly) The Economic Theory of the Multinational Enterprise: selected papers, 1985; (jtly) Multinationals and World Trade: vertical integration and the division of labour in world industries, 1986; The Firm and the Market: studies in multinational enterprise and the scope of the firm, 1987; Enterprise and Competitiveness: a systems view of international business, 1990; (ed) Entrepreneurship, 1990; (ed) Multinational Corporations, 1990; Economics of Business Culture: game theory, transaction costs and economic performance, 1991; (ed) Global Research Strategy and International Competitiveness, 1991; (ed) International Business and Global Integration, 1992; (ed jtly) Multinational Enterprise in the World Economy: essays in honour of John Dunning, 1992; (ed jtly) Industrial Concentration and Economic Inequality: essays in honour of Peter Hart, 1993; Entrepreneurship and Business Culture, 1995; The Organization of International Business, 1995; (ed) The Theory of the Firm, 1996; Information and Organization: a new perspective on the theory of the firm, 1997; (ed) Culture, Social Norms and Economic Performance, 1997; (ed jtly) Institutions and the Evolution of Modern Business, 1997; (ed jtly) The Economics of Marketing, 1998; (ed jtly) Cultural Factors in Economic Growth, 2000; Economics of International Business, 2000; Enterprise and Leadership, 2000; (ed jtly) Oxford Handbook of Entrepreneurship, 2005; (ed jtly) Economics of Networks, 2008; The World's First Railway System, 2009; The Multinational Enterprise Revisited: the essential Buckley and Casson, 2009; Entrepreneurship: theory, networks, history, 2010; (ed) Markets and Market Institutions: their origin and evolution, 2011; (jtly) The Entrepreneur in History, 2013; (ed jtly) History of Entrepreneurship: innovation and risk-taking 1200–2000, 2013; (ed jtly) Large Databases in Economic History: research methods and case studies, 2013; Theory of International Business: economic models and methods, 2016; The Multinational Enterprise: theory and history, 2017. *Recreations:* collecting old books, studying old railways, visiting old churches, drawing in pastel. *Address:* 6 Wayside Green, Woodcote, Reading RG8 0QJ. *T:* (home) (01491) 681483, (office) (0118) 931 8227.

**CASSY, John Aldren;** Chief Executive Officer, Factory 42 Ltd, since 2016; *b* Winchester, 23 March 1974; *s* of Stuart Cassy and Rosamond Cassy; *m* Mary O'Reilly; one *s* one *d*. *Educ:* King Edward VI Sch., Southampton; St John's Coll., Cambridge (BA Social and Political Sci. 1996). Hon. Prof. of Humanities, Univ. of Exeter, 2018–. *Recreations:* music, yoga. *Address:* Factory 42 Ltd, New Wing, Somerset House, Strand, WC2R 1LA. *E:* info@factory42.uk. *Club:* Soho House.

**CASTAGNA, Alexis Anne;** *see* Campbell, A. A.

**CASTALDI, Dr Peter;** Chief Medical Officer, Scottish Equitable, 2004–10 (Company Medical Officer, 1997–2004); *b* 13 Jan. 1942; *s* of Frank and Sarah Jane Castaldi; *m* 1967, Joan Sherratt; one *s* one *d*. *Educ:* Grammar Sch. for Boys, Neath; Welsh Nat. Sch. of Medicine (MB, BCh 1966). Resident hosp. posts, N Wales, 1966–69; Principal in General Practice, Bangor, Gwynedd, 1969–79; MO 1979–84, SMO 1984–86, DHSS; PMO, DSS, 1986–92. Chief Med. Advr, DSS, and Dir of Med. Services, Benefits Agency, 1992–95. Company Medical Officer: UNUM UK, 1996–99; AEGON UK (formerly Guardian Royal Exchange), Lytham, 1997–2014; UNUM Ltd, 2001–04 (CMO, 1999–2001); Med. Mem., Ind. Tribunal Service, MoJ, 1996–2014. CStJ 1993. *Recreation:* armchair Rugby critic. *Address:* 24 Cavendish Road, Lytham St Annes, Lancs FY8 2PX.

**CASTELL, Sir William (Martin),** Kt 2000; LVO 2004; FCA; Chairman, Wellcome Trust, 2006–15; *b* 10 April 1947; *s* of William Gummer Castell and Gladys (*née* Doe); *m* 1971, Renice Mendelson; one *s* two *d*. *Educ:* St Dunstan's Sch.; City of London Coll. (BA). ACA 1974, FCA 1980. Various posts in marketing, finance and admin, Wellcome Foundn, 1975–86; Co-founding Dir, Biomedical Res. Centre, Vancouver, 1983; Man. Dir, Wellcome Biotech., 1984–87; Commercial Dir, Wellcome plc, 1987–89; Chief Exec., Amersham Internat., then Nycomed Amersham, subseq. Amersham plc, later Pres. and CEO, GE Healthcare, 1990–2006. Non-executive Director: Marconi (formerly GEC), 1997–2003; BP plc, 2006–12 (Sen. Ind. Dir, 2010–12); a Vice-Chm., 2004–06, External Dir, 2006–11, General Electric; Mem., Adv. Bd, Ondra Partners, 2009–13 (Chm., 2012–13). Chairman: Cttee on Design Bursaries Health and Envmt, RSA, 1986–88; Design Dimension, 1994–99 (Dep. Chm., 1988–94); Regeneration Through Heritage, BITC, 1997–2000; Prince's Trust, 1998–2003. Member: MRC, 2001–04; Royal Commn for the Exhibn of 1851, 2011– (Mem. Bd of Mgt, 2011–; Chm., Finance Cttee, 2012–). Trustee: Natural Hist. Mus., 2004–08; Educn and Employers' Taskforce, 2009–. Mem. Bd, Life Scis Inst., Michigan Univ., 2003–07; non-exec. Dir, Nat. Bureau of Asian Res., 2006–11. Mem. Bd, Chichester Festival Th., 2009– (Chm., 2012–). Hon. Mem., Russian Academia Europaea, 1996. Hon. FMedSci 2004; Hon. Fellow: Green Coll., Oxford, 2005 (Vis. Fellow, 1993–2005); Univ. of Cardiff, 2005; Hon. FKC 2006. Hon. DSSc Brunel, 2004; Hon. DCL Oxford, 2005; Hon. DSc: Imperial Coll. London, 2008; London Metropolitan, 2016. *Recreations:* international affairs, theatre, shooting, golf, tennis. *Club:* Athenæum.

**CASTLE, Andrew Nicholas;** lead commentator, BBC Tennis, since 2003; Presenter, LBC Radio; *b* Epsom, 15 Nov. 1963; *s* of Frank James Castle and Lyn Castle (later Mathers); *m* 1991, Sophia Runham; two *d*. *Educ:* Millfield Sch.; Richard Hulsh Sch., Taunton; Seminole Jun. Coll., Orlando, Florida; Wichita State Univ., Kansas (BA Mktg and Business 1985). Professional tennis player, 1986–92: Mem., GB Team, Davis Cup and Eur. Cup, 1986–92; Mem., GB Olympic Team, Seoul, 1988, Barcelona, 1992. Presenter: Skysports: tennis, 1992–2000; basketball, 1994–96; golf, 1995–2000; GMTV, 2000–10; LBC Radio, 2013–14; Andrew Castle Breakfast, 2014–16, The Great American Songbook, then The Smooth Sanctuary, 2016–18, Smooth Radio. *Publications:* squash, golf, tennis, running, yoga. *Clubs:* All England Lawn Tennis, International Lawn Tennis of GB.

**CASTLE, Rt Rev. Dr Brian Colin;** Bishop Suffragan of Tonbridge, 2002–15; an Honorary Assistant Bishop, Diocese of Bath and Wells, since 2016; *b* 7 Sept. 1949; *s* of Ernest and Sarah Castle; *m* 1979, Jane Richmond; one *s* two *d*. *Educ:* UCL (BA (Hons) Classics 1972); Cuddesdon Theol Coll. (MA Theol. Oxford 1980); Birmingham Univ. (PhD Theol. 1989). Social worker, 1972–74; teacher, Lesotho, Southern Africa, 1974. Ordained deacon, 1977, priest, 1978; Assistant Curate: St Nicholas, Sutton, 1977; Limpsfield, Surrey, 1977–81; Priest i/c, Chingola, Chililabombwe and Solwezi, Zambia, 1981–84; Vis. Lectr, Ecumenical Inst., Geneva, 1984–85; Vicar, N Petherton and Northmoor Green, Somerset, 1985–92; Vice-Principal and Dir of Pastoral Studies, Ripon Coll. Cuddesdon, Oxford, 1992–2001. Archbps' Advr in alternative spiritualities and new religious movements, 2005–15. Vis. Scholar, Sarum Coll., 2015–; Hon. Res. Fellow, Exeter Univ., 2016–. *Publications:* Hymns: the making and shaping of a theology for the whole people of God, 1990; Sing a New Song to the Lord, 1994; Unofficial God: voices from beyond the walls, 2004; Reconciling One and All: God's gift to the world, 2008; Reconciliation: the journey of a lifetime, 2014; articles in various theol jls. *Recreations:* fly fishing, cross country ski-ing. *Address:* Pound Cottage, Wootton Courtenay, Som TA24 8RH. *E:* brianc@briancastle.org. *W:* www.briancastle.org.

**CASTLE, Dawn Elizabeth;** *see* Ohlson, D. E.

**CASTLE, Enid,** OBE 1997; JP; Principal, The Cheltenham Ladies' College, 1987–96; *b* 28 Jan. 1936; *d* of Bertram and Alice Castle. *Educ:* Hulme Grammar Sch. for Girls, Oldham; Royal Holloway Coll., Univ. of London. BA Hons History. Colne Valley High Sch., Yorks, 1958–62; Kenya High Sch., Nairobi, 1962–65; Queen's Coll., Nassau, Bahamas, 1965–68; Dep. Head, Roundhill High Sch., Leicester, 1968–72; Headmistress: High Sch. for Girls, Gloucester, 1973–81; Red Maids' Sch., Bristol, 1982–87. Pres., GSA, 1990–91. JP Glos, 1989. *Recreations:* travel, tennis, bridge, music.

**CASTLE, (John) Mark,** OBE 2004; Chief Executive Officer, Field Studies Council, since 2018; *b* Irvine, 15 July 1960; *s* of John Castle and Patricia Castle; *m* 1988, Frances Evans; one *s* two *d*. *Educ:* Irvine Royal Acad.; Royal Mil. Acad. Sandhurst; Army Staff Coll., Camberley. Commnd officer RHF, 1979–99; CO KOSB, 2000–03; Dep. Dir Army Personnel Strategy, 2003–07; Chief of Campaign Plans, Iraq, 2007–08; Comdr Mission Support, Warminster, 2008; Dep. Commanding Gen. Min. of Interior Transition Team, Iraq, 2008–09. Chief Executive: Assoc. of Police Authorities, 2009–12; Assoc. of Police and Crime Comrs, 2012–14; CEO, Victim Support, 2014–18. Mem., Sentencing Council, 2015–. Trustee, Soc. for Protection of Animals Abroad, 2010–15. QCVS 2001. Bronze Star (USA), 2009; Legion of Merit (USA), 2010. *Recreations:* horse riding, ski-ing, gardening, military history, family. *Address:* Field Studies Council, Preston Montford, Montford Bridge, Shrewsbury, Shropshire SY4 1HW. *T:* (01743) 852100. *E:* mark.castle@field-studies-council.org.

**CASTLE, Rt Rev. Merwyn Edwin;** Bishop of False Bay, 2006–12; *b* 2 Nov. 1942; *s* of Ernest Edwin and Catherine Castle. *Educ:* Federal Theol Seminary, Alice (DipTh). Ordained deacon, 1969, priest, 1970; Rector, Christ the King, Coronationville, 1977–82; Dean, Johannesburg, 1982–87; Rector: Gambleville, Uitenhage, 1987–90; Matroosfontein, Cape Town, 1990–92; Chaplain, Archbishop of Cape Town, 1992–93; Rector, St Saviour's, Claremont, 1993–94; Bishop Suffragan of Cape Town, 1994–2006, Southern Reg., 1994–98, False Bay Reg., 1998–2006. Chairman: Provincial Liturgical Cttee, 2000–; Anglican AIDS and Healthcare Trust, 2007–; Liaison Bishop, Council for the Religious Life, 2000–; Mem., Provincial Pensions Bd, 2009–. Bishop Protector, African Province, Third Order of St Francis, 2005. *Recreations:* gardening, music, reading.

**CASTLE, Pamela Margaret,** OBE 2005; Chair, Castle Debates, since 2010; *b* Hornsey, London; *d* of Ernest Smith and Margaret Smith; *m* David Castle; two *s* one *d*. *Educ:* Hornsey High Sch.; Queen Mary Coll., Univ. of London (BSc 1st Cl. Hons Chem.); Coll. of Law, London; Oriel Coll., Oxford. Admitted as solicitor, 1988; Partner and Hd of Envmtl Law, CMS Cameron McKenna, 1994–2002. Chair: Thames Reg., Envmt Agency Adv. Cttee, 1998–2004; London Sustainable Develt Commn, 2001–05; UK Envmtl Law Assoc., 2001–03; Envmtl Law Foundn, 2003–10; Nat. Non-Food Crops Centre, 2005–13. Mem., Art Fund. Hon. LLD City, 2013. *Recreations:* walking, swimming, family and friends, reading, crosswords. *Address:* Castle Debates, 19 South Hill Park Gardens, NW3 2TD. *T:* (020) 7435 5700. *E:* chair@castledebates.org.uk. *Club:* Athenæum.

**CASTLE STEWART,** 8th Earl *cr* 1800 (Ireland); **Arthur Patrick Avondale Stuart;** Viscount Castle Stewart, 1793; Baron, 1619; Bt (NS) 1628, of Castle Stewart; farming and countryside management, now retired; *b* 18 Aug. 1928; 3rd but *e* surv. *s* of 7th Earl Castle Stewart, MC, and Eleanor May (*d* 1992), *er d* of late S. R. Guggenheim, New York; *S* father, 1961; *m* 1st, 1952, Edna Fowler (*d* 2003); one *s* one *d*; 2nd, 2004, Gillian, DL, *d* of Frederick William Savill, Blaby, Leics; three step *d*. *Educ:* Brambletye; Eton; Trinity Coll., Cambridge (BA). Lieut Scots Guards, 1949. Vice-Pres., S. R. Guggenheim Mus., NY, 1967–97; Peggy Guggenheim Museum, Venice: Vice-Pres., Adv. Bd, 1980–2011; Pres., 2011–13; Pres. Emeritus, 2013; Mem., Bd of Trustees, Guggenheim UK Charitable Trust, 2001–13. Trustee, Christian Community in UK, 1973–2003. FCMI. *Heir: s* Viscount Stuart, *qv*. *Address:* Stuart Hall, Stewartstown, Co. Tyrone BT71 5AE. *T:* (028) 8773 8208. *Club:* Carlton.

**CASTLEMAINE,** 8th Baron *cr* 1812; **Roland Thomas John Handcock,** MBE (mil.) 1981; *b* 22 April 1943; *s* of 7th Baron Castlemaine and Rebecca Ellen (*d* 1978), *o d* of William T. Soady, RN; *S* father, 1973; *m* 1st, 1969, Pauline Anne (marr. diss.), *e d* of John Taylor Bainbridge; 2nd, 1989, Lynne Christine, *e d* of Maj. Justin Michael Gurney, RAEC; one *s*. *Educ:* Campbell Coll., Belfast. psc, ph (cfs). Lt-Col, AAC, retd 1992. *Heir: s* Hon. Ronan Michael Edward Handcock, *b* 27 March 1989.

**CASTLES, Prof. Stephen,** DPhil; FASSA; Research Professor in Sociology, University of Sydney, 2009–16, now Honorary Professor; Research Associate, International Migration Institute, Oxford Martin School (formerly James Martin 21st Century School), University of Oxford, since 2011 (Associate Director and Senior Researcher, 2009–11); *b* Melbourne, 9 Nov. 1944; *s* of Heinz and Fay Castles; *m* 2000, Ellie Vasta. *Educ:* Oxted Co. Grammar Sch.; Univ. of Frankfurt am Main (Vor-Diplom); Univ. of Sussex (MA; DPhil). FASSA 1997. Res. Fellow, Res. Inst. Friedrich Ebert Foundn, Bonn, 1971–72; Lectr, 1972–75, Sen. Lectr, 1975–78, Prof. of Political Econ., 1978–79, Fachhochschule Frankfurt am Main; Co-ordinator, Totterdown Children's Community Workshop, Bristol, 1979–80; Lectr (pt-time) in Sociol., Bristol Poly., 1979–80; Co-ordinator, Design and Media, Foundn for Educn with Prodn, Botswana, 1981; Prof. of Political Econ. and Sociol., Fachhochschule Frankfurt am Main, 1982–86; Director: Centre for Multicultural Studies, Univ. of Wollongong, 1986–96; Centre for Asia Pacific Social Transformation Studies (jt venture of Univs of Wollongong and Newcastle), 1996–2001; University of Oxford: Prof. of Migration and Refugee Studies, 2001–09; Dir, Refugee Studies Centre, 2001–06; Sen. Res. Fellow, Internat. Migration Inst., James Martin 21st Century Sch., 2006–09. Vis. Prof. of Migration Studies, Univ. of Sussex, 1998–2000; Vis. Fellow, Centre d'Etudes et Recherches Internat., Paris, 1995; Visiting Scholar: Cornell Univ., 1988; Eur. Univ. Inst., Florence, 1991–92. Dir Secretariat, UNESCO-MOST Asia Pacific Migration Res. Network, 1995–2000. Chm., UK Home Office Adv. Panel on Country Information, 2003–05. Member: Nat. Population Council, 1987–91; Multicultural and Population Res. Adv. Bd, Australian Bureau of Immigration, 1989–96. *Publications:* (with G. Kosack) Immigrant Workers and Class Structure in Western Europe, 1973 (Italian edn 1976, Spanish edn 1984); (with W. Wüstenberg) The Education of the Future, 1979 (Spanish edn 1982); Here for Good: Western Europe's new ethnic minorities, 1984 (German edn 1987); (jtly) Mistaken Identity: multiculturalism and the demise of nationalism in Australia, 1988, 3rd edn 1992; (with M. Miller) The Age of Migration: international population movements in the modern world, 1993, (with M. Miller and H. de Haas) 5th edn 2014 (Japanese edn 1996, Spanish edn 2004, Turkish and Chinese edns 2005, Korean edn 2013); (jtly) A Shop Full of Dreams: ethnic small businesses in Australia, 1995; (jtly) Immigration and Australia, 1998; (with A. Davidson) Citizenship and Migration: globalization and the politics of belonging, 2000; Ethnicity and Globalization: from migrant worker to transnational citizen, 2000; (jtly) Migration, Citizenship and the European Welfare State: a European dilemma, 2006; *edited jointly:* Australia's Italians, 1992; The Teeth are Smiling… the persistence of racism in multicultural Australia, 1996; Migration in the Asia Pacific, 2003; Migration and Development: perspectives from the South, 2008 (Spanish edn 2007); Social Transformation and Migration: national and local experiences in South Korea, Turkey,

Mexico and Australia, 2015. *Recreations:* swimming, walking, photography, yoga. *Address:* School of Social and Political Sciences, University of Sydney, NSW 2006, Australia. *T:* (2) 93512650, *Fax:* (2) 90369380. *E:* stephen.castles@sydney.edu.au.

**CASTRO, Alicia Amalia;** Ambassador of Argentina to the Court of St James's, 2012–15; Permanent Representative to International Maritime Organization, 2012–15; *b* Bahia Blanca, Argentina, 27 July 1949; *d* of Juan Manuel Castro Justo and Alicia Beatriz Altube; one *d*. Cabin Crew, Aerolineas Argentinas, 1970–91; Gen. Sec., Argentine Flight Crew Mems' Assoc., 1991–2000; Founder, Argentine Workers' Union, 1994; Vice Pres., Internat. Transport Workers' Fedn, 2000–06. MP Argentina, 1997–2005; Mem., MERCOSUR Parly Cttee; drafted MERCOSUR Parly Protocol; Vice Pres., Transport Cttee; Spokesperson, Workers' Legislation Cttee; Pres., Friendship Parly Gp with Venezuela; Internat. Parly Rep for MERCOSUR, UNASUR, World Social Forum, G15 Summit of the Americas (Mar del Plata), 2001–05; Ambassador to Venezuela, 2006–11. Mem., Exec. Bd, Internat. Transport Workers' Fedn, 2002–14. Founder, UK Pro-Dialogue Gp on Malvinas Question, 2012. Order del Libertador (Venezuela), 2007; Order Antonio José de Sucre (1st Cl.) (Venezuela), 2011; Order Francisco de Miranda (1st Cl.) (Venezuela), 2012.

**CASTRO, Susan Rochford;** *see* Bickley, S. R.

**CATCHPOLE, Nancy Mona,** OBE 1987; Chairman, Board of Trustees, Bath Royal Literary and Scientific Institution, 2002–06 (a Trustee, since 1997); *b* 6 Aug. 1929; *d* of George William Page and Mona Dorothy Page (*née* Cowin), New Eltham; *m* 1959, Geoffrey David Arthur Catchpole; one *s* one *d*. *Educ:* Haberdashers' Aske's Hatcham Girls' Sch.; Bedford Coll., Univ. of London (BA Hons Hist.). Asst mistress, Gravesend Grammar Sch. for Girls, 1952–56; i/c History, Ipswich High Sch. GPDST, 1956–62; part time lectr in History and General Studies, Bath Tech. Coll., 1977–96. Sec., Bath Assoc. of University Women, 1970–75; Regional Rep. on Exec., BFUW, 1975–77, Vice-Pres., 1977–80, Pres., 1981–84. Women's National Commission: Co-Chairman, 1983–85; Immediate Past Co-Chairman, 1985–86; part-time Sec. with special responsibility for Women's Trng Roadshow prog., 1985–88; Actg Sec., March–Dec. 1988; Consultant for Women's Trng Roadshow prog. to RSA Women's Wkg Gp/Industry Matters, 1989–90; Vice-Chm., RSA Women's Adv. Gp (formerly Women's Working Group for Industry Year 1986), 1985–95; British Federation of Women Graduates Charitable Foundation (formerly Crosby Hall): Gov., 1992–98, 2002–04; Vice-Chm. of Govs, 1992–95, Chm., 1995–98; Chm., Grants Cttee, 1992–95; Archivist, 2012–. Chm., U3A, Bath, 2001–03. Chm., Bath Branch, Historical Assoc., 1993–96 (Sec., 1975–79; Hon. Treas., 2001–04). A Governor, Weston Infants' Sch., Bath, 1975–85 (Chm., 1981–83; Vice-Chm., 1983–86); Member: Managers, Eagle House Community Sch., Somerset CC, 1979–82; Case Cttee, Western Nat. Adoption Soc., 1975–77; Wessex RHA, 1986–90; Avon FHSA Service Cttee, 1990–96; Discipline Cttee, Avon HA, 1997–2003. FRSA 1986. Hon FHA (Jubilee Fellow), 2013. *Recreations:* listening, viewing, talking, writing. *Address:* 66 Leighton Road, Weston, Bath BA1 4NG. *T:* (01225) 423338.

**CATCHPOLE, Stuart Paul;** QC 2002; international arbitrator, since 2004; *b* 21 July 1964; *s* of Robert James Catchpole and Celia Catchpole; *m* 1995, Rebecca (marr. diss. 2013); one *s* two *d*; *m* 2015, Rachel; three *s*. *Educ:* Univ. of Durham; Inns of Court Sch. of Law. Called to the Bar, Inner Temple, 1987, Bencher, 2008; in practice at the Bar, 1988–. Treasury Supplemental Panel (Common Law), 1992–98; Jun. Counsel to the Crown, 1998–2002; a Recorder, 2004–14; a Dep. High Court Judge, 2010–14; Mem., States of Jersey Complaints Bd, 2013–. Part-time Legal Mem., Proscribed Orgns Appeal Commn, 2001–. *Publications:* (ed) Crown Proceedings, Halsbury's Laws, 4th edn, vol. 12 (1), 1998; (contrib.) Extradition, Halsbury's Laws, 4th edn, vol. 17 (2), 2000. *Recreations:* cinema, theatre, reading, wine, horse riding, sailing. *Address:* 39 Essex Chambers, 81 Chancery Lane, WC2A 1DD. *T:* (020) 7832 1111, *Fax:* (020) 7353 3978. *E:* stuart.catchpole@39essex.com. *Club:* Royal Automobile.

**CATER, Dr John Charles,** CBE 2015; DL; Vice-Chancellor, Edge Hill University (formerly Principal, Edge Hill College of Higher Education), since 1993; *b* Northampton, 3 Feb. 1953; *s* of William Ernest and Frances Brenda Cater; *m* 1981, Sue Lawlor; one *s* one *d*. *Educ:* Univ. of Wales, Lampeter (BA Hons Geog. 1974); Council for Nat. Academic Awards (PhD 1984). Res. Asst, Lectr and Res. Fellow, Liverpool Poly., 1974–79; Edge Hill College of Higher Education: Lectr, Sen. Lectr, then Hd of Dept of Urban Policy and Race Relns, 1979–86; Dep. Dean, 1986–90; Hd, Policy Res. and Develt, 1990–92; Dir of Resources, 1992–93. Chair: Higher Educn NW, 1999–2001; Gtr Merseyside and W Lancs Lifelong Learning Network, 2006–11. Director: Higher Educn Careers Service, 1994–2013; Standing Conf. of Principals, 1994–2004 (Vice-Chm., 1997–2001; Chm., 2001–03); TTA, 1999–2005 (Chairman: Audit Cttee, 2001–03; Accreditation Cttee, 2003–05); Graduate Prospects, 1999–2013; Trng and Develt Agency for Schs, 2005–06 (Chm., Accreditation Cttee, 2005–06). Mem., Adv. Cttee on Degree-Awarding Powers, QAA, 2006–12. Universities UK: Mem., Health and Social Care Cttee, 2004–; Mem., 2007–, Chm., 2014–, Teacher Educn Adv. Gp; Mem., DFE/DoH Social Work Reform Bd, 2010–16. Dir, 1994–2013, Chm., 2003–05, Liverpool City of Learning. DL Lancs 2019. Hon. Fellow, Liverpool John Moores Univ., 2016. *Publications:* (with T. P. Jones) Social Geography, 1989; contrib. articles and chapters on residential segregation, black and Asian business, housing and public policy. *Recreations:* most sports (Rugby, cricket, golf, squash), current affairs, reading, travel. *Address:* Edge Hill University, St Helens Road, Ormskirk, Lancs L39 4QP. *T:* (01695) 584234, *Fax:* (01695) 577137.

**CATES, Prof. Michael Elmhirst,** PhD; FRS 2007; FRSE; Lucasian Professor of Mathematics, University of Cambridge, since 2015; *b* 5 May 1961. *Educ:* Trinity Coll., Cambridge (BA 1982, MA; PhD 1986; Hon. Fellow, 2013). Cavendish Laboratory, Cambridge: Asst Lectr, 1989–92; Univ. Lectr, 1992–95; Prof. of Natural Philosophy, Sch. of Physics, Univ. of Edinburgh, 1995–2015; Royal Soc. Res. Prof., Univ. of Edinburgh, later at Univ. of Cambridge, 2007–. Sen. Res. Fellow, Trinity Coll., Cambridge, 2016–. FRSE 2005. *Publications:* articles in learned jls. *Recreations:* hill-walking, painting, music. *Address:* Faculty of Mathematics, Centre for Mathematical Sciences, Wilberforce Road, Cambridge CB3 0WA.

**CATHCART,** family name of **Earl Cathcart**.

**CATHCART, 7th Earl** *cr* 1814; **Charles Alan Andrew Cathcart,** ACA; Lord Cathcart (Scot.) 1447; Viscount Cathcart, Baron Greenock 1807; *b* 30 Nov. 1952; *s* of 6th Earl Cathcart, CB, DSO, MC and Rosemary (*d* 1980), *yr d* of Air Cdre Sir Percy Smyth-Osbourne, CMG, CBE; *S* father, 1999; *m* 1981, Vivien Clare, *o d* of F. D. McInnes Skinner; one *s* one *d*. *Educ:* Eton. Commnd Scots Guards, 1972–75. Whinney Murray, 1976–79; Ernst & Whinney, 1979–83; Gardner Mountain and Capel-Cure Agencies Ltd, 1983–94; Director: Murray Lawrence Members Agencies Ltd, 1995–96; RGA Holdings Ltd, 1996–2011; RGA Capital Ltd, 1996–2011; RGA Reinsurance UK Ltd, 1996–2011; Vivien Greenock Ltd, 2007–; Spring Garden Eggs Ltd, 2011–. Mem. (C) Breckland DC, 1997–2007. Elected Mem., H of L, 2007. Mem., Queen's Bodyguard for Scotland, Royal Co. of Archers. *Recreations:* ski-ing, sailing, country pursuits. *Heir:* s Lord Greenock, *qv*. *Address:* Gateley Hall, Norfolk. *Club:* Pratt's.

**CATHCART, Samuel;** Sheriff of Glasgow and Strathkelvin at Glasgow (formerly Floating Sheriff), 2000–17; *b* 5 March 1950; *s* of Samuel Cathcart and Margaret Gordon or Cathcart; *m* 1985, Sandra Fullarton; one *s* one *d*. *Educ:* Dalry High Sch.; Edinburgh Univ. (LLB). Admitted Solicitor, 1974, in practice, 1974–77; Procurator Fiscal Depute, 1977–88; called to the Scottish Bar, 1989; Advocate, 1989–99; Advocate Depute, Crown Office, 1996–99. *Recreations:* sailing, fishing. *Address:* 43 Douglas Street, Largs, Ayrshire KA30 8PT. *T:* (01475) 672478.

**CATHERWOOD, Andrea Catherine, (Mrs R. G. Smith);** television and radio broadcaster; journalist; *b* 27 Nov. 1967; *d* of late Henry Robert Courtney Catherwood and of Adrienne Catherwood; *m* 2002, Richard Gray Smith; three *s* (of whom two are twins). *Educ:* Strathearn Sch., Belfast; Manchester Univ. (LLB Hons). Reporter, Ulster TV, 1991–93; reporter, 1994–96, news anchor, 1996–98, CNBC Asia, in Hong Kong; corresp. and newscaster, ITV News, 1998–2000; evening newscaster, Channel 5 News, 2000–01; Internat. Corresp. and newscaster, ITV News, 2001–06; Presenter: Sunday Edition, 2006–07; Bloomberg Television, 2009–12; BBC Radio 4, 2013–. *Recreations:* watching a lot of cricket, time with family and friends, cooking, reading, theatre, sailing in Mallorca. *W:* andreacatherwood.com, www.twitter.com/acatherwoodnews. *Clubs:* Soho House; Royal North of Ireland Yacht; Reial Club Nautic (Port de Pollença).

**CATLIN, John Anthony,** CB 2004; Director (Legal Services), Departments of Health and for Work and Pensions (formerly of Social Security), 1996–2007; *b* 25 Nov. 1947; *s* of John Vincent Catlin and Kathleen Glover Catlin (*née* Brand); *m* 1974, Caroline Jane Goodman; one *s* two *d*. *Educ:* Ampleforth Coll., York; Birmingham Univ. (LLB 1969). Solicitor of the Supreme Court, 1972. Articled Clerk, 1970–72, Asst Solicitor, 1972–75, Gregory Rowcliffe & Co.; Legal Asst, 1975–78, Sen. Legal Asst, 1978–84, Treasury Solicitor's Dept; Asst Solicitor, 1984–89, Dep. Solicitor, 1989–96, Dept of the Envmt. *Recreations:* opera and music, languages, history. *E:* jcatlin0@googlemail.com.

**CATLIN, Stephen John Oakley;** Executive Deputy Chairman, XL Catlin, 2015–17 (Chief Executive and Deputy Chairman, Catlin Group Ltd, 1995–2015); *b* Aldershot, 25 June 1954; *s* of Robin John Oakley Catlin and Rita Fortune Catlin; *m* 1975, Helen Margaret Gill; two *d*. ACII 2011. Dep. underwriter, B. L. Evens and Others, 1982–84; Founder and Chief Exec., Catlin Underwriting Agencies Ltd, 1984–95, Chm., 1987–95. Lloyd's Nominated Dir, Equitas Hldgs Ltd, 1996–2002. Chm., Lloyd's Market Assoc., 2000–03; Member: Council, Lloyd's, 2002–04; Lloyd's Franchise Bd, 2003–06. Pres., Insce Inst. of London, 2010–11. Chm., Assoc. Bermuda Insurers and Reinsurers, 2015–16; Vice Chm., Internat. Insce Soc., 2015–; Chair, Insce Develt Forum, 2015–. Vis. Fellow, Oxford Univ. Centre for Corporate Reputation, 2008–. Chm., Sick Children's Trust, 1999–2015. Ernst & Young Entrepreneur of the Year, 2011. *Recreations:* fishing, shooting.

**CATLING, Charlotte Merilyn S.;** *see* Skene Catling.

**CATLING, Christopher Paul;** Secretary, Royal Commission on the Ancient and Historical Monuments of Wales, since 2015; *b* Stamford, Lincs, 11 Oct. 1955; *s* of Harry Catling and Elizabeth Catling; *m* 1983, Katharine Owen; one *s* one *d*. *Educ:* Cirencester Comp. Sch.; St Catharine's Coll., Cambridge (BA 1979). FSA 2004; MCIfA (MIfA 2004). PR consultant, 1979–85; independent author and heritage advocate, 1985–2015. Founder Dir, Heritage Alliance, 2002–05; Director: Cotswold Archaeol., 2005–15; Marc Fitch Fund, 2010–. Chair: Welsh Historic Places of Worship Forum, 2017–; Historic Wales Strategic Partnership, 2017–. Mem. Council, NT, 2017– (Mem., Wales Adv. Bd, 2017–). *Publications:* Cirencester: the development and buildings of a Cotswold town, 1975; Eyewitness Travel: Florence and Tuscany, 1990, 22nd edn 2018; Eyewitness Travel: Venice and the Veneto, 1992, 22nd edn 2018; National Geographic Amsterdam, 2000, 2nd edn 2014; Eyewitness Travel: Madeira, 2005, 15th edn 2018; Practical Archaeology, 2009, 3rd edn 2011. *Recreations:* Radio 3, real books, running, exploring Portugal. *Address:* Royal Commission on the Ancient and Historical Monuments of Wales, Plas Crug, Aberystwyth SY23 1NJ. *T:* (01970) 621201. *E:* christopher.catling@rcahmw.gov.uk.

**CATLOW, Prof. (Charles) Richard (Arthur),** DPhil; FRS 2004; FRSC, FInstP; Professorial Research Associate, Department of Chemistry, University College London, since 2014 (Professor of Solid State Chemistry and Dean, Mathematics and Physical Sciences Faculty, 2007–14; Head, Department of Chemistry, 2007–08); *b* 24 April 1947; *s* of Rolf M. Catlow and Constance Catlow (*née* Aldred); *m* 1978, Carey Anne Chapman; one *s*; *m* 2000, Nora de Leeuw. *Educ:* Clitheroe Royal Grammar School; St John's College, Oxford (MA, DPhil). FRSC 1990; FInstP 1995. Research Fellow, Oxford Univ., 1973–76; Lectr, Dept of Chemistry, UCL, 1976–85; Prof. of Physical Chemistry, Univ. of Keele, 1985–89; Wolfson Prof. of Natural Philosophy, 1989–2007, Dir, Davy Faraday Lab., 1998–2007, Royal Instn of GB. Member: CCLRC, 2006–07; Council, Royal Soc., 2009–11 (Foreign Sec. and Vice Pres., 2016–). Liversidge Lect., RSC, 2009. Medal for Solid State Chem., 1992, Award for Interdisciplinary Science, 1998, RSC. *Publications:* (jtly) Point Defects in Materials, 1988; ed jtly and contrib. to works on computational and materials sciences; 700 papers in learned jls. *Recreations:* reading, music, walking. *Address:* Mathematics and Physical Sciences Faculty, University College London, Gower Street, WC1E 6BT. *E:* c.r.a.catlow@ucl.ac.uk. *Club:* Athenæum.

**CATON, Martin Philip;** *b* 15 June 1951; *s* of William John Caton and Pauline Joan Caton; *m* 1996, Bethan, *d* of late Hermus Evans and of Menai Evans; two step *d*. *Educ:* Newport Grammar Sch., Essex; Norfolk Sch. of Agriculture; Aberystwyth Coll. of FE (HNC). Scientific Officer, Welsh Plant Breeding Stn, Aberystwyth, 1974–84; Political Researcher, David Morris, MEP, 1984–97. Mem. (Lab) Swansea CC, 1988–97. MP (Lab) Gower, 1997–2015.

**CATON, Dr Valerie, (Mrs D. M. Harrison);** HM Diplomatic Service, retired; Ambassador to Finland, 2006–10; *b* 12 May 1952; *d* of Robert Caton and Florence Amy Caton (*née* Aspden); *m* 1987, David Mark Harrison; one *s* one *d*. *Educ:* Blackburn High Sch. for Girls; Bristol Univ. (BA, PhD); Grad. Sch. of European Studies, Univ. of Reading (MA). Lectrice, Univ. of Sorbonne, Paris, 1977–78; Tutor in French, Exeter Univ., 1978–80; joined HM Diplomatic Service, 1980: FCO, 1980–82; Second, later First Sec., EC Affairs, Brussels, 1982–84; First Sec. (Chancery), Paris, 1988–92; Dep. Head of Mission, Stockholm, 1993–96; Counsellor (Financial and Economic), Paris, 1997–2001; Head: Envmt Policy Dept, FCO, 2002–04; Climate Change and Energy Gp, FCO, 2004–06. Dir, UK Nordic Baltic Summit, 2010–11; Dir and Trustee, CAMFED Internat., 2013–. St Antony's College, Oxford: Sen. Associate Mem., 2001–02, 2012–13; Sen. Common Room Mem., 2013–. Vis. Fellow, Sch. of Politics, Econs and Internat. Relations, Univ. of Reading, 2013–; Associate, Centre for Political and Diplomatic Studies, 2015–. *Publications:* France and the Politics of European Economic and Monetary Union, 2015; various articles in jls on France and EU issues, and on works of French writer, Raymond Queneau. *Recreations:* reading, theatre, collecting humorous books, walking, riding. *Address:* School of Politics, Economics and International Relations, University of Reading, Whiteknights, Reading RG6 6AA.

**CATOVSKY, Prof. Daniel,** MD, DSc; FRCP, FRCPath, FMedSci; Professor of Haematology, and Head of Department of Haematology and Cytogenetics, Institute of Cancer Research, 1988–2004, now Professor Emeritus; Hon. Consultant, Royal Marsden Hospital, 1988–2004; *b* 19 Sept. 1937; *s* of Felix Catovsky and Ana Kabanchik; *m* 1960, Julia Margaret Polak (Dame Julia Polak, DBE) (*d* 2014); two *s* (one *d* decd). *Educ*: Faculty of Medicine, Buenos Aires Univ. (MD 1961); London Univ. (DSc Med. 1985). FRCPath 1986; FRCP 1990. Royal Postgraduate Medical School: Fellow, 1967–76; Hon. Sen. Lectr in Haematol. and Medicine, 1976–87; Prof. of Haematol Oncology, 1987–88; Consultant, Hammersmith Hosp., 1976–88. Visiting Professor: Mount Sinai Med. Sch., NY, 1981; M. D. Anderson Cancer Center, Univ. of Texas, 2004–05. Ham-Wasserman Lecture (first annual), Amer. Soc. of Hematology, 1984. FMedSci 1999. British Soc. for Haematology Medal, 2000; Binet-Rai Medal, Internat. Workshop on Chronic Lymphocytic Leukaemia, 2005. *Publications*: The Leukemic Cell, 1981, 2nd edn 1991; (with A. Polliack) Chronic Lymphocytic Leukaemia, 1988; (with R. Foa) The Lymphoid Leukaemias, 1990; (ed with A. V. Hoffbrand and E. G. Tuddenham) Postgraduate Haematology, 5th ed 2005, (ed with A. V. Hoffbrand, A. R. Green and E. G. Tuddenham) 6th ed 2010; 900 articles in learned jls. *Recreations*: walking, films, theatre. *Address*: Division of Molecular Pathology, Institute of Cancer Research, 15 Cotswold Road, Sutton, Surrey SM2 5NG. *T*: (020) 8722 4461.

**CATTANACH, Bruce Macintosh,** PhD, DSc; FRS 1987; Senior Scientist, MRC, 1970–98; *b* 5 Nov. 1932; *s* of James and Margareta Cattanach; *m* 1st, 1966, Margaret Bouchier Crewe (*d* 1996); two *d*; 2nd, 1999, Josephine Peters. *Educ*: King's Coll., Univ. of Durham (BSc, 1st Cl. Hons); Inst. of Animal Genetics, Univ. of Edinburgh (PhD, DSc). Scientific Staff, MRC Induced Mutagenesis Unit, Edinburgh, 1959–62, 1964–66; NIH Post Doctoral Res. Fellow, Biology Div., Oak Ridge Nat. Lab., Tenn, USA, 1962–64; Sen. Scientist, City of Hope Med. Center, Duarte, Calif, 1966–69; Scientific Staff, 1969–86, Hd of Genetics Div., 1987–96, MRC Radiobiology Unit, Chilton, Oxon; Actg Dir, MRC Mammalian Genetics Unit, Harwell, 1996–97. *Publications*: contribs to several learned jls on X-chromosome inactivation, sex determination, mammalian chromosome imprinting, and genetics generally. *Recreations*: squash; breeding, showing and judging pedigree dogs; investigating inherited disease in dogs and devising control schemes for elimination. *Address*: Downs Edge, Reading Road, Harwell, Oxon OX11 0JJ. *T*: (01235) 835410.

**CATTERALL, Dr John Ashley,** OBE 1995; FIMMM, FInstP; Senior Executive, Engineering Council, 1997–99; *b* 26 May 1928; *s* of John William Catterall and Gladys Violet Catterall; *m* 1960, Jennifer Margaret Bradfield (*d* 2010); two *s*. *Educ*: Faculty of Science and Technol., London (BSc, PhD, DIC). ARSM; FIMMM (FIM 1964); FInstP 1968; CPhys 1965; CEng 1978. National Physical Lab., 1952–74; Dept of Industry, 1974–81; Head, Energy Technology Div., and Dep. Chief Scientist, Dept of Energy, 1981–83; Sec., SERC, 1983–88; Sec., Inst. of Metals, 1988–91, then Sec. and Chief Exec., Inst. of Materials, 1991–97. Inst. of Metals Rosenhain Medal for Physical Metallurgy, 1970. *Publications*: (with O. Kubaschewski) Thermochemical Data of Alloys, 1956; contrib. Philos. Mag., Jl Inst. of Physics, Jl Inst. of Metals. *Recreation*: reading. *Address*: Hill House, The Doward, Whitchurch, Ross-on-Wye, Herefordshire HR9 6DU. *T*: (01600) 890341.

**CATTERALL, John Stewart;** novelist; Director, C&T Partnerships, 2012–15 (Managing Director, 1993–2001, Director, 2002–12, C&T (formerly Conferences and Training Ltd)); *b* 13 Jan. 1939; *s* of John Bernard and Eliza Catterall; *m* 1965, Ann Beryl Hughes; two *s*. *Educ*: Blackpool Tech. Coll. and Sch. of Art. Mem. CIPFA. Posts in local authorities, 1961–70; Management Accountant, Cambridgeshire and Isle of Ely CC, 1970–72, Chief Accountant, 1972–73; Asst County Treasurer, Financial Planning and Accounting, Cambs CC, 1973–76; Dist Treasurer, Southampton and SW Hants DHA, 1976–78, Area Treasurer, 1978–82; Regional Treasurer, NE Thames RHA, 1982–85; Dep. Dir, Finance, NHS Mgt Bd, 1985–89; Head of Health Services, 1985–89, Head of Health Adv. Services, 1989, CIPFA. Chm. and Chief Exec., C International Ltd, 1990–92; Director: Capita PLC, 1992–93; Agenda Planning Res. Ltd, 2001–10. *Publications*: novels: The Price of Fear, 2013; Bellman's Folly, 2013; The Anderton Legacy, 2015; contribs to professional jls. *Recreations*: golf, swimming, reading. *Address*: 22 Ainslie Place, Lymington, Hants SO41 9PX. *T*: 07926 435673.

**CATTERSON, Her Honour Marie Thérèse;** a Circuit Judge, 2001–18; *b* 14 Oct. 1948; *e d* of late James Joseph Catterson and Rosemary Catterson; *m* 1984; two *d*. *Educ*: Wyggeston Girls' Grammar Sch., Leicester; University Coll. London (LLB 1970). Called to the Bar, Gray's Inn, 1972; in practice as barrister, S Eastern Circuit, 1972–2001; a Recorder, 1996–2001. *Recreations*: gardening, travel.

**CATTO,** family name of **Baron Catto**.

**CATTO, 3rd Baron** *cr* 1936, of Cairncatto, co. Aberdeen; **Innes Gordon Catto;** Bt 1921; *b* 7 Aug. 1950; *e s* of 2nd Baron Catto; *S* father, 2001; *m* 2014, Ali Farhan Negyal. *Educ*: Grenville Coll.; Shuttleworth Agric. Coll. *Heir*: *b* Hon. Alexander Gordon Catto [*b* 22 June 1952; *m* 1981, Elizabeth Scott, twin *d* of Maj. T. P. Boyes; two *s* one *d*].

**CATTO, Sir Graeme (Robertson Dawson),** Kt 2002; MD; DSc; FRCP, FRCPE, FRCPGlas, FMedSci; FRSE; Professor of Medicine, University of Aberdeen, 2005–09, now Emeritus; *b* 24 April 1945; *s* of William Dawson Catto and Dora Elizabeth (*née* Spiby); *m* 1967, Joan Sievewright (MBE 2016); one *s* one *d*. *Educ*: Robert Gordon's Coll., Aberdeen; Univ. of Aberdeen (MB ChB Hons 1969; MD Hons 1975; DSc 1988). FRCPGlas 1982; FRCP 1984; FRCPE 1988; FRSE 1996. House Officer, Aberdeen Royal Infirmary, 1969–70; Res. Fellow, then Lectr, Univ. of Aberdeen, 1970–75; Harkness Fellow, Commonwealth Fund of NY; Fellow in Medicine, Harvard Univ., 1975–77; University of Aberdeen: Sen. Lectr, then Reader, 1977–88; Dean, Faculty of Medicine and Med. Scis, 1992–98; Prof. of Medicine and Therapeutics, 1988–2000; Vice Principal, 1995–2000; Hon. Consultant Physician and Nephrologist, Aberdeen Royal Infirmary, 1977–2000; Pro-Vice Chancellor (Medicine), Univ. of London, 2003–05, Prof. Emeritus, 2015; Vice Principal, KCL and Dean, GKT, 2000–05; Hon. Consultant Nephrologist, Guy's and St Thomas' NHS Trust, 2000–05; Hon. Consultant Physician and Nephrologist, NHS Grampian, 2005–09. Vice-Chm., Aberdeen Royal Hosps NHS Trust, 1992–99. Chief Scientist, Scottish Executive (formerly Scottish Office) Health Dept, 1997–2000. Member: GMC, 1994–2009 (Pres., 2002–09; Chm. Educn Cttee, 1999–2002); SHEFC, 1996–2002; Specialist Trng Authority, 1999–2002; Standing Medical Adv. Cttee, 2002–05; Council, Regulation of Healthcare Professionals, 2003–08; Scottish Stem Cell Network, 2006–11 (Chm., 2008–11); Commn on Assisted Dying, 2010–11; Chm., 2012–15, Patron, 2015–, Dignity in Dying. Member: Lambeth, Southwark and Lewisham HA, 2000–02; SE London Strategic HA, 2003–05; Qatar Council for Healthcare Practitioners, 2013–; Jt Adv. Bd, Weill-Cornell Med. Sch., Qatar, 2017–. Chm., HE Better Regulation Gp, Universities UK, 2009–12. Pres., ASME, 2009–13; Vice Pres., Acad. of Experts, 2009–. Founder FMedSci 1998 (Treas., 1998–2001); Fellow, Acad. of Med. Educators, 2012. Patron, Med. Council on Alcohol, 2007–. Chairman: Robert Gordon's Coll., Aberdeen, 1995–2005; Lathallan Sch., 2012–17; Gov., Qatar Sci. and Technol. Park, 2005–07; Pres., Coll. of Med., 2010–15. Hon. FRCGP 2000; Hon. FRCSE 2002; Hon. FFPM 2008. FRSA 1996. FKC 2005. Hon. LLD Aberdeen, 2002; Hon. DSc: St Andrews, 2003; Robert Gordon's Univ., 2004; Kent, 2007; South Bank, 2008; London, 2009. Hon. MD: Southampton, 2004; Brighton, 2010; Buckingham, 2015. *Publications*: (ed) Clinical Transplantation: current practice and future prospects, 1987; (with D. A. Power) Nephrology, 1988; (ed) Calculus Disease, 1988; (ed) Chronic Renal Failure, 1988; (ed) Haemodialysis, 1988; (ed) Management of Renal Hypertension, 1988; (ed) Pregnancy and Renal Disorders, 1988; (ed) Drugs and the Kidney, 1989; (ed) Glomerulo-nephritis, 1989; Multisystem Diseases, 1989; Transplantation, 1989; (ed) Urinary Tract Infections, 1989; (with A. W. Thomson) Immunology of Renal Transplantation, 1993; contrib. to learned jls on aspects of renal disease. *Recreation*: hills and glens. *Address*: 4 Woodend Avenue, Aberdeen AB15 6YL. *T*: (01224) 310509; Maryfield, Glenbuchat, Aberdeenshire AB36 8TS. *T*: (01975) 641317. *Clubs*: Athenæum; Royal Northern and University (Aberdeen).

**CAU, Antoine Emond André;** Founding President, Antedman SA, Switzerland, since 2006; *b* 26 Aug. 1947; *s* of Henri and Laure Cau; *m* 1978, Patricia Stamm. *Educ*: Lycée Mignet, Aix-en-Provence; Institut d'Etudes Commerciales de Grenoble (diplôme de direction et de gestion des entreprises; maîtrise de gestion). Hertz: Station Manager, Avignon, 1970–75; station manager posts, 1975–77; District Manager: Nice, 1977; Côte d'Azur, 1978–80; Zone Manager, S of France, 1980–82; Ops Manager, Italy, 1982–84; Corporate Accounts Manager, Hertz Europe, 1984; Gen. Manager, France, 1985–90; Vice Pres., Hertz Europe, 1990; Vice Pres., Hertz Corp., and Pres., Hertz International, 1990–97; Chief Executive: Forte Hotels, 1998–2001; W Eur. Div., Compass Gp, 2001–05. Chevalier: de l'Ordre National du Mérite (France), 1992; de la Légion d'Honneur (France), 2004. *Recreations*: motorsport, music. *Address*: Antedman, 6 Place des Perrières, 1296 Coppet, Switzerland. *E*: antoine.cau@antedman.ch.

**CAUDWELL, John David;** Founder, Chairman and Chief Executive, Caudwell Group, 1978–2006; *b* 7 Oct. 1952; *s* of Walter and Beryl Caudwell; partner, Claire Johnson; two *s* three *d*. *Educ*: Berryhill Jun. High Sch.; Stoke-on-Trent Polytech. (HNC Mech. Engrg). With Michelin Tyre Co., 1970–80. Founder and Chm., The Caudwell Charity, later Caudwell Children, 2000–. *Recreations*: charity fundraising, cycling, flying, diving, motorcycling, antiques. *Address*: Caudwell Children, Minton Hollins Building, Shelton Old Road, Stoke-on-Trent, Staffs ST4 7RY. *T*: 0845 3001348, *Fax*: (01782) 600639. *E*: charity@caudwellchildren.com.

**CAULCOTT, Thomas Holt;** Chief Executive, Birmingham City Council, 1982–88; *b* 7 June 1927; *s* of late L. W. Caulcott and Doris Caulcott; *m* 1st, 1954, C. Evelyn Lowden (marr. diss. 1987); one *d* (and one *s* decd); 2nd, 1988, Jane Marguerite Allsopp. *Educ*: Solihull Sch.; Emmanuel Coll., Cambridge. Asst Principal, Central Land Bd and War Damage Commn, 1950–53; transferred to HM Treasury, 1953; Private Sec. to Economic Sec. to the Treasury, 1955; Principal, Treasury supply divs, 1956–60; Private Sec. to successive Chancellors of the Exchequer, Sept. 1961–Oct. 1964; Principal Private Sec. to First Sec. of State (DEA), 1964–65; Asst Sec., HM Treasury, 1965–66; Min. of Housing and Local Govt, 1967–69; Civil Service Dept, 1969–70; Under-Sec., Machinery of Govt Gp, 1970–73; Principal Finance Officer, Local Govt Finance Policy, DoE, 1973–76; Sec., AMA, 1976–82. Chm., Royal Shrewsbury Hosps NHS Trust, 1998–2003; non-exec. Dir, Heart of Birmingham PCT, 2006–11. Mem., S Shropshire DC, 1991–95 (Chm., Policy and Resources Cttee, 1993–95). Mem. Cttee of Mgt, Hanover Housing Assoc., 1988–94. Mem. Bd, W Midlands Arts, 1996–97. Harkness Fellowship, Harvard and Brookings Instn, 1960–61; Vis. Fellow, Dept of Land Economy, Univ. of Cambridge, 1984–85; Hon. Fellow: Inst. of Local Govt Studies, Univ. of Birmingham, 1979–; Birmingham City Univ. (formerly Birmingham Polytechnic, later Univ. of Central England), 1990–. *Publications*: Management and the Politics of Power, 1996. *Address*: 12 Dinham, Ludlow, Shropshire SY8 1EJ. *T*: (01584) 875154.

**CAULFEILD,** family name of **Viscount Charlemont**.

**CAULFIELD, Ian George,** CBE 2000; DL; Clerk of the Council and Chief Executive, Warwickshire County Council, and Clerk to the Warwickshire Lieutenancy, 1986–2005; *b* 14 Dec. 1942; *s* of William and Elizabeth Caulfield; *m* 1967, Geraldine Mary Hind; three *s*. *Educ*: Liverpool Inst. High Schs for Boys; Univ. of Manchester (BA Hons Geography); Liverpool Poly. (DipTP). Jun. Planning Assistant, Liverpool City, 1964–65; Planning Assistant, Lancs CC, 1965–69; Sen. Planning Officer, Hants CC, 1969–74; Asst Hd, Res. and Intelligence Unit, 1974–76, Prin. Assistant to Chief Exec., 1976–78, Oxford CC; Asst Exec., 1978–83, Dep. Clerk and Asst Chief Exec., 1983–86, Warwicks CC. DL Warwicks, 2005. *Publications*: (jtly) Planning for Change: strategic planning and local government, 1989. *Recreations*: sport, particularly soccer.

**CAULFIELD, Rev. James Edward;** Principal Roman Catholic Chaplain to the Royal Air Force, since 2012; *b* Downpatrick, NI, 10 May 1961; *s* of William Caulfield and Margaret Mary Caulfield. *Educ*: Mount St Mary's Coll., Spinkhill; Rutland Sixth Form Coll., Oakham; Southfields Coll. of FE, Leicester (OND Catering); All Hallows Coll., Dublin (Dip. Philosophy; BD). Assistant Priest: Our Lady and the English Martyrs Church, Cambridge, 1989–92; Lowestoft, 1992–94; Parish Priest, Huntingdon, 1994–97; RAF Chaplain, 1997–. Mem., Standing Cttee, Nat. Conf. of Priests for Eng. and Wales, 2001–06. Provincial Chaplain, Knights St Columba, East Anglia, 1992–97. *Recreations*: photography, hill-walking, reading, exploring history, travel. *E*: cardinal-biggles@hotmail.co.uk. *Club*: Royal Air Force.

**CAULFIELD, Maria Colette;** MP (C) Lewes, since 2015. Nurse and Research Sister, Royal Marsden Hosp. An owner and shareholder, Lewes FC. Non-exec. Dir, BHT Sussex. Mem. (C) Brighton and Hove CC, 2007–11. Contested (C) Caerphilly, 2010. *Address*: House of Commons, SW1A 0AA.

**CAULFIELD, Sir Mark Jonathan,** Kt 2019; MD; FRCP, FMedSci; Chief Scientist, Genomics England, since 2013 (interim Chief Executive, 2019); Professor of Clinical Pharmacology, since 1999 and Co-Director, William Harvey Research Institute, since 2002, Barts and The London School of Medicine and Dentistry, Queen Mary University of London; Director, National Institute for Health Research Barts Biomedical Research Centre, since 2008; *b* 16 July 1960; *s* of Michael Caulfield and Patricia Caulfield (*née* Cox); *m* 1991, Frances; two *d*. *Educ*: Bishop Douglass Sch.; London Hosp. Med. Coll., Univ. of London (MB BS; MD). MRCP 1988, FRCP 2000. Barts and The London School of Medicine and Dentistry, Queen Mary University of London: Sen. Lectr in Clin. Pharmacol., 1996–98; Reader in Clin. Pharmacol., 1998–99. Hon. Consultant Physician, Barts Health NHS Trust (formerly Royal Hosps Trust, subseq. Barts and The London NHS Trust), 1996–. Pres., British Hypertension Soc., 2009–11. Member: British and Irish Hypertension Soc., 1993–; British Pharmacol. Soc., 1996–; Eur. Soc. of Hypertension, 2000–; Internat. Soc. of Hypertension, 2000–. MInstD 2006. FMedSci 2008. *Publications*: over 200 articles in scientific jls. *Recreations*: walking, golf. *Address*: William Harvey Research Institute, Queen Mary University of London, Charterhouse Square, EC1M 6BQ. *T*: (020) 7882 3402. *E*: m.j.caulfield@qmul.ac.uk; 35 Sandiland Crescent, Hayes, Kent BR2 7DP.

**CAUSTON, Richard John;** composer; *b* London, 12 March 1971; *s* of John and Ann Causton; *m* 2005, Jessica Summers; one *s* one *d*. *Educ*: William Ellis Sch.; Univ. of York (BA 1st Cl. Hons 1993; MA 1994); Royal Coll. of Music (Postgrad. ARCM 1995). Fellow Commoner in Creative Arts, Trinity Coll., Cambridge, 2003–05; Composition Tutor,

Birmingham Conservatoire, 2006–12; Lectr in Composition, 2012–15, Reader in Composition, 2015–, Univ. of Cambridge; Fellow in Music, King's College, Cambridge, 2012–. Work with ensembles incl. City of Birmingham SO, BBC SO, Philharmonia Orch., Orch. of Age of Enlightenment, Sinfonie-Orchester Basel, Rundfunksinfonieorchester Saarbrücken, Halle Orch., EU Youth Orch., London Sinfonietta, Birmingham Contemp. Music Gp, Nash Ensemble and Ensemble Recherche. Has made recordings. 1st prize, 3rd Internat. Nuove Sincronie Composition Award, 1996; British Composer Award, BASCA, 2004; Royal Philharmonic Soc. Award, 2006. *Publications:* The Persistence of Memory, 1995; Notturno, 1998, rev. edn 2001; Millennium Scenes, 1999, rev. edn 2001; Seven States of Rain, 2002; Between Two Waves of the Sea, 2004; Phoenix, 2006, rev. edn 2007; La Terra Impareggiabile, 2007; As Kingfishers Catch Fire, 2007, rev. edn 2008; Chamber Symphony, 2009, rev. edn 2010; Twenty-Seven Heavens, 2012; Out of Your Sleep, 2012; Ricercare, 2012; De Profundis, 2014; Night Piece, 2014; The Flight, 2015, Psalm 27, 2017; Ik Zeg: NU, 2019. *Address:* c/o Music Department, Oxford University Press, Great Clarendon Street, Oxford OX2 6DP. *T:* (01865) 355020/355019, *Fax:* (01865) 355060. *E:* repertoire.promotion.uk@oup.com.

**CAUTE, (John) David,** MA, DPhil; FRSL, FRHistS; writer; *b* 16 Dec. 1936; *m* 1st, 1961, Catherine Shuckburgh (marr. diss. 1970); two *s*; 2nd, 1973, Martha Bates (*d* 2019); two *d*. *Educ:* Edinburgh Academy; Wellington; Wadham Coll., Oxford. Scholar of St Antony's Coll., 1959. Spent a year in the Army in the Gold Coast, 1955–56, and a year at Harvard Univ. on a Henry Fellowship, 1960–61. Fellow of All Souls Coll., Oxford, 1959–65; Visiting Professor, New York Univ. and Columbia Univ., 1966–67; Reader in Social and Political Theory, Brunel Univ., 1967–70. Regents' Lectr, Univ. of Calif., 1974; Vis. Prof., Bristol Univ., 1985. Literary Editor, New Statesman, 1979–80. Co-Chm., Writers' Guild, 1981–82; Chm., Sinclair Fiction Prize, 1984. FRSL 1998. JP Inner London, 1993. *Plays:* Songs for an Autumn Rifle, staged by Oxford Theatre Group at Edinburgh, 1961; The Demonstration, Nottingham Playhouse, 1969; The Fourth World, Royal Court, 1973; Brecht and Company, BBC TV, 1979; BBC Radio: Fallout, 1972; The Zimbabwe Tapes, 1983; Henry and the Dogs, 1986; Sanctions, 1988; Animal Fun Park, 1995. *Publications:* At Fever Pitch (novel), 1959 (Authors' Club Award and John Llewelyn Rhys Prize, 1960); Comrade Jacob (novel), 1961; Communism and the French Intellectuals, 1914–1960, 1964; The Left in Europe Since 1789, 1966; The Decline of the West (novel), 1966; Essential Writings of Karl Marx (ed), 1967; Fanon, 1970; The Confrontation: a trilogy, 1971 (consisting of The Demonstration (play), 1970; The Occupation (novel), 1971; The Illusion: an essay on politics, theatre and the novel, 1971); The Fellow-Travellers, 1973, rev. edn 1988, as The Fellow-Travellers, Intellectual Friends of Communism; Collisions, 1974; Cuba, Yes?, 1974; The Great Fear: the anti-communist purge under Truman and Eisenhower, 1978; Under the Skin: the death of white Rhodesia, 1983; The K-Factor (novel), 1983; The Espionage of the Saints, 1986; News from Nowhere (novel), 1986; Sixty Eight: the year of the barricades, 1988; Veronica or the Two Nations (novel), 1989; The Women's Hour (novel), 1991; Joseph Losey: a revenge on life, 1994; Dr Orwell and Mr Blair (novel), 1994; Fatima's Scarf (novel), 1998; The Dancer Defects: the struggle for cultural supremacy during the cold war, 2003; Marechera and the Colonel, 2009; Politics and the Novel During the Cold War, 2010; Isaac and Isaiah: the covert punishment of a cold war heretic, 2013; Doubles (novel), 2016; (ed) Perlzweig: pioneer of British Zionism, 2019; *as John Salisbury: novels:* The Baby-Sitters, 1978; Moscow Gold, 1980. *Address:* 41 Westcroft Square, W6 0TA.

**CAUTHEN, Stephen Mark;** jockey, 1976–93; *b* Covington, Kentucky, 1 May 1960; *e s* of Ronald (Tex) Cauthen and Myra Cauthen; *m* Amy Kathrine Roth Fuss; three *d*. Apprentice jockey, 1976, Churchill Downs, Kentucky; first win, Red Pipe, 1976; raced at Aqueduct and Santa Anita; champion jockey, USA, 1977; won US Triple Crown on Affirmed, 1978; moved to Lambourn, 1979; champion jockey, UK, 1984, 1985, 1987; races won include: with Tap on Wood, 2,000 Guineas, 1979; with Slip Anchor, Derby, 1985; with Oh So Sharp, Oaks, 1,000 Guineas and St Leger, 1985; with Reference Point, Derby, St Leger and King George V and Queen Elizabeth Diamond Stakes, 1987; with Diminuendo, Oaks, 1988; with Michelozzo, St Leger, 1989; with Old Vic, French Derby and Irish Derby, 1989; Champion Stakes 3 times (Cormorant Wood, Indian Skimmer, In the Groove); Grand Prix de St Cloud (Atcatanango, Diamond Shoal); Prix de Diane (Indian Skimmer). *Address:* 167 S Main Street, Walton, KY 41094, USA.

**CAUTLEY, (Edward) Paul (Ronald),** CMG 2001; OBE 2015; DL; Founder, Helping People Win Ltd, since 2011; *b* 1 March 1940; *s* of Ronald Lockwood Cautley and Ena Lily Medwin; *m* 1966, Sandra Elizabeth Baker; two *d*. *Educ:* Downside Sch. Syndication Manager, Central Press Features, 1958–60; Retail Marketing Manager, ICI Paints, 1960–62; Finance Negotiator, GDM Finance, 1962–64; General Manager, Marling Industries, 1964–66; Account Dir, S. H. Benson, 1966–70; Dir, New Product Development, BRB, 1971–73; Chief Executive and Founder Chairman: Strategy Ltd, 1974–94; The D Group, 1994–2011. HAC, 1958–61; RM Reserve, 1961–68. Hon. Col, RM Reserve, London, 1999–2011; Pres., Chatham Royal Marine Cadets, 2000–09; Col Comdt, Royal Marine Cadets, 2011– (Col, 2004–11). Trustee, Marine Soc. and Sea Cadets (formerly Sea Cadet Assoc.), 2001–09. Freeman, City of Ionclucts, 2008. DL Greater London, 2001. FRGS 1991; life mem., 15 railway preservation socs. *Publications:* The Cautley Chronicle, 1986. *Recreations:* photography (mainly landscapes), 00 gauge model railway owner (pre-1948, Southern Railway). *Address:* 5 Warden Court, Cuckfield, W Sussex RH17 5DN. *E:* paulcautley@gmail.com. *Club:* Honourable Artillery Company.

**CAVACO SILVA, Anibal;** President of Portugal, 2006–16; *b* 15 July 1939; *s* of Teodoro Silva and Maria do Nascimento Cavaco; *m* 1963, Maria Alves; one *s* one *d*. *Educ:* Superior Inst. Econs and Financial Scis, Lisbon; York Univ. (PhD 1973). Teacher of public economics and political economy: Inst. Econ. and Financial Studies, Lisbon, 1966–78; Catholic Univ., Lisbon, 1975–2006 (Prof., 1979–2006); New Univ. of Lisbon, 1978–2001 (Prof., 1979–2001); Res. Fellow, Calouste Gulbenkian Foundn, 1967–77; Dir, Res. and Statistical Dept, Bank of Portugal, 1977–80 and 1981–85; Minister of Finance and Planning, 1980–81; Pres., Council for Nat. Planning, 1981–84; Prime Minister of Portugal, 1985–95. Leader, PSD, 1985–95. Econ. Advr to Bank of Portugal, 1995–2004. Member: Scientific Soc., Catholic Univ. of Portugal; Inst. of Public Finance; Royal Acad. of Moral and Pol Scis of Spain; Club of Madrid on Democratic Transition and Consolidation. Hon. Dr: York, 1993; Coruña, Spain, 1996; Goa, India, 2007; Léon, Spain, 2008; Heriot-Watt, Edinburgh, 2009. Joseph Bech Prize, 1991; Freedom Prize, Schmidheiny Foundation, 1995; Carl Bertelsmann Prize, Bertelsmann Foundn, 1995; Mediterranean Award for Instns, Fondazione Mediterraneo, 2009. *Publications:* Budget Policy and Economic Stabilization, 1976; Economic Effects of Public Debt, 1977; Public Finance and Macroeconomic Policy, 1992; A Decade of Reforms, 1995; Portugal and the Single Currency, 1997; The European Monetary Union, 1999; Autobiografia Política, vol. 1 2002, vol. 2, 2017; Portugal and the Future of the European Union, 2018; numerous articles on financial mkts, public econs, Portuguese econ. policy and European integration. *Address:* Rua do Sacramento a Alcântara 49R, 1350–278, Lisbon, Portugal.

**CAVADINO, Paul Francis;** freelance consultant in criminal justice and penal affairs, since 2010; Chief Executive, Nacro, 2002–09; Member, Parole Board for England and Wales, since 2010; *b* 5 Dec. 1948; *s* of John Joseph and Mary Patricia Cavadino; *m* 1970, Maria Claire Carrack; two *s*. *Educ:* St Michael's Coll., Leeds; Balliol Coll., Oxford (BA Jurisprudence). Univs and Colls Sec., Christian Aid, 1970–72; National Association for the Care and Resettlement of Offenders: NE Regl Orgnr, 1972–75; Sen. Inf. Officer, 1975–82; Sen. Press Officer, 1982–90; Principal Officer (Criminal Justice Policy), 1990–94; Director: of Communications, 1997–99; of Policy and Inf., 1999–2001; of Policy, Race and Resettlement, 2001–02. Chairman: Penal Affairs Consortium, 1989–2001 (full-time, 1994–97); Voluntary Sector Community Engagement Project, 2005–08. Sec., New Approaches to Juvenile Crime, 1978–84; Clerk, Parly All-Party Penal Affairs Gp, 1980–2001; Mem., Reducing Reoffending Third Sector Adv. Gp, MoJ, 2009–11. Advr, Sentencing Council of England and Wales, 2010–15. Trustee: Coalition for Racial Justice (UK), 2010–14; African Prisons Project, 2011– (Vice Chm., 2012–13; Chm., 2013–15); User Voice, 2011–15. *Publications:* Bail: the law, best practice and the debate, 1993; Introduction to the Criminal Justice Process, 1995, 3rd edn, 2008; Children Who Kill, 1996. *Recreations:* cricket, jazz music, Italian food and drink. *Address:* 136 Onslow Gardens, Wallington, Surrey SM6 9QE. *T:* (020) 8274 2382. *E:* pc003f3813@blueyonder.co.uk.

**CAVALIER-SMITH, Prof. Thomas,** PhD; FRS 1998; FRSC 1997; Professor of Evolutionary Biology, Department of Zoology, University of Oxford, 2000–07, now Emeritus; *b* 21 Oct. 1942; *s* of Alan Hailes Spencer Cavalier-Smith and Mary Maude Cavalier-Smith; *m* 1st, 1964, Gillian Glaysher; one *s* one *d*; 2nd, 1991, Ema E-Yung Chao; one *d*. *Educ:* Kenninghall Primary Sch.; Norwich Sch.; Gonville and Caius Coll., Cambridge (MA 1967); King's Coll., London (PhD 1967); Open Univ. (BA). FLS; FRSB. Tutorial Student, King's Coll., London, 1964–67; Guest Investigator, and Damon Runyon Meml Res. Fellow, Rockefeller Univ., NY, 1967–69; Lectr, 1969–82, Reader, 1982–89, in Biophysics, King's Coll., London; Prof. of Botany, Univ. of BC, 1989–99; NERC Professorial Fellow, Dept of Zool., Univ. of Oxford, 1999–2007. Vis. Fellow, Res. Sch. of Biol. Scis, ANU, 1981, 1985–86; Fellow, Canadian Inst. for Advanced Res. (Evolutionary Biol. Prog.), 1988–2007; Vis. Scientist, Univ. of Cape Town, 1995–96. Pres., British Soc. for Protist Biol., 2006–09. Internat. Prize for Biol., Japan Soc. for Promotion of Sci., 2004; Linnean Medal for Zool., Linnean Soc. of London, 2007; Frink Medal, Zool Soc. of London, 2008. *Publications:* (ed with J. P. Hudson) Biology, Society and Choice, 1982; (ed) The Evolution of Genome Size, 1985; over 250 scientific articles in jls, contribs to books. *Recreations:* reading, natural history, travel. *Address:* Department of Zoology, University of Oxford, South Parks Road, Oxford OX1 3PS. *T:* (01865) 281065.

**CAVAN, 13th Earl of,** *cr* 1647 (Ire.); **Roger Cavan Lambart;** Baron Cavan 1618; Baron Lambart 1618; Viscount Kilcoursie 1647; *b* 1 Sept. 1944; *s* of Frederick Cavan Lambart (*d* 1963) and Audrey May, *d* of Albert Charles Dunham; *S* kinsman, 1988, but has not yet established his right to the Peerage. *Educ:* Wilson's School, Wallington, Surrey.

**CAVANAGH, Diana Lesley;** Director of Educational Studies (formerly Strategic Director of Education), City of Bradford Metropolitan District Council, 1996–2001; *b* 19 Nov. 1944; *d* of Arthur and Nellie Eggleston; *m* 1973, Michael Cavanagh. *Educ:* Fairfield High Sch.; Westfield Coll., London (BA Hons 1966); Univ. of Liverpool (PGCE 1967); Univ. of Edinburgh (Dip. Applied Linguistics 1973); Sheffield Poly. (MSc 1982); Leeds Univ. (MA 2006). German Teacher, Cumberland, 1967–70; English Teacher, Sulingen Gymnasium, W Germany, 1970–73; Lectr in English Lang./Educn, Univ. of Birmingham, 1973–75; British Council Project Co-ordinator, Medical Coll., Jeddah, 1975–77; Section Hd, ESOL, Abraham Moss Centre, Manchester, 1977–83; Professional Asst, and Dep. Area Educn Officer, Derbyshire, 1983–85; Asst Educn Officer (Reorgn and Curriculum), Rochdale, 1985–89; Chief Asst Exec. Officer (Policy Develt), 1989–91, Mem. Bd, 1992–93, Inst. of Citizenship Studies; Chief Educn Officer, Rochdale MBC, 1991–96. Chair, Assessment and Qualifications Alliance, 2003–07 (Dep. Chair, 1999–2003). Sec., Glossop Guild, 2010–. FRSA 1991–2015. *Publications:* Introducing PET, 1980; Power Relations in the Further Education College, 1983; Staff Development in the Further Education College, 1984. *Recreations:* hill walking, polar travel, reading. *Address:* 4 Cross Cliffe, Glossop, Derbys SK13 8PZ.

**CAVANAGH, Hon. Sir John Patrick,** Kt 2019; **Hon. Mr Justice Cavanagh;** a Judge of the High Court, Queen's Bench Division, since 2019; *b* 17 June 1960; *s* of Dr Gerry Cavanagh and Anne Cavanagh (*née* Kennedy); *m* 1989, Suzanne Tolley; one *s* three *d*. *Educ:* Mt Carmel Convent Sch., Stratford-on-Avon; Warwick Sch.; New Coll., Oxford (MA); Clare Coll., Cambridge (LLM); Univ. of Illinois Coll. of Law. Residential social worker, St Philip's Sch., Airdrie, 1979–80; Instructor in Law, Univ. of Illinois Coll. of Law, Urbana-Champaign, 1983–84; part-time Lectr in Law, New Coll., Oxford, 1984–87; called to the Bar, Middle Temple, 1985, Bencher, 2015; in practice at the Bar, 1986–2019; Jun. Counsel to Crown, B Panel, 1997–2001; QC 2001; Recorder, 2004–19; Jt Head of Chambers, 11 King's Bench Walk, 2013–19; Dep. High Court Judge, 2017–19. Chm., Employment Law Bar Assoc., 2005–07. Judge, Administrative Tribunal, Bank for Internat. Settlements, 2009–. Pres., Old Warwickian Assoc., 2009; Governor: Warwick Sch., 2009–; Aldwickbury Sch., 2009–. *Publications:* (ed and contrib.) Tolley's Employment Handbook, 9th edn 1985 to 15th edn 2001; (contrib.) Butterworth's Local Government Law, 1998–2006; (ed jtly and contrib.) Harvey on Industrial Relations and Employment Law, annually 2000–04. *Recreations:* family, reading, football (Celtic from afar), tennis, avoiding gardening. *Address:* Royal Courts of Justice, Strand, WC2A 2LL.

**CAVANAGH, Lorraine;** QC 2019; *b* Liverpool, 11 March 1976; *d* of John Cavanagh and Hazel Cavanagh. *Educ:* St Gregory's RC High Sch., Cheshire; Univ. of Manchester (LLB Hons 1999). BVC 2000. Called to the Bar, Gray's Inn, 2000; in practice as a barrister, specialising in child law and mental capacity law, St John's Bldgs (formerly 28 St John St), 2000–. Member: Greater Manchester Regl Cttee, Family Law Bar Assoc.; Exec. Cttee, Court of Protection Practitioners Assoc., 2012–; Exec. Cttee, Assoc. of Lawyers for Children, 2018–. *Recreations:* cinema, theatre, family and friends, travelling, dancing. *Address:* St John's Buildings, 24a–28 St John Street, Manchester M3 4DJ. *T:* (0161) 214 1500. *E:* clerks@stjohnsbuildings.co.uk.

**CAVE, Rt Hon. Sir Charles Anthony H.;** *see* Haddon-Cave.

**CAVE, Sir George Charles,** 6th Bt *cr* 1896, of Sidbury Manor, Sidbury, co. Devon; *b* 8 Sept. 1987; *s* of Sir John Charles Cave, 5th Bt and Carey Diana Cave (*née* Lloyd); *S* father, 2018, but his name does not appear on the Official Roll of the Baronetage.

**CAVE, Maj. Gen. Ian John;** Chief of Staff, Field Army, since 2018; *b* 22 May 1966; *s* of Richard Cave and Diane Chick; *m* 1994, Caroline Frearson; two *d*. *Educ:* Liverpool Poly.; Cranfield Univ. (MDA 1999). Commnd RWF, 1988; Rifle Platoon Comdr, NI, 1988–89; OC Recce Platoon, Berlin, 1989–92; Zimbabwe, 1993; Adjt; Ops Officer, RWF; Observer/Controller with US Army Jt Readiness Trng Centre, 1996–97; J5 Plans, UK Perm. Jt HQ; i/c rifle coy., 22nd Cheshire Regt; served NI, 2002, Iraq, 2004; Iraq Information Strategy, MoD, 2005; CO, 1 Mercian Regt, 2006–08; Asst Dir, Commitments, Army HQ, 2008–11; Comdr, Initial Trng Gp, 2011–12; Chief CJ5 Plans, HQ ISAF, Kabul, 2013–14; Dir Trng, Army HQ, 2014–15; Dep. COS (Plans), Jt Force Comd Naples, 2015–18. *Recreations:* road cycling, exploring Italy.

**CAVE, Prof. Martin Edward**, OBE 2009; DPhil; Chairman, Office of Gas and Electricity Markets, since 2018; *b* 13 Dec. 1948; *s* of D. T. and S. M. Cave; *m* 1st, 1972, Kathryn Wilson (marr. diss. 2004); one *s* two *d*; 2nd, 2016, Juliet Weale. *Educ:* Balliol Coll., Oxford (BA 1969); Nuffield Coll., Oxford (BPhil 1971; DPhil 1977). Res. Fellow, Birmingham Univ., 1971–74; Brunel University: Lectr, 1974–81; Sen. Lectr, 1981–86; Prof. of Economics, 1986–2001; Vice-Principal, 1996–2001; Prof., and Dir, Centre for Mgt Under Regulation, Warwick Business Sch., Univ. of Warwick, 2001–10; BP Centennial Prof., LSE, 2010–11. Visiting Professor: Business Sch., Imperial Coll. London, 2011–17; LSE, 2018–. Economic Consultant: HM Treasury, 1986–90; OFTEL, subseq., OFCOM, 1990–2006. Mem., 1996–2002, Dep. Chm. and Mem. Council, 2012–14, Competition (formerly Monopolies and Mergers) Commn; Dir, Payments Council, 2007–11; Inquiry Chm., CMA, 2014–18. *Publications:* Computers and Economic Planning: the Soviet experience, 1980; (with Paul Hare) Alternative Approaches to Economic Planning, 1981; (jtly) The Use of Performance Indicators in Higher Education, 1988, 3rd edn 1997; (ed jtly) Output and Performance Measurement in Government, 1990; (ed with Saul Estrin) Competition and Competition Policy: a comparative analysis of Central and Eastern Europe, 1993; (ed jtly) Reconstituting the Market: the political economy of microeconomic transformation, 1999; (with Robert Baldwin) Understanding Regulation, 1999, 2nd edn 2011; (ed jtly) Handbook of Telecommunications Economics, vol. 1, 2002, vol. 2, 2005; Every Tenant Matters, 2007; Review of Competition and Innovation in the Water Sector, 2009; (ed jtly) Oxford Handbook of Regulation, 2010; (with W. Webb) Spectrum Management, 2015; contrib. to jls on regulatory economics and other subjects. *Recreations:* theatre, cinema. *Address:* Ofgem, 10 South Colonnade, Canary Wharf, E14 4PU.

**CAVE, Prof. Terence Christopher**, CBE 2013; FBA 1991; Professor of French Literature, Oxford University, 1989–2001, now Emeritus; Fellow and Tutor in French, St John's College, Oxford, 1972–2001, now Emeritus Fellow; *b* 1 Dec. 1938; *s* of Alfred Cyril Cave and Sylvia Norah (*née* Norman); *m* 1965, Helen Elizabeth Robb (marr. diss. 1990); one *s* one *d*; *m* 2013, Kirsti Sellevold. *Educ:* Winchester Coll.; Gonville and Caius Coll., Cambridge (MA; PhD; Hon. Fellow 1997). University of St Andrews: Assistant, 1962–63; Lectr, 1963–65; University of Warwick: Lectr, 1965–70; Sen. Lectr, 1970–72. Dir, Balzan Interdisciplinary Seminar, Res. Centre, St John's Coll., Oxford, 2010–14. Visiting Professor: Cornell Univ., 1967–68; Univ. of California, Santa Barbara, 1976; Univ. of Virginia, Charlottesville, 1979; Univ. of Toronto, 1991; Univ. of Alberta, 1992; Univ. of Paris VII, 1995; UCLA, 1997; RHUL, 2001–04; Visiting Fellow: All Souls Coll., Oxford, 1971; Princeton Univ., 1984; Royal Norwegian Soc. of Scis and Letters, Trondheim, 1991 (Mem., 1993); Hon. Sen. Res. Fellow, Inst. of Romance Studies, Univ. of London, 1990; Hon. Fellow, QMUL, 2010. MAE 1990; Mem., Norwegian Acad. of Sci. and Letters, Oslo, 2015. Hon. DLit London, 2007. Balzan Prize for Literature since 1500, 2009. Chevalier, l'Ordre Nat. du Mérite (France), 2001. *Publications:* Devotional Poetry in France, 1969; Ronsard the Poet, 1973; The Cornucopian Text: problems of writing in the French Renaissance, 1979; Recognitions: a study in poetics, 1988; (trans.) Madame de Lafayette, The Princesse de Clèves, 1992; (ed) George Eliot, Daniel Deronda, 1995; (ed) George Eliot, Silas Marner, 1996; Pré-histoires: textes troublés au seuil de la modernité, 1999; Pré-histoires II: langues étrangères et troubles économiques, 2001; (with S. Kay and M. Bowie) A Short History of French Literature, 2003; How to Read Montaigne, 2007; (ed) Thomas More's 'Utopia' in Early Modern Europe: paratexts and contexts, 2008; Mignon's Afterlives: crossing cultures from Goethe to the twenty-first century, 2011; Retrospectives: essays in literature, poetics and cultural history, 2009; Thinking with Literature: towards a cognitive criticism, 2016; (ed with D. Wilson) Reading Beyond the Code: literature and relevance theory, 2018; articles and essays in learned jls, collective vols, etc. *Recreations:* music, languages. *Address:* St John's College, Oxford OX1 3JP.

**CAVE-BROWNE-CAVE, Sir John Robert Charles**, 17th Bt *cr* 1641, of Stanford, Northamptonshire; *b* 22 June 1957; *o s* of Sir John Chalmers Huggard; *S* father, 2011; *m* 2001, Jennifer Angelica Fong. *Address:* 7701 Barrymore, Delta, BC V4C 4C8, Canada.

**CAVELL, His Honour John James**; a Circuit Judge, 1994–2012; *b* 1 Oct. 1947; *s* of Eric Essery Cavell and Edith Emma Doreen (*née* Jose); *m* 1977, Philippa Julia Frances (*née* Kelly); one *s* one *d*. *Educ:* King Edward's Sch., Stourbridge; Churchill Coll., Cambridge (MA). Called to the Bar, Middle Temple, 1971. Practising Barrister on Midland and Oxford Circuit, 1971–94; a Recorder, 1991–94. *Recreations:* playing the piano, music generally, walking, bridge, gardening. *Address:* c/o Midland Circuit Secretariat Judicial Team, 6th Floor, Temple Court, 33 Bull Street, Birmingham B4 6DW.

**CAVENDER, David John**; QC 2010; *b* Erith, Kent, 17 Sept. 1964; *s* of Kenneth and Maureen Cavender; *m* 1995, Naomi Taylor; one *s* three *d*. *Educ:* Glyn Grammar Sch.; King's Coll. London (LLB 1st Cl. Hons; AKC). Served RM Commandos, 1982–86. Trainee Solicitor, Herbert Smith, 1991–93; called to the Bar, Middle Temple, 1993; in practice as barrister, specialising in commercial litigation, 1993–. *Recreations:* ski-ing, tennis, running, music festivals. *Address:* 1 Essex Court, Temple, EC4Y 9AR. *E:* dcavender@oeclaw.co.uk.

**CAVENDISH**, family name of **Duke of Devonshire** and **Barons Cavendish of Furness, Chesham**, and **Waterpark**.

**CAVENDISH, Lord; James William Patrick Cavendish**; *b* 12 Dec. 2010; *s* and *heir* of Earl of Burlington, *qv*.

**CAVENDISH OF FURNESS**, Baron *cr* 1990 (Life Peer), of Cartmel in the County of Cumbria; **Richard Hugh Cavendish**; Chairman, Holker Estate Group of Companies (interests including agricultural and urban property, leisure, mineral extraction, export, construction, national hunt racing and forestry), 1971–2015; *b* 2 Nov. 1941; *s* of late Richard Edward Osborne Cavendish and of Pamela J. Lloyd Thomas; *m* 1970, Grania Mary Caulfeild; one *s* one *d*. *Educ:* Eton. International banking, 1961–71. Dir, UK Nirex Ltd, 1993–99. A Lord in Waiting (Govt Whip), 1990–92. Member, House of Lords Select Committee: on Croydon Tramlink Bill, 1992–93; on EU Sub-Cttee B, 1999–2003; on EU, 2001–03; on Natural Envmt and Rural Communities Act 2006, 2017–18; on EU Financial Affairs Cttee, 2018. Mem., Hist. Buildings and Monuments Commn for England, 1992–98. Chm., Lancs & Cumbria Foundn for Med. Res., 1994–2000. Chm., Morecambe and Lonsdale Conservative Assoc., 1975–78. Chm. Governors, St Anne's Sch., Windermere, 1983–89. Mem., Cumbria CC, 1985–90. High Sheriff 1978, DL 1988, Cumbria. FRSA. *Publications:* A Time to Plant, 2012. *Recreations:* gardening, National Hunt racing, collecting drawings, reading, travel, fly fishing. *Address:* Low Frith, Cark-in-Cartmel, Cumbria LA11 7PP. *T:* (015395) 59998. *Clubs:* Brooks's, Pratt's, White's, Beefsteak.

**CAVENDISH OF LITTLE VENICE**, Baroness *cr* 2016 (Life Peer), of Mells in the County of Somerset; **Hilary Camilla Cavendish**; Head, Policy Unit, No 10 Downing Street, 2015–16; *b* London, 20 Aug. 1968; *d* of late Richard Cavendish and of Jean Mavis Hay; *m* 1999, Huw John van Steenis, *qv*; three *s*. *Educ:* Putney High Sch.; Brasenose Coll., Oxford (BA 1st Cl. Hons PPE 1989); John F. Kennedy Sch. of Govt, Harvard Univ. (Kennedy Meml Trust Schol.; MPA 1991). Business analyst, McKinsey & Co., 1991–93; Dir of Progs, London First, 1993–95; Chief Exec., S Bank Employers Gp, 1995–99; Advr to CEO, Pearson plc, 1999–2002; The Times: leader writer, 2002–13; op-ed columnist, 2004–13; Chief Leader Writer, 2010–13; Associate Ed., 2011–13; Associate Ed. and columnist, Sunday Times, 2013–15; Contrib. Ed. and columnist, Financial Times, 2018–. Leader, Cavendish Rev. into Care Assts, 2013 (report pubd, 2013). Sen. Fellow, Mossavar-Rahmani Center for Business and Govt, Harvard Kennedy Sch., 2018–. Non-exec. Dir, Care Quality Commn, 2013–15. Chair, Frontline for Social Work, 2017–. *Publications:* Extra Time: 10 lessons for an ageing world, 2019. *Recreations:* reading crime thrillers, playing piano, tennis, architecture. *Address:* House of Lords, SW1A 0PW.

**CAVENDISH, Mark Simon**, MBE 2011; professional cyclist, Team Dimension Data, since 2016; *b* Douglas, IOM, 21 May 1985; *s* of David Cavendish and Adele Towns; *m* 2013, Peta Todd; one *s* one *d*. *Educ:* Ballkermeen High Sch., IOM. Track cyclist: Gold Medal, Madison, Union Cycliste Internat. World Championships, 2005, 2008, 2016; Gold Medal, Men's Scratch, Commonwealth Games, Melbourne, 2006; Silver Medal, Men's Omnium, Rio de Janeiro Olympics, 2016; road cyclist: T-Mobile Team, 2007; Team High Road, 2008; Team Columbia High Road, 2009; Team HTC-Columbia, 2010; HTC High Road, 2011 (winner, Union Cycliste Internat. Road Race World Championships); Team Sky, 2012; Etixx (formerly Omega Pharma)-Quick-Step Team, 2013–15; winner, British National Road Race Championship, 2013. Winner of 30 Tour de France stages (2008, 2009, 2010, 2011, 2012, 2013, 2015, 2016). BBC Sports Personality of Year, 2011. *Publications:* Boy Racer, 2009; At Speed, 2013. *Recreations:* cars, music. *Address:* c/o Wasserman, 7th Floor, Aldwych House, Aldwych, WC2B 4HN. *E:* clhinde@teamwass.com. *Club:* Velo Rocacorba (Girona, Spain).

**CAVENDISH, Dr Michael William Patrick, (Will)**, CB 2014; Global Leader, Digital Services, Arup, since 2018; *b* Windsor, 9 Dec. 1964; *s* of Patrick Cavendish and Pamela Cavendish; *m* 1994, Cavelle Creightney; one *s* one *d*. *Educ:* Magdalen Coll., Oxford (BA Hons PPE 1986); MSc Develt Econs 1987; PhD 1997). Jun. Res. Fellow, St John's Coll., Oxford, 1994–99; Lectr in Envmtl Econs, Imperial Coll., London, 1999–2000; Hd of Policy, Labour Party, 2000–01; Special Adviser: DFES, 2001–02; Prime Minister's Strategy Unit, 2003–05; Dir, Strategy, 2005–07, Dir, Health and Wellbeing, 2008–09, DoH; Dir Gen., Internat. Energy and Climate Change, DECC, 2009–11; Dir Gen., Red Tape Challenge, Efficiency and Reform Gp, then Implementation Gp, Cabinet Office, 2011–14; Dir Gen., Innovation, Growth and Technol., DoH, 2014–16; Dir Gen., Cabinet Office, 2016 (on secondment); Strategy Lead, DeepMind Applied, 2016–17. *Publications:* (jtly) Adjusting Privatization, 1992. *Address:* Arup, 13 Fitzroy Street, W1T 4BQ.

**CAVENDISH, Ruth;** *see* Glucksmann, M. A.

**CAVENDISH, Will;** *see* Cavendish, M. W. P.

**CAVIN, Paul René;** QC 2018; *b* Bristol, 29 March 1968; *s* of Gerry Cavin and Madeleine Perigueux; *m* 2009, Kate Blumgart; one *s* one *d*. *Educ:* Univ. of East Anglia (BA Hons Amer. Hist. and Politics 1990); Coll. of Law (CPE 1991). Solicitor, Denton Hall, 1992–94; called to the Bar, Gray's Inn, 1995; Hd of Chambers, 2 Harcourt Bldgs, 2018–. Treas., SE Circuit, 2017–. *Recreations:* US politics, history, my children. *Address:* 2 Harcourt Buildings, Temple, EC4Y 9DB. *T:* (020) 7353 2112. *E:* pcavin@2hb.co.uk.

**CAWDOR**, 7th Earl *cr* 1827; **Colin Robert Vaughan Campbell**; Baron Cawdor, 1796; Viscount Emlyn, 1827; Vice Lord-Lieutenant for the Area of Nairn, 2013–17; *b* 30 June 1962; *s* of 6th Earl and of his 1st wife, Cathryn, *d* of Maj.-Gen. Sir Robert Hinde, KBE, CB, DSO; *S* father, 1993; *m* 1994, Lady Isabella Stanhope, *y d* of 11th Earl of Harrington; one *s* three *d*. *Educ:* Eton; St Peter's College, Oxford. Member, James Bridal Meml Soc., London. DL Nairn, 1996. *Heir: s* Viscount Emlyn, *qv*. *Address:* Carnoch, The Streens, Nairn IV12 5RQ.

**CAWLEY**, family name of **Baron Cawley**.

**CAWLEY**, 4th Baron *cr* 1918; **John Francis Cawley**; Bt 1906; *b* 28 Sept. 1946; *s* of 3rd Baron Cawley and Rosemary Joan (*née* Marsden); *S* father, 2001; *m* 1979, Regina Sarabia, *d* of late Marqués de Hazas, Madrid; three *s* one *d*. *Educ:* Eton. *Heir: s* Hon. William Robert Harold Cawley, *b* 2 July 1981. *Address:* Castle Ground, Ashton, Leominster, Herefordshire HR6 0DN. *T:* (01584) 711209.

**CAWLEY, Prof. Peter**, PhD; FRS 2010; CEng, FREng, FIMechE; Professor of Mechanical Engineering, since 1996, and Head of Department, since 2012, Imperial College London; *b* Sheffield, 25 Nov. 1953; *s* of Bernard and Florence Cawley; partner, Wendy Quill. *Educ:* St Michael's Coll., Leeds; St Ignatius Coll., Enfield; Univ. of Bristol (BSc 1975; PhD 1979). CEng 1985; FIMechE 2001; FREng 2006. Vibration engr, Lucas CAV, 1979–81; Imperial College, London: Lectr, 1981–89; Sen. Lectr, 1989–92; Reader, 1992–96. Chm., Permasense, 2009–16; Director: Guided Ultrasonics Ltd, 1999–; Rheon Labs Ltd, 2018–; Cognition Energy Ltd, 2018–. *Publications:* contrib. papers to jls. *Recreations:* watching football (Sheffield Wednesday) and cricket, walking, theatre, cinema. *Address:* Department of Mechanical Engineering, Imperial College London, SW7 2AZ. *T:* (020) 7594 7000. *E:* p.cawley@imperial.ac.uk.

**CAWLEY, Stephen Ingleby**, CVO 2007 (LVO 2003); FCA; Deputy Treasurer to the Queen, 2003–07; *b* 14 March 1947; *s* of Joe Cawley and Madge (*née* Ingleby); *m* 1971, Mariquet Scott; two *s*. *Educ:* Hull Grammar Sch.; Edinburgh Univ. (MA 1970). FCA 1973. Joined KPMG, 1970; Partner, 1984–94; Sen. Partner, Sussex, 1992–94; financial consultancy and Lectr, Univ. of Brighton, 1994–96; Dir of Finance, Property Services and Royal Travel, Royal Household, 1996–2003. *Recreations:* wine, opera, gardening, hill-walking, sports, travelling. *Address:* Robin Post, Firle Road, Seaford, E Sussex BN25 2HJ.

**CAWSEY, Ian Arthur;** *b* 14 April 1960; *s* of Arthur Henry Cawsey and Edith Morrison Cawsey; *m* 1987, Linda Mary, *d* of Henry and Joy Kirman; one *s* two *d*. *Educ:* Wintringham Sch. Computer operator, 1977–78; computer programmer, 1978–82; systems analyst, 1982–85; IT consultant, 1985–87; PA to Elliot Morley, MP, 1987–97. Member (Lab): Humberside CC, 1989–96; N Lincs Unitary Council, 1995–97 (Leader, 1995–97); Chm., Humberside Police Authy, 1993–97. MP (Lab) Brigg and Goole, 1997–2010; contested (Lab) same seat, 2010. PPS to Leader of House of Lords, 2001–02; an Asst Govt Whip, 2005–07. Chm., All Party Gp on Animal Welfare, 1998–2010.

**CAWSON, (Peter) Mark;** QC 2001; a Recorder, since 2000; a Deputy High Court Judge, Chancery Division, since 2004; *b* 4 June 1959; *s* of late Frederick Helenus Peter Cawson and Patricia Mary Cawson; *m* 1986, Julia Louise Hoe; two *s* one *d*. *Educ:* Wrekin Coll., Telford; Liverpool Univ. (LLB Hons). Called to the Bar, Lincoln's Inn, 1982, Bencher, 2010; Junior, Northern Circuit, 1987; Asst Recorder, 1998–2000. Chairman: Northern Circuit Commercial Bar Assoc., 2008–13; Northern Chancery Bar Assoc., 2013–. Mem. Council, Church Soc., 2013–. *Recreations:* church affairs, armchair politics, travel, watching sports. *Address:* Exchange Chambers, 201 Deansgate, Manchester M3 3NW. *T:* (0161) 833 2722, *Fax:* (0161) 833 2789. *E:* Cawsonqc@exchangechambers.co.uk. *Club:* Royal Birkdale Golf.

**CAWTHRA, David Wilkinson**, CBE 1997; FREng; FICE; Principal, Cawthra & Co., 1995–2005; *b* 5 March 1943; *s* of Jack and Dorothy Cawthra; *m* 1967, Maureen Williamson; one *s* one *d*. *Educ*: Heath Grammar Sch., Halifax; Univ. of Birmingham (BSc Hons). Mitchell Construction Co., 1963–73; Tarmac Construction, 1973–78; Balfour Beatty Ltd, 1979–91; Chief Executive: Balfour Beatty, 1988–91; Miller Group, 1992–94. Dir, BICC, 1988–91. Chm., Nat. Rail Contractors' Gp, 1999–2005. Vice-Pres., ICE, 1996–99. FREng (FEng 1990). *Recreations*: second home in rural France, genealogical one name study of Cawthras, medieval history. *Address*: Willow House, Riverside Close, Oundle, Peterborough PE8 4DN.

**CAYFORD, Philip John Berkeley**; QC 2002; *b* 28 July 1952; *s* of late Berkeley Cayford and Christabel Cayford (*née* Robson); partner, Tanya; one *s*. *Educ*: Marlborough Coll.; University Coll., Cardiff (LLB). Called to the Bar, Middle Temple, 1975, Bencher, 2013; in practice as barrister, 1978–; Hd of Chambers, 2016–. Mem., Bar Standards Bd Complaints Cttee, 2005–11. Photographer and conservation film maker: producer, African Hunters, 1984; producer/director: The Rhino War, 1987; Ivory Wars, 1989; The Last Show on Earth, 1992; Vicuña, the Golden Fleece, 2009. Dir, Tusk USA, 2008–15; Trustee, Tusk Trust, 2003–15; Tusk Global Ambassador, 2015–. FRGS; FZS. Ed., 2007–14, Consultant Ed., 2014–, Family Affairs, Family Law Bar Assoc. *Publications*: (contrib. illus.) The Percy Bass Book of Traditional Decoration, 2005. *Recreations*: country sports, cricket, flying, classic car rallying. *Address*: (chambers) 29 Bedford Row, WC1R 4HE. *E*: pcayford@29br.co.uk. *Clubs*: Garrick, Royal Automobile, Chelsea Arts, Royal Air Force, MCC; Refreshers Cricket (Club Captain, 2009–16; Pres., 2016–), I Zingari.

**CAYGILL, Hon. David Francis**, CNZM 1997; Councillor, Environment Canterbury Regional Council, since 2016 (Deputy Chair of Commissioners, 2010–16); *b* 15 Nov. 1948; *s* of Bruce Allott Caygill and Gwyneth Mary Caygill; *m* 1974, Eileen Ellen Boyd; one *s* three *d*. *Educ*: St Albans Primary Sch.; Christchurch Boys' High Sch.; Univ. of Canterbury (BA, LLB). Pres., Univ. of Canterbury Students' Assoc., 1971. Barrister and Solicitor, 1974–78; Partner, Buddle Findlay, 1996–2004. Christchurch City Councillor, 1971–80; MP (Lab) St Albans, NZ, 1978–96; Minister of Trade and Industry, Minister of Nat. Develt, Associate Minister of Finance, 1984–87; Minister of Health, Dep. Minister of Finance, 1987–88; Minister of Finance, 1988–90; Dep. Leader of the Opposition, 1994–96. Dep. Chair, Commerce Commn, 2004–09; Chm., Electricity Commn, NZ, 2007–10. *Recreations*: collecting and listening to classical records, following American politics.

**CAYLEY, Andrew Thomas**, CMG 2014; QC 2012; Director of Service Prosecutions, since 2013; *b* E Preston, W Sussex, 24 March 1964; *s* of Granville Cayley and Elizabeth Mary Cayley (*née* Cook); *m* 1996, Andrea Maria Matačić; two *s* two *d*. *Educ*: University Coll. London (LLB 1985; LLM 1986); RMA, Sandhurst (Professionally Qualified Officers' Course 1991). Admitted as solicitor, 1989; commnd Army Legal Services (Adjt Gen.'s Corps), 1991; served in Belize, Germany, UK and The Hague; retd as Major, 1998; Prosecuting Counsel and Sen. Prosecuting Counsel, Internat. Criminal Tribunal for Former Yugoslavia, 1995–2005; Sen. Prosecuting Counsel, Internat. Criminal Court, The Hague, 2005–07; called to the Bar, Inner Temple, 2007, Bencher, 2015; Defence Counsel, Special Court for Sierra Leone and Internat. Criminal Tribunal for Former Yugoslavia, 2007–09; Internat. Co-Prosecutor, Extraordinary Chambers in the Courts of Cambodia (Khmer Rouge Tribunal), 2009–13. *Recreations*: history, running, a decent, thoughtful and respected life. *Address*: Service Prosecuting Authority, RAF Northolt, West End Road, Ruislip HA4 6NG. *E*: acayley@tgchambers.com. *Club*: Reform.

**CAYLEY, Sir Digby (William David)**, 11th Bt *cr* 1661; MA; Head of Latin, St Francis School, Pewsey, 2016–17; *b* 3 June 1944; *s* of Lieut-Comdr W. A. S. Cayley, RN (*d* 1964) (*ggs* of 7th Bt), and Natalie Maud Cayley, BA (*d* 1994); *S* kinsman, 1967; *m* 1st, 1969, Christine Mary Gaunt (marr. diss. 1987); two *d*; 2nd, 1993, Cathryn Mary Russell, MA Cantab; two *s*. *Educ*: Malvern Coll.; Downing Coll., Cambridge (MA; PGCE). Assistant Classics Master: Portsmouth Grammar Sch., 1968–73; Stonyhurst Coll., 1973–81; dealer in antiques, 1981–89; Assistant Classics Master: Marlborough Coll., 1989–90 and 1994–97; Abingdon Sch., 1990–94; Master i/c Shooting, Marlborough Coll., 1994–2000; Hd of Classics, Pinewood Sch., Bourton, 2003–08; private tutor/supply teacher in Classics, 2009–15. *Recreations*: English Longcase clocks (collector and occasional dealer), bridge, my family. *Heir*: *s* Thomas Theodore William Cayley, *b* 17 Feb. 1997. *Address*: Meadowside, Hyde Lane, Marlborough, Wilts SN8 1JN. *T*: 07716 010666. *E*: digbycayley@gmail.com.

**CAYLEY, Michael Forde**; Director, Personnel and Support Services, Department of Social Security, 1998–2000; *b* 26 Feb. 1950; *s* of late Forde Everard De Wend Cayley and Eileen Lilian Cayley; *m* 1987, Jennifer Athalie Jeffcoate (*née* Lytle). *Educ*: Brighton Coll.; St John's Coll., Oxford (MA English). Admin. Trainee, Inland Revenue, 1971–73; Private Sec. to Chm., Price Commn, 1973–75; Inland Revenue: Principal, 1975; Asst Sec., 1982; Under Sec., 1991; Dir, Financial Instns Div., 1994–98, Company Tax Div., 1995–98. *Publications*: *poems*: Moorings, 1971; (ed) Selected Poems of Richard Crashaw, 1972; The Spider's Touch, 1973; poems and articles on modern poets in various mags. *Recreations*: piano and organ-playing, art, genealogy. *Address*: 7 The Strand, Hayling Island, Hants PO11 9UB.

**CAYTON, William Henry Rymer, (Harry)**, CBE 2014 (OBE 2001); Chief Executive, Professional Standards Authority for Health and Social Care (formerly Council for Healthcare Regulatory Excellence), since 2007; *b* 27 March 1950; *s* of late Dr Henry Rymer Cayton and Marion Cromie (*née* Young). *Educ*: Bristol Cathedral Sch.; New Univ. of Ulster (BA Hons 1971; Dist. Grad. Award, 2003); Univ. of Durham (Dip. Anth. 1973); Univ. of Newcastle upon Tyne (BPhil 1979). Teacher: King's Sch., Rochester, 1972; Dame Allan's Sch., Newcastle upon Tyne, 1973–76; Northern Counties Sch. for the Deaf, 1976–80; National Deaf Children's Society: Educn Officer, 1980–82; Dir, 1982–91; Exec. Dir, Alzheimer's Disease Soc., subseq. Chief Exec., Alzheimer's Soc., 1991–2003; Nat. Dir, Patients and the Public, DoH, 2003–07. Canadian Commonwealth Fellow, 1983. Chairman: Nat. Information Governance Bd for Health and Social Care, 2008–12; Patient and Public Expert Adv. Gp, Commn on Human Medicines, 2012–; Member: Sec. of State for Health's Adv. Gp on Youth Treatment Service, 1991–96; Central R&D Cttee, NHS, 1999–; NHS Modernisation Bd, 2000–02; Human Genetics Commn Sub-Cttee, 2000–03; Vice Chm., Consumers in NHS Research, 1996–2003. Mem., Press Recognition Regulation Panel, 2014–. Chm., Voluntary Council for Handicapped Children, 1986–91. Trustee: Hearing Res. Trust, 1985–2005; Nat. Children's Bureau, 1987–91; Age Concern England, 1992–94; Comic Relief, 2005– (Chair, UK Grants Cttee, 2015–). Mem. Bd, Alzheimer Europe, 1998–2003; Patron, Arts4Dementia, 2015–. Pres. and Hon. Life Mem., European Fedn of Deaf Children's Assocs, 1990–91. Frequent broadcasts. FFPH (through distinction) 2007. Alzheimer Europe Award, 2003; Life-Time Achievement Award, RCPsych, 2007. *Publications*: Dementia: Alzheimer's and other dementias, 2002; numerous essays and articles. *Recreations*: art, music, food. *Address*: 24 Barlby Gardens, North Kensington, W10 5LW. *T*: (office) (020) 7389 8030. *Club*: Athenæum.

**CAYZER**, family name of **Baron Rotherwick**.

**CAZALET, Hon. Lady; Camilla Jane**; *b* 12 July 1937; *d* of 6th Viscount Gage, KCVO, and Hon. Alexandra Imogen Clare Grenfell (*d* 1969); *m* 1965, Sir Edward Stephen Cazalet, *qv*; two *s* one *d*. *Educ*: Benenden Sch. Dir, Lumley Cazalet, 1967–2001. Trustee, Glyndebourne Arts Trust, 1978–2004; Member: Royal Nat. Theatre Bd, 1991–97; Exec. Cttee, Friends of Covent Garden, 1994–2000; Royal Nat. Theatre Develt Council, 1996–2008; Gov., Royal Ballet, 2000–08. *Recreations*: theatre, music, dance. *Address*: Flat 10, 41 Stanhope Gardens, SW7 5QY. *T*: (020) 7244 6182.

**CAZALET, Sir Edward (Stephen)**, Kt 1988; DL; a Judge of the High Court of Justice, Family Division, 1988–2000; *b* 26 April 1936; *s* of late Peter Victor Ferdinand Cazalet and Leonora Cazalet (*née* Rowley, then Wodehouse); *m* 1965, Camilla Jane (*née* Gage) (*see* Hon. Lady Cazalet); two *s* one *d*. *Educ*: Eton Coll. (Fellow, 1989–2004); Christ Church, Oxford (MA Jurisprudence). Called to the Bar, Inner Temple, 1960, Bencher, 1985. QC 1980; a Recorder, 1985–88; Family Division Liaison Judge for SE Circuit, 1990–96. Chairman: Horserace Betting Levy Appeal Tribunal, 1977–88; Sussex Assoc. for Rehabilitation of Offenders, 1991–98; CAB, Royal Courts of Justice, 1992–98; British Agencies for Adoption and Fostering, 2000–05; Jockey Club Appeal Bd, 2001–05; Injured Jockeys' Fund, 2002–06 (Trustee, 1987–2006). Chm. Trustees, Charles Douglas-Home Award, 1986–96; Trustee, Winston Churchill Meml Fund, 2004–11. DL E Sussex, 1989. *Recreations*: riding, ball games, chess. *Address*: Shaw Farm, Plumpton Green, Lewes, East Sussex BN7 3DG. *Club*: Garrick.

**CEARNS, Kathryn**, OBE 2017; independent consultant, since 2014; *b* Harrogate, Yorks, 30 April 1964; *d* of Michael Verity and Vicki Verity (later Clifford); *m* 1989, Simon Justin Cearns. *Educ*: Leeds Girls' High Sch.; Goldsmiths' Coll., London (BA Hons Eng. Lit. 1995). ACA 1990; FCA 2001; FCCA 2002. Auditor, Ernst and Young, 1987–91; Tech. Author, BPP plc, 1991–98; Project Dir, Accounting Standards Bd, 1998–2000; Consultant Accountant, Herbert Smith Freehills (formerly Herbert Smith) LLP, 2000–14. Chairman: Financial Reporting Cttee, ICAEW, 2008–17; Financial Reporting Adv. Bd to HM Treasury, 2010–16; Office of Tax Simplification, 2019–; Mem., Ext. Audit Cttee, IMF, 2017–. Non-executive Director: Companies House, 2017–; UK Supreme Court, 2017–; Highways England, 2018–. Mem. Council, ICAEW, 2016–19. Trustee, RBL Industries, 2017–. *Recreations*: bridge, theatre, opera, ballet, literature, needlework.

**CECIL**; *see* Gascoyne-Cecil, family name of Marquess of Salisbury.

**CECIL**, family name of **Marquess of Exeter**, and **Barons Amherst of Hackney** and **Rockley**.

**CECIL, Charles Anthony**, MBE 2011; Founder and Chief Executive, Revolution Software, since 1990; *b* London, 11 Aug. 1962; *s* of Charles David Cecil and Veronica Mary Cecil (*née* Lawley); *m* 1991, Noirin Carmody; one *s* one *d*. *Educ*: Bedales Sch.; Univ. of Manchester (BSc/BEng Hons Engrg, Manuf. and Mgt 1985). Dir, Artic Computing, 1981–86; Founder and Man. Dir, Paragon Programming, 1986–87; Develt Dir, US Gold, 1987–88, Activision (UK), 1988–90; Director/Designer, computer game projects including: Broken Sword adventure series, 1996–; Da Vinci Code, Imagine Entertainment/ Take 2, 2006; Doctor Who Adventure Games, 2006 (BAFTA Wales Award). Director: Screen Yorkshire, 2004–; BFI, 2013–16. Member: BAFTA, 2000; Co. of Merchant Adventurers, York, 2011. *Recreations*: competing in national and international rowing events, travel, history (popular, medieval and biblical). *E*: charlesc@revolution.co.uk.

**CECIL, Clementine**; Executive Director, Pushkin House, since 2016; *b* London, 22 Oct. 1975; *d* of Hugh and Mirabel Cecil. *Educ*: Cheltenham Ladies' Coll.; Glasgow Univ. (MA Double 1st Jt Hons Russian and Scottish Lit.); Birmingham Univ. (MA Historic Envmt Conservation). Moscow corresp., The Times, 2001–04; freelance journalist, 2001–: World of Interiors, Cornerstone mag. (SPAB), Blueprint, TLS. Director: SAVE Britain's Heritage, 2012–16; SAVE Europe's Heritage, 2012–16 (Trustee, 2016–); Trustee, SAVE Trust, 2016–. Moscow Architecture Preservation Society: Co-Founder, 2004; Trustee, 2005–; Chm., 2012–16. Member: Internat. Melnikov Hse Cttee, 2007–11; Tbilisi Heritage Gp, 2011–. *Publications*: editor and compiler: Moscow Heritage at Crisis Point (Russian and English), 2007, 2nd edn 2009; Samara: endangered city on the Volga (Russian and English), 2009; St Petersburg Heritage at Risk (Russian and English), 2012. *Recreation*: swimming and drawing in North Norfolk. *Address*: 6 Basterfield House, Golden Lane Estate, Golden Lane, EC1Y 0TN. *E*: clemcecil@gmail.com.

**CECIL, Desmond Hugh**, CMG 1995; arts charity trustee, international political and funding adviser; *b* 19 Oct. 1941; *s* of Dr Rupert Cecil, DFC, and Rosemary Cecil (*née* Luker); *m* 1964, Ruth Elizabeth Sachs; three *s* one *d*. *Educ*: Headington Co. Primary Sch.; Magdalen Coll. Sch., Oxford; Queen's Coll., Oxford (MA); studied oboe with Joy Boughton, London, and violin/viola with Sascha Lasserson, London and Max Rostal, Berne. Violinist and oboist in Switzerland; Leader, Neuchâtel Chamber Orchestra, 1965–70; joined HM Diplomatic Service, 1970; Second Sec., FCO, 1970–73; First Secretary: Bonn, 1973–74; FCO, 1974–76; also Press Officer, Mission to UN, Geneva, 1976–80; FCO, 1980–85; Counsellor and Chargé d'Affaires, Vienna, 1985–89; FCO, 1989–92; on secondment with Board of P&O European Ferries, 1992; Under Sec., FCO, 1992–95. Senior Advisor: British Telecom, 1996–97; BNFL, 1996–2006; GEC/Marconi Communications, subseq. Marconi, 1998–2001. Chm., Arena Pal Ltd, 2002–03. Antiquarian book dealer, 1997–. Council Mem., Britain Russia Centre, 1998–2000; Member Board: Germany Project, Panel 2000, 1999–2000; Internat. Mendelssohn Foundn, Leipzig, 2001– (Chm., UK Friends, 2005–). Council Mem., Royal Philharmonic Soc., 1995–2005 (Chm., Sponsorship Cttee, 1998–2005; Hon. Co-Treas., 1999–2005); Dir and Trustee, Jupiter Orch., 1996–2002; Trustee, later Dir, LPO, 2005–; Adviser: Russian Arts Help Charity, Moscow, 2000–05; Nuclear Management Partners Ltd Bd, 2008, 2014–16; UK Rep., AREVA, then Sen. Vice-Pres., AREVA UK, 2006–12 (Expert Chair, 2012–16); Mem. Bd, Nuclear Industry Assoc., 2010– (Mem., Nominations Cttee, 2010–); Mem. Adv. Bd, OMFIF, 2013–; Internat. Rep., Gstaad Menuhin Fest. and Acad., 2001–; Mem., Adv. Council, Park Lane Gp, 2015–. Trustee: Voices for Hospices, 2000–04; Norbert Brainin Foundn, Asolo, 2003–09; Oxford Philharmonic Orch., 2017–18. Mem., Develt Cttee (formerly Appeal Cttee), Queen's Coll., Oxford, 2005–. Member: Mensa, 1968–2005; Sherlock Holmes Soc. of London, 1970–; Kingston Chamber Music Soc., 1990–; British-German Assoc., 2001–05. Freeman, 2015, Liveryman, 2017, Musicians' Co. Distinguished Friend of Oxford Univ. Award, 2012. *Publications*: A Violin by Antonio Stradivari 1724, 2017. *Recreations*: playing music and cricket, downhill ski-ing, chess, antiquarian travel books. *Address*: 38 Palace Road, East Molesey, Surrey KT8 9DL. *T*: (020) 8783 1998. *Clubs*: Athenæum (Chm., Wine Cttee, 1999–2001; Chm., Gen. Cttee, 2003–06; Trustee, 2008–18; Life Mem., 2018), MCC (Eur. Cricket Advr, 1998–2002); Claygate Cricket (Life Vice Pres.).

**CEENEY, Natalie Anna**, CBE 2010; Director, ICENI Associates LLP, since 2016; *b* 22 Aug. 1971; *d* of Anthony and Jacky Ceeney; *m* 2007, Dr Simon David John Chaplin, *qv*. *Educ*: Newnham Coll., Cambridge (MA 1st Cl. Maths/Social and Pol Sci.). NHS Manager: Northwick Park Hosp., 1992–94; Herts Health Agency, 1994–96; Gt Ormond St Hosp., 1996–98; Strategy Consultant, McKinsey, 1998–2001; Dir, Ops and Services, British Liby, 2001–05; Chief Exec., Nat. Archives, Keeper of the Public Records and Historical MSS Comr, 2005–10; Chief Exec. and Chief Ombudsman, Financial Ombudsman Service, 2010–13; Head of Customer Standards, HSBC UK, 2014–15; Chief Exec., HM Courts and Tribunals Service, 2015–16. Chair: Innovate Finance, 2017–; Ind. Access to Cash Rev.,

2018–; non-executive Director: Countrywide PLC, 2017–; Anglian Water Services Ltd, 2018–. Mem. Bd, Sport England, 2018–. *Recreations:* cycling, literature, theatre, Rugby union. *E:* nceeney@gmail.com.

**CEFAI, Dame Sally (Anne);** *see* Coates, Dame S. A.

**CELLAN-JONES, Diane;** *see* Coyle, D.

**CELLAN-JONES, (Nicholas) Rory;** Technology Correspondent, BBC News, since 2007; *b* London, 17 Jan. 1958; *s* of late Alan James Gwynne Cellan Jones and of Sylvia Margaret Rich; *m* 1990, Dr Diane Coyle, *qv*; two *s*. *Educ:* Dulwich Coll.; Jesus Coll., Cambridge (BA Mod. and Medieval Langs 1981). BBC: researcher, BBC Leeds, 1981–83; producer, BBC TV News, 1983–86; reporter: Wales Today, 1986–88; BBC TV News, 1988–98; Business Correspondent, BBC TV, 1998–2007. *Publications:* Dot.Bomb, 2001. *Address:* c/o BBC News Centre, Broadcasting House, Portland Place, W1A 1AA.

**CERF, Vinton Gray,** PhD; Vice-President and Chief Internet Evangelist, Google Inc., since 2005; *b* New Haven, Conn, 23 June 1943; *s* of Vinton Thruston Cerf and Muriel Cerf (*née* Gray); *m* 1966, Sigrid L. Thorstenberg; two *s*. *Educ:* Van Nuys High Sch., Calif; Stanford Univ. (BS 1965); UCLA (MS 1970; PhD 1972). Systems Engr, IBM Corp., 1965–67; Principal Programmer, Computer Sci. Dept, UCLA, 1967–72; Asst Prof. of Elec. Engrg and Computer Sci., Stanford Univ., 1972–76; Prog. Manager, 1976–81, Principal Scientist, 1981–82, Defense Advanced Res. Projects Agency; Vice-Pres. of Engrg, MCI Digital Inf. Services Co., 1982–86; Vice-Pres., Corp. for Nat. Res. Initiatives, 1986–94; Sen. Vice-Pres. for Data Architecture, MCI Telecoms Corp., 1994–95; Senior Vice-President: for Internet Architecture and Engrg, MCI Communications Corp., 1996–98; for Internet Architecture and Technol. Strategy, MCI WorldCom Corp., subseq. MCI, 1998–2005. Mem. Bd, Cttee on Sci. and Engrg Indicators, Nat. Sci. Bd, 2013–. Dist. Vis. Scientist, Jet Propulsion Lab., CIT, 1998–. Internet Society: Founder Mem., 1992; Founder Pres., 1992–95; Chm., 1998–99; Trustee, 1992–2002; Chm., Internet Societal Task Force, 1999–2000. FAAAS, 1990. Foreign Mem., Royal Soc., 2016. (Jtly) Queen Elizabeth Prize for Engrg, Royal Acad. of Engrg, 2013. Presidential Medal of Freedom (USA), 2005.

**CESCAU, Patrick Jean-Pierre;** Chevalier, Légion d'Honneur, 2005; Group Chief Executive Officer, Unilever, 2005–08; Chairman, InterContinental Hotels Group, since 2013; *b* Paris, 27 Sept. 1948; *s* of Pierre and Louise Cescau; *m* 1974, Ursula Kadansky; one *s* one *d*. *Educ:* ESSEC Business Sch., Paris (business degree); INSEAD (MBA dist.). Unilever, 1973–2008: consultant, 1973–76, sen. consultant, 1976–77, Unilever France; Commercial Manager, Astra Calve, France, 1977–81; Chief Accountant, Union Deutsche Lebensmittelwerke GmbH, 1981; Germany, 1984; Commercial Mem., Unilever Edible Fats and Dairy Netherlands, 1984; Financial Dir, PT Unilever Indonesia, 1986–89; Nat. Manager, Unilever Portugal, 1989–91; Chm., PT Unilever Indonesia, 1991–95; Pres. and CEO, Van den Bergh Foods, USA, 1995–97; Mem. Bd Dirs, Unilever US, Inc., 1995–96; Pres., Lipton USA, 1997–98; Gp Financial Controller and Dep. Chief Financial Officer, 1998–99; Financial Dir, 1999–2000; Foods Dir, 2001–04; Chm., Unilever plc and Dep. Chm., Unilever NV, 2004–05. Non-executive Director: Pearson plc, 2002–12 (Sen. Ind. Dir, 2010–12); Tesco plc, 2009–15 (Sen. Ind. Dir, 2010–15); Internat. Airlines Gp, 2010–. Conseiller du Commerce Extérieur de la France, Netherlands, 2002–. Chm., Nat. Assoc. of Margarine Manufacturers, USA, 1996–98; Mem. Bd and Exec. Cttee, Tea Council, USA, 1997–98. Trustee, Leverhulme Trust, 2005–09. Chm., St Jude Children Charity, 2009–13. *Recreations:* arts, photography, reading, theatre. *Address:* Intercontinental Hotels Group, Broadwater Park, Denham, Bucks UB9 5HR.

**CEZAR, Aaron Garfield;** Founding Director, Delfina Foundation, since 2007; *b* Louisiana, 18 June 1977; *s* of Lucius Cezar, Jr and Marita Victorian. *Educ:* Oberlin Jun. and Sen. High Sch.; Princeton Univ. (BA Econs 1999; Cert. Dip. Theatre and Dance 1999); King's Coll. London (MA Cultural and Creative Industries (Dist.) 2003). Mgt Consultant, Consulting Gp, Computer Sciences Corp., 1999–2002; Prog. Manager, Metal Culture, 2003–05; Man. Dir, Metal Space, 2005–07. Special Projects Manager, London 2012 Olympics, 2004–05; Co-Curator, Performance Art Prog., 58th Venice Biennale, 2019. Dir, Visual Arts, Beyond Borders Scotland, 2010–16; Advr at Large, Art Jameel, 2018–. Mem. Cttee, Nat. Meml to British Victims of Overseas Terrorism, 2016–17. Trustee: All Change Arts, 2009–; Shubbak, 2014–. Hon. FRCA 2017. *Publications:* (ed with Dani Burrows) Politics of Food, 2019. *Recreations:* dancing, cinema, writing, travelling. *Address:* Delfina Foundation, 29/31 Catherine Place, SW1E 6DY. *T:* (020) 7233 5344. *E:* aaron@delfinafoundation.com.

**CHACKSFIELD, Mark Andrew;** QC 2019; *b* King's Lynn, 14 Sept. 1974; *s* of Christopher Chacksfield, MBE and Elizabeth Chacksfield; *m* 2002, Felicity Kay Seymour; two *s* one *d*. *Educ:* Royal Grammar Sch., High Wycombe; Clare Coll., Cambridge (BA 1997). Called to the Bar, Middle Temple, 1999; in practice as barrister, specialising in intellectual property, 8 New Square, 2000–. *Recreations:* running, modern pentathlon, the environment, travel, my fabulous family. *Address:* 8 New Square, Lincoln's Inn, WC2A 3QP. *T:* (020) 7405 4321. *E:* mark.chacksfield@8newsquare.co.uk.

**CHADHA, Prof. Jagjit Singh;** Director, National Institute of Economic and Social Research, since 2016; *b* W Yorks, 1 Dec. 1966; *s* of Manmohan Chadha and Manjit Chadha (*née* Anand); *m* 1992, Sahar Khosrovi-Azerbaijani; one *s* one *d*. *Educ:* John Lyon Sch., Harrow; University Coll. London (BSc Econ 1985); London Sch. of Econs and Political Sci. (MSc Econ 1990). Official, Bank of England, 1992–98; Fellow, Clare Coll., Cambridge 1999–2003; Prof. of Econs, Univ. of St Andrews, 2003–05; Chief Quantitative Economist, BNP Paribas, 2005–07; Prof. of Econs, Univ. of Kent, 2008–15. *Publications:* Parables, Trade-offs and Lags, 2017; articles in learned jls. *Recreations:* photography, walking, cinema, music, football. *Address:* National Institute of Economic and Social Research, 2 Dean Trench Street, SW1P 3HE. *E:* j.chadha@niesr.ac.uk.

**CHADLINGTON,** Baron *cr* 1996 (Life Peer), of Dean in the county of Oxfordshire; **Peter Selwyn Gummer;** Chief Executive, 2000–15, Group Senior Advisor, 2015–16, Huntsworth plc; Senior Partner, Chadlington Consultancy, since 2016; *b* 24 Aug. 1942; *s* of late Rev. Canon Selwyn Gummer and Sybille (*née* Mason); *m* 1982, Lucy Rachel, *er d* of A. Ponsonby Dudley-Hill; one *s* three *d*. *Educ:* King's Sch., Rochester, Kent; Selwyn Coll., Cambridge (BA, MA). Portsmouth and Sunderland Newspaper Gp, 1964–65; Viyella International, 1965–66; Hodgkinson & Partners, 1966–67; Industrial & Commercial Finance Corp., 1967–74; Founder, 1974–94, Chm., 1994–98, Shandwick Internat. plc; Internat. Public Relations, 1998–2000. Non-executive Director: CIA Group PLC, 1990–94; Halifax plc (formerly Halifax Building Soc.), 1994–2001 (non-exec. Mem., London Bd, 1990–94); Britax Childcare Hldgs Ltd, 2005–11; Director: Black Box Music Ltd, 1999–2001; Oxford Resources, 1999–2002; Chairman: hotcourses.com, 2000–04; guideforlife.com, 2000–02. Marketing Gp of GB, 1993–95. Chairman: Royal Opera House, Covent Gdn, 1996–97; LAPADA, 2011–17. Member: NHS Policy Bd, 1991–95; Arts Council of England (formerly of GB), 1991–96 (Chm., Nat. Lottery Advr Bd for Arts and Film, 1994–96). Mem., EU Select Sub-Cttee B (Energy, Industry and Transport), H of L, 2000–03. Chm., Action on Addiction, 2000–07; Mem. Bd, Mending Broken Hearts Appeal, British Heart Foundn, 2010–. Chm., Understanding Industry Trust, 1991–96; Trustee, Atlantic Partnership, 1999–; Mem. Bd of Trustees, Amer. Univ., 1999–2001;

Mem. Council, Cheltenham Ladies' Coll., 1998–2003. Gov., Ditchley Foundn, 2008–. FRSA. Hon. Fellow, Bournemouth Univ., 1999–. *Publications:* various articles and booklets on public relations and marketing. *Recreations:* opera, Rugby, cricket. *Clubs:* White's, Carlton, MCC, Walbrook (Dir, 1999–2004).

*See also* Baron Deben, Baron Hindlip.

**CHADWICK, Charles McKenzie,** CBE 1992 (OBE 1984); British Council Director (formerly Representative), Poland, 1989–92; *b* 31 July 1932; *s* of late Trevor McKenzie Chadwick and Marjory Baron; *m* 1st, 1965, Evelyn Ingeborg Ihlenfeldt (marr. diss.); one *s*; 2nd, 1999, Mary Christina Beatrice Teale; one *s*. *Educ:* Charterhouse School; Trinity Coll., Toronto (BA). Army service, 1950–52; HMOCS Provincial Administration, Northern Rhodesia, 1958–64; Lectr, 1964–66, and Head, Administrative Training, 1966–67, Staff Trng Coll., Lusaka; British Council Officer, 1967–92; service in Kenya, Nigeria, Brazil, London; British Election Supervisor, Zimbabwe, 1980; British Council Rep., Canada, 1981–88. Member: Commonwealth Observer Gp, Ghanaian Presidential elections, 1992, Pakistan National elections, 1993, Cameroon Parly elections, 1997; EU observer team, S African election, 1994; FCO Observer, Uganda elections, 1996; OSCE Supervisor, Bosnia elections, 1996. Gov., Hampstead Sch., 1992–2000. *Publications:* It's All Right Now, 2005; A Chance Acquaintance, 2009; Brief An Sally, 2010; Die Frau, die zu viel fühlte, 2013; Josefa, 2014. *Address:* c/o United Agents Ltd, 12–26 Lexington Street, W1F 0LE.

**CHADWICK, Derek James,** DPhil; CChem, FRSC; Director, Novartis (formerly Ciba) Foundation, 1988–2008; *b* 9 Feb. 1948; *s* of Dennis Edmund and Ida Chadwick; *m* 1980, Susan Reid (*d* 2002); two *s*. *Educ:* St Joseph's Coll., Blackpool; Keble Coll., Oxford (BA, BSc, MA, DPhil). FRSC 1982. ICI Fellow, Cambridge Univ., 1972–73; Prize Fellow, Magdalen Coll., Oxford, 1973–77; Lectr and Sen. Lectr, Liverpool Univ., 1977–88. Vis. Prof., Univ. of Trondheim, Norway, 1995–2012. Member: Sci. Cttee, Louis Jeantet Foundn, Geneva, 1989–98; Hague Club of European Foundn Dirs, 1989–2008 (Sec., 1993–97); Sci. Adv. Cttee, 1990–96, Exec. Council, 1991–2000 (Vice-Pres., 1994–2000), AMRC; CCLRC, 2002–07. Mem., Soc. of Apothecaries, 1990. Hon. FRCP 2009. *Publications:* chapters in: Aromatic and Heteroaromatic Chemistry, 1979; Comprehensive Heterocyclic Chemistry, 1984; The Research and Academic Users' Guide to the IBM PC, 1988; Pyrroles, Pt 1, 1990; ed many vols in Novartis (formerly Ciba) Foundn symposium series; many papers in chemistry jls, e.g. Jl Chem. Soc., Tetrahedron, Tet. Letters, etc. *Recreations:* music, gardening, playing bridge. *Address:* 4 Bromley Avenue, Bromley, Kent BR1 4BQ. *T:* (020) 8460 3332. *E:* derekchadwick@hotmail.com.

**CHADWICK, Fiona Jane;** Ballet Administrator, Junior Royal Ballet School, 1996–99; *b* 13 May 1960; *d* of late William Chadwick and of Anne Chadwick; *m* 1st, 1990, Anthony Peter Dowson (marr. diss.); one *d*; 2nd, 1996, Robert Cave; one *s* one *d*. *Educ:* Royal Ballet Sch. Joined Royal Ballet Co., 1978; Soloist, 1981–84; Principal, 1984–96. Leading rôles included: Swan Lake, Romeo and Juliet, Sleeping Beauty, Cinderella, La Fille Mal Gardée, Giselle, Prince of the Pagodas, La Bayadère, Pursuit, Firebird. Patron, London Children's Ballet, 2001–. DLitt Lancaster, 2009.

**CHADWICK, Rear Adm. John,** CB 2001; Director, Greenwich Hospital, 2003–07; *b* 26 March 1946; *s* of Alec and Elsie Chadwick; *m* 1970, Jacqueline Cosh; two *s*. *Educ:* Cheadle Hulme Sch. CEng 1973; FIET (FIEE 1996). BRNC Dartmouth, 1966; RNC Greenwich (electronic engrg), 1967–69; submarine service, 1970; served in HM Submarines Otter, Ocelot, Spartan, 1970–82; Sqdn Weapon Engr, 3rd Submarine Sqdn, 1984–86; Submarine Weapon System Manager, MoD(PE), 1987–89; Captain 1989; Asst Dir, Operational Requirements, MoD, 1990–93; Dir, Underwater Weapons, MoD(PE), 1993–96; i/c HMS Collingwood, 1996–98; Chief Naval Engr Officer, 1999–2001; FO Trng and Recruiting, 1998–2001. Pres., RN Rugby League, 1997–2001. Chm., RN & RM Charity, 2008–12. *Recreations:* walking, gardening, house renovation.

**CHADWICK, Rt Hon. Sir John (Murray),** Kt 1991; ED; PC 1997; a Lord Justice of Appeal, 1997–2007; *b* 20 Jan. 1941; *s* of Hector George Chadwick and Margaret Corry Chadwick (*née* Laing); *m* 1975, Diana Mary Blunt; two *d*. *Educ:* Rugby School; Magdalene Coll., Cambridge (MA). Called to the Bar, Inner Temple, 1966 (Bencher, 1986; Treasurer, 2004). Standing Counsel to DTI, 1974–80; QC 1980; Judge of Courts of Appeal of Jersey and Guernsey, 1986–93; a Recorder, 1989–91; Judge of the High Court, Chancery Div., 1991–97; Chancery Supervising Judge, Birmingham, Bristol and Cardiff, 1995–97. Pres., Court of Appeal of Cayman Is, 2008–15. A Lieut Bailiff of Guernsey, 2008–May 2020; a Judge, Dubai Internat. Financial Centre Court, 2008–17 (Dep. Chief Justice, 2013–16); Mem., Special Tribunal Related to Dubai World, 2009–. Vice-Pres., Corp. of the Sons of the Clergy, 2004–16. Dir, Utd Services Trust, 2005–14. Visitor, Green Templeton Coll., Oxford, 2010–. *Address:* One Essex Court, Temple, EC4Y 9AR. *Clubs:* Athenæum, Beefsteak, Garrick; Royal Yacht Squadron (Cowes).

**CHADWICK, Sir Joshua Kenneth B.;** *see* Burton-Chadwick.

**CHADWICK, Dr Priscilla;** education consultant; Principal, Berkhamsted Collegiate School, 1996–2008; Chair, Dioceses Commission, 2008–10; *b* 7 Nov. 1947; *d* of Prof. Henry Chadwick, KBE, FBA. *Educ:* Oxford High Sch.; Clarendon Sch., N Wales; Girton Coll., Cambridge (BA Theol Tripos 1970); Oxford Univ. (PGCE); London Univ. (MA Curriculum Studies 1983; PhD 1993). Head of Religious Education: St Helen's Sch., Northwood, 1971–73; Putney High Sch., 1973–78; St Bede's C of E/RC Comprehensive, Redhill, 1979–82; Dep. Head, Twyford C of E High Sch., Acton, 1982–85; Headteacher, Bishop Ramsey C of E Sch., Ruislip, 1986–91; Dean, Educnl Develt, South Bank Univ., 1992–96. Chm., HMC, 2005. Member: English Anglican/RC Cttee, 1981–2006; BBC/ITC Central Religious Adv. Cttee, 1983–93; Youth Crime Cttee, NACRO, 1988–94; Goldsmiths' Coll. Council, 1991–97; Southwark Cathedral Council, 2009–16; Council, Nat. Soc., C of E, 2015–. Chairman: Culham St Gabriel's Trust (formerly St Gabriel's Trust), 1987–2018; School Chaplains and Leaders Assoc. (formerly Bloxham Project), 2011–17; Church Sch. of the Future Rev., 2011–12. Chm. Govs, Wren Acad., London, 2008–14; Governor: Westminster Sch., 1997–; Uppingham Sch., 2009–19 (Vice-Chm., 2013–19); Harris Westminster Sixth Form, 2014–. FRSA 1992. Hon. DEd Herts 2006; Hon. DLaws Roehampton 2011. *Publications:* Schools of Reconciliation, 1994; Shifting Alliances: the partnership of Church and State in English education, 1997; (contrib.) Anglican Church School Education, 2013; (contrib.) Education across the United Kingdom 1944–2017: local government, accountability and partnerships, 2018; articles in various educnl jls. *Recreations:* music and the arts, world travel. *Club:* East India.

**CHADWICK-JONES, Prof. John Knighton,** PhD, DSc(Econ); Research Professor, University of Fribourg, Switzerland, 1993–2002; *b* 26 July 1928; *s* of Thomas Chadwick-Jones and Cecilia Rachel (*née* Thomas); *m* 1965, Araceli Carceller y Bergillos, PhD; two *s* one *d*. *Educ:* Bromsgrove Sch.; St Edmund Hall, Oxford (MA). PhD Wales, 1960; DSc(Econ) Wales, 1981. CPsychol, FBPsS. Scientific Staff, Nat. Inst. of Industrial Psychol., London, 1957–60; Lectr, then Sen. Lectr, in Industrial Psychol., UC, Cardiff, 1960–66; Reader in Social Psychol., Flinders Univ. of South Australia, 1967–68; Dir, Occupational Psychol. Res. Unit, UC, Cardiff, 1968–74; Prof. of Psychology, Saint Mary's Univ., Halifax, Canada, 1974–93, now Emeritus (Mem., Exec. Cttee, Bd of Governors, 1975–78). Canada Soc. Scis and Humanities Res. Council Leave Fellow: Darwin Coll., Cambridge,

1980–81; MRC Unit on Develt and Integration of Behaviour, Cambridge, 1984–85; Visiting Fellow: Clare Hall, Cambridge, 1982; Wolfson Coll., Cambridge, 1984–85; Wolfson Coll., Oxford, 1988–89; St Edmund's Coll., Cambridge, 1990–91. Dir, Cambridge Canadian Trust (Toronto), 1988–94. Fellow, Amer. Psychol Assoc.; Hon. Fellow, Canadian Psychol Assoc. *Publications:* Automation and Behaviour: a social psychological study, 1969; Social Exchange Theory: its structure and influence in social psychology, 1976; (jtly) Brain, Environment and Social Psychology, 1979; Absenteeism in the Canadian Context, 1979; (jtly) Social Psychology of Absenteeism, 1982; Developing a Social Psychology of Monkeys and Apes, 1998; articles in academic jls. *Address:* Clare Hall, Herschel Road, Cambridge CB3 9AL.

**CHADWYCK-HEALEY, Sir Charles (Edward),** 5th Bt *cr* 1919, of Wyphurst, Cranleigh, Co. Surrey and New Place, Luccombe, Somerset; DL; Chairman, Chadwyck-Healey Ltd, 1973–99; President, Chadwyck-Healey Inc., 1975–99; *b* 13 May 1940; *s* of Sir Charles Arthur Chadwyck-Healey, 4th Bt, OBE, TD, and of Viola, *d* of late Cecil Lubbock; *S* father, 1986; *m* 1967, Angela Mary, *e d* of late John Metson; one *s* two *d*. *Educ:* Eton; Trinity Coll., Oxford (MA; Hon. Fellow, 2006). Member: Marshall Aid Commemoration Commn, 1994–2000; Liby and Inf. Commn, 1995–2000; Lord Chancellor's Adv. Council on Nat. Records and Archives (formerly Public Records), 2001–06. Dir, openDemocracy Ltd, 2001–09. Mem., Ely Cathedral Council, 2001–07. Chm., Cambs Police Shrievalty Trust, 2005–10. Chm., Beds, Cambs and Northants (formerly Beds, Cambs, Northants and Peterborough) Wildlife Trusts, 2009–13; Pres., CPRE Cambs, 2008–13. High Sheriff, 2004–05, DL, 2004, Cambs. *Heir: s* Edward Alexander Chadwyck-Healey [*b* 2 June 1972; *m* 1999, Denise Suzanne, (Denny), *e d* of Caroline Osborne; two *d*]. *Address:* 5 Madingley Road, Cambridge CB3 0EE. *T:* (01223) 316766. *Clubs:* Athenæum, Brooks's.

**CHAFFEY, Ven. Jonathan Paul Michael,** CB 2018; Director General Chaplaincy Services, Headquarters Air Command and Chaplain-in-Chief and Archdeacon, Royal Air Force, 2014–18; *b* London, 1962; *s* of Rev. Michael Chaffey and Shirley Chaffey; *m* 1988, Jane Frances Page, (Rev. Jane Chaffey); three *d*. *Educ:* Worksop Coll.; Univ. of Durham (BA Hons Sociol. 1983; CTh 1987); Nottingham Univ. (MA Theol. 2007). Ordained deacon, 1987, priest, 1988; Curate, St Stephen's Gateacre, Liverpool, 1987–90; RAF Chaplain, 1990–2018; rcds 2013–14. QHC 2012–18. Hon. Canon, Lincoln Cathedral, 2015–. *Recreations:* historical biographies, several sports, flute, family. *Club:* Royal Air Force.

**CHAHAL, Saimo;** Senior Partner, since 1995, and Joint Head of Public and International Law, since 2012, Bindmans LLP; First-tier Tribunal Judge (Mental Health), since 2004; a Judge of the Court of Protection, since 2018; *b* Punjab, India, 18 July 1958; *d* of Shere and Chanan Chahal; *m* 2016, Stephen Pierce; one *s* one *d*. *Educ:* Twickenham Green Primary Sch.; Knellar Girls' Secondary Sch.; Sussex Univ. (BA Hons Sociol.). Legal Advr, Deptford Law Centre, 1984–89; trainee solicitor with Hornby and Levy Solicitors, 1989–90; admitted as solicitor, 1990; Legal Advr, Wandsworth Law Centre, 1990–92; Housing, Civil and Employment Law Solicitor, HCL Hanne and Co., 1992–94. Associate Fellow, Centre for Public Law, Univ. of Cambridge, 2018. Legal Aid Lawyer of Year, Mental Health, Legal Aid Practitioners Gp, 2006; Solicitor of Year, Law Soc. Excellence Award, 2008; Public Law and Human Rights Lawyer of Year, Soc. of Asian Lawyers, 2011; Hot Campaigning Lawyer, The Lawyer, 2007. Hon. QC 2014. *Recreations:* reading group, film club, walking, art, architect, interior design, gardening. *Address:* Bindmans LLP, 236 Gray's Inn Road, WC1X 8HB. *T:* 07919 307115. *E:* s.chahal@bindmans.com.

**CHAILLY, Riccardo;** conductor; Musical Director, La Scala, Milan, since 2017 (Principal Conductor, 2015–17); Music Director, Lucerne Festival Orchestra, since 2016; *b* 20 Feb. 1953; *s* of late Luciano Chailly and of Anna Maria Chailly; *m* 1987, Gabriella Terragni; two *s*. *Educ:* Conservatory of Music, Perugia; St Cecilia, Rome; Giuseppe Verdi, Milan. Chief Conductor, Berlin Radio Symph. Orch., 1982–89; Principal Conductor and Music Dir, Teatro Comunale, Bologna, 1986–93; Principal Conductor: Royal Concertgebouw Orch., Amsterdam, 1988–2004, now Conductor Emeritus; Orch. Giuseppe Verdi, Milan, 1999–2005, now Conductor Laureate; Kapellmeister, Gewandhaus Orch., Leipzig, 2005–16; has conducted world's leading orchestras, including Vienna and Berlin Philharmonic, Chicago Symphony, Philadelphia and Cleveland; has performed in major opera houses, including: La Scala, Milan, Vienna State Opera, Covent Garden, Munich, Metropolitan Opera, NY. Hon. RAM 1996. Numerous recordings. Grand Prix du Disque, Acad. Charles Cros, 1984, 1985, 1987, 1992, and other recording awards. Grande Ufficiale, Italian Republic, 1994. *Address:* c/o Teatro alla Scala, Via Filodrammatici 2, 20121 Milano, Italy.

**CHAISTY, Paul;** QC 2001; a Recorder, since 2000; a Deputy High Court Judge, since 2006; *b* 12 March 1958; *s* of Dora Cranston (*née* Preston); *m* 1987, Margaret Judith Lewis; one *s* one *d*. *Educ:* Parrs Wood High Sch., Manchester; Nottingham Univ. (LLB); Exeter Coll., Oxford (BCL). Called to the Bar, Lincoln's Inn, 1982; in practice as barrister, Manchester, 1982–, London, 2006–, specialising in commercial and Chancery law. *Recreations:* fishing, family, football, friends. *Address:* Kings Chambers, 36 Young Street, Manchester M3 3FT. *T:* (0161) 832 9082; Serle Court, 6 New Square, Lincoln's Inn, WC2A 3QS. *T:* (020) 7242 6105.

**CHAKRABARTI,** Baroness *cr* 2016 (Life Peer), of Kennington in the London Borough of Lambeth; **Shami Chakrabarti,** CBE 2007; PC 2018; Director, Liberty, 2003–16; *b* 16 June 1969; *d* of Shyamalendou and Shyamali Chakrabarti; one *s*. *Educ:* London Sch. of Econs and Pol Sci. (LLB). Called to the Bar, Middle Temple, 1994, Bencher, 2006; lawyer, Legal Advr's Br., Home Office, 1996–2001; In-house Counsel, Liberty, 2001–03. Shadow Attorney Gen., 2016–. Vis. Fellow, Nuffield Coll., Oxford, 2006–. Member: Tate Members Council, 2006–15; Leveson Inquiry, 2011–12. Chancellor: Oxford Brookes Univ., 2008–15; Univ. of Essex, 2014–17. Hon. Fellow, Mansfield Coll., Oxford, 2009–. Governor: LSE, 2005–11; BFI, 2006–13. *Publications:* On Liberty, 2014; Of Women: in the 21st century, 2017; contribs to Public Law and European Human Rights Law Review, and various newspapers and magazines. *Recreations:* friends, popular cinema. *Address:* House of Lords, SW1A 0PW.

**CHAKRABARTI, Reeta;** journalist; News Presenter and Correspondent, BBC, since 2014; *b* 12 Dec. 1964; *d* of Bidhan Kumar and Ruma Chakrabarti; *m* 1992, Paul Hamilton; two *s* one *d*. *Educ:* King Edward VI High Sch., Birmingham; Internat. Sch., Calcutta; Exeter Coll., Oxford (BA Hons English and French; Hon. Fellow 2017). BBC: current affairs producer, Today, The World at One and PM, Radio 4, 1992–94; reporter, Radio 5 Live Breakfast Prog., 1994–96; Community Affairs Corresp., 1997–99; Political Corresp., 1999–2010; Educn and Social Affairs Corresp., 2010–14. Patron: Naz Project, 2001–14; Nat. Mentoring Consortium, 2003–15; Pan Intercultural Arts; Media Soc., Chartered Univ. 2019. Hon. Fellow: UEL, 2003; UCL, 2019. DLitt York St John, 2018. *Recreations:* reading, swimming, tennis, visiting beautiful European cities, enjoying my children! *Address:* Zone D, Floor B1, Lower Ground Floor Newsroom, BBC Broadcasting House, Portland Place, W1A 1AA.

**CHAKRABARTI, Sir Sumantra,** KCB 2006; President, European Bank for Reconstruction and Development, since 2012; *b* 12 Jan. 1959; *s* of Hirendranath Chakrabarti and Gayatri Chakrabarti (*née* Rudra); *m* 1983, Mari Sako, *qv*; one *d*. *Educ:* City of London Sch. for Boys; New Coll., Oxford (BA PPE 1981; Hon. Fellow 2004); Sussex Univ. (MA Econ 1984). ODI Fellow and Economist, Govt of Botswana, 1981–83; Sen. Economic Asst and Economic Advr, ODA, 1984–88; Asst to UK Exec. Dir, IMF and World Bank, Washington, 1988–90; Private Sec. to Rt Hon. Lynda Chalker, 1990–92; Assistant Secretary: Aid Policy and Resources Dept, ODA, 1992–96; Envmt, Transport, and Regions Team, Spending Directorate, HM Treasury, 1996–98; Dep. Dir, Budget and Public Finances, HM Treasury, 1998; Dir, Performance and Innovation Unit, 1998–2000, Head, Econ. and Domestic Affairs Secretariat, 2000–01, Cabinet Office; Dir Gen. for Regl Progs, 2001–02, Perm. Sec., 2002–07, DFID; Perm. Sec., MoJ, 2007–12; Clerk of the Crown in Chancery, 2007–12. Hon. Bencher, Middle Temple, 2009. Hon. LLD Sussex, 2004; Hon. DCL E Anglia, 2010; Dr *hc* Bucharest Univ. Econ. Studies, 2013. *Recreations:* Indian history, soul music, football. *Address:* European Bank for Reconstruction and Development, One Exchange Square, EC2A 2JN.

**CHALAYAN, Hussein,** MBE 2006; RDI 2013; fashion designer; artist; *b* Nicosia, Cyprus, 12 Aug. 1970. *Educ:* Central Saint Martins, London (BA Hons Fashion Design 1993; Hon. Fellow 2011). Founder, own label, 1994; Creative Director: TSE New York, 1998–2000; Asprey, 2001–04; Puma, 2008–10; Designer, Vionnet, 2015–. Exhibitions include: From Fashion and Back, Design Mus., London, 2009, Mus. of Contemporary Art, Tokyo, 2010; 1994–2010, Modern Mus., Istanbul, 2010; Fashion Narratives, Les Arts Décoratifs, Paris, 2011. Designer of the Year, British Fashion Awards, 1999, 2000; Outstanding Lifetime Achievement to Design, FX Internat. Interior Design Awards, London, 2009. *Publications:* Hussein Chalayan, 2005; *relevant publication:* Hussein Chalayan, 2011. *E:* press@chalayan.com.

**CHALFIE, Prof. Martin,** PhD; William R. Kenan Jr Professor of Biological Sciences, Columbia University, since 2002 (Chair, Department of Biological Sciences, 2007–10); *b* Chicago, 15 Jan. 1947; *s* of Eli and Vivian Chalfie; *m* 1989, Tulle Hazelrigg; one *d*. *Educ:* Harvard Univ. (PhD 1977). Teacher, Hamden Hall County Day Sch., Connecticut, 1970–72; Research Scientist, MRC Laboratory of Molecular Biology, Cambridge, 1977–82; Columbia University: Asst Prof., 1982–89; Associate Prof., 1989–93; Prof., 1994–. Foreign Mem., Royal Soc., 2018. (Jtly) Nobel Prize in Chemistry, 2008. *Publications:* contrib. articles in jls. *Address:* Columbia University, Department of Biological Sciences, 1018 Fairchild Center, MC 2446, New York, NY 10027, USA.

**CHALFONT,** Baron *cr* 1964 (Life Peer); **Alun Arthur Gwynne Jones;** PC 1964; OBE 1961; MC 1957; Chairman: Marlborough Stirling Group, 1994–99; Southern Mining Corp., 1997–99; *b* 5 Dec. 1919; *s* of Arthur Gwynne Jones and Eliza Alice Hardman; *m* 1948, Dr Mona Mitchell, MB ChB (*d* 2008); one *d* decd. *Educ:* West Monmouth Sch. Commissioned into South Wales Borderers (24th Foot), 1940; served in: Burma 1941–44; Malayan campaign 1955–57; Cyprus campaign 1958–59; various staff and intelligence appointments; Staff Coll., Camberley, 1950; Jt Services Staff Coll., 1958; Russian interpreter, 1951; resigned commission, 1961, on appt as Defence Correspondent, The Times; frequent television and sound broadcasts and consultant on foreign affairs to BBC Television, 1961–64. Mem., H of L, 1964–2015. Minister of State, Foreign and Commonwealth Office, 1964–70; UK Permanent Rep. to WEU, 1969–70; Foreign Editor, New Statesman, 1970–71. Dep. Chm., IBA, 1989–90; Chm., Radio Authy, 1991–94. Director: W. S. Atkins International, 1979–83; IBM UK Ltd, 1973–90 (Mem. IBM Europe Adv. Council, 1973–90); Lazard Bros & Co. Ltd, 1983–90; Shandwick plc, 1985–95; Triangle Holdings, 1986–90; Dep. Chm., Television Corp. plc, 1996–2001; Chairman: Industrial Cleaning Papers, 1979–86; Peter Hamilton Security Consultants Ltd, 1984–86; VSEL Consortium, later VSEL, 1987–95; President: Abington Corp. (Consultants) Ltd, 1981–; Nottingham Bldg Soc., 1983–90. Pres., All Party Defence Gp, H of L, 1995 (Chm., 1980–94). President: Hispanic and Luso Brazilian Council, 1975–80; RNID, 1980–87; Llangollen Internat. Music Festival, 1979–90; Freedom in Sport, 1982–88; Chairman: UK Cttee for Free World, 1981–89; Eur. Atlantic Gp, 1983–; Member: Nat. Defence Industries Council, 1992–; IISS; Bd of Governors, Sandle Manor Sch. MRI; MInstD. FRSA. Hon. Fellow UCW Aberystwyth, 1974. Hon. Col, Univ. of Wales OTC, 1991–94. Liveryman, Worshipful Co. of Paviors. Freeman, City of London. *Publications:* The Sword and The Spirit, 1963; The Great Commanders, 1973; Montgomery of Alamein, 1976; (ed) Waterloo: battle of three armies, 1979; Star Wars: suicide or survival, 1985; Defence of the Realm, 1987; By God's Will: a portrait of the Sultan of Brunei, 1989; The Shadow of My Hand (autobiog.), 2000; contribs to The Times, and other national and professional journals. *Recreations:* formerly Rugby football, cricket, lawn tennis; now music and theatre. *Clubs:* Garrick, MCC, City Livery.

**CHALISE, Dr Suresh Chandra;** Ambassador of Nepal to the Court of St James's and to Ireland, 2010–14; *b* Rajbiraj, Nepal, 24 Oct. 1957; *s* of late Ram Nath Chalise and of Chet Kumari Chalise; *m* 1996, Dr Milan Adhikary; two *d*. *Educ:* Banaras Hindu Univ., India (PhD Pol Sociol. 1990); Univ. of Justus Liebig, Giessen, Germany (postdoctoral studies in Develt Sociol. 2005); Asia Pacific Centre for Security Studies, Honolulu (Sen. Exec. Course 2006). Sec. on Internat. Affairs to Rt Hon. K. P. Bhattarai, 1991–96; Sen. Res. Fellow, Inst. of Sociol., Univ. of Justus Liebig, 1996–97; Alexander von Humboldt Foundn Postdoctoral Res. Fellow, Inst. of Political Sci., Univ. of Dortmund, 1998–99; Foreign Relns Advr to Hon. G. P. Koirala, 2003–06; leader of team of Nepalese generals to encourage interaction with Maoist rebels, July 2006; assisted Hd of Nepalese Govt and hd of Maoist rebels in Nepal's Peace Process, Aug. 2006; Advr to Prime Minister of Nepal on Foreign Affairs (with Minister of State status), 2006–07; Ambassador to USA, 2007–08; Policy Advr to former Prime Minister and Pres. of Nepali Congress, Hon. G. P. Koirala, 2008–09. Consultant, US Nat. Democratic Inst., DFID, Friedrich Ebert Foundn, Berlin, UNDP, Nexant/SARI (energy) and WHO. Hon. Citizen, Galveston City, Texas, 1992. Mahendra Vidhya Bhusan (Gold Medal) Grade A (Nepal), 1994. *Publications:* Sociology of the Legislative Elite in a Developing Society, 1995; (jtly) Women in Politics in Nepal: their socioeconomic, health, legal and political constraints, 1996; Coalition Governments and Political Acculturation in Germany, 1997. *Recreations:* light music, movies.

**CHALK, Alexander John Gervase;** MP (C) Cheltenham, since 2015; *b* 8 Aug. 1976; *s* of Gilbert Chalk and Gillian Miller (*née* Blois); *m* 2011, Sarah Beslee; two *d*. *Educ:* Winchester Coll.; Magdalen Coll., Oxford (BA Mod. Hist. 1998); City Univ. (DipLaw Dist. 2000). Called to the Bar, Middle Temple, 2001; barrister, 6 King's Bench Walk, then 6KBW College Hill, 2001–. Mem. (C), Hammersmith and Fulham Council, 2006–14. Mem., Justice Cttee, H of C, 2015–19. *Recreations:* cycling, playing guitar, reading, family. *Address:* House of Commons, SW1A 0AA. *E:* alex.chalk.mp@parliament.uk. *Club:* MCC.

**CHALK, Gerald Anthony;** a District Judge (Magistrates' Courts), since 2004; *b* 26 Nov. 1950; *s* of William Pickering Chalk and Winifred Chalk (*née* James); one *s*. *Educ:* Univ. of Newcastle upon Tyne (LLB Hons 1973). Admitted as solicitor, 1978; articled to McKenzie Bell & Sons, (Solicitors), Sunderland, later Asst Solicitor, 1975–79; Asst Prosecutor to Prosecuting Solicitors' Dept, Northumbria Police, 1979–83; Asst Solicitor, then Partner, Hawley & Rodgers, (Solicitors), Nottingham, 1983–2001; Partner, Johnson Partnership, (Solicitors), Nottingham, 2001–04. Actg Stipendiary Magistrate, 1999. *Recreations:* sport, history, literature. *Address:* c/o Carlisle Magistrates' Court, Rickergate, Carlisle, Cumbria CA3 8QH. *T:* (01228) 518838.

**CHALKE, Rev. Canon Stephen John,** MBE 2004; charity founder, educationalist, Baptist minister, author, and television and radio broadcaster; *b* 17 Nov. 1955; *s* of Victor Joseph Chalke and Ada Elizabeth (*née* Wroth); *m* 1980, Cornelia Maria Reeves; two *s* two *d*. *Educ:* Spurgeon's Coll., London (DipTh 1981). Ordained Minister, 1981; Minister, Tonbridge Baptist Ch, 1981–85; Founder: Oasis Trust, 1985–; Oasis Community Learning, 2005–); Faithworks, 2001–; Sen. Minister, Oasis Church Waterloo (formerly church.co.uk, Waterloo), 2003–; Founder, Stop the Traffik, 2006–; UN Special Advr, Community Action Against Human Trafficking, 2008–. Ecumenical Canon, Southwark Cathedral, 2017–. Dir, Parentalk, 1998–2011. FRSA 1998. Hon. Fellow Sarum Coll., 2005. Templeton UK Award, 1997. DUniv Staffs, 2015. *Publications:* books include: More Than Meets the Eye, 1995, rev. edn 2003; The Parentalk Guide to Your Child and Sex, 2000; He Never Said, 2000; Faithworks, 2001; The Parentalk Guide to Great Days Out, 2001; Faithworks Stories of Hope, 2001; Faithworks Unpacked, 2002; Intimacy and Involvement, 2003; Faithworks 100 Proven Ways for Community Transformation, 2003; (jtly) The Lost Message of Jesus, 2003; Trust: a radical manifesto, 2004; Intelligent Church, 2006; Change Agents, 2007; Stop the Traffik, 2009; (jtly) Apprentice: walking the way of Christ, 2009; Different Eyes: the art of living beautifully, 2010; Being Human: becoming the best version of yourself, 2015; The Lost Message of Paul, 2019. *Recreations:* gym, running, football, Crystal Palace FC. *Address:* The Oasis Centre, 1 Kennington Road, SE1 7QP. *T:* (020) 7921 4200, *Fax:* (020) 7921 4201. *E:* steve.chalke@oasisuk.org. *Club:* Riverside.

**CHALKER OF WALLASEY,** Baroness *cr* 1992 (Life Peer), of Leigh-on-Sea in the County of Essex; **Lynda Chalker;** PC 1987; President, Africa Matters Ltd, since 2016 (Chairman, 1998–2016); independent consultant on Africa and development to business and governments; company director; *b* 29 April 1942; *d* of late Sidney Henry James Bates and Marjorie Kathleen Randell; *m* 1st, 1967, Eric Robert Chalker (marr. diss. 1973); no *c*; 2nd, 1981, Clive Landa (marr. diss. 2003). *Educ:* Heidelberg Univ.; London Univ.; Central London Polytechnic. Statistician with Research Bureau Ltd (Unilever), 1963–69; Dep. Market Research Manager with Shell Mex & BP Ltd, 1969–72; Chief Exec. of Internat. Div. of Louis Harris International, 1972–74. MP (C) Wallasey, Feb. 1974–1992; Opposition Spokesman on Social Services, 1976–79; Parly Under-Sec. of State, DHSS, 1979–82, Dept of Transport, 1982–83; Minister of State, Dept of Transport, 1983–86; Minister of State, 1986–97, and Minister for Overseas Develt, 1989–97, FCO. Non-executive Director: Freeplay Energy plc, 1997–2006; Capital Shopping Centres plc, 1997–2000; Develt Consultants Internat., 1999–2003; Ashanti Goldfields Co. Ltd, 2000–04; Group 5 (Pty) Ltd, 2001–12; Unilever plc and Unilever NV, 2004–07 (Adv. Dir, 1998–2004); Member, International Advisory Board: LafargeHolcim (formerly Lafarge et Cie), 2004–17; Merchant Bridge & Co., 2005–. Member: BBC Gen. Adv. Cttee, 1975–79; RIIA, 1977–. Pres., BESO, 1998–2005 (Chm., 1998–2004); Chm., Medicines for Malaria Venture, 2006–11; Member, Board: Sentebale, 2010–; Elimination 8, 2016–18. Chm. Mgt Bd, LSHTM, 1998–2006. Hon. Fellow and Mem., RGS, 1998 (Pres., 2018–). Hon. Col, 156(NW) Transport Regt, RLC(V), 1995–2000. *Publications:* (jtly) Police in Retreat (pamphlet), 1967; (jtly) Unhappy Families (pamphlet), 1971; (jtly) We are Richer than We Think, 1978; Africa: turning the tide, 1989. *Recreations:* music, cooking, theatre, driving, wildlife protection and anti-poaching initiatives. *Address:* House of Lords, SW1A 0PW.

**CHALKLEY, Richard;** a Judge of the Upper Tribunal (Immigration and Asylum Chamber) (formerly a Vice President, Immigration Appeal Tribunal, later a Senior Immigration Judge, Asylum and Immigration Tribunal), 2002–16; a Deputy Tribunal Judge, since 2016; *b* 23 March 1949; *s* of late Kenneth Arthur Chalkley and Vera Chalkley; *m* 1st, 1973 (marr. diss. 2007); one *s* one *d*; 2nd, 2011, Caroline Maud, BA (Hons), *widow* of Henry Macintosh MacPhee, Scarinish, Isle of Tiree. *Educ:* College of Law. Articled to Ormsby Izzard-Davies, Woburn, 1969; admitted solicitor, 1974; Asst Solicitor, Graham Withers & Co., Solicitors, Shrewsbury, 1974–77; Partner: Bradfield & Howson, Solicitors, Maidstone, 1977–87; Thomson Snell & Passmore, Solicitors, Tunbridge Wells, 1987–99. Pt-time, 1995–99, full-time, 1999–2000, Immigration Adjudicator; pt-time Chm., Immigration Appeal Tribunal, 2000–02; Legal Mem., Special Immigration Appeals Commn, 2005–16. Chm., Kent Dental Services Cttee, 1985–95; Dep. Chm., Kent Medical Services Cttee, 1985–94; Member: Kent FPC, 1985–90; Bd, Kent Family Health Services Cttee, 1990–95. Trustee: Shropshire Scouts, 2018–; Student Union, Harper Adams Univ., 2019–. Freeman, City of London, 2010. *Publications:* Professional Conduct: a hand book for chartered surveyors, 1990, 2nd edn 1994; contrib. various articles to Chartered Surveyor Weekly. *Recreations:* reading, bridge, fly fishing, clay shooting, motorcycles and motorcycling. *E:* Jurist@nym.hush.com. *Club:* Bearsted and Thurnham (Life Mem.).

**CHALLACOMBE, Prof. Stephen James,** PhD; FRCPath; FDSRCS, FDSRCSE; FMedSci; educator and medical researcher; Professor of Oral Medicine, King's College London, since 1988; Director of External Strategy, 2004–11, and Vice Dean, 2005–11, King's College London Dental Institute; Dean for External Affairs, King's College London Health Schools, 2008–11; Consultant in Diagnostic Microbiology, Guy's and St Thomas' NHS Foundation Trust, 1984–2011; *b* London, 5 April 1946; *s* of late Kenneth Vivian Challacombe, Sudbury, Suffolk, and Caryl Graydon (*née* Poore); *m* 1969, Christine Barbara, (Tina), *d* of Rt Rev. Francis William Cocks, CB; one *s* one *d*. *Educ:* Culford Sch.; Guy's Hosp. Dental Sch. (BDS 1969); PhD London 1976. LDSRCS 1968; FRCPath 1992; FDSRCSE 1994; FDSRCS 2004. Department of Immunology, Guy's Hospital Medical and Dental Schools: Res. Fellow, 1971–72; Lectr, 1972–76; Sen. Lectr, 1976–85; Reader in Oral Immunol., Univ. of London, 1985–88; King's College London Dental Institute: Sub-dean of Dental Studies, 1983–87; Hd, Dept of Oral Medicine and Pathol., 1986–2003; Postgrad. Sub-dean (Dental), 1992–2002. Sen. Res. Fellow, Dept of Immunol., Mayo Clinic, Rochester, Minn, 1978–79 (Edward C. Kendall Res. Fellow); Vis. Prof., Dept of Oral Biol., UCSF, 1995. Hon. Consultant in Oral Medicine to UK Armed Forces, 1998–2012. President: British Soc. for Oral Medicine, 1995–97; Odontological Section, RSM, 1996–97; Metropolitan Br., BDA, 1999; British Soc. for Dental Res. (British Div. of IADR), 2000–02; Internat. Assoc. Dental Res., 2003–04; Eur. Assoc. Oral Medicine, 2008–10. FKC 2010. FMedSci 1998. Mem., Hunterian Soc. (Pres., 2007–08). Hon. DSc Athens, 2011. Colgate Res. Prize, British Div., 1977, Basic Res. in Oral Sci. Award, 1981, Dist. Scientist Award for Exptl Pathol., 1997, IADR. *Publications:* edited jointly: Food Allergy and Intolerance, 1985, 2nd edn 2002; Practical and Theoretical Aspects of ELISA, 1988; Mucosal Immunology, 1990; Oral AIDS Research, 1997, 3rd edn 2011; Immunology of Oral Diseases, 1998; Oral Health and Disease in AIDS, 2006; The Mouth and AIDS, 2011; Global Challenges in Oral HIV, 2016; contrib. 300 acad. papers on mucosal immunity, oral medicine, immunological, dermatological and microbiol aspects of oral diseases. *Recreations:* golf, tennis, ski-ing, sailing, theatre, formerly Rugby (Pres., Guy's Hosp. RFC, 1991–2001), water polo (Pres., Guy's Hosp. Swimming and Water Polo Club, 1985–98), being a grandfather, dog walking. *Address:* 101 Mycenae Road, Blackheath, SE3 7RX. *T:* (020) 8858 7933; King's College London Dental Institute, Guy's Hospital, SE1 9RT. *T:* (020) 7188 4399, *Fax:* (020) 7188 1159. *E:* stephen.challacombe@kcl.ac.uk. *Clubs:* Athenæum, Savage, MCC, Pilgrims; Nobody's Friends.

**CHALLEN, Colin Robert;** artist; *b* 12 June 1953; *s* of late Grenfell Stephen William Challen and of Helen Mary Challen (*née* Swift). *Educ:* Hull Univ. (BA Hons Philosophy 1982). Served RAF, 1971–74. Postman, 1974–78; publisher and printer, Hull, 1983–94; Labour Party Organiser, Leeds and W Yorks, 1994–2000. Member (Lab): Hull CC, 1986–94; Scarborough BC, 2011–15 (Leader, Lab Gp, 2014–15). MP (Lab) Morley and Rothwell, 2001–10. Member: Envmtl Audit Select Cttee, 2001–10; Energy and Climate Change Select Cttee, 2009–10; Chairman, All Party Parliamentary Group: on Climate Change, 2005–10; on Intelligent Energy, 2005–10. FRSA 2007. Hon. Fellow, Soc. for Envmt, 2008; Hon. FCIWEM 2009. *Publications:* Price of Power: the secret funding of the Conservative Party, 1998; Too Little, Too Late: the politics of climate change, 2009. *Recreations:* rambling, art, music. *E:* colinchallen@gmail.com. *W:* www.colinchallen.org.

**CHALLEN, David John,** CBE 2002; Chairman, EMEA Governance Committee, Citigroup, 2010–14 (Co-Chairman, Schroder Salomon Smith Barney, then Vice-Chairman, European Investment Bank, Citigroup, 2000–10); *b* 11 March 1943; *s* of Sydney Albert Challen and Doris Ellen Challen (*née* Hardy); *m* 1967, Elizabeth McCartney; one *s* one *d*. *Educ:* The High Sch., Dublin; Trinity Coll., Dublin; Harvard Univ. (MBA). With J. Walter Thompson, 1964–72; J. Henry Schroder & Co. Ltd, 1972–2000: Dir, 1979–2000; Hd, Corporate Finance, 1990–94; Vice Chm., 1995–97; Chm., 1997–2000. Non-executive Director: Anglian Water PLC, 1993–2002; Thomson Travel Group plc, 1998–2000; Anglo American plc, 2002–14; Amersham plc, 2003–04; Smiths Group plc, 2004–15. Chm., Financial Services Practitioner Panel, 1998–2001; Member: Adv. Cttee on Business and the Envmt, 1991–92; Panel on Takeovers and Mergers, 1993–94, 1999–2018 (Dep. Chm., 2006–18); Financial Reporting Council, 1995–2003. Gov., Morley Coll., 1993–99. *Club:* Athenæum.

**CHALLEN, Rt Rev. Michael Boyd,** AM 1988; Executive Director, Brotherhood of St Laurence, 1991–99; Adjunct Professor of Ethics, Curtin University of Technology, Perth, since 2000; *b* 27 May 1932; *s* of late B. Challen; *m* 1961, Judith, *d* of A. Kelly; two *d*. *Educ:* Mordialloc High School; Frankston High School; Univ. of Melbourne (BSc 1955); Ridley College, Melbourne (ThL 1956). Deacon 1957, priest 1958; Curate of Christ Church, Essendon, 1957–59; Member, Melbourne Dio. Centre, 1959–63; Director, 1963–69; Priest-in-charge, St Luke, Fitzroy, 1959–61; St Alban's, N Melbourne, 1961–65; Flemington, 1965–69; Dir, Anglican Inner-City Ministry, 1969; Dir, Home Mission Dept, Perth, 1971–78; Priest-in-charge, Lockridge with Eden Hill, 1973; Archdeacon, Home Missions, Perth, 1975–78; Asst Bp, dio. of Perth, WA, 1978–91; Exec. Dir, Anglican Health and Welfare Service, Perth, 1977–78. *Address:* Unit 7, 30 Kwong Alley, North Fremantle, WA 6159, Australia. *T:* and *Fax:* (8) 94336784.

**CHALLINOR, Robert Michael; His Honour Judge Challinor;** a Circuit Judge, since 2004; *b* 10 July 1950; *s* of Henry Clive Challinor and Gladys Violet Challinor (*née* Chapman); *m* 1984, Jill; two *s*. *Educ:* St Peter's Sch., Bournemouth; Trent Polytech. (LLB London 1973). Called to the Bar, Gray's Inn, 1974; Asst Recorder, 1991–97; Recorder, 1997–2004. *Recreations:* art, walking, music, being with my family. *Address:* c/o Wolverhampton Crown Court, Pipers Row, Wolverhampton WV1 3LQ.

**CHALMERS, Lt Gen. Douglas McKenzie,** DSO 2013; OBE 2010 (MBE 2003); Deputy Chief of the Defence Staff (Military Strategy and Operations), since 2018; *b* Belfast, 26 Feb. 1966; *s* of David and Elizabeth Chalmers; *m* 1992, Helen Evans. *Educ:* Bearwood Coll.; US Sch. of Advanced Mil. Studies, Fort Leavenworth, Kansas (MA 2001); Trinity Hall, Cambridge (MPhil Internat. Relns 2007). Commnd 1st Bn, Royal Irish Rangers, 1986; SO2, G5 Plans, 1st (UK) Armd Div., 2001–03; Bn 21C, 1st Royal Irish Rangers, 2003–04; MA to Chief of Jt Ops, Perm. Jt HQ, 2004–06; CO, 2nd Bn, Princess of Wales's Royal Regt, 2007–09; COS, 3rd (UK) Armd Div., 2009–11; HCSC 2011; Comdr, 12 Mechanized Bde, 2011–13; Liaison Officer for CDS to Chm., US Jt Chiefs of Staff, 2013–14; ACOS (Ops), UK Perm. Jt HQ, 2014–15; Dep. Comdg Gen., III (US) Corps, 2015–18. Col, Princess of Wales's Royal Regt, 2016. Commander, Order of Dannebrog (Denmark), 2016; Officer, Legion of Merit (USA), 2017. *Recreations:* fly fishing, general aviation, rowing, walking in circles. *Address:* c/o Army Personnel Centre, Kentigern House, 65 Brown Street, Glasgow G2 8EX.

**CHALMERS, Sir Iain (Geoffrey),** Kt 2000; FRCP, FRCPE, FFPH, FCOG(SA); Articles Editor, James Lind Library, since 2003; Co-ordinator, James Lind Initiative, 2003–19; Director, UK Cochrane Centre, 1992–2002; *b* 3 June 1943; *s* of Hamish and Lois Chalmers; *m* 1972, Jan Skitmore; two *s*. *Educ:* Middlesex Hosp. Med. Sch., London Univ. (MB BS 1966; MSc Social Medicine 1975). MRCS 1966; LRCP 1966; DCH 1973; MRCOG 1973, FRCOG 1985; FFPH (FFPHM 1986); FRCPE 1996; FCOG(SA) 2001; FRCP 2002. House Physician, House Surgeon, Middlesex Hosp.; House Physician, Welsh Nat. Sch. of Medicine; House Surgeon, Raigmore Hosp., Inverness; MO, UNRWA for Palestinian Refugees, Gaza; Registrar, Dept of Obst. and Gynaecol., then MRC Fellow, Dept of Med. Stats, Welsh Nat. Sch. of Medicine, Cardiff; Oxford University: Dir, Nat. Perinatal Epidemiology Unit, 1978–92; Clin. Lectr in Obst. and Gynaecol., 1978–92; Archie Cochrane Res. Fellow, Green Coll., 1992–94; Hon. Consultant in Public Health Medicine, Oxfordshire HA, 1978–2002; Hon. Specialist in Public Health Medicine, Milton Keynes PCT, 2003–13; Hon Mem., Sen. Scientific Staff, MRC Clin. Trials Unit, 2003–; Specialist in Public Health Medicine, Oxford Univ. Hosp. NHS Trust, 2013–. Visiting Professor: Univ. of Liverpool, 1993–; Inst. of Child Health, 1997–2003, Sch. of Public Policy, 1998–2003, UCL; Exeter Univ., 2000–03; Hon. Professor: Cardiff Univ., 2006; Univ. of Edinburgh, 2008. Editor: Oxford Database of Perinatal Trials, 1988–92; Testing Treatments Interactive, 2012–. FMedSci 1999. Hon. FRSocMed 2005; Hon. Fellow, Royal Statistical Soc. 2006. Hon. DSc Aberdeen, 1999; London, 2004; Plymouth, 2008; Oxford Brookes, 2008; Hon. MD Liverpool, 2001; DUniv York, 2001; Hon. Dr, Free Univ., Amsterdam, 2006. *Publications:* (ed jtly) Effectiveness and Satisfaction in Antenatal Care, 1982; (ed jtly) Effective Care in Pregnancy and Childbirth, 1989; (ed jtly) Systematic Reviews, 1995; (ed jtly) Non-random Reflections on Health Services Research, 1997; (jtly) Testing Treatments, 2006, 2nd edn 2011; contribs to learned jls incl. Lancet, Jl RSocMed, BMJ Evidence Based Medicine. *Address:* c/o Cochrane UK, Summertown Pavilion, Middle Way, Oxford OX2 7LG. *T:* (01865) 516300.

**CHALMERS, Prof. James Peter,** FRSE; Regius Professor of Law, University of Glasgow, since 2012; *b* Dundee, 4 Nov. 1976; *s* of John Macdonald Chalmers and Margaret Ann Chalmers (*née* Watt). *Educ:* Inverurie Acad.; Univ. of Aberdeen (LLB Hons 1998; DipLP 2000); Tulane Univ. of Louisiana (LLM 1999). Lectr in Law, 2000–06, Sen. Lectr, 2006–07, Univ. of Aberdeen; Sen. Lectr in Law, Univ. of Edinburgh, 2007–12. Visiting Professor: Univ. of Baltimore, 2001; Univ. of Maryland, 2001; Vis. Jun. Res. Fellow, QMUL, 2007; Vis. Researcher, Uppsala Univ., 2014. Ed., Edinburgh Law Rev., 2011–13. Mem., Criminal Courts Rules Council, 2008–19. Trustee, HIV Scotland, 2010–13. FRSE 2019. *Publications:* Trusts: cases and materials, 2002; (with F. Leverick) Criminal Defences and Pleas in Bar of Trial, 2006; Legal Responses to HIV and AIDS, 2008; (with M. L. Ross) Walker and Walker: the law of evidence in Scotland, 4th edn 2015; (ed jtly) Essays in Criminal Law in Honour of Sir Gerald Gordon, 2010; The New Law of Sexual Offences in Scotland, 2011; contrib. articles to learned jls. *Recreations:* Swedish language, cinema. *Address:* School of Law, University of Glasgow, 5–9 Stair Building, Glasgow G12 8QQ. *T:* (0141) 330 5408. *E:* james.chalmers@glasgow.ac.uk.

**CHALMERS, Very Rev. John Pearson**; Moderator of the General Assembly of the Church of Scotland, 2014–15; a Chaplain in Ordinary to the Queen, since 2013; *b* Bothwell, 5 June 1952; *s* of Isaac Macmillan Chalmers and Mary Ann Pearson; *m* 1976, Elizabeth Barbara Boning; two *s* one *d*. *Educ*: Univ. of Strathclyde; Univ. of Glasgow (BD; CPS). Ordained Minister, 1979; Minister, Renton Trinity, 1979–86; Clerk, Dumbarton Presbytery, 1982–86; Minister, Palmerston Place, Edinburgh, 1986–95; Church of Scotland: Depute Gen. Sec., Bd of Ministry, 1995–2001; Pastoral Advr and Associate Sec., Ministries Council, 2001–10; Principal Clerk to the Gen. Assembly, 2010–17. Hon. DD Aberdeen, 2016. *Recreations*: golf, bee-keeping, reading, gardening. *Address*: Church of Scotland, 121 George Street, Edinburgh EH2 4YN. *T*: (0131) 225 5722. *E*: jchalmers@churchofscotland.org.uk. *Club*: Royal Troon Golf.

**CHALMERS, Prof. John Philip**, AC 1991; FAA, FAAHMS; Professor of Medicine, since 1996, and Senior Director at the George Institute for Global Health (formerly the Institute for International Health, then the George Institute for International Health), since 2000 (Professorial Fellow, 1999–2000), University of Sydney; *b* 12 Jan. 1937; *m* 1977, Dr Alexandra Bune; four *s* one *d*. *Educ*: King's Sch., Parramatta; St Paul's Coll., Univ. of Sydney (BSc, MB BS); Univ. of NSW (PhD). FRCP, FRCPGlas, FRCPE, FACP, FRACP, FRACMA. Medical appts, Royal Prince Alfred Hosp., to 1968; Research Fellow: Nat. Heart Foundn, Univ. of NSW, 1965–66; MIT, 1969–70; RPMS, 1970–71; University of Sydney: Sen. Lectr, 1971–72; Assoc. Prof. of Medicine, 1973–75; Prof. of Medicine, Flinders Univ., 1975–96. Hon. Physician, Royal Prince Alfred Hosp., 1971–75; Vis MO, Repatriation Gen. Hosp., Concord, 1972–75; Mem., Bd of Management, Flinders Med. Centre, 1977–; Dean, Sch. of Medicine, Flinders Univ., 1991–92; Res. Chm., Royal N Shore Hosp., 1996–2000; Chm., Res. Develt for Faculty of Medicine, Sydney Univ., 2000–02. Royal Australian College of Physicians: Chm., State Cttee for SA, 1982–86; Chm., Bd of Censors, 1984–88; Vice-Pres., 1988–90; Pres., 1990–92; Pres., Internat. Soc. of Hypertension, 1992–94; Chm., Scientific Adv. Bd, Internat. Soc. and Fedn of Cardiology, 1997–; former mem. and chm., numerous sci. adv. cttees and govt med. bodies. FAA 1987; FAAHMS 2015; Hon. FRACS. Hon. MD: Queensland, 1991; NSW, 1994; Flinders, 1999; Sydney, 2007; Lund, 2018. Wellcome Medal for contrib. to Med. Res., 1981; Volhard Award, Internat. Soc. of Hypertension, for contrib. to Hypertension Res., 1998; Zanchetti Award, Eur. Soc. of Hypertension, 2008; Res. Medal, Nat. Heart Foundn of Australia, 2009. Officer, Order of Merit (France), 2010. Mem., editl bds of learned jls. *Publications*: over 750 articles in medical jls, on pharmacology, physiology, blood pressure, hypertension and other medical research. *Recreations*: cricket, cooking, theatre, reading, travel. *Address*: George Institute for Global Health, PO Box M201, Missenden Road, Camperdown, Sydney, NSW 2050, Australia; 3A Dettmann Avenue, Longueville, NSW 2066, Australia.

**CHALMERS, Michael John**; Director, Children and Families, Scottish Government, since 2017; *b* Dundee, 20 June 1974; *s* of David Chalmers and Elizabeth Chalmers; *m* 2008, Leigh Davidson; three *s* one *d*. *Educ*: James Gillespie's High Sch.; Univ. of Edinburgh (LLB Hons 1996; DipLP 1997; LLM Dist. Internat. Law and Human Rights 2011). Admitted as solicitor, 1998. Dundas & Wilson CS, 1997–2005; Solicitor, Office of the Advocate Gen., 2005–07; Branch Hd, Litigation, Scottish Govt, 2007–09; Solicitor (Scotland) to HM Revenue and Customs, 2009–11; Hd, Adv. and Legislation Div., Office of the Advocate Gen., 2011–12; Dir, Office of Advocate Gen. and Solicitor to Advocate Gen. for Scotland, 2012–17. *Recreations*: spending time with family, reading, following Dundee United FC, listening to music, attempting to improve a high golf handicap. *Address*: Scottish Government, St Andrew's House, Regent Road, Edinburgh EH1 3DG.

**CHALMERS, Sir Neil (Robert)**, Kt 2001; Warden, Wadham College, Oxford, 2004–12; *b* 19 June 1942; *s* of William King and Irene Margaret Chalmers (*née* Pemberton); *m* 1970, Monica Elizabeth Byanjeru (*née* Rusoke); two *d*. *Educ*: King's College Sch., Wimbledon; Magdalen Coll., Oxford (MA); St John's Coll., Cambridge (PhD). Lectr in Zoology, Makerere University Coll., Kampala, 1966–69; Scientific Dir, Nat. Primate Res. Centre, Nairobi, 1969–70; Open University: Lectr, subseq. Sen. Lectr, then Reader in Biology, 1970–85; Dean of Science, 1985–88; Dir, British Mus. (Natural History), then Natural History Mus., 1988–2004. Chm., Nat. Biodiversity Network Trust, 2005–12. President: Marine Biol Assoc. UK, 2002–07; Inst. of Biology, 2004–06. Fellow, Birkbeck Coll., Univ. of London, 2002. Hon. Fellow: King's College Sch., Wimbledon, 2003; Wadham Coll., Oxford, 2013. Hon. DSc Plymouth, 2004. *Publications*: Social Behaviour in Primates, 1979; numerous papers on animal behaviour in Animal Behaviour and other learned jls. *Recreations*: music, golf, astronomy.

**CHALMERS, Patrick Edward Bruce**; JP; Chairman: Upper Deeside Access Trust, 2003–09; Cairngorms Outdoor Access Trust, 2008–10; *b* Chapel of Garioch, Aberdeenshire, 26 Oct. 1939; *s* of L. E. F. Chalmers, farmer, Lethenty, Inverurie, and Helen Morris Campbell; *m* 1st, 1963, Ailza Catherine Reid (*d* 2004), *d* of late William McGibbon, Advocate in Aberdeen; three *d*; 2nd, 2008, Rosemary Newsome (*née* Larkins). *Educ*: Fettes Coll., Edinburgh; N of Scotland Coll. of Agriculture (NDA); Univ. of Durham (BScA). Joined BBC as radio talks producer, BBC Scotland, 1963; television producer, 1965; sen. producer, Aberdeen, 1970; Head of Television, Scotland, 1979–82; Gen. Man., Co-Productions, London, 1982; Controller, BBC Scotland, 1983–92; Dir, BBC World Service Television, Asia, 1992–93, retd 1994; Dir, Scottish Ensemble, 1995–2002. Director: Hutchvision News Ltd, 1992–93; Grampian Venture Capital Fund, 1996–. President: Edinburgh Television Fest., 1984–92; BAFTA, Scotland, 1990–92. Dir, Scottish Film Production Fund, 1988–91. Mem., Aberdeenshire Council, 1995–99 (Chm., Lib Dem Gp); Convenor, Grampian Police Bd, 1998–99. Chm., Marr Area Cttee, 1996–99. Mem., Grampian Region Children's Panel, 1974–79. FRSA 1990. Bailie of Bennachie, 1975. JP Aberdeenshire, 1996. *Recreations*: ski-ing, gardening. *Address*: The Bridge House, Bibury, Glos GL7 5NP. *T*: and *Fax*: (01285) 740749. *Clubs*: New (Edinburgh); Royal Northern (Aberdeen); Foreign Correspondents' (Hong Kong); Kandahar Ski.

**CHALONER**, family name of **Baron Gisborough**.

**CHALSTREY, Sir (Leonard) John**, Kt 1996; MD; FRCS; JP; Lord Mayor of London, 1995–96; Consultant Surgeon, St Bartholomew's Hospital, 1969–96, now Surgeon Emeritus, St Bartholomew's and the Royal London Hospitals; Senior Lecturer, St Bartholomew's Hospital Medical College, University of London, 1969–96; *b* 17 March 1931; *s* of late Leonard Chalstrey and Frances Mary (*née* Lakin); *m* 1958, Aileen Beatrice Bayes; one *s* one *d*. *Educ*: Dudley Grammar Sch., Worcs; Queens' Coll., Cambridge (BA Hons 1954; MA 1958); Med. Coll., St Bartholomew's Hosp. (MB, BChir 1957; MD 1967). MRCS, LRCP 1957; FRCS 1962. Nat. Service, RAEC, 1949–51. Jun. med. and surgical posts, St Bartholomew's Hosp., 1958–59; Lectr in Anatomy, Middx Hosp. Med. Sch., 1959–61; Jun. Surgical Registrar, St Bartholomew's Hosp., 1962; Registrar, then Sen. Surgical Registrar, Royal Free Hosp., 1963–69; Hon. Consultant Surgeon, St Luke's Hosp. for Clergy, 1975–93. Examiner in Surgery: Univ. of London, 1976–95; Univ. of Cambridge, 1989–94. Non-exec. Mem., City and Hackney HA, 1992–93. City University: Mem. Court, 1986–92; Mem. Council, 1992–2001; Chancellor, 1995–96. Maj., 357 Field Surgical Team, RAMC(V), TA, 1991–96; Hon. Col, 256 (City of London) Field Hosp., RAMC(V), 1996–2000; Member: City of London TAVRA, 1992–2000 (Pres., 1995–96); Gtr London TAVRA, 1992–2000. Governor, Corp. of Sons of the Clergy, 1992–. Mem., Court of Common Council, City of London Corp., 1981–84; Alderman (Vintry Ward), City of London, 1984–2001; Sheriff, City of London, 1993–94; HM Lieut, City of London, 1995–2001; JP 1984. Member, Court of Assistants: Soc. of Apothecaries (Sen. Warden, 1992–93 and 1993–94; Master, 1994–95); Barbers' Co. (Master, 1998–99); Member: Parish Clerks' Co., 1993–2007; HAC, 1995– (Hon. Mem., Ct of Assts, 1984–2001). Vice-Pres., City of London Sect., BRCS, 1992–. Trustee, Morden Coll., 1995–2005; Special Trustee: St Bartholomew's Hosp., 1998–2001; Royal London Hosp., 1999–2001; Life Gov., Christ's Hosp., 1996–; Trustee, St Bartholomew's and The Royal London Hosps Charitable Foundn, 2001–08. Pres., Guildhall Historical Assoc., 2000–07. FRSocMed 1965; Fellow, Assoc. of Surgeons of GB and Ireland, 1969; FRSA 1996. Hon. GSM 1996; Hon. FRSPH (Hon. FRSH 1996); Hon. Fellow, QMW, 1996. Hon. DSc City, 1995. KStJ 1995 (Mem., Chapter-Gen., 1994–99); Surgeon-in-Chief, and Chm. Med. Bd, St John Ambulance, 1993–99; Hospitaller, Priory of England, 1999–2002 (Mem., Priory Council and Chapter, 1999–2002). Grand Officier, Ordre National du Merité (France), 1996. *Publications*: (with Coffman and Smith-Laing) Gastro-Intestinal Disorders, 1986; (contrib.) Cancer in the Elderly, 1990; (contrib.) Maingot's Abdominal Operations, 7th edn 1980, 8th edn 1986; The Aldermen of the City of London, 1900–2010, 2011; papers on surgical subjects in Brit. Jl Surgery, Brit. Jl Cancer and Jl RSM; contribs to Jl of Cambridge Univ. Heraldic and Genealogical Soc. *Recreations*: painting in oils, history of City of London. *Address*: Danebury, 113 The Chine, N21 2EG. *T*: (020) 8360 8921. *Clubs*: Oxford and Cambridge, East India, Guildhall, City Pickwick (Pres., 2007–); Honourable Artillery Company Mess.

**CHAMBERLAIN, Very Rev. Father George Ford, (Leo)**, OSB; Parish Priest, St John the Evangelist, Easingwold, York, 2008–18; *b* 13 Aug. 1940; *s* of Brig. Noel Joseph Chamberlain, CBE and Sarah (Sally) (*née* Ford). *Educ*: Ampleforth Coll.; University Coll., Oxford (BA 1961; MA 1965). Novitiate, Ampleforth Abbey, 1961, solemn profession, 1965; ordained priest, 1968; Ampleforth College: Housemaster, St Dunstan's House, 1972–92; Sen. History Master, 1973–92; Headmaster, 1992–2003; Master, St Benet's Hall, Oxford, 2004–07. Involved with aid to Church in Central and Eastern Europe under Communism, 1968–90; organised A Time for Change Conf., Ampleforth Coll., 1990. Member: Council of Management, Keston Inst. (formerly Keston Coll.), 1985–2003; Catholic Bishops' Cttee for European Affairs, 1992–2000; HMC, 1993–2003; Catholic Ind. Schs Conf., 1993–2003 (Mem. Cttee, 1994–2000). Gov., St Gregory the Great Sch., Oxford, 2005–07. Titular Cathedral Prior of St Peter, Glos, 2008–. Hon. Fellow, St Benet's Hall, Oxford, 2008–16. *Address*: Ampleforth Abbey, York YO62 4EN.

**CHAMBERLAIN, Kevin John**, CMG 1992; Deputy Legal Adviser, Foreign and Commonwealth Office, 1990–99; *b* 31 Jan. 1942; *s* of late Arthur James Chamberlain and Gladys Mary (*née* Harris); *m* 1967, Pia Rosita Frauenlob; one *d*. *Educ*: Wimbledon Coll.; King's Coll., London (LLB). Called to the Bar, Inner Temple, 1965. HM Diplomatic Service, 1965–99: Asst Legal Adviser, FCO, 1965–74; Legal Adviser: British Mil. Govt, Berlin, 1974–76; British Embassy, Bonn, 1976–77; Asst Legal Adviser, FCO, 1977–79; Legal Counsellor, FCO, 1979–83; Counsellor (Legal Advr), Office of UK Perm. Rep. to EC, Brussels, 1983–87; Legal Counsellor, FCO, 1987–90. Mem., NATO Appeals Bd, 2004–13. Legal Advr, Ministerial Adv. Panel on Illicit Trade in Cultural Objects, 2000–04; Consultant to DCMS on applications for immunity for cultural property, 2008–. Chm., Ind. Remuneration Panel, Reigate and Banstead BC, 2001–09. Mem., Cultural Heritage Law Cttee, 2007–16, Mem., Cttee on Participation in Global Cultural Heritage Governance, 2017–, ILA. CEDR Accredited Mediator, 2002; Mediator, E Surrey Community Mediation Service, 2002–. Vis. Sen. Lectr in Laws, KCL, 2006–08. Hon. Sen. Lectr in Laws, UCL, 2004–05. Fellow, Soc. of Advanced Legal Studies, 2001–. *Publications*: War and Cultural Heritage, 2004, 2nd edn 2013; (contrib.) Protecting Cultural Property in Armed Conflict, 2010; (contrib.) Research Handbook on the Law of Cultural Heritage and Trade, 2013; (contrib.) Yearbook of International Humanitarian Law, 2014; (contrib.) Heritage, Ancestry and Law: principles, policies and practices in dealing with historical human remains, 2015. *Recreations*: opera, tennis, antiques, choral singing. *Address*: Fairfield, Warren Drive, Kingswood, Tadworth, Surrey KT20 6PY.

**CHAMBERLAIN, Very Rev. Father Leo**; see Chamberlain, Very Rev. Father G. F.

**CHAMBERLAIN, (Leslie) Neville**, CBE 1990; Chairman, The Northern Way, 2006–09; Deputy Chairman, British Nuclear Fuels plc, 1995–99 (Chief Executive, 1986–96); *b* 3 Oct. 1939; *s* of Leslie Chamberlain and Doris Anne Chamberlain (*née* Thompson); *m* 1971, Joy Rachel Wellings; one *s* three *d*. *Educ*: King James I Grammar School, Bishop Auckland; King's College, Univ. of Durham (BSc 1961; MSc 1962). FInstP. UKAEA, 1962–71; Urenco Ltd, 1971–77; British Nuclear Fuels: Fuel Production, 1977–81; Enrichment Business Manager, 1981–84; Dir, Enrichment Div., 1984–86. Dir, 1981–2005, Chm., 2002–05, Urenco Ltd; non-executive Director: Dennis Gp plc, 1994–98; Manchester 2002 Ltd, 1999–2002; New East Manchester Ltd, 1999–2002; RBG Resources plc, 2001–02; AMEC Nuclear Ltd, 2005–14; Essar Oil UK Ltd, 2013–14; Chm., Structure Vision Ltd, 2007–. Chm., Nat. Council, TEC, 1999–2001; Mem., NACETT, 1999–2001. Mem. Bd, NW Develt Agency, 2001–04. Chairman: British Energy Assoc., 1999–2001; Internat. Nuclear Energy Acad., 2001–04; Manufg Inst., 2002–; Cheshire and Warrington Econ. Alliance, 2005–10; Nat. Centre for Zoonosis Res., 2008–13; Cheshire Business Leaders, 2011–; Co-Chm., Trans-Atlantic Nuclear Energy Forum, 2005–10. Trustee, N of England Zool Soc., 2004–13. Mem., Council, Salford Univ., 2000–09. Freeman, Fuellers' Co., 1997– (Master, 2014–15). FInstE; CCMI; FRSA. Hon. FINucE 1994; Hon. Fellow, European Nuclear Soc., 1994. Hon. DSc: Salford, 1989; Chester, 2012. Melchett Lectr and Medal, Inst. of Energy, 1989. *Recreations*: horse racing, swimming, music, endangered animals, regional politics. *Address*: Oaklands, 2 The Paddock, Hinderton Road, Neston, South Wirral, Cheshire CH64 9PH. *T*: (0151) 353 1980. *Club*: Athenæum.

**CHAMBERLAIN, Ven. Malcolm Leslie**; Archdeacon of Sheffield and Rotherham, since 2014; *b* Newmarket, 1 Dec. 1969; *s* of Alan Leslie Chamberlain and Marylyn Sandra Chamberlain; *m* 1994, Joanne Eckersley; one *s* one *d*. *Educ*: Univ. of York (BA Hons 1992); Wycliffe Hall, Oxford (BTh 1996); Univ. of Liverpool (MPhil 2011). Ordained deacon, 1996, priest, 1997; Curate: St John's, Pleck and Bescot, Walsall, 1996–99; St Matthew and St James, Mossley Hill, 1999–2002; Associate Chaplain, 1999–2002, Anglican Chaplain, 2002–07, Univ. of Liverpool; Emerging Church Consultant, Dio. of Liverpool, 2002–07; Rector, St Mary's, Wavertree, 2008–13; Area Dean, Toxteth and Wavertree, 2012–13. *Recreations*: family, football, cinema, music. *Address*: 34 Wilson Road, Sheffield S11 8RN; Diocesan Church House, 95–99 Effingham Street, Rotherham S65 1BL. *T*: (01709) 309110. *E*: malcolm.chamberlain@sheffield.anglican.org.

**CHAMBERLAIN, Hon. Sir Martin Daniel**, Kt 2019; **Hon. Mr Justice Chamberlain**; a Judge of the High Court, Queen's Bench Division, since 2019; *b* Edinburgh, 25 Nov. 1973; *s* of David and Maria Chamberlain; *m* 2001, Samantha Louise Broadfoot, *qv*; one *s* two *d*. *Educ*: Stewart's Melville Coll., Edinburgh; University Coll., Oxford (BA 1994; BCL 1996); City Univ., London (DipLaw 1995); Inns of Court Sch. of Law. Called to the Bar, Middle Temple, 1997; in practice as barrister, specialising in public law and human rights, 1998–2019; QC 2013; a Dep. High Court Judge, 2016–19. Mem., Attorney Gen.'s Panels of Jun. Counsel to Crown, 2001–13. *Address*: Royal Courts of Justice, Strand, WC2A 2LL.

**CHAMBERLAIN, Prof. Mary Christina,** FRHistS; Professor of Modern History, Oxford Brookes University, 1995–2009, now Emeritus; *b* 3 Sept. 1947; *d* of Arthur James Chamberlain and Gladys Mary Chamberlain (*née* Harris); *m* 1st, 1971, Carey Harrison (marr. diss. 1977); one *d*; 2nd, 1980, Peter Lane (marr. diss. 1997); two *d*; 3rd, 2002, Prof. Stein Ringen, *qv*. *Educ*: Univ. of Edinburgh (MA Hons); London Sch. of Econs and Pol Sci. (MSc); Royal Holloway, Univ. of London (MA 2010). Researcher, Arms Control and Disarmament Res. Unit, FCO, 1970–71; Lecturer: Norfolk Coll. of Art and Technol., 1973–74; London Coll. of Fashion, 1974–75; Ipswich Civic Coll., 1975–77; Sen. Lectr, London Coll. of Printing (London Inst.), 1977–87; Lectr (pt-time), Univ. of WI (Cave Hill, Barbados), 1988–91; Fellow, Univ. of Essex, 1991–93; Sen. Lectr, Oxford Brookes Univ., 1993–95. Visiting Professor: Univ. of WI, 2004, 2006; NY Univ., 2004. Founding Ed., Studies in Memory and Narrative, 1997–2008. Mem., Adv. Gp, Virago Press, 1976–91. Member: UK Govt Caribbean Adv. Gp, 1998–2002; Panel of Assessors, Big Lottery Fund, 2001–06. Consultant, Barbados Nat. Oral Hist. Project, 1999; Trustee: Nat. Life Story Collection, Nat. Sound Archive, BL, 1991–2004; Raphael Samuel History Centre, 2016– (Mem., Adv. Gp, 2002–07). FRHistS 2002. *Publications*: Fenwomen, 1975, 3rd edn 2011; Old Wives' Tales, 1981, 2nd edn 2006; (ed) Writing Lives, 1988; Growing Up in Lambeth, 1989; Narratives of Exile and Return, 1997, 2nd edn 2004; (ed with P. Thompson) Narrative and Genre, 1998, 2nd edn 2004; (ed) Caribbean Migration: globalised identities, 1998; (ed with H. Goulbourne) Caribbean Families in Britain and the Atlantic World, 2001; Family Love in the Diaspora: migration and the Anglo-Caribbean experience, 2006; Empire and Nation-building in the Caribbean: Barbados 1937–1966, 2010; The Mighty Jester, 2014; The Dressmaker of Dachau, 2015 (19 edns worldwide); The Hidden, 2019. *Recreations*: walking, ski-ing, travel, cooking, grandchildren, gardening, cinema. *Address*: c/o Juliet Mushens, CaskieMushens, 18 Soho Square, W1D 3QL. *T*: (020) 7025 8802. *E*: marychamberlain100@gmail.com.

**CHAMBERLAIN, Matthew James;** Chief Executive Officer, London Metal Exchange, since 2017; *b* Reading, 27 Jan. 1982; *s* of Michael John and Susan Mary Chamberlain; *m* 2012, Solange Helene Jeannine Dive; two *d*. *Educ*: Reading Sch.; Trinity Coll., Cambridge (MA). Analyst, Citigroup Global Markets Ltd, 2004–06; Dir and Founding Mem., financial instns coverage team, Perella Weinberg, 2006–10; Dir and Hd, Eur. financial technol., UBS, 2010–12; Hd of Strategy and Implementation, London Metal Exchange, 2012–13; Co-Hd, Business Develt, London Metal Exchange and LME Clear, 2013–16; Chief Operating Officer and Hd of Strategy, 2016–17. *Recreations*: sporadic parenting, contact sports (observing from a safe distance), running slowly. *Address*: London Metal Exchange, 10 Finsbury Square, EC2A 1AJ. *T*: (020) 7113 8888.

**CHAMBERLAIN, Michael Aubrey,** OBE 2007; FCA; Consultant, KPMG, Leicester, 1994–2004; *b* 16 April 1939; *s* of George Thomas Everard Chamberlain and Doris (*née* Arden). *Educ*: Repton Sch., Derbys. FCA 1963. Sen. Partner, KPMG Peat Marwick, 1974–93. Pres., Inst. of Chartered Accountants in England and Wales, 1993–94 (Vice-Pres., 1991–92; Dep. Pres., 1992–93); Chm., Chartered Accountants Compensation Scheme, 1998–2009. Chairman: Leicester Diocesan Bd of Finance, 1983–98; Corp. of Church House, 2008–14 (Chm. Council, 2009–14); Audit Cttee, Corp. of Sons of Clergy, 2010–16; Member: Archbishops' Council, 1999–2007 (Chm. Finance Cttee, 1999–2007); Adv. Bd, RSCM, 2000–15. Dir, Allchurches Trust Ltd, 2006–16. Mem. Council, Univ. of Leicester, 1996–2008 (Treas., 1999–2008). Lay Canon, 1988–2014, Canon Emeritus, 2015, Mem. Council, 2012–, Leicester Cathedral. Hon. Dist. Fellow, Univ. of Leicester, 2009. Hon. LLD Leicester, 1993. *Address*: Willow End, 3 Spinney Nook, Main Street, Tugby, Leics LE7 9EY. *T*: (0116) 259 8064.

**CHAMBERLAIN, Neville;** *see* Chamberlain, L. N.

**CHAMBERLAIN, Rt Rev. Nicholas Alan;** *see* Grantham, Bishop Suffragan of.

**CHAMBERLAIN, Dr Nira Cyril;** Principal Consultant for Data and Decision Sciences (formerly for Data Science and Mathematical Modelling), Babcock Analytical Solutions, Babcock International, since 2015; Senior Data Scientist, Holland and Barrett International, since 2018; *b* Birmingham, 17 June 1969; *s* of Sylvester Chamberlain and Esmeralda Chamberlain; two *s*; *m* 2016, Jacqueline Rhule. *Educ*: Coventry Poly. (BSc Maths 1991); Loughborough Univ. (MSc Industrial Mathematical Modelling 1993); Univ. of Portsmouth (PhD Maths 2013). CMath 1998; CSci 2005. Mathematical Simulation Engineer: T and N, 1994–97; EDS, 1998–2001; Mathematical Engr, Advantica, 2002; Modelling Consultant, LSC Gp, 2002–12; Analytics Modeller, RWE npower, 2012–13; Chief Mathematician, LSC Gp, 2014–15. Mem. Council, IMA, 2008–14 (Vice Pres., 2017; Pres., Jan. 2020–). Association Fellow, Operational Res. Soc., 2015; Vis. Fellow, Loughborough Univ., 2017–. Speaker, Speakers for Schs, 2014–; BBC Expert Voice, 2015–. Hon. DSc Greenwich, 2019. *Recreations*: cycling, cricket, pool, table football, cinema, researching the modern history of black mathematicians. *E*: nira.chamberlain@yahoo.com.

**CHAMBERLAIN, Paul Arthur;** Headmaster, Cheltenham College, 1997–2004; *b* 10 June 1948; *s* of Arthur and Lilian Amy Chamberlain; *m* 1970, Kathleen Eleanor Hopley; one *s* one *d*. *Educ*: Verdin Grammar Sch., Winsford, Cheshire; Univ. of Durham (BSc Hons Zoology 1969; PGCE 1970). Haileybury College: Asst Master, 1970–83; Housemaster, 1983–88; Headmaster, St Bees Sch., Cumbria, 1988–97. *Recreations*: fell walking, fly-fishing, music, photography. *Address*: Drumlins, Lowick Green, Ulverston, Cumbria LA12 8DY. *T*: (01229) 885424.

**CHAMBERLAIN, Peter Edwin,** FREng; FRINA; producer of fine wine and olive oil, central Italy; Director, Pai Faena Srl, 2003–16; *b* 25 July 1939; *s* of late Dr Eric Alfred Charles Chamberlain, OBE, FRSE, and Winifred Louise, (Susan) (*née* Bone); *m* 1963, Irene Frew (separated 2010; she *d* 2018); two *s* one *d*; partner, 2011, Annamaria Tarallo (*d* 2016); partner, 2018, Ursula Liebing. *Educ*: Royal High Sch.; Edinburgh Univ. (Keasby Schol., BSc); RN Colls Manadon and Greenwich (MSc Naval Architecture UCL). RCNC. Asst Constructor, ship and submarine design, ME and Bath, 1963–68; Constructor: submarine design, Bath, 1968–69; submarine construction, Birkenhead, 1969–72; ship structures R&D, Dunfermline, 1972–74; postgrad. programmes in Naval Architecture, UCL, 1974–77; ship design, Bath, 1977–78; Chief Constructor: Hd of Secretariat, Bath, 1978–80; Surface Ship Forward Design, Bath, 1980–82; RCDS 1983; Asst Sec., Hd of Secretariat to Master Gen. of Ordnance, London, 1984–85; Under Sec., Dir Gen. Future Material Programmes (Naval), London, 1985–87; Dep. Controller Warship Equipments, MoD, 1987–88; Chief Underwater Systems Exec., MoD, 1988–89; creation of Defence Res. Agency, MoD, 1989–92; Engr Dir, System and Services Div., BAe, 1992–98; Dir, ANZAC WIP Project, BAe Australia, 1999. Director: Timely Solutions Ltd, 2000–06; Xienta, 2001–03. Mem., Internat. Council on Systems Engrg, 1995–. FREng (FEng 1988); FRINA 1988. *Recreations*: visual arts, poetry, music, maintaining a part of rural Italy. *Address*: via San Martino 7, 06057 Monte Castello di Vibio (PG), Italy. *E*: petercham@icloud.com.

**CHAMBERLAIN, Samantha Louise;** *see* Broadfoot, S. L.

**CHAMBERLAYNE, Julian Charles;** Partner, since 2003, Head, Knowledge Management and Compliance, Compliance Officer for Legal Practice, and Head, Aviation and International Injuries, since 2007, Stewarts Law LLP; *b* Maisemore, Glos, 21 Nov. 1970; *s* of Jeremy Chamberlayne and Valerie Chamberlayne; *m* 2005, Kate Cordier-Verreck; two *d*. *Educ*: Queen Mary and Westfield Coll., London (LLB Hons 1991); Coll. of Law (Solicitors Final Exams 1992). Admitted solicitor, 1994; trainee solicitor, 1992–94, Solicitor, 1994–99, Hutchins & Co.; career break (cycled from Fairbanks, Alaska to Tierra del Fuego), 1999–2000; Solicitor, Stewarts Law LLP, 2000–03. Chm., Forum of Complex Injury Solicitors, 2013–; Mem., Ogden Wkg Party, 2019–. *Publications*: (contrib.) Personal Injury Schedules: calculating damages, 3rd edn 2010 to 4th edn 2018. *Recreations*: cycling, snowboarding, country walks with Kate, Ella, Pippa and our trusty Border Terrier, gardening. *Address*: Stewarts, 5 New Street Square, EC4A 3BF. *T*: (020) 7822 8000. *E*: jchamberlayne@stewartslaw.com.

**CHAMBERS, Aidan,** FRSL; writer; *b* 27 Dec. 1934; *m* 1968, Nancy Lockwood. Teacher, 1957–68; Jt Founder, Thimble Press, 1969, publisher of Signal: Approaches to Children's Books, 1970–2003. Pres., Sch. Library Assoc., 2003–06. Hon. PhD Umeå, 2003; Hon. LLD Gloucestershire, 2008; Hon. DLitt Oxford Brookes, 2011. FRSL 2009. Children's Lit. Assoc. award, USA, 1979; Eleanor Farjeon Award, Children's Book Circle, 1982; Hans Andersen Award, Internat. Bd on Books for Young People, 2002; Lifetime Achievement Award for Services to English Educn, Nat. Assoc. for Teaching of English, 2010. *Publications*: The Reluctant Reader, 1969; Introducing Books to Children, 1973; Booktalk, 1985; The Reading Environment, 1991; Tell Me: children, reading and talk, 1993; Reading Talk, 2001; *novels*: Breaktime, 1978; Dance on my Grave, 1982; Now I Know, 1987; The Toll Bridge, 1992; Postcards from No Man's Land, 1999 (Carnegie Medal, LA, 1999; Michael Printz Award, USA, 2003); This Is All: the pillow book of Cordelia Kenn, 2005; Dying to Know You, 2012; Blindside, 2015; *short stories*: The Kissing Game, 2011; *for children*: Seal Secret, 1980; The Present Takers, 1983; (with Peppo Bianchessi) Il Vermo, 2017; *plays for young people*: Johnny Salter, 1966; The Car, 1967; The Chicken Run, 1968; The Dream Cage, 1981; Only Once, 1998; The Toll Bridge, 1998; ed. of anthologies etc. *Address*: Lockwood, Station Road, South Woodchester, Stroud, Glos GL5 5EQ. *W*: www.aidanchambers.co.uk.

**CHAMBERS, Alan;** Member (UU) North Down, Northern Ireland Assembly, since 2016; *b* Belfast, 15 Oct. 1947; *s* of Andrew and Mary, (May), Chambers; *m* 1969, Linda Murdie; two *s* three *d*. *Educ*: Avoniel Primary Sch., Belfast; Annadale Grammar Sch., Belfast. Self-employed businessman, 1970–. Mem., Pt-time Reserve, RUC, 1972–86. Mem. (Ind Unionist), N Down BC, 1991–2014 (Mayor, 2000); Mem., Ards and N Down BC, 2014–16 (Ind Unionist, 2014–15, UU, 2015–16). Mem., Econ. Cttee, NI Assembly, 2016–. Mem., NI Policing Bd, 2018–. UUP spokesperson on economy and policing, 2016–. Service Medal, RUC (GC), 1985. *Recreations*: football and most sports. *Address*: (office) 1A Donaghadee Road, Groomsport, Co. Down BT19 6LG. *T*: (028) 9147 7555. *E*: alcham49@aol.com.

**CHAMBERS, Prof. Andrew David,** PhD; consultant in board practice and in internal auditing; Academic Director, FTMS Global, 2014–16; *b* 7 April 1943; *s* of Lewis Harold and Florence Lilian Chambers; *m* 1st, 1969, Mary Elizabeth Ann Kilbey (marr. diss. 1984); two *s*; 2nd, 1987, Celia Barrington (*née* Pruen) (*d* 2016); two *s* two *d* (incl. twin *s* and *d*), and one step *s*. *Educ*: St Albans Sch.; Hatfield Coll., Univ. of Durham (BA Hons); London South Bank Univ. (PhD 2013). CEng; EurIng; CITP; FCA, FBCS, FCCA, FIIA. Arthur Andersen & Co., 1965–69; Barker & Dobson, 1969–70; United Biscuits, 1970–71; City University Business School; Lectr in Computer Applications in Accountancy, 1971–74; Leverhulme Sen. Res. Fellow in Internal Auditing, 1974–78; Sen. Lectr in Audit and Management Control, 1978–83; Prof. of Internal Auditing, 1983–93, then Emeritus; Administrative Sub-Dean, 1983–86; Acting Dean, 1985–86; Dean, 1986–91; Head of Dept of Business Studies, 1986–89; Warden, Northampton Hall, City Univ., 1983–86 (Dep. Warden, 1972–76); Prof. of Audit and Control, Univ. of Hull, 1994–98; Academic Dir, FTMS, 1999–2001; Prof. of Corporate Governance (formerly of Internal Auditing), London S Bank Univ., 2004–13. Vis. Professor: in Computer Auditing, Univ. of Leuven, Belgium, 1980–81, 1992–93; of Internal Auditing, Birmingham City Univ. (formerly Univ. of Central England), 2006–11. Mem., Mgt Audit LLP (formerly Dir, Mgt Audit Ltd), 1991–2014. Chm., Harlequin IT Services Ltd, 1998–99. Consultant: MacIntyre Hudson, Chartered Accountants, 1987–89; BBHW, Chartered Accountants, 1990–92; Director: Paragon Gp of Cos (formerly Nat. Home Loans Hldgs), 1991–2003 (Chm., Remuneration Cttee, 1992–95, Audit Cttee, 1995–2003); Nat. Mortgage Bank, 1991–92; IIA Inc., 1993–96 (Mem. Internat. Standards Bd, 1992–95, 2008–); Pilgrim Health NHS Trust, 1996–99; FTMS Online, 1999–2002. Mem. Auditing Practices Bd, 2006–09. Specialist Advr, Inquiry into Auditors: Market Concentration and their Role, H of L Economic Affairs Select Cttee, 2010–12. Institute of Internal Auditors–UK: Mem. Council, 1985–86; Mem., Professional Standards and Guidelines Cttee (Chm., 1991–95); Association of Chartered Certified Accountants: Mem., Auditing Cttee, 1994–2011; Chm., Internal Auditing Cttee, 2002–06; Chm., Corporate Governance and Risk Mgt Cttee, 2006–10; Mem., Governance, Risk and Perf. Forum, 2011–. Member: Council, BCS, 1979–83 (Mem., Tech. Bd, 1979–82; Chm., Meetings Cttee, 1980–82); IT Cttee, 1986–91, Internal Audit Cttee, 1998–2003 and 2011–14, Corporate Governance Cttee, 2004–06, ICAEW; Educn, Training and Technol. Transfer Cttee, British Malaysian Soc., 1987–90; MBA Adv. Bd, Ashridge Management Coll., 1986–92; UK Cttee on Internal Audit Guidance for Financial Services, 2012–13; Council, Tavistock Inst., 2004–08 (Chm., Audit Cttee, 2006–08); Corporate Governance and Co. Law Cttee, Accountancy Europe (formerly Fédération des Experts Comptables Européen), 2004– (Chair, 2014–17). Director: Council of Univ. Management Schs, 1988–92; Med. Defence Union, 2004–06 (Chm., Audit Cttee, 2004–06); Hon. Auditor, RSAA, 1986–91. External Examr, Dundee Univ., 1998–2002. MInstD 1986; FRSA. Governor: Islington Green Comprehensive Sch., 1989–91; Chapel St Leonard's Primary Sch., 2018–. Liveryman, Loriners' Co., 2003–. Member, Editorial Board: Computer Fraud and Security, 1981–87; Managerial Auditing Jl, 1986–9; Gen. Editor, Internat. Jl of Auditing, 1995–2003; Editor: Internal Control, 1997–2005; Corporate Governance, 1998–2004; Fraud, 2000–01. *Publications*: (with O. J. Hanson) Keeping Computers Under Control, 1975; (ed) Internal Auditing: developments and horizons, 1979; Internal Auditing: theory and practice, 1981, 2nd edn (with G. M. Selim and G. Vinten) 1987; Computer Auditing, 1981, 3rd edn (with J. M. Court) 1991; Effective Internal Audits: how to plan and implement, 1992; (with G. Rand) Auditing the IT Environment, 1994; (with G. Rand) Auditing Contracts, 1994; (ed) Internal Auditing, 1996; (with G. Rand) The Operational Auditing Handbook: auditing business processes, 1997, 2nd edn 2010; (with J. Ridley) Leading Edge Internal Auditing, 1998; Tolley's Corporate Governance Handbook, 2002, 7th edn 2017 as Chambers' Corporate Governance Handbook; Tolley's Internal Auditor's Handbook, 2005, 2nd edn 2009; papers in learned jls. *Recreation*: family. *Address*: The Water Mill, Moat Lane, Old Bolingbroke, Spilsby, Lincs PE23 4ES. *T*: (01790) 763350. *E*: ProfAChambers@outlook.com. *Club*: Reform.

**CHAMBERS, Daniel;** Joint Company Director, Blink Films (formerly Blink Film and Television) Ltd, since 2007; *b* 13 Sept. 1968; *s* of Michael Earnest Chambers and Florence Ruth Cooper; partner, Rebecca Claire Eisig Cotton. *Educ*: William Ellis Sch.; University Coll. Sch.; Brasenose Coll., Oxford (BA Hons). Journalist, Evening Standard, 1991–92; researcher/asst producer, Panorama, Dispatches and Equinox, 1992–96; Director: Equinox

Sun Storm, 1996; Equinox Russian Roulette, 1997; Science Department, Channel 4: Dep. Commng Ed., 1998–99; Editor, 1999–2001: devised Secrets of the Dead; commnd Escape from Colditz, Cannibal, Extinct and Salvage Squad; responsible for Scrapheap Challenge; jtly responsible for Big Brother; Controller of Factual Progs, Channel 5, subseq. Five, 2001–03: devised History Strand Revealed; commnd World War I in Colour, Kings & Queens, Britain's Worst Driver, Fifth Gear; Dir of Programmes, Five, 2003–06; Blink: Exec. Producer of Great Sperm Race, When Boris Met Dave, Ancients Behaving Badly, Chinese Food in Minutes, True Stories, Extraordinary Animals, The Lion Cub from Harrods, Monty Don's Italian Gardens, Classic Car Rescue, Treasures Decoded, My Wild Affair, Rebuilding Noah's Ark, Super Skyscrapers, Mexican Food Made Simple, The Woman Raised by Monkeys, Nazi Titanic: What Destroyed the Hindenberg?, The Missing Evidence, Shut-Ins, Meet the Orangutans. Gov., London Film Sch., 2006–. Trustee, Freud Mus., 2014–. Mem., BAFTA. Author of play, Selling Out (first dir. by Alan Ayckbourn, Scarborough, 1992). *Recreations:* cinema, playing the piano. *Address:* Blink Films Ltd, Bankstock Building, 42–44 De Beauvoir Crescent, N1 5SB. *T:* (020) 3150 0777. *Club:* Shoreditch House.

**CHAMBERS, Dominic Kern;** QC 2008; *b* Solihull, 28 Feb. 1963; *s* of Martin Royston Chambers and Marcia Parsons Chambers; *m* 1992, Georgina Kent, *qv* (marr. diss. 2009); one *s* two *d*. *Educ:* Sandroyd Sch.; Harrow Sch.; King's Coll. London (LLB Hons). Called to the Bar: Gray's Inn, 1987; British Virgin Islands, 2011; full rights of audience DIFC Cts, Dubai, 2016; in practice as barrister, 1988–, specialising in internat. and commercial litigation and arbitration. Freeman, City of London, 1983; Liveryman, 1992, Mem., Ct of Assts, 2009, Co. of Pewterers. *Recreations:* horology, wine, shooting, Brazil rainforest. *Address:* Maitland Chambers, 7 Stone Buildings, Lincoln's Inn, WC2A 3SZ.

**CHAMBERS, Ernest George Wilkie;** Managing Director, Beattie Communications Group (formerly Beattie Media), 2001–08; *b* 10 May 1947; *s* of Ernest and Ada Chambers; *m* 1971, Jeanette; one *s* one *d*. *Educ:* Harris Acad., Dundee; Dundee Univ. (BSc 1st Cl. Hons Applied Sci. 1969); Strathclyde Univ. (MBA 1987). Graduate civil engr, E of Scotland Water Bd, 1969–73; Asst Engr, Lower Clyde Water Bd, 1973–75; Area Engr (Renfrew), 1975–78; Lower Clyde Division: Divl Ops Engr, 1978–84; Asst Divl Manager, 1984–86; Asst Dir (Ops and Maintenance), 1986–88; Dir of Water, 1988–94; Dir, Water Services, Strathclyde Regl Council, 1994–95; Chief Exec., West of Scotland Water, 1995–2001. *Recreations:* DIY, gardening.

**CHAMBERS, Fredrick Rignold H.;** *see* Hyde-Chambers.

**CHAMBERS, John T.;** Founder and Chief Executive Officer, JC2 Ventures, since 2018; *m* Elaine; two *c*. *Educ:* West Virginia Univ. (BS/BA business; JD); Indiana Univ. (MBA). IBM (incl. Exec. Vice-Pres.), 1976–82; Wang Labs (latterly Sen. Vice-Pres. of US Ops), 1982–90; Sen. Vice-Pres. for Worldwide Ops, 1991–94, Exec. Vice-Pres., 1994–95, Pres. and CEO, 1995–2006, Chm. and Chief Exec., 2006–15, Exec. Chm., 2015–17, Cisco Systems Inc. Mem., US President's Adv. Cttee for Trade Policy and Negotiations and Nat. Security Adv. Cttee, 1997–99. Outstanding Civil Service Medal, US Army; Edison Achievement Award, 2016; Nat. Defence Gold Medal (France), 2017. *Publications:* Connecting the Dots: lessons for leadership in a start-up world, 2018.

**CHAMBERS, Prof. Jonathon Arthur,** PhD, DSc; CEng, FREng, FIET, FIEEE; Professor of Digital Communications, Signal Processing and Intelligent Sensing, and Head, Department of Engineering, Leicester University, since 2017; *b* Peterborough, 10 March 1960; *s* of Arthur Chambers and Dr Betty Chambers, MBE. *Educ:* Orton Longueville Sch., Peterborough; Peterborough Regl Coll.; HMS Fisgard and HMS Collingwood; Poly. of Central London (BSc 1st Cl. Electrical Engrg 1985); Imperial Coll. London (PhD Signal Processing 1990; DSc 2014). CEng 1994; FIET 2005; FIEEE 2011; FREng 2012. Lectr, Poly. of Central London, 1985–86; res. scientist, Schlumberger Cambridge Res., 1991–93; Lectr, 1994–98, Reader, 1998–2000, Imperial Coll. London; Prof. of Signal Processing, KCL, 2001–04; Professorial Res. Fellow, Cardiff Univ., 2004–07; Professor of Communications and Signal Processing, Univ. of Loughborough, 2007–14; of Signal and Information Processing, Newcastle University, 2015–17. *Publications:* (jtly) Recurrent Neural Networks for Prediction: learning algorithms, architectures and stability, 2001; (jtly) EEG Signal Processing, 2007. *Recreations:* classical music, cycling, motor vehicles. *Address:* Department of Engineering, University of Leicester, University Road, Leicester LE1 7RH. *E:* Jonathon.Chambers@leicester.ac.uk.

**CHAMBERS, Michael Laurence;** QC 2003; **His Honour Judge Michael Chambers;** a Circuit Judge, since 2011; *b* 3 Dec. 1956; *s* of late Lawrence Chambers, CEng and Maureen Chambers; *m* 1989, Verity Susan Stowell Hunt; one *s* one *d*. *Educ:* Cheltenham Coll.; St Peter's Coll., Oxford (MA). Called to the Bar, Lincoln's Inn, 1980; in practice, Wales and Chester Circuit, 1981–2011; Circuit Jun., 2002. An Asst Recorder, 1997–2000; a Recorder, 2000–11; Standing Counsel to HM Customs and Excise, 2001. Legal Assessor, GMC, 2002–. *Address:* Birmingham Crown Court, 1 Newton Street, Birmingham B4 7NA. *Club:* Chester City.

**CHAMBERS, His Honour Nicholas Mordaunt;** QC 1985; mediator and arbitrator, since 2012; a Circuit Judge (a Specialist Judge), 1999–2012; Mercantile Judge for Wales and Chester, 1999–2007, for Wales, 2007–12; *b* 25 Feb. 1944; *s* of late Marcus Mordaunt Bertrand Chambers and Lona Margit Chambers (*née* Gross); *m* 1966, Sally Elizabeth, *er d* of T. H. F. (Tony) Banks; two *s* one *d*. *Educ:* King's School, Worcester; Hertford College, Oxford (BA 1965). Called to the Bar, Gray's Inn, 1966, Bencher, 1994; a Recorder, 1987–99; a Dep. High Court Judge, 1994–99. Member: Civil Procedure Rule Cttee, 1997–99; Civil Cttee, Judicial Studies Bd, 2002–08. Chm., Incorporated Council of Law Reporting, 2001–13. Qualified mediator 1999; FCIArb 2012. *Publications:* (author and illustrator) Missed Moments in Legal History, 2012; Case Handling; an illustrated view from the Bench, 2014. *Recreations:* illustration, sketching, writing. *Address:* Brick Court Chambers, 7–8 Essex Street, WC2R 3LD. *Club:* Garrick.

**CHAMBERS, Maj.-Gen. Peter Antony,** CB 2002; MBE 1982; Director, McWhirter Foundation, 2009–15; *b* 23 April 1947; *s* of Mary Eugenie Chambers and Vincent Gerard Chambers; *m* 1968, Valerie Anne Straker; one *d* (and one *d* decd). *Educ:* De La Salle Grammar Sch.; Liverpool Univ. (BA Hons). Commissioned RAOC, 1969; Staff Coll. 1979 (psc); OC 51 Ordnance Co., 1982–83; CO 1 Ordnance Bn, 1985–88; Col Ordnance 1, 1988–90; Higher Comd and Staff Course, 1990; Comdr Supply, 1st (BR) Corps, 1990–93; Mem., RCDS, 1993; Dir, Logistic Support Policy, 1995–97; Sen. Army Mem., RCDS, 1997–98; DCS, HQ Land Command, 1998–2002. Dir, Hill Homes, 2002–06; Interim CEO, Richmond upon Thames Council for Voluntary Services, 2006–07. Rep. Col Comdt, RLC, 2003–04, 2006–07. Chm., RAOC Assoc., 1997–2014 (Pres., Council, 2013–17). *Recreations:* walking, voluntary charity work, family. *Address:* RAOC Secretary, RHQ the RLC, Dettingen House, The Princess Royal Barracks, Deepcut, Camberley, Surrey GU16 6RW.

**CHAMBERS, Robert Alexander H.;** *see* Hammond-Chambers.

**CHAMBERS, Prof. Ruth Margaret,** OBE 2012; DM; FRCGP; general practitioner; Clinical Lead for Technology Enabled Care Services for Staffordshire, Stoke-on-Trent Clinical Commissioning Group, since 2016 (Clinical Associate, 2011–16; Clinical Lead for Telehealth, 2013–16; Clinical Chair, 2016–18); *b* Gloucester, 13 March 1952; *d* of Ronald Campbell and Hilda Campbell (*née* Probyn); *m* 1977, Christopher Chambers; two *s* one *d*. *Educ:* Altrincham Grammar Sch. for Girls; Nottingham Univ. (BMedSci 1973; BM BS 1975; DM 1995). FRCGP 1992. General Practitioner: Mobberley, 1982–85; Stone, 1985–96; Tunstall, 1997– (now pt-time). Prof. of Primary Care, Staffs Univ., 1996–2005, now Hon. Prof.; Dir, Gen. Practice Educn, W Midlands SHA, 2005–06; Clin. lead for practice develt, NHS Stoke on Trent, 2008–11; Long Term Conditions Priority Lead, W Midlands Academic Health Sci. Network, 2014–18. Mem., Governing Council, Coll. of Medicine, 2010–11. *Publications:* Clinical Effectiveness Made Easy, 1998, 4th edn (jtly) as Clinical Effectiveness and Clinical Governance Made Easy, 2007; (with M. Davies) What Stress!, 1999; (with M. Davies) What Stress in Primary Care!, 1999; Survival Skills for GPs, 1999; Fertility Problems: a simple guide, 1999; Involving Patients and the Public: how to do it better, 1999, 2nd edn 2003; (jtly) Survival Skills for Nurses, 1999; (jtly) Teaching Made Easy: a manual for health professionals, 1999, 3rd edn 2011 (Korean edn 2008); (jtly) Opportunities and Options in Medical Careers, 2000; (with G. Wakley) Making Clinical Governance Work for You, 2000 (Japanese edn 2004); (jtly) Continuing Professional Development in Primary Care, 2000; (ed with M. Baker) A Guide to General Practice Careers, 2000; (with K. Mohanna) Risk Matters in Healthcare: communicating, explaining and managing risk, 2000; (jtly) Tackling Teenage Pregnancy: sex, culture and needs, 2000; (jtly) Occupational Health Matters in General Practice, 2000; (jtly) Back Pain Matters in Primary Care, 2001; (jtly) Diabetes Matters in Primary Care, 2001; (jtly) Implementing the National Service Framework for Coronary Heart Disease in Primary Care, 2001; (jtly) Clinical Effectiveness and Clinical Governance for Midwives, 2001, 2nd edn 2008; (jtly) Mental Healthcare Matters in Primary Care, 2001; (jtly) Musculoskeletal Matters in Primary Care, 2001; (jtly) Cardiovascular Disease Matters in Primary Care, 2001; (with G. Wakley) Obesity and Overweight Matters in Primary Care, 2001; (with G. Wakley) Sexual Health Matters in Primary Care, 2001; (jtly) Prescription for Learning: techniques, games and activities, 2002; (ed) A Guide to Accredited Professional Development: pathway to revalidation, 2002; (ed) A Guide to the Accredited Professional Development Modules File: evidence of learning, 2002; (jtly) Clinical Governance in General Dental Practice, 2002; (jtly) Beating Stress in the NHS, 2002; (jtly) Appraisal for the Apprehensive, 2002; (jtly) Smoking Cessation Matters in Primary Care, 2002; (jtly) Infertility Matters in Healthcare, 2003; (jtly) Survival Skills for Doctors and their Families, 2003; (jtly) Make Your Healthcare Organisation a Learning Organisation, 2003; (jtly) Improving Sexual Health Advice, 2003; (jtly) Demonstrating Your Competence 1: healthcare teaching, 2004; (jtly) Demonstrating Your Competence 2: women's health, 2004; (jtly) Demonstrating Your Competence 3: cardiovascular and neurological conditions, 2004; (jtly) The Good Appraisal Toolkit for Primary Care, 2004; (jtly) The Good Mentoring Toolkit for Healthcare, 2004; (jtly) Demonstrating your Clinical Competence in Women's Health, 2004; (jtly) Demonstrating your Competence 4: respiratory disease, mental health, diabetes and dermatology, 2004; Beat Back Pain, 2004; (ed with K. Licence) Looking after Children in Primary Care: a companion to the Children's National Service Framework, 2005; (jtly) Demonstrating your Clinical Competence in Cardiovascular and Neurological Conditions, 2005; (jtly) Demonstrating your Competence 5: substance abuse, palliative care, musculoskeletal conditions, prescribing practice, 2005; (with G. Wakley) Chronic Disease Management in Primary Care: quality and outcomes, 2005; (jtly) Demonstrating your Competence in Reproductive Health: a guide for hospital doctors, their trainers and practitioners with a special interest, 2005; (jtly) Demonstrating your Clinical Competence in Respiratory Disease, Diabetes and Dermatology, 2005; (ed) Career Planning for Everyone in the NHS: the toolkit, 2005; (with G. Wakley) Clinical Audit in Primary Care: demonstrating quality and outcomes, 2005; Healthy Heart, 2005; (jtly) Demonstrating your Clinical Competence in Depression, Dementia, Alcoholism, Palliative Care and Osteoporosis, 2005; (jtly) Guiding Doctors in Managing their Careers, 2006; (jtly) Supporting Self Care in Primary Care, 2006; (jtly) How to Succeed in Writing a Book, 2006; (ed) Making an Effective Bid, 2007; (ed jtly) How to Succeed as a Leader, 2007; (jtly) Your Teaching Style, 2007; (jtly) Revalidation: prepare now and get it right, 2008; (jtly) Digital Healthcare: the essential guide, 2016; articles in jls. *Recreations:* theatre, walking, family, especially husband and grandchildren. *Address:* Stoke-on-Trent Clinical Commissioning Group, One Smithfield, Leonard Coates Way, Hanley, Stoke-on-Trent ST1 4FA. *T:* (01782) 291439. *E:* ruth.chambers@stoke.nhs.uk.

**CHAMBERS, Ruth Marian;** *see* Arlow, R. M.

**CHAMBERS, Sarah Penelope;** independent consultant; Chair, Legal Services Consumer Panel, since 2018; Member; Electoral Commission, since 2018; Pensions Regulator Determinations Panel, since 2018; *b* 8 Nov. 1958; *d* of Sir (Stanley) Paul Chambers, KBE, CB, CIE and of Edith Chambers; *m* 1985, Andrew Hearn; three *s*. *Educ:* Channing Sch., N London; Somerville Coll., Oxford (BA Hons PPE). Department of Trade and Industry, 1979–2004: on loan to OFT, 1980–81; on loan to Oftel as Dir, Licensing, 1994–98; Dir, Strategy and Competitiveness Unit, 1999–2001; Dir, Automotive Unit, 2001–04; Chief Exec., Postal Services Commn, 2004–08; Dir, Consumer and Competition Policy, BERR, subseq. BIS, 2008–11; Dir, Office for Renewable Energy Deployment, DECC, 2011–13. Panel Member: Judicial Appts Commn, 2012–; Bar Standards Bd, 2012–17; CAA Consumer Panel, 2012–; Renewable Energy Consumer Code, 2013–; CMA, 2013–18 (non-exec. Dir, 2016–18). Ind. Dir, UK Payments Council, 2014–15. Mem., Adv. Bd, Centre for Competition Policy, UEA, 2009–14. Chm. Trustees, Shepherds Bush Families Project, 2013–14; Trustee: Zamcog, 2013–18; Greenhouse Sports, 2018–. *Recreations:* tennis, running.

**CHAMBERS, Stephen Lyon,** RA 2005; artist; *b* 20 July 1960; *s* of John Tangye Chambers and Gillian Mure Chambers; *m* 1991, Denise de Cordova; three *s*. *Educ:* Winchester Sch. of Art (Fellow 1986); St Martin's Sch. of Art (BA 1st Cl. Hons 1982); Chelsea Sch. of Art (MA 1983). Rome Schol., 1983–84; Fellow, Downing Coll./Kettle's Yard, Cambridge, 1998–99. Trustee: Bryan Robertson Trust, 2003–; Arthur Koestler Trust, 2013–. Hon. Fellow, Downing Coll., Cambridge, 2016. Solo exhibitions include: Flowers East Gall., London, 1989, 1992, 1995, 1998, 2000, 2003, 2006; Flowers Graphics, London, 1995, 1997, 2003, 2005; Flowers West, Santa Monica, 1998, 2000; Ikon Gall., Birmingham, 1993; Kettle's Yard, Cambridge, 1998, 1999; Gal. Kemper, Munich, 2000, 2001; Frissiras Mus., Athens, 2002; Gal. Frank Pages, Baden-Baden, 2005, 2015; Kings Place Gall., 2010; RA, 2012; Gall. 10, Milan, 2013; Pera Mus., Istanbul, 2014; Ca' Dandolo, 57th Venice Biennale, 2017; Heong Gall., Cambridge, Petronilla Silver Fine Art, London, 2018; *group exhibitions* include: Flowers East Gall.; RCA; Winchester Gall.; Plymouth Arts Centre; Riverside Studios; London Inst.; Flowers, NY; Nigel Greenwood Gall., London; Eagle Gall., London; Fitzwilliam Mus., Cambridge. Set designs for Royal Ballet, 2001. *Publications:* Long Pig, 1994; Four Heads, 1994; Healing Poems for the Great Ape, 1997; A Year of Ranting Hopelessly, 2007; The Long Feast, 2010; *relevant publication:* Stephen Chambers (monograph), by Andrew Lambirth, 2008; Stephen Chambers: the big country, by Rod Mengham, 2012; The Big Country and Other Stories, by Alison Wilding, Rod Mengham and Randy Lerner, 2014; The Court of Redonda, by Rod Mengham and

Kathleen Soriano, 2017. *Recreations:* cryptic crosswords, avoiding listening to speeches, Middle Eastern cooking, growing vegetables, Liverpool Football Club, sea kayaking. *Address:* c/o Royal Academy of Arts, Burlington House, Piccadilly, W1J 0BD. *E:* info@stephenchambers.com.

**CHAMBERS, Stuart John;** Chairman: Anglo American plc, since 2017; Travis Perkins plc, since 2017; President and Chief Executive, NSG Group (formerly Nippon Sheet Glass Co. Ltd), 2008–09 (Director, 2006–09; Executive Vice President, 2007–08; Chief Executive, Pilkington Group, 2006–07); *b* 25 May 1956; *s* of Reginald and Eileen Chambers; *m* 1984, Nicolette Horrocks; one *s* two *d*. *Educ:* Friends Sch., Great Ayton; UCL (BSc Hons). Shell, 1977–88; Mars Corp., 1988–96; Pilkington: Gp Vice Pres. Marketing, Building Products, 1996–97; Gen. Manager, Pilkington UK Ltd, 1997–98; Man. Dir, Primary Products Europe, 1998–2000; Pres., Building Products Worldwide, 2000–07; Gp Chief Exec., Pilkington plc, 2002–06. Chairman: Rexam PLC, 2012–16; ARM Hldgs plc, 2014–16; non-executive Director: ABP Hldgs plc, 2002–06 (Chm., Remuneration Cttee, 2005–06); Smiths Gp plc, 2006–12 (Chm., Remuneration Cttee, 2006–12); Tesco plc, 2010–15 (Chm., Remuneration Cttee, 2010–15); Manchester Airport Gp plc, 2010–12; Tesco Personal Finance, 2012–14. Member: NorthWest Business Leadership Team, 1997–2009 (Chm., 2006–08); Hearings Cttee, Takeover Panel, 2016–. Vis. Fellow, Univ. of Oxford, 2008–. *Recreations:* sailing, supporting Rugby Union.

**CHAMBERS, Timothy Lachlan,** OBE 2009; JP; FRCP; Consultant Physician (general and renal medicine), Bristol Royal Hospital for Children (formerly Royal Hospital for Sick Children, Bristol), 1979–2010; Vice Lord-Lieutenant of the County of Bristol, since 2012; *b* 11 Feb. 1946; *né* Seamus Rory Dorrington; *s* of late Mary Teresa Dorrington, Moate, Co. Westmeath, and adopted *s* of late Victor Lachlan Chambers and Elsie Ruth (*née* Reynolds); *m* 1971, (Elizabeth) Joanna Ward, DL, FRCP; one *s* one *d* (and one *d* decd). *Educ:* Wallington County Grammar Sch.; King's College London; King's Coll. Hosp. Med. Sch. (MB BS 1969). FRCP 1983; FRCPE 1985; FRCPI 1995 (Fellow, Faculty of Paediatrics, RCPI, 1989). Jun. med. posts, London and SE England, 1969–73; Tutor in paed. and child health, Univ. of Leeds, 1973–76 (Sen. Registrar in (renal) medicine, St James's Hosp., Leeds, 1974–75); Physician and nephrologist, Derbyshire Children's Hosp. and Nottingham Hosps, 1976–79; Physician (gen. and renal medicine), paediatric depts, Southmead Hosp., Bristol, and Weston-super-Mare Gen. Hosp., 1979–2010; Sen. Clinical Lectr in Child Health, Univ. of Bristol, 1979–2010; Clinical Dean, Southmead Hosp., 1983–90; Mem. Court, Univ. of Bristol, 1994–99; Member: Governing Body, Inst. of Child Health, 1987–97; Bd of Govs, Hosps for Sick Children (London) SHA, 1993–94. Dep. Med. Dir, Southmead Health Services NHS Trust, 1994–96. Consultant in paediatrics to MoD, 1985–2010; Civilian Consultant Advr (Paediatrics) to Medical Dir. Gen. (Navy), 1993–2012. Medicines and Healthcare Products Regulatory Agency (formerly Medicines Control Agency): Member: Cttee on Safety of Medicines, 1999–2005; Expert Adv. Gp on Paediatric Medicines (formerly Paediatric Medicines Working Gp), 2000–05, 2008–12; Adv. Bd on Registration of Homoeopathic Products, 2000–14 (Chm., 2003–14); Alternate UK Delegate, Paediatric Cttee, European Medicines Agency, 2008–12. Mem., SW Adv. Sub Cttee on Clinical Excellence Awards, 2003–09 (Med. Vice Chm., 2006–09). Royal College of Physicians: Mem. Council, 1990–92; Censor, 1992–94. Regl (SW England) Advr, RCPE, 1996–2001; Mem., BMA 1979–2014 (Chm., Paed. Sub-Cttee, Central Consultants and Specialists Cttee, 1989–94); Associate (perf. assessor), GMC, 1998–2010; Mem., 1976–97, Hon. Asst Sec., 1981–84, Hon. Sec., 1984–89, BPA, subseq. CPCH, then RCPCH; FRSocMed 1977 (a Vice-Pres., 2001–03; Mem. Council, 1995–2003; Pres., Sect. of Paediatrics, 1994–95; Hon. Editor, 1997–2001; Pres., United Services Section, 2001–03); President: Union of Nat. Eur. Paed. Socs and Assocs, 1990–94; Bristol Medico-Chirurgical Soc., 1996–97; Bristol Div., BMA, 1999–2000; SW Paediatric Club, 2004–06; Bristol Medico-Legal Soc., 2007–09. Sometime examr to med. bodies and univs at home and abroad; chm. and mem., other prof. and govtl cttees and adv. bodies in UK and Europe. Member: Philosophical, Oxford; British Assoc. for Paed. Nephrology (Hon. Mem. 2011); Corresp. Mem., Société Française de Pédiatrie, 1994. Mem., Editl Bd, Sri Lanka Jl of Child Health, 2002–. Trustee: St John's Home, Bristol, 1985–93; Royal Med. Benevolent Fund, 1988–2004; Educn and Resources for Improving Childhood Continence, 2006–14 (Acting Chm., 2012–14); Ammerdown Centre, Som, 2017–; Chm., Bristol, NSPCC, 2011–14 (Vice Pres., 2014–). Ambassador: Alabaré Charity, 2010–19 (Vice Chm., Bristol Ambassadors, 2011–19); Girlguiding Bristol and S Glos, 2010–. Gov., Redland High Sch. for Girls, Bristol, 2011–16 (Chm., 2012–16). Commnd Capt., 1984, retired Lt Col, 2010, RAMC(V); O/C Clin. Sqdn 243 (The Wessex) Field Hosp. (V), 2006–08 (Hon. Mem., Officers' Mess); MO, Lt Col, Somerset Cadet Bn The Rifles (formerly Light Infantry) (ACF), 1999–2012; non-regtl Mem., HAC, 2013; Mem., Co. and City of Bristol Cttee, 2008–, Vice Chm., 2015–18, Wessex RFCA; Hon. Mem., Officers' Mess, RM Reserve Bristol, 2013–; VR 2016. Eucharistic Minister and Reader, RC Cathedral Church of SS Peter and Paul, Clifton, 1991–; Oblate of Downside, 2010–. Master, Bristol Br., Guild of Catholic Doctors, 2006–08. Freeman, City of London, 1982; Liveryman: Apothecaries' Soc., 1985– (Master, 2011–12); Member: Court of Assts, 2000–); Barbers' Co., 2012–. JP Bristol, 1993; High Sheriff, Co. of City of Bristol, 2009–10; DL 2012. Hon. FSLCPaed 2002; Hon. FRCPCH 2014. CFM 2011. Hon. DSc Bristol, 2016. Diamond Jubilee Medal, 2012; Good Samaritan Medal, Pontifical Council for Health Care Workers, 2013. KLJ (Justice) 2017 (CLJ 2013). *Publications:* Fluid Therapy in Childhood, 1987; contribs to med. and lay jls and collective works. *Recreation:* bruising the serpent's head. *Address:* 4 Clyde Park, Bristol BS6 6RR. *T:* (0117) 974 2814. *Clubs:* Athenæum, MCC, Victory Services; Clifton (Bristol); Bristol Savages (Green Feather); Lido (Bristol); Galle Face Hotel (Colombo).

**CHAMBERS, Tony;** Brand and Content Director, Wallpaper\*, since 2017 (Editor-in-Chief, 2007–17); *b* Liverpool, 4 Sept. 1963; *s* of Joseph and Anne Chambers; *m* 2012, Georgia Dehn; one *d*. *Educ:* Central St Martin's Coll. of Art and Design (BA 1st Cl. Hons Graphic Design 1987). Art Ed., Sunday Times, 1987–97; Art Dir, GQ, 1997–2002; Creative Dir, Wallpaper\*, 2003–07. *Address:* Wallpaper\*, Blue Fin Building, 110 Southwark Street, SE1 0SU. *T:* (020) 3148 7706. *E:* contact@wallpaper.com. *Clubs:* Walbrook, Soho House.

**CHAMIER, Michael Edward Deschamps,** FCA; European Financial Consultant, Molitor Europe, since 2003; Secretary General, Fondation Mérite Européen, since 2012; *b* 4 Feb. 1941; *s* of late Saunders Edward Chamier and Mary Frances (*née* Chapman); *m* 1977, Deborah Mary Unwin; one *s* two *d*. *Educ:* Ampleforth Coll., York. FCA 1975. Sen. Audit Mgr, Arthur Young, Paris, 1965–68; Dep. Dir, Finance and Admin, Reckitt & Coleman, France, 1968–72; Asst Financial Controller for Europe, Squibb Europe, 1972–77; Dep. Dir of Financial Admin, Europe, CABOT Europe, 1977–83; Dir of Finance, EP, 1983–2002. KHS 2016. Silver Medal, European Foundn of Merit, 2006. *Publications:* Property Purchasing in France, 1981. *Recreations:* worldwide travel, opera, Anglo-French theatre and films. *Address:* 1 rue de Limpach, Reckange-sur-Mess, 4980 Luxembourg. *E:* chamier@europe.com.

**CHAMP, Andrea Helen;** see Quinn, A. H.

**CHAMPION, Prof. Justin Adrian Ivan,** PhD; FRHistS; Professor of History of Early Modern Ideas, Royal Holloway, University of London, 2003–17, now Emeritus Professor, and Hon. Fellow, 2018 (Head, Department of History, 2005–10); President, Historical Association, 2014–17; *b* 22 Dec. 1960; *s* of late Ivan Champion and Anne (*née* Davies); *m* 2014, Sylvia Carter; one *d*. *Educ:* Churchill Coll., Cambridge (BA 1983; MA 1985; PhD 1989). FRHistS 1995. Lectr in Early Modern Hist., La Sainte Union, Southampton, 1990–92; Lectr, 1992–95, Sen. Lectr, 1995–99, Reader, 1999–2003, Royal Holloway, Univ. of London. John Hinckley Chair of British Hist., Johns Hopkins Univ., 2003. Leverhulme Emeritus Fellow, 2018. Trustee, Egham Mus., 2014–18. FRSA 2005. Hon. FHA 2013. Presenter, television programmes: The Great Plague of London, 1999; Secrets of the Palace, 2002; Kings and Queens, 2003; consultant and contrib., Shakespeare Uncovered, 2014–18; also radio broadcasts for In Our Time, Making History, Night Waves and Free Thinking. Medlicott Medal for History, Historical Assoc., 2018. *Publications:* The Pillars of Priestcraft Shaken, 1992; (ed) Epidemic Disease in London, 1993; London's Dreaded Visitation, 1995; John Toland's Nazarenus, 1999; Republican Learning, 2003; (ed) Robert Molesworth's An Account of Denmark, 2011; contrib. learned jls. *Recreations:* racquet sports, cycling, collecting fine art and ceramics, especially Wedgwood liberty works. *Address:* Department of History, Royal Holloway, University of London, Egham Hill, Egham TW20 0EX. *T:* (01784) 443749. *Club:* Royal Ascot Cricket.

**CHAMPION, Sarah Deborah;** MP (Lab) Rotherham, since Nov. 2012; *b* Maldon, Essex, 10 July 1969. *Educ:* Prince William Sch., Oundle; Sheffield Univ. (BA Hons Psychol. 1991). Manager, Rotherham Arts Centre, Rotherham MBC, 1992–94; Arts Officer, Ashfield DC, 1994–96; CEO, Chinese Arts Centre, Manchester, 1996–2008; Chief Exec., Bluebell Wood Children's Hospice, 2008–12. Shadow Minister for Home Affairs, 2015–16; Shadow Minister, then Shadow Sec. of State for Women and Equalities, 2016–17; Mem., Select Cttee for Women and Equalities, 2017–; Chair, All Party Parliamentary Group: for survivors of childhood abuse; for sexual violence; for prostitution and global sex trade. *Publications:* Representing the People, 1999; Made in China, 2001; Vital: international artists of Chinese descent, 2008; (jtly) 21: discussions with artists of Chinese descent in the UK, 2009. *Recreations:* gardening, food, travel, wine, endurance horse riding, pets. *Address:* House of Commons, SW1A 0AA. *T:* (constituency office) (01709) 331035. *E:* sarah.champion.mp@parliament.uk.

**CHAN, Cho-chak John,** GBS 1999; CBE 1993 (OBE 1985); LVO 1986; JP; Managing Director: Transport International Holdings Ltd (formerly Kowloon Motor Bus Holdings Ltd), 1997–2008 (non-executive Director, 2008–11; Independent non-executive Director and Deputy Chairman, since 2012); Kowloon Motor Bus Co. (1933) Ltd, 1993–2007 (non-executive Director, since 2008); *b* 8 April 1943; *s* of late Kai Kit Chan and Yuk Ying Wong; *m* 1965, Wai-chun Agnes Wong; one *s* one *d*. *Educ:* St Rose of Lima's Sch.; Wah Yan Coll., Kowloon; La Salle Coll., Univ. of Hong Kong (BA (Hons), DMS). Commerce and Industry Dept, 1964; Economic Br., Govt Secretariat, 1970; Private Sec. to Gov., 1973; City Dist Comr (Hong Kong), 1975; Asst Dir of Home Affairs, 1976; Dep. Dir of Trade, 1977; Exec. Dir and Gen. Man., Sun Hung Kai Finance Co. Ltd, 1978; Principal Assistant Secretary: for Security, Govt Secretariat, 1980; for CS, 1982; Dep. Dir of Trade, 1983; Dep. Sec. (Gen. Duties), 1984; Dir of Inf. Services, 1986; Dep. Chief Sec., 1987; Sec. for Trade and Industry, 1989; Sec. for Educn and Manpower, 1991. Non-executive Director and Chairman: RoadShow Hldgs Ltd, 2001–17; Hong Kong News Expo Ltd, 2013–; non-exec. Dir, Long Win Bus Co. Ltd, 2008–; Independent non-executive Director: Hang Seng Bank Ltd, 1995–; Guangdong Investments Ltd, 1998–; Swire Properties Ltd, 2010–17; Fordwell Internat. Hldgs Ltd, 2011–14. Chm. Court, Hong Kong Univ. of Sci. and Technol., 2008–. JP Hong Kong, 1984. CCMI 2006. Hon. Fellow, Univ. of Hong Kong, 2000. Hon. DBA Internat. Management Centres, 1997; Hon. DSocSc: Hong Kong Univ. of Sci. and Technol., 2009; Univ. of Hong Kong, 2011; Lingnan, 2012. *Recreations:* swimming, music, reading. *Address:* Room A, 7/F Glory Heights, 52 Lyttelton Road, Hong Kong. *T:* 90138883. *Clubs:* Hong Kong Jockey (Chm., 2006–10); Hong Kong (Chm., 2007–08).

**CHAN FANG, Anson Maria Elizabeth, (Mrs Anson Chan),** GBM 1999; Hon. GCMG 2002; CBE 1992; JP; Chief Secretary for Administration, Government Secretariat, Hong Kong Special Administrative Region, 1997–2001; Convenor, Hong Kong 2020, since 2013; *b* 17 Jan. 1940; *d* of Howard Fang and Fang Zhao Ling; *m* 1963, Archibald John Chan Tai-wing, MBE, QPM, CPM (*d* 2010); one *s* one *d*. *Educ:* Univ. of Hong Kong (BA Hons). Admin. Officer, Hong Kong Govt, 1962–70; Asst Financial Sec., 1970–72; Asst Sec. for New Territories, 1972–75; Principal Asst Sec. for Social Services, 1975–79; Dep. Dir, 1979–84, Dir, 1984–87, Social Welfare; Sec. for Econ. Services, 1987–93; Sec. for CS, April–Nov. 1993; Chief Sec., 1993–97. Mem. (HK Island), Legislative Council of HK, 2007–08. JP Hong Kong, 1975. Jean Mayer Global Citizenship Award, Tufts Univ., 2005; O'Connor Justice Prize Honoree, 2018. Chevalier, Ordre National de la Légion d'Honneur (France), 2009. *Recreation:* music. *Address:* 22nd Floor, 3 Lockhart Road, Wan Chai, Hong Kong. *Clubs:* Zonta (Hong Kong East); Hong Kong Jockey, Hong Kong Country (Hong Kong).

**CHAN, Jeremy;** Co-Founder and Head Chef, Ikoyi Restaurant, since 2017 (one Michelin star, 2018); *b* UK, 11 April 1987; *s* of Roy Chan and Lorna Chan. *Educ:* Winchester Coll.; Princeton Univ. (BA *magna cum laude*). Worked in finance and investment banking; began to cook, 2013; Restaurant Noma, 2014; Dinner by Heston, 2015–16. *Recreations:* art, cinema, music, running. *Address:* Ikoyi, 1A, 1 St James's Market, SW1Y 4AH.

**CHAN, Rt Hon. Sir Julius,** GCMG 1994; KBE 1980 (CBE 1975); PC 1981; GCL 2005; MP (People's Progress), Papua New Guinea, 1968–97 and since 2007; Governor of New Ireland, since 2007; *b* 29 Aug. 1939; *s* of Chin Pak and Tinkoris Chan; *m* 1966, Stella Ahmat. *Educ:* Marist Brothers Coll., Ashgrove, Qld; Univ. of Queensland, Australia (Agricl Science). Co-operative Officer, Papua New Guinea Admin, 1960–62; private business, coastal shipping and merchandise, 1963–70. Minister for Finance, 1972–77; Dep. Prime Minister and Minister for Primary Industry, 1977–78; Prime Minister, 1980–82; Minister for Finance and Planning, 1985–86; Dep. Prime Minister, 1985–88; Minister for Trade and Industry, 1986–88; Dep. Opposition Leader, 1988–92; Dep. Prime Minister and Minister for Finance and Planning, 1992–94; Prime Minister and Minister for Foreign Affairs, 1994–97; Parly Leader, People's Progress Party, 1970–97, 2007–14. Hon. Dr Dankuk, S Korea, 1977; Hon. Dr Technol., Univ. of Technol., PNG, 1983. *Publications:* Playing the Game: life and politics in Papua New Guinea (memoir), 2016. *Recreations:* swimming, walking, boating, bicycling. *Address:* Parliament House, Waigani, NCD, Papua New Guinea.

**CHAN, Dr Margaret F. C.,** OBE 1997; FFPHM 1997; Director-General, World Health Organization, 2007–17; *b* Hong Kong, 1947; *m* David Chan; one *s*. *Educ:* Northcote Coll. of Educn, Hong Kong; Univ. of Western Ontario (BA 1973; MD 1977); National Univ. of Singapore (MSc Public Health 1985); Harvard Business Sch. Hong Kong Department of Health: MO, Maternal and Child Health Services, 1978–85; SMO, Family Health Services, 1985–87; PMO, Health Admin, 1987–89; Asst Dir, Personal Health Services, 1989–92; Dep. Dir, 1992–94; Dir, 1994–2003; World Health Organization: Dir, Dept for Protection of Human Envmt, 2003–05; Dir, Communicable Diseases Surveillance and Response, and Rep. of Dir-Gen. for Pandemic Influenza, 2005; Asst Dir-Gen. for Communicable Diseases, 2005–06. Prince Mahidol Award in Public Health (Thailand), 1999.

**CHAN SEK KEONG, Hon.;** Senior Judge, Supreme Court of Singapore, 2015–18 (Chief Justice, 2006–12); *b* Ipoh, Perak, 5 Nov. 1937; *m* 1965, Elisabeth Albyn Eber; three *d*. *Educ:* Univ. of Malaya in Singapore (LLB Hons). Legal Asst, Bannon & Bailey, Fedn of Malaya, 1962–63; Legal Asst, 1963–66, Partner, 1966–69, Braddell Bros, Singapore; Partner, Shook Lin & Bok, Singapore and Malaya, 1969–86; Judicial Comr of the Supreme Court, 1986–88; Judge of the Supreme Court, 1988–92; Attorney-Gen. of Singapore, 1992–2006; Sen. Counsel 1996. Mem., Mil. Ct of Appeal, Singapore, 1971–86. Pres., Legal Service Commn, 2006–12. Chm., Presidential Council for Minority Rights, 2006–. Pres., Singapore Acad. of Law, 2006–12. Dist. Fellow, Nat. Univ. of Singapore, 2013–. Hon. Bencher, Lincoln's Inn, 2008. Hon. LLD Nat. Univ. of Singapore, 2010. DSO, Darjah Utama Bakti Cemerlang (Singapore), 1999; Darjah Dato' Seri Paduka Mahkota Perak (Malaysia), 1999; Order of Temasek (2nd Class) Darjah Utama Temasek (Singapore), 2008. Internat. Jurists' Award, Internat. Council Jurists, 2009. *Recreation:* reading. *Address:* c/o Supreme Court of Singapore, 1 Supreme Court Lane, Singapore 178879.

**CHAN, Siu-Oi, Patrick,** GBM 2013; Hon. Mr Justice Chan; Non-Permanent Judge, Court of Final Appeal, Hong Kong, since 2013 (Permanent Judge, 2000–13); *b* 21 Oct. 1948; *s* of late Chan Chu-Yau and Li Man-Yee; *m* 1990, Lisa Chiang Miu-Chu. *Educ:* Univ. of Hong Kong (LLB 1974; Postgrad. Cert. in Laws, 1975; Hon. Fellow 2003). Barrister in private practice, Hong Kong, 1977–87; Judge of District Court, 1987–91; Dep. Registrar of Supreme Court, 1991–92; Judge, 1992–97, Chief Judge, 1997–2000, High Court of Hong Kong. Hon. Bencher, Inner Temple, 2001. Hon. Fellow, Chinese Univ. of Hong Kong, 2011. Hon. LLD: City Univ. of Hong Kong, 2008; Univ. of Hong Kong, 2011. *Address:* Court of Final Appeal, 8 Jackson Road, Central, Hong Kong. *T:* 21230033.

**CHAN, Dr Stephen Ming Tak;** HM Coroner, Inner North London, 1995–2002; *b* 16 Oct. 1948; *s* of late Kwok Kong Chan and Fun Ching Cheung; *m* 1972, Margaret Ann Small, *y d* of Francis Shadrack Small and Edith May Small. *Educ:* Bishop Hall Jubilee Sch., Hong Kong; RMN 1970; Kent Univ.; Charing Cross Hosp. Med. Sch., Univ. of London (MB, BS 1978; DMJ 1988); Cardiff Law Sch., Univ. of Wales (LLM 1992). Psychiatric nurse, St Augustine's Hosp., near Canterbury, 1967–70; jun. med. posts, Radcliffe Infirmary and John Radcliffe Hosp., Oxford and Charing Cross Hosp., 1979–80; postgrad. medical trng, Hammersmith Hosp., RPMS, Univ. of London, 1980–83; Principal in general practice, Epsom, 1983–86; Forensic Medical Examr, 1984–90, Sen. Forensic Medical Examr, 1990–94, Metropolitan Police; Forensic Medical Consultant in private practice, 1986–94; Asst Dep. Coroner, 1989–93, Dep. Coroner, 1993–94, Southern Dist, Gtr London; Asst Dep. Coroner, City of London, 1990–93. Member: Coroners' Soc. for England & Wales, 1989–2002; Council, Medico-Legal Soc., 1994–2002 (Hon. Treas., 1990–94); British Acad. Forensic Sci., 1988–2002; RSAA, 1992– (Trustee and Mem. Council, 2006–10; Benefactor, 2010–); RIIA, 1993– (Founder Mem. and Donor, Life Membership Legacy Fund, 2005–). Mem., Pugin Soc., 2002–. Patron, NACF, 2000–. *Publications:* Suicide Verdict: the coroner's dilemma, 1992; papers on medico-legal subjects. *Recreations:* Italian opera, Victorian antiques, Chinese history, song writing. *Address:* 1 Foreland Heights, Broadstairs, Kent CT10 3FU. *Clubs:* Lansdowne, Royal Over-Seas League.

**CHANCE, Sir (John) Sebastian,** 5th Bt *cr* 1900, of Grand Avenue, Hove; artist, since 2015; Teacher of Art, Bedford Sch., 1993–2015; *b* Kenilworth, Warwickshire, 1954; *s* of Sir (George) Jeremy (ffolliott) Chance, 4th Bt and Cecilia Mary Elizabeth Chance; *S* father, 2017; *m* 1977, Victoria Mary, *d* of Denis McClean; two *s* one *d*. *Educ:* Dartington Hall Sch.; Stourbridge Coll. of Art (BA Hons Fine Art); Birmingham Poly. (PGCE Art Educn). *Recreations:* walking, gardening. *Heir: s* Thomas Hugh Jeremy Chance [*b* 1983; *m* 2011, Rachel Mary Fleming]. *E:* jschance98@gmail.com.

**CHANCE, Michael Edward Ferguson,** CBE 2009; counter-tenor; Artistic Director, The Grange Festival, since 2015; *b* Penn, Bucks, 7 March 1955; *s* of John Wybergh Chance and Wendy Muriel (*née* Chance); *m* 1991, Irene, *d* of late Hon. Francis Edward Noel-Baker; one *s* one *d*. *Educ:* St George's Sch., Windsor; Eton Coll.; King's Coll., Cambridge (MA English 1977; Mem., King's Coll. Choir, 1974–77). Stockbroker, Mullens & Co., 1977–80. Founder Mem., The Light Blues, 1977–83; Mem., Monteverdi Choir, 1980–83; solo career, 1983–: operatic débuts: Buxton Fest, 1983; Kent Opera, Opéra de Lyon, Göttingen Handel Fest., 1985; Paris Opera, 1988; Glyndebourne Fest., 1989; ENO, Netherlands Opera, 1991; Covent Garden, Scottish Opera, 1992; Australian Opera, 1993; Buenos Aires, 1996; WNO, 1997; San Francisco Opera, 1998; Maggio Musicale, Florence, 1999; Leipzig Opera, 2000; Munich State Opera, 2003; rôles include: Oberon in A Midsummer Night's Dream; Apollo in Death in Venice; Julius Caesar; Andronico in Tamerlano; Bertardo in Rodelinda; Orfeo in Orfeo ed Euridice; Ottone in Agrippina; Ottone in L'incoronazione di Poppea; Military Governor in A Night at the Chinese Opera; Orpheus in The Second Mrs Kong; concert performances in Europe, USA and Japan. Prof. Royal Conservatorium, Den Haag, 2004–; Prof. of Singing, Royal Acad. of Music, 2010–. Numerous recordings of oratorio, opera and recitals. *Recreations:* card games (mainly bridge), golf, cooking, chaotic boating. *T:* (020) 8874 3222.

**CHANCE, Michael Spencer;** Executive Counsel, Joint Disciplinary Scheme for Accountants, 1993–97; *b* 14 May 1938; *s* of Florence and Ernest Horace Chance; *m* 1962, Enid Mabel Carter; three *d*. *Educ:* Rossall School. Solicitor. With Challinor & Roberts, Warley, 1962–70; Senior Asst Prosecuting Solicitor, Sussex Police Authy, 1970–72; Office of Director of Public Prosecutions, 1972–86: Asst Dir, 1981–86; Chief Crown Prosecutor, North London, 1986–87; Asst Head of Legal Services, Crown Prosecution Service, 1987; Dep. Dir, Serious Fraud Office, 1987–90; Consultant, Cameron Markby Hewitt, 1991–93. *Address:* 28 Beaufort Place, Cambridge CB5 8AG.

**CHANCE, Sir Sebastian;** *see* Chance, Sir J. S.

**CHAND, Ravi Parkash,** CBE 2011; QPM 2002; Chief People Officer, Department for International Development, since 2018; *b* Bedford, 23 Dec. 1969; *s* of late Mehar Chand and of Charan Kaur; *m* 2002, Elizabeth Mary Rose White; two *s* one *d*. FCIPD 2009. With Police Service, 1989–2003, incl. Head of Equality, Bedfordshire Police, 1999–2001; Mgt Consultant, Veredus Exec. Resourcing, 2003–06; estabd small financial services co.; Home Office: Dir, Strategic Diversity Action Team, 2006–07; Dir, Gp Equality and Diversity, 2006–12; Dir, Capability, Talent and Diversity, 2012–14; Dir, Workforce and HR, HMRC, 2014–18. Mem., Home Sec.'s Stephen Lawrence Steering Gp, 2000–03. Comr, Formal Investigation into Police Service in England and Wales under Race Relns Act, 2004–05. Pres., Nat. Black Police Assoc., 2001–03. Advr on equality issues, nationally and internationally. *Publications:* (jtly) The Police Service in England and Wales, 2005. *Recreations:* golf, travelling, DIY, entertaining my children. *Address:* Department for International Development, 22 Whitehall, SW1A 2EG. *T:* 07917 177693. *E:* Ravichand1@sky.com.

**CHANDE, Manish Jayantilal,** FRICS; Senior Partner, Clearbell Capital LLP, since 2013; *b* 23 Feb. 1956; *s* of late Jayantilal Keshavji Chande, Hon. KBE; one *s* one *d*. *Educ:* City Univ. (Dip. Accountancy). ACA 1980. FRICS 2008. Chief Exec. and Finance Dir, Imry Plc, 1985–97; Chief Exec., Trillium plc, then Land Securities Trillium, 1997–2002; Chief Exec. and Co-founder, Mountgrange Capital plc, 2002–09; Sen. Partner, Mountgrange Investment Mgt LLP, 2009–13. Non-exec. Chm., Nat. Car Parks Ltd, 2003–05; non-exec. Dir, Mitie plc, 2003–06. Comr, English Heritage, 2004–11. Mem., ICAEW, 1980–. Trustee: Windsor Leadership Trust, 2005–09; London Clinic, 2009–; Canal and River Trust, 2012–. *Address:* Clearbell Capital LLP, 2 Harewood Place, W1S 1BX. *T:* (020) 7494 7620, *Fax:* (020) 7494 7626. *E:* manish@clearbell.com. *Clubs:* Lansdowne, Arts.

**CHANDLER, Sir Colin (Michael),** Kt 1988; FRAeS, FCMA; Chairman, easyJet plc, 2002–09; *b* 7 Oct. 1939; *s* of Henry John Chandler and Mary Martha (*née* Bowles); *m* 1964, Jennifer Mary Crawford; one *s* one *d*. *Educ:* St Joseph's Acad.; Hatfield Polytechnic. FRAeS 1994. Commercial Apprentice, De Havilland Aircraft Co., 1956; Hawker Siddeley Aviation, later British Aerospace, Kingston: Commercial Manager, 1967–72; Exec. Dir, Commercial, 1973–78; Divl Man. Dir, 1978–82; Gp Marketing Dir, 1983–85; Hd of Defence Export Services, MoD, 1985–89; Vickers plc: Man. Dir, 1990–92; Chief Exec., 1992–98; Chm., 1997–2000; Chm., Vickers Defence Systems Ltd, 2000–02. Chairman: TI Automotive Ltd, 2003–07; Automotive Technik Ltd, 2004–08; Clarity Commerce Solutions, 2009–11 (Dep. Chm., 2007–09); Future Film, 2010–. Non-executive Director: Siemens Plessey Electronic Systems, 1990–95; TI Group, subseq. Smiths Group, 1992–2007 (Dep. Chm., 1999–2004); Guardian Royal Exchange, 1995–99; Racal Electronics plc, 1999–2000 (Chm., 2000); Thales plc, 2000–02; Holiday Taxis.com, 2009–19. Vice Pres., EEF, 1991; Member: NDIC, 1992–2002; Cttee, DTI Priority Japan Campaign, 1992–2001. Pro-Chancellor, Cranfield Univ., 2001–07. Gov., Reigate GS, 2004–17 (Vice-Chm., Bd of Govs, 2010–17; Chm., Finance and Foundn Cttee, 2008–17). FCMA 1987. Commander, Order of the Lion of Finland, 1982. *Recreations:* playing tennis, reading, gardening, listening to music. *Address:* Camp Farm Cottage, Camp Road, Wimbledon, SW19 4UW. *Clubs:* Reform, Mark's; Harbour.

**CHANDLER, Ven. Ian Nigel;** Archdeacon of Plymouth, 2010–18; *b* Stockton on Tees, 9 Nov. 1965; *s* of Kenneth Chandler and Marian Chandler. *Educ:* Bishopsgarth Sch., Stockton on Tees; Stockton Sixth Form Coll.; King's Coll. London (BD; AKC 1989); Chichester Theological Coll. Ordained deacon, 1992, priest, 1993; Asst Curate, All Saints, Hove, 1992–96; Domestic Chaplain to Bishop of Chichester, 1996–2000; Vicar, St Richard's, Haywards Heath, 2000–10; Rural Dean, Cuckfield, 2004–06; Proctor in Convocation, 2005–10. *Recreations:* theatre, music, art, travel. *Club:* Nikæan.

**CHANDLER, Very Rev. Michael John;** Dean of Ely, 2003–11, now Dean Emeritus; Prior, Hospital of St John, Canterbury and Hospital of St Nicholas, Harbledown, since 2016; *b* 27 May 1945; *s* of late John Godfrey Chandler and Ena Doris (*née* Holdstock); *m* 1966, Janet Mary (*née* Raines); one *s* one *d*. *Educ:* Brasted Place Coll.; Lincoln Theol Coll.; KCL (PhD 1987); Dip. Theol. London Univ. (ext.) 1975; Dip. Theol. (STh) Lambeth (ext.) 1980. FR.HistS 2017. Ordained deacon, 1972, priest, 1973; Curate: St Dunstan's, Canterbury, 1972–75; St John the Baptist, Margate, 1975–78; Vicar of Newington, 1978–88 (with Bobbing and Iwade, 1978–80, with Hartlip and Stockbury, 1980–88); Rector, St Stephen's, Hackington, 1988–95; Canon Res., Canterbury Cathedral, 1995–2003. Rural Dean: Sittingbourne, 1984–88; Canterbury, 1994–95. *Publications:* The Life and Work of John Mason Neale, 1995; The Life and Work of Henry Parry Liddon, 2000; An Introduction to the Oxford Movement, 2003; Queen Victoria's Archbishops of Canterbury, 2019; contrib. Oxford DNB. *Recreations:* walking, birdwatching, reading, sailing, boating about in mud. *Address:* 218 Tankerton Road, Whitstable, Kent CT5 2AT. *T:* (01227) 262937.

**CHANDLER, Paul Geoffrey;** Chief Executive, Traidcraft, 2001–13; Chairman: Durham Cathedral Council, since 2011 (Member, since 2008); William Leech Foundation, since 2014; non-executive Director, Co-operative Group, since 2015; *b* 13 Oct. 1961; *s* of late Dr David Geoffrey Chandler and Gillian Chandler; *m* 1993, Sarah Gillian Munro-Faure; three *d*. *Educ:* Wellington Coll., Berks; St John's Coll., Oxford (Stanhope Histl Essay Prize, 1983; BA Mod. Hist. 1983; MA 1987); Henley Mgt Coll. (MBA 1987). ACIB 1985. Joined Barclays Bank, 1983: Manager, Moorgate Br., 1986–87; on secondment to Church Urban Fund, 1987; Manager, Gp Strategic Planning, 1987–89; Asst Personal Sector Dir, London Western Reg., 1990–92; Gen. Sec., SPCK, 1992–2001 (Vice-Pres., 2001–). Non-exec. Dir, Engage Mutual Assce, 2012–15. Mentor (formerly Tutor), 2005–, Fellow, 2009–, Gov., 2015–, Vice-Chair, 2017–, St Chad's Coll., Durham Univ. Member: Council, Overseas Bishoprics Fund, 1992–2001; Bd of Mission, C of E, 1994–2001; Exec. Cttee, Feed the Minds, 1996–2001; Trustee, C of E Pensions Bd, 1998–2001. Trustee, SPCK-USA, 1992–2001; Member: Cttee of Mgt, Assoc. for Promoting Christian Knowledge (Ireland), 1995–2001; Exec. Cttee, Indian SPCK, 1998–2001; Exec. Cttee, European Fair Trade Assoc., 2002– (Pres., 2007–10); Gen. Council, S American Mission Soc., 2002–06; IPPR North, 2005–10; NE Regl Council, CBI, 2008–12. Dir, Cafédirect Guardian Share Co., 2006–11 (Chm., 2007–08); Chair, UK Fair Trade Leaders Forum, 2011–12. Churchwarden: St Stephen's, S Lambeth, 2000–01 (Mem. PCC, 1984–94, 1996–2001); St John's, Neville's Cross, 2013–15 (Mem. PCC, 2007–11, 2013–15); Mem. PCC, St Nicholas, Durham, 2002–05; Lay Canon, Durham Cathedral, 2008–. Gov., St Martin-in-the-Fields High Sch. for Girls, 1997–2001 (Vice-Chm., 1993–2001); Lay Adv. Gov., Chorister Sch., Durham, 2005–. Trustee: All Saints Educnl Trust, 1992–2005; Co. Durham Community Foundn, 2013– (Vice-Chair, 2017–); Bible Soc., 2015–; Interhealth Worldwide, 2016–17. Director: William Leech Foundn, 2001– (Mem., Research (formerly Professorial) Fellowship Mgt Cttee, 2006–14); Shared Interest, 2013–. *Recreations:* time with my family, reading, history, walking on Yorkshire Moors, collecting works of John Buchan.

**CHANDLER, Prof. Sara Jean Mary;** solicitor; Professor of Clinical Legal Education, College of Law, 2003–12; Visiting Professor of Clinical Legal Education, London South Bank University, since 2012; *b* Clovelly, Devon, 15 May 1946; *d* of Rev. Arthur Chandler and Jeannette Chandler; *m* 1996, José Olivares; two *s*. *Educ:* St Brandon's Sch.; Ilfracombe Grammar Sch.; University Coll. of Swansea (BA Hons Politics 1969); Univ. of Newcastle upon Tyne (MA Latin American Studies 1970); London Sch. of Econs and Pol Sci.; Poly. of the South Bank (CQSW and DipASS 1982); City Poly. (CPE 1992). Univ. of Glasgow, 1973; voluntary work, 1973–74, social worker, 1974–80, Jt Wkg Gp for Refugees from Chile; caseworker, N Lewisham Law Centre, 1982–92; articled clerk, Glazer Delmar Solicitors, 1993–95; admitted as solicitor, 1995; Solicitor: Hanne & Co. Solicitors, 1995–98; Plumstead Law Centre, 1998–2003; Solicitor, 2003–12, Dir of Pro Bono, 2005–08, Coll. of Law. Mem. Council, Law Soc., 2002–. Pres., Fedn of Eur. Bar Assocs, 2017–18. Hon. QC 2016. FRSA. *Recreations:* theatre, Latin American music, art, reading, swimming. *Address:* London South Bank University, Law Department, 103 Borough Road, SE1 0AA. *T:* (020) 7815 5788. *E:* sarachandler.lawsociety@gmail.com.

**CHANDLER, Victor William;** Chairman, Victor Chandler International Ltd, 1996–2014; *b* 18 April 1951; *s* of late Victor and Elizabeth Chandler; *m* 1st (marr. diss. 2010); three *s*; 2nd, 2012, Caroline Villar. *Educ:* Millfield Sch. Chm. and Man. Dir, Victor Chandler Ltd, 1974–96. *Recreation:* equestrian pursuits.

**CHANDLER, Dame Wendy**; see Hall, Dame W.

**CHANDOS,** 3rd Viscount *cr* 1954, of Aldershot; **Thomas Orlando Lyttelton;** Baron Lyttelton of Aldershot (Life Peer) 2000; *b* 12 Feb. 1953; *s* of 2nd Viscount Chandos and of Caroline Mary (who *m* 1985, Hon. David Hervey Erskine), *d* of Rt Hon. Sir Alan Lascelles, GCB, GCVO, CMG, MC; *S* father, 1980; *m* 1985, Arabella Sarah, *d* of Adrian Bailey and Lady Mary Russell; two *s* one *d*. *Educ*: Eton; Worcester College, Oxford (BA). Banker, 1974–93, Dir, 1985–93, Kleinwort Benson. Opposition spokesman on Treasury matters, 1995–97. Chief Exec., Northbridge Ventures Ltd; Chairman: Lopex plc, 1997–99; Capital & Regional plc, 2000–10; Director: Botts Co. Ltd, 1993–97; Cine-UK Ltd, 1995–2004; Middlesex Hldgs; Global Natural Energy plc, 2000; Northbridge (UK) Ltd, 2001–11. Chm., Television Corporation, 2004–06. Director: ENO, 1995–2004; Education 2000; Gov., Nat. Film and Television Sch., 1996–2001. Chm. Trustees, Esmée Fairbairn Foundn. *Heir: s* hon. Oliver Antony Lyttelton, *b* 21 Feb. 1986. *Address*: Valley Farm House, Boyton, Woodbridge IP12 3LF.

**CHANEY, Prof. Edward Paul de Gruyter,** PhD; FSA, FRHistS; Professor of Fine and Decorative Arts, and Chair, History of Collecting Research Centre, Solent University (formerly Southampton Institute, then Southampton Solent University), since 1998; *b* 11 April 1951; *s* of Edward Robert Dell Chaney and Maaike Louise Chaney (*née* de Gruyter); *m* 1973, Lisa Maria Jacka (writes as Lisa Chaney) (marr. diss. 2002); two *d*. *Educ*: Leighton Park Sch., Reading; Ealing Sch. of Art; Reading Univ. (BA Hist. of Art); Warburg Inst. (MPhil 1977; PhD 1982); Eur. Univ. Inst., Florence. Lectr, Univ. of Pisa, 1979–85; Adjunct Asst Prof., Georgetown Univ. in Florence, Villa Le Balze, 1982–83; Associate, Harvard Univ. Center for Italian Renaissance Studies, Villa I Tatti, Florence, 1984–85; Shuffrey Res. Fellow in Architectural Hist., Lincoln Coll., Oxford, 1985–90; Lectr in Hist. of Art (pt-time), Oxford Poly., 1990–91; Historian to London Div., English Heritage, 1991–93; Lectr in Hist. of Art (pt-time), Oxford Brookes Univ., 1993–; Sen. Lectr in Fine Arts Valuation, Southampton Inst., 1996. Res. Fellow, Huntington Liby, San Marino, Calif, 1994; Leverhulme Maj. Res. Fellow, 2010–12; Fernand Braudel Fellow, Eur. Univ. Inst., Florence, 2015. Visiting Prof. of Art History, New College of Humanities, London, 2014–. FSA 1993; FRHistS 2006. Commendatore, Stella della Solidarietà (Italy), 2003. *Publications*: (ed with N. Ritchie) Oxford, China and Italy: writings in honour of Sir Harold Acton, 1984; The Grand Tour and the Great Rebellion: Richard Lassels and "The Voyage of Italy" in the Seventeenth Century, 1985; A Traveller's Companion to Florence, 1986, 3rd edn 2018; (ed with P. Mack) England and the Continental Renaissance: essays in honour of J. B. Trapp, 1990; (ed with J. Bold) English Architecture Public and Private: essays for Kerry Downes, 1993; The Evolution of the Grand Tour: Anglo-Italian cultural relations since the Renaissance, 1998, rev. edn 2000; (with G. Worsdale) The Stuart Portrait: status and legacy, 2001; (with C. Clearkin) Richard Eurich (1903–1992): visionary artist, 2003; The Evolution of English Collecting: receptions of Italian art in the Tudor and Stuart periods, 2003; Inigo Jones's 'Roman Sketchbook', 2 vols, 2006; William Rose: tradition and an individual talent, 2009; (with T. Wilks), The Jacobean Grand Tour: Early Stuart travellers in Europe, 2014; Genius Friend: G. B. Edwards and The Book of Ebenezer Le Page, 2015; contribs to books, jls, newspapers, exhibition catalogues, etc. *Address*: School of Art, Design and Fashion, Solent University, East Park Terrace, Southampton SO14 0YN. *E:* edward.chaney@solent.ac.uk.

**CHANG, Dr Jung;** author; *b* Sichuan, China, 25 March 1952; *d* of Shou-yu Chang and De-Hong Xia; *m* 1991, John Arthur George Halliday. *Educ*: Sichuan Univ., China; Univ. of York (PhD Linguistics 1982). Dir of Chinese Studies, External Services, SOAS, 1986–91. Hon. Fellow, SOAS, 2018. Hon. DLit: Buckingham, 1993; Warwick, 1997; York, 1997; Open, 1998; Bowdoin Coll., USA, 2005; Dundee, 2015. *Publications*: Wild Swans: three daughters of China, 1991; (with J. Halliday) Mao: the unknown story, 2005; Empress Dowager Cixi: the concubine who launched modern China, 2013; Big Sister, Little Sister, Red Sister: three women at the heart of 20th century China, 2019. *Recreations*: ski-ing, snorkelling. *Address*: c/o Aitken Alexander Associates, 291 Gray's Inn Road, WC1X 8EB.

**CHANG, Prof. Ruth Elizabeth,** JD, DPhil; Professor of Jurisprudence, University of Oxford, since 2019; Fellow, University College, Oxford, since 2019; *b* USA; partner, Kit Fine. *Educ*: Dartmouth Coll., USA (AB 1985); Harvard Univ. (JD 1988); Balliol Coll., Oxford (DPhil 1998). Lecturer in Philosophy: Magdalen Coll., Oxford, 1990; Worcester Coll., Oxford, 1990–91; Jun. Res. Fellow, Balliol Coll., Oxford, 1991–93, 1995–96; Rutgers University: Asst Prof., 1998–2004; Associate Prof., 2004–14; Prof. of Philosophy, 2014–19. Visiting Assistant Professor: UCLA, 1993–94; Univ. of Chicago Law Sch., 1994–95; Vis. Res. Prof., ANU, 2010; Vis. Prof., NYU Abu Dhabi Univ., 2014–19. *Address*: University College, High Street, Oxford OX1 4BH. *E*: ruth.chang@law.ox.ac.uk.

**CHANG, Sarah Young Joo;** violinist; *b* Philadelphia, 10 Dec. 1980; *d* of Min Soo Chang and Myoung Jun Chang (*née* Lee). *Educ*: Juilliard Sch. of Music, NY. Began violin studies at age of 4; engagements at age of 8 with NY Philharmonic and Philadelphia Orch.; recorded first album at age of 10; has performed with orchestras in Asia, Europe and the Americas, incl. NY Philharmonic, Philadelphia Orch., Berlin Philharmonic, Vienna Philharmonic, Royal Concertgebouw Orch., Amsterdam, LSO, LPO, NHK SO, Tokyo, Hong Kong SO, Washington Nat. SO; recitals incl. performances at Kennedy Center, Washington, Carnegie Hall, NY, Orchestra Hall, Chicago, Symphony Hall, Boston and Barbican Centre, London. Has made numerous recordings. Young Artist of Year, Gramophone mag., 1993; Nan Pa Award, S Korea, 1993; Newcomer of Year, Internat. Classical Music Awards, 1994; Avery Fisher Prize, 1999; Internazionale Accademia Musicale Chigiana Prize, 2005; Young Global Leader, WEF, 2008. *Address*: c/o IMG Artists, Capital Tower, 91 Waterloo Road, SE1 8RT. *T*: (020) 7957 5800, *Fax*: (020) 7957 5801.

**CHANG-HIM, Most Rev. French Kitchener,** Hon. OBE 2014; Bishop of the Seychelles, 1979–2004; Archbishop of the Indian Ocean, 1984–95; Archbishop Emeritus, 2013; *m* 1975, Susan Talma; twin *d*. *Educ*: Lichfield Theol Coll.; St Augustine's Coll., Canterbury; Trinity Coll., Univ. of Toronto (LTh 1975); Oxford Centre for Mission Studies (MPhil Univ. of Wales 2010). Deacon, Sheffield, 1962; priest, Seychelles, 1963; Curate of Goole, 1962–63; Rector of Praslin, Seychelles, 1963–66 and 1969–71; Asst Priest, St Leonard's, Norwood, Sheffield, 1967–68; Vicar General, Seychelles, 1972–73; Rector, S Mahé Parish, 1973–74; Archdeacon of Seychelles, 1973–79; Priest-in-charge, St Paul's Cathedral, Mahé, 1977–79; Dean, Province of the Indian Ocean, 1983–84. DD (*hc*) Trinity Coll., Toronto, 1991. *Address*: PO Box 44, Victoria, Mahé, Seychelles. *T*: 4248151. *E*: bishop@seychelles.net.

**CHANNER, Jillian;** independent historic building and architectural glass consultant, since 2011; *b* 2 July 1949; *d* of Eric David Kerr, MC and Betty (*née* Knight); *m* 1988, Donal Gilbert O'Connell Channer (*d* 2015). *Educ*: Univ. of York (BA Hons 1970, MA 1971). Dept of MSS and Early Printed Books, TCD, 1971–72; Photo-Archives, Courtauld Inst. of Art, Univ. of London, 1973–75; Sec., Corpus Vitrearum Medii Aevii, GB, 1975–84; English Heritage: Inspector, Ancient Monuments and Historic Buildings, 1984–88; Head of SW and W Midlands, Historic Buildings Div., 1988–91; Head of SW Team, 1991–98; Project Dir, 1998–2002; Phoenix Trust, later Prince of Wales's Regeneration Trust: Dir, 2002–07; Heritage Policy Advr, English Partnerships, subseq. Homes and Communities Agency (on secondment), 2007–11. Member: Stained Glass Adv. Cttee, Council for Care of Churches, 1984–91; Inst. of Historic Buildings Conservation, 1997–; Church Buildings Council, 2016–. AABC Register Lay Assessor, 1999– (Mem. Bd, 2009–). Member: Council, British Soc. of Master Glass Painters, 1969–86 (Jt Ed., Jl, 1983–86); British Archaeol Assoc., 1972–85 (Mem. Council, 1981–85); Assoc. for Studies in Conservation of Historic Buildings, 1984– (Mem. Council, 1988–2002); Wells Cathedral Fabric Adv. Cttee, 2007–; Salisbury DAC, 2009–; Coventry Cathedral Fabric Adv. Cttee, 2017–; Bath and Wells DAC, 2019–. FRSA 2002; FSA 2003. Hon. Sec. to Trustees, Ely Stained Glass Mus., 1978–84; Trustee: Ancient Monuments Soc., 2002–; Woodchester Mansion Trust, 2007–10; Internat. Monuments Trust, 2012–17; St Andrew's Conservation Trust, 2016–. Freeman, City of London, 1984; Liveryman, Co. of Glaziers, Painters and Stainers of Glass, 1984–. *Publications*: various contribs to specialist pubns on historic buildings conservation and stained glass. *Recreations*: gardening, talking. *Address*: The Notch, 50 Tower Hill, Hisomley, Westbury, Wilts BA13 4DA. *T*: (01373) 824895. *E*: jill.channer@gmail.com.

**CHANNING, Alastair;** see Channing, R. A.

**CHANNING, Jeffrey Paul;** self-employed consultant; Programme Manager (Solent Enterprise Zone), Solent Local Enterprise Partnership, 2012–18; *b* 8 Aug. 1950; *s* of Leonard Herbert Channing and Joy Channing; *m* 1994, Kate Munson. *Educ*: Aylesbury Grammar Sch.; University Coll. London (BSc Geog.). Joined Civil Service as trainee, 1974; Hd of Central Policy, 1989–92, Hd of Urban Develt Corps, 1992–94, DoE, Cabinet Office, 1994–96; Hd of Construction Policy, DoE, 1996–99; Hd of Planning Policy, DETR, 1999–2003; Dir, Thames Gateway, later Thames Gateway, Olympics and Sustainable Bldgs, ODPM, later DCLG, 2003–06; consultant, 2006–09; Develt (formerly Prog.) Manager, Partnership for Urban S Hants, 2009–12. Mem. of Bd, First Wessex Housing Gp Ltd, 2007–17. *Recreations*: ceramics, yoga. *E*: jchanning1@btinternet.com.

**CHANNING, (Raymond) Alastair,** FCILT; Managing Director, Associated British Ports, 1995–97; *b* 2 May 1943; *s* of late Geoffrey Channing, FRCS and Kathleen Channing; *m* 1976, Victoria Margaret Nish. *Educ*: Clifton Coll.; Clare Coll., Cambridge (MA; athletics Blue, 1965, and competed for Oxford and Cambridge against various American Univs, 1965). Various posts in Depts of Transport and Envmt, incl. Asst Private Sec. to successive Ministers of Transport; British Transport Docks Board, later Associated British Ports: Sec., 1979–84; Dir, 1984; Dep. Man. Dir, 1991–95; Dir, ABP Hldgs plc, 1992–97. FCILT (FCIT 1994 (Chm., 1996–98)). *Recreation*: music. *Address*: The Old Manor House, Hampnett, Cheltenham, Glos GL54 3NW. *T*: (01451) 860795. *Club*: Reform.

**CHANNON, Prof. Keith Michael,** MD; FRCP; FMedSci; Field Marshal Earl Alexander Professor of Cardiovascular Medicine, since 2014, and Deputy Head, Medical Sciences Division, since 2018, University of Oxford; Fellow, Exeter College, Oxford, since 2014; Hon. Consultant Cardiologist, Oxford University Hospitals, since 1999; *b* Lincoln, 17 Nov. 1963; *m* Dr Elizabeth Orchard; one *s* two *d*. *Educ*: University of Manchester (BSc 1st Cl. Hons Med. Biochem. 1985; MD 1997). Univ. of Manchester Med. Sch. (MB ChB Hons Medicine 1988). MRCP 1991, FRCP 2003. Fellow in Cardiol., Duke Univ. Medical Centre, USA, 1993–97; Prof. of Cardiovascular Medicine, Univ. of Oxford, 2002–14; Fellow, Lady Margaret Hall, Oxford, until 2014; Dir, R&D, Oxford Univ. Hosps NHS Trust, and Associate Hd for Clin. Res., Med. Scis Div., Univ. of Oxford, 2012–. Dir, NIHR Oxford Biomed. Res. Centre, 2008–. FMedSci 2009. *Publications*: contrib. book chapters; contribs to scientific jls on basic sci. of vascular biol. and clin. res. in coronary artery disease. *Address*: Division of Cardiovascular Medicine, University of Oxford, John Radcliffe Hospital, Oxford OX3 9DU. *T*: (01865) 572783, *Fax*: (01865) 572784. *E*: keith.channon@cardiov.ox.ac.uk.

**CHANT, Ann;** see Chant, E. A.

**CHANT, Christopher Marc;** independent consultant, since 2015; Executive Director, and Director, Government G-Cloud Programme (formerly Government Cloud and Data Centre Consolidation Programme), Cabinet Office, 2010–12; Executive Director, Government Digital Service, 2010–11; *b* 3 July 1955; *s* of Frank and Olive Chant; *m* 1977, Beryl; one *s* one *d*. *Educ*: Dane Court Tech. High Sch. Inland Revenue: Ops and Investigation, 1976–99; E Service Delivery Dir, 1999–2002; Hd of Service Delivery, Cabinet Office, 2002–05; Chief Inf. Officer, DEFRA, 2005–08; Govt Chief Inf. Officer for London 2012 Olympics, DCMS, 2008–10. *Recreations*: ski-ing, photography, cooking, travel. *E*: chrischant@mac.com. *W*: www.twitter.com/cantwaitogo.

**CHANT, (Elizabeth) Ann,** CB 1997; Deputy Director of Charities to TRH the Prince of Wales and the Duchess of Cornwall, 2005–10; *b* 16 Aug. 1945; *d* of late Capt. Harry Charles Chant and Gertrude Chant (*née* Poel). *Educ*: Blackpool Collegiate Sch. for Girls. Nat. Assistance Bd, Lincoln, 1963–66; Min. of Social Security, Lincoln, 1966–70; NHS Whitley Council, DHSS London, 1970–72; DHSS, Lincoln, 1972–74; DHSS Regl Office, Nottingham, 1974–82; Manager, DHSS Sutton-in-Ashfield, 1982–83; DHSS HQ, London, 1983–85; Prin. Private Sec. to Permanent Sec., DHSS, 1985–87; Head: Records Br., DSS, Newcastle upon Tyne, 1987–89; Contribns Unit, 1990–91; Chief Executive: Contributions Agency, DSS, 1991–94; Child Support Agency, DSS, 1994–97; Man. Dir for Corporate Social Responsibility, BITC, 1997–99; Reviews of Public Trust Office and Legal Services Ombudsman's Office for Lord Chancellor's Dept, 1999; a Comr and Dep. Chm., Bd of Inland Revenue, 2000–04; acting Chm., Bd of Inland Revenue, 2004; Dir Gen., HM Revenue and Customs, 2005. Exec. Council Mem., Industrial Soc., 1993–2000. Trustee: Citizens Advice, 2005–07; Garfield-Weston Trust for St Paul's Cathedral, 2012–16; Foundn Years Trust, 2012–18. Lay Gov., London South Bank (formerly S Bank) Univ., 2001–09. Hon. LLD London South Bank, 2010. *Recreations*: friends, music (especially opera), theatre. *Club*: Athenæum.

**CHANTLER, Sir Cyril,** GBE 2017; Kt 1996; MD; FRCP; Emeritus Chairman and Honorary Fellow, University College London Partners, since 2014 (Chairman, 2009–14); Children Nationwide Medical Research Fund Professor of Paediatric Nephrology, London University, 1990–2000, Emeritus Professor, since 2001; *b* 12 May 1939; *s* of Fred Chantler and Marjorie Chantler (*née* Clark); *m* 1963, Shireen Saleh; two *s* one *d*. *Educ*: Wrekin Coll.; St Catharine's Coll., Cambridge (BA 1960; MB BChir 1963; MD 1973); Guy's Hosp. Med. Sch. MRC Travelling Fellow, Univ. of California, 1971; Guy's Hospital: Sen. Lectr and Consultant Paediatrician, 1972–80; Prof. of Paediatric Nephrology, 1980–2000; General Manager, 1985–88; Clinical Dean, Principal, 1989–92, 1992–98, UMDS, Guy's and St Thomas' Hosps; Vice Principal, KCL, and Dean, GKT Hosps' Med. and Dental Sch. of KCL, 1998–2000; Pro-Vice-Chancellor, London Univ., 1997–2000. Med. Dir, Well Child, 2001–05. Member: NHS Policy Bd, 1989–95; GMC, 1994–2003 (Chm., Standards Cttee, 1997–2002). Chairman: Sci. Adv. Cttee, Foundn for the Study of Infant Deaths, 1988–90; Council of Heads of UK Med. Schs, 1998–99; Beit Meml Fellowships for Med. Res., 2003–09; Complex Primary Care Practice Prog. Bd, 2014–; Mem. Council, St George's Med. Sch., 2000–03. Chairman: Gt Ormond St Hosp. for Sick Children NHS Trust, 2001–08; King Edward VII Hosp. Fund for London, 2004–10 (Sen. Associate, 2001–04); non-executive Director: Guy's and Lewisham NHS Trust, 1991–92; Guy's and St Thomas' NHS Trust, 1993–97; Lambeth, Southwark, Lewisham HA, 1998–2000; Private Health Information Network, 2015–. Pres., British Assoc. of Medical Managers,

1991–97. Advr, Associate Parly Health Gp, 2005–; Mem., Public Sector Adv. Panel, Doctors.net.uk, 2007–14; Co-Chm., SARS Expert Adv. Enquiry, Hosp. Authy of Hong Kong, 2003; Chairman: Clinical Adv. Gp, NHS London, 2007–08; NHS England Quality and Clinical Risk Audit Cttee, 2013–14; Review of Standardised Packing of Tobacco Products, HM Govt, 2014. Trustee: Dunhill Med. Trust, 2001–09; Media Standards Trust, 2006–16; British Kidney Patients Assoc., 2007–10; non-exec. Dir, By the Bridge, 2006–15. Mem. Council, Southwark Cathedral, 2000–. Gov., South Bank Univ., 2002–05. Teale Lectr, 1987, Censor, 1989–90, Harveian Orator, 2002, RCP. FKC 1998. Founder FMedSci 1998. Hon. FRCS 2018. Hon. Fellow, Inst. of Child Health. Foreign Associate, Inst. of Medicine, Nat. Acad. of Scis, USA, 1999; Hon. Mem., Amer. Paed. Assoc., 1992. James Spence Medal, RCPCH, 2005; Ira Greifer Award, Internat. Ped. Nephrol. Assoc., 2007. Co-Editor, Pediatric Nephrology Jl, 1986–96; Mem., Editl Bd, Jl Amer. Med. Assoc., 2002–11. Dr *hc* Lille, 1998; Hon. DSc London South Bank, 1999; Hon. DSc(Med): London, 2005; Kent, 2009; UCL, 2012. Otto Wolff Medal, RSocMed, 2015. *Recreations:* golf, opera, reading. *Address:* 32 Benbow House, 24 New Globe Walk, Bankside, SE1 9DS. *T:* (020) 7401 3246. *Club:* Athenæum.

**CHAPLIN, Edward Graham Mellish,** CMG 2004; OBE 1988; HM Diplomatic Service, retired; Appointments Secretary to the Prime Minister for senior ecclesiastical appointments, since 2014; *b* 21 Feb. 1951; *s* of late James and Joan Chaplin; *m* 1983, Nicola Helen Fisher; one *s* two *d. Educ:* Queens' Coll., Cambridge (BA 1st Cl. Hons Oriental Studies 1973). Entered FCO, 1973; Muscat, 1975–77; Brussels, 1977–78; Ecole Nat. d'Admin, Paris, 1978–79; on secondment to CSD as Private Sec. to Lord Pres. of the Council and Leader of H of L, 1980–81; FCO, 1981–84; Head of Chancery, Tehran, 1985–87; FCO, 1987–89; on secondment to Price Waterhouse Management Consultants, 1990–92; Dep. Perm. Rep., UKMIS Geneva, 1992–96; Hd, ME Dept, FCO, 1997–99; Ambassador to the Hashemite Kingdom of Jordan, 2000–02; Dir, Middle East and N Africa, FCO, 2002–04; Ambassador to Iraq, 2004–05; Ambassador to Italy, 2006–11. Vis. Fellow, Centre of Internat. Studies, Univ. of Cambridge, 2005–06. Sen. Advr, Good Governance Gp, 2011–17. Associate, Darwin Coll., Cambridge, 2011–. Comr, Commonwealth War Graves Commn, 2011–19. Trustee: Mowgli Foundn, 2011–18; British Inst. for Study of Iraq, 2012–18. Gov., Wellington Coll., 2011–. *Recreations:* music, tennis, hill/mountain walking. *E:* egmc51@gmail.com.

**CHAPLIN, John Cyril,** CBE 1988; FREng; FRAeS; Member, Civil Aviation Authority and Group Director, Safety Regulation (formerly Safety Services), 1983–88; *b* 13 Aug. 1926; *s* of late Ernest Stanley Chaplin and Isabel Chaplin; *m* 1st, 1949, Ruth Marianne Livingstone (*d* 2004); two *s* two *d*; 2nd, 2005, Margaret Bronwen Nelson (*née* Evans), *widow* of William Nelson. *Educ:* Keswick School. Miles Aircraft, 1946; Vickers-Supermarine, 1948; Handley Page, 1950; Somers-Kendall Aircraft, 1952; Heston Aircraft, 1956; Air Registration Board, 1958; Civil Aviation Authority, 1972, Dir-Gen. Airworthiness, 1979. FREng (FEng 1987). *Publications:* papers to RAeS, incl. Concorde airworthiness certification and safety regulation, in Jl of Aeronautical Hist. *Recreations:* sailing, photography, travel. *Club:* Cruising Association (Vice-Pres., 1995–98; Pres., 2003–04).

**CHAPLIN, Laura Susan;** *see* McGillivray, L. S.

**CHAPLIN, Sir Malcolm (Hilbery),** Kt 1991; CBE 1984; FRICS; Chairman, Hilbery Chaplin, chartered surveyors, Romford and Essex (formerly Senior Partner, Hilbery Chaplin Porter, chartered surveyors, London, W1); *b* 17 Jan. 1934; *s* of Sir George Chaplin, CBE, FRICS and Lady Chaplin, (Doris Evelyn, *née* Lee); *m* 1959, Janet Gaydon; three *s. Educ:* Summer Fields, Oxford; Rugby Sch.; Trinity Hall, Cambridge (MA Est. Mgt 1961; Athletics Blue, 440 yds). Former Member: Barking, Havering and Brentwood DHA; Essex AHA. Treasurer: Billericay Cons. Assoc., 1970–73; Brentwood and Ongar Cons. Assoc., 1973–79 (Pres., 1988–92); Eastern Area Cons. Assocs, 1980–88 (Vice Pres., 1988–98); Mem., Nat. Union Exec. and Gen. Purposes Cttees, 1980–98; Chm., Cons. Bd of Finance, 1993 (Dep. Chm., 1988–93); Conservative Party: Mem. Bd of Mgt, 1993–98; Treasurer, 1993–2000; Association Chm., 1994–2011; Trustee, Cons. Agents Superannuation and Benevolent Funds, 1992–2000. Former Governor: Brentwood Sch; St Martins Schs, Hutton. Trustee, Romford War Meml Old Folks Club and other trusts. Freeman, City of London. Liveryman: Innholders' Co. (Master, 1992–93); Chartered Surveyors' Co. *Recreations:* dairy farming (retired), golf, watching cricket and Rugby. *Address:* c/o 84 Market Place, Romford, Essex RM1 3JE. *Clubs:* Carlton, Oxford and Cambridge, MCC; Hawks (Cambridge); Gentlemen of Essex CC.

**CHAPLIN, Dr Simon David John,** FDSRCS; Director of Culture and Society, Wellcome Trust, since 2014; *b* Dagenham, 17 March 1969; *s* of David John Chaplin and Diane Elizabeth Chaplin (*née* Lewis); *m* 2007, Natalie Anna Ceeney, *qv. Educ:* Hitchin Boys' Sch.; Fitzwilliam Coll., Cambridge (BA Natural Scis 1991; MA 1995); King's Coll. London (PhD Hist. 2009). FDSRCS 2010. Asst Curator, 1992–95, Associate Curator, 1995–98, Science Mus.; Sen. Curator, 1998–2007, Dir, Museums and Special Collections, 2007–10, RCS; Hd, Wellcome Liby, 2010–14. Menzies Campbell Lectr, 2006, Hunterian Orator, 2010, RCS. Hon. Secretary: Soc. for Hist. of Natural Hist., 2005–08; British Soc. for Hist. of Sci., 2010–14. *Publications:* contrib. book chapters and articles to learned jls on hist. of medicine. *Address:* Pearson's Cottage, Frittenden, Kent TN17 2DD.

**CHAPMAN, Angela Mary, (Mrs I. M. Chapman);** Headmistress, Central Newcastle High School (GDST), 1985–99; *b* 2 Jan. 1940; *d* of Frank Dyson and Mary Rowe; *m* 1959, Ian Michael Chapman; two *s. Educ:* Queen Victoria High Sch., Stockton; Univ. of Bristol (BA Hons French); Sorbonne (Dip. de Civilisation Française). Teacher of French, Bede Sch., Sunderland, 1970–80; Dep. Headmistress, Newcastle upon Tyne Church High Sch., 1980–84. *Recreations:* military history, walking, tennis. *Address:* 14 Alpine Way, Sunderland, Tyne and Wear SR3 1TN.

**CHAPMAN, Prof. Antony John,** OBE 2018; PhD; CPsychol, FBPsS; FAcSS; President and Vice-Chancellor (formerly Vice-Chancellor and Principal), Cardiff Metropolitan University (formerly University of Wales Institute, Cardiff), 1998–2016; Professor, University of Wales, 1998–2016, now Emeritus (Senior Vice-Chancellor and Chief Executive, 2004–07); *b* 21 April 1947; *s* of Arthur Charles Chapman and Joan Muriel Chapman (*née* Brown); *m* 1985, Dr Siriol David, OBE; two *s* two *d. Educ:* Milford Haven Grammar Sch.; Bexley Grammar Sch.; Univ. of Leicester (BSc 1968; PhD 1972). FBPsS 1978; CPsychol 1988. University of Wales Institute of Science and Technology, Cardiff: Lectr, 1971–78; Sen. Lectr, 1978–83; University of Leeds: Prof. of Psychol., 1983–98 (on secondment, pt-time, to CVCP Acad. Audit Unit, 1990–94); Dir, Centre for Applied Psychol Studies, 1987–90; Dean of Sci., 1992–94; Pro-Vice-Chancellor, 1994–98; Vis. Prof., 1998–2003. Associate Ed., British Jl Develtl Psychol., 1983–88; Ed.-in-Chief, Current Psychol., 1985–89; Mem., Editl Bd, Jl of Organizational Behavior, 1988–92; Ed., British Jl Psychol., 1989–95; Mem., Editl Cttee, British Jl Educnl Psychol., 1991–95; Senior Editor, book series: Psychol. for Professional Gps, 1981–88; Psychol. in Action, 1985–89; Internat. Liby of Critical Writings in Psychol., 1991–95; Mem. Bd, BPS Communications, 1979–; Founding Co-Dir, Sound Alert Ltd, 1994 (winner, Prince of Wales Award for Innovation, 1997); Member: Council, CBI Wales, 1999–2004, 2006–12, 2013–16; Bd, Cardiff Business Technol. Centre, 2000–16; Council, Cardiff Chamber of Commerce, 2004–07; Prince's Trust, Wales, Public Sector Partnerships, 2012–15; Adv. Bd, Cardiff Business Council, 2013–16. Economic and Social Research Council: Vice-Chm., Trng Bd, 1995–96; Chairman: Res. Recognition Exercise, 1993–96; Policy Rev. Gp, 1994–96; Psychol Subject Panel, 1996–2001. Chairman: Assoc. of UK Heads of Psychol. Depts, 1990–92; UK Deans of Sci. Cttee, 1992–94; Mem., Cttee Eur. Assoc. Deans of Sci., 1993–94; a Vice-Pres., UUK, 2002–04 (Mem. Bd, 2002–06); Chm., Higher Educn Wales, 2002–04. Member: RAE Psychol. Panel, HEFCE, 1992, 1996; Northern Exams and Assessment Bd, 1994–98; Bd, QAA, 2000–06, 2011–16 (Chairman: Access Recognition and Licensing Cttee, 2003–06, 2015–16; Cttee for Wales, 2004–06, 2013–16); Council for Ind. and Higher Educn, 2002–12; Bd, Univs and Colls Employers' Assoc., 2002–05; Bd, Leadership Foundn for Higher Educn, 2003–07; Council, Parly Univ. Gp (formerly All Party Parly Gp), 2004–16; Bd, Univs and Colls Admissions Service, 2007–13; Adv. Bd, London Sch. of Commerce, 2007–11; Bd, Higher Educn Acad., 2009–16 (Chm., Academic Council, 2009–11); Leadership Council, Nat. Centre for Univs and Business, 2012–16; Remuneration Cttee, Cardiff and Vale FE Coll., 2016–. Member, Court: Cardiff Univ., 1993–2016; Univ. of Wales, Aberystwyth, later Aberystwyth Univ., 1998–2016. Chm., Academic Accreditation Cttee, Singapore Assoc. Private Schs and Colls, 2009–12; Advr to Bd of Govs, S Australian Mgt Inst., 2009–12; UUK Internat. Policy Network, 2011–16; Governance and Adv. Bd, Arab European Leadership Bd, Assoc. Arab Univs, 2014–. Trustee, Buttle UK, 2016–. British Psychological Society: Chm., Bd of Examrs, Qualifying Exam, 1986–90; Pres., 1988–89; Chm., Jls Cttee, 1995–98; Hon. Fellow, 1999; President: Psychol. Section, BAAS, 1993–94; Assoc. of Learned Socs for the Social Scis, 1995–98. Vice-Pres., Cardiff Business Club, 2007–16. Gov., Bramhope Primary Sch., 1997–98. Fellow, Inst. of Welsh Affairs, 2007–08, 2010–. FAcSS (AcSS 1999); FRSA 1997; FInstD 2015; FLSW 2016. Mem., NY Acad. of Scis, 1992–. Liveryman, Livery Co. of Wales, 2014–17. Hon. DSc Leicester, 2008; Hon. DLitt Cardiff Metropolitan, 2016. *Publications:* jointly: Humour and Laughter: theory, research and applications, 1976, 2nd edn 1995; It's a Funny Thing, Humour, 1977; Friendship and Social Relationships in Children, 1980, 2nd edn 1995; Models of Man, 1980; Children's Humour, 1980; Road Safety: research and practice, 1981; Pedestrian Accidents, 1982; Psychology and People, 1983; Psychology and Social Problems, 1984; Elements of Applied Psychology, 1984, 2nd edn 2016; Psychology and Law, 1984; Noise and Society, 1984; Cognitive Processes in the Perception of Art, 1984; Cognitive Science, Vols I, II and III, 1995; Biographical Dictionary of Psychology, 1997; guest co-ed., collections of papers in various jls; contrib. articles to jls and chapters in books. *Recreations:* family, music, cricket, soccer. *Address:* Hill House, 95 Cyncoed Road, Cardiff CF23 6AE. *E:* antonyjchapman@gmail.com. *Clubs:* Athenæum; Cardiff and County (Cardiff).

**CHAPMAN, Ben;** *see* Chapman, J. K.

**CHAPMAN, Charles Cyril Staplee;** corporate development consultant; Member for Corporate Development and Finance, UK Atomic Energy Authority, 1988–90; *b* 9 Aug. 1936; *s* of Thomas John Chapman and Gertrude Gosden Chapman; *m* 1963, Lorraine Dorothy Wenborn; two *s. Educ:* St Peter's Sch., York; Univ. of Sheffield (BSc Hons). British Petroleum Co., 1958, Manager, Chemicals, Corporate Planning, Minerals, 1962–85; Senior Strategy Advisor, British Telecom, 1986–88. *Recreation:* growing rhododendrons.

**CHAPMAN, Maj. Gen. Chip;** *see* Chapman, Maj. Gen. Clive.

**CHAPMAN, Christine;** Member (Lab) Cynon Valley, National Assembly for Wales, 1999–2016; *b* 7 April 1956; *d* of late John Price and Edith Jean Price; *m* 1981, Dr Michael Chapman; one *s* one *d. Educ:* Porth County Girls' Sch.; UCW, Aberystwyth (BA Hons); South Bank Poly. (Dip. Careers Guidance 1989); UWCC (MSc Econ 1992; MPhil 2001); Univ. of Wales Swansea (PGCE 1995). Mid Glamorgan County Council: Community Services Agency, 1979–80; Mid Glamorgan Careers, 1980–93; Educn Business Partnership (on secondment), 1993–94; teaching and consultancy posts, 1995–96; Co-ordinator, Torfaen Educn Business Partnership, 1996–99. Mem. (Lab) Rhondda Cynon Taff Council, 1995–99. Dep. Minister for Educn and Lifelong Learning and for Local Govt, Welsh Assembly Govt, 2005–07. Chair, Petitions Cttee, 2009–11, Children and Young People's Cttee, 2011–16, Nat. Assembly for Wales. Nat. Assembly for Wales Rep., Cttee of Regions, 2008–12. *Recreations:* theatre, walking and women's history.

**CHAPMAN, Prof. Christopher Hugh;** Scientific Consultant, Schlumberger Cambridge Research (formerly Schlumberger Cambridge Research, later Schlumberger Gould Research), since 2005 (Scientific Adviser, 1991–2005); *b* 5 May 1945; *s* of late John Harold Chapman and Margaret Joan Weeks; *m* 1974, Lillian Tarapaski; one *s* one *d. Educ:* Latymer Upper School; Christ's College, Cambridge (MA); Dept of Geodesy and Geophysics, Cambridge (PhD). Asst Prof., Univ. of Alberta, 1969–72, Associate Prof., 1973–74; Asst Prof., Univ. of California, Berkeley, 1972–73; University of Toronto: Associate Prof., 1974–80; Prof., 1980–84; Killam Research Fellow, 1981–83; Adjunct Prof., 1984–88; Prof. of Physics, 1988–90; Prof. of Geophysics, Dept of Earth Scis, and Fellow, Christ's Coll., Cambridge, 1984–88. Hon. Prof. of Theoretical Seismology, Univ. of Cambridge, 2005–12; Emeritus Hon. Prof. of Theoretical Seismology, Univ. of Cambridge, 2012–. Green Scholar, Univ. of California, San Diego, 1978–79, 1986. Gold Medal, RAS, 2013. *Publications:* Fundamentals of Seismic Wave Propagation, 2004; research papers in sci. jls. *Recreations:* sailing, photography, woodwork. *Address:* Schlumberger Cambridge Research, High Cross, Madingley Road, Cambridge CB3 0EL. *T:* (01223) 315576.

**CHAPMAN, Clare Fiona Louise;** *see* Stanley, C. F. L.

**CHAPMAN, Maj. Gen. Clive, (Chip),** CB 2012; Senior British Military Advisor, United States Central Command, 2010–12; Consultant, Skarbek Associates, since 2013; television/ radio media analyst on terrorism, since 2015; *b* Launceston, 27 March 1959; *s* of Peter and Fay Chapman; *m* 1987, Geinor Bolton; one *s* one *d. Educ:* Lancaster Univ. (BA Hons 1980); Royal Military Acad. Sandhurst. COS, 5 Airborne Bde, 1992–94; JSSC, 1996–98; SO1 Ops/Trng HQ NI, 1998–99; in command 2nd Bn, Parachute Regt, 1999–2001; Col Mil. Ops 2, MoD, 2001–04; in command 19 Light Bde, 2004–05; COS NI, 2006–07; Hd, Counter Terrorism and UK Ops, 2007–10. Chm., Home Office rev. of police discipline, 2014. *Publications:* Notes from a Small Military, 2013. *Recreations:* country walks, football, ski-ing, theatre. *Address:* c/o NatWest Bank, Plymouth PL6 5FH. *T:* 07808 520118. *E:* chipchapman@hotmail.co.uk.

**CHAPMAN, Sir David (Robert Macgowan),** 3rd Bt *cr* 1958, of Cleadon, Co. Durham; DL; Consultant, UBS AG (formerly Laing & Cruickshank Investment Management, then UBS Laing & Cruickshank, later UBS Wealth Management (UK) Ltd), 2002–12; *b* 16 Dec. 1941; *s* of Sir Robert Macgowan Chapman, 2nd Bt, CBE, TD and Barbara May, *d* of Hubert Tonks; *S* father, 1987; *m* 1965, Maria Elizabeth de Gosztonyi-Zsolnay, *o d* of late Dr N. de Mattyasovsky-Zsolnay; one *s* one *d. Educ:* Marlborough; McGill Univ., Montreal (BCom). Wise Speke Ltd, then Wise Speke Div., Brewin Dolphin Securities Ltd, stock and share brokers, Newcastle upon Tyne: Partner, 1971–87; Dir, 1987–99; First Vice-Pres. and Sen. Relationship Manager for NE England, Merrill Lynch Internat. Bank, 1999–2002. Chairman: Team General Partner Ltd, 1994–2012; Northern Enterprise General Partner Ltd, 2000–13; North East Finance (Holdco) Ltd, 2019–; Dep. Chm., Adv. Bd, North East Finance Ltd, 2010–18; Director: Northern Rock plc (formerly North of England Building

Soc. then Northern Rock Building Soc.), 1974–2004 (Chm., Trustees, Northern Rock Pension Schemes, 2004–13); Breathe North Appeal Ltd, 1988–2001; British Lung Foundation Ltd, 1989–95; Gordon Durham & Co. Ltd, 1994–98; High Gosforth Park Ltd, 1999–2004; NE Regl Investment Fund Ltd, 1999–2009; NES General Partner Ltd, 1999–2017; Zytronic plc, 2000–18; Salle Farms Ltd, 2000–15; Guestwick Farms Ltd, 2000–15; NE Regl Investment Fund Two Ltd, 2001–09; Three Ltd, 2002–09; CNE General Partner Ltd, 2001–16; Farmstar Polska Sp. z o.o. Co., 2006–15; NE Regl Investment Fund Partner Ltd, 2006–09. Chairman: Virgin Money Retirement Savings Scheme (formerly Pension Scheme), 2011–; Virgin Money Ind. Governance Cttee, 2015–. Stock Exchange: Mem. Council, 1979–88; Chairman: Northern Unit, 1988–91; NE Reg. Adv. Gp, 1991–98. MCSI (MSI 1991) (NE Pres., 1993–2008). Mem. Council, CBI, 2001–03; Chm., 2001–03, Dep. Chm., 2003–05, NE Reg., CBI. Chm., Northumbria Coalition Against Crime, 1995–2000. Mem., Greenbury Cttee, 1995. Dir, Shrievalty Assoc. Ltd, 1999–2001. Trustee: Northern Rock Foundn, 2002–16; Industrial Trust, 2004–10; Patron, Hospitality and Hope, 2014– (Trustee, 2017–). Governor: St Aidan's Coll., Durham, 1987–97; UC, Durham, 1998–2000 (Chm., Graduates' Soc., 2001–04); Mem. Council, Univ. of Durham, 1997–2003. Tyne and Wear: High Sheriff, 1993–94; DL 1997. *Heir: s* Michael Nicholas Chapman [*b* 21 May 1969; *m* 1998, Eszter, *y d* of Dr Attila Perlényi; two *s*]. *Address:* Pinfold House, 6 West Park Road, Cleadon, Sunderland, Tyne and Wear SR6 7RR.

**CHAPMAN, Douglas;** MP (SNP) Dunfermline and West Fife, since 2015; *b* Edinburgh, 1955; *m*; two *c. Educ:* W Calder High Sch.; Napier Coll. Branch banking, then personnel mgt, TSB Scotland; work for Bruce Crawford, MSP, 1999–2005; Campaign Manager, SNP, 2006–07. Mem. (SNP) Fife Council, 1997–98 and 2007–15 (Chm., Educn and Children's Services Cttee, 2007–12). Educn spokesman, COSLA, 2012. Contested (SNP): Dunfermline and W Fife, 2005, Feb. 2006; Kirkcaldy and Cowdenbeath, 2010. *Address:* House of Commons, SW1A 0AA.

**CHAPMAN, (Francis) Ian,** CBE 1988; Chairman, Radiotrust PLC, 1997–2001; Chairman, 1991–96, Deputy Chairman, 1997–99, Guinness Publishers Ltd; Chairman, Scottish Radio Holdings (formerly Radio Clyde) PLC, 1972–96 (Hon. President, 1996–2001); *b* 26 Oct. 1925; *s* of late Rev. Peter Chapman and Frances Burdett; *m* 1953, Marjory Stewart Swinton; one *s* one *d. Educ:* Shawlands Academy, Glasgow; Ommer Sch. of Music, Glasgow. Served RAF, 1943–44; worked in coal mines as part of national service, 1945–47. Joined Wm Collins Sons & Co. Ltd, 1947 as management trainee; Sales Manager, 1955; Gp Sales Dir, 1960; Jt Man. Dir, 1968–76; Dep. Chm., William Collins Hldgs, 1976–81; Chm., William Collins Publishers Ltd, 1979–81; Chm. and Gp Chief Exec., William Collins Hldgs plc, 1981–89. Chairman: Harvill Press Ltd, 1976–89; Hatchards Ltd, 1976–89; Ancient Home Bookshop (Ipswich) Ltd, 1976–89; Co-Chm. and Actg Chief Exec., Harper & Row, NY, 1987–89; Chm. and Man. Dir, Chapmans Publishers, 1989–94. Chm., The Listener Publications PLC, 1988–93; Dep. Chm., Orion Publishing Gp, 1993–94; Director: Independent Radio News, 1984–85; Pan Books Ltd, 1962–84 (Chm., 1974–76); Book Tokens Ltd, 1981–94; Stanley Botes Ltd, 1985–89; (non-exec.) Guinness PLC, 1986–91; (non-exec.) United Distillers PLC, 1987–91; Pres.-Dir Gen., Guinness Media SAS, Paris, 1996–99. Publishers' Association: Mem. Council, 1963–76, 1977–82; Vice Pres., 1978–79 and 1981–82; Pres., 1979–81; Trustee, 1993–97. Chm., Nat. Acad. of Writing, 2000–03; Member: Bd, Book Develt Council, 1967–73; Governing Council, Scottish Business in the Community, 1983–98; Dir, Scottish Opera, Theatre Royal Ltd, 1974–79; Trustee, Book Trade Benevolent Soc., 1982–2003. Chm. Council, Strathclyde Univ. Business School, 1985–88. FRSA 1985; CCMI (CBIM 1982). Hon. DLitt Strathclyde, 1990. Scottish Free Enterprise Award, 1985. *Publications:* various articles on publishing in trade jls. *Recreations:* music, golf, reading, grandchildren. *Address:* Kenmore, 46 The Avenue, Cheam, Surrey SM2 7QE. *T:* (020) 8642 1820, *Fax:* (020) 8642 7439. *E:* fichapman25@googlemail.com. *Clubs:* Garrick, MCC; Royal Wimbledon Golf; Walton Heath Golf.
See also I. S. Chapman.

**CHAPMAN, His Honour Frank Arthur;** a Senior Circuit Judge, 2003–09 (a Circuit Judge, 1992–2009); *b* 28 May 1946; *s* of Dennis Arthur Chapman and Joan Chapman; *m* 1968, Mary Kathleen Jones; one *s* one *d. Educ:* Newton-le-Willows Grammar School; University College London (LLB, LLM; Brigid Cotter Prize). Called to the Bar, Gray's Inn, 1968; practice at Birmingham. Resident Judge, Wolverhampton, 1997–2007; Hon. Recorder, Birmingham, 2007. Practising Anglican. *Recreations:* travel, mountaineering, antiques, theatre, good food, wine and company.

**CHAPMAN, Sir Frank (Joseph),** Kt 2011; CEng, FIMechE, FREng; Chief Executive, BG Group plc, 2000–12; *b* 17 June 1953; *s* of Frank William Chapman and Clara Minnie Chapman; *m* 1st, 1975, Evelyn Mary Hill (marr. diss. 1995); two *d*; 2nd, 1996, Kari Elin Theodorsen; one *s* one *d. Educ:* East Ham Tech. Coll. (OND (Dist.) 1971); Queen Mary Coll., London Univ. (BSc 1st Cl. Hons Mech. Engrg 1974). CEng 1999; FIMechE 1999; FREng 2012. Engr, BP, 1974–78; various engrg and mgt appts, Shell, 1978–96; joined British Gas, 1996; Man. Dir, BG Exploration and Production, 1996–99; Dir, BG Gp (formerly BG) plc, 1997–2012; Pres., BG Internat., 1999–2000. Non-exec. Dir, Rolls-Royce, 2011–; Vice-Chm., Myeloma UK, 2016–. FRSA 2000. CCMI (CIMgt 2001). *Recreations:* yachting, ski-ing, music.

**CHAPMAN, Frederick John;** Group Treasurer, LucasVarity, 1996–98; *b* 24 June 1939; *s* of late Reginald John Chapman and Elizabeth Chapman; *m* 1964, Paula Brenda Waller; one *s* two *d. Educ:* Sutton County Grammar Sch. Joined ECGD, 1958; Principal, 1969; Asst Sec., 1977; Under Sec., 1982; Principal Estabt and Finance Officer, 1985–88; Varity Corporation: Treas. (Europe), 1988–89; Treas. and Vice-Pres., 1990–96. *Recreations:* reading, music. *Address:* 17136 Wrigley Circle, Fort Myers, FL 33908, USA.

**CHAPMAN, Sir George (Alan),** Kt 1982; FCA; FCIS; Senior Partner, Chapman Upchurch, Chartered Accountants, 1958–2000; *b* 13 April 1927; *s* of late Thomas George Chapman and Winifred Jordan Chapman; *m* 1950, Jacqueline Sidney (*née* Irvine) (*d* 2009); two *s* five *d. Educ:* Trentham Sch.; Hutt Valley High Sch.; Victoria University. Fellow, Chartered Inst. of Secretaries, 1969 (Mem., 1948–); Fellow, Inst. of Chartered Accountants of NZ (formerly NZ Soc. of Accountants), 1969 (Mem., 1948–). Joined Chapman Ross & Co., subseq. Chapman Upchurch, 1948. Chairman: Norwich Union General Insurance (formerly Norwich Winterthur) (NZ), 1985–92 (Dir, 1982–92); BNZ Finance, 1979–88 (Dir, 1977–88); Mitel Telecommunications, 1984–91; Pilkington (formerly Pilkington Brothers) (NZ), 1989–94 (Dir, 1982–94); Director: Bank of New Zealand, 1968–86 (Dep. Chm., 1976–86); Maui Developments Ltd, 1979–85; Offshore Mining Co. Ltd, 1979–85; Liquigas Ltd, 1981–85 (Chm., 1982–84); NZ Bd, Norwich Union Life Insurance Soc., 1982–92; Skellerup Industries Ltd, 1982–90 (Dep. Chm., 1984–87); Skellerup Industries, Malaysia, 1986–90; State Insurance Ltd, 1990–99 (Vice Chm., 1992–99); Norwich Union Holdings (NZ) Ltd, 1990–99 (Vice Chm., 1992–99); Vice Chm., Norwich Union Life Insurance (NZ) Ltd, 1993–98. Chairman: NZ Building Industry Authority, 1992–2000; Housing New Zealand Ltd, 1992–95 (Chm. Housing Corp. of NZ and Housing NZ Estabt Bd, April–July 1992). NZ National Party: Member, 1948–; Vice-Pres., 1966–73; Pres., 1973–82. Councillor, Upper Hutt Bor. Council, 1952–53, Deputy Mayor, Upper Hutt, 1953–55; Member: Hutt Valley Drainage Bd, 1953–55; Heretaunga Bd of Governors, 1953–55; Pres., Upper Hutt Chamber of Commerce, 1956–57. MInstD 1970, FInstD 1979. *Publications:* The Years of Lightning, 1980. *Recreations:* golf, reading, tennis. *Address:* 53 Barton Avenue, Heretaunga, Wellington, New Zealand. *T:* (4) 5283512. *Clubs:* Royal Wellington Golf, Wellington Racing (Life Mem.).

**CHAPMAN, Graham Andrew;** QC 2014; *b* Basildon, 28 Dec. 1975; *s* of Michael Chapman and Sheila Chapman; *m* 2002, Wendy Appleby; one *s* one *d. Educ:* Westcliff High Sch. for Boys; Oriel Coll., Oxford (BA Hons 1st Cl. Juris.). Called to the Bar, Inner Temple, 1998, Bencher, 2014; in practice as barrister, specialising in commercial litigation and arbitration, 4 New Square, 1999–. Jun. Bench Auditor, Inner Temple, 2015–. *Publications:* (ed) Jackson and Powell on Professional Liability, 5th edn 2002, 6th edn 2007. *Recreations:* family, music, art, theatre, motor sport, cricket, football, golf. *Address:* 4 New Square, Lincoln's Inn, WC2A 3RJ. *T:* (020) 7822 2000. *E:* g.chapman@4newsquare.com.

**CHAPMAN, Prof. Dame Hilary (Anne), (Dame Hilary Neil),** DBE 2018 (CBE 2012); FRCN; DL; independent professional consultant; Chief Nurse and Chief Operating Officer, Sheffield Teaching Hospitals NHS Foundation Trust, 2010–13 (Chief Nurse, 2006–10 and 2013–18); *b* Sheffield, 16 Aug. 1963; *d* of Alec and Jeanne Margaret Brown; *m* 2010, Anthony Neil. *Educ:* Sheffield Sch. of Nursing (RN 1985); Leeds Metropolitan Univ. (BSc Hons 1992); Sheffield Business Sch. (MBA 1997). FRCN 2018. Staff Nurse: Cardiothoracic, 1985–86, Intensive Care Areas, 1986–87, Northern Gen. Hosp., Sheffield; Intensive Care Unit, Leicester Royal Infirmary, 1987; Staff Nurse, 1987–89, Sister, 1989–92, Intensive Care Areas, Northern Gen. Hosp., Sheffield; Sen. Nurse Manager, Theatre and Critical Care, Leicester Royal Infirmary, 1992–95; Dep. Chief Nurse, Queen's Med. Centre, Nottingham, 1995–99; Director of Nursing and Midwifery: Kettering Gen. Hosp., 1999–2001; Univ. Hosps Coventry and Warwickshire, 2001–06. Vis. Prof., Faculty of Health and Wellbeing, Sheffield Hallam Univ., 2008–. Hon. DMed Sheffield 2015. DL S Yorks, 2017. *Recreations:* walking, travel, fine cuisine, friends and family.

**CHAPMAN, Ian;** *see* Chapman, F. I.

**CHAPMAN, Ian Stewart;** Chief Executive and Publisher, Simon and Schuster UK Ltd, since 2013 (formerly Managing Director and Chief Executive Officer, 2000–13); *b* 15 Jan. 1955; *s* of (Francis) Ian Chapman, *qv*; *m* 1978, Maria Samper; one *s* two *d. Educ:* Cranleigh Sch., Surrey; Univ. of Durham (BA (French and Spanish) 1980). Bookseller: Hatchards, Oxford St, 1973–74; WH Smith, Paris, 1974–75; trainee: Doubleday and Co. Inc., NY, 1980–81; Berkley Publishers, Putnam Gp, NY, 1981; editl asst, William Morrow Inc. NY, 1981–82; Ed., then Editl Dir, Hodder and Stoughton Ltd, 1983–88; Pan Macmillan: Publishing Dir, 1988–94; Man. Dir, 1994–2000. *Recreations:* golf, walking, ski-ing, gym. *Address:* Benedict House, Staplecross Road, Northiam, E Sussex TN31 6JJ. *T:* (01580) 830222, *Fax:* (01580) 830027; Simon and Schuster UK Ltd, 222 Gray's Inn Road, WC1X 8HB. *T:* (020) 7316 1910, *Fax:* (020) 7316 0331. *E:* ian.chapman@simonandschuster.co.uk. *Clubs:* Garrick, MCC.

**CHAPMAN, James Keith, (Ben);** *b* 8 July 1940; *s* of John Hartley and Elsie Vera Chapman; *m* 1st (marr. diss.); three *d*; 2nd, 1999, Maureen Ann (*née* Byrne), pharmacist; one step *s. Educ:* Appleby Grammar Sch., Appleby in Westmorland. Pilot Officer, RAFVR, 1959–61. Min. of Pensions and Nat. Insce, 1958–62; Min. of Aviation/BAA, 1962–67; Rochdale Cttee of Inquiry into Shipping, 1967–70; BoT, 1970–74; First Sec. (Commercial), Dar es Salaam, 1974–78; First Sec. (Econ.), Accra, 1978–81; Asst Sec., DTI, 1981–87; Commercial Counsellor, Peking, 1987–90; Dep. Regl Dir, NW, and Dir, Merseyside, 1991–93; Regl Dir, Northwest, 1993–94; DTI; Dir, Trade and Industry, Govt Office for NW, 1994–95. Founder Consultant, Ben Chapman Associates, 1995–97. MP (Lab) Wirral S, Feb. 1997–2010. PPS to Minister of State, DETR, 1997–99, DTI, 1999–2001, DCMS, 2001–05. Member: Intelligence and Security Cttee, 2005–10; Ecclesiastical Cttee, 2005–10. All-Party Parliamentary Groups: Chairman: China, 1997–2010 (Pres., 2010–); Britain-Turkey, 1998–2001; Soap and Detergents Industry, 1999–2001; Cleaning and Hygiene Products Industry, 2001–10; Vietnam, 2003–10 (Pres., 2010–); Vice-Chair, Turkish Northern Cyprus, 2006–10; Sec., Chile, 2005–10. Mem., Commonwealth Parly Assoc. Exec. Cttee, 2005–10. Fellow, Industry and Parlt Trust, 2006–10. Dir, Wirral Chamber of Commerce, 1995–96; Chm., Adv. Bd, China Gateway-North West, 1996–97; Pres., Wirral Investment Network, 2007–10 (Hon. Vice-Pres., 1997–2007). Pres., Vietnam-UK Network, 2018– (Exec. Chm., 2013–18). Member: Adv. Bd, China Britain Law Inst., 2010–; Bd, Univ. of Central Lancs, 2011–12 (Special Internat. Advr, 2011–14). Patron; Wirral Fund for Children with Special Needs, 2010–; Dep. Patron, BESO, 2003–05. Trustee, Historic Cheshire Churches Preservation Trust, 2011–16. Hon. Ambassador: for Cumbria, 1995–; for Merseyside, 1997–. Fellow, 48 Gp Club (Vice Pres., 2011–). Friendship Order (Vietnam), 2018. *Recreations:* opera, music, walking, theatre, art appreciation, travel. *Address:* 9 Darlington Place, Bath BA2 6BX.

**CHAPMAN, Jeffrey Paul;** QC 2010; *b* London, 23 Aug. 1963; *s* of Cliff and Joyce Chapman; *m* 2000, Annette Caseley; two *d. Educ:* Wakeman Sch., Shrewsbury; Univ. of Sussex (BA Hons 1985); Trinity Hall, Cambridge (LLM 1986). Called to the Bar, Middle Temple, 1989; in practice as barrister, 1990–. *Recreations:* playing squash and chess, watching football, scuba diving, being at home with family and friends. *Address:* Fountain Court, Temple, EC4Y 9DH. *T:* (020) 7583 3335. *E:* jpc@fountaincourt.co.uk. *Clubs:* Blacks; West Ham; Shrewsbury Town.

**CHAPMAN, Jennifer;** MP (Lab) Darlington, since 2010; *b* 25 Sept. 1973; *m* 2014, Nicholas Desmond John Smith, *qv*; two *s* by a previous marriage. *Educ:* Hummersknott Sch., Darlington; Queen Elizabeth Sixth Form Coll., Darlington; Brunel Univ. (BSc Psychol. 1996); Durham Univ. (MA Medieval Archaeol. 2004). Sen. Parly researcher to Alan Milburn, MP, 1997–2005. Mem. (Lab) Darlington BC, 2007–10. Shadow Minister for Justice, 2011–16, for Educn, 2016, for Exiting the EU, 2016–. *Address:* House of Commons, SW1A 0AA.

**CHAPMAN, Rt Rev. John Holland;** *see* Ottawa, Bishop of.

**CHAPMAN, Prof. John Newton,** PhD; FRSE; FIEEE, FInstP; Professor of Physics, 1988–2014, and Vice Principal and Head, College of Science and Engineering, 2010–14, University of Glasgow (Dean of Physical Sciences, 2008–10), now Emeritus Vice Principal; *b* 21 Nov. 1947; *s* of John Avi Chapman and Nora Chapman; *m* 1972, Judith Margaret Brown; one *s* one *d. Educ:* St John's Coll., Cambridge (BA 1st Cl. Hons Natural Scis 1969); Fitzwilliam Coll., Cambridge (PhD 1973). FInstP 1988; FIEEE 2011. Res. Fellow, Fitzwilliam Coll., Cambridge, 1971–74; Lectr, 1974–84, Reader, 1984–88, Univ. of Glasgow. Mem., EPSRC, 2003–08. FRSE 1991. *Recreations:* tennis, hill walking, photography, music. *Address:* Kelvin Building, University of Glasgow, Glasgow G12 8QQ. *T:* (0141) 330 4462, *Fax:* (0141) 330 4464. *E:* john.chapman@glasgow.ac.uk.

**CHAPMAN, Jonathan;** *see* Chapman, S. J.

**CHAPMAN, Ven. Justine Penelope Heathcote A.;** *see* Allain Chapman.

**CHAPMAN, Keith Vincent;** Founder, Keith Chapman Productions, since 2012; b 12 Dec. 1958; s of Roy Kenneth Chapman and Patricia Margaret Chapman (née Rose); m 1984, Kirsty Jane Asher (marr. diss. 2017); three s. Educ: St Nicholas Comp. Sch., Basildon; Great Yarmouth Art Coll. (Graphics Distn and Coll. Award). Art Dir, Garrat Baulcombe Advertising Agency, 1980–82; Creative Dir, McCarthy Oswin Advertising, 1982–85; Art Dir, Jim Henson Entertainment, 1985–88; Art Dir, Bastable Daley, 1988–95; freelance art dir/illustrator, 1995–2000; Co-Founder and Creative Dir, Chapman Entertainment, 2001–12. Children's television shows: Creator: Bob the Builder, 1999; Fifi and the Flowertots, 2005; Paw Patrol, 2013; Co-Creator, Roary the Racing Car, 2007; Producer: Little Charley Bear, 2011; Raa Raa the Noisy Lion, 2015. Hon. DA Norwich Univ. Coll. of the Arts, 2009. Recreations: writing, painting, football, golf. Address: Keith Chapman Productions, c/o MHA Macintyre Hudson, 30–34 New Bridge Street, New Bridge Street House, EC4V 6BJ. T: 07885 765674.

**CHAPMAN, Mark Fenger,** CVO 1979; HM Diplomatic Service, retired; Member, Police Complaints Authority, 1991–95; b 12 Sept. 1934; er s of late Geoffrey Walter Chapman and Esther Marie Fenger; m 1959, Patricia Mary Long; three s (and one s decd). Educ: Cranbrook Sch.; St Catharine's Coll., Cambridge. Entered HM Foreign Service, 1958; served in: Bangkok, 1959–63; FO, 1963–67; Head of Chancery, Maseru, 1967–71; Asst Head of Dept, FCO, 1971–74; Head of Chancery, Vienna, 1975–76; Dep. High Comr and Counsellor (Econ. and Comm.), Lusaka, 1976–79; Diplomatic Service Inspector, 1979–82; Counsellor, The Hague, 1982–86; Ambassador to Iceland, 1986–89. Club: Norfolk (Norwich).

**CHAPMAN, Mary Madeline, (Mrs A. R. Pears);** Member, Archbishops' Council, Church of England, since 2010 (Chairman, Audit Committee, since 2010); b 9 March 1949; d of Kenneth F. Chapman, MBE and Agnes G. B. Chapman (née Thompson); m 1st, 1976, Robert Henry Lomas (marr. diss. 1986); 2nd, 1990, Andrew Roger Pears; one d. Educ: Sutton High Sch.; Univ. of Bristol (BA Hons). Dip CIM 1975; CDir 2005. Mkting Exec., BTA, 1971–76; Mkting Manager, L'OREAL (Golden Ltd), 1976–82; General Manager: Nicholas Labs Ltd, 1982–86; Biotherm, 1986–88; Man. Dir, Helena Rubinstein, 1988–90; Dir, Personnel Ops, L'OREAL (UK), 1990–93; Chief Exec., Investors in People UK, 1993–98; Dir Gen., Inst. of Mgt, later Chief Exec., Chartered Mgt Inst., 1998–2008. Non-executive Director: Royal Mint, 2008–14; Insolvency Service, 2017–. Chairman: Inst. of Customer Service, 2009–16; Gen. Chiropractic Council, 2017–. Member: Nat. Lottery Commn, 2008–13; Gambling Commn, 2013–15. Mem. Council, Brunel Univ., 2009–17. Trustee, Girls' Day Sch. Trust, 2005–14. FInstD. Recreations: walking, sailing, theatre, church and community projects.

**CHAPMAN, Matthew James;** QC 2017; b Croydon, 4 July 1971; s of Terry John Chapman and Christine Chapman. Educ: Shirley High Sch., Croydon; John Ruskin Sixth Form Coll., Croydon; Univ. of Bristol (LLB Hons 1992); King's Coll. London (LLM 1993). Called to the Bar, Gray's Inn, 1994; Res. Asst, Criminal Law Team, Law Commn, 1994–96; in practice as a barrister, Barnard's Inn Chambers, 1997–2000, 1 Serjeants' Inn and 1 Chancery Lane, 2000–. Pt-time Tutor in Contract Law, City Univ., 1994–95. Pegasus Scholar, 1999. Publications: The Snail and the Ginger Beer: the singular case of Donoghue v. Stevenson, 2009; (jtly) Munkman on Employers' Liability, 16th edn 2013; (jtly) Saggerson on Travel Law and Litigation, 5th edn 2013, 6th edn 2017. Recreations: horses, English countryside, East Sussex, Isles of Greece, 20th century English literature. Address: 1 Chancery Lane, WC2A 1LF. T: (020) 7092 2900. E: mchapman@1chancerylane.com.

**CHAPMAN, Nicholas John;** Managing Director, The Irish Times Ltd, 1999–2001; b 17 June 1947; s of Frank and Elizabeth Chapman; m 1995, Louise Shaxson; two d. Educ: Merchant Taylors' Sch.; Clare Coll., Cambridge (MA); Exeter Univ. (MA 2003). With Hodder and Stoughton: Graduate Trainee, 1969; European Sales, 1970; Editor, 1973; Publishing Dir, Associated Business Press, 1975; Editor-in-Chief, Futura Paperbacks, 1979; Publishing Director: Macdonald Futura, 1980; Macmillan London, 1983; Head of BBC Books and Educn, 1986–89, Dir, Consumer Products Gp, 1989–94, BBC Enterprises; Man. Dir, BBC Worldwide Publishing, 1994–97; Director: BBC Worldwide Ltd, 1994–97; BBC Americas Inc., 1994–97; Mem., BBC Bd of Management, 1994–96; Man. Dir & Publisher, Orion Military, subseq. Cassell Mil. Publishing, Orion Publishing Gp, 1998–99. Pres., Publishers Assoc., 1994–96. Non-exec. Dir, Dorset Healthcare Univ. NHS Foundn Trust, 2011–14. Chm., Trustee Bd, St Margaret's Hospice, Somerset, 2008–12. Gov., Norwood Sch., 1998–99. Recreations: walking, natural history, reading, mountain climbing. Address: Ferncroft House, Walton Elm, Marnhull, Dorset DT10 1QG.

**CHAPMAN, Nigel Conrad,** CMG 2008; Chief Executive, Plan International, 2009–15; b 14 Dec. 1955; s of late Prof. Norman Bellamy Chapman; m 1984, Margaret Farrar; two d. Educ: Hymers Coll., Hull; Magdalene Coll., Cambridge (MA Hons English Lit.). Joined BBC, 1977: researcher and producer, BBC News and Current Affairs, incl. Nationwide, Newsnight and Breakfast News, 1979–89; Editor, Public Eye, 1989–92; Head: Regl and Local Progs, SE, 1992–94; Broadcasting, Midlands and East, 1994–96; Controller, English Regions, 1996–98; Dir, BBC Online, 1999–2000; Dep. Dir, 2000–04, Dir, 2004–09, BBC World Service; Chairman: BBC World Service Trust, 2002–09; Plan UK, 2003–09. Chm. Trustees, NACRO, 2016–; Trustee: Shelter UK, 2012–18; Care International UK, 2016–. Non-exec. Dir, S Central Ambulance Service NHS Foundn Trust, 2016–. Mem. (Lab), Oxford CC, 2016–. Gov., New Marston Primary Sch., 2017–. Recreations: sport (football and cricket), music, walking, reading. Address: 34 Chalfont Road, Oxford OX2 6TH. T: (01865) 554757.

**CHAPMAN, Patricia Maud;** journalist; b 3 May 1948; d of Arthur and Elizabeth Chapman; m 1970, David Clark; one s. Educ: Rochford Secondary Sch., Essex. Tea-girl, sub-ed. and columnist, Boyfriend mag., 1964–67; reporter, Romford Times and Havering Express, then sub-ed., Western Daily Press, Bristol, 1967–71; sub-ed., The Sun, 1971–79; sub-ed., Daily Mirror, 1979–82; Asst Night Ed., 1982–86, Dep. Ed., 1986–88, The Sun; Ed., News of the World, 1988–94. A Founder Mem., Press Complaints Commn, 1991–93 (Chm., Code of Practice Cttee, 1991). Recreations: painting, ephemera, cooking and eating! Address: c/o News UK, 1 London Bridge Street, SE1 9GF.

**CHAPMAN, Peter John;** Member (C) Scotland North East, Scottish Parliament, since 2016; b Ellon, 13 May 1950; s of Peter Chapman and Elizabeth Chapman; m 1995, Edith Watson; one s one d. Educ: Peterhead Acad.; Aberdeen Agricl Coll. (HND Agric.). Started farming (beef cattle, dairy, laying hens, cereals) with father and brothers, 1974; partnership with son (farming 850 acres with beef cattle, dairy, broiler chickens, cereals, later 1,100 acres with beef cattle, cereals, wind turbines), 1998–. Vice-Pres., NFU Scot., 1998–2000. Non-exec. Dir, SNH, 2001–07. Shadow Cabinet Sec. for rural econ. and connectivity, 2016–. Recreations: classic cars, dog walking, Doric poetry and literature, Robert Burns. Address: Scottish Parliament, Edinburgh EH99 1SP. T: (0131) 348 6149. E: peter.chapman.msp@parliament.scot.

**CHAPMAN, Rev. Canon Rex Anthony;** Residentiary Canon of Carlisle Cathedral, 1978–2004, now Canon Emeritus; Diocesan Director of Education, 1985–2004; Chaplain to the Queen, 1997–2008; b 2 Sept. 1938; s of Charles Arthur Chapman and Doris Chapman (née Eldred); m 1964, Margaret Anne (née Young); one s one d. Educ: Leeds Grammar Sch.; UCL (BA Classics 1962); St Edmund Hall, Oxford (BA Theol. 1964; MA 1968); Wells Theol Coll.; Univ. of Birmingham (DPS 1967). National Service, RAF, 1957–59 (Chinese linguist). Ordained deacon, 1965, priest, 1966; Asst Curate, St Thomas', Stourbridge, 1965–68; Associate Chaplain, Univ. of Aberdeen, 1968–78; Hon. Canon, St Andrew's Cathedral, Aberdeen, 1976–78; Vice-Dean, Carlisle Cathedral, 1980, 1982, 1984, 1989, 1994, 1998, 2002; Bishop's Advr for Educn, dio. of Carlisle, 1978–85; Bishops' Selector for Ministry in C of E, 1985–2004 (Sen. Selector, 1997–2004); warrant, dio. of Aberdeen and Orkney, 2006–. Chm., Vacancy-in-See Cttee, dio. of Carlisle, 1997–2003; Mem., Crown Appts Commn for See of Carlisle, 1988, 2000. Member: Gen. Synod of C of E, 1985–2000 (Mem., Bd of Educn, 1985–96; Chm., Schs Cttee, 1990–96); Carlisle Diocesan Synod, 1978–2003; Chm., House of Clergy, dio. of Carlisle, 1996–2003. Member: Cumbria Educn Cttee, 1978–98; Cumbria Educn Forum, 1999–2004; Standing Adv. Council for Religious Educn, Cumbria, 1978–2003 (Chm., 1989–2003); Cumbria Learning and Recreation Scrutiny Panel, 2001–04; Standing Cttee, Nat. Soc. for Promoting Religious Educn, 1982–97; Chm. Orgn Cttee, Cumbria Schs, 2001–04 (Vice-Chm., 1999–2001). Governor: Trinity Sch., Carlisle, 1978–2003 (Chm., 1989–2003); Carlisle and Blackburn (formerly Carlisle) Dio. Trng Inst., 1979–2004 (Vice-Chm., 2001–04); St Martin's Coll. (formerly UC of St Martin), Lancaster, 1985–2004; St Chad's Coll., Durham, 1989–94. Trustee, Carlisle Educnl Charity, 1978–2004 (Chm. of Trustees, 1998–99). Chm., Carlisle and Eden Valley Marriage Guidance Council, 1984–87; Mem., Cumbria Cttee, Royal Jubilee and Prince's Trust, 1985–87. Publications: A Kind of Praying, 1970; Out of the Whirlwind, 1971; A Glimpse of God, 1973; The Cry of the Spirit, 1974; The Glory of God, 1978; contrib. to A Dictionary of Christian Spirituality, 1983. Recreation: variable. Address: Myreside Cottage, Finzean, Banchory, Aberdeenshire AB31 6NB. T: (01330) 850485. Club: Royal Over-Seas League.

See also Rev. Canon M. J. Everitt.

**CHAPMAN, Hon. Rhiannon Elizabeth,** FCIPD; Managing Director, Plaudit, 1994–2010; b 21 Sept. 1946; d of 2nd Viscount St Davids and Doreen Guinness Jowett; m 1974, Donald Hudson Chapman (marr. diss. 1992); two step s. Educ: Tormead Sch., Guildford; King's Coll., London Univ. (LLB Hons 1967; AKC). FCIPD (FIPM 1972). Industrial Soc., 1968; LWT, 1968–70; Philips Electronics Industries, 1970–77; CPI Data Peripherals Ltd, 1977–80; Personnel Dir, London Stock Exchange, 1980–90; business consultant, 1990–91; Dir, Industrial Soc., 1991–93; Mem., WDA, 1994–98. Chairman: National Australia CIF Trustee Ltd, 1994–96; Fleming Managed Growth plc, 1999–2002; Visions Consulting, 2004–05; non-executive Director: S. R. Gent plc, 1994–97; Bibby Financial Services, 2002–03. Dir, South West of England Urban Regeneration Fund, 2003–. Member: UFC, 1989–93; Employment Appeal Tribunal, 1991–2016; Council, PSI, 1993–98; Technical Mem., BUPA, 1997–. External Reviewer of Complaints, TTA, 1998–2004; Advr, People and Skills Agenda, SBAC, 2005–07. CCMI. Recreations: yoga, drawing, handcrafts. Address: 3 Church Green, Great Wymondley, Hitchin, Herts SG4 7HA. T: (01438) 759102.

**CHAPMAN, Richard Harold;** QC 2019; b Manchester, 29 Oct. 1975; s of Malcolm and Angela Chapman; m 2003, Melissa Julie Rosenfield; two d. Educ: Manchester Grammar Sch.; Brasenose Coll., Oxford (BA Juris. 1997). Called to the Bar, Gray's Inn, 1998; pupillage, 1998–99, in practice as a barrister, specialising in commercial and chancery law, 1999–, Hd of Chambers, 2019–, 18 St John Street Chambers; a Fee-Paid Judge, First-tier Tribunal (Tax Chamber), 2015–. Recreations: family, synagogue, school governor, numerous committees, photography. Address: 18 St John Street Chambers, Manchester M3 4EA. T: (0161) 278 1800. E: rchapman@18sjs.com.

**CHAPMAN, Roger Ralph,** CBE 2007; Chairman, GARS Search and Recovery Ltd, since 2015; b 29 July 1945; s of Ralph Aubrey Hector Chapman and Hilda Bisset Chapman; m 1971, Patricia June Nelson Sansom; two s. Educ: Chesterton Sch., Seaford; Bedford Sch.; BRNC, Dartmouth. Royal Navy Submarines, 1963–71: 2nd i/c conventional submarine (Long (N) Specialist); invalided out due to poor eyesight; submersible pilot and Survey Manager, Vickers Oceanics Ltd, 1971–76 (with co-pilot, rescued from submersible at 1575ft in Atlantic, 1973); Managing Director: Subsea Surveys Ltd, 1976–84 (pioneering robotics in North Sea and worldwide); James Fisher Rumic Ltd (specialising in submarine rescue services for RN, incl. rescue of 7 Russian sailors trapped in submarine in Russian Far East, 2005), 1984–2003; James Fisher Defence Ltd: Vice Chm., 2003–12; Chm., 2012–14; non-exec. Dir, 2014. Fellow, Soc. for Underwater Technol., 1985. Pres., Barrow Br., RNLI, 1998–2003. Founder, with wife, Rumic Foundn Trust (helping young disadvantaged people in Cumbria), 2003 (Chm.). Gov., Chetwynde Sch., Barrow, 2005–09. Publications: No Time on Our Side, 1975. Recreations: golf, sailing (Clipper Round World Race, 1998–99), rock-climbing, music, Italian food and red wine at lunchtime, laughing and having fun with my family, ski-ing. Address: Low Hencroft, Woodland, Broughton in Furness, Cumbria LA20 6AG. T: 07850 953654. E: chapman_roger@hotmail.com. Club: Sloane.

**CHAPMAN, Roy de Courcy;** Headmaster of Malvern College, 1983–96; b 1 Oct. 1936; s of Edward Frederic Gilbert Chapman and Aline de Courcy Ireland; m 1959, Valerie Rosemary Small; two s one d. Educ: Dollar Academy; St Andrews Univ. (Harkness Schol.: MA 1959); Moray House Coll. of Educn, Edinburgh. Asst Master, Trinity Coll., Glenalmond, 1960–64; Marlborough College: Asst Master, 1964–68; Head of Mod. Langs, 1968–75; OC CCF, 1969–75; Rector of Glasgow Acad., 1975–82. Chairman: Common Entrance Bd, 1988–93; HMC, 1994. Publications: Le Français Contemporain, 1971; (with D. Whiting) Le Français Contemporain: passages for translation and comprehension, 1975. Recreations: cruising, France, snorkelling. Address: 41 North Castle Street, St Andrews, Fife KY16 9BG.

**CHAPMAN, Prof. (Stephen) Jonathan,** DPhil; FIMA; Professor of Mathematics and its Applications, since 1999, and Director, Oxford Centre for Industrial and Applied Mathematics, since 2008, University of Oxford; Fellow of Mansfield College, Oxford, since 1999; b 31 Aug. 1968; s of Stephen Cyril Chapman and Pauline Mary Chapman; m 1996, Aarti Chand; one s one d. Educ: Merton Coll., Oxford (BA Maths 1989); St Catherine's Coll., Oxford (DPhil Applied Maths 1991). FIMA 2007. Research Fellow: Stanford Univ., Calif, 1992–93; St Catherine's Coll., Oxford, 1993–95; Royal Soc. Res. Fellow, Univ. of Oxford, 1995–99. Richard C. Diprima Prize, 1994, Julian Cole Prize, 2002, SIAM; Whitehead Prize, 1998, Naylor Prize, 2015, London Mathematical Society. Publications: papers in learned jls. Recreations: music, walking. Address: Mathematical Institute, University of Oxford, Andrew Wiles Building, Radcliffe Observatory Quarter, Woodstock Road, Oxford OX2 6GG. T: (01865) 270507.

**CHAPMAN, Prof. Stephen Kenneth,** CBE 2016; PhD; FRSC, FRSE; President and Vice-Chancellor, Edith Cowan University, Western Australia, since 2015; b 12 May 1959. Educ: Univ. of Newcastle upon Tyne (BSc 1st Cl. Hons Chem. 1980; PhD 1983). FRSC 2005. NATO Postdoctoral Fellow, MIT, 1983–85; University of Edinburgh: Lectr, then Reader, 1985–96; Prof. of Biol Inorganic Chem., 1996–2009; Hd of Chem., 2000–05; Vice

Principal for Planning, Resources and Res. Policy, 2006–09; Principal and Vice-Chancellor, Heriot Watt Univ., 2009–15. FRSE 2005. *Address:* Edith Cowan University, 270 Joondalup Drive, Joondalup, WA 6027, Australia.

**CHAPMAN, Timothy James Patrick,** FREng; Director, Arup, since 2004; *b* Dublin, Ireland, 19 May 1965; *s of* Dr David Chapman and Dr Valerie Chapman; *m* 1989, Dr Marisa Fernandez; three *d*. *Educ:* University Coll. Dublin (BE Civil Engrg 1986); Imperial Coll. London (MSc DIC Soil Mechanics 1987). CEng 1992; FICE 2002. Graduate Engr, 1987, Associate Dir, 2000–04, Arup. FREng 2014. *Publications:* (ed) ICE Manual of Geotechnical Engineering, 2012; ICE and CIRIA reports. *Recreations:* reading, socialising. *Address:* Arup, 13 Fitzroy Street, W1T 4BQ. *T:* (020) 7755 3238. *E:* tim.chapman@arup.com.

**CHAPMAN, Gen. Sir Timothy John G.;** *see* Granville-Chapman.

**CHAPMAN, Tony;** film maker and writer; architecture critic and consultant, since 2016; architectural judge in awards and competitions, since 2000; *b* York, 23 Dec. 1950; *s of* James Chapman and Mary Chapman (*née* Alcock); *m* 1979, Jane Bentley (annulled 1992); *m* 2011, Wendy Akers. *Educ:* Pocklington Sch., Yorks; Univ. of Nottingham (BA Hons English). Researcher/writer, BBC TV Comedy, 1979–82: Not the Nine O'Clock News, Q9, Q10 (There's a Lot of it About); researcher/producer, BBC TV Current Affairs and Features, 1982–92: That's Life, Nationwide, 60 Minutes, Friday Report, First Sight, documentaries on early flying, architecture, envmtl and planning issues; Producer, 7 Days, ITV Meridian, 1992–93; Dir, Time Code Prodns, 1992–; Hd of Press, 1996–99, Hd of Awards, 1996–2016, RIBA. Artistic Dir, Man in the Moon, Chelsea, 1978–82. Mem., Twentieth Century Soc., 2007–. Author of performed plays, incl. Pilate, Essay on Nam, 1926 and All That, Seven Deadly Sins, On the Road, There'll Always be a Brentford. Hon. FRIBA 2011. *Publications:* Architecture 98, 1998; Architecture 99, 1999; Architecture 00, 2000; Architecture 01, 2001; Architecture 02, 2002; Architecture 03, 2003; Architecture 04, 2004; Architecture 05, 2005; The Stirling Prize: a decade of architecture and innovation, 2006; Architecture 06, 2006; Architecture 07, 2007; Architecture 08, 2008; Architecture 09, 2009; Architecture 10, 2010; Architecture 11, 2011; Buildings of the Year 2012, 2012; Building, Bridges and Landmarks, 2016; The RIBA Stirling Prize: 20, 2016; (contrib.) Contexts: the work of Hodder + Partners, 2017; (contrib.) Spirit of Place: 100 houses 100 years, 2017; articles in Architects' Jl, RIBA Jl, 20th Century Mag. *Recreations:* travel and travel writing, theatre, writing, acting, cycling, walking. *Address:* 14 Fairlawns, Cambridge Park, Twickenham TW1 2JY. *T:* 07921 767139. *E:* tonytimecode@me.com. *W:* www.thestuffofarchitecture.com. *Club:* Questors (Acting Mem., 1976–).

**CHAPMAN, William Edward,** CVO 2008; Private Secretary and Chief of Staff to the Lord Mayor of London, 2009–17; *b* 20 March 1952; *s of* late Philip and Pam Chapman. *Educ:* High Wych Primary Sch.; Bishop's Stortford Coll.; St Peter's Coll., Oxford (MA); Hertford Coll., Oxford (MLitt). Joined DoE (subseq. DETR), 1976; Information Directorate and speech writer for two Secs of State, 1988–91; Private Sec. for Home Affairs, then Parly Affairs, to the Prime Minister, 1991–94; Head: Planning Policies Div., 1994–98; Regeneration Div., 1998–99; Sec. for Appts to the Prime Minister and Ecclesiastical Sec. to the Lord Chancellor, 1999–2008; PM's Advr on Sen. Church and Lord-Lieut Appts, 2008; Dir of Policy, Tony Blair Faith Foundn, 2008–09. Mem., Adv. Council, McDonald Centre for Theology, Ethics and Public Life, 2008–; Mem. Council, Westcott House, Cambridge, 2019–. Trustee: Mitzvah Trust, 1998–2008; S Hackney Parochial Sch. Charity, 1998–2008; Lord Mayor's Trust for Charities, 2009–19; Soc. of the Faith, 2018–; Mansion House Scholarship Scheme, 2019–; Making the Leap, 2019–. Publisher: Sion Coll., 2009–18 (Hon. Fellow, 2018); Goodenough Coll., 2017–. *Recreations:* books, art, music, daydreams, night life. *Address:* 10 Atherton Road, E7 9AJ.

**CHAPPELL, Julie Louise Jo, (Mrs Bradley Porter),** OBE 2005; Managing Director, Business, London and Partners, since 2018; *b* Poole, 2 April 1978; *d of* John Chappell and Kathryn Chappell; *m* 2014, Bradley Porter; two *d*. *Educ:* Brasenose Coll., Oxford (BA PPE). Joined FCO, 1999; Central Africa Desk, Africa Directorate, FCO, 1999–2000; Second Sec., Amman, 2000–03; seconded to Coalition Provisional Authy, Baghdad, 2003; seconded to State Dept, Washington, DC, 2004; Hd, NATO Section, FCO, London, 2005–06; Regl Conflict Advr, Addis Ababa, 2006–09; Ambassador to Guatemala and (non-resident) to Honduras and El Salvador, 2009–12; Hd, Emerging Powers Prog. and GREAT Britain Campaign, FCO, 2012–14; Partner, Hawthorn London, 2014–18. Young Global Leader, WEF, 2015. *Recreations:* travel, sports. *E:* juleschappell@londonandpartners.com.

**CHAPPELOW, Peter Raymond;** company chairman; *b* 23 March 1947; *s of* Raymond and Stella Chappelow and step *s of* James Tillett; *m* 1990, Tina Margaret Jones; two *d*. *Educ:* Hanson Grammar Sch., Bradford. Mktg Dir, Grattan, 1969–89; CEO, The Marketing Co., 1989–91; Dir, Racing Green, 1991–96; Man. Dir, Country Holidays, 1992–94; Dir, Thomson Travel Gp, 1994–2001. Chairman: Supreme Imports, 2003–06; M and M Direct, 2004–07; Bounty, 2004–07; School-Safe, 2004–08; Graphic-Inline, 2005–08; Advantage Healthcare, 2005–07; Kingswood, 2006–08; Travelsphere, 2006–12; Hotter, 2007–14; Baker Ross, 2008–10; CVS, 2010–; OKA, 2014–18; Pure Collection, 2014–; Linley & Simpson, 2018–. Member: Bd, English Tourism Council, 1995–2003; Cabinet Office Honours Cttee (Economy), 2005–13. *Recreations:* squash, tennis, golf, real music. *E:* chappelow@hotmail.com. *Clubs:* Lansdowne; Bradenton Country (Florida); Otley Golf, Ilkley Lawn Tennis and Squash.

**CHAPPLE, Prof. Iain L. C.,** PhD; FDSRCPSGlas, FDSRCSE; Professor of Periodontology, since 2001, and Head, School of Dentistry, and Director of Research, Institute of Clinical Sciences, since 2016, University of Birmingham; Honorary Consultant in Restorative Dentistry, Birmingham Community Healthcare NHS Foundation Trust (formerly South Birmingham Primary Care Trust), since 1996; *b* Sunderland, 4 June 1963; *s of* Arthur Chapple and Beryl Chapple; *m* 1990, Elizabeth Gough; two *d*. *Educ:* Univ. of Newcastle (BDS Dentistry 1986); Univ. of Birmingham (PhD 1993); Jt Royal Colls of Surgeons (Cert. of Completion of Specialist Trng Restorative Dentistry 1996). FDSRCPSGlas 1989; FDSRCSE 2004. House Surgeon, Newcastle Dental Hosp., 1986–87; Sen. House Surgeon, Maxillofacial Surgery, Sunderland Gen. Hosp., 1987–88; Registrar, Leeds Dental Inst. and St James's Univ. Hosp., Leeds, 1988–90; University of Birmingham: Clin. Lectr in Restorative Dentistry, 1990–96; Sen. Lectr, 1996–2001. Sec. Gen., Eur. Fedn of Periodontology, 2016–; Treas., Oral and Dental Res. Trust, 2009–. Charles Tomes Medal, RCS, 2012; Dist. Scientist, Internat. Assoc. of Dental Res., 2018. *Publications:* The Periodontium and Orthodontics in Health and Disease, 1996; Understanding Periodontal Diseases: assessment and diagnostic procedures in dental practice, 2002; Decision-Making for the Periodontal Team, 2003; Successful Periodontal Therapy: a non-surgical approach, 2003; Periodontal Management of Children and Adolescents, 2003; Periodontal Medicine in Practice, 2004; Contemporary Periodontal Surgery: an illustrated guide to the art behind the science, 2008; 19 textbook chapters; 202 scientific articles in peer-reviewed jls. *Recreations:* family, running, cycling, table tennis, musical theatre, theatre, walking, ski-ing. *Address:* School of Dentistry, University of Birmingham, 5 Mill Pool Way, Edgbaston, Birmingham B5 7EG. *T:* (0121) 466 5129. *E:* i.l.c.chapple@bham.ac.uk.

**CHAPPLE, Field Marshal Sir John,** GCB 1988 (KCB 1985); CBE 1980 (MBE 1969); DL; Vice Lord-Lieutenant of Greater London, 1997–2005; *b* 27 May 1931; *s of* C. H. Chapple; *m* 1959, Annabel Hill; one *s* three *d*. *Educ:* Haileybury; Trinity Coll., Cambridge (MA). Joined 2nd KEO Goorkhas, 1954; served Malaya, Hong Kong, Borneo; Staff Coll., 1962; jssc 1969; Commanded 1st Bn 2nd Goorkhas, 1970–72; Directing Staff, Staff Coll., 1972–73; Services Fellow, Fitzwilliam Coll., Cambridge, 1973; Commanded 48 Gurkha Infantry Bde, 1976; Gurkha Field Force, 1977; Principal Staff Officer to Chief of Defence Staff, 1978–79; Comdr, British Forces Hong Kong, and Maj.-Gen., Brigade of Gurkhas, 1980–82; Dir of Military Operations, 1982–84; Dep. Chief of Defence Staff (Progs and Personnel), 1985–87; C-in-C, UKLF, 1987–88; CGS, 1988–92; Gov. and C-in-C, Gibraltar, 1993–95. ADC Gen. to the Queen, 1987–92. Col, 2nd Goorkhas, 1986–94. Hon. Col, Oxford Univ. OTC, 1988–95. Chm., UK Trust for Nature Conservation in Nepal (formerly King Mahendra UK Trust), 1993–; Trustee, King Mahendra Trust, Nepal, 1993–2006. Mem. Council, WWF UK, 1984–99 (Trustee, 1988–93; Amb., 1999– (Chm. of Ambs, 2003–11)). Vice Patron: Army Mus. Ogilby Trust, 1995–; Gurkha Mus., 2003– (Trustee, 1973–2003); Nat. Army Mus., 2003– (Trustee, 1981–2002); President: Indian Mil. Hist. Soc., 1991–; Mil. Hist. Soc., 1992–2013; Soc. for Army Histl Res., 1993–2012; Trekforce, 1998–2006; Stoll Foundn (formerly Sir Oswald Stoll Foundn), 1998–2012; BSES Expeditions, 1999–2009; Cobra (formerly Bilimoria) Foundn, 2005–; Kipling Soc., 2008–11; Friends of Imperial War Mus., 2008–13; Friends of Nat. Army Mus., 2009–; Vice Pres., British Assoc. for Cemeteries in S Asia, 2013–. Pres., Combined Services Polo Assoc., 1991–2006. FZS (Life Fellow 1946; Pres., 1992–94); FRGS 1947 (Life Fellow 1967; Mem. Council, 1980–2000); FLS, FSA, FRSA. DL Greater London, 1996. KStJ. *Clubs:* Beefsteak, Cavalry and Guards, Army and Navy, Honourable Artillery Company.

**CHAPPLE, Keith,** FIET; Chairman, Alliance for Electronic Business, 2001–02; *b* 11 Aug. 1935; *s of* Reginald Chapple and Gladys Evelyn (*née* Foster); *m* 1962, Patricia Margaret Aitchison; one *s* two *d*. *Educ:* City of Bath Boys' Sch.; Rugby Coll. of Technol. FIET (FIEE 1984). Engrg Manager, Gen. Precision Systems Ltd, 1961–66; Sales Engr, SGS-Fairchild Ltd, 1966–69; Mktg Manager, SGS-Fairchild SpA (Italy), 1969–70; Sales Manager, Intel Corp. (Belgium), 1970–72; Chm. and Man. Dir, Intel Corp. (UK) Ltd, 1972–2000. President: Fedn of Electronics Industry, 1996–97 (Vice-Pres., 1997–99); Swindon Chamber of Commerce, 1996–98; Chm., EU Cttee, American Chamber of Commerce in Belgium, 1998–2001. Mem., Oxford Isis Br., Rotary Club. MCMI (MIMgt 1976); FRSA 1999. Hon. DTech Loughborough, 1986. *Recreations:* music, family. *Club:* Clarendon (Oxford) (Pres., 2003–04).

**CHAPPLE, His Honour Roger Graham;** a Circuit Judge, 2004–16; a Senior Circuit Judge, 2007–16; Deputy Judge of Upper Tribunal, Health, Education and Social Care Chamber, since 2017; *b* 28 Aug. 1951; *s of* Robert William Chapple and Elsie Mary Chapple (*née* Hubbard). *Educ:* Univ. of Leeds (LLB Hons). Called to the Bar, Gray's Inn, 1974, Bencher, 2009; in practice as a barrister, specialising in common law, 1974–94; Dep. JA, 1994–95; an Asst JAG, 1995–2004; Asst Recorder, 1999–2000, Recorder, 2000–04; Resident Judge: Middlesex Guildhall Crown Court, 2005–07; Inner London Crown Court, 2007–16; Sen. Judge, Sovereign Base Areas, Cyprus, 2007–16; Actg Judge, Grand Court of Cayman Is, 2017–. Mem., Parole Bd for England and Wales, 2016–. Hon. Recorder of Southwark, 2012–17. Trustee, Nat. Justice Mus. *Recreations:* travel, music (particularly opera), combining the two. *Club:* Athenæum.

**CHARALAMBOUS, Bambos;** MP (Lab) Enfield Southgate, since 2017. *Educ:* Chase Boys' Comp. Sch.; Tottenham Coll.; Liverpool Poly. (LLB 1990). Trainee solicitor, Saunders & Co., 1994–97; housing caseworker, Hodge Jones & Allen, 1998; solicitor, Housing Litigation Team, Hackney LBC, 1998–. Mem. (Lab) Enfield LBC, 1994–2018. Mem., Justice Cttee, H of C, 2017–. *Address:* House of Commons, SW1A 0AA.

**CHAREST, Hon. Jean;** Partner, McCarthy Tétrault, since 2013; Premier of Quebec, 2003–12; *b* 24 June 1958; *s of* Claude Charest and Rita Charest (*née* Leonard); *m* 1980, Michèle Dionne; one *s* two *d*. *Educ:* Univ. of Sherbrooke (LLB 1980). Called to the Bar, Quebec, 1981; Lawyer: Legal Aid Office, 1980–81; Beauchemin, Dussault, 1981–84. MP (PC), Sherbrooke, 1984–98; Asst Dep. Speaker, 1984–86; Minister of State for Youth, 1986–90; Dep. Govt Leader; Minister: for Fitness and Amateur Sport, 1988–90; of Envmt, 1991–93; Dep. Prime Minister, 1993; Minister: for Industry, Sci. and Technol., 1993; responsible for Federal Business Develt Bank, 1993. Mem. (Quebec L) for Sherbrooke, Nat. Assembly of Quebec, 1998–2012. Leader: Progressive Conservative Party, 1993–98; Quebec Liberal Party, 1998; Leader of Official Opposition, 1998–2003. *Address:* McCarthy Tétrault, Suite 2500, 1000 De La Gauchetière Street West, Montréal, QC H3B 0A2, Canada.

**CHARETTE, Janice Maria;** High Commissioner for Canada in the United Kingdom, since 2016; *b* Ottawa, 11 July 1962; *d of* Leo Villeneuve and Wilhelmina Villeneuve Emmerson; *m* 1984, Reginald Charette; one *s* one *d*. *Educ:* Carleton Univ. (BComm). Officer, Dept of Finance, Canada, 1984–89; Policy Analyst, Office of Privatization and Regulatory Affairs, 1989–91; Sen. Deptl Asst, Office of Minister of Finance, 1989–91; Sen. Policy Advr, Federal-Provincial Relns Office, 1991–92; Sen. Deptl Asst, Office of Minister of Finance, then Exec. Asst to COS, Office of Prime Minister, 1992–93; Coordinator, Base Closures Task Force, then Dir of Ops, Program Review Secretariat, later Exec. Dir, Strategic Projects Unit, Privy Council Office, 1994–96; Principal, Public Sector/Strategy Practice, Ernst & Young, 1996–97; COS, Leader of Progressive Conservative Party of Canada, 1997–98; Dir, Transition Team, Canada Pension Plan Investment Bd, 1998–99; Sen. Asst Dep. Minister, Policy Sector, Justice, 1999–2000; Privy Council Office: Asst Sec. to Cabinet (Priorities and Planning), then Dep. Sec. to Cabinet (Plans and Consultations), 2000–03; Associate Dep. Minister of Health, 2003–04; Deputy Minister: of Citizenship and Immigration Canada, 2004–06; of Human Resources and Skills Develt, 2006–10; of Intergovtl Affairs, 2010–12; Dep. Clerk of Privy Council and Associate Sec. to Cabinet, 2010–13; Clerk of the Privy Council and Sec. to Cabinet, 2014–16. *Address:* High Commission of Canada, Canada House, Trafalgar Square, SW1Y 5BJ.

**CHARKHAM, Rev. Rupert Anthony;** Vicar, Holy Trinity Church, Cambridge, since 2003; a Chaplain to the Queen, since 2016; *b* London, 15 July 1959; *s of* late Jonathan Philip Charkham, CBE and of Moira Elizabeth Frances Charkham; *m* 1987, Elizabeth Janet Sykes Wilson; one *s* one *d*. *Educ:* Haileybury Coll.; Univ. of Exeter (BA 1981); Wycliffe Hall, Oxford. Insurance Broker, Sedgwick plc, 1981–83. Ordained deacon and priest, 1989; Curate, St Aldates Church, Oxford, 1989–92; Rector, St Paul's Church, Salisbury, 1992–2003. *Recreations:* photography, classical music, playing piano, waking up at Lords. *Address:* Holy Trinity Church, Market Street, Cambridge CB2 3NZ. *T:* (01223) 355397. *E:* Rupert.charkham@htcambridge.org.uk. *Club:* MCC.
*See also* Baroness Shackleton of Belgravia.

**CHARKIN, Richard Denis Paul;** Executive Director, Bloomsbury Publishing plc, 2007–18; Founder, Mensch Publishing; *b* 17 June 1949; *s of* Frank Charkin and Mabel Doreen Charkin (*née* Rosen); *m* 1972, Susan Mary Poole; one *s* two *d*. *Educ:* Haileybury and ISC; Trinity College, Cambridge (MA); Harvard Business Sch. (AMP). Science Editor, Harrap & Co., 1972; Sen. Publishing Manager, Pergamon Press, 1973; Oxford University Press: Medical Editor, 1974; Head of Science and Medicine, 1976; Head of Reference,

1980; Managing Dir, Academic and General, 1984; Octopus Publishing Group (Reed International Books), 1988; Chief Exec., Reed Consumer Books, 1989–94; Exec. Dir, 1988–96 and Chief Exec., 1994–96, Reed Internat. Books; CEO, Current Science Gp, 1996–97; Chief Exec., Macmillan Ltd, 1998–2007. Mem., Bd of Mgt, John Wisden & Son, 1995–2009; non-executive Director: Scoot.com plc, 2000–02; Xrefer Ltd, 2000–04 (Chm., 2003–04); Melbourne University Publishing, 2006–08; Inst. of Physics Publishing, 2009–; Liverpool Univ. Press, 2017–; Amphio, 2017–; Cricket Properties Ltd, 2018–; Chm., Macmillan India Ltd, 2004–07. Executive Director: Internat. Publishers Assoc., 2011– (Vice Pres., 2013–14; Pres., 2015–16); Fedn of European Publishers, 2011–14. Member: Wkg Gp on UK Literary Heritage, 2006–12; Adv. Council, Inst. of English Studies, 2008–; Internat. Adv. Bd, Frankfurt Book Fair, 2008–. Vice-Pres., 2004–05, 2006–07, Pres., 2005–06, Publishers Assoc. Chm., 2007–08, Pres., 2015–20, Book Soc. (formerly Soc. of Bookmen). Vis. Fellow, Green College, Oxford, 1987; Vis. Prof., Univ. of the Arts, London (formerly London Inst.), 2003–; Hon. Sen. Res. Associate, UCL, 2016–20. Chm. Trustees, Whitechapel Art Gall., 1997–2000; Chm., Common Purpose UK, 1998–2007; Trustee, Common Purpose Charitable Trust, 2007– (Chair, 2017–); Mem. Strategy Adv. Cttee, BL, 2004–11. Mem., Editl Bd, Logos, 2019–. *Publications:* Charkin Blog: the archive, 2008; Top Tips for Wannabe CEOs, 2009. *Recreations:* music, cricket, eight grandchildren. *E:* rcharkin@gmail.com.

**CHARLEMONT**, 15th Viscount *cr* 1665 (Ire.); **John Dodd Caulfeild**; Baron Caulfeild of Charlemont 1620 (Ire.); *b* 15 May 1966; *o s* of 14th Viscount Charlemont and Judith Ann (*née* Dodd); *S* father, 2001; *m* 1991, Nadea Stella, *d* of Wilson Fortin; two *s*. *Heir:* s Hon. Shane Andrew Caulfeild, *b* 19 May 1996.

**CHARLES, Hon. Sir (Arthur) William (Hessin)**, Kt 1998; a Judge of the High Court of Justice, Queen's Bench Division, 2014–18 (Family Division, 1998–2014); President, Upper Tribunal (Administrative Appeals Chamber), 2012–18; Vice President, Court of Protection, 2014–18; President, First-tier Tribunal (War Pensions and Armed Forces Compensation Chamber), 2016–18; *b* 25 March 1948; *s* of late Arthur Attwood Sinclair Charles and May Davies Charles (*née* Westerman); *m* 1974, Lydia Margaret Ainscow; one *s* one *d. Educ:* Malvern College; Christ's College, Cambridge (MA Hons). Called to the Bar, Lincoln's Inn, 1971; Junior Counsel to the Crown (Chancery), 1986; First Junior Counsel to HM Treasury on Chancery Matters, 1989–98. *Recreation:* golf. *Clubs:* Hawks (Cambridge); Denham Golf.

**CHARLES, Caroline, (Mrs Malcolm Valentine)**, OBE 2002; fashion designer; Founder, Caroline Charles, 1963; *b* 18 May 1942; *m* 1966, Malcolm Valentine (*d* 2016); one *s* one *d. Educ:* Sacred Heart Convent, Woldingham; Swindon Art Sch. *Recreations:* gardening, tennis, theatre, travel. *Address:* 56/57 Beauchamp Place, SW3 1NY. *T:* (020) 7225 3197.

**CHARLES, Deborah Ann; Her Honour Judge Charles;** a Circuit Judge, since 2016; *b* 26 Aug. 1972; *d* of late Alan Charles and of Sheila Charles; *m* 2001, Paul Wiltshire; three *s. Educ:* Univ. of Warwick (BA Hons Eng. and Eur. Lit.); Middlesex Univ. (CPE Law). Called to the Bar, Lincoln's Inn, 1996; in practice as barrister, 1996–2016; a Recorder, 2012–16. *Recreations:* dance, family, theatre, travel. *Address:* Croydon Crown Court, The Law Courts, Altyre Road, Croydon CR9 5AB. *E:* croydoncrowncourt@hmcts.gsi.gov.uk.

**CHARLES, Jonathan James;** District Judge (Magistrates' Courts), South Wales, 2003–14; *b* 4 Sept. 1946; *s* of William Robert Charles and Elizabeth Charles; *m* 1970, Linda Ann Llewellyn; two *s* one *d. Educ:* Bridgend Boys' Grammar Sch.; Bristol Poly. Admitted Solicitor, 1980; Justices' Clerk: Merthyr Tydfil, 1981–85; Lower Rhymney Valley, 1985–88; Bridgend, 1988–97; Consultant Solicitor, Keith Evans & Co., Newport, 1997–2001; District Judge (Magistrates' Courts), Wolverhampton, 2001–03. Sec., Lord Chancellor's Adv. Cttee for Mid-Glamorgan, 1995–97. *Recreations:* travel, Rugby football, cricket.

**CHARLES, Michael Geoffrey A.;** *see* Audley-Charles.

**CHARLES, Nicola;** *see* Perry, J. A.

**CHARLES, Sir Robert (James)**, ONZ 2011; KNZM 1999; CBE 1992 (OBE 1972); golf professional, 1960–2010; *b* 14 March 1936; *s* of Albert Ivor Charles and Phyllis Irene Charles; *m* 1962, Verity Joan Aldridge; one *s* one *d. Educ:* Wairarapa Coll. Nat. Bank of NZ, 1954–60. Golf tournament victories include: NZ Open, 1954 (amateur), 1966, 1970, 1973; NZ PGA, 1961, 1979, 1980; Swiss Open, 1962, 1974; British Open, 1963; Atlanta Classic, USA, 1967; Canadian Open, 1968; Piccadilly World Match Play, England, 1969; John Player Classic and Dunlop Masters, England, 1972; S African Open, 1973; joined Senior Tour, 1986: 75 victories incl. Sen. British Open, 1989 and 1993. *Publications:* Left Handed Golf, 1965; The Bob Charles Left Handers Golf Book, 1985, 2nd edn 1993; Golf for Seniors, 1994. *Recreations:* farming, golf course architecture, tennis, boating. *Address:* Lytham, 456 Burnt Hill Road, Oxford 7495, New Zealand. *Club:* Christchurch Golf (New Zealand).

**CHARLES, Hon. Sir William;** *see* Charles, Hon. Sir A. W. H.

**CHARLES-EDWARDS, Prof. Thomas Mowbray**, DPhil; FBA 2001; Jesus Professor of Celtic, University of Oxford, 1997–2011, now Emeritus Professor of Celtic; Fellow of Jesus College, Oxford, 1997–2011, now Emeritus; *b* 11 Nov. 1943; *s* of Thomas Charles-Edwards and Imelda Charles-Edwards (*née* Bailey); *m* 1975, Davina Gifford Lewis (pen name Gifford Lewis) (*d* 2008); two *s. Educ:* Ampleforth Coll.; Corpus Christi Coll., Oxford (BA, MA, DPhil, Dip. Celtic Studies). Scholar, Dublin Inst. for Advanced Studies, 1967–69; P. S. Allen Jun. Res. Fellow in History, 1969–71, Fellow and Tutor in Modern Hist., 1971–96, Corpus Christi Coll., Oxford, Emeritus Fellow, 1997. Hon. MRIA 2006. *Publications:* Bechbretha (with Fergus Kelly), 1983; The Welsh Laws, 1989; Early Irish and Welsh Kinship, 1993; Early Christian Ireland, 2000; (ed) After Rome, 2003; The Chronicle of Ireland, 2006; Wales and the Britons, 350–1064, 2013; (with Julian Reid) Corpus Christi College, Oxford: a history, 2017. *Address:* 32 Harbord Road, Oxford OX2 8LJ. *T:* (01865) 556943; Corpus Christi College, Oxford OX1 4JF. *T:* (01865) 616789. *E:* thomas.charles-edwards@jesus.ox.ac.uk.

**CHARLESTON, Bryan**, PhD; Director, Pirbright Institute, since 2015; *b* Halton, 7 May 1959; *s* of Lewis Stuart Charleston and Annie Violet Charleston; *m* 1984, Janet Lesley Rust; two *s. Educ:* Royal Veterinary Coll., London (BVetMed 1982; PhD 1991); University Coll. London (MSc Molecular Biol. and Applied Biotechnol. 1988). MRCVS 1982. Wellcome Trust Vet. Post-doctoral Fellow, 1991–94; Inst. for Animal Health, subseq. Pirbright Inst., 1994–, Res. Gp Leader, 1994–2009. *Publications:* over 110 primary scientific papers and reviews in field of infectious disease res.; one patent. *Recreations:* cycling, photography. *Address:* Pirbright Institute, Ash Road, Pirbright, Woking, Surrey GU24 0LZ. *T:* (01483) 231001, *Fax:* (01483) 232448. *E:* bryan.charleston@pirbright.ac.uk.

**CHARLESWORTH, Anita Rose**, CBE 2017; Chief Economist, Health Foundation, since 2014; *b* 17 Jan. 1967; *d* of Terry and Jean Bird; *m* 1998, Nick Charlesworth; one *s* three *d. Educ:* PCL (BA Hons Social Sci.); Univ. of York (MSc Health Econs). Economist: DoH, 1990–95; HM Treasury, 1995–96; Associate Dir, SmithKline Beecham, 1996–98; Team Leader, Welfare to Work and various public services, 1998–2003, Dir, Public Services, 2003–06, HM Treasury; Dir, 2006–08, Dir, Evidence and Analysis Unit, and Chief Analyst, 2008–10, DCMS; Chief Economist, Nuffield Trust, 2010–14. Non-executive Director: Islington PCT, 2007–11; The Whittington, 2011–16. Hon. Prof., Health Services Mgt Centre, Univ. of Birmingham, 2017–. Trustee: Tommy's; Office of Health Econs. *Recreations:* spending time with my husband and children, camping, theatre, tennis. *Address:* The Health Foundation, 8 Salisbury Square, EC4Y 8AP. *T:* (020) 7257 8000, *Fax:* (020) 7257 8001. *E:* info@health.org.uk.

**CHARLESWORTH, Prof. Brian**, PhD; FRS 1991; FRSE; Senior Honorary Professorial Fellow, Institute of Evolutionary Biology (formerly Institute of Cell, Animal and Population Biology), University of Edinburgh, since 2010 (Royal Society Research Professor, 1997–2007; Professorial Fellow, 2007–10); *b* 29 April 1945; *s* of Francis Gustave Charlesworth and Mary (*née* Ryan); *m* 1967, Deborah Maltby (*see* D. Charlesworth); one *d. Educ:* Queens' Coll., Cambridge (BA Natural Scis; PhD Genetics). FRSE 2000. Post-Doctoral Fellow, Univ. of Chicago, 1969–71; Lectr in Genetics, Univ. of Liverpool, 1971–74; Lectr, 1974–82, Reader, 1982–84, in Biology, Univ. of Sussex; Prof., 1985–92, Chm., 1986–91, G. W. Beadle Distinguished Service Prof., 1992–97, Dept of Ecology and Evolution, Univ. of Chicago. President: Soc. for Study of Evolution, 1999; Genetics Soc., 2006–09; Eur. Soc. for Evolution and Biology, 2011–13. Fellow, Amer. Acad. of Arts and Scis, 1996. Foreign Associate, Nat. Acad. of Scis, USA, 2013. Darwin Medal, Royal Soc., 2000; Darwin-Wallace Medal, Linnean Soc., 2010; Thomas Hunt Morgan Medal, Genetics Soc. of America, 2015. *Publications:* Evolution in Age-Structured Populations, 1980, 2nd edn 1994; (with Deborah Charlesworth) Evolution: a very short introduction, 2003; (with Deborah Charlesworth) Elements of Evolutionary Genetics, 2010; papers in Nature, Science, Genetics, Genetical Res., Evolution, Amer. Naturalist, Procs Roy. Soc. *Recreations:* reading, listening to classical music, walking. *Address:* Institute of Evolutionary Biology, School of Biological Sciences, University of Edinburgh, Charlotte Auerbach Road, Edinburgh EH9 3FL.

**CHARLESWORTH, Prof. Deborah**, PhD; FRS 2005; FRSE; Professorial Research Fellow, Institute of Evolutionary Biology (formerly Institute of Cell, Animal and Population Biology), University of Edinburgh, 1997, now Emeritus Professor, *née* Maltby; *m* 1967, Brian Charlesworth, *qv;* one *d. Educ:* Newnham Coll., Cambridge (BA 1965; PhD 1968). FRSE 2001. MRC Jun. Res. Fellow, Univ. of Cambridge, 1968–69; Postdoctoral Fellow, Univ. of Chicago, 1969–71; Hon. Res. Fellow, Univ. of Liverpool, 1971–74; temp. Lectr, Univ. of Sussex, 1974–84; Res. Associate, 1984–88, Asst Prof., 1988–92, Prof., 1992–97, Univ. of Chicago. *Publications:* (with Jonathan Silvertown) Introduction to Plant Population Biology, 2001; (with Brian Charlesworth) Evolution: a very short introduction, 2003; (with Brian Charlesworth) Elements of Evolutionary Genetics, 2010. *Address:* Institute of Evolutionary Biology, University of Edinburgh, Charlotte Auerbach Road, Edinburgh EH9 3FL.

**CHARLESWORTH, His Honour Peter James;** a Circuit Judge, 1989–2004; *b* 24 Aug. 1944; *s* of late Joseph William Charlesworth and Florence Mary Charlesworth; *m* 1967, Elizabeth Mary Postill (*d* 2010); one *s* one *d. Educ:* Hull Grammar Sch.; Leeds Univ. (LLB 1965, LLM 1966). Called to the Bar, Inner Temple, 1966. In practice on North-Eastern Circuit, 1966–89; a Recorder, 1982–89. Judicial Mem., Parole Bd, 2005–09. Rugby Football League: Mem., Adv. Panel, 1994–2004; Sen. Mem., Judiciary Panel, 2004–07; Chairman: Disciplinary Cttee, 1998–; Operational Rules Tribunal, 2007– (Sen. Mem., 2016–). Member: Yorks Dales Nat. Park Authy, 2008–16 (Dep. Chm., 2012–13, Chm., 2013–16; Dep. Chm., Planning Cttee, 2009–12); Yorks Dales Local Access Forum, 2017– (Chm., 2018–). Member: Council, Bodington Hall, Univ. of Leeds, 2001–10; Council of Mgt, Yorkshire Dales Soc., 2005–13. Trustee: Yorks Dales Millennium Trust, 2003– (Chm., 2006–09); Yorks Dales Soc., 2016–. Mem., Bramhope Parish Council, 2006–10. *Recreations:* reading, Rugby League football (spectating), walking in the Yorkshire dales, travel. *Address:* 2 Goodwood, Ilkley, W Yorks LS29 0BY.

**CHARLETON, Peter Mitchel Andrews; Hon. Mr Justice Charleton;** a Judge of the Supreme Court of Ireland, since 2014; *b* 11 April 1956; *s* of John Charleton and Evelyne Charleton (*née* Butler); *m* 1988, Fiona Day; one *s* two *d. Educ:* St Mary's Coll., Rathmines; Trinity Coll. Dublin (BA (Mod) 1980). Called to the Bar, King's Inns, Dublin, 1979; in practice as barrister, 1979–2006; a Judge of the High Court of Ireland, Commercial Court Div., 2006–14. *Publications:* Controlled Drugs and the Criminal Law, 1986; Irish Criminal Law: cases and materials, 1992; Offences Against the Person, 1992; (with P. A. McDermott) Criminal Law, 1999; Lies in a Minor: an essay on evil and deceit, 2006; contrib. articles to law jls. *Recreations:* piano, reading, tennis. *Address:* Supreme Court, The Four Courts, Inns Quay, Dublin 7, Ireland. *T:* 8886000. *E:* supremecourt@courts.ie.

**CHARLIER, Rear Adm. Simon Boyce**, CBE 2013; FRAeS; Senior Defence and Political Advisor, MBDA UK, since 2013; *b* Pembury, Kent, 15 March 1958; *s* of Wing Comdr Dennis Claude Charlier, MC and Mary Pepper Charlier; *m* 1990, Margaret Anna Johns; two *s* one *d. Educ:* Dover Coll. FRAeS 2008. Royal Navy, 1978–: CO HMS Sheraton, 1990–91; Sen. Pilot, 815 Sqdn, 1992–95; CO HMS Northumberland, 1996–98; MoD DN Plans, then MoD NATO and EU Policy Directorate, 1998–2002; CO HMS Cornwall, 2002–04; COS (Aviation and Carriers) to C-in-C Fleet, and Rear Adm. Fleet Air Arm, 2008–10; Dir, Operating Airworthiness, Mil. Aviation Authy, 2010–12. ADC to the Queen, 2006–09. President: RN Equestrian Soc., 2008–; Armed Forces (formerly Combined Services) Equestrian Assoc., 2011–17; RN Winter Sports, 2012–13. *Recreations:* eventing, golf, mountain biking, ski-ing, clarinet. *Address:* Sydling St Nicholas, Dorset. *Club:* Naval and Military.

**CHARLTON, Alan**, CMG 1996; CVO 2007; HM Diplomatic Service, retired; trainer, writer; *b* 21 June 1952; *s* of Henry and Eva Charlton; *m* 1974, Judith Angela Carryer; two *s* one *d. Educ:* Nottingham High Sch.; Gonville and Caius Coll., Cambridge (MA); Leicester Univ. (PGCE); Manchester Univ. (BLing). Teacher, Gesamtschule, Gelsenkirchen, Germany, 1975–77; West Africa Dept, FCO, 1978–79; Amman, 1981–84; Near East and North Africa Dept, FCO, 1984–86; BMG Berlin, 1986–90; Dep. Chief, Assessments Staff, Cabinet Office, 1991–93; Head, Eastern Adriatic Unit, FCO, 1993–95; Bosnia Contact Group Rep., 1995–96; Political Counsellor, 1996–98, Dep. Hd of Mission, 1998–99, Bonn; Dep. Hd of Mission, Berlin, 1999–2000; Dir, SE Europe, FCO, 2001; Dir, Personnel, then HR Dir, FCO, 2002–04; Dep. Hd of Mission, Washington, 2004–07, and Ambassador to Orgn of American States, 2006–07; Ambassador to Brazil, 2008–13. Founder, British-Brazilian Conversa, 2014. Trustee: Canning House, 2017–; Canning Liby, 2018–. Mem., Adv. Bd, Brazil Inst., KCL, 2015–. Robin Humphreys Fellow, Inst. of Latin American Studies, Univ. of London, 2013–; Hon. Prof., Univ. of Nottingham, 2013–. Gov. and Advr, De Montfort Univ., 2013–; Gov., Sherborne Sch., 2013–18; Vice-Chm., Bd of Govs, Sherborne Qatar, 2015–18. Lectr on cruise ships incl. Black Watch, 2015, Queen Mary, 2015, Crystal Symphony, 2016, Black Watch, 2016, Crystal Cruises, 2017, Viking Sun, 2017, 2019. *Publications:* Shaking My Briefcase: diplomatic stories, 2016. *Recreations:* history, genealogy, football, cricket.

**CHARLTON, Alexander Murray;** QC 2008; *b* Herts, 13 March 1958; *s* of Murray Anthony Charlton and Pamela Charlton; *m* 1989, Emma Marie Clezy; one *s* two *d. Educ:* Tonbridge Sch.; St Andrews Univ. (MA Hons English); City Univ. (Dip. Law). Called to the Bar, Middle Temple, 1983. Contributing Ed., Professional Negligence and Liability. *Recreations:* sailing, ski-ing, Rugby. *Address:* 4 Pump Court, EC4Y 7AN. *T:* (020) 7842 5555, *Fax:* (020) 7583 2036. *E:* acharlton@4pumpcourt.com.

**CHARLTON, Sir Bobby;** *see* Charlton, Sir R.

**CHARLTON, Celia Anne;** *see* Dawson, C. A.

**CHARLTON, Prof. David,** PhD; FRS 2014; FInstP; Poynting Professor of Physics, University of Birmingham, since 2017 (Professor of Particle Physics, 2005–17); Spokesperson, ATLAS Collaboration at Large Hadron Collider, CERN, Geneva, 2013–17 (Deputy Spokesperson, 2009–13). *Educ:* Univ. of Oxford (BA 1st Cl Hons Physics 1985); Univ. of Birmingham (PhD Particle Physics 1989). FInstP 2009. Trigger, then Physics Coordinator, OPAL Collaboration, Large Electron-Positron Collider, CERN, Geneva, then at Univ. of Birmingham, 1989–2000; work on semiconductor tracker, 2001–04, on trigger, 2004–07, ATLAS, Univ. of Birmingham; Deputy Physics Coordinator, 2007–08, Physics Coordinator, 2008–09, ATLAS Collaboration, CERN. Richard Glazebrook Medal, Inst. of Physics, 2017. *Address:* School of Physics and Astronomy, University of Birmingham, Edgbaston, Birmingham B15 2TT.

**CHARLTON, Prof. Graham,** MDS; FDSRCSE; Professor of Conservative Dentistry, University of Edinburgh, 1978–91, now Emeritus Professor (Dean of Dental Studies, 1978–83); *b* 15 Oct. 1928; *s* of Simpson R. Charlton and Georgina (*née* Graham); *m* 1956, Stella Dobson (*d* 2005); two *s* one *d*. *Educ:* Bedlington Grammar Sch., Northumberland; St John's Coll., York (Teaching Cert.); King's Coll., Univ. of Durham (BDS); Univ. of Bristol (MDS). Teacher, Northumberland, 1948–52; National Service, 1948–50; Dental School, 1952–58; General Dental Practice, Torquay, 1958–64; University of Bristol: Lecturer, 1964–72; Cons. Sen. Lectr, 1972–78; Dental Clinical Dean, 1975–78. *Address:* 17 Northumberland Avenue, Forest Hall, Newcastle upon Tyne NE12 9NR.

**CHARLTON, Henry Marshall,** DPhil; FMedSci; FRS 1994; Reader in Neuroendocrinology, University of Oxford, 1990–2006, now Emeritus; Fellow of Linacre College, Oxford, 1970–2006, now Emeritus; *b* 10 March 1939; *s* of Joseph Douglass Charlton and Lilian Charlton; *m* 1965, Margaret Jeffrey; one *s* one *d*. *Educ:* Corpus Christi Coll., Oxford (MA, DPhil). Mem., MRC Neuroendocrinology Unit, Oxford, 1964–68; Lectr, Oxford Univ., 1968–90. Founder FMedSci 1998. *Publications:* contrib. scientific jls. *Recreations:* Real tennis, hill walking, gardening. *Address:* 61 Plantation Road, Oxford OX2 6JE. *T:* (01865) 554248.

**CHARLTON, John, (Jack),** OBE 1974; DL; Manager, Republic of Ireland Football Team, 1986–95; broadcaster; *b* 8 May 1935; *s* of late Robert and Elizabeth Charlton; *m* 1958, Patricia; two *s* one *d*. *Educ:* Hirst Park Sch., Ashington. Professional footballer, Leeds United, 1952–73; 35 England caps, 1965–70; Manager: Middlesbrough, 1973–77; Sheffield Wednesday FC, 1977–83; Newcastle United FC, 1984–85. Mem., Sports Council, 1977–82. DL Northumberland, 1997. *Publications:* Jack Charlton's American World Cup Diary, 1994; The Autobiography, 1996. *Recreations:* shooting, fishing, gardening.
*See also* Sir Robert Charlton.

**CHARLTON, John,** CBE 2007; JP; Director and Chairman, JCC Consultancy Ltd, 1996–2001; Chairman, University Hospital Birmingham NHS Foundation Trust (formerly NHS Trust), 1998–2006; *b* 11 Oct. 1940; *s* of late F. E. Charlton and Esther (*née* Lakin); *m* 1965, Carol Rosemary Shaw; two *s*. *Educ:* King Edward's Grammar Sch., Five Ways; Birmingham Univ. (BDS, LDS). DDH, DDPH 1970. Area Dental Officer, Oldbury, 1964–66; Dep. Chief Dental Officer, 1966, Chief Dental Officer, 1966–74, Warley; Area Dental Officer, Sandwell, 1974–82; Sandwell Health Authority: Dist Dental Officer, 1982–92; Consultant in Dental Public Health, 1992–96; Exec. Dir, 1993–96. Mem., Birmingham AHA, 1974–82; Dental Advr, W Midlands RHA, 1977–80; Chm., S Birmingham HA, 1981–91. Chm., Arden Gp Sec., Weoley Ward Lab. Party, 1967–83. Birmingham District Council: Mem. (Lab), Weoley Ward, 1980–82, Bartley Gn Ward, 1982–90; Hon. Alderman, 1990. Dir, British Fluoridation Soc., 1993–. Founder Member: Bournville Village Lessees Assoc.; SW Birmingham Assoc. for Advancement of State Educn; Lunar Soc., 1990. Trustee, University Hosp. Birmingham Charities, 1999–2011. Gov., Birmingham City Univ., 2007–15. JP Birmingham, 1992–2000. *Recreations:* racketball, travelling, politics. *Address:* 48 Middle Park Road, Selly Oak, Birmingham B29 4BJ. *T:* (0121) 475 7700.

**CHARLTON, Louise;** Co-founder, 1987, and Vice Chairman, since 2012, Brunswick Group LLP (Group Senior Partner, 2004–12); *b* Wakefield, 25 May 1960; *d* of John Charlton and Patricia Crawford (*née* Hulme); *m* 1985, Andrew Durant; two *s* one *d*. *Educ:* Univ. of Reading (BA Hons French). Non-exec. Dir, RPS Gp, 2008–18. Dir and Trustee, Natural Hist. Mus., 2006–14. *Recreations:* family, fishing, cinema, travel, reading. *Address:* c/o Brunswick Group LLP, 16 Lincoln's Inn Fields, WC2A 3ED. *T:* (020) 7396 7437. *E:* lcharlton@brunswickgroup.com.

**CHARLTON, Richard McKenzie,** AM 1996; FTS; FInstPet; Chairman, South East Water Ltd, 1995–2002; *b* 20 March 1935; *s* of Richard Rutherford Charlton and Yvonne Gladys Charlton (*née* McKenzie); *m*; two *s* two *d*. *Educ:* Sydney Univ. (BE Mining 1957; MESc 1959). Joined Shell as trainee petroleum engr, 1959: various posts in The Hague, UK, Nigeria, Kuwait, Trinidad and Brunei, 1959–75; Shell Australia: Gen. Manager, Exploration & Prodn, 1975–76; Exec. Dir, NW Shelf Project, 1976–80; Dir Ops, Shell UK Exploration & Prodn, Aberdeen, 1980–83; Chm., Shell Cos in Malaysia, 1983–86; Hd, Exploration & Prodn Ops & Liaison, The Hague, 1986–91; Chm. and Chief Exec. Officer, Shell Gp of Cos in Australia, 1991–95, retd. Director: Fujitsu Australia Ltd, 1994–97; Coles-Myer Ltd, 1995–2003; Hongkong Bank of Australia, 1996–2001; Chm., Adcorp Australia Ltd, 1999–2005. Chancellor, Univ. of Newcastle, NSW, 1994–2004. Chairman: Art Foundn, Victoria, 1994–97 (Dep. Chm., 1992–94); Hunter Symphony Orch., 1995–97; Australia-Malaysia Soc., 1995–. Chm., Nat. Basketball League, 1997–2000. Mem., Soc. Petroleum Engrs, 1971; FAICD; FInstD; FAIM. *Publications:* papers on petroleum industry. *Recreations:* horse racing, Rugby, snow ski-ing, surfing, tennis. *Clubs:* Melbourne, Australia (Melbourne); Victoria Racing, Moonee Valley Racing.

**CHARLTON, Sir Robert, (Sir Bobby),** Kt 1994; CBE 1974 (OBE 1969); Director, Manchester United Football Club, since 1984; *b* 11 Oct. 1937; *s* of late Robert and Elizabeth Charlton; *m* 1961, Norma Ball; two *d*. *Educ:* Bedlington Grammar Sch., Northumberland. Professional Footballer with Manchester United, 1954–73, for whom he played 751 games and scored 245 goals; FA Cup Winners Medal, 1963; FA Championship Medals, 1956–57, 1964–65 and 1966–67; World Cup Winners Medal (International), 1966; European Cup Winners medal, 1968. 100th England cap, 21 April 1970; 106 appearances for England, 1957–73. Manager, Preston North End, 1973–75. Mem., Cttee, FIFA. Founder, Find a Better Way, landmine charity, 2011. Hon. Freeman, City of Manchester, 2009. Hon. Fellow, Manchester Polytechnic, 1979. Hon. MA, 1985, DUniv, 2013, Manchester; Hon. D Hiroshima Univ. of Econs, 2013; Hon. LLD Bath, 2016. Sir Stanley Matthews Award, 2000; Lifetime Achievement Award, BBC Sports Personality of the Year, 2008; Lifetime Achievement Award, Laureus World Sports Awards, 2012; Order of Rising Sun, Gold Rays with Rosette (Japan), 2012; UEFA Order of Merit in Diamond, 2016.

*Publications:* My Soccer Life, 1965; Forward for England, 1967; This Game of Soccer, 1967; Book of European Football, Books 1–4, 1969–72; My Manchester United Years: the autobiography, 2007; My England Years: the autobiography, 2008; 1966: my world cup story, 2016. *Recreation:* golf.
*See also* John Charlton.

**CHARLTON-WEEDY, Maj. Gen. Michael Anthony,** CBE 1997 (OBE 1993); DL; Assistant Director, International Resilience, Cabinet Office, since 2017; *b* 11 June 1950; *s* of late Kenneth Charlton Weedy and of Valerie (*née* Reed); *m* 1979, Julia Redfern; two *s* one *d*. *Educ:* Millfield; Sandhurst. Commnd RA, 1971; sc 1982; CO 4th Regt RA, 1990–92 (despatches 1992); rcds 1995; Chief Faction Liaison Officer, Bosnia, 1995–96; Dir, OR (Land CIS), MoD, 1997–2000; Sen. Directing Staff (Army), RCDS, 2001–02; Dep. Adjt Gen., MoD, 2002–03. Chief Exec., Emergency Planning Coll., 2003–10, Dir, UK Resilience Trng, 2010–17, Cabinet Office. DL N Yorks, 2010. *Recreation:* country sports. *Address:* c/o HSBC, Kingsbridge, Devon TQ7 1PB.

**CHARMLEY, Prof. John Denis,** DPhil; FRHistS; Professor of History, and Pro Vice-Chancellor, Academic Strategy, St Mary's University, Twickenham, since 2016; *b* 9 Nov. 1955; *s* of John Charmley and Doris Charmley; *m* 1st, 1977, Ann Dorothea Bartlett (marr. diss. 1992); three *s* (incl. twins); 2nd, 1992, Lorraine Fegan (marr. diss. 2003; she *d* 2012); 3rd, 2004, Rachael Heap. *Educ:* Rock Ferry High Sch., Birkenhead; Pembroke Coll., Oxford (BA 1977; MA 1982; DPhil 1982). FRHistS 1987. University of East Anglia: Lectr in English Hist., Sch. of English and American Studies, 1979–92; Sen. Lectr in Hist., Sch. of Hist., 1992–96; Reader in Hist., 1996–98; Prof. of Modern History, 1998–2016; Head: Sch. of Hist., 2002–12; Sch. of Music, 2009–14; Interdisciplinary Inst. for the Humanities, 2014–16; Associate Dean, Res., 2005–10, Enterprise, 2010–16, Faculty of Arts and Humanities; Director: E Anglian Film Archive, 2010–14; Employability, 2011–16; Centre of E Anglian Studies, 2012–14. Fulbright Prof., Westminster Coll., Fulton, Mo, 1992–93. Chm., Mid-Norfolk Cons. Assoc., 2000–03; Election Agent: Mid Norfolk, 2000–02; S Norfolk, 2005, 2010. Dir, Low Carbon Innovation Fund, 2011–14. Pres., Norfolk and Norwich Br., Historical Assoc., 2000–16; Vice Chm., Cons. Hist. Gp, 2003–. Dir, Norwich Heritage and Regeneration Trust, 2009–16. Editor, History, 2010–15. Fellow, Historical Assoc., 1980. *Publications:* Duff Cooper, 1986; Lord Lloyd and the Decline of the British Empire, 1987; (ed) Descent to Suez: the diaries of Sir Evelyn Shuckburgh, 1987; Chamberlain and the Lost Peace, 1989; Churchill: the end of glory, 1993; Churchill's Grand Alliance, 1995; A History of Conservative Politics 1990–1996, 1996; Splendid Isolation?: Britain and the balance of power 1874–1914, 1999; The Princess and the Politicians, 2005; A History of Conservative Politics since 1830, 2008. *Recreations:* reading, walking, dining out. *Address:* Pro Vice-Chancellor's Office, St Mary's University, Waldegrave Road, Twickenham TW1 4SX. *T:* (020) 8240 4191. *Club:* Norfolk (Norwich).

**CHARNLEY, Sir (William) John,** Kt 1981; CB 1973; MEng, FREng, FRAeS, FRIN; *b* 4 Sept. 1922; *s* of George and Catherine Charnley; *m* 1945, Mary Paden (*d* 2007); one *s* one *d*. *Educ:* Oulton High Sch., Liverpool; Liverpool Univ. MEng 1945; FREng (FEng 1982); FRIN 1963; FRAeS 1966. Aerodynamics Dept, RAE Farnborough, 1943–55; Supt, Blind Landing Experimental Unit, 1955–61; Imperial Defence Coll., 1962; Head of Instruments and Electrical Engineering Dept, 1963–65, Head of Weapons Dept, 1965–68, RAE Farnborough; Head of Research Planning, Min. of Technol., 1968–69; Dep. Controller, Guided Weapons, Min. of Technology, later MoD (PE), 1969–72; Controller, Guided Weapons and Electronics, MoD (PE), 1972–73; Chief Scientist (RAF), 1973–77, and Dep. Controller, R&D Establishments and Res. C, MoD, 1977–77; Controller, R&D Establishments and Res., MoD, 1977–82. Director: Fairey Holdings Ltd, 1983–86; Winsdale Investments Ltd, 1985–88. Technical Advr, Monopolies and Mergers Commn, 1982; Specialist Advr to House of Lords Select Cttee on Science and Technology, 1986. Chm., Civil Aviation Res. and Develt Programme Bd, 1984–92; Mem., Air Traffic Control Bd, 1985–96. President: Royal Inst. of Navigation, 1987–90; European Orgn for Civil Aviation Equipment, 1993–97. Trustee, Richard Ormonde Shuttleworth Remembrance Trust, 1987–98. Hon. FRAeS 1992. Hon. DEng Liverpool, 1988. Bronze Medal, 1960, Gold Medal, 2001, RIN, Silver Medal, 1973, Gold Medal, 1980, RAeS. *Publications:* papers on subjects in aerodynamics, aircraft all weather operation, aircraft navigation, defence R&D. *Club:* Royal Air Force.

**CHARONE, Barbara;** Director, MBC PR, since 2000; *b* Chicago, 22 March 1952; *d* of Rose Charone. *Educ:* New Trier High Sch.; Northwestern Univ. (BA Hons). Journalist, Sounds mag., 1974–77; Dep. Ed., until 1977; freelance journalist, Daily Mail, Rolling Stone, Cream, Crawdaddy, 1979–81; with Warner Bros Records, 1981–2000, Dir of Press, until 2000. *Publications:* Life as a Rolling Stone: authorised biography of Keith Richards, 1978 (also German, Japanese and US edns). *Recreations:* tennis, Chelsea Football Club (season ticket holder, since 1980), music, theatre. *Address:* MBC PR, Warm Seas House, 23 Wellington Road, NW8 9SL. *T:* (020) 7449 4333. *E:* bc@mbcpr.com. *Clubs:* Groucho, Home House, Ivy.

**CHART, Jennifer Ann,** CBE 2004; Head Teacher, Portland College (formerly Portland School), Sunderland, 1996–2011; *b* 23 April 1951; *d* of John and Edna Hunt; *m*; one *s* one *d*. *Educ:* Univ. of Newcastle upon Tyne (Cert Ed SEN; Dip. Adv. Educnl Studies SEN; BPhil). Teacher, 1972–75; class teacher, 1980–89, Dep. Head Teacher, 1989–96, Ashleigh Sch., N Tyneside. Asst Sec., Thompson Hall (Tyneside MENCAP), 1968–72; Chm., N Tyneside Toy Liby, 1977–89. Trustee, Adventure Holidays (for disabled/disadvantaged children in Tyneside), 2001– (Chm. Trustees, 2012–). *Recreations:* outdoor activities, including walking and golf; needlecraft, painting. *Address:* Lianachan, Scott Street, East Hartford, Northumberland NE23 3AW.

**CHARTERIS,** family name of **Earl of Wemyss**.

**CHARTRES,** family name of **Baron Chartres**.

**CHARTRES, Baron** *cr* 2017 (Life Peer), of Wilton in the County of Wiltshire; **Richard John Carew Chartres,** GCVO 2019 (KCVO 2009); PC 1995; Bishop of London, 1995–2017; Prelate of the Order of the British Empire, 1995–2017, Prelate Emeritus, 2017; Dean of the Chapels Royal, 1995–2019; *b* 11 July 1947; *s* of Richard and Charlotte Chartres; *m* 1982, Caroline Mary, *d* of Sir (Charles) Alan McLintock; two *s* two *d*. *Educ:* Hertford Grammar Sch.; Trinity Coll., Cambridge (BA 1968; MA 1973; Hon. Fellow, 2017); Cuddesdon Theol Coll., Oxford; Lincoln Theol Coll. Ordained: deacon, 1973; priest, 1974; Asst Curate, St Andrew's, Bedford, Dio. of St Albans, 1973–75; Bishop's Domestic Chaplain, St Albans, 1975–80; Archbishop of Canterbury's Chaplain, 1980–84; Vicar, St Stephen with St John, Westminster, 1984–92; Area Bishop of Stepney, 1992–95. Chairman: C of E Church Bldgs Div. (formerly C of E Heritage Forum), 1998–2015; C of E Shrink the Footprint Envmtl Campaign, 2006–14; Actg Chm., Bd of Govs, Church Comrs, 2005–17. Gresham Prof. of Divinity, 1986–92. Six Preacher, Canterbury Cathedral, 1991–96. Founder and Chm. of Trustees, 1997–2011, St Ethelburga's Centre for Reconciliation and Peace (Life Pres., 2011); Co-Chm., Partner and Trustee, St Mellitus Coll., 2007–17. Ind. Mem., H of L Appts Commn, 2019–. Hon. Bencher, Middle Temple, 1998. Liveryman: Merchant Taylors' Co., 1997; Drapers' Co., 2000; Hon. Freeman: Weavers' Co., 1998; Leathersellers' Co., 1999; Woolmen's Co., 2000; Vintners' Co., 2001;

Grocers' Co., 2008; Water Conservators' Co., 2009; Pewterers' Co., 2015; Arts Scholars' Co., 2017. FSA 1999. Ehrendomprediger, Berliner Dom, 2001. BD Lambeth, 1983. Hon. DLitt London Guildhall, 1998; Hon. DD: London, 1999; City, 1999; Brunel, 1999; KCL, 2010. *Publications:* The History of Gresham College 1597–1997, 1998; Tree of Knowledge, Tree of Life, 2005. *Address:* House of Lords, SW1A 0PW.

**CHASE, Graham Frank;** Chairman, Chase and Partners, since 1995; President, Royal Institution of Chartered Surveyors, 2006–07; *b* 5 Jan. 1954; *s* of late Frank Augustus Chase, FSVA and of Joan Lynette Chase (*née* Hibbert); *m* 1980, Fiona Anderson Batley; two *d*. *Educ:* Mill Hill Sch.; Willesden Coll. of Professional Building (DipEstMan 1976). FRICS 1988; FCIArb 1999; FICPD 2005; Chartered Arbitrator 2009. Estates Surveyor, BBC, 1976–79; Estates Manager, Ladbroke Racing Ltd, 1978–79; Clive Lewis and Partners: Shops Surveyor, 1980–84; Partner, 1984–86; Dir, 1986–93; Dir, Colliers Erdman Lewis, 1993–94. Non-exec. Dir, Assura Gp Ltd (formerly Med. Property Investment Fund plc), 2003–10. Royal Institution of Chartered Surveyors: Chairman: Internat. Cttee, 1991–94; Metrication Cttee, 1993–94; Commercial Mkt Panel, 1995–99; Commercial Property Fac., 2000–04; Review Cttee, Code of Practice for Commercial Leases, 2004; Conflicts of Interest Working Gp, Dispute Resolution Service, 2010–11; Wkg Gp on Practice Statement and Guidance Notes for chartered surveyors actg as expert witnesses, RICS, 2012–. Representative: on H of C Select Cttee on future of shopping, 1993; Retail Property, 1996–99; on Modernising Stamp Duty Cttee, HM Treasury, 2003–04; to H of L Select Cttee on property taxation reform, 2004; Member: Code of Measuring Practice, 1993–94; Commercial Property Policy Panel, 1996–99. Royal Institution of Chartered Surveyors: President's Arbitrators Panel, 1998–; President's Ind. Experts Panel, 2000–; Leadership Team, 2004–07; Gen. Council, 1999–2000; Governing Council, 2001–03, 2004–; Nominations Cttee, 2010–; Gen. Practice Divl Pres., 2000; Vice Pres., 2004–05; Sen. Vice Pres., 2005–06; Valuers Registration Scheme Rev. Gp, 2014–15; Registered Valuer, 2014–. External Examiner: Northumbria Univ., 2008–12; Kingston Univ., 2009–13; Vis. Prof., Westminster Univ., 2015–. Pres., Assoc. of Town and City Mgt (formerly Assoc. of Town Centre Mgt), 2011– (Chm., 2008–11); Member: Shops Agents Soc., 1980–; Accessible Retail, 1987–; Investment Property Forum, 1995–; British Council of Shopping Centres, 1995– (Mem., Adv. Panel, 2012–); Property Industry Forum, 1996–99, Property Adv. Gp, 1999–2004, DETR; Property Forum, Bank of England, 2000–04; Empty Property Gp, ODPM, 2003–06; Bd, Expert Advisors in Planning Services, 2009–; Bd, Assoc. of British Crime Partnership, 2010–11. Pres., Old Millhillians in Property, 2014–. Jt Chm., Property Mktg Awards. Governor: Woodhouse VI Form Coll., 1996–2000; Mill Hill Sch., 2000–08; Trustee, Alford House Youth Club, Lambeth, 1999–; Trustee, Gov. and Dir of Bd, Coll. of Estate Mgt, 2004– (Chm., Educn and Res. Cttee, 2010–11); Trustee and Gov., King's Ely Sch., 2015–; Chm., Saracens Multi Acad. Trust, 2017–. Trustee: Maritime Heritage Mus., 2012–; Covent Garden Area Trust, 2014–18 (Chm., 2016–18). Freeman, City of London, 1991; Liveryman: Co. of Chartered Surveyors, 1991– (Master, 2014–15); Co. of Arbitrators, 2015–; Mem., Educn Cttee, 2016–; Mem. Ct, 2017–); Hon. Surveyor, Information Technologists' Co., 2019–. Mem., Old Millhillians Club, 1972–. Hon. Fellow, South Bank Univ., 2012. *Publications:* Business Tenancy Renewal Handbook, 2006; (ed and contrib.) Handbook of Rent Review, by Reynolds and Fetherstonhaugh, 2017. *Recreations:* Rugby, cricket, hockey, wine, food, disc jockey (as Fat Boy Fat), cycling, reading, sailing, UK history, UK geography, walking, curry. *Address:* 146 Green Dragon Lane, Winchmore Hill, N21 1ET. *T:* (020) 8364 0738; Chase and Partners LLP, 6 Maiden Lane, Covent Garden, WC2E 7NW. *T:* (020) 7462 1340. *E:* gfc@chaseandpartners.co.uk. *Clubs:* Old Millhillians Rugby Football (player, 1972–97); Saracens; Totteridge Millhillians Cricket (player, 1972–86); Arsenal Football; Winchmore Hill and Enfield Hockey (player, 1997–2012); Enfield Cricket; Hazelwood Lawn Tennis and Squash.

**CHASE, Prof. Howard Allaker,** PhD, ScD; FREng, CEng; CSci; FIChemE; Fellow and Director of Studies in Chemical Engineering, Magdalene College, Cambridge, 1984–2018, now Emeritus Fellow; Professor of Biochemical Engineering, University of Cambridge, 2000–15, now Emeritus Professor; Director of Research and Development, Enval Ltd, since 2005 (Chairman, 2005–08); *b* 17 Nov. 1954; *s* of Peter Howard Chase and Phoebe Farrar Chase (*née* Winn); *m* 1st, 1982, Penelope Jane Lewis (marr. diss. 2003); one *s* one *d*; 2nd, 2003, Dawn Christine Leeder. *Educ:* Westminster Sch., London; Magdalene Coll., Cambridge (Exhibnr; BA 1975, MA 1978; PhD 1979, ScD 2001, Cantab. CChem, MRSC 1987; FIChemE 1998; CEng 1998, FREng 2005; CSci 2005. Hirst Res. Centre, GEC, Wembley, 1971–72; University of Cambridge: Bye Fellow, Magdalene Coll., 1977; Res. Fellow, St John's Coll., 1978; post-doctoral res. asst, Dept of Biochem., 1978–81; Department of Chemical Engineering: Res. Associate, 1982–83; Royal Soc. Res. Fellow, 1983–84; Asst Lectr in Chem. Engrg, 1984–86; Lectr, 1986–96; Reader in Biochem. Engrg, 1996–2000; Hd of Dept, 1998–2006; Hd, Sch. of Technol., 2010–13; Magdalene College: Lectr in Natural Sci., 1984–2000; Tutor for Grad. Students, 1987–93; Sen. Tutor, 1993–96; Tutor, 1996–98. University College London: Vis. Prof., Dept of Chem. and Biochem. Engrg, 1991–92; Hon. Res. Fellow, 1993–. Mem. editl cttees and bds of scientific jls. External Examiner: Dept of Chem. Engrg, Univ. of Bradford, 2001–05; Dept of Chem. Engrg, Univ. of Newcastle upon Tyne, 2003–05; Dept of Biochem. Engrg, UCL, 2007–10; Dept of Chem. Engrg, Univ. of Manchester, 2008–10. Sir George Beilby Medal and Prize, Soc. Chem. Ind., RSC and Inst. Metals, 1993; BOC Envmtl Award, 2001, Donald Medal, 2010, IChemE Awards. *Publications:* contribs to scientific jls specialising in biotechnol., biochem. engrg, microbiol., envmtl engrg, waste treatment technol., etc. *Recreations:* food and drink, public transport, hot beaches. *Address:* Magdalene College, Cambridge CB3 0AG. *T:* (01223) 332128. *E:* hac1000@cam.ac.uk.

**CHASE, Prof. Mark Wayne,** PhD; FRS 2003; Keeper of the Jodrell Laboratory, since 2006, and Distinguished Senior Researcher, since 2014, Royal Botanic Gardens, Kew (Head of Molecular Systematics, 1992–2006); *b* 17 Jan. 1951; *s* of Wayne Marshall Chase and Helen Louise Chase (*née* Andrews). *Educ:* Paw Paw High Sch., Mich; Albion Coll., Albion, Mich. (BA Hons Hist. 1973); Univ. of Michigan, Ann Arbor (MS Biology 1980; PhD Botany 1985). Postdoctoral Res. Fellow, Dept of Biol., 1986–88, Lectr, Botany (Plant Systematics), 1987, Univ. of Mich., Ann Arbor; Asst Prof., 1988–92, Dir, Univ. Herbarium, 1990–92, Univ. of N Carolina, Chapel Hill. *Publications:* (ed jtly) Genera Orchidacearum: vol. 1, Introduction, Apostasioideae, and Cypripedioideae, 1999; vol. 2, Orchidoideae I, 2001; vol. 3, Orchideae II and Vanilloideae, 2003; (ed jtly) Plants of the World, 2017; contribs to books and many articles in professional jls. *Recreation:* gardening. *Address:* Jodrell Laboratory, Royal Botanic Gardens, Kew, Richmond, Surrey TW9 3DS.

**CHASE, Robert John;** HM Diplomatic Service, retired; Secretary General, International Aluminium Institute (formerly International Primary Aluminium Institute), 1997–2008; *b* 13 March 1943; *s* of late Herbert Chase and of Evelyn Chase; *m* 1966, Gillian Ann Chase (*née* Shelton); one *s* two *d*. *Educ:* Sevenoaks Sch.; St John's Coll., Oxford. MA (Mod. Hist.). Entered HM Diplomatic Service, 1965; Third, later Second Sec., Rangoon, 1966–69; UN Dept, FCO, 1970–72; First Sec. (Press Attaché), Brasilia, 1972–76; Hd Caribbean Section, Mexico and Caribbean Dept, FCO, 1976–80; on secondment as a manager to Imperial Chemical Industries PLC, 1980–82; Asst Hd, S American Dept, FCO, 1982–83; Asst Hd, Maritime, Aviation and Environment Dept, FCO, 1983–84; Counsellor (Commercial), Moscow, 1985–88; Overseas Inspector, FCO, 1988–89; Hd, Resource Mgt Dept, FCO, 1989–92; Consul-Gen., Chicago, 1993–96; Dir Gen. of Trade and Investment, and Consul-Gen., Milan, 1996–97. Chm., 2012–15, Vice Pres., 2015–, Westminster Decorative and Fine Arts Soc. *Recreations:* lecturing on military history, visiting historic sites, National Trust guide. *Address:* Flat 14, St Thomas Wharf, 78 Wapping High Street, E1W 2NB. *T:* (020) 7709 7376. *Club:* Oxford and Cambridge.

**CHASE, Rodney Frank,** CBE 2001; Chairman, Genel Energy plc (formerly Vallares), 2011–15; *b* 12 May 1943; *s* of late Norman Maxwell Chase, MBE and of Barbara Chase (*née* Marshall). *Educ:* Liverpool Univ. (BA Hons Hist.). Joined British Petroleum, 1964: various posts in marketing, oil trading and shipping distribn, 1964–81; Dir (Exploration and Prodn), BP Australia, 1982–85; Gp Treas., BP, 1986–89; Chief Exec. Officer, BP Exploration (USA), 1989–92; a Man. Dir, BP, 1992–98; Chm. and Chief Exec. Officer, BP America, 1992–94; Dep. Gp Chief Exec., BP, 1998–2003. Dep. Chm. and Sen. non-exec. Dir, Tesco plc, 2004–10 (non-exec. Dir, 2002–10); Chm., Petrofac, 2005–11; non-executive Director: BOC, 1995–2001; Diageo, 1999–2004; Computer Sciences Corp., 2001 (Chm., 2012); Nalco Co., 2005–11; Tesoro Corp., 2006; Hess Corp., 2013–; Sen. Advr, Lehman Brothers, 2003–08. Chm., UK Emissions Trading Gp, 1998–2002; Mem., Adv. Cttee on Business and the Envmt, 1993–2000. Mem., Amer. Petroleum Inst., 2000–02. *Recreations:* golf, ski-ing. *E:* rodney@rfchase.com.

**CHASE, Roger Robert;** Director of Personnel, BBC, 1989–91; *b* 19 Sept. 1928; *s* of Robert Joseph Chase and Lillian Ada (*née* Meredith); *m* 1958, Geraldine Joan Whitlamsmith; three *d*. *Educ:* Gosport Grammar Sch. Served RN, 1947–49. Joined BBC, 1944; Engrg Div., 1944–47 and 1949–67; Television Personnel Dept, 1967–74; Head, Central Services Dept, 1974–76; Controller, Personnel, Television, 1976–82; Dep. Dir of Personnel, 1982–89. Chm., BBC Club, 1979–91. *Recreation:* sailing. *Address:* Vernons, Vernons Road, Chappel, Colchester, Essex CO6 2AQ. *T:* (01206) 240143. *Club:* Royal Naval Sailing Association.

**CHATELIER, Trevor Mansel;** a District Judge (Magistrates' Courts), Liverpool, 2001–13; a Recorder, 2006–13; *b* 5 Oct. 1950; *s* of Dr Mansel Frederick Chatelier and Barbara Winifred Chatelier; *m* 2012, Cornelia Petronella Bax; one step *d*; twin *s* from a previous marriage. *Educ:* Uxbridge Tech. Coll.; Mid-Essex Tech. Coll. (LLB); Coll. of Law. Admitted solicitor, 1974; asst solicitor posts, 1974–79; Solicitor, Messrs Wilson Houlder & Co., Southall, 1979–2001; Actg Stipendiary Magistrate, Leeds Magistrates' Court, 1998–2001. Member: YHA; NT; Cruising Assoc.; Westerly Owners Assoc. *Publications:* Criminal Advocacy in the Magistrates' Court, 1981; article in Law Soc. Gazette. *Recreations:* coastal sailing, angling, cycle touring, camping, motor-cycling, classical guitar, languages, good food, good company and going out. *T:* 07802 208955. *E:* smart.alec@sky.com.

**CHATER, Prof. Keith Frederick,** PhD; FRS 1995; Head, Department of Molecular Microbiology, John Innes Centre, 2001–04, Emeritus Fellow, 2004–18; *b* 23 April 1944; *s* of Frederick Ernest Chater and Marjorie Inez Chater (*née* Palmer); *m* 1966, Jean Wallbridge; three *s* one *d*. *Educ:* Trinity Sch. of John Whitgift, Croydon; Univ. of Birmingham (BSc 1st Cl. Hons Bacteriol. 1966; PhD Genetics 1969). John Innes Institute, later John Innes Centre: research scientist in Streptomyces genetics, 1969–2018; Dep. Head, 1989–96, Head, 1998–2001, Dept of Genetics. Fulbright Scholar, Harvard Univ., 1983; Hon. Professor: UEA, 1988–2016; Chinese Acad. of Scis, Inst. of Microbiology, 1999; Huazhong Agricl Univ., Wuhan, 2000; Univ. of Newcastle upon Tyne, 2006–09. *Publications:* (jtly) Genetic Manipulation of Streptomyces: a laboratory manual, 1985; (ed jtly) Genetics of Bacterial Diversity, 1989; (jtly) Practical Streptomyces Genetics, 2000. *Recreations:* painting, gardening, bird-watching. *Address:* 6 Coach House Court, Norwich NR4 7QR. *T:* 07966 006092. *E:* keithchater@yahoo.com.

**CHATER, Prof. Nicholas John,** PhD; FBA 2012; Professor of Behavioural Science, since 2010, and Head, Behavioural Science Group, since 2011, Warwick Business School, University of Warwick; *b* Salisbury, 8 July 1965; *s* of Robert John Chater and Dorothy Chater; partner, Louie Fooks; two *d*. *Educ:* Trinity Coll., Cambridge (BA 1986); Univ. of Edinburgh (PhD 1990). Lecturer in Psychology: UCL, 1989–90; Univ. of Edinburgh, 1990–94; Lectr in Exptl Psychol., Univ. of Oxford, 1994–96; Fellow, Somerville Coll., Oxford, 1994–96; Professor of Psychol., Univ. of Warwick, 1996–2005; of Cognitive and Decision Scis, UCL, 2005–10. Fellow, Cognitive Sci. Soc., 2011. *Publications:* with Michael Oaksford: Rationality in an Uncertain World, 1998; Rational Models of Cognition, 1998; Bayesian Rationality, 2007; The Probabilistic Mind, 2008; Cognition and Conditionals, 2010; (with Morten Christiansen) Connectionist Psycholinguistics, 2001; (with Susan Hurley) Perspectives on Imitation, 2005; (with Morten Christiansen) Creating Language, 2016; The Mind is Flat, 2018. *Recreations:* reading, philosophy. *Address:* Behavioural Science Group, Warwick Business School, University of Warwick, Coventry CV4 7AL. *E:* nick.chater@wbs.ac.uk.

**CHATTERJEE, Prof. (Vengalil) Krishna (Kumar),** FRS 2017; FRCP, FMedSci; Professor of Endocrinology, University of Cambridge, 1998–2018, now Emeritus; Fellow of Churchill College, Cambridge, since 1990; *b* 23 April 1958. *Educ:* Wolfson Coll., Oxford (BA, BM BCh). FRCP 1996. SHO, Hammersmith, Brompton and St Thomas' Hosps, 1983–85; Registrar, Hammersmith Hosp., 1985–87; Res. Fellow, Massachusetts Gen. Hosp., 1987–90; Wellcome Sen. Fellow and Hon. Cons. Physician, Addenbrooke's Hosp., 1994–. NIHR Sen. Investigator, 2009–; Wellcome Trust Sen. Investigator, 2011–. FMedSci 2000. *Recreations:* travel, music. *Address:* Wellcome-MRC Institute of Metabolic Science, University of Cambridge, Metabolic Research Labs, PO Box 289, Addenbrooke's Hospital, Hills Road, Cambridge CB2 0QQ.

**CHATTERJI, Prof. Joya,** PhD; FBA 2018; Professor of South Asian History, University of Cambridge, since 2014; Fellow, Trinity College, Cambridge, since 2007; *b* New Delhi, 27 Feb. 1964; *d* of Jognath Chatterji and Valerie Ann Sawyer; one *s*; *m* 2004, Anil Seal. *Educ:* Lawrence Sch., Sanawar; Lady Sri Ram Coll., Delhi Univ. (BA Hons); Trinity Coll., Cambridge (BA 1987; PhD 1992). Jun. Res. Fellow, Trinity Coll., Cambridge, 1989–94; Lectr in Hist., 2000–04, Reader in Hist., 2004–07, LSE; Lectr in Hist., 2007–09, Reader in Hist., 2009–14, Univ. of Cambridge. Editor, Modern Asian Studies, 2009–. *Publications:* Bengal Divided, 1995; The Spoils of Partition, 2007; (ed jtly) The Routledge Handbook of the South Asian Diaspora, 2013; (jtly) The Bengal Diaspora, 2016; Partition's Legacies, 2018; articles in jls incl. Modern Asian Studies, Comparative Studies in Soc. and Hist. *Recreations:* reading, writing, cooking. *Address:* Trinity College, Cambridge CB2 1TQ. *T:* (01223) 338577. *E:* jc280@cam.ac.uk.

**CHATTERTON DICKSON, Robert Maurice French;** HM Diplomatic Service; High Commissioner to Bangladesh, since 2019; *b* 1 Feb. 1962; *s* of Capt. W. W. F. Chatterton Dickson, RN and Judith Chatterton Dickson (*née* French); *m* 1995, Teresa Bargielska Albor; two *d* and one step *s* one step *d*. *Educ:* Wellington Coll.; Magdalene Coll., Cambridge (Exhibnr; BA 1984, MA 1988). Investment analyst, subseq. instnl and internat. portfolio manager, Morgan Grenfell Asset Mgt Ltd, 1984–90; entered FCO, 1990; 2nd Sec. (Chancery/Inf.), Manila, 1991–94; First Secretary: FCO, 1994–97; Washington, 1997–2000; FCO, 2000–03; Counsellor, FCO, 2003–04; Ambassador to Republic of Macedonia, 2004–07; Hd of Counter-Terrorism Policy, later Counter Terrorism, Dept,

2007–10; Consul Gen., Chicago, 2010–13; Dep. Ambassador to Afghanistan, 2013–15; Dir, Foreign Policy, 2015–17, Dir, Secretariat and Progs, 2017–18, Nat. Security Secretariat, Cabinet Office (on secondment); Addnl Dir, Western Balkans Prog., FCO, 2018–19. Chm., Diplomatic Service Assoc., 2002–04. *Recreations:* history, recreational running, messing about in boats. *Address:* Foreign and Commonwealth Office, King Charles Street, SW1A 2AH. *Club:* Bosham Sailing (W Sussex).

**CHATTY, Prof. Dawn**, PhD; FBA 2015; Professor of Anthropology and Forced Migration, University of Oxford, 2010–15, now Emeritus; Fellow, St Cross College, Oxford, 2002–15, now Emeritus; *b* New York, 16 Oct. 1947; *d* of Diaeddine Chatty and Eleonora Swanson (*née* Dorfman); *m* 1979, Oliver Nicholas Patrick Mylne; one *s* one *d*. *Educ:* Univ. of Calif, Los Angeles (BA Anthropol.; PhD Anthropol.); Inst. of Social Studies, The Hague (MA Social Develt). Fulbright Prof., Univ. of Damascus, Syria, 1977–79; UNDP Tech. Assistance Expert, Oman, 1979–88; Associate Prof., Sultan Qaboos Univ., Oman, 1988–94; Dulverton Sen. Fellow, Queen Elizabeth House, Univ. of Oxford, 1994–2002; Reader of Anthropol. of Forced Migration, 2002–10, Dir, Refugee Studies Centre, 2011–14, Univ. of Oxford. Chair, Commn on Nomadic Peoples, Internat. Union of Anthropol and Ethnol Scis, 1998–2013. Founder, Dana Declaration on Conservation and Nomadic Peoples, Jordan, 2002. Pres., Syrian Studies Assoc., 2002–05. *Publications:* From Camel to Truck, 1986, 2nd edn 2013; Mobile Pastoralist: development planning in the Sultanate of Oman, 1996; Displacement and Dispossession in the Modern Middle East, 2010; Syria: the making and unmaking of a refuge state, 2018. *Recreations:* travel, photography, hill walking. *Address:* Refugee Studies Centre, University of Oxford, Queen Elizabeth House, 3 Mansfield Road, Oxford OX1 3TB. *T:* (01865) 281715, *Fax:* (01865) 281230. *E:* dawn.chatty@qeh.ox.ac.uk.

**CHATWANI, Jaswanti;** Legal Chairman, Immigration Appeal Tribunal, 2000–03 (Vice President, 1992–2000); *b* 23 Nov. 1933; *d* of Keshavji Ramji Tanna and Shantaben Tanna; *m* 1953, Rajnikant Popatlal Chatwani; one *s* one *d*. *Educ:* Government Sch., Dar-es-Salaam, Tanzania. Called to the Bar, Lincoln's Inn, 1959; attached to Chopra & Chopra, Legal Practice, Mwanza, Tanzania, 1959–60; in private practice, Zanzibar, 1960–65; Sec. and Legal Aid Counsel, Tanganyika Law Soc., 1965–68; in private practice, Dar-es-Salaam, Tanzania, 1968–70; Sen. Immigration Counsellor, UKIAS, 1971–78; Legal Officer, then Sen. Complaints Officer, CRE, 1979–87; part-time Adjudicator, Immigration Appeals, 1980–87, full-time Adjudicator 1987–92. Mem., Judicial Studies Bd, Ethnic Minorities Adv. Cttee, 1991–94. *Recreations:* walking, travel, reading.

**CHATWIN, (John) Malcolm**, CEng, FIET; Chairman, Warrington Homes, since 2003; *b* 19 July 1945; *s* of John Edward Chatwin and Louie Valerie Chatwin; *m* 1969, Elizabeth Joy West; one *s* two *d*. *Educ:* City of London Sch.; University College London (BSc(Eng) Elect. Eng.). Operations Engr, LEB, 1969–73; Commercial Economist, Seeboard, 1973–77; Pricing Policy Manager, Electricity Council, 1977–79; Dep. Commercial Dir and Commercial Dir, N of Scotland Hydro-Electric Bd, 1980–87; Yorkshire Electricity: Dir, Business Planning, 1987–90; Commercial Dir, 1990–92; Chief Exec., 1992–97. Dir, Electricity Assoc., 1992–97; Chm., Regional Power Generators, 1992–94, 1996–97. Dir, Century Inns, 1995–99. *Recreations:* ski-ing, sailing.

**CHAUDHRY, Mahendra Pal;** MP, Fiji, 1987, 1992–99 and 2001–06; Prime Minister of Fiji, 1999–2000; Leader of the Opposition, 2004–06; *b* 2 Sept. 1942; *m* Virmati Frank; two *s* one *d*. *Educ:* Tavua Indian Sch.; Shri Vivekananda High Sch. Assistant, Res. Lab., Emperor Gold Mines, 1959–60; Office of the Auditor Gen., 1960–75 (Sen. Auditor, 1973–75); General Secretary: Fiji Public Service Assoc., 1970–99; Nat. Farmers' Union, 1978–. Asst Nat. Sec., 1975–87, Nat. Sec., 1988–92, Fiji TUC. Minister: of Finance, April–May 1987; of Finance, Public Enterprises, Sugar Industry and Information, 1999–2000; of Finance, Nat. Planning, Sugar Industry and Public Utilities (Water and Energy) in Interim Admin, 2007–08. Fiji Labour Party: Founder Mem., 1985; Asst Sec.-Gen., 1985–94; Sec.-Gen. and Parly Leader, 1994–.

**CHAUDHURI, Prof. Kirti Narayan**, PhD; FBA 1990; External Professor of History, European University Institute, Florence; *b* 8 Sept. 1934; *s* of late Nirad C. Chaudhuri, CBE, FRSL, FRAS; *m* 1961, Surana Chaudhuri; one *s*. *Educ:* privately in India; London Univ. (BA Hons Hist., 1959; PhD 1961). Derby Reginald Schol., London Univ., 1959–61; School of Oriental and African Studies, London University: Res. Fellow in Econ. Hist., 1961–63; Lectr in Econ. Hist. of Asia, 1963–74; Reader, 1974–81; Prof. of Econ. Hist. of Asia, 1981–91; Chairman: S Asia Area Studies Centre, 1982–85; History Exam. Bd, 1982–87; Vasco da Gama Prof. of Hist. of European Expansion, European Univ. Inst., Florence, 1991–99; Director: Centre for Comparative Studies, Provence, 1999; Gallery Schifanoia, Mas de San Vitale, 1999. FRHistS 1993; MAE 1994. D. João de Castro Internat. History Prize. Producer, director and scriptwriter: Four Nights in Tunis (audio play), 2007; Twelve Days of Summer in Benito Juarez (audio story), 2008; Jaguar of Chaco (film story), 2010; Dolor de Rosita Valdez (film story), 2010; Night Blooming Flower of the Poison Tree (film story in three parts), 2011; Nostos Algos? Nostalgia? (film story), 2012; Guilt from a Night of the Full Moon (film story), 2013; producer, director, script and screenplay writer: Downfall and Redemption of Dr John Faustino (film story), 2010; Striped Fish and Cosmic Turtle: General in his Equinoctial Maze (narrative film), 2016; dir and script writer: Dr Johannes von Faust: a kinematic interlace (feature film), 2013; Personal journey to the equinoctial regions of New Continent (narrative film), 2014; Fiesta de Buleria: a day under the Cordillera in the life of a failed revolutionary (feature film), 2014; Kurdistan: at War or Peace 2017? (documentary), 2017; producer, director, screenplay writer and narrator: Alexander von Humboldt, Racist German, Scientist or Liberal European? (documentary), 2018; Humboldt and the Amazon Forests, Part II, 1799–1803 and 2004–2013 (documentary), 2018; War & Peace between the Euphrates, Syria and the High Caucasus (film story), 2018; producer, director, script writer and narrator: Syria: In a Global Conflict? (documentary), 2017; Syria Lebanon Iraq War (documentary), 2017; producer, director and screenplay writer: Themes on Surrealism before Surrealism: a fireball summer in the short life of Comte de Lautréamont (art film), 2019; Mellifluence: a handful of honey: yielding architecture or what they saw. Themes on Surrealism (art film), 2019; A Nuclear Event at Three Roman Towns: a tale of absolute terminus (art film), 2019. *Publications:* The English East India Company: the study of an early joint-stock company 1600–1640, 1965; The Economic Development of India under the East India Company 1814–58: a selection of contemporary writings, 1971; The Trading World of Asia and the English East India Company 1660–1760, 1978; Trade and Civilisation in the Indian Ocean: an economic history from the rise of Islam to 1750, 1985; Asia before Europe: the economy and civilisation in the Indian Ocean from the rise of Islam to 1750, 1990; From the Atlantic to the Arabian Sea, 1995; The Dream of the Unicorn in the Year of Geneviève, 1996; A Mediterranean Triptych, 1998; The Landscape of the Corvo, 1998; (ed jtly) Historia Expansão Portuguesa, 5 vols, 1998–99; The Sacrifice, 2000; Venezia, the Vision of the Blind Gladiator, 2000; Interlace, Variations on Ornamental Space, 2001; Polyphony, 2002; Notre Dame sous la Neige, 2002; Sea & Civilisation: a visual archive, 3 vols, 2003; Veneto, 2003; Capri: resurrection of the drowned Aphrodite, 2003; Avignon in July: a midnight and two afternoons in the life of Lady Georgina Saville, 2004; Form in an Arid Land: Sahara and the Maghreb, 2004; Tango in San Telmo, 2005; A Purple Land, 2005; Tree of Blood, 2005; Cleopatra in Tripolitania: an imaginary text in images, 2005; Islam and Space: a transcontinental visual narrative of space and architectonics, 3 vols, 2005; Roman Mediterranean and the Passion of Perpetua, 2006; Forms of Perception: point, straight line, curve, solid, monochrome, and colour, 2006; Garden of the Tuareg, 2006; Bodas de Sangre, 2006; Jaguar of Chaco, 2007; Entre Primavera y Invierno, 2007; Bailarinas del Camba, 2007; Jane and Idle Days in Patagonia, 2007; El Asesino del Rio Grande, 2007; South America 2008: Cinco Tierras, 2009; contribs to Econ. Hist. Rev., Eng. Histl Rev., Jl of European Econ. Hist., Jl of RAS, Modern Asian Studies, TLS. *Recreations:* exploration, making professional feature films, printing and designing limited edition livres d'artistes, collecting 20th century graphic prints, wine tasting and gastronomic cuisine. *E:* kncfilmproduction@gmail.com. *Club:* Athenæum.

**CHAUNY de PORTURAS-HOYLE, Gilbert;** Director General, Treaties and other International Agreements, Ministry of Foreign Affairs, Peru, 2011–13; *b* Lima, 8 March 1944; *m* 1971, Carmen Loreto y Laos; two *s* one *d*. *Educ:* UNI (BA Arch 1966); Pontificia Universidad Católica, Peru (BA Arts 1967); Peruvian Diplomatic Acad. (Dip. and Licentiate Internat. Relns 1969). Joined Peruvian Diplomatic Service, 1970: Third Secretary: Under-Secretariat for Political and Diplomatic Affairs, Dept of Europe, Africa, Asia and Oceania, Min. of Foreign Affairs, Lima, 1970–72; Bogotá, 1972–75; Second Sec., Perm. Representation to Internat. Orgns, Geneva, and Consul Gen., Geneva and Vaud, 1975–78; First Secretary: Head: of Ceremonials, Protocol Dept, 1978–79; OAS Dept, Dept for Internat. Orgns and Confs, 1979–80; Counsellor, Hd of Political Dept, Washington, 1980–84; Minister Counsellor: and Consul Gen., Toronto, 1984–86; Asst Dir for America, Min. of Foreign Affairs, 1986–88; Minister, Dir of Aeronautical and Space Affairs, Min. of Foreign Affairs, 1988–89 (Delegate to Internat. Civil Aviation Orgn, Montreal); Minister and Hd of Chancery, London, and Perm. Rep. to IMO, 1989–93 (Chargé d'Affaires, March–June 1989 and March–Nov. 1993); Ambassador: Dir Gen. of Special Pol Affairs, Min. of Foreign Affairs, 1993–95; to Austria, and concurrently to Slovenia, Slovakia and Turkey, 1995–2000; Perm. Rep. of Peru to UN Office, Vienna, UNIDO, IAEA and Comp. Nuclear Test-Ban Treaty Orgn, 1995–2000; Ambassador to UK and to Ireland, 2000–01; Nat. Dir for Frontier Develt, Min. of Foreign Affairs, 2002–03; Under-Sec. for Internat. Cultural Affairs, Min. of Foreign Affairs, 2003–05; Ambassador: to Hungary, and concurrently to Croatia and Bosnia-Herzegovina, 2005–07; to The Netherlands, Perm. Rep. to OPCW, and Gov. to Common Fund for Commodities, 2007–08; to Kingdom of Sweden, and concurrently to Republic of Iceland, 2008–11, and to Kingdoms of Denmark and Norway, 2009–11. President, National Commission: for Antarctic Affairs, 1993–95; for Biol Diversity, 1993–95; for Climatic Changes and Ozone, 1993–95. Member: Peruvian Inst. for Genealogical Res., 1962–; Peruvian Inst. Aerospace Law, 1994–2000. Mem., Confrérie des Chevaliers du Tastevin. Pres., Peruvian Assoc. of Kts of SMO, Malta, 1973–. Kt 1988, Grand Cross of Merit, 2001, SMO Malta; Kt Comdr with Star, Constantinian Order of St George, 2000. Kt Comdr, Orden de Bogotá (Colombia), 1974; Official: Order of San Carlos (Colombia), 1975; Orden de Isabel la Católica (Spain), 1978; Grand Cross, Orden del Condor de los Andes (Bolivia), 1995; Gold Grand Cross, Honour Badge for Merit (Austria), 2000; Grand Cross, Orden al Mérito por Servicios Distinguidos (Peru), 2005; Grand Cross, Order of Polar Star (Sweden), 2010. *Publications:* contrib. books and periodicals on internat. diplomatic relns, protocol, hist. of art, hist., and genealogy. *Recreations:* art and old map collecting, historical and genealogical research, tennis, bridge. *Address:* Lima Los Cedros 475, San Isidro, Lima 27, Peru. *T:* (1) 4410941, 0990319390, *Fax:* (1) 2214555; Ministerio de Relaciones Exteriores del Peru, Jirón Lampa 545, Lima 1, Peru. *T:* (1) 2042400. *Clubs:* Canning, Nacional, Regatas, Lima Golf (Lima); St Johanns (Vienna); Haagsche Club-Plaats Royaal (The Hague); Nya Sällskapet (Stockholm).

**CHAVEZ, Victor Manuel**, CBE 2015; Chief Executive, Thales UK, since 2011; *b* Barrow-in-Furness, 19 Jan. 1963; *s* of Victor Chavez and Janet Chavez; *m* 1992, Fiona Mary Black; two *d*. *Educ:* Barrow Boys' Grammar Sch.; Univ. of York (BSc Hons Phys 1984); Univ. of Surrey (MSc Satellite Engrg and Telecommunications 1993). Systems Engr, GEC Telecommunications, 1984–86; Principal Consultant, Systems Designers Ltd, 1986–92; Business Manager, EDS-Scicon, 1992–99; Business Develt Dir, Thomson-CSF, 1999–2000; Thales UK: Sales and Mktg Dir, 2000–09; Dep. Chief Exec., 2009–11. Pres., techUK, 2013–15; Member: Bd, Engineering UK, 2014–; Manufacturing Council, CBI, 2017–. *Recreations:* cycling, photography, hiking, travel. *Address:* Thales UK, 4 Carlton Gardens, SW1Y 5AA.

**CHAYTOR, Sir Bruce Gordon**, 9th Bt *cr* 1831, of Croft, Yorkshire and Witton Castle, Durham; *b* 31 July 1949; *s* of Herbert Gordon Chaytor and Mary Alice Chaytor (*née* Craven); *S* kinsman, Sir George Reginald Chaytor, 8th Bt, 1999, but his name does not appear on the Official Roll of the Baronetage; *m* 1st, 1969, Rosemary Lea Stephen (marr. diss. 1978); one *s* one *d*; 2nd, 2011, Donnalaine Marie Hruby. *Heir: s* John Gordon Chaytor, *b* 17 Jan. 1973. *Address:* 2785 Sooke Road, Victoria, BC V9B 1Y8, Canada.

**CHAYTOR, David Michael;** *b* 3 Aug. 1949; *m*; one *s* two *d*. *Educ:* Bury Grammar Sch.; Royal Holloway Coll., London (BA Hons 1970); Leeds Univ. (PGCE 1976); London Univ. (MPhil 1979). Sen. Staff Tutor, Manchester Coll. of Adult Educn, 1983–90; Hd, Dept of Continuing Educn, Manchester Coll. of Arts and Technology, 1993–97. Mem., Calderdale MBC, 1982–97. Contested (Lab) Calder Valley, 1987, 1992. MP (Lab) Bury North, 1997–2010.

**CHAZOT, Georges-Christian;** international consultant; *b* 19 March 1939; *s* of late Raymond Chazot, banker and Suzanne Monnet; *m* 1962, Marie-Dominique Tremois, painter; one *s* two *d*. *Educ:* Lycée Gauthier; Lycée Bugeaud Algiers; Ecole Polytechnique, Paris; Univ. of Florida (MSEE 1964); Internat. Marketing Inst., Harvard, 1972; Wharton Sch., Univ. of Philadelphia. Joined Schlumberger Group, 1962; Electro-Mechanical Research, USA, 1962–65; Schlumberger Instrument and Systems, 1965–76; Alcatel Alsthom, 1977–92; Saft, 1977–88; Chairman and Chief Executive: Saft, 1984–88; Alcatel Business Systems, 1989–92; ADIA France, 1992–93; Gp Man. Dir, Eurotunnel, 1994–2000; Chairman: Prosegur France, 2003–05; Eurotunnel Development Ltd, 2002–04. Mem. Adv. Council, X-PM Transition Partners, 2001–; Mem. Bd, Giat Industries, 2002–10. Dir, Actim, Paris, 1988–92. Treas., Fondn Franco Japonaise Sasakawa, 1990–; Vice-Chm., FM Radio Notre-Dame, 2001–; Dir and former Dir, internat. cos. Mem., Adv. Council, World Economic Forum, Switzerland, 1983–87; Vice-Pres., French Chamber of Commerce in London, 1995–2002. Chairman: Hôpital Paris St Joseph Foundn, 2008–; Assoc. Marie-Thérèse, 2017. Chevalier, Ordre de St Grégoire Le Grand, 2007; Officier, Ordre National du Mérite (France), 1996; Légion d'honneur, 2015 (Chevalier, 1990). *Recreation:* sailing. *Address:* 24 rue des Réservoirs, Versailles 78000, France. *E:* georgeschazot@orange.fr. *Club:* UNCL (Union Nationale pour la Course au Large) (Paris).

**CHEADLE, Rear Adm. Richard Frank**, CB 2005; DL; Member (Ind), West Devon Borough Council, since 2015; *b* 27 Jan. 1950; *s* of Marcus and Marion Cheadle; *m* 1972, Sonja Arntzen; one *s* one *d*. *Educ:* Peter Symonds Sch.; RNEC (MSc Marine Engrg). Joined RN, 1968; engrg appts in nuclear submarines, Renown, Dreadnought and Splendid, 1975–85; Dep. Sqn Engr, 1985–87; Hd, In Service Submarine Propulsion Systems, 1987–90; jsdc 1991–92; CSO (Nuclear), Rosyth, 1992–95; Director: Naval Manpower Develt, 1995–97; Nuclear Propulsion, 1997–2000; Comdr, Devonport Naval Base,

2000–02; COS, Second Sea Lord and Chief Naval Engrg Officer, 2003; Controller of the Navy and Dir, Land Maritime, 2003–06. Pres., SSAFA Plymouth, 2016–. DL Devon, 2008. *Recreations:* painting, golf, repairing broken machinery.

**CHECKETTS, Sir David (John),** KCVO 1979 (CVO 1969; MVO 1966); Squadron Leader, retired; an Extra Equerry to the Prince of Wales, since 1979; *b* 23 Aug. 1930; 3rd *s* of late Reginald Ernest George Checketts and late Frances Mary Checketts; *m* 1958, Rachel Leila Warren Herrick; one *s* three *d*. Flying Training, Bulawayo, Rhodesia, 1948–50; 14 Sqdn, Germany, 1950–54; Instructor, Fighter Weapons Sch., 1954–57; Air ADC to C-in-C Malta, 1958–59; 3 Sqdn, Germany, 1960–61; Equerry to Duke of Edinburgh, 1961–66, to the Prince of Wales, 1967–70; Private Sec. to the Prince of Wales, 1970–79. *Recreation:* ornithology. *Address:* Forges, Fulford Barnyard, Cullompton, Devon EX15 1TJ. *T:* (01884) 839779.

**CHECKETTS, Guy Tresham,** CBE 1982; Deputy Chairman and Managing Director, Hawker Siddeley International, 1975–90, retired; *b* 11 May 1927; *s* of John Albert and Norah Maud Checketts; *m* 1957, Valerie Cynthia Stanley; four *s*. *Educ:* Warwick Sch.; Birmingham Univ. (BScEng Hons). British Thompson Houston Co., Rugby, 1948–51; Brush Group, 1951–57; Hawker Siddeley International, 1957–90. Chm., SE Asia Trade Adv. Gp, 1979–83; Mem., BOTB, 1981–84. *Recreation:* sailing. *Club:* Royal Over-Seas League.

**CHECKLAND, Sir Michael,** Kt 1992; Director-General, BBC, 1987–92; Chairman, Higher Education Funding Council for England, 1997–2001; *b* 13 March 1936; *s* of Leslie and Ivy Florence Checkland; *m* 1st, 1960, Shirley Frances Corbett (marr. diss. 1983); two *s* one *d*; 2nd, 1987, Sue Zetter. *Educ:* King Edward's Grammar Sch., Five Ways, Birmingham; Wadham Coll., Oxford (BA Modern History; Hon. Fellow, 1989). FCMA; CCMI. Accountant: Parkinson Cowan Ltd, 1959–62; Thorn Electronics Ltd, 1962–64; BBC: Senior Cost Accountant, 1964; Head of Central Finance Unit, 1967; Chief Accountant, Central Finance Services, 1969; Chief Accountant, Television, 1971; Controller, Finance, 1976; Controller, Planning and Resource Management, Television, 1977; Director of Resources, Television, 1982; Dep. Dir-Gen., 1985; Director: BBC Enterprises, 1979–92 (Chm., 1986–87); Visnews, 1980–85; Nynex Cable Communications, 1995–97. President: Commonwealth Broadcasting Assoc., 1987–88; Birmingham & Midland Inst., 1994; Vice-President: RTS, 1985–94 (FRTS 1987); EBU, 1991–92; Methodist Conf., 1997; Mem., ITC, 1997–2003. Chairman: NCH, 1991–2001; Brighton Internat. Fest., 1993–2002; CBSO, 1995–2001; Director: Nat. Youth Music Theatre, 1992–2002; Wales Millennium Centre, 2003–09. Chm., Horsham YMCA, 2005–11. Trustee, Reuters, 1994–2009. Governor: Westminster Coll., Oxford, 1993–97; Birkbeck Coll., 1993–97; Brighton Univ., 1996–97 and 2001–07 (Chm., 2002–06); Wesley House, 2002–08. *Recreations:* sport, music, travel. *Address:* Orchard Cottage, Park Lane, Maplehurst, near Horsham, West Sussex RH13 6LL.

**CHECKLEY, Prof. Stuart Arthur,** FRCPsych, FRCP; Consultant Psychiatrist, Maudsley Hospital, 1981–2001; Dean, 1989–2001, and Professor of Psychoneuroendocrinology, 1994–2001, now Emeritus, Institute of Psychiatry; Assistant Principal, King's College London, 2001–03; *b* 15 Dec. 1945; *s* of Arthur William George Checkley and Hilda Dorothy Checkley; *m* 1970, Marilyn Jane Evans, BA; one *s* one *d*. *Educ:* St Albans Sch.; Brasenose Coll., Oxford (BA, BM BCh). FRCP, FRCPsych. House appts, London Hosp. and St Charles Hosp., 1970–73; Registrar in Psych., London Hosp., 1973–74; Maudsley Hospital: Registrar, 1974–76; Hon. Sen. Registrar, 1977–78; Hon. Consultant, 1980–81; research worker, supported by Wellcome Trust, 1978–81; Mapother Travelling Fellow, USA, 1979; Institute of Psychiatry: Sen. Lectr, 1979–81; Sen. Lectr, Metabolic Unit, 1985–94. Non-exec. Dir, S London and Maudsley NHS Trust, 1999–2001. FKC 2001. *Publications:* (ed) The Management of Depression, 1998; papers on treatment of depression and hormones in relation to depression. *Recreation:* bird watching.

**CHEDZEY, Ven. Derek Christopher;** Archdeacon of Hereford, since 2018; *b* 1967. *Educ:* Trinity Coll., Bristol (BA 1993); Univ. of Wales (MA 2012). Ordained deacon, 1993, priest, 1994; Curate: Holy Spirit, Bedgrove, 1993–95; St Mary the Virgin, Haddenham, with Cuddington, Kingsey and Aston Sandford, 1995–98; Team Vicar, St Birinus, High Wycombe, 1998–2001; Deanery Trng Officer and Curate, Exe Valley Team, Tiverton, 2001–04; Priest-in-charge, St John the Baptist, Frenchay and All Saints, Winterbourne Down, Bristol, 2004–06; Diocese of Bristol: Dir of Lay Ministries, 2004–08; Warden of Readers, 2004–15; Advr for Initial Ministerial Educn, 2008–15; Asst Archdeacon, 2013–15; Dir of Ordinands and Hd, Ministry Develt, 2015–18; Canon Residentiary, Bristol Cathedral, 2015–18. Hon. Curate, St Mary, Yate, 2009–15; Hon. Canon, Bristol Cathedral, 2011–15. *Address:* The Diocesan Office, The Palace, Hereford HR4 9BL. *T:* (01432) 373316. *E:* derek.chedzey@hereford.anglican.org.

**CHEEMA-GRUBB, Hon. Dame Bobbie,** DBE 2015; **Hon. Mrs Justice Cheema-Grubb;** a Judge of the High Court, Queen's Bench Division, since 2015; Presiding Judge, South Eastern Circuit, since 2019; *b* Derby, 6 Oct. 1966; *d* of Darshan Singh and Harbans Kaur Cheema; *née* Parmjit-Kaur Cheema; changed name by deed poll to Bobbie Cheema-Grubb, 2015; *m* 1990, Russell Paul Stephen Grubb; one *s* two *d*. *Educ:* City of Leeds Sch., Leeds; King's Coll. London (LLB Hons; AKC). Called to the Bar, Gray's Inn, 1989; barrister in private practice, specialising in criminal and administrative law, 1989–2015; a Recorder, 2006–15; a Dep. High Court Judge, 2010–15; QC 2013; Jun. Treasury Counsel, 2006–11; Sen. Treasury Counsel, 2011–15. *Recreations:* art, architecture, theatre, walking. *Address:* Royal Courts of Justice, Strand, WC2A 2LL. *E:* susan.riley2@justice.gov.uk.

**CHEESMAN, Dr Clive Edwin Alexander;** Richmond Herald of Arms, since 2010; Earl Marshal's Secretary, since 2012; *b* London, 21 Feb. 1968; *s* of Wilfrid Henry Cheesman, architect, and Elizabeth Amelia Cheesman (*née* Hughes), bio-chemist; *m* 2002, Roberta, *d* of Ciro Suzzi Valli, of Chiesanuova, San Marino. *Educ:* Latymer Upper Sch.; Oriel Coll., Oxford (BA 1st Cl. Hons Lit.Hum. 1989; MA 1995); Univ. degli Studi, San Marino (PhD 1993). Called to the Bar, Middle Temple, 1996 (Harmsworth Maj. Exhibnr and Astbury Schol.); British Museum: Special asst, 1990–91, 1994; full-time curator, 1995; pt-time curator, 1995–2000; Rouge Dragon Pursuivant, Coll. of Arms, 1998–2010. Lectr in Roman Hist., Birkbeck Coll., London, 2002–03. Advr, Portable Antiquities Scheme, DCMS, 2006–; Mem., Lord Chancellor's Forum on Histl Manuscripts and Academic Res., 2011–. Trustee: Oriel Coll. Develt Trust, 2006–; Thames Explorer Trust, 2006–. FSA 2011. *Publications:* (with J. H. C. Williams) Rebels, Pretenders and Imposters, 2000; (ed) The Armorial of Haiti, 2007. *Address:* College of Arms, 130 Queen Victoria Street, EC4V 4BT. *T:* (020) 7236 2191, *Fax:* (020) 7248 6448. *E:* richmond@college-of-arms.gov.uk.

**CHEESMAN, Colin;** Chief Executive, Cheshire County Council, 1998–2002; *b* 8 Nov. 1946; *s* of John Hamilton Cheesman and Elsie Louisa Cheesman; *m* 1969, Judith Mary Tait; one *s* three *d*. *Educ:* Alleyn's Sch., Dulwich; Liverpool Univ. (LLB Hons). Admitted Solicitor, 1971. Portsmouth County BC, 1969–71; Notts CC, 1971–73; joined Cheshire CC, 1973; Group Director: Support Services, 1991–94; Information and Leisure Services, 1994–97. Clerk, Cheshire Lieutenancy and Sec. to Cheshire Adv. Cttee, 1998–2002; Sec. and Solicitor, Cheshire Fire Authy, 1998–2002; Sec., Cheshire Probation Bd, 1998–2002. Mem. Court, Univ. of Liverpool, 1999–2002. Gov., Walton Centre NHS Foundn Trust, 2012–. Hon. Sec., Parkinson's Disease Soc., 2007–15. *Recreations:* reading, hill walking, keeping fit, theatre. *Address:* 7 Radnor Drive, Westminster Park, Chester CH4 7PS. *T:* (01244) 678866.

**CHEETHAM, Anthony John Valerian;** Founder and Chairman, Head of Zeus Ltd, since 2012; *b* 12 April 1943; *s* of Sir Nicolas John Alexander Cheetham, KCMG; *m* 1st, 1969, Julia Rollason (marr. diss.); two *s* one *d*; 2nd, 1979, Rosemary de Courcy (marr. diss.); two *d*; 3rd, 1997, Georgina Capel. *Educ:* Eton Coll.; Balliol Coll., Oxford (BA). Editorial Dir, Sphere Books, 1968; Managing Director: Futura Publications, 1973; Macdonald Futura, 1979; Chm., Century Publishing, 1982–85; Man. Dir, Century Hutchinson, 1985; Chm. and Chief Exec., Random Century Gp, 1989–91; Chief Exec., Orion Books, subseq. Orion Publishing Gp Ltd, 1991–2003; Consultant to CEO of Random House UK and Publisher of Knopf, USA, 2004–05; Chm. and Publisher, Quercus Publishing plc, 2005–09; Associate Publisher and Dir, Grove Atlantic Ltd, 2009–11. *Publications:* Richard III, 1972. *Recreations:* gardening, oak trees, forestry, early medieval history. *Address:* 8 Morpeth Mansions, Morpeth Terrace, SW1P 1ER. *T:* (020) 7834 3684.

**CHEETHAM, Prof. Anthony Kevin,** FRS 1994; FRSC; FIMMM; Distinguished Research Fellow, Department of Materials Science and Metallurgy, University of Cambridge, since 2017; Research Professor, Materials Research Laboratory, University of California at Santa Barbara, since 2018; Professor of Solid State Chemistry, Royal Institution, 1986–2007; Emeritus Student, Christ Church, Oxford, since 1991; *b* 16 Nov. 1946; *s* of Norman James Cheetham and Lilian Cheetham; *m* 1984, Janet Clare (*née* Stockwell); one *s* one *d*, and one *d* (one *s* decd) from a previous marriage. *Educ:* Stockport Grammar Sch.; St Catherine's Coll., Oxford (Hon. Scholar); Wadham Coll., Oxford (Sen. Scholar). BA (Chem.) 1968; DPhil 1971. FIMMM 2008. University of Oxford: Cephalosporin Fellow, Lincoln Coll., 1971–74; Lectr in Chemical Crystallography, 1974–90; Tutor in Inorganic Chem., Christ Church, 1974–91; Reader in Inorganic Materials, 1990–91; University of California at Santa Barbara: Prof. of Materials, 1991–2007; Prof. of Chemistry, 1992–2007; Dir, Materials Res. Lab., 1992–2004; Dir, Internat. Center for Materials Res., 2004–07; Emeritus Prof., 2007–18; University of Cambridge: Prof. of Materials Sci., 2007–08; Goldsmiths' Prof. of Materials Sci., 2008–17; Fellow, Trinity Coll., Cambridge, 2007–14 (Hon. Fellow, 2017). Visiting Professor: Arizona State Univ., 1977; Univ. of California, Berkeley, 1979; Dist. Vis. Prof., Nat. Univ. of Singapore, 2016–. Blaise Pascal Internat. Res. Prof., Paris, 1997–99; Vis. Foreign Scientist, Amer. Chem. Soc., 1981; Francqui Internat. Chair, Brussels, 2001–02; Raman Chair, Indian Acad. Scis, 2011. Humphrey Davy Lectr, Royal Soc., 2003. Mem. Council, 2010–12, Treas. and Vice-Pres., 2012–17, Royal Soc. Member: Scientific Council, Institut Laue-Langevin, Grenoble, 1988–90; Scientific Advisory Board: Max-Planck-Institut für Festkörperforschung, Stuttgart, 1999–; Center for Advanced Interdisciplinary Res. in Materials Sci., Universidad de Chile, Santiago, 2000–; Materials Creation Trng Prog., Integrative Grad. Educn and Res. Traineeship, UCLA, 2002–06; Nat. High Magnetic Field Lab., Florida, 2003–07; Dept of Chem., Southampton Univ., 2004–09; African Insts for Sci. and Technol., 2004–; Dept of Chem., UCL, 2006–; Internat. Centre for Materials Sci., Bangalore, 2008–; International Advisory Board: CSIRO Div. of Manufacturing and Infrastructure Technol., Australia, 2003–06; Nat. Inst. for Materials Res., Tsukuba, Japan, 2006–; King Abdulla Univ. of Sci. and Technol., Saudi Arabia, 2010–. Dir, Gen. Funds Investment Trust plc, 1984–87; Founder, NGEN Enabling Technologies Fund, 2001. Science Adviser: Bd, Unilever, 2000–08; Deutsche Bank Asset Mgt, 2009–. MAE 2009. Member: German Nat. Acad. Scis (Leopoldina), 2011; German Acad. of Engrg, 2013; Foreign Member: Indian Nat. Acad. of Scis, 1998; Mongolian Acad. of Scis, 2008; Foreign Fellow, Pakistan Acad. of Scis, 1997; Distinguished Fellow, Nehru Center for Advanced Scientific Res., Bangalore, 1999; Fellow (formerly Associate Fellow), World Acad. of Scis (formerly Third World Acad. of Scis, then Acad. of Scis for the Developing World), 1999; Fellow, Amer. Acad. of Arts and Scis, 2014; Hon. Fellow, Singapore Nat. Acad. of Sci., 2018; Foreign Fellow, Indian Nat. Acad., 2019. Dr hc Versailles Saint-Quentin-in-Yvelines, 2006; Hon. DSc: St Andrews, 2011; Tumkur, India, 2011; Warwick, 2015. Corday-Morgan Medal and Prize, 1982, Solid State Chemistry Award, 1988, Structural Chemistry Award, 1996, RSC; Bonner Chemiepreis, Univ. of Bonn, 2001; (jtly) Somiya Award, Internat. Union of Materials Res. Socs, 2004; Wolfson Merit Award, Royal Soc. 2007; Advanced Investigator Award, Eur. Res. Council, 2008; Leverhulme Medal, Royal Soc., 2008; TWAS Medal Lectr, Acad. of Scis for the Developing World, 2011; Körber Eur. Sci. Award, Trustee Cttee, Körber Foundn, 2011; Platinum Medal, IMMM, 2011; Nyholm Prize for Inorganic Chem., RSC, 2012; Chemical Pioneer Award, Amer. Inst. of Chemists, 2014; Humboldt Res. Award, 2014; Internat. Gold Medal for Materials Sci. and Technol., Materials Res. Soc. of India, 2017; Basolo Medal, Northwestern Univ., 2017. *Publications:* Solid State Chemistry: techniques (with P. Day), 1986; Solid State Chemistry: compounds (with P. Day), 1992; contribs to sci. jls. *Recreations:* international affairs, golf, cricket. *Address:* Department of Materials Science and Metallurgy, University of Cambridge, 27 Charles Babbage Road, Cambridge CB3 0FS. *T:* (01223) 334300. *E:* akc30@cam.ac.uk; (home) 1695 East Valley Road, Montecito, CA 93108, USA. *T:* (805) 5651211.

**CHEETHAM, Julia Ann;** QC 2015; a Recorder, since 2008; *b* Niagara Falls, Canada, 21 Sept. 1967; *d* of Dr John Cheetham and Pamela Cheetham; *m* 1991, Marc Paul Bernard Albert Willems, *qv*; two *s* one *d*. *Educ:* Wilmslow High Sch.; Nottingham Univ. (LLB Hons). Called to the Bar, Lincoln's Inn, 1990. *Recreations:* travel, cooking, cycling. *Address:* Deans Court Chambers, 24 St John's Street, Manchester M3 4DF. *T:* (0161) 214 6000. *Club:* Bareges Cycling.

**CHEETHAM, Prof. Juliet,** OBE 1995; Member, Mental Health Tribunal for Scotland, since 2005; Sessional Inspector, Care Inspectorate, Scotland (formerly Social Work Inspection Agency), since 2006; *b* 12 Oct. 1939; *d* of Harold Neville Blair and Isabel (*née* Sanders); *m* 1965, Christopher Paul Cheetham; one *s* two *d*. *Educ:* St Andrews Univ. (MA); Oxford Univ. (Dip. in Social and Admin. Studies). Qual. social worker. Probation Officer, Inner London, 1960–65; Lectr in Applied Social Studies, and Fellow of Green Coll., Oxford Univ., 1965–85; Prof. and Dir, Social Work Res. Centre, Stirling Univ., 1986–95, now Prof. Emeritus; Contract Res. Co-ordinator, SHEFC, 1996–97; Develt Officer, E Lothian Council, 1998; Social Work Comr, Mental Welfare Commn for Scotland, 1998–2005. Member: Cttee of Enquiry into Immigration and Youth Service, 1966–68; Cttee of Enquiry into Working of Abortion Act, 1971–74; NI Standing Adv. Commn on Human Rights, 1974–77; Central Council for Educn and Trng in Social Work, 1973–89; Commn for Racial Equality, 1977–84; Social Security Adv. Cttee, 1983–88; CNAA Social Scis Cttee, 1989–91; ESRC Res. Resources Bd, 1993–96. Vice-Chm., Social Policy and Social Work Panel, HEFCE Res. Assessment Exercise, 1996. Volunteer, CAB, 2018–. *Publications:* Social Work with Immigrants, 1972; Unwanted Pregnancy and Counselling, 1977; Social Work and Ethnicity, 1982; Social Work with Black Children and their Families, 1986; (jtly) Evaluating Social Work Effectiveness, 1992; (jtly) The Working of Social Work, 1998; contrib. collected papers and prof. jls. *Recreation:* canal boats. *Address:* October House, 14 Abbey Close, Abingdon, Oxon OX14 3JD. *T:* (01235) 532132.

**CHEETHAM, Rt Rev. Richard Ian;** *see* Kingston-upon-Thames, Area Bishop of.

**CHEFFINGS, (Charles) Nicholas;** Partner and Head, Real Estate Disputes, Hogan Lovells (formerly Lovell White Durrant, then Lovells), since 1999 (Global Chair, 2012–18); *b* Laceby, 24 Jan. 1960; *s* of Charles Ronald and Eden Eileen Cheffings; *m* 1983, Ann Elizabeth Thiess. *Educ:* Univ. of Leicester (LLB Hons). Qualified as lawyer, 1983; with NCB, 1983–90; Partner, Nabarro Nathanson, 1990–99. Member: Law Soc.; Property Litigation Assoc.; Council, Heart of the City, 2014–; Members and Communications Cttee, Real Estate Balance, 2015–; Adv. Panel, Women in Law London, 2016–; Profit-with-Purpose Working Gp for UK Nat. Adv. Bd, 2016–. Founder Mem., Sen. Leaders Forum, Lord Mayor's Power of Diversity prog., 2014–; Chairman: PRIME, 2016–; Making the Leap, 2018–. Hon. Mem., ARBRIX, 2012. Hon. MRICS, 2010. Trustee: Internat. Sen. Lawyers Project-UK, 2012–; CareTech Charitable Foundn, 2018–. Freeman, Solicitors' Co., 2016–. *Publications:* (Gen. Ed.) Sweet & Maxwell's Commercial Property Disputes: Law and Practice, 1999; contribs to learned and professional jls. *Recreations:* travelling, photography, watching most sports, theatre, sporadic periods of inactivity. *Address:* Hogan Lovells International LLP, Atlantic House, Holborn Viaduct, EC1A 2FG. *T:* (020) 7296 2000, *Fax:* (020) 7296 2001. *E:* nicholas.cheffings@hoganlovells.com.

**CHEFFINS, Prof. Brian Robert,** FBA 2018; S. J. Berwin Professor of Corporate Law, and Fellow of Trinity Hall, University of Cambridge, since 1998; *b* 21 Jan. 1961; *s* of Ronald Ian Cheffins and Sylvia Joy Cheffins; *m* 1992, Joanna Hilary Thurstans; two d. *Educ:* Univ. of Victoria, BC (BA, LLB); Trinity Hall, Cambridge (LLM). Faculty of Law, University of British Columbia, Vancouver: Asst Prof., 1986–91; Associate Prof., 1991–97; Prof., 1997. Visiting Professor: Harvard Law Sch., 2002; Columbia Law Sch., 2016; Visiting Fellow: Duke Univ., 2000; (also Lectr) Stanford Law Sch., 2003; UBC (Fasken Martineau Vis. Sen. Scholar), 2013; Harvard Business Sch. (Thomas K. McCraw Fellowship in US Business History), 2014. John S. Guggenheim Meml Fellow, 2002–03; J. M. Keynes Fellow in Financial Econs, Univ. of Cambridge, 2014–; Leverhulme Maj. Res. Fellow, 2016–18. *Publications:* Company Law: theory, structure and operation, 1997 (SPTL Prize, 1998); The Trajectory of (Corporate Law) Scholarship, 2004; Corporate Ownership and Control: British business transformed, 2008; (ed) The Modern History of US Corporate Governance, 2011; The Public Company Transformed, 2018. *Address:* Faculty of Law, University of Cambridge, 10 West Road, Cambridge CB3 9DZ. *T:* (01223) 330084. *E:* brc21@cam.ac.uk.

**CHELMSFORD,** 4th Viscount *cr* 1921, of Chelmsford, co. Essex; **Frederic Corin Piers, (Kim), Thesiger;** Baron Chelmsford 1858; *b* 6 March 1962; *o* s of 3rd Viscount Chelmsford and Clare Rendle, *d* of Dr G. R. Rolston; *S* father, 1999; *m* 2002, Charlotte, *d* of Patrick Robin and Madeleine de Gerault de Langalarie; one s. *Heir:* s Hon. Frederic Thesiger, *b* 9 Feb. 2006. *Address:* 4/4 Hampstead Hill Gardens, NW3 2PL.

**CHELMSFORD, Bishop of,** since 2010; **Rt Rev. Stephen Geoffrey Cottrell;** *b* 31 Aug. 1958; *s* of John Geoffrey and Eileen Beatrice Cottrell; *m* 1984, Rebecca Jane Stirling; three s. *Educ:* Belfairs High Sch. for Boys; Poly. of Central London (BA (Hons) Media Studies, 1979); St Stephen's House, Oxford. Ordained deacon, 1984, priest, 1985; Curate, Christ Ch, Forest Hill, 1984–88; Priest-in-charge, St Wilfrid's, Chichester, and Asst Dir of Pastoral Studies, Chichester Theol Coll., 1988–93; Diocesan Missioner, Wakefield, 1993–98; Springboard Missioner, 1998–2001; Canon Pastor, Peterborough Cathedral, 2001–04; Area Bishop of Reading, 2004–10. Entered H of L, 2014. *Publications:* (ed jtly) Follow Me: a programme of Christian nurture for all ages, 1991; Sacrament, Wholeness and Evangelism: a Catholic approach, 1996; (jtly) Emmaus: the way of faith, 1996; Catholic Evangelism, 1998; Praying Through Life: at home, at work and in the family, 1998; Travelling Well: a companion guide to the Christian life, 2000; (jtly) Vital Statistics, 2002; (jtly) Youth Emmaus, 2003; On This Rock: Bible foundations for Christian living, 2003; I Thirst: the cross-the great triumph of love, 2003; From the Abundance of the Heart: Catholic evangelism for all Christians, 2006; Do Nothing to Change Your Life, 2007; Do Nothing Christmas is Coming: an advent calendar with a difference, 2008; The Things He Carried: a journey to the cross, 2008; Hit the Ground Kneeling: seeing leadership differently, 2008; The Things He Said: the story of the first Easter Day, 2009; How to Pray, 2011; The Nail: being part of the Passion, 2011; Christ in the Wilderness: reflecting on the paintings by Stanley Spencer, 2012; Walking Backwards to Christmas, 2014; The Things He Did: the story of Holy Week, 2016; Striking Out: poems and stories from the Camino, 2018. *Recreations:* reading poetry, cooking, playing the guitar, trying to play the ukulele banjo, lino printing. *Address:* Bishopscourt, Main Road, Margaretting, Ingatestone, Essex CM4 0HD. *T:* (01277) 352001, *Fax:* (01277) 355374.
    *See also* D. J. Cottrell.

**CHELMSFORD, Dean of;** *see* Henshall, Very Rev. N. J.

**CHELMSFORD, Archdeacon of;** *see* Snowden, Ven. E.

**CHELSEA, Viscount; Edward Charles Cadogan;** DL; *b* 10 May 1966; *s* and *heir* of 8th Earl Cadogan, *qv*; *m* 1990, Katharina Johanna Ingeborg (marr. diss. 2017), *d* of Rear-Adm. D. P. A. Hülsemann; two s one d. *Educ:* St David's Coll., Llandudno. Joined RAF, 1987; served Germany, UK and Cyprus; Flt Lt. Gulf War Medal with Clasp, 1991. DL Greater London, 2012. *Recreations:* country pursuits, ski-ing, rock climbing, hill walking. *Heir:* s Hon. George Edward Charles Diether Cadogan, *b* 24 Sept. 1995. *Club:* Royal Air Force.

**CHELTENHAM, Archdeacon of;** *see* Andrew, Ven. P. J.

**CHELTON, Captain Lewis William Leonard,** RN; Secretary, Engineering Council, 1987–97; *b* 19 Dec. 1934; *s* of Lewis Walter Chelton and Doris May Chelton (*née* Gamblin); *m* 1957, Daphne Joan (*d* 2019), *oc* of Lt Col R. P. Landon, MC, RA and Betty Landon (*née* Eden); three s. *Educ:* Royal Naval College, Dartmouth. Called to the Bar, Inner Temple, 1966. Entered RN as Cadet, 1951; served in ships and shore estabts, home and abroad; Fleet Supply Officer, 1979–81; Captain, 1981; Chief Naval Judge Advocate, 1982–84; retired (voluntarily), 1987. Sec., 1997–2007, Treas., 1997–2015, Hatch Beauchamp and Dist Cons. Assoc.; Dep. Chm., Taunton Constituency Cons. Assoc., 1999–2004. Mem., Exec. Cttee, R. S. Surtees Soc., 1984–. Gov., Bruton Sch. for Girls, 1999–2018. Mem., Hatch Beauchamp PCC, 1997–2019. *Recreations:* reading, country life. *Address:* Palmers Green House, Hatch Beauchamp, near Taunton, Som TA3 6AE. *T:* (01823) 480221. *Club:* Farmers.

**CHEN, Prof. Min,** PhD; Professor of Scientific Visualization, University of Oxford, since 2011; Fellow, Pembroke College, Oxford, since 2011; *b* Shanghai, 25 May 1960; *s* of Junning Chen and Feng-yu Kong; *m* 1985, Rona Chen; one s one d. *Educ:* Fudan Univ. (BSc 1982); Univ. of Wales, Swansea (PhD 1991). University of Wales, Swansea, later Swansea University: Res. Asst, 1987–90; Lectr, 1990–98; Sen. Lectr, 1998–2001; Prof., 2001–11; Dep. Hd, 2009–10, Actg Hd, 2010–11, Dept of Computer Scis. FBCS; FLSW; Fellow, European Computer Graphics Assoc. *Publications:* High Performance Computing for Computer Graphics and Visualisation, 1996; Volume Graphics, 2000; Information Theory Tools for Visualization, 2016. *Recreations:* family, reading, gardening, walking. *Address:* Department of Engineering Science, University of Oxford, 7 Keble Road, Oxford OX1 3QG. *T:* (01865) 610600, *Fax:* (01865) 610612. *E:* min.chen@oerc.ox.ac.uk.

**CHEN, Prof. Sheng,** PhD, DSc; FIEEE, FREng; Professor of Intelligent System and Signal Processing, University of Southampton, since 2005; *b* Qianzhou, Fujian, China, 20 Sept. 1957; *s* of Zuoying Chen and Manyun Wang; *m* 1995, Qian Yao; one s. *Educ:* China Petroleum Inst. (BEng 1982); City Univ., London (PhD 1986); Southampton Univ. (DSc 2005). FIET 2005; FIEEE 2008; FREng 2014. Sen. Lectr, 1993–96, Reader, 1996–99, Portsmouth Univ.; Reader, Southampton Univ., 1999–2005. ISI highly cited research, 2004. *Publications:* contrib. res. papers to learned jls. *Address:* Electronics and Computer Science, University of Southampton, Highfield, Southampton SO17 1BJ. *T:* (023) 8059 6660, *Fax:* (023) 8059 4508. *E:* sqc@ecs.soton.ac.uk.

**CHENERY, Peter James;** Chief Executive, The Royal Anniversary Trust, since 2010 (General Manager, 2007–10); *b* 24 Oct. 1946; *s* of late Dudley James Chenery and Brenda Dorothy (*née* Redford); *m* 1979, Alice Blanche Faulder; three d. *Educ:* Forest Sch.; Christ Church, Oxford (MA); SOAS, London Univ. (Cert. in Arabic and Islamic Studies). Teacher, Ghana Teaching Service, 1967–70; joined British Council, 1970: Amman, 1971–73; Middle East Dept, 1973–76; Iran, 1976; Riyadh, 1977; Freetown, 1978–80; Jedda, 1981–84; Representative, Sana'a, Yemen Arab Republic, 1984–88; Munich, 1988–90; Sec. of the Council and Hd of Public Affairs, 1990–97; Director and Cultural Counsellor: Greece, 1997–2000; Canada, 2000–06. Member: British Cttee, UK-Canada Council (formerly UK-Canada Colloquia), 2006–; MECAS Assoc., 2017–. Associate Mem., St Antony's Coll., Oxford, 2000. FRSA 1996. Freeman, City of London, 2015; Liveryman, Broderers' Co., 2015–. *Publications:* (contrib.) The International Encyclopaedia of Cheese, 2007. *Recreations:* books, amusing conversation, lunch, history, numismatics, light recreational travel in the Mediterranean. *Address:* The Royal Anniversary Trust, Sanctuary Buildings, 20 Great Smith Street, SW1P 3BT. *Clubs:* Travellers; Leander.

**CHENEVIX-TRENCH, Jonathan Charles Stewart;** Co-founder and Partner, African Century Group, since 2008; *b* 24 March 1961; *s* of Anthony Chenevix-Trench and Elizabeth (*née* Spicer); *m* 1998, Lucy Ward; two s two d. *Educ:* Eton Coll.; Merton Coll., Oxford (BA Lit.Hum. 1984). Morgan Stanley International, 1984–2007: Vice Pres., Financial Engrg, 1990–92; Exec. Dir, Overall Risk Manager for Eur. Derivative Products, 1992–94; Man. Dir, 1994–99; Hd, Fixed Income in Europe, 1999–2004; Global Hd, Interest Rates and Foreign Exchange, 2000–05; Chm., 2006–07; Chief Operating Officer, Institutional Securities Gp, 2007. Gov., Royal Ballet Sch., 2007–. *Recreations:* reading, outdoor activities, gardening, natural history, ballet. *Clubs:* Pratt's, White's.

**CHENEY, Richard Bruce;** Vice-President of the United States of America, 2001–09; *b* 30 Jan. 1941; *s* of Richard H. Cheney and Marjorie Dickey Cheney; *m* 1964, Lynne Ann Vincent; two d. *Educ:* Casper Elementary Sch.; Natrona County High Sch.; Univ. of Wyoming (BA 1965; MA 1966); Univ. of Wisconsin. Public service, Wyoming, 1965–69; Federal service, 1969–73; Vice-Pres., Bradley Woods, 1973–74; Dep. Asst to Pres. Ford, 1974–75; Asst to Pres. Ford and White House Chief of Staff, 1975–77; Mem. (Republican) for Wyoming House of Representatives, 1978–89; Chm., Repub. Policy Cttee, 1981, Repub. House Conf., 1987; Repub. House Whip, 1988; Mem., Cttees on Interior and Insular Affairs, Intelligence, Iran Arms Deals; Sec. of Defense, USA, 1989–93. Sen. Fellow, Amer. Enterprise Inst., 1993–95. Chm. Bd, and CEO, Halliburton Co., 1995–2000. *Publications:* (with Lynne V. Cheney) Kings of the Hill, 1983; (with Liz Cheney) In My Time: a personal and political memoir, 2011; (with Jonathan Reiner) Heart: an American medical odyssey, 2013; (with Liz Cheney) Exceptional: why the world needs a strong America, 2015. *Address:* c/o American Enterprise Institute, 1150 17th Street NW, Washington, DC 20036, USA.

**CHENG, Prof. Kar Keung,** PhD; FRCGP, FFPH, FMedSci; Professor of Public Health and Primary Care, since 1995, and Director, Institute of Applied Health Research, since 2016, University of Birmingham; Founding Head, Department of General Practice, Peking University Health Science Center, since 2011; *b* Hong Kong, 20 Aug. 1958; *s* of Yiu Chiu Cheng and Yuk Kung Cheng; *m* 1986, Jane Tam; one s one d (and one s decd). *Educ:* St Paul's Co-educnl Coll., Hong Kong; Univ. of Hong Kong (BSc 1982; MB BS 1984); Hughes Hall, Cambridge (PhD 1994). FRCGP 1991; FFPH 1997. Lectr, Univ. of Hong Kong, 1986–93; Sen. Lectr, Univ. of Birmingham, 1993–95. Guest Prof., Peking Univ. Health Sci. Center, 2011–. FMedSci 2012. *Recreations:* family, listening to classical music, watching football. *Address:* Institute of Applied Health Research, Murray Learning Centre, University of Birmingham, Birmingham B15 2TT. *E:* k.k.cheng@bham.ac.uk.

**CHÉRIF, Taïeb,** PhD; Secretary General, International Civil Aviation Organization, 2003–09; *b* 29 Dec. 1941; *m* 1971, Meryem Elkaouakibi; three s. *Educ:* Univ. d'Alger, Algiers (BMaths); École nationale de l'aviation civile, Toulouse (Dip. Aeronautical Engrg); Cranfield Inst. of Technology (MSc Air Transport; PhD Air Transport Econs). Various positions of responsibility, Civil Aviation Authy, Algeria, 1971–92; State Sec. for Higher Educn, Algeria, 1992–94; civil aviation consultant, 1995–97; Rep. of Algeria, Council, ICAO, 1998–2003. *Address:* c/o International Civil Aviation Organization, 999 University Street, Montreal, QC H3C 5H7, Canada.

**CHERN, Dr Cyril,** RIBA; FCIArb; barrister, architect and arbitrator; *b* Los Angeles, 17 June 1946; *s* of George and Lola Chern. *Educ:* Univ. of S Calif (BArch 1969; JD 1972). CIArb 2000, FCIArb 2000; RIBA 2002. Captain/Ship Master, Merchant Navy, 1976–97. Called to the Bar: Gray's Inn, 1972; Calif, 1972; US Supreme Court, 1975; Partner: Acquaro, Chern, Cooper & Wright, Architects, 1970–73; Chern & Brown, 1973–80; Chern & Culver, 1980–83; Musick, Peeler & Garrett, 1984–86; Judge, *pro tem*, Calif Superior Court, 1986–93; Gen. Counsel and Dir, Maritime Ops, Turner Marine & Shipping, Hong Kong, London, 1993–98; Partner, Clinton, Clinton & Chern, London, 1998–2000; barrister: 5 Pump Court Chambers, 2002–05; Crown Office Chambers, 2006–18; 4 New Square Chambers, 2018–. Dispute Board Federation: Fellow, 2002; Hon. Sec., 2005–; Chair, Internat. Cttee on Dispute Resolution in Immediate Post-Conflict Countries, 2009–; Mem., 2000, Fellow, 2006, and Mem., Adjudicators' Assessment Panel, 2008–, Fédn Internat. des Ingénieurs-conseils, Geneva. Member: President's List of Adjudicators, Internat. Mediation Council, Paris, 1975; Civil Mediation Council, London, 2017–. Fellow, Centre for Internat. Legal Studies, Austria, 1981. Freeman, City of London, 2002. *Publications:* (jtly) Emden's Construction Law (annually), 2006–; Chern on Dispute Boards, 2007, 4th edn 2019; International Commercial Mediation, 2008; (contrib.) Atkin's Encyclopaedia of Court Forms in Civil Proceedings, 2008; The Law of Construction Disputes, 2010, 3rd edn 2019; The Commercial Mediator's Handbook, 2014; Nuclear Infrastructure Development, 2019. *Recreations:* sailing, fly fishing. *Address:* 4 New Square Chambers, Lincoln's Inn, WC2A 3RJ. *T:* (020) 7822 2000, *Fax:* (020) 7900 6909. *E:* c.chern@4newsquare.com.

**CHERNAIK, Judith Sheffield,** Hon. OBE 2002; PhD; writer; Founder and Co-Editor, Poems on the Underground, since 1986; *b* 24 Oct. 1934; *d* of Reuben Sheffield and Gertrude Lapidus; *m* 1956, Warren Lewis Chernaik; one s two d. *Educ:* Cornell Univ. (BA); Yale Univ. (PhD). Instr in English, Columbia Univ., 1963–65; Asst Prof. of English, Tufts Univ., 1965–69 (Scholar, Radcliffe Inst., 1966–68); Lectr, QMW, Univ. of London, 1975–88. Writer: features and documentaries for BBC Radio; The Two Marys (play), perf. in London and Bologna, 1997. Dir, Underground Poems CIC, 2008–. Fellow, Amer. Council of Learned Socs, 1972. *Publications:* The Lyrics of Shelley, 1972; *novels:* Double

Fault, 1975; The Daughter, 1979; Leah, 1987; Mab's Daughters, 1991 (US title, Love's Children, 1992; trans. Italian, 1997); *poetry anthologies:* (ed jtly) 100 Poems on the Underground, 1991, 10th edn 2001; (ed) Reflecting Families, 1995; (ed jtly) New Poems on the Underground, 2004, new edn 2006; (ed) Carnival of the Animals, 2005; (ed) Best Poems on the Underground, 2009; (ed) Poems on the Underground: a new edition, 2012; *biography:* Schumann: the faces and the masks, 2018; reviews and essays in TLS, The Times, New York Times, Guardian, Musical Opinion, PN Review, Musical Times, etc. *Recreations:* piano, chamber music, opera. *Address:* 124 Mansfield Road, NW3 2JB.

**CHERRY, Bridget Katherine**, OBE 2003; FSA; Editor: Buildings of England, 1983–2002; Buildings of Scotland, Ireland and Wales, 1991–2002; *b* 17 May 1941; *d* of Norman Stayner Marsh, CBE, QC and Christiane Marsh (*née* Christinnecke); *m* 1966, John Cherry, *qv*; one *s* one *d*. *Educ:* Oxford High Sch. for Girls; Lady Margaret Hall, Oxford (BA Modern Hist.); Courtauld Inst. of Art, Univ. of London (Dip. Hist. of Art). FSA 1980. Asst Librarian, Conway Library, Courtauld Inst., 1964–68; Res. Asst to Sir Nikolaus Pevsner, Buildings of England, 1968–83. Mem., Royal Commn on Historical Monuments of England, 1987–94; English Heritage: Comr, 1992–2001; Mem., Adv. Cttee, 2003–09; Mem., London Adv. Cttee, 1985–99; Mem., Historic Built Environment (formerly Buildings) Adv. Cttee, 1986–2003. Mem. Council, London Topographical Soc., 1999–. Trustee: Sir John Soane's Mus., 1994–2015; Historic Royal Palaces, 2003–08; Southern Marches Area Quaker Meeting, 2015–; Chair, Heritage of London Trust, 2008–10; Ironbridge Heritage Foundn, 2014–. Hon. FRIBA 1993. *Publications:* reviser or part author, 2nd edns, Buildings of England series, incl. Wiltshire, 1975, Hertfordshire, 1977, London 2: South, 1983, Devon, 1989, London 3: North West, 1991, London 4: North, 1998, London 5: East, 2005; Ivy-Mantled Tower: a history of the church and churchyard of St Mary Hornsey, 2015; articles and reviews on arch. subjects in learned jls. *Recreations:* walking, gardening. *Address:* Bitterley House, Cleestanton Road, Bitterley, near Ludlow, Shropshire SY8 3HJ.

**CHERRY, Joanna Catherine**; QC (Scot.) 2009; MP (SNP) Edinburgh South West, since 2015; *b* Edinburgh, 18 March 1966; *d* of Thomas Alastair Cherry and Mary Margaret Cherry (*née* Haslette). *Educ:* Holy Cross Sch., Edinburgh; St Margaret's Convent Sch. for Girls, Edinburgh; Univ. of Edinburgh (LLB Hons 1988; LLM 1989; DipLP 1990). Called to the Bar, 1995; Standing Jun. to Scottish Govt, 2003–09; Advocate Depute, 2008–11. Bencher, Middle Temple, 2019. *Recreations:* travel, reading, swimming. *Address:* House of Commons, SW1A 0AA.

**CHERRY, John**, FSA; Keeper, Department of Medieval and Modern Europe, British Museum, 1998–2002; *b* 5 Aug. 1942; *s* of Edwin Lewis Cherry and Vera Edith Blanche (*née* Bunn); *m* 1966, Bridget Katherine Marsh (*see* B. K. Cherry); one *s* one *d*. *Educ:* Portsmouth Grammar Sch.; Christ Church, Oxford (Open Scholar 1960, MA). British Museum: Asst Keeper, Dept of British and Medieval Antiquities, 1964–69; Asst Keeper, 1969–81, Dep. Keeper, 1981–98, Dept of Medieval and Later Antiquities. Dir, British Archaeological Assoc., 1977–82; Vice Pres., Soc. of Antiquaries of London, 1996–2000 (Sec., 1986–96); Pres., Soc. of Jewellery Historians, 2006–10. Vis. Fellow, All Souls Coll., Oxford, 2003. Mem., Treasure Valuations Cttee, DCMS, 2006–14. Chm., Emery Walker Trust, 2007–14 (Trustee, 1999–2015); Trustee: York Museums Trust, 2002–07; Friends of Ludlow Mus., 2014–. *Publications:* (jtly) The Ring from Antiquity to the 20th Century, 1981; (ed with I. H. Longworth) Archaeology in Britain since 1945, 1986; Medieval Decorative Art, 1991; Goldsmiths, 1992; The Middleham Jewel and Ring, 1994; (ed) Mythical Beasts, 1995; (ed with M. Caygill) Sir Augustus Wollaston Franks: Collecting and the British Museum, 1997; Medieval Love Poetry, 2005; (jtly) Good Impressions: image and authority in medieval seals, 2008; The Holy Thorn Reliquary, 2010; Richard Rawlinson and his Seal Matrices, 2016; articles in learned jls on topics of archaeology and collecting.

**CHERRY, John Mitchell**; QC 1988; a Recorder, 1987–2003; *b* 10 Sept. 1937; *s* of John William and Dorothy Mary Cherry; *m* 1972, Eunice Ann Westmoreland; one *s* two *d* (and one *s* decd). *Educ:* Cheshunt Grammar Sch.; Council of Legal Education. Called to the Bar, Gray's Inn, 1961. Mem., Criminal Injuries Compensation Bd, 1989–2002; Legal Mem., Mental Health Review Tribunals, 2002–07. *Recreations:* cricket, Rugby, food, wine. *Address:* Winterton, Turkey Street, Bulls Cross, Enfield, Middx EN1 4RJ. *T:* (01992) 719018.

**CHERRY, Michael Hugh**, OBE 2017; National Chairman, Federation of Small Businesses, since 2016 (Policy Director, 2010–16); *b* London, 1 Nov. 1953; *s* of Harold Hugh Cherry and Joan Cherry; *m* 1988, Janet Theresa Mills; two *s* one *d*, and one *s* one *d* from previous marriage. *Educ:* Yarlet Hall Prep. Sch.; Repton Public Sch. AIMMM (CMIWSc 1974). W. H. Mason & Son (Timber Merchants) Ltd, 1970–: Dir, 1973; Man. Dir, 1987–. Dir, M.H.C. Industrials Ltd, 1985–. Member: Prime Minister's Business Adv. Council, 2017–; Adv. Council, Thriving at Work, 2019–; Trustee, RAF Heraldry Trust, 2014–. Joined T&AVR Mercian Volunteers, 1972, commnd, 1973–77. FRSA 2006. *Recreations:* family, classic cars, forestry and woodlands, Armed Forces and Reservists. *Address:* W. H. Mason & Son (Timber Merchants) Ltd, The Old Sawmills, Wetmore Road, Burton on Trent DE14 1QN. *T:* (01283) 563455, *Fax:* (01283) 511526. *Club:* Army and Navy.

**CHESHAM, 7th Baron** *cr* 1858; **Charles Gray Compton Cavendish**; *b* 11 Nov. 1974; *er s* of 6th Baron Chesham and of Suzanne Adrienne (*née* Byrne); *S* father, 2009; *m* 2002, Sarah Elizabeth, *d* of Bruce Dawson; one *s* two *d*. *Educ:* King's Sch., Parramatta; Durham Univ.; City Univ. *Heir: s* Hon. Oliver Nicholas Bruce Cavendish, *b* 15 Feb. 2007.

**CHESHER, Prof. Andrew Douglas**, FBA 2001; FAcSS; William Stanley Jevons Professor of Economics and Economic Measurement, University College London, since 2013 (Professor of Economics, 1999–2013); *b* 21 Dec. 1948; *s* of late Douglas George Chesher and Eileen Jessie Chesher (*née* Arnott); *m* 1st, 1971, Janice Margaret Elizabeth Duffield (marr. diss.); two *s*; 2nd, 2000, Valérie Marie Rose Jeanne Lechene; two *d*. *Educ:* Whitgift Sch.; Univ. of Birmingham (BSocSc Maths, Econs and Stats). Res. Associate, Acton Soc., 1970–71; Lectr in Econometrics, Univ. of Birmingham, 1972–83; Prof. of Econometrics, 1984–99, Hd, Dept of Econs, 1987–90 and 1996–98, Univ. of Bristol; Dir, Centre for Microdata Methods and Practice, Inst. for Fiscal Studies and Dept of Econs, UCL, 2000–. Vis. Prof., Univ. of Bristol, 2000–10; Res. Fellow, Inst. for Fiscal Studies, 2001–; Hon. Prof., Beihang Univ., Beijing, 2017–. Mem. Council, ESRC, 2001–05 (Mem., 1996–2000, Vice-Chm., 1997–2000, Res. Resources Bd; Chm., Res. Grants Bd, 2001–05). Mem. Cttee, Nat. Food Survey, 1987–. Mem. Council, 1998–2004, Pres., 2016–17, Life Vice-Pres., 2018, REconS. Governor, NIESR, 2002–. Fellow, Econometric Soc., 1999 (Mem. Council, 2011–15); FAcSS 2018. Foreign Hon. Mem., Amer. Economic Assoc., 2011. Hon. DSc Birmingham, 2017. Associate Editor: Econometrica, 1990–96 and 2000–03; Jl Econometrics, 1995–2003; Econ. Jl, 1997–2000; Jl Royal Statistical Soc., Series A, 1999–2001; Co-Ed., Econometric Soc. Monograph Series, 2001–09. *Publications:* (with R. Harrison) Vehicle Operating Costs in Developing Countries, 1987; contribs to learned jls in econs and stats. *Address:* Glebe Lodge, 289 Hills Road, Cambridge CB2 8RP.

**CHESHIRE, Dr (Christopher) Michael**, FRCP, FRCGP, FACP; Medical Advisor, Broughton House Nursing Home, since 2012; *b* 18 July 1946; *s* of Gordon Sydney Cheshire and Vera Cheshire; *m* 1970, Jane Mary Cordle; one *s* one *d*. *Educ:* Manchester Univ. (BSc Hons 1969; MB ChB Hons 1976). DCH 1979; FRCP 1990; FRCGP 2010; FACP 2010. House Officer, Medicine and Surgery, Manchester Royal Infirmary, 1976–77; Senior House Officer: Cardiothoracic Medicine, Wythenshawe, 1977–78; Paediatrics, Univ. Hosp., S Manchester, 1978–79; SHO, Medicine, 1979–80, Consultant Physician, 1983–2010, Manchester Royal Infirmary; Lectr in Geriatric Medicine, Univ. Hosp., S Manchester, 1980–83; Med. Dir, 1993–97, Dir of Educn, 1997–2005, Central Manchester Healthcare NHS Trust; Clinical Dir of Service Redesign, 2005–06, Clinical Head of Intermediate Care, 2006–07, Central Manchester PCT; Med. Dir, NHS N of England (formerly NW SHA), 2009–13; secondary care doctor, Central Manchester Commng Gp, 2012–13; Clinical Leader, Patient and Family Centred Care, King's Fund, 2012–13; Sen. Med. Advr, Haelo, 2013–14. Non-exec. Dir, Stockport Foundn Trust, 2013–. Censor, 2006–07, Clin. Vice-Pres., 2007–10, RCP. Chairman: NW, British Geriatrics Soc., 1998–2001; Educn Gp, British Assoc. of Med. Managers, 1998–2001. Patron, METrust, 2011–; Trustee, Beth Johnson Foundn, 2017–. *Publications:* contribs on topics of medicine and management. *Recreations:* swimming, reading novels, garden, family. *Address:* Long Ridge, Derwent Lane, Hathersage S32 1AS.

**CHESHIRE, Lt Col Colin Charles Chance**, OBE 1993; Vice President, International Confederation of Fullbore Rifle Associations, 2011–19 (Secretary General, 2003–11); *b* 23 Aug. 1941; *s* of Air Chief Marshal Sir Walter Graemes Cheshire, GBE, KCB and Mary Cheshire (*née* Chance), DL; *m* 1st, 1968, Cherida Evelyn (marr. diss. 1975), *d* of Air Chief Marshal Sir Wallace Hart Kyle, GCB, KCVO, CBE, DSO, DFC; one *s* one *d*; 2nd, 1976, Angela, *d* of D. Fulcher. *Educ:* Worksop Coll. Royal Tank Regiment: served Borneo, Singapore, Malaysia, BAOR, NI, UK; Armour Sch., Bovington Camp, 1968; RMCS, 1972–73; Staff Coll., Camberley, psc† 1974; Bde Major, RAC, HQ 1 (BR) Corps, 1978–80; Lt Col, 1980; GSO1 (W) (Principal Quality Engr) Quality Assurance Directorate, MoD, 1980–81; retd 1981. Sales and Marketing Manager: Vickers Instruments Ltd, 1981–83; Army Systems, Ferranti Computer Systems, 1983–85; Sales and Mktg Dir, Wallop Gp, and Man. Dir, Walloptronics Ltd, 1985–87; Bursar, Oundle Sch., 1987–95; Chief Exec., NRA, 1995–2002. Mem., Exec. Cttee, Independent Schs Bursars Assoc., 1992–95. Chm., GB Target Shooting Fedn, 1994–97; Member: British Rifle Team, 1971–2006 (Captain, 1991, 1992, 1994, 1995, Vice Captain, 1982, 1999); GB Veterans Rifle Team, 2001–15 (Captain, 2014–15); Winner, World Long Range Rifle Team Championships, Palma Match, 1992, 1995. Mem., HAC, 1960–. Mem., Guild of Sports Internationalists, 1998–2002 (Middle Warden, 2001). FCMI (FIMgt 1985). *Publications:* History and Records of the World Long Range Rifle Championships - the Palma Match 1876 to date, 1992. *Recreations:* rifle shooting, golf, Freemasonry. *Address:* 1 Westcroft House, Conigre Mews, Trowbridge, Wilts BA14 8RF.
*See also* Sir J. A. Cheshire.

**CHESHIRE, Sir Ian (Michael)**, Kt 2014; Chief Executive, Kingfisher plc, 2008–15; *b* 6 Aug. 1959; *s* of Donald and Pamela Cheshire; *m* 1984, Kate Atherton; two *s* one *d*. *Educ:* King's Sch., Canterbury; Christ's Coll., Cambridge (Schol.; BA 1st Cl. Hons Law and Econs 1980; MA). Kingfisher plc, 1998–2015, Dir, 2000–15; Chief Exec., B&Q plc, 2005–08. Chairman: Debenhams plc, 2016–19; Barclays UK, 2017–; non-executive Director: Bradford & Bingley plc, 2003–08; Whitbread plc, 2011–17 (Sen. non-exec. Dir, 2013–17). Lead non-exec. Dir, DWP, 2011–14; Govt Lead non-exec. Dir, 2015–; Chm., Adv. Bd, Cambridge Prog. for Sustainability Leadership, 2011–15; Chairman: British Retail Consortium, 2012–14; Prince of Wales Corporate Leaders Gp on Climate Change, 2012–15; Heads Together, 2016–. Chm. Trustees, Medicinema (charity), 2003–16; Trustee: Prince of Wales Charitable Foundn, 2016– (Chair); Inst. for Govt, 2017–; Pres., Business Disability Forum, 2011–. Chm., Ernest Bevin Coll., 2000–08. FRSA 1999; MInstD 1992. Chevalier, Ordre Nat. du Mérite (France), 2012. *Recreations:* reading, arts, music, sailing, ski-ing. *E:* siriancheshire@gmail.co.uk. *Clubs:* Reform, Hurlingham; Bembridge Sailing.

**CHESHIRE, Prof. Jennifer Lilian**, PhD; FBA 2011; Professor of Linguistics, Queen Mary University of London, since 1996; *b* 26 Feb. 1946; *d* of Sydney Harold Russell and Elsie Millicent Russell; *m* 1970, Paul Charles Cheshire; one *s* one *d*. *Educ:* London Sch. of Econs (BA Hons 1st cl. French and Linguistics 1971); Univ. of Reading (PhD 1979). Lectr, Univ. of Bath, 1980–83; Lectr, then Sen. Lectr, Birkbeck Coll., London, 1983–91; Prof. of English Linguistics, Univ. of Fribourg, 1991–96. Member: ESRC Bd of Examiners, 1999–2003; ESRC Recognition Exercise, Linguistics, 2001, 2005; Linguistics Panel, 2001 and 2008 RAEs; NZ Peer-based Review Funding Exercise, Humanities and Law Panel, 2003, 2006 and 2012; Mod. Langs Panel, 2014 REF; Chair, Humanities Panel, HK RAE, 2020. Ed., Language in Society, 2013–. Gov., Raines Foundn Sch., 1998–2011. *Publications:* Variation in an English Dialect, 1982; English Around the World: sociolinguistic perspectives, 1991; (with P. Trudgill) A Reader in Sociolinguistics, 1998; (with D. Britain) Social Dialectology, 2003; articles in Jl of Sociolinguistics, Language and Educn, Language in Society, Language Variation and Change, Lingua, etc. *Recreations:* mountain walking, cinema. *Address:* Department of Linguistics, School of Languages, Linguistics and Film, Queen Mary University of London, Mile End Road, E1 4NS. *T:* (020) 7882 8923, *Fax:* (020) 8980 5400. *E:* J.L.Cheshire@qmul.ac.uk. *W:* www.jennycheshire.com.

**CHESHIRE, Air Chief Marshal Sir John (Anthony)**, KBE 1995 (CBE 1991; OBE 1982); CB 1994; FRAeS; Lieutenant-Governor and Commander-in-Chief, Jersey, 2001–06; *b* 4 Sept. 1942; *s* of Air Chief Marshal Sir Walter Cheshire, GBE, KCB and Lady Cheshire; *m* 1964, Shirley Ann Stevens (*d* 2016); one *s* one *d*. *Educ:* Ipswich Sch.; Worksop Coll.; RAF Coll., Cranwell. Operational Flying Duties, UK and Singapore, 1964–70; Air Ops Officer, Special Forces, 1971–73; Canadian Forces Staff Coll., 1973–74; Operational Flying Duties, Special Forces, 1975–76; Air Plans, MoD, 1976–79; Commander: Air Wing, Brunei, 1980–82; RAF Lyneham, 1983–85; Plans Br., HQ Strike Command, 1986–87; Defence and Air Attaché, Moscow, 1988–90; Dep. Comdt, RAF Staff Coll., 1991–92; ACOS (Policy), SHAPE, 1992–94; UK Mil. Rep., HQ NATO, 1995–97; C-in-C, Allied Forces NW Europe, 1997–2000. Chm., RAF Charitable Trust, 2009–13. Pres., Royal Internat. Air Tattoo, 2009–13. KStJ 2002. *Recreations:* golf, field shooting, writing an historical novel. *Address:* The Retreat, 15b Notton, Lacock, Wilts SN15 2NF. *Club:* Royal Air Force.
*See also* C. C. C. Cheshire.

**CHESHIRE, Michael**; *see* Cheshire, C. M.

**CHESSELL, Amanda Elizabeth**, CBE 2015; FREng; IBM Distinguished Engineer, since 2007; *b* Bath, 11 April 1965; *d* of Raymond Sidney Tee and Mary Theresa Tee. *Educ:* Plymouth Poly. (BSc Hons Computing and Informatics 1987); Univ. of Brighton (MSc Software Engrg 1997). FREng 2002. IBM: Software Engr, 1987–2001; Sen. Technical Staff Mem., 2001–07. ODPi Egeria Lead, 2018–. Visiting Professor: Univ. of Sheffield, 2009–; Univ. of Surrey, 2016–. Hon. DSc: Plymouth, 2013; Bath, 2017; Hon. DTech: Brighton, 2015; S Wales, 2016. *Publications:* Patterns of Information Management, 2013; Common

Information Models for an Open, Analytical and Agile World, 2015. *Recreation:* photography. *Address:* IBM UK Ltd, Hursley Park, Winchester, Hants SO21 2JN. *E:* mandy_chessell@uk.ibm.com.

**CHESSELLS, Sir Arthur David, (Sir Tim),** Kt 1993; Chairman of Trustees, British Telecommunications Pension Scheme, 1999–2007; *b* 15 June 1941; *s* of late Brig. Arthur Chessells and Carmel Mary (*née* McGinnis); *m* 1966, Katharine, *d* of Dick and Rachel Goodwin; two *s* two *d*. *Educ:* Stonyhurst Coll. CA 1965. Partner, Arthur Young, 1972–89; Mem., Kent AHA, 1979–82; Vice-Chm., Tunbridge Wells HA, 1982–88; Mem., SE Thames RHA, 1988–90; Chairman: NE Thames RHA, 1990–92; London Implementation Gp, 1992–95; Legal Aid Bd, 1995–2000. Non-exec. Mem., NHS Policy Bd, 1992–95. Director: Odgers and Co. Ltd, 1989–95; Price and Pierce Inc., 1993–97; Dixons Gp, 1995–2001; Care UK, 1995–2005; Hermes Pension Mgt, 1999–2007 (Chm., 1999–2004), and other cos. Chm., Nat. Approval Council for Security Systems, 1995–99. Mem. Council, St Christopher's Hospice, 1989–92. Gov., Heythrop Coll., Univ. of London, 2009–13. Trustee: Kent Community Housing Trust, 1990–95; Stonyhurst Charitable Fund, 1980–93; Chatham Historic Dockyard, 1992–97; Charities Aid Foundn, 1998–2005; Chairman, Trustees: Guy's and St Thomas' Charitable Foundn, 1996–2006; Horder Centre for Arthritis, 2000–09, 2012–17. *Recreations:* reading, shooting, gardening. *Address:* Coach House Cottage, North Street, Mayfield TN20 6AN. *Club:* Carlton.
See also J. M. Chessells.

**CHESSELLS, Prof. Judith Mary,** OBE 2004; MD; FRCP, FRCPath; Leukaemia Research Fund Professor of Haematology and Oncology, Institute of Child Health, London University, 1988–2002; *b* 30 Dec. 1938; *d* of late Brig. Arthur Edgar Chessells and Carmel Mary Chessells (*née* McGinnis); *m* 1969, Dr Gerald McEnery; one *d*. *Educ:* Sacred Heart Convent, Brighton; London Hosp. Med. Coll., London Univ. (MB BS Hons; MD). Lectr in Haematology, Inst. of Child Health, 1972–73; Consultant Haematologist, Hosp. for Sick Children, Great Ormond St, 1973–87, Hon. Consultant, 1988–2002. FRCPCH 1997. *Publications:* contrib. to learned jls. *Recreations:* theatre, literature.
See also Sir A. D. Chessells.

**CHESSELLS, Sir Tim;** see Chessells, Sir A. D.

**CHESSHYRE, (David) Hubert (Boothby),** CVO 2004 (LVO 1988); Clarenceux King of Arms, 1997–2010; Secretary, Most Noble Order of the Garter, 1988–2003; *b* 22 June 1940; *e s* of late Col Hubert Layard Chesshyre and Katharine Anne (*née* Boothby). *Educ:* King's Sch., Canterbury; Trinity Coll., Cambridge (Choral Clerk; MA); Christ Church, Oxford (DipEd 1967). FSA 1977; FHS 1990. Wine merchant (Moët et Chandon and Harvey's of Bristol), 1962–65; Green Staff Officer at Investiture of the Prince of Wales, 1969; Rouge Croix Pursuivant, 1970–78, and on staff of Sir Anthony Wagner, Garter King of Arms, 1971–78; Chester Herald of Arms, 1978–95; Norroy and Ulster King of Arms, 1995–97. Mem., Westminster Abbey Fabric Commn (formerly Architectural Adv. Panel), 1985–2003. Member: Council, Heraldry Soc., 1973–85; Bach Choir, 1979–93; Madrigal Soc., 1980–. Hon. Genealogist to Royal Victorian Order, 1987–2010. Lectr, NADFAS, 1982–2002. Lay Clerk, Southwark Cathedral, 1971–2003. Freeman: City of London, 1975; Musicians' Co., 1994 (Liveryman, 1995–). *Publications:* (Eng. lang. editor) C. A. von Volborth, Heraldry of the World, 1973; The Identification of Coats of Arms on British Silver, 1978; (with A. J. Robinson) The Green: a history of the heart of Bethnal Green, 1978; (with Adrian Ailes) Heralds of Today, 1986, 2nd edn 2001; (ed with T. Woodcock) Dictionary of British Arms, vol. I, 1992; Garter Banners of the Nineties, 1999; (with P. J. Begent) The Most Noble Order of the Garter, 650 Years, 1999.

**CHESSUN, Rt Rev. Christopher Thomas James;** see Southwark, Bishop of.

**CHESTER, Bishop of;** no new appointment at time of going to press.

**CHESTER, Dean of;** see Stratford, Very Rev. Dr T. R.

**CHESTER, Archdeacon of;** see Gilbertson, Ven. M. R.

**CHESTER, Dr Peter Francis,** FREng; FInstP; FIET; Chairman, National Wind Power Ltd, 1991–95; *b* 8 Feb. 1929; *s* of late Herbert and of Edith Maud Chester (*née* Pullen); *m* 1953, Barbara Ann Collin; one *s* four *d*. *Educ:* Gunnersbury Grammar Sch.; Queen Mary College, London (BSc 1st Physics 1950); PhD London 1953. Post-doctoral Fellow, Nat. Research Council, Ottawa, 1953–54; Adv. Physicist, Westinghouse Res. Labs, Pittsburgh, 1954–60; Head of Solid State Physics Section, CERL, 1960–65; Head of Fundamental Studies Section, CERL, 1965–66; Res. Man., Electricity Council Res. Centre, 1966–70; Controller of Scientific Services, CEGB NW Region, 1970–73; Dir, Central Electricity Res. Labs, 1973–82; a Dir, Technol. Planning and Res., Div., CEGB, 1982–86; Dir, Environment, CEGB, 1986–89; Exec. Dir, Technology and Environment, Nat. Power, 1990–92. Science Research Council: Mem., 1976–80; Mem., Science Bd, 1972–75; Chm., Energy Round Table and Energy Cttee, 1975–80. Mem., ACORD, DTI, 1992–93. Vice-Pres., Inst. of Physics, 1972–76. A Dir, Fulmer Res. Inst., 1976–83. Faraday Lectr, IEE, 1984–85. Robens Coal Science Medal, 1985. *Publications:* original papers in solid state and low temperature physics, reports on energy and the environment, acid rain, clean technology, renewable energy and windpower.

**CHESTERFIELD, Archdeacon of;** see Coslett, Ven. C. A.

**CHESTERMAN, Alexander Edward,** OBE 2016; Founder and Chief Executive Officer, Cazoo Ltd, since 2018; *b* London, 9 Jan. 1970; *s* of John and Carole Chesterman; *m* 2001, Angela; two *s*. *Educ:* St Paul's Sch.; University Coll. London (BSc Hons Econ). Exec. Vice Pres., Planet Hollywood Internat. Inc., 1991–99; Founder and Chief Executive Officer, Bagelmania plc, 2000–03; Founder, ScreenSelect, subseq. LoveFilm Internat., 2003–07; Founder and CEO, Zoopla.co.uk, then Zoopla Property Gp, later ZPG plc, 2007–18. *Recreations:* art, travel, tennis, ping pong.

**CHESTERMAN, Rev. Canon (George) Anthony,** PhD; Chaplain to the Queen, 1998–2008; Continuing Ministerial Education Adviser to Bishop of Derby and Residentiary Canon (later Canon Theologian), Derby Cathedral, 1989–2003; *b* 22 Aug. 1938; *s* of late Francis John Chesterman and Frances Annie Chesterman; *m* 1964, Sheila Valerie Wilkinson; one *s* one *d*. *Educ:* Lancaster Royal Grammar Sch.; Univ. of Manchester (BSc); Nottingham Univ. (DipAE 1974; PhD 1989); Coll. of the Resurrection, Mirfield. Ordained deacon, 1964, priest, 1965; Curate, St John the Evangelist, Newbold, Chesterfield, 1964–67; Litchurch Gp Ministry, Derby (youth and adult educn specialist), 1967–70; Rector, All Saints, Mugginton and Kedleston, 1970–89; Diocesan Adult Educn Officer, Derby, 1970–79; Vice-Principal, E Midlands Ministry Trng Course, 1979–88. Mem., Gen. Synod, 1990–95. *Publications:* occasional articles and book reviews. *Recreations:* cooking, gardening, music, the visual arts, golf. *Address:* 7 Hillside, Lesbury, Alnwick, Northumberland NE66 3NR.

**CHESTERMAN, Gordon,** Director, Careers Service, University of Cambridge, 2002–18 (Senior Proctor, 2016–17; Deputy Senior Proctor, 2019); Fellow and Tutor, St Edmund's College, Cambridge, since 2012; letterpress printer, since 1974; *b* 14 March 1957; *s* of Frederick and Marie Chesterman; *m* 1984, Deirdre McCormack; two *s* one *d*. *Educ:* University College Sch., Hampstead; London Coll. of Printing (HND Printing). Graduate trainee, then Personnel Officer, De La Rue Company, 1978–83; Graduate Recruitment Manager, Deloitte Haskins & Sells, 1983–86; Account Manager, Publishing Resources Ltd, Cambridge, 1986–90; self employed, 1990–95; Careers Advr, then Dep. Dir, Careers Service, Univ. of Cambridge, 1995–2002. Member: Steam Boat Assoc.; UK Letterpress Exchange. *Recreations:* fine letterpress printing, oil painting, historic ship preservation. *Address:* St Edmund's College, Mount Pleasant, Cambridge CB3 0BN. *E:* gc214@cam.ac.uk. *Club:* Oxford and Cambridge.

**CHESTERS, Rt Rev. Alan David,** CBE 2007; Bishop of Blackburn, 1989–2003; an Hon. Assistant Bishop: of Chichester, since 2011; of Southwark, 2011–14; of Chester, 2003–10; of St Asaph, 2009–10; *b* 26 Aug. 1937; *s* of Herbert and Catherine Rebecca Chesters; *m* 1975, Jennie Garrett (*d* 2011); one *s*. *Educ:* Elland Grammar Sch., W Yorks; St Chad's Coll., Univ. of Durham (BA Mod. History; Hon. Fellow, 2010); St Catherine's Coll., Oxford (BA Theol., MA); St Stephen's House, Oxford (Hon. Fellow, 2008). Curate of St Anne, Wandsworth, 1962–66; Chaplain and Head of Religious Education, Tiffin School, Kingston-upon-Thames, 1966–72; Director of Education and Rector of Brancepeth, Diocese of Durham, 1972–84; Hon. Canon of Durham Cathedral, 1975–84; Archdeacon of Halifax, 1985–89. A Church Comr, 1982–98 (Mem., Bd of Governors, 1984–89, 1992–98). Mem., General Synod, 1975–2003 (Mem., Standing Cttee, 1985–89, 1990–95); Chm., C of E Bd of Educn, and Council, Nat. Soc., 1999–2003. Mem. Cathedral Chapter, Chester, 2003–10. Member: Countryside Commn, 1995–99; Countryside Agency, 1999–2001; Chm., NW Rural Affairs Forum, 2002–06. Pres., Cheshire Assoc. of Local Councils, 2005–10. Chairman: Govs, St Martin's Coll. of Higher Educn, Lancaster, 1990–2002; Council, St Stephen's House, Oxford, 1995–2003; Mem. Council, Univ. of Chester, 2005–10. House of Lords, 1995–2003. Hon. Fellow: Univ. of Central Lancs, 2001; St Martin's Coll. of HE, 2003; Blackburn Coll., 2004; Myerscough Coll., 2004; Univ. of Cumbria, 2007. DTheol Chester, 2010. *Recreations:* railways, classical music, reading. *Address:* 14 Pegasus Court, Deanery Close, Chichester PO19 1EA.

**CHESTERS, Pamela Joy,** CBE 2013; Chair, Anchor Trust, 2013–18; *b* 28 April 1956; *d* of late Ian Storrie Beveridge and Kathleen Mary Beveridge; *m* 1991, Alan Chesters. *Educ:* St Andrews Univ. (MA Hons Mediaeval Hist.; Pres., Students' Rep. Council, 1977–78). British Petroleum: various posts in UK and USA, latterly CEO, Duckhams Oils, 1979–98. Chair, Royal Free Hampstead NHS Trust, 2001–09; Advr to Mayor of London on Health and Youth Opportunities, GLA, 2009–12; Chair, Central London Community Healthcare NHS Trust, 2012–16. Non-exec. Dir, MHCLG (formerly DCLG), 2017–. Contested (C) Bristol W, 2001. Mem. (C) London Borough of Camden, 1990–2000 (Leader of Opposition, 1998–2000). Mem., Nat. Educn Exec., LGA, 1997–2000. Chair, English Churches Housing Gp, 2003–09. Dir, Opera della Luna, 1994–2004. Trustee: Common Purpose, 2005–09; Action for Children (formerly NCH), 2006–12 (Chm., 2007–12); Chair, Prince's Initiative for Mature Enterprise, 2014. Non-exec. Mem. Ct, Univ. of St Andrews, 2016–19; Chm. Council, Bath Univ., 2019–. *Recreations:* theatre, travel. *Address:* 62 Redington Road, NW3 7RS. *T:* (020) 7435 4190.

**CHESTERTON, David,** CB 1999; Chief Executive, UK Sports Council, 1998–99 (on secondment); *b* 30 Nov. 1939; *s* of Raymond and Joyce Chesterton; *m* 1st, 1965, Ursula Morgan; one *s* three *d*; 2nd, 1977, Lindsay Fellows; three step *d*. *Educ:* Reading Sch.; St Catherine's Coll., Oxford (BA). Editorial Assistant: Financial World, 1961–62; Fleet Street Letter, 1962–65; Producer, BBC External Services, 1965–68, Exec. Producer, 1968–74; Northern Ireland Office: Principal, 1974–80; Asst Sec., 1980–85; Under Sec., 1985–92; Hd of Heritage and Tourism Gp, DNH, 1992–96; Head of Sport, Tourism, Millennium and Nat. Lotteries Charities Bd Gp, DNH, then DCMS, 1996–98. *Recreations:* food and drink, France.

**CHETWODE,** family name of **Baron Chetwode**.

**CHETWODE, 2nd Baron** *cr* 1945, of Chetwode; **Philip Chetwode**; Bt, 1700; *b* 26 March 1937; *s* of Capt. Roger Charles George Chetwode (*d* 1940; *o s* of Field Marshal Lord Chetwode, GCB, OM, GCSI, KCMG, DSO) and Hon. Molly Patricia Berry, *d* of 1st Viscount Camrose (she *m* 2nd, 1942, 1st Baron Sherwood, from whom she obtained a divorce, 1948, and *m* 3rd, 1958, Sir Richard Cotterell, 5th Bt, CBE); *S* grandfather, 1950; *m* 1st, 1967, Mrs Susan Dudley Smith (marr. diss. 1979); two *s* one *d*; 2nd, 1990, Mrs Fiona Holt. *Educ:* Eton. Commissioned Royal Horse Guards, 1956–66. *Heir:* *s* Hon. Roger Chetwode [*b* 29 May 1968; *m* 1998, Miranda, *d* of Comdr Graeme Rowan-Thomson; two *s* one *d*]. *Address:* Oaktrees, Drift Road, Winkfield, Windsor, Berks SL4 4QQ. *Club:* White's.

**CHETWYND,** family name of **Viscount Chetwynd**.

**CHETWYND, 11th Viscount** *cr* 1717 (Ire.); **Adam Douglas Chetwynd**; Baron Rathdown 1717 (Ire.); *b* 26 Feb. 1969; *er twin s* of 10th Viscount Chetwynd and Celia Grace Chetwynd (*née* Ramsay); *S father*, 2015; *m* 2000, Johanna Marie Karatau; two *s* one *d*. *Heir:* *s* Hon. Connor Adam Chetwynd, *b* 18 Oct. 2001.

**CHETWYND, Sir Peter James Talbot,** 10th Bt *cr* 1795, of Brocton Hall, Staffordshire; *b* 21 Sept. 1973; *o s* of Sir Robin John Talbot Chetwynd, 9th Bt and Heather Helen Chetwynd (*née* Lothian); *S father*, 2012, but his name does not appear on the Official Roll of the Baronetage.

**CHETWYND-TALBOT,** family name of **Earl of Shrewsbury and Waterford**.

**CHEVALIER, Tracy,** FRSL; author; *b* Washington, DC, 19 Oct. 1962; *d* of Douglas Chevalier and Helen Chevalier (*née* Werner); *m* 1994, Jonathan Drori (CBE 2007); one *s*. *Educ:* Oberlin Coll. (BA English); Univ. of E Anglia (MA Creative Writing). Literary ed., St James Press, 1988–93; freelance ed., 1994–97. Mem. Bd, BL, 2015–. Pres., Royal Literary Fund, 2015–18. FRSL 2008. Hon. DLitt E Anglia, 2013; Hon. DFA Oberlin, 2013. *Publications:* The Virgin Blue, 1997; Girl with a Pearl Earring, 1999; Falling Angels, 2001; The Lady and the Unicorn, 2004; Burning Bright, 2007; Remarkable Creatures, 2010; The Last Runaway, 2013; At the Edge of the Orchard, 2016; (ed) Reader, I Married Him, 2016; New Boy, 2017; A Single Thread, 2019. *Recreations:* quilting, guerrilla gardening, Venice. *Address:* c/o Curtis Brown, Haymarket House, 28–29 Haymarket, SW1Y 4SP. *E:* hello@tchevalier.com.

**CHEWTON, Viscount; Edward Robert Waldegrave;** *b* 10 Oct. 1986; *e s* of 13th Earl Waldegrave, *qv*. *Educ:* Eton Coll.; Christ Church, Oxford (BA Hist. 2009). Called to the Bar, Lincoln's Inn, 2011. *Address:* Chewton House, Chewton Mendip, Radstock, Som BA3 4LL.

**CHEYNE, David Watson;** Senior Adviser, Akira Partners LLP, since 2015; *b* 30 Dec. 1948; *s* of Brig. W. W Cheyne, DSO, OBE and L. A. Cheyne; *m* 1978, J. Gay Passey; three *s*. *Educ:* Stowe Sch.; Trinity Coll., Cambridge (BA Law 1971; MA). Admitted solicitor, 1974; Linklaters: Asst Solicitor, 1974–80; Partner, 1980–2011; Hd of Corporate, 2000–05; Sen. Partner, 2006–11; Consultant, 2011–15. Vice Chm., EMEA, Moelis & Co., 2011–14.

Non-exec. Dir, Blackrock World Mining Trust plc, 2012–. *Recreations:* shooting, fishing, collecting antiques. *Address:* 19 Ladbroke Gardens, W11 2PT. *T:* (020) 7229 0096. *E:* davidcheyne1@hotmail.com.

**CHEYNE, Iain Donald,** CBE 1995; Member, Professional Oversight Board, Financial Reporting Council, 2009–12; *b* 29 March 1942; *s* of Andres Delporte Gordon Cheyne and Florence Muriel Cheyne; *m* 1st, 1969, Amelia Martinez Arriola (marr. diss. 2008); two *s* one *d*; 2nd, 2011, Susan Souter. *Educ:* Hertford Coll., Oxford (MA English Lit. 1963); Coll. of Law, London; Stanford Univ. (Exec. Prog. 1987); London Business Sch. (Corporate Finance Prog. 1989); London Univ. (MPhil Archaeol. 1994). Articled Clerk, Droogleever and Co., Solicitors, 1964–68; admitted solicitor, 1967; Partner, Alfille and Co., Solicitors, 1968–72; Lloyds Bank, subseq. Lloyds TSB, plc: Legal Advr, 1972–86; General Manager: Corporate Communications, 1986–88; Strategic Planning, 1988–91; Corporate and Instnl Banking, 1991–97; Man. Dir, Internat. Banking, 1997–2000; Dir of Private Affairs to HH the Aga Khan, 2000–05; Dir Gen., Aga Khan Agency for Microfinance, 2005–07. Dir, Habib Bank, Pakistan, 2004–09; Vice-Chm., Habib and Allied Bank, UK, 2004–09; Exec. Dir, R M Walkden and Co. Investment Mgrs, 2011–12. *Recreations:* archaeology, game shooting, vintage car racing. *Address:* Gooselands, Aldbourne Road, Baydon, Marlborough, Wilts SN8 2HZ; 39 Quai D'Anjou, 75004 Paris, France. *Clubs:* Garrick, Lansdowne; Cercle de l'Union interalliée (Paris).

**CHEYNE, Sir Patrick (John Lister),** 4th Bt *cr* 1908, of Leagarth, Fetlar; *b* 2 July 1941; *s* of Sir Joseph Lister Watson Cheyne, 3rd Bt, OBE and Mary Mort Allen; *S* father, 2007; *m* 1968, Helen Louise Trevor (*née* Smith); one *s* three *d*. *Educ:* Lancing Coll. FRICS 1997 (ISVA 1973). Cadet Seaman, British India Steam Navigation Co. Ltd, 1959; Seaman Cadet, RN, 1963; completed Commn as Lt Torpedo Anti-Submarine Officer, 1973. *Recreations:* fell walking, photography, gardening, croquet. *Heir: s* Louis Richard Patrick Lister Cheyne, *b* 25 March 1971. *Address:* Laurel Bank, 34 Stamford Road, Bowdon, Altrincham, Cheshire WA14 2JX. *T:* (0161) 928 0448. *E:* louisecheyne@btinternet.com.

**CHIBNALL, Christopher Antony;** writer and producer, since 1999; *b* Watford, 21 March 1970; *s* of Robert and Gill Chibnall; birth mother, Veronica Oxley; *m* 2002, Madeline Joinson; two *s*. *Educ:* Range High Sch., Formby; St Mary's Coll., Strawberry Hill (BA 1st Cl. Hons Drama and English Univ. of Surrey); Sheffield Univ. (MA Theatre and Film). Videotape Librarian, Sky TV, 1991–93; Administrator, Théâtre de Complicité, 1996–99. Writer and producer for television: Born and Bred, 2001–04; Life on Mars, 2005–06; Torchwood, 2006–08; Doctor Who (5 episodes), 2007–13, lead writer, 2017–; Law & Order UK, 2009; United, 2011; Broadchurch, 2013 (Best Writer Award, BPG, 2014), 2015, 2017; The Great Train Robbery, 2013. Writer in Residence, Grip Th., 1998–99; writer on attachment: NT Studio, 1999; Soho Th., 2000–01; writer and producer of plays: Best Daze, Grip Th., 1997; Gaffer, Grip Th., 1999, Southwark Playhouse, 2004; Kiss Me Like You Mean It, Soho Th., 2002; Worst Wedding Ever, Salisbury Playhouse, 2014. Mem., BAFTA, 2014–. *Publications:* Kiss Me Like You Mean It, 2002; Worst Wedding Ever, 2014. *Recreations:* music, cinema, theatre, football, long walks by the sea. *Address:* c/o Cathy King, Independent Talent Group Ltd, 40 Whitfield Street, W1T 2RH. *T:* (020) 7636 6565.

**CHIBWA, Anderson Kaseba;** High Commissioner of Zambia to Malaysia, 2010; *b* 24 March 1950; *s* of Chulu and Sarah Chibwa; *m* 1990, Grace Mwewa Kasese; three *s* three *d*. *Educ:* Univ. of Zambia (BA 1974); Univ. of Miami (MA 1979). Sen. Researcher, Nat. Council for Scientific Res., Zambia, 1974–82; Sen. Lectr, Pan African Inst. for Develt, 1982–99; Project Manager, CARE Internat., Zambia, 1999–2003; High Comr for Zambia in the UK, 2003–09. *Publications:* Population Atlas of Zambia, 1974; Internal Migrations in the Commonwealth of the Bahamas 1970–75, 1980. *Recreations:* reading, meeting people.

**CHICHESTER,** family name of **Marquess of Donegall**.

**CHICHESTER, 9th Earl of,** *cr* 1801; **John Nicholas Pelham;** Bt 1611; Baron Pelham of Stanmer, 1762; *b* (posthumously) 14 April 1944; *s* of 8th Earl of Chichester (killed on active service, 1944) and Ursula (*d* 1989) (she *m* 2nd, 1957, Ralph Gunning Henderson; marr. diss. 1971), *o d* of late Walter de Pannwitz, de Hartekamp, Bennebroek, Holland; *S* father, 1944; *m* 1975, Mrs June Marijke Hall; one *d*. *Recreations:* music, flying. *Heir:* kinsman Richard Anthony Henry Pelham [*b* 1 Aug. 1952; *m* 1987, Georgina, *d* of David Gilmour; two *s*]. *Address:* Little Durnford Manor, Salisbury, Wilts SP4 6AH.

See also E. A. Conway.

**CHICHESTER, Bishop of,** since 2012; **Rt Rev. Martin Clive Warner,** PhD; *b* 24 Dec. 1958; *s* of John Warner and Anona Warner (now McGeorge). *Educ:* King's Sch., Rochester; Maidstone Grammar Sch.; Durham Univ. (BA 1980, MA 1985; PhD 2003); St Stephen's House, Oxford. Ordained deacon, 1984, priest, 1985; Asst Curate, St Peter, Plymouth, 1984–88; Team Vicar, Parish of the Resurrection, Leicester, 1988–93; Priest Administrator, Shrine of Our Lady of Walsingham, 1993–2002; Associate Vicar, St Andrew, Holborn, 2002–03; Canon Residentiary, St Paul's Cathedral, 2003–10; Bishop Suffragan of Whitby, 2010–12. A Church Comr, 2014–. Master of Guardians, Shrine of Our Lady of Walsingham, 2006–16. *Publications:* Walsingham: an ever-circling year, 1996; Say Yes to God, 1999; (ed) The Habit of Holiness, 2004; Known to the Senses, 2005; Between Heaven and Charing Cross, 2009. *Recreations:* medieval and Renaissance art, contemporary architecture, cinema, modern fiction, travel. *Address:* The Palace, Chichester, W Sussex PO19 1PY. *T:* (01243) 782161.

**CHICHESTER, Dean of;** see Waine, Very Rev. S. J.

**CHICHESTER, Archdeacon of;** see Irvine-Capel, Ven. L. T.

**CHICHESTER, Giles Bryan;** Member (C) South West England and Gibraltar, European Parliament, 2004–14 (Devon and East Plymouth, 1994–99; South West Region, England, 1999–2004); *b* 29 July 1946; *s* of Sir Francis Chichester, KBE and Sheila Mary (*née* Craven); *m* 1979, Virginia Ansell; two *s* one *d*. *Educ:* Westminster Sch.; Christ Church, Oxford (BA Hons Geography; MA). FRGS 1972. Trainee, Univ. of London Press and Hodder & Stoughton, publishers, 1968–69; Francis Chichester Ltd: Production Manager, 1969–71; Co. Sec., 1970–89; Dir, 1971–2013; Man. Dir, 1983–2013; Chm., 1989–2013. Chm., Foreign Affairs Forum, 1987–90. European Parliament: Cons. spokesman: on Research, Technol Develt and Energy Cttee, 1994–99; on Industry, External Trade, Res. and Energy Cttee, 1999–2004; Chm., Industry, Research and Energy Cttee, 2004–07; Leader, Cons. MEPs, 2007–08; Pres., Delegn for Relns with Australia and NZ, 2007–08 and 2008–09; Vice-Pres., 2011–12. Pres., European Energy Forum (formerly Foundn), 2004–14 (Vice Pres., 1995–2004). Mem. Council, Air League, 1995–99. *Publications:* pamphlets on nuclear energy, small business, opportunities for young people in Europe, sustainable energy. *Recreations:* rowing, sailing, vegetarian cooking. *Address:* (office) 9 St James's Place, SW1A 1NP. *T:* (020) 7493 0932; Longridge, West Hill, Ottery St Mary, Devon EX11 1UX. *E:* gbchichester@gmail.com. *Clubs:* Pratt's; London Rowing; Royal Western Yacht (Plymouth); Royal Yacht Squadron (Cowes).

**CHICHESTER, Sir James (Henry Edward),** 12th Bt *cr* 1641, of Raleigh, Devonshire; founder and Chairman, Chichester Trees and Shrubs Ltd; *b* 15 Oct. 1951; *s* of Sir (Edward) John Chichester, 11th Bt and Hon. Anne Rachel Pearl, *d* of 2nd Baron Montagu of Beaulieu; *S* father, 2007; *m* 1990, Margaret Anne, *o d* of late Major John Walkelyne Chandos-Pole, Radbourne Hall, Derbys; two *s*. *Educ:* Eton. Chm., Batsford Foundn, 2000–. *Recreations:* dendrology, stalking, shooting, ornithology. *Heir: s* Edward John Chandos-Pole Chichester, *b* 27 July 1991. *Address:* (office) The Mill Studio, Beaulieu, Hampshire SO42 7YG. *T:* (01590) 612198, *Fax:* (01590) 612194. *Clubs:* Pratt's, Shikar; Beaulieu River Sailing.

**CHICHESTER CLARK, Emma, (Mrs C. R. Wace);** freelance illustrator and author, since 1983; *b* 15 Oct. 1955; *d* of Sir Robin Chichester-Clark; *m* 2008, C. Rupert Wace. *Educ:* Chelsea Sch. of Art (BA Hons); Royal Coll. of Art (MA Hons). Teacher, 1983–85: foundn students, City & Guilds Sch. of Art; Middx Poly. *Publications: author and illustrator:* Catch that Hat!, 1986; The Story of Horrible Hilda and Henry, 1988; Myrtle, Tertle and Gertle; The Bouncing Dinosaur, 1990; Tea with Aunt Augusta, 1991; Miss Bilberry's New House, 1993; Piper; Little Miss Muffet counts to Ten, 1997; More!, 1998; I Love you, Blue Kangaroo!, 1998; Follow my Leader, 1999; Where are you, Blue Kangaroo?, 2000; It was you, Blue Kangaroo!, 2001; No more kissing!, 2001; I'll show you, Blue Kangaroo!, 2003; Up in Heaven, 2003; No more teasing!, 2004; Just for you, Blue Kangaroo!, 2004; Will and Squill, 2005; Melrose and Croc, 2005; Amazing Mr Zooty!, 2006; Melrose and Croc Find a Smile, 2006; Melrose and Croc Friends for Life, 2006; Happy Birthday to You, Blue Kangaroo!, 2006; Eliza and The Moonchild, 2007; Melrose and Croc By the Sea, 2007; Melrose and Croc Go to Town, 2007; Minty and Tink, 2008; Melrose and Croc: a hero's birthday, 2008; Mummy and Me, 2009; My Baby Sister, 2009; Goldilocks and the Three Bears, 2009; Plum, Rabbit and Me, 2010; Lulu and the best cake ever!, 2012; Come to School Too, Blue Kangaroo!, 2012; Lulu and the Treasure Hunt, 2013; Bears Don't Read!, 2014; Plumdog, 2014; Love is My Favourite Thing!, 2015; When I First Met You, Blue Kangaroo, 2015; Plenty of Love to Go Round, 2016; The Plumdog Path to Perfection, 2016; Another Year of Plumdog, 2017; The Rescue of Bunny Wunny, 2018; All You Need is Love, 2019; *illustrated books include: Laura Cecil:* Listen to this!, 1987; Stuff and Nonsense, 1989; Boo!, 1990; A Thousand Yards of Sea, 1992; Preposterous Pets, 1994; The Frog Princess, 1994; Noah and the Space Ark, 1998; The Kingfisher Book of Toy Stories, 2000; Cunning Cat Tales, 2001; Wicked Wolf Tales, 2001; *Geraldine McCaughren:* The Orchard Book of Greek Myths, 1992; The Orchard Book of Greek Gods and Goddesses, 1997; The Orchard Book of Roman Myths, 1999; *Adele Geras:* Sleeping Beauty, 2000; Giselle, 2000; Swan Lake, 2000; The Nutcracker, 2000; *Michael Morpurgo:* Aesop's Fables, 2004; Hansel and Gretel, 2008; The Best of Times, 2009; The Pied Piper of Hamelin, 2011; Pinocchio, 2013; Toto: the dog-gone amazing story of the Wizard of Oz, 2017; *Allan Ahlberg:* Mrs Vole and the Vet, 1996; Baby on Board, 2018; *Lewis Carroll:* Alice in Wonderland (abridged), 2009; Alice Through the Looking Glass, 2013; *Quentin Blake:* Three Little Monkeys, 2016; Three Little Monkeys on Holiday, 2019; Primrose Lockwood, Cissy Lavender, 1989; Margaret Ryan, Fat Witch Rides Again, 1990; James Reeves, Ragged Robin, 1990; Pat Thomson, Beware of the Aunts!, 1991; Margaret Mahy, The Queen's Goat, 1991; Roald Dahl, James and the Giant Peach, 1991; Ben Frankel, Tertius and Pliny, 1992; D. J. Enright, The Way of the Cat, 1992; Peter Dickinson, Time and the Clockmice, 1993; Ann Turnbull, Too Tired, 1993; Anne Fine, The Haunting of Pip Parker, 1994; Gina Pollinger, Something Rich and Strange, 1995; Sam McBratney, Little Red Riding Hood, 1996; John Yeoman, The Glove Puppet Man, 1997; Jane Falloon, Thumbelina, 1997; Adrian Mitchell, The Adventures of Robin Hood and Marian, 1998; Naomi Lewis, Elf Hill, 1999; Kevin Crossley-Holland, Enchantment, 2001; Rosemary Sutcliff, The Minstrel and the Dragon Pup, 2001; Diana Wynne Jones, Wild Robert, 2001; Oxford First Illustrated Dictionary, 2004; Reinhardt Jung, Bambert's Book of Missing Stories, 2008; Oscar Wilde, A Picture of Dorian Grey, 2009; Colin McNaughton, Not Last Night But The Night Before, 2009; Martin Waddell, The Orchard Book of Hans Christian Andersen, 2010; Nanette Newman, What Will You Be, Grandma?, 2011; Colin McNaughton, Have You Ever Ever Ever?, 2011; Enid Blyton, Magical Treasury, 2015; Ben Manley, The Misadventures of Frederick, 2019. *Recreations:* walking, cinema, music, friends. *Address:* c/o Caroline Walsh, David Higham Associates, 7–12 Noel Street, W1F 8GQ. *Club:* Chelsea Arts.

**CHICK, John Stephen;** HM Diplomatic Service, retired; educational consultant, 1994–2005; *b* 5 Aug. 1935; *m* 1966, Margarita Alvarez de Sotomayor; one *s* three *d*. *Educ:* St John's Coll., Cambridge (BA 1959); Univ. of Pennsylvania (MA 1960). Entered FO, 1961; Madrid, 1963–66; First Sec., Mexico City, 1966–69; FCO, 1969–73; First Sec. and Head of Chancery, Rangoon, 1973–76; Head of Chancery, Luxembourg, 1976–78; Commercial Counsellor and Consul-Gen., Buenos Aires, 1978–81; Head of Arms Control Dept, FCO, 1981–83; Head of S Pacific Dept, FCO, 1983–85. Consul-Gen., Geneva, 1985–89. Dir of Internat. Affairs, Sallingbury Casey Ltd, 1990–91; Associate Dir, Rowland Public Affairs, 1991. *Address:* 21 Ranelagh Avenue, SW13 0BL. *T:* (020) 8876 5916.

**CHICKEN, Maj. Gen. Simon Timothy,** OBE 2003 (MBE 1996); Head of Distribution Development and Transport, Waitrose, 2016–19; *b* Blyth, Northumberland, 24 April 1955; *s* of Joseph Leonard and Isobel Chicken; *m* 1987, Charlotte Kate Davies; two *s*. *Educ:* King Edward VI Sch., Morpeth; King's Coll. London (MA Defence Studies). Royal Marines: Young Officer Trng, 1977; Regtl Duty, 1978–90; Royal Netherlands Marine Corps (on exchange), 1990–92; RNSC, 1993; Officer Comdg K Co., 42 Commando, 1993–95; Staff Officer, Operational Requirements, 1995–97; Officer Comdg, 539 Assault Sqdn, 1997–2000; CO, 45 Commando Gp, 2000–02; British Defence Staff, Washington, 2003–06; COS, Jt Force HQ, 2006–08; ACOS, Perm. Jt HQ, 2008–10; Sen. Directing Staff (Navy), RCDS, 2011–13. Sen. Responsible Owner, Stock Operating Model Prog., 2014–15, Hd of Nat. Distribution, 2015–16, Waitrose. *Recreations:* walking, running, cycling, playing guitar. *Address:* c/o Corps Secretary, Whale Island, Portsmouth PO2 8ER. *T:* (023) 9254 7214. *E:* Ed.Musto287@mod.gov.uk. *Club:* Victory Services.

**CHIDDICK, Prof. David Martin,** CBE 2010; Chairman, Leicestershire Partnership NHS Trust, 2011–15; *b* 26 Oct. 1948; *s* of Derek and Jeanette Chiddick; *m* 1973, Jane Elizabeth Sills; one *s* two *d*. *Educ:* Poly. of Central London; Cranfield Univ. (MSc). FRICS 1975; MRTPI 1979. Sen. Planning Officer, Herts CC, 1977–79; Prof. of Land Econ., 1985–87, Sen. Dean, 1987–89, Dep. Dir, 1989–93, Leicester Poly., then De Montfort Univ.; Pro-Vice Chancellor, De Montfort Univ., 1993–2000; Vice Chancellor, Univ. of Lincoln, 2000–09, now Prof. Emeritus. Chm., NHS E Midlands Strategic HA, 2010–11 (non-exec. Dir, 2004–10); non-exec. Dir, Leicester Royal Infirmary, 1993–2000. Chm., HEFCE Space Mgt Gp. Mem. Council, Lincs Agricl Soc. (Pres., 2010). Founding Ed., Jl of Property Mgt, 1984–95. Liveryman, Merchant Taylors' Co. FRSA 1992. *Publications:* (ed with A. Millington) Land Management: new directions, 1983; Lincoln 2020, 2006. *Recreations:* mountain walking, watching Rugby Union, golf, reading, music. *Address:* 64 Dalby Avenue, Bushby, Leicester LE7 9RD.

**CHIDGEY,** family name of **Baron Chidgey**.

**CHIDGEY,** Baron *cr* 2005 (Life Peer), of Hamble-le-Rice in the county of Hampshire; **David William George Chidgey,** CEng, FICE, FCIHT, FIEI; *b* 9 July 1942; *s* of Cyril Cecil Chidgey and Winifred Hilda Doris Chidgey (*née* Weston); *m* 1965, April Carolyn

Idris-Jones; one s two d. Educ: Royal Naval Coll., Portsmouth; Portsmouth Poly. CEng 1971; MCIT 1985; FCIHT (FIHT 1990); FIEI 1990; FICE 1993; MConsEI 1993. Mech. and aeronautical engr, Admiralty, 1958–64; Highways and Civil Engr, Hants CC, 1965–72; Brian Colquhoun and Partners: Chartered Engr and Project Manager, UK, ME and W Africa, 1973–85; Associate Partner and Man. Dir, Ireland, 1981–88; Associate Partner, Central Southern England, 1988–93; Thorburn Colquhoun: Associate Dir, Southern England and Project Dir, Engrg Facilities Management, mil. estabts in Hants, 1994–. Mem. Adv. Bd, UK Br., Transparency Internat., 2008–. Chairman: Internat. Adv. Bd, Commonwealth Policy Studies Unit, 2008–11; Commonwealth Policy Develt Cttee, 2018–. Mem. Council, 2007–, Political Coordinator for Aid Effectiveness Progs., 2011–17, Eur. Parliamentarians for Africa. Contested: (SLD) Hampshire Central, Eur. Parlt, Dec. 1988 and 1989; (Lib Dem) Eastleigh, 1992. MP (Lib Dem) Eastleigh, June 1994–2005. Lib Dem spokesman for: employment, 1994–95; transport, 1995–97; trade and industry, 1997–99; for Internat. Develt and Foreign and Commonwealth Affairs (Africa), H of L, 2010–; for Africa, H of L, 2017–; Lib Dem dep. spokesman for defence, 2006–07; Lib Dem delegate to Council of Europe and WEU, 2009–10. Member: Foreign Affairs Cttee, 1999–2005; Chairmen's Panel, 2001–05; Jt Cttee on Human Rights, 2003–05; EU Sub Cttee C, Foreign Affairs, Defence and Develt, H of L, 2006–09; Co-Chairman: Lib Dem Parly Party Cttee on Internat. Develt, 2010–13; Commonwealth All-Party Parly Gp, 2013–; Chm., 2013–16, Co-Chm., 2016–, Africa All-Party Parly Gp. Trustee, Africa Europe Parly Initiative, 2019–. CRAeS 2004. MInstD. *Publications*: papers in technical jl, Traffic Engineering and Control. *Recreations*: walking, reading. *Address*: House of Lords, SW1A 0PW. *Clubs*: National Liberal, Royal Over-Seas League.

**CH'IEN, Dr Raymond Kuo Fung,** GBS 1999; CBE 1994; JP; Chairman, Hang Seng Bank Ltd, since 2007; b 26 Jan. 1952; s of James Ch'ien and Ellen Ma; m Whang Hwee Leng; one s two d. *Educ*: Rockford Coll., Illinois (BA 1973); Univ. of Pennsylvania (PhD Econs 1978). Gp Man. Dir, Lam Soon Hong Kong Gp, 1984–97; Chm., China.com Inc., 1999–2013. Dir, MTR Corporation Ltd, 1998–2015 (Chm., 2003–15). MEC, Hong Kong, then HKSAR, 1992–2002. Trustee, Univ. of Pennsylvania, 2006–16. JP Hong Kong, 1993. Young Industrialist Award, Hong Kong, 1988. *Recreations*: scuba diving, hiking, tennis, Chinese paintings and ceramics. *Address*: Suites 28 & 30, 2/F., Casey Building, 38 Lok Ku Road, Hong Kong. *T*: (office) 25430887. *Clubs*: Hong Kong, Hong Kong Jockey.

**CHIENE, John;** b 27 Jan. 1937; s of John and Muriel Chiene; m 1st, 1965, Anne; one s one d; 2nd, 1986, Carol; one d. *Educ*: Rugby; Queens' Coll., Cambridge (BA). Wood Mackenzie: joined, 1962; Man. Partner, 1969; Sen. Partner, 1974; Jt Chief Exec., Hill Samuel & Co. Ltd (who had merged with Wood Mackenzie), 1987; Chm., County NatWest Securities, on their merger with Wood Mackenzie, 1988–89; Dep. Chm., County NatWest Ltd, 1989–90; Chm., Gartmore Capital Strategy Fund, 1996–2002. *Recreations*: golf, opera, ski-ing. *Clubs*: City of London; New (Edinburgh).

**CHIGNELL, Anthony Hugh,** MBE 2009; FRCS; FRCOphth; Consulting Ophthalmic Surgeon: St Thomas' Hospital, 1973–99; King Edward VII Hospital, 1985–2000; Hospitaller, St John of Jerusalem, 2002–08; b 14 April 1939; s of Thomas Hugh Chignell and Phyllis Una (née Green); m 1962, Phillippa Price Brayne-Nicholls; one s two d. *Educ*: Worth Sch.; Downside Sch.; St Thomas' Hosp. (MB BS 1962). DO 1966; FRCS 1968; FRCOphth 1989 (Hon. FRCOphth 2006). Registrar, Moorfields Eye Hosp., 1966–69; Sen. Registrar, Retinal Unit, Moorfields Eye Hosp. and St Thomas' Hosp., 1969–73; Teacher in Ophthalmology, London Univ., 1980–99. Civilian Consultant in Ophthalmology to Army, 1983–99; Consultant Advr in Ophthalmology to Metropolitan Police, 1988–99. Scientific Advr, Nat. Eye Inst., 1991–99; International Advisor: Dept of Ophthalmology, Hong Kong Univ., 2011–16; Lifeline Express Foundn, Hong Kong, 2012–16; Rwanda Inst. of Internat. Ophthalmology, 2012–16. Chm., World Sight Foundn, 2012–. Gov., Royal Nat. Coll. for Blind, 1987–97; Mem. Council, GDBA, 1989–2002 (Dep. Chm., 2001–02). Mem., Jules Gonin Club, 1972. Trustee: Ridley Eye Foundn (formerly Ridley Foundn), 1988–2012 (Chm., 2001–04); Fight for Sight, 1992–95; British Humane Assoc., 2008– (Chm., 2010–). Mem. Court, Spectacle Makers' Co., 1988–2010 (Master, 1999–2000). GCStJ 2008 (OStJ 1987; KStJ 2002). *Publications*: Retinal Detachment Surgery, 1979, 2nd edn 1988; Vitreo-Retinal Surgery, 1998; numerous articles related to retinal detachment surgery. *Recreations*: fly-fishing, golf, Herefordshire. *Address*: 3 Tedworth Square, SW3 4DU. *Clubs*: MCC; New Zealand Golf (Weybridge); Seniors Golfing Soc.

**CHILCOT, Rt Hon. Sir John (Anthony),** GCB 1998 (KCB 1994; CB 1990); PC 2004; Chairman, B & CE Group, 1999–2013; President, Police Foundation, 2011–19 (Chairman of Trustees, 2001–11); b 22 April 1939; s of Henry William Chilcot and Catherine Chilcot (née Ashall). *Educ*: Brighton Coll. (Lyon Scholar); Pembroke Coll., Cambridge (Open Scholar; MA; Hon. Fellow, 1999). Joined Home Office, 1963; Asst Private Sec. to Home Secretary (Rt Hon. Roy Jenkins), 1966; Private Sec. to Head of Civil Service (late Baron Armstrong of Sanderstead), 1971–73; Principal Private Secretary to Home Secretary (Rt Hon. Merlyn Rees; Rt Hon. William Whitelaw), 1978–80; Asst Under-Sec. of State, Dir of Personnel and Finance, Prison Dept, 1980–84; Under-Sec., Cabinet Office (MPO), 1984–86; Asst Under Sec. of State, 1986 (seconded to Schroders, 1986–87), Dep. Under Sec. of State, 1987–90, Home Office; Permanent Under Sec. of State, NI Office, 1990–97. Staff Counsellor: Security and Intelligence Agencies, 1999–2004; Nat. Criminal Intelligence Service, 2002–06. Member: Ind. Commn on the Voting System, 1997–98; Lord Chancellor's Adv. Council on Public Records, 1999–2003; Nat. Archives Council, 2003–04; Review of Intelligence on Weapons of Mass Destruction, 2004; Chairman: Privy Council Cttee on Intercept as Evidence, 2007–09, Adv. Cttee, 2009–; Iraq Inquiry, 2009–16 (Chilcot Report publd 2016). Director: RTZ Pillar, 1986–90; NBW Ltd, 2002–12. Pres., First Div. Pensioners' Gp, 1998–2002. Trustee, The Police Rehabilitation Trust, 2002–19. Mem., Awards Council, Royal Anniversary Trust, 2003–. Vice-Pres. and Fellow, Brighton Coll., 2005–. Hon. FBA 2019. *Recreations*: reading, music and opera, travel.

**CHILCOTT, Sir Dominick (John),** KCMG 2018 (CMG 2003); HM Diplomatic Service; Ambassador to Turkey, since 2018; b 17 Nov. 1959; s of Michael and Rosemary Chilcott; m 1983, Jane Elizabeth Bromage; three s one d. *Educ*: St Joseph's Coll., Ipswich; Greyfriars Hall, Oxford (BA Hons (Philosophy and Theol.) 1982). Midshipman, RN, 1978–79; entered FCO, 1982; Southern African Dept, FCO, 1982–83; Turkish lang. trng, 1984; Third, later Second, Sec., Ankara, 1985–88; First Sec., Central African Dept, then EC Dept (Internal), FCO, 1988–92; Hd, Political Section, Lisbon, 1993–95; Private Sec. to Foreign Sec., 1996–98; Counsellor, Ext. Relns, UK Perm. Repn to EU, Brussels, 1998–2002; Dir, Iraq Policy Unit, 2002–03; Dir, EU Directorate, FCO, 2003–06: High Comr, Sri Lanka, 2006–07; Dep. Hd of Mission, Washington, 2008–11; Middle East and N Africa Directorate, FCO, 2011; Ambassador: Iran, 2011; Ireland, 2012–16. *Recreations*: reading, walking, watching sport, music, theatre. *Address*: c/o Foreign and Commonwealth Office, King Charles Street, SW1A 2AH. *E*: dominick.chilcott@fco.gov.uk.

**CHILCOTT, Robert Lionel;** tenor; conductor; full-time composer, since 1997; b Plymouth, 9 April 1955; m 1st, Polly (marr. diss.); one s three d; 2nd, 2005, Kate Ledger; one d. *Educ*: King's Coll., Cambridge (choral scholar; BA 1976). Mem., King's Singers, 1986–97. Principal Guest Conductor, BBC Singers; former Conductor, Royal Coll. of Music Chorus; conductor of choirs worldwide incl. World Youth Choir, RIAS Kammerchor, Orphei Drangar, Jauna Musika, Taipei Chamber Singers and Tower NZ Youth Choir. Composer of choral music, esp. for youth choirs. *Compositions include*: Can you hear me?, 1998; The Making of the Drum, 1999; Jubilate, 1999; Canticles of Light, 2000; A Little Jazz Mass, 2004; Advent Antiphons, 2005; Weather Report, 2006; Missa Cantate, 2006; This Day, 2007; Salisbury Vespers, 2009; Requiem, 2010; On Christmas Night, 2011; Jazz Songs of Innocence, 2011; Nidaros Jazz Mass, 2012; Angry Planet, 2012; St John Passion, 2013; Five Days that Changed the World, 2013; Move him into the sun, 2018; Christmas Oratorio, 2018. *Address*: c/o Choral Connections, 14 Stevens Close, Prestwood, Great Missenden, Bucks HP16 0SQ. *W*: www.bobchilcott.com.

**CHILD, Sir (Coles John) Jeremy,** 3rd Bt cr 1919; actor; b 20 Sept. 1944; s of Sir Coles John Child, 2nd Bt, and Sheila (d 1964), e d of Hugh Mathewson; S father, 1971; m 1971, Deborah Jane (née Snelling) (marr. diss. 1976); one d; m 1978, Jan (marr. diss. 1986), y d of B. Todd, Kingston upon Thames; one s one d; m 1987, Elizabeth (d 2019), y d of Rev. Grenville Morgan, Canterbury, Kent; one s one d. *Educ*: Eton; Univ. of Poitiers (Dip. in French). Trained at Bristol Old Vic Theatre Sch., 1963–65; Bristol Old Vic, 1965–66; repertory at Windsor, Canterbury and Colchester; Conduct Unbecoming, Queen's, 1970; appeared at Royal Court, Mermaid and Bankside Globe, 1973; Oh Kay, Westminster, 1974; Donkey's Years, Globe, 1977; Hay Fever, Lyric, Hammersmith, 1980; Out of Order, Far and Middle East tour, 1995; Plenty, Albery, 1999; Pride and Prejudice, UK tour, 2000; The Circle, UK tour, 2002; Ying Tong, New Ambassadors, 2005; An English Tragedy, Palace Th., Watford, 2008; Balmoral, UK tour, 2009; Artist Descending a Staircase, Old Red Lion, 2009; *films include*: Privilege, 1967; Oh What a Lovely War!, 1967; The Breaking of Bumbo, 1970; Young Winston, 1971; The Stud, 1976; Quadrophenia, 1978; Sir Henry at Rawlinson's End, 1979; Chanel Solitaire, 1980; High Road to China, 1982; Give my Regards to Broad Street, 1983; Taffin, 1987; A Fish called Wanda, 1989; The Madness of King George, 1994; Regeneration, 1996; Don't Go Breaking My Heart, 1997; Whatever Happened to Harold Smith?, 1999; Lagaan, 2000; Laissez Passer, South Kensington, 2001; Wimbledon, Separate Lies, 2003; Porter, 2010; The Iron Lady, 2011; Darkest Hour, 2018; *television includes*: 'Tis Pity She's a Whore; Diana, Her True Story; Falklands Play, 2002; *series*: Father, Dear Father, Edward and Mrs Simpson, The Jewel in the Crown, Bergerac, The Glittering Prizes, Wings, Fairly Secret Army, Oxbridge Blues, Edge of Darkness, First Among Equals, Game, Set and Match, Lovejoy, Perfect Scoundrels, Gravy Train Goes East, Headhunters, Harnessing Peacocks, Sharpe's Enemy, Frank Stubbs Promotes, A Dance to the Music of Time, Mosley, A Touch of Frost, Love in a Cold Climate, Doc Martin, Midsomer Murders, Judge John Deed, Amnesia, East Enders, Doctors, The Little Drummer Girl. *Heir*: s Coles John Alexander Child, b 10 May 1982. *Club*: Garrick.

**CHILD, Denis Marsden,** CBE 1987; Director, Eurotunnel plc, 1985–98; b 1 Nov. 1926; s of late Percival Snowden Child and Alice Child (née Jackson); m 1973, Patricia Charlton (d 2015); two s one d by previous marr. *Educ*: Woodhouse Grove Sch., Bradford. Joined Westminster Bank, Leeds, 1942; RN, 1944–48; rejoined Westminster Bank; National Westminster Bank: Asst Area Manager, Leeds, 1970; Area Manager, Wembley, 1972; Chief Manager, Planning and Marketing, 1975; Head, Management Inf. and Control, 1977; Gen. Manager, Financial Control Div., 1979; Dir, NatWest Bank, 1982–96; Dep. Gp Chief Exec., 1982–87; Dir, Coutts & Co., 1982–97; Chm., Lombard North Central, 1991–96. Chairman: Exec. Cttee, BBA, 1986–87; Council, Assoc. for Payment Clearing Services, 1985–86; Financial Markets Cttee, Fedn Bancaire, EC, 1985–87; Director: Internat. Commodities Clearing House, 1982–86 (Chm., 1990–93); Investors Compensation Scheme Ltd, 1988–92. Bd Mem., CAA, 1986–90. Mem., IBM UK Pensions Trust, 1984–97 (Chm., 1994–97). Member: Accounting Standards Cttee, 1985–90; Securities and Investments Bd, 1986–92. FCIB; FCIS. *Recreations*: golf, gardening. *Address*: Fairways, Park Road, Farnham Royal, Bucks SL2 3BQ. *T*: (01753) 648096. *Club*: Stoke Park Golf.

**CHILD, Sir Jeremy;** see Child, Sir C. J. J.

**CHILD, Prof. John,** FBA 2006; Professor of Commerce, University of Birmingham, 2000–09 and since 2013; b 10 Nov. 1940; s of late Clifton James Child, OBE and Hilde Child (née Hurwitz); m 1965, Marianne Ann Mitchiner; one s one d. *Educ*: St John's College, Cambridge (scholar; MA, PhD, ScD). Rolls-Royce, 1965–66; Aston Univ., 1966–68; London Business Sch., 1968–73; Prof. of Organizational Behaviour, Aston Univ., 1973–91 (Dean, Aston Business Sch., 1986–89); Dean and Dir, China-Europe Management Inst., Beijing, 1989–90; Diageo Prof. of Mgt Studies, Univ. of Cambridge, and Fellow of St John's Coll., Cambridge, 1991–2000. Vis. Fellow, Nuffield Coll., Oxford, 1973–78; Visiting Professor: Univ. of Hong Kong, 1998–2000; Lingnan Coll., Sun Yat-Sen Univ., Guangzhou, China, 2012–17. Editor-in-Chief, Organization Studies, 1992–96. Hon. Dr: Helsinki Sch. of Econs, 1996; Corvinus, Budapest, 2009; Aalborg, Denmark, 2016; DLit Aston, 2013. *Publications*: British Management Thought, 1969; The Business Enterprise in Modern Industrial Society, 1969; Organization, 1977; (jtly) Lost Managers, 1982; (ed) Reform Policy and the Chinese Enterprise, 1990; (jtly) Reshaping Work, 1990; (jtly) New Technology in European Services, 1990; Management in China, 1994; (jtly) Co-operative Strategy, 1998, 3rd edn 2019; (jtly) The Management of International Acquisitions, 2001; Organization, 2005, 2nd edn 2015; (jtly) Corporate Co-evolution, 2008 (George R. Terry Award, Acad. of Mgt, 2009); (ed) The Evolution of Organizations, 2012; (ed) Knowledge and the Study of Organization and Management, 2013; (jtly) The Dynamics of Corporate Co-evolution, 2013; Hierarchy, 2019; numerous contribs to learned jls. *Recreations*: sailing, mountain walking, bridge. *Address*: Birmingham Business School, University House, University of Birmingham, Birmingham B15 2TT. *T*: (0121) 414 8322. *E*: j.child@bham.ac.uk. *Club*: Earlswood Sailing.

**CHILD, Prof. Mark Sheard,** PhD; FRS 1989; Coulson Professor of Theoretical Chemistry, University of Oxford, 1994–2004, and Fellow of University College, Oxford, 1994–2007; b 17 Aug. 1937; s of George Child and Kathleen (née Stevenson); m 1964, Daphne Hall; one s two d. *Educ*: Pocklington Sch., Yorks; Clare Coll., Cambridge (BA, PhD). Vis. Scientist, Berkeley, California, 1962–63; Lectr in Theoretical Chem., Glasgow Univ., 1963–66; Oxford University: Lectr in Theoretical Chem., 1966–89; Aldrichian Praelector in Chemistry, Oxford Univ., 1989–92; Prof. of Chemical Dynamics, 1992–94; Fellow, St Edmund Hall, 1966–94, Emeritus Fellow, 1994–. *Publications*: Molecular Collision Theory, 1974; Semiclassical Methods with Molecular Applications, 1991, 2nd edn 2014; Theory of Molecular Rydberg States, 2011. *Recreations*: gardening, walking, local history. *Address*: 50 Ashley Drive, Swinton, Manchester M27 0AX.

**CHILD VILLIERS,** family name of **Earl of Jersey.**

**CHILDS, Darren Michael;** Chief Executive, Premiership Rugby, since 2019; b Doncaster, March 1966; s of Alan Childs and Sonia Childs; m 2000, Dr Jacqueline; one s one d. *Educ*: Doncaster Grammar Sch.; Stanford Graduate Sch. of Business (Exec. Prog. in Internat. Mgt). Dir, Business Develt, Star TV, Hong Kong, 1991–98; Sen. Vice Pres., Sony Pictures Television Internat., 1998–2005; Man. Dir, Global Networks, BBC Worldwide, 2005–10;

CEO, UKTV, then UKTV Media, 2010–19. Non-exec. Dir, Antenna Gp Adv. Bd, 2014–. Mem., Angel Investor Network, London Business Sch. Enterprise 100, 2013–. Mem., BAFTA, 2011–. *Recreations:* TV (of course), Rugby, technology, cycling. *Address:* Premiership Rugby, 7th Floor, Regal House, 70 London Road, Twickenham TW1 3QS.

**CHILDS, David Robert;** Managing Partner, Clifford Chance, 2006–14; *b* 28 June 1951; *s* of late Robert and of Gwenifer Childs; *m* 1993, Julie Meyer; two *s* one *d*. *Educ:* Sheffield Univ. (LLB); University Coll. London (LLM). Admitted solicitor, 1976; Clifford Chance: Partner, 1981–2014; Hd, Global Corporate Practice Area, 2000–05; Chief Operating Officer, 2003–06. Non-exec. Dir and Chm., Conduct Cttee, Financial Reporting Council, 2014–. Hon. LLD Sheffield, 2016. *Recreations:* good restaurants, reading, woodland, travel.

**CHILDS, Richard John Nicholas,** QPM 1998; Chairman, Lincolnshire West Clinical Commissioning Group, since 2013; *b* Plymouth, 20 Sept. 1954; *s* of John Peter Childs and Daphne Rosamond Childs (*née* Whiter); *m* 1984, Caroline Mary Cocks; one *s*, and one step *s* one step *d*. *Educ:* Plymouth Coll.; Open Univ. (BSc Psychol. and Stats 1996). Metropolitan Police, 1973–87; Asst Chief Constable, Sussex Police, 1987–97; Dep. Chief Constable, Crime Prevention Agency, Home Office, 1997–98; Chief Constable, Lincolnshire Police, 1998–2003. Man. Dir, Community Safety Consultancy Ltd, 2003–15. Chm., NHS Lincs, 2007–13. Member: Prison Service Pay Review Body, 2006–12; Commn for Rural Communities, 2009–13; GDC Fitness to Practise Panel, 2011–; Police Remuneration Rev. Body, 2018–; Nat. Crime Agency Remuneration Rev. Body, 2018–. *Recreations:* railways, book binding, travelling.

**CHILDS, Robert Simon;** Chairman, Hiscox Ltd, since 2013 (Chief Underwriting Officer, 2001–13); *b* Brentwood, 21 June 1951; *m* 1977, Mary; two *s* one *d*. *Educ:* Bedford Coll., Univ. of London (BA Hons Hist.). Joined Hiscox, 1986; Active Underwriter, Hiscox Lloyd's Syndicate 33, 1993–98; Chm., Hiscox USA, 1998–; CEO, Hiscox Insce Co. (Bermuda) Ltd, 2005–09. Chairman: Lloyd's War, Civil War and Financial Guarantee Sub-Cttee, 2000; Lloyd's Market Assoc., 2003–05; Mem., Council, Lloyd's, 2012– (a Dep. Chm., 2017–). Non-exec. Dir, HIM Capital Hldgs Ltd, 2009. Chm., Adv. Bd, Mgt Sch., Royal Holloway, Univ. of London, 2004–12. Trustee, Enham, 2010–. Chm., Bermuda Soc., 2010–. *Recreations:* sailing, tennis, golf. *Address:* Hiscox Ltd, 45 Reid Street, Hamilton, HM12, Bermuda. *T:* 2788300. *E:* lauren.kane@hiscox.com. *Club:* Royal Bermuda Yacht.

**CHILLINGWORTH, Rt Rev. David Robert;** Bishop of St Andrews, Dunkeld and Dunblane, 2005–17; Primus of the Scottish Episcopal Church, 2009–17; *b* 23 June 1951; *s* of David Andrew Richard Chillingworth and Sheila Margaret (*née* Bateman); *m* 1975, Alison Penney; two *s* one *d*. *Educ:* Portora Royal Sch., Enniskillen; Royal Belfast Academical Instn; Trinity Coll., Dublin (BA Classics 1973); Oriel Coll., Oxford (BA Theol. 1975, MA 1981); Ripon Coll., Cuddesdon. Ordained deacon, 1976, priest, 1977; Curate-Asst, Holy Trinity, Joanmount, 1976–79; C of I Youth Officer, 1979–83; Curate-Asst, Bangor Abbey, 1983–86; Rector, Seagoe Parish Ch, Portadown, 1986–2005; Dean of Dromore, 1995–2002; Archdeacon of Dromore, 2002–05. Hon. DD South, Sewanee, Tenn, 2014. *Recreations:* music, reading, cycling, sailing, travel. *Address:* 9 Almondhill Steading, Kirkliston, Edinburgh EH29 9LA. *E:* david@chillingworth.org.uk. *W:* www.bishopdavid.net.

**CHILSTON,** 4th Viscount *cr* 1911, of Boughton Malherbe; **Alastair George Akers-Douglas;** Baron Douglas of Baads, 1911; film producer; *b* 5 Sept. 1946; *s* of Ian Stanley Akers-Douglas (*d* 1952) (*g s* of 1st Viscount) and of Phyllis Rosemary (who *m* 2nd, John Anthony Cobham Shaw, MC), *d* of late Arthur David Clere Parsons; *S* cousin, 1982; *m* 1971, Juliet Anne, *d* of Lt-Col Nigel Lovett, Glos Regt; three *s*. *Educ:* Eton College; Madrid Univ. *Recreation:* sailing. *Heir:* *s* Hon. Oliver Ian Akers-Douglas [*b* 13 Oct. 1973; *m* 2005, Camilla Elizabeth Haldane Edwards; two *s* one *d*]. *Address:* Tichborne Cottage, Tichborne, Alresford, Hants SO24 0NA. *T:* (01962) 734010.

**CHILVERS, Prof. Clair Evelyn Druce,** DSc; Founder Trustee and Chair, Mental Health Research UK, since 2008; published poet; *b* 8 Feb. 1946; *d* of Air Cdre Stanley Edwin Druce Mills, CB, CBE and Joan Mary Mills (*née* James); *m* 1st, 1965, Antony Stuart Chilvers, MA, MChir, FRCS (marr. diss. 1995); one *s* one *d*; 2nd, 1998, Bill Crampin (marr. diss. 2007). *Educ:* Cheltenham Ladies' Coll.; LSE (BSc Econ); LSHTM (MSc); DSc Nottingham 1995. Scientist, Inst. of Cancer Res., 1979–90; Prof. of Epidemiology, Med. Sch., 1990–99, now Emeritus, and Dean of Grad. Sch., 1996–99, Nottingham Univ.; Department of Health: Dir of R & D, Trent Region, NHS Exec., 1999–2002; Head of R & D, Directorate of Health and Social Care, Midlands and E of England, 2002–04; Dir, NHS R & D, Mental Health, 2004–06; Research Director: Nat. Inst. for Mental Health, 2004–06; Care Services Improvement Partnership, DoH, 2006–07; Mental Health Act Commission, 2006; Chm., Notts Healthcare NHS Trust, 2007–10; Chair, Glos Hosps NHS Foundn Trust, 2011–16. Mem., Royal Commn on Envmtl Pollution, 1994–98. Mem., Cttee on Carcinogenicity of Chemicals in Food, Consumer Products and Envmt, DoH, 1993–2000. Non-executive Director: Nottingham Community Health NHS Trust, 1991–96; Learning and Skills (formerly Further Education) Develt Agency, 1998–2001. Trustee: Lloyds TSB Foundn, 2005–10; Centre for Mental Health, 2010–14; Barnwood Trust, 2012–18; McPin Foundn, 2017–. Member, Council: Nottingham Univ., 1994–99; Cheltenham Coll., 2011–15; Chm. Council, Southwell Cathedral, 2000–06. MRSocMed 2011. DL Notts, 2007–10. *Publications:* numerous in learned jls, mainly in field of cancer epidemiology. *Recreations:* writing poetry, opera, classical music, cinema, walking, food and wine, travel.

**CHILVERS, Prof. Edwin Roy,** PhD, ScD; FRCP, FRCPE; FMedSci; Professor of Medicine and Head, National Heart and Lung Institute, Imperial College London, since 2018; *b* 17 March 1959; *s* of Derek John Chilvers and Marjorie Grace Chilvers; *m* 1982, Rowena Joy Tyssen; two *s* one *d*. *Educ:* Univ. of Nottingham Med. Sch. (BMedSci 1980; BM BS Hons 1982); PhD London 1991; MA 2002, ScD 2016, Cantab. MRCP 1985, FRCP 1999; FRCPE 1995. Registrar, Ealing and Hammersmith Hosps, 1985–87; MRC Clinical Trng Fellow, 1987–90; Edinburgh University: Lectr in Respiratory Medicine, 1990–92; Wellcome Trust Sen. Res. Fellow in Clinical Sci., 1992–98; Reader in Medicine, 1997–98; Prof. of Respiratory Medicine, 1998–2018, Dir, Graduate Educn, Sch. of Clinical Medicine, 2017–18, Univ. of Cambridge; Fellow, St Edmund's Coll., Cambridge, 1999–2018. Hon. Consultant Physician: Royal Infirmary, Edinburgh, 1992–98; Addenbrooke's and Royal Papworth Hosps, 1998–2018. Non-exec. Dir, Papworth Hosp. NHS Trust, 2002–06. FMedSci 2007; FHEA 2007. *Publications:* (ed jtly) Davidson's Principles and Practice of Medicine, 17th edn 1995 to 19th edn 2002; contrib. scientific papers on inflammatory cell biol. and intracellular signalling. *Recreations:* wine, music, cycling. *Address:* 4 Mallows Close, Comberton, Cambridge CB23 7GN. *T:* (01223) 331531.

**CHIN, Prof. Jason William Karl,** PhD; FMedSci; Head, Centre for Chemical and Synthetic Biology, since 2010, and Joint Head, Division of Protein and Nucleic Acid Chemistry, since 2018, Medical Research Council Laboratory of Molecular Biology; Professor of Chemistry and Chemical Biology, University of Cambridge, since 2012; Fellow in Natural Sciences, Trinity College, Cambridge, since 2007; *b* London, 9 July 1973; *s* of Edgar Chin and Margaret Chin; *m* 2005, Stacey Erin Rutledge; one *s* one *d*. *Educ:* William Ellis Sch.; Lincoln Coll., Oxford (BA Chem. 1996); Yale Univ. (PhD Organic Chem. 2001). Postdoctoral Fellow, Scripps Research Inst., La Jolla, 2001–03; Prog. Leader, MRC-LMB, Univ. of Cambridge, 2003–; Dir of Studies in Biochem., Trinity Coll. Cambridge, 2007–. Lectures incl. Andrew E. Derome Meml, Univ. of Oxford, 2013. FMedSci 2016. Mem. and Gold Medal, EMBO, 2010. Francis Crick Prize, Royal Soc., 2009; Corday-Morgan Prize, RSC, 2010; Sackler Prize in Phys. Scis, Tel Aviv Univ., 2019. *Publications:* approx. 100 articles in scientific jls. *Address:* Medical Research Council Laboratory of Molecular Biology, Francis Crick Avenue, Cambridge CB2 0QH. *E:* chin@mrc-lmb.cam.ac.uk.

**CHINERY, David John;** District Judge (Magistrates' Courts), Thames Valley, 2013–16; a Recorder, since 2002; *b* 10 Aug. 1950; *s* of Oliver John Chinery and Gladys Alberta Chinery; *m* 1973, Jeannette Elizabeth Owens; two *d*. *Educ:* Alleyne's Sch., Stevenage; Coll. of Law. Justices' Clerk's Asst, Hitchin Magistrates' Court, 1969–75; Asst Clerk to Justices, Northampton Magistrates' Court, 1975–79; admitted solicitor, 1979; Asst Solicitor, 1979–82, Partner, 1982–90, Borneo, Martell & Partners, Northampton; sole practitioner, 1990–98. Deputy Stipendiary Magistrate: Nottingham, 1993–98; Doncaster, 1996–98; Birmingham, 1997–98; Stipendiary Magistrate, later District Judge (Magistrates' Court), W Midlands, 1998–2013. *Recreations:* Rugby Union football, cricket, music, Victorian poetry. *Address:* Midlands Regional Support Unit, Floor 4, Priory Court, 33 Bull Street, Birmingham B4 6DS.

**CHING, Henry,** CBE 1982; Secretary General, Caritas-Hong Kong, 1990–91; *b* 2 Nov. 1933; *s* of Henry Ching, OBE and Ruby Irene Ching; *m* 1963, Eileen Frances Peters; two *d*. *Educ:* Diocesan Boys' School, Hong Kong; Hong Kong Univ. (BA Hons); Wadham Coll., Oxford (MA, DipEd). Schoolmaster, 1958–61; Hong Kong Civil Service: various appts, 1961–73; Principal Asst Financial Sec., 1973–76; Dep. Financial Sec., 1976–83; Sec. for Health and Welfare and MLC, Hong Kong, 1983–85, retired. Chief Administrator, Hong Kong Foundn, 1989. Chm., Hong Kong Volunteer and ex-POW Assoc. of NSW, 2006–10. *Recreations:* cricket, rowing. *Address:* 39 Saiala Road, East Killara, NSW 2071, Australia.

**CHINKIN, Prof. Christine Mary,** CMG 2017; PhD; FBA 2009; barrister; Professor of International Law, now Emerita, and Director, Centre for Women, Peace and Security, 2015–18, London School of Economics and Political Science; William W. Cook Global Law Professor, University of Michigan. *Educ:* Univ. of London (LLB 1971; LLM 1972); Yale Univ. (LLM 1981); Univ. of Sydney (PhD 1990). Mem., Law Faculty, Univ. of Sydney; Prof. and Dean, Faculty of Law, Univ. of Southampton, 1993. Called to the Bar, 2003; Member, Matrix Chambers. Visiting Professor: AHRC, Australian Nat. Univ., 2003; Columbia Univ., 2004; Dir of Studies, Internat. Law Assoc., 2004–; Scholar in Residence, Amnesty Internat., 2005. Consultant on human rights and human trafficking, UN Office of High Comr of Human Rights, 2002; Expert Consultant on violence against women, UN Div. for the Advancement of Women, 2005; Mem., Kosovo Human Rights Adv. Panel, 2010–16. Cert. of Merit, 2001, Goler T. Butcher Medal (jtly), 2006, Amer. Soc. of Internat. Law. *Publications:* Third Parties in International Law, 1993; (jtly) The Boundaries of International Law: a feminist analysis, 2000 (trans. Japanese, 2004); (contrib.) Halsbury's Laws of Australia, vol. 14, 1994; (jtly) Dispute Resolution in Australia, 2nd edn 2002; (jtly) The Making of International Law, 2007. *Address:* Department of Law, London School of Economics and Political Science, Houghton Street, WC2A 2AE.

**CHINN, Antony Nigel Caton;** QC 2003; a Recorder, since 2000; *b* 20 May 1949; *s* of Edward William Chinn and Barbara Ursula Neene Chinn (*née* Tilbury); *m* 1973, Margot Susan Elizabeth Emery; two *s*. *Educ:* Ardingly Coll.; Inns of Court Sch. of Law. Called to the Bar, Middle Temple, 1972; in practice, specialising in criminal law; Asst Recorder, 1996–2000. *Recreations:* motor sport, football, music. *Address:* Westgate Chambers, 64 High Street, Lewes, E Sussex BN7 1XG. *T:* (01273) 480510. *Club:* Goodwood Road Racing.

**CHINN, Susan Avril, (Lady Chinn),** CBE 2012; *b* Cobham, 4 April 1943; *d* of late Louis Speelman and of Meryl Speelman; *m* 1965, Sir Trevor Edwin Chinn, *qv*; two *s*. *Educ:* The Warren, Worthing. PR Consultant, 1983–95. Mem. Bd, 2005–15, and Chm., Develt Council, 2003–15, RNT. Vice Chm., Royal Marsden Cancer Appeal, 1990–93. Special Trustee, Gt Ormond St Hosp. for Sick Children, 1990–2000; Trustee: Child Psychotherapy Trust, 1993–96; The Silverline, 2012–; Mountview Acad. of Th. Arts, 2018. JP Inner London, 1980–2009. *Recreations:* theatre, gardening, fly fishing. *E:* susan@chinn.com.

**CHINN, Sir Trevor (Edwin),** Kt 1990; CVO 1989; Senior Adviser, CVC Capital Partners, since 2002; *b* 24 July 1935; *s* of late Rosser and Susie Chinn; *m* 1965, Susan Avril Speelman (*see* S. A. Chinn); two *s*. *Educ:* Clifton Coll.; King's Coll., Cambridge. Lex Service, subseq. RAC plc: Dir, 1959–2003; Man. Dir, 1968–73; Chief Exec., 1973–96; Chm., 1973–2003; Chm., Kwik-Fit, 2002–05; Chm., AA, 2004–07. Chairman: ITIS, 2000–11; Streetcar Ltd, 2007–11; Tesco Cars, 2010–12; Tusker, 2011–15; Who Can Fix My Car, 2015–. Vice-Chm., Commn for Integrated Transport, 1999–2004; Chm., Motorists' Forum, 2000–10. Chm., Mayor's Fund for London, 2008–11. Chm., Jt Israel Appeal, 1973–93; Pres., United Jewish Israel Appeal, 1993–; Mem., Exec. Cttee, Jewish Leadership Council, 2006–; Vice Pres., Jewish Assoc. for Business Ethics, 1995–2011; Pres., Norwood Ravenswood, subseq. Norwood, 1996–2006; Vice Chm., Wishing Well Appeal, Gt Ormond St Hosp. for Sick Children, 1985–89. Vice Chm., Hampstead Th., 1990–2004. Trustee, Royal Acad. Trust, 1989–2004 (Dep. Chm., 1996–2004). Trustee, Duke of Edinburgh's Award, 1978–88. Freeman of the City of London. Chief Barker, Variety Club of GB, 1977, 1978. *Recreations:* fishing, theatre, antique glass, antique maps of the Holy Land. *Clubs:* Garrick, Royal Automobile.

**CHINNERY, Prof. Patrick Francis,** PhD; FRCP, FRCPath, FMedSci; Professor of Neurology and Head, Department of Clinical Neurosciences, University of Cambridge, since 2015; *b* Leeds, 11 Feb. 1968; *s* of late Brendan Chinnery and of Mary Chinnery; *m* 1991, Rachel Mary Kean; one *s* three *d*. *Educ:* Univ. of Newcastle (BMedSci 1st Cl. Hons 1989; MB BS Hons 1992; PhD 2000); Specialist Training Authy (Cert. of Completion of Higher Specialist Trng Neurol. 2002). MRCP 1995, FRCP 2006; MRCPath 2001, FRCPath 2001. House Physician, Royal Victoria Infirmary, Newcastle upon Tyne, 1992–93; SHO, Newcastle Teaching Hosps, 1993–95; University of Newcastle upon Tyne, later Newcastle University: Wellcome Clinical Res. Trng Fellow, 1995–98; Wellcome Advanced Clinical Res. Fellow, 1998–2000; Clinical Lectr in Neurol., 2000–02; Sen. Lectr in Neurogenetics, 2002–04; Prof. of Neurogenetics, 2004–15; Dir, Inst. of Human Genetics, then Inst. of Genetic Medicine, 2010–15; Wellcome Trust Sen. Fellow in Clinical Sci., 2003–18; Wellcome Trust Principal Res. Fellow, 2018–; Public Orator, 2007–13; Specialist Registrar in Neurol., Northern Region, 1997–2002; Newcastle Hospitals NHS Foundation Trust: Hon. Consultant Neurologist, 2008–15; Dir, NIHR Biomedical Res. Centre, 2008–15. Sen. Investigator, NIHR, 2010. FMedSci 2009; Fellow, American Neurol Assoc., 2011. Foulkes Foundn Medal, Acad. of Med. Scis, 2011. Associate Ed., Brain: a Jl of Neurology, 2004–13. *Publications:* over 500 articles in medical and scientific jls incl. Lancet, Science, Nature, JAMA and Nature Genetics. *Recreations:* fell running, flute. *Address:* Department of Clinical Neurosciences, Addenbrooke's Hospital, Cambridge Biomedical Campus, Hills Road, Cambridge CB2 0QQ.

**CHINUBHAI, Sir Prashant**, 4th Bt *cr* 1913, of Shahpur, Ahmedabad, India; *b* 15 Dec. 1955; *o s* of Sir Udayan Chinubhai (formerly Ranchhodlal), 3rd Bt and of Muneera Khodadad Fozdar; *S* father, 2006, but his name does not appear on the Official Roll of the Baronetage; *m* 1977, Swati Hrishikesh Mehta; three *d*. *Heir: uncle* Kirtidev Chinubhai [*b* 15 March 1932; *m* 1967, Meera Ratilal Nanavati]. *Address*: Chinubhai House, Lal Darwaja, Ahmedabad 380001, India.

**CHIPMAN, Dr John Miguel Warwick**, CMG 1999; Director General and Chief Executive, The International Institute for Strategic Studies, since 1993; Director, IISS-US and IISS-Asia, since 2001; *b* 10 Feb. 1957; *s* of Lawrence Carroll Chipman and Maria Isabel (*née* Prados); *m* 1997, Lady Theresa Helen Margaret Manners, *yr d* of 10th Duke of Rutland, CBE; twin *s*. *Educ*: Harvard Coll. (BA Hons); London Sch. of Economics (MA Dist.); Balliol Coll., Oxford (MPhil, DPhil). Research Associate: IISS, 1983–84; Atlantic Inst. for Internat. Affairs, Paris, 1985–87; The International Institute for Strategic Studies: Asst Dir for Regl Security, 1987–90; Dir of Studies, 1990–93; Shangri-La Dialogue, Singapore, 2002; Manama Dialogue, Bahrain, 2004. Mem., Internat. Adv. Bd, Reliance Industries Ltd (Mumbai), 2006– (Special Advr to Chm.). Founder, Strategic Comments jl, 1995. *Publications*: Vième République et Défense de l'Afrique, 1986; (ed and jt author) NATO's Southern Allies, 1988; French Power in Africa, 1989; numerous contribs to edited vols, learned jls and newspapers. *Recreations*: tennis, ski-ing, scuba diving, riding, collecting travel books. *Address*: The International Institute for Strategic Studies, Arundel House, 6 Temple Place, Temple Place, WC2R 2PG. *T*: (020) 7379 7676. *Clubs*: White's, Garrick; Harvard (New York).

**CHIPPERFIELD, Sir David (Alan)**, Kt 2010; CBE 2004; RDI 2006; RA 2007; RIBA; Principal, David Chipperfield Architects, since 1984; *b* 18 Dec. 1953; *s* of Alan John Chipperfield and Peggy Chipperfield (*née* Singleton); partner, Dr Evelyn Stern; two *s* one *d*, and one *s* from previous relationship. *Educ*: Wellington Sch., Somerset; Kingston Poly.; Architectural Assoc. (AA Dip). RIBA 1982. Designer, Douglas Stephens & Partners, 1977–78; Architect, Richard Rogers & Partners, 1978–79; Project Architect, Foster Associates, 1981–84. Projects include: Toyota Auto, Kyoto, Japan, 1990; Gotoh Museum, Chiba, Japan, 1991; Matsumoto Corp. HQ, Okayama, Japan, 1992; River and Rowing Mus., Henley-on-Thames, 1997 (Best Building in England, RFAC Trust/BSkyB Bldg of the Year Award, 1999); Ernsting Service Center, Coesfeld-Lette, Germany, 1998; Gormley Studio, London, 2003; Private House, NY, 2004; Housing Villaverde, Madrid, 2005; Figge Art Mus., Davenport, 2005; Hotel Puerta America, Madrid, 2005; Mus. of Modern Lit., Marbach am Neckar, Germany, 2006 (RIBA Stirling Prize, 2007); Des Moines Public Liby, Iowa, 2006; America's Cup Bldg, Valencia, 2006; BBC Scotland, Glasgow, 2006; Liangzhu Culture Mus., China, 2007; Empire Riverside Hotel, Hamburg, 2007; Gall. 'Am Kupfergraben 10', Berlin, 2007; Rena Lange HQ, Munich, 2007; Ninetree Village, Hangzhou, China, 2008; Kivik Pavilion, Kivik, Sweden, 2008; Neues Museum, Berlin, 2009; City of Justice, Barcelona, 2009; Anchorage Mus. at Rasmuson Center, Alaska, 2009; Mus. Folkwang, Essen, 2010; Kaufhaus Tyrol Dept Store, Innsbruck, 2010; Lab. Bldg, Basel, 2010; Rockbund Art Mus., Shanghai, 2010; Turner Contemp., Margate, 2011; Hepworth Wakefield, 2011; HEC Paris MBA Bldg, Jouy-en-Josas, 2012; St Louis Art Mus., Missouri, 2013; Museo Jumex, Mexico City, 2013; One Pancras Square, London, 2013; Fayland House, Bucks, 2014; One Kensington Gardens, London, 2015; Villa Eden, Gardone, Italy, 2015; Xixi Wetland Estate, Hangzhou, 2015; Westkaai Towers, Antwerp, 2016; Royal Academy, London, 2018; Amorepacific HQ, Seoul, 2018; James Simon Gall., Berlin, 2018. Founder and Dir, 9H Gall., London. Curator, Internat. Architecture Exhibn, Venice Biennale, 2012. Design Tutor, RCA, 1988–89; Prof. of Architecture, Staatliche Akad. der Bildenden Künste, Stuttgart, 1995–2000; Mies van der Rohe Chair, Escuela Técnica, Barcelona, 2001; Visiting Professor: Harvard Univ., 1987–88; Graz Univ., 1992; Naples Univ., 1992; Ecole Polytechnique, Lausanne, 1993–94. Trustee, Architecture Foundn, 1992–97. Awards include: Andrea Palladio Prize, 1993; RIBA Award, 1998, 1999, 2002, 2003, 2004, 2007, 2008, 2009, 2010; Tessenow Gold Medal, 1999; Civic Trust Award, 1999; Royal Gold Medal, RIBA, 2011; Praemium Imperiale (Japan), 2013. Order of Merit (Germany), 2009. *Publications*: Theoretical Practice, 1994; (jtly) David Chipperfield Architects: form matters, 2009; (jtly) Neues Museum Berlin, 2009; *relevant publications*: El Croquis (monograph), 1998, 2001, 2004, 2006, 2010; David Chipperfield, Architectural Works 1990–2002, 2003; David Chipperfield, Idea e Realta, 2005; David Chipperfield 1984–2009, 2009; David Chipperfield Architects, 2013; (ed with S. Kretz) On Planning, 2018; David Chipperfield Architects Works, 2018. *Recreations*: reading, drawing, swimming. *Address*: (office) 1 Surrey Street, WC2R 2ND. *T*: (020) 7620 4800. *Club*: Royal Automobile.

**CHIPPERFIELD, Sir Geoffrey (Howes)**, KCB 1992 (CB 1985); Deputy Chairman, 2000–03, and Director, 1993–2003, Pennon Group (formerly South West Water plc); *b* 20 April 1933; *s* of Nelson Chipperfield and Eleanor Chipperfield; *m* 1959, Gillian James; two *s*. *Educ*: Cranleigh; New Coll., Oxford. Called to the Bar, Gray's Inn, 1955. Joined Min. of Housing and Local Govt, 1956; Harkness Fellow, Inst. of Govtl Studies, Univ. of Calif, Berkeley, 1962–63; Principal Private Sec., Minister of Housing, 1968–70; Sec., Greater London Develt Plan Inquiry, 1970–73; Under Sec., 1976, Dep. Sec., 1982–87, DoE; Dep. Sec., Dept of Energy, 1987–89; Perm. Under-Sec. of State, Dept of Energy, 1989–91; Perm. Sec. and Chief Exec., PSA Services, 1991–93. Chm., Heliodynamics Ltd, 2000–. Chairman: DTI Energy Adv. Panel, 1996–2001; British Cement Assoc., 1996–2001. Pro-Chancellor, Univ. of Kent, 1998–2005. Mem. Council, Foundn of Sci. and Technol., 2005–. *Recreations*: reading, gardening. *Clubs*: Oxford and Cambridge, Athenæum.

**CHIPPINDALE, Christopher Ralph**, PhD; Reader in Archaeology, University of Cambridge, at University Museum of Archaeology and Anthropology, 2001–13, now Emeritus; *b* 13 Oct. 1951; *s* of Keith and Ruth Chippindale; *m* 1976, Anne Lowe (marr. diss. 2008); two *s* two *d*; civil partnership 2008, Justice Oleka. *Educ*: Sedbergh School; St John's College, Cambridge (BA Hons); Girton Coll., Cambridge (PhD). MCIfA; FSA. Editor, freelance, Penguin Books, Hutchinson Publishing Group, 1974–82; Res. Fellow in Archaeology, 1985–88, Bye-Fellow, 1988–91, Girton Coll., Cambridge; Asst Curator, 1988–93, Sen. Asst Curator, 1993–2013, Cambridge Univ. Mus. of Archaeol. Vis. Prof., Univ. of Witwatersrand, 2002–11. Richard Colt Hoare Prize, 1984. Editor, Antiquity, 1987–97. *Publications*: Stonehenge Complete, 1983 (British Archaeological Book Award, 1984), 4th edn 2012; (ed jtly) The Pastmasters, 1989; (jtly) Who owns Stonehenge?, 1990; A High Way to Heaven, 1998; (ed jtly) The Archaeology of Rock Art, 1999; (ed jtly) Landscapes of European Rock-art, 2002; articles in jls. *Recreations*: gardening, taking things easier, worrying. *Address*: 46 High Street, Chesterton, Cambridge CB4 1NG.

**CHIPPING, Hilary Jane**; Chief Executive, South East Midlands Local Enterprise Partnership, since 2018 (Head of Infrastructure, 2013–15; Acting Chief Executive, 2015); *b* 31 Jan. 1955; *d* of late Clarence John Watts and Alice Mary Watts; *m* 1975, Richard Frank Chipping; one *s* one *d*. *Educ*: Bletchley Grammar Sch.; Univ. of Manchester (BA Econ) 1975, MA (Econ) 1977. Joined Civil Service, 1977; Head: Local Govt Finance Div., 1990–94, Water Services Div., 1994–95, DoE, Local Authy Housing Div., DETR, 1995–2000; Roads Policy Div., DTLR, 2000–01; Dir, Network Strategy, Highways Agency, 2001–07; Dir, mksm Inter-Regional Bd, 2008–11; Consultant, Hilary Chipping Consulting Ltd, 2011–13. *Recreations*: walking, cookery.

**CHIRAC, Jacques René**; Grand Croix de la Légion d'Honneur; Grand Croix de l'Ordre National du Mérite; President of the French Republic, 1995–2007; Member, Constitutional Council of France, 2007–11; *b* Paris, 29 Nov. 1932; *s* of François Chirac, company manager and Marie-Louise (*née* Valette); *m* 1956, Bernadette Chodron de Courcel; one *d* (and one *d* decd). *Educ*: Lycée Carnot and Lycée Louis-le-Grand, Paris; Diploma of Inst. of Polit. Studies, Paris, and of Summer Sch., Harvard Univ., USA. Served Army in Algeria. Ecole Nat. d'Admin, 1957–59; Auditor, Cour des Comptes, 1959; Head Dept: Sec.-Gen. of Govt, 1962; Private Office of Georges Pompidou, 1962–67; Counsellor, Cour des Comptes, 1965; State Secretary: Employment Questions, 1967–68; Economy and Finance, 1968–71; Minister for Parly Relations, 1971–72; Minister for Agriculture and Rural Development, 1972–74; Home Minister, March–May 1974; Prime Minister, 1974–76 and 1986–88. Deputy from Corrèze, elected 1967, 1968, 1973, 1976 (UDR), 1978 (RPR), 1981, 1986, 1988 and 1993; Sec.-Gen., UDR, Dec. 1974–June 1975; Pres., Rassemblement pour la République, 1976–81 and 1982–94. Mayor of Paris, 1977–95. Member from Meymac, Conseil Général of Corrèze, 1968–88, Pres. 1970–79. Mem., European Parlt, 1979–80. Treasurer, Claude Pompidou Foundn (charity for elderly and for handicapped children), 1969. Founder, Jacques Chirac Foundation for Sustainable Develt and Cultural Dialogue, 2008. Croix de la valeur militaire; Chevalier du Mérite agricole, des Arts et des Lettres, de l'Etoile noire, du Mérite sportif, du Mérite touristique; Médaille de l'Aéronautique. *Publications*: a thesis on development of Port of New Orleans, 1954; Discours pour la France à l'heure du choix, 1978; La lueur de l'espérance: réflexion du soir pour le matin, 1978; Une Nouvelle France, 1994; La France pour Tous, 1995; Chaque pas doit être un but (memoir), 2009.

**CHISHOLM**, family name of **Baroness Chisholm of Owlpen**.

**CHISHOLM OF OWLPEN**, Baroness *cr* 2014 (Life Peer), of Owlpen in the County of Gloucestershire; **Hon. Caroline Elizabeth Chisholm**; *b* 23 Dec. 1951; *d* of 1st Baron Egremont, MBE; *m* 1976, Colin Chisholm, *qv*; two *s* one *d*. Co-Chm., Conservatives Candidates Committee. A Baroness in Waiting (Govt Whip), 2015–16, 2017–18 and 2019–; Spokesperson on Cabinet Office, H of L, 2016.

**CHISHOLM, Alex**; Permanent Secretary, Department for Business, Energy and Industrial Strategy, since 2016; *b* London, 2 Jan. 1968; *s* of late Duncan Chisholm and of Annabelle Chisholm; *m* 1993, Eliza Pakenham; three *s*. *Educ*: Downside Sch., Som; Merton Coll., Oxford (MA Hist.); INSEAD, Fontainebleau (MBA). Civil Servant, DTI and OFT, 1990–97; Sen. Exec., media, technol. and services businesses, 1997–2007; Chm. and Mem., Commn for Communication Regulation, 2007–13; Chief Exec., Competition and Markets Authy, 2013–16; Perm. Sec., DECC, 2016. Trustee, Breadline Africa, 2003–. *Recreations*: travel, history, gardening, cycling. *Address*: Department for Business, Energy and Industrial Strategy, 1 Victoria Street, SW1H 0ET.

**CHISHOLM, Catherine Alexandra, (Kitty), (Lady Chisholm)**; Director, Boardwalk Leadership, since 2012; *b* 19 April 1946; *d* of Gregory Panas and Aleca Panas, Athens; *m* 1969, Sir John Alexander Raymond Chisholm, *qv*; one *s* one *d*. *Educ*: Girton Coll., Cambridge (BA 1969); Open Univ. (BSc 2001); Henley Business Sch. (MSc Coaching and Behavioural Change 2012). Open University: Res. Asst in Classics, 1976–82; Course Co-ordinator in Contg Educn, 1982–83; Adminr, Sci. and Technol. Updating, 1983–89; Business Develt Manager, 1989–91; Dir of Develt, 1991–2002; Dir of Develt, Brunel Univ., 2003–07. Member: Bd, British Telecom Acad., 2000–02; Borderless Educn Observatory Bd, 2001–10; Adv. Bd, Vosper Thorneycroft Educn Services, 2003–06; Adv. Bd, JRBH Strategy Mgt, 2007–13; Adv. Bd, Magna Carta Inst., 2010–; Chair, 2012–15, Mem., 2015–, Adv. Bd, RHUL. Trustee: CASE Europe, 1995–2001 (Chm., 1998–2001); Reach, 2003–11 (Dep. Chm., 2009–11; Chm., 2011); Nat. Mus. of Sci. and Industry, 2007–15. FRSA 2000. *Publications*: Political and Social Life in the Great Age of Athens, 1978; Rome, the Augustan Age, 1981; (jtly) Neuroscience for Leadership: harnessing the brain gain advantage, 2015; (jtly) Championing Women Leaders, 2015; contrib. IEDP Developing Leaders. *Recreations*: pink roses, reading, grandchildren, classic car race photography. *Club*: Reform.

**CHISHOLM, Colin**; Investment Director, Rathbones, 2014–17; *b* London, 4 Oct. 1949; *s* of late Archibald Hugh Tennent Chisholm, CBE and Josephine Chisholm; *m* 1976, Hon. Caroline Elizabeth Wyndham (*see* Baroness Chisholm of Owlpen); two *s* one *d*. *Educ*: Eton; Christ Church, Oxford (MA PPE). Jardine Matheson, 1971–74; Schroders, 1974–79; Hambros Bank, 1979–85; Thornhill, 1985–94; Rothschilds, 1994–95; Hd, Private Clients and Charities, Jupiter Fund Mgt, 1996–2014. Non-exec. Dir, City of Oxford Geared Income Trust, 1998–2006. Trustee: Nelson Trust, 2006–16; RSL, 2012–; Chelsea Physic Garden, 2015–. Hon. FRSL 2018. *Address*: Lampern House, Owlpen, Dursley, Glos GL11 5BX. *T*: (01453) 861314. *Clubs*: Beefsteak, Pratt's, Turf.

**CHISHOLM, Sir John (Alexander Raymond)**, Kt 1999; FREng; Chairman: Medical Research Council, 2006–12; Genomics England, 2013–19; *b* 27 Aug. 1946; *s* of late Ruari Ian Lambert Chisholm and of Pamela Harland Chisholm; *m* 1969, Catherine Alexandra (*née* Pana) (*see* C. A. Chisholm); one *s* one *d*. *Educ*: Queens' Coll., Cambridge (BA 1968). CEng 1974, FREng (FEng 1996); FIET (FIEE 1995); FRAeS 2007; FInstP 1999. Vauxhall Motors, 1964–69; Scicon Ltd, 1969–79; Cap Scientific Ltd, 1979–91: Man. Dir, 1981–86; Chm., 1986–91; Chm., Yard Ltd, 1986–91; UK Man. Dir, Sema Group plc, 1988–91; Chief Executive: DRA, subseq. DERA, 1991–2001; QinetiQ plc, 2001–05; Chm., QinetiQ Group plc, 2005–10. Chm., NESTA, subseq. Nesta, 2009–16. Non-executive Director: Expro Internat. plc, 1994–2003; Bespak plc, 1999–2005; Health and Social Care Inf. Centre, 2014–17; Historic Grand Prix Cars Assoc., 2015–. Mem., UK Foresight Steering Gp, 1993–2000. President: Electronic and Business Equipment Assoc., 1989–90; IEE, 2005–06; IET, 2006. Hon. Fellow, QMUL, 2015. Mem. Council, Cranfield Univ., 1995–2002. *Recreations*: participative sports, old cars. *Address*: Batchworth Hill House, London Road, Rickmansworth WD3 1JS.

**CHISHOLM, John William**, CBE 2000; FRCGP; Director, Concordia Health Ltd, 2006–18; Adviser, NHS Working in Partnership Programme, since 2005; *b* 29 Dec. 1950; *s* of late William Chisholm and of Olive Chisholm (*née* Tomlinson); *m* 1977, Caroline Mary Colyer (*née* Davis) (marr. diss. 2006); two *d*, and one step *s*; partner, Prof. Ann Marie Sommerville (*née* Pryal). *Educ*: Clifton Coll. Prep. Sch.; Clifton Coll.; Peterhouse, Cambridge (exhibnr; BA 1971, BChir 1974, MB 1975); Westminster Med. Sch. DRCOG 1977; MRCGP 1978, FRCGP 1995. House surgeon, 1974–75, house physician, 1975, Croydon Gen. Hosp.; GP trainee, Reading Vocational Trng Scheme, 1976–79; GP, Twyford, 1979–2004. Member Board: DPP 2000, 2004–; BMJ Pubns Gp, 2002–04. Member: Jt Cttee on Postgrad. Trng for Gen. Practice, 1980–90, 1995–2005; Supervisory Bd, NHS Centre for Coding and Classification, 1990–97; Standing Med. Adv. Cttee, 1998–2005; Partners' Council, NICE, 1998–2001; Expert Patients Task Force, 1999–2000; Patient Care (Empowerment) Modernisation Action Team, 2000; NHS IT Task Force, 2002–04; Primary Care Task Gp, 2003; Nat. Primary Care Develt Team Adv. Bd, 2004–06. Observer, Clinical Standards Adv. Gp, 1993–96. Mem., GMC, 1999–2003 (Mem., Standards Cttee, 1999–2002); British Medical Association: Chm., Junior Members Forum, 1981–82; Mem. Council, 1981–82, 1988–; Member: Finance Cttee, 2002–06, 2007–; Med. Ethics Cttee, 2004– (Dep. Chm., 2007; Chm., 2014–); Gen. Med. Services Cttee, subseq. GPs Cttee, 1977– (Negotiator, 1990–97; Jt Dep. Chm., 1991–97; Chm., 1997–2004; Chairman: Trainees Subcttee, 1978–80; Jt (with RCGP) Computing Gp, 1984–86; Practice Orgn Subcttee, 1986–90; Nurse Prescribing Wkg Gp, 1988–89); Mem. Council, RCGP, 2005– (Observer, 2004–05). Chairman: Gen. Med. Services Defence Fund, 1997–2001; Gen. Practitioners Defence Fund, 2001–04. Observer, Acad. of Med. Royal Colls, 2002–04. Rep., European Union of GPs (UEMO), 1988–2004. Patron, Men's Health Forum, 2004–. *Publications:* (ed jtly) Micros in Practice: report of an appraisal of GP microcomputer systems, 1986; (ed) Making Sense of the Red Book, 1989, (with N. D. Ellis) 2nd edn 1993, 3rd edn 1997; (ed) Making Sense of the New Contract, 1990; (ed) Making Sense of the Cost Rent Scheme, 1992; articles esp. concerning gen. practice orgn. *Recreations:* reading, art, photography, music (former amateur flautist, singer, conductor). *Address:* 5 Elmers End Road, Anerley, SE20 7ST. *T:* (020) 8778 2550. *E:* john.chisholm@john-chisholm.demon.co.uk.

**CHISHOLM, Kitty;** see Chisholm, C. A.

**CHISHOLM, Malcolm George Richardson;** Member (Lab) Edinburgh Northern and Leith, Scottish Parliament, 2011–16 (Edinburgh North and Leith, 1999–2011); *b* 7 March 1949; *s* of late George and Olive Chisholm; *m* 1975, Janet Broomfield, writer; two *s* one *d*. *Educ:* George Watson's Coll.; Edinburgh Univ. (MA Hons, Dip Ed). Formerly Teacher of English, Castlebrae High School and Broughton High School. MP (Lab) Edinburgh, Leith, 1992–97, Edinburgh North and Leith, 1997–2001. Parly Under-Sec. of State, Scottish Office, 1997. Scottish Executive: Dep. Minister, 2000–01, Minister, 2001–04, for Health and Community Care; Minister for Communities, 2004–06. *Recreations:* cinema, swimming, literature.

**CHISHOLM, Prof. Michael Donald Inglis,** FBA 2002; FSA; Professor of Geography, University of Cambridge, 1976–96, now Emeritus; Professorial Fellow, St Catharine's College, Cambridge, 1976–96; *b* 10 June 1931; *s* of M. S. and A. W. Chisholm; *m* 1st, 1959, Edith Gretchen Emma (*née* Hoof) (marr. diss. 1981); one *s* two *d*; 2nd, 1986, Judith Carola Shackleton (*née* Murray). *Educ:* St Christopher Sch., Letchworth; St Catharine's Coll., Cambridge (MA; ScD 1996). Nat. Service Commn, RE, 1950–51. Deptl Demonstrator, Inst. for Agric. Econs, Oxford, 1954–59; Asst Lectr, then Lectr in Geog., Bedford Coll., London, 1960–64; Vis. Sen. Lectr in Geog., Univ. of Ibadan, 1964–65; Lectr, then Reader in Geog., Univ. of Bristol, 1965–72; Prof. of Economic and Social Geography, Univ. of Bristol, 1972–76. Associate, Economic Associates Ltd, consultants, 1965–77. Geography Editor for Hutchinson Univ. Lib., 1973–82. Mem. SSRC, and Chm. of Cttees for Human Geography and Planning, 1967–72; Member: Local Govt Boundary Commn for England, 1971–78; Rural Develt Commn, 1981–90; English Adv. Cttee on Telecommunications, 1990–92; Local Govt Commn for England, 1992–95. Mem. Council, IBG, 1961 and 1962 (Jun. Vice-Pres., 1977; Sen. Vice-Pres., 1978; Pres. 1979). Conservator of River Cam, 1979–2007 (Chm., 1991–2007); Bd Mem., Cambridge Preservation Soc., 2000–08; Vice-Chm., Cambs ACRE, 2001–02. Pres., Spalding Gentlemen's Soc., 2016–19 (Hon. Sec., 2013–16). FSA 2019. Gill Memorial Prize, RGS, 1969. *Publications:* Rural Settlement and Land Use: an essay in location, 1962; Geography and Economics, 1966; (ed jtly) Regional Forecasting, 1971; (ed jtly) Spatial Policy Problems of the British Economy, 1971; Research in Human Geography, 1971; (ed) Resources for Britain's Future, 1972; (jtly) Freight Flows and Spatial Aspects of the British Economy, 1973; (jtly) The Changing Pattern of Employment, 1973; (ed jtly) Studies in Human Geography, 1973; (ed jtly) Processes in Physical and Human Geography: Bristol Essays, 1975; Human Geography: Evolution or Revolution?, 1975; Modern World Development, 1982; Regions in Recession and Resurgence, 1990; (ed jtly) Shared Space: Divided Space, 1990; Britain on the Edge of Europe, 1995; (ed jtly) A Fresh Start for Local Government, 1997; Structural Reform of British Local Government: rhetoric and reality, 2000; (jtly) Botched Business: the damaging process of reorganising local government 2006–2008, 2008; In the Shadow of the Abbey: Crowland, 2013; papers in Farm Economist, Oxford Econ. Papers, Trans Inst. British Geographers, Geography, Geographical Jl, Applied Statistics, Area, Envmt and Planning, Jl of Local Govt Law, Jl of Histl Geography, Proceedings of Cambridge Antiquarian Soc., etc. *Recreations:* gardening, theatre, opera, interior design. *Address:* 5 Clarendon Road, Cambridge CB2 8BH.

**CHISHOLM, (Peter) Nicolas,** MBE 2011; Headmaster, Yehudi Menuhin School, 1988–2010; *b* 7 Dec. 1949; *s* of David Whitridge Chisholm and Marjorie Chisholm; *m* 1977, Auriol Mary Oakeley. *Educ:* Christ's Hospital, Horsham; St John's Coll., Cambridge (MA). Tenor Lay Vicar, Chichester Cathedral, 1972–76; Asst Master, Prebendal Sch., Chichester, 1972–76; Hurstpierpoint College: Hd Classics, 1976–88; Housemaster, Eagle Hse, 1982–88. Chairman: Sussex Assoc. of Classical Teachers, 1982–88; Trustees, SE Music Schemes, 1996–2009; Nat. Assoc. of Music and Dance Schools, 2001–09. Member: Performing Arts Panel, SE Arts Bd, 1990–96; Music and Dance Scheme Expert Panel, DCSF, 2007–09 (Chm., Excellent! Gala Steering Cttee, 2007–09); Mem., 2008–10, Chm., 2008–10, Sports, Arts, Recreation Cttee, Soc. of Heads of Ind. Schs (Mem., Educn Cttee, 1996–2003). Member: Council, Eur. String Teachers Assoc., 2008–11; Council, ISM, 2011–18 (Pres., 2016–17; Trustee, 2018–); Council, Brighton Early Music Fest., 2011–; Trustee, Brighton Philharmonic Soc., 2011–19 (Chm., 2014–19). Pres., Surrey Philharmonic Orch., 2000–01. Governor: Royal Ballet Sch., 1997–2014 (Chm., Academic and Pastoral Cttee, 2000–14); St Paul's Girls' Sch., 2011– (Chm., Educn Cttee, 2013–). Mem., Iford PCC, 1988–. Dir, Iford Village Choir, 2012–. FRSA. Freeman: Co. of Musicians, 2006 (Yeoman, Coordination Cttee, 2010–15 (Chm., 2013–14); Liveryman, 2012); City of London, 2010. Churchwarden, St Nicholas, Ilford, 2018–. *Publications:* Menuhin's Vision: fifty years of the Yehudi Menuhin School, 2013. *Recreations:* music, classic cars, walking, photography, archaeology, gardening, watercolour painting, linocut printing. *Address:* 2 Iford Manor Cottages, Iford, Lewes, E Sussex BN7 3EP. *T:* (01273) 471733, 07710 179599.

**CHISHTI, Rehman;** MP (C) Gillingham and Rainham, since 2010; Prime Minister's Special Envoy for Freedom of Religion or Belief, since 2019; *b* Muzaffarabad, Pakistan, 4 Oct. 1978; *s* of Abdul Rehman Chishti and Zarina Chishti. *Educ:* Fort Luton High Sch. for Boys; Chatham Grammar Sch. for Girls; University of Wales, Aberystwyth (LLB Hons 2000). Called to the Bar, Lincoln's Inn, 2001; in practice as a barrister, Goldsmith Chambers, 2003–09. Special Adviser: to Benazir Bhutto, 1999–2007; to Rt Hon. Francis Maude, MP, 2006–07. Mem., Medway Council, 2003– (Lab, 2003–06, C, 2006–) (Mem. Cabinet, 2007–10). PPS to Minister for Schools, 2014–15, to Attorney General, 2015–16; PM's Trade Envoy to Pakistan, 2017–18. Vice Chm. (Communities), Cons. Party, 2018. Contested (Lab) Horsham, 2005. *Recreations:* running, cricket, tennis, football, theatre, cinema. *Address:* House of Commons, SW1A 0AA. *T:* (020) 7219 3000. *E:* rehman.chishti.mp@parliament.uk.

**CHISLETT, Derek Victor;** Warden, Sackville College, 1988–96; *b* 18 April 1929; *s* of Archibald Lynn Chislett and Eva Jessie Chislett (*née* Collins); *m* 1954, Joan Robson (*d* 2018); two *d*. *Educ:* Christ's Hospital. Admiralty, 1946–53; HM Forces, 1947–49; Nat. Assistance Board, 1953–66; Min. of Social Security, 1966–68; Department of Health and Social Security, 1968–88; Under Sec., 1983; Controller, Newcastle Central Office, 1983–86; Dir of Finance (Social Security), 1986–88. Mem. Exec. Cttee, Nat. Assoc. of Almshouses, 1989–2001 (Vice-Chm., 1995–2001). Trustee, Motability Tenth Anniversary Trust, 1989–2000. Freeman, City of London, 1998; Mem., Guild of Freemen, City of London, 1999. *Publications:* Sackville College: a short history and guide, 1995. *Recreations:* opera, listening to the 'cello, growing vegetables. *Address:* Boswell House, High Street, Bexhill on Sea, East Sussex TN40 2HA. *T:* (01424) 733755.

**CHISM, Nicholas James;** Chief Business Adviser, Department for Business, Energy and Industrial Strategy, since 2019 (Director General, Enterprise, 2018–19); *b* London, 8 Oct. 1968; *s* of Michael Chism and Jennifer Chism; *m* 1995, Deborah Wilkin; one *s* one *d*. *Educ:* Mansfield Coll., Oxford (MA). FCA 2003. KPMG: KPMG UK, 1990–95; Corporate Finance, 1995–2008; Partner, 2001–18; UK Hd, Infrastructure, 2004–08; Global Hd, Infrastructure, 2008–13; Global Chair, Infrastructure, Govt and Healthcare, 2013–18; Global Hd, Sectors, 2015–18. AMICE 2018. *Recreations:* football, theatre, cinema, travel, family. *Address:* Department for Business, Energy and Industrial Strategy, 1 Victoria Street, SW1H 0ET. *T:* (020) 7215 5000. *E:* nick.chism@beis.gov.uk. *Club:* Reform.

**CHISNALL, Air Vice-Marshal Steven,** CB 2008; Teaching Fellow, Strategy and International Security, Southampton University, since 2016 (Director of Strategy, 2012–16); *b* Urmston, Manchester, 12 June 1954; *s* of Eric and Muriel Chisnall; *m* 1980, Elizabeth Ennis; three *s*. *Educ:* Urmston Grammar Sch.; Univ. of Sheffield (BA English 1976; PGCE 1977); St John's Coll., Cambridge (MPhil Internat. Relns 1989). English Teacher, Hinde House, Sheffield, 1977–79; RAF, 1980–2008: tours incl. Germany, 1981–84, NI, 1991–93; Cabinet Office, 1993–95; Dep. Dir, Defence Policy, MoD, 1996–98; Station Comdr, RAF Halton, 1998–99; Liaison Officer, Islamabad, 2002; Sen. Directing Staff (Air), RCDS, 2004–08; Chief Operating Officer, Simulstrat Ltd, 2008–09; Strategic Relns Dir, Xchanging, 2009–11; CEO and Dir, Andrews Outcomes Internat., 2011–12. Vis. Prof. in War Studies, KCL, 2009–. Trustee: Victory Services Club, 2014–; Officers' Assoc., 2015–. Patron, RAF Holmpton, 2006–. Chm., RAF Oxford and Cambridge Soc., 2012–. *Recreations:* sport, reading and writing—history, international relations, fiction, jazz. *Address:* The Chilterns. *Club:* Royal Air Force (Chm., 2005–08).

**CHISWELL, Maj. Gen. James Robert,** CB 2018; CBE 2011; MC 2002; Director, UK Special Forces, 2015–18; *b* Berlin, 29 March 1964; *s* of Maj.-Gen. Peter Irvine Chiswell, *qv*; *m* 2006, Linda Metcalf; one *s* one *d*. *Educ:* Allhallows Sch.; King's Coll. London (MA Defence Studies). Commnd Parachute Regt, 1983; CO 2nd Bn, 2004; Comdr, 16 Air Assault Bde, 2009; Hd, Overseas Ops, MoD, 2011–12; GOC 1st (UK) Armoured Div., then 1st (UK) Div., 2012–15. *Recreations:* sailing, walking, family.

**CHISWELL, Maj.-Gen. Peter Irvine,** CB 1985; CBE 1976 (OBE 1972; MBE 1965); Chairman, Buckland Leadership Development Centre, 1996–2006; *b* 19 April 1930; *s* of late Col Henry Thomas Chiswell, OBE (late RAMC) and Gladys Beatrice Chiswell; *m* 1958, Felicity Philippa, *d* of R. F. Martin; two *s*. *Educ:* Allhallows School; RMA Sandhurst. Commissioned Devonshire Regt, 1951; served Kenya Emergency, 1953–55; served Cyprus and Suez; transf. Parachute Regt, 1958; DAAG HQ Berlin Inf. Bde, 1963–65; Brigade Major, 16 Para Bde, 1967–68; GSO1 (DS), Staff Coll., 1968–69; CO 3 PARA, 1969–71; Col GS (Army Training), 1971–74; Comd British Contingent DCOS UN Force Cyprus, 1974–76; Comd, 44 Para Bde, 1976–78; ACOS (Operations), HQ Northern Army Gp, 1978–81; Comd, Land Forces NI, 1982–83; GOC Wales, 1983–85. Gov., Christ Coll., Brecon, 1987–2008. DL Powys, 1989–95. *Recreation:* travel.
See also Maj. Gen. J. R. Chiswell.

**CHITTENDEN, Rear Adm. Timothy Clive,** CEng, FIMechE, FNucI; non-executive Director, Sellafield Ltd, 2008–16; *b* 25 May 1951; *s* of late Frederick William John Chittenden and Pauline Beryl (*née* Cockle); *m* 1974, Anne Clare Style; three *d*. *Educ:* Chatham House Grammar Sch.; Churchill Coll., Cambridge (MA Engrg Sci.); MSc Marine Engrg RNEC; Royal Naval Coll., Greenwich (Dip. Nuclear Technol.). MINucE 1982; CEng 1988; MIMechE 1988, FIMechE 2001; FNucI (FINucE 2005). Marine Engineer Officer: HMS Warspite, 1982–85; HMS Talent, 1988–90; Asst Dir, Nuclear Safety, MoD (PE), 1990–93; Prodn Manager, Clyde Submarine Base, 1993–94; Captain 1994; Assistant Director: Business and Safety, Chief Strategic Systems Exec., MoD (PE), 1995–97; Swiftsure & Trafalgar Update, Defence Procurement Agency, MoD, 1997–99; Dir, Inservice Submarines, Ship Support Agency, MoD, Naval Support Comd, 1999–2000; Submarine Support Integrated Project Team Leader and Dir, Warship Support Agency, 2000–03; COS (Support) to C-in-C Fleet, 2003–05. BAE Systems Submarines Solutions, subseq. BAE Systems Maritime Submarines: Prog. Dir, Astute, 2005–07; Safety Assurance Dir, 2007–10; Proj. Mgt Dir, 2011; Associate, 2011–15. Pres., Nuclear Inst., 2013–15 (Vice Pres., 2012–13). Freeman, Co. of Carmen, 2004–. *Recreations:* sailing and dinghy racing, hill-walking, 0.22 target rifle shooting, reading, listening to music. *T:* (01946) 861089. *E:* tcchittenden@aol.com. *Clubs:* Hawks (Cambridge); Bassenthwaite Sailing.

**CHITTICK, Carolyn Julie;** see Fairbairn, C. J.

**CHITTY, Alison Jill,** OBE 2004; RDI 2009; theatre designer; *b* 16 Oct. 1948; *d* of late Ernest Hedley Chitty, Prebendary of St Paul's Cathedral and of Irene Joan Waldron. *Educ:* King Alfred School, London; St Martin's School of Art; Central School of Art and Design (Degree in Theatre Design); Arts Council Scholarship. Victoria Theatre, Stoke-on-Trent, 1970–79 (designed over 40 productions; Head of Design 4 years); designer, 1970–, for *theatre: RNT* incl. A Month in the Country, Don Juan, Much Ado About Nothing, The Prince of Homburg, Danton's Death, Major Barbara, Kick for Touch, Tales from Hollywood, Antigone, Martine, Venice Preserv'd, Fool for Love, Neaptide, Antony and Cleopatra, The Tempest, The Winter's Tale, Cymbeline, Cardiff East, Remembrance of Things Past, 2000 (Olivier Award, 2001), Luther, 2001, Scenes from the Big Picture, 2003, Two Thousand Years, 2005, The Voysey Inheritance, 2006 (Best Costume Designer, Olivier Award, 2007), Grief, 2011; *RSC* incl. Tartuffe, Volpone, Breaking the Silence, Romeo and Juliet, Hamlet, 2001; other productions include: Old King Cole (Th. Royal Stratford East); Orpheus Descending (Haymarket); The Rose Tattoo (Playhouse); Uncle Vanya (Hampstead Th.); Measure for Measure, Julius Caesar (Riverside Studios); The Way South (Bush); Carmen Jones, Lennon (Crucible Sheffield); Merchant of Venice, The Master and Margherita, 2004, King Lear, 2005 (Chichester); Days of Wine and Roses (Donmar Warehouse); The Vortex (UK tour and Apollo Th.), 2007–08; Uncle Vanya (Rose Th., Kingston and UK tour), 2008; Ecstasy (Hampstead and West End), 2011; A Provincial Life (Nat. Th. Wales), 2012; for *opera:* Marriage of Figaro (Opera North); New Year (Houston Grand Opera); Bow Down/Down By the Riverside (Southbank); Siege of Calais (Wexford); The Vanishing Bridegroom (St Louis Opera Th.); Gawain (Royal Opera House); Falstaff (Göteborg Music Theatre); Jenufa (Dallas Opera, 1994, 2004; San Francisco Opera, 2000); Billy Budd (Grand Th. Geneva, 1994; Royal Opera House, 1995; Bastille Opera Paris, 1996; Dallas Opera and Houston Grand Opera, 1997–98; Seattle Opera, Tel Aviv Opera, 2000; Washington, 2004; LA Opera, 2014); Khovanshchina (ENO, 1994, 2003); Blond Eckbert (Santa Fe Opera, 1994); Modern Painters (Santa Fe Opera, 1995); Arianna (Royal Opera House, 1995); Mask of Orpheus (Royal Fest. Hall, 1996); Die Meistersinger von Nürnberg (Danish Royal Opera Copenhagen, 1996); Misper (Glyndebourne, 1997); Turandot (Bastille Opera Paris, 1997); The Flying Dutchman (Bordeaux Opera, 1998; Vilnius, 2004; Bergen, 2008); Tristan and Isolde (Seattle Opera, 1998; Lyric Opera Chicago, 2000); The Bartered Bride (Royal Opera House at Sadlers

Wells, 1998); Julius Caesar (Bordeaux Opera, 1999); Otello (Bavarian State Opera, Munich, 1999, 2013); Dialogues of the Carmelites (Santa Fe Opera, 1999); Aida (Grand Th. Geneva, 1999); The Last Supper (Staats Oper Berlin and Glyndebourne, 2000); Ion (Aldeburgh Fest. and Almeida Opera, 2000); La Vestale (ENO, 2002); Bacchae (RNT, 2002); Original Sin (Crucible Sheffield, 2002); Cavalleria Rusticana, Pagliacci (Royal Albert Hall, 2002); L'Enfant et les Sortilèges (Maastricht, 2003); Cosi Fan Tutti (ENO, 2003); The Io Passion (Aldeburgh Fest., Almeida Opera, Bregenz and UK tour, 2004); Tangier Tattoo (Glyndebourne, 2005); Midsummer Marriage (Chicago Lyric Opera, 2005); Carmen (Greek Nat. Opera, 2007); The Minotaur (Royal Opera House, 2008, 2013); Adrianna's Fall (Cologne, 2008); Hippolyte et Aricie (Reis Opera, Holland, 2009); Semper Dolors, Semper Dowland/The Corridor (Aldeburgh, QEH and Bregenz, 2009); Forza del Destino (Holland Park Opera, 2010); Rigoletto (La Fenice, Venice and Reggio Emelia, 2010; Venice, 2012); Betrothal in a Monastery (Paris, 2011; Toulouse, 2015); Madame Butterfly (Oslo, 2012); Nabucco (La Scala, Milan, Royal Opera House, 2013); Parsifal (Royal Opera House, 2013); Billy Budd (LA, 2014); The Pirates of Penzance (ENO, Luxembourg, Caen, Saarbrucken, 2015); The Corridor/The Cure (Aldeburgh, Royal Opera House Linbury), 2015; Theodora, Théâtre Champs Elysées, Paris, 2015); The Corridor/The Cure (Royal Opera House Linbury, Holland Fest., 2016); Das Rheingold (Gothenburg Opera, 2018); for *films*: Blue Jean, Aria, Life is Sweet, Black Poppies (BBC), Naked, 1993; Secrets & Lies, 1995 (Palme d'Or, 1996); The Turn of the Screw (BBC), 2004. Retrospective exhibition, Alison Chitty Design Process 1970–2010, NT, 2010. Dir, Motley Theatre Design Sch., 2000– (Co-Dir, 1992–2000); Associate, NT, 2003–11; Design Consultant, Rose Th., Kingston, 2007–08. Fellow: Birkbeck, Univ. of London, 2011; Univ. of the Arts, London, 2013. DUniv Staffordshire, 2005. Misha Black Medal, CSD, 2007; Young Vic Award, 2008. *Publications*: (contrib.) Theatre in a Cool Climate. *Address*: c/o Rayfield Allied, Unit 26 China Works, Black Prince Road, SE1 7SJ.

**CHITTY, Sir Andrew Edward Willes**, 4th Bt *cr* 1924, of The Temple; DPhil; Senior Lecturer in Philosophy, University of Sussex; *b* 20 Nov. 1953; *s* of Sir Thomas Willes Chitty, 3rd Bt and of Susan Elspeth Chitty, *qv*; *S* father, 2014, but his name does not yet appear on the Official Roll of the Baronetage. *Educ*: Univ. of Sussex (BA Develtl Psychol.; MA Philos.); Univ. of Oxford (DPhil). Lecturer in Philosophy: Birkbeck Coll., Univ. of London and Univ. of Bristol, 1990–94; Univ. of Sussex, 1994. *Heir*: *uncle* Michael Willes Chitty [*b* 10 June 1929; *m* 1954, Janet Leonora Messenger; one *s* one *d*].

**CHITTY, Dr Anthony**; retired; Director of Corporate Engineering, Rolls-Royce Power Engineering Ltd (formerly Northern Engineering Industries, R-R Industrial Power Group), 1989–93 (Deputy Director, 1988–89); *b* 29 May 1931; *s* of Ashley George Chitty and Doris Ellen Mary Buck; *m* 1956, Audrey Munro; two *s* one *d*. *Educ*: Glyn Grammar Sch., Epsom; Sir John Cass Coll. (BSc); Imperial Coll., London. (PhD, DIC). CEng. GEC Res. Labs, 1955; Hd, Creep of Steels Lab., ERA, 1959; GEC Power Gp, 1963; Chief Metallurgist (Applications), C. A. Parsons, 1966; Dir, Advanced Technol. Div., Clarke Chapman-John Thompson, 1973; Internat. Res. and Develt, 1978; Gen. Manager, Engrg Products, N. E. I. Parsons, 1979; Regional Industrial Adviser, NE Region, DTI, 1984–88. Vis. Prof., Univ. of Aston in Birmingham, 1977–84. Chairman: Bd of Newcastle Technol. Centre, 1988–90 (Dep. Chm., 1985–88); Centre for Adhesive Technol., 1990–93); Member, Board: Newcastle Univ. New Ventures Ltd, 1989–93; Newcastle Polytechnic Products Ltd, 1989–93. *Publications*: research publications in the fields of materials and welding for power generation. *Recreations*: hill walking, gardening. *Address*: 2 The Pound, Westcott Street, Westcott, Dorking, Surrey RH4 3NU.

**CHITTY, Susan Elspeth, (Lady Chitty)**; author; *b* 18 Aug. 1929; *d* of Rudolph Glossop and Mrs E. A. Hopkinson (writer, as Antonia White); *m* 1951, Sir Thomas Willes Chitty, 3rd Bt (*d* 2014); one *s* three *d*. *Educ*: Godolphin Sch., Salisbury; Somerville Coll., Oxford. Mem. editorial staff, Vogue, 1952–53; subseq. journalist, reviewer, broadcaster and lecturer. *Publications*: *novels*: Diary of a Fashion Model, 1958; White Huntress, 1963; My Life and Horses, 1966; *biographies*: The Woman who wrote Black Beauty: a life of Anna Sewell, 1972; The Beast and the Monk: a life of Charles Kingsley, 1975; Charles Kingsley and North Devon, 1976; Gwen John 1876–1939, 1981; Now to My Mother, 1985; That Singular Person Called Lear, 1988; Playing the Game: a biography of Sir Henry Newbolt, 1997; *non-fiction*: (with Thomas Hinde) On Next to Nothing, 1976; (with Thomas Hinde) The Great Donkey Walk, 1977; The Young Rider, 1979; *edited*: The Intelligent Woman's Guide to Good Taste, 1958; The Puffin Book of Horses, 1975; As Once in May, by Antonia White, 1983; Antonia White: Diaries 1926–1957, vol. I, 1991, vol. II, 1992. *Recreations*: riding, travel.

*See also* Sir A. E. W. Chitty, Bt.

**CHIVERS, Rev. Canon Christopher Mark**; Principal, Westcott House, Cambridge, since 2015; Affiliated Lecturer, Faculty of Divinity, University of Cambridge, since 2018; *b* Bristol, 16 July 1967; *s* of Rev. Ernest Alfred John Chivers and Margaret-Rose Lilian Chivers; *m* 1998, (Elizabeth) Mary Rumble (*née* Philpott); three *s*. *Educ*: Bristol Cathedral Sch. (chorister); Magdalen Coll., Oxford (Academical Clerk; BA Hons Music 1988; MA 1992); Selwyn Coll., Cambridge (BA Hons Theol. and Religious Studies 1996 (Univ. Theol Studies Prize); MA 1999); Westcott House, Cambridge (CTM 1997). Asst Master and Lay Clerk, St Michael's Coll., Tenbury, 1984–85; Dir of Music, New Coll. Sch., Oxford, 1988; Asst to Dir of Music and Hd of Music, Cheltenham Ladies' Coll., 1989; Lay Chaplain, Housemaster and Choristers' Tutor, King's Coll. Sch., Cambridge, 1989–94; ordained deacon, 1997, priest, 1998; Asst Curate, St James' and St John's Churches, Friern Barnet, 1997–99; Canon Precentor, St George's Cathedral, Cape Town, 1999–2001; Minor Canon, 2001–05, Precentor, 2002–05, Priest Vicar, 2012–, Westminster Abbey; Canon Chancellor and Founding Dir of ExChange, Blackburn Cathedral, 2005–10, now Canon Emeritus; Vicar, John Keble Church, Mill Hill, 2010–15; Asst Priest, St Michael's Church, Mill Hill, 2011–15; Area Dean, W Barnet, 2014–15. Hon. Canon, Dio. of Saldanha Bay, S Africa, 2014–. Pres., Cambridge Theol Fedn, 2018–19; Trustee: Kay Mason Foundn, 2002–15; S African Church Develt Trust, 2003–15; USPG, 2005–18 (Chair of Trustees, 2012–18; Hon. Vice Pres., 2018–); Anglican Communion Fund, 2012–; Montgomery Trust Lectr, 2013–; Christopher Robin Foundn, 2015–; Teape Trust, 2015–. Presenter, Daily Service and Act of Worship, BBC Radio 4, 2006–. *Publications*: Echoes of a Rainbow Song, 1999; The Hard Road to Glory, 2001; Rumours of God Amidst the Ruins, 2001; The Open Window, 2004; Dear Dom and Greg…, 2007; Jerusalem Haiku, 2007; South African Haiku, 2008; Fully Alive, 2010, Faith from the Belly of the Whale, 2012; Telling it Slant: broadcasting faith in a contemporary world, 2013; Letters to Jonny, 2015; contrib. The Times, Independent, Guardian, Church Times, C of E Newspaper, The Tablet, Cape Times, Cape Argus, Pretoria News, Johannesburg Star, Sunday Independent (S Africa); compositions include antiphons, carols, canticles and responses. *Recreations*: writing and reading poetry, composing choral music, lawn tennis, Western Province Rugby, Glos CCC, Blackburn Rovers, Asian and African travel. *Address*: Westcott House, Jesus Lane, Cambridge CB5 8BP. *T*: (01223) 741000. *E*: principal@westcott.cam.ac.uk.

**CHIVERS, Rear Adm. Paul Austin**, CBE 2019 (OBE 2002); Director, Military Aviation Authority, 2015–18; *b* Bristol, 30 April 1962; *s* of Austin Chivers and Margaret Chivers; one *s* one *d*. *Educ*: Wellington Sch.; King's Coll. London (MA Defence Studies). Joined RN, 1981; at sea, 1982–99; CO HMS Lancaster, 2002–04; MoD/operational, 2005–10; CO RNAS Yeovilton, 2011–12; Hd, Oversight and Approvals, Mil. Aviation Authy, 2013–15. Mem., Royal Navy Club of 1765 and 1785. FRAeS 2017. *Recreation*: yachting.

**CHIVERS, (Tom) David**; QC 2002; *b* 17 Nov. 1960; *s* of Tom Alan Chivers and Anneliese Chivers (*née* Ungar); *m* 1996, Helen Lorraine Searle; one *s* one *d*. *Educ*: Millfield Sch.; Downing Coll., Cambridge (BA Hons Law). Called to the Bar, Lincoln's Inn, 1983, Bencher, 2013. Acting Judge, Commercial Ct, BVI, 2018. *Publications*: (contrib.) Co-operatives That Work, 1988; (contrib.) Practice and Procedure in the Companies Court, 1997; The Law of Majority Shareholder Power, 2008, 2nd edn 2017. *Address*: Erskine Chambers, 33 Chancery Lane, WC2A 1EN. *T*: (020) 7242 5532, *Fax*: (020) 7831 0125. *Club*: Athenæum.

**CHO, Yoon-Je**; Ambassador of Republic of Korea to United States of America, since 2017; *b* 22 Feb. 1952; *s* of Yong-Chan Cho and Kwi-Ju Chung; *m* 1980, Sun-Ae Woo; one *s* two *d*. *Educ*: Seoul Nat. Univ. (BA Econs); Stanford Univ. (MA; PhD Econs 1984). Sen. Economist, World Bank, 1984–88 and 1992–93; Economist, IMF, 1989–92; Vice Pres., Korea Inst. of Public Finance, 1994–95; Sen. Advr to Minister of Finance and Dep. Prime Minister, Republic of Korea, 1995–97; Chief Econ. Advr to Pres. of Republic, 2003–05; Ambassador of Republic of Korea to Court of St James's, 2005–08; Prof. of Econs, 1997–2017, now Emeritus, Dean, 2009–11, Grad. Sch. of Internat. Studies, Sogang Univ. Mem., Nat. Econ. Adv. Council, Republic of Korea, 2013–15. *Publications*: Lessons of Financial Liberalization from Asia and Latin America, 1987; Industrialization of Korea, 1992; State Governance Structure and Economic Policies in Korea, 2009; contrib. numerous articles to Jl Money, Credit Banking, Jl Develt Econs, World Econ., World Develt, World Bank Econ. Rev., World Bank Res. Observer, etc. *Address*: Embassy of the Republic of Korea, 240 Massachussetts Avenue, NW Washington, DC 20008, USA. *Club*: Travellers.

**CHOLERTON, Dr Simon Derrick**; Director, Defence Science and Technology, Ministry of Defence, since 2016; *b* Sheffield, 7 Jan. 1968; *s* of Vernon and Brenda Cholerton. *Educ*: Henry Fanshawe Sch., Dronfield; Imperial Coll. London (BSc; ARCS; MBA; DIC); Pembroke Coll., Cambridge (PhD 1994). Joined MoD, 1993; Private Sec. to Under Sec. of State for Defence, 1996–98; Hd, Middle East Section, 2001–03; Policy Advr, Baghdad, 2003; Hd, Equipt Capability Secretariat, 2009–11; COS, Defence Equipment and Support, MoD, 2011–13; Ops Dir, Defence and Security Orgn, UKTI, 2013–16; Interim Chief Scientific Advr, 2018–19. LGBT Champion, MoD, 2012–16. *Recreations*: Radio 4, travel, Charlton Athletic. *Address*: Ministry of Defence, Main Building, Whitehall, SW1A 2HB.

**CHOLMELEY, Sir (Hugh John) Frederick (Sebastian)**, 7th Bt *cr* 1806, of Easton, Lincolnshire; *b* 3 Jan. 1968; *o s* of Sir Montague Cholmeley, 6th Bt and of Juliet Auriol Sally (*née* Nelson); *S* father, 1998; *m* 1993, Ursula Anne, *d* of Hon. Sir H. P. D. Bennett, *qv*; one *s* one *d*. *Educ*: Eton Coll.; RAC Cirencester. MRICS (ARICS 1992). *Recreation*: the countryside. *Heir*: *s* Montague Hugh Peter Cholmeley, *b* 19 May 1997.

**CHOLMONDELEY**, family name of **Marquess of Cholmondeley**, and of **Baron Delamere**.

**CHOLMONDELEY, 7th Marquess of**, *cr* 1815; **David George Philip Cholmondeley**, KCVO 2007; Bt 1611; Viscount Cholmondeley (Ire.), 1661; Baron Cholmondeley of Namptwich (Eng.), 1689; Earl of Cholmondeley, Viscount Malpas, 1706; Baron Newborough (Ire.), 1715; Baron Newburgh (Gt Brit.), 1716; Earl of Rocksavage, 1815; DL; Joint Hereditary Lord Great Chamberlain of England (acting for the reign of Queen Elizabeth II); *b* 27 June 1960; *s* of 6th Marquess of Cholmondeley, GCVO, MC and Lavinia Margaret (DL Cheshire), *d* of late Col John Leslie, DSO, MC; *S* father, 1990; *m* 2009, Rose, *d* of Timothy Hanbury; two *s* (twins) one *d*. DL Norfolk 2016. *Heir*: *s* Earl of Rocksavage, *qv*. *Address*: Cholmondeley Castle, Malpas, Cheshire SY14 8AH.

**CHOMSKY, Prof. (Avram) Noam**, PhD; Institute Professor, Massachusetts Institute of Technology, 1976–2002, now Emeritus (Ferrari P. Ward Professor of Modern Languages and Linguistics, 1966–76); Laureate Professor of Linguistics, University of Arizona, since 2017; *b* Philadelphia, 7 Dec. 1928; *s* of late William Chomsky and of Elsie Simonofsky; *m* 1st, 1949, Carol Doris Schatz (*d* 2008); one *s* two *d*; 2nd, 2014, Luisa Valeria Galvao-Wasserman. *Educ*: Central High Sch., Philadelphia; Univ. of Pennsylvania (BA 1949; MA 1951; PhD 1955); Society of Fellows, Harvard, 1951–55. Massachusetts Institute of Technology: Asst Prof., 1955–58; Associate Prof., 1958–61; Prof. of Modern Langs, 1961–66. Res. Fellow, Harvard Cognitive Studies Center, 1964–65. Vis. Prof., Columbia Univ., 1957–58; Nat. Sci. Foundn Fellow, Inst. for Advanced Study, Princeton, 1958–59; Linguistics Soc. of America Prof., Univ. of Calif, LA, 1966; Beckman Prof., Univ. of Calif, Berkeley, 1966–67; Vis. Watson Prof., Syracuse Univ., 1982; Lectures: Shearman, UCL, 1969; John Locke, Oxford, 1969; Bertrand Russell Meml, Cambridge 1971; Nehru Meml, New Delhi, 1972; Whidden, McMaster Univ., 1975; Huizinga Meml, Leiden, 1977; Woodbridge, Columbia, 1978; Kant, Stanford, 1979. Member: Nat. Acad. of Scis; Amer. Acad. of Arts and Scis; Linguistic Soc. of America; Amer. Philosophical Assoc.; Bertrand Russell Peace Foundn; Utrecht Soc. of Arts and Scis; Deutsche Akademie der Naturforscher Leopoldina; Corresp. Mem., British Acad., 1974; Hon. Mem., Ges. für Sprachwissenschaft, Germany, 1990. Fellow, Amer. Assoc. for Advancement of Science; William James Fellow, Amer. Psychological Assoc., 1990. Hon. FBPsS; Hon. FRAI 1990. Hon. DLitt: London, 1967; Visva-Bharati, West Bengal, 1980; Cambridge, 1995; Harvard, 2000; Calcutta, 2001; Hon. DHL: Chicago, 1967; Loyola Univ., Chicago, 1970; Swarthmore Coll., 1970; Bard Coll., 1971; Delhi, 1972; Massachusetts, 1973; Pennsylvania, 1985; Maine, 1992; Gettysburg Coll., 1992; Amherst Coll., 1995; Buenos Aires, 1996; Rovira i Virgili, Tarragona, 1998; Guelph, 1999; Columbia, 1999; Connecticut, 1999; Scuola Normale Superiore, Pisa, 1999; Toronto, 2000; Western Ontario, 2000; Free Univ. of Brussels, 2003; Central Conn State, 2003; Athens, 2004; Florence, 2004; Bologna, 2005; Ljubljana, 2005; Santo Domingo Inst. of Technol., 2006; Dr *hc*: Univ. Nacional del Comahue, Argentina, 2002; Univ. Nacional de Colombia, 2002; Univ. of Cyprus, 2006; Univ. de Chile, Santiago, 2006; Univ. de la Frontera, Temuco, 2006. Distinguished Scientific Contribution Award, Amer. Psychological Assoc., 1984; Kyoto Prize in Basic Science, Inamori Foundn, 1988; Orwell Award, Nat. Council of Teachers of English, 1987, 1989; Killian Award, MIT, 1992; Lannan Literary Award, for non-fiction, 1992; Homer Smith Award, New York Univ. Sch. of Medicine, 1994; Loyola Mellon Humanities Award, Loyola Univ., Chicago, 1994; Helmholtz Medal, Berlin-Brandenburgische Akad. Wissenschaften, 1996; Rabindranath Tagore Centenary Award, Asiatic Soc., Calcutta, 2000. *Publications*: Syntactic Structures, 1957; Current Issues in Linguistic Theory, 1964; Aspects of the Theory of Syntax, 1965; Cartesian Linguistics, 1966; Topics in the Theory of Generative Grammar, 1966; Language and Mind, 1968; (with Morris Halle) Sound Pattern of English, 1968; American Power and the New Mandarins, 1969; At War with Asia, 1970; Problems of Knowledge and Freedom, 1971; Studies on Semantics in Generative Grammar, 1972; For Reasons of State, 1973; The Backroom Boys, 1973; Peace in the Middle East?, 1974; (with Edward Herman) Bains de Sang, 1974; Reflections on Language, 1975; The Logical Structure of Linguistic Theory, 1975; Essays on Form and Interpretation, 1977; Human Rights and American Foreign Policy, 1978; Language and Responsibility, 1979; (with

Edward Herman) Political Economy of Human Rights, 1979; Rules and Representations, 1980; Radical Priorities, 1981; Lectures on Government and Binding, 1981; Towards a New Cold War, 1982; Some Concepts and Consequences of the Theory of Government and Binding, 1982; Fateful Triangle: the United States, Israel and the Palestinians, 1983; Modular Approaches to the Study of the Mind, 1984; Turning the Tide, 1985; Barriers, 1986; Pirates and Emperors, 1986; Knowledge of Language: its nature, origin and use, 1986; Generative Grammar: its basis, development and prospects, 1987; On Power and Ideology, 1987; Language in a Psychological Setting, 1987; Language and Problems of Knowledge, 1987; The Chomsky Reader, 1987; The Culture of Terrorism, 1988; (with Edward Herman) Manufacturing Consent, 1988; Necessary Illusions, 1989; Deterring Democracy, 1991; Chronicles of Dissent, 1992; Year 501: the conquest continues, 1993; Rethinking Camelot: JFK, the Vietnam war, and US political culture, 1993; Letters from Lexington: reflections on propaganda, 1993; World Orders, Old and New, 1994; The Minimalist Program, 1995; Powers and Prospects, 1996; Class Warfare (interviews), 1996; The Common Good (interviews), 1998; Profit Over People, 1998; The New Military Humanism, 1999; New Horizons in the Study of Language and Mind, 2000; Rogue States, 2000; A New Generation Draws the Line, 2000; 9–11, 2001; Understanding Power, 2002; On Nature and Language, 2002; Hegemony or Survival, 2003; Middle East Illusions, 2003; Imperial Ambitions, 2005; Failed States, 2006; (with Gilbert Achcar) Perilous Power, 2006; What We Say Goes, 2008; Hopes and Prospects, 2010; Occupy, 2012. *Address*: Department of Linguistics and Philosophy, Massachusetts Institute of Technology, 32–D808, 77 Massachusetts Avenue, Cambridge, MA 02139–4307, USA. *T*: (617) 2537819.

**CHOPE, Sir Christopher (Robert),** Kt 2018; OBE 1982; MP (C) Christchurch, since 1997; barrister; *b* 19 May 1947; *s* of late His Honour Robert Charles Chope and Pamela Durell; *m* 1987, Christo Hutchinson; one *s* one *d*. *Educ*: St Andrew's Sch., Eastbourne; Marlborough Coll.; St Andrews Univ. (LLB Hons). Called to the Bar, Inner Temple, 1972. Mem., Wandsworth Borough Council, 1974–83; Chm., Housing Cttee, 1978–79; Leader of Council, 1979–83. Consultant, Ernst & Young, 1992–98. MP (C) Southampton, Itchen, 1983–92; contested (C) Southampton, Itchen, 1992. PPS to Minister of State, HM Treasury, 1986; Parly Under-Sec. of State, DoE, 1986–90; Parly Under-Sec. of State (Minister for Roads and Traffic), Dept of Transport, 1990–92; front bench spokesman on trade and industry, 1998–99, on Treasury, 2001–02, on Transport, 2002–05. Jt Sec., Cons. Backbench Environment Cttee, 1983–86; Member: Select Cttee on Procedure, 1984–86, 2005–10; Select Cttee on Trade and Industry, 1999–2001; H of C Admin Cttee, 2006–10; Speaker's Panel of Chairmen, 2005–; Select Cttee on Constitutional and Political Reform, 2010–15; Standards Cttee, 2013–15; Privileges Cttee, 2013–15; Select Cttee on Scottish Affairs, 2015–17; Cttee on Standards, 2015–17; Cttee on Privileges, 2015–17; Procedure Cttee, 2017–; Home Affairs Cttee, 2017–; Cttee on Exiting the EU, 2017–. Member: Exec., 1922 Cttee, 2005–12 (Jt Sec., 2006–12); Delegn, Council of Europe, 2005– (Chm., Legal Affairs and Human Rights Cttee, 2012–13; Leader, European Cons. Gp, 2014–15). Chm., Cons. Parly Candidates Assoc., 1995–97. A Vice Chm., Cons. Party, 1997–98. Chm., Cons. Way Forward, 2002–09. Member: HSC, 1993–97; Local Govt Commn for England, 1994–95; Vice-Pres., LGA, 2000. Mem. Exec. Cttee, Soc. of Cons. Lawyers, 1983–86. *Address*: House of Commons, SW1A 0AA. *T*: (020) 7219 5808. *Clubs*: Royal Southampton Yacht; Christchurch Conservative.

**CHOPRA, Preet Kaur;** *see* Gill, P. K.

**CHORLEY,** family name of **Baron Chorley**.

**CHORLEY,** 3rd Baron *cr* 1945, of Kendal, Westmorland; **Nicholas Rupert Debenham Chorley;** Director, Europe, Middle East and Africa, for Public Safety and Security, Hexagon Safety and Infrastructure, since 2015; *b* 15 July 1966; *er s* of 2nd Baron Chorley and of Ann Chorley (*née* Debenham); *S* father, 2016; *m* 1996, Morag Jane Smith; one *s* one *d*. *Educ*: Marlborough Coll.; Durham Univ. (BSc 1988); Univ. of Edinburgh (MSc 1989). Intergraph: Technical Lead, CAD Projects, 1989–94; Hong Kong, 1994–95; Australia and NZ, 1994–97; Technical Manager, Kuala Lumpur, 1997–98; Projects Manager, UK, 1998–2002; Sales and Account Manager UK, Hexagon Safety and Infrastructure (formerly Intergraph), 2002–14. FRGS. *Recreations*: photography, cycling, hill walking, running, writing and travel, in search of contrast. *Heir*: *s* Hon. Patrick Alexander Carmichael Chorley, *b* 14 March 2000.

**CHOTE, Robert William;** Chairman, Office for Budget Responsibility, since 2010; *b* 24 Jan. 1968; *s* of Morville Vincent William Chote and Mary Isabel Chote (*née* Davis); *m* 1997, Sharon Michele White, *qv*; two *s*. *Educ*: Queens' Coll., Cambridge (MA Econs; Hon. Fellow 2015). Econs corresp. and commentator, The Independent and Independent on Sunday, 1990–94; Econs Ed., FT, 1995–99; Advr and speechwriter to First Dep. Man. Dir, IMF, Washington, 1999–2002; Dir, Inst. for Fiscal Studies, 2002–10. Chair: Adv. Gp on Public Data Literacy, Royal Statistical Soc., 2015–; OECD Network of Parly Budget Offices and Ind. Fiscal Instns, 2018–; Ext. Adv. Panel, Irish Parly Budget Office, 2018–. Gov., NIESR, 1997–. Member: Stats Adv. Cttee, ONS, 1998–99; Adv. Bd, UK Centre for Measurement of Govt Activity, ONS, 2006–10; Acad. and Policy Bd, Oxford Inst. for Econ. Policy, 2003; Finance Cttee, Cambridge Univ., 2009–18. DUniv York, 2015. *Publications*: (with J. Cremona) Exploring Nature in the Wilds of Europe, 1988; (with J. Cremona) Exploring Nature in North Africa, 1989; (contrib.) Insight Guide to Tunisia, 1990; An Expensive Lunch: the political economy of Britain's new monetary framework, 1997; (ed jtly) IFS Green Budget (annual report), 2003–10. *Address*: Office for Budget Responsibility, 14T, 102 Petty France, SW1H 9AJ. *T*: (020) 3334 6337. *E*: obrenquiries@obr.gsi.gov.uk.

**CHOTE, Sharon Michele;** *see* White, S. M.

**CHOTHIA, Cyrus Homi,** PhD; FRS 2000; Member of Scientific Staff, MRC Laboratory of Molecular Biology, Cambridge, 1990–2007, now Emeritus; Senior Research Fellow, Wolfson College, Cambridge, 2003–09, now Emeritus; *b* 19 Feb. 1942; *s* of Homi and Betty Chothia; *m* 1967, Jean Sandham; one *s* one *d*. *Educ*: Alleyn's Sch., London; Univ. of Durham (BSc 1965); Birkbeck Coll., London Univ. (MSc 1967); UCL (PhD 1970). Mem., Scientific Staff, MRC Lab. of Molecular Biology, Cambridge, 1970–73; EMBO Fellow, Dept of Molecular Biochemistry and Biophysics, Yale Univ., and Dept of Chemical Physics, Weizmann Inst. of Science, Israel, 1974; Chargé de Recherche, Service du Biochimie Cellulaire, Institut Pasteur, Paris, 1974–76; Res. Associate, Dept of Chemistry, UCL, 1976–80; Royal Soc. EPA Cephalosporin Fund Sen. Res. Fellow, MRC Lab. of Molecular Biology, Cambridge, and Dept of Chemistry, UCL, 1980–90; Mem., Scientific Staff, Cambridge Centre for Protein Engrg, 1990–93. Mem., EMBO, 1988. Dan David Prize, Dan David Foundn/Tel Aviv Univ., 2015; Sen. Scientist Accomplishment Award, Internat. Soc. for Computational Biol., 2015. *Publications*: papers on molecular biology in scientific jls. *Recreations*: cinema, books, conversation. *Address*: MRC Laboratory of Molecular Biology, Francis Crick Avenue, Cambridge CB2 0QH; 26 Clarendon Street, Cambridge CB1 1JX.

**CHOUDHURY, Hon. Sir Akhlaq Ur-Rahman,** Kt 2017; **Hon. Mr Justice Choudhury;** a Judge of the High Court, Queen's Bench Division, since 2017; *b* Winchester, 1967; *s* of Azizur Rahman Choudhury and Sultana Choudhury; *m* 1993, Safina Rahman; two *s* one *d*. *Educ*: Univ. of Glasgow (BSc Hons 1988); Sch. of Oriental and African Studies, Univ. of London (LLB Hons 1991); Inns of Court Sch. of Law (BVC 1992). Called to the Bar, Inner Temple, 1992; in practice as a barrister, 11 King's Bench Walk, 1992–2017; a Recorder, 2009–17; QC 2015; a Dep. High Court Judge, 2016–17; Pres., Employment Appeal Tribunal, 2019–; Mem., Attorney Gen.'s Panel of Counsel, B Panel, 2000, A Panel, 2013. Gov., W Herts Coll., 2012–. *Publications*: (contrib.) Tolley's Employment Law Handbook, 1996–. *Recreations*: cycling, hiking, music, cinema. *Address*: Royal Courts of Justice, Rolls Building, Fetter Lane, EC4A 1NL.

**CHOUDHURY, Anwar Bokth;** HM Diplomatic Service; Governor, Cayman Islands, 2018; *b* 15 June 1959; *s* of Afruz Bokth Choudhury and Ashrafun Nessa Choudhury; *m* 2001, Momina Laskar; one *s* two *d*. *Educ*: Salford Univ. (BSc Engrg); Durham Univ. (MBA). Principal Design Engr, Siemens and Plessey Radar, 1985–90; Design Engr/Strategist, RAF, 1990–93; Asst Dir, MoD, 1994–99; Dir, Policy, Cabinet Office, 2000–03; Dir, Policy/Strategy, FCO, 2003–04; High Comr, Bangladesh, 2004–08; Dir, Internat. Security and Institutions, FCO, 2008–11; Dir, FCO, 2011–13; Ambassador to Peru, 2014–18. Hon. DSc Salford. *Recreations*: cricket, bridge, addicted to Bengali Baul music. *Address*: c/o Foreign and Commonwealth Office, King Charles Street, SW1A 2AH.

**CHOUDHURY, Sumit P.;** *see* Paul-Choudhury.

**CHOW, Sir Chung Kong,** Kt 2000; GBS 2015; FREng; FIChemE; FHKEng, FCILT; Chairman, Hong Kong Exchanges and Clearing Ltd, 2012–18; *b* 9 Sept. 1950. *Educ*: Univ. of Wisconsin (BS Chem. Engrg 1972); Univ. of California (MS Chem. Engrg 1974); Chinese Univ. of Hong Kong (MBA 1981); Harvard (AMP 1991). CEng; FIChemE 1997; FREng 2001. Res. Engr, Climax Chemical Co., New Mexico, 1974–76; Process Engr, Sybron Asia Ltd, Hong Kong, 1976–77; with BOC Group, 1977–96: Hong Kong Oxygen, Hong Kong and BOC, Australia, 1977–84; Man. Dir, Hong Kong Oxygen, 1984–86; Pres., BOC Japan, 1986–89; Gp Manager, Gases Business Develt, BOC Gp plc, England and USA, 1989–91; Regl Dir, N Pacific, based in Tokyo and Hong Kong, 1991–93; Chief Exec., Gases, 1993–96; joined Main Bd, 1994; Man. Dir, 1994–97; Chief Executive: GKN plc, 1997–2001; Brambles Industries, 2001–03; Mass Transit Railway Corporation, Hong Kong, 2003–11. Non-executive Director: Standard Chartered plc, 1997–2008; Anglo American plc, 2008–14; AIA Gp Ltd, 2010–; Chairman: Standard Chartered Bank (Hong Kong) Ltd, 2004–10; Hong Kong Gen. Chamber of Commerce, 2012–14; Mem., Financial Leaders Forum, 2017–. Non-official Member: Exec. Council, HKSAR, 2012–; Human Resources Planning Commn, Hong Kong, 2018–; Chairman: Adv. Cttee on Corruption, ICAC, 2013–; Adv. Cttee on Admission of Quality Migrants and Professionals, Hong Kong, 2016–; Mem. Bd, Community Chest of Hong Kong, 2017–. Pres., 1999–2000, Dep. Pres., 2000–01, SBAC. FCGI 2000; FCILT 2004; FHKEng 2005. Hon. FHKIE 2004. Hon. DEng Bath, 2001.

**CHOWDHURY, Ajay;** Partner and Managing Director, BCG Digital Ventures London, since 2015; *b* 29 April 1962; *s* of Micky and Indira Chowdhury; *m* 1st, 1995, Liz McDonnell (marr. diss. 2010); two *d*; 2nd, 2015, Angelina Melwani. *Educ*: Sydenham Coll., Bombay (BCom 1st Cl.); Wharton Sch., Univ. of Penn (MBA); Central Sch. of Speech and Drama; Metropolitan Film Sch. Manager, Bain & Co., 1986–91; Gp Develt Manager, MAI PLC, 1991–92; Develt Dir, MAI Media, 1993–94; Man. Dir, United Interactive, 1994–99; Chief Executive Officer: Lineone, 1999–2000; NBC Internet Europe, 2000; Man. Partner, IDG Ventures Europe, 2000–06; Gen. Partner, Acacia Capital, 2006–07; Chief Executive Officer: ComQi Group (formerly EnQii Hldgs plc), 2007–13; Seatwave, 2013–14. Chm., Shazam Entertainment, 2001–07; Director: Index on Censorship, 1994–2000; Empower Interactive, 2002–06; Lionhead Games, 2004–06. Mem. Council, Arts Council London, 2009–13. Director: MLA (formerly Resource: Council for Mus, Archives and Libraries), 2000–06; British Screen Adv. Council, 2003–16 (Dep. Chm., 2013–16); DCMS, 2013–16. Trustee: 24 Hour Museum, 2002–06; Historic Royal Palaces, 2016–; Riverside Studios, 2016–17; Mem. Bd, Enacte, 2014–. Non-exec. Dir, FairFX, 2014–. Artistic Dir, Rented Space Th. Co., 1988–. *Recreations*: directing plays, theatre, films, music, bridge, diving. *Address*: 4 Duke's Head Yard, N6 5JQ.

**CHOWN, John Francis;** independent international tax and economic adviser, since 2015; Investor and Adviser, NCL Technology Ventures Ltd, since 2017; *b* Hutton Rudby, 12 Dec. 1929; *s* of Walter Redvers and Mary Elizabeth Chown; *m* 1969, Vera Marie Luise Wohl; two *d*. *Educ*: Gordonstoun; Selwyn Coll., Cambridge (Wrenbury Schol.; Adam Smith Prize; BA Econs 1954; Hon. Fellow 1997). Nat. Service, RAF, 1949–51. Mgt trainee, Pye Ltd, 1956–58; Asst to Chm., Robinson Frere, 1958–60; Dir, Maxwell Stamp, 1960–62. Co-Founder and Mem., Exec. Cttee, Inst. for Fiscal Studies, 1969–; Mem., OMFIF, 2012–. Internat. Tax Advr, Chown Dewhurst LLP, 1992–2015. Mem., Cttees, Internat. Tax Specialist Gp. Mem., Tax Cttee, IoD, 1972–2002, now Hon. Life Fellow; former Member: Taxation and Tech. Cttee, Assoc. of Corporate Treasurers; London Cttee, Internat. Fiscal Assoc.; Internat. Financial Services, London; Cttees, Political Econ. Club. Former Mem. Cttee, London Handel Soc.; Hon. Financial Advr and Hon. Mem., Royal Soc. Musicians. Tax corresp., FT; reviewer of books, TLS. Former Trustee, Handel Opera Gp. *Publications*: (with R. Valentine) International Bond Market in the 1960s, 1968; (ed) International Fund Year Book, 1970; VAT Explained, 1972, 2nd edn 1973; Taxation and Multinational Enterprise, 1974; A Guide to Capital Transfer Tax, 1975; Offshore Financial Centres, 1975, 4th edn, 1981; (with L. Halpern) Taxation of Direct Investment in the United States, 1980; Foreign Exchange Risk: a tax and financial analysis, 1983; Tax Efficient Forex Management, 1986; Tax Efficient Foreign Exchange Management, 1990; A History of Money - from AD 800, 1994; (with K. Desai) The Taxation of Foreign Exchange and Derivatives, 1997; A History of Monetary Unions, 2004; articles, reviews and contribs on tax and money, mainly financial and currency crises, Eurozone and conflicts of interest within banking system, incl. contrib. to Trusts and Trustees. *Recreations*: music, monetary history, walking. *Address*: 7 Acacia Road, NW8 6AB. *T*: (020) 7722 9916. *E*: john@johnchown.co.uk. *W*: www.johnchown.co.uk. *Club*: Reform.

**CHRÉTIEN, Rt Hon. Jean;** CC 2007; OM 2009; PC (Canada) 1967; QC (Canada) 1980; Prime Minister of Canada, 1993–2003; Counsel, Dentons Canada LLP, since 2014; *b* 11 Jan. 1934; *s* of Willie Chrétien and Marie Chrétien (*née* Boisvert); *m* 1957, Aline Chaîné; two *s* one *d*. *Educ*: Trois-Rivières; Joliette; Shawinigan; Laval Univ. (BA, LLL). Called to the Bar, and entered Shawinigan law firm of Chrétien, Landry, Deschênes, Trudel and Normand, 1958; Counsel, Lang Michener Lawrence and Shaw, 1986–90; Director: Shawinigan Sen. Chamber of Commerce, 1962; Bar of Trois-Rivières, 1962–63. Government of Canada: MP (L): St Maurice, 1963–86; Beauséjour, New Brunswick, 1990–93; St Maurice, 1993–2003; Parly Sec. to Prime Minister, 1965, and to Minister of Finance, 1966; Minister of State, 1967; Minister of National Revenue, Jan. 1968; Minister of Indian and Northern Affairs, July 1968; Pres., Treasury Bd, 1974; Minister of Industry, Trade and Commerce, 1976; Minister of Finance, 1977–79; Minister of Justice, responsible for constitutional negotiations, Attorney General, Minister of State for Social Develt, 1980–82; Minister of Energy, Mines and Resources, 1982–84; Deputy Prime Minister and External Affairs Minister, 1984; External Affairs Critic for official Opposition, 1984–86; Leader of the Opposition, 1990–93. Elected Leader, Liberal Party of Canada, June 1990. Counsel, Heenan Blaikie, 2004–14. Hon LLD: Wilfred Laurier, 1981; Laurentian, 1982; W

Ontario, 1982; York, Ont., 1986; Alberta, 1987; Lakehead, 1988; Ottawa, 1994; Meiji, Tokyo, 1996; Warsaw Sch. of Econs, Michigan State, 1999; Hebrew Univ. of Jerusalem, Meml, St Johns, 2000. *Publications:* Straight from the Heart, 1986; My Years as Prime Minister, 2007; My Stories, My Times, 2018. *Recreations:* ski-ing, fishing, golf, reading, classical music. *Address:* Dentons Canada LLP, 99 Bank Street, Suite 1420, Ottawa, ON K1P 1H4, Canada.

**CHRÉTIEN, Prof. Michel,** OC 1986; OQ 1994; MD; FRS 2009; FRSC; Emeritus Senior Scientist, Chronic Disease, Ottawa Hospital Research Institute (formerly Ottawa Health Research Institute); *b* Shawinigan, Quebec, 26 March 1936; *s* of Willie Chrétien and Marie Chrétien (*née* Boisvert); *m* Micheline Ruel; two *d*. *Educ:* Séminaire de Joliette (BA cum laude 1955); Univ. of Montreal (MD cum laude 1960); McGill Univ. (MSc 1962). CSPQ (Endocrinology) 1969; FACP 1971; FRCP&S (Canada) 1973. Clinical Research Institute of Montreal: Dir, Lab. of Molecular Neuroendocrinol., 1967–99; Scientific Dir and CEO, 1984–94; EJLB Foundn Prof., 1994–98; Physician, Dept of Medicine and Endocrine Div., 1967–99, Chief of Endocrinol., 1978–84, Hôtel-Dieu Hosp., Montreal; Prof. of Medicine, Univ. of Montreal, 1975–99, Prof. Emeritus, 2002; Physician, Dept of Endocrinol., Ottawa Hosp., 1998–; Scientific Dir and CEO, Loeb Health Res. Inst., Ottawa Civic Hosp., 1998–2001; Prof., Dept of Medicine, Univ. of Ottawa, 1998–; Ottawa Health Research Institute: Dir, Regl Protein Chemistry Centre and Diseases of Ageing Unit, 2001–06; Sen. Scientist, Hormone, Growth and Develt, 2006. FRSC 1981; Fellow: AAAS, 1996; Molecular Medicine Soc., 1999. Adjunct Prof., Fac. of Medicine, McGill Univ., Montreal, 1970–; Hon. Prof., Chinese Acad. of Med. Scis and Peking Union Med. Coll., 1986. Chevalier, Légion d'Honneur (France), 2004. *Publications:* articles in scientific jls. *Address:* Ottawa Hospital Research Institute, 725 Parkdale Avenue, Ottawa, ON K1Y 4E9, Canada.

**CHRIMES, Neil Roy;** Director, Ursus Economicus Ltd, since 2017; *b* 10 June 1954; *er s* of Geoffrey Richard Chrimes and Dorothy Enid Chrimes (*née* Wyatt); *m* 1982, Anne Margery, (Henny), Barnes; one *s* one *d*. *Educ:* Queen Mary's Grammar Sch., Basingstoke; Univ. of Exeter (BA 1975); MIT (SM 1979). Economic Assistant, MAFF, 1975–77; Harkness Fellow, MIT, 1977–79; Sen. Economic Assistant, MAFF, 1979–81; HM Diplomatic Service, 1981–2006: Economic Advr, FCO, 1981–87; Economist, Res. Dept, IMF, Washington, 1987–89; Sen. Econ. Advr, FCO, 1989–94; Dep. UK Perm. Rep. and Counsellor (Econ. and Financial), OECD, Paris, 1994–98; Economic Counsellor, Jakarta, 1998; Hd, African Dept (Southern), FCO, 1999–2001; Counsellor (Econ., Sci. and Trade), Ottawa, 2001–06; Head of Programmes, Lord Mayor's Office, City of London, 2006–17. Trustee, Florence Nightingale Foundn, 2011–17. Liveryman, Horners' Co., 1980. Church Warden, St Peter and St Paul Hawkley with Priors Dean, 2011–18; Mem. Synod, Portsmouth Dio., 2018–. FRSA 2006. *Recreations:* travel, wine, music (especially mediaeval), gardening, cricket. *Address:* Walnut Cottage, Lower Green, Hawkley, Liss, Hants GU33 6NR. *Club:* MCC.

**CHRIST CHURCH, Dublin, Dean of;** *see* Dunne, Very Rev. D. P. M.

**CHRIST CHURCH, Oxford, Dean of;** *see* Percy, Very Rev. Canon Prof. M. W.

**CHRISTCHURCH, Bishop of,** since 2019; **Rt Rev. Dr Peter Ruane Carrell;** *b* Christchurch, NZ, 16 Nov. 1959; *s* of Brian Ruane Carrell and May Pauline Carrell; *m* 1988, Teresa Kundycki; one *s* three *d*. *Educ:* Univ. of Canterbury, NZ (BSc Hons); Univ. of Otago (BD); Univ. of Durham (PhD). Ordained deacon, 1986, priest, 1987; Asst Curate, Shirley, 1987–90; Asst Priest, Stoke, 1993–95; Vicar, Blenheim South, 1995–2001; Ministry Educator, Dio. of Nelson, 2001–10; Dir of Educn, Dio. of Christchurch, and Dir of Theology House, Christchurch, 2010–19; Archdeacon of South Canterbury, 2014–18, of Mid Canterbury, 2015–18, of Pegasus, 2018. *Publications:* Jesus and the Angels, 1997. *Recreations:* walking, cycling, gardening, politics, Rugby, cricket. *Address:* PO Box 4438, Christchurch 8140, New Zealand. *T:* (3) 3486960. *E:* bishopsea@anglicanlife.org.nz. *Clubs:* Christchurch, Riccarton Rotary (Christchurch).

**CHRISTENSEN, Jayne, (Mrs P. L. Christensen);** *see* Torvill, J.

**CHRISTENSEN, Jens;** Commander First Class, Order of the Dannebrog; Hon. GCVO; Ambassador of Denmark to Organization for Economic Co-operation and Development, 1989–91; *b* 30 July 1921; *s* of Christian Christensen and Sophie Dorthea Christensen; *m* 1st, 1950, Tove (*née* Jessen) (*d* 1982); one *s* two *d*; 2nd, 1983, Vibeke Pagh. *Educ:* Copenhagen Univ. (MPolSc 1945). Joined Danish Foreign Service, 1945; Head of Section, Econ. Secretariat of Govt, 1947; Sec. to OEEC Delegn in Paris, 1949 and to NATO Delegn, 1952; Hd of Sect., Min. of Foreign Affairs, 1952, Actg Hd of Div., 1954; Chargé d'Affaires a.i. and Counsellor of Legation, Vienna, 1957; Asst Hd of Econ.-Polit. Dept, Min. of For. Affairs, 1960; Dep. Under-Sec., 1961; Under-Sec. and Hd of Econ.-Polit. Dept, 1964–71; Hd of Secretariat for Eur. Integration, 1966; Ambassador Extraord. and Plenipotentiary, 1967; State Sec. for Foreign Econ. Affairs, 1971; Ambassador to the Court of St James's, 1977–81; Pres., Danish Oil and Natural Gas Co., 1980–84; Ambassador to Austria, 1984–89. Governor for Denmark, The Asian Development Bank, 1967–73. Chm., Cross Cultures Project Assoc., 1999–2006. Knight Grand Cross: Order of Icelandic Falcon; Order of Northern Star, Sweden; Order of St Olav, Norway; Royal Victorian Order; Austrian Order of Honour. *Address:* Strandvejen 647, 2930 Klampenborg, Denmark.

**CHRISTENSEN, Lisa Ellen Buch;** Improvement Manager (social care), NHS Improvement, since 2018; *b* Preston, 11 Sept. 1956; *d* of late Poul Buch Christensen and Marjorie Christensen (later Hayes); *m* 1992, Jack Prescott (*d* 2009); two *d*. *Educ:* Ackworth Sch.; Shrewsbury High Sch. for Girls; Imberhorne Sch.; Univ. of Kent at Canterbury (BA Hons English and Philosophy 1978). Various admin. posts, Islington Council, 1979–85; Develt Officer, then Dir, Haringey Assoc. for Ind. Living, 1986–89; Wakefield Case Mgt Project, 1989–91; Develt Officer, Carers Project, Yorks RHA, 1991–92; Dir, Community Services, Bradford Community Health NHS Trust, 1992–97; Exec. Dir, Hackney Council, 1997–99; Dir, Social Services, Lambeth Council, 1999–2002; Dir, Social Services, 2002–05, Children's Services, 2005–13, Norfolk CC; Dir, Lisa Christensen Consulting Ltd, 2013–18. Consultant, health and social care, 2013–. *Recreations:* cinema, theatre, reading, walking, having dinner with friends. *Address:* Flat 14, Langbourne House, Effra Parade, SW2 1PJ. *T:* 07540 566186.

**CHRISTIAN, Louise;** Co-Founder, 1985, Senior Partner, 1985–2010, Senior Consultant, 2010–14, Christian Khan (formerly Christian Fisher), Solicitors; Senior Consultant, Public Law Project, since 2015; *b* Oxford, 22 May 1952; *d* of late John, (Jack) and Maureen Christian. *Educ:* St Anne's Coll., Oxford (BA Hons Hist. 1973). Solicitor: Lovell White & King, 1976–79; Plumstead Law Centre, 1979–81; Legal Advr to Police Cttee, GLC, 1981–84. Chair: Inquest, 1998–2007 (Mem. Bd, 2007–); Liberty, 2007–09; Member Bd, Centre for Corporate Accountability, 2007–09; Article 19, 2006–08; Mem., Adv. Bd, Kurdish Human Rights Project, 1997–. Has undertaken human rights missions to ME, Turkey, etc. Hon. Dr Staffs, 2003. Legal Aid Personality of Year Award, Legal Aid Practitioners Gp, 2004; Human Rights Award, Liberty/Law Soc./Justice, 2004. *Publications:* (jtly) Inquests: a practitioner's guide, 2002. *Address:* Public Law Project, 150 Caledonian Road, N1 9RD. *T:* (020) 7843 1260, 07884 363630, *Fax:* (020) 7837 7048. *E:* louisec022@gmail.com.

**CHRISTIANI, Alexander,** Dr jur; Ambassador of Austria to the Court of St James's, 2000–05; *b* 31 May 1940; *s* of Dr Alfred Christiani-Kronwald, (Baron von Christiani-Kronwald), and Rose Christiani-Kronwald; *m* 1968, Renate Sedlmayer, PhD; one *s* one *d*. *Educ:* Univ. of Vienna (Dr jur 1964); Diplomatic Acad., Vienna. Federal Ministry for Foreign Affairs, Austria: Political Dept, 1966–69; Asst to Sec.-Gen. for Foreign Affairs, 1969; UN Mission, NY, 1970–75; Alternate Rep. of Austria to Security Council, 1973–74; Dir, Div. i/c of Vienna Internat. Centre, 1976–81; Consul Gen., Austrian Delegn, Berlin, 1981–86; Ambassador to South Africa, 1986–90; Dir, Dept for ME and Africa, 1990–96; Ambassador to the Netherlands, 1996–2000. Mem., Austrian Delegns to UN Gen. Assemblies, 1967–81. Mem. Bd, Austrian Foreign Policy Assoc. Vice-Pres., Austro-British Soc., 2005–. Cross, KM. Grand Cross: Order of Oranje-Nassau (Netherlands), 2000; Al-Istiqlal Order (Jordan); Grand Officer, Order of Merit (Syria); Comdr, Order of Oak Crown (Luxembourg); Grand Decoration of Honour in Gold (Austria). *Recreations:* music, travelling, theatre. *Address:* Reithlegasse 9, 1190 Vienna, Austria. *T:* and *Fax:* (1) 3681525. *E:* achristiani@hotmail.com. *Clubs:* Rotary, St Johann's (Vienna).

**CHRISTIANSON, Rev. Canon Rodney John, (Bill);** Vicar, St Michael Paternoster Royal, 2000–09; Secretary General, The Mission to Seafarers, 2001–09; *b* S Africa, 19 March 1947; *s* of late Kenneth Alfred John Christianson and Jessie Winifred Nelson (*née* Kelly). *Educ:* Glenwood High Sch., Durban; Officer Trng Sch., S Africa; St Paul's Theol Coll., Grahamstown (DipTh); Open Univ. Ordained deacon 1972, priest 1973; Curate, Pietermaritzburg, SA, 1972–75; Missions to Seamen, subseq. Mission to Seafarers: Asst Chaplain, Gravesend, 1976–81; Sen. Chaplain, Port of London, 1981–82; Port Chaplain, Richards Bay, SA, 1982–91; also Parish Priest, St Andrew, Richards Bay and St Aidan, Kwambonambi, 1982–91; Trng Chaplain, Hull, 1991–93; Ministry Sec., 1993–2000. Mem., Archbp of Cape Town's Commn to conduct investigation into work amongst young people in the Church of SA, 1974. Guild Chaplain, St Bride's Ch, London, 1990; Chaplain, Innholders' Co., 2002–14 (Mem., Ct of Assts, 2013–); Liveryman, Tallow Chandlers' Co., 2011. Hon. Chaplain, Shipwrights' Co., 2012. Hon. Canon: Bloemfontein Cathedral, SA, 1993–; Anglican Church of Canada, 2009. Hon. Master Mariner, SA, 1988. Hon. FNI 2009. *Recreations:* painting/art, music, theatre, photography. *Address:* 45 Wimbledon Park Court, Wimbledon Park Road, SW19 6NN.

**CHRISTIE, Aidan Patrick;** QC 2008; a Recorder, since 2009; *b* Edinburgh, 26 Oct. 1962; *s* of late William James Christie and Maeve Patricia Christie (*née* Gallacher); *m* 1991, Claire Elliott; one *s* one *d*. *Educ:* Edinburgh Acad.; Hertford Coll., Oxford (BA Lit.Hum. 1985); Downing Coll., Cambridge (MA Law 1987). Called to the Bar, Middle Temple, 1988, Bencher, 2018. Bar Standards Board: Mem., 2015–; Mem., Professional Conduct Cttee, 2011– (Barrister Vice-Chair, 2014–15; Chair, 2015–). Panel Deemster, Isle of Man High Court, 2012–. *Recreation:* reading. *Address:* 4 Pump Court, Temple, EC4Y 7AN. *T:* (020) 7842 5555. *E:* achristie@4pumpcourt.com. *Club:* New (Edinburgh).

**CHRISTIE, Andrew George,** CBE 2017; Chairman: Birmingham Children's Trust, since 2016; Adoption and Special Guardianship (formerly Adoption) Leadership Board, since 2016; *b* Bristol, 10 Oct. 1953; *s* of Michael George Christie and Mary Shirley Christie; *m* 2008, Deborah Jane Hickland; one *s* one *d* and two step *s*. *Educ:* George Watson's Coll., Edinburgh; Manchester Univ. (BA Econs 1974); Sussex Univ. (MSW, CQSW 1979). With MENCAP, 1974–76; trainee social worker, 1977–79, social worker, 1979–83, E Sussex CC; Asst Team Manager, 1984–86, Team Manager, 1986–88, Actg Divl Manager, 1988–89, London Borough of Lewisham; Surrey County Council: Asst Area Dir, W Surrey, 1989–93; Gen. Manager, Children's Services, 1993–96; Actg Jt Hd of Children's Services, 1996–97; Children's Services Manager, 1997–98; London Borough of Hammersmith and Fulham: Asst Dir (Community Services), 1998–2000; Asst Dir (Children's Services), 2000–02; Jt Actg Dir, Social Services, 2002–03; Dir, Hammersmith and Fulham Children's Trust, 2003–06; Dir, Children's Services, 2006–11; Tri-borough Exec. Dir of Children's Services, London Bor. of Hammersmith and Fulham, Royal Bor. of Kensington and Chelsea and City of Westminster, 2011–16. *Recreations:* golf, snowboarding, hill walking.

**CHRISTIE, Augustus Jack;** Executive Chairman, Glyndebourne Productions Ltd, since 2000 (Director, since 1989); *b* 4 Dec. 1963; *s* of Sir George William Langham Christie, CH; *m* 1993, Imogen Lycett Green (marr. diss. 2006); four *s*; *m* 2009, Danielle de Niese; one *s*. *Educ:* St Aubyns, Rottingdean; Eton Coll.; King's Coll., London (2nd Cl. Hons Zool). Worked in various theatres, incl. Tricycle, NT, Batignano Opera, Robert Fox Associates, 1987; asst ed. and asst cameraman, Partridge Films, 1989–91; freelance cameraman, 1991–; documentaries include: A Puffin's Tale, Halloween, 1991; A New Fox in Town, 1993; The Lion's Share, Lions, 1994; Hugo's Diary, 1995; Red Monkeys of Zanzibar, 1996; The Battle of the Sexes, The Tale of Two Families, 1998; Buffalo: the African boss, Triumph of Life, 1999. Hon. FKC. *Recreations:* sport, music, nature. *Address:* Glyndebourne, Lewes, E Sussex BN8 5UU.

**CHRISTIE, David;** Warden, St Edward's School, Oxford, 1988–2004; *b* 22 Feb. 1942; *s* of William and Jean Christie, Bannockburn; *m* 1969, Elsa Margaret Shearer; one *s* two *d*. *Educ:* Dollar Acad.; Univ. of Strathclyde; Univ. of Glasgow. Lektor, British Centre, Folkuniversity of Sweden, 1965–66; Asst Master, George Watson's Coll., 1966–71; Lectr in Economics, Moray House Coll., Edinburgh, 1971–77; Res. Associate (part-time), Esmée Fairbairn Research Centre, Heriot-Watt Univ., 1972–77; Teacher, European Sch., Luxembourg, 1977–83; pt-time Faculty Mem., Miami Univ. European Center, Luxembourg, 1980–83; Head of Econs, Winchester Coll., 1983–88. Member: Econs and Business Studies Panel, Scottish Cert. of Educn Exam. Bd, 1973–77 (Convenor, 1975–77); Scottish Cttee, IBA, 1973–77; Dep. Chm., HMC Wkg Party on Inspection, 1993–97; Chm., Oxford Conf. in Educn, 1997–2002. Educn Adviser, Haberdashers' Co., 2005–11. Dir, Ecclesiastical Insurance Gp plc, 2001–16 (Dep. Chm. and Sen. Ind. Dir, 2013–16). Mem., Council of Mgt, Hebridean Trust, 1998–2009; Trustee, Allchurches Trust Ltd, 2013–16. *Publications:* (contrib.) Curriculum Development in Economics, 1973; (contrib.) Teaching Economics, 1975; (with Prof. A. Scott) Economics in Action, 1976; articles, reviews and entries in jls. *Recreations:* books, golf, hills, gardens. *Address:* Sunnybank, Blebo Craigs KY15 5UF. *Club:* Royal & Ancient (St Andrews).

**CHRISTIE, Elizabeth Mary, (Mrs Stuart Christie);** *see* Steel, Her Honour E. M.

**CHRISTIE, Herbert;** Director General, European Investment Bank, 1995–99, now Hon. Director General (Director, Research Department, 1983–95); *b* 26 Sept. 1933; *s* of Brig.-Gen. H. W. A. Christie, CB, CMG, and Mary Ann Christie; *m* 1982, Gilberte F. M. V. Desbois; one *s*. *Educ:* Methodist Coll., Belfast; Univ. of St Andrews (MA). Asst Lectr, Univ. of Leeds, 1958–60; Econ. Asst, HM Treasury, 1960–63; First Sec., Washington, DC, 1963–66; Econ. Adviser, J. Henry Schroder Wagg and Co. Ltd, 1966–71, with secondment as Econ. Adviser, NBPI, 1967–71; Sen. Econ. Adviser, Min. of Posts and Telecommunications, 1971–74, and Dept of Prices and Consumer Protection, 1974–76; Econ. Adviser, EEC Commn, Brussels, 1976–78; Under Sec., HM Treasury, 1978–83. Hon. Vis. Prof., Middlesex Univ., 1990–95. Order of European Merit, 2005. *Publications:* contrib. to books and learned jls. *Recreations:* languages, foreign travel. *Address:* 47 Rue J-B Esch, 1473 Luxembourg. *Club:* Reform.

**CHRISTIE, Prof. Ian Leslie,** FBA 1994; Anniversary Professor of Film and Media History, Birkbeck College, University of London, since 1999; *b* 23 Feb. 1945; *s* of late Robert Christie and Ethel Christie; *m* 1979, Patsy Nightingale; one *s* three *d*. *Educ:* Belfast Royal Acad.; Queen's Univ., Belfast (BA 1966). Lectr in Complementary Studies, Derby Coll. of Art, 1969–73; Sen. Lectr in Art Hist. and Film Studies, Derby Coll. of Higher Educn, 1973–75; British Film Institute: Regl Prog. Advr, then Hd of Programming, 1976–84; Hd of Distribn, 1984–92; Head of Special Projects, 1993–94; Associate Ed., Sight and Sound, 1995–97; Prof. of Film Studies, Univ. of Kent at Canterbury, 1997–99. Vis. Dir, Film Centre, Art Inst. of Chicago, 1985–86; Visiting Professor: Univ. of S Florida, 1989; Palacky Univ., Olomouc, Czech Republic, 2012–15; Gresham Coll., London, 2017–; Dist. Vis. Fellow, European Humanities Res. Centre, 1995–98, Vis. Lectr in Film and Fellow, Magdalen Coll., 1995–98, Oxford Univ.; Slade Prof. of Fine Art, Cambridge Univ., 2005–06; Founder and Dir, London Screen Study Collection, Birkbeck Coll., 2006–. Dir, Connoisseur Video, 1990–97. Vice-Pres., 1993–2012, Pres., 2012–14, Europa Cinemas. Mem. Exec. Cttee, GB-USSR Assoc., 1983–89. Jt Ed., Film Studies jl, 1999–2009. Co-curator of exhibitions: Eisenstein: his life and art, MOMA, Oxford, and Hayward Gall., 1988; Spellbound: art and film, Hayward Gall., 1996; The Director's Eye, MOMA, Oxford, 1996; Modernism: designing a new world, V&A Mus., 2006; Lights, Camera, London!, London Film Mus., 2012–13; All that Life Can Afford?, London Screen Study Collection archive, Birkbeck, Univ. of London, 2013; Unexpected Eisenstein, Gall. for Russian Arts and Design, London, 2016; Revolution: Russian art 1917–1932, RA, 2017; Animatograph! How cinema was born in Haringey, Bruce Castle, London and touring to London Metropolitan Archives, Nat. Sci. and Media Mus., Bradford, 2019. Frequent radio and television broadcaster on cinema; consultant on film policy, archiving and programming. *Publications:* Powell, Pressburger and Others, 1978; Arrows of Desire: the films of Michael Powell and Emeric Pressburger, 1985, 2nd edn 1994; (ed) The Life and Death of Col Blimp, 1994; The Last Machine, 1995; (ed) Gilliam on Gilliam, 1999; A Matter of Life and Death, 2000; The Art of Film: John Box and production design, 2009; (ed) Audiences: defining and researching screen entertainment reception, 2012; Doctor Zhivago, 2015; Robert Paul and the Origins of British Cinema, 2019; *edited jointly*: FEKS, Formalism, Futurism, 1978; The Film Factory, 1988, 2nd edn 1994; Eisenstein at 90, 1988; Scorsese on Scorsese, 1989, 3rd edn 2003; Inside the Film Factory, 1991; Eisenstein Rediscovered, 1993; Protazanov and the Continuity of Russian Cinema, 1993; Spellbound: art and film, 1996; Law's Moving Image, 2004; The Cinema of Michael Powell: international perspectives on an English film-maker, 2005; Stories We Tell Ourselves: the cultural impact of film in the UK, 2009; Opening Our Eyes: how film contributes to the culture of the UK, 2011; Living Politics, Making Music: the writings of Jan Fairley, 2014; Where is History Today?: new ways of representing the past, 2015; Stories: screen narrative in the digital era, 2018; Sculpture and Film, 2019; Time Traveller: Robert Paul and the Invention of Cinema, 2019. *Recreations:* running, ski-ing, occasional carpentry, stereoscopy and magic lanterns, affordable wine, unaffordable opera, new media. *Address:* 131 Mount View Road, N4 4JH. *T:* (020) 8348 3656. *W:* www.ianchristie.org, https://paulsanimatographworks.wordpress.com.

**CHRISTIE, Very Rev. John Cairns;** Church of Scotland Minister; Moderator of the General Assembly of the Church of Scotland, 2010–11; *b* Glasgow, 9 July 1947; *s* of John Cairns Christie and Agnes Christie (*née* Ritchie); *m* 1st, 1972, Elizabeth McDonald McIntosh (*d* 1993); one *d*; 2nd, 1995, Annette Cooke Carnegie Evans (*née* Hamill). *Educ:* Hermitage Sch., Helensburgh; Univ. of Strathclyde (BSc 1971); Jordanhill Coll. of Educn, Glasgow (PGCE 1973); Univ. of Glasgow (BD Hons 1989). CBiol 1976; MRSB (MIBiol 1976). Teacher, Albert Secondary Sch., Glasgow, 1973–78; Principal Teacher of Sci., Tiree High Sch., 1978–84; Warden, Dalneigh Hall of Residence, Inverness Royal Acad., 1984–86; ordained minister, 1990; Minister, Hyndland Parish Ch, Glasgow, 1990–2004; Interim Minister: Cumnock Trinity, 2004–05; Kilmacolm Old, 2005–07; North West Lochaber, 2007–08; Scots Kirk Lausanne and West Kilbride, 2008–09; Greenock Finnart St Paul's, 2009–10; Paisley Oakshaw Trinity, 2011–12; (and Locum) Renfrew North Ch, 2013–14; Clerk to Presbytery of Dumbarton, 2018. Convener, Bd of Parish Educn, 2001–05, Safety and Protection of Children, 2001–05, Safeguarding, 2005–10, Theol. of Forgiveness and Proportionality, 2007–09, Church of Scotland. Qualified Mediator, Church Congregations, 2010. Regular contrib. to Thought for the Day, BBC Radio Scotland. *Recreations:* hill-walking, gardening. *E:* JChristie@ChurchofScotland.org.uk.

**CHRISTIE, Julie (Frances),** actress; *b* 14 April 1940; *d* of Frank St John Christie and Rosemary Christie (*née* Ramsden). *Educ:* Convent; Brighton Coll. of Technology; Central Sch. of Speech and Drama. *Films:* Crooks Anonymous, 1962; The Fast Lady, 1962; Billy Liar, 1963; Darling, 1964 (Oscar, NY Film Critics Award, Br. Film Academy Award, etc); Young Cassidy, 1964; Dr Zhivago, 1965 (Donatello Award); Fahrenheit 451, 1966; Far from the Madding Crowd, 1966; Petulia, 1967; In Search of Gregory, 1969; The Go-Between, 1971; McCabe and Mrs Miller, 1972; Don't Look Now, 1973; Shampoo, 1974; Heaven Can Wait, 1978; Memoirs of a Survivor, 1981; The Animals Film, 1982; Return of the Soldier, 1982; Heat and Dust, 1983; The Gold Diggers, 1984; Power, 1987; Miss Mary, 1987; Fools of Fortune, 1990; The Railway Station Man, 1992; Hamlet, 1997; Afterglow, 1998; No Such Thing, 2001; The Phantom of the Louvre, 2001; Troy, Finding Neverland, 2004; The Secret Life of Words, 2005; Away From Her, 2007 (Golden Globe and Screen Actors Guild awards for Best Actress, 2008); Glorious 39, 2009; Red Riding Hood, 2011; The Company You Keep, 2012; *stage:* Old Times, Wyndham's, 1995; Suzanna Andler, Chichester, 1997. Fellow, BAFTA, 1997. Motion Picture Laurel Award, Best Dramatic Actress, 1967; Motion Picture Herald Award, Best Dramatic Actress, 1967.

**CHRISTIE, Linford,** OBE 1998 (MBE 1990); athlete; athletics coach; Managing Director, Nuff Respect, sports management company; *b* Jamaica, 2 April 1960; *s* of James and late Mabel Christie. *Educ:* Wandsworth Tech. Coll. Competed as a runner over 50 times for Great Britain, 1980–97. *European indoor championships:* Gold medal (200 m), 1986; Gold medal (60 m), 1988 and 1990; *European championships:* Gold medal (100 m), 1986 and 1990; *Commonwealth Games:* Silver medal (100 m), 1986; Gold medal (100 m), 1990 and 1994; *European Cup:* Gold medals (100 and 200 m), 1987; Gold medal (100 m), 1991, 1992 and 1994; Gold medals (100 and 200 m), 1997 (Men's Team Captain); *Olympic Games:* Silver medal (100 m), 1988; Gold medal (100 m), 1992 (British Men's Team Captain); *World indoor championships:* Silver medals (60 and 200 m), 1991; *World Cup:* Silver medal (200 m), 1992; Gold medal (100 m), 1989 and 1992; *World championships:* Gold medal (100 m), 1993; Silver medal (100 m relay), 1993. British and European 100 m record (9.87 seconds), and British 200 m record (20.09 seconds), 1988; British 100 yards record (9.30 seconds), Edinburgh, 1994; European 60 m record (6.47 seconds) and World indoor 200 m record (20.25 seconds), 1995. British Athletics Writers' Assoc., Male Athlete of the Year, 1988 and 1992. Hon. MSc Portsmouth Univ., 1993. *Publications:* Linford Christie (autobiog.), 1989; To Be Honest With You (autobiog.), 1995. *Address:* Nuff Respect, No.1 Constable's Boatyard, 15 Thames Street, Hampton, Middx TW12 2EW. *T:* (020) 8891 4145. *E:* nuff_respect@msn.com. *Club:* Thames Valley Harriers (Pres., 1997).

**CHRISTIE, Richard Hamish;** QC 2006; a Recorder, since 2009; *b* 17 April 1963; *s* of Martin and Phoebe Christie; *m* 1989, Jane; three *d*. *Educ:* Clifton Coll.; Manchester Univ. (LLB 1984). Called to the Bar, Inner Temple, 1986; Head of Chambers, 2 Pump Court, 2008–14; Jt Head of Chambers, 187 Fleet Street, 2014–. *Recreations:* cinema, Scotland, walking. *Address:* 187 Fleet Street, EC4A 2AT.

**CHRISTIE, Sally Ann;** *see* Shuttleworth, S. A.

**CHRISTIE, Sarah Katrina;** *see* Lambert, S. K.

**CHRISTIE, Prof. Thomas;** Director, The Aga Khan University Examination Board, 2003–14; Professor of Educational Assessment and Evaluation, University of Manchester, 1994–2003, now Professor Emeritus; *b* 12 May 1939; *s* of John Frew Christie and Margaret Watson Christie; *m* 1962, Patricia Ray Bozie; two *s* one *d*. *Educ:* Univ. of Edinburgh (MA, BEd). Res. Associate, 1963–66, Lectr in Educn, 1966–73, Sen. Lectr, 1973–76 and 1978–86, Dept of Educn, Univ. of Manchester; Sen. Lectr in Educnl Res., Dept of Educn, Univ. of Guyana, and Commonwealth Fund for Tech. Co-operation Consultant to Caribbean Exams Council, Barbados, 1976–78; University of Manchester: Dir, Centre for Formative Assessment Studies, Sch. of Educn, 1986–96; Dean, Fac. of Educn and Dir, Sch. of Educn, 1997–2002. Sen. Assessment Consultant, Adam Smith Internat., Lahore, 2014–16. Distinguished Prof., Aga Khan Univ., 2013. Hon. DSc National Univ. of Mongolia, 1998. *Publications:* (jtly) Creativity: a selective review of research, 1968, 2nd edn 1971; (with G. M. Forrest) Standards at GCE A Level: 1963 and 1973, 1980; (with G. M. Forrest) Defining Public Examination Standards, 1981; A Guide to Teacher Assessment (3 vols), 1990; (ed with B. Boyle) Issues in Setting Standards: establishing comparabilities, 1996. *Recreations:* reading, crossword puzzles, desert travel. *Address:* 24 Blenheim Road, Moseley, Birmingham B13 9TY. *T:* (0121) 449 7939.

**CHRISTIE, William Lincoln;** harpsichord player, organist and conductor; Founder and Director, Les Arts Florissants, since 1979; *b* Buffalo, New York State, 19 Dec. 1944; *s* of William Lincoln Christie and Ida Jones Christie; adopted French citizenship. *Educ:* Harvard Coll. (BA 1966); Yale Univ. (MusM 1969). Student of piano and harpsichord in US, 1957–70; Asst in Hist. of Music and Dir, Collegium Musicum, Dartmouth Coll., USA, 1970–71; moved to France, 1971; Collaborator, Soc. de musique d'autrefois, Paris, 1972–75; Visiting Professor: Conservatoires of Paris, Lyon and The Hague, and GSMD, 1977–81; Sommer Akademie für Musik, Innsbrück, 1978–83; Prof., Paris Conservatoire, 1982–95. Musical Dir, Hippolyte et Aricie, L'Opéra de Paris, 1985; regularly conducts orchs in France, Switzerland, UK and USA; Glyndebourne début, Handel's Theodora, 1996. Mem., Vis. Cttee for Music, Harvard Univ., 1993–96; Artist in Residence, Les Arts Florissants, Juilliard Sch., 2007–. Mem., Acad. des Beaux Arts, 2008. Has made numerous recordings, 1976–, esp. works for harpsichord, and vocal works of 17th and 18th centuries with Les Arts Florissants. Hon. DMus NY at Buffalo, 1997. Prix Georges Pompidou, 2005. Officier des Arts et des Lettres (France); Commandeur de la Légion d'Honneur (France), 2010. *Publications:* Sonate Baroque, 1989; Purcell au Coeur du Baroque, 1995. *Recreations:* gardening, cooking. *Address:* Les Arts Florissants, 221 avenue Jean Jaurès, 75019 Paris, France. *T:* (1) 43879888; Le Logis du Bâtiment, 85210 Thiré, France. *W:* www.jardindewilliamchristie.fr.

**CHRISTO AND JEANNE-CLAUDE;** artist; Christo Javacheff, *b* Gabrovo, Bulgaria, 13 June 1935; *m* Jeanne-Claude de Guillebon (*d* 2009); one *s*. Emigrated to USA 1964. Completed works include: Wrapped Objects, 1958; Stacked Oil Barrels and Dockside Packages, Cologne Harbour, 1961; Iron Curtain-Wall of Oil Barrels, blocking Rue Visconti, Paris, 1962; Store Fronts, NYC, 1964; Wrapped Kunsthalle, Berne, and Wrapped Fountain and Wrapped Medieval Tower, Spoleto, Italy, 1968; 5,600 Cubicmeter Package, Documenta 4, Kassel, 1968; Wrapped Floor and Stairway, Mus. of Contemporary Art, Chicago, 1969; Wrapped Coast, Little Bay, Sydney, Australia, 1969; Wrapped Monuments, Milan, 1970; Wrapped Floors and Covered Windows and Wrapped Walk Way, Krefeld, Germany, 1971; Valley Curtain, Grand Hogback, Rifle, Colo, 1970–72; The Wall, Wrapped Roman Wall, Via V. Veneto and Villa Borghese, Rome, 1974; Ocean Front, Newport, RI, 1974; Running Fence, Sonoma and Marin Counties, Calif, 1972–76; Wrapped Walk Ways, Kansas City, Mo, 1977–78; Surrounded Islands, Biscayne Bay, Miami, Fla, 1980–83; The Pont Neuf Wrapped, Paris, 1975–85; The Umbrellas, Japan-USA, 1984–91; Wrapped Floors and Stairways and Covered Windows, Mus. Würth, Künzelsau, Germany, 1995; Wrapped Reichstag, Berlin, 1971–95; Wrapped Trees, Switzerland, 1997–98; The Wall - 13,000 Oil Barrels, Gasometer Oberhausen, Germany, 1999; The Gates, Central Pk, NYC, 2005; Big Air Package, Gasometer Oberhausen, Germany, 2013; The Floating Piers, Lake Iseo, Italy, 2016; Mastaba, Serpentine Gall., 2018. *Fax:* (212) 9662891. *W:* www.christojeanneclaude.net.

**CHRISTOPHER,** Baron *cr* 1998 (Life Peer), of Leckhampton in the co. of Gloucestershire; **Anthony Martin Grosvenor Christopher,** CBE 1984; President, TU Fund Managers Ltd (formerly Trades Union Unit Trust), since 2012 (Director, 1981–2012; Chairman, 1983–2012); public and political affairs consultant, since 1989; General Secretary, Inland Revenue Staff Federation, 1976–88; *b* 25 April 1925; *s* of George Russell Christopher and Helen Kathleen Milford Christopher (*née* Rowley); *m* 1962, Adela Joy Thompson. *Educ:* Cheltenham Grammar Sch.; Westminster Coll. of Commerce. Articled Pupil, Agric. Valuers, Gloucester, 1941–44; RAF, 1944–48; Inland Revenue, 1948–57; Asst Sec. 1957–60, Asst Gen. Sec. 1960–74, Jt Gen. Sec. 1975, Inland Revenue Staff Fedn. Member: TUC General Council, 1976–89 (Chm., 1988–89); TUC Economic Cttee, 1977–89; TUC Education Cttee, 1977–85; TUC Educn and Training Cttee, 1985–86; TUC Employment Policy and Orgn Cttees, 1985–89; TUC International Cttee, 1982–89; TUC Finance and General Purposes Cttee, 1983–89; TUC Media Working Group, 1979–89 (Chm., 1985–89); TUC Employment Policy and Orgn Cttee, 1979–85; TUC Social Insurance Cttee, 1986–89; Mems Auditor, ICFTU, 1984–2004. House of Lords: Member, Select Committees: Audit, 2003–06; Consolidation of Bills, 2003–14; Mem., European Cttee on Envmt and Agric., 2000–03, 2005–06. Member: Tax Reform Cttee, 1974–80; Tax Consultative Cttee, 1980–88; Royal Commn on Distribution of Income and Wealth, 1978–79; IBA, 1978–83; Council, Inst. of Manpower Studies, 1984–89; ESRC, 1985–88; GMC, 1989–94. Chm., Tyre Industry EDC, 1983–86; Vice Pres., Building Socs Assoc., 1985–90; Director: Civil Service Building Soc., 1958–87 (Chm., 1978–87); Birmingham Midshires Building Soc., 1987–88; Policy Studies Inst. Council, 1983–91; Member: Bd, Civil Service Housing Assoc., 1958–96 (Vice-Chm., 1988–96); Council, NACRO, 1956–98 (Chm., 1973–98); Home Sec.'s Adv. Council for Probation and After-care, 1967–77; Inner London Probation and After-care Cttee, 1966–79; Audit Commn, 1989–95; Broadcasting Complaints Commn, 1989–97; Council, 1985–90, Assembly, 1990–, SCF; Chm., Alcoholics Recovery Project, 1970–76; Member: Home Sec.'s Working Party on Treatment of Habitual Drunken Offenders, 1969–71; Inquiry into Rover Cowley Works Closure, 1990; Trustee: Commonwealth Trades Union Council Charitable Trust, 1985–89; Inst. for Public Policy Res., 1989–94 (Treas., 1990–94). Vis. Fellow, Univ. of Bath, 1981–; Mem. Council, Royal Holloway and Bedford New Coll., 1985–89. FRSA 1989. *Publications:* (jtly) Policy for Poverty, 1970; (jtly) The Wealth

Report, 1979; (jtly) The Wealth Report 2, 1982. *Recreations:* gardening, reading, walking dogs. *Address:* c/o TU Fund Managers Ltd, Congress House, Great Russell Street, WC1B 3LQ. *Club:* Beefsteak.

**CHRISTOPHER, Ann,** RA 1989 (ARA 1980); FRSS; sculptor; *b* 4 Dec. 1947; *d* of late William and Phyllis Christopher; *m* 1969, Kenneth Cook. *Educ:* Harrow School of Art (pre-Diploma); West of England College of Art (DipAD Sculpture). RWA, 1983–2010; FRSS (FRBS 1992). Represented by Pangolin London. Prizewinner, Daily Telegraph Young Sculptors Competition, 1971; Arts Council grants, 1973–76; Silver Medal for Sculpture of Outstanding Merit, RBS, 1994. *Exhibitions include:* RA Summer Exhibns, 1971–; Oxford Gallery, Oxford, 1973, 1974, 1978; Dorset County Mus. and Art Gall. (retrospective), 1989; Victoria Art Gall., Bath, 1992; Courcoux & Courcoux, 1991, 1999; Sculpture 93, London, 1993; Summer Exhibns, Redfern Gall., 1995, 1996; solo exhibitions: Redfern Gall., 1997; Jubilee Park, Canary Wharf, 2004; The Power of Place, RA, 2008; Pangolin, London, 2010, 2013, 2016, 2019; The Lines of Time, RA, 2016; Ballinglen Arts Foundn, Co. Mayo, 2018; Rosenberg & Co., NY, 2019. *Work in Collections:* Bristol City Art Gallery; Contemporary Arts Soc.; Chantrey, London; Glynn Vivian Art Gall., Swansea; RWA; British Mus.; Gruss & Co., NY; RA; Corcoran Art Gall., Washington; Pallant House Gall., Chichester; Royal Collection, Windsor Castle. *Commissions:* 3½m bronze, Tower Bridge Rd, London, 1990; 4½m bronze, Castle Park, Bristol, 1993; 2.3m bronze, Washington, USA, 1994; 4.8m corten steel, Plymouth, 1996; 2.3m bronze, Linklaters & Paines, London, 1997; 3m bronze, Great Barrington, Mass, USA, 1998; 5.5m corten steel, Portmarine, 2001; 2.2m bronze, Cordes, France, 2002; medal for British Art Soc., 2004; 12 bronzes, Kings Place, London, 2008; 2m bronze, Rwenzori Sculpture Foundn, Uganda, 2017. *Publications:* Ann Christopher, 2016; Drawing Lines, 2016. *Recreation:* cinema.

**CHRISTOPHER, Sir (Duncan) Robin (Carmichael),** KBE 2000; CMG 1997; HM Diplomatic Service, retired; *b* 13 Oct. 1944; *m* 1980, Merril Stevenson; two *d. Educ:* Keble Coll., Oxford (BA); Fletcher Sch., Tufts Univ., USA (MA). FCO, 1970; Second, then First, Sec., New Delhi, 1972; First Sec., FCO, 1976; Dep. Hd of Mission, Lusaka, 1980; FCO, 1983; on secondment to Cabinet Office, 1985; Counsellor: Madrid, 1987; FCO, 1991; Ambassador: to Ethiopia, 1994–97; to Indonesia, 1997–2000; to Argentina, 2000–04. Sec. Gen., 2007–11, Projects Dir, 2011–15, Global Leadership Foundn. Dir, Rurelec plc, 2005–10. Trustee: The Brooke Hosp., 2005–13; St Matthew's Children's Fund, Ethiopia, 2005–; Prospect Burma, 2005–; Redress, 2005–14. *Recreations:* ski-ing, motorcycling, music. *E:* rchristopher2@yahoo.co.uk.

**CHRISTOPHER, Sir Robin;** *see* Christopher, Sir D. R. C.

**CHRISTOPHERS, Richard Henry Tudor, (Harry),** CBE 2012; conductor; Founder and Conductor, The Sixteen, since 1979; Artistic Director, Handel and Haydn Society, Boston, since 2008; *b* 26 Dec. 1953; *s* of Richard Henry Christophers and Constance Clavering Christophers (*née* Thorp); *m* 1979, Veronica Mary Hayward; two *s* two *d. Educ:* Canterbury Cathedral Choir Sch.; King's Sch., Canterbury; Magdalen Coll., Oxford (Mods Classics, BA Music, MA; Hon. Fellow, 2009). Conducting débuts: BBC Prom. concert, 1990; Salzburg Fest., 1989; Lisbon Opera, 1994; ENO, 2000; freelance conductor: BBC Philharmonic, City of London Sinfonia, Acad. of St Martin in the Fields, Hallé, London Symphony, San Francisco Symphony, Deutsches Kammerphilharmonie, etc. Principal Guest Conductor, Granada Symphony Orchestra, 2008–. Numerous recordings. FRWCMD 2009; FRSCM 2014. Hon. DMus: Leicester, 2008; Canterbury Christ Church, 2016; Northumbria, 2017. Grand Prix du Disque, 1988; Deutschen Schallplattenkritik, 1992 and 1993; Gramophone Award, 1992; Diapason d'or, 1995 and 1996; Classical Brit Award, 2005; Gramophone Artist of the Year, 2009. *Recreations:* cooking, Arsenal FC. *Address:* The Sixteen, Quadrant House, 10 Fleet Street, EC4Y 1AU.

**CHRUSZCZ, Charles Francis;** QC 1992; a Recorder, 1990; *b* 19 Nov. 1950; *s* of Janick Francis Chruszcz and Kathleen Whitehurst Chruszcz; *m* 1972, Margaret Olivia Chapman; three *s. Educ:* Queen Mary Coll., London (LLB Hons). Called to the Bar, Middle Temple, 1973; Asst Recorder, 1985–90. *Recreations:* reading, music, building renovation, the outdoors.

**CHU, Prof. Steven,** PhD; William R. Kenan, Jr Professor of Physics and Professor of Molecular and Cellular Physiology, Stanford University, since 2013; *b* 28 Feb. 1948; *s* of Ju Chin Chu and Ching Chen Li; *m* Dr Jean Fetter; two *s* by a previous marriage. *Educ:* Univ. of Rochester (AB Maths 1970, BS Physics 1970); Univ. of Calif, Berkeley (PhD Physics 1976). Postdoctoral Res. Fellow, Univ. of Calif, Berkeley, 1976–78; Mem., Technical Staff, Bell Labs, Murray Hill, 1978–83; Hd, Quantum Electronics Res. Dept, AT&T Bell Labs, Holmdel, 1983–87; Prof. of Physics and Applied Physics, 1987, Theodore and Frances Geballe Prof. of Physics and Applied Physics, 1990–2004, Chm., Physics Dept, 1990–93, 1999–2001, Stanford Univ.; Prof. of Physics and of Molecular and Cell Biology, Univ. of Calif, Berkeley, 2004–09; Dir, Lawrence Berkeley Nat. Lab., 2004–09; Sec. of Energy, USA, 2009–13. Vis. Prof., Collège de France, 1990. American Association for the Advancement of Science: Mem., 1995; Fellow, 2000; Pres., 2019–Feb. 2020; Chm., Bd of Dirs, Feb. 2020–. Fellow: APS, 1987; Optical Soc. of America, 1988; Amer. Acad. Arts and Scis, 1992. Member: NAS, 1993; Academia Sinica, 1994; Amer. Philosophical Soc., 1998; Foreign Member: Chinese Acad. Scis, 1998; Korean Acad. Scis and Technol., 1998; Royal Soc., 2014. Internat. FREng 2011. Broida Prize for Laser Spectroscopy, 1987, Schawlow Prize for Laser Sci., 1994, APS; King Faisal Internat. Prize for Sci., 1993; Meggers Award for Spectroscopy, Optical Soc. of America, 1994; Humboldt Sen. Scientist Award, 1995; Science for Art Prize, LVMH, 1995; (jtly) Nobel Prize for Physics, 1997. *Recreations:* swimming, cycling, tennis. *Address:* Department of Physics, Stanford University, Stanford, CA 94305, USA.

**CHUA, Nam-Hai,** FRS 1988; Andrew W. Mellon Professor and Head of Laboratory of Plant Molecular Biology, Rockefeller University, 1981, now Professor Emeritus; Deputy Chairman, Temasek Life Sciences Laboratory, Singapore, since 2013; *b* 8 April 1944; *m* 1970, Suat Choo Pearl; two *d. Educ:* Univ. of Singapore (BSc Botany and Biochem.); Harvard Univ. (AM, PhD Biol.). Lectr, Biochem. Dept, Univ. of Singapore, 1969–71; Rockefeller University, Cell Biology Department: Res. Associate, 1971–73; Asst Prof., 1973–77; Associate Prof., 1977–81. Chm., Management Bd, 1995, Scientific Adv. Bd, 1995, Inst. of Molecular Agrobiology, Nat. Univ. of Singapore. Fellow, Acad. Sinica, Taipei, 1988; Associate Fellow, Third World Acad. of Scis, 1988; Hon. Member: Japanese Biochemical Soc., 1992; Japanese Soc. of Plant Physiologists; Foreign Mem., Chinese Acad. of Scis. Nat. Sci. and Technol. Medal, Singapore, 1998; Singapore Public Admin Gold Medal, 2002; Internat. Prize in Biol., Japan Soc. for Promotion of Sci., 2005; Lawrence Bogorad Award for Excellence in Plant Biol. Res., Amer. Soc. for Plant Biologists, 2010. *Publications:* Methods in Chloroplast Molecular Biology, 1982; Plant Molecular Biology, 1987; Methods in Arabidopsis Research, 1992; 317 pubns in professional jls. *Recreations:* squash, ski-ing. *Address:* Rockefeller University, 1230 York Avenue, New York, NY 10065-6399, USA. *T:* (212) 3278126, *Fax:* (212) 3278327.

**CHUAN LEEKPAI;** MHR, Trang Province, Thailand, 1969–2007; Leader of the Opposition, 1995–97 and 2001–03; *b* 28 July 1938. *Educ:* Trang Wittaya Sch.; Silpakorn Pre-Univ.; Thammasat Univ. (LLB 1962). Barrister-at-Law, Thai Bar, 1964; lawyer. Thailand, Dep. Minister of Justice, 1975; Minister to Prime Minister's Office, 1976; Minister: of Justice, 1976 and 1980–81; of Commerce, 1981; of Agric. and Co-operatives, 1982–83; of Educn, 1983–86; Speaker, House of Reps, 1986–88; Minister of Public Health, 1988–89; Dep. Prime Minister and Minister of Agric. and Co-operatives, 1990–92; Prime Minister, 1992–95; Prime Minister and Minister of Defence, 1997–2001. Chm., Adv. Cttee, Democrat Party. Vis. Lectr, Forensic Medicine Dept, Faculty of Medicine, Chulalongkorn Univ. Hon. Dr Political Science: Srinakharinwirot, 1985; Ramkhamhaeng, 1987; Hon. LLD: Philippines, 1993; Vongchavalitkul, 1998; Hon. LitD: (Painting) Silpakorn, 1994; Nat. Univ. of San Marcos, Lima, 1999. Kt Grand Cross (First Cl.), 1979, Kt Grand Cordon, 1981, Order of Crown (Thailand); Kt Grand Cross (First Cl.), 1980, Kt Grand Cordon (Special Cl.), 1982, Order of White Elephant (Thailand). *Address:* c/o Democrat Party, 67 Setsiri Road, Samsen NI Phaya Thai, Bangkok 10400, Thailand.

**CHUBB,** family name of **Baron Hayter**.

**CHUBB, Anthony Gerald Trelawny,** FCA; Chairman, Foseco (formerly Foseco Minsep) PLC, 1986–90; *b* 6 April 1928; *s* of Ernest Gerald Trelawny Chubb and Eunice Chubb; *m* 1951, Beryl Joyce (*née* Cross); two *s. Educ:* Wylde Green Coll., Sutton Coldfield. FCA 1962 (ACA 1951); ACMA 1956. CBIM 1981. Joined Foundry Services Ltd, 1951; Man. Dir, Foseco UK, 1964–69; Dir, Foseco Ltd, 1966; Man. Dir, Foseco International, 1969–78; Dep. Gp Man. Dir, 1974–79, Gp Man. Dir, 1979–86, Foseco Minsep PLC; Chm., Electrocomponents PLC, 1986–90 (Dep. Chm., 1983–86; Dir, 1980–90). *Recreations:* golf, gardening, reading.

**CHUBB, Prof. Ian William,** AC 2006 (AO 1999); Chief Scientist of Australia, 2011–16; *b* 17 Oct. 1943; *s* of Ian and Lillian Chubb; *m* 1971, Claudette Maes; three *d. Educ:* Christ Church, Oxford (MSc, DPhil 1975). Heyman's Res. Fellow, Univ. of Ghent, 1969–71; Wellcome Schol., Christ Church, Oxford, 1971–74; Res. Fellow, St John's Coll., Oxford, 1974–77; Lectr, Sen. Lectr, then Associate Prof., Flinders Univ., 1977–85; Dep. Vice-Chancellor, 1986–90, Emeritus Prof., 1990, Univ. of Wollongong; Chair, Commonwealth Higher Educn Council, 1990–95; Dep. Vice-Chancellor, Monash Univ., 1993–95; Vice Chancellor: Flinders Univ., 1995–2000; ANU, 2001–11, now Prof. Emeritus. Chm., Australian Vice-Chancellors' Cttee, 2000–01; Pres., Gp of Eight Univs, 2005–09. Mem. Bd, CSIRO, 2008–11. Fellow: Aust. Coll. of Educn, 2008; Aust. Acad. of Technol Scis and Engrg, 2014; Royal Soc. of NSW, 2014; Aust. Acad. of Sci., 2017. Hon. Dr Flinders, 2000; DUniv: ANU, 2011; Sunshine Coast, 2014; Hon. DLitt Charles Darwin Univ., 2011; Hon. LLD: Monash, 2012; Melbourne, 2015. Academy Medal, Aust. Acad. of Sci., 2016. *Address:* College of Asia and the Pacific, 132 Lennox Crossing, J. G. Crawford Building, Australian National University, Canberra, ACT 2601, Australia.

**CHUGG, Daniel Patrick Brendon;** HM Diplomatic Service; Ambassador to Burma, since 2018; *b* Berkeley, Glos, 26 Jan. 1973; *s* of William David Chugg and Elizabeth Chugg; *m* 1999, Alison Fiona Cubie; one *s* one *d. Educ:* St Thomas High Sch., Exeter; Atlantic Coll.; Glasgow Univ. (MA Hons 1996); Emmanuel Coll., Cambridge (MPhil 1997); Exeter Univ. (DipLaw 1998). Entered FCO, 1998; Desk Officer, Central Eur. Dept, 1998–99; Chinese lang. trng, 1999–2000; Vice-Consul, Hong Kong, 2000–05; First Sec., FCO, 2005–07; Hd of Communications, New Delhi, 2007–10; Political Counsellor, Beijing, 2010–14; Head: ISIL Taskforce and Iraq Dept, FCO, 2014–15; Counter-Daesh Communications Dept, FCO, 2015–17. *Recreations:* jazz, opera, Britpop, photography, watching England lose at football and cricket, entertaining my children. *Address:* c/o Foreign and Commonwealth Office, King Charles Street, SW1A 2AH. *E:* dan.chugg@fco.gov.uk.

**CHUNG, Kyung-Wha,** Korean Order of Merit; concert violinist; *b* 26 March 1948; *d* of Chun-Chai Chung and Won-Sook (Lee) Chung; *m*; two *s. Educ:* Juilliard Sch. of Music, New York. Moved from Korea to New York, 1960; 7 years' study with Ivan Galamian, 1960–67; New York début with New York Philharmonic Orch., 1967; European début with London Symphony Orch., Royal Festival Hall, London, 1970. Mem. Faculty, Juilliard Sch. of Music, NY, 2007–. First prize, Leventritt Internat. Violin Competition, NY, 1967. *Address:* c/o Opus 3 Artists, 470 Park Avenue South, 9th Floor North, New York, NY 10016, USA.

**CHUNN, Louise Frances, (Mrs A. J. Anthony);** Founder and Editor, welldoing.org, since 2013; Editor, Planet Mindful, since 2018; *b* Auckland, NZ, 24 July 1956; *d* of late Jeremiah Alfred Chunn and Yvonne Chunn; *m* 2001, Andrew John Anthony; one *s* two *d. Educ:* Baradene Coll.; Univ. of Auckland (BA Hist. 1977). Reporter, Fashion Weekly, 1982–83; Features Ed., then Dep. Ed., 1983–85, Ed., 1985–86, Just Seventeen; Dep. Ed., Elle, 1986–89; Women's Page Ed., Guardian, 1989–94; Associate, then Features Ed., 1995–98, Dep. Ed., 1998, Vogue; Ed., ES Mag., Evening Standard, 1998–2000; Dep. Ed., 2000–02, Ed., 2002–06, In Style; Editor: Good Housekeeping, 2006–08; Psychologies, 2009–12. *Recreations:* fantasy travel, family, friends, books. *Address:* 4 Dunmore Road, NW6 6TR. *T:* 07817 011806. *E:* louisechunn@btinternet.com.

**CHURCH, Ian David,** CBE 2002; Editor, Official Report (Hansard), House of Commons, 1989–2002; *b* 18 Oct. 1941; *s* of John Jasper and Violet Kathleen Church; *m* 1964, Christine Stevenson; one *d. Educ:* Roan School. Journalist with: Dundee Courier and Advertiser, 1958–64; Press Association, 1964; The Scotsman, 1966; The Times, 1968; joined Hansard, 1972; Dep. Editor, 1988. Sec., Commonwealth Hansard Editors Assoc., 1990–2002 (Pres., 1996–99). Ind. Mem., Standards Cttee, Mid-Sussex DC, 2007–11 (Vice Chm., 2010–11). *Publications:* Hansard Centenary Volume, 2009; The Remains of the Living (fiction), 2013; Harvest of Blood (fiction), 2016.

**CHURCH, John Carver,** CMG 1986; CVO 1988; MBE 1970; HM Diplomatic Service, retired; *b* 8 Dec. 1929; *s* of Richard Church, CBE, FRSL, and Catherina Church; *m* 1953, Marie-Geneviève Vallette; two *s* two *d. Educ:* Cranbrook Sch., Kent; Ecole Alsacienne, Paris; Christ's Coll., Cambridge (MA 1953). Reuters News Agency, 1953–59; Central Office of Information, 1959–61; Commonwealth Relations Office: Information Officer, Calcutta, 1961–65; Foreign and Commonwealth Office: Second Secretary (Commercial) Rio de Janeiro, 1966–69; First Sec. (Information) Tel Aviv, 1969–74; First Sec., News Dept, FCO, 1974–77; Consul (Commercial) Milan, 1977–78; Consul-General: São Paulo, 1978–81; Naples, 1981–86; Barcelona, 1986–89. *Address:* La Métairie, Le Maine, 24510 Ste Alvère, France.

**CHURCH, John George,** CBE 1998; DL; FCA; President, Church & Co. plc, since 2002 (Chairman, 1991–2001); *b* 14 May 1936; *s* of Dudley Ross Church and Louise Elizabeth Church; *m* 1965, Rhona Elizabeth Gibson; one *s* one *d. Educ:* Stowe Sch. FCA 1959. Mgt Consultant, Annan Impey Morrish, 1961–64; joined Church & Co. plc, 1964: Asst Co. Sec., 1964–67; Co. Sec., 1967–76; Dir, 1968–2001; Man. Dir, 1976–97. Non-executive Director: Babers Ltd, 1972– (Chm., 1996–); James Southall and Co. Ltd, 1985–98 and 2000–06 (Dep. Chm., 2002–06); Start Rite Ltd, 1985–98 and 2000–06; Kingsley Park Properties (formerly St Matthew's Hosp.) Ltd, 1981–2003. President: British Footwear Mfrs Fedn, 1988–89; Boot Trade Benevolent Soc., 1984–85. St Andrew's Group of Hospitals, Northampton: Gov., 1995–; Mem. Bd Mgt, 1999–2010; non-exec. Dir, 2004–10. Member: Ct, Univ. of Northampton (formerly Nene Coll., Northampton, subseq. UC of Northampton), 1994–; Bd of Mgmt, Cordwainers' Coll., 1976–2000. Liveryman,

Cordwainers' Co., 1958– (Mem. of Ct, 1992–; Master, 1998–99). High Sheriff, Northants, 1993–94; DL Northants, 1997. FRSA 1995. Hon. Fellow, UC of Northampton, 2002. *Recreation:* country pursuits. *Club:* Royal Automobile.

**CHURCH, Jonathan,** CBE 2015; Founder and Director, Jonathan Church Productions, since 2015; *b* Nottingham, 4 March 1967; *s* of Tony Church and Marielaine Church (*née* Douglas); *m* Yvonne Thompson; four *d. Educ:* Frank Weldon Comprehensive Sch., Nottingham; Clarendon Coll. of Further Educn, Nottingham. Asst Dir, 1990–91, Asst Producer, 1992, Nottingham Playhouse; Associate Dir, Derby Playhouse, 1994–95; Artistic Dir, Salisbury Playhouse, 1995–99; Associate Dir, Hampstead Th., 1999–2001; Artistic Director: Birmingham Rep. Th., 2001–06; Chichester Fest. Th., 2006–16; Sydney Theatre Co., 2015–16; Summer Season, Theatre Royal, Bath, 2016–. *Director:* The Ballad of Reading Gaol, The Bear, 1988, Crucible Th., Sheffield; Saint Oscar, 1992, Angels Rave On, 1998, Nottingham Playhouse; Derby Playhouse: Frankie & Johnny, Two, 1993; Someone Who'll Watch Over Me, Absurd Person Singular, Importance of Being Earnest, 1994; Oleanna, Derby 100, 1995; Salisbury Playhouse: Comic Cuts, The Rover, The Banished Cavaliers, Oleanna, Educating Rita, The Merchant of Venice, 1996; Time and the Conways, The Rehearsal, The Double Inconstancy, Disappearances, The Cherry Orchard, Racing Demon, 1997; Romeo and Juliet (and nat. tour), The Alchemical Wedding, Top Girls (and Plymouth Th. Royal), 1988; Colombe, Just Between Ourselves, 1999; Birmingham Repertory Theatre: The Crucible, 1995; Private Lives, Closer, 2001; Of Mice and Men, 2001 (and Liverpool, Savoy, 2003, Old Vic, 2004); Peter Pan, Elizabeth Rex, 2002; Murmuring Judges, Absence of War, Racing Demon, 2003; The Witches, transf. Wyndham's Th., 2005; Promises and Lies, 2006; Chichester Festival Theatre: Oleanna/Educating Rita, 1996; Pravda, 2006; (Co-Dir) Nicholas Nickleby Part I and Part II, 2006 and 2007, transf. Gielgud Th., 2007; Hobson's Choice, 2007; The Circle, 2008; The Grapes of Wrath, 2009; The Critic, Master Class, (Co-Dir) The Real Inspector Hound, 2010; Singin' in the Rain, 2011, transf. Palace Th., 2012; The Resistible Rise of Arturo Ui, transf. Duchess, 2013; Amadeus, 2014; Taken at Midnight, 2014, transf. Th. Royal, Haymarket, 2015; Mack & Mabel, 2015; *other productions:* Mirror of the Moon (Man in the Moon), In Lambeth, Ensemble Th., Vienna, 1992 and Lyric Hammersmith, 1993; Magnetic North, W Yorks Playhouse, 1993; The Broken Heart, Lyric Hammersmith, 1994; You Be Ted and I'll be Sylvia, Hampstead Th., 1999; A Busy Day, Bristol Old Vic and Lyric Shaftesbury Ave, 2000; Red Velvet, Hampstead Th., 2000; God and Stephen Hawking, Bath Th. Royal and tour, 2000; The Diary of Anne Frank, tour, 2000; Hobson's Choice, Plymouth Th. Royal and tour, 2002, Th. Royal, Bath, transf. Vaudeville Th., 2016; The Lady in the Van, Th. Royal, Bath, 2017; An Ideal Husband, Vaudeville, 2018; The Price, Th. Royal, Bath, 2018; In Praise of Love, Ustinov Th., Bath, 2018; *co-producer:* Macbeth, Gielgud Th., 2007; The Last Confession, Haymarket Th., 2007; Taking Sides, Collaboration, Duchess Th., 2009; ENRON, Noël Coward Th., 2010; Top Girls, Trafalgar Studios, 2011; Rosencrantz and Guildenstern are Dead, Haymarket Th., 2011; South Downs, The Browning Version, Harold Pinter Th., 2012; Sweeney Todd, Adelphi Th., 2012.

**CHURCH, Judith Ann;** *b* 19 Sept. 1953; *d* of late Edmund Church and of Helen Church; two *s. Educ:* Leeds Univ. (BA Hons Maths and Phil.); Huddersfield Poly. (PGCE Technical); Aston Univ. (Postgrad. Dip. Occupational Health and Safety); Thames Valley Coll. (DMS). Teacher, VSO, 1975–77; Process Research, Mars UK, 1979–80; HM Inspector of Factories, HSE, 1980–86; Nat. Health and Safety Officer, MSF, 1986–94. Contested (Lab) Stevenage, 1992; MP (Lab) Dagenham, June 1994–2001. *Recreation:* keeping fit.

**CHURCH, Sarah Persephone Sutherland,** CB 2017; Director, Future Farming and Countryside Programme, Department for Environment, Food and Rural Affairs, since 2017; *b* Epping, Essex, 28 June 1973; *d* of Richard Thomas and Angela Thomas. *Educ:* Alton Convent Sch.; Peter Symonds Coll.; St John's Coll., Cambridge (BA 1995). Civil Service, 1995–; Dir, Food and Farming, DEFRA, 2015–16. *Address:* Department for Environment, Food and Rural Affairs, 2 Marsham Street, SW1P 4DF.

**CHURCHILL;** *see* Spencer-Churchill.

**CHURCHILL,** 6th Baron *cr* 1815, of Wychwood in the County of Oxford; **Richard Harry Ramsay Spencer;** *b* London, 11 Oct. 1926; *s* of late Col Richard Augustus Spencer, DSO, OBE and Maud Evelyn Spencer; *S* kinsman, 2017; *m* 1st, 1958, Antoinette Rose-Marie de Charrière (*d* 1994); two *s*; 2nd, 1999, Cressida Josephine Alice Sykes (*née* Van Halle). *Educ:* Wellington Coll., Crowthorne; Architectural Assoc. (RIBA, AA Dip.). Lieut, Coldstream Guards, 1944–47. Practised as an architect, Smith Street, Chelsea. *Recreations:* parachuting, diving, drawing and painting. *Heir: s* Hon. Michael Richard de Charrière Spencer [*b* 9 Nov. 1960; *m* 1995, Elizabeth Monk]. *Address:* Craven Cottage, Redenham, Andover, Hants SP11 9AS. *E:* rhspencer@btinternet.com.

**CHURCHILL, Caryl, (Mrs David Harter);** playwright; *b* 3 Sept. 1938; *d* of Robert Churchill and Jan (*née* Brown); *m* 1961, David Harter; three *s. Educ:* Trafalgar Sch., Montreal; Lady Margaret Hall, Oxford (BA 1960). Student prodns of early plays, 1958–61; *radio plays:* The Ants, 1962; Lovesick, 1966; Identical Twins, 1968; Abortive, 1971; Not… not… not… not enough oxygen, 1971; Schreiber's Nervous Illness, 1972; Henry's Past, 1972; Perfect Happiness, 1973; *television plays:* The Judge's Wife, 1972; Turkish Delight, 1973; The After Dinner Joke, 1978; The Legion Hall Bombing, 1978; Crimes, 1981; (with Ian Spink) Fugue, 1987; *stage plays:* Owners, 1972; Moving Clocks Go Slow, 1975; Objections to Sex and Violence, 1975; Light Shining in Buckinghamshire, 1976; Vinegar Tom, 1976; Traps, 1977; (contrib.) Floorshow, 1977; Cloud Nine, 1979; Three More Sleepless Nights, 1980; Top Girls, 1982; Fen, 1983; Softcops, 1984; (collaborator) Midday Sun, 1984; (with David Lan and Ian Spink) A Mouthful of Birds, 1986; Serious Money, 1987; Ice cream, 1989; Hot Fudge, 1989; Mad Forest, 1990; (with Ian Spink and Orlando Gough) Lives of the Great Poisoners, 1991; The Skriker, 1994; (trans.) Seneca's Thyestes, 1994; Blue Heart, 1997; This is a Chair, 1997; Far Away, 2000; A Number, 2002; Drunk Enough to Say I Love You?, 2006; Love and Information, 2012; Here We Go, 2015; Escaped Alone, 2016; Pigs and Dogs, 2016; Glass. Kill. Bluebeard. Imp., 2019. *Publications:* Owners, 1973; Light Shining in Buckinghamshire, 1976, new edn 1989; Traps, 1977, new edn 1989; Vinegar Tom, 1978; Cloud Nine, 1979, new edn 1989; Top Girls, 1982; Fen, 1983; Fen and Softcops, 1984; A Mouthful of Birds, 1986; Serious Money, 1987; Plays I, 1985; Plays II, 1988; Objections to Sex and Violence in Plays by Women, vol. 4, 1985; Ice cream, 1989; Mad Forest, 1990; Lives of the Great Poisoners, 1992; The Skriker, 1994; Thyestes, 1994; Blue Heart, 1997; This is a Chair, 1999; Far Away, 2000; A Number, 2002; Drunk Enough to Say I Love You?, 2006; Love and Information, 2012; Here We Go, 2015; Escaped Alone, 2016; Pigs and Dogs, 2016; Glass. Kill. Bluebeard. Imp., 2019; anthologies. *Address:* c/o Casarotto Ramsay & Associates Ltd, Waverley House, 7–12 Noel Street, W1F 8GQ. *T:* (020) 7287 4450.

**CHURCHILL, Emma Jane;** Director, Process Transformation, HM Revenue and Customs, since 2015; *b* Swindon, 3 May 1975; *d* of Lawrence Churchill and Ann Churchill; one *d. Educ:* Cheltenham Ladies' Coll.; St John's Coll., Oxford (BA Lit.Hum. 1st Cl. 1996). Policy Advr, DSS, 1996–98; Private Sec. to Sec. of State for Social Security, 1998–99; Operational Policy and Judicial Support Manager, Appeals Service, 1999–2001; Policy Advr to the Prime Minister, 2001–03; Hd, Domestic Violence Unit, 2003–04, Prin. Private Sec. to Sec. of State, 2004–07, Home Office; UK Border Agency: Dir, Immigration Policy, 2008–10; Dir, Asylum, 2010–11; Dir, Strategy and Assurance, 2011–13; Dir, Civil Service, Cabinet Office, 2013–15. *Recreations:* watching England win the Ashes, supporting Liverpool FC, taking daughter Jennifer on fast rollercoasters, eating and drinking with family. *Address:* HM Revenue and Customs, 1st Floor, 100 Parliament Street, SW1A 2HQ. *T:* 0300 055 1177. *E:* emma.churchill@hmrc.gsi.gov.uk.

**CHURCHILL, Johanna Peta;** MP (C) Bury St Edmunds, since 2015; Parliamentary Under-Secretary of State, Department of Health and Social Care, since 2019; *m* 1992, Peter Ian Churchill; four *d. Educ:* Dame Alice Harpur Sch., Bedford; Univ. of Lincoln (BSc); Univ. of Nottingham (MSc). Retail work for regl and global brands, then site develt and building industry; director of contracting cos, 1994–2015. Mem. (C) Lincs CC, 2013–15. An Asst Govt Whip, 2018–19. *Address:* House of Commons, SW1A 0AA.

**CHURCHILL, Lawrence,** CBE 2010; Chairman, Independent Governance Committee, Prudential Assurance Company, since 2015; *b* 5 Aug. 1946; *s* of Austin and Kathleen Churchill; *m* 1991, Karen Darcy; twin *d*, and one *s* one *d* from previous marriage. *Educ:* Birkenhead Sch.; St John's Coll., Oxford (MA). Systems Analyst, Proctor & Gamble, 1969–73; Sen. Systems Designer, then Exec. Dir, Hambro Life Assce, 1973–85; Exec. Dir, Allied Dunbar Assce, 1985–91; Chief Exec., NatWest Life, 1991–95; Man. Dir, NatWest Life Investments, 1995–98; Chm., Unum Ltd, 1998–2002; CEO, Zurich Financial Services, 2002–04. Chairman: Pension Protection Fund, 2004–10; NEST Corp., 2010–15; Applegate Marketplace Ltd, 2015–; Clara-Pensions, 2018–. Senior Independent Director: Good Energy (formerly Monkton) plc, 2004–12; Children's Mutual, 2005–10; BUPA, 2015–18 (non-exec. Dir, 2009–18); non-exec. Dir, Huntswood, 2005–06. Non-executive Director: PIA, 1994–98; ABI, 1995–98; Employers' Forum on Disability, 2000–03; Financial Ombudsman Service, 2002–05. Chairman: Raising Standards Quality Mark Scheme, 2000–02; Financial Services Compensation Scheme, 2012–18; Mem., Bd for Actuarial Standards, 2006–12; Trustee, Prudential Corporate Trustee Ltd, 2015–. Vice Pres., Employment Opportunities, 2004–08; Prince's Initiative for Mature Enterprise: Ambassador, 2009–15; Member: Thought Leadership Gp, 2013–15; Nat. Leadership Team, Business in the Community Age at Work Campaign, 2015–18; Chm., Commissioning Gp, 2014–15. Trustee: RSA, 2000–02; Internat. Longevity Centre - UK, 2007–; Age UK, 2015–17. Gov., Pension Policy Inst., 2010– (Chm., 2016–). *Publications:* (jtly) A Changing Nation, 1997; (jtly) New Beginnings, 2000; (jtly) The Concept of Value, 2007. *Recreations:* Rugby, theatre, opera, family. *Address:* 4 Lansdown Crescent, Bath BA1 5EX. *E:* lawrence.churchill@thechurchillsonline.com. *Club:* Oxford and Cambridge.

**CHURCHILL, Neil Gareth,** OBE 2018; PhD; Director for Patient Experience, Participation and Equalities (formerly for Patient Experience), NHS England (formerly NHS National Commissioning Board), since 2013; *b* Carshalton, 6 Sept. 1966; *s* of Ronald and Shirley Churchill; *m* 1996, Anna Barlow; two *d. Educ:* Fitzwilliam Coll., Cambridge (BA Hist. 1988); London South Bank Univ. (MBA 2000); Univ. of Sussex (PhD Art Hist. 2016). Head of Communications: Barnardo's, 1991–96; PSI, 1996–98; Dep. Chief Exec., Crisis, 1998–2001; Ext. Affairs Dir, Age Concern, 2001–07; Chief Exec., Asthma UK, 2007–13. Non-exec. Dir, NHS South of England (formerly NHS SE Coast), 2009–13. Member: Nat. Information Governance Bd, 2011–13; Exec. Bd, Beryl Inst., 2015–. Res. Fellow, Smith Inst., 2010–13. Trustee: Cardboard Citizens, 2001–07; Crisis, 2005–08; Prisoners' Advice Service, 2010–14; Students' Union, London S Bank Univ., 2013–16; Tavistock Centre for Couple Relationships, 2014–16; Future Care Capital, 2019–. Member, Editorial Board: Cultural Trends, 2000–10; Research Involvement and Engagement Jl, 2014–. *Publications:* (ed) Advancing Opportunity: older people and social care, 2008; (ed) Health Futures, 2009; (ed) More For Less in Health, 2010; (ed) Prospects for Health and Wellbeing Boards, 2013. *Recreations:* reading, playing the violin, trying to write art history whilst vicariously enjoying daughters' academic studies. *Address:* NHS England, Nursing Directorate, Skipton House, 80 London Road, SE1 6LH. *T:* (0113) 807 0106. *E:* neilchurchill@nhs.net. *W:* www.twitter.com/neilgchurchill.

**CHURCHILL, Sophie,** OBE 2011; PhD; Chair, Potato Sector Board, Agriculture and Horticulture Development Board, since 2017; *b* Braintree, Essex, 15 May 1963; *d* of John Race and Eva Race; two *s* one *d. Educ:* Corpus Christi Coll., Oxford (BA Hons PPE 1984); Univ. of Birmingham (PhD 1995). Dir, Birmingham City Pride, 2001–03; Chief Exec., West Midlands Centre for Excellence in Regeneration, 2003–06; Chief Exec. and Dir, National Forest Co., 2006–14; Founder and Dir, The Corpse Proj., 2015–. Chair, TREE AID, 2011–17. Pres., Royal Forestry Soc., 2015–17. Tutor, Pembroke-Kings Prog., Univ. of Cambridge, 2017. Non-exec. Dir, Trent and Dove Housing, 2017. Hon. FICFor 2012. *Publications:* The Art of the Chief Executive, 2017. *Address:* 16 Bevin House, Butler Street, E2 0RW. *T:* 07973 529603. *E:* sophiechurchill1505@gmail.com.

**CHURSTON,** 5th Baron *cr* 1858; **John Francis Yarde-Buller;** Bt 1790; *b* 29 Dec. 1934; *s* of 4th Baron Churston, VRD and Elizabeth Mary (*d* 1951), *d* of late W. B. du Pre; *S* father, 1991; *m* 1973, Alexandra Joanna, *d* of A. G. Contomichalos; one *s* two *d. Educ:* Eton Coll. 2nd Lt RHG, 1954. A Freemason. *Heir: s* Hon. Benjamin Anthony Francis Yarde-Buller [*b* 13 Sept. 1974; *m* 2000, Sophie Frances, *e d* of Brian Duncan]. *Address:* Yowlestone House, Puddington, Tiverton, Devon EX16 8LN. *T:* (01884) 860328. *Clubs:* Buck's, White's.

**CICCONE, Madonna Louise Veronica, (Madonna);** singer and actress; *b* 16 Aug. 1958; *d* of Sylvio, (Tony), Ciccone and late Madonna Ciccone; *m* 1st, 1985, Sean Penn (marr. diss. 1989); one *d* by Carlos Leon; 2nd, 2000, Guy Ritchie (marr. diss. 2008); one *s* and one adopted *s*; three adopted *d. Educ:* Adams High Sch.; Univ. of Michigan (dance scholarship); Alvin Alley Studios, NY. Formed Maverick Records Co., 1992; *recordings* include: first hit single, Holiday, 1983; albums: Madonna, 1983; Like a Virgin, 1984; True Blue, 1986; Like a Prayer, 1989; Erotica, 1992; Bedtime Stories, 1994; Ray of Light, 1998; Music, 2000; American Life, 2003; Confessions on a Dance Floor, 2005; I'm Going to Tell You a Secret, 2006; The Confessions Tour, 2007; Hard Candy, 2008; Celebration, 2009; MDNA, 2012; Rebel Heart, 2015; Madame X, 2019. *Films:* A certain Sacrifice, 1979; Vision Quest, 1985; Desperately seeking Susan, 1985; Shanghai Surprise, 1986; Who's that Girl?, 1987; Bloodhounds of Broadway, 1989; Dick Tracy, 1989; Soap-Dish, 1990; Shadows and Fog, 1991; A League of their Own, 1991; In Bed with Madonna, 1991; Truth or Dare, 1991; Body of Evidence, 1992; Snake Eyes, 1994; Dangerous Game, 1994; Blue in the Face, 1995; Girl 6, 1996; Evita (Golden Globe Award for best actress), 1996; Four Rooms, 1996; The Next Best Thing, 2000; Swept Away, 2002; Die Another Day, 2002; dir, Filth and Wisdom, 2008; writer and exec. prod., I Am Because We Are, 2008; dir and co-writer, W. E., 2012; *theatre:* Up For Grabs, Wyndham's, 2002. *Publications:* Sex, 1992; *for children:* The English Roses, 2003; Mr Peabody's Apples, 2003; Yakov and the Seven Thieves, 2004; The Adventures of Abdi, 2004.

**CICUTTO, Francis John;** Chairman, Chord Capital Pty Ltd, 2005; *b* 9 Nov. 1950; *s* of Francesco Cicutto and Ultima (*née* Margaritta); *m* 1982, Christine Bates; one *s. Educ:* Univ. of NSW. Chief Manager, Central Business Dist, Victoria Nat. Australia Bank Ltd, 1986–88; Exec. Vice Pres., Americas, NAB, USA, 1988–89; NAB Australia: Gen. Manager, Credit Bureau, 1989–92; State Manager, NSW and ACT, 1992–94; Dir and Chief Exec.,

Clydesdale Bank PLC, 1994–96; Chief Gen. Manager, 1996–99, Man. Dir and CEO, 1999–2004, Nat. Australia Bank Ltd; Chairman: ORIX Australia, 2004–08; Run Corp., 2005–07. Dir, St Vincent Health, 2004–. Dir, Melbourne Business Sch., 1999. *Recreations:* Rugby, golf, cricket, theatre. *Clubs:* Union, Killara Golf (Sydney); Australian (Melbourne).

**CIECHANOVER, Prof. Aaron J.**, MD, DSc; Professor, since 1992, and Distinguished Research Professor, since 2002, Faculty of Medicine, Technion-Israel Institute of Technology, Haifa, Israel; *b* 1 Oct. 1947; *s* of Yitzhak and Bluma Ciechanover; *m* 1975, Dr Menucha Siletzky; one *s*. *Educ:* Hebrew Univ., Jerusalem (MSc 1970; MD 1974); Technion-Israel Inst. of Technol., Haifa (DSc 1982). Nat. Compulsory Service, Israel Defence Forces, 1974–77: Mil. Physician, Israeli Navy and Unit for R&D, Surgeon-Gen. HQ. Department of Biochemistry, Faculty of Medicine, Technion-Israel Institute of Technology: Res. Fellow, 1977–79; Lectr, 1979–81; Sen. Lectr, 1984–87; Associate Prof., 1987–92; Dir, Rappaport Family Inst. for Res. in Med. Scis, 1993–2000. Vis. Scientist, Inst. for Cancer Res., Fox Chase Cancer Center, Philadelphia, 1978, 1979, 1980, 1981; Postdoctoral Fellow, Dept of Biol., MIT and Whitehead Inst. for Biomed. Res., Cambridge, Mass, 1981–84; Visiting Professor: Dana Farber Cancer Inst. and Harvard Med. Sch., 1985, 1986; Div. of Haematol.-Oncology, Dept of Pediatrics, Children's Hosp., Washington Univ. Sch. of Medicine, St Louis, annually, 1987–99 and 2001; Univ. of Kyoto Sch. of Medicine, 2000; Northwestern Univ. Sch. of Medicine, 2002, 2003; Microbiol. and Tumor Biol. Center, Karolinska Inst., Stockholm, 2003; City Univ. of Osaka Sch. of Medicine, 2003–04, 2005; Rockefeller Univ., NY, 2004; Distinguished Vis. Res. Prof., Nat. Cheng Kung Univ., Taiwan, 2007; Amer. Cancer Soc. Eleanor Roosevelt Meml Fellow, 1988–89. Mem., EMBO, 1996. Hon. FRSC 2005. Hon. PhD: Tel Aviv, 2002; Ben Gurion, 2004; City Univ. of Osaka, 2005. Holds numerous awards and prizes, including: (jtly) Albert and Mary Lasker Award for Basic Med. Res., 2000; (jtly) Nobel Prize in Chemistry, 2004. *Publications:* contrib. numerous original articles, book chapters and review articles on intracellular proteolysis. *Address:* The Ruth and Bruce Rappaport Faculty of Medicine, Technion-Israel Institute of Technology, Efron Street, PO Box 9649 Bat Galim, Haifa 31096, Israel. *T:* 48295379, *Fax:* 48513922. *E:* c_tzachy@netvision.net.il.

**CIMA, Maj. Gen. Keith Harington**, CB 2007; CEng; various executive and non-executive positions in France, UK and Australia; *b* 28 May 1951; *s* of late Peter Harington Cima and Ivy Rose Cima; *m* 1985, Susan Diane Rook; three *s* one *d* (and one *d* decd). *Educ:* Brasenose Coll., Oxford (MA); Open Univ. (MBA); RMA Sandhurst; RMCS Shrivenham; RAF Staff Coll. CEng, MIMechE 1992. Grad. trainee, Babcock and Wilcox Ltd, 1973–74. Troop Commander: 1 Trng Regt, RE, 1975–76; 20 Field Sqn, 1977–78; Intelligence Officer, HQ RE, 2nd Div., 1978; Adjt 25 Engr Regt, 1979–80; psc(a)† 1981; SO2 MoD, 1982–83; OC 3 Field Sqn, 1984–85; SO2 RE, HQ UK Mobile Force, 1986–87; SO1 Directing Staff, RMCS, 1988–90; CO 38 Engr Regt, 1991–93; Project Manager, Mines and Demolitions, 1994, Gen. Engrg Equipt, 1995, Procurement Exec.; Col Personnel Br. 7, Mil. Sec., 1995; rcds 1996; Director: Engr Support (Army), 1997–99; Manning (Army), 1999–2000; COS, Adjt Gen., 2001–02; Sen. Army Mem., RCDS, 2002–05; Team Leader, Project Hyperion - the co-location and integration of HQ Land and Adjt Gen., MoD, 2005–06; Resident Gov. and Keeper of the Jewel House, HM Tower of London, 2006–10. Consultant, ES-KO Internat., 2011–15; case worker, 2011–, Chm., 2019–, SSAFA France; secouriste, Fedn Nationale de Protection Civile, Lamballe, 2015– (Treas., 2018–). Non-exec. Dir, Ex-Forces Jobs, 2012–13. Chairman: Cosmissus, 2013–14; Lakeside Resources Ltd, 2014–; Tech. Dir, Cole Construction (Aus) Ltd. FCMI 2004–16. Pres., Instn of RE, 2007–12. Col Comdt, RE, 2003–; Hon. Col, Royal Monmouthshire RE (Militia), 2006–14 (Chm., Regtl Trust, 2006–14). Freeman: City of London, 2007; Carpenters' Co., 2010; Comr of Lieutenancy for City of London, 2010; Liveryman, Engineers' Co., 2015–16. Volunteer crew and Helmsman, Thames Crew, subseq. Tower Lifeboat Stn, Central London, RNLI, 2007–18 (Staff Helmsman, 2012–16). *Publications:* Reflections from the Bridge, 1994. *Recreations:* dinghy and offshore sailing, marathons, gardening, philately (GB), DIY, building a $1/8$ scale steam railway. *Address:* c/o RHQ Royal Engineers, Brompton Barracks, Chatham, Kent ME4 4UG.

**CIPOLLA, Prof. Roberto**, DPhil; FIET; CEng, FREng; Professor of Information Engineering, University of Cambridge, since 2000; Managing Director, Cambridge Research Laboratory, Toshiba Research Europe, since 2007; Fellow, Jesus College, Cambridge, since 1992; Professor of Computer Vision, Royal Academy of Arts, since 2004; *b* Solihull, 3 May 1963; *s* of Salvatore Cipolla and Concetta Criminisi; *m* 2000, Maria Cristina Bordin; one *d*. *Educ:* Queens' Coll., Cambridge (BA Engrg 1984); Univ. of Pennsylvania (MSE 1985); Univ. of Electro-communications, Tokyo (MEng Robotics 1988); Balliol Coll., Oxford (DPhil 1991). FIET 2009; CEng 2010; FREng 2010. Res. Asst, Valley Forge Res. Center, Penn, 1984–85; Vis. Researcher, Electrotech. Lab., Tsukuba, Japan, 1987–88; Lady Wolfson Res. Fellow, St Hugh's Coll., Oxford, 1990–92; Toshiba Fellow, Toshiba R&D Centre, Kawasaki, Japan, 1991–92; Lectr, 1992–97, Reader, 1997–2000, Univ. of Cambridge. *Publications:* Active Visual Inference of Surface Shape, 1995; (ed jtly) Computer Vision: ECCV '96 (2 vols), 1996; (ed jtly) New Geometric Techniques in Computer Vision, 1998; (ed) Computer Vision for Human-Machine Interaction, 1998; (ed jtly) Shape, Contour and Grouping in Computer Vision, 1999; (with P. J. Giblin) Visual Motion of Curves and Surfaces, 2000; (ed jtly) The Mathematics of Surfaces IX, 2000; (ed jtly) Computer Vision: detection, recognition and reconstruction, 2010; contrib. papers to jls on computer vision. *Recreations:* Japanese language and culture, photography, art. *Address:* Department of Engineering, University of Cambridge, Cambridge CB2 1PZ. *T:* (01223) 332849. *E:* cipolla@eng.cam.ac.uk.

**CITARELLA, Victor Thomas;** social care, children's services and management consultant; Director, CPEA Ltd, since 2001; *b* 8 May 1951; *s* of Thomas and Evelyn R. M. Citarella; *m* 1975, Jacqueline Hopley; three *s* one *d*. *Educ:* Sweyne Grammar Sch., Essex; University Coll., Cardiff (BSc Hons Econs 1973, Cert. Social Work 1978). Residential Child Care Officer, S Glamorgan, 1974–80; Team Manager, Hillingdon Social Services, 1980–82; Day and Residential Care Officer, W Sussex, 1982–85; Area Manager, Bristol, Avon, 1985–88; Dep. Dir of Social Services, 1988–91, Dir of Social Services, 1991–2000, City of Liverpool. Pres., Social Care Assoc., 1992. *Address:* 5 New Acres, Newburgh, Wigan, Lancs WN8 7TU. *T:* (01257) 462698. *E:* vic.citarella@cpea.co.uk.

**CIUMEI, Charles Gregg;** QC 2014; *b* London, 1 April 1964; *s* of Arminio Ciumei and Elizabeth Whatley (née Cusworth); *m* 2007, Anne Schädle; one *s* two *d*. *Educ:* Queen Elizabeth's Comprehensive Sch., Wimborne; Wadham Coll., Oxford (BA Exptl Psychol. 1987); City Univ., London (DipLaw 1990). Scientist, ARE, 1987–89; called to the Bar, Middle Temple, 1991; in practice as barrister, 1991–. *Recreation:* rock climbing. *Address:* Essex Court Chambers, 24 Lincoln's Inn Fields, WC2A 3EG. *T:* (020) 7813 8000. *E:* cciumei@essexcourt.com.

**CLACK, Amanda Georgina**, FRICS; Executive Director, Head of Strategic Advisory, Member, UK Board, and Chair, Strategy Board, CBRE Group Inc., since 2017; President, Royal Institution of Chartered Surveyors, 2016–17; *b* Ongar, Essex, 10 May 1968; *d* of Peter Charles Clack and Olive Frances Clack. *Educ:* Brentwood Ursuline Convent High Sch.; Anglia Poly. Univ. (BSc Quantity Surveying (with distinction) 1991); Univ. of Reading (MSc Prog. Mgt 1994). FRICS 1992. Chartered Surveyor and Proj. Manager, BDB Surveying, 1986–92; Partner: Hornagold and Hills, 1992–2006; PwC, 2006–15; EY, 2015–17. Member: East of England Develt Bd, 2000–02; Expert Panel, Major Progs, NAO, 2012–14; Commn of Inq. into Brexit and Skills, All-Party Parly Gp for Excellence in Built Envmt, 2016–17, for Women in Construction, 2019; Chm., Brexit Infrastructure Gp - Skills, 2016–17; Mem., Expert Adv. Panel on immediate building safety measures after Grenfell Tower fire, DCLG, then MHCLG, 2017–. Chm., Women in Proj. Mgt Specific Interest Gp, 1994–96, Vice Chm., Editl Bd, Project Mag., 1995–98, Assoc. for Project Managers. Dir, Royal Burnham Yacht Club, 2002–04; Chm. and Mem., Friends of London Festival Orch., 2006–14. Member: Bd, Univ. Coll. of Estate Mgt, 2019; Bd, Chartered Surveyors Trng Trust, 2019; Develt Bd, LSO, 2019. Associate School Gov., Brentwood Ursuline High Sch., 2014–16. FAPM 1994; FCMI (FIMgt 1999), CCMI 2015; FIC 2006; FRSA 2014; FICE 2018. Freeman, City of London, 2007; Liveryman, Surveyors' Co., 2007 (Ct Asst, 2017). *Publications:* (jtly) Diversity Management in der Immobilienbrache, 2017; (with Judith Gabler) Managing Diversity and Inclusion in the Real Estate Sector, 2019. *Recreations:* sailing, ski-ing, music, art, interior design, self build, photography. *T:* 07976 403438. *E:* amanda.clack@btinternet.com. *Club:* Royal Automobile.

**CLACK, Prof. Jennifer Alice**, PhD, ScD; FRS 2009; Curator in Vertebrate Palaeontology, 2005–15, and Professor, 2006–15, now Professor Emeritus of Vertebrate Palaeontology, University Museum of Zoology, Cambridge; Fellow, Darwin College, Cambridge, 1997–2015; *b* Manchester, 3 Nov. 1947; *d* of Ernest and Alice Agnew; *m* 1980, Robert Neil Garfield Clack. *Educ:* Bolton Sch. (Girls' Div.); Univ. of Newcastle upon Tyne (PhD 1984); MA 1989, ScD 2000 Cantab; Univ. of Leicester (Grad. Cert. Museum Studies); Museums Dip., Museums Assoc. Display technician, 1971–75, Asst Mus. Educn Officer, 1975–78, Birmingham City Museums and Art Gall.; University Museum of Zoology, Cambridge: Asst Curator, 1981–95; Sen. Asst Curator, 1995–2000; Reader in Vertebrate Palaeontol., 2000–05. FLS 1986. Foreign Hon. Mem., Amer. Acad. of Arts and Scis, 2009; Hon. Mem., Royal Swedish Acad. of Scis, 2014. Hon. DSc: Chicago, 2013; Leicester, 2014. Daniel Giraud Elliot Medal, NAS, 2008; T. Neville George Medal, Glasgow Geol Soc., 2013; Lapworth Medal, Palaeontol Assoc., 2015. *Publications:* Gaining Ground: the origin and evolution of early tetrapods, 2002, 2nd edn 2012; contrib. papers, book chapters and articles. *Recreations:* choral singing, especially chamber choirs and English Church music, gardening, wine, cooking. *Address:* University Museum of Zoology, Cambridge, Downing Street, Cambridge CB2 3EJ. *T:* (01223) 336613, *Fax:* (01223) 336679. *E:* j.a.clack@zoo.cam.ac.uk.

**CLACKSON, Prof. James Peter Timothy**, PhD; Professor of Comparative Philology, University of Cambridge, since 2016; Fellow, Jesus College, Cambridge, since 1998; *b* Gloucester, 13 Sept. 1966; *s* of Andrew Peter Clackson and late Anne Claire Clackson (née Bramley); *m* 1st, 1991, Dr Sarah Joanne Quinn (*d* 2003); 2nd, 2005, Véronique Mottier. *Educ:* Loughborough Grammar Sch.; Trinity Coll., Cambridge (BA 1988; MA; PhD 1992). Jun. Res. Fellow, Trinity Coll., Cambridge, 1991–95; Lectr in Classics, 1997–2012, Reader in Comparative Philol., 2012–16, Univ. of Cambridge. Hugh Last Fellow, British Sch. at Rome, 2005–06. Ed., Trans Philological Soc., 2014–. Philip Leverhulme Prize, Leverhulme Trust, 2001. *Publications:* The Linguistic Relation Between Armenian and Greek, 1994; Indo-European Linguistics, 2007; (with G. Horrocks) The Blackwell History of the Latin Language, 2007; Language and Society in the Greek and Roman Worlds, 2015; contrib. articles to learned jls. *Recreations:* ski-ing, punting. *Address:* Jesus College, Cambridge CB5 8BL. *T:* (01223) 339415. *E:* jptc1@cam.ac.uk.

**CLAES, Willy;** Secretary General, NATO, 1994–95; *b* Hasselt, Belgium, 24 Nov. 1938; *m*; one *s* one *d*. *Educ:* Free Univ., Brussels. Asst Sec., then Provincial Sec., De Voorzorg, 1962–65; Local Councillor, Hasselt, 1964–94; MHR (Socialist), Hasselt, 1968–94; Minister of: Nat. Educn, Flemish Reg., 1972–73; Econ. Affairs, 1973–74 and 1977–79; Deputy Prime Minister and Minister of: Econ. Affairs, 1979–81; Econ. Affairs and Planning and Nat. Educn, 1987; Foreign Affairs, 1992–94. Belgian Socialist Party: Mem., Exec. Cttee, 1965–94; Co-Pres., 1975–77. Pres., Flemish Council for High Schs and Universities, 2014–. Numerous decorations from Europe, Mexico and Bolivia. *Publications:* Tussen droom en werkelijkheid: bouwstenen voor en ander Europa, 1979; La Chine et l'Europe, 1980; Livre Blanc de l'Energie, 1980; Quatre Années aux Affaires Economiques, 1980; Elementen voor een nieuw energiebeleid, 1980; Belgie … quo vadis?: un conte moderne, 1980; De Derde Weg: beschouwingen over de Wereldcrisis, 1987. *Recreations:* piano music, conducting orchestras. *Address:* Berkenlaan 62, 3500 Hasselt, Belgium.

**CLAGUE, Joan;** Director of Nursing Services, Marie Curie Memorial Foundation, 1986–90; *b* 17 April 1931; *d* of James Henry Clague and Violet May Clague (née Johnson). *Educ:* Malvern Girls' Coll.; Guy's Hosp.; Hampstead Gen. Hosp.; Simpson Meml Maternity Pavilion. Asst Regional Nursing Officer, Oxford Regional Hosp. Bd, 1965–67; Principal, then Chief Nursing Officer, St George's Hosp. Bd of Governors, 1967–73; Area Nursing Officer, Merton, Sutton and Wandsworth AHA, 1973–81; Regl Nursing Officer, NE Thames RHA, 1981–86. Pres., Assoc. of Nurse Administrators, 1983–85. Trustee, WRVS Trustees Ltd, 1991–96. WHO Fellow, 1969; Smith and Nephew EEC Scholar, 1981. *Recreations:* walking, domestic pursuits. *Address:* 7 Tylney Avenue, SE19 1LN. *T:* (020) 8670 5171.

**CLAHSEN, Prof. Harald**, PhD; FBA 2008; Alexander von Humboldt Professor of the Psycholinguistics of Multilingualism and Founding Director, Potsdam Research Institute for Multilingualism, University of Potsdam, since 2011; *b* Germany, 2 July 1955. *Educ:* Univ. of Wuppertal (MA 1978; PhD 1981); Univ. of Düsseldorf (Habilitation 1987). Lectr, Univ. of Düsseldorf, 1983–93; Prof., Dept of Lang. and Linguistics, Univ. of Essex, 1993–2011. Gerhard Hess Award, German Sci. Foundn. *Publications:* (ed jtly) Language Development and Language Disorders (series); (contrib.) The Handbook of Clinical Linguistics, 2008; articles in jls. *Address:* Human Sciences Faculty, Universität Potsdam, Karl-Liebknecht-Str. 24–25, 14476 Potsdam, Germany.

**CLANCARTY**, 9th Earl of, *cr* 1803; **Nicholas Power Richard Le Poer Trench;** Baron Kilconnel 1797; Viscount Dunlo 1801; Baron Trench (UK) 1815; Viscount Clancarty (UK) 1823; Marquess of Heusden (Kingdom of the Netherlands) 1818; *b* 1 May 1952; *s* of Hon. Power Edward Ford Le Poer Trench (*d* 1975), *y s* of 5th Earl of Clancarty, and Jocelyn Louise Courtney (*d* 1962); *S* uncle, 1995; *m* 2005, Victoria Frances Lambert; one *d*. *Educ:* Westminster Sch.; Ashford Grammar Sch.; Plymouth Polytech.; Univ. of Colorado; Sheffield Polytech. Elected Mem., H of L, 2010.

**CLANCY, Dame Claire (Elizabeth)**, DCB 2017; DL; Chief Executive and Clerk, National Assembly for Wales, 2007–17; *b* 14 March 1958; *d* of Douglas and Teresa Coates; *m* 1994, Michael John Clancy (*d* 2010). *Educ:* Dartford Grammar Sch. for Girls; Open Univ. (BA 1st Cl. Psychol.). Manpower Services Commn, 1977–88; Dept of Employment, 1988–90; Chief Exec., Powys TEC, 1990–92; Govt Office for SW, 1992–96; Dir of Policy and Planning, Companies House, 1996–97; Dir, Patent Office, 1999–2002; Registrar of Companies and Chief Exec., Companies House, 2002–07. Gwent: DL 2017; High Sheriff 2019–20. DUniv Wales, 2017. *Recreations:* dressage, walking, photography. *E:* clancyc@btinternet.com.

**CLANCY, Deirdre V., (Mrs Clancy Steer);** costume and set designer; painter; writer; b 31 March 1943; adopted d of Julie M. Clancy; m 1975, Michael Maxwell Steer; one s two d. Educ: Convent of the Sacred Heart, Tunbridge Wells; Birmingham Coll. of Art (NDD 1st Cl. Hons). Arts Council Asst, Lincoln Rep., 1965; House Designer, Royal Court Theatre, 1966–68: productions include costumes for D. H. Lawrence Trilogy, 1966; sets and costumes for: Early Morning, 1967; The Sea, 1973; has designed for RNT, RSC, ENO, Scottish Opera, New Sadlers Wells Opera, Chichester Fest. Theatre; costumes for Oliver, Tivoli, 2007, Napoli, Stanislavski Th., Moscow, 2009; numerous prodns in Europe, N America, Japan and Australia, incl. Marriage of Figaro, LA Opera, 2004; Opéra Lyon: Così fan Tutte, Marriage of Figaro, Don Giovanni, 2007–10; Old Globe, San Diego: King Lear, The Madness of George III, Triumph of Love, Taming of the Shrew, 2010, Shakespeare Fest. (12 prodns); Amadeus, The Tempest (transf. Th. Royal Bath, 2012), Much Ado About Nothing, 2011; Aarhus: Die Tote Stadt, 2010, Tristan and Isolde, 2012; Die Fledermaus, WNO, 2011. Founder dir, Cherubim Music Trust, 2001–. Films include: The Virgin and The Gypsy, 1969; Mrs Brown, 1997 (Best Film Costumes, BAFTA Award, 1998); Tom's Midnight Garden, 1998; television: Wives and Daughters, 1999. Has exhibited designs; exhibitions include: Red Brick Bldg, Glastonbury, 2018; Arts Centre, Salisbury, 2018. Speaker on costume and fashion history and practice. DUniv UCE, 2003. Green Room Award, Vic, Australia, for Best Costume (opera), 1990 and 1991; Olivier Award for Best Costume Design (for A Month in the Country, Triumph Prodns, and Loves Labours Lost, RSC), 1997, (for All's Well That Ends Well, RSC), 2005. Publications: Costume Since 1945, 1996, 2nd edn 2015; Costumes of Colonial America, 2009; Costumes of the 1980s and 90s, 2009; Designing Costume for Stage and Screen, 2014. Recreations: infrequent domesticity, family pursuits, more painting, hopefully. Address: 125 Duck Street, Tisbury, Wilts SP3 6LJ. E: dcs@clancy.uk.com. W: www.clancy.uk.com.

**CLANCY, Richard Francis Stephen;** District Judge (Magistrates' Courts), Liverpool, 2005–18; b 2 Sept. 1948; s of Francis Gerrard Clancy and Evaline Margaret Clancy; m 1976, Anne Margaret Lawless; one s one d. Educ: St Ambrose Coll., Altrincham; Coll. of Law, Guildford. Articled to John Arthur Wheeler, OBE, Solicitor, Warrington, 1969–74; admitted solicitor, 1974; prosecuted, W Midlands and Merseyside, 1974–83; in private practice as partner, Ridgway Greenall, Warrington, and E. Rexmakin & Co., Liverpool, 1983–2000; Acting Stipendiary Magistrate for Staffs, 1998–2000; District Judge (Magistrates' Cts), Birmingham, 2001–05. Member: Risley Prison Visitors' Centre Cttee, 1990–2000 (Chm., 1998–2000); Merseyside Criminal Justices Strategy Cttee, 1997–2000; Merseyside Justices' Issues Cttee, 2005. Mem., Warrington Sports Council (Chm., 1996–99); former Auditor, Warrington Athletic Club. Recreations: sport, piano, accordion, history, literature.

**CLANFIELD, Viscount; Ashton Robert Gerard Peel;** Managing Director, Stifel Nicolaus Europe Ltd, since 2015; b 16 Sept. 1976; s and heir of 3rd Earl Peel, qv; m 2004, Matilda Rose Aykroyd; one s three d. Educ: Ampleforth; Durham Univ. (BA Hons 1999); Univ. of Buckingham (MBA 2004). With Cazenove Fund Management, 2000–02; Dir, Panmure Gordon and Co., 2006–10; Partner, Oriel Securities, 2010–15. Heir: s Hon. Nicholas Robert William Peel, b 4 May 2015.

**CLANMORRIS, 8th Baron cr 1800 (Ire.); Simon John Ward Bingham,** MA; FCA; b 25 Oct. 1937; s of 7th Baron Clanmorris and of Madeleine Mary, d of late Clement Ebel; S father, 1988; m 1971, Gizella Maria, d of Sandor Zverkó; one d. Educ: Downside; Queens' College, Cambridge (MA). ACA 1965, FCA 1975. Chm., Campaign for Lower Electricity Prices, 2017–. Heir: cousin Robert Derek de Burgh Bingham [b 29 Oct. 1942; m 1969, Victoria Mary, yr d of P. A. Pennant-Rea; three d]. Address: c/o Coutts & Co., 440 Strand, WC2R 0QS.

See also Hon. C. M. T. Bingham.

**CLANWILLIAM, 8th Earl of, cr 1776 (Ire.); Patrick James Meade;** Bt 1703 (Ire.); Viscount Clanwilliam, Baron Gillford 1766; Baron Clanwilliam (UK) 1828; Founding Partner, 1995, Chairman, since 1996, Meade Hall (formerly The Policy Partnership, later Gardant Communications); b 28 Dec. 1960; s of 7th Earl of Clanwilliam and Maxine (née Hayden-Scott); S father, 2009; m 1st, 1989, Serena Emily (marr. diss. 1994), d of late Lt-Col B. J. Lockhart; one d; 2nd, 1995, Cara de la Peña (marr. diss. 2009); one s one d. Educ: Eton Coll. 1 Bn, Coldstream Guards, 1979–83. Exec., Hanson plc, 1983–90; attached Home Office as special advr to Home Sec., 1986–88; with Ian Greer & Associates, 1990–93; Man. Dir, Westminster Policy Partnership Ltd, 1993–95; Chairman: Cleveland Bridge UK Ltd, 2001–04; Eurasia Drilling Co. Ltd, 2008–; Director: Polyus Gold, 2006–13; CBM Oil plc, 2007–11; Otkritie OUCP, 2008–09; NMC Health Gp, 2012–; SOMA Oil and Gas, 2013–. Councillor (C) Royal Bor. of Kensington and Chelsea, 1990–98 (Chm., Traffic and Highways Cttee). Mem. Bd of Trustees, British Sch. of Osteopathy, 1997–2000; Trustee, Benevolent Soc. of St Patrick, 1993–. Gov., Knightsbridge Sch., 2006–08. Recreations: helicopter flying, prison reform and prison sentencing policy, free fall parachuting, sub-aqua diving, Palladian architecture, golf, fishing, motorbiking. Heir: s Lord Gillford, qv. Address: 1 Meade Mews, SW1P 4EG. T: (020) 7976 5555. Clubs: White's, Turf, Chatham Dining; Mill Reef (Antigua, WI); New Zealand (Weybridge).

**CLAPHAM, Michael;** b 15 May 1943; s of late Thomas Clapham and of Eva Clapham; m 1965, Yvonne Hallsworth; one s one d. Educ: Leeds Polytechnic (BSc); Leeds Univ. (PGCE); Bradford Univ. (MPhil). Miner, 1958–70; Lectr, 1974–77; Dep. Head, Yorks NUM Compensation Dept, 1977–83; Head of Industrial Relations, NUM, 1983–92. MP (Lab) Barnsley West and Penistone, 1992–2010. PPS to Minister of State for Health, 1997. Member: Trade and Industry Cttee, 1992–97, 2003–05; DTI, then BERR Select Cttee, 2004–10; Vice Chm., back-bench Trade and Industry Gp, 1996–97; Chairman, All-Party Group: on Occupational Safety and Health, 1996–2010; on Coalfield Communities, 1997–2008; on NATO Parly Assembly, 2000; Jt Chm., All-Party Gp on Fire Safety, 2001–10; Hon. Sec., All-Party Gp on Energy Studies, 1997–2010; Chm., Minister's Adv. Panel on Mines Compensation, 1999–2010. Chair, NATO Civil Dimensions of Security, 2004–08. Chairman: Barnsley Community Safety Partnership (formerly Barnsley Crime Prevention Partnership), 1995–2007; Multi Agency Panel, 1999–2007; Construction Skills and Certification Scheme, 2011–18. Chm., review of coalfield regeneration, 2010. Trustee, Coalfields Regeneration Trust, 2012–. Recreations: reading, walking, gardening, construction, health and safety, regeneration of mining communities, politics.

**CLAPHAM, Peter Brian,** CB 1996; PhD; CEng, FInstP; Consultant on technology and public administration reform, since 1996; Director, National Physical Laboratory, 1990–95; b 3 Nov. 1940; s of Wilfred Clapham and Una Frances (née Murray); m 1965, Jean Margaret (née Vigil); two s. Educ: Ashville Coll., Harrogate; University Coll. London (BSc, PhD; Fellow, 1996). Research in optics and metrology, NPL, 1960–70; Sec., Adv. Cttee on Res. on Measurements and Standards, 1970–71; res. management and head of marketing, NPL, 1972–81; Res. and Technology Policy, DoI, 1981–82; Supt of Div. of Mech. and Optical Metrology, NPL, 1982–84; Dir 1985, Chief Exec. 1989, Nat. Weights and Measures Lab. Chm., W European Legal Metrology Cooperation, 1989–90; Member: Presidential Council of Internat. Orgn of Legal Metrology, 1985–90; Internat. Cttee of Weights and Measures, 1991–96; British Hallmarking Council, 2001–09. Dir, Bushy Park Water Gardens Trust, 1997–2002. Publications: numerous sci. contribs to learned jls. Recreations: peregrination, crafts, Catenians.

**CLAPP, Cdre Michael Cecil,** CB 1982; RN retired; b 22 Feb. 1932; s of Brig. Cecil Douglas Clapp, CBE and Mary Elizabeth Emmeline Palmer Clapp; m 1975, Sarah Jane Alexander; one s two d. Educ: Chafyn Grove Sch., Salisbury; Marlborough College. Joined Royal Navy, 1950 (despatches, 1965); commanded HM Ships Puncheston, Jaguar and Leander, and 801 Buccaneer Mk2 Sqdn; Commander, Falklands Amphibious Task Gp, 1982. Mem., Stock Exchange, 1987–95. Gov., Kelly Coll., 1985–2010. Publications: Amphibious Assault, Falklands, 1996. Recreations: sailing, shooting, fishing, country life. Clubs: Royal Cruising; Exeter White Ensign (Pres., 1994–).

**CLAPP, Susannah,** FRSL; Theatre Critic, The Observer, since 1997; b 9 Feb. 1949; d of Ralph James Clapp and Marion (née Heeremans). Educ: Ashford Co. Grammar Sch.; Univ. of Bristol (BA Hons). Sub-editor, The Listener, 1970–74; reader and ed., Jonathan Cape, 1974–79; radio critic, Sunday Times, 1978–80; Asst Ed., London Rev. of Books, 1979–92; Theatre Critic: Nightwaves, Radio 3, 1994–2013; New Statesman, 1996–97. FRSL 2013. Publications: With Chatwin: portrait of a writer, 1997; A Card from Angela Carter, 2012. Address: 37 Granville Square, WC1X 9PD. T: (020) 7837 1686. Club: Cranium.

**CLAPPISON, (William) James;** b 14 Sept. 1956; m 1984, Helen Margherita Carter; one s three d. Educ: St Peter's Sch., York; Queen's Coll., Oxford (Schol.; PPE). Called to the Bar, Gray's Inn, 1981. Contested (C): Barnsley E, 1987; Bootle, May and Nov. 1990. MP (C) Hertsmere, 1992–2015. Parly Under-Sec. of State, DoE, 1995–97; Opposition frontbench spokesman on home affairs, 1997–2001; Shadow Minister for Work, 2001–02; Opposition front bench spokesman, Treasury affairs, 2002; Shadow Minister for Work and Pensions, 2007–10. Mem., Select Cttee on Home Affairs, 2002–15, on European Scrutiny, 2007–15. Recreations: bridge, walking. Club: Carlton.

**CLAPTON, Eric Patrick,** CBE 2004 (OBE 1995); singer, guitarist and songwriter; b 30 March 1945; s of Patricia Clapton; m 1979, Patricia Ann Harrison (née Boyd) (marr. diss. 1988); (one s decd by Lori Del Santo); one d by Yvonne Kelly; m 2002, Melia McEnery; three d. Educ: St Bede's Sch., Surrey; Kingston Coll. of Art. Guitarist with: Roosters, 1963; Yardbirds, 1963–65; John Mayall's Bluesbreakers, 1965–66; Cream, 1966–68; Blind Faith, 1969; Delaney and Bonnie, 1970; Derek and the Dominoes, 1970; solo performer, 1972–. Albums include: (with Yardbirds): Five Live Yardbirds, 1964; For Your Love, 1965; (with Bluesbreakers) Blues Breakers, 1966; (with Cream): Fresh Cream, 1967; Disraeli Gears, 1967; Wheels of Fire, 1968; Goodbye, 1969; (with Blind Faith) Blind Faith, 1969; (with Derek and the Dominoes) Layla and Other Assorted Love Songs, 1970; solo: Eric Clapton, 1970; 461 Ocean Boulevard, 1974; There's One in Every Crowd, 1975; E. C. Was Here, 1975; No Reason to Cry, 1976; Slowhand, 1977; Backless, 1978; Just One Night, 1980; Another Ticket, 1981; Money and Cigarettes, 1983; Behind the Sun, 1985; August, 1986; Journeyman, 1989; 24 Nights, 1992; Unplugged, 1992; From the Cradle, 1994; Pilgrim, 1998; Blues, 1999; (with B. B. King) Riding with the King, 2000; Reptile, 2001; One More Car One More Rider, 2002; Me and Mr Johnson, 2004; Sessions for Robert J, 2004; Back Home, 2005; (with J. J. Cale) The Road to Escondido, 2006; Clapton, 2010; Old Sock, 2013; The Breeze, 2014; Slowhand at 70, 2015; I Still Do, 2016; Happy Xmas, 2018. Co-owner and Design Dir, Cordings of Piccadilly, 2003–. Founder, Crossroads Centre, Antigua, 1997. Numerous awards. Publications: Eric Clapton: the autobiography, 2007.

**CLARE, John Charles,** CBE 2005; non-executive Chairman: JobCentre Plus, 2007–11; Dreams plc, 2008–11; Capital and Regional plc, 2010–17; b 2 Aug. 1950; s of Sidney Charles and Joan Mildred Clare; m 1974, Anne Ross; two s. Educ: Edinburgh Univ. (BSc Hons Applied Maths). Sales and marketing roles in UK, Switzerland, Denmark, Sweden, Mars Ltd, 1972–82; Business Develt Dir and Marketing Dir, Racing Div., Ladbroke Gp plc, 1982–85; Dixons Group plc: Marketing Dir 1985–86, Man. Dir 1986–88, Dixons Ltd; Gp Dir, 1988–92; Man. Dir, Dixons Stores Gp, 1988–92; Gp Man. Dir, 1992–94; Chief Exec., Dixons Gp, later DSG Internat. plc, 1994–2007. Non-executive Director: Dyson Ltd, 2007–12; JJB Sports plc, 2009–10 (Chm., 2010). Recreations: cricket, music, family, Tottenham Hotspur supporter.

**CLARE, Michael George;** DL; Founder, and President, since 2008, Dreams plc (Executive Chairman and Managing Director, 1987–2008); Chairman, Clarenco LLP, since 2008; b 8 Feb. 1955; s of late Thomas Isaac Clare and Betty Clare (née Jeffries); m 1979, Carol Ann Ballingall; two s two d. Educ: Davenies Sch.; Chalfonts Community Coll.; High Wycombe Coll.; Buckinghamshire New Univ. Br. Manager, Williams Furniture, 1976–78; Area Manager: Hardys Furniture, then Queensway, 1978–80; Perrings Furniture, 1980–83; Sales Dir, Deanes Furniture, 1983–85; Proprietor, Sofa Bed Centres, 1985–87. Dir, British Retail Consortium, 2006–08. Pres., Furniture Trade Benevolent Assoc., 2006–07; Patron, Retail Trust, 2007–08. FInstD 1990. Freeman, City of London, 2001; Liveryman, Co. of Furniture Makers, 2001–. DL Bucks 2011. Chm. of Trustees, Clare Foundn, 2009–17. Gov., Bucks Chiltern UC, 2006–08; Patron: Chalfonts Community Coll., 2008–11; Clare Business Sch., 2012–. Bucks Ambassador, 2007–. DUniv Buckingham, 2009. Regl Entrepreneur of Year, Ernst & Young, 2002. Recreation: travelling the world and making my dreams a reality. Address: c/o Clarenco LLP, 6 Lancaster Court, Coronation Road, High Wycombe, Bucks HP12 3TD. T: (01494) 682000. E: mike@clarenco.com.

**CLARE, Pauline Ann,** CBE 2002; QPM 1996; DL; executive coach, since 2002; Chief Constable of Lancashire, 1995–2002; b 26 July 1947; d of Kathleen and Thomas Rostron; m 1983, Reginald Stuart Clare; two step d. Educ: St Mary's Secondary Modern Sch., Leyland, Lancs; Open Univ. (BA Hons). CCMI (CIMgt 1996). Lancashire Constabulary: Police Cadet, 1964; Constable to Inspector, Policewomen's Dept, Juvenile Liaison, 1966; Merseyside Police: Inspector Uniform Patrol and Computer Project Team, 1973; Chief Inspector, Uniform Patrol, Community Services Dept, 1983; Supt, Community Services Dept, Sub Divl and Dep. Divl Comd, Sefton, 1987; Chief Supt, Divl Comd, Sefton, 1991; Asst Chief Constable, Crime and Ops, 1992–94; Dep. Chief Constable, Cheshire Constabulary, 1994–95. Hon. Col, Lancs ACF, 1996–2002. Pres., Lancs Assoc. of Clubs for Young People (formerly Lancs Assoc. of Boys' Clubs), 1995–2002; Chair, Rainbow House charity, Mawdesley, 2016–. Comdr, St John Ambulance, Lancs, 2004–07. DL Lancs 1998. FRSA 2002. Hon. Fellow, Univ. of Central Lancashire, 1994. DUniv Open, 1999. Police Long Service and Good Conduct Medal, 1988; Lancashire Woman of the Year, 1993. SSStJ 1985 (Mem. Council, Lancs, 1998–2009). Recreations: gardening, charity work, reading novels, entertaining at home. Address: Bolton-by-Bowland, Clitheroe, Lancs.

**CLARE, Rebecca Mary S.;** see Sabben-Clare.

**CLARE, Rear Adm. Roy Alexander George,** CBE 2007; DL; Director, Auckland War Memorial Museum, New Zealand, 2011–16; b 30 Sept. 1950; s of late John Arnold Clare and Ludmilla Clare (née Nossoff); m 1st, 1979, Leonie (Mimi) Hutchings (d 1979); 2nd, 1981, Sarah Catherine Jane Parkin; one s two d. Educ: St George's Grammar Sch., Cape Town; BRNC, Dartmouth (Queen's Sword, 1972). Joined Royal Navy, 1966; jun. rating, HMS Ganges and HMS Decoy, 1966–68; Upperyardman Cadet, Dartmouth, 1968; Midshipman, HMS Ashanti, 1970–71; Sub-Lieut, Yacht Adventure, Whitbread Round

The World Race, 1973–74; Lieut, HMS Diomede, 1974–75; First Lieut, HMS Bronington (HRH The Prince of Wales), 1975–77; Principal Warfare Officer, HMS Juno, 1978–80; CO, HMS Bronington, 1980–81; Ops Officer, HMS Glamorgan (Lt Comdr), 1982–83; Staff of Flag Officer Sea Trng, 1984–85; rnsc, Greenwich (Comdr), 1985–86; CO, HMS Birmingham, 1987–89; MA to Minister of State for Armed Forces, 1989–91; CO, HMS York and Capt., Third Destroyer Sqdn, 1991–92; rcds, 1993; Asst Dir, Naval Plans and Programmes Div., MoD, 1993–96; CO, HMS Invincible, 1996–97; Commodore, BRNC, 1998–99; Rear-Adm. 1999; Dir Operational Mgt, NATO Regl Comd North, 1999–2000; Dir, Nat. Maritime Mus., 2000–07; Chief Exec., Museums, Libraries and Archives Council, 2007–11. Member, Board: Creative and Cultural Skills, 2005–07; MLA, 2006–07; Qualifications and Curriculum Develt Agency, 2009–11; Heritage Alliance, 2018–; Chm., Museums Aotearoa, 2015–16 (Mem. Bd, 2014–16). Trustee: Bronington Trust, 1990–99 (Vice Pres., 1999–2002); Naval Review, 1990–2011; Britannia Assoc., 2001–04. Chm., Midland Naval Officers' Assoc., 2000–02; Member: Greenwich Forum, 2000–07; Univ. of Greenwich Assembly, 2000–07; RNSA. Vice Pres. and Hon. Mem., Assoc. of Yachting Historians, 2010–. Chair: Chelmsford Cultural Develt Trust, 2017–; Friends of St Mary's Tollesbury, 2018–. Member Board: Good Things Foundn, 2017–; Robert Tailler (or Taylor) Charity, 2018–. Mem. Court, Univ. of Essex, 2019–. Freeman: City of London, 2001; Clockmakers' Co., 2004; Shipwrights' Co., 2005– (Liveryman, 2002–05). DL Essex, 2018. CCMI, until 2011 (CIMgt 2001); FRSA 2005–08; MInstD 2006–11; FRIN 2006–07. Hon. DLitt Greenwich, 2007. *Publications:* (ed) HMS Bronington: a tribute to one of Britain's last wooden walls, 1996; contrib. to Naval Rev. *Recreations:* family (two granddaughters), sailing, walking, maritime research, blogger, photographer. *Address:* Tollesbury, Essex. *E:* roylarenz@gmail.com. *Clubs:* Anchorites, Royal Navy of 1765 and 1785, City Naval; Royal Yacht Squadron (Naval Mem.).

**CLARENDON,** 8th Earl of, 2nd *cr* 1776; **George Edward Laurence Villiers;** Baron Hyde 1756; Partner, Knight Frank, since 2006; *b* 12 Feb. 1976; *s* of 7th Earl of Clarendon and Jane Diana, *d* of late E. W. Dawson; *S* father, 2009; *m* 2007, Bryonie, *d* of Maj.-Gen. Anthony de C. L. Leask, *qv;* three *s*. *Educ:* Milton Abbey Sch.; Royal Agricl Coll. (BSc Hons). MRICS. Liveryman, Fishmongers' Co., 2008. Page of Honour to the Queen, 1987–89. *Heir: s* Lord Hyde, *qv. Address:* c/o Holywell House, Swanmore, Hants SO32 2QE. *Club:* Boodle's.

**CLARIDGE, Prof. Michael Frederick;** Emeritus Professor of Entomology, Cardiff University; *b* 2 June 1934; *s* of Frederick William Claridge and Eva Alice (*née* Jeffery); *m* 1967, Lindsey Clare Hellings; two *s* one *d*. *Educ:* Lawrence Sheriff Sch., Rugby; Keble Coll., Oxford (MA, DPhil). Lectr in Zoology 1959–74, Sen. Lectr in Zoology 1974–77, Univ. Coll., Cardiff; Reader in Entomology, 1977–83, Prof. of Entomology, 1983–99, Head of Sch. of Biol., 1989–94, Univ. of Wales, Cardiff. President: Linnean Soc. of London, 1988–91; Systematics Assoc., 1991–94; Royal Entomol Soc., 2000–02 (Hon. Fellow, 2006). Linnean Medal for Zool., Linnean Soc., 2000. *Publications:* Handbook for the Identification of Leafhoppers and Planthoppers of Rice, 1991; chapters in: The Leafhoppers and Planthoppers, 1985; Organization of Communities—Past and Present, 1987; Prospects in Systematics, 1988; The Biodiversity of Micro-organisms and Invertebrates, 1991; Evolutionary Patterns and Processes, 1993; Planthoppers: their ecology and management, 1993; Identification of Pest Organisms, 1994; Species—the Units of Biodiversity, 1997; Insect Sounds and Communication: physiology, behaviour, ecology and evolution, 2006; Contemporary Debate on the Philosophy of Biology, 2009; Insect Biodiversity: science and society, 2009; papers in Biol Jl of Linnean Soc., Ecological Entomology, Amer. Naturalist. *Recreations:* classical music, cricket, natural history. *Address:* School of Biosciences, Cardiff University, Cardiff CF10 3TL. *E:* claridge@cardiff.ac.uk.

**CLARK;** *see* Chichester Clark and Chichester-Clark.

**CLARK;** *see* Gordon Clark.

**CLARK,** family name of **Baron Clark of Windermere**.

**CLARK, Hon. Lord; Alistair MacDonald Clark;** a Senator of the College of Justice in Scotland, since 2016; *b* Glasgow, 3 Dec. 1955; *s* of John and Matilda Clark; *m* 1980, Jacqueline Wright; one *s* one *d*. *Educ:* Univ. of Glasgow (LLB); Univ. of Strathclyde (PhD). Lectr, Glasgow Coll. of Technol., 1978; Lectr, Sen. Lectr, then pt-time Lectr and Tutor, Univ. of Strathclyde, 1978–96; Advocate, 1994; QC (Scot.) 2007. *Publications:* Product Liability, 1989; contrib. legal jls. *Recreations:* reading, hill-walking, music, football, golf. *Address:* Court of Session, Parliament House, Edinburgh EH1 1RQ. *E:* alistair.clark@advocates.org.uk.

**CLARK OF CALTON,** Baroness *cr* 2005 (Life Peer), of Calton in the City of Edinburgh; **Lynda Margaret Clark;** PC 2013; PhD; a Senator of the College of Justice in Scotland, 2006–19; Chairman, Scottish Law Commission, 2012–14; *b* 26 Feb. 1949. *Educ:* St Andrews Univ. (LLB Hons); Edinburgh Univ. (PhD). Lectr, Univ. of Dundee, 1973–76; admitted Advocate, Scots Bar, 1977; QC (Scot.) 1989; called to the English Bar, Inner Temple, 1988, Bencher, 2000. Advocate Gen. for Scotland, 1999–2006. Contested (Lab) Fife North East, 1992. MP (Lab) Edinburgh Pentlands, 1997–2005. Member, Court: Edinburgh Univ., 1995–97; Dundee Univ., 2018–; Chancellor's Assessor, Edinburgh Napier Univ., 2008–13.

**CLARK OF WINDERMERE,** Baron *cr* 2001 (Life Peer), of Windermere in the County of Cumbria; **David George Clark,** LVO 2016; PC 1997; DL; Chairman, Forestry Commission, 2001–09; *b* 19 Oct. 1939; *s* of George and Janet Clark; *m* 1970, Christine Kirkby; one *d*. *Educ:* Manchester Univ. (BA(Econ), MSc); Sheffield Univ. (PhD 1978). Forester, 1956–57; Laboratory Asst in Textile Mill, 1957–59; Student Teacher, 1959–60; Student, 1960–63; Pres., Univ. of Manchester Union, 1963–64; Trainee Manager in USA, 1964; University Lecturer, 1965–70. Non-executive Director: Homeowners Friendly Soc., 1987–97, 1999–2010; Thales plc, 1999–2011; Carlisle Utd Ltd, 2001–; Sellafield Ltd, 2007–15. Contested Manchester (Withington), 1966; MP (Lab) Colne Valley, 1970–Feb. 1974; contested same seat, Oct. 1974; MP (Lab) South Shields, 1979–2001. Opposition spokesman on Agriculture and Food, 1973–74, on Defence, 1980–81, on the Environment, 1981–86; Opposition front bench spokesman on: environmental protection and develt, 1986–87; food, agriculture and rural affairs, 1987–92; defence, disarmament and arms control, 1992–97; Chancellor, Duchy of Lancaster, 1997–98. Mem., Parly Assembly, NATO, 1981–2005 (Leader, UK delegn, 2001–05); Chm., Atlantic Council of UK, 1998–2003. Pres., Open Spaces Soc., 1979–88. Vis. Prof. of Hist. and Politics, Univ. of Huddersfield, 2013–. Hon. Fellow, Univ. of Cumbria, 2009. DL Cumbria, 2007. Freedom, Borough of S Tyneside, 1989. *Publications:* The Industrial Manager, 1966; Colne Valley: Radicalism to Socialism, 1981; Victor Grayson, Labour's Lost Leader, 1985; We Do Not Want The Earth, 1992; The Labour Movement in Westmorland, 2012; Voices from Labour's Past, 2015; Victor Grayson: the man and the mystery, 2016; various articles on Management and Labour History. *Recreations:* fell-walking, ornithology, watching football, gardening. *Address:* House of Lords, SW1A 0PW.

**CLARK, Alan Richard;** HM Diplomatic Service, retired; *b* 4 Sept. 1939; *s* of George Edward Clark and Norah Ivy Maria Clark (*née* Hope); *m* 1961, Ann Rosemary (*née* Hosford); (one *s* decd). *Educ:* Chatham House Grammar Sch., Ramsgate. Foreign Office, 1958; HM Forces, 1960–62; FO 1962; served Tehran, 1964–66; Jedda, 1966–68; Second Sec. (Economic), later First Sec., Paris, 1969–71; FCO, 1972–76; Dep. Hd of Mission, Freetown, 1976–80; FCO, 1980–84; secondment (with rank of Counsellor) to Vickers Shipbuilding and Engineering Ltd, 1984–86; Counsellor and Head of Chancery, Bucharest, 1986–90; Consul-Gen., Montreal, 1990–93; Sen. Overseas Inspector, FCO, 1994–96. Vice-Chm., Thanet Community Housing Assoc., 1999–2003. Complaint Convenor, Kent and Medway HA, 2002–05; Perf. Assessor, GMC, 2002–14. Non-exec. Dir, E Kent Hosps Univ. NHS Foundn Trust, 2003–10; Interim Chm., Shepway PCT, 2004–05. Trustee, Michael Yoakley's Charity, 2000–15 (Chm. of Trustees, 2005–11); Dir, Yoakley Care Trustee Ltd and Yoakley Share Care Ltd, 2016–. *Recreations:* swimming, walking, reading. *Address:* 9 Dane End Road, Westgate-on-Sea, Kent CT8 8PH.

**CLARK, Alistair MacDonald;** *see* Clark, Hon. Lord.

**CLARK, Prof. Andrew,** DPhil; FBA 2015; FRSE; Professor of Cognitive Philosophy, University of Sussex, since 2019; *b* London, 1957; *s* of James Henderson Clark and Christine Clark (*née* Russell); *m* 2014, Dr Alexandra Morcom. *Educ:* Bp Thomas Grant Secondary Modern Sch., Streatham; Stirling Univ. (BA 1st Cl. Hons Philosophy 1981; DPhil Philosophy 1984). Temp. Lectr in Philosophy, Univ. of Glasgow, 1984–85; Lectr, then Reader, in Philosophy with Cognitive Scis, Univ. of Sussex, 1985–93; Prof. of Philosophy, and Dir, Philosophy/Neurosci./Psychol. Prog., Washington Univ., St Louis, 1993–2000; Prof. of Philosophy and Cognitive Sci., Univ. of Sussex, 2000–02; Prof. of Philosophy and Dir, Cognitive Sci. Prog., Indiana Univ., 2002–04; Prof. of Logic and Metaphysics, Univ. of Edinburgh, 2004–18. Chandaria Laureate, Sch. of Advanced Study, Univ. of London, 2016. FRSE 2007. Member: Scotch Malt Whisky Soc.; Scotch Perspectives. *Publications:* Microcognition: philosophy, cognitive science and parallel distributed processing, 1989; Associative Engines: connectionism, concepts and representational change, 1993; Being There: putting brain, body and world together again, 1997; Mindware: an introduction to the philosophy of cognitive science, 2001, 2nd edn 2014; Natural-Born Cyborgs: minds, technologies and the future of human intelligence, 2003; Supersizing the Mind: embodiment, action, and cognitive extension, 2008; Surfing Uncertainty: prediction, action, and the embodied mind, 2016. *Recreations:* collector of American comics and pulp fiction, co-owner of narrowboat, Love and Rockets; music: techno, electronica and lounge. *Address:* Department of Philosophy, Arts A, University of Sussex, Brighton BN1 9QN. *E:* andy.clark@sussex.ac.uk.

**CLARK, Andrew George;** Chief Music Critic, Financial Times, 1996–2014; *b* 30 Nov. 1952; *s* of George Clark and Georgina Brenda Clark (*née* Gibson); *m* 1987, Alison Gibson; one *s*. *Educ:* Sedbergh Sch.; Durham Univ. (BA Hons Modern Hist.). Eur. Arts Corresp., Financial Times, 1981–95. Mem., Editl Bd, Opera mag., 1990–. Critic Prize, Cultural Foundn of City of Salzburg, 1998; Special Prize, Anglo-German Foundn, 2000. *Publications:* Il Verdi del Centenario, 2003; Old Millport, 2006; A World Apart: the story of Hebridean shipping, 2010; Pleasures of the Firth: two hundred years of the Clyde steamers, 2012.

**CLARK, Antony Roy;** Rector, Michaelhouse, South Africa, since 2019; *b* 7 Nov. 1956; *s* of Roger and Betty Clark; *m* 1981, Dr Brigitte Jennifer Lang; one *s* two *d*. *Educ:* St Andrew's Coll., S Africa; Rhodes Univ. (BA; HDE); Downing Coll., Cambridge (Douglas Smith Scholar, MA 1981). Teacher, Westerford High Sch., Cape Town, 1984–90; investment business, 1990–91; Headmaster: St Joseph's Marist Coll., Cape Town, 1992–93; St Andrew's Coll., Grahamstown, 1994–2002; Gresham's Sch., Holt, 2002–08; Malvern Coll., 2008–19. Mem., Old Andrean Club. *Recreations:* cricket, squash, chess, reading, hiking. *Address:* Michaelhouse, Balgowan 3275, South Africa. *Clubs:* Quidnuncs; Hawks.

**CLARK, Brian Robert,** FRSL 1985; playwright; *b* 3 June 1932; *s* of Leonard and Selina Clark; *m* (marr. diss.); two *s*; *m* 1990, Cherry Potter. *Educ:* Merrywood Grammar Sch., Bristol; Redland Coll. of Educn, Bristol; Central Sch. of Speech and Drama, London; Nottingham Univ. BA Hons English. Teacher, 1955–61, and 1964–66; Staff Tutor in Drama, Univ. of Hull, 1966–70. Since 1971 has written some thirty television plays, incl. Whose Life Is It Anyway? and The Saturday Party; television film, (with Cherry Potter) House Games; also series: Telford's Change; Late Starter. Stage plays: Whose Life Is It Anyway? (SWET award for Best Play, 1977; filmed, 1982); Can You Hear Me At the Back?, 1978; Campions Interview; Post Mortem; Kipling, London and NY, 1985; The Petition, NY and Nat. Theatre, 1986; (with Kathy Levin) Hopping to Byzantium, Germany 1989, Sydney, Aust., 1990; In Pursuit of Eve (also acted), London, 2001. Founded Amber Lane Press, publishing plays and books on the theatre, 1978. *Publications:* Group Theatre, 1971; Whose Life Is It Anyway?, 1978; Can You Hear Me At the Back?, 1979; Post Mortem, 1979; The Petition, 1986; In Pursuit of Eve, 2001. *Address:* c/o Judy Daish Associates, 2 St Charles Place, W10 6EG. *T:* (020) 8964 8811.

**CLARK, Brodie;** *see* Clark, Robert B.

**CLARK, Rt Rev. Bruce Quinton;** Bishop of Riverina, 1993–2004; *b* Brisbane, Qld, 22 May 1939; *s* of Quinton Clark; *m* 1965, Elizabeth Shufflebotham. *Educ:* Brisbane Boys' Coll.; St Francis Theol Coll., Brisbane (ThL). Ordained deacon and priest, 1963; Assistant Curate: All Saints, Chermside, 1963–65; St Matthew's, Groveley, 1965–67; Vicar, St Luke's, Miles, 1967–70; Rector: St Matthew's, Gayndah, 1970–76; St Peter's, Gympie, 1976–83; St Paul's, Maryborough, 1983–89; Surfers Paradise Parish, 1989–93. Archdeacon: Wide Bay, Burnett, 1985–89; Moreton, 1989–91; Gold Coast and Hinterland, 1991–93. *Recreations:* restoring furniture, music, photography.

**CLARK, Charles Anthony, (Tony),** CB 1994; higher education consultant; Director, Student Support, Department for Education and Employment, 1999–2000; *b* 13 June 1940; *s* of late Stephen and Winifred Clark; *m* 1968, Penelope Margaret (*née* Brett); one *s* two *d*. *Educ:* King's Coll. Sch., Wimbledon; Pembroke Coll., Oxford (MA Nat. Sci.). Pressed Steel Co., 1961; Hilger & Watts Ltd, 1962–65; DES, subseq. DFE, later DFEE, 1965–2000; seconded to UGC, 1971–73; Under Sec., 1982; Hd of Finance Br. and Prin. Finance Officer, 1987–89; Dir (formerly Under Sec.), Higher Educn, 1989–99. Mem., Effingham Parish Council, 2003–05. Mem. Council, Surrey Univ., 1999–2006; Gov., Southampton Solent Univ. (formerly Southampton Inst.), 2000–09. Hon. LLD Nottingham Trent, 2000. *Recreations:* gardening, golf, travel, long distance walking. *Address:* The Paddock, Guildford Road, Effingham, Surrey KT24 5QA.

**CLARK, Rt Hon. Charles Joseph, (Joe),** CC 1995; PC (Canada) 1979; President, Joe Clark & Associates (Principal Partner, 1994); company director; Professor of Practice, Institute for the Study of International Development, McGill University, since 2005; Vice-President, Global Leadership Foundation, since 2010; *b* 5 June 1939; *s* of Charles and Grace Clark; *m* 1973, Maureen Anne McTeer (she retained her maiden name); one *d*. *Educ:* High River High Sch.; Univ. of Alberta (BA History; MA Polit. Sci.). Journalist, Canadian Press, Calgary Herald, Edmonton Jl, High River Times, 1964–66; Lectr in Political Science, Univ. of Alberta, Edmonton, 1966–67; Exec. Asst to Hon. Robert L. Stanfield, Leader of the Opposition, 1967–70. MP (Progressive C): Rocky Mountain, later Yellowhead,

1972–93; Kings-Hants, 2000; Calgary Centre, 2000–04; Leader of the Opposition, Canada, 1976–79; Prime Minister of Canada, 1979–80; Leader of the Opposition, 1980–83; Sec. of State for External Affairs, 1984–91; Minister for Constitutional Affairs, 1991–93, Leader, Progressive Cons. Party of Canada, 1976–83 and 1998–2002. UN Special Rep. for Cyprus, 1993–95. Pres., Queen's Privy Council for Canada, 1991–93. Hon. LLD: New Brunswick, 1976; Calgary, 1984; Alberta, 1985; King's Coll., Halifax, 1994; Concordia, 1994; St Thomas, Minn, 1999; York, 2009; Carleton, 2010; UBC, 2012; McGill 2015. Alberta Order of Excellence, 1983. *Publications*: How We Lead: Canada in a century of change, 2013. *Recreations*: riding, reading, walking, film going.

**CLARK, Prof. Christopher David,** PhD; FRGS; Sorby Professor of Geoscience, University of Sheffield, since 2009; *b* Hampton Court, 3 July 1963; *s* of late Robin Cresswell Howes and of Pauline Ruby Howes (*née* Russell, now Clark) and step *s* of Terence Charles Clark; *m* 2000, Margaret Rose Stuckey; one *d*. *Educ*: Otford Primary Sch.; Wildernesse Sch.; University Coll. of Wales, Aberystwyth (BSc 1985); Univ. of Edinburgh (PhD 1990). Mountaineer (made first ascent of Shimshall Whitehorn, Karakorum, 1986). University of Sheffield: Lectr in Remote Sensing, 1990–97; Sen. Lectr, 1998–2002; Reader, 2002–04; Prof., 2004–09. Mem., Editl Adv. Bd, Earth Surface Processes and Landforms, 2008–. Member: Peer Rev. Coll., NERC, 2006–10; Assessment Bd, Res. Council of Norway, 2010–11; Geog. sub-panel, REF 2014 and REF 2021, 2011–. Mem. Council, Remote Sensing Soc., 1993–96. Mem., Nat. Sheep Assoc. FRGS 2009. *Publications*: (jtly) Remote Sensing Handbook for Tropical Coastal Management, 2000; contrib. articles to learned jls on glacial geomorphol., glaciol. and Quaternary sci., and also on remote sensing of corals, mangroves, snow and archaeol. *Recreations*: mountaineering (regrettably, now armchair), white water kayaking, Landrover trialling, and sheep farming with the ambition to make enough money to pay for the fences to keep them in. *Address*: Brough Lea Farm, Brough, Hope Valley, Derbys S33 9HG. *T*: (01433) 623646. *E*: c.clark@sheffield.ac.uk. *Clubs*: Alpine; XABA Mountaineering.

**CLARK, His Honour Christopher Harvey;** QC 1989; a Circuit Judge, 2005–16; Resident Judge, Truro Combined Court, 2012–16; *b* 20 Dec. 1946; *s* of Harvey Frederick Beckford Clark and Winifred Julia Clark; *m* 1st, 1972, Gillian Elizabeth Ann Mullen (marr. diss. 2004); one *s* two *d*; 2nd, 2004, Mrs Wendy Gay Keith. *Educ*: Taunton's Grammar Sch., Southampton; The Queen's Coll., Oxford (BA 1968; MA 1987). Called to the Bar, Gray's Inn, 1969, Bencher, 2000–11; Mem., Western Circuit, 1969–2005; an Asst Recorder, 1982–86; a Recorder, 1986–2005. Head of Pump Court Chambers, 2001–05. Hon. Recorder, City of Truro, 2015–16. President: Dorset Magistrates' Assoc., 2007–11; City of Winchester Trust, 2007–11. Chancellor: dio. of Winchester, 1993–2016; dio. of Portsmouth, 2003–14 (Dep. Chancellor, 1994–2003); Deputy Chancellor: dio. of Chichester, 1995–2006; dio. of Salisbury, 1997–2007. Lay Reader, C of E, 1998–2017. Pres., Stockbridge Amateur Dramatic Soc., 2007–11 (Chm., 1977–2007). Cornwall Co. Organiser, Nat. Garden Scheme, 2017–. *Recreations*: golf, cricket, gardening, walking, fly-fishing, exploring Cornwall, visiting old churches, enjoying his grandchildren's company, acting in pantomime. *Club*: Flyfishers'.

**CLARK, Sir Christopher Munro,** Kt 2015; PhD; FBA 2010; Regius Professor of History, University of Cambridge, since 2014; Fellow and Director of Studies, St Catharine's College, Cambridge, since 2007; *b* Sydney, Australia, 14 March 1960; *m* 1993, Dr Nina Lübbren; two *s*. *Educ*: Sydney Grammar Sch.; Sydney Univ.; Freie Univ., Berlin; Univ. of Cambridge (PhD 1992). Formerly Reader in European History, then Prof. of Modern European History, 2007–14, Univ. of Cambridge. FAHA 2008. Officer's Cross, Order of Merit (Germany), 2011. *Publications*: The Politics of Conversion: missionary protestantism and the Jews in Prussia, 1728–1947, 1995; (contrib.) The Napoleonic Legacy, 2000; Kaiser Wilhelm II: a life in power, 2000; (contrib) Confessional Conflict in Nineteenth-Century Germany, 2001; (ed with W. Kaiser) Culture Wars: secular-Catholic conflict in nineteenth century Europe, 2004; Iron Kingdom: the rise and downfall of Prussia, 1600–1947, 2006 (Wolfson Hist. Prize, 2007; Deutscher Historikerpreis, 2010); The Sleepwalkers: how Europe went to war in 1914, 2012; Time and Power, 2019; contribs to jls incl. Past & Present, Jl Modern Hist., Comparativ, Correspondence. *Address*: St Catharine's College, Trumpington Street, Cambridge CB2 1RL.

**CLARK, Christopher Richard Nigel,** CBE 2011; Chairman, JSC Severstal, 2007–15; *b* 29 Jan. 1942; *s* of late Rev. Vivian George Clark and Aileen Myfanwy Clark (*née* Thompson); *m* 1964, Catherine Ann Mather; two *s* one *d* (and one *s* decd). *Educ*: Marlborough Coll.; Trinity Coll., Cambridge; Brunel Univ. MIMMM (MIM 1967). Johnson Matthey plc, 1962–2004: Mem. Bd, 1990–2004; Chief Operating Officer, 1996–98; Chief Exec., 1998–2004. Chairman: Associated British Ports Holdings Ltd, 2004–11; Urenco Ltd, 2006–11; RusPetro, 2011–13; non-executive Director: Trinity Holdings (Dennis), 1993–98; FKI plc, 2000–06; Rexam plc, 2003–06 (Dep. Chm., 2003–06); Mem., Adv. Bd, Citicorp Venture Capital, 2009–16. Governor: Harris Acad. Merton, 2017–; Harris Acad. Morden, 2017–. Student of history, Open Univ., 2015–19. MInstD 1990; CCMI 2001. Centenary Medal, SCI, 2002. *Recreations*: opera, ballet, watching Rugby and cricket. *Address*: 30 Marryat Road, SW19 5BD. *T*: (020) 8946 5887. *E*: christopher.clark64@gmail.com. *Club*: Jesters.

**CLARK, Claire Madeleine Ridgway,** MBE 2011; patisserie consultant; Owner, Claire Clark Ltd, since 2010; *b* Swindon, 1964; *d* of Rev. David Ridgway Hemsley and Grace Ridgway Hemsley; *m* Stephen Peter Clark (marr. diss.). *Educ*: Waddesdon C of E Secondary Sch.; Aylesbury Coll. of Further Educn (City & Guilds); Thames Valley Univ. (City & Guilds 706/3 pt 1 and pt 2). Commis Chef, Randolph Hotel, Oxford, 1982–84; Commis Pastry Chef: Ritz Hotel, London, 1984–85; Intercontinental Hotel, London, 1985–88; Head Pastry Chef: Sutherlands Restaurant, London, 1988–90; Portman Intercontinental Hotel, London, 1990–93; teaching and compiling pastry progs, Le Cordon Bleu, London, 1993–95; Pastry Consultant, H of C, 1995–97; Head Pastry Chef: Bluebird Restaurant, London, 1995–97; Claridge's Hotel, London, 1997–2000; Dir, Claire Clark Ltd, pastry mgt co. and consultancy, 2000–01; Head Pastry Chef: Hilton Metropole Hotel, London, 2001–03; Wolseley, London, 2003–05; French Laundry, Calif, 2005–09; Pastry Consultant, Sandy Lane Hotel, Barbados, 2009–10; pop-up shop, Harvey Nicholls, London, 2010. Examr for Advanced Pastry, City & Guilds, 1995. Master of Culinary Arts (Meilleur Ouvrier de GB 1996). *Publications*: Indulge, 2007; 80 Cakes from Around the World, 2014. *E*: claire@claire-clark.com.

**CLARK, Colin James;** MP (C) Gordon, since 2017; Parliamentary Under Secretary of State, Scotland Office, since 2019; a Lord Commissioner of HM Treasury (Government Whip), since 2019; *b* Aberdeen, 20 May 1969; *s* of Robert and Marion Clark; *m* 2005, Philippa Jones; two *s*. *Educ*: Turriff Acad.; Heriot-Watt Univ. (BA Business 1990). Man. Dir and owner, DGM Growers, 1993–2005; owner, R&M Clark Farmers, 2005–; Chm., Nessgro Ltd, 2005–. Mem. (C), Aberdeenshire CC, 2016–17. Contested (C) Gordon, 2015. *Address*: House of Commons, SW1A 0AA. *T*: (020) 7219 1542. *E*: colin.clark.mp@parliament.uk.

**CLARK, Prof. Colin Whitcomb,** PhD; FRS 1997; FRSC 1988; Professor of Mathematics, University of British Columbia, 1969–94, Professor Emeritus, since 1994; *b* 18 June 1931; *s* of George Savage Clark and Irene (Stewart) Clark; *m* 1955, Janet Arlene Davidson; one *s* two *d*. *Educ*: Univ. of BC (BA 1953); Univ. of Washington (PhD 1958). Instructor, Univ. of Calif, Berkeley, 1958–60; Asst Prof., then Associate Prof. of Maths, Univ. of BC, 1960–69. Regent's Lectr in Maths, Univ. of Calif, Davis, 1986; Visiting Professor: of Ecology and Systematics, Cornell Univ., 1987; of Ecology and Evolutionary Biol., Princeton Univ., 1997. Hon. DSc Victoria, BC, 2000. *Publications*: Mathematical Bioeconomics, 1976, 3rd edn 2010; Bioeconomic Modelling and Fisheries Management, 1985; (with M. Mangel) Dynamic Modelling in Behavioral Ecology, 1988; (with M. Mangel) Dynamic State Variable Models in Ecology, 2000; The Worldwide Crisis in Fisheries, 2007; Math Overboard! (Basic Math for Adults), Pt 1, 2012, Pt 2, 2013. *Recreations*: natural history, ski-ing, hiking. *Address*: Institute of Applied Mathematics, University of British Columbia, Vancouver, BC V6T 1Z2, Canada. *T*: (604) 2745379.

**CLARK, Dr Cynthia Zang Facer;** Executive Director, Council of Professional Associations on Federal Statistics, since 2018; Administrator, National Agricultural Statistics Service, US Department of Agriculture, 2008–14; *b* 1 April 1942; *d* of Joseph Elmer Facer and Flora Burnell Zang Facer (*née* Zang); *m* 1963, Glenn Willet Clark; three *s* three *d*. *Educ*: Mills Coll. (BA Maths 1963); Univ. of Denver (MA Maths 1964); Iowa State Univ. (MS 1974; PhD Stats 1977). Mathematical Statistician, Statistical Res. Div., US Census Bureau, 1977–79; Econ. Statistician, Statistical Policy Office, Office of Mgt and Budget, 1979–83; Asst Div. Chief for Res. and Methodology, Agric. Div., US Census Bureau, 1983–90; Dir, Survey Methods Div., Nat. Agricl Stats Service, US Dept of Agriculture, 1990–96; Associate Dir for Methodology and Standards, Census Bureau, US Dept of Commerce, 1996–2004; Exec. Dir for Methodology, ONS, 2004–07; internat. statistical consultant, 2007–08, 2015–. Member: Statistics Canada Adv. Cttee on Statistical Methods, 2016–; NAS Cttee on Nat. Statistics Panel on Re-engineering Census Bureau Annual Econ. Surveys, 2015–18; Adv. Cttee on Lab. for Interdisciplinary Statistical Analysis 2020, 2015–; Co-Chair, Amer. Statistical Assoc./Amer. Assoc. of Public Opinion Res. Task Force on Survey Climate, 2016–. Member, Board: Council of Professional Assocs for Federal Statistics, 2015–; Council of Food and Agricl Resource Econs, 2017–. Vice-Pres., Internat. Assoc. of Survey Statisticians, 2017–. Fellow, Amer. Statistical Assoc., 1997; FSS 2005. Member: Amer. Assoc. of Public Opinion Res., 1994; (elected) ISI, 1997– (Chair, Cttee on Women in Statistics, 2003–11); Friends of Agricl Statistics and Analysis, 2015–. Meritorious Presidential Rank Award, 2011; Dist. Alumnae Award, Iowa State Univ., 2014. *Publications*: (ed jtly) Computer Assisted Survey Information Collection, 1998; Training for the Future: addressing tomorrow's survey tasks, 1998; (jtly) Understanding American Agriculture: challenges for the Agricultural Resource Management Survey, 2007; (with F. Nolan) Quality Improvement in the Office for National Statistics, 2007; (contrib.) Leadership and Women in Statistics, 2016. *Recreations*: genealogy, ice-skating, travel, cultural events, family activities with spouse, siblings, 6 children and 20 grandchildren, Church service. *Address*: 6628 McLean Court, McLean, VA 22101, USA. *T*: (703) 6638746. *E*: czfclark@cox.net.

**CLARK, David Beatson,** CBE 1986; TD 1966; DL; Chairman, Rotherham District Health Authority, 1993–96 (Member, 1985–96); *b* 5 May 1933; *s* of late Alec Wilson Clark, OBE, JP, DSc(Tech) and Phyllis Mary Clark; *m* 1959, Ann Morgan Mudford; two *s* one *d*. *Educ*: Wrekin College; Keele Univ. (BA Hons Physics and Econs). Beatson Clark: joined 1958; Managing Dir, 1971; Chm. and Managing Dir, 1979; Exec. Chm., 1984–88. Non-executive Director: Royal Bank of Scotland, 1988–91; Yorkshire Electricity Gp, 1990–94 (Mem., Yorkshire Electricity Bd, 1980–90); Rotherham TEC, 1990–92. President: Rotherham Chamber of Commerce, 1975–76; Sheffield Br., BIM, 1983–86; Glass Manufacturers' Fedn, 1982–83; Mem. Council, Univ. of Sheffield, 1984–2000. Chm., Rotherham Hospice Trust, 2007–10. Liveryman, Glass Sellers' Co., 1967; Freeman, Cutlers' Co. in Hallamshire, 1980. DL S Yorks, 1990; High Sheriff, S Yorks, 1992. Hon. Fellow, Sheffield City Polytechnic, 1988. *Address*: 19 Beech Avenue, Rotherham, South Yorks S65 3HN.

**CLARK, Prof. David Millar,** CBE 2013; DPhil; FMedSci; FBA 2003; FBPsS, FAcSS; Professor of Experimental Psychology, University of Oxford, since 2011; Fellow, Magdalen College, Oxford, since 2011; *b* 20 Aug. 1954; *s* of Herbert Clark and Doris Alice Millar; *m* 1994, Prof. Anke Ehlers, *qv*; two *s*. *Educ*: Christ's Hosp.; Oxford Univ. (MA Exptl Psychol.; DPhil); London Univ. (MPhil Clinical Psychol.). Lectr, 1983–93, Prof., 1996–2000, Dept of Psychiatry, Univ. of Oxford; Wellcome Principal Res. Fellow, 1993–2000; Fellow, University Coll., Oxford, 1987–2000; Prof. of Psychology, Inst. of Psychiatry, 2000–11; Head, Dept of Psychology, 2000–06, KCL. President: British Assoc. of Behavioural and Cognitive Psychotherapies, 1992–93; Internat. Assoc. of Cognitive Psychotherapy, 1992–95. Nat. Clinical and Informatics Advr, Government's Improving Access to Psychological Therapies Initiative, 2008–. FMedSci 1999; FBPsS 2009; FAcSS 2016. Hon. DSc: LSE, 2011; Roehampton, 2013. Distinguished Scientist Award: for the Application of Psychol., Amer. Psychol. Soc., 2010; Soc. for Sci. in Clin. Psychol., 2016; Lifetime Achievement Award: BPsS, 2014; Amer. Assoc. of Behavioral and Cognitive Therapies, 2015. *Publications*: Cognitive Behaviour Therapy for Psychiatric Problems, 1989; Science and Practice of Cognitive Behaviour Therapy, 1996; (with Richard Layard) Thrive, 2014; contrib. numerous articles on causes and treatment of anxiety disorders to learned jls. *Recreations*: travel, wine, modern art. *Address*: Oxford Centre for Anxiety Disorders and Trauma, Department of Experimental Psychology, The Old Rectory, Paradise Square, Oxford OX1 1TW.

**CLARK, Prof. (David) Stuart (Thorburn),** PhD; FBA 2000; FRHistS; FLSW; Professor of Early Modern History, Swansea University (formerly University of Wales, Swansea), 1998–2008, now Emeritus; *b* 22 Nov. 1942; *m* 1965, Janet Stephanie Gaze; one *s* two *d*. *Educ*: UC Swansea (BA 1964); Trinity Hall, Cambridge (PhD 1971). Lectr, 1967–95, Sen. Lectr, 1995–98, Dept of History, UC Swansea, subseq. Univ. of Wales, Swansea. Fellow: IAS, Princeton, 1988–89; Nat. Humanities Centre, NC, 1999–2000; British Acad. Reader, 1998–2000; Vis. Prof., Univ. of Richmond, Va, 2003; Vis. Fellow, 2004–05, Vis. Prof., 2008–09, Princeton Univ. FRHistS 1985; FLSW 2010. *Publications*: Thinking with Demons: the idea of witchcraft in early modern Europe, 1997; (ed) Annales School: critical assessments in history, 4 vols, 1999; (ed) The Athlone History of Witchcraft and Magic in Europe, 6 vols, 1999–2002; (ed) Languages of Witchcraft: narrative, ideology and meaning in early modern culture, 2001; Vanities of the Eye: vision in early modern European culture, 2007. *Recreations*: music, Arsenal FC. *Address*: 44 Manselfield Road, Murton, Swansea SA3 3AR.

**CLARK, His Honour Denis;** a Circuit Judge, 1988–2007; *b* 2 Aug. 1943; twin *s* of John and Mary Clark; *m* 1967, Frances Mary (*née* Corcoran); four *d*. *Educ*: St Anne's RC Primary, Rock Ferry, Birkenhead; St Anselm's Coll., Birkenhead; Sheffield Univ. LLB. Called to the Bar, Inner Temple, 1966; practised Northern Circuit, 1966–88; a Recorder, 1984–88. *Recreations*: medieval history, cricket, theatre.

**CLARK, Derek Roland;** Member (UK Ind) East Midlands, European Parliament, 2004–14; *b* 10 Oct. 1933; *m* 1973, (Rosemary) Jane Purser. *Educ*: Univ. of Bristol (Teaching Cert.); Univ. of Exeter (Dip. Sci.). ACP 1971. Teacher of Sci., Air Balloon Hill Secondary Sch., Bristol, 1954–62; Hd of Sci. Dept, 1962–74, Sen. Master, 1970–74, Cherry Orchard Sch., Northampton; Sen. Hd of House, Lings Upper Sch., Northampton, 1974–85;

Teacher of Sci., Falcon Manor Sch., Northants, 1985–93. Chm., Physics Subject Panel, CSE, E Midlands, 1970–76. UK Independence Party: Chm., Northants Br., 1995–2004; Chm., E Midlands Regl Cttee, 1996–2003 and 2008–12; Mem., NEC, 2001–04; Party Sec., 2002–04.

**CLARK, Prof. (Edith) Gillian**, DPhil; FBA 2012; Professor of Ancient History, University of Bristol, 2000–10, now Emerita; *b* Denbigh, N Wales, 30 Dec. 1946; *d* of late Prof. John Callan James Metford and Edith Metford (*née* Donald); *m* 1972, Stephen R. L. Clark; one *s* two *d*. *Educ:* Clifton High Sch., Bristol; Somerville Coll., Oxford (MA; DPhil 1973). Lectr in Ancient Hist., Univ. of Leicester, 1970–71; Mary Ewart Jun. Res. Fellow, Somerville Coll., Oxford, 1972–74; Lectr in Classics, 1989–95, Sen. Lectr, 1995–2000, Univ. of Liverpool. Part-time posts: Tutor in Moral Philosophy and in NT Studies, Univ. of Glasgow, and in Classical Civilisation, Open Univ. in Scotland, 1980–83; Tutor in Ancient Hist., St Andrews Univ., 1981–82; Tutor, Dept of Greek, 1983–86, Hon. Lectr in Greek and Ancient Hist., 1986–89, Univ. of Liverpool; Lectr in Ecclesiastical Hist., Manchester Univ., 1986–89. Chair, Council of Univ. Classical Depts, 2001–03. Convenor, AHRC Res. Panel 1, 2002–06. Member, Advisory Council: Inst. for Classical Studies, Univ. of London, 2004–09; Inst. for Advanced Studies, Univ. of Durham, 2006–13. Dir, Internat. Conf. on Patristic Studies, Oxford, 2003–; Mem., Internat. Organising Cttee, Fédn Internat. des Assocs d'Etudes Classiques, 2011–14. Mem. Council, Classical Assoc., 1998–2003. Co-editor: Translated Texts for Historians 300–800, 1989–; Oxford Early Christian Studies, 1996–; Member: Editl Cttee, Jl Roman Studies, 2000–11; Editl Adv. Bd, Jl Ecclesiastical Hist., 2009–; Consulting Ed., Jl Late Antiquity, 2009–. *Publications:* Iamblichus: On the Pythagorean Life, 1989; Augustine: Confessions, 1993, rev. edn 2005; Women in Late Antiquity, 1993; Augustine: Confessions 1–4, 1995; Porphyry: On Abstinence from Killing Animals, 2000; Christianity and Roman Society, 2004; Late Antiquity: a very short introduction, 2011; Body and Gender, Soul and Reason in Late Antiquity, 2011; Monica: an ordinary saint, 2015; contrib. papers to jls and ed vols; *festschrift:* Being Christian in Late Antiquity: a festschrift for Gillian Clark, ed C. Harrison, C. Humfress and B. Sandwell, 2014. *Recreations:* walking, music, art and architecture. *Address:* 49 Bellevue Crescent, Bristol BS8 4TF. *E:* gillian.clark@bristol.ac.uk.

**CLARK, Sir Francis (Drake)**, 5th Bt *cr* 1886, of Melville Crescent, Edinburgh; *b* 16 July 1924; *yr s* of Sir Thomas Clark, 3rd Bt and Ellen Mercy (*d* 1987), *d* of late Francis Drake; *S* brother, 1991; *m* 1958, Mary (*d* 1994), *yr d* of late John Alban Andrews, MC, FRCS; one *s*. *Educ:* Edinburgh Acad. RN 1943–46. Dir, Clark Travel Service Ltd, London, 1948–80. *Recreations:* tennis, cricket, music, gardening. *Heir: s* Edward Drake Clark [*b* 27 April 1966; *m* 2000; three *d*].

**CLARK, Frank**, CBE 1991; Chair, Care Inspectorate, Scotland, 2011–13; Member: Healthcare Improvement, Scotland, 2011–13; Scottish Social Services Council, 2011–13; *b* 17 Oct. 1946; *m*; two *d*. MHSM 1974; DipHSM 1974. Clerical Trainee, Bd of Mgt for Royal Cornhill and Associated Hosps, 1965–67; Higher Clerical Officer, Kingseat Hosp., 1967–69; Dep. Hosp. Sec., 1969–70, Hosp. Sec., 1970–71, Canniesburn and Schaw Hosps; Dep. Hosp. Sec., Glasgow Royal Infirmary and Sub-Gp, 1971–74; Administrator, Glasgow Royal Infirmary, 1974–77; Greater Glasgow Health Board Eastern District: Asst Dist Administrator, 1977–81; Dist Gen. Administrator, 1981–83; Hamilton and E Kilbride Unit, Lanarkshire Health Board: Dist Administrator, 1983–84; Dir of Admin. Services, June–Sept. 1984; Sec. to Bd, Lanarks Health Bd, 1984–85; General Manager: Lanarks Health Bd, 1985–96; Lothian Health Bd, May–Dec. 1990; Dir, Strathcarron Hospice, 1996–2006. Vis. Prof., Health Fac., Glasgow Caledonian Univ., 1993–; Hon. Prof., Dept of Nursing and Midwifery, Univ. of Stirling, 1997–. Chairman: W of Scotland Health Service Res. Network, 1990–95; Scottish Health Bd Gen. Managers Gp, 1993–95 (Vice Chm., 1995–96); Lanarks Drugs Action Team, 1995–96; Scottish Hospices Forum, 1998–2001; Central Scotland Health Care NHS Trust, Jan.–March 1999; Forth Valley Primary Care Trust, April–Sept. 1999; Ministerial Task Force, NHS Tayside, 2000; Bd, NHS Forth Valley, 2001–02; Scottish Partnership for Palliative Care, 2003–06; Social Care and Social Work Improvement, Scotland, 2010–11; Vice Chm., Scottish Partnership Agency for Palliative and Cancer Care, 1998–2001; Member: Chief Scientist's Health Service Res. Cttee, 1989–93; Scottish Health Service Adv. Council, 1990–93; Scottish Overseas Health Support Policy Bd, 1990–96; Jt Wkg Gp on Purchasing, 1992–96; Scottish Implementation Gp, Jun. Doctors' and Dentists' Hours of Work, 1992–96; Scottish Council for Postgrad. Med. and Dental Educn, 1993–96; Implementation Gp, Scottish Health Services Mgt Centre, 1993–96; Strategy Gp, R&D Strategy for NHS in Scotland, 1994–96; Ind. Hospices Representative Cttee, Help the Hospices, 1998–2001; Convenor, Scottish Commn for the Regulation of Care, 2006–10. Mem. Bd, New Lanarkshire Ltd, 1992–98. Non-exec. Dir, Voluntary Assoc. for Mental Welfare, 1997–2006. Consultant in Corporate Governance, 2013–. Mem. Editl Adv. Bd, Health Bulletin, 1993–96. Pres., Cumbernauld Rotary Club, 2000–01, 2005–06; Community Services Convenor, Kilsyth Rotary Club, 2018–. Paul Harris Fellow, Rotary Internat., 2011. *Address:* 7 Southerness Drive, Cumbernauld G68 0HU.

**CLARK, Gabrielle Seal;** *see* Hinsliff, G. S.

**CLARK, Gerald Edmondson**, CMG 1989; Chairman, International Nuclear Energy Academy, 2013–14 (Secretary, 2000–12); General Secretary, Energy Strategists Consultancy Ltd, 2001–14; Consultant, Pell Frischmann, since 2006; *b* 26 Dec. 1935; *s* of Edward John Clark and Irene Elizabeth Ada Clark (*née* Edmondson); *m* 1967, Mary Rose Organ; two *d*. *Educ:* Johnston Grammar School, Durham; Jt Services Sch. for Linguists; New College, Oxford (MA). FEI (FInstE 1998). HM Diplomatic Service, 1960–93: Foreign Office, 1960; Hong Kong, 1961; Peking, 1962–63; FO, 1964–68; Moscow, 1968–70; FCO, 1970–73; Head of Chancery, Lisbon, 1973–77; Asst Sec., Cabinet Office, 1977–79; seconded to Barclays Bank International, 1979–81; Commercial Counsellor, Peking, 1981–83; FCO, 1984–87; UK Perm. Rep. to IAEA, UNIDO, and to UN in Vienna, 1987–92; Sen. DS, RCDS, 1993; Sec. Gen., Uranium Inst., 1994–2000. Patron, New London Orchestra, 1993–2006. Chm., London Gp, Henley Alumni Assoc., 1997–2007. *Publications:* articles and speeches on the civil nuclear fuel cycle and related subjects. *Recreations:* conversation with my wife and friends, long distance walking. *Address:* 4 Sanditon, Station Road, Sidmouth, Devon EX10 8LL. *T:* (01395) 488605. *E:* geraldeclark@aol.com. *Club:* Athenæum.

**CLARK, Gillian;** *see* Clark, E. G.

**CLARK, Hon. Glen David;** President, since 2011, and Chief Operating Officer, since 2017, Jim Pattison Group (Executive Vice-President, 2005–11; Member, Board of Directors, since 2009); Premier of British Columbia, 1996–99; *b* 22 Nov. 1957; *m* 1980, Dale Babish; one *s* one *d*. *Educ:* Simon Fraser Univ. (BA Pol Sci. & Canadian Studies); Univ. of BC (MA Community & Regl Planning). MLA (NDP) Vancouver East, 1986–91, Vancouver-Kingsway, 1991–2001. Minister of: Finance and Corporate Relns, 1991–93; Employment and Investment, 1993–96; Leader, NDP, BC, 1996–2001. Pacific NW Manager, 2001, then Vice-Pres., Jim Pattison Sign Gp. Member, Board of Directors: Canfor Corp., 2009–; Westshore Terminals, 2009–. *Recreation:* spending time with family. *Address:* Jim Pattison Group, Suite 1800-1067 West Cordova Street, Vancouver, BC V6C 1C7, Canada.

**CLARK, Prof. Gordon Leslie**, DSc; FBA 2005; Professor and Director, 2013–18, now Emeritus Professor, and Co-Director, Zurich Programme, since 2018, Smith School of Enterprise and the Environment, University of Oxford; Professorial Fellow, St Edmund Hall, Oxford, since 2013; Research Fellow, Institute of Ageing, University of Oxford, since 2001; Sir Louis Matheson Distinguished Visiting Professor, Department of Banking and Finance (formerly Faculty of Business and Economics), Monash University, Melbourne, since 2009; *b* 10 Sept. 1950; *s* of Bryan Clark and Florence Lesley Clark (*née* Cowling); *m* 1972, Shirley Anne Spratling; one *s*. *Educ:* Monash Univ. (BEcon, MA); McMaster Univ. (PhD 1978; Dist. Alumni Award, 1998); MA, DSc 2002, Oxon. Asst Prof., Harvard Univ., 1978–83; Associate Prof., Univ. of Chicago, 1983–85; Prof., Carnegie Mellon Univ., 1985–91; Monash University: Prof., 1989–95; Hd of Dept, 1990–93; Associate Dean, 1991–94; Actg Dean, 1993–94; Dir, Inst. of Ethics and Public Policy, 1991–95; University of Oxford: Halford Mackinder Prof. of Geography, 1995–2012; Chm., Faculty Bd of Anthropology and Geography, 1999–2001; Professorial Fellow: St Peter's Coll., 1995–2012; Saïd Business Sch., 2000–03, 2013–18; Head, Centre for the Envmt (incl. Sch. of Geog. and the Envmt), 2003–08; Sen. Res. Fellow, Harvard Law Sch., 2005–08. Nat. Research Council Fellow, US Nat. Acad. of Sci., 1981–82; Fellow, Lincoln Land Inst., 1981–82. FASSA 1993. Chancellor's Medal, UCSB, 2000. *Publications:* Interregional Migration, National Policy and Social Justice, 1983; (jtly) State Apparatus, 1984; Judges and the Cities, 1985; (jtly) Regional Dynamics, 1986; Unions and Communities Under Siege, 1989; Pensions and Corporate Restructuring in American Industry, 1993; (ed jtly) Multiculturalism, Difference and Postmodernism, 1993; (ed jtly) Management Ethics, 1995; (ed jtly) Asian Newly Industrialised Economies in the Global Economy, 1996; (ed jtly) Accountability and Corruption: public sector ethics, 1997; Pension Fund Capitalism, 2000; (ed jtly) Oxford Handbook of Economic Geography, 2000; European Pensions & Global Finance, 2003; (ed jtly) Pension Security in the 21st Century, 2003; (jtly) Global Competitiveness and Innovation, 2004; (ed jtly) The Oxford Handbook of Pensions and Retirement Income, 2006; (jtly) The Geography of Finance, 2007; (ed jtly) Managing Financial Risk, 2009; (jtly) Saving for Retirement: intention, context and behaviour, 2012; (jtly) Sovereign Wealth Funds: legitimacy, governance and global power, 2013; (jtly) Institutional Investors in Global Markets, 2017; (jtly) New Oxford Handbook of Economic Geography, 2018. *Recreations:* walking, reading, music, holidays. *Address:* Smith School of Enterprise and the Environment, University of Oxford, South Parks, Oxford OX1 3QY. *Club:* Athenæum.

**CLARK, Prof. Graeme Milbourne**, AC 2004 (AO); PhD; FAA, FRS 2004; Laureate Professor Emeritus, since 2006, Adjunct Professor of Electrical Engineering, since 2014, Member, Graeme Clark Institute for Biomedical Engineering, since 2017 and Professorial Fellow, School of Engineering, since 2018, University of Melbourne; Otolaryngologist Emeritus, Eye and Ear Hospital, Melbourne since 2007; *b* 16 Aug. 1935; *s* of Colin and Dorothy Clark; *m* 1961, Margaret Burtenshaw; one *s* four *d*. *Educ:* Univ. of Sydney (MB BS Hons 1957; MS 1968; PhD 1969). FRCSE 1961; FRCS 1962 (Hon. FRCS 2004); FRACS 1966. University of Melbourne: Foundn Prof. of Otolaryngology and Chm., 1970–2004; Hd and Founder, Cochlear Implant Prog., 1970–2004; Laureate Prof., 1999–2004; Laureate Professorial Fellow, 2004; Founder and Dir, Bionic Ear Inst., Melbourne, 1984–2005, Dir Emeritus, 2006–; Dist. Researcher, ICT 4 Life Scis in Electl and Electronic Engrg, 2012–14; Hd and Founder, Cochlear Implant Clinic, Royal Victoria Eye and Ear Hosp., 1985–2004; Principal Scientist, St Vincent's Hosp., Melbourne, 2006–09; Adjunct Prof., Univ. of Wollongong, 2006–12; Dist. Prof., La Trobe Univ., 2008–12. Leader, Bionics Prog., Aust. Res. Council Centre of Excellence for Electromaterials Sci., 2005–12. Director: Human Communication Res. Centre, Aust. Res. Council, 1988–96; Co-op. Res. Centre for Cochlear Implant, Speech and Hearing Res., Melbourne, 1992–98. Mem., Adv. Council for Children with Impaired Hearing, 1982–; Exec. Mem., Deafness Foundn of Victoria, 1973–91. Mem., 2008–, and Principal Scientist, Graeme Clark Foundn (Chm., 2008). Life Mem., Aust. Soc. of Otolaryngol. Head and Neck Surgery, 2016. FAA 1998; FTSE 1998. Hon. FRSocMed 2003. Hon. MD: Medizinische Hochschule, Hannover, 1988; Sydney, 1989; Hon. DSc Wollongong, 2002; Hon. DEng Chung Yuan Christian Univ., Taiwan, 2003; Hon. LLD Monash, 2004; DUniv Zargoza, 2010; Hon. Dr Health Scis, Univ. of Technol., Sydney, 2013. Ian Wark Medal, Aust. Acad. of Sci., 2006; Zülch Prize, Max Planck Soc., 2007; Lister Medal, RCS, 2010; Florey Medal, Aust. Inst. of Policy and Sci. and Commonwealth Serum Labs, 2011; Zotterman Medal, Nobel Inst. for Neurophysiol., 2011; Lasker-DeBakey Clinical Med. Res. Award, Lasker Foundn, 2013; Fritz J. and Dolores H. Russ Prize, NAE and Ohio Univ., 2015; Shambaugh Prize, CORLAS, 2018. Asst Ed., Jl of Otolaryngol Soc. of Aust., 1973–80; Mem., Editl Bd, Cochlear Implants Internat., 2007–. *Publications:* Sounds from Silence, 2000; Cochlear Implants: fundamentals and applications, 2003; 52 book chapters, more than 420 refereed contribs to scientific jls, 1 monograph and 5 edited books and jl supplements. *Recreations:* surfing, science and theology, bush walking. *Address:* Graeme Clark Institute for Biomedical Engineering, Level 1, Building 261, University of Melbourne, 203 Bouverie Street, Carlton, Vic 3053, Australia. *E:* gclark@unimelb.edu.au. *Club:* Melbourne (Melbourne).

**CLARK, Greg**, CBE 2015; FAcSS; global advisor on cities; *b* Wimbledon, London, 13 April 1962; *s* of Paul Clark and Clare Houlihan; *né* Gregory Adrian Clark; changed name to Greg Clark by deed poll, 2009; *m* 1997, Julia Franks; two *s*. *Educ:* Wimbledon Coll.; Homerton Coll., Cambridge (BEd 1986); Columbia Univ.; London Sch. of Econs and Political Sci. Man. Dir, Econ. Develt, Gtr London Enterprise, 1995–2000; Exec. Dir, Strategy and Communications, London Develt Agency, 2000–04; Lead Advr, Office of Dep. Prime Minister, 2004–10. Chm., The Business of Cities Gp, 2010–. Chair, OECD Forum of Cities and Regions, 1998–2008. Member, Board: TfL, 2016– (Chm., Investment and Progs Cttee, 2016–); London Econ. Action Partnership, 2017–. Sen. Fellow, Urban Land Inst., 2007–; Global Fellow: Metropolitan Prog. and Global Cities Initiative, Brookings Instn, Washington, DC, 2010–; LSE, 2015. Hon. Prof., UCL, 2014–. Chm., Jones Lang LaSalle Cities Res. Centre, 2013–. Harkness Fellow, 1995. FAcSS 2017; FRSA. Freeman, City of London, 2017. Hon. Ambassador, City of Brisbane, 2010. John Shield's Prize, City of Barcelona, 2010. *Publications:* (ed jtly) Investment Strategies and Financial Tools for Local Development, 2007; Local Development Benefits from Staging Global Events, 2008; Recession, Recovery and Reinvestment: the role of economic leadership in a global crisis, 2008; (jtly) Organising Local Economic Development: the role of development agencies and companies, 2010; (with Tim Moonen) Delivering Local Development: new growth and investment strategies, 2013; The Making of a World City: London 1991 to 2021, 2014; (jtly) Local Economic Leadership, 2015; (with Tim Moonen) World Cities and Nations States, 2016; The Short History of Global Cities, 2016; The Business of Cities, 2017; more than 100 articles and reports for global organisations incl. OECD, Brookings Instn, World Bank, Urban Land Inst. *Recreations:* tennis, poetry, kite flying. *Address:* c/o UCL City Leadership Laboratory, STEaPP, University College London, Boston House, 36–38 Fitzroy Square, 2nd Floor, W1T 6EY. *E:* gregclark@thebusinessofcities.com, g.clark@ucl.ac.uk. *Club:* Arsenal Football.

**CLARK, Gregor Munro**, CB 2006; Parliamentary Counsel to the Scottish Law Commission, 1995–2000 and since 2006; *b* 18 April 1946; *s* of late Ian Munro Clark and Norah Isobel Joss; *m* 1st, 1974, Jane Maralyn Palmer (*d* 1999); one *s* two *d*; 2nd, 2000,

Alexandra Plumtree (née Miller). *Educ:* Queen's Park Senior Secondary Sch., Glasgow; St Andrews Univ. (LLB Hons). Admitted Faculty of Advocates, 1972; entered Lord Advocate's Dept, London, 1974; Asst Parly Draftsman, then Dep. Parly Draftsman, 1974–79; Asst Legal Sec. to Lord Advocate, and Scottish Parly Counsel, 1979–99; Scottish Exec., 1999–2002 and 2004–06; Scottish Parly Counsel (UK), Scotland Office, 2002–04. *Recreations:* piano, opera, Scandinavian languages and literature. *Address:* 18 Rocheid Park, Inverleith, Edinburgh EH4 1RU. *T:* (0131) 315 4634. *Club:* New (Edinburgh).

**CLARK, Rt Hon. Greg(ory David);** PC 2010; PhD; MP for Tunbridge Wells, since 2005 (C, 2005–19; Ind, since 2019); *b* 28 Aug. 1967; *s* of John and Patricia Clark; *m* 1999, Helen Fillingham; one *s* two *d*. *Educ:* St Peter's Comprehensive Sch., S Bank, Middlesbrough; Magdalene Coll., Cambridge (MA Econs); LSE (PhD 1992). Consultant, Boston Consulting Gp, 1991–94; res. and teaching, LSE and Open Univ. Business Sch., 1994–96; Special Advr to Sec. of State for Trade and Industry, 1996–97; Chief Advr, 1997–99, Controller, 1999–2001, Commercial Policy, BBC; Dir of Policy, 2001–03, of Policy and Res., 2003–05, Cons. Party. Shadow Minister: for Charities, Social Enterprise and Volunteering, 2006–08; for Cabinet Office, 2007–08; Shadow Energy and Climate Change Sec., 2008–10; Minister of State: DCLG, 2010–12; BIS, 2011–12; Financial Sec., HM Treasury, 2012–13; Minister of State, Cabinet Office, 2013–15; Minister of State (Minister for Univs and Sci.), BIS, 2014–15; Sec. of State for Communities and Local Govt, 2015–16; Sec. of State for Business, Energy and Industrial Strategy, 2016–19. Mem. (C) Westminster CC, 2002–05 (Cabinet Mem., 2003–05). Vis. Fellow, Nuffield Coll., Oxford, 2007–15 (Hon. Fellow, 2017). *Address:* House of Commons, SW1A 0AA.

**CLARK, Guy Wyndham Nial Hamilton,** CVO 2018; Lord-Lieutenant, Renfrewshire, 2007–19 (Vice Lord-Lieutenant, 2002–07); *b* 28 March 1944; *s* of late Capt. George Hubert Wyndham Clark and Lavinia Mariquita Smith (née Shaw Stewart); *m* 1967, Brighid Lovell Greene; two *s* one *d*. *Educ:* Eton Coll.; Mons Officer Cadet Sch. Commnd Coldstream Guards, 1962–67; Investment Manager, Murray Johnstone, 1973–77; Partner, R. C. Greig & Co. (Glasgow), 1977–86; Dir, Greig, Middleton & Co. Ltd, 1986–97; Managing Director: Murray Johnstone Private Investors Ltd, 1997–2001; Aberdeen Private Investors Ltd, 2001–06; Sen. Divl Dir, Bell Lawrie, 2006–08. Mem., Internat. Stock Exchange, 1983; MSI 1992, FCSI (FSI 2005). Mem. Exec. Cttee, Erskine Hosp. for Ex Servicemen, 1981–97. Vice Pres., W Lowland Bn Army Cadet Force League, 2007–; Pres., Lowland Reserve Forces and Cadets Assoc., 2014–. Pres., E Renfrewshire and Inverclyde Br., SSAFA (formerly SSAFA Forces Help) Renfrewshire, 2007–; Patron, Accord Hospice, 2007–; Hon. Patron, Incorporated Glasgow Renfrewshire Soc., 2007–; Hon. Pres., St Columba's Sch., 2008–. Inverclyde: JP 1981–2007; DL 1987–2007. Vice Chm., JP Adv. Cttee for Inverclyde, 1990–2003. *Recreations:* country sports, gardening. *Address:* (home) Braeton House, Inverkip, Renfrewshire PA16 0DU. *T:* (01475) 520619, *Fax:* (01475) 521030. *E:* g.clark282@btinternet.com. *Clubs:* Turf, MCC; Western (Glasgow).

**CLARK, Rt Hon. Helen Elizabeth,** ONZ 2010; PC 1990; Commissioner, Global Commission on the Economy and Climate; Prime Minister of New Zealand, 1999–2008; *b* 26 Feb. 1950; *d* of George and Margaret Clark; *m* 1981, Dr Peter Byard Davis. *Educ:* Epsom Girls' Grammar School; Auckland Univ. (BA 1971; MA Hons 1974). Junior Lectr in Political Studies, Auckland Univ., 1973–75; UGC Post Graduate Scholar, 1976; Lectr, Political Studies Dept, Auckland Univ., 1977–81. MP (Lab): Mount Albert, NZ, 1981–96 and 1999–2009; Owairaka, 1996–99. Minister: of Housing, of Conservation, 1987–89; of Health, of Labour, 1989–90; Dep. Prime Minister, 1989–90; Dep. Leader of the Opposition, 1990–93, Leader, 1993–99; Minister of Arts, Culture and Heritage, 1999–2008; Minister in Charge of Security Intelligence Service and Govt Commns Security Bureau, 1999–2008; Minister for Ministerial Services, 1999–2008; Administrator, UNDP, 2009–17. *Publications:* Women, Equality, Power: selected speeches from a life of leadership, 2018. *Recreations:* theatre, opera, ballet, film music, ski-ing, trekking, reading.

**CLARK, Helen Rosemary;** writer, since 2005; policy adviser and consultant specialising in climate change and health, since 2007; educational examiner and assessor, since 2009; associate consultant on youth, 2010; Associate Director, Royal Public Affairs, since 2013; *b* 23 Dec. 1954; *d* of George Henry Dyche and Phyllis May Dyche (née James); *m* (marr. diss.); two *c*; *m* 2001, Alan Clark. *Educ:* Spondon Park Grammar Sch.; Bristol Univ. (BA Hons Eng Lit. 1976; MA Medieval Lit. 1978; PGCE 1979). English Teacher, 1979–97. Examr, English Lit. and Lang., London, Cambridge, Southern and Northern Exam. Bds, 1985–97. MP (Lab) Peterborough, 1997–2005; contested (Lab) same seat, 2005. Lead author, 9 reports for All-Party Gp on A Fit and Healthy Childhood, 2014–. Assessor, scrutineer, examiner and nat. trainer, OCR Exam. Bd, 2007–. Dir, Heritage Lottery Fund Proj. Unexamined Lives, 2011–17. Associate Ed., New Jurist mag., 2017–. *Publications:* contrib. to various political jls, national newspapers, specialist mags and policy documents; contrib. to jls on health and nutrition, 2016–. *Recreations:* reading novels, political and historical biography, modern films and theatre.

**CLARK, Prof. Ian,** PhD; FBA 1999; FLSW; Professor of International Relations, University of Queensland, 2014–16, Hon. Professor, Sch. of Political Sci. and Internat. Studies, since 2017; *b* 14 March 1949; *m* 1970, Janice (née Cochrane); one *s* one *d*. *Educ:* Glasgow Univ. (MA); Australian National Univ. (PhD 1975). Lectr, 1974–81, Sen. Lectr, 1981–84, Univ. of Western Australia; Fellow, Selwyn Coll., Cambridge, 1985–97, Hon. Fellow, 2000; Dep. Dir, Centre of Internat. Studies, Cambridge, 1993–97; University of Wales, Aberystwyth, later Aberystwyth University: Prof. of Internat. Politics, 1998–2008; E. H. Carr Prof., 2008–14; Emeritus Prof., 2014. Leverhulme Major Res. Fellow, 2002–04; Vis. Fellow, ANU, 2003; Professorial Fellow, ESRC, 2007–10; Vis. Prof., S. Rajaratnam Sch. of Internat. Studies, Singapore, 2014–16. British Academy: Mem. Council, 2001–04; Chair, Political Studies, 2005–08, Posts, 2005–11. Founding FLSW 2010. *Publications:* The Hierarchy of States, 1989; Nuclear Diplomacy and the Special Relationship, 1994; Globalization and Fragmentation: international relations in the twentieth century, 1997; Globalization and International Relations Theory, 1999; The Post-Cold War Order, 2001; Legitimacy in International Society, 2005; International Legitimacy and World Society, 2007; Hegemony in International Society, 2011; The Vulnerable International Society, 2013; Waging War: a new philosophical introduction, 2015. *Recreations:* swimming, cycling, grandfather. *Address:* School of Political Science and International Studies, University of Queensland, St Lucia Campus, Brisbane, Qld 4072, Australia.

**CLARK, Ian Robertson,** CBE 1979; PhD; former Chairman, Clark & Associates Ltd; *b* 18 Jan. 1939; *s* of Alexander Clark and Annie Dundas Watson; *m* 1961, Jean Scott Waddell Lang; one *s* one *d*. *Educ:* Dalziel High Sch., Motherwell; Univ. of Wales Trinity St David (PhD 2010). FCCA, CPFA. Trained with Glasgow Chartered Accountant; served in local govt, 1962–76, this service culminating in the post of Chief Executive, Shetland Islands Council; full-time Mem., BNOC, from 1976 until privatisation in 1982; Jt Man. Dir, Britoil plc, 1982–85; Chm., Ventures Div., Costain Gp, subseq. Urban Enterprises Ltd, 1987–93; former Chm., C & M (Hydraulics) Ltd. Hon. LLD Glasgow, 1979. *Publications:* Reservoir of Power, 1980; contribs to professional and religious periodicals. *Recreations:* theology, general reading, walking. *Address:* Bellfield House, High Askomil, Campbeltown, Argyll PA28 6EN. *T:* (01586) 553905.

**CLARK, James Frame;** HM Diplomatic Service, retired; Managing Director, Clear Coaching & Consulting Ltd, since 2007; *b* 12 March 1963; *s* of James F. Clark and Anne Clark (née Wilson); partner, Anthony J. Stewart. *Educ:* Edinburgh Univ. (BSc Hons Geog.). Teacher, W Berlin, 1985–87; entered FCO, 1988; Mexico and Central America Dept, 1988–89; Arabic lang. trng, 1989; Cairo, 1990; ME Dept, FCO, 1990–91; UK Rep., Brussels, 1991–93; First Secretary: Econ. Relns Dept, FCO, 1994–95; Press Office, FCO, 1995–97; on loan to German Foreign Min., Bonn, 1997–98; EU, Bonn, 1998–99; Hd, Conf. and Visits Gp, FCO, 1999–2003; Commercial Dir, FCO Services, 2003–04; Ambassador to Luxembourg, 2004–07; Consul Gen., Chicago, 2007–10. Dir, UK Internat. Coach Fedn, 2012–13. *Recreations:* friends, food, fitness, reading, writing, travel.

**CLARK, Dame Jill M.;** *see* Macleod Clark.

**CLARK, Rt Hon. Joe;** *see* Clark, Rt Hon. C. J.

**CLARK, John Hunter Somerville,** OBE 2016; Chairman, John Clark Motor Group, since 2015; *b* Edinburgh, 8 July 1947; *s* of Thomas Somerville and Jessie Clark; *m* 2014, Emma-Jane Gilbart-Smith; one *s* one *d*; one *s* one *d* by a previous marriage. *Educ:* Melville Coll., Edinburgh. Partner, Lothian Sports Cars, 1970–77; Founder, John Clark Motor Gp, 1977; Man. Dir, John Clark Hldgs Ltd, 1977–2015. Dir, Historic Grand Prix Assoc., 2015–. FIMI 2000. *Recreations:* historic motor sport, golf, outdoor pursuits. *Address:* Falfield House, Peat Inn, Cupar, Fife KY15 5LJ. *T:* (01224) 407407, *Fax:* (01224) 330910. *E:* j-clark@johnclark.co.uk. *Clubs:* Royal Automobile; Royal Northern and University (Aberdeen); Royal Aberdeen Golf, Royal Burgess Golfing Society.

**CLARK, John Mullin;** Director, Mission and Public Affairs, Archbishops' Council, Church of England, 2002–07; *b* 19 April 1946; *s* of James and Margaret Clark; *m* 1975, Jenny Brown; one *s*. *Educ:* St Peter's Coll., Oxford (MA); Inst. of Educn, London Univ. (PGCE 1974); King's Coll., London (MA 1999); Heythrop Coll., Univ. of London (MA Psychol. of Religion 2009). Operation Mobilisation, Iran, 1967–73; Iran Literature Assoc., Tehran, 1976–80; Church Missionary Society: Regl Sec., ME and Pakistan, 1980–86; Communications Sec., 1987–91; Sec., Overseas Bishoprics' Fund, and Partnership Sec., Partnership for World Mission, Bd of Mission, C of E, 1992–2000; Chief Sec. for Mission, Archbishops' Council, C of E, 2000–02. Mem., Anglican Communion Mission Commns, 1989–2005. Chairman: Friends of Dio. of Iran, 1994–; United Soc. for Christian Literature, 1996–2016; Jerusalem and E Mission Trust, 2008–. Anglican Lay Reader, 1974–. *Recreations:* opera, walking, church history, T. E. Lawrence, Iran. *Address:* 32 Weigall Road, Lee, SE12 8HE. *T:* (020) 8852 2741.

**CLARK, Sir John S.;** *see* Stewart-Clark.

**CLARK, Rt Rev. Jonathan;** *see* Croydon, Area Bishop of.

**CLARK, Prof. Jonathan Charles Douglas,** PhD; historian; Hall Distinguished Professor of British History, University of Kansas, 1995–2018; *b* 28 Feb. 1951; *s* of Ronald James Clark and Dorothy Margaret Clark; *m* 1996, Katherine Redwood Penovich. *Educ:* Downing Coll., Cambridge (BA 1972); Corpus Christi Coll., Cambridge (MA 1976); Peterhouse, Cambridge (PhD 1981). Research Fellow: Peterhouse, Cambridge, 1977–81; Leverhulme Trust, 1983; All Souls Coll., Oxford, 1986–95 (Sen. Res. Fellow, 1995). Vis. Prof., Cttee on Social Thought, Univ. of Chicago, 1993; Dist. Vis. Lectr, Univ. of Manitoba, 1999; Vis. Fellow, Forschungszentrum Europäische Aufklärung, Potsdam, 2000; Visiting Professor: Univ. of Northumbria, 2001–03; Oxford Brookes Univ., 2009–13. Initiated Oxford American Inst. (now Rothermere Amer. Inst.), 1990. Gov., Pusey House, Oxford, 1991–98. *Publications:* The Dynamics of Change, 1982; English Society 1688–1832, 1985, 2nd edn, as English Society 1660–1832, 2000; Revolution and Rebellion, 1986; (ed) The Memoirs and Speeches of James, 2nd Earl Waldegrave, 1988; (ed) Ideas and Politics in Modern Britain, 1990; The Language of Liberty 1660–1832, 1994; Samuel Johnson, 1994; (ed) Edmund Burke, Reflections on the Revolution in France, 2001; (ed jtly) Samuel Johnson in Historical Context, 2002; Our Shadowed Present, 2003; (ed) A World by Itself: a history of the British Isles, 2010; (ed jtly) The Politics of Samuel Johnson, 2012; (ed jtly) The Interpretation of Samuel Johnson, 2012; Restoration to Reform: British history 1660–1832, 2014; Thomas Paine: Britain, America and France in the age of enlightenment and revolution, 2018; (ed jtly) British and Irish Diasporas, 2019; articles in learned jls. *Recreation:* more history. *Address:* South Wing, Callaly Castle, Alnwick, Northumberland NE66 4TA. *Club:* Beefsteak.

**CLARK, Sir Jonathan (George),** 5th Bt *cr* 1917, of Dunlambert, City of Belfast; Managing Director, DC Training and Recruitment Solutions, since 2002; *b* 9 Oct. 1947; *o s* of Sir Colin Douglas Clark, 4th Bt and Margaret Coleman Clark (née Spinks); *S* father, 1995; *m* 1971, Susan Joy, *d* of Brig. T. I. G. Gray; one *s* two *d*. *Educ:* Eton. Royal Green Jackets, 1966–78. Various appts within private health care industry, 1978–2001. *Recreations:* horse trials, hunting. *Heir: s* Simon George Gray Clark [*b* 3 Oct. 1975; *m* 2010 Aoife Sisk]. *Address:* Somerset House, Threapwood, Malpas, Cheshire SY14 7AW. *T:* (01948) 770205.

**CLARK, Judy Anne M.;** *see* MacArthur Clark.

**CLARK, Dame June;** *see* Clark, Dame M. J.

**CLARK, Karen;** *see* Nicol, K.

**CLARK, Kathryn Sloan, (Katy);** Political Secretary to Leader of the Opposition, since 2015; *b* 3 July 1967; one *d*. *Educ:* Kyle Acad., Ayr; Univ. of Aberdeen (LLB 1990); Univ. of Edinburgh (DipLP 1991). Admitted solicitor, 1992; in private practice as solicitor, 1992–98; Legal Officer, 1998, Hd of Membership Legal Services, 1999–2005, UNISON. Contested (Lab) Galloway and Upper Nithsdale, 1997. MP (Lab) N Ayrshire and Arran, 2005–15; contested (Lab) same seat, 2015. Member: Scottish Affairs Select Cttee, 2005–10; Procedure Cttee, 2005–10; European Scrutiny Cttee, 2006–10; Envmtl Audit Cttee, 2010–15; Speaker's Panel of Chairmen, 2010–15; BIS Select Cttee, 2010–15; Cttee on Arms Control, 2010–15. Mem., Labour Party, 1985–. Hd, Labour Party Democracy Rev., 2018. Contested (Lab) London, EP, 2019.

**CLARK, Keith;** International General Counsel, Morgan Stanley, 2002–09; *b* 25 Oct. 1944; *s* of Douglas William Clark and Evelyn Lucy (née Longlands); *m* 2001, Helen Paterson; one *s* one *d* by a previous marriage. *Educ:* Chichester High Sch. for Boys; St Catherine's Coll., Oxford (MA Jurisprudence; BCL). Joined Clifford Chance, 1971; Partner, 1976; Sen. Partner, 1993; Chm., 2000–02. Trustee, Pallant House Gall., Chichester, 2007–17. *Publications:* (jtly) Syndicated Lending Practice Documentation, 1993; articles on banking and financial topics. *Recreations:* walking, ballet, theatre, novels.

**CLARK, Malcolm,** CB 1990; Inspector General, Insolvency Service, Department of Trade and Industry, 1984–89, retired; *b* 13 Feb. 1931; *s* of late Percy Clark and Gladys Helena Clark; *m* 1956, Beryl Patricia Dale; two *s*. *Educ:* Wheelwright Grammar Sch., Dewsbury, Yorks. FCCA 1980. Department of Trade and Industry Insolvency Service: Examiner, 1953–62; Sen. Examiner, 1962–66; Asst Official Receiver, Rochester, 1966–70; Official Receiver, Lytham St Annes, 1970–79; Principal Inspector of Official Receivers, 1979–81; Dep. Inspector Gen., 1981–84. *Recreations:* theatre, gardening, reading. *Address:* 67 Evering Avenue, Alderney, Poole BH12 4JF.

**CLARK, Dr Malcolm Brian,** OBE 2001; Chairman, Grant & Cutler, 2000–11; Director, Queen Elizabeth's Foundation for Disabled People, 1980–2001; *b* 17 May 1934; *s of* Herbert Clark and Doris May Clark (*née* Waples); *m* 1st, 1960, Jennifer Anne Thonger (*d* 1985); one *s* one *d*; 2nd, 1988, Lorna Stephanie Killick (marr. diss. 1995); 3rd, 2009, Helen Patricia Farr. *Educ:* Univ. of Birmingham (BSc Chem. Engrg; PhD 1958). Chemical Engineer: Albright & Wilson, 1958–62; A. Boake Roberts, 1962–66; Marketing Manager, Bush Boake Allen, 1966–68; Albright & Wilson: Res. Manager, 1968–70; Personnel Dir, 1970–72; Personnel and Prodn Dir, 1972–74; Man. Dir, Bush Boake Allen, 1975–80. Mem. Council, Grange Centre, 2001–14. *Recreations:* books, walking, theatre, music, wine. *Address:* The Birches, 13 Cleveland Road, Worcester Park, Surrey KT4 7JQ.

**CLARK, Margaret Anita, (Mrs P. D. Walton),** CBE 2015 (OBE 1999); Chairman, Plunkett Foundation, since 2013; Chair: Rural Coalition, since 2016; Rural England CIC Stakeholder Group, since 2016; *b* London, 1947; *d of* Reginald and Maud Clark; *m* 1998, Peter David Walton, *qv*. *Educ:* Trinity Grammar Sch.; Wood Green Sch.; Holborn Coll. of Law, Langs and Commerce. Various appts from Exec. Officer to Dir of Policy, Rural Develt Commn, 1967–99; Countryside Agency: Dir, 1999–2001; Dep. Chief Exec., 2001–06; Actg Chief Exec., 2005; Dep. Chief Exec., Commn for Rural Communities, 2006–07. Mem. Bd, 1998–2008, Chm., 2008–15, Hastoe Housing Assoc. Member: Prince of Wales's Affordable Rural Housing Initiative, 2003–09; Commn for Rural Community Develt and Rural Cttee, Carnegie UK Trust, 2004–10; Rural Affairs Cttee, BBC, 2007–11; Policy Cttee, CPRE, 2008–14 (Mem., Trustee Bd, 2015–). Chair, Wkg Party on Territorial Policy in Rural Areas, OECD, 2000–07. Trustee, Arkleton Trust, 2001–14. Hon. Fellow, Centre for Rural Economy, Univ. of Newcastle upon Tyne. FRSA. *Recreations:* theatre, opera, ballet, cinema, entertaining friends and family, walking the dog, shopping. *Address:* Tolpuddle, Dorchester, Dorset. *Club:* Army and Navy.

**CLARK, Dame (Margaret) June,** DBE 1995; FRCN; FAAN; FLSW; Professor of Community Nursing, University of Wales, Swansea, 1997–2003, now Emeritus; *b* 31 May 1941; *d of* Ernest Harold Hickery and Marion Louise Hickery (*née* Walters); *m* 1966, Roger Michael Geoffrey Clark; one *s* one *d*. *Educ:* Pontywaun Grammar Sch.; University College London (BA Hons Classics 1962); University College Hosp. (SRN 1965); Royal College of Nursing (RHV 1967); Univ. of Reading (MPhil 1972); PhD South Bank Polytechnic 1985. FRCN 1982. Nurse, 1965; health visitor, 1967; clinical nursing appts, combined with teaching and research while bringing up a family; resumed as health visitor, Berks, 1981; Senior Nurse (Research), 1983; Health Authority posts: Special Projects Co-ordinator, Lewisham and N Southwark, 1985–86; Dir, Community Nursing Services, W Lambeth, 1986–88; Chief Nursing Adviser, Harrow, 1988–90; Prof. of Nursing, Middlesex Poly., later Univ., 1990–96. Member: Royal Commn on Long Term Care of the Elderly, 1997–98; Bevan Commn on NHS Wales, 2009–11. Pres., RCN, 1990–94. Mem. Court, Swansea Univ., 1997– (Mem. Council, 2005–17; Hon. Gov., 2018). Council of Europe Fellow, 1981; Churchill Fellow, 1996. Mem., Sigma Theta Tau Internat. the Honor Soc. of Nursing, 1997. Special interests incl. nursing informatics and services for older people. OStJ 2019. FAAN 2010; FLSW 2012. *Publications:* A Family Visitor, 1973; (with R. Hiller) Community Care, 1975; What Do Health Visitors Do?, 1981; (with S. Parsonage) Infant Feeding and Family Nutrition, 1981; (with J. Henderson) Community Health, 1983; (with M. Baly) District Nursing, 1981; (contrib.) Nursing Practice and Health Care, 5th edn 2008; (contrib.) Policy and Politics in Healthcare, 6th edn 2011; Nursing: an exquisite obsession (autobiog.), 2015; contrib. numerous papers to med. and nursing jls. *Recreations:* grandchildren, charity organisations (Age Cymru, St John Ambulance Brigade).

**CLARK, Air Vice-Marshal Martin Adrian,** CB 2016; CEng, FIET; FRAeS; Director, Berryfield Farm Consulting Ltd, since 2016; *b* Hillingdon, 17 Feb. 1961; *s of* David and Frances Clark; *m* 1987, Valerie Hillyard; one *s* one *d*. *Educ:* St George's Sch., Hong Kong; Queen Mary Coll., Univ. of London (BSc (Eng) Electrical and Electronic Engrg 1982); Open Univ. (MBA 1999). CEng 1991; MIET 1991, FIET 2011; FRAeS 2013. Joined RAF, 1979; Jun. Engrg Officer, 55 Sqn, RAF Marham, 1984–85; OC Aircraft Servicing Flight, 1985–87, Aircraft Systems Gp, Nimrod Engrg Develt and Investigation Team, 1987–89, RAF Kinloss; Sen. Engrg Officer, 27 Sqn, RAF Marham, 1989–91; SO to AO Engrg and Supply, HQ Strike Comd, 1991–94; acsc 1994; Harrier Engrg Authy, RAF Wyton, 1994–98; OC Engrg and Supply Wing, RAF Kinloss, 1998–2000; Military Asst 2 to Chief of Defence Logistics, 2000–01; Asst Dir, Prog. Mgt, 2001–05, HQ Defence Logistics Orgn; Gp Capt. Support, HQ 2 Gp, 2005–06; Dep. Team Leader, Nimrod MRA4 Project, Defence Procurement Agency, 2006–07; Head: Air ISTAR Defence Equipment and Support, 2007–11; Tech. Certification, 2011–12, Tech. Dir, 2012–16, Mil. Aviation Authy; Chief Tech. Officer, Defence Safety Authy, 2015–16. President: RAF Ice Hockey Assoc., 2013–17; RBL, Trowbridge, 2015–; Pres., Trowbridge and W Wilts, 2015–, Area Pres., Wales, Midlands and SW, 2018–, RAF Assoc. Trustee, Alabaré, 2015–. Gov., Wilts Coll., 2015– (Chm., 2018–). *Recreations:* family, ski-ing, following Bath Rugby, reading historical novels, theatre, ballet, cycling. *E:* maclark61@icloud.com. *Club:* Royal Air Force.

**CLARK, Martin Charles;** Director, Camden Arts Centre, since 2017; *b* Chelmsford, 15 Jan. 1976; *s of* John and Ann Clark; *m* 2002, Rosie Hill; one *s* one *d*. *Educ:* Sheffield Hallam Univ. (BA Hons Fine Art 1998); Royal Coll. of Art (MA Curating and Commng Art 2001). Record buyer and disc jockey, The Store, Sheffield, 1996–99; Exhibns Curator, and Tutor, Kent Inst. of Art and Design, 2001–05; Curator, Exhibns, Arnolfini, Bristol, 2005–07; Artistic Dir, Tate St Ives, 2007–13; Dir, Bergen Kunsthall, 2013–17; Artistic Dir, Art Sheffield, 2016. *Recreations:* reading magazines, buying books, collecting records, drinking in pubs, dancing hard. *Address:* Camden Arts Centre, Arkwright Road, NW3 6DG.

**CLARK, Maxwell Robert Guthrie Stewart S.;** *see* Stafford-Clark.

**CLARK, Dr Michael;** Executive Chairman, MAT Group, 2002–04 (Director, 1992–2002); *b* 8 Aug. 1935; *s of* late Mervyn Clark and of Sybilla Norma Clark (*née* Winscott); *m* 1958, Valerie Ethel (*d* 2017), *d of* C. S. Harbord; one *s* one *d*. *Educ:* King Edward VI Grammar School, East Retford; King's College London (BSc (1st cl. Hons) Chemistry, 1956; FKC 1987); Univ. of Minnesota (Fulbright Scholar, 1956–57); St John's College, Cambridge (PhD 1960). FRSC 1988. Research Scientist, later Factory Manager, ICI, 1960–66; Smith's Industries Ltd, 1966–69; PA International Management Consultants, 1969–73; Marketing Manager, St Regis Paper Co., 1973–78; Dir, Courtenay Stewart International, 1978–81; PA International Management Consultants, 1981–93 (Trustee, 1994–2000). Treasurer, 1975–78, Chm., 1980–83, Cambs Cons. Assoc.; Cons. Eastern Area Exec., 1980–83. Contested (C) Ilkeston, 1979; MP (C) Rochford, 1983–97, Rayleigh, 1997–2001. Chm., Sci. and Technol. Select Cttee, 1997–2001; Member: Select Cttee for Energy, 1983–92 (Chm., 1989–92); Select Cttee on Trade and Industry, 1992–94; Council, Parly IT Cttee, 1984–90; Speaker's Panel of Chairmen, 1997–2001; Chairman: All Party Gp for the Chemical Industry, 1994–97 (Hon. Sec. 1985–90; Vice-Chm., 1990–94); Parly Gp for Energy Studies, 1992–97; Bd, Parly Office of Sci. and Technol., 1993–97; Parly British-Russian Gp, 1994–2001; Parly British-Venezuelan Gp, 1995–2001; Hon. Secretary: Parly and Scientific Cttee, 1985–88; Parly Anglo-Nepalese Soc., 1985–90; Parly Anglo-Malawi Gp, 1987–90; Parly Space Cttee, 1989–91; Cons. Backbench Energy Cttee, 1986–87 (Vice-Chm., 1987–90); Mem., 1922 Exec. Cttee, 1997–2001; Chm., IPU, 1990–93 (Mem. Exec., 1987–94). Mem., Adv. Panel, Conservation Foundn, 1995–2000. Mem., Adv. Bd, Fulbright Commn, 1995–2001. Governor, Melbourn Village Coll., 1974–83 (Chm., 1977–80). *Publications:* The History of Rochford Hall, 1990; Clark of the House, 2005. *Recreations:* gadding about, golf, grandchildren. *Address:* 5 Moorgarth, New Road, Ingleton, Carnforth, N Yorks LA6 3PR. *T:* (015242) 41856.

**CLARK, Michael Duncan,** CBE 2014; choreographer; Artistic Director, Michael Clark Company; Artistic Associate, Barbican, since 2005; *b* 2 June 1962; *s of* late William Clark and Elizabeth Duncan. *Educ:* Kintore Primary Sch.; Rubislaw Acad., Aberdeen; Royal Ballet Sch. Resident choreographer, Riverside Studios, London, 1982; launched Michael Clark Company, 1984. Key works: New Puritan, 1984; Do You Me? I Did, 1984; not H.air, 1985; Because We Must, 1987; I Am Curious, Orange, 1988; Mmm…, 1992; "O", 1994; current/SEE, 1998; OH MY GODDESS, 2003; I Do, 2007; come, been and gone, 2009; th, 2011; WHO'S ZOO?, 2012; The Barrowlands Project, 2012; New Work, 2012; animal / vegetable / mineral, 2013; to a simple, rock 'n' roll . . . song, 2016. Hon. Fellow, Trinity Laban, 2016. Hon. DArts Robert Gordon Univ., Aberdeen, 2011. *Address:* Michael Clark Company, Barbican Centre, Silk Street, EC2Y 8DS.

**CLARK, Neil Andrew; His Honour Judge Neil Clark;** a Circuit Judge, since 2012; *b* Sunderland, 1964; *s of* Andrew Clark and Margaret Rosannia Clark (*née* Rae); *m* 1998, Susan Godley. *Educ:* Bede Sch., Sunderland; Univ. of Leeds (LLB). Called to the Bar, Inner Temple, 1987, Bencher, 2012; in practice as a barrister, 1987–2012; a Recorder, 2005–12; Judge (pt-time), Mental Health Review Tribunals, 2008–12. *Recreations:* sports particularly football (Sunderland AFC), cricket and equestrian, all things related to Scotland, reading. *Club:* Durham County Cricket.

**CLARK, Paul Anthony Mason;** a District Judge (Magistrates' Courts) (formerly Metropolitan Stipendiary Magistrate), since 1996; Designated District Judge for West London, 2007–12; a Recorder, since 2003; *b* 19 Aug. 1952; *s of* Thomas James, (Tony), Clark and Winifred Mary Clark (*née* Mason); *m* 1979, Jane Ann; one *s* two *d*. *Educ:* John Leggott GS, Scunthorpe; Jesus Coll., Oxford (MA). Called to the Bar, Middle Temple, 1975 (Astbury Schol.); in practice, 1975–96. Chm., Inner London Youth Courts, 1997–2000. Mem., Council of Dist Judges for England and Wales, 2001–13. Lectr, Gen. Council of the Bar, 1998–2004. Mem. Bd, Internat. Inst. on Special Needs Offenders, 2003–07. Pres., David Isaacs Fund, 2004–18 (Vice Pres., 1998–2004). Contributing Ed., Archbold Magistrates' Courts Criminal Practice, 2011–19. *Recreations:* anything Italian, cricket, painting, gardening, book and ceramics collecting. *Address:* Office of the Senior District Judge, Westminster Magistrates' Court, 181 Marylebone Road, NW1 5BR. *Club:* Oxford and Cambridge.

**CLARK, Air Vice-Marshal Paul Derek,** CB 1993; CEng, FRAeS; Vice President, Homeland Security, BAE SYSTEMS North America, Arlington, Virginia, 2003–05, retired 2006; *b* 19 March 1939; *s of* John Hayes Clark and Kathleen Clark; *m* 1963, Mary Elizabeth Morgan; two *d*. *Educ:* Orange Hill Grammar Sch.; RAF Henlow Technical Coll.; BA Open Univ., 1985. CEng 1970; FRAeS 1987. Commnd Engr Br., RAF, 1961; RAF Wittering, 1961–63, Topcliffe, 1963, Wittering, 1964–69, Cranwell, 1969–70; RAF Staff Coll., Bracknell, 1971; HQ Logistics Comd, USAF, 1972–74; HQ Strike Comd, 1974–76; Nat. Defence Coll., 1977; OC Engrg Wing, RAF Leuchars, 1977–79; HQ No 1 Gp, RAF Bawtry, 1980–81; Stn Comdr No 30 Maintenance Unit, RAF Sealand, 1981–83; RCDS, 1984; MoD, 1985–86; Directorate Electronics Radar Air, MoD (PE), 1986–87; Dir, European Helicopter 101 Project, MoD (PE), 1987–89; Comdt RAF Signals Engrg Estabt, 1990–91; AO, Engrg and Supply, HQ Strike Comd, 1991–93; retd, 1994; Dir of Mil. Support, Support Div., GEC-Marconi Avionics, 1994–95; RMPA Prog. Dir, GEC-Marconi Aerospace Systems Ltd, 1995–97; Pres. and CEO, GEC-Marconi Avionics Inc., Atlanta, 1997–98; Vice President: GEC Account Dir for Lockheed Martin, 1998–99; C–130 Avionics Modernization Prog., BAE SYSTEMS Aerospace Sector, Austin, Texas, 2000–01; Inf. and Electronics System Integration Sector, BAE SYSTEMS Nashua, New Hampshire, 2001–03. *Recreations:* gardening, volunteer work. *Club:* Royal Air Force.

*See also* Prof. T. J. H. Clark.

**CLARK, Paul Gordon;** Director, Gateway Associates (UK) Ltd, since 2010; *b* 29 April 1957; *s of* Gordon Thomas Clark and Sheila Gladys Clark; *m* 1980, Julie Hendrick; one *s* one *d*. *Educ:* Gillingham Grammar Sch.; Keele Univ. (BA Hons 1980; Sec., Students' Union, 1977–78); Univ. of Derby (DMS 1996). Res. Assistant to Pres., then Educn Adminr, AEU, 1980–86; Admin. Asst Sec., then Manager, Nat. Educn Centre, TUC, 1986–97. Mem., Gillingham BC, 1982–90 (Leader, Lab. Gp, 1989–90). Contested (Lab) Gillingham, 1992. MP (Lab) Gillingham, 1997–2010; contested (Lab) Gillingham and Rainham, 2010, 2015. PPS, LCD, 1999–2001, to Minister for Housing and Planning, 2001–02, to Minister for Criminal Justice, 2002–03, to Dep. Prime Minister, 2005–07; an Asst Govt Whip, 2003–05; Parly Under-Sec. of State, DfT, 2008–10. Member, Board: Thames Gateway Kent Partnership, 2000; Groundwork Kent and Medway, 2001–13; Medway CAB, 2011– (Chm., 2012–). Director: Sunlight Development Trust, 2010–; Grassroot Diplomat, 2012–14. Mem. Council, Univ. of Keele, 2012–.

**CLARK, His Honour Peter Charles Lister;** a Circuit Judge, 1995–2017; a Senior Circuit Judge, Employment Appeal Tribunal, 2006–17; *b* 16 June 1948; *s of* Charles Lister Clark and Mary Isobel Clark; *m* 1973, Josephine Neilson Hogg; one *s* one *d*. *Educ:* Repton Sch.; Southampton Univ. (LLB). Called to the Bar, Gray's Inn, 1970, Bencher, 2012; in practice at the Bar, 1971–95; a Recorder, Midland and Oxford Circuit, 1994–95. *Recreations:* various. *Address:* Devereux Chambers, Queen Elizabeth Building, Temple, EC4Y 9BS. *T:* (020) 7353 7534. *Club:* Reform.

**CLARK, Prof. Peter Irving,** MD; FRCP; Consultant Medical Oncologist, Clatterbridge Cancer Centre, 1989–2017; Chair, NHS England Chemotherapy Clinical Reference Group, since 2013; National Clinical Lead, Cancer Drugs Fund, NHS England, since 2016 (Chair, 2013–16); *b* Worthing, 1 July 1956; *s of* Denis and Beth Clark; *m* 1985, Cecile Messent; three *s*. *Educ:* Worthing High Sch.; Gonville and Caius Coll., Cambridge (BA 1978); Univ. of London (MB BS 1981; MD 1989). FRCP 1995. Med. Dir, Clatterbridge Cancer Centre, Merseyside, 1993–2000. Chair: Assoc. of Cancer Physicians, 2000–06; Nat. Chemotherapy Adv. Gp, 2004–13; Technol. Appraisal Cttee, NICE, 2009–13. *Publications:* contrib. papers to med. jls. *Recreations:* family, wine, viticulture, walking, jazz, reading, Everton Football Club.

**CLARK, Petula, (Sally Olwen),** CBE 1998; singer, actress; *b* 15 Nov. 1932; *d of* Leslie Clark; *m* 1961, Claude Wolff; one *s* two *d*. Own BBC radio series, Pet's Parlour, 1943; early British films include: Medal for the General, 1944; I Know Where I'm Going, 1945; Here Come the Huggetts, 1948; Dance Hall, 1950; White Corridors, 1951; The Card, 1951; Made in Heaven, 1952; The Runaway Bus, 1953; That Woman Opposite, 1957. Began career as singer in France, 1959. Top female vocalist, France, 1962; Bravos du Music Hall award for outstanding woman in show business, France, 1965; Grammy awards for records Downtown and I Know A Place. Numerous concert and television appearances in Europe and USA including her own BBC TV series; world concert tour, 1997; UK tour, 2013, 2016; US tour, 2017; Canadian tour, 2018. *Films:* Finian's Rainbow, 1968; Goodbye Mr Chips, 1969; Second to the Right and Straight on till Morning, 1982; *musicals:* The Sound of Music, Apollo Victoria, 1981; (also composer and creator) Someone Like You, Strand, 1990; Blood Brothers, NY, 1993, nat. tour, 1994–95; Sunset Boulevard, Adelphi, 1995, 1996, NY, 1998, nat. US tour, 1998–2000. Commandeur des Arts et des Lettres (France), 2012. *Address*: c/o Claude Wolff, 15 chemin Rieu, 1208 Geneva, Switzerland.

CLARK, Ramsey; lawyer in private practice, New York City, since 1969; *b* Dallas, Texas, 18 Dec. 1927; *s* of late Thomas Clark, and of Mary Ramsey; *m* 1949, Georgia Welch (*d* 2010), Corpus Christi, Texas; one *s* one *d*. *Educ*: Public Schs, Dallas, Los Angeles, Washington; Univ. of Texas (BA); Univ. of Chicago (MA, JD). US Marine Corps, 1945–46. Private practice of law, Dallas, 1951–61; Asst Attorney Gen., Dept of Justice, 1961–65; Dep. Attorney Gen., 1965–67, Attorney Gen., 1967–69. UN Human Rights Award, 2008. *Address*: 37 West 12th Street, New York, NY 10011–8503, USA.

CLARK, Prof. Raymond Peter, OBE 2005; FRSocMed; Chairman, Fravalet Co. Ltd, since 1998; Chief Executive, Society of Environmental Engineers, since 2002; *b* Handborough, Oxon, 1 May 1944; *s* of late Bernard Frederick Clark and Mabel Lillian Clark; *m* 2006, Prof. Mervyn Leonardo de Calcina-Goff. *Educ*: Thames Valley Grammar Sch., Twickenham; Univ. of Manchester (BSc); City Univ. London (PhD 1973; DSc 2016). CEng 2003; CEnv 2009. SO, Div. of Human Physiol., NIMR, 1969–74; Hd, Thermal Biol. and Aerobiol. Unit, MRC Clin. Res. Centre, 1974–90; Hon. Sen. Res. Fellow, KCL, 1990–96; Prof., and Chm., Biomed. Centre, Cranfield Univ., 1996–98. Mem. Council, Foundn for Sci. and Technol., 1989–95; Mem. Bd and Trustee, Engrg Council, 2010–16. Chm., Soc. for Envmt, 2011–12 (Hon. Fellow, 2014). Pres., RPS, 1998–2001 (Fellow, 1990; Hon. Fellow, 2001). Fellow, Soc. Envmtl Engrs, 1994 (Hon. Fellow, 2006); FRSocMed 2006. Freeman, City of London, 1994; Liveryman, Engrs' Co., 2006; Master, Educators' Co., 2010–11. *Publications*: (with O. G. Edholm) Man and His Thermal Environment, 1985; contrib. papers and articles to jls and magazines. *Recreations*: cars - owning and driving, City of London Livery Movement. *Address*: 48 Spencer Heights, 28 Bartholomew Close, EC1A 7ES. *T*: 07775 657865. *E*: ray@medi.demon.co.uk. *Club*: National Liberal.

CLARK, Rebecca Faye; *see* Pow, R. F.

CLARK, Rebecca Louise; Director, Churches and Cathedrals, and Secretary to Church Buildings Council and Cathedrals Fabric Commission for England, Church of England, since 2017; *b* Exeter, 2 June 1983; *d* of Barry Clark and Jane Clark. *Educ*: Regent's Park Coll., Oxford (BA Classical Archaeol. and Ancient Hist. 2004); Ironbridge Inst., Univ. of Birmingham (MA Heritage Mgt 2006); Warwick Business Sch. (MBA 2018). Asst Visitor Services Manager, Stourhead, Nat. Trust, 2006–07; Strategy and Policy Projects Officer, Surrey CC, 2007–08; English Heritage: Policy and Guidance Delivery Manager for Heritage Protection Reform, 2009–10; Exec. Asst to Chief Exec., 2010–13; Sen. Cathedrals Officer and Dep. Sec., Cathedrals Fabric Commn for England, C of E, 2013–17. Treas., Soc. for Church Archaeol., 2015–. *Recreations*: ancient history, archaeology, Agatha Christie, C20th female novelists, country walks, Champagne (not enough), gin, foreign travel, real ale pubs. *Address*: Church House, Great Smith Street, SW1P 3AZ. *T*: (020) 7898 1887. *E*: becky.clark@churchofengland.org.

CLARK, Reginald Blythe, FCSI; Chief Executive, Rhino Sport & Leisure, since 2006; *b* 15 March 1958; *s* of Thomas Harold Clark and Catherine Clark; *m* 1983, Judith Anne Brown; one *s* one *d*. *Educ*: Brinkburn Comprehensive Sch., Hartlepool; Christ Church, Oxford (MA). Capital markets career with Yamaichi Securities, Swiss Bank Corp. and J P Morgan, then European Finance Dir, Kobe steel, Japan, 1988–97; Man. Dir, Loxko Venture Managers Ltd, 1991–2005; Director: London & Oxford Gp, 1993–2011; Darwin Rhodes Gp, 2005–07. Party Treasurer, Liberal Democrats, 2000–05; Contested (Lib Dem) Hartlepool, 1997 and 2010. Vis. Prof., Nippon Univ., Tokyo, 2018–20. FIC (FIBC 1999); FCSI (FSI 2005); CMC; FRSA. Foreign Minister's Commendation Award, Japan, 2016. *Recreations*: reading, Rugby (Oxford Blue 1978, 1979; founder, Kew Occasionals RFC), Japanese culture. *Clubs*: Garrick, National Liberal; Vincent's (Oxford) (Pres., 1979–80).

CLARK, Richard David; Chief Executive, Devon County Council, 1989–96; Clerk to Devon and Cornwall Police Authority, 1993–97 (Associate Clerk, 1989–93); *b* 2 Sept. 1934; *s* of David and Enid Clark; *m* 1958, Pamela Mary (*née* Burgess); two *d*. *Educ*: Luton Boys' Grammar Sch.; Keele Univ. (BA, DipEd); Univ. de Paris, Sorbonne. Teaching, Woodberry Down Comprehensive School, 1957–61; Education Admin, Herts CC, 1961–69; Asst Educn Officer, Lancs CC, 1969–71; Second Dep. County Educn Officer, Hants CC, 1972–76; Chief Educn Officer, Glos CC, 1976–83; County Educn Officer, Hants CC, 1983–88. Dir, Devon and Cornwall TEC, 1989–95. Mem., Adv. Cttee on Supply and Educn of Teachers. Adviser to: Burnham Cttee, 1982–87; Educn Cttee, ACC, 1982–89, 1990–95; Council of Local Educn Authorities, 1983–89. Governor: Plymouth Univ., 1995–2000; Sidmouth Coll., 1995–2000. Fellow Commoner, Churchill Coll., Cambridge, 1983; Vis. Fellow, Southampton Univ., 1986–88; Hon. Fellow, Exeter Univ., 1992–98. FRSA 1977. *Recreations*: books, gardening, wood turning, croquet. *Address*: Glendale House, Rannoch Road, Crowborough, East Sussex TN6 1RB.

CLARK, Richard Jeffrey; Chairman, Michael Grandage Company, since 2012; *b* Yorkshire, 20 Nov. 1959; *s* of late Jeffrey Clark and of Patricia Clark (*née* Halls). *Educ*: Bingley Beckfoot Grammar Sch.; Univ. of Hull (LLB; Lionel Rosen and Sweet & Maxwell Prize). MCIArb 2005; CEDR Accredited Mediator, 2006. Admitted Solicitor, 1984. Slaughter and May, 1982–2017: Partner, 1991; Hd, Dispute Resolution, 2008–13; Exec. Partner, 2013–17. Chm., Coll. of Legal Practice, 2019–. Mem., Adv. Council, Tate St Ives, 2004–10; Comr, Royal Hosp. Chelsea, 2017–. Gov., Falmouth Coll. of Arts, 1996–2004. Mem., Bd of Regents, 2016–, Hon. Fellow 2017, Harris Manchester Coll., Oxford. Ed., Dispute Resolution Rev., 2009–12. *Publications*: contrib. articles to legal jls. *Recreations*: art, jazz, theatre, walking. *Address*: Michael Grandage Company, Fourth Floor, Wyndham's Theatre, Charing Cross Road, WC2H 0DA. *Clubs*: Boodle's, Two Brydges, Groucho.

CLARK, (Robert) Brodie, CBE 2010; consultant in security, risk and border operations, since 2012; Director, Clark Advisory Ltd, since 2012; *b* Glasgow, 16 June 1951; *s* of David Clark and Mary Clark; *m* 1976, Jennifer Taylor; one *s* one *d*. *Educ*: Hutchesons' Grammar Sch., Glasgow; Univ. of Glasgow (MA Hons Philos. and Sociol.). HM Prison Service, 1973–2004: Gov., HM Prisons Bedford, 1988–91, Woodhill, 1991–94, and Whitemoor, 1994–97; Hd of Industrial Relations, 1997–99; Dir, High Security Prisons, 1999–2000; Dir, Security, Prisons Bd, 2000–04; Sen. Dir, Immigration and Nationality Directorate, 2004–07; Strategic Dir, Border and Immigration Agency, 2007–08; Hd, Border Force, UK Border Agency, 2008–11. Nat. and internat. prison expert, 2016–. Non-executive Director: Leeds Community Healthcare Trust, 2014–; Compass, 2014–. Contrib., Government training experts, Dods, 2013–. *Recreations*: walking, sport, reading.

CLARK, Roderick David; Chief Executive, Prisoners' Education Trust, since 2013; *b* 10 May 1961; *s* of Sydney Clark and Mary Anne Clark (*née* Kellas); *m* 1995, Kate Paul; one *d*. *Educ*: Corpus Christi Coll., Oxford (BA Lit.Hum.). Civil Servant, 1984–2012, posts mainly in field of social security; Dir Gen. Strategy, DCA, then MoJ, 2005–08; Principal and Chief Exec., Nat. Sch. of Govt, 2008–12. *Recreations*: cooking, walking, running.

CLARK, Stuart; *see* Clark, D. S. T.

CLARK, Sir Terence (Joseph), KBE 1990; CMG 1985; CVO 1978; HM Diplomatic Service, retired; Senior Consultant, MEC, 1995–2008; *b* 19 June 1934; *s* of Joseph Clark and Mary Clark; *m* 1960, Lieselotte Rosa Marie Müller; two *s* one *d*. *Educ*: Thomas Parmiter's, London. RAF (attached to Sch. of Slavonic Studies, Cambridge), 1953–55; Pilot Officer, RAFVR, 1955. HM Foreign Service, 1955; ME Centre for Arab Studies, 1956–57; Bahrain, 1957–58; Amman, 1958–60; Casablanca, 1961–62; FO, 1962–65; Asst Pol Agent, Dubai, 1965–68; Belgrade, 1969–71; Hd of Chancery, Muscat, 1972–73; Asst Hd of ME Dept, FCO, 1974–76; Counsellor (Press and Information), Bonn, 1976–79; Chargé d'Affaires, Tripoli, Feb.–March 1981; Counsellor, Belgrade, 1979–82. Dep. Leader, UK Delegn, Conf. on Security and Co-operation in Europe, Madrid, 1982–83; Hd of Information Dept, FCO, 1983–85; Ambassador to Iraq, 1985–89; Ambassador to Oman, 1990–94. Dir, Internat. Crisis Gp Bosnia Project, Sarajevo, 1996. Chm., Anglo-Omani Soc., 1995–2004 (Vice-Pres., 2004–); Mem., Exec. Cttee of Mgt, ME Assoc., 1998–2004. Member: Council, British Sch. of Archaeology in Iraq, later British Inst. for the Study of Iraq, 2003–08 (Patron, 2018–); Adv. Bd, Iraq Infrastructure Fund, 2009–18; Chm. Trustees, 2010–19, Trustee, 2019–, Friends of Basrah Mus. Member: RSAA, 1991 (Mem. Council, 2001–07); RIIA, 1995–2007; FRGS 1993. Chm., Saluki Coursing Club, 2000–05; Vice Chm., British Iraqi Friendship Soc., 2008–12. Commander's Cross, Order of Merit (Fed. Republic of Germany), 1978. *Publications*: (jtly) The Saluqi: coursing hound of the East, 1995; (jtly) Oman in Time, 2001; (jtly) Al-Mansur's Book on Hunting, 2001; (jtly) Dogs in Antiquity, 2001; Underground to Overseas: the story of Petroleum Development Oman, 2007; (jtly) British Missions around the Gulf 1575–2005, 2008; Oman's Invisible Energy, 2014; The Salukis in my Life, 2018; articles on Salukis and coursing in magazines. *Recreations*: Salukis, walking. *Club*: Hurlingham.

CLARK, Sir Timothy (Charles), KBE 2014; President, Emirates Airline, since 2004; *b* Aruba, 22 Nov. 1949; *s* of late Capt. J. F. G. Clark, MBE and of Mrs R. Granville; *m* 1997, Geraldine; one *s* two *d*. *Educ*: Kent Coll., Canterbury; London Univ. (Econs degree 1971). Planner, British Caledonian, 1972–75; Cost Economist, Gulf Air, 1975–85; Emirates Airline, 1985–, various directorships. Founder and Chm., Emirates Airline Foundn. FRAeS. Officier de la Légion d'Honneur (France), 2009. *Recreations*: ski-ing, aeronautical history, maritime history, interior design.

CLARK, Timothy Elwyn, QC 2017; a Recorder, since 2010; *b* Ely, 28 June 1968; *s* of Bryan Clark and Mary Clark-Glass; *m* 2007, Mary Tmaira; one *s* one *d*. *Educ*: Methodist Coll., Belfast; Univ. of Bristol (LLB Hons); Inns of Court Sch. of Law. Pres., Univ. of Bristol Union, 1989–90. Called to the Bar, Inner Temple, 1993. *Recreations*: reading, watching Rugby. *Address*: 23 Essex Street, WC2R 3AA. *E*: clerks@23es.com. *Club*: Reform.

CLARK, Timothy Howard, OBE 2008; Chairman, ie:music, since 2016 (Joint Managing Director, 2002–16); *b* Kitale, Kenya, 20 May 1945; *s* of Rev. Canon Robert Clark and Doris Clark; *m* 1973, Jane Andrea Vincent Johns; three *d*. *Educ*: Prince of Wales Sch., Nairobi. Island Records: Sales Rep., 1968–70; Production Manager, 1970–72; Mktg Dir, 1972–76; Man. Dir, 1976–80; Man. Dir, Telling Editions, 1985–2004. Vice Pres., UNICEF, 2002–. *Recreations*: literature, music, Rugby, swimming. *Address*: 52 Lebanon Park, Twickenham, Middx TW1 3DG. *T*: (020) 8892 2190. *E*: tc@iemusic.co.uk. *Clubs*: Soho House; Lensbury (Teddington); Harlequins Rugby.

CLARK, Prof. Timothy John Hayes, FRCP; Professor of Pulmonary Medicine, Imperial College Faculty of Medicine at the National Heart and Lung Institute, since 1990; *b* 18 Oct. 1935; *s* of John and Kathleen Clark; *m* 1961, Elizabeth Ann Day; two *s* two *d*. *Educ*: Christ's Hospital; Guy's Hospital Medical Sch. BSc 1958; MB BS (Hons) 1961, MD 1967 London. FRCP 1973 (LRCP 1960, MRCP 1962); MRCS 1960. Fellow, Johns Hopkins Hosp., Baltimore USA, 1963; Registrar, Hammersmith Hosp., 1964; Lecturer and Sen. Lectr, Guy's Hospital Med. Sch., 1966; Consultant Physician: Guy's Hosp., 1968–90; Royal Brompton Hosp., 1970–98; Prof. of Thoracic Med., Guy's Hosp. Med. Sch., later UMDS, 1977–89; Dean: Guy's Hosp., 1984–89; UMDS, 1986–89; Pro-Vice-Chancellor for Medicine and Dentistry, Univ. of London, 1987–89; Dean, Nat. Heart and Lung Inst., 1990–97; Pro-Rector (Medicine), 1995–97, (Educnl Qly), 1997–2000, Imperial Coll.; Pro-Rector and Provost, Imperial Coll. at Wye, 2000–01; Pro-Rector (Admission), Imperial Coll., 2001–02. Mem., Council of Governors, UMDS, 1982–89, 1990–95. Specialist Adviser to Social Services Cttee, 1981 and 1985. Special Trustee, Guy's Hosp., 1982–86. Pres., British Thoracic Soc., 1990–91; Chm., Global Initiative for Asthma, 2000–04; Vice-Chairman: Nat. Asthma Campaign, 1993–2000; ICRF, 1997–2002; Trustee and Mem. Council, Stroke Assoc., 2002–11. FKC 1995. *Publications*: (jtly) Asthma, 1977, 4th edn 2000; (ed) Small Airways in Health and Disease, 1979; (jtly) Topical Steroid Treatment of Asthma and Rhinitis, 1980; (ed) Clinical Investigation of Respiratory Disease, 1981; (jtly) Practical Management of Asthma, 1985, 3rd edn 1998; articles in British Medical Jl, Lancet, and other specialist scientific jls. *Recreation*: cricket. *Address*: 8 Lawrence Court, NW7 3QP. *T*: (020) 8959 4411. *Club*: MCC.

*See also* Air Vice-Marshal P. D. Clark.

CLARK, Timothy Nicholas; Senior Adviser, G3 Group, since 2009; Senior Partner, Slaughter and May, 2001–08; *b* 9 Jan. 1951; *s* of Sir Robert Anthony Clark, DSC and of Andolyn Marjorie Clark (*née* Lewis); *m* 1974, Caroline Moffat; two *s*. *Educ*: Sherborne Sch.; Pembroke Coll., Cambridge (MA Hist.). Admitted solicitor, 1976; with Slaughter and May (Solicitors), 1974–2008, Partner, 1983–2008. Non-executive Director: Big Yellow Gp plc, 2008–18; COIF Funds, 2008–13; Mint Partners Ltd, 2008–10. Member: Governing Body, ICC UK, 2003–; Adv. Bd, Uria Menendez, 2008–; Bd of Sen. Advrs, Chatham House, 2008–; Bd of Sen. Advrs, Centre for Eur. Reform, 2011–; Vice Chm., Business for New Europe, 2008–. Member: Develt Cttee, Nat. Gall., 2001–; Bd, RNT, 2008–17; Audit Cttee, Wellcome Trust, 2011–18. Trustee, Economist Trust, 2009– (Chm., 2010–); Chairman: WaterAid UK, 2013–; HighTide Th., 2016–. *Recreations*: flying, football, cricket, theatre. *E*: timnclark@gmail.com. *Club*: Royal Air Squadron (Chm., 2010–17).

CLARK, Tony; *see* Clark, C. A.

CLARK, Gen. Wesley Kanne, Hon. KBE 2000; Chairman and Chief Executive Officer, Wesley K. Clark & Associates, since 2003; Supreme Allied Commander, Europe, 1997–2000; Commander-in-Chief, United States European Command, 1997–2000; *m* Gert; one *s*. *Educ*: US Military Acad.; Magdalen Coll., Oxford (Rhodes Schol.; BA 1968). Served in Vietnam (Silver and Bronze Stars); Sen. Military Asst to Gen. Alexander Haig; Head, Nat. Army Trng Centre; Dir of Strategy, Dept of Defense; Mem., American negotiating team, Bosnian peace negotiations, Dayton, Ohio, 1995; Head, US Southern Comd, Panama. Consultant, 2000–01, Man. Dir, Merchant Banking, 2001–03, Stephens Gp Inc. Vice-Chm. and Sen. Advr, James Lee Witt Associates, 2004; Chm., Rodman & Renshaw, 2006; Mem., Adv. Bd, Mutualink, 2009–. Co-Chm., Growth Energy, 2009–; Dir, Juhl Wind Inc., 2009–. Presidential Medal of Freedom (USA), 2000. *Publications*: Waging Modern War, 2001; Winning Modern Wars, 2003; A Time to Lead, 2007. *Address*: Wesley K. Clark & Associates, PO Box 3276, Little Rock, AR 72203, USA. *T*: (501) 2449522, *Fax*: (501) 2442203.

**CLARKE,** family name of **Barons Clarke of Hampstead** and **Clarke of Stone-cum-Ebony**.

**CLARKE OF HAMPSTEAD,** Baron *cr* 1998 (Life Peer), of Hampstead in the London Borough of Camden; **Anthony James Clarke,** CBE 1998; *b* 17 April 1932; *s* of Henry Walter and Elizabeth Clarke; *m* 1954, Josephine Ena (*née* Turner); one *s* one *d*. *Educ:* New End Primary Sch., Hampstead; St Dominic's RC Sch., Kentish Town; Ruskin Coll., Oxford (TU educn course, 1954). Nat. Service, Royal Signals, 1950–52; TA and AER, 1952–68. Joined PO as Telegraph Boy at 14; worked as Postman until elected full-time officer, Union of Post Office Workers, 1979; Nat. Editor, The Post, UPW jl, 1979–82; Dep. Gen. Sec., UPW, later CWU, 1982–93. Member: Hampstead Lab Party, 1954–86; St Albans Lab Party, 1986–; Lab Party NEC, 1983–93; Chm., Lab Party, 1992–93. Mem. (Lab) Camden LBC, 1971–78. Contested (Lab) Camden, Hampstead, Feb. and Oct. 1974. Member: Exec. Cttee, Camden Cttee for Community Relns, 1974–81; Camden Council of Social Services, 1978–87. Mem., Labour Friends of Israel, 1972–. Governor, Westminster Foundn for Democracy, 1992–98. Trustee, RAF Mus., 2001–. Trustee, Wells and Campden Charitable Trust; Founder Mem., and Trustee, One World Action (formerly One World), 1984–. KSG 1994. *Recreations:* Arsenal FC, The Archers, reading. *Address:* 83 Orchard Drive, St Albans, Herts AL2 2QH. *T:* (01727) 874276; House of Lords, SW1A 0PW.

**CLARKE OF STONE-CUM-EBONY,** Baron *cr* 2009 (Life Peer), of Stone-cum-Ebony in the County of Kent; **Anthony Peter Clarke;** Kt 1993; PC 1998; a commercial and maritime arbitrator, since 2018; a Justice of the Supreme Court of the United Kingdom (formerly a Lord of Appeal in Ordinary), 2009–17; a non-permanent Judge, Court of Final Appeal, Hong Kong, since 2013; *b* 13 May 1943; *s* of late Harry Alston Clarke and Isobel Corsan Clarke (*née* Kay); *m* 1968, Rosemary (*née* Adam); two *s* one *d*. *Educ:* Oakham Sch.; King's Coll., Cambridge (Econs Pt I, Law Pt II; MA). Called to the Bar, Middle Temple, 1965, Bencher, 1987 (Master Treas., 2012); QC 1979; a Recorder, 1985–92; a Judge of the High Court of Justice, QBD, 1993–98; Admiralty Judge, 1993–98; a Lord Justice of Appeal, 1998–2005; Master of the Rolls, 2005–09; Head of Civil Justice, 2005–09. Prime Warden, Shipwrights' Co., 2014–15. *Recreations:* golf, tennis, holidays, bridge. *Address:* Arbitrators at 10 Fleet Street, Quadrant Chambers, Quadrant House, 10 Fleet Street, EC4Y 1AU. *Club:* Garrick.

See also C. A. Clarke.

**CLARKE, Rt Hon. Lord; Matthew Gerard Clarke;** PC 2008; a Senator of the College of Justice in Scotland, 2000–13 (a Judge of the Inner House of the Court of Session, 2008–13); *s* of Thomas Clarke and Ann (*née* Duddy). *Educ:* Holy Cross High Sch., Hamilton; Univ. of Glasgow (MA; LLB; Francis T. Hunter Scholar; Cunnighame Bursar). Solicitor, 1972. Lectr, Dept of Scots Law, Edinburgh Univ., 1972–78; admitted to Faculty of Advocates, 1978; Standing Junior Counsel to Scottish Home and Health Dept, 1983–89; QC (Scot.) 1989; a Judge of the Courts of Appeal of Jersey and Guernsey, 1995–2000. Member: Consumer Credit Licensing Appeal Tribunal, 1976–2000; Estate Agents Tribunals, 1980–2000; Trademarks Tribunal, 1995–2000; Chm. (part-time), Industrial Tribunals, 1987–2000. Leader, UK Delegn, Council of the Bars and Laws Socs of EC, 1992–96 (Mem., 1989–99). British Council: Mem., Scottish Cttee, 2001–08; Chm., Scottish Law Cttee, 2001–07. Hon. Fellow, Europa Inst., Univ. of Edinburgh, 1995–. *Publications:* (Scottish Editor) Sweet & Maxwell's Encyclopaedia of Consumer Law, 1980; (contrib.) Corporate Law: the European dimension, 1991; (contrib.) Butterworth's EC Legal Systems, 1992; (contrib.) Green's Guide to European Laws in Scotland, 1995; (contrib.) McPhail, Sheriff Court Practice, 1999; (contrib.) A True European: essays for Judge David Edward, 2004; (contrib.) Court of Session Practice, 2005. *Recreations:* cooking, opera, chamber music, the music of Schubert, travel. *Address:* 92 Whitehouse Loan, Edinburgh EH9 1BD.

**CLARKE, Prof. Adrienne Elizabeth,** AC 2004 (AO 1991); PhD; FTSE, FAA; Chancellor, La Trobe University, 2011–17; Personal Chair in Botany, 1985, and Laureate Professor, 1999, University of Melbourne; *b* Melbourne, 6 Jan. 1938; *d* of Valentine Clifford and Alice Louise Petty; *m* (marr. diss.); two *d* one *s*. *Educ:* Ruyton Grammar Sch.; Univ. of Melbourne (PhD). Melbourne University: Reader in Botany, 1981–85; Dir, Plant Cell Biol. Res. Centre, 1982–99; Dep. Head, Sch. of Botany, 1992–2000. Chm., CSIRO, 1991–96; Mem., Sci. Adv. Bd, Friedrich Meischer Inst., 1991. Director: Alcoa of Australia, 1993–96; AMP Ltd, 1994–99; Woolworths Ltd, 1994–2007; WMC Ltd, 1996–2002; WMC Resources Ltd, 2002–05; Fisher & Paykel Healthcare Corp. Ltd, 2002–08; Chief Sci. Advr, 2006–10, Dep. Chm., 2006–10, Hexima Ltd. Lt-Governor, Victoria, 1997–2001. Victoria's first Ambassador for Biotechnology, 2001–02. Member: PM's Supermarket to Asia Cttee, 1996–2002; Innovation Econ. Adv. Bd Vic, 2002–06. Member, Board: Mental Health Res. Inst., 2002–06 (Mem., Cttee for Melbourne, 1994–2003); Inst. for Commercialisation, 2002–04. Pres., Internat. Soc. for Plant Molecular Biology, 1997–98. Foreign Associate, Nat. Acad. of Scis, USA, 1993; Comp., Inst. of Engrs, Australia, 1993; Fellow, Amer. Coll. of Arts and Scis, 1998. Mueller Medal, ANZAAS, 1992; Outstanding Achievers Award, Nat. Aust. Day, 1994; Centenary Medal, 2003. *Publications:* (ed with I. Wilson) Carbohydrate-Protein Recognition, 1988; (with B. A. Stone) Chemistry and Biology of (1–3)-B-glucans, 1992; (jtly) Genetic Control of Self-Incompatibility and Reproductive Development in Flowering Plants, 1994; (jtly) Cell and Developmental Biology of Arabinogalactan-Proteins, 2002; chapters in numerous books; over 140 papers in learned jls. *Recreations:* swimming, bush walking, ski-ing. *E:* aeclarke@unimelb.edu.au. *Club:* Lyceum (Melbourne).

**CLARKE, Alan,** CBE 2011; Chief Executive, One NorthEast Regional Development Agency, 2003–12; *b* 18 Aug. 1953; *s* of late Neville Clarke and Jean Clarke; *m* 1977, Deborah Anne Hayes; one *s* two *d*. *Educ:* Univ. of Lancaster (BA Hons Econs 1974); Univ. of Liverpool (MCD 1977). MRTPI 1980. Policy Officer, South Ribble BC, 1974–75; Planning Asst, S Tyneside Council, 1977–79; Newcastle City Council: Planning Asst, 1979–83; Sen. Econ. Develt Asst, 1983–86; Hd, Econ. Develt, 1986–91; Chief Econ. Develt Officer, 1991–95; Asst Chief Exec., Sunderland CC, 1995–2000; Chief Exec., Northumberland CC, 2000–03. Non-exec. Dir, South Tyneside NHS Foundn Trust, 2012–. *Recreations:* cycling, football, hill-walking. *Address:* 13 Langholm Road, East Boldon, Tyne and Wear NE36 0ED.

**CLARKE, Andrew Bertram;** QC 1997; *b* 23 Aug. 1956; *s* of Arthur Bertram Clarke and Violet Doris Clarke; *m* 1981, Victoria Clare Thomas; one *s* two *d*. *Educ:* Crewe Grammar Sch.; King's Coll., London (LLB; AKC); Lincoln Coll., Oxford (BCL). Called to the Bar, Middle Temple, 1980; in practice at the Bar, 1981–; Co-Hd, Littleton Chambers, 2006–14. Gov., Goffs Foundn Sch., Cheshunt, 1996–2011; non-exec. Dir, Goffs Acad., 2011–. Chm., Friends of St Mary's Church, Cheshunt, 1994–. *Recreations:* supporter of Crewe Alexandra FC, Gloucestershire CCC; collector of European ceramics and modern prints. *Address:* 38 Albury Ride, Cheshunt, Herts EN8 8XF. *T:* (020) 7797 8600.

**CLARKE, Anthony Richard;** Teacher in Public Services, Milton Keynes College, since 2018; National Spokesperson on foreign affairs, Green Party, 2013–15; *b* 6 Sept. 1963; *s* of Walter Arthur Clarke and Joan Ada Iris Clarke; *m* Carole Chalmers; one *s* one *d*. *Educ:* Lings Upper Sch., Northampton. Social Work Trainer, Northamptonshire CC, then Disability Trng Officer, 1983–97. Dir, 1999–2010, Gen. Manager, 2005–08, Northampton Town FC; Chief Exec., Northampton Town Football in the Community, 2008–10; Projects Manager, D. C. Clarke Roofing Ltd, 2011–15; Teacher in Public Services, Northampton Coll., 2016–18. MP (Lab) Northampton South, 1997–2005; contested same seat (Lab) 2005, (Ind), 2010, (Green), 2015. Member: (Ind) Northampton BC, 2007–11; (Ind) Northants CC, 2009–13.

**CLARKE, Rt Rev. Barry Bryan;** Bishop of Montreal, 2004–15; *b* Montreal, 10 Oct. 1952; *m* 1997, Leslie James; one *d* from previous marriage. *Educ:* McGill Univ. (BTh 1977); Montreal Theol Coll. (Dip. Min. 1978). Ordained 1978; Asst Curate, St Matthias, Westmount, 1978–80; Rector: Trinity Church, St Bruno, 1980–84; St Michael and All Angels, 1984–93; St Paul's, Lachine, 1993–2004. Regional Dean: Ste Anne, 1988–92; Pointe Claire, 1997–2003; Archdeacon, St Lawrence, 2003–04.

**CLARKE, Prof. Barry Goldsmith,** PhD; CEng, Eur Ing; FICE; Professor of Civil Engineering Geotechnics, University of Leeds, 2008–19; *b* Newcastle upon Tyne, 13 July 1950; *s* of Denis Goldsmith Clarke and Eileen Clarke; *m* 1997, Sandra Elsie Tindale. *Educ:* S Shields Grammar Sch.; Univ. of Newcastle upon Tyne (BSc 1971); Gonville and Caius Coll., Cambridge (PhD 1978). CEng 1988; Eur Ing 1990; FICE 1999. VSO, W Indies, 1971–73. Dir, PM Insitu Techniques, 1977–84; University of Newcastle upon Tyne: Lectr, 1984–98; Prof., 1998–2008; Hd, Civil Engrg, 1998–2002. President: Engrg Profs' Council, 2009–11; ICE, 2012–13. *Publications:* Pressuremeters in Geotechnical Design, 1994; Engineering of Glacial Soils, 2017; contrib. papers to Geotechnique, ICE Geotech. Engrg, ICE Civil Engrg, ASTM Geotech. Testing, ASCE Geotechnics and Geoenvmtl, Qly Jl Engrg Geol. *Recreations:* walking, gardening. *Address:* Harrogate, N Yorks HG2 9AB. *E:* b.g.clarke@leeds.ac.uk.

**CLARKE, Barry James;** Regional Employment Judge (Wales), since 2015; Deputy Chair, Central Arbitration Committee, since 2016; National Director of Training for Employment Tribunals (England and Wales), since 2017; a Recorder, since 2019; *b* Derby, 10 May 1970; *s* of Robert Ian Clarke and Carol Joan Clarke; *m* 1992, Dr Kathryn Sian Walters, PsyD, CPsychol; one *s* two *d*. *Educ:* Redbourne Upper Sch. and Community Coll., Ampthill, Beds; Univ. of Manchester (Bradford Schol.: BA 1st Cl. Hons Hist. 1991; Thomas Frederick and Mary Tout Prize); London Sch. of Econs and Pol Sci. (MSc Econ. Political Theory (Dist.) 1994). Trainee solicitor, Frere Cholmeley, 1994–96; admitted as solicitor, 1996; Solicitor: Rowe & Maw, 1996–98; Pattinson & Brewer, 1998–2000; Solicitor and Partner, Russell Jones & Walker, 2000–07; ACAS arbitrator, 2007–10. Fee paid Employment Judge, 2005–10; Fee Paid Immigration Judge, 2006–10; Employment Judge, 2010–15. Mem., Wales Cttee, Equality and Human Rights Commn, 2007–10. Nat. Chm., Employment Lawyers' Assoc., 2006–08. Trustee, Cardiff Law Centre, 2003–08. Wig & Pen Prize, City of London Law Soc., 1996. *Publications:* Challenging Racism, 2003. *Recreations:* long distance running, squash, ski-ing, technology, guitar, history. *Address:* Wales Employment Tribunal, Third Floor, Cardiff and The Vale Magistrates' Court, Fitzalan Place, Cardiff CF24 0RT.

**CLARKE, Dr Belinda Rosanna;** Director, Agri-Tech East, since 2014; *b* Norwich. *Educ:* Norwich High Sch. for Girls; Newnham Coll., Cambridge (BA Hons Natural Scis Tripos 1995; MA 1998); John Innes Centre (PhD 1999). CBiol 2004; FRSB 2011; ARAgS 2017. Science Liaison Manager, Norwich Res. Park, 1999; Nuffield Schol., 2001. Internat. Trade Advr (biotech and pharma), UKTI, 2005–07; Life Scis Manager, One Nucleus, 2007–11; Dir, Innovation Ecosystems, Ideaspace, Univ. of Cambridge, 2011–12; Lead Technologist, Bioscis, Innovate UK, 2012–14. Director: Leatherhead Food Res., 2012–15; Agrimetrics, 2017–. Mem., UKRI-BBSRC (formerly BBSRC), 2015–. Trustee, Royal Norfolk Agricl Assoc., 2014–. *E:* belinda.clarke@agritech-east.co.uk.

**CLARKE, Brian;** see Clarke, J. B.

**CLARKE, Brian;** artist; *b* 2 July 1953; *s* of late Edward Ord Clarke and of Lilian Clarke (*née* Whitehead); *m* 1972, Elizabeth Cecilia (marr. diss. 1996; remarried 2013), *d* of Rev. John Finch; one *s*. *Educ:* Clarksfield Sch., Oldham; Oldham Sch. of Arts and Crafts (Jr Schol.); Burnley Sch. of Art; North Devon Coll. of Art and Design (Dip. Art and Design). Vis. Prof., Archtl Art, UCL, 1993–. Executor, Estate of Francis Bacon, 1998–. Trustee and Mem. Cttee, Robert Fraser Foundn, 1990–; Trustee: Ely Stained Glass Mus.; Capital City Acad. (formerly Lowe Educnl Charitable Foundn), 2001–; Architecture Foundn, 2002– (Chm., 2007–13); Winston Churchill Meml Trust, 2007– (Mem. Council, 1985–); Zaha Hadid Foundn, 2016– (Executor, 2016). *Major exhibitions* include: Glass/Light Exhibn, Fest. of City of London, 1979; Der Architektur der Synagogue, Deutsches Architektur Mus., Frankfurt, 1980; New Paintings, Constructions and Prints, RIBA, 1981; Paintings, Robert Fraser Gall., 1983; 1976–86, Seibu Mus. of Art, Tokyo, 1987; Malerei und Farbfenster 1977–88, Hessisches Landesmuseum, 1988; Paintings, Indar Pasricha Gall., New Delhi, 1989; Intimations of Mortality, Galerie Karsten Greve, Köln; Into and Out of Architecture, 1990, New Paintings, 1993, Mayor Gall., London; Architecture and Stained Glass, Sezon Mus. of Art, Tokyo, 1990; Designs on Architecture, Oldham Art Gall., 1993; Paintings and Stained Glass Works in Architecture, 1995, The Glass Wall, 1998, Transillumination, 2003, Tony Shafrazi Gall., NY; Brian Clarke Linda McCartney, Musée Suisse du Vitrail au Château de Romont and German Mus. for Stained Glass, Linnich, 1997–98; 80 Artistes autour du Mondial, Galerie Enrico Navarra, Paris, 1998; Fleurs de Lys, Faggionato Fine Arts, London, 1999; Flowers for New York, Corning Gall., Steuben, NY, 2002; Lamina, Gagosian Gall., London, 2005; Don't Forget the Lamb, Phillips de Pury, NY, 2008; Brian Clarke, Life and Death, Vitromusée Romont, Switzerland, 2011; Love Him More, Kristy Stubbs Gall., Texas, 2011; Atlantes and Astragals, Christie's, London, 2011; Brian Clarke Works on Paper 1969–2011, The Old and the Dead, Gemeentemuseum den Haag, Netherlands, 2011; Phillips De Pury at the Saatchi Gall., London, 2011; Brian Clarke Born Oldham 1953, Oldham Gall., 2013; Between Extremities, Pace Gall., New York, 2013; Piper & Clarke. Stained Glass: art or anti-art, Verey Gall. and Eton Coll., 2014; Spitfires and Primroses, 2015, Night Orchids, 2016, Pace London; Summer Solstice Screens, Heni Gall., 2017; Art of Light, Sainsbury Centre for Visual Arts, UEA, 2018; *major stained glass works* include: St Gabriel's Ch, Blackburn, 1976; All Saints Ch, Habergham, 1976; Queen's Med. Centre, Nottingham, 1978; Laver's & Barraud Building, London, 1981; Olympus Optical Europa GmbH HQ Building, Hamburg, 1981; King Kahled Internat. Airport, Riyadh, 1982; Buxton Thermal Baths, 1987; Lake Sagami Country Club, Yamanashi, 1988; New Synagogue, Darmstadt, 1988; Victoria Quarter, Leeds, 1989; Cibreo Restaurant, Tokyo, 1990; Glaxo Pharmaceuticals, Uxbridge, 1990; Stansted Airport, 1991; Spindles Shopping Centre, Oldham, 1991–93; España Telefonica, Barcelona, 1991; Number One America Square, London, 1991; 35–38 Chancery Lane, London, 1991; Carmelite, London, 1992; 100 New Bridge St, London, 1992; (with Will Alsop) facade of Hotel de Ville des Bouches-du-Rhone, Marseille, 1992–94; Glass Dune, Hamburg, 1992; EAM Building, Kassel, Germany, 1992–93; New Synagogue, Heidelberg, 1993; Hammersmith Hosp., London, 1993; WH Smith & Sons, Abingdon, 1994; The Grace Building, NY, 1994; Crossrail Paddington, London, 1994; Cliveden Hotel, 1994; Frankfurter Allee Plaza, Berlin, 1994; New Synagogue, Aachen, 1994; Norte Shopping, Rio de Janeiro, 1995; (with Linda McCartney) Rye Hosp., 1995; Valentino Village, Noci, 1996; Center Villa-Lobos (design), São Paulo, 1997; Offenbach Synagogue, 1997; Future Systems Tower NEC, 1997; Praça

Norte Clock Tower, 1997; Heidelberg Cathedral, 1997; New Catholic Church, Obersalbach, 1997; Pfizer Pharmaceuticals, NY, 1997, 2001, 2003; Chep Lap Kok Airport, Hong Kong; Chicago Sinai, 1997; Warburg Dillon Read (stained glass cone), Stamford, Conn, 1998; (with Lord Foster) Al Faisaliah Centre, Riyadh, 2000; West Winter Garden (design), Heron Quays, London, 2001; Hotel and Thalassotherapy Centre, Nova Yardinia, Italy, 2002; Ascot Racecourse (stained glass façade), 2003; (with Lord Foster) Pyramid of Peace (stained glass apex), Astana, Kazakhstan, 2006; Linköping Cathedral (stained glass), Sweden, 2010; Papal Nunciature, London (stained glass), 2010; bldg, Lexington St, Soho, London, 2015; Immanuel Chapel (windows), Virginia Theol Seminary, 2018; spa, Beaverbrook Country Club, 2019; stage designs for Paul McCartney World Tour, 1990; designed: stadia sets for Paul McCartney New World Tour, 1993; stage sets for: The Ruins of Time (ballet), Dutch Nat. Ballet, 1993; The Crucible, Staatstheater Braunschweig, Germany, 2016; Yaguara Cachaça bottle, 2013; fellowship medal for Winston Churchill Meml Trust; curator: A Strong Sweet Smell of Incense: a portrait of Robert Fraser, Pace London, 2015; Summer Solstice Spitfires, Heni Gall., 2016. FRSA 1988. Hon. FRIBA 1993; Hon. DLitt Huddersfield, 2007; DHL Virginia Theological Seminary, 2018. Hon. Liveryman, Glaziers' and Master Glass Painters' Co., 2012. Churchill Fellow in architectl art, 1974; special commendation award, Art and Work, Arts Council, 1989; Europa Nostra award, 1990; Special Award for Stained Glass, Leeds Award for Architecture, 1990; special commendation award, Working for Cities, British Gas, 1992; Eur. Shopping Centre Award, 1995; BDA Auszeichnung guter Bauten, Heidelberg, 1996; Cttee of Honour, Fondation Vincent van Gogh, Arles, 2001. *Recreations:* reading, hoarding. *W:* www.brianclarke.co.uk.

**CLARKE, (Charles) Giles,** CBE 2012; DL; entrepreneur and financier; President, England and Wales Cricket Board, 2015–18 (Chairman, 2007–15; Director, 2004–18); *b* Bristol, 29 May 1953; *s* of Charles Nigel Clarke and Stella Rosemary Clarke, *qv*; *m* 1983, Judy Gould; one *s*. *Educ:* Rugby Sch.; Oriel Coll., Oxford (BA Hons Persian with Arabic); Damascus Univ. Chm. and Founder, Majestic Wine Warehouses, 1981–89; Chief Exec. and Co-founder, Pet City plc, 1990–98; Chairman: Fosters Rooms, 1989–2007; Safestore plc, 2001–03; Westleigh Investments, 2002–; WCBS, 2004–; CCI Internat., 2004–; Boston Tea Party Ltd, 2006–; Amerisur Resources plc, 2007–; Ironveld plc, 2012–; Kazeera Global plc (formerly Kennedy Ventures plc), 2014–; Promatic Internat., 2017–. Mem. Council, LSC, 2002–07 (Mem., Adult Learning Cttee, 2002–07). Dir, Internat. Cricket Council, 2007–18 (Chm., Pakistan Task Team, 2010–18; Chm., Finance and Commercial Cttee, 2012–18). Chm., Somerset CCC, 2002–08. Mem., Chief Execs Orgn, 2003–. President: Canynges Soc., 1990; Young Presidents Orgn, London Chapter, 1997; Dolphin Soc., 2005. Conseil, Commanderie de Bordeaux, 2009– (Regent, 2015–). Master, Soc. of Merchant Venturers, 2010. DL Wilts, 1998–2002, Som, 2004. *Recreations:* Persian poetry, wine, military history, coral reef marine fish, cricket, shooting. *E:* giles.clarke@westleighuk.com. *Clubs:* MCC; Somerset County Cricket.

**CLARKE, Sir (Charles Mansfield) Tobias,** 6th Bt *cr* 1831; *b* Santa Barbara, California, 8 Sept. 1939; *e s* of Sir Humphrey Orme Clarke, 5th Bt, and Elisabeth (*d* 1967), *d* of Dr William Albert Cook; *S* father, 1973; *m* 1971, Charlotte (marr. diss. 1979), *e d* of Roderick Walter; *m* 1984, Teresa L. A. de Chair, *d* of late Somerset de Chair; one *s* two *d*. *Educ:* Eton; Christ Church, Oxford (MA); Univ. of Paris; New York Univ. Graduate Business Sch. Bankers Trust Co., NY, 1963–80 (Vice-Pres., 1974–80). Associate Dir, Swiss Bank Corp., London, 1992–94. Underwriting Mem., Lloyds, 1984–; MCSI (MSI 1993). Chm., Standing Council of the Baronetage, 1993–96 (Vice-Chm., 1990–92; Hon. Treas., 1980–92; Vice Pres.); Editor and founder, The Baronets Journal, 1987–99; Chm. Trustees, Baronets Trust, 1996–2002 (Trustee, 1989); Publisher, The Official Roll of the Baronetage, 1997. Lord of the Manor of Bibury. *Recreations:* accidental happenings, riding, gardening, photography, stimulating conversation; Pres., Bibury Cricket Club. *Heir:* s (Charles Somerset) Lawrence Clarke, *b* 12 March 1990. *Clubs:* White's, Boodle's, Beefsteak, Pratt's, Pilgrims, MCC; Jockey (Paris); The Brook, Racquet and Tennis (New York).

**CLARKE, Rt Hon. Charles (Rodway);** PC 2001; *b* 21 Sept. 1950; *s* of Sir Richard Clarke, KCB, OBE and Brenda Clarke (*née* Skinner); *m* 1984, Carol Marika Pearson; two *s*. *Educ:* Highgate Sch.; King's Coll., Cambridge (BA Hons 1973). Pres., NUS, 1975–77; various admin. posts, 1977–80; Head, Office of Rt Hon. Neil Kinnock, MP, 1981–92; Chief Exec., Quality Public Affairs, 1992–97. Mem. (Lab) Hackney LBC, 1980–86. MP (Lab) Norwich South, 1997–2010; contested (Lab) same seat, 2010. Parly Under-Sec. of State, DfEE, 1998–99; Minister of State, Home Office, 1999–2001; Minister without Portfolio and Chm., Labour Party, 2001–02; Sec. of State for Educn and Skills, 2002–04, for the Home Dept, 2004–06. Mem., Treasury Select Cttee, 1997–98. Visiting Professor: Sch. of Pol, Social and Internat. Studies, UEA, 2010–17; Sch. of Politics and Philosophy, Univ. of Lancaster, 2010–; Sch. of Econs, UCL, 2012–14; Policy Inst., KCL, 2015–; Dist. Fellow, USC, 2018–. *Publications:* (ed) The Too Difficult Box: the big issues politicians can't crack, 2014; (ed jtly) British Labour Leaders, 2015; (ed jtly) British Conservative Leaders, 2015. *Recreations:* chess, reading, walking, supporting Norwich City Football Club. *E:* charlesclarke2109@gmail.com. *W:* www.charlesclarke.org.

**CLARKE, Christopher Alan;** Member, 2001–10, a Deputy Chairman, 2004–10, Competition Commission; *b* 14 May 1945; *s* of late Harry Alston Clarke and Isobel Corsan Clarke (*née* Kay); *m* 1st, 1971, Jessica Pearson (marr. diss. 1976); 2nd, 1978, Charlotte Jenkins; one *s* one *d*. *Educ:* Oakham Sch.; Selwyn Coll., Cambridge (BA Econs 1967, MA); London Business Sch. (MSc/MBA 1972). With Shell Internat. Petroleum Co. Ltd, 1967–73; IDJ Ltd, 1973–74; Man. Dir, Arbuthnot Latham Asia Ltd, 1979–82; Arbuthnot Latham & Co. Ltd, 1974–82 (Dir, 1978–82); Director: Samuel Montagu & Co. Ltd, 1982–96; HSBC Investment Banking, 1996–98. Non-executive Director: Weir Gp, 1999–2008; Omega Underwriting Hldgs, 2005–06; Omega Insurance Hldgs, 2006–10. Mem., Privatisation Project Bd, Cabinet Office, 2005–12. Dir, Trustee and Hon. Treas., Classics for All, 2014–. *Recreations:* golf, fishing, reading, wine, theatre, ballet. *Club:* Berkshire Golf.
*See also Baron Clarke of Stone-cum-Ebony.*

**CLARKE, (Christopher) Michael,** CBE 2009; FRSE; Director, Scottish National Gallery, 2001–16; *b* 29 Aug. 1952; *s* of Patrick Reginald Clarke and Margaret Catherine Clarke (*née* Waugh); *m* 1978, Deborah Clare Cowling; two *s* one *d*. *Educ:* Felsted; Manchester Univ. (BA (Hons) History of Art). FRSE 2008. Art Asst, York City Art Gall., 1973–76; Res. Asst, British Mus., 1976–78; Asst Keeper in Charge of Prints, Whitworth Art Gall., Manchester Univ., 1978–84; Asst Keeper, 1984–87, Keeper, 1987–2000, Nat. Gall. of Scotland. Vis. Fellow: Yale Center for British Art, 1985; Clark Art Inst., 2004. Hon. Prof., Edinburgh Coll. of Art, Univ. of Edinburgh, 2016–. Chevalier, Ordre des Arts et des Lettres (France), 2004; Comdr, Order of the Dannebrog (Denmark), 2012. *Publications:* Pollaiuolo to Picasso: Old Master prints in the Whitworth Art Gallery, 1980; The Tempting Prospect: a social history of English watercolours, 1981; (ed with N. Penny) The Arrogant Connoisseur: Richard Payne Knight, 1982; The Draughtsman's Art: Master Drawings in the Whitworth Art Gallery, 1983; Lighting up the Landscape: French Impressionism and its origins, 1986; Corot and the Art of Landscape, 1991; Eyewitness Art: watercolour, 1993; (ed jtly) Corot, Courbet und die Maler von Barbizon, 1996; Oxford Concise Dictionary of Art Terms, 2001; The Playfair Project, 2004; The Art of Golf, 2014; articles, reviews, etc, in Apollo, Art Internat., Burlington Magazine, Museums Jl. *Recreations:* golf, travel, cycling slowly. *Club:* Royal and Ancient (St Andrews).

**CLARKE, Rt Hon. Sir Christopher (Simon Courtenay Stephenson),** Kt 2005; PC 2013; a Lord Justice of Appeal, 2013–17; *b* 14 March 1947; *s* of late Rev. John Stephenson Clarke and Enid Courtenay Clarke; *m* 1974, Caroline Anne Fletcher; one *s* two *d*. *Educ:* Marlborough College; Gonville and Caius College, Cambridge (MA). Called to the Bar, Middle Temple, 1969, Bencher, 1991 (Treas., 2016); Attorney of Supreme Court of Turks and Caicos Islands, 1975; QC 1984; a Recorder, 1990–2004; a Deputy High Ct Judge, 1993–2004; a Judge of the Cts of Appeal of Jersey and Guernsey, 1998–2004; a Judge of the High Ct of Justice, QBD, 2005–13. Judge, Ct of Ecclesiastical Causes Reserved, 2015–; Judge, Ct of Appeal, Bermuda, 2017– (Pres., 2019–). Counsel to Bloody Sunday Inquiry, 1998–2004. Councillor, Internat. Bar Assoc., 1988–90; Chm., Commercial Bar Assoc., 1993–95; Mem., Bar Council, 1993–99. Internat. Arbitrator, 2017–. Mem., Archbishop of Canterbury's Commn on the Relationship of Channel Islands to wider C of E, 2018–19. FRSA 1995. *Clubs:* Brooks's, Garrick, Hurlingham.

**CLARKE, Darren Christopher,** OBE 2012; professional golfer, since 1990; *b* 14 Aug. 1968; *m* Heather (*d* 2006); two *s*; *m* 2012, Alison Campbell. Amateur wins include: Spanish, Irish, N of Ireland and S of Ireland Championships, 1990; has played on European Tour, 1991–, PGA Tour, 2005–; wins include: Alfred Dunhill Open, 1993; Benson and Hedges Internat., Volvo Masters, 1998; Compass Gp Eur. Open, 1999; Compass Gp English Open, 1999, 2000, 2002; World Golf Championships (WGC) Accenture Match Play, 2000 (first European to win a WGC event); Smurfit Eur. Open, Chunichi Crowns, Japan, 2001; WGC NEC-Invitational, NI Masters, 2003; Mitsui Sumitomo VISA Taiheijo Masters, Japan, 2004, 2005; BMW Asian Open, KLM Open, 2008; Open, Royal St George's, 2011: Member: Alfred Dunhill Cup team, 1994, 1995, 1996, 1997, 1998, 1999; World Cup team, 1994, 1995, 1996; Ryder Cup team, 1997, 1999, 2002, 2004, 2006, 2010, 2012 (a Vice-Captain), 2016 (Captain); Seve Trophy team, 2000, 2002; Royal Trophy team, 2007. Founder, Darren Clarke Foundn, 2002. *Publications:* The Mind Factor, 2005; Darren Clarke: my Ryder Cup story, 2006; An Open Book: my autobiography, 2012. *Recreations:* films, reading, cars, fishing, Liverpool FC. *Address:* c/o ISM Ltd, Cherry Tree Farm, Cherry Tree Lane, Rostherne, Cheshire WA14 3RZ. *T:* (01565) 832100, *Fax:* (01565) 832200. *E:* ism@sportism.net.

**CLARKE, Hon. Sir David (Clive),** Kt 2003; DL; a Judge of the High Court of Justice, Queen's Bench Division, 2003–10; a Presiding Judge, Northern Circuit, 2006–09; *b* 16 July 1942; *s* of Philip George Clarke and José Margaret Clarke; *m* 1969, Alison Claire, *d* of Rt Rev. Percy James Brazier; two *s* (and one *s* decd). *Educ:* Winchester Coll.; Magdalene Coll., Cambridge (BA 1964, MA 1968). Called to the Bar, Inner Temple, 1965, Bencher, 1992; in practice, Northern Circuit, 1965–93 (Treas., 1988–92); a Recorder, 1981–93; QC 1983; a Circuit Judge, 1993–97; a Sen. Circuit Judge, and Hon. Recorder of Liverpool, 1997–2003; Asst Surveillance Comr, 2010–17. Member: Criminal Justice Consultative Council, 1999–2003; UK Donation Ethics Cttee, 2014–16. DL Merseyside, 2011. Hon. Fellow, Liverpool John Moores Univ., 2007. Hon. LLD Liverpool, 2004. *Recreations:* walking, sailing, swimming, canals. *Club:* Trearddur Bay Sailing (Anglesey).

**CLARKE, Prof. David William,** DPhil; FRS 1998; FREng, FIET; Professor of Control Engineering, Oxford University, 1992–2008, now Emeritus; Fellow, New College, Oxford, 1969–2008, now Emeritus; *b* 31 May 1943; *s* of Norman William Clarke and Laura (*née* Dewhurst); *m* 1967, Lynda Ann Weatherhead; two *s*. *Educ:* Balliol Coll., Oxford. MA, DPhil Oxon. FIET (FIEE 1984); FREng (FEng 1989). Oxford University: Astor Res. Fellow, New Coll., 1966–69; Lectr, 1969–86; Reader in Information Engrg, 1986–92; Hd, Dept of Engrg Sci., 1994–99. Former Dir, now Consultant, Invensys UTC for Advanced Instrumentation. Sir Harold Hartley Silver Medal, Inst. of Measurement and Control, 1983; Gold Medal of Achievement (Sen. Award), IEE, 2002. *Publications:* Advances in Model-Based Predictive Control, 1994; papers in learned jls. *Recreations:* gardening, historical ship models, learning C++ for Windows API. *Address:* New College, Oxford OX1 3BN. *T:* (01865) 279507.

**CLARKE, Donald Roberts;** Finance Director, 3i (formerly Investors in Industry) Group plc, 1988–91; *b* 14 May 1933; *s* of Harold Leslie Clarke and Mary Clarke; *m* 1959, Susan Charlotte Cotton (*d* 2014); one *s* three *d*. *Educ:* Ealing Grammar Sch.; The Queen's Coll., Oxford (MA). Articled Peat Marwick Mitchell & Co., 1957–62; Accountant, The Collingwood Group, 1962–64; Industrial and Commercial Finance Corporation: Investigating Accountant, 1964; Controller, 1964–67; Br. Manager, 1967–68; Co. Sec., 1968–73; Investors in Industry Gp (formerly Finance for Industry): Sec./Treasurer, 1973–76; Asst Gen. Manager, 1976–79; Gen. Manager, Finance, 1979–88. Dir, Consumers' Assoc. Ltd, 1990–92. Member: UGC, 1982–85; Industrial, Commercial and Prof. Liaison Gp, National Adv. Body for Local Authority Higher Educn, 1983–85; Continuing Educn Standing Cttee, Nat. Adv. Body for Local Authority Higher Educn and UGC, 1985–89; Council, Royal Holloway, Univ. of London (formerly RHBNC), 1987–2002 (Hon. Fellow, 2005). Trustee, Hestercombe Gardens Trust, 2001–14 (Patron, 2014–). *Publications:* (jtly) 3i: 50 years investing in industry, 1995. *Club:* Oxford and Cambridge.

**CLARKE, Elaine Denise;** *see* Watson, E. D.

**CLARKE, Prof. Eric Fillenz,** PhD; FBA 2010; Heather Professor of Music, University of Oxford, since 2007; *b* 31 July 1955; *s* of John Clarke and Marianne (*née* Fillenz); *m* Catherine Ferreira; one *s* one *d*. *Educ:* Univ. of Sussex (BA Music 1977, MA Music 1978); Univ. of Exeter (PhD Psychol. 1984). Lectr, 1981–88, Sen. Lectr, 1988–91, Reader, 1991–93, in Music, City Univ., London; James Rossiter Hoyle Prof. of Music, Univ. of Sheffield, 1993–2007. *Publications:* Empirical Musicology (ed with Nicholas Cook), 2004; Ways of Listening, 2005; (with N. Dibben and S. Pitts) Music and Mind in Everyday Life, 2010; (ed with David Clarke) Music and Consciousness, 2011; contrib. numerous papers to jls of Music Perception, Psychology of Music, Musicae Scientiae, Music Analysis, Popular Music. *Recreations:* cycling, gardening, walking, playing music. *Address:* Music Faculty, University of Oxford, St Aldate's, Oxford OX1 1DB. *T:* (01865) 276125, *Fax:* (01865) 276128. *E:* eric.clarke@music.ox.ac.uk.

**CLARKE, Eric Lionel;** *b* 9 April 1933; *s* of late Ernest and Annie Clarke; *m* 1955, June Hewat; two *s* one *d*. *Educ:* St Cuthbert's Holy Cross Acad.; W. M. Ramsey Tech. Coll.; Esk Valley Tech. Coll. Coalminer: Roslin Colliery, 1949–51; Lingerwood Colliery, 1951–69; Bilston Glen Colliery, 1969–77; Trade Union Official, 1977–89; Gen. Sec., NUM Scotland; redundant, unemployed, 1989–92. Mem., Midlothian CC and then Lothian Regl Council, 1962–78. MP (Lab) Midlothian, 1992–2001. An Opposition Whip, 1994–97. *Recreations:* fly fishing, gardening, carpentry, football spectator. *Address:* 32 Mortonhall Park Crescent, Edinburgh EH17 8SY. *T:* (0131) 664 8214. *Club:* Danderhall Miners' Welfare.

**CLARKE, Frank**; Hon. Mr Justice Clarke; Chief Justice of Ireland, since 2017; *b* Dublin, 10 Oct. 1951; *s* of Bernard Clarke and Sheila Clarke (*née* Bailey); *m* 1977, Prof. Jacqueline Hayden; one *s* one *d*. *Educ*: Drimnagh Castle Christian Brothers Sch., Dublin; University Coll. Dublin (BA). Called to the Bar, King's Inns, Dublin, 1973, Bencher, 1994; in practice as barrister, 1973–2004; Sen. Counsel, 1985–2004; a Judge of the High Court, 2004–12; a Judge, Supreme Court of Ireland, 2012–17. Chair, Referendum Commn on Lisbon Treaty, 2010. Chair, Irish Legal Terms Adv. Cttee, 2014–. Mem., Panel on Article 255 of Treaty on Functioning of EU, 2018–. Adjunct Professor: TCD, 2012–; University Coll. Cork, 2014–. Judge in Residence, Griffith Coll., Dublin, 2010–. Bencher, Middle Temple, 2018. Chairman: Bar Council, 1993–95; Council of King's Inns, 1999–2004. Mem. Council, IBA, 1992–2004 (Co-Chair, Barristers and Advocates, 1998–2002). Pres., Irish Soc. for European Law, 2015–. Vice Pres., Network of Presidents of Supreme Judicial Courts of EU, 2019–. Hon. Member: Canadian Bar Assoc., 1994; Australian Bar Assoc., 2002. Dist. Fellow, Griffith Coll., 2017. *Recreations*: horse racing, Rugby, music, theatre. *Address*: Supreme Court, Four Courts, Inns Quay, Dublin 7, Ireland. *T*: (1) 8886540. *Club*: Turf (Dep. Sen. Steward, 2003–05).

**CLARKE, Garth Martin**; Chief Executive, Transport Research Laboratory, 1997–2001; *b* 1 Feb. 1944; *s* of Peter Oakley Clarke and Ella Audrey (*née* Jenner); *m* 1966, Carol Marian Trimble; three *d*. *Educ*: Duke's Grammar Sch., Alnwick, Northumberland; Liverpool Univ. (BSc Hons). FCIHT (FIHT 1996). Research Physicist, 1966–73, Ops Dir, 1983–87, Plessey Research (Caswell) Ltd; Dir, Commercial Ops, Plessey Res. and Technology Ltd, 1987–89; Business Develt Dir, Business Systems Gp, GPT Ltd, 1990–93; Business Dir, TRL, 1993–97. Chief Exec., Transport Res. Foundn, 1997–2001; Chm., Viridis, 1999–2001. Dir, Parly Adv. Council for Transport Safety, 2001–05. Fellow, Transport Res. Foundn, 1998. CCMI. *Recreations*: birdwatching, water colour painting, photography.

**CLARKE, Geoff James**; QC (Scot.) 2008; *b* Edinburgh, 3 May 1966; *s* of Owen Clarke, CBE and Elizabeth Clarke; *m* 2002, Kelly Loughran; two *s*. *Educ*: N Berwick High Sch.; Edinburgh Univ. (LLB Hons). Solicitor, 1989–93, Advocate, 1994–2008, specialising in personal injury, valuation for rating, Simpson & Marwick, Edinburgh. *Recreations*: walking, reading, judo. *Address*: Stair Park, North Berwick, E Lothian EH39 4DD. *T*: (01620) 890754, *Fax*: (01620) 890758. *E*: geoff.clarke@compasschambers.com. *Club*: North Berwick Golf.

**CLARKE, Georgina Ann**; *see* Byrne, G. A.

**CLARKE, Giles**; *see* Clarke, C. G.

**CLARKE, Giles Colin Scott**, PhD; museums and heritage consultant; Head, Department of Exhibitions and Education, Natural History Museum, 1994–2001; *b* 9 Jan. 1944; *s* of Colin Richard Clarke and Vera Joan, (Georgie), Clarke (*née* Scott); *m* 1967, Helen Parker (*see* Helen Clarke); one *s*. *Educ*: Sevenoaks Sch.; Keble Coll., Oxford (MA 1970); Birmingham Univ. (PhD 1970). VSO, Gambia, 1963; Mem., Internat. Biological Prog. Bipolar Expeditions, 1967–68; Asst Keeper of Botany, Manchester Mus., 1970–73; Head, Pollen Section, 1973–79, Dep. Head, Dept of Public Services, 1979–94, British Mus. (Natural History), later Natural History Mus. Member: Council, British Bryological Soc., 1971–2001 (Pres., 1998–99; Hon. Mem., 2005); Cttee, Trends in Leisure and Entertainment Conf. and Exhibn, 1993–2005 (Chair, 1998). Chair, Cttee, Wildlife Photographer of the Year, 1984–2001. Trustee, Eureka! Children's Mus., 1999–2011; Mem. Cttee, Royal Tunbridge Wells SO, 2010– (Chm., 2013–). Japanese Soc. for Promotion of Sci. Fellow, Nagoya Univ. Mus., 2008; Exec. Advr to Nagoya Univ., 2015–. Hon. Mem., Kennel Club, 2008 (Chair, Liby and Gall. Panel, 2012–). FLS 1971; FMA 1996; FRSA 1997. *Publications*: numerous papers in prof. jls on botany and museums. *Recreations*: opera, organ music, art galleries, reading, making things. *Address*: Kynance, Clarence Road, Tunbridge Wells, Kent TN1 1HE.

**CLARKE, Graham Neil**; Chairman, Hamdene Horticultural Publishing Services Ltd, 2006–18; *b* 23 July 1956; *s* of late Henry Charles Owen Clarke, RVM and Doris May Clarke; *m* 1980, Denise Carole (*née* Anderson); two *d*. *Educ*: Rutherford Sch., N London; Wisley School of Horticulture (WisCertHort). Staff gardener, Buckingham Palace, 1975–76; Nurseryman, Hyde Park, 1976; Amateur Gardening: Sub-Editor, 1976–79; Chief Sub-Editor, 1979–81; Dep. Editor, 1981–86; Editor, 1986–98; Editor, Home Plus Magazine, 1984–85; IPC gardening titles: Gp Editor, 1993–95; Special Projects Editor, 1995–98; Editor-at-Large, 1998–99; Editor: Exotic & Greenhouse Gardening, 2000–01; Garden Calendar, 2000–01; Develt Ed., 1999–2001, Man. Ed., 2000–02, Guild of Master Craftsman Pubns; Editor: Water Gardening, 1999–2002; Business Matters, 2002–03; Guild News, 2003–04, 2007–14; Horticulture Week, 2004–05; publishing and horticulture consultant, 2002–04 and 2005–; gardening presenter, Ideal World TV, 2012; official blog author, Westland Horticulture, 2015–16. FLS 1990; FCIHort (FIHort 2011) (AIHort 1991; MIHort 1995). *Publications*: Step by Step Pruning, 1985; Autumn and Winter Colour in the Garden, 1986; Complete Book of Plant Propagation, 1990; The Ultimate House Plant Handbook, 1997; Beginner's Guide to Water Gardening, 2002; Collins Practical Guide: Water Gardening, 2004; Collins Practical Guide: Pruning, 2005; Success with Roses, 2007; Success with Shade-Loving Plants, 2007; Success with Sun-Loving Plants, 2007; Success with Water Gardens, 2007; Success with Water-Saving Gardens, 2007; Success with Acid-Loving Plants, 2008; Success with Alkaline-Loving Plants, 2008; The Organic Gardener's Year, 2008; Coastal Gardening, 2009; Success with Small-Space Gardening, 2009; Success with Alpine Gardening, 2009; The Organic Herb Gardener, 2010; Growing for Food and Colour, 2012; Amateur Gardening Yearbook, 2015; Gardener's Book of Tips, 2017; Gardener's Book of Trivia, 2017. *Recreations*: gardening, philately, family history, script and screenplay writing. *Address*: Hamdene House, 127 Magna Road, Bournemouth, Dorset BH11 9NE. *Club*: Royal Horticultural Society Garden (Surrey).

**CLARKE, Gregory**; Chairman, Football Association, since 2016; *b* 27 Oct. 1957; *s* of George and Mary Clarke; *m* 1984, Anne Wilson; four *d*. *Educ*: Gateway Grammar Sch., Leicester; Wolverhampton Poly. (BA Hons 1980); City Univ. Business Sch. (MBA 1983). Vice Pres., Global Cellular, Nortel, 1992–95; Chief Exec., Cable & Wireless Mobile, 1995–97; Chief Operating Officer, 1997–99, Chief Exec., 1999–2000, Cable & Wireless Communications plc; Chief Executive Officer: ICO Teledisc, 2000–02; Lend Lease Corp., Sydney, 2002–09; O3b, 2009–10. Chairman: Eteach UK Ltd, 2000–02; Football League, 2010–16; UK2, 2011; Redefine Internat., later RDI REIT plc, 2011–18; Met Office, 2012–17; Easynet, 2012; non-executive Director: Leicester City, 2000–07; BUPA Ltd, 2001–07. A Vice-Pres., FIFA, 2019–. *Recreations*: family, football, Leicester City FC, opera, Rugby, reading.

**CLARKE, Dr Helen**, FSA; Director, Society of Antiquaries, 1990–94; *b* 25 Aug. 1939; *d* of George Parker and Helen (*née* Teare); *m* 1967, Giles Colin Scott Clarke, *qv*; one *s*. *Educ*: Univ. of Birmingham (BA; PhD); Univ. of Lund, Sweden. FSA 1972. Dir of Excavations, King's Lynn, 1963–67; Res. Fellow, Sch. of History, Birmingham Univ., 1965–67; Lecturer in Medieval Archaeology: Glasgow Univ., 1967–69; UCL, 1976–90. Visiting Professor in Medieval Archaeology: Lund Univ., Sweden, 1991; Århus Univ., Denmark, 1992; Kiel Univ., Germany, 1993. Hon. Sen. Lectr (formerly Hon. Res. Associate), Inst. of Archaeol., UCL, 2000–. Editor and Translator: Royal Swedish Acad. of Letters, History and Antiquities, 1975–2008; Bd of National Antiquities, Sweden (also Consultant), 1990–95; Consultant, English Heritage, 1987–94. Trustee, Council for British Archaeol., 2004–07. Member: Svenska Arkeologiska Samfundet, 1988; Vetenskapssocieteten i Lund, 1988. Hon. Fil Dr Lund, 1991. Silver Medal for services to Swedish archaeol., Royal Swedish Acad. of Letters, History and Antiquities, 2012. *Publications*: Regional Archaeologies: East Anglia, 1971; Excavations in King's Lynn, 1963–1970, 1977; The Archaeology of Medieval England, 1984, 2nd edn 1986; Towns in the Viking Age, 1991, 2nd edn 1995; Sandwich: the 'completest medieval town in England', 2010; Walks Through Historic Sandwich, 2011; Discover Medieval Sandwich: a guide to its history and buildings, 2012; Helgö Revisited: a new look at the excavated evidence for Helgö, central Sweden, 2017. *Recreations*: attending opera, watching cricket, investigating the landscape.

**CLARKE, Henry Benwell**; Board Member, Rail Estate Consultancy, since 1998; *b* 30 Jan. 1950; *yr s* of late Stephen Lampard Clarke and Elinor Wade Clarke (*née* Benwell); *m* 1973, Verena Angela Lodge; four *s* one *d*. *Educ*: St John's Sch., Leatherhead; South Bank Polytechnic (BSc Estate Management 1972); Imperial College London (MSc Management Science 1977; DIC 1977). ARICS 1973, FRICS 1986; ACIArb 1979. British Rail Property Board: S Region, 1972–78; NW Region, 1978–82; E Region, 1982–85; Regional Estate Surveyor and Manager, Midland Region, 1985–86; Chief Estate Surveyor, HQ, 1986–87; Nat. Develt Manager, 1987–88; Dep. Chief Exec., Crown Estate Comrs, 1988–92, Acting Chief Exec. and Accounting Officer, 1989. Mem., Gen. Council, British Property Fedn, 1989–92. Dir, Henry Clarke Associates, 2004–. Member, Board: People and Places Internat., 1993–2004; Telecom Property Ltd, 1999–2010; Crownmead Properties Ltd, 2001–; Kings Yard Developments, 2003–04; Intelligent Business Space Ltd, 2004–08; The Model Bus Co., 2006–; Jackson Green Ltd (formerly Jackson-Green Partnership), 2006–; Revetment Ltd, 2008–; Aquobex Ltd, 2013–. Mem. Council, Christian Union for Estate Profession, 1983–88; Member, Board: Youth with a Mission (England), 1990–; Mercy Ships (UK), 1995–; Moggerhanger House Preservation Trust, 1997–2005; Railway Children Trust, 2002–17; Lindow Ministry Trust Ltd, 2002–; Mercy Ships Internat., 2015–; Apsley Paper Trail, 2017–; advisor to various Christian trusts. Freeman: City of London, 2008; Plumbers' Co., 2008. *Recreations*: reading, walking, transport, architecture, Church. *Address*: 42 Wordsworth Road, Harpenden, Herts AL5 4AF.

**CLARKE, Hilda Mary Maude**; Headteacher, Tiffin School, 2009–15; *b* Loughborough, 9 Nov. 1954; *d* of Frederick Clarke and Rosie Clarke (*née* de Taranto). *Educ*: Kelvin Hall Sch., Hull; Sussex Univ. (BA Hons Hist.); Hull Univ. (PGCE); Inst. of Educn, London (NPQH). Teacher, then Sen. Teacher and Hd of History, Alsager Sch., Cheshire, 1977–92; Dep. Head, Tiffin Girls' Sch., 1992–2000; Headteacher, Langley Grammar Sch., 2000–09. Chm., Berks Assoc. of Secondary Hds, 2007–09. *Recreations*: classical music, sport.

**CLARKE, Ian James**; QC 2016; *b* London, 3 Dec. 1967; *s* of John Eric Clarke and Joan Roberts Clarke; *m* 1997, Charlotte Rosemary Matthews; one *s* one *d*. *Educ*: Ryde Sch., IoW; Newcastle Univ. (LLB Hons). Called to the Bar, Lincoln's Inn, 1990 (Hardwicke Scholar), Bencher, 2013; in practice as barrister, Selborne Chambers; Dep. Adjudicator to HM Land Registry, 2004–13; a Judge of First-tier Tribunal (Property Chamber) (Land Registration), 2013–. Chm., Inns of Court Conduct Cttee, 2018–. *Publications*: (ed) Cousins: Law of Mortgages, 2nd edn 2001 to 4th edn 2017; Wolstenholme and Cherry's Annotated Land Registration Act 2002, 2003. *Recreations*: ski-ing, sailing, food, wine, family and friends. *Address*: Selborne Chambers, 10 Essex Street, WC2R 3AA. *T*: (020) 7420 9500. *E*: ian.clarke@selbornechambers.co.uk. *Clubs*: Bar Yacht; Sea View Yacht.

**CLARKE, (James) Brian**; author and journalist; Fishing Correspondent, The Times, 1991–2018; *b* 28 May 1938; *s* of Thomas Clarke and Annette Clarke (*née* Vickers); *m* 1968, (Edith Isobel) Anne Farley; three *d*. *Educ*: St Mary's Grammar Sch., Darlington; Darlington Tech. Coll. Reporter and sub-ed., Northern Echo, Darlington, 1955–59; Dep. Features Ed., Evening Gazette, Middlesbrough, 1959–61; home news sub-ed., Scottish Daily Mail, Edinburgh, 1961–62; home news and Parly sub-ed., The Guardian, 1962–67; Nat. Press Officer, IBM UK, 1967–68; Public Affairs Advr, Nat. Computing Centre, 1968–69; indep. mgt consultant, 1969–74; various corporate communications and envmtl mgt posts, IBM UK, 1974–91 (on secondment to BBC, 1988–90: series producer, In the Name of the Law (television), 1988–89; Consultant, BBC Bd of Mgt, 1989–90); consultant, envmtl progs, IBM UK, 1990–91; Fishing Corresp., Sunday Times, 1975–96. Vice-Pres., Wild Trout Trust, 2009– (Pres., 2004–09). *Publications*: The Pursuit of Stillwater Trout, 1975, 8th edn 2014; (contrib.) The Masters on the Nymph (US), 1976; (contrib.) Stillwater Trout Fisheries, 1976; (contrib.) The Complete Salmon and Trout Fisherman, 1978; (jtly) The Trout and the Fly, 1980, 7th edn 2005; (contrib.) West Country Fly Fishing, 1983; (contrib.) The Fly-Fishers, 1984; (contrib.) The One That Got Away, 1991; (jtly) Flyfishing for Trout (US), 1993; Trout etcetera: selected writings 1982–1996, 1996; (contrib.) Lessons from the Fish, 1996; (contrib.) Trout and Salmon, 1999; (contrib.) Fly-Fishers' Progress, 2000; The Stream (novel), 2000 (Natural World Book Prize, 2000; Authors' Club Best First Novel Award, 2000); (jtly) Understanding Trout Behaviour (US), 2002; (contrib.) The World of Fly-Fishing, 2003; (contrib.) The Literary Non-Fiction Collection, 2005; (contrib.) Richard Walker: a biography, 2007; On Fishing: journalism and essays 1996–2007, 2007. *Recreations*: fishing, walking, photography, table tennis, sitting still in the countryside watching and listening. *Address*: c/o Watson, Little Ltd, 22 Highbury Grove, N5 2ER. *Club*: Flyfishers'.

**CLARKE, Jane**; author (as Jane Lythell); *d* of Michael David Hilborne-Clarke and Margaret Lythell; one *d* by Howard Austin Trevette. *Educ*: Norwich High Sch. for Girls; University College London (BA Hons English Lang. and Lit. 1975); Slade Sch. of Fine Art. Film Programmer, BFI, 1980–82; Features Prod., TV-am, 1982–88: Ed., Henry Kelly Saturday Show, 1984–85; Features Ed., Good Morning Britain, 1985–87; Ed., After Nine, 1987–88; Independent Prod., Pithers, Clarke and Ferguson, 1988–89 (prod., Children First for Granada TV, 1989); Series Ed., New Living for British Satellite Broadcasting, 1990–91; Controller, Features, West Country TV, 1992–95; Dep. Dir, BFI, 1995–97; Chief Exec., BAFTA, 1998; Foreign and Commonwealth Office: Head: Broadcast and Allied Media, subseq. TV and Radio, Public Diplomacy Dept, 1999–2002; Strategy and Progs, then Strategy and Campaigns, Public Diplomacy Team, 2002–05; Internal Communications, 2005–06; Head of Communications: Sport England, 2006–08; Kent CC, 2008–11. Writer (full-time), 2011–. Bd Mem., London Fest. of Literature, 2000–01. *Publications*: (with Diana Simmonds) Move Over Misconceptions: Doris Day reappraised, 1981; as Jane Lythell: The Lie of You, 2014; After the Storm, 2015; Woman of the Hour, 2016; Behind Her Back, 2018. *Recreations*: Tottenham Hotspur FC, reading, walking, cricket, astronomy. *E*: clarke.jane22@gmail.com. *W*: http://janelythellamwriting.blogspot.com, www.twitter.com/janelythell, www.instagram.com/jane_lythell_writer.

**CLARKE, Prof. Jane**, PhD; FRS 2015; FRSC; FMedSci; President, Wolfson College, Cambridge, since 2017; Professor of Molecular Biophysics, University of Cambridge, 2009–17, now Emerita; *b* London, 10 Sept. 1950; *d* of Cyril Morgan and Shirley Morgan (*née* Jenkins); *m* 1973, Christopher Clarke; one *s* one *d*. *Educ*: Univ. of York (BA 1st Cl. Hons Biochem. 1972); Univ. of Cambridge (PGCE 1973); Georgia Inst. of Technol., Atlanta (MSc Applied Biol. 1990); Univ. of Cambridge (PhD 1994). FRSC 2013; FMedSci 2013. Science teacher in secondary schs, incl. Hd of Sci., Northumberland Park Sch.,

Tottenham, 1973–86; Postdoctoral Fellow, Centre for Protein Engrg, MRC Centre, Cambridge, 1994–97; Wellcome Trust Career Develt Fellow, 1997–2001, Wellcome Trust Sen. Res. Fellow, 2001–17, Reader in Molecular Biophysics, 2007–09, Dept of Chemistry, Univ. of Cambridge; Fellow, Trinity Hall, Cambridge, 2010–17. Mem., EMBO, 2012. *Publications:* contribs to learned jls incl. Biochem., Structure, Jl Biol Chem., Biophysics Jl, Nature, Proc. NAS, Jl Amer. Chem. Soc., Current Opinion Structural Biol., Jl Molecular Biol. *Address:* Wolfson College, Barton Road, Cambridge CB3 9BB. *T:* (01223) 336426. *E:* jc162@cam.ac.uk.

**CLARKE, Prof. John,** FRS 1986; Professor of Physics, since 1973, and Luis W. Alvarez Memorial Chair for Experimental Physics, since 1994, University of California, Berkeley; *b* 10 Feb. 1942; *s* of Victor Patrick and Ethel May Clarke; *m* 1979, Grethe F. Pedersen; one *d. Educ:* Christ's Coll., Cambridge (BA, MA 1968; Hon. Fellow, 1997); Darwin Coll., Cambridge (PhD 1968; ScD 2003). Postdoctoral Scholar, 1968, Asst Prof., 1969, Associate Prof., 1971–73, Univ. of California, Berkeley. Alfred P. Sloan Foundn Fellow, 1970; Adolph C. and Mary Sprague Miller Inst. for Basic Research into Science Prof., 1975, 1994, 2007; John Simon Guggenheim Fellow, 1977; Vis. Fellow, Clare Hall, Cambridge, 1989; By-Fellow, Churchill Coll., Cambridge, 1998; Faculty Res. Lectr, Univ. of California, Berkeley, 2005; 150th Anniv. Vis. Prof., Chalmers Univ. of Technol., Gothenburg, 2009–13, 2015, 2016; Chair Prof., Nat. Taiwan Normal Univ., Taipei, 2012–. For. Mem., Royal Soc. of Arts and Scis in Gothenburg, Sweden, 2007; For. Associate, Nat. Acad. of Scis, USA, 2012. FAAAS 1982; Fellow, Amer. Phys. Soc., 1985; FInstP 1999; Fellow, Amer. Acad. of Arts and Scis, 2015; Mem., Amer. Philosophical Soc., 2017. Charles Vernon Boys Prize, Inst. of Physics, 1977; Calif. Scientist of the Year, 1987; Fritz London Meml Award for Low Temperature Physics, 1987; Joseph F. Keithley Award, APS, 1998; Comstock Prize for Physics, NAS, 1999; IEEE Council on Superconductivity Award, 2002; Scientific American 50 Award, 2002; Lounasmaa Prize, Finnish Acad. of Arts and Scis, 2004; Hughes Medal, Royal Soc., 2004; Outstanding Performance Award, Lawrence Berkeley Nat. Lab., 2010; Berkeley Citation, Univ. of Calif, Berkeley, 2011. *Publications:* approx. 475 contribs to learned jls. *Address:* Department of Physics, University of California, 366 Le Conte Hall, Berkeley, CA 94720–7300, USA. *T:* (510) 6423069.

**CLARKE, John Francis;** Chief Executive, Welsh European Funding Office, National Assembly for Wales, 2000–03; *b* 10 June 1947; *s* of Francis William Clarke and Joan Margaret Clarke; *m* 1969, Lynda Mary Hudson; three *s. Educ:* Windermere Grammar Sch.; Manchester Univ. (BA Hons); Harvard Business Sch. (PMD 1984). ACIB. Barclays Bank: Mgt Trainee, 1968–75; Asst Manager, 1975–78; Asst District Manager, 1978–81; Sen. Corporate Manager, 1981–84; Corporate Finance Dir, 1986–91; Regl Dir, 1991–99; Sen. Vice Pres., Barclays USA, 1984–86. Chm., Greater Nottingham TEC, 1997–98; Mem., East Midlands Regl IDB, 1992–97. Chairman: The Stables Theatre, Wavendon, 1977–91; St Donats Arts Centre Ltd, 2006–10; Dir, Amelia Methodist Trust Co. Ltd, 2016–. Pres., Llantwit Major Rotary Club, 2002–03 and 2012–13 (Mem., 1999–); Vice-Pres., Cardiff Business Club, 1998–2011. Mem., Audit Cttee, Univ. of Wales Inst., Cardiff, 2006–11; Gov., Llantwit Major Comprehensive Sch., 2005–. Trustee, World at Play, 2011–12. *Recreations:* golf, gardening. *Address:* The Old Vicarage, St Donats, Llantwit Major, Vale of Glamorgan CF61 1ZB. *T:* (01446) 793180. *Club:* Cottrell Park Golf.

**CLARKE, Very Rev. John Martin;** Dean of Wells, 2004–15; *b* 20 Feb. 1952; *s* of Roland Ernest Clarke and Edna Lucy Hay; *m* 1985, Constance Elizabeth Cressida Nash; two *s* one *d. Educ:* West Buckland Sch.; Hertford Coll., Oxford (MA); Edinburgh Theol Coll. (BD). Ordained deacon, 1976, priest, 1977; Asst Curate, The Ascension, Kenton, Newcastle, 1976–79; Precentor, St Ninian's Cathedral, Perth, 1979–82; Information Officer and Communications Advr to the Gen. Synod of the Scottish Episcopal Church, 1982–87; Philip Usher Scholarship, Greece, 1987–88; Vicar, St Mary, Battersea, 1989–96; Principal, Ripon Coll., Cuddesdon, 1997–2004; Canon and Preb., Lincoln Cathedral, 2000–04. *Recreations:* walking, reading, music, cricket. *Address:* 1 Blackbridge Road, Chippenham, Wilts SN15 3LS.

**CLARKE, Rear-Adm. John Patrick,** CB 1996; LVO 1986; MBE 1978; Chief Executive, British Marine Federation, 2001–06; Hydrographer of the Navy and Chief Executive, United Kingdom Hydrographic Office (formerly Hydrographic Agency), 1996–2001; *b* 12 Dec. 1944; *s* of Frank and Christine Clarke; *m* 1st, 1969, Ann Parham (marr. diss. 1997); one *s* two *d*; 2nd, 1998, Mrs Jeffy J. Salt. *Educ:* Epsom Coll.; BRNC. Commanding Officer, HM Ships: Finwhale, 1976; Oberon, 1977; Dreadnought, 1979–80; CO, Submarine CO's Qualifying Course, 1983–84; Exec. Officer, HM Yacht Britannia, 1985–86; Captain: Submarine Sea Training, 1986–89; Seventh Frigate Squadron, 1989–90; Asst Dir, Naval Staff Duties, 1990–92; Dir, Naval Warfare, 1992; Dir, Naval Management, Communications and Inf. Systems, 1993–94; Flag Officer Trng and Recruiting, 1994–96. Adjudicator, Solicitors' Regulation Authy, 2008–13. Younger Brother, Trinity House, 1997. QDR 2007. Hon. Mem., RICS. *Recreations:* golf, sailing. *Club:* Yeovil Golf.

**CLARKE, Most Rev. John Robert;** Archbishop of Athabasca, 2003–09; Metropolitan of the Ecclesiastical Province of Rupert's Land, 2003–09; *b* 27 July 1938; *s* of Rt Rev. Neville and Alice Clarke; *m* 1964, Nadia Juliann Slusar; one *s* two *d. Educ:* Univ. of W Ontario (BA); Huron Coll., London, Ontario (LTh; DD *jure dignitatis,* 1992). Ordained: deacon, 1963; priest, 1964; Curate, St Michael and All Angels, Toronto, 1964–66; Priest-in-charge, Church of the Apostles, Moosonee, 1966–84; Exec. Archdeacon and Treas., Dio. of Athabasca, 1984–91; Bishop of Athabasca, 1992–2009. *Recreations:* woodworking, travelling, canoeing, gardening.

**CLARKE, His Honour Sir Jonathan (Dennis),** Kt 1981; a Circuit Judge, 1982–93; *b* 19 Jan. 1930; *e s* of late Dennis Robert Clarke, Master of Supreme Court, and of Caroline Alice (*née* Hill); *m* 1956, Susan Margaret Elizabeth (*née* Ashworth); one *s* three *d. Educ:* Kidstones Sch.; University Coll. London. Admitted Solicitor, 1956; partner in Townsends, solicitors, 1959–82; a Recorder of the Crown Court, 1972–82. Mem. Council, Law Soc., 1964–82, Pres., 1980–81; Sec., Nat. Cttee of Young Solicitors, 1962–64; Member: Matrimonial Causes Rule Cttee, 1967–78; Legal Studies Bd, CNAA, 1968–75; Judicial Studies Bd, 1979–82; Criminal Injuries Compensation Bd, 1993–2004; Criminal Injuries Compensation Appeals Panel, 1996–2004. Governor, College of Law, 1970–90, Chm. of Governors, 1982. *Recreations:* sailing, ski-ing. *Clubs:* Garrick, Farmers; Royal Western Yacht.

**CLARKE, Rt Hon. Kenneth Harry;** CH 2014; PC 1984; QC 1980; MP for Rushcliffe, since 1970 (C, 1970–2019; Ind, since 2019); Father of the House, since 2017; *b* 2 July 1940; *e c* of Kenneth Clarke and Doris (*née* Smith), Nottingham; *m* 1964, Gillian Mary Edwards (*d* 2015); one *s* one *d. Educ:* Nottingham High Sch.; Gonville and Caius Coll., Cambridge (BA, LLB; Hon. Fellow, 1997). Chm., Cambridge Univ. Conservative Assoc., 1961; Pres., Cambridge Union, 1963; Chm., Fedn Conservative Students, 1963. Called to Bar, Gray's Inn 1963, Hon. Bencher, 1989, Bencher, 1998; Mem., Midland Circuit. Research Sec., Birmingham Bow Group, 1965–66. Contested Mansfield, 1964 and 1966. PPS to Solicitor General, 1971–72; an Asst Govt Whip, 1972–74 (Govt Whip for Europe, 1973–74); a Lord Comr, HM Treasury, 1974; Parly Sec., DoT, later Parly Under Sec. of State for Transport, 1979–82; Minister of State (Minister for Health), DHSS, 1982–85; entered Cabinet as Paymaster General and Minister for Employment, 1985–87; Chancellor of Duchy of Lancaster and Minister for Trade and Industry (with addnl responsibility to co-ordinate Govt policy on Inner Cities), 1987–88; Secretary of State: for Health, 1988–90; for Educn and Science, 1990–92; for the Home Dept, 1992–93; Chancellor of the Exchequer, 1993–97; Minister of State (Minister without Portfolio), 2012–14. Mem., Parly delegn to Council of Europe and WEU, 1973–74; Sec., Cons. Parly Health and Social Security Cttee, 1974; Opposition Spokesman on: Social Services, 1974–76; Industry, 1976–79; Shadow Sec. of State for Business (formerly Business, Enterprise and Regulatory Reform), 2009–10; Lord Chancellor and Sec. of State for Justice, 2010–12. Liveryman, Clockmakers' Co., 2001–. Hon. LLD: Nottingham, 1989; Huddersfield, 1993; DUniv Nottingham Trent, 1996. *Publications:* New Hope for the Regions, 1969; Kind of Blue: a political memoir, 2016; pamphlets published by Bow Group, 1964–. *Recreations:* modern jazz music; watching Association Football and cricket, bird-watching. *Address:* House of Commons, SW1A 0AA. *Clubs:* Garrick; Nottinghamshire CC (Pres., 2002–04).

**CLARKE, Rt Rev. Kenneth Herbert;** Bishop of Kilmore, Elphin and Ardagh, 2001–12; Mission Director, South American Mission Society Ireland, 2013–18; *b* 23 May 1949; *s* of Herbert Clarke and Anne Clarke (*née* Gage); *m* 1971, Helen Good; four *d. Educ:* Holywood Primary Sch.; Sullivan Upper Sch., Holywood, Co. Down; TCD (BA 1971; Div. Testimonium 1972). Ordained deacon, 1972, priest, 1973; Curate: Magheralin, 1972–75; Dundonald, 1975–78; served in Chile with S Amer. Mission Soc., 1978–81; Incumbent: Crinken Ch, Dublin, 1982–86; Coleraine Parish, 1986–2001; Archdeacon of Dalriada, 1998–2001. *Publications:* Called to Minister?, 1990; Going for Growth, 2011. *Recreations:* walking, reading, golf. *Address:* SAMS House, 1 Irwin Crescent, Lurgan, Craigavon BT66 7EZ. *T:* (28) 3831 0144. *E:* kenclarkefanta@hotmail.com.

**CLARKE, Laura Mary;** HM Diplomatic Service; High Commissioner to New Zealand and non-resident Governor, Pitcairn, Henderson, Ducie and Oeno Islands, since 2018; *b* London, 3 June 1978; *d* of late Charles James Richmond Clarke and of Anne Mary Clarke; *m* 2006, Toby Fisher; one *s* two *d. Educ:* Colchester Girls' High Sch.; Colchester Sixth Form Coll.; Queens' Coll., Cambridge (BA Double 1st Cl. Hons German and Russian 2001); London Sch. of Econs and Pol Sci. (MSc Internat. Relns 2003). Trainee, Enlargement Directorate Gen., EC, 2002; Policy Officer, Mental Capacity Bill Team, 2004–05, Human Rights Policy Advr, 2005–06, DCA; joined FCO, 2006; Hd, EU Justice and Home Affairs, Germany, Bulgaria and Romania, FCO, 2006–08; COS to Minister for Europe, FCO, 2008–10; Hd, FCO-DFID Sudan Unit, 2011; Counsellor (Politics, Prosperity, Communications), Pretoria, 2012–15; Hd, S Asia Dept and Whitehall India Coordinator, FCO, 2015–17; High Comr to Samoa, 2018–19. *Recreations:* (when not working or kid-wrangling) travel, theatre, walking, eating with friends. *Address:* c/o British High Commission Wellington, BFPO 5608 HA4 6EP. *T:* (New Zealand) (4) 9242858. *E:* laura.clarke@fco.gov.uk.

**CLARKE, Laurence;** *see* Clarke, S. L. H.

**CLARKE, Prof. Malcolm Alistair,** PhD; Professor of Commercial Contract Law, Cambridge University, 1999–2010, now Emeritus; Fellow, St John's College, Cambridge, since 1970; *b* 1 April 1943; *s* of Kenneth Alfred William Clarke and Marian Florence Clarke (*née* Rich); *m* 1968, Eva Olga Bergman; two *s. Educ:* Kingswood Sch., Bath; L'Ecole des Roches, Verneuil-sur-Avre, France; St John's Coll., Cambridge (LLB 1965; MA 1968; PhD 1973). Asst, Institut de Droit Comparé, Paris, 1965–66; Research Fellow, Fitzwilliam Coll., Cambridge, 1966–68; Lectr, Univ. of Singapore, 1968–70; Cambridge University: Asst Lectr in Law, 1970–75; Lectr, 1975–93; Reader in Commercial Contract Law, 1993–99; Dir of Studies, St John's Coll., Cambridge, 1972–92. *Publications:* Aspects of the Hague Rules, 1976; (jtly) Shipbuilding Contracts, 1981, 2nd edn 1992; The International Carriage of Goods by Road: CMR, 1982, 6th edn 2014; The Law of Insurance Contracts, 1989, 6th edn 2009, and bi-annually, 1999–2016; Policies and Perceptions of Insurance, 1997; Contracts of Carriage by Air, 2002, 2nd edn 2010; (jtly) Butterworths Law of Contract, 2nd edn 2003, 4th edn 2010; Contracts of Carriage by Land and Air, 2004, 2nd edn 2008; Policies and Perceptions of Insurance in the Twenty-First Century, 2005; (ed and contrib.) Principles of European Insurance Contract Law, 2009, 2nd edn 2015; (jtly) Palmer on Bailment, 3rd edn 2009; (jtly) Insurance: the laws of Australia, 2009; (jtly) Contractual Duties: performance, breach, termination and remedies, 2011. *Recreations:* cycling, music, photography, walking. *Address:* St John's College, Cambridge CB2 1TP. *T:* (01223) 338600, *Fax:* (01223) 337720.

**CLARKE, Mark Galbraith,** FCA; Director General, Finance and Strategy, Department for Business, Enterprise and Regulatory Reform (formerly Department of Trade and Industry), 2006–08; *b* 19 June 1953; *s* of Sir Richard William Barnes Clarke, KCB, OBE and Brenda Clarke; *m* 1982, Dr Alexandra Macleod; one *s* two *d. Educ:* Jesus Coll., Oxford (MA PPE). Arthur Andersen & Co., 1975–82; TSB Gp plc, 1982–89; Coopers & Lybrand, then PricewaterhouseCoopers, mgt consultants, 1989–2000; Barclays plc, 2000–03; Abbey National plc, 2003–05; Bank of Ireland, 2005–06. Non-executive Director: British Chambers of Commerce, 2010–16 (Chm., Audit and Risk Cttee, 2011–16); Kent Reliance Provident Soc., 2011–13 (Chm., Audit and Risk Cttee, 2011–13); One Housing Gp, 2013–14 (Chm., Audit and Controls Cttee, 2013–14); Community Savings Bank Assoc., 2015–. Member: Exchequer Funds Audit Cttee, HM Treasury, 2007–10; Members Estimate Audit Cttee and Admin Estimate Audit Cttee, H of C, 2009–13; Finance Cttee, 2009–14, Investment Cttee, 2009–14, Enterprise Ext. Adv. Bd, 2011–15, UCL; Risk and Audit Cttee, Jesus Coll., Oxford, 2012–18. Gov., Highgate Sch., 2007–17.

**CLARKE, Martin Gerald,** FIA; Government Actuary, since 2014; *b* Urmston, 17 March 1956; *s* of Rev. Roland Clarke and Eva Mary Clarke; two *s* one *d*; *m* 2015, Julia Clare Heaton. *Educ:* Canon Slade Grammar Sch., Bolton; Jesus Coll., Cambridge (BA Maths 1977); Harvard Business Sch. (Gen. Manager Prog. 2003). FIA 1982. Co-operative Insurance Society: Actuary, 1980–85; Mktg Manager, 1985–97; Mktg Dir, 1997–2002; Life & Savings Dir, Co-operative Financial Services, 2002–06; Exec. Dir, Pension Protection Fund, 2006–14. Chm., UK Sustainable Investment and Finance Assoc., 2010–14. Trustee, Lankelly Chase Foundn, 2013–17. Non-exec. Dir, Civil Service Insce Soc., 2019–. Gov., Pension Policy Inst., 2019–. Mem., Actuaries' Co., 2014. *Publications:* contrib. papers to professional actuarial bodies. *Recreations:* music, art, sport. *Address:* Government Actuary's Department, Finlaison House, 15–17 Furnival Street, EC4A 1AB. *T:* (020) 7211 2620. *E:* martin.clarke@gad.gov.uk. *Club:* Actuaries.

**CLARKE, Martin Peter;** Publisher and Editor, MailOnline, since 2008; *b* 26 Aug. 1964; *s* of Robert William Clarke and Doris May (*née* Snowden); *m* 1998, Veronica (*née* Gilfedder); one *s. Educ:* Gravesend Grammar Sch. for Boys; Bristol Univ. (BA Hons). Daily Mail Executive, 1988–94; News Ed., Daily Mirror, 1995; Editor: Scottish Daily Mail, 1995–97; The Scotsman, 1997–98; Editor-in-Chief: Daily Record and Sunday Mail Ltd, 1998–2000; Ireland on Sunday, 2001–04; Exec. Ed., Mail on Sunday, 2004–05; Associate Ed., The Daily Mail, 2005–08. *Address:* The Daily Mail, Northcliffe House, 2 Derry Street, W8 5TS. *T:* (020) 7938 6000.

**CLARKE, Matthew Gerard;** *see* Clarke, Rt Hon. Lord.

**CLARKE, Melissa Sophia; Her Honour Judge Melissa Clarke;** a Senior Circuit Judge, and Designated Civil Judge for Thames Valley, Bedfordshire and Hertfordshire, since 2017; *b* Ontario, Canada; *d* of James Hoey and Mariana Goulandris; *m* 1997, (Stephen) Matthew Clarke; two *s* two *d. Educ:* Sherborne Sch. for Girls; Univ. of Manchester (BA Hons 1990); Coll. of Law, Lancaster Gate (CPE 1991; Law Soc. Finals 1992); Univ. of Bristol (Postgrad. Dip. Intellectual Property Law 1994). Admitted solicitor, 1994; Linklaters & Paines, subseq. Linklaters LLP: trainee solicitor, 1992–94; solicitor, 1994–2002; Vice Pres. Business Affairs, Incomit AB, 2002–05; career break, 2005–08; Dep. District Judge, 2008–11; District Judge, 2011–15; Recorder, 2012–15; Circuit Judge, 2015–17; Dep. High Court Judge, 2015–. *Recreations:* family, piano, cars, Greece. *Address:* Oxford Combined Court, St Aldates, Oxford OX1 1TL. *T:* (01865) 264200. *Club:* Royal Over-Seas League.

**CLARKE, Michael;** *see* Clarke, C. M.

**CLARKE, Prof. Michael,** CBE 2003; FRCP, FRCPE, FFPH, FMedSci; Professor of Epidemiology, University of Leicester, 1981–2002; Hon. Consultant, Leicestershire Health, 1974–2002; *b* 2 Nov. 1940; *s* of late Leslie Frederick Clarke and Gertrude Mary Clarke (*née* Dring); *m* 1966, Susan Jenkins Thompson (marr. diss. 1994); one *s* one *d. Educ:* Middlesex Hosp. Med. Sch., Univ. of London (MB BS 1965). MRCS, LRCP 1965; DPH 1968; MFPHM 1974, FFPH (FFPHM 1979); FRCP 1991; FRCPE 1996. Lectr, St Thomas' Hosp., London, 1968–74; Vis. Scientist, R&D, Nat. Centre for Health Services, 1972–73; Sen. Lectr, Dept of Community Health, Univ. of Leicester, 1974–80. Dir, Trent Inst. for Health Services Res., 1993–2002. Member: MRC Public Health & Health Services Res. Bd, 1990–94; Chair, Strategic Review of the NHS R&D Levy, 1998–2000. Vice Pres., FPHM, 1995–2000. FMedSci 2002. *Publications:* articles on epidemiology and health services res., particularly in relation to reproduction, care of the elderly and urinary incontinence. *Recreations:* cooking, interior design. *Address:* The Stables, Coombes Yard, Welland Rise, Sibbertoft, Northants LE16 9UP.

**CLARKE, Prof. Michael;** Director General (formerly Director), Royal United Services Institute, 2007–15, now Distinguished Fellow; *b* Wallasey, Cheshire, 29 July 1950; *s* of Leonard George Clarke and Evelyn Clarke (*née* Stanley); *m* 1977, Janet Reynolds. *Educ:* Cardinal Wiseman Secondary Modern Sch.; Churchfields Comprehensive Sch.; University Coll. of Wales, Aberystwyth (BSc (Econ) 1971; MSc (Econ) 1973; Fellow 2012). Lecturer: Dept of Govt, Univ. of Manchester, 1975–79; Dept of Politics, Univ. of Newcastle upon Tyne, 1979–90; King's College London: Dir, Centre for Defence Studies, 1990–2001; Prof. of Defence Studies, 1995–2007; Dir, Internat. Policy Inst., 2001–05; Dir of Res. Develt and Dep. Vice-Principal, 2005–07; Vis. Prof. of Defence Studies, 2007–. FKC 2015. Hon. Prof., Univ. of Exeter, 2012. Freeman, Barbers' Co., 2017–. MInstD 2000. *Publications:* British External Policy-making in the 1990s, 1992; Global Development and Human Security, 2007; The Challenge of Defending Britain, 2019; (ed jtly) Tipping Point: Britain, Brexit and security in the 2020s, 2019; contrib. articles to Internat. Affairs, RUSI Jl, Conflict, Security and Develt. *Recreations:* running very slowly, theatre, cricket, sailing. *Address:* 88 Rope Street, SE16 7TF. *Club:* Reform.

**CLARKE, Canon Prof. Michael Gilbert,** CBE 2000; DL; Professor, School of Public Policy, 1993–2008, now Emeritus, Pro-Vice-Chancellor, 1998–2003, and Vice-Principal, 2003–08, University of Birmingham; *b* 21 May 1944; *s* of Rev. Canon Reginald Gilbert Clarke and Marjorie Kathleen Clarke; *m* 1967, Angela Mary Cook; one *s* two *d. Educ:* Queen Elizabeth Grammar Sch., Wakefield; Sussex Univ. (BA 1966; MA 1967). Teaching Assistant, Essex Univ., 1967–69; Lectr and Dir of Studies in Politics, Edinburgh Univ., 1969–75; Asst Dir and Depute Dir, Policy Planning, Lothian Regl Council, 1975–81; Dir, LGTB, 1981–90; Chief Exec., Local Govt Mgt Bd, 1990–93; Head, Sch. of Public Policy, Univ. of Birmingham, 1993–98. Chm., Birmingham Royal Ballet, 2009–18. Trustee: Worcs Community Foundn, 2004–; Elgar Foundn, 2008–; Barber Inst., 2008–; Three Choirs Fest., 2014–; Hult Internat. Business Sch., 2015–; Pres., Herefordshire and Worcs Community First, 2005–; Governor: King's Sch., Worcester, 2006–; Univ. of Worcester, 2007; Chm., Univ. of Birmingham Sch., 2012–15. Fellow, Ashridge Coll., 2015–. Mem., Gen. Synod of C of E, 1990–93, 1995–; Dioceses Commission, 2008– (Chm., 2010–); Lay Canon and Mem. Chapter, 2001–10, Canon Emeritus, 2010, Worcester Cathedral. DL Worcs, 2000. Hon. MA Worcester, 2000; Hon. DLitt Aston, 2009; DUniv Birmingham, 2014. *Publications:* Getting the Balance Right, 1990; Choices for Local Government: the 1990s and beyond, 1991; How Others See Us, 1995; Breaking Down the Barriers, 1995; Renewing Public Management, 1996; articles on UK public policy and management issues esp. local govt and central-local relns. *Recreations:* music, reading, grandchildren, gardening. *Address:* Millington House, 15 Lansdowne Crescent, Worcester WR3 8JE. *T:* (01905) 617634. *Club:* Reform.

**CLARKE, Maj.-Gen. Michael Hugo Friend;** Immigration Appeals Adjudicator, 1993–2004; *b* 22 Sept. 1936; *s* of Patrick Joseph Clarke and Catherine Amy Clarke (*née* Friend); *m* 1962, Gerritje van der Horst; one *s* one *d. Educ:* Rutland House Sch.; Allhallows Sch. Called to the Bar, Lincoln's Inn, 1959; enlisted RASC, 1959; commissioned 2nd Lieut RASC, 1960; Captain, Army Legal Services, 1961; served BAOR, Singapore, Nairobi, Hong Kong, Cyprus, N Ireland; HQ Army Legal Aid, 1981; MoD, 1983; Army Legal Aid, BAOR, 1986; Army Legal Group UK, 1987; Brig., Legal HQ BAOR, 1989; Dir, Army Legal Services, 1992–94. Trustee, Inst. of Obs and Gyn., 1995–2003. *Recreations:* gardening, walking, sport.

**CLARKE, Michael John,** PhD; Chief Executive, Royal Society for the Protection of Birds, 2010–19; *b* Dartford, Kent, 2 Jan. 1960; *s* of George Fredrick Albert Clarke and Barbara Patricia Clarke; *m* 1982, Naomi Joan; two *d. Educ:* Gravesend Grammar Sch.; Hertford Coll., Oxford (BA Zoology 1981; MA); Southampton Univ. (PhD 1988). Nature Conservancy Council, 1981–88; Royal Society for the Protection of Birds: Conservation Manager, 1988–91, Regl Dir, 1991–98, SE England; Ops Dir, 1998–2010. Member: England Forestry Forum, 2001–06; Ind. Forestry Panel, 2011–12; REFIT Platform, EC, 2016–19. Mem. Council, Southampton Univ., 1996–99; Dir, N Beds Schs Trust, 2009–10. FRSA. *Publications:* papers on envmtl sci. *Recreations:* birds and wildlife, archaeology, slow food. *W:* www.twitter.com/mike__clarke.

**CLARKE, Nicholas Stephen;** QC 2006; a Recorder, since 2000; *b* Rochdale, 30 Dec. 1959; *s* of Thomas Clarke and Marjorie Clarke; *m* 2014, Barbara Louise Webster. *Educ:* Sheffield Univ. (LLB Hons 1980). Called to the Bar, Middle Temple, 1981; Asst Recorder, 1999–2000. *Recreations:* walking three dogs, growing orchids, playing golf and snooker. *Address:* 9 St John Street, Manchester M3 4DN. *T:* (0161) 955 9000, *Fax:* (0161) 955 9001. *E:* clerks@9stjohnstreet.co.uk.

**CLARKE, Nicky,** OBE 2007; hair stylist; Co-Founder and Co-Director, Nicky Clarke Salon, Mayfair, and Nicky Clarke Haircare Products; *b* 17 June 1958; *m* 1982, Lesley Anne Gale; one *s* one *d*; partner, Kelly Simpkin; one *s*. Director: Southern Tropics Ltd; Nicky Clarke Products Ltd. Has made numerous TV appearances as expert and spokesperson on matters related to hair. Numerous awards, including: British Hairdresser of Year Award; London Hairdresser of Year Award. *Publications:* Hair Power, 1999; contribs to newspapers and magazines, incl. Vogue, Tatler, Marie Claire and Harpers Bazaar. *Recreations:* ski-ing, water ski-ing, contemporary music. *Address:* 11 Carlos Place, W1K 3AX.

**CLARKE, Oz;** wine writer, author, television presenter and broadcaster. *Educ:* Pembroke Coll., Oxford. Actor: theatre: various roles with RSC, NT, Old Vic, Chichester Festival Th.; Billy, 1974, Sweeney Todd, 1979, Theatre Royal, Drury Lane; The Mitford Girls, Globe, 1981; Evita, Prince Edward, 1982–83; television, A Man of Feeling, 1980; radio, The Lord of the Rings, BBC Radio 4, 1981; films: Superman, 1978; Superman II, 1980; Who Dares Wins, 1982; Much Ado About Nothing, 1984; presenter/wine expert, television: Food and Drink, 1982–2001; James May's Road Trip, 2006–07; Christmas Cooks, 2007; Oz and James's Big Wine Adventure, 2006–07; Oz and James Drink to Britain, 2009; Oz and Hugh Drink to Christmas, 2009; Toy Stories, 2009–14; Oz and Hugh Raise the Bar, 2010–11; James May's Man Lab, 2010–13; Let's Do Christmas with Gino and Mel, 2012–13; Timeshift: Spicing Up Britain (also writer), 2015; Greatest Ever Christmas Ads, 2016; Secrets of the National Trust with Alan Titchmarsh, 2016–17; host and performer, theatre, Oz and Armonico Drink to Music, UK tour with Armonico Consort, 2016–17. Co-chair: Internat. Wine Challenge, 2007–; UK Wine Awards, 2017–. British Wine Taster of the Year, 1973; winner: World Wine Tasting Championship, 1982; Internat. World Wine Tasting Championships, LA, 1982; Le Prix du Champagne Lanson Special Millennium Award, 1999; Internat. Wine and Spirit Competition Communicator of the Year, 2006; (jtly) Internat. Wine Challenge Personality of the Year, 2009; Lifetime Achievement Award, Drinks Retailing Awards, 2015; Communicator of the Year, English Wine Producers, 2016. Officier, Ordre du Mérite Agricole (France), 2010. *Publications:* Webster's Wine Guide, subseq. Oz Clarke's Wine Guide, then 250 Best Wines: wine buying guide, annually, 1984–2011 (Wine Guild of UK Wine Writer, 1984); Sainsbury's Book of Wine, 1987 (Wine Guild of UK Wine Writer, 1989); The Essential Wine Book, 1988; Sainsbury's Regional Wine Guides (series), 1988; Sainsbury's Pocket Wine Guide, 1993; Oz Clarke's Pocket Wine Book, annually, 1993–; Oz Clarke's New Classic Wines, 1991 (Wine Guild of UK Wine Writer, Glenfiddich Drink Award, André Simon Drink Book Award, James Beard Wine and Spirits Award, 1992); Oz Clarke's New Encyclopedia of French Wines, 1991; Oz Clarke's Wine Atlas, 1995, 2nd edn 2007 (Julia Child Cookbook Award, 1996); Clarke and Spurrier's Fine Wine Guide, 1998, 2nd edn 2001; Vinopolis World Wine Guide, 1999; Oz Clarke's Encyclopedia of Wine, 1999, 2nd edn 2003; Oz Clarke's Introducing Wine, 2000, 2nd edn 2003; (with Margaret Rand) Grapes and Wines, 2001, 2nd edn 2015 (Le Prix Lanson Wine Book of the Year, 2002; Gourmand Drink Award for Best Drinks Educn Book, 2015); Oz Clarke's Australian Wine Companion, 2004; (with Julie Arkell) Oz and James's Big Wine Adventure, 2006; Bordeaux, 2006, 3rd edn 2012 (Roederer Internat. Wine Book of the Year, 2009); 101 Best White and Rosé Wines, 2008; Let Me Tell You About Wine, 2009; Oz and James Drink to Britain (Gourmand Drink Award for Wine Lit.), 2009; My Top Wines for 2013, 2012; The History of Wine in 100 Bottles (Gourmand Drink Award for Best Wine Book), 2015; Wine A-Z, 2015; Oz Clarke's World of Wine: wines grapes vineyards, 2017. *Address:* c/o Limelight Celebrity Management Ltd, 10 Filmer Mews, 75 Filmer Road, SW6 7JF. *T:* (020) 7384 9950, *Fax:* (020) 7384 9955. *E:* mail@limelightmanagement.com.

**CLARKE, Sir Paul (Robert Virgo),** KCVO 2013 (CVO 2009); Chief Executive, Clerk of the Council, Keeper of the Records and Surveyor General, Duchy of Lancaster, 2000–13; independent mentor, since 2013; *b* 13 Aug. 1953; *s* of Robert Charles Houghton Clarke and Joan Clarke (*née* Stanton); *m* 1978, Vanessa Carol Pike; two *d. Educ:* Abingdon Sch.; W London Coll. FRICS 1988. Valuation Surveyor and Tech. Asst to Exec. Trustee, Grosvenor Estate, 1974–82; Equity Partner, Clarke & Green, Chartered Surveyors, 1982–96; Property Investment Manager, Wellcome Trust, 1996–2000. Property Adv. Mem., Greenwich Hosp. Adv. Panel, 2002–12; Chm., Adv. Panel, CBRE Global Investors (formerly ING) UK Property Income Fund, 2006–14; Vice-Chm., Northbank BID, 2012–13; non-executive Director: Berkshire Investment Capital, 2013–16; Rural Estates Cttee, Grosvenor Estate, 2014–; Ind. Mem., Knight Frank Investment Mgt Investment Cttee, 2014–. Member: Estates Cttee, Oxford Univ. Endowment Mgt, 2013–17. Trustee: Duke of Lancaster Housing Trust, 2008–14; Addington Fund, 2013–18; Ind. Trustee, 69 Brook Street Trust, 2014–. Chm. and Trustee, Assoc. of Lancastrians in London, 2016–18 (Pres., 2014–16). *Recreations:* walking, ski-ing, drawing/painting, travel, writing. *E:* prvclarke@gmail.com.

**CLARKE, Prof. Peter Frederick,** LittD; FBA 1989; Master of Trinity Hall, Cambridge, 2000–04 (Hon. Fellow, 2005); Professor of Modern British History, Cambridge University, 1991–2004; *b* 21 July 1942; *s* of late John William Clarke and Winifred Clarke (*née* Hadfield); *m* 1st, 1969, Dillon Cheetham (marr. diss. 1990); two *d*; 2nd, 1991, Dr Maria Tippett, FRS(Can), British Columbia. *Educ:* Eastbourne Grammar Sch.; St John's Coll., Cambridge (BA 1963; MA 1967; PhD 1967; LittD 1989). FR.HistS 1972. Asst Lectr and Lectr in History, 1966–78, Reader in Modern Hist., 1978–80, UCL; Cambridge University: Fellow, St John's Coll., 1980–2000 (Tutor, 1982–87); Lectr in History, 1980–87; Reader in Modern History, 1987–91; Sec., Faculty Bd of Hist., 1985–86. Vis. Prof. of Modern British Hist., Harvard Univ., 1974; Vis. Fellow, Res. Sch. of Social Scis, ANU, 1983; Heath Dist. Vis. Prof., Grinnell Coll., Iowa, 1995; Dir's Visitor, Inst. for Advanced Study, Princeton, 2009. Lectures: Creighton, London Univ., 1998; Ford's, Univ. of Oxford, 2002; Del Grauer Meml, Vancouver Inst., 2008; Frank Turner Meml, Univ. of Texas at Austin, 2011; Kemper, Westminster Coll., Fulton, 2013. Member: Council, RHistS, 1979–83; Adv. Council on Public Records, 1995–2000; Royal Commn on Historical MSS, 2000–03; Adv. Council on Nat. Records and Archives, 2003–05. Chm., S Cambs Area Party, SDP, 1981–82. Jt Review Ed., History, 1967–73; Chm., Editl Bd, Twentieth Century British History, 1988–98. *Publications:* Lancashire and the New Liberalism, 1971, 2nd edn 1993; Liberals and Social Democrats, 1978, 3rd edn 1993; The Keynesian Revolution in the Making, 1988, 2nd edn 1990; A Question of Leadership: from Gladstone to Thatcher, 1991, 2nd edn 1992, new edn, from Gladstone to Blair, 1999; Hope and Glory: Britain 1900–1990, 1996, 2nd edn as Hope and Glory: Britain 1900–2000, 2004; The Keynesian Revolution and its Economic Consequences, 1998; The Cripps Version: the life of Sir Stafford Cripps, 2002; The Last Thousand Days of the British Empire, 2007; Keynes: the twentieth century's most influential economist, 2009; Mr Churchill's Profession: statesman, orator, writer, 2012; The Locomotive of War: money, empire, power and guilt, 2017; articles in learned jls; contribs to TLS, London Rev. of Books, FT, etc. *Recreations:* walking, cooking. *Address:* 3 The Light Building, Brooklands Avenue, Cambridge CB2 8DG; 9919 Gowlland Point Road, Pender Island, BC V0N 2M3, Canada. *Club:* Union (Victoria, BC).

**CLARKE, Peter Henry,** FRICS; Member of the Lands Tribunal, part time, 1993–96, full time, 1996–2005; *b* 22 Sept. 1935; *s* of late Henry George Clarke and Winifred Eva Clarke (*née* Sharp); *m* 1964, May Connell; one *d. Educ:* Ealing Technical Coll.; Coll. of Estate Management; LLB 1972, MPhil 1993, London. ARICS 1957, FRICS 1973; ACIArb 1976. With G. L. Hearn & Partners, 1952–57, 1959–60; Cubitt Estates, 1960–64; Eldonwall Ltd, 1964–69; Donaldsons, 1969–96 (Partner, 1972–96). *Publications:* (jtly) Land Values, 1965; (jtly) Valuation: Principles into Practice, 1980, 5th edn 2000; The Surveyor in Court, 1985; articles on compensation and rent reviews in various jls. *Recreations:* music, opera, reading, walking, dogs. *Address:* 65 Brittains Lane, Sevenoaks, Kent TN13 2JS. *T:* (01732) 456437.

**CLARKE, Peter John Michael,** CVO 2001; OBE 2006; QPM 2002; HM Chief Inspector of Prisons, since 2016; *b* Epsom, Surrey, 27 July 1955; *s* of Ernest John Wallace Clarke and Doris Louisa Emma Clarke (*née* Wakeham); *m* 1983, Deborah Ann Bazalgette; two *s* one *d*. *Educ:* Glyn Grammar Sch., Epsom; Univ. of Bristol (LLB Hons 1977); Cabinet Office Top Mgt Prog., 1998. Joined Metropolitan Police, 1977; Inspector, 1984–89; Chief Inspector, 1989–92; Superintendent, 1992–94; Staff Officer to Comr, 1993–94; Divl Comdr, Brixton Div., 1994–96; Comdr, Royalty and Diplomatic Protection Dept, 1997–2000; Dep. Asst Comr, HR, 2001; rcds 2002; Dep. Asst Comr, Hd of Anti-Terrorist Br. and Nat. Co-ordinator of Terrorist Investigations, 2002–08. Non-executive Director: Knightsbridge Guarding Ltd, 2008–15; SOCA, 2009–13; Senior Adviser: Olive Gp, 2008–12; Kellogg, Brown and Root, 2011–15. Member: Bd of Trustees, Crimestoppers, 2008–; Nat. Security Forum, 2009–10; Bd, Charity Commn, 2013–16. Terrorism and Security Consultant, CBS News, 2008–16. Educn Comr, Birmingham, 2014 (Report into allegations concerning Birmingham schs arising from Trojan Horse letter). Fellow, Center for Law and Security, NY Univ., 2008–12; Vis. Prof., Cranfield Univ., 2010–12. Patron, Internat. Centre for the Study of Radicalisation, KCL, 2011–. Pres., Metropolitan and City Police Relief Bd, 1997–2008. Chm., Metropolitan Police Cricket Club, 2002–08. Hon. LLD Bristol, 2008. *Publications:* (contrib.) Investigating Terrorism: current political, legal and psychological issues, 2015. *Recreations:* watching cricket, walking, cycling. *E:* peterjmclarke@aol.com. *Clubs:* Special Forces, MCC.

**CLARKE, Peter William;** QC 1997; **His Honour Judge Peter William Clarke;** a Circuit Judge, since 2009; *b* 29 May 1950; *s* of His Honour Edward Clarke, QC, and Dorothy May Clarke (*née* Leask); *m* 1978, Victoria Mary, *d* of Michael Francis Gilbert, CBE, TD; one *s* one *d*. *Educ:* Sherborne Sch.; Inns of Court Sch. of Law. Called to the Bar, Lincoln's Inn, 1973, Bencher, 2003; in practice at the Bar, specialising in criminal law, 1974–; Asst Recorder, 1987–91; Recorder, 1991–2009. *Recreations:* losing at tennis to my children, ski-ing, golf, digital photography, enjoying my wife's paintings. *Address:* Blackfriars Crown Court, 1–15 Pocock Street, SE1 0BJ. *Club:* Garrick.

**CLARKE, Philip Brian;** Managing Director, Various Artists Ltd, since 2017; *b* Watford, 14 May 1961; *s* of Brian and Hazel Clarke; *m* 1992, Isabel Katharine Lloyd; two *s*. *Educ:* Rickmansworth Sch.; Univ. of Manchester (BA Hons Combined Studies (Mil. and American)). Sub Ed., Hammerville Publishers, 1984; Press Officer, Nat. Army Mus., 1985–86; stand-up comedian, 1986–90; Producer, Light Entertainment, BBC Radio, 1990–97; TV Producer, Absolutely Prodns, 1997–98; TV Producer, 1999–2001, Editor, Comedy, 2001–03, Talkback Prodns; Head of Comedy: Objective Prodns, 2003–13; Channel 4, 2013–17. Non-exec. Dir, Improbable Th. Co., 2013–. *Recreations:* kickboxing, gardening. *Club:* Chiswick House.

**CLARKE, Rachel Emma;** *see* Cusk, R. E.

**CLARKE, Rebecca Astley, (Bec Astley Clarke),** MBE 2013; Founder, Astley Clarke, 2006; *b* Islington, 3 Feb. 1973; *d* of Dr Charles Clarke and late Dr Ruth Seifert; *m* 2009, Chris Pearson; one *s* one *d*. *Educ:* City of London Sch. for Girls; Edinburgh Univ. (MA Hons Politics and Philosophy). Andersen Consulting, 1996–99; Commercial Dir, iVillage.co.uk, 2000–03; Hd, Non-Retail Strategy, Tesco.com, 2003–05. *Recreations:* cooking, running, Seinfeld. *Address:* Italy.

**CLARKE, Richard Ian;** HM Diplomatic Service, retired; Director, Child Soldiers International, 2012; *b* 7 Sept. 1955; *s* of Sydney Thomas Reginald Clarke and Joan Clarke; *m* 1st, 1978, Anne Elizabeth Menzies (marr. diss. 1993); one *s*; 2nd, 1993, Sheenagh Marie O'Connor; two *s* one *d*. *Educ:* Market Harborough Upper Sch.; Univ. of E Anglia (BSc). Joined FCO, 1977: 3rd, later 2nd, Sec., Caracas, 1978–83; 2nd, later 1st, Sec., FCO, 1983–87; 1st Sec., Washington, 1987–91; Asst Hd, Planning Staff, FCO, 1991–93; Dep. Hd, UN Dept, FCO, 1993–96; Counsellor and Dep. Hd of Mission, Dublin, 1996–98; Hd, Policy Planning Staff, FCO, 1998–2001; High Comr, Tanzania, 2001–03. Mem., Audit Commn, 2004–11. Ian St James Award for short fiction, 1991. *Publications:* (contrib.) Midnight Oil, 1991. *Recreations:* Leicester City, reading, Wars of the Roses, American Civil War, cheese straws, Glam and Punk and R and B, early 20th century art, ethnographic art.

**CLARKE, Most Rev. Richard Lionel;** *see* Armagh, Archbishop of, and Primate of All Ireland.

**CLARKE, Dr Richard William John;** Director General for Policy, Research and Humanitarian, Department for International Development, since 2018; *b* Chatham, 28 April 1976; *s* of John David Clarke and Jill Kelland Bruford Clarke; *m* 2004, Elise Shearing; two *s*. *Educ:* King's Sch., Rochester; Pembroke Coll., Cambridge (BA Archaeol. and Anthropol. 1997); St John's Coll., Cambridge (PhD Social Anthropol. 2001). Dep. Dir, Policing Policy, Home Office, 2001; Dep. Dir, Third Sector Policy, Cabinet Office; Sen. Policy Advr, HM Treasury; Dir, Strategy and Improvement, Metropolitan Police Service, 2009–11; Home Office: Dir, Counter Terrorism Strategy, 2011–14; Prog. Dir for Digital Services, Border Prog., 2014–16; Internat. Dir, 2016–18. *Publications:* (contrib.) Human Rights in Global Perspective: anthropological studies of rights, claims and entitlements, 2003; (contrib.) Boundless Worlds: an anthropological approach to movement, 2008. *Recreation:* spending time in the fresh air with my sons. *Address:* Department for International Development, 22 Whitehall, SW1A 2EG.

**CLARKE, Rev. Robert Sydney,** OBE 2000; Secretary and Director of Training, Hospital Chaplaincies Council, 1994–2000; Chaplain to HM the Queen, 1987–2005; *b* 31 Oct. 1935; *s* of George Sydney and Elizabeth Clarke. *Educ:* St Dunstan's College; King's Coll., Univ. of London (AKC 1964; MA 1965). Chaplain: New Cross Hospital, Wolverhampton, 1970–74; Herrison and West Dorset County Hosp., Dorchester, 1974–79; Westminster Hosp. and Westminster Medical School, Univ. of London, 1979–85; Winchester HA, 1985–94. Sen. Hon. Chaplain, Winchester and Eastleigh NHS Trust, 1994–2000. *Recreations:* breeding and showing dogs, music, travel, DIY. *Address:* c/o 3 Brook Court, Middlebridge Street, Romsey, Hants SO51 8HR. *E:* robertsclarke@tiscali.co.uk. *Club:* Kennel.

**CLARKE, Roger Eric;** literary translator and editor; Director of Shipping and Ports, Department of the Environment, Transport and the Regions, 1997–99; *b* 13 June 1939; *s* of late Frederick Cuérel Clarke and Hilda Josephine Clarke; *m* 1983, Elizabeth Jane, *d* of late Gordon W. Pingstone and Anne Ellen Pingstone; one *d*. *Educ:* UCS, Hampstead; Corpus Christi Coll., Cambridge (MA). Various posts in Min. of Aviation, BoT and Depts of Trade and Transport, 1961–72 and 1974–85; Air Traffic Rights Advr to Govt of Fiji, 1972–74; Under Sec., Civil Aviation Policy Directorate, 1985–89, Public Transport Directorate, 1989–91, Shipping Policy Directorate, 1991–97, Dept of Transport. Reader, Rochester Dio., C of E, 1976–. *Publications:* The Trawler Gaul: why was no search made for the wreck?, 2000; The Trawler Gaul: the search for bodies of the crew in northern Russia, 2000; (trans.) M. Benoît, Prisoner of God, 2008; (ed) Pushkin: The Queen of Spades and other stories, 2011, rev. edn 2017; (ed) Pushkin, The Captain's Daughter and History of Pugachov, 2012, rev. edn 2017; (translations with commentaries): Pushkin, Eugene Onegin, 1999, new trans. and commentary 2011, rev. edn 2015; Pushkin, Boris Godunov, 1999; Pushkin, Ruslan and Lyudmila, 2005, new edn 2009, rev. edn 2017; Pushkin, Eugene Onegin and other works, 2005; Erasmus, Praise of Folly and Pope Julius Barred from Heaven, 2008, new edn 2013; Pushkin, Boris Godunov and Little Tragedies, 2010, rev. edn 2017; Pushkin, Love Poems, 2013, rev. edn 2014; Pushkin, Belkin's Stories and A History of Goryukhino Village, 2014; Thomas More, Utopia, 2017; Pushkin, Complete Lyrics and Shorter Poems, vol. 1, 1809–17, 2018, rev. edn 2019, vol. 2, 1817–24, 2019. *Recreations:* family, friends, church, philately, garden, theatre, music, languages, travel. *Address:* 64 Scotts Lane, Shortlands, Bromley, Kent BR2 0LX. *Club:* Reform.

**CLARKE, Roger Howard,** CBE 2005; PhD; Director, National Radiological Protection Board, 1987–2003; *b* 22 Aug. 1943; *s* of late Harold Pardoe and Laurie Gwyneth Clarke; *m* 1966, Sandra Ann (*née* Buckley); one *s* one *d*. *Educ:* King Edward VI Sch., Stourbridge; Univ. of Birmingham (BSc, MSc); Polytechnic of Central London (PhD). Res. Officer, Berkeley Nuclear Laboratories, CEGB, 1965–77; Hd of Nuclear Power Assessments, NRPB, 1978–83; Bd Sec., 1983–87. Deleg. to UN Sci. Cttee on the Effects of Atomic Radiation, 1979–2004; Chairman: OECD Nuclear Energy Agency Cttee on Radiation Protection and Public Health, 1987–92; Internat. Commn on Radiol Protection, 1993–2005 (Mem., 1989–93; Emeritus Mem., 2005); Mem., Gp of Experts, Article 31, Euratom, 1988–2004. Visiting Professor: Imperial Coll. of Science, Technol. and Medicine, 1993–2002; Univ. of Surrey, 1994–. Lindell Lectr, Swedish Risk Kollegiat, 1999. Hon. FRCR 1994; Hon. FSRP 1995; Hon. FINucE 2002. DUniv Surrey, 2004. G. William Morgan Award, US Health Physics Soc., 1994; Ellison-Cliffe Medal, RSocMed, 1996; Hanns Langendorff Medal, Voreinigung deutscher Strahlenschutzärtze, 2002; Medal, French Nat. Assembly, 2005. *Publications:* Carcinogenesis and Radiation Risk (with W. V. Mayneord), 1975; Evolution of ICRP Recommendations 1977, 1990 and 2007, 2011; numerous papers in sci. and technical literature. *Recreations:* gardening, theatre, travel. *Address:* Corner Cottage, Woolton Hill, Newbury, Berks RG20 9XJ. *T:* (01635) 253957.

**CLARKE, Roy,** OBE 2002; writer, since 1965; *b* 28 Jan. 1930; *s* of Austin and Alice Clarke; *m* 1953, Enid Kitching; one *s* one *d*. *Educ:* badly during World War II. Soldier, salesman, policeman and teacher until I was able to persuade people I was actually a writer. *Television series:* The Misfit, 1970–72; Last of the Summer Wine, 1972–2010 (31 series); Open All Hours, 1975–82; Potter, 1979–83; Pulaski, 1987; Single Voices, 1990; The World of Eddie Weary, 1990; Keeping Up Appearances, 1990–96; Ain't Misbehaving, 1994; Still Open All Hours, 2013, 2014, 2015; *films:* Hawks, 1988; A Foreign Field, 1993; *stage:* Mr Wesley, Lincoln Cathedral, Southwell Minster etc, 2003. Freeman of Doncaster, 1994. Hon. DLitt: Bradford, 1988; Huddersfield, 1997; DUniv Sheffield Hallam, 2001. Best Series Award, Writers' Guild, 1970; Pye TV Award, 1982, Denis Potter Award, 1996, BAFTA; Lifetime Achievement Award, British Comedy Awards, 2010. *Publications:* Summer Wine Chronicles, 1986; The Moonbather, 1987; Summer Wine Country, 1995; (with J. Rice) Hyacinth Bucket's Hectic Social Calendar, 1995. *Recreations:* walking, reading, hiding. *Address:* c/o The Agency, 24 Pottery Lane, Holland Park, W11 4LZ. *T:* (020) 7727 1346.

**CLARKE, Sir Rupert (Grant Alexander),** 4th Bt *cr* 1882, of Rupertswood, Colony of Victoria; *b* 12 Dec. 1947; *s* of Major Sir Rupert Clarke, 3rd Bt, AM, MBE and Kathleen Clarke (*née* Hay); *S* father, 2005; *m* 1978, Susannah, *d* of Sir Robert Law-Smith, CBE, AFC; one *s* two *d*. *Educ:* Melbourne Univ. (LLB). *Heir: s* Rupert Robert William Clarke, *b* 24 June 1981. *Address:* Bolinda Vale, Clarkefield, Vic 3430, Australia.

**CLARKE, (Samuel) Laurence (Harrison),** CBE 1988; CEng, FIET; Assistant Technical Director, GEC plc, 1981–91; Director: Sira Ltd, 1989–95; Filtronic Ltd, 1989–93; *b* 16 Dec. 1929; *s* of late Samuel Harrison Clarke, CBE; *m* 1952, Ruth Joan Godwin, *yr d* of Oscar Godwin, OBE and Muriel Godwin; one *s* three *d*. *Educ:* Westminster Sch.; Trinity Coll., Cambridge (BA). Technical Dir, GEC-Elliott Automation Ltd, 1970–74; Technical Dir (Automation), GEC-Marconi Electronics Ltd, 1974–81; Director, GEC Computers Ltd, 1971–83. Dep. Dir, 1983–87, Dir, 1987, Alvey Programme, DTI. *Publications:* various papers in learned and technical jls. *Recreations:* tapestry, church kneeler, church choir singing, accordion playing, family history. *Address:* Sarum End, Salisbury Road, Southwold, Suffolk IP18 6LG. *T:* (01502) 725116.

**CLARKE, Sarah,** OBE 2018; Lady Usher of the Black Rod and Serjeant-at-Arms, House of Lords, Officer of the Garter, and Secretary to the Lord Great Chamberlain, since 2018; *b* Wolverhampton, 12 Oct. 1965; *d* of Geoffrey Clarke and Dianne Clarke. *Educ:* Wolverhampton Girls' High Sch.; Roehampton Inst. of Educn (BSc Hons Univ. of Surrey 1988); Inst. of Mktg (cert. 1993); Univ. of Leicester (MSc 2005). Account Dir, BH Associates, 1989–91; consultancy work, 1991–93; Sen. Communications Dir, Women's Tennis Assoc., 1994–97; Events Manager: FA, 1997–98; CARE Internat. 1998–99; Ops Manager, Wembley Stadium, 1999–2000; Sen. Manager, Major Events Dept, UK Sport, 2000–05; All England Lawn Tennis Club: Press Ops Manager, Championships, 2003–09; Championships Manager, 2009–11; Championships Dir, 2013–18 (Championships Dir Designate, 2012). Various event roles: London Marathon, 2003–; FA, 2003–08; Athens Olympics, 2004; Commonwealth Games, 2004; Turin Olympics, 2006; Asian Games, 2006; Beijing Olympics, 2008; Ride London, 2013–. Hon. DLitt Wolverhampton, 2018. *Recreations:* happily getting lost on long countryside walks, drawing cartoons, walking dogs at Battersea Dogs Home, watching team sports, visiting old buildings. *Address:* Black Rod, House of Lords, SW1A 0PW. *Club:* Reform.

**CLARKE, Sarah Anne;** QC 2017; a Recorder, since 2012; *b* London, 3 Nov. 1970; *d* of Angela and Peter Clarke; one *s* one *d*. *Educ:* Durham Univ. (BA Hons Law); Inns of Court Sch. of Law (BVC 1994). Called to the Bar, Inner Temple, 1994, Bencher 2013. Mem., Bar Standards Bd, 2011–15. Inns of Court Coll. of Advocacy. *Publications:* Insider Dealing: law and practice, 2013, 2nd edn 2019. *Recreations:* ski-ing, scuba diving, classical music, theatre. *Address:* Serjeants' Inn Chambers, 85 Fleet Street, EC4Y 1AE. *T:* (020) 7427 5000, *Fax:* (020) 7353 0425. *E:* sclarkeqc@serjeantsinn.com.

**CLARKE, Simon Richard;** MP (C) Middlesbrough South and East Cleveland, since 2017; Exchequer Secretary to HM Treasury, since 2019; *b* Middlesbrough, 28 Sept. 1984; *s* of Richard Clarke and Jill Clarke; *m* 2012, Hannah Levy; one *s*. *Educ:* Red House Sch., Norton; Yarm Sch.; University Coll., Oxford (BA Mod. Hist.); BPP Law Sch., Holborn (Legal Practice Course). Joined Slaughter and May, 2008; admitted solicitor, 2010; Sen. Parly Asst to Dominic Raab, MP, 2010–13; Advr to Graham Stuart, MP, 2013–17. *Recreations:* history, travel, sport. *Address:* House of Commons, SW1A 0AA. *T:* (020) 7219 2674. *E:* simon.clarke.mp@parliament.uk.

**CLARKE, Mrs Stella Rosemary,** CBE 1997; JP; President, Community Self Build Agency Ltd, since 2017 (Chairman, 1989–2017); Vice President, Lord-Lieutenant, County of Bristol, 2004–07; *b* 16 Feb. 1932; *d* of John Herbert and Molly Lord-Isabel Bruce King; *m* 1952, Charles Nigel Clarke; four *s* one *d*. *Educ:* Cheltenham Ladies' Coll.; Trinity Coll. Dublin. Long Ashton RDC: Councillor, Chm. Council, Housing and Public Health Cttees, 1955–73; Mem., Woodspring Dist Council, 1973–76; co-opted Mem., Somerset CC, Social Services and Children's Cttee, 1957–73. A Governor, BBC, 1974–81. Purchased and restored Theatre Royal, Bath, with husband, 1974–76. Dir, Fosters Rooms Ltd, 1975–96. Member: Housing Corp., 1988–95; Bristol Develt Corp., 1989–96; Lord Chancellor's Lay Interviewers Panel for Judges, 1994–2001; Nat. Lottery Charities Bd, 1995–99 (Chm., England Cttee, 1997–99). Member, Board: Knightstone Housing Assoc., 1976–2000

(Chm., 1997–2000); At-Bristol (formerly The Exploratory), 2000–09. Pro-Chancellor, Bristol Univ., 1997–2007 (Chm. Council, 1987–97; Hon. Fellow, 2008). JP Bristol, 1968 (Chm., Bench, 1991–95); DL Bristol (formerly Avon), 1986. *Recreations:* family and the variety of life. *Address:* Gatcombe Court, Flax Bourton, Bristol BS48 3QT. *T:* (01275) 393141.
See also C. G. Clarke.

**CLARKE, His Honour Stephen Patrick;** a Circuit Judge, 1995–2013; *b* 23 March 1948; *s* of Leslie Clarke and Anne Mary Clarke; *m* 1974, Margaret Roberta Millar; two *s*. *Educ:* Rostrevor Coll., Adelaide, SA; Univ. of Hull (LLB Hons). Called to the Bar, Inner Temple, 1971; practised as barrister on Wales and Chester Circuit, 1971–95; Circuit Junior, 1988–89; Asst Recorder, 1988–92; Recorder, 1992–95; Liaison Judge: N Powys Magistrates, 2000–07; Chester and Ellesmere Port Magistrates, and Vale Royal Magistrates, 2007–11. Asst Parly Boundary Comr for Wales, 1994–95. Member: Probation Bd, Cheshire, 2001–11; HM Council of Circuit Judges, 2005–09. *Recreations:* rambling, watching cricket, theatre.

**CLARKE, Rt Hon. Thomas,** CBE 1980; PC 1997; JP; *b* 10 Jan. 1941; *s* of James Clarke and Mary (*née* Gordon). *Educ:* All Saints Primary Sch., Airdrie; Columba High Sch., Coatbridge; Scottish College of Commerce. Started working life as office boy with Glasgow Accountants' firm; Asst Director, Scottish Council for Educational Technology, before going to Parliament. Councillor: (former) Coatbridge Council, 1964; (reorganised) Monklands District Council, 1974; Provost of Monklands, 1975–77, 1977–80, 1980–82. Vice-President, Convention of Scottish Local Authorities, 1976–78, President, 1978–80. MP (Lab) Coatbridge and Airdrie, June 1982–1983, Monklands W, 1983–97, Coatbridge and Chryston, 1997–2005, Coatbridge, Chryston and Bellshill, 2005–15; contested (Lab) same seat, 2015. Opposition front bench spokesman on: Scottish Affairs, 1987; health and social security (personal social services), 1987–90; Scotland, 1992–93; overseas aid, 1993–94; disabled people's rights, 1994–97; Minister of State (Minister for Film and Tourism), Dept of Culture, Media and Sport, 1997–98. Chm., PLP Foreign Affairs Cttee, 1983–86. Author and main sponsor: Disabled Persons (Consultation, Representation and Services) Act, 1986; Internat. Develt (Reporting and Transparency) Act, 2006. Director, award winning amateur film, Give Us a Goal, 1972; former President, British Amateur Cinematographers' Central Council. JP County of Lanark, 1972. *Recreations:* films, reading, walking. *Address:* 37 Blair Road, Coatbridge, Lanarkshire ML5 1JQ. *T:* (01236) 602813.

**CLARKE, Timothy;** Chief Executive, Mitchells & Butlers plc, 2003–09; *b* 24 March 1957; *s* of David Clarke and Molly Clarke; *m* 1986, Fiona Haigh (*d* 2014); two *s*. *Educ:* Corpus Christi Coll., Oxford (BA 1978, MA). Panmure Gordon & Co., 1979–90; Bass plc, subseq. Six Continents plc, 1990–2003: Chief Exec., Bass Retail, 1995–2000; Chief Exec., 2000–03. Non-executive Director: Associated British Foods plc, 2004–17 (Sen. Ind. non-exec. Dir, 2007–17); Hall & Woodhouse Ltd, 2010–; Timothy Taylor & Co. Ltd, 2010– (Chm., 2017–); Triplepoint VCT 2011 plc, 2011–; Chm., Birmingham Airport Hldgs Ltd, 2017–. Dir, British Beer and Pub Assoc., 1995–2007 (Chm., 2002). Trustee, Drinkaware Trust, 2007–09. Trustee Director: Birmingham Royal Ballet, 2006–14; Elgar Foundn, 2009–17. Gov., 2010–, Vice-Chm., 2015–19, Schs of King Edward VI in Birmingham Foundn (Chm., Ind. Schs Governing Body, 2014–).

**CLARKE, Sir Tobias;** *see* Clarke, Sir C. M. T.

**CLARKE, Tracey Norma Beatrice L.;** *see* Lloyd-Clarke.

**CLARKE, William Michael;** *b* 13 Oct. 1966; *s* of Patrick and Margaret Clarke; *m* 2001, Paula Sloan; one *d*. *Educ:* St Malachy's High Sch., Castlewellan, Co. Down. Mem. (SF), Down DC, 2001– (Chm., 2006–07). Mem. (SF) S Down, NI Assembly, 2003–April 2012. *Recreations:* hill walking, reading, cycling. *Address:* 37 King Street, Newcastle, Co. Down BT33 0HD. *T:* (028) 4377 0185, *Fax:* (028) 4377 1826.

**CLARKE-HACKSTON, Fiona;** Consultant, Memini, since 2016; Chief Executive, British Screen Advisory Council, 2010–16 (Secretary, 1987–90; Director, 1990–2010); *b* 30 April 1954; *d* of Donald Gordon Hackston and Muriel Lesley Hackston (*née* Glover); *m* 1984, Norman Malcolm Clarke; one *s* one *d*. *Educ:* UC of S Wales and Monmouthshire, Cardiff (BA Hons); Univ. of Southampton (MA 1977). Sec. to Marketing Dir, Grants of St James, 1978–79; Editor, and Head of Book Dept, Truman & Knightley, 1979–81; Personnel Advr, Ernst & Whinney, Middle East, 1981–84; Asst, Film, TV and Video, British Council, 1986. Voting Mem., BAFTA. Hon. Fellow, BKSTS, 2015. *Recreations:* family, hiking, bridge, film, travel, dance. *Address:* 353 Wimbledon Park Road, SW19 6NS.

**CLARKSON, Rt Hon. Adrienne;** PC (Can.) 1999; CC 1999 (OC 1992); CMM; CD; Co-Founder and Co-Chair, Institute for Canadian Citizenship, since 2006; Governor General and Commander-in-Chief of Canada, 1999–2005; *b* Hong Kong, 10 Feb. 1939; naturalised Canadian citizen; *m* John Ralston Saul, CC, writer. *Educ:* Trinity Coll., Univ. of Toronto (BA Hons English Lit.; MA 1961); Sorbonne, Univ. of Paris. Interviewer-host, CBC TV: Take Thirty, 1965–75; Fifth Estate, 1975–82; Agent-Gen. for Ontario, Paris, 1982–87; Pres. and Publisher, 1987–88, Publisher, Adrienne Clarkson Books, 1988–99; McClelland and Stewart; Exec. Producer and Host, CBC TV: Adrienne Clarkson's Summer Festival, 1988–98; Adrienne Clarkson Presents, 1988–98; Something Special. Chair, Bd of Trustees, Canadian Mus. of Civilization, Quebec, 1995–99; Pres., Exec. Bd, IMZ, Vienna, 1995–99; Chair, Man Asia Literary Prize, 2007–08; Dir, Global Centre for Pluralism, 2009–. Lay Bencher, Law Soc. of Upper Canada, 1999. CBC Massey Lectr, 2014. Sen. Fellow, Massey Coll., 1993. Col-in-Chief, Princess Patricia's Canadian Light Infantry, 2007–. Gen. Editor, New Woman series, 1970–72. Hon. Mem., Kainai Chieftainship (Hon. Chief, Blood Tribe), 2005. Hon. Fellow: Royal Conservatory of Music, Toronto, 1993; Univ. of Trinity Coll., Toronto, 1996. Hon. Dr: Dalhousie, 1988; Acadia, 1991; PEI, 1996; Victoria, 2000; Toronto, 2001; McGill, 2001; Laval, 2002; York, Mt Allison, Queen's, Western Ontario, Ottawa, Law Soc. of Upper Canada, 2003; Concordia, 2004; McMaster, Guelph, Ryerson, OCAD, 2006; St Vincent, 2008; Queen's, Carleton, 2009; Royal Roads, 2011; Hon. DCL Lakehead, 1992; Hon. DLitt: Manitoba, 2001; Bishop's, 2003; Thorneloe, 2011; Dr *hc* Siena, 2002. Best TV Journalist, 1974, 1982, Gordon Sinclair Award, 1975, Best Writer, TV Documentary, 1977, ACTRA; Canada 125 Medal, 1992; Prix Gémeaux, 1992; ANIK Award, 1994. Centennial Medal, 1967; Queen's Golden Jubilee Medal, 2002; Order of Friendship (Russian Fedn), 2005; Queen's Diamond Jubilee Medal, 2012. *Publications:* A Lover More Condoling, 1968; Hunger Trace, 1970; True To You In My Fashion, 1971; Heart Matters (memoirs), 2006; Norman Bethune (biog.), 2009; Room for All of Us, 2011; Belonging: the paradox of citizenship, 2014.

**CLARKSON, Ven. Alan Geoffrey;** Archdeacon of Winchester, 1984–99, Archdeacon Emeritus, since 1999; *b* 14 Feb. 1934; *s* of Instructor Captain Geoffrey Archibald Clarkson, OBE, RN and Essie Isabel Bruce Clarkson; *m* 1959, Monica Ruth (*née* Lightburne); two *s* one *d*. *Educ:* Sherborne School; Christ's Coll., Cambridge (BA 1957, MA 1961); Wycliffe Hall, Oxford. Nat. Service Commn, RA, 1952–54. Curate: Penn, Wolverhampton, 1959–60; St Oswald's, Oswestry, 1960–63; Wrington with Redhill, 1963–65; Vicar, Chewton Mendip with Emborough, 1965–74; Vicar of St John Baptist, Glastonbury with Godney, 1974–84; Priest in Charge: West Pennard, 1981–84; Meare, 1981–84; St Benedict, Glastonbury, 1982–84; Vicar of Burley, Ringwood, 1984–99. Proctor in Convocation, 1970–75, 1990–95. Hon. Canon, Winchester Cathedral, 1984–99. *Recreations:* music, gardening, carpentry, wood-turning. *Address:* 4 Harefield Rise, Linton, Cambridge CB21 4LS. *T:* (01223) 892988. *E:* a.clarkson@talktalk.net.
See also P. J. Clarkson.

**CLARKSON, Prof. Brian Leonard,** DSc; FREng; Principal, University College of Swansea, 1982–94; Vice-Chancellor, University of Wales, 1987–89; *b* 28 July 1930; *s* of L. C. Clarkson; *m* 1953, Margaret Elaine Wilby; three *s* one *d*. *Educ:* Univ. of Leeds (BSc, PhD). FREng (FEng 1986); FRAeS; Hon. FIOA. George Taylor Gold Medal, RAeS, 1963. Dynamics Engineer, de Havilland Aircraft Co., Hatfield, Herts, 1953–57; Southampton University: Sir Alan Cobham Research Fellow, Dept of Aeronautics, 1957–58; Lectr, Dept of Aeronautics and Astronautics, 1958–66; Prof. of Vibration Studies, 1966–82; Dir, Inst. of Sound and Vibration Res., 1967–78; Dean, Faculty of Engrg and Applied Science, 1978–80; Deputy Vice-Chancellor, 1980–82. Sen. Post Doctoral Research Fellow, Nat. Academy of Sciences, USA, 1970–71 (one year's leave of absence from Southampton). Chm., ACU, 1992–93 (Vice-Chm., 1990–92). Sec., Internat. Commn on Acoustics, 1975–81. Pres., Fedn of Acoustical Socs of Europe, 1982–84. Member: SERC, 1984–88; CNAA, 1988–91. Hon. DSc: Leeds, 1984; Southampton, 1987; Universiti Sains Malaysia, 1990; Hon. LLD Wales, 1996. *Publications:* author of sections of three books: Technical Acoustics, vol. 3 (ed Richardson) 1959; Noise and Acoustic Fatigue in Aeronautics (ed Mead and Richards), 1967; Noise and Vibration (ed White and Walker), 1982; (ed) Stochastic Problems in Dynamics, 1977; technical papers on Jet Noise and its effect on Aircraft Structures, Jl of Royal Aeronautical Soc., etc. *Recreations:* walking, gardening, travelling, golf. *Address:* 17 Southgate Road, Southgate, Swansea SA3 2BT.

**CLARKSON, His Honour Derek Joshua;** QC 1969; a Circuit Judge, 1977–95; Middlesex Liaison Judge, 1985–95; *b* 10 Dec. 1929; *o s* of Albert and Winifred Charlotte Clarkson (*née* James); *m* 1960, Peternella Marie-Luise Ilse Canenbley; one *s* one *d*. *Educ:* Pudsey Grammar Sch.; King's Coll., Univ. of London. LLB (1st cl. Hons) 1950. Called to Bar, Inner Temple, 1951; Nat. Service, RAF, 1952–54 (Flt Lt). In practice as Barrister, 1954–77; Prosecuting Counsel to Post Office on North-Eastern Circuit, 1961–65; Prosecuting Counsel to Inland Revenue on North-Eastern Circuit, 1965–69; Recorder of Rotherham, 1967–71; Recorder of Huddersfield, 1971; a Recorder of the Crown Court, 1972–77. Mem., Gen. Council of the Bar, 1971–73. Inspector of companies for the Department of Trade, 1972–73, 1975–76. Pres., Middlesex Magistrates' Assoc., 1994–95. *Recreations:* theatre-going, giving talks, book collecting. *Address:* 2 Harlow Oval Court, Harlow Oval, Harrogate HG2 0DT.

**CLARKSON, Prof. Geoffrey Peniston Elliott,** PhD; Chairman, Circle L Ltd, 1990; Professor of Business Administration, Trident (formerly Touro) University International, 2003; *b* 30 May 1934; *s* of George Elliott Clarkson and Alice Helene (*née* Manneberg); *m* 1960, Eleanor M. (*née* Micenko); two *d*. *Educ:* Carnegie Mellon Univ., Pittsburgh, Pa (BSc, MSc, PhD). Asst Prof., Sloan Sch. of Management, MIT, 1961–65, Associate Prof., 1965–67, Vis. Prof., 1975–77. Vis. Ford Foundn Fellow, Carnegie-Mellon Univ., 1965–66; Vis. Prof., LSE, 1966–67; Nat. Westminster Bank Prof. of Business Finance, Manchester Business Sch., Univ. of Manchester, 1967–77; Prof. of Business Admin, 1977–89, and Dean, Coll. of Business Admin, 1977–79, Northeastern Univ., Boston. Dir of and consultant to public and private manufg and financial services cos, 1969–; Chairman: Polymerics Inc., 1983–89; Sealcorp Ltd, 1990–94. MInstD 1973. *Publications:* Portfolio Selection: a simulation of trust investment, USA 1962 (Ford Dissertation Prize, 1961); The Theory of Consumer Demand: a critical appraisal, USA 1963; Managerial Economics, 1968; (with B. J. Elliott) Managing Money and Finance, 1969, 3rd edn 1982; Jihad (novel) 1981; Day Trader (novel), 2000. *Recreations:* fishing, sailing, reading, USA.

**CLARKSON, Gerald Dawson,** CBE 1990; QFSM 1983; Chief Fire Officer and Chief Executive, London Fire and Civil Defence Authority, 1987–91, retired; Chairman, Dawson Usher International Ltd, 1994–2002; *b* 4 June 1939; *s* of Alexander Dickie Clarkson and Agnes Tierney Price; *m* 1959, Rose Lilian Hodgson; one *s* one *d*. *Educ:* Westminster Technical Coll.; Polytechnic of Central London (BA Hons). FIMS, FCMI, FRSPH. Served Royal Engineers, 1960–61. Joined London Fire Bde, 1961; Dep. Chief Officer, 1983; Reg. Fire Comdr No 5, Greater London Region, 1987–91. Member: Central Fire Bdes Adv. Council, 1987–91; Fire Service Central Examinations Bd, 1987–91; Ind. Mem., Kent Police Authy, 1995–2003; Mem., Kent Police and Crime Panel, 2012–14; Adviser: Nat. Jt Council for Local Authorities Fire Bdes, 1987–91; Assoc. of Metropolitan Authorities, 1987–91; Chairman: Fedn of British Fire Orgns, 1990–91; London Fire Brigade Retired Members Association, 1991–2010 (Pres. Emeritus, 2010); President: London Fire Brigade Widows' and Orphans' Friendly Soc., 1987–91; Commonwealth and Overseas Fire Service Assoc., 1990–2000; Dir, Nat. Fire Protection Assoc., USA, 1990–93. Founder Chm., Firefighters Meml Charitable Trust, 1990–2013 (granted Royal Charter, 2010) (Life Pres., 2014). Mem. (C), Ashford BC, 2006– (Mem., Planning Cttee, 2006–10; Exec. Portfolio Holder for Cultural Services, 2007–10, for Envmtl Services, 2010–11; Dep. Leader, 2011–13; Leader, 2013–). Chairman: Charing Rd Safety and Traffic Mgt Cttee, 2005–10; Charing Playing Fields Managing Trustees, 2007–11 (Vice Chm., 2005–07). Freeman: City of London, 1983; Glasgow, 2004; Founder Mem., Worshipful Co. of Firefighters (formerly Guild of Firefighters, then Co. of Firefighters), 1988– (Founder Master, 1988); Mem., HAC, 2004–. OStJ 1989. Hon. FIFireE 1989. *Recreations:* reading, sailing, fishing, music. *Address:* Charing Lodge, Pett Lane, Charing, Kent TN27 0DL. *Club:* East India.

**CLARKSON, Harriet;** *see* Green, H.

**CLARKSON, Jeremy Charles Robert;** journalist and broadcaster, since 1978; *b* 11 April 1960; *m* 1993, Frances Catherine Cain (marr. diss. 2014), *d* of Major Robert Henry Cain, VC and Mary Denise Addison; one *s* two *d*. *Educ:* Repton Sch. Rotherham Advertiser, 1978–81; family co., selling Paddington Bears, 1981–84; established Motoring Press Agency, 1984–94; columnist: Performance Car magazine, 1986–93; Top Gear magazine, 1993–; Esquire magazine, 1992–93; Sunday Times, 1993–; The Sun, 1996–; television: presenter: Top Gear, 1989–99, and 2002–15; Jeremy Clarkson's Motorworld, 1995, 1996; Extreme Machines, 1998; Robot Wars, 1998; Clarkson, 1998, 1999, 2000; Clarkson's Car Years, 2000; Speed, 2001; Meet the Neighbours, 2002; Great Britons: Brunel, 2003; The Victoria Cross: For Valour, 2003; Inventions That Changed the World, 2004; The Greatest Raid of All Time, 2006; PQ17: An Arctic Convoy Disaster, 2014; The Grand Tour, 2016, 2017, 2019; Who Wants to Be a Millionaire, 2018, 2019. *Publications:* Clarkson on Cars, 1996; Clarkson Hot 100, 1997; Planet Dagenham, 1998; Born to be Riled, 1999; Jeremy Clarkson on Ferrari, 2000; The World According to Jeremy Clarkson, 2004; I Know You Got Soul, 2004; And Another Thing: the world according to Clarkson, vol. 2, 2006; Don't Stop Me Now, 2007; For Crying Out Loud!: the world according to Clarkson, vol. 3, 2008; Driven to Distraction, 2009; How Hard Can it Be?: the world according to Clarkson, vol. 4, 2010; Is It Really Too Much To Ask?: the world according to Clarkson, vol. 5, 2013.

**CLARKSON, John;** *see* Clarkson, P. J.

**CLARKSON, Patrick Robert James**; QC 1991; a Recorder, since 1996; *b* 1 Aug. 1949; *s* of Commander Robert Anthony Clarkson, LVO, RN and Sheila Clarissa Neale; *m* 1975, Bridget Cecilia Doyne (*d* 2013); two *s* one *d*. *Educ:* Winchester. Called to the Bar, Lincoln's Inn, 1972. *Recreation:* country. *Address:* Landmark Chambers, 180 Fleet Street, EC4A 2HG. *T:* (020) 7430 1221. *Clubs:* Boodle's, MCC.
See also Lord Irwin.

**CLARKSON, Dr Peter David**, MBE 2010; Executive Secretary, Scientific Committee on Antarctic Research, 1989–2005; Emeritus Associate, Scott Polar Research Institute, since 2005; *b* 19 June 1945; *s* of late Maurice Roland Clarkson and Jessie Yoxall (*née* Baker); *m* 1974, Rita Margaret Skinner; one *d*. *Educ:* Epsom Coll.; Univ. of Durham (BSc 1967); Univ. of Birmingham (PhD 1977). FGS 1980. Geologist with British Antarctic Survey, 1967–89: wintered in Antarctica, Halley Bay, 1968 and 1969; Base Comdr, 1969; Antarctic field seasons in Shackleton Range (leader 3 times), 1968–78; in S Shetland Is, 1974–75; in Antarctic Peninsula, 1985–86 (leader). UK adviser to PROANTAR, Brazil, 1982. Chm., Trans-Antarctic Assoc., 2006–17 (Hon. Sec., 1980–93; Grants Sec., 1993–96; Trustee, 1996–2017). Polar Medal, 1976. *Publications:* (jtly) Natural Wonders of the World: 100 spectacular wonders of the natural world, 1995; Volcanoes, 2000; (jtly) 100 Great Wonders of the World, 2004; (jtly) Science in the Snow: fifty years of international collaboration through the Scientific Committee on Antarctic Research, 2011, 2nd edn as Science in the Snow: sixty years of international collaboration through the Scientific Committee on Antarctic Research, 2018; articles on Antarctic geology. *Recreations:* walking, woodwork, photography, music, lecturing on Antarctic cruise ships, all matters Antarctic. *Address:* Scott Polar Research Institute, Lensfield Road, Cambridge CB2 1ER. *T:* (01223) 336531; 35 King's Grove, Barton, Cambridge CB23 7AZ. *T:* (01223) 263417. *Club:* Antarctic.

**CLARKSON, Prof. (Peter) John**, PhD, ScD; CEng, FREng; FIET, FIED; Professor of Engineering Design, since 2004, and Director, Cambridge Engineering Design Centre, since 1997, University of Cambridge; Fellow, Trinity Hall, Cambridge, since 1995 (Vice Master, 2009–13); *b* Oswestry, 11 Nov. 1961; *s* of Ven. Alan Geoffrey Clarkson, *qv*; *m* 1988, Mary Susan Joan Moore; two *s* two *d*. *Educ:* Wells Cathedral Sch.; Trinity Hall, Cambridge (BA 1984; MA 1988; PhD 1988; ScD 2017). CEng 1990, FREng 2012; FIET 2004; FIED 2011. Student engr, English Electric Valve Co., UK, 1980–84; Consulting Engr, PA Consulting Gp, UK, 1988–95; Lectr in Engrg Design, 1995–2001, Reader in Engrg Design, 2001–04, Univ. of Cambridge. Dr *hc* Katholieke, Leuven, 2012. Sir Misha Black Medal, 2018. *Publications:* (with S. Keates) Countering Design Exclusion, 2003; (ed jtly) Inclusive Design, 2003; (jtly) Design for Patient Safety, 2004; (ed with C. Eckert) Design Process Improvement, 2005; (ed jtly) Design for Inclusivity, 2007; (jtly) Inclusive Design Toolkit, 2007; (jtly) Engineering Better Care, 2017; contrib. papers to design jls. *Recreations:* music, cycling, church. *Address:* Department of Engineering, University of Cambridge, Trumpington Street, Cambridge CB2 1PZ. *T:* (01223) 748246. *E:* pjc10@eng.cam.ac.uk.

**CLARRICOATS, Prof. Peter John Bell**, CBE 1996; FRS 1990; FREng; Professor of Electronic Engineering, Queen Mary and Westfield (formerly Queen Mary) College, University of London, 1968–97, now Emeritus Professor, Queen Mary, University of London (Head of Department, 1979–97); *b* 6 April 1932; *s* of John Clarricoats and Cecilia (*née* Bell); *m* 1st, 1955, Gillian (*née* Hall) (marr. diss. 1962); one *s* one *d*; 2nd, 1968, Phyllis Joan (*née* Lloyd); two *d*, and one step *s* one step *d*. *Educ:* Minchenden Grammar Sch.; Imperial Coll. (BSc (Eng), PhD, DSc (Eng) 1968). FInstP 1964; FIET (FIEE 1967); FIEEE 1967; FCGI 1980; FREng (FEng 1983). Scientific Staff, GEC, 1953–58; Lectr, Queen's Univ. Belfast, 1959–62; Sheffield Univ., 1962–63; Prof. of Electronic Engineering, Univ. of Leeds, 1963–67; Mem., Governing Body, QMC, 1976–79, Dean of Engineering, 1977–80; Fellow, QMW, 1999. Founder Editor, Electronics Letters (IEE Jl), 1964–. Chm., Defence Scientific Adv. Council, MoD, 1997–2000. Chm., British Nat. Cttee for Radio Sci., subseq. UK Panel for URSI, 1985–93; Vice-Pres., URSI, 1993–99. Chairman: 1st Internat. Conf. on Antennas and Propagation, IEE, 1978; European Microwave Conf., 1979; Mil. Microwaves Conf., 1988; Microwaves and RF Conf., 1994. Distinguished Lectr, IEEE, 1987–8. Institution of Electrical Engineers: Vice-Pres., 1989–91; Mem. Council, 1964–67, 1977–80; Chm., Electronics Div., 1978–79; Hon. Fellow, 1993; awards: Premia, Electronics Section, 1960, 1961; Marconi, 1974; Measurement Prize, 1989; J. J. Thomson Medal, 1989; Oliver Lodge, 1992. FRAS 2015; FRSA 2017; Fellow, URSI, 2017. Hon DSc: Kent, 1993; Aston, 1995. Coopers Hill Meml Prize, IEE, 1964; European Microwave Prize, 1989, Dist. Achievement Medal, 2005, European Microwave Assoc.; Cert. of Appreciation, 1989, Millennium Medal, 2000, Distinguished Achievement Award, 2001, IEEE; Sir Frank Whittle Gold Medal, RAEng, 2015. *Publications:* Microwave Ferrites, 1960; (with A. D. Olver) Corrugated Horns for Microwave Antennas, 1984; (with A. D. Olver) Microwave Horns and Feeds, 1994; papers on antennas and waveguides. *Recreations:* music, history. *Address:* The Red House, 3 Grange Meadows, Elmswell, Suffolk IP30 9GE. *T:* (01359) 240585.

**CLARY, Sir David (Charles)**, Kt 2016; FRS 1997; President, Magdalen College, Oxford, 2005–Aug. 2020; Professor of Chemistry, University of Oxford, since 2002; *b* Halesworth, Suffolk, 14 Jan. 1953; *s* of late Cecil Raymond Clary and Mary Mildred Clary; *m* 1975, Heather Ann Vinson; three *s*. *Educ:* Colchester Royal Grammar Sch.; Sussex Univ. (BSc 1974); Corpus Christi Coll., Cambridge (PhD 1977); ScD Cantab 1998. CChem, FRSC 1997; CPhys, FInstP 1997. IBM World-Trade Postdoctoral Fellow, San Jose, Calif, 1977–78; Postdoctoral Fellow, Manchester Univ., 1978–80; Research Lectr in Chemistry, UMIST, 1980–83; Department of Chemistry, Cambridge University: Demonstrator, 1983–87; Lectr, 1987–93; Reader in Theoretical Chem., 1993–96; Magdalene College, Cambridge: Fellow, 1983–96 (Hon. Fellow, 2005); Dir of Studies in Natural Scis, 1988–96; Sen. Tutor, 1989–93; Fellow Commoner, 1996–2002; Prof. of Chem. and Dir, Centre for Theoretical and Computational Chem., UCL, 1996–2002; Hd, Div. of Mathematical and Physical Scis, Univ. of Oxford, and Fellow, St John's Coll., Oxford, 2002–05. Chief Scientific Advr, FCO, 2009–13. Visiting Fellow: Univ. of Colo, 1987–88; Canterbury Univ., NZ, 1992; Univ. of Sydney, Australia, 1994; Hebrew Univ. of Jerusalem, 1994; Université de Paris Sud, 1995; Miller Vis. Prof., Univ. of Calif at Berkeley, 2001; Vis. Prof., Nat. Univ. of Singapore, 2002; Einstein Prof., Chinese Acad. of Scis, 2014. Lectures: George B. Kistiakowsky, Harvard Univ., 2002; Kenneth Pitzer, Univ. of Calif at Berkeley, 2004; Burton Meml, Imperial Coll., London, 2004; Paul Grandpierre, Columbia Univ., 2004; Thomas Graham, UCL and RSC, 2004; Charles Coulson, Univ. of Georgia, 2009; IBM Hursley, Univ. of Southampton, 2009; Noel Hush, Univ. of Sydney, 2014. Trustee, Henry Fund, 2007–. Mem. Council, Royal Soc., 2003–05; Royal Society of Chemistry: Mem. Council, 1990–93 and 1994–2001, Vice-Pres., 1997–2001; Pres., 2006–09, Faraday Div.; Meldola Medal, 1981; Marlow Medal, Faraday Div., 1986; Corday-Morgan Medal, 1989; Tilden Medal and Lectr, 1998; Chemical Dynamics Prize, 1998; Polanyi Medal, 2004; Liversidge Award, 2010; Spiers Meml Award, 2018. Fellow: AAAS, 2003; APS, 2003; FRSA 2005; Foreign Hon. Mem., Amer. Acad. of Arts and Scis, 2003; Hon. Fellow, Chemical Res. Soc. of India, 2019. Hon. DSc Sussex, 2011 (50th Anniversary Fellow, 2012). Annual Medal, Internat. Acad. of Quantum Molecular Scis, 1989 (Mem., 1998–). Editor, Chemical Physics Letters, 2000–. *Publications:* papers on chemical physics and theoretical chemistry in learned jls. *Recreations:* family, football, foreign travel. *Address:* Magdalen College, Oxford OX1 4AU. *T:* (01865) 276100.

**CLASPER, Michael**, CBE 1995; Chairman: Coats plc, since 2013; Coats Group (formerly Guinness Peat Group) plc, since 2014; *b* 21 April 1953; *s* of Douglas and Hilda Clasper; *m* 1975, Susan Rosemary Shore; two *s* one *d*. *Educ:* Bede Sch., Sunderland; St John's Coll., Cambridge (1st cl. Hons Engineering). British Rail, 1974–78; joined Procter & Gamble 1978, Advertising Dir, 1985–88; Gen. Manager, Procter & Gamble Holland, 1988–91; Man. Dir and Vice-Pres., Procter & Gamble UK, 1991–95; Regl Vice-Pres., Laundry Products, Procter & Gamble Europe, 1995–99; Pres., Global Home Care and New Business Develt, Procter & Gamble, 1999–2001; Dep. Chief Exec., 2001–03, Chief Exec., 2003–06, BAA plc; Operational Man. Dir, Terra Firma, 2007–08; Chm., HM Revenue and Customs, 2008–12. Chairman: Which? Ltd, 2008–17; BIOSS Internat. Ltd, 2017–; non-exec. Dir, ITV plc, 2006–14 (Sen. Ind. Dir, 2010–14); Sen. Ind. Dir, Serco, 2014–18; Mem., Investor Bd, EMI, 2007–08. Member: Adv. Council on Business and the Envmt, 1993–99; Mgt Cttee, Business and Envmt Prog., Univ. of Cambridge Prog. for Industry, 2000–07; Nat. Employment Panel, 2006–08; Chair, BITC Marketplace Taskforce, 2005–07. Gov., RSC, 2011–. Pres., Chartered Mgt Inst., 2014–17. *Recreations:* walking, ski-ing, tennis, golf, theatre.

**CLAUGHTON, John Alan**; Senior Counsel, Graham Pelton Consulting; *b* 17 Sept. 1956; *s* of Ronald Patterson and Patricia Claughton (*née* Dobell); *m* 1993, Alexandra Dyer; three *s*. *Educ:* King Edward's Sch., Birmingham; Merton Coll., Oxford (MA 1st Cl. Lit. Hum.). Professional cricketer, Warwickshire CCC, 1979–80; corp. finance advr, N. M. Rothschild & Sons, 1980–82; schoolmaster: Bradfield Coll., 1982–84; Eton Coll., 1984–2001; Headmaster, Solihull Sch., 2001–05; Chief Master, King Edward's Sch., Birmingham, 2006–16. Governor: Selly Oak Trust Sch., 2015–; West House Sch., 2016–; British Sch. of Milan, 2018–. *Recreations:* sport, travel, ballet, reading. *Address:* 170 Rotton Park Road, Birmingham B16 0LN.

**CLAXTON STEVENS, Christopher Paul**; consultant in antique and contemporary furniture, since 2009; *b* Pinner, 15 May 1952; *s* of Edward Arthur George Stevens and Barbara Joan Stevens (*née* Claxton); *m* 1976, Patricia Mary Payne (marr. diss. 1982); one *s* by Diana Lindsay Halliwell; *m* 2019, Gladys Joseph Zakana. *Educ:* Haileybury Coll.; Christ Church, Oxford (MA). With Christie's Auctioneers, 1975–81; Norman Adams Ltd, London, 1981–2009 (Dir, 1986–2009); Course Advr and Lectr, W Dean Coll., W Sussex, 1998–. Chairman: Regl Furniture Soc., 1993–2001 (Life Vice-Pres., 2011); London Appreciation Soc., 2016–. Trustee: Chiltern Open Air Mus. of Buildings, 1980–; Geffrye Mus., 1997–2012; Frederick Parker Foundn, 1997–; Art Workers' Guild, 2008–14; Patron, British Antique Furniture Restorers' Assoc., 2009– (Vice-Pres., 2014–). Master: Furniture Makers' Co., 2002; Arts Scholars' Co., 2012. *Publications:* 18th Century English Furniture: the Norman Adams collection, 1983; (jtly) British Furniture 1600–2000, 2005; The Frederick Parker Collection: a selection of chairs, 2006; contrib. articles to magazines, jls and exhibn catalogues. *Recreations:* England, architecture. *Address:* 24 Shandon Road, Clapham, SW4 9HR. *E:* c.claxtonstevens@normanadams.com.

**CLAY, Sir Edward**, KCMG 2005 (CMG 1994); HM Diplomatic Service, retired; High Commissioner, Kenya, 2001–05; *b* 21 July 1945; *m* 1969, Anne Stroud; three *d*. FO, later FCO, 1968; Nairobi, 1970; Second, later First, Sec., Sofia, 1973; FCO, 1975; First Secretary: Budapest, 1979; FCO, 1982; Counsellor: Nicosia, 1985; FCO, 1989; Ambassador (non-resident) to Rwanda, 1994–95, to Burundi, 1994–96; High Comr to Uganda, 1993–97; Dir, Public Diplomacy and Public Services, FCO, 1997–99; High Comr to Cyprus, 1999–2001. Associate Dir, Centre for Political and Diplomatic Studies, 2007–; Mem., Adv. Bd, Governance and Justice Gp, 2009–. Trustee: Leonard Cheshire Disability, 2005–11; Constant Gardener Trust, 2005–; RODI-UK, 2005–16; Kitchen Table Charities Trust, 2008–17; Internat. Alert, 2010–16; Patron, Excellent Develt, 2006–. *Recreation:* seven grandchildren.

**CLAY, Lindsey Anne**; Chief Executive Officer, Thinkbox, since 2013; *b* Workington, Cumbria, 28 Nov. 1965; *d* of late Michael John Clay and Patricia Anne Clay (*née* Dunn); *m* 2000, Matthew Richard White; two *d*. *Educ:* St Bees Sch., Cumbria; Jesus Coll., Cambridge (BA Hons 1988). Account manager, Clarke Hooper Consulting, 1988–92; Director: McCann Erickson, 1992–97; J Walter Thompson, 1997–2007; Mktg Dir, 2007–10, Man. Dir, 2010–12, Thinkbox. Non-exec. Dir, Somethin' Else, 2016–. Member: Steering Cttee, Rank Fellowship, 2007– (Chair, 2016–); Bd, British Arrows (formerly British TV Advertising) Awards, 2008–. Trustee, Rank Foundn, 2016–. Member: WACL, 2005– (Pres., 2015–16); Mktg Gp of GB, 2014–; Pres., Global TV Gp, 2019–. Fellow, Mktg Soc., 2014. *Recreations:* netball playing for Weston Park, N London Netball League, running, reading, theatre, television. *Address:* Thinkbox TV, Manning House, 22 Carlisle Place, SW1P 1JA. *T:* (020) 7630 2320. *E:* Lindsey.Clay@thinkbox.tv.

**CLAY, Sir Richard (Henry)**, 7th Bt *cr* 1841, of Fulwell Lodge, Middlesex; *b* 2 June 1940; *s* of Sir Henry Felix Clay, 6th Bt, and Phyllis Mary (*d* 1997), *yr d* of late R. H. Paramore, MD, FRCS; *S* father, 1985; *m* 1963, Alison Mary, *d* of late Dr James Gordon Fife; three *s* two *d*. *Educ:* Eton. FCA 1966. *Recreation:* sailing. *Heir: s* Charles Richard Clay [*b* 18 Dec. 1965; *m* 2000, Janette Maria, *o d* of Steve Carothers, USA; one *s* one *d*]. *Address:* The Copse, Shiplate Road, Bleadon, N Somerset BS24 0NX.

**CLAY, Robert Alan**; Member (Lab), City and County of Swansea Council, 2013–17; *b* 2 Oct. 1946; *s* of Albert Arthur Clay, OBE and Joyce Doris (*née* Astins); *m* 1980, Uta Christa. *Educ:* Bedford Sch.; Gonville and Caius Coll., Cambridge. Bus driver, Tyne and Wear PTE, 1975–83. Branch Chm., GMBATU, 1977–83. MP (Lab) Sunderland North, 1983–92. Treas., 1983–86, Sec., 1986–87, Campaign Gp of Labour MPs. Chief Exec., Pallion Engrg Ltd, 1992–93; Partner, Roots Music, 1993. *Recreations:* walking, reading.

**CLAYDON, David John**; Chairman and Chief Executive Officer, D. Claydon Advisers, since 2013; Co-Founder, 2013, and Co-Chief Executive Officer, Macro Advisory Partners LLP; *b* Chipping Sodbury, Glos, 17 Dec. 1970; *s* of Terry John and Joan Elizabeth Claydon; *m* 2000, Tabitha Lockwood Estabrook; two *s* one *d*. *Educ:* Ridings Sch., Winterbourne, Bristol; Univ. of Essex (BA 1st Cl. Govt). ESU Congressional Schol., US House of Reps, Washington, Office of the Majority Leader, 1993–94; Associate, Chem. Banking Corp., New York, NY, 1995–97; Vice Pres., J. P. Morgan, NY, 1997–2000; Man. Dir, Morgan Stanley, London, 2000–08; Econ. Advr to Foreign Sec., FCO, 2008–10; Hd, Macro Strategy, FICC, UBS Securities Co. Ltd, 2010–12. Mem. Bd, Gt Ormond St Hosp. Mem., ESU. Trustee, IPPR. FRSA. *Recreations:* yoga, cycling, charitable work, current affairs, classic cars, relaxing! *Address:* Ashton Hill Farm, Corston, Bath BA2 9EY. *T:* (01225) 872935. *E:* claydon123@btinternet.com.

**CLAYDON, Geoffrey Bernard**, CB 1990; Member, Legal Directorate, Department of Transport, 1990–95; *b* 14 Sept. 1930; *s* of Bernard Claydon and Edith Mary (*née* Lucas); unmarried. *Educ:* Leeds Modern; King Edward's, Birmingham; Birmingham Univ. (LLB). Articled at Pinsent & Co., Birmingham, 1950; admitted Solicitor, 1954. Legal Asst, 1959, Sen. Legal Asst, 1965, Treasury Solicitor's Dept; Asst Solicitor, DTI, 1973; Asst Treasury Solicitor, 1974; Principal Asst Treasury Solicitor and Legal Advr, Dept of Energy, 1980. Mem., Editorial Bd, Jl of Energy and Natural Resources Law, 1983–90. National Tramway Museum: Sec., 1958–84; Vice-Chm., 1969–99; Vice-Pres., 1998–2005 and 2006–; Pres., 2005–06. Light Rail Transit Association (formerly Light Railway Transport League): Chm.

of League, 1963–68; Vice-Pres., 1968–2008; Pres., 2008–11; Patron, 2011–. Pres., Tramway and Light Railway Soc., 1996–2001 and 2011– (Chm., 1967–93; Vice-Pres., 1993–96); Dir, Heritage Railway Assoc., 2003– (Chairman: Legal and Parly Affairs (formerly Legal Services) Cttee, 2002–; Heritage Tramways Cttee, 2006–); Dir, UKTram, 2015–. Chm., Consultative Panel for Preservation of British Transport Relics, 1982–; Member: Inst. of Transport Admin, 1972–; Fixed Track Section, Confedn of Passenger Transport, 1996–2014; CIT Working Party on transport legislation, 1996–98. CMILT (MCIT 1997; MILT 1999). *Publications:* (contrib. on tramways) Halsbury's Laws of England, 2000; (ed) British Tramway Accidents, 2006. *Recreations:* rail transport, travel. *Address:* 3 The Park, Duffield, Derbys DE56 4ER. *T:* (01332) 841007. *Club:* Royal Automobile.

CLAYDON, Nick; Senior Partner, Brunswick Group LLP, since 2010 (Partner, 2001–10); *b* London, 24 Feb. 1967; *s* of Ralph and Valerie Claydon; *m* 1st, 2000, Manisha Vadhia (*d* 2007); one *s*; 2nd, 2013, Charlotte Wheeler; one *d*. *Educ:* Caterham Sch.; Univ. of Leeds (BA Hons Politics). Researcher for Chris Smith, MP, 1990; Editl, The House Mag., 1991; Political Consultant: Advocacy Partnership, 1991–92; Ian Greer Associates, 1992–95; Associate Partner, Brunswick Gp LLP, 1995–98; Hd, Ext. Communications, British Airways, 1998–2001. Member: Corporate Bd, ENO, 2012–16; Corporate Bd, ENB, 2016–; Bd, Maggie's, 2016–. Trustee, Demos, 2006–. *Address:* Brunswick Group LLP, 16 Lincoln's Inn Fields, WC2A 3ED. *T:* (020) 7404 5959. *E:* nclaydon@brunswickgroup.com. *Club:* Ivy.

CLAYSON, His Honour Timothy; a Circuit Judge, 2004–18; Honorary Recorder of Bolton, 2012–18; *b* 19 Aug. 1952; *s* of Victor Clayson and Elsie Clayson (*née* Cryer); *m* 1st, 1976, Anita Morton (marr. diss. 1995); two *s* one *d*; 2nd, 1997, Heidi Svensgaard (marr. diss. 2002); 3rd, 2009, Joanne Lowe. *Educ:* Christ's Hosp.; University Coll. London (LLB 1973). Called to the Bar, Gray's Inn, 1974; a Recorder, 1996–2004; International Judge, UN, Kosovo, 2001–03: Dist Court, Gjilan, 2001, Mitrovica, 2002; Supreme Court, 2003. *Recreations:* sailing, classical music.

CLAYTON, Rear Adm. Christopher Hugh Trevor; Assistant Director Intelligence, NATO International Military Staff, 2004–07; *b* 21 May 1951; *s* of Arthur Henry Trevor Clayton and Patricia June Norma Clayton; *m* 1997, Deirdre Hannah; one *s* two *d*, and two step *s*. *Educ:* Bishop McKenzie's Sch., Lilongwe, Nyasaland; Wells House, Malvern Wells, Worcs; St John's Sch., Leatherhead. Entered BRNC as naval aviator, 1970; Commanding Officer: HMS Beaver (T22 Frigate), 1993–94; HMS Chatham (T22 Frigate), 1996–97; Commodore Naval Aviation, i/c Naval Air Comd, 2000–02; HCSC 2003; CO, HMS Ocean (Helicopter Carrier), 2003–04; Rear Adm. 2004. Chairman: RN Winter Sports Assoc., 1997–2004, Pres., 2004; Combined Services Winter Sports Assoc., 2003. *Recreations:* squash, golf, winter sports, modern history, carpentry and cabinet making, tending 6 acres. *Address:* c/o Naval Secretary, Fleet Headquarters, Whale Island, Portsmouth PO2 8BY. *Club:* Naval and Military.

CLAYTON, Captain Sir David (Robert), 12th Bt *cr* 1732, of Marden; Shipmaster, retired; *b* 12 Dec. 1936; *s* of Sir Arthur Harold Clayton, 11th Bt, DSC, and of Alexandra, Lady Clayton, *d* of late Sergei Andreevsky; *S* father, 1985; *m* 1971, Julia Louise, *d* of late Charles Henry Redfearn; two *s*. *Educ:* HMS Conway. Joined Merchant Service, 1953; promoted to first command as Captain, 1970. *Recreations:* shooting, sailing. *Heir:* *s* Robert Philip Clayton [*b* 8 July 1975; *m* 2004, Rachel Kathleen Hughes; one *s* two *d*]. *Address:* Rock House, Kingswear, Dartmouth, Devon TQ6 0BX. *T:* (01803) 752433. *Club:* Royal Dart Yacht (Kingswear).

CLAYTON, Jeremy Paul; Director, Knowledge and Innovation Strategy and International, Department for Business, Innovation and Skills, 2014–16 (Director, Research Base, 2011–14); *b* 3 Feb. 1956; *s* of Giles Conrad Clayton and late Anne Margaret Clayton (*née* Crennell); *m* 1990, Mary Lucille Hindmarch. *Educ:* Bedales Sch.; Christ Church, Oxford (MA Physics). Department of Energy, 1978–91: Private Sec. to Norman Lamont, MP, David Mellor, MP, and Rt Hon. Nigel Lawson, MP, 1981–83; Secretariat, Sizewell B Public Inquiry, 1984–87; electricity privatisation, 1989–91; Dir, Building Mgt Privatisation Unit, PSA Services, 1991–94; Department of Trade and Industry: Director: Prog. Finance and Public Expenditure Survey, 1994–97; Radiocommunications Agency Third Generation Mobile Communications Auction Team, 1997–2000; Export Control, 2000–03; Gp Dir, Transdeptl Sci. and Technol., OST, subseq. Office of Sci. and Innovation, 2003–07; Dep. Head, Govt Office for Science, DIUS, later BIS, 2007–11. UK/US Fulbright Comr, 2014–16. Mem. Council, UEA, 2016–. Gov., Walcot Foundn, 2016–. Trustee, Campaign for Sci. and Engrg, 2017–. Member: Glyndebourne Fest. Soc.; Benslow Music Trust; Ramblers Assoc.; Friend: Covent Gdn; Aldeburgh Fest.; Wigmore Hall; RA; Lake Dist. *Recreations:* cello, piano, singing, walking, reading, classical music, theatre and film. *Address:* 25 Fitzwilliam Road, SW4 0DW.

CLAYTON, Margaret Ann; *b* 7 May 1941; *d* of late Percy Thomas Clayton and of Kathleen Clayton (*née* Payne). *Educ:* Christ's Hospital, Hertford; Birkbeck Coll., London (BA, MSc). Entered Home Office, 1960; Executive Officer/Asst Principal, 1960–67; Asst Private Secretary to Home Secretary, 1967–68; Principal, 1968–75 (seconded to Cabinet Office, 1972–73); Asst Sec., 1975–82; Asst Under Sec. of State, 1983–95; Resident Chm., CSSB, 1983; Dir of Services, Prison Service, 1986–90; Police Dept, 1990–93; Personnel Dept, 1994. Dir, Butler Trust, 1996–99; Chm., Mental Health Act Commn, 1999–2002. Chm., Farriers Registration Council, 2001–06. Mem., Lambeth, Southwark and Lewisham HA, 1995–99. Freeman, City of London, 1984; Liveryman, Farriers' Co., 1984–. *Recreations:* gardening, theatre, reading, bell-ringing.

CLAYTON, Michael Aylwin; Editor of Horse and Hound, 1973–96; Editor-in-Chief, IPC country titles, 1994–97; *b* 20 Nov. 1934; *s* of late Aylwin Goff Clayton and Norah (*née* Banfield); *m* 1988, Marilyn Crowhurst (*née* Orrin); one *s* one *d* from a previous marriage. *Educ:* Bournemouth Grammar School. National Service, RAF, 1954–56. Reporter: Lymington Times and New Milton Advertiser, 1951–54; Portsmouth Evening News, 1956–57; London Evening News, 1957–61; reporter/feature writer, New Zealand Herald, 1961; reporter, London Evening Standard, 1961, Dep. News Editor, 1962–64; News Editor, Southern Ind. Television, 1964–65; staff correspondent, BBC TV and radio (incl. Vietnam, Cambodia, India, Pakistan and Middle East), 1965–73; Presenter, Today, BBC Radio 4, 1973–75. Dir, IPC Magazines, 1994–97. Chm., British Soc. of Magazine Editors, 1986. Mem., Press Complaints Commn, 1991–93. Chairman: BHS, 1998–2001; British Horse Industry Confedn, 1999–2004; Trustees, Mus. of Hunting, 2006–. *Publications:* A Hunting We Will Go, 1967; (with Dick Tracey) Hickstead—the First Twelve Years, 1972; (ed) The Complete Book of Showjumping, 1975; (ed) Cross-Country Riding, 1977; The Hunter, 1980; The Golden Thread, 1984; Prince Charles: horseman, 1987; The Chase: a modern guide to foxhunting, 1987; Foxhunting in Paradise, 1993; Endangered Species, 2004; The Glorious Chase, 2005; Peterborough Royal Foxhound Show—a history, 2006; The Duke of Rutland's Hounds, the Belvoir, 2011; (with Alastair Jackson) A Short History of Foxhunting, 2013; The Ride of My Life, 2016. *Recreations:* foxhunting, music, bridge.

CLAYTON, Prof. Nicola Susan, PhD; FRS 2010; Professor of Comparative Cognition, University of Cambridge, since 2005; Fellow of Clare College, Cambridge, since 2000; Scientist in Residence, Rambert Dance Company, since 2011 (Scientific Adviser, 2009–11); *b* 22 Nov. 1962; *d* of Colin and Angela Clayton; *m* 2001, Dr Nathan Jon Emery. *Educ:* Pembroke Coll., Oxford (BA Hons Zoology 1984; Domus Scholarship); Univ. of St Andrews (PhD Bird Song 1987). University of California, Davis: Asst Prof., 1995–98; Associate Prof., 1998–2000; Chair, Animal Behavior Grad. Gp, 1999–2000; Full Prof., 2000; University of Cambridge: Univ. Lectr, 2000–02, Reader in Comparative Cognition, 2002–05, Dept of Experimental Psychol.; Co-founder, The Captured Thought, Dept of Psychology, 2012–; Tutor and Dir of Studies, Clare Coll., Cambridge, 2000–. Perry Gilbert Lectr, Univ. of Cornell, 2014; with Clive Wilkins: Floyd Clarke Lectr, Univ. of Wyoming, 2013; The Captured Thought Lecture series, Florida Univ., 2015; Medawar Lect., UCL, 2015; SAGE Dist. Lect, UCSB, 2016. Member: Cognitive Neurosci. Section, Fac. of 1000 Biology, 2002–; Animal Scis Cttee, 2003–05, 2008–11, Res. Cttee A (Animal Systems, Health and Well Being), 2009–12, BBSRC; Adv. Bd, Culture and Mind Proj., AHRC, 2004–; Dorothy Hodgkin Fellowship Selection Panel B Side, Royal Soc., 2008–10; Ecol. and Evolution Panel, Eur. Res. Cttee FP8, 2008–14. Member: Council, Assoc. for Study of Animal Behaviour, 2009–12; British Neurosci. Assoc. (Mem., Organizing Cttee, 2002–03); Eur. Psychological Soc.; Council, Eur. Brain and Behaviour Soc., 2009–. FRSB (FSB 2010). Internat. Affiliate, Amer. Psychol Assoc.; Fellow, Assoc. for Psychol Scis, 2010. Consulting Editor: Behavioural Neuroscience, 1999–2002; Learning and Behavior, 2007–; Associate Editor: Learning and Motivation, 2000–03; Qly Jl of Experimental Psychology, 2001–04; Animal Behaviour, 2001–04; Mem., Editl Cttee, Biological Reviews, 2003–06; Member, Editorial Board: Public Library of Science One, 2006–; Procs of Royal Soc. B, 2007–. Frank Beach Award, Amer. Psychol Assoc., 2000; Klaus Immelmann Prize in animal behaviour, Bielefeld Univ., 2003; Jean-Marie Delwart Award in Comparative and Evolutionary Neurosci., Belgium Acad. of Scis, 2010; Mid-career Award, Experimental Psychol. Soc., 2012. *Publications:* (jtly) Social Intelligence: from brain to culture, 2007; 268 articles in scientific jls incl. Nature and Science. *Recreations:* dancing, especially Argentine tango and salsa but also jazz and ballet, yoga, bird watching, playing clarinet and saxophone. *Address:* Department of Psychology, University of Cambridge, Downing Street, Cambridge CB2 3EB. *T:* (01223) 333559, *Fax:* (01223) 333564. *E:* nsc22@cam.ac.uk, nickyclayton@rambert.org.uk.

CLAYTON, Richard Anthony; QC 2002; a Recorder, since 2006; *b* 25 May 1954; *s* of Dennis Lloyd and Patricia Estelle Clayton; *m* 1st, 1980, Isabel Glen Japp (marr. diss.); one *s*; 2nd, 1992, Anne Bernadette Burns (marr. diss.); one *s*; 3rd, 2010, Claer Lloyd-Jones. *Educ:* New Coll., Oxford (BA PPE). Called to the Bar, Middle Temple, 1977, Bencher, 2010. South Islington Law Centre, 1980–82; Osler, Hoskin Harcourt, Toronto, 1982–83; in Chambers, 1984–. UK Rep., Venice Commn, 2011–19. Associate Fellow, Centre for Public Law, Univ. of Cambridge, 2001–. *Publications:* Practice and Procedure at Industrial Tribunals, 1987; (jtly) Civil Actions Against the Police, 1987, 3rd edn 2004; Judicial Review Procedure, 1993, 2nd edn 1996; Police Actions, 1993, 2nd edn 1996; The Law of Human Rights, 2000, 2nd edn 2009. *Recreations:* theatre, reading, ski-ing. *Address:* 7 Bedford Row, WC1R 4BS.

CLAYTON, Stanley James; Town Clerk of the City of London, 1974–82; *b* 10 Dec. 1919; *s* of late James John Clayton and late Florence Clayton; *m* 1955, Jean Winifred, *d* of late Frederick Etheridge; one *s* one *d*. *Educ:* Ensham Sch.; King's Coll., London (LLB). Served War of 1939–45, commnd RAF. Admitted Solicitor 1958. City of Westminster, 1938–52; Camberwell, 1952–60; Asst Solicitor, Holborn, 1960–63; Deputy Town Clerk: Greenwich, 1963–65; Islington, 1964–69; City of London, 1969–74. Comdr, Order of Dannebrog (Denmark); holds other foreign orders. *Address:* Fairfield, Purston Lane, High Ackworth, W Yorks WF7 7EQ.

CLEARY, (Anthony) Shaun; HM Diplomatic Service; High Commissioner to Mozambique, 2010–14; *b* Brigg, 27 Oct. 1965; *s* of Michael Cleary and Marlene Cleary; *m* Kathryn Anne Douglas; two *s* four *d*. *Educ:* Clare Coll., Cambridge (BA 1987; MPhil Internat. Relns 1988; MBA 2009; MSc Finance 2013). Joined HM Diplomatic Service, 1988; S America Dept, FCO, 1989–90; Pol Officer, S Africa, 1990–93; Hd, NATO Team, then Hd, Baltic/Balkans Team, FCO, 1994–97; Energy, Envmt and Budget Counsellor, OECD, Paris, 1998–2002; Dep. Hd, Aviation, Maritime and Energy Dept, FCO, 2003–04; Dep. Consul Gen., Basra, 2004–05; Spending Review Team, then Hd, Capability Review Team, FCO, 2005–07; Financial Planning Dir, E Sussex NHS Trust (on secondment), 2007; Asst Dir of Protocol, FCO, 2008; Dep. Leader, Stabilisation Review Team, Cabinet Office (on secondment), 2008; Actg High Comr, Suva, 2009; Hd, Flu Crisis Unit, Consular Crisis Gp, FCO, 2009; Actg Hd of Mission, Monrovia, 2014; Actg Dep. High Comr, Freetown, 2014. *Publications:* contrib. article in African Affairs. *Recreation:* cooking. *Address:* c/o Foreign and Commonwealth Office, King Charles Street, SW1A 2AH. *E:* shaun.cleary@fco.gov.uk.

CLEARY, His Honour Anthony Simon Lissant; a Circuit Judge, 2006–19; a Deputy High Court Judge, Family Division, 2011–19; a Deputy Circuit Judge, since 2019; *b* 21 Jan. 1946; *s* of Bruce and Patricia Cleary; *m* 1st, 1968, Georgina Clark (marr. diss 1973); one *s* two *d*; 2nd, 1974, Carmel Briddon; one *s*. *Educ:* Fettes Coll.; Sheffield Univ. (LLB Hons). Account Exec., Benton & Bowles Advertising Agency, 1968–70; admitted solicitor, 1971; Registrar, then Dist Judge, 1986–2006; Asst Recorder, 1989–92, Recorder, 1992–2006. Civil Tutor Judge, 2001–10, IT Liaison Judge, 2003–10, Judicial Studies Bd. Member: Lord Chancellor's Matrimonial Causes Rules Cttee, 1984–86; Lord Chancellor's Children Act Procedure Adv. Gp, 1989–91; Lord Chancellor's Children Act Adv. Cttee, 1991–93; Judicial Liaison Panel, CAFCASS, 2004–06. Chm., Sheffield Family Conciliation Service, 1984–86 (Chm., Steering Cttee); Mem. Cttee, Birmingham Family Mediation Service, 1987–89. Mem., Family Law Cttee, Law Soc., 1984–86. Lecturer in Family Law: for Jordans (publishers of Family Law Jl), Birmingham Law Soc. and FLBA, 1987–2006; for Judicial Studies Bd, 1999–2010. Contributing Ed., Butterworth's County Court Precedents and Pleadings, 1988–93; Gen. Ed., Family Court Practice, annually, 1993–. *Publications:* Nobody Comes, 2014. *Recreations:* music (choral clerk, Coventry Cathedral; Mem., Armonico Consort, 2005–09), rifle shooting, planning, with occasional success, return trips to homeland, NZ.

CLEARY, Prof. Mark Christopher, PhD; Vice Chancellor and Principal, University of Bradford, 2007–13; *b* Birmingham, 27 Dec. 1954; *s* of Michael and Dorothy Cleary; *m* 1980, Marie Frances Brophy; two *s*. *Educ:* Jesus Coll., Cambridge (BA Hons Geog. 1977; PhD 1983). Lectr, Univ. of Exeter, 1980–89; Senior Lecturer: Univ. of Brunei, 1989–92; Univ. of Waikato, NZ, 1992–93; University of Plymouth: Reader, 1995–99; Prof. of Geog., 1999–2003; Dean of Social Sci. and Business, 2003–04; Dep. Vice-Chancellor, 2005–07. *Publications:* Peasants, Politicians and Producers: the organisation of agriculture in France since 1918, 1989, repr. 2006; (with P. Eaton) Borneo: change and development, 1992; (with S. Y. Wong) Oil, Economic Development and Diversification in Brunei Darussalam, 1994; (with P. Eaton) Tradition and Reform: land tenure and rural development in Southeast Asia, 1996; (with Goh Kim Chuan) Environment and Development in the Straits of Malacca, 2000. *Recreations:* cycling, walking.

**CLEARY, Shaun**; see Cleary, A. S.

**CLEAVE, Brian Elseley**, CB 1995; Solicitor of Inland Revenue, 1990–99; *b* 3 Sept. 1939; *s* of Walter Edward Cleave and Hilda Lillian Cleave (*née* Newman); *m* 1979, Celia Valentine Williams. *Educ*: Eastbourne Coll. (Duke of Devonshire's schol.); Exeter Univ. (LLB 1961); Kansas Univ.; Manchester Univ. Admitted Solicitor, 1966; called to the Bar, Gray's Inn, 1999. Asst Solicitor, Wilkinson Howlett and Durham, 1966–67; Inland Revenue Solicitor's Office, 1967–99: Asst Solicitor, 1978; Prin. Asst Solicitor, 1986. Senior Consultant: EU/Tacis Taxation Reform Project, Moscow, 2000–05; EU/Tacis Assistance to the State Tax Administration, Ukraine Project, 2006–07; Consultant, Govt of Tanzania and Govt of Zanzibar on sharing profits from oil prodn, 2008–09. Hon. QC 1999. FRSA 1995. *Publications*: (contrib.) The Impact of the OECD and UN Model Conventions on Bilateral Tax Treaties, 2012; (contrib.) Tax Rules in Non-Tax Agreements, 2012; case notes and other contribs to tax periodicals incl. British Tax Rev., European Taxation and Bulletin for Internat. Taxation. *Recreations*: theatre, travel, walking my Parson Russell terrier. *Address*: 15 Bellevue Road, Barnes, SW13 0BJ. *E*: brianecleave@gmail.com.

**CLEAVER, Sir Anthony (Brian)**, Kt 1992; Chairman, Novia Financial plc (formerly Novia Financial Holdings Ltd), since 2008; *b* 10 April 1938; *s* of late William Brian Cleaver and Dorothea Early Cleaver (*née* Peeks); *m* 1st, 1962, Mary Teresa Cotter (*d* 1999); one *s* one *d*; 2nd, 2000, Mrs Jennifer Guise Lloyd Graham, widow. *Educ*: Berkhamsted Sch.; Trinity Coll., Oxford (Schol.; MA; Hon. Fellow 1989). FBCS 1976; FRCM 2008. Joined IBM United Kingdom, 1962; IBM World Trade Corp., USA, 1973–74; Dir, DP Div., IBM UK, 1977; Vice-Pres. of Marketing, IBM Europe, Paris, 1981–82; Gen. Man., 1984, Chief Exec., 1986–91, Chm., 1990–94, IBM United Kingdom Holdings Ltd; Chairman: General Cable PLC, 1995–98 (Dir, 1994–98); IX Europe plc, 1999–2007. Chairman: UKAEA, 1993–96; AEA Technology plc, 1996–2001; MRC, 1998–2006; Nuclear Decommissioning Authy, 2004–07; Engrg and Technol. Bd, subseq. EngineeringUK, 2007–10; NERC, 2014–18. Chairman: The Strategic Partnership Ltd, 1997–2000; Baxi Partnership, 1999–2000; SThree plc, 2000–10; UK eUnivs Worldwide Ltd, 2001–04; Asia Pacific Advisers (UK Trade & Investment, formerly Trade Partners UK), 2000–03; Working Links (Employment) Ltd, 2003–09. Director: General Accident plc (formerly General Accident, Fire & Life Assurance Corp.), 1988–98; Smith & Nephew PLC, 1993–2002; Loral Europe Ltd, 1995–96; Cable Corp., 1995–96; Lockheed Martin Tactical Systems UK Ltd, 1996–99; Lockheed Martin UK Ltd, 1999–2006. Dir, Nat. Computing Centre, 1976–80. Member Board: UK Centre for Econ. and Environmental Develt, 1985–98 (Dep. Chm., 1992–98); BITC, 1985–2000 (Chm., Business in the Envmt Target Team, 1988–99; Mem., President's Cttee, 1988–91; Dep. Chm., 1991–2000); RIPA, 1985–90; Mem., Council, ABSA, 1985–97 (Dir, 1991–97); Pres., Involvement and Participation Assoc., 1997–2002. Chairman: Industrial Develt Adv. Bd, DTI, 1993–99; TEC Ind. Assessors Cttee, 1994–98; Council for Excellence in Mgt and Leadership, 2000–02; Member: Nat. Adv. Council for Educn and Trng Targets, 1993–98; Electronics EDC, NEDO, 1986–92; CBI, 1986–97 (Mem., President's Cttee, 1988–92); BOTB, 1988–91; Nat. Trng Task Force, 1989–92; Adv. Council, Centre for Dispute Resolution, 1996–2007; Partnership Korea, 1997–99; PPARC Appointments Cttee, 1996–2000; Cttee on Standards in Public Life, 1997–2003; British Government Panel on Sustainable Develt, 1998–2000; Singapore British Business Council, 1999–2000, 2003–04. Dir, American Chamber of Commerce, 1989–91. Member: HRH Duke of Edinburgh's Seventh Commonwealth Study Conf. Council, 1990–92; Council for Industry and Higher Educn, 1991–94; Carnegie Inquiry into Third Age, 1991–93. Chm., Portsmouth Univ. Business Adv. Bd, 1992–99; Member: Oxford Univ. Adv. Council on Continuing Educn, 1993–99; Oxford Univ. Develt Prog. Adv. Bd, 1999–2005; President's Cttee, Oxford Univ. Appeal, 1988; Appeal Chm., Trinity Coll., Oxford, 1989–98; Chm., RCM, 1999–2007 (Mem. Council, 1998–99; Vice-Pres., 2008–); Member Council: Templeton Coll., Oxford, 1982–93; PSI, 1985–88; Pres., Inst. of Mgt, 1999–2000; Chm. Govs, Birkbeck Coll., 1989–98; Mem., Cttee of Chm. of Univ. Councils, 1992–98; Trustee, Oxford Univ. Higher Studies Fund, 1994–2009. Dep. Chm., ENO, 1998–2000 (Dir, 1988–2000). Pres., Classical Assoc., 1995–96. Pres., Business Commitment to the Envmt, 2000–14. Freeman, City of London, 1987; Co. of Information Technologists, 1985– (Liveryman, 1994); Co. of Musicians, 2003– (Liveryman, 2005; Master, 2013–14). FCGI 2004. Hon. FCIM 1989 (Hon. Vice-Pres., 1989–); Hon. FCIPS 1996; Hon. FREng 2011; Hon. FIChemE 2013. FRSA 1987 (Chm., RSA Inquiry into Tomorrow's Co., 1993–95). Mem. Council, WWF, 1988–92. Patron, Friends of Classics, 1991–. Hon. Fellow: Birkbeck Coll., London, 1999; Univ. of Central Lancashire, 2007. Hon. LLD: Nottingham, 1991; Portsmouth, 1996; Hon. DSc: Cranfield, 1995; Hull, 2002; City, 2002; Hon. DTech London Metropolitan, 2003; DUniv Middx, 2003. UN Envmt Program Global 500 Roll of Honour, 1989. *Recreations*: music, especially opera; sport, especially cricket, golf. *E*: sirabc01@gmail.com. *Clubs*: Athenæum, Royal Automobile, MCC, Serpentine Swimmers.

**CLEE, Christopher**; QC 2009; a Recorder, since 2005; *b* Cardiff, 20 July 1961; *s* of Bernard Clee and Gaye Clee; *m* 1987, Kim Wibberley; two *s* two *d*. *Educ*: Bishop Vaughan Comp. Sch., Swansea; University Coll., Cardiff (LLB Hons); Inns of Court Sch. of Law. Called to the Bar, Gray's Inn, 1983. *Recreations*: football, Rugby, cricket, 1970s new wave music. *Address*: 18 Withy Park, Bishopston, Swansea SA3 3EY. *T*: (01792) 232020. *E*: christopherclee471@hotmail.com.

**CLEESE, John Marwood**; writer and actor; *b* 27 Oct. 1939; *s* of late Reginald and Muriel Cleese; *m* 1st, 1968, Connie Booth (marr. diss. 1978); one *d*; 2nd, 1981, Barbara Trentham (marr. diss. 1990; she *d* 2013); one *d*; 3rd, 1993, Alyce Faye Eichelberger (marr. diss. 2009); 4th, 2012, Jennifer Wade. *Educ*: Clifton Sports Acad.; Downing College, Cambridge (MA). Founder and former Dir, Video Arts Ltd. Started making jokes professionally, 1963; started on British television, 1966; TV series have included: The Frost Report, 1966–67; At Last the 1948 Show, 1967; Monty Python's Flying Circus, 1969–73; Fawlty Towers, 1975, 1979; The Human Face (documentary); Hold the Sunset, 2018, 2019. Films include: Interlude, 1968; And Now For Something Completely Different, 1970; The Magic Christian, 1971; Monty Python and the Holy Grail, 1974; Romance with a Double Bass, 1974; Life of Brian, 1978; Privates on Parade, 1982; The Meaning of Life, 1982; Yellowbeard, 1983; Silverado, 1985; Clockwise, 1986; A Fish Called Wanda, 1988; Erik the Viking, 1989; Splitting Heirs, 1993; Mary Shelley's Frankenstein, 1994; Rudyard Kipling's The Jungle Book, 1995; Fierce Creatures, 1997; The Out of Towners, 1998; Isn't She Great, 1998; The World Is Not Enough, 1999; Rat Race, 2002; Die Another Day, 2002; Harry Potter and the Chamber of Secrets, 2002; Scorched, 2005; The Pink Panther 2, 2009. Solo show: The Alimony Tour, UK, 2011. *Live show*: Monty Python Live (Mostly), O2 Arena, 2014; Fawlty Towers Live, Sydney, Australia and tour, 2016. Adapted: Bang Bang, Mercury Th., Colchester, 2017. Andrew D. White Prof.-at-Large, Cornell Univ., 1999–. Hon. LLD St Andrews. *Publications*: (with Robin Skynner) Families and How to Survive Them, 1983; The Golden Skits of Wing Commander Muriel Volestrangler FRHS and Bar, 1984; The Complete Fawlty Towers, 1989; (with Robin Skynner) Life and How to Survive It, 1993; (with Brian Bates) The Human Face, 2001; (jtly) The Pythons Autobiography by the Pythons, 2004; So, Anyway… (autobiog.), 2014. *Recreations*: gluttony, sloth. *Address*: c/o Independent Talent, 40 Whitfield Street, W1T 2RH.

**CLEGG, Prof. John Brian**, PhD; FRS 1999; Professor of Molecular Medicine, University of Oxford, 1996–2001, now Emeritus; *b* 9 April 1936; *s* of John Richard and Phyllis Clegg. *Educ*: Arnold Sch., Blackpool; Fitzwilliam House, Cambridge (MA 1963; PhD 1963). Univ. of Washington, Seattle, 1963; Johns Hopkins Univ., 1964–65; MRC Lab. of Molecular Biology, 1965; Department of Medicine, University of Liverpool: Lectr, 1966–68; Sen. Lectr, 1969–74; University of Oxford: Lectr, Dept of Medicine, 1974–79; Reader in Molecular Haematology, 1987–96; Asst Dir, Inst. of Molecular Medicine, 1989–2001; MRC Sen. Scientific Staff, 1979–2001. Hon. MRCP 1986, Hon. FRCP 1999. *Publications*: (with D. J. Weatherall) The Thalassaemia Syndromes, 1965, 4th edn 2001; scientific contribs to learned jls. *Recreations*: gardening, travel in France. *Address*: Institute of Molecular Medicine, John Radcliffe Hospital, Oxford OX3 9DS. *T*: (01865) 222398.

**CLEGG, Judith Caroline**; Founder and Chief Executive Officer: Takeout (formerly Venturing Unlimited), since 2006; The Glasshouse, since 1998; angel investor, since 1998; *b* Reading; *d* of (Geoffrey) Peter (Scott) Clegg and (Caroline) Jane Clegg. *Educ*: Warkworth C of E Primary Sch., Northumberland; Amble Middle Sch.; St Anne's Sch. for Girls, Windermere; Warwick Univ. (BSc 1st Cl. Hons Mgt Sci.). With Arthur Andersen Business Consulting, 1993–97; Operational Develt Manager, Pret, 1997–98; Co-founder and Chief Operating Officer, Moonfruit.com, 1999–2001; Advr, Philip Gould Associates, 2002–04; Associate Dir, Egremont, 2004–06. Founder, Battersea Courage Trust, 1998; Co-Founder, HANDSOFF Campaign, 2017–. *Recreations*: sailing in everything from tiny dinghies to ocean-going yachts (sailed across Pacific Ocean from Tahiti to Auckland), horse-riding, yoga, running, cooking, drinking earl grey tea. *Address*: Takeout, Second Home, 47–49 Princes Place, W11 4QA.

**CLEGG, Rt Hon. Sir Nicholas (William Peter)**, Kt 2018; PC 2008; Vice-President of Global Affairs and Communications, Facebook, since 2018; *b* 7 Jan. 1967; *s* of Nicholas P. Clegg and Hermance Eulalie van den Wall Bake; *m* 2000, Miriam Gonzalez Durantez; three *s*. *Educ*: Westminster Sch.; Robinson Coll., Cambridge (MA Anthropol.); Univ. of Minnesota (post grad. res., Political Theory); Coll. of Europe, Bruges (MA European Studies). Trainee journalist, The Nation mag., NY, 1990; Consultant, GJW Govt Relns, London, 1992–93; Official, Relns with New Independent States, EC, 1994–96; Mem. of Cabinet, Office of Sir Leon Brittan, EC, 1996–99; MEP (Lib Dem) E Midlands, 1999–2004. MP (Lib Dem) Sheffield Hallam, 2005–17; contested (Lib Dem) same seat, 2017. Lib Dem Home Affairs spokesman, 2006–07; Leader, Liberal Democrats, 2007–15; Dep. Prime Minister and Lord President of the Council, 2010–15. Political Columnist, Guardian Unlimited, 2000–05. Pt-time Lectr, Sheffield Univ., 2004–05. Trustee, NPG, 2012–15. David Thomas Prize, Financial Times, 1993. *Publications*: Politics: between the extremes, 2016; How to Stop Brexit (And Make Britain Great Again), 2017. *Recreations*: outdoors, arts. *Club*: National Liberal.

**CLEGG, Peter Alexander**, RDI 2010; RIBA; Senior Partner, Feilden Clegg Bradley Studios (formerly Architects), since 1978; *b* 29 Aug. 1950; *s* of Alexander Bradshaw Clegg and Jessie Coverdale Clegg (*née* Phillips); *m* 1975, Elizabeth Derry Watkins; two *s*. *Educ*: Tadcaster Grammar Sch.; Clare Coll., Cambridge (BA 1972, MA); Yale Univ. Sch. of Architecture (MED 1974). Worked for Herbert Newmann Associates, New Haven, Conn, 1974–75; Cambridge Design Architects, 1975–78. Vis. Prof., Bath Univ., 1998–; Sir Arthur Marshall Vis. Prof. of Sustainable Urban Design, Univ. of Cambridge, 2012–13. Major projects include: envmtl office, BRE; gall. and visitor facilities, Yorks Sculpture Park, 2006; Central Office, Nat. Trust, Swindon; Woodland Trust HQ, Grantham; housing, Accordia, Cambridge (RIBA Stirling Prize, 2008); Chelsea Academy; Broadcasting Place, Leeds; Visitor Centre, Jodrell Bank, 2011. *Publications*: (with D. Watkins) The Complete Greenhouse Book, 1975; (with D. Watkins) Sunspaces, 1978; (jtly) Feilden Clegg Bradley: the environmental handbook, 2007; contribs to UK-based architectural jls. *Recreations*: walking, music, gardening, work. *Address*: Hill Farm Barn, Cold Ashton, Chippenham, Wilts SN14 8LA; Feilden Clegg Bradley Studios, Bath Brewery, Tollbridge Road, Bath BA1 7DE.

**CLEGG, His Honour Philip Charles**; DL; a Circuit Judge, 1987–2009; a Deputy Circuit Judge, 2009–13; *b* 17 Oct. 1942; *s* of Charles and Patricia Clegg; *m* 1st, 1965, Caroline Frances Peall (marr. diss. 1996); one *s* two *d*; 2nd, 1997, Fiona Cameron. *Educ*: Rossall; Bristol Univ. (LLB Hons). Called to the Bar, Middle Temple, 1966; in practice on Northern Circuit; Asst Recorder, 1980–83; Recorder, 1983–87; Resident Judge, Basildon Combined Crown Court, 1996–2007; Itinerant Murder Judge, SE Circuit, 2008–09. Mem., Sentencing Adv. Panel, 2005–08. Mem., Vintage Austin Trans-Africa Expedn, 1963. Trustee, WW1 Aviation Heritage Trust, 2014–. DL Essex, 2009. *Recreations*: sailing, vintage cars, steam boating.

**CLEGG, Richard Ninian Barwick**; QC 1979; a Recorder of the Crown Court, 1978–93; *b* 28 June 1938; *s* of Sir Cuthbert Clegg, TD; *m* 1963, Katherine Veronica, *d* of A. A. H. Douglas; two *s* one *d*. *Educ*: Aysgarth; Charterhouse; Trinity Coll. Cambridge (MA). Captain of Oxford Pentathlon Team, 1959. Called to Bar, Inner Temple, 1960, Bencher, 1985. Chm., NW section of Bow Group, 1964–66; Vice-Chm., Bow Group, 1965–66; Chm., Winston Circle, 1965–66; Pres., Heywood and Royton Conservative Assoc., 1965–68. *Publications*: (jtly) Bow Group pamphlet, Towards a New North West, 1964; Forged by Fire (memoir), 2009; *poetry*: The Secret Room, 2013; Give Me a Vision; Shadow Across the Moon, 2014; The Curlew Cries, 2015. *Recreations*: sport, music, travel. *Address*: Ford Farm, Wootton Courtenay, Minehead, Somerset TA24 8RW. *T*: (01643) 841669. *Club*: Lansdowne.

**CLEGG, Richard P.**; see Plumbly-Clegg, R.

**CLEGG, Simon Paul**, CBE 2006 (OBE 2001); Executive Director, 2019 European Games, since 2018; Managing Director, Zeus International Management, since 2014; *b* 11 Aug. 1959; *s* of Peter Vernon Clegg and Patricia Anne Clegg (*née* Long); *m* 1985, Hilary Anne Davis; one *s* one *d*. *Educ*: Stowe Sch. Commnd RA, 1981; OC Battery, 7th Parachute Regt, RHA, 1989. Manager, British Biathlon Team, 1984–85; British Olympic Association: Asst Gen. Sec., 1989–91; Dep. Gen. Sec., 1991–96; Chief Exec., 1997–2009; Olympic Quartermaster, Summer and Winter Olympic Games, 1988 (on secondment); Great Britain Team: Dep. Chef de Mission, Olympic Games, 1992 and 1996, Olympic Winter Games, 1994; Chef de Mission: Olympic Winter Games, 1998, 2002 and 2006; Olympic Games, 2000, 2004 and 2008; Chief Executive: European Youth Olympic Games, Bath, 1995; Ipswich Town Football Club, 2009–13 (Dir, Ipswich Town plc, 2009–13). Director: London Olympic Bid, 2003–05; LOCOG, 2005–08; Dir and Mem. Exec. Bd, British Olympic Assoc., 2013–16; Exec. Dir, European Olympic Cttees, European Games, 2013–14; Chief Operating Officer: European Games Organising Cttee, Azerbaijan, 2014–15; Expo 2020, Dubai, 2016–17. Chm., Sport:80, 2018–. Chm., Great British Badminton, 2013–16. Trustee, Royal Artillery Charitable Fund, 2006–16. Hon. Dr University Campus Suffolk, 2011. Dostlug Order (Azerbaijan), 2015. *Clubs*: Leander, Cavalry and Guards.

**CLEGG, William**; QC 1991; a Recorder, since 1992; *b* 5 Sept. 1949; *s* of Peter Hepworth Clegg and Sheila Clegg; *m* 1st, 1974, Wendy Doreen Chard (marr. diss. 2002); one *s* one *d*; 2nd, 2008, Judith Gay Matthews. *Educ*: St Thomas More High School; Bristol Univ.

(LLB). Called to the Bar, Gray's Inn, 1972; in practice, SE Circuit. Head of Chambers, 1995–. *Publications:* Under the Wig (memoir), 2018. *Recreations:* squash, cricket. *Address:* 2 Bedford Row, WC1R 4BU. *T:* (020) 7440 8888. *Clubs:* Garrick, MCC.

**CLEGG-HILL,** family name of **Viscount Hill**.

**CLEGHORN, Bruce Elliot,** CMG 2002; HM Diplomatic Service, retired; High Commissioner, Malaysia, 2001–06; *b* 19 Nov. 1946; *s* of Ivan Robert Cleghorn and Margaret (*née* Kemplen); *m* 1976, Sally Ann Robinson; three *s*. *Educ:* Sutton Valence Sch., Kent; St John's Coll., Cambridge (BA Hons, MA). Commonwealth Fellow, Panjab Univ., 1970–72; Jun. Res. Fellow, Inst. of Commonwealth Studies, Univ. of London, 1972–74; joined HM Diplomatic Service, 1974; Delegn to CSCE, 1974–75; FCO, 1975–76; First Secretary: Delegn to NATO, 1976–79; New Delhi, 1980–83; FCO, 1983–87; Counsellor, CSCE Delegn, Vienna, 1987–89; Dep. Hd, UK Delegn to negotiations on conventional arms control, Vienna, 1989–91; Dep. High Comr and Counsellor (Econ. and Commercial), Kuala Lumpur, 1992–94; Head of Non-Proliferation Dept, FCO, 1995–97; Minister and Dep. Perm. Rep., UK Delegn to NATO, Brussels, 1997–2001. Staff Performance Assessor, 2007–08, Records Sensitivity Reviewer, 2008–, FCO. Mem., Mgt Cttee, SE Asia Rainforest Res. Prog., Royal Soc., 2006–11. *Publications:* (with V. N. Datta) A Nationalist Muslim and Indian Politics, 1974. *Recreations:* walking, potting, gardening, birdwatching.

**CLEIN, Natalie;** 'cellist; *b* 25 March 1977; *d* of Peter Clein and Channa Clein (*née* Salomonson). *Educ:* Royal Coll. of Music; Hochschule Vienna (with Heinrich Schiff). BBC Proms début, 1997; has performed as a soloist with all major orchestras in the UK, and as a recitalist in UK, Europe, New York and Tokyo; participates in internat. chamber festivals; has premiered works by Peter Maxwell Davies, Elvis Costello and John Tavener; recordings include Elgar Cello Concerto and Sonatas by Brahms, Schubert and Rachmaninov. Artist in Association, 2005, now Vis. Prof., RCM; Prof., Trinity Laban Conservatoire, 2009–; Dir of Performance, Faculty of Music, Univ. of Oxford, 2016–20. Young Musician of Year, BBC, 1994; Eurovision Young Musician, 1994; Ingrid zu Zolms Kultur Preis, 2003; Young Artist Brit Award, 2005.

**CLELAND, Helen Isabel;** Headteacher, Woodford County High School, 1991–2010; *b* 3 July 1950; *d* of John Douglas Cleland and Hilda Malvina Cleland; *m* 1973, Dr Robin Hoult (*d* 2001); one *s* one *d*. *Educ:* King Edward VI High Sch. for Girls, Birmingham; Exeter Univ. (BA Hons English); Homerton Coll., Cambridge (PGCE). English Teacher, Dame Alice Owen's Sch., London, 1972–76; English Teacher, 1976–79, Sen. Teacher, 1979–86, Haverstock Sch., London; Dep. Head, Edmonton Sch., Enfield, 1986–91. *Recreations:* reading, theatre, hill walking, horse-riding, travel.

**CLELAND, Prof. John Goodhart,** CBE 2008; FBA 2003; Professor of Medical Demography, London School of Hygiene and Tropical Medicine, 1992–2010, now Emeritus; *b* 9 March 1942; *s* of late William Paton Cleland; *m* 1st, 1969, Susan Gilbert Harman (marr. diss. 1990); one *s* one *d*; 2nd, 2004, Sandra Carr. *Educ:* Charterhouse Sch.; Selwyn Coll., Cambridge (MA). Res. Officer, LSE, 1966–69; Sociologist, Population Bureau, ODA, 1969–72; Demographer, Med. Dept, Fiji, 1972–74; Demographic Analyst, World Fertility Survey, ISI, 1975–87; Sen. Res. Fellow, LSHTM, 1988–92. Mem., Scientific and Adv. Gp, Dept of Reproductive Health and Res., WHO, 1999–2005; Chm., Population Investigation Cttee, 2003–14. President: British Soc. for Population Studies, 1997–99; Internat. Union for Scientific Study of Population, 2006–09. *Publications:* (with J. Hobcraft) Reproductive Change in Developing Countries: insights from the World Fertility Survey, 1985; (with C. Scott) The World Fertility Survey: an assessment, 1987; (with A. Hill) The Health Transition: methods and measures, 1991; (jtly) The Determinants of Reproductive Change in Bangladesh, 1994; (with B. Ferry) Sexual Behaviour and AIDS in the Developing World, 1995. *Recreations:* fishing, woodland management. *Address:* The Manor House, Silver Street, Barton St David, Somerset TA11 6DB. *T:* and *Fax:* (01458) 851266. *E:* John.Cleland@lshtm.ac.uk.

**CLELAND, Victoria Mary Florence;** Executive Director, Banking, Payments and Innovation (formerly Banking, Payments and Financial Resilience), Bank of England, since 2018; *b* England; *d* of Robert Francis Doxford Cleland and Joan Cleland. *Educ:* Malvern Coll.; Hereford VI Form Coll.; St Hilda's Coll., Oxford (BA PPE 1991; MA); Imperial Coll. Mgt Sch. (MBA). BDO Binder Hamlyn, 1991–92; Bank of England: Analyst, Business Finance Div., 1992–95, Wholesale Markets Supervision Div., 1995–96; Graduate Recruitment Manager, 1996–98; Manager, Domestic Finance Div., 1999–2001, Market Infrastructure Div., 2001–03; Private Sec. to Dep. Gov., 2003–06; Sen. Manager, Payment and Settlement Systems, 2006–08; Dep. Hd, Special Resolution Unit, 2008–10; Hd, Notes Div., 2010–14; Chief Cashier and Dir of Notes, 2014–18. *Recreations:* road cycling, hiking, wine tasting, theatre, art history, charity trustee. *Address:* Bank of England, Threadneedle Street, EC2R 8AH. *T:* (020) 7601 4402.

**CLELLAND, David Gordon;** *b* 27 June 1943; *s* of Archibald, (Clem), Clelland and Ellen, (Nell), Clelland (*née* Butchart); *m* 2004, Brenda; two *d* from former marr. *Educ:* Kelvin Grove Boys' School, Gateshead; Gateshead and Hebburn Technical Colleges. Apprentice electrical fitter, 1959–64; electrical tester, 1964–81. Gateshead Borough Council: Councillor, 1972–86; Recreation Chm., 1976–84; Leader of Council, 1984–86. Nat. Sec., Assoc. of Councillors, 1981–85. MP (Lab) Tyne Bridge, Dec. 1985–2010. An Asst Govt Whip, 1997–2000; a Lord Comr of HM Treasury (Govt Whip), 2000–01. Member: Home Affairs Select Cttee, 1986–88; Energy Select Cttee, 1989–90; OPDM Select Cttee, 2001–05; Transport Select Cttee, 2005–10. Chairman, All Party Group: on non-profit-making Members' Clubs; on Turks and Caicos Is, 2005–10; Chairman: Backbench Envmt Cttee, 1990–97; PLP Regl Govt Gp, 1992–97; PLP Trade Union Gp, 1994–97; Vice-Chm., Northern Gp of Lab MPs (Sec., 1990–98). Parly Advr, Working Men's Club and Institute Union, 2011–17. Chm., Trustees Bd, Gateshead Carers Assoc., 2014–. Hon. Alderman, 2004, Hon. Freeman, 2010, Gateshead. *Recreations:* power boating, reading, playing guitar.

**CLEMENT, David James,** OBE 2006; Chairman, Systems Network, 1997–2013; *b* 29 Sept. 1930; *s* of James and Constance Clement; *m* 1958, Margaret Stone; two *s* one *d*. *Educ:* Chipping Sodbury Grammar Sch.; Univ. of Bristol (BA). CPFA 1957. Internal Audit Asst, City of Bristol, 1953–56; Accountancy/Audit Asst, 1956–60, Chief Accountancy Asst, 1960–65, City of Worcester; Dep. Chief Finance Officer, Runcorn Develt Corp., 1965–68; Chief Finance Officer, Antrim and Ballymena Develt Commn, 1968–72; Asst Sec., Dept of Finance, NI, 1972–75, Dep. Sec., 1975–80; Under Sec., DoE, NI, 1980–84. Financial consultant, 1985–90; Chm., HELM Corp., 1990–98. Mem., Investigations Cttee, CIPFA, 2001–11. Dir, NI Council for Integrated Educn, 2007–16. Chm. Trustees, Ulster Historical Foundn, 2000–08. Hon. Treas., NI Council for Voluntary Action, 2000–05. *Recreations:* lawn tennis, Association football, contract bridge, philately.

**CLEMENT, Marc;** *see* Clement, R. M.

**CLEMENT, Richard, (Dick),** OBE 2007; freelance writer, director and producer; *b* 5 Sept. 1937; *s* of Frederick and Alice Eleanor Clement; *m* 1st, Jennifer F. Sheppard (marr. diss. 1981); three *s* one *d*; 2nd, 1982, Nancy S. Campbell; one *d*. *Educ:* Bishop's Stortford Coll.; Westminster Sch., Conn, USA. Co-writer (with Ian La Frenais): *television:* The Likely Lads, 1964–66; Whatever Happened to the Likely Lads, 1972–73; Porridge, 1974–76 (stage version, 2009), new series, 2017; Thick as Thieves, 1974; Going Straight, 1978; Auf Wiedersehen, Pet, 1983–84, 2002–04; Freddie and Max, 1990; Full Stretch, 1993; The Rotters' Club (adaptation), 2005; Archangel (adaptation), 2005; Spies of Warsaw (adaptation), 2013; Henry IX, 2017; *films:* The Jokers, 1967; Otley, 1968; Hannibal Brooks, 1968; Villain, 1971; Porridge (also dir), 1979; Water (also dir), 1984; Vice Versa, 1987; The Commitments, 1991; Still Crazy, 1998; Honest, 2000; Goal, 2005; Flushed Away, 2006; Across the Universe, 2007; The Bank Job, 2008; Killing Bono, 2011; My Generation (also co-producer), 2018. Director: *films:* Otley, 1968; A Severed Head, 1969; Bullshot, 1983; co-producer (with Ian La Frenais) Vice Versa, 1987; The Commitments, 1991 (jtly, Evening Standard Peter Sellers Award, 1992); *stage:* Billy, 1974; Anyone for Denis?, 1981; Chasing Bono, 2018; Jukebox Hero, 2019. *Publications:* (with Ian La Frenais) More than Likely: a memoir, 2019. *Recreations:* work, tennis, backgammon; Chelsea FC. *Address:* 9700 Yoakum Drive, Beverly Hills, CA 90210, USA. *Clubs:* Garrick; Mulholland Tennis (LA).

**CLEMENT, Prof. (Robert) Marc,** PhD; CPhys, FIET, FInstP; Vice President, since 2014, and Dean, School of Management, since 2015, Swansea University; *b* Llwynhendy, Llanelli, 19 Nov. 1953; *s* of Gerald Edmund Clement and Eira Mary Clement; one *d*. *Educ:* Univ. of Wales, Swansea (BSc 1st cl. Hons Physics 1976; Postgrad. Dip. Ionisation Physics 1977); Univ. of Wales (PhD Laser Physics 1979). CPhys, MInstP 1984; FIET 2002; FInstP 2007. Teacher of Maths and Physics, Ystalyfera Sch., 1980; Royal Soc. Scholarship for Postdoctoral Study, Centre d'Etudes Nucléaire de Saclay, Paris, 1981–82; West Glamorgan Institute of Higher Education: Temp. Lectr, 1982, Lectr I, 1983, Lectr II, 1984, in Maths; transfer to Fac. of Electronic Engrg, 1985; Sen. Lectr in Microelectronics, 1986; Principal Lectr and Hd, Sch. of Electrical Engrg, 1987; Dean, Fac. of Electronic Engrg, 1988; University of Wales, Swansea: Chair of Innovation, Sch. of Engrg, 2000; Sen. Exec. to Vice Chancellor's Office, 2004; Vice-Chancellor and Chief Exec., 2007–11, Pres., 2011–12, Univ. of Wales; Swansea University: Prof. of Medical Devices, 2012; Dir, Enterprise and Innovation, Inst. of Life Sci., 2012. Founding FLSW 2010. P. M. Davidson Prize for Theoretical Physics, Univ. of Wales, Swansea, 1976; Business Award, HTV/Western Mail, 1990. *Publications:* books and articles in academic jls. *Recreations:* ski-ing, squash, weight training, choral singing, Sunday school teacher, adjudicator at many National and Urdd Eisteddfodau. *Address:* Dean's Office, School of Management, Swansea University, Bay Campus, Fabian Way, Swansea SA1 8EN. *E:* r.m.clement@swansea.ac.uk.

**CLEMENT-JONES,** family name of **Baron Clement-Jones**.

**CLEMENT-JONES,** Baron *cr* 1998 (Life Peer), of Clapham in the London Borough of Lambeth; **Timothy Francis Clement-Jones,** CBE 1988; Consultant, DLA Piper UK LLP, since 2018; International Business Relations Partner, 2010–11, and London Managing Partner, 2011–17, Global Government Relations (formerly Upstream), government and media relations practice of DLA Piper UK LLP (formerly Dibb Lupton Alsop, later DLA Piper Rudnick Gray Carey) (Chairman, 1999–2009); *b* 26 Oct. 1949; *s* of late Maurice Llewelyn Clement-Jones and Margaret Jean Clement-Jones (*née* Hudson); *m* 1st, 1973, Dr Vicky Veronica Yip (*d* 1987); 2nd, 1994, Jean Roberta Whiteside; one *s*. *Educ:* Haileybury; Trinity Coll., Cambridge (Economics Pt I, Law Tripos Pt II); MA). Admitted Solicitor, 1974. Articled Clerk, Coward Chance, 1972–74; Associate, Joynson-Hicks, 1974–76; Corporate Lawyer, Letraset Internat. Ltd, 1976–80; Hd Legal Services, LWT, 1980–83; Legal Dir, Grand Metropolitan Retailing, 1984–86; Gp Co. Sec. and Legal Advr, Woolworth Hldgs, then Kingfisher plc, 1986–95; Dir, Political Context Ltd, 1996–99; Chm., Envmtl Context, later Context Gp Ltd, 1997–2009; Dir, British American Business Inc., 2006–. Lib Dem spokesman on health, H of L, 1998–2004, on culture, media and sport, 2004–10, on creative industries, 2015–16; on Digital Economy, 2017–. Chm., Select Cttee on Artificial Intelligence, H of L, 2017–18; Mem., Select Cttee on Communications, H of L, 2010–15, on Built Envmt, 2015–16; Vice-Chairman: All-Party Autism Gp, 2003–10; All-Party China Gp, 2005–; All-Party Turkey Gp, 2010–17; All-Party UAE Gp, 2010–15; All-Party Ovarian Cancer Gp, 2010–16; Co-Chm., All Party Gp on Artificial Intelligence, 2017–. Introduced Tobacco Advertising and Sponsorship Act 2002 and Live Music Act 2012 as private members' bills. Chm., Assoc. of Liberal Lawyers, 1982–86. Chairman: Liberal Party, 1986–88; Lib Dem Finance Cttee, 1991–98; Dir, Lib Dem EP election campaign, 1994; Chm., Lib Dem Mayoral and Assembly campaign, London, 2000, 2004; Federal Treas., Lib Dems, 2005–10. Trustee and Dir, Cancer BACUP, subseq. Cancerbackup (founded by Dr V. V. Clement-Jones), 1986–2008. Chairman: Crime Concern, 1991–95; Lambeth Crime Prevention Trust, 2004–09; Bd of Dirs, Ombudsman Services, 2016–; Trustee, CentreForum (formerly Centre for Reform), 1998–2009. Chairman, Council: Sch. of Pharmacy, Univ. of London, 2008–12; QMUL, 2017–; Mem. Council, UCL, 2012–17; Mem., Corporate Finance Faculty Bd, ICAEW, 2016–. Chair, Adv. Council, Inst. for Ethical AI in Educn, 2018–; Mem., Adv. Council, Airmic, 2016–. Pres., Ambitious About Autism (formerly Treehouse, educnl charity for autistic children), 2011– (Chm. Trustees, 2001–08); Trustee, Barbican Centre Trust, 2013–16; Mem. Council, Heart of the City, 2013–. Law Soc. City Ambassador, 2014–; Barts Charity Ambassador, 2014–. Gov., Haileybury, 2001–. FRSA. *Recreations:* reading, eating, talking, the arts, travelling, walking. *Address:* c/o House of Lords, SW1A 0PW. *T:* (020) 7622 4205. *E:* clementjonest@parliament.uk.

**CLEMENTI, Sir David (Cecil),** Kt 2004; Chairman, King's Cross Central General Limited Partnership, since 2008; Chairman, BBC Board, since 2017; *b* 25 Feb. 1949; *s* of Air Vice-Marshal Cresswell Montagu Clementi, CB, CBE and Susan (*née* Pelham); *m* 1972, Sarah Louise, (Sally), Cowley; one *s* one *d*. *Educ:* Winchester Coll.; Lincoln Coll., Oxford; Harvard Business Sch. (MBA 1975). With Arthur Andersen & Co., 1970–73; qualified as CA 1973; with Kleinwort Benson Ltd, 1975–97: Dir, 1981–97; Man. Dir, KB Securities, 1987–89; Head, Corporate Finance, 1989–94; Chief Exec., 1994–97; Vice Chm., 1997; Dep. Gov., Bank of England, 1997–2002; Chairman: Prudential plc, 2002–08; Virgin Money, 2011–15; World First, 2011–18. Non-executive Director: Rio Tinto plc, 2003–10; Foreign & Colonial Investment Trust, 2008–12; Dep. Chm., Ruffer LLP, 2010–17. Conducted reviews: of regulation of legal services in England and Wales, 2004; of BBC governance, 2016. Trustee, Royal Opera House, 2006–14. Warden, Winchester Coll., 2008–14. *Recreations:* sailing, ballet. *Club:* Royal Yacht Squadron.

**CLEMENTS, Andrew;** *see* Clements, F. A.

**CLEMENTS, Andrew Joseph;** Music Critic, Guardian, since 1993; *b* 15 Sept. 1950; *s* of Joseph George Clements and Linda Helen Clements; *m* 1977, Kathryn Denise Coltman (marr. diss. 2007); two *d*. *Educ:* Crypt Sch., Gloucester; Emmanuel Coll., Cambridge (BA). Music Critic: New Statesman, 1977–88; Financial Times, 1979–93; Editor, Musical Times, 1987–88. Dir, Holst Foundn, 1992–. *Publications:* Mark-Anthony Turnage, 2000. *Recreation:* birding. *Address:* c/o Guardian, Kings Place, 90 York Way, N1 9AG.

**CLEMENTS, Dr (Frederick) Andrew;** Chief Executive (formerly Director), British Trust for Ornithology, since 2007; *b* Morecambe, Lancs, 25 Oct. 1954; *s* of Frederick George Clements and Clarice Clements (*née* Hartley); *m* 1997, Susannah Burton (marr. diss. 2008); one *s* one *d*. *Educ:* Haberdashers' Aske's Sch.; University Coll. of Wales, Bangor (BSc Hons Zool.); Univ. of Wales (PhD Zool. 1980). Conservation Officer, NCC, 1982–87; Chief Wildlife Inspector, DoE, 1987–91; Manager, 1991–2000, Dir, Protected Areas, 2000–06,

English Nature; Dir, Ferrypath Consulting Ltd (own co.), 2006–08. Mem. Bd, Natural England, 2014–. Trustee, Nat. Biodiversity Network, 2013–. Pres., Norfolk and Norwich Naturalists' Soc., 2014–15. Wildlife Tour Leader (pt-time), Himalayas, Ethiopia, Namibia, 1990–2002. *Publications*: (contrib.) AA Field Guide to the Birds of Britain and Europe, 1998; (contrib.) Silent Summer, 2010; contrib. scientific papers to New Scientist, Animal Behaviour, Behaviour, Zeitschrift für Tierpsychologie, Science, Plosone, The Auk. *Recreations*: birding, watching wildlife round the world, sculling, veggie cooking. *Address*: c/o British Trust for Ornithology, The Nunnery, Thetford, Norfolk IP24 2PU. *T*: (01842) 750050, (01842) 750030. *E*: andy.clements@bto.org, andy.clements@ferrypath.co.uk.

**CLEMENTS, John Rodney**; Finance Manager, People & Planet Ltd, 2006–15; *b* 19 Jan. 1947; *s* of late Peter Larby Clements and of Ethel Blanche Lillian Clements (*née* Steele); *m* 1st, 1969, Janet Sylvia Mallender (marr. diss. 1992); two *d*; 2nd, 1999, Georgina Margaret Eckles (marr. diss. 2005); 3rd, 2012, Caroline Mary Kramer. *Educ*: Univ. of Manchester (BA Hons Mod. Hist. with Econs and Politics 1968). ACA 1973, FCA 1978. Auditor, KPMG Peat Marwick, Accountants, 1968–73; Financial Accountant, Co-operative Bank, 1973–74; Asst to Chief Accountant, Stock Exchange, 1974–79; Dep. Finance Officer, UCL, 1979–85; Dep. Dir of Finance, Univ. of Sheffield, 1985–92; Dir of Finance, Univ. of Leeds, 1992–94; independent consultant, 1994–95; Sec. of the Chest, then Dir of Finance and Sec. of the Chest, Univ. of Oxford, 1995–2004; Fellow, Merton Coll., Oxford, 1995–2004. *Recreations*: history, literature, hill walking, model railways. *Address*: 19 Raleigh Park Road, Oxford OX2 9AZ.

**CLEMENTS, Judith M.**; independent consultant and executive coach, since 2016; Chief Executive, Mental Health Foundation of New Zealand, 2005–16; *b* 27 June 1953; *d* of Robert and Margaret Dunn; *m* 1st, 1975, Paul Clements (marr. diss. 1979); 2nd, 1998, Rex Hewitt. *Educ*: Birmingham Univ. (LLB Hons 1974); Brunel Univ. (MA Public and Social Admin 1979). Dip. Inst. Housing 1976. London Borough of Camden: Estate Manager, 1974–76; Sen. Estate Manager, 1976–79; Tenancy Services Officer, 1979–81; Business System Analyst, 1981–82; Asst Dir of Housing, 1982–87; Dep. Chief Housing Officer, Brighton BC, 1987–91; Hd of Management Practice, Local Govt Management Bd, 1991–92; Chief Exec., Mind (Nat. Assoc. of Mental Health), 1992–2001; ind. consultant, 2001–05. Trustee, Mentality, 2001–03; Mem., UK Grants Cttee, Comic Relief, 2003–05. Member: Bd of Govs, Brighton Univ., 2000–05; Council, UCL, 2001–03. FRSA 1999. Hon. DSocSci Brunel, 1997. *Recreations*: reading, especially crime fiction and feminist fiction, yoga. *E*: judimclements@gmail.com.

**CLEMENTS, Judy**, OBE 2000; Independent Adjudicator and Chief Executive, Office of the Independent Adjudicator for Higher Education, 2016–17; *b* Guyana, 20 Feb. 1958; *d* of Vernon Clements and Annette Clements; *m* (marr. diss.); one *d*. *Educ*: Open Univ. (BA Hons Social Scis); Univ. of Central England (LLB). Police officer, West Midlands Police, 1978–89; Co-ordinator, Safer Cities Crime Prevention Project, Home Office, 1989–94; Race and Equalities Advr to HM Prison Service, 1999–2003 (report, Investigation into Racism, Brixton Prison, 2001); Dir, SE England, 2003–08, Dir, Customer Services and Communications, 2008–09, Ind. Police Complaints Commn; Adjudicator, HMRC, 2009–16. Chm., Diana Princess of Wales NHS Children's Hosp. Trust, Birmingham, 1998–99. Mem., Video Appeals Panel, BBFC, 2011–. Trustee, Turning Point, 2004–08; Vice Chm., Barnardo's, 2011–15. *Publications*: various reports; (section ed.) British Jl of Leadership in Public Services. *Recreations*: theatre, walking, cooking, reading, committed Seventh Day Adventist Christian.

**CLEMENTS, Rev. Keith Winston**, PhD; General Secretary, Conference of European Churches, 1997–2005; *b* Sichuan, China, 7 May 1943; *s* of Harry Clements and Alfreda (*née* Yarwood); *m* 1967, Margaret Hirst; two *s*. *Educ*: King Edward VII Sch., Lytham; King's Coll., Cambridge (MA 1969); Regent's Park Coll., Oxford (MA 1972, BD 1980); PhD Bristol 1997. Ordained to Baptist Ministry, 1967; Associate Minister, Mid-Cheshire Fellowship of Baptist Chs, 1967–71; Minister, Downend Baptist Ch, Bristol, 1971–77; Tutor, Bristol Baptist Coll., 1977–90; Sec. for Internat. Affairs, CCBI, 1990–97. Part-time Lectr, Dept of Theol. and Religious Studies, Univ. of Bristol, 1984–90; Select Preacher, Univ. of Cambridge, 1993; Adjunct Lectr, Whitley Coll., Melbourne, 2008–. Hon. Fellow, New Coll., Edinburgh, 1990–99. Ed., Baptist Historical Soc., 1980–85. *Publications*: Faith, 1981; A Patriotism for Today: dialogue with Dietrich Bonhoeffer, 1984; The Theology of Ronald Gregor Smith, 1986; Friedrich Schleiermacher, 1987; Lovers of Discord, 1988; What Freedom?: the persistent challenge of Dietrich Bonhoeffer, 1990; Learning to Speak: the Church's voice in public affairs, 1995; Faith on the Frontier: a life of J. H. Oldham, 1999; The Churches in Europe as Witnesses to Healing, 2003; Bonhoeffer and Britain, 2006; (ed) Dietrich Bonhoeffer Works, Vol. 13 (London 1933–35), 2007; (ed) The Moot Papers: faith, freedom and society 1938–44, 2009; The SPCK Introduction to Bonhoeffer, 2010; Ecumenical Dynamic: living in more than one place at once, 2013; We Will Remember, 2014; Dietrich Bonhoeffer's Ecumenical Quest, 2015; Look Back in Hope: an ecumenical life, 2017; numerous articles in learned jls on theol. and religion. *Recreations*: grandchildren, ornithology, reading, listening to music, walking, choral singing. *Address*: 67 Hillcrest Road, Portishead, N Somerset BS20 8HN. *T*: (01275) 845242.

**CLEMENTS, Kirsty Anne**; *see* Wark, K. A.

**CLEMENTS, Michael Alan**; a Judge of the Upper Tribunal (Immigration and Asylum Chamber) (formerly Resident Senior Immigration Judge, Asylum and Immigration Tribunal), since 2007; President, First-tier Tribunal (Immigration and Asylum Chamber), since 2011; *b* 25 Nov. 1954; *s* of Philip and Gwendoline Clements; *m* 1978, Carol Mary; three *s*. *Educ*: King Edward VI Sch., Bath. Admitted solicitor, 1983; NP; articled clerk, solicitor, then Partner, Giffin Couch & Archer, Leighton Buzzard, 1979–90; Solicitor, Horwood & James, Aylesbury, 1990–2001; Immigration Adjudicator, 2001–; Sen. Immigration Judge, 2006. Legal Mem., Tribunals Service, 1993–. *Address*: President's Office, Field House, Bream's Buildings, EC4A 1DZ. *T*: (020) 7073 4221.

**CLEMENTS, Prof. Ronald Ernest**; Samuel Davidson Professor of Old Testament Studies, King's College, University of London, 1983–92, now Professor Emeritus; *b* 27 May 1929; *m* 1955, Valerie Winifred (*née* Suffield); two *d*. *Educ*: Buckhurst Hill County High Sch.; Spurgeon's Coll.; Christ's Coll., Cambridge; Univ. of Sheffield. MA, DD Cantab. Asst Lectr 1960–64, Lectr 1964–67, Univ. of Edinburgh; Lectr, Univ. of Cambridge, 1967–83. Hon. For. Sec., SOTS, 1973–83 (Pres., 1985); Hon. Mem., OTWSA, 1979–. Hon. DLitt Acadia, Nova Scotia, 1982. Burkitt Medal for Biblical Studies, British Acad., 2013. *Publications*: God and Temple, 1965; Prophecy and Covenant, 1965; Old Testament Theology, 1978; Isaiah 1–39, 1979; A Century of Old Testament Study, 1976, 2nd edn 1983; Prayers of the Bible, 1986; Jeremiah, 1988; (ed) The World of Ancient Israel, 1989; Wisdom in Theology, 1993; Old Testament Prophecy: from oracles to canon, 1996; Israel and the Nations, 2011; contrib. Vetus Testamentum, Jl of Semitic Studies. *Recreations*: reading, travel, photography, aeromodelling. *Address*: 8 Brookfield Road, Coton, Cambridge CB23 7PT.

**CLEMITS, John Henry**, RIBA; Managing Director, PSA Projects Cardiff, 1990–92; *b* 16 Feb. 1934; *s* of late Cyril Thomas Clemits and Minnie Alberta Clemits; *m* 1958, Elizabeth Angela Moon; one *s* one *d*. *Educ*: Sutton High Sch.; Plymouth College of Art; Bucks New Univ. (BA Hons Creative Arts 2010); Open Univ. (BA Hons Humanities with Art Hist. 2012). RIBA (ARIBA 1962 (Dist. in Thesis)). National Service, RAF, 1959–61; Captain, RE (TA), 43 Wessex Div. and Royal Monmouthshire RE (Militia), 1964–69. Plymouth City Architects Dept, 1954–59; Watkins Gray & Partners, Architects, Bristol, 1961–63; SW RHB, 1963–65; Architect, MPBW, Bristol, 1965–69; Sen. Architect, MPBW, Regional HQ, Rheindahlen, Germany, 1969–71; Naval Base Planning Officer, MPBW, Portsmouth, 1971–73; Suptg Architect, PSA, Directorate of Bldg Develt, 1973–75; Suptg Planning Officer, PSA, Rheindahlen, 1975–79; Dir of Works (Army), PSA, Chessington, 1979–85; Dir for Wales, PSA, Central Office for Wales, DoE, 1985–90. Chairman: Cowbridge Choral Soc., 1988–90; Vale of Glamorgan Buildings Preservation Trust, 1994–97; Dewi Sant Housing Assoc., 1995–2001. Member: Nat. Council, Welsh Fedn of Housing Assocs, 1996–99; Dio. of Llandaff Parsonage Bd, 2009–14. Chm., S Wales Art Soc., 2005–06 (Prog. Sec., 2002–05). *Recreations*: music, life-long learning, painting, travel. *Address*: The Lodge, Hendrescythan, Creigiau, Cardiff CF15 9NN. *T*: (029) 2089 0559.

**CLEMITSON, Julie; Her Honour Judge Clemitson**; a Circuit Judge, since 2019; *b* Alnwick, Northumberland, 1968; *d* of Robert Clemitson and Lynn Clemitson; *m* 1998, Frazer McDermott; two *s* one *d*, and one step *d*. *Educ*: Ponteland Co. High Sch.; Univ. of Newcastle upon Tyne (Law). Called to the Bar, Inner Temple, 1991; a Recorder, 2016–19.

**CLEMMOW, Jana Eve**; *see* Bennett, J. E.

**CLEMMOW, Simon Phillip**; Founder, CHI & Partners (formerly Clemmow Hornby Inge Ltd), advertising agency, since 2001; *b* Cambridge, 30 June 1956; *s* of late Dr Phillip Charles and Joan Alicia Clemmow; *m* 1987, Elizabeth Danuta Kaminska; one *s* and one step *d*. *Educ*: Univ. of Reading (BA Hons Typography and Graphic Communication). Trainee, Benton & Bowles, 1982; Account Planner, Gold Greenlees Trott, 1983–88; Founder, Simons Palmer Denton Clemmow & Johnson, 1988–97; CEO, TBWA, 1997–2001. *Recreations*: cycling, reading, river boating, keeping fit (swimming and going to gym), restoring an old house in Italy, walking, playing golf, listening to rock music, playing the drums, studying local history, doing the Times crossword, watching Arsenal FC and England cricket team. *Address*: CHI & Partners, 7 Rathbone Street, W1T 1LY. *T*: (020) 7462 8580, *Fax*: (020) 7462 8501. *E*: simon.clemmow@chiandpartners.com. *Club*: Union.

**CLEOBURY, Nicholas Randall**, MA; FRCO; conductor; *b* 23 June 1950; *s* of John and Brenda Cleobury; *m* 1978, Heather Kay; one *s* one *d*. *Educ*: King's Sch., Worcester; Worcester Coll., Oxford (MA Hons). Assistant Organist: Chichester Cathedral, 1971–72; Christ Church, Oxford, 1972–76; Chorus Master, Glyndebourne Opera, 1977–79; Asst Director, BBC Singers, 1977–79; Conductor: main BBC, provincial and London orchestras and opera houses, also in Albania, Australia, Austria, Belgium, Canada, Denmark, Finland, France, Germany, Holland, Hong Kong, Italy, Lithuania, Macedonia, Norway, Poland, Singapore, Slovenia, S Africa, Spain, Sweden, Switzerland, USA; regular BBC TV appearances; numerous CD recordings. Principal Opera Conductor, Royal Academy of Music, 1981–88; Artistic Director: Aquarius, 1983–92; Cambridge Symphony Soloists, 1990–92; Britten Sinfonia, 1992–2005; Britten in Oxford, 2012–13; Music Dir, Oxford Bach Choir, 1997–2015; Founder and Artistic Dir, Sounds New, 1997–2006; Associate Dir, Orchestra of the Swan, 2004–08; Artistic Dir and Principal Conductor, Mid Wales Opera, 2010–17; Principal Conductor, John Armitage Meml, 2010–17; Head of Opera, Qld Conservatorium, 2016–19. Principal Guest Conductor, Gävle, Sweden, 1989–91; Guest Conductor, Zürich Opera, 1993–2005. Music Dir, Broomhill Arts, 1990–94; Artistic Director: Cambridge Fest., 1992; Mozart Now, 2004–06; Artistic Advr, Berks Choral Fest., USA, 2002–08. Fellow, Canterbury Christ Church Univ., 2006. Hon. RAM 1985. *Recreations*: cricket, food, reading, theatre, walking, wine. *E*: NicholasCleobury@btinternet.com. *W*: www.NicholasCleobury.net. *Clubs*: MCC, Lord's Taverners.

*See also* Sir S. J. Cleobury.

**CLEOBURY, Sir Stephen (John)**, Kt 2019; CBE 2009; FRCM; FRCO; Fellow, since 1982, and Director of Music and Organist, 1982–2019, King's College, Cambridge; Organist, Cambridge University, 1991–2016; *b* 31 Dec. 1948; *s* of John Frank Cleobury and Brenda Julie (*née* Randall); *m*; two *d*; *m* 2004, Emma Sian, *d* of late John Ivor Disley, CBE; two *d*. *Educ*: King's Sch., Worcester; St John's Coll., Cambridge (MA, MusB). FRCO 1968; FRCM 1993. Organist, St Matthew's, Northampton, 1971–74; Sub-Organist, Westminster Abbey, 1974–78; Master of Music, Westminster Cathedral, 1979–82; Cambridge University Musical Society: Conductor, 1983–2009; Chorus Dir, 2009–16; Conductor Laureate, 2016–. Chief Conductor, 1995–2007, Conductor Laureate, 2007–, BBC Singers. President: IAO, 1985–87; Cathedral Organists' Assoc., 1988–90; RCO, 1990–92 (Hon. Sec., 1981–90); Friends of Cathedral Music, 2016–; Herbert Howells Soc., 2016–; Mem. Council, RSCM, 1982–2000. FRSCM 2008; FRSA 2016. Hon. FGCM 2015. Hon. DMus Anglia Poly., 2001; Hon. Dr York, 2018. *Recreation*: reading. *Address*: 12 Park Grove, York YO31 8LG.

*See also* N. R. Cleobury.

**CLERK, Sir Robert (Maxwell)**, 11th Bt cr 1679, of Penicuik (NS); OBE 1995; Lord-Lieutenant, Midlothian, since 2013 (Vice Lord-Lieutenant, 2011–13); *b* 3 April 1945; *er s* of Sir John Dutton Clerk, 10th Bt, CBE, VRD and Evelyn Elizabeth Clerk (*née* Robertson); *S* father, 2002; *m* 1970, Felicity Faye Collins; two *s* one *d*. *Educ*: Winchester Coll.; Wye Coll., London Univ. (BScAgric). Partner, Smiths Gore, Chartered Surveyors, 1980–2003. Chairman: Council, Assoc. of Salmon Fishery Bds, 1989–95; Atlantic Salmon Trust, 2005–10. Ensign, Queen's Body Guard for Scotland (Royal Company of Archers). DL Midlothian, 1995. *Recreations*: bee-keeping, landscape gardening, salmon fishing. *Heir*: *s* George Napier Clerk, *b* 27 May 1975. *Club*: New (Edinburgh).

**CLERKE, Sir Francis Ludlow Longueville**, 13th Bt cr 1660, of Hitcham, Buckinghamshire; *b* 25 Jan. 1953; *e s* of Sir John Edward Longueville Clerke, 12th Bt, and Mary, *d* of Lt-Col Ivor Reginald Beviss Bond, OBE, MC; *S* father, 2009; *m* 1st, 1982, Vanessa Anne (marr. diss. 2011), *o d* of Charles Cosman Citron and Olga May Citron; one *s* one *d*; 2nd, 2014, Louise, *d* of late Martin Louis Botha and Margaret Bell Botha. *Educ*: Diocesan Coll., Cape Town; Stellenbosch Univ. (BA); Witwatersrand Univ. (LLB); Cape Town Univ. (LLM). *Heir*: *s* William Francis Talbot Clerke, *b* 17 Jan. 1987. *Address*: 5 Lourens River Estate, 7 Bizweni Avenue, Somerset West, 7130 Cape Town, South Africa.

**CLERKIN, Natasha Genia**; *see* Pearlman, N. G.

**CLEVELAND, Archdeacon of**; *see* Rushton, Ven. S. J.

**CLEVELAND, Alexis Jane**, CB 2004; *b* 28 Jan. 1954; *d* of late Arthur and Peggy Cleveland. *Educ*: Brighton and Hove High Sch.; Univ. of Salford. Business Develt Dir, IT Services Agency, 1989–93; Benefits Agency, Department of Social Security, subseq. Department for Work and Pensions: Territorial and Jobseekers Allowance Dir, 1993–97; Ops Support Dir, 1997–2000; Chief Exec., 2000–02; Chief Exec., Pension Service, 2002–07; Cabinet Office: Dir Gen., Transformational Govt and Cabinet Office Mgt, 2007–09; Dir Gen., Corporate Services, 2009–11. Non-exec. Advr, HM Treasury, 2011–15; non-exec. Chm., Food and Envmt Res. Agency, 2013–15 (non-exec. Dir, 2011–13); Chair, Animal and Plant Health Agency, 2014–15. Ind. consultant, 2013–. Lay

Mem. Council, 2011–, Chair, UC Council, 2012–18, Durham Univ. Trustee and Co. Dir, Barnardo's, 2011–. Non-exec. Dir, Northumbria, Tyne and Wear NHS Foundn Trust, 2015–. *Recreations:* travel, walking, opera, theatre, cinema, gardening.

**CLEVERDON, Dame Julia (Charity), (Dame Julia Garnett),** DCVO 2008 (CVO 2003); CBE 1996; Chair: National Literacy Trust, since 2014; Transform Alliance, since 2016; *b* 19 April 1950; *d* of late Thomas Douglas James Cleverdon, BBC producer and Elinor Nest Lewis; *m* 1st, 1973, Martin Christopher Ollard (marr. diss. 1978); 2nd, 1985, (William) John (Poulton Maxwell) Garnett, CBE (*d* 1997); two *d*. *Educ:* Newnham Coll., Cambridge (BA Hons History). Communication Adviser, British Leyland and Anglo-American Mining Corp., S Africa, 1972–75; Industrial Society: Head, Eastern and Public Services Dept, 1975–77; Head, Common Purpose Campaign, 1977–79; Dir, Communication and Publicity Div., 1979–81; founded Pepperell Dept for Inner Cities and Educn work, 1981–88; Man. Dir, Develt, BITC, 1988–92; Chief Exec., 1992–2008, Vice Pres., 2008–18, Business in the Community. Chair, Teach First, 2006–13 (Vice Patron, 2014–); Business Leader, Nat. Council of Educn Excellence, 2007–09; Mem. Bd, NCVO, 2011–16. Chm., Building Stronger Communities Taskforce, 2009 (Report, 2009); Co-Chair, ind. rev. into youth social action, 2012–13 (Report, In the Service of Others: a vision for youth social action by 2020, 2013). Chm., Campaign Bd, Newnham Coll., Cambridge, 2009; Member, Board: Teach for All, 2009; Careers and Enterprise Co., 2015–; UK Holocaust Meml Foundn, 2015–; Nat. Citizen Service Trust, 2018–; Co-Founder and Trustee, Step Up To Serve, 2013–; Patron: Helena Kennedy Bursary Scheme; Volunteer Reading Help. Hon. LLB Warwick, 2003; Hon. DLit Harper Adams, 2008; Hon. Dr: Middlesex, 2009; Central Lancashire, 2010; Aston, 2011; Exeter, 2011; Open, 2016. *Publications:* Why Industry Matters, 1978. *Recreations:* children, gardening, collecting pink lustre, entertaining. *Address:* (office) 8 Alwyne Road, Islington, N1 2HH.

**CLEVERLY, James Spencer,** TD; MP (C) Braintree, since 2015; Minister without Portfolio, Cabinet Officer, since 2019; Co-Chairman, Conservative Party, since 2019; *b* Lewisham, 4 Sept. 1969; *s* of James Philip Cleverly and Evelyn Suna Cleverly; *m* 2000, Susannah Janet Temple Sparks; two *s*. *Educ:* Colfe's Sch. for Boys; Thames Valley Univ. (BA Hons Hospitality Mgt). Sales Manager, VNU, 1996–2002; Internat. Advertising Manager, Informa, 2002–04; mobilised service, British Army, 2004; Gp Advertising Manager, Crimson Publishing, 2005–06; Online Commercial Manager, Caspian Publishing, 2006–07; Dir, Point & Fire Media Ltd, 2007–11. Mem. (C) Bexley and Bromley, London Assembly, GLA, 2008–16; Mem. Bd, London Develt Agency, 2008–12; Chairman: London Waste and Recycling Bd, 2010–12; London Fire and Emergency Planning Authy, 2012–15; London Local Resilience Forum, 2012–15. Dep. Chm., Cons. Party, 2018–19; Parly Under-Sec. of State, DExEU, 2019. Served Army Reserves (formerly TA), 1989–. *Recreations:* Rugby, triathlon, spending time with my family. *Address:* House of Commons, SW1A 0AA. *T:* (020) 7219 3000. *E:* james.cleverly.mp@parliament.uk. *Club:* Carlton.

**CLEWS, Richard Anthony;** a District Judge (Magistrates' Courts), since 2016; *b* Kendal, 16 Aug. 1963; *s* of David Clews and late Eileen Clews (*née* Madden); *m* 1st, 1995, Kitty Colley (marr. diss. 2003); 2nd, 2011, Anne MacKenzie; one *s*, and one step *d*. *Educ:* Kingston Poly. (LLB Hons 1985). Called to the Bar, Gray's Inn, 1986; barrister, 1986–2016; Dep. Dist Judge (Magistrates' Courts), 2006–16. *Recreations:* walking, football, cricket, motoring, motorcycling. *Address:* Bradford and Keighley Magistrates' Court and Family Court, The Tyrls, Bradford, W Yorks BD1 1LA. *T:* (01274) 390111, *Fax:* 0870 739 4466. *E:* wy-bradfordmags@hmcts.gsi.gov.uk.

**CLIFF, Prof. Andrew David,** FBA 1996; FSS; CGeog; Professor of Theoretical Geography, 1997–2010, now Emeritus, and Pro-Vice-Chancellor, 2004–10, University of Cambridge; Fellow, Christ's College, Cambridge, since 1974; *b* 26 Oct. 1943; *s* of Alfred Cliff and Annabel Cliff (*née* McQuade); *m* 1964, Margaret Blyton; three *s*. *Educ:* King's Coll. London (BA 1964); Northwestern Univ. (MA 1966); Univ. of Bristol (PhD 1969; DSc 1982); MA Cantab 1973. FSS 1968; CGeog 2002. Teaching Asst in Geog., Northwestern Univ., 1964–66; Res. Associate in Geog., 1968–69, Lectr, 1969–72, Bristol Univ.; Lectr in Geog., 1973–91, Reader in Theoretical Geog., 1991–97, Univ. of Cambridge. MAE 2002. Victoria Medal, RGS, 2017. *Publications:* jointly: Spatial Autocorrelation, 1973; Elements of Spatial Structure: a quantitative approach, 1975; Locational Analysis in Human Geography, 2nd edn 1977; Locational Models, 1977; Locational Methods, 1977; Spatial Processes: models and applications, 1981; Spatial Diffusion: an historical geography of epidemics in an island community, 1981; Spatial Components in the Transmission of Epidemic Waves through Island Communities: the spread of measles in Fiji and the Pacific, 1985; Spatial Aspects of Influenza Epidemics, 1986; Atlas of Disease Distributions: analytical approaches to epidemiological data, 1988; London International Atlas of AIDS, 1992; Measles: an historical geography of a major human viral disease from global expansion to local retreat 1840–1990, 1993; Deciphering Global Epidemics: analytical approaches to the disease records of world cities 1888–1912, 1998; Island Epidemics, 2000; War and Disease, 2004; World Atlas of Epidemic Diseases, 2004; Poliomyelitis: a world geography - emergence to eradication, 2006; Infectious Diseases: emergence and re-emergence. A geographical analysis, 2009; An Atlas of Epidemic Britain, 2012; The Control of Epidemic Communicable Diseases, 2013; Atlas of Refugees, Displaced Populations and Communicable Disease: decoding global geographical patterns and processes since 1901, 2018. *Recreations:* watching Grimsby Town FC, old roses, theatre. *Address:* Department of Geography, University of Cambridge, Downing Place, Cambridge CB2 3EN. *T:* (01223) 333366.

**CLIFF, Anita,** OBE 2007; Executive Headteacher, Manor Multi Academy Trust, since 2016; National Leader of Education, since 2009; *b* Bilston, Wolverhampton, 15 Sept. 1964; *d* of David Moss and Mary Ivy Moss; *m* 1987, David Edward Cliff. *Educ:* Moseley Park Sch., Wolverhampton; Univ. of Birmingham (BEd 1986; MEd Sch. Improvement 1996). Teacher, Lozells Primary Sch., Birmingham, 1986; Dep. Hd, 1998, Actg Hd, 1999, Manor Primary Sch., Coseley; Headteacher, Manor Primary Multi Acad. Teaching Sch. (formerly Primary Teaching Sch.), 1999–2016. *Recreations:* reading, writing. *Address:* 5 Canalside Close, Penkridge, Stafford ST19 5TX. *T:* (school) (01902) 556460. *E:* acliff@manorprimary.com.

**CLIFF, Ian Cameron,** CMG 2016; OBE 1991; HM Diplomatic Service, retired; Chargé d'Affaires, Croatia, 2015–16; international affairs consultant, since 2017; *b* 11 Sept. 1952; *s* of late Gerald Shaw Cliff and Dorothy Cliff; *m* 1988, Caroline Mary Redman; one *s* two *d*. *Educ:* Hampton Grammar Sch.; Magdalen Coll., Oxford (MA Modern Hist.). Asst Master (Hist.), Dr Challoner's GS, Amersham, 1975–79; joined HM Diplomatic Service, 1979: SE Asia Dept, 1979–80; Arabic lang. trng, St Andrews Univ. and Damascus, 1980–82; First Sec., Khartoum, 1982–85; Head, Arabian Peninsula Section, ME Dept, FCO, 1985–87; Perm. Under Sec.'s Dept, FCO, 1987–89; First Sec., UK Mission to UN, NY, 1989–93; Counsellor, on loan to DTI as Dir, Exports to ME, Near East and N Africa, 1993–96; Deputy Hd of Mission, Consul-Gen. and Dir of Trade Promotion, Vienna, 1996–2001; Ambassador to: Bosnia and Herzegovina, 2001–05; Sudan, 2005–07; UK Perm. Rep. to OSCE, Vienna, 2007–11; Ambassador to Kosovo, 2011–15. Member, Board of Trustees: Slynn Foundn, 2017–; SOS Sahel UK, 2018–. *Publications:* occasional articles in railway magazines. *Recreations:* railways, philately, music.

**CLIFF, Rt Rev. William Grant;** *see* Brandon, Bishop of.

**CLIFFE, Air Vice-Marshal John Alfred,** CB 2008; OBE 1994; Chairman, Royal Air Forces Association, since 2016; Managing Director, JacAero Ltd, since 2013; *b* Hyde, Cheshire, 14 June 1953; *s* of Kenneth Cliffe and Mary Vickerman Cliffe (*née* Ellor); *m* 1975, Amanda Penelope Barr. *Educ:* Hyde Co. Grammar Sch. Commnd RAF, 1972; flying trng, 1972–74; Pilot, XI, 19, 23 and 43 Sqdns and Lightning Trng Flight, 1974–88; RNSC, 1988; Personal Staff Officer to AOC 11 Gp, 1989–90; OC XI Sqdn, 1991–94; Air Plans, MoD, 1994–95; Plans, HQ RAF Stike Comd, 1995–97; rcds, 1998; OC RAF Leeming, 1999–2000; Comdr, British Forces, Falkland Is, 2001; Dir, Flying Trng, 2002–03; COS Ops, HQ RAF Strike Comd, 2003–05; Dir Gen., Trng and Educn, MoD, 2005–07. Gen. Manager, Special Mission Business Gp, 2008–11, Dir, Sales and Business Develt, 2011–13, Cobham Aviation Services. *Recreations:* fly-fishing, ornithology, hill walking, golf. *Club:* Royal Air Force.

**CLIFFORD,** family name of **Baron Clifford of Chudleigh**.

**CLIFFORD OF CHUDLEIGH,** 14th Baron *cr* 1672; **Thomas Hugh Clifford;** Count of The Holy Roman Empire; DL; *b* 17 March 1948; *s* of 13th Baron Clifford of Chudleigh, OBE and Hon. Katharine Vavasseur Fisher, 2nd *d* of 2nd Baron Fisher; S father, 1988; *m* 1st, 1980, (Muriel) Suzanne (marr. diss. 1993), *d* of Major Campbell Austin and Mrs Campbell Austin; two *s* one *d*; 2nd, 1994, Clarissa, *er d* of His Honour A. C. Goodall, MC. *Educ:* Downside Abbey. Commnd Coldstream Guards, 1967; stationed British Honduras, 1967–68; Instructor, Guards Depot, 1968–69; Northern Ireland, 1969, 1971, 1972; ADC to Chief of Defence Staff, 1972–73; served with ACE Mobile Force, 1973; Adjutant, Guards Depot, 1974–75. Royal Agricultural College, Cirencester, 1977–79. DL Devon, 1998. *Recreations:* fishing, croquet and crolf. *Heir: s* Hon. Alexander Thomas Hugh Clifford, *b* 24 Sept. 1985. *Address:* The Old Stables, Ugbrooke, Chudleigh, Devon TQ13 0AD. *T:* (01626) 853460.

**CLIFFORD, Daniel;** Chef/Patron: Midsummer House Restaurant, Cambridge, since 1998; Flitch of Bacon, Little Dunmow, Essex, since 2015; *b* Canterbury, Kent, 6 Aug. 1973; *s* of Tony Clifford and Denise (*née* Wynn); *m* Valerie Arnou; five *d*. *Educ:* Canterbury High Sch. Commis chef, Howfield Manor Hotel and Restaurant, Canterbury, 1989–92; first commis chef, Bell Inn, Aston Clinton, 1992; Demi-chef de Partie, Box Tree, Ilkley, 1992–93; Chef de Partie, Millers, Harrogate, 1993; Sous Chef, Provence Restaurant, Hordle, 1993–95; Chef de Partie, Jean Bardet Restaurant, Tours, 1995–96; Sen. Sous Chef, Rascasse, Leeds, 1996–98. Michelin Stars, 2002, 2005. *Address:* Midsummer House Restaurant, Midsummer Common, Cambridge CB4 1HA. *T:* (01223) 369299. *E:* reservations@midsummerhouse.co.uk.

**CLIFFORD, Most Rev. Dermot,** PhD, DD; Archbishop of Cashel and Emly, (RC), 1988–2014, now Emeritus; *b* 25 Jan. 1939. *Educ:* St Brendan's Coll., Killarney, Co. Kerry; St Patrick's Coll., Maynooth (BSc 1960); Irish Coll., Rome; Lateran Pontifical Univ., Rome (STL 1964); NUI (HDipE 1966); LSE (MSc 1974); Loughborough (PhD 1989). Ordained priest, Rome, 1964; Dean of Studies, St Brendan's Coll., Killarney, 1964–72; Diocesan Sec., Kerry, 1974–86; Lectr, Univ. Coll., Cork, 1975–81; Chaplain, St Mary of the Angels Home for Children with Intellectual Disabilities, Beaufort, Co. Kerry, 1976–86; ordained Archbishop, Thurles, 1986; Coadjutor Archbishop of Cashel and Emly, 1986–88; Apostolic Administrator, Cloyne Diocese, 2009–12. Chm., Dept of Planning and Communications, Council for R&D of Irish Episcopal Commn, 1991–2014. Trustee: Mary Immaculate Teachers' Trng Coll., Limerick, 1987–2014; Bothar, Third World Aid Orgn, 1991–. Patron, Gaelic Athletic Assoc., 1989–2014. *Publications:* The Social Costs and Rewards of Caring, 1990. *Recreations:* reading, walking, sport. *Address:* The Green, Holycross, Thurles, Co. Tipperary, Ireland. *T:* (504) 43802.

**CLIFFORD, Nigel Richard;** Operating Partner, Marlin Equity Partners, since 2018; *b* 22 June 1959; *s* of Dr John Clifford and Barbara Dorothy Clifford; *m* 1989, Jeanette Floyd; two *s* one *d*. *Educ:* Portsmouth Grammar Sch.; Downing Coll., Cambridge (MA 1983); Strathclyde Univ. (MBA 1994); DipCAM 1986; Dip. Inst. Mkting 1984. FRICS 2017. British Telecom, 1981–92: Head, Internat. Operator Services, 1987–90; Sen. Strategy Advr, Chm.'s Office, 1990; Head, Business Strategy and Develt, Mobile Communications, 1990–92; Chief Exec., Glasgow Royal Infirmary Univ. NHS Trust, 1992–98; Sen. Vice Pres., Service Delivery, Cable & Wireless Communications, 1998–2000; Chief Executive: Tertio Ltd, 2000–05; Symbian, 2005–10; Micro Focus Internat. plc, 2010–11; Procserve Holdings Ltd, 2012–15; Sen. Vice Pres., Nokia, 2008–10; Chief Exec., Ordnance Survey, 2015–18. Dep. Chm., Geospatial Commn, 2018–. Founding Dir, Herald Foundn for Women's Health, 1994. FCMI (FIMgt 1995); FRSA 1996; FRGS 2012. *Recreations:* family life, walking, running. *Club:* Morpeth Comrades Social (Morpeth).

**CLIFFORD, Sir Roger (Joseph),** 7th Bt *cr* 1887; *b* 5 June 1936; *s* of Sir Roger Charles Joseph Gerard Clifford, 6th Bt and Henrietta Millicent Kiver (*d* 1971); S father, 1982; *m* 1968, Joanna Theresa, *d* of C. J. Ward, Christchurch, NZ; two *d*. *Educ:* Beaumont College, England. *Recreations:* golf, Rugby football. *Heir: b* Charles Joseph Clifford [*b* 5 June 1936; *m* 1983, Sally Green (marr. diss. 1990)]. *Clubs:* Blenheim (Blenheim, NZ); Christchurch, Christchurch Golf.

**CLIFFORD, Stephen Mark;** General Director, Evangelical Alliance, 2009–19; *b* Bradford, May 1954; *s* of Rev. Albert Clifford and Joyce Clifford; *m* 1976, Ann Mary Alford; one *s* one *d*. *Educ:* Grange Boys Grammar Sch., Bradford; London Bible Sch. (BA Theology 1976). Secondary Sch. Teacher, 1980–85; Team Mem. and Church Leader, Pioneer Network, 1985–2008. Internat. Chair, March for Jesus, 1988–2000; Chair: Soul in the City, 2003–04; Hope 08, 2006–08; Member, Board: Evangelical Alliance; Spring Harvest. Co-founder, Leader and Lecturer: DNA; Equipped to Lead. *Recreations:* ski-ing, diving, tennis, cycling, films, theatre, art - particularly portraits.

**CLIFFORD, Susan Merlyn,** MBE 1994; Founder Director, 1982, Honorary Director, 1983–88, Joint Executive Director, 1988–2012, Common Ground (initiated Apple Day annual festival, 21 October); *b* 16 April 1944; *d* of Bernard Clifford and Hilda Clifford (*née* Moorley). *Educ:* Brincliffe Grammar Sch., Nottingham; Univ. of Hull (BSc Hons); Edinburgh Coll. of Art (DipTP). Work in planning consultancy, Edinburgh, 1966–68; landscape architecture practice, 1968–69; Lectr in Extra-Mural Studies, Edinburgh Univ., 1968–69; Lectr, then Sen. Lectr in Planning and Natural Resource Mgt, PCL, 1970–74; Lectr, Bartlett Sch. of Architecture and Planning, UCL, 1975–90. Friends of the Earth (UK), 1971–82 (Hon. Dir); Founder Trustee, Earth Resources Res., 1972; Hon. Mem., Culture SW (Regl Cultural Consortium), 2000–03; Mem., Design Review Cttee, CABE, 2000–02. Has initiated and toured exhibns, including: The Tree of Life, with S Bank Centre, 1989–90; Out of the Wood, with Crafts Council, 1989–90; Leaves by Andy Goldsworthy, Natural Hist. Mus., 1989; from place to PLACE, Barbican Centre, 1996. *Publications:* (ed jtly) Second Nature, 1984; (ed jtly) Pulp!, 1989; Places: the city and the invisible, 1993; with Angela King: Holding Your Ground: an action guide to local conservation, 1985; The Apple Source Book, 1991, enlarged edn 2007; Celebrating Local Distinctiveness, 1994; A Manifesto for Fields, 1997; Rivers, Rhynes and Running Brooks, 2000; England in Particular: a celebration of the commonplace, the local, the vernacular and the distinctive, 2006; Community Orchards Handbook, 2008, 2nd edn 2011; Journeys Through England in Particular: on foot, 2014; Journeys Through England in Particular: coasting, 2014; edited with Angela King: Trees Be Company: an anthology of tree poetry, 1989, 3rd edn 2001; Local Distinctiveness: place particularity and identity, 1993; from place to PLACE: maps and parish maps, 1996; Field Days: an anthology of poetry about fields, 1998; The River's Voice: an anthology of poetry about rivers, 2000; The Common Ground Book of Orchards, 2000. *Recreation:* looking at the land. *Address:* c/o Common Ground, Lower Dairy, Toller Fratrum, Dorchester, Dorset DT2 0EL. *T:* (01300) 321778.

**CLIFFORD, Sir Timothy (Peter Plint),** Kt 2002; Director-General, National Galleries of Scotland, 2001–06 (Director, 1984–2000); *b* 26 Jan. 1946; *s* of late Derek Plint Clifford and Anne (*née* Pierson); *m* 1968, Jane Olivia, *yr d* of Sir George Paterson, OBE, QC; one *d. Educ:* Sherborne, Dorset; Perugia Univ. (Dip. Italian); Courtauld Inst., Univ. of London (BA Hons, History of Art). Dip. Fine Art, Museums Assoc., 1972; AMA. Asst Keeper, Dept of Paintings, Manchester City Art Galleries, 1968–72, Acting Keeper, 1972; Asst Keeper, Dept of Ceramics, Victoria and Albert Mus., London, 1972–76; Asst Keeper, Dept of Prints and Drawings, British Mus., London, 1976–78; Dir, Manchester City Art Galls, 1978–84. Member: Manchester Diocesan Adv. Cttee for Care of Churches, 1978–84; NACF Cttee (Cheshire and Gtr Manchester Br.), 1978–84; North Western Museum and Art Gall. Service Jt Adv. Panel, 1978–84; Cttee, ICOM (UK), 1980–82; Chm., Internat. Cttee for Museums of Fine Art, ICOM, 1980–83 (Mem., Exec. Cttee, 1983–88); Board Member: Museums and Galleries Commn, 1983–88; British Council, 1987–92 (Fine Arts Adv. Cttee, 1988–92), Founder, Museo di Castedilago, Umbria, 2012; Founder and Committee Member: Friends of Manchester City Art Galls, 1978–84; Patrons and Associates, Manchester City Art Galls, 1979–; Mem. Exec. Cttee, Scottish Museums Council, 1984–2006; Mem. Adv. Council, Edinburgh Internat. Fest., 2012–; Consultant, Simon C. Dickinson Ltd, London, 2007–. Cttee Mem., Derby Internat. Porcelain Soc., 1983–86; Vice-Pres., Turner Soc., 1984–86, and 1989–; Pres., NADFAS, 1996–2006; Mem., Adv. Cttee, Come and See Scotland's Churches, 1989–90. Member Consultative Committee: Sculpture Jl, 1998–; Gazette des Beaux-Arts, 1999–. Vice-Pres., Frigate Unicorn Preservation Soc., 1987–2003. Trustee: Lake Dist Art Gall. and Mus. Trust, 1989–97; Royal Yacht Britannia, 1998–2011; Hermitage Develt Trust, 1999–2003; Stichting Hermitage aan de Amstel, 1999–2005; Wallace Collection, 2003–11. Patron: Friends of Sherborne House, 1997–; Art and Antiques Fair, Olympia, 2008–10; Attingham Summer Sch. Member: Accademia Italiana delle Arti Applicate, 1988; Ateneo Veneto, Italy, 1997; Opificio delle Pietre Dure, Florence; Comitato Scientifico, Foundn of the Civic Museums of Venice. FRSA; FRSE 2001; FSAScot 1986. Freeman: Goldsmiths' Co., 1989 (Liveryman, 2007–); City of London, 1989. Hon. LLD: St Andrews, 1996; Aberdeen, 2005; Hon. DLitt Glasgow, 2001. Special Award, BIM, 1991. Commendatore: al Ordine della Repubblica Italiana, 1999 (Cavaliere, 1988); Ordine de S Maurizio e Lazzaro, 2000; Grand Ufficiale della Solidarietà Italiana, 2004. *Publications:* (with Derek Clifford) John Crome, 1968; (with Dr Ivan Hall) Heaton Hall, 1972; (with Dr T. Friedmann) The Man at Hyde Park Corner: sculpture by John Cheere, 1974; Vues Pittoresques de Luxembourg … par J. M. W. Turner, (Luxembourg) 1977; Ceramics of Derbyshire 1750–1975 (ed, H. G. Bradley), 1978; J. M. W. Turner, Acquerelli ed incisioni, (Rome) 1980; Turner at Manchester, 1982; (with Ian Gow) The National Gallery of Scotland: an architectural and decorative history, 1988; (jtly) Raphael: the pursuit of perfection, 1994; (with Ian Gow) Duff House, 1995; (with A. Weston-Lewis) Effigies and Ecstasies: Roman Baroque sculpture and design in the age of Bernini, 1998; Designs of Desire: architectural and ornament prints and drawings 1500–1850, 2000; (with Nicholas Barker and Hugh Brigstocke) A Poet in Paradise: Lord Lindsay and Christian Art, 2000; (jtly) The Age of Titian, 2004; Choice: twenty-one years of collecting in Scotland, 2005; (contrib.) Croatia: aspects of Art & Architecture, 2009; contrib. Burlington Magazine, Apollo, etc. *Recreations:* bird watching, entomology. *Address:* Ampthill Park House, Ampthill, Beds MK45 2HF. *Clubs:* Turf, Beefsteak, Garrick, Pratt's; New (Edinburgh).

**CLIFT, Richard Dennis,** CMG 1984; HM Diplomatic Service, retired; *b* 18 May 1933; *s* of late Dennis Victor Clift and Helen Mildred Clift (*née* Evans); *m* 1st, 1957, Barbara Mary Travis (marr. diss. 1982); three *d;* 2nd, 1982, Jane Rosamund Barker (*née* Homfray) (*d* 2014). *Educ:* St Edward's Sch., Oxford; Pembroke Coll., Cambridge. BA 1956. FO, 1956–57; Office of British Chargé d'Affaires, Peking, 1958–60; British Embassy, Berne, 1961–62; UK Delegn to NATO, Paris, 1962–64; FO, 1964–68; Head of Chancery, British High Commn, Kuala Lumpur, 1969–71; FCO, 1971–73; Counsellor (Commercial), Peking, 1974–76; Canadian Nat. Defence Coll., 1976–77; seconded to NI Office, 1977–79; Hd of Hong Kong Dept, FCO, 1979–84; High Comr in Freetown, 1984–86; Political Advr, Hong Kong Govt, 1987–89. Advr and Social Policy Co-ordinator, CAB, Twickenham CAB, 2000–11. Student, London Coll. of Furniture, 1989–91. Trustee and Advr, Richmond Aid, 2015–. *Recreations:* sailing, walking. *Address:* Winkleigh, Old Farm Road, Hampton TW12 3QT.

**CLIFT, Prof. Roland,** CBE 2006 (OBE 1994); FREng, FIChemE; Professor of Environmental Technology and Director, Centre for Environmental Strategy, 1992–2005, Distinguished Professor, 2005–08, Emeritus Professor, 2008, University of Surrey; Adjunct Professor, University of British Columbia, since 2009; *b* 19 Nov. 1942; *s* of Leslie William Clift and Ivy Florence Gertrude Clift (*née* Wheeler); *m* 1st, 1968, Rosena Valory (*née* Davison); one *d;* 2nd, 1979, Diana Helen (*née* Manning); one *s* (and one *s* decd). *Educ:* Trinity Coll., Cambridge (BA 1963; MA 1967); PhD McGill 1970. CEng, FIChemE 1984; FREng (FEng 1986). Technical Officer (Chem. Engr), ICI, 1964–67; Lectr, Asst Prof. and Associate Prof., McGill Univ., 1967–75; Lectr, Imperial Coll., London, 1975–76; Lectr, Univ. of Cambridge, 1976–81; Fellow, Trinity Coll., Cambridge, 1976–81 (Praelector, 1980–81); University of Surrey: Prof. of Chem. Engrg, 1981–92; Dir, Centre for Envmtl Strategy, 1992–2005. Visiting Professor: Univ. di Napoli, 1973–74; Chalmers Univ. of Technol., Gothenburg, 1989–; Univ. of Coimbra, 2015–. Editor in Chief, Powder Technology, 1987–95. Director: ClifMar Associates, 1986–2007; Blackrock New Energy Investment Trust (formerly Merrill Lynch New Energy Technologies), 1999–2010. Chairman: Clean Technology Management Cttee, SERC, 1990–94; Engrg Bd, AFRC, 1992–94; Member: UK Ecolabelling Bd, 1992–98; Royal Commn on Envmtl Pollution, 1996–2005; Sci. Adv. Council, DEFRA, 2006–11; specialist advr to H of L on energy efficiency, 2004–05. Exec. Dir, Internat. Soc. for Industrial Ecology, 2011–13 (Pres., 2009–10). Rev. Ed. and Contrib., Intergovtl Panel on Climate Change, Wkg Gp III, 2012–14. Mem., Governing Body, Charterhouse Sch., 1982–91. Hon. Citizen of Augusta, Georgia, 1987. FRSA 1986. Hon. FCIWEM 2011. Sir Frank Whittle Medal, Royal Acad. of Engrg, 2003; P. V. Danckwerts Award, IChemE and AIChE, 2010; Society Award, Internat. Soc. for Industrial Ecology, 2015; George E. Davis Medal, IChemE, 2017. *Publications:* (jtly) Bubbles, Drops and Particles, 1978, repr. 2005; (ed jtly) Fluidization, 1985; (jtly) Slurry Transport using Centrifugal Pumps, 1992, 3rd edn 2005; (jtly) Processing of Particulate Solids, 1997; (ed jtly) Sustainable Development in Practice, 2004; (ed jtly) Taking Stock of Industrial Ecology, 2015. *Recreations:* arguing and thinking. *Address:* Department of Chemical Biological Engineering, University of British Columbia, 2360 East Mall, Vancouver, BC V6T 1Z3, Canada. *Club:* Athenæum.

**CLIFTON, Lord;** Henry Robert Stuart Bligh; *b* 23 April 1999; *s* and heir of 12th Earl of Darnley, *qv. Educ:* Radley Coll.

**CLIFTON, Bishop of, (RC),** since 2001; **Rt Rev. Declan Lang;** *b* 15 April 1950; *s* of Francis and Mai Lang. *Educ:* Ryde Sch., IoW; Allen Hall, St Edmund's Coll., Ware; Royal Holloway Coll., Univ. of London (BA Hons). Ordained priest, 1975; Asst Priest, St John's Cathedral, Portsmouth, 1975–79; Sec. to Bishop of Portsmouth, 1979–82; Diocesan Advr for Adult Religious Educn, 1982–90; Parish Priest: Our Lady of the Apostles, Bishop's Waltham, Hants, 1982–86; Sacred Heart, Bournemouth, 1986–90; Administrator, St John's Cathedral, Portsmouth, 1990–96; VG, Dio. Portsmouth and Parish Priest, St Edmund, Abingdon, 1996–2001. *Publications:* (jtly) Parish Project: a resource book for parishes to review mission, 1992. *Recreations:* walking, travel, cinema, theatre. *Address:* St Ambrose, North Road, Leigh Woods, Bristol BS8 3PW. *T:* (0117) 973 3072.

**CLIFTON, His Honour Gerald Michael;** a Circuit Judge, 1992–2012; *b* 3 July 1947; *s* of Frederick Maurice Clifton and Jane Clifton; *m* 1973, Rosemary Anne Vera Jackson; two *s. Educ:* Liverpool Coll. (Schol.); Brasenose Coll., Oxford (Open Classical Schol., MA). Called to the Bar, Middle Temple, 1970, Bencher, 2006; joined Northern Circuit, 1970; Asst Recorder, 1982; Recorder, 1988; Mem., Manx Bar, 1992. Pres., NW Area, Mental Health Review Tribunal (Restricted Cases), 1997–2004; Tutor Judge, Judicial Studies Bd, 2003–12; Liaison Judge for Liverpool Magistrates, 2003–12; Additional Judge, Central Criminal Court, 2003–12; Mem., Parole Bd, 2004–10. Foundn Mem., 1992–, and Vice-Pres., 2001–, Liverpool Coll. *Recreations:* walking, philately, sailing, water colouring, genealogy. *Clubs:* Bar Yacht; Athenæum (Liverpool).

**CLIFTON, Sir (Hervey) Hamish (Peter) B.;** *see* Bruce-Clifton.

**CLIFTON, Richard Francis;** Head, UK Delegation, Channel Tunnel Safety Authority, 2003–11; *b* 18 Sept. 1946; *s* of Joseph Walter Clifton and Georgina Clifton (*née* Naughton); *m* 1970, Gloria Christine Hugill; two *d. Educ:* Univ. of Warwick (BA Econs 1969; MA Industrial Relns 1970). Policy Advr, Dept of Employment, 1974–86; Health and Safety Executive, 1986–2006: Head of Med. Admin, 1986–90; Head of Finance and Planning, 1990–96; Head of Policy Unit, 1996–2001; Dir, Railway Policy, 2001–03. Chm. Bd, European Agency for Safety and Health at Work, Bilbao, 2000–01. Chm., wkg party on Obstruction of the Railway by Road Vehicles, reported 2002. Mem. (Lib Dem), Sutton LBC, 2010– (Chair, Planning Cttee, 2014–16; Mayor, 2016–17). *Recreations:* Mem., Phoenix Concert Band, Sutton. *Address:* 55 The Ridgway, Sutton, Surrey SM2 5JX. *T:* (020) 8643 5603. *E:* rfclifton@btinternet.com.

**CLIFTON, Rita Ann,** CBE 2014; Chairman, BrandCap, since 2013; *b* 30 Jan. 1958; *d* of late Arthur Leonard Clifton and Iris Mona Clifton (*née* Hill); *m* Brian Martin Astley; two *d. Educ:* Newnham Coll., Cambridge (MA Hons Classics). Sen. Account Rep., J. Walter Thompson, 1983–86; Strategic Planning Dir, then Vice Chm. and Exec. Planning Dir, Saatchi & Saatchi, 1986–97; CEO, 1997–2001, Chm., 2002–12, Interbrand. Non-exec. Chm., Populus Ltd, 2004–17; non-executive Director: Dixons Retail (formerly Dixons Gp, then DSG Internat.) plc, 2003–12; EMAP plc, 2005–08; Bupa, 2010–16; Nationwide Bldg Soc., 2012–; ASOS plc, 2014–; Ascential plc, 2016–. Vis. Prof., Henley Business Sch. (formerly Henley Mgt Coll.), 2006–. Mem., Sustainable Develt Commn, 1999–2005. President: WACL, 1997–98; Market Res. Soc., 2010–14; Mem., Mktg Gp of GB, 1999–. Mem., Adv. Bd, Judge Inst. of Mgt Studies, Cambridge, 2000–06. Trustee: WWF-UK, 2007–13; Green Alliance, 2018–; Chm., TCV (formerly BTCV), 2011–17. Dir, Henley Fest., 2010–18. FRSA 1997; Fellow, Mktg Soc., 2004. *Publications:* How to Plan Advertising, 1997; The Future of Brands, 2000; Brands and Branding, 2004, 2nd edn 2009. *Recreations:* dance, environment, fashion, media. *Address:* c/o BrandCap, Northburgh House, 10 Northburgh Street, EC1V 0AT. *T:* (020) 7780 7600.

**CLIFTON, Shaw,** PhD; General of The Salvation Army, 2006–11; *b* 21 Sept. 1945; *s* of Albert Clifton and Alice Jane Clifton (*née* Shaw); *m* 1st, 1967, Helen Ashman (*d* 2011); two *s* one *d;* 2nd, 2013, Birgitte Brekke. *Educ:* Latymer Sch., Edmonton; King's Coll., London (LLB Hons, BD 1st Cl. Hons, AKC 1968; Relton Prize for Histl and Biblical Theol.; PhD 1988). Lecturer in Law: Inns of Court Sch. of Law, 1968–70; Univ. of Bristol, 1970–71; commnd and ordained Officer of The Salvation Army, 1973; Salvation Army appointments: Burnt Oak, London, 1973; Mazoe, 1975, Bulawayo, 1978, Rhodesia; Enfield, London, 1979; Legal and Parly Sec., Internat. HQ, London, 1982–89; Bromley, Kent, 1989–92; Divisional Commander: Durham and Tees, 1992–95; Mass, USA, 1995–97; Territorial Commander: Pakistan, 1997–2002; NZ, Fiji and Tonga, 2002–04; UK with Republic of Ireland, 2004–06. Principal Lectr, Samuel Logan Brengle Insts, UK, Pakistan, India, Australia, NZ; Frederick Coutts Meml Lectr, Sydney, 2003. Member: Vis. Faculty, Internat. Coll. for Officers, London, 1982–; Internat. Doctrine Council, 1980–83; Internat. Moral and Social Issues Council, 1983–93. Freeman, City of London, 2007. *Publications:* What Does the Salvationist Say?, 1977; Growing Together, 1984; Strong Doctrine, Strong Mercy, 1985; Never the Same Again, 1997; Who Are These Salvationists?, 1999; New Love - Thinking Aloud About Practical Holiness, 2004; Selected Writings, Vol. 1, 1974–1999, Vol. 2, 2000–2010, 2010; From Her Heart: the preaching and teaching of Helen Clifton, 2012; Something Better: autobiographical essays, 2014; Crown of Glory, Crown of Thorns, 2015; The History of The Salvation Army, vol. 9, 1995–2015, 2019. *Recreations:* music, reading, walking, family. *Address:* The Salvation Army, 101 Queen Victoria Street, EC4V 4EH. *T:* (020) 7332 8001. *E:* shaw_clifton@salvationarmy.org.

**CLIFTON-BROWN, Sir Geoffrey (Robert),** Kt 2018; MP (C) The Cotswolds, since 2010 (Cirencester and Tewkesbury, 1992–97, Cotswold, 1997–2010); chartered surveyor and farmer; *b* 23 March 1953; *s* of late Robert and Elizabeth Clifton-Brown; *m* 1979, Alexandra Peto-Shepherd (marr. diss. 2004); one *s* one *d. Educ:* Tormore Sch., Kent; Eton Coll.; RAC, Cirencester. FRICS 2002. Chm., N Norfolk Cons. Assoc., 1986–91. PPS to Minister of Agric., Fisheries and Food, 1995–97; an Opposition Whip, 1999–2001, 2003, Opposition Asst Chief Whip, 2005; Opposition front bench spokesman on local and devolved govt, 2003–04; Shadow Minister: for Foreign Affairs and Trade, 2005–07; for Internat. Develt and Trade, 2007–10. Member: Envmt Select Cttee, 1992–95; Public Accounts Commn, 1997–99; Public Accounts Cttee, 1997–99, 2017– (Dep. Chm., 2017–); Finance and Services Cttee, 2005–15; Cttee of Selection, 2005–15; Liaison Cttee, 2010–15; Finance Cttee, 2015–17, 2017–. Vice Chm., Euro Atlantic Gp, 1996–2015; Chm., Cons. Party Internat. Office, 2010–15. Freeman, City of London, 1981; Liveryman, Farmers' Co., 1984. *Recreations:* fishing, all country pursuits. *Address:* House of Commons, SW1A 0AA. *T:* (020) 7219 3000. *Clubs:* Carlton, Farmers.

**CLIMER, Naomi Wendy,** CBE 2018; Co-Chair, Institute for the Future of Work, since 2018; President, Institution of Engineering and Technology, 2015–16; *b* London, 18 Dec. 1964; *d* of Benjamin Climer and Wendy Climer; *m* 2008, Carl Schofield; one *d. Educ:* Imperial Coll. London (BSc Jt Hons Chem. with Mgt Sci. 1986). Engr, BBC, 1987–90; Proj. Manager, Island Technical, 1990–93; yr travelling, 1993–94; BBC: Manager, Engrg and Ops Trng, BBC World Service, 1994–97; Controller, Technol., BBC News, 1997–2000; Dir, Ops, ITV Digital, 2000–02; Dir, Professional Services, Sony Europe Ltd, 2002–06; Dir, Sony UK Ltd, 2005–10; Vice Pres., Sony Europe Ltd, 2006–12; Pres., Sony Media Cloud Services, 2012–15. Non-executive Director: Sony UK Technol. Centre Ltd, 2016–; Focusrite plc, 2018–. Chair, Future Communications Challenge Gp, DCMS, 2016–17; Chair, Council, Internat. Broadcasting Convention, 2016–; Mem., Sci. and Technol. Hons Cttee, 2017–Jan. 2020. Dir, Parliamentary Broadcasting Unit Ltd, 1998–2000. Trustee, IET, 2010–17 (Dep. Pres., 2012–14); Gov., Nat. Film and Television Sch., 2017–18. FREng 2013 (Trustee, 2017–Sept. 2020). DUniv Huddersfield, 2016; Hon. DEng: Southampton Solent, 2016; Bradford, 2017; Wolverhampton, 2018. *Recreations:* family, sailing, cycling, motorbiking, theatre, cello, piano.

**CLINCH, David John, (Joe),** OBE 1997; Secretary, Open University, 1981–98; *b* 14 Feb. 1937; *s* of Thomas Charles Clinch and Madge Isabel Clinch (née Saker); *m* 1963, Hilary Jacques; one *s* one *d*. *Educ:* Nautical Coll., Pangbourne; St Cuthbert's Soc., Univ. of Durham (BA); Indiana Univ. (MBA); Open Univ. (BSc 2009). National Service, Royal Navy (Sub-Lieut), Supply and Secretariat, 1955–57. Administrator, Univ. of Sussex, 1963–69; Deputy Secretary and Registrar, Open University, 1969–81; Registrar Counterpart, Allama Iqbal Open Univ., Pakistan, 1976–77. Consultant: Univ. for Industry, 2000–02; UNESCO, 2003–04; Consultant Higher Education Adviser: Milton Keynes Econ. and Learning Partnership, 2001–10; University Centre Milton Keynes, 2010–13. Member: Conf. of Univ. Administrators, 1973–99; British Fulbright Scholars Assoc., 1978–; Conf. of Registrars and Secs, 1981–98 (Chm., 1990–91); Bd of Govs (formerly Council of Foundn), Internat. Baccalaureate Orgn, 1999–2005 (Treas., 2000–05; Sec., 2003–05; Hon. Life Mem., 2005); Trustee and Secretary: Internat. Baccalaureate Fund Inc., USA, 2004–07; Internat. Baccalaureate Fund, Canada, 2004–07; Internat. Baccalaureate Fund UK, 2006–07. Dir, Nat. Educnl Resources Information Service Trust, 1989–93; Bd Mem., COUNTEC, 2005–11. Trustee, Open Univ. Superannuation Scheme, 1989–97; Hon. Vice Pres., Open Univ. Students Assoc., 2000–05 (Hon. Life Mem., 2005). Mem. Ct, Univ. of Surrey, Roehampton, 2000–04. Dir, Milton Keynes City Orch., 2001–08; Trustee, Milton Keynes City Orch. Foundn, 2010–13. Treas., Milton Keynes Natural Hist. Soc., 2017–. FRSA 1997. DUniv Open, 2000. *Recreations:* music, natural history, reading, walking. *Address:* 39 Tudor Gardens, Stony Stratford, Milton Keynes MK11 1HX. *T:* (01908) 562475.

**CLINCH, Stephen David;** Founder and Director, ClinchMaritime Ltd, since 2018; Chief Inspector of Marine Accidents, Marine Accident Investigation Branch, Department for Transport, 2010–18; *b* London, 16 June 1955; *s* of David and Mary Clinch; *m* 1983, Susan Maria Cullen; one *s* one *d*. *Educ:* City of London Poly.; Merchant Navy Coll. (Master Mariner). Deck Officer, P&O Bulk Shipping, 1971–85; Ops Superintendent, P&O Bulk Carriers, 1985–88; Ship Master, P&O Bulk Shipping, 1988–89; Ops Manager, P&O Bulk Carriers, 1989–91; Gen. Manager, 1991–94, Marine Dir, 1994–98, P&O Bulk Shipping; Marine Dir, Associated Bulk Carriers, 1998–2001; Dep. Dir, Bahamas Maritime Authy, 2002–04; Dep. Chief Inspector, Maritime Accident Investigation Br., DfT, 2004–10. Chairman: Marine Accident Investigator's Internat. Forum, 2012–16; EU Permanent Co-op. Framework, 2012–18. Trustee: CHIRP, 2010–18; Royal Alfred Seafarer's Soc., 2019–; Trustee Dir, Nautilus Internat., 2018–. Merchant Navy Medal for Meritorious Service, 2017. *Recreations:* theatre, walking, fine art.

**CLINES, Prof. David John Alfred;** Professor of Biblical Studies, University of Sheffield, 1985–2003, now Emeritus; Director: Dictionary of Classical Hebrew Ltd, since 2001; Sheffield Phoenix Press, since 2004; *b* 21 Nov. 1938; *s* of Alfred William and Ruby Coral Clines; *m* 1st, 1963, Dawn Naomi Joseph; one *s* one *d*; 2nd, 1989, Heather Ann McKay. *Educ:* Univ. of Sydney (BA Hons 1960); St John's Coll., Cambridge (BA 1963; MA 1967). University of Sheffield: Asst Lectr in Biblical History and Literature, 1964–67; Lectr, 1967–73, Sen. Lectr, 1973–79, Reader, 1979–85, in Biblical Studies. Co-Founder and Partner, JSOT Press, 1976–87; Dir, Sheffield Acad. Press, 1987–2001 (Chm., 1987–92). President: SOTS, 1996; Soc. of Biblical Literature, 2009. Hon. PhD Amsterdam, 2001. Burkitt Medal in Biblical Studies, British Acad., 2015. *Publications:* I, He, We and They: a literary approach to Isaiah 53, 1976; The Theme of the Pentateuch, 1978, 2nd edn 1997; Ezra, Nehemiah, Esther, 1984; The Esther Scroll: the story of the story, 1984; Job 1–20, 1990; What Does Eve Do to Help? and Other Readerly Questions to the Old Testament, 1990; Interested Parties: the ideology of writers and readers of the Hebrew Bible, 1995; The Bible and the Modern World, 1997; The Sheffield Manual for Authors and Editors in Biblical Studies, 1997; On the Way to the Postmodern: Old Testament essays 1967–1998, 1998; Job 21–37, 2006; On Psalms, 2008; Job 38–42, 2011; *edited:* The Dictionary of Classical Hebrew: vol. 1, 1993, vol. 2, 1995, vol. 3, 1996, vol. 4, 1998, vol. 5, 2001, vol. 6, 2006, vol. 7, 2010, vol. 8, 2011, vol. 9, 2016, rev. edn as The Dictionary of Classical Hebrew Revised: vol. 1, 2018, vol. 2, 2019; The Poetical Books: a Sheffield reader, 1997; The Concise Dictionary of Classical Hebrew, 2009; *edited jointly:* Art and Meaning: rhetoric in biblical literature, 1982; Midian, Moab and Edom: the history and archaeology of late Bronze and Iron Age Jordan and North-West Arabia, 1983; The Bible in Three Dimensions (essays), 1990; Telling Queen Michal's Story: an experiment in comparative interpretation, 1991; Among the Prophets: imagery, language and structure in the prophetic writings, 1993; Of Prophets' Visions and the Wisdom of Sages (essays), 1993; The New Literary Criticism and the Hebrew Bible, 1993; The Bible in Human Society (essays), 1995; The World of Genesis: persons, places, perspectives, 1998; Auguries: the Jubilee volume of the Department of Biblical Studies, 1998; Weisheit in Israel, 2003; The Centre and the Periphery, 2010; A Critical Engagement, 2011; Making a Difference, 2012; Biblical Reception: vol 1, 2012, vol. 2, 2013, vol. 3, 2015, vol. 4, 2016, vol. 5, 2018; The Reception of the Hebrew Bible in the Septuagint and the New Testament, 2013; articles in learned jls. *Recreations:* congresses, databases. *Address:* 96 Ashland Road, Sheffield S7 1RJ. *T:* (0114) 255 0562.

**CLINK, Rear Adm. John Robert Hamilton,** CBE 2017 (OBE 2002); Clerk, Merchant Taylors' Company, since 2018; *b* Hillingdon, 18 Feb. 1964; *s* of Michael and Jennifer Clink; *m* 1988, Jacqueline Sayce; two *s*. *Educ:* Cheltenham Grammar Sch.; Britannia Royal Naval Coll.; King's Coll. London (MA Internat. Security and Strategy 2012). Joined RN, 1983; in Command: HMS Archer, 1991–93; HMS Kent, 1999–2002; HMS Ark Royal, 2008–10; Dep. Comdr, UK Maritime Forces, 2011–12; Comdr, British Forces Gibraltar, 2012–14; Flag Officer, Scotland and NI, 2014–15; Flag Officer Sea Trng, 2015–18. Younger Brother, Trinity House. Liveryman, Shipwrights' Co. FRIN. *Recreations:* golf, sailing, ski-ing, cycling. *Clubs:* Royal Navy of 1765 and 1785; Saunton Golf.

**CLINTON;** see Fiennes-Clinton, family name of Earl of Lincoln.

**CLINTON, 22nd Baron** *cr* 1299 (title abeyant 1957–65); **Gerard Nevile Mark Fane Trefusis;** DL; landowner; *b* 7 Oct. 1934; *s* of Capt. Charles Fane (killed in action, 1940); assumed by deed poll, 1958, surname of Trefusis in addition to patronymic; *m* 1959, Nicola Harriette Purdon Coote; one *s* two *d*. *Educ:* Gordonstoun. Took seat in House of Lords, 1965. Mem., Prince of Wales's Councils, 1968–79. JP Bideford, 1963–83; DL Devon, 1977. *Recreations:* shooting, fishing, forestry. *Heir: s* Hon. Charles Patrick Rolle Fane Trefusis [*b* 21 March 1962; *m* 1992, Rosanna, *yr d* of John Izat; three *s*]. *Address:* Heanton Satchville, near Okehampton, North Devon EX20 3QE. *T:* (01805) 804224. *Clubs:* Boodle's, Royal Yacht Squadron, Turf.

**CLINTON, Bill;** *see* Clinton, W. J.

**CLINTON, Hillary Diane Rodham,** JD; Secretary of State, United States of America, 2009–13; *b* Chicago, 26 Oct. 1947; *d* of late Hugh Ellsworth and Dorothy Howell Rodham; *m* 1975, William Jefferson, (Bill) Clinton, *qv*; one *d*. *Educ:* Wellesley Coll.; Yale Univ. Law Sch. (JD 1973). Attorney, Children's Defense Fund, Cambridge, Mass and Washington, 1973–74; legal consultant, Carnegie Counsel on Children, New Haven, 1973–74; legal counsel, Nixon impeachment inquiry, Judiciary Cttee, US House of Reps, 1974; Asst Prof. of Law and Dir, Legal Aid Clinic, Univ. of Arkansas, Fayetteville, 1974–77; Partner, Rose Law Firm, 1977–92; Asst Prof. of Law, Univ. of Arkansas, Little Rock, 1979–80. Hd, Presidential Task Force on Nat. Health Care Reform, 1993. US Senator from NY State, 2001–09. Democratic Candidate for Presidency of USA, 2016. Numerous awards for humanitarian work. *Publications:* It Takes a Village, 1996; Dear Socks, Dear Buddy, 1998; Living History, 2003; Hard Choices, 2014; What Happened, 2017; (with C. Clinton) The Book of Gutsy Women: favourite stories of courage and resilience, 2019; contribs to professional jls.

**CLINTON, Robert George,** CVO 2008; Senior Partner, Farrer & Co., 2002–08; *b* 19 Aug. 1948; *s* of George Thomas and Mary Josephine Clinton; *m* 1981, Annita Louise Bennett; one *s* one *d*. *Educ:* Beaumont Coll.; Brasenose Coll., Oxford (MA 1975). Admitted solicitor, 1975; Partner, Farrer & Co., 1979–2008. Dir, Early Resolution CIC, 2011–. Chm., Tony Blair Faith Foundn, 2007–14. Trustee, Wessex Youth Trust, 2002–. *Recreations:* sailing, travel. *Address:* 85 Richmond Avenue, N1 0LX. *T:* (020) 7609 8336. *Club:* Garrick.

**CLINTON, William Jefferson, (Bill),** JD; President of the United States of America, 1993–2001; *b* 19 Aug. 1946; *s* of late Virginia Kelly; *m* 1975, Hillary Diane Rodham (*see* H. D. R. Clinton); one *d*. *Educ:* Georgetown Univ. (BS 1968); University Coll., Oxford (Rhodes Schol.; Hon. Fellow, 1993; DCL by Diploma, 1994); Yale Univ. Law Sch. (JD 1973). Prof., Univ. of Arkansas Law Sch., 1974–76; Attorney Gen., Arkansas, 1977–79; with Wright, Lindsey & Jennings, law firm, 1981–83; Governor of Arkansas, 1979–81 and 1983–92. Chairman: Educn Commn of the States, 1986–87; Nat. Governors' Assoc., 1986–87 (Co-Chm., Task Force on Educn, 1990–91); Democratic Governors' Assoc., 1989–90 (Vice Chm., 1987–88); Democratic Leadership Council, 1990–91. UN Special Envoy to Haiti, 2009–. Democrat. Hon. DCL Oxford, 1994. *Publications:* Between Hope and History, 1996; My Life, 2004; Giving: how each of us can change the world, 2007; Back to Work: why we need smart government for a strong economy, 2011; (jtly) The President is Missing (novel), 2018. *Address:* (office) 55 West 125th Street, New York, NY 10027, USA.

**CLINTON-DAVIS,** family name of **Baron Clinton-Davis**.

**CLINTON-DAVIS, Baron** *cr* 1990 (Life Peer), of Hackney in the London Borough of Hackney; **Stanley Clinton Clinton-Davis;** PC 1998; *b* 6 Dec. 1928; *s* of Sidney Davis; name changed to Clinton-Davis by deed poll, 1990; *m* 1954, Frances Jane Lucas; one *s* three *d*. *Educ:* Hackney Downs Sch.; Mercers' Sch.; King's Coll., London University (LLB 1950; FKC 1996). Admitted Solicitor, 1953; in practice, 1953–70; consultant, S. J. Berwin & Co., later S. J. Berwin LLP, 1989–97, 1998–. Mem. Exec. Council, Nat. Assoc. of Labour Student Organisations, 1949–50. Councillor, London Borough of Hackney, 1959; Mayor of Hackney, 1968. Contested (Lab): Langstone Div. of Portsmouth, 1955; Yarmouth, 1959 and 1964. MP (Lab) Hackney Central, 1970–83; Parly Under-Sec. of State, Dept of Trade, 1974–79; Opposition spokesman on trade, prices and consumer protection, 1979–81, on foreign affairs, 1981–83. Mem., H of L, 1990–2018. Opposition frontbench spokesman on transport, H of L, 1990–97; Minister of State, DTI, 1997–98. Vice Chm., Parly Envmt Gp. Mem., Commn of EC, 1985–89. Chm., Adv. Cttee on Protection of the Sea, 1984–85, 1989–97; Pres., Refugee Council, 1989–97. Pres., AMA, 1992–97. Vice Pres., Lab. Finance and Industry Gp, 1993–. Member: RIIA; Council and Exec. Cttee, Justice; UN Selection Cttee for Sasakawa, Envmt Project; Adv. Bd, Centre of European Law, KCL; formerly Mem., Bd of Deputies of British Jews; Parly Relations Sub-Cttee of the Law Soc.; Hon. Mem., London Criminal Courts Solicitors' Assoc. Mem: Council, British Maritime League, 1989–97. Jt Pres., Soc. of Labour Lawyers, 1991–; President: UK Pilots Assoc. (Marine), 1991; BALPA, 1994; Inst. of Travel Management; Aviation Envmt Fedn; Vice-Pres., Chartered Instn of Envmtl Health Officers, 1991–. Pres., Hackney Br., Multiple Sclerosis Soc.; Vice-Pres., Hackney Assoc. for Disabled; Hon. Mem. Rotary Club, Hackney. Hon. Mem., 1979, and former Trustee, NUMAST (formerly Merchant Navy and Airline Officers' Assoc.); Hon. Fellow, QMW, 1993; Hon. FCIWEM; FRSA 1992 (Mem. Acad. Bd for Internat. Trade). Hon. Dr *hc* Polytechnical Inst., Bucharest, 1993. First Medal for Outstanding Services to Animal Welfare in Europe, Eurogroup for Animal Welfare, 1988. Grand Cross, Order of Leopold II, Belgium (for services to EC), 1990. *Recreations:* golf, Association football, reading biographical histories.

**CLITHEROE, 2nd Baron** *cr* 1955, of Downham; **Ralph John Assheton;** Bt 1945; Chairman, Yorkshire Bank, 1990–99; Vice Lord-Lieutenant of Lancashire, 1995–99; *b* 3 Nov. 1929; *s* of 1st Baron Clitheroe, KCVO, PC, FSA, and Sylvia Benita Frances, Lady Clitheroe, FRICS, FLAS, (*d* 1991), *d* of 6th Baron Hotham; *S* father, 1984; *m* 1961, Juliet, *d* of Lt-Col Christopher Lionel Hanbury, MBE, TD; two *s* one *d*. *Educ:* Eton; Christ Church, Oxford (Scholar, MA). FCIB 1991. Served as 2nd Lieut Life Guards, 1948–49. Chairman: RTZ Chemicals Ltd, 1973–87; RTZ Borax Ltd, 1979–89; US Borax and Chemical Corp., 1980–89; RTZ Oil & Gas Ltd, 1983–88; Director: Borax Consolidated, 1960–89; RTZ Corp., 1968–89; First Interstate Bank of California, 1981–89; TR Natural Resources Investment Trust, 1982–87; American Mining Congress, 1982–89; Halliburton Co., Texas, 1987–2002. Mem., Council, Chemical Industries Assoc., 1984–88. Liveryman, Skinners' Co. DL Lancs, 1986. *Heir: s* Hon. Ralph Christopher Assheton [*b* 19 March 1962; *m* 1996, Olivia, *o d* of Anthony Warrington]. *Address:* The Lidgett House, Downham, Clitheroe, Lancs BB7 4BL. *Clubs:* Boodle's, Royal Automobile.

**CLITHEROW, Rev. Canon Andrew;** Chaplain to the Queen, 2007–Nov. 2020; Chaplain, University of Central Lancashire, 2012–Nov. 2020; *b* Guildford, 18 Nov. 1950; *s* of late Rt Rev. Richard George Clitherow and of Diana Clitherow; *m* 2002, Rebekah Clare Eames (marr. diss.); two *s* two *d*; *m* 2011, Nicola Howard. *Educ:* Ellesmere Coll., Shropshire; St Chad's Coll., Durham Univ. (BA Hons 1972); Salisbury and Wells Theol Coll.; Exeter Univ. (MPhil 1987). Ordained deacon, 1979, priest, 1980; Hon. Curate, Christ Church, Bedford, 1979–84; Asst Chaplain, Bedford Sch., 1979–84; Chaplain, Caldicott Sch., 1984–85; Res. Minister, St James, Acton Trussell and All Saints', Bednall, and Curate, St Michael and All Angels, Penkridge, 1985–88; Chaplain and Hd of Religious Studies, Rossall Sch., 1989–94; Vicar, St Paul's, Scotforth, 1994–2000; Res. Canon, Blackburn Cathedral, 2000–07; Dir of Trng, Dio. of Blackburn, 2001–07; Priest in Charge: St Cuthbert's, Lytham, 2007–11; St John's, Lytham, 2008–11. *Publications:* Into Your Hands: prayer and the call to holiness in everyday ministry and life, 2001; Renewing Faith in Ordained Ministry, 2004; Creative Love in Tough Times, 2007; Desire, Love and the

Rule of St Benedict, 2008; Prayer: the embrace of love, 2009. *Recreations:* walking, cycling, music, reading, fishing, cooking. *Address:* 31 Mythrop Avenue, Lytham, Lancs FY8 4HZ. *E:* andrewclitherow1@gmail.com.

**CLIVE, Viscount; Jonathan Nicholas William Herbert;** *b* 5 Dec. 1979; *s* and *heir* of Earl of Powis, *qv*.

**CLIVE, Eric McCredie,** CBE 1999; FRSE; Honorary Professor, University of Edinburgh, since 2014 (Visiting Professor, 1999–2014); *b* 24 July 1938; *s* of Robert M. Clive and Mary L. D. Clive; *m* 1962, Kay M. McLeman; one *s* two *d* (and one *d* decd). *Educ:* Univs of Edinburgh (MA, LLB with dist.); Michigan (LLM); Virginia (SJD). Solicitor. Lecturer 1962–69, Sen. Lectr 1969–75, Reader 1975–77, Professor of Scots Law 1977–81, Univ. of Edinburgh; a Scottish Law Comr, 1981–99. FRSE 1999. Hon. Dr Osnabrück, 2008. *Publications:* Law of Husband and Wife in Scotland, 1974, 4th edn 1997; (ed jtly) Principles, Definitions and Model Rules of European Contract Law, 2009; articles and notes in legal jls. *Address:* 14 York Road, Edinburgh EH5 3EH. *T:* (0131) 552 2875.

**CLOGGIE, Angela Thomson;** *see* Grahame, A. T.

**CLOGHER, Bishop of,** since 2011; **Rt Rev. (Francis) John McDowell;** *b* Belfast, 20 Jan. 1956; *s* of James McDowell and Elizabeth McDowell; *m* 1986, Dorothy Mary Jackson; one *d*. *Educ:* Annadale Grammar Sch.; Queen's Univ., Belfast (BA Hons Hist. 1978); London Sch. of Econs and Pol Sci. (DBS 1984); Trinity Coll., Dublin (BTh 1996). Ordained deacon, 1996, priest, 1997; Sen. Mgt, Short Brothers Missile Div., 1980–87; Asst Dir, CBI, NI, 1987–91. Curate, Antrim Parish, 1996–99; Rector: Kildollagh and Ballyrashane, 1999–2002; Dundela, 2002–11. Hon. Sec., Gen. Synod of C of I, 2008–11. *Recreations:* literature, theology, history, walking, admiring other people's gardens. *Address:* The See House, Fivemiletown, Co. Tyrone BT75 0QP. *E:* bishop@clogher.anglican.org.

**CLOKE, Prof. (Frederick) Geoffrey (Nethersole),** DPhil; FRS 2007; Professor of Chemistry, University of Sussex, since 1994; *b* 12 April 1953; *s* of late Frederick and Cecelia Cloke; partner, Siobhan Mehaffy. *Educ:* Balliol Coll., Oxford (BA Hons 1975; DPhil 1978; MA 1981). SERC Postdoctoral Fellow, Inorganic Chemistry Lab., Oxford, 1978–79; Jun. Res. Fellow, Balliol Coll., Oxford, 1979–83; Postdoctoral Associate, MIT, Cambridge, 1981–82; University of Sussex: SERC Advanced Fellowship, 1983–84; New Blood Lectr in Inorganic Chem., 1984–89; Sen. Lectr in Chem., 1989–90; Reader in Chem., 1990–94. *Publications:* over 150 res. papers in learned jls inc. Science, Jl of Amer. Chemical Soc., Angewandte Chemie, Chemical Communications. *Recreations:* sport—golf (playing), cricket (now only watching!), mountain walking/scrambling, woodworking, movies, jazz and 70s music. *Address:* Department of Chemistry, Chichester Building, University of Sussex, Brighton BN1 9QJ. *T:* (01273) 678735, *Fax:* (01273) 677196. *E:* f.g.cloke@sussex.ac.uk.

**CLOKE, Prof. Paul John,** PhD; DSc; FBA 2009; Professor of Geography, University of Exeter, since 2006; *b* 17 Feb. 1953; *s* of William and Iris Cloke (*née* Tinton); *m* 1974, Vivien Jane Hewitt; one *s* one *d*. *Educ:* Southampton Univ. (BA); Wye Coll., London (PhD); Bristol Univ. (DSc). Lectr, Reader, then Prof. of Geog., Univ. of Wales, Lampeter, 1977–92; Reader, 1992–93, Prof. of Geog., 1993–2005, Univ. of Bristol. Founder Ed., Jl of Rural Studies. *Publications:* Key Settlements in Rural Areas, 1979; Introduction to Rural Settlement Planning, 1983; (with C. Park) Rural Resource Management, 1985; Rural Planning, 1987; Policies and Plans for Rural People, 1988; Rural Land Use Planning, 1989; (with P. Bell) Deregulation and Transport, 1990; (with J. Little) The Rural State, 1990; (with C. Philo and D. Sadler) Approaching Human Geography, 1991; Policy and Change in Thatcher's Britain, 1992; (jtly) Writing the Rural, 1994; (ed jtly) Contested Countryside Cultures, 1997; Rural Wales, 1997; (ed jtly) Introducing Human Geographies, 1999, 3rd edn 2013; (with P. Milbourne and R. Widdowfield) Rural Homelessness, 2002; (with O. Jones) The Culture of Trees, 2002; Country Visions, 2003; (jtly) Practising Human Geography, 2004; (ed jtly) Envisioning Human Geographies, 2004; (ed jtly) Spaces of Geographic Thought, 2005; (ed jtly) Handbook of Rural Studies, 2006; (ed jtly) International Perspectives on Rural Homelessness, 2006; (with J. May and S. Johnsen) Swept Up Lives, 2010; (with C. Barnett, N. Clarke and A. Malpass) Globalizing Responsibility, 2011; (with V. del Casino, M. Thomas and R. Panelli) A Companion to Social Geography, 2011; (with J. Beaumont) Faith-Based Organisations, Welfare and Exclusion in European Cities, 2012; (with J. Beaumont and A. Williams) Working Faith, 2013; (with M. Pears) Mission In Marginal Places: the theory, 2016; (with M. Pears) Mission in Marginal Places: the praxis, 2016. *Recreations:* Contemporary Christian worship music, countryside walking, Tottenham Hotspur Football Club. *Address:* College of Life and Environmental Sciences, University of Exeter, Amory Building, Rennes Drive, Exeter EX4 4RJ. *T:* (01392) 724522, *Fax:* (01392) 263342. *E:* p.cloke@exeter.ac.uk.

**CLOONEY, George Timothy;** actor, director and producer; *b* 6 May 1961; *s* of Nicholas Clooney and Nina Bruce Clooney (*née* Warren); *m* 1989, Talia Balsam (marr. diss. 1993); *m* 2014, Amal Alamuddin; one *s* one *d* (twins). *Educ:* Northern Kentucky Univ. *Television series: actor:* E/R, 1984–85; The Facts of Life, 1985–86; Roseanne, 1988–89; Sunset Beat, 1990; Baby Talk, 1991; Bodies of Evidence, 1992; Sisters, 1992–94; ER, 1994–99; Catch-22 (also co-dir and co-prod.), 2019; *director and producer:* K Street, 2003; Unscripted, 2005; *actor in television films:* Combat High, 1986; Fail Safe (also prod.), 2000. *Films: actor:* Return of the Killer Tomatoes, 1988; Red Surf, 1990; Unbecoming Age, 1993; From Dusk Till Dawn, One Fine Day, 1996; Batman and Robin, 1997; The Peacemaker, Out of Sight, The Thin Red Line, 1998; Three Kings, 1999; The Perfect Storm, O Brother, Where Art Thou? (Best Actor, Golden Globe Awards, 2001), 2000; Spy Kids, 2001; Ocean's Eleven, Welcome to Collinwood (also prod.), 2002; Solaris, Confessions of a Dangerous Mind (also dir), Intolerable Cruelty, 2003; Ocean's Twelve, 2005; Syriana (also prod.) (Best Supporting Actor, Golden Globe and Academy Awards, 2006), Good Night, and Good Luck (also writer and dir), 2006; The Good German (also prod.), Ocean's Thirteen, Michael Clayton, 2007; Leatherheads (also dir), Burn After Reading, 2008; The Men Who Stare at Goats, 2009; Up in the Air, The American, 2010; The Descendants, 2011 (Best Actor, Golden Globe Awards, 2012); Gravity, 2013; The Monuments Men (also co-writer, dir and prod.), 2014; Tomorrowland: a world beyond, 2015; Hail, Caesar!, Money Monster (also prod.), 2016; *producer:* Rock Star, 2001; Insomnia, Far From Heaven, 2002; Criminal, 2004; The Jacket, The Big Empty, Rumour Has It, 2005; PU-239, A Scanner Darkly, 2006; Our Brand is Crisis, 2016; *director, co-producer and co-writer:* Suburbicon, 2017. *Address:* c/o Creative Artists Agency, 2000 Avenue of the Stars, Los Angeles, CA 90067, USA.

**CLORE, Melanie;** Co-founder, Clore Wyndham Fine Art Ltd, since 2016; *b* 28 Jan. 1960; *d* of Martin and Cynthia Clore; *m* 1992, Yaron Meshoulam; one *s* one *d*. *Educ:* Channing Sch., Highgate; Univ. of Manchester (BA Hons Hist. of Art 1981). Became an auctioneer, 1985; Sotheby's: Hd, Impressionist and Modern Art Dept, 1991–2016; Member: European Bd, 1995–2016; Exec. Mgt Cttee, 1995–2016; Dep. Chm., 1997–2011, Chm., 2011–16, Sotheby's Europe; Co-Chm. Worldwide, Impressionist and Modern Art Dept, Sotheby's, 2000–16. Trustee: Whitechapel Art Gall., 1988–98; Tate, 2004–08; Clore Duffield Foundn, 2012–; RA Develt Trust, 2016–; Hon. Trustee, Tate Foundn, 2009–. *Recreations:* going to the movies, pottering in the garden, visiting museums and art galleries.

**CLOSE, Prof. Francis Edwin,** OBE 2000; FInstP; Professor of Theoretical Physics, University of Oxford, 2001–10, now Emeritus; Fellow, Exeter College, Oxford, 2001–10, now Emeritus; *b* 24 July 1945; *s* of Frederick Archibald Close and Frances Moreton Close; *m* 1969, Gillian Matilda Boyce; two *d*. *Educ:* King's Sch., Peterborough; St Andrews Univ. (BSc 1967); Magdalen Coll., Oxford (DPhil 1970). FInstP 1991. Research Fellow: Stanford Linear Accelerator, Calif, 1970–72; Daresbury Lab., 1973; CERN, Geneva, 1973–75; Res. Scientist, 1975–2000, and Head of Theoretical Physics Div., 1991–2000, Rutherford Appleton Lab. Dist. Scientist, Oak Ridge Nat. Lab. and Univ. of Tennessee, 1988–90; Vis. Prof., Birmingham Univ., 1996–2002; Sen. Scientist, CERN, 1997–2000; Gresham Prof. of Astronomy, 2000–03. Mem. Council, Royal Instn, 1997–99 (Christmas Lectr, 1993); Vice-Pres., BAAS, 1993–99. Chm., British Physics Olympiad, 2003–05. Fellow, APS, 1992; Fellow in Public Understanding of Physics, Inst. Physics, 1995–97. Kelvin Medal, Inst. Physics, 1996; Faraday Medal, Royal Soc., 2013. *Publications:* Introduction to Quarks and Partons, 1979; The Cosmic Onion, 1983; The Particle Explosion, 1987; End, 1988; Too Hot to Handle, 1991; Lucifer's Legacy, 2000; The Particle Odyssey, 2002; The Void, 2007; Antimatter, 2009; Neutrino, 2010; The Infinity Puzzle, 2012; Half-Life, 2015; Eclipse, 2017; Theories of Everything, 2017; Trinity, 2019; numerous res. papers on theoretical physics, and articles on science in The Guardian. *Recreations:* writing, singing, travel, Real tennis, chasing solar eclipses. *Address:* Exeter College, Oxford OX1 3DP. *Club:* Radley College Real Tennis.

**CLOSE, Glenn;** actress; *b* 19 March 1947; *d* of William and Bettine Close; *m* 1st, 1969, Cabot Wade (marr. diss.); 2nd, 1984, James Marlas (marr. diss.); 3rd, 2006, David Shaw; one *d* by John Starke. *Educ:* William and Mary Coll. (BA 1974). With New Phoenix Repertory Co., 1974–75; *theatre* includes: New York: Love for Love, 1974; A Streetcar Named Desire; The Crucifer of Blood, 1978–79; Barnum, 1980–81; The Real Thing, 1984 (Tony Award); Benefactors, 1986; Death and the Maiden, 1992 (Tony Award); Sunset Boulevard, LA, 1993–94, NY, 1994–95 (Tony Award), ENO, 2016; A Streetcar Named Desire, NT, 2002; A Delicate Balance, NY, 2014; *films* include: The World According to Garp, 1982; The Natural, 1984; Fatal Attraction, 1987; Dangerous Liaisons, 1989; Hamlet, 1991; The House of Spirits, 1994; Serving in Silence: the Margarethe Cammermeyer story, 1995; Air Force One, 1997; Paradise Road, 1997; Cookie's Fortune, 1999; Things You Can Just Tell by Looking at Her, 2000; 102 Dalmatians, 2000; The Safety of Objects, 2003; The Stepford Wives, 2004; The Chumscrubber, Evening, 2007; Albert Nobbs, 2012 (also prod. and co-writer); The Girl with All the Gifts, 2016; The Wife, 2018 (Golden Globe and Screen Actors Guild awards for Best Actress, 2019); numerous TV appearances incl. The Shield (series), 2005; Damages (series), 2007–12; Agatha Christie's Crooked House, 2017. *Address:* c/o CAA, 2000 Avenue of the Stars, Los Angeles, CA 90067, USA.

**CLOSE, James Russell;** chef owner, Raby Hunt restaurant, since 2009 (one Michelin star, 2012; two Michelin stars, 2016); *b* Bishop Auckland, 17 Oct. 1979; *s* of Russell Close and Helene Close; one *d*. *Educ:* Barnard Castle Sch. *Recreations:* golf, eating in Michelin star restaurants around the world. *Address:* c/o Raby Hunt Restaurant, Summerhouse, Darlington, Co. Durham DL2 3UD.

**CLOSE, Seamus Anthony,** OBE 1996; Member (Alliance) Lagan Valley, Northern Ireland Assembly, 1998–2007; *b* 12 Aug. 1947; *s* of late James and of Kathleen Close; *m* 1978, Deirdre McCann; three *s* one *d*. *Educ:* St Malachy's Coll.; Belfast Coll. of Business Studies. Company Sec., 1970–85; Financial Dir, 1985–2017. Mem. (Alliance), Lisburn CC (formerly Lisburn BC), 1973–2011 (Mayor, 1993–94); Mem. (Alliance) NI Assembly, 1982–86; Negotiator: Brooke/Mayhew Talks, 1991–92; Good Friday Agreement, 1998. Dep. Leader, Alliance Party, 1991–2001. Contested (Alliance): Fermanagh and S Tyrone, Aug. 1981; S Antrim, 1983; Lagan Valley, 1987, 1992, 1997, 2001, 2005. Chm., Lisburn City Dist Policing Partnership, 2005–06. Freedom, City of Lisburn, 2010. *Recreations:* sports, family, current affairs. *Address:* 123 Moira Road, Lisburn, Northern Ireland BT28 1RJ. *T:* (028) 9267 0639.

**CLOTHIER, Richard John;** Chairman, Aqua Bounty Technologies plc, since 2006; *b* 4 July 1945; *s* of J. Neil Clothier and Barbara Clothier; *m* 1st, 1972, Ingrid Hafner (*d* 1994); two *s*; 2nd, 1995, Sarah (*née* Riley). *Educ:* Peterhouse, Zimbabwe; Univ. of Natal (BSc Agric.); Harvard (AMP). Milk Marketing Board, 1971–77; Dalgety Agriculture, 1977–88; Chief Executive: Pig Improvement Co., 1988–92; Dalgety plc, 1993–97; Plantation & Gen. Investments, later PGI Gp, 1998–2005; Director: Granada Gp, 1996–2004; PGI Gp, 2005–06; Chairman: Robinson plc, 2004–18; Spearhead Internat. Ltd, 2005–15; Exosect Ltd, 2012–15. *Publications:* The Bundu Book, 1969. *Recreations:* yacht racing, field sports, painting and drawing. *Address:* 19 Broomhouse Road, SW6 3QU. *T:* 07771 644962. *Clubs:* Farmers, Royal Thames Yacht, Royal Ocean Racing.

**CLOTHIER, Rosemary Harriet;** *see* Millard, R. H.

**CLOUDER, Fiona Jennifer;** HM Diplomatic Service; Ambassador to Chile, 2014–18. *Educ:* University Coll. London (BSc Human Sci. and Neurosci. 1985); Henley Mgt Coll. (Dip. Mgt). Science and Engineering Research Council: Cttee Sec., Physical Sci., 1985–88; Co-ordinator, Manufg Engrg, 1988–91; Private Sec. to Chm. and Chief Exec., 1991–94; Dep. Hd, Internat. Relns, BBSRC, 1994–96; Hd, UK Office, UK Res. Office, Brussels, 1996–97; Hd, Internat. Relns, 1997–2001, Hd of Strategy, 2001, BBSRC; entered FCO, 2001; Dep. Hd, Sci. and Technol., 2001–02, Hd, Sci. and Innovation, 2002–06, FCO; Dir, Corporate Services, New Delhi, 2006–09; Dep. Dir, 2009–11, Actg Dir, 2011, Migration, FCO; Dep. Dir, Americas and Hd, S America Dept, FCO, 2011–13. *Address:* c/o Foreign and Commonwealth Office, King Charles Street, SW1A 2AH.

**CLOUGH, Christopher George,** FRCP; Consultant Neurologist, King's College Hospital, since 1995; Chairman, National Clinical Advisory Team; *b* 30 Aug. 1953; *s* of George and Daisy Clough; *m* 1979, Lyn Sylvia Griffiths; two *s* one *d*. *Educ:* Manchester Univ. (MB ChB). FRCP 1992. Royal Alexandra Hosp., Rhyl, 1975–76; Hull Royal Infirmary, 1976–79; Leeds Gen. Infirmary, 1979–80; Mount Sinai Med. Centre, 1980–81; Queen Elizabeth Med. Centre, Birmingham, and Midlands Centre for Neurology and Neurosurgery, Smethwick, 1981–89; Cons. Neurologist, Brook Regl Neuroscience Centre and Bromley Hosps, 1989–95; Dir, Regl Neurosci Centre, 1991–98; Med. Dir, KCH, 1998–2003; Chief Med. Advr, SE London Strategic HA, 2003–06; Dir, Jt Cttee on Higher Med. Trng, RCP, later RCP Trng Bd, 2005–08. Hon. Sen. Lectr, KCL, Neurology Advr, DoH. Member: Fabian Soc.; Labour Party. *Publications:* pubns on Parkinson's Disease, headache and restless legs. *Recreations:* tennis, music, lifelong Spurs fan. *Address:* 66 Graystone Road, Whitstable CT5 2JU.

**CLOUGH, Mark Gerard;** QC 1999; Senior Counsel, Dentons Europe LLP, Brussels, since 2014; independent consultant, since 2014; *b* 13 May 1953; *s* of late Philip Gerard Clough and of Mary Elizabeth Clough (*née* Carter); one *d*; *m* 1989, Joanne Elizabeth Dishington; two *s*. *Educ:* Ampleforth Coll.; St Andrews Univ. (MA 1976). Called to the Bar, Gray's Inn, 1978; admitted Solicitor, 1995, Scotland, 2013; Solicitor Advocate, 1996; Partner: Ashurst Morris Crisp, then Ashurst, 1995–2006; Addleshaw Goddard, 2006–10; Brodies LLP, 2011–13. CEDR Accredited Mediator, 2016. Chm., Solicitors Assoc. of Higher Ct Advocates, 2003–06; Member: Adv. Bd, British Inst. of Internat. and Comparative Law Competition Law Forum, 2003–10; Bd, European Maritime Law Orgn, 2004–; Scottish

Competition Law Forum, 2011–. Owner, Wynd Th., Melrose, 2009–15. Trustee: Slynn Foundn, 1997–; Camden People's Th., 2000–; Melrose Arts Trust, 2009–15. Mem., Editl Bd, Internat. Trade Law and Regulation Jl, 1996–. *Publications:* EC Competition Law and Shipping, 1990; EC Merger Regulation, 1995; (contrib.) Vaughan's Laws of the European Communities, 1997; Trade and Telecoms, 2002; (ed) Collective Dominance: the contribution of the Community Courts, 2003; (contrib.) A True European—essays for Judge David Edward, 2004; articles on EU Law and competition law. *Recreations:* theatre, poetry, shooting, tennis, golf. *Club:* New (Edinburgh).

**CLOUGH, Susanna Patricia;** *see* FitzGerald, S. P.

**CLOUT, Prof. Hugh Donald,** PhD, DLit; FBA 1997; Professor of Geography, University College London, 1987–2007, now Emeritus; *b* 29 April 1944; *s* of Donald Clout and Florence (*née* Allwood). *Educ:* University College London (BA, MPhil, PhD 1979, DLit 2000); Univ. de Paris I (Dr de l'Université 1983). Lectr, 1967–81, Reader, 1981–87, in Geography, UCL. Fellow, UCL, 2008. Hon. Dr Geog. Paris IV, 2004. *Publications:* (ed) Regional Development in Western Europe, 1975, 3rd edn 1987; (ed) Themes in the Historical Geography of France, 1977; Agriculture in France on the Eve of the Railway Age, 1980; The Land of France 1815–1914, 1982; (ed) Western Europe: geographical perspectives, 1985, 3rd edn 1994; (ed) Times London History Atlas, 1991, 5th edn, as The Times History of London, 2007; After the Ruins: restoring the countryside of northern France after the Great War, 1996; (ed) Contemporary Rural Geographies, 2007; Patronage and the Production of Geographical Knowledge in France, 2009. *Address:* Department of Geography, University College London, Gower Street, WC1E 6BT.

**CLOVER, (Anne) Sarah;** Partner specialising in lawyers' professional liability, regulation and discipline, Clyde & Co. LLP (formerly Barlow Lyde & Gilbert), since 1989; *b* London, 9 Sept. 1958; *d* of John Pinder and Sheila Pinder (*née* Keogh); *m* 1993, Anthony Clover; three *d*. *Educ:* St Leonards-Mayfield Sch.; University Coll. London (LLB 1981). Admitted as solicitor, 1983. Mem. Cttee, City of London Law Soc. *Address:* Clyde & Co. LLP, St Botolph Building, 138 Houndsditch, EC3A 7AR. *T:* (020) 7876 5000. *E:* Sarah.Clover@clydeco.com.

**CLOW, Sarah Jane;** *see* Mitchell, S. J.

**CLOWES, Alfred William;** General Secretary, Ceramic and Allied Trades Union, 1980–95; *b* 17 Dec. 1931. Joined the Industry on leaving school; Asst Gen. Sec., Ceramic and Allied Trades Union, 1975–80. Hon. Freeman, City of Stoke-on-Trent, 1995. *Address:* 22 Meadow Avenue, Wetley Rocks, Stoke-on-Trent ST9 0BD.

**CLUCKIE, Prof. Ian David,** FREng, FCIWEM; FICE; Pro-Vice-Chancellor (Science and Engineering), Swansea University, 2008–15, now Emeritus Professor of Engineering; *b* Edinburgh, 20 July 1949; *m* 1972; one *s* one *d*. *Educ:* Univ. of Surrey (BSc); Univ. of Birmingham (MSc, PhD). CEng, FREng (FEng 1997); FIWEM 1983; FICE 1988; FRMetS 1979. W. S. Atkins, Swansea, 1966–72; Central Water Planning Unit, Reading, 1974–76; Lectr, Univ. of Birmingham, 1976–88; Salford University: Prof. of Water Resources, 1988–97; Chm., Dept of Civil Engrg, 1991–96; Dir, Telford Res. Inst., 1993–94, 1996–97; Acad. Dir, Salford Civil Engineering Ltd, 1989–97; Prof. of Hydrology and Water Mgt, and Dir, Water and Envmtl Mgt Res. Centre, Bristol Univ., 1997–2007. Visiting Professor: Sun Yat-Sen Univ., 2004–; Anhui Univ., 2014–; Hohai Univ., 2014; Vis. Chair, Nat. Inst. of Hydraulic Res., Nanjing, 2012–. Natural Environment Research Council: Mem., AAPS Res. Grants and Trng Awards Cttee, 1988–91; Chm., AAPS Cttee, 1991–94; Mem., Terrestrial and Freshwater Scis, Marine Scis, Atmospheric Scis and Higher Educn Affairs Cttees, 1991–94; Chm., EPSRC Flood Risk Mgt Res. Consortium, 2004–12. Chm., UK IAHS Cttee, 2006–12; Pres., Internat. Commn on Remote Sensing, IAHS, 2009–14. FRSA 1993. For. Academician, Chinese Acad. of Engrg, 2015. Friendship Award (China), 2015. *Publications:* (with C. G. Collier) Hydrological Applications of Weather Radar, 1991; (jtly) Radar Hydrology for Real-time Flood Forecasting, 2001; contribs to learned jls. *Recreations:* sailing, hill walking.

**CLUFF, Blondel Bernadette Rosceilia,** CBE 2018; Chief Executive, West India Committee, since 2010 (Fellow, 2013); Representative of Anguilla to the United Kingdom and European Union, since 2016 and Special Adviser to the Chief Minister; *b* Farnham Common, Bucks, 29 May 1960; *d* of late Joseph Hodge and Cora Hodge; *m* 1993, John Gordon, (Algy), Cluff, *qv*; three *s*. *Educ:* Sir William Herschel Grammar Sch.; Westminster Univ. (LLB Hons). Admitted solicitor, England and Wales, 1983; Asst Co. Solicitor and Sec., Gulf + Western (Associates Capital), 1983–86; Hd, Legal Dept, and Asst Co. Sec., Lazard Bros and Co. Ltd, 1986–93. Chair, London and SE Cttee, NLHF, 2019– (Chair, London Cttee, HLF, 2014–19); Mem., Adv. Cttee, 2014–; Themes Selection Sub-Cttee, 2014–, Royal Mint. Trustee: Prince's Trust, 2016–; Prince's Trust Internat., 2016–19. Freeman, City of London, 2016; Liveryman, Goldsmiths' Co., 2018. FKC 2012; FRSA 2017. Diamond Jubilee Medal, 2012. *Publications:* (with Alexander Marshall) 100 Things You Didn't Know About the Caribbean, 2015; (with David Wells) The Caribbean's Great War, 2016; 50 Things You Didn't Know About Anguilla, 2018. *Recreations:* family, reading, writing, travel, heritage, music, collecting art and antiques, farming. *Address:* c/o West India Committee, Suite 53, 4 Whitehall Court, SW1A 2EL. *T:* (020) 7799 5441. *E:* blondelcluff@westindiacommittee.org. *Clubs:* Royal Yacht Squadron, Turf, Farmers.

**CLUFF, John Gordon, (Algy),** OBE 2017; DL; Chairman, Cluff Natural Resources plc, 2012–19 (Chief Executive, 2012–18); Chairman: Cluff Geothermal, 2009–14; The Spectator, 1985–2005 (Proprietor, 1981–85); *b* 19 April 1940; *o s* of late Harold Cluff and Freda Cluff, Waldeshare House, Waldeshare, Kent; *m* 1993, Blondel Bernadette Rosceilia Hodge (*see* B. B. R. Cluff); three *s*. *Educ:* Stowe Sch. 2/Lieut, Grenadier Guards, 1959; Captain, Guards Independent Parachute Co., 1963; served W Africa, Cyprus, Malaysia, retd 1965. Founded Cluff Oil, subseq. Cluff Resources, 1971, Chief Exec., 1971, Chm., 1979; founded Cluff Mining, 1996, Chm., 1996–2004, Chief Exec., 1996–2003; founded Cluff Gold, 2004, Chief Exec., 2004–10, Exec. Chm., 2004–11, non-exec. Chm., 2011–12. Contested (C) Ardwick Div. of Manchester, 1966. Chm., Cons. Commn on the Commonwealth, 2000. A Dir, Centre for Policy Studies, 1998–2005. Governor: Commonwealth Inst., 1994–2009; Stowe Sch., 1998–2010. Chm., Nat. Army Mus. Foundn, 2013–15; Mem. Council, Nat. Army Mus., 2013–15; Pres., ATC, Kent, 2007–; Vice Pres., Army Benevolent Fund, Kent, 2007–. Trustee, Stowe House Preservation Trust, 1999–2011; Chm. Trustees, War Memorials Trust, 2003–14; Trustee, Commonwealth Educn Trust, 2009–15; Founder Trustee, Remembrance Trust, 2018–. Hon. Col, 3rd Bn, Princess of Wales's Royal Regt, 2010–. DL Kent, 2009. Chevalier de l'Ordre Nat. (Burkina Faso), 2009. *Publications:* Get On With It (memoirs), 2016; Unsung Heroes, 2018; By The Way…, 2019. *Clubs:* White's, Beefsteak, Brooks's, Pratt's; Royal Yacht Squadron; Brook, Racquet and Tennis (New York).

**CLUNAS, Prof. Craig,** PhD; FBA 2004; Professor of the History of Art, University of Oxford, 2007–18, now Professor Emeritus; Fellow of Trinity College, Oxford, 2007, now Honorary Fellow; *b* 1 Dec. 1954; *s* of Charles Clunas and Elizabeth Clunas (*née* Robertson); one *s*. *Educ:* Aberdeen Grammar Sch.; King's Coll., Cambridge (BA 1st cl. (Chinese Studies) 1977); SOAS, Univ. of London (PhD 1983). Res. Asst, Far Eastern Dept, 1979–93, Sen. Res. Fellow in Chinese Studies, 1993–94, V&A Mus.; Sen. Lectr in Hist. of Art, 1994–97, Prof. of Hist. of Art, 1997–2003, Univ. of Sussex; Percival David Prof. of Chinese and East Asian Art, SOAS, Univ. of London, 2003–07. A. W. Mellon Lectr in Fine Arts, Center for Advanced Study in Visual Arts, Nat. Gall. of Art, Washington, DC, 2012. MAE 2013. Hon. DLitt Warwick, 2010. *Publications:* Chinese Export Watercolours, 1984; Chinese Furniture, 1989; Superfluous Things: social status and material culture in Early Modern China, 1991; Fruitful Sites: garden culture in Ming Dynasty China, 1996; Art in China, 1997; Pictures and Visuality in Early Modern China, 1997; Elegant Debts: the social art of Wen Zhengming, 2004; Empire of Great Brightness: visual and material cultures of Ming China, 2007; Screen of Kings: royal art and power in Ming China, 2013; Ming: 50 years that changed China, 2014; Chinese Painting and its Audiences, 2017; numerous articles in learned jls. *Address:* History of Art Department, Littlegate House, St Ebbe's, Oxford OX1 1PT. *E:* craig.clunas@hoa.ox.ac.uk.

**CLUNES, (Alexander) Martin,** OBE 2015; DL; actor; *b* 28 Nov. 1961; *s* of late Alec Sheriff de Moro Clunes and Daphne (*née* Acott); *m* 1st, Lucy Aston (marr. diss. 1993); 2nd, 1997, Philippa Braithwaite; one *d*. Founder: Big Arts, 1990; Buffalo, prodn co. *Theatre includes:* The Henrys, ESC; The Admirable Crichton, Th. Royal, Haymarket; Much Ado About Nothing, Julius Caesar, Open Air Th., Regent's Park; Party Tricks, Nottingham Playhouse (dir), 1995; Tartuffe, NT, 2002. *Television includes:* No Place Like Home, 1983; All At Number 20, 1986; Men Behaving Badly, 1991–98; Jeeves and Wooster, 1991; If You See God, Tell Him, 1993; Demob, 1993; Harry Enfield and Chums, 1994; An Evening with Gary Lineker, 1994; Born to Be Wild, 1999; Gormenghast, 2000; Men Down Under, 2000; Lorna Doone, 2000; William and Mary, 2003; Doc Martin, 2004, 2005, 2007, 2009, 2011, 2013, 2015, 2017, 2019; Reggie Perrin, 2009; A Mother's Son, The Town, 2012; Arthur and George, 2015; Vanity Fair, 2018; Manhunt, Warren, 2019; presenter: Martin Clunes: The Lemurs of Madagascar, 2012; Islands of Australia, 2017; Islands of America, 2019; My Travels and Other Animals, 2019; *television films:* Over Here, 1996; Neville's Island, 1998; Touch and Go, 1998; Hunting Venus (also dir), 1999; Sex 'n' Death, 1999; Dirty Tricks, 2000; A is for Acid, 2002; Goodbye Mr Chips, 2002; Beauty, 2004. *Films:* The Russia House, 1990; Carry on Columbus, 1992; Swing Kids, 1993; Staggered (also dir), 1994; Sweet Revenge, 1998; Shakespeare in Love, 1998; The Acid House, 1998; Saving Grace, 2000; Global Heresy, 2002. DL Dorset, 2019.

**CLUNIES ROSS, Prof. Margaret Beryl, (Mrs J. R. Green);** McCaughey Professor of English Language and Early English Literature, 1990–2007, now Emeritus, and Honorary Professor, Medieval and Early Modern Studies Centre (formerly Centre for Medieval Studies), since 2009, University of Sydney; Adjunct Professor, School of Humanities, University of Adelaide, since 2015; President, National Academies Forum, 1998; *b* 24 April 1942; *d* of Ernest Phillips Tidemann and Beryl Chudleigh Tidemann (*née* Birch); *m* 1st, 1964, Bruce Axel Clunies Ross; 2nd, 1971, Lester Richard Hiatt; one *s* one *d*; 3rd, 1990, John Richard Green. *Educ:* Walford Girls' Grammar Sch., Adelaide; Univ. of Adelaide (BA Hons 1963); Somerville Coll., Oxford (MA 1970; BLitt 1973). George Murray Overseas Scholar, Univ. of Adelaide at Somerville Coll., Oxford, 1963–65; Lectr in Medieval English Lang. and Lit., St Hilda's Coll. and LMH, Oxford, 1965–68; Alice B. Horsman Travelling Fellow, Somerville Coll., Oxford, at Arnamagnaean Inst. for Icelandic Studies, Copenhagen Univ., 1968–69; University of Sydney: Lectr, Dept of Early Eng. Lit. and Lang., 1969–73; Sen. Lectr, English Dept, 1974–83; Associate Prof., 1984–90; Head, Dept of English, 1993–94; Dir, Centre for Medieval Studies, 1997–2007. Vis. Mem., Linacre Coll., Oxford and Hon. Res. Associate, UCL, 1979–80; Guest researcher, Univ. of Munich, 1986–87; Vis. Scholar, Univ. of N Carolina, Chapel Hill, 1991–92; Visiting Professor: McMaster Univ., Ont and Vis. Scholar, Pontifical Inst. of Mediaeval Studies, Toronto, 1995; Centre for Medieval Studies, Univ. of Bergen, 2011; Exchange scholar, Kungl. Vitterhetsakademien, Sweden 1996; Quatercentenary Vis. Fellow, Emmanuel Coll., Cambridge, 1997; Vis. Scholar, Humboldt Univ., Berlin, 2002–03; Vis. Fellow, All Souls Coll., Oxford, 2003; Hon. Res. Associate, Dept of Anglo-Saxon, Norse and Celtic, Univ. of Cambridge, 2011–14. Mem., Australian Res. Council, 1995–97. Mem., Nat. Bd of Employment, Educn and Trng, 1995–97. Pres., Aust. Acad. of Humanities, 1995–98. Fellow, Royal Gustavus Adolphus Acad., Uppsala, 2001. Hon. DPhil Göteborg Univ., 2000. Centenary Medal, Commonwealth of Australia, 2003. Kt, Order of the Falcon (Iceland), 2018. *Film:* (jtly) Waiting for Harry, 1980 (1st Prize, RAI film comp., 1982). *Publications:* (with S. A. Wild) Djambidj: an Aboriginal song series from Northern Australia, 1982; (ed jtly) Songs of Aboriginal Australia, 1987; Skáldskaparmál: Snorri Sturluson's ars poetica and medieval theories of language, 1987; (with J. Mundrugmundrug) Goyulan the Morning Star: an Aboriginal clan song series from North Central Arnhem Land, 1988; Prolonged Echoes: Old Norse myths in Medieval northern society, Vol. 1: The Myths, 1994; Vol. 2: The Reception of Myth in Medieval Iceland, 1998; (ed jtly) Old Norse Studies in the New World, 1994; The Norse Muse in Britain 1750–1820, 1998; (ed) Old Icelandic Literature and Society, 2000; The Old Norse Poetic Translations of Thomas Percy, 2001; (ed) Old Norse Myths, Literature and Society, 2003; (ed jtly) The Correspondence of Edward Lye, 2004; A History of Old Norse Poetry and Poetics, 2005; (ed) Skaldic Poetry of the Scandinavian Middle Ages, vol. 7: poetry on Christian subjects (2 parts), 2007, vol. 8: poetry in Fornaldarsögur (2 parts), 2017; The Cambridge Introduction to the Old Norse-Icelandic Saga, 2010; (ed with Jonas Wellendorf) The Fourth Grammatical Treatise, 2014; (ed) The Pre-Christian Religions of the North: research and reception, vol. 1: From the Middle Ages to c. 1830, 2017, vol. II: From c. 1830 to the Present, 2019; contrib. numerous articles in learned jls and chapters in books of essays. *Recreations:* family history, walking, visiting children and grandchildren. *Address:* PO Box 7319, Hutt Street, Adelaide, SA 5000, Australia.

**CLUTTERBUCK, Andrew Maurice Gray;** QC 2014. *Educ:* Worth Sch.; Lincoln Coll., Oxford (BA). Served RM, 1986–90. Called to the Bar: Middle Temple, 1992. *Address:* 4 Stone Buildings, Lincoln's Inn, WC2A 3XT. *Club:* Buck's.

**CLUTTON, James Charles;** Director of Opera, and Producer, Opera Holland Park, since 2000; *b* London, 18 Jan. 1966; *s* of Ernest James Clutton and Margaret Rose Clutton; *m* 2007, Angela Edwards. *Educ:* St Francis de Sales, Tottenham; St Ignatius Coll., Enfield. Ind. theatre producer, London, 1995–97; Associate Producer: Bill Kenwright Ltd, 1998–2000; UNICEF Fest., Kosovo, 1999. Producer of over 120 operatic prodns; commnd and produced Alice's Adventures in Wonderland, over 90 perfs incl. at Royal Opera House; producer, Verdi Requiem for Grenfell, 2017. Compositions include: Oscar (musical, co-written with Damian Landi), 1995; Great Things (Thomas Hardy poem set to music), 1997. Outstanding Achievement in Opera award, Internat. Inst. of Dance and Theatre, 2015; Internat. Opera Award, 2018; Broadway World Award, 2018. *Recreations:* running (London Marathon, 2012), mixology, 'The West Wing', The Beatles, Bob Dylan, painting, walking in Lake District, family history, Tottenham Hotspur FC. *Address:* Opera Holland Park, 37 Pembroke Road, W8 6PW. *E:* james.clutton@operahollandpark.com.

**CLUTTON-BROCK, Prof. Timothy Hugh,** PhD; ScD; FRS 1993; Prince Philip Professor of Ecology and Evolutionary Biology, University of Cambridge, 2007–14, Director of Research, since 2014 (Professor of Animal Ecology, 1994–2007); *b* 13 Aug. 1946; *s* of Hugh Alan Clutton-Brock and late Eileen Mary Stableforth; *m* 1980, Dafila Kathleen Scott; one *s* one *d*. *Educ:* Rugby Sch.; Magdalene Coll., Cambridge (BA, MA,

PhD, ScD). NERC res. fellowship, Animal Behaviour Res. Gp, Oxford, 1972; Lectr in Ethology, Univ. of Sussex, 1973; Cambridge University: Sen. Res. Fellow in Behavioural Ecology, King's Coll., 1976; SERC Advanced Fellow, Dept of Zoology, 1981; Royal Soc. Res. Fellow in Biology, 1983; Lectr in Zoology, 1987–91; Reader in Animal Ecology, 1991–94. Extraordinary Prof., Mammal Res. Inst., Univ. of Pretoria, 2000; Hon. Prof., Univ. of Exeter, 2011. Chm., IUCN Deer Specialist Gp, 1980–90. Jt Editor, Princeton Monographs in Behavioral Ecology, 1982–. Hon. Mem., Amer. Soc. of Mammalogists, 2009. Hon. Dr: Zurich, 2013; Pretoria, 2013. Scientific Medal, 1984, Frink Medal, 1998, Zoological Soc. of London; Hart Merriam Award, Mammal Soc. of America, 1991; Marsh Award, British Ecol Soc., 1998; William Bate Hardy Prize, Cambridge Philosophical Soc., 1999; Darwin Medal, Royal Soc., 2013; Assoc. for Study of Animal Behaviour Medal 2014. *Publications:* (ed) Primate Ecology, 1977; (ed) Readings in Sociobiology, 1978; Red Deer: the behaviour and ecology of two sexes, 1982; (ed) Rhum, Natural History of an Island, 1987; (ed) Reproductive Success, 1988; Red Deer in the Highlands, 1989; The Evolution of Parental Care, 1991; Meerkat Manor: flower of the Kalahari, 2007; Mammal Societies, 2016; approx. 380 sci. papers on animal behaviour, ecology and evolution in Nature, Jl Animal Ecol., Evolution, Amer. Naturalist, Jl of Zoology, Animal Behaviour, Behaviour, Behavioral Ecol. and Sociobiol., Folia Primatologica and other jls. *Recreations:* bird watching, fish watching, fishing. *Address:* Department of Zoology, Downing Street, Cambridge CB2 3EJ. *T:* (01223) 336618.

**CLWYD**, 4th Baron *cr* 1919, of Abergele, co. Denbigh; **John Murray Roberts**; Bt 1908; *b* 27 Aug. 1971; *e s* of 3rd Baron Clwyd and of Geraldine (*née* Cannons); *S* father, 2006; *m* 2004, Lea-Anne Margaret Henry; one *s* one *d*. *Heir: s* Hon. John David Roberts, *b* 16 June 2006.

**CLWYD**, Rt Hon. Ann; PC 2004; MP (Lab) Cynon Valley, since May 1984; journalist and broadcaster; *b* 21 March 1937; *d* of Gwilym Henri Lewis and Elizabeth Ann Lewis; *m* 1963, Owen Dryhurst Roberts (*d* 2012), TV director and producer. *Educ:* Halkyn Primary Sch.; Holywell Grammar Sch.; The Queen's Sch., Chester; University Coll., Bangor. Former: Student-teacher, Hope Sch., Flintshire; BBC Studio Manager; freelance reporter, producer; Welsh corresp., The Guardian and The Observer, 1964–79; Vice-Chm., Welsh Arts Council, 1975–79. Member: Welsh Hospital Board, 1970–74; Cardiff Community Health Council, 1975–79; Royal Commn on NHS, 1976–79; Working Party, report, Organisation of Out-Patient Care, for Welsh Hosp. Bd; Working Party, Bilingualism in the Hospital Service; Labour Party Study Gp, People and the Media; Arts Council of Gt Britain, 1975–80; Labour Party NEC, 1983–84; PLP Exec., 1997–2006 (Vice Chm., 2001–05; Chm., 2005–06); Chm., Cardiff Anti-Racialism Cttee, 1978–80. Chm., Labour back bench cttee on Health and Social Security, 1985–87; Vice-Chm., Labour back bench cttee on Defence, 1985–87; Opposition front bench spokesperson on women, 1987–88, on educn, 1987–88, on overseas develt and co-operation, 1989–92, on Wales, 1992, on Nat. Heritage, 1992–93, on employment, 1993–94, on foreign affairs, 1994–95. Member: Shadow Cabinet, 1989–93; Select Cttee on Internat. Develt, 1997–2005, on Foreign Affairs, 2010–. Chm., All Party Gp on Human Rights, 1997–; Special Envoy to the Prime Minister on Human Rights in Iraq, 2003–10; apptd by the Prime Minister to lead review into NHS, 2013. Chair, Indict, 2003–. Member: NUJ; TGWU. Contested (Lab): Denbigh, 1970; Gloucester, Oct. 1974; Mem. (Lab) Mid and West Wales, European Parlt, 1979–84. Hon. Fellow: Univ. of Wales, Bangor; N Wales Inst. of Higher Educn. Hon. Dr Wales; Hon. LLD Trinity Coll., Carmarthen. White Robe, Gorsedd of Bards, Nat. Eisteddfod of Wales, 1991. Backbencher of the Year, House Magazine and Spectator Parly Awards, 2003; Campaigning MP of the Year, Channel 4 Political Awards, 2003. *Address:* (office) 4th Floor, Crown Buildings, Aberdare, Mid Glam CF44 7HU. *T:* (01685) 871394.

**CLYDE**, Joseph; *see* Walden, G. G. H.

**CLYDESMUIR**, 3rd Baron *cr* 1948, of Braidwood, co. Lanark; **David Ronald Colville**; *b* 8 April 1949; *e s* of 2nd Baron Clydesmuir, KT, CB, MBE, TD and Joan Marguerita, *d* of late Lt-Col E. B. Booth, DSO; *S* father, 1996; *m* 1978, Aline Frances, *er d* of Peter Merriam; two *s* two *d*. *Educ:* Charterhouse. Dir, BDB Ltd, Lloyd's Brokers, 2001–. *Heir: s* Hon. Richard Colville, *b* 21 Oct. 1980. *Address:* 40 Ritherdon Road, SW17 8QF.

**COACKLEY, Richard James**, CBE 2014; CEng; FICE; FCIWEM; Director: URS Corporation Ltd, 2012–14; AECOM Infrastructure & Environment UK Ltd, 2014–17, Independent Adviser, since 2017; President, Institution of Civil Engineers, 2011–12; Chair, Reservoirs Panel, Institution of Civil Engineers, since 2019; *b* Hexham, Northumberland, 8 Dec. 1954; *s* of Dr Peter Coackley and Marion Coackley; *m* 1978, Isabella Margaret Christina McArthur; two *s*. *Educ:* Bearsden Acad.; Univ. of Glasgow (BSc 1st Cl. Hons Civil Engrg). CEng 1980; FICE 1998; FCIWEM (CWEM 1998). Vice Pres., Binnie Black & Veatch, 1975–2000; Director: Mouchel Parkman, 2000–06; White Young Green, 2006–10; Scott Wilson, 2010–12. Chm., CEEQUAL Ltd, 2013–15. Chairman: Nuclear Construction Best Practice Forum, 2012–17; Smoothing Financial Cyclicality in the Water Industry AMP Cycle, 2012–17. Pres., British Section, Société des Ingénieurs et Scientifiques de France, 2019–Feb. 2020; UK Nat. Mem. Rep., WFEO, 2019–. Freeman: Water Conservators' Co., 1999; City of London, 2000. Mem., Smeatonian Soc. of Civil Engrs, 2014. *Recreations:* sailing, vine growing, double bass playing. *Address:* Institution of Civil Engineers, One Great George Street, Westminster, SW1P 3AA. *T:* 07753 628126. *E:* coackleyrj@gmail.com.

**COAD**, Emma D.; *see* Dent Coad.

**COADY, Frances Rachel**; Literary Agent, Aragi Inc., since 2015; *b* 16 June 1958; *d* of Matthew and Patricia Coady; *m* 2007, Peter Philip Carey, *qv*. *Educ:* Streatham Hill and Clapham High Sch.; Bromley High Sch.; Univ. of Sussex (BA Hons English Lit. 1980); Univ. of Essex (MA English Lit. 1981). Faber and Faber, 1982–86, Sen. Non-Fiction Commng Editor, 1983–86; Researcher for Alan Yentob, Head of Dept of Music and Arts, BBC TV, 1986; Random House, 1986–95: Editl Dir, Jonathan Cape, 1986–89; Founder Publisher, Vintage Paperbacks, 1989–93; Publisher, overseeing Jonathan Cape, Chatto & Windus, Pimlico and Vintage, 1993–95; Publisher, Granta Books, 1995–99; Vice-Pres. and Publisher, Picador USA, 2000–12; Editor At Large, Macmillan, 2007–12; Pres. and Publisher, Atavist Books, 2012–15. *Recreations:* looking at art, theatre, cinema, reading.

**COAKER, Vernon Rodney**; MP (Lab) Gedling, since 1997; *b* 17 June 1953; *s* of Edwin Coaker; *m* 1978, Jacqueline Heaton; one *s* one *d*. *Educ:* Drayton Manor Grammar Sch., London; Warwick Univ. (BA Hons); Trent Poly. (PGCE). Hist. Teacher, Manvers Pierrepont Sch., 1976–82; Hd of Dept, Arnold Hill Sch., 1982–88; Sen. Teacher, Bramcote Pk Sch., 1989–95; Dep. Headteacher, Big Wood Sch., 1995–97. Mem., Rushcliffe BC, 1983–97 (Leader, 1987–97). PPS to Minister of State for Social Security, 1999, to Financial Sec. to HM Treasury, 1999–2001, to Minister of State (Minister for School Standards), DfES, 2001–02, to Sec. of State for Culture, Media and Sport, 2002–03; an Asst Govt Whip, 2003–05; a Lord Comr of HM Treasury (Govt Whip), 2005–06; Parly Under-Sec. of State, 2006–08, Minister of State, 2008–09, Home Office; Minister of State (Minister for Schs and Learners), DCSF, 2009–10; Shadow Sec. of State for NI, 2011–13, 2015–16, for Defence, 2013–15. Contested (Lab): Rushcliffe, 1983; Gedling, 1987, 1992. *Address:* House of Commons, SW1A 0AA.

**COAKLEY, Rev. Canon Prof. Sarah Anne**, FBA 2019; Norris-Hulse Professor of Divinity, University of Cambridge, 2007–18 (Deputy Chair, Arts and Humanities, 2011–14); Fellow, Murray Edwards College (formerly New Hall), 2007–18, now Emeritus; *b* 10 Sept. 1951; *d* of late (Frank) Robert Furber and Anne Wilson Furber; *m* 1975, Dr James Farwell Coakley; two *d*. *Educ:* Blackheath High Sch.; New Hall, Cambridge (BA 1973; MA, PhD 1983); Harvard Divinity Sch. (ThM 1975). Harkness Fellow, 1973–75; Univ. Lectr in Religious Studies, 1976–90, Sen. Lectr, 1990–91, Lancaster Univ.; Tutorial Fellow in Theology, Oriel Coll., and Univ. Lectr in Theology, Oxford, 1991–93; Prof. of Christian Theology, 1993–95, Edward Mallinckrodt, Jr, Prof. of Divinity, 1995–2007, Vis. Prof. of Systematic and Philosophical Theology, 2007–08, Harvard Univ. Vis. Professorial Fellow, Princeton Univ., 2003–04; Hon. Prof., Univ. of St Andrews, 2018–20; Professorial Fellow, Australian Catholic Univ., Melbourne, 2019–. Select Preacher, Oxford Univ., 1991, 2014; Hulsean Lectr, Cambridge Univ., 1991–92, 2010; Henry Luce III Fellow, 1994–95; Hulsean Preacher, Cambridge Univ., 1996, 2010; Mulligan Preacher, Gray's Inn, 2003. Lectures: Samuel Ferguson, Manchester Univ., 1997, 2010; Riddell, Newcastle Univ., 1999; Tate-Willson, Southern Methodist Univ., 1999; Prideaux, Exeter Univ., 2000; Jellema, Calvin Coll., 2001; Stone, Princeton Theol Seminary, 2002; Cheney, Berkeley Divinity Sch. at Yale, 2002; Hensley Henson, Oxford Univ., 2005; J. A. Hall, Univ. of Victoria, BC, 2007; Paddock, Gen. Theol Seminary, NY, 2009; Gifford, Aberdeen Univ., 2012; Warfield, Princeton Theol Seminary, 2015; DuBose, Sewanee, 2015; Stob, Calvin Coll., 2015; Richards, Univ. of Virginia, 2016. Pres., British Soc. for Philos. of Religion, 2013–15. Ordained deacon, 2000, priest, 2001; Asst Curate, SS Mary and Nicholas, Littlemore, 2000–07; Assoc. Priest, The Good Shepherd, Waban, MA, 2001–08; licensed to officiate, Ely Dio., 2008–; Asst Priest, 2008–10, Minor Canon, 2010, Hon. Canon, 2011–18, Ely Cathedral. Consultant to C of E Doctrine Commn, 1982–84, Mem., 1984–92. Hon. Life Fellow, Oriel Coll., Oxford, 2018. ThD *hc* Lund, 2006; DD *hc* Gen. Theol Seminary, NY, 2008; St Andrews, 2014; Heythrop Coll., London, 2017; DSL *hc* Toronto (St Michael's Coll.), 2015. *Publications:* Christ Without Absolutes: a study of the Christology of Ernst Troeltsch, 1988; (ed with David A. Pailin) The Making and Remaking of Christian Doctrine, 1993; (ed) Religion and the Body, 1997; Powers and Submissions: spirituality, philosophy and gender, 2002; (ed) Re-thinking Gregory of Nyssa, 2003; (ed with Kay Kaufman Shelemay) Pain and Its Transformations: the interface of biology and culture, 2007; (ed with Samuel Wells) Praying for England: priestly presence in contemporary culture, 2008; (ed with Charles M. Stang) Re-thinking Dionysius the Areopagite, 2009; (ed with Paul Garilyuk) The Spiritual Senses, 2011; Sacrifice Regained: reconsidering the rationality of Christian belief, 2011; (ed with F. Ward) Fear and Friendship: Anglicans engaging with Islam, 2012; God, Sexuality and the Self: an essay on the Trinity, 2013; (ed with Martin A. Nowak) Evolution, Games and God: the principle of cooperation, 2013; The New Asceticism: sexuality, gender and the quest for God, 2015; (ed with Jessica Martin) For God's Sake: re-imagining priesthood and prayer in a changing church, 2016; contrib. to C of E reports and to theol. jls. *Recreations:* musical activities, thinking about the garden, picking up litter.
*See also* R. J. Furber, W. J. Furber.

**COATES, Prof. Andrew John**, DPhil; FRAS; Professor of Physics, since 2007, and Deputy Director (formerly Co-Director) (Solar System), since 2011, Mullard Space Science Laboratory, University College London; *b* Heswall, 26 Aug. 1957; *s* of late Thomas Theodore Coates and of Audrey Coates; *m* 1983, Katherine Ann Cooke; two *d*. *Educ:* Bancroft's Sch., Woodford Green, Essex; Univ. of Manchester Inst. of Sci. and Technol. (BSc Pure Applied Physics 1978); Keble Coll., Oxford (MSc Sci. and Application of Electric Plasmas 1979; DPhil Plasma Physics 1982). FRAS 1993. Mullard Space Science Laboratory, University College London: post doctoral res. asst, 1982–88; Sen. Exptl Officer, 1988–89; Royal Soc. Univ. Res. Fellow, 1989–99; Reader in Physics, 1996–2007; Head: Space Plasma Physics, 1999–2005; Planetary Science, 2005–15 (space mission contribs incl. Cassini Plasma Spectrometer (lead co-investigator, electron spectrometer), ExoMars Rover (principal investigator, PanCam), JUICE, Venus Express, Mars Express, Rosetta, Bepi Colombo, Cluster, Double Star, Magnetospheric Multiscale, Beagle 2, Active Magnetospheric Particle Tracer Explorer, Giotto (co-investigator)); Dep. Dir, 2007–11. Hon. Prof. of Physics, Univ. of Aberystwyth, 2007–; Visiting Scientist: Max Planck Inst. for Solar System Physics, 1987–88; Bartol Res. Inst., Univ. of Delaware, 1994. Mem., ESA Solar System Wkg Gp, 1999–2001. BA Media Fellow, BBC World Service, 1994. *Publications:* contribs to learned jls on plasma interaction with solar system objects, magnetospheres and ionospheres, planetary surfaces and space instrumentation. *Recreations:* family, travel, ski-ing, popularising science, Leyton Orient. *Address:* Mullard Space Science Laboratory, University College London, Holmbury St Mary, Dorking, Surrey RH5 6NT. *T:* (01483) 204145. *E:* a.coates@ucl.ac.uk.

**COATES, Sir Anthony Robert M.**; *see* Milnes Coates.

**COATES, David**; HM Diplomatic Service, retired; independent analyst, money laundering and sanctions requirements, since 2008; *b* 13 Nov. 1947; *s* of late Matthew Coates and Margaret Ann Davies Coates (*née* Ross); *m* 1974, Joanna Kay Weil (marr. diss. 2010); two *d*. *Educ:* Dame Allan's Boys' Sch., Newcastle; Univ. of Bristol (BA Hist.); Univ. of Hawaii; Joint University Centre, Taiwan. FCO, 1974–77; language training, Hong Kong, 1977–78; First Sec., Peking, 1978–81; Iran Desk, FCO, 1981–83; Asst Head, S America Dept, 1983–86; First Sec., UKMIS, Geneva, 1986–89; Counsellor and Head, Political Section, Peking, 1989–92; Head, Jt Assistance Unit, Central and E Europe, FCO, 1993–95; Head, Far Eastern and Pacific Dept, FCO, 1995–98; Dir Gen., British Trade and Cultural Office, Taipei, 1999–2002; Estate Modernisation Man., FCO, 2002–04; Ambassador to Côte d'Ivoire, 2004–06. Dir, Financial Crime, BBA, 2006–08. Associate Prof., later Asst Prof., Tamkang Univ., Taiwan, 2008–17. Guest Lectr, Noble-Caledonian Cruises, 2018. *Recreations:* ski-ing, theatre, hill-walking, leeks. *E:* david.coates@live.co.uk.

**COATES, David**, MBE 2017; PhD; CBiol, FRSB, FLS; Professor of Life Sciences, University of Dundee, since 2009; *b* Wallsend upon Tyne, 8 May 1957; *s* of Jack and Eva Coates; *m* 1981, Janice Whatley; one *s* one *d*. *Educ:* Ipswich Sch.; Univ. of Leeds (BSc Hons Genetics 1978); Univ. of E Anglia (PhD 1983). Res. Fellow, Purdue Univ., Indiana, 1983–85; Demonstrator in Genetics, Oxford Univ., 1985–89; Snow Tutorial Fellow in Plant Develt, Magdalen Coll., Oxford, 1988–89; Lectr in Applied Biol., 1989–99, Hd, Sch. of Biol., 2000–04, Univ. of Leeds; Dean, Sch. of Life Scis, Univ. of Bradford, 2004–09; University of Dundee: Dean, Sch. of Learning and Teaching, Coll. of Life Scis, subseq. Dir, Life and Biomed. Scis Educn, Sch. of Life Scis, 2009–17; Dep. Principal, Learning and Teaching, 2011–13. Vis. Prof., Coll. de France and INSERM 36, Paris, 1986–87. Chair, Heads of Univ. Biol Scis, 2005–12. Vice Pres., Inst. of Biol., 2004–09. Hon. Sec., Soc. of Biol., 2009–12. FRSA. *Recreations:* reading, history, supporting Diabetes UK. *Address:* D'Arcy Thompson Unit, School of Life Sciences, University of Dundee, Nethergate, Dundee DD1 4HN. *E:* d.coates@dundee.ac.uk.

**COATES, Sir David (Charlton Frederick)**, 3rd Bt *cr* 1921, of Haypark, City of Belfast; *b* 16 Feb. 1948; *o s* of Sir Frederick Gregory Lindsay Coates, 2nd Bt and Joan Nugent, *d* of Maj.-Gen. Sir Charlton Spinks, KBE, DSO; *S* father, 1994; *m* 1973, Christine Helen, *d* of

Lewis F. Marshall; two s. Educ: Millfield. Heir: s James Gregory David Coates [b 12 March 1977; m 2004, Laura Claire, er d of Gordon and Margaret Bennett; one s]. Address: Launchfield House, Briantspuddle, Dorchester, Dorset DT2 7HN.

**COATES, Dudley James;** consultant and writer; Head of Environment Group, Ministry of Agriculture, Fisheries and Food, 1996–2001; Vice President, Methodist Conference, 2006; b 15 Sept. 1946; o s of late Edward and Margot Coates; m 1969, Rev. Canon Dr Jean Walsingham; two d. Educ: Westcliff High School for Boys; Univ. of Sussex (BA (Hons)); STETS (MA Univ. of Surrey). Joined MAFF as Asst Principal, 1968; Second Sec., UK Delegn to the EC, Brussels, 1970–72; Principal, MAFF, 1973; Lectr, Civil Service Coll., 1978–81; Head of Animal Health Div. II, 1981–83, Head of Financial Management Team, 1983–87, MAFF; Dir Gen. of Corporate Services, Intervention Bd for Agricultural Produce, 1987–89; Dir, Regl Services, MAFF, 1989–96. Public Mem., Network Rail, 2002–10. Methodist local preacher, 1970–; Member: Methodist Conf., 1988, 1989, 1993–2004, 2006–08, 2010, 2012, 2014–16; Methodist Council, 2004–08, 2009–10; Chair, Methodist Publishing House, 1996–2004; Methodist ecumenical representative: Gen. Synod of C of E, 2001–07; Baptist Union Council, 2012–13; Southampton Methodist District: Mem., Ecumenical Team (formerly Ecumenical Action Team), 2009–; Dist Ecumenical Officer, 2010–; Sec., Policy Cttee (formerly Policy Exec.), 2010–18. Gov., 2002–11, Trustee, 2011–15, STETS. Pt-time student in Christian Liturgy, Sarum Coll. Publications: (contrib.) Policies into Practice (ed David Lewis and Helen Wallace), 1984; Shades of Grey, 2006. Recreations: Christian activities, singing, cycling, model railways. E: coatesdudley@gmail.com.

**COATES, James Richard,** CB 1992; FCILT; Under Secretary, Urban and Local Transport Directorate, Department of Transport, 1994; b 18 Oct. 1935; s of William Richard Coates and Doris Coral (née Richmond); m 1969, Helen Rosamund Rimington; one s one d. Educ: Nottingham High Sch.; Clare Coll., Cambridge (MA). Joined Ministry of Transport, 1959; Private Sec. to Permanent Sec., 1962–63; Principal, 1963; Private Sec. to Secretary of State for Local Govt and Regional Planning, 1969, and to Minister of Transport, 1970–71; Asst Sec., DoE, 1971; Under Secretary, 1977; Dir, London Reg., PSA, 1979–83; Department of Transport: Highways Policy and Prog. Directorate, 1983–85; Rlys Directorate, 1985–91; Urban and Gen. Directorate, 1991–93. FCILT (FCIT 1996; Mem., Policies Cttee). Recreations: reading, listening to music, looking at buildings, gardening. Address: 10 Alwyne Road, N1 2HH.

**COATES, John Dowling,** AC 2006 (AO 1995; AM 1989); President, Australian Olympic Committee, since 1990; Member, International Olympic Committee, since 2001 (Executive Board Member, 2009–13; Vice President, 2013–17); Chairman, William Inglis & Son Ltd, since 2007; b 7 May 1950; s of Sidney Dowling Coates and Valerie Irene Coates; m 1981, Pauline Frances Kahl (marr. diss. 2005); five s one d; m 2017, Orieta Pires. Educ: Homebush Boys' High Sch.; Sydney Univ. (LLB). Joined Greaves Wannan & Williams, 1971: Partner, 1977–87 and 1991–2001; Consultant, 1987–91; Kemp Strang Lawyers: Partner, 2001–09; Special Counsel, 2010–18. Man. Dir, Austus Properties Ltd, 1987–90 (Dir, 1990–91); Chairman: Reef Casino Trust, 1993–97; Triplecee Retail Investment Trust, 1994–99; Accord Pacific Hldgs Ltd, 1994–2002; Australian Olympic Foundn Ltd, 1996–; Burson-Marsteller Australia, 2000–04; Dep. Chm., Kengfu Properties Pte Ltd, 1997–2002; Dir, 1995–2012, Dep. Chm., 2003–12, David Jones Ltd; Member: Grant Samuel Adv. Bd, 2002–17 (Dir, managers, Grant Samuel Laundy Pub Fund, 2005–07); Sydney Olympic Park Authy, 2005–16; Director: United Customer Solutions Pty Ltd, 2004–06; Grosvenor Australia Properties Pty Ltd, 2005–10 (Consultant, 2004–05); Grosvenor Australia Investments Ltd, 2005–10; Events NSW Pty Ltd, 2007–09. Mem., Eur. Australian Business Council, 2009–. Dir, Australian Inst. of Sport, 1985–86 (Dep. Chm., 1986–89); Dep. Chm., Australian Sports Commn, 1989–98 (Mem., 1987–89); Mem. Council, Internat. Rowing Fedn, 1992–2014; President: Internat. Council of Arbitration for Sport, 2011– (Vice Pres., 1994–2011); Court of Arbitration for Sport, 2011–. Australian Olympic Committee: Mem., Exec. Bd, 1982–85; Vice-Pres., 1985–90; Exec. dir, 1992 Olympic Games Bid, Brisbane CC, 1985–86; Vice Pres., Sydney Olympics 2000 Bid Ltd, 1991–93; Sen. Vice Pres., Sydney Organising Cttee for Olympic Games, 1993–2000. International Olympic Committee: Member: Olympic Games Study Commn, 2002–03; TV Rights and New Media Commn, 2005–15; Chair: Legal Affairs Comm (formerly Juridical Commn), 2014– (Mem., 2002–14); Sport and Law Commn, 2014–15; Member, Co-ordination Commission: Games of XXX Olympiad, London 2012, 2005–12; Games of XXXI Olympiad, Rio de Janeiro 2016, 2010–16; Games of XXXII Olympiad, Tokyo, 2020, 2013– (Chair, 2013–); Delegate Mem., Broadcast Rights Negotiations for Oceania, 2015–. Dir, Roseville Coll. Foundn Ltd, 1997–2003. Rowing Manager, Australian Team, Montreal Olympics, 1976; Admin. Dir, Australian Team, Moscow Olympics, 1980; Asst Gen. Manager, Australian Team, Los Angeles Olympics, 1984; Chef de Mission, Australian Olympic Team: Seoul, 1988; Barcelona, 1992; Atlanta, 1996; Sydney, 2000; Athens, 2004; Beijing, 2008. Hon. Life Member: NSW Olympic Council Inc., 1990; Australian Rowing Council Inc., 1993; NSW Rowing Assoc. Inc., 1994; Australian Olympic Cttee, 1997. IOC Centennial Trophy, 1994; Olympic Order in Gold, 2000; FISA Medal of Honour, 2000; Australian Sports Medal, 2001; Centenary Medal, Australia, 2003. Recreations: golf, swimming, rowing, other sports, the Olympic movement. Address: c/o Australian Olympic Committee Inc., Level 4, Museum of Contemporary Art, 140 George Street, Sydney, NSW 2000, Australia. Clubs: Commonwealth (Canberra); Sydney Rowing (Hon. Life Mem.), Carbine (past Chm.), Australian Turf; Drummoyne Sailing, Concord Golf.

**COATES, Prof. John Henry,** FRS 1985; Sadleirian Professor of Pure Mathematics, Cambridge University, 1986–2012; Fellow of Emmanuel College, Cambridge, since 1986; b 26 Jan. 1945; s of J. H. Coates and Beryl (née Lee); m 1966, Julie Turner; three s. Educ: Australian National Univ. (BSc); Trinity Coll., Cambridge (PhD). Assistant Prof., Harvard Univ., 1969–72; Associate Prof., Stanford Univ., 1972–74; Univ. Lectr, Cambridge, and Fellow, Emmanuel Coll., 1974–77; Prof., ANU, 1977–78; Prof. of Maths, Univ. de Paris, Orsay, 1978–86, Ecole Normale Supérieure, Paris, 1985–86; Hd of Dept of Pure Maths and Math. Stats, Cambridge Univ., 1991–97. Pres., London Math. Soc., 1988–90; Vice-Pres., Internat. Mathematical Union, 1991–95; Mem. Council, Royal Soc., 1992–94. Dr hc: Ecole Normale Supérieure, 1997; Heidelberg, 2012. Address: Emmanuel College, Cambridge CB2 3AP; 104 Mawson Road, Cambridge CB1 2EA. T: (01223) 740260.

**COATES, His Honour Marten Frank;** a Circuit Judge, 1997–2013; a Judge of the Mental Health Tribunal, since 2013; b 26 March 1947; s of Frank and Violet Coates; m 1973, Susan Anton-Stephens; three d. Educ: Pocklington Sch., York; Durham Univ. (BA Hons 1972); Cert. Biblical Studies. Called to the Bar, Inner Temple, 1972; Asst Recorder, Midland and Oxford Circuit, 1989–93; Recorder, 1993–97. Chancellor, Dio. Lichfield, 2006–11.

**COATES, Prof. Nigel Martin;** Professor of Architectural Design and Head of Department of Architecture, Royal College of Art, 1995–2011, now Professor Emeritus; Founder and Director, Nigel Coates Ltd, since 2009; Art Director, Slamp, 2009–15; b 2 March 1949; s of Douglas Coates and Margaret Coates (née Trigg). Educ: Hanley Castle Grammar Sch., Malvern; Univ. of Nottingham (BA Arch Hons); Architectural Assoc. (AA Dip (Year Prize)); Univ. of Rome (Italian Govt Scholar). Unit Master, AA, 1979–89. Course Master, Bennington Coll., Vt, 1980–81. Jt Founder and Co-dir, Branson Coates Architecture Ltd, 1985–2006. Founder Mem., Narrative Architecture Today, 1979–89. Mem., Adv. Bd, ICA, 1987–89; Chair, Academic Court, London Sch. of Architecture, 2015–. Architecture columnist, Independent on Sunday, 2003–05. Trustee, Architecture Foundn, 2000–13. External Examiner: Bartlett Sch. of Architecture and AA, 1993–94; Dept of Architecture, Univ. of Cambridge, 2000–02. Presenter, 1989, advr and subject, 1992, TV documentaries. Lectures world-wide. Branson Coates' projects include: Katharine Hamnett shop, London, 1988; Caffè Bongo 1985, Arca di Noe 1988, Hotel Otaru Marittimo 1989, Nishi Azabu Wall 1990 and Art Silo 1993, in Japan; (built projects) Taxim Nightpark 1991 and Key fihan 1999, in Turkey; shops for Jigsaw in UK, Ireland and Japan, 1988–96; new depts for Liberty, Regent St, branches and airport shops, 1992–96; La Forêt and Nautilus Restaurants, Schiphol Airport, Amsterdam, 1993; Bargo Bar, Bass Taverns, 1996; Oyster House and Powerhouse::uk, London, 1998; New Gall. Bldg, Geffrye Mus., 1998; Nat. Centre for Popular Music, Sheffield, 1998; British Expo Pavilion, Lisbon 98; Body Zone, Millennium Dome, London, 2000; Inside Out, travelling exhibn, British Council, 2001; Mktg Suite and Roman Amphitheatre display, Guildhall, London, 2002; House to Home, Houses of Parliament, 2004; (shop design) Charles Fish, London, 2006. Branson Coates' exhibition design projects include: (contrib.) Living Bridges Exhibn, RA, 1996; (contrib.) Erotic Design Exhibn, Design Mus., 1997; Look Inside! New British Public Interiors, internat. tour, 1997; Colani Exhibn, Design Mus., 2007. Nigel Coates Ltd's projects include: Middle and Over Wallop Restaurant, Glyndebourne, 2009; Slamp Euroluce stands, 2009, 2011, 2013, 2015. Nigel Coates designs include: Metropole and Jazz furniture collections, 1986; Noah collection, 1988; Female, He-man and She-woman mannequins, 1988; Tongue chair, 1989; Carpet collection, 1990; Gallo collection, Poltronova, 1991; Slipper chair, 1994; glass vase collection, Simon Moore, 1996; Oxo furniture, Hitch Mylius; Oyster furniture, Lloyd Loom; Fiesolani vases, Salviati; Slamp:ville, Slamp; Big Shoom, Alessi; Tête-a-Tête collection, Fornasetti; G-love chair, Contempo, 2006; Bodypark Tiles, Bardelli, 2006; lighting collections, Slamp, 2005–; Veneziani collections, AV Mazzega, 2008–; Scubism collection, Fratelli Boffi, 2008–; Pandada table, Pandamonium auction, WWF; Cloudelier, Swarovski Crystal Palace; Rollover and Loop collections, Varaschin; Tulipino vases, Simon Moore, 2009; Animalia, Fratelli Boffi, 2010; Faretto and Chapeau collections, Slamp, Rome, 2011; Angel Falls, Terzani Spa, 2012; Carry Artid Vases, Secondo Me Edizioni, 2012; Illuminati, Crocco and Punctum Collections, Slamp, 2013; Tetrapetal, Xilo, 2014; Combacio Sofa System, Fornasetti, 2014; Baciamano Easy Chair, 2014; Lehnstuhl, Gebrüder Thonet Vienna, 2014; Feral collection, Nigel Coates, 2015; Potentino collection, 2015; Stöcker, Bodystuhl, Gebrüder Thonet Vienna, 2015; Heads Up collection, Nude Glass, 2015; Bump chair, L'Abbate, 2015; Tassonomia collection, Glamora, 2016; Cafestuhl, Gebrüder Thonet Vienna, 2016; Potentino II, Potentino, 2017; Nigel Coates Eyewear, 2017. Exhibitions: Gamma City, Air Gall., 1985; (one-person) Ark Albion, AA, 1984; Ecstacity, AA, 1992; British Pavilion, Venice Biennale, 2000; Latent Utopias, Graz, 2002; Micro Utopias, Valencia Biannual, 2003; Vextacity, Fabbrica Europa, Florence, 2003; Greetings from London, Selfridges and Architecture Foundn, 2004; Babylon:don, 10th Internat. Architecture Exhibn, Venice Biennale, 2006; FutureCities, Barbican Art Gall., 2006; Hypnerotosphere, Venice Biennale, 2008; Battersea Gods Home, Super Contemp. Exhibn, Design Mus., 2009; (one-person) Baroccabilly, Nigel Coates Studio, London, Galleria Carlo Madesami, Milan, 2010, Cristina Grajales Inc., NY, 2011; Poltronova Connection, Nigel Coates Studio, 2010; Postmodernism, V&A, 2011; Neo-mio Chandelier, Superdesign, London, 2011; British Design, V&A, 2012; Handblown, 2013; Exploded, London Design Fest., 2013; Springboard, Nigel Coates Studio, London, 2014; (co-curator) Pavilion of Art and Design, RCA, 2010; (contrib.) Sleep, London, 2014; Paracastello and (contrib.) Wallpaper Handmade, Fuori Salone, Milan, 2015; work in collections of V&A Mus.; Casa Reale, Entratalibera, Milano, 2012, London Design Fest., 2012; Kama: Sesso, E Design, Triennale Design Mus., Milano, 2012–13; Fonds Régional d'Art Contemporain du Centre, Orléans, France; work exhibited in UK, Europe, US and Japan. Mem., Soc. of Authors; Editor, NATO magazines 1, 2 and 3, Architectural Assoc., 1984–86. Inter-Design Award for Contribution to Japanese cities, Japan Inter-Design Forum, 1990; Outstanding Lifetime Contribn to Design Award, FX mag., 2011; Annie Spink Award, RIBA, 2012. Publications: Ecstacity, 1992; Guide to Ecstacity, 2003; Collidoscope, 2004; Narrative Architecture, 2011; (contrib.) Educating Architects, 2014. Recreations: contemporary art, video-making, Italian culture, riding. Address: Nigel Coates Ltd, 1 Glendower Place, SW7 3DU. W: www.nigelcoates.com. Clubs: Chelsea Arts, Groucho.

**COATES, Ralph Douglas;** Chief Financial Officer, TSB Banking Group, since 2016; b Cape Town, SA, 28 Oct. 1972; s of John Coates and Jennifer Cluver; m 2002, Alexa Morrell; two d. Educ: Univ. of Cape Town (BCom; Postgrad. Dip. Accountancy). ACA CA (SA). With Price Waterhouse, then PricewaterhouseCoopers: SA, 1996–99; Sen. Manager in Transaction Services, London, 2000–04; Finance Dir, UK Retail and Business Bank, Barclays Bank, 2004–13; Finance Dir, Bank of England, 2013–16.

**COATES, Dame Sally (Anne), (Dame Sally Cefai),** DBE 2013; Director, Southern Academies, United Learning Trust, since 2014; b London, 15 April 1953; d of Francis Coates and Emilie Coates (née McConnell); m 1995, Serge Cefai; three s one d. Educ: Convent of the Sacred Heart, Maidstone; Maidstone Girls' Grammar; Furzedown Coll. (Cert Ed); Inst. of Educn, Univ. of London (BEd); South Bank Univ. (MA). Dep. Hd, 1989–2004, Headteacher, 2004–08, Sacred Heart Sch.; Principal, Burlington Danes Acad., 2008–14. Mem. Bd, Nat. Citizen Service Trust, 2018–. Recreations: reading, travelling. Address: 124 Amyand Park Road, Twickenham, Middx TW1 3HP. T: (020) 8891 3388, 07824 368526.

**COATES, Her Honour Suzanne;** a Circuit Judge, 1998–2013; b 2 Aug. 1949; d of late Jack Coates and of Elsie Coates (now Brown); m 1980, John Brian Camille Tanzer, qv; two s. Educ: Skipton Girls' High Sch.; Guy's Hosp.; South Bank Poly. (HVCert 1972); Queen Mary Coll., London Univ. (LLB 1977). SRN, Guy's Hosp., 1968–71; Health Visitor, Bromley LBC, 1972–74; called to the Bar, Gray's Inn, 1978; Asst Recorder, 1992–96; a Recorder, 1996–98. Recreations: music, reading, walking, football (watching), gardening, travel, cooking.

**COATS, Sir Alexander James,** 5th Bt cr 1905, of Auchendrane, Maybole, co. Ayr; b 6 July 1951; o s of Sir Alastair Francis Stuart Coats, 4th Bt and Lukyn Coats (née Gordon); S father, 2015, but his name does not appear on the Official Roll of the Baronetage; m 1999, Clara, d of Ernesto Abril de Vivero. Educ: Eton. Heir: uncle Ivor Paul Coats [b 25 Jan. 1923; m 1959, Caroline Gay Pinckney; two s one d (and one d decd)].

**COATS, David Richard Graham;** Director, WorkMatters Consulting Ltd, since 2010; Research Fellow, Smith Institute, since 2010; Visiting Professor, Centre for Sustainable Work and Employment Futures, University of Leicester, since 2014; b 28 Aug. 1962; s of Frank Alexander Coats and Doreen Coats. Educ: Portway Sch., Bristol; University Coll. London (LLB 1983; LLM 1986); Inns of Court Sch. of Law. Called to the Bar, Inner Temple, 1985; Trades Union Congress: Policy Officer, Orgn and Industrial Relns Dept, 1989–94; Sen. Policy Officer, 1994–99, Head, 1999–2004, Econ. and Social Affairs Dept. Mem., Low Pay Commn, 2000–04; Associate Dir – Policy, Work Foundn, 2004–10. Member: Partnership Fund Assessment Panel, DTI, 2000–04; Central Arbitration Cttee, 2005–; Nat. Stakeholder Council on Health, Work and Well-Being, DWP, 2006–10.

Member, Advisory Board: ESRC Future of Work Prog., 2000–05; Industrial Relns Res. Unit, Univ. of Warwick, 2000–; Mem., Exec. Cttee, Involvement and Participation Assoc., 2000–; Mem., Global Agenda Council on Employment, WEF, 2012–14. Mem. (Lab) Haringey BC, 1990–98. *Recreations:* walking, travel, reading, cooking. *Address:* WorkMatters Consulting Ltd, 10 Albion Drive, Haggerston, E8 4ET. *T:* (020) 7241 1587. *E:* dcoats@workmattersconsulting.co.uk.

**COATS, Prof. Karen,** PhD; Professor of Education and Director, Centre for Research in Children's Literature, University of Cambridge, since 2019; *b* Penn, USA, 21 Nov. 1963; *d* of Joseph Moser and Dawn Moser; *m* 1988, William Coats; two *d*. *Educ:* Virginia Polytechnic Inst. and State Univ. (BA English, MA English); George Washington Univ. (PhD Human Scis 1998). Illinois State University: Asst Prof., 1998–2004; Associate Prof., 2004–09; Prof. of English, 2009–19. Vis. Associate Prof., Grad. Prog. in Children's Lit., Hollis Univ., 2015–. *Publications:* Looking Glasses and Neverlands: Lacan, desire, and subjectivity in children's literature, 2004; (ed jtly) The Gothic in Children's Literature: haunting the borders, 2007; (ed jtly) Handbook of Research on Children's and Young Adult Literature, 2011; Children's Literature and the Developing Reader, 2013; (ed with Lisa Rowe Fraustino) Mothers in Children's and Young Adult Literature: from the eighteenth century to postfeminism, 2016; The Bloomsbury Introduction to Children's and Young Adult Literature, 2017; (ed jtly) MLA Options for Teaching Young Adult Literature, 2020. *Address:* Faculty of Education, University of Cambridge, 184 Hills Road, Cambridge CB2 8PQ. *E:* kscoat2@ilstu.edu.

**COBB, Henry Nichols;** Partner, Pei Cobb Freed & Partners, Architects, since 1960; *b* 8 April 1926; *s* of Charles Kane Cobb and Elsie Quincy Cobb; *m* 1953, Joan Stewart Spaulding; three *d*. *Educ:* Harvard College (AB 1947); Harvard Graduate Sch. of Design (MArch 1949). Architectural Div., Webb & Knapp, 1950–60; Pei Cobb Freed & Partners (formerly I. M. Pei & Partners), 1960–. Sch. of Architecture, Yale University: William Henry Bishop Vis. Prof., 1973, 1978; Charlotte Sheperd Davenport Vis. Prof., 1975; Graduate School of Design, Harvard: Studio Prof. and Chm., Dept of Architecture, 1980–85; Adjunct Prof. of Architecture and Urban Design, 1985–88. Hon. DFA: Bowdoin Coll., 1985; Fordham Univ., 2016; Dr Technical Scis *hc*, Swiss Fed. Inst. of Technol., 1990. Topaz Medallion for Excellence in Architectural Educn, Assoc. of Collegiate Schs of Architecture/AIA, 1995; Lynn S. Beedle Lifetime Achievement Award, Council on Tall Buildings and Urban Habitat, 2013; Gold Medal for Architecture, Amer. Acad. of Arts and Letters, 2014. *Publications:* Where I Stand, 1980; Architecture and the University, 1985. *Address:* Pei Cobb Freed & Partners, 88 Pine Street, New York, NY 10005–1801, USA. *T:* (212) 8724020.

**COBB, Prof. Justin Peter,** FRCS; Professor of Orthopaedics, Imperial College London, since 2005; Orthopaedic Surgeon to the Queen at King Edward VII Hospital and Imperial College NHS Trust, since 2008; *b* 15 March 1958; *s* of late Capt. Peter Cobb, OBE and Jennifer Cobb (*née* Martin); *m* 1985, Iona Stormonth Darling; three *s* one *d*. *Educ:* Sherborne Sch.; Magdalen Coll., Oxford (BM BCh 1982; MCh 1991). FRCS 1986. Registrar, St Thomas' Hosp., 1985–87; Sen. Registrar, Middlesex Hosp. and Royal Nat. Orthopaedic Hosp., 1987–91; Consultant Orthopaedic Surgeon: UCL Hosps NHS Trust, 1991–2005; King Edward VII's Hosp. Sister Agnes (formerly King Edward VII's Hosp. for Officers), 1995–. Founder and Director: Acrobot Co. Ltd, 2001–10; Embody-Orthopaedic Ltd, 2015–. *Publications:* pubns in diseases of the hip and knee, corrective surgery, assistive technologies incl. 3D printing, robotics and navigation. *Recreations:* sailing, ski-ing, golf, but mainly work. *Address:* St Johns House, Chiswick Mall, W4 2PS. *E:* j.cobb@imperial.ac.uk. *Clubs:* Athenæum, Hurlingham; St Albans Medical; Swinley Forest Golf (Ascot).

**COBB, Piers Andrew Conrad R.;** *see* Russell-Cobb.

**COBB, Hon. Sir Stephen (William Scott),** Kt 2013; **Hon. Mr Justice Cobb;** a Judge of the High Court, Family Division, since 2013; Family Division Liaison Judge, North Eastern Circuit, since 2015; *b* 12 April 1962; *s* of Hon. Sir John Francis Scott Cobb and Lady (Joan Mary) Cobb; *m* 1989, Samantha Cowling; two *s* one *d*. *Educ:* Winchester Coll.; Liverpool Univ. (LLB Hons 1984). Called to the Bar, Inner Temple, 1985, Bencher, 2011; QC 2003; a Recorder, 2004–13; Head of Chambers, One Garden Court, 2007–13; a Dep. High Ct Judge, 2009–13. Mem., Family Justice Council, 2004–09, 2013–18. Chm., Family Law Bar Assoc., 2010–11. Fellow, Internat. Acad. of Matrimonial Lawyers, 2007. Fellow, Winchester Coll., 2017. Consultant Ed., Family Law Reports and Family Law Jl, 2015–. Hon. DLaws Liverpool, 2019. *Publications:* (ed) Essential Family Practice, 2000; (ed) Clarke, Hall and Morrison, On Children, 2004–09; (contrib.) A Handbook for Expert Witnesses in Children Act Cases, 2nd edn, 2007; (contrib.) Halsbury's Laws of England, vol. 3, 2008; (contrib.) Civil Appeals, 2nd edn, 2013. *Recreation:* family. *Address:* Royal Courts of Justice, Strand, WC2A 2LL. *Clubs:* Hurlingham; Bembridge Sailing.

**COBBETT, David John,** ERD 1962; TD 1973; FCILT; railway and transportation management consultant; *b* 9 Dec. 1928; *m* 1952, Beatrix Jane Ogilvie Cockburn (*d* 2013); three *s*. *Educ:* Royal Masonic Sch. FCILT (FILT 1999). Gen. Railway admin. and managerial positions, 1949–67; Divl Movements Manager, Liverpool Street, 1967; Divl Manager, Norwich (British Railways Bd), 1968–70; Asst Managing Dir, Freightliners Ltd, 1970–73; Dep. Gen. Manager, British Railways Bd Scottish Region, 1973; Gen. Manager, British Railways Scottish Region, 1974–76; Chm., British Transport Ship Management, Scotland, 1974–76; Gen. Manager, BR Eastern Region, 1976–77; British Railways Board: Export Dir (Special Projects), 1977–78; Dir, Strategic Studies, 1978–83; Dir, Information Systems and Technology, 1983–85. Dir, Transmark, 1978. Mem. Bd, Railway Benevolent Instn, 1979–99 (Dep. Chm., 1981–84; Chm., 1984–98; Vice Pres., 2000–). Dir, Dachaidh Respite Care, Kingussie (formerly Aviemore), 1993–2017 (Sec. and Treas., 1993–2008; Finance Dir, 2012–16). Bt Col, Royal Corps of Transport (RARO), 1974. *Recreations:* military matters, historical reading, games. *Address:* Cockburn House, 3 Kinchurdy Court, Boat of Garten PH24 3BB. *T:* and *Fax:* (01540) 673269. *E:* david_cobbett@yahoo.com. *Clubs:* Army and Navy, MCC; Probus (Badenoch).

**COBBOLD;** *see* Lytton Cobbold, family name of Baron Cobbold.

**COBBOLD, 2nd Baron** *cr* 1960, of Knebworth; **David Antony Fromanteel Lytton Cobbold;** DL; Chairman and Managing Director, Lytton Enterprises Ltd, Knebworth House, since 1971; farmer, 2018; *b* 14 July 1937; *s* of 1st Baron Cobbold, KG, GCVO, PC, and Lady Hermione Bulwer-Lytton, *er d* of 2nd Earl of Lytton, KG, GCSI, GCIE, PC; assumed by deed poll, 1960, additional surname of Lytton; *S* father, 1987; *m* 1961, Christine Elizabeth, 3rd *d* of Major Sir Dennis Frederic Bankes Stucley, 5th Bt; three *s* one *d*. *Educ:* Eton College; Trinity Coll., Cambridge (BA Hons Moral Sciences). Fellow, Assoc. of Corporate Treasurers. PO, RAF, 1955–57. NATO Flying Training Scheme, Canada, 1956–57. Morgan Guaranty Trust Co., New York, 1961–62; Bank of London and South America Ltd, London, Zürich, Barcelona, 1962–72; Treasurer, Finance for Industry Ltd, 1974–79; Manager Treasury Div., BP Finance International, The British Petroleum Co. plc, 1979–87; Gen. Manager Financial Markets, TSB England & Wales plc, 1987–88; Dir, Hill Samuel Bank Ltd, and Head of TSB-Hill Samuel Treasury Div., 1988–89; Man. Dir, Gaiacorp Currency Managers, 1991–94 (Dir, 1989–94); Director: Close Brothers Gp plc, 1993–2000; Stevenage Leisure Ltd, 1999–2002. Mem., Assoc. for Monetary Union in Europe, 1992–2002. Mem., Finance and Policy Cttee, HHA, 1973–97 (Hon. Treas., 1988–97); Gov., Union of European HHAs, 1993–97. Chm., Stevenage Community Trust, 1990–2006; Trustee, Pilgrim Trust, 1993–2010; Director: Shuttleworth Trust, 1998–2002; English Sinfonia Orch. Ltd, 1998–2002. Elected Mem., H of L, 2000–14, crossbencher. Contested (L): Bishop Auckland, Oct. 1974; Hertfordshire, European Parly Election, 1979. DL Herts, 1993. *Recreation:* travel. *Heir: s* Hon. Henry Fromanteel Lytton Cobbold [*b* 12 May 1962; *m* 1987, Martha Frances, *d* of James Buford Boone, Jr; one *s* one *d*].

**COBBOLD, Rear-Adm. Richard Francis,** CB 1994; Chief Executive Officer, C2S2, since 2008; *b* 25 June 1942; *s* of Geoffrey Francis and Elizabeth Mary Cobbold; *m* 1975, Anne Marika Hjörne (marr. diss. 1995); one *s* one *d*. *Educ:* Bryanston Sch.; BRNC Dartmouth. Early service, RN: HMS Kent; Staff of FO Naval Flying Training; HMS Juno; HMS Hermes; loan to RAN: RN Staff College 1973; Arctic Flight in comd, 1973–74; 820 Sqdn, Sen. Observer, 1974–75; MoD, 1975–77; HMS Mohawk in comd, 1977–79; MoD, 1979–83; RCDS 1984; HMS Brazen in comd, 1985–86; Dir of Defence Concepts, MoD, 1987–88; Captain 2nd Frigate Sqdn, 1989–90; ACDS Op. Requirements (Sea), 1991–94, and for Jt Systems, 1992–94; Dir, RUSI, 1994–2007. Specialist Adviser: H of C Defence Cttee, 1997–2007; H of C Foreign Affairs Cttee, 2003; Sen. Policy Advr, Ocean Security Initiative, 2005–08. Vice Pres., Strategic Develt, Duos Technologies Internat. Inc., 2007–08. FRAeS 1994. Governor, London Nautical Sch., 1997–. *Recreations:* gardening, naval and military history. *Club:* Army and Navy.

**COBHAM, 12th Viscount** *cr* 1718; **Christopher Charles Lyttelton;** DL; landowner; Bt 1618; Baron Cobham 1718; Lord Lyttelton, Baron of Frankley 1756 (renewed 1794); Baron Westcote (Ire.) 1776; *b* 23 Oct. 1947; 2nd *s* of 10th Viscount Cobham, KG, GCMG, GCVO, TD, PC and Elizabeth Alison, *d* of J. R. Makeig-Jones, CBE; *S* brother, 2006; *m* 1973, Tessa Mary, *d* of late Col A. G. Readman, DSO; one *s* one *d*. *Educ:* Eton. Wood Gundy Ltd, 1969–85; Chm. and Chief Exec., NCL Investments, 1985–2002; Dep. Chm., 2002–07, Consultant, 2007–11, Smith & Williamson. Elder Brother, Trinity House, 2003–. DL Worcs, 2010. *Heir: s* Hon. Oliver Christopher Lyttelton, *b* 24 Feb. 1976.
*See also Hon. R. C. Lyttelton.*

**COBHAM, Penelope, Viscountess; Penelope Ann Lyttelton,** CBE 2014; Chairman, VisitEngland, 2009–17 (Deputy Chairman, VisitBritain, 2005–09); Director General, The 5% Club, since 2017; *b* 2 Jan. 1954; *d* of late Roy and Dorothy Cooper; *m* 1974, 11th Viscount Cobham (marr. diss. 1995; he *d* 2006). *Educ:* St James's Sch., Malvern. Chairman: British Casino Assoc., 1999–2009; Civic Trust, 1999–2003. Commissioner: English Heritage, 1989–92; Countryside Commn, 1991–92; Museums and Galls Commn, 1993–2000; Trustee, V&A, 1993–2003; Member: Exec. Council, Historic Houses (formerly HHA), 1985–; Bd, British Waterways, 1993–95; LDDC, 1993–98; Historic Royal Palaces Ministerial Adv. Bd, 1990–98; Council, Nat. Trust, 2004–10. Co. Dir and Consultant incl. Chm., Heart of England Radio Ltd, subseq. Chrysalis Radio Midlands, 1993–2007. Consultant: Ernst & Young, 1997–2009; Farrer & Co. Solicitors, 2001–04; GI Partners (UK) Ltd, 2007–08; Advr, Citi Pvte Bank, 2010–11; Chm., Adv. Bd, Highland Gp Internat., 2010–13; Dep. Chm., Adv. Bd, Pagefield Communications Ltd, 2015–17; Member: Strategy Bd, Linley, 2015–17; Adv. Bd, Urban Legacies, 2017–. Guardian, Birmingham Assay Office, 1990–2015. Pres., Midlands Woman of the Year, 1994–; Chm., Mus. Prize Trust, 2001–. Trustee: Birmingham Mus Trust, 2012–16; Shakespeare Birthplace Trust, 2013–; Great War Symphony, 2017–. Pres., governor and patron, numerous civic, charitable and educnl bodies. Freeman: City of London; Goldsmiths' Co. DL West Midlands, 1994–95. FRSA. *Address:* (office) 198 Hagley Road, Stourbridge, W Midlands DY8 2JN. *T:* (01384) 377517.

**COBURN, David Adam;** Member for Scotland, European Parliament, 2014–19 (UK Ind, 2014–18; Ind, 2018–19); *b* Glasgow, 11 Feb. 1959; *s* of Adam Coburn and Matilda Coburn (*née* Sprott Black); partner, Crawford Austin. *Educ:* Glasgow High Sch.; Univ. of Leeds. Former trader, London and NY commodity and financial futures markets, 1981–92; co-founder and co-owner, air freight forwarding company. Freeman, City of Glasgow, 1980. Contested (UK Ind) Falkirk, 2015. Mem., Gadfly Club. *Recreations:* arts and antiques, archaeology, country pursuits, gardening, vintage cars, bibliophile.

**COBURN, Michael Jeremy Patrick;** QC 2010; barrister; *b* Manila, 28 March 1966; *s* of Jeremy Coburn and Rosemary Coburn; *m* 2006, Jennifer Manuel; two *d*. *Educ:* Charterhouse; Worcester Coll., Oxford (BA Lit.Hum.); City Univ., London (DipLaw). Called to the Bar, Inner Temple, 1990; in practice as a barrister, specialising in commercial law, 1991–. *Recreations:* cooking, cycling. *Address:* 20 Essex Street, WC2R 3AL. *T:* (020) 7842 1200. *E:* mcoburn@20essexst.com.

**COCHRANE,** family name of **Earl of Dundonald** and **Baron Cochrane of Cults.**

**COCHRANE, Lord; Archie Iain Thomas Blair Cochrane;** *b* 14 March 1991; *s* and heir of Earl of Dundonald, *qv*. *Educ:* Ampleforth Coll.; Univ. of Nottingham. Work in Fintech sector; then in Bogotá, Colombia, and subseq. in Amsterdam. *Recreations:* sailing, ski-ing, trial biking, country sports, travelling. *Address:* Lochnell Castle, Benderloch, Argyll PA37 1QT.

**COCHRANE OF CULTS, 5th Baron** *cr* 1919; **Thomas Hunter Vere Cochrane;** *b* 7 Sept. 1957; *s* of 4th Baron Cochrane of Cults and of Janet Mary Watson (*née* Cheyne); *S* father, 2017; *m* 2008, Silke, *d* of late Peter Quandt. *Educ:* Eton Coll.; Exeter Univ. (LLB). Called to the Bar, Inner Temple, 1980. Mem., Queen's Body Guard for Scotland (Royal Co. of Archers). Liveryman, Fanmakers' Co., 2007–. *Recreations:* horse racing, theatre, opera, Scottish country dancing. *Heir: b* Hon. Michael Charles Nicholas Cochrane, OBE [*b* 4 March 1959; *m* 2000, Janet Lilias, *d* of Capt. J. H. Murray; one *s* one *d*].

**COCHRANE, Alannah Elizabeth;** *see* Weston, A. E.

**COCHRANE, Sir (Henry) Marc (Sursock),** 4th Bt *cr* 1903; *b* 23 Oct. 1946; *s* of Sir Desmond Oriel Alastair George Weston Cochrane, 3rd Bt, and of Yvonne Lady Cochrane (*née* Sursock); *S* father, 1979; *m* 1969, Hala (*née* Es-Said); two *s* one *d*. *Educ:* Eton; Trinity Coll., Dublin (BBS, MA). Director: Hambros Bank Ltd, 1979–85; GT Management PLC, subseq. LGT Asset Management, 1985–98; INVESCO, 1998–99; Henderson Global Investors, 2000–05. Hon. Consul General of Ireland in Beirut, 1979–84. Trustee, Chester Beatty Library and Gall. of Oriental Art, Dublin. *Recreations:* ski-ing, target shooting, electronics. *Heir: s* Alexander Desmond Sursock Cochrane [*b* 7 May 1973; *m* 2007, Alannah Elizabeth Weston, *qv*; two *d*]. *Address:* Woodbrook, Bray, Co. Wicklow, Ireland. *T:* (1) 2821421; Beit as-Saifi, Mar Maroun Street, Mar Maroun/Saifi District, Beirut, Lebanon. *T:* (1) 565368/9.

**COCHRANE, Keith Robertson,** CBE 2016; FRSE; Chief Executive, Schenck Process Group, since 2019 (Chairman, 2017–19); *b* 11 Feb. 1965; *m* 1998, Fiona Margaret Armstrong; one *s* one *d*. *Educ:* Dunblane High Sch.; Univ. of Glasgow (BAcc 1st Cl. Hons). CA 1989; Arthur Andersen, 1986–93, Audit Manager, 1990–93; Gp Financial Controller and Co. Sec., 1993–96, Gp Financial Dir, 1996–2000, Stagecoach Holdings plc; Chief Exec., Stagecoach Gp, 2000–02; Dir of Gp Financial Reporting, 2003–04, Gp Controller,

2004–05; Gp Dir of Finance, 2005–06; Scottish Power plc; Finance Dir, 2006–09; Chief Exec., 2009–06, Weir Gp PLC. Sen. Ind. Dir, Carillion plc, 2015–18 (Interim Chief Exec., 2017); UK Govt Lead non-exec. Dir, Scotland Office and Office of Advocate Gen., 2015–18; Chairman: Third Energy, 2017–18; Score Gp, 2018–. Mem. Council, Glenalmond Coll., 2013–. Trustee, Duke of Edinburgh's Study Confs (UK Fund) Bd, 2015–. FRSE 2016. Hon. DSc Strathclyde, 2013. *Recreations:* golf, music, travel, reading.

**COCHRANE, Malcolm Ralph**, MBE 2012; Vice Lord-Lieutenant of Oxfordshire, 1999–2009; *b* 8 Aug. 1938; *s* of Air Chief Marshal Hon. Sir Ralph Cochrane, GBE, KCB, AFC and Hilda (*née* Wiggin); *m* 1972, Mary Anne Scrope, *d* of Ralph Scrope and Lady Beatrice Scrope, *d* of 6th Earl of Mexborough; one *s* two *d*. *Educ:* Eton Coll.; Balliol Coll., Oxford. Nat. Service, Scots Guards, 1957–58. Design Research Unit, 1962–65; Design Panel, BRB, 1965–72; Director: Cochranes of Oxford Ltd, 1972–2007; Cults Lime Ltd, 1976–. High Sheriff, 1996, DL 1998, Oxon. *Recreations:* arts, gardening, watching sport. *Address:* Grove Farmhouse, Shipton-under-Wychwood, Oxon OX7 6DG. *T:* (01993) 830742.

**COCHRANE, Sir Marc;** *see* Cochrane, Sir H. M. S.

**COCHRANE, Prof. Peter**, OBE 1999; PhD, DSc; FREng, FIET, FIEEE; Co-Founder and Chairman, Cochrane Associates, since 2006; consultant to government and international companies; Professor of Sentient Systems, University of Suffolk, since 2017; *b* 11 July 1946; *s* of Colin Cochrane and Gladys Cochrane; *m* 1971, Brenda Cheetham (*d* 2003); two *s* two *d*; *m* 2005, Jane Tromans. *Educ:* Trent Poly. (BSc Electrical Engrg 1973); Essex Univ. (MSc Telecommunications 1976; PhD Transmission Systems 1979; DSc Systems Design 1991). CGIA 1975; CEng 1977; FIET (FIEE 1987; MIEE 1977); FIEEE 1992 (MIEEE 1983); FREng (FEng 1994). General Post Office: Technician, System Maintenance, 1962–69; Student Engr, 1969–73; Exec. Engr, GPO Res. Labs, 1973–79; BT Laboratories: Head of Gp, 1979–83; Head of Section, 1983–87; Head, Optical Networks Div., 1987–91; Head, Systems Res., 1991–93; Head, Advance Res., 1993–94; Head of Res., 1994–99; Chief Technologist, BT, 1999–2000; Co-Founder and CEO, ConceptLabs, Calif., 2000–06. Mem. Adv. Bd, Computer Scis Corp. Vanguard Prog., 1996–98. Technical Advr, Motorola, 2002–08; Adviser: IRDETO, 2004–12; PMC Sierra, 2005–09; Qatar Computing Res. Inst., 2013–. Visiting Professor: CNET, Lannion Univ., France, 1978; NE London Poly., 1980–90; Essex Univ., 1988–99; Southampton Univ., 1991–94; Kent Univ., 1991–96; UCL, 1994–99; QMUL (formerly QMW), 1999–2006; Univ. of Hertfordshire, 2012–17; Univ. of Suffolk, 2012–17. Mem., NY Acad. of Scis, 1995. FRSA. Hon. DTech Stafford, 1996. Holds 14 original patents. *Publications:* (with J. E. Flood) Transmission Systems, 1991; (with D. J. T. Heatley) Modelling Telecommunication Systems, 1995; Tips for Time Travellers, 1997; Uncommon Sense, 2004; numerous professional papers and articles in IEE, IEEE, and other jls, newspapers, magazines, columns and blogs on educn, mgt, technol., sci. and society. *Recreations:* music, running, mathematics, philosophy, my family, fly fishing, reading, cycling. *Address:* Cochrane Associates, c/o Ensors, Cardinal House, 46 St Nicholas Street, Ipswich, Suffolk IP1 1TT.

**COCHRANE-DYET, Fergus John**, OBE 2015; HM Diplomatic Service; High Commissioner to Zambia, 2016–19; *b* 16 Jan. 1965; *s* of late Lt-Col Iain Cochrane-Dyet and of Rosemary Cochrane-Dyet; *m* 1987, Susie Emma Jane Aram; three *s*. *Educ:* Felsted Sch.; Jesus Coll., Oxford; Durham Univ. (BA Hons); Sch. of Oriental and African Studies, Univ. of London; Univ. of Exeter. Joined HM Diplomatic Service, 1987; Third Sec. (Political), Lagos, 1990–93; Second Sec. (Political), Abuja, 1993–94; First Secretary: Hd, N Africa Section, FCO, 1994–96; Hd, British Interests Section, Tripoli, 1996–97; Hd, Commercial, Jakarta, 1998; Dir, Trade and Investment Promotion for Australia, and Dep. Consul Gen., Sydney, 1998–2001; Chargé d'Affaires, Conakry, 2001–02; Dep. Hd of Mission, Kabul, 2002; Dep. Hd, Africa Dept (Southern), FCO, 2002–04; Dep. High Comr, Lusaka, 2004–07; Dep. Hd, Helmand, Afghanistan, 2007; High Comr to Seychelles, 2007–09, to Malawi, 2009–11; Dep. Hd of Mission, Helmand, Afghanistan, 2012; Ambassador to Liberia, 2013–15. *Recreations:* running, scuba diving, films. *Address:* c/o Foreign and Commonwealth Office, King Charles Street, SW1A 2AH.

**COCKBURN, Sir Charles (Christopher)**, 13th Bt of that Ilk, *cr* 1671; Chairman, Portcullis Group Ltd, 2015; *b* Ross-on-Wye, Herefordshire, 19 Nov. 1950; *s* of Sir John Elliot Cockburn, 12th Bt of that Ilk and Glory Patricia Cockburn (*née* Mullings); *S* father, 2015, but his name does not appear on the Official Roll of the Baronetage; *m* 1st, 1978, Beverly Jane Stangroom (marr. diss. 1984; she *d* 1999); 2nd, 1985, Margaret Ruth, *d* of Samuel Bell; two *s* one *d* (of whom one *s* one *d* are twins). *Educ:* Lindisfarne Coll.; Emanuel Sch.; City of London Poly. (BA Govt and Politics); Garnet Coll. (PGCE). Rock 'n' roll (the lost years), 1970–78; teacher in further educn, 1981–84; with Lloyd Hughes Associates, public policy consultants, 1984–87; founding Ed., Financial Regulation Review, 1987–89; Chm., Portcullis Research Ltd, 1989–2016. MInstD. *Recreations:* cycling, song-writing. *Heir:* *s* Christopher Samuel Alexander Cockburn, *b* 24 March 1986. *Club:* Twickenham Rowing.

**COCKBURN, David;** The Certification Officer for Trade Unions and Employers' Associations, 2001–16; (part-time) Employment Judge (formerly Chairman, Employment Tribunals), 2001–12; *b* 30 Nov. 1948; *s* of John William Cockburn and Nora Cockburn (*née* Carr); *m* 1976, Polly Dickey; one *s* two *d*. *Educ:* King's Sch., Pontefract; LSE (LLB 1970; MSc (Econ) 1972). Admitted solicitor, 1975; Partner, Pattinson & Brewer, solicitors, 1978–2001. Chm., Code Compliance Panel, PhonepayPlus, 2008–14. Chairman: Industrial Law Soc., 1983–86 (Vice-Pres., 1986–); Employment Lawyers' Assoc., 1994–96; Employment Law Cttee, Law Soc., 1995–99; Treas., Inst. of Employment Rights, 1995–2001. Vis. Prof., Middlesex Univ., 2002–. Member, Editorial Committee: Industrial Law Jl, 1986–; Encyclopaedia of Employment Law, 1990–. *Publications:* (contrib.) Justice for a Generation, 1985; (contrib.) Labour Law in Britain, 1986; (jtly) Know-how in Employment Law, 1995; (contrib.) The Changing Institutional Face of British Employment Relations, 2006; articles on labour law in learned jls. *Recreations:* jogging, cycling, sailing, ski-ing, jazz, theatre.

**COCKBURN, Prof. Forrester**, CBE 1996; MD; FRCPE, FRCPGlas; FRSE; Samson Gemmell Professor of Child Health, University of Glasgow, 1977–96, now Emeritus Professor; Chairman, Yorkhill NHS Trust, 1997–2001; *b* 13 Oct. 1934; *s* of Forrester Cockburn and Violet E. Bunce; *m* 1960, Alison Fisher Grieve; two *s*. *Educ:* Leith Acad.; Univ. of Edinburgh (MB ChB 1959; MD *cum laude* 1966); DCH Glasgow 1961. FRCPE 1971; FRCPGlas 1978; FRSE 1999. Med. trng, Royal Infirmary of Edinburgh, Royal Hosp. for Sick Children, and Simpson Memorial Maternity Pavilion, Edinburgh, 1959–63; Huntingdon Hertford Foundn Res. Fellow, Boston Univ., Mass, 1963–65; Nuffield Sen. Res. Fellow, Univ. of Oxford, 1965–66; Wellcome Trust Sen. Med. Res. Fellow, Univ. of Edin. and Simpson Meml Maternity Pavilion, 1966–71; Sen. Lectr, Dept of Child Life and Health, Univ. of Edin., 1971–77. Chm., Panel on Child Nutrition and Wkg Gp on Weaning Diet, Cttee on Med. Aspects of Food Policy (Report, 1994). Founder FRCPCH 1996, Hon. FRCPCH 1997; Hon. FRCSE 2000. James Spence Medal, RCPCH, 1998. *Publications:* Neonatal Medicine, 1974; The Cultured Cell in Inherited Metabolic Disease, 1977; Inborn Errors of Metabolism in Humans, 1980; (with O. P. Gray) Children—A Handbook for Children's Doctors, 1984; (with J. H. Hutchison) Practical Paediatric Problems, 6th edn 1986; (with T. L. Turner and J. Douglas) Craig's Care of the Newly Born Infant, 8th edn 1988; Fetal and Neonatal Growth, 1988; (ed jtly and contrib.) Diseases of the Fetus and Newborn, 1989, 2nd edn 1995; (jtly) Children's Medicine and Surgery, 1996; around 200 articles mainly on fetal and neonatal nutrition and inherited metabolic disease. *Recreations:* walking, gardening, painting.

**COCKBURN, Patrick Oliver;** Iraq correspondent, The Independent, since 2003; *b* Cork, 5 March 1950; *s* of late Claud Cockburn, journalist and Patricia Cockburn; *m* 1981, Jan Montefiore; two *s*. *Educ:* St Stephen's, Dublin; Glenalmond, Perth; Trinity Coll., Oxford (BA Hist.). Financial Times: on Middle East staff, 1980–84; Moscow corresp., 1984–87; Associate, Carnegie Endowment for Internat. Peace, 1988–89; The Independent: Middle East Ed., 1990–92; Washington corresp., 1992–95; Jerusalem corresp., 1995–99; Moscow corresp., 1999–2002. *Publications:* (with Andrew Cockburn) Out of the Ashes: the resurrection of Saddam Hussein, 1999; The Broken Boy, 2005; The Occupation: war and resistance in Iraq, 2006; Muqtada al-Sadr and the Battle for the Future of Iraq, 2008; (with Henry Cockburn) Henry's Demons, 2011; The Jihadis Return: Isis and the New Sunni uprising, 2014, 2nd edn as The Rise of Islamic State: Isis and the new Sunni revolution, 2015. *Address:* The Independent, 2 Derry Street, W8 5HF. *T:* (020) 7005 2810. *E:* patrickcockburn2@gmail.com. *Clubs:* Reform, Frontline, Groucho.

**COCKBURN, William**, CBE 1989; TD 1980; Deputy Chairman, UK Mail Group (formerly Business Post) plc, 2002–12; *b* 28 Feb. 1943. Entered Post Office, 1961; held various junior and middle management positions; apptd Mem., PO Board, 1981, Mem. for Finance, Counter Services and Planning, 1982–84; Mem. for Royal Mail Operations, 1984–86; Man. Dir, Royal Mail, 1986–92; Chief Executive: The Post Office, 1992–95; W. H. Smith Gp PLC, 1996–97; Gp Man. Dir, BT UK, 1997–2001; Chm., Parity Gp plc, 2001–03; Dep. Chm., AWG, 2003–06. Chm., Internat. Post Corp., 1994–95; non-executive Director: Lex Service plc, 1993–2002; Centrica plc, 1997–99; Army Bd, 2008–11. Member: Bd, BITC, 1990–2003; Council, Industrial Soc., 1992–2002; Chairman: Sch. Teachers' Review Body, 2002–08; Senior Salaries Review Body, 2008–14. Pres., Inst. of Direct Marketing, 2001–06. Col, RE Postal and Courier Service (V), 1986–91; Hon. Col, RE Postal and Courier Service, 1992–94; Hon. Col Comdt, RLC, 1996–2006. FCIT 1993; FRSA; CCMI (CIMgt 1993). Freeman, City of London.

**COCKBURN-CAMPBELL, Sir Alexander (Thomas)**, 7th Bt *cr* 1821, of Gartsford, Ross-shire; Facilities Manager, Colliers International, 2012–14; *b* 16 March 1945; *o s* of Sir Thomas Cockburn-Campbell, 6th Bt and of Josephine Zoi Cockburn-Campbell (*née* Forward); *S* father, 1999; *m* 1969, Kerry Ann, *e d* of Sgt K. Johnson; one *s* one *d*. *Educ:* Edwards Business Coll. (Adv. Cert. Mktg/Mgt). Prodn Mgr, 1980–90; Maintenance Manager, Uniting Church Homes, 1995–2000; Building Ops Supervisor, Knight Frank Facilities Managers, Perth, WA, 2000–12. Protestant Lay Minister, 1980– (Dip. Ministry). *Recreation:* surf-board riding. *Heir:* *s* Thomas Justin Cockburn-Campbell, *b* 10 Feb. 1974. *Address:* 103 Waterperry Drive, Canning Vale, WA 6155, Australia. *T:* (8) 92562049.

**COCKCROFT, Barry Michael**, CBE 2010; dental surgeon; Chief Dental Officer, Department of Health, 2006–15, Health Education England, 2012–15, NHS England, 2013–15; *b* 6 Nov. 1950; *s* of late Harry and Margaret Cockcroft; *m* 1973, Diane Lay; one *s* two *d*. *Educ:* De La Salle Coll., Salford; Univ. of Birmingham (BDS 1973; Charles Greene Prize, 1973). Sen. House Officer, Coventry & Warwickshire Hosp., 1974; general dental practitioner: Coventry, 1975–79; Rugby, 1979–2002; Dep. Chief Dental Officer, DoH, 2002–06. Non-exec. Dir, Mydentist, 2015–. JP Rugby, 1992–2000. Hon. FDS RCS 2007; Hon. FFGDP(UK) 2011. Hon. Fellow, Univ. of Central Lancashire, 2008. Hon. DDSc Plymouth, 2014. *Recreations:* proud grandparent to Arthur, Theo, Xander, Edie, Sadie, Ivy, Clara and number 8 (pending!), live music and theatre, watching Rugby RFC, supporting Bolton Wanderers FC. *Address:* Highview, Hillmorton Lane, Clifton Upon Dunsmore, Rugby CV23 0BL. *E:* bmc397237@gmail.com.

**COCKCROFT, John Hoyle;** author and journalist; Consultant, International Conflict Resolution, 1990–2006; writer and political and computer adviser; various electronics directorships, since 1977; *b* 6 July 1934; *s* of late Lionel Fielden Cockcroft and Jenny Hoyle; *m* 1971, Tessa Fay Shepley; three *d*. *Educ:* Primary, Trearddur House; Oundle; St John's Coll., Cambridge (Sen. Maj. Scholar (History), 1953). MA Hons History and Econs 1958; Pres., Cambridge Union, 1958. Royal Artillery, 2nd Lieut, 1953–55. Feature writer, Financial Times, 1959–61; Economist, GKN, 1962–67; seconded to Treasury, Public Enterprises Div. (transport), 1965–66; Econ. Editor, Daily Telegraph, 1967–74. MP (C) Nantwich, Feb. 1974–1979; Mem. Select Cttee on Nationalised Industries (transport), 1975–79; Company Secretaries Bill (Private Member's), 1978. Duff Stoop & Co., stockbrokers (corporate finance), 1978–86; Laurence Prust, stockbrokers (corporate finance), 1986–90; Dir, BR (Eastern Region), 1984–89; Consultant: GKN, 1971–76; Mail Users' Assoc., 1976–79; Commed Ltd, 1976–93; Inst. of Chartered Secretaries, 1977–79; BR, 1979–84; Cray Electronics, 1982–84; Dowty, 1983–86; Wedgwood, 1983–84; Crystalate, 1983–86; MAP Securities (corporate finance), 1992–95; Heathmere (UK), 1996–; ESL & N, 2006–. Consultant: NEI History Archives, 1980–85; GKN History Archives, 2002–. Member Council: European Movement, 1973–74, 1983–84; Conservative Gp for Europe, 1980–87. Member: RUSI; UNA/European-Atlantic Gp. Trustee, Sanderson Trust (Oundle), 1992–2010. Leader-writer, Sunday Telegraph, 1981–86; Columnist: Microscope, 1982–85; electronic money transmission, Banking World, 1984–86; Westminster Watch, Electronics Times, 1985–90; contrib., Order! Order!, 2015–. *Publications:* (jtly) Reforming the Constitution, 1968; (jtly) Self-Help Reborn, 1969; Why England Sleeps, 1971; (jtly) An Internal History of Guest Keen and Nettlefolds, 1976; Microelectronics, 1982; Microtechnology in Banking, 1984; articles in The European, The Scotsman, Jl of Contemp. British Hist., Essex Chronicle, 1979–. Politics interviewer, BBC Radio Essex, 2011–. Probus Luncheon Club speaker, 2014–. *Recreations:* walking, reading, writing, entertaining. *Address:* 315 Broomfield Road, Chelmsford CM1 4DU.

**COCKELL, Sir Merrick (Richard)**, Kt 2010; Chairman: London Pensions Fund Authority, since 2015 (Member, Board, since 2011; Deputy Chairman, 2013–15); UK Municipal Bonds Agency, since 2015; Executive Chairman, Cratus Communications Ltd, since 2014; *b* 16 June 1957; *s* of late Peter Colvile Cockell and of Hildegard Christina Gaskell (*née* Kern); *m* 1986, Karen Libby; two *d*. *Educ:* Pierrepont Sch. Trader, F. M. Barshall Ltd, Ghana, Togo, Sierra Leone, The Gambia, then in China, 1977–82; Founder Dir, Abingdon Cockell Ltd, 1982–2006. Sen. Advr, PA Consulting Gp, 2014–. Royal Borough of Kensington and Chelsea: Mem. (C), 1986–2015; Chm., Educn Authy, 1992–95; Chief Whip, 1995–2000; Leader of Council, 2000–13. Member: London Governance Commn, 2004–06; Audit Commn, 2009–11. Chairman: London Councils (formerly Assoc. of London Govt), 2006–10; LGA, 2011–14; Crossrail 2 Growth Commn, 2015–16. Chairman: Cons. Councillors' Assoc., 2008–11 (Dep. Chm., 2005–08); Bd, Cons. Party, 2008–11. Chm., Localis Res. Ltd, 2009–. Trustee, 2020 Public Services Trust (formerly Public Services Res. Gp), 2008–11. Gov., Kensington Aldridge Acad., 2014–. Freeman, City of London, 2008. Kensington Col 31 (Middx Yeomanry and Princess

Louise's Kensington) Signal Sqdn, 2015–. *Recreations:* opera, travel (reading and actual), family and dogs. *Address:* c/o London Pensions Fund Authority, 2nd Floor, 169 Union Street, SE1 0LL. *T:* (020) 7369 6006. *E:* mrc@cockell.co. *Club:* Chelsea Arts.

**COCKELL, Michael Henry;** a Deputy Chairman of Lloyd's, 1986; *b* 30 Aug. 1933; *s* of Charles and Elise Seaton; *m* 1961, Elizabeth Janet Meikle; one *s* three *d. Educ:* Harrow School. Survey officer, 1st Regt HAC (RHA), 1955–59. Underwriter for G. N. Rouse Syndicate 570, 1968–90; Chm., M. H. Cockell & Co., 1978; Senior Partner, M. H. Cockell & Partners, 1986; Chm., Atrium Cockell Underwriting Ltd, 1997–98; Dir, Medway plc, 1997–2000. Dep. Chm., Lloyd's Non-Marine Assoc., 1982, Chm., 1983–; Mem. Council, Lloyd's, 1984–87, 1990–93 and 1995–96. *Recreations:* all sport (especially cricket), ornithology, melodic music, gardening, countryside. *Address:* Court Horeham, Cowbeech, Herstmonceaux, E Sussex BN27 4JN. *T:* (01323) 833171. *Clubs:* MCC; IZ.

**COCKER, (Peter) Mark;** author, naturalist and tutor; *b* Buxton; *s* of Peter Cocker and Anne Cocker; *m* 1989, Mary Muir; two *d. Educ:* Buxton Coll.; Univ. of East Anglia (BA Eng. 1982). Conservation work, RSPB, Nature Conservancy Council, Birdlife Internat., 1985–88; wildlife tour guide, Naturetrek, Limosa, 1988–2001; freelance journalism, mainly for Guardian, Guardian Weekly, Times Newspapers, Eastern Daily Press, New Statesman, Spectator, 1988–. Founder Mem. Council, Oriental Bird Club, 1984–88; Mem. Council, African Bird Club, 1994–2000; Pres., Norfolk and Norwich Naturalists' Soc., 2007–08. Co-Founder: New Networks for Nature, 2008–13; Norfolk Fest. of Nature, 2015–18; Mem. Council, Norwich Science Fest., 2016. Trustee, Ted Ellis Trust, 2018–. Ambassador, Friends of the Peak District, 2018–. Hon. DLitt E Anglia, 2016. *Publications:* A Himalayan Ornithologist: the life and work of Brian Houghton Hodgson (with Carol Inskipp), 1988; Richard Meinertzhagen: soldier, scientist and spy, 1989; Loneliness and Time, 1992; Rivers of Blood, Rivers of Gold: Europe's conflict with tribal peoples, 1998; Birders: tales of a tribe, 2001; Birds Britannica, 2005; A Tiger in the Sand, 2006; Crow Country, 2007 (New Angle Prize for Literature, 2009); (with David Tipling) Birds and People, 2013; Claxton: field notes from a small planet, 2014; Our Place: can we save Britain's wildlife before it is too late?, 2018; A Claxton Diary: further field notes from a small planet, 2019. *Recreations:* birds, insects, flowers, photography, reading, growing things, filling notebooks with scribble. *Address:* c/o PEW Literary Agency Ltd, 46 Lexington Street, W1F 0LP. *W:* www.markcocker.com.

**COCKER, Victor,** CBE 2000; Chairman, Aga Foodservice Group, 2004–08; *b* 30 Oct. 1940; *s* of Harold Nathan Cocker and Marjorie Cocker; *m* 1963, Jennifer Nicholls; two *d. Educ:* King Edward VII Sch., Sheffield; Nottingham Univ. (BA Econ Hons); Harvard Business Sch. (Internat. SMP 1990). FCIWEM. NW Gas Board, 1962–68; West Midlands Gas, 1968–74; Severn Trent Water Authy, 1974–89; Man. Dir, Severn Trent Water Ltd, 1991–95; Gp Chief Exec., Severn Trent plc (formerly Chief Exec., Severn Trent Water), 1995–2000. Non-executive Director: Aquafin NV, 1993–2000; Railtrack Gp, 1999–2002; Aga Foodservice Gp (formerly Glynwed Internat.), 2000–08; Modern Waste, 2008. Founder Chm., Waste and Resources Action Prog., 2000–08. Water Aid: Trustee, 1996–2007; Vice Chm., 1998–2001; Chm., 2001–07; Chm., Severn Trent Region, 1997–2000. Dir, Midlands Excellence, 1996–2000. Member: Adv. Cttee on Business in Environment, 1996–2003; World Business Council for Sustainable Develt, 1997–2000. Chm., Forward Birmingham RNLI Lifeboat Campaign, 1994–96; Member: RNLI Cttee of Mgt, 1996–2002; RNLI Council, 2003–10 (Vice Pres., 2010–); RSA Council, 2004–10; Norfolk Local Access Forum, 2016–. Birmingham City University: Mem., 2009–16, Dep. Chm., 2011–15, Bd of Govs; Pro Chancellor, 2011–15. CCMI. Hon. FCIWM 2004. DUniv Central England, 2006; Hon. DLaws Nottingham, 2019. *Recreations:* Fakenham Ramblers (Gp Sec.), North Norfolk U3A (Chm.). *Address:* Aldercarr, Bayfield, Holt, Norfolk NR25 7JW. *T:* (01263) 713613.

**COCKERAM, Eric (Paul);** JP; *b* 4 July 1924; *er s* of Mr and Mrs J. W. Cockeram; *m* 1949, Frances Irving; two *s* two *d. Educ:* The Leys Sch., Cambridge. Served War, 1942–46: Captain The Gloucestershire Regt; "D Day" landings (wounded and later discharged). MP (C): Bebington, 1970–Feb. 1974; Ludlow, 1979–87. PPS: to Minister for Industry, 1970–72; to Minister for Posts and Telecommunications, 1972; to Chancellor of Exchequer, 1972–74. Mem., Select Cttee on Corporation Tax, 1971, on Industry and Trade, 1979–87; Mem., Public Accounts Cttee, 1983–87. Pres., Menswear Assoc. of Britain, 1964–65. Mem., Bd of Governors, United Liverpool Hosps, 1965–74; Chm., Liverpool NHS Exec. Council, 1970. Chairman: Watson Prickard Ltd, 1966–2001; Johnson Fry (Northern) Ltd, 1988–94; Director: TSB (NW), 1968–83; TSB (Wales & Border Counties), 1983–88; Liverpool Building Soc., 1975–82 (Vice-Chm., 1981–82); Midshires Building Soc., 1982–88; Muller Group (UK) Ltd, 1983–94. Member of Lloyd's. Liveryman, Worshipful Co. of Glovers, 1969–, Mem. Court, 1979–89. Freeman: City of London; City of Springfield, Ill. JP, City of Liverpool, 1960. *Recreations:* bridge, golf, shooting, country walking. *Address:* Fairway Lodge, Caldy, Wirral, Cheshire CH48 1NB. *T:* (0151) 625 1100. *Clubs:* Carlton, Army and Navy.

**COCKERELL, Michael Roger Lewis;** political documentary maker, author, broadcaster; *b* 26 Aug. 1940; *s* of Prof. Hugh Cockerell and Fanny Cockerell (*née* Jochelman); *m* 1st, 1970, Anne Faber (marr. diss. 1980); one *s* one *d*; 2nd, 1984, Bridget Heathcoat-Amory (marr. diss. 1990); two *d*; 3rd, 2011, Anna Lloyd; three *d. Educ:* Kilburn Grammar Sch.; Heidelberg Univ.; Corpus Christi Coll., Oxford (MA PPE; Hon. Fellow, 2012). Magazine journalist, 1962–66; Producer, BBC African Service, 1966–68; Current Affairs, BBC TV, 1968–87: Producer, 24 Hours, 1968–72; reporter: Midweek, 1972–75; Panorama, 1975–87; freelance TV reporter and documentary maker, 1987–: *programmes* include: investigations into political lobbying, the Honours system, the Whips, and the Cabinet; How to Be series; profiles of Alan Clark, James Callaghan, Edward Heath, Enoch Powell, Barbara Castle, Roy Jenkins, Betty Boothroyd, Stella Rimington, The Rivals (Gordon Brown and Michael Portillo); Tony Blair's Thousand Days, 2000; News from Number Ten: Alastair Campbell and the media, 2000; Trust Me, I'm a Politician, 2003; With Friends Like These: Britain's relations with France, Germany and US, 2003; The Downing Street Patient: Health of PMs, 2004; Do You Still Believe in Tony?, 2004; The Brown-Blair Affair, 2004; Michael Howard: No More Mr Nasty, 2005; How We Fell for Europe, 2005; How to be Tory Leader, 2005; Tony's Tight Spot, 2006; Blair: the inside story (three-part series), How to be ex-Prime Minister, 2007; Dave Cameron's Incredible Journey, 2007; The Making of the Iron Lady, 2008; Great Offices of State (trilogy on Treasury, Home Office and FCO), 2010; How to Win the TV Debate, 2010; The Secret World of Whitehall (trilogy on Prime Minister's Office, Cabinet Office and Special Political Advrs), 2011; The Lost World of the Seventies, 2012; Boris Johnson: The Irresistible Rise, 2013; Inside the Commons (4-part series), 2015; EU Referendum Campaign, 2016; Ronald Reagan and Donald Trump, 2017; Theresa May's Downfall, What Makes Boris Tick?, 2019; BBC Radio 4 documentaries: The Trial of David Irving, 2004; Tales from the Cutting Room, 2006; Profile: Conrad Black, 2007 and 2010; Speaker Michael Martin, 2008. Vis. Prof. of Politics, Nottingham Univ., 2011–; Vis. Lectr, LSE, 1998–, Nuffield Coll., Oxford, 2001–04. Huw Wheldon Lect., BBC2, 2000. Consultant, Oxford DNB, 2000–. Hon. DCL UEA, 2007. Emmy Award, 1980; Best Documentary Award, RTS, 1982; Golden Nymph Award, Monte Carlo, 1988; Judges' Award for Special Contrib. to Politics, Pol Studies Assoc., 2008; James Cameron Special Award, 2010. *Publications:* (jtly) Sources Close to the Prime Minister, 1984; Live from Number Ten: the inside story of Prime Ministers and TV, 1988; (contrib.) The Blair Effect, 2001; (contrib.) Where the Truth Lies, 2006; articles in newspapers. *Recreations:* cricket, tennis, merry-making. *Address:* 27 Arundel Gardens, W11 2LW. *T:* (020) 7727 8035, 07747 031940. *E:* michael.cockerell@gmail.com. *Clubs:* MCC (playing mem.), Lord's Taverners, Bushmen.

**COCKERHAM, David,** CBE 1995; HM Diplomatic Service, retired; International Director, Invest.UK (formerly Invest in Britain Bureau), 1999–2001; *b* 14 May 1944; *s* of late Henry Cockerham and Eleanor Cockerham (*née* Nicholls); *m* 1967, Ann Lesley Smith; two *s. Educ:* Leeds Central High Sch. Joined FO, 1962; Saigon, 1967–68; Japanese studies, Tokyo, 1969–71; Vice-Consul: Yokohama, 1971–72; Tokyo, 1972–75; FCO, 1975–79; Vice-Consul (Commercial Inf.), British Inf. Services, NY, 1979–81; Consul (Commercial) and Exec. Asst to Dir-Gen. of Trade Develt, USA, British Trade Develt Office, NY, 1981–83; First Sec. (Commercial), Tokyo, 1983–87; Hd, Exports to Japan Unit, DTI, 1987–90 (on secondment); Dir of Ops, Migration and Visa Dept, FCO, 1990–91; Dep. High Comr, Madras, 1991–94; Consul-Gen. and Dir of Trade Promotion, Osaka, 1994–98. Member: FCO Assoc., 2000–; Bearsted and Thurnham Soc. (Vice-Chm. and Sec., 2005–07). *Recreations:* jazz clarinet, banjo and saxophone.

**COCKERILL, Hon. Dame Sara Elizabeth, (Hon. Dame Sara Eaton),** DBE 2017; Hon. Mrs Justice Cockerill; a Judge of the High Court, Queen's Bench Division, since 2017; *b* Weston Super Mare, 7 Nov. 1968; *d* of Alan Cockerill and Lilian Cockerill; *m* 1997, Nigel Trevor Eaton, QC. *Educ:* Lady Eleanor Holles Sch.; St Anne's Coll., Oxford (BA 1989; Eldon Schol.). Called to the Bar, Lincoln's Inn, 1990; in practice as a barrister, specialising in commercial law, 1990–2017; QC 2011; a Dep. High Court Judge, 2016–17. *Publications:* (Contributing Ed.) (Commercial Court and Arbitration) Civil Procedure (The White Book), 2011–; The Law and Practice of Compelled Evidence in Civil Proceedings, 2011; Eleanor of Castile: the shadow queen, 2014. *Recreations:* medieval history, cycling, running, C19 fiction, waiting on cat. *Address:* Royal Courts of Justice, Rolls Building, Fetter Lane, EC4A 1NL. *W:* www.saracockerill.com.

**COCKETT, Ven. Elwin Wesley;** Archdeacon of West Ham, since 2007; *b* Kotagiri, Tamil Nadu, India, 24 May 1959; *s* of late Dr Norman Cockett and Janet Cockett (*née* Graham, then Slade); *m* 1977, Susan Mary Jones; one *s* two *d. Educ:* St Paul's Cath. Choir Sch.; Forest Sch., Snaresbrook; Oak Hill Theological Coll. (BA Theol. and Pastoral Studies 1991). Practice Manager, Bethnal Green Med. Mission, 1983–88; ordained deacon, 1991, priest, 1992; Curate, St Chad's, Chadwell Heath, 1991–94; Curate i/c, 1994–95, Priest i/c, 1995–97, Vicar, 1997–2000, St Paul's, Harold Hill; Team Rector, Billericay and Little Burstead, 2000–07; Rural Dean, Basildon, 2004–07. Chair, Chelmsford Diocesan Bd of Educn, 2014–18. Club Chaplain, West Ham UFC, 1992–2011. Dir, Aston Mansfield, 2009–. Gov., Forest Sch., Snaresbrook, 2011–; Mem., Genesis Educnl Trust, 2017–. *Recreations:* music, motorcycling, following the fortunes of West Ham United, enjoying the delights of Exmoor. *Address:* 86 Aldersbrook Road, E12 5DH. *T:* (020) 8989 8557, *Fax:* (020) 8530 1311. *E:* a.westham@chelmsford.anglican.org, elwin@cockett.org.

**COCKING, Prof. Edward Charles Daniel,** FRS 1983; Professor of Botany, University of Nottingham, 1969–97, now Professor Emeritus; *b* 26 Sept. 1931; *y s* of late Charles Cocking and Mary (*née* Murray); *m* 1960, Bernadette Keane; one *s* one *d. Educ:* Buckhurst Hill County High Sch., Essex; Univ. of Bristol (BSc, PhD, DSc). FRSB. Civil Service Commission Research Fellow, 1956–59; Nottingham University: Lectr in Plant Physiology, 1959–66; Reader, 1966–69; Head of Dept of Botany, 1969. Leverhulme Trust Res. Fellow, 1995–97. S. Yoshida Meml Lecture, Hangzhou Univ., China, 1987. Member: Lawes Agricl Trust Cttee, Rothamsted Experimental Stn, 1987–91 (Mem., Governing Body, 1991–2013; Chm., 1999–2003); Adv. Cttee on Forest Res., Forestry Commn, 1987–95; Council, Royal Soc., 1986–88; AFRC, 1990–94 (Royal Soc. Assessor, 1988–90); Lawes Agriculture Trust Co., 2000–17. Trustee, Royal Botanic Gardens, Kew, 1983–93; Member, Governing Body: Glasshouse Crops Res. Inst., 1983–87; British Soc. Horticultural Res., 1987–89. Pres., Sect. K, BAAS, 1983. Royal Soc. Trustee, Uppingham Sch., 1997–2007. MAE 1993. Hon. Mem., Hungarian Acad. Scis, 1995; Fellow: Indian Acad. of Agricl Scis, 2000; World Innovation Foundn, 2003. Hon. DSc Nottingham, 2017. Lifetime Achievement Award, Univ. of Toledo, USA, 2004. *Publications:* Introduction to the Principles of Plant Physiology (with W. Stiles, FRS), 3rd edn 1969; numerous scientific papers in botanical/genetics jls on plant genetic manipulations and nitrogen fixation. *Recreations:* walking, travelling, especially by train, occasional chess. *Address:* Centre for Crop Nitrogen Fixation, Life Sciences Building, School of Biosciences, University of Nottingham, University Park, Nottingham NG7 2RD. *T:* (0115) 951 3056, *Fax:* (0115) 951 6334. *E:* edward.cocking@nottingham.ac.uk; 30 Patterdale Road, Woodthorpe, Nottingham NG5 4LQ. *T:* (0115) 926 2452.

**COCKINGS, Giles Francis Sacheverell;** QC 2016; *b* Olney, Bucks, 20 Jan. 1969; *s* of Dr Garth Cockings and Gerda Cockings; *m* 2004, Charlotte Yarrow; one *s* three *d. Educ:* Bedford Sch., Bedford; Univ. of Reading (BSc Hons Econ. 1991); City Univ., London (LLB Hons 1995); Inns of Court Sch. of Law. Credit Lyonnais Alexander Laing & Cruickshank Institutional Equities, 1987–88; called to the Bar, Middle Temple, 1996; in practice as barrister, specialising in criminal law, 1996–. Member: Criminal Bar Assoc., 1996–; South Eastern Circuit, 1996–. *Publications:* (contrib.) Criminal Procedure and Investigation Act 1996: disclosure provisions, 1999. *Recreations:* family, Rugby, fly fishing, motor sport, classic car restoration, golf, gardening, cooking, dogs, cricket. *Address:* Furnival Chambers, 30–32 Furnival Street, EC4A 1JQ. *T:* (020) 7405 3232. *E:* gcockings@furnivallaw.co.uk, clerks@furnivallaw.co.uk. *Club:* Latimer Lakes Fishing.

**COCKLE, Alexandra Helen;** see Depledge, A. H.

**COCKLE, Edward John, (Ted);** President, Virgin EMI, since 2013; *b* Wendover, Bucks; *s* of John Cockle and Josie Cockle; *m* 2011, Joanne Reid; one *s* one *d. Educ:* Aylesbury Grammar Sch.; Univ. of Bristol (BSocSci 1995). Mktg Dir, Sony Music Ops, 1995–2005; Mktg Dir, 2005–07, Co-Pres., 2007–13, Island Records. *Address:* Virgin EMI, Universal Music, 4 St Pancras Square, N1C 4AG.

**COCKROFT, His Honour (Peter) John;** a Circuit Judge, 1993–2013; *b* 24 Sept. 1947; *s* of late Walter Philip Barron Cockroft and Nora Cockroft (*née* Collett); *m* 1975, Maria Eugenia Coromina Perandones; one *s* two *d. Educ:* Queen Elizabeth I Grammar Sch., Darlington; Queens' Coll., Cambridge (BA, LLB). Called to the Bar, Middle Temple, 1970 (Astbury Scholar); practised NE Circuit; Asst Recorder, 1985–89; Recorder, 1989–93. *Recreations:* visiting Spain, gardening. *Address:* Brackenwell Cottage, North Rigton, N Yorks LS17 0DG. *T:* (01423) 734585. *Clubs:* Yorkshire County Cricket; Yorkshire Rugby Football Union.

**COCKS,** family name of **Baron Somers.**

**COCKS, Hon. Anna Gwenllian S.;** see Somers Cocks.

**COCKS, Clifford Christopher,** CB 2008; FRS 2015; Chief Mathematician, Government Communications Headquarters, 2001–09; *b* Cheshire, 28 Dec. 1950; *s* of William Cocks and Joan Cocks; *m* 1979, Gillian White; one *s* one *d. Educ:* King's Coll., Cambridge (BA

1971). CMath 1998; FIMA 1998. Civil Service: SO, 1973; SSO, 1979; Sen. Civil Service, 1998. Visiting Fellow: Univ. of Bristol, 2005; Merton Coll., Oxford, 2006; Vis. Prof., KCL, 2015–18. Hon. DSc: Bristol, 2008; UEA, 2008; Birmingham, 2015. *Recreations:* Reader (Anglican), amateur dramatics. *E:* cliffcocks@outlook.com.

**COCKS, Dr Leonard Robert Morrison, (Dr Robin Cocks),** OBE 1999; TD 1979; Keeper of Palaeontology, Natural History Museum (formerly British Museum (Natural History)), 1986–98; *b* 17 June 1938; *s* of late Ralph Morrison Cocks and Lucille Mary Cocks (*née* Blackler); *m* 1963, Elaine Margaret Sturdy; one *s* two *d*. *Educ:* Felsted School; Hertford College, Oxford (BA, MA, DPhil, DSc). FGS; CGeol. Commissioned Royal Artillery 1958; active service Malaya, 1958–59; DSIR Research Student, Oxford Univ., 1962–65; British Museum (Nat. Hist.), 1965–; Dep. Keeper of Palaeontology, 1980–86. Geologist, Royal Engineers, 1970–83. President: Palaeontographical Soc., 1994–98; GA, 2004–06 (Vice-Pres., 2003–04, 2006–07); Member: Council, Palaeontological Assoc., 1969–82, 1986–88 (Editor, 1971–82, Pres., 1986–88; Lapworth Medal, 2010); Council, Geological Soc., 1982–89, 1997–2000 (Sec., 1985–89; Pres., 1998–2000; Coke Medal, 1995); NERC Geological Res. Grants Cttee, 1978–81, 1984. Comr, Internat. Commn on Zoological Nomenclature, 1982–2000. Vis. Fellow, Southampton Univ., 1988–95; Vis. Prof., Imperial Coll., London, 1997–2001. Visitor, Oxford Univ. Mus. of Natural Hist., 1997–2008. Dumont Medal, Belgian Geol Soc., 2003. *Publications:* The Evolving Earth, 1979; (ed) Encyclopedia of Geology, 5 vols, 2005; (with T. H. Torsvik) Earth History and Palaeogeography, 2017; papers in sci. jls, on Ordovician-Silurian biostratigraphy and brachiopods, esp. from Britain, Canada, Norway, Russia, China. *Recreation:* country pursuits. *Address:* Department of Earth Sciences, Natural History Museum, Cromwell Road, SW7 5BD. *T:* (020) 7942 5140. *E:* r.cocks@nhm.ac.uk.

**COCKSHAW, Sir Alan,** Kt 1992; FREng; FICE; Chairman, English Partnerships (formerly English Partnerships, and Commission for New Towns), 1998–2001; *b* 14 July 1937; *s* of John and Maud Cockshaw; *m* 1960, Brenda Payne; one *s* three *d*. *Educ:* Farnworth Grammar Sch.; Leeds Univ. (BSc). FICE 1985; FREng (FEng 1986). Chief Executive: Fairclough Civil Engrg, 1978–85; Fairclough Parkinson-Mining, 1982–85; Fairclough Engrg, 1983–84; Gp Chief Exec., 1984–88, Chm., 1988–97, AMEC plc; Chairman: Manchester Millennium Ltd, 1996–2003; Roxboro Gp, 1997–2005; British Airways Regl, 2000–03; New East Manchester Ltd, 2000–02. Non-exec. Dir, Norweb plc, 1992–95; non-executive Director: New Millennium Experience Co., 1997–2000; Pidemco Land, then CapitaLand, Singapore, 1999–2005. Chairman: Overseas Projects Bd, DTI, 1992–95; Oil and Gas Projects and Supplies Office, DTI, 1994–97; Mem., BOTB, 1992–95; Dep. Chm., NW Business Leadership Team, 1990–97 (Life Pres., 1997). Chm., Major Projects Assoc., 1998–2004. Pres., ICE, 1997–98. Hon. DEng UMIST, 1997; Hon. DSc Salford, 1998. *Recreations:* Rugby (both codes), cricket, walking, gardening. *Address:* Hanover House, 30–32 Charlotte Street, Manchester M1 4FD.

**COCKSWORTH, Rt Rev. Christopher John;** see Coventry, Bishop of.

**CODD, Geoffrey;** see Codd, R. G.

**CODD, Michael Henry,** AC 1991; Chancellor, University of Wollongong, 1997–2009; *b* 26 Dec. 1939; *s* of Ernest Applebee Codd and Nell Gregory (*née* Pavy). *Educ:* Univ. of Adelaide (BEc Hons). Statistician, 1962–69; joined Dept of Prime Minister, Australia, 1969; Under-Sec., Dept of Prime Minister and Cabinet, 1979–81; Sec., Dept of Employment and Ind. Relns, 1981–83; Chm., Industries Assistance Commn, 1983–85; Sec., Dept of Community Services, 1985–86; Head, Dept of Prime Minister and Cabinet and Sec. to Cabinet, 1986–91. Non-executive Director: Qantas, 1992–2009; Telstra Ltd, 1992–99; Australian Nuclear Science and Technol. Orgn, 1996–2001; MLC Ltd, 1996–2011; CitiPower, 1999–2002; Ingeus, 2003–09 (Chm., 2006–09). *Address:* 586 Williamsdale Road, Williamsdale, NSW 2620, Australia. *T:* 04286 28880.

**CODD, (Ronald) Geoffrey,** CEng; CITP; FBCS; change professional, since 1957; author, since 2004; *b* 20 Aug. 1932; *s* of Thomas Reuben Codd and Betty Leyster Codd (*née* Sturt); *m* 1960, Christine Ellen Léonide Robertson; one *s* two *d*. *Educ:* Cathedral Sch., Llandaff; The College, Llandovery; Presentation Coll., Cobh. CEng 1990. Dip. in Company Direction, 1989. Served RAF, Transport Comd, 1952–57. Rolls Royce, Aero-Engine Div., 1957–58; International Computers, 1958–61; Marconi Co., 1961–70; J. Bibby & Sons, Liverpool, 1970–74; Weir Gp, Glasgow, 1974–80; Brooke Bond Gp, 1981–86; Under Sec. and Dir, Information and Risks Management, ECGD, 1986–90; Managing Partner, InterChange Associates, 1990–2004. Dir, Randolph Enterprise, 1992–98. Advr to Bd, HM Customs and Excise, 1992–96. Associate, Wentworth Res., 1992–. Mem., ELITE Forum, BCS, 1991–. Chairman: Community Plan Steering Gp, 2009–11; Osmington Soc., 2009–11, 2016–; White Horse Ancient Monument Restoration Gp, 2009–12; Church Reordering Gp, 2015–. FInstD 1984. Freeman, City of London, 1990; Liveryman, Co. of Inf. Technologists, 1990. *Publications:* The Drowning Director, 2007; The Diligent Director in a Digital Business World, 2014, 2nd edn 2016; Skomer Memories, 2016, 2nd edn as Skomer Memories: a story of the trials, tribulations, and joys experienced by the last family to own and farm this enchanting island, 2018; contributor to business magazines. *Recreations:* competitive and leisure sailing, theatre, practical pastimes. *Address:* The White House, Church Lane, Osmington, Dorset DT3 6EJ. *Clubs:* City Livery; Royal Dorset Yacht; Goodwood Aero.

**CODRINGTON, Sir Christopher (George Wayne),** 4th Bt *cr* 1876, of Dodington, Gloucestershire; *b* 20 Feb. 1960; *s* of Sir Simon Codrington, 3rd Bt and of Pamela Joy Halliday Codrington (*née* Wise); *S* father, 2005; *m* 1991, Noelle Lynne, *d* of Dale Leverson; one *s* one *d* (and one *s* decd). *Educ:* Millfield; RAC Cirencester. *Heir:* *s* William George Bethell Codrington, *b* 14 April 2003. *Address:* Springfield House, Fordwells, Witney, Oxon OX29 9PP.

**CODRINGTON, Sir (Giles) Peter,** 9th Bt *cr* 1721, of Dodington, Gloucestershire; *b* 28 Oct. 1943; *s* of Sir William Richard Codrington, 7th Bt, and Joan Kathleen Birelli, *e d* of Percy E. Nicholas; *S* brother, 2006; *m* 1989, Shirley Linda Duke; two *s* one *d*. *Recreation:* yachting. *Heir:* (to Btcy) *s* Daniel Peter Codrington, *b* 8 Feb. 1993. *Clubs:* Monaco Yacht; Antigua Yacht.

**CODRINGTON, Richard John;** HM Diplomatic Service, retired; *b* 18 Dec. 1953; *s* of Capt. Christopher Thomas Codrington, RN and Anna Maria (*née* Hanscomb); *m* 1985, Julia Elizabeth Nolan; two *s*. *Educ:* Ampleforth; Lincoln Coll., Oxford (MA). MoD, 1975–78; entered HM Diplomatic Service, 1978: FCO, 1978–79; 2nd, later 1st. Sec., Dar es Salaam, 1980–82; FCO, 1983–85; 1st Sec., New Delhi, 1985–88; Asst Hd, S Asian Dept, FCO, 1989–92; on loan to S. G. Warburg & Co. Ltd, 1992–94; on loan, as Hd, Cross-media ownership review team, DNH, 1994; Dir of Trade Promotion and Investment, Paris, 1995–99; Dep. High Comr, Ottawa, 1999–2003; Hd, Online Communications Dept, FCO, 2003–04; RCDS, 2004; Hd, Afghanistan Gp, FCO, 2005–08; reviewed UK Trade & Investment's worldwide inward investment activity, 2008; based in Jakarta, 2009–13, Ottawa, 2013–17. *Publications:* Cyril Bleaden, MC, Soldier and Vicar, 2016. *Recreations:* photography, family history, diving, ski-ing.

**CODRON, Sir Michael (Victor),** Kt 2014; CBE 1989; theatrical producer; *b* 8 June 1930; *s* of I. A. Codron and Lily (*née* Morgenstern). *Educ:* St Paul's Sch.; Worcester Coll., Oxford (MA; Hon. Fellow 2012). Director: Aldwych Theatre; Cameron Mackintosh Prof. of Contemporary Theatre, Oxford Univ., 1993. Emeritus Fellow, St Catherine's Coll., Oxford, 2003. Productions include: Share My Lettuce, Breath of Spring, 1957; Dock Brief and What Shall We Tell Caroline?, The Birthday Party, Valmouth, 1958; Pieces of Eight, 1959; The Wrong Side of the Park, The Caretaker, 1960; Three, Stop It Whoever You Are, One Over the Eight, The Tenth Man, Big Soft Nellie, 1961; Two Stars for Comfort, Everything in the Garden, Rattle of a Simple Man, 1962; Next Time I'll sing to You, Private Lives (revival), The Lovers and the Dwarfs, Cockade, 1963; Poor Bitos, The Formation Dancers, Entertaining Mr Sloane, 1964; Loot, The Killing of Sister George, Ride a Cock Horse, 1965; Little Malcolm and his Struggle against the Eunuchs, The Anniversary, There's a Girl in my Soup, Big Bad Mouse, 1966; The Judge, The Flip Side, Wise Child, The Boy Friend (revival), 1967; Not Now Darling, The Real Inspector Hound, 1968; The Contractor, Slag, The Two of Us, The Philanthropist, 1970; The Foursome, Butley, A Voyage Round my Father, The Changing Room, 1971; Veterans, Time and Time Again, Crown Matrimonial, My Fat Friend, 1972; Collaborators, Savages, Habeas Corpus, Absurd Person Singular, 1973; Knuckle, Flowers, Golden Pathway Annual, The Norman Conquests, John Paul George Ringo... and Bert, 1974; A Family and A Fortune, Alphabetical Order, A Far Better Husband, Ashes, Absent Friends, Otherwise Engaged, Stripwell, 1975; Funny Peculiar, Treats, Donkey's Years, Confusions, Teeth 'n' Smiles, Yahoo, 1976; Dusa, Stas, Fish & Vi, Just Between Ourselves, Oh, Mr Porter, Breezeblock Park, The Bells of Hell, The Old Country, 1977; The Rear Column, Ten Times Table, The Unvarnished Truth, The Homecoming (revival), Alice's Boys, Night and Day, 1978; Joking Apart, Tishoo, Stage Struck, 1979; Dr Faustus, Make and Break, The Dresser, Taking Steps, Enjoy, 1980; Hinge and Bracket at the Globe, Rowan Atkinson in Revue, House Guest, Quartermaine's Terms, 1981; Season's Greetings, Noises Off, Funny Turns, The Real Thing, 1982; The Hard Shoulder, 1983; Benefactors, 1984; Why Me?, Jumpers, Who Plays Wins, Look, No Hans!, 1985; Made in Bangkok, Woman in Mind, 1986; Three Sisters, A View from the Bridge, 1987; Hapgood, Uncle Vanya, Re: Joyce, The Sneeze, Henceforward, 1988; The Cherry Orchard, 1989; Man of the Moment, Look Look, Hidden Laughter, Private Lives, 1990; What the Butler Saw, 70 Girls 70, The Revengers' Comedies, 1991; The Rise and Fall of Little Voice, 1992; Time of My Life, Jamais Vu, 1993; Kit and the Widow, Dead Funny, Arcadia, The Sisters Rosensweig, 1994; Indian Ink, Dealer's Choice, 1995; The Shakespeare Revue, A Talent to Amuse, 1996; Tom and Clem, Silhouette, Heritage, 1997; Things We Do for Love, Alarms and Excursions, The Invention of Love, 1998; Copenhagen, Comic Potential, 1999; Peggy for You, 2000; Blue/Orange, 2001; Life After George, Bedroom Farce, Damsels in Distress, 2002; My Brilliant Divorce, Dinner, 2003; Democracy, 2004; Ying Tong, Losing Louis, 2005; Glorious!, 2006; Entertaining Angels, 2006; The Bargain, 2006; Quartermaine's Terms, 2013; Mr Foote's Other Leg, 2015; *film:* Clockwise, 1986. *Recreation:* collecting Caroline of Brunswick memorabilia. *Address:* Aldwych Theatre Offices, Aldwych, WC2B 4DF. *Club:* Garrick.

**COE,** family name of **Baron Coe**.

**COE,** Baron *cr* 2000 (Life Peer), of Ranmore in the co. of Surrey; **Sebastian Newbold Coe**, CH 2013; KBE 2006 (OBE 1990; MBE 1982); President, International Association of Athletics Federations, since 2015 (Council Member, since 2003; Vice President, 2007–15); *b* 29 Sept. 1956; *s* of late Peter and Angela Coe; *m* 1990, Nicola McIrvine (marr. diss.); two *s* two *d*; *m* 2011, Mrs Carole Annett, *d* of M. J. K. Smith. *Educ:* Loughborough University (BSc Hons Economics and Social History). Won gold medal for running 1500m and silver medal for 800m at Moscow Olympics, 1980; gold medal for 1500m and silver medal for 800m at Los Angeles Olympics, 1984; European Champion for 800m, Stuttgart, 1986; set world records at 800m, 1000m and mile, 1981. Research Assistant, Loughborough Univ., 1981–84. Sports Council: Mem., 1983–89; Vice-Chm., 1986–89; Chm., Olympic Review Gp, 1984–85. Member: HEA, 1987–92; Olympic Cttee, Medical Commn, 1987–93; Athletes Commn, IOC, Lausanne (first Chm., 1981–92); Olympic Cttee, Sport for All Commn, 1997–. Chairman: London 2012 Olympic Bid, 2004–05 (Vice-Chm., 2003–04); LOCOG, 2005–13; British Olympic Assoc., 2012–16; Olympic Legacy Ambassador, 2012–. Steward, BBB of C, 1995–97; Chm., FIFA Ethics Cttee, 2006–10; Mem. Bd, England 2018 FIFA World Cup Bid, 2009. Chairman: Diadora (UK), 1987–94; Complete Leisure Group Ltd, 2005–13; CSM Sport & Entertainment, 2013–; non-exec. Dir, Chime Communications, 2014–; Global Advr, Nike Internat., 2001–15. Sebastian Coe Health Clubs, Jarvis Hotel Group, 1994. MP (C) Falmouth and Camborne, 1992–97; contested (C) same seat, 1997. PPS to Ministers of State for Defence Procurement and for Armed Forces, MoD, 1994–95, to Dep. Prime Minister, 1995–96; a Govt Whip, 1996–97. Dep. Chief of Staff, 1997, Private Sec., 1997–2001, to Leader of Conservative Party. Pres., AAA of England, 2000–; Founder Mem., Laureus World Sports Acad., 2000–; Assoc. Mem., Académie des Sports, France. Sports columnist, The Daily Telegraph, 2000–. Chancellor, Loughborough Univ., 2017–. Hon. DTech Loughborough, 1985; Hon. DSc Hull, 1988. Lifetime Achievement Award, BBC Sports Personality of the Year Awards, 2012. Principe de Asturias award (Spain), 1987. *Publications:* (with David Miller) Running Free, 1981; (with Peter Coe) Running for Fitness, 1983; (with Nicholas Mason) The Olympians, 1984, 2nd edn 1996; Running My Life (autobiog.), 2012. *Recreations:* listening to recorded or preferably live jazz, theatre. *Clubs:* East India, Sportsman's.

**COE, Albert Henry, (Harry);** Chairman: Travelsphere Holdings Ltd, 2000–06; Jaycare Holdings Ltd, 2000–04; Leisure Ventures plc, 2002–04; *b* 28 May 1944; *m* Beryl Margaret; two *d*. Supervisor, Coopers & Lybrand, 1967–70; Gp Financial Controller, Aerialite Ltd, 1970–72; Gp Finance Dir, London Scottish Bank, 1972–75; Finance Director: (print and packaging), Smurfit Ltd, 1975–81; Granada TV, 1981–88; Airtours plc: Gp Finance Dir, 1988–96; Dep. Chief Exec., 1996–97; Gp Man. Dir, 1997–99; non-exec. Dir, 1999–2001. Non-executive Director: Britannia Bldg Soc., 2000–03; Capital Ideas plc, 2004–07. *Recreations:* cricket, tennis, golf, ski-ing, stock market, current affairs. *Address:* Finvara, Wilmslow Road, Mottram St Andrew, Cheshire SK10 4QT.

**COE, Jonathan,** PhD; FRSL; writer, since 1987; *b* 19 Aug. 1961; *s* of Roger and Janet Coe; *m* 1989, Janine McKeown; two *d*. *Educ:* Trinity Coll., Cambridge (BA); Warwick Univ. (MA, PhD 1986). FRSL 2012. Hon. Dr: UCE, 2002; Birmingham, 2006; Hon. DLitt Wolverhampton, 2006. Officier, Ordre des Arts et des Lettres (France), 2016 (Chevalier, 2004). Premio Letterario Citta de Vigevano, 2017. *Publications:* The Accidental Woman, 1987; A Touch of Love, 1989; The Dwarves of Death, 1990; Humphrey Bogart: take it and like it, 1991; James Stewart: leading man, 1994; What a Carve Up!, 1994 (Prix du Meilleur Livre Etranger, 1995); The House of Sleep, 1997 (Prix Médicis Etranger, 1998); The Rotters' Club, 2001 (Bollinger Everyman Wodehouse Prize, 2001; Premio Arcebispo Juan de San Clemente, 2004) (televised 2005); Like a Fiery Elephant: the story of B. S. Johnson, 2004 (Samuel Johnson Prize, 2005); The Closed Circle, 2004; The Rain Before It Falls, 2007; The Terrible Privacy of Maxwell Sim, 2010; The Story of Gulliver, 2013; Marginal Notes, Doubtful Statements, 2013; Expo 58, 2013; Loggerheads and Other Stories, 2014;

Number 11, 2015 (Premio internazionale Ennio Flaiano, 2016); The Broken Mirror, 2017; Middle England, 2018. *Recreation:* music. *Address:* c/o Peake Associates, PO Box 66726, NW5 9FE. *T:* (020) 7681 4307.

**COE, Rosalind;** QC 2008; **Her Honour Judge Coe;** a Circuit Judge, since 2011; *b* Nottingham, 2 Sept. 1959; *d* of late James Thompson; *m* 1980, David Lockhart Coe; one *s* one *d*. *Educ:* Nottingham Univ. (LLB 1981); Inns of Court Sch. of Law. Called to the Bar, Middle Temple, 1983, Bencher, 2013; Recorder, 2003–11. *Recreations:* family, films, holidays. *Address:* Nottingham Crown Court, 60 Canal Street, Nottingham NG1 7EL.

**COELHO, Paulo;** writer; *b* Rio de Janeiro, 28 Aug. 1947; *m* Christina Oiticica. Composer of popular songs, with Raul Seixas, 1973–82. Special Counsellor for Intercultural Dialogues and Spiritual Convergences, UNESCO, 2007; UN Messenger of Peace, 2007. Mem., Brazilian Acad. of Letters, 2002. *Publications:* The Pilgrimage, 1987; The Alchemist, 1988; Brida, 1990; O Dom Supremo: the gift, 1991; The Valkyries, 1992; Maktub, 1994; By the River Piedra I Sat Down and Wept, 1994; The Fifth Mountain, 1996; Love Letters from a Prophet, 1997; The Manual of the Warrior of Light, 1997; Veronika Decides to Die, 1998; The Devil and Miss Prym, 2000; Father, Sons and Grandsons, 2001; Eleven Minutes, 2003; The Genie and the Roses, 2004; The Zahir, 2005; Like the Flowing River, 2006; The Witch of Portobello, 2006; The Winner Stands Alone, 2008; Aleph, 2010; Manuscript Found in Accra, 2012; Adultery, 2014; The Spy, 2016; Hippie, 2018. *Recreations:* reading, travelling, computers, the Internet, music, football, walking, practising Kyudu. *Address:* Sant Jordi Asociados Agencia Literaria S. L. U., Paseig de Gràcia 89, 1° 1ª, 08008 Barcelona, Spain. *T:* and *Fax:* (93) 2240107. *E:* post@santjordi-asociados.com.

**COELLO, Judith Elaine; Her Honour Judge Coello;** a Circuit Judge, since 2010; *b* 7 Jan. 1959; *d* of Anthony John Banks and Avrielle Doreen Mary Banks; *m* 1st, 1986, Timothy William Nichols (*d* 1999); 2nd, 2010, Kenneth R. Coello. *Educ:* Bridlington High Sch. for Girls; Liverpool Poly. (BA Hons); Christleton Coll. of Law, Chester. Admitted solicitor, 1983; Asst Solicitor, London Bor. of Sutton, 1983–85; Prosecuting Solicitor, Cambs CC, 1985–87; Principal Legal Advr, Richmond upon Thames Magistrates' Court, 1987–93; Hd of Legal Services, Uxbridge Magistrates' Court, 1993–2000; Dep. Dist Judge (Magistrates' Courts), 1997–2007; pt-time Immigration Adjudicator, 1997–2000; Immigration Judge, 2000–05, Designated Immigration Judge, 2005–06; a Judge of the Upper Tribunal (Immigration and Asylum Chamber) and Sen. Immigration Judge (formerly a Sen. Immigration Judge, Asylum and Immigration Tribunal), 2006–10; Recorder, 2007–10. Pres., Council of Immigration Judges, 2004–05. *Recreations:* gardening, walking, theatre, ballet. *E:* HHJ.Judith.Coello@ejudiciary.net.

**COEN, Prof. Enrico Sandro,** CBE 2003; PhD; FRS 1998; John Innes Professor, John Innes Centre and School of Biology, University of East Anglia, since 1999; *b* 29 Sept. 1957; *s* of Ernesto Coen and Dorothea Coen (*née* Cattani); *m* 1984, Lucinda, *d* of late Alexander Poliakoff, OBE; two *s* one *d*. *Educ:* King's Coll., Cambridge (BA 1979; PhD Genetics 1982). SERC Postdoctoral Fellow, Cambridge, 1982–84; Res. Fellow, St John's Coll., Cambridge, 1982–85; Res. Scientist, John Innes Centre, BBSRC, 1984–99. Foreign Associate, US Nat. Acad. of Scis, 2001. EMBO Medal, Rome, 1996; Science for Art Prize, LVMH, Moët Hennessy, Paris, 1996; Linnean Medal, 1997; Darwin Medal, Royal Soc., 2004. *Publications:* papers in Nature, Cell, Science. *Recreation:* painting. *Address:* Department of Cell and Developmental Biology, John Innes Centre, Norwich Research Park, Norwich NR4 7UH. *T:* (01603) 450274.

See also Sir M. Poliakoff, S. Poliakoff.

**COEN, (Thomas) Paul;** Director, Paul Coen Ltd, 2014–16; *b* 21 Dec. 1953; *s* of Patrick Coen and Anne Coen (*née* O'Neil); *m* 1974, Kate Knox (*d* 2009); two *s* two *d*. *Educ:* Manchester Univ. (BA Econ Hons Govt). NCB, later British Coal, 1977–89; Hertfordshire County Council, 1990–95: Dir, Commercial Services, 1990–91; Dir, Business Services, 1991–94; Dep. Chief Exec., 1995; Chief Executive: Surrey CC, 1995–2004; Essex CC, 2005–06; Local Govt Assoc., 2006–09; Man. Dir and Vice-Chm., UK Public Sector Gp, Citigroup, 2010–13. Chm., Ashridge Business Sch., 2014–15 (Vice-Chm., 2012–14). *Recreations:* reading, cycling, walking, cooking.

**COEN, Yvonne Anne, (Mrs John Pini);** QC 2000; a Recorder, 2000–14; *d* of John and Bernadette Coen; *m* 1991, John Peter Julian Pini, *qv;* one *s* one *d*. *Educ:* Loreto Coll., St Albans; St Catherine's Coll., Oxford (MA Hons Jurisp.). Called to the Bar, Lincoln's Inn, 1982 (Hardwicke School. and Eastham Schol.), Bencher, 2008; criminal practitioner, Midland and Oxford Circuit, 1982–2014; an Asst Recorder, 1997–2000. Mem., Bar Council, 1987–90. *Recreations:* Stamford Shoestring Theatre, swiping at a golf ball, exploring, savouring husband's cuisine, *qv*.

**COETZEE, Prof. John Maxwell;** writer; Professor of Literature, University of Adelaide, since 2011; *b* 9 Feb. 1940; one *d* (one *s* decd). *Educ:* Univ. of Cape Town (MA); Univ. of Texas (PhD). FRSL 1988. Assistant Professor of English, State University of New York at Buffalo, 1968–71; Lectr in English, 1972–82, Prof. of Gen. Lit., 1983–98, Dist. Prof. of Lit., 1999–2001, Univ. of Cape Town; Res. Fellow, Univ. of Adelaide, 2002–10. Butler Prof. of English, State Univ. of New York at Buffalo, 1984; Hinkley Prof. of English, Johns Hopkins Univ., 1986, 1989; Visiting Professor of English: Harvard Univ., 1991; Univ. of Texas, 1995; Dist. Service Prof. of Social Thought, Univ. of Chicago, 1996–2003. Hon. Fellow, MLA, 1989. Hon. DLitt: Strathclyde, 1985; SUNY, 1989; Cape Town, 1995; Natal, 1996; Rhodes, 1999; Oxford, 2002; La Trobe, 2004; Adelaide, 2005. Nobel Prize for Literature, 2003. Order of Mapungubwe (Gold) (S Africa), 2005. *Publications:* Dusklands, 1974; In the Heart of the Country, 1977 (CNA Literary Award, 1977; filmed as Dust, 1986); Waiting for the Barbarians, 1980 (CNA Literary Award, 1980; James Tait Black Prize, 1980; Geoffrey Faber Award, 1980); Life and Times of Michael K, 1983 (CNA Literary Award, 1983; Booker-McConnell Prize, 1983; Prix Femina Etranger, 1985); Foe, 1986 (Jerusalem Prize, 1987); (ed with André Brink) A Land Apart, 1986; White Writing, 1988; Age of Iron, 1990 (Sunday Express Award, 1990); Doubling the Point, 1992; The Master of Petersburg, 1994 (Irish Times Internat. Fiction Award, 1995); Giving Offence, 1996; Boyhood, 1997; The Lives of Animals, 1999; Disgrace, 1999 (Booker Prize, 1999); Stranger Shores, 2001; Youth, 2002; Elizabeth Costello, 2003 (Qld Premier's Literary Award, 2004); Slow Man, 2005; Inner Workings: essays, 2007; Diary of a Bad Year, 2007; Summertime, 2009; Scenes from Provincial Life, 2011; The Childhood of Jesus, 2013; (with A. Kurtz) The Good Story: exchanges on truth, fiction and psychotherapy, 2015; The Schooldays of Jesus, 2016; Late Essays, 2017; essays in Comp. Lit., Jl of Mod. Lit., Linguistics, Mod. Lang. Notes, Pubns of MLA, etc. *Address:* PO Box 3045, Newton, SA 5074, Australia.

**COEY, Prof. (John) Michael (David),** PhD; FRS 2003; Erasmus Smith's Professor of Natural and Experimental Philosophy, 2007–12, Professor Emeritus, 2013, and Fellow, since 1982, Trinity College, Dublin (Professor of Experimental Physics, 1987–2007); *b* 24 Feb. 1945; *s* of David Stuart Coey and Joan Elizabeth Coey (*née* Newsam); *m* 1973, Wong May; two *s*. *Educ:* Jesus Coll., Cambridge (BA 1966); Univ. of Manitoba (PhD 1971). Chargé de Recherche, CNRS, Grenoble, 1971–78; Trinity College, Dublin: Lectr, 1978–84; Associate Prof., 1984–87. Visiting Scientist: IBM, Yorktown Heights, 1979; CEN Grenoble, 1985; Applied Physics Lab., Johns Hopkins, 1986; Visiting Professor: Inst. of Physics, Peking, 1980; McGill Univ., 1982; Univ. of Bordeaux, 1984; Univ. of Paris VI, 1992; UCSD, 1997; Florida State Univ., 1998; Univ. of Paris XI, 1998; Le Mans Univ., 1999, 2001, 2003; Univ. of Strasbourg, 2006, 2015 (Gutenberg Prize, 2015); Nat. Univ. of Singapore, 2013; Beihang Univ., 2014; Albert Einstein Prof., Chinese Acad. of Scis, 2011; NUS, 2012. Fulbright Fellow, 1997. Founder/Dir, Magnetic Solutions Ltd, 1994–2006. Chm., Magnetism Commn, Internat. Union of Pure and Applied Physics, 2002–05. Co-ordinator, Concerted European Action on Magnets, 1985–94. MRIA 1982 (Vice Pres., 1989–90; Gold Medal, 2005); Mem., Eur. Acad. Sci., 2013. FInstP 1984 (Charles Chree Medal and Prize, 1997; Max Born Medal and Prize, 2019). Fellow: American Mineralog. Soc., 1995; APS, 2000. Foreign Associate, Nat. Acad. of Scis, USA, 2005. Dr *hc* Inst. Nat. Poly., Grenoble, 1994. Advisory Editor: Jl of Magnetism and Magnetic Materials, 1990–; Physical Rev. Letters, 1999–2005. Humboldt Prize, Alexander von Humboldt Foundn, 2013. *Publications:* (with K. Moorjani) Magnetic Glasses, 1984; Rare Earth Iron Permanent Magnets, 1996; (with R. Skomski) Permanent Magnetism, 1999; Magnetism and Magnetic Materials, 2010; numerous articles on magnetism and electronic properties of solids in learned jls. *Recreation:* gardening. *Address:* School of Physics and CRANN, Trinity College, Dublin 2, Ireland. *T:* (1) 8961470. *E:* jcoey@tcd.ie.

**COFFEY, Ann;** see Coffey, M. A.

**COFFEY, Rev. David Roy,** OBE 2008; General Secretary, Baptist Union of Great Britain, 1991–2006; Global Ambassador, BMS World Mission, since 2010; *b* 13 Nov. 1941; *s* of Arthur Coffey and Elsie Maud Willis; *m* 1966, Janet Anne Dunbar; one *s* one *d*. *Educ:* Spurgeon's Coll., London (BA). Ordained, 1967; Minister: Whetstone Baptist Church, Leicester, 1967–72; North Cheam Baptist Ch, London, 1972–80; Sen. Minister, Upton Vale Baptist Ch, Torquay, 1980–88; Sec. for Evangelism, BUGB, 1988–91. President: BUGB, 1986–87; European Baptist Fedn, 1997–99; Vice Pres., 2000–05, Pres., 2005–10, Baptist World Alliance; Free Churches Moderator and a co-Pres., Churches Together in England, 2003–07; Vice Pres., CCJ, 2009–. Gov., 2007–15, Chm. Council, 2012–15, Spurgeon's Coll. Patron: Embrace (formerly Biblelands), 2009–; SAT-7, 2009–. Hon. DD: Dallas Baptist Univ., Texas, 2007; Palmer Seminary, Philadelphia, 2008. *Publications:* Build that Bridge—a Study in Conflict and Reconciliation, 1986; Discovering Romans, 2000; Joy to the World, 2008; All One in Christ Jesus: a passionate appeal for Evangelical Unity, 2009. *Recreations:* Elgar Society, Chelsea FC, armchair sportsman, grandchildren, music, political biography. *Address:* 129 Broadway, Didcot, Oxon OX11 8XD. *T:* (01235) 517700.

**COFFEY, John Joseph;** QC 1996; a Recorder, since 1989; *b* 29 July 1948; *s* of John and Hannah Coffey; *m* 1970, Patricia Anne Long; three *s* (and one *s* decd). *Educ:* Bishop Ward Secondary Modern Sch., Dagenham; Mid-Essex Coll. of Technology (LLB Hons London). Called to the Bar, Middle Temple, 1970; Asst Recorder, 1985. Hd of Chambers, 1993–2017. *Recreation:* supporting West Ham United.

**COFFEY, (Margaret) Ann;** MP for Stockport, since 1992 (Lab, 1992–2019; Ind Gp for Change (formerly Change UK), since 2019); *b* 31 Aug. 1946; *d* of late John Brown, MBE, and of Marie Brown; *m* 1973 (marr. diss. 1989); one *d*; *m* 1998, Peter Saraga. *Educ:* Poly. of South Bank (BSc); Manchester Univ. (MSc). Trainee Social Worker, Walsall Social Services Dept, 1971–72; Social Worker: Birmingham, 1972–73; Gwynedd, 1973–74; Wolverhampton, 1974–75; Stockport, 1977–82; Cheshire, 1982–88; Team Leader, Fostering, Oldham Social Services Dept, 1988–92. Mem. (Lab) Stockport MBC, 1984–92 (Leader, Labour Group, 1988–92). Contested (Lab) Cheadle, 1987. An Opposition Whip, 1995–96; Opposition spokeswoman on health, 1996–97; PPS to Prime Minister, 1997–98, to Sec. of State for Social Security, 1998–2001, to Sec. of State for Work and Pensions, 2001–02, to Sec. of State for Transport, 2002–06, to Sec. of State for Trade and Industry, 2006–07, to Chancellor of the Exchequer, 2007–10. Mem., Trade and Industry Select Cttee, 1993–95. *Address:* House of Commons, SW1A 0AA.

**COFFEY, Matthew James,** CB 2018; Chief Operating Officer and Deputy Chief Inspector, Ofsted, since 2014; *b* Lincoln, 27 May 1967; *s* of Terence James Coffey and Margaret Mary Hearmon (*née* Hardwick); *m* 1993, Louise Brockes; two *d*. *Educ:* Branston Sch. and Community Coll.; Exeter Coll.; Univ. of Lincoln (MA Criminol. and Social Policy 2006). Regl Manager, Hotel and Catering Trng Co., 1991–95; Quality Manager, Hospitality Trng Foundn, 1995–97; Sen. Inspector, Trng Standards Council, 1997–2001; Inspection Manager, Adult Learning Inspectorate, 2001–07; HM Inspector, Ofsted, 2007–. *Recreations:* family, travel, cinema, motor sport, music. *Address:* Ofsted, 70 Petty France, SW1H 9EX. *T:* 0300 013 0095. *E:* matthew.coffey@ofsted.gov.uk.

**COFFEY, Dr Therese Anne;** MP (C) Suffolk Coastal, since 2010; Secretary of State for Work and Pensions, since 2019; *b* Billinge, 18 Nov. 1971; *d* of late Tom Coffey and of Sally Coffey. *Educ:* St Mary's Coll., Crosby; St Edward's Coll., Liverpool; University Coll., London (BSc 1993; PhD Chem. 1997). Mgt Accountant. Various posts with Mars UK Ltd, 1997–2007; Finance Dir, Mars Drinks UK, 2007–09; Property Finance Manager, BBC, 2009–10. Mem. (C) Whitchurch Town Council, 1999–2003. An Asst Govt Whip, 2014–15; Parly Sec. (Dep. Leader), Office of the Leader of the H of C, 2015–16; Parly Under-Sec. of State, 2016–19, Minister of State, 2019, DEFRA. Contested (C): SE England, EP, 2004, 2009; Wrexham, 2005. *Recreations:* dog walking, sudoku, pub quizzes, live music. *Address:* House of Commons, SW1A 0AA. *T:* (020) 7219 7164. *E:* therese.coffey.mp@parliament.uk.

**COFFIN, Rt Rev. Peter Robert;** Bishop Ordinary (Anglican) to Canadian Forces, 2004–16; *b* 31 May 1946; *s* of Gerald R. A. Coffin and Jean Mary Thorburn Coffin (*née* Edwards); *m* 1972, Deborah Creighton; one *d*. *Educ:* Univ. of King's Coll., Halifax, NS (BA); Trinity Coll., Toronto (STB); Carleton Univ., Ottawa (MA Internat. Affairs). Ordained deacon, 1971, priest 1971; Asst Curate, St Matthew's, Ottawa, 1971–73; Lectr, House of the Epiphany, Kuching, Sarawak, E Malaysia, 1973–76; Incumbent, Parish of Hull, Quebec, 1976–84; Archdeacon of W Quebec, 1978–84; Incumbent, Christ Church, Bell's Corners, Ottawa (Nepean), 1984–90; Archdeacon of Carleton, 1986–90; Rector of Christ Church Cathedral, Ottawa and Dean of Ottawa, 1990–99; Bishop of Ottawa, 1999–2007. Chm., Interfaith Cttee on Canadian Military Chaplaincy, 2008–10. Hon. DD: Univ. of King's Coll., Halifax, NS, 1998; Trinity Coll., Toronto, 2004. *Address:* 42 Bridle Park Drive, Kanata, Ottawa, ON K2M 2E2, Canada.

**COGBILL, Vivienne Margaret;** see Dews, V. M.

**COGDELL, Prof. Richard John,** PhD; FRS 2007; FRSE; Hooker Professor of Botany, University of Glasgow, since 1993 (Titular Professor, 1988–93); *b* 4 Feb. 1949; *s* of Harry William Frank Cogdell and Evelyn Cogdell; *m* 1970, Barbara Lippold; one *s* one *d*. *Educ:* Royal Grammar Sch., Guildford; Univ. of Bristol (BSc Hons Biochem. 1970; PhD Biochem. 1973). Postdoctoral res., Cornell Univ., Ithaca, and Univ. of Washington, Seattle, 1973–75; Lectr, Dept of Botany, Univ. of Glasgow, 1975–88. Visiting Professor: UCLA, 1979; Univ. of Paris-Sud, 2004; Adjunct Prof., Chinese Nat. Acad. of Scis Inst. of Biophysics, Beijing, 2005–07. Mem., BBSRC, 2014–18. FRSE 1991; FRSA 2009. Alexander von Humboldt Res. Prize, 1995; Daiwa-Adrian Prize for Anglo-Japanese Res.,

2002. *Publications:* over 250 scientific papers in learned jls. *Recreations:* playing cricket, going to opera and theatre, Scottish country dancing. *Address:* 152 Hyndland Road, Glasgow G12 9PN. *T:* (0141) 330 4232, *Fax:* (0141) 330 4620. *E:* R.Cogdell@bio.gla.ac.uk.

**COGGINS, Prof. John Richard,** OBE 2008; PhD; FRSE; FRSB; Professor of Molecular Enzymology, 1995–2009, now Emeritus, and Vice-Principal, Life Sciences, Medicine and Veterinary Medicine, 2006–09, University of Glasgow; *b* 15 Jan. 1944; *s* of Cecil Rex Coggins and Pamela Mary Coggins (*née* Burnet); *m* 1970, Lesley Frances Watson; one *s* one *d*. *Educ:* Bristol GS; Queen's Coll., Oxford (MA); Univ. of Ottawa (PhD). FRSE 1988. Research Fellow: Brookhaven Nat. Lab., USA, 1970–72; Cambridge Univ., 1972–74; Glasgow University: Lectr, 1974–78; Sen. Lectr, 1978–86; Prof. of Biochemistry, 1986–95; Dir, Grad. Sch. of Biomedical and Life Scis, 1995–97; Hd, Div. of Biochemistry and Molecular Biology, 1997–98; Res. Dir, 1998–2000, Dir and Dean, 2000–05, Inst. of Biomed. and Life Scis; Chm., Hds of Univ. Biol Sci. Depts, 2003–07. Chm., Biochem. and Biophys. Cttee, 1985–88, Mem., Biotechnol. Directorate Management Cttee, 1987–90, SERC; Member: Liby and Inf. Services Cttee, Scotland, 1982–88; Biotechnol. Jt Adv. Bd, 1989–94; Wkg Party on Biotechnol., NEDO, 1990–92; AFRC, 1991–94; Council, Hannah Res. Inst., 1994–2005; Scottish Sci. Adv. Cttee, 2002–07; BBSRC, 2008–14; Governing Mem., 1994–2007, Chm., 2007–10, Caledonian Res. Foundn; Advr for Biochem., UFC, 1989–92; Chm., HEFCE RAE Panel for Biochemistry, 1995–96; Vice-Pres. (Life Scis), RSE, 2003–06 (Res. Awards Convener, 1999–2002); Treas., Bioscis Fedn 2007–09. Chm., Molecular Enzymol. Gp, 1981–85, Policy Cttee, 2004–08, Biochemical Soc.; Mem. Council, Royal Soc. of Biol., 2010–18. Chm., Portland Press Ltd, 2009–13. Dir, Ops and Strategy, Glasgow City of Sci., 2011–13. Trustee, 2004–10, Vice Chm., 2010–16, Glasgow Sci. Centre. Mem. Adv. Bd, Research Inf. Network, 2005–12. *Publications:* Multidomain Proteins: structure and evolution, 1986; contribs on enzymes and on plant and microbial biochem. to Biochem. Jl, Jl of Biol Chem., Jl Molecular Biol., etc. *Recreations:* sailing, travel, good food, reading. *Address:* 5 Chapelton Gardens, Bearsden, Glasgow G61 2DH. *T:* (0141) 942 5082.

**COGGON, Prof. David Noel Murray,** OBE 2002; PhD, DM; FRCP, FFOM, FFPH, FMedSci; Professor of Occupational and Environmental Medicine, MRC Lifecourse Epidemiology Unit (formerly Environmental Epidemiology Unit, then Epidemiology Resource Centre), University of Southampton, 1997–2015, now Emeritus; *b* 25 Dec. 1950; *s* of Frederick and Annette Coggon; *m* 1976, Sarah (*née* Cole); one *s* four *d*. *Educ:* Clare Coll., Cambridge (BA 1972; MA 1976); New Coll., Oxford (BM BCh 1976; DM 1993); Univ. of Southampton (PhD 1984). MRCP 1978, FRCP 1992; FFOM 1993; FFPH 2005. Clinical Scientist, MRC Envmtl Epidemiol. Unit, 1980–97, Dir, Arthritis Res. UK/MRC Centre for Musculoskeletal Health and Work, 2014–15, Univ. of Southampton. Chairman: Depleted Uranium Oversight Bd, 2001–07; Mobile Telecommns and Health Res. Prog. Mgt Cttee, 2008–12; Member: Industrial Injuries Adv. Council, 1988–2003; Adv. Cttee on Pesticides, 1997–2000 (Chm., 2000–05); Ind. Expert Gp on Mobile Phones, 1999–2000; Adv. Gp on Non-ionising Radiation, 2001–09; Plant Protection Products and Residues Panel, Eur. Food Safety Authy, 2006–09; Cttee on Toxicity of Chemicals in Food, Consumer Products and the Envmt, 2007–15 (Chm., 2008–15). Pres., Faculty of Occupational Medicine, RCP, 2008–11. FMedSci 1998. *Publications:* Statistics in Clinical Practice, 1995, 2nd edn 2002; (jtly) Epidemiology for the Uninitiated, 3rd edn 1993 to 5th edn 2003. *Recreations:* rambling, gardening, cabinet making, choral singing. *Address:* MRC Lifecourse Epidemiology Unit, Southampton General Hospital, Southampton SO16 6YD. *T:* (023) 8077 7624, *Fax:* (023) 8070 4021. *E:* dnc@mrc.soton.ac.uk.

**COGHER, Michael Patrick;** Comptroller and City Solicitor, City of London Corporation, since 2012; *b* Prestatyn, Denbighshire, 1 Nov. 1966; *s* of Anthony and Eileen Cogher; *m* 1994, Penelope Martin; two *d*. *Educ:* Ruthin Sch., Denbighshire; Manchester Poly. (LLB Hons); Coll. of Law. Dip. Local Govt Law and Practice. Trainee solicitor, London Bor. of Richmond upon Thames, 1989–91; admitted as solicitor, 1991; London Borough of Merton: Asst Solicitor, 1991–95; Sen. Solicitor, 1995–96; Principal Solicitor, 1996–98; Hd, Legal Services, 1998–2000; Hd, Legal Services, Peterborough CC, 2000–01; Dir, Legal and Democratic Services, London Bor. of Hammersmith and Fulham, 2001–09; Shared Dir of Legal Services, RBKC, 2009–12. *Recreations:* sailing, ski-ing, hill-walking, theatre. *Address:* City of London, PO Box 270, Guildhall, EC2P 2EJ. *T:* (020) 7332 3699, *Fax:* (020) 7332 1634. *E:* michael.cogher@cityoflondon.gov.uk.

**COGHILL, Clare Elizabeth;** Member (Lab), since 2010 and Leader, since 2017, Waltham Forest London Borough Council; *b* Birmingham, 7 July 1979; *d* of Ian Sinclair Coghill and Lynda Clare Coghill. *Educ:* Leasowes High Sch. and Community Coll.; King Edward VI Coll., Stourbridge; Univ. of York (BA). Cabinet Mem., Children and Young People, 2012–14, Regeneration, 2014–17, Waltham Forest LBC. Mem., Exec., London Councils, 2017–. Dep. Chair, LGA, 2019–. Mem., London Bd, Arts Council, 2018–. *Recreations:* tennis, travel, fluent French speaker. *Address:* Waltham Forest Council, Waltham Forest Town Hall, Forest Road, Walthamstow, E17 4JF. *T:* 07725 528625. *E:* leader@walthamforest.gov.uk.

**COGHILL, Sir Patrick Kendal Farley,** 9th Bt *cr* 1778, of Coghill, Yorkshire; *b* 3 Nov. 1960; *o s* of Sir Toby Coghill, 8th Bt; *S* father, 2000; *m* 2016, Annabel Baddeley. *Heir:* none.

**COGHLAN, Terence Augustine;** QC 1993; *b* 17 Aug. 1945; *s* of late Austin Francis Coghlan and of Ruby Coghlan (*née* Comrie); *m* 1973, Angela Agatha Westmacott; one *s* two *d*. *Educ:* Downside; Perugia; New Coll., Oxford; Inns of Court. Called to the Bar, Inner Temple, 1968 (Scholar; Bencher, 2004); Recorder, 1989–2009. Pt-time Judge, Mental Health Review Tribunal, 2000–15. Film extra, 1968 (incl. German Heinkel bomber pilot in film, Battle of Britain, 1969); Director: City of London Sinfonia, 1975–2010; Temple Music Foundn, 2004–13. Chairman: St Endellion Fests Trust, 2007–18; Temple Church Cttee, 2011–13. *Publications:* Meningitis, 1998; medico-legal articles. *Recreations:* wandering around buildings with Pevsner, wine, walking, bird-watching, cycling, theatre, opera, performing choral music badly, fine art, grandchildren, travel. *Address:* 1 Crown Office Row, Temple, EC4Y 7HH. *Clubs:* Les Six, MCC.

**COGHLIN, Rt Hon. Sir Patrick,** Kt 1997; PC 2009; a Lord Justice of Appeal, Supreme Court of Judicature, Northern Ireland, 2008–15; President, Lands Tribunal, Northern Ireland, 1999–2015; *b* 7 Nov. 1945; *s* of late James Edwin Coghlin and Margaret Van Hovenberg Coghlin; *m* 1971, Patricia Ann Elizabeth Young; one *s* three *d*. *Educ:* Royal Belfast Academical Instn; Queen's Univ., Belfast (LLB Hons); Christ's Coll., Cambridge (Dip. Criminology). Called to the Bar: NI, 1970; Gray's Inn, 1975 (Hon. Bencher 2000); NSW, 1992; Republic of Ireland, 1995; Jun. Crown Counsel for NI, 1983–85; QC (NI) 1985; Dep. County Court Judge, 1983–94; Sen. Crown Counsel, NI, 1993–97; Judge, High Ct of Justice, NI, 1997–2008. Vice-Chm., Mental Health Review Tribunal, 1987–97; Mem., Law Reform Adv. Cttee, NI, 1988–93; Vice-Pres., VAT Tribunal, NI, 1990–93; Dep. Chm., Boundary Commn, NI, 1999–2008. Chm., NI Bar Council, 1991–93. *Recreations:* Rugby, soccer, squash, reading, music, travel. *Clubs:* Kildare Street and University (Dublin); Royal Ulster Yacht; Ballyholme Yacht; Bangor Rugby, Perennials Rugby; Ballyholme Bombers FC.

**COGHLIN, Thomas Ashley;** QC 2018; *b* Cuckfield, Sussex, 11 Sept. 1973; *s* of Terence Coghlin and Claire Coghlin; *m* 2006, Lisa Sullivan; four *d*. *Educ:* Worth Sch.; Worcester Coll., Oxford (MA Juris. 1995; BCL 1996). Called to the Bar, Inner Temple, 1998; in practice as a barrister, Cloisters, 1998–; a Fee-paid Employment Judge, 2013–. Dir, Bar Mutual Indemnity Fund Ltd, 2017–. *Recreations:* family, cricket. *Address:* Cloisters, 1 Pump Court, Temple, EC4Y 7AA. *T:* (020) 7827 4000. *E:* tac@cloisters.com.

**COGLEY, Stephen William;** QC 2011; *b* Hants, 13 Aug. 1961; *s* of William and Loretta Cogley; *m* Sally Jane; two *s* two *d*. *Educ:* Ripon Grammar Sch.; Newcastle Univ. (LLB Hons). Called to the Bar, Gray's Inn, 1984; in practice as a barrister, specialising in commercial law. *Recreations:* marching to my own drum, tinkering with the engine on my ship. *Address:* XXIV Old Buildings, Lincoln's Inn, WC2A 3UP. *E:* stephen.cogleyqc@xxiv.co.uk.

**COHAN, Sir Robert (Paul),** Kt 2019; CBE 1989; Founder Artistic Director, Contemporary Dance Trust; *b* 27 March 1925; *s* of Walter and Billie Cohan; British citizen, 1989. *Educ:* Martha Graham Sch., NYC. Joined Martha Graham Co., 1946; Partner, 1950; Co-Dir, Martha Graham Co., 1966; Artistic Dir, Contemporary Dance Trust Ltd, 1967; Artistic Dir and Principal Choreographer, 1969–87, Dir, 1987–89, London Contemporary Dance Theatre; Artistic Advr, Batsheva Co., Israel, 1980–90; Director: York Univ., Toronto Choreographic Summer Sch., 1977; Gulbenkian Choreographic Summer Sch., Univ. of Surrey, 1978, 1979, 1982; Banff Sch. of Fine Arts Choreographic Seminar, Canada, 1980; New Zealand Choreographic Seminar, 1982; Choreographic Seminar, Simon Fraser Univ., Vancouver, 1985; Internat. Dance Course for Professional Choreographers and Composers, Surrey Univ., 1985, 1989. With London Contemporary Dance Theatre toured Britain, E and W Europe, S America, N Africa and USA; major works created: Cell, 1969 (recorded for BBC TV, 1982); Stages, 1971; Waterless Method of Swimming Instruction, 1974 (recorded for BBC TV); Class, 1975; Stabat Mater, 1975 (recorded for BBC TV); Masque of Separation, 1975; Khamsin, 1976; Nympheas, 1976 (recorded for BBC TV, 1983); Forest, 1977 (recorded for BBC TV); Eos, 1978; Songs, Lamentations and Praises, 1979; Dances of Love and Death, 1981; Agora, 1984; A Mass for Man, 1985 (recorded for BBC TV); Ceremony, 1986; Interrogations, 1986; Video Life, 1986; Phantasmagoria, 1987; A Midsummer Night's Dream, 1993; The Four Seasons, 1996; Aladdin, 2000. Editor, Choreography and Dance, 1988–2000. Hon. Fellow, York Univ., Toronto. Hon. DLitt: Exeter, 1993; Kent, 1996; DUniv: Middlesex, 1994; Winchester, 2006. Evening Standard Award for most outstanding achievement in ballet, 1975; Soc. of West End Theatres Award for most outstanding achievement in ballet, 1978; UK Dance Critics' Circle Cttee Award for Lifetime Achievement, 2005. *Publications:* The Dance Workshop, 1986. *Recreation:* dancing. *Address:* The Place, 17 Dukes Road, WC1H 9PY. *T:* (020) 7121 1000.

**COHEN,** family name of **Baroness Cohen of Pimlico.**

**COHEN OF PIMLICO,** Baroness *cr* 2000 (Life Peer), of Pimlico in the City of Westminster; **Janet Cohen;** Senior Advisor, BPP Holdings, 2010–18; *b* 4 July 1940; *d* of late George Edric Neel and Mary Isabel Neel (*née* Budge); *m* 1971, James Lionel Cohen; two *s* one *d*. *Educ:* Newnham Coll., Cambridge (BA Hons Law 1962; Associate Fellow, 1988–91). Articled clerk, Frere Cholmeley, 1963–65; admitted solicitor, 1965; Consultant: ABT Associates, USA, 1965–67; John Laing Construction, 1968–69; Department of Trade and Industry: Principal, 1969–78; Asst Sec., 1978–82; Asst Dir, 1982–88, Dir, 1988–2000, Charterhouse Bank Ltd. Chm., Café Pelican Ltd, 1984–90; Vice Chm., Yorks Building Soc., 1994–99 (Dir, 1991–94); non-executive Director: Waddington plc (formerly John Waddington), 1994–97; London & Manchester Gp plc, 1997–98; United Assce Gp, 1998–99; BPP Hldgs, 1994–2006 (Chm., 2002–06); London Stock Exchange, 2001–13; MCG plc, 2003–11; Chairman: InviseoMedia Hldgs Ltd, 2007–09; Trillium Hldgs, 2008–10. Mem., Schools Exam. and Assessment Council, 1990–93. Mem. Bd, Sheffield Develt Corp., 1993–97. Pres., BPP University Coll. (formerly Coll.) of Professional Studies, 2008–13; Chancellor, BPP Univ., 2013–. Trustee, City of Cambridge Educn Foundn, 2015–16; Bd Mem., Parkside Fedn Multi Acad. Trust, 2015–. A Governor, BBC, 1994–99. Member: EU Scrutiny Cttee, H of L, 2006– (Chm., Sub Cttee A); H of L Audit Cttee, 2013–18. Chairman: Parlt Choir, 2006–08; Cambridge Arts Th., 2007–15. Gov., University Tech. Coll., Cambridge, 2015–. Hon. Fellow: St Edmund's Coll., Cambridge, 2000; Lucy Cavendish Coll., Cambridge, 2007. Hon. DLitt Humberside, 1995. *Publications:* as Janet Neel: Death's Bright Angel, 1988; Death on Site, 1989; Death of a Partner, 1991; Death among the Dons, 1993; A Timely Death, 1996; To Die For, 1998; O Gentle Death, 2000; Ticket to Ride, 2005; as Janet Cohen: The Highest Bidder, 1992; Children of a Harsh Winter, 1994. *Recreation:* writing.

**COHEN, Amanda Jane;** *see* Ridout, A. J.

**COHEN, Prof. Anthony Paul,** CBE 2008; PhD; FRSE; Principal and Vice-Chancellor, Queen Margaret University (formerly Queen Margaret University College), 2003–09, now Emeritus Professor of Social and Cultural Anthropology; Hon. Professor of Social Anthropology, University of Edinburgh, since 2003; *b* 3 Aug. 1946; *s* of Mark Cohen and Mary Cohen (*née* Nissenbaum); *m* 1968, Prof. Bronwen J. Steel, OBE; three *s*. *Educ:* Univ. of Southampton (BA Hons; MSocSc; PhD 1973). Res. Fellow, Meml Univ. of Newfoundland, 1968–70; Asst Prof., Queen's Univ. at Kingston, Ont., 1970–71; Lectr, then Sen. Lectr in Social Anthropol., Univ. of Manchester, 1971–89; University of Edinburgh: Prof. of Social Anthropol., 1989–2003; Provost of Law and Social Scis, and Dean of Social Scis, 1997–2002. Convener, Scottish Forum for Grad. Educn, 1994–96; Founding Convener, Health Cttee, Universities Scotland, 2006–09. FRAI 1979; FRSE 1995. Hon. DSc Edinburgh, 2005; Hon. DSc St Andrew's, 2017. *Publications:* The Management of Myths: the politics of legitimation in a Newfoundland community, 1975; (ed) Belonging: identity and social organisation in British rural cultures, 1982; The Symbolic Construction of Community (CHOICE Award for Outstanding Book of the Year), 1985 (trans. Turkish and Japanese); (ed) Symbolising Boundaries: identity and diversity in British cultures, 1986; Whalsay: symbol, segment and boundary in a Shetland Island community, 1987; (ed with K. Fukui) Humanising the City?: social contexts of urban life at the turn of the Millennium, 1993 (trans. Japanese); (jtly) Villages Anglais, Ecossaises, Irlandaises, 1993; Self Consciousness: an alternative anthropology of identity, 1994 (trans. Danish); (ed with N. J. Rapport) Questions of Consciousness, 1995; (ed) Signifying Identities: anthropological perspectives on boundaries and contested values, 2000; papers and chapters in books. *Recreations:* music, reading. *Club:* New (Edinburgh).

**COHEN, Prof. Bernard Woolf;** Slade Professor, and Chair of Fine Art, University of London, 1988–2000, now Emeritus Slade Professor; *b* 28 July 1933; *s* of Victor and Leah Cohen; *m* 1959, Jean Britton; one *s* one *d*. *Educ:* Slade School of Fine Art, University Coll. London (Dip. Fine Art). Head of Painting, Wimbledon Sch. of Art, 1980–85. Vis. Prof., Univ. of New Mexico, USA, 1969–70. Fellow: UCL, 1992; Kent Inst. of Art and Design, 1998. First one man exhibn, Gimpel Fils Gall., 1958, again in 1960; other exhibitions: Molton Gall., 1962; Kasmin Gall., Bond Street, 1963, 1964, 1967; Waddington Gall., 1974, 1977, 1979, 1990; First New York exhibn, Betty Parsons Gall., 1967; major retrospective, Hayward Gall., 1972; print retrospective, Tate Gall., 1976; drawing retrospective, Ben Uri Gall., 1994; paintings, Tate Gall., 1995; paintings of the 90s, Flowers East Gall., London,

1998, Flowers West Gall., Santa Monica, 1999; Flowers Central, London, 2001, 2004, six new large lithographs, 2002; paintings, 2006, paintings retrospective, 2011, Flowers Gall., NY; paintings from the 60s, Flowers East Gall., 2007; paintings of six decades, Flowers East Gall., 2009; 80th birthday, Flowers Central, London, 2013; About Now, Paintings and Prints 2000–2015, Flowers East, 2015; 13 paintings from 55 years, Tate Britain, 2017–18; (with Nathan Cohen) Two Journeys, Flowers East, 2018; Post POP, Gulbenkian Gall., Lisbon, 2018; Louis Stern Fine Art, LA, 2018; represented GB at Venice Biennale, 1966. Work in collections of Tate Gall., Mus. of Modern Art, New York; Fogg Mus., Mass; Minneapolis Walker Art Centre; Carnegie Inst., Pittsburgh, and others. *Relevant publication:* Bernard Cohen: work of six decades, by Norbert Lynton and Ian McKay, 2009; About Now, by Ian McKay, 2015. *Recreations:* travel, music. *Address:* 80 Camberwell Grove, SE5 8RF.

COHEN, Betty; *see* Jackson, B.

COHEN, Daniel; President, Access Entertainment, since 2016; *b* London, 15 Jan. 1974; *s* of Ernie and Rosalind Cohen; *m* 2012, Prof. Noreena Tamar Hertz, *qv. Educ:* City of London Sch.; Lady Margaret Hall, Oxford (BA Hons Double First English Lit.). Channel 4: Commissioning Ed., Documentaries, 2001–04; Head of Documentaries, 2004–06; Head of E4, 2006–07; Controller: BBC Three, 2007–10; BBC One, 2010–13; Dir of Television, BBC, 2013–15. Mem., BAFTA. *Recreations:* football, cricket, English literature, TV and new media, pickle, current affairs, meditation, giraffes, contemporary art. *Club:* Groucho.

COHEN, Frank; art collector; Co-Founder, The Dairy Art Centre, 2013–17; *b* Manchester, 15 Oct. 1943; *s* of Louis and Minnie Cohen; *m* 1972, Cherryl Garson; one *s* one *d. Educ:* Chorlton Grammar Sch. Founder and Owner, Glyn Webb Home Improvement Stores, 1977–99; Dir, Home Improvement Co. Ltd, 1997. Founder, Initial Access, 2007–12. Member, Advisory Board: Bonhams, 2008–; Art 13, 2012–; Art 14, 2013–14. Judge: Jerwood Prize, 2002; Turner Prize, 2003. *Recreations:* art, opera, wine, boxing. *Address:* Brindlow House, 32 Prestbury Road, Wilmslow, Cheshire SK9 2LL. *T:* (01625) 527100, 07768 875522. *E:* frankc@1st4arts.com. *Clubs:* Arts, Academicians, 5 Hertford Street, Annabel's, George, Ivy, Harry's Bar, Alfred's.

COHEN, Gabrielle Ann; an Assistant Auditor General, National Audit Office, 2005–15; *b* 25 May 1961; *d* of David Michael Cowell and Gloria Ethel Cowell; three *s. Educ:* Univ. of Kent (BA Hons Hist. and Pol.). CPFA. National Audit Office, 1987–2015: Head of Press Office, 1996–2000; Dir, Communications and Corporate Affairs, 2000–05. Non-exec. Dir, Southend Univ. Hosp. Foundn Trust, 2016–. *Recreations:* current affairs, reading, theatre, cinema, football.

COHEN, Harry Michael; accountant; *b* 10 Dec. 1949; *m* 1978, Ellen Hussain; one step *s* one step *d*. Mem., Waltham Forest Borough Council, 1972–83 (formerly Chm., Planning Cttee and Sec., Labour Group). MP (Lab) Leyton, 1983–97, Leyton and Wanstead, 1997–2010. Mem., Select Cttee on Defence, 1997–2001; Sec., All-Party Parly Gp on Race and Community. Mem., N Atlantic Assembly, 1992–2010 (Rapporteur; Chm. sub-cttee for Economic Co-operation and Convergence with Central & Eastern Europe, 1996–2000). Mem., UNISON. Vice Pres., Royal Coll. of Midwives.

COHEN, Sir Ivor (Harold), Kt 1992; CBE 1985; TD 1968; Chairman: Remploy Ltd, 1987–93; Japan Electronics Business Association, 1991–2002; *b* 28 April 1931; *s* of Jack Cohen and Anne (*née* Victor); *m* 1963, Betty Edith, *yr d* of Reginald George and Mabel Appleby; one *d. Educ:* Central Foundation Sch., EC2; University Coll. London (BA (Hons) Mod. Hist.; Fellow, 1987). Nat. Service, Royal Signals, 1952–54 (2nd Lieut); TA, Royal Signals, 1954–69 (Major 1964). Engrg industry, 1954–57; range of managerial posts, Mullard Ltd (subsid. of Philips (UK)), 1957–77; Dir, Philips Lighting, 1977–79; Man. Dir, Mullard Ltd, 1979–87; Dir, Philips Electronics (UK) Ltd, 1984–87. Non-executive Director: AB Electronic Products Gp plc, 1987–93; Océ (UK) Ltd, 1988–2001; PA Holdings Ltd, 1989–2001; Redifon Holdings Ltd, 1989–94; Magnetic Materials Gp plc, 1992; Electron Technologies Ltd, 1994–97; Deltron Electronics, 1995–2003; Russell Partnership Ltd, 1996–97; Chairman: Optima Group Ltd, 1995–96; Sira Ltd, 1998–2001; Cons., Comet Gp plc, 1987–90; Advr, Apax & Co. Ventures (formerly Alan Patricof Associates), 1987–93; Mem., Adv. Cttee, Mitsubishi Electric Europe BV (formerly Mitsubishi Electric (UK) Ltd), 1991–2002. Member: IT Adv. Panel, 1981–86; Teletext and Viewdata Steering Gp, DTI, 1981–87; Electronic Components EDC, NEDO, 1980–88; Electronics Ind. EDC, NEDO, 1982–86; Steering Cttee, Telecom. Infrastructure, DTI, 1987–88; Computing Software and Communications Requirements Bd, DTI, 1984–88; Steering Bd, Radiocommunications Agency, DTI, 1990–95; Electronics Ind. Sector Gp, NEDO, 1988–92 (Chm., 1990–92); Chairman: Electronic Applications Sector Gp, NEDO, 1988–90; Measurement Adv. Cttee, DTI, 1994–97; Member Council: Electronic Components Ind. Fedn, 1980–87; European Electronic Components Assoc., 1985–87; Dir, Radio Industries Council, 1980–87. Mem., Schs Examinations and Assessment Council, 1988–90; British Schools Technology: Mem. Council of Management, 1984–87, Trustee Dir, 1987–89; Mem., Management Adv. Gp IT Res. Inst., Brighton Poly., 1987–90; FIET (CompIEE 1988); CompInstMC 1997; Hon. Mem. CGLI, 1989; FInstD 1988–2003; FRSA 1984; Hon. FREng (Hon. FEng 1992). Freeman, City of London, 1982; Liveryman, Sci. Instrument Makers' Co., 1982– (Master, 1997). Hon. DSc City, 1998. Mem., Editl Bd, Nat. Electronics Review, 1987–90. *Publications:* articles on electronics policy and marketing and use of inf. technology in the technical press. *Recreations:* opera, reading, occasional sculpting, walking in towns, video film making. *Address:* c/o Lloyds Bank, 137 North End, Croydon CR0 1TN. *Clubs:* East India, Reform.

COHEN, Janet; *see* Baroness Cohen of Pimlico.

COHEN, Prof. Jonathan, FRCP, FRCPE, FRCPath; FMedSci; FFICM; Foundation Dean, Brighton and Sussex Medical School, University of Sussex, 2003–13, now Emeritus Professor; *b* 11 Oct. 1949; *s* of Norman and Ruth Cohen; *m* 1973, Noëmi Weingarten; one *s* one *d. Educ:* William Ellis Grammar Sch., London; Charing Cross Hosp. Med. Sch. (MB, BS). FRCP 1987; FRCPath 1992; FRCPE 1997; FFICM 2014. Jun. trng appts at Whittington Hosp., LSHTM, and Duke Univ. Med. Center, NC, USA, 1975–85; Wellcome Sen. Lectr in Infectious Diseases, RPMS, 1985–92; Prof. and Hd of Dept of Infectious Diseases, 1992–2002, Vis. Prof., 2002–, RPMS, later Imperial Coll., London. Forbes Fellow, Univ. of Melbourne, 2011. Member: Jt Commn on Vaccination and Immunisation, 2000–05; Nat. Expert Panel on New and Emerging Infections, 2004–07. Member: SE England Sci. and Technol. Adv. Council, 2003–08; Infections and Immunity Bd, MRC, 2004–07. Academy of Medical Sciences: Fellow, 2000; Mem. Council, 2002–05. Chm., Clin. Trials Adv. and Awards Cttee, CRUK, 2006–09; Panel Mem., RAE, 2008; Member: Exec. Cttee, Med. Schs Council, 2008– (Vice Chm., 2009–12); Undergrad. Bd, GMC, 2009–12; Clinical Med. Panel, REF, 2011–14; Med. Vice Chm., SE Region, Adv. Cttee on Clin. Excellence Awards, 2009–13. President: Eur. Congress Clin. Microbiol. and Infectious Diseases, 2012–13; Internat. Soc. of Infectious Diseases, 2014–18 (Mem. Council, 2006–; Mem. Exec., 2008–). Non-executive Director: Brighton and Sussex Univ. Hosps Trust, 2004–10; Sussex Partnership NHS Trust, 2010–13; E Sussex NHS Trust, 2014–15; King's Coll. Hosp. NHS Foundn Trust, 2015–. Chairman: British Med. and Dental Students' Trust, 2012–; Fellowship Cttee, Arthritis Res. UK, 2013–14 (Trustee and Chair, Scientific Cttee, 2014–); Appeals Panel, NICE, 2017–; Member: Scientific Adv. Bd, Lister Inst., 2013–18; Adv. Council, Coll. of Medicine, 2015–; WHO Expert Adv. Gp on Sepsis, 2017–. MAE 2017. Fellow, Eur. Soc. of Clin. Microbiol. and Infectious Diseases, 2017. Hon. MD Brighton and Sussex Med. Sch., 2016. Member Editorial Board: Lancet Infectious Diseases, 2000–19; PLoS Medicine, 2004–12; Ed.-in-Chief, Internat. Jl Infectious Diseases, 2001–06. *Publications:* (ed jtly) Infectious Diseases, 1999, 4th edn 2016; contrib. scientific papers on infection, immunity and sepsis. *Recreations:* family, photography, ski-ing, pipe-smoking. *Address:* Brighton and Sussex Medical School, University of Sussex, Brighton, E Sussex BN1 9PX. *T:* (01273) 877577. *E:* j.cohen@bsms.ac.uk.

COHEN, Hon. Sir Jonathan (Lionel), Kt 2017; Hon. Mr Justice Cohen; a Judge of the High Court, Family Division, since 2017; *b* 8 May 1951; *s* of late Hon. Leonard Harold Lionel Cohen, OBE and Eleanor Lucy Quixano Cohen (*née* Henriques); *m* 1983, Bryony Frances Carfrae; two *s* one *d. Educ:* Eton Coll.; Univ. of Kent at Canterbury (BA Hons). Called to the Bar, Lincoln's Inn, 1974, Bencher, 2004; SE Circuit; QC 1997; a Recorder, 1997–2017; Hd of Chambers, 4 Paper Buildings, 2003–12; a Dep. High Ct Judge, Family Div., 2005–17. Mem., Mental Health Review Tribunal, 2000–17. Liveryman, Skinners' Co., 1978– (Master, 2005–06). Governor: Skinners' Co.'s Sch. for Girls, Hackney, 1994–2002; Judd Sch., Tonbridge, 2002–06; Tonbridge Sch., 2006– (Chm., 2007–17); Mem., Develt Bd, LAMDA, 2004–07. *Recreations:* playing sport badly, theatre. *Address:* Royal Courts of Justice, Strand, WC2A 2LL. *Clubs:* Garrick, MCC; Swinley Forest Golf; Refreshers Cricket.

COHEN, Jonathan Michael; QC 2016; *b* Manchester, 10 Aug. 1977; *s* of Philip and Maureen Cohen; *m* 2016, Rose Michelson. *Educ:* Manchester Grammar Sch.; St Anne's Coll., Oxford (MA Juris.). Called to the Bar, Gray's Inn, 1999. *Recreation:* fast cars. *Address:* Littleton Chambers, 3 King's Bench Walk North, Temple, EC4Y 7HR. *E:* jcohen@littletonchambers.co.uk.

COHEN, Sir Philip, Kt 1998; PhD; FRS 1984; FRSE 1984; Professor of Enzymology, since 2010, Director, Medical Research Council Protein Phosphorylation Unit, 1990–2012, and Director, Scottish Institute for Cell Signalling, 2008–12, University of Dundee; *b* 22 July 1945; *s* of Jacob Davis Cohen and Fanny (*née* Bragman); *m* 1969, Patricia Townsend Wade; one *s* one *d. Educ:* Hendon County Grammar Sch.; University Coll. London (BSc 1st Cl. Hons (Biochemistry Special), 1966; PhD Biochem., 1969; Fellow, 1993). SRC/NATO Postdoctoral Res. Fellow, Dept of Biochem., Univ. of Washington, Seattle, USA, 1969–71; Univ. of Dundee: Lectr in Biochem., 1971–78; Reader in Biochem., 1978–81; Prof. of Enzymology, 1981–84; Royal Soc. Res. Prof., 1984–2010; Dir, Wellcome Trust Biocentre, 1997–2007. Croonian Lectr, Royal Soc., 1998. Pres., British Biochemical Soc., 2006–08 (Hon. Mem., 2003). Mem., Eur. Molecular Biology Orgn, 1982–; MAE 1990. Hon. Mem., Amer. Soc. of Toxicol., 2010. Founder FMedSci 1998. Hon. FRCPath 1998. Foreign Associate, US NAS, 2008; Corresp. Fellow, Aust. Acad. of Sci., 2013. Hon. DSc: Abertay, 1998; Strathclyde, 1999; St Andrews, 2005; Autonoma de Madrid, 2016; Hon. MD Linköping, 2004; Hon. LLD: Debrecen, 2004; Dundee, 2007. Anniversary Prize, Fedn of Eur. Biochemical Socs, 1977; Colworth Medal, 1978, CIBA medal and prize, 1992, British Biochem. Soc.; Prix van Gysel, Belgian Royal Acads of Medicine, 1992; Dundee City of Discovery Rosebowl Award, 1993; Bruce Preller Prize, RSE, 1993; Special Achievement Award, 1996, Dist. Service Award, 2005, Miami Biotech. Winter Symposium; Louis-Jeantet Prize for Medicine, 1997; Pfizer Award for Innovative Sci., 1999; Sir Hans Krebs Medal, Fedn of Eur. Biochem. Socs, 2001; Bristol Myers Squibb Dist. Achievement Award in Metabolic Res., 2002; Royal Medal, RSE, 2004; Debrecen Award for Molecular Medicine, 2004; Rolf Luft Prize, Karolinska Inst., Stockholm, 2006; Royal Medal, Royal Soc., 2008; Achievement Award, Soc. for Biomolecular Sci., 2009; Award for Leading Individual Contribn to Life Scis in Scot., Scottish Enterprise Life Scis, 2009; Millennium Medal, MRC, 2013; Albert Einstein World Award of Sci., World Cultural Council, 2014. Hon. Mem., Dundee Rotary Club, 2006. Man. Editor, Biochimica et Biophysica Acta, 1981–92. *Publications:* Control of Enzyme Activity, 1976, 2nd edn 1983; (ed series) Molecular Aspects of Cellular Regulation: vol. 1, 1980; vol. 2, 1982; vol. 3, 1984; vol. 4, 1985; vol. 5, 1988; vol. 6, 1991; over 500 original papers and revs in scientific jls. *Recreations:* chess, bridge, golf, natural history. *Address:* MRC Protein Phosphorylation and Ubiquitylation Unit, The Sir James Black Centre, University of Dundee, Dow Street, Dundee DD1 5EH; Inverbay Bramblings, Waterside, Invergowrie, Dundee DD2 5DQ. *T:* (01382) 562328. *Clubs:* Isle of Harris Golf; Dundee Bridge; Royal & Ancient Golf (St Andrews).

COHEN, Robert; cellist, conductor and teacher, lecturer and broadcaster; *b* London, 15 June 1959; *s* of late Raymond Cohen, violinist and of Anthya Cohen (*née* Rael); *m* 1987, Rachel Smith; four *s. Educ:* Purcell Sch.; Guildhall Sch. of Music; cello studies with William Pleeth, André Navarra, Jacqueline du Pré and Mstislav Rostropovich. Started playing cello, aged 5; début at RFH (Boccherini Concerto), aged 12; London recital début, Wigmore Hall, aged 17; ESU scholarship to Tanglewood Fest., USA, 1978; recording début, 1979; concerts with major orchestras in USA, Europe and worldwide, 1979–; cellist, Fine Arts Quartet, 2011–18. Conductor: various chamber orchestras, 1990–; symphony orchestras, 1997–. Dir, Charleston Manor Fest., E Sussex, 1989–. Prof., Royal Acad. of Music, 1998–; Prof. of Advanced Cello Studies, Conservatorio della Svizzera Italiana di Lugano, 2000–11; Fellow, Purcell Sch. for Young Musicians, 1992–. Curator, HiBrow.TV, 2009–; radio series, On That Note, USA, 2014. Launched Cello Clinic and Cohen Pod Talks, 2009–; lectr, Royal Acad. of Music, 2014. Has made numerous recordings; internat. radio broadcasts and TV appearances. Hon. RAM 2009. Winner: Suggia Prize, Musicians Benevolent Fund, UK, 1970–75 (annually); Young Concert Artists Internat. Comp., NY, 1978; Piatigorsky Prize, Tanglewood Fest., 1978; UNESCO Internat. Comp., Czechoslovakia, 1981; Robert Helpmann Award, Live Performance Australia, 2004. *Recreations:* photography, alternative medicine, healing, philosophy. *E:* office@robertcohen.info. *W:* www.robertcohen.info.

COHEN, Sir Ronald (Mourad), Kt 2001; Chairman, The Portland Trust, since 2005; Founder, 1972, Chairman, 1972–2005, Apax Partners Worldwide LLP (formerly Apax Partners Holdings Ltd); *b* 1 Aug. 1945; *s* of late Michel Mourad Cohen and of Sonia Sophie Cohen (*née* Douek); *m* 1st, 1972, Carol Marylene Belmont (marr. diss. 1975); 2nd, 1983, Claire Whitmore Enders (marr. diss. 1986); 3rd, 1987, Sharon Ruth Harel; one *s* one *d. Educ:* Orange Hill GS; Exeter Coll., Oxford (Exhibnr, MA; Hon. Fellow, 2000; Pres., Oxford Union Soc.); Harvard Business Sch. (MBA; Henry Fellowship). Consultant, McKinsey & Co. (UK and Italy), 1969–71; Chargé de mission, Institut de Développement Industriel France, 1971–72. Founder Director: British Venture Capital Assoc., 1983 (Chm., 1985–86); Eur. Venture Capital Assoc., 1985; City Gp for Smaller Cos, 1992; a Founder and Vice-Chm., Eur. Assoc. Securities Dealers Automated Quotation, 1995–2001; Dir, NASDAQ Europe, 2001–03. Chairman: Social Investment Task Force, 2000–10; Bridges Ventures Ltd, 2002–12; Commn on Unclaimed Assets, 2005–10; Portland Capital LLP, 2006–10; Big Society Capital Ltd, 2012–13; Social Impact Investment Task Force, 2013–15; Global Social Impact Investment Steering Gp, 2015–; Founder and Dir, Social Finance Ltd, 2009–11; Dir, Social Finance US, 2011–; Dir, Social Finance Israel, 2013–; Member: Wkg Party on Smaller Cos, Stock Exchange, 1993; UK Competitiveness Cttee,

DTI, 1998–2000. Member: Exec. Cttee, Centre for Econ. Policy Res., 1996–99; Finance Cttee, Inst. for Social and Econ. Policy in ME, Kennedy Sch., Harvard Univ., 1997–98; Adv. Bd, Fulbright Commn, 1997–99; Franco-British Council, 1997–99; Dean's Adv. Bd, Harvard Business Sch., 2005; Bd of Overseers, Harvard Univ., 2007–13; Dir, Harvard Mgt Co., 2012–15; Chancellor's Bd of Benefactors, 2003–, Investment Cttee, 2007–14, Oxford Univ.; Trustee Mem., Exec. Cttee, IISS, 2005–10. Mem., Internat. Council, Tate Gall., 2004–; Trustee, BM, 2005–12. Mem., Adv. Bd, InterAction, 1986–; Hon. Pres., Community Develt Finance Assoc., 2005–07. Contested (L): Kensington N, 1974; London W, EP elecn, 1979. Vice-Chm., Ben-Gurion Univ. Innovation Award for innovation in social finance, Rockefeller Foundn, 2012. *Publications:* The Second Bounce of the Ball: turning risk into opportunity, 2007. *Recreations:* music, art, theatre, cinema, tennis. *T:* (020) 7182 7800. *Clubs:* Athenæum, Royal Automobile, Queen's.

COHEN, Samantha Louise; Her Honour Judge Cohen; a Circuit Judge, since 2019; *b* Ipswich, 16 Jan. 1970; *d* of Lawrence Paul Cohen and Jeanne Cohen; *m* 2000, David Stephen Toube; one *s* one *d*. *Educ:* Aylesbury High Sch.; Univ. of Southampton (BA Eng. and Philos. 1992); City Univ. (DipLaw 1994). Called to the Bar, Inner Temple, 1995; in practice as a barrister, 4 Brick Court, then 9 Bedford Row, 1995–2019; a Recorder, 2016–19. *Recreations:* cooking, sailing, family. *Address:* Basildon Crown Court, The Gore, Basildon SS14 2EW. *T:* (01268) 458000.

COHEN, Prof. Simon B.; *see* Baron-Cohen, S.

COHEN, Prof. Stanley; Distinguished Professor, Department of Biochemistry, Vanderbilt University School of Medicine, 1986–2000, now Emeritus; *b* 17 Nov. 1922; *s* of Louis Cohen and Fruma Feitel; *m* 1st, 1951, Olivia Larson; three *s*; 2nd, 1981, Jan Elizabeth Jordan. *Educ:* Brooklyn Coll., NY; Oberlin Coll., Ohio; Univ. of Michigan (BA, PhD). Teaching Fellow, Dept of Biochem., Univ. of Michigan, 1946–48; Instructor, Depts of Biochem. and Pediatrics, Univ. of Colorado Sch. of Medicine, 1948–52; Fellow, Amer. Cancer Soc., Dept of Radiology, Washington Univ., St Louis, 1952–53; Associate Prof., Dept of Zoology, Washington Univ., 1953–59; Vanderbilt University School of Medicine, Nashville: Asst Prof. of Biochem., 1959–62; Associate Prof., 1962; Prof. 1967–86. Mem., Editl Bds of learned jls. Mem., Nat. Acad. of Science, and other sci. bodies. Hon. DSc Chicago, 1985. Nobel Prize for Physiology or Medicine, 1986 (jtly); other prizes and awards. *Publications:* papers in learned jls on biochemistry, cell biology, human developmental biology, embryology.

COHEN, Stephen Benedict; Member, Gambling Commission, since 2016 (Chair, National Lottery Committee, since 2018); Venture Partner, Piedmont Partners Group Ventures, since 2017; *b* Dundee, 1956; two *s* two *d*. *Educ:* University Coll., Oxford (BA Physiol.); University Coll. London. Mercury Asset Mgt, 1980–99; Man. Dir, Zurich Scudder, 2001–02; CEO, EMEA, Putnam, 2002–05; Man. Dir, Troika Dialog AM, 2005–08; Dir and Chief Operating Officer, Montanaro Asset Mgt, 2008–10; CEO, Governance for Owners LLP, 2012–14. Chm., Future Route Ltd, 2015–18; non-executive Director: Highgate Capital Fund, 2015–; J P Morgan Japan Investment Trust plc, 2016–; EG Capital Advrs, 2017–; Woodford Patient Capital Trust plc, 2019–; Adviser to Chief Executive Officer: Denville Hall, 2014–; Pestival, 2016–. Mem. Council, UK Health and Care Professionals Council, 2014– (Acting Chair, 2018–19). Chm., Beacon Fellowship Charitable Trust, 2005–14. *Recreations:* tennis, gardening, bridge. *Address:* 24a Groom Place, SW1X 7BA. *T:* 07776 172145. *E:* Stephen_cohen2002@yahoo.co.uk.

COHEN, Sir Stephen Harry W.; *see* Waley-Cohen.

COHEN, Prof. Stephen Michael, PhD; FRS 2008; Professor, Department of Biological Sciences, National University of Singapore, since 2010; Research Director, Institute of Molecular and Cell Biology, Singapore, since 2010 (Acting Director, 2010–11); Professor, Department of Cellular and Molecular Medicine, University of Copenhagen, since 2014; *b* Ottawa, 29 Oct. 1956; *m* Pernille Rørth. *Educ:* Univ. of Toronto (BSc 1977); Princeton Univ. (MA 1980; PhD 1983). Postdoctoral Fellow: MIT, 1983–86; Max Planck Inst. for Develtl Biol., Germany, 1986–89; Asst Prof., Baylor Coll. of Medicine, Houston, 1989–93; Asst Investigator, Howard Hughes Med. Inst., 1990–93; Gp Leader, 1993–2007, Sen. Scientist, 1995–2007, Co-ordinator, Develtl Biol. Unit, 1996–2007, EMBL, Germany; CEO and Temasek Sen. Investigator, Temasek Life Scis Lab., Singapore, 2007–10; Adjunct Prof., Dept of Biol Scis, Nat. Univ. of Singapore, 2007–10. *Publications:* articles in jls. *Address:* Department of Cellular and Molecular Medicine, Panum Institute, 18.4, University of Copenhagen, Biegdamsvej 3, 2200 Copenhagen, Denmark.

COHEN-TANNOUDJI, Prof. Claude, PhD; Grand Croix, Légion d'Honneur; Commandeur, Ordre National du Mérite; Professor of Atomic and Molecular Physics, Collège de France, Paris, 1973–2004; *b* 1 April 1933; *s* of Abraham Cohen-Tannoudji and Sarah Sebbah; *m* 1958, Jacqueline Veyrat; one *s* one *d* (and one *s* decd). *Educ:* Ecole Normale Supérieure, Paris; Univ. of Paris (PhD Physics 1962). Researcher, CNRS, 1960–64; Associate Prof., 1964–67, Prof., 1967–73, Univ. of Paris. Member: Académie des Sciences, Paris, 1981; NAS, USA, 1994. (Jtly) Nobel Prize for Physics, 1997. *Publications:* (jtly) Quantum Mechanics, Vols I and II, 1977; Atoms in Electromagnetic Fields, 1994; with J. Dupont-Roc and G. Grynberg: Photons and Atoms: introduction to Q.E.D., 1989; Atom-photon Interactions, 1992; Advances in Atomic Physics: an overview, 2011. *Recreation:* music. *Address:* Laboratoire Kastler-Brossel, Département de Physique de l'ENS, 24 rue Lhomond, 75231 Paris Cedex 05, France. *T:* (1) 45350218.

COHN, Prof. Anthony George, PhD; CEng, FREng, FIET, FBCS; Professor of Automated Reasoning, School of Computing, University of Leeds, since 1996; *b* Cardiff, 19 Aug. 1954; *s* of Peter and Lieselott Cohn; *m* 1986, Gillian Margaret Liggat; one *s* one *d*. *Educ:* Chesham Prep. Sch.; Dr Challoner's Grammar Sch.; Univ. of Essex (BSc 1st Cl. Hons Computing Sci.; PhD Computer Sci. 1983). FIET 2005; FBCS 2005; CITP 2005; CEng 2015; FREng 2015. Systems Programmer, GEC Marconi, 1975–76; Lectr, Univ. of Warwick, 1979–89; University of Leeds: Sen. Lectr, 1990–94; Reader, 1995–96; Hd, Sch. of Computing, 1999–2004. Adjunct Prof., Univ. of Technol., Sydney, 2012–14; Distinguished Visiting Professor: Tongji Univ., China, 2018–; Qingdao Univ. of Sci. and Technol., China; Turing Fellow, Alan Turing Inst., 2018–20. Dir, KR Inc., 2000–. Editor-in-Chief: Spatial Cognition and Computation, 2003–; Artificial Intelligence, 2007–14. Trustee, Internat. Jt Conf. on Artificial Intelligence, 1997–2007 (Pres., 2003–05). Fellow: Eur. Assoc. for Artificial Intelligence, 1999; Assoc. for Study of Artificial Intelligence and Simulation of Behaviour, 2005; Assoc. for Advancement of Artificial Intelligence, 2006. Dist. Service Award, Assoc. for Advancement of Artificial Intelligence, 2012; Donald E. Walker Dist. Service Award, Internat. Jt Conf. on Artificial Intelligence, 2015. *Recreations:* my family, food, wine, tennis, badminton, swimming, travel, walks. *Address:* School of Computing, University of Leeds, Leeds LS2 9JT. *T:* (0113) 343 5482, *Fax:* (0113) 343 5468. *E:* a.g.cohn@leeds.ac.uk.

COHN-SHERBOK, Rabbi Prof. Dan; Professor of Judaism, University of Wales, Lampeter, 1997–2009, Professor Emeritus, 2010; *b* 1 Feb. 1945; *s* of Dr Bernard Sherbok and Ruth Sherbok (*née* Goldstein), Denver, Colo; *m* 1976, Lavinia Charlotte Heath. *Educ:* Williams Coll., Mass (BA); Hebrew Union Coll., Ohio (BHL, MAHL); Wolfson Coll., Cambridge (MLitt, PhD). Served as rabbi in US, Australia, SA and England, 1970–75; Chaplain, Colorado Hse of Representatives, 1971; Lectr in Jewish Theology, Univ. of Kent, 1975–97; Dir, Centre for Study of Religion and Society, Univ. of Kent, 1982–90; Dir, Centre for Study of World's Religions, Univ. of Wales, Lampeter, 2003–08. Mem., AHRC Peer Review Coll., 2007–. Visiting Professor: Univ. of Essex, 1993–94; of Inter-Faith Dialogue, Univ. of Middx, 1995–; of Judaism, Univ. of Wales at Lampeter, 1995–97; Univ. of St Andrews, 1995; Univ. of Wales, Bangor, 1998; Vilnius Univ., 2000; Univ. of Durham, 2002; Trinity Univ. Coll. (formerly Trinity Coll.), Carmarthen, 2007–10, Univ. of Wales Trinity St David, 2010–; St Mary's Univ. (formerly UC), Twickenham, 2007–; Charles Univ., Prague, 2008; York St John Univ., 2011–; Vis. Schol., Sarum Coll., 2005–; Visiting Research Fellow: Heythrop Coll., Univ. of London, 2011–; Centre of Religions for Peace and Reconciliation, Univ. of Winchester, 2013–; Hon. Prof., Aberystwyth Univ., 2010–. Pres., London Soc. for Study of Religion, 2014–16. Hon. DD Hebrew Union Coll., 1996. Hon. Col ADC, New Mexico, 1957. *Publications:* The Jews of Canterbury, 1984; (ed) World Religions and Human Liberation, 1984; On Earth as it is in Heaven, 1987; (ed) Exploring Reality, 1987; The Jewish Heritage, 1988; Holocaust Theology, 1989; Jewish Petitionary Prayer, 1989; God and the Holocaust, 1989; Rabbinic Perspectives on the New Testament, 1990; (ed) The Canterbury Papers, 1990; (ed) The Salman Rushdie Controversy, 1990; (ed) Essays on Religion and Society, 1990; (ed) Using the Bible Today, 1991; (ed) A Traditional Quest, 1991; (ed) The Sayings of Moses, 1991; (ed) Tradition and Unity, 1991; (ed) Problems in Contemporary Jewish Philosophy, 1991; A Dictionary of Judaism and Christianity, 1991; Issues in Contemporary Judaism, 1991; (ed) Islam in a World of Diverse Faiths, 1991; The Blackwell Dictionary of Judaica, 1992; Israel: the history of an idea, 1992; Exodus, 1992; (ed) Many Mansions, 1992; (ed) World Religions and Human Liberation, 1992; (ed) Religion in Public Life, 1992; (ed) Torah and Revelation, 1992; Atlas of Jewish History, 1993; The Jewish Faith, 1993; Not a Job for a Nice Jewish Boy, 1993; Judaism and Other Faiths, 1994; The Future of Judaism, 1994; Jewish and Christian Mysticism, 1994; The American Jew, 1994; (ed) Glimpses of God, 1994; (jtly) A Short History of Judaism, 1994; Jewish Mysticism, 1995; (jtly) A Popular Dictionary of Judaism, 1995; (ed) Beyond Death: theological and philosophical reflections on life after death, 1995; (ed) Divine Interventions and Miracles, 1996; Medieval Jewish Philosophy, 1996; The Hebrew Bible, 1996; Modern Judaism, 1996; Biblical Hebrew for Beginners, 1996; (ed) The Liberation Debate, 1996; (jtly) A Short Reader in Judaism, 1996; Atlas of Jewish History, 1996; Fifty Key Jewish Thinkers, 1997; The Jewish Messiah, 1997; After Noah, 1997; (ed) Theodicy, 1997; The Crucified Jew, 1997; (jtly) A Short Introduction to Judaism, 1997; Concise Encyclopedia of Judaism, 1998; Understanding the Holocaust, 1999; (ed) The Future of Jewish Christian Dialogue, 1999; (ed) The Future of Religion, 1999; Judaism, 1999; Jews, Christians and Religious Pluralism, 1999; Messianic Judaism, 2000; Interfaith Theology, 2001; (jtly) The Palestine-Israeli Conflict, 2001; (ed) Voices of Messianic Judaism, 2001; (ed) Religious Diversity in the Graeco-Roman World, 2001; Anti-Semitism, 2002; Holocaust Theology: a reader, 2002; Interfaith Theology: a reader, 2002; (jtly) The Palestine-Israeli Conflict, 2002; Judaism: history, belief and practice, 2003, 2nd edn 2017; What's a Nice Jewish Boy Like You Doing in a Place Like This?, 2003; (ed) A Life of Courage: Sherwin Wine and Humanistic Judaism, 2003; The Vision of Judaism: wrestling with God, 2004; (jtly) An Encyclopedia of Judaism and Christianity, 2004; Dictionary of Jewish Biography, 2005; (jtly) Pursuing the Dream: a Jewish-Christian conversation, 2005; The Paradox of Antisemitism, 2006; The Politics of Apocalypse, 2006; Kabbalah and Jewish Mysticism, 2006; What Do You Do When Your Parents Live Forever?, 2007; Dictionary of Kabbalah and Kabbalists, 2009; Judaism Today, 2010; Introduction to Zionism and Israel, 2011; The Palestinian State: a Jewish justification, 2012; The Illustrated History of Judaism, 2013; (jtly) Love, Sex and Marriage: insights from Judaism, Christianity and Islam, 2013; Eternal Angels, 2013; The Athenæum: sketches, 2014; (jtly) Why Can't They Get Along?, 2014; (jtly) Sensible Religion, 2014; (jtly) Debating Palestine and Israel, 2014; Animals are People Too, 2014; (cartoonist) Williams College Alumni Cartoons, 2014; Illustrated History of the Jewish Faith, 2015; (jtly) Terror and Religion, 2016; Judaism: belief and practice, 2017; Dictionary of Jews and Judaism, 2017; Jews: everything you wanted to know but were too afraid to ask, 2018; (jtly) People of the Book, 2018; (jtly) Interfaith Prayer and Worship, 2019; numerous articles to learned jls. *Recreations:* keeping cats, walking, drawing cartoons. *Address:* 89 Winchester Court, Vicarage Gate, W8 4AF. *E:* cohnsherbok@googlemail.com. *Clubs:* Athenæum, Oxford and Cambridge.

COHRS, (William) Michael; Member of Court, Bank of England, 2011–15; *b* Midland, Mich; *s* of William and Lois Cohrs; *m* 1984, Arlene; two *s*. *Educ:* Harvard Univ. (BA Econs; MBA). Deutsche Bank, 1995–2010: Hd, Global Banking, 2004–10; Mem., Mgt Bd, 2009–10. Non-exec. Dir, Surfcast, 2010–; Industrial Advr, EQT, 2012–. *Recreations:* football, fishing.

COIA, Dame Denise (Assunta), (Dame Denise Macdonald), DBE 2016; Chair, Scottish Government Taskforce on Mental Health and Wellbeing of Children in Scotland, since 2018; Convenor, Children in Scotland, since 2017; *b* Glasgow, 1952; *d* of Guistino, (Joseph), Coia and Winnifred Jill Coia; *m* 1977, Archibald Nicholson Macdonald; two *s*. *Educ:* Notre Dame High Sch. for Girls, Glasgow; Univ. of Glasgow (MB ChB 1976). DRCOG 1978; MRCPsych 1981, FRCPsych 1996. Doctor, then Consultant Psychiatrist, Glasgow, 1987–2011. Mental Health Advr, Gtr Glasgow Health Bd, 1986–2006; PMO, Mental Health, Scottish Govt, 2006–11; Chair, Healthcare Improvement Scotland, 2010–18. Hon. Sen. Lectr, Dept of Psychological Medicine, Univ. of Glasgow, 1987–2011. Dir, Tannoch Loch Co., 2015–. Member: Bd, Professions Supplementary to Medicine, London, 1997–2001; Clin. Standards Bd, Quality Improvement Scotland, 1999–2003; Scientific Bd, Med. Res., Scotland, 2006–12; Care Inspectorate, Scotland, 2010–. Med. Associate, 1990–, Chm., Quality Scrutiny Gp, 2013–, GMC. Chair, Royal Coll. of Psychiatrists Scotland, 2001–05; Vice-Pres., RCPsych, 2005–10. Sec., Acad. of Royal Med. Colls and Faculties in Scotland, 2003–06. MInstD 2015. FRSE 2018. Hon. FRCGP 2006. Sen. Fellow Award, RCPsych, 2013. *Publications:* (with J. M. Atkinson) Families Coping with Schizophrenia, 1995; contribs to psychiatric jls. *Recreations:* walking, ski-ing, horse riding, tennis, theatre, art, literature. *Address:* Mental Health Directorate, Scottish Government, Floor 3, St Andrews House, 2 Regent Road, Edinburgh EH1 3DG.

COID, Dr Donald Routledge; consultant and specialist in medical administration and public health medicine, since 1985; Director, Donald Coid Consultants Pty Ltd, since 2012; *b* 13 June 1953; *s* of late Charles Routledge Coid and Marjory Macdonald Coid (*née* Keay); *m* 1985, Susan Kathleen Ramus (*née* Crocker); three *d*. *Educ:* Bromley Grammar Sch. for Boys; Harrow County Sch. for Boys; Univ. of Nottingham (BMedSci; BM, BS); LSHTM (MSc 1981). MRCP 1979; MFCM 1985, MFPHM 1989, FFPH (FFPHM 1996); FRACMA 1985; FAFPHM 1991; FRCPE 1998; FRSPH (FRIPHH 1998). Hse Physician, Nottingham City Hosp., 1976; Hse Surgeon, Nottingham Gen. Hosp., 1977; Sen. Hse Officer, Brook Gen. Hosp., London, 1977–78; Res. Asst, Middlesex Hosp. Med. Sch., 1979; Field Med. Officer, Royal Flying Doctor Service, Australia, Eastern Goldfields, 1979–80; MO, Community Health Services, WA, 1981–82; Regl Dir of Public Health, Eastern Goldfields, WA, 1982–85; Med. Supt, Kalgoorlie Reg. Hosp., WA, 1984–85; Fife Health Board: Cons. in Public Health, 1985–92; Asst Gen. Manager, 1992–93; Chief Admin. MO, Dir of Public Health and Exec. Dir, Tayside Health Bd, 1994–98; Consultant in Health Services Res., Ninewells Hosp. and Med. Sch., Dundee, 1998–2000; Public Health Consultant, Grampian Health Bd, 2000–01; Dir of Med. Services, Armadale Health Service, WA, 2001–06, 2017–18; Exec. Dir of Med. Services, Wide Bay Health Service (formerly Wide Bay Health Service Dist), Qld, 2006–09; Public Health Physician, Population Health Services, Qld, 2009–10; Med. Advr, Travel Doctor—TMVC, Perth, WA, 2010–18; Med. Dir, Clinics and Assistance, Internat. SOS, Beijing, 2010–11; Regl Med. Dir, Mainland China, Taiwan and Remote Territories, International SOS, 2011–12; Director of Medical Services: Bentley Hosp., Perth, WA, 2012–14; NW Tasmania Health Orgn, 2012–14; St John of God Murdoch Hosp., WA, 2014–17; Dir of Clinical Services, N Metropolitan Health Service, Perth, 2018–19. Consultant to: Govt of Qatar, 1999; WHO, 2000; overseas projects, Corp. of Victoria, 2003. Hon. Sen. Lectr, Dundee Univ., 1994–2001. *Publications*: on public health and related topics in learned jls. *Recreations*: golf, cricket, piano, singing, cycling, swimming, pilates. *Address*: 131 Churchill Avenue, Subiaco, WA 6008, Australia. *T*: (61) 893822496, 457115881. *Clubs*: Royal & Ancient Golf, New Golf (St Andrews); Cottesloe Golf (WA).

**COJOCARU, Alina;** ballet dancer; Principal, English National Ballet, since 2013; *b* Bucharest, 27 May 1981; *d* of Gheorge Cojocaru and Nina Cojocaru. *Educ*: Ukrainian State Ballet Sch.; Royal Ballet Sch. With Kiev Ballet, 1998; joined Royal Ballet, 1999, Principal, 2001–13. Guest dancer with Mariinsky Ballet, American Ballet Th., Royal Danish Ballet, Hungarian Nat. Ballet, Paris Opera Ballet, Romanian Nat. Ballet, Bolshoi Ballet, Hamburg Ballet, Nat. Ballet of Cuba, Teatro Colon, South African Ballet, Kremlin Ballet, Sarasota Ballet, Zagreb Ballet, Australian Ballet. Performances include main rôles in The Nutcracker, Romeo and Juliet, Giselle, Don Quixote, Swan Lake, Sleeping Beauty, Cinderella, Onegin, Manon, Coppelia, Mayerling and Le Corsaire, Lady of the Camellias, A Month in the Country, A Midsummer Night's Dream, Etudes, La Bayadère, Jewels, Symphonic Variations, La Sylphide, In the Night, Las Hermanas, Scènes de Ballet, Gong, Symphony in C, Daphnis and Chloe, No Man's Land, La Fille mal gardée, Second Breath, The Lesson, Duo Concertant, The Leaves are Fading, Other Dances, Voices of Spring, Beyond Bach, Tombeaux, Ondine, Vertiginous Thrill Of Exactitude, Raymond act 3, Dances at a Gathering, Radio and Juliet, No Man's Land. Trustee, Hospices of Hope, 2008–. Prix de Lausanne, 1997; Best Female Dancer, Critics' Circle Dance Award, 2002; Ballerina of the Decade, Moscow, 2010; Dancer of the Year, German Dance Critics Award, 2012; Best Female Dancer, Benois de la Danse, 2004, 2012. Cavalier of Romania, 2002. *Address*: c/o English National Ballet, Markova House, 39 Jay Mews, SW7 2ES.

**COKAYNE,** family name of **Baron Cullen of Ashbourne**.

**COKE,** family name of **Earl of Leicester**.

**COKE, Viscount;** Edward Horatio Coke; *b* 11 June 2003; *s* and *heir* of Earl of Leicester, *qv*.

**COKER, Jane Elizabeth;** a Judge of the Upper Tribunal, Immigration and Asylum Chamber, since 2011; *b* Saltburn, 11 July 1954; *d* of Frank Percival Charles Coker and Mary Coker; one *s* two *d*. *Educ*: Cheadle Hulme Sch.; Westfield Coll., Univ. of London (BSc Biol Scis). Admitted as solicitor, 1980; Founder Partner, Coker Vis Solicitors, 1982–2002; Immigration Judge (formerly Immigration Adjudicator), 2002–11 (pt-time, 2002–07). *Address*: Immigration and Asylum Chamber, Field House, 15–25 Breams Buildings, EC4A 1DZ. *E*: UpperTribunalJudge.Coker@eJudiciary.net.

**COKER, Paul;** Managing Director, Ranks Hovis McDougall, 1992–93; *b* 27 July 1938; *s* of Leslie and Mabel Coker; *m* 1966, Delphine Rostron Baden; twin *s* one *d*. *Educ*: Merchant Taylors' Sch. Joined Ranks Hovis McDougall (Cerebos Group), 1964: Man. Dir, General Products, 1982–87; Planning Dir, 1987–89; Dep. Man. Dir, 1989–91; Finance Dir, 1991–92. *Recreations*: golf, cricket, gardening, theatre. *Address*: Courtlands, Nightingales Lane, Chalfont St Giles, Bucks HP8 4SL. *T*: (01494) 762040.

**COKER, William John;** QC 1994; *b* 19 July 1950; *s* of Edgar and Peggy Coker; *m* 1977, Ruth Elaine Pull; one *s* one *d*. *Educ*: Bedford Sch.; Manchester Univ. (LLB). Called to the Bar, Gray's Inn, 1973. *Recreations*: golf, fishing.

**COLBORN, (Leslie) Nigel;** freelance writer and journalist, since 1986; *b* Nottingham, 20 Feb. 1944; *s* of late Leslie Colborn and Anne Colborn; *m* 1972, Rosamund Hewlett; two *s* two *d*. *Educ*: King's Sch., Ely; Cornell Univ. (BS). Dir, Colborn Gp, 1972–76; farmer, 1976–86. Presenter, Gardeners' World, BBC TV, 1988–91; Panellist, Gardeners' Question Time, BBC Radio, 1996–2003. Gardening Corresp., Daily Mail, 2009–. Royal Horticultural Society: Trustee, 2002–10; Vice-Chm., Council, 2006–09 (Mem., 1998–). FRSA. Lifetime Achievement Award, Garden Media Guild, 2012; VMH 2013. *Publications*: (with Ursula Buchan) The Classic Horticulturist, 1987; This Gardening Business, 1988; Exposed Gardens, 1989; Leisurely Gardening, 1989; Family Piles, 1990; The Container Garden, 1990; The Good Old Fashioned Gardener, 1993; Annuals and Bedding Plants, 1994; A Flower for Every Day, 1996; Great Plants for Small Gardens, 1997; Nigel Colborn's Garden Magic, 1998; The Garden Floor, 2000; Wisley: inspiration for all seasons, 2006; Plant Solutions, 2006; A Garden Under Glass, 2007; *novels*: The Kirkland Acres, 1994; The Congregation, 1996; Weather of the Heart, 1997. *Recreations*: nature, theatre, photography, ornithology, travel, music. *E*: ncolborn@btinternet.com. *Club*: Farmers.

**COLCHESTER, Area Bishop of,** since 2014; **Rt Rev. Roger Anthony Brett Morris;** *b* Hereford, 18 July 1968; *s* of Anthony Edward Morris and Eirwen Morris; *m* 1991, Sally Jane; two *d*. *Educ*: Imperial Coll. London (BSc; ARCS 1987); Trinity Coll., Cambridge (BA 1992; MA); Ridley Hall Theol Coll. Ordained deacon, 1993, priest, 1994; Asst Curate, Northleach Gp of Parishes, 1993–96; Rector, Coln River Gp of Parishes incl. Sevenhampton, 1996–2003; Dir of Parish Develt and Evangelism, Dio. of Coventry, 2003–08; Archdeacon of Worcester, 2008–14. *Recreations*: supporting Bristol Rovers, music, films, Greenbelt Festival, walking the dog. *Address*: The Bishop's Office, 1 Fitzwalter Road, Lexden, Colchester CO3 3SS. *E*: roger.morris@me.com.

**COLCLOUGH, Rt Rev. Michael John;** an Honorary Assistant Bishop, Diocese of London and Diocese in Europe, since 2013; *b* 29 Dec. 1944; *s* of Joseph and Beryl Colclough; *m* 1983, Cynthia Flora Mary De Sousa; two *s*. *Educ*: Leeds Univ. (BA Hons English and Religious Studies); Cuddesdon Coll., Oxford. Ordained deacon, 1971, priest, 1972; Curate: St Werburgh, Burslem, 1971–75; St Mary, S Ruislip, 1975–79; Vicar, St Anselm, Hayes, 1979–86; Area Dean of Hillingdon, 1985–92; Team Rector, Uxbridge, 1986–92; Archdeacon of Northolt, 1992–94; personal asst to Bp of London (Archdeacon at London House), 1994–96; Priest-in-Charge: St Vedast-alias-Foster, 1994–96; St Magnus the Martyr, London Bridge, 1995–96; Dep. Priest in Ordinary to the Queen, 1995–96; Area Bishop of Kensington, 1996–2008; a Residentiary Canon, St Paul's Cathedral, 2008–13; Bishop in Residence, St Paul Knightsbridge, 2013–. Chaplain to Mercers' Co., 2010–. Chm. Mission, Evangelism and Renewal in England Cttee, C of E, 1999–2003. Patron: Micro Loan Foundn, 1999–2008; London Care Connections, 2003–08; Shooting Star Trust, 2005–08; W London Action for Children, 2005–08; Hoffman Foundn for Autism, 2005–. *Recreations*: travel, walking in the English countryside, reading, people. *Address*: 12 Grosvenor Court, Sloane Street, SW1X 9PF. *T*: (020) 3612 3135. *E*: michaeljcolclough@gmail.com.

**COLDSTREAM, John Richard Francis;** writer; Literary Editor, The Daily Telegraph, 1991–99; *b* 19 Dec. 1947; *s* of Gerald Coldstream and Marian Gatehouse; *m* 1977, Susan Elizabeth Pealing. *Educ*: Bradfield Coll.; Univ. of Nice; Univ. of Sussex. Evening Echo, Hemel Hempstead, 1971–74; joined Daily Telegraph, Peterborough column, 1974; Dep. Literary Editor, Daily Telegraph, 1984–91 and Sunday Telegraph, 1989–91. Member: Arts Council Literature Adv. Panel, 1992–97; Man Booker (formerly Booker) Prize Adv. Cttee, 1996–2004. *Publications*: (ed) The Daily Telegraph Book of Contemporary Short Stories, 1995; Dirk Bogarde: the authorised biography, 2004; (ed) Ever, Dirk: the Bogarde letters, 2008; Victim, 2011; Restored, Refreshed, Renewed, 2015. *Recreation*: theatre. *E*: johncoldstream@btinternet.com. *Club*: Garrick.

**COLE,** family name of **Earl of Enniskillen**.

**COLE, Ailsa Jane A.;** *see* Anderson-Cole.

**COLE, Allan Gordon Halliwell,** FRCA; Consultant Anaesthetist, University Hospitals of Leicester NHS Trust (formerly Glenfield Hospital and Leicester Royal Infirmary), since 1985; *b* 20 Feb. 1949; *s* of late Robert Randle Cole and Anne Dorothy Cole; *m* 1st, 1974, Stacey Elizabeth Gregg (marr. diss.); 2nd, 1979, Penelope Gaye Cole (marr. diss.); one *s* one *d*; 3rd, 2007, Jennifer, *widow* of Prof. David Marsden, FRS. *Educ*: Marlborough Coll.; St Bartholomew's Hosp. (MB BS 1973). MRCS, LRCP 1973; FRCA (FFARCS 1979). SHO, then Registrar in Anaesthesia, St Bartholomew's Hosp., 1976–80; Sen. Registrar in Anaesthesia, John Radcliffe Hosp., Oxford, 1980–85; Medical Director: Glenfield Hosp., Leicester, 1993–2000; University Hosps of Leicester NHS Trust, 2000–09. Med. Examiner, Leics, 2016–; Special Advr, Defence and Nat. Rehab. Centre, 2019–. Chm., British Assoc. of Med. Managers, 2003–05. *Publications*: papers in peer-reviewed jls of anaesthesia and med. mgt. *Recreations*: golf, singing (choir), gliding. *Address*: 42 Groby Lane, Newtown, Linford, Leics LE6 0HH. *T*: (01530) 244375. *E*: coleallan@doctors.org.uk.

**COLE, Caroline Louise;** *see* Flint, Rt Hon. C. L.

**COLE, Gordon Stewart;** QC 2006; *b* 25 March 1956; *s* of Dermott and Jean Cole; *m* 1989, Sarah, (Sally), Cooper; one *s* one *d*. *Educ*: John Moores Univ., Liverpool (BA Hons Law); Inns of Court Sch. of Law. Called to the Bar, Inner Temple, 1979; in practice as barrister, 1979–, specialising in criminal law. *Recreations*: fly fishing, tennis, golf, shooting, Liverpool FC, ski-ing, tractor driving. *Address*: c/o Exchange Chambers, One Derby Square, Liverpool L2 9XX. *T*: (0151) 236 7747. *E*: coleqc@exchangechambers.co.uk; c/o Farrar's Building, Temple, EC4Y 7BD. *T*: (020) 7583 9241.

**COLE, Harry;** Deputy Political Editor, Mail on Sunday, since 2018; *b* Kent, 27 April 1986; *s* of Robert and Denise Cole. *Educ*: Tonbridge Sch.; Univ. of Edinburgh (MA 2009). News Ed., Guido Fawkes Blog, 2009–15; Columnist: Daily Star, 2011–12; GQ and Sun on Sunday, 2012–15; Contributing Ed., The Spectator, 2012–15; Westminster Correspondent, The Sun, 2015–18. *Recreations*: countryside, Pomerol and politics. *Address*: Mail on Sunday, Northcliffe House, 2 Derry Street, SW8 5HY. *T*: 07826 855190. *Club*: 5 Hertford Street.

**COLE, Prof. John Peter;** Professor of Human and Regional Geography (formerly of Regional Geography), University of Nottingham, 1975–94; Emeritus since 1994; *b* Sydney, Australia, 9 Dec. 1928; *s* of Philip and Marjorie Cecelia Cole; *m* 1st, 1952, Isabel Jesús (*née* Urrunaga) (*d* 2007); two *s*; 2nd, 2008, Karen Jean (*née* De Bres). *Educ*: Bromley Grammar Sch.; Univ. of Nottingham (State School., BA, MA, PhD, DLitt); Collegio Borromeo, Pavia Univ., Italy (British Council Schol.). Demonstrator, Univ. of Nottingham, 1951–52; Nat. Service with RN, Jt Services Sch. for Linguists, Russian Language Interpreter, 1952–54 (Lt Comdr RNR, retired); Oficina Nacional de Planeamiento y Urbanismo, Lima, Peru, 1954–55; Lectr in Geography, Univ. of Reading, 1955–56; Lectr in Geography, Univ. of Nottingham, 1956–69. Reader, 1969–75; Vis. Lectr or Prof., Univs of Washington, Columbia, Mexico, Valparaíso, Nanjing, Beijing. *Publications*: Geography of World Affairs, 1959, 6th edn 1983; (with F. C. German) Geography of the USSR, 1961, 2nd edn 1970; Italy, 1964; Latin America, 1965, 2nd edn 1975; (with C. A. M. King) Quantitative Geography, 1968; (with N. J. Beynon) New Ways in Geography, 1968, 2nd edn 1982; Situations in Human Geography, 1975; The Development Gap, 1981; Geography of the Soviet Union, 1984; China 1950–2000 Performance and Prospects, 1985; The Poverty of Marxism in Contemporary Geographical Applications and Research, 1986; Development and Underdevelopment, 1987; (with T. Buck) Modern Soviet Economic Performance, 1987; (with F. J. Cole) The Geography of the European Community, 1993, 2nd edn 1997; Geography of the World's Major Regions, 1996; Global 2050: a basis for speculation, 1999; Geography at Nottingham 1922–1970: a record, 2000; contribs to learned jls, UK and overseas. *Recreations*: travel, languages, pen drawing and painting, gardening. *Address*: 10 Ranmore Close, Beeston, Nottingham NG9 3FR. *T*: (0115) 925 0409.

**COLE, Justin Mark; His Honour Judge Cole;** a Circuit Judge, since 2014. *Educ*: Univ. of Nottingham (LLB); Chester Coll. of Law (Solicitor's Finals). Admitted solicitor, 1990; called to the Bar, Inner Temple, 1992; a Dep. Dist Judge, Magistrates' Court, 2005–10; a Recorder, 2009–14. *Address*: Aylesbury Crown Court, Walton Street, Aylesbury, Bucks HP21 7FT.

**COLE, Margaret Rose, (Mrs Graeme Cooke);** Chief Risk Officer and General Counsel, PricewaterhouseCoopers LLP UK, since 2012 (Member, UK Executive Board, since 2012); *b* Preston, Lancs, 17 June 1961; *d* of late Herbert and Patricia Cole; *m* 1998, Graeme Cooke. *Educ*: Winckley Sq. Convent Sch., Preston; New Hall, Cambridge (BA 1982); Coll. of Law, Lancaster Gate. Admitted solicitor, 1985. Stephenson Harwood: articled clerk, 1983; Asst Solicitor, 1985–90; Partner, 1990–95; Partner, White & Case, 1995–2005; Dir, Enforcement, 2005–10, Man. Dir, Enforcement, Financial Crime and Markets, 2010–12, FSA. Mem., Inst. for Fiscal Studies, 2012. Hon. Dr of Laws Coll. of Law, 2012. *Publications*: (contrib.) A Practitioner's Guide to FSA Investigations and Enforcement, 2nd edn 2007. *Recreations*: horse riding, travel, opera. *Address*: PricewaterhouseCoopers LLP, 1 Embankment Place, WC2N 6RH.

**COLE, Martina;** author; *b* Aveley, Essex, 30 March 1959; *d* of Christopher and Ellen Whiteside; one *s* one *d*. Hon. DLitt Anglia Ruskin, 2008. *Publications*: Dangerous Lady, 1992 (adapted for TV, 1995); The Ladykiller, 1993; Goodnight Lady, 1994; The Jump, 1995 (adapted for TV, 1996); The Runaway, 1997 (adapted for TV, 2010); Two Women, 1999; Broken, 2000; Faceless, 2001; Maura's Game, 2002; The Know, 2003; The Graft, 2004; The Take, 2005 (adapted for TV, 2009); Close, 2006; Faces, 2007; The Business, 2008; Hard Girls, 2009; The Family, 2010; The Faithless, 2011; The Good Life, 2015; Get Even, 2015; Betrayal, 2016; Damaged, 2017. *Recreation*: voracious reader. *Address*: c/o Darley Anderson Literary, TV & Film Agency, Estelle House, 11 Eustace Road, SW6 1JB. *T*: 07917 335263. *E*: chris@littlefreddie.com.

**COLE, Nathan James;** Headmaster, Wilson's School, Wallington, since 2014; *b* Sheffield, 1980; *s* of Carl and Jennifer Cole. *Educ*: Univ. of Nottingham (BA Hons Hist. 2001); Hughes Hall, Cambridge. Saffron Walden County High School: Teacher of Hist., 2002–04; Asst Sen. Tutor, 2004–05; Hd of Hist., 2005–06; Wilson's School: Year Manager, 2006–08;

Asst Hd, 2008–10; Dep. Hd, 2010–14. *Recreations:* obsessing about the causes of Edward VIII's abdication, spending time on cruise ships, dining in and out. *Address:* Wilson's School, Mollison Drive, Wallington, Surrey SM6 9JW.

COLE, Nicholas Arthur; His Honour Judge Nicholas Cole; a Circuit Judge, since 2015; *b* Nottingham, 21 March 1968; *s* of late John C. P. Cole and Moira J. Cole (née Holton); *m* 1995, Joanne Elizabeth Ellis; two *s*. *Educ:* Nottingham High Sch.; Univ. of Birmingham (BSc Hons Biol Scis); Nottingham Law Sch. (CPE); Inns of Court Sch. of Law. Called to the Bar, Lincoln's Inn, 1993; in practice as barrister, St Ives Chambers, Birmingham, specialising in family and regulatory law, 1994–2015 (Hd of Chambers, 2013–15); a Recorder, 2009–15. *Recreations:* Italian cars, old buildings, keeping sheep. *Address:* Worcester Combined Court, Shirehall, Foregate Street, Worcester WR1 1EQ.

COLE, Prof. Peter Geoffrey; journalist; Professor of Journalism, University of Sheffield, 2000–10, now Emeritus; *b* 16 Dec. 1945; *s* of Arthur and Elizabeth Cole; *m* 1982, Jane Ellison; three *s* one *d*. *Educ:* Tonbridge Sch.; Queens' Coll., Cambridge. Reporter, Evening News, 1968–72; Diary Editor, Evening Standard, 1976–78; News Editor, Deputy Editor, The Guardian, 1978–88; Editor, Sunday Correspondent, 1988–90; News Review Editor, The Sunday Times, 1990–93; Prof. of Journalism, Univ. of Central Lancs, 1993–2000. *Publications:* (with Peter Pringle) Can You Positively Identify This Man?, 1975; (with Tony Harcup) Newspaper Journalism, 2010. *Address:* Department of Journalism, University of Sheffield, 9 Mappin Street, Sheffield S1 4DT. *Clubs:* Garrick; Plymouth Argyle Supporters' (London Branch); Lancashire County Cricket.

COLE, His Honour Richard Raymond Buxton; DL; a Circuit Judge, 1984–2007; *b* 11 June 1937; *s* of late Raymond Buxton Cole, DSO, TD, DL, and Edith Mary Cole; *m* 1962, Sheila Joy Rumbold; one *s* one *d*. *Educ:* Dragon School; St Edward's, Oxford. Admitted as solicitor 1960; Partner in Cole & Cole Solicitors, Oxford, 1962–84; Recorder, 1976–84; Hon. Recorder, City of Coventry, 1999–2007. Mem., Parole Bd, 1981–83. President: Berks, Bucks and Oxon Law Soc., 1981–82; Council of HM Circuit Judges, 2001. Mem. Governing Body, Dragon Sch., 1975–92, Chm., 1986–92. Chm., Burford Parish Council, 1976–79, first Town Mayor, 1979. Master, Upholders' Co., 1992–93. Hon. Pres., Assoc. of Master Upholsterers, later Assoc. of Master Upholsterers and Soft Furnishers, 1993– (Hon. Fellow, 2015). DL Warwickshire, 2001. Chancellor's Medal, Univ. of Warwick, 2011. *Publications:* Bunny Cole: an Oxford man, 2010. *Recreations:* sport, gardening. *Club:* Frewen (Oxford).

COLE, Simon; Chief Executive Officer, 7digital Group plc (formerly Unique Broadcasting Company, then UBC Media Group plc), since 1989; *b* Newark, 20 Feb. 1958; *s* of Samuel Cole and Elizabeth Cole; *m* 2010, Amanda McArthur. *Educ:* Queen Elizabeth's Grammar Sch., Blackburn; Univ. of Manchester (BA Hons Drama 1981). BBC; Producer, 1983–85, Hd of Programming, 1985–87, Piccadilly Radio, Manchester; Chief Exec., PPM Radiowaves, 1986–89; Co-Founder, Unique Broadcasting Co., 1989. Dir, Audioboo Ltd, subseq. AudioBoom Ltd, 2010–15; Chm., IdeaDrop Ltd, 2016–; non-exec. Dir, MelodyVR Ltd, 2016–. Gov., Central Sch. of Ballet, 2010–. *Recreation:* running - Great North Run. *Address:* 7digital Group plc, 69 Wilson Street, EC2A 2BB. *T:* (020) 7099 7777. *E:* simon.cole@7digital.com. *Club:* Soho House.

COLE, Stephanie, (Mrs Peter Birrel), OBE 2005; actress; *b* 5 Oct. 1941; *d* of June Sheldon; *m* 1st, 1973, Henry Marshall (marr. diss.); one *d*; 2nd, 1998, Peter Birrel (*d* 2004). *Educ:* Clifton High Sch., Bristol; Bristol Old Vic Sch. Work in repertory theatre, and with Old Vic, etc; *television:* Soldiering On (Alan Bennett Talking Heads monologue), 1988; The Lady Vanishes (TV film), 2013; *series:* Tenko, 1980–84; Waiting for God, 1989–94; Keeping Mum, 1997–99; Life As We Know It, 2001; Doc Martin, 2004–09; Coronation Street, 2011–13 (Best Comedy Actress, British Soap Awards, 2012); Still Open All Hours, 2014–19; Man Down, 2014–17; Scarborough, 2019; *theatre* includes: A Passionate Woman, Comedy, 1995; Quartet, Albery, 1999; So Long Life, Th. Royal, Bath, 2001; The Shell Seekers, tour, 2003–04; Blithe Spirit, Savoy, 2005; The Rivals, Th. Royal, Bath, 2005; Born in the Gardens, Th. Royal, Bath, 2008; Separate Tables, 2009, Pygmalion, 2010, Chichester Festival Th.; This May Hurt a Bit, tour and London, 2014; Talking Heads, Th. Royal, Bath, 2015; Fool in King Lear, Bristol Old Vic, 2016; *films* include: Grey Owl, 2000; *radio* includes: Cabin Pressure (4 series), 2008–14; Ed Rearden's Week (8 series), 2005–17. Best TV Comedy Actress, 1992; Best TV Comedy Performance, 1999. *Publications:* A Passionate Life, 1998. *Recreations:* reading, gardening, painting, walking, theatre-going. *Address:* c/o John Grant, Conway van Gelder Grant Ltd, 8–12 Broadwick Street, W1F 8HW. *T:* (020) 7287 0077.

COLE, Prof. Stewart Thomas, PhD; FRS 2007; President, Institut Pasteur, Paris, since 2018; *b* 14 Jan. 1955; *s* of Leonard Thomas Cole and Jean Margaret Cole; *m* 1980, Lesley Curnick; one *s* one *d*. *Educ:* University Coll., Cardiff (BSc Hons 1976); Univ. of Sheffield (PhD 1979). Res. Asst, Max-Planck Institute for Biology, Tübingen, 1980–83; Institut Pasteur, Paris: staff scientist, 1984–89; Hd, Unité de Génétique Moléculaire Bactérienne, 1989–2007; Dir, Strategic Technol., 2000–04; Scientific Dir, 2004–05; Dir, Global Health Inst., Ecole Polytechnique Fédérale de Lausanne, Switzerland, 2007–17. Associate Mem., Nat. Acad. of Pharmacy (France), 2014. Kochon Prize, Stop TB Partnership, 2009; Behring Prize, Philipps-Univ. Marburg, 2014; Gardner Middlebrook Lifetime Achievement Award, 2016. Chevalier de la Légion d'Honneur (France), 2004. *Publications:* (ed jtly) Tuberculosis and the Tubercle Bacillus, 2005; over 350 scientific articles. *Recreations:* fly fishing, ski-ing, opera, Rugby. *Address:* Institut Pasteur, 25–28 rue du Docteur Roux, 75015 Paris, France. *T:* (33) 145688001. *E:* stewart.cole@pasteur.fr.

COLE, Timothy Marcus; Executive Director, Europe, ONE, since 2019; *b* Cuckfield, 2 May 1965; *s* of John Chantler Cole and Elsie Anne Cole; *m* 1997, Clare Elizabeth Parkes; one *s* one *d*. *Educ:* Durham Univ. (BA Hons). Christian Aid: Asst Eur. Community Officer, 1993–95; Sen. Prog. Officer, then Hd, Great Lakes Reg., 1995–99; Prog. Dir, Democratic Republic of Congo, Save the Children, 1999–2001; entered FCO, 2001; Head: Global Econ. Issues, FCO, 2001–02; Pan-African Policy Unit, FCO, 2003–05; Deputy Head of Mission: Mozambique, 2006–09; Zimbabwe, 2009–12; Ambassador to Cuba, 2012–16; UK Envoy to the Commonwealth, 2016–17; Hd, Internat. Orgns Dept, FCO, 2016–17; Migration Envoy, FCO, 2017. Gov., Internat. Sch. Havana, 2012–13. *Recreations:* golf, Rugby, ski-ing.

COLE-HAMILTON, Alexander Geoffrey; Member (Lib Dem) Edinburgh Western, Scottish Parliament, since 2016; *b* Welwyn Garden City, 22 July 1977; *s* of David and Liz Cole-Hamilton; *m* 2005, Gillian; two *s* one *d*. *Educ:* Madras Coll., St Andrews; Univ. of Aberdeen. Pres., Aberdeen Univ. Students' Rep. Council, 1999–2000; Constituency Organiser for John Barrett, MP, 2000–01; Communications Officer, Scottish Lib Dems, 2001–04; Policy Manager, Fairbridge, 2004–08; Hd, Policy, Aberlour Child Care Trust, 2008–16. *Recreations:* surfing, cooking, scuba diving. *Address:* Scottish Parliament, Edinburgh EH99 1SP. *T:* (0131) 348 5000. *E:* alex.cole-hamilton.msp@parliament.scot. *Club:* Scottish Liberal.

COLE-HAMILTON, (Arthur) Richard, CBE 1993; BA; CA; FCIBS; Chairman, Stakis PLC, 1995–98 (Deputy Chairman, 1994–95); Chief Executive, Clydesdale Bank PLC, 1982–92; *b* 8 May 1935; *s* of late John Cole-Hamilton, CBE; *m* 1963, Prudence Ann; one *s* two *d*. *Educ:* Ardrossan Academy; Loretto School; Cambridge Univ. (BA). Commissioned Argyll and Sutherland Highlanders, 1960–62. Brechin Cole-Hamilton & Co. (Chartered Accountants), 1962–67; Clydesdale Bank, 1967–92: Manager, Finance Corp. and Money Market, 1971; Asst Manager, Chief London Office, 1971; Supt of Branches, 1974; Head Office Manager, 1976; Asst Gen. Manager, 1978; Gen. Manager, 1979; Dep. Chief Gen. Manager, Feb. 1982; Dir, 1984–92. Chm., Cttee of Scottish Clearing Bankers, 1985–87, and 1991–92; Vice-Pres., Scottish Council for Develt and Industry, 1992–96; Dir, Glasgow Chamber of Commerce, 1985–91; Pres., Ayrshire Chamber of Commerce and Industry, 1992–96. Pres., Inst. of Bankers in Scotland, 1988–90. Mem. Council, Inst. of Chartered Accts of Scotland, 1981–85. Trustee: Nat. Galls of Scotland, 1986–96; Princess Royal Trust for Carers, 1991–98; Mem. Exec. Cttee, Erskine Hosp., 1976–2004. *Recreation:* golf. *Address:* 28 South Beach, Troon, Ayrshire KA10 6EF. *T:* (01292) 310603. *Clubs:* Western (Glasgow); Highland Brigade; Royal and Ancient Golf (Capt., 2004–05), Prestwick Golf.

COLEBY, Anthony Laurie; Executive Director, Bank of England, 1990–94; *b* 27 April 1935; *s* of Dr Leslie James Moger Coleby and Laurie Coleby (née Shuttleworth); *m* 1966, Rosemary Melian Elisabeth, *d* of Sir Peter Garran, KCMG; one *s* two *d*. *Educ:* Winchester; Corpus Christi, Cambridge (BAEcon, MA). Bank of England: joined, 1961; Personal Asst to Man. Dir, IMF, 1964–67; Assistant Chief, Overseas Dept, 1969; Adviser, Overseas Dept, 1972; Dep. Chief Cashier, 1973; Asst Dir, 1980–86; Chief Monetary Advr to the Governor, 1986–90; Exec. Dir, 1990–94. Non-executive Director: Halifax Building Soc., subseq. Halifax plc, 1994–2001; Anglo Irish Bank Corp., 1994–2001; Italian Internat. Bank, 1994–99. *Recreations:* choral singing, railways and transport. *Address:* 1 Maynard House, Moat Park, Great Easton, Essex CM6 2DL.

COLEGATE, Isabel Diana, (Mrs Michael Briggs); writer; *b* 10 Sept. 1931; *d* of Sir Arthur Colegate, sometime MP, and Winifred Mary, *d* of Sir William Worsley, 3rd Bt; *m* 1953, Michael Briggs; two *s* one *d*. *Educ:* Runton Hill Sch., Norfolk. Worked as literary agent at Anthony Blond (London) Ltd, 1952–57. FRSL 1981. Hon. MA Bath, 1988. *Publications:* The Blackmailer, 1958; A Man of Power, 1960; The Great Occasion, 1962 (re-issued as Three Novels, 1983); Statues in a Garden, 1964; Orlando King, 1968; Orlando at the Brazen Threshold, 1971; Agatha, 1973 (re-issued as The Orlando Trilogy, 1984); News from the City of the Sun, 1979; The Shooting Party, 1980 (W. H. Smith Literary Award, 1980; filmed, 1985); A Glimpse of Sion's Glory, 1985; Deceits of Time, 1988; The Summer of the Royal Visit, 1991; Winter Journey, 1995; A Pelican in the Wilderness: hermits, solitaries and recluses, 2002. *Recreation:* walking the dog. *Address:* Rashwood Cottage, Mells, Frome, Somerset BA11 3PX.

COLELLA, Anton; Chief Executive, Moore Stephens International, since 2018; Hon. Professor of Education, University of Glasgow, since 2012; *b* 25 May 1961; *s* of Dominic Colella and Anna Colella (née Bruno); *m* 1988, Angela Cooney; two *s* two *d*. *Educ:* St Mungo's Acad., Glasgow; Stirling Univ. (BA Hons 1983; DipEd). Teacher of RE, Holyrood Secondary Sch., Glasgow, 1983–87; Principal Teacher of RE, St Columba's High Sch., Gourock, 1987–92; Principal Teacher of RE, 1992–96, Asst Hd Teacher, 1996–99, Holyrood Secondary Sch.; Depute Hd Teacher, St Margaret Mary's Secondary Sch., Glasgow, 1999–2001, seconded to SQA, 2001; Dir of Qualifications, 2002–03, Chief Exec., 2003–06, SQA; Chief Exec., ICAS, 2006–18. Chairman: Scottish Council of Ind. Schs, 2010–16; Global Accounting Alliance, 2011–; Exec. Bd, Scottish Catholic Educn Service, 2015–. Mem., QAA Scotland Cttee, 2001–09; Member Board: Scottish Further Educn Unit, 2001–07; CBI Scotland, 2008– (Mem. Council, 2011–15). Member: Bd, Glasgow Coll. of Nautical Studies, 1998–2007; Bd of Trustees, Columba 1400, 2007– (Chm., Audit Cttee, 2014–); Adv. Bd, Adam Smith Business Sch., 2011–. Trustee, Scottish Internat. Educn Trust, 2013–. Hon. DBA BPP Univ., 2014. *Recreations:* family, playing guitar, Rugby, fishing, eating out. *Address:* Moore Stephens International, 150 Aldersgate Street, EC1A 4AB.

COLEMAN, Prof. Alice Mary; Professor of Geography, King's College, London, 1987–96, now Emeritus; *b* 8 June 1923; *d* of Bertie Coleman and Elizabeth Mary (née White). *Educ:* Clarendon House Sch.; Furzedown Training Coll. (Cert. of Educn); Birkbeck Coll., Univ. of London (BA Hons 1st Cl.); King's Coll., Univ. of London (MA with Mark of Distinction). FKC 1980. Geography Teacher, Northfleet Central Sch. for Girls, 1943–48; Geography Dept, King's Coll., London: Asst Lectr, 1948; Lectr, 1951; Sen. Lectr, 1963; Reader, 1965. Vis. Prof. for Distinguished Women Social Scientists, Univ. of Western Ontario, 1976; BC/Mombusho Prof. of Geog., Hokkaido Univ. of Educn at Asahikawa, 1985. Initiated and directed Second Land Utilisation Survey of Britain, 1960–; Dir, Design Improvement Controlled Experiment, 1988–94. Editor, Graphological Magazine, 1995. Gill Meml Award, RGS, 1963; The Times-Veuve Clicquot Award, 1974; Busk Award, RGS, 1987. *Publications:* The Planning Challenge of the Ottawa Area, 1969; Utopia on Trial, 1985; PACE Graphological Thesaurus, 1985; Scapes and Fringes: environmental territories of England and Wales, 2000; (English lang. ed. and designer) Graphology Across Cultures, 2003; (with Mona McNee) The Great Reading Disaster, 2007; 120 land-use maps in eleven colours at the scale of 1:25,000; over 300 academic papers. *Recreations:* reading, graphology.

COLEMAN, Brian John; local government and planning consultant; occasional broadcaster; Member (C) Barnet London Borough Council, 1998–2014; *b* 25 June 1961; *s* of John Francis Coleman and Gladys Coleman (née Cramp). *Educ:* Queen Elizabeth Boys' Sch., Barnet. Mills Allen Ltd, advertising co., 1989–99. Mem., Barnet CHC, 1991–94. Barnet London Borough Council: Cabinet Mem. for Envmt, 2002–04, for Community Safety and Community Engagement, 2006–08, for Envmt and Transport, 2010–12; Dep. Mayor, 2004–05; Mayor, 2009–10. London Assembly, Greater London Authority: Mem. (C) Barnet and Camden, 2000–12; contested (C) same seat, 2012; Chm., 2004–05 and 2006–07; Dep. Chm., 2005–06 and 2007–May 2008. Dep. Leader, Cons. Gp, GLA, 2002–04; Conservative Group Leader: London Fire and Emergency Planning Authy, 2000–12 (Dep. Chm., 2000–05; Vice Chm., 2005–08; Chm., 2008–12); N London Waste Authy, 2002–08 and 2010–12 (Chm., 2006–08; Vice Chm., 2012–). Chairman: Fire Services Mgt Cttee, LGA, 2009–; Local Govt Fire Service Employers, 2009–10. Asst Dist Gov., Rotary London Dist, 2016–. Hon. Pres., London Home and Water Safety Council, 2001–. Vice President: Chipping Barnet Cons. Assoc., 2002; Hendon Cons. Assoc., 2002. Vice Chm., Finchley Council of Christians and Jews, 2015–18; Mem., Exec. Cttee, London Mayors' Assoc., 2016–. Governor: Christchurch Secondary Sch., 1993–2005 (Chm., 1999–2000); Ravenscroft Sch., 1996–2011; Queen Elizabeth's Boys' Sch., 2005–10. Vice Pres., Friern Barnet Summer Show (Chm., 1995–99); Trustee: Finchley Charities, 2000–; Eleanor Palmer Trust, 2012–14. President: Hendon and Edgware Dist Scouts, 2004–08; Bor. of Barnet Dist Scouts, 2008–11. FRSA 2004. Freeman: City of London, 2003; Farriers' Co., 2008. Paul Harris Fellow, Rotary Internat., 2006. Hon. Dr Middlesex, 2008. *Recreations:* opera, theatre. *Club:* Barnet Rotary (Pres., 2014–15, 2017–18).

**COLEMAN, Christopher Lewis;** Global Partner (formerly Managing Director), and Group Head of Banking, Rothschild, since 2015; *b* London, 25 June 1968; *s* of John and Anne Marie Coleman; *m* 1997, Vivienne Lundgren; two *s*. *Educ:* Westminster Sch.; London Sch. of Econs and Pol Sci. (BSc Econ.). With Rothschild, 1989–: Financial Services, Banking, 1990–93; Treasury Credit, 1993–94; Acquisition Finance, Banking, 1994–99; Hd, Natural Resources, Banking, 1999–2004; Chief Operating Officer, Banking, 2002–08; Co-Head of Banking, 2008–13; Hd of Banking, 2013–15. Non-executive Director: Merchant Bank of Central Africa, 2001–08; Randgold Resources, 2008–14 (non-exec. Chm., 2014–18); Papa John's Internat., Inc., 2012–; Barrick Gold Corp., 2019–. *Address:* Rothschild, New Court, St Swithin's Lane, EC4N 8AL. *T:* (020) 7280 5000. *E:* christopher.coleman@rothschild.com, christopher.coleman@randgold.com.

**COLEMAN, David Frederick,** QPM 2004; DL; Chief Constable, Derbyshire Constabulary, 2001–07; *b* 4 Oct. 1952; *s* of Frederick and Margaret Elizabeth Coleman; *m* 1974, Hilary Grace Taylor; two *s*. *Educ:* Univ. of Manchester (BA Hons Geog.). Joined Derbyshire Constabulary, 1975; Divl Comdr, Derby, 1994–95; Asst Chief Constable, Leics Constabulary, 1996–2000. Pres., Peak Dist Mt Rescue Orgn, 2007–. DL Derbys, 2007, High Sheriff Derbys, 2014–15. DUniv Derby, 2016. *Recreations:* golf, reading, watching football, gardening, sailing, hill walking.

**COLEMAN, Iain;** *b* 18 Jan. 1958; *m* 1996, Sally Powell (see Dame S. A. V. Powell); one *s*. *Educ:* Tonbridge Sch. Former Local Govt Officer. Mem. (Lab), Hammersmith and Fulham BC, 1986–97 and 2010–14 (Leader, 1991–96; Mayor, 1996–97). MP (Lab) Hammersmith and Fulham, 1997–2005.

**COLEMAN, Isobel Mary;** *see* Plumstead, I. M.

**COLEMAN, Jeremy Barrington;** a District Judge (Magistrates' Courts) (formerly Metropolitan Stipendiary Magistrate), 1995–2016; *b* 9 June 1951; *s* of late Neville Coleman and Pauline Coleman; *m* 1975, Margot; one *s* one *d*. *Educ:* Coll. of Law, London. Admitted solicitor, 1975; Partner in family firm, Samuel Coleman, 1975–95. Mem., Law Soc. Children's Panel, 1990. Mem., RPS (LRPS 1982). *Publications:* (contributing ed.) Archbold Magistrates' Court Criminal Practice, 2004. *Recreations:* photography, cricket, archaeology. *Club:* Middlesex CC.

**COLEMAN, Hon. Dr Jonathan David;** Chief Executive Officer, Acurity Health Group Ltd, since 2018; *b* Auckland, 23 Sept. 1966; *s* of Ronald Douglas Coleman and Patricia Kathleen Ruby Coleman; *m* 2006, Sandra Jane Keaney; one *s* one *d*. *Educ:* Auckland Grammar Sch.; Auckland Univ. (BHB; MB ChB 1991; DObst 1993); London Business Sch. (MBA 2000). Jun. hosp. doctor, various posts in NZ and UK, 1991–94; GP Registrar, Oxford Vocational Trng Scheme, Oxford, 1995–96; Royal Flying Doctors Service, Broken Hill, NSW, 1996; Gen. Med. Practitioner, Islington, 1997–99; Mgt Consultant, Booz Allen and Hamilton, London, 2000–01; Med. Practitioner, Auckland, 2002–05; Mgt Consultant, PricewaterhouseCoopers, Auckland, 2003–05. MP (Nat.) Northcote, NZ, 2005–18. Minister of Immigration, Minister of Broadcasting, Associate Minister of Health and Associate Minister of Tourism, 2008–11; Minister of Defence, Minister of State Services and Associate Minister of Finance, 2011–14; Minister of Health and Minister for Sport and Recreation, 2014–17. *Recreations:* travel, reading, tennis, fitness, Rugby, cricket, cycling.
*See also* R. J. L. Coleman.

**COLEMAN, Katharine,** MBE 2009; freelance glass artist and engraver; *b* 30 Jan. 1949; *d* of Hector Colin Beardmore Mackenzie and Frances Mackenzie; *m* 1974, David Edward Coleman; one *s* one *d*. *Educ:* Roedean Sch.; Girton Coll., Cambridge (BA Geog 1970; MA 1974). Regd Artist/Maker, Crafts Council. Solo exhibitions: Scottish Gall., Edinburgh, 2008, 2011; Galerie Porée, Paris, 2009, 2012. Work in public collections: V&A Mus.; Corning Mus. of Glass, USA; Cheltenham Art Gall. and Mus.; Nat. Mus of Scotland, Edinburgh; Shipley Art Gall., Gateshead; Birmingham City; Lybster, Caithness; Kamenicky Senov, Czech Republic; Broadfield House Glass Mus.; Kunstsammlungen Veste Coburg, Germany; Alexander Tutsek Collection, Munich; MUDAC, Lausanne; Nat. Mus. of NI; Norwich Castle Mus.; Glasmuseum Frauenau (Bavarian State Mus. of Glass), Germany. Chm., Guild of Glass Engravers, 2002–05; FGE (FGGE 1992). Member: Contemp. Applied Arts, 2004; Art Workers Guild, 2004. Freeman, City of London, 2015; Hon. Liveryman, Glass Sellers' Co., 2015. Adrian Sassoon Prize for Arts of the Kiln, 2004; Hon. Mention Prize, Coburg Glass Prize, 2006; (first) Glass Sellers' Prize for Engraving on Glass, 2007; Pearsons Prize for Best Use of Engraving on Glass, 2008; People's Prize, British Glass Biennale, 2015. *Recreations:* other people's gardens, opera, antique glass, films. *Address:* 261 Cromwell Tower, Barbican, EC2Y 8DD. *T:* (020) 7628 6552. *E:* katharine@katharinecoleman.co.uk. *W:* www.katharinecoleman.co.uk.

**COLEMAN, Lucy Madeline;** *see* Stone, L. M.

**COLEMAN, Martin Andrew;** Partner, 1991–2017, and Global Head, Antitrust, Regulation and Competition, 1997–2017, Norton Rose Fulbright LLP (formerly Norton Rose Group); *b* London, 19 Nov. 1952; *s* of Joseph Coleman and Betty Coleman; *m* 1991, Ishbel; one *s* two *d*. *Educ:* Preston Manor High Sch., Wembley; Worcester Coll., Oxford (BA, BCL). Lectr in Law, Brunel Univ., 1979–89; Associate, Norton Rose, 1989–91. Member, Board: Solicitors Regulatory Authy, 2010–15; HEFCE, 2017–18; Dep. Chair, Office for Students, 2017–. Mem., ESRC, 2010–16. Non-exec. Dir, CMA, 2017– (Inquiry and Panel Chair, 2018–). Mem. Council, Kent Univ., 2015–. Trustee, Police Now, 2016–. Fellow, Hughes Hall, Cambridge, 2018–. *Publications:* (with Michael Grenfell) The Competition Act 1998: law and practice, 1999. *Recreations:* reading, travel, cinema. *E:* martina.coleman@btinternet.com.

**COLEMAN, His Honour Nicholas John;** a Circuit Judge, 1998–2015; *b* 12 Aug. 1947; *s* of late Leslie Ernest Coleman and Joyce Coleman; *m* 1971, Isobel Mary Plumstead, *qv*; one *s* two *d*. *Educ:* Royal Pinner Sch.; Liverpool Univ. (LLB Hons). Called to the Bar, Inner Temple, 1970, Bencher, 2004; practised SE Circuit, 1972–98; a Recorder, 1989–98; Resident Judge, Peterborough Combined Court, 2001–09. Lectr, 1970–72, Examr, 1972–76, Inns of Court Sch. of Law. Judicial Member: Parole Bd, 2004–14, 2017–; Restricted Patients Panel, 2007–. *Recreations:* sport, travel, theatre, cinema. *Clubs:* MCC; Hampstead and Westminster Hockey; Hunstanton Golf; Royal West Norfolk Golf.

**COLEMAN, Peter Anthony;** Secretary General, European Parliamentary Labour Party, 1997–2004; *b* 10 Oct. 1945; *s* of late William and Maggie Coleman; *m* 1966, Dorothy Edith Lawrence; two *d*. *Educ:* Avenue Primary Sch., Wellingborough; Park Road Junior Sch., Kettering; Kettering Sch. for Boys; Kettering Boot and Shoe Tech. Coll. (ABBSI). Progress chaser: Holyoake Footwear, 1961–64; Wilson & Watsons, 1964–66; Labour Party: organiser: Peterborough, 1967–71; Nottingham, 1972–76; SE Derbys, 1976–78; Asst Regl Organiser, E Midland, 1978–83, Regl Dir, 1983–93; Nat. Dir of Orgn and Develt, 1993–97. Nat. Vice-Pres., Nat. Union of Labour Organisers, 1977–78; Nat. Chair, Computing for Labour, 2003–06. Member: Exec. Cttee, Fabian Soc., 1994–95; Mgt Cttee, H. S. Chapman Soc., 2000–04. Trustee, 2009–, Nat. Vice Chair, 2012–, Labour Party Superannuation Soc. Chm., Friends of Shanklin Th., 2011–16; Dir, Shanklin Th., 2016–. *Publications:* (ed) Labour's Fundraising Guide, 1984; pamphlets on electoral law, Labour Party regeneration and polling-day systems. *Recreations:* theatre, travel, watching cricket and football. *Address:* 27 Orchard Road, Shanklin, Isle of Wight PO37 7NX. *Clubs:* Hampshire CC; Newclose CC.

**COLEMAN, Richard James Lee;** QC 2012; *b* Auckland, NZ, 1968; *s* of Ronald Douglas Coleman and Patricia Kathleen Ruby Lee; *m* 2007, Rachel Jane Avery; two *s* one *d*. *Educ:* Auckland Grammar Sch.; Corpus Christi Coll., Cambridge (MA); Yale Univ. (LLM 1991). Called to the Bar: Lincoln's Inn, 1994; NY, 1995; in practice as a barrister specialising in commercial law. *Publications:* (contrib.) Law of Bank Payments, 1996, 5th edn 2017. *Recreations:* spending time with family and friends, reading, following the All Blacks. *Address:* Fountain Court Chambers, Temple, EC4Y 9DH. *T:* (020) 7583 3335, *Fax:* (020) 7353 0329. *E:* rjc@fountaincourt.co.uk.
*See also* Hon. J. D. Coleman.

**COLEMAN, Sir Robert (John),** KCMG 2005; Visiting Professor, University of Plymouth, 2006–16; *b* 8 Sept. 1943; *s* of Frederick and Kathleen Coleman; *m* 1966, Malinda Tigay Cutler; two *d*. *Educ:* Univ. of Oxford (MA); Univ. of Chicago (JD). Called to the Bar, Inner Temple, 1969. Lectr in Law, Univ. of Birmingham, 1967–70; Barrister at Law, 1970–73; European Commission: Administrator, subseq. Principal Administrator, 1974–82; Dep. Head of Div., safeguard measures and removal of non-tariff barriers, 1983; Head of Div., Intellectual Property and Unfair Competition, 1984–87; Dir, Public Procurement, 1987–90; Dir, Approximation of Laws, Freedom of Estabt, and Freedom to Provide Services, 1990–91; Director General: Transport, 1991–99; Health and Consumer Protection, 1999–2003. EU Liaison Officer, Baltic and Internat. Maritime Council, 2005–13; Mem., Admin. Bd, Eur. Maritime Safety Agency, 2007–12. Sen. Practitioner Fellow, 2003–04, Sen. Res. Fellow, 2004–06, Inst. of Governance, QUB. Visiting Professor: Univ. of East London, 1997–2003; World Maritime Univ., Malmo, 2006–12; Maritime Law Inst., Malta, 2006–12. Mem. Adv. Bd, Sch. of Mgt, Univ. of Bath, 2001–03. *Publications:* contribs and articles on legal and policy issues, concerning corporate accounting, employee participation, intellectual property and transport. *Recreations:* cycling, music. *Address:* Flete House, Apt 3, Ivybridge, Devon PL21 9NX.

**COLEMAN, Roger,** FRCA; Co-Director, Helen Hamlyn Centre for Design (formerly Research Centre), 1999–2008, and Professor of Inclusive Design, 2002–08, now Emeritus, Royal College of Art; *b* 20 March 1943; *s* of Ronald Charles Coleman and Margaret Grace Coleman (née Thomas); *m* 1st, 1965, Alison Fell (marr. diss. 1967); one *s*; 2nd, 1995, Sally Reilly. *Educ:* Ealing Grammar Sch. for Boys; Edinburgh Sch. of Art and Edinburgh Univ. (Andrew Grant Schol.; MA Hons Fine Art). Lectr, Leeds Sch. of Art and Design, and Vis. Lectr, Bradford Sch. of Art and Design, 1967–70; Sen. Lectr, St Martin's Sch. of Art and Design, 1970–72; Partner, Community Press, London, 1972–73; freelance designer and maker, 1973–84; Director: Community, Construction and Design Ltd, 1984–91; London Innovation Ltd, 1985–2003; Dir, DesignAge prog., RCA, 1991–98. Co-ordinator, Eur. Design for Ageing Network, 1994–98. Jury Chm., RSA Student Design Awards, 1992–2008. Founder and Mem. Council, Welfare State Internat. (perf. community arts gp), 1968–2008. Exhibitions: One Rock, Lanternhouse, Ulverston, 2003; Flat Earth, 2006, A Short Walk on the Lark, 2008, New Departures, 2012, Between Countries, 2014, Old Fire Engine House, Ely; Flat Earth 2007, EXHIBIT, London, 2007; Vendanges des Images, Sancerre, France, 2010; travelling exhibn, A Husk of Hares, Wisbech, March and Ely, 2013. FRCA 1996; FRSA 2000. Hon. Dr Catholic Univ. Leuven, 2012. Sir Misha Black Award for Innovation in Design Educn, 2001. *Publications:* The Art of Work: an epitaph to skill, 1988, rev. Japanese edn 1998; Designing for our Future Selves, 1993; Design Research for our Future Selves, 1994; Working Together: a new approach to design, 1997; (jtly, also ed) Design für die Zukunft, 1997; Living Longer: the new context for design, 2001; (jtly) Inclusive Design: design for the whole population, 2003; (jtly) Design for Patient Safety: a system-wide design-led approach to tackling patient safety in the NHS, 2003; (jtly) Design for Patient Safety: future ambulances, 2007; (jtly) Design for Inclusivity, 2007. *Recreation:* fen watching and imaginary punt-gunning - waiting for the seas to rise. *Address:* c/o Helen Hamlyn Centre for Design, Royal College of Art, Kensington Gore, SW7 2EU. *E:* roger.coleman@hon.rca.ac.uk. *W:* www.rogercolemanphotography.com.

**COLEMAN, Terry, (Terence Francis Frank);** reporter and author; *b* 13 Feb. 1931; *s* of Jack and D. I. B. Coleman; *m* 1st, 1954, Lesley Fox-Strangeways Vane (marr. diss.); two *d*; 2nd, 1981, Vivien Rosemary Lumsdaine Wallace (MBE 2019); one *s* one *d*. *Educ:* 14 schs incl. Poole Grammar Sch. LLB London. Formerly: Reporter, Poole Herald; Editor, Savoir Faire; Sub-editor, Sunday Mercury, and Birmingham Post; Reporter and then Arts Corresp., The Guardian, 1961–70. Chief Feature Writer, 1970–74; Special Writer with Daily Mail, 1974–76; The Guardian: Chief Feature Writer, 1976–79, writing mainly political interviews, incl. last eight British Prime Ministers; NY Correspondent, 1981; special corresp., 1982–89; Associate Editor, The Independent, 1989–91. FRSA. Feature Writer of the Year, British Press Awards, 1982; Journalist of the Year, Granada Awards, 1987. *Publications:* The Railway Navvies, 1965 (Yorkshire Post prize for best first book of year), rev. edn 2015; A Girl for the Afternoons, 1965; (with Lois Deacon) Providence and Mr Hardy, 1966; The Only True History: collected journalism, 1969; Passage to America, 1972, rev. edn 2000; (ed) An Indiscretion in the Life of an Heiress (Hardy's first novel), 1976; The Liners, 1976; The Scented Brawl: collected journalism, 1978; Southern Cross, 1979; Thanksgiving, 1981; Movers and Shakers: collected interviews, 1987; Thatcher's Britain, 1987; Empire, 1993; Nelson: the man and the legend, 2001, US edn as The Nelson Touch, 2002; Olivier: the authorised biography, 2005; The Old Vic: the history of a great theatre, 2014. *Recreations:* cricket, opera, circumnavigation. *Address:* c/o Peters, Fraser & Dunlop, 55 New Oxford Street, WC1A 1BS. *T:* (020) 7344 1000. *E:* colemanterry@hotmail.co.uk. *Club:* MCC.

**COLEMAN, Victor Paul;** freelance travel and features writer, 2007–14; Deputy Director, Corporate Science and Analytical Services, Health and Safety Executive, 2006–07; *b* 28 Feb. 1952; *s* of Richard William Coleman and Edna Grace Coleman; *m* 1978, Eleanor Jane Kirkwood. *Educ:* Greenford Co. Grammar Sch.; King's Coll., Cambridge (MA); Univ. of Aston in Birmingham (Dip. Occupational Safety and Health). HM Inspector of Factories, 1973–83; Health and Safety Executive: Principal Inspector of Factories, 1983–92; Hd, Railway Safety Policy, 1992–94; Dep. Chief Inspector of Railways, 1995–98; Chief Inspector of Railways, 1998–2002; Hd of Policy for Hazardous Industries, 2002–03; Hd of Finance and Planning, 2003–06. Chm., Railways Industry Adv. Cttee, HSC, 1998–2001; Mem., Channel Tunnel Safety Authy, 1995–98. *Recreations:* theatre, walking, writing.

**COLENSO-JONES, Maj. (Gilmore) Mervyn (Boyce);** one of HM Body Guard, Honourable Corps of Gentlemen-at-Arms, 1982–2000 (Harbinger, 1997–2000); *b* 4 Sept. 1930; *s* of late Dr Gilmore Leonard Colenso Colenso-Jones and Kathleen Edwina Colenso-Jones (née Macartney); *m* 1968, Rosamond Anne Bowen. *Educ:* Rugby Sch. Commnd Royal Welch Fusiliers, 1950: served at home and abroad; jssc, Latimer, 1968–69; Brit. Exchange Officer, US Continental Army Comd, Va, 1969–70; retd 1972, in rank of Maj., Regtl Sec., RWF, 1972–81. Mem., S Glamorgan HA, 1981–84. CStJ 1981 (Priory Sec. for Wales, 1981–84). *Recreations:* country pursuits, oil and water-colour painting. *Address:* 18 Bearwater, Hungerford, Berks RG17 0NN. *T:* (01488) 683250.

**COLERAINE**, 2nd Baron *cr* 1954, of Haltemprice; **James Martin Bonar Law;** *b* 8 Aug. 1931; *s* of 1st Baron Coleraine, PC, *y s* of Rt Hon. Andrew Bonar Law, and Mary Virginia (*d* 1978), *d* of A. F. Nellis, Rochester, NY; *S* father, 1980; *m* 1st, 1958, Emma Elizabeth Richards (marr. diss.); two *d*; 2nd, 1966, Anne Patricia, (Tomt) (*d* 1993), *yr d* of Major-Gen. R. H. Farrant, CB; one *s* one *d* (and one *d* decd); 3rd, 1998, Marion Robina, (Bobbie), *d* of Sir Thomas Ferens, CBE and *widow* of Peter Smyth. *Educ:* Eton; Trinity College, Oxford. Formerly in practice as a solicitor. Hon. Consultant, Fedn of Private Residents' Assocs, 1994–. *Heir: s* Hon. James Peter Bonar Law, *b* 23 Feb. 1975. *Address:* The Dower House, Sunderlandwick, Driffield, E Yorks YO25 9AD. *T:* (01377) 253535. *E:* jamescoleraine123@btinternet.com.
*See also Baron Ironside, J. R. O'Grady.*

**COLERIDGE**, family name of **Baron Coleridge**.

**COLERIDGE**, 5th Baron *cr* 1873, of Ottery St Mary; **William Duke Coleridge;** *b* 18 June 1937; *s* of 4th Baron Coleridge, KBE, and Cecilia Rosamund (*d* 1991), *d* of Adm. Sir William Wordsworth Fisher, GCB, GCVO; *S* father, 1984; *m* 1st, 1962, Everild Tania (marr. diss. 1977), *d* of Lt-Col Beauchamp Hambrough, OBE; one *s* two *d*; 2nd, 1977, Pamela (*d* 2018), *d* of late G. W. Baker, CBE, VRD; two *d*. *Educ:* Eton; RMA Sandhurst. Commissioned into Coldstream Guards, 1958; served King's African Rifles, 1962–64; commanded Guards Independent Parachute Company, 1970–72. Director: Abercrombie & Kent, 1978–90; Larchpark Properties Ltd, 1987–92; Chairman: Universal Energy Ltd, 1984–90; European Leisure Estates plc, 1988–90; Advr, Nat. Marine Aquarium, 1990–. Gov., Royal West of England Residential Sch. for the Deaf, 1984–. *Heir: s* Hon. James Duke Coleridge, *b* 5 June 1967. *Address:* The Manor House, Ottery St Mary, Devon EX11 1DR. *T:* (01404) 812564.

**COLERIDGE, David Ean;** Chairman of Lloyd's, 1991, 1992 (Deputy Chairman, 1985, 1988, 1989); *b* 7 June 1932; *s* of Guy Cecil Richard Coleridge, MC and Katherine Cicely Stewart Smith; *m* 1955, Susan Senior; three *s*. *Educ:* Eton. Glanvill Enthoven, 1950–57; R. W. Sturge & Co., 1957–95: Dir, 1966–95; Chm., A. L. Sturge (Holdings) Ltd (now Sturge Holdings PLC), 1978–95. Chm., Oxford Agency Hldgs Ltd, 1987–90; Director: R. A. Edwards (Holdings) Ltd, 1985–90; Wise Speke Hldgs Ltd, 1987–94; Ockham Hldgs, subseq. Highway Insurance, 1995–2006 (Chm., 1995). Mem., Council and Cttee of Lloyd's, 1983–92. *Recreations:* golf, racing, gardening, family. *Address:* 37 Egerton Terrace, SW3 2BU. *T:* (020) 7581 1756.
*See also N. D. Coleridge.*

**COLERIDGE, Geraldine Margaret, (Gill), (Mrs D. R. Leeming);** Chairman, Rogers Coleridge and White, Literary Agency, since 2014 (Director, since 1988); *b* 26 May 1948; *d* of Antony Duke Coleridge and June Marian Caswell; *m* 1974, David Roger Leeming; two *s*. *Educ:* Queen Anne's School, Caversham; Marlborough Secretarial College, Oxford. BPC Partworks, Sidgwick & Jackson, Bedford Square Book Bang, to 1971; Publicity Manager, Chatto & Windus, 1971–72; Dir and Literary Agent, Anthony Sheil Associates, 1973–88. Pres., Assoc. of Authors' Agents, 1988–91. Dir, Deborah Rogers Foundn, 2015–. Mem. Cttee, Royal Literary Fund, 2008–15. *Recreations:* music, reading, gardening. *Address:* The Warrens, Hartest, Bury St Edmunds, Suffolk IP29 4EB.

**COLERIDGE, Most Rev. Mark Benedict;** *see* Brisbane, Archbishop of, (RC).

**COLERIDGE, Nicholas David,** CBE 2009; Chairman, Condé Nast Britain, since 2017; President, Condé Nast International Ltd, 2012–17 (Vice-President, 1999–2011); Managing Director: Condé Nast Publications, 1992–2017 (Editorial Director, 1989–91); Condé Nast Digital (formerly CondéNet) Ltd, 1999–2017; Director: Les Publications Condé Nast, 1994–2017; Condé Nast Zao, 2012–17; Chairman, Condé Nast India, since 2017 (Director, 2006–17); *b* 4 March 1957; *s* of David Ean Coleridge, *qv*; *m* 1989, Georgia Metcalfe; three *s* one *d*. *Educ:* Eton; Trinity Coll., Cambridge. Associate Editor, Tatler, 1979–81; Columnist, Evening Standard, 1981–84; Features Editor, Harpers and Queen, 1985–86, Editor, 1986–89. Chm., Periodical Publishers Assoc., 2004–06; Dir, Press Bd of Finance, 2006–. Chairman: British Fashion Council, 2000–03; Fashion Rocks for the Prince's Trust, RAH, 2003; Director: Prince's Trust Trading Bd, 2004–07; Adv. Bd, Concert for Diana, Wembley Stadium, 2007; Ambassador: Creative Industries, c&binet, DCMS, 2008–10; Landmark Trust, 2014–; Chairman: Campaign for Wool, 2013– (Vice Chm., 2009–13); Gilbert Trust for the Arts, 2015–. Council Mem., RCA, 1995–2000; Trustee, V&A Mus., 2013– (Chm., 2015–). Patron, Elephant Family, 2013–. Young Journalist of the Year, British Press Awards, 1983; Mark Boxer Award, BSME, 2001; Marcus Morris Award, 2013, Hall of Fame, 2017, PPA. *Publications:* Tunnel Vision, collected journalism, 1982; Around the World in 78 Days, 1984; Shooting Stars, 1984; The Fashion Conspiracy, 1988; How I Met My Wife and other stories, 1991; Paper Tigers, 1993; With Friends Like These, 1997; Streetsmart, 1999; Godchildren, 2002; A Much Married Man, 2006; Deadly Sins, 2009; The Adventuress, 2012; The Glossy Years: magazines, museums and selective memoirs, 2019. *Address:* Wolverton Hall, Pershore, Worcs WR10 2AU; 29 Royal Avenue, SW3 4QE. *T:* (020) 7730 5998.

**COLERIDGE, Hon. Sir Paul (James Duke),** Kt 2000; a Judge of the High Court, Family Division, 2000–14; Founder and Chairman, Marriage Foundation, since 2012; *b* 30 May 1949; *s* of late James Bernard and Jane Evelina Coleridge; *m* 1973, Judith Elizabeth Rossiter; two *s* one *d*. *Educ:* Cranleigh Sch., Surrey; College of Law, London. Called to the Bar, Middle Temple, 1970, Bencher, 2000; in practice at the Bar, 1970–85; Internat. Legal Advr to Baron Hans Heinrich Thyssen-Bornemisza, Switzerland, 1985–89; private practice, 1989–2000; QC 1993; a Recorder, 1996–2000; Family Div. Liaison Judge, Western Circuit, 2002–11. *Recreations:* Dorset, gardening, motor-bikes. *Address:* Marriage Foundation, PO Box 1230, Cambridge CB1 0XD. *E:* p.coleridge@marriagefoundation.org.uk. *Club:* MCC.

**COLES, Adrian Michael,** OBE 2011; Director-General, Building Societies Association, 1993–2013; *b* 19 April 1954; *s* of Kenneth Ernest Coles and Constance Mary (*née* Sykes); *m* 1981, Marion Alma Hoare; one *s* one *d*. *Educ:* Holly Lodge Grammar Sch., Smethwick; Univ. of Nottingham (BA Hons); Univ. of Sheffield (MA). Economist, Electricity Council, 1976–79; Building Societies Association: Economist, 1979–81; Head: Econs and Stats, 1981–86; External Relns, 1986–93; Dir-Gen., Council of Mortgage Lenders, 1993–96. Chm., Thames Valley Housing Assoc., 1990–93; Director: Housing Securities Ltd, 1994–; Banking Code Standards Bd Ltd, 1999–2009; Parsons Mead Educnl Trust Ltd, 2000–07; Communicate Mutuality Ltd, 2001–13; Independent Housing Ombudsman, 2001–04; Lending Standards Bd Ltd, 2009–13; Reclaim Fund Ltd, 2011–; Progressive Bldg Soc., 2014–; BSA Pension Trustees Ltd, 2014–. Chm., Consumer Adv. Bd, Fairer Finance, 2015–. Sec. Gen., Internat. Union for Housing Finance, 2001–09; Chm., Commn on Co-operative and Mutual Housing, 2007–09. Member: Financial Services Commn, Gibraltar, 2014–; Adv. Bd, Corporate Governance Res. Gp, Cardiff Business Sch., 2016–. Trustee: Money Advice Trust, 1994–2004; Funding Network, 2017–; Soc. of Friends, Imperial War Mus., 2017–18. *Publications:* (with Mark Boleat) The Mortgage Market, 1987; numerous articles in housing and housing finance jls. *Recreations:* long distance walking, reading, family, National Trust volunteer, Tottenham Hotspur FC season ticket holder. *Club:* Surrey County Cricket.

**COLES, Rev. Prof. Alasdair John,** PhD; FRCP; Professor of Neuroimmunology, University of Cambridge, since 2014; *b* London, 18 Nov. 1966; *s* of Sir (Arthur) John Coles, *qv*; *m* 1991, Olivia Mary Collingwood; one *s* one *d*. *Educ:* Walhampton Sch.; Westminster Sch.; Pembroke Coll., Oxford (BA 1987); Green Coll., Oxford (BM BCh 1990); Corpus Christi Coll., Cambridge (PhD 1997). MRCP 1993, FRCP 2008. House roles, Gloucestershire Royal Hosp. and John Radcliffe Hosp., Oxford, 1991; SHO rotation, Queen's Med. Centre, Nottingham, 1992–93; SHO, Nat. Hosp. for Neurol. and Neurosurgery, 1993; MO, Vom Hosp., Nigeria, 1993–94; East Anglian Neurology rotation, 1994–2004, Consultant Neurologist, 2004–, Addenbrooke's Hospital; Lectr in Clin. Neuroimmunology, Univ. of Cambridge, 2004–14. Ordained deacon, 2008, priest, 2009. *Recreations:* bread baking, fixie construction. *Address:* Department of Neurology, Box 165, Addenbrooke's Hospital, Hill's Road, Cambridge CB2 2QQ.

**COLES, Alec,** OBE 2010; Chief Executive Officer, Western Australian Museum, since 2010; Adjunct Associate Professor, School of Social Sciences, University of Western Australia, since 2014; *b* Wolverhampton, 3 Jan. 1959; *s* of William John and Kathleen Audrey Coles. *Educ:* Univ. of Leicester (BSc Hons Biol Scis); Univ. of Newcastle upon Tyne (Post Grad. Cert. Cultural Mgt); Univ. of E Anglia (Mus. Leadership Prog.). AMA (by Dip.) 1986. Asst Curator, 1980–86, Dep. Curator, 1986–88, Woodspring Mus.; Sen. Museums Officer, Tyne & Wear Museums, 1988–92; Curator, Hancock Mus., Newcastle upon Tyne, 1992–96; Sen. Curator, Tyne & Wear Museums, 1996–2000; Chief Exec., Northumberland Wildlife Trust, 2000–02; Director: Tyne & Wear Museums, 2002–09; Tyne & Wear Archives & Museums, 2009–10. Hon. Treas., Museums Assoc., 2006–. MAICD 2014. FLS 1990; FRSA 2009. Hon DLitt UWA, 2017. *Recreations:* natural history (botany), music. *Address:* Western Australian Museum, Locked Bag 49, Welshpool DC, WA 6986, Australia. *T:* (8) 65527800. *E:* reception@museum.wa.gov.au.

**COLES, Sir (Arthur) John,** GCMG 1997 (KCMG 1989; CMG 1984); HM Diplomatic Service, retired; Permanent Under-Secretary of State, Foreign and Commonwealth Office, and Head of the Diplomatic Service, 1994–97; *b* 13 Nov. 1937; *s* of Arthur Strixton Coles and Doris Gwendoline Coles; *m* 1965, Anne Mary Sutherland Graham; two *s* one *d*. *Educ:* Magdalen Coll. Sch., Brackley; Magdalen Coll., Oxford (BA 1960, MA). Served HM Forces, 1955–57. Joined HM Diplomatic Service, 1960; Middle Eastern Centre for Arabic Studies, Lebanon, 1960–62; Third Sec., Khartoum, 1962–64; FO (later FCO), 1964–68; Asst Political Agent, Trucial States (Dubai), 1968–71; FCO, 1971–75; Head of Chancery, Cairo, 1975–77; Counsellor (Developing Countries), UK Perm. Mission to EEC, 1977–80; Head of S Asian Dept, FCO, 1980–81; Private Sec. to Prime Minister, 1981–84; Ambassador to Jordan, 1984–88; High Commissioner to Australia, 1988–91; Dep. Under-Sec. of State, FCO, 1991–94. Non-exec. Dir, BG plc, 1998–2008. Chm., Sight Savers Internat., 2001–07. Trustee, Imperial War Mus., 1999–2004. Vis. Fellow, All Souls Coll., Oxford, 1998–99. Gov., Ditchley Foundn, 1997–2012; Mem. Council, Atlantic Coll., 2001–03. President, FCO Assoc., 2000–02. Gov., Sutton's Hosp. in Charterhouse, 2003–05. *Publications:* British Influence and the Euro, 1999; Making Foreign Policy: a certain idea of Britain, 2000; Blindness and The Visionary: the life and work of John Wilson, 2006. *Recreations:* walking, cricket, bird-watching, reading, music. *Address:* Kelham, Dock Lane, Beaulieu, Hants SO42 7YH.
*See also A. J. Coles.*

**COLES, Prof. Bryony Jean,** FBA 2007; FSA; Professor of Prehistoric Archaeology, University of Exeter, 1996–2008, now Emeritus; *b* 12 Aug. 1946; *d* of John Samuel Orme, CB, OBE, and Jean Esther Orme (*née* Harris); *m* 1985, John Morton Coles, *qv*. *Educ:* High Wycombe High Sch.; Univ. of Bristol (BA Hist. 1968); Inst. of Archaeology, Univ. of London (Postgrad. Dip. Archaeol. 1970); University Coll. London (MPhil Anthropol. 1972). FSA 1975. University of Exeter: Lectr, 1972–89; Sen. Lectr, 1989; Reader, 1990; British Acad. Res. Readership, 1991–94. Co-Dir (with J. M. Coles), Somerset Levels Proj., 1973–89; Dir, Wetland Archaeol. Res. Proj., 1989–. Editor, Jl of Wetland Archaeol., 2000–. Mem., Archaeol. Adv. Panel, Nat. Mus. and Galls of Wales, 1991–2003; Vice Pres., Prehistoric Soc., 1994–97; Chm., NW Wetland Survey, 1994–98. Mem., Scientific Adv. Council, Netherlands Archaeol. Res. Sch., 1997–2008. Pres., Devon Archaeol Soc., 2006–08. Baguley Award, Prehistoric Soc., 1990, 1999; George Stephenson Medal, ICE, 1995; (jtly) British Archaeol Award, 1986, 1988, 1998. *Publications:* Anthropology for Archaeologists, 1981; Beavers in Britain's Past, 2006; with J. M. Coles: Prehistory of the Somerset Levels, 1980; Sweet Track to Glastonbury: the Somerset Levels in prehistory, 1986; People of the Wetlands, 1989; Enlarging the Past: the contribution of wetland archaeology (Rhind Lects 1994–95), 1996; Avanke, Bever, Castor: the story of beavers in Wales, 2019; contribs to Wetland Archaeol. Res. Proj. occasional papers, British and Europ. conf. procs and learned jls. *Recreations:* walking, wildlife and wetlands, gardening, reading. *Address:* c/o Department of Archaeology, University of Exeter, Laver Building, North Park Road, Exeter EX4 4QE. *T:* (01392) 264350.
*See also J. D. Orme.*

**COLES, Rt Rev. Dr David John;** Bishop of Christchurch, 1990–2008; Vicar of Heathcote-Mount Pleasant, 2015–18; *b* 23 March 1943; *s* of Samuel Arthur and Evelyn Ann Coles; *m* 1st, 1970, Ceridwyn Mary Parr (marr. diss.); one *s* one *d*; 2nd, 2001, Joy Woodley. *Educ:* Auckland Grammar Sch.; Univ. of Auckland (MA Hons 1967); Univ. of Otago (BD 1969; MTh 1971); Univ. of Manchester (PhD 1974); Melbourne Coll. of Divinity (Dip. Religious Educn). Deacon 1968, priest 1969; Curate, St Mark, Remuera, Auckland, 1968–70; Asst Chaplain, Selwyn Coll., Dunedin, 1970–71; Curate, Fallowfield, 1972–73; Chaplain, Hulme Hall, Univ. of Manchester, 1973–74; Vicar of: Glenfield, 1974–76; Takapuna, 1976–80; Examining Chaplain to Bp of Auckland, 1974–80; Dean and Vicar of St John's Cathedral, Napier, Dio. of Waiapu, 1980–84; Dean of Christchurch and Vicar-General, Dio. of Christchurch, 1984–90; Locum Chaplain, Copenhagen, 2014–15; Vicar, Wakatipu, Queenstown, 2008–14. Pres., Conf. of Churches of Aotearoa-NZ, 1991. *Recreations:* music, ski-ing, tramping. *Address:* 88 Canon Street, St Albans, Christchurch 8014, New Zealand.

**COLES, Dominic Peter;** independent consultant across media, sport and technology, since 2018; *b* London, 22 Dec. 1964; *s* of Peter and Dianne Coles; *m* 1991, Karen Ash; one *s* one *d*. *Educ:* Keele Univ. (BA Hons PPE 1987); Harvard Business Sch. (AMP 2010). ACA 1991. Manager, Touche Ross & Co., 1988–92; Sen. Manager, Deloitte & Touche Corporate Finance, 1993–96; Investment Manager, Baltic Investments, 1996–97; BBC: Hd of Investment, 1997–99; Dir, Sports Rights and Finance, BBC Sport, 1999–2007; Chief Operating Officer: News and Nations, 2007–12; London 2012 Olympics, 2008–12; Dir of Ops, 2012–14; Exec. Vice Pres. of Strategy, Discovery Networks Internat., and Chief Operating Officer and Chief Financial Officer, Discovery Networks Northern Europe, 2014–17. Mem., Adv. Cttee, Sport Relief, 2008–. Olympic torchbearer, London 2012. *Recreations:* family, fitness, walks, restaurants, cars, chilli harvesting, Liverpool FC, Harlequins RFC, life and the rest….

**COLES, Prof. Harry James,** PhD, DSc; FInstP; Professor of Photonics of Molecular Materials, and Director, Centre of Molecular Materials for Photonics and Electronics, Electrical Engineering Division, University of Cambridge, 2002–13, now Professor Emeritus; Fellow of St Catharine's College, Cambridge, 2006–13; *b* 28 Aug. 1946; *s* of

William and Audrey Joan Coles; *m* 1st, 1968, Janet Phillips (marr. diss. 2008); one *s*; 2nd, 2009, Leona Marie Hope (*née* Averis). *Educ*: Tal Handaq Grammar Sch., Malta; Trowbridge Boys' High Sch.; Queen Elizabeth Coll., Univ. of London (BSc Hons); Brunel Univ. (PhD 1975); Victoria Univ. of Manchester (DSc 1985). FInstP 1985. Maître de Recherche, Univ. Louis Pasteur, Strasbourg, 1975–79; Victoria University of Manchester: Lectr, 1980–85; Sen. Lectr, 1985–87; Reader, 1988–90; Prof., 1991–95; Prof., Univ. of Southampton, and Dir, Southampton Liquid Crystal Inst., 1995–2002. Visiting Professor: Berlin, 1990; Tokyo, 1990; Directeur de Recherche, Strasbourg, 1991. George Gray Medal, British Liquid Crystal Soc., 2003. *Publications*: (jtly) Liquid Crystal Handbook, Vol. IIB, 1998; contrib. over 350 papers to learned jls; 35 internat. patents; over 450 presentations to scientific confs. *Recreations*: dog walking, gardening, reading, music. *Address*: CMMPE, Electrical Engineering Division, Department of Engineering, University of Cambridge, 9 JJ Thompson Avenue, Cambridge CB3 0FA. *E*: hjc37@cam.ac.uk.

**COLES, Sir John;** *see* Coles, Sir A. J.

**COLES, John David,** CB 2005; FREng; RCNC; Consultant, Harcourt Coles Ltd, 2006; *b* 10 May 1945; *s* of William Frederick Coles and Alice Marie Coles; *m* 1967, Judith Ann Baker (*d* 1992); two *d*. *Educ*: University Coll. London (BSc 1969; MSc 1970). FRINA 1998; FREng 2004. RCNC 1971–2005; Staff Constructor to Flag Officer Submarines, 1978–82; Head of British Admiralty Office, USA, 1982–85; Assistant Director: Future Projects, 1985–88; Dir Gen. Submarines, 1988–92; Dir of Works, Strategic Systems, 1992–94; rcds, 1994; Supt Ships, Devonport, MoD, 1995–97; Dir Gen., Equipment Support (Sea), Chief Exec., Ships, then Warship, Support Agency, and Head of RCNC, 1998–2007; Carrier Vehicle Future Integrated Project Team Leader, Defence Procurement Agency, MoD, 2005–07. Hon. DEng Bath.

**COLES, John Morton,** ScD, PhD; FBA 1978; Professor of European Prehistory, University of Cambridge, 1980–86; Fellow of Fitzwilliam College, since 1963, Hon. Fellow, 1987; *b* 25 March 1930; *s* of Edward John Langdon Coles and Alice Margaret (*née* Brown); *m* 1985, Bryony Jean Orme (*see* B. J. Coles); two *s* two *d* of previous marr. *Educ*: Woodstock, Ontario; Univ. of Toronto (BA; tennis colours 1952); Univ. of Cambridge (MA, ScD); Univ. of Edinburgh (PhD; Scottish Tennis Cup 1959). Carnegie Scholar and Research Fellow, Univ. of Edinburgh, 1959–60; Asst Lectr, 1960–65, Lectr, 1965–76, Reader, 1976–80, Univ. of Cambridge. Fellow, McDonald Inst. for Archaeological Res., Univ. of Cambridge, 1992–96; Hon. Res. Prof., Univ. of Exeter, 1993–2003. President, Prehistoric Soc., 1978–82. Member: Royal Commn on Ancient and Historical Monuments of Scotland, 1992–2002; Directorate, Discovery Prog. Ireland, 2001–06. MAE 1989; Hon. Corresp. Mem., Deutsches Archäologisches Institut, 1979; Hon. MIFA 1991; Hon. MRIA 2005. FSA 1963 (Vice-Pres., 1982–86); Hon. FSAScot 2000. Hon. FilDr Uppsala Univ., 1997. Grahame Clark Medal, British Acad., 1995; ICI Medal, British Archaeol Awards, 1998; Europa Prize for Prehistory, Prehistoric Soc., 2000; Gold Medal, Soc. of Antiquaries of London, 2002; European Archaeol Heritage Prize, 2006; Rajewski Medal, Nat. Mus., Warsaw, 2007; Gold Medal, Royal Swedish Acad. of Letters, History and Antiquities, 2009. *Publications*: The Archaeology of Early Man (with E. Higgs), 1969; Field Archaeology in Britain, 1972; Archaeology by Experiment, 1973; (with A. Harding) The Bronze Age in Europe, 1979; Experimental Archaeology, 1979; (with B. Orme) Prehistory of the Somerset Levels, 1980; The Archaeology of Wetlands, 1984; (with B. J. Coles) Sweet Track to Glastonbury: the Somerset Levels in prehistory, 1986; (ed with A. Lawson) European Wetlands in Prehistory, 1987; Meare Village East, 1987; (with B. J. Coles) People of the Wetlands, 1989; Images of the Past, 1990; From the Waters of Oblivion, 1991; (with A. Goodall and S. Minnitt) Arthur Bulleid and the Glastonbury Lake Village 1892–1992, 1992; (with D. Hall) Fenland Survey, 1994; Rock Carvings of Uppland, 1994; (with S. Minnitt) Industrious and Fairly Civilised: the Glastonbury lake village, 1995; (with B. Coles) Enlarging the Past: the contribution of wetland archaeology, 1996; (with S. Minnitt) The Lake Villages of Somerset, 1996; (with D. Hall) Changing Landscapes: the ancient Fenland, 1998; (ed jtly) World Prehistory: studies in memory of Grahame Clark, 1999; (ed jtly) Bog Bodies, Sacred Sites and Wetland Archaeology, 1999; Patterns in a Rocky Land: rock carvings in South West Uppland, Sweden, 2000; (jtly) Ceremony and Display: the South Cadbury Bronze Age shield, 2000; Shadows of a Northern Past: rock carvings of Bohuslän and Østfold, 2005; (ed jtly) Grahame Clark and his Legacy, 2010; contrib. Proc. Prehist. Soc., Antiquaries Jl, Antiquity, Somerset Levels Papers, etc. *Recreations*: music, ancient art, wetlands, woodlands. *Address*: Fursdon Mill Cottage, Cadbury, Devon EX5 5JS. *T*: (01392) 860125.

**COLES, Sir Jonathan Andrew,** Kt 2019; Chief Executive, United Learning (formerly United Church Schools Trust and United Learning Trust), since 2012; *b* 5 May 1972; *s* of Robert and Josephine Coles; *m* 1995, Rachel Brooks; one *s* two *d*. *Educ*: Judd Sch., Tonbridge; Mansfield Coll., Oxford (BA); St Catharine's Coll., Cambridge (PGCE); York Univ. (MA). Head, Class Size Unit, DfEE, 1998–99; Perf. and Innovation Unit, Cabinet Office, 1999–2000; Head, Educn Green Paper, White Paper and Bill, 2000–02, Dir, London Challenge, 2002–05, DfES; Dir, 14–9 Reform, DfES, later DCSF, 2005–08; Dir Gen., Schs, DCSF, later DFE, 2008–10; Dir Gen., Educn Standards, DFE, 2010–11. Vis. Prof., UCL Inst. of Educn, 2016–. Chm., Challenge Partners, 2012–. Trustee: Prince's Teaching Inst., 2012–; Educn Media Centre, 2013–18. FIMA 2013; FCollT (Hon. FCOT) 2014. *Address*: (office) Fairline House, Nene Valley Business Park, Oundle, Peterborough PE8 4HN. *E*: jon.coles@unitedlearning.org.uk.

**COLES, Kenneth George,** AM 2000; BE; FIEAust; CEng, FIMechE; Chairman, Conveyor Co. of Australia Pty Ltd, 1957–91; *b* Melbourne, 30 June 1926; *s* of Sir Kenneth Coles; *m* 1st, 1950, Thalia Helen Goddard (marr. diss. 1980); one *s* two *d*; 2nd, 1985, Rowena Danziger. *Educ*: The King's Sch., Parramatta, NSW; Sydney Univ. (BE 1948). FIE(Aust) 1986; FIMechE 1969; FAIM 1959. Gained engrg experience in appliance manufacturing and automotive industries Nuffield Aust. Pty Ltd, Gen. Motors Holdens Pty Ltd and Frigidaire, before commencing own business manufacturing conveyors, 1955; Chm. and Man. Dir, K. G. Coles & Co. Pty Ltd, 1955–76, Chm. 1976–95; Chm. and Man. Dir, KGC Magnetic Tape Pty Ltd, 1973–80. Director: Australian Oil & Gas Corp. Ltd, 1969–89 (Dep. Chm., 1984–89); A. O. G. Minerals Ltd, 1969–87 (Dep. Chm., 1984–87); Coles Myer Ltd (formerly G. J. Coles & Coy Ltd), 1976–94; Electrical Equipment Ltd, 1976–84; Permanent Trustee Co. Ltd, 1978–94 (Vice Chm., 1990–91; Chm., 1991–94); Chatham Investment Co. Ltd, 1987–94; NRMA Insurance Ltd, 1989–90; Stockland Trust Group, 1990–95; Chairman: Innovation Council of NSW Ltd, 1984–89 (Dir, 1982–89); Metal and Engrg (formerly Nat. Engrg) Training Bd, 1988–99. Metal Trades Industry Association: Gen. Councillor, NSW Br., 1976–94; Nat. Councillor, 1988–94; Mem. Bd, Sir William Tyree MTIA Foundn, 1995–2002. Chm., Lizard Island Reef Res. Foundn, 1994–2012 (Dir, 1992– ). Member: Internat. Solar Energy Soc., 1957–97; Science & Industry Forum, Australian Academy of Science, 1983–94; Mem. and Employers' Rep., NSW Bd of Secondary Educn, 1987–90. Mem. Council, Nat. Roads and Motorists Assoc., NSW, 1986–90. Councillor and Mem. Bd of Governors, Ascham Sch., 1972–82; Employers' Rep., NSW Secondary Schs Bd, 1979–83. Sydney University: Fellow, Senate, 1983–97; Chairman: Internat. House, 2001–03 (Mem. Council 1993–2003); Save Sight Inst., 2001–10 (Mem. Council, 1998–2010); Mem., Bd of Advice, Sydney Conservatorium of Music, 2007–11. Hon. Associate, Med. Sch., Sydney Univ., 2011– . Dir, Visionsearch Pty Ltd, 2011–15. Hon. Dr Univ. Sydney, 1999. *Publications*: Branching Out: the George Coles family tree, 2001, 2nd edn 2015. *Address*: 501/170 Ocean Street, Edgecliff, NSW 2027, Australia. *T*: (2) 93286084. *Clubs*: Union, Australian, Sydney Rotary; Royal Sydney Golf; Rose Bay Surf.

**COLES, Rev. Richard Keith Robert;** Vicar of St Mary the Virgin, Finedon, since 2011; *b* Northampton, 26 March 1962; *s* of Nigel Coles and Elizabeth Coles (*née* Davey); civil partnership 2010, David. *Educ*: Wellingborough Sch.; South Warwickshire Coll. of Further Educn; King's Coll. London (BA 1994; FKC 2017); Univ. of Leeds (MA 2005); Coll. of the Resurrection, Mirfield. Band Member: Bronski Beat, 1984–85; The Communards, 1985–88. Presenter, Night Waves, BBC Radio 3, 1994–2003. Ordained deacon, 2005, priest, 2006; Curate and Lectr, St Botolph, Boston, 2005–07; Curate, St Paul's, Knightsbridge, 2007–10, Chaplain to RAM, 2007–08. Presenter: Saturday Live, BBC Radio 4, 2010– ; The Big Painting Challenge, 2017– . Chancellor, Univ. of Northampton, 2017– . Patron, Wellingborough Homes, 2017– . Hon. PhD Northampton, 2012; Hon. DLitt Warwick, 2016. *Publications*: Lives of the Improbable Saints, 2012; Legends of the Improbable Saints, 2013; Fathomless Riches, 2014; Bringing in The Sheaves, 2016. *Recreation*: walking around looking at things. *Address*: The Vicarage, Church Hill, Finedon NN9 5NR. *Club*: Groucho.

**COLES, Sadie;** Proprietor, Sadie Coles HQ gallery, since 1997; *b* Portsmouth, 13 Feb. 1963; *m* 2004, Juergen Teller; one *s*. *Educ*: Middlesex Poly. (BA). Jun. asst to Sir John Tooley, Royal Opera Hse, 1986–87; Mktg Asst, NT, 1987–89; Asst Dir, Arnolfini Art Centre, 1989–90; Dir, Anthony D'Offay Gall., 1990–96. *Publications*: (contrib.) Some Kind of Heaven, 1997; (contrib.) Art, Money, Parties: new institutions in the political economy of contemporary art, 2005; (contrib.) Collecting Contemporary, 2006. *Address*: Sadie Coles HQ, 62 Kingly Street, W1B 5QN. *T*: (020) 7493 8611, *Fax*: (020) 7499 4878. *E*: info@sadiecoles.com.

**COLES, Sir Sherard (Louis) C.;** *see* Cowper-Coles.

**COLEY, Dr Graham Douglas;** Group Director Compliance, QinetiQ Ltd, 2006–08 (Business Continuity Director, 2001–06); *b* 16 Nov. 1946; *s* of late Douglas Leonard Coley and Phyllis Adeline Coley (*née* Hughes); *m* 1972, Susan Elizabeth Thackery. *Educ*: Halesowen Grammar Sch.; Birmingham Univ. (BSc 1st Cl. Hons); Darwin Coll., Cambridge (PhD 1971). FIET (FIEE 1994); FInstP 1998. Midlands Res. Station, Gas Council, 1967–68; Atomic Weapons Research Establishment, Aldermaston, 1968–87: Supt, Explosives Technol. Br., 1982–85; Head, Chemical Technol. Div., 1985–87; Dir, Nuclear Resources, MoD PE, 1987–90; Dep. Head, Efficiency Unit, Prime Minister's Office, 1990–92; Asst Chief Scientific Advr (Projects), MoD, 1992–94; Man. Dir, Protection and Life Scis Div., 1994–97, Man. Dir, Science, 1997–2000, Business Continuity Div, 2000–01, DERA. Trustee, Wild Trout Trust, 2003– . Non-executive Director: Upper Oykel Ltd, 2010–; Oykel Bridge Hotel Ltd, 2011– . *Publications*: papers in technical jls and internat. conf. proc. *Recreations*: flyfishing, shooting, gardening (auriculas). *Club*: Flyfishers'.

**COLFER, Eoin;** author; *b* 14 May 1965; *s* of Billy and Noreen Colfer; *m* 1991, Jacqueline Power; two *s*. *Educ*: Carysfort Coll. of Educn (BEd). Teacher: Scoil Mhuire Primary Sch., Wexford, 1986–94; Jeddah Private Acad., Saudi Arabia, 1994–95; Internat. Sch. of Martina Franca, Italy, 1995–96; Sfat Internat. Sch., Tunisia, 1996–98; Scoil Mhuire Primary Sch., 1998–2002. Irish Children's Laureate, 2014–16. *Publications*: Benny and Omar, 1998; Benny and Babe, 1999; Going Potty, 1999; The Wish List, 2000; Ed's Funny Feet, 2000; Ed's Bed, 2001; Artemis Fowl, 2001; Artemis Fowl and the Arctic Incident, 2002; Artemis Fowl and the Eternity Code, 2003; Spud Murphy, 2004; The Supernaturalist, 2004; Artemis Fowl and the Opal Deception, 2005; Half Moon Investigations, 2006 (adapted for television, 2009); Captain Crow's Teeth, 2006; Artemis Fowl and the Lost Colony, 2006; The Worst Boy in the World, 2007; Airman, 2008; Artemis Fowl and the Time Paradox, 2008; And Another Thing…: Douglas Adams's Hitchhiker's Guide to the Galaxy: Part Six of Three, 2009; Artemis Fowl and the Atlantis Complex, 2010; Plugged, 2011; The Reluctant Assassin, 2013; The Hangman's Revolution, 2014; The Forever Man, 2015; Imaginary Fred, 2015; Iron Man: the gauntlet, 2016; My Real Life (play), 2017; (jtly) Illegal, 2017; Mariella, Queen of the Skies, 2018; (ed) Once Upon a Place, 2018.

**COLFOX, Sir Philip John,** 3rd Bt *cr* 1939; businessman and campaigner; Chairman, Symondsbury Estate, since 2019 (Chief Executive, 1997–2019); *b* 27 Dec. 1962; *s* of Sir (William) John Colfox, 2nd Bt and Frederica Loveday Colfox, of Adm. Sir Victor Crutchley, VC, KCB, DSC; *S* father, 2014; *m* 1993, Julia Schomberg; one *s* three *d* (incl. twins). Building contractor, 1988–93; farmer, 1993– . With Lloyd's Market (Jardine Thompson Graham), 1982–85; Mem., Lloyd's 1985–99. Campaigned for victims of Lloyd's insurance market crisis of 1995–2000; political lobbyist, European Landowners Orgn, Brussels, 2006. Mem. (Lib Dem), Bridport Town Council, 2005–15. Treas., W Dorset Lib Dems, 2006–08. Member: Council, Western Union of Unitarian Churches, 2010– ; Exec. Cttee, Gen. Assembly of Unitarian and Free Christian Churches, 2015– . Trustee: John Colfox Trust, 1999–2005; Walbridge Trust, 2000–16; Chm., St Ronan's Sch., 1995–97; Chm. Trustees, Bridport Unitarian Chapel, 2010– . Co-founder: Red Squirrel SW Project, 2009; Bridport Gig Racing Club, 2009. FRSA. *Publications*: The Case for Environmental Medicine, 1987. *Heir*: *s* John Alfred Colfox, *b* 4 June 2000. *Address*: The Estate Office, Symondsbury, Dorset DT6 6HG.

**COLGAN, Michael Anthony,** Hon. OBE 2010; Artistic Director and Member Board, Gate Theatre, Dublin, 1983–2017; *b* Dublin, 17 July 1950; *s* of James Colgan and Josephine Colgan (*née* Geoghegan). *Educ*: Trinity Coll., Dublin (BA). Dir, Abbey Th., Dublin, 1974–78; Co-Manager, Irish Th. Co., 1977–78; Dublin Theatre Festival: Manager, 1978–80; Artistic Dir, 1981–83; Mem., Bd of Dirs, 1983–2015. Exec. Dir, Little Bird Films, 1986–; Co-Founder, Blue Angel Films Co., 1999. Artistic Dir, Parma Fest., 1982; Chm., St Patrick's Fest., 1996–99; Mem. Bd, Millennium Festivals Ltd, Laura Pels Foundn, NY, 2000–04. Mem., Irish Arts Council, 1989–94. Mem., Gov. Authy, Dublin City Univ. Theatre productions include: Faith Healer, Dublin, NY and Edinburgh; No Man's Land, Dublin and London; I'll Go On; Juno and the Paycock; Salomé; Krapp's Last Tape, Edinburgh; 19 Beckett Stage Plays; six Beckett Fests, Dublin, NY, London and Sydney; four Pinter Fests, Dublin and NY. World premières incl. The Birds, Molly Sweeney, Afterplay, Shining City, The Home Place. Director: First Love; Faith Healer; Krapp's Last Tape. Television Producer: Troubles, 1986; Two Lives, 1993; Beckett Film Project, 2000; Celebration, 2006. Member, Board of Directors: Lir Acad. of Dramatic Arts; Dublin Festival Th.; Blue Angel Films Ltd. Hon. LLD TCD. Sunday Independent Arts Award, 1985, 1987; Nat. Entertainment Award, 1996; People of the Year Award, 1999; Irish Times Theatre Lifetime Achievement Award, 2006. Chevalier, Ordre des Arts et des Lettres, 2007. *Recreations*: middle distance running, chamber music. *Clubs*: Ivy; Residence (Dublin).

**COLGAN, His Honour Samuel Hezlett;** a Circuit Judge, 1990–2010; *b* 10 June 1945; *s* of late Henry George Colgan and of Jane Swan Hezlett. *Educ*: Foyle College, Londonderry; Trinity College Dublin (MA, LLB). Called to the Bar, Middle Temple, 1969; a Recorder, SE Circuit, 1987. *Recreations*: travelling, the arts, reading, tennis.

**COLGRAIN**, 4th Baron cr 1946, of Everlands, co. Kent; **Alastair Colin Leckie Campbell**; DL; b 16 Sept. 1951; s of 3rd Baron Colgrain and of Veronica Margaret, d of late Lt-Col William Leckie Webster, RAMC; S father, 2008; m 1979, Annabel Rose, yr d of late Hon. Robin Hugh Warrender; two s. Educ: Eton; Trinity Coll., Cambridge (BA 1973). High Sheriff, Kent, 2013–14. Elected Mem., H of L, 2017. DL Kent, 2017. Heir: s Hon. Thomas Colin Donald Campbell, b 9 Feb. 1984.

**COLIN, Kimberlee**, RDI 2015; Co-founder and Partner: Industrial Facility, since 2002; Retail Facility, since 2009; Future Facility, since 2016; m 2001, Samuel Hecht, qv; two s. Educ: Univ. of Calif, Los Angeles (BA Art Hist.); Southern Calif Inst. of Architecture (MArch). Artist's Asst to Mike Kelley, 1995; Commng Editor (arch. and design), Phaidon Press, 1998–2000. Design Advr to Herman Miller, 2008–. Tutor: AA, 2001–03; RCA, 2001–05; École cantonale d'art de Lausanne, 2017, 2019. FRSA 2015. Publications: jointly: Fabrications, 2001; Extra Spatial, 2002; Things That Go Unseen, 2003; Product as Landscape, 2005; Usefulness in Small Things, 2011; Industrial Facility, 2018. Address: Industrial Facility, 20 Britton Street, EC1M 5UA. E: mail@industrialfacility.co.uk.

**COLIN-THOMÉ, David Geoffrey**, OBE 1997; FRCGP, FFPH, FRCP; General Practitioner, Castlefields, Runcorn, 1971–2007; National Director for Primary Care, 2001–10, and Medical Director for Commissioning and System Management Directorate, 2007–10, Department of Health; independent healthcare consultant, since 2010; b 5 Oct. 1943; s of William James Charles Colin-Thomé and Pearl Erin Colin-Thomé; m 1969, Christine Mary Simpson; one s one d. Educ: Hutton Grammar Sch., Preston; Newcastle upon Tyne Medical Sch. (MB BS 1966). FRCGP 1990; MHSM 1998; FFPH (FFPHM 2002); FRCP 2006. Dir Primary Care, NW Regl Office, NHS Exec., DoH, 1994–96; SMO, Scottish Office, 1997–98; Dir Primary Care, London Region, DoH, 1998–2001. Hon. Visiting Professor: Centre for Public Policy and Mgt, Manchester Univ., 2002–; Sch. of Health, Durham Univ., 2004–. Hon. FFGDP(UK) 2005; Hon. FQNI 2009. Recreations: eclectic interests in theatre, dance, books and sport; devoted grandfather to Amber, Jacob, Luca, Ryan, Beth and Zachary; supporter of Everton FC. Address: Hunter House, Bainbridge Lane, Eshott, Northumberland NE65 9FD.

**COLL, Dame Elizabeth Anne Loosemore E.**; see Esteve-Coll.

**COLLARBONE, Dame Patricia**, DBE 1998; EdD; consultant, since 2018; Director, Creating Tomorrow Ltd, 2009–17; Executive Director for Development, Training and Development Agency, 2006–07 (on secondment from Institute of Education). Educ: MBA 1995; EdD Lincolnshire and Humberside Univ. 1999. Headteacher, Haggerston Sch., Hackney, 1990–96; Founding Dir, London Leadership Centre, Inst. of Education, Univ. of London, 1997–2002; Dir of Leadership Progs, Nat. Coll. for Sch. Leadership, Nottingham, 2002–04; Dir, Nat. Remodelling Team, Nat. Coll. for Sch. Leadership, then TTA, 2003–06. Manager, London Regl Assessment Centre, 1996–98, London Regl Trng and Development Centre, 1998–99, NPQH. Advr, on rôle of the Headteacher, Govt 9th Select Cttee, 1998; Special Advr, on headship and leadership issues, DfEE, 1999–2001. Former Member: SCAA Key Stage 3 Adv. Gp; DfEE Adv. Cttee on Improving Schs; Educn Summit. Member: DfEE Sch. Improvement Team; NPQH Mgt Develt Gp, TTA. London Pres., NAHT. Fellow: Univ. of Lincolnshire and Humberside; Hull Univ., 2000. FRSA. Publications: Understanding Systems Leadership, 2008; (with John West-Burnham) Creating Tomorrow: planning, developing and sustaining change in education and other public services, 2009.

**COLLARD, Dr Ian Frank**; HM Diplomatic Service; Ambassador to Panama, 2013–17; b 13 April 1976; m Tamara Renée; four d. Educ: King Edward VI Grammar Sch., Chelmsford; King's Coll., Cambridge (BA 1st Cl. Physical and Biol Anthropol. 1997; PhD Ecol. and Evolutionary Biol. 2002). Paralegal Associate, Imperial Oil, Canada, 1997; reporter, Lloyd's List, 1998; Res. Associate, Human Diversity Project, King's Coll. Res. Centre, Univ. of Cambridge, 1998–99; entered FCO, 2002; Desk Officer, ME Dept, 2002–03; UN/Internat. Orgns Dept, 2003–04, FCO; Second Sec. (Pol), UKMIS to UN, NY, 2005–08; First Sec. (Pol), Washington, 2008–11; Hd, N America Dept, FCO, 2011–12; Silver Comd, Olympics Security, Counter-Terrorism Dept, FCO, 2012; Hd, N America Dept, FCO, 2012–13. Address: c/o Foreign and Commonwealth Office, King Charles Street, SW1A 2AH.

**COLLARD, Paul Anthony Carthew**; Chief Executive, Creativity, Culture and Education, since 2009; b 17 Aug. 1954; s of late Douglas Reginald Collard, OBE and Eleni Cubitt; m 1983, Hilary Porter; three s one d. Educ: Ampleforth Coll., York; Trinity Coll., Cambridge (BA Hons). Exec. Sec., Friends of Cyprus, 1976–80; Administrator, Aga Khan Award for Architecture, 1980–82; Gen. Manager, ICA, 1983–87; Dep. Controller, BFI, South Bank, 1988–92; Director: UK Year of Visual Arts, 1993–97; Internat. Fest. of Arts and Ideas, New Haven, CT, 1997–2001; Hd, Programme Develt, Newcastle Gateshead Initiative, 2001–04; Nat. Dir, Creative Partnerships, 2005–09. Programme Co-ordinator, Newcastle Gateshead Bid for European Capital of Culture, 2001–03. David Goldman Prof. of Business Innovation, Univ. of Newcastle upon Tyne, 2003–04; Hon. Prof., Univ. of Nottingham, 2015–. Mem., Arts Council of England, subseq. Arts Council England, 2002–04 (Chm., NE Regl Arts Council, 2002–04). Recreation: arguing with the children. Address: Creativity, Culture and Education, 20 Portland Terrace, Newcastle upon Tyne NE2 1QQ.

**COLLAS, Sir Richard (John)**, Kt 2014; Bailiff of Guernsey, since 2012 (Deputy Bailiff, 2005–12); a Judge of the Court of Appeal of Jersey, since 2012; Acting Deemster, Isle of Man, since 2014; b 27 May 1953; s of Peter Renouf Collas and Nora Kathleen Collas (née Turner); m 1986, Amanda Judith Kenmir (d 2010); two s one d. Educ: Jesus Coll., Oxford (BA Engrg Sci. 1975); City Univ., London (Dip. Law 1981). Lever Brothers Ltd, 1975–80. Called to the Bar, Gray's Inn, 1982, Guernsey, 1983; Collas Day Advocates, 1983–2005. Recreations: family, boating. Address: Bailiff's Chambers, Royal Court House, St James Street, St Peter Port, Guernsey GY1 2NZ. T: (01481) 726161. Clubs: United (Guernsey); Guernsey Yacht, Royal Channel Islands Yacht.

**COLLECOTT, Dr Peter Salmon**, CMG 2002; HM Diplomatic Service, retired; consultant on international diplomacy and business, since 2009; Founding Partner, since 2011, and Co-Chairman, since 2016, Ambassador Partnership (formerly ADRg Ambassadors LLP); b 8 Oct. 1950; s of late George William Collecott and Nancie Alice Collecott (née Salmon); m 1982, Judith Patricia Pead. Educ: Chigwell Sch., Essex; St John's Coll., Cambridge (MA 1976; PhD 1976); MIT (Kennedy Schol. 1972). Royal Soc. Fellow, Max Planck Inst. for Physics and Astrophysics, Munich, 1976–77; joined HM Diplomatic Service, 1977; FCO, 1977–78; MECAS, Lebanon, later London, 1978–80; 1st Secretary: (Political), Khartoum, 1980–82; (Econ., Commercial, Agricl), Canberra, 1982–86; Head, Iran/Iraq Section, ME Dept, FCO, 1986–88; Asst Head, EC Dept (Ext.), FCO, 1988–89; Counsellor, Head of Chancery and Consul Gen., later Dep. Head of Mission, Jakarta, 1989–93; Counsellor (EU and Econ.), Bonn, 1994–98; Hd, Admin. Restructuring Rev. Team, FCO, 1998–99; Dir, Resources, FCO, 1999–2001; Dep. Under-Sec. of State and Chief Clerk, subseq. Dir Gen., Corporate Affairs, FCO, 2001–03; Ambassador to Brazil, 2004–08. Special Advr to Internat. Sustainability Unit, Prince of Wales' Charities, 2010–15.

Diplomatic Advr to Govt of Catalonia, 2013–16. Trustee: Sir Heinz Koeppler Trust, 2010–; Canning House, 2011–17 (Chm., 2016–17). Publications: papers on theoretical physics in learned jls. Recreations: gardening, reading.

**COLLENDER, His Honour Andrew Robert**; QC 1991; a Circuit Judge, 2006–16; b 11 Aug. 1946; s of John and Kathleen Collender; m 1974, Titia Tybout (d 2013); two s. Educ: Mt Pleasant Boys High Sch., Zimbabwe; Univ. of Bristol (LLB Hons). Called to the Bar, Lincoln's Inn, 1969, Bencher, 2000; a Recorder, 1993–2006; a Dep. High Ct Judge, 1998–2016; Head of Chambers, 2 Temple Gardens, 2002–05; a Sen. Judge, 2007–16; Presiding Sen. Judge, 2014–16, Sovereign Base Areas, Cyprus. Recreations: playing the violin, sailing. Address: 57 Clarendon Drive, Putney, SW15 1AW. Club: Bosham Sailing.

**COLLENETTE, Hon. David (Michael)**; PC (Canada) 1983; FCILT; Senior Counsel, Hill & Knowlton, Canada, since 2008; Distinguished Fellow, Glendon College, York University, Toronto, 2004–09; b 24 June 1946; s of David Henry and Sarah Margaret Collenette; m 1975, Penny Hossack; one s. Educ: Glendon Coll., York Univ. (BA Hons) MA). FCILT 2009. Admin. Officer, Marketing Div., Internat. Life Assurance Co., UK, 1970–72; Exec. Vice-Pres., Mandrake Management Consultants, Canada, 1987–93. Advr, Intergraph Corp., 2005–12. MP (L): York East, 1974–79 and 1980–84; Don Valley East, 1993–2004; Minister of State for Multiculturalism, 1983–84; Minister of Nat. Defence and of Veterans' Affairs, 1993–96; Minister of Transport, 1997–2003. Sec.-Gen., Liberal Party of Canada, 1985–87 (Exec. Dir, Toronto, 1969–70, Ontario, 1972–74). Chm., CILT (N America), 2011–15; Vice-Pres., CILT (Internat.), 2010–16. Dir, Harbourfront Corp., Toronto, 2009–. Special Advr on High Speed Rail to Govt of Ont, 2015–17. Member: Internat. Adv. Council, Inst. for Internat. Studies, Stanford Univ., 1999–2005; Canadian Adv. Bd, Parsons Brinckerhoff, 2011–15. Hon. LLD York Univ., Toronto, 2016. Recreations: swimming, theatre, classical music. Address: Hill & Knowlton, 50 O'Connor Street, Suite 1115, Ottawa, ON K1P 6L2, Canada. E: david.collenette@hillandknowlton.ca, dcollenette@glendon.yorku.ca. Clubs: National, University (Toronto).

**COLLENS, Rupert**; see Mackeson, Sir R. H.

**COLLERY, Shane Edward**; QC 2018; a Recorder, since 2004; b London, 1964; s of Shane Francis Collery and Anne Elizabeth Collery; m 2007, Elizabeth Webster; two s two d. Educ: Univ. of Nottingham (LLB Law 1987); Inns of Court Sch. of Law (Bar finals); Sch. of Advanced Studies, Univ. of London (MA Taxation 2012). Called to the Bar, Lincoln's Inn, 1988; in practice as a barrister, Red Lion Chambers, 1991–; Standing Counsel: HM Customs and Excise, subseq. HMRC, 2002–05; Revenue Customs Prosecution Office, 2006–11; BIS, subseq. BEIS, 2011–17; Insolvency Service, 2017–18. Recreations: Rugby, family, travel. Address: Red Lion Chambers, 18 Red Lion Court, EC4A 3EB. E: shane.collery@18rlc.co.uk.

**COLLETT, Sir Ian (Seymour)**, 3rd Bt cr 1934; b 5 Oct. 1953; s of David Seymour Collett (d 1962), and of Sheila Joan Collett (who m 1980, Sir James William Miskin, QC), o d of late Harold Scott; S grandfather, 1971; m 1982, Philippa, o d of late James R. I. Hawkins, Preston St Mary, Suffolk; one s one d. Educ: Lancing College, Sussex. Mem., Internat. Inst. of Marine Surveyors, 1998. Recreations: golf, fishing, cricket, shooting. Heir: s Anthony Seymour Collett [b 27 Feb. 1984; m 2011, Sophie Elizabeth Mary Williams]. Clubs: MCC; Aldeburgh Golf; Aldeburgh Yacht.

**COLLETT, Michael John**; QC 2013; b Bristol, 11 Dec. 1971; s of John and Bridget Collett; m 1998, Melissa Manes; one s one d. Educ: Queen Elizabeth's Hosp., Bristol; St John's Coll., Oxford (BA 1st Cl. Hons Lit. Hum.); City Univ. (DipLaw (Dist.)). MCIArb 2005. Called to the Bar, Gray's Inn, 1995, Bencher, 2019; in practice as barrister, specialising in commercial law, 1997–. Chm., London Common Law and Commercial Bar Assoc., 2018–19. Publications: (contrib.) Arbitration in England, 2013; (jtly) London Maritime Arbitration, 4th edn, 2018; (contrib.) Practitioner's Handbook on International Commercial Arbitration, 3rd edn, 2019. Recreation: classic cars. Address: 20 Essex Street, WC2R 3AL. T: (020) 7842 1200, Fax: (020) 7842 1270. E: clerks@20essexst.com.

**COLLEY, Kitty**; see Ussher, K.

**COLLEY, Prof. Linda Jane**, CBE 2009; PhD; FRHistS; FBA 1999; FRSL; Shelby M. C. Davis 1958 Professor of History, Princeton University, since 2003 (Old Dominion Professor in the Humanities, 2013–14); b 13 Sept. 1949; d of Roy Colley and Marjorie (née Hughes); m 1982, David Nicholas Cannadine (see Sir David Cannadine); one d decd. Educ: Bristol Univ. (BA); Cambridge Univ. (MA, PhD). University of Cambridge: Eugenie Strong Research Fellow, Girton Coll., 1975–78; Fellow: Newnham Coll., 1978–79; Christ's Coll., 1979–81 (Hon. Fellow, 2006); Yale University: Dir, Lewis Walpole Liby, 1982–96; Asst Prof., History, 1982–85; Associate Prof., 1985–90; Prof., History, 1990–92; Richard M. Colgate Prof. of History, 1992–98. Sch. Prof. in History and Leverhulme Personal Res. Prof., European Inst., LSE, 1998–2003. Hooker Distinguished Vis. Prof., McMaster Univ., 1999; Glaxo Smith Kline Sen. Fellow, Nat. Humanities Center, NC, 2006; Adjunct Prof., Humanities Res. Centre, ANU, 2006–; Fletcher Jones Distinguished Fellow, Huntington Liby, Calif, 2010; Birkelund Fellow, Cullman Center for Scholars and Writers, NY Public Liby, 2013–14; Long-term Fellow, Swedish Collegium for Advanced Study, Uppsala, 2017– (Fellow, 2016–17); John Simon Guggenheim Meml Fellow, 2017. Journalism and work on radio and TV; writer and presenter, Acts of Union and Disunion series, BBC Radio 4, 2014. Lectures: Anstey, Univ. of Kent, 1994; William Church Meml, Brown Univ., 1994; Dist. (in British Hist.), Univ. of Texas at Austin, 1995; Trevelyan, Cambridge Univ., 1997; Wiles, QUB, 1997; Hayes Robinson, Royal Holloway, Univ. of London, 1998; Ford Special, Oxford Univ., 1998; Bliss Carnochan, Stanford Humanities Center, 1998; Prime Minister's Millennium, 1999; Ena H. Thompson, Pomona Coll., Calif, 2001; Raleigh, British Acad., 2002; Nehru, London, 2003; Bateson, Oxford Univ., 2003; Chancellor Dunning Trust, Queen's Univ., Ont., 2004; Byrn, Vanderbilt Univ., 2005; Annual Internat. Hist., LSE, 2006; C. P. Snow, Christ's Coll., Cambridge, 2007; Political Sci. Quarterly, 2007; Victoria County Hist., 2007; President's, Princeton Univ., 2007; Gordon B. Hinkley in British Studies, Univ. of Utah, 2010; Bosley-Warnock, Univ. of Delaware, 2010; Martin Wright, Univ. of Sussex, 2011; Kayser, George Washington Univ., 2011; Indian Social and Econ. Hist. Rev., Delhi, 2011; Ubbelohde, Case Western Univ., 2011; Max Weber, Eur. Univ., Florence, 2012; John Coffin Meml, Univ. of London, 2012; Iredell, Univ. of Lancaster, 2012; Macmillan, Univ. of Toronto, 2013; Ralph Miliband, LSE, 2014; Gomes, Emmanuel Coll., Cambridge, 2015; Robbs, Univ. of Auckland, 2015; Aylmer, Univ. of York, 2015; Donald W. Sutherland Lect. in Legal Hist., Univ. of Iowa, 2015; Jefferson Foundn, Univ. of Virginia, 2016; Lowell Humanities, Boston Coll., 2016; John Mackintosh, Univ. of Edinburgh, 2016; Biennial Gen., Royal Swedish Acad. of Scis, Stockholm, 2018; Winter, London Rev. of Books, 2018; Castle, Univ. of Durham, 2018; Arts and Humanities, UCD, 2018; Dist. Lect. in History, Wesleyan Univ., 2018. Mem., Steering Gp, Rev. of REF UK, BIS, 2016. Guest Curator, exhibn, Taking Liberties: the struggle for Britain's freedoms and rights, BL, 2008–09. Member: Council, Tate Gall. of British Art, 1999–2003; BL Bd, 1999–2003; Adv. Council, Paul Mellon Centre for British Art, 1998–2003; Bd, Princeton Univ. Press, 2007–; Res. Cttee, BM, 2012–. MAE 2010. FRHistS 1988; FRSL 2004. Hon. DLitt: South Bank, 1998;

UEA, 2005; Bristol, 2006; Hull, 2012; DUniv Essex, 2004; Hon. Dr QUB, 2019. *Publications:* In Defiance of Oligarchy: The Tory Party 1714–60, 1982; Namier, 1989; Crown Pictorial: art and the British monarchy, 1990; Britons: forging the nation 1707–1837, 1992 (Wolfson History Prize, 1993); Captives: Britain, Empire and the world 1600–1850, 2002; The Ordeal of Elizabeth Marsh, 2007; Taking Stock of Taking Liberties, 2008; Acts of Union and Disunion, 2014; The Constitutions of Danger: war and the writing of a modern world, 2020; numerous articles and reviews in UK and USA jls. *Recreations:* travel, looking at art, politics. *Address:* Department of History, Princeton University, 129 Dickinson Hall, Princeton, NJ 08544–1017, USA; c/o Natasha Fairweather, 20 Powis Mews, W11 1JN. *W:* www.lindacolley.com.

**COLLIER,** family name of **Baron Monkswell.**

**COLLIER, Andrew James,** CB 1976; Deputy Secretary, Department of Health and Social Security, 1973–82; *b* 12 July 1923; *s* of Joseph Veasy Collier and Dorothy Murray; *m* 1950, Bridget (*d* 2012), *d* of George and Edith Eberstadt, London; two *d. Educ:* Harrow; Christ Church, Oxford. Served Army, RHA, 1943–46. Entered HM Treasury, 1948; Private Sec. to successive Chancellors of the Exchequer, 1956–59; Asst Sec., 1961; Under-Sec., 1967; Under-Secretary: Civil Service Dept, 1968–71; DHSS, 1971–73. *Club:* Athenæum.

**COLLIER, Andrew John,** CBE 1995; Schools Adjudicator, 1999–2005; General Secretary, Society of Education Officers, 1996–99 (Treasurer, 1987–92; President, 1990); *b* 29 Oct. 1939; *s* of Francis George Collier and Margaret Nancy (*née* Nockles); *m* 1964, Gillian Ann (*née* Churchill); two *d. Educ:* University College Sch.; St John's Coll., Cambridge (MA). Assistant Master, Winchester Coll., 1962–68; Hampshire County Educn Dept, 1968–71; Buckinghamshire County Educn Dept, 1971–77; Dep. Chief Educn Officer, 1977–80, Chief Educn Officer, 1980–96, Lancashire CC. Member: Open Univ. Vis. Cttee, 1982–88; Council for Accreditation of Teacher Educn, 1984–89; Nat. Training Task Force, 1989–92; Gen. Synod Bd of Educn, 1993–2001; Educn Cttee, Royal Soc., 1995–2000; Chm., County Educn Officers' Soc., 1987–88; Treas., Schools Curriculum Award, 1987–92. Chm., Assoc. of Educn Cttees Trust, 2010–17. Liveryman, Worshipful Company of Wheelwrights, 1972–2002. Mem. Council, Univ. of Lancaster, 1981–86, 1988–94, 1996–99; Governor: Myerscough Coll., 1996–2003; St Martin's Coll., Lancaster, 2001–07; Whitechapel Primary Sch., 2002–05 (Chm. of Govs, 2003–04); Univ. of Cumbria, 2007–10. Pres., Lancs Fedn of Young Farmers' Clubs, 1985–88. Blackburn Diocesan Synod, 2018–. *Publications:* (contrib.) New Directions for County Government, 1989; articles in jls. *Recreations:* music, walking, boating. *Clubs:* Athenæum; Leander (Henley-on-Thames); Salcombe Yacht; Warrington Rowing.

**COLLIER, Air Vice-Marshal Andy;** *see* Collier, Air Vice-Marshal J. A.

**COLLIER, Prof. Christopher George,** MBE 2018; PhD, DSc; CMet; Professor of Atmospheric Science, 2009–15, now Emeritus, and Head of Strategic Partnerships, National Centre for Atmospheric Science, 2009–15, University of Leeds; *b* 10 Sept. 1946; *s* of George and Barbara Collier; *m* 1969, Cynthia Dawson; two *s. Educ:* Hyde County Grammar Sch.; Imperial Coll., London (BSc Hons Physics 1968; ARCS); Univ. of Salford (PhD 1999; DSc 2008). CMet 1995. Meteorological Office, 1968–95; University of Salford, 1995–2009: Dir, Telford Res. Inst., 1997–98; Dean, Fac. of Sci., Engrg and Envmt, 1999–2003; Prof. of Envmtl Remote Sensing, 1995–2009. Chm., EU COST-73 Internat. Radar Networking Mgt Cttee, 1986–91. FRMetS 1967 (Pres., 2004–06; Hon. FRMetS 2012); Member: British Hydrological Soc.; CIWEM; Amer. Meteorological Soc. Robert Hugh Mill Medal, RMetS, 1982; L. G. Groves Prize, Met. Office, 1984; first Vaisala Prize, WMO, 1986. *Publications:* Applications of Weather Radar Systems, 1996; Hydrometeorology, 2016; over 90 refereed scientific pubns and over 200 conf. papers and reports. *Recreations:* swimming, reading, gardening, writing, Church of England. *Address:* School of Earth and Environment, Maths/Earth and Environment Building, University of Leeds, Leeds LS2 9JT.

**COLLIER, David Gordon,** OBE 2015; Chief Executive, Rugby League International Federation, 2015–18; *b* 22 April 1955; *s* of John and Pat Collier; *m* 1980, Jennifer Pendleton; two *s* one *d. Educ:* Loughborough Grammar Sch.; Loughborough Univ. (BSc Hons Sports Sci. and Recreation Mgt). Dep. Manager, Adams Sports Centre, Wem, 1979–80; Dep. Sec. Gen. and Manager, Essex CCC, 1980–83; Chief Exec., Glos CCC, 1983–86; Mktg Manager, Sema Gp plc, 1986–88; Sen. Vice-Pres., American Airlines, 1988–92; Man. Dir, Servisair plc, 1992–93; Chief Executive: Leics CCC, 1993–99; Notts CCC, 1999–2004; ECB, 2005–14. Internat. hockey umpire, 1985–2002. Member: European Hockey Fedn, 2000–04; Fedn of Internat. Hockey, 2002– (Mem. Exec. Bd, 2008–12; Chm., Audit Cttee, 2011); Ind. Mem., Major Events Panel, UK Sport, 2011–16. Chm., Internat. Hockey Rules Bd, 2008–. Pres., Club Cricket Conf., 2015–16. Chairman: HIX Mgt Gp Ltd, 2016–19; Lord's Taverners, 2017–. Sydney Friskin Award, Hockey Writers, 2003. DUniv: Loughborough, 2014; Nottingham Trent, 2018. *Recreations:* cricket, hockey, golf.

**COLLIER, Declan;** Chief Executive Officer, London City Airport, 2012–17; *b* Dublin, 14 June 1955; *s* of John and Margaret Collier; *m* 1985, Jan Winter; one *d. Educ:* Catholic Univ. Sch., Dublin; Trinity Coll., Dublin (BA Mod (Econ); MSc (Econ) Econs). Sen. exec. and mgt posts with ExxonMobil, 1980–99; Chm., Esso Ireland, 1999–2002; Alternative Fuels Manager/Eur. Dist Heating Manager, ExxonMobil, 2002–05; CEO, Dublin Airport Authy, 2005–12; Chm., AerRianta Internat., 2005–12. Chm., Office of Rail and Road, 2019– (non-exec. Dir, 2018–). Non-executive Director: Allied Irish Bank plc, 2009–12; Allied Irish Banks (UK) plc, 2012–18; Schiphol Airports Gp, 2018–; CrowdVision, 2018–; Chair, TCR Internat. NV, 2018–. President: Airports Council Internat., Europe, 2011–13; Airports Council Internat., World, 2015–17 (Vice-Chair, 2013–15); Mem. Bd, Airport Operators Assoc., UK, 2012–18. Mem. Council, CBI, 2015–18. Chairman: Dublin Th. Fest., 2011–16; Irish Th. Trust, 2011–18. *Recreations:* cycling, hill walking, Rugby, theatre, family. *Clubs:* Naval and Military; Dun Laoghaire Golf.

**COLLIER, Air Vice-Marshal James Andrew, (Andy),** CB 2005; CBE 1995; Deputy Commander-in-Chief Personnel and Training Command and Chief of Staff to Air Member for Personnel, 2003–05; *b* 6 July 1951; *s* of late Charles Robert Collier and Cynthia Collier (*née* Walsh), and step *s* of late Paul Scott; *m* 1972, Judith Arnold; one *d. Educ:* Headlands Sch., Swindon; Univ. of Durham (BSc 1972). Commnd RAF 1972; Sqn Ldr 1980; Wing Comdr 1987; Gp Capt. 1991; Air Cdre 1998; Air Vice-Marshal 2003. *Recreations:* golf, following sport (especially international Rugby and cricket), reading science, philosophy, religion, historical fiction. *Club:* Royal Air Force.

**COLLIER, John Spencer,** FCA; artist; Consultant, Grosvenor Clive & Stokes, 2014–16 (Partner, 2011–13); *b* 4 March 1945; *s* of James Bradburn Collier and Phyllis Mary Collier; *m* 1972, Theresa Mary Peers; two *s* one *d. Educ:* Trinity Coll., Cambridge (BA Geography 1967). FCA 1973. Tutor, King's Coll., London, 1967–69; joined Price Waterhouse, 1969: various posts, incl. Sen. Manager, 1969–81; Partner, 1981–92; Chief Executive: Newcastle Initiative, 1992–95; Lowes Gp plc, 1995–96; Finance Dir, Earth Centre, 1996–97; Sec. Gen., ICAEW, 1997–2002. Dir, Clive & Stokes Internat., 2004–11. Dir, Tyne and Wear Enterprise Agency, 1992–97; Chm., Dance City, Newcastle upon Tyne, 1994–97. Chm.,

Practice Regulation Directorate, ICAEW, 1993–97. Gov., Newcastle Coll., 1994–97. Chm., Friends of Richmond Park, 2004–07; Treas., Wordsworth Trust, 2004–; Trustee, British Pregnancy Adv. Service, 2013–. *Publications:* The Corporate Environment: the financial consequences for business, 1995. *Recreations:* mountains, marathons, painting, drawing. *Address:* 114 Lupus Street, SW1V 4AJ. *T:* (020) 7828 3412. *Club:* Travellers.

**COLLIER, Lesley Faye,** CBE 1993; Répétiteur, Royal Ballet, since 2000; Principal Dancer with the Royal Ballet, 1972–95; *b* 13 March 1947; *d* of Roy and Mavis Collier; twin *s. Educ:* The Royal Ballet School, White Lodge, Richmond. Joined Royal Ballet, 1965; has danced most principal roles in the Royal repertory; Ballet Mistress, 1995–99, Mem., Classical Ballet Staff, 1999–2000, Royal Ballet Sch. Evening Standard Ballet Award, 1987. *Address:* Royal Ballet, Royal Opera House, Covent Garden, WC2E 9DD.

**COLLIER, Prof. Melvyn William;** Director, Leuven University Library, Belgium, 2005–12, now Emeritus Professor, Leuven University; Chairman, Flanders Heritage Library, since 2016; *b* 31 July 1947; *s* of late James Collier and Jessie Collier (*née* Siddall); *m* 1st, 1968, Anne Nightingale (*d* 2004); one *s* one *d*; 2nd, 2010, Hedwig Schwall. *Educ:* Bolton Sch.; Univ. of St Andrews (MA); Strathclyde Univ. (DipLib). FCLIP (ALA 1981; MIInfSc 1990, FIInfSc 1997). Academic Librarian posts at St Andrews Univ., UC, Cardiff and Hatfield Poly., 1970–79; Dep. Hd, Liby Services, PCL, 1980–84; Librarian, Leicester Poly., 1985–89; Hd, Div. of Learning Develt, and Prof. of Information Mgt, De Montfort Univ., 1989–97; Director: Strategic and Operational Planning, Dawson Hldgs, 1997–2000; Tilburg Univ. Liby, Netherlands, 2001–03. Vis. Prof., De Montfort Univ., 1997–2001; part-time Prof., Univ. of Northumbria, 2000–06. Mem., Liby and Inf. Commn, 1996–2000 (Chm., Res. Cttee, 1996–2000); Chairman: Liby and Inf. Adv. Cttee, British Council, 1995–2001; UK Office for Liby Networking, 1995–97; Mem., Jt Inf. Systems Cttee, HEFCs, 1996–97. Director: Open Learning Foundn, 1995–97; Information For All, 1997–99. Hon. DLitt Strathclyde, 2006. Medal, Hungarian Liby Assoc., 1992. *Publications:* Local Area Networks: the implications for library and information science, 1984; (ed) Case Studies in Software for Information Management, 1986; (ed) Telecommunications for Information Management and Transfer, 1987; (jtly) Decision Support Systems in Academic Libraries, 1991; (jtly) Decision Support Systems and Performance Assessment in Academic Libraries, 1993; (ed) Electronic Library and Visual Information Research: ELVIRA 1, 1995, ELVIRA 2, 1996; (ed) Business Planning for Digital Libraries: international approaches, 2010; numerous jl articles and res. reports. *Recreations:* golf, hill-walking. *Address:* Naamsestraat 145, 3000 Leuven, Belgium.

**COLLIER, Sir Paul,** Kt 2014; CBE 2008; DPhil; FBA 2017; Professor of Economics, Oxford University, since 1993 (on leave of absence, 1998–2003); Fellow, St Antony's College, Oxford, since 1986; *b* 23 April 1949; *s* of Charles and Doris Collier; *m* 1998, Pauline Boerma; one *s. Educ:* King Edward VII Grammar Sch., Sheffield; Trinity Coll., Oxford (MA 1970); Nuffield Coll., Oxford (DPhil 1975). Oxford University: Fellow, Keble Coll. and Research Officer, Inst. of Econs and Stats, 1976–86; Univ. Lectr in Econs, 1986–89; Reader in Econs, 1989–92; Dir, Centre for Study of African Economies, 1991; Dir, Res. Dept, World Bank, Washington, 1998–2003. Prof. Invité, Centre d'Études et de Recherches sur le Développement Internat., Univ. d'Auvergne, 1989–; Vis. Prof., Kennedy Sch. of Govt, Harvard, 1992–96; Fellow, Centre for Economic Policy Res., 1993–; Associate, Tinbergen Inst., 1994–95. Lectures: Rausig, Moscow, 2000; Summers, Pa, 2001. Member: Overseas Develt Council, Program Associates Gp, Washington, 1994–96; Africa Panel, SSRC, NY, 1993–96; ESCOR Cttee, ODA then DFID, 1996–98. Man. Editor, Jl of African Economies, 1992–. Edgar Graham Prize, SOAS, 1988; Distinction Award, 1996, 1998; President's Medal, British Acad., 2014. *Publications:* Labour and Poverty in Kenya, 1986; Labour and Poverty in Rural Tanzania, 1986, 2nd edn 1991; Peasants and Governments, 1989; Controlled Open Economies, 1990, 2nd edn 1994; The Bottom Billion: why the poorest countries are failing and what can be done about it, 2007; Wars, Guns and Votes: democracy in dangerous places, 2009; The Plundered Planet: how to reconcile prosperity with nature, 2010; Exodus: immigration and multiculturalism in the 21st century, 2013; (jtly) Refuge: transforming a broken refugee system, 2017; The Future of Capitalism: facing the new anxieties, 2018. *Address:* Blavatnik School of Government, University of Oxford, Radcliffe Observatory Quarter, Woodstock Road, Oxford OX2 6GG.

**COLLIER, His Honour Peter Neville;** QC 1992; a Senior Circuit Judge, 2007–18; Resident Judge, Leeds Combined Court Centre, 2007–18; *b* 1 June 1948; *s* of late Arthur Neville Collier and of Joan Audrey Collier (*née* Brewer); *m* 1972, Susan Margaret Williamson; two *s. Educ:* Hymers Coll., Hull; Selwyn Coll., Cambridge (MA). Called to the Bar, Inner Temple, 1970, Bencher, 2002; Leader, NE Circuit, 2002–05. A Recorder, 1988–2007; a Dep. High Court Judge (Family Div.), 1998–2007; Hon. Recorder of Leeds, 2007–18. Chancellor: dio. of Wakefield, 1992–2006; dio. of Lincoln, 1998–2006; dio. of York, 2006–. Mem., Bar Council, 2000–07. Lay Canon, York Minster, 2001–; Chm., York Minster Council, 2005–. Vicar Gen., Province of York, 2008–. *Recreations:* long distance walking, reading, music.

**COLLIER-KEYWOOD, Richard David;** Network Vice Chairman, PricewaterhouseCoopers, 2011–17; *b* Nottingham, 21 July 1961; *s* of John Richard Collier-Keywood and Eirwen Harris; *m* 1984, Karen Ann Bradford; two *s* two *d. Educ:* Warwick Univ. (LLB). FCA 1986. Called to the Bar. PricewaterhouseCoopers: Partner, 1992–2017; UK Hd of Tax, 2003–08; UK Man. Partner, and Global Hd of Tax, 2008–11. Chairman: New Forest Care Ltd, 2016–; Harris Scott Investments Ltd, 2017–; School for Social Entrepreneurs, 2017–. Comr, Dormant Assets Commn, 2016–. Trustee: NGM; Mango; Chasan Trust. *Recreations:* tennis, sailing.

**COLLIN, Jack,** MA, MD; FRCS; Consultant Surgeon, John Radcliffe Hospital, Oxford, 1980–2010; Fellow of Trinity College, Oxford, since 1980; *b* 23 April 1945; *s* of John Collin and Amy Maud Collin; *m* 1971, Christine Frances Proud; three *s* one *d. Educ:* Univ. of Newcastle (MB BS, MD); Mayo Clinic, Minn. University of Newcastle: Demonstrator in Anatomy, 1969–70; Sen. Res. Associate, 1973–75; Registrar in Surgery, Royal Victoria Infirmary, Newcastle, 1971–80; Clin. Reader in Surgery, 1980–2001, Chm., Faculty of Clin. Medicine, 1990–92, Univ. of Oxford. Mayo Foundn Fellow, Mayo Clinic, Minn, 1977. Moynihan Fellow, Assoc. of Surgeons of GB and Ire., 1980; James IV Fellow, James IV Assoc. of Surgeons Inc., NY, 1993. Royal College of Surgeons: Arris and Gale Lectr, 1976; Jacksonian Prize, 1987; Hunterian Prof., 1988–89. Non-exec. Dir, Nuffield Orthopaedic Centre NHS Trust, 1990–93. Member: Internat. Soc. of Surgery, 1994–; European Surgical Assoc., 1994–. Jobst Prize, Vascular Surgical Soc. of GB and Ireland, 1990. *Publications:* papers on vascular surgery, intestinal myoelectrical activity and absorption, parenteral nutrition and pancreatic and intestinal transplantation. *Recreations:* gardening, walking, cycling. *Address:* Trinity College, Oxford OX1 3BH.

**COLLIN, (John) Richard (Olaf),** FRCS; Consultant Oculoplastic Surgeon: Harley Street Clinic, since 1981; King Edward VII's Hospital, Sister Agnes (formerly King Edward VII Hospital for Officers), since 1993; Honorary Professor of Ophthalmology, Institute of Ophthalmology, University College London, since 2008; *b* 1 May 1943; *s* of late John Olaf Collin and Ellen Vera (*née* Knudsen); *m* 1st, 1979, Theresa Pedemonte (marr. diss. 1982); 2nd, 1993, Geraldine O'Sullivan (*d* 2013); two *d. Educ:* Charterhouse; Sidney Sussex Coll.,

Cambridge (MA); Westminster Med. Sch. (MB BChir). FRCS 1972. House surgeon and house physician, Westminster Hosp., 1967–68; ship's surgeon, P&O, 1969–70; Ophthalmology Registrar, Moorfields Eye Hosp., 1972–75; Fellow in Ophthalmic Plastic and Reconstructive Surgery, Univ. of Calif, San Francisco, 1976–77; Lectr, then Sen. Lectr, Professorial Unit, 1978–81, Consultant Surgeon, 1981–2017, Moorfields Eye Hosp. Hon. Consultant, Gt Ormond St Hosp. for Sick Children, 1983–2017. Master, Oxford Ophthalmol Congress, 1997–98. President: British Ocular Plastic Surgery Soc., 2002–05; European Soc. Oculo Plastic and Reconstructive Surgery, 2003–05. *Publications:* A Manual of Systematic Eyelid Surgery, 1983, 3rd edn 2006; (with A. G. Tyers) A Colour Atlas of Ophthalmic Plastic Surgery, 1995, 3rd edn 2008; articles on ophthalmic, plastic and reconstructive surgery topics. *Recreations:* sailing, shooting, tennis, hunting, fishing, theatre, opera. *Address:* 67 Harley Street, W1G 8QZ. *T:* (020) 7486 2699; 32 Old Queen Street, SW1H 9HP. *T:* (020) 7222 0582. *Clubs:* Royal Ocean Racing, Hurlingham; Beaulieu River Sailing (Beaulieu).

**COLLINGE, Prof. John,** CBE 2004; FRS 2005; Professor of Neurology, since 2001, Director, Institute of Prion Diseases, since 2017, and Director, MRC Prion Unit at UCL (formerly MRC Prion Unit), since 1998, University College London (Founder and Head, Department of Neurodegenerative Disease, 2001–17); *b* 25 Jan. 1958; *s* of late Robert Collinge and Edna Collinge; *m* 1986, Donna Anne Keel (marr. diss. 1990). *Educ:* Burnley Grammar Sch.; St John's Coll., Cambridge; Univ. of Bristol (BSc Hons 1981; MB ChB 1984; MD 1992). MRCP 1988, FRCP 1998; FRCPath 1999. Bristol Royal Infirmary: House Surg., 1984–85; House Physician, 1985; Hon. Sen. House Officer in Pathology, 1985–86; Demonstrator in Pathology, Univ. of Bristol, 1985–86; Med. Rotation, Westminster Hosp., 1986–87; Senior House Officer: in Medicine, Hammersmith Hosp., 1987; in Neurology, Nat. Hosp. for Neurology and Neurosurgery, 1987–88; Merck, Sharp and Dohme Fellow, 1988, Clin. Scientific Staff, 1988–90, MRC Div. of Psychiatry, Clin. Res. Centre, Harrow; Hon. Registrar in Psychiatry, Northwick Park Hosp., 1988–90; Clin. Res. Fellow, Dept of Biochemistry and Molecular Genetics, St Mary's Hosp. Med. Sch., 1990–91; St Mary's Hospital: Hon. Registrar, 1990–91, Hon. Sen. Registrar, 1991–94, in Neurology; Hon. Consultant in Neurology and Molecular Genetics, 1994–; Imperial College School of Medicine at St Mary's (formerly St Mary's Hospital Medical School): Wellcome Sen. Res. Fellow, 1992–96, Prin. Res. Fellow, 1996–2000, in Clin. Scis; Prof. of Molecular Neurogenetics and Hd, Dept of Neurogenetics, 1994–2001; Hon. Consultant Neurologist, 1996–, Dir, Nat. Prion Clinic, 2001–, Nat. Hosp. for Neurology and Neurosurgery. Inaugural Sen. Investigator of Faculty, Nat. Inst. for Health Res., 2008–17, now Sen. Investigator Emeritus. Vis. Prof. of Neurology, Harvard Med. Sch., 2017–. Member: Neurosci Panel, Wellcome Trust, 1994–97; Spongiform Encephalopathy Adv. Cttee, 1996–2002, 2007–11; Dep. Chm., High-level Gp on BSE, EU, 1996–97; Chm., Res. Adv. Panel, MND Assoc., 1997–2000 (Mem., 1994–97). Mem. Council, Royal Soc., 2011–13. Hon. Fellow, Amer. Neurological Assoc., 2013; Member: Clin. Genetics Soc., 1993; Assoc. of British Neurologists, 1995. Founder FMedSci 1998. Hon. DSc Bristol, 2008. Linacre Medal, 1992, Graham Bull Prize in Clin. Sci., 1993, Jean Hunter Prize, 2004, RCP; Alfred Meyer Medal, British Neuropathol Soc., 1997; Howard Taylor Ricketts Medal, Univ. of Chicago, 2001. *Publications:* (ed jtly) Prion Diseases of Humans and Animals, 1992; (ed jtly) Prion Diseases, 1997; papers on prion diseases, Alzheimer's and other neurodegenerative diseases and neurogenetics. *Recreations:* mountain walking, sailing. *Address:* MRC Prion Unit at UCL, Institute of Prion Diseases, Courtauld Building, 33 Cleveland Street, W1W 7FF. *T:* (020) 7837 4888. *Clubs:* Athenæum, Little Ship.

**COLLINGE, John Gregory;** High Commissioner for New Zealand in the United Kingdom, 1994–97, and concurrently High Commissioner in Nigeria and Ambassador to the Republic of Ireland; *b* 10 May 1939; *s* of Norman Gregory Collinge and Hilary Winifred Fendall; *m* 2003, Margaret Elaine Postlethwaite; two *d* by a previous marriage. *Educ:* Auckland Univ. (LLB); University Coll., Oxford (MLitt). Called to the Bar, 1963, and admitted Solicitor, 1963, High Court of NZ; called to the Bar, 1966, and admitted Solicitor, 1966, High Court of Australia. Sen. Lectr in Law, Melbourne Univ., 1967–70; Partner, law firm, Melbourne, Wellington and Auckland, 1969–2005. Pres., NZ National Party, 1989–94. Chairman: Policy and Finance Cttee, Auckland Regl Authy, 1983–86; Commerce Commn, 1984–89; Alcohol Adv. Council of NZ, 1991–94; Nat. Civil Defence Energy Planning Cttee, 1992–94. Member: Auckland Electric Power Bd, 1977–80, 1992–93 (Chm., 1980–92); Electrical Develt Assoc. of NZ, 1990–91 (Pres., 1991–94); Council, Electricity Supply Assoc. of NZ, 1991–92. Chairman: New Zealand Pelagic Fisheries Ltd, 1975–81; United Distillers (NZ) Ltd, 1991 (Dir, 1986–91); Director: Mercury Energy Ltd, 1998–99; Vector Ltd, 2002–04 (Dep. Chm., 2002–04). Pres., Auckland Citizens and Ratepayers Inc., 1999–2004; Trustee, Auckland Energy Consumer Trust, 2000–06 (Dep. Chm., 2001–04). Alternate Gov., EBRD, 1994–97. Comr, Commonwealth War Graves Commn, 1994–97; Gov., Commonwealth Foundn, 1994–97; Mem. Bd of Govs, Commonwealth Inst., 1994–97. Vice-Pres., Royal Over-Seas League, 1994–97; Trustee: Waitangi Foundn, 1994–97; Dame Sister Mary Leo Foundn, 1998–; Chip-in Foundn for Disaster Relief, 2016–; Pres., Auckland Rotary, 2017–18; Patron: Captain Cook Birthplace Trust, 1994–97; Shakespeare Globe Trust, 1994–97; British NZ Business Assoc. (formerly British/NZ Trade Council), 1997–. Commemoration Medal, NZ, 1990. *Publications:* Restrictive Trade Practices and Monopolies in New Zealand, 1969, 2nd edn 1982; Tutorials in Contract, 1985, 4th edn 1989; The Law of Marketing in Australia and New Zealand, 1989, 2nd edn 1990; An Identity for New Zealand?, 2010. *Recreations:* New Zealand history, restoring colonial houses and colonial antiques, Rugby, cricket. *Address:* 10 London Street, St Mary's Bay, Auckland, New Zealand. *T:* 93608951; Frog Pond Farm, Ansty, Wilts SP3 5PY. *Clubs:* Vincent's (Oxford); Wellington (NZ); Royal NZ Yacht Squadron (Auckland).

**COLLINGRIDGE, Prof. Graham Leon,** CBE 2019; PhD; FRS 2001; Professor of Neuroscience in Anatomy, School of Physiology, Pharmacology and Neuroscience (formerly School of Physiology and Pharmacology), University of Bristol, since 1994; Ernest B. and Leonard B. Smith Chair, Department of Physiology, University of Toronto, since 2015; Senior Investigator, Lunenfeld-Tanenbaum Research Institute, Mount Sinai Hospital, Toronto, since 2015; *b* 1 Feb. 1955; *s* of Cyril Leon Collingridge and Marjorie May Caesar; *m* 1st, 1992, Catherine Rose (marr. diss. 2009); one *s* two *d*; 2nd, 2011, Clarrisa Ann Bradley; one *s*. *Educ:* Enfield GS; Univ. of Bristol (BSc 1977); Sch. of Pharmacy, London Univ. (PhD 1980). CBiol, FRSB (FIBiol 1997). Res. Fellow in Physiology, Univ. of British Columbia, 1980–82; Sen. Res. Officer, Dept of Physiology and Pharmacology, Univ. of NSW, 1983; Lectr, 1983–90, Reader, 1990, Dept of Pharmacology, Univ. of Bristol; Prof., and Head of Dept of Pharmacology, Univ. of Birmingham, 1990–94; University of Bristol: Head of Dept of Anatomy, 1996–98; Dir, MRC Centre for Synaptic Plasticity, 1999–2012. WCU Prof., Dept of Brain and Cognitive Scis, Seoul Nat. Univ., 2009–13. Founder, European Dana Alliance for the Brain, 1997. Pres., British Neurosci. Assoc., 2007–09. Founder FMedSci 1998. Editor-in-Chief, Neuropharmacology, 1993–2010. *Publications:* numerous papers in scientific jls, such as Nature, Neuron, Nature Neuroscience on the neural basis of learning and memory and other aspects of neuroscience. *Recreations:* ski-ing, snow-boarding, soccer, running, golf, travel. *Address:* Department of Physiology, Medical Sciences Building, 1 King's College Circle, Room 3207, University of Toronto, Toronto, ON M5S 1A8, Canada. *T:* (416) 9782674.

**COLLINGS, Juliet Jeanne d'Auvergne;** *see* Campbell, J. J. d'A.

**COLLINGS, Matthew Glynn Burkinshaw;** QC 2006; *b* 13 Aug. 1961; *s* of Frederick, (Burke), Collings and Beryl Collings; *m* 1984, Amanda Maine-Tucker; two *s*. *Educ:* Colston's Sch., Bristol; London Sch. of Econs (LLB). Called to the Bar: Lincoln's Inn, 1985, Bencher, 2017; BVI, 2011; Cayman, 2012; in practice as barrister, 1986–, specialising in company, insolvency and commercial law. Former Mem., Insolvency Rules Adv. Cttee. Chm., Oxfordshire and Bucks Cons. Party, 2006–09. Contested (C) Newport E, 2005. *Recreations:* vintage cars, opera, ski-ing. *Address:* Maitland Chambers, 7 Stone Buildings, Lincoln's Inn, WC2A 3SZ. *T:* (020) 7406 1200, *Fax:* (020) 7406 1300. *E:* mcollings@maitlandchambers.com.

**COLLINI, Prof. Stefan Anthony,** PhD; FRHistS; FBA 2000; Professor of Intellectual History and English Literature, Cambridge University, 2000–14, now Emeritus; Fellow, Clare Hall, Cambridge, 1986–2014, now Emeritus; *b* 6 Sept. 1947; *s* of Raymond Collini and Hilda May (*née* Brown); *m* 1971, Ruth Karen Morse. *Educ:* St Joseph's Coll., Beulah Hill; Jesus Coll., Cambridge (BA 1969, MA 1973; Thirlwall Prize and Seeley Medal 1973; PhD 1977); Yale Univ. (MA 1970). FRHistS 1981. Res. Fellow, St John's Coll., Cambridge, 1973–74; University of Sussex: Lectr in Intellectual Hist., 1974–82; Reader, 1982–86; Cambridge University: Asst Lectr in English, 1986–90; Lectr, 1990–94; Reader, 1994–2000. Visiting Fellow: History of Ideas Unit, ANU, 1982–83 and 1987; Clare Hall, Cambridge, 1986; Vis. Fellow, All Souls Coll., Oxford and James Ford Lectr, Univ. of Oxford, 2017; Visiting Professor: Inst. Internacional de Estudios Avanzados, Caracas, 1983; in Humanities, Radboud Univ., Nijmegen, 2019; Dir d'études associé, Ecole des Hautes Etudes en Scis Sociales, Paris, 1986 and 1991; Mem., Inst. for Advanced Study, Princeton, 1994–95; British Studies Fellow, Ransom Humanities Res. Center, Austin, Tex., 1995; Sen. Res. Fellowship, British Acad., 1999–2000; Leverhulme Major Res. Fellowship, 2007–10; Birkelund Fellowship, Nat. Humanities Center, NC, 2012–13. Co-ed., Cambridge Rev., 1986–93. *Publications:* Liberalism and Sociology, 1979; (jtly) That Noble Science of Politics, 1983; Arnold, 1988, 2nd edn 1994; (ed) On Liberty, by J. S. Mill, 1989; Public Moralists, 1991; (ed) Interpretation and Overinterpretation, by Umberto Eco, 1992; (ed) Culture and Anarchy, by Matthew Arnold, 1993; (ed) The Two Cultures, by C. P. Snow, 1993; English Pasts: essays in history and culture, 1999; (ed jtly) Economy, Polity, and Society, 2000; (ed jtly) History, Religion, and Culture: British Intellectual History 1750–1950, 2000; Absent Minds: intellectuals in Britain, 2006; Common Reading: critics, historians, publics, 2008; That's Offensive!: criticism, identity, respect, 2011; What Are Universities For?, 2012; (ed) Two Cultures?, by F. R. Leavis, 2013; Common Writing: essays on literary culture and public debate, 2016; Speaking of Universities, 2017; The Nostalgic Imagination: history in English criticism, 2019; contrib. essays and reviews in jls, incl. TLS, London Rev. of Books, etc. *Address:* Faculty of English, Cambridge University, 9 West Road, Cambridge CB3 9DP. *T:* (01223) 335070.

**COLLINS,** family name of **Baron Collins of Mapesbury.**

**COLLINS OF HIGHBURY,** Baron *cr* 2011 (Life Peer), of Highbury in the London Borough of Islington; **Raymond Edward Harry Collins;** *b* Newport, IoW, 21 Dec. 1954; *s* of late Harry Collins and Isobel Collins; civil partnership 2005, *m* 2014, Rafael Ballesteros. *Educ:* Univ. of Kent, Canterbury (BA Hons Industrial Relns and Pols 1980). Transport and General Workers' Union: Asst Librarian, 1972–74; Specialist Asst, Educn, 1974–77; Policy Advr and Special Asst to Gen. Sec., 1980–85; Nat. Admin. Officer, 1985–98; Asst Gen. Sec., TGWU, subseq. Unite, 1998–2008; Gen. Sec., Labour Party, 2008–11. An Opposition Whip, 2011–; opposition spokesman on foreign affairs and internat. develt, H of L, 2012–. Labour Party: Mem., 1970–; Mem., Nat. Policy Forum, 1997–2003, Nat. Constitution Cttee, 2001–08. Mem., Unite (formerly TGWU), 1972–. Patron: Positive East, 2011–; LGBT Labour, 2011–. *Recreations:* Spanish history, swimming, Arsenal FC. *Address:* House of Lords, SW1A 0PW. *W:* www.twitter.com/Lord_Collins.

**COLLINS OF MAPESBURY,** Baron *cr* 2009 (Life Peer), of Hampstead Town in the London Borough of Camden; **Lawrence Antony Collins,** Kt 2000; PC 2007; LLD; FBA 1994; a Justice of the Supreme Court of the United Kingdom, 2009–11, Acting Justice, 2011–16 (formerly a Lord of Appeal in Ordinary); non-permanent Judge, Hong Kong Court of Final Appeal, since 2011; Fellow of Wolfson College, Cambridge, 1975–2008, now Emeritus (Honorary Fellow, 2009); Professor of Law, University College London, since 2011; international arbitrator, since 2011; *b* 7 May 1941; *s* of late Sol Collins and Phoebe (*née* Barnett); *m* 1st, 1982, Sara Shamni (marr. diss. 2003); one *s* one *d*; 2nd, 2012, Patti Langton. *Educ:* City of London Sch.; Downing Coll., Cambridge (BA, George Long Prize, McNair Schol., 1963; LLB, Whewell Schol., 1964; LLD 1994; Hon. Fellow, 2000); Columbia Univ. (LLM 1965). Mem. Inst de Droit Internat., 1989. Admitted solicitor, 1968; Partner, Herbert Smith, solicitors, 1971–2000 (Hd, Litigation and Arbitration Dept, 1995–98); QC 1997; a Dep. High Court Judge, 1997–2000; a Judge of High Court of Justice, Chancery Div., 2000–07; a Lord Justice of Appeal, 2007–09. Bencher, Inner Temple, 2001. Visiting Professor: QMUL (formerly QMC, then QMW), 1982–; Columbia Law Sch., 2012; Vis. Prof., 2012, 2014, Adjunct Prof., 2015–, NY Univ. Sch. of Law. Lectr, Hague Acad. of Internat. Law, 1991, 1998, 2007; Graveson Meml Lectr, KCL, 1995; F. A. Mann Lectr, British Inst. of Internat. and Comparative Law, 2001; Lionel Cohen Lectr, Hebrew Univ., Jerusalem, 2007; Freshfields Arbitration Lectr, 2009; Chancery Bar Assoc. Lectr, 2010; Commercial Bar Assoc. Lectr, 2010; Ian Borrin Vis. Fellow, Victoria Univ. of Wellington, NZ, 2011; Clarendon Law Lectr, 2012; Herbert Smith Freehills Internat. Arbitration Lectr, Singapore, 2013. Member: Lord Chancellor's Wkg Party on Foreign Judgments, 1979–81; Bar and Law Soc. Jt Wkg Party on UK-US Judgments Convention, 1980–82; Law Commn Jt Wkg Party on Torts in Private Internat. Law, 1982–84; Ministry of Justice (formerly DCA) Adv. Cttee on Private Internat. Law, 2004–. Chm., Takeover Appeal Bd, 2015– (Dep. Chm., 2013–15). Hon. Sec., British Br., 1983–88, Chm., Cttee on Internat. Securities Regulation, 1988–94, Internat. Law Assoc. Member: Adv. Council, Centre for Commercial Law Studies, QMUL (formerly QMW), 1989–; Adv. Bd, Cambridge Univ. Centre for European Legal Studies, 1993–97; Council of Advrs, Singapore Internat. Arbitration Centre, 2010–. Mem., Amer. Law Inst., 2010–. Hon. Member: SPTL, 1993; British Inst. of Internat. and Comparative Law, 2008– (Mem., Council of Mgt, 1992–2006); Mem., Adv. Council, 2006–10; Vice-Pres., 2011–); Hon. Life Mem., 2000, Lifetime Achievement Award, 2011, Law Soc. Lifetime Achievement Award, Solicitors' Co., 2009. Member: Editl Adv. Cttee, Law Qly Rev., 1988–; Bd of Eds, Internat. and Comparative Law Qly, 1988–2009; Editl Cttee, British Yearbook of Internat. Law, 1991– (Chair, 2011–); Editl Bd, Civil Justice Qly, 2005–; Adv. Ed., Civil Procedure, 2002–09. *Publications:* European Community Law in the United Kingdom, 1975, 4th edn 1990; Civil Jurisdiction and Judgments Act 1982, 1983; Essays in International Litigation and the Conflict of Laws, 1994; (Gen. Ed.) Dicey & Morris (now Dicey, Morris & Collins), Conflict of Laws, 11th edn 1987 to 15th edn 2012. *Address:* Essex Court Chambers, 24 Lincoln's Inn Fields, WC2A 3EG.

**COLLINS, Sir Alan (Stanley),** KCVO 2005; CMG 1998; HM Diplomatic Service, retired; Managing Director, Olympic Legacy, UK Trade & Investment, 2011–12; *b* 1 April 1948; *s* of Stanley Arthur Collins and Rose Elizabeth Collins; *m* 1971, Ann Dorothy Roberts; two *s* one *d*. *Educ:* Strand GS; London School of Economics and Political Science

(BSc Econs). Joined MoD, 1970; Private Sec. to Vice Chief of Air Staff, 1973–75; joined FCO, 1981; Deputy Head of Mission: Addis Ababa, 1986–90; Manila, 1990–93; Counsellor, FCO, 1993–95; Dir-Gen., British Trade and Cultural Office, Taipei, 1995–98; Ambassador, Philippines, 1998–2002; (on secondment) Vice-Pres. for Internat. Relns, Shell, 2002–03; High Comr, Singapore, 2003–07; Consul-Gen., New York and Dir-Gen., Trade and Investment in the US, 2007–11. *Recreations*: sport, antiques, reading, walking.

**COLLINS, Hon. Sir Andrew (David),** Kt 1994; a Judge of the High Court of Justice, Queen's Bench Division, 1994–2017; *b* 19 July 1942; *s* of late Rev. Canon Lewis John Collins, MA, and Dame Diana Clavering Collins, DBE; *m* 1970, Nicolette Anne Sandford-Saville; one *s* one *d*. *Educ*: Eton; King's Coll., Cambridge (BA, MA). Called to the Bar, Middle Temple, 1965, Bencher, 1992; QC 1985; a Recorder, 1986–94. Pres., Immigration Appeal Tribunal, 1999–2002; Lead Judge, Administrative Court, 2004–07.

**COLLINS, Anne-Marie;** *see* Curtis, A.-M.

**COLLINS, Arthur John,** OBE 1973; HM Diplomatic Service, retired; Representative of the Secretary of State, Foreign and Commonwealth Office, 1988–2006; *b* 17 May 1931; *s* of Reginald and Margery Collins; *m* 1952, Enid Maureen (*d* 2015), *d* of Charles Stableford, FRIBA and Sarah Stableford; one *s* one *d*. *Educ*: Purley Grammar Sch. Served RAF, 1949–51. Min. of Health, 1951–68 (Private Sec. to Perm. Sec., 1960–61, and to Parly Sec., 1962–63); transf. to HM Diplomatic Service, 1968; FCO, 1968–69; First Secretary and Head of Chancery: Dhaka, 1970–71; Brasilia, 1972–74; Asst Head of Latin America and Caribbean Depts, FCO, 1974–77; Counsellor, UK Delegn to OECD, Paris, 1978–81; High Comr, Papua New Guinea, 1982–85; adviser on management, FCO, 1986–88; Consultant, EBRD, 1991; Assessor, VSO, 1993–99. Pres., Brighton and Hove Archaeol Soc., 1996–99. Chm., Brighton, Hove and Dist, 1998–2004 and 2012–15, SE Region, 2009–14, ESU. *Publications*: papers on early colonialism in New Guinea. *Address*: 60 Dean Court Road, Rottingdean, Sussex BN2 7DJ. *Club*: Hove (Hove).

**COLLINS, Benjamin Roger;** QC 2016; a Recorder, since 2018; *b* Coventry, 5 March 1972; *s* of David Andrew Collins and Ruth Collins; *m* 1996, Michelle Elizabeth Lancefield; two *s*. *Educ*: King Henry VIII Sch., Coventry; Queens' Coll., Cambridge (BA 1995; MA 1998). Called to the Bar: Middle Temple, 1996; NI, 2016; in practice as a barrister, 1 Crown Office Row, 1996–2012, Old Square Chambers, 2012–. Mem., Qualifications Cttee, Bar Standards Bd, 2010–13; Reviewer Mem., Bar Pro Bono Unit, 2013–. Consulting Ed., Criminal Injuries Compensation. *Publications*: (contrib. ed) Professional Negligence and Liability; contrib. to New Law Jl, Occupational Medicine, Judicial Rev., Legal and Medical, Jl of Personal Injury Law. *Recreations*: Rugby Union, taxi driving for sons, Mario Kart. *Address*: Old Square Chambers, 10–11 Bedford Row, WC1R 4BU. *T*: (020) 7269 0300. *E*: collinsqc@oldsquare.co.uk.

**COLLINS, Prof. Brian Stanley,** CB 2011; DPhil; CEng, FREng, FInstP, FIET, FICE, FBCS; Professor of Engineering Policy, University College London, since 2011; *b* 3 Oct. 1945; *s* of James and Maud Collins; *m* 1st (marr. diss.); one *s* one *d*; *m* 2nd (marr. diss.); partner, Gillian Sowerby. *Educ*: Chislehurst and Sidcup Grammar Sch.; St Peter's Coll., Oxford (Open Schol.; BA Physics 1967, MA); DPhil Astrophysics Oxon 1971. FInstP 1984; CEng 1988; FIET (FIEE 1988); FBCS 2000; CITP 2000; FREng 2009; FICE 2009. Res. Scientist, 1973–85, Dep. Dir, 1987, RSRE; rcds 1986; Chief Scientist and Dir, Technol. (Grade 3), GCHQ, 1987–91; Partner, KPMG, 1991–92; IT Dir, Wellcome Trust, 1994–97; Global Chief Inf. Officer, Clifford Chance, 1999–2001; Prof. of Information Systems, Cranfield Univ., 2003–11. Chief Scientific Adviser: DfT, 2006–11; BERR, then BIS, 2008–11. Vice President: IEE, 1999–2002; BCS, 2003–06. Mem., Court of Assts, Co. of Information Technologists, 2004–. FRSA 1997. *Publications*: (ed with Prof. R. Mansell) Trust and Crime in Information Societies, 2004. *Recreations*: golf (learning), cricket and Rugby (watching), country walks, ballet, music, reading. *Address*: Department of Civil, Environmental and Geomatic Engineering, University College London, Gower Street, WC1E 6BT. *E*: brian.collins@ucl.ac.uk.

**COLLINS, Sir Bryan (Thomas Alfred),** Kt 1997; OBE 1989; QFSM 1983; HM Chief Inspector of Fire Services, 1994–98; *b* 4 June 1933; *m* 1959, Terry Skuce; one *s* one *d*. *Educ*: Queen Mary's Sch. RAF, 1951–53; with Fire Service, 1954–98; Chief Fire Officer, Humberside, 1979–89; Inspector of Fire Services: Northern Area, 1989–93; Midlands and Wales, 1993–94. *Address*: Gwelo, Thatcher Stanfords Close, Melbourn, S Cambs SG8 6DT.

**COLLINS, Christopher Douglas;** Chairman, Hanson plc, 1998–2005 (Director, 1991–2005; Vice-Chairman, 1995–97); *b* 19 Jan. 1940; *s* of Douglas and Patricia Collins; *m* 1976, Susan Ann Lumb; one *s* one *d*. *Educ*: Eton Coll. Chartered Accountant. Articled clerk, Peat Marwick Mitchell, 1959–65; Goya Ltd: Man. Dir, 1968–75; Dir, 1975–80; with Hanson plc, 1989–2005. Chairman: Forth Ports PLC, 2000–09; Old Mutual plc, 2005–09 (non-exec. Dir, 1999–2005). Amateur steeplechase jockey, 1965–75; represented GB in 3-day equestrian events, 1974–80; Chm., British Team Selection Cttee, 1981–84; Jockey Club Steward, 1980–81; Mem., Horse Race Betting Levy Bd, 1982–84. Chairman: Aintree Racecourse Ltd, 1983–88; National Stud, 1986–88; Jockey Club Racecourses (formerly Racecourse Hldgs Trust), 2005–08. *Recreations*: reading, gardening, equestrian sport. *Clubs*: Jockey, White's, Pratt's.

**COLLINS, Crispian Hilary Vincent;** Chairman, Schroder Global Real Estate Securities Ltd (formerly ING Global Real Estate Securities Ltd, then Investors in Global Real Estate Ltd), 2006–16; *b* 22 Jan. 1948; *s* of late Bernard John Collins, CBE, and Gretel Elisabeth Collins (*née* Piehler); *m* 1974, Diane Barbara Bromley; one *s* two *d*. *Educ*: Ampleforth Coll.; University Coll., Oxford (BA Hons Modern History). Joined Phillips & Drew, 1969; Fund Manager, Pension Funds, 1975–98; Partner, 1981–85; Dir, 1985–2002; Chief Exec., 1998–2000; Chm., 1999–2002; Mem., Mgt Cttee, Phillips & Drew Fund Mgt, 1994–00. Chm., European (formerly Matrix) Real Estate Investment Trust Ltd, 2007–14; Vice Chm., UBS (later UBS Global) Asset Management, 2000–03. Director: Salvation Army Trustee Co., 2003–08; The Children's Mutual, 2003–09; Chm., Safe Child Thailand (formerly Thai Children's Trust), 2009–. Chm. of Govs, St Leonards-Mayfield Sch., 2003–09. *Recreations*: golf, watching sport, opera, gardens. *E*: crispiancollins@btinternet.com.

**COLLINS, Damian Noel Thomas;** MP (C) Folkestone and Hythe, since 2010; *b* Northampton, 4 Feb. 1974; *s* of Fearghal and Diane Collins; *m* 2004, Sarah Richardson; one *s* one *d*. *Educ*: St Mary's High Sch., Herefordshire; Belmont Abbey Sch., Hereford; St Benet's Hall, Oxford (BA Hons Modern Hist.). Cons. Res. Dept and Press Officer, 1996–99; Dir, M & C Saatchi, 1999–2008; Sen. Counsel, Lexington Communications, 2008–10. PPS to Sec. of State for NI, 2012–14, to Foreign Sec., 2014–15. Mem., H of C Select Cttee on Culture, Media and Sport, 2010–12 and 2015– (Chm., 2016–). Pres., Oxford Univ. Cons. Assoc., 1995. *Publications*: (contrib.) Conservative Revival, 2006; (contrib.) The New Blue, 2008; Charmed Life: the phenomenal world of Philip Sassoon, 2016. *Recreations*: cricket, football, Rugby (watching), walking in Kent, cooking with Jamie Oliver. *Address*: House of Commons, SW1A 0AA. *T*: (020) 7219 7072. *E*: damian.collins.mp@parliament.uk. *Clubs*: Lord's Taverners, MCC; Manchester United.

**COLLINS, Prof. David John,** PhD; CPsychol, CSci; Director, Grey Matters Performance Ltd, since 2010; Professorial Fellow, Human Performance, University of Edinburgh, since 2019; *b* 31 Dec. 1953; *s* of Arthur and Ivy Collins; *m* 2003, Helen Brooker; two *d*, and one *s* two *d* from previous marriage. *Educ*: Borough Rd Coll. (CertEd, BEd Hons); Pennsylvania State Univ. (MSc); Univ. of Surrey (PhD 1990); BASES accredited Sport Psychologist; BASES High Perf. Sport Accreditation, 2001; BOA registered Sport Psychologist; Practitioner Psychologist, Health and Care Professionals Council, 2009; Reg. Applied Psychol. Supervisor, BPsS, 2010. CPsychol 2009; CSci 2009; AFBPsS 2010. Commn RM, 1972–76. Teacher: Stowe Sch., 1978–79; Bucks CC, 1979–80 and 1981–85; Sen. Lectr, St Mary's Coll., Twickenham, 1985–93; Reader, then Prof., Manchester Metropolitan Univ., 1993–98; Prof. of Physical Educn and Sport Performance, Univ. of Edinburgh, 1998–2005; Performance Dir, UK Athletics, 2005–08; Prof. and Dir, Inst. of Coaching and Performance, Univ. of Central Lancs, 2009–19. Sport Psychologist: RFU, 1990–91; Olympic Weightlifting, 1992–97; Short Track Speed Skating, 1993–99; Scottish Judo, 1999–2004; Scottish Curling, 1999–2004; UK Athletics, 1999–2005; Chelsea FC Acad., 2009–; Dir of Coaching, iZone Driver Performance, 2012–. Director: $P^2E$, 2002–09; Rugby Coaches Assoc., 2012–. Founding Fellow, British Soc. of Martial Arts, 1998; Fellow, BASES, 2010. Godan Karate, 2016. *Publications*: The Use of Physiological Measures in Sport Psychology: a handbook, 1982; (jtly) Working with Teams, 1990; (jtly) Get Ready for Squash, 1990; Sport Psychology and Motor Control, 1992; Applying Psychological Research for Coaching and Performance Enhancement, 1993; (jtly) Talent Identification and Development: an academic review, 2002; (jtly) Rugby Tough, 2002; (ed jtly) Performance Psychology: a practitioners' guide, 2008; (jtly) Talent Development: a practitioner guide, 2017; (ed jtly) The Routledge Handbook of Elite Performance, 2018; over 70 books and book chapters; over 300 peer rev. papers; contrib. learned jls. *Recreations*: scuba and technical diving, outdoor pursuits, curry consumption. *Clubs*: Romford Rugby, Saracens, Bedford Rugby, Northampton and Brackley Rugby; Royal Canoe (Teddington); Busen Martial Arts (Twickenham).

**COLLINS, Deborah;** Chief Operating Officer, Cardiff University, since 2019; *b* 18 April 1963; *d* of Brig. Kenelm John and Angela Charlotte Hathaway; *m* 1991, Tim Collins (marr. diss. 2013); one *s* one *d*. *Educ*: Worcester Coll., Oxford (BA (Jurisprudence) 1984). Articled Clerk, Coward Chance, 1985–87, Solicitor, Clifford Chance, 1987–88; merchant banker, J. Henry Schroder Wagg & Co. Ltd, 1988–91; Govt Legal Service: DTI, 1991–97; European Secretariat, Cabinet Office Legal Advrs, 1997–99; Divl Manager, DFEE Legal, 1999–2002; Legal Advr to Highways Agency, 2002–03; Dir, Legal Services Gp, DTI, 2003–06; Dir, Legal (Ops), HMRC, 2006–07; Strategic Dir, Communities, Law and Governance (formerly Dir, Legal and Democratic Services), 2007–12, Strategic Dir, Envmt and Social Regeneration (formerly Envmt and Leisure), 2012–18, Southwark Council. *Recreations*: mountains, walking, cooking, watching plants grow in my garden. *Address*: Cardiff University, Cardiff CF10 3AT. *T*: (029) 2087 0954.

**COLLINS, Dee,** CBE 2018; QPM 2013; Chief Constable, West Yorkshire Police, since 2016 (Temporary Chief Constable, 2014–16); *b* Altrincham, Feb. 1965; *m* 2017, Derin John Rose. *Educ*: Manchester High Sch. for Girls; Univ. of Manchester Inst. of Sci. and Technol. (BSc Jt Hons). Police officer, Cleveland Police, 1987–2005; Comdr, S Basic Comd Unit, Cumbria Constabulary, 2005–07; Derbyshire Police: Asst Chief Constable Support, 2007–10; seconded to Nat. Police Improvement Agency as a Syndicate Dir, 2010; Strategic Comd Course, 2010; Asst Chief Constable Operational Support; Dep. Chief Constable, West Yorks Police, 2014. *Recreations*: walking, ski-ing, being outdoors. *Address*: West Yorkshire Police Headquarters, PO Box 9, Laburnum Road, Wakefield, W Yorks WF1 3QP. *T*: (01924) 292002. *E*: ccoffice@westyorkshire.pnn.police.uk.

**COLLINS, Francis Sellers,** MD; PhD; Director, National Institutes of Health, USA, since 2009; *b* 14 April 1950; *s* of Fletcher and Margaret Collins; *m* 1998, Diane Lynn Baker; two *d*. *Educ*: Univ. of Virginia, Charlottesville (BS Highest Hons 1970); Yale Univ. (MPhil, PhD Physical Chem. 1974); Univ. of N Carolina Sch. of Medicine (MD Hons 1977). University of Michigan: Asst Prof. of Internal Medicine and Human Genetics, Med. Sch., Ann Arbor, 1984–88; Chief, Div. of Med. Genetics, Dept of Internal Medicine and Human Genetics, 1988–91; Prof. of Internal Medicine and Human Genetics, 1991–93 (on leave, 1993–2003); Dir, Nat. Human Genome Res. Inst., Bethesda, Maryland, 1993–2008. Asst Investigator, 1987–88, Investigator, 1991–93, Howard Hughes Med. Inst., Ann Arbor, Mich. Presidential Medal of Freedom (USA), 2007; Nat. Medal of Sci. (USA), 2009. *Publications*: The Language of Life: DNA and the revolution of personalised medicine, 2010. *Address*: National Institutes of Health, 9000 Rockville Pike, Bethesda, MD 20892, USA.

**COLLINS, Ven. Gavin Andrew;** Archdeacon of The Meon, since 2011; *b* 31 Dec. 1966; *s* of John Collins and Margaret Collins; *m* 1994, Christina Kidd; one *s* two *d*. *Educ*: Trinity Hall, Cambridge (BA 1989; MA 1993); Trinity Coll., Bristol (BA 1996; MA 1997). Ordained deacon, 1997, priest, 1998; Asst Curate, St Barnabas, Cambridge, 1997–2002; Vicar, Christ Church, Chorleywood, 2002–11; Rural Dean, Rickmansworth, 2006–11. Hon. Canon, St Albans Cathedral, 2009–11. *Recreations*: cycling, running, time with my family, engagement in political debate. *Address*: Victoria Lodge, 36 Osborn Road, Fareham PO16 7DS. *T*: (01329) 608895.

**COLLINS, Gerard;** *see* Collins, J. G.

**COLLINS, Prof. Harold Maurice,** PhD; FBA 2012; FLSW; Distinguished Research Professor, and Director, Centre for Study of Knowledge, Expertise and Science, School of Social Sciences, Cardiff University, since 1997; *b* Hitchin, 13 June 1943; *s* of Sidney and Sadie Collins; *m* 2010, Susan Carter; one *s* one *d* and one step *s* one step *d*. *Educ*: Hitchin Grammar Sch.; BSc (Econ) London ext. 1967; Univ. of Essex (MA 1971); Univ. of Bath (PhD 1981). Lectr in Sociol., Liverpool Coll. of Commerce, 1968–70; University of Bath: Lectr, Sen. Lectr, then Reader in Sociol., 1973–89; Dir, Sci. Studies Centre, 1981–85; Prof. of Sociol., 1989–95; Hd, Sch. of Social Scis, 1990–92; Prof. of Sociol., Univ. of Southampton, 1995–97; Affiliated Res. Schol., Dept of Hist. and Philosophy of Sci., Cambridge Univ., 1999. Guest, Xerox Park, Palo Alto, 1987; Visiting Professor: Univ. of Limburg, 1988–90; UCSD, 1993; Tayuan Univ., China, 2006; Univ. of Minas Gerais, Belo Horizonte, Brazil, 2008; Andrew W. Mellon Vis. Prof. of Hist., CIT, 2003; Visiting Research Fellow: Dept of Sci. and Technol. Studies, Cornell Univ., 2001; Max Planck Inst. for Hist. of Sci., Berlin, 2002. Beller Lectr, APS, Boston, 2019. Pres., Soc. for Social Studies of Sci., 1991–93. FLSW 2013. J. D. Bernal Award, Soc. for Social Studies of Sci., 1997. *Publications*: (with T. J. Pinch) Frames of Meaning: the social construction of extraordinary science, 1982; Changing Order: replication and induction in scientific practice, 1985, 2nd edn 1992; Artificial Experts: social knowledge and intelligent machines, 1990; (with T. J. Pinch) The Golem: what everyone should know about science, 1993, 2nd edn 1998 (Robert K. Merton Book Prize, Amer. Sociol Assoc., 1995); (with M. Kusch) The Shape of Actions: what humans and machines can do, 1998; (with T. J. Pinch) The Golem at Large: what you should know about technology, 1998; (ed jtly) The One Culture?: a conversation about science, 2001; Gravity's Shadow: the search for gravitational waves, 2004; (with T. J. Pinch) Dr Golem: how to think about medicine, 2005; (with R. Evans) Rethinking Expertise, 2007; Tacit and Explicit Knowledge, 2010; Gravity's Ghost: scientific discovery in the twenty-first century, 2011; Gravity's Ghost and Big Dog:

scientific discovery and social analysis in the twenty-first century, 2013; Are We All Scientific Experts Now?, 2014; (with R. Evans and C. Higgins) Ball Call: technology's attack on referees and umpires and how to fix it, 2016; Gravity's Kiss: the detection of gravitational waves, 2017; (with R. Evans) Why Democracies Need Science, 2017; Artifictional Intelligence: against humanity's surrender to computers, 2018; Forms of Life: the method and meaning of sociology, 2019. *Recreations:* making unnecessary things with wood taken from skips, banter. *Address:* School of Social Sciences, Cardiff University, Cardiff CF10 3WT. *T:* (029) 2140 9637. *E:* CollinsHM@cf.ac.uk.

COLLINS, Prof. Hugh Graham, FBA 2006; Vinerian Professor of English Law, University of Oxford, since 2013; Fellow, All Souls College, Oxford, since 2013; *b* 21 June 1953; *s* of Richard and Joan Collins; *m* 1983, Prof. Emily Simonoff; two d. *Educ:* Pembroke Coll., Oxford (MA, BCL); Hon. Fellow, 2015); Harvard Law Sch. (LLM). Fellow, Brasenose Coll., Oxford, 1976–91; Prof. of English Law, 1991–2013, Hd, Dept of Law, 1994–97 and 2006–09, LSE; Acting Dean, Faculty of Law, Univ. of Oxford, 2015. Mem., Adv. Forum on Impact of Employment Policies, DTI, later BERR, then BIS, 2006–10. Academic Bencher, Middle Temple, 2014. Member, Editorial Committee: Industrial Law Jl, 1982–; Modern Law Rev., 1992–2015; Eur. Rev. of Contract Law, 2005–. *Publications:* Marxism and Law, 1982; The Law of Contract, 1986, 4th edn 2003; Justice in Dismissal, 1992; Regulating Contracts, 1999; (jtly) Labour Law: texts and materials, 2001, 2nd edn 2005; Employment Law, 2003, 2nd edn 2010; The European Civil Code, 2008; (with G. Teubner) Networks as Connected Contracts, 2011; (jtly) Labour Law, 2012; (jtly) Philosophical Foundations of Labour Law, 2018; (jtly) Foundations of Indirect Discrimination Law, 2018. *Recreations:* opera, theatre, modern art, painting, sailing, building walls, gardening. *Address:* All Souls College, Oxford OX1 4AL. *T:* (01865) 279379.

COLLINS, James Douglas; QC 2012; *b* Bristol, 8 Dec. 1969; *s* of Charles Douglas Collins and Jhoann Temlett Collins; *m* 2001, Sharmila Vijayanti Nikapota; four d. *Educ:* Sherborne Sch., Dorset; Downing Coll., Cambridge (BA 1993). Called to the Bar, Gray's Inn, 1995; in practice as barrister, specialising in commercial litigation and arbitration, 1995–. *Address:* Essex Court Chambers, 24 Lincoln's Inn Fields, WC2A 3EG.

COLLINS, (James) Gerard; Member, European Parliament, 1994–2004 (Vice President, 1998–99); *b* Abbeyfeale, Co. Limerick, 16 Oct. 1938; *s* of late James J. Collins, TD and Margaret Collins; *m* 1969, Hilary Tattan. *Educ:* University Coll., Dublin (BA). Teacher. Asst Gen. Sec., Fianna Fáil, 1965–67. TD (FF) Limerick W, 1967–97; Parly Sec. to Ministers for Industry and Commerce and for the Gaeltacht, 1969–70; Minister for Posts and Telegraphs, 1970–73; opposition front-bench spokesman on agriculture, 1973–75; spokesman on justice, 1975–77; Minister for Justice, 1977–81; Minister for Foreign Affairs, March–Dec. 1982; opposition front-bench spokesman on foreign affairs, 1983–87; Minister for Justice, 1987–89; Minister for Foreign Affairs, 1989–92. Mem., Consultative Assembly, Council of Europe, 1973–77; Chm., Parly Cttee on Secondary Legislation of European Communities, 1983–87. Mem., Limerick CC, 1974–77. *Address:* The Hill, Abbeyfeale, Co. Limerick, Ireland.

COLLINS, Dr Jane Elizabeth, (Mrs David Evans), FRCP, FRCPCH; Chief Executive, Marie Curie (formerly Marie Curie Cancer Care), 2012–19; *b* 19 Oct. 1954; *d* of Thomas and Betsy Collins; *m* 1978, David Evans; one *s* one d. *Educ:* Portsmouth High Sch.; Univ. of London (MSc Clin. Biochem. 1985); Univ. of Birmingham (MB ChB 1978; MD 1988). FRCP 1994; FRCPCH 1996. Consultant Paediatric Neurologist, Guy's Hosp., 1991–94; Consultant Paediatric Neurologist, 1994–96, Consultant in Metabolic Medicine, 1996–2001, Gt Ormond St Hosp.; Med. Dir, Gt Ormond St Hosp. NHS Trust, 1999–2001; Chief Exec., Great Ormond Street Hosp. NHS Trust and Great Ormond Street Hosp. Children's Charity, 2001–12. Paediatric consultant (formerly Children's Doctor columnist), The Times, 1999–2007. Non-exec. Dir, University Coll. London Hosps NHS Foundn Trust, 2019–. Chm., London Clinical Senate Council, 2013–18; Mem., Gen. Adv. Council, 2013–16, Trustee, 2017–, King's Fund. Hon. Fellow: UCL, 2011; UCL Inst. of Child Health, 2016.

COLLINS, Jane Maria; Member (UK Ind) Yorkshire and the Humber Region, European Parliament, 2014–19; *b* East Hardwick, near Pontefract, 17 Feb. 1962. *Educ:* Pontefract Girls' High Sch. Head Girl, with Robert Ward, racehorse trainer, Doncaster, 1980–85; with Alex Stewart, trainer, Newmarket, 1985, subseq. at family stable yard, Selby; equine physiotherapist, 1995–2004. Contested (UK Ind): Scunthorpe, 2010; Barnsley, March 2011; Rotherham, Nov. 2012, 2015.

COLLINS, Dame Joan (Henrietta), DBE 2015 (OBE 1997); actress and writer; *b* 23 May; *er* d of late Joseph Collins and Elsa (*née* Bessant); *m* 1st, 1954, Maxwell Reed (marr. diss. 1957; he d 1974); 2nd, 1963, (George) Anthony Newley (marr. diss. 1970; he d 1999); one *s* one d; 3rd, 1972, Ronald S. Kass (marr. diss. 1983; he d 1986); one d; 4th, 1985, Peter Holm (marr. diss. 1987); 5th, 2002, Percy Gibson. *Educ:* Francis Holland Sch.; RADA. *Films include:* Lady Godiva Rides Again, I Believe in You, 1952; Our Girl Friday, The Square Ring, 1953; The Good Die Young, Turn the Key Softly, 1954; Land of the Pharaohs, The Virgin Queen, The Girl in the Red Velvet Swing, 1955; The Opposite Sex, 1956; The Wayward Bus, Island in the Sun, Sea Wife, 1957; The Bravados, 1958; Rally Round the Flag, Boys, 1959; Esther and the King, Seven Thieves, 1960; Road to Hong Kong, 1962; Warning Shot, The Subterfuge, 1967; Can Hieronymus Merkin Ever Forget Mercy Humppe and Find True Happiness?, Drive Hard Drive Fast, 1969; Up in the Cellar, The Executioner, 1970; Quest for Love, Revenge, 1971; Tales from the Crypt, Fear in the Night, 1972; Tales that witness Madness, 1973; Dark Places, Alfie Darling, 1974; The Call of the Wolf, I don't want to be born, 1975; The Devil within Her, 1976; Empire of the Ants, 1977; The Big Sleep, 1978; Sunburn, The Stud, 1979; The Bitch, 1980; The Nutcracker, 1984; The Cartier Affair, 1985; Decadence, 1994; In the Bleak Midwinter, 1995; The Clandestine Marriage, 1998; Joseph and the Amazing Technicolor Dreamcoat, 1999; The Flintstones in Viva Rock Vegas, 2000; Those Old Broads, 2000; Ellis in Glamourland, 2005; Fetish, 2010 (Best Actress, NY City Internat. Film Fest.); The Time of Their Lives, 2017; Gerry, 2018 (Best Actress Award, LA Shorts Fest.); *stage includes:* The Last of Mrs Cheyney, Cambridge Th., 1980; Private Lives, Aldwych, 1990, US tour and NY, 1992; Love Letters, US, 2000; Over the Moon, Old Vic, 2001; Full Circle, UK tour, 2004; An Evening with Joan Collins, UK tour, 2006, NY, 2010; Legends, US tour, 2006–07; Dick Whittington, Birmingham Hippodrome, 2010; One Night with Joan Collins, Leicester Sq. Th., 2013, 2014; Joan Collins Unscripted, UK tour, 2019; *television includes:* serials: Dynasty, 1981–89; Sins, 1986; Monte Carlo, 1986; Pacific Palisades, 1997; Guiding Light, 2002; Footballers' Wives, 2006; Benidorm, 2014; American Horror Story, 2018; Hawaii Five-O, 2019; series: Tonight at 8.30, 1991; film: Annie: A Royal Adventure, 1995; documentary: Joan Does Glamour, 2009; also appearances in plays and series. Awards: Best TV Actress, Golden Globe, 1982; Hollywood Women's Press Club, 1982; Favourite TV Performer, People's Choice, 1985. *Publications:* Past Imperfect (autobiog.), 1978; The Joan Collins Beauty Book, 1980; Katy: a fight for life, 1982; My Secrets, 1994; Second Act (autobiog.), 1996; My Friends' Secrets, 2000; Joan's Way, 2002; The Art of Living Well, 2007; The World According to Joan, 2011; Passion for Life (autobiog.), 2013; *novels:* Prime Time, 1988; Love and Desire and Hate, 1990; Too Damn Famous, 1995; Star Quality, 2002; Misfortune's Daughters, 2004; The St Tropez Lonely Hearts Club, 2015.

COLLINS, Sir John (Alexander), Kt 1993; Chairman, DSG international (formerly Dixons Group) plc, 2002–09 (Deputy Chairman, 2001–02); *b* 10 Dec. 1941; *s* of John Constantine Collins and Nancy Isobel Mitchell; *m* 1965, Susan Mary Hooper. *Educ:* Campbell Coll., Belfast; Reading Univ. Joined Shell, 1964; various appointments in Shell in Kenya, Nigeria, Colombia and UK; Chm. and Chief Exec., Shell UK, 1990–93; Chief Exec., Vestey Gp, 1994–2001; Chm., National Power, 1997–2000. Non-executive Director: BSkyB, 1994–97; N. M. Rothschild & Sons, 1995–2005; LSO, 1997–2000; P&O, 1998–2006; Stoll Moss Theatres Ltd, 1999–2000; Rothschild Continuation Hldgs AG, 1999–2010; 3i Infrastructure plc, 2009–14; Blue Diamond Gp, 2014–. Chm., Cantab Pharmaceuticals plc, 1996–99. Chairman: Adv. Cttee on Business and Envmt, 1991–93; Energy Adv. Panel, DTI, 2001–03; Sustainable Energy Policy Adv. Bd, DTI/DEFRA, 2004–07. Mem., Supervisory sub-cttee, Treasury and Resources, States of Guernsey Govt Dept., 2013–16. Pres., The Energy Institute, 2005–07. Chm., Guernsey Employment Trust, 2015–. Gov., Wellington Coll., 1995–99. *Recreations:* theatre, sailing. *Address:* Le Repos Au Coin, La Fosse, St Martin, Guernsey GY4 6EB. *Clubs:* Royal Yacht Squadron (Cowes); United (Guernsey); Royal Guernsey Golf.

See also R. Collins.

COLLINS, John Morris; barrister; a Recorder of the Crown Court; 1980–98; *b* 25 June 1931; *s* of late Emmanuel Cohen, MBE, and Ruby Cohen; *m* 1968, Sheila Brummer; one d. *Educ:* Leeds Grammar Sch.; The Queen's Coll., Oxford (MA LitHum). Called to Bar, Middle Temple, 1956, Member of North Eastern Circuit; Hd of Chambers, 1966–2001, Jt Hd of Chambers, 2001–02; a Deputy Circuit Judge, 1970–80. Pres., Leeds Jewish Representative Council, 1986–89. Nat. Pro Bono Award, 2016. *Publications:* Summary Justice, 1963; various articles in legal periodicals, etc. *Recreations:* walking, travelling. *Address:* (home) 14 Sandhill Oval, Leeds LS17 8EA. *T:* (0113) 268 6008; (chambers) Zenith Chambers, 10 Park Square, Leeds LS1 2LH. *T:* (0113) 245 5438, *Fax:* (0113) 242 3515.

COLLINS, John Vincent, MD; FRCP; Consultant Physician, since 1973; Consultant Physician and Director of Education and Professional Development, Benenden Hospital, Kent, 2007–12; Medical Director, Lister Hospital, 2008–15; *b* 16 July 1938; *s* of Thomas Ernest Vincent Collins and Zillah Phoebe Collins; *m* 1st, 1963, Helen Eluned Cash (marr. diss. 2008); one *s* one d; 2nd, 2009, Hilary Anne Booker. *Educ:* Guy's Hosp. Med. and Dental Sch. (BDS 1961; MD 1974). FRCP 1981. Dental and Medical Schs, Guy's Hosp., 1956–66; Guy's, St Mary's, Royal Brompton and Westminster Hosps, 1967–72; Hon. Consultant Physician and Sen. Lectr, St Bartholomew's Hosp. Med. Sch., London, 1973–76; Consultant Physician: Royal Brompton Hosp., 1976–2003; St Stephen's Hosp., 1979–89; Westminster Hosp., 1989–93; Chelsea & Westminster Hosp., 1993–2003 (Med. Dir, 1994–2003); Hon. Consultant, In Pensioners, Royal Hosp., Chelsea, 1980–2003. Sen. Med. Advr, Benenden Healthcare Soc., 1979–2011; Gp Med. Advr, Smith & Nephew plc, 1987–2010. Chm., Clinical Standards Cttee, RCP, 2000–03. Mem., Soc. of Apothecaries. *Publications:* more than 150 papers, two monographs, and contribs to books. *Recreations:* painting, travel, tennis. *Address:* The Lister Hospital, Chelsea Bridge Road, SW1W 8RH.

COLLINS, Judith, (Mrs R. J. H. Collins); see McClure, J.

COLLINS, Kama Louise; see Melly, K. L.

COLLINS, Kathleen Joyce, (Kate), (Mrs D. A. L. Cooke); Director, Career Development and Assessment, Home Office, 2006–07; *b* 12 March 1952; *d* of Norman Jeffrey Collins and Phyllis Laura Collins (*née* Yardley); *m* 1984, David Arthur Lawrence Cooke, *qv*. *Educ:* Lady Margaret Hall, Oxford (BA Mod. Langs 1973; MA 1974). Joined Home Office as Immigration Officer, 1975; Admin. Trainee, 1977; Principal, 1982; Dep. Chief Insp., 1988–91, Dir (Ports), 1991–94, Immigration Service; Cabinet Office, 1994–96; Home Office: Police Dept, 1997; Dep. Dir Gen., Immigration and Nationality Directorate, 1998–2000; Director: Organised Crime, 2000–03; Adelphi Prog., 2003–06. *Recreations:* music, reading, countryside.

COLLINS, Sir Kenneth Darlingston, (Sir Ken), Kt 2003; Chairman, Scottish Environment Protection Agency, 1999–2007; *b* 12 Aug. 1939; *s* of Nicholas Collins and Ellen Williamson; *m* 1966, Georgina Frances Pollard; one *s* one d. *Educ:* St John's Grammar Sch.; Hamilton Acad.; Glasgow Univ. (BSc Hons); Strathclyde Univ. (MSc). FRSGS 1993. Left school, 1956; steelworks apprentice, 1956–59; univ., 1960–65; planning officer, 1965–66; WEA Tutor-Organiser, 1966–67; Lecturer: Glasgow Coll. of Bldg, 1967–69; Paisley Coll. of Technol., 1969–79. MEP (Lab) Strathclyde E, 1979–99. European Parliament: Dep. Leader, Labour Gp, 1979–84; Socialist spokesman on envmt, public health and consumer protection, 1984–89; Chm., Cttee on Envmt, Public Health and Consumer Protection, 1979–84 and 1989–99 (Vice Chm., 1984–87); Chm., Conf. of Cttee Chairmen, 1993–99. Dir, Inst. for Eur. Envmt Policy, London, 1991–99 (Bd Mem., 1999–2006). Member: EU High-Level Gp on Competitiveness, Energy and the Envmt, 2005–08; Adv. Bd, ESRC Genomics Policy and Res. Forum, 2006–08; Professional Practices Panel, Eur. Public Affairs Consultancies' Assoc., 2006–09. Member: East Kilbride Town and Dist Council, 1973–79; Lanark CC, 1973–75; East Kilbride Develt Corp., 1976–79; Bd, Forward Scotland, 1996–2003; Bd, EEA, 2000–05; Chairman: NE Glasgow Children's Panel, 1974–76; Central Scotland Forest (formerly Countryside) Trust, 1998–2001; Adv. Cttee, Scottish Alliance for Geoscis, Envmt and Society, 2008–10. Hon. Sen. Res. Fellow, Dept of Geography, Lancaster Univ., 1991–98; Associate Fellow, Eur. Centre for Public Affairs, 1999–. Vice-Pres., Assoc. of Drainage Authorities. Hon. Mem., Landscape Inst. Member: Fabian Soc.; Amnesty Internat.; Labour Movement in Europe; Hon. Pres., Scottish Assoc. of Geography Teachers, 2003–06; Hon. Vice-President: Royal Envmtl Health Inst. of Scotland, 1983–2009; Internat. Fedn on Envmtl Health, 1987; Inst. of Trading Standards Admin; Inst. of Environmental Health Officers; Nat. Soc. for Clean Air; Town and Country Planning Assoc. Chm., Tak Tent Cancer Support Charity, 1999–2002; Ambassador, Nat. Asthma Campaign Scotland, 2002. Fellow, Industry and Parlt Trust, 1984. Hon. FCIWEM 1994; Hon. FCIWM 2001. Mem. Adv. Bd, Jl Water Law. DUniv Paisley, 2004; Hon. DSc Glasgow, 2009. *Publications:* contributed to European Parliament reports; various articles on European envmt policy. *Recreations:* listening to music, playing the piano, dog walking, gardening. *Address:* 11 Stuarton Park, East Kilbride, Lanarkshire G74 4LA. *T:* (01355) 221345.

COLLINS, Lesley Elizabeth; see Appleby, L. E.

COLLINS, Margaret Elizabeth, CBE 1983; RRC; Matron-in-Chief, Queen Alexandra's Royal Naval Nursing Service, 1980–83; *b* 13 Feb. 1927; *d* of James Henry Collins and Amy Collins. *Educ:* St Anne's Convent Grammar Sch., Southampton. RRC 1978 (ARRC 1965). Royal Victoria Hosp., Bournemouth, SRN 1949; West Middlesex Hosp., CMB Part 1; entered QARNNS as Nursing Sister, 1953; accepted for permanent service, 1958; Matron, 1972; Principal Matron, 1976. SSStJ 1978. QHNS, 1980–83. *Recreations:* gardening, theatre-going. *Address:* Lancastria, 5 First Marine Avenue, Barton-on-Sea, Hants BH25 6DP. *T:* (01425) 612374.

COLLINS, Mark; see Collins, N. M.

**COLLINS, Prof. Matthew,** PhD; FBA 2014; McDonald Professor in Palaeoproteomics, University of Cambridge, since 2018; Niels Bohr Professor in Palaeoproteomics, University of Copenhagen, since 2016. *Educ:* Univ. Coll. of N Wales (BSc Zool. with Marine Zool. 1982); Univ. of Glasgow (PhD Geol. 1986). NERC Res. Fellow, Dept of Geol., Univ. of Glasgow and Dept of Biochem., Univ. of Leiden, 1986–89; Royal Soc. Eur. Fellow, Dept of Chem., Univ. of Leiden, 1989–90; Postdoctoral Res. Asst, NERC Biomolecular Palaeontol. Special Topic, Dept of Geol., Univ. of Bristol, 1990–92; Lectr in Biogeochem., 1992–2001, Reader in Biogeochem., 2001–03, Univ. of Newcastle upon Tyne; University of York: Reader in Archaeol., 2003–05; Co-Founder, BioArCh, 2003; Prof. of Biomolecular Archaeol., 2006–18. Prof. in Biomolecular Archaeol., Vrije Univ., Amsterdam, 2005–14. *Publications:* contribs to learned jls. *Address:* Department of Archaeology, University of Cambridge, Cambridge CB2 3DZ.

**COLLINS, Michael;** aerospace consultant; Vice President, LTV Aerospace and Defense Company (formerly Vought Corporation), 1980–85; former NASA Astronaut; Command Module Pilot, Apollo 11 rocket flight to the Moon, July 1969; *b* Rome, Italy, 31 Oct. 1930; *s* of Maj.-Gen. and Mrs James L. Collins, Washington, DC, USA; *m* 1957, Patricia M. Finnegan (*d* 2014), Boston, Mass; two *d* (one *s* decd). *Educ:* St Albans Sch., Washington, DC (grad.). US Mil. Academy, West Point, NY (BSc); advanced through grades to Colonel; Harvard Business Sch. (AMP), 1974. Served as an experimental flight test officer, Air Force Flight Test Center, Edwards Air Force Base, Calif; he was one of the third group of astronauts named by NASA in Oct. 1963; served as backup pilot for Gemini 7 mission; as pilot with John Young on the 3-day 44-revolution Gemini 10 mission, launched 18 July 1966, he shared record-setting flight (successful rendezvous and docking with a separately launched Agena target vehicle; completed two periods of extravehicular activity); Command Module Pilot for Apollo flight, first lunar landing, in orbit 20 July 1969, when Neil Armstrong and Edwin Aldrin landed on the Moon. Asst Sec. of State for Public Affairs, US, 1970–71; Dir, Nat. Air and Space Museum, Smithsonian Institution, 1971–78; Under Sec., Smithsonian Inst., 1978–80. Maj. Gen. Air Force Reserve, retired. Fellow, Soc. of Experimental Test Pilots. Member, Order of Daedalians. Hon. degrees from: Stonehill Coll.; St Michael's Coll.; Northeastern Univ.; Southeastern Univ. Presidential Medal of Freedom, NASA; FAI Gold Space Medal; DSM (NASA); DSM (AF); Exceptional Service Medal (NASA); Astronaut Wings; DFC; Congressional Gold Medal, 2011. *Publications:* Carrying the Fire (autobiog.), 1974; Flying to the Moon and Other Strange Places (for children), 1976; Liftoff, 1988; Mission to Mars, 1990. *Recreations:* fishing, painting.

**COLLINS, Michael Brendan,** OBE 1983 (MBE 1969); HM Diplomatic Service, retired; HM Consul-General, Istanbul, 1988–92; *b* 9 Sept. 1932; *s* of Daniel James Collins, GM and Mary Bridget Collins (*née* Kennedy); *m* 1959, Maria Elena Lozar. *Educ:* St Illtyd's College, Cardiff; University College London. HM Forces, 1953–55. FO 1956; Santiago, Chile, 1959; Consul, Santiago, Cuba, 1962; FO, 1964; Second, later First, Sec. (Admin.) and Consul, Prague, 1967; Dep. High Comr, Bathurst, The Gambia, 1970; Head of Chancery, Algiers, 1972; First Sec., FCO, 1975; Consul Commercial, Montreal, 1978; Consul for Atlantic Provinces of Canada, Halifax, 1981; Counsellor (Economic and Commercial), Brussels, 1983. *Recreations:* walking, reading, music.

**COLLINS, Michael Geoffrey;** QC 1988; barrister, arbitrator and mediator; *b* 4 March 1948; *s* of late Francis Geoffrey Collins and Margaret Isabelle Collins; *m* 1985, Bonnie Gayle Bird. *Educ:* Peterhouse, Rhodesia (now Zimbabwe); Exeter Univ. (LLB). Called to the Bar, Gray's Inn, 1971, Bencher, 1999. A Recorder, 1997–2001. Special Legal Consultant: Fulbright & Jaworski LLP, Washington, 2002–06; Hanscom, Collins and Hall (formerly Crandall, Hanscom & Collins) PA, Rockland, ME, 2006–. *Publications:* contributor, Private International Litigation, 1988. *Recreations:* golf, tennis, watercolours, amateur dramatics. *Address:* 9304 Belmart Road, Potomac, MD 20854, USA. *T:* (301) 9830024; Essex Court Chambers, 24 Lincoln's Inn Fields, WC2A 3EG. *T:* (020) 7813 8000.

**COLLINS, Michael John,** MBE 2015; clarinettist; Professor, Royal College of Music, since 1983; *b* 27 Jan. 1962; *s* of Gwendoline Violet and Fred Allenby Collins; *m* 1997, Isabelle van Keulen (marr. diss. 2008); one *s* one *d. Educ:* Royal Coll. of Music (ARCM, Clarinet and Piano with Hons). FRCM 2010. BBC Young Musician of the Year, 1978. Principal clarinet: London Sinfonietta, 1982–2002; Nash Ensemble, 1982–2002; Philharmonia Orchestra, 1988–95; Dir, London Winds Ensemble, 1988–; Principal Conductor, City of London Sinfonia, 2010–. Many solo recordings. Hon. RAM 1997. Musicians' Co. Medal, 1980; competition winner: Leeds, 1980; Concert Artists' Guild, NY, 1982 (Amcon Award); Internat. Rostrum of Young Performers, Unesco, 1985; Tagore Gold Medal, 1982. *Recreations:* walking, driving, wildlife.

**COLLINS, Neil Adam;** Columnist, Financial Times, since 2012; *s* of late Clive and Joan Collins; *m* 1981, Vivien Goldsmith (marr. diss. 1994); one *d*; *m* 1999, Julia Frances Barnes; one *s* one *d. Educ:* Uppingham School; Selwyn College, Cambridge (MA). City Editor: Evening Standard, 1979–84; Sunday Times, 1984–86; Daily Telegraph, 1986–2005; Flyfishing correspondent, The Spectator, 2002–04; Columnist: Evening Standard, 2005–09; Reuters, 2009–10; FT Alphaville, 2010–12. Director: Templeton Emerging Markets Investment Trust plc, 2006–16; Dyson James Ltd, 2006–07; Finsbury Growth & Income Trust, 2008–. Gov., St Andrew's School, Eastbourne, 1999–2003. Financial Journalist of the Year, British Press Awards, 2002. *Recreations:* walking, wine, fly fishing, opera, model railways. *Address:* 12 Gertrude Street, SW10 0JN. *T:* (020) 7352 9595, 07836 256674.

**COLLINS, (Nicholas) Mark,** PhD; Chairman: Galapagos Conservation Trust, since 2012 (Trustee, since 2006); Swallowtail and Birdwing Butterfly Trust, since 2017; *b* 23 April 1952; *s* of late John Anthony Collins and of Mary Collins (*née* Humphries); *m* 1982, Melanie Margaret Stephens; one *s* one *d. Educ:* Wadham Coll., Oxford (BA 1973, MA 1974); Imperial Coll., London (DIC 1977; PhD 1977); MBA Open Univ. 1999. Centre for Overseas Pest Res., Nigeria and Sarawak, 1974–80; Internat. Centre for Insect Physiol. and Ecol., Kenya, 1980–82; IUCN, 1982–88; World Conservation Monitoring Centre, 1988–2000 (Dir, 1994–2000); UNEP, Cambridge and Kenya, 2000–05; Dir, Commonwealth Foundn, 2005–11. Vis. Fellow, Univ. of Westminster, 2011–12. HM Inspector of Zoos, 1990–2000. Trustee: FFI, 1989–98; Wildscreen Trust, 1997–2004; Total Foundn, 2003–06; Member: Darwin Initiative Adv. Cttee, 2001–06; Darwin Expert Cttee, 2012–16. Chairman: Cambridge Sustainable City, 1996–2002; Cambridge and Peterborough Sustainable Develt Round Table, 2003–04. Mem., Commonwealth Scholarship Commn, 2008–11. Trustee, Earthwatch Europe, 2011–18. Gov., Meridian Co. Primary Sch., 1996–99. Member: Royal Entomol Soc.; RGS. Busk Medal, RGS, 2000. *Publications:* (jtly) The IUCN Invertebrate Red Data Book, 1983; (with M. G. Morris) Threatened Swallowtail Butterflies of the World, 1985; (ed jtly) Kora: an ecological inventory of the Kora National Reserve, Kenya, 1986; (ed jtly) Insect-Fungus Interactions, 1988; (ed) The Management and Welfare of Invertebrates in Captivity, 1989; The Last Rainforests, 1990; (ed jtly) The Conservation of Insects and their Habitats, 1991; The Conservation Atlas of Tropical Forests: (ed jtly) Asia, 1991, (ed jtly) Africa, 1992; (editl advr and co-ordinator) Encyclopedia of the Biosphere, Vol. II, Tropical Rainforests, 2000; (ed jtly) From Hook to Plate: the state of marine fisheries, 2010; numerous contribs to learned jls. *Recreations:* boating, countryside. *Address:* 49 West Street, Comberton, Cambridge CB23 7DS. *T:* (01223) 262458. *E:* collinsmark@gmail.com.

**COLLINS, Patrick Michael;** Chief Sports Writer, Mail on Sunday, 1982–2014; *b* 23 Nov. 1943; *s* of Patrick and Julia Collins (*née* Canty); *m* 1969, Julie Kathleen Grundon; three *s* one *d. Educ:* St Joseph's Acad., Blackheath, London. Reporter, Kentish Mercury, 1962–65; sports writer: Sunday Citizen, 1965–67; News of the World, 1967–78; sports columnist: London Evening News, 1978–80; London Evening Standard, 1980–82; Punch, 1990–92. Mem., English Sports Council, 1999–2002. Pres., Sports Journalists' Assoc. of GB, 2015–. British Sports Journalism Awards: British Sports Journalist of the Year, 1989, 1990, 1997, 2002, 2008; Sports Feature Writer of the Year, 1993, 2002; Sports Columnist of the Year, 1999, 2000, 2004, 2006, 2012. *Publications:* (with Pat Pocock) Percy, 1987; The Sportswriter, 1996; Among the Fans: a year of watching the watchers, 2011. *Recreations:* watching cricket, reading modern history, family.

**COLLINS, His Honour Paul Howard,** CBE 1999; a Circuit Judge, 1991–2010; Senior Circuit Judge, Central London Civil Justice Centre, 2001–10; a Deputy Circuit Judge, 2010–12; *b* 31 Jan. 1944; *s* of Michael and Madie Collins; *m* 1987, Sue Fallows; one step *s. Educ:* Orange Hill Grammar Sch.; St Catherine's Coll., Oxford (MA). Called to the Bar, Lincoln's Inn, 1966 (Bencher, 2000); a Recorder, 1989. Designated Civil Judge for London Gp of County Cts, 2001–08. Mem., Parole Bd, 2010–14. Dir of Studies, Judicial Studies Bd, 1997–99. Chm., Council, Inns of Court Disciplinary Tribunals, 2010–13. *E:* paulhowardcollins@gmail.com. *Clubs:* Athenæum, Questors.

**COLLINS, Pauline,** OBE 2001; actress (stage and television); *b* Exmouth, Devon, 3 Sept. 1940; *d* of William Henry Collins and Mary Honora Callanan; *m* John Alderton, *qv*; two *s* one *d. Educ:* Convent of the Sacred Heart, Hammersmith, London; Central Sch. of Speech and Drama. *Stage:* 1st appearance in A Gazelle in Park Lane, Theatre Royal, Windsor, 1962; 1st London appearance in Passion Flower Hotel, Prince of Wales, 1965; The Erpingham Camp, Royal Court, 1967; The Happy Apple, Hampstead, 1967, and Apollo, 1970; Importance of Being Earnest, Haymarket, 1968; The Night I chased the Women with an Eel, 1969; Come As You Are (3 parts), New, 1970; Judies, Comedy, 1974; Engaged, National Theatre, Old Vic, 1975; Confusions, Apollo, 1976; Rattle of a Simple Man, Savoy, 1980; Romantic Comedy, Apollo, 1983; Shirley Valentine, Vaudeville, 1988, NY, 1989 (Tony Award, Best Actress, 1989); Shades, Albery, 1992; *television,* 1962–: series: Upstairs Downstairs; No Honestly; P. G. Wodehouse; Thomas and Sarah; The Black Tower; Forever Green; The Ambassador; Mount Pleasant; Dickensian; plays: Long Distance Information, 1979; Knockback, 1984; Man and Boy, 2002; Sparkling Cyanide, 2003; Famous Last, 2009; *film:* What We Did on Our Holiday, 2006; *films:* Shirley Valentine, 1989 (Evening Standard Film Actress of the Year, 1989; BAFTA Best Actress Award, 1990); City of Joy, 1992; My Mother's Courage, 1997; Paradise Road, 1997; Mrs Caldicot's Cabbage War, 2002; You Will Meet a Tall Dark Stranger, 2011; Albert Nobbs, 2012; Quartet, 2013; The Time of Their Lives, 2017. Dr *hc* Liverpool Poly., 1991. *Publications:* Letter to Louise, 1992. *Address:* c/o Independent Talent Group Ltd, 40 Whitfield Street, W1T 2RH.

**COLLINS, Peter;** *see* Collins, V. P.

**COLLINS, Peter G.,** RSA 1974 (ARSA 1966); painter in oil; *b* Inverness, 21 June 1935; *s* of E. G. Collins, FRCSE; *m* 1959, Myra Mackintosh (marr. diss. 1978); one *s* one *d. Educ:* Fettes Coll., Edinburgh; Edinburgh Coll. of Art. Studied in Italy, on Andrew Grant Major Travelling Scholarship, 1957–58. Work in permanent collections: Aberdeen Civic; Glasgow Civic; Holyrood Palace. *Recreations:* music, art-historical research. *Address:* Royal Scottish Academy, The Mound, Edinburgh EH2 2EL; The Cottage, Hilltown of Ballindean, Inchture, Perthshire PH14 9QS.

**COLLINS, Philip,** LVO 1994; singer, drummer, songwriter, actor and record producer; Trustee, Prince's Trust, since 1983; patron of numerous charities; *b* 30 Jan. 1951; *s* of Greville and June Collins; *m* 1st, 1975 (marr. diss.); one *s* one *d*; 2nd, 1984, Jill Tavelman (marr. diss. 1995); one *d*; 3rd, 1999, Orianne Cevey (marr. diss. 2008); two *s. Educ:* primary and secondary schs; Barbara Speake Stage Sch. Played parts in various television, film and stage productions, 1965–67; mem. of various rock groups, 1967–70; drummer, 1970–96, lead singer, 1975–96, Genesis; started writing songs, 1976; toured Japan, USA and Europe, 1978, 1987; reunion tour, Europe and N America, 2007; first solo album, 1981; solo world tours, 1985, 1990; started producing records for other artists, 1981. Albums include: *with Genesis:* Nursery Cryme, 1971; Foxtrot, 1972; Genesis Live, 1973; Selling England by the Pound, 1973; The Lamb Lies Down on Broadway, 1974; A Trick of the Tail, 1976; Genesis Rock Roots, 1976; Wind and Wuthering, 1977; Genesis Seconds Out, 1977; And Then There Were Three, 1978; Duke, 1980; Abacab, 1981; Three Sides Live, 1982; Genesis, 1983; Invisible Touch, 1986; We Can't Dance, 1991; *solo:* Face Value, 1981; Hello … I must be Going, 1982; No Jacket Required, 1985; But Seriously, 1989; Both Sides, 1993; Dance into the Light, 1996; Hits, 1998; Testify, 2002; Going Back, 2010. *Films:* Buster (lead role), 1988; Frauds, 1993. Numerous awards, incl. Grammy (eight), Ivor Novello (six), Brit (four), Variety Club of GB (two), Silver Clef (two), Academy Award, and Elvis awards. *Publications:* Not Dead Yet (autobiog.), 2016.

**COLLINS, Philip James;** columnist, The Times, since 2009 (Deputy Chief Leader Writer, 2009–13, Chief Leader Writer, 2013–15); Associate Editor, Prospect, since 2015; Founder and Writer-in-Chief, The Draft, since 2018; *b* 16 May 1967; *s* of late Frederick John Collins and Jennifer Anne Collins (*née* Taylor, now Dawson); *m* 2002, Geeta Guru-Murthy; two *s. Educ:* Birmingham Univ. (BA Hons 1988); Birkbeck Coll., London (MSc Dist. 1991); St John's Coll., Cambridge. Res. Officer, London Weekend TV, 1988–89; Political Asst to Frank Field, MP, 1989–92; Research Officer: Inst. of Educn, London Univ., 1992; Fleming Investment Mgt, 1995–97; Equity Strategist: HSBC James Capel, 1997–99; Dresdner Kleinwort Benson, 1999–2000; Dir, Social Mkt Foundn, 2000–05; Chief Speech Writer, Prime Minister's Policy Directorate, 2005–07; Sen. Vis. Fellow, LSE, 2007–09; Visiting Fellow: Dept of Public Policy, Univ. of Oxford, 2010–; University Coll., Oxford, 2016. Chm. Trustees, Demos, 2008–18. FRSA. *Publications:* (ed) An Authority in Education, 2001; The Men from the Boys, 2002; (ed) Culture or Anarchy?, 2002; Bobby Dazzler, 2003; (ed) Reinventing Government Again, 2004; (with R. Reeves) Liberal Republic, 2009; The Art of Speeches and Presentations, 2012; When They Go Low, We Go High: speeches that shape the world - and why we need them, 2017; Start Again: how we can fix our broken politics, 2018. *Recreations:* music, cricket, football, poetry, television, philosophy. *Address:* The Times, 1 London Bridge Street, SE1 9GF. *E:* phil.collins@thetimes.co.uk.

**COLLINS, Richard Edward Charles,** FRCS; Vice President, Royal College of Surgeons of England, 2009–11; *b* Moncton, NB, 9 Jan. 1943; *s* of Edward Collins and Jessie Collins (*née* Charles); *m* 1971, Valerie Margaret Celba; three *d. Educ:* Chigwell Sch.; St George's Hosp. Med. Sch., London (MB BS 1967); Harvard Med. Sch. MRCS 1967, FRCS 1971; LRCP 1967. Consultant Surgeon, Kent and Canterbury, and Thanet Hosps, then East Kent Hosps NHS Trust, 1976–2008. Member, Council: Assoc. of Surgeons of GB and Ire., 1996–2002; RCS, 2002–11; Pres., British Assoc. of Endocrine Surgeons, 2002–03. Chm., Gen. Surgery, Intercollegiate Exam. Bd, 1998–2001. Kent Ambassador, 2007 (Chm., 2012–). FRCSEd *ad hominem* 2000; FRSocMed 1977. Freeman, City of London, 2002; Liveryman, Barbers' Co., 2006. Member: Kent Ornithological Soc., 1971–; Lord's Taverners, 2012–. *Publications:* (contrib.) Birds of Kent, 1981; chapters in various surgical textbooks on thrombosis prophylaxis, endocrine surgery; papers on endocrine surgery, surgical trng and orgn of surgical and trauma services. *Recreations:* cricket, birdwatching, fly-fishing. *Address:* Seatonden, Ickham, Canterbury, Kent CT3 1SL. *Clubs:* MCC; Kent County Cricket (Pres., 2005; Vice-Chm., 2013–); Surgical 60 Travelling.

**COLLINS, Robert;** Managing Director, Waitrose Ltd, since 2016; *b* Nairobi, 1970; *s* of Sir John (Alexander) Collins, *qv; m* 1997, Fleur Benton Jones; two *s* one *d. Educ:* Wellington Coll.; Univ. of Edinburgh (MA Spanish and Business Studies). Joined John Lewis Partnership, 1993; Waitrose Ltd: e-Commerce Dir, 2007–09; Personnel Dir, 2009–11; Retail Dir, 2011–16. *Recreations:* sailing, tennis. *Address:* Waitrose Ltd, Waite House, Doncastle Road, Bracknell RG12 8YA. *T:* (01344) 424680.

**COLLINS, Sir Rory (Edwards),** Kt 2011; FMedSci; FRS 2015; Co-director, Clinical Trial Service Unit and Epidemiological Studies Unit, since 1986, British Heart Foundation Professor of Medicine and Epidemiology, since 1996, Nuffield Professor of Population Health, since 2016, and Head, Nuffield Department of Population Health, since 2013, University of Oxford; Fellow, St John's College, Oxford, since 2016; *b* Hong Kong, 3 Jan. 1955; *s* of Jack Collins and Catherine Collins (*née* Burke). *Educ:* Dulwich Coll., London; George Washington Univ., USA (BSc Stats 1977); St Thomas's Hosp. Med. Sch., London (MB BS 1981); St Peter's Coll., Oxford (MSc Stats 1983). FRCPE 2002. Hon FBPhS 2017. Res. Fellow, Dept of Cardiovascular Medicine and Clin. Trial Service Unit, Univ. of Oxford, 1981–86. FMedSci 2004. *Recreation:* tennis. *Address:* Clinical Trial Service Unit and Epidemiological Studies Unit, Nuffield Department of Population Health, Richard Doll Building, Old Road Campus, Roosevelt Drive, Oxford OX3 7LF. *T:* (01865) 743743, *Fax:* (01865) 743985. *E:* rory.collins@ndph.ox.ac.uk.

**COLLINS, Sarah;** *see* Veale, S.

**COLLINS, Simon C.;** *see* Crawford Collins.

**COLLINS, Simon Jeremy;** Principal, Simon J. Collins & Associates Ltd, since 2017; Partner, 1999–2017, and Chairman and Senior Partner, 2012–17, KPMG LLP, now Senior Partner Emeritus; *b* London, 13 April 1960; *s* of Bernard and Sylvia Collins; *m* 1986, Simone Bersinski; one *s* one *d. Educ:* Haberdashers' Aske's Sch., Elstree; Victoria Univ. of Manchester (BA (Econ) 1982). ACA 1986. Trng contract, Price Waterhouse, 1982–87; Sen. Manager, S. G. Warburg & Co., 1987–91; Man. Dir and Hd, Debt Structuring, Nat West, 1991–98. Trustee, Pancreatic Cancer UK, 2012–. Chm., RAF100 Appeal Bd, 2016–. Mem., Chartered Accountants' Co., 2013–. Mem., Global Leadership Bd, Manchester Univ., 2013–. *Recreations:* family, opera, motoring, art deco objects. *E:* simon@simonjcollins.com.

**COLLINS, Prof. Susan Alexis Regine,** PhD; artist; Professor of Fine Art, since 2010, and Director, Slade Centre for Electronic Media in Fine Art, since 1995, Slade School of Fine Art, University College London (Slade Professor, 2013–18; Slade Director, 2010–18); *b* London, 15 Jan. 1964; *d* of Dennis S. Collins and Helene M. Collins (*née* Davis); partner, 1998, Tim Head. *Educ:* St Paul's Girls' Sch.; Chelsea Coll. of Art (Foundn); Slade Sch. of Fine Art, University Coll. London (BA Hons Fine Art 1987); Univ. of Reading (PhD Fine Art 2001). Amer. Assoc. of Univ. Women Rose Sidgwick Meml Fellow, Sch. of Art Inst. of Chicago, 1990–91 (Fulbright Travel Award); Lectr in Computer Arts and Animation, Columbia Coll., Chicago, 1991–92; Res. Fellow in Interactive Media, W Surrey Coll. of Art and Design, 1992–94; Sessional Lectr (pt-time) in Fine Art, Univ. of Reading, 1994–95; Hd, Electronic Media, Slade Centre for Electronic Media in Fine Art, 1995–2010, Hd, Undergrad. Fine Art Media, 2005–10, Slade Sch. of Fine Art, UCL. *Works include:* Woolwich Foot Tunnel, 1993; Pedestrian Gestures, 1994; Touched, 1996; In Conversation, Brighton, Amsterdam, Helsinki, Cardiff, Berlin, 1997–2001; Transporting Skies, 2002; Tate in Space, commnd for Tate Online, 2002; The Spectrascope, 2004; Fenlandia, 2004–05; Glenlandia, 2005–06; Underglow, 2005; Seascape, De La Warr Pavilion, 2009; Love Brid, 2009; Brighter Later, 2013; LAND, 2017. Mem., BAFTA. Zainul Award, Faculty of Fine Art, Dhaka Univ., 2018. *Publications:* contributor: A Directory of British Film and Video Artists, 1996; New Media: practice and content in Britain 1994–2004, 2004; Networked Narrative Environments, 2004; Spatialities: geographies of art and architecture, 2012. *Recreations:* art, film, books, travel, food, social media. *Address:* Slade School of Fine Art, University College London, Gower Street, WC1E 6BT. *T:* (020) 7679 2313, *Fax:* (020) 7679 7801. *E:* susan.collins@ucl.ac.uk.

**COLLINS, Terence;** Chief Executive, Durham County Council, since 2016; *b* Guisborough, N Yorks, 30 Nov. 1960; *s* of Terry and Vilma Collins. *Educ:* Sacred Heart Sch., Redcar, N Yorks; Univ. of Teesside (MBA 2000). Leisure Officer, 1979–80, Eston Leisure Centre Supervisor, 1980–81, Redcar and Cleveland Council; Cultural Events Manager, Brighton and Hove Council, 1981–84; Leisure Services Officer, Eastleigh BC, 1984–86; Darlington Borough Council: Asst Manager, 1986–90, Manager, 1990–92, Dolphin Centre; Leisure Contract Manager, 1992–98; Hd, Leisure and Cultural Services, 1998–2002; Asst Dir, Envmt, 2002–04; Hd, Envmtl Services, S Tyneside Council, 2004–06; Dir, Neighbourhood Services, and Asst Chief Exec., City of York Council, 2006–09; Corporate Dir, Neighbourhood Services, Durham CC, 2009–16. *Recreations:* fitness, golf, season ticket holder at Middlesbrough FC. *Address:* Durham County Council, County Hall, Durham DH1 5UL. *T:* 0300 026 8062. *E:* terry.collins@durham.gov.uk.

**COLLINS, His Eminence Cardinal Thomas;** *see* Toronto, Archbishop of, (RC).

**COLLINS, Timothy William George,** CBE 1996; Partner, Vico Partners, since 2017; *b* 7 May 1964; *s* of late William and Diana Collins; *m* 1997, Clare, *d* of Geoffrey and Auriel Benson; one *s. Educ:* Chigwell Sch., Essex; LSE (BSc); KCL (MA). Cons. Res. Dept, 1986–89; Advr to Secs of State for the Envmt, 1989–90, for Employment, 1990–92; Press Sec. to Prime Minister, 1992; Dir of Communications, Cons. Party, 1992–95; Mem., Prime Minister's Policy Unit, 1995; Sen. Strategy Consultant, WCT Ltd, 1995–97. MP (C) Westmorland and Lonsdale, 1997–2005; contested (C) same seat, 2005. An Opposition Whip, 1998–99; Shadow Minister for the Cabinet Office, 2001–02; Shadow Secretary of State: for Transport, 2002–03; for Educn, 2003–05. Vice-Chm., Cons. Party, 1999–2001. Man. Dir, 2009–12, Chm., 2012–13, Bell Pottinger Public Affairs Ltd; Chm., Bell Pottinger Political, 2013–17; Partner, Bell Pottinger LLP, 2013–17. *Address:* (office) 31 Southampton Row, Holborn, WC1B 5HJ.

**COLLINS, Prof. (Vincent) Peter,** MD, PhD; FRCPath, FMedSci, FHEA; Professor of Histopathology, University of Cambridge, 1997–2014, now Emeritus; Hon. Consultant Pathologist, Addenbrooke's Hospital, 1997–2014; *b* 3 Dec. 1947; *s* of James Vincent Collins and Mary Ann Collins (*née* Blanche). *Educ:* University Coll., Dublin (MB, BCh, BAO 1971); Karolinska Inst., Stockholm (MD; PhD 1978); MA (Cantab) 2013. MRCPath 1988, FRCPath 1996; Fellow, Faculty of Pathology, RCPI, 1989. House appts, Mater Hosp., Dublin, 1972–73; junior appts, 1974–82, Cons. Pathologist, 1982–90, Sen. Cons. Pathologist, 1994–97, Karolinska Inst.; Head of Clin. Res., Ludwig Inst. for Cancer Res., Stockholm Br., 1986–98; Prof. of Neuropathology, Univ. of Gothenburg, 1990–94; Sen. Cons. Pathologist, Sahlgrenska Univ. Hosp., Gothenburg, 1990–94; Prof. of Tumour Pathology, Karolinska Inst., 1994–97. Foreign Adjunct Prof., Karolinska Inst., 1998–. FMedSci 2002; FHEA 2008. *Publications:* over 300 papers on human brain tumours. *Recreations:* sailing, ski-ing, music. *Address:* c/o Department of Histopathology, Box 235, Addenbrooke's Hospital, Cambridge CB2 0QQ. *T:* (01223) 336072.

**COLLINS, William Janson,** MBE 2004; Chairman, William Collins Sons & Co. (Holdings) Ltd, 1976–81; *b* 10 June 1929; *s* of late Sir William Alexander Roy Collins, CBE, and Lady Collins (Priscilla Marian, *d* of late S. J. Lloyd); *m* 1951, Lady Sara Elena Hely-Hutchinson (*d* 2013), *d* of 7th Earl of Donoughmore; one *s* three *d. Educ:* Magdalen Coll., Oxford (BA). Joined William Collins Sons & Co. Ltd, 1952; Dir, then Man. Dir, 1967; Vice-Chm., 1971; Chm., 1976. *Recreations:* Royal tennis, shooting, fishing, tennis, golf. *Club:* All England Lawn Tennis and Croquet.

**COLLINS RICE, Rowena;** Director-General, Attorney General's Office, since 2013; a Deputy High Court Judge, since 2017; *b* 24 April 1960; *d* of John Frederick, (Jack), Collins and Hilda Collins (*née* Campbell); *m* 1986, Hugh Robert Collins Rice; two *s. Educ:* Westbourne Sch., Glasgow; Hertford Coll., Oxford (BA 1st Cl. Hons Jurisprudence 1981). Home Office, 1985–91; Treasury Solicitor's Dept, 1992–95; admitted solicitor, 1995; Home Office, 1995–2003; DCA, 2003–05; HMRC, 2005–07, Dir, Legal (Tax Law); Legal Dir, 2007–08, Dir Gen., Democracy, Constitution and Law, and Chief Legal Officer, 2008–10, DCA, later MoJ; Dir Gen., Constitutional, Dep. Prime Minister's Gp, Cabinet Office, 2010–11; Sec., Leveson Inquiry, 2011–12. *Address:* Attorney General's Office, 5–8 The Sanctuary, SW1P 3JS. *T:* (020) 7271 2401. *E:* rowena.collins-rice@attorneygeneral.gsi.gov.uk.

**COLLINSON, Anne Elizabeth;** *see* Aitken, A. E.

**COLLINSON, Rev. Nigel Thomas;** Methodist Minister; Secretary, Methodist Conference, 1999–2003 (President, 1996–97); *b* 14 March 1941; *s* of Tom and Agnes Collinson; *m* 1964, Lorna Ebrill; two *d. Educ:* Forster Street Sch., Tunstall; Hanley High Sch., Stoke on Trent; Hull Univ. (BA Theol 1962); Wesley House, Cambridge (MA Theol 1964). Ordained 1967; Methodist Minister: Clifton and Redland Circuit, Bristol, 1964–67; Stroud and Cirencester Circuit, 1967–72; Wolverhampton Trinity Circuit, 1972–80; Supt, Oxford Circuit and Methodist Chaplain to Univ. students, 1980–88; Chm., Southampton Dist, 1988–98. Hon. Chaplain, British and Internat. Sailors' Soc., 2005. Hon. DD Hull, 1997. *Publications:* The Opening Door, 1986; (with David Matthews) Facing Illness, 1986; The Land of Unlikeness, 1996. *Recreations:* golf, fishing, gardening, the arts.

**COLLINSON, Prof. Simon Charles,** DPhil; Professor of International Business and Strategy, since 2012, Deputy Pro-Vice-Chancellor, since 2016 and Director, City-REDI Research Institute, since 2016, University of Birmingham (Director and Dean, Birmingham Business School, 2012–16); *b* Mwanza, Tanzania, 23 April 1964; *s* of Michael and Norma Collinson; *m* 1993, Carol Bryce; three *s. Educ:* Univ. of Leeds (BA Jt Hons); Univ. of Florida (MA Hons); Sussex Univ. (DPhil 1991). University of Edinburgh: Asst Dir and Sen. Res. Fellow, Inst. for Japanese-Eur. Technol. Studies, 1991–98; Lectr in Internat. Business Studies, Mgt Sch. and Dept of Business Studies, 1998–2000; Warwick Business School, University of Warwick: Sen. Lectr, 2000–05; Associate Dean, MBAs, 2004–05; Reader in Internat. Business, 2006–08; Hd, Mktg and Strategy Gp, 2007–09; Prof. of Internat. Business and Innovation, 2008–11; Dep. Dean, 2009–10; Prof. of Internat. Business and Innovation, Henley Business Sch., Univ. of Reading, 2011–12. Guangbiao Prof., Sch. of Econs and Mgt, Zhejiang Univ., China, 2010–13; Academic Associate, Centre for Internat. Business and Mgt, Judge Business Sch., Univ. of Cambridge, 2008–. Mem., ESRC, 2011–18. Member: Bd of Dirs, Advanced Inst. of Mgt, 2007–11; Council, British Acad. of Mgt, 2011–13; Exec. Bd, Chartered Assoc. (formerly UK Assoc.) of Business Schs, 2013– (Chm., 2015–18); Bd, Gtr Birmingham Chamber of Commerce, 2014–. FRSA 2014; FBAM 2017; FAcSS 2017. *Publications:* Small and Successful in Japan, 1995; (with M. Jay) From Complexity to Simplicity, 2012; (with A. Rugman) International Business, 5th edn 2008 to 7th edn 2017; (ed with G. Morgan) Images of the Multinational Firm, 2009; contrib. papers to learned jls. *Recreations:* squash, ski-ing, sailing, golf, tennis, travel. *Address:* Birmingham Business School, University House, Edgbaston Park Road, Birmingham B15 2TY.

**COLLIS, His Honour Ian;** a Circuit Judge, 2000–09; *b* 21 Feb. 1946; *s* of late Harold Collis and Florence Collis; *m* 1968, Julia Georgina Cure; three *s. Educ:* Dartford Grammar Sch.; LLB (Hons) London. Admitted Solicitor, 1970; District Judge, 1987–2000; a Recorder, 1996–2000. *Recreations:* gardening, grandchildren.

**COLLIS, Peter George,** CB 2005; Chief Land Registrar and Chief Executive, HM Land Registry, 1999–2010; *b* 13 Oct. 1953; *s* of Martin Arthur Collis and Margaret Sophie Collis; *m* 1978, Linda Jean Worssam (marr. diss. 1999); one *s* one *d; m* 2000, Jan Morgan; one step *s. Educ:* Univ. of Aston in Birmingham (BSc 1st Cl. Hons Communication Sci. and Linguistics 1975). Joined Civil Service, 1975; admin trainee, Depts of Trade, Industry and Prices and Consumer Protection, 1975–78; Personal Asst to Chm. and Dep. Chm., NEB, 1978–80; Principal, Dept of Trade, 1980–83; Mktg Exec., Balfour Beatty, 1983–85 (on secondment); Principal, Dept of Transport, 1985–88; Head, Driver Licensing Div., DVLA, 1988–91; Head, Finance Exec. Agencies 2 Div., 1991–92, Highways Resource Mgt Div., 1992–94, Dept of Transport; Strategy and Private Finance Dir, Highways Agency, 1994–97; Business Develt Dir, Dept of Transport, 1997; Finance and Commercial Policy Dir, Employment Service, 1997–99. Non-exec. Dir, Newable Ltd (formerly GLE Gp), 2012–. Lay Mem., Governance, and Dep. Chm., Surrey Downs CCG, 2013–18; Dep. Lay Mem., Surrey Heartlands CCGs, 2018–. Hon. RICS 2003 (Mem., Governing Council, 2006–12). *Recreations:* family, enjoying the coast and the countryside, railways, Germany.

**COLLIS, Sarah Lilian;** *see* Anderson, S. L.

**COLLIS, Simon Paul,** CMG 2014; HM Diplomatic Service; Ambassador to Saudi Arabia, since 2015; *b* 23 Feb. 1956. *Educ:* King Edward VII Sch., Sheffield; Christ's Coll., Cambridge (BA Hons). Joined HM Diplomatic Service, 1978: FCO, 1978–80; Arabic lang. trng, 1980–81; 3rd, later 2nd, Sec., Bahrain, 1981–83; 1st Secretary: FCO, 1984–85; UK Mission to UN, NY, 1986; Head, India Section, S Asia Dept, FCO, 1987–88; Head of Chancery, Tunis, 1988–90; Gulf War Emergency Unit, FCO, 1990–91; New Delhi, 1991–94; Asst Head, Near East and N Africa Dept, FCO, 1994–96; Dep. Hd of Mission, Amman, 1996–99; on secondment to BP, 1999–2000; Consul General: Dubai, 2000–04; Basra, 2004–05; Ambassador to Qatar, 2005–07; Ambassador to Syria, 2007–12; Ambassador to Iraq, 2012–14. *Address:* c/o Foreign and Commonwealth Office, King Charles Street, SW1A 2AH.

**COLLON, Nicholas William Hyde;** Principal Conductor and Artistic Director, Aurora Orchestra, since 2005; Chief Conductor and Artistic Adviser, Residentie Orkest, The Hague, since 2018 (Principal Conductor, 2016–18); *b* Kingston-upon-Thames, 7 Feb. 1983; *s* of Michael and Jo Collon; *m* 2010, Jane Mitchell; one *s. Educ:* Eton Coll.; Clare Coll., Cambridge (BA Music). Guest conducting debuts: BBC Proms, Opera North, BBC SO, Aldeburgh Fest., 2009; Glyndebourne, LSO, 2010; London Philharmonic, BBC Scottish SO, Bregenz Fest., Stavanger SO, Royal Northern Sinfonia, Birmingham Contemp. Music Gp, 2011; Philharmonia Orch., London Mozart Players, BBC Nat. Orch. of Wales, Munich Chamber Orch., ENO, Bremen Music Fest., BBC Philharmonic Orch.,

Bournemouth SO, 2012; Hallé Orch., RPO, Spanish Nat. Orch., Acad. Ancient Music, Auckland Philharmonia, Ensemble Intercontemporain, Lucerne Fest., Glyndebourne on Tour, 2013; Bamberg SO, Orch. du Capitole de Toulouse, Orch. Nat. de Lyon, Zurich Tonhalle, Residentie Orch., Brussels Philharmonic Orch., Wroclaw Philharmonic Orch., Ulster Orch., Prague Radio SO, Les Violons du Roy, Trondheim SO, 2014. *Address:* c/o Intermusica, 9 Kingsway, WC2B 6XF.

**COLLYEAR, Sir John (Gowen),** Kt 1986; FREng; Chairman, AE plc, 1981–86; *b* 19 Feb. 1927; *s* of John Robert Collyear and late Amy Elizabeth Collyear (*née* Gowen); *m* 1953, Catherine Barbara Newman (*d* 2019); one *s* two *d*. *Educ:* Leeds Univ. (BSc). FIMechE (Hon. FIMechE 1995); FIMMM (Hon. FIMMM 2002), FIET; FREng (FEng 1979). Served RE Lieut 6th Airborne Div., Far and Middle East, 1944–48. Graduate apprentice and Production Engr, Joseph Lucas Industries, 1951; Glacier Metal Company Ltd: Production Engr, 1953; Production Manager, 1956; Chief Production Engr, 1956; Factory Gen. Manager, 1959; Managing Director, 1969; Bearings Div. Man. Dir, Associated Engineering Ltd, 1972; Group Man. Dir, AE plc, 1975. Chairman: MK Electric Gp PLC, 1987–88; Fulmer Ltd, 1987–91; USM Texon Ltd (formerly United Machinery Gp), 1987–95. Chm., Technology Requirements Bd, DTI, 1985–88. President: Motor Industry's Res. Assoc., 1987–97; Inst. of Materials, 1992–94. Hon. Bencher, Gray's Inn, 2000. *Publications:* Management Precepts, 1975; The Practice of First Level Management, 1976. *Recreations:* golf, bridge, piano music. *Address:* Donnington House, Cotswold Heights, Lower Swell Road, Stow-on-the-Wold, Cheltenham, Glos GL54 1LT. *T:* (01451) 830565. *Club:* Athenæum.

**COLMAN, Anthony John,** PhD; Research Associate, since 2013 and Visiting Fellow, since 2014, University of East Anglia; non-executive Chairman, PupilAsset.com, since 2016; *b* 24 July 1943; *s* of late William Benjamin Colman and Beatrice (*née* Hudson); *m* Juliet Annabelle, *d* of Alec and June Owen; two *s*, and four *s* two *d* by prev. marriages. *Educ:* Paston Grammar Sch.; Magdalene Coll., Cambridge (BA 1964; MA); Univ. of E Africa, 1964–66; LSE, 1966; Univ. of East Anglia (MA 2009; PhD 2013). Unilever (United Africa Co.), 1964–69; Burton Group, 1969–90: Merchandise Manager, 1971–74, Buying and Merchandising Dir, 1974–76, Top Shop; Asst Man. Dir, Womenswear Sector, 1976–81; Director: Burton Menswear, 1976–81; Top Man, 1976–81; Dorothy Perkins, 1979–81; Dir, 1981–90. Director: GLE, 1990–97 (Chm., GLE Development Capital, 1990–97); Aztec, 1990–98; London First Centre Ltd, 1994–2002. Mem. (Lab) Merton LBC, 1990–98 (Leader of Council, 1991–97). Chair, Local Govt Superannuation Funds Cttee (incl. Police, Fire Bde and Teachers), 1992–98. Vice-Chm., ALA, 1991–95. Contested (Lab), SW Herts, 1979. MP (Lab) Putney, 1997–2005; contested (Lab) same seat, 2005. PPS to Minister of State, NI Office, 1998–2000. Member: Treasury Select Cttee, 1997–98; Internat. Develt Select Cttee, 2000–05; Chairman: All Party Gp on Socially Responsible Investment, 1998–2005; All Party UN Gp, 2001–05; All Party UN Gp, 2002–05; PLP Trade and Industry Cttee, 1997–99. Chairman: Low Pay Unit, 1990–98; London Res. Centre, 1994–97; Dir, Public Private Partnerships Prog. Ltd, 1998–2001 (Chm., 1996–98); Member: Price Commn, 1977–79; Labour Finance & Industry Gp, 1973– ; Labour Party Enquiry into Educn & Trng in Europe, 1991–93; Exec. Cttee, UNED, subseq. Stakeholder Forum for Our Common Future, 1995–2005; Adv. Bd, African Venture Capital Assoc., 2005–08. Assoc. Dir, 2005–09, non-exec. Dir, 2009–, Africa Practice Ltd. Pres., UNA UK SE Reg., 2005–07 (Deleg. to UN Gen. Assembly Millennium Develt Goals, 2005); Smart Partner, Commonwealth Partnership for Technology Mgt, 2008– . Member of Council: VSO, 2000–07; Chatham House, 2001–07; ODI, 2006–14; World Future Council, 2007–. Chm., One World Trust, 2007–10; Trustee, New Economics Foundn, 2005–08. One People Oration, Westminster Abbey, 2006. Chm., Wimbledon Theatre Trust, 1991–96; Dir, London Arts Bd, 1994–98; Trustee, Nelson Mus., 2009–. Patron: Friends of Africa, 2004–07; Friends of Ahmadiyya Muslim Assoc., 2005–07. Local preacher, Methodist Ch, 2005–. Industrial Fellow, Kingston Univ. (formerly Poly.), 1983–; Fellow, Southlands Coll., Roehampton Univ., 2003; Associate Fellow, Governance of Clean Develt Proj., ESRC/UEA, 2010–; Vis. Scholar, New Sch., NY, 2013–. Adjunct Sen. Res. Scientist, Earth Inst., Columbia Univ., NY, 2012–; Hon. Vis. Res. Fellow, Univ. of Cape Town, 2015–. Liveryman, Horners' Co., 2009. FRSA 1983; FRGS 2003; CCMI 2003. *Publications:* Missing Power, 2009; (ed jtly) The Oxford Handbook of Food, Water and Society, 2019. *Clubs:* Reform; N Norfolk Rotary; Norfolk.

**COLMAN, (Bernard) Trevor;** Member (UK Ind) South West, European Parliament, Oct. 2008–2014; *b* St Breward, Cornwall, 27 Aug. 1941. *Educ:* Camelford Grammar Sch.; Tavistock Grammar Sch. Court clerk, Magistrate's Clerks office, Tavistock, 1958–62; police officer, Devon Constabulary, then Devon and Cornwall Constabulary, 1962–95. Script advisor to Wycliffe, TV series, 1994–99. *Publications:* Incident into Evidence, 1989; short stories; articles in magazines.

**COLMAN, Jeremy Gye;** Auditor General for Wales, 2005–10; *b* 9 April 1948; *s* of Philip Colman and Georgina Maude Colman (*née* Gye); *m* 1st, 1978, Patricia Ann Stewart, *qv* (marr. diss. 1996); 2nd, 1997, Gillian Margaret Carless. *Educ:* John Lyon Sch., Harrow; Peterhouse, Cambridge (BA Mathematical Tripos 1969, MA 1973); Imperial Coll., London (MSc; DIC 1972); Open Univ. (PGDCCI 2001). Home Civil Service, 1971–88: CSD, 1971–75, Private Sec. to Second Perm. Sec., 1973–74; Principal, Industrial Policy: HM Treasury, 1975–78; CSD, 1978–81; Private Sec. to successive heads of Home Civil Service, 1980–82; Principal, Health Finance, 1982–84, Asst Sec., Public Enterprises, 1984–88, HM Treasury; Dir, Co. NatWest Ltd, 1988–90; Partner, Privatisation Services, London, 1991, Head of Corp. Finance practice, Prague, 1992–93; Price Waterhouse; Dir, 1993–98, Asst Auditor Gen., 1999–2005, National Audit Office. Freeman, Ironmongers' Co., 1991. *Recreations:* cookery, fine furniture-making. *Club:* Oxford and Cambridge (Chm., 1992–94).

**COLMAN, Sir Michael (Jeremiah),** 3rd Bt *cr* 1907; Chairman, Reckitt and Colman plc, 1986–95; First Church Estates Commissioner, 1993–99; *b* 7 July 1928; *s* of Sir Jeremiah Colman, 2nd Bt, and Edith Gwendolyn Tritton; *S* father, 1961; *m* 1955, Judith Jean Wallop, JP, DL, *d* of Vice-Adm. Sir Peveril William-Powlett, KCB, KCMG, CBE, DSO; two *s* three *d*. *Educ:* Eton. Director: Reckitt & Colman plc, 1970–95; Foreign and Colonial Ventures Advisors Ltd, 1988–99; Foreign and Colonial Private Equity Trust, 1995–2002. Member: Council of Royal Warrant Holders, 1977–2012, Pres., 1984–85; Trinity House Lighthouse Bd, 1985–94 (Younger Brother, 1994). Member: Council, Chemical Industries Assoc., 1982–84; Bd, UK Centre for Econ. and Environmental Develt, 1985–99 (Chm., 1996–99). Mem., Council, Scout Assoc., 1985–2000. Mem. Gen. Council and Mem. Finance Cttee, King Edward's Hosp. Fund for London, 1978–2004; Special Trustee, St Mary's Hosp., 1988–99; Trustee: Royal Foundn of Grey Coat Hosp., 1989–2004; Allchurches Trust Ltd, 1994–2008. Capt., Yorks Yeomanry, RARO, 1967. Mem. Ct, Skinners' Co., 1985–2008 (Master, 1991–92). Hon. LLD Hull, 1993. Cross of St Augustine, 1999. *Recreations:* farming, shooting. *Heir:* s Jeremiah Michael Powlett Colman [*b* 23 Jan. 1958; *m* 1981, Susan Elizabeth, *yr d* of John Henry Britland, York; two *s* one *d*]. *Address:* Dairy Hill House, Malshanger, Basingstoke, Hants RG23 7ET; 40 Chester Square, SW1W 9HT; Tarvie, Bridge of Cally, Blairgowrie, Perthshire PH10 7PJ. *Clubs:* Cavalry and Guards, Boodle's.

**COLMAN, Dr Peter Malcolm,** AC 2017; FRS 2014; FAA, FTSE; Structural Biology Division, Walter and Eliza Hall Institute of Medical Research, Melbourne, since 2001; *b* 3 April 1944; *s* of Clement Colman and Kathleen Colman (*née* Malcolm); *m* 1967, Anne Elizabeth Smith; two *s*. *Educ:* University of Adelaide (BSc 1st Cl. Hons 1966; PhD 1970). FAA 1989; FTSE 1997. Postdoctoral Fellow: Univ. of Oregon, 1969–72; Max Planck Inst., Munich, 1972–75; Queen Elizabeth II Fellow, 1975–77, Principal Investigator, NH&MRC, 1977–78, Univ. of Sydney; Scientist, 1978–89, Chief, Div. of Biomolecular Engrg, 1989–97, CSIRO; Dir, Biomolecular Res. Inst., Melbourne, 1991–2000. Scientific Founder and non-exec. Dir, Biota Hldgs Ltd, 1985–91. Performed res. which determined the 3-dimensional structure of influenza virus neuraminidase and established and led the group which subsequently discovered Relenza, the first neuraminidase inhibitor to be approved for use in treatment of influenza. Mem., Asia-Pacific Internat. Molecular Biol. Network, 1998–. Vice Pres., Internat. Union of Crystallography, 2008–11. Hon. DSc Sydney, 2000; DUniv Adelaide, 2010. (Jtly) Australia Prize, 1996; Victoria Prize, Govt of Vic, Australia, 2008. *Publications:* contribs to scientific jls on structural biol., influenza virus and drug discovery, apoptosis. *Recreation:* music. *Address:* PO Box 321, E Melbourne, Vic 8002, Australia.

**COLMAN, Sir Timothy (James Alan),** KG 1996; Lord-Lieutenant for Norfolk, 1978–2004; *b* 19 Sept. 1929; 2nd but *o* surv. *s* of late Captain Geoffrey Russell Rees Colman and Lettice Elizabeth Evelyn Colman, Norwich; *m* 1951, Lady Mary Cecilia (Extra Lady in Waiting to Princess Alexandra), twin *d* of late Lt-Col Hon. Michael Claude Hamilton Bowes Lyon and Elizabeth Margaret, Glamis; two *s* three *d*. *Educ:* RNC, Dartmouth and Greenwich. Lieut RN, 1950, retd 1953. Chm., Eastern Counties Newspapers Group Ltd, 1969–96; Director: Reckitt & Colman plc, 1978–89; Whitbread & Co. PLC, 1980–86; Anglia Television Group PLC, 1987–94; Life Trustee, Carnegie UK Trust, 1966–2000 (Chm., 1982–87). Member: Countryside Commn, 1971–76; Water Space Amenity Commn, 1973–76; Adv. Cttee for England, Nature Conservancy Council, 1974–80; Eastern Regional Cttee, National Trust, 1967–71. Pro-Chancellor, Univ. of E Anglia, 1974–2000 (Chm. Council, 1973–86). Chairman: Trustees, Norfolk and Norwich Festival, 1974–2002; Royal Norfolk Agricl Assoc., 1985–96 (Pres., 1982, 1997); Trustees, E Anglia Art Foundn, 1993–2005; Trustees, Norwich Cathedral Trust, 1998–2009. President: Norfolk Naturalists Trust, 1962–78; Friends of Norwich Museums, 1978–2009. Pres., E. Anglian TAVRA, 1989–95. FRSA 1995. JP 1958, DL 1968, High Sheriff, 1970, Norfolk. Hon. Fellow, UEA, 2004. Hon. DCL UEA, 1973; DUniv Anglia Poly., 1999. KStJ 1979. *Address:* Bixley Manor, Norwich, Norfolk NR14 8SJ. *T:* (01603) 625298. *Clubs:* Turf, Pratt's; Norfolk (Norwich).

*See also* S. R. Troughton.

**COLMAN, Trevor;** *see* Colman, B. T.

**COLMER, Ven. Malcolm John;** Archdeacon of Hereford, 2005–10, now Archdeacon Emeritus; *b* 15 Feb. 1945; *s* of late Frederick Colmer, OBE and Gladys Colmer; *m* 1966, Kathleen Elizabeth Colmer (*née* Wade); one *s* three *d*. *Educ:* Sussex Univ. (BSc (Maths); MSc (Fluid Mechs)); Nottingham Univ. (BA (Theol.)). Scientific Officer, RAE, 1967–71; ordained deacon, 1973, priest, 1974; Assistant Curate: St John the Baptist, Egham, 1973–76; St Mary, Chadwell, 1976–79; Vicar: St Michael, S Malling, Lewes, 1979–85; St Mary, Hornsey Rise, 1985–87; Team Rector, Hornsey Rise, Whitehall Park Team, 1987–96; Archdeacon of Middx, 1996–2005. Area Dean of Islington, 1990–95. *Recreations:* music, painting, natural history, gardening. *E:* malcolm_colmer@hotmail.com.

**COLQUHOUN, Andrew John,** PhD; Chairman, National Horticultural Forum, 2002–13; Director General, Royal Horticultural Society, 1999–2006; *b* 21 Sept. 1949; *s* of late Kenneth James Colquhoun, MC, and of Christine Mary Colquhoun (*née* Morris); *m* 1st, 1975, Patricia Beardall (marr. diss. 2010); one *s* one *d*; 2nd, 2011, Stephanie Donaldson. *Educ:* Tiffin Sch.; Nottingham Univ. (BSc 1st Cl. Hons 1971); Glasgow Univ. (PhD 1974); City Univ. Business Sch. (MBA Dist. 1987); Roehampton Univ. (Postgrad. Dip. Counselling and Psychotherapy 2009). Joined HM Diplomatic Service, 1974; Third Sec., FCO, 1974–75; Second Sec., MECAS, 1975–77; Second, later First, Sec., Damascus, 1977–79; First Sec., Tel Aviv, 1979–81; Principal, Cabinet Office, 1981–83; Planning Staff, FCO, 1983–84; Shandwick Consultants (on secondment to ICA), 1984–86; Dir of Educn and Trng, 1987–90; Sec. and Chief Exec., 1990–97, ICAEW. Sec., Consultative Cttee of Accountancy Bodies, 1990–97. Chm., Investigation Cttee, ICAEW, 2009–15. Non-executive Director: NERC, 2007–12; Office of the Health Professions Adjudicator, 2009–12. Member: Audit Cttee, Edexcel Foundn, 1997–2002; BITC Headteacher Mentoring Prog., 1998–2013; Mid Sussex Literacy Project, 1998–2004; Rail Passengers (formerly Rail Users Consultative) Cttee for Southern England, 1999–2003; Chairman: SEEDA Horticulture Wkg Gp, 2006–10; Farming and Rural Issues Gp for the SE, 2010–15. Trustee: Hastings and Rother Mediation Service, 2009–18; Action in Rural Sussex, 2013–. Mem. Council, Nottingham Univ., 1999–2006. *Publications:* various articles on accountancy, professions, educn, horticulture and recruitment in nat., educnl and professional press. *Recreations:* bird watching, gardening, country life, reading. *Address:* Studio House, 64 Croft Road, Hastings, Sussex TN34 3HE.

**COLQUHOUN, Prof. David,** FRS 1985; Professor of Pharmacology, since 1983 (A. J. Clark Professor of Pharmacology, 1985–2004), Director, Wellcome Laboratory for Molecular Pharmacology, 1993–2004, and Hon. Fellow, 2004, University College London; *b* 19 July 1936; *s* of Gilbert Colquhoun and Kathleen Mary (*née* Chambers); *m* 1976, Margaret Ann Boultwood; one *s*. *Educ:* Birkenhead Sch.; Liverpool Technical Coll.; Leeds Univ. (BSc); Edinburgh Univ. (PhD). Lectr, Dept of Pharmacol., UCL, 1964–70; Vis. Asst, then Associate Prof., Dept of Pharmacol., Yale Univ. Med. Sch., 1970–72; Sen. Lectr, Dept of Pharmacol., Univ. of Southampton Med. Sch., 1972–75; Sen. Lectr, Dept of Pharmacol., St George's Hosp. Med. Sch., 1975–79; Reader, Dept of Pharmacol., UCL, 1979–83. Guest Prof., Max-Planck-Institut für Medizinische Forschung, Heidelberg, 1990–91. Lectures: Krantz, Univ. of Maryland, 1987; Tony Birmingham Meml, Univ. of Nottingham, 2011. Trustee, Sir Ronald Fisher Meml Cttee, 1975–. Alexander von Humboldt Prize, 1990; HealthWatch Award, 2010; (jtly) UK Sci. Blog Prize, Good Thinking Soc., 2012. Member Editorial Board: Jl of Physiology, 1974–81; Jl Gen. Physiology, 1998–; Series B, Proceedings of Royal Soc. Blog, DC's Improbable Science, www.dscience.net. Wellcome Gold Medal, British Pharmacol Soc., 2015. *Publications:* Lectures on Biostatistics, 1971; articles in Jl of Physiology, Nature, British Jl of Pharmacology, Proc. of Royal Soc., etc. *Recreations:* walking, linear algebra, blogging, investigative journalism. *Address:* Chiddingstone, Common Lane, Kings Langley, Herts WD4 8BL. *T:* (01923) 266154. *E:* d.colquhoun@ucl.ac.uk.

**COLQUHOUN of Luss, Sir Malcolm;** *see* Colquhoun, Sir R. M.

**COLQUHOUN, Ms Maureen Morfydd;** political researcher and writer; Chief Executive, North West Government Relations, since 1994; *b* 12 Aug. 1928; *m* 1949, Keith Colquhoun (marr. diss. 1980); two *s* one *d*; partner, 1975, *m* 2015, Barbara Todd; extended family, two *d*. Mem. Labour Party, 1945–; Member: Shoreham UDC, 1965–74; Adur District Council, 1973–74; West Sussex CC, 1971–74; Hackney BC, 1982–90; Lakes Parish Council, 1994–98, 2006–. MP (Lab) Northampton North, Feb. 1974–1979. Information Officer, Gingerbread, 1980–82. Hon. Sec., All-Party Parly Gp on AIDS, 1987–88; Chm.,

Secretaries and Assistants' Council, H of C, 1992–93. Mem., Assoc. of Former MPs, 2005– (Mem., Exec. Cttee, 2006–). Founder and Chairman: Historic Ambleside Trust, 1992–; Pensions Lobbying, 1996–; Co-Founder, Lakes Vision Gp, 1997; Mem. Exec. Cttee, Ambleside Civic Trust, 1993–; Sec. of State Appointee, Lake Dist Nat. Park Authy, 1998–2006. Co-Founder and Chairperson to Trustees, Harriet Martineau Foundn, 2000. *Publications:* A Woman In the House, 1980; Inside the Westminster Parliament, 1992; New Labour–New Lobbying, 1998. *Recreations:* jazz, opera, theatre. *Address:* South Knoll, Rydal Road, Ambleside, Cumbria LA22 9AY. *E:* maureencolquhoun@btopenworld.com. *Club:* University Women's.

**COLQUHOUN of Luss, Sir (Rory) Malcolm,** 9th Bt *cr* 1786, of Luss, Dumbarton; Chief of the Clan; Joint Principal, Broomwood Hall and Northcote Lodge Schools, since 1984; Chairman, Luss Estates Co., since 2008; *b* 20 Dec. 1947; s of Sir Ivar Iain Colquhoun, 8th Bt and Kathleen Colquhoun (*née* Duncan); *S* father, 2008; *m* 1st, 1978, Susan Timmerman (marr. diss. 1983); one s; 2nd, 1989, Katharine Mears; one s one d. *Educ:* Eton; Univ. of Reading (BSc Est. Man.). Founding Trustee, Northwood Education Foundn, 2013–. *Recreations:* opera, travel, piano, beautifying things. *Heir: s* Patrick John Colquhoun [*b* 17 Dec. 1980; *m* 2010, Charlotte Murphy; two s]. *Address:* 74 Nightingale Lane, SW12 8NR. *E:* m.colquhoun@northwoodschools.com; Camstraddan, Luss, Argyllshire G83 8NX. *E:* sirmalcolm@lussestates.co.uk. *Clubs:* White's, Turf; New (Edinburgh).

**COLSTON, His Honour Colin Charles;** QC 1980; a Circuit Judge, 1983–2003; *b* 2 Oct. 1937; *yr s* of late Eric Colston, JP, and Catherine Colston; *m* 1963, Edith Helga, *d* of late Med. Rat Dr Wilhelm and Frau Gisela Hille, St Oswald/Freistadt, Austria; two s one d. *Educ:* Rugby Sch.; The Gunnery, Washington, Conn, USA; Trinity Hall, Cambridge (MA). National Service, RN, 1956–58; commissioned, RNR, 1958–64. Called to the Bar, Gray's Inn, 1962; Midland and Oxford Circuit (formerly Midland Circuit); Recorder of Midland Circuit, 1968–69; Member, Senate of Inns of Court and Bar, 1977–80; Recorder of the Crown Court, 1978–83; Resident Judge, St Albans, 1989–2000. Lay Judge, Court of Arches, Canterbury, 1992–2012. Member: Criminal Cttee, Judicial Studies Bd, 1989–92; Parole Bd for England & Wales, 2004–07. Chm., St Albans Diocesan Bd of Patronage, 1987–2000. Hon. Canon, St Albans Cathedral, 2002–07, Canon Emeritus, 2007–.

**COLSTON, Michael;** Chairman, Ewelme Park Farm Ltd, since 1996; *b* 24 July 1932; s of Sir Charles Blampied Colston, CBE, MC, DCM, FCGI and Lady (Eliza Foster) Colston, MBE; *m* 1st, 1956, Jane Olivia Kilham Roberts (marr. diss.); three *d*; 2nd, 1977, Judith Angela Briggs (*d* 2016). *Educ:* Ridley Coll., Canada; Stowe; Gonville and Caius Coll., Cambridge. Joined 17th/21st Lancers, 1952; later seconded to 1st Royal Tank Regt for service in Korea. Founder Dir, Charles Colston Group Ltd (formerly Colston Appliances Ltd) together with late Sir Charles Colston, 1955, Chm. and Man. Dir, 1969–89; Chm. and Man. Dir, Colston Domestic Appliances Ltd, 1969–79. Chairman: Colston Consultants Ltd, 1989–93; Tallent Engineering Ltd, 1969–89; Tallent Holdings plc, 1989–90; ITS Rubber Ltd, 1969–85; Quit Ltd, 1989–93; Dishwasher Council, 1970–75. Dir, Farming and Wildlife Adv. Gp, 1991–2002. Chm., Assoc. Manufrs of Domestic Electrical Appliances, 1976–79. Member Council: Inst. of Directors, 1977–93 (Pres., Thames Valley Br., 1983–93); CBI, 1984–90 (Chm., S Regl Council, 1986–88); British Electrotechnical Approvals Bd, 1976–79; SMMT, 1987–90. Chm., Dogwatch, 2006–13. Trustee, Hawk and Owl Trust, 1991–96. *Recreations:* fishing, shooting, tennis; founder Cambridge Univ. Water Ski Club. *Address:* Ewelme Park, Park Corner, Nettlebed, Henley-on-Thames RG9 6DZ. *T:* (01491) 641668.

**COLT, Sir Edward (William Dutton),** 10th Bt *cr* 1694; MB, FRCP, FACP; Attending Physician, Mount Sinai-St Luke's Roosevelt Hospital, New York, until 2015; *b* 22 Sept. 1936; *s* of Major John Rochfort Colt, North Staffs Regt (*d* 1944), and of Angela Miriam Phyllis (*née* Kyan; she *m* 1946, Capt. Robert Leslie Cock); *S* uncle, 1951; *m* 1st, 1966, Jane Caroline (marr. diss. 1972), *d* of James Histed Lewis, Geneva and Washington, DC; 2nd, 1979, Suzanne Nelson (*née* Knickerbocker); one *d* (one s decd). *Educ:* Stoke House, Seaford; Douai Sch.; University Coll., London. Lately: Medical Registrar, UCH; House Physician, Brompton Hosp.; Associate Clinical Prof. of Medicine, Columbia Univ., NY, until 2015. *Publications:* contribs, especially on body composition, sports medicine, particularly running, to British and American med. jls. *Recreations:* ski-ing, bicycling. *Heir:* none.

**COLTART, Christopher McCallum;** QC 2014; *b* London, 19 March 1968; s of Timothy McCallum Coltart and Eileen Elizabeth Anne Coltart; *m* 2003, Kirsty Ealand; two s one d. *Educ:* Dulwich Coll.; St Edmund Hall, Oxford (MA PPE 1990). Admitted Solicitor, 1993; Trainee solicitor, 1993–95, Solicitor, 1995–98, Manches & Co.; called to the Bar, Inner Temple, 1998–; in practice as barrister, specialising in business crime and regulatory law, 1998–. *Recreations:* armchair sportsman, walking, fishing, ski-ing, birdwatching, cooking. *Address:* 2 Hare Court, Temple, EC4Y 7BH. *T:* (020) 7353 5324, 07866 628136. *E:* christophercoltartqc@2harecourt.com.

**COLTART, His Honour Simon Stewart;** a Circuit Judge, 1991–2018; *b* 3 Sept. 1946; *s* of late Gilbert McCallum Coltart and Mary Louise (*née* Kemp); *m* 1973, Sarah Victoria Birts; two s (and one s decd). *Educ:* Epsom Coll.; Leeds Univ. (LLB). Called to the Bar, Lincoln's Inn, 1969 (Eastham Scholar); a Recorder, 1987–91. Mem., Parole Bd, 1997–2003. Mem., Court of Assts, Grocers' Co., 1991– (Master, 1999). Governor: Stoke Brunswick Sch., 1991–2006; Oundle Sch., 2003–09. *Recreations:* sailing, golf, shooting, fishing. *Address:* Moat Park Farmhouse, Rose Hill, Uckfield, E Sussex TN22 5UQ. *Clubs:* Boodle's; Sussex; Bar Yacht, Royal Yacht Squadron; Rye Golf.

**COLTHURST, Sir Charles (St John),** 10th Bt *cr* 1744, of Ardrum, co. Cork; *b* 21 May 1955; *s* of Sir Richard La Touche Colthurst, 9th Bt and Janet Georgina (*née* Wilson-Wright) (*d* 2007); *S* father, 2003; *m* 1987, Nora May (marr. diss. 2019), *d* of Mortimer Kelleher; one s three d. *Educ:* Eton; Magdalene Coll., Cambridge (MA); University Coll., Dublin. Solicitor. *Heir: s* John Conway La Touche Colthurst, *b* 13 Oct. 1988. *Address:* Blarney Castle, Blarney, Co. Cork, Ireland. *Clubs:* MCC; Royal Irish Automobile, Kildare Street (Dublin).

**COLTMAN, Anne Clare, (Mrs T. C. Coltman);** *see* Riches, A. C.

**COLTON, Hon. Sir Adrian George Patrick,** Kt 2015; **Hon. Mr Justice Colton;** a Judge of the High Court of Justice in Northern Ireland, since 2015; Presiding Coroner, since 2016; Senior Criminal Judge, since 2017; *b* Dromore, Tyrone, 13 March 1959; *s* of Hugh James and Margaret Colton; *m* 1987, Carmel Ferguson; two s one d. *Educ:* St Michael's Coll., Enniskillen; Queen's Univ. Belfast (LLB Hons; Cert. Inst. Professional Legal Studies). Called to the Bar, NI, 1983; QC (NI) 2006. Motor Insurers' Bureau Panel Arbitrator, 2014–15. Chm., Gen. Council of the Bar, NI, 2009–11; Co-Chm., Forum for Barristers and Advocates, Internat. Bar Assoc., 2014–15. Mem., Panel of Chairmen, Anti-Doping Panels, Irish Sports Council, 2008–. *Recreations:* Gaelic football, cycling. *Address:* Royal Courts of Justice, Chichester Street, Belfast BT1 3JF.

**COLTON, Simon David;** QC 2017; a Recorder, since 2018; *b* London, 1976; *s* of late Nicholas Colton and of Kay Colton; *m* 2000; three s one d. *Educ:* St Paul's Sch., Hammersmith; Trinity Hall, Cambridge (BA Mod. Langs and Law with Eur. option 1998). Called to the Bar, Inner Temple, 1999; in practice as barrister, specialising in commercial litigation, 1999–. Vice Chm., Professional Conduct Cttee, Bar Standards Bd, 2016–. *Publications:* (specialist ed. on procedure) McGregor on Damages, 20th edn 2017. *Recreation:* coastal walking. *Address:* One Essex Court, Temple, EC4Y 9AR.

**COLTON, Rt Rev. (William) Paul;** *see* Cork, Cloyne and Ross, Bishop of.

**COLTRANE, Robbie,** OBE 2006; actor and director; *b* Glasgow, 31 March 1950; *m* 1999, Rhona Irene Gemmell; one s one d. *Educ:* Trinity Coll., Glenalmond; Glasgow Sch. of Art (DA Drawing and Painting). *Television* includes: Laugh? I nearly paid my licence fee!, 1985; Hooray for Holyrood, 1986; Tutti Frutti, 1986; The Miners' Strike, 1987; Mistero Buffo, 1990; Coltrane in a Cadillac, 1992; Cracker (3 series), 1993, 1994, 1995, (TV films) White Ghost, 1996, Cracker, 2006; The Ebb Tide, 1997; Coltrane's Planes and Automobiles, 1997; The Plan Man, 2003; Frazier, 2004; Robbie Coltrane: B-Road Britain (2 series), 2007, 2008; Murderland, 2009; The Gruffalo (voice), 2009; National Treasure, 2016; Critical Evidence, 2016–17; *films* include: Absolute Beginners, 1985; Mona Lisa, 1985; Danny Champion of the World, 1988; Henry V, 1988; Nuns on the Run, 1989; The Pope Must Die, 1990; Oh, What A Night, 1991; Huck Finn, 1992; Goldeneye, 1995; Buddy, 1996; Montana, 1997; Frogs for Snakes, 1997; Message in a Bottle, 1999; The World Is Not Enough, 1999; Harry Potter and the Philosopher's Stone, 2001; From Hell, 2002; Harry Potter and The Chamber of Secrets, 2002; Harry Potter and the Prisoner of Azkaban, 2004; Ocean's Twelve, 2005; Harry Potter and the Goblet of Fire, 2005; Harry Potter and the Order of the Phoenix, 2006; Provoked, 2007; Bloom Brothers, 2007; Harry Potter and the Half-Blood Prince, 2009; Harry Potter and the Deathly Hallows, Pt 1, 2010, Pt 2, 2011; Great Expectations, 2012; Brave, 2012; Effie Gray, 2014; *theatre:* has appeared and toured with Traverse Theatre Co. and Borderline Theatre Co., 1976–, incl. Mistero Buffo, 1990; Yr Obedient Servant, Lyric, 1987. Silver Rose Award, Montreux TV Fest., 1987; Evening Standard Peter Sellers Award, 1991; TV Best Actor Awards: BAFTA, 1994, 1995, 1996; Silver Nymph, Monte Carlo, 1994; BPG, 1994; RTS, 1994; FIPA (French Acad.), 1994; Cable Ace, 1994; Cannes TV Fest., 1994. *Publications:* Coltrane in a Cadillac, 1993; (with John Binias) Planes and Automobiles, 1997; Robbie Coltrane's B-Road Britain, 2008; newspaper and magazine articles. *Recreations:* politics, drawing, vintage cars, reading, sailing, piano, fishing, film, ships. *Address:* c/o CDA, 167–169 Kensington High Street, W8 6SH. *T:* (020) 7937 2749. *Clubs:* Groucho, Soho House, Chelsea Arts, Marzipan; Glasgow Arts.

**COLVER, Hugh Bernard,** CBE 1991; public affairs and business development consultant; Group Communications Director, BAE SYSTEMS, 2000–05; *b* 22 Aug. 1945; s of late Rev. Canon John Lawrence Colver and Diana Irene (*née* Bartlett); *m* 1970, Gillian Ogilvie (marr. diss. 2001), *y d* of late Morris and Dorothy Graham, Christchurch, NZ; one s one d; one s by Penny Studholme; *m* 2013, Winnie Marques, *e d* of Helge and Ulla Pedersen, Odense, Denmark. *Educ:* King Edward VI Grammar Sch., Louth, Lincs. Reporter: Market Rasen Mail, 1961–63; Hereford Times and Hereford Evening News, 1963–67; Asst Editor, Helicopter World and Hovercraft World, 1967–68; Journalist, FT Surveys, Financial Times, 1968–71; freelance journalist, writer and PR consultant, 1971–75; Press Officer, MoD, 1975–78; PRO, RAE, 1978–79; Staff PRO to Flag Officer, Scotland and NI, 1979–81; Press Officer, Prime Minister's Office, 1981–82; Chief Press Officer, Dept of Employment, 1982–84; Dep. Dir of Information, Metropolitan Police, 1984–85; Ministry of Defence: Dep. Chief of PR, 1985–87; Chief of PR, 1987–92; Public Affairs Dir, British Aerospace Defence Ltd, 1992–95; Dir of Communications, Cons. Central Office, 1995. Non-executive Chairman: Europac Gp Ltd, 2000–10 (Dir, 1997–2010); Defence Public Affairs Consultants, 2000–10 (Dir, 1997–2010); The Good and Gift Co. Ltd, 2017–; Dir, Mackland Res. and Marketing Services, 2017–; Mem., Steering Gp, Conservative Alumni, 2014–. Hon. Col, Media Ops Gp (Vols), TA, 2002–06. FRAeS 1998; FR.SA. Pres., Pen and Sword Club, 2006–. Liveryman, Bowyers' Co., 2005 (Court Asst, 2011); Hon. Freeman, Co. (formerly Guild) of PR Practitioners, 2015. *Publications:* This is the Hovercraft, 1972. *Recreations:* motoring, motor racing, walking.

**COLVILE, Oliver Newton;** *b* 26 Aug. 1959. *Educ:* Stowe Sch. Agent, Cons. Party, 1981–93; Account Dir, Rowland Sallingbury Casey, 1993, 1995–96; Dir, PR co., 1993–95; Proprietor, Oliver Colvile and Associates, 1996–2010. Dir, Polity Communications, 2005–10, 2017–. MP (C) Plymouth, Sutton and Devonport, 2010–17; contested (C) same seat, 2017. Mem., NI Select Cttee, 2010–17; Chm., All Party Parly Gp for Excellence in the Built Envmt, 2012–17 (Vice Chm., 2010–12); Vice Chairman: All Party Parly Gp: for the Armed Forces (RM), 2010–17; on Pharmacy, 2010–17; for Zambia and Malawi, 2011–17; for Zimbabwe; Sec., All Party Parly Gp on Integrated Health, 2010–17. Contested (C) Plymouth Sutton, 2001, 2005.

**COLVILE, Robert Raleigh;** Director, Centre for Policy Studies, since 2017 (Research Fellow, 2008–13); *b* Oxford, 23 June 1980; s of Robert and Rosemary Colvile; *m* 2014, Andrea Coleman (*d* 2019); two s. *Educ:* Eton Coll.; Peterhouse, Cambridge (BA Hons Hist. 2002; MA; MPhil Internat. Relns 2003). Daily Telegraph: trainee, 2004–05; jun. reporter, 2005–06; Features Sub-Ed., 2006–07; Dep. Features Ed., 2007–09; Dep. Comment Ed., Daily Telegraph and Comment Ed., Sunday Telegraph, 2009–12; Comment Ed., Daily Telegraph, 2012–13; Hd of Comment, 2013–14, Asst Ed. (Comment), 2014–15, Telegraph Media Gp; News Dir, Buzzfeed UK, 2015; Dep. Dir, Centre for Policy Studies, 2016–17; Ed., CapX, 2016–17. Dir, Direct Democracy (pt-time), 2006–07. *Publications:* The Great Acceleration, 2016; contribs to Commonwealth Jl Internat. Affairs. *Recreations:* reading, writing, fomenting the salvation of capitalism. *Address:* Centre for Policy Studies, 57 Tufton Street, SW1P 3QL. *T:* (020) 7222 4488. *E:* robert@cps.org.uk. *Club:* House of St Barnabas.

**COLVILLE,** family name of **Viscount Colville of Culross** and of **Baron Clydesmuir**.

**COLVILLE OF CULROSS,** 5th Viscount *cr* 1902; **Charles Mark Townshend Colville;** Lord (Scot.) 1604; Baron (UK) 1885; *b* 5 Sept. 1959; *e s* of 4th Viscount Colville of Culross, QC and of Mary Elizabeth (*née* Webb-Bowen); *S* father, 2010. *Educ:* Rugby; Univ. of Durham. Producer, BBC, 1994–2016; series producer: ITN, 2017–18; Smithsonian Channel, 2018–19; CNN, 2019–. Elected Mem., H of L, 2011. Mem., Communications Select Cttee, H of L, 2017–. Trustee, Tree Council, 2014–. *Heir: b* Hon. (Richmond) James Innys Colville [*b* 9 June 1961; *m* 1993, Aurea Katherine Dowson; two s].

**COLVILLE, Col (Raeburn) Murray (Longair),** TD 1996; Vice Lord-Lieutenant of Leicestershire, since 2013; Managing Director, Leicester Office Furnishers, since 1979; *b* 16 June 1952; *s* of Robert Stirling Colville and Eileen Rowe Colville; *m* 1992, Karen Ewart; one s two d. *Educ:* Magdalen Coll. Sch.; Royal Mil. Acad., Sandhurst. Commnd Duke of Wellington's Regt, Londonderry; served 1973–2008; Col, TA, 2000–13, incl. i/c Royal Anglian Inf. Unit in Bosnia; Dep. Comdr, 49 Bde TA, Nottingham, 2003–05. Director: Stirling Interiors, 1992–; LofDirect.co.uk, 2007–. Chairman: E Midlands RFCA, 2012–; Leics World War I Centenary Ref. Gp, 2014–. Mem., Leics and Rutland Cttee, ABF the Soldiers' Charity, 2000–15. Trustee, Queen's Royal Lancers and Notts Yeomanry Mus., 2010–. DL Leics, 1997. *Address:* White House Farm, Main Street, Barkby, Leicester LE7 3QG.

**COLVIN, Andrew James;** Comptroller and City Solicitor, City of London Corporation (formerly Corporation of London), 1989–2012; *b* 28 April 1947; s of Gilbert Russell Colvin, OBE, MA, and Dr Beatrice Colvin, MRCS, LRCP, DPH; *m* 1971, Helen Mary

Ryan; one s three d. *Educ*: qualified Solicitor, 1975; LLM Leicester Univ., 1996. Articled to Borough Solicitor, subseq. Asst Town Clerk, London Borough of Ealing, 1971–82; Dep. Town Clerk and Borough Solicitor, Royal Borough of Kensington and Chelsea, 1982–89. Legal Advr, Assoc. of London Govt, subseq. London Councils, 1996–2012 (London Boroughs' Assoc., 1984–96); Advr, English Nat. Stadium Trust, 1997–2012. Governor: St Gregory's RC Sch., 1989–93; Cardinal Wiseman RC Sch., 1992–99 (Chm., 1994–99). Freeman: City of London, 1989; City of London Solicitors' Co., 1996. *Recreations*: sailing, music, cycling.

**COLVIN, David Hugh**, CMG 1993; HM Diplomatic Service, retired; *b* 23 Jan. 1941; 3rd *s* of late Major Leslie Hubert Boyd Colvin, MC, and of Edna Mary (*née* Parrott); *m* 1971, (Diana) Caroline Carew, *y d* of Gordon MacPherson Lang Smith and Mildred (*née* Carew-Gibson); one *s* one *d*. *Educ*: Lincoln Sch.; Trinity Coll., Oxford (MA). Assistant Principal, Board of Trade, 1966. Joined HM Foreign (later Diplomatic) Service, 1967; Central Dept, FO, 1967; Second Secretary, Bangkok, 1968–71; European Integration Dept, FCO, 1971–75; First Sec., Paris, 1975–77; First Sec. (Press and Inf.), UK Permanent Representation to the European Community, 1977–82; Asst Sec., Cabinet Office, 1982–85; Counsellor and Hd of Chancery, Budapest, 1985–88; Hd, SE Asian Dept, FCO, 1988–91; Minister, Rome, 1992–96; Ambassador to Belgium, 1996–2001. Diplomatic Communications Consultant, Adam Smith Inst., 2001–03. Consultant, SCS Ltd, 2003–06; Exec. Dir, Jordan Internat. Bank plc, 2005–10. Mem., New Europe Adv. Council, 2001–06; Vice-Pres., European-Atlantic Gp, 2001–06. Chairman: British-Italian Soc., 2001–06; Anglo-Belgian Soc., 2001–13; Patron, Drones Club of Belgium (P. G. Wodehouse Soc.), 1997–2001. Trustee, Prospect Burma, 2001–17. Freeman, City of London, 2002. Commendatore, Ordine della Stella della Solidarietà Italiana (Italy), 2003; Commandeur de l'Ordre de la Couronne (Belgium), 2009. *Recreations*: military history, cycling, rallying old cars. *Address*: 15 Westmoreland Terrace, SW1V 4AG. *T*: (020) 7630 8349. *Club*: Travellers.

**COLVIN, Kathryn Frances**, CVO 2002; FCIL; HM Diplomatic Service, retired; Special Representative of Secretary of State for Foreign and Commonwealth Affairs, since 2015; *b* 11 Sept. 1945; *d* of Ernest Osborne and Frances Joy Osborne; *m* 1971, Prof. Brian Colvin. *Educ*: Walthamstow Hall, Sevenoaks; Bristol Univ. (BA Hons 1967); Bordeaux Univ. (Diplôme d'Etudes Supérieures 1965). FCIL (FIL 1968). Joined FO (later FCO), 1968; Res. Analyst, Western and Central Europe, 1968–94: Inf. Res. Dept, 1968–77; Res. Dept, 1977–94; Mem., UK Delegn to UN Commn on Human Rights, 1980–90; Temp. Duty as 1st Sec., Political, Rome, 1988 and 1991, and Paris, 1992; Deputy Head: OSCE Dept, 1994–95; Western Eur. Dept, 1995–98; Whitehall Liaison Dept, 1998–99; Vice-Marshal of the Diplomatic Corps, and Head, Protocol Div., FCO, 1999–2002; Ambassador to the Holy See, 2002–05. Sen. Clerk to EU Foreign Affairs, Defence and Develt Policy Sub-Cttee, H of L, 2006–13. Mem., London Cttee, 2006–11, Trustee/Dir, 2007–16, Co-Chair, 2015–16, UN Women UK (formerly UNIFEM UK). Ind. Mem., Hons and Awards Cttee, Order of St John, 2007–. Officier, Légion d'Honneur (France), 1996. *Recreations*: art, design, opera, theatre, cinema, swimming.
See also Ven. H. J. Osborne.

**COLVIN, Prof. Sarah Jean**, DPhil; Schröder Professor of German, University of Cambridge, since 2014; Fellow, Jesus College, Cambridge, since 2014; *b* Singapore, 13 July 1967; *d* of Charles Alexander and Jean Colvin; partner Cary Parker; one *s*. *Educ*: Dauntsey's Sch., Devizes; Exeter Coll., Oxford (BA 1st Cl. Hons); Christ Church, Oxford (DPhil 1995). Jun. Res. Fellow, St John's Coll., Oxford, 1995–97; University of Edinburgh: Lectr, 1997–2002; Reader, 2002–04; Eudo C. Mason Chair of German, 2004–10; Prof. in Study of Contemp. Germany and Dir, Inst. for German Studies, Univ. of Birmingham, 2010–12; Prof. of German, Univ. of Warwick, 2013–14. *Publications*: The Rhetorical Feminine: gender and orient on the German stage, 1999; Women and German Drama, 2002; Ulrike Meinhof and West German Terrorism, 2009; The Routledge Handbook of German Politics and Culture, 2015. *Recreations*: theatre, National Alliance for Arts in Criminal Justice. *Address*: Jesus College, Cambridge CB5 8BL. *E*: sjc269@cam.ac.uk.

**COLWYN, 3rd Baron** *cr* 1917; **Ian Anthony Hamilton-Smith**, CBE 1989; Bt 1912; dental surgeon, 1966–2006; bandleader, 1970–2004; *b* 1 Jan. 1942; *s* of 2nd Baron Colwyn and Miriam Gwendoline (*d* 1996), *d* of Victor Ferguson; *S* father, 1966; *m* 1st, 1964, Sonia Jane (marr. diss. 1977; she *d* 2006), *d* of P. H. G. Morgan; one *s* one *d*; 2nd, 1977, Nicola Jeanne, *d* of Arthur Tyers, The Avenue, Sunbury-on-Thames; two *d*. *Educ*: Cheltenham Coll.; St Bartholomew's Hosp. and Royal Dental Hosp., Univ. of London. BDS London 1965; LDS, RCS 1966. Dir, Dental Protection Ltd, 1990–2001 (Chm., 1996–2001). Non-exec. Dir, Project Hope UK, 1998–2001; Chm., Campbell Montague Internat., 2005–08; Dir, London Sedation Services Ltd, 2007–08. President: Natural Medicines Soc., 1989–2005; Huntington's Disease Assoc., 1991–98; Arterial Health Foundn, 2004–12; Soc. for Advancement of Anaesthesia in Dentistry, 1994–97; Mem. Council, Med. Protection Soc., 1994–2001. Mem., H of L Sci. and Technol. Select Cttee, 2006–10; Pres., All Party Parly Gp for Complementary and Integrated Healthcare (formerly Alternative and Complementary Medicine), 1989–; Co-Chm., All Party Parly Jazz Gp, 1994–; Vice Chm., All Party Parly Gp on Dentistry, 1998–; Chm., All Party Parly Gp for Emergency Ambulance and Paramedic Services, 2010–12; Chm., 1997–2004, Mem., 2012–, Refreshment Cttee, H of L; a Dep. Speaker and Dep. Chm. of Cttees, 2007–; elected Mem., H of L, 1999. Patron: Res. Council for Complementary Medicine; Blackie Foundn. Fellow, BDA, 2007. *Recreations*: riparian activities, music, jazz, golf, Rugby. *Heir*: *s* Hon. Craig Peter Hamilton-Smith [*b* 13 Oct. 1968; *m* 2003, Louise Vanessa, *d* of Callum Barney; one *s* one *d*]. *Address*: House of Lords, SW1A 0PW. *T*: (020) 7219 3184.

**COLYER, His Honour John Stuart**; QC 1976; a Circuit Judge, 1991–2000; *b* 25 April 1935; *s* of late Stanley Herbert Colyer, MBE, FHA, and Louisa (*née* Randle); *m* 1961, Emily Warner (*d* 2019), *o d* of late Stanley Leland Dutrow and Mrs Dutrow, Blue Ridge Summit, Pa, USA; two *d*. *Educ*: Dudley Grammar Sch.; Shrewsbury; Worcester Coll., Oxford (Open History Scholarship; BA 1958, MA 1961). 2nd Lieut RA, 1954–55; Lieut RA (TA), 1955–59. Called to the Bar, Middle Temple, 1959 (Bencher, 1983); Instructor, Univ. of Pennsylvania Law Sch., Philadelphia, 1959–60, Asst Prof., 1960–61; practised English Bar, Midland and Oxford Circuit (formerly Oxford Circuit), 1961–91; a Recorder, 1986–91. Hon. Reader, 1985–91, and Mem. Council, 1985–91, Council of Legal Educn (Lectr (Law of Landlord and Tenant), 1970–89); Vice-Pres., Lawyers' Christian Fellowship, 1993–2010 (Chm., 1981–89); Mem., Anglo-American Real Property Inst., 1980– (Treasurer, 1984). Blundell Meml Lectr, 1977, 1982, 1986. Chm., Selection Cttee, Margaret Parkinson Scholarship, RCN, 1998–2009, RCN Foundn, 2009–16; Trustee and Gov., Royal Sch. for Deaf Children, Margate, 2000– (Chm., 2005–08, 2009–; Chm., 2008–09, 2014–15, Dir, 2009–15, John Townsend Trust); Trustee, RCN Foundn, 2010–17. *Publications*: (ed jtly) Encyclopaedia of Forms and Precedents (Landlord and Tenant), vol. XI, 1965, vol. XII, 1966; A Modern View of the Law of Torts, 1966; Landlord and Tenant, in Halsbury's Laws of England, 4th edn, 1981, new edn, 1994; Gen. Ed., Megarry's The Rent Acts, 11th edn, 1988; articles in Conveyancer and other professional jls. *Recreations*: entertaining my family, opera, cultivation of cacti and of succulents (esp. Lithops), gardening generally, travel, education and welfare of the profoundly deaf. *Address*: c/o Falcon Chambers, Falcon Court, EC4Y 1AA. *T*: (020) 7353 2484, *Fax*: (020) 7353 1261.

**COLYTON, 2nd Baron** *cr* 1956, of Farway, Devon and of Taunton, Somerset; **Alisdair John Munro Hopkinson;** *b* 7 May 1958; *s* of Hon. Nicholas Henry Eno Hopkinson (*d* 1991), *o s* of 1st Baron Colyton, PC, CMG and Fiona Margaret (*d* 1996), *o d* of Sir Thomas Torquil Alphonso Munro, 5th Bt; *S* grandfather, 1996; *m* 1980, Philippa, *d* of P. J. Bell; two *s* one *d*. *Heir*: *s* Hon. James Patrick Munro Hopkinson, *b* 8 May 1983. *Address*: Lindertis, by Kirriemuir, Angus DD8 5NT.

**COMBER, Ven. Anthony James;** Archdeacon of Leeds, 1982–92, now Archdeacon Emeritus; *b* 20 April 1927; *s* of late Norman Mederson Comber and Nellie Comber. *Educ*: Leeds Grammar School; Leeds Univ. (MSc Mining); St Chad's Coll., Durham (DipTh); Munich Univ. Colliery underground official, 1951–53. Vicar: Oulton, 1960–69; Hunslet, 1969–77; Rector of Farnley, 1977–82. *Publications*: (contrib.) Today's Church and Today's World, 1977. *Recreations*: politics; walking in Bavaria. *Address*: 28 Blayds Garth, Woodlesford, Leeds LS26 8WN. *T*: (0113) 288 0489.

**COMBERMERE, 6th Viscount** *cr* 1827; **Thomas Robert Wellington Stapleton-Cotton;** Bt 1677; Baron 1814; *b* 30 Aug. 1969; *o s* of 5th Viscount Combermere; *S* father, 2000; *m* 2005, Caroline Sarah, *o d* of late Charles Leonard Anthony Irby; one *s* one *d*. *Heir*: *s* Hon. Laszlo Michael Wellington Stapleton-Cotton, *b* 20 Aug. 2010.

**COMBES, Ven. Roger Matthew;** Archdeacon of Horsham, 2003–14; *b* 12 June 1947; *m* 1983, Christine Mary Keiller; two *d*. *Educ*: King's Coll., London (LLB 1969); Ridley Hall, Cambridge. Ordained deacon, 1974, priest, 1975; Curate: St Paul's, Onslow Square, 1974–77; Holy Trinity, Brompton, 1976–77; Holy Sepulchre with All Saints, Cambridge, 1977–86; Rector, St Matthew's, Silverhill, 1986–2003; RD, Hastings, 1998–2002. *Address*: 3 Aldingbourne Close, Ifield, Crawley RH11 0QJ.

**COMINS, David;** Rector, Glasgow Academy, 1994–2005; *b* 1 March 1948; *s* of Jack Comins and Marjorie Mabel (*née* Rowbotham); *m* 1972, Christine Anne Speak; one *s* two *d*. *Educ*: Scarborough Boys' High Sch.; Downing Coll., Cambridge (BA, MA, PGCE). Assistant Mathematics Teacher: Mill Hill Sch., 1971–75; Strathallan Sch., Perthshire, 1975–76; Glenalmond College, Perthshire: Asst Maths Teacher, 1976–80; Head of Maths, 1980–85; Dir of Studies, 1985–89; Dep. Head, Queen's Coll., Taunton, 1989–94. Teacher of Maths, Shenzhen Coll. of Internat. Educn, Shenzhen, 2005–07. Churchill Fellow, 1981. *Recreations*: mountaineering, ballet, music, crosswords, sudoku. *Address*: Flat 6, Block 8, Kirklee Gate, Glasgow G12 0SZ. *Club*: Alpine.

**COMNINOS, Sophie Henrietta;** see Turner Laing, S. H.

**COMPAGNONI, Marco;** Partner, since 2006, and Global Co-Head of Private Equity, since 2013, Weil Gotshal & Manges (Member, Management Committee, since 2015); *b* Haltwhistle, Northumberland, 3 May 1962; *s* of Peter Compagnoni and Santina Margherita Compagnoni. *Educ*: Queen Elizabeth Grammar Sch., Hexham; Univ. of Newcastle upon Tyne (LLB Hons). Admitted solicitor, 1987; joined Lovell, White & King, later Lovell White Durrant, then Lovells, 1985, Partner, 1993–2006 (Hd, Internat. Private Equity Practice, 2002–06); Mem., Partnership Bd, 1996–99 and 2001–04). Trustee: Serpentine Gall., 2000–15; Royal Opera Hse, Covent Gdn, 2000–07; Royal Opera Hse Benevolent Fund, 2000–07; The Foundation Foundn, 2018–; Gov., Royal Ballet Co., 2001–07; Dir, Sadler's Wells Trust Ltd, 2009–16; Pres., Serpentine Galleries of the Americas, 2014–16; Chair, Contemporary Art Soc., 2018–. Mem. Council, Friends of Covent Gdn, 1995– (Chm., 2000–07). Mem., Law Panel, The Times, 2006–09. *Recreations*: opera, contemporary art, shooting, Parson Jack Russell terriers, eating, wine, Scotland, Belted Galloway cattle, Zwartble sheep. *Address*: c/o Weil, Gotshal & Manges, 110 Fetter Lane, EC4A 1AY.

**COMPSTON, Alastair;** see Compston, D. A. S.

**COMPSTON, His Honour Christopher Dean**, MA; a Circuit Judge, 1986–2013; *b* 5 May 1940; *s* of Vice Adm. Sir Peter Maxwell Compston, KCB and Valerie Bocquet; *m* 1st, 1968, Bronwen Henniker Gotley (marr. diss. 1982); one *d* (and two *s* decd); 2nd, 1983, Caroline Philippa, *d* of Paul Odgers, CB, MBE, TD; two *s* one *d*. *Educ*: Epsom Coll. (Prae Sum.); Magdalen Coll., Oxford (MA). Called to the Bar, Middle Temple, 1965, Bencher, 2006; a Recorder, 1982–86. Mem. Senate, Inns of Court, 1983–86. Trustee: Fund for Epilepsy, 2000–05; Prison Fellowship, 1997–2007; ZANE, 2012–; Patron: Second Chance, 2008–; Compassionate Friends, 2014–. *Publications*: Recovery from Divorce: a practical guide, 1993; (contrib.) Relational Justice, 1994; Cracking up without Breaking up, 1998. *Recreations*: the arts, writing, family, travel, gardening, selling second hand books for good causes. *Address*: c/o Royal Courts of Justice, Strand, WC2A 2LL. *Club*: Seaview Yacht.

**COMPSTON, Prof. (David) Alastair (Standish)**, CBE 2016; FRCP; FRS 2016; FMedSci, FRSB; Professor of Neurology, University of Cambridge, 1989–2015, now Emeritus; Fellow of Jesus College, Cambridge, 1990–2015, now Emeritus; *b* 23 Jan. 1948; *s* of late Nigel Dean Compston and Diana Mary Compston (*née* Standish); *m* 1973, Juliet Elizabeth Page (*see* J. E. Compston); one *d*. *Educ*: Rugby Sch.; Middlesex Hospital Med. Sch., London Univ. (MB BS (Hons); PhD). FRCP 1986. Jun. Hosp. appts, Nat. Hosp. for Nervous Diseases, 1972–82; Cons. Neurologist, University Hosp. of Wales, 1982–87; Prof. of Neurology, Univ. of Wales Coll. of Medicine, 1987–88. Editor, 2004–13, Editor Emeritus, 2014, Brain. Pres., Assoc. of British Neurologists, 2009–11. For. Mem., Nat. Acad. of Scis, Germany, 2008; For. Associate Mem., Nat. Acad. of Medicine (formerly Inst. of Medicine, Nat. Academies), USA, 2012. Founder FMedSci 1998; FRSB (FIBiol 2000). FRSA 1997. Internat. Prize for Multiple Sclerosis Res., Sobek Foundn, 2002; Charcot Award, Multiple Sclerosis Internat. Fedn, 2007; Zülch Prize, Max Planck Soc., 2010; Medal for Scientific Achievement in Neurol., World Fedn of Neurol., 2013; John Dystel Prize, Amer. Acad. of Neurology, 2015; Hughlings Jackson Medal, RSocMed, 2015; Galen Medal, Soc. of Apothecaries, 2016; Assoc. of British Neurologists Medal, 2016; Jean Hunter Prize, RCP, 2018. *Publications*: (ed) McAlpine's Multiple Sclerosis, 4th edn 2005; Simples and Rarities Suitable and Honourable to the College, 2018; (jtly) Queen Square: a history of the National Hospital and its Institute of Neurology, 2018; contribs to human and experimental demyelinating diseases, in learned jls. *Recreations*: being outside, antiquarian books. *Address*: Mead House, West Wickham Road, Horseheath, Cambridge CB21 4QA. *T*: (01223) 893414. *Club*: Garrick.

**COMPSTON, Prof. Juliet Elizabeth**, OBE 2014; MD; FRCP, FRCPath, FRCPE, FMedSci; Professor of Bone Medicine, University of Cambridge, 2003–12, now Emeritus; *b* 18 Dec. 1945; *d* of Sir Denys Lionel Page, FBA and Katharine Elizabeth Page; *m* 1973, (David) Alastair (Standish) Compston, *qv*; one *d*. *Educ*: Middlesex Hosp. Med. Sch., London Univ. (BSc 1967; MB BS 1970; MD 1979). FRCP 1988; FRCPath 1996; FRCPE 2011. Sen. Lectr and Hon. Consultant, Univ. Hosp. of Wales; Lectr in Medicine, then Reader in Metabolic Bone Disease, 1999–2003, Univ. of Cambridge. Hon. Consultant Physician, Addenbrooke's Hospital, Cambridge. Ed.-in-Chief, Jl Bone and Mineral Res., 2013–17. Sec. and Treas., Amer. Soc. for Bone and Mineral Res., 2019–. FMedSci 1999. Kohn Foundn Award, Nat. Osteoporosis Soc., 2006; John G. Haddad Award, Internat. Bone and Mineral Soc., 2009; Frederic C. Bartter Award, Amer. Soc. for Bone and Mineral Res., 2009. *Publications*: (ed) Osteoporosis: new perspectives on causes, prevention and treatment, 1996; (with Clifford Rosen) Osteoporosis, 1997, 2nd edn 2001; Understanding

Osteoporosis, 1998; (with Ignac Fogelman) Key Advances in the Effective Management of Osteoporosis, 1999; (ed jtly) HRT and the Menopause: current therapy, 2002; (jtly) Osteoporosis: best medicine for osteoporosis, 2005; (ed jtly) Bone Disease of Organ Transplantation, 2005; 420 articles in peer-reviewed jls. *Address:* Department of Medicine, University of Cambridge Clinical School, Addenbrooke's Hospital, Hills Road, Cambridge CB2 0QQ; Mead House, West Wickham Road, Horseheath, Cambridge CB21 4QA.

**COMPSTON, Prof. William,** PhD; FRS 1987; FAA; FTSE; Australian National University: Professor in Isotope Geochemistry, 1987–96, now Emeritus; Consultant, Research School of Earth Sciences, 1997–99 and since 2002; University Fellow, 2000–01, Visiting Fellow, since 2002; *b* 19 Feb. 1931; *s* of late J. A. Compston; *m* 1952, Elizabeth Blair; three *s* one *d*. *Educ:* Christian Brothers' Coll., Fremantle; Univ. of WA (BSc (Hons); PhD). Res. Fellow, CIT, 1956–58; Res. Fellow, Dept of Terrestrial Magnetism, Carnegie Inst. of Washington, 1958; Lectr, Univ. of WA, 1959–60; Australian National University: Fellow, then Sen. Fellow, 1961–74; Professorial Fellow, 1974–87. Lectures: Mawson, 1988, Flinders, 1998, Australian Acad. of Sci.; Hallimond, Mineralogical Soc., 1998. Hon. Fellow, Chinese Acad. of Geol Scis, 2006. Hon. DSc Western Australia, 1988. Stillwell Award, Geol Soc. of Australia, 1990; Clunies Ross Award, Clunies Ross Meml Foundn, 1995; Friendship Award, State Admin of Foreign Experts Affairs, China, 2006. *Address:* Research School of Earth Sciences, Australian National University, Canberra, ACT 0200, Australia; 8 Wells Gardens, Manuka, ACT 2603, Australia.

**COMPTON,** family name of **Marquess of Northampton**.

**COMPTON, Earl; Daniel Bingham Compton;** *b* 16 Jan. 1973; *s* and *heir* of Marquess of Northampton, *qv*; *m* 2001, Lucy (marr. diss. 2008), 5th *d* of Lt-Col Benedict Cardozo; two *d*; *m* 2017, Emilia, 2nd *d* of Captain John Hungerford; one *s*. *Heir: s* Hon. Henry Douglas Hungerford Compton, *b* 24 Oct. 2018.

**COMPTON, Benjamin Edward;** QC 2011; *b* Taunton, 11 May 1956; *s* of David Compton and Susan Compton; *m* 1991, Belinda Grice; one *s* two *d*. *Educ:* Harrow Sch.; Inns of Court Sch. of Law. Called to the Bar, Lincoln's Inn, 1979; in practice as barrister, specialising in health and safety and clinical negligence. *Recreations:* walking in mountains, ski-ing, running a small farm in Wiltshire. *Address:* Corsley House, Corsley, Warminster, Wilts BA12 7PH. *T:* (01373) 832229; Outer Temple Chambers, 222 The Strand, WC2R 1BA. *T:* (020) 7353 6381. *E:* Ben.Compton@outertemple.com. *Club:* Soho House.

**COMPTON, Prof. Richard Guy,** DPhil; Professor of Chemistry, since 1996, and Aldrichian Praelector, since 2011, University of Oxford; Tutorial Fellow, St John's College, Oxford, since 1985; *b* Scunthorpe, 10 March 1955; *s* of Joseph Compton and Doreen Compton. *Educ:* Frome Grammar Sch.; University Coll., Oxford (MA; DPhil 1981). Lecturer in Chemistry: Univ. of Liverpool, 1981–85; Univ. of Oxford, 1985–96. Lifelong Hon. Prof., Sichuan Univ., 2004–; Vis. Prof., Ecole Normale Superiore, Paris, 2017. MAE 2015. Fellow: Internat. Soc. of Electrochemistry, 2010; Internat. Union of Pure and Applied Chemistry, 2014. *Publications:* Electrode Potentials, 1996; Foundations of Physical Chemistry, 1996; Understanding Voltammetry, 2007, 3rd edn 2018; A G Stromberg: first class scientist, second class citizen, 2011; Understanding Voltammetry: problems and solutions, 2012; Simulation of Electrode Processes, 2014; over 1500 papers in jls incl. Electroanalysis, ChemPhysChem, Angewandte Chimie. *Recreations:* reading, travel. *Address:* St John's College, Oxford OX1 3JP. *T:* (01865) 275957, *Fax:* (01865) 275410. *E:* richard.compton@chem.ox.ac.uk.

**COMYNS, Jacqueline Roberta;** a District Judge (Magistrates' Courts) (formerly a Metropolitan Stipendiary Magistrate), 1982–2013; *b* 27 April 1943; *d* of late Jack and Belle Fisher; *m* 1963, Malcolm John Comyns, medical practitioner; one *s*. *Educ:* Hendon County Grammar Sch.; London Sch. of Econs and Pol Science (LLB Hons 1964). Called to the Bar, Inner Temple, 1969; practised on South Eastern Circuit; a Recorder, 1991–2002. *Recreations:* theatre, travel, swimming.

**CONAGHAN, Geoffrey;** Agent General for Victoria, Australia, in London, 2013–16; *b* Australia, 1958; *s* of John Conaghan and Amirisa, (Amy), Conaghan (*née* Stavrianou); partner, Mathew Erbs. *Educ:* Holy Cross Coll., Ryde, Sydney; Australian Nat. Univ. (BA). Exec. Dir, Tourism Trng, Victoria, 1987–94; Gen. Manager, Corporate Affairs, Melbourne Airport, 1994–2009; Comr of Victoria to India, Victorian Govt Business Office, 2009–13. Comr, Tourism Victoria Bd, 1998–2009. *Clubs:* Royal Over-Seas League; Castellorizian (Melbourne).

**CONALTY, Ven. Julie Anne;** Archdeacon of Tonbridge, since 2017; *b* 1963. *Educ:* SE Inst. of Theol Educn. Ordained deacon, 1999, priest, 2000; non-stipendiary Minister: St Michael the Archangel, East Wickham, 1999–2004; St Luke with Holy Trinity, Charlton, 2004–10; Curate, St Mark and St Margaret, Plumstead Common, 2010–12; Vicar, Christ Church, Erith, 2012–17; Bishop's Advr for Ordained Ministry, Dio. of Rochester, 2013–17; Area Dean, Erith, 2014–17. Mem., Gen. Synod, C of E. Hon. Canon, Rochester Cathedral, 2016–. *Address:* c/o Diocese of Rochester, St Nicholas Church, Boley Hill, Rochester ME1 1SL. *T:* (01634) 560000.

**CONANT, Sir John (Ernest Michael),** 2nd Bt *cr* 1954; farmer and landowner, since 1949; *b* 24 April 1923; *s* of Sir Roger Conant, 1st Bt, CVO, and Daphne, Lady Conant, *d* of A. E. Learoyd; *S* father, 1973; *m* 1st, 1950, Periwinkle Elizabeth (*d* 1985), *d* of late Dudley Thorp, Kimbolton, Hunts; two *s* two *d* (and one *s* decd); 2nd, 1992, Mrs Clare Attwater, *yr d* of W. E. Madden. *Educ:* Eton; Corpus Christi Coll., Cambridge (BA Agric). Served in Grenadier Guards, 1942–45; at CCC Cambridge, 1946–49. Farming in Rutland, 1950–; High Sheriff of Rutland, 1960. *Recreations:* fishing, shooting, tennis. *Heir: s* Simon Edward Christopher Conant [*b* 13 Oct. 1958; *m* 2000, Justine Sarah Preston]. *Address:* Periwinkle, Lyndon, Oakham, Rutland LE15 8TU. *T:* (01572) 737275.

**CONCANNON, Dr Harcourt Martin Grant;** President, Pensions Appeal Tribunals for England and Wales, 1998–2008; *s* of Edwin Martin Joseph Concannon and Caroline Elizabeth Margaret Concannon (*née* Grant); *m* 1978, Elaine Baldwin; one *s* one *d*. *Educ:* University Coll. Sch.; University College London (LLB, LLM, PhD). Solicitor. Articled to Town Clerk, London Borough of Bexley, 1960–64; Lectr in Law, Nottingham Poly., 1964–68; Senior Lecturer: Sheffield City Poly., 1968–71; Univ. of Salford, 1972–93; Full-time Chm., Independent Tribunal Service, 1993–98. *Recreations:* languages, painting, walking.

**CONDON,** family name of **Baron Condon**.

**CONDON,** Baron *cr* 2001 (Life Peer), of Langton Green in the County of Kent; **Paul Leslie Condon,** Kt 1994; QPM 1989; DL; Commissioner, Metropolitan Police, 1993–2000; Chairman, Anti-Corruption and Security (formerly Anti-Corruption) Unit, International Cricket Council, 2003–10 (Director, 2000–03); *m*; two *s* one *d*. *Educ:* St Peter's Coll., Oxford (Bramshill Scholar; MA; Hon. Fellow). Joined Metropolitan Police, 1967; Inspector, 1975–78; Chief Inspector, 1978–81; Superintendent, Bethnal Green, 1981–82; Staff Officer to Comr as Superintendent, then as Chief Superintendent, 1982–84; Asst Chief Constable, Kent Constabulary, 1984–87; Dep. Asst Comr, 1987–88, Asst Comr, 1988–89, Metropolitan Police; Chief Constable, Kent Constabulary, 1989–92. Mem., H of L,

2001–17. Pres., BSIA, 2003–06. Non-exec. Dir, G4S (formerly Securicor, then Group 4 Securicor), 2000–13 (Dep. Chm., 2006). CCMI (CIMgt 1991); FRSA 1992. DL Kent, 2001.

**CONDRY, Rt Rev. Dr Edward Francis;** Bishop Suffragan of Ramsbury, 2012–18; an Honorary Assistant Bishop, Diocese of Peterborough, since 2018; *b* 25 April 1953; *s* of Roy and Muriel Condry; *m* 1977, Sarah Louise Long; two *s* two *d*. *Educ:* Latymer Upper Sch.; Univ. of E Anglia (BA 1974); Exeter Coll., Oxford (BLitt 1977); DPhil Oxon 1980; Lincoln Theol Coll.; Univ. of Nottingham (DipTh 1981); MBA Open Univ. 2002. Ordained deacon, 1982, priest, 1983; Asst Curate, Weston Favell, Northampton, 1982–85; Vicar, Bloxham with Milcombe and S Newington, 1985–93; Rector, Rugby Team Ministry, 1993–2002; Canon Treas., Canterbury Cathedral, 2002–12; Hon. Canon, Salisbury Cathedral, 2012–18. *Recreations:* running, cycling, canoeing, rowing, walking, laughing at my own jokes, planning adventures.

**CONEFREY, Stella;** *see* Bruzzi, Stella.

**CONGDON, David Leonard;** Head of Campaigns and Policies (formerly Director of Public Affairs, then Head of External Relations), MENCAP, 1998–2012; *b* 16 Oct. 1949; *s* of Archibald George Congdon and late Marjorie Congdon; *m* 1972, Teresa Winifred Hill; one *d*. *Educ:* Alleyn's Sch.; Thames Polytechnic (BSc Hons Econ.). Graduate Systems Analyst, ICL, 1970; Philips Electronics: Systems Analyst, 1973–85; Computer Consultant, 1985–92. London Borough of Croydon: Councillor, 1976–92; Vice-Chm., Educn Cttee, 1979–83; Chm., Social Services, 1983–86, 1990–91; Dep. Leader, 1988–92; Chm., Finance Sub-Cttee. Vice-Chm., local Cons. Assocs, 1979–82. MP (C) Croydon North East, 1992–97; contested (C) Croydon Central, 1997, 2001. PPS to Minister of State for Social Security, 1995–97. Mem., Select Cttee on Health, 1992–95. Lay Mem., E Surrey CCG, 2013–. Governor, Croydon Coll., 1979–92. Trustee: Action on Elder Abuse, 2012–; Croydon Mencap, 2012–. Voluntary advr, Challenging Behaviour Foundn, 2012–. *Recreations:* tennis, badminton, reading political biographies, listening to music; lapsed Fulham fan. *Address:* 56 Keston Avenue, Old Coulsdon, Surrey CR5 1HN.

**CONGDON, Prof. Timothy George,** CBE 1997; Chairman (formerly Director), Institute of International Monetary Research and Professor of Economics, University of Buckingham, since 2014; Founder and Chief Executive, International Monetary Research Ltd, 2009–13; *b* 28 April 1951; *s* of D. G. Congdon and Olive Emma Congdon (*née* Good); *m* 1988, Dorianne Preston-Lowe; one *d*. *Educ:* Univ. of Oxford (BA 1st cl. Hons Mod. Hist. and Econs). MCSI. On economics staff, The Times, 1973–76; Chief Economist, L. Messel & Co., 1976–86 (Partner, 1980–86); Chief London Economist, Shearson Lehman, 1986–88; Founder, Man. Dir, 1989–2001, Chief Economist, 2001–05, Lombard Street Research. Non-exec. Chm., SBW Insurance Research, 1994–97. Mem., Treasury Panel of Independent Forecasters, 1993–97. Hon. Prof., Cardiff Business Sch., 1990–2006; Vis. Prof., Sir John Cass Business Sch., City of London (formerly City Univ. Business Sch.), 1998–2004; Vis. Fellow, LSE, 2005–07. Econs columnist, Standpoint mag., 2008–. Econs spokesman, UKIP, 2010–14. Contested (UK Ind) Forest of Dean, 2010. Chm., Freedom Assoc., 2011–14. Hon. Sec., Political Economy Club, 1999–2011. FRSA 1991; Fellow, Soc. of Business Economists, 2000. Hon. FIA 2002. *Publications:* Monetary Control in Britain, 1982; The Debt Threat, 1988; Reflections on Monetarism, 1992; Money and Asset Prices in Boom and Bust, 2005; Keynes, the Keynesians and Monetarism, 2007; Central Banking in a Free Society, 2009; How to Stop the Recession, 2009; Money in a Free Society, 2011; (ed) Money in the Great Recession, 2017. *Recreations:* reading, walking, chess, opera. *Address:* Huntley Manor, Huntley, Glos GL19 3HQ. *Club:* Royal Automobile.

**CONGLETON,** 9th Baron *cr* 1841, of Congleton, co. Chester; **John Patrick Christian Parnell;** Bt 1766; *b* 17 March 1959; *er s* of 8th Baron Congleton and of Anna Hedvig Parnell (*née* Sommerfelt); *S* father, 2015; *m* 1985, Marjorie-Anne, *o d* of John Hobdell, Cobham, Surrey; two *s* one *d*. *Educ:* Eton; Univ. of Edinburgh. *Heir: s* Hon. Christopher John Edward Parnell, *b* 1987.

**CONGO, Sonia, (Mrs C. W. Congo);** *see* Lawson, S.

**CONINGHAM, Prof. Robin Andrew Evelyn,** PhD; FRAS; FSA; Professor of Early Medieval Archaeology, since 2005, and UNESCO Professor in Archaeological Ethics and Practice in Cultural Heritage, since 2014, Durham University; *b* Pembury, 2 Dec. 1965; *s* of late Simon Coningham and of Stephanie Coningham; *m* 1990, Paula Geake; two *s*. *Educ:* Tunbridge Wells Tech. High Sch.; Tonbridge Sch.; King's Coll., Cambridge (Coll. Schol.; BA Archaeol. and Anthropol. 1988; PhD Archaeol. 1994). FRAS 1994. Grad. Schol., British Inst. in Eastern Africa, Nairobi, 1989–94; Department of Archaeological Sciences, University of Bradford: Lectr, 1994–99; Sen. Lectr, 1999–2001; Reader, 2001–04; Prof. of S Asian Archaeol., 2004–05; Hd of Dept, 2004–05; Durham University: Hd, Dept of Archaeol., 2007–08; Pro Vice Chancellor and Hd, Faculty of Social Scis and Health, 2008–15. Consultant, World Heritage Centre, 1997–2002 and 2009–, Expert Mem., Internat. Scientific Steering Cttee for Lumbini, 2010–, UNESCO. Mem., Editl Bd, S Asian Studies, 2010–15. Quality Assurance Agency for Higher Education: Specialist Reviewer, 1995–2001; Rev. Chair, 2000–02; Mem., Pearson World Class Qualifications Expert Panel, 2012–15. Arts and Humanities Research Council: Mem., Peer Rev. Coll., 2004–06, 2009–; Mem., Res. Panel 1, 2006–08; Mem., Global Challenges Res. Fund Strategic Adv. Gp, 2017–. British Academy: Mem., Sponsored Insts and Socs Cttee, 2009–17; Mem., Internat. Engagement Cttee, 2011–17; For. Corresp. Mem., Assoc. Internazionale di Studi sul Mediterraneo e l'Oriente, 2017–. Hon. Sec., British Inst. Persian Studies, 2006–09. Gov., N Tees and Hartlepool NHS Foundn Trust, 2011–14. Trustee: Ancient Indian and Iran Trust, 1999–2010; Antiquity Trust, 2010–. FSA 2016. *Publications:* Anuradhapura: the British-Sri Lankan Excavations at Anuradhapura Salgaha Watta, vol. 1, The Site, 1999, vol. 2, The Artefacts, 2006, (with P. Gunawardhana) vol. 3, The Hinterland, 2013; (with J.-F. Milou) UNESCO Reactive Monitoring Mission to Lumbini, Birthplace of Lord Buddha: report and recommendations of a UNESCO mission to Nepal, 2001; (with P. Gunawardhana) Essays in Archaeology, 2005; (with I. Ali) Charsadda: the British-Pakistani excavations at the Bala Hisar, 2007; (with P. Gunawardhana) Essays in Archaeology 2, 2010; (with G. Scarre) The Ethics of Archaeology: appropriating the past, 2013; (with R. Young) The Archaeology of South Asia: from the Indus to Asoka, 2015; (with N. Lewer) Archaeology, Cultural Heritage Protection and Community Engagement in South Asia, 2019; contrib. popular, learned and scientific articles and book chapters on archaeol. of Buddhism, S Asia and Iran, and on post-disaster and post-conflict heritage protection. *Recreations:* table-tennis, table-football, lap-dogs, typing with two fingers. *Address:* Department of Archaeology, Durham University, South Road, Durham DH1 3LE. *T:* (0191) 334 2904, *Fax:* (0191) 334 2905. *E:* r.a.e.coningham@durham.ac.uk. *Club:* Travellers.

**CONINGSBY, His Honour Thomas Arthur Charles;** QC 1986; a Circuit Judge, 1992–2006; Designated Civil Judge, 1999–2006; Vicar General of the Province of York, 1980–2008; *b* 21 April 1933; *s* of Francis Charles and Eilleen Rowena Coningsby; *m* 1959, Elaine Mary Coningsby; two *s* three *d*. *Educ:* Epsom; Queens' Coll., Cambridge (MA). Called to the Bar, Gray's Inn, 1957; Mem., Inner Temple, 1988. A Recorder, 1986–92; Head of Chambers, 3 Dr Johnson's Building, Temple, 1988–92; Dep. High Court Judge,

1992–2006; Liaison Judge, 1995–2005. Chancellor: Dio. of York, 1977–2006; Dio. of Peterborough, 1989–2006. Member: Lord Chancellor's Matrimonial Causes Rule Cttee, 1986–89; Gen. Council of the Bar, 1988–90; Supreme Court Procedure Cttee, 1988–92; Chm., Family Law Bar Assoc., 1988–90 (Sec., 1986–88); Pres., SE London Magistrates' Assoc., 1996–2006. Member, General Synod, 1970–2008 (Member: Legal Adv. Commn, 1975–2008; Fees Adv. Commn, 1979–2008). Mem. Governing Body, SPCK, 1990–92. Pres., Chipstead Decorative and Fine Arts Soc., 2014–18 (Chm., 2011–14). *Recreation:* lawn tennis. *Address:* Leyfields, Chipstead, Surrey CR5 3SG. *T:* (01737) 553304. *Club:* Athenæum.

CONLEY, **Brian Paul**; entertainer, host, actor and singer; *b* Paddington, London, 7 Aug. 1961; *s* of Colin and Pauline Conley; *m* 1996, Anne-Marie Aindow; two *d*. *Educ:* Wembley High Sch.; Barbara Speakes Stage Sch. *Television:* as host: Brian Conley This Way Up, 1989–90; Brian Conley Show, 1992–95 and 2000–02; Brian Conley Alive & Dangerous, 1996; National Lottery: We've Got Your Number, 1999; Royal Variety Performance, 1999; An Audience With…, 2002; Judgement Day, 2003; Let Me Entertain You, 2006–07; Dirty Rotten Cheater, 2007; Timeline, 2014; The TV That Made Me, 2015–; as actor: Survivors, 1977; Outside Chance, 1993; Time after Time, 1994–95; The Grimleys, 1999–2000; The Life and Times of Vivienne Vyle, 2007; *film:* Circus, 2000; Dream, 2001; Arthur's Dyke, 2001; Cruise of the Gods, 2002; Equilibrium, 2002; I am Bob, 2007; for television: Hotel!, 2001; *theatre:* eight Royal Variety Performances, 1988–99; pantomimes, 1991–; Me and My Girl, Adelphi, 1991; Jolson (as Jolson), Victoria Palace, 1995–98; Elton John's Glasses, Queen's, 1998; Chitty Chitty Bang Bang, Palladium, 2005; The Music Man, Chichester, 2008 (Best Performance in a Musical, Theatrical Mgt Assoc.); Hairspray, Shaftesbury, 2009–10; Brother Love's Travelling Salvation Show, UK tour, 2011; Oliver!, UK tour, 2012; Barnum, UK tour, 2014; Alive & Dangerous tour, 2016; *albums:* Stage to Stage, 1996; Songs from the Shows, 2002; Brian Conley Sings, 2002; Let the Good Times Roll, 2002. Patron, Hire a Hero, 2014–. Nat. TV Award for Most Popular Comedy Performer, 1995; Most Popular Performer, Manchester Evening News Th. Awards, 2004. *Recreations:* walking the dogs, cinema and theatre, being a dad. *Address:* c/o Sue Latimer, ARG Talent, 4a Exmoor Street, W10 6BD. *T:* (020) 7436 6400. *E:* latimer@argtalent.com.

CONLEY, **Rosemary Jean Neil**, CBE 2004; DL; diet and fitness expert; Partner, Rosemary Conley Enterprises, since 1986; Chairman, Digital Wellbeing Ltd, since 2015; Managing Director, Facial Toning Solutions Ltd, since 2018; *b* 19 Dec. 1946; *d* of Oswald Neil Weston and Edith Cecilia Weston; *m* 1st, 1968, Philip Conley (marr. diss. 1983); one *d*; 2nd, 1986, Michael John Rimmington. *Educ:* Bushloe High Sch., Wigston. RSA Exercise to Music. Secretary, then founded own slimming club business, Slimming and Good Grooming, 1971; sold business to IPC Magazines, 1981; Man. Dir, Successful Slimming and Good Grooming Clubs Ltd, subsid. of IPC, 1981–85; (with Mike Rimmington): founder: Rosemary Conley Enterprises, 1986; Rosemary Conley Diet and Fitness Clubs Ltd, 1993 (Chm., 1993–2014); Rosemary Conley Diet and Fitness magazine, Quorn House Publishing Ltd, 1996 (Chm., 1996–2014); Rosemary Conley Licences Ltd, 2003 (Chm., 2003–17); Quorn House Media, 2008 (Chm., 2008–14). Patron: Mildmay; Send a Cow; Laura Centre, Leicester; STEPS Conductive Educn Sch., Shepshed, Leics; FareShare E Midlands, 2015–. Pres., Leics. Young Enterprise, 2005–. DL Leics, 1999. Hon. Freeman, City of Leicester, 2001. *Publications:* Eat Yourself Slim, 1982; Eat and Stay Slim, 1983; Positive Living, 1984; Rosemary Conley's Hip and Thigh Diet, 1988, 2nd edn 1992; Rosemary Conley's Complete Hip and Thigh Diet, 1989, 2nd edn 2002; Looking Good, Feeling Great, 1989; Rosemary Conley's Inch Loss Plan, 1990, 2nd edn 1998; Whole Body Programme, 1992; Rosemary Conley's Metabolism Booster Diet, 1991; (with Patricia Bourne) Rosemary Conley's New Hip and Thigh Diet Cookbook, 1993; Shape Up For Summer, 1993; Rosemary Conley's Flat Stomach Plan, 1994; Rosemary Conley's Beach Body Plan, 1994; Be Slim, Be Fit, 1995; Rosemary Conley's Complete Flat Stomach Plan, 1996, 2nd edn 2002; Rosemary Conley's New Body Plan, 1997, 2nd edn 2002; Rosemary Conley's Low Fat Cookbook, 1999; Rosemary Conley's Low Fat Cookbook 2, 2000; Rosemary Conley's Red Wine Diet, 2000; Eat Yourself Slim, 2001; Rosemary Conley's GI Jeans Diet, 2006; Rosemary Conley's Ultimate GI Jeans Diet, 2007; GI Hip and Thigh Diet, 2008; Slim to Win: diet and cookbook, 2008; Rosemary Conley's Amazing Inch Loss Plan, 2010; My Kitchen Table, 2011; The Secrets of Staying Young, 2011; The FAB Diet, 2013; The 3-2-1 Diet, 2015; presented 31 fitness videos. *Recreations:* ice skating (celebrity contestant, Dancing on Ice, ITV, 2012), walking dogs, home making, writing, speaking about diet and fitness and sharing Christian testimony. *Address:* Rosemary Conley Enterprises, PO Box 10470, Markfield, Leics LE67 9XP. *T:* (01530) 249396. *E:* rosemary@rosemaryconleyenterprises.com.

CONLON, **Michael Anthony**; QC 2002; *b* 26 Nov. 1951; *s* of Thomas Reginald Conlon and Barbara (*née* Capper); *m* 1974, Pamela Carter; one *d*. *Educ:* Enfield Grammar Sch.; Queens' Coll., Cambridge (BA 1973, MA 1977). Called to the Bar, Inner Temple, 1974; in practice at the Bar, 1974–76; government lawyer, 1976–86; tax partner in accounting firms, 1986–91; solicitor, 1992–97; Partner, Allen & Overy, 1993–97; returned to the Bar, 1997; Hd of Indirect Tax, Hogan Lovells Internat. LLP, 2012–15; returned to the Bar, 2015. Mem., Tax Law Rev. Cttee, 1994–2007. Nat. Pres., VAT Practitioners Gp, 1998–; Pres., Inst. of Indirect Taxation, 1999–2012 (Fellow, 1998). FTII 1997; Fellow, Soc. of Advanced Legal Studies, 1999. Liveryman: Co. of Tax Advisers, 2006– (Mem., Ct of Assts, 1999–2008); Co. of Spectacle Makers, 2006– (Mem., Ct of Assts, 2008–12). Exec. Ed., VAT Intelligence, 1993–2006; Member Editorial Board: De Voil Indirect Tax Service, 1999–; Tax Jl, 2000–. *Publications:* numerous technical articles. *Recreations:* art, music, literature. *Address:* Temple Tax Chambers, 3 Temple Gardens, EC4Y 9AU.

CONN, **Edith**, OBE 2000; JP; Vice Lord-Lieutenant of Greater Manchester, 2014–17; *b* Manchester, 1948; *m* 1970, Stephen Leonard Conn; one *s* one *d*. *Educ:* Manchester Poly. (BA Hons Humanities 1991). British Red Cross: joined Gtr Manchester br., 1978; Pres., 2000; Life Mem., 2000; counsellor, CAB, 1978–85; Treas., NSPCC, 1980–88; Chairman: Heart Res. Gtr Manchester, 1980–88; Reclaim Proj., 2009–13; Crimestoppers Gtr Manchester, 2010–; assessor: North West War Pensions, 1985–90; Queen's Award for Voluntary Service, 2002–; Member, Committee: Christie Against Cancer, 2000–04; Breakthrough Breast Cancer NW, 2009–14; Trustee: Gtr Manchester High Sheriff's Police Trust, 2008–; Bolton Octagon Th. Trust, 2009–14; Mem. Cttee, Royal Exchange Th., Manchester, 2009–14; Patron, Manchester City Art Gall. Greater Manchester: JP; DL 2001; High Sheriff 2008. DUniv Bolton, 2008. Badge of Honour, 1989, Distinguished Service, 1993, Exceptional Service, 2000, Red Cross. *Recreations:* family, cooking, reading, art history, tennis, football, good company and good wine (Comdr, Ordre des Coteaux de Champagne). *Address:* 17 Oakley Park, Heaton, Bolton BL1 5XL. *T:* 07703 190792. *E:* eydieconn@hotmail.com. *W:* www.twitter.com/edith_conn.

CONNAGHAN, **John**, CBE 2015; Director General, Irish Health Service, 2018; *b* Glasgow, 2 Sept. 1954; *s* of John Connaghan and Mary Connaghan; *m* 1983, Evelyn Joyce Steven; three *s* one *d*. *Educ:* Glasgow Caledonian Univ. (BA Business Studies 1976); Univ. of Strathclyde (DMS 1980; MBA 1984); Cabinet Office Top Mgt Prog. 2008. Gen. Manager, Charles Letts & Co. Ltd, 1979–87; Chief Executive: Victoria Infirmary NHS Trust, 1987–94; Western General NHS Trust, 1995–2000; Fife Acute Hosps Trust, 2000–04; Dir of Health Delivery, then of Workforce and Performance, later of Perf. and Delivery, Scottish Exec., then Scottish Govt, 2004; Interim Dir Gen. for Health and Social Care, Scottish Govt, 2013–14; Chief Operating Officer, NHS Scotland, 2014–17. Leader, Govt Task Force on waiting times, 2002–06, on NHS perf., 2008–. Chm., OPEX Ltd, 1998–. Dir, Maggie's Centres, 1994–2005. *Recreations:* golf, photography, hockey (current member Scotland Men's Veterans team). *Address:* 54A St Albans Road, Edinburgh EH9 2LX. *T:* 07836 704107. *E:* connaghan2000@yahoo.com. *Clubs:* Blairgowrie Golf, Fidra Lions Hockey, Scotland Masters Hockey.

CONNAL, (**Robert**) **Craig**; QC (Scot.) 2002; Partner, Pinsent Masons LLP (formerly McGrigor Donald, then McGrigors), since 1980 (Head of Advocacy in Litigation and Compliance, 2014–16); *b* 7 July 1954; *s* of James Brownlee Connal and Jean Elizabeth Polley or Connal; *m* 1976, Mary Ferguson Bowie; two *d*. *Educ:* Hamilton Acad.; Glasgow Univ. (LLB 1st Cl. Hons). Admitted Solicitor, Scotland, 1977, England and Wales, 2006; Solicitor Advocate: (civil), 1996, (criminal), 2004, Scotland; (all courts), England and Wales, 2006; reg. to appear in Dubai Internat. Financial Centre Courts, 2015. McGrigor Donald, then McGrigors: Hd, Commercial Litigation, 2002–07; Senior Litigation Partner, 2007–12; Hd of Advocacy, 2007. Accredited advocacy trainer, Nat. Inst. for Trial Advocacy, 2010; certified specialist in arbitration, Law Soc. of Scotland, 2011. Ext. Examr in Law, Dept of Land Econ., Aberdeen Univ., 2001–05. Mem., Wkg Party on Partnership Law, Scottish Law Commn, 2000–03. Vice Chm. (Scotland), 2015–19, UK Chm., 2019–, British and Irish Commercial Bar Assoc. Member, Council: Royal Faculty of Procurators in Glasgow, 1995–98; SSC, 1999–. Convenor, Rights of Audience Course (Civil), Law Soc. of Scotland, 2004–. Solicitor Advocate of the Year, Law Soc. of England and Wales, 2012. *Publications:* (contrib.) Stair Memorial Encyclopaedia of Scots Law, 1986; contrib. articles to learned jls incl. Jl Law Soc. of Scotland, Jl Planning & Envmtl Law, Estates Gazette, Scottish Planning and Envmt Law, Scots Law Times, Tax Advr, Scottish Criminal Law, Juridical Rev., Edinburgh Law Rev.; contribs to general press incl. IBA Litigation News. *Recreations:* Rugby referee, food and wine, gardens (but not gardening). *Address:* Pinsent Masons LLP, 141 Bothwell Street, Glasgow G2 7EQ. *T:* (0141) 567 8400, *Fax:* (0141) 567 8401. *E:* craig.connal@pinsentmasons.com. *Club:* Whitecraigs Rugby.

CONNARTY, **Michael**; *b* 3 Sept. 1947; *m* 1969, Margaret Doran; one *s* one *d*. *Educ:* St Patrick's High Sch., Coatbridge; Stirling and Glasgow Univs (Student Pres., Stirling Univ., 1970–71); Jordanhill Coll. of Educn (BA; DCE). Teacher of econs and modern studies (secondary and special needs), 1976–92. Exec. Mem., Central region, EIS, 1978–84 (Pres., 1982–83). Rector, Stirling Univ., 1983–84. Mem. (Lab) Stirling DC, 1977–90 (Leader of Council, 1980–90); Chm., Lab. Party Scottish Local Govt Cttee, 1988–90. Mem., Lab. Party Scottish Exec., 1981, 1983–92. Contested (Lab) Stirling, 1983, 1987. MP (Lab) Falkirk E, 1992–2005, Linlithgow and E Falkirk, 2005–15; contested (Lab) same seat, 2015. PPS to Minister of State for Film and Tourism, 1997–98. Member: Information Select Cttee, 1997–2001; European Scrutiny Select Cttee, 1998–2015 (Chm., 2006–10); Parly Assembly, Council of Europe, 2010–15 (Hon. Associate, 2016; Mem., Educn, Culture and Scis Cttee, 2010–15; Chm., 2012–14, Vice Chm., 2014–15, Educn, Youth and Sport Sub Cttee). Chm., Parly Jazz Appreciation Gp, 2001–15; Secretary: Parly Humanist Gp, 1998–2001; Offshore Oil & Gas Industry Gp, 1998–2015; All Party Parly Gp on Nuclear Energy; Vice-Chm., All-Party Parly Gp on Chemical Industries, 2010–15 (Treas., 1994–97; Chm., 1997–2000; Sec., 2000–10); Sec., PLP Sci. and Technol. Cttee, 1992–97; Co-ordinator, PLP Scottish Task Force, Skills and Trng, Youths and Students, 1994–97; Vice Chm., Scottish PLP Gp, 1996–98 (Chm., 1998–99). Chair, Scottish Nat. Jazz Orch., 2007–17. Mem. Bd, POST, 1997–2015; Mem., Humanist Soc. Scotland, 2015–. Patron, Humanists UK (formerly British Humanist Assoc.), 2010. Trustee, Envmtl Projects in Clackmannan, 2017–. JP 1977–90.

CONNELL, **Edward Samuel; His Honour Judge Connell**; a Circuit Judge, since 2019; *b* Consett, Co. Durham, 28 Jan. 1972; *s* of William Connell and Teresa Connell. *Educ:* Salesian Coll., Farnborough; Keele Univ. (BA Jt Hons French and Geog.); Coll. of Law (CPE). Called to the Bar, Middle Temple, 1996; barrister, 5 St Andrew's Hill, 1996–2019; a Recorder, 2009–19. *Recreations:* sport (particularly football), travel, cinema, photography. *Address:* Isleworth Crown Court, Ridgeway Road, Isleworth TW7 5LP.

CONNELL, **Prof. John Jeffrey**, CBE 1985; PhD; FRSE; FIFST; Director, Torry Research Station, Aberdeen (Ministry of Agriculture, Fisheries and Food), 1979–87 (Assistant Director, 1969–79); Emeritus Professor, Aberdeen University, 1987; *b* 2 July 1927; *s* of John Edward Connell and Margaret Connell; *m* 1950, Margaret Parsons; one *s* two *d* (and one *d* decd). *Educ:* Burnage High Sch.; Univ. of Manchester (BSc 1947); Univ. of Edinburgh (PhD 1950). FIFST 1970; FRSE 1984. Torry Research Station: Scientific Officer, 1950; Sen. Sci. Officer, 1955; Principal Sci. Officer, 1961; Dep. Chief Sci. Officer, 1979; Officer i/c Humber Lab., Hull (Sen. Principal Sci. Officer), 1968–69. Res. Associate, 1969–79 and Hon. Res. Lectr, 1979–83, Aberdeen Univ. Mem., Fisheries Res. and Develt Bd, 1979–84. *Publications:* Control of Fish Quality, 1975, 4th edn 1995 (Spanish edn 1978); Trends in Fish Utilisation, 1982; scientific and technical papers related to use of fish as food. *Recreations:* music, hill walking. *Address:* 61 Burnieboozle Crescent, Aberdeen AB15 8NR. *T:* (01224) 315852.

CONNELL, **Prof. John Muir Cochrane**, MD; FRCPE, FMedSci; FRSE; Chairman, NHS Tayside 2015–18; *b* 10 Oct. 1954; *s* of William and Betty Connell; *m* 1978, Lesley Elizabeth Armstrong; three *s* one *d*. *Educ:* Spiers Sch., Beith, Ayrshire; Hutchesons' Grammar Sch., Glasgow; Univ. of Glasgow (MB ChB 1977; MD 1986). MRCP 1979; FRCPGlas 1989; FRCPE 2002. Clin. Scientist, 1983–87, Sen. Clin. Scientist, 1987–94, MRC Blood Pressure Unit, Western Infirmary, Glasgow; MRC Travelling Fellow, Howard Florey Inst., Melbourne, 1986–87; University of Glasgow: Hon. Prof. in Medicine, 1994–95; Prof. of Endocrinol., 1995–2009; Hd, Grad. Sch., 2006–09, Faculty of Medicine; University of Dundee: Prof. of Endocrinology, 2009–15; Dean of Medicine, 2009–11; Vice Principal and Hd, Coll. of Medicine, Dentistry and Nursing, 2012–15. Chm., Educn Trng Adv. Bd, GMC, 2013–18. Sec., 2000–03, Treas., 2003–07, Assoc. of Physicians of GB and Ireland; Member, Council: Acad. of Med. Scis, 2008–11; (also Fellowship Sec.) RSE, 2015–19; RCPE, 2016–. Gov., Hutchesons' GS, 2001–04. FMedSci 1999; FRSE 2002. *Publications:* (contrib. with A. F. Dominiczak) Handbook of Hypertension, Vol. 44, 2007; contrib. learned articles on aspects of endocrinology and genetics of cardiovascular disease. *Recreations:* family, golf, travel, literature. *Clubs:* New (Edinburgh); New Golf (St Andrews).

CONNELL, **Margaret Mary**, MA; Principal, Queen's College, London, 1999–2009; *b* 3 Jan. 1949; *d* of late Leo Connell and Margaret Isobel Connell. *Educ:* Lady Margaret Hall, Oxford (MA). Physics teacher, Headington Sch., Oxford, 1970–76; maths teacher, North London Collegiate Sch., 1976–86; Dep. Headmistress, Bromley High Sch. (GPDST), 1986–91; Headmistress, More House Sch., 1991–99. *Recreations:* music, travel, reading. *Address:* 3 Cranford Mews, Bromley, Kent BR2 8GA. *T:* (020) 8295 1572. *Club:* University Women's.

CONNELL, **Rear Adm. Martin John**; Assistant Chief of Naval Staff (Aviation, Amphibious Capability and Carriers), and Rear Admiral Fleet Air Arm, since 2019; *b* Rotherham, Yorks, 18 Dec. 1968; *s* of William and Teresa Connell; *m* 1993, Penny Vincent; one *s* one *d*. *Educ:* Salesian Coll., Farnborough. Joined RN, 1987; CO, HMS

Severn, 2003–04; Directorate of Operational Capability, MoD, 2005–06; CO, HMS Chatham, 2006–09; MoD Plans, 2009–11; CO, HMS Illustrious, 2012–13; Dep. Principal SO to CDS, 2013–14; Comdr, UK Amphibious Task Gp, 2015–16; Naval Attaché, Washington, 2016–18. Internat. Fellow, US Naval War Coll., 2005. Younger Brother, Trinity House. Pres., RN Football Assoc., 2019–. *Recreations:* mountain biking, football. *Address:* Havant, Hants. *E:* connellmartin@hotmail.com.

**CONNELLY, Brian Norman,** OBE 2002; HM Diplomatic Service, retired; High Commissioner, Kingdom of Tonga, and Consul for Pacific Islands under American sovereignty South of the Equator, 1999–2001; *b* 25 Dec. 1941; *s* of late Bernard Connelly and Julia Connelly (*née* Murphy); *m* 1965, Theresa, (Terrie), Hughes; one *s* one *d. Educ:* Holycross Acad., Edinburgh. Joined FO, 1967; Budapest, 1969–71; Montevideo, 1971–74; FCO, 1974–76; Kuwait, 1976–80; Seoul, 1980–84; First Sec., FCO, 1984–86; First Sec. (Commercial), Dhaka, 1987–90; Admnr and Chief Magistrate, Ascension Island, 1991–95; High Comr, Solomon Is, 1996–98. *Recreations:* golf, snorkelling. *Address:* 24 Latimer, Stony Stratford, Bucks MK11 1HY.

**CONNELLY, Christine Kerr;** Director General Informatics, Department of Health, 2008–11; *b* Hamilton, 28 Dec. 1958; *d* of Thomas Connelly and Margaret Connelly (*née* Kerr); *m* 1985, Derek Ball. *Educ:* Holy Cross High Sch., Hamilton; Aberdeen Univ. (BSc Hons 1980). BP plc, 1984–2004; Chief Information Officer, Cadbury Schweppes, 2004–07. *Recreations:* netball, golf, theatre. *Club:* Stoke Park (Stoke Poges).

**CONNELLY, Iain Miller;** President, Royal Incorporation of Architects in Scotland, 2013–15; *b* Dunfermline, Fife, 2 Nov. 1954; *s* of Dr James Connelly and Susanne Connelly; partner, Christine Harper; two *s* one *d. Educ:* Dunfermline High Sch.; Edinburgh Coll. of Art (BArch Hons 1977, DipArch 1978, Heriot-Watt Univ.). Architect: Sir Frank Mears & Partners, 1978–79; Kenneth Oliver Architects, Dunfermline, 1979–83; Architect, then Principal Architect, Dunfermline DC, 1983–96; Property Services Manager, Fife Council, 1996–2012. Mem. Bd, Kingdom Housing Assoc., 2016–; Dir, Kingdom Initiatives Ltd, 2016–. Editorial, RIAS Qly mag., 2013–15. Scottish Pres., Soc. of Chief Architects in Local Authorities, 2004–06. Mem. Council, RIAS, 2004–18 (Hon. Treas., 2016–18). Mem., Scottish Soc. of Architect Artists, 2012–. *Recreations:* golf, cycling, music (playing piano), reading, photography, watching world go by with a glass of red. *Address:* 5 Adia Road, Torryburn, Dunfermline, Fife KY12 8LB. *T:* (01383) 881763, 07711 993430. *E:* iainconnelly1@sky.com.

**CONNER, Rt Rev. David John,** KCVO 2010; Dean of Windsor, since 1998; Register, Order of the Garter, since 1998; Domestic Chaplain to the Queen, since 1998; *b* 6 April 1947; *s* of late William Ernest Conner and Joan Millington Conner; *m* 1969, Jayne Maria Evans; two *s. Educ:* Erith Grammar School; Exeter College, Oxford (Symes Exhibnr; MA); St Stephen's House, Oxford. Asst Chaplain, St Edward's School, Oxford, 1971–73, Chaplain, 1973–80; Team Vicar, Wolvercote with Summertown, Oxford, 1976–80; Senior Chaplain, Winchester College, 1980–86; Vicar, St Mary the Great with St Michael, Cambridge, 1987–94; RD of Cambridge, 1989–94; Bishop Suffragan of Lynn, 1994–98; Bishop to the Forces, 2001–09. Hon. Fellow, Girton Coll., Cambridge, 1995. Hon. Chaplain, The Pilgrims, 2002–12. *Address:* The Deanery, Windsor Castle, Berks SL4 1NJ. *T:* (01753) 848707. *E:* deansprivatesecretary@stgeorges-windsor.org.

**CONNERY, Sir Sean,** Kt 2000; actor; *b* 25 Aug. 1930; *s* of Joseph and Euphamia Connery; named Thomas; adopted stage name of Sean, 1953; *m* 1st, 1962, Diane Cilento (marr. diss. 1974; she *d* 2011); one *s;* 2nd, 1975, Micheline Roquebrune; two step *s* one step *d.* Served Royal Navy. Has appeared in films: No Road Back, 1956; Action of the Tiger, 1957; Another Time, Another Place, 1957; Hell Drivers, 1958; Tarzan's Greatest Adventure, 1959; Darby O'Gill and the Little People, 1959; On the Fiddle, 1961; The Longest Day, 1962; The Frightened City, 1962; Woman of Straw, 1964; The Hill, 1965; A Fine Madness, 1966; Shalako, 1968; The Molly Maguires, 1968; The Red Tent (1st Russian co-production), 1969; The Anderson Tapes, 1970; The Offence, 1973; Zardoz, 1973; Ransom, 1974; Murder on the Orient Express, 1974; The Wind and the Lion, 1975; The Man Who Would Be King, 1975; Robin and Marian, 1976; The First Great Train Robbery, 1978; Cuba, 1978; Meteor, 1979; Outland, 1981; The Man with the Deadly Lens, 1982; Wrong is Right, 1982; Five Days One Summer, 1982; Highlander, 1986; The Name of the Rose, 1987 (BAFTA Award for Best Actor, 1988); The Untouchables, 1987 (Best Supporting Actor, Academy Awards, 1988; Golden Globe Award); The Presidio, 1989; Indiana Jones and the Last Crusade, 1989; Family Business, 1990; The Hunt for Red October, 1990; The Russia House, 1991; Highlander II–The Quickening, 1991; Medicine Man, 1992; Rising Sun, 1993; A Good Man in Africa, 1994; First Knight, 1995; Just Cause, 1995; The Rock, 1996; Dragonheart, 1996; The Avengers, 1998; Entrapment, 1999; Playing by Heart, 1999; Finding Forrester, 2001; League of Extraordinary Gentlemen, 2003; as James Bond: Dr No, 1963; From Russia With Love, 1964; Goldfinger, 1965; Thunderball, 1965; You Only Live Twice, 1967; Diamonds are Forever, 1971; Never Say Never Again, 1983. Producer, Art, Wyndhams, 1996 (Tony Award, 1998). FRSAMD 1984. Fellow, BAFTA, 1998. Freedom of City of Edinburgh, 1991. Hon. DLitt: Heriot-Watt, 1981; St Andrews, 1988. BAFTA Life Time Achievement Award, 1990; Man of Culture Award, 1990; Scot of the Year Award, BBC Scotland, 1991; American Cinematique Award, 1992; Rudolph Valentino Award, 1992; Nat. Board of Review Award, 1994; Golden Globe Cecil B. De Mille Award, 1996; Lifetime Achievement Award, European Film Awards, 2005. Commander, Order of Arts and Literature (France), 1987; Légion d'Honneur. *Publications:* (with Murray Grigor) Being A Scot, 2008. *Recreations:* golf, tennis, reading.

**CONNING, David Michael,** OBE 1994; FRCPath; FRSB; Director-General, British Nutrition Foundation, 1985–94; *b* 27 Aug. 1932; *s* of Walter Henry Conning and Phyllis Elsie Conning (*née* Lovell); *m* 1st, 1956, Betty Sleightholme (marr. diss. 1991); three *s* one *d;* 2nd, 1991, Lesley Myra Yeomans (*née* Beresford). *Educ:* Dame Allan's Boys' Sch., Newcastle upon Tyne; Med. Sch., King's Coll., Univ. of Durham (MB, BS). FRCPath 1982; FRSB (FIBiol 1984); FIFST 1988. RAMC, 1956–59. SMO Pathology, Middlesbrough Gen. Hosp., 1959–61; Lectr in Pathology, Royal Victoria Infirmary, 1961–65; Hon. Consultant Pathologist, Newcastle and Dist Hosps, 1963–65; Dep. Dir, Central Toxicol. Lab., ICI plc, 1966–78; Dir, BIBRA, 1978–85. Chm., Brit. Toxicol Soc., 1981. Hon. Mem., European Toxicol Soc. (Pres., 1983–86). Hon. Prof. of Toxicology, Surrey Univ., 1977–86. *Publications:* Toxic Hazards in Foods, 1983; Experimental Toxicology, 1988, 2nd edn 1993; contrib. book chapters and articles in jls of toxicol. and nutrition. *Recreation:* mending things. *Address:* Blacksmith's Cottage, Totnor, Brockhampton, Hereford HR1 4TJ. *T:* (01989) 740303.

**CONNOCK, Dr Alexander;** Managing Director, Missile, digital content creation, since 2017; *b* June 1965; *s* of late Michael and Caroline Connock; *m* 1998, Sumitra; one *d. Educ:* Manchester Grammar Sch.; St John's Coll., Oxford (BA Hons Politics and Econs); Columbia Univ. (MA Journalism); INSEAD (MBA); Salford Univ. (PhD 2018). Researcher, Granada TV, 1990–92; asst producer, BBC, 1990–92; Planet TV: producer, 1992–96; Man. Dir, Planet TV Radio, 1996–99; Co-Founder and Chief Exec., Ten Alps plc, 1999–2011; Man. Dir, Shine North, then Endemol Shine North, 2012–17. Member: RTS 2007– (Chm., RTS North West, 2010–17); BAFTA, 2013–. Visiting Professor: Univ. of Sunderland, 2012; Univ. of Salford, 2016–; Vis. Fellow, Reuters Inst., Univ. of Oxford, 2012–13; Prof. of Digital Innovation, 2015, Vis. Prof., 2016–, Manchester Metropolitan Univ.; Sen. Tutor, Nat. Film and Television Sch., 2018–; Associate Fellow, Saïd Sch. of Business, Oxford Univ., 2018–. Entrepreneur-in-Residence, INSEAD, 2011–. Trustee: Unicef UK, 2017–; Hallé Orchestra, 2018–. *Recreations:* piano, photography. *Club:* Soho House.

**CONNOLLY, Barbara Winifred;** QC 2011; *b* London, 12 Oct. 1955; *d* of John Thomas Murphy and Brigid, (Delia), Joyce; *m* (marr. diss.); two *s. Educ:* LLB Hons. Called to the Bar, Inner Temple, 1986; in practice as a barrister, specialising in family and civil law. *Recreations:* family, friends, walking, books, theatre, film, music, art. *Address:* 7 Bedford Row, WC1R 4BS. *T:* (020) 7242 3555, *Fax:* (020) 7242 2511. *E:* bconnolly@7br.co.uk.

**CONNOLLY, Sir Billy,** Kt 2017; CBE 2003; stand-up comedian, actor; *b* 24 Nov. 1942; *m* 1st, Iris (marr. diss. 1985); one *s* one *d;* 2nd, 1990, Pamela Stephenson; three *d.* Welder, Clyde shipyards; (with Gerry Rafferty) formed folk duo, Humblebums; first solo concert, 1971; *theatre* includes: writer, The Red Runner, Edinburgh, 1979; performer: Die Fledermaus, Scottish Opera, 1978; The Pick of Billy Connolly, Cambridge, 1981; The Beastly Beatitudes of Balthazar B, Duke of York's, 1982; one-man show, London Palladium, 1985; Hammersmith Apollo, 2004; Billy Connolly Live In New York, 2005; What About Dick?, 2007; tours: Rebel Without a Clue, world tour, 1987; UK, 1992; Northern UK, 1997; Hammersmith Apollo, Australia, NZ, 1999; Aberdeen, Canada, 2000; England, Ireland, 2001; Scotland, 2005; Too Old to Die Young, Australia, 2006; NY, Canada, 2006; Montreal, UK, 2007; Ireland, San Francisco, 2008; Scotland, NZ, 2009; Seattle, Hammersmith Apollo, 2010; Canada, 2010; The Man, Australia, 2011, England and Wales, 2012; High Horse, Scotland, 2014, Australia, Canada, 2015, London, 2016; *films* include: Big Banana Feet, 1976; Absolution, 1979; Bullshot, 1983; Water, 1985; The Big Man, 1990; Down Among the Big Boys, 1993; Pocahontas, 1995; Muppet Treasure Island, 1996; Mrs Brown, Ship of Fools, Paws, Deacon Brodie, 1997; Still Crazy, The Changeling, Boon Dock Saints, 1998; The Debt Collector, The Imposters, 1999; Beautiful Joe, 2000; Cletis Tout, 2000; An Everlasting Piece, Gabriel and Me, 2001; The Man Who Sued God, Timeline, 2003; The Last Samurai, Lemony Snicket's A Series of Unfortunate Events, 2004; Good Sharma, 2005; Fido, Open Season, Garfield 2, 2006; The X-Files: I Want to Believe, 2008; Boondock Saints II, 2008; Gulliver's Travels, 2010; Brave, The Hobbit, 2012; Quartet, 2013; What We Did on our Holiday, The Hobbit: The Battle of the Five Armies, 2014; *television* includes: Head of the Class (series, USA), 1990–92; Billy (series, USA), 1992; Billy Connolly's World Tour of Scotland (series), 1994; A Scot in the Arctic, 1995; Pearl (US series), 1997; Billy Connolly's World Tour of Australia (series), 1996; Erect for 30 Years, 1998; Gentlemen's Relish, 2000; White Oleander, 2001; Billy Connolly's World Tour of England, Ireland and Wales, 2002; Billy Connolly's World Tour of New Zealand (series), 2004; Billy Connolly: Journey to the Edge of the World (series), 2009; Billy Connolly's Route 66 (series), 2011; Billy Connolly's Big Send Off, 2014; Tracks Across America (series), 2016; Billy Connolly: portrait of a lifetime, 2017; Billy Connolly's Ultimate World Tour (series), 2018; Billy Connolly: made in Scotland, 2018; Billy Connolly's Great American Trail, 2019; presenter, The Bigger Picture, 1994; *play:* Androcles and the Lion, 1984. Numerous recordings and DVDs. *Publications:* Gullible's Travels, 1982; Billy Connolly's World Tour of Australia, 1996; Journey to the Edge of the World, 2009; Made In Scotland: my grand adventures in a wee country, 2018; Tall Tales and Wee Stories, 2019.

**CONNOLLY, Edward Thomas;** Regional Chairman of Industrial Tribunals, Manchester, 1988–98; *b* 5 Sept. 1935; *s* of Edward Connolly and Alice Joyce; *m* 1962, Dr Pamela Marie Hagan; one *s* one *d. Educ:* St Mary's Coll., Crosby; Prior Park Coll.; Liverpool Univ. (LLB). Qualified as solicitor, 1960. Asst Solicitor, Lancs CC, 1960–63; Asst Prosecuting Solicitor, Liverpool City Council, 1963–65; Dep. Chief Legal Officer, Skelmersdale Develt Corp., 1965–68; Asst Clerk of the Peace, Lancs CC, 1968–71; Dep. Circuit Administrator, Northern Circuit, 1971–76; Chm. of Industrial Tribunals, 1976–88.

**CONNOLLY, John;** full-time writer and novelist, since 1998; *b* Dublin, 31 May 1968; *s* of Desmond Connolly and Brid Connolly; partner, Jennifer Ridyard; two *s. Educ:* Synge Street CBS, Dublin; Trinity Coll., Dublin (BA; Dist. Alumnus 2015); Dublin City Univ. (MA). Journalist, The Irish Times, 1993–98. *Publications:* Charlie Parker series: Every Dead Thing, 1999 (Shamus Award for Best First P.I. Novel, Private Eye Writers of America, 2000); Dark Hollow, 2000; The Killing Kind, 2001; The White Road, 2002 (Barry Award for Best British Crime Novel, 2003); The Reflecting Eye, 2004; The Black Angel, 2005; The Unquiet, 2007; The Reapers, 2008; The Lovers, 2009; The Whisperers, 2010; The Burning Soul, 2011; The Wrath of Angels, 2012; The Wolf in Winter, 2014; A Song of Shadows, 2015; A Time of Torment, 2016; Parker: a miscellany, 2016; A Game of Ghosts, 2017; The Woman in the Woods, 2018; A Book of Bones, 2019; Samuel Johnson series: The Gates, 2009; The Infernals, 2011; The Creeps, 2013; The Chronicles of the Invaders Trilogy: Conquest, 2013; Empire, 2015; Dominion, 2016; *other novels:* Bad Men, 2003; The Book of Lost Things, 2006; he, 2017; *short stories:* Nocturnes (collection), 2004; Night Music: Nocturnes 2 (collection), 2015 (Edgar Award, Best Short Story, 2014); *non-fiction:* (ed with Declan Burke) Books to Die For, 2012 (Agatha Award for Best Non-fiction, 2012; Anthony Award, Macavity Award, 2013); Horror Express, 2018. *Recreations:* unofficial ambassador for impoverished eighties musicians through weekly radio show ABC to XTC on 2XM, supporter of coffee shops and vineyards, tirer-out of dogs. *Address:* Box 53, 113 Lower Rathmines Road, Dublin 6, Ireland. *E:* contact@johnconnollybooks.com.

**CONNOLLY, John Patrick,** FCA; non-executive Chairman: Metric Capital Partners, since 2011; G4S, since 2012; Co-founder and Executive Chairman, CogitalGroup, since 2016; Global Chairman, Deloitte Touche Tohmatsu, 2007–11 (Global Managing Director, 2003–07); *b* 29 Aug. 1950; *s* of John Connolly and Mary Connolly (*née* Morrison); *m* 1992, Odile Lesley Griffith; one *s* one *d* (and one *s* decd) from former marriage. *Educ:* St Bede's Coll., Manchester. FCA 1971. Partner: Mann Judd, Chartered Accountants, 1977; Touche Ross, 1980: Regl Partner i/c North, 1983–87; Man. Partner, Regl Offices, 1987–90, London and South, 1990–95; Man. Partner, Deloitte & Touche, 1995–99; Sen. Partner and CEO, Deloitte UK, 1999–2011. Non-executive Chairman: AMEC, then Amec Foster Wheeler plc, 2011–17; Quest Topco Ltd, 2011–; Elian, 2014–; Man. Partner, Sports Investment Partners, 2011–. Mem., Bd of Trustees and Chm., Finance Cttee, London Business Sch., 2010–15. Chm., Gt Ormond St Hosp. Children's Charity, 2014– (Chm., Rare Disease Centre Appeal, 2011–14). *Recreations:* family, building businesses, Manchester United (season ticket holder), horseracing (owner of 8 racehorses), shooting, The White Horse Inn on the Sussex Downs, author (first children's book, The Blue Monkey). *Address:* CogitalGroup, 1st Floor, 2 Babmaes Street, St James's, SW1Y 6HD.

**CONNOLLY, Joseph;** novelist and author; *b* 23 March 1950; *s* of Joseph Connolly and Lena Connolly (*née* Forte); *m* 1970, Patricia Quinn; one *s* one *d. Educ:* Oratory Sch. Apprentice, then Ed., Hutchinson Publishers, 1969–71; owner, Flask Bookshop, Hampstead, 1975–88; columnist, The Times, 1984–88; regular contributor, The Times, Daily Telegraph and other nat. newspapers, 1984–; occasional writer, Spectator, Garrick, Independent, Daily Telegraph, Daily Mail, Sunday Times, Sunday Telegraph and others; Restaurant Critic, 2009–15, columnist, 2015–17, Hampstead & Highgate Express;

Restaurant Critic, Daily Telegraph, 2015–16. Founder Mem., Useless Inf. Soc., 1994–. Member: Soc. of Authors, 1983; RSL, 2007. Hon. Life Mem., Wodehouse Soc. Mem., Devonshire Soc., 2009–. Patron, Royal Free Charity, 2011–. *Publications:* Collecting Modern First Editions, 1977; P. G. Wodehouse: an illustrated biography, 1979; Jerome K. Jerome: a critical biography, 1981; Modern First Editions: their value to collectors, 1984; The Penguin Book Quiz Book, 1985; Children's Modern First Editions, 1988; Beside the Seaside, 1999; All Shook Up: a flash of the Fifties, 2000; Christmas and How to Survive It, 2003; Wodehouse, 2004; Faber and Faber: eighty years of book cover design, 2009; The A–Z of Eating Out, 2014; *novels:* Poor Souls, 1995; This Is It, 1996; Stuff, 1997; Summer Things, 1998 (filmed as Embrassez qui vous voudrez, and, in English, as Summer Things, 2002); Winter Breaks, 1999; It Can't Go On, 2000; SOS, 2001; The Works, 2003; Love is Strange, 2005; Jack the Lad and Bloody Mary, 2007; England's Lane, 2012; Boys and Girls, 2014; Style, 2015; This is 64, 2017; *contributor:* My Life and Times, by Jerome K. Jerome, 1992; Booker 30: a celebration of 30 years of the Booker Prize for Fiction 1969–1998, 1998; British Greats, 2000; The Book of Useless Information, 2002; The Man Booker Prize: 35 years of the best in contemporary fiction 1969–2003, 2003; British Comedy Greats, 2003; Icons in the Fire: the decline and fall of almost everybody in the British film industry 1984–2000, by Alexander Walker, 2004; Private Passions, by Michael Berkeley, 2005; Folio 60: a bibliography of the Folio Society 1947–2006, 2007; A Hedonist's Guide to Life, 2007; On the Art of Making Up One's Mind, by Jerome K. Jerome, 2009; Christmas Pudding, by Nancy Mitford, 2011; The Times Diary at 50: the antidote to the news, by Patrick Kidd, 2016. *Recreations:* books, Times crossword, wine, lunching and loafing. *Address:* c/o Jonathan Lloyd, Curtis Brown Group Ltd, Haymarket House, 28–29 Haymarket, SW1Y 4SP. *T:* (020) 7393 4400, *Fax:* (020) 7393 4401. *E:* cb@curtisbrown.co.uk. *W:* www.josephconnolly.co.uk. *Clubs:* Garrick, Chelsea Arts, Ivy.

**CONNOLLY, Prof. Patricia,** PhD; CEng, FREng, FIET; FRSocMed; FRSE; Professor of Bioengineering, since 1999, and Director, Strathclyde Institute of Medical Devices, since 2006, University of Strathclyde; Chief Executive Officer, Ohmedics Ltd, since 2009; *b* Glasgow, 11 Aug. 1958; *d* of John and Patricia Connolly; *m* 2003, Alistair John MacWilliam. *Educ:* St Saviour's Primary Sch., Govan; Notre Dame High Sch., Glasgow; Univ. of Strathclyde (BSc 1st Cl. Hons Electrical and Electronic Engrg 1981; PhD 1984). CEng; FIET 2002; FREng 2014. Lectr, then Sen. Lectr, Univ. of Glasgow, 1984–92; Res. Dir, Byk Gulden Italia (Altana Pharma), Milan, 1992–97; Tech. Dir, Nycomed Amersham, Lausanne, 1997–99. FRSE 2005; FRSocMed 2009. *Publications:* contribs to biomed., engrg, biosensors and med. jls. *Recreations:* reading, gardening, windsurfing. *Address:* Department of Biomedical Engineering, Wolfson Centre, 106 Rottenrow, University of Strathclyde, Glasgow G4 0NW. *T:* (0141) 548 3034. *E:* patricia.connolly@strath.ac.uk.

**CONNOLLY, Dame Sarah (Patricia),** DBE 2017 (CBE 2010); opera singer; mezzo-soprano; *b* 13 June 1963; *d* of Gerald Connolly and Jane Connolly (*née* Widdowson); *m* Carl Randolph Talbot; one *d. Educ:* Raventhorpe Sch., Darlington; Queen Margaret's Sch., Escrick; Royal Coll. of Music (Dip RCM Piano; Dip RCM Singing). Rôles include: English National Opera: Dido in The Trojans, 2004; Sesto in La clemenza di Tito, 2005; title rôle in Agrippina, 2007; title rôle in Medea, 2013; title rôle in Giulio Cesare, Glyndebourne, 2005; début, Metropolitan Opera, as Annio in La clemenza di Tito; début, La Scala, Milan as Dido; Octavian in Der Rosenkavalier, Scottish Opera, 2006; Romeo in I Capuleti e i Montecchi, Opera North, 2008; Nerone in L'incoronazione de Poppea, Barcelona, 2009; Dido in Dido and Aeneas, ROH, 2009; Der Komponist in Ariadne auf Naxos, Metropolitan Opera, 2010; Mary Queen of Scots in Mary Stuart, Opera North, 2010; David in Saul, Barbican, 2011; Phaedra in Hippolyte et Aricie, Glyndebourne, 2013; Brangane in Tristan und Isolde, ROH, 2014; Jocaste in Oedipe, ROH, 2016; Gertrude in Hamlet, Glyndebourne, 2017; Fricka in Das Rheingold, ROH, 2018; concert appearances include: Salzburg Fest., Tanglewood Fest., Vienna Konzertaus, Berlin Philharmonie, Zankel Hall, NY and Concertgebouw, Amsterdam; soloist in Last Night of the Proms, 2009. *Recreations:* reading, teaching, cooking, gardening. *Address:* c/o Askonas Holt Ltd, 15 Fetter Lane, EC4A 1BW. *E:* keiron.cooke@askonasholt.co.uk.

**CONNOLLY, Prof. Sean Joseph,** DPhil; FBA 2016; Professor of Irish History, Queen's University, Belfast, 1996–2017, now Emeritus; *b* Dublin, 9 Dec. 1951; *s* of Thomas Connolly and Mary Connolly; *m* 1977, Mavis Bracegirdle; one *s* one *d. Educ:* University Coll. Dublin (BA 1972); Univ. of Ulster (DPhil 1977). Archivist, Public Record Office of Ireland, 1977–80; Lectr in Hist., St Patrick's Coll., Dublin, 1980–81; Lectr, 1981–90, Reader, 1990–96, in Hist., Univ. of Ulster. Visiting Fellow: Folger Liby, Washington, DC, 1998; European University Inst., Florence, 2012. MRIA 1996. *Publications:* Priests and People in Pre-Famine Ireland 1780–1945, 1982; Religion, Law and Power: the making of Protestant Ireland 1660–1760, 1982; (ed) The Oxford Companion to Irish History, 1998; Contested Island: Ireland 1460–1630, 2007; Divided Kingdom: Ireland 1630–1800, 2008. *Recreations:* cinema, Italian language and culture. *Address:* School of History, Anthropology, Philosophy and Politics, Queen's University, Belfast BT7 1NN. *T:* (028) 9097 3850. *E:* s.connolly@qub.ac.uk.

**CONNOR, Bishop of,** since 2007; **Rt Rev. Alan Francis Abernethy;** *b* 12 April 1957; *s* of Walter Abernethy and Margaret (*née* Sloan); *m* 1983, Liz Forster; one *s* one *d. Educ:* Harding Meml Primary, Belfast; Grosvenor High Sch., Belfast; Queen's Univ., Belfast (BA 1978; BD 1989); Trinity Coll., Dublin (DipTh 1981). Ordained deacon, 1981, priest, 1982; Assistant Curate: St Elizabeth's, Dundonald, 1981–84; Lecale Gp of Parishes, 1984–87; Officiating Chaplain, RAF Bishopscourt, 1984–87; Rector: St John's, Helen's Bay, 1987–90; St Columbanus, Ballyholme, 1990–2007. Canon, Down Cath., 2000–07. Religious Advr, Downtown Radio, 1985–90. *Publications:* Fulfilment and Frustration, 2002; Shadows on the Journey, 2011. *Recreations:* tennis, cycling, family holidays, reading, cooking. *Address:* Bishop's House, 3 Upper Malone Road, Belfast BT8 6TD. *T:* (office) (028) 9082 8870, *Fax:* (028) 9031 0138. *E:* bishop@connor.anglican.org.

**CONNOR, Clare;** Chief Executive, The Place, since 2017; *b* Cambridge, 13 Feb. 1970; *d* of Barrie Keith Connor and Jennifer Rosemary Connor (*née* Doggett); *m* 1999, Evroy Deer; one *s* one *d. Educ:* London Contemp. Dance Sch. (BA 1st Cl. Hons Contemp. Dance 1991); De Montfort Univ. (PGCE Secondary - Dance 1994). Professional dancer, Phoenix Dance Th., 1991–93; teacher of dance and drama, Islington Green, 1994–96; Sen. Lectr in Dance and Performing Arts, Newham Sixth Form Coll., 1996–2002; Creative Dir, Momentum Arts, 2002–05; Dir, Stratford Circus Arts Centre, 2005–14; Dir, Business Develt, Southbank Centre, 2014–17. *Address:* The Place, 17 Dukes Road, WC1H 9PY. *T:* (020) 7121 1071/2. *E:* clare.connor@theplace.org.uk.

**CONNOR, Clare Joanne,** CBE 2018 (OBE 2006; MBE 2004); Managing Director, Women's Cricket, England and Wales Cricket Board, since 2019 (Director, England Women's Cricket, 2008–19); *b* Brighton, 1 Sept. 1976; *d* of Michael and Norma Connor; *m* 2006, Roger Nicholson (marr. diss. 2013). *Educ:* Brighton Coll.; Manchester Univ. (BA Hons English 1998). Neuro-Linguistic Programming Practitioner, 2011. Mem., England Women's Cricket team, 1995–2006 (Captain, 2000–06; team regained The Ashes, 2005). English teacher, Housemistress and Hd of PR, Brighton Coll., 1999–2007; on sabbatical, 2003–05, as presenter, The Cricket Show, Channel 4, columnist, The Observer and radio cricket summariser, Test Match Special, BBC Radio 4. Mem., Commn on Future of Women's Sport, 2009–12. Member, Board: Sussex CCC, 2008–; Sport England, 2010; Mem., Women's Cttee, 2008– (Chair, 2011–), Cricket Cttee, 2009–, ICC. *Recreations:* keeping fit, reading, time with family, cinema, theatre. *Address:* 6A Amesbury Crescent, Hove, E Sussex BN3 5RD. *T:* 07721 728394. *E:* clare.connor@ecb.co.uk. *Club:* MCC (Hon. Life Mem. 2009).

**CONNOR, Rt Rev. George Howard Douglas;** Bishop of Dunedin, 2005–09; *b* 27 Feb. 1942; *s* of George Sherwood Connor and Elizabeth Agnes (*née* Gordon); step *s* of John Edward Marshall Ball; *m* 1967, Nonie Saxby; two *s* two *d. Educ:* St John's Coll., Auckland; LTh (1st cl. Hons) 1965, LTh (Aotearoa) 1992; Massey Univ. (Postgrad. Dip. Arts (History) 2011; MA History 2012). Ordained deacon, 1965, priest, 1966; Theol Tutor, Ch of Melanesia, 1967–73; Maori Mission priest, Waiapu dio., 1975–86; Archdeacon of Waiapu, 1981–86, Canon Theologian Emeritus, 1986; Regional Bishop in the Bay of Plenty, 1989–2005. Protector Gen., SSF, 2001–08. *Address:* 47 Pacific Parade, Surfdale, Waiheke Island 1081, New Zealand.

**CONNOR, Prof. James Michael,** MD, DSc; FRCPGlas; Burton Professor of Medical Genetics, Glasgow University, 1987–2011; *b* 18 June 1951; *s* of James Connor and Mona Connor (*née* Hall); *m* 1979, Dr Rachel Alyson Clare Brooks; two *d. Educ:* Liverpool Univ. (BSc (Hons); MB ChB (Hons); MD; DSc). MRCP 1977; FRCPGlas 1988; FRCPE 1990. Gen. med. professional trng in various Liverpool hosps, 1975–77; Resident in Internal Medicine, Johns Hopkins Hosp., Baltimore, 1977–78; Univ. Res. Fellow, Dept of Medicine, Liverpool Univ., 1978–81; Instr in Med. Genetics, John Hopkins Hosp., 1981–82; Cons. in Med. Genetics, 1982–84, Wellcome Trust Sen. Lectr in Med. Genetics, 1984–87, Duncan Guthrie Inst. of Med. Genetics, Glasgow. *Publications:* Essential Medical Genetics, 1984, 6th edn 2011; Prenatal Diagnosis in Obstetric Practice, 1989, 2nd edn 1995; (ed jtly) Emery and Rimoin's Principles and Practice of Medical Genetics, 3rd edn 1996 to 5th edn 2007; articles on pathophysiology and prevention of genetic disease. *Recreations:* fly fishing, sea kayaking, mountain biking.

**CONNOR, His Honour Jeremy George;** a Circuit Judge, 1996–2004; *b* 14 Dec. 1938; *s* of Joseph Connor and Mabel Emmeline (*née* Adams), ARCA. *Educ:* Beaumont; University Coll., London (LLB; DRS); Heythrop Coll., Univ. of London (MA 2005); King's Coll. London (DTh 2011). Called to the Bar, Middle Temple, 1961, Bencher, 2003 (Reader, 2018); S Eastern Circuit. Apptd to Treasury List, Central Criminal Court, 1973; Metropolitan Stipendiary Magistrate, 1979–96; a Recorder, 1986–96; a Chm., Inner London Youth Cts (formerly Juvenile Cts), 1980–96; Chairman: Family Proceedings Court, 1991–94; Inner London and City Probation Cttee, 1989–96; Member: Exec. Cttee, Central Council of Probation for England and Wales, 1982–89; Parole Bd, 1998–2004; Lord Chancellor's Adv. Cttee on Legal Educn and Conduct, 1996–99; Student Conduct Cttee, Inns of Court, 2005–10. Referee, Mental Health Foundn, 1993–2004. Mem., Judicial Studies Bd, 1990–95. Pres., British Acad. of Forensic Scis, 1989–90 (Chm., Exec. Council, 1983–86; Mem. Council, 1982–93); Chm., Inst. for Study of Treatment of Delinquency, 1992–93. Trustee: Grubb Inst. of Social Studies, 1995–2004; Stapleford Trust for Drug Treatment and Res., 1995–98; London Action Trust, 1996–2005; Assoc. of Blind Catholics, 1996–2004; Rainer Foundn, 1997–98 (Mem. Council, 1996–97); New Lease Trust, 1997–99; Royal Philanthropic Soc., 1998–99; Frontiers Th. Ltd, 2013–18. Vice-Patron, Blind in Business, 1999–. Fellow, Soc. of Advanced Legal Studies, 1999. Freeman, City of London, 1980; Liveryman, Fanmakers' Co., 1981 (Mem., Livery Cttee, 1987–90; Master, 2007–08). *Publications:* chapter in Archbold, Criminal Pleading, Evidence and Practice, 38th and 39th edns. *Recreations:* travel, theatre, occasional broadcasting. *Clubs:* Garrick, Royal Society of Medicine.

**CONNOR, John William,** PhD; FRS 2010; CPhys, FInstP; Senior Consultant in plasma theory, Culham Centre for Fusion Energy, 2007–15, now Honorary Consultant; *b* Crewe, Cheshire, 6 Nov. 1942; *s* of John Connor and Mabel Connor, Cheshire; *m* 1965, Rachel Christine Hicks; one *s* one *d. Educ:* Crewe Co. Grammar Sch.; Univ. of Birmingham (BSc 1st Cl. 1964; PhD 1967). CPhys 1992, FInstP 1992. Research in field of theoretical plasma physics, UKAEA Culham Lab., 1967–89; Hd, Theory and Modelling Dept, UKAEA Fusion Culham Lab., 1989–2007. Vis. Scientist, Princeton Plasma Physics Lab., NJ, 1980; Vis. Prof., 2007–13, Dist. Res. Fellow, 2013–, Imperial Coll. London. Mem., Scientific Adv. Bd and Consultant, Tokamak Energy Ltd, 2010–. Hannes Alfven Prize, Eur. Phys. Soc., 2004; Payne-Gaposchkin Prize, Inst. of Physics, 2007. *Publications:* approx. 170 papers in Nature, Procs Royal Soc., Physics of Fluids, Physics of Plasmas, Physical Rev. Letters, Plasma Physics and Controlled Fusion, Nuclear Fusion, Jl Plasma Physics, etc. *Recreations:* amateur history, reading, crosswords, art history, walking. *Address:* Culham Centre for Fusion Energy, Culham Science Centre, Abingdon OX14 3DB. *T:* (01235) 466922, 07854 044258, *Fax:* (01235) 466435. *E:* jack.connor@ukaea.uk, rachel@pennsbury.co.uk.

**CONNOR, Michael Henry;** HM Diplomatic Service, retired; Director of Trade Promotion, and Commercial Counsellor, Madrid, 1995–2000; *b* 5 Aug. 1942; *s* of late Henry Connor and Agnes Cecilia Connor (*née* Lindsey); *m* 1964, Valerie Jannita Cunningham; three *s. Educ:* St John's Coll., Portsmouth. Joined HM Diplomatic Service, 1964; FO, 1964–68; Attaché, Cairo, 1968–70; Commercial Officer, Vienna, 1970–73; Second Sec. (Commercial/Aid), Kathmandu, 1973–76; FCO, 1976–81; First Sec., 1979; Havana: First Sec. (Commercial) and Consul, 1981–82; First Sec. and Hd of Chancery, 1982–83; Hd of Chancery, Ottawa, 1983–88; First Sec., FCO, 1988–91; Ambassador, El Salvador, 1991–95. *Recreations:* swimming, photography, trekking, theatre.

**CONNOR, His Honour Roger David;** DL; a Circuit Judge, 1991–2005; *b* 8 June 1939; *s* of Thomas Bernard Connor and Susie Violet Connor (*née* Spittlehouse); *m* 1967, Sandra Home Holmes; two *s. Educ:* Merchant Taylors' School; Brunel College of Advanced Science and Technology; The College of Law. Solicitor; articled to J. R. Hodder, 1963–68; Asst Solicitor, 1968–70; Partner, Hodders, 1970–83; Metropolitan Stipendiary Magistrate, 1983–91; a Recorder, 1987–91. DL Bucks, 2005. *Recreations:* music, golf, gardening. *Address:* Bourn's Meadow, Little Missenden, Amersham, Bucks HP7 0RF. *Club:* Beaconsfield Golf.

**CONNOR, (Ryan) Stephen,** OBE 2013; non-executive Chairman, National Centre for Domestic Violence, since 2016 (Chief Executive Officer, 2002–16); *b* Aylesbury, 6 March 1974. *Educ:* Aylesbury Grammar Sch.; Surrey Univ. (LLB Hons 2006); City Univ. London (BVC; Postgrad. Dip. Legal Skills). Called to the Bar, Inner Temple, 2007; Trainer, Judicial Studies Bd, 2009–. Chm., Hate Crime Scrutiny Panel, Crown Prosecution, 2009–12. Fellow, City Univ. London, 2008. *Recreations:* carp fishing, motor-cross. *Address:* National Centre for Domestic Violence, Edgeborough House, Upper Edgeborough Road, Guildford, Surrey GU1 2BJ. *T:* 0844 8044999, 07961 199999. *E:* steve.connor@ncdv.org.uk.

**CONNOR, Prof. Steven Kevin,** DPhil; FBA 2016; Grace 2 Professor of English, University of Cambridge, since 2012; Fellow, Peterhouse, Cambridge, since 2012; *b* Chichester, 11 Feb. 1955; *s* of George Leslie Connor and Geraldine Vivien Connor; *m* 1st, 1984, Lindsey Richardson (marr. diss. 1988); one *d*; 2nd, 2005, Prof. Lynda Nead; two *s. Educ:* Christ's Hosp., Horsham; Bognor Regis Comprehensive Sch.; Wadham Coll., Oxford (BA English 1976; DPhil 1979). Birkbeck College, University of London: Lectr in

English, 1979–89; Sen. Lectr in English, 1990–91; Reader in Modern English Lit., 1991–93; Prof. of Modern Lit. and Theory, 1994–2012. *Publications:* Charles Dickens, 1985; Samuel Beckett: repetition, theory and text, 1988; Postmodernist Culture: an introduction to theories of the contemporary, 1989, 2nd rev. and enlarged edn 1996; Theory and Cultural Value, 1992; (ed) Samuel Beckett's Waiting for Godot and Endgame: a new casebook, 1992; (ed) Charles Dickens, Oliver Twist, 1994; The English Novel in History, 1950 to 1995, 1995; James Joyce, 1996, 2nd edn 2012; (ed) Charles Dickens, The Mystery of Edwin Drood, 1996; (ed) Charles Dickens, 1996; Dumbstruck: a cultural history of ventriloquism, 2000; The Book of Skin, 2004; (ed) The Cambridge Companion to Postmodernism, 2004; Fly, 2006; The Matter of Air: science and art of the ethereal, 2010; Paraphernalia: the curious lives of magical things, 2011; A Philosophy of Sport, 2011; Beyond Words: sobs, hums, stutters and other vocalizations, 2014; Beckett, Modernism and the Material Imagination, 2014; Living by Numbers: in defence of quantity, 2016; Dream Machines, 2017; The Madness of Knowledge: on wisdom, ignorance and fantasies of knowing, 2019; Giving Way: thoughts on unappreciated dispositions, 2019. *Recreations:* gardening, running. *Address:* Peterhouse, Trumpington Street, Cambridge CB2 1RD.

**CONNOR, Sir William Joseph, (Sir Bill),** Kt 2003; General Secretary, Union of Shop Distributive and Allied Workers, 1997–2004; Chair, British Acupuncture Federation, since 2013; *b* 21 May 1941; *s* of William and Mary Connor; *m* 1962, Carol Ann Beattie; one *s* one *d*. Union of Shop Distributive and Allied Workers: Area Organiser, 1971–78; Nat. Officer, 1978–89; Dep. Gen. Sec., 1989–97. Member: TUC Gen. Council and Exec. Cttee, 1997–2004; Partnership Fund Assessment Panel, 1998–2004; Central Arbitration Cttee, 2000–10. Dir, Unity Bank, 1997–2004. Chairman: Nat. Register of Hypnotherapists and Psychotherapists, 2004–09; Supervisory Bd, Union Modernisation Fund, 2005–10. *Recreations:* music, reading, computers, digital photography. *Address:* 25 Abington Drive, Banks, Southport, Merseyside PR9 8FL.

**CONNORS, James Scott, (Jimmy);** tennis player; tennis commentator, CBS television; *b* 2 Sept. 1952; *s* of late James Scott Connors and Gloria Thompson Connors; *m* 1978, Patti McGuire; one *s* one *d*. *Educ:* Univ. of California at Los Angeles. Amateur tennis player, 1970–72, professional, 1972; major Championships won: Australia, 1974; Wimbledon, 1974, 1982; USA, 1974, 1976, 1978, 1982, 1983; South Africa, 1973, 1974; WCT, 1977, 1980; Grand Prix, 1978; played for USA, Davis Cup, 1976, 1981. Champions Tour, 1993–99. BBC Overseas Sports Personality, 1982. *Publications:* The Outsider: my autobiography, 2013.

**CONOLLY, Mrs Yvonne Cecile;** consultant in primary education; Head of Inspection and Monitoring, London Borough of Islington, 1995–99 (Senior Inspector for Primary Education, 1989–95); *b* 12 June 1939; *d* of Hugh Augustus and Blanche Foster; *m* 1965, Michael Patrick Conolly (marr. diss. 1996); one *d*. *Educ:* Westwood High Sch., Jamaica; Shortwood Coll., Jamaica (Teachers' CertEd); Polytechnic, N London (BEd Hons Primary Educn). Primary school teacher: Jamaica, 1960–63; London, 1963–68; Head Teacher, London, 1969–78; ILEA Inspector, Multi-ethnic Education, 1978–81; Inspector of Primary Schools, 1981–90, Dist Primary Inspector, 1988–90, ILEA. Member: Home Secretary's Adv. Council on Race Relations, 1977–86; IBA, 1982–86; Consumer Protection Adv. Cttee, 1974–75. Governor, former Centre for Information and Advice on Educnl Disadvantage, 1975–80; (first) Chm., Caribbean Teachers' Assoc., 1974–76. Registered Inspector, OFSTED, 1993–2000. Governor: Stroud Green Primary Sch., 1992–2004; Park View Community Coll. (formerly Langham Sch.), 1997–2004. Chaplaincy Visitor, Whittington Hosp., 2007–11. Mem., Soroptimist Internat. of Gtr London, 2001–13 (Hon. Sec., 2003–04; Pres., 2005–06). *Publications:* (contrib.) Mango Spice, book of 44 Caribbean songs for schools, 1981; (contrib.) Against the Tide—Black Experience in the ILEA, 1990. *Recreations:* writing, theatre, classical music.

**CONOLLY-CAREW,** family name of **Baron Carew**.

**CONRAD, Alan David;** QC 1999; **His Honour Judge Conrad;** a Circuit Judge, since 2013; *b* 10 Dec. 1953; *s* of Maurice and Peggy Conrad; *m* 1st, 1982 (marr. diss. 1998); one *s* one *d*; 2nd, 2002, Julie Whittle. *Educ:* Bury Grammar Sch.; Brasenose Coll., Oxford (BA Hons Jurisp.). Called to the Bar, Middle Temple, 1976; Asst Recorder, 1993–97; Recorder 1997–2013. *Recreations:* travel, reading, music, motor cars, cricket, cookery, dogs. *Address:* Courts of Justice, Crown Square, Manchester M3 3FL. *Club:* Lancashire County Cricket.

**CONRAD, Peter John;** writer; Student, and Tutor in English Literature, Christ Church, Oxford, 1973–2011; *b* 11 Feb. 1948; *s* of Eric and Pearl Conrad. *Educ:* Hobart High Sch.; Univ. of Tasmania (BA); New Coll., Oxford (MA). Fellow, All Souls Coll., Oxford, 1970–73. Boyer Lectr, ABC, 2004. Hon. DLitt Tasmania, 1993. *Publications:* The Victorian Treasure-House, 1973; Romantic Opera and Literary Form, 1977; Shandyism, 1978; Imagining America, 1980; Television: the medium and its manners, 1982; The Art of the City: views and versions of New York, 1984; The Everyman History of English Literature, 1985; A Song of Love and Death: the meaning of opera, 1987; Down Home: revisiting Tasmania, 1988; Where I Fell to Earth, 1990; Underworld, 1992; Feasting with Panthers, 1994; To Be Continued, 1995; Modern Times, Modern Places, 1998; The Hitchcock Murders, 2000; Orson Welles: the stories of his life, 2003; At Home in Australia, 2003; Tales of Two Hemispheres, 2004; Creation: artists, gods and origins, 2007; Islands, 2009; Verdi and/or Wagner, 2011; How the World Was Won, 2014; Mythomania, 2016; Shakespeare, 2018. *Address:* 19 Offley Road, SW9 0LR. *T:* (020) 7735 1422.

**CONRAD, Elizabeth Margaret,** OBE 1994; MA, FMA; Curator, The Bowes Museum, Barnard Castle, 1979–2001; *b* 5 May 1939; *d* of James Johnston and Elizabeth Russell Wilson; *m* 1970, George Loraine Conran (*d* 1986); (one *d* decd). *Educ:* Falkirk High Sch.; Glasgow Univ. (MA). FMA 1969. Res. Asst, Dept of History of Fine Art, Glasgow Univ., 1959–60; Asst Curator, The Iveagh Bequest, Kenwood, 1960–63; Keeper of Paintings, City Art Galls, Manchester, 1963–74; Arts Adviser, Greater Manchester Council, 1974–79. FRSA 1987. *Publications:* exhibn catalogues; articles in art and museum jls. *Recreations:* gardens, ballet. *Address:* 31 Thorngate, Barnard Castle, Co. Durham DL12 8QB. *T:* (01833) 631055.

**CONRAN, Jasper Alexander Thirlby,** OBE 2008; Designer (clothing, accessories and bridalwear, ceramics, crystal, furniture, fragrances, luggage, theatre), Chairman and Chief Executive Officer, Jasper Conran Holdings Ltd; Director, 2009–15, and Chairman, 2014–15, Conran Holdings; Creative Director, 2011–15, and Chairman, 2012–15, The Conran Shop Ltd; *b* 12 Dec. 1959; *s* of Sir Terence Orby Conran, *qv* and Shirley Ida Conran, *qv*. *Educ:* Bryanston School, Dorset; Parsons School of Art and Design, New York. First womenswear collection, 1978; menswear introd 1985; J by Jasper Conran collection at Debenhams, launched 1996; L'Hôtel Marrakech, opened 2016 (Gold List, Condé Nast Traveler, 2018, 2019). Costumes for: The Rehearsal, 1991 (Laurence Olivier Award, 1991); My Fair Lady (also sets), 1992; Tombeaux, ROH, 1993; Sleeping Beauty, Scottish Ballet, 1994; Brahms/Handel Variations, Birmingham Royal Ballet, 1994; Stravinsky Symphony in C, Bayerisches Staatsoper, Munich, 1994; The Complete Consort, Bayerisches Staatsballet (also sets), Munich, 1994; Swan Lake, Scottish Ballet, 1995; Edward II, 1995, The Nutcracker Sweeties, 1996, The Shakespeare Suite, 1999, Arthur, Part 1, 2000, Part II, 2001, Birmingham Royal Ballet; Maria Stuarda, ENO, 1998; Within the Golden Hour, ROH, 2019. Vis. Prof., Univ. of the Arts London, 2007–. Trustee: Wallace Collection, 2007–15; Architecture Foundn, 2010–12. Gov., Bryanston Sch., 2007–09. Hon. DLitt Heriot-Watt, 2004; Hon. DCL East Anglia, 2006. Fil d'Or (Internat. Linen Award), 1982 and 1983; British Fashion Council Designer of the Year Award, 1986–87; Fashion Group of America Award, 1987; British Collections Award, 1991; Prince's Medal, Homes and Gardens Classic Design Awards, 2003 and 2006; Outstanding Design Award, British Interior Design Assoc., 2004; Design and Decoration Award, 2005; Innovation and Design Award, Condé Nast Traveler, 2011; Retailer of Year, Homes & Gardens Designer Awards, 2013. *Publications:* (with Andrew Montgomery) Country, 2010. *Address:* 1–7 Rostrevor Mews, Fulham, SW6 5AZ. *T:* (020) 7384 0800. *E:* info@jasperconran.com.

**CONRAN, Sebastian Orby;** industrial designer; Chief Executive Officer: Sebastian Conran Associates, since 2009; Consequential Robotics Ltd, since 2016; *b* London, 5 April 1956; *s* of Sir Terence Orby Conran, *qv* and Shirley Ida Conran, *qv*; *m* 2008, Gertrude Maria Thoma; two *s*. *Educ:* Bryanston Sch.; Central Sch. of Art and Design (Industrial Design Engrg). Wolff Olins, 1978–81; Hd of Design, Mothercare, 1981–86; Founder, Sebastian Conran Associates, 1986, later merged with Conran Gp to form Conran & Partners, 1999; Dir, Conran & Partners Ltd, 1999–2009 and 2014–; Man. Dir, Studio Conran, 2008–09. Director: Inclusiviti Ltd, 2015–; Bike Republic Ltd, 2015–. Taught furniture design, RCA, 1994–97; Visiting Professor: Univ. of the Arts, London, 2009–12; Bristol Robotics Lab., 2016–; Designer in Residence, Sheffield Univ. Sci. Faculty, 2011–13. Leader, Design and Technol. Alliance against Crime, 2008–; Chairman: Adv. Bd, Creative Industries Technols Innovation Network, 2009–; Design in Action Scotland, 2012–; Design Special Interest Gp, 2013–. Trustee: Design Council; D&AD; Design Mus.; Conran Foundn. Patron, Alex Moulton Trust. Ambassador for: ICAN; ACID; Turquoise Mt Trust; Bristol Aerospace Design Mus. Gov., Bryanston Sch., Dorset, 2011–. FCSD 2008; FRSA. Hon. FRCA 2008; Hon. Fellow: Univ. of the Arts, London; Arts Univ., Bournemouth. Hon. DTech Loughborough, 2012; Hon. DArts Hertfordshire, 2012; Hon. PhD Engrg Sheffield; Hon. PhD Design West of England. Liveryman, Pewterers' Co. *Publications:* Contemporary Furniture, 1999; Contemporary Lighting, 1999. *Address:* 2 Munden Street, W14 0RH. *E:* sconran@sebastianconran.com.
*See also J. A. T. Conran.*

**CONRAN, Shirley Ida,** OBE 2004; writer; *b* 21 Sept. 1932; *d* of W. Thirlby Pearce and Ida Pearce; *m* 1955, Sir Terence Conran (marr. diss. 1962); two *s*. *Educ:* St Paul's Girls' Sch.; Southern College of Art, Portsmouth; Chelsea Poly.; Central St Martins Coll. of Art and Design. Fabric Designer and Director of Conran Fabrics, 1956–62; Member, Selection Cttee, Design Centre, 1961–69. Journalist; (first) Woman's Editor, Observer Colour Magazine, 1964; Woman's Editor, Daily Mail, 1969 (founded Femail); Life and Style Editor, Over 21, 1972–74. Founder Pres., Mothers in Management, later Work-Life Balance Trust, 1998–2005; Founder: Maths Action, 2004; Maths Anxiety Trust, 2018. Advr to DfEE, 2000–02, DFE, 2014–. Hon. Fellow, UCL, 2016. *Publications:* Superwoman, 1975, revd edn as Down with Superwoman, 1990; Superwoman Year Book, 1976; Superwoman in Action, 1977; (with E. Sidney) Futurewoman, 1979; The Magic Garden, 1983; The Amazing Umbrella Shop, 1990; *novels:* Lace, 1982; Lace 2, 1985; Savages, 1987; Crimson, 1991; Tiger Eyes, 1994; The Revenge, 1997. *Recreations:* reading, iPad.
*See also J. A. T. Conran, S. O. Conran.*

**CONRAN, Sir Terence (Orby),** CH 2017; Kt 1983; RDI 2010; Chairman: The Conran Shop Ltd, 1976–2012; Conran Ltd, 1990–2014; Conran Holdings Ltd, 1993–2014; Conran & Partners (formerly C. D. Partnership), 1993–2014; *b* 4 Oct. 1931; *m*; two *s*; *m* 1963, Caroline Herbert (marr. diss. 1996); two *s* one *d*; *m* 2000, Vicki Davis. *Educ:* Bryanston, Dorset. Chm., Conran Holdings Ltd, 1965–68; Jt Chm., Ryman Conran Ltd, 1968–71; Chairman: Habitat Group Ltd, 1971–88; RSCG Conran Design (formerly Conran Design Group/Conran Associates), 1971–92; Habitat France SA, 1973–88; Conran Stores Inc., 1977–88; J. Hepworth & Son Ltd, 1981–83 (Dir, 1979–83); Habitat Mothercare Ltd, 1982–88; Jasper Conran Ltd, 1982–99; Heal & Sons Ltd, 1983–87; Richard Shops, 1983–87; Storehouse plc, 1986–90 (Chief Exec., 1986–88; non-exec. Dir, 1990); Butlers Wharf Ltd, 1984–90; Bibendum Restaurant Ltd, 1986–; Benchmark Woodworking Ltd, 1989–; Blue Print Café Ltd, 1989–2006; Conran Shop Holdings Ltd, 1990; Le Pont de La Tour Ltd, 1991–2006; Conran Shop SA, 1991; Butlers Wharf Chop House Ltd, 1993–2006; Quaglino's Restaurant Ltd, 1991–2006; Bluebird Store Ltd, 1994–2006; Conran Restaurants Ltd, 1994; Mezzo Ltd, 1995–2006; Conran Shop Marylebone, 1995–2014; Gustavino's Inc., 1997–; Conran Collection Ltd, 1997–2010; Conran Shop Manhattan Inc., 1997; Coq d'Argent Ltd, 1997–2006; Orrery Restaurant Ltd, 1997–2006; The Great Eastern Hotel Co. Ltd, 1997–2006; Sartoria Restaurant Ltd, 1997–2006; Zinc Bar & Grill Ltd, 1997–2005; Atlantic Blue SNC, 1998–; Conran Finance Ltd, 1998–2014; Almeida Restaurant Ltd, 2001–; Boundary Hotel, 2009–; Director: Conran Ink Ltd, 1969–; The Neal Street Restaurant, 1972–89; Conran Octopus, 1983–98; Bhs plc, 1986–88; Savacentre Ltd, 1986–88; Michelin House Investment Co. Ltd, 1989–; Vice-Pres., FNAC, 1985–89. Launched: Conran Exclusive Design for Marks & Spencer, 2011; Paint by Conran, with Master Paintmakers, 2014. Estabd Conran Foundn for Design Educn and Research, 1981–. Mem., Royal Commn on Environmental Pollution, 1973–76. Member: Council, RCA, 1978–81, 1986– (Provost); Adv. Council, V&A Mus., 1979–83; Trustee: V&A Museum, 1984–90; Design Museum, 1989– (Chm., 1992). Gov., Bryanston Sch., 1992–2005. RSA Presidential Medal for Design Management to Conran Group; RSA Presidential Award for Design Management to Habitat Designs Ltd, 1975; SIAD Medal, 1981; Assoc. for Business Sponsorship of the Arts and Daily Telegraph Award to Habitat Mothercare, 1982; RSA Bicentenary Medal, 1982; President's Award, D&AD, 1989. Hon. FRIBA 1984. Commandeur de l'Ordre des Arts et des Lettres (France), 1991. *Publications:* The House Book, 1974; The Kitchen Book, 1977; The Bedroom & Bathroom Book, 1978; (with Caroline Conran) The Cook Book, 1980, rev. edn as The Conran Cookbook, 1997; The New House Book, 1985; Conran Directory of Design, 1985; Plants at Home, 1986; The Soft Furnishings Book, 1986; Terence Conran's France, 1987; Terence Conran's DIY by Design, 1989; Terence Conran's Garden DIY, 1990; Toys and Children's Furniture, 1992; Terence Conran's Kitchen Book, 1993; Terence Conran's DIY Book, 1994; The Essential House Book, 1994; Terence Conran on Design, 1996; (with Dan Pearson) The Essential Garden Book, 1998; Easy Living, 1999; Chef's Garden, 1999; Terence Conran on Restaurants, 2000; Terence Conran on London, 2000; Terence Conran on Small Spaces, 2001; Q & A: a sort of autobiography, 2001; Kitchens: the hub of the home, 2002; Classic Conran, 2003; (with M. Fraser) Designers on Design, 2005; (with Peter Prescott) Eat London, 2007, 3rd edn 2017; Eco House Book, 2009; Plain Simple Useful: the essence of Conran style, 2014; My Life in Design, 2016. *Recreations:* gardening, cooking, cigar smoking. *Address:* Design Museum, 224–238 Kensington High Street, W8 6AG. *T:* (020) 3862 5900.
*See also J. A. T. Conran, S. O. Conran.*

**CONROY, Paul Martin;** music consultant; Chief Executive Officer, Adventure Records Ltd, since 2002; *b* Surbiton, 14 June 1949; *s* of late D. and M. Conroy; *m* 1st, 1980, Maxine Felstead (marr. diss. 1989); one *s*; 2nd, 1993, Katie Rennie; one *d*. *Educ:* John Fisher Sch., Purley; Ewell Technical Coll.; Newman Coll., Birmingham. Has worked in various areas of music business, 1971–: agent: Terry King Associates, 1971–73; Charisma Artistes,

1973–75; Manager, Kursaal Flyers, 1975–77; Gen. Manager, Stiff Records, 1977–83; Man. Dir, US Div., WEA Records, 1983–89; President: Chrysalis Records, 1989–92; Virgin Records UK Ltd, 1992–2002. Director: Matey Boys Prodns Ltd, 2007–17; Adventures in Living, 2010–17. Chm., BRIT Awards, 1998, 1999, 2000. Mem. Cttee, Mus. of Childhood, Bethnal Green, 2004–10. Patron, Tech Music Sch., Acton, 2009. President's Award, Country Music Assoc. of USA, 1987. *Recreations:* cycling, supporting Chelsea, cricket, antique collecting. *E:* paul@adventuresin-music.com.

**CONRY, Rt Rev. Kieran Thomas;** Bishop of Arundel and Brighton, (RC), 2001–14, now Emeritus; *b* 1 Feb. 1951. *Educ:* Cotton Coll., N Staffs; Ven. English Coll., Rome; Gregorian Univ., Rome (PhB, STB). Ordained 1975; Teacher, Cotton Coll., 1976–80; Private Sec. to Apostolic Delegate to the Court of St James's, 1980–88; Parish Priest, Leek, 1988–90; Administrator, St Chad's Cathedral, 1990–94; Dir, Catholic Media Office, 1994–2001; Parish Priest, St Austin's, Stafford, 2001. Ecumenical Associate, Guildford Cath., 2013–. Mem., 1988–93, Vice-Chm., 1992–93, Nat. Conf. of Priests; Chm., Birmingham City Centre Churches, 1992–93.

**CONS, Sir Derek,** Kt 1990; SPMB; President, Court of Appeal, Brunei, 2003–06; *b* 15 July 1928; *s* of Alfred Henry Cons and Elsie Margaret (*née* Neville); *m* 1952, Mary Roberta Upton Wilkes. *Educ:* Rutlish; Birmingham Univ. (LLB (Hons)). Called to Bar, Gray's Inn, 1953. RASC (2nd Lieut), 1946–48. Hong Kong: Magistrate, 1955–62, Principal Magistrate, 1962–66; District Judge, 1966–72; Judge of Supreme Court, 1972–80, Justice of Appeal, 1980–86, Vice Pres., Court of Appeal, 1986–93, Comr of the Supreme Court, Brunei, 1974–2003; Justice of Appeal, Bermuda, 1994–2002; Mem., Court of Final Appeal, Hong Kong, 1997–2006. SPMB (Negara Brunei Darussalam), 2003. *Recreation:* walking. *Address:* Mulberry Mews, Church Street, Fordingbridge, Hants SP6 1BE; RS2, Rosalp, 1972 Anzere, Switzerland. *Club:* Bramshaw Golf (Hants).

**CONSIDINE, Craig Anthony;** Chief Executive Officer, Tanglin Trust School, Singapore, since 2018; *b* Traralgon, Australia, 18 June 1959; *s* of Francis John and Pamela Joy Considine; *m* 1991, Penelope; one *s* four *d*. *Educ:* Royal Melbourne Inst. of Technol. (BASc); Melbourne Univ. (DipEd); Charles Sturt Univ. (MEd). Redden Coll., 1981–83; Geelong Coll., 1984–99; Hd of Boarding, Scotch Oakburn Coll., 1999–2000; Dir, Co Curriculum, Geelong GS, 2001–03; Headmaster: Wanganui Collegiate Sch., 2004–08; Millfield Sch., 2008–18. *Recreations:* golf, restaurants. *Address:* Tanglin Trust School, 95 Portsdown Road, Singapore 139299.

**CONSTABLE, Adam Michael;** QC 2011; a Recorder, since 2010; *b* Croydon, 26 Jan. 1973; *s* of Paul Constable and Katrina Constable; *m* 1999, Lucy (*née* Rutherford); three *d*. *Educ:* Trinity Sch., Croydon; Balliol Coll., Oxford (BA 1st cl. Juris.; MA). Called to the Bar, Inner Temple, 1995, Bencher, 2012; Treasury Counsel, 2002–07. Chm., Putney Common Assoc., 2012–. Chm., Bd of Govs, Fairley House Sch., 2012–. Co-Editor, Construction Law Reports, 2010–. *Publications:* (ed) Keating on JCT Contracts, 2006; Building Defects, 2006; Construction Claims, 2007; (contrib.) Keating on NEC, 2012; (ed) Keating on Offshore Construction and Marine Engineering, 2015; (jtly) Litigation in the Technology and Construction Court, 2018. *Recreations:* family, Rugby, golf, magic. *Clubs:* 67 Pall Mall, Roehampton, Two Brydges, Winchester House.

**CONSTABLE, Sir Frederic S.;** *see* Strickland-Constable.

**CONSTABLE, John Derek;** Headteacher, Langley Grammar School, since 2010; *b* Ipswich, 8 Feb. 1963; *s* of Derek Constable and Peggy Constable; *m* 1997, Sandra Marshal; one *s* one *d*. *Educ:* Northgate High Sch., Ipswich; Univ. of Durham (BSc Engrg Sci. and Mgt 1984); Univ. of Nottingham (PGCE 1988). NPQH 2003. Engrg trainee, Unilever, 1985–87; Teacher of Physics, Aylesbury Grammar Sch., 1988–90; Hd of Physics, Watford Boys' Grammar Sch., 1990–98; Hd of Sci., Asst Hd, Sir William Borlase's Grammar Sch., 1998–2003; Dep. Hd, Wycombe High Sch., 2003–09. Gov., Ditton Park Acad., 2014–. Trustee, Bury Lake Young Mariners, 2015–. *Recreations:* dinghy sailing and instructing, photography, travel, walking, cycling. *Address:* Langley Grammar School, Reddington Drive, Langley, Berks SL3 7QS. *T:* (01753) 598300. *E:* johnconstable@lgs.slough.sch.uk.

**CONSTABLE, John Robert;** Principal Pianist, London Sinfonietta, 1968–2017, now Principal Emeritus; Principal Harpsichordist, Academy of St Martin in the Fields, since 1984; Professor, Royal College of Music, since 1984; *b* 5 Oct. 1934; *s* of Ernest Charles William Constable and May Jane Constable (*née* Rippin); *m* 1956, Kate Ingham (*d* 2016); two *d*. *Educ:* Leighton Park Sch., Reading; Royal Acad. of Music (pupil of Harold Craxton; LRAM and Recital Dip.; FRAM 1986). Pianist, piano accompanist and harpsichordist, music from medieval and baroque to modern; repetiteur, Royal Opera House, 1960–72; concerts at Wigmore Hall, Queen Elizabeth Hall, Royal Opera House and in major European, USA and Japanese cities; numerous TV and radio appearances; many records incl. lieder, chansons, Spanish songs, Victorian ballads, song cycles, chamber music, harpsichord concertos and harpsichord continuo in operas. *Recreations:* travel, looking at paintings, watching cricket. *Address:* 13 Denbigh Terrace, W11 2QJ. *T:* (020) 7229 4603.

**CONSTABLE, Neil Ernest Alexander;** Chief Executive, Shakespeare's Globe, since 2010; *b* Frimley, 15 Aug. 1965; *s* of late Ernest and of Patricia Constable; civil partnership 2010, Christopher Martin. *Educ:* Clifton Coll., Bristol; Guildhall Sch. of Music and Drama (FGS (FGSM 1985)). Royal Shakespeare Company: stage and co. manager, 1985–96; London Manager, 1997–2000; Gen. Adminr, 2000–02; Exec. Dir, Almeida Th., 2003–10. Governor: GSMD, 2008–17; Clifton Coll., 2010–. Mem., Soc. of London Theatres, 2002–. Trustee: Shakespeare's Birthplace, 2012–18; Royal Theatrical Support Trust, 2013–. CCMI 2012. *Recreations:* gardening, vintage cars, 20th century architecture. *Address:* Shakespeare's Globe, 21 New Globe Walk, Bankside, SE1 9DT. *T:* (020) 7902 1440. *E:* neil.c@ shakespearesglobe.com. *Clubs:* Soho House, Garrick.

**CONSTABLE, Paule;** lighting designer; Associate Director, Royal National Theatre, since 2015 (Technical Associate, 2006–15); Associate: Lyric Theatre, Hammersmith, since 2005; New Adventures, since 2007; *b* 9 Nov. 1966; *d* of Paul and Lyn Constable; partner, Ian Richards; one *s* one *d*. *Educ:* Stamford High Sch.; Goldsmiths' Coll., Univ. of London (BA Drama and English; Hon. Fellow, 2008). Productions for: RNT; Glyndebourne; Royal Opera House; ENO; RSC; Donmar Th.; productions include: Street of Crocodiles, 1993, The 3 Lives of Lucie Cabrol, 1995, Théâtre de Complicité; His Dark Materials, RNT 2005 (Olivier Award for Best Lighting Design, 2005); Don Carlos, Gielgud, 2005 (Olivier Award for Best Lighting Design, 2006); Evita, Adelphi, 2006; Satyagraha, ENO, 2007; St Joan, RNT, 2007 (Kt of Illumination Award, 2007); Warhorse, RNT, 2007, Broadway, 2011 (Tony Award for Best Lighting; Outer Circle Critics Award, LA, 2012 (LA Critics Circle Award, 2013); Othello, Donmar Warehouse, 2007; Ivanov, Wyndham's, 2008; Chalk Garden, Donmar, 2008 (Olivier Award for Best Lighting Design, 2009); Oliver, Drury Lane, 2009; Phedre, RNT, 2009; Billy Budd, Glyndebourne, 2010; Les Miserables 25th Anniv. concert, O2 and tour, 2010 (LA Critics Circle Award, 2012); Meistersinger, Glyndebourne, 2011; The Curious Incident of the Dog in the Night-Time, RNT, 2012 (White Light Award for Best Lighting Design, Olivier Awards, 2013), NY, 2014 (Tony Award for Best Lighting Design, Outer Critics Circle Award, NY Drama Desk Award, 2015), LA, 2017 (LA Critics Circle Award, 2018); Britten Canticles, Aldeburgh and ROH, 2013; The Light Princess, RNT, 2013; Sleeping Beauty, Matthew Bourne and New Adventures, 2013 (LA Critics Circle Award, 2014); Wolf Hall, RSC, 2014; Entführung, Glyndebourne, 2015; Cavalleria Rusticana and Pagliacci, Metropolitan Opera, 2015; 25th Anniv. global prodn of Les Miz, 2015 (Helpmann Award); Nothing, Glyndebourne, 2016; The Red Shoes, Matthew Bourne and New Adventures, 2016; The Threepenny Opera, NT, 2016; Angels in America, Follies (Kt of Illumination Award, 2018), RNT, 2017; Heisenberg: The Uncertainty Principle, Wyndham's, 2017; Pericles, Public Acts, NT, 2018; Ear for Eye, Royal Court, 2018; Romeo and Juliet, Curve Th., Leicester, 2019 (and UK tour); for BBC: Carmen, 2003; Magic Flute, 2003; Giulio Cesare, 2005; Marriage of Figaro, 2006; Cosi Fan Tutti, 2006. Founder, Women in Stage Entertainment, 2011–. Mem., Assoc. Lighting Designers. Hon. Fellow: Rose Bruford Coll., 2010; Central Sch. of Speech and Drama, 2010. Hospital Award for Contribn to Theatre, Hosp. Club, 2006; Internat. Opera Award for Best Lighting, 2013. *Recreations:* surfing, cycling, walking, digging the allotment, being with the kids, running, mountains, the ocean. *Address:* c/o Davina Shah, Macnaughton Lord Representation, 2nd Floor, 16 Crucifix Lane, SE1 3JW. *T:* (020) 7407 9201. *E:* davina@mlrep.com.

**CONSTANCE, Angela;** Member (SNP) Almond Valley, Scottish Parliament, since 2011 (Livingston, 2007–11); *b* 15 July 1970; *d* of Sonny Constance and Mary (*née* Colquhoun); *m* 2000, Garry Knox; one *s*. *Educ:* Univ. of Glasgow (MA Soc. Sci.); Univ. of Stirling (MSocSc Soc. Work). Social Worker (Criminal Justice): Clackmannanshire Council, 1998; Perth and Kinross Council, 1999; Social Worker (Mental Health), S Lanarks Council, 2001–07. Mem. (SNP), W Lothian Council, 1997–2007. Scottish Parliament: Minister for Skills and Lifelong Learning, 2010–11, for Children and Young People, 2011, for Youth Employment, 2011–14; Cabinet Sec. for Educn and Lifelong Learning, 2014–16, for Communities, Social Security and Equalities, 2016–18. *Recreations:* jogging, eating out, cinema. *Address:* Scottish Parliament, Edinburgh EH99 1SP. *T:* (01506) 460403. *E:* angela.constance.msp@parliament.scot.

**CONSTÂNCIO, Vítor;** Vice-President, European Central Bank, 2010–18 (Member, Governing Council, 2000–09); *b* Lisbon, Portugal, 12 Oct. 1943. *Educ:* Technical Univ. of Lisbon (Econs degree 1965); Univ. of Bristol (postgrad. studies). Asst Prof. of Econs, Technical Univ. of Lisbon, 1965–73; Hd of Dept, Econ. Models and Global Programming, Centre of Planning Studies, and Prof., Instituto Superior do Serviço Social, 1972–73; Prof., Catholic Univ. of Portugal, 1980–81. Banco de Portugal: Hd, Res. Dept, 1975; Dep. Gov., 1977, 1979, 1981–84; Gov., 1985–86; Sen Advr, 1989–94; Exec. Dir, Banco Português de Investimento, 1995–2000; Gov., Banco de Portugal, 2000–10. MP, Portugal, 1976, 1980–81, 1987–88. Sec. of State, Planning, 1974–75; Budget and Planning, 1976; Minister of Finance, 1978. President: Commn for Eur. Integration, 1977, 1979; Parly Commn on Eur. Affairs, 1980–81; Portuguese Sect., Eur. Movement, 1980–81. Mem., Conselho de Estado, 1995–99. Non-exec. Dir, EDP, 1998–2000. Guest Prof., Univ. Nova de Lisbon, 1982–84; Guest Prof. of Econs, Instituto Superior de Economia e Gestão, Technical Univ. of Lisbon, 1989–2009.

**CONSTANT, Charles Kenvyn ff.;** *see* ffrench-Constant.

**CONSTANTINE, David Peter,** MBE 2010; DL; Co-Founder Director (formerly Executive Officer), Motivation Charitable Trust, since 1992; *b* 14 July 1960; *s* of William Geoffrey Constantine and Jean Virginia Constantine. *Educ:* Writtle Agricl Coll. (DipAgr 1982); Oxford Brookes Univ. (BSc Hons 1986); Royal Coll. of Art (MDes 1990; Hon. FRCA 1999; Sen. FRCA 2008). Programmer, IBM, 1986–88. Founded Motivation to help people with mobility disabilities, creating sustainable projects in low-income, countries. Mem., Internat. Cttee, Leonard Cheshire, 1997–2006; Trustee and Director: Design Mus., 1999–2017; Calvert Trust, Exmoor, 2004–10; Arnolfini Gall., Bristol, 2007–14. DL City of Bristol, 2014. Hon. FRSA and Bicentenary Medal for Design, RSA, 2010. Hon. MA Bristol, 2003; DUniv Oxford Brookes, 2006; Hon. Dr: Essex, 2014; Bath, 2016. *Recreations:* photography, travel, cinema, modern history, kite flying, rowing, watercolour painting. *Address:* Motivation, Unit 2, Sheene Road, Bedminster, Bristol BS3 4EG. *T:* (0117) 966 0398. *E:* info@motivation.org.uk.

**CONT, Prof. Rama,** PhD; Professor of Mathematical Finance, University of Oxford, since 2018; Fellow of St Hugh's College, Oxford, since 2018; *b* Tehran, 30 June 1972; *s* of Gholam Hossein Cont and Mansoureh Danesh-Kazemi; *m* 1999, Rokhsaneh Ghandi; one *s* one *d*. *Educ:* Ecole Polytechnique, Paris (BSc 1994); Ecole Normale Supérieure, Paris (MSc 1995); Université Paris Sud (PhD 1998); Univ. of Paris (Habilitation in Maths 2004). CNRS Res. Fellow, Dept of Applied Maths, Ecole Polytechnique, Paris, 1998–2006; Associate Prof., Dept of Ops Res., Columbia Univ., NY, 2007–11; Prof. of Maths and Chair, Mathematical Sci., Imperial Coll. London, 2012–18. CNRS Sen. Res. Scientist, Sorbonne Univ., Paris, 2010–. Scientific Advr, Financial Stability Div., Norges Bank, Oslo, 2014–; Res. Economist, IMF, 2017–18; Consultant, Eur. Central Bank, 2018. Fellow, SIAM, 2017. Louis Bachelier Prize, French Acad. of Scis, 2010; APEX Award for Excellence in Interdisciplinary Res., Royal Soc., 2017. *Publications:* Financial Modelling with Jump Processes, 2004; (Ed.-in-Chief) Encyclopedia of Quantitative Finance, 2010; (jtly) Stochastic Integration by Parts and Functional Ito Calculus, 2016. *Recreation:* classical Chinese literature. *Address:* Mathematical Institute, Andrew Wiles Building, University of Oxford, Oxford OX2 6GG. *E:* Rama.Cont@maths.ox.ac.uk.

**CONTE-HELM, Marie Theresa,** (Mrs A. W. Purdue), OBE 2011; Executive Director, UK-Japan 21st Century Group, 2011–17; *b* 13 Nov. 1949; *d* of Angelo and Santa Conte; *m* 1979, Arthur William Purdue; one *d*. *Educ:* CUNY (BA Art History 1971); East-West Center, Univ. of Hawaii (MA Asian Art 1973). Cultural Officer, Embassy of Japan, 1975–79; Lectr in Art History, Sunderland Poly., 1979–86; Head of Japanese Studies Div., and Reader in Japanese Studies, Sunderland Poly., subseq. Univ. of Sunderland, 1986–94; Reader in Japanese Studies and Dir, East Asian Affairs, Univ. of Northumbria at Newcastle, 1994–99. Dir Gen., Daiwa Anglo-Japanese Foundn, 2000–11. Vis. Prof., Univ. of Northumbria at Newcastle, 1999–. Mem., Bd of Govs, Univ. for Creative Arts, 2011–. Commendation, Japanese Minister of Foreign Affairs, 2009. *Publications:* Japan and the North East of England: from 1862 to the present day, 1989 (trans. Japanese 1991); The Japanese and Europe: economic and cultural encounters, 1996; academic papers, articles and book reviews. *Recreations:* theatre, film, outdoor swimming, walking. *Address:* The Old Rectory, Allendale, near Hexham, Northumberland NE47 9DA. *T:* (01434) 683350; 176A Leighton Road, NW5 2RE. *E:* marie@conte-helm.co.uk.

**CONTI, Most Rev. Mario Joseph;** Archbishop of Glasgow, (RC), 2002–12, now Archbishop Emeritus; *b* Elgin, Moray, 20 March 1934; *s* of Louis Joseph Conti and Josephine Quintilia Panicali. *Educ:* St Marie's Convent School and Springfield, Elgin; Blairs Coll., Aberdeen; Pontifical Gregorian Univ. (Scots College), Rome. PhL 1955, STL 1959. Ordained, Rome, 1958; Curate, St Mary's Cathedral, Aberdeen, 1959–62; Parish Priest, St Joachim's, Wick and St Anne's, Thurso (joint charge), 1962–77; Bishop of Aberdeen, 1977–2002. Chairman: Scottish Catholic Heritage Commn, 1980–2014; Commn for the Pastoral Care of Migrant Workers and Tourists (incl. Apostleship of the Sea, Scotland), 1978–85; Pres.-Treasurer, Scottish Catholic Internat. Aid Fund, 1978–85; Pres., National Liturgy Commn, 1981–85; Scottish Mem., Episcopal Bd, Internat. Commn for English in the Liturgy, 1978–87; Mem., Bishops' Jt Bio-ethics Cttee (formerly Cttee for Bio-ethical

Issues), 1982–2012; Catholic Bishops' Conference of Scotland: Pres., Commn for Christian Doctrine and Unity, 1985–2012; Vice Pres., 2002–12; Chair, Cttee for Inter-religious Dialogue, 2006–; Consultor-Mem., Secretariat, later Council, for Promotion of Christian Unity (Rome), 1984–2014; Convener, Action of Churches Together in Scotland, 1990–93; Co-moderator, Jt Working Gp, WCC and RC Church, 1996–2006; Hd, Catholic Delegn, 8th Assembly of WCC, Harare, 1998; Member: Pontifical Commn for Cultural Heritage of the Church, Rome, 1994–2004; Health Appts Adv. Cttee, 1994–2000; Jt Commn on Doctrine (RC Church and C of S), 2000–15; Historic Bldgs Council of Scotland, 2000–03. Founder Mem., Medieval Glasgow Trust, 2016–. Conventual Chaplain *ad honorem*, British Assoc., SMO Malta, 1991– (Principal Chaplain, 1995–2000, 2005–15). FRSE 1995. Hon. Mem., Merchants' House of Glasgow, 2012. Hon. DD: Aberdeen, 1989; Glasgow, 2010; Hon. DLitt Glasgow Caledonian, 2015. KCHS 1989. Grand Prior, Scottish Lieutenancy, 2013–. Commendatore, Order of Merit of the Italian Republic, 1981; Grande Ufficiale, Ordine della Stella della Solidarietà Italiana, 2007. *Publications:* Oh Help!: the making of an Archbishop, 2003; It's Late!: final pages of a Bishop's journal, 2015; numerous articles in defence of the tradition of faith and Christian morality. *Recreations:* music, art, book browsing, TV, travel, swimming. *Address:* 40 Newlands Road, Glasgow G43 2JD. *E:* mario.conti@rcag.org.uk.

**CONTI, Tom;** actor, since 1960; director; *b* Scotland, 1942; *m* Kara Wilson; one *d*. London appearances include: Savages, Royal Court and Comedy, 1973; Other People, The Black and White Minstrels, Hampstead; The Devil's Disciple, RSC Aldwych, 1976; Whose Life is it Anyway?, Mermaid and Savoy, 1978, NY 1979 (SWET Award for Best Actor in a new play, Variety Club of GB Award for Best Stage Actor, 1978, Tony Award for Best Actor, 1979); They're Playing Our Song, Shaftesbury, 1980; Romantic Comedy, Apollo, 1983; An Italian Straw Hat, Shaftesbury, 1986; Otherwise Engaged (also dir), Theatre Royal, Windsor, 1990; The Ride Down Mount Morgan, Wyndham's, 1991; Present Laughter (also dir), Globe, 1993; Chapter Two, Gielgud, 1996; Jesus, My Boy, Apollo, 1998; Jeffrey Bernard is Unwell, Garrick, 2006; Romantic Comedy (also dir), UK tour, 2007; Wife After Death, UK tour, 2010; Smash, Menier Chocolate Factory, 2011; Rough Justice, UK tour, 2012; Twelve Angry Men, Garrick, 2014, UK tour, 2015; Before the Party (also dir), UK tour, 2016; The Patriotic Traitor, Park Th., 2016; *directed:* Last Licks, Broadway, 1979; Before the Party, Oxford Playhouse and Queen's, 1980; The Housekeeper, Apollo, 1982; Treats, Hampstead, 1989; *films include:* Galileo, Flame, 1974; Eclipse, 1975; Full Circle, The Duellists, 1977; The Wall, 1980; Merry Christmas, Mr Lawrence, 1983; Reuben, Reuben, 1983; American Dreamer, 1985; Miracles, 1985; Saving Grace, 1986; Heavenly Pursuits, 1987; Beyond Therapy, 1987; The Dumb Waiter (USA); White Roses; Shirley Valentine, 1989; Two Brothers Running; Someone Else's America, 1997; Sub Down, 1997; Out of Control, 1997; Something To Believe In, 1997; Don't Go Breaking My Heart, 1998; A Closed Book, 2010; The Tempest, 2010; Streetdance 2, 2012; City Slackers, 2012; The Dark Knight Rises, 2012; Paddington 2, 2017; *television appearances include:* Madame Bovary, The Norman Conquests, Glittering Prizes, The Beate Klarsfeld Story, Fatal Dosage, The Quick and the Dead, Blade on the Feather, Wright Verdicts, Friends, The Cosby Show, I Was a Rat, Deadline, Donovan; Four Seasons, Ten Days to War, 2008. *Publications:* The Doctor (novel), 2004. *Club:* Garrick.

**CONTRERAS, Dame (Carmen) Marcela,** DBE 2007; MD; FRCP, FRCPE, FRCPath; Professor of Transfusion Medicine, UCL Medical School (formerly Royal Free and University College Medical School), University College London, 1998; Director, Diagnostics, Development and Research, National Blood Service, 1999–2007; *b* 4 Jan. 1942; *d* of Dr Juan Eduardo Contreras and Elena Mireya (*née* Arriagada); *m* 1968, Dr Roberto Jaime Guiloff (marr. diss. 1997); one *s* one *d*. *Educ:* Dunalastair British Sch. for Girls, Santiago; Sch. of Medicine, Univ. of Chile (BSc 1963; LMed 1967; MD 1972). MRCPath 1988, FRCPath 1997; FRCPE 1992; FRCP 1998. British Council Schol., RPMS and MRC Blood Gp Unit, London, 1972–74; SSO, 1974–76, Med. Asst in Blood Transfusion, 1976–78, N London Blood Transfusion Centre, Edgware; Sen. Registrar in Haematology, St Mary's Hosp., London, 1978–80; Dep. Dir, 1980–84, Chief Exec. and Med. Dir, 1984–95, N London Blood Transfusion Centre; Exec. Dir, London and SE Zone, Nat. Blood Service, 1995–99. Vis. Prof., Faculty of Applied Scis, UWE, 2004–. Hon. Mem., MRC Blood Gp Unit, 1987–95. President: Internat. Soc. of Blood Transfusion, 1996–98; British Blood Transfusion Soc., 2001–03. Review Editor, Vox Sanguinis, 1989–96, 2003– (Ed.-in-Chief, 1996–2003); Member, Editorial Board: Transfusion Medicine, 1990–; Transfusion Medicine Reviews, 1993–; Blood Reviews, 1995–; Transfusion Alternatives in Transfusion Medicine, 1999–. FMedSci 2003. *Publications:* (jtly) Blood Transfusion in Clinical Medicine, 8th edn 1987, 10th edn 1997; ABC of Transfusion, 1990, 3rd edn 1998; Blood Transfusion: the impact of new technologies, 1990; contrib. numerous papers and chapters in the field of transfusion medicine. *Recreations:* theatre, travelling, opera, horse riding, walking, training in developing countries.

**CONVILLE, Clare Benedicta;** literary agent; Director, C&W (formerly Conville & Walsh), since 2000; *b* London, 14 Oct. 1959; *d* of late David Henry Conville, OBE and Jean Margaret Bury; two *s* one *d*. *Educ:* Garden House; Bute House; Cranbourne Chase Sch. for Girls; Westminster Sch.; Bristol Univ. (BA Hons). Publicity Officer, Penguin Books, 1986–87; Editor, Random House, 1987–93; agent, AP Watt, 1993–2000. *Publications:* (jtly) Dangerous Women: a guide to modern life, 2011. *Recreations:* organising arts festivals, going to prison, throwing poetry parties too big for my house. *Address:* C&W, 5th Floor, Haymarket House, 28–29 Haymarket, SW1Y 4SP. *Clubs:* Academy, Quo Vadis Upstairs, Chelsea Arts, Mortimer House.

**CONWAY, (David) Martin;** President, Selly Oak Colleges, Birmingham, 1986–97; *b* 22 Aug. 1935; *s* of Geoffrey S. and Dr Elsie Conway; *m* 1962, Ruth, *d* of Rev. Richard Daniel; one *s* two *d*. *Educ:* Sedbergh Sch.; Gonville and Caius Coll., Cambridge (BA, MA); and by friends and fellow Christians in many different cultures. Internat. Sec., SCM of GB and Ire., 1958–61; Study Sec., World Student Christian Fedn, Geneva, 1961–67; Sec. for Chaplaincies in Higher Educn, Gen. Synod of C of E, 1967–70; Publications Sec., WCC, 1970–74; Asst Gen. Sec. for Ecumenical Affairs, BCC, 1974–83; Dir, Oxford Inst. for Church and Society, and Tutor, Ripon Coll., Cuddesdon, Oxford, 1983–86. Simultaneous interpreter at assemblies and major world confs of WCC, 1961–2006; Consultant, Faith and Order Commn, WCC, 1971–82; Consultant, 1974–83, and Mem., 1986–91, C of E Bd for Mission and Unity. Chairman: Bd for Social Responsibility, Dio. of Oxford, 2000–10; Soc. of Ecumenical Studies, 2001–10; Trustees, Centennial Fund, World Student Christian Fedn, 2009–11. DLitt Lambeth, 1994. Editor: The Ecumenical Review, 1972–74; Christians Together, 1983–91; Oxford Papers on Contemporary Society, 1984–86. *Publications:* The Undivided Vision, 1966; (ed) University Chaplain?, 1969; The Christian Enterprise in Higher Education, 1971; Seeing Education Whole, 1971; Look Listen Care, 1983; That's When the Body Works, 1991; Journeying Together Towards Jubilee, 1999; Introducing the World Council of Churches, 2001; World Christianity in the 20th Century, 2 vols, 2008; contribs to Student World, New Christian, Audenshaw Papers, Internat. Rev. of Mission, etc. *Recreations:* other people—family, friends, colleagues; travel, music. *Address:* 63 Tuckers Court, Coral Springs Way, Richmond Village, Witney OX28 5DG. *T:* (01993) 358732.
See also Very Rev. J. A. Conway.

**CONWAY, Derek Leslie,** TD 1990; *b* 15 Feb. 1953; *s* of Leslie and Florence Conway; *m* 1980, Colette Elizabeth Mary (*née* Lamb); two *s* one *d*. *Educ:* Beacon Hill Boys' School. Principal Organiser, Action Research for the Crippled Child, 1974–83; Chief Exec., Cats Protection League, 1998–2003. Borough Councillor and Dep. Leader of the Opposition, Gateshead Metropolitan Borough Council, 1974–78; Mem., Tyne and Wear Metropolitan County Council, 1977–83 (Leader, 1979–82); Member Board: Washington Develt Corp., 1979–83; North of England Develt Council, 1979–83; Newcastle Airport, 1980–83; Northern Arts, 1980–83. Non-exec. Dir, Foreign & Colonial Gp Investment Fund, 1997–2001. MP (C) Shrewsbury and Atcham, 1983–97; contested (C) same seat, 1997; MP Old Bexley and Sidcup, 2001–10 (C, 2001–08; Ind C, 2008–10). PPS to Minister of State: Welsh Office, 1988–91; Dept of Employment, 1992–93; an Asst Govt Whip, 1993–94; a Lord Comr of HM Treasury (Govt Whip), 1994–96; Vice Chamberlain of HM Household, 1996–97. Mem., Speaker's Panel of Chairmen, 2001–08; Member, Select Committee: on Agric., 1987; on Transport, 1987–88; on Armed Forces Discipline, 1991; Liaison, 2001–08; Finance and Services, 2001–08; on Defence, 2005–07; Chm., Select Cttee on Accommodation and Works, 2001–08. Chairman: British-Morocco Parly Gp, 1984–92, 2001–10; British-Venezuelan Gp, 1987–93; Mem. Exec., British American Parly Gp, 2001–08; Vice Chm., Cons. backbench Defence Cttee, 1991–97. Treas., IPU, 2001–08 (Mem. Exec. Cttee, 1986–97; Vice-Chm., British Gp, 1992–93); Vice-Chm., CPA, 2004–08. Member, Conservative Party Committees: Nat. Exec. Cttee, 1971–81; Nat. Gen. Purposes Cttee, 1972–74; Nat. Local Govt Cttee, 1979–83; Nat. Vice-Chm., Young Conservatives, 1972–74. Mem. Exec. Cttee, British Venezuela Soc., 1987–93. Crown Estates Paving Comr, 1994–96. Commnd RMA Sandhurst into Royal Regt of Fusiliers; Major, 5th Bn (TA) Light Infantry. MInstD. Grand Officer, Al Wissam Al Alaoui Order (Morocco), 2016 (Kt Comdr, 2004). *Recreation:* historical fiction.

**CONWAY, Donald Hugh Stevenson;** a Judge of the Upper Tribunal (Immigration and Asylum Chamber), since 2010, and Resident Judge of the First-tier Tribunal, since 2011; *b* Paisley, 31 Oct. 1954; *s* of Dr Hugh Conway, FRCP and Dr Lilian Conway (*née* Donald); *m* 1998, Isabella Sutherland; two *s*. *Educ:* Paisley Grammar Sch.; Glasgow Acad.; Cardonald Coll.; Univ. of Edinburgh (BA 1976; LLB 1978); Univ. of Glasgow (MPhil 1992). Admitted solicitor, 1980, NP, 1981; Reporter, Children's Panel, Glasgow, 1980–83; Procurator Fiscal Depute, Hamilton, Kilmarnock, Glasgow, 1983–89; admitted Faculty of Advocates, 1991; in practice as an advocate, 1991–96; Immigration Adjudicator, pt-time, 1994–96, full-time, 1996–2003; Regl Immigration Adjudicator, N Shields, 2003–05; Resident Senior Immigration Judge: N Shields, 2005–07; Manchester, 2007–11; Resident Judge: Hatton Cross, 2011–17; Scotland and NI, 2017–. *Recreations:* books, dogs, walking. *Address:* (office) Eagle Building, 215 Bothwell Street, Glasgow G2 7EZ. *T:* (0141) 242 7553. *E:* TribunalJudge.Conway@ejudiciary.net.

**CONWAY, Edmund Alexander;** Economics Editor, Sky News, since 2011; columnist, The Times, since 2014; *b* London, 10 Nov. 1979; *s* of late Dr Cyril Conway and of Dr Caroline Conway; *m* 2015, Lady Eliza Pelham, *d* of Earl of Chichester, *qv*; two *d*. *Educ:* Westminster Cathedral Choir Sch.; Oratory Sch.; Pembroke Coll., Oxford (BA English); Harvard Univ. (Fulbright Alistair Cooke Schol.; Shorenstein Schol.; MPA 2011). Reporter, Daily Telegraph, 2003–05; Econs Corresp., Daily Mail, 2005–06; Econs Ed., Daily Telegraph and Sunday Telegraph, 2006–10. Gov., NIESR, 2014–. *Publications:* 50 Economics Ideas You Really Need to Know, 2009; The Summit, 2014. *Recreations:* reading economic history, DJing (tech house, disco). *Address:* Sky News, Four Millbank, SW1P 3JA. *E:* ed.conway@sky.uk.

**CONWAY, Sir Gordon (Richard),** KCMG 2005; FRS 2004; FRSB; Professor of International Development, Imperial College, London, since 2005; Chief Scientific Adviser, Department for International Development, 2005–09; *b* 6 July 1938; *s* of Cyril Conway and Thelma (*née* Goodwin); *m* 1965, Susan Mary Mumford; one *s* two *d*. *Educ:* Kingston Grammar Sch.; Kingston Polytechnic; University Coll. of North Wales, Bangor (BSc 1959). DipAgricSci, Cambridge, 1960; DTA University Coll. of West Indies, Trinidad, 1961; PhD Univ. of California, Davis, 1969; FIBiol 1978, Hon. FRSB (Hon. FIBiol 2001). Research Officer (Entomology), Agric. Res. Centre, State of Sabah, Malaysia, 1961–66; Statistician, Inst. Ecology, Univ. of California, Davis, 1966–69; Imperial College, London: Res. Fellow and Lectr, Dept of Zoology and Applied Entomology, 1970–76; Dir, 1977–80, Chm., 1980–86, Centre for Envmtl Technol.; Reader in Environmental Management, Univ. of London, 1976–80; Prof. of Environmental Technol., 1980–88; Rep. for India, Nepal and Sri Lanka, Ford Foundn, 1989–92; Vice-Chancellor, 1992–98, Emeritus Prof., 2003–, Univ. of Sussex. Pres., Rockefeller Foundn, 1998–2004. Vis. Prof., Imperial Coll., 1989–2004. Pres., RGS, 2006–09. Director: Sustainable Agric. Prog., Internat. Inst. for Envmt and Develt, 1986–88; BOC Foundn, 1994–97; Sussex Enterprise, 1995–98; RSA, 2005–06; African Agricl Technol. Foundn, 2009–15; Lawes Agricl Trust, 2011–17. Mem., Royal Commn on Environmental Pollution, 1984–88. Chm. Bd, Inst. Develt Studies, 1992–98; Member: Internat. Inst. for Envmt and Develt, 1993–97; Bd, Internat. Food Policy Res. Inst., Washington, 1994–97; Council, World Food Prize, 2002–18; Bd, Meridian Inst., 2013–; Kirkhouse Trust, 2013–17; Bd, Liby of Alexandria, Cairo, 2016–. Chairman: Runnymede Trust Commn on Muslims in Britain, 1996–97; Living Cities (formerly Nat. Community Develt Initiative), 2000–04; Visiting Arts, 2004–09; UK Collaborative on Develt Scis, 2007–09; Montpellier Panel, 2010–16; Sen. Advr, Malabo Montpellier Panel, 2017–. DL E Sussex, 2006. FCGI 2006; Fellow, Amer. Acad. of Arts and Scis, 2000; Hon. FREng 2077. Hon. Fellow, Univ. of Wales, Bangor, 1997. Hon. LLD Sussex, 1998; Hon. DSc: W Indies, 1999; Brighton, 2001; DUniv Open, 2004. Founder's Medal, RGS, 2017. *Publications:* Pest and Pathogen Control, 1984; (jtly) After the Green Revolution, 1990; (jtly) Unwelcome Harvest, 1991; Doubly Green Revolution: food for all in the 21st century, 1997; (jtly) Science and Innovation for Development, 2010; One Billion Hungry: can we feed the world?, 2012; (jtly) African Farmers in the Digital Age, 2016; papers and reports on agricl ecology. *Recreations:* travel, movies, music. *Address:* Imperial College, SW7 1NA. *Club:* Reform.

**CONWAY, James Leo;** General Director, English Touring Opera, since 2002; *b* Granby, Quebec, Canada, 10 Feb. 1956; *s* of Frederick L. Conway and Catherine P. Conway (*née* McBride); partner, 2006, Jonathan Peter Kenny. *Educ:* Univ. of Toronto (BA Hons; Gold Medallist in Philosophy; MA Hons English); University Coll. Dublin (DipEd); City Univ., London (MA Arts Policy/Mgt). Gen. Dir, Opera Th. Co., Dublin, 1987–2003. Opera Specialist, Arts Council Ireland, 2003–06. Hon. RCM, 2014. *Publications:* The Christians of Malabar, 1991. *Recreations:* theatre, music, visual art, history, philosophy. *Address:* English Touring Opera, 50 Britton Street, EC1M 5UP. *T:* (020) 7833 2555. *E:* jconway@englishtouringopera.org.uk.

**CONWAY, Very Rev. John Arthur;** Provost, St Mary's Cathedral, Edinburgh, since 2017; *b* Farnborough, Kent, 6 Dec. 1967; *s* of (David) Martin Conway, *qv*; *m* 1993, Dr Susannah Gibbs; three *d*. *Educ:* Eliot Sch., Putney; Oxford Sch., Oxford; Univ. of Leeds (BEng 1990); Univ. of Edinburgh (BD 1997). Ordained deacon, 1997, priest, 1998; Chaplain, St Mary's Episcopal Cathedral, Edinburgh, 1997–2001; Rector, St Martin's Episcopal Church, Edinburgh, 2001–17. Initial Ministerial Educn Co-ord., Dio. of

Edinburgh, 2004–07, 2009–11. *Recreations:* cycling, walking, cooking, reading. *Address:* St Mary's Cathedral, Palmerston Place, Edinburgh EH12 5AW. *T:* (0131) 225 6293. *E:* provost@cathedral.net.

**CONWAY, Prof. John Horton,** FRS 1981; John von Neumann Professor of Mathematics, Princeton University, USA, 1987–2013, now Emeritus. *Educ:* Gonville and Caius Coll., Cambridge (BA 1959; MA 1963; PhD 1964). Cambridge University: Lectr in Pure Maths, to 1973; Reader in Pure Mathematics and Mathematical Statistics, 1973–83; Prof. of Maths, 1983–87; Fellow: Sidney Sussex Coll., 1964–70; Gonville and Caius Coll., 1970–87. Hon. DSc Liverpool, 2001. Polya Prize, London Mathematical Soc., 1987; Frederic Esser Nemmers Prize, Northwestern Univ., 1999; Steele Prize, AMS, 1999; Joseph Priestley Award, 2001. *Publications:* Regular Algebra and Finite Machines, 1971; On Numbers and Games, 1976; Atlas of Finite Groups, 1985; The Book of Numbers, 1996; The Sensual Quadratic Form, 1997. *Address:* Department of Mathematics, Princeton University, Fine Hall, Washington Road, Princeton, NJ 08544-1000, USA.

**CONWAY, Martin;** see Conway, D. M.

**CONWAY, Rt Rev. Stephen David;** see Ely, Bishop of.

**CONWAY MORRIS, Prof. Simon,** PhD; FRS 1990; Professor of Evolutionary Palaeobiology, University of Cambridge, 1995–2019, now Emeritus; Fellow of St John's College, Cambridge, since 1987; *b* 6 Nov. 1951; *s* of Richard Conway Morris and Barbara Louise Maxwell; *m* 1975, Zoë Helen James; two *s. Educ:* Univ. of Bristol (BSc Hons); Univ. of Cambridge (PhD). Research Fellow, St John's Coll., Cambridge, 1975–79; Lectr, Open Univ., 1979–83; Lectr in Palaeontology, 1983–91, Reader in Evolutionary Palaeobiology, 1991–95, Cambridge Univ. Gallagher Vis. Scientist, Univ. of Calgary, 1981; Nuffield Sci. Res. Fellowship, 1987–88; Merrill W. Haas Vis. Dist. Prof., Univ. of Kansas, 1988; Selby Fellow, Aust. Acad. of Scis, 1992; Cecil H. and Ida Green Vis. Prof., Univ. of British Columbia, 2008–. Member Council: Systematics Assoc., 1981–85; NERC, 1996–2002; Cambridge Philosophical Soc., 2014– (Pres., 2018–19). Royal Instn Christmas Lectr, 1996; Gifford Lectr, Univ. of Edinburgh, 2007. Hon. Fellow, Eur. Union of Geoscis, 1997. Hon. DPhil Uppsala, 1993; Hon. DSc Hull, 2008. Walcott Medal, Nat. Acad. of Scis, 1987; Charles Schuchert Award, Paleontol. Soc., 1989; George Gaylord Simpson Prize, Yale Univ., 1992; Lyell Medal, Geol Soc. of London, 1998; Kelvin Medal, Royal Philosophical Soc. of Glasgow, 2007; Ide and Luella Prize, Coll. of Sci., A&M Univ., Texas, 2007; William Bate Hardy Prize, Cambridge Philosophical Soc., 2010. *Publications:* The Crucible of Creation, 1998; Life's Solution, 2003; The Runes of Evolution, 2015; contribs to professional jls. *Recreations:* G. K. Chesterton, wine, punting. *Address:* Department of Earth Sciences, University of Cambridge, Downing Street, Cambridge CB2 3EQ. *T:* (01223) 333400.

**CONYNGHAM,** family name of **Marquess Conyngham**.

**CONYNGHAM, 8th Marquess** *cr* 1816; **Henry Vivian Pierpoint Conyngham;** *b* 23 May 1951; *s* of 7th Marquess Conyngham and Eileen Wren (*née* Newsam); *S* father, 2009; *m* 1st, 1971, Juliet Ann, *yr d* of Robert Kitson (marr. diss. 1985); one *s* one *d*; 2nd, 1985, Lady Iona Grimston, *yr d* of 6th Earl of Verulam; one *d. Educ:* Harrow; Harvard Univ. Irish Rep., 1976–78, Consultant, 1978–84, Sotheby's; Chairman: Slane Castle Ltd; Slane Castle Productions. Dir, CityArts (formerly Grapevine Arts Centre), Dublin. Columnist, Irish Daily Mirror, 2002–. *Heir: s* Earl of Mount Charles, *qv. Address:* Slane Castle, Co. Meath, Eire; Beau Parc House, Navan, Co. Meath, Eire. *Club:* Kildare Street and University (Dublin).

**COODE-ADAMS, (John) Giles Selby,** OBE 1998; DL; President, Royal Horticultural Society, 2008–10 (Member, Council, 2002–10; Treasurer, 2006–08); *b* 30 Aug. 1938; *s* of Geoffrey Coode-Adams and Cynthia Mildred Coode-Adams (*née* Selby-Bigge); *m* 1960, Sonia Elizabeth, *d* of Laurence Frederick York; one *s* one *d. Educ:* Eton. 2nd Lieut, 16/5 Queen's Royal Lancers, 1956–58. Joined L. Messel, 1959, Partner, 1967–86; Man. Dir, then Sen. Advr, Lehman Bros, 1986–99; Director: Guardian Media Gp plc, 1999–2008; Rathbone Bros plc, 1999–2008; Trades Media Gp plc, 2003–07. Chm., Westonbirt and Bedgebury Adv. Cttee, Forestry Commn, 2006–; Mem., Adv. Cttee, Hillier Arboretum, 2010–. Chief Exec., Royal Botanic Gdns Kew Foundn, 1991–97 (Trustee, 2011–); Mem., Gdns Cttee, English Heritage, 1997–2002. Former Mem. Council, Univ. of Essex. High Sheriff, 2000–01, DL, Essex. Freeman: City of London; Merchant Taylors' Co. *Recreations:* fishing, music, gardening. *Address:* Feeringbury Manor, Feering, Colchester, Essex CO5 9RB. *T:* (01376) 561946, *Fax:* (01376) 562481. *E:* jgsca@btinternet.com. *Club:* Boodle's.

**COOGAN, Ven. Robert Arthur William;** Archdeacon of Hampstead, 1985–94, now Archdeacon Emeritus; *b* 11 July 1929; *s* of Ronald Dudley Coogan and Joyce Elizabeth Coogan (*née* Roberts). *Educ:* Univ. of Tasmania (BA); Univ. of Durham (DipTheol). Asst Curate, St Andrew, Plaistow, 1953–56; Rector of Bothwell, Tasmania, 1956–62; Vicar: North Woolwich, 1962–73; St Stephen, Hampstead, 1973–77; Priest in Charge, All Hallows, Gospel Oak, 1974–77; Vicar of St Stephen with All Hallows, Hampstead, 1977–85; Priest in Charge: Old St Pancras with St Matthew, 1976–80; St Martin with St Andrew, Gospel Oak, 1978–81; Area Dean, South Camden 1975–81, North Camden 1978–83; Prebendary of St Paul's Cathedral, 1982–85. Commissary for Bishop of Tasmania, 1968–88; Exam. Chaplain to Bishop of Edmonton, 1985–94. *Recreations:* reading, gardening, travel. *Address:* Salters Hall West, Stour Street, Sudbury, Suffolk CO10 2AX. *T:* (01787) 370026. *Club:* Oriental.

**COOGAN, Steve;** actor, writer and producer; *b* 14 Oct. 1965; one *d* by Anna Cole; *m* 2002, Caroline Hickman (marr. diss. 2005). *Educ:* Manchester Poly. Sch. of Theatre. Partner, Baby Cow Prodns Ltd, 1999–. *Radio:* On The Hour, 1992; Knowing Me, Knowing You, with Alan Partridge, 1992; *television* includes: Spitting Image, 1984; The Day Today (also writer), 1994; Knowing Me, Knowing You, with Alan Partridge (also writer), 1995; Coogan's Run (also writer), 1995; I'm Alan Partridge (also writer), 1997, 2002; The Fix, 1997; Alice Through the Looking Glass, 1998; Dr Terrible's House of Horrible (also writer and prod.), 2001; The Private Life of Samuel Pepys (also prod.), 2003; Saxondale (also writer and prod.), 2006, 2007; The Trip, 2010 (Best Male Perf. in a Comedy Role, BAFTA, 2011); Mid Morning Matters with Alan Partridge, 2010–11, 2016; Moone Boy, 2012; Welcome to the Places of My Life, 2013 (Best Male Perf. in a Comedy Prog., BAFTA, 2013); The Trip to Italy, 2014; Happyish, 2015; Alan Partridge's Scissored Isle, 2016 (Best Male Perf. in a Comedy Prog., BAFTA, 2017); The Trip to Spain, 2017; This Time with Alan Partridge, 2019; *films:* The Wind in the Willows, 1996; The Parole Officer (also writer), 2001; 24 Hour Party People, 2002; Coffee and Cigarettes, 2003; Around the World in 80 Days, 2004; Happy Endings, A Cock and Bull Story, 2005; The Alibi, Marie Antoinette, Night at the Museum, 2006; Hot Fuzz, 2007; Night at the Museum 2, 2009; The Look of Love, Alan Partridge: Alpha Papa, Philomena (also prod. and co-writer), 2013; Northern Soul, Night at the Museum: Secret of the Tomb, 2014; Mindhorn, The Dinner, 2017; Ideal Home, 2018; Stan & Ollie, Greed, 2019; *theatre:* The Man Who Thinks He's It (tour), 1998. *Publications:* (jtly) I, Partridge: we need to talk about Alan, 2011; Easily Distracted, 2015. *Address:* Baby Cow Productions Ltd, 5–6 Portland Mews, W1F 8JG; c/o Independent Talent Group Ltd, 40 Whitfield Street, W1T 2RH.

**COOK;** see Curnock Cook.

**COOK, Alan Ronald,** CBE 2006; FCII; Chairman: LV=, since 2017 (non-executive Director, since 2017); Chetwood Financial Ltd, since 2017; *b* 23 Sept. 1953; *s* of Ronald Joseph Cook and Dorothy May Cook; *m* 1975, Anita Patricia Kelleher; two *s* one *d. Educ:* Ealing Grammar Sch. for Boys. FCII 1975. Prudential Assce Co. Ltd, 1970–93; Sen. Vice Pres., Jackson Nat. Life, USA, 1993–96; Prudential Assurance Co. Ltd: Acquisitions Dir, 1996–97; Man. Dir, Gen. Insce, 1997–99; Man. Dir, Retail Insce Ops, 1999–2000; Chief Exec., Insce Services, 2000–01; Chief Operating Officer, UK and Europe, 2001–02; CEO, Nat. Savings & Investments, 2002–06; Man. Dir, Post Office Ltd, 2006–10. Chm., Permanent TSB Gp Hldgs (formerly Irish Life and Permanent Gp Hldgs), 2011–17; Dep. Chm., Sainsbury's Bank, 2014–16 (non-exec. Dir, 2011–13); non-exec. Dir, MetLife Europe, 2013–16. Chm., Highways Agency, 2011–14; Gov., Inst. of Financial Services, 2005–08; non-executive Director: Financial Ombudsman Service, 2008–11; DfT, 2009–14; OFT, 2010–11. Chm., 2010–16, Patron, 2016–, Action for ME. Vice-Chm. Govs, Luton Univ., 2003–05; Ind. Gov., Univ. of Bedfordshire, 2010–18 (Chm., 2011–18). FRSA 2000; FCMI 2005. Freeman, City of London, 2003; Mem., Co. of Insurers, 2005–. Hon. DBA Bedfordshire, 2006. *Recreations:* fell-walking, swimming. *Address:* Orchard Grange, 28 Church End Road, Shenley Brook End, Milton Keynes MK5 7AB. *E:* Alan.Cook@orchard-grange.co.uk.

**COOK, Allan Edward,** CBE 2008; FREng; FRAeS; Chairman: Helios Towers, since 2018; HS2 Ltd, since 2018; *b* 27 Sept. 1949; *s* of late Stanley Livingston Porter and of Sarah Neve; *m* 1970, Kathleen Pegg; two *d. Educ:* Sunderland Coll. of FE; Sunderland Poly. (DMS; Full Technol. Cert); Sunderland Univ. (BSc Hons Electronics). Chief Exec., Hughes Aircraft (Europe), 1995; Man. Dir, GEC-Marconi Avionics, 1998–2000; Gp Man. Dir Progs and Man. Dir Eurofighter, BAE Systems, 2000–01; Chief Exec., Cobham plc, 2001–09. Chairman: W. S. Atkins, 2010–17; Selex ES (formerly Selex Galileo), 2011–14; Finmeccanica UK, 2012–14; Dep. Chm., Marshalls of Cambridge (Hldgs) Ltd, 2011–15. Director: Manufg Forum, 2006; Ministerial Adv. Gp for Manufg, 2008–; Chairman: Nat. Skills Acad. for Manufg, 2008–; SEMTA, 2010–; Skills and Job Retention Gp, BIS, then BEIS, 2010–; Lead non-exec. Mem. Bd, BIS, 2014–16; Co-Chair, Defence Growth Partnership, 2016–. President: SBAC, 2007–09; AeroSpace and Defence Industries Assoc. of Europe, 2008–09; Vice Pres., Royal Acad. of Engrg, 2014–. FREng 2010; FRAeS 1998. Hon. DSc Cranfield, 2016. *Recreations:* squash, music, walking, theatre, wine. *Clubs:* Royal Automobile, Royal Air Force.

**COOK, Sir Andrew (John),** Kt 2016; CBE 1996; Chairman, William Cook Holdings Ltd, since 1982 (Chief Executive, 1982–2017); *b* 11 Oct. 1949; *s* of late Andrew McTurk Cook and Barbara Jean (*née* Gale); *m* 1st, 1987, Alison Jane Lincoln (marr. diss. 2011); one *s* three *d*; 2nd, 2013, Angelika Hirsch-Stronstorff (marr. diss. 2017). *Educ:* High Storrs Grammar Sch., Sheffield; University Coll. London (LLB). Called to the Bar, Gray's Inn, 1972. Dir, William Cook & Sons (Sheffield) Ltd, 1974–82. *Publications:* Thrice Through the Fire: the history of the William Cook company 1985–1998, 1999; Ashes and Dust: a business autobiography 1997–2009, 2010; (with Andrew Rhys Thompson) Coal, Steam and Comfort: 141R568 and the Swiss classic train, 2010; The Doctors of Ulm and other stories, 2015. *Recreations:* boats, mountains, history, trains, planes, bikes. *Address:* William Cook Holdings Ltd, Parkway Avenue, Sheffield S9 4UL. *Clubs:* Royal Thames Yacht; Gstaad Yacht.

**COOK, Ann;** see Christopher, A.

**COOK, Sir Christopher Wymondham Rayner Herbert,** 5th Bt *cr* 1886; company director, since 1979; Director, Diamond Guarantees Ltd, 1980–91; *b* 24 March 1938; *s* of Sir Francis Ferdinand Maurice Cook, 4th Bt and Joan Loraine, *d* of John Aloysius Ashton-Case; *S* father, 1978; *m* 1st, 1958, Mrs Malina Gunasekera (from whom he obtained a divorce, 1975; she *d* 2010); one *s* one *d*; 2nd, 1975, Mrs Margaret Miller, *d* of late John Murray; one *s* one *d. Educ:* King's School, Canterbury. *Recreations:* reading, philately, painting. *Heir: s* Richard Herbert Aster Maurice Cook [*b* 30 June 1959; *m* 1996, Corinne Solange Andrée, *d* of René Daniel Dayras; one *s* two *d*].

**COOK, Colin Simon Bult;** Director, Digital, Scottish Government, since 2017 (Acting Director, Digital, 2016–17); *b* Hythe, 23 Sept. 1965; *s* of Simon Hugh Bult Cook and Erica Cook; *m* 2010, Patricia Mary Quinn; two *s* one *d. Educ:* King Alfred Sch., Highbridge; Peter Symonds Coll., Winchester; Durham Univ. (BA Hons Politics); Internat. Mgt Centres (MBA). Metal Box plc, 1987–92; Applied Chemicals, 1992–93; Royal Mail, 1993–2003: Controller, Chm. and Chief Exec.'s Office, The Post Office, 1997–99; Mktg Dir, Royal Mail, 1999–2003; Sen. Civil Servant, Scottish Govt, 2003–09; Mktg Dir, British Army, 2009–12; Dep. Dir, Digital, Scottish Govt, 2012–16. Trustee: Poppy Factory, 2011–17; Royal Caledonian Educn Trust, 2018–. *Address:* Digital Directorate, Scottish Government, Victoria Quay, Leith, Edinburgh EH6 6QQ. *T:* (0131) 244 2389. *E:* directordigital@gov.scot.

**COOK, Daniel Thomas Victor;** Master of the Choristers and Organist, Durham Cathedral, since 2017; *b* Newcastle-upon-Tyne, 7 Sept. 1979; *s* of Graham Cook and Jill Cook (*née* Andrews, now Barrett); *m* 2007, Miriam Taylor; two *s. Educ:* Royal Coll. of Music (ARCM 1999); Royal Coll. of Organists (FRCO 2000; Dip. in Choral Directing 2002); Royal Acad. of Music (LRAM 2002; BMus Hons 2003; ARAM 2013). Organ Scholar: Worcester Cathedral, 1998–99; Southwark Cathedral, 2000–02; Organ Scholar, 2002–03, Asst Organist, 2003–05, Westminster Abbey; Asst Dir of Music, Salisbury Cathedral, 2005–11; Organist and Master of the Choristers, St Davids Cathedral, 2011–13; Sub-organist, Westminster Abbey, 2013–17. Musical Director: Grange Choral Soc., 2008–11; Farrant Singers, 2009–11; Durham Univ. Choral Soc., 2018–; Artistic Dir, Mousai, 2010–. *Recreations:* theatre, opera, walking. *E:* daniel@danielcookorganist.com.

**COOK, David;** see Cook, J. D.

**COOK, David Julian,** CB 2015; Second Parliamentary Counsel, since 2007; *b* 15 July 1962; *s* of Stanley and late Dorothy Mary Cook; *m* 1988, Christine Margaret Alice Barnard; two *s* one *d. Educ:* Merton Coll., Oxford (BA Classics 1985, MA); Coll. of Law (CPE 1986; Law Finals 1987). Articled Clerk, then Solicitor, Freshfields, 1988–91; Office of Parliamentary Counsel: Asst Parly Counsel, 1991–95; Sen. Asst Parly Counsel, 1995–99; Dep. Parly Counsel, 1999–2003; Parly Counsel, 2003–; Hd of Drafting Team, Tax Law Rewrite Project, Bd of Inland Revenue, 2003–05 (on secondment). *Recreations:* archaeology, walking, Victorian novels.

**COOK, David Somerville;** solicitor; Senior Partner, Messrs Sheldon & Stewart, Solicitors, Belfast; Chairman, Police Authority for Northern Ireland, 1994–96; Lord Mayor of Belfast, 1978–79; *b* 25 Jan. 1944; *s* of late Francis John Granville Cook and Jocelyn McKay (*née* Stewart); *m* 1972, Mary Fionnuala Ann Deeny (see M. F. A. Cook); four *s* one *d. Educ:* Campbell Coll., Belfast; Pembroke Coll., Cambridge (MA). Alliance Party of Northern Ireland: Founder Member, 1970; Hon. Treasurer, 1972–75; Central Executive Cttee, 1970–78, 1980–85; Dep. Leader, 1980–84; Pres., 1992–93. Chm., NI Voluntary Trust, 1979–99. Mem., Belfast City Council, 1973–85; Mem. (Alliance) for Belfast S, NI Assembly, 1982–86; contested (Alliance): Belfast South, Feb. 1974, by-elections March

1982 and Jan. 1986, gen. election, 1987; N Ireland, European Parly elecn, 1984. Trustee: Ulster Museum, 1974–85; The Buttle Trust, 1991–2001; Brontë Memorial Cottage, Drumballyroney, Co. Down, 1995–; Vice Pres., NI Council on Alcohol, 1978–83; Member: NI Council, European Movement, 1980–84; Cttee, Charity Know How Fund, 1991–94; Exec. Cttee, Assoc. of Community Trusts and Foundns, 1992–98 (Chm., 1994–95); Exec. Cttee, Clanmil Housing Assoc. (formerly RBL Housing Assoc. Ltd), 1994–99; Chm., Craigavon and Banbridge Community Health and Social Services Trust, 1994–2001. Director: Ulster Actors' Co. Ltd, 1981–85; Crescent Arts Centre, Belfast, 1994–96; C21 Theatre Co., 2008–. Pres., Belfast Lit. Soc., 2012–13. Mem., Royal Naval Assoc. Gov., Brownlow Coll. (Integrated Secondary Sch.), 1994–98. Obtained Orders of Mandamus and fines for contempt of court against Belfast City Council, following its unlawful protest against the Anglo-Irish Agreement, 1986, 1987. Chm., West Down Beagles Hunt Club, 2003–13. Mem., Friends of HMS Caroline, 2016–. *Publications:* Blocking the Slippery Slope, 1997; (contrib.) The Republican Ideal, ed Norman Porter, 1998. *Recreations:* marmalade making, observing politicians. *Address:* 8 Main Street, Loughbrickland, Banbridge, Co. Down BT32 3NQ.

**COOK, Fionnuala;** *see* Cook, M. F. A.

**COOK, Gordon Charles,** DSc, MD; FRCP; physician with special interest in tropical and infectious diseases, and medical historian; Visiting Professor, University College London, since 2002; *b* Wimbledon, 17 Feb. 1932; *e s* of late Charles Francis Cook and Kate Cook (*née* Kraninger, then Grainger); *m* 1963, Elizabeth Jane, *d* of late Rev. Stephen Noel Agg-Large; one *s* three *d*. *Educ:* Wellingborough, Kingston-upon-Thames and Raynes Park Grammar Schs; Royal Free Hosp. Sch. of Medicine, London Univ. (BSc Physiol 1955; MB BS 1957; MD 1965; Charlotte Brown Prize, 1965; Cunning Award, 1967; Legg Award, 1969; DSc 1976). MRCS; LRCP 1957, MRCP 1960, FRCP 1972; FRACP 1978; FLS 1989; FRCPE 2002. Commissioned RAMC (Capt.), seconded to Royal Nigerian Army, 1960–62. Hosp. appts, Royal Free, Hampstead Gen., Royal Northern, Brompton, St George's, 1958–63; Lectr, Royal Free Hosp. Sch. of Medicine and Makerere Univ. Coll., Uganda, 1963–69; Prof. of Medicine and Cons. Physician, Univs of Zambia, 1969–74, Riyadh, 1974–75, Papua New Guinea, 1978–81; Sen. MO, MRC, 1975–76; Sen. Lectr in Clinical Scis, LSHTM, 1976–97; University College London: Hon. Sen. Lectr in Medicine (Infectious Diseases), 1981–2002; Sen. Res. Fellow, Wellcome Trust Centre for History of Medicine, 1997–2002. Hon. Consultant Physician: Hosp. for Trop. Diseases and UCL Hosps, 1976–97; St Luke's Hosp. for the Clergy, 1988–2009; Hon. Lectr in Clinical Parasitology, St Bart's Hosp. Med. Coll., 1992–. Vis. Prof., Univs of Basra, Mosul, Doha. Consultant, advr and mem., professional and learned bodies; Mem., Jt Cttee on Higher Med. Trng, 1987–93. Member: Assoc. of Physicians of GB and Ireland, 1973–; Exec. Council, Med. Writers Gp, Soc. of Authors, 1994–99 (Chm., 1997–99); Mem. Exec. Cttee and Examiner, Faculty of Hist. and Philosophy of Medicine and Pharmacy, Soc. of Apothecaries, 1997–; Examiner for membership of RCP, 1977–84. Lectures: Ahmed Hafez Moussa Meml, 1994; Stanley Browne Meml, 1995; Monckton Copeman, Soc. of Apothecaries, 2000; Denny, Barber-Surgeons' Co., 2003. President: RSTM&H, 1993–95; Osler Club, London, 1993–95; Baconian Club of St Albans, 1995–96; History of Medicine Sect., RSM, 2003–04 (Vice-Pres., 1994–96); Fellowship of Postgrad. Medicine, 2000–07; Founder and Chm., Erasmus Darwin Foundn, Lichfield, 1994–2011 (Vice-Pres., 2011–); Trustee, BookPower (formerly Educnl Low-priced Sponsored Texts), 1996–2011; Member: Council, Galton Inst., 2005–10; Cttee, Friends of Florence Nightingale Mus., 2005–09 (Vice-Chm., 2006–09). Hon. Archivist, Seamen's Hosp. Soc., 2002– (Hon. Life Gov., 2007–); Hon. Res. Associate, Greenwich Maritime Inst., 2003–. Mem. Council, Cathedral and Abbey Church of St Alban, 1983–88. Liveryman, Apothecaries' Co., 1981–. Editor, Jl of Infection, 1995–97; mem., editl bds, med. jls. Frederick Murgatroyd Meml Prize, RCP, 1973; Hugh L'Etang Prize, RSM, 1999. *Publications:* (ed jtly) Acute Renal Failure, 1964; Tropical Gastroenterology, 1980; (jtly) 100 Clinical Problems in Tropical Medicine, 1987, 2nd edn 1998; Communicable and Tropical Diseases, 1988; Parasitic Disease in Clinical Practice, 1990; From the Greenwich Hulks to Old St Pancras: a history of tropical disease in London, 1992, reissued 2015; (ed) Gastroenterological Problems from the Tropics, 1995; (ed) Travel-associated disease, 1995; (ed) Manson's Tropical Diseases, 20th edn, 1996 to 22nd edn, 2009; Victorian Incurables: a history of the Royal Hospital for Neuro-Disability, Putney, 2004; John MacAlister's Other Vision: a history of the Fellowship of Postgraduate Medicine, 2005; The Incurables Movement: an illustrated history of the British Home, 2006; Tropical Medicine: an illustrated history of the pioneers, 2007; Disease in the Merchant Navy: a history of the Seamen's Hospital Society, 2007; Health-Care for All: history of a third-world dilemma, 2009; Caribbean Diseases: Doctor George Low's expedition in 1901–02, 2009; Twenty-Six Portland Place: the early years of the Royal Society of Tropical Medicine and Hygiene, 2011; Torrid Disease: memoirs of a tropical physician in the late twentieth century, 2011; Origin of a Medical Specialty: the Seamen's Hospital Society and tropical medicine, 2012; The Tropical Disease that never existed: a history of 'Sprue', 2013; The Rise and Fall of a Medical Specialty: London's clinical tropical medicine, 2014; National Service Fifty Years Ago: life of a medical conscript in West Africa, 2014; Disease and Sanitation in Victorian Britain: lessons for the 'Third World', 2015; Before the 'Germ Theory': a history of cause and management of infectious disease before 1900, 2015; The Milk Enzyme: adventures with the human lactase polymorphism, 2016; History of Malabsorption in a Warm Environment, 2016; Greenwich and its Lost Hospitals: havens of maritime welfare, 2017; Sugar and Obesity: is fructose the culprit?, 2017; Zambia, and creation of the first Department of Medicine, 2019; Ebola, and other epidemics, 2019; numerous research papers, chapters, reviews and editorials. *Recreations:* cricket, walking, listening to baroque and classical music, medical/scientific history. *Address:* 11 Old London Road, St Albans, Herts AL1 1QE. *T:* (01727) 869000. *Clubs:* Athenæum, MCC.

**COOK, (Jeremy) David;** Master of the Senior Court, Queen's Bench Division, since 2011; *b* 18 May 1958; *s* of Brian and Pauline Cook; *m* 1990, Katherine Bayer; two *d*. *Educ:* Keele Univ. (BA Hons 1981). Accredited Mediator, Sch. of Psychotherapy and Counselling, 2005. Called to the Bar, Gray's Inn, 1982, Bencher, 2009; in practice at the Bar, specialising in common law, 1983–2011. Legally Qualified Mem., CICAP, later Tribunal Judge (Criminal Injuries), 2005–11. Mem., Civil Procedure Rules Cttee, 2018. *Publications:* (contrib.) Civil Appeals, 2nd edn, 2013; (contrib.) Powers and Harris Clinical Negligence, 5th edn, 2015; (contrib.) Civil Procedure, 2014–. *Recreations:* theatre, literature, sailing. *Address:* Royal Courts of Justice, Strand, WC2A 2LL.

**COOK, John,** FRCSEd; FRSE 1970; Consultant Surgeon, Eastern General Hospital, Edinburgh, 1964–87; *b* 9 May 1926; *s* of George Cook and Katherine Ferncroft (*née* Gauss); *m* 1st, 1953, Patricia Mary Bligh (*d* 1998); one *s* four *d*; 2nd, 2005, Judith Mary Strangward Hill. *Educ:* Fettes Coll., Edinburgh; Edinburgh Univ. (MB 1949, ChM 1963). FRCSEd 1954. Served Med. Br., RAF, 1950–52 (Flt Lieut). House Surgeon, Royal Infirmary, Edinburgh, 1949; Res. Asst, Radcliffe Infirm., Oxford, 1954–55; First Asst, Dept of Surg., Makerere University Coll., Uganda, 1955–64 (Reader in Surg., 1962–64). Royal Coll. of Surgeons of Edinburgh: Hon. Sec., 1969–72; Mem. Council, 1974–84. Representative Mem., GMC, 1982–86; Hon. Sec., Internat. Fedn of Surgical Colls, 1974–84. *Publications:* contrib. surgical jls. *Recreation:* music.

**COOK, Dr John Barry;** Headmaster, Epsom College, 1982–92; *b* 9 May 1940; *er s* of late Albert Edward and Beatrice Irene Cook, Gloucester; *m* 1964, Vivien Margaret Roxana Lamb, *o d* of late Victor and Marjorie Lamb, St Albans; two *s* one *d*. *Educ:* Sir Thomas Rich's Sch., Gloucester; King's Coll., Univ. of London (BSc 1961, AKC 1961); Guy's Hosp. Med. Sch. (PhD 1965). Guy's Hospital Medical School: Biophysics research, 1961–64; Lectr in Physics, 1964–65; Haileybury College: Asst Master, 1965–72; Senior Science Master and Head of Physics Dept, 1967–72; Headmaster, Christ Coll., Brecon, 1973–82. Dir, Inner Cities Young People's Project, 1992–95; Principal, King George VI & Queen Elizabeth Foundn of St Catharine's at Cumberland Lodge, 1995–2000; educnl consultant, 2000–. Church in Wales: Mem. Governing Body, 1976–83; Coll. of Episcopal Electors, 1980–83. Chairman: S Wales ISIS, 1978–82; Academic Policy Cttee, HMC, 1988–88. Children's Hospice Association for South-East: Chm., 1995–97; Trustee, 1995–2002. Chm. Governors, Royal School, Great Park, Windsor, 1998–2000. Liveryman, Barbers' Co., 1999– (Chm., 700th Anniv. Appeal, 2008–). Pres., Copped Hall Golf Soc., 2017–. *Publications:* (jtly) Solid State Biophysics, 1969; Multiple Choice Questions in A-level Physics, 1969; Multiple Choice Questions in O-level Physics, 1970; papers in Nature, Molecular Physics, Internat. Jl of Radiation Biology, Jl of Scientific Instruments, Educn in Science, Conference and Trends in Education. *Recreations:* sports, photography, philately. *Address:* 6 Chantry Road, Bagshot, Surrey GU19 5DB. *T:* (01276) 475843.

**COOK, Prof. Jon;** Professor of Literature, University of East Anglia, 2005, now Professor Emeritus (Dean, Faculty of Arts and Humanities, 2004–10); *b* Bristol, 14 March 1949; *s* of late Max William Jesse Cook and of Phylis Cook (*née* Jackman); *m* 1st, 1977 (separated 2007; marr. diss. 2012); one *d*; 2nd, 2012, Katherine Hope Skala. *Educ:* Sevenoaks Sch.; Queens' Coll., Cambridge (BA Hons Eng. 1970; MA 1974); Univ. of East Anglia (MA Studies in Fiction 1971). Lectr, 1972–92, Sen. Lectr, 1992–2005, in English, UEA. Vis. Associate Prof., Dept of English, Univ. of Minnesota, 1976; Vis. Lectr, English Seminar, Free Univ. of Berlin, 1983; Hurst Vis. Prof., Dept of English, Univ. of Washington, 2006. Member: Arts Council England, 2008–17 (Chairman: East, 2008; South East, 2013–17); Arts and Humanities Res. Council Strategy Gp, 2011–13. Judge: Caine Prize for African Writing, 2009–10; Ind. Foreign Fiction Prize, 2011–12; Mem., Academy, Folio Prize for Literature, 2013–. *Publications:* Romanticism and Ideology, 1981; William Hazlitt: selected writings, 1991; Poetry in Theory, 2004; Hazlitt in Love, 2007; After Sebald: essays and illuminations, 2014. *Recreations:* walking, music, wandering in cities. *Address:* School of Literature, Drama and Creative Writing, Faculty of Arts and Humanities, University of East Anglia, Norwich NR4 7TJ. *T:* (01603) 592793, *Fax:* (01603) 507721. *E:* j.cook@uea.ac.uk.

**COOK, Leonard Warren,** CBE 2005; CRSNZ 2005; National Statistician and Registrar General for England and Wales, 2000–05; *b* 13 April 1949; *s* of late Archie Cook and Jean (*née* Paterson). *Educ:* Univ. of Otago, New Zealand (BA Hons Maths and Stats). Department of Statistics, New Zealand: Res. Officer, 1971–79; Dir, Statistical Methods, 1979–82; Asst Govt Statistician, 1982–86; Dep. Govt Statistician, 1986–91; Govt Statistician, 1992–2000. Secretariat, Task Force on Tax Reform, NZ, 1981; Mem., Royal Commn on Social Policy, NZ, 1987–88; Chm., Medical Training Bd, 2007–09; Families Comr and Chm. Bd, Families Commn, 2015–; Mem., Remuneration Authy, 2016–. Vis. Prof., UCL, 2005–10. *Publications:* contribs to NZ Population Review, Proceedings of ISI. *Recreations:* fly fishing, travel. *Address:* 71 Glen Road, Kelburn, Wellington, New Zealand.

**COOK, Lucy L.;** *see* Lumsden-Cook.

**COOK, Prof. Malcolm Charles,** PhD; Professor of French Eighteenth-Century Studies, University of Exeter, 1994–2008, now Emeritus; *b* 19 May 1947; *s* of Francis H. Cook and Betty J. G. Cook; *m* 1974, Odile Jaffré; two *s* one *d*. *Educ:* Univ. of Warwick (BA 1969; PhD 1974). Assistant associé, Université de Paris X, Nanterre, 1972–76; Lectr in French, Westfield Coll., London, 1977–78; Exeter University: Lectr in French, 1978–88; Sen. Lectr, 1988–93; Reader, 1993–94; Dep. Vice-Chancellor, 2001–04. Chm., MHRA, 1999–. Hon. Fellow, Heythrop Coll., Univ. of London, 2015. Gen. Editor, MLR, 1994–2001 (French Ed., 1987–93). Officier, Ordre des Palmes Académiques (France), 2008. *Publications:* Fictional France, 1993; (ed) French Culture since 1945, 1993; (ed) Journalisme et Fiction au 18e siècle, 1999; (ed) Modern France: society in transition, 1999; (ed) Anecdotes, Faits-Divers, Contes, Nouvelles, 1700–1820, 2000; Critical Inventory of the Correspondence of Bernardin de Saint-Pierre, 2001; (ed) Réécritures 1700–1820, 2002; Bernardin de Saint-Pierre: a life of culture, 2006; (ed) Critique, Critiques, 2006; La Correspondance de Bernardin de Saint-Pierre, édition critique, 2007; (ed) Bernardin de Saint-Pierre, Voyage en Normandie, 2015. *Recreations:* swimming, walking, watching soccer and cricket. *Address:* Westfield House, 2 Westfield Road, Budleigh Salterton, Devon EX9 6SS. *T:* (01395) 446854.

**COOK, Margaret Stella;** *see* Singh, M. S.

**COOK, (Mary) Fionnuala (Ann),** OBE 2002; Chairwoman, Southern Health and Social Services Board, Northern Ireland, 2003–09; Vice Lord-Lieutenant, Co. Down, since 2009; *b* 3 May 1946; *d* of late Dr Donnell McLarnon Deeny and Annie Deeny (*née* McGinley); *m* 1972, David Somerville Cook, qv; four *s* one *d*. *Educ:* Loreto Abbey, Rathfarnham, Dublin; University Coll., Dublin (BA 1968). Member: Gen. Adv. Council, BBC, 1979–85; Bd, NI Housing Exec., 1985–91; Gen. Consumer Council, NI, 2002–08. Chairwoman, Southern HSS Council, NI, 1991–2001. Mem., Gen. Osteopathic Council of UK, 2002–09 (Actg Chair, 2003–05). Pres., Hosp. Caterers Assoc., 2012–17; Trustee, British Red Cross, 2014–. Founding Gov., Integrated Educn Fund, 1992–97. Chairwoman, Bd of Govs, Bridge Integrated Primary Sch., 2003–08. High Sheriff, Co. Down, 2006. Mem., Loughbrickland WI. *Recreations:* gardening, gossip. *Address:* 8 Main Street, Loughbrickland, Banbridge, Co. Down BT32 3NQ. *T:* (028) 4066 9669.
*See also* Rt Hon. Sir D. J. P. Deeny, M. E. McL. Deeny.

**COOK, Michael Edgar,** CMG 2000; HM Diplomatic Service, retired; High Commissioner, Kampala, 1997–2000; *b* 13 May 1941; *s* of FO Aubrey Edgar Cook, RAFVR (killed in action, 1944) and late Muriel Constance Molly Bateman (*née* Wemyss); *m* 1st, 1970, Astri Edel Wiborg (marr. diss. 1983); one *s* one *d*; 2nd, 1983, Annebritt Maria Aslund (*d* 2013); two step *d*; 3rd, 2014, Patricia Ann Dearlove; one step *d*. *Educ:* Bishop's Stortford Coll.; Fitzwilliam Coll., Cambridge (MA Hons). Regent St Poly. (Dip. Mgt Studies). Export Manager, Young's Sea Foods, 1964–66; joined FCO, 1966; 3rd Sec., Commercial, Oslo, 1967–70; FCO, 1970–73; 1st Sec. then Head of Chancery, Accra, 1973–77; 1st Sec., Commercial, Stockholm, 1977–81; Head of Chancery and Dep. High Comr, Port of Spain, 1981–84; Counsellor and Dep. High Comr, Dar es Salaam, 1984–87; FCO, 1987–92; Consul Gen., Istanbul, 1992–97. Non-executive Chairman: Orient Bank Ltd, Uganda, 2006–; AREPL Ltd, 2015–; Dir/Trustee, Concordia (YSV) Ltd, 2006–10. Area Dir for Brighton and Hove, Sussex Enterprise, 2001–03. Mem., Conservative Party Globalisation and Global Poverty Gp, 2006–07. Mem. Cttee, Hove Civic Soc., 2018–. *Recreations:* wine, cooking, jazz, travel. *Address:* 17 Denmark Villas, Hove, E Sussex BN3 3TD.

**COOK, His Honour Michael John;** a Circuit Judge, 1986–2003; consultant solicitor, 2005–11; legal author and speaker; *b* 20 June 1930; *s* of George Henry Cook and Nora Wilson Cook (*née* Mackman); *m* 1st, 1958, Anne Margaret Vaughan; three *s* one *d*; 2nd,

1974, Patricia Anne Sturdy; one d. *Educ:* Leeds Grammar Sch.; Worksop Coll.; Univ. of Leeds (LLB 2(1) Cl. Hons). Admitted Solicitor, 1953. National Service, commnd Royal Artillery, 1954. Willey Hargrave & Co., Solicitors, to 1957; Ward Bowie, Solicitors, 1957–86 (Senior Partner, 1965–86); a Recorder, 1980–86; Designated Family Judge for Surrey (formerly Designated Child Care Judge), Guildford County Ct, 1995–2003. Consultant, Horsey Lightly Fynn, Solicitors, 2007–11. Founder Mem., Holborn and City of Westminster Law Socs, 1962–; Past Hon. Sec. and Pres., London Solicitors' Litigation Assoc.; Hon. Pres., Assoc. of Law Costs Draftsmen, 1997–2003; Member: Solicitors Disciplinary Tribunal, 1975–86; Law Society sub-cttees and working parties. Chm., 2000–06, Mem. Bd, 2006–12, Royal Med. Foundn. Gov., Epsom Coll., 1990–2007. Patron: Assoc. for Families who have Adopted from Abroad, 1995–2012; Surrey Family Mediation Service, 2003–12. Freeman, City of London, 1990. General Editor: The Litigation Letter, 1981–2016; Butterworths Costs Service, 1991–2013. *Publications:* The Courts and You, 1976; The Taxation of Contentious Costs, 1979; The Taxation of Solicitors Costs, 1986; Cook on Costs, 1991, annually, 2000–13; (jtly) The New Civil Costs Regime, 1999; contrib. to: Cordery on Legal Services (formerly Cordery on Solicitors), 1995–; Butterworths Personal Injury Litigation Service, 1995–2013; Civil Justice Qly, 2002–13; The Civil Court Practice, 2012–13. *Recreations:* gardening, theatre, swimming, Ranger at Painshill Park. *Clubs:* Law Society; St George's Hill Tennis.

**COOK, Michael John,** PhD; CEng; FREng, FIStructE; Director, BuroHappold Engineering (formerly BuroHappold Engineers Ltd), since 2008; Partner, Happold LLP, since 2017 (Chairman and Senior Partner, 2011–17); *b* Epsom, 19 Feb. 1955; *s* of Jack Cook and Mary Cook; *m* 1981, Sue Martin. *Educ:* Rutlish Sch., Merton; Gonville and Caius Coll., Cambridge (BA Mechanical Scis 1977; MA); Univ. of Bath (PhD 1983). CEng 1987; FIStructE 2004; FREng 2010. Buro Happold, subseq. BuroHappold Engineering, 1982–: Dir (London), 1996–2003; Dir of Structural Engrg, 2003–08; Dir of Buildings, 2008. Adjunct Prof., Dept of Civil and Envmtl Engrg, Imperial Coll. London, 2007–. Chm., Timber Res. and Develt Assoc., 2010–12. Trustee: IStructE Educnl Trust, 2005–13; Happold Foundn (formerly Happold Trust), 2011–. Vice-Pres., IStructE, 2015–16. FRSA 2016. Hon. DEng Bath, 2016. Milne Medal, IABSE, 2009. *Publications:* articles in Structural Engineer and NCE Jl. *Recreations:* live performance (especially opera), travel (cities), buildings, cooking, playing piano. *Address:* BuroHappold Engineering, 17 Newman Street, W1T 1PD. *T:* (020) 7927 9700. *E:* mike.cook@burohappold.com. *Club:* Athenæum.

**COOK, Prof. Nicholas (John),** PhD; FBA 2001; 1684 Professor of Music, University of Cambridge, 2009–17, now Emeritus; *b* Athens, 5 June 1950; *s* of late Prof. John Manuel Cook, FBA and Enid May Cook (née Robertson); *m* 1975, Catherine Bridget Louise Elgie; one *s* one *d*. *Educ:* King's Coll., Cambridge (BA 1971, MA 1976; PhD 1983); Univ. of Southampton (BA 1977). Lectr in Music, Univ. of Hong Kong, 1982–90; Prof. of Music, 1990–99, Dean of Arts, 1996–98, Res. Prof. of Music, 1999–2003, Univ. of Southampton; Prof. of Music, 2004–05, Professorial Res. Fellow in Music, 2005–09, Royal Holloway, Univ. of London; British Acad. Wolfson Res. Prof., 2014–17. Dir, AHRC (formerly AHRB) Res. Centre for the History and Analysis of Recorded Music, 2004–09. Chair, Music Panel, HEFC RAE 2001. MAE 2010. Hon. DHL Chicago, 2013; Dr *hc* Gheorghie Dima Music Acad., Cluj-Napoca, Romania, 2015. Ed., Jl Royal Musical Assoc., 1999–2004. *Publications:* A Guide to Musical Analysis, 1987; Music, Imagination and Culture, 1990; Beethoven: Symphony No 9, 1993; Analysis Through Composition: principles of the classical style, 1996; Analysing Musical Multimedia, 1998; Music: a very short introduction, 1998; (ed jtly) The Cambridge History of Twentieth-Century Music, 2004; (ed jtly) Empirical Musicology: aims, methods, prospects, 2004; The Schenker Project: culture, race, and music theory in fin-de-siècle Vienna, 2007 (Wallace Berry Award, Soc. for Music Theory, 2010); (ed jtly) The Cambridge Companion to Recorded Music, 2009; Beyond the Score: music as performance, 2013; Music as Creative Practice, 2018; contrib. articles in most major musicological jls. *Address:* Old School House, School Hill, Alderbury, Salisbury SP5 3DR. *T:* (01722) 710012. *E:* NJC69@cam.ac.uk.

**COOK, Prof. Paul Derek,** MBE 1985; PhD; CEng; Chairman and Managing Director, Scientifica-Cook Ltd, since 1962; Professor of Laser Science, Brunel University, 1986–97; *b* 12 March 1934; *s* of James Walter Cook and Florence Jefferay; *m* 1954, Frances Ann James; four d. *Educ:* Queen Mary Coll., London (BSc Hons; PhD 1963; Sir John Johnson Scholar, 1959). Res. Scientist: MRC, 1960–62; Middlesex Hosp. Med. Sch., 1962–65. Prof. of Laser Physics, Brunel Univ., 1986–91. Scientific Adviser to: Minister for the Envmt and Countryside, DoE, 1990–92; British Gas, 1990–92; Laser Consultant, BAe, 1986–; former Consultant, W Midlands Police, 1991–92; Scientific Advr to Lady Olga Maitland, 1992–96. Responsible for design and develt of numerous laser systems used in med. and mil. estabts throughout world, incl. ophthalmic LaserSpec; originator and inventor of Laser Guidance Systems for weapon alignment in each Tornado; major contrib. to Europe's first laser gyroscope in 1970s; invention of laser instrument that improves safety of motorists by detecting and correcting night myopia; estab. world's first Night Vision Clinic for treating night blindness disorders. Dep. Chm., Conserve, 1990–93; Founder/President: British Science and Technol. Trust, 1985–96; Science and Technol. Trust, 2002–; UK Pres., Japanese Zen Nippon Airinkai, 1978–81. *Recreations:* breeding and rearing exotic Japanese carp, cultivating Japanese bonsai, inventing, experimenting with ideas, especially those related to improving safety on the roads, passion for early automobile number plates. *Address:* 252A Acton Lane, Chiswick, W4 5DJ.

**COOK, Paul Graham Whalley; His Honour Judge Cook;** a Circuit Judge, since 2018; *b* Exeter, 25 Oct. 1967; *s* of Dr Michael Edward Massey Cook and Gillian Margaret Cook (née Whalley). *Educ:* Exeter Sch.; Haileybury Coll.; Univ. of Kent, Canterbury (BA Hons 1989). Called to the Bar, Middle Temple, 1992; in practice as a barrister, Albion Chambers, 1993–2017; a Recorder, 2012–18. *Recreations:* creative property restoration, reading (historical biographies), cycling. *Address:* Taunton Crown Court, Shire Hall, Taunton, Somerset TA1 4EU.

**COOK, Sir Peter (Frederic Chester),** Kt 2007; RA 2003; RIBA; Bartlett Professor of Architecture, University College London, 1990–2005, now Emeritus (Chairman, Bartlett School of Architecture, 1990–2004); Joint Professor of Architecture, Royal Academy, 2005–10, now Emeritus; Design Principal, HOK International, since 2004; Director, Cook-Robotham Architectural Bureau, since 2004; *b* 22 Oct. 1936; *s* of Major Frederick William Cook and Ada Cook (née Shaw); *m* 1st, 1960, Hazel Aimee Fennell (marr. diss. 1989); 2nd, 1990, Dr Yael Reisner; one *s*. *Educ:* Bournemouth Coll. of Art; Architectural Assoc. (AA Dip. 1960). Tutor, Architectural Assoc., 1964–90; Prof. of Arch., HBK Städelschule, Frankfurt am Main, 1984–2002. Director: ICA, 1969–71; Art Net, 1972–79. Visiting Professor: UCLA, 1968–69; Southern Calif Inst. of Arch., 1980, 1983, 1992; Oslo Sch. of Arch., 1982; Univ. of Qld, 1993; Nihon Univ., Tokyo, 1994; Tech. Univ., Vienna, 1997, 1999, 2001, 2002; Lund Univ., 2004–. Nat. Coll. of Art, Tokyo, 2016; Kenzo Tange Vis. Prof., Harvard Grad. Sch. of Design, 2015. Cook-Robotham Architecture Bureau projects: (completed) Verbania Th., Italy, 2008; Law and Admin Bldg, Univ. of Economics, Vienna, 2014; Abedian Sch. of Arch., Bond Univ., Qld, 2014; Drawing Studio, Arts Univ. Bournemouth, 2016. Founder Mem., Archigram, 1961–76. Mem., European Acad. of Sci. and Art; Bund Deutscher Architekten. FRCA 2006; FRSA. Fellow, Bournemouth Arts Inst., 2008; Hon. Fellow, UCL, 2009. Hon. Dr Lund, 2009. Royal Gold Medal in Arch., RIBA, 2002; Gustav Eiffel Prize, Ecole Spéciale d'architecture, Paris, 2005; Mario Pani Award for Arch., Mexico City, 2010. Commandeur, Ordre des Arts et des Lettres (France), 2002. *Publications:* Architecture: action and plan, 1972; Experimental Architecture, 1982; (with R. Llewellyn-Jones) New Spirit in Architecture, 1992; Peter Cook: six conversations, 1993; Primer, 1996; (with N. Spiller) The Power of Contemporary Architecture, 1999; (with N. Spiller) The Paradox of Contemporary Architecture, 2001; The City: as a garden of ideas, 2003; Drawing: the motive force of architecture, 2008; Peter Cook Workbook, 2015. *Recreations:* music, observing towns. *Address:* 54 Compayne Gardens, NW6 3RY. *T:* and *Fax:* (020) 7372 3784. *E:* peter.cook@ucl.ac.uk; Cook-Robotham Architectural Bureau, 81 Essex Road, N1 2SF. *E:* info@crabstudio.net.

**COOK, Prof. Peter John,** CBE 1996; FTSE; Professorial Fellow, since 2012, and Senior Advisor, since 2015, Peter Cook Centre for CCS Research, University of Melbourne; Director, PJC International, since 1998; *b* 15 Oct. 1938; *s* of John and Rose Cook; *m* 1961, Norma Irene Walker; two *s*. *Educ:* Durham Univ. (BSc Hons, DSc); ANU (MSc); Univ. of Colorado (PhD). FTSE 1998. Geologist to Sen. Geologist, BMR, Canberra, 1961–76; Sen. Res. Fellow, ANU Res. Sch. of Earth Sci., 1976–82 (Vis. Fellow, 1982–90); Chief of Div./Chief Res. Scientist, BMR, 1982–90 (Prof., Univ. Louis Pasteur, Strasbourg, 1989); Dir, British Geol Survey, 1990–98; Dir, Australian Petroleum Co-op. Res. Centre, 1998–2003; Chief Exec., Co-op. Res. Centre for Greenhouse Gas Technologies, 2003–11. Adrian Fellow, Univ. of Leicester, 1992–98. Chairman: Consortium for Ocean Geosci., 1980–82; Commonwealth/State Hydrogeol. Cttee, 1983–88; Intergovtl Oceanographic Commn, Prog. Ocean Sci. and Non-Living Resources, 1984–2001; Dir, MineXchange, 1999–2015; Member: Adv. Cttee, Aust. Nuclear Sci. and Tech. Orgn, 1984–90; Geol. Adv. Panel, BM (Nat. Hist.), 1990–98; Earth Scis Cttee, 1990–94, Earth Scis Tech. Bd, 1995–98, NERC; Chm., Forum of European Geol Surveys, 1996–97. President: EuroGeoSurveys, 1995–96; Aust.-French Assoc. of Scientists, 2000–03; Member: Council, MIRO, 1991–98; Adv. Cttee for Protection of the Seas, 1997–99; Nat. Carbon Capture and Storage Council, 2010–12. Chm., report on engrg energy, Aust. Council of Learned Acads, 2013. Fellow, Geol. Soc. of Aust., 2007. Major John Coke Medal, Geol. Soc., London, 1997; Lewis G. Weeks Gold Medal, Australian Petroleum and Exploration Assoc., 2004; Leopold von Buch Medal, Geol Soc., Germany, 2004. Centenary Medal, Australia, 2001; Greenman Award, Internat. Energy Agency (GHG Prog.), 2010. Order of Merit, France, 2005. *Publications:* Clean Energy, Climate and Carbon, 2012; Geologically Storing Carbon, 2014; more than 100 contribs to books and learned jls, on energy and sustainability, greenhouse gas technologies, phosphate deposits, marine mineral resources, coastal zone studies, palaeogeography, science management and science policy. *Recreations:* ski-ing, hiking, travel, history, farming. *T:* (2) 62396504, *Fax:* (2) 62396049. *E:* pjcook@co2crc.com.au. *Club:* Commonwealth (Canberra).

**COOK, Robert Barclay;** UK Managing Director, Virgin Active Ltd, since 2016; *b* Torphins, Aberdeenshire, 30 Jan. 1966; *s* of Thomas Barclay Cook and Ethel Cook; *m* 1995, Deborah Anne Elisabeth; one *s*. *Educ:* Robert Gordon's Inst. of Technol. (HND Hotel and Catering 1987). Ops Dir, Malmaison, 1998–2000; Man. Dir, Columbus and Dakota Hotels, 2000–04; CEO, Malmaison and Hotel du Vin Gps, 2004–11; Chief Exec., Village Hotels, De Vere Group, 2012–14; Chief Operating Officer, Macdonald Hotels and Resorts, 2015–16. Member: Global Scot; l'Académie du Champagne. Hon. DBA Robert Gordon, 2007. *Recreations:* golf (6 handicap), shooting.

**COOK, Robert Edward L.;** see Longley-Cook.

**COOK, Roger James;** investigative journalist; broadcaster: The Cook Report, ITV, 1985–97; Cook Report Specials, ITV, 1998–2004; *b* 6 April 1943; *s* of Alfred and Linda Cook; *m* 1st, 1966, Madeline Koh (marr. diss. 1974); 2nd, 1982, Frances Alice Knox; one d. *Educ:* Hurlstone Agricl Coll.; Sydney Univ. TV and radio reporter, ABC (Australia), 1960–66; TV and radio dir, Warnock Sandford Advertising (Aust.), 1966–68; reporter, BBC Radio 4, World at One, World This Weekend, PM, 1968–76; freelance documentary dir, 1968–72; creator and presenter, Checkpoint, Radio 4, 1973–85; presenter and reporter, Radio 4 documentary series: Time for Action; Real Evidence; investigative reporter, BBC TV: Nationwide; Newsnight, 1972–84. Vis. Prof., Centre for Broadcast Journalism, Nottingham Trent Univ., 1997–2011, now Emeritus. Hon. DLitt Nottingham Trent, 2004. BPG Award, for outstanding contrib. to radio, 1978; Pye (now Sony) Radio Personality of the Year, 1979; Ross McWhirter Foundn Award, for courageous reporting, 1980; Valiant for Truth Award, 1988; TV and Radio Industries Award, for best ITV prog., 1993, and Special Award, for outstanding contrib. to broadcasting, 1998; RTS (Midlands) Best On-Screen Personality, 1996; Houston Worldfest Silver Award, for best interview, 1997; Charleston Worldfest Gold Award, for best investigative prog., 1997; Brigitte Bardot Internat. Award (Genesis Awards), for best campaigning wildlife prog., 1997; British Acad. Special Award, for outstanding investigative reporting, 1998. *Publications:* (with Tim Tate) What's Wrong With Your Rights?, 1988; (with Howard Foster) Dangerous Ground, 1999; More Dangerous Ground, 2011. *Recreations:* film, music, motor sport.

**COOK, Rosemary Grace,** CBE 2008; Chief Executive Officer, Institute of Physics and Engineering in Medicine, since 2012; *b* London, 24 Feb. 1959; *d* of late John Rogers and Gladys Rogers; civil partnership 2006, Alison Norman; two d. *Educ:* Stafford Girls' High Sch.; Bradford Sch. of Nursing; Aston Univ. (MA Public Sector Mgt (Dist.)); Univ. of Manchester (Postgrad. Dip. Applied Social Res.). SRN 1980; RGN 1989; FQNI 2013. Registered Nurse, St Luke's Hosp., Bradford, and Stafford Dist Gen. Hosp., 1980–91; Primary Care Facilitator, N Staffs HA/Staffs Family HSA, 1991–97; Audit and Quality Manager, Manchester Audit and Quality Gp, 1997–99; Nursing Officer, DoH, 1999–2003; Hd, Working Time Directive Prog., NHS Modernisation Agency, DoH, 2003–05; Dir, Queen's Nursing Inst., 2005–12. Vis. Prof. of Enterprise, Northumberland Univ., 2008–11; Hon. Prof., Buckinghamshire New Univ., 2012. Hon. DLitt Manchester Metropolitan, 2008. *Publications:* A Nurse's Survival Guide to Primary Care, 1999; The Writer's Manual, 2004; Awareness and Influence in Health and Social Care, 2006; The Nightingale Shore Murder, 2011, 2nd edn 2015. *Recreations:* reading, writing, theatre, local history research. *Address:* Institute of Physics and Engineering in Medicine, Fairmount House, 230 Tadcaster Road, York YO24 1ES. *T:* (01904) 610821, *Fax:* (01904) 612279. *E:* rosemary.cook@ipem.ac.uk. *Club:* Penn.

**COOK, Prof. Stephen Arthur,** OC 2015; OOnt 2013; PhD; FRS 1998; FRSC 1984; University Professor, Department of Computer Science, University of Toronto, 1985–2005, now Emeritus; *b* 1939; *s* of Gerhard A. Cook and Lura Cook; *m* 1968, Linda; two *s*. *Educ:* Univ. of Michigan (BSc Math. 1961); Harvard Univ. (SM Math. 1962; PhD Math. 1966). Asst Prof., Math. and Computer Science, Univ. of Calif at Berkeley, 1966–70; University of Toronto: Associate Prof., 1970–75, Prof., 1975–85, Dept of Computer Science. Member: Nat. Acad. of Scis (US), 1985; Amer. Acad. of Arts and Scis, 1986. A. M. Turing Award, ACM, 1982. *Publications:* numerous papers in jls. *Recreation:* sailing. *Address:* Department of Computer Science, University of Toronto, Toronto, ON M5S 3G4, Canada. *T:* (416) 9785183. *Club:* Royal Canadian Yacht.

**COOK, Timothy,** OBE 1997; Clerk to the Trustees, City Parochial Foundation, 1986–98; *b* 25 April 1938; *s* of late Stephen Cook and Kathleen (née Henwood); *m* 1967, Margaret Taylor; one *s* one d. *Educ:* Loughborough Grammar Sch.; Trinity Hall, Cambridge (BA);

Brunel Univ. (MA). Called to the Bar, Middle Temple, 1961. Asst Lectr in Law, Sheffield Univ., 1960–61; Asst Warden, Norman House, 1962–64; Prison Welfare Officer, HM Prison, Blundeston, 1964–66; Dir, Alcoholics Recovery Project, 1966–74; Hd, Cambridge House and Talbot, 1975–77; Dir, Family Service Units, 1978–85. *Publications*: Vagrant Alcoholics, 1975; (ed jtly) The Drunkenness Offence, 1969; (ed) Vagrancy, 1979; Merfyn Turner: practical compassion, 1999; (jtly) A Management Companion for the Voluntary Sector, 2000; Reflections on Good Grant Making, 2000; History of the Carers' Movement, 2007; (jtly) The Cohen Interviews, 2013. *Recreations*: cinema, reading, theatre. *Address*: 26 Criffel Avenue, SW2 4AZ. *T*: (020) 8674 3141.

**COOK, Tina Gail, (Mrs Justin Goad);** QC 2011; *b* Lancs, 23 Sept. 1964; *d* of Peter Cook and Pauline Cook; *m* 1997, Justin Goad; one *s* two *d*. *Educ*: Queen Elizabeth Grammar Sch., Blackburn; Exeter Coll., Oxford (BA Jurisprudence; MA). Called to the Bar, Middle Temple, 1988; in practice as a barrister, specialising in public law child care, 1988–; Hd of Chambers, 2016–. Dir, Giraffe Media, 2011–14. Trustee: Families for Children, 2008–; Law Foundn, Univ. of Oxford, 2019–. *Recreations*: buying wine, theatre, my children, my husband, lunching and parties (any kind). *Address*: 42 Bedford Row, WC1R 4LL. *E*: tc@42br.com.

**COOK, William Birkett,** MA; Master of Magdalen College School, Oxford, 1972–91; *b* 30 Aug. 1931; *e s* of late William James and Mildred Elizabeth Cook, Headington, Oxford; *m* 1958, Marianne Ruth, *yr d* of late A. E. Taylor, The Schools, Shrewsbury; one *s* one *d* (and one *d* decd). *Educ*: Dragon Sch.; Eton (King's Schol.); Trinity Coll., Cambridge (Schol.). National Service, 1950–51 (commnd in RA). Porson Prizeman, 1953; 1st cl. Classical Tripos Pt I, 1953, Pt II, 1954; Henry Arthur Thomas Student, 1954; MA Oxon by incorporation, 1972. Asst Master, Shrewsbury Sch., 1955–67, and Head of Classical Faculty, 1960–67; Headmaster of Durham Sch., 1967–72. Governor: Oxford High Sch., 1979–2000; Bedford Modern Sch., 1992–2001. Administrator, Choir Schools' Assoc. Bursary Trust, 1987–92; Dir, Thomas Wall Trust, 1992–2002; Gov., Ewelme Exhibn Endowment, 1993–2008 (Chm., 1999–2008). *Recreations*: music, gardening, Scottish country dancing. *Address*: Hunter's Moon, 96A Oxford Road, Old Marston, Oxford OX3 0RD. *T*: (01865) 250882.

**COOKE, Andrew James,** QPM 2014; Chief Constable, Merseyside Police, since 2016; *b* Liverpool, 10 March 1964; *s* of Joseph Cooke and Beryl Cooke; *m* 1989, Deborah Maxfield; two *d*. *Educ*: St Francis Xavier's Coll., Liverpool; Univ. of Nottingham (BA Hons Politics 1985). Merseyside Police: Constable, 1985–89; Detective Constable, 1989–97; Detective Sergeant, 1997–99; Detective Inspector, 1999–2001; Detective Chief Inspector, 2001–03; Detective Superintendent, 2003–05; Detective Chief Superintendent, 2005–08; Asst Chief Constable, Lancashire Constabulary, 2008–12; Dep. Chief Constable, Merseyside Police, 2013–16. National Policing Lead: for Witness Protection, 2008–17; for Serious and Organised Crime, 2017–. *Recreations*: Liverpool FC supporter, dog walking, St Helens RLFC supporter, family. *Address*: Merseyside Police Headquarters, PO Box 59, Liverpool L69 1JD. *T*: (0151) 777 8000. *E*: andrew.j.cooke@merseyside.police.uk.

**COOKE, Prof. Anne,** DPhil; FMedSci, FRSB; Professor of Immunobiology, University of Cambridge, 2000–13, now Emeritus; Fellow, King's College, Cambridge, 1992–2013, now Emeritus; *b* South Shields, 14 Nov. 1945; *d* of William and Margaret Syme; *m* 1969, Jonathan Cooke; two *s*. *Educ*: Univ. of Glasgow (BSc Hons 1967); Univ. of Sussex (DPhil 1970). SRC Postdoctoral Fellow, Univ. of Sussex, 1970–72; Postdoctoral Fellow, Univ. of Illinois, 1972–73; ARC Postdoctoral Fellow, Middx Hosp., 1973–78; Wellcome Trust Sen. Res. Fellow, Middx Hosp. Medical Sch., 1978–81; Wellcome Trust Sen. Lectr, University Coll. and Middx Schs of Medicine, 1981–88; Reader in Exptl Immunol., UCL, 1988–90; Lectr, 1990–96, Reader in Immunol., 1996–2000, Cambridge Univ. Poll Vis. Prof., Univ. of Seattle, 1999. Member, Grant Committees for: Arthritis Res. UK (formerly Arthritis Res. Campaign), 1988– (Mem., Adv. Bd, Centre for Adolescent Rheumatol., 2012–); Diabetes UK, 1992–95; Leukaemia Res. Fund, 1993–96; Action Res., 1998–; MRC Fellowship, 1999–2004; Finnish Acad. of Scis, 2003–07; Hong Kong Univ., 2006–10; Member: Res. Grants Council of HK, 2009–15; Cttee, Collaborative Res. Fund and Theme Based Res. Scheme, Hong Kong, 2011–17; Dorothy Hodgkin Fellowship Selection Cttee, 2010–13; CORE Biomed. and Health Scis Panel, Luxembourg, 2016–; Council, Internat. Union of Immunol. Socs, 2017–18; Adv. Bd, Invest in ME, 2017–; Wkg Gp, Phase II Rev. of Res. Grants Council, Hong Kong, 2018. Chair, Forum and Trustee, British Soc. for Immunology, 2014–18. FMedSci 2007; FRSB (FSB 2011). Hon. Fellow UCL, 2006. Hon. Dr Copenhagen, 2010. Member, Editorial Board: Trends in Parasitology; Autoimmunity; Scandinavian Jl Immunol.; Internat. Jl of Exptl Path.; Biology Direct; Rev. of Diabetic Studies; Assoc. Ed., Frontiers in Immunol. *Publications*: (jtly) Advanced Immunology, 1987, 3rd edn 1995; (ed jtly) Encyclopedia of Immunobiology, vol. 5, 2016; contrib. res. articles to jls incl. Nature, Jl Clin. Investigation, Diabetes, Jl Immunol., reviews for jls incl. Trends in Immunol., Parasitol. *Recreations*: walking in mountains, listening to music, reading, photography, travel, art. *Address*: Department of Pathology, University of Cambridge, Tennis Court Road, Cambridge CB2 1QP. *T*: (01223) 333907, *Fax*: (01223) 333914. *E*: ac416@cam.ac.uk; 10 Danvers Road, N8 7HH.

**COOKE, Rear-Adm. Anthony John,** CB 1980; Private Secretary to Lord Mayor of London, 1981–92; *b* 21 Sept. 1927; *s* of Rear-Adm. John Ernest Cooke, CB and late Kathleen Mary Cooke; *m* 1st, 1951, Margaret Anne (marr. diss. 1994; she *d* 2010), *d* of late Frederick Charles Hynard; one *s* three *d* (and one *s* decd); 2nd, 1995, Patricia Sinclair Stewart, *d* of late William Sinclair Stewart and of Margaret Jane Stewart; one step *s* two step *d*. *Educ*: St Edward's Sch., Oxford. Entered RN 1945; specialised in navigation, 1953; Army Staff Coll., 1958; Sqdn Navigating Officer, HMS Daring, Second Destroyer Sqdn, 1959–61; Staff Navigating Officer to Flag Officer, Sea Trng, 1961; Comdr 1961; Directorate of Naval Ops and Trade, 1961–63; i/c HMS Brighton, 1964–66; Directorate of Navigation and Tactical Control, 1966; Captain 1966; Captain of Dockyard and Queen's Harbourmaster, Singapore, 1967–69; Captain 1st Destroyer Sqdn, Far East, later DivI Comdr 3rd Div. Western Fleet, i/c HMS Galatea, 1969–71; Dir, Royal Naval Staff Coll., 1971–73; Cdre Clyde i/c Clyde Submarine Base, 1973–75; Rear-Adm. 1976; Senior Naval Mem., Directing Staff, RCDS, 1975–78; Adm. Pres., RNC Greenwich, 1978–80, retd. Police Foundn, 1980–81. A Younger Brother, Trinity House, 1974. Freeman: City of London, 1979; Shipwrights' Co., 1980. OStJ 1990. *Recreation*: keeping up with twenty-two grandchildren. *Address*: 11 Elm Grove Road, Ealing, W5 3JH. *T*: (020) 3067 0031.

**COOKE, Anthony Roderick Chichester Bancroft;** Director, 1999–2007, and Chairman, 2005–07, Baltic Exchange Ltd; *b* 24 July 1941; *s* of Maj.-Gen. Ronald Basil Bowen Bancroft Cooke, CB, CBE, DSO and Joan, *d* of Maj. Claude O. Chichester; *m* 1972, Daryll, *d* of David Aird Ross; two *s* one *d*. *Educ*: Ampleforth Coll.; London Business Sch. (MSc 1970). FCA 1964. With Binder Hamlyn & Co., 1960–68; Manager, Jessel Securities plc, 1970–72; Man. Dir, London Australian & Gen. Exploration Co., 1972–75; Ellerman Lines plc, 1975–91: Chief Exec., Investment Services, 1975–78; Chief Exec., City Liners, 1978–85; Chief Executive and Chairman: Ellerman Lines plc, 1985–87; Cunard Ellerman, 1987–91; Gp Chief Exec., Andrew Weir & Co. Ltd, 1991–99. Director: James Fisher & Sons plc, 2002–11; West of England Shipowners Insce Assoc. Ltd, 2002–12. Mem., Adv. Bd, Inst. of Statecraft, 2013–. President: Chamber of Shipping, 1996–97; Inst. of Chartered Shipbrokers, 2002–04. Chm., NE Hants Cons. Assoc., 2012–13. Trustee, Inst. of Statecraft, 2017–. High Sheriff, Hampshire, 2001–02. FRSA 1980. *Recreation*: active sports. *Address*: Poland Court, Odiham, Hampshire RG29 1JL. *T*: (01256) 702060. *Club*: Boodle's.

**COOKE, Brian;** Circuit Administrator, South Eastern Circuit, 1989–95; *b* 16 Jan. 1935; *s* of Norman and Edith Cooke; *m* 1958, Edith Mary Palmer; two *s* one *d*. *Educ*: Manchester Grammar Sch.; University Coll. London (LLB). Served Royal Air Force, 1956–59. Called to Bar, Lincoln's Inn, 1959; Dept of Director of Public Prosecutions, 1960–68; Deputy Clerk of the Peace, Inner London Quarter Sessions, 1968–71; Dep. Circuit Administrator, North Eastern Circuit, 1971–81, Circuit Administrator, 1981–82; Sec. of Commissions, 1982–88, Hd of Judicial Appointments Gp, 1987–88, Lord Chancellor's Dept. Part-time Pres., Mental Health Rev. Tribunals, 1996–2003. JP Middx, 1985–99. *Recreations*: golf, walking, theatre, music, the arts. *Address*: 12 The Pryors, East Heath Road, NW3 1BS. *Club*: Hampstead Golf.

**COOKE, Colin Ivor;** non-executive Chairman: Fenner PLC, 1993–2011; Dowlis Corporate Solutions plc, 2005–13; Energybuild Group plc, 2007–10; *b* 17 Dec. 1939; *m* 1983, Sheila Handley; four *s* one *d*. *Educ*: Cardiff High Sch.; Advanced Coll. of Technology, Newport (HND Metallurgy). GKN, 1956–63; Hepworth Ceramic, 1963–71; RTZ, 1971–72; Du-Port, 1972–80, Main Bd Dir, 1982–86; Dir, WDA, 1987–89; Dir, 1989–98, Chm., 1991–98, Triplex Lloyd. Dir, Dynacast Internat., 1999–2003; non-executive Director: Ash & Lacy, 1987–97; British Dredging, 1990–93; Yorkshire Water, 1995–97; Oystertec plc, 2002. Chm., Tipton City Challenge, 1993–98. FIMMM (FIM 1996). Freeman, City of London, 1996; Liveryman, Founders' Co., 1996–. *Recreations*: golf, swimming, military history. *Clubs*: Royal Porthcawl Golf; Cardiff County.

**COOKE, David Arthur Lawrence;** Director, British Board of Film Classification, 2004–16; *b* 11 March 1956; *s* of James Robert Cooke and Verity Cooke (*née* Brandrick); *m* 1984, Kathleen Joyce Collins, *qv*. *Educ*: University Coll., Oxford (BA 1st Cl. Hons Mod Hist.; MA). Home Office: admin trainee, 1977–81; Private Sec. to Patrick Mayhew, MP (Minister of State), 1981–82; Principal, Prisons, Drugs and Broadcasting Depts, 1982–89; G5, Broadcasting Dept, 1990; on loan to other govt depts, 1990–93; Dir, Asylum, and Immigration Service Enforcement, Home Office, 1994–97; G3, Constitution Secretariat, Cabinet Office, 1997; Director: Central Inf. Technol. Unit, Cabinet Office, 1997–2000; Criminal Policy Gp, Home Office, 2000–02; Associate Pol Dir, NI Office, 2002–04. Non-exec. Dir, Office of Information Comr, 2016–. Vis. Prof., UCL, 2016–. *Recreations*: film, music, sport, cooking. *E*: dcooke1927@gmail.com. *Club*: Athenæum.

**COOKE, David Charles;** Consultant, Pinsent Masons (formerly Pinsents), Solicitors, 2002–06; *b* 22 March 1938; *s* of F. J. E. Cooke and Hilda Cooke. *Educ*: Bolton Sch.; Accrington Grammar Sch.; Manchester Univ. (LLB). Hall Brydon & Co., Manchester, 1961–64; King & Partridge, Madras, 1964–67; Pinsent & Co., Birmingham, then Pinsent Curtis, subseq. Pinsent Curtis Biddle, solicitors: Asst Solicitor, 1967; Partner, 1969–86; Sen. Partner, 1986–94. *Recreations*: classical music, fell walking, theatre, reading. *Address*: c/o Pinsent Masons, 55 Colmore Row, Birmingham B3 2FG. *T*: (0121) 629 1553. *Club*: Oriental.

**COOKE, David John,** OBE 1995; Director, British Council, Brazil, 2002–05; *b* 4 Jan. 1947; *s* of late Dennis and of Bessie Cooke; *m* 1970, Lindsey Ram; two *d*. *Educ*: Oxford Coll. of Technology (ONC 1967, HNC Applied Biology 1968); Univ. of Leicester (BSc Biological Sci. 1971; PhD Genetics 1974). Jun. Technician, Dept of Biochemistry, Oxford Univ., 1963–65; Site Services Operator, UKAEA Culham, 1965–66; Scientific Asst, UKAEA Harwell, 1966–68; SRC/NATO Res. Fellow, Univ. of Tromsø, Norway, 1974–76; Res. Fellow and Lectr in Genetics, Univ. of Sheffield, 1976–78; British Council: Sci. Advr, London, 1978–81; Sci. Officer, Belgrade, 1981–84; First Sec. (Sci.), British High Commn, New Delhi, 1984–87; Dir, Project Develt Dept, 1989–91; Educn Attaché, British Embassy, Washington, 1991–94; Dep. Dir, Manchester, 1994–99; Dir, Develt and Training Services, and Mem., Sen. Mgt Strategy Team, 1999–2002. Chm., Eastbourne Br., Eur. Movt, 2013–18 (Vice Chm., 2010–13). *Recreations*: walking, cycling, cross-country ski-ing, gardening. *E*: cooke.dave@gmail.com.

**COOKE, David John; His Honour Judge David Cooke;** Specialist Chancery Judge, since 2008; *b* Rugby, 23 Aug. 1956; *s* of Matthew and Margaret Cooke; *m* 1979, Susan George; one *s* one *d*. *Educ*: Lawrence Sheriff Sch., Rugby; Trinity Coll., Cambridge (BA 1978). Admitted Solicitor, 1981; Partner, Pinsent & Co., Solicitors, 1983–2001; Dep. Dist Judge, 1997–2001; Dist Judge, 2001–08. Hon. Bencher, Lincoln's Inn, 2016. *Recreations*: competitive swimming, sailing, golf. *Address*: Birmingham Civil Justice Centre, Bull Street, Birmingham B4 6DS.

**COOKE, Del;** *see* Cooke, S. D.

**COOKE, Dominic,** CBE 2014; Associate Artist, Royal Shakespeare Company, since 2012 (Associate Director, 2002–07); Associate Director, National Theatre, since 2013; *b* 1966; *s* of Malcolm Cooke and Gloria Solomon (*née* Turower). *Educ*: Westminster City Sch.; Univ. of Warwick (BA Hons Eng. and Theatre Studies 1988). Associate Dir, 1998–2002, Artistic Dir, 2007–13, Royal Court Th.; productions include: *Royal Court*: Other People, Fireface, 2000; Spinning into Butter, Redundant, Fucking Games, 2001; Plasticine, The People are Friendly, This is a Chair (co-dir), Identical Twins, 2002; Rhinoceros, The Pain and the Itch, 2007; Now or Later, Wig Out!, 2008; Seven Jewish Children, The Fever, Aunt Dan and Lemon, 2009; Clybourne Park, 2010; Chicken Soup with Barley, 2011; In Basildon, Choir Boy, In the Republic of Happiness, 2012; The Low Road, 2013; Pigs and Dogs, 2016; *Royal Shakespeare Co.*: The Malcontent, 2002; Cymbeline, 2003; Macbeth, 2004; As You Like It, Postcards From America, 2005; The Crucible, The Winter's Tale, Pericles, 2006; Noughts and Crosses, 2007; Arabian Nights, 2009; The Comedy of Errors, NT, 2011; Teddy Ferrara, Donmar Warehouse, 2015; Here We Go, NT, 2015; Ma Rainey's Black Bottom, NT, 2016; Follies, NT, 2017, 2019; *film*: On Chesil Beach, 2018; *for television*: The Hollow Crown: The Wars of the Roses, 2016. *Publications*: Arabian Nights (adaptation), 1998; Noughts and Crosses (adaptation), 2007.

**COOKE, Prof. Elizabeth Jane;** Judge of the Upper Tribunal (Lands Chamber), since 2019; *b* Uxbridge, 29 April 1962; *d* of Jean Finney (*née* Pegler), and adopted *d* of Gerald Coppin and Mary Coppin (*née* Netherwood); *m* 1985, John Cooke; one *s* one *d* (and one *s* one *d* decd). *Educ*: Magdalen Coll., Oxford (BA); Univ. of Reading (LLM). Admitted solicitor, 1988; Assistant Solicitor: Withers, 1988; Barrett & Thomson, 1989–91; University of Reading: Lectr, 1992–2001; Reader, 2001–03; Prof. of Law, 2003–15; Principal Judge, Land Registration Div., First-tier Tribunal (Property Chamber), 2015–19. A Law Comr, 2008–15. Hon. Prof., Univ. of Cambridge, 2015–19; Hon. Vis. Prof., Univ. of Oxford, 2019–. *Publications*: (jtly) The Family, Law and Society, 4th edn 1996 to 6th edn 2008; The Modern Law of Estoppel, 2000; The New Law of Land Registration, 2003; Land Law, 2006, 2nd edn 2012; Modern Studies in Property Law, 2001, 4th edn 2007; (ed jtly) Megarry and Wade: The Law of Real Property, 9th edn, 2019. *Recreations*: running, climbing, making music, gardening, family and friends. *Address*: Royal Courts of Justice, Strand, WC2A 2LL.

**COOKE, Graeme Robert Daryl**; Deputy UK Chief Veterinary Officer, Department for Environment, Food and Rural Affairs, since 2017; *b* Fermanagh; *s* of Cecil Cooke and Olive Cooke; *m* 1998, Margaret Rose Cole. *Educ:* Selwyn Coll., Cambridge (BA 1986, VetMB 1989); JSCSC; Cass Business Sch., London (MBA Dist. 2009). Clin. practice, 1990–2001; Policy Adviser, DEFRA, 2001–07; Dir, FEI, 2009–16; Concepts, MoD, 2016–17. Mem. Bd, Brooke Action for Working Horses and Donkeys, 2016–. *Recreations:* horse owner and sport, running, music, travel, Army Reserve Officer, opera, charity work, theatre. *E:* graemerdcooke@gmail.com. *Clubs:* Hawks; Leander.

**COOKE, Gregory Alan**; Chairman, BNP Paribas Real Estate UK (formerly ATIS Real Weatheralls, then Atisreal), 2001–14 (Senior Partner, Weatherall Green & Smith, 1998–2001); *b* 28 April 1949; *m* Elizabeth; one *s* two *d*. *Educ:* Trent Coll. (BSc). MRICS. Henley Sch. of Business Studies. Capital & Counties Property Co. Ltd, 1972–73; with Weatherall Green & Smith, subseq. ATIS Real Weatheralls, then Atisreal, later BNP Paribas Real Estate UK, 1973–2014. Mem., Mgt Bd, BNP Paribas Real Estate, 2004–14. *Recreations:* ski-ing, sailing, tennis.

**COOKE, Helen Jane**; freelance nutritional health adviser and therapist; Director, Helen Cooke Nutrition, since 2010; *b* 20 Sept. 1963; *d* of Dr Michael Cooke and Mary Cooke (now Brash). *Educ:* Orme Girls' Sch., Newcastle, Staffs; St Bartholomew's Hosp., London (RGN Cert.); Univ. of Exeter (MA Complementary Health Studies 2001); Thames Valley Univ. (BSc Nutritional Medicine 2009). Staff Nurse, St Bartholomew's Hosp., London, 1987; Hd of Nursing, Promis Recovery Centre, 1988–90; Sister, Abbotsleigh Nursing Home, 1990–92; Bristol Cancer Help Centre, later Penny Brohn Cancer Care: Therapy Manager, 1992–2000; Dir of Therapy, 2000–05; Hd, Inf. and Res., 2005–08. Integrative Health Advr, Sixpartswater. Non-exec. Dir, and Nutrition Lead, Portland Centre for Integrative Medicine, 2014–. Co-founder, HealthHive, 2019–. *Publications:* The Bristol Approach to Living with Cancer, 2003. *Recreations:* stained glass design, art, travel, walking, laughing. *E:* helen.cooke2@btinternet.com. *W:* www.helencookenutrition.co.uk.

**COOKE, Hon. Sir Jeremy (Lionel)**, Kt 2001; international commercial arbitrator, since 2016; Judge of the Dubai International Centre, since 2016; Judge of Singapore International Commercial Court, since 2018; *b* 28 April 1949; *s* of late Eric Edwin Cooke and Margaret Lilian Cooke; *m* 1972, Barbara Helen Willey; one *s* two *d*. *Educ:* Whitgift Sch., Croydon; St Edmund Hall, Oxford (Open Exhibn, 1967; MA Jurisprudence, 1st cl. Hons 1970; Rugby blue, 1968, 1969). Harlequins RFC, 1970–75. Admitted Solicitor, 1973; with Coward Chance, 1973–76; called to the Bar, Lincoln's Inn (Droop Schol.), 1976, Bencher, 2001; QC 1990; an Asst Recorder, 1994–98; a Recorder, 1998–2001; Hd of Chambers, 7 King's Bench Walk, 1999–2001; a Judge of the High Ct, QBD, 2001–16; a Judge of the Commercial Ct, 2003–16 (Judge in Charge, 2012–14); Presiding Judge, S Eastern Circuit, 2007–11. Dir, Edward Connor Ltd, 2018–. Pres., E Sussex Magistrates' Assoc., 2009–13. Vice-Pres., Lawyers' Christian Fellowship, 2003–11; Vice Chm., LICC Ltd (formerly London Inst. for Contemp. Christianity), 2004–14 (Mem. Council, 1997–2014). Chm. Council, London Shipping Law Centre, 2019–; Member, Council: WBT Ltd, 1977–89; Internat. Assoc. of English in Law and Insurance, 2013–. Trustee, Egerton Rothesay, 2017–. Youth club leader, 1972–92; Elder and congregation leader, 1992–97. Asst leader, LDN Camps, 2014–. Reader, C of E, 2001–. *Recreations:* amusing eight grandchildren, foozling at golf, learning to sing. *Address:* 7 King's Bench Walk, Temple, EC4Y 7DS. *Clubs:* National (Vice Pres., 2007–); Vincent's (Oxford); Capital (Dubai).

**COOKE, John Arthur**; international economic relations consultant, since 2003; *b* 13 April 1943; *er s* of late Dr Arthur Hafford Cooke, MBE and Ilse Cooke (*née* Sachs); *m* 1970, Tania Frances, 2nd *d* of A. C. Crichton; one *s* two *d*. *Educ:* Dragon Sch.; Magdalen Coll. Sch., Oxford; Univ. of Heidelberg; King's Coll., Cambridge (Exhibnr, Sen. Scholar, BA History 1964, MA 1968); LSE. Mem., Cambridge Univ. expedition to Seistan, 1966. Asst Principal, Board of Trade, 1966; Second, later First, Sec., UK Delegn to European Communities, 1969–73; DTI, 1973–76; Office of UK Perm. Rep. to European Communities, 1976–77; Dept of Trade, 1977–80 (at Inst. Internat. d'Administration Publique, Paris, 1979); Asst Sec., Dept of Trade, 1980–84; seconded to Morgan Grenfell & Co. as Asst Dir, 1984–85; Department of Trade and Industry, 1985–97: Under Sec., Overseas Trade Div. 2, 1987–89; Head of Central Unit, 1989–92; Dir, Deregulation Unit, 1990–92; Head of Internat. Trade Policy Div., 1992–96; Dir and Advr on Trade Policy, 1996–97; Leader, UK delegn to 9th UN Conf. on Trade and Develt, 1996; Chm., OECD Trade Cttee, 1996–97; Hd of Internat. Relations, ABI, 1997–2003. Non-executive Director: RTZ Pillar Ltd, 1990–93; W Middx Univ. Hosp. NHS Trust, 1996–98; Bd Sec., ENO, 1996–. Chairman: Financial Leaders' Wkg Gp Insurance Evaluation Team, 2002–13; Liberalisation of Trade in Services Cttee, TheCityUK (formerly Internat. Financial Services, London), 2006–; European Co-Chm., Financial Leaders' Wkg Gp, 2006–13; Dep. Chm., SITPRO Ltd, 2006–11. Member: Exec. Bd, Anglo-Irish Encounter, 2004–08; Adv. Council, Federal Trust, 2004– (Treas., 2009–15); Adv. Bd, Eur. Centre for Internat. Political Economy, 2008–. Trustee, St Luke's Community Trust, 1983–93 and 1996–2000 (Vice-Chm., 1991–93; Patron, 2000–); Member: Council, Marie Curie Cancer Care (formerly Marie Curie Meml Foundn), 1992–2008 (Vice Pres., 2008–); Bd, Marie Curie Trading Ltd, 1999–2002. Trustee, ENO Benevolent Fund, 2001– (Chm., 2008–18). Mem. Editl Bd, Internat. Trade Law Reports, 1997–2012. *Publications:* articles and contribs to seminars, mainly on internat. trade in financial services. *Recreations:* reading, travelling, looking at buildings. *Address:* 29 The Avenue, Kew, Richmond, Surrey TW9 2AL. *T:* (020) 8940 6712. *Clubs:* Oxford and Cambridge; Cambridge Union.

**COOKE, Kathleen Joyce**; *see* Collins, K. J.

**COOKE, Margaret Rose**; *see* Cole, M. R.

**COOKE, Michael John**, CBE 2011; executive mentor and coach, since 2015; Chief Executive, Nottinghamshire Healthcare NHS Trust, 2007–14; *b* Coalville, 25 Oct. 1959; *s* of Albert Cooke and Dorothy Cooke; *m* 2001, Amanda Claire Blackwood; one *d*. *Educ:* Leeds Grammar Sch.; Loughborough Univ. (BSc 1983); Sheffield Univ. (DipHSM 1986). AHSM 1986. Dep. Chief Exec., Huddersfield NHS Trust, 1993–99; Chief Executive: Halton Gen. Hosps, 1999–2001; S Staffordshire and Shropshire NHS Foundn Trust, 2001–07. Special Prof. in Healthcare Innovation and Learning, Nottingham Univ., 2009–14; Prof. of Practice, Healthcare Leadership and Innovation, Warwick Business Sch., 2015. Chair, MindTech NIHR Health Technol. Co-operative, 2013–16; Advr, NIHR, 2014–; non-exec. Dir, Humber NHS Foundn Trust, 2016–. Chair: Embedded Steering Gp, UCL, 2017–; Knowledge and Impact Gp, Univ. of York, 2019–. Trustee, Yorks Wildlife Trust, 2015– (Dep. Chm., 2016–18; Chm., 2018–). Hon. DLitt Staffordshire. *Recreations:* family, sport, Italy, wine, birdwatching, gardening. *Address:* Hagg Bridge House, Storwood, York YO42 4TF. *E:* mikecooke7@icloud.com.

**COOKE, His Honour Nicholas Orton**; QC 1998; a Senior Circuit Judge, 2007–18; a Deputy High Court Judge, Queen's Bench Division, 2010–18; a Judge of the Central Criminal Court, 2012–18; *b* 1 July 1955; 2nd and *o* surv. *s* of B. O. Cooke and V. Cooke; *m* 1979, Jean Ann Tucker; two *d*. *Educ:* King Edward's Sch., Birmingham; UC Wales, Aberystwyth (Sweet and Maxwell Prize; LLB 1st Cl. Hons 1976). Called to the Bar, Middle Temple, 1977 (Blackstone Entrance Exhibn 1976), Bencher, 2010; in practice at the Bar, 1978–2007; Asst Recorder, 1994–97; Recorder, 1997–2007; Leader, Wales and Chester Circuit, 2007; Recorder of Cardiff, 2008–12. Dep. Pres., then Legal Mem. (Restricted Patient Panel), Mental Health Review Tribunal, Wales, 1999–. Judge of the Provincial Court of the Church in Wales, 2004–; Chancellor, Dio. of St Davids, 2005–. Co-opted Mem., City of London Standards Cttee, 2019–. Freeman, City of London, 2014; Liveryman, Fan Makers' Co., 2014–. *Recreations:* hockey, theatre, association football (Newport County AFC).

**COOKE, Peter**; *see* Cooke, W. P.

**COOKE, Peter Raymond; His Honour Judge Peter Cooke**; a Circuit Judge, since 2016; *b* Newcastle-under-Lyme, Staffs; *s* of late Raymond Cooke and Megan Cooke; *m* 2006, Tracy Vernum; one *s* one *d* by a previous marriage. *Educ:* Newcastle High Sch.; Manchester Univ. (LLB); De Montfort Univ. (LLM Envmtl Law). Called to the Bar, Lincoln's Inn, 1985; barrister, 6 Fountain Court, subseq. Cornwall Street Chambers, Birmingham, 1988–2016, Hd of Chambers, 2014–16; a Recorder, 2003–16. *Recreations:* flying, scuba diving (PADI staff instructor, trimix and rebreather qualified technical diver). *Address:* c/o Derby Crown Court, Morledge, Derby DE1 2XE.

**COOKE, Prof. Richard William Ingram**, MD; FRCP, FRCPCH, FMedSci; Professor of Neonatal Medicine, University of Liverpool, 1988–90 and 1998–2012, now Emeritus; *b* 23 May 1947; *s* of Edward Ingram Cooke and Pauline Ellen Ross Cooke (*née* Foster); *m* 1977, Theresa Elizabeth Reardon Garside; one *s* three *d*. *Educ:* Colfe's Sch.; Charing Cross Hosp. Med. Sch. (qual. 1971; MD 1979); Univ. of Exeter (MA Medieval Studies 2014). DCH 1973; FRCP 1986; FRCPCH 1997. Research Fellow, then Lectr, Oxford Univ., 1976–78; Staff Paediatrician, Sophia Kinderziekenhuis, Rotterdam, 1978–79; University of Liverpool: Sen. Lectr in Child Health, 1980–83; Reader, 1983–87; Prof. of Paediatric Medicine, 1991–98. President: British Assoc. Perinatal Paediatrics, 1990–92; Neonatal Soc., 1997–2000; Vice-Pres., RCPCH, 1997– (Actg Pres., 1999–2000). Founder FMedSci 1998. *Publications:* (ed jtly) Chemical Trade Names and Synonyms, 1978; (jtly) The Very Immature Infant, 1989; (ed jtly) The Baby under 1000 grams, 1989; (ed jtly) Practical Perinatal Care, 1999; numerous articles and papers on neonatal medicine. *Recreations:* jazz, contemporary painting, sailing, Richard III Society, medieval history. *Address:* 6 Market Street, Dartmouth TQ6 9QE.

**COOKE, Roger Malcolm**; Partner in charge, Administration, Arthur Andersen, 1995–98; *b* 12 March 1945; *s* of Sidney and Elsie Cooke; *m* 1st, 1968, Antoinette (*d* 2012); one *s* one *d*; 2nd, 2013, Susan. FCA, CTA (Fellow). Qualified Chartered Accountant, 1968; Arthur Andersen & Co.: joined 1968, Tax Div.; Partner, 1976; Head, London Tax Div., 1979–89; area co-ordinator, tax practice, Europe, Middle East, Africa and India, 1989–93; Dep. Man. Partner, UK, 1989–93; Man. Partner-Chief Financial Officer, Chicago, 1993–95. Mem., Exec. Bd, 2006–19, Dep. Chm., 2010–13, Chm., 2013–19, Glos CCC (Hon. Treas., 2007–10). Vice-Pres., Wooden Spoon Soc., 2012– (Hon. Treas., 1999–2006; Trustee, 1999–2012). *Publications:* Establishing a Business in the United Kingdom, 1978. *Recreations:* playing tennis, travel, ski-ing, cricket, football, good food. *Address:* Madoreen, Larch Avenue, Sunninghill SL5 0AP. *Club:* Royal Berkshire Racquets and Health.

**COOKE, Prof. Sir Ronald Urwick**, Kt 2002; PhD, DSc; FAcSS; Vice-Chancellor, University of York, 1993–2002 (Member, Court, since 2003); *b* 1 Sept. 1941; *y s* of Ernest Cooke and Lillian (*née* Mount), Maidstone, Kent; *m* 1968, Barbara Anne, *d* of A. Baldwin; one *s* one *d*. *Educ:* Ashford Grammar Sch.; University College London, Univ. of London (BSc 1st Cl. Hons, MSc, PhD, DSc; Fellow, 1994). Lectr, UCL, 1961–75; Prof. of Geography, 1975–81, Dean of Science, 1978–80, and Vice-Principal, 1979–80, Bedford Coll., Univ. of London; Prof. and Hd of Dept of Geography, 1981–93, Dean of Arts, 1991–92, and Vice-Provost, 1991–93, UCL. Dir, UCL Press, 1990–95. Amer. Council of Learned Societies Fellow, UCLA, 1964–65 and 1973; Visiting Professor: UCLA, 1968; Univ. of Arizona, Tucson, 1970; Arizona State Univ., Tempe, 1988. Desert research in N and S America, N Africa and ME. Chm. and co-Founder, Geomorphological Services Ltd, 1986–90. Member: US-UK Fulbright Commn, 1995–2000; HEFCE, 1996–2003; Chm., Jt Information Systems Cttee, 2003–08. Chm., British Geomorphological Res. Group, 1979; Pres., RGS, 2000–03 (Mem. Council, 1980–83; Back Grant, 1977; Founder's Medal, 1994); Mem. Council, Inst. of British Geographers, 1973–75 (Pres., 1991–92). Hon. Sec., York Archaeological Trust, 1994–96; Chairman: Yorks Arboretum (formerly Castle Howard Arboretum Trust), 2002–11 (Trustee, 2011–17); York Local Strategic Partnership, 2007–12 (Dep. Chm., 2012–16); Yorks and Humber Cttee, HLF, 2017–19; Dep. Chm., England N Area Cttee, NLHF, 2019–; Dir, Visit York, 2012–15; Ind. Chm., Reinvigorate York, 2011–15. Trustee: Laurence Sterne Trust, 1994–2006; Nat. Mus. of Science and Industry, 2002–10; York Museums Trust, 2002–08; York Civic Trust, 2002–17 (Chm., 2009–12; Vice-Chm., 2012–17); St Leonard's Hospice, York, 2003–08. Patron: York Early Music Fest., 1995–; Elvington Air Mus., 1999–; York Musical Soc., 2016–; Dir, Ryedale Fest., 2015–. Mem., Co. of Merchant Adventurers of City of York. DL N Yorks, 2004–17. Hon. Freeman, City of York, 2006. Fellow, RHBNC, 1993. Hon. DCL Kent, 2004; Hon. DPhil Glos, 2004; DUniv York, 2005. *Publications:* (ed with J. H. Johnson) Trends in Geography, 1969; (with A. Warren) Geomorphology in Deserts, 1973; (with J. C. Doornkamp) Geomorphology in Environmental Management, 1974, 2nd edn 1990; (with R. W. Reeves) Arroyos and Environmental Change in the American Southwest, 1976; (contrib.) Geology, Geomorphology and Pedology of Bahrain, 1980; (contrib.) Urban Geomorphology in Drylands, 1982; Geomorphological Hazards in Los Angeles, 1984; (with A. Warren and A. S. Goudie) Desert Geomorphology, 1993; (with G. B. Gibbs) Crumbling Heritage?, 1993; Why York is Special, 2006; Sustaining the City Beautiful, 2015; York: changing the face of the city, 2016; (contrib.) The Streets of York: four centuries of change, 2018; contribs mainly on desert and applied geomorphology in prof. jls.

**COOKE, (Sally) Del**; Head, Henrietta Barnett School, since 2014; *b* London, 3 Sept. 1958; *d* of Eirwyn and Marlene Rowlands; *m* 1980, David Cooke; three *s*. *Educ:* Godolphin and Latymer Sch.; Bristol Univ. (BSc Maths and Stats 1979); Nottingham Univ. (PGCE 1980); Leicester Univ. (MBA Educnl Leadership 2005); Nat. Coll. of Sch. Leadership (NPQH 2006). Teacher, 1980–81, Hd of Year, 1981–82, T. P. Riley Community Sch.; private tutor, maths and clarinet, 1983–; teacher: adult educn, Horsham, 1989–93; Coll. of Richard Collyer, 1990–96; Cranleigh School: teacher, 1993–98; Hd of Maths, 1998–2001; Housemistress, 2001–02; Dep. Hd (and Actg Hd), 2002–07; Hd, Sir William Perkins's Sch., 2007–14. Team Inspector, Ind. Schs Inspectorate, 2007–14. Vice-Chair, Educn Cttee, Girls Schs Assoc., 2010–14; Mem., Jt Assocs Curriculum Gp, 2010–14. Gov., Halstead Prep. Sch., 2007–14. *Recreations:* family, books, competitive games, bassoon, church. *Address:* Henrietta Barnett School, Central Square, Hampstead Garden Suburb, NW11 7BN. *E:* dcooke@hbschool.org.uk.

**COOKE, Sarah Helen**; *see* Crowther, S. H.

**COOKE, Stephen John**; Senior Partner, Slaughter and May, since 2016; musician and composer for film and television; *b* London, 7 March 1959; *s* of Robert and Barbara Cooke; two *s* one *d*. *Educ:* Lincoln Coll., Oxford (MA). Joined Slaughter and May, 1982; Partner, 1991–; Hd, Mergers and Acquisitions, 2001–16. Non-exec. Dir, PRS for Music Ltd, 2018–. Composer and musician: for films: China's Stolen Children, 2007; A Love that

Never Dies, 2018; for television, including: The Dying Rooms, 1995; Innocents Lost, 1997; Slavery, 2000; Old, 2002; Reporters at War, 2003; Bulgaria's Abandoned Children, 2007; Chosen, 2008; War Child, 2011; Kashmir's Torture Trail, 2012; Land of Hope and Glory - a Life in the Country, 2016; The Queen's Green Planet, 2018; music for radio. *Publications:* Takeovers, 1997; The Morning of Our Lives, 2017; various articles. *Recreations:* music, reading, sports. *Address:* Slaughter and May, One Bunhill Row, EC1Y 8YY. *T:* (020) 7090 3261. *E:* steve.cooke@slaughterandmay.com. *Clubs:* Athenæum, Groucho, MCC.

**COOKE, (William) Peter,** CBE 1997; *b* 1 Feb. 1932; *s* of late Douglas Edgar Cooke, MC and Florence May (*née* Mills); *m* 1st, 1957, Maureen Elizabeth (*d* 1999), *er d* of late Dr E. A. Haslam-Fox; two *s* two *d*; 2nd, 2005, Mrs Julia Mary Bain (*née* Warrack). *Educ:* Royal Grammar Sch., High Wycombe; Kingswood Sch., Bath; Merton Coll., Oxford (MA; Hon. Fellow 1997). Entered Bank of England, 1955; Bank for Internat. Settlements, Basel, 1958–59; Personal Asst to Man. Dir, IMF, Washington, DC, 1961–65; Sec., City Panel on Takeovers and Mergers, 1968–69; First Dep. Chief Cashier, Bank of England, 1970–73; Adviser to Governors, 1973–76; Hd of Banking Supervision, 1976–85; Associate Dir, 1982–88; Chm., Price Waterhouse Regulatory Adv. Practice, 1989–96; Advr, Price Waterhouse, subseq. PricewaterhouseCoopers, 1997–2002. Housing Corporation: Mem. Bd, 1988–97; Dep. Chm., 1994–97; Chm., 1997. Chairman: City EEC Cttee, 1973–80; Group of Ten Cttee on Banking Regulations and Supervisory Practices at BIS, Basel, 1977–88. Director: Safra Republic Holdings SA, 1989–99; Financial Holdings (UK), 1994–2009; Alexander & Alexander Services Inc., 1994–96; Bank of China Internat. Hldgs Ltd, 1997–98; Housing Finance Corp., 1997–2003; State Street Bank (Europe) Ltd, 1998–2006; Bank of China Internat. UK Ltd, 1999–2018; HSBC Republic Holdings SA, 2000–01; Bank of China Ltd, 2004–07; Medi Capital Hldgs, 2006–10; Assured Guaranty (UK), 2009–12; BMCE Internat. (Hldgs), 2010–11; Dir, Church Housing Trust, 1984–2006. Member: Nat. Cttee, English Churches Housing Group, 1977–94; Council, Chatham House (RIIA), 1992–2005 (Dep. Chm., 1998–2005). Governor: Pangbourne Coll., 1982–2002; Kingswood Sch., 1991–2002; Gayhurst Sch., 2010–14 (Chm., 2011–14). Pres., Merton Soc., 1995–98. *Recreations:* music, golf, travel. *Address:* Oak Lodge, Maltmans Lane, Gerrards Cross, Bucks SL9 8RP. *Club:* Denham Golf.

**COOKE-PRIEST, Rear Adm. Colin Herbert Dickinson,** CB 1993; CVO 2009; Chief Executive, The Trident Trust, 1994–99; an Extra Gentleman Usher to the Queen, since 2009 (a Gentleman Usher to the Queen, 1994–2009); *b* 17 March 1939; *s* of Dr William Hereward Dickinson Priest and Harriet Lesley Josephine Priest (*née* Cooke); *m* 1965, Susan Mary Diana Hobler; two *s* two *d*. *Educ:* St Piran's, Maidenhead; Marlborough Coll.; BRNC, Dartmouth. Entered RN, 1957; Lieut, 1960; exchange service with RAN, 1968–70; commanded: HMS Plymouth, 1975–76; HMS Berwick, 1976; Airwarfare Directorate, Naval Staff, MoD, 1977–79; Naval Asst to C-in-C Fleet, 1979–81; Asst Dir, Naval Air Warfare, 1981–82; CO, HMS Boxer, 1983–85; Dir, Maritime Tactical Sch., 1985–87; CO, HMS Brilliant and Capt. Second Frigate Sqn, 1987–89; Dep. Asst Chief of Staff (Ops) to Supreme Allied Comdr Europe, 1989–90; Flag Officer, Naval Aviation, 1990–93. Chm., FAA Officers' Assoc., 1998–2005. Pres., Fly Navy Heritage Trust, 2014–. FRAeS 1992. Freeman, City of London, 1985; Hon. Liveryman, Coachmakers' and Coach Harness Makers' Co., 1985; Liveryman, Hon. Co. of Air Pilots (formerly GAPAN), 1999– (Master, 2009–10). *Address:* Tasman House, 18A Beechworth Road, Havant, Hants PO9 1AX.

**COOKE-YARBOROUGH, Sir Anthony Edmund,** 13th Bt *cr* 1661; Private Banking Chairman, EFG International AG, since 2019; *b* Oxford, 6 Aug. 1956; *s* of late Edmund Henry Cooke-Yarborough and Anthea Katharine Cooke-Yarborough; *S* cousin, 2017; *m* 1990, Joanna Susan Northrop; one *s* two *d*. *Educ:* Eton; Gonville and Caius Coll., Cambridge (BA Econs 1978). Account Exec., Lloyds Bank Internat., Madrid, 1982–85; Hd of Private Banking, New York, Lloyds TSB Bank plc, 1992–94; Dir, Internat. Investments, Lloyds Bank Brazil, 1994–97; Exec. Dir, Merrill Lynch Internat. Bank, 1997–2002; CEO, Barclays Private Bank Ltd, 2002–04; CEO, Mourant Private Wealth, 2005–09; Hd of Private Banking, 2009–11, Man. Dir, 2011, Chief Exec., 2011–18, EFG Private Bank Ltd. FRGS. *Recreations:* rowing, hillwalking, family. *Heir: s* George Edmund Cooke-Yarborough, *b* 11 June 1991. *Address:* EFG Private Bank Ltd, Leconfield House, Curzon Street, W1J 5JB. *T:* (020) 7872 3647. *E:* anthony.cooke-yarborough@efgl.com. *Club:* Leander.

**COOKSEY, Sir David (James Scott),** GBE 2007; Kt 1993; Chairman: Bechtel Ltd, since 2008; Francis Crick Institute, 2008–17; *b* 14 May 1940; *s* of Dr Frank S. Cooksey, CBE, and Muriel M. Cooksey; *m* 1st, 1973, Janet Wardell-Yerburgh (marr. diss. 2003); one *s* one *d*; 2nd, 2011, Mrs Mary Ann Lutyens. *Educ:* Westminster Sch.; St Edmund Hall, Oxford Univ. (MA; Hon. Fellow 1995). Dir of Manufacturing, Formica International, 1969–71; Man. Dir, Intercobra Ltd, 1971–80; Man. Dir, 1981–87, Chm., 1987–2006, Advent Venture Partners; Director: Advent International Corp., 1985–90; Electra Risk Capital, 1981–90; Bespak plc, 1993–2004 (Chm., 1995–2004); William Baird plc, 1995–2002; Establishment Investment Trust plc, 2002–15 (Chm., 2011–15); Resolution plc (formerly Resolution Life Gp), 2004–08; Chairman: Diamond Light Source Ltd, 2002–08; London & Continental Railways Ltd, 2006–11; Quadrille Publishing Ltd, 2007–13; Eurasian Natural Resources Corp. plc, 2007–09; UK Financial Investments Ltd, 2009–12. Chairman: Audit Commn, 1986–95; Local Govt Commn for England, 1995–96; Dir, Bank of England, 1994–2005 (Chm., non-exec. Dirs Cttee, 2001–05). Member: Council, CBI, 1976–88; Scottish Economic Council, 1980–87; Council, British Venture Capital Assoc., 1983–89 (Chm., 1983–84; Hon. Life Pres., 2012); Innovation Adv. Bd, DTI, 1988–93; Adv. Bd, SVP Global, 2012–18; Dir, Eur. Private Equity and Venture Capital Assoc., 2004–07 (Chm., 2005–06); Chairman: MRC/DoH Jt Health Res. Delivery Gp, 2004–06; DoH UK Clinical Res. Collaboration Industry Reference Gp, 2004–10; HM Treasury Cooksey Review of UK Health Res., 2006; UK Govt Rep., Dementia Discovery Fund, 2015–. Chairman: Small Business Investment Taskforce, DTI, 2000–04; Bioscis Innovation and Growth Taskforce, DoH/DTI, 2003–09. Chm., State Honours Cttee, 2005–10; Mem., Main Honours Cttee, 2005–10. Mem. Council, 1993–2003, Pro Chancellor, 2008–13, Southampton Univ. Trustee: Mary Rose Trust, 1994–2001 (Chm., 1996–2001); Gov., Wellcome Trust, 1995–99. Hon. FMedSci 2004; Hon. Fellow, BAAS, 2004. Hon. Fellow: Univ. of Wales, Cardiff, 1998; Imperial Coll. London, 2007; Hon. FKC 2012. Hon. DBA Kingston, 1996; Hon. DSc: Southampton, 2008; UCL, 2011. *Recreations:* sailing (Round Britain and Ireland 2-handed Yacht Race: 2nd, 1966, 1970; 3rd, 1974, 1978), music, theatre, wine. *Address:* c/o Bechtel Ltd, 11 Pilgrim Street, EC4V 6RN. *Clubs:* Boodle's; Royal Yacht Squadron; Royal and Ancient Golf.

**COOKSEY, Ian Alexander;** Headmaster, Watford Grammar School for Boys, since 2015; *b* Sutton Coldfield, 25 Oct. 1974; *s* of Geoff Cooksey and Diana Cooksey (later Hillcox); *m* 2001, Eleanor Croft; one *s* one *d*. *Educ:* Queen Mary's Grammar Sch.; Magdalen Coll., Oxford (MA 1st Cl. Biol Scis 1997; PGCE 1998); Inst. of Educn, Univ. of London (NPQH 2007; MA with Dist. 2010). Teacher of Science, Furamera Secondary Sch., Zimbabwe (Project Trust), 1993–94; Teacher of Biology and Rowing, 1998–2003, Asst Hd, 2003–07, Tiffin Sch.; Vice Principal, Tomlinscote Sch., 2007–10; Hd of Coll., King's Internat. Coll., 2010–11; Hd, Dr Challoner's High Sch., 2011–15. Nat. Leader of Educn, 2016. FRGS 1999. *Publications:* (contrib.) Mkomazi: the ecology, biodiversity and conservation of a Tanzania savanna, 1999. *Recreations:* Munro-bagging (201 completed), bird-watching (world list - 751), opera, cinema, cricket, travel. *Address:* Watford Grammar School for Boys, Rickmansworth Road, Watford, Herts WD18 7JF. *T:* (01923) 208900, *Fax:* (01923) 208901. *E:* head@watfordboys.org.

**COOKSEY, Janet Clouston Bewley, (Poppy), (Lady Cooksey),** OBE 2004; PhD; art historian and picture restorer, since 1978; *b* 15 Feb. 1940; *d* of late Dr Ian Aysgarth Bewley Cathie and Dr Marian Josephine Cunning; *m* 1966, Hugh Arthur Wardell-Yerburg (*d* 1970); one *d*; *m* 1973, Sir David Cooksey, *qv* (marr. diss. 2003); one *s* one *d*. *Educ:* Cheltenham Ladies' Coll.; Univ. of London (BSc ext.); Univ. of St Andrews (PhD Fine Arts). Amateur fencer, 1956–72, 1998–: Jun. Schs Champion, 1954 and 1955; Sen. Schs and under-20 Champion, 1956; British Ladies Foil Champion, 1965, 1967 and 1969–72; winner: De Beaumont International, 1967, 1971 and 1972; Desprez Cup, 1964–67, 1969 and 1972; Jubilee Bowl, 1964–67, 1970–72; double gold medallist, Commonwealth Games, 1966 and 1970; repr. GB in Olympic fencing teams, 1964, 1968, 1972 and in World Championships, 1963–72; veteran competitions include: double gold medallist (foil and epée individual and team) Commonwealth Games, Johannesburg, 1999, Wales, 2001; double gold medallist (foil and epée), World Championships, Budapest, 2000, Martinique, 2001, Tampa, Fla, 2002, Porec, 2010; double gold medallist (foil and epée), European Champs, Cologne, 2001 and France, 2011 (also silver medal, sabre); double gold medallist (foil and epée), World Championships, Croatia, 2011; triple gold medallist (foil, epée, sabre), Commonwealth Games, Singapore, 2012; double gold medallist (foil and epée), Commonwealth Games, Glasgow, 2014, NZ, 2016; gold medallist, epée, Commonwealth Games, Canberra, 2018. Lectr, extra-mural studies, Univ. of St Andrews, 1975–78, and Dir, Alexander Nasmyth exhibn, 1979; Dir, Special Projects, Univ. of Southampton, 1993–96. Mem., Bd of Trustees, Royal Armouries, 1993–99 (Mem., Design Cttee, 1994–99). Chairman: RNLI Crew Training Appeal, 1996–2000; Countess Mountbatten Hospice Appeal, 1996–2000; Gift of Sight Appeal, Southampton Gen. Hosp., 1998–2001; Area Chm., Children's Hospice Appeal, 1994–96. Member: Corporate Develt Bd, NSPCC, 1997–2008; Bd Trustees, Mental Health Foundn, 1997–2000; Nat. Appeal Bd, Marie Curie Cancer Care, 1997–2000; Scrutiny Panel for N and Mid Hants HA, 2000. Trustee, British Fencing Assoc., 2000–. FRSA 1986. Freeman, City of London, 2004; Guild of Freemen: Mem. Ct, 2002–; Mem., Finance and Gen. Purposes Cttee, 2011–19 (Chm., 2016–19); Master, 2015–16; Mem., Ct Nominations Cttee, 2016–; Chm., Investments Cttee, 2018–; Liveryman, Arts Scholars' Co., 2016. DL Hants, 1998–2005. *Publications:* The Pleasure of Antiques, 1973; Alexander Nasmyth 1758–1840 (exhibn catalogue), 1979; Alexander Nasmyth: a man of the Scottish Renaissance, 1991; contributed to: The Dictionary of Art, 1996; Oxford DNB, 2004. *Recreations:* entertaining, reading, gardens, the arts, travel, tennis, fencing. *Address:* Uplands House, Upton, Banbury, Oxon OX15 6HJ. *Club:* Salle Paul Fencing.

**COOKSLEY, Nigel James;** QC 2002; *b* 2 April 1953; *s* of Norman Cooksley and Diana Margaret Barnes Cooksley; *m* 1980, Stephanie Jupe; one *s* one *d*. *Educ:* Felsted Sch.; Queens' Coll., Cambridge (MA Law). Called to the Bar, Inner Temple, 1975; in practice, specialising in personal injury, clinical negligence, professional negligence, health and safety work; Jt Hd of Chambers, 2009–15. Mem., Civil Justice Council, 2002–04; former Chm., Personal Injuries Bar Assoc. *Recreations:* travel, golf, football, cricket, Rugby, horse racing. *Clubs:* Chesfield Downs Golf, Weston Cricket.

**COOKSON, Brian;** *see* Cookson, M. B.

**COOKSON, Clive Michael;** Science Editor, Financial Times, since 1991; *b* London, 13 Feb. 1952; *s* of Prof. Richard Clive Cookson, FRS and Ellen Amin Cookson; *m* 1978, Caroline Davidson; one *s* one *d*. *Educ:* Winchester Coll.; Brasenose Coll., Oxford (BSc 1st Cl. Hons Chem.). Trainee journalist, Luton Evening Post, 1974–76; Sci. corresp., THES, 1976–77; American Ed., Times supplements, 1977–81; Technol. corresp., The Times, 1981–83; Sci. corresp., BBC Radio, 1983–87; Technol. Ed., 1987–90, Pharmaceuticals corresp., 1990–91, FT. *Address:* Financial Times, Bracken House, 1 Friday Street, EC4M 9BT. *E:* clive.cookson@ft.com.

**COOKSON, (Michael) Brian,** OBE 2008; President, Union Cycliste Internationale, 2013–17; *b* Preston, 22 June 1951; *s* of Kenneth and Dorothy Cookson; *m* 1973, Sian Talbot; two *s* one *d*. *Educ:* Hutton Grammar Sch.; Manchester Poly. (Dip. Landscape Architecture 1973). Chartered Landscape Architect 1975. Landscape architect and regeneration manager, 1973–2004; Exec. Dir (Regeneration), Pendle BC, 2004–13. Pres., British Cycling, 1996–2013 (Life Mem.); Mem., Swiss Cycling, 2014–17. Hon Fellow, Univ. of Central Lancs, 2009. Hon. DCL European, 2015; Hon. DBA Manchester Metropolitan, 2015. *Recreations:* cycling, playing guitar (improving).

**COOKSON, Thomas Richard,** MA; Headmaster, Winchester College, 2003–05; *b* 7 July 1942; *s* of Samuel Harold Cookson, MD, FRCP and Elizabeth Mary Cookson; *m* 1972, Carol Hayley (*d* 2009); three *d*. *Educ:* Winchester Coll.; Balliol Coll., Oxford (MA Eng. Lit.). Assistant Master: Winchester, 1964–65; Hopkins Grammar Sch., New Haven, USA, 1965–67; Winchester, 1967–72; Manchester Grammar Sch., 1972–74; Head of English, Winchester, 1974–83, Housemaster, 1983–90; Headmaster: King Edward VI Sch., Southampton, 1990–96; Sevenoaks School, 1996–2001; Principal, British Sch. in Colombo, 2002. Governor: Rugby Sch., 2005–12; English Coll. in Prague, 2005–09; New Sch. at W Heath, 2006–10; Wellington Coll., 2011–16; Dorton Coll. (formerly Dorton House Sch.), 2011–. Chm., Physics Partners (formerly Physics-S3), 2007–. *Publications:* John Keats, 1972; Bernard Shaw, 1972. *Recreation:* golf. *Address:* Chapel Cottage, Kemsing Road, Wrotham, Kent TN15 7BU.

**COOLING, Vice Adm. Robert George,** CB 2011; FCMI; business consultant and advisor/mentor; *b* 11 July 1957; *s* of Edwin and Rosalind Cooling; *m* 1984, Helen Smith; two *s*. *Educ:* Christ Church Cathedral Sch., Oxford; King's Sch., Canterbury; Keele Univ. (BA Hons Internat. Relns 1978); BRNC, Dartmouth, 1978; Manchester Business Sch., Univ. of Manchester (Advanced Mgt Achievement Course 2012). Commnd RN, 1978; comd, HMS Sandpiper, 1985–86; Instructor in Navigation, US Naval Acad., Annapolis, 1990–92; comd HMS Battleaxe, 1992–93; jssc 1993; COS to Comdr UK Task Gp, 1997–98; comd HMS Montrose and 6th Frigate Sqn, 1998–2000; Dir Naval Staff, MoD, 2002–03; hcsc 2004; comd HMS Illustrious, 2004–06 (Carrier Strike Gp Comdr); has served in ops in Arctic Circle, ME and Gulf reg., Indian Ocean, Mediterranean, S China Sea and Atlantic; comd UK Task Gp evacuation operation from Beirut, 2006; Dep. Comdr, Striking and Support Force, NATO, 2006–08; ACNS, MoD, 2008–09; COS to NATO Supreme Allied Comdr Transformation, 2009–11. Dir, Northfield Leadership. Non-exec. dir in financial services, logistics and technol. sectors. Pres., HMS Illustrious Assoc., 2012–. Voluntary work in support of Reserve and Cadet Forces; volunteer RNLI crewman, Humber Lifeboat stn, 2017–. FCMI 2012. Freeman, City of London, 2004; Hon. Mem., Co. of Lightmongers, 2004. *Recreations:* travel, country pursuits, anti-poaching and conservation work in Africa. *Club:* Royal Navy of 1765 and 1785.

**COOMBE, Andrew Jackson**, FCA; Lord-Lieutenant of South Yorkshire, since 2015; *b* Sheffield, 5 Nov. 1946; *s* of Major Richard Jackson Coombe, TD and Anne Jocelyn Coombe; *m* 1973, Susan Mary Lockwood; one *s* one *d*. *Educ*: Glengorse Prep. Sch., Battle; Wellington Coll., Crowthorne; Caer Rhun Hall, Conway; Coll. of Law, Guildford and Christelton. ACA 1969, FCA 1979. Chartered Accountant, Cooper Brothers & Co., 1965–71; trainee solicitor, Wake Smith & Co., 1971–76; admitted solicitor, 1976; Wagon Finance Corporation plc: first in-house Solicitor, 1976–80; Dir, Bank of Europe and Wagon Finance Ltd, 1980–86; Dir, 1982–86; Dep. Man. Dir, 1984–86; Man. Dir, 1986; Keeble Hawson, solicitors: Partner, 1986–2008; Finance Partner, 1986–2008; Hd, Corporate Finance Dept, 1991–2006. HM Tax Comr, 1986–2001. Dir, Propland Hldgs Ltd, 1990–97; non-exec. Dir, VHE plc, 1998–2002. Secretary: Claremont Nursing Home Th. Appeal, 1974–2000; S Yorks Muslim Community Forum, 2014–15; Trustee: St Luke's Hospice, 1976–2011 (Chm., 2001–09; Vice Pres., 2012–); Bluecoat Educnl Trust, 1983–2000; Freshgate Foundn, 1987–2000; Ashdell Prep. Sch., 1990–95 (Chm., 1993–95); Broomgrove Trust, 2005–10 (Chm., 2005–09). Chairman: Mgt Cttee, Claremont Hosp., 1991–98; Our Story Our Community - Cohesion Gp, 2012–15; Council, Sheffield Cathedral, 2013–. Non-executive Director: Sheffield (Students in Free Enterprise) Ltd, 2005–09; Univ. of Sheffield Students Union, 2007–10. Vice President: S and W Yorks, RBL, 2015–; Sheffield Chamber of Commerce and Ind., 2015–; Friends of Sheffield Cathedral, 2015–; President: S Yorks Community Foundn, 2015–; Sheffield Sea Cadets, 2015–; RFCA for Yorks and Humber, 2017– (Vice Pres., 2015–17); Jt Pres., S and W Yorks, Order of St John, 2018–. Patron: Yorks Historic Churches Trust, 2015; Emmeus Sheffield, 2018–. Lieut, B Sqdn (SRY), Royal Yeo. Regt and Royal Yeo., TA, 1970–76. DL 1995, High Sheriff 2011, S Yorks. *Recreations*: golf, fishing (trout and salmon), cooking, hill walking, visiting house and family in SW France, reading. *Address*: 79 Slayleigh Lane, Sheffield S10 3RG. *T*: (0114) 230 5515, 07932 152365. *E*: drewcoombe@gmail.com. *Clubs*: Cavalry and Guards; Lindrick Golf (Hon. Treas., 1988–91), Royal and Ancient Golf (St Andrews); Derwent Fly Fishing.

**COOMBE, Gary Andrew**; Chief Executive Officer, Gillette Co., since 2019; *b* Barnet, 28 Feb. 1964; *s* of Brian Coombe and Doreen Taylor; *m* 1989, Heidi; one *s* one *d*. *Educ*: St Columba's Coll., St Albans; Aston Univ., Birmingham (BSc Business Mgt). Sales Exec., 1986–93, Brand Manager, 1993–97, Procter & Gamble UK; Mktg Dir, Procter & Gamble Europe, 1997–2003; Vice President: Procter & Gamble UK, 2003–06; Procter & Gamble, USA, 2006–10; Vice Pres., 2010–14, Pres., 2014–17, Procter & Gamble Europe; Pres., Procter & Gamble Global Gillette, 2018–19. Freeman, City of London; Mem., Poulters' Co. *Recreations*: ski-ing, wine collecting, running, family, travelling, fundraising (Willow Foundation). *Address*: Procter & Gamble Europe SA, 47 route de Saint-Georges, 1213 Petit-Lancy 1, Switzerland. *T*: (58) 0045522, *Fax*: (58) 0037520. *E*: coombe.ga@pg.com. *Club*: Morton's.

**COOMBE, His Honour Gerald Hugh**; a Circuit Judge, 1986–98; *b* 16 Dec. 1925; *s* of William Stafford Coombe and Mabel Florence Coombe; *m* 1957, Zoë Margaret Richards; one *s* one *d*. *Educ*: Alleyn's School, Dulwich; Hele's School, Exeter; Exeter College, Oxford. MA 1950. RAF (Navigator), 1944–48; Solicitor, 1953; Partner, Whitehead Monckton, Maidstone, 1956–86; HM Coroner, Maidstone, 1962–86; a Recorder, 1983–86. *Club*: Royal Air Force.

**COOMBE, John David**, FCA; Chairman, Home Retail Group plc, 2012–16 (non-executive Director, 2005–12); *b* London, 17 March 1945; *s* of Sidney and Phyllis Coombe; *m* 1970, Gail Alicia Brazier; three *d*. *Educ*: Haberdashers' Aske's Sch., Elstree; City of London Coll. (BSc Econ.). FCA 1970. Dixon Wilson & Co., Chartered Accountants, 1966–71; Mgt Accountant, Head Office, 1971–72, Investment Analyst, 1972–73, British Oxygen Gp Ltd; Asst Chief Accountant, 1973–76, Gp Treas., 1976–84, Charterhouse Gp Ltd; Finance Manager, Charter Consolidated plc, 1984–86; Gp Financial Controller, Glaxo Hldgs plc, 1986–92; Gp Finance Dir, Glaxo Hldgs, later Glaxo Wellcome plc, 1992–2000; Chief Financial Officer, GlaxoSmithKline plc, 2000–05. Chm., Hogg Robinson Gp plc, 2006–16; Mem., Supervisory Bd, Siemens AG, 2003–08; non-exec. Dir, HSBC Holdings plc, 2005–14. Member: UK Accounting Standards Bd, 1996–2003; Code Cttee, Panel on Takeovers and Mergers, 2001–07. Mem., Cttee on Corporate Governance, ICAEW, 2003–09. Mem., Hundred Gp, 1992– (Chm., 1999–2001). Mem. Council, Royal Acad. of Arts, 2007–12; Trustee, Royal Acad. Trust, 2004–11. *Recreations*: golf, bridge.

**COOMBER, Judith Amanda Jane**; *see* Gleeson, J. A. J.

**COOMBES, Prof. (Raoul) Charles (Dalmedo Stuart)**, MD; PhD; FRCP, FMedSci; Professor of Medical Oncology, and Imperial Lead, Cancer Research Centre of Excellence, Imperial College London, since 2016; *b* 20 April 1949; *s* of late Raoul Coombes and Doreen Coombes; *m* 1984, Caroline Sarah Oakes; two *s* two *d*. *Educ*: Douai Sch.; St George's Hosp. Med. Sch. (MB BS); Inst. of Cancer Res., London (PhD 1978; MD 1981). MRCP 1973, FRCP 1990. MRC Clinical Res. Fellow, 1974–77; Sen. Registrar, 1977–80, Hon. Consultant, 1980–83, Royal Marsden Hosp.; Sen. Clinical Scientist, Ludwig Inst. for Cancer Res., 1980–83; Consultant Physician, St George's Hosp., 1983–90; Prof. and Hd of Dept of Med. Oncology, 1990–97, Dean of Res., 1993–97, Charing Cross and Westminster Med. Sch.; Dir of Cancer Services, Hammersmith Hosps NHS Trust, 1995–2006; Imperial College Faculty of Medicine, Hammersmith Hospital: Prof. of Med. Oncology, 1997–2012; Hd, Dept of Cancer Med., 1997–2012; Dir, CRUK (formerly Imperial Coll. Cancer Res. (UK)) Labs, 1999–2016; Hd, CRUK and Biomed. Res. Centre Theme Leader for Cancer, 2009–16. Civilian Consultant, RAF, 1993–. FMedSci 2001. Ed., *Therapeutic Advances in Med. Oncology*, 2009–. *Publications*: *Breast Cancer Management*, 1981; *The New Endocrinology of Cancer*, 1987; *New Targets in Cancer Therapy*, 1994; numerous papers and articles in professional jls. *Recreations*: painting, walking. *Address*: 30 Wingate Road, W6 0UR. *Club*: Chelsea Arts.

**COOMBS, Anthony Michael Vincent**; Chairman, S & U plc, since 2008 (Managing Director, 1999–2008); Director, Grevayne Properties Ltd, since 1972; *b* 18 Nov. 1952; *s* of late Clifford Keith Coombs and of Celia Mary Gostling (*née* Vincent); *m* 1984, Andrea Caroline (*née* Pritchard); one *s*. *Educ*: Bilton Grange Sch.; Charterhouse; Worcester Coll., Oxford (MA). Birmingham City Council: Mem., 1978–88: Deputy Chairman: Educn Cttee, 1982–84; Social Services Cttee, 1982–84; Cons. spokesman on educn, Birmingham MDC, 1984–86. MP (C) Wyre Forest, 1987–97; contested (C) same seat, 1997. PPS to Rt Hon. David Mellor, MP, 1989–92, to Rt Hon. Gillian Shephard, MP, 1995–96; an Asst Govt Whip, 1996–97. Vice-Chairman: Cons. Back-Bench Educn Cttee, 1993–96 (Sec., 1987–93); Cons. Parly Educn Cttee, 1993–96; All Party Parly Sports Cttee, 1993–96; Parly Human Rights Gp, 1993–96 (Sec., 1987–93); Parly Social Scis Gp, 1994–96; Sec., Cons. Parly Finance Cttee, 1994–96. Mem., Exec. Cttee, Conservative Team 1000, 1997–2001; Treas., Cons. Party, 2004–05; Chm., Productivity Forum, Cons. Policy Forum, 2013–14. Chairman: Businessesforsale.com plc, 2000–02; Cubana Restaurants Ltd, 2002–17. Chm., PR Cttee, Consumer Credit Assoc., 2006–15. Member: Bd, Develt Cttee, Worcester Coll., Oxford, 1996–98; Bd, Birmingham Royal Ballet Develt Trust, 1998–2006; Business Council, Politeia, 2011–. Dir, Schools Outreach, 1997–2003. Pres., Wyre Forest "Solidarity" Campaign, 1987–97; Mem., One Nation Gp. Vice-Chm., Friends of Cyprus,

1992–97. Chm. of Governors, Perry Common Sch., Birmingham, 1978–93; Governor: King Edward Foundn, 1982–88; Birmingham Coll. of Tourism, 1982–88; Ind. Primary and Secondary Educn Trust, 1997–2007. Chm. of Trustees, Nat. Inst. for Conductive Educn, 2001–15 (Trustee, 1998–); Trustee: Scholarships for Kids (Kenya), 2008–14; Keith Coombs Trust, 2012–; Premier Christian Media Trust, 2014–; Dir and Trustee, Birmingham Royal Ballet, 2017–. *Publications*: Bow Group papers, numerous articles in newspapers and jls. *Recreations*: golf, tennis, occasional football, music, theatre, ballet, yoga. *Address*: 18 Cheyne Walk, SW3 5RA. *Clubs*: Royal Automobile, Annabel's; Little Aston Golf.

**COOMBS, Kay**, OBE 2005; HM Diplomatic Service, retired; Ambassador to Honduras, 2002–04; *b* 8 July 1945; *d* of late William Tom Coombs and Beatrice Mabel Coombs (*née* Angel). *Educ*: Univ. of Newcastle upon Tyne (BA Hons). Joined FCO, 1967; Bonn, 1971–73; Latin American floater, 1974–75; Zagreb, 1976–79; FCO, 1979–82; La Paz, 1982–86; Rome, 1987–91; FCO, 1991–95; Beijing, 1995–98; Ambassador to Mongolia, 1999–2001. Hon. Mem., Queen's Messenger Corps, 2001. *Recreations*: listening to classical music, reading, flora.

**COOMBS, Ven. Peter Bertram**; Archdeacon of Reigate, 1988–95, now Emeritus; *b* 30 Nov. 1928; *s* of Bertram Robert and Margaret Ann Coombs; *m* 1953, Catherine Ann (*née* Buckwell); one *s* one *d*. *Educ*: Reading Sch.; Bristol Univ. (MA 1960); Clifton Theological Coll. Curate, Christ Church, Beckenham, 1960–64; Rector, St Nicholas, Nottingham, 1964–68; Vicar, Christ Church, New Malden, 1968–75; Rural Dean of Kingston upon Thames, 1970–75; Archdeacon of Wandsworth, 1975–88. *Recreations*: walking, sketching. *Address*: 92 Locks Heath Park Road, Locks Heath, Southampton SO31 6LZ. *T*: (01489) 577288.

**COOMBS, Simon Christopher**; Managing Agent, South Swindon Conservative Association, 2001–04; *b* 21 Feb. 1947; *s* of late Ian Peter Coombs and Rachel Robins Coombs; *m* 1st, 1983, Kathryn Lee Coe Royce (marr. diss. 2003; she *d* 2011); 2nd, 2017, Laura Ann Holiday (*d* 2018). *Educ*: Wycliffe Coll.; Reading University (BA, MPhil). Marketing Executive, British Telecom and Post Office, Data and Telex, 1970–82; Marketing Manager, Telex Networks, British Telecom, 1982–83; Business Develt Advr, Inst. of Customer Service, 1997–2001. Mem., Southern Electricity Consultative Council, 1981–84. Reading Borough Council: Mem., 1969–84; Chm., Transportation Cttee, 1976–83; Vice-Chm., Policy Cttee, 1976–83; Dep. Leader, 1976–81; Chief Whip, 1983. MP (C) Swindon, 1983–97; contested (C) Swindon South, 1997, 2001. PPS to Minister of State for Industry and IT, 1984–85, to Parly Under-Sec. of State DoE, and Minister of State for the Environment, 1985, to Sec. of State for Scotland, 1993–95, to Pres. of BoT, 1995–97. Member: Select Cttee on Employment, 1987–92; British-American Parly Gp, 1983–; CPA, 1983–97; Chairman: Cable TV Gp, 1987–97 (Sec., 1986–87); British Malawi Parly Gp, 1985–93 (Sec., 1985–89); Pres., Parly Food and Health Forum, 1993–97 (Chm., 1989–93), Sec., 1985–89); Treasurer: Parly IT Cttee, 1987–97; Anglo-Malta Parly Gp, 1994–97; Sec., Anglo-Tunisia Parly Gp, 1994–97. Vice-Chairman: Cons. Tourism Cttee, 1988–92 (Chm., 1992–97); All Party Tourism Cttee, 1992–97; All Party Manuf. Gp, 1993–97; All Party Exports Gp, 1993–97; Sec., Cons. Employment Cttee, 1991; Chm., Cons. Party, Wessex Area, 1980–83; Chm., Wessex Area Young Conservatives, 1973–76; Pres., Wilts Young Conservatives, 1984–97. Pres., Swindon Music Fest., 1987–2004; Vice-Chm., 1997–2014, Chm., 2014–, Ralph Vaughan Williams Soc.; Mem. Cttee, English Music Fest., 2002–05. Gov., Wycliffe Coll., 1995–2006. Proj. Manager, Blandford Railway Arches Trust, 2014–17. *Recreations*: music, cricket, philately, reading, book-collecting, photography. *Address*: 24 Wellsworth Lane, Rowlands Castle, Hants PO9 6BY. *Club*: Hampshire Cricket.

**COONEY, David John**; Ambassador of Ireland to Italy, Libya and San Marino, 2017; *b* London, 29 April 1954; *m* Geraldine O'Kelly; one *s* three *d*. *Educ*: Univ. of Keele (BA Hons Politics and Hist.). Exec. Officer, Dept of Agric., Ireland, 1976–78; Admin. Officer, Dept of Public Service, 1978–79; Department of Foreign Affairs: Third Secretary: Inf. Sect., 1979–80; Develt Cooperation Div., 1980–81; Sec., Embassy to the Holy See, 1981–85; Third Sec., Political Div., 1985–86; Private Sec. to Sec.-Gen., 1986–88; Sec., Embassy of Ireland, Vienna, 1988–89; First Secretary: Econ. Div., 1989–90; (Antici), Perm. Repn to EU, Brussels, 1990–93; Counsellor, Eur. Corresp., 1994; Coordinator of White Paper on Irish For. Policy, 1994–95; Counsellor: Hd, Political Sect., Anglo-Irish Div. (participated in negotiation of Good Friday Agreement), 1995–98; Dep. Perm. Rep. to OECD, Paris, 1998–2000; Minister-Counsellor, Paris, 2000; Ambassador, Dep. Perm. Rep. to UN, NY, 2000–01; Political Dir, Asst Sec.-Gen., 2001–05; Perm. Rep. to UN, NY, 2005–07; Ambassador to Court of St James's, 2007–09; Sec. Gen., Dept of For. Affairs and Trade (formerly Dept of For. Affairs), 2009–14; Ambassador: to the Holy See, 2012–14; to Spain, Tunisia and Andorra, 2014–17.

**COONEY, Lorna**; *see* Fitzsimons, L.

**COONEY, Raymond George Alfred, (Ray)**, OBE 2005; actor, author, director, theatrical producer; created Theatre of Comedy at Shaftesbury Theatre, and Little Theatre of Comedy at Ambassadors Theatre, 1983; purchased The Playhouse, London, 1992; *b* 30 May 1932; *s* of Gerard Cooney and Olive (*née* Clarke); *m* 1962, Linda Dixon; two *s*. *Educ*: Alleyn's Sch., Dulwich. First appeared in *Song of Norway*, Palace, 1946; toured in Wales, 1954–56; subseq. played in: *Dry Rot* and *Simple Spymen*, Whitehall; *Mousetrap*, *Ambassador*; *Charlie Girl*, *Adelphi*; *Not Now Darling*, *Savoy* (also film); *Not Now Comrade* (film); *Run for your Wife*, Guildford; *Two into One*, Leicester and Guildford; *Caught in the Net*, Windsor; (and dir) *It Runs in the Family*, Playhouse, 1992; (and dir) *Funny Money*, Playhouse, 1995; *The Chiltern Hundreds*, Vaudeville, 1999. Productions (some jointly) include: *Thark* (revival); *Doctor at Sea*; *The Queen's Highland Servant*; *My Giddy Aunt*; *Move Over Mrs Markham* (revival, 2018); *The Mating Game*; *Lloyd George Knew My Father*; *That's No Lady-That's My Husband*; *Say Goodnight to Grandma*; *Two and Two Make Sex*; *At the End of the Day*; *Why Not Stay for Breakfast?*; *A Ghost on Tiptoe*; *My Son's Father*; *The Sacking of Norman Banks*; *The Bedwinner*; *The Little Hut*; *Springtime for Henry*; *Saint Joan*; *The Trials of Oscar Wilde*; *The Dame of Sark*; *Jack the Ripper*; *There Goes the Bride* (and played leading role, Ambassadors, 1974); *Ipi Tombi*; *What's a Nice Country Like US Doing In a State Like This?*; *Some of My Best Friends Are Husbands*; *Banana Ridge*; *Fire Angel*; *Elvis*; *Whose Life is it Anyway?* (London and NY); *Clouds*; *Chicago*; *Bodies*; *Beatlemania*; *Not Now Darling* (revival); *Hello Dolly* (revival); *Duet for One* (London and NY); *They're Playing Our Song*; *Children of a Lesser God*; *Run for your Wife*; *Aladdin*; *See How They Run*; *Pygmalion*; *Two Into One* (revival, 2014); *Passion Play*; *Loot* (revival); *Intimate Exchanges*; *Wife Begins at Forty*; *An Italian Straw Hat* (revival); *It Runs in the Family*; *Out of Order*; *Fools Rush In*; *Run for your Wife 2*; *Caught in the Net*; *Over the Moon*; *Twice Upon a Time*; *Stop Dreamin'*. *Publications*: (with H. and M. Williams) *Charlie Girl*, 1965; *plays*: (with Tony Hilton) *One for the Pot*, 1961; *Chase Me Comrade*, 1964; (with Tony Hilton) *Stand by your Bedouin*, 1966; (with John Chapman) *Not Now Darling*, 1967; (with John Chapman) *My Giddy Aunt*, 1968; (with John Chapman) *Move Over Mrs Markham*, 1969; (with Gene Stone) *Why Not Stay for Breakfast?*, 1970; (with John Chapman) *There Goes the Bride*, 1973; *Run for Your Wife*, 1981; *Two into One*, 1983; *Wife Begins at Forty*, 1986; *It Runs in the Family*, 1989;

Out of Order, 1990; Funny Money, 1996; Caught in the Net, 2000; (with Michael Cooney) Tom, Dick and Harry, 2003; Twice in a Lifetime, 2010. *Recreations:* tennis, swimming. *Address:* Ridge House, Forest Side, Epping, Essex CM16 4ED.

**COOPER**; *see* Ashley-Cooper, family name of Earl of Shaftesbury.

**COOPER**, family name of **Viscount Norwich** and **Baron Cooper of Windrush**.

**COOPER OF WINDRUSH**, Baron *cr* 2014 (Life Peer), of Chipping Norton in the County of Oxfordshire; **Andrew Timothy Cooper**; Founder and Director, Populus Group Ltd, since 2003; *b* Twickenham, Middx, 9 June 1963; *s* of late Ian Roger and Brenda Muriel Cooper; *m* 2000, Elizabeth Fiona (*née* Campbell); three *d*. *Educ:* Reigate Grammar Sch.; London Sch. of Econs and Political Sci. (BSc Econ 1985). Policy Researcher, SDP, 1986–87; Political Advr to Rt Hon. David Owen, MP, 1987–90; Hd of Res., Social Market Foundn, 1994–95; Dep. Dir of Res., 1995–97, Dir of Political Strategy, 1997–99, Cons. Party; Dir, Live Strategy Ltd, 2000; Dir of Strategy, Prime Minister's Office, 2011–13. *Publications:* contributed to: Blue Tomorrow, 2001; The Blue Book on Health, 2002; The Blue Book on Transport, 2002; Philip Gould: an unfinished life, 2012. *Recreations:* watching Manchester Utd, visiting the USA, cooking Spanish food. *Address:* House of Lords, SW1A 0PW; Populus, 10 Northburgh Street, EC1V 0AT. *T:* (020) 7253 9900, *Fax:* (020) 7253 9911.

**COOPER, Adam**; dancer, choreographer and actor; *b* 1971; *m* 2000, Sarah Wildor, *qv*; one *s* one *d*. *Educ:* Arts Educational Sch.; Royal Ballet Sch. Royal Ballet, 1989–97: Principal Dancer, 1994; main rôles include: Prince Rudolf, in Mayerling; Kings of the North and South, in Prince of the Pagodas; Romeo, and Tybalt, in Romeo and Juliet; Lescaut, in Manon; Espada, in Don Quixote; created rôles in Bloodlines, Ebony Concerto, Tombeaux, Firstext, Room of Cooks; with Adventures in Motion Pictures: The Swan, in Swan Lake, 1995; The Pilot, in Cinderella, 1998; On Your Toes (also choreog.), Leicester Haymarket, 2002, RFH, 2003; Singin' in the Rain, Sadler's Wells, 2004, Chichester, 2011, Palace Th., 2012; Sky Masterson, in Guys and Dolls, Piccadilly, 2006; The Wizard of Oz, RFH, 2008; Shall We Dance (also choreog.), Sadler's Wells, 2009; with Adam Cooper Productions, Les Liaisons Dangereuses (also choreog.), Japan, then Sadler's Wells, 2005; *choreography* includes, Grand Hotel, Donmar Warehouse, 2004; Candide, Menier Chocolate Factory, 2013, Geneva, 2016; for Scottish Ballet: Elegy for Two; Reflections for Images of Dance; Sunny Afternoon, Harold Pinter Th., 2014; Evita, Copenhagen, 2014; Gefährliche Liebschaften (also Dir), Munich, 2016; *television:* Madame Bovary, 2000. Dir, musical, Simply Cinderella, Curve, Leicester, 2008. Dir of Boys, London Studio Theatre. *Address:* c/o Jean Diamond, Diamond Management, 31 Percy Street, W1T 2DD.

**COOPER, Sir Adrian**; *see* Cooper, Sir R. A.

**COOPER, Prof. Aldwyn John Richard**, PhD; Vice Chancellor and Chief Executive, Regent's University London, since 2013; *b* Dulwich, 27 May 1949; *s* of Robert and May Cooper; *m* 1973, Rosalind Patricia Meyer; one *s* one *d*. *Educ:* Dulwich Coll.; Sir John Cass Coll., subseq. City of London Poly. (BSc 1st Cl. Special Hons Psychol. 1972); Bristol Univ. (PhD Cognitive Psychol. 1975). Jun. Engr, Mott, Hay and Anderson, 1969; Demonstrator in Psychol., Bristol Univ., 1973–75; Harkness Fellow, Stanford and Berkeley Univs, 1975–76; Sen. Lectr, Open Univ., 1976–80; Prof. of Information Systems, Henley Mgt Coll., 1980–87; Man. Dir, Henley Distance Learning, 1983–87; Business Gp Dir, Open Coll., 1987–90; Man. Dir, Workhouse Television, 1990–99; Pro Vice Chancellor, Univ. of Glamorgan, 2000–07; Dean, Glamorgan Business Sch., 2004–06; Principal, Regent's Coll., London, 2007–13. Mem., Crown Estates Paving Commn, 2016–. FRSA. *Publications:* (with M. Blakstad) The Communicating Organisation, 2005. *Recreations:* reading, theatre, travel, wine, gastronomy, perfumes, teddy bears, flying. *Address:* South Lodge, Regent's University London, Inner Circle, Regent's Park, NW1 4NS. *T:* (020) 7487 7506. *E:* coopera@regents.ac.uk.

**COOPER, Sir Alexander (Paston Astley)**, 7th Bt *cr* 1821, of Gadebridge, Hertfordshire; *b* 1 Feb. 1943; *o s* of Sir Patrick Graham Astley Cooper, 6th Bt and Audrey Anne Jervoise, *d* of Major D. P. J. Collas; *S* father, 2002; *m* 1974, Minnie Margaret, *d* of Charles Harrison. *Heir: kinsman* Gerald Nigel Astley Cooper [*b* 8 June 1916; *m* 1st, 1941, Mary Constance Piercy (marr. diss. 1945); one *d*; 2nd, 1951, Joan Ryland, *d* of Dr Bernard Wall; one *s* one *d*]. *Address:* 8 Berkshire Close, Leigh-on-Sea, Essex SS9 4RT.

**COOPER, Prof. Andrew Ian**, PhD; FRS 2015; Professor of Chemistry, since 2003, Founding Director, Centre for Materials Discovery, since 2007, and Academic Director, Materials Innovation Factory, since 2016, University of Liverpool; *m* Julie; two *s*. *Educ:* Univ. of Nottingham (BSc Chem. 1991; PhD 1994). 1851 Fellow and Royal Soc. NATO Fellow, Univ. of N Carolina at Chapel Hill, 1995–97; Ramsay Meml Res. Fellow, Melville Lab. for Polymer Synthesis, Univ. of Cambridge, 1997–99; Fellow, Darwin Coll., Cambridge, 1997–99; University of Liverpool: Royal Soc. Res. Fellow, 1999; Hd of Chem., 2007–09; Hd, Sch. of Physical Scis, 2010–11. Award in Environmentally Friendly Polymers, 2005, McBain Medal, 2007, Corday-Morgan Prize, 2009, Tilden Prize, 2014, RSC. *Address:* Department of Chemistry, University of Liverpool, Crown Street, Liverpool L69 7ZD.

**COOPER, Ven. Annette Joy**; Archdeacon of Colchester, 2004–19, now Archdeacon Emeritus; *b* 15 Nov. 1953; *d* of Harry Whitaker and Grace Mary Whitaker (*née* Parnham, later James); *m* 1972, Andrew John Cooper; two *s*. *Educ:* Lilley and Stone Newark Girls' High Sch.; Open Univ. (BA 1980); London Univ. (CQSW, DipSW 1985, ext.); Dip. Religious Studies, Southwark Ordination Course, 1988; Durham Univ. (MA Theol. and Ministry 2013). Local Authority social worker, 1979–88. Ordained deacon, 1988, priest, 1994; NSM, St Peter, Pembury, and full-time Asst Chaplain, Tunbridge Wells HA, 1988–91; full-time Chaplain, Bassetlaw Hosp. and Community Services NHS Trust, 1991–96; Priest i/c Edwinstowe St Mary, 1996–2004. Chaplain: Center Parcs, Sherwood, 1996–2000; Southwell Diocesan Mothers' Union, 1996–99; Area Dean, Worksop, 1999–2004. Hon. Canon: Southwell Minster, 2002–04; Chelmsford Cathedral, 2004–. Regl Rep. to House of Bishops, 2013–16. Non-exec. Dir, Allchurches Trust Ltd, 2008–18. Permission to Officiate: Dio. of Chelmsford, 2019–; Dio. of St Edmundsbury and Ipswich, 2019–. *Publications:* It's Hard to Say Goodbye, 1994. *Recreations:* sailing, singing, entertaining family and friends. *Address:* 1 Fox Hill, Hollesley, Woodbridge, Suffolk IP12 3RD.

**COOPER, Anthony**; *see* Cooper, Derek A.

**COOPER, Anthony William**, CBE 2003; Principal, Aldercar Community Language College, 1995–2014; *b* 22 Sept. 1952; *s* of Lawrence and Mary Cooper; *m* 1985, Susan Margaret Howard; four *d*. *Educ:* Leeds Univ. (BEd Hons 1975); Nottingham Univ. (MEd 1982). Teacher of Geog., 1975–81, Hd of Humanities, 1981–89, Western Mere Sch., Derbys; Hd of Humanities, High View Community Tech. Sch., Derbys, 1989–90; Dep. Hd, Aldercar Sch., Derbys, 1990–95. Mem., E Midlands Judging Panel, The Teaching Awards, 2001–. FRSA 2003. Nat. Award for Secondary Sch. Leadership, The Teaching Awards, 2000. *Recreations:* reading, antique collections, theatre and concerts, playing an active rôle in supporting grandchildren.

**COOPER, Artemis Clare Antonia**, FRSL; writer; *b* London, 22 April 1953; *d* of 2nd Viscount Norwich, CVO; *m* 1986, Antony James Beevor (*see* Sir A. J. Beevor). *Educ:* Camden Sch. for Girls; St Hugh's Coll., Oxford (BA English Lang. and Lit.). Administrator, Duff Cooper Prize, 1993–. Trustee, 999 Club, Deptford, 2006–13. Dr *hc* York, 2015. FRSL 2016. Chevalier, Ordre des Arts et des Lettres (France), 1997. *Publications:* (ed) A Durable Fire: the letters of Duff and Diana Cooper, 1913–1950, 1983; Cairo in the War, 1939–1945, 1989; Mr Wu and Mrs Stitch: the letters of Evelyn Waugh and Diana Cooper, 1991; Watching in the Dark: a child's fight for life, 1992; (with Antony Beevor) Paris After the Liberation, 1944–49, 1994; Writing at the Kitchen Table: the authorized biography of Elizabeth David, 1999; (ed) Words of Mercury: Patrick Leigh Fermor, 2003; Patrick Leigh Fermor: an adventure, 2012; (ed jtly) The Broken Road: from the Iron Gates to Mount Athos, by Patrick Leigh Fermor, 2013; Elizabeth Jane Howard: a dangerous innocence, 2016. *Recreations:* reading, cooking, walking, peering into other people's windows. *Address:* c/o Felicity Bryan Literary Agency, 2A North Parade, Oxford OX2 6LX. *T:* (01865) 513816. *E:* agency@felicitybryan.com. *W:* www.artemiscooper.com.
*See also* Viscount Norwich.

**COOPER, Air Cdre Barbara**, CBE 2003 (OBE 2001); Senior Member of Council, National Trust, 2016–18 (Member, 2013–16); *b* Kingston, Ont, 23 Nov. 1958; *d* of William Donald and Eva Paxton; *m* 1981, William Cooper. *Educ:* Staffordshire Univ. (Postgrad. Dip. HR 2013). Commnd Air Traffic Control Br., RAF, 1978–85; on sabbatical, 1985–87; personnel rôles, RAF Admin (Sec.) Br., 1987–93; SO to CAS, 1993–97; ascs 1998; OC, Base Support Wing, RAF Lyneham, 1998–2000; Directing Staff, Advanced Comd and Staff Course, Shrivenham, 2000–02; Dep. Dir, Service Personnel Policy (Operational Welfare) and Hd, UK Prisoner of War Inf. Bureau, 2002–05; Dir, RAF Div., JSCSC, Shrivenham, 2005–06; rcds 2007; ACOS Personnel Strategy and Manpower, 2008–10; Comdt, Air Cadets, 2010–12. RAF Volunteer ex-Regular Reserve (Air Cdre), 2013–. Hon. Pres., Stroud, Tetbury and Cirencester Air Cadets, 2012. FCIPD 2012. Trustee, Defence Med. Welfare Service, 2017–. *Recreations:* family and friends, visiting NT properties, theatre, cycling, gardening and growing more veg than the family can politely eat. *Club:* Royal Air Force (Trustee, 2015–).

**COOPER, Rt Rev. Carl Norman**; Chief Executive Officer, Powys Association of Voluntary Organisations, since 2008; *b* 4 Aug. 1960; *s* of Joseph and Kathleen Mary Cooper; *m* 2011, Amanda Clare Williams; one *s* two *d* by a former marriage. *Educ:* St David's University Coll., Lampeter (BA Hons French 1982); Wycliffe Hall, Oxford; Trinity Coll., Carmarthen (MPhil Wales 1999); Univ. of Wales Inst., Cardiff (Postgrad. Cert. Leadership for Collaboration 2010). Ordained deacon, 1985, priest, 1986; Curate, Llanelli, 1985–87; Priest i/c, 1987–88, Rector, 1988–93, Ciliau Aeron, Llannerch Aeron, Dihewyd and Mydroilyn; Rector, Rectorial Benefice of Dolgellau, 1993–2002; Diocesan Warden of Ordinands, Bangor, 1999–2001; Archdeacon of Meirionnydd, 2000–02; Bishop of St Davids, 2002–08. Student in Professional Practice, Univ. of Wales Trinity St David. *Address:* Powys Association of Voluntary Organisations, 30 Ddole Road Industrial Estate/ Ystâd Ddiwydiannol Heol Ddole, Llandrindod Wells, Powys LD1 6DF.

**COOPER, Sir Cary (Lynn)**, Kt 2014; CBE 2001; 50th Anniversary Professor of Organizational Psychology and Health, Alliance Manchester Business School (formerly Manchester Business School), University of Manchester, since 2015; *b* 28 April 1940; adopted British nationality, 1993; *s* of Harry and Caroline Cooper; *m* 1984, Rachel Faith Cooper; two *d*; one *s* one *d* from previous marr. *Educ:* Univ. of California, Los Angeles (BS, MBA); Univ. of Leeds (PhD). FBPsS 1982. Lectr in Psychology, Univ. of Southampton, 1967–73; University of Manchester Institute of Science and Technology: Prof. of Organizational Psychol., subseq. BUPA Prof. of Organizational Psychol. and Health, 1975–2003; Pro-Vice-Chancellor, 1995–2000; Dep. Vice-Chancellor, 2000–02; Prof. of Organizational Psychol. and Health, Lancaster Univ. Mgt Sch., 2003–08, now Dist. Prof.; Pro Vice-Chancellor, Lancaster Univ., 2004–10, 2012–15. Advr to WHO and ILO, 1982–84. Founding Editor, Jl of Organizational Behavior, 1980–; Co-Ed., Internat. Jl Mgt Reviews, 1999–2001; Ed., Stress and Health (formerly Stress Medicine), 2009–15 (Associate Ed., 1987–92; Co-Ed., 1992–2009). Member: Bd of Trustees, Amer. Inst. of Stress, 1984–; Adv. Council, Nat. Inst. of Clin. Applications of Behavioral Medicine, USA; ESRC Research Priorities Bd, 1998–2000; Pres., British Acad. of Management, 1987–90, 1997–2004, 2015–19 (Fellow, 1995); Chm., Sunningdale Inst., Nat. Sch. of Govt, 2004–09; Chm., Global Agenda Council on Chronic Disease and Wellbeing, 2009–10, Mem., Global Agenda Council on Mental Health, 2011–17, World Econ. Forum. President: Inst. of Welfare Officers, 1998–; Internat. Stress Mgt Assoc. (UK), 2000–11; British Assoc. of Counselling and Psychotherapy, 2007–12 (Vice Pres., 2000–06); Relate, 2009–17; CIPD, 2016–. Ambassador, The Samaritans, 2000–10. Myers Lectr, BPsS, 1986; Apothecaries Lect., Soc. of Occupational Medicine, 2001. FRSA 1990; FRSocMed 1995; FRSPH (FRSH 1997); Fellow, Amer. Acad. of Mgt, 1997 (Mem. Bd of Govs, 2000–03; Dist. Service Award, 1998); CCMI (CIMgt 1997); FAcSS (AcSS 2001) (Chm., 2009–15). Hon. Mem., Soc. of Psychosom. Res.; Hon. FFOM 2005; Hon. FRCP 2006; Hon. FRCPI 2008; Hon. FBPsS 2010; Hon. Fellow: Eur. Acad. of Occupational Health Psychol., 2010; IOSH, 2012. MSc Manchester, 1979; Hon. DLitt Heriot-Watt, 1998; Hon. DBA Wolverhampton, 1999; Hon. DSc: Aston, 2002; Sheffield, 2011; Chester, 2017; DUniv Middx, 2003; DLaws Bath, 2014. Lifetime Achievement Award, Div. of Occupational Psychol., BPsS, 2007; Lord Dearing Lifetime Achievement Award for Higher Educn, Times Higher Educn Awards, 2010; HR's Most Influential Thinker, 2015. Series Ed., Advances in Mergers and Acquisitions, 2000–. *Publications:* (jtly) T-Groups, 1971; Group Training for Individual and Organizational Development, 1973; Theories of Group Processes, 1975; Developing Social Skills in Managers, 1976; OD in the US and UK, 1977; (jtly) Understanding Executive Stress, 1978; Advances in Experiential Social Processes, vol. 1, 1978, vol. 2, 1980; (jtly) Stress at Work, 1978; (jtly) Executives under Pressure, 1978; Behavioural Problems in Organizations, 1979; (jtly) The Quality of Working Life in Western and Eastern Europe, 1979; Learning from Others in Groups, 1979; The Executive Gypsy, 1979; Current Concerns in Occupational Stress, 1980; Developing Managers for the 1980's, 1980; (jtly) Combating Managerial Obsolescence, 1980; The Stress Check, 1980; White Collar and Professional Stress, 1981; Improving Interpersonal Relations, 1981; (jtly) Groups at Work, 1981; Executive Families Under Stress, 1981; (jtly) After Forty, 1981; Coping with Stress at Work, 1982; Psychology and Management, 1982; (jtly) Management Education, 1982; (jtly) Introducing Organization Behaviour, 1982; (jtly) High Pressure, 1982; Stress Research, 1983; (jtly) Human Behaviour in Organizations, 1983; (jtly) Stress and the Woman Manager, 1983; Public Faces, Private Lives, 1984; (jtly) Working Women, 1984; (jtly) Psychology for Managers, 1984; Psychosocial Stress and Cancer, 1984; (jtly) Women in Management, 1984; (jtly) The Change Makers, 1985; (jtly) Job Stress and Blue Collar Work, 1985; (jtly) International Review of Industrial and Organizational Psychology, annually 1986–2004; (jtly) Man and Accidents Offshore, 1986; (jtly) Stress and the Nurse Manager, 1986; (jtly) Pilots under Stress, 1986; (jtly) Psycho-social Factors at Work, 1987; (jtly) Retirement in Industrialized Societies, 1987; Living with Stress, 1988; Stress and Breast Cancer, 1988; (jtly) High Fliers, 1988; (jtly) Early Retirement, 1989; (jtly) Career Couples: contemporary lifestyles and how to manage them, 1989; (jtly) Understanding Stress: health care professionals, 1990; (jtly) Managing People at Work, 1990; Industrial and Organizational Psychology: critical writings, 1991; (jtly) Stress

Survivors, 1991; (jtly) Cancer and Stress, 1991; (jtly) Work Psychology, 1991, 2nd edn 1997; (jtly) Stress and Accidents in the Offshore Oil and Gas Industry, 1991; Managing Organizations in 1992, 1991; (jtly) On the Move: the psychology of change and transitions, 1991; Personality and Stress, 1991; (jtly) Mergers and Acquisitions: the human factor, 1992; (jtly) Shattering the Glass Ceiling: the woman manager, 1992; (jtly) Relax: dealing with stress, 1992; (jtly) Women's Career Development, 1992; (jtly) Total Quality and Human Resources, 1992; (jtly) Successful Stress Management, 1993; (jtly) Stress in the Dealing Room, 1993; (jtly) The Workplace Revolution, 1993; (jtly) No Hassle: taking the stress out of work, 1994; (jtly) Business Elites, 1994; Handbook on Stress Medicine and Health, 1995; Trends in Organizational Behaviour, 1995; (jtly) Stress and Employer Liability, 1996, 2nd edn 2001; (jtly) Organizations and the Psychological Contract, 1996; (ed jtly) Blackwell Encyclopedia of Management, 1997; (jtly) Creating Tomorrow's Organizations, 1997; (jtly) Balancing Work, Life and Family, 1998; (ed jtly) Concise Encyclopedia of Management, 1998; (ed) Theories of Organizational Stress, 1998; (jtly) Stress and Strain, 1999; (ed) Who's Who in the Management Sciences, 2000; (ed jtly) Cancer and the Family, 2000; (jtly) Conquer your Stress, 2000; (ed) Classics in Management Thought, 2000; (jtly) Strategic Stress Management, 2000; (jtly) Organizational Stress, 2001; (jtly) Occupational Health Psychology, 2001; (jtly) New World of Work, 2001; (jtly) Emotions at Work, 2001; (ed jtly) International Handbook of Organizational Culture and Climate, 2001; Fundamentals of Organizational Behaviour (4 vols), 2002; (jtly) FT Guide to Executive Health, 2002; (jtly) Workplace Bullying, 2002; (ed jtly) Bullying and Emotional Abuse in the Workplace, 2003; (jtly) Creating a Balance, 2003; (jtly) Destressing Doctors, 2003; (jtly) The Employment Relationship, 2003; (jtly) Managing the Risk of Workplace Stress, 2004; (jtly) Stress: a brief history, 2004; (jtly) Work-Life Integration, 2005; (ed) Leadership and Management in the 21st Century, 2005; (ed) Handbook of Stress Medicine and Health, 2005; (ed jtly) Work, 6 vols, 2005; (ed jtly) Workplace Violence, 2005; (ed jtly) Reinventing Human Resource Management, 2005; Managing Emotions in Mergers and Acquisitions, 2005; (ed jtly) Inspiring Leaders, 2006; (jtly) Managing Value-based Organizations, 2006; (jtly) Happy Performing Managers, 2006; (ed jtly) Positive Organizational Behavior, 2007; (jtly) How to Deal with Stress, 2007, 2010; (jtly) Detox Your Desk, 2007; (jtly) Managing Executive Health, 2008; (jtly) Positively Responsible, 2008; (jtly) Organizational and Work Psychology, 2008; (ed jtly) Research Companion to Emotions in Organizations, 2008; (ed jtly) Building More Effective Organizations, 2008; (ed jtly) Employee Wellbeing Support, 2008; (ed jtly) Long Working Hours Culture, 2008; (jtly) Open Source Leadership, 2009; (jtly) Workplace Psychological Health, 2009; (jtly) Missing Pieces: employee wellbeing, 2009; (jtly) Employee Morale, 2009; (ed jtly) Oxford Handbook of Organizational Wellbeing, 2009; (ed jtly) Oxford Handbook of Personnel Psychology, 2009; (ed jtly) Handbook of Organizational Behavior, 2 vols, 2009; (ed) New Directions in OB, 4 vols, 2009; (ed jtly) Research Companion to Corruption in Organizations, 2009; (ed jtly) International Handbook of Work and Organizational Psychology, 2009; (ed jtly) Handbook of Managerial Behavior and Occupational Health, 2009; (jtly) Leading HR, 2010; (jtly) Coping with Work Stress, 2010; (jtly) Organizational Stress Management, 2010; (jtly) The Science of Occupation Health, 2010; (ed jtly) Risk Business, 2010; (ed jtly) Bullying and Harassment in the Workplace, 2011; (ed jtly) Women and Management, 2011; (ed jtly) Crime and Corruption in Organizations, 2011; (jtly) Wellbeing: productivity and happiness at work, 2011, 2nd edn 2018; (jtly) Doing the Right Thing, 2011; (jtly) Stress in Turbulent Times, 2012; (jtly) Wellbeing and Work, 2012; (jtly) High Engagement Work Culture, 2012; (jtly) OB for Dummies, 2012; (jtly) Downsizing, 2012; (jtly) From Stress to Wellbeing, 2013; (ed jtly) How Can HR Drive Success, 2013; (ed jtly) Building Resilience for Success, 2013; (ed jtly) Wellbeing (6 vols), 2014; (jtly) Solving the Strategy Delusion, 2015; The Economic Crisis and Occupational Stress, 2015; (jtly) Do We Need HR, 2015; (jtly) Why the Social Sciences Matter, 2015; (jtly) Stress Management in the Construction Industry, 2015; (jtly) Handbook on Work-life Balance in Asia, 2015; (jtly) The Outstanding Middle Manager, 2016; (jtly) Routledge Companion to Wellbeing at Work, 2017; (jtly) Myths of Management, 2017; (jtly) Handbook of Stress and Health, 2017; (jtly) Managing Health and Wellbeing in the Public Sector, 2017; (jtly) The Spartan Worker, 2018; (jtly) The Wellbeing Workout, 2019; (jtly) Wellbeing at Work, 2019; articles on social science and medicine, stress medicine. *Recreations:* reading 19th century Russian fiction, living in hope with Manchester City football, enjoying my four children and six grandchildren! *Address:* Alliance Manchester Business School, University of Manchester, Booth Street West, Manchester M15 6PB; 25 Lostock Hall Road, Poynton, Cheshire SK12 1DP. *T:* (01625) 871450.

**COOPER, Prof. Cyrus**, OBE 2015; DL; DM; FRCP, FFPH, FMedSci; Professor of Rheumatology, since 1997 and Director, MRC Lifecourse Epidemiology Unit (formerly MRC Epidemiology Resource Centre), since 2003, University of Southampton; Professor of Epidemiology, University of Oxford, since 2011 (Norman Collisson Professor of Musculoskeletal Sciences, 2007–11); Fellow of St Peter's College, Oxford, since 2007; *b* 14 Feb. 1957; *s* of Dr Sarosh Cooper and Khorshed Cooper; *m* 1984, Margaret O'Donovan; two *s*. *Educ:* Gonville and Caius Coll., Cambridge (BA 1977); St Bartholomew's Hosp., London (MB BS 1980); DM Soton 1985. FRCP 1996; FFPH 2005. Sen. Registrar, Bristol Royal Infirmary, 1988–90; Asst Prof., Mayo Clinic, Minn, 1990–92; Sen. Lectr in Rheumatol., Univ. of Southampton, 1992–97. Chm., Bd of Trustees, Nat. Osteoporosis Soc., 2004–07. FMedSci 2000. DL Hants, 2016. *Publications:* (jtly) Prevention and Treatment of Osteoporosis: a clinician's guide, 2005; original res. contribs to learned jls on epidemiology of osteoporosis, osteoarthritis and other rheumatic disorders, studies into develt origins of coronary heart disease and metabolic syndrome; over 800 research papers with h-index of 119. *Recreations:* cricket, football. *Address:* MRC Lifecourse Epidemiology Unit, University of Southampton, Southampton General Hospital, Southampton SO16 6YD; c/o Nuffield Department of Orthopaedics, Rheumatology and Musculoskeletal Sciences, University of Oxford, Nuffield Orthopaedic Centre, Windmill Road, Oxford OX3 7LD. *Clubs:* Hampshire County Cricket; Southampton FC.

**COOPER, David Antony**; a District Judge (Magistrates' Courts) (formerly Metropolitan Stipendiary Magistrate), 1991–2010; a Deputy District Judge (Magistrates' Courts), 2010–14; *b* 12 June 1945; *s* of Rev. Stanley Francis Cooper and Jane Anne Cooper; *m* 1968, Françoise Armandine Henriette Fourré; three *s*. *Educ:* Sandown Grammar Sch., IoW; Exeter Univ. (LLB); College of Law. Articled clerk, Freshfields, London, 1966–69; admitted Solicitor, 1969; with Heppenstalls, Lymington, 1969–71; Partner, Ellison & Co., Colchester, 1971–91. *Recreations:* life on the Isle of Mull, learning French and staying in France.

**COOPER, Prof. David Edward**; author; Professor of Philosophy, University of Durham, 1986–2008; *b* 1 Oct. 1942; *s* of late Edward Cooper and Lilian Doris Cooper (*née* Turner); *m* 1st, 1971, Patricia Patterson; 2nd, 1980, Sheila Ann Armstrong, *qv* (marr. diss. 1998); 3rd, 2000, Joy Palmer. *Educ:* Highgate Sch.; St Edmund Hall, Oxford; Nuffield Coll., Oxford (MA, BPhil). Lectr in Philosophy, Pembroke and Jesus Colls, Oxford, 1966–69; Asst Prof. of Philosophy, Univ. of Miami, 1969–72; Lectr in Phil. of Educn, Univ. of London Inst. of Educn, 1972–74; Reader in Phil., Univ. of Surrey, 1974–85. Associate Dir, Project Sri Lanka, Durham Univ., 2008–11; Sec. and Trustee, Project Sri Lanka Charity, 2010–. Visiting Professor, Universities of: Khartoum, 1975; Minnesota, 1977; Cape Town, 1979; Heidelberg and Tübingen, 1985; Trinity (Texas), 1986; Alberta, 1987; Vanderbilt, 1990; Malta, 1994; Ruhuna, Sri Lanka, 2006–09; Rivers Distinguished Vis. Prof. of the Humanities, E Carolina Univ., 1998; Vis. Sen. Res. Fellow, KCL, 1991–94; Leverhulme Res. Fellow, 1996–97; AHRB Res. Fellow, 1999–2000; Leverhulme res. grant, 2002–03, 2006–07. Fellow, Internat. Soc. for Intercultural Studies and Res., India, 1993–. Chairman: Phil. of Educn Soc., 1987–90; Friedrich Nietzsche Soc., 1991–94; President: Mind Assoc., 1991; Aristotelian Soc., 1993–94; Member: Council, Royal Inst. of Philosophy, 1995–2014; Exec. Cttee, Royal Inst. of Phil., 1997–2009. Hon. Diploma, Univ. Nacional de Educación a Distancia, Madrid, 1992. *Publications:* Philosophy and the Nature of Language, 1973; Presupposition, 1974; Knowledge of Language, 1975; (ed) The Manson Murders, 1975; Illusions of Equality, 1980; Authenticity and Learning, 1983; Metaphor, 1986; (ed) Education, Values and Mind, 1986; Existentialism: a reconstruction, 1994, 2nd rev. edn 1999; (ed jtly) The Environment in Question, 1992; (ed) Blackwell's Companion to Aesthetics, 1993; (ed jtly) Just Environments, 1995; World Philosophies: an historical introduction, 1995, 2nd edn 2002; Heidegger, 1996; (ed) Aesthetics: the classic readings, 1997, 2nd edn 2019; (ed) Ethics: the classic readings, 1998; (ed) Epistemology: the classic readings, 1998; (ed jtly) Spirit of the Environment, 1998; (ed) Metaphysics: the classic readings, 1999; The Measure of Things: humanism, humility and mystery, 2002; Meaning, 2003; (with S. P. James) Buddhism, Virtue and Environment, 2005; A Philosophy of Gardens, 2006; (ed jtly) Philosophy: the classic readings, 2009; Convergence with Nature: a Daoist perspective, 2012; Sunlight on the Sea: reflecting on reflections, 2013; (ed jtly) Key Thinkers on the Environment, 2017; Senses of Mystery: engaging with nature and the meaning of life, 2017; Animals and Misanthropy, 2018; Street Dog: a Sri Lankan story, 2018; Old Stripe, 2019. *Recreations:* music, walking, wildlife. *E:* david.cooper001@yahoo.com.

**COOPER, (Derek) Anthony**; Member, Nuclear Decommissioning Authority, 2005–11; *b* 11 Dec. 1943; *s* of Donald Cooper and Freda Cooper (*née* Sheridan); *m* 1967, June Iley; one *s* two *d*; one *s*. *Educ:* Whitehaven Grammar Sch.; Edinburgh Univ. (BSc Forestry and Wild Life Mgt). Forest Officer, Forestry Commn, 1967–76; Institution of Professionals, Managers and Specialists: Negotiations Officer, 1976–79; Asst Sec., 1979–82; Asst Gen. Sec., 1982–87; Dep. Gen. Sec., 1987–91; Gen. Sec., Engrs and Managers Assoc., 1991–2001; Jt Gen. Sec., Prospect, 2001–02; Chm., Nuclear Industry Assoc. (formerly British Nuclear Industry Forum), 2002–05. Chairman: Aid Tspt Ltd, 1993–98; 4U@work Ltd, 2000–03; PPP Consultancy Ltd, 2002–06; Chairman of Trustees: Combined Nuclear Industry Pension Plan Ltd, 2006–13; Magnox Electric Gp of Electricity Supply Pension Scheme Ltd, 2009–15; Trustee, BNFL Gp Pension Scheme Ltd, 2008–12; Dir, Way Ahead Training Ltd, 1999–2003. Commissioner: Postal Services Commn, 2000–10; Forestry Commn, 2001–06. Member: Govt Energy Adv. Panel, 1993–2003; EU Energy Consultative Cttee, 1998–2001; Strategy Bd, 2002–04, Investment Cttee, 2003–04, Nuclear Decommissioning Agency Prog. Bd, 2003–04, DTI. Mem., Gen. Council, TUC, 1997–2000. Trustee: Power Aid Logistics, 1993–98; Royal Hosp. for Neuro-disability, Putney, 1995–97. *Recreations:* reading, sailing, walking. *Address:* 55 Rivulet Apartments, Devan Grove, N4 2GS.

See also Rt Hon. Y. Cooper.

**COOPER, Wing Comdr Donald Arthur**, CBE 1990; AFC 1961; Chief Inspector, Air Accidents Investigation Branch, Department of Transport, 1986–90; *b* 27 Sept. 1930; *s* of A. A. Cooper and E. B. Cooper (*née* Edmonds); *m* 1958, Belinda, 3rd *d* of Adm. Sir Charles Woodhouse, KCB and Lady Woodhouse; three *s*. *Educ:* Queen's Coll., British Guiana; RAF Coll., Cranwell; BA Open. ATPL (H) 1961, ATPL (A) 1972. FRAeS. Served on fighter and trng sqdns, 1952–56; Empire Test Pilot's Sch., 1957; RAF Farnborough, 1958–60; RAF sc 1961; Sqdn Comdr CFS Helicopter Wing, 1962–64; HQ FTC, 1964–66; Defence Operational Requirements Staff, MoD, 1966–70; joined Accidents Investigation Br., BoT, on retirement, 1970. *Recreations:* walking, ballroom dancing, amateur dramatics. *Address:* 7 Lynch Road, Farnham, Surrey GU9 8BZ.

**COOPER, Edward James Oswald**; Head of Practice, OMS Employment, Slater & Gordon Lawyers; *b* London, 12 June 1959; *s* of Derek Oswald Cooper and Julia Mary Cooper; *m* 1993, Atinuke Olubunmi Alake, (Bobbie); three *s*. *Educ:* Winchester House Sch., Sevenoaks; Tonbridge Sch.; Bristol Univ. (LLB). Admitted solicitor, 1984; Trainee Solicitor, then Asst Solicitor, Simmons & Simmons, 1982–85; Russell Jones & Walker, then Slater & Gordon Lawyers: Asst Solicitor, 1985–88; Nat. Hd, Employment Dept, 1990; Partner, 1988; Nat. Practice Gp Leader (Employment), 2012. Member: Employment Lawyers' Assoc.; Industrial Lawyers' Assoc. Mem., Mange Tout Book Club. *Recreations:* cricket, reading, jazz. *Address:* Slater & Gordon Lawyers, 90 High Holborn, WC1V 6LJ. *T:* (020) 7657 1506, *Fax:* (020) 7657 1546. *E:* Edward.Cooper@slatergordon.co.uk. *Clubs:* MCC; Crocodiles Cricket.

**COOPER, (Edward) John**; Chief Executive, Hammersmith Hospitals NHS Trust, 1994–2001; *b* 21 April 1943; *s* of John and Rosalind Cooper; *m* 1977, Susan Hitchin. *Educ:* Malvern Coll.; Nottingham Univ. (BA); Manchester Business Sch. (MBA 1971). AHSM 1969. Nat. Admin. Trng Scheme, NHS, 1965–66; United Liverpool Hosps, 1966–67; Univ. Hosp., S Manchester, 1967–69; various posts, Llewelyn-Davies Internat., 1971–78; S Australian Health Commn, 1978–85 (Dep. Chm. and Comr, 1983–85); Dist Gen. Manager, Hampstead HA, 1985–91; Chief Exec., Royal Free Hampstead NHS Trust, 1991–94. Mem. Council, RCP, 2004–08. Hon. FRCP 2008. *Recreations:* performing arts, travel. *Address:* 74 High Street, Hemingford Grey, Cambs PE28 9BN.

**COOPER, Eileen**, OBE 2016; RA 2001; RE 2002; artist; Keeper of the Royal Academy, 2011–17; *b* 10 June 1953; *d* of John Lawrence and Marjorie Cooper; *m* 1983, David Malcolm Southward; two *s*. *Educ:* Goldsmiths' Coll., London (DipAD); RCA (MA Painting; FRCA 2006, Hon. FRCA 2011). Part-time Tutor, Printmaking: RCA, 1994–2008; Royal Acad. Schs, 2005–; Artist in Residence, Dulwich Picture Gall., 1998–99. Solo exhibitions include: at Art First, London: Open Secrets, 1998; Second Skin: Eileen Cooper in the 80's and 90's, touring show, 1999; Raw Material Part I and Part II, Dulwich Picture Gall., 2000; Works on Paper, 2002; Passions: new work on paper, Art First, NY, 2002; A Celebration, Art First Projects, NY, 2003; Eileen Cooper 50 New Works, 2003; Time of Your Life, 2005; Deeper Water, 2007; Dreams of Elsewhere, 2009; Collages, Royal Acad. Friends Room, 2010; Showing Off, 2011; Edge to Edge, 2013; In the Garden, Rabley Drawing Centre, 2015; Hide and Seek, work on paper 1977–2014, RA, 2015, Swindon Mus. and Art Gall., Mercer Art Gall., Harrogate, 2016; Love-In-Idleness, Rook and Raven Gall., London, 2016; Between the Lines, Galerie Miro, Prague, 2016; A Woman's Skin, Wolfson Coll., Cambridge, 2017; Till the Morning Comes, Fine Art Soc., London, 2017; Under the Same Moon, Letitia Gall., Beirut, 2018; Forest, Rabley Gall., Wilts, 2018; Short Stories, Sims Reed Gall., London, 2019. Numerous gp exhibns in Britain, Europe, USA and Asia; works in public and private collections worldwide. Curator: Confluence, APT Gallery, 2009; RA Summer Show, 2009–14; Encounter, Royal Acad. in Asia, 2012, Royal Acad. in Middle E, Doha, 2013; Co-ordinator, RA Summer Show, 2017. Hon. Fellow, Murray Edwards Coll., Cambridge, 2016. Hon. DArt Southampton Solent, 2013. *Publications:* (cover) Women who Run with the Wolves, by Clarissa Pinkola Estés, 1998; (cover and illus.) Meeting Midnight, by Carol Ann Duffy, 1999; *relevant publication:* Between the Lines, by Martin Gayford and Sara Lee, 2015. *Recreations:* reading, walking. *Address:* Royal Academy of Arts, Burlington House, Piccadilly, W1J 0BD.

**COOPER, Prof. (Elizabeth) Helen,** PhD, DLitt; FBA 2006; Professor of Medieval and Renaissance English, University of Cambridge, 2004–14, now Emeritus; Fellow, Magdalene College, Cambridge, 2004–14, now Life Fellow; *b* 6 Feb. 1947; *d* of Sir Percy Edward, (Sir Peter), Kent, FRS and (Margaret) Betty Kent; *m* 1970, Michael George Cooper (*d* 2007); two *d*. *Educ*: New Hall, Cambridge (BA 1968, MA; PhD 1972); DLitt Oxford 1996. Jun. Res. Fellow, New Hall, Cambridge, 1971–74; Beaverbrook Tutorial Fellow in English and Univ. CUF Lectr, University Coll., Oxford, 1978–2004, now Emeritus Fellow (Hon. Fellow, 2014). Editor for Old and Middle English, Medium Ævum, 1989–2002. Pres., New Chaucer Soc., 2000–02. Trustee: Prince's Teaching Inst. 2013–; Shakespeare's Birthplace Trust, 2013–17. Hon. DLitt Washington and Lee, 2001. *Publications*: Pastoral: Mediaeval into Renaissance, 1978; Great-Grandmother Goose, 1978; The Structure of the Canterbury Tales, 1983; Oxford Guides to Chaucer: The Canterbury Tales, 1989, 2nd edn 1996; (ed) Sir Thomas Malory: Le Morte Darthur, 1998; The English Romance in Time, 2004; Shakespeare and the Medieval World, 2010; numerous articles in books and periodicals. *Address*: Magdalene College, Cambridge CB3 0AG. *E*: ehc31@cam.ac.uk.

**COOPER, Sir (Frederick Howard) Michael C.;** *see* Craig-Cooper.

**COOPER, Gareth;** *see* Cooper, W. G.

**COOPER, Gen. Sir George (Leslie Conroy),** GCB 1984 (KCB 1979); MC 1953; DL; Chief Royal Engineer, 1987–93; *b* 10 Aug. 1925; *s* of late Lt-Col G. C. Cooper and Mrs Y. V. Cooper, Bulmer Tye House, Sudbury; *m* 1957, Cynthia Mary Hume; one *s* one *d*. *Educ*: Downside Sch.; Trinity Coll., Cambridge (wartime short course). Commnd 1945; served with Bengal Sappers and Miners, 1945–48; Korea, 1952–53; psc 1956; jssc 1959; Instructor, RMA Sandhurst, 1959–62 and Staff Coll., Camberley, 1964; Brevet Lt-Col, 1964; GSO1, 1st Div., 1964–66; CRE, 4th Div., 1966–68; MoD, 1968–69; Comdr, 19th Airportable Bde, 1969–71; Royal Coll. of Defence Studies, 1972; Dep. Dir Army Trng, 1973–74; GOC W District, 1974–75; Dir, Army Staff Duties, 1976–79; GOC SE District, 1979–81; Adjt-Gen., 1981–84, retd. ADC General to the Queen, 1982–84. Mem., UK Bd of Management, and Dir of Management Develt, GEC, 1985–86. Colonel Commandant: RE, 1980–93; RPC, 1981–85; Col, Queen's Gurkha Engineers, 1981–91. Mem. Council, Nat. Army Mus., 1981–95. Chm., Knightstone Syndicate Management (formerly HGP Managing Agency), 1991–93 (Dir, 1990–91). Lay Rep., Senate and Bar Council Disciplinary Bodies, 1984–90. Chm., 1980–95, Jt Pres., 1995–2002, Jt Patron, 2002–, Infantile Hypercalcæmia Foundn, later Williams Syndrome Foundation; Chm., Princess Alexandra's NHS Hosp. Trust, 1994–96; Mem. Council, Action Research (formerly Nat. Fund for Res. into Crippling Diseases), 1982–95; Trustee, Harlow War Meml Inst., 1990–2014; Patron, Pahar Trust, 1993–2010. DL Essex, 1990. *Publications*: (with D. A. Alexander) The Bengal Sappers 1803–2003, 2003; Fight, Dig and Live: the story of the Royal Engineers in the Korean War, 2011; articles and book reviews. *Recreations*: writing, gardening, fighting old age. *Address*: 37 Mulberry Green, Old Harlow, Essex CM17 0EY. *T*: (01279) 427214. *Club*: Army and Navy.

**COOPER, Gilead Patrick;** QC 2006; *b* 24 April 1955; *s* of Lionel and Lily Cooper; *m* 2016, Geneviève Helleringer; one *s* one *d*. *Educ*: Haileybury; Christ Church, Oxford (MA); City Univ. (Dip. Law). Called to the Bar, Middle Temple, 1983; in practice specialising in Chancery law. *Publications*: contributed: Tolley's Pensions Law; Palmer on Bailment, 2009. *Recreations*: anything other than sport. *Address*: Wilberforce Chambers, 8 New Square, Lincoln's Inn, WC2A 3QP. *T*: (020) 7306 0102. *E*: sibyl@cumae.me. *Club*: Garrick.

**COOPER, Helen;** *see* Cooper, E. H.

**COOPER, Imogen,** CBE 2007; concert pianist; *b* 28 Aug. 1949; *d* of late Martin Du Pré Cooper, CBE and Mary Cooper (*née* Stewart); *m* 1982, John Alexander Batten (marr. diss. 2002). *Educ*: Paris Conservatoire, with Jacques Février and Yvonne Lefébure, 1961–67 (Premier Prix, 1967); Vienna, with Alfred Brendel, 1970. Plays regularly with all major British orchestras; regular appearances at Proms, 1975–; first British pianist, and woman, to have appeared in South Bank Piano Series, 1975; British festivals include Bath, Cheltenham, Harrogate, Brighton, Edinburgh and Aldeburgh. Overseas engagements incl. concerts with London Symphony Orch., Berlin, Vienna, New York, Los Angeles, Boston, Philadelphia and Cleveland Philharmonic Orchestras, and regular tours to Australasia, Holland, France, Scandinavia, USA and Japan. Humanitas Vis. Prof. of Classical Music and Music Educn, St John's Coll., Oxford, 2012–13. Recordings include: Schubert Live; Schumann solo and lieder (with Wolfgang Holzmair); solo Mozart concerti; Wigmore Hall Live Series Wolf lieder and solo; Chopin, Liszt/Wagner solo. Hon. RAM, 1997. Mozart Meml Prize, 1969. *Recreations*: sea swimming, architecture, gastronomy. *Address*: c/o Askonas Holt, 15 Fetter Lane, EC4A 1BW. *T*: (020) 7400 1700.

**COOPER, Jane Elizabeth Louise;** communications consultant; Senior External Communications Adviser, Crown Agents, 2016–18; *b* New York City, 9 Aug. 1958; *d* of Bryan Cooper and Patricia Cooper; *m* 2005, David Robertson; one *s* one *d*. *Educ*: Leeds Univ. (BA Hons Eng. Lit. 1979); Law Soc. Finals 1993; Univ. of London (MA Hist. of Art 2007). Editl Asst, BT Batsford, 1981–87; Sec., All Party Human Rights Gp, 1987–89; Hd, Govt Relns, Amnesty Internat., 1989–95; Dir, Westminster Strategy, 1995–2001; communications consultant, 2001–05; Head of Communications: Leigh Day & Co., 2001–05; Enforcement and Compliance, HMRC, 2005–08; Director of Communications: DCSF, 2008–09; DCMS, 2009–10; Dir of Communications, then Dir of Communications and Brand, UNICEF UK, 2011–16. Dir, Death Penalty Proj., 2007–13. Trustee: Internat. Broadcast Trust, 2013–15; ShareAction, 2017–. Gov., City Lit, London, 2011– (Dep. Chm., 2017–). *Publications*: International Human Rights (with David Mepham), 2004. *Recreations*: swimming, scuba diving. *Address*: 69 Queen Elizabeth's Walk, N16 5UG. *T*: (020) 8800 4906. *E*: jane.cooper4@btinternet.com.

**COOPER, Jilly, (Mrs Leo Cooper),** CBE 2018 (OBE 2004); author; *b* 21 Feb. 1937; *d* of Brig. W. B. Sallitt, OBE, and Mary Elaine Whincup; *m* 1961, Leo Cooper (*d* 2013); one *s* one *d*. *Educ*: Godolphin Sch., Salisbury. Reporter, Middlesex Independent, Brentford, 1957–59; followed by numerous short-lived jobs as account executive, copy writer, publisher's reader, receptionist, puppy fat model, switchboard wrecker, and very temporary typist. Columnist: Sunday Times, 1969–82; Mail on Sunday, 1982–87. Hon. DLitt: Gloucester, 2009; Anglia Ruskin, 2011. Outstanding Achievement Award, Romantic Novelists' Assoc., 2018; Lifetime Achievement Award, Comedy Women in Print, 2019. *Publications*: How to Stay Married, 1969, rev. edn 2011; How to Survive from Nine to Five, 1970 (new edn as Work and Wedlock, 1978); Jolly Super, 1971; Men and Super Men, 1972; Jolly Super Too, 1973; Women and Super Women, 1974 (new edn as Super Men and Super Women, 1977); Jolly Superlative, 1975; Super Jilly, 1977; Class, 1979; The British in Love, 1980; (with Tom Hartman) Violets and Vinegar, 1980; Supercooper, 1980; Intelligent and Loyal, 1981, re-issued as Mongrel Magic, 1981; Jolly Marsupial, 1982; (with Imperial War Museum) Animals in War, 1983; The Common Years, 1984; Leo and Jilly Cooper on Cricket, 1985; (with Patrick Lichfield) Hot Foot to Zabrieskie Point, the Unipart Calendar Book, 1985; How to Survive Christmas, 1986; Leo and Jilly Cooper on Horse Mania, 1986; Turn Right at the Spotted Dog, 1987; Angels Rush In, 1990; *novels*: Emily, 1975; Bella, 1976; Harriet, 1976; Octavia, 1977; Prudence, 1978; Imogen, 1978; Riders, 1985 (televised, 1993); Rivals, 1988; Polo, 1991; The Man who made Husbands Jealous, 1993 (televised, 1995); Araminta's Wedding, 1993; Appassionata, 1996; Score, 1999; Pandora, 2002; Wicked!, 2006; Jump!, 2010; Mount!, 2016; *short stories*: Love and Other Heartaches, 1981, re-printed as Lisa and Co., 1982; *for children*: Little Mabel, 1980; Little Mabel's Great Escape, 1981; Little Mabel Wins, 1982; Little Mabel Saves the Day, 1985. *Recreations*: merry-making, wild flowers, music, mongrels, greyhounds. *Address*: c/o Curtis Brown, Haymarket House, 28–29 Haymarket, SW1Y 4SP.

**COOPER, John;** *see* Cooper, E. J.

**COOPER, John Gordon;** QC 2010; barrister; writer and broadcaster; Hon. Visiting Professor of Law, Cardiff University, since 2010; *b* Wolverhampton, 15 Sept. 1958; *s* of John Cooper and Mary Cooper. *Educ*: Regis Comp. Sch., Wolverhampton; Univ. of Newcastle (LLB Hons; Butterworth's Law Prizeman 1980). Called to the Bar: Middle Temple, 1983, Bencher, 2012; NSW and Vic, Australia, 1989; Gibraltar, 2013; lawyer, Clifford Chance, London, 1988–89. Member: Crime, Criminal Bar Assoc., 2001–12; Bar Council, 2007–14 (Vice-Chm., Public Affairs Cttee, 2008–11); Cttee, SE Circuit, 2010–15; Dir of Educn, 2012–15. Chm., Iran Tribunal, 2010–13. Pres., League Against Cruel Sports, 2011–15 (Chm., 1992–2012). Member: Working Pty, Nudge Global, 2012–15; Working Party on Assistance Dogs, DEFRA, 2017–. Chm., Adv. Bd, Trust the Mkt, 2015–19; Mem., Adv. Bd, Big Brother Watch, 2016–18. Mem., Bd of Trustees, Prisoners of Conscience, 2010–; Trustee, Citizenship Foundn, 2017–. Sen. Legal Advr to Home Affairs Select Cttee, 2014–18; Legal Advr to Shadow Attorney Gen., 2015–18; Special Advr, Access to Justice Commn, 2015–17. Mem., Adv. Bd, Newcastle Univ. Law Sch., 2012–. Patron, Born Innocent, 2016–. Mem. Labour Party, 1984–. Contested (Lab): NW Surrey, 1987; Amber Valley, 1992. Mem. (Lab) Watford BC, 1991–94 (Vice Chm., Civic Amenities, 1993–94). FRSA 2009. Freeman, City of London, 2011–; Mem., Coopers' Co. Broadcaster on TV and radio, 1982–, incl. presenter and contrib. to progs on BBC, ITV, Sky, Channel 4, Al Jazeera, Radio 4. Writer: plays: The Cure, Royal Court, 1982; Burning Point, Tricycle, 1987; television: The Law Lord, 1991; The Advocates, 1992. Columnist: The Times, 1999–2009; Independent, 2012–15; Dogs Today, 2017–; writer, Observer, 2009–. Ed., Criminal Bar Qly, 2004–19; Consultant Ed., Criminal Law and Justice Weekly, 2010–18. *Publications*: Encyclopedia of Data Protection and Privacy (contrib.), 1998–; Cruelty: an analysis of Article 3, 2003; The Link Between Animal Abuse and Human Violence, 2009; Inquests, 2010; (contrib.) Cases That Changed our Lives, 2010; (contrib.) Sentencing Guidelines, 2013; contrib. articles and feature writer for most legal pubns incl. New Law Jl, Criminal Law Rev., Solicitors Jl and nat. newspapers. *Recreations*: photography, history, Wolverhampton Wanderers, pedalling on a bicycle in the gym but going nowhere. *Address*: Parsonage Farm, Dairy Way, Abbots Langley, Herts WD5 0QJ. *T*: 07973 908288; 25 Bedford Row, WC1R 4HD; (literary) c/o Paul Stevens, Independent Talent, 40 Whitfield Street, W1T 2RH. *E*: johncooperqc@sky.com. *W*: www.johncooperqc.com, www.twitter.com/john_cooper_qc. *Clubs*: Groucho, Chelsea Arts, Home House.

**COOPER, Rev. Canon John Leslie;** Archdeacon of Coleshill, 1990–93; *b* 16 Dec. 1933; *s* of Iris and Leslie Cooper; *m* 1959, Gillian Mary Dodds; two *s* one *d*. *Educ*: Tiffin School, Kingston, Surrey; Chichester Theological Coll. BD 1965, MPhil 1978, London Univ. (External Student). National Service, RA; commissioned, 1952–54. General Electric Co. management trainee, 1954–59; Chichester Theol Coll., 1959–62; Asst Curate, All Saints, Kings Heath, Birmingham, 1962–65; Asst Chaplain, HM Prison, Wandsworth, 1965–66; Chaplain: HM Borstal, Portland, Dorset, 1966–68; HM Prison, Bristol, 1968–72; Research Fellow, Queen's Coll., Birmingham, 1972–73; Priest-in-Charge 1973–81, Vicar 1981–82, St Paul's, Balsall Heath, Birmingham. Examining Chaplain to Bishop of Birmingham, 1981–82; Archdeacon of Aston, and Canon Residentiary, St Philip's Cathedral, Birmingham, 1982–90; Asst Curate, Holy Trinity, Sutton Coldfield, 1993–96. Hon. Canon, Birmingham Cathedral, 1993–97, now Canon Emeritus. *Recreations*: music, reading, travel, carpentry, photography, cookery, painting. *Address*: Flat 9, Ramsay Hall, 9–13 Byron Road, Worthing, W Sussex BN11 3HN. *T*: (01903) 207939.

**COOPER, John Michael;** QC 2014; *b* Newcastle upon Tyne, 14 Aug. 1960; *s* of Michael and Angela Cooper; *m* 1993, Romina; two *d*. *Educ*: Mt St Mary's Coll., Spinkhill; Reading Univ. (LLB). Called to the Bar, Inner Temple, 1985; in practice as barrister, specialising in health and safety and envmtl law, London, 1986–99, Manchester, 1999–2003, London, 2003–. *Recreations*: running marathons, cricket, shooting, wine. *Address*: Crown Office Chambers, 2 Crown Office Row, Temple, EC4Y 7HJ. *T*: (020) 7797 8100. *E*: cooper@crownofficechambers.com. *Club*: MCC.

**COOPER, Rear-Adm. John Spencer,** OBE 1974; *b* 5 April 1933; *s* of Harold Spencer Cooper and Barbara (*née* Highet); *m* 1966, Jacqueline Street (*née* Taylor); two *d*. *Educ*: St Edward's Sch., Oxford; Clare Coll., Cambridge (MA 1959). Joined RN, 1951; served as Lieut on HM Ships Ceylon and Ark Royal; joined Submarines 1966, Polaris Systems Officer in HMS Renown; Comdr 1969; MoD, 1970–73; Flag Officer, Submarines Staff, 1974–76; Captain 1976; Director, Trials, Chevaline programme, 1976–78; Special Proj., RN, Washington, 1978–80; Cdre 1981; Dir, Weapons (Strategic Systems), 1981–83; Dir Gen., Strategic Weapon Systems, 1983–85; Chief Strategic Systems Exec., MoD, 1985–88. Operations Manager: Naval Command and Control Div., Ferranti International, 1988–90; Ferranti Naval Systems, 1990–93.

**COOPER, Julie Anne Margaret Joan;** a District Judge (Magistrates' Courts), since 2018; *b* Perivale, London, 23 March 1960; *d* of Don Ramsey and Joan Ramsey; one *d*. *Educ*: Kneller Girls' Sch., Twickenham; Lancaster Univ. (LLB). Trained at Peters and Peters, 1988–90; founded Maclaverty Cooper Atkins, 1996, specialised in criminal law; a Dep. Dist Judge (Magistrates' Courts), 2000–18. Founder Mem., Spelthorne Domestic Violence Forum. *Recreations*: dog training, theatre, cinema. *Address*: Croydon Magistrates' Court, Barclay Road, Croydon CR9 3NG.

**COOPER, Julie Elizabeth;** MP (Lab) Burnley, since 2015; *b* 20 June 1960; *d* of Robert Calder and Teresa Fletcher (*née* Smith); *m* 1984, Brian Cooper; one *s* one *d*. *Educ*: Colne Park High Sch., Colne; Edge Hill Coll., Ormskirk (BA Hons Eng. Lang. and Lit.). English teacher, Birkdale High Sch., Dewsbury, 1982–84; Librarian, Hagergham High Sch., Burnley, 1990–92; Dir, Coopers Chemist, Burnley, 1992–2010. Shadow Minister: Health, 2016–18; Health and Social Care, 2018–. Mem. (Lab), Burnley BC, 2005–16 (Leader, 2012–14). *Recreations*: travel, film, music, reading. *Address*: House of Commons, SW1A 0AA. *T*: (01282) 425744.

**COOPER, Kenneth Reginald,** CB 1991; Chief Executive, The British Library, 1984–91; *b* 28 June 1931; *s* of Reginald and Louisa May Cooper; *m* 1955, Olga Ruth (*née* Harvey); two *s* two *d*. *Educ*: Queen Elizabeth's Grammar Sch., Barnet; New Coll., Oxford (MA). FIPM; FITD (Pres., 1981–83); FIInfSc (Pres., 1988–89). Various appointments, Min. of Labour, 1954–62; Principal, HM Treasury, 1962–65; Principal Private Secretary to Minister of Labour, 1966–67; Asst Sec. for Industrial Training, Min. of Labour, 1967–70; Chief Executive: Employment Services Agency, 1971–75; Training Services Agency, 1975–79; Dir Gen., Nat. Fedn of Building Trades Employers, 1979–84. Vis. Prof., Strathclyde Univ.,

1987–91. Dep. Chm., CICI, 1988–92; Dir, Book Trust, 1988–93. Pres., Old Elizabethans' Assoc., 2016–19. CCMI (CBIM 1989); FRSA 1987. Hon. Fellow, Brighton Poly., 1991. Hon. FCLIP 2002. *Recreations:* music, Rugby football.

**COOPER, Prof. Leon N.,** PhD; Thomas J. Watson, Sr, Professor of Science, Brown University, Providence, RI, since 1974; Director, Institute for Brain and Neural Systems, since 1991, and Director, Brain Science Program, since 2000, Brown University; *b* NYC, 28 Feb. 1930; *s* of Irving Cooper and Anna Cooper (*née* Zola); *m* 1969, Kay Anne Allard; two *d*. *Educ:* Columbia Univ. (AB 1951, AM 1953, PhD 1954). Nat. Sci. Foundn postdoctoral Fellow, and Mem., Inst. for Advanced Study, 1954–55; Res. Associate, Univ. of Illinois, 1955–57; Asst Prof., Ohio State Univ., 1957–58; Associate Prof., Brown Univ., 1958–62, Prof., 1962–66, Henry Ledyard Goddard Prof., 1966–74. Consultant, various governmental agencies, industrial and educational organizations. Lectr, Summer Sch., Varenna, Italy, 1955; Visiting Professor: Brandeis Summer Inst., 1959; Bergen Internat. Sch. Physics, Norway, 1961; Scuola Internazionale di Fisica, Erice, Italy, 1965; Ecole Normale Supérieure, Centre Universitaire Internat., Paris, 1966; Cargèse Summer Sch., 1966; Radiation Lab., Univ. of Calif at Berkeley, 1969; Faculty of Scis, Quai St Bernard, Paris, 1970, 1971; Brookhaven Nat. Lab., 1972; Chair of Math. Models of Nervous System, Fondation de France, 1977–83; Mem., Conseil Supérieur de la Recherche, l'Université René Descartes, Paris, 1981–87. Alfred P. Sloan Foundn Res. Fellow, 1959–66; John Simon Guggenheim Meml Foundn Fellow, 1965–66. Co-Chm., Bd of Dirs, Nestor Inc. Fellow: Amer. Physical Soc.; Amer. Acad. of Arts and Sciences. Member: Amer. Philosoph. Soc.; National Acad. of Sciences; Sponsor Fedn of Amer. Scientists; Soc. for Neuroscience, Amer. Assoc. for Advancement of Science; Defense Science Bd, 1989–93. Mem. Bd of Govs, Internat. Neural Network Soc., 1989–94. (Jtly) Comstock Prize, Nat. Acad. of Scis, 1968; (jtly) Nobel Prize for Physics, 1972; Award of Excellence, Grad. Fac. Alumni, Columbia Univ., 1974; Déscartes Medal, Acad. de Paris, Univ. René Déscartes, 1977; Yrjö Reenpää Medal, Finnish Cultural Foundn, 1982; John Jay Award, 1985, Award for Distinguished Achievement, 1989, Columbia Univ.; Alexander Hamilton Award, Columbia Coll., 1996; Rosenberger Medal, Brown Univ., 2013. Hon. DSc: Columbia, 1973; Sussex, 1973; Illinois, 1974; Brown, 1974; Gustavus Adolphus Coll., 1975; Ohio State Univ., 1976; Univ. Pierre et Marie Curie, Paris, 1977. Public lectures, internat. confs, symposia. *Publications:* Introduction to the Meaning and Structure of Physics, 1968; (contrib.) The Physicist's Conception of Nature, 1973; How We Learn, How We Remember: toward an understanding of brain and neural systems, 1995; contrib. The Many Body Problem, 1963; (jtly) Theory of Cortical Plasticity, 2004; (ed jtly) BCS: 50 years, 2011; Science and Human Experience, 2014; contrib. to numerous jls incl. Physics Rev., Amer. Jl Physics, Biological Cybernetics, Jl of Neurosci., Jl of Neurophysiol., Procs of the US Nat. Acad. of Scis. *Recreations:* music, theatre, ski-ing. *Address:* Physics Department, Brown University, Providence, RI 02912–1843, USA. *T:* (401) 8632172. *Clubs:* University, Faculty (Providence, RI).

**COOPER, Léonie Alison;** Member (Lab) Merton and Wandsworth, London Assembly, Greater London Authority, since 2016; *b* Hertford; *d* of Albert and Rosa Cooper. *Educ:* Broxbourne Sch., Broxbourne, Herts; University Coll. London (BA Hons). Consultant, L'Eau Ltd, 2005–10; Sustainability Manager, Longhurst Gp, 2010–12; Sustainability Consultant, 2012–16. Mem. (Lab), Wandsworth LBC, 2006–. London Assembly, Greater London Authority: Dep. Chair, Envmt Cttee, 2018– (Chair, 2016–18); Member: Housing Cttee, 2016–; Budget and Perf. Cttee, 2016–. Member: London Fire and Emergency Planning Authy, 2016–18; Fire, Resilience and Emergency Planning Cttee, 2018–. *Recreations:* walking, reading, cooking. *Address:* Greater London Authority, City Hall, Queen's Walk, SE1 2AA. *T:* (020) 7983 6536. *E:* leonie.cooper@london.gov.uk. *Club:* Rotary (Battersea Park).

**COOPER, Mark;** Head of Music Television, BBC Studios, since 2013; *b* London, 14 Nov. 1952; *s* of Rt Hon. Sir Frank Cooper, GCB, CMG, PC and Peggie Cooper; *m* 2003, Sian Davies; three *s* one *d*. *Educ:* Cranbrook Sch.; Jesus Coll., Cambridge (BA English Lit. 1974); Sussex Univ. (MA American Studies 1976); Univ. of Calif, Santa Barbara. Music journalist, Record Mirror, Number 1, 1980–84; freelance music journalist, Q, Mojo, Word, Guardian, Telegraph, 1984–2000; Press Officer, Virgin Records, 1984–86; Internat. Liaison, Polygram, 1987–88; Researcher, Initial TV, 1988–89; joined BBC TV 1990; Asst Prod., The Late Show (music); est. and Exec. Prod., Later with Jools Holland, 1992–2019, Jools' Hootenanny, 1993–2019; est. and oversees BBC TV Glastonbury coverage, 1997–; Creative Hd, BBC Music Entertainment, 2001–13; Executive Producer: BBC 4 music documentaries, incl. Britannia strand (jazz, punk, reggae etc), Rock 'n' Roll/Folk/Blues America, The Joy of Abba/Country/Disco/Easy Listening, The Joy of Mozart, Gregory Porter's Popular Voices, The Story of Top of the Pops 1976–1987, The Joy of the Bee Gees, Go West, Guitar, Bass and Drums; BBC 2 documentary series, incl. Girls and Boys, I'm in a Rock n Roll Band!, Reginald D. Hunter's Songs of the South; BBC 1 documentaries and performances, incl. Fleetwood Mac, Agnetha, The Carpenters, Top of the Pops Christmas and New Year's Eve; BBC 1 and BBC 4 music sessions and Songwriters Circle; BBC Classical output incl. The Proms on TV, 2013–18 and documentaries incl. Tamara Rojo's Giselle, Tony Pappano's Greatest Arias and Thomas Quasthoff: Becoming a Lied Singer. *Recreations:* cricket, supporting QPR, literature. *Address:* 6 Layer Gardens, Acton, W3 9PR. *T:* (020) 8993 3021. *E:* mark.cooper@bbc.co.uk. *Club:* Millfields Cricket.
See also V. Glastonbury.

**COOPER, Mary Helen;** see Lazarus, M. H.

**COOPER, Michael John;** Director General, British Diabetic Association, 1992–98; *b* 24 July 1937; *s* of Frederick Walton Cooper and Ivy Kathleen (*née* Harris); *m* 1961, Kathy Cockett; two *s* one *d*. *Educ:* King's Sch., Rochester; Univ. of Exeter (BA 1960); Oberlin Coll., Ohio; Internat. Management Develt Inst., Switzerland (MBA 1970). RAF, 1955–57. Shell Internat. Petroleum Co. Ltd, 1961–69; Panocean-Anco Ltd, 1970–83 (Man. Dir, 1980–83); Dir, Burmah Castrol PLC, 1983–91. Vice-Chm., E Sussex HA, 1996–2000 (Dir, 1992–2000). Vis. Prof., Univ. of Westminster, 1992–2001. Chm., Care for the Carers, Sussex, 2000–07. Vice-Chm., Queen's Nursing Inst., 2003–13 (Trustee, 2002–); Trustee: Music in Hosps (formerly Council for Music in Hosps), 2001–17; Diabetes Network Internat., 2002–07. Member: Exec. Cttee, Lib Dem Wealden Constituency, 2000–08 (Vice Chm., 2004–06); Exec. Cttee, Lib Dem European Gp, 2006–17. Mem. Bd, Conservators of Ashdown Forest, 2002–. Gov., High Hurstwood C of E Primary Sch., 1995–2018 (Chm., 1998–2007). *Recreations:* music, walking, cricket, tennis, travel. *Address:* Old Hall Cottage, High Hurstwood, Uckfield, E Sussex TN22 4AD. *T:* (01825) 733268, 07836 221261; Flat 5, 130 Belgrave Road, SW1V 2BL; Le Gouttat, 71520 Clermain, France. *Club:* Oriental.

**COOPER, Michael John,** OBE 1997; CBiol; Staff Development Adviser and Trainer, Voluntary Service Overseas, 2005–07; *b* 5 April 1949; *s* of Stanley and Evelyn Cooper; *m* 1975, Gillian Isted; two *s*. *Educ:* Sutton High Sch., Plymouth; York Univ. (BA). CBiol, MRSB (MIBiol 1971). VSO, Chassa Secondary Sch., Zambia, 1972; Mill Hill Sch., London, 1973–78 (Dir of Biol., 1974–78); Dep. Head, Upper Sch., Moulsham High Sch., Chelmsford, 1978–81; Dep. Headteacher, Valley Sch., Worksop, 1982–85; Headmaster,

Hillcrest Sch., Hastings, 1985–90; Principal, British Sch. in the Netherlands, 1990–99; Headmaster, Latymer Sch., 1999–2005. Selector, VSO, 1975–90. Governor: Middx Univ., 2003–06; Enfield Coll., 2003–06; Truro Coll., 2014–. Chm., Peninsula Learning Trust, St Austell, 2016–; Director: Tudor Acad. Trust, Feltham, 2016–; King's Acad. Trust, Portsmouth, 2016–. Trustee: CAB Cornwall, 2014–. *Recreations:* walking, gardening, swimming, reading. *Address:* Blue Ocean, Chapel Point Lane, Cornwall PL26 6PP. *T:* (01726) 842955. *Club:* Victory Services.

**COOPER, Morris;** a District Judge (Magistrates' Court), 2004–15; *b* 10 Oct. 1948; *s* of Arthur Cooper and Elsie Cooper; *m* 1989, Vivien Joy Hallam; one *s* two *d*. Called to the Bar, Gray's Inn, 1979; Clerk to the Justices: for Burton-on-Trent and Uttoxette, 1980–88; for N Staffs, 1988–89; in practice as a barrister, 1991–2004; actg Stipendiary Magistrate, 1999, subseq. Dep. Dist Judge (Magistrates' Court), 2000–04. *Recreation:* playing guitar.

**COOPER, Nigel Cookson;** Co-ordinator, Wimbledon Tennis Championships, 1988–95; *b* 7 May 1929; *s* of Richard and Violet Sarah Cooper; *m* 1972, Elizabeth Gillian Smith; two *s* one *d*. *Educ:* Leeds Training Coll., Leeds Univ. (LLB); State Univ. of Iowa, USA (MA). Teacher, primary and secondary schools, 1950–59; Lecturer: Trent Park Training Coll., 1959–61; Loughborough Training Coll., 1961–64; Provincial Supervisor (Schools and Community) for Nova Scotia, Canada, 1964–65; County Organiser of Schools for Norfolk, 1965–68; Asst Education Officer for Oldham, 1970–72; Asst Director of Educn for British Families Educn Service in Europe, 1972–78; Registrar, Kelvin Grove College of Advanced Education, Brisbane, Australia, 1978–82; Gen. Sec., BAAB, 1982–87. Mem., Elmbridge BC, 1999 (Dep. Mayor, 2007–08, Mayor, 2008–09). *Recreations:* playing the trumpet, squash, jogging. *Address:* 24 Southfields, East Molesey, Surrey KT8 0BP. *T:* and *Fax:* (020) 8224 0712.

**COOPER, Sir (Richard) Adrian,** 6th Bt *cr* 1905, of Shenstone Court, co. Stafford; *b* 21 Aug. 1960; *o s* of Sir Richard Powell Cooper, 5th Bt and Angela Marjorie (*née* Wilson); S father, 2006; *m* 1994, Belinda Potter. *Educ:* Millfield Sch. *Heir:* none. *Address:* Hill Farm, Swalcliffe, Banbury, Oxon OX15 5EN.

**COOPER, Rev. Canon Richard Thomas;** Rector of Richmond, North Yorkshire, 1998–2009; Chaplain to the Queen, 2003–16; *b* 7 March 1946; *s* of Frank and Margaret Cooper, Littlethorpe; *m* 1978, Janet Johnston; one *s* one *d*. *Educ:* Ripon Grammar Sch.; Leeds Univ. (BA 1969); Coll. of the Resurrection, Mirfield. Ordained deacon, 1971, priest, 1972; Assistant Curate: Rothwell, 1971–75; Adel, Leeds, 1975–78; Priest i/c, Holy Trinity, Knaresborough, 1978–81; Vicar: Middleton Tyas, Croft and Eryholme, 1981–90; Aldborough with Boroughbridge and Roecliffe, 1990–98. RD, Richmond, 1986–90; Area Dean, Ripon, 1990–93; Chaplain, The Green Howards, 2002–; Regtl Chaplain, Yorks Regt, 2007–12; Officiating Chaplain to the Military, 2009–12. Hon. Canon, Ripon Cathedral, 1997–. Proctor in Convocation and Mem., Gen. Synod of C of E, 1986–90; Chm., House of Clergy, dio. Ripon, 1993–2001. Freeman and Chaplain: Mercers', Grocers' and Haberdashers' Co., Richmond, 1991– (Warden, 2007); Fellmongers' Co., Richmond, 1998– (Master, 2016–17). *Recreations:* choral singing, cycling, fishing. *Address:* 13 Ash Bank Road, Ripon, N Yorks HG4 2EQ.

**COOPER, Sir Robert (Francis),** KCMG 2013 (CMG 1997); MVO 1975; HM Diplomatic Service, retired; Counsellor, European External Action Service, European Union, 2010–12; *b* 28 Aug. 1947; *s* of late Norman and Frances Cooper. *Educ:* Delamere Sch., Nairobi; Worcester Coll., Oxford (BA); Univ. of Pennsylvania (MA). Joined FCO 1970; Tokyo 1972; London 1977; seconded to Bank of England, 1982; UK Rep. to EC, 1984; Head of Management Review Staff, FCO, 1987; Head of Far Eastern Dept, FCO, 1987; Hd of Policy Planning Staff, FCO, 1989; Counsellor, 1993, Minister and Dep. Hd of Mission, 1996–98, Bonn; Dir, Asia, FCO, 1998–99; Hd, Defence and Overseas Secretariat, Cabinet Office (on secondment), 1999–2001; Govt's special rep. for Afghanistan, 2001–02; Dir Gen. for Ext. Affairs, Council Secretariat of EU, 2002–10. Special Advr to EU High Rep., 2012–. Vis. Prof., LSE, 2012–. *Publications:* The Postmodern State and the World Order, 1996; The Breaking of Nations, 2003. *Recreations:* Shakespeare, ballroom dancing, bicycling.

**COOPER, Ven. Robert Gerard;** Archdeacon of Sunderland, since 2018; *b* Oldham, 26 July 1968; *s* of Terence Cooper and Eileen Cooper; *m* 1991, Katy Elizabeth; three *s* one *d*. *Educ:* Bluecoat Sch., Oldham; Univ. of Wales, Aberystwyth (BD 1991); Lincoln Theol Coll. (Postgrad. Cert. Mission and Ministry). Ordained deacon, 1993, priest, 1994; Curate: Whitkirk, Leeds, 1993–96; St Hilda's, Leeds, 1996–97; Chaplain, Chigwell Sch., Essex, 1997–98; Vicar: St Matthew's, Lightcliffe, 1998–2005; St Giles with St Mary and All Saints, Pontefract, 2005–18; Rural, later Area Dean of Pontefract, 2006–18. Canon: Wakefield Cathedral, 2007–18; Musoma, Tanzania, 2017–; Durham Cathedral, 2018–. Member: Gen. Synod, 2008–18; Church Bldgs Council, 2015–. Chm., Coal Industry Social Welfare Orgn, 2014–. *Recreations:* film, family, travel, education, Land Rovers, claret. *Address:* St Nicholas' Vicarage, Hedworth Lane, Boldon Colliery, Tyne and Wear NE35 9JA. *T:* (0191) 536 2300. *E:* archdeacon.of.sunderland@durham.anglican.org.

**COOPER, Prof. Robin Hayes,** PhD; FBA 1993; Professor of Computational Linguistics, University of Gothenburg, 1995–2012, now Emeritus; Director, Swedish National Graduate School of Language Technology, 2001–12; *b* 23 Dec. 1947; *s* of Dennis J. Cooper and Marjorie (*née* Wilding); *m* 1985, Elisabet B. Engdahl; two *d*. *Educ:* Corpus Christi Coll., Cambridge (MA); Univ. of Massachusetts at Amherst (PhD). Lektor, Universität Freiburg, 1969–71; Assistant Professor: Univ. of Texas at Austin, 1975–76; Univ. of Massachusetts at Amherst, 1976–77; Univ. of Wisconsin, Madison, 1977–81, Associate Prof., 1981–87; Docent, Lund Univ., 1984–87; University of Edinburgh: Lectr, 1986–89; Reader in Cognitive Sci., 1989–96. Mellon Fellow, Stanford Univ., 1980–81; Fellow, Center for Advanced Study in Behavioral Scis, Stanford, 1981–82; Guggenheim Fellow, Edinburgh and Stanford, 1986–87. Fellow, Royal Soc. of Arts and Scis, Gothenburg, 1996. MAE 2009. FilDr *hc* Uppsala, 2006. *Publications:* Quantification and Syntactic Theory, 1983; (ed jtly) Situation Theory and its Applications, Vol. 1, 1990; (ed jtly) Language in Flux: dialogue coordination, language variation, change and evolution, 2008; contribs to numerous books, contrib. Computational Intelligence, Ethnomusicology, Jl Logic, Lang. and Information, Jl Logic and Computation, Lang., Linguistics and Philosophy, Musique en Jeu, Nordic Jl Linguistics, Res. on Lang. and Computation, Dialogue and Discourse. *Recreations:* yoga, music. *Address:* Department of Philosophy, Linguistics and Theory of Science, University of Gothenburg, Box 200, 40530 Göteborg, Sweden; Bigatan 1, 43139 Mölndal, Sweden.

**COOPER, Rosemary;** see Martin, R.

**COOPER, Rosemary Elizabeth;** MP (Lab) West Lancashire, since 2005; *b* 5 Sept. 1950; *d* of William and Rose Cooper. *Educ:* Bellerive Convent GS; Liverpool Univ. W. Cooper Ltd, 1973–80; Littlewoods Organisation: merchandiser, 1980–92; PR Manager, Littlewoods Internat., 1994–95; Gp Corporate Communications Manager, 1995–2001; Project Co-ord., Equal Opportunities Commn Taskforce on Women and Pay, 1999–2000. Mem. and Vice-Chm., Liverpool HA, 1994–96; Chm., Liverpool Women's Hosp. NHS Trust, 1996–2005. Mem. (Lib Dem, then Lab), Liverpool CC, 1973–2000; Lord Mayor of Liverpool, 1992–93 (Hon. Alderman, 2011). Contested (Lib Dem): Knowsley N, Nov.

1986, 1987; Liverpool Garston, 1983; Liverpool Broadgreen, 1992; contested (Lab) NW Reg., EP elecns, 2004. Former Director: Merseyside Centre for Deaf People; Roy Castle Foundn. *Address:* House of Commons, SW1A 0AA.

**COOPER, Russell;** *see* Cooper, T. R.

**COOPER, Maj.-Gen. Sir Simon (Christie),** GCVO 2000 (KCVO 1991); Master of HM's Household, 1992–2000; *b* 5 Feb. 1936; *s* of Maj.-Gen. Kenneth Christie Cooper, CB, DSO, OBE and Barbara Harding-Newman; *m* 1967, Juliet Elizabeth Palmer; one *s* one *d. Educ:* Winchester College; rcds, psc. Commissioned Life Guards, 1956; served Aden, London, BAOR, 1957–63; Captain-Adjt, Household Cavalry Regt, 1963–65; ADC to CDS Earl Mountbatten of Burma, 1965–66; Borneo, Malaya, 1966–67; Staff Coll., 1968; BAOR, 1969–75; CO Life Guards, 1974–76; GSO1, Staff Coll., 1976–78; OC Household Cavalry and Silver Stick in Waiting, 1978–81; Commander, RAC Centre, 1981–82; RCDS, 1983; Dir, RAC, 1984–87; Comdt, RMA, Sandhurst, 1987–89; GOC London Dist and Maj.-Gen. Commanding Household Div., 1989–91. Trustee, Royal Armouries, 2004–11. Pres., 2005–12, Vice Pres., 2012–, SSAFA (formerly SSAFA Forces Help), Wilts. Hon. Colonel: Westminster Dragoons, 1987–97; Royal Yeomanry, 1987–97. *Recreations:* cricket, ski-ing, sailing, shooting. *Clubs:* Army and Navy, MCC.

**COOPER, Simon Nicholas;** DL; a District Judge (Magistrates' Courts), 2002–18; *b* 2 Sept. 1953; *s* of Lt Comdr Alan Geoffrey Cooper and Wendy Anne Cooper (*née* Mcleod); *m* 1998, Philippa Mason. *Educ:* Kelly Coll.; Bristol Univ. (LLB Hons); RNC Dartmouth; Inns of Court Sch. of Law. Joined RN, 1972; served HMS Wilton, Rhyl, Intrepid, Hecate and Yarmouth; called to the Bar, Middle Temple, 1982; RN Judge Advocate, 1988; Comdr 1994; Dep. Chief Naval Judge Advocate, 1994–97 and 2001–02; retd from RN, 2002. Recorder, 2002–12. DL Wilts, 2018. *Recreations:* fly fishing, golf, choral singing. *Club:* Army and Navy.

**COOPER, Dr Tarnya,** FSA; Curatorial and Collections Director, National Trust, since 2018; *b* Moseley, 28 Dec. 1967. *Educ:* De Stafford Comprehensive Sch., Surrey; Reigate Sixth Form Coll.; Camberwell Sch. of Arts (BA 1st Cl. Hons Hist. of Drawing and Printmaking 1989); Courtauld Inst. of Art (MA Hist. of Art 1995); Univ. of Sussex (DPhil Hist. of Art 2001). Asst Curator, Res. and Educn, Coll. Art Collections, UCL, 1991–2004; Res. Curator, Elizabeth I Exhibn, Nat. Maritime Mus., 2000–02; National Portrait Gallery: 16th Century Curator, 2002–11; Chief Curator, and Curator, 16th Century Collections, 2011–15; Curatorial Dir, 2016–17. FSA 2013. *Publications:* Tudor and Jacobean Portraiture: a short introductory guide, 2008; Citizen Portrait, 2012; (with C. Bolland) The Real Tudors: kings and queens rediscovered, 2014; (ed) A Portrait of Britain, 2014; (ed jtly) Painting in England: artistic practice, patronage and display, 2015; (jtly) The Encounter: portrait drawings from Leonardo to Rembrandt, 2017; contrib. to books and exhibn catalogues; contrib. Renaissance Studies, British Art Jl. *Address:* National Trust, Heelis, Kemble Drive, Swindon SN2 2NA. *E:* tarnya.cooper@nationaltrust.org.uk.

**COOPER, Hon. (Theo) Russell,** AM 2012; MLA (National Party) Crows Nest, Queensland, 1992–2001 (Roma, Queensland, 1983–92); *b* 4 Feb. 1941; *s* of Theo Beverley Cooper and Muriel Frances Cooper; *m* 1965, Penelope Anne Parkinson; one *s* three *d. Educ:* Surfers Paradise State Sch.; Correspondence Sch.; Toowoomba Prep. Sch.; King's Sch., Parramatta. Councillor, 1976–88, Dep. Chm., 1982–86, Bendemere Shire Council; Dep. Chm., Roma Electorate NP Council, 1980–83; Chm., Wallumbilla-Yuleba Branch, NP, 1974–83. Minister for: Corrective Services and Admin. Services, 1987–89; Police and Emergency Services, 1989; Premier of Qld, Sept.–Dec. 1989; Leader of the Opposition, 1989–91; Opposition spokesman for police and corrective services, 1992–96; Minister for Police and Corrective Services and for Racing, 1996–98; Opposition spokesman on Primary Industries, 1998–2000. Vice-Pres., Maranoa Graziers Assoc., 1979–80 (Chm., Wallumbilla Br.); Pres., Roma and Dist Amateur Race Club, 1981–83. *Recreations:* golf, tennis (active), Rugby League, Rugby Union, cricket. *Address:* 10 Somerset Drive, Buderim, Qld 4556, Australia. *Clubs:* Queensland; Headland Golf.

**COOPER, Dame Trelise (Pamela),** DNZM 2014 (MNZM 2004); fashion designer; Director, Trelise Cooper Group, since 1997; *b* Auckland, 21 Dec. 1957; *d* of Joseph and Pamela Neill; *m* 1984, Jack Cooper; one *s* and one step *s* one step *d. Educ:* Henderson High Sch. Estabd Trelise Cooper Ltd Editions, 1985–89 (two boutiques, Auckland and Wellington); estabd Trelise Cooper Gp, 1997. *Recreations:* family, travel, opera, charity. *Address:* Trelise Cooper Group, 8 Lion Place, Newmarket, Auckland 1023, New Zealand. *T:* 93795005. *E:* enquiry@trelisecooper.co.nz.

**COOPER, Hon. Warren Ernest,** CNZM 1997; MP (National Party) Otago, 1975–96; Minister of Defence and Minister responsible for War Pensions, New Zealand, 1990–96, also Minister of Civil Defence and of Internal Affairs, 1993–96; *b* Dunedin, 21 Feb. 1933; *s* of William Cooper; *m* 1959, Lorraine Margaret, *d* of Angus T. Rees; three *s* two *d. Educ:* Musselburgh Sch.; King's High Sch., Dunedin. Formerly Minister of Tourism, Minister of Regional Develt, Minister in charge of Publicity and in charge of Govt Printing Office; Postmaster Gen., 1980; Minister of Broadcasting and Assoc. Minister of Finance, 1981; Minister of Foreign Affairs and Overseas Trade, 1981–84; Minister of Local Govt and of Radio and Television, 1990–93. Mem., Cabinet Cttees on Expenditure Control and Revenue, State Sector, Appts and Honours, Social and Family Policy, Treaty of Waitangi Issues, 1990–96. Member Executive: S Island Publicity Assoc., 1971; NZ Municipal Assoc. Life Mem. and former Pres., Queenstown Jaycees. Mayor of Queenstown, 1968–75 and 1995–2001. JP Queenstown. Silver Jubilee Medal, 1977. *Address:* 8 Park Street, Queenstown 9300, New Zealand.

**COOPER, Sir William (Daniel Charles),** 6th Bt *cr* 1863, of Woollahra; *b* 5 March 1955; *s* of Sir Charles Eric Daniel Cooper, 5th Bt, and Mary Elisabeth (*d* 1999), *e d* of Captain J. Graham Clarke; *S* father, 1984; *m* 1988, Julia Nicholson. *Educ:* Northease Manor, Lewes, Sussex. *Heir: b* George John Cooper, *b* 28 June 1956.

**COOPER, (William) Gareth,** FCILT; Chairman, Stena Line, 1997–2006; *b* 19 Aug. 1943; *s* of William Alderson Cooper and Florence Morwen Cooper (*née* Matthews); *m* 1966, Carole Roberta Davies; one *s* one *d. Educ:* University Coll., Swansea (BScEng). Managing Director: Wallington Weston Co. Ltd, 1977–83; Weston Hyde Products Ltd, 1983–87; Crown Berger Ltd, 1987–91; Stena Line UK Ltd, 1991–97; Managing Director: White Young Green plc, 1997–2004; E Midlands Electricity; Chm., Arriva plc, 1999–2004; Dir, Simon Gp. *Recreations:* opera, travel, photography. *Address:* 5 Oak Park, Alderley Edge, Cheshire SK9 7GS.

**COOPER, William Robert Patrick W.;** *see* White-Cooper.

**COOPER, Rt Hon. Yvette;** PC 2007; MP (Lab) Normanton, Pontefract and Castleford, since 2010 (Pontefract and Castleford, 1997–2010); *b* 20 March 1969; *d* of (Derek) Anthony Cooper, *qv* and June Cooper (*née* Iley); *m* 1998, Rt Hon. Edward Michael Balls, *qv*; one *s* two *d. Educ:* Eggars Comprehensive Sch., Balliol Coll., Oxford (BA 1st Cl. Hons PPE 1990); Harvard Univ.; London Sch. of Econs (MSc Econs 1995). Economic researcher for Rt Hon. John Smith, MP, 1991–92; Domestic Policy specialist, Clinton Presidential Campaign, Arkansas, 1992; Policy Advr to Labour's Treasury Team, 1992–95; leader writer and economic columnist, The Independent, 1995–97. Parliamentary Under-Secretary of State: for Public Health, DoH, 1999–2002; Lord Chancellor's Dept, 2002–03; (Social Exclusion Minister), ODPM, 2003–05; Minister of State (Minister for Housing and Planning), ODPM, later DCLG, 2005–07; Minister for Housing, DCLG, 2007–08; Chief Sec. to HM Treasury, 2008–09; Sec. of State for Work and Pensions, 2009–10; Shadow Sec. of State for Work and Pensions, 2010; Shadow Minister for Women and Equalities, 2010–13; Shadow Sec. of State for Foreign and Commonwealth Affairs, 2010–11, for the Home Dept, 2011–15. Member: Select Cttee on Educn and Employment, 1997–99; Intelligence and Security Cttee, 1997–99; Chm., Home Affairs Select Cttee, 2016–. *Address:* House of Commons, SW1A 0AA. *T:* (020) 7219 5080.

**COOTE, Anna;** policy analyst and writer; Principal Fellow, New Economics Foundation, since 2016 (Head of Social Policy, 2008–16); Member, London Sustainable Development Commission, since 2017; *b* 1 April 1947; *d* of Capt. J. O. Coote and Sylvia Coote; one *d. Educ:* Edinburgh Univ. (MA). Feature Writer, Observer, 1968–72; Dep. Editor, New Statesman, 1978–82; Editor, Diverse Reports, Channel 4, 1982–86; Res. Fellow, IPPR, 1989–91; Sen. Lectr, Goldsmiths' Coll., London Univ., 1991–93; Dep. Dir, IPPR, 1993–98; Dir of Health Policy, King's Fund, 1998–2005; Hd of Patient and Public Involvement, Healthcare Commn, 2005–08. Mem., London Health Commn, 2000–05; Comr for Health, UK Sustainable Develt Commn, 2000–09. Trustee, Help the Aged, 2001–06. Hon. DLitt Bath, 1999. *Publications: include:* (jtly) Civil Liberty: the NCCL guide, 1972; (jtly) Women's Rights: a practical guide, 1974; (jtly) Sweet Freedom, 1987; (jtly) Power and Prejudice, 1990; (ed) The Welfare of Citizens, 1992; New Gender Agenda, 2000; (ed) Time on Our Side, 2013. *Recreations:* cycling, tennis, walking, cinema, theatre.

**COOTE, Sir Nicholas Patrick,** 16th Bt *cr* 1621; *b* 28 July 1953; *s* of Sir Christopher John Coote, 15th Bt and of Anne Georgiana Coote (*née* Handford); *S* father, 2016; *m* 1980, Mona Rebecca, *d* of late Moushegh Bedelian; one *s* one *d. Educ:* Winchester Coll. *Heir: s* Rory Alasdair Coote, *b* 3 April 1987.

**COPE,** family name of **Baron Cope of Berkeley**.

**COPE OF BERKELEY,** Baron *cr* 1997 (Life Peer), of Berkeley in the co. of Gloucestershire; **John Ambrose Cope,** Kt 1991; PC 1988; *b* 13 May 1937; *s* of George Cope, MC, FRIBA, Leicester; *m* 1969, Djemila Lovell Payne, *d* of late Col P. V. L. Payne, Martinstown, Dorset and Mrs Tanetta Blackden, Amer. Colony of Jerusalem; two *d. Educ:* Oakham Sch., Rutland. Chartered Accountant; Company Director. Commnd RA and RE, Nat. Service and TA. Contested (C) Woolwich East, 1970; MP (C) South Gloucestershire, Feb. 1974–1983, Northavon, 1983–97; contested (C) Northavon, 1997. A Govt Whip, 1979–87, and Lord Comr of HM Treasury, 1981–83; Treas. of HM Household and Dep. Chief Whip, 1983–87; Minister of State: Dept of Employment and Minister for Small Businesses, 1987–89; NI Office, 1989–90; Dep. Chm. and Jt Treas., Cons. Party, 1990–92; HM Paymaster Gen., 1992–94; Opposition spokesman on NI, 1997–98, on home affairs, 1998–2001, H o L; Opposition Chief Whip, H of L, 2001–07. Chm., H of L Select Cttee on Small and Medium Sized Enterprises, 2012–13. Mem., British-Irish Parly Assembly, 2008–11. Sen. Comr, Royal Hospital Chelsea, 1992–94. Pres., Inst. of Business Counsellors, 1988–90; Dep. Chm., Small Business Bureau, 1995–2001; Pres., S Glos Chamber of Commerce, 1993–2001. Chm., Horse and Pony Taxation Cttee, 1994–2000. Vice Pres., Royal Soc. of St George, 1998–. Mem. Cttee, British Sch. of Archaeol. in Jerusalem, 1998–2001; Trustee: War Memls Trust (formerly Friends of War Memls), 1997–2017 (Pres., 2018–); Conservative Party Archive, Bodleian Liby, 2008–15; Friends of Edward Said Nat. Conservatory of Music UK, 2013– (Chm., 2013–18). Patron: Avon Riding for the Disabled, 1985–2012; Friends of Royal Nat. Hosp. for Rheumatic Diseases, Bath, 2003–18. *Publications:* (with Bernard Weatherill) Acorns to Oaks (Policy for Small Business), 1967; (ed) A Funny Thing Happened, 1991; I'm sorry you were in when I called, 1992. *Recreations:* woodwork, a Derby Bentley motor car, church bell ringing. *Address:* House of Lords, SW1A 0PW. *Clubs:* Carlton (Chm., 2004–10), Pratt's; Tudor House (Chipping Sodbury).

**COPE, Alan,** CPFA, FCCA; County Treasurer, Cheshire County Council, 1997–2001; *b* 8 Oct. 1946; *s* of John William Cope and Bertha Cope; *m* 1969, Gillian Mary Kirk; two *s. Educ:* Swanwick Hall Grammar Sch.; Univ. of Liverpool (MA 2004). CPFA 1968; FCCA 1981. Accountant, Derbyshire CC, 1963–69; Cheshire County Council: Sen. Auditor, 1969–72; Technical Accountant, 1972–74; Gp Accountant, 1974–78; Chief Accountant, 1978–85; Asst Dir, Policy Unit, 1985–87; Asst Co. Treas., 1987–89; Co. Finance Officer, 1989–97. Treasurer: Cheshire Fire Authy, 1997–2001; Cheshire Probation Service, 1997–2001; Cheshire Police Authy, 1998–2001. Non-exec. Mem., Finance Cttee, Royal Mencap Soc., 2004–12. *Address:* The Meadows, 19 Dee Crescent, Farndon, Chester CH3 6QJ. *T:* (01829) 270602.

**COPE, David Robert,** MA; international education and recruitment consultant; *b* 24 Oct. 1944; *yr s* of late Dr Cuthbert Cope, FRCP and Eileen Cope (*née* Putt); *m* 1st, 1966, Gillian Margaret Peck (marr. diss. 1994); one *s* two *d*; 2nd, 1996, Juliet Caroline, *e d* of Prof. Richard Swinburne, *qv*; two *s. Educ:* Winchester Coll. (Scholar); Clare Coll., Cambridge (Scholar). 1st Cl. Hons Hist. Tripos Part II, 1965; BA 1965; MA 1972. Asst Master, Eton Coll., 1965–67; Asst British Council Rep. (Cultural Attaché), Mexico City, 1968–70; Asst Master, Bryanston Sch., 1970–73; Headmaster: Dover College, 1973–81; British Sch. of Paris, 1981–86; Master of Marlborough Coll., 1986–93; Field Dir, Zambia, VSO, 1994–97. Director: Ashoka (UK) Trust, 1998–2001; Application Research Ltd, 2002–08; Sen. Associate, Search Associates, 2002– (Vice-Pres., 2009–13; Exec. Vice-Pres., 2013–18; Dir, Sch. Relns, 2018–). Trustee: Assoc. for Educn and Guardianship of Internat. Students, 2005–17; SoundAffects, 2008–12. FRSA. *Recreations:* music, running, books, travel. *Address:* Berry House, 41 High Street, Over, Cambridge CB24 5NB. *T:* (01954) 231130. *Club:* Athenæum.

**COPE, David Robert;** Director, Parliamentary Office of Science and Technology, 1998–2012; *b* 7 July 1946; *s* of Lawrence William and Ethel Anne Cope; *m* 1992, Reiko Takashina. *Educ:* Fitzwilliam Coll., Cambridge Univ. (MA); London School of Economics (MScEcon, with dist.). Res. Officer, University Coll. London, 1969–70; Lectr, Nottingham Univ., 1970–81; Environment Team Leader, Internat. Energy Agency Coal Unit, 1981–86; Exec. Dir, UK CEED, 1986–97; Prof. of Energy Econs, Doshisha Univ., Kyoto, Japan, 1997–98. Special Lectr in Energy and Environment Studies, Nottingham Univ., 1985–94; Vis. Lectr, Cambridge Univ., 1988–95; First Caltex Green Fund Fellow, 1992, and Ext. Examiner, 1992–, Centre of Urban Planning and Envmtl Mgt, Univ. of Hong Kong; Associate, Clare Hall, Cambridge Univ., 2005–. Member: Council, Nat. Soc. for Clean Air, 1990–98; Standing Cttee on the Envmt, ACOST, 1990–92; Climate Change Wkg Gp, 1993; Packaging Standards Council (formerly Packaging Council), 1992–96; Envmtl Stats Adv. Cttee, DoE, later DETR, 1994–98. Chm., Europe-Japan Experts' Assoc., 2002. Hon. PhD N London, 2001. *Publications:* (with P. Hills and P. James) Energy Policy and Land Use Planning, 1984; (with S. Owens) Land Use Planning Policy and Climate Change, 1992; numerous papers on energy and environmental policy topics. *Recreations:* amateur volcanology, hill walking, woodworking.

**COPE, Jeremy Ewart**; Managing Director, UK, Royal Mail Group, 2002–03; b 30 Nov. 1951; s of late Michael Ewart Cope and Maureen Ann Cope (née Casey); m 1985, Dianne Elizabeth Gilmour; one s. *Educ*: St Paul's Sch.; Jesus Coll., Cambridge (MA); Warwick Univ. (MSc). MCIPD. Joined Post Office as management trainee, 1973; Asst Head Postmaster, Southend, 1980; Dir of Personnel, Royal Mail, 1986; Gen. Manager, London, 1988; Dir of Strategy, Royal Mail, 1989; Dir of Strategy and Commercial Develt, Post Office, 1992; Man. Dir, Strategy and Personnel, Post Office, 1995; Mem. for Strategy and Personnel, Post Office Bd, 1996–99; Gp Man. Dir, Post Office, subseq. Consignia, then Royal Mail Gp, 1999–2003. Dir, Camelot plc, 2000–03; Chairman: Celyn Hldgs (formerly HRS Ltd, then T-Three Ltd), 2004–; One Croydon Health Alliance, 2018–; non-exec. Dir, GCDA, 2007–12. Chairman: Prison Service Pay Review Body, 2005–11, (interim) 2018–19; NHS Pay Review Body, 2011–17. Trustee, Royal Mail Sen. Exec. Pension Plan, 2015–. Chm., London Regl Cttee, FEFC, 2000–01. Dir, English Bridge Union, 2011– (Treas., 2015–); Chm., English Bridge Educn and Develt, 2014–15. Gov., Kingston Univ., 1999–2007 (Chm., 2002–07); Chm., London South Bank Univ., 2015–. *Recreations*: bridge, supporting Fulham FC, cooking, theatre, avoiding the gardening. *Address*: 24 Auckland Road, SE19 2DJ. *Club*: Hurlingham.

**COPE, Jonathan**, CBE 2003; Répétiteur, Royal Ballet Company, since 2005 (Principal, 1987–90 and 1992–2006); b 1963; m Maria Almeida; one s one d. *Educ*: Royal Ballet Sch. Joined Royal Ballet Co., 1982; Soloist, 1985–86; property business, 1990–92. Leading rôles include: Cinderella, Pursuit, Giselle, Swan Lake, Prince of the Pagodas, Fearful Symmetries, The Sons of Horus, Romeo and Juliet, Sleeping Beauty, La Bayadère, Different Drummer, Frankenstein, Fleeting Figures, The Modern Prometheus, Words Apart, Manon, The Nutcracker, Ondine, Mayerling, The Judas Tree, Aminta, in Sylvia. *Address*: c/o Royal Ballet Company, Royal Opera House, Covent Garden, WC2E 9DD.

**COPE, Wendy Mary**, OBE 2010; FRSL; writer, freelance since 1986; b 21 July 1945; d of Fred Stanley Cope and Alice Mary (née Hand). *Educ*: Farringtons Sch.; St Hilda's Coll., Oxford (MA); Westminster College of Education, Oxford (DipEd). Teacher in London primary schs, 1967–81 and 1984–86; Arts editor, ILEA Contact, 1982–84; Television columnist, The Spectator, 1986–90. FRSL 1992. Hon. Fellow, Goldsmiths, Univ. of London, 2013. Hon. DLitt: Southampton, 1999; Oxford Brookes, 2003. Cholmondeley Award for Poetry, 1987; Michael Braude Award, Amer. Acad. of Arts and Letters, 1995. *Publications*: Making Cocoa for Kingsley Amis (poems), 1986; Twiddling Your Thumbs (rhymes for children), 1988; (ed) Is That The New Moon?, 1989; The River Girl, 1991; Serious Concerns (poems), 1992; (ed) The Orchard Book of Funny Poems, 1993; (ed) The Funny Side, 1998; (ed) The Faber Book of Bedtime Stories, 2000; If I Don't Know (poems), 2001; (ed) Heaven on Earth: 101 happy poems, 2001; (ed) George Herbert, Verse and Prose, 2002; Two Cures for Love: selected poems 1979–2006, 2008; The Audience (with music by Roxanna Panufnik), 2009; Going for a Drive (poems for children), 2010; Family Values (poems), 2011; Time for School (poems for children), 2013; Life, Love and The Archers: recollections, reviews and other prose, 2014; Christmas Poems, 2017; St Hilda of Whitby (with music by Nicola Lefanu), 2018; Anecdotal Evidence (poems), 2018. *Recreations*: playing the piano, gardening. *Address*: c/o Faber and Faber, Bloomsbury House, 74–77 Great Russell Street, WC1B 3DA.

**COPELAND, Maj. Gen. Ian Martin**, CB 2013; FCILT; Chairman, Foreland Shipping Ltd, since 2018; b Weston-super-Mare, 6 Oct. 1959; s of Peter Wilfred Norman Copeland and Ann Copeland; m 1982, Sallyann Horlick; one s one d. *Educ*: Bristol Grammar Sch.; Royal Military Acad. Sandhurst. FCILT 2013. Joined Army, 1979; Troop Comdr, 1 Sqdn, 1980–81, Jun. Leaders' Regt, 1981–83, RCT; Transport Control Officer (New Territories Hong Kong), Gurkha Transport Regt, 1984–86; Regtl Ops Officer, 4 Armd Div., Transport Regt, RCT, 1986–88; Adjutant, 155 (Wessex) Transport Regt RCT (Vol.), 1988–89; Army Command and Staff Course, 1990; psc 1991; Dep. COS 19 Mechanised Bde, 1992–94; Directing Staff, Army Comd and Staff Coll., 1997–99; CO 10 Transport Regt RLC and Comdr Queen's Own Gurkha Logistic Regt, 1999–2001; Dep. Asst COS Orgn, HQ Land Forces, 2001–04; hcsc 2004; Comdr 101 Logistic Bde, 2004–06; Dir Logistics (Army), 2006–09; Hd Defence Support Chain Ops and Movements, 2009–10; Dir Jt Support Chain, Defence Equipment and Support, 2010–13; Man. Dir and Vice Pres., DynCorp Internat. UK, 2014–15. Dir, Copeland Adv. Ltd, 2015–. Hon. Col, 155 (Wessex) Transport Regt RLC (Vol.), 2010–14. President: RLC Cricket Club, 2005–; RLC Shooting Club, 2005–; RLC Golf Soc., 2008–; RLC Regtl Assoc., 2012–. *Recreations*: golf, keeping fit, walking the dog, gardening, travel. E: ian.copeland59@gmail.com.

**COPELAND, Michael Stewart**; Member (UU) Belfast East, Northern Ireland Assembly, 2003–07 and 2011–15; b Belfast, 23 June 1954; s of George and Emily Copeland; m Sonia; one s one d. *Educ*: Lisnasharragh High Sch.; RMA, Sandhurst. Apprentice joiner, then site manager, William Copeland & Son Ltd; Dir, then Man. Dir, Modarc, Copeland Gp. Rifleman, then Commnd Officer, UDR. Mem. (UU) Castlereagh BC, 2001–13. GSM Clasp (NI).

**COPINGER-SYMES, Maj. Gen. Tom Richardson**, CBE 2017 (OBE 2012); QCVS 2008; Director, Military Digitisation, Joint Forces Command, since 2019; b Singapore; s of Wilfred James Charles Griffith Copinger-Symes and Susan Joy Copinger-Symes; m 2008, Helen Clare Archer; two d. *Educ*: Pangbourne Coll.; RMA Sandhurst; Univ. of Warwick (BA Hons); Cranfield Univ. (MSc). Joined Army, 1992; CO 5th Bn The Rifles, 2010–12; Comdr 1st Intelligence, Surveillance and Reconnaissance Bde, 2014–16; GOC Force Troops Comd (6th (UK) Div.), 2017–19. Asst Col Comdt, The Rifles, 2019–. Hon. Col, FANY, 2018–. *Recreations*: ball games, winter and field sports, theatre, family, Chelsea FC. *Address*: c/o Regimental Headquarters, The Rifles, Peninsula Barracks, Romsey Road, Winchester, Hants SO23 8TS. T: (01962) 828527. *Clubs*: Cavalry and Guards; St Moritz Tobogganing; Campden Hill Tennis.

**COPLAND, Geoffrey Malcolm**, CBE 2007; DPhil; CPhys, FInstP; consultant on higher education, since 2007; Rector and Vice-Chancellor, University of Westminster, 1996–2007; b 28 June 1942; s of late Cyril Charles Copland and Jessie Palmer Copland; m 1st, 1967, Janet Mary Todd (marr. diss. 1985); one s one d; 2nd, 1985, Dorothy Joy Harrison. *Educ*: Fitzmaurice Grammar Sch., Bradford-on-Avon; Merton Coll., Oxford (MA, DPhil 1967). MInstP 1973; CPhys 1985; FInstP 2003. Post-doctoral scientist, Yale Univ., 1967–69; University of London: Researcher and Lectr in Physics, QMC, 1969–71; Lectr in Physics, Queen Elizabeth Coll., 1971–80; Dean of Studies, Goldsmiths' Coll., 1981–87; Dep. Rector, Poly. of Central London, later Univ. of Westminster, 1987–95. Mem. Council, UUK (formerly CVCP), 1998–2007 (Vice-Pres. and Chm., England and NI Council, 2003–07). Member Board: Edexcel Foundn, 1998–2003; PSI, 1998–2007; Central London Partnership, 2001–07; Central London LSC, 2005–07; Chm. Bd, Univs and Colls Employers Assoc., 2002–06. Pres., Assoc. of ASET, 2006–. Mem., Council for Industry and Higher Educn, 1999–2007 (Trustee, 2001–07); Chm., Thomas Wall Trust, 1999–; Trustee: Regent St Polytechnic Trust, 1996–2007; Quintin Hogg Trust, 1996–; Quintin Hogg Meml Fund, 1996–; Internat. Student House, 2000– (Chm., 2017–18); Learning from Experience Trust, 2000– (Chair, 2011–17); Helena Kennedy Foundn, 2008–13; Mem., Alban Acads Trust, 2018–. Governor: Trinity Laban, 2007– (Vice-Chm., 2012–); Univ. of Bedfordshire, 2008–14. Mem. Council, Trinity Coll. London, 2012– (Vice-Chm., 2015–). FRSA 1991; FGCL 2000; Hon. FTCL 2000. Hon. Fellow, Univ. of Bedfordshire, 2014. Hon DSc Westminster, 2008. *Publications*: research papers in physics and higher educn in various jls. *Recreations*: walking, cricket, gardening. *Address*: 24 The Broadway, Wheathampstead, St Albans AL4 8LN. T: (01438) 833663. *Club*: Oxford and Cambridge.

**COPLEY, John (Michael Harold)**, CBE 2014; opera director; b 12 June 1933; s of Ernest Harold Copley and Lilian Forbes; civil partnership 2006, John Hugh Chadwyck-Healey (d 2014). *Educ*: King Edward's, Five Ways, Birmingham; Sadler's Wells Ballet Sch.; Central Sch. of Arts and Crafts, London (Dip. with Hons in Theatre Design). Appeared as the apprentice in Britten's Peter Grimes for Covent Garden Opera Co., 1950; stage managed: both opera and ballet companies at Sadler's Wells, in Rosebery Avenue, 1953–57; also various musicals, plays, etc, in London's West End, incl. The World of Paul Slickey and My Fair Lady. Joined Covent Garden Opera Co.: Dep. Stage Manager, 1960; Asst Resident Producer, 1963; Associate Resident Producer, 1966; Resident Producer, 1972; Prin. Resident Producer, 1975–88. *Productions include*: *at Covent Garden*: Suor Angelica, 1965; Così fan Tutte, 1968, 1981; Orpheo ed Euridice, 1969; Le Nozze di Figaro, 1971, 1985; Don Giovanni, 1973; La Bohème, 1974, 1985, 2012, 2015; Faust, 1974; L'elisir d'amore, 1975, 1981, 1985; Benvenuto Cellini, 1976; Ariadne auf Naxos, 1976; Maria Stuarda; Royal Silver Jubilee Gala, 1977; Werther, 1979; La Traviata, Lucrezia Borgia, 1980; Alceste, 1981; Semele, 1982, 1988, 1996; Norma, 1987; L'elisir d'amore, 1992; *at London Coliseum (for Sadler's Wells, subseq. ENO)*: Carmen, Il Seraglio, Il Trovatore, La Traviata, Mary Stuart; Rosenkavalier, La Belle Hélène, 1975; Werther, 1977; Manon, Aida, Julius Caesar, Les Mamelles de Tirésias, 1979; The Merry Widow, 2008; *Athens Festival*: Macbeth; *Netherlands Opera*: Lucia; *Opera National de Belge*: Lucia; *Wexford Festival*: La Clemenza di Tito; L'Infedeltà delusa; *Dallas Civic Opera*: Lucia; Hansel and Gretel, 1991; Elektra, Il Trovatore, 1996; Ariodante, 1998; *Chicago Lyric Opera*: Lucia; La Bohème, 1983; Orlando, 1986; Tancredi, 1989; The Barber of Seville, 1989; Peter Grimes, Idomeneo, 1997; Gioconda, 1998; Die Fledermaus, 1999; *Canadian Opera, Toronto*: Lucia; Falstaff; La Bohème, 1984; Adriana Lecouvreur, La Forza del Destino, 1987; *Greek Nat. Opera*: Madame Butterfly; *Australian Opera*: Fidelio, Nozze di Figaro, Rigoletto, Magic Flute, Jenufa, Ariadne auf Naxos, Madame Butterfly, Fra Diavolo, Macbeth, La Traviata, Manon Lescaut, Lucia di Lammermoor, Tosca, Manon; Adriana Lecouvreur, 1984; Peter Grimes, 1986; Carmen, 1987; La Forza del Destino, 1988; *Victoria State Opera*: Don Carlos, 1984; La Bohème, 1985; *WNO*: La Traviata, Falstaff, Peter Grimes, Tosca; Peter Grimes, 1983; *Opera North*: Les Mamelles de Tirésias, Madama Butterfly; *Scottish Opera*: Lucia, Ballo in Maschera, Dido and Aeneas; Acis and Galatea for English Opera Group in Stockholm, Paris, Aldeburgh Fest.; *New York City Opera*: Le Nozze di Figaro; Der Freischutz; Don Quichotte; *Santa Fé Opera*: Ariodanie, 1987; Così fan tutte, 1988; Der Rosenkavalier, La Traviata, 1989; La Bohème, 1990; Tosca, 1994; Semele, 1997; Idomeneo, 1999; *Ottawa Festival*: Midsummer Night's Dream; Eugene Onegin, 1983 *Vancouver Opera*: Carmen; *San Francisco Opera*: Julius Caesar; The Midsummer Marriage, 1983; Don Giovanni, 1984; Orlando, 1985; Le Nozze di Figaro, Eugene Onegin, 1986; La Traviata, 1987; Idomeneo, 1989; Midsummer Night's Dream, 1992; Pique Dame, 1993; Peter Grimes, 1998; *San Diego Opera*: Eugene Onegin, 1985; Le Nozze di Figaro, 1986; Così fan tutte, 1991; *Staatsoper Munich*: Adriana Lecouvreur, 1984; Teatro La Fenice, Venice: Semele, 1991 and 1992; *Deutsche Oper, Berlin*: L'Elisir d'amore, 1988; *Metropolitan Opera, NY*: Julius Caesar, 1988; Semiramide, 1990, 2018; L'Elisir d'amore, 1991; Norma, 2001; Le Pirata, 2002; *Opera Theatre of St Louis*: La Rondine, 1996; *Grange Festival*: The Abduction from the Seraglio, 2018. Sang as soloist in Bach's St John Passion, Bremen, Germany, 1965; appeared as Ferdy in John Osborne's play, A Patriot for Me, at Royal Court Theatre, 1965. Co-directed (with Patrick Garland): Fanfare for Europe Gala, Covent Garden, 3 Jan. 1973; Fanfare for Elizabeth gala, Covent Garden, 21 April 1986. Hon. RAM 1999; Hon. RCM 2002. *Recreation*: cooking. *Address*: 9D Thistle Grove, SW10 9RR.

**COPLEY, Tom Phillip**; Member (Lab) London Assembly, Greater London Authority, since 2012; b 11 May 1985. *Educ*: Univ. of Nottingham (BA Politics). Worked for Labour Party, HPA and Searchlight Educnl Trust. Greater London Authority: Member: Econ. Cttee, 2012–13; Housing and Regeneration Cttee, 2012–13; Transport Cttee, 2012–; Planning Cttee, 2013–; Dep. Chair, Housing Cttee, 2013–14 and 2016–19 (Chair, 2014–16, 2019–20). Mem., London Fire and Emergency Planning Authy, 2015–16. Mem. (Lab), Lewisham LBC, 2018–. Trustee: Humanists UK (formerly British Humanist Assoc.), 2013–; New Diorama Th., 2014–. Patron, LGBT Labour, 2012–. *Address*: Greater London Authority, City Hall, Queen's Walk, SE1 2AA.

**COPP, Prof. Andrew John**, DPhil; FRCPath; FMedSci, FRSB; Professor of Developmental Neurobiology, since 1996, and Director (London), Human Developmental Biology Resource, since 1999, Institute of Child Health, University College London; b 27 Feb. 1954; s of Frederick John Copp and Doreen Ann Copp (née Crouch). *Educ*: St Peter's Coll., Oxford (BA 1st Cl. Hons (Zool.) 1975); Wolfson Coll., Oxford (DPhil (Exptl Embryol.) 1978); Guy's Hosp. Med. Sch., London Univ. (MB BS 1983). FRCPath 2003. Fogarty Internat. Res. Fellow, Dept of Paediatrics, Stanford Univ. Med. Sch., Calif, 1984–86; Res. Scientist, ICRF, Univ. of Oxford, 1986–92; Sen. Lectr, then Reader, Inst. of Child Health, UCL, and Wellcome Sen. Res. Fellow in Clin. Sci., 1992–96; Dir, Inst. of Child Health, UCL, 2003–12. Member: Neuroscis & Mental Health Bd, 2003–07; Career Develt Award and Sen. Non-clinical Fellowship Panel, 2012–16, MRC; Grants and Fellowship Panel, Mason Med. Res. Foundn, 2019–. Non-exec. Dir, Gt Ormond St Hosp. NHS Trust, 2003–12. Mem., Med. Adv. Bd, SPARKS, 1999–2004. Pres., Develtl Pathol. Soc., UK, 1993–97. Mem. Bd of Advrs, Foulkes Foundn, 2000–; Mem. Bd, 2004–07, Hon. Dir of Res., 2007–14, Children's Trust Tadworth; Mem. Bd, Bo Hjelt Foundn, 2010–. FMedSci 2000; FRSB (FSB 2012). Man. Ed., Anatomy and Embryology, 1998–2003; Associate Ed., Birth Defects Res. A: Clinical and Molecular Teratology, 2002–12. *Publications*: (with D. L. Cockcroft) Postimplantation Mammalian Embryos: a practical approach, 1990; more than 200 peer-reviewed articles in acad. jls on birth defects, esp. neural tube defects such as spina bifida, develtl biol., genetics. *Address*: UCL Institute of Child Health, 30 Guilford Street, WC1N 1EH. T: (020) 7905 2355, Fax: (020) 7905 2953. E: a.copp@ucl.ac.uk.

**COPPEL, Andrew Maxwell**, CBE 2008; FCA; Chairman, Dolphin Capital Investors Ltd, since 2016; b 22 Aug. 1950; s of Isaac Coppel and Marjorie Coppel; m 1974, June Vanessa Gillespie; one s one d. *Educ*: Belfast Royal Acad.; Queen's Univ., Belfast (LLB Hons). FCA 1982. With Coopers & Lybrand, 1973–77; Asst Dir, Morgan Grenfell & Co. Ltd, 1977–86; Finance Dir, Ratners Gp plc, 1986–90; Chief Executive: Sale Tilney plc, 1990–92; Queens Moat Houses plc, 1993–2003; Racecourse Hldgs Trust, later Jockey Club Racecourses, 2004–07; McCambridge Gp, 2008–10; Chm., Alternative Hotel Gp, later De Vere Gp, 2010–11; Gp Chief Exec., De Vere Gp, 2011–15. Ind. Dir, Crest Nicholson Hldgs Ltd, 2009–11; non-exec. Dir, Bannatyne Gp, 2016–19. Mem., Adv. Bd on Ireland, Lloyds Bank, 2012. Chairman: Tourism Ireland Ltd, 2001–07; London Irish Hldgs Ltd, 2008–11. Vice Pres., Queen's Univ. Assoc., London, 2000–12 (Mem. Council, 1980–). Chm., Shooting Star Children's Hospices, 2019–. Associate Mem., Glyndebourne, 2015–; Patron,

RA, 2017–. *Recreations:* Rugby, golf, tennis, cinema, reading action novels. *E:* acop@btinternet.com. *Clubs:* Hurlingham; Claygate Tennis, St George's Hill Golf (Surrey); Surrey County Cricket.

**COPPEL, Philip Antony;** QC 2009; *b* London, 5 Jan. 1960; *s* of William Andrew and Maria Antonietta Coppel; *m* 1991, Francesca Maria Gallo; one *s* two *d. Educ:* Daramalan Coll., Canberra; Australian Nat. Univ. (BA Hons Hist., LLB). Barrister and solicitor, Canberra, 1984–91; Solicitor, McKenna & Co., London, 1991–94; called to the Bar, Lincoln's Inn, 1994; barrister, Gray's Inn, specialising in commercial and govtl disputes, 1994–. *Publications:* Information Rights, 2004, 5th edn 2018; (contrib.) Halsbury's Laws of England, 2001, 2002; (contrib.) Atkin's Court Forms, 2007, 2008, 2011, 2012, 2015; (contrib.) Jordan's Tribunal Practice, 2012; Cornerstone's Electoral Legislation, 2016. *Recreation:* classical music. *Address:* 2–3 Gray's Inn Square, Gray's Inn, WC1R 5JH. *T:* (020) 7421 1860, *Fax:* (020) 7405 1166. *E:* pcqc@2-3gis.co.uk.

**COPPEL, Yvonne Ruth; Her Honour Judge Coppel;** a Circuit Judge, since 2007; *b* Salford, 24 July 1954; *d* of Hyman and Hilda Coppel; *m* 1988; one *s* one *d. Educ:* N Manchester High Sch. for Girls; Univ. of Birmingham (LLB Hons). Called to the Bar, Inner Temple, 1976; Asst Recorder, 1996–2000; Recorder, 2000–07. *Recreations:* cinema, fell walking, theatre. *Address:* Liverpool Civil and Family Courts, 35 Vernon Street, Liverpool L2 2BX. *T:* (0151) 296 2200.

**COPPEN, Luke Benjamin Edward;** Editor, The Catholic Herald, since 2004; *b* 8 Feb. 1976; *s* of Rev. Canon Martin Coppen and Christine Coppen (*née* Stevens); *m* 2004, Marlena Marciniszyn; two *d. Educ:* Testbourne Community Sch., Whitchurch, Hants; Cricklade Coll., Andover; Sch. of Oriental and African Studies, Univ. of London (BA Study of Religions and Politics); Univ. of Wales, Cardiff (Postgrad. Dip. Journalism Studies). Film Ed., London Student mag., 1996–97; reporter, 1998–2000, Dep. Ed., 2000–04, Catholic Herald; Faith in Brief columnist, The Times, 2001–05. *Recreations:* cinema, cycling, rabbit-keeping. *Address:* The Catholic Herald, Herald House, Lambs Passage, Bunhill Row, EC1Y 8TQ. *T:* (020) 7448 3606, *Fax:* (020) 7256 9728. *E:* luke@catholicherald.co.uk.

**COPPIN, Alan Charles;** Chairman, Sports Grounds Safety Authority, since 2015; *b* 4 June 1950; *s* of Charles and Vera Coppin; *m* 1975, Gaynor Hilary Wareham; one *s. Educ:* Westlain Grammar Sch., Brighton; Brighton Poly. Mgt posts with cos incl. Strutt & Parker, THF Leisure, Associated Leisure and Bembom Group, 1971–86; Sen. Mgt Consultant, KPMG, 1986–88; Chief Exec., Wembley Stadium Ltd, 1988–95, Wembley plc, 1995–98; Chief Exec., Historic Royal Palaces, 1999–2003. Associate, Prime Minister's Delivery Unit, Cabinet Office, 2002–04. A Crown Representative, Cabinet Office, 2013–16. Chairman: Danoptra Hldgs, 2002–06; Redstone plc, 2006–09; Timeless Mgt Gp, 2009–12; Aeternum Ltd, 2010–14; Venue Retail Ltd, 2010–12; The Coffee Mob CIC, 2011–; Mem. Exec. Bd, Compass Gp plc, 1998–99; non-executive Director: Metroline plc, 1997–2000; Carillion plc, 1999–2002; Expocentric plc, 2000–02; Protocol n. v., 2002–04; Capital & Regional plc, 2004–10; Berkeley Gp Hldgs plc, 2006–13; Marshalls plc, 2010–. Non-executive Director: Air Force Operating and Performance Gp (formerly Air Comd), RAF, 2007–13; RAF Bd, 2009–13; Ind. Mem., Air Rank Appts Bd, RAF, 2011–13; Ind. Panel Mem., Public Appts, DCMS, 2015– (Sen. Ind. Panel Mem., 2017–). Chairman: NW London TEC, 1990–92; Stadium and Arena Mgt Project, 1994–95. Chairman: Include, nat. children's charity, 1997–2000; Robinia Care Gp, 2003–04; Prince's Foundn for Built Envmt, 2004–06 (Trustee, 2003–04); Campaign Bd, RAF Mus., 2013– (Trustee, 2013–); Spirit of 2012, 2017–19; Trustee, Greenwich Foundn, 2003–04. Mem., Adv. Forum, Saïd Business Sch., Oxford Univ., 2002–07. Patron, Windsor Leadership Trust, 2003–17 (Fellow 2017). Hon. Vis. Prof., Business Sch., Univ. of N London, 1998–2003. CCMI (CIMgt 1997). FRSA 2003–05. *Publications:* (jtly) Timeless Management, 2002; Great Britons on Success, 2009; The Human Capital Imperative, 2017. *Recreations:* family activities, cinema, writing, Chelsea FC season ticket holder, fitness. *Club:* Royal Air Force.

**COPPLE, Philip;** Director General, Prisons, HM Prison and Probation Service, since 2019; *b* Ashton under Lyne, Manchester, 30 May 1969; *s* of Anthony and Eleanor Copple; *m* 1992, Gabrielle Reddington; two *s* one *d. Educ:* St Joseph's RC High Sch., Whitefield; Holy Cross Sixth Form Coll., Bury; Univ. of Durham (BA 1st Cl. Hons Politics). Prison Officer, HMP Leeds, 1990–92; Principal Officer, HMP Wakefield, 1992–94; Gov. 5, Office of Dir of Security and Progs, HM Prison Service HQ, 1994–95; Gov. 5, HMP Wealstun, 1995–96; Gov. 4, 1997–98, Dep. Gov., 1999–2000, HMP Frankland; Governor: HM YOI Deerbolt, 2000–02; HMP Frankland, 2002–06; Area Manager, NE Prisons, 2006–09; National Offender Management Service, Ministry of Justice: Dir, Offender Mgt, NE, 2009–11; Dir, Nat. Operational Services, 2011; Dir, High Security, 2011–12; Dir of Public Sector Prisons, 2013–16; Chief Operating Officer, 2016–17; Exec. Dir, Prisons, HM Prison and Probation Service, 2017–18. *Recreations:* family, friends, swimming, cycling. *Address:* HM Prison and Probation Service, 102 Petty France, SW1H 9AJ. *T:* (020) 3334 3555. *E:* DirectorGeneralPrisons@noms.gsi.gov.uk.

**COPPOLA, Francis Ford;** Artistic Director, American Zoetrope (formerly Zoetrope Studios), since 1969; *b* 7 April 1939; *s* of late Carmine Coppola and of Italia Pennino; *m* 1963, Eleanor Neil; one *s* one *d* (and one *s* decd). *Educ:* Hofstra Univ. (BA); Univ. of Calif, LA (MFA). Films directed: Dementia 13, 1963; You're a Big Boy Now, 1967; Finian's Rainbow, 1968; The Rain People, 1969; The Godfather, 1972 (2 Acad. Awards, 1973); The Conversation, 1974; The Godfather Part II, 1974 (3 Acad. Awards, 1975); Apocalypse Now, 1979; One From the Heart, 1981; The Outsiders, 1983; Rumble Fish, 1983; The Cotton Club, 1984; Peggy Sue Got Married, 1987; Gardens of Stone, 1988; Tucker: The Man and His Dream, 1988; New York Stories (Life Without Zoe), 1989; The Godfather Part III, 1991; Bram Stoker's Dracula, 1993; Jack, 1996; John Grisham's The Rainmaker, 1998; Apocalypse Now Redux, 2001; Youth Without Youth, 2007; Tetro (also prod. and writer), 2010; executive producer: Black Stallion, 1979; Hammett, 1983; Lionheart, 1987; The Secret Garden, 1993; Mary Shelley's Frankenstein, 1994. Irving G. Thalberg Meml Award, Academy Awards, 2011. Commandeur, Ordre des Arts et des Lettres, 1983. *Publications:* The Godfather Notebook, 2016. *Recreations:* reading, writing, scientific discovery. *Address:* American Zoetrope, 916 Kearny Street, San Francisco, CA 94133–5138, USA. *T:* (415) 7887500.

**COPPS, Hon. Sheila Maureen,** OC 2012; PC (Can.) 1993; President, Sheila Copps & Associates; radio and television presenter; newspaper columnist; actress; *b* 27 Nov. 1952; *d* of Vic Copps and Geraldine (*née* Guthro); one *d. Educ:* Univ. of Western Ontario (BA Hons English and French); Univ. of Rouen; McMaster Univ. Journalist, 1974–77. MPP (L) Ontario, 1981–84; MP (L) Hamilton E, Canada, 1984–2004. Official Opposition Critic for: Housing and Labour, 1984–87; Health and Welfare and Fitness and Amateur Sport, 1987–89; Envmt and Co-Critic for Social Policy, 1989–90; Industry, 1990–91; Dep. Leader of Opposition, 1991–93; Minister of the Envmt, 1993–96; Dep. Prime Minister, 1993–97; Minister of Canadian Heritage, 1996–2003. *Publications:* Nobody's Baby, 1986; Worth Fighting For, 2004.

**COPSON, Andrew James William;** Chief Executive, Humanists UK (formerly British Humanist Association), since 2010; *b* Nuneaton, 19 Nov. 1980; *s* of David Copson and Julia Heather Cunningham; civil partnership 2011, Mark John Wardrop. *Educ:* King Henry VIII Sch., Coventry; Balliol Coll., Oxford (BA Hons 1st cl. Ancient and Mod. Hist. 2004); Chartered Inst. of Public Relations (Dip. Public Relns 2008). Vice Pres., Welfare and Equal Opportunities, Oxford Univ. Student Union, 2002–03; Parly Liaison Officer, Citizenship Foundn, 2004–05; British Humanist Association: Educn and Public Affairs Officer, 2005–07, on part-time secondment as Researcher, Office of Baron Macdonald of Tradeston, 2005–07; Hd, Educn and Public Affairs, 2007–09. Member: RE Consultants Gp, QCA, 2006–10; Standing Adv. Council on RE, City of Westminster, 2006–16 (Chm., 2010–16); Census Diversity Adv. Gp, ONS, 2007–09; Steering Gp for New Guidance on RE, DCSF, 2008–09; Humanities Diploma Adv. Gp, 2008–10; Standing Adv. Conference on Religion and Belief, BBC, 2009–14; Steering Gp on Spiritual, Moral, Social and Cultural Educn in FE, Learning and Skills Improvement Service, 2009–10; Ind. Schs Practitioners' Gp on Spiritual, Moral, Social and Cultural Educn, DCSF, 2009–10; Equality Reference Gp, DWP, 2010–11; Faith, Belief and Meaning Gp, Nat. Council for Palliative Care, 2010–12; Non-religion and Secularity Res. Network, 2010–; Nat. Adv. Panel, Equality Matters for Children, 2011–12; Community Accountability Forum, CPS, 2011–13; Adv. Panel on Equality and Inclusion, Ofqual, 2011–15; Steering Gp, Religious Educn (England) Subject Review, 2011–13; Commn on Religion and Belief in British Public Life, 2013–15; Freedom of Religion and Belief Adv. Gp, FCO, 2014–15; Strategic Ref. Gp, Equality and Human Rights Commn, 2015–17; Adv. Bd, Religion Media Centre, 2018–. Mem. Council, Electoral Reform Soc., 2017–. Trustee: Oxford Pride, 2004–05; Values Educn Council, 2005–08 (Chm., 2006–08); Gay and Lesbian Humanist Assoc., 2005–10 (Chm., 2008–10); Pink Triangle Trust, 2006–08; Religious Educn Council of England and Wales, 2006–15, 2018– (Treas., 2018–); Conway Hall Ethical Soc. (formerly South Place Ethical Soc.), 2007–13; Eur. Humanist Fedn, 2007–10; Nat. Council of Faiths and Beliefs in Further Educn, 2008–13 (Vice Chm., 2008–13); Internat. Humanist Trust, 2011–; All Faiths and None, 2011–13; Actors of Dionysus, 2014–17 (Mem., Inner Circle, 2018–); Humanist International (formerly International Humanist and Ethical Union): Delegate to Council of Europe, 2008–12 (Hd of Delegn, 2010–11); Vice Pres., 2010–15; First Vice Pres., 2012–15; Pres., 2015–; Delegate of Eur. Humanist Fedn to OSCE, 2008–10. Mem., Exec. Cttee, Labour Humanists, 2007–09. Associate: Centre for Law and Religion, Cardiff Univ., 2008–; Equality and Diversity Forum Res. Network, 2012–15. Accredited practitioner, Non-Religious Pastoral Support Network, 2017. MCIPR 2005; FCMI 2014; FRSA 2006. Gov., Seven Sisters Primary Sch., Haringey, 2007–09 (Chm., Curriculum Cttee, 2008–09). *Publications:* The Wiley-Blackwell Handbook on Humanism (ed with A. C. Grayling), 2015; Secularism: politics, freedom, and religion, 2017; A Very Short Introduction to Secularism, 2019. *Recreations:* American science fiction, English novels, Roman and Greek history, Greek drama, gardening. *Address:* Humanists UK, 39 Moreland Street, EC1V 8BB. *T:* (020) 7324 3066. *E:* andrew@humanists.uk. *Club:* Athenæum.

**CORBET, Dr Gordon Barclay;** zoologist; *b* 4 March 1933; *s* of George and Mary Corbet; *m* 1959, Elizabeth Urquhart; one *s* one *d. Educ:* Morgan Acad., Dundee; Univ. of St Andrews. BSc, PhD. Asst Lectr in Biology, Sir John Cass Coll., London, 1958–59; British Museum (Natural History): Sen., later Principal, Scientific Officer, Dept of Zoology, 1960–71; Dep. Keeper of Zoology, 1971–76; Hd, Dept of Central Services, 1976–88. *Publications:* The Terrestrial Mammals of Western Europe, 1966; Finding and Identifying Mammals in Britain, 1975; The Handbook of British Mammals, 2nd edn (with H. N. Southern), 1977, 3rd edn (with S. Harris), 1991; The Mammals of the Palaearctic Region, 1978; The Mammals of Britain and Europe, 1980; A World List of Mammalian Species (with J. E. Hill), 1980, 3rd edn 1991; The Mammals of the Indomalayan Region (with J. E. Hill), 1992; The Nature of Fife, 1998. *Recreations:* wildlife on sand dunes, family history. *Address:* 8 Hillhead Lane, Lundin Links, Leven, Fife KY8 6DE. *T:* (01333) 329524.

**CORBETT,** family name of **Baron Rowallan.**

**CORBETT, Air Vice-Marshal (Anthony) Sean,** CB 2018; MBE 1999; Director, Defence, Security and Intelligence, Earth-i, since 2018; *b* Duxford, 19 Aug. 1964; *s* of Anthony Corbett and Adele Corbett; *m* 1993, Gaynor Jones; two *s. Educ:* Hayfield Sch., Doncaster; Keele Univ. (BA Hons Biol. and Geog. 1986); King's Coll. London (MA Defence Studies 2001). Commnd RAF, 1988; Comdr Jt Service Signals Orgn, 2005–08; UK Chief of Intelligence, Afghanistan, 2010–11; UK Dep. Mil. Rep. to NATO, 2011–13; ACOS, Intelligence, PJHQ, 2014–15; Dep. Dir, Commonwealth Integration, Defense Intelligence Agency, USA, 2015–18. *Recreations:* angling, photography, Rugby, ski-ing. *T:* 07490 525888. *E:* corbett.anthony.sean@gmail.com.

**CORBETT, Dame Antoinette;** *see* Sibley, Dame A.

**CORBETT, Bernie;** General Secretary, 2000–16, Finance and Business Manager, 2016–17, Writers' Guild of Great Britain; *b* Cuckfield, Sussex, 17 Sept. 1952; *s* of Wally Corbett and Liz Corbett (*née* Smoker); partner, Jane Pickard; one *s. Educ:* Haywards Heath Grammar Sch., Sussex. Reporter: W Sussex County Times, 1969–73; Evening Argus, Brighton, 1973–74; Dep. Chief Sub-Ed., Birmingham Post, 1974–80; Chief Sub-Ed., Guardian, 1980–85; Ed., The Journalist (NUJ), 1985–87; freelance journalist, 1987–90; Chief Features Sub-Ed., Independent, 1990–94; Nat. Organiser, NUJ, 1995–2000.

**CORBETT, Gerald Michael Nolan;** DL; Chairman: Britvic PLC, 2005–17; Segro plc, since 2016; *b* 7 Sept. 1951; *s* of late John Michael Nolan Corbett and of Pamela Muriel Corbett (*née* Gay); *m* 1976, Virginia Moore Newsum; one *s* three *d. Educ:* Tonbridge Sch.; Pembroke Coll., Cambridge (Foundn Schol.; MA); London Business Sch. (MSc with Dist.); Harvard Business Sch. (Exchange Schol.). Boston Consulting Gp, 1975–82; Dixons Group plc: Gp Finance Controller, 1982–85; Corporate Finance Dir, 1985–87; Group Finance Director: Redland plc, 1987–94; Grand Metropolitan plc, 1994–97; Chief Exec., Railtrack Gp plc, 1997–2000. Chairman: Woolworths Gp plc, 2001–07; Holmes Place plc, 2003–06; SSL International PLC, 2005–10; Moneysupermarket.com plc, 2007–14; Towry Hldgs, 2012–14; Betfair, 2012–16; Numis Securities plc, 2014–17 (non-exec. Dir, 2009–14); non-executive Director: MEPC Plc, 1995–98; Burmah Castrol Plc, 1998–2000; Greencore Gp plc, 2004–10. Chm., RNID, 2007–13. Chm. Govs, Abbot's Hill Sch., 1997–2002; Gov., Luton Univ., 2002–05. Vice Chm., Herts Community Foundn, 2010–13 (Chm., 2013–); Chm., St Albans Cathedral Music Trust, 2010–. Mem. Council, High Sheriffs Assoc., 2008–11. Freeman, City of London, 1989. High Sheriff, 2018, DL, 2015, Herts. FRSA 2006. *Recreations:* country pursuits, golf, ski-ing, bridge. *Address:* Holtsmere End Farm, Redbourn, Herts AL3 7AW. *Clubs:* Oxford and Cambridge, MCC (Chm., 2015–).

**CORBETT, Prof. Greville George,** PhD; FBA 1997; FAcSS; Distinguished Chair (formerly Professor) of Linguistics, University of Surrey, since 1988; *b* 23 Dec. 1947; *s* of George Pilsbury Corbett and Elsie Mary Bates; three *s. Educ:* Univ. of Birmingham (BA 1970; MA 1971; PhD 1976). Lectr, 1974–85, Reader, 1985–88, Univ. of Surrey. Pres., Linguistics Assoc. of GB, 1994–97. FAcSS (AcSS 2000). MAE 2008. Hon. Mem., Linguistic Soc. of America, 2014. *Publications:* Predicate Agreement in Russian, 1979; Hierarchies, Targets and Controllers: agreement patterns in Slavic, 1983; (jtly) Computers, Language Learning and Language Teaching, 1985; Gender, 1991; (ed jtly) Heads in Grammatical Theory, 1993; (ed jtly) The Slavonic Languages, 1993; Number, 2000; (jtly) The Syntax-Morphology Interface: a study of syncretism, 2005; Agreement, 2006; (ed jtly) Deponency and Morphological Mismatches, 2007; (jtly) A Dictionary of Archi: Archi-Russian-English,

2007; (ed jtly) Defective Paradigms: missing forms and what they tell us, 2010; (ed jtly) Case and Grammatical Relations: studies in honor of Bernard Comrie, 2008; (ed jtly) Features: perspectives on a key notion in linguistics, 2010; Features, 2012; (ed jtly) Canonical Morphology and Syntax, 2012; (ed jtly) Periphrasis: the role of syntax and morphology in paradigms, 2013; (ed) The Expression of Gender, 2014; (ed jtly) Understanding and measuring morphological complexity, 2015; (ed jtly) Archi: complexities of agreement in cross-theoretical perspective, 2016; (jtly) Morphological Complexity, 2017. *Recreation*: music. *Address*: Surrey Morphology Group, School of Literature and Languages, Faculty of Arts and Social Sciences, University of Surrey, Guildford, Surrey GU2 7XH.

**CORBETT, James Patrick**; QC 1999; FCIArb; a Deputy High Court Judge and Deputy Mercantile Judge, since 2007; *b* 10 May 1952; *s* of late Patrick Francis Corbett and Kathleen Mary Corbett (*née* O'Callaghan); *m* 1979, Barbara Janet Willett; one *s* four *d*. *Educ*: Squire Sch., Chelsea; Univ. of Exeter (LLB 1973; LLM European Legal Studies 1975); Inns of Court Sch. of Law; Inst. of Law, Jersey. FCIArb 1997; Chartered Arbitrator, 2001. Called to the Bar, Inner Temple, 1975, Bencher, 2008, Lincoln's Inn, *ad eundem*, 1998; Lectr in Law, Univ. of Leicester, 1975–77; in practice at the Bar, 1977–2010; joined Midland and Oxford Circuit, 1979; called to Irish Bar, 1981, Northern Irish Bar, 1994, NSW Bar, 2002, Anguilla Bar, 2002, St Kitts and Nevis Bar, 2004, BVI Bar, 2004, Turks and Caicos Bar, 2007, Cayman Is Bar, 2010, Gibraltar Bar, 2013, Bahamas Bar, 2015; in practice with Kobre & Kim LLP, 2010–18, with Baker & Partners, St Helier, Jersey, 2018–. Asst Recorder, 1996–2000; Recorder, 2000–10. CEDR Registered Mediator, 2000. Mem., Soc. of Trust and Estate Practitioners, 2005–. Contested (SDP): Erewash, Derbys, 1983; Cheshire E, 1984; Staffs Moorlands, 1987. Liveryman: Arbitrators' Co., 2000–; Bowyers' Co., 2003–. *Publications*: articles in legal and arbitration jls. *Recreations*: jazz, the cinema, Rugby League, cricket. *Address*: Baker & Partners, Midland Chambers, 2–10 Library Place, St Helier, Jersey, Channel Islands JE1 2BP. *Clubs*: Garrick; Ronnie Scott's Jazz.

**CORBETT, Michelle Jane, (Mrs Michael O'Gorman); Her Honour Judge Corbett**; a Circuit Judge, since 2009; *b* Salford, 9 Feb. 1965; *d* of Michael Corbett and Carol Lowry (*née* Seddon); *m* 1993, Michael O'Gorman, JP; two *d*. *Educ*: Manchester High Sch. for Girls; Univ. of Leeds (LLB Hons). Called to the Bar, Inner Temple, 1987 (Profumo Award), Bencher, 2015; barrister, 1987–2009; Recorder, 2007–09. *Recreations*: my two children, marmalade making, running, Manchester United Football Club, learning to play golf. *Address*: West London Family Court, Dukes Green Avenue, Feltham, Middx TW14 0LR. *E*: HHJ.Michelle.Corbett@ejudiciary.net.

**CORBETT, Dr Richard Graham**; Member (Lab) Yorkshire and the Humber Region, European Parliament, 1999–2009 and since 2014 (Merseyside West, Dec. 1996–1999); Leader, European Parliamentary Labour Party, since 2017; *b* 6 Jan. 1955; *s* of Harry Graham Corbett and Kathleen Zita Corbett (*née* Bryant); *m* 1st, 1984, Inge van Gaal (marr. diss.); one *s*; 2nd, 1989, Anne de Malsche (marr. diss.); two *d*; 3rd, 2017, Lorraine Kirkwood. *Educ*: Farnborough Rd Sch., Southport; Internat. Sch., Geneva; Trinity Coll., Oxford (BA Hons PPE); Univ. of Hull (Extra Mural Doctorate 1995). Stagiare, Socialist Gp, European Parlt, 1976; UK Labour Delegn, 1977; Commn (Regl Policy), 1977; Sec. Gen., European Co-ordination Bureau, Internat. Youth Orgns, 1977–81; European civil servant, 1981–89; European Parliament: political advr, 1989–94, Dep. Gen. Sec., 1995–96, Socialist Gp; Vice Pres., Cttee on Instnl Affairs, 1997–99; Labour Party and Socialist Gp spokesman on constitutional affairs, 1999–2009; Dep. Leader, Labour MEPs, 2006–09 and 2014–17; Mem. Bd, Britain in Europe, 2001–05; Vice Chair, UK European Movement, 2014–. Mem., Cabinet of Herman Van Rompuy, Pres. of European Council, 2010–14. Mem. Regl Bd, Yorks, 1999–2001 and 2007–09, Mem., Nat. Policy Forum, 2008–09 and 2014–, Labour Party. *Publications*: A Socialist Policy for Europe, 1985; The European Parliament, 1990, 9th edn 2016; The Treaty of Maastricht: from conception to ratification, 1993; The European Parliament's Role in closer EU integration, 1998; The European Union: how does it work?, 4th edn, 2015; contrib. Annual Rev. on Instnl Develts in EU for Jl Common Mkt Studies. *Recreations*: ski-ing, watching football, reading. *Address*: European Parliament, 60 Rue Wiertz, 1047 Brussels, Belgium.

**CORBETT, Maj.-Gen. Sir Robert (John Swan)**, KCVO 1994; CB 1991; lecturer in history, since 2003; Director: Hart International, since 2003; Chelsea Group, since 2015; *b* 16 May 1940; *s* of Robert Hugh Swan Corbett and Patricia Elizabeth Corbett (*née* Cavan-Lambart); *m* 1966, Susan Margaret Anne O'Cock; three *s*. *Educ*: Woodcote House; Shrewsbury School; Royal Mil. Coll. of Sci., 1972; Army Staff Coll., 1973; US Armed Forces Staff Coll., 1980. Joined Army in ranks, 1958, commissioned Irish Guards, 1959; served UK, Cyprus, Hong Kong, Falkland Is, Belize, BAOR; Brigade Major, HQ Household Div., 1980–81; CO, 1st Bn Irish Guards (4 Armoured Brigade, BAOR), 1981–84; Chief of Staff and Dep. Comdr, British Forces Falkland Is, 1984–85; Comdr, 5th Airborne Brigade, 1985–87; rcds 1987; Dir, Defence Programme, MoD, 1987–89; GOC Berlin (British Sector) and British Comdt, Berlin, 1989–3 Oct. 1990 (German re-unification); attached HQ BAOR, 1990–91; GOC London Dist, and Maj. Gen. Comdg Household Div., 1991–94. Mem. Adv. Bd, Deutsche Bank Berlin AG, 1991–2000. Chairman: Guards Chapel Adv. Cttee, 1993–2011; Berlin Infantry Bde Meml Trust Fund, 1992–99. Dir, Dulverton Trust, 1994–2003. Regtl Lt-Col, Irish Guards, 1988–91. Hon. Col, London Irish Rifles, 1993–2000. Liveryman, Vintners' Co., 1968. Hon. Citizen, 1993, Mem., Conseil Municipal, 2000–04, Pierrefeu, France. Order of Merit, Berlin, 1990; Hon. Grand Officier, Ordre de Mérite (Luxembourg), 1994; Hon. Grande Oficial, Ordem do Infante Dom Henrique (Portugal), 1994; Hon. Dato Paduka, Order of Crown of Brunei, 1993. *Publications*: Berlin and the British Ally 1945–1990, 1993. *Recreations*: travel, reading (especially military history), walking, English church history and architecture. *Address*: c/o RHQ Irish Guards, Wellington Barracks, SW1E 6HQ. *Clubs*: Pratt's, Buck's.

**CORBETT, Air Vice-Marshal Sean**; *see* Corbett, Air Vice-Marshal A. S.

**CORBIN, Christopher John**, OBE 2014; hotelier and restaurateur; *b* 1 March 1952; *s* of Frederick Christopher Corbin and Vera Corbin (*née* Copperwaite); *m* 1982, Francine Checinski; one *s* one *d* (twins). *Educ*: St Christopher's, Bournemouth; Westminster Tech. Coll. Co-founder and Director (with Jeremy King): Caprice Hldgs Ltd, 1982–2002; Caprice Events Ltd, 1995–2000; Dir, Rex Restaurant Associates, 2003–; co-proprietor (with Jeremy King): restaurants: Le Caprice, 1981–2004; The Ivy, 1990–2004; J. Sheekey, 1998–; The Wolseley, 2003–; St Alban, 2006–09; bar, Monkey Bar, NY, 2009–10; The Delaunay, 2011–; Brasserie Zédel, 2012–; Colbert, 2012–; Fischer's, 2014–; hotel, The Beaumont, 2014–; co-founder, Bellanger, 2015. Restaurateur of Year, Caterer and Hotelkeeper, 1993. *Recreations*: eating, British modern art, art history, France and the French, modern music. *Clubs*: Royal Automobile, Groucho.

**CORBITT, Air Vice Marshal Ian Stafford**; Chief Executive, RAF Training Group Defence Agency, and Air Officer Commanding, RAF Training Group, 1999–2002; *b* 30 July 1947; *s* of John Kellock Corbitt and Hilda Mary Corbitt; *m* 1976, Anne Lucille Worthy; two *d*. *Educ*: Simon Langton Grammar Sch., Canterbury; Quaid-i-Azam Univ., Islamabad (MSc Defence and Strategic Studies 1993). ACCA; CDipAF 1999. No 48 Sqdn, RAF Changi, Singapore, 1970–72; qualified Flying Instructor, RAF Leeming, 1973; ADC to AOC 46 Gp, RAF Upavon, 1973–75; Flt Comdr, No 30 Sqdn, 1976–77, OC Hercules Conversion Sqdn, 1977–79, RAF Lyneham; Staff Coll., Bracknell, 1980; HQ British Forces, Hong Kong, 1981–83; OC 242 OCU, RAF Lyneham, 1983–86; Flt Examr, USAF, Scott AFB, Ill, 1986–88; OC RAF Lyneham, 1989–91; HCSC, 1992; Nat. Defence Coll., Rawalpindi, 1992–93; Contingency Plans, HQ STC, 1993–95; Air Cdre, Policy and Plans, HQ PTC, 1995–99. *Club*: Royal Air Force.

**CORBOULD, Christopher Charles**, OBE 2014; special effects supervisor and 2nd unit director in film industry, since 1988; *b* London, 5 March 1958; *s* of Clifford and Jean Corbould; *m* 1986, Lynne Margaret Buckley; three *d*. *Educ*: Colfe's Grammar Sch. MIExpE 2003. Special effects asst, 1975–80; special effects technician/sen. technician, 1980–88; *films* include: Superman II, 1980; For Your Eyes Only, 1981; Superman III, 1983; A View to Kill, 1985; The Living Daylights, 1987; Willow, 1988; special effects supervisor/director, 1988–; *films* include: Licence to kill, 1989; Shadowlands, 1993; Interview with a Vampire: The Vampire Chronicles, 1994; GoldenEye, 1995; Tomorrow Never Dies, 1997; The Mummy, The World is Not Enough, 1999; Lara Croft: Tomb Raider, 2001; Die Another Day, 2002; Lara Croft Tomb Raider: The Cradle of Life, 2003; Casino Royale, 2006; The Dark Knight, Quantum of Solace, 2008; Inception, 2010 ((jtly) Academy Award, BAFTA Award, 2011); X Men: First Class, 2011; The Dark Knight Rises, Skyfall, 2012. Hon. DTech Southampton Solent, 2009; Hon. DA Hertfordshire, 2010. *Recreations*: guitar, horse riding, theatre, music, family.

**CORBY, Mary Margaret**; *see* Reilly, M. M.

**CORBYN, Rt Hon. Jeremy (Bernard)**; PC 2015; MP (Lab) Islington North, since 1983; Leader of the Labour Party and Leader of the Opposition, since 2015; *b* 26 May 1949; *s* of David Benjamin Corbyn. *Educ*: Adams Grammar Sch., Newport, Shropshire. NUPE Official, 1975–83; sponsored NUPE, then UNISON, MP. Mem., Haringey Borough Council, 1974–84 (Chm., Community Develt Cttee 1975–78, Public Works 1978–79, Planning Cttee 1980–81, 1982–83). Member: Select Cttee on Social Security, 1990–97; Justice Select Cttee, 2011–15; Chair, London Gp of Lab MPs, 1993–96 (Vice-Chair, 1985–93); All Party Parliamentary Groups: Chair, Mexico, Chagos Islands; Jt Vice Chair, Human Rights; Vice Chair, Latin America, African Great Lakes; Sec., Bolivia, Dalits; Mem., traveller law reform, cycling; Member, Parliamentary Groups: RMT; CWU; Justice Unions; Socialist Campaign; CND (Chair). Chair: Liberation; Stop the War Coalition; Vice Chair, Nat. Council, CND. Trustee: Highbury Vale Blackstock Trust; Dalit Solidarity Campaign. Patron, Mitford Under Fives. *Address*: House of Commons, SW1A 0AA. *T*: (020) 7219 3545.

**CORBYN, Stuart Alan**; Chief Executive, Cadogan Estates Ltd, 1986–2008; *b* Inverness, 9 Feb. 1945; *s* of late Gp Capt. Donald Corbyn, CBE and Frances Corbyn (*née* Anderson); *m* 1st, 1985, Mary Moolan Feroze (*d* 2003); 2nd, 2005, Gillian Louise Nunn. *Educ*: Haileybury. FRICS 1982. Gooch & Wagstaff, 1972–82; Sole Principal, Surveyors Consultancy Services, 1982–86. Chairman: Pollen Estate Trustee Co., 2008–14; Get Living London, 2013–18; non-executive Director: Derwent London plc, 2006–17; Long Acre Estates, 2008–. Pres., British Property Fedn, 1997–98. Church Comr, 2001–06; Mem., Royal Commn for the Exhibn of 1851, 2009–. Mem., Property Adv. Gp, Revitalise, 2017–; Co-opted Mem., Property Investment Bd, City of London Corp., 2017–. Trustee: Royal Parks Foundn, 2003–06; Chelsea Physic Garden, 2008–15; Sloane Stanley Estate, 2009–11; Somerset House Trust, 2009–12; Naunton Dovecote Trust (formerly Naunton Village Trust), 2011–; Young Dementia UK Homes, 2014–17; Queen Alexandra's House Assoc., 2015–; Opera Holland Park, 2018–; Comr, Royal Hosp. Chelsea, 2008–17. Chm., Chelsea Soc., 2009–12. Non playing Dir, RPO, 2006–12. Mem. Council, Royal Albert Hall, 2010–. *Recreations*: architecture, art, fishing, gardening, music, travel. *Clubs*: Chelsea Arts, Sloane.

**CORCORAN, Alexander Martin Desmond**; Chairman, Lefevre Fine Art Ltd, since 2001; *b* London, 28 Feb. 1968; *s* of Desmond Corcoran and Judith Keppel; *m* (marr. diss.); one *s* one *d*. *Educ*: Ampleforth Coll., Yorks; British Inst., Florence; City & Guilds of London Art Sch. Waddington Galls, London, 1986–88; Partner, Alex Reid and Lefevre Ltd (Lefevre Gall.), 1995–2000. *Address*: Lefevre Fine Art Ltd, 31 Bruton Street, W1J 6QS. *T*: (020) 7493 2107. *E*: amdc@lefevrefineart.com.

**CORCORAN, Prof. Neil**, FEA; King Alfred Professor of English Literature, University of Liverpool, 2004–10, now Emeritus; *b* 23 Sept. 1948; *s* of John Patrick Corcoran and Angela (*née* Attwood); *m* 1979, Gillian Anne Jeffs; three *s*. *Educ*: Austin Friars Sch., Carlisle; St Edmund Hall, and Wolfson Coll., Oxford (MA, MLitt). Lectr, then Sen. Lectr in English, Sheffield Univ., 1974–94; Professor of English: Univ. of Wales, Swansea, 1994–96; Univ. of St Andrews, 1996–2004. FEA 2001. *Publications*: The Song of Deeds: a study of The Anathemata of David Jones, 1982; Seamus Heaney, 1986; (ed) The Chosen Ground: essays on the contemporary poetry of Northern Ireland, 1992; English Poetry since 1940, 1993; After Yeats and Joyce, 1997; The Poetry of Seamus Heaney: a critical study, 1998; Poets of Modern Ireland: text, context, intertext, 1999; (ed) Do You, Mr Jones?: Bob Dylan with the poets and professors, 2002; Elizabeth Bowen: the enforced return, 2004; (ed) Cambridge Companion to Twentieth-Century English Poetry, 2007; Shakespeare and the Modern Poet, 2010; Poetry & Responsibility, 2014; Reading Shakespeare's Soliloquies: text, theatre, film, 2018. *Recreations*: swimming, cycling, listening to various kinds of music, looking at paintings. *Address*: School of English, University of Liverpool, Liverpool L69 7ZR. *T*: (0151) 794 2720. *E*: nc23@liverpool.ac.uk.

**CORDARA, Roderick Charles**; QC 1994; *b* 26 March 1953; *s* of Carlo and Silvia Cordara; *m* 1997, Tsambika Anastasas; one *d*. *Educ*: City of London Sch.; Trinity Hall, Cambridge. Called to the Bar: Middle Temple, 1975; NSW, 1999; Sen. Counsel (NSW) 2001. *Address*: Essex Court Chambers, 24 Lincoln's Inn Fields, WC2A 3EG. *Clubs*: Oxford and Cambridge, Royal Automobile, h, 67 Pall Mall.

**CORDER, Vice Adm. Sir Ian Fergus**, KBE 2016; CB 2013; Lieutenant Governor, Bailiwick of Guernsey, since 2016; *b* Nuneaton, 6 Aug. 1960; *s* of William and Colleen Corder; *m* 1984, Kathryn Alison Snoad; two *s*. *Educ*: Rugby Sch.; Peterhouse, Cambridge (BA Maths 1981; MA; Hon. Fellow, 2016). Joined RN, 1978; various operational submarine appts, 1982–88; Submarine Comd Course, 1989; EO, HMS Sceptre, 1990–91; Commanding Officer: HMS Oracle, 1991–92; HMS Splendid, 1996–98; Naval Asst to First Sea Lord, 1999–2001; CO, HMS Cumberland, 2001–02; Dep. Dir, Policy on Internat. Orgns, MoD, 2002–03; Chief of Strategic Systems Exec., 2004–06; Dir, Naval Personnel Strategy, 2006–08; Dep. Comdr Striking Force NATO, 2009–11; Comdr Ops and Rear Adm. Submarines as Hd of Fighting Arms, 2011–13; UK Mil. Rep. to NATO, 2013–16. *Recreations*: reading, music, running, travel, flying.

**CORDEROY, Rev. Graham Thomas**; Minister, Hutton and Shenfield Union Church, 1987–96; *b* 15 April 1931; *s* of Thomas and Gladys Corderoy; *m* 1957, Edna Marian Barnes; six *d*. *Educ*: Emanuel Sch., London; Manchester Univ. (BA Theology 1957). Ordained 1957; King's Lynn, 1957–62; commissioned RAF Chaplain, 1962; Principal Chaplain, Church of Scotland and Free Churches, and Hon. Chaplain to the Queen, 1984–87. Inst. of Alcohol Studies Bd, 1986–2006. *Recreations*: Rugby referee 1964–87, Gilbert and Sullivan buff. *Address*: Longmead, 66 Hardwick Lane, Bury St Edmunds, Suffolk IP33 2RB. *Club*: Royal Air Force.

**CORDINGLEY, David;** Director South Africa, British Council, 2010–13; *b* 27 Oct. 1952; *s* of Robert and Annie Burrell Cordingley; *m* 1992, Patricia Lobo; one *s. Educ:* Lancaster Royal Grammar Sch.; St Peter's Coll., Oxford (BA Physics 1973, MA 1977; PGCE 1974); Univ. of E Anglia (MA Develt Studies 1993). VSO, St Kitts, WI, 1974–76; teacher, Tonbridge Sch., 1977–79; Hd of Sci., Navrongo Secondary Sch., Ghana, 1979–81; teacher, Island Sch., Hong Kong, 1981–86; joined British Council, 1986: Asst Rep., Malawi, 1987–88; First Sec. (Sci. and Health), British Council Div., High Commn, New Delhi, 1988–92; Contract Dir, Manchester, 1993–97; Project Manager, Nairobi, 1997–2000; Dir, Vietnam, 2000–04; Regl Dir, Americas and Australasia, 2004–05; Dir, Brazil, 2005–09. *Recreations:* transport (railways, motoring, aviation), sport (walking, cycling, soccer), travel, photography. *Address:* Billingshurst, West Sussex. *E:* dcordingley@btinternet.com.

**CORDINGLEY, Maj.-Gen. Patrick Anthony John,** DSO 1991; OBE 2017; Chairman, MMI Research, 2001–08; *b* 6 Oct. 1944; *s* of Maj.-Gen. John Edward Cordingley, OBE and Ruth Pamela St John Carpendale; *m* 1968, Melissa Crawley; two *d. Educ:* Sherborne School. Commissioned into 5th Royal Inniskilling Dragoon Guards, 1965; commanded, 1984–87; commanded 7th Armoured Brigade, 1988–91; served Libya, Cyprus, UK, BAOR, Gulf; Comdr, Combined Arms Trng Centre, 1991–92; GOC Eastern Dist, 1992–95; GOC 2nd Div., 1995–96; Sen. British Loan Service Officer, Sultanate of Oman, 1996–2000. Col, Royal Dragoon Guards, 2000–05; Hon. Col, Bristol Univ. OTC, 2000–05. Chm., Defence and Security Forum, 2002–. Chm. Trustees, Gilbert White House and Oates Mus., 2002–08; Chm., Nat. Meml Arboretum Future Foundns Appeal, 2007–17; Pres., Romsey Show, 2014; Patron: Romsey War Horse Meml Proj., 2015; Esclusham War Meml Proj., 2016–. Gov., Sherborne Sch., 2001–16 (Chm., Internat. Coll., 2007–16). Mem. Ct, Ironmongers' Co., 2000– (Master, 2010–11). FRGS 1986. Hon. DSc Hull, 2007. OStJ 1993. USA Bronze Star, 1991; Order of Oman, 2000. *Publications:* Captain Oates: soldier and explorer, 1984, 4th edn 2012; In the Eye of the Storm, 1996, 3rd edn 2009. *Recreations:* country pursuits, whale-watching. *Club:* Cavalry and Guards (Chm., 2002–04).

**CORDINGLY, David Michael Bradley,** DPhil; writer; *b* 5 Dec. 1938; *s* of late Rt Rev. Eric Cordingly, MBE, sometime Bishop of Thetford, and of Mary Mathews; *m* 1971, Shirley Elizabeth Robin; one *s* one *d. Educ:* Christ's Hosp., Horsham; Oriel Coll., Oxford (MA); Univ. of Sussex (DPhil). Graphic designer, 1960–68; Exhibn designer at BM, 1968–71; Keeper of Art Gall., Royal Pavilion and Museums, Brighton, 1971–78; Asst Dir, Mus. of London, 1978–80; National Maritime Museum: Asst Keeper, 1980–82; Dep. Keeper, 1982–86; Keeper of Pictures, 1986–88; Head of Exhibns, 1988–93. Guest Curator, Mariners' Mus., Va, 2000–01. Exhibns organised include: Looking at London, 1980; Sea Finland, 1986; Captain Cook, Brisbane Expo, 1988; Mutiny on the Bounty, 1989; Henry VIII at Greenwich, 1991; Pirates: Fact and Fiction, 1992. FRSA 1974. Order of the White Rose of Finland, 1986. *Publications:* Marine Painting in England, 1974; Painters of the Sea, 1979; (with W. Percival Prescott) The Art of the Van de Veldes, 1982; Nicholas Pocock, 1986; Captain James Cook, Navigator, 1988; Pirates: fact and fiction, 1992; Life Among the Pirates, 1995; Pirates: an illustrated history, 1996; Ships and Seascapes, 1997; Heroines and Harlots: women at sea in the great age of sail, 2001; Billy Ruffian: the Bellerophon and the downfall of Napoleon, 2003; Cochrane the Dauntless: the life and adventures of Thomas Cochrane, 2007; Spanish Gold: Captain Woodes Rogers and the Pirates of the Caribbean, 2011. *Recreations:* sailing, carpentry. *Address:* 2 Vine Place, Brighton, Sussex BN1 3HE. *Clubs:* Athenæum; Chichester Yacht.

**CORDY-SIMPSON, Lt-Gen. Sir Roderick (Alexander),** KBE 1998 (OBE 1984); CB 1993; President, Royal British Legion, 2000–04; Vice Lord-Lieutenant of Wiltshire, 2016–19; *b* 29 Feb. 1944; *s* of late Col John Roger Cordy-Simpson, CBE, MC and Ursula Margaret Cordy-Simpson; *m* 1974, Virginia Rosemary Lewis; one *s* one *d. Educ:* Radley College. Commissioned 1963, commanded, 1983–86, 13th/18th Royal Hussars (QMO); Comd 4th Armoured Brigade, 1988–90; COS, UN Bosnia Hercegovina, 1992–93; COS BAOR, 1993–94; GOC 1st (UK) Armd Div., 1994–96; Dep. Force Comdr, Bosnia Hercegovina, 1996–97; retd 1998. Lieut, HM Tower of London, 2001–04. Hon. Colonel: Light Dragoons, 2000–08; Wilts ACF, 2014–17. Chairman: Regular Forces Employment Assoc., 2002–07; Services Sound and Vision Corp., 2004–08. DL Wilts, 2004. US Legion of Merit, 1997; Order of Al Istiqlal (1st Class) (Jordan), 2008. *Recreations:* ski-ing, reading, fishing. *Address:* The Coach House, Bishopstrow, Warminster, Wilts BA12 9HJ. *Club:* Cavalry and Guards.

**COREN, Giles Robin Patrick;** opinion columnist, since 1999, Restaurant Critic, since 2002, The Times; *b* 29 July 1969; *s* of late Alan Coren, writer and broadcaster, and of Anne Coren (*née* Kasriel); *m* 2010, Esther Walker; one *s* one *d. Educ:* Westminster Sch.; Keble Coll., Oxford (BA Hons English Lit.). The Times: feature writer, 1993–96; Ed., Times Diary, 2000–01; columnist, Tatler, and Ed., Tatler About Town, 1998–99; columnist: Match of the Day mag., 1996–99; Mail on Sunday, 1997–98; Sunday Times, 2002–06; GQ mag., 2004–07; Esquire mag., 2011–; Time Out, 2014–; restaurant critic, Independent on Sunday, 1999–2000; television: co-presenter: The F-word, 2005–06; Animal Farm, 2007; Edwardian Supersize Me, 2007; The Supersizers Eat…, 2007–09; Giles and Sue Live the Good Life, 2010; Our Food, 2012; 12 Drinks of Christmas, 2013; Pressure Cooker, 2014–15; Back in Time for Dinner, 2015; Back in Time for Christmas, 2015; Back in Time for the Weekend, 2016; Back in Time for Brixton, 2016; Further Back in Time for Dinner, 2017; Amazing Hotels: life beyond the lobby, 2017–; presenter: Movie Lounge, 2006; Million Dollar Critic, 2014–15; Giles Coren: my failed novel, 2016; writer and presenter: Tax the Fat, 2006; Eat to Live Forever with Giles Coren, 2015. *Publications:* Against the Odds: James Dyson, an autobiography, 1997; Winkler, 2005; Anger Management for Beginners, 2010; How to Eat Out, 2012; (ed jtly) Chocolate and Cuckoo Clocks: the essential Alan Coren, 2008. *Recreations:* Eton fives, cricket, writing fiction, daily afternoon naps. *Address:* The Times, 1 London Bridge Street, SE1 9GF. *T:* (020) 7782 5000. *Clubs:* Groucho, Soho House; MCC (Assoc. Mem.); Old Westminster Cricket.
*See also* D. J. S. Mitchell.

**COREY, Prof. Elias James,** PhD; Professor of Chemistry, 1959–68, Sheldon Emory Professor of Chemistry, 1968–98, Harvard University, now Emeritus; *b* 12 July 1928; *s* of Elias Corey and Tina Corey (*née* Hasham); *m* 1961, Claire Higham; two *s* one *d. Educ:* MIT (BS 1948; PhD 1951). University of Illinois, Urbana-Champaign: Instructor, 1951; Asst Prof., 1953–55; Prof. of Chemistry, 1955–59. Former Member: Bd of Dirs, physical sciences, Alfred P. Sloan Foundn; Sci. Adv. Bd, Robert A. Welch Foundn. Foreign Mem., Royal Soc., 1998. Hon. DSc: Chicago, 1968; Hofstra, 1974; Oxford, 1982; Liège, 1985; Illinois, 1985; Hon. ScD Cantab, 2000; Hon. AM Harvard, 1959. Numerous awards, medals and prizes from univs and learned bodies in USA, Europe and Asia, incl. US Nat. Medal of Science, 1988 and Nobel Prize for Chemistry, 1990. *Publications:* numerous papers in learned jls on pure and synthetic chemistry, esp. on development of methods of organic synthesis, making possible mass production of medicinal and other products, based on natural materials. *Address:* Department of Chemistry, Harvard University, 12 Oxford Street, Cambridge, MA 02138, USA.

**CORK AND ORRERY,** 15th Earl of, *cr* 1620; **John Richard Boyle, (Jonathan);** Baron Boyle of Youghal, 1616; Viscount Dungarvan, 1620; Baron Boyle of Broghill, 1621; Viscount Boyle of Kinalmeaky and Baron of Bandon Bridge, 1627; Earl of Orrery, 1660 (all Ire.); Baron Boyle of Marston (GB) 1711; Chairman, Maritime Investment Holdings Pte Ltd, Singapore, 1986–2014; *b* 3 Nov. 1945; *e s* of 14th Earl of Cork and Orrery, DSC, VRD; *S* father, 2003; *m* 1973, Hon. Rebecca Juliet Noble, *y d* of Baron Glenkinglas (Life Peer), PC; one *s* two *d* (of whom one *s* one *d* are twins). *Educ:* Harrow; RNC Dartmouth. Lt-Comdr RN, retd. Dir, E. D. & F. Man Sugar Ltd, London, 1994–2006. Life Governor, Soc. for the Advancement of the Christian Faith. Mem. Council, Internat. Dendrol. Soc., 2007–. Chm., Chichester Cathedral Restoration and Develt Trust, 2008–15; Trustee, MapAction, 2007–14. Elected Mem., H of L, 2016–. *Recreations:* country pursuits, sailing, ski-ing, classic cars, cathedrals. *Heir: s* Viscount Dungarvan, *qv. Address:* Lickfold House, Petworth, West Sussex GU28 9EY. *Clubs:* Boodle's; Royal Yacht Squadron, Royal Northern and Clyde Yacht; Castaways.
*See also* Baron Middleton.

**CORK, CLOYNE, AND ROSS, Bishop of,** since 1999; **Rt Rev. (William) Paul Colton;** *b* 13 March 1960; *s* of George Henry Colton and Kathleen Mary Colton (*née* Jenkins); *m* 1984, Susan Margaret Good; two *s. Educ:* Ashton Sch., Cork; Lester B. Pearson Coll. of the Pacific, BC, Canada; University Coll., Cork (BCL Hons); Trinity Coll., Dublin (DipTh, MPhil); Univ. of Wales, Cardiff (LLM 2006); Cardiff Univ. (PhD 2013). Curate, St Paul, Lisburn, dio. Connor, 1984–87; Domestic Chaplain to Bp of Connor, 1985–90; Vicar Choral, Belfast Cathedral, 1987–90, Minor Canon, 1989–90; Priest Vicar, Registrar and Chapter Clerk, Christ Church Cathedral, Dublin, 1990–95; Co-ordinator of Religious Programmes (Protestant), RTE, 1993–99; Incumbent of Castleknock and Mulhuddart with Clonsilla, dio. Dublin, 1990–99; Canon, Christ Church Cathedral, Dublin, 1997–99. Associate, Centre for Law and Religion, 2006–14, Hon. Res. Fellow, Sch. of Law and Politics, 2014–, Cardiff Univ. Clerical Hon. Sec., Gen. Synod of C of I, 1999. *Recreations:* piano, organ, music, walking, reading, computers, Manchester United Football Club, hockey. *Address:* The Palace, Bishop Street, Cork T12 WEY1, Ireland. *T:* (21) 5005080. *Club:* Kildare Street and University (Dublin).

**CORK, Adam James;** freelance composer, since 1997; Associate Artist, Royal Shakespeare Company, since 2012; *b* London, 16 Jan. 1974; *s* of Richard Graham Cork, *qv*; one *s. Educ:* Hampstead Sch.; Camden Sch. for Girls (6th Form); Trinity Hall, Cambridge (BA Hons Music 1995). Composer: *radio* includes: Losing Rosalind, 2000; Don Carlos, 2005; The Luneberg Variation, 2006; Othello, The Chalk Garden, 2008; *television* includes: Re-ignited, 2003; Frances Tuesday, 2004; Macbeth, 2010; The Hollow Crown: Richard II, 2012; *films:* Bust, 2002; Tripletake, 2003; The Three Rules of Infidelity, 2004. *Theatre:* composer and sound designer: Don Carlos, Sheffield Crucible, Gielgud, 2004; Suddenly Last Summer, Sheffield Crucible, Albery, 2004; The Late Henry Moss, Tom and Viv, Almeida, 2006; The Tempest, RSC, 2006; Frost/Nixon, Gielgud, 2006, transf. NY, 2007; The Cherry Orchard, Sheffield Crucible, 2007; Macbeth, Chichester, Gielgud, transf. NY, 2007; No Man's Land, Duke of York's, 2008; Ivanov, Wyndhams, 2008; The Last Days of Judas Iscariot, Almeida, 2008; The Chalk Garden, Creditors, Donmar, 2008; (and lyricist) Enron, Chichester, Royal Court, Noël Coward, 2009, transf. NY, 2010; Time and the Conways, Phèdre, NT, 2009; A View from the Bridge, Duke of York's, 2009; A Streetcar Named Desire, Donmar, 2009; Madame de Sade, Wyndhams, 2009; Hamlet, Wyndhams, transf. NY, 2009; Red, Donmar, 2009, transf. NY, 2010 (Tony Award for Best Sound Design of a Play); Romeo and Juliet, RSC, 2010, transf. NY, 2011; Danton's Death, NT, 2010; King Lear, Donmar, 2010 (Olivier Award for Best Sound, 2011); Evening Standard Award for Best Design, 2011); Luise Miller, Donmar, 2011; Anna Christie, Donmar, 2011 (Evening Standard Award for Best Design); Decade, Headlong, 2011; Richard II, Donmar, 2011; Cat on a Hot Tin Roof, Broadway, 2013; Peter & Alice, Henry V, Noël Coward, 2013; The Exorcist, Birmingham Rep, 2016; Travesties, Apollo, 2017; Ink, Almeida, 2017; composer: All's Well That Ends Well, NT, 2009; (and co-lyricist) London Road, Cottesloe, 2011, transf. Olivier, 2012 (Critics Circle Award for Best Musical); The Merchant of Venice, RSC, 2011; (and lyricist and sound score) The Lion, the Witch and the Wardrobe, Kensington Gardens, 2012. *Publications:* London Road, 2011. *Address:* c/o United Agents, 12–26 Lexington Street, W1F 0LE. *T:* (020) 3214 0873. *E:* RCobbe@unitedagents.co.uk.

**CORK, Richard Graham;** art critic, art historian, broadcaster and exhibition organiser; *b* 25 March 1947; *s* of Hubert Henry Cork and Beatrice Hester Cork; *m* 1970, Vena Jackson; two *s* two *d. Educ:* Kingswood Sch., Bath; Trinity Hall, Cambridge (MA, PhD). Art critic, Evening Standard, 1969–77, 1980–83; Editor, Studio International, 1975–79; art critic, The Listener, 1984–90; Chief Art Critic, The Times, 1991–2002; Art Critic, New Statesman, 2003–06. Slade Prof. of Fine Art, Cambridge, 1989–90; Lethaby Lectr, RCA, 1974; Durning-Lawrence Lectr, UCL, 1987; Henry Moore Foundn Sen. Fellow, Courtauld Inst. of Art, 1992–95. Former Member: Hayward Gall. Advisory Panel; Fine Arts Advisory Cttee, British Council; Cttee, Contemp. Art Soc.; Art Adv. Cttee, St Mary's Hosp.; Mem., Arts Council of England, 1995–98 (Chm., Visual Art Panel, 1995–98). Curator: Critic's Choice, 1973; Vorticism and its Allies, 1974; Beyond Painting and Sculpture, 1974; Sculpture Now: Dissolution or Redefinition?, 1974; Arte Inglese Oggi, 1976; Art for Whom?, 1978; Art for Society, 1978; Un Certain Art Anglais, 1979; British Art in the 20th Century, 1987; David Bomberg retrospective, 1988; A Bitter Truth: Avant-Garde Art and the Great War, 1994; British Art Show, 1995; A Life of Their Own, Lismore Castle, 2008; Wild Thing: Jacob Epstein, Henri Gaudier-Brzeska and Eric Gill, RA, 2009–10; Young Bomberg and the Old Masters, Nat. Gall., 2019–20; Selector: Turner Prize, 1988; Citibank Photography Prize, 1997; Natwest Art Prize, 1998; North Meadow Millennium Dome Sculpture Project, 1998–2000; Sunderland Gateway Commn, 1999–; John Moores Painting Prize, 1999; Times/Artangel Open, 1999–2000; Jerwood Drawing Prize, 2001; Elector, Slade Professorship of Fine Art, Univ. of Cambridge, 1999–2004; Member: Trafalgar Sq. Plinth Adv. Gp, 1999–2000; Selection Cttee, New St Paul's Cathedral Font, 1999; Adv. Council, Paul Mellon Centre for British Art, 1999–2005; Design Cttee, Diana, Princess of Wales Meml Fountain, 2000–02; BBC Churchill Commn, 2003–; St Martin-in-the-Fields East Window Cttee, 2004; Maggie's Arts Gp, 2009–; Internat. Adv. Bd, Ben Uri Mus., 2011–; Editl Bd, RA Mag., 2009–; Chm. of Judges, Rouse Kent Public Art Award, 2006 and 2007; Judge: BlindArt, 2006; St Martin-in-the-Fields East Window, 2006; Chichester Open Art Exhibn, 2007; Darwin Ceiling Commn, Nat. History Mus., 2008; Sculpture Shock, Royal British Soc. of Sculptors, 2012–13; British Watercolour Soc. Competition, 2015; Daiwa Foundn Art Prize, 2017–18. Syndic, Fitzwilliam Mus., Cambridge, 2002–14. Patron, Paintings in Hosps, 2012–. Trustee: Public Art Develt Trust, 1988–95; Wyndham Lewis Meml Trust, 1998–2016. Organiser of many exhibns, incl. shows in Milan, Paris, Berlin and at Hayward Gall., Tate Gall. and RA. Frequent broadcaster on radio and television. Hon. FRA 2011. John Llewellyn Rhys Meml Prize, 1976; Sir Banister Fletcher Award, 1986; Art Fund Award, 1995. *Publications:* Vorticism and Abstract Art in the First Machine Age, vol. I: Origins and Development, 1975, vol. II: Synthesis and Decline, 1976; The Social Role of Art, 1979; Art Beyond the Gallery in Early Twentieth Century England, 1985; David Bomberg, 1987; Architect's Choice, 1992; A Bitter Truth: Avant-Garde Art and the Great War, 1994; Bottle of Notes: Claes Oldenburg and Coosje van Bruggen, 1997; Jacob Epstein, 1999; Everything Seemed Possible: art in the 1970s, 2003; New Spirit, New Sculpture, New Money: art in the 1980s, 2003; Breaking

Down the Barriers: art in the 1990s, 2003; Annus Mirabilis?: art in the year 2000, 2003; Michael Craig-Martin, 2006; Wild Thing: Epstein, Gaudier-Brzeska, Gill, 2009; The Healing Presence of Art: a history of Western art in hospitals, 2012; Peter Prendergast, 2013; Face to Face: interviews with artists, 2015; contribs to art magazines and exhibn catalogues. *Recreations:* enjoying family, looking at art, walking. *Address:* 24 Milman Road, NW6 6EG. *T:* (020) 8960 2671.
See also A. J. Cork.

**CORKE, Donald Stevenson**; Sheriff of Lothian and Borders at Edinburgh, since 2013; *b* Salisbury, Southern Rhodesia, 5 Aug. 1959; *s* of Robert and Marion Corke; *m* 1989, Helen White; one *s* two *d*. *Educ:* Mount Pleasant Sch., Salisbury, Southern Rhodesia; Univ. of Cape Town (BA); Univ. of the Witwatersrand (LLB). Advocate of Supreme Court of SA, 1985; Mem., Faculty of Advocates, Edinburgh, 1988; Advocate, Scottish Bar, 1988–2000; called to the Bar, Middle Temple, 1995; pt-time Immigration Adjudicator, 1997–2000; Immigration Adjudicator, 2000–05; Immigration Judge, 2005–09; pt-time Sheriff, 2005–09; Sheriff of: S Strathclyde, Dumfries and Galloway at Airdrie, 2009–11; Lothian and Borders at Jedburgh, 2011–13. Dep. Dist Chm., Appeals Service, 1998–2001. *Address:* Sheriff Court House, 27 Chambers Street, Edinburgh EH1 1LB.

**CORKUM, Prof. Paul Bruce,** OC 2007; PhD; FRSC 1996; FRS 2005; Canada Research Chair in Attosecond Photonics and Director, Attosecond Science Program, National Research Council of Canada, since 2008; Professor of Physics, University of Ottawa, since 2008; *b* 30 Oct. 1943. *Educ:* Acadia Univ., Nova Scotia (BSc 1965); Lehigh Univ., Penn (MS 1967; PhD 1972). Postdoctoral Fellow, 1973–75, Scientist, 1975–2008, Nat. Research Council of Canada. Gold Medal, Canadian Assoc. of Physicists, 1996; Tory Award, RSC, 2003; Quantum Electronics Award, IEEE, 2005; Killam Prize, 2006; Harvey Prize, Technion - Israel Inst. of Technol., 2013; King Faisal Internat. Prize for Sci., 2013; Frederic Ives Medal, Optical Soc. of America, 2014, 2015. Golden Jubilee Medal, 2002. *Publications:* articles in learned jls. *Address:* Joint Attosecond Science Laboratory, University of Ottawa and National Research Council of Canada, Advanced Research Complex, Room 464, 25 Templeton Street, Ottawa, K1N 6N5, Canada; 15 Rothwell Drive, Ottawa, ON K1J 7G3, Canada.

**CORLETT, Andrew Thomas Kaneen; His Honour Deemster Corlett;** HM First Deemster, Isle of Man, since 2018 (Second Deemster, 2011–18); *b* Douglas, I of M, 2 March 1959; *s* of William Thomas Kaneen Corlett and Jean Mary Corlett; *m* 1989, Angelina Tehan; one *s* one *d*. *Educ:* King William's Coll., Isle of Man; Pembroke Coll., Oxford (MA). Called to the Bar, Gray's Inn, 1984; admitted to the Manx Bar, 1984; Partner, Dickinson Cruickshank & Co., Advocates, 1985–95; Government Advocate, Attorney General's Chambers, Douglas, 1995–2001; Dir, Simcocks, Advocates, 2001–07; Dep. Deemster, 2007–11. *Recreations:* walking, sporadic gym attendance, cinema, theatre, visual arts, London. *Address:* Isle of Man Courts of Justice, Deemsters Walk, Bucks Road, Douglas, Isle of Man IM1 3AR.

**CORLETT, Clive William,** CB 1995; Deputy Chairman, Board of Inland Revenue, 1994–98 (Under Secretary, 1985–92; Director General, 1992–94); *b* 14 June 1938; *s* of F. William and Hanna Corlett; *m* 1964, Margaret Catherine Jones; one *s*. *Educ:* Birkenhead Sch.; Brasenose Coll., Oxford (BA PPE). Merchant Navy, 1957. Joined Inland Revenue, 1960; seconded to: Civil Service Selection Bd, 1970; HM Treasury, 1972–74 (as Private Sec. to Chancellor of Exchequer) and 1979–81. Mem. Cttee, Friends of Greenwich Park, 2001–. Hon. Treas., Old Colfeians RFC, 2000–13.

**CORLETT, Gerald Lingham;** Chairman, Higsons Brewery plc, 1980–88; *b* 8 May 1925; *s* of Alfred Lingham Corlett and Nancy Eileen Bremner; *m* 1957, Helen Bromfield Williamson; three *s* one *d*. *Educ:* Rossall School; Aberdeen University (short war-time course). RA, 1943–47 (Lieut, Royal Indian Artillery). Higsons Brewery, 1947–88. Director: Westminster (Liverpool) Trust Co., 1960–2001 (Chm., 1995–2001); Midshires Building Soc. (Northern Bd), 1977–87; Radio City (Sound of Merseyside), 1982–88 (Chm., 1985–88); Boddingtons Gp, 1985–88; Watson Prickard, 1991–96 (Chm., 1991–96). Member, Council: Brewers' Soc., 1964–88; Scottish Sch., 1956–95. Mem., Brewers' Co., 1983–2006. *Recreation:* family. *Club:* Royal Liverpool Golf.

**CORLETT, William John Howarth;** QC (I of M) 1999; Attorney General, Isle of Man, 1998–2011; *b* 25 March 1950; *s* of William Thomas Kaneen Corlett and Jean Mary Corlett; *m* 1974, Janice Mary Crowe; one *s*. *Educ:* King William's Coll., Isle of Man; Univ. of Nottingham (LLB). Called to the Bar, Gray's Inn, 1972; admitted to Manx Bar, 1974; Partner, Dickinson Cruickshank & Co., Advocates, 1975–92; Sen. Partner, Corlett Bolton & Co., Advocates, 1992–98. *Recreations:* golf, salmon fishing. *Address:* Close Jairg, Old Church Road, Crosby, Isle of Man IM4 2HA. *T:* (01624) 852119.
See also A. T. K. Corlett.

**CORLEY, Dame Elizabeth (Pauline Lucy),** DBE 2019 (CBE 2015); Senior Adviser, Allianz Global Investors, since 2018 (Chief Executive Officer, 2012–16; Vice Chairman, 2016–17); *b* Luton, 19 Oct. 1956; *d* of Robert Cooper Trown and Yvonne Celina-Rose Trown; *m* 1986, Michael Charles Corley; one step *d*. *Educ:* Horsham High Sch. for Girls; Postgrad. Dip. Mgt 1984. FCII 1980. Sun Alliance Life & Pensions, 1975–85; Consultant, then Partner, Coopers & Lybrand Mgt Consultancy, 1985–93; Dir, 1993–98, Man. Dir, 1998–2004, Mercury Asset Mgt, subseq. Merrill Lynch Investment Managers; CEO, Europe, Allianz Global Investors, 2005–12. Non-executive Director: Financial Reporting Council, 2011–17; Pearson plc, 2014–; BAE Systems, 2016–; Morgan Stanley, 2018–. Gov., CFA Inst., 2016–18. Trustee, British Mus., 2016–. FRSA. *Publications:* Requiem Mass, 1998; Fatal Legacy, 2000; Grave Doubts, 2006; Innocent Blood, 2008; Dead of Winter, 2014. *Recreations:* thriller writing, music, travel, gardening. *Address:* Allianz Global Investors, 199 Bishopsgate, EC2M 3TY.

**CORLEY, Paul John;** media consultant, since 2008; *b* 23 Dec. 1950; *s* of Robert Charles Corley and Margaret Dorothy Corley. *Educ:* Worcester Coll., Oxford (BA Hons Modern Hist.). Journalist, Westminster Press, 1972–76; News and Current Affairs, BBC TV, 1976–81; Producer, The Tube, Tyne Tees TV, 1982–84; Director of Programmes: Border TV, 1984–91; Granada Gp, NE TV, 1991–92; Controller: Factual Progs, Carlton TV, and Man. Dir, Carlton Broadcasting, 1992–96; Network Factual Progs, ITV Network Centre, 1996–98; Chief Exec., Border TV, 1998–2000; Man. Dir, GMTV, 2001–08. *Recreations:* television, music, ski-ing. *Clubs:* Groucho, Soho House.

**CORLEY, Peter Maurice Sinclair;** Chairman, Community Library, Painswick, 2011–13; *b* 15 June 1933; *s* of Rev. James Maurice Corley, MLitt and Mrs Barbara Shearer Corley; *m* 1961, Dr Marjorie Constance Doddridge; two *d*. *Educ:* Marlborough Coll.; King's Coll., Cambridge (MA). Min. of Power, 1957–61; Min. of Transport, 1961–65; BoT, 1965–69; Commercial Sec., Brussels, 1969–71; Asst Sec., DTI, 1972–75; Dir Gen., Econ. Co-operation Office, Riyadh, 1976–78; Dept of Industry, 1978–81; Under Sec., DTI, 1981–93. Consultant, Year of Engineering Success, 1993–96. *Recreations:* music, painting, travel. *Club:* Oxford and Cambridge.

**CORLEY, Roger David,** CBE 1993; Director, Clerical, Medical and General Life Assurance Society, 1975–97 (Managing Director, 1982–95); *b* 13 April 1933; *s* of Thomas Arthur and Erica Trent Corley; *m* 1964, Brigitte (*née* Roeder), PhD, FSA, FRSA; three *s*. *Educ:* Hymers College, Hull; Univ. of Manchester (BSc). FIA 1960. Joined Clerical Medical, 1956: Investment Manager, 1961–72; Actuary, 1972–80; Dep. Gen. Manager and Actuary, 1980–82. Chairman: Pharos SA, 1995–2006; St Andrew's Gp, 1995–2003; Director: Korea Asia Fund Ltd, 1990–2000; Nat. Westminster Life Assce Ltd, 1992–95; Lands Improvement Hldgs, 1994–99; City of Westminster Arts Council, 1994–2003; British Heart Foundn, 1995–2004; Medical Defence Union Ltd, 1996–2004; FIL (formerly Fidelity Investments) Life Insurance Ltd, 1997–2012; RGA Reinsurance UK Ltd, 1999–2012. Mem., Financial Services Commn of Gibraltar, 1995–2000. Pres., Inst. of Actuaries, 1988–90 (Mem. Council, 1976–94; Hon. Sec., 1980–82; Vice-Pres., 1985–88); Vice Pres., Internat. Actuarial Assoc., 1990–98 (Mem. Council, 1983–98; Nat. Correspondent for England, 1984–90); Mem., Deutsche Gesellschaft für Finanz- und Versicherungsmathematik (formerly für Versicherungsmathematik), 1975–. Master, Actuaries' Co., 1992–93 (Mem. Court, 1985–2006). FRSA 1990. *Recreations:* theatre, travel, music.

**CORMACK,** family name of **Baron Cormack**.

**CORMACK,** Baron *cr* 2010 (Life Peer), of Enville in the County of Staffordshire; **Patrick Thomas Cormack,** Kt 1995; DL; *b* 18 May 1939; *s* of Thomas Charles and Kathleen Mary Cormack, Grimsby; *m* 1967, Kathleen Mary McDonald; two *s*. *Educ:* St James' Choir School and Havelock School, Grimsby; Univ. of Hull. Second Master, St James' Choir School, Grimsby, 1961–66; Company Education and Training Officer, Ross Group Ltd, Grimsby, 1966–67; Assistant Housemaster, Wrekin College, Shropshire, 1967–69; Head of History, Brewood Grammar School, Stafford, 1969–70. Vis. Lectr, Univ. of Texas, 1984. Dir, Historic House Hotels Ltd, 1981–89; Chm., Aitken Dott Ltd (The Scottish Gallery), 1983–89. Trustee, Tradescant Trust, 1980–2001; President: Staffs Historic Buildings Trust, 1983–; Staffs Historic Churches Trust, 1997–2012; Staffs Parks and Gdns Trust, 2006–14; Prayer Book Soc., 2011–; Lincolnshire Heritage Trust, 2018–; Vice-President: Lincs Old Churches Trust, 1997–; Nat. Churches Trust (formerly Historic Churches Preservation Trust, 2005– (Trustee, 1972–2006); Member: Historic Buildings Council, 1979–84; Faculty Jurisdiction Commn, 1979–84; Heritage in Danger (Vice-Chm., 1974–2000); Council for British Archaeology, 1979–89; Royal Commn on Historical Manuscripts, 1981–2003; Council for Independent Educn (Chm.), 1979–97; Lord Chancellor's Adv. Cttee on Public Records, 1979–84; Council, Georgian Gp, 1985–; Council, Winston Churchill Meml Trust, 1983–93; Adv. Council on Nat. Records and Archives, 2003–06. Chairman: William Morris Craft Fellowship, 1988–; Adv. Council, Nat. Fisheries Mus., 1997–2000; Historic Lincoln Trust, 2012–; Ambassador, Nat. Forest, 2005–10. MP (C) Cannock, 1970–74, Staffs SW, 1974–83, Staffs S, 1983–2010. Dep. Shadow Leader of H of C and spokesman on constitutional affairs, 1997–2000. Member: Select Cttee on Educn, Science and Arts, 1979–84; Select Cttee on Foreign Affairs, 2001–03; Home Affairs Sub-cttee (F), Select Cttee on EU, H of L 2015–17; Chairman's Panel, H of C, 1983–97; Chairman: H of C Works of Art Cttee, 1987–2001; NI Affairs Select Cttee, 2005–10; Mem., H of C Commn, 2001–05. Member: All Party Arts and Heritage Gp (Chm. 1979–2010; Pres. 2010–); Cons. Party Arts and Heritage Cttee, 1979–84 (Chm.); H of L Works of Art Cttee, 2012–15; Chm., Cons. Party Adv. Cttee on Arts and Heritage, 1988–99; Treas., CPA, 2000–03; Mem. Exec., 1922 Cttee, 2002–05; Dir, Parly Broadcasting Unit, 2002–10; Chm., Campaign for an Effective Second Chamber, 2003–. Chairman: British-Finnish Parly Gp, 1992–2010; British-Bosnian Parly Gp, 1992–97, 2001–10; British-Croatian Parly Gp, 1992–97. Sen. Associate Mem., St Antony's Coll., Oxford, 1996– (Vis. Parly Fellow, 1994–95); Vis. Schol., Hull Univ., 1995–. Trustee, 1983–2016, Chm., 2001–16, Patron, 2016–, History of Parlt Trust. Chm. Editorial Bd, Parliamentary Publications, 1983–; Ed., The House Magazine, 1983–2005 (Chm. Editl Bd, 1978–; Life Pres., 2005); Internat. Pres., First mag., 1994–. FSA 1978 (Vice Pres., 1994–98). Rector's Warden, 1978–90, Parly Warden, 1990–92, St Margaret's Church, Westminster; Churchwarden, St Mary's, Enville, 1992–2009; Mem., Gen. Synod of C of E, 1995–2005; Dep. High Steward, Lincoln Cathedral, 2018–. Governor, ESU, 1999–2006 (Vice-Pres., Lincs Br., 2013–). Vice-President: Royal Stuart Soc., 2002–; Tennyson Soc., 2012–; Sen. Vice Pres., Public Monuments and Sculpture Assoc., 2010–. Patron, Internat. Bomber Command Centre, 2015–. Mem. Ct, Univ. of Lincoln, 2018–. FRHistS 2010. Mem., Worshipful Co. of Glaziers, 1979–; Freeman, City of London, 1979. DL Staffs, 2011. Hon. FHA 2010. Hon. Dr Catholic Univ. of America, 2010; Hon. DLitt Hull, 2010. Hon. Citizen of Texas, 1985. Churchwarden, St Mary and St Chad, Brewood, 1971–77. Commander, Order of the Lion (Finland), 1998. *Publications:* Heritage in Danger, 1976; Right Turn, 1978; Westminster: Palace and Parliament, 1981; Castles of Britain, 1982; Wilberforce—the Nation's Conscience, 1983; Cathedrals of England, 1984; Responsible Capitalism, Vol. I, 2010, Vol. II, 2017. *Recreations:* fighting philistines, walking, visiting old churches, avoiding sitting on fences. *Address:* House of Lords, SW1A 0PW. *Clubs:* Athenæum; Lincolnshire.

**CORMACK, Ann Catherine;** Executive Head, Human Resources, De Beers Group, since 2017; *b* Inverness, 30 March 1962; *d* of William Cormack and Margaret Cormack; *m* 1991, James Murray Grant; two *d*. *Educ:* Univ. of Edinburgh (MA Hons Mod. Langs 1984); Univ. of Strathclyde (Post-grad. Dip. Russian 1985). Network Planner, Supply and Distribn, Shell UK, 1985–87; Communications Co-ordinator, Shell Traveller's Check Retail, Shell UK, 1987–89; Area Asst, USSR, Bulgaria, Poland, Romania, E Germany, E Eur. Div., Shell Internat., 1989–91; Man. Dir, Cory South, then Exec. Dir, Shell Direct, 1992–95; Customer Interfaces Project Manager, Shell UK, 1995–96; Change Manager, Shell Retail, Netherlands, 1996–97; Leadership and Performance Team Associate, Global Transformation of Shell Gp, 1998–99; Manager, B2B and Lubricants, Shell Internal Consultancy, 1999–2001; Man. Dir, Euroshell Fleet Cars, 2002–04; Man. Dir, Small Business Service, DTI, 2005–07; CEO, D1-BP Fuel Crops, 2007–09; Managing Director: Darach Consulting, 2009–11; Energy, Xyntéo, 2011–13; Dir Internat., Rolls-Royce plc, 2013–17. Member, Council: BIEE, 2005–16 (Chair, 2006–07); RIIA (Chatham House), 2017–; non-exec. Dir, Audit Risk Assce Cttee, FCO, 2011–. *Recreations:* scuba-diving, swimming, ski-ing, learning to fly helicopters. *Address:* De Beers Group, 20 Carlton House Terrace, SW1Y 5AN. *T:* (020) 7430 3050.

**CORMACK, Dr Douglas;** independent consultant on environment and management; *b* 10 Jan. 1939; *s* of Douglas Cormack and Mary Hutton (*née* Bain); *m* 1966, Barbara Ann Jones (*d* 2004); two *s*. *Educ:* Gourock High Sch.; Greenock High Sch.; Univ. of Glasgow (BSc 1961; PhD Physical Chemistry 1964). Res. Associate, Chemical Oceanography, Woods Hole Oceanographic Instn, Mass, USA, 1964–67; Warren Spring Laboratory, Department of Trade and Industry: SSO, 1967–72; PSO, 1972–74; Sen. Principal and Hd, Oil Pollution Div., 1974–79; Scientific Advr, Marine Pollution Control Unit, Depts of Trade and Industry and Transport, 1979–86; Warren Spring Laboratory, Department of Trade and Industry: Dep. Dir with responsibility for Envmtl Res. and Personnel, 1986–89; Dep. Dir and Business Manager, 1989–92; Chief Exec., 1992–94; Dir, Envmt, British Maritime Technology, 1994–96. Chm., British Oil Spill Control Assoc., 2000–04; Mem., UK Accreditation Exec. Gp, 2003–04; Chm., ISAA, 2003–. Mem. Bd, Soc. of Maritime

Industries (formerly British Marine Equipment Council), 2000–04. Vice-Chm., Adv. Cttee on Protection of the Sea, 1992–95. Associate, Paragon Associates, Envmtl Consultants, 1994–97; Ind. Consultant, Cormack Associates, 1997–. Hon. Fellow, Internat. Spill Control Orgn, 2009. Mem., Council, RNLI, 2003–. FRSA 1988; Founding Fellow, Inst. of Contemp. Scotland, 2001. Editor, Jl of Oil and Chem. Pollution, 1985–91. *Publications*: Response to Oil and Chemical Marine Pollution, Applied Science, 1983; Response to Marine Oil Pollution—Review and Assessment, 1999; The Rational Trinity: imagination, belief and knowledge, 2010; numerous scientific papers and reports on catalytic processes, atmospheric pollution abatement, marine pollution prevention and response, waste recycling, final disposal and remediation of contaminated land. *Recreations*: sailing, beagling, reading philosophy, politics, history and science. *Address*: 1 Flint Copse, Redbourn, Herts AL3 7QE. *Clubs*: Civil Service; Royal Gourock Yacht.

**CORMACK, James Shearer**; QC 2018; Partner, Pinsent Masons LLP, since 2001; *b* Inverness, 11 Nov. 1968; *s* of James Cormack and Jean Cormack; *m* 2012, Emma Christine Pashley; one *s* two *d*. *Educ*: Lochaber High Sch., Fort William; Univ. of Edinburgh (LLP Hons; DipLP). Admitted solicitor: Scotland, 1993; England and Wales, 2006. Trainee solicitor, then Solicitor, McGrigor Donald, 1991–95; Mem., Faculty of Advocates, 1996–2001. *Recreations*: family, dog, walking, cycling, reading. *Address*: Pinsent Masons LLP, Princes Exchange, 1 Earl Grey Street, Edinburgh EH3 9AQ. *T*: (0131) 777 7356, *Fax*: (0131) 777 7003. *E*: jim.cormack@pinsentmasons.com.

**CORMACK, John**, CB 1982; Director, Parliamentary and Law, Institute of Chartered Accountants of Scotland, 1987–88 (Assistant Director, 1984–87); Fisheries Secretary, Department of Agriculture and Fisheries for Scotland, 1976–82; *b* 27 Aug. 1922; *yr s* of late Donald Cormack and Anne Hunter Cormack (*née* Gair); *m* 1947, Jessie Margaret Bain; one *s* one *d* (and one *d* decd). *Educ*: Royal High Sch., Edinburgh. Served RAPC, 1941–46; Captain and Command Cashier, CMF, 1946. Entered Department of Agriculture for Scotland, 1939; Principal, 1959; Private Sec. to Sec. of State for Scotland, 1967–69; Asst Sec., 1969; Under Sec., 1976. *Recreations*: golf, music. *Address*: 9/1 Murrayfield Road, Edinburgh EH12 6EW.

**CORMACK, Robert Linklater Burke**, CMG 1988; DL; HM Diplomatic Service, retired; *b* 29 Aug. 1935; *s* of late Frederick Eunson Cormack, CIE, and Elspeth Mary (*née* Linklater), Dounby, Orkney; *m* 1962, Eivor Dorotea Kumlin; one *s* two *d*. *Educ*: Trinity Coll., Glenalmond; Trinity Hall, Cambridge (BA Agric.). National Service, 2nd Lieut, The Black Watch, 1954–56. Dist Officer, Kenya (HMOCS), 1960–64; entered CRO (subseq. Diplomatic Service), 1964: Private Sec. to Minister of State, 1964–66; 1st Secretary: Saigon, 1966–68; Bombay, 1969–70; Delhi, 1970–72; FCO, 1972–77; Counsellor and Consul-Gen., Kinshasa, 1977–79; RCDS, 1980; Counsellor (Economic and Commercial), Stockholm, 1981–85; Hd of Information Technology Dept, FCO, 1985–87; Ambassador, Zaire and (non-resident) Rwanda and Burundi, 1987–91; Ambassador, Sweden, 1991–95. Hon. Consul for Sweden in Orkney, 1996–2006. Mem. (Ind.), Orkney Is Council, 1997–2003. DL Orkney, 1996; JP Orkney, 2002–07. Comdr, Order of North Star (Sweden), 1983. *Address*: Westness House, Rousay, Orkney KW17 2PT. *Club*: Hawks' (Cambridge).

**CORMACK, Prof. Robin Sinclair**, PhD; FSA; Professor in the History of Art, Courtauld Institute of Art, London University, 1991–2004, now Emeritus; *b* 27 Sept. 1938; *s* of James Menzies Cormack and Meryl Joyce Cormack (*née* Pendred); *m* 1st, 1961, Annabel Shackleton (marr. diss. 1985); one *s* one *d*; 2nd, 1985, (Winifred) Mary Beard (*see* Dame W. M. Beard); one *s* one *d*. *Educ*: Bristol Grammar Sch.; Exeter Coll., Oxford (BA Lit.Hum. 1961; MA 1965); Courtauld Inst. of Art, London Univ. (AcDip 1964; PhD 1968). FSA 1975. Gall. Manager, ICA, 1961–62; Lectr in History of Slavonic and E European Art, SSEES and Courtauld Inst. of Art, London Univ., 1966–73; Vis. Fellow, Dumbarton Oaks, Center for Byzantine Studies, Harvard Univ., 1972–73; Lectr in History of Art, Courtauld Inst., London Univ., 1973–82; British Academy Reader, Warburg Inst., London Univ., 1982–85; Bye Fellow, Robinson Coll., Cambridge, 1984–85 (Sen. Mem., 1985–); Reader in History of Art, 1986–90, Dep. Dir, 1999–2002, Courtauld Inst., London Univ. Geddes-Harrower Prof. of Greek Art and Archaeology, Aberdeen Univ., 2001–02; Leverhulme Emeritus Fellow, 2004–06; Getty Scholar, Res. Inst., The Getty, Los Angeles, 2005–06; Special Prof. in Classics, Univ. of Nottingham, 2005–08; Lecturing Asst, Faculty of Classics, Univ. of Cambridge, 2010–. Vis. Schol. in Byzantine Studies, Dumbarton Oaks, Washington DC, 2011. Consultant: to RA for Byzantium 330–1453 exhibn, 2008–09, for El Greco in Italia, exhibn at Casa di Carraresi, Treviso, 2015–16. *Publications*: Writing in Gold, 1985 (trans. French, Icônes et Société à Byzance, 1993); The Church of S Demetrios of Thessaloniki, 1985; The Byzantine Eye, 1989; Painting the Soul, 1998 (Runciman Award, Anglo-Hellenic League and Onassis Foundn); Byzantine Art, 2000, 2nd edn 2018; Icons, 2007, 2nd edn 2014; Byzantium 330–1453, 2008; Oxford Handbook of Byzantine Studies, 2008. *Recreations*: learning to play the spinet and use Photoshop. *Address*: 120 Huntingdon Road, Cambridge CB3 0HL. *T*: (01223) 312734.

**CORMACK, Dame (Winifred) Mary**; *see* Beard, Dame W. M.

**CORNELIUS, David Frederick**, FCIHT; transport and research consultant; *b* 7 May 1932; *s* of Frederick M. N. and Florence K. Cornelius; *m* 1956, Susan (*née* Austin); two *s* two *d*. *Educ*: Teignmouth Grammar Sch.; Exeter University Coll. (BSc (Hons) Physics). Royal Naval Scientific Service, 1953–58; UKAEA, 1958–64; Research Manager, Road Research Laboratory, 1964–72; Asst Director, Building Research Estabt, 1973–78; Head, Research, Transport and Special Programmes, 1978–80, Transport Science Policy Unit, 1980–82, Dept of Transport; Asst Dir, 1982–84, Dep. Dir, 1984–88, Actg Dir, 1988–89, Dir, 1989–91, Transport and Road Res. Lab. Initiated formation of European Forum of Highway Res. Labs in 1990, leading to successful collaboration between members in highway res., road safety and traffic engrg. FRSA. *Publications*: Path of Duty (biog.), 2000, 2nd edn 2014; scientific papers to nat. and internat. confs and in jls of various professional instns on range of topics in tribology, highway transportation and internat. collaboration in res. *Recreations*: touring Europe, Africa and the Antipodes by motorhome, world travel by container ships, sea and river cruises, swimming and cycling, observing and taking pleasure from the career progression of offspring in fields of commerce, science, the arts and academia and the development of our six grandchildren, member of Emsworth Methodist Church Council, member of Hayling Island U3A. *Address*: White Poplars, 40 Webb Lane, Hayling Island, Hants PO11 9JE. *T*: (023) 9246 7212.

**CORNELL, Eric Allin**, PhD; Adjoint Professor, Department of Physics, University of Colorado, Boulder, since 1995 (Assistant Adjoint Professor, 1992–95); Fellow, Joint Institute for Laboratory Astrophysics and National Institute of Standards and Technology, since 1994; *b* Palo Alto, Calif, 1961; *s* of Prof. Allin Cornell and Elizabeth Cornell (*née* Greenberg); *m* 1995, Celeste Landry; two *d*. *Educ*: Stanford Univ. (BS 1985); MIT (PhD 1990). Postdoctoral res. asst, Jt Inst. for Lab. Astrophysics, Boulder, 1990–92; Sen. Scientist, Nat. Inst. of Standards and Technol., Boulder, 1992–. (Jtly) Nobel Prize for Physics, 2001. *Publications*: articles in jls. *Address*: Joint Institute for Laboratory Astrophysics, University of Colorado, Campus Box 440, Boulder, CO 80309–0440, USA.

**CORNELL, Jim Scott**, CEng, FREng; FICE; FCILT; Executive Director, Railway Heritage Trust, 1996–2009; *b* 3 Aug. 1939; *s* of James William Cornell and Annie Cornell (*née* Scott); *m* 1962, Winifred Eileen Rayner; one *s* one *d*. *Educ*: Thirsk Grammar Sch.; Bradford Inst. of Technol. CEng 1967; FICE 1983; FCILT (FCIT 1986); FREng (FEng 1992). With British Rail, 1959–96: jun. and middle mgt civil engrg posts, 1959–76; Divisional Civil Engineer: King's Cross, 1976–78; Newcastle, 1978–81; Asst Regl Civil Engr, York, 1981–83; Regl Civil Engr, Scotland, 1983–84; Dep. Gen. Manager, 1984–86, Gen. Manager, 1986–87, ScotRail; Dir, Civil Engrg, 1987–92; Man. Dir, Regl Railways, 1992–93; Man. Dir, BR Infrastructure Services, 1993–96. Non-exec. Dir, Railtrack plc, subseq. Network Rail, 2002–09. FCMI (FIMgt 1987). Chm., Railway Heritage Trust, 2018–. *Recreations*: tennis, gardening. *T*: (01525) 851070.

**CORNELL, Peter**; Founder, Cornell Partners, 2011; Founding Partner, Metric Capital, since 2011; *b* 5 Oct. 1952; *s* of Dr Sydney Page Cornell and Marjorie Joan Cornell; *m* 1981, Bernadette Conway; one *s* three *d*. *Educ*: Tonbridge Sch., Kent; Exeter Univ.; Chester Law Coll. SSC. Admitted solicitor, 1975; joined Clifford Chance, 1975: on secondment to Philip Morris, Lausanne, 1978–79; opened Singapore office, 1981; returned to London office, 1986; Man. Partner, Madrid office, 1989–2001; opened Barcelona office, 1993; Eur. Man. Partner, 1996–2001; Global Managing Partner, 2001–07; Man. Dir, Stakeholder Relations, Terra Firma Capital Partners Ltd, later Terra Firma Capital Mgt Ltd, 2007–11. Mem. Council, 2009–11, Vice-Chm., Global Buyout Cttee, 2009–11, BVCA. Non-executive Director: F&CP Hldgs Ltd; Schroders (CI) Ltd; Ceiba Investments Ltd, 2018–; Breedon Gp PLC, 2018–. Chairman: Legal Bd, Ogier, 2011–; Augusta Securities Ltd, 2013–; Lexington Consultants, 2016–; Grant Thornton (CI), 2017–. Mem., Internat. Adv. Bd, IE Business Sch., Madrid, 2006–. Accredited Mediator, CEDR, 2010. Legal Business Lawyer of the Year, 2007. *Recreations*: family, sport, tennis, golf, squash, ski-ing, surfing. *Address*: Horizons, York Way, Fort George, St Peter Port, Guernsey GY1 2SY. *Clubs*: Royal Automobile, Royal Channel Yacht; Royal Guernsey Golf; La Moraleja (Madrid).

**CORNER, Diane Louise**, OBE 2018; HM Diplomatic Service; Counsellor, Foreign and Security Policy, Washington, since 2019; *b* 29 Sept. 1959; *d* of Captain Alaric John Corner and late Marjorie Corner (*née* Ashcroft); *m* 1986, Peter Timothy Stocker; four *d*. *Educ*: Winchester Co. High Sch. for Girls; Peter Symonds Coll.; Univ. of Bristol (BA Hons French and Politics); King's Coll. London (MA Internat. Relns 2019). Entered FCO, 1982; Second Sec. (Chancery), Kuala Lumpur, 1985–88; First Sec., FCO, 1989–91; Cabinet Office (on secondment), 1991–93; Dep. Hd of Mission, Berlin, 1994–98; First Sec., FCO, 1998–2000; NATO Defence Coll., Rome, 2000; Counsellor and Dep. High Comr, Harare, 2001–03; Counsellor, FCO, 2003–04; on loan to Cabinet Office as Chief Assessor, CSSB, 2004–05; Dir, Prism Change Prog., 2005–06, Shared Services Prog., 2007–08, FCO; Catlin Underwriting (on loan), 2008; Actg High Comr, Sierra Leone, 2008–09; High Comr, Tanzania, 2009–13; Ambassador to Democratic Republic of Congo and Republic of Congo, 2013–14; Asst Sec.-Gen. and Dep. Special Rep. (Political and Protection), UN Multidimensional Integrated Stabilization Mission in Central African Republic, 2014–17; ind. consultant on peacekeeping, 2017–18. *Recreations*: reading, keeping fit. *Address*: c/o Foreign and Commonwealth Office, King Charles Street, SW1A 2AH.

**CORNER, Prof. Frances Marie**, OBE 2009; DPhil; Warden, Goldsmiths, University of London, since 2019; *b* Aden, 25 Feb. 1959; *d* of Ernest James Agnew and Joanna Southworth Agnew (*née* Kelly); *m* 1980, Anthony Peter Corner; one *s*. *Educ*: St Maurs Convent, Weybridge; St Martin's Sch. of Art (BA Hons 1981); Chelsea Coll. of Art (MA Fine Art 1984); Kellogg Coll., Oxford (DPhil 2004). University of Gloucestershire: Sen. Lectr, 1991–94; Hd, Div. of Arts, 1994–95; Hd, Dept of Arts, 1995–98; Associate Dean, Faculty of Arts and Humanities, 1998–2001; Hd, Sir John Cass Dept of Art, Media and Design, London Metropolitan Univ., 2001–05; Hd of Coll., 2005–19, Prof. of Arts and Design Educn, 2009–19, London Coll. of Fashion; Pro Vice-Chancellor, UAL, 2013–19. London Leader, Sustainability, London Sustainable Develt Commn, 2008. Member: Steering Gp, Gp for Learning in Art and Design, 2002–07; Adv. Bd, British Fashion Council, 2011–; Exec. Cttee, Internat. Foundn of Fashion Technology Institutes, 2011– (Chair, 2014–). Chair, Council for Higher Educn in Art and Design, 2006–09 (Vice Chair, 2005–06). Individual Internat. Consultant, Orange Heart UN Trust Fund; Trustee, Wallace Collection, 2009–17; Chair of Trustees, House of Illustration, 2015–. Dist. Prof., Beijing Inst. of Fashion Technol., 2016–. FRSA. Hon. Fellow, Univ. of Gloucestershire, 2017. *Publications*: Why Fashion Matters, 2014. *Recreations*: yoga, running, reading, travel. *Address*: Goldsmiths, University of London, New Cross, SE14 6NW. *Clubs*: h, House of St Barnabas.

**CORNER, Dame Jessica (Lois)**, DBE 2014; PhD; FMedSci; Professor of Cancer and Supportive Care, and Pro-Vice-Chancellor for Research and Knowledge Exchange, University of Nottingham, since 2016; *b* 22 March 1961; *d* of Rodney, (Bunny), Corner and Judith Corner; *m* 1st, 1985, Cameron Findlay (marr. diss. 1998); one *d*; 2nd, 1999, Christopher Bailey; one *d*. *Educ*: Chelsea Coll., London (BSc Hons Nursing Studies 1983); King's Coll., London (PhD 1990). RN 1983; Oncology Nurse Cert. 1985; Mem. Inst. for Learning and Teaching. 2002. Staff Nurse: Cardiothoracic Unit, St George's Hosp., London, 1983–84; Royal Marsden Hosp., London, 1984–85; Nursing Studies Department, King's College, London: Res. Asst, 1985; Postgrad. Researcher, 1985–87; Macmillan Lectr in Cancer and Palliative Care, 1987–90; Sen. Macmillan Lectr and Hd, Academic Nursing Unit, Inst. of Cancer Res. and Royal Marsden Hosp., 1990–94; Institute of Cancer Research, London: Dir and Dep. Dean (Nursing), Centre for Cancer and Palliative Care Studies, 1994–2002; Prof. of Cancer Nursing, 1996–2002; University of Southampton: Prof. of Cancer and Palliative Care, 2002–08; Dean of Health Scis, 2008–15; Dir for Improving Cancer Services, 2005–08, Chief Clinician, 2008–16, Macmillan Cancer Support. Member, Council: Research England, 2018; Acad. of Med. Scis, 2018–. FHEA 2002; FMedSci 2015. *Publications*: Becoming a Staff Nurse, 1991; Cancer Nursing: care in context, 2001, 2nd edn 2008; Researching Palliative Care, 2001; over 100 acad. papers in books and jls. *Recreations*: a very amateur gardener and flautist, walking in the Lake District, chaotic family life with two daughters born 12 years apart. *Address*: Executive Office, University of Nottingham, Trent Building, University Park, Nottingham NG7 2RD. *E*: jessica.corner@nottingham.ac.uk.

**CORNER, Timothy Frank**; QC 2002; a Recorder, since 2004; a Deputy High Court Judge, since 2008; *b* 25 July 1958; *s* of Frank and June Corner. *Educ*: Bolton Sch.; Magdalen Coll., Oxford (Demy (Open Scholar); BCL; MA (Jurisprudence). Called to the Bar, Gray's Inn, 1981, Bencher, 2007; Junior Counsel to the Crown, A Panel, 1999–2002. Chm., Adv. Panel on Standards for the Planning Inspectorate, 2006–10. Chm., Planning and Envmt Bar Assoc., 2008–12. *Publications*: contrib. Jl of Planning and Envmt Law. *Recreations*: singing, walking, books, travel. *Address*: Landmark Chambers, 180 Fleet Street, EC4A 2HG. *T*: (020) 7430 1221. *E*: tcorner@landmarkchambers.co.uk. *Club*: Athenæum.

**CORNESS, Sir Colin (Ross)**, Kt 1986; Chairman, Glaxo Wellcome plc, 1995–97; *b* 9 Oct. 1931; *s* of late Thomas Corness and Mary Evelyne Corness. *Educ*: Uppingham Sch.; Magdalene Coll., Cambridge (BA 1954, MA 1958; Hon. Fellow, 2001). Graduate Sch. of Business Admin, Harvard, USA (Advanced Management Program Dip. 1970). Called to the Bar, Inner Temple, 1956. Dir, Taylor Woodrow Construction Ltd, 1961–64; Man. Dir,

Redland Tiles Ltd, 1965–70; Redland PLC: Man. Dir, 1967–82; Chief Exec., 1977–91; Chm., 1977–95. Chm., Nationwide Building Soc., 1991–96. Director: Chubb & Son PLC, 1974–84 (Dep. Chm., 1984); W. H. Smith & Son (Holdings) PLC, 1980–87; Gordon Russell PLC, 1985–89; Courtaulds PLC, 1986–91; S. G. Warburg Gp, 1987–95; Unitech, 1987–95; Union Comp Corp., 1991–99; Chubb Security, 1992–97; Taylor Woodrow plc, 1997–2001. A Dir, Bank of England, 1987–95. Chm., Building Centre, 1974–77; Pres., Nat. Council of Building Material Producers, 1985–87; Member: EDC for Building, 1980–84; Industrial Develt Adv. Bd, 1982–84. Trustee, Uppingham Sch., 1996–99; Observer/Trustee, Nottingham RC Dio., 2007–12. Hon. DBA Kingston, 1994. *Recreations:* gardening, travel, music. *Address:* 54 Chesterfield House, Chesterfield Gardens, W1J 5JU.

**CORNICK, Rev. Dr David George;** General Secretary, Churches Together in England, 2008–18; Fellow of Robinson College, Cambridge, since 1997; *b* 12 Sept. 1954; *s* of Cecil George Cornick and Thelma (*née* Le Brun); *m* 1977, Mary Hammond; two *s*. *Educ:* Hertford and Mansfield Colls, Oxford (MA); King's Coll., London (BD; PhD 1982); Open Univ. (MBA 2008). United Reformed Church: Minister, Radlett and Borehamwood, 1981–84; Chaplain, Robinson Coll., Cambridge, 1984–87; Trng Officer, South-Western Province, 1987–92; Dir of Studies in Church Hist., 1992–2001, Principal, 1996–2001, Westminster Coll., Cambridge; Gen. Sec., URC, 2001–08. Select Preacher, Univ. of Cambridge, 2003. Congregational Lect., Through Eric Routley's Eyes, 2018. *Publications:* Under God's Good Hand, 1998; (contrib. and ed jtly) From Cambridge to Sinai: the worlds of Agnes Smith Lewis and Margaret Dunlop Gibson, 2006; Letting God be God: the reformed tradition, 2008. *Recreations:* music, walking, embroidery. *Address:* Robinson College, Grange Road, Cambridge CB3 9AN.

**CORNISH, Charles T.;** Group Chief Executive, Manchester Airports Group, since 2010; *b* Hamilton, Scotland; *s* of Charlie Cornish and Isabel Cornish; *m* 1992, Margo; one *s* three *d*. *Educ:* Hamilton Grammar Sch.; Univ. of Strathclyde (BA 1980); Postgrad. Dip. Personnel and Develt. Customer Services Dir, 1997–99, Chief Exec., 1999–2000, West of Scotland Water; Global Business Performance Dir, 2000–01, Chief Operating Officer, 2001–02, Thames Water, later RWE/Thames Water; Man. Dir and Bd Dir, United Utilities plc, 2002–10. *Recreations:* golf, football. *E:* Charlie.Cornish@manairport.co.uk. *Club:* Oriental.

**CORNISH, Francis;** *see* Cornish, R. F.

**CORNISH, Iain Charles Andrew;** Chairman, St James's Place, since 2018 (Independent non-executive Director, since 2011); *m* Josette; two *d*. *Educ:* Univ. of Southampton (BSc 1982). Statistician, DTI; Sen. Consultant, Strategy Services Consultancy Practice, KPMG; Corporate Planner, Bradford & Bingley Bldg Soc.; Corporate Develt Manager, 1992, later Gen. Mktg Manager, Chief Exec., 2003–11, Yorks Bldg Soc. Dep. Chm., 2006–07, Chm., 2007–08, Building Societies' Assoc. Chm., Financial Services Practitioner Panel, 2009–11; non-exec. Dir, Prudential Regulation Authy, 2013–15; Chm., Shawbrook Bank, 2015–18. Treas., Macmillan Cancer Support, 2017–.

**CORNISH, James Easton;** Director and European Market Strategist, BT Alex. Brown (formerly NatWest Securities), 1990–99; *b* 5 Aug. 1939; *s* of Eric Easton Cornish and Ivie Hedworth (*née* McCulloch); *m* 1968, Ursula Pink; one *s*. *Educ:* Eton Coll.; Wadham Coll., Oxford (BA); Harvard. Joined FO, 1961; Bonn, 1963; British Mil. Govt, Berlin, 1965; FCO, 1968; Washington, 1973; Dep. Head of Planning Staff, FCO, 1977; Central Policy Rev. Staff, 1980; seconded to Phillips & Drew, 1982; resigned HM Diplomatic Service, 1985; Manager, Internat. Dept, Phillips & Drew, 1982–87; Asst Dir, subseq. Associate Dir, County Securities Ltd, 1987–90.

**CORNISH, (Robert) Francis,** CMG 1994; LVO 1978; HM Diplomatic Service, retired; Chairman, South West Tourism Ltd, 2003–09; *b* 18 May 1942; *s* of late Charles Derrick Cornish and Catherine Cornish; *m* 1964, Alison Jane Dundas; three *d*. *Educ:* Charterhouse; RMA Sandhurst. Commissioned 14th/20th King's Hussars, 1962–68; HM Diplomatic Service 1968; served Kuala Lumpur, Jakarta and FCO, 1969–76; First Sec., Bonn, 1976–80; Asst Private Sec. to HRH the Prince of Wales, 1980–83; High Comr, Brunei, 1983–86; Counsellor (Inf.), Washington, and Dir, British Inf. Services, NY, 1986–90; Head of News Dept, and Spokesman, FCO, 1990–93; Sen. British Trade Comr, Hong Kong, 1993–97; Consul-Gen., HKSAR, 1997; Sen. Directing Staff, RCDS, 1998; Ambassador to Israel, 1998–2001. FRSA 2003. Director: Gross Hill Properties Ltd, 2002–10; Sydney & London Properties Ltd, 2003–10. Chm., Taunton Town Centre Co., 2003–12; Trustee, Brewhouse Th., Taunton, 2010–13. *Club:* Cavalry and Guards.

**CORNISH, Sophie,** MBE 2013; entrepreneur and business advisor; Co-Founder, notonthehighstreet.com, since 2006 (Director, 2006–16); Managing Partner, Busby & Fox, since 2017; *b* London, 11 Aug. 1965; *d* of late Paul and Penny Vincenzi; *m* 2001, Simon Cornish; one *s* one *d*. *Educ:* Kingston Grammar Sch. Writer and ed., Cosmopolitan, Hearst Mags, 1984–86; Creative Brand Manager, No 7 and 17 Cosmetics, BA Associates, 1986–88; beauty writer and ed., Good Housekeeping, Hearst Mags, 1988–90; New Business Manager, GGK London, 1990–94; Account Dir, Publicis London, 1994–99; Channel Ed., BEME.com, IPC Media/Time Inc. UK, 2000; freelance writer, stylist, mktg consultant, 2001–05; Business Growth Advr, Boom Ents, 2017–. Director: Clay Lane Ltd, 2017–; Emma Vowles Ltd, 2017–; Doodle Prodns Ltd, 2017–; Penny Vincenzi Ltd, 2019–. Mem. Bd, CRUK Women of Influence, 2012–16. Gov., Surbiton High Sch., 2012– (Dep. Chm., 2016–). *Publications:* Your Wedding Your Way, 2003; (jtly) Build a Business From Your Kitchen Table, 2012; (jtly) Shape Up Your Business, 2014. *Recreation:* CrossFit.

**CORNISH, Prof. William Rodolph,** CMG 2013; FBA 1984; Herchel Smith Professor of Intellectual Property Law, Cambridge University, 1995–2004, now Emeritus (Professor of Law, 1990–95); Fellow, Magdalene College, Cambridge, since 1990 (President, 1998–2001); *b* 9 Aug. 1937; *s* of Jack R. and Elizabeth E. Cornish, Adelaide, S Australia; *m* 1964, Lovedy E. Moule; one *s* two *d*. *Educ:* Univs of Adelaide (LLB) and Oxford (BCL); LLD Cantab, 1996. Lectr in Law, LSE, 1962–68; Reader in Law, Queen Mary Coll., London, 1969–70; Prof. of English Law, LSE, 1970–90. Ext. Acad. Mem., Max Planck Inst. for Innovation and Competition (formerly for Patent, Copyright and Competition Law, then for Intellectual Property, Competition and Tax Law, subseq. for Intellectual Property and Competition Law), Munich, 1989–. Hon. QC 1997; Bencher, Gray's Inn, 1998. Hon. Mem., Chartered Inst. of Patent Agents, 2005. Hon. Fellow, LSE, 1996. Hon. LLD Edinburgh, 2005. *Publications:* The Jury, 1968; (Jt Editor) Sutton and Shannon on Contracts, 1970; (jtly) Encyclopedia of United Kingdom and European Patent Law, 1977; Intellectual Property, 1981, 8th edn (jtly) 2013; Law and Society in England 1750–1950, 1989; (jtly) Oxford History of the Laws of England, vols XI–XIII 1820–1914, 2010; articles etc in legal periodicals. *Address:* Magdalene College, Cambridge CB3 0AG.

**CORNOCK, Maj.-Gen. Charles Gordon, (Bill),** CB 1988; MBE 1974; Bursar, Cranleigh School, 1989–95; *b* 25 April 1935; *s* of Gordon Wallace Cornock and Edith Mary (*née* Keeley); *m* 1963, Kay Smith; two *s*. *Educ:* King Alfred Sch., Plön, Germany; RMA, Sandhurst. Commnd RA, 1956; served, 1957–71: 33 Para Lt Regt; 1 RHA; RMA, Sandhurst; Staff Coll., Camberley; BMRA; Armed Forces Staff Coll., Norfolk, Va; Second in Comd, 1972–74 and CO 1974–76, 7 Para RHA; GSO1 DS Staff Coll., Camberley, 1977–78; Col GS HQ UKLF, 1979; CRA 3rd Armoured Div., 1980–81; RCDS, 1982; Dep. Comdt, Staff Coll., Camberley, 1983; Dir, RA, 1984–86; C of S and Head of UK Delegn, Live Oak, SHAPE, 1986–89. Col Comdt RA, 1986–94; Rep. Col Comdt, RA, 1991–92. Chm., Confedn of British Service and Ex-Service Orgns, 1996–99. Comdr, St John Ambulance (Jersey), 1999–2004. Mem., Police Complaints Authy (Jersey), 2001–05. President: RA Golfing Soc., 1989–98; Jersey Scout Assoc., 2005–11; Mem. Cttee, Jersey Blind Soc., 2006–; Vice-Pres., Combined Services and Army Hockey Assoc. Trustee, Jersey Army Cadet Force, 2010–. Mem., Sen. Golfers' Soc. FCMI. *Recreations:* hockey, tennis, golf, ski-ing, water ski-ing. *Address:* Upton, Trinity, Jersey JE3 5DT. *Clubs:* Army and Navy; La Moye Golf (Jersey).

**CORNS, Prof. Thomas Nicholas,** DPhil; FBA 2015; Professor of English Literature, Bangor University (formerly University College of North Wales, then University of Wales, Bangor), 1994–2014, now Emeritus; *b* Prescot, Lancs; *s* of Joseph Richard Corns and Martha Lily Corns; *m* 1972, Patricia Allen; two *s*. *Educ:* Prescot Grammar Sch.; Brasenose Coll., Oxford (BA 1972); Maximilianeum Foundn, Munich; University Coll., Oxford (DPhil 1978). University College of North Wales, subseq. University of Wales, Bangor: Lectr, 1975–87, Sen. Lectr, 1987–92, Reader, 1992–94, of English Lit.; Pro-Vice-Chancellor, 2004–07. Founder and Co-Convener, British Milton Seminar, 1990–2014; Hon. Sec., Standing Cttee, Internat. Milton Symposium, 1995–2015. *Publications:* The Development of Milton's Prose Style, 1982; Milton's Language, 1990; Uncloistered Virtue: English political literature, 1640–1660, 1992; (ed) The Cambridge Companion to English Poetry, Donne to Marvell, 1993; Regaining Paradise Lost, 1994; John Milton: the prose works, 1998; (ed) The Royal Image: representations of Charles I, 1999; (ed) Blackwell Companion to Milton, 2001; A History of Seventeenth-Century English Literature, 2006; (jtly) John Milton and the Manuscript of De Doctrina Christiana, 2007; John Milton: life, work and thought, 2008; (ed jtly) The Complete Works of Gerrard Winstanley, 2009; (ed) The Milton Encyclopedia, 2012; (ed) A New Companion to Milton, 2016; (ed jtly) Milton and Catholicism, 2017. *Recreations:* golf, bird watching, dog walking. *Address:* School of English Literature, Bangor University, Gwynedd LL57 2DG. *T:* (01248) 382102. *E:* els009@bangor.ac.uk. *Club:* Henllys Golf (Beaumaris).

**CORNWALL, Archdeacon of;** *see* Bryer, Ven. P. D.

**CORNWALL, His Honour Christopher John;** a Circuit Judge, 2002–16; *b* 20 Dec. 1950; *s* of Geoffrey and Joan Cornwall; *m* 1977, Elizabeth Dunbar Cliff; two *s* one *d*. *Educ:* Shrewsbury Sch.; St Catherine's Coll., Oxford (BA Hons). Called to the Bar, Lincoln's Inn, 1975; Asst Recorder, 1990–94; a Recorder, 1994–2002. *Recreations:* hill-walking, gardening, European literature, classical music, the visual arts.

**CORNWALL, Hugo;** *see* Sommer, P. M.

**CORNWALL-LEGH,** family name of **Baron Grey of Codnor**.

**CORNWALLIS,** family name of **Baron Cornwallis**.

**CORNWALLIS,** 4th Baron *cr* 1927, of Linton, Kent; **(Fiennes Wykeham) Jeremy Cornwallis;** *b* Tunbridge Wells, 25 May 1946; *s* of 3rd Baron Cornwallis, OBE and Judith Lacy Scott (*d* 2009); *S* father, 2010; *m* 1969, Sara Gray de Neufville, *d* of Lt-Col Nigel Stockwell, Benenden, Kent; one *s* two *d*. *Educ:* Eton; Royal Agricultural Coll., Cirencester. *Recreations:* golf, cricket. *Heir:* *s* Hon. (Fiennes) Alexander (Wykeham Martin) Cornwallis, *b* 25 Nov. 1987. *Address:* Spratts Cottage, Stone, Tenterden, Kent TN30 7JH. *E:* cornwallis46@btinternet.com. *Clubs:* MCC, I Zingari, Eton Ramblers; Rye Golf, Machrihannish Golf.

**CORNWELL, Alison Margaret;** creative industries finance executive; Chief Financial Officer, Vue Entertainment International Group, since 2014; *b* Glasgow, 30 June 1966; *d* of Dr Harold John Campbell Cornwell and Jane Helen Cornwell (*née* Begg); *m* 1993, Norman Macleod; three *s* one *d*. *Educ:* Univ. of Glasgow (BAcc 1987). CA 1990. Sen. Manager, Coopers & Lybrand Corporate Finance, 1990–95; Sen. Vice Pres. Finance, Walt Disney TV Internat., 1995–2005; Chief Financial Officer: Sparrowhawk Media Gp, 2005–08; Alliance Films Gp, 2008–13. Chm., Oversight Bd, ICAS, 2018–. Gov., BFI, 2013–18 (Chm., Audit Cttee, 2013–18). Non-exec. Dir, Centre for the Moving Image and Edinburgh Internat. Film Fest., 2016– (Mem., Audit Cttee, 2018–). Columnist, ICAS mag., 2013–14. Mem. Council, ICAS, 2018–. *Recreations:* music, photography, film, cycling, genealogy. *Address:* Frieth, Henley on Thames; Bharcasaig, Isle of Skye. *E:* alison_cornwell@msn.com.

**CORNWELL, Bernard,** OBE 2006; novelist, since 1980; *b* 23 Feb. 1944; *s* of William Oughtred and Dorothy Rose Cornwell and adopted *s* of late Joseph and Margery Wiggins; *m* 1st, 1967, Lindsay Leworthy (marr. diss. 1976); one *d*; 2nd, 1980, Judy Cashdollar. *Educ:* Monkton Combe Sch.; London Univ. (BA ext.). Producer, BBC TV, 1970–76; Hd, Current Affairs TV, BBC NI, 1976–78; Ed., Thames TV News, 1978–80. Dir, Amer. Associates of Nat. Army Mus. Mem., Charleston Liby Soc. *Publications:* Sharpe's Eagle, 1981; Sharpe's Gold, 1981; Sharpe's Company, 1982; Sharpe's Sword, 1983; Sharpe's Enemy, 1984; Sharpe's Honour, 1985; Sharpe's Regiment, 1986; Sharpe's Siege, 1987; Redcoat, 1987; Sharpe's Rifles, 1988; Wildtrack, 1988; Sharpe's Revenge, 1989; Sea Lord, 1989; Sharpe's Waterloo, 1990; Crackdown, 1990; Stormchild, 1991; Sharpe's Devil, 1992; Scoundrel, 1992; Rebel, 1993; Copperhead, 1994; Sharpe's Battle, 1995; Battle Flag, 1995; The Winter King, 1995; The Bloody Ground, 1996; Enemy of God, 1996; Sharpe's Tiger, 1997; Excalibur, 1997; Sharpe's Triumph, 1998; Sharpe's Fortress, 1999; Stonehenge, 2000 BC, 1999; Sharpe's Trafalgar, 2000; Harlequin, 2000; Sharpe's Prey, 2001; Gallows Thief, 2001; Vagabond, 2002; Sharpe's Havoc, 2003; Heretic, 2003; Sharpe's Escape, 2004; The Last Kingdom, 2004; The Pale Horseman, 2005; Sharpe's Fury, 2006; Lords of the North, 2006; Sword Song, 2007; Azincourt, 2008; The Burning Land, 2009; The Fort, 2010; Death of Kings, 2011; 1356, 2012; The Pagan Lord, 2013; The Empty Throne, 2014; Warriors of the Storm, 2015; The Flame Bearer, 2016; Fools and Mortals, 2017; War of the Wolf, 2018; *non-fiction:* Waterloo: the true story of four days, three armies and three battles, 2014. *Recreations:* sailing, acting with Monomy Theatre (Chatham, Mass). *Address:* PO Box 168, West Chatham, MA 02669, USA. *Clubs:* Stage Harbor Yacht (Chatham, Mass), Carolina Yacht (Charleston, SC).

**CORNWELL, David John Moore, (John le Carré);** writer; *b* 19 Oct. 1931; *s* of late Ronald Thomas Archibald Cornwell and Olive (*née* Glassey); *m* 1954, Alison Ann Veronica Sharp (marr. diss. 1971; she *d* 2009); three *s*; *m* 1972, Valerie Jane Eustace; one *s*. *Educ:* Sherborne; Berne Univ.; Lincoln Coll., Oxford (1st cl. Modern Languages; Hon. Fellow 1984). Taught at Eton, 1956–58. Mem. of HM Foreign Service, 1960–64. Hon. DLitt: Exeter, 1990; St Andrews, 1996; Southampton 1997; Bath, 1998; Hon. Dr Berne, 2008; Hon. DLitt Oxford, 2012. Cartier Diamond Dagger, CWA, 1988; Goethe Medal, Goethe Inst., 2011. Comdr, Ordre des Arts et des Lettres (France), 2005. *Publications:* Call for the Dead, 1961 (filmed as The Deadly Affair, 1967); A Murder of Quality, 1962; The Spy Who Came in from the Cold, 1963 (Somerset Maugham Award; Crime Writers' Assoc. Gold Dagger, 1963, Dagger of Daggers, 2005) (filmed); The Looking-Glass War, 1965 (filmed); A Small Town in Germany, 1968; The Naïve and Sentimental Lover, 1971; Tinker, Tailor, Soldier, Spy, 1974 (televised 1979; filmed 2011); The Honourable Schoolboy, 1977 (James

Tait Black Meml Prize; Crime Writers' Assoc. Gold Dagger); Smiley's People, 1980 (televised 1982); The Little Drummer Girl, 1983 (filmed 1985; televised 2018); A Perfect Spy, 1986 (televised 1987); The Russia House, 1989 (filmed 1991); The Secret Pilgrim, 1991; The Night Manager, 1993 (televised 2016); Our Game, 1995; The Tailor of Panama, 1996 (filmed 2001); Single & Single, 1999; The Constant Gardener, 2001 (filmed 2005); Absolute Friends, 2003; The Mission Song, 2006; A Most Wanted Man, 2008 (filmed 2014); Our Kind of Traitor, 2010 (filmed 2016); A Delicate Truth, 2013; The Pigeon Tunnel, 2016; A Legacy of Spies, 2017; Agent Running in the Field, 2019. *Address:* c/o Jonny Geller, Curtis Brown Group Ltd, Haymarket House, 28–29 Haymarket, SW1Y 4SP.

**CORNWELL, Patricia D(aniels);** American crime novelist; *b* 9 June 1956; *d* of Sam and Marilyn Daniels; *m* 1980, Charles Cornwell (marr. diss. 1990). *Educ:* Davidson Coll., N Carolina (BA English 1979). Crime Reporter, Charlotte Observer, 1979–81 (N Carolina Press Assoc. Award, 1980); Technical Writer, then Computer Analyst, Office of Chief Med. Examr, Richmond, Va, 1984–90; Volunteer Police Officer. *Publications: non-fiction:* A Time For Remembering: the story of Ruth Bell Graham, 1983, re-issued as Ruth—a Portrait, 1997; Scarpetta's Winter Table, 1998; Portrait of a Killer: Jack the Ripper—case closed, 2002; Food to Die For, 2002; Ripper: the secret life of Walter Sickert, 2017; *fiction:* Hornet's Nest, 1997; Southern Cross, 1999; Isle of Dogs, 2001; At Risk, 2006; The Front, 2007; Dr Kay Scarpetta novels: Postmortem, 1990 (John Creasey Meml Award, CWA; Edgar Award, MWA; Anthony Award, Boucheron Award, World Mystery Convention; Macavity Award, Mystery Readers Internat.); Body of Evidence, 1991; All That Remains, 1992; Cruel and Unusual, 1993; The Body Farm, 1994; From Potter's Field, 1995; Cause of Death, 1996; Unnatural Exposure, 1997; Point of Origin, 1998; Black Notice, 1999; The Last Precinct, 2000; Blow Fly, 2003; Predator, 2005; Trace, 2005; Book of the Dead, 2007; Scarpetta, 2008; The Scarpetta Factor, 2009; Port Mortuary, 2010; Red Mist, 2011; The Bone Bed, 2012; Dust, 2013; Flesh and Blood, 2014; Depraved Heart, 2015; Chaos, 2016. *Address:* c/o Curtis Brown Group Ltd, Haymarket House, 28–29 Haymarket, SW1Y 4SP; c/o ICM Partners, 65 East 55th Street, New York, NY 10022, USA.

**CORP, Maj.-Gen. Philip James Gladstone,** CB 1996; CEng, FIMechE; *b* 23 June 1942; *s* of Wilfred James Corp and Janet Maude Corp (*née* Gladstone); *m* 1st, 1965, Penelope Joan Smith (marr. diss.); two *s*; 2nd, 1978, Dawn Phyllis Durrant (*née* Holder); one step *s* two step *d*. *Educ:* Warwick Sch.; Queen Elizabeth GS, Crediton; Pembroke Coll., Cambridge (MA Mech. Scis and Law). Commissioned REME from RMA Sandhurst, 1962; RMCS and Staff Coll., 1973–74; Op. Requirements, MoD, 1975–76; Comd 3 Field Workshop, 1977–78; REME Combat Develt, 1979–80; Dep. Project Manager, MoD (PE), 1981–83; Comd 7 Armd Workshop, BAOR, 1984–86; QMG Staff, MoD, 1987–89; Comdt, REME Officers' Sch., 1990; Dir, Equipment Engrg, MoD, 1990–93; Dir-Gen. Equipment Support (Army), 1993–97; Chief Exec., IRTE, subseq. Soc. of Ops Engrs, 1998–2002. Col Comdt, REME, 1996–2000. Mem. Bd, Engrg Council (UK), 2002–08. Vice-Pres., C&G, 2008–11. Trustee: Army Rifle Assoc., 1996–2011; Council for Cadet Rifle Shooting, 1998–. Hon. FSOE 2001; Hon. FCGI 2011. *Recreations:* music, choral singing. *Address:* RHQ REME, MoD Lyneham, Lyneham, Chippenham SN15 9HB.

**CORP, Rev. Ronald Geoffrey,** OBE 2012; SSC; freelance conductor and composer; *b* 4 Jan. 1951; *s* of Geoffrey Charles Corp and Elsie Grace (*née* Kinchin). *Educ:* Blue Sch., Wells; Christ Church, Oxford (MA); Southern Theol Educn and Trng Scheme (DipTheol). Librarian, producer and presenter, BBC Radio 3, 1973–87; freelance, 1987–: Conductor: Highgate Choral Soc., 1984–; London Chorus (formerly London Choral Soc.), 1985–; New London Orch., 1988–; New London Children's Choir, 1991–; has conducted: BBC Singers, BBC Concert Orch., Cape Philharmonic Orch., Leipzig Philharmonic Orch., Brussels Radio and TV Orch., Royal Scottish Nat. Orch., BBC Scottish SO and at BBC Promenade concerts. Numerous recordings. Life Vice Pres., Help Musicians UK (formerly Musicians Benevolent Fund), 2016– (Trustee, 2000–16); Vice-Pres., Sullivan Soc., 2001–; President: Bracknell Choral Soc., 2006–11 (Patron); Nat. Assoc. of Choirs, 2015–; Patron: Oundle Fest., 2014–; Chantry Dance Co. Ordained deacon, 1998, priest, 1999; NSM, St James, Hampstead and St Mary with All Souls, Kilburn, 1998–2002; Assistant Curate (non-stipendiary): Christ Church, Hendon, 2002–07; St Alban's, Holborn, 2007–. Freeman: City of London, 2007; Musicians' Co., 2007. *Compositions:* And All The Trumpets Sounded (cantata), 1989; Laudamus, 1994; Cornucopia, 1997; Piano Concerto, 1997; A New Song (cantata), 1999; Mary's Song, 2001; Adonai Echad, 2001; Kaleidoscope, 2002; Missa San Marco, 2002; Dover Beach, 2003; Forever Child, 2004; Waters of Time, 2006; String Quartet no 1, 2007, no 2, 2009, no 3, 2011; Jubilate Deo, 2008; Symphony, 2009; The Hound of Heaven, 2009; The Ice Mountain (children's opera), 2010; Dhammapada, 2010; The Wayfarer, 2011; Things I Didn't Say, 2011; Songs of the Elder Sisters, 2011; The Yellow Wallpaper, 2011; Crawhall (clarinet quintet), 2012; Lullaby for a Lost Soul, 2012; Cello Concerto, 2014; The Pelican (chamber opera), 2014; Fields of the Fallen (WW1 song cycle), 2014; Behold, the Sea, 2015; Letters from Lony (song cycle), 2016; Letters from Lony (song cycle), 2016, performed Berlin, 2019. Hon. DMus Anglia Ruskin, 2012; Hon. DMus Hull, 2014. *Publications:* The Choral Singer's Companion, 1987, 3rd edn 2006. *Recreations:* reading, opera, ballet, theatre. *Address:* Bulford Mill, Bulford Mill Lane, Cressing, Essex CM77 8NS.

**CORRALL, Prof. Sheila Mary, (Mrs R. G. Lester);** Professor, Library and Information Science, University of Pittsburgh, since 2012; *b* 11 Sept. 1950; *d* of Baron Lowry, PC, PC (NI) and Mary Audrey Lowry (*née* Martin); *m* 1st, 1974, Jonathan Austyn Corrall (marr. diss. 1995); 2nd, 1996, Raymond George Lester. *Educ:* Richmond Lodge Sch., Belfast; Girton Coll., Cambridge (BA Classical Tripos 1974, MA 1977); Poly. of N London (Postgrad. DipLib (CNAA) 1976); Roffey Park Mgt Inst. (MBA Sussex 1992); Univ. of Southampton (MSc Inf. Systems 2002); Univ. of Sheffield (Postgrad. Cert. Higher Educn 2006). ALA 1977, FLA 1999, MIInfSc 1986, FCLIP 2002, Hon. FCLIP 2012. Hd, Inf. Services, Sci. Ref. and Inf. Service, BL, 1988–90; Dir, Liby and Inf. Services, Aston Univ., 1991–95; Librarian, Univ. of Reading, 1995–2001; Dir, Acad. Services, Univ. of Southampton, 2001–03; Prof. of Librarianship and Inf. Mgt, 2004–12, Hd, Dept of Inf. Studies, Univ. of Sheffield, 2006–10. Chairman: Adv. Cttee, UKOLN, 1995–98; Inf. Services NTO, 1999–2001; Mgt Bd, MIMAS (formerly Manchester Inf. and Associated Services), 2006–10; Hds of Schs and Depts Cttee, British Assoc. for Inf. and Liby Educn and Res., 2006–10; Member: Cttee on Electronic Inf., 1994–98, Learning and Teaching Cttee, 2005–08, JISC; Libraries and Inf. Adv. Cttee, British Council, 1995–98; AHRC Peer Rev. Coll., 2006–. Mem., Presidential Cttee for Internat. Agenda on Lifelong Literacy, IFLA, 2005. Pres., Chartered Inst. of Liby and Inf. Professionals, 2002–03. FRSA 1996; MIMgt 1998; FCMI 2003. Lifetime Achievement Award, Internat. Inf. Industries, 2014. *Publications:* (ed) Collection Development: options for effective management, 1988; Strategic Planning for Library and Information Services, 1994; (with A. Brewerton) The New Professional's Handbook: your guide to information services management, 1999; Strategic Management of Information Services: a planning handbook, 2000; contrib. numerous articles and book chapters on liby and inf. mgt. *Recreations:* walking, theatre. *Address:* University of Pittsburgh, 135 North Bellefield Avenue, Information Sciences Building, Room 614, Pittsburgh, PA 15260, USA. *T:* (412) 6249317, *Fax:* (412) 6487001.

**CORRAN, Anne Jane;** *see* Mills, Dame A. J.

**CORRIE, John Alexander;** farmer; consultant on African affairs and development, and financial advisor to developing countries, since 2004; Member (C) West Midlands Region, European Parliament, 1999–2004 (Worcestershire and South Warwickshire, 1994–99); *b* 29 July 1935; *s* of John Corrie and Helen Brown; *m* 1965, Sandra Hardie; one *s* two *d*. *Educ:* Kirkcudbright Acad.; George Watson's Coll.; Lincoln Agric. Coll., NZ. Commnd NZ Army, 1956. Farming in NZ, 1955–59, in Selkirk, 1959–65 and in Kirkcudbright, 1965–. Lectr for British Wool Marketing Bd and Agric. Trng Bd, 1966–74; Mem. Cttee, NFU, SW Scotland, 1964–74 (Vice-Chm. Apprenticeship Council, 1971–74); Nuffield Scholar in Agriculture, 1972. Dist Officer, Rotary Internat., 1973–74 (Community service). Nat. Chm., Scottish Young Conservatives, 1964. Contested (C): North Lanark, 1964; Central Ayr, 1966; Cunninghame N, 1987; Argyll and Bute, 1992. MP (C): Bute and N Ayr, Feb. 1974–1983; Cunninghame N, 1983–87. Opposition spokesman on educn in Scotland, Oct. 1974–75; an Opposition Scottish Whip, 1975–76 (resigned over Devolution); PPS to Sec. of State for Scotland, 1979–81; Mem., Council of Europe and WEU, 1982–87. Treas., Scottish Cons. Back Bench Cttee, 1980, Chm. 1981–82; Leader, Cons. Gp on Scottish Affairs, 1982–84; Sec., Cons. Back Bench Fish-farming Cttee, 1982–86; brought in Pvte Mem.'s Bill, Diseases of Fish, 1983. Exec. Mem., Assoc. of Former Mems of Parlt, 2015–. Mem. European Parlt, 1975–76 and 1977–79 (Mem. Cttees of Agriculture, Reg. Develt and Transport, 1977–79). Vice-President: EEC-Turkey Cttee, 1975–76; EEC Fisheries Cttee, 1977–79; EEC Mediterranean Agricl Cttee, 1977–79; Rapporteur for EEC Fisheries Policy, 1977–78. European Parliament: Chief Whip of Cons. Gp, 1997–99; Member: Employment and Social Affairs, 1998–99; Agric. and Budgets Cttees, 1999; Chm., 1979 Back Bench Cttee; Dir, Human Rights Cttee, 1994–99; Dir, Animal Rights and Sustainable Develt Intergp, 1994–99; Chm., Pensions Cttee, 1999–2004; Co-ordinator, Develt Cttee, 1999–2004; Co-Pres., ACP/EU Jt Parly Assembly, 1999–2002 (Vice-Pres., 2002–04, Hon. Life Pres., 2002–). Pres., European Sustainable Develt Gp, 2004–14; Mem., Council, AWEPA European Parliamentarians for Africa, 2004–17. Mem., N/S Cttee, Council of Europe. Chm., Transport Users' Consultative Cttee for Scotland, 1989–94; Mem., Central Transport Consultative Cttee, 1989–94 (Vice Chm., 1992–94; Mem., Railways Industry Adv. Cttee, 1993–94; Mem., Health Safety Cttee, 1993–94). Chm., Polymer Trng Ltd, 2007–10. Vice Pres., Scottish Former MPs Assoc., 2018–; Pres., African-Eur. Parliamentarians Initiative, 2018–. Member: Council, Scottish Landowners Fedn, 1990–94 (Vice Chm., SW Reg., 1992–94); Judges Panel for Belted Galloway Soc., 1991– (Council Mem., 2004–; Vice Chm., 2008–11; Chm., 2011–14; Vice Pres., 2016–); Timber Growers UK (SW), 1991–94; Dir, Ayr Agricl Soc., 1990–95; Pres., Rigget Cattle Soc., 2008–14. Industry and Parlt Trust Fellowship with Conoco (UK) Ltd, 1986–87. *Publications:* (jtly) Towards a European Rural Policy, 1978; Towards a Community Forestry Policy, 1979; Fish Farming in Europe, 1979; The Importance of Forestry in the World Economy, 1980. *Recreations:* shooting, fishing. *Address:* Park House, Tongland, Kirkcudbright DG6 4NE. *T:* (01557) 820232. *E:* j.corrie126@btinternet.com.

**CORRIE, His Honour Thomas Graham Edgar;** a Circuit Judge, 1994–2014; a Deputy Circuit Judge, 2014–18; *b* 18 Dec. 1946; *s* of late John Alexander Galloway Corrie, OBE, MC and Barbara Phyllis Corrie (*née* Turner); *m* 1971, Anna Cathinca Logsdail; one *s* two *d*. *Educ:* Eton (King's Schol.); Brasenose Coll., Oxford (MA). Called to the Bar, Gray's Inn, 1969; Midland and Oxford Circuit, 1971–94; a Recorder, 1988–94; Designated Family Judge, Oxford, 2001–05. Trustee, Oxfordshire Family Mediation, 1996–2007. Chm., 1999–2011, Pres., 2011–, Oxford Med. and Legal Soc. *Recreation:* cycling. *Address:* c/o 2 Harcourt Buildings, Temple, EC4Y 9DB. *Club:* Frewen (Oxford).

**CORRIE, Timothy David;** Chairman, Bob & Co, 2014–17; *b* 8 Dec. 1940; *s* of Robert Corrie and Peggy Rose Corrie; *m* 1966, Helene Desgouilles (*d* 2017); two *s* one *d*. *Educ:* Reed's Sch.; Univ. of Bristol (BA Hons French and Drama). Paramount Pictures, 1970–71; Agent: at Fraser & Dunlop, subseq. Peters, Fraser & Dunlop, 1971–2008; United Agents, 2008–13. Chm., BAFTA, 2010–12 (Dep. Chm., 2009–10, 2012–13; Life Mem.). *Recreations:* playing awful golf and watching films, good, bad and indifferent. *Address:* Top of the Hill, 29 South Road, Chorleywood, Herts WD3 5AS. *T:* (01923) 283540. *Clubs:* Groucho; Chorleywood Golf.

**CORRIGAN, Prof. (Francis) Edward,** PhD; FRS 1995; Professor of Mathematics, University of York, since 2011 (part-time, since 2016); *b* 10 Aug. 1946; *s* of late Anthony Corrigan and Eileen Corrigan (*née* Ryan); *m* 1970, Jane Mary Halton; two *s* two *d*. *Educ:* St Bede's Coll., Manchester; Christ's Coll., Cambridge (MA, PhD). A. J. Wheeler Fellow, Durham, 1972–74; CERN Fellow, Geneva, 1974–76; Durham University: Lectr, Sen. Lectr and Reader, 1976–92; Prof. of Maths, 1992–99; Hd, Dept of Math. Scis, 1996–98; University of York: Prof. of Maths, 1999–2007; Hd, Dept of Maths, 1999–2004, 2005–07; Prof. of Maths and Principal, Collingwood Coll., Durham Univ., 2008–11; Hd, Dept of Maths, Univ. of York, 2011–15. Joliot-Curie Fellow, ENS Paris, 1977–78; Vis. Associate, CIT, 1978–79; Vis. Fellow, Dept of Applied Maths and Theoretical Physics, Cambridge, 1983; Derman Christopherson Fellow, Durham Univ., 1983–84; Visiting Professor: Centre for Particle Theory, Durham Univ., 1999–2002; Kyoto Univ., 2005. Life Mem., Clare Hall, Cambridge. Hon. Ed., Jl of Physics A, 1999–2003. *Publications:* articles on elementary particle theory and mathematical physics in learned jls. *Recreations:* playing and listening to music, visiting grandchildren. *Address:* Department of Mathematics, University of York, York YO10 5DD. *T:* (01904) 323074. *E:* edward.corrigan@york.ac.uk.

**CORRIGAN, Margaret Mary;** Teacher: of children with special needs, Beechwood School, Aberdeen, 2007–08; of children with additional support needs, Mile End School, Aberdeen, 2010–11; *d* of Joseph Hamilton and Mary Anna (*née* Monaghan); *m* 1979, Gerard Michael Corrigan; one *s* two *d*. *Educ:* Univ. of Strathclyde (BA Hons English); Edinburgh Univ. (PGCE 2005). Trainee journalist with newspaper/magazine publishers D. C. Thomson, Dundee, 1977–78; Advertising Copywriter and Acct Exec., Austin Knight Advertising, Glasgow, 1978–81; Depute Dir of Public Relns, Cumbernauld Devilt Corp., 1981–83; Mktg and Communications Officer/Lectr, Falkirk Coll. of Further and Higher Educn, 1999–2004; Teacher of English, Mearns Acad., Aberdeenshire, 2005–07. Mem., Radio Authority, 1990–95. *Recreations:* swimming, music, theatre, dancing.

**CORRIGAN, Thomas Stephen,** OBE 1999; Chairman, 2change, 2003–10; *b* 2 July 1932; *s* of late Thomas Corrigan and Renée Victorine Corrigan (*née* Chaborel); *m* 1963, Sally Margaret Everitt; two *d*. *Educ:* Beulah Hill; Chartered Accountant (Scottish Inst.). Nat. Service, Army (2nd Lieut), 1955–57. Chief Accountant, Lobitos Oilfields, 1957–62; Exec., Keyser Ullmann, 1962–64; Inveresk Group: Finance Dir, 1964–71; Man. Dir, 1971–74; Chm., 1974–83. Chairman: Havelock Europa, 1983–89; Rex Stewart Gp Ltd, 1987–90; dir of other cos. Pres., British Paper and Board Industry Fedn, 1975–77; Vice-Pres., European Confedn of Pulp, Paper and Board Industries, 1982–83; Mem., NEDC (Tripartite Sector Working Party on paper industry), 1976–77. Chairman: POUNC, 1984–94; Direct Mail Accreditation and Recognition Centre, 1995–97. Advr and Chief Assessor, 1994–2000, Mem. Ind. Panel of Judges, 2001–03, Charter Mark Awards, Cabinet Office; Chief Assessor, Queen's Awards for Internat. Trade, 2007–11; Mem., London Award Panel, Prince's Trust, 2002–; Mem., Investment Cttee, Printing Charity (formerly Printers' Charitable Corp.), 2006–18. Master: Makers of Playing Cards Co., 1978–79; Stationers and Newspaper Makers' Co., 1990–91; Marketors' Co., 1995. FRSA. *Recreations:* golf, bridge, tennis, travel. *Address:* 57 Marsham Court, Marsham Street, SW1P 4JZ. *T:* (020) 7828 2078. *Clubs:* MCC, Royal Automobile, City Livery; Royal & Ancient Golf (St Andrews); Walton Heath Golf.

**CORRIGAN-MAGUIRE, Mairead;** Co-Founder, Northern Ireland Peace Movement, later Community of the Peace People, 1976 (Hon. Life President); *b* 27 Jan. 1944; *d* of Andrew and Margaret Corrigan; *m* 1981, Jackie Maguire; two *s* and three step *c*. *Educ:* St Vincent's Primary Sch., Falls Road, Belfast; Miss Gordon's Commercial Coll., Belfast. Secretarial qualification. Confidential Sec. to Managing Director, A. Guinness Son & Co. (Belfast) Ltd, Brewers, Belfast. Initiator of Peace Movement in Northern Ireland, Aug. 1976; Chm., Peace People Organisation, 1980–81; Co-founder, Nobel Women's Initiative. Hon. Dr of Law, Yale Univ., 1976; Nobel Prize for Peace (jtly), 1976; Carl-Von-Ossietzky Medaille for Courage, Berlin, 1976. *Publications:* The Vision of Peace: faith and hope in Northern Ireland, 1999. *Address:* c/o The Peace People, 224 Lisburn Road, Belfast, N Ireland BT9 6GE. *T:* (028) 9066 3465, *Fax:* (028) 9068 3947. *E:* info@peacepeople.com.

**CORRIN, His Honour John William,** CBE 1995; Chairman, BlackRock (Isle of Man) Ltd (formerly Merrill Lynch Investment Managers (Isle of Man) Ltd), 1998–2008; *b* 6 Jan. 1932; *s* of Evan Cain Corrin and Dorothy Mildred Corrin; *m* 1961, Dorothy Patricia, *d* of late J. S. Lace; one *d*. *Educ:* Murrays Road Primary Sch., Douglas; King William's Coll., IOM. Admitted to Manx Bar, 1954. Attorney Gen., IOM, 1974–80; Second Deemster, 1980–88; HM's First Deemster, Clerk of the Rolls, and Dep. Governor, IOM, 1988–98. Chairman (all IOM): Criminal Injuries Compensation Tribunal, 1980–88; Licensing Appeal Court, 1980–88; Prevention of Fraud (Unit Trust) Tribunal, 1980–88; Income Tax Appeal Comrs, 1988–2007; Tynwald Ceremony Arrangements Cttee, 1988–98. Chairman: Manx Blind Welfare Soc., 1980–2012; Manx Workshop for the Disabled, 1982–2010; Hon. Member: IOM Med. Soc.; IOM Law Soc.; President: IOM Br., Crossroads Care, 1988–2013; Lon Dhoo Male Voice Choir; IOM Br., SSAFA, 1989–2009; IOM Alcohol Adv. Council; Patron: Cruse Bereavement Care (IOM), 1988–2013; Sailing for the Disabled, 2000–09. Freeman, Borough of Douglas, 1998. Paul Harris Fellow, Rotary Internat., 2007. Tynwald Honour, I of M, 2012. *Recreations:* music, gardening, bridge. *Address:* Cummal Cheh, 11 Devonshire Road, Douglas, Isle of Man IM2 3QY. *T:* (01624) 621806.

**CORRIS, Prof. Paul Anthony,** FRCP; Professor of Thoracic Medicine, Newcastle University, since 2000; Deputy Director, Institute of Transplantation, Newcastle University and Newcastle Hospitals NHS Foundation Trust, since 2012; Senior Medical Scientific Officer, Pulmonary Vascular Research Institute, since 2018; *b* Bebington, Cheshire, 20 May 1953; *s* of Ronald George and Gladys Corris; *m* 1980, Elizabeth Ann Hill; one *s* one *d*. *Educ:* Birkenhead Sch.; University Coll. and Westminster Med. Sch., Univ. of London (MB BS 1976). FRCP 1991. House Physician, Westminster Hosp., 1976; Postgrad. Trng, London, Leicester and Newcastle, 1976–86; Consultant Respiratory Physician, Newcastle upon Tyne Hosps, 1986–. Clinical Respiratory Lead, NHS North (formerly Respiratory Lead, NHS NE), 2010–; Chm., Clinical Ref. Gp, 2010–, Res. Lead, 2012–, Nat. Pulmonary Hypertension Service. Mem., Noncommunicable Disease Alliance, WHO, 2018. President: Eur. Soc. for Heart and Lung Transplantation, 2006; Internat. Soc. for Heart and Lung Transplantation, 2007; British Thoracic Soc., 2009; N of England Thoracic Soc., 2010; Pulmonary Vascular Res. Inst., 2016–17. Gov., Newcastle Hosps NHS Foundn Trust, 2013–17. Mem., Literary and Philosophical Soc. of Newcastle. British Thoracic Soc. Medal, 2018; Lifetime Achievement Award, Pulmonary Vascular Res. Inst., 2018. *Publications:* (ed) Heart and Heart Lung Transplantation, 1999; contrib. 350 papers to jls incl. New England Jl Medicine, Lancet, BMJ, Amer. Jl Respiratory and Critical Care Medicine, Thorax; 50 book chapters. *Recreations:* cinema, theatre, opera, wine, Rugby, soccer, ski-ing, mountain walking, literature, art and design, classic cars, fly fishing. *Address:* Department of Respiratory Medicine, Freeman Hospital, High Heaton, Newcastle upon Tyne NE7 7DN. *T:* (0191) 223 1084, *Fax:* (0191) 223 1321. *E:* paul.corris@ncl.ac.uk. *Club:* Athenæum.

**CORRY;** *see* Lowry-Corry, family name of Earl of Belmore.

**CORRY, Viscount; John Armar Galbraith Lowry-Corry;** *b* 2 Nov. 1985; *s* and *heir* of Earl of Belmore, *qv*; *m* 2016, Francesca, *o d* of Guido Vasapolli. *Address:* The Garden House, Castle Coole, Enniskillen, N Ireland BT74 6JY.

**CORRY, Daniel Richard;** Chief Executive, New Philanthropy Capital, since 2011; *b* London, 4 Dec. 1959; *s* of Bernard Corry and Marilyn Corry; one *s* one *d* by Dinah Roake. *Educ:* University Coll., Oxford (BA 1st Cl. PPE); Queen's Univ., Canada (MA Econs). Economist, Dept of Employment and HM Treasury, 1984–89; Hd, Labour Party Econ. Secretariat, 1989–92; Sen. Economist, IPPR, 1992–97; Special Adviser: DTI, 1997–2001; DTLR, 2001–02; Dir, New Local Govt Network, 2002–05; Special Advr to Sec. of State for Educn, 2005–06; Chm., Council of Econ. Advrs, HM Treasury, 2006–07; Hd, Downing St Policy Unit, 2007–08; Sen. Econ. Advr to the Prime Minister, 2007–10; Dir in Econs Segment, FTI Consulting, 2011. Vis. Fellow, Univ. of Southampton, 2011–. Mem., Financial Adv. Cttee, FA, 2002–07; Member, Advisory Board: Centre for Public Scrutiny, 2005–; CentreForum, 2010–15; Big Society Capital, 2012–. Trustee: 19 Princelet Street, 2011–; What Works Centre for Wellbeing, 2015–; St Mungo's, 2017–. *Publications:* (with Gerry Holtham) Growth With Stability: progressive macroeconomic policy, 1995; Public Expenditure: effective management and control, 1997; (jtly) Public/Private Partnerships, 1997; (with Gerry Stoker) New Localism, 2002; (jtly) UK Economic Performance since 1997, 2011. *Recreations:* Chelsea FC, jazz, writing. *E:* dan.corry@thinknpc.org.

**CORRY, Sir James (Michael),** 5th Bt *cr* 1885, of Dunraven, co. Antrim; *b* 3 Oct. 1946; *e s* of Sir William James Corry, 4th Bt and of Diana Pamela Mary Corry (*née* Lapsley); *S* father, 2000; *m* 1973, Sheridan Lorraine, *d* of A. P. Ashbourne; three *s*. *Educ:* Downside Sch. Joined Shell-Mex and BP Ltd, 1966; British Petroleum Co. Ltd, 1976; BP Nederland BV, 1992; Manager, LPG Ops, BP Nederland VOF, Netherlands, 1992–2001. Admin Officer, DWP, 2009–13. *Heir:* *s* William James Alexander Corry, *b* 7 Dec. 1981. *Address:* 73 Wand Road, Wells, Somerset BA5 1RN. *T:* 01749 679068. *E:* james.corry@btopenworld.com.

**CORSAR, Hon. Dame Mary (Drummond),** DBE 1993; FRSE; Chairman: TSB Foundation Scotland, 1994–97 (Trustee, 1992–97); Women's Royal Voluntary Service, 1988–93; *b* 8 July 1927; *o d* of Lord Balerno, CBE, TD, DL and Mary Kathleen Smith; *m* 1953, Col Charles Herbert Kenneth Corsar, LVO, OBE, TD (*d* 2012); two *s* two *d* (and one *d* decd). *Educ:* Westbourne, Glasgow; St Denis, Edinburgh; Edinburgh Univ. (MA Hons). Dep. Chief Comr, Girl Guides, Scotland, 1972–77; Chm., Scotland WRVS, 1981–88. Member: Vis. Cttee, Glenochil Young Offenders Instn, 1976–94; Parole Bd for Scotland, 1982–89. Hon. Pres., Scottish Women's AAA, 1973–91. Member: Exec. Cttee, Trefoil Centre for Handicapped, 1975–2002; Convocation, Heriot-Watt Univ., 1986–96; Royal Anniversary Trust, 1990–93. Gov., Fettes Coll., 1984–99. FRSE 1997. *Recreations:* countryside, hand crafts. *Address:* Flat 4, 85 South Oswald Road, Edinburgh EH9 2HH. *T:* (0131) 662 0194. *Clubs:* New (Edinburgh); Scottish Ladies Climbing.

**CORSTON, Baroness** *cr* 2005 (Life Peer), of St George in the County and City of Bristol; **Jean Ann Corston;** PC 2003; *b* 5 May 1942; *d* of late Charles Lawrence Parkin and Eileen Ada Parkin; *m* 1st, 1961, Christopher John Davy Corston; one *s* one *d* (and one *d* decd); 2nd, 1985, Prof. Peter Brereton Townsend, FBA (*d* 2009). *Educ:* LSE (LLB 1989); Open Univ. Labour Party posts: Asst Regl Organiser, 1976, Regl Organiser, 1981, South West; Asst National Agent, London, 1985–86. Called to the Bar, Inner Temple, 1991; Bristol chambers. MP (Lab) Bristol East, 1992–2005 (sponsored by TGWU). PPS to Sec. of State for Educn and Employment, 1997–2001. Mem., Select Cttee on Agric., 1992–95, on Home Affairs, 1995–97; Chair: Jt Cttee on Human Rights, 2001–05; Select Cttee on Social Mobility, 2015–16; Member: Jt Cttee on Privacy and Injunctions, 2011–12; EU Cttee on Justice, Institutions and Consumer Protection, 2013–14 (Chair, 2013–14); Constitution Cttee, H of L, 2017–; Chair, All Party Parly Gp for Women in Penal System, 2009–. Co-Chm., PLP Women's Gp, 1992–97; Chairman: PLP Civil Liberties Gp, 1997–2005; PLP, 2001–05 (Dep. Chm., 1997–98 and 1999–2000; Mem., Parly Cttee, 1997–2005). Chm., Commonwealth Women Parliamentarians, 2000; Mem., Exec. Cttee, 1998–2005, Mem., UK Exec. Cttee, 2011–, CPA. Vice Chair, Parliament Choir, 2011–17. FRSA 2008. *Recreations:* gardening, reading, knitting. *Address:* House of Lords, SW1A 0PW.

**CORVEDALE, Viscount; Benedict Alexander Stanley Baldwin;** *b* 28 Dec. 1973; *s* and heir of 4th Earl Baldwin of Bewdley, *qv*. *Educ:* Newcastle Univ. (BMus 1996).

**CORY, Sir (Clinton Charles) Donald,** 5th Bt *cr* 1919, of Coryton, Whitchurch, Glamorgan; *b* 13 Sept. 1937; *s* of Sir Clinton James Donald Cory, 4th Bt and Mary, *o d* of Dr Arthur Douglas Hunt; *S* father, 1991. *Educ:* Brighton Coll.; abroad. *Recreations:* collecting antiques, travel, gardening. *Heir:* kinsman James Maurice Perkins-Cory [*b* 10 May 1966; *m* 1998, Alexandra Dudfield; two *d*]. *Address:* 18 Cloisters Road, Letchworth Garden City, Herts SG6 3JS. *T:* (01462) 677206; PO Box 167, Mpemba, Malawi, Central Africa.

**CORY, Prof. Suzanne,** AC 1999; PhD; FRS 1992; FAA; Honorary Distinguished Professorial Fellow, Blood Cells and Blood Cancer Division, Walter and Eliza Hall Institute of Medical Research, University of Melbourne, since 2009 (Vice Chancellor's Fellow, 2010–15); *b* 11 March 1942; *d* of Desmond and Joy Cory; *m* 1969, Prof. Jerry Adams; two *d*. *Educ:* Univ. of Melbourne (BSc, MSc); Wolfson Coll., Cambridge (PhD 1968; Hon. Fellow, 2000). Rothmans Fellow, Univ. of Geneva, 1969–71; Walter and Eliza Hall Institute of Medical Research, 1971–: Sen. Principal Res. Fellow, 1988–; Jt Head, Molecular Genetics of Cancer Div., 1988–2005; Dir, 1996–2009; Prof. of Medical Biol., Univ. of Melbourne, 1996–2009. Internat. Res. Schol., Howard Hughes Med. Inst., 1992–97. FAA 1986 (Pres. 2010–14); FAACR 2013. Foreign Mem., NAS, USA, 1997; Foreign Hon. Mem., Amer. Acad. of Arts and Scis, 2001; Assoc. Foreign Mem., French Acad. Sci., 2002; Academician, Pontifical Acad. of Scis, 2004; Assoc. Mem., EMBO, 2007; Hon. Mem., Japan Acad., 2013. Hon. DSc: Sydney, 2000; Oxford, 2004; Rockefeller, 2016; Hon. DLaws Melbourne, 2015. Lemberg Medal, Australian Soc. Biochem. and Molecular Biol., 1995; Burnet Medal, Australian Acad. Sci., 1997; (jtly) Australia Prize, 1998; (jtly) Charles S. Mott Prize, General Motors Cancer Res. Foundn, 1998; Women in Science Award, L'Oréal-UNESCO, 2001; Royal Medal, Royal Soc., 2002; Pearl Meister Greengard Prize, Rockefeller Univ., 2009; Colin Thomson Medal for Cancer Res., Assoc. for Internat. Cancer Res., UK, 2011; Eureka Prize for Leadership in Sci., Australian Mus., 2012; Lifetime Achievement Award, Fac. of Medicine, Nursing and Health Scis, Monash Univ., 2014. Chevalier de la Légion d'Honneur (France), 2009. *Publications:* numerous scientific papers and reviews. *Recreations:* camping, hiking, swimming, wilderness photography, ski-ing. *Address:* Walter and Eliza Hall Institute of Medical Research, 1G Royal Parade, Parkville, Vic 3052, Australia. *T:* (3) 93452492.

**CORY-WRIGHT, Katherine Elizabeth;** *see* Grange, K. E.

**CORY-WRIGHT, Sir Richard (Michael),** 4th Bt *cr* 1903; *b* 17 Jan. 1944; *s* of Capt. A. J. J. Cory-Wright (killed in action, 1944), and Susan Esterel (*d* 1993; she *m* 2nd, 1949, Lt-Col J. E. Gurney, DSO, MC), *d* of Robert Elwes; *S* grandfather, 1969; *m* 1st, 1976, Veronica Bolton (marr. diss. 1994); three *s*; 2nd, 1998, Helga Wright, *e d* of George Godfrey. *Educ:* Eton; Birmingham Univ. *Heir:* *s* Roland Anthony Cory-Wright, *b* 11 March 1979.

**COSCELLI, Dr Andrea;** Chief Executive, Competition and Markets Authority, since 2017 (Executive Director, Markets and Mergers, 2013–16; Acting Chief Executive, 2016–17); *b* Parma, Italy, 11 Feb. 1969; *s* of Carlo and Brenna Alinovi Coscelli; *m* 1996, Giovanna Bertazzoni; one *s*. *Educ:* Bocconi Univ. (Laurea in Econs 1992); Stanford Univ. (PhD Econs 1998). Trng and Mobility of Researchers Fellow, UCL, 1997–98; Consultant, Nat. Economic Res. Associates, 1998–2002; Associate Dir, Lexecon Ltd, 2002–05; Vice Pres., Charles River Associates, 2005–08; Dir, Competition Economics, Ofcom, 2008–13. *Address:* Competition and Markets Authority, The Cabot, 25 Cabot Square, E14 4QA. *E:* andrea.coscelli@cma.gov.uk.

**COSFORD, Paul Anthony,** CB 2016; FFPHM; Director for Health Protection and Medical Director, Public Health England, 2013–19; *b* 20 May 1963; *s* of Brian and Judith Cosford; *m* 2006, Dr Gillian Catherine Leng, *qv*; two step *d*, and one *s* one *d* (and one *s* decd) from a previous marriage. *Educ:* Exmouth Ch Primary Sch.; Exeter Sch.; St Mary's Hosp. Med. Sch., Univ. of London (BSc Hons 1984; MB BS (Hons in Pathol.) 1987); St George's Hosp. Med. Sch., Univ. of London (MSc Public Health 1994). MRCPsych 1991; MFPHM 1995, FFPHM 2001; Cert. of Completion of Specialist Trng 1996. Lectr and Hon. Registrar in Psychiatry, St Mary's Hosp. Med. Sch., 1990–92; Consultant in Public Health: Herts, 1996–97; Beds, 1997–2000; Dir of Public Health, Northants HA, 2000–02; Dir, Health Strategy and Public Health, Leics, Northants and Rutland Strategic HA, 2002–06; Medical Dir, E of England Strategic HA, 2006–10; Regl Dir of Public Health, East of England, DoH, 2006–10; Exec. Dir of Health Protection Services, HPA (on secondment), 2010–13 (Acting Chief Exec., 2012–13). Hon. Sen. Lectr, Univ. of Leicester, 2005–09; Hon. Sen. Fellow, Univ. of Cambridge, 2007–13; Vis. Prof. of Public Health, Univ. of Chester, 2014–. *Publications:* contribs on health protection, screening and public health to learned jls. *Recreations:* amateur dramatics, gardening, walking, audax cycling. *Address:* 3 Park Palings Walk, Haynes, Beds MK45 3PY. *E:* paulcosford@doctors.org.uk.

**COSGROVE, Rt Hon. Lady; Hazel Josephine Cosgrove,** CBE 2004; PC 2003; a Senator of the College of Justice in Scotland, 1996–2006; *b* 12 Jan. 1946; *d* of late Moses Aron Aronson and Julia Tobias; *m* 1967, John Allan Cosgrove, dental surgeon; one *s* one *d*. *Educ:* Glasgow High Sch. for Girls; Univ. of Glasgow (LLB). Advocate at the Scottish Bar. Admitted to Fac. of Advocates, 1968; QC (Scot.) 1991; Standing Junior Counsel to Dept of Trade, 1977–79; Sheriff of Glasgow and Strathkelvin, 1979–83; Sheriff of Lothian and Borders at Edinburgh, 1983–96. Temporary Judge, High Court and Court of Session, Scotland, 1992–96. Mem., Parole Bd for Scotland, 1988–91; Chairman: Mental Welfare Commn for Scotland, 1991–96; Expert Panel on Sex Offending, Scotland, 1997–2001; Dep. Chm., Boundary Commn for Scotland, 1997–2006. Hon. Fellow, Harris Manchester Coll., Oxford, 2001. Hon. LLD: Napier, 1997; Glasgow, 2002; Strathclyde, 2002; St Andrews, 2003; DUniv Stirling, 2004. *Recreations:* foreign travel, opera, swimming, walking, reading, being a grandmother. *E:* hazelcosgrove@uk2.net.

**COSGROVE, Brian Joseph**, OBE 2018; artist, sculptor and writer; *b* 6 April 1934; *s* of Denis Cosgrove and Martha Cosgrove (*née* Hesketh); *m* 1963, Angela Helen Dyson; two *d*. *Educ*: Manchester Coll. of Art. Nat. Service, Army, 1952–54 (Malayan campaign). TV Graphic Designer, 1967–72; TV Programme Dir, 1972–76; Founder (with Mark Hall), Cosgrove Hall Productions, to produce animated films, 1976–95, Jt Man. Dir, 1995–2002 (BAFTA Award, 1982, 1983, 1985, 1986, 1987, 2000, 2004; Prix Jeunesse, Munich Film Fest., 1982; Internat. Emmy, 1984, 1991; Prix Danube, Bratislava Film Fest., 1990; 2 Observer Children's Film Awards, 1990; RTS Award, 1999, 2002). Wrote and produced, The Cosgrove Hall Story: the history of the animation studio, 2018. Mem., MENSA. Hon. DA Manchester Metropolitan, 2010; Hon. DLitt Chester, 2015. Special Award, 2012, Lifetime Achievement Award, 2013, BAFTA; Fellowship Award, Manchester Animation Fest., 2015. *Recreations*: writing, painting, sculpture, gardening, computer graphic art. *Address*: B. & A. Cosgrove Ltd, Longlea Cottage, Kidderton Lane, Brindley, Nantwich, Cheshire CW5 8JD. *T*: (01270) 524550.

**COSGROVE, Hazel Josephine**; *see* Cosgrove, Rt Hon. Lady.

**COSGROVE, Gen. Hon. Sir Peter (John)**, AK 2014 (AM 1985; AC 2000); CVO 2019; MC 1970; CNZM 2000; Governor-General of Australia, 2014–19; *b* Sydney, NSW, 28 July 1947; *s* of John Francis and Ellen Mary Cosgrove; *m* 1976, Lynne Elizabeth Payne; three *s*. *Educ*: Waverley Coll., Sydney; RMC, Duntroon (Dip. Mil. Studies); US Marine Corps Comd and Staff Coll., Quantico; Nat. Defence Coll., New Delhi. Platoon Comdr, 9th Bn, Royal Australian Regt, S Vietnam, 1969; ADC to Gov.-Gen., 1972; Adjt and Co. Comdr, 5th/7th Bn, Royal Australian Regt, 1973–75; Instructor, Inf. Centre, 1976–78; psc (US) 1979; SO, HQ Field Force Command, 1979–82; CO, 1st Bn, Royal Australian Regt, 1983–84; Instructor, British Army Staff Coll., 1984–86; MA to CGS, 1987; jssc, Canberra, 1988; Dir Infantry, and Comdt, Infantry Centre, 1990–91; Comdr, 6th Bde, 1992–93; Comdt, Australian Defence Force Warfare Centre, 1995–96, RMC, 1997; Commander: 1st Div. and Deployable Jt Force HQ Australian Army, 1998–99; InterFET Force (E Timor), 1999–2000; Land Comdr, Australia, 2000; Chief of Army, 2000–02; Chief, Australian Defence Force, 2002–05. Hd, Operation Recovery Taskforce after Cyclone Larry, Qld, 2006. Chm., SA Defence Adv. Bd, 2006–14. Chm., Australian War Meml Council, 2007–12. Chm., Augusta Westland Australia, 2006–13; Director: Qantas Airways Ltd, 2005–14; Qantas Superannuation Plan, 2005–14; Cardno Ltd, 2007–14; Commonwealth Superannuation Corp. Chancellor, Australian Catholic Univ., 2010–14. FAICD 2009; Paul Harris Fellow, Rotary Internat., 2001. DUniv: Northern Territory, 2001; Griffith, 2006; Australian Catholic, 2009. GCSG 2013; KStJ 2014. Order of Nat. Merit Tong-Il Medal (Republic of Korea), 2001; Legion of Merit Medal (USA), 2001; Order of Prince Henry (Portugal), 2001; Centenary Medal (Australia), 2003; DSO (Singapore), 2004; Officier, Légion d'Honneur (France), 2005; Kt Grand Cross, Order of Crown (Tonga), 2015; Grand Chain, Order of Timor Leste, 2016: Collar, Order of Liberator Gen. San Martin (Argentina), 2016; Grand Cross, Order of Liberty (Portugal), 2018. Australian of Year, 2001. *Publications*: My Story (autobiog.), 2006; Boyer Lectures, 2009. *Recreations*: golf, cricket, Rugby, music, literature.

**COSGROVE, Thomas James**; QC 2017; *b* London, 15 Dec. 1970; *s* of John and Sally Cosgrove. *Educ*: St Edward's Sch., Oxford; Sidney Sussex Coll., Cambridge (BA 1993). Called to the Bar, Inner Temple, 1994; in practice as barrister, specialising in planning and public law, 1994–. Mem., Professional Conduct Cttee, Bar Standards Bd, 2013–17. Dep. Commissary for Public Notaries, 2017–. *Publications*: (jtly and Gen. Ed.) Cornerstone on the Planning Court, 2015. *Recreations*: golf, cricket, walking, Isle of Mull (Hebrides), painting, nature conservation, travel. *Address*: Cornerstone Barristers, 2–3 Gray's Inn Square, WC1R 5JH. *T*: (020) 7242 4986. *E*: tcosgrove@cornerstonebarristers.com. *Clubs*: MCC; Beaconsfield Golf.

**COSLETT, Ven. Carol Ann**; Archdeacon of Chesterfield, since 2018; *b* Epsom, 18 Aug. 1963; *d* of Christopher Slater and Ruth Slater; *m* 1992, Martin Coslett; one *s* one *d*. *Educ*: University Coll. of N Wales (BD Hons 1985); Jesus Coll., Cambridge (PGCE 1986); Inst. of Educn, Univ. of London (MA 1992); Ripon Coll., Cuddesdon. Teacher, Uckfield Community Coll., 1986–89; Hd of Music, Kings Manor, Guildford, 1989–94; Hd of RE/Collective Worship, Woodcote High Sch., 1994–2000; Dir of Music, St Teresa's, Effingham, 2001; ordained deacon, 2003, priest, 2004; Curate, St Mary the Virgin, Horsell, Guildford, 2003–07; Rector, Utd Benefice of Betchworth and Buckland, Mole Valley, 2007–18; Area Dean and Asst Archdeacon, 2013–18; Interim Team Rector, Merstham and Gatton, Reigate, 2014–16. *Recreations*: walking, swimming, theatre-going, reading, travel, music (playing clarinet and piano, singing). *Address*: 4 Woodnook Close, Ashgate, Chesterfield S42 7JB. *T*: (01246) 569764. *E*: ccoslett@btinternet.com.

**COSSONS, Sir Neil**, Kt 1994; OBE 1982; Director, Science Museum, 1986–2000; Chairman, English Heritage, 2000–07; *b* 15 Jan. 1939; *s* of Arthur Cossons and Evelyn (*née* Bettle); *m* 1965, Veronica Edwards (MBE 2015; DL); two *s* one *d*. *Educ*: Henry Mellish Grammar Sch., Nottingham; Univ. of Liverpool (MA). FSA 1968 (Life Fellow 2018); FMA 1970. Curator of Technology, Bristol City Museum, 1964; Dep. Dir, City of Liverpool Museums, 1969; Dir, Ironbridge Gorge Museum Trust, 1971; Dir, Nat. Maritime Mus., 1983–86. Comm, Historic Buildings and Monuments Commn for England (English Heritage), 1989–95, and 1999–2000 (Mem., Ancient Monuments Adv. Cttee, 1984–98); Mem., Adv. Cttee, English Heritage, later Historic England, 2013–); Chm., RCHME, 2000–03. Member: Curatorium Internat. Committee for the Conservation of the Industrial Heritage, 1973–78; BBC General Adv. Council, 1987–90; NEDO Tourism and Leisure Industries Sector Gp (formerly Leisure Industries EDC), 1987–90; Council, RCA, 1989–2015 (Pro-Provost and Chm. of Council, 2007–15); Design Council, 1990–94; Comité Scientifique, Conservatoire Nat. des Arts et Métiers, 1991–2000. President: Assoc. for Industrial Archaeology, 1977–80; Assoc. of Independent Museums, 1983– (Chm., 1978–83); Museums Assoc., 1981–82; ASE, 1996; RGS-IBG, 2003–06; Member, Council: Newcomen Soc. for Study of Hist. of Engrg and Technol., 1992–2006 (Mem., 1963; Pres., 2001–03; Fellow 2010); FMI, 1993–98. Mem., British Waterways Bd, 1995–2001. Trustee: Civic Trust, 1987–93; Nat. Heritage Meml Fund, 2016–19; Heritage Lottery Fund, 2016–19. Gov., Imperial Coll. of Sci., Technology and Medicine, 1989–93. Collier Prof. in the Public Understanding of Sci., Univ. of Bristol, 2001–02. Hon. Prof., Univ. of Birmingham, 1994–. FIIC 2017; Fellow, Sci. Mus., 2019. Hon. FRCA, 1987, Sen. FRCA, 2015; Hon. FRIBA 2002; Hon. FCIWEM 2002; Hon. Fellow, BAAS, 2007; Comp IEE, 1991; CCMI (CIMgt 1996); Hon. Mem., SCI, 2002; Hon. CRAeS 1996. Hon. DSocSc Birmingham, 1979; DUniv: Open, 1984; Sheffield Hallam, 1995; York, 1998; Hon. DLitt: Liverpool, 1989; Bradford, 1991; Nottingham Trent, 1994; UWE, 1995; Bath, 1997; Greenwich, 2004; Chester, 2018; Hon. DSc: Leicester, 1995; Nottingham, 2000; Hon. DArts De Montfort, 1997. Norton Medlicott Medal, Historical Assoc., 1991; President's Medal, Royal Acad. of Engrg, 1993; Dickinson Meml Medal, Newcomen Soc., 2001; Maitland Medal, IStructE, 2002; Tercentenary Medal, Soc. of Antiquaries, 2008. Series Editor, England's Landscape, 2006. *Publications*: (with R. A. Buchanan) Industrial Archaeology of the Bristol Region, 1968; (with K. Hudson) Industrial Archaeologists' Guide, 1969, 2nd edn 1971; Industrial Archaeology, 1975, 3rd edn 1993; (ed) Transactions of the First International Congress on the Conservation of Industrial Monuments, 1975; (ed) Rees's Manufacturing Industry, 1975; (with H. Sowden) Ironbridge—Landscape of Industry, 1977; (with B. S. Trinder) The Iron Bridge—Symbol of the Industrial Revolution, 1979, 2nd edn (Japanese) 1989, (English) 2002; (ed) Management of Change in Museums, 1985; (ed) Making of the Modern World, 1992; (ed) Perspectives on Industrial Archaeology, 2000; (with M. Jenkins) Liverpool: seaport city, 2011; numerous papers, articles and reviews. *Recreations*: travel, design, industrial archaeology. *Address*: The Old Rectory, Rushbury, Shropshire SY6 7EB. *T*: (01694) 771603. *E*: nc@cossons.org.uk. *Club*: Athenæum.

**COSTA, Alberto Castrenze**; MP (C) South Leicestershire, since 2015.

**COSTA, Antonio Maria**, PhD; Under-Secretary General, United Nations, 2002–10; Executive Director, United Nations Office on Drugs and Crime, and Director-General, United Nations Office, Vienna, 2002–10; Editor-in-Chief, Journal of Policy Modeling, since 1975; *b* 16 June 1941; *s* of Francesco Costa and Maria (*née* Contratto); *m* 1971, Patricia Wallace; two *s* one *d*. *Educ*: Turin Univ. (degree in political sci. 1964); Acad. of Scis, Moscow (Math. Econs 1967); Univ. of Calif at Berkeley (MA Econs 1969; PhD Econs 1971). Sen. Economic Advr, UN, NY, 1971–83; Dep. Sec. Gen. (Special Counsellor), OECD, 1983–87; Dir Gen. for Econs and Finance, Special Advr to Pres., and Mem., Monetary Cttee, EU, Brussels, 1987–92; Dir Gen. for Strategic Planning, Ferrero Gp, 1992–93; Sec. Gen., EBRD, 1994–2002. Member: Wkg Party for Co-ordination of Macroeconomic Policies of G10 Countries, OECD; Bd of Dirs, EIB; EU Rapporteur to EP; financial Sherpa for G8 meetings, 1987–92. Vis. Prof. of Econs, Moscow Univ. and Acad. of Scis, Moscow, 1963–64; Adjunct Professor of Economics: Univ. of Calif at Berkeley, 1968–70; CU NY, 1970–76; New York Univ., 1976–87; Vis. Prof., Free Univ., Brussels, 1990–94. Chm. Bd, Internat. Award Premio Res Publica. *Publications*: Checkmate Pendulum (novel) (trans. Italian as Scaccomatto all'Occidente, 2015) (Cerruglio literary prize, 2016). *E*: Editor@EconModels.com, autore@scaccomatto-all-occidente.com.

**COSTA, Kenneth Johann**; Chairman, Ken Costa Strategic; Co-Chairman and Partner, Alvarium Investments (formerly LJ Partnership), since 2018; *b* 31 Oct. 1949; *s* of late Joseph Costa and of Martha Costa; *m* 1982, Fiona Morgan Williams; two *s* two *d*. *Educ*: Univ. of Witwatersrand (BA, LLB); Queens' Coll., Cambridge (LLM, Cert. in Theology). Joined S. G. Warburg, subseq. UBS Investment Bank, 1976: Dep. Chm., 1993; Chm., Investment Banking Bd, Hd of Global Mergers and Acquisitions, 1995; Vice-Chm., 1996–2007; Chm., Investment Banking for Europe, ME and Africa, 2004–07; Chm., Lazard Internat., 2007–11. Dir, Songbird Estates plc, 2014–15; Chairman: Oxford Place Capital; Adv. Bd, Gemcorp, 2016–. Gresham Prof. of Commerce, Gresham Coll., 2009–12. Chm., London Connection, St Paul's Inst., 2011–13. Chm. Adv. Bd, LSO, 2000–09. Fundraising Patron, Gt Ormond Street Hosp., 2006–16; Trustee, Nelson Mandela Children's Trust UK. Chm., Alpha Internat., 2001–16; Church Warden, Holy Trinity, Brompton, 2001–16. *Publications*: God at Work, 2007; Know Your Why, 2016; contrib. articles to Wall St Jl, FT, The Times. *Recreations*: country activities, politics, music, theology.

**COSTAIN, Janice Elizabeth**; *see* Hall, J. E.

**COSTAIN, Peter John**, FCA; Deputy Chairman, Costain Group Plc, 1995–97 (Group Chief Executive, 1980–95); Director: Pearl Group, 1989–2005; London Life Ltd, 1994–2005; Hendersons (formerly AMP UK, then HHG) plc, 1994–2005; *b* 2 April 1938; *s* of Sir Albert Costain; *m* 1963, Victoria M. Pope; three *s*. *Educ*: Charterhouse. Peat Marwick Mitchell & Co., 1956–63; Richard Costain Ltd, 1963–65; Costain Australia Ltd, 1965–92: Board Member, 1967; Managing Director, 1971; Chief Executive, 1973. Dir, Wessex Water Services Ltd, 1999–2014. Mem., London Adv. Bd, Westpac Banking Corp., 1981–86. Mem. Bd, CITB, 1989–93. Chm., Tenterden Day Care Centre for the Disabled and Elderly, 2007–16. FAIB. Prime Warden, Basketmakers' Co., 1998–99. *Recreations*: sailing, ski-ing, golf. *Clubs*: Royal Thames Yacht; Rye Golf, Royal St George's Golf.

**COSTELLO, Elvis**; *see* McManus, D. P. A.

**COSTELLO, John Francis**, MD; FRCP, FRCPI; Consultant Physician: Cromwell Hospital, SW5, since 1983; London Clinic, since 2005; Chairman, Capital Hospitals Ltd, 2006–17; Consultant, Skanska (UK), 2015–17; *b* 22 Sept. 1944; *s* of late William and Sarah Costello; *m* 1972, Dr Christine Ellen McGregor White (marr. diss.); three *s*; *m* 1996, Susanna Clarke; two *s*. *Educ*: Belvedere Coll., Dublin; University Coll., Dublin (MB BCh, BAO Hons 1968; MD 1987). MRCP 1972, FRCP 1982; MRCPI 1995, FRCPI 1996. Hospital appts, Mater Hosp., Dublin, St Stephen's, and Royal Northern; RPMS, 1970–72; Registrar, Brompton Hosp., 1972–73; Lectr, Univ. of Edinburgh, Edinburgh Royal Infirmary, 1973–75; Asst Prof. of Medicine, and attending physician, Univ. of California, San Francisco, 1975–77; King's College Hospital: Consultant Physician, 1977–2003, now Hon. Consultant Physician; Chm. of Consultants, 1989–91; Med. Clinical Dir, Acute Services, 1989–93; Dir, Respiratory Medicine, King's Coll. Sch. of Medicine and Dentistry, 1982–98; Med. Dir, King's Healthcare NHS Trust, 1991–94; Dir of Medicine, King's Healthcare, subseq. KCH, NHS Trust, 1997–2003. Vis. Fellow, KCL, 2003–. Mem. Bd, Health Care Projects, 2008–12. Examr in Medicine, Conjoint Bd, 1979–83; Examr, MRCPI, 2004–12; Med. Vice Chm., SE Thames/S London Regl Cttee for Distinction Awards, 1997–2002. Chm., Educn Trust, Ind. Doctors Fedn, 2007–15. Founder Pres., Respiratory Sect., RSocMed, 1991–93; Mem. Council, British Thoracic Soc., 1996. *Publications*: (ed jtly) Beta Agonists in the Treatment of Asthma, 1992; (ed) Methylxanthines and Phosphodiesterase Inhibitors, 1994; (jtly) A Colour Atlas of Lung Infections, 1996; (ed) Sympathomimetic Enantiomers in the Treatment of Asthma, 1997; (contrib.) Horizons in Medicine, 2002; papers, reviews and chapters on lung disease, esp. asthma, and early detection of lung cancer, bowel cancer and coronary heart disease. *Recreations*: opera, golf. *Address*: 12 Melville Avenue, Wimbledon, SW20 0NS. *T*: (020) 8879 1309. *E*: jfcostello@btinternet.com. *Clubs*: Garrick; Royal Wimbledon Golf.

**COSTELLO, Hon. Peter Howard**, AC 2011; Chairman, Australian Future Fund, since 2014 (Guardian, 2009–13); *b* 14 Aug. 1957; *s* of Russell and Anne Costello; *m* 1982, Tanya Pamela Coleman; one *s* two *d*. *Educ*: Carey Baptist Grammar Sch.; Monash Univ. (LLB Hons, BA). Solicitor, 1981–84; Barrister, 1984–90. MP (L) Higgins, Vic, 1990–2009; Shadow Minister for Corporate Law Reform and Consumer Affairs, 1990–92; Shadow Attorney Gen. and Shadow Minister for Justice, 1992–93; Shadow Minister for Finance, 1993–94; Shadow Treasurer, 1994–96; Dep. Leader of Opposition, 1994–96; Treasurer, 1996–2007; Dep. Leader, Liberal Party, 1994–2007. Man. Dir, BKK Partners, 2009–12; Chm., ECG Financial Pty Ltd, 2013–. Chm., Qld Commn of Audit, 2012–13. Chairman: OECD, 2000; G20 Finance Ministers and Central Bankers, 2006. World Bank: Gov., 1996–2007; Mem., 2008–11, Chm., 2011–14, Ind. Adv. Bd; Governor: IMF, 1996–2007; Asian Develt Bank, 1996–2007. Mem., Internat. Adv. Bd, Allianz SE, 2011–; Dir, Nine Entertainment Co., 2013–16 (Chm., 2016–). Trustee, Melbourne Cricket Ground, 2013–. Co-Chairman: Third Australia-China Forum, 2013; Australia-China High Level Dialogue, 2014–17. Hon. LLD Monash, 2013. *Publications*: (jtly) Arbitration in Contempt, 1986; (with P. Coleman) The Costello Memoirs, 2008. *Recreations*: swimming, football, reading. *Clubs*: Melbourne Cricket (Trustee, 2013–); Essendon Football.

**COTRUBAS, Ileana, (Mme Manfred Ramin);** opera singer, retired 1990; *b* Rumania; *d* of Vasile and Maria Cotrubas; *m* 1972, Manfred Ramin. *Educ:* Conservatorul Ciprian Porumbescu, Bucharest. Opera and concert engagements all over Europe, N America and Japan. Formerly permanent guest at Royal Opera House, Covent Garden; Member, Vienna State Opera (Hon. Mem., 1991); also frequently sang in Scala, Milan, Munich, Berlin, Paris, Chicago, NY Metropolitan Opera. Main operatic roles: Susanna, Pamina, Gilda, Traviata, Manon, Tatyana, Mimi, Melisande, Amina, Elisabetta, Nedda, Marguerite. Has made numerous recordings. Hon. Citizen, Bucharest, 1993. Kammersängerin, Austria, 1981; Grand Officer: Sant Iago da Espada (Portugal), 1990; Steaua României (Romania), 2000. *Publications:* Opernwahrheiten, 1998; (with M. Ramin) Die manipulierte Oper, 2018.

**COTTAGE, Rosina;** QC 2011; a Recorder, since 2012; *b* London, 29 Dec. 1965; *d* of Peter Cottage and Josephine Cottage; partner, Andrew Davidson; one *s* one *d*. *Educ:* Dunottar Sch. for Girls; Epsom Coll.; Univ. of Bristol (LLB); Coll. of Law. Called to the Bar, Inner Temple, 1988; in practice as a barrister, specialising in crime and family, 9–12 Bell Yard, 1989–98, 9 Gough Square, 1998–2013, Red Lion Chambers, 2013–. Mem., Sentencing Council for England and Wales, 2016–. *Recreations:* family, friends, domestic animal husbandry. *Address:* 18 Red Lion Court, EC4A 3EB.

**COTTAM, Harold;** Founding Partner, Investor Relations Development LLP, 2002–08; Managing Director, Pentwyn Renewables Ltd, since 2012; *b* 12 Oct. 1938; *s* of Rev. Canon Frank and Elizabeth Cottam; *m* 1962, Lyn Minton; two *d*. *Educ:* Bedford School. FCA. Deloitte & Co., Tanganyika and Peru, 1960–64; Smith Kline UK, 1964–66; Simon Engineering Group, Spain, 1966–68; Ernst & Whinney, subseq. Ernst & Young, 1968–92; UK Man. Partner, 1987–92; Chairman: Ernst & Young Case Services (Internat.), 1992–93; Ernst & Young Pan-European Consulting Gp, 1992–93; Haden MacLellan Hldgs, 1992–97; Anglo United (Coalite Products, Charrington and Falkland Is Gp), 1993–96; Rebus Gp, 1996–99; Britannic plc, subseq. Britannic Gp plc, 1996–2004. Dir, Allied Colloids Gp, 1992–97. *Recreations:* piano, opera, tennis. *Address:* 8a Burton Mews, SW1W 9EP.

**COTTAM, Maj.-Gen. Nicholas Jeremy,** CB 2007; OBE 1990; Registrar, St Paul's Cathedral, 2009–15; *b* 17 Feb. 1951; *s* of late Brig. H. W. Donald Cottam, OBE and Diana Cottam; *m* 1982, Susan Habberfield-Bateman; one *s* one *d*. *Educ:* Univ. of Durham (BA Hons). VSO, 1969. Commnd Royal Green Jackets, 1973: CO, 2nd RGJ, 1990–93 (despatches 1993); Comd, 8th Inf. Bde, 1995–96; rcds 1997; Director: Intelligence, MoD, 1998–2000; Personal Services (Army), MoD, 2000–02; GOC 5th Div., 2003–05; Mil. Sec., 2005–08; Reserve Forces Study Team Leader, 2008. Col Comdt, 2nd RGJ, 2002–07. *Recreation:* mountaineering. *Club:* Alpine.

**COTTENHAM,** 9th Earl of, *cr* 1850; **Mark John Henry Pepys;** Bt 1784 and 1801; Baron Cottenham 1836; Viscount Crowhurst 1850; Partner, Bridging the Gap China LLP, since 2011; Chief Executive Officer, Times Education, since 2016; *b* 11 Oct. 1983; *s* of 8th Earl of Cottenham; *S* father, 2000; *m* 2015, Juan Du. *Educ:* Eton; Bristol Univ. Dir, VCP Advisors, 2017–. *Heir: b* Hon. Sam Richard Pepys, *b* 26 April 1986.

**COTTER,** family name of **Baron Cotter**.

**COTTER,** Baron *cr* 2006 (Life Peer), of Congresbury in the County of Somerset; **Brian Joseph Michael Cotter;** *b* 24 Aug. 1936; *s* of Michael Joseph Cotter and Mary Cotter; *m* 1963, Eyleen Patricia Wade; two *s* one *d*. *Educ:* Downside Sch., Somerset. Sales Manager, then Man. Dir, Plasticable Ltd, 1989–2003. MP (Lib Dem) Weston-super-Mare, 1997–2005; contested (Lib Dem) same seat, 2005. Lib Dem spokesman on small businesses, 1997–2005. Lib Dem spokesman in H of L for small businesses, 2006–, for skills and apprenticeships, 2007–. Sec., All-Party Parly China Gp. Nat. Patron, YMCA, 1998–; Patron, Somewhere To Go (charity for homeless people, N Som). *Recreations:* reading, gardening, films. *Address:* 52 Eddington Court, 30 Beach Road, Weston-Super-Mare, Som BS23 1DH. *T:* (01934) 418866; House of Lords, SW1A 0PW.

**COTTER, Barry Paul;** QC 2006; **His Honour Judge Cotter;** a Circuit Judge, since 2010; Designated Civil Judge for Avon, Somerset and Gloucester, since 2017; a Deputy High Court Judge, since 2010; Designated Civil Judge, Senior Circuit Judge, Bristol Civil and Family Justice Centre, since 2018; *b* 30 July 1963; *s* of Austin and Angela Cotter; *m* 1996, Catherine Maskell; one *s* two *d*. *Educ:* St Theresa's Primary Sch., St Helens; West Park High Sch., St Helens; University Coll. London (LLB 1984). Called to the Bar, Lincoln's Inn, 1985, Bencher, 2018; Recorder, 2002–10; Dep. Hd, Old Sq. Chambers, 2003–10; Designated Civil Judge for Devon and Cornwall, 2010–17. Mem., Civil Justice Council, 2016–. Mem. Cttee, Personal Injury Bar Assoc., 1995–99 and 2001–03. Vis. Fellow, Univ. of Bristol, 2016–; Visitor, Bath Univ., 2017. Personal Injury Barrister of Yr, Eclipse Proclaim Personal Injury Awards, 2009. *Publications:* Cotter: Defective and Unsafe Products: Law and Practice, 1996; (Gen. Ed.) Munkman on Employer's Liability, 14th edn 2006, 15th edn 2009. *Recreations:* family life, running, walking, Rugby, cycling. *Address:* Bristol Civil Justice Centre, 2 Redcliff Street, Bristol BS1 6GR.

**COTTER, Mark James;** QC 2017; a Recorder, since 2019; *b* Cardiff, 30 July 1971; *s* of James Anthony Cotter and Violet May Cotter; *m* 2018, Sarah Elizabeth Paul. *Educ:* Llanishen High Sch., Cardiff; Kingston Univ. (LLB Hons); Univ. of Wales, Cardiff (LLM). Called to the Bar, Middle Temple, 1994; in practice as a barrister, specialising in criminal law, Holborn Chambers, 1995–2001, 5 St Andrew's Hill, 2001–. *Recreations:* ballet (Friend of Royal Opera House), military history (Friend of Imperial War Museum), football (season ticket at Cardiff City Football Club). *Address:* 5 St Andrew's Hill, EC4V 5BZ. *T:* (020) 7332 5400. *E:* clerks@5sah.co.uk.

**COTTER, Sir Patrick Laurence Delaval,** 7th Bt *cr* 1763, of Rockforest, Cork; *b* 21 Nov. 1941; *s* of Laurence Stopford Llewelyn Cotter; *S* uncle, 2001; *m* 1967, Janet, *d* of George Potter, Barnstaple; one *s* two *d*. *Educ:* Blundell's; RAC Cirencester. *Heir: s* Julius Laurence George Cotter, *b* 5 Jan. 1968.

**COTTER, Suzanne Maree;** Director, Mudam Luxembourg - Musée d'Art Moderne Grand-Duc Jean, since 2018; *b* Melbourne, Australia, 20 April 1961; *d* of James and Elaine Cotter; *m* 1987, Bruce Manson. *Educ:* Star of the Sea High Sch., Southport, Qld; Queensland Inst. of Technol., Brisbane (Dip. Applied Sci. 1981); Univ. of Melbourne; École du Louvre, Paris (Dip. du Premier Cycle 1994); Courtauld Inst. of Art (MA 1995); City Univ. (Post-grad. Dip. Cultural Leadership 2007). Asst to Australian Cultural Attaché, Paris, 1991–94; Exhibn Organiser, Serpentine Gall., London, 1996–98; Curator, Whitechapel Gall., London, 1998; Exhibns Curator, Hayward Gall., London, 1998–2002; Sen. Curator, Modern Art Oxford, 2002–07; Dep. Dir and Sen. Curator, then Curator at Large, Modern Art Oxford, 2008–09; Curator, Abu Dhabi Project, Solomon R. Guggenheim Foundn, 2010–12; Dir, Mus. of Contemp. Art, Serralves Foundn, Porto, 2013–18. Co-Curator, Sharjah Biennial 10, 2011. Ext. Examr, MA in Curating Contemp. Art, RCA, 2007–10. Member: Bd, Internat. Cttee for Mus and Collections of Modern Art, 2017–19; Bd, Mophradat, Brussels; Prog. Cttee, Documenta 14. Trustee: Paris Calling charity, 2005–10; Peer, London, 2005–09. Judge, Turner Prize, 2008; Jury Member: Wolfgang Hahn Prize, Mus. Ludwig, Cologne, 2017; Edward Steichen Award, 2019. FRSA 2005. Chevalier, Ordre des Arts et des Lettres (France), 2005. *Publications:* (contrib.) Vox Populi, by Fiona Tan, 2006; (ed) Out of Beirut, 2006; (ed) Transmission Interrupted, 2009; (ed) Michael Clark, 2011; (contrib) Defining Contemporary Art: 25 years in 200 pivotal artworks, 2011; Joana Hadjithomas and Khalil Joreige, 2013; Imran Qureishi: artist of the year, 2013; exhibn catalogues. *Recreations:* tennis, ski-ing, swimming, reading, theatre, films, art.

**COTTERELL, Sir Henry Richard Geers, (Sir Harry),** 7th Bt *cr* 1805; OBE 2015; farmer; Chairman, Fisher German LLP, since 2015; *b* Cirencester, 22 Aug. 1961; *s* of Sir John Henry Geers Cotterell, 6th Bt and Vanda Alexandra Clare Cotterell, MBE; *S* father, 2017; *m* 1st, 1986, Carolyn Beckwith-Smith (*d* 1999); two *s* one *d*; 2nd, 2002, Katherine Bromley; one *s* one *d*. *Educ:* Eton Coll.; RMA, Sandhurst. Partner, Garnons Estate, 1986–. Pres., CLA, 2011–13. Chm., Inst. of Cancer Vaccines and Immunotherapy, 2000–. *Recreations:* motorcycling, shooting. *Heir: s* Richard John Geers Cotterell, *b* 1 May 1990. *Address:* Garnons, Herford HR4 7JU. *T:* (01981) 590235. *Club:* Whites.

**COTTERELL, Prof. Roger Brian Melvyn,** LLD; FBA 2005; FAcSS; Anniversary Professor of Legal Theory, Queen Mary University of London, since 2005; *b* 30 Nov. 1946; *s* of Walter Leslie Cotterell and Hilda Margaret Cotterell (*née* Randle); *m* 1969, Ann Zillah Poyner; one *s* one *d*. *Educ:* King Edward VI Camp Hill Sch., Birmingham; University Coll. London (LLB 1968; LLM 1969); Birkbeck Coll., Univ. of London (MScSoc 1977); LLD London 1988. Lectr in Law, Univ. of Leicester, 1969–74; Queen Mary College, then Queen Mary and Westfield College, subseq. Queen Mary, University of London: Lectr in Law, 1974–78; Sen. Lectr in Law, 1978–85; Reader in Legal Theory, 1985–90; Prof. of Legal Theory, 1990–2005; Actg Hd, 1989–90, Hd, 1990–91, Dept of Law; Dean, Faculty of Laws, 1993–96. Vis. Prof. and Jay H. Brown Centennial Faculty Fellow in Law, Univ. of Texas, Austin, 1989; George Lurcy Lectr, Amherst Coll., Mass, 1989; Visiting Professor: Univ. of Lund, 1996; Katholieke Univ. Brussel and Facultés Universitaires St Louis, Brussels, 1996, 1997; Internat. Inst. for the Sociol. of Law, Onati, Spain, 2003, 2004. Mem. Panel, Eur. Res. Council, 2017–19. Mem., Cttee of Hds of Univ. Law Schs, 1993–96. Mem., Law Panel, RAE, 1999–2001, 2005–08. Trustee, 1996–99, Chm., Articles Prize Cttee, 1999–2000, Law and Soc. Assoc. Mem. Ct, Univ. of Leicester, 2000–03. FAcSS 2014. *Publications:* The Sociology of Law: an introduction, 1984 (trans. Chinese 1989, Spanish 1991, Korean 1992), 2nd edn 1992 (trans. Lithuanian 1997, Chinese 2015); (ed jtly) Law, Democracy and Social Justice, 1988; The Politics of Jurisprudence: a critical introduction to legal philosophy, 1989, 2nd edn 2003 (trans. Chinese 2013); (ed) Law and Society, 1994; (ed) Process and Substance: Butterworth lectures on comparative law, 1994; Law's Community: legal theory in sociological perspective, 1995; Emile Durkheim: law in a moral domain, 1999; (ed) Sociological Perspectives on Law, 2 vols, 2001; (with Coleridge Goode) Bass Lines: a life in jazz, 2002; Law, Culture and Society: legal ideas in the mirror of social theory, 2006; (ed) Law in Social Theory, 2006; Living Law: studies in legal and social theory, 2008; (ed) Emile Durkheim: justice, morality and politics, 2010; (ed jtly) Authority in Transnational Legal Theory: theorising across disciplines, 2016; Sociological Jurisprudence: juristic thought and social inquiry, 2018; contribs to symposia and jls on law, social sci. and phil. *Recreations:* listening to and writing about music, exploring cities, European cinema. *Address:* Law School, Queen Mary University of London, Mile End Road, E1 4NS. *T:* (020) 7882 3946, *Fax:* (020) 8981 8733. *E:* r.b.m.cotterell@qmul.ac.uk.

**COTTESLOE,** 6th Baron (UK) *cr* 1874; **Thomas Francis Henry Fremantle;** *b* 17 March 1966; *s* of 5th Baron Cottesloe and Elizabeth Ann (*née* Barker); *S* father, 2018. *Educ:* St Edward's Sch., Oxford; Royal Agricl Coll., Cirencester.

**COTTHAM, (George) William;** Chairman, CentreWest London Buses Ltd, 1995–97; *b* 11 July 1944; *s* of George William and Elizabeth Cottham; *m* 1967, Joan Thomas; two *d*. *Educ:* Univ. of London; Polytechnic of Liverpool; Liverpool Coll. of Commerce. BSc 1st Cl. Hons, LLB 2nd Cl. Hons. FCILT. Various posts, Liverpool City Transport, 1960–74; District Transport Manager, St Helens, 1974–77; Transport General Manager, Newport, 1977–80; Gen. Manager, Cleveland Transit, 1980–83; Dir Gen., W Yorks PTE, 1983–86; Chairman and Managing Director: Yorkshire Rider, 1986–94; Rider Hldgs, 1988–94; Rider York, 1990–94. *Recreations:* family, home, garden, music, photography, writing poetry. *Address:* Bismarckia, 1438 Palm Grove Villas, Four Seasons Resort Estates, Nevis, West Indies; Vila Fonte, Algarve, Portugal; Naples Lakes, Naples, FL 34112, USA.

**COTTINGHAM, Barrie,** MBE 2017; FCA; Deputy Chairman, Pinelog Group Ltd, 1997–2013; *b* 5 Oct. 1933; *s* of John and Eleanor Cottingham; *m* 1st, 1957, Kathleen Morton (marr. diss. 2008); one *s* (and one *d* decd); 2nd, 2012, Nicola Lesley Scahill McMullan; one step *s* one step *d*. *Educ:* Carfield Sch. ATII. Coopers & Lybrand: joined, 1957; Partner, 1964–95; Exec. Partner, i/c Regl Practice, 1986–93; Mem. UK Bd, 1974–93. Chairman: SIG plc, 1993–2004; Cattles plc, 1995–2006; Dep. Chm., Dew Pitchmastic plc, 1997–2005; non-exec. Dir, VP plc, 1996–2009. Pres., Sheffield and District, Soc. of Chartered Accountants, 1964. Mem., Investment Gp and Pension Fund Sub-cttee, Univ. of Sheffield, 2002–13. Dir and Trustee, Autism Plus, 2010–12. Pres., Boys and Girls Clubs S Yorks (formerly S Yorks and Hallamshire Clubs for Young People), 1964–. *Recreations:* golf, watching Rugby and soccer, theatre, opera. *Address:* Waterstones, 2 Beckside, Cawthorne, Barnsley S75 4EP. *T:* (01226) 791395.

**COTTON;** *see* Stapleton-Cotton, family name of Viscount Combermere.

**COTTON, Christopher John Pott;** DL; Chief Executive, Royal Albert Hall, 2010–17; *b* Edinburgh, 27 Jan. 1950; *s* of Tom and Phyllis Alexander Cotton; *m* 1983, Elizabeth Meriol Trevor; one *d* and one step *s*. *Educ:* Malvern Coll.; Architectural Assoc. RIBA. Whinney Mackay Lewis Partnership, 1974–2000; Aros Architects, 2000–05; Royal Albert Hall: Building and Ops Dir, 2005–10; Chair, Exhibition Rd Cultural Gp, 2012–17. Dir, Julie's Bicycle, 2011–19. Chair, Jerwood Space, 2013–; Trustee: Foundling Mus., 2017–; Gerald Coke Handel Foundn, 2018–; Mem. Adv. Bd, Tickets for Troops, 2013–18. Hon. RCM 2015. DL Greater London, 2018. *Recreations:* sailing, architecture, music, visual arts. *Address:* 66 Rodenhurst Road, SW4 8AR. *T:* 07831 340323. *E:* Chris@ChrisCotton.co.uk. *Club:* Hurlingham.

**COTTON, Danielle Amara,** QFSM 2004; Commissioner, London Fire Brigade, 2017–April 2020; *b* Horley, Surrey, 11 June 1969; *d* of Roy Cotton and Marguerite Cotton (*née* Johnson). London Fire Brigade, 1988–April 2020: Area Manager, Central Service Delivery/Central Ops, 2007; Dep. Asst Comr, 2007–12; Asst Comr, 2012–16; Dir, Safety and Assurance, 2015–16. *Recreations:* walking, cycling, ski-ing. *Address:* London Fire Brigade Headquarters, 169 Union Street, SE1 0LL. *T:* (020) 8555 1200. *E:* dany.cotton@london-fire.gov.uk.

**COTTON, Diana Rosemary, (Mrs R. B. Allan);** QC 1983; a Recorder, 1982–2011; *b* 30 Nov. 1941; *d* of Arthur Frank Edward and Muriel Cotton; *m* 1966, Richard Bellerby Allan; two *s* one *d*. *Educ:* Berkhamsted School for Girls; Lady Margaret Hall, Oxford (MA). Joined Middle Temple, 1961; called to Bar, 1964; Bencher, 1990; Member, Midland Circuit; a Dep. High Ct Judge, 1993–2011. Mem., Criminal Injuries Compensation Bd, 1989–2000; a Judge of First-tier Tribunal: Criminal Injuries Compensation (formerly

**COTTON, Jane Catherine;** Human Resources Director, Oxfam, 1999–2014; *b* 10 Jan. 1959; *d* of Tony and Jean Alderson; *m* 1980, Stephen Paul Cotton. *Educ:* Girton Coll., Cambridge (MA). Department of Transport: graduate trainee posts, 1979–83; Aviation Policy, 1983–88; Personnel, 1989–92; Railways Policy/Finances, 1992–93; Hd of Resources, Charity Commn, 1993–96; Sec. to Board, Dept of Transport, 1996–97; Personnel Dir, DETR, 1997–99. Trustee: Canal and River Trust, 2012–17; WWF, 2014–19; Bucks, Berks and Oxon Wildlife Trust, 2015–; One YMCA, 2017–. *Recreations:* gardening, walking, football (spectator), theatre.

**COTTON, His Honour John Anthony;** a Circuit Judge, 1973–93; *b* 6 March 1926; *s* of Frederick Thomas Hooley Cotton and Catherine Mary Cotton; *m* 1960, Johanna Aritia van Lookeren Campagne; three *s* two *d*. *Educ:* Stonyhurst Coll.; Lincoln Coll., Oxford. Called to the Bar, Middle Temple, 1949; Dep. Chm., W Riding of Yorks QS, 1967–71; Recorder of Halifax, 1971; a Recorder and Hon. Recorder of Halifax, 1972–73. Mem., Parole Bd, 1995–2001. *Recreation:* golf. *Address:* Myrtle Garth, Rossett Beck Close, Harrogate HG2 9NU.

**COTTON, Richard Selkirk;** Commercial Adviser, Iraq Britain Business Council, since 2014; *b* 29 March 1947; *s* of Albert George Cotton and Vera May Cotton. *Educ:* Coll. of Estate Mgt (BSc (Estate Mgt) London); Wye Coll., London Univ. (Dip. Farm Business Admin). Cluttons, subseq. Cluttons LLP, 1970–2009: Partner, 1976; Sen. Partner, 2003–09; Dir, Cluttons Private Finance Ltd, 2006–09. Property Dir, Residential Land, 2010–12; Hd, Mktg and Leasing, Basra Internat. Oil and Gas Free Zone, 2012–14. Non-exec. Dir, Go Native, 2009–16; Chairman: First Penthouse plc, 2009–14; AHR Gp, 2019–. Chm., UAE Br., 1980–83, Mem., Brooke Rev. Cttee, 2004, Mem., Mgt Bd, 2009–16, RICS. Mem., Chartered Surveyors' Co., 1997– (Master, 2006–07). *Recreations:* golf, walking, bridge, travel, theatre. *Address:* 21C Sunderland Terrace, W2 5PA. *T:* 07885 807816.

**COTTRELL, Amanda Arianwen Cecilia,** OBE 2011; DL; Patron, Visit Kent, since 2015 (Chairman, 2007–15); *b* Windsor, Berks, 22 Sept. 1941; *d* of Stafford Vaughan Stephen Howard and Mary Gracia Howard (*née* Neville); *m* 1967, Michael Noel Francis Cottrell; two *s* two *d*. *Educ:* St George's Sch., Clarens, Montreux; Sch. of Mus. of Fine Arts, Boston, Mass (Dip.). Magistrate, 1983–2006, High Sheriff 2006–07, DL 2011, Kent. Patron: Produced in Kent, 2006–; Hadlow Coll., 2013–; Trustee, Canterbury Cath., 2007–; Mem. Bd, Visit England, 2011–14. Chm., Communities and Partnerships Framework, Dio. of Canterbury, 2013–. Kent Ambassador, 2006–. Hon. Fellow, Canterbury Christchurch Univ., 2010. Hon. DCL Kent, 2011. Liveryman, Fruiterers' Co., 2007; Freeman, City of Canterbury, 2015. *Recreations:* painting, gardening, walking. *Address:* Visit Kent, 28–30 St Peter's Street, Canterbury, Kent CT1 2BQ. *T:* (01227) 812900.

**COTTRELL, Prof. David John,** FRCPsych; Professor of Child and Adolescent Psychiatry, since 1994, and Dean of Medicine, 2008–13, University of Leeds; *b* Leigh-on-Sea, 22 June 1956; *s* of John Geoffrey and Eileen Beatrice Cottrell; *m* 1985, Amanda Caroline Stroud; two *s*. *Educ:* Westcliff High Sch. for Boys; Hertford Coll., Oxford (BA Hons Physiol Sci. 1976; MA 1984); Westminster Med. Sch., Univ. of London (MB BS 1979). MRCPsych 1983, FRCPsych 1999. Lectr in Child and Adolescent Psychiatry, St George's Hosp. Med. Sch., Univ. of London, 1984–87; Sen. Lectr in Child and Adolescent Psychiatry, London Hosp. Med. Coll., 1987–93; Dir, Learning and Teaching, Sch. of Medicine, Univ. of Leeds, 1999–2006. Non-exec. Dir, Bradford Teaching Hosps Foundn Trust, 2008–12. Trustee and Director: YoungMinds, 2005–16; Nat. Youth Adv. Service, 2013–15. *Publications:* (jtly) What Works for Whom: a critical review of treatments for children and adolescents, 2002, 2nd edn 2014; (jtly) Developing Multi-professional Teamwork for Integrated Children's Services, 2006, 2nd edn 2010; contrib. articles to scientific med. jls on child and adolescent psychiatry. *Recreations:* rowing, reading, France.

*See also Bishop of Chelmsford.*

**COTTRELL, Peter John Waraker,** AO 1987; OBE 1978; Director, SAHF Enterprises, 2004–08; *b* 25 May 1928; *s* of Knowles Waraker Cottrell and Elmira Grenfell Cottrell; *m* 1952, Barbara Jean Wheeler (*d* 2011); two *s* two *d*. *Educ:* Sydney Univ. (BEng, MEng; Univ. Medal (Mech. Eng) 1951); Birmingham Univ. (Postgrad. Dip. in Mgt). Cadet, Qld Irrigation Commn, 1945–46; cadet, then engr, Australian Dept of Munitions, 1947–60; Email Ltd: Manager, 1960–74; Man. Dir, 1974–92; Chm., 1993–98. Chairman: Export Finance & Insurance Corp., 1983–86; Pacifica Gp Ltd, 1989–95; Scania Australia Pty Ltd, 1991–2003; Adelaide Steamship Co. Ltd, 1992–99; Boral Ltd, 1994–2000; Adsteam Marine Ltd, 1997–2001; Dep. Chm., Australian Telecommunications Commn, 1982–87; Dir, Nat. Australia Bank, 1985–98. Vice-Pres., Business Council of Australia, 1991–92. Hon. FIEAust 1994. Hon. Life Mem., Sydney Adventist Hosp. Fedn, 2008. Hon. DBus Charles Sturt Univ., 1996. Sir James Kirby Medal, IProdE, 1986; Sir Charles McGrath Award, Aust. Marketing Inst., 1989. *Recreation:* family activities. *Address:* 4 Canberra Avenue, Turramurra, NSW 2074, Australia. *T:* 0414 601988.

**COTTRELL, Richard John;** author and internet journalist; *b* 11 July 1943; *s* of John Cottrell and Winifred (*née* Barter); *m* 1st, 1965, Dinah Louise (*née* David) (marr. diss. 1986); two *d*; 2nd, 1987, Tracy Katherine (*née* Wade) (marr. diss. 1996); one *d*; 3rd, 1997, Liliana (*née* Velitchkova) (marr. diss. 2000); 4th, 2001, Diana (*née* Kiebdoj); two *d*. *Educ:* Court Fields Sch., Wellington, Somerset. Journalist: Wellington Weekly News, 1958; South Devon Jl, 1960; Topic (internat. news weekly), 1962; Evening Argus, Brighton, 1963; Lincolnshire Standard, 1964; Evening Post, Bristol, 1965; TWW, subseq. HTV, 1967–79. Chairman: RCA Ltd, 1989–94; Rail Central Europe, 1994–2002. Contested (C) Bristol, European Parly elecn, 1989. MEP (C) Bristol, 1979–89; Sec., backbench cttee, European Dem. Gp, 1979; Member: Transport Cttee, 1979–83; External Econ. Relns Cttee, 1979–82; Information Cttee, 1981–84; ACP-EEC Convention, 1981–84; Agriculture Cttee, 1982–86; Rules Cttee, 1982–89; Environment Cttee, 1983–89; Budget Cttee, 1983–86; Energy Cttee, 1986–88; delegate to ASEAN, 1983, to ACP, 1985, to China, 1987. Pres., Euroconsult Ltd, 2002–08. Ed., Warsaw Business Jl, 2003–04. *Publications:* Energy, the Burning Question for Europe (jtly), 1981; (ed and contrib.) Transport for Europe, 1982; Blood on their Hands: the killing of Ann Chapman, 1987; The Sacred Cow, 1987; Gladio: NATO's dagger at the heart of Europe, 2011; Doctor Who?: atomic bomber Beeching and his war on the railways, 2013; contribs to Encounter, Contemporary Review, Foreign Policy Jl, End the Lie, Russia Today. *Recreations:* travel, reading, transport studies, appreciation of real ale, astronomy, ornithology, maintenance of a large private library, philosophy, psychoanalysis, cooking, economics.

**COTTRELL, Rt Rev. Stephen Geoffrey;** *see* Chelmsford, Bishop of.

**COTTRELL-BOYCE, Frank,** FRSL; writer; Professor of Reading and Communication, Liverpool Hope University, since 2012; *b* Liverpool, 23 Sept. 1959; *s* of Francis and Joan Boyce; *m* 1983, Denise Cottrell; four *s* three *d*. *Educ:* W Park High Sch., St Helens; Keble Coll., Oxford (BA, DPhil). Screenplays: Forget About Me, 1990; Butterfly Kiss, 1995; Welcome to Sarajevo, 1997; Hilary and Jackie, 1998; The Claim, 2000; 24 Hour Party People, 2002; Code 46, 2003; Millions, 2004 (Best Screenplay, BIFA, 2005); A Cock and Bull Story, 2005; Grow Your Own, 2007; The Railway Man, 2013; Goodbye Christopher Robin, 2017; Sometimes Always Never, 2019; scriptwriter, London 2012 Olympics opening ceremony; *television* includes: God on Trial, 2008; Framed, 2009; *radio play*, The Door in the Pillow, 2019. FRSA; FRSL 2012. *Publications:* The Claim (play), 2001; novels for children: Millions, 2004 (Carnegie Medal, CILIP, 2004); Framed, 2005; Cosmic, 2008; Desirable, 2008; The Unforgotten Coat, 2011 (Guardian Children's Fiction Prize, 2012); Chitty Chitty Bang Bang Flies Again, 2011; Chitty Chitty Bang Bang and the Race Against Time, 2013; Chitty Chitty Bang Bang Over the Moon, 2014; The Astounding Broccoli Boy, 2015; Sputnik's Guide to Life on Earth, 2017; Runaway Robot, 2018. *Recreations:* running, fencing, desk avoidance, involved in many community projects including Plaza Community Cinema, Liverpool. *Address:* c/o Greg Hunt, Independent Talent Group, 40 Whitfield Street, W1T 2RH.

**COTTS, Sir Richard Crichton Mitchell,** 4th Bt *cr* 1921, of Coldharbour Wood, Rogate, Sussex; *b* 26 July 1946; *er s* of Sir Robert Crichton Mitchell Cotts, 3rd Bt and Barbara Mary Winifrede (*d* 1982), *o d* of Captain H. J. A. Throckmorton, RN; *S* father, 1995, but his name does not appear on the Official Roll of the Baronetage. *Educ:* Oratory Sch. *Heir:* *b* Hamish William Anthony Mitchell Cotts [*b* 15 Sept. 1951; *m* 1995, Merlyn Mattiuzzo; three *s* three *d*].

**COUCHER, Iain Michael;** Chief Executive, AWE plc, since 2016; *b* 22 Aug. 1961; *s* of Brian and Daphne Coucher; *m* 1993, Tanya Nightingale (separated); one *s* one *d*. *Educ:* Ashville Coll., Harrogate; Imperial Coll., London (BSc Eng Hons Aeronautical Engrg); Henley Mgt Coll. (MBA); Open Univ. (MSc Envmtl Decision Making 2015). Defence project design, Hunting Engrg, and Marconi, 1982–85; project manager and dir, then Head of Transport, EDS, then SD-Scicon, 1985–97; Chief Executive: TranSys Consortium, 1997–99; Tube Lines Gp, 1999–2001; Network Rail: Man. Dir, Jan.–Sept. 2002; Dep. Chief Exec., 2002–07; Chief. Exec., 2007–10; Man. Dir, Alvarez & Marsal Corporate Solutions (Europe) LLP, 2012–15; Chief Exec., LBC Tank Terminals, 2014–15. Dir, Rly Safety and Standards Bd, 2003–10. Dir, Cadent Gas Ltd, 2018–. *Recreations:* cycling, birdwatching, films. *Address:* AWE plc, Aldermaston, Reading, Berks RG7 4PR.

**COUCHMAN, James Randall;** *b* 11 Feb. 1942; *s* of Stanley Randall Couchman and Alison Margaret Couchman; *m* 1967, Barbara Jean (*née* Heilbrun); one *s* one *d*. *Educ:* Cranleigh School; King's College, Newcastle upon Tyne; Univ. of Durham. Oil industry, 1964–70; Public House Manager, family company, 1970–74; Gen. Manager, family licensed trade co., 1974–80, Director, 1980–95. Member (C): Bexley LBC, 1974–82 (Chm., Social Services, 1975–78, 1980–82); Oxford CC, 2005–13 (Cabinet Mem. for Adult Social Services, 2006–10, for Finance and Property, 2010–12). Chm., Bexley HA, 1981–83. Member: Assoc. of Metropolitan Authorities Social Services Cttee, 1975–80; Central Council for Educn and Training of Social Workers, 1976–80; Governor, Nat. Inst. for Social Workers, 1976–80. MP (C) Gillingham, 1983–97; contested (C) same seat, 1997. PPS to Minister of State for Social Security, 1984–86, to Minister of Health, 1986–88, to Chancellor of Duchy of Lancaster, 1988–89, to Sec. of State for Social Security, 1989–90, to Lord Pres. of the Council and Leader of the House, 1995–97. Member: Social Services Select Cttee, 1983–85; Select Cttee on Health, 1990–92; Public Accounts Cttee, 1992–95; Select Cttee on NI, 1995–97. Fellow, Industry and Parlt Trust, 1987. Mem., Vintners' Co. *Recreations:* travel, reading, listening to music, politics. *Address:* 4 Shelley Close, Banstead, Surrey SM7 1EE. *T:* (01737) 363020.

**COUCHMAN, Martin,** OBE 2005; Deputy Chief Executive, British Hospitality Association, 1993–2016; *b* 28 Sept. 1947; *s* of late Frederick Alfred James Couchman and Pamela Mary Couchman (*née* Argent); *m* 1983, Carolyn Mary Constance Roberts; three *s* one *d*. *Educ:* Sutton Valence Sch.; Exeter Coll., Oxford (BA Jurisprudence). Building Industry, 1977–77; National Economic Development Office, 1977–92: Industrial Advr, 1977–84; Hd of Administration, 1984–87; on secondment as UK Dir of European Year of the Environment, 1987–88; Sec., NEDC, 1988–92. Chm., Social Affairs, HOTREC, Hospitality Europe (formerly European Confedn of Nat. Assocs of Hotels, Restaurants, Cafés and Similar Estabts), 2001–13 (Mem. Exec. Cttee, 1997–2000); Chm., CBI Sectoral Employment Issues Cttee, 2000–10. Mem., Green Alliance, 1988–. FRSA 1988. *Recreations:* Anglo-Saxon history, armchair archaeology, amateur dramatics. *E:* Martin.Couchman@oxfordalumni.org.

**COUCHMAN, Nicholas Duncan;** sports lawyer, investor and entrepreneur; Partner and Head of Sport, Charles Russell Speechlys LLP, since 2018; *b* Toulouse, France, 21 July 1965; *s* of Mark Couchman and Françoise Caseau; *m* 1995, Yvonne Gilleece; one *s* one *d*. *Educ:* Devonvik High Sch. for Boys; Univ. of Nottingham (BA Hons Law); Manchester Metropolitan Univ. (Post Grad. Dip.). Admitted solicitor, 1990. Partner, Townleys, 1989–2000; Founder and Chm., Couchmans LLP, 2001–18; Partner, then consultant, Sports Investment Partners LLP, 2010–. Editor, Sports and Character Licensing Jl, 1999–2002. *Recreations:* piano, Brighton, opera, cricket, guitar. *Address:* Charles Russell Speechlys LLP, 5 Fleet Place, EC4M 7RD. *T:* (020) 7438 2296, 07740 465044. *E:* nic.couchman@crsblaw.com. *Club:* Soho House.

**COUGHLAN, John Joseph,** CBE 2009; Chief Executive, Hampshire County Council, since 2015; *b* Birmingham, 19 April 1960; *s* of James Coughlan and Philomena Coughlan (*née* Swann); *m* 1994, Madeleine O'Connor; one *s* one *d*. *Educ:* Univ. of Leeds (BA Jt Hons 1982); Selly Oak Colls, Birmingham (CQSW 1988); Univ. of Birmingham (MBA 2001). Birmingham CC, 1982–97; Asst Dir, Social Services Dept, Dudley MBC, 1997–2001; Corporate Dir, Telford and Wrekin Council, 2001–05; on secondment as Interim Dir, Children and Young People, Haringey LBC, 2008; Dir of Children's Services, 2005–15, Dep. Chief Exec., 2009–15, Hampshire CC; Dir of Children's Services, IoW Council, 2013–15. Commissioner for Children's Services: Torbay BC, 2016–; Bucks CC, 2018–. Pres., ADSS, 2006–07; Jt Pres., Assoc. of Dirs of Children's Services, 2007–08. Chm. Trustees, BookTrust, 2018–. *Recreations:* swimming, reading, walking, Birmingham City Football Club. *Address:* Hampshire County Council, Castle Avenue, Winchester SO23 8UG. *E:* john.coughlan@hants.gov.uk.

**COUGHLIN, Michael Charles;** Executive Director for Customers, Digital and Transformation, Surrey County Council, since 2018; *b* London, 13 May 1959; *s* of Dennis and Jean Louise Dorothy Coughlin; *m* 1986, Christine Ann Hance; two *s* one *d*. *Educ:* Thomas Bennett Sch.; Portsmouth Poly. (BA Hons Social Admin); Loughborough Univ. (Dip. ILAM); Croydon Coll. (Dip. Mgt Studies, Dip. CI Mktg). Recreation Officer, Crawley BC, 1981–84; Leisure Manager, Bexley London Bor., 1984–87; Hd of Leisure and Community Services, Elmbridge BC, 1987–97; Dir, Leisure and Cultural Services, 1997–2000, Planning and Envmt, 2000–02, Royal Bor. Windsor and Maidenhead; Chief Executive: Crawley BC, 2002–08; Reading BC, 2008–12; Exec. Dir, LGA, 2012–14; Gp Man. Dir (UK), Bathroom Brands Ltd, 2014–17; Global HR Dir, Bathroom Brands Gp Ltd, 2017–18. *Recreations:* music - playing guitar and bass, songwriting, performing, singing, squash - team and league, ballroom and latin dancing, family, friends and holidays, cooking. *Address:* Surrey County Council, County Hall, Penrhyn Road, Kingston-upon-Thames, Surrey KT1 2DN. *T:* 07722 158115. *E:* michael.coughlin@surreycc.gov.uk.

**COUGHLIN, Vincent William;** QC 2003; Chief Criminal Counsel, Financial Conduct Authority, since 2017; b 6 May 1957; s of Cornelius and Maureen Coughlin; m 1988, Elizabeth Anne Ray; one s two d. Educ: Christ's Hospital, Horsham; Queen Mary Coll., London (LLB Hons). Called to the Bar, Middle Temple, 1980; in practice as barrister, SE Circuit and Wales and Chester Circuit, specialising in criminal law, 1980–2017. Recreations: jazz guitar, cycling.

**COULING, Neil William,** CBE 2013; Director General, Universal Credit, Department for Work and Pensions, since 2014; b Ware, Herts, 12 Feb. 1964; s of Donald and Valerie Couling; m 1993, Kate Lloyd Jones; three s one d. Educ: Richard Hale Sch., Hertford; Univ. of Manchester (BA Hons Politics and Modern Hist. 1985). Admin. rôles, DHSS, then DSS, 1986–99; Principal Private Sec. to Sec. of State for DSS, then DWP, 2000–03; Director: Jobcentre Plus SE, 2003–06; Jobcentre Plus Benefit and Fraud, 2006–09; Benefit Strategy, 2009–12; Work Services and Hd, Jobcentre Plus, 2012–14. Non-executive Director: Govt Office of SE, 2004–06; Pension and Disability Carers Service, 2009–11. Recreations: walking in the Welsh hills and South Downs, my children, watching sci-fi; Secretary of Milland Tractor Appreciation Soc., 2014–. Address: Department for Work and Pensions, Caxton House, Tothill Street, SW1H 9NA. E: neil.couling@dwp.gov.uk.

**COULL, Prof. Alexander,** PhD; DSc; FRSE; FICE; Regius Professor of Civil Engineering, University of Glasgow, 1977–92; b 20 June 1931; s of William Coull and Jane Ritchie (née Reid); m 1962, Frances Bruce Moir; one s two d. Educ: Peterhead Acad.; Univ. of Aberdeen (BScEng, PhD; DSc 1983). FRSE 1971; FICE 1972, FIStructE 1973; Res. Asst, MIT, USA, 1955; Struct. Engr, English Electric Co. Ltd, 1955–57; Lectr in Engrg, Univ. of Aberdeen, 1957–62; Lectr in Civil Engrg, Univ. of Southampton, 1962–66; Prof. of Struct. Engrg, Univ. of Strathclyde, 1966–76. Chm., Clyde Estuary Amenity Council, 1981–86. Publications: Tall Buildings, 1967; Fundamentals of Structural Theory, 1972; (with B. Stafford Smith) Tall Building Structures: Planning Analysis and Design, 1991; author or co-author of 130 res. papers in scientific jls. Recreations: golf, hill walking. Address: 4 Monaltrie Way, Ballater, Aberdeenshire AB35 5PS. T: (01339) 755766.

**COULL, Maj.-Gen. John Taylor,** CB 1992; FRCS; FRCSE; Medico-Legal Adviser, Army Medical Directorate, Ministry of Defence, 1992–97; b 4 March 1934; s of late John Sandeman Coull and Ethel Marjory (née Taylor); m 1958, Mildred Macfarlane; three s. Educ: Robert Gordon's College; Aberdeen Univ. Med. Sch. MB ChB. House appts, Aberdeen Royal Infirmary, 1958–60; Commissioned RAMC, 1960; Surgeon: Colchester Mil. Hosp., 1960–63; Queen Alexandra Mil. Hosp., 1963; Sen. Registrar, Edinburgh East Gen. Hosp., 1963–65; Royal Herbert Hosp., 1965–67; Sen. Registrar, Birmingham Accident Hosp., 1967; Consultant Surgeon, BMH Singapore, 1967–70; Lectr, Dept of Orthopaedics, Univ. of Edinburgh, 1970–71; Consultant Orthopaedic Surgeon, BAOR, 1971–77; Consultant Adviser in Orthop. Surgery and Sen. Consultant, Queen Elizabeth Mil. Hosp., 1977–86; Consulting Surgeon, HQ BAOR, 1986–88; Dir of Army Surgery, 1988–92. Hon. Col 202 (Midland) Field Hosp. RAMC (V), 1992–97; Col Comdt, RAMC, 1994–99. Mitchiner Meml Lectr, RAMC, 2001. QHS 1988–92. Mitchiner Medal, RCS, 1980. OStJ. GSM N Ireland, 1976. Publications: chapters in: Field Pocket Surgery, 1981; R. Smith's The Hand, 1985; Trauma, 1989; articles in learned jls. Recreations: home maintenance, carpentry, gardening, travel. Address: Sheigra, 25 Braemar Road, Ballater AB35 5RL. Club: Royal Northern and University (Aberdeen).

**COULSHED, Brian Thomas;** Headmaster, Parmiter's School, Hertfordshire, 1993–2010, now Emeritus Headmaster; b St Helens, Lancs, 11 March 1950; s of Thomas Cyril and Mary Ann Coulshed; m 1982, Gillian Margaret Dunsire; two s. Educ: West Park Grammar Sch., St Helens; Univ. of Manchester (BA Hons, PGCE). Asst teacher, then Hd of Year, Longdean Sch., Hemel Hempstead, 1972–79; Hd of Dept, then Hd of Year, Hemel Hempstead Sch., 1979–86; Dep. Headmaster, Goffs Sch., 1986–92. Vis. Fellow, St Catharine's Coll., Cambridge, 2000. Chm., SW Herts Heads' Assoc., 1999–2010. Pres., Herts Schs FA, 2004–. Trustee, Parmiter's Almshouse Foundn, 1993–. Mem., 1912 Club. Gov., St Margaret's Sch., Bushey, 2011–. Freeman, City of London, 2015. Headteacher of the Year, 2007. Publications: The History of the Parmiter's Estates Foundation, 1997; The History of the Parmiter's Foundation, 2000, 2nd edn 2008. Recreations: cricket (playing mem., Leverstock Green CC, 1973–2017; mem., Herts Over 60s County XI, 2011–, Capt., 2017–), football, Rugby League (lifelong supporter of Liverpool FC and St Helens Rugby League FC). E: briancoulshed@hotmail.co.uk. Clubs: Leverstock Green Cricket (Pres., 2003–), Middx County Cricket, Herts County Cricket.

**COULSON, Mrs Ann Margaret;** Chairman, Leamington Hastings Consolidated Charity, 1998–2011 (Trustee, 1992–2011); b 11 March 1935; d of Sidney Herbert Wood and Ada (née Mills); m 1958, Peter James Coulson; two s one d. Educ: The Grammar Sch., Chippenham, Wilts; UCL (BScEcon); Univ. of Manchester (DSA); Wolverhampton Technical Teachers' Coll. (CertEd). Hosp. Admin, 1956–62; Lectr in Econs and Management, Bromsgrove Coll. of Further Educn, 1968–76; Asst Dir, North Worcestershire Coll., 1976–80; Service Planning and Develt Co-ordinator, 1980–83, Regl Planning Administrator, 1983–88, Dir of Planning, 1988–91, W Midlands RHA; Gen. Manager, Age Concern, Solihull, 1991–94. City of Birmingham Dist Council, 1973–79; special interest in Social Services. Mem., IBA, 1976–81. Trustee, Age Concern, Warwicks, 1996–2007. Recreations: sailing, cooking, music, theatre. Address: Rowans, Leamington Hastings, near Rugby, Warwicks CV23 8DY. T: (01926) 633264.

**COULSON, Frances Elaine;** Managing Partner, since 2000, and Senior Partner, since 2014, Moon Beever, Solicitors (Partner, since 1988); b Sheffield, 23 Dec. 1961; d of late Richard and of Faith Gilbert; m 1983, Philip Coulson; three d. Educ: Sheffield High Sch. for Girls; King's Coll. London (LLB Hons 1983; Dip. EC Law 1991). Admitted as solicitor, 1986. Chm., Appeals Cttee, ACCA, 2006–12. Mem., Charity Cttee, Co. of Blacksmiths, 2009–. Pres., R3, 2011–12 (Chm., Fraud Gp, 2011–). Trustee, Fraud Adv. Panel, 2012–. Mem. and Chair, Ind. Remuneration Panel, Braintree DC, 2014–. Freeman, City of London, 2007–; Liveryman, Blacksmiths' Co., 2007–. Recreations: equestrian, hockey, walking, reading. Address: Moon Beever, Bedford House, 21a John Street, WC1N 2BF. T: (020) 7400 7770, Fax: (020) 7400 7799. E: fcoulson@moonbeever.com. Club: Carlton.

**COULSON, Rt Hon. Sir Peter (David William),** Kt 2008; PC 2018; **Rt Hon. Lord Justice Coulson;** a Lord Justice of Appeal, since 2018; b 31 March 1958; s of David Coulson and Pamela Coulson (née Shorter); m 1985, Veronica Lachkovic; one s two d; partner, Rachael Harrison, qv. Educ: Lord Wandsworth Coll.; Univ. of Keele (BA Hons 1980). Called to the Bar, Gray's Inn, 1982 (Sir Malcolm Hilbery Award, 1982; Bencher, 2006); in practice, 1984–2004; QC 2001; Recorder, 2002–04; Sen. Circuit Judge, 2004–07; Presiding Judge, NE Circuit, 2011–14; a Judge of the High Court of Justice, QBD, 2008–18; Judge in Charge of Estates, until 2017; Dep. Hd, Civil Justice, 2018–. Mem. Bd, Acad. of St Martin in the Fields, 2009–16. Contributor, Lloyd's Law Reports: Professional Negligence, 1999–2000. Hon. DLaws Keele, 2012. Publications: (jtly) Professional Negligence and Liability, 2000; The Technology and Construction Court, 2006; Construction Adjudication, 2007, 4th edn 2018. Recreations: British art 1750–1950, comedy, music, cricket, Watford FC. Address: Royal Courts of Justice, Strand, WC2A 2LL. Club: Garrick.

**COULSON, Sarah April Louise;** see Baxter, S. A. L.

**COULSON, Prof. Timothy Neal,** PhD; Professor of Zoology, since 2013, and Associate Head, Department of Zoology, since 2016, University of Oxford; Fellow, Jesus College, Oxford, since 2013; b Cambridge, 31 July 1968; s of Patrick Coulson and Anne Coulson; one s two d. Educ: Barton C of E Prim. Sch.; Comberton Village Coll., Cambridge; Hill Road Sixth Form Coll., Cambridge; Univ. of York (BSc Biol. 1990); Imperial Coll. London (PhD 1994). Res. Fellow, Inst. of Zool., 1994–2000; Res. Fellow, 2000–03, Lectr in Zool., 2003–04, Univ. of Cambridge; Imperial College London: Sen. Lectr, 2004–05; Reader, 2005–07; Prof. of Population Biol., 2007–12. Mem. Council, Univ. of Oxford, 2017–; Chair, IT Cttee, Univ. of Oxford. Chief Ed., Ecology Letters, 2016–. Publications: 250 articles in scientific jls. Recreations: cycling, hiking, cooking, fieldwork. Address: 122 Southfield Road, Oxford OX4 1PA. T: 07872 850090. E: tim.coulson@zoo.ox.ac.uk.

**COULTER, Rev. Dr David George,** CB 2016; QHC 2010; Minister, St Andrew's in the Grange, St Peter Port, Guernsey, since 2019; b Belfast, 29 Dec. 1957; s of George Coulter and Elizabeth Coulter; m 1981, Grace Woods; two s. Educ: Regent House Sch.; Queen's Univ., Belfast (BA Hons); Univ. of St Andrews (BD Hons); Cranfield Univ. (MDA); Univ. of Edinburgh (PhD 1998). Officer, Royal Irish Rangers, 1976–85; Minister, C of S, 1989–; Chaplain, Royal Army Chaplains' Dept, 1989–2018; Chaplain Gen. HM Land Forces, 2014–18. QCVS 1996. SBStJ 2011. Recreations: sailing, Nordic walking. Club: Royal Air Force.

**COULTON, Very Rev. Canon Nicholas Guy;** Residentiary Canon and Sub-Dean, Christ Church, Oxford, 2003–08, Canon Emeritus, since 2012; b 14 June 1940; s of Nicholas Guy Coulton and Audrey Florence Furneaux Coulton (née Luscombe); m 1978, Edith Mary Gainford; one s two d. Educ: Blundell's School, Tiverton; Cuddesdon Coll., Oxford; BD London (ext.) 1972; MA Oxon 2007. Admitted Solicitor, 1962; Asst Solicitor, Burges, Salmon & Co., Bristol, 1962–65. Ordination training, 1965–67; Curate of Pershore Abbey with Birlingham, Wick and Pinvin, 1967–71; Domestic Chaplain to Bishop of St Albans, 1971–75; Vicar of St Paul's, Bedford, 1975–90; part-time Industrial Chaplain, 1976–89; Provost, subseq. Dean, St Nicholas' Cathedral, Newcastle upon Tyne, 1990–2003, now Dean Emeritus. Proctor in Convocation, 1985–90; Hon. Canon of St Alban's Cathedral, 1989–90. Member: Gen. Synod of C of E, 1998–2003; Legal Adv. Commn of C of E, 2001–11. Mem., USPG Delegn to Province of West Indies, 1999. Chm., NE CCJ, 1991–2002; Member: NE Assembly, 2002–03; Churches' Refugee Network, 2008–. Dir, Ecclesiastical Insurance Gp, 1997–2005. Governor: Newcastle upon Tyne Church High Sch., 1990–2003; Dame Allan's Schs, 1990–2003; Ripon Coll., Cuddesdon, 2002–08; Christ Church Cathedral Sch., 2003–08. Pres., Friends of Pershore Abbey, 2006–11. OStJ 2002. Publications: Twelve Years of Prayer, 1989; (ed) The Bible, The Church and Homosexuality, 2005; contrib. articles and book reviews in Ecclesiastical Law Jl, 2010–19. Recreations: gardening, reading, listening to music, historical exploration, national asylum work for the churches, annual visits to Mathieson Music School, Kolkata. Address: 123 Merewood Avenue, Oxford OX3 8EQ.

**COUNSELL, Her Honour Hazel Rosemary;** see Fallon, Her Honour H. R.

**COUNSELL, James Henry;** QC 2017; b Bristol, 11 Feb. 1961; s of Henry Counsell and Pamela Counsell (née Westhead); m 1991, Lisa Maria Rodway; two s one d. Educ: Marlborough Coll.; Magdalene Coll., Cambridge (MA). Called to the Bar, Inner Temple, 1984; in practice as a barrister, 2 King's Bench Walk, 1986–2003, Outer Temple Chambers, 2003–. Dir, Lympsham Manor Farm, 2011–. Chm., Lympsham Sports Club, 2016–; President: Lympsham CC, 2013–16; Lympsham and Belvedere CC, 2017–. Recreations: cricket, Rugby, farming, gardening. Address: Outer Temple Chambers, 222 Strand, WC2R 1BA. E: james.counsell@outertemple.com; The Manor, Lympsham, near Weston-super-Mare, Somerset BS24 0DT. T: (01934) 750943, 07770 752329. Clubs: Farmers, MCC.

**COUNT, Dr Brian Morrison;** Chairman: Jacoma Estates Ltd, since 2008; InfraCo Africa Ltd, since 2014; b 18 Feb. 1951; s of Douglas John Count and Ethel Sarah Count; m 1975, Jane Elizabeth Hudson; three s. Educ: King's College, Cambridge (MA Maths); Exeter Univ. (PhD Physics). Central Electricity Generating Board: Research Dept, 1974–84; Planning Dept, 1984–90; National Power: Project Develt Dir, 1990–95; Dir of Ops, 1995–96; Mem. Bd, 1996–2000; Man. Dir, UK, 1999–2000; Innogy Holdings: Chief Operating Officer, 2000–01; Chief Exec., 2001–03; CEO, RWE Trading, 2003–05. Non-executive Director: Eskom, 2002–08; Sterecycle Ltd, 2008–12. Mem., Industrial Develt Adv. Bd, DTI, later BERR, then BIS, 2004–10. Recreations: golf, Rugby, entertaining. Address: Oakwood House, Blindmans Gate, Woolton Hill, Newbury, Berks RG20 9XD.

**COUPER, Heather Anita,** CBE 2007; CPhys, FInstP; FRAS; science broadcaster and author, since 1983; Director, Pioneer TV Productions, 1988–99; b 2 June 1949; o d of late George Couper Elder Couper and Anita Couper (née Taylor). Educ: St Mary's Grammar Sch., Northwood, Middx; Univ. of Leicester (BSc Hons Astronomy and Physics); Linacre Coll., Oxford. FRAS 1970; CPhys 1999; FInstP 1999. Management trainee, Peter Robinson Ltd, 1967–69; Res. Asst, Cambridge Observatories, 1969–70; Lectr, Greenwich Planetarium, Old Royal Observ., 1977–83. Gresham Prof. of Astronomy, 1993–96. Mem., Millennium Commn, 1994–2006. President: Brit. Astron. Assoc., 1984–86; Jun. Astron. Soc., 1987–89. Presenter on television: Heavens Above, 1981; Spacewatch, 1983; The Planets, 1985; The Stars, 1988; The Neptune Encounter, 1989; A Close Encounter of the Second Kind, 1992; Stephen Hawking: a profile, 2002; producer/narrator: ET—Please Phone Earth, 1992; Space Shuttle Discovery, 1993; Electric Skies, 1994; Arthur C. Clarke: the Visionary, 1995; On Jupiter, 1996; Black Holes, 1997; narrator/presenter: Rendezvous in Space, and Avalanche, 1995; Raging Planet, 1997; The Sci-Fi Files, Killer Earth, and Stormforce, 1998; producer, Universe, 1999; presenter/producer, Space Shuttle: human time bomb?, 2003; presenter on radio: Science Now, 1983; Cosmic Pursuits, 1985; Seeing Stars, 1991–2001; ET on Trial, 1993; Starwatch, 1996; Sun Science, 1999; The Essential Guide to the 21st Century (series), 2000; Red Planet (series), 2003; Worlds Beyond (series), 2005; Arthur C. Clarke: the Science Behind the Fiction, 2005; A Brief Guide to Infinity, 2006; Britain's Space Race, 2007; Cosmic Quest (series), 2008; also appearances and interviews on wide variety of television and radio progs. Astronomy columnist, The Independent. Hon. DLitt Loughborough, 1991; Hon. DSc: Hertfordshire, 1994; Leicester, 1997. Publications: Exploring Space, 1980; (jtly) Heavens Above, 1981; Journey into Space, 1984; (jtly) Starfinder, 1984; (jtly) The Halley's Comet Pop-Up Book, 1985; (jtly) The Universe: a 3-dimensional study, 1985; Space Scientist series, 1985–87: Comets and Meteors; The Planets; The Stars; jointly: The Sun; The Moon; Galaxies and Quasars; Satellites and Spaceprobes; Telescopes and Observatories; with Nigel Henbest: Space Frontiers, 1978; The Restless Universe, 1982; Physics, 1983; Astronomy, 1983; The Planets, 1985; The Stars, 1988; The Space Atlas, 1992; Guide to the Galaxy, 1994; How the Universe Works, 1994; Black Holes, 1996; Big Bang, 1997; Is Anybody Out There?, 1998; To the Ends of the Universe, 1998; Space Encyclopedia, 1999; Universe, 1999; Mars: the inside story of the red planet, 2001; Extreme Universe, 2001; Philip's Stargazing, annually 2004–; Out of this World, 2007; Universe, 2007; The History of Astronomy, 2007; The Story of Astronomy, 2012; The Secret Life of Space, 2015; The Astronomy Bible, 2015; The Universe Explained - a cosmic Q & A, 2018; numerous articles in nat.

newspapers and magazines. *Recreations:* travel, the English countryside, classical music; wine, food and winemaking. *Address:* David Higham Associates, 7th Floor, Waverley House, 7–12 Noel Street, W1F 8GQ. *Club:* Groucho.

**COUPER, Sir James George,** 7th Bt *cr* 1841; *b* 27 Oct. 1977; *o s* of Sir Nicholas Couper, 6th Bt and of his 1st wife, Kirsten Henrietta, *d* of Major George Burrell MacKean; *S father,* 2002. *Heir: cousin* Jonathan Every Couper [*b* 26 Feb. 1931; *m* 1986, Heather Agnes Heath].

**COUPLAND, George,** PhD; FRS 2007; Director, Max Planck Institute for Plant Breeding Research, Cologne, since 2001; *b* 20 Dec. 1959; *s* of Walter Archibald Coupland and Margaret Coupland; *m* 1991, Jane Parker; one *s* one *d. Educ:* Univ. of Glasgow (BSc 1st Cl. Hons Microbiol. 1981); Univ. of Edinburgh (PhD 1984). Postdoctoral experience, Inst. for Genetics, Univ. of Cologne and Max Planck Inst. for Plant Breeding Res., Cologne, 1985–88; res. gp leader, Plant Breeding Inst., Cambridge and Cambridge Lab., John Innes Centre, Norwich, 1987–2001. Hon. Lectr, UEA, 1993–2001; Hon. Prof., Univ. of Cologne, 2003–. Cttee, Genetical Soc. of UK, 1997–2001; Cttee, UK RAE, 2007–08. Mem., EMBO, 2001; Associate Member: Class of Scis, Royal Acad. of Belgium, 2006; NAS, USA, 2012. *Publications:* articles in learned jls incl. Nature, Science, Cell. *Recreations:* ornithology, travel. *Address:* Max Planck Institute for Plant Breeding Research, Plant Developmental Biology, Carl von Linné Weg 10, 50829 Köln, Germany. *T:* (221) 5062205, *Fax:* (221) 5062207. *E:* coupland@mpipz.mpg.de.

**COUPLAND, Steven Michael Edward; His Honour Judge Coupland;** a Circuit Judge, since 2016; *b* Sheffield, 16 Oct. 1969; *s* of Michael Howard Coupland and Naomi Edwina Coupland; *m* 1992, Natalie Millard; one *s* one *d. Educ:* Montsaye Comprehensive Sch., Rothwell, Northants; University Coll. of Wales, Aberystwyth (LLB Hons); Inns of Court Sch. of Law. Called to the Bar, Lincoln's Inn, 1993; in practice as barrister, 1993–2016; a Recorder, 2012–16.

**COURAGE, Maj.-Gen. Walter James,** CB 1994; MBE 1979; Director, The Risk Advisory Group plc (formerly Ltd), since 1997; *b* 25 Sept. 1940; *s* of late Walter Henry Phipps and of Nancy Mary Courage (*née* Reeves, who *m* 3rd, John Frederick Gardner), and step *s* of late Lt-Col Nigel Anthony Courage, MC; *m* 1964, Lavinia Patricia, *d* of late John Emerson Crawhall Wood; one *s* one *d. Educ:* Abingdon Sch.; RMA, Sandhurst. Commnd 5th Royal Inniskilling Dragoon Guards, 1961; served BAOR, Libya and Canada, 1961–81; commanded Regt, 1982–84; Div. Col Staff Coll., 1985; Comdr 4th Armoured Bde, 1985–88; Chief of Staff, UN Force in Cyprus, 1988–90; Chief Joint Services Liaison Officer, BAOR, Bonn, 1990–94; Chief, Ext. Affairs Div., Germany, 1994–95; Dir-Gen., TA, 1995–96. Member: Bd, British American Business Inc., 2001–17; Adv. Bd, Moore, Clayton & Co., 2002–07; Dir, Janusian Security Risk Mgt, 2002–07; Chm., Future Digital Footprint, 2015–18. Consultant: AMEC Project Investments Ltd, 1997–2004; DLA, 2000–04; Investor and Consultant, Viramal Ltd, 2014–; Sen. Advr, IW Capital, 2017–. Trustee, Shotover Estate, 2005–. FCMI. *Recreations:* shooting, cricket, ski-ing, polo, fine art. *Address:* Brigmerston Farm House, Brigmerston, Salisbury, Wilts SP4 8HX. *Clubs:* Cavalry and Guards, MCC; I Zingari.

**COURCY;** see de Courcy, family name of Baron Kingsale.

**COURT, Rt Rev. David;** see Grimsby, Bishop Suffragan of.

**COURT, Hon. Richard Fairfax,** AC 2003; Ambassador of Australia to Japan, since 2017; *b* 27 Sept. 1947; *s* of Hon. Sir Charles Walter Michael Court, AK, KCMG, OBE; *m* 1989, Joanne, *d* of B. Moffat; one *d*, and one *s* one *d* by previous marriage. *Educ:* Univ. of Western Australia (BCom). Man. Dir, Court Marine Pty, 1974–82. MLA (L) Nedlands, WA, 1982–2001; Shadow Minister for Small Business, 1986; Dep. Leader, Parly Lib. Party, 1987–90; Shadow Minister for: Resources, Develt, Mines, Fuel and Energy, NW and Goldfields, 1990–91; Resource and Industrial Develt, Mines and Aboriginal Affairs, 1991–92; Public Sector Management, also Leader of the Opposition and Shadow Treas., 1992–93; Premier of WA, Treasurer and Minister for Public Sector Mgt and for Federal Affairs, 1993–2001; Minister for: Tourism, 1994–95; Youth, 1996–97. Chm., Resource Investment Strategy Consultants, 2001–16; Consultant, Australian Capital Equity Pty Ltd, 2001–16. Non-exec. Dir, Iron Ore Hldgs Ltd, 2007–14.

**COURT, Robert Vernon;** Managing Director, Global Stakeholder Strategies, since 2015; *b* 28 Jan. 1958; *s* of Derrick and Catherine Court; *m* 1983, Rebecca Ophelia Sholl; three *s* one *d. Educ:* Churchill Coll., Cambridge (MA). Entered FCO, 1981; Bangkok, 1983–86; First Sec., FCO, 1986–88; Private Sec. to Minister of State, 1988–90; First Secretary: UK Delegn to NATO, 1990–93; UK Perm. Repn to EU, 1993–96; PA to Chm. and CEO, 1997–99, Gp Co-ordinator for Sustainable Develt, 2000–01, Rio Tinto plc; Dep. High Comr, Canberra, 2001–05; Vice-Pres., Govt Affairs Internat., GlaxoSmithKline, 2005–09; Global Hd of External Affairs, Rio Tinto, 2009–15. Partner, DRD Partnership, 2017–; Sen. Advr, Critical Resource, 2017–. *Recreations:* sub-aqua diving, swimming, travel. *Address:* Ashtead, Surrey. *E:* robert.v.court@gmail.com. *Club:* Royal Automobile.

**COURTAULD, George,** OBE 2016; Vice Lord-Lieutenant of Essex, 2003–13; landowner and farmer; *b* 2 May 1938; *s* of George Courtauld and Claudine Suzanne (*née* Booth); *m* 1962, Dominie Jennifer Faith Mirren Riley-Smith; two *s* two *d. Educ:* Gordonstoun; Pembroke Coll., Cambridge (BA 1961). Commnd Grenadier Guards, 1957. With textile manufacturer, Courtaulds Ltd, 1962–83. Queen's Messenger, 1985–2000. Chairman: Haven Gateway Partnership, 2002–08 (Pres., 2008–); NE Essex Strategic LSC, 2004; Harwich Regeneration Gp, 2005–10; Essex Br., Prince's Trust, 2005–08; Essex Envmt Trust, 2005–16; Essex Women's Adv. Gp, 2007–; Rural Community Council, Essex, 2008–16 (Pres., 2016–); Harwich and Stour Valley Area Bd, 2010–12. President: Friends of Essex Churches, 2002–14; Chelmsford and Mid Essex Samaritans, 2003–14; Halstead Allotment Holders and Leisure Gardeners Assoc., 2006–; Essex Br., SSAFA, 2008–; Vice President: Essex Co. Scout Council, 2002–13; Essex Community Foundn, 2004–. Master Patron, Public Catalogue Foundn, Essex, 2006–. Member: Halstead RDC, 1967–74; Braintree DC, 1974–85. Freeman, City of London, 1959; Liveryman: Weavers' Co., 1961–; Goldsmiths' Co., 1970–. High Sheriff, 2001–02, DL 2002, Essex. *Publications:* An Axe, A Spade and Ten Acres, 1983; Odd Noises from the Barn, 1985; The Travels of a Fat Bulldog, 1995; The Fat Bulldog Roams Again, 1998; The Last Travels of a Fat Bulldog, 2000; (ed) Essex Girl's Limericks, 2010; An Alphabet of Awful Animals, 2016. *Recreations:* travel, plant collecting, forestry. *Address:* Knight's Barn, Colne Engaine, Earls Colne, Essex CO6 2JG. *Clubs:* White's, Special Forces; Essex.

**COURTENAY,** family name of Earl of Devon.

**COURTENAY, Lord; Jack Haydon Langer Courtenay;** *b* 16 Aug. 2009; *s* and *heir* of Earl of Devon, *qv*.

**COURTENAY, Ralph Andrew,** RIBA; FCSD; Managing Director, 1992–2007, Senior Vice President, 1998–2007, HOK Europe; *b* 21 Feb. 1943; *s* of Reginald William James Courtenay and Joyce Louisa Courtenay; *m* 1969, Brenda Ruth Caudle; two *d. Educ:* Abbey Sch., London; NE London Poly. (Dist. in Thesis). RIBA 1972; FCSD 1984. Austin-Smith, London, 1978–89: Partner, 1980–89; Man. Partner, 1984–89; own practice, Ralph Courtenay Associates, 1989–92; joined HOK, London, 1992, Man. Dir, 1995–2007; Dir, HOK Worldwide, 1996–2007; Chm., HOK European Architects Network, 2000–07. Mem., Soc. of Architectural Illustrators, 1982. *Publications:* contrib. articles to Building Design, Architects Jl and Architectural Rev. *Recreations:* marathon running, golf, tennis, ski-ing, painting, music, opera. *Address:* 1 The Orchards, Mill Road, Winchelsea, E Sussex TN36 4HJ. *Clubs:* Royal Automobile, Arts; Hemstead Forest Golf, Sissinghurst Tennis.

**COURTENAY, Sir Thomas Daniel, (Sir Tom),** Kt 2001; actor; *b* 25 Feb. 1937; *s* of late Thomas Henry Courtenay and Annie Eliza Quest; *m* 1st, 1973, Cheryl Kennedy (marr. diss. 1982); 2nd, 1988, Isabel Crossley. *Educ:* Kingston High Sch., Hull; University Coll., London (Fellow 1994). RADA, 1958–60; started acting professionally, 1960; Old Vic, 1960–61: Konstantin Treplieff, Poins, Feste and Puck; Billy Liar, Cambridge Theatre, June 1961–Feb. 1962 and on tour; Andorra, National Theatre (guest), 1964; The Cherry Orchard, and Macbeth, Chichester, 1966; joined 69 Theatre Co., Manchester, 1966: Charley's Aunt, 1966; Romeo, Playboy of the Western World, 1967; Hamlet (Edinburgh Festival), 1968; She Stoops to Conquer, (transferred to Garrick), 1969; Peer Gynt, 1970; Charley's Aunt, Apollo, 1971; Time and Time Again, Comedy, 1972 (Variety Club of GB Stage Actor Award, 1972); The Norman Conquests, Globe, 1974; The Fool, Royal Court, 1975; Prince of Homburg, The Rivals, Manchester (opening prods of The Royal Exchange), 1976; Otherwise Engaged, NY, 1977; Clouds, Duke of York's, 1978; Crime and Punishment, Manchester, 1978; The Dresser, Manchester and Queen's, 1980 (Drama Critics Award and New Standard Award for best actor, 1980), NY 1981; The Misanthrope, Manchester and Round House, 1981; Andy Capp, Manchester and Aldwych, 1982; Jumpers, Manchester, 1984; Rookery Nook, Shaftesbury, 1986; The Hypochondriac, Lyric, Hammersmith, 1987; Dealing with Clair, Richmond, 1988; The Miser, Manchester, 1991; Moscow Stations (one-man show), Traverse Theatre, Edinburgh, 1993, 1994, Garrick, 1994 (Evening Standard and Critics' Circle Award), NY, 1995; Poison Pen, Manchester, 1993; Uncle Vanya, NY, 1995, Manchester, 2001; Art, Wyndham's, 1996; King Lear, Manchester, 1999; Pretending to be Me (one-man show), W Yorks Playhouse, 2002, Comedy, 2003; The Home Place, Gate, Dublin, transf. Comedy, 2005; UK and Ireland tour, Pretending to be Me, 2010–11. Began acting in films, 1962. *Films:* The Loneliness of the Long Distance Runner, Private Potter, 1962; Billy Liar, 1963; King and Country, 1964 (Volpi Cup, 1964); Operation Crossbow, King Rat, Dr Zhivago, 1965; The Night of the Generals, The Day the Fish Came Out, 1967; A Dandy in Aspic, 1968; Otley, 1969; One Day in the Life of Ivan Denisovich, 1970; Catch Me a Spy, 1971; The Dresser, 1983 (Golden Globe Award); The Last Butterfly, 1990; Let Him Have It, 1991; The Boy from Mercury, 1996; Whatever Happened to Harold Smith?, 1999; Last Orders, 2002; Nicholas Nickleby, 2003; The Golden Compass, 2007; Gambit, 2012; Quartet, 2013; Night Train to Lisbon, 2014; 45 Years, 2015 (Silver Bear for best actor, Berlin Film Fest., 2015; Best Actor, Critics' Circle Film Awards, 2016); Dad's Army, 2016; The Guernsey Literary and Potato Peel Pie Society, King of Thieves, 2018; The Aeronauts, 2019; *television* includes: Redemption, 1991; Old Curiosity Shop (film), 1995; A Rather English Marriage, 1998 (BAFTA Award); The Flood, 2007; Little Dorrit, Royle Family Christmas Special, 2008; Unforgotten, 2015 (Best Supporting Actor, BAFTA, 2016); Grandpa's Great Escape, 2018. Best Actor Award, Prague Festival, 1968; TV Drama Award (for Oswald in Ghosts), 1968. *Publications:* Dear Tom: letters from home (memoirs), 2000. *Recreations:* listening to music (mainly classical, romantic and jazz), watching sport (and occasionally taking part in it, in a light-hearted manner), the countryside, playing the ukelele. *Address:* Putney. *Club:* Garrick.

**COURTICE, Dame Veronica Anne, (Dame Polly),** DBE 2016; LVO 2008; Director, Institute for Sustainability Leadership, University of Cambridge, since 2000; *b* Johannesburg, 3 June 1952; *d* of Henry Albert Scott and Edith Vera Scott; *m* 1982, Dr Giles Robert Moorsom Courtice; one *s* one *d. Educ:* Sans Souci Girls' High Sch., Cape Town; Univ. of Cape Town (BA); New Hall, Cambridge (BA Hons 1978). Curator, S African Mus., 1974–76; Dep. Academic Mktg Manager, Penguin Books Ltd, 1978–81; Longman Group Ltd: Promotion Manager, 1981–83; Mktg Manager, 1983–86; Gp Mktg Manager, 1986–89; Dir of Mktg, 1989–90, Dep. Dir, 1990–2000, Prog. for Industry, Univ. of Cambridge. Dir, Jupiter Green Investment Trust plc, 2007–; non-exec. Dir, Anglian Water Services Ltd, 2015–. *Address:* Institute for Sustainability Leadership, University of Cambridge, 1 Trumpington Street, Cambridge CB2 1QA.

**COURTNEY, Prof. Edward,** MA; Gildersleeve Professor of Classics, University of Virginia, 1993–2002, now Emeritus; *b* 22 March 1932; *s* of George and Kathleen Courtney; *m* 1962, Brenda Virginia Meek; two *s. Educ:* Royal Belfast Academical Instn; Trinity Coll., Dublin (BA); BA (by incorporation) 1955, MA 1957, Oxford. University studentship, Dublin, 1954–55; Research Lectr, Christ Church, Oxford, 1955–59; Lectr in Classics, 1959, Reader in Classics, 1970, Prof. of Latin, 1977, King's Coll., London; Prof. of Classics, 1982–93; Leonard Ely Prof. of Humanistic Studies, 1986–93, Stanford Univ. *Publications:* (ed) Valerius Flaccus, Argonautica (Leipzig), 1970; (ed jtly) Juvenal, Satires 1, 3, 10, 1977; (ed jtly) Ovid, Fasti (Leipzig), 1978, 4th edn 1997; A Commentary on the Satires of Juvenal, 1980, repr. 2014; (ed) Juvenal, The Satires, a text, 1984; (ed) Statius, Silvae, 1990; The Poems of Petronius, 1991; The Fragmentary Roman Poets, 1993, 2nd edn 2003; Musa Lapidaria: a selection of Latin verse inscriptions, 1995; Archaic Latin Prose, 1999; A Companion to Petronius, 2002; many articles and reviews. *Recreation:* chess (schoolboy champion of Ireland, 1950). *Address:* 2306 Tarleton Drive, Charlottesville, VA 22901–1827, USA.

**COURTNEY, Kevin George;** Joint General Secretary, National Education Union, since 2017; *b* Pontypridd, 16 Aug. 1959; *s* of Elwyn and Joan Courtney; *m* 1989, Polly Donnison; one *s* one *d. Educ:* Coed-Y-Lan Comprehensive Sch.; Imperial Coll. London (BSc Physics); Chelsea Coll. (PGCE). Teacher of Physics, Camden Sch. for Girls, 1983–92; Associate Sec., Camden NUT, 1990–2010; Dep. Sec. Gen., 2010–16, Gen. Sec., 2016–17, NUT. *Recreations:* cinema, walking, museums, cycling, camping. *Address:* National Education Union, Hamilton House, Mabledon Place, WC1H 9BD. *E:* kevin.courtney@neu.org.uk.

**COURTNEY, Roger Graham,** CPhys, FInstP; CEng, FCIBSE; consultant, construction research and innovation; *b* 11 July 1946; *s* of late Ronald Samuel Courtney and Marjorie Dixon Courtney; *m* 1973, Rosemary Madeleine Westlake; four *d. Educ:* Roan School for Boys, SE3; Trinity Coll., Cambridge (MA); Univ. of Bristol (MSc); Brunel Univ. (MTech(OR)). CPhys 1991, FInstP 1991; MCIOB 1993; FCIBSE 1993; CEng 1994. Building Research Station, later Building Research Establishment, 1969–77: res. on bldg and urban services and energy conservation; Sci. Officer, 1969–72; Sen. Sci. Officer, 1972–75; PSO, 1975–81; Inner Cities Directorate, DoE, 1977–78; Sci. and Technology Secretariat, Cabinet Office, 1978–84 (Sec. to ACARD and IT Adv. Panel); SPSO, 1981–83; DCSO, 1983–86; Technical Dir, Energy Efficiency Office, Dept of Energy, 1984–86; Dep. Dir, 1986–88, Dir, 1988–90, Chief Exec., 1990–97, BRE, DoE; Dep. Chm., BRE Ltd, 1997–99. Chm., Dacortium Ltd, 2013–17. Professorial Fellow in Construction Innovation, 2001–08, Professorial Res. Fellow, Sch. of Mechanical, Aerospace and Civil Engrg, 2008–12, Univ. of Manchester (formerly UMIST); Vis. Prof., Bartlett Sch. of Construction and Project Mgt, 2005–12, Bartlett Sch. of Graduate Studies, 2013–16, UCL. *Publications:* papers in sci. and professional jls. *Address:* 89 Parkside Drive, Watford WD17 3AY. *T:* (01923) 221715.

**COURTOWN,** 9th Earl of, *cr* 1762; **James Patrick Montagu Burgoyne Winthrop Stopford;** Baron Courtown (Ire.), 1758; Viscount Stopford, 1762; Baron Saltersford (GB), 1796; Captain of the Yeoman of the Guard (Deputy Chief Whip, House of Lords), since 2016; *b* 19 March 1954; *s* of 8th Earl of Courtown, OBE, TD, DL, and Patricia, 3rd *d* of Harry S. Winthrop, Auckland, NZ; *S* father, 1975; *m* 1985, Elisabeth, *yr d* of I. R. Dunnett, Broad Campden, Glos; one *s* two *d. Educ:* Eton College; Berkshire Coll. of Agriculture; RAC, Cirencester. A Lord in Waiting (Govt Whip), 1995–97, 2015–16; an Opposition Whip, 1997–2000; elected Mem., H of L, 1999. *Heir: s* Viscount Stopford, *qv. Address:* House of Lords, SW1A 0PW.
 *See also* Lady E. C. Godsal.

**COURTS, Robert Alexander;** MP (C) Witney, since Oct. 2016; *b* 21 Oct. 1978; *s* of Ian and Sheila Courts; *m* 2011, Kathryn Lewis; one *s. Educ:* Berkhamsted Sch.; Univ. of Sheffield (LLB). Called to the Bar, Lincoln's Inn, 2003; in practice as barrister, specialising in crime, personal injury and clin. negligence, 2003–16. Pegasus Schol., Crown Law Office, Wellington, NZ, 2009. Mem. (C), W Oxon DC, 2014–17 (Cabinet Mem. for Housing and Communities, 2015; Dep. Leader, 2016–17). *Address:* House of Commons, SW1A 0AA.

**COUSE, Philip Edward,** FCA; Partner, Coopers & Lybrand, 1966–91; *b* 24 March 1936; *s* of Oliver and Marion Couse; *m* 1st (marr. diss. 1973); two *s* one *d*; 2nd, Carol Ann Johannessen Pruitt; one step *d. Educ:* Uppingham Sch.; Hackley Sch., USA. Qualified as Chartered Accountant, 1961. Birmingham Chartered Accountants' Students Society: Sec., 1958–59; Chm., 1967–69; Pres., 1977–78; Birmingham and West Midlands Soc. of Chartered Accountants: Mem. Cttee, 1974–92, Pres., 1982–83; Institute of Chartered Accountants: Mem. Council, 1978–92; Chm. of various cttees; Pres., 1989–90; Chartered Accountants' Dining Club: Mem. Cttee, 1981–92, Treas., 1985–89, Pres., 1989–91. Director: Birmingham Heartlands and Solihull Hosp. NHS Trust, 1991–2000; William King Ltd, 1993–99. Part-time Comr, Friendly Socs Commn, 1992–97. Dir, Hillstone Sch. Trust, Malvern, 1971–86; Chairman: Edgbaston C of E Coll. for Girls, 1982–88; Birmingham Rep. Theatre Foundn, 1991–96; Dir, Birmingham Rep. Th., 1991–96; Chm., Birmingham Dio. Bd of Finance, 1992–2000, and Mem. of various cttees; Mem., C of E Pensions Bd, 1998–99. Mem., Council of Management, Ironbridge Heritage Foundn, 1991–2005 (Treas., 1991–2003); Trustee, Birmingham Eye Foundn, 1981–91 (Treas., 1981–91). Liveryman, Co. of Chartered Accountants in England and Wales, 1977–2014 (Mem., Court, 1987–90). *Recreations:* music, horse racing, woodwork, theatre going. *Address:* 23 Frederick Road, Edgbaston, Birmingham B15 1JN; 715 Greenwood Manor Circle, West Melbourne, FL 32904, USA.

**COUSINS, Air Chief Marshal Sir David,** KCB 1996 (CB 1991); AFC 1980; Air Member for Personnel, and Air Officer Commanding-in-Chief, Personnel and Training Command, 1995–98; *b* 20 Jan. 1942; *s* of late Peter and Irene Cousins; *m* 1st, 1966, Mary Edith McMurray (marr. diss. 2003); two *s* one *d*; 2nd, 2006, Maggie Broadbent. *Educ:* St Edward's Coll., Malta; Prince Rupert's Sch., Wilhelmshaven; RAF College; Open Univ. (BA 1992). 92 Sqn (Lightnings), 1965–68; ADC to CAS, 1968–70; 15 Sqn (Buccaneers), 1970–73; Air Plans, HQ RAF Germany, 1973; RAF Staff Coll., 1974; Staff Officer to ACAS (OR), 1975–77; OC 16 Sqn (Buccaneers), 1977–80; Central Trials and Tactics Orgn, 1980; PSO to CAS, 1981–83; OC RAF Laarbruch, 1983–85; RCDS 1986; Dir, Air Offensive, MoD, 1987–89; Dir Gen. Aircraft 2, MoD (PE), 1989–91; AOC and Comdt, RAF Coll. Cranwell, 1992–94; AOC No 38 Gp, and SASO Strike Comd, 1994–95. Controller, RAF Benevolent Fund, 1998–2006. ADC to the Queen, 1984–85. *Recreations:* dinghy sailing, golf, horology. *Clubs:* Royal Air Force; Henley Golf.

**COUSINS, James Mackay;** *b* 23 Feb. 1944; *m*; two *s*, and one step *s* one step *d. Educ:* New Coll., Oxford (Schol.); London School of Economics. Contract Researcher, and Lectr in job markets, Commn on Industrial Relns and Depts of Employment and the Environment. Member: Wallsend Borough Council, 1969–73; Tyne and Wear County Council, 1973–86 (Dep. Leader, 1981–86). MP (Lab) Newcastle upon Tyne Central, 1987–2010. Mem., Treasury Select Cttee, 1997–2010.

**COUSINS, Jeremy Vincent;** QC 1999; a Recorder, since 2000; *b* 25 Feb. 1955; *s* of Eric Cousins and Joyce Cousins; *m* 1993, Jane Owens; two *s* one *d. Educ:* Oxford Sch.; Warwick Univ. Called to the Bar, Middle Temple, 1977; in practice at the Bar, 1977–; an Asst Recorder, 1996–2000; a Dep. High Ct Judge, 2007–. Chm., Midland Chancery and Commercial Bar Assoc., 2002–05. *Publications:* (consultant ed.) Third Party Litigation Funding, 2014. *Recreations:* walking in Scotland, travelling in Europe. *Address:* Radcliffe Chambers, 11 New Square, Lincoln's Inn, WC2A 3QB.

**COUSSINS, Baroness** *cr* 2007 (Life Peer), of Whitehall Park in the London Borough of Islington; **Jean Elizabeth Coussins;** independent consultant on corporate responsibility, since 2006; *b* 26 Oct. 1950; *d* of Walter Leonard Coussins and Jessica Coussins (*née* Hughes); *m* 1976, Roger Hamilton (marr. diss. 1985); one *s* one *d*; one *d. Educ:* Godolphin and Latymer Girls' Sch.; Newnham Coll., Cambridge (BA (Medieval and Modern Langs) 1973; MA 1976; Hon. Fellow, 2014). Sec., UN Youth and Student Assoc., 1973–75; Women's Rights Officer, NCCL, 1975–80; Dep. Dir, Child Poverty Action Gp, 1980–83; Sen. Educn Officer, ILEA, 1983–88; Dir, Social Policy Div., 1988–94, Equality Assurance Div., 1994–96, CRE; Chief Exec., Portman Gp, 1996–2006. Non-exec. Dir and Council Mem., ASA, 2003–09. Founder Mem. and Chm., Maternity Alliance, 1980–81. Member: Crime Prevention Panel, Foresight Prog., DTI, 2000–03; Scottish Ministerial Adv. Cttee on Alcohol Problems, 2001–06; Adv. Gp on alcohol harm reduction, PM's Strategy Unit, 2003–04; Expert Taskforce on Consumers and Markets, DoH, 2004. Ind. Mem. Adv. Council, BBFC, 2002–05; Comr, Better Regulation Commn, 2004–07. Co-Chm., All-Party Parly Gp on Modern Langs, 2016– (Chm., 2008–16); Vice-Chair, All-Party Parly Gp on UN, on British Council; Member: H of L Information Cttee, 2007–12; Sub-Cttee on External Affairs, H of L EU Select Cttee, 2013–; H of L Select Cttee on Internat. Relns, 2016–. Mem., Corporate Responsibility Bd (formerly Adv. Panel on Corporate Responsibility), Camelot Gp, 2011–16. Trustee: Inst. for Citizenship, 1994–99; Drinkaware Trust, 2001–06; Alcohol Educn and Res. Council, 2004–07; President: Money Advice Trust, 2010–; Speak to the Future, 2015–. Parent Gov., Ashmount Sch., 1980s; Associate Fellow and Mem. Governing Body, Newnham Coll., Cambridge, 2002–05; Mem., Bd Govs, Channing Sch., 2007–12. Pres., Peru Support Gp, 2012–. Patron, On the Shoulders of Giants Th. Co.; Vice-Patron, British Sch. of Osteopathy. Hon. Fellow: Chartered Inst. of Linguists, 2010 (Vice-Pres., 2012–); UCL, 2010. Hon. Dr Open, 2019. President's Medal, British Acad., 2013. *Publications:* Taking Liberties, 1978; (jtly) Shattering Illusions: West Indians in British politics, 1986; (contrib.) Policing Black People, 1990; pamphlets and booklets on equality and maternity rights. *Recreations:* family, travel, food, swimming, football, crosswords. *Address:* House of Lords, SW1A 0PW. *T:* (020) 7219 5353. *E:* coussinsj@parliament.uk. *Club:* Fulham Football.

**COUSSIOS, Prof. Constantin-Cassios,** PhD; Professor of Biomedical Engineering, since 2011, and Director, Institute of Biomedical Engineering, since 2016, University of Oxford; Fellow of Magdalen College, Oxford, since 2004; *b* Athens, 21 March 1977; *s* of Dimitrios Coussios and Elissabet Coussiou; *m* 2005, Agathoniki Trigoni; three *s. Educ:* Pembroke Coll., Cambridge (BA 1998; MEng 1998; MA 2001; PhD 2002). Engrg undergrad. trainee, Balfour Beatty Civil Engrg Ltd, 1995; engrg intern, Centre d'Essais Aéronautique de Toulouse, 1995; military service, Hellenic Air Force, 1997 and 1998; Post-doctoral Res. Fellow, Dept of Biomed. Engrg, Univ. of Cincinnati, 2001–02; Lectr and Res. Associate, Dept of Aerospace and Mechanical Engrg, Boston Univ., 2002–03; University of Oxford: Lectr in Biomed. Engrg, Dept of Engrg Sci., 2004–06; Founder and Hd, Biomed. Ultrasonics, Biotherapy and Biopharmaceuticals Lab., Oxford Inst. of Biomed. Engrg, 2004–; Bellhouse Foundn Reader in Biomed. Engrg, 2006–10; Founder and Dir, Oxford Centre for Drug Delivery Devices, 2014–. Tech. Dir, OrganOx Ltd, 2008–; Co-founder, OxSonics Ltd, 2014–. Sec. Gen. and Mem. Bd, Internat. Soc. for Therapeutic Ultrasound, 2006–10. Fellow, Acoustical Soc. of Amer., 2009 (F. V. Hunt Postdoctoral Fellow, 2002–03; R. Bruce Lindsay Award, 2012). Hamilton Prize, Univ. of Cambridge, 2001; Young Person's Award for Innovation in Acoustical Engrg, Inst. of Acoustics, 2007; Frederic Lizzi Early Career Award, Internat. Soc. for Therapeutic Ultrasound, 2012. *Publications:* (contrib.) Methods in Engineering, 2011; articles in learned jls. *Recreations:* piano, basketball, tennis. *Address:* Institute of Biomedical Engineering, Old Road Campus Research Building, Headington, Oxford OX3 7DQ. *T:* (01865) 617727, *Fax:* (01865) 617728. *E:* constantin.coussios@eng.ox.ac.uk.

**COUTTIE,** family name of **Baroness Couttie.**

**COUTTIE, Baroness** *cr* 2016 (Life Peer), of Downe in the County of Kent; **Philippa Marion Couttie;** a Baroness in Waiting (Government Whip), since 2017; *b* 25 Sept. 1962; *d* of late James Kenneth Roe and of Dame Marion Audrey Roe, *qv; m* 2002, Stephen Couttie; one *s* one *d. Educ:* Roedean Sch.; St Andrews Univ. (BSc Hons). Co-Founder, Wearne Public Relations, 1987–90; Chief Exec., Cornerstone Communications, 1990–92; Proprietor and CEO, PR Consultants, 1992–99; Associate Dir, J. Henry Schroder, 1999–2000; Dir, Citigroup Securitisation Div., 2000–06. Westminster City Council: Mem. (C), 2006–18 (Leader, 2012–17); Member: Children's Services Overview and Scrutiny Cttee, 2006–07; Planning and City Develt Cttee, 2006–07; Sch. Govs Appt Cttee, 2007–08; Resources and Corp. Services Overview and Scrutiny Cttee, 2007–08; Dep. Cabinet Member, Children's Services, 2007–08; Cabinet Member: for Housing, 2008–11; for Strategic Finance, 2011–12. Conservative Party: Hd, Educn Team, Private Finance Panel, 1997–99; Hd, Treasury Team, James Cttee, 2004–05; Chm., Public Sector Efficiency subgp, Econ. Competitive Policy Gp, 2006–07; Advr on Benefit Caps to DWP, 2011–. Member: Polling and Digital Media Select Cttee, 2017–18; Work and Pensions Gp, H of L, 2018–. Deputy Leader: LGA, 2014– (Mem. Exec., Cons. Gp, 2013–17); London Councils Exec., 2012–17 (Lead, Public Sector Reform and Devolution, 2014–17). Chairman: Westminster Health and Wellbeing Bd, 2012–13; West End Partnership, 2013–17. Member: London Crime Reduction Bd, 2012–14; Bd, Royal Parks, 2012–17; Bd, London LEP, 2014–16; London Infrastructure Delivery Bd, 2014–16. Non-exec. Dir, Mitie Gp plc, 2017–. Non-exec. Sen. Advr, FTI Consulting, 2014–17. Mem. Council, Imperial Coll. London, 2006–14 (Chm. Audit Cttee, 2006–14). Vice Chm., London Events, MacMillan Cancer Support, 2004–11; Patron, Breast Cancer Haven, 2004–11. *Recreations:* ski-ing, travelling, reading, ancient history, antiquities, opera. *Address:* House of Lords, SW1A 0PW.

**COUTTS;** *see* Money-Coutts, family name of Baron Latymer.

**COUTTS, Anne Jane,** MEd; Principal, Canberra Girls' Grammar School, 2011–18; *b* Watford, 9 April 1956; *d* of Alistair and Mysie Sutherland; *m* 1978, Rt Rev. Ian Alexander Coutts (*see* Bishop of Bunbury); two *d. Educ:* King's High Sch., Warwick; Aspley Grammar Sch.; Univ. of Warwick (BSc, PGCE, MEd). Res. Asst, Nuffield Inst. for Med. Res. and Oxford Inst. of Virol., 1978–80; Teacher of Chemistry: Coventry LEA, 1981–83; Hereford and Worcester LEA, 1983–86; Hd of Gen. Studies, Trent Coll., 1986–88; Dep. Hd, then Actg Hd, Edgbaston Coll. of Educn, 1988–92; Head: Eothen Sch., Caterham, 1992–95; Sutton High Sch., 1995–2003; Headington Sch., 2003–10. Mem., QCDA (formerly QCA) Adv. Gp for Res. in Assessment and Qualifications Cttee, HMC Council, 2007–12. *Recreations:* photography, singing, saxophone, cooking, reading.

**COUTTS, Herbert,** MBE 2008; FSAScot; FMA; Director of Culture and Leisure (formerly of Recreation), City of Edinburgh Council, 2001–07; *b* 9 March 1944; *s* of late Herbert and Agnes Coutts, Dundee; *m* 1970, Angela Elizabeth Mason Smith; one *s* three *d. Educ:* Morgan Acad., Dundee. FSAScot 1965; AMA 1970, FMA 1976. Asst Keeper of Antiquities and Bygones, Dundee City Museums, 1965–68, Keeper, 1968–71; Supt, Edinburgh City Museums, 1971–73; City Curator, City of Edinburgh Museums and Art Galls, 1973–96; City of Edinburgh Council: Hd of Museums and Galls, 1996–97; Hd of Heritage and Arts, 1997–99; Dir of Recreation, 1999–2001. Vice Pres., Museums Assts Gp, 1967–70; Member: Bd, Scottish Museums Council, 1971–74, and 1986–88; Govt Cttee on Future of Scotland's Nat. Museums and Galleries, 1979–80 (report pub. 1981); Bd, Museums Trng Inst., 1995–2000; Bd, Cultural Heritage NTO, 2000–04; Bd of Trustees, Nat. Galleries of Scotland, 2007–11. Member, Council: Museums Assoc., 1977–78, 1987–88; Soc. of Antiquaries of Scotland, 1981–82; Museums Advr, COSLA Arts and Recreation Cttee, 1985–90, 1995–99. Member: Paxton House Trust, 1988–2002, 2006–; E Lothian Community Develt Trust, 1989–2010; Scottish Catholic Heritage Commn, 2006–14; Bd, Order of Malta Dial-a-Journey Trust, 2007–17 (Chm., 2011–17) (Mem. Bd, 2010–16, Chm., 2011–16, Wheelchair Vehicle Enterprise Ltd); Dunbar Community Council, 2007–; Bd, Dunbar Community Develt Co., 2007–; Bd, Battle of Prestonpans Heritage Trust, 2007– (Jt Chm., 2017–). Trustee, Scottish Catholic Heritage Collections Trust, 2011–; Chm., Scottish Battlefields Trust, 2015–. External Examr, St Andrews Univ., 1993–97. Building Projects: City of Edinburgh Art Centre (opened 1980); Museum of Childhood Extension (opened 1986); People's Story Museum (opened 1989); City of Edinburgh Art Centre Extension (opened 1992); Makars' Court, Scotland's Poets' Corner (opened 1998); Scott Monument Restoration (completed 1999); Usher Hall Renovation (completed 2000). Exhibitions at City of Edinburgh Art Centre: The Emperor's Warriors, 1985; Gold of the Pharaohs, 1988; Gold of Peru, 1990; Golden Warriors of the Ukrainian Steppes, 1993; Star Trek—The Exhibition, 1995; Quest for a Pirate, 1996; Gateway to the Silk Road, 1996. Contested (Lab) Angus South, 1970. Founding Fellow, Inst. of Contemp. Scotland, 1999. SBStJ 1977; KM 2009. Bailie in the Barony of Dolphinstoun, 2008–. *Publications:* (jtly) Broughty Castle, 1970; Ancient Monuments of Tayside, 1970; Tayside Before History, 1971; (with Robin Hill) Edinburgh Crafts, 1974; Aince a Bailie, Aye a Bailie, 1974; Edinburgh: an illustrated history, 1975; (ed) Amber in Polish History, 1978; (with John Heyes) Museum of Childhood, 1980; Huntly House, 1980; Lady Stair's House, 1980; (ed) The Emperor's Warriors, 1985; (ed) Gold of the Pharaohs, 1988; The Pharaoh's Gold Mask, 1988; (ed) Dinosaurs Alive, 1990; (ed) Gold of Peru, 1990; (ed) Golden Warriors of the Ukrainian Steppes, 1993; (ed) Star Trek—The Exhibition, 1995; (ed) Gateway to the Silk Road, 1996; (ed) Quest for a Pirate, 1996; (ed) Faster, Higher, Stronger, 1997; exhibn catalogues; contrib. Museums Jl and archaeol jls. *Recreations:* relaxing with family, gardening, going to the opera, writing, reading, walking. *Address:* Kirkhill House, Queen's Road, Dunbar, East Lothian EH42 1LN. *T:* (01368) 863113.

**COUTTS, Rt Rev. Ian Alexander;** *see* Bunbury, Bishop of.

**COUTTS, Sir Russell,** KNZM 2009 (DCNZM 2000); CBE 1995 (MBE 1985); yachtsman; *b* 1 March 1962; *s* of late Allan and Beverley Coutts; *m* 1999, Jennifer Little; three *s* one *d. Educ:* Auckland Univ. (BEng). Gold Medal, Finn Cl., Olympic Games, LA,

1984; World Champion, Match Racing, 1992, 1993 and 1996; ranked No 1, Match Racing Circuit, 1994; winner, Brut Sailing series, 1996; Helmsman: Admiral's Cup winner, Pinta, 1993; America's Cup winners, Black Magic, San Diego, 1995 and Team NZ, Auckland, 2000; World Title, S Australia, 2001; 1st Swedish Match Cup, Marstrand, 2001; winner, World Title, Farr 40, 2001 and 2006; Skipper and Exec. Dir, America's Cup winner, Alinghi Team, Switzerland, 2003; designer, new boat, RC 44, 2005; winner, World Title, TP 52, 2007; CEO, Oracle Team USA (formerly BMW Oracle Racing), 2008 (winner, America's Cup in Yacht USA, 2010); Chief Executive: America's Cup Event Authy, 2014–17; SailGP, 2018–. Yachtsman of the Year, NZ, 1984; Sperry World Sailor of the Year, 1995; Trophée Fabergé, Match Racing, 1996. *Publications*: The Course to Victory, 1996; America's Cup 2000, 1999; Challenge 2000: the race to win the America's Cup, 1999. *Recreation*: golf. *Clubs*: Société Nautique de Genève; New York Yacht; Royal New Zealand Yacht; North Shore Golf, Titirangi Golf (Auckland).

**COUTTS, William Walter B.;** *see* Burdett-Coutts.

**COUTURIER, Hernán Antonio;** Ambassador of Peru to the Court of St James's, 2010–11; *b* 9 Dec. 1943; *s* of Hernán Couturier and Josefina Mariátegui; *m* 1996, Sonia Labarthe; two *s* two *d*. *Educ*: Champagnat Marist Sch., Peru; Leoncio Prado Military Sch.; Catholic Univ. of Peru; San Marcos Univ. of Peru; Diplomatic Acad. of Peru (Bachelor Internat. Relns). Joined Min. of Foreign Affairs as Third Sec., 1968; Third Sec., 1968, Chile, 1968; Second Sec., Perm. Mission to OAS, 1971; Second, then First Sec., USA, 1973–74; First Sec., Foreign Policy Under-Secretariat, 1975, Hd, S Amer. Dept of Pol and Diplomatic Div., 1976, Min. of Foreign Affairs; First Sec., then Counsellor, Colombia, 1977–80; Counsellor, Perm. Mission to UN, 1980; Minister Counsellor, Dep. Perm. Rep. to UN, 1981; Dir, 1984–86, Dir Gen., 1986–87, Policy Planning, Min. of Foreign Affairs; Ambassador to Zimbabwe, 1987–89; Consul Gen., NY, 1989–92; Dir Gen. for Special Pol Affairs, 1993, for Pol Affairs, 1994, Sec.-Gen., 1994, Min. of Foreign Affairs; Ambassador to Canada, 1994–2000; Nat. Dir for Border Develt and Borderlines, 2000, Under-Sec. for Multilateral and Special Affairs, 2000–01, Min. of Foreign Affairs; Ambassador to Bolivia, 2001–04, to Brazil, 2004–07, and non-resident to Guyana, 2005–07; Ministry of Foreign Affairs: Under-Sec. for Eur. Affairs, 2007–08; Gen. Co-ordinator, Latin Amer., Caribbean–EU V Summit, 2007; Under-Sec. for Amer. Affairs, 2009–10. Mem., Peruvian Soc. of Internat. Law, 1977; Associated Mem., Peruvian Centre for Internat. Studies, 1993. Professor: Diplomatic Acad. of Peru, 1975–76, 1985–86, 2009–10; San Martin de Porres Univ., Peru, 2008; Peruvian Univ. of Applied Scis, 2009–10; lectr on internat. issues in academic, professional and mil. instns. Mem. of Soc. of Founders of Independence of Peru, 1993. Officer: Orden Bernardo O'Higgins (Chile), 1975; Orden Rio Branco (Brazil), 1976; Grand Cross: Orden de San Carlos (Colombia), 1979; Orden, Libertador Simón Bolívar (Bolivia), 1995; Orden del Cóndor de los Andes (Bolivia), 2004; Orden al Mérito por Servicios Distinguidos (Peru), 2004; Orden Cruzeiro do Sul (Brazil), 2007; Orden del Mérito Civil (Spain), 2008; Orden José Gregorio Paz Soldán (Peru), 2008. *Publications*: articles, monographs and lectures on foreign policy issues in newspapers and mags. *Recreations*: tennis, cycling, hunting, reading. *Clubs*: Travellers; Tennis Las Terrazas, Los Inkas Golf (Lima).

**COUZENS, Air Vice-Marshal David Cyril,** CEng, FIMechE, FRAeS; Senior Directing Staff (Air), Royal College of Defence Studies, 2003–04; *b* 15 Oct. 1949; *s* of Cyril Couzens and Joyce Couzens (*née* Walker); *m* 1977, Deborah Cawse; one *s* one *d*. *Educ*: Ecclesbourne Sch.; Churchill Coll., Cambridge (MA); Open Univ. Business Sch. (MBA); Loughborough Univ. (Postgrad. Dip). CEng 1979; FIMechE 1991; FRAeS 1995. Joined Royal Air Force, 1968: initial and professional trng, 1968–72; practical aircraft/weapon system appts, 1972–88; personnel mgt, 1988–89; Gp Captain 1990; Superintendent of Armament, 1990–91; Dep. Dir Support Policy (Op. Requirements) (RAF), MoD Policy, 1991–94; rcds 1994; Air Cdre 1995; Air Cdre, CIS, HQ Strike Comd, 1995–97; Dir, Logistic Inf. Strategy (RAF), MoD, 1997–98; AO, Logistic Inf. Strategy and Industrial Interface Study, MoD, 1998–99; Air Vice-Marshal 1999; Dir Gen., Defence Logistics (Communications and Inf. Systems), 1999–2001, Defence Logistics Capability, 2001–02, MoD; COS to Surgeon Gen., MoD, 2002–03. Pres., RAeS, 2010–11 (Mem. Council, 2006–12; Chm., Professional Standards Bd, 2006–09); Mem. Bd, Engrg Council, 2008–15. Trustee, RAF Benevolent Fund, 2003–04, 2006–14. President: RAF Rugby League, 1999–2004; Combined Services Rugby League, 2002–04. *Recreations*: hill-walking, gardening, music. *Club*: Royal Air Force (Chm., 2003–04).

**COVE, Sarah Louise; Her Honour Judge Cove;** a Circuit Judge, since 2019; *b* London, 1969; *d* of John Cove and Susanne Cove. *Educ*: Queen Mary and Westfield Coll., Univ. of London (LLB 1990); Coll. of Law, London. Admitted a solicitor, 1993; a Dep. District Judge, 2010–16; a District Judge, 2016–19.

**COVENEY, Michael William;** theatre critic and author; *b* 24 July 1948; *s* of William Coveney and Violet Amy Coveney (*née* Perry); *m* 1977, Susan Monica Hyman; one *s*. *Educ*: St Ignatius College, London; Worcester College, Oxford. Editor, Plays and Players, 1975–78; theatre critic: Financial Times, 1981–89; The Observer, 1990–97; Daily Mail, 1997–2004. *Publications*: The Citz, 1990; Maggie Smith, 1992; The Aisle is Full of Noises, 1994; (with Robert Stephens) Knight Errant: memoirs of a vagabond actor, 1995; The World According to Mike Leigh, 1996; Cats on a Chandelier: the Andrew Lloyd Webber story, 1999; Ken Campbell: the great caper, 2011; Maggie Smith: a biography, 2015; (with Peter Dazeley) London Theatres, 2017. *Recreations*: music, running, travel. *Address*: c/o United Agents, 12–26 Lexington Street, W1F 0LE.

**COVENTRY,** family name of Earl of Coventry.

**COVENTRY,** 13th Earl of, *cr* 1697; **George William Coventry;** Viscount Deerhurst 1697; *b* 5 Oct. 1939; *s* of Comdr Cecil Dick Bluett Coventry, DSC, RD, RNR; *S* kinsman, 2004; *m* 1965, Gillian Frances, *d* of F. W. R. Randall; one *d*. *Educ*: Prince of Wales Sch., Nairobi. *Heir*: *nephew* David Duncan Sherwood Coventry [*b* 5 March 1973; *m* 2003, Sarah Sadie Bishop; one *s*].

**COVENTRY, Bishop of,** since 2008; **Rt Rev. Dr Christopher John Cocksworth;** *b* 12 Jan. 1959; *s* of Stanley John Cocksworth and Auriol Gwyneth Cocksworth; *m* 1979, Charlotte Mary Pytches; five *s*. *Educ*: Manchester Univ. (BA (1st cl. Hons) Theol., 1980; PhD 1989); Didsbury Sch. of Educn, Manchester Poly. (PGCE 1981); St John's Theol Coll., Nottingham. Teacher and House Tutor, King Edward's Sch., Witley, Surrey, 1981–84; doctoral res. student, 1986–88. Ordained deacon, 1988, priest, 1989; Asst Curate, Christ Church, Epsom, 1988–92; Chaplain, RHBNC, Univ. of London, 1992–97; Dir, STETS, 1997–2001; Principal, Ridley Hall, Cambridge, 2001–08. Hon. Canon, Guildford Cathedral, 2000–01, now Canon Emeritus. Mem., C of E Liturgical Commn, 1996–2006; Jt Chair, Jt Implementation Commn of Anglican-Methodist Covenant, 2009–14; Chair, Co-ordinating Gp for Episcopal Teaching Document on Marriage and Sexuality, 2017–; Chairman: C of E Faith and Order Commn, 2012–; Reformation 500th Anniversary Planning Gp, 2015–; Member: House of Bps' Standing Cttee, 2012–; Ct of Ecclesiastical Causes Reserved, 2015–. Mem., H of L, 2013–. Hon. DD Royal Holloway, Univ. of London, 2009. *Publications*: Evangelical Eucharistic Thought in the Church of England, 1993; (with Paul Roberts) Renewing Daily Prayer, 1993; (with Alan Wilkinson) An Anglican Companion, 1996, 2nd edn 2001; Holy, Holy, Holy: worshipping the Trinitarian God, 1997; Prayer and the Departed, 1997; (with Jeremy Fletcher) The Spirit and Liturgy, 1998; (with Rosalind Brown) Being a Priest Today, 2002, 2nd edn 2006; Wisdom: the Spirit's gift, 2003; Holding Together: Gospel, Church and Spirit, 2008; Seeing Jesus and Being Seen by Him, 2014; various articles in bks and learned jls. *Recreations*: hill-walking, cycling, swimming, film watching, organic fruit and vegetable gardening. *Address*: Bishop's House, 23 Davenport Road, Coventry CV5 6PW. *T*: (024) 7667 2244.

**COVENTRY, Dean of;** *see* Witcombe, Very Rev. J. J.

**COVENTRY, Archdeacon of;** *see* Field, Ven. S. E.

**COVEY, Donna May,** CBE 2014; Chief Executive, Against Violence and Abuse, since 2014; Executive Chair, IRIS Interventions, since 2017; *b* 20 June 1961; *d* of Mrs Cynthia Covey. *Educ*: Univ. of Warwick (BSc); Birkbeck Coll., London (Postgrad. Dip. Mgt). Nat. Officer, GMB, 1988–98; Dir, Assoc. of CHCs for England and Wales, 1998–2001; Chief Executive: Nat. Asthma Campaign, subseq. Asthma UK, 2001–07; Refugee Council, 2007–12. Chm., London Food Commn, 1986–87; Vice Chm., Wandsworth CHC, 1987–88. Member: Gen. Council, TUC, 1988–98; Nat. Women's Cttee, Labour Party, 1992–98; Migration Impacts Forum, 2007–09. Mem. Bd, Eur. Fedn of Allergy and Airway Diseases Patients Assocs, 2003–07 (Vice-Pres. 2006–07); Trustee: Long Term Conditions Alliance, 2005–07; Equality and Diversity Forum, 2010–12; Counterpoints Arts, 2012–. FRSA. *Publications*: contributed to: Waiting for Change, 1986; Visions of Primary Care, 1999; NHS Frontline: visions for 2010, 2000; A Practical Guide to Primary Care Groups and Trusts, 2001. *Recreations*: rambling, murder mysteries, Tate Gallery, yoga. *E*: donna_covey@hotmail.com.

**COVILLE, Air Marshal Sir Christopher (Charles Cotton),** KCB 2000 (CB 1995); Chairman, C4 Defence & Security Ltd, since 2010; *b* 2 June 1945; *s* of Henry and Anna Coville; *m* 1967, Irene Johnson; one *s* two *d*. *Educ*: De La Salle Grammar Sch., Liverpool; RAF Coll., Cranwell. BA Open. Lightning Pilot and Instructor, 1969–73; Phantom Pilot and Instructor, 1973–78; Central Tactics and Trials Orgn, 1978–80; Personal Staff Officer to UK Mil. Rep., Brussels, 1981–83; OC Ops Wing, RAF Stanley, 1983; OC 111 Fighter Sqn, 1983–85; Gp Capt. Air, HQ 11 Fighter Group, 1985–86; OC RAF Coningsby, 1986–88; RCDS 1989; Air Cdre Flying Training, HQ RAF Support Command, 1990–92; AO Trng and AOC Trng Gp, 1992–94; Chief Exec., Trng Gp Defence Agency, Apr.–Sept. 1994; ACDS, Op. Requirements (Air), 1994–98; Dep. C-in-C, AFCENT, 1998–2000; Dep. C-in-C, AFNORTH, 2000–01; Air Mem. for Personnel, and C-in-C, PTC, 2001–03. Chairman: Westland Helicopters, 2005–11; Forces Pension Soc., 2011–14; Sen. Defence and Security Advr, EMC UK, 2007–15; Sen. Defence Advr, Secure Cloud Plus, 2019–; non-exec. Dir, Arizona Gp Ltd, 2011–12. President: RAF Microlight Assoc., 1992–2000; RAF Football Assoc., 1996–2002; Vice-Pres., RAFA, 2001–. FCIPD (FITD 1993); FRAeS 1994. *Recreations*: gliding, fishing. *Clubs*: Royal Air Force, Mosimann's.

**COVINGTON, Nicholas;** Director, Office of Manpower Economics, 1986–89; *b* 9 June 1929; *s* of late Cyril Tim Covington and Margaret Joan (*née* Bray); *m* 1st, 1953, Pat Sillitoe; one *s* two *d*; 2nd, 1983, Kathy Hegarty. *Educ*: Cranleigh Sch.; Oriel Coll., Oxford. RAF, 1947–49; TA Commn, 1952. Metal Box Co. Ltd, South Africa, 1952–57; Gen. Manager and Dir, Garnier & Co. Ltd, 1957–66; entered Min. of Labour, 1966; Asst Sec., 1971; Industrial Relns Div., Dept of Employment, 1976–86. *Address*: Dovecote House, Lower Slaughter, near Cheltenham, Glos GL54 2HY.

**COWAN, Annella Marie;** Sheriff of Grampian, Highland and Islands at Aberdeen, 1997–2016; *b* 14 Nov. 1953; *m* 1979, James Temple Cowan (*marr*. diss. 1995). *Educ*: Elgin Acad.; Edinburgh Univ. (LLB 1976; MSc 1984). Admitted Solicitor, 1978; Procurator Fiscal Depute, 1978–86; seconded to Scottish Law Commn, 1984–86; admitted Faculty of Advocates, 1987; Temp. Sheriff, 1991; Sheriff of Tayside, Central and Fife at Stirling, 1993–97. *Recreations*: equestrianism, foreign travel, painting.

**COWAN, Dr George Osborne,** OBE 1986; FRCP, FRCPE; Medical Director, Joint Committee on Higher Medical Training, Royal Colleges of Physicians of UK, 2001–05; *b* 5 Sept. 1939; *s* of late John Jardine Cowan and Marion Ramsay Cowan (*née* Corrie); *m* 1981, Beatrice Mary Hill, MA, MPhil, MLitt, *d* of late Leonard Charles Hill, OBE, DSC, FRGS and Joyce (*née* Snelus). *Educ*: Merchiston Castle Sch., Edinburgh; Univ. of St Andrews (MB ChB 1963); Open Univ. (Dip. Music, 2004); BA 1st Cl. Hons Humanities with Music, 2007). MRCPE 1967, FRCPE 1978; DTM&H 1968; MRCP 1967, FRCP 1983. Commissioned RAMC, 1962; served Australia, Hong Kong, Malaysia, Singapore, Nepal, The Gambia, Germany and NI; Consultant Physician in Army Hosps, 1973–96; Prof. of Mil. Medicine, RAMC, 1987–92; Dir of Army Medicine, 1992–93; Comdt and Post-Grad. Dean, Royal Army Med. Coll., 1993–96; QHP 1992–96; retired in rank of Maj.-Gen., 1996. Dean of Postgrad. Medicine, Univ. of London (N Thames) (formerly N Thames (E) Region), 1996–2001. Hon. Sen. Lectr, Bute Med. Sch., subseq. Sch. of Med. and Biol Scis, Univ. of St Andrews, 2008–14. Cohen Lectr, Univ. of Liverpool, 1991; Grundy Lectr (and Medal), RCP and RAMC, 2013. Pres., RSTM&H, 1995–97 (Vice-Pres., 1993–95). Hon. FRCPI 2003; Hon. FRCPGlas 2005; Hon. Life Fellow, Soc. for Acute Medicine, 2011. MD *hc* St Andrews, 2008. Mitchiner Medal, RCS, 1992. OStJ 1994. *Publications*: (ed) Atlas of Medical Helminthology and Protozoology, 3rd edn, 1991; (with B. J. Heap) Clinical Tropical Medicine, 1993; (with N. R. H. Burgess) Atlas of Medical Entomology, 1993; The Most Fatal Distemper: typhus in history, 2016. *Recreations*: golf, music, medical history. *Clubs*: Army and Navy; Royal & Ancient Golf (St Andrews).

**COWAN, Maj. Gen. James Michael,** CBE 2013 (OBE 2005; MBE 1999); DSO 2010; Chief Executive, Halo Trust, since 2015; *b* Tidworth, Wilts, 28 April 1964; *s* of Col Edward Cowan and Janet Cowan (*née* Spurling); *m* 1992, Hon. Mary Louise Manningham-Buller, *d* of Viscount Dilhorne, *qv*; two *s* one *d*. *Educ*: Wellington Coll.; Pembroke Coll., Oxford (MA Hons Modern Hist.); Christ's Coll., Cambridge (MPhil Internat. Relns); RMA, Sandhurst. Commnd Black Watch (Royal Highland Regt), 1987; served: Berlin, 1987–89; NI, 1989–91 (despatches 1991); Zimbabwe, 1991–92; Hong Kong, 1993–94; Army Staff Coll., 1996; MoD, 1996–99; Germany, 1999–2001; MoD, 2001–03; HCSC 2006; Iraq, 2004 and 2006–07; Afghanistan, 2009–10; MoD, 2010–12; GOC 3rd (UK) Div., 2013–15. QCVS 2007. *Recreations*: hill walking, military history. *Address*: Halo Trust, Carronfoot, Thornhill, Dumfriesshire DG3 5BF.

**COWAN, Lionel David, (Nick Cowan);** Chairman, West Lambeth Health Authority, 1982–86; *b* 18 Dec. 1929; *m* 1953, Pamela Ida, *e d* of Hubert and Winifred Williams, Totton, Hants; one *s* two *d*. *Educ*: Surbiton County Grammar Sch.; King's Coll., London (BA Hons Spanish, 1995); Univ. of Salamanca (Dip. in Hispanic Studies, 1994). CCIPD (CIPM 1979; AMIPM 1965). Served Royal Navy, 1945–61: Fleet Air Arm Aircrew (Lieut), 1953; Sen. Instr, RAN, 1958–60. Training Officer, Shoe and Allied Trades Res. Assoc., 1961–62; Perkins Engines Gp, 1962–72; Dir of Personnel, Philips Electronic and Associated Industries, 1972–78; Gp Personnel Dir, Unigate Ltd, 1978–79; Dir and Sec., Fedn of London Clearing Bank Employers, 1980–87; Personnel Dir, TSB England & Wales, 1987–89. Personnel mgt consultant, 1989–2005. Member: Employment Appeal Tribunal, 1976–2000; Editorial Panel, Industrial Relns Law Reports, 1977–; Civil Service

Arbitration Tribunal, 1979–; Central Arbitration Cttee, 1984–2000; Equal Opportunities Commn, 1988–91; NEDO Enquiry, Industrial Relns Trng for Managers, 1976, Supply and Demand for Skilled Manpower, 1977. Vice-Pres. (Employee Relations), IPM, 1977–79. Director, Oxford Univ. Business Summer Sch., 1980. *Publications:* Personnel Management and Banking, 1983; The Clearing Banks and the Trade Unions, 1984. *Recreations:* things Spanish, music and opera, bridge. *Address:* 3 Oaks Way, Ripley, Woking, Surrey GU23 6LT. *T:* (01483) 479665.

**COWAN, Robert Charles;** writer and broadcaster; *b* 14 April 1948; *s* of Maurice Bernard Cowan and Vera Cowan; *m* 1971, Georgina Gilmour; two *d. Educ:* Fern Bank Primary Sch.; Leas House Sch.; Pitman's Coll. Asst, Lewis Cranston Public Relns, 1965; Advertising Dept, Pergamon Press, 1966–68; Asst Librarian, BBC Record Liby and Concerts Mgt, 1968–69; Advertising Manager, 1970–78, Archivist, 1978–89, Boosey & Hawkes Music Publishers Ltd. Ed., Music Diary, 1982–89; contrib. 1985–, Ed., 1989–91, CD Rev. mag.; Ed., Classics mag., 1991–93; contrib., 1993–, Contributing Ed., 1999–, Gramophone; writer, The Independent, 1993–; Classic FM: co-presenter, Classic Verdict, 1992–95; presenter: Our Musical Yesterdays, 1993; Off the Record, 1996; CD Choice, 1998–2000; presenter, BBC Radio 3: CD Masters, 2001–07; The Cowan Collection, 2003–07; Radio 3 (formerly Rob Cowan) Breakfast, 2007–11; Essential Classics, 2011–17; Sunday Morning, 2011–16; Rob's Gold Standard on Saturday Classics, 2016–17; Cowan's Classics on classicfm.com, 2018–. Blog, Rob's Retro Classical, robccowan.wordpress.com. Mem., Royal Soc. of Musicians, 2014. Grammy Award, 1995. *Publications:* The Guinness Classical 1000, 1997. *Recreations:* walking, listening, reading, CD and book collecting, writing (for fun), sketching, studying the work of John Ruskin, spending time with my family. *Address:* 2 Merry Hill Mount, Bushey, Herts WD23 1DJ.

**COWAN, Ronald Jack;** MP (SNP) Inverclyde, since 2015; *b* Greenock, 6 Sept. 1959; *s* of James Clews Cowan and May Harper Cowan; one *s* two *d. Educ:* Greenock Acad. Systems Analyst, Playtex, 1978–86; IT Consultant, Campbell Lee Computer Services, 1986–2001; Man. Dir, Ronnie Cowan Solutions, 2001–15. FRSA. *Recreations:* art (appreciation), sport (watching), sleeping (with optional snoring). *Address:* House of Commons, SW1A 0AA. *E:* ronnie.cowan.mp@parliament.uk. *Club:* Greenock Wanderers Rugby Football.

**COWAN, Gen. Sir Samuel,** KCB 1997; CBE 1988 (OBE 1983); Chief of Defence Logistics, Ministry of Defence, 1998–2002; Aide-de-camp to the Queen, 2000–02; *b* 9 Oct. 1941; *s* of late Samuel Cowan and Rachel Cowan; *m* 1971, Anne Gretton; one *s* one *d. Educ:* Lisburn Technical Coll.; Open Univ. (BA 1980). Commissioned Royal Signals, 1963; CO 2 Armd Div. HQ and Signal Regt, 1980–82; Comdr Communications and Comdr 1 Signal Brigade, 1 (BR) Corps, 1985–87; Director of Public Relations (Army), 1987–88; Comdt, RMCS, 1989–91; ACDS OR (Land), 1991–94; Inspector Gen. Training, MoD, 1995–96; QMG, MoD, 1996–98. Col Comdt, Brigade of Gurkhas, 1994–2003; Master of Signals, 2003–08. President: Gurkha Bde Assoc., 2004–13; Oxfordshire Br., SSAFA (formerly SSAFA-Forces Help), 2008–; Dep. Grand Pres., Royal Commonwealth Ex-Services League, 2003–13. Trustee, Racing Welfare, 2009–13. Hon. FCIPS 2000; Hon. FCILT (Hon. FILT 2000). Hon. DSc Cranfield, 1999. *Recreations:* sport, walking. *Address:* c/o RHQ Royal Signals, Blandford Camp, Dorset DT11 8RH. *T:* (01258) 482082.

**COWANS, David;** Chief Executive, Places for People Group, since 1999; *b* 3 May 1957; *s* of Harry and Margaret Cowans; *m* 1st, 1997, Julie Brewerton (*d* 2011); one *s* two *d*; 2nd, 2016, Jane Barker. *Educ:* St Cuthbert's Grammar Sch., Newcastle upon Tyne; New Coll., Durham (Dip. Housing Studies); Birmingham Univ. (MBA). CDir 2010; FRICS 2013; MIRPM 2014. Neighbourhood Officer, Walsall MBC, 1979–82; Area Manager, Sheffield CC, 1982–86; Asst Dir of Housing, Leicester CC, 1986–88; Gen. Manager, 1988–94, Dir of Housing, 1994–97, Birmingham CC; Gp Chief Exec., N British Housing Gp, 1997–99. Mem. Exec. Council, Nat. Housing Fedn, 1998–2001. Vis. Fellow, Dept of Land Economy, Univ. of Cambridge, 2016. FRSA 2009. *Recreations:* cinema, music, my children, social history, gardening, walking, economic history, architecture and design, social media. *Address:* Galtres House, 11 Rawcliffe Lane, Clifton, York YO30 6NP. *T:* (01904) 650150. *E:* david.cowans@placesforpeople.co.uk.

**COWARD, Lt Gen. Sir Gary (Robert),** KBE 2012 (OBE 1996); CB 2008; Chairman: Redline Aviation Security Ltd, since 2013; Museum of Army Flying, since 2016; SSAFA - the Armed Forces charity, since 2017; *b* 26 Aug. 1955; *s* of Robert Vacey and Marion Avril Coward; *m* 1978, Chrissie Hamerton; one *s. Educ:* Duke of York's Royal Mil. Sch.; RMA Sandhurst. Served RA, 1974–82; transf. to AAC, 1983; OC 656 Sqdn, 1991–93; UN mil. spokesman (UNPROFOR), 1994–95; CO 1 Regt, 1996–98; Sec., Chiefs of Staff Cttee, MoD, 1998–2000; Dep. Comdr, Jt Helicopter Comd, 2000–03; Dir, Equipt Capability (Air and Littoral Manoeuvre), MoD, 2003–05; Comdr, Jt Helicopter Command, 2005–08; COS (Jt Welfare Develt), 2008–09; Chief of Materiel (Land), Defence Equipment and Support, 2009–12; Quartermaster Gen., 2009–12. Dep. Col. Comdt, AAC, 2010–. Comr, then Gov., Duke of York's Royal Military Sch., 2008–18. Vice Chm., Sandhurst Trust, 2013–19. CGIA 1988.

**COWARD, Vice Adm. Sir John (Francis),** KCB 1990; DSO 1982; Lieutenant Governor and Commander-in-Chief of Guernsey, Channel Islands, 1994–2000; *b* 11 Oct. 1937; *s* of Reginald John Coward and Isabelle (*née* Foreman); *m* 1963, Diana (*née* Taylor); two *s. Educ:* Downside; RNC, Dartmouth. Served submarines, 1959–76, i/c HMS Oracle and HMS Valiant; Naval Asst to First Sea Lord, 1978–80; i/c HMS Brilliant, 1980–82; S Atlantic, 1982; Dir, Naval Operational Requirements, 1984; Flag Officer: Sea Trng, 1987–88; Flotilla One, 1988–89; Submarines, and Comdr Submarines Eastern Atlantic, 1989–91; Comdt, RCDS, 1992–94. Rear Adm. 1987; Vice Adm. 1989; retd 1994. Mem. Bd, N. M. Rothschild (CI) Ltd, 2000–07; Chm., Luxury Brands Gp, 2001–02. Underwriting Mem. of Lloyd's, 1978–. Mem., Council, RNLI, 1998–2008. *Recreations:* sailing, gardening, cricket, golf. *Clubs:* Royal Navy of 1919, Royal Navy of 1765 and 1785; Royal Yacht Squadron.

**COWARD, Nicholas;** Chairman, England Golf Partnership, since 2016; *b* 13 Feb. 1966; *s* of John and Jane Coward; *m* 2007, Vivien Lyle; one *s* one *d. Educ:* Shrewsbury Sch.; Bristol Univ. (LLB 1989); Guildford Coll. of Law. Solicitor, Freshfields, 1990–96; Football Association: Co. Solicitor, 1996–98; Dir, Legal and Corporate Affairs, 1998–2004; Actg Chief Exec., 1998–2000 and 2002–03; Dir, Wembley Stadium, 1999–2001; Dep. Chm., A. S. Biss & Co., 2004–07; Chief Exec., British Horseracing Authy, 2007–11; Gen. Sec., Premier League, 2011–15. Chm., Sports Rights Owners Coalition, 2005–10; Director: European Professional Football Leagues, 2013–15; FA, 2014–15; Mem., UEFA Professional Football Strategy Council, 2014–. Treas., CCPR, 2004–07. *Clubs:* Ivy, MCC; Royal Cinque Ports Golf (Deal).

**COWARD, Dame Pamela (Sarah),** DBE 2003; education consultant, 2004–09; Headteacher, Middleton Technology School, 1991–2004; *b* 18 Jan. 1944; *d* of late Henry and Faith Coward; one *s*, and one step *s* one step *d. Educ:* City of Leeds Trng Coll. (Teachers' Cert. 1969); Open Univ. (BA 1979; Advanced Dip. in Mgt 1988). Manchester Univ. (Advanced Dip. in Guidance in Educn 1981). Special Needs Co-ordinator, Heywood Community Sch., 1984–88. Council Mem., Specialist Schools' Trust, 1998–2004. Chair, Altus Multi-Academy Trust, Rochdale Sixth Form Coll., 2016– (Chm. of Govs, 2009–16); Vice-Chair, Govs, Kingsway Park High Sch., 2009–. Trustee, Rossendale, Hyndburn and Burnley Home-Start, 2014–. FRSA 1993. *Recreations:* theatre, evenings out, reading, three granddaughters.

**COWARD, Richard Edgar;** retired; Director for Library Planning, OCLC Inc., 1980–81; *b* 19 April 1927; *s* of Edgar Frank Coward and Jean (*née* McIntyre); *m* 1949, Audrey Scott Lintern; one *s* two *d. Educ:* Richmond Grammar Sch., Surrey. FCLIP. Dir Gen., Bibliographic Servs Div., British Library, 1975–79. Member: Adv. Cttee on BBC Archives, 1976–79; Library Adv. Council (England), 1976–. *Address:* Allfarthings, West Street, Mayfield, E Sussex TN20 6DT.

**COWBURN, Norman;** Chairman, Britannia Building Society, 1987–90 (Managing Director, 1970–84; Deputy Chairman, 1986–87); *b* 5 Jan. 1920; *s* of Harold and Edith Cowburn; *m* 1945, Edna Margaret Heatley; two *s* one *d. Educ:* Queen Elizabeth's Grammar Sch., Blackburn. FCIS, FCIB. Burnley Building Soc., 1936. Served War, 1940–46. Burnley Building Soc., 1946; Leek and Westbourne Building Soc., 1954 (re-named Britannia Building Soc., Dec. 1975). *Recreations:* golf, gardening. *Address:* Greywoods, Cheddleton Road, Birchall, Leek, Staffs ST13 5QZ. *T:* (01538) 383214.

**COWBURN, Prof. Russell Paul,** PhD; FRS 2010; Professor of Experimental Physics, University of Cambridge, since 2015 (Director of Research, Cavendish Laboratory, 2010–15); *b* Newcastle-upon-Tyne, 1971; *s* of Frank and Dorothy Cowburn; *m* 1996, Rebecca Wade. *Educ:* Dame Allan's Boys' Sch., Newcastle-upon-Tyne; St John's Coll., Cambridge (BA Natural Scis 1993; PhD Exptl Condensed Matter Physics 1996). Res. Fellow, St John's Coll., Cambridge, 1997–2000; Reader, Durham Univ., 2000–04; Prof. of Nanotechnol., Imperial Coll. London, 2005–10. *Publications:* contribs to Nature, Science, Physical Rev. Letters, Applied Physics Letters. *Address:* Department of Physics, Cavendish Laboratory, University of Cambridge, J. J. Thomson Avenue, Cambridge CB3 0HE. *E:* rpc12@cam.ac.uk.

**COWDRAY,** 4th Viscount *cr* 1917; **Michael Orlando Weetman Pearson;** Bt 1894; Baron 1910; *b* 17 June 1944; *s* of 3rd Viscount Cowdray and of his 1st wife, Lady Anne Pamela Bridgeman, *d* of 5th Earl of Bradford; *S* father, 1995; one *s* by Barbara Page; *m* 1st, 1977, Ellen (marr. diss. 1984), *d* of Hermann Erhardt; 2nd, 1987, Marina Rose, *d* of late John H. Cordle and of Mrs H. J. Ross Skinner; two *s* three *d. Educ:* Gordonstoun. *Recreation:* historic motor racing. *Heir: s* Hon. Peregrine John Dickinson Pearson, *b* 27 Oct. 1994. *Address:* Greenhill House, Vann Road, Fernhurst, Haslemere GU27 3NL. *Club:* White's.

**COWELL, Andrew Graham,** FIMechE, FREng; Managing Director, Mercedes AMG High Performance Powertrains Ltd, since 2013; *b* Blackpool, 12 Feb. 1969; *s* of Dr Geoffrey Cowell and Doreen Cowell (now Suffell); partner, Sarah Dillon; four *s. Educ:* Univ. of Lancaster (BEng 1st Mech. Engrg 1991). FIMechE 2010; FREng 2017. Sen. Engr, Cosworth Racing Ltd, 1991–99; Hd, Pre-Develt, BMW Motorsport F1, 1999–2000; Principal Engr, Cosworth Racing Ltd, 2000–04; Chief Engr, 2004–08, Engrg and Prog. Dir, 2008–13, Mercedes AMG High Performance Powertrains Ltd. *Recreations:* being amazed at the development rate of my four young sons, walking, cycling, amateur motor sport, gardening. *Address:* Mercedes AMG High Performance Powertrains Ltd, Morgan Drive, Brixworth, Northants NN6 9GZ. *T:* (01604) 880100. *E:* andy.cowell@mercedes-amg-hpp.com.

**COWELL, (Andrew John Hulke) Hamish,** CMG 2017; HM Diplomatic Service; Ambassador to Oman, since 2017; *b* Richmond, N Yorks, 31 Jan. 1965; *s* of Barry Hulke Cowell and Anne Roberta Cowell (*née* Menzies); *m* 2000, Shadi Akhtar Khankasmai; three *d. Educ:* Madras Coll., St Andrews; Wadham Coll., Oxford (BA 1st Cl. Hons Oriental Studies (Persian and Islamic Studies); Oriental Studies Faculty Prize). Entered FCO, 1987; ME Dept, 1987–88; Second Sec., Colombo, 1989–92; First Sec. and Dep. Hd of Mission, Tehran, 1992–94; EU Directorate, 1994–96; Hd, Pol and Econ. Sections, Cairo, 1996–99; Foreign Sec.'s Speechwriter, 1999–2000; Press Office, 10 Downing St, 2000; First Sec., UK Representation, Brussels (ME/N Africa), 2001–04; on secondment to Quai d'Orsay, 2004; Hd, Internat. Policy, Paris, 2005–09; Private Sec. to Minister of State, FCO, 2010–11; Head: Libya Crisis Unit, 2011–12; N Africa Dept, 2012–13; Ambassador to Tunisia, 2013–16. *Recreations:* fishing, reading, tennis, walking. *Address:* c/o Foreign and Commonwealth Office, King Charles Street, SW1A 2AH. *E:* Hamish.cowell@fco.gov.uk.

**COWELL, Hamish;** *see* Cowell, A. J. H. H.

**COWELL, His Honour Peter Reginald;** a Circuit Judge, 1996–2012; *b* 9 March 1942; *s* of Reginald Ernest Cowell and Philippa Eleanor Frances Anne Cowell (*née* Prettejohn); *m* 1975, Penelope Jane Bowring; two *s* one *d. Educ:* Bedford Sch.; Gonville and Caius Coll., Cambridge. Called to the Bar, Middle Temple, 1964, Bencher, 1997 (Master of the Revels, 2001–13; Autumn Reader, 2008); Asst Recorder, 1985–92; Recorder, 1992–96. Mem. Senate, Inns of Court, 1975–78. *Recreations:* acting (Mem., Old Stagers, 1970–), sculling, genealogy. *Address:* c/o Middle Temple Treasury, Middle Temple Lane, EC4Y 9AT. *Club:* Garrick.

**COWELL, Prof. Raymond,** CBE 2004; Vice-Chancellor, Nottingham Trent University, 1992–2003 (Director and Chief Executive, Trent Polytechnic, Nottingham, then Nottingham Polytechnic, 1987–92); *b* 3 Sept. 1937; *s* of Cecil Cowell and Susan Cowell (*née* Green); *m* 1963, Sheila (*née* Bolton); one *s* one *d. Educ:* St Aidan's Grammar Sch., Sunderland; Bristol Univ. (BA, PhD); Cambridge Univ. (PGCE). Head of English, Nottingham Coll. of Educn, 1970–73; Dean of Humanities 1974–81, Dep. Rector 1981–87, Sunderland Polytechnic. Member: CNAA, 1974–77 and 1981–85; Unit for Develt of Adult and Continuing Educn, 1986–90; British Council Cttee for Internat. Co-op. in Higher Educn, 1990–2000; Bd, Greater Nottingham TEC, 1990–93; Directing Gp, Prog. on Instnl Management in Higher Educn, OECD, 1990–97; Council, NCVQ, 1991–97; Bd, Higher Educn Business Enterprise, 1993–95; Policy Liaison Gp, Open Learning Foundn, 1993–95; Adv. Panel, Nat. Reading Initiative, DNH, 1996–97; E Midlands Business Leadership Team, BITC, 2001–03. Chairman: Staff and Educnl Develt Assoc., 1993–96; CVCP working gp on vocational higher educn, 1993–96; Management Bd and Members Adv. Gp, Univs and Colls Staff Develt Agency (formerly Univs Staff Develt Unit), 1993–95; E Midlands Arts Bd Ltd, 1995–2001 (Mem., Arts Council of England, 1996–98). Board Member: Nottingham City Challenge, 1991–93; Opera North, 2000–10; Nottingham Bldg Soc., 2003–08 (Vice-Chm., 2004–08); Chair, Bd, Viva Chamber Orch., 2005–09. Trustee: Djanogly City Acad., 2008–16 (Mem. Bd of Govs, 2005–08); Nottingham Contemporary, 2008–12. FRSA 1996. DL Notts, 1996. Midlander of the Year, Carlton TV, 2002. *Publications:* Twelve Modern Dramatists, 1967; W. B. Yeats, 1969; (ed) Richard II, 1969; Critics on Yeats, 1971; Critics on Wordsworth, 1973; The Critical Enterprise, 1975; articles and reviews on higher education. *Recreations:* books, music, theatre.

**COWELL, Simon Phillip;** music executive and television and film producer; *b* London, 7 Oct. 1959; *s* of late Eric Cowell and Julie Cowell; one *s* by Lauren Silverman. Various posts, EMI Music Publishing; co-founder, E&S Music; co-founder, Fanfare Records; A&R Consultant, BMG, later Sony BMG, then Sony Music, 1989–; founder, S Records; signed acts incl. Curiosity Killed the Cat, Five, Robson and Jerome, Westlife; founder, Syco Entertainment, 2004; artists incl. Il Divo, Leona Lewis, Susan Boyle, One Direction, Little Mix, James Arthur, Ella Henderson and Fifth Harmony; producer and judge of TV talent shows; creator of Got Talent and The X Factor formats; *judge*: Pop Idol, 2001–03; American Idol, 2002–10; *executive producer*: American Inventor, 2006–07; *creator and executive producer*: America's Got Talent, 2006–09; Australia's Got Talent, 2007; *creator and judge*: The X Factor, 2004–10, 2014–; Britain's Got Talent, 2007–; The X Factor USA, 2011–13; America's Got Talent, 2016–; *creator*: La Banda, 2015; *producer*: One Chance, 2013; One Direction: This is Us, 2013. Special Achievement Award, BAFTA, 2010; Internat. Emmy Founders Award, 2010; Rose d'Or Golden Jubilee Award, 2010; Personality of the Year Award, MipCom, 2014; Music Industry Trust Award, 2015. *Publications*: I Don't Mean to be Rude, but…, 2003. *Address*: c/o Syco Entertainment, Sony Music, 9 Derry Street, W8 5HY.

**COWEN, Brian;** Member (FF) of the Dáil (TD) for Laois-Offaly, June 1984–2011; Taoiseach (Prime Minister of Ireland), 2008–11; President, Fianna Fáil, 2008–11; Director, Cowen Consulting, since 2013; *b* 10 Jan. 1960; *s* of late Bernard Cowen; *m* 1990, Mary Molloy; two *d*. *Educ*: Cistercian Coll., Roscrea; University Coll., Dublin. Solicitor. Minister: for Labour, 1991–92; for Transport, Energy and Communications, 1992–94; for Health and Children, 1997–2000; for Foreign Affairs, 2000–04; for Finance, 2004–08; Tánaiste (Dep. Prime Minister), 2007–08. *Recreation*: all sports.

**COWEN, Prof. Philip John,** MD; FRCPsych; FMedSci; MRC Clinical Scientist and Hon. Consultant Psychiatrist, Department of Psychiatry, since 1983, and Professor of Psychopharmacology, since 1997, University of Oxford; *b* Romford, Essex, 26 April 1951; *s* of Dr Dennis D. Cowen and Mrs Judith Cowen, JP (*née* Elks); *m* 1983, Stephanie Ruth Marsh; one *s* three *d*. *Educ*: Brentwood Sch.; University Coll. London (BSc 1971); University Coll. Hosp. (MB BS 1974); Univ. of London (MD 1984). FRCPsych 1991. Hse Physician, UCH, 1974–75; Hse Surgeon, Wycombe Gen. Hosp., 1975–76; Registrar, Rotational Trng Scheme in Psychiatry, KCH, 1976–79; Fellow in Clin. Pharmacol., MRC Clin. Pharmacol. Unit, Oxford, 1979–83. Member: Guideline Panel on Generalized Anxiety Disorder, NICE, 2010–11; MRC Neurosci. and Mental Health Bd, 2011–15. FMedSci 2000. Lifetime Achievement Award, British Assoc. of Psychopharmacol., 2014. *Publications*: (jtly) Shorter Oxford Textbook of Psychiatry, 1995, 7th edn 2018; contribs to learned jls on psychopharmacol. and psychiatry. *Recreations*: sport (spectator), philosophy, family. *Address*: Department of Psychiatry, Warneford Hospital, Oxford OX3 7JX. *T*: (01865) 226394. *E*: phil.cowen@psych.ox.ac.uk.

**COWGILL, Peter Alan;** Executive Chairman, JD Sports Fashion plc, since 2004; *b* 18 March 1953; *s* of John Cowgill and Kathleen Cowgill; *m* Lindsay; one *s* two *d*. *Educ*: De La Salle Grammar Sch., Manchester; Hull Univ. (BSc). FCA 1981. Sen. Partner, Cowgill Holloway LLP, chartered accountants, 1983–; Finance Dir, JD Sports plc, 1996–2001. Non-executive Chairman: United Carpets plc, 2005–; MBL Gp plc, 2006–14. *Address*: JD Sports Fashion plc, Hollinsbrook Way, Pilsworth, Bury BL9 8RR. *T*: (0161) 767 1620, *Fax*: (0161) 767 1759. *E*: peter.cowgill@jdplc.com.

**COWIE, Hon. Lord; William Lorn Kerr Cowie;** a Senator of the College of Justice in Scotland, 1977–94; a Judge of the Court of Appeal, Botswana, 1995–98; *b* 1 June 1926; *s* of late Charles Rennie Cowie, MBE and Norah Slimmon Kerr; *m* 1958, Camilla Henrietta Grizel Hoyle; twin *s* two *d*. *Educ*: Fettes Coll.; Clare Coll., Cambridge; Glasgow Univ. Sub-Lieut RNVR, 1944–47; Cambridge, 1947–49; Glasgow Univ., 1949–51; Mem., Faculty of Advocates, 1952; QC (Scotland) 1967. *Address*: 61/6 Grange Loan, Edinburgh EH9 2EG. *T*: (0131) 667 8238. *Club*: New (Edinburgh).

**COWIE, Andrew Graeme;** Assistant Chief Constable, Local Policing North, Police Scotland, 2016–18; *b* Edinburgh, 1 July 1966; *s* of Alan Cowie and Eleanor Cowie; *m* 1988, Alison Macleod; one *s* two *d*. *Educ*: Onthank Prim. Sch., Kilmarnock; Mile End Prim. Sch., Aberdeen; Aberdeen Grammar Sch.; Univ. of Aberdeen (MA Hons Internat. Relns and Politics 1987); Open Univ. (MBA 2003). Patrol Officer, then Sgt, Metropolitan Police, 1988–94; Northern Constabulary: Patrol Officer, 1994–97; Patrol Sgt, 1997–99; Emergency Planning Officer, 2000; Partnership Develt, 2002; Area Comdr, Shetland, 2003–06; Supt, Corporate Services, 2006–09; Chief Supt, 2009–11; Dep. Chief Constable, 2011–13; Asst HM Inspector of Constabulary for Scotland, 2013–16. *Recreations*: family, cycling, time trialling, cinema, travelling.

**COWIE, Ian McGregor;** journalist; columnist, Sunday Times, since 2013; *b* 15 Sept. 1958; *s* of Joseph Cowie and Mary (*née* Proctor); *m* 1987, Susan Carole Fleming; one *s*. *Educ*: William Ellis Sch.; Univ. of York (BA Hons); City Univ. (Postgrad. Dip.). Daily Telegraph: City Reporter, 1986–89; Personal Finance Ed., 1989–2010; Head of Personal Finance, 2008–13. Columnist, Spectator Business, 2008–10. Mem., Soc. for Nautical Res., 2016. Personal Finance Journalist of the Year: Golden Pen Awards, 1996; Wincott Award, 2007; Consumer Journalist of the Year, London Press Club Awards, 2011; Financial Commentator of the Year, Headline Money Awards, 2015; Best Freelance Journalist, Assoc. of Investment Companies Awards, 2017. *Publications*: Daily Telegraph Guides series on savings and investments, 1996–2013; contrib. Spectator. *Recreation*: sailing close to the wind. *E*: ian.cowie@sunday-times.co.uk. *Club*: Royal Ocean Racing.

**COWIE, Dr Lennox Lauchlan,** FRS 2004; Astronomer, University of Hawaii, since 1997; *b* 18 Oct. 1950. *Educ*: Edinburgh Univ. (BSc 1st cl.); Harvard Univ. (PhD 1976). Res. Astronomer, with rank of Associate Prof., Princeton Univ., 1979–81; Associate Prof. of Physics, MIT, 1981–84; Chief, Acad. Affairs Br., Space Telescope Sci. Inst., and Prof., Johns Hopkins Univ., 1984–86; Associate Dir, Inst. for Astronomy, Univ. of Hawaii, 1986–97. *Publications*: numerous papers in refereed learned jls. *Address*: Institute for Astronomy, University of Hawaii, 2680 Woodlawn Drive, Honolulu, HI 96822–1839, USA.

**COWIE, William Lorn Kerr;** *see* Cowie, Hon. Lord.

**COWLEY, 8th Earl** *cr* 1857; **Garret Graham Wellesley, (Jr);** Baron Cowley 1828; Viscount Dangan 1857; Group Chief Executive, Wellesley Group, since 2013; Chairman, since 2012, and Chief Executive, since 2015, Wellesley & Co. (Joint Chief Executive, 2012–15); *b* 30 March 1965; *o s* of 7th Earl Cowley and Suzanne Wellesley (*née* Lennon); *S* father, 2016; *m* 1990, Claire Lorraine, *d* of P. W. Brighton, Stow Bridge, Norfolk; two *s* one *d*. *Educ*: Franklin Coll., Switzerland (Associate of Arts degree). Traded Options, Hoare Govett, 1985–88; Manager, Ing (London) Derivatives Ltd, 1991–94; CEO, IFX Ltd, 1995–2003; Gp Chief Exec., Zetters plc, then IFX Gp plc, 2000–03; Sen. Vice Pres., Index Futures Gp, 1995–2002; Chief Executive: ODL Securities Ltd, 2003–10; ODL Gp Ltd, 2003–10; Vice-Chm., FXCM Securities Ltd, 2010–13. Non-executive Chairman: Prestige Asset Management Ltd, 2008–; Eastern Counties Finance, 2008–. Non-exec. Chm., Children's Miracle Network UK, 2007–; Trustee, Redwings Horse Sanctuary, 2004–. *Heir*: *s* Viscount Dangan, *qv*.

**COWLEY, Prof. Alan Herbert,** FRS 1988; FRSC; Robert A. Welch Professor of Chemistry, University of Texas at Austin, 1991–2015, now Emeritus; *b* 29 Jan. 1934; *s* of late Herbert Cowley and Dora Cowley; *m* 1975, Deborah Elaine Cole; two *s* three *d*. *Educ*: Univ. of Manchester (BSc, MSc; Dalton Chem. Schol., 1956–58; PhD 1958). Technical Officer, ICI, 1960–61; University of Texas at Austin: Asst Prof. of Chemistry, 1962–67; Associate Prof., 1967–70; Prof., 1970–84; George W. Watt Centennial Prof., 1984–88; Richard J. V. Johnson Regents Prof. of Chemistry, 1989–91; Sir Edward Frankland Prof. of Inorganic Chem., Imperial Coll., London, 1988–89. Deutsche Akademische Austauschdienst Fellow, 1973; Guggenheim Fellow, 1976–77; von Humboldt Sen. Fellow, 1996; Lectures: Jeremy I. Musher Meml, Hebrew Univ., Jerusalem, 1979; Mobay, Univ. of New Hampshire, 1985; Karcher, Univ. of Oklahoma, 1985; Reilly, Univ. of Notre Dame, 1987; Fischel, Vanderbilt Univ., 1991; Baxter, Northern Illinois Univ., 1992; Etter Meml, Univ. of Minnesota, 1995; Vis. Prof., Univ. of Western Ont., 1987; Gauss Prof., Göttingen Acad. of Scis, 2005. Member: Chem. Soc., subseq. RSC, 1961 (Award for Main-Gp Element Chem., 1980; Centenary Medal and Lectureship, 1986); Amer. Chem. Soc., 1962 (Southwest Regl Award, 1986); Eur. Acad. of Scis, 2009; Corresp. Member: Mexican Acad. of Scis, 2004; Göttingen Acad. of Scis, 2007; Eur. Acad. of Scis and Arts, 2009. Stiefvater Meml Award and Lectureship, Univ. of Nebraska, 1987; Chemical Pioneer Award, Amer. Inst. of Chemists, 1994; C. N. R. Rao Award, Chem. Res. Soc. of India, 2007; Award for Dist. Service in Advancement of Inorganic Chem., ACS, 2009. Mem. Bd of Trustees, Gordon Res. Confs, 1989–98 (Chm., 1994–95). Member, Editorial Board: Inorganic Chemistry, 1979–83; Chemical Reviews, 1984–88; Polyhedron, 1984–2000; Jl of Amer. Chem. Soc., 1986–91; Jl of Organometallic Chemistry, 1987–2008; Organometallics, 1988–91; Dalton Trans., 1997–2000; Mem. Bd, Inorganic Syntheses, 1983– (Ed.-in-Chief, vol. 31). FRSC 2004. Dr hc Bordeaux I, 2003. *Publications*: over 500 pubns in learned jls. *Recreations*: squash, sailing, music. *Address*: Department of Chemistry and Biochemistry, University of Texas at Austin, 1 University Station A5300, Austin, TX 78712–0165, USA. *Clubs*: Athenæum; Headliners (Austin).

**COWLEY, Jason;** journalist, magazine editor and writer; Editor-in-chief, New Statesman, since 2018 (Editor, 2008–18); *b* Harlow, Essex, 19 June 1965; *s* of Anthony Frank Cowley and Lilian Ella Edith Cowley (*née* Shears); *m* 1998, Sarah Jane Kernohan; one *s*. *Educ*: various state schs; Univ. of Southampton (BA 1st Cl. Hons English and Philosophy). Reporter, then News Ed., The Bookseller, 1992–95; staff feature writer, The Times, 1996–98; Literary Ed., New Statesman, 1999–2002; Sen. Ed. and writer, Observer, 2003–07; Ed., Granta, 2007–08. Founder Mem. Council, Caine Prize for African Writing, 1997; Booker Prize judge, 1997. Ed. of Year, current affairs and specialist mags, 2009, Ed. of Year, current affairs and newspaper magazines, 2011, Ed. of Year, current affairs and politics, 2017, British Soc. of Mag. Editors. *Publications*: Unknown Pleasures: a novel, 2000; The Last Game: love, death and football, 2009; (ed) The New Statesman Century: a celebration of the best and boldest writing from the magazine's history, 2013; Reaching for Utopia: making sense of an age of upheaval, 2018. *Recreations*: reading, writing, walking, good food, football, cricket. *Address*: New Statesman, John Carpenter House, 7 Carmelite Street, Blackfriars, EC4Y 0BS. *E*: Jceditor@newstatesman.co.uk. *Clubs*: Garrick; Arsenal; Hatfield Heath Cricket.

**COWLEY, Kenneth Edward,** AO 1988; Chairman, R. M. Williams Holdings Ltd, 1994–2015; *b* 17 Nov. 1934; *s* of Edward Clegg Cowley and Patricia Bertha (*née* Curran); *m* 1958, Maureen Yvonne Manahan; one *s* one *d*. Sen. Exec., The Australian, 1964–97; Director: News Ltd, 1976–97; Internat. Bd, News Corp., 1980–2011; Chief Exec., 1980–97, Chm., 1992–96, Exec. Chm., 1996–97, News Ltd; Chairman: PMP Communications (formerly Pacific Magazines and Printing) Ltd, 1991–2001; Ansett Transport Industries, then Ansett Australia Hldgs, 1992–98 (Dir, 1997–2000); Ansett Internat., 1997–2000; Tasman Pacific Airways (traded as Ansett NZ, then Qantas NZ), 1997–2000; Ind. Newspapers Ltd (NZ), 2001–04 (Dir, 1990–2005). Director: Qld Press Ltd, 1987–97; Commonwealth Bank of Australia, 1997–2001; Tower Estate plc, 1998–. Councillor, Royal Agricl Soc. of NSW, 1979–. Life Gov., Art Gall. of NSW, 1997 (Trustee, 1986–97); Patron, Australian Stockman's Hall of Fame & Outback Heritage Centre, 2009– (Chm., 1976–2009). Hon. DBus NSW, 2008. *Club*: Union (Sydney).

**COWLEY, Lesley Ruth,** OBE 2011; Chair: Driver and Vehicle Licensing Agency, since 2014; Companies House, since 2017; *b* Bristol, 30 June 1960; *d* of John Mawson and Heather Mawson; *m* 1989, David Cowley; one *s*. *Educ*: St Ursula's High Sch., Bristol; Univ. of West of England, Bristol (MBA Dist.). Asst to Insolvency Partner, Monahans, 1988–90; Dir, New Coll., Swindon, 1990–99; Nominet: Ops Dir, 1999–2001; Man. Dir, 2002–04; CEO, Nominet, 2004–14. Non-exec. Dir, Public Policy, AQL, 2014–; Lead non-exec. Dir, Nat. Archives, 2016–. Member: Council, Country Code Names Supporting Orgn, 2007–16; Policy and Public Affairs Bd, BCS, 2013–16; Surveillance Rev. Panel, RUSI, 2014–15. FCMI 2005; FCICM (FICM 2005); FBCS 2008; FRSA 2010; FInstD 2011; CCMI 2016. *Recreations*: Tiffany glass and glass fusing, competitive gardening. *E*: lesley@lesleycowley.com. *W*: www.lesleycowley.com.

**COWLEY, Dame Sarah (Ann),** DBE 2013; PhD; Professor of Community Practice Development, Florence Nightingale School (now Faculty) of Nursing and Midwifery, King's College London, 1997–2012, now Emeritus Professor; *b* St Helier, Jersey, 6 Feb. 1948; *d* of Charles Lyn and Margaret Handley; *m* 1971, Ernest Michael Leonard Cowley (marr. diss. 1974); one *s*. *Educ*: Perse Sch. for Girls, Cambridge; St Mary's Hosp., London (RN 1969); Brighton Poly. (RHV 1981); Open Univ. (BA Hons 1984); Brighton Poly. (PhD 1991). Staff Nurse, St Mary's Hosp., 1969–70; Ward Sister, Marple Dale Hosp., 1971; Night Sister, Bromley Hosp., 1972–74; Clinical Teacher, Farnborough Sch. of Nursing, 1975–80; Health Visitor, 1981–86, Field Work Teacher, 1986–92, Eastbourne HA; Lectr, Dept of Nursing Studies, 1992–95, Sen. Lectr, 1995–97, KCL. Trustee, Inst. of Health Visiting, 2012–. *Publications*: (ed with I. Norman) The Changing Nature of Nursing in a Managerial Age, 1999; (ed with J. Appleton) The Search for Health Needs: research for health visiting practice, 2000; (ed) Public Health Policy and Practice: a sourcebook for health visitors and community nurses, 2002; (with M. Frost) The Principles of Health Visiting, 2006; (ed) Public Health in Policy and Practice: a sourcebook for health visitors and community nurses, 2002, 2nd edn as Policy and Practice in Community Public Health: a sourcebook, 2008; contrib. peer-reviewed acad. papers. *Recreation*: walking on Bournemouth beach and in New Forest with dog and grandchildren. *Address*: Florence Nightingale Faculty of Nursing and Midwifery, King's College London, 57 Waterloo Road, SE1 8WA. *E*: sarah.cowley@kcl.ac.uk.

**COWLEY, Sarah Julie;** HM Diplomatic Service; Head, Prosperity Fund Department, Foreign and Commonwealth Office, since 2017; *b* Norfolk, 19 Nov. 1977; *d* of Paul and Julie Cowley; *m* 2007, Paul Hamilton Boschi; two *d*. *Educ*: Wisbech Grammar Sch.; University Coll. London (BA Hons Hist.); Open Univ. (MBA). With KPMG, 2003–04; DLA Piper, 2004–05; entered FCO, 2005; Asst Private Sec. to Minister of State, 2007–09; Private Sec. to UK Special Rep. for Afghanistan and Pakistan, 2009–10; Political Advr to Hd, EU Delegn in Kabul, 2010–11; Head: of Communications, Islamabad, 2011–12; of Olympic and Paralympic Co-ordination Centre, FCO, 2012; Commercial Diplomacy, FCO, 2012–13; Ambassador to Latvia, 2013–17. *Recreation*: travel. *Address*: c/o Foreign and Commonwealth Office, King Charles Street, SW1A 2AH. *E*: sarah.cowley@fco.gov.uk.

**COWLEY, Prof. Stanley William Herbert**, FRS 2011; Professor of Solar-Planetary (formerly Space Plasma) Physics, and Head, Radio and Space Plasma Physics Group, Department of Physics and Astronomy, University of Leicester, 1996–2015, now Emeritus Professor; *b* 11 April 1947; *s* of late Herbert William Leslie Cowley and Annie Jenny Cowley (*née* Clark); *m* 1970, Lynn Doreen Moore; two *s* one *d*. *Educ:* Imperial Coll., Univ. of London (BSc, ARCS, PhD, DIC). FBIS 1975; MInstP 1975, FInstP 2011; FRAS 1986; CPhys 1989. Imperial College, University of London: SERC Advanced Fellow, 1977–82; Lectr, 1982–85; Reader, 1985–88; Prof. of Physics, 1988–95; Head, Space and Atmospheric Physics Gp, Blackett Lab., 1990–95; PPARC Sen. Fellow, 2001–04; Royal Soc. Leverhulme Trust Sen. Res. Fellow, 2006–07. Mem., PPARC, 1994–96. Fellow, Amer. Geophysical Union, 1995. Chapman Medal, 1991, Gold Medal, 2006, RAS; Bartels Medal, Eur. Geoscis Union, 2006. *Publications:* contrib. numerous papers in solar system plasma physics in learned jls. *Recreation:* walking the dog. *Address:* Department of Physics and Astronomy, University of Leicester, University Road, Leicester LE1 7RH. *T:* (0116) 223 1331, (0116) 252 3563.

**COWLEY, Sir Steven**, Kt 2018; PhD; FRS 2014; FInstP, FREng; Director, Princeton Plasma Physics Laboratory, since 2018. *Educ:* Corpus Christi Coll., Oxford (BA Physics 1981); Princeton Univ. (MA 1983; PhD 1985). FInstP 2004; FREng 2014. Harkness Fellow, 1981–83; postdoctoral res., Culham Lab., 1985–87; Princeton Univ., 1987–93; UCLA, 1993–2001 (Prof., 2000–01); Leader, Plasma Physics Gp, Imperial Coll. London, 2001–03; Dir, Center for Multi-scale Plasma Dynamics, UCLA, 2004–08; Dir, Culham Centre for Fusion Energy, 2008–16; Prof. of Plasma Physics (pt-time), Imperial Coll. London; CEO, UKAEA, 2009–16; Pres., Corpus Christi Coll., Oxford, 2016–18. Mem., Prime Minister's Council for Sci. and Technol., 2011–. Fellow, Amer. Physical Soc., 1998. Hon. FIET 2015. Glazebrook Medal, Inst. of Physics, 2012. *Publications:* contribs to learned jls incl. Physical Rev. Letters, Physics of Plasmas, Nuclear Fusion, New Jl of Physics. *Address:* Princeton Plasma Physics Laboratory, 100 Stellarator Road, Princeton, NJ 08540, USA.

**COWLING, Gareth;** see Cowling, His Honour T. G.

**COWLING, Peter John;** Director, Falmouth Quay Consultants, 2003–13; *b* 11 Nov. 1944; *s* of Harold Cowling and Irene (*née* Phillips); *m* 1979, Sara Fox; one *d* (and one *d* decd). *Educ:* Bletchley Grammar Sch.; Britannia Royal Naval Coll. Joined RN 1963; commanded: HMS Naiad, 1979; HMS York and 3rd Destroyer Sqdn, 1988; Sen. Naval Officer, Middle East, 1991; Dir, Naval Ops, MoD, 1992; retired 1994. Dir, RSA, 1994–96; Head of Corporate Relns, Proshare, 1997–98; Dir, Nat. Maritime Mus. Cornwall, 1998–2003. Chm., Cornwall SSAFA, 2006–15; Mem. Council, Trustee and SW Regl Rep., SSAFA, 2015–. Younger Brother, Trinity House, 1981– (Pilgrim, 1996–). Queen's Gold Medal, 1967. *Recreations:* sailing, gardening, tennis. *Address:* Little Court, Gold Hill, Batcombe, Somerset BA4 6HF.

**COWLING, Sharon Katherine;** see Phillips, S. K.

**COWLING, Very Rev. Simon Charles;** Dean of Wakefield, since 2018; *b* 1959. *Educ:* Gonville and Caius Coll., Cambridge (BA 1980); King's Coll. London (PGCE 1982); Lincoln Theol Coll. (BTh 1991). Teacher; ordained deacon, 1991, priest, 1992; Curate: St Martin, Potternewton, Leeds, 1991–94; St Chad, Far Headingley, Leeds, 1994–96; Vicar, St Edmund King and Martyr, Roundhay, 1996–2007; Area Dean, Allerton, 2004–07; Canon Residentiary and Precentor, Sheffield Cathedral, 2007–13; Rector, Bolton Abbey, Skipton, 2013–18. Hon. Canon, Ripon Cathedral, 2015–. *Address:* Cathedral Centre, 8–10 Westmorland Street, Wakefield WF1 1PJ.

**COWLING, His Honour (Thomas) Gareth;** a Circuit Judge, 2004–09; *b* 12 Nov. 1944; *s* of late Clifford Cowling and Beryl Elizabeth Cowling (*née* Thomas); *m* 1970, Jill Ann Stephens; one *s* one *d*. *Educ:* Eastbourne Coll.; College of Law. Articled to Clifford Cowling, of Clifford Cowling & Co., Hampshire, 1964; admitted Solicitor of Supreme Court, 1969; Solicitor, Solicitor's Dept, New Scotland Yard, 1969–72; called to Bar, Middle Temple, 1972; private practice at Bar, London and Winchester, Western Circuit, 1972–88; Metropolitan Stipendiary Magistrate, 1988–89; Stipendiary Magistrate, subseq. Dist Judge (Magistrates' Courts), Hampshire, 1989–2004; a Recorder, 1998–2004. Mem., Parole Bd, 2007. *Recreations:* eating and drinking with family and friends, trying to play golf.

**COWMAN, Prof. Alan Frederick**, AC 2019; PhD; FRS 2011; Head, Division of Infection and Immunity, Walter and Eliza Hall Institute of Medical Research, since 1999; *b* Brisbane, 27 Dec. 1954. *Educ:* Griffith Univ. (BSc Hons 1979); Univ. of Melbourne (PhD Molecular Parasitol. 1984). FAA 2001. Postdoctoral res. at Univ. of Calif, Berkeley, 1984–86; Walter and Eliza Hall Inst. Med. Res., 1986–. Wellcome Trust Australian Sen. Res. Fellow, 1988; Internat. Res. Schol., 1992, 1993–97, 2000–10, Sen. Internat. Res. Schol., 2012–, Howard Hughes Med. Inst. NHMRC Australia Fellow, 2011. Boehringer-Mannheim Medal, 1994, Lemberg Medal, 2006, Australian Soc. Biochem. and Molecular Biol. *Publications:* contribs to scientific jls incl. Nature, Cell, Blood, Science, Traffic. *Address:* Walter and Eliza Hall Institute of Medical Research, WEHI Biotechnology Centre, 4 Research Avenue, La Trobe R&D Park, Bundoora, Vic 3086, Australia.

**COWPER-COLES, Sir Sherard (Louis)**, KCMG 2004 (CMG 1997); LVO 1991; Group Head of Public Affairs, HSBC Holdings plc, since 2017 (Senior Adviser to Group Chairman and Group Chief Executive, 2013–15; Group Head of Government Affairs, 2015–17); Chairman, HSBC Bank, Oman, since 2017; *b* 8 Jan. 1955; *s* of late Sherard Hamilton Cowper-Coles and Dorothy (*née* Short); *m* 1st, 1982, Bridget Mary Elliott (marr. diss. 2011); four *s* one *d*; 2nd, 2012, Jasmine Zerinini; one *d*. *Educ:* Freston Lodge Sch.; New Beacon Sch.; Tonbridge Sch. (Scholar); Hertford Coll., Oxford (Classical Scholar; MA; Hon. Fellow, 2002). HM Diplomatic Service, 1977–2010: Third, later Second, Sec., Cairo, 1980–83; First Sec., Planning Staff, FCO, 1983–85; Private Sec. to Perm. Under-Sec. of State, 1985–87; First Sec., Washington, 1987–91; Asst, Security Policy Dept, FCO, 1991–93; Res. Associate, IISS, 1993–94; Head, Hong Kong Dept, FCO, 1994–97; Counsellor (Political) Paris, 1997–99; Prin. Private Sec. to Sec. of State for For. and Commonwealth Affairs, 1999–2001; Ambassador to: Israel, 2001–03; Saudi Arabia, 2003–07; Afghanistan, 2007–09; Special Rep. for Afghanistan and Pakistan, FCO, 2009–10; Business Devlt Dir, Internat., BAE Systems, 2011–13. Chm., Financial Inclusion Commn, 2014–. Chm., Saudi-British Soc., 2011–16; UK Chm., Omani-British Friendship Assoc., 2014–; Member: Bd, China Britain Business Council, 2014– (Chair, 2019–); Saudi-British Jt Business Council, 2015–; Egyptian-British Business Council, 2015–. Member: Winston Churchill Meml Trust Appeal Cttee, 2013–15; Internat. Engagement Cttee, British Acad., 2014–. Pres., Jane Austen Soc., 2015–. Chm., Pitzhanger Manor and Gallery Trust, 2012–. Hon. Prof., Nottingham Univ., 2011–; Hon. Fellow, Exeter Univ., 2011–. CRAeS 2011. Liveryman, Skinners' Co., 1988. Hon. DLitt Westminster, 2014. *Publications:* Cables from Kabul: the inside story of the West's Afghanistan campaign, 2011; Ever the Diplomat: confessions of a Foreign Office mandarin, 2012; contrib. Survival (IISS jl). *Address:* HSBC Holdings plc, 8 Canada Square, E14 5HQ. *Club:* Brooks's.

**COWTON, Catherine Judith;** QC 2019; a Recorder, since 2018; *b* Lichfield, 11 May 1972; *d* of Mervyn Cowton and Janine Cowton; *m* 2002, Gordon Baker; three *c*. *Educ:* Alice Ottley Sch., Worcester; Magdalene Coll., Cambridge (BA Hons Law 1994; MA). Called to the Bar, Middle Temple, 1995; in practice as a barrister, specialising in family law, Queen Elizabeth Bldg, 1996–. *Recreations:* family, rowing, violin. *Address:* Queen Elizabeth Building, Temple, EC4Y 9BS. *T:* (020) 7797 7837. *E:* c.cowton@qeb.co.uk.

**COX,** family name of **Baroness Cox**.

**COX**, Baroness *cr* 1982 (Life Peer), of Queensbury in Greater London; **Caroline Anne Cox;** a Deputy Speaker, House of Lords, 1986–2006; Chief Executive Officer, Humanitarian Aid Relief Trust, 2004–16 and since 2017 (President, 2016–17); *b* 6 July 1937; *d* of Robert John McNeill Love, MS, FRCS and Dorothy Ida Borland; *m* 1959, Dr Murray Cox, FRCPsych (*d* 1997); two *s* one *d*. *Educ:* Channing School; London Univ. (BSc (Sociology, 1st Cl. Hons) 1967, MSc (Economics) 1969). FRCN 1985. SRN, London Hosp., 1958; Staff Nurse, Edgware Gen. Hosp., 1960; Research Associate, Univ. of Newcastle upon Tyne, 1967–68; Department of Sociology, Polytechnic of North London: Lecturer, Senior Lectr, Principal Lectr, 1969–74; Head of Department, 1974–77; Dir, Nursing Educn Res. Unit, Chelsea Coll., London Univ., 1977–84. Dir, Centre for Policy Studies, 1983–85; Co-Dir, Educnl Res. Trust, 1980–2010. A Baroness in Waiting, April–Aug. 1985. Chancellor: Bournemouth Univ., 1992–2001; Liverpool Hope Univ., 2006–13. Vice President: RCN, 1990–; Liverpool Sch. of Tropical Medicine, 2006–. Chm., Exec. Bd, Internat. Islamic Christian Orgn for Reconciliation and Reconstruction. Pres., Tushinskaya Children's Hosp. Trust; Patron: Medical Aid for Poland Fund; Barnabas Fund, 2016–. Fellow, Goodenough Coll., 2005. Hon. FRCS 1996. Hon. PhD Polish Univ. in London, 1988; Hon. LLD CNAA; DUniv: Surrey; UCE, 1998; Hon. DH Utah; Hon. Dr Yerevan; Hon. DSS QUB, 1996; Hon. DSc: City, 1999; Wolverhampton, 1999. Internat. Mother Teresa Award, All India Christian Council, 2005; Mkhitar Gosh Medal, Republic of Armenia, 2005; 25th Anniv. Medal, Polish Solidarity Movt, 2005; Medal of Gratitude, Eur. Solidarity Centre, Poland 2012. Commander's Cross, Order of Merit (Poland), 1990. *Publications:* (ed jtly) A Sociology of Medical Practice, 1975; (jtly) Rape of Reason: the corruption of the Polytechnic of North London, 1975; (jtly) The Right to Learn, 1982; Sociology: a guide for nurses, midwives and health visitors, 1983; (jtly) The Insolence of Office, 1989; (jtly) Choosing a State School: how to find the best education for your child, 1989; Trajectories of Despair: misdiagnosis and maltreatment of Soviet orphans, 1991; (with John Eibner) Ethnic Cleansing in Progress: war in Nagorno Karabakh, 1993; (jtly) Made to Care: the case for residential and village communities for people with a mental handicap, 1995; (contrib.) Remorse and Reparation, ed Murray Cox, 1998; (jtly) The West, Islam and Islamism, 2003, 2nd edn 2006; (with Catherine Butcher) Cox's Book of Modern Saints and Martyrs, 2006; (with John Marks) This Immoral Trade: slavery in the 21st century, 2006, 2nd edn 2013; (with B. Rogers) The Very Stones Cry Out: the persecuted Church: pain, passion and praise, 2011. *Recreations:* campanology, hill walking. *Address:* House of Lords, SW1A 0PW. *T:* (office) (020) 8205 4608. *Club:* Royal Over-Seas League.

**COX, Sir Alan (George)**, Kt 1994; CBE 1988; FCA; FCMA; Chief Executive, ASW Holdings PLC, 1981–96; *b* 23 Aug. 1936; *s* of late George Henry Cox and Florence Ivy Cox; *m* 1994, Rosamund Shelley. *Educ:* Oldbury Grammar Sch. FCA 1959; ACMA 1961. Chm. and Chief Exec., GKN Rolled and Bright Steel Ltd, 1978–80; Corporate Management Dir, GKN, PLC, 1980–81; Director: Morgan Crucible Co. plc, 1995–2004; Meggitt plc, 1996–2011; Henry Ivy Associates Ltd, 2000–. Founder Chairman: Wales Millennium Centre Ltd, 1996–2001; The Public Ltd (formerly Jubilee/c/Plex Arts), 2001–04. Member: Bd, Cardiff Bay Devlt Corp., 1987–2000; School Teachers Review Body, 1991–95; Financial Reporting Council, 1996–99. Chm., Mountview Acad. of Theatre Arts Ltd, 2004–07. *Recreations:* cookery, opera, walking. *Address:* PO Box 27, Chepstow, Monmouthshire NP16 6EY. *Club:* Savile.

**COX, Alistair Richard;** Chief Executive, Hays plc, since 2007; *b* 25 Feb. 1961; *s* of Gerald and Jean Cox; *m* 1988, Merete Oftedahl; two *s*. *Educ:* Univ. of Salford (BSc Hons Aeronautical Engrg, Dip. Engrg); Stanford Grad. Sch. of Business (MBA). Aeronautical Engr, British Aerospace UK, 1978–83; Engr and Manager, Schlumberger Wireline Services, Norway and USA, 1983–90; Consultant and Manager, McKinsey & Co., 1990–94; Gp Strategy Dir, 1994–98, Regl Pres. Asia, 1998–2002, Blue Circle Industries, subseq. Lafarge; Chief Exec., Xansa plc, 2002–07. Non-exec. Dir, 3i, 2009–15. *Recreations:* scuba diving, mountaineering, sailing, wake boarding, motorsports. *Address:* Hays plc, 250 Euston Road, NW1 2AF. *T:* (020) 7383 2266, *Fax:* (020) 7388 4367.

**COX, Alister Stransom**, MA; Headmaster, Royal Grammar School, Newcastle upon Tyne, 1972–94; *b* 21 May 1934; *s* of Rev. Roland L. Cox and F. Ruth Cox; *m* 1960, Janet (*née* Williams); one *s* two *d*. *Educ:* Kingswood School, Bath; New College, Oxford (Scholar). Hon. Mods (1st Class); Lit. Hum. BA 1957, MA 1961. Sixth Form Master, Clifton Coll., 1957–63; Head of Classics, Wellington Coll., 1963–69; Dep. Head, Arnold Sch., Blackpool, 1969–72. Vis. Lectr in Greek, Bristol Univ., 1968. Founder Mem., Sinfonia Chorus, Northern Sinfonia of England, 1973–94 (Mem., Management Cttee, 1980–85). FRSA 1982. *Publications:* Lucretius on Matter and Man, 1967; Didactic Poetry, in Greek and Latin Literature (ed Higginbotham), 1969; articles in Greece and Rome, Times Educnl Supp. and educnl jls. *Recreations:* music, especially singing; French life and politics; touring lecturer Alliance Française. *Address:* 3 Lower Gale, Ambleside, Cumbria LA22 0BD. *T:* (015394) 32634.

**COX, Gen. André;** General of the Salvation Army, 2013–18; *b* Salisbury, Fedn of Rhodesia and Nyasaland, 12 July 1954; *s* of Ronald Cox and Hilda Cox; *m* 1976, Silvia Volet; three *d*. *Educ:* Nat. Retail Distribution Cert. Salvation Army: Corps Officer, Switzerland, 1979–87; PR Officer, Zimbabwe, 1987–92; Financial Officer, Zimbabwe, 1992–97; PR Officer, Switzerland, 1997–2001; Business Officer, Switzerland, 2001–05; Territorial Commander: Finland and Estonia, 2005–08; S Africa, 2008–12; UK and Ire., 2012–13; COS, 2013. Dr *hc*: UCES Buenos Aires 2016; Univ. William Booth Kinshasa, 2018. *Recreations:* photography, reading, walking.

**COX, Anthony Robert**, PhD, CEng; adviser on science and technology, since 1998; *b* 30 Nov. 1938; *s* of Robert George Cox and Gladys Cox; *m* 1963, Constance Jane Hammond; one *s* two *d*. *Educ:* Brockley County School; Imperial College, London. BScEng (Metallurgy). ARSM, MIMMM. RARDE, 1960–69; Exchange Scientist, US Naval Research Lab., Washington, 1969–71; Dep. Materials Supt, RARDE, 1971–75; Asst Dir, Armour and Materials, Military Vehicle Engineering Estab., 1975–80; MoD Central Staffs Defence Science, 1980–83; Counsellor, Science and Technol., Washington, 1983–87; Superintendent, Radiation Sci. and Acoustics, NPL, 1988–92; Counsellor, Sci. and Technol., Tokyo, 1993–98. Dir, Asia Pacific Technology Network, 1999–2003. Business Mentor, Prince's Trust, 2001–05. *Publications:* papers on refractory metals, structure and strengthening mechanism on high strength steel, fractography, explosive effects, archaeological artefacts corrosion, composites, space, robotics, science policy, metrology. *Recreations:* sailing, foreign travel, gardening, industrial archaeology, University of the Third Age.

**COX, Archibald, Jr**; Chairman: Sextant Group Inc., since 1993; Ayablu Inc., since 2011; *b* 13 July 1940; *s* of late Prof. Archibald Cox and Phyllis Ames; *m* 1962, Cornelia Sharp; one *s* one *d*; *m* 2005, Judy Gordon. *Educ*: Harvard Coll. (ABEcon 1962); Harvard Business Sch. (MBA 1964). Associate 1964–70, Vice Pres. 1971–72, Man. Dir, 1973–88, Morgan Stanley & Co. Incorp.; Man. Dir and Head of London Office, Morgan Stanley Internat., 1977–88; President and Chief Executive Officer: First Boston Corp., 1990–93; Magnequench Internat., 1995–2005. Chairman: Neo Material Technologies Inc., 2005–06; Precision Magnetics Singapore, 2007–10; Barclays Americas, 2008–11. Director: Diamar Interactive Corp., 1995–2000; Hutchinson Technol. Inc., 1996–2009; Harris Chemical Gp, 1997–98; BidClerk Inc., 2004–14; Micell Technologies Inc., 2007–; Unifi Inc., 2008–; Simphotek Inc., 2010–15; SponsorHub Inc., 2011–15; Madaket Inc., 2013–; Inea Internat. Ltd, 2015–; Element Data Inc., 2016–; Adranos Energetics, 2017–. Man. Mem., Courant Capital Mgt LLC, 2010–15. Dir, Amer. Mus. of Natural Hist., 2011–15. Member: Securities and Investments Board, 1986–88; Bd, Securities Industry Assoc., 1990–93; Chm., Foreign Policy Assoc., 2010–14. Trustee, St Paul's Sch., Concord, NH, 2012–. *Recreations*: cycling, rowing, hiking, sailing. *Clubs*: Links (New York); Bucks Harbor Yacht (Brooksville, Maine); Kollegewidgwok Yacht (Blue Hill, Maine); Blue Hill Country (Blue Hill, Maine); Lyford Cay (Nassau).

**COX, Barry**; see Cox, C. B.

**COX, Barry Geoffrey**, CBE 2013; Chairman: Digital UK, 2005–12; Deputy Chairman, Channel Four, 1999–2006; *b* 25 May 1942; *s* of Leonard William Cox and Daisy Miriam; *m* 1st, 1963, Pamela Ann Doran (marr. diss. 1977); two *s* two *d*; 2nd, 1984, Kathryn Diane Kay (marr. diss. 1994); 3rd, 2001, Fiona Pamela Hillary. *Educ*: Tiffin Sch., Kingston-upon-Thames; Magdalen Coll., Oxford (BA Hons). Reporter: The Scotsman, 1965–67; Sunday Telegraph, 1967–70; Producer and Dir, Granada TV, 1970–74; London Weekend Television: Editor, then Controller, 1974–87; Dir, Corporate Affairs, 1987–94; Dir, ITV Assoc., 1995–98; Chairman: Digital TV Stakeholders' Gp, 2002–05; Digital Radio Working Gp, 2008. News Internat. Vis. Prof. of Broadcast Media, Oxford Univ., 2003. Treas., Inst. of Educn, London Univ., 2000–08. Chm., Oval House Theatre, 2001–07. Life Mem., BAFTA. *Publications*: Civil Liberties in Britain, 1975; The Fall of Scotland Yard, 1977; Free For All?, 2004. *Address*: Mapledene TV Productions Ltd, 72 Wilton Road, SW1V 1DE. *E*: Barry.cox3@btopenworld.com.

**COX, Brian Denis**, CBE 2003; actor, director, teacher and writer; *b* 1 June 1946; *s* of Charles Mcardle Campbell Cox and Mary Ann Gillerline (*née* Mccann); *m* 1st, 1968, Caroline Burt (marr. diss. 1987); one *s* one *d*; 2nd, 2001, Nicole Elisabeth Ansari; two *s*. *Educ*: LAMDA. *Stage appearances*: début, Dundee Rep., 1961; Royal Lyceum, Edinburgh, 1965–66; Birmingham Rep., 1966–68; As You Like It, Birmingham and Vaudeville (London début), 1967; title rôle, Peer Gynt, Birmingham, 1967; When We Dead Awaken, Edinburgh Fest., 1968; In Celebration, Royal Court, 1969; The Wild Duck, Edinburgh Festival, 1969; The Big Romance, Royal Court, 1970; Don't Start Without Me, Garrick, 1971; Mirandolina, Brighton, 1971; Getting On, Queen's, 1971; The Creditors, Open Space, 1972; Hedda Gabler, Royal Court, 1972; Playhouse, Nottingham: Love's Labour's Lost, title rôle, Brand, What The Butler Saw, The Three Musketeers, 1972; Cromwell, Royal Court, 1973; Royal Exchange, Manchester: Arms and the Man, 1974; The Cocktail Party, 1975; Pilgrims Progress, Prospect Th., 1975; Emigrés, Nat. Theatre Co., Young Vic, 1976; Olivier Theatre: Tamburlaine The Great, 1976; Julius Caesar, 1977; The Changeling, Riverside Studios, 1978; National Theatre: title rôle, Herod, The Putney Debates, 1978; On Top, Royal Court, 1979; Macbeth, Cambridge Th. and tour of India, 1980; Summer Party, Crucible, 1980; Have You Anything to Declare?, Manchester then Round House, 1981; title rôle, Danton's Death, Nat. Theatre Co., Olivier, 1982; Strange Interlude, Duke of York, 1984 (Drama Mag. Best Actor Award, 1985), Nederlander, NY, 1985; Rat in the Skull, Royal Court, 1984 (Drama Mag. and Olivier Best Actor Awards, 1985) and NY, 1985; Fashion, The Danton Affair, Misalliance, Penny for a Song, 1986, The Taming of the Shrew, Titus Andronicus (title rôle), 1987, The Three Sisters, 1989, RSC, and Titus Andronicus on tour, Madrid, Paris, Copenhagen, 1988 (Olivier Award, Best Actor in a Revival, and Drama Mag. Best Actor Award for RSC 1988 season); Frankie and Johnny in the Clare-de-Lune, Comedy, 1989; Richard III, and title rôle, King Lear, National and world tour, 1990–91; The Master Builder, Edinburgh, 1993, Riverside, 1994; St Nicholas, Bush, 1997, NY, 1998 (Lucille Lortel Award, 1998); Skylight, LA, 1997; Art, NY, 1998; Dublin Carol, Old Vic, and Royal Court, 2000; Uncle Varrick, Edinburgh Royal Lyceum, 2004; Rock 'n' Roll, Royal Court, 2006, NY, 2007; Lolita, NT, 2009; That Championship Season, NY, 2011; The Weir, Donmar Warehouse, 2013, transf. Wyndhams, 2014; Waiting for Godot, Royal Lyceum, Edinburgh, 2015; *films*: Nicholas and Alexandra, 1971; In Celebration, 1975; Manhunter, Shoot for the Sun, 1986; Hidden Agenda, 1990; Braveheart, The Cutter, 1994; Rob Roy, 1995; Chain Reaction, The Glimmer Man, Long Kiss Goodnight, 1996; Desperate Measures, Food for Ravens, Poodle Spring, 1997; The Boxer, The Corruptor, Mad About Mamba, The Minus Man, Rushmore, 1998; The Biographer, 2000; Saltwater, Strictly Sinatra, The Affair of the Necklace, 2001; Morality Play, The Rookie, Adaptation, The Bourne Identity, L.I.E., Super Troopers, 2002; 25th Hour, X-Men 2, The Ring, 2003; Troy, The Reckoning, The Bourne Supremacy, 2004; Red-eye, Woman in Winter, The Ringer, 2005; Match Point, Fourth Wall, Running with Scissors, 2006; The Flying Scotsman, Zodiac, Terra, The Waterhorse: legend of the deep, 2007; The Escapist, Agent Crush, Shoot on Sight, 2008; Tell-Tale, The Good Heart, 2009; Red, Wide Blue Yonder, 2010; Ironclad, Rise of the Planet of the Apes, 2011; Coriolanus, The Campaign, Blood, 2012; Theatre of Dreams, Red 2, 2013; Believe, Forsaken, 2014; The Anomaly, 2014; Pixels, 2015; The Carer, The Autopsy of Jane Doe, 2016; Churchill, 2017; Super Troopers 2, 2018; Rory's Way, 2019; *TV appearances*: Churchill's People: The Wallace, 1972; The Master of Ballantrae, 1975; Henry II, in The Devil's Crown, 1978; Thérèse Raquin, 1979; Dalhousie's Luck, Bothwell, 1980; Bach, 1981; Pope John Paul II, 1984; Florence Nightingale, 1985; Beryl Markham: a shadow in the sun, 1988; Secret Weapon, Acting in Tragedy (BBC Masterclass), 1990; The Lost Language of Cranes, The Cloning of Joanna May, The Big Battalions, 1992; The Negotiator, 1994; Witness for Hitler, Blow Your Mind See A Play, 1995; Nuremberg (best supporting actor, Emmy Award), 2001; Frasier, 2002; The Strange Case of Sherlock Holmes and Arthur Conan Doyle, Blue/Orange, 2005; Deadwood, 2006; The Outsiders, The Secret of the Nutcracker, 2007; The Day of the Triffids, Marple: They Do It with Mirrors, 2009; On Expenses, 2010; Brian Cox's Jute Journey, 2010; The Sinking of the Laconia, 2011; The Straits, A Touch of Cloth, Addicted to Pleasure, 2012; An Adventure in Space and Time, 2013; Bob Servant, 2013–15; Shetland, The Game, 2014; War and Peace, 2015; The Slap, 2015; Penny Dreadful, 2016; Medici: Masters of Florence, 2016; Brian Cox's Russia, 2017; Urban Myths, 2017; Succession, 2018, 2019; *radio*: McLevy, 2001–15; *directed*: Edinburgh Festival: The Man with a Flower in his Mouth, The Stronger, 1973; Orange Tree, Richmond: I Love My Love, 1982; Mrs Warren's Profession, 1989; The Crucible, Moscow Art Theatre, London and Edinburgh, 1988–89; The Philanderer, Hampstead Th. Club, 1991 (world première of complete version); Richard III, Regent's Park Open Air Th., 1995. Rector, Dundee Univ., 2010–16. Hon. LLD Dundee, 1994; Hon. DLitt: Queen Margaret, 2007; Kingston, 2011; Hon. DDra, RSAMD, 2007; Hon. Dr Napier, 2008. Internat. Theatre Inst. Award, 1990. *Publications*: Salem to Moscow: an actor's Odyssey,

1991; The Lear Diaries, 1992. *Recreations*: keeping fit, tango. *Address*: c/o Conway van Gelder Grant Ltd, 8–12 Broadwick Street, W1F 8HW. *T*: (020) 7287 0077. *Clubs*: Garrick, Groucho.

**COX, Prof. Brian Edward**, OBE 2010; PhD; FRS 2016; Professor of Particle Physics, University of Manchester, since 2009; Royal Society Professor for Public Engagement in Science, since 2015; *b* Oldham, 3 March 1968; *m* 2003, Gia Milinovich; one *s*, and one step *s*. *Educ*: Hulme Grammar Sch.; Univ. of Manchester (BSc 1st Cl. Hons Physics; PhD). Keyboard player, rock band: Dare, 1986–92; D:Ream, 1993–97. University of Manchester: Mem., High Energy Physics Gp; PPARC Advanced Fellow; Royal Soc. Univ. Res. Fellow, 2005; researcher, ATLAS experiment, Large Hadron Collider, CERN, 2004–. Television: presenter: Wonders of the Solar System, 2010; Wonders of the Universe, 2011; Wonders of Life, 2013; Science Britannica, 2013; Human Universe, 2014; Six Degrees of Separation, 2015; The 21st Century Race for Space, 2017; The Planets, 2019; co-presenter, Stargazing Live, 2011–; Forces of Nature with Brian Cox, 2016; radio: co-presenter, The Infinite Monkey Cage, 2009–. Michael Faraday Award, Royal Soc., 2012. *Publications*: (with Jeff Forshaw) Why Does E=mc$^2$?, 2010; (with Andrew Cohen) Wonders of the Solar System, 2010; (with Andrew Cohen) Wonders of the Universe, 2011; (with Jeff Forshaw) The Quantum Universe: everything that can happen does happen, 2012; (with Andrew Cohen) Wonders of Life, 2013; (with Andrew Cohen) Human Universe, 2014; (with Andrew Cohen) The Planets, 2019. *Address*: School of Physics and Astronomy, University of Manchester, Oxford Road, Manchester M13 9PL; c/o Northbank Talent Management, Cameo House, 11 Bear Street, WC2H 7AS.

**COX, Brian (Robert) Escott**; QC 1974; a Recorder of the Crown Court, 1972–98; *b* 30 Sept. 1932; *yr s* of late George Robert Escott Cox, solicitor, and Doris Cox; *m* 1st, 1956, one *s* two *d*; 2nd, 1969, Noelle Gilormini; one *s* one *d*. *Educ*: Rugby Sch.; Oriel Coll., Oxford (BA Jurisprudence). Called to the Bar, Lincoln's Inn, 1954, Bencher, 1985; Midland and Oxford Circuit; a Dep. High Court Judge, 1980–98. *Recreation*: listening to and playing jazz.

**COX, Rt Hon. (Charles) Geoffrey**; PC 2018; QC 2003; MP (C) Torridge and West Devon, since 2005; Attorney General, since 2018; *b* 30 April 1960; *s* of Michael and Diane Cox; *m* 1985, Jeanie (*née* McDonald); two *s* one *d*. *Educ*: Downing Coll., Cambridge (BA). Called to the Bar, Middle Temple, 1982; in practice, specialising in criminal law, human rights, constitutional, commercial and defamation law; Hd of Chambers, Thomas More Chambers, 2003–. Contested (C) Torridge and W Devon, 2001. *Recreations*: walking, swimming, theatre, literature, political history, enjoying rural life. *Address*: Thomas More Chambers, 7 Lincoln's Inn Fields, WC2A 3BP. *T*: (020) 7404 7000, *Fax*: (020) 7831 4606. *E*: clerks@thomasmore.co.uk; House of Commons, SW1A 0AA.

**COX, Prof. (Christopher) Barry**, PhD, DSc; Professor, Division of Life Sciences, and Assistant Principal, King's College London, 1989–96; *b* 29 July 1931; *s* of Herbert Ernest Cox and May Cox; *m* 1st, 1961, Sheila (*née* Morgan) (*d* 1996); two *s* one *d*; 2nd, 1998, Marie-Hélène (*née* Forges). *Educ*: St Paul's Sch., Kensington (Sen. Foundn Scholar); Balliol Coll., Oxford (MA); St John's Coll., Cambridge (PhD); DSc London. Asst Lectr in Zoology, King's Coll. London, 1956–59; Harkness Fellow of Commonwealth Fund, at Mus. of Comparative Zoology, Harvard, 1959–60; King's College London: Lectr in Zoology, 1959–66; Sen. Lectr, 1966–69; Reader, 1969–76; Prof., 1976–96; Head: Dept of Zoology, 1982–85; Dept of Biology, 1985–88; Fulbright Schol., Stanford Univ., Calif, 1988–89. Mem. Council, Palaeontological Assoc., 1967–69, 1974 (Vice-Pres., 1969–81). Editor: Palaeontology, 1975–79; Proc. of Leatherhead & Dist Local Hist. Soc., 2005–. Palaeontological collecting expedns to Central Africa, 1963; Argentina, 1967; N Brazil, 1972; Qld, Aust., 1978. *Publications*: Prehistoric Animals, 1969; (with P. D. Moore) Biogeography—an ecological and evolutionary approach, 1973, 9th edn 2016; (jtly) The Prehistoric World, 1975; (jtly) Illustrated Encyclopedia of Dinosaurs and Prehistoric Animals, 1988; (jtly) Atlas of The Living World, 1989; research papers on vertebrate palaeontology and historical biogeography, in Phil. Trans. Royal Soc., Proc. Zool. Soc., Nature, Bull. Brit. Mus. (Nat. Hist.), Jl Biogeog., etc. *Recreations*: theatre, old Surrey buildings (Chm., Domestic Bldgs Res. Gp, 2000–05; Sec., Surrey Dendrochronology Project, 2002–).

**COX, Prof. Sir David (Roxbee)**, Kt 1985; PhD; FRS 1973; FRSC; Warden of Nuffield College, Oxford, 1988–94, Hon. Fellow, 1994; *b* 15 July 1924; *s* of S. R. Cox, Handsworth, Birmingham; *m* 1948, Joyce (*née* Drummond), Keighley, Yorks; three *s* one *d*. *Educ*: Handsworth Grammar Sch., Birmingham; St John's Coll., Cambridge (MA). PhD Leeds, 1949. Posts at Royal Aircraft Establishment, 1944–46; Wool Industries Research Assoc., 1946–50; Statistical Laboratory, Cambridge, 1950–55; Visiting Prof., University of N Carolina, 1955–56; Reader in Statistics, 1956–60, Professor of Statistics, 1961–66, Birkbeck Coll. (Fellow, 2001); Prof. of Statistics, 1966–88 and Head of Dept of Maths, 1970–74, Imperial Coll. of Sci. and Technology. SERC Sen. Res. Fellow, 1983–88. President: Bernoulli Soc., 1979–81; Royal Statistical Soc., 1980–82; Pres., ISI, 1995–97. Foreign Member: Royal Danish Acad. of Scis and Letters, 1983; Indian Acad. of Scis, 1997; For. Hon. Mem., Amer. Acad. of Arts and Sciences, 1974; For. Associate, Nat. Acad. of Scis, USA, 1988. FIC 1994; FRSC 2010. Hon. FIA 1991; Hon. FBA 1997; Hon. FRSE 2013. Hon. DSc: Reading, 1982; Bradford, 1982; Helsinki, 1986; Heriot-Watt, 1987; Limburg's Univ. Centrum, 1988; Queen's Univ., Kingston, Ont, 1989; Waterloo, 1991; Neuchâtel, 1992; Padua, 1994; Minnesota, 1994; Toronto, 1994; Abertay Dundee, 1995; Tech. Univ. of Crete, 1996; Athens Univ. of Economics, 1998; Bordeaux II, 1999; Harvard, 1999; Elche, 1999; Rio de Janeiro, 2000; Leeds, 2005; Southampton, 2006; Gothenburg, 2007; Glasgow, 2011. Weldon Meml Prize, Univ. of Oxford, 1984; Kettering Medal, General Motors Cancer Foundn, 1990; (jtly) Max Planck Forschungspreis, 1993; Copley Medal, Royal Soc., 2010; BBVA Foundn Frontiers of Knowledge Award in Basic Scis, 2016; Internat. Prize for Statistical Res., 2016. Editor of Biometrika, 1966–91. *Publications*: Statistical Methods in the Textile Industry, 1949 (jt author); Planning of Experiments, 1958; (jtly) Queues, 1961; Renewal Theory, 1962; (jtly) Theory of Stochastic Processes, 1965; (jtly) Statistical Analysis of Series of Events, 1966; Analysis of Binary Data, 1970, 2nd edn 1989; (jtly) Theoretical Statistics, 1974; (jtly) Problems and Solutions in Theoretical Statistics, 1978; (jtly) Point Processes, 1980; (jtly) Applied Statistics, 1981; (jtly) Analysis of Survival Data, 1984; (jtly) Asymptotic Methods, 1989; (jtly) Inference and Asymptotics, 1994; (jtly) Multivariate Dependencies, 1996; (jtly) Theory of Design of Experiments, 2000; (jtly) Components of Variance, 2002; Selected Papers, two vols, 2005; Principles of Statistical Inference, 2006; (jtly) Principles of Applied Statistics, 2011; (jtly) Case-Control Studies, 2014; papers in Jl of Royal Statistical Society, Biometrika, etc. *Address*: Nuffield College, Oxford OX1 1NF.

**COX, Rt Hon. Geoffrey**; see Cox, Rt Hon. C. G.

**COX, Sir George (Edwin)**, Kt 2005; Chairman, Design Council, 2004–07; *b* 28 May 1940; *s* of George Herbert Cox and Beatrice Mary Cox; *m* 1st, 1963, Gillian Mary Mannings (marr. diss. 1996); two *s*; 2nd, 1996, Lorna Janet Peach; two *d*. *Educ*: Quintin Sch.; Queen Mary Coll., Univ. of London (BScAeEng). Engineer, BAC, 1962–64; Molins Machine Co.: Systems Designer, 1964–67; Manufacturing Manager, 1967–69; Management Consultant, Urwick Orr & Partners, 1969–73; UK Dir, Diebold Gp,

1973–77; Man. Dir, Butler Cox, 1977–92; Chm., 1992–94, Chief Exec., 1993–94, P-E International; Chief Exec., 1995–96, Chm., 1996–99, Unisys Ltd; Man. Dir, Unisys Inf. Services, Europe, 1996–99; Dir Gen., Inst. of Dirs, 1999–2004 (Hon. Life Fellow, 2004). Non-exec. Dir, 2000–07, Sen. Ind. Dir, 2003–07, Bradford & Bingley plc; Member: Bd, Shorts, 2000–; Supervisory Bd, Euronext, 2002–07; Bd, NYSE-Euronext, 2007–13. Cox Review of Creativity in Business, for HM Treasury, reported 2005; Author, Overcoming Short-termism within British Business, reported 2013. Chm., Merlin (Med. Emergency Relief Internat.), 2001–07. Mem. Bd, LIFFE, 1995–2002. Mem. Bd of Inland Revenue, 1996–99. Vis. Prof., Royal Holloway, Univ. of London, 1995–98. Pres., Management Consultancies Assoc., 1991. President: Royal Coll. of Speech and Lang. Therapists, 2008– (Hon. Fellow, 2011); IED, 2010–14 (Hon. FIED 2007). Mem. Adv. Bd, Warwick Business Sch., 2001– (Chm., 2006–10); Pro-Chancellor, 2010–, Chm. Council, 2011–17, Univ. of Warwick. Trustee: VSO, 2004–07; Culham Languages and Sci. Sch., 2009–11. Mem., Information Technologists Co., 1992–; Master, Guild of Mgt Consultants, 1997–98. CCMI (CIMgt 1992); CRAeS 2008. Hon. Fellow, Queen Mary, Univ. of London, 2007. DUniv Middlesex, 2002; Hon. DBA Wolverhampton, 2004; Hon. DDes De Montfort, 2007; Hon. DCL Northumbria, 2007; Hon. DSc: Huddersfield, 2008; Cranfield, 2011. *Publications*: American Secret Projects 2: US Airlifters 1941 to 1961, 2019; American Secret Projects 3: US Airlifters since 1962, 2019; contribs to various jls. *Recreations*: theatre, rowing (Chief Coach, Univ. of London Boat Club, 1976–78, Chm. of Selectors, GB Men's Rowing, 1978–80), history of aviation. *Clubs*: Leander (Pres., 2008–13), University of London Boat (Pres., 2014–).

COX, Gilbert Kirkwood, CVO 2010; MBE 1996; JP; Lord-Lieutenant of Lanarkshire, 2000–10; *b* 24 Aug. 1935; *s* of William and Mary Bryce Cox; *m* 1959, Marjory Moir Ross Taylor; two *s* one *d*. *Educ*: Airdrie Acad.; Glasgow Royal Tech. Coll. NCB, 1953–63; David A. McPhail & Sons Ltd, 1963–71; Gen. Manager, Scotland, Associated Perforators & Weavers Ltd, 1971–97. Dir, Airdrie Savings Bank, 1985–2012 (Chm., 1995–97). Chair, St Andrew's Hospice Airdrie Major Appeal, 2014–. Chm. Bd of Mgt, Coatbridge Coll., 1996–2000. JP N Lanarks, 1984; DL, 1989, Hon. Sheriff, 2002–, Lanarks. *Recreations*: golf, photography, travel. *Address*: Bedford House, 29 Commonhead Street, Airdrie, N Lanarkshire ML6 6NS. *T*: (01236) 763331.

COX, John; freelance director of plays, opera, revue and musicals in Britain and abroad; *b* 12 March 1935; *s* of Leonard John Cox and Ethel Minnie May Cox (*née* McGill). *Educ*: Queen Elizabeth's Hosp., Bristol; St Edmund Hall, Oxford (MA; Hon. Fellow, 1991). Vis. Fellow, European Humanities Res. Centre, Oxford, 1995. Freelance dir, 1959–; Dir of Prodn, Glyndebourne Festival Opera, 1971–81; Gen. Adminr, 1981–85, Artistic Dir, 1985–86, Scottish Opera; Prodn Dir, Royal Opera House, Covent Gdn, 1988–94. Productions include: *Glyndebourne*: Richard Strauss cycle (notably Capriccio, Intermezzo, Der Rosenkavalier), Rake's Progress, The Magic Flute, La Cenerentola; *ENO*: Così fan tutte, Patience, Merry Widow, Lucky Peter's Journey; *Scottish Opera*: L'Egisto, Manon Lescaut, Marriage of Figaro, Lulu, Don Giovanni; *Royal Opera*: Manon, Die Fledermaus, Guillaume Tell, Capriccio, Die Meistersinger, Il Viaggio a Reims, Die Frau ohne Schatten, Tosca, Eugene Onegin; *Garsington Opera*: Così fan tutte, Nozze di Figaro, Philosopher's Stone, Fidelio; *Australian Opera*: Barber of Seville, Albert Herring, Patience, Masked Ball, Capriccio (Olympic Arts Fest.), Arabella; *Santa Fe Opera*: L'Egisto, La Calisto, Marriage of Figaro, Arabella; *Monte Carlo Opera*: Rake's Progress, Hamlet, Eugene Onegin, Picture of Dorian Gray (world première), Vanessa, Così fan tutte, Otello; *Salzburg Opera*: Il Re Pastore, Ariadne auf Naxos (original version), Rake's Progress, Der Freischutz, La Traviata; *Madrid*: Eugene Onegin, La Cenerentola, Rake's Progress, Capriccio; *Drottningholm*: Zemire et Azor, Tom Jones; *San Francisco*: Arabella, Magic Flute, Rake's Progress, Capriccio, Don Carlos, Ariadne auf Naxos, Così fan tutte; *Metropolitan, NY*: Barber of Seville, Magic Flute, Capriccio, Werther, Thaïs; *La Scala, Milan*: Rake's Progress, Magic Flute; *Amsterdam*: Der Rosenkavalier, Tannhäuser, Intermezzo; *Chicago Lyric Opera*: Thaïs, Capriccio, Ariadne auf Naxos, Così fan tutte; *Copenhagen*: Hamlet, Falstaff; *Munich*: Daphne; also opera in Brussels, Stockholm, Cologne, Frankfurt, Florence, Turin, Parma, Nice, Strasbourg, Toulouse, Lisbon, Vienna, Leeds, Dallas, San Diego, Los Angeles, Washington, Houston, Wexford, Melbourne, Vancouver, etc. Jt Librettist, Oscar, Santa Fe Opera, 2013 (world première). Mem., Adv. Bd, Youth At Risk, 2005–. *Address*: 7 West Grove, SE10 8QT. *T*: (020) 8692 2450.
*See also* S. J. Cox.

COX, John Colin Leslie, CBE 1994; Chairman: London Europe Gateway Ltd, since 1996; Alsitek Ltd, since 2012; *b* 23 Oct. 1933; *s* of late Dr Leslie Reginald Cox, OBE, FRS, and Hilda Cecilia Cox; *m* 1983, Avril Joyce Butt; one *s* one *d*. *Educ*: University College Sch., London; Queens' Coll., Cambridge (BA). National Service, 2nd Lieut, 2nd 10th Princess Mary's Own Gurkha Rifles, 1956–58 (GSM Malaya 1958). Joined Shell Group, 1958: Executive positions in Shell Ghana, 1962–65, and in Shell Gp in London, 1966–77; Shell Chemicals UK: Personnel Dir, 1978–81; Dir, Business Develt, and chm. of subsid. cos, 1981–86; Dir Gen., CIA, 1987–95; Chief Exec., London First Centre, 1995–96. Member: Armed Forces Pay Review Body, 1993–99; Steering Bd, Lab. of the Govt Chemist, 1992–96; Adv. Cttee, European Movement, 1994–98; Bd, UK CEED, 1996 (Chm., 1999–2013); Bd, PHLS, 1997–2003; Standards Bd, Edexcel Foundn, 1997; Envmt Cttee, Knightsbridge Assoc., 1997–98; Vice Chm., Defence and Security Forum, 1996; Chief Exec., Pensions, Protection and Investment Accreditation Bd, 2000–08. Mem. (C), Westminster CC, 1998–2006 (Vice Chm., PFI Cttee, 1998, Planning and Licensing Cttee, 2000). Chairman: Governing Body, Westminster Adult Educn Service, 1998; Edge Foundn, 2009–10; Gov., City of Westminster Coll., 2000. Mem., Caux Round Table, 1991–. FRSA 1989. *Recreations*: sailing, antiques, country pursuits, photography. *Clubs*: Army and Navy, Hurlingham, Reform; Leander (Henley on Thames); Royal Solent Yacht (IoW).

COX, Ven. John Stuart; Archdeacon of Sudbury, 1995–2006, now Archdeacon Emeritus; *b* 13 Sept. 1940; *s* of Arthur F. W. Cox and Clarice M. Cox; *m* Mary Diane Williams; one *s* one *d*. *Educ*: Fitzwilliam House, Cambridge (MA); Linacre Coll., and Wycliffe Hall, Oxford (BA); Birmingham Univ. (DPS). Ordained deacon, 1968, priest, 1969; Assistant Curate: St Mary's, Prescot, 1968–71; St George, Newtown, Birmingham, 1971–73; Rector, St George, Newtown, Birmingham, 1973–78; Selection Sec., ACCM, 1978–83 (Sen. Selection Sec., 1979–83); Canon Residentiary, Southwark Cathedral, 1983–91; Diocesan Dir of Ordinands and Dir of Post-Ordination Training, Southwark, 1983–91; Vicar, Holy Trinity Church in the Ecumenical Parish of Roehampton, 1991–95; Diocesan Dir of Educn, St Edmundsbury and Ipswich, 2006–10. *Publications*: (contrib.) Religion and Medicine, Vol. 1, 1970; (contrib.) Say One for Me, 1992; A Risk Worth Taking, 2007; In All Senses, 2008; Fast and Feast, 2008; Cross Examined, 2009; Relationships, 2010; More than Caring and Sharing, 2011; The Voice of the Prophet, 2011; Dreams and Visions, 2011; Life is Not a Game of Perfect, 2012; The Week That Changed the World, 2012; Critical Friend, 2013; Light to the Nations, 2013; What do Christians Believe?, 2014; It's Not Your Fault You're Stressed, 2014; Not Another… Meeting, 2015; Growing in the Faith, 2015; Body Language, 2015; Being a Better PCC, 2016; Hard Pews, Boring Sermons, No Loos, 2016; The Challenge of the Lord's Prayer, 2017; Happy Talk, 2018; Happy and Blessed, 2019. *Recreations*: music, reading, theatre, golf, wine-making. *Address*: 2 Bullen Close, Bury St Edmunds, Suffolk IP33 3JP. *T*: and *Fax*: (01284) 766796.

COX, Jonathan Mark, PhD; Headmaster, Royal Grammar School, Guildford, since 2007; *b* 25 Feb. 1966; *s* of Darrell and Nita Cox; *m* 1993, Rosemary Bruce; one *s* two *d*. *Educ*: Charlton Prep. Sch.; St Mary's Coll., Southampton; Univ. of Southampton (BSc Hons Physiol. with Pharmacol. 1987; PhD Biochem. 1992); Royal Coll. of Music (Cert. Advanced Performance 1988). Whitgift School: Biology Teacher, 1992–98; Hd of Sixth Form, 1998–2001; Second Master, 2001–06. *Recreations*: classical music and close-up magic, enjoying the company of my children, listening to opera, visiting auctions, drinking my father-in-law's fine wine. *Address*: c/o The Royal Grammar School, High Street, Guildford, Surrey GU1 3BB. *T*: (01483) 880608, *Fax*: (01483) 306127. *E*: headmaster@rgsg.co.uk. *Clubs*: East India, MCC, Lansdowne.

COX, Jonson; Chairman, Water Services Regulation Authority, since 2012; Adviser, I Squared Capital, since 2013; *b* 11 Oct. 1956; *s* of Peter Cox and Bobbie Cox (*née* Sutton); partner, Barbara Kennedy Wight; one *s* two *d*. *Educ*: King Edward VI Sch., Totnes; Clare Coll., Cambridge (MA Econs). Royal Dutch/Shell Gp, 1979–92; Man. Dir and Chm., Yorkshire Envmtl, 1993–96; Managing Director: and Mem. Bd, Kelda Gp plc, 1994–2000; Yorkshire Water, 1996–2000; Chief Operating Officer, Railtrack plc, 2000–01; Chief Exec., Valpak Ltd, 2002–04; Gp Chief Exec., Anglian Water Gp plc, 2004–10 (Dep. Chm., 2010). Chairman: UK Coal plc, subseq. Coalfield Resources plc, 2010–12; Harworth Gp, 2012–18; Cory Gp, 2015–18; non-exec. Dir, Wincanton plc, 2006–. *Recreation*: outdoor activities. *Address*: Water Services Regulation Authority, 21 Bloomsbury Street, WC1B 3HF. *T*: (0121) 644 7750. *E*: jonson.cox@ofwat.gov.uk.

COX, Josephine; writer; *b* 15 July 1940; *d* of Bernard and Mary Jane Brindle; *m* Kenneth George Cox; two *s*. Formerly: clerk, Milton Keynes Develt Council; secretarial and teaching posts, incl. Lectr in Sociol. and History, Bletchley Coll., Milton Keynes; Partner, family landscaping co. *Publications*: as Josephine Cox: Her Father's Sins, 1986; Let Loose the Tigers, 1988; Take This Woman, 1989; Angels Cry Sometimes, 1990; Whistledown Woman, 1990; Outcast, 1991; Alley Urchin, 1991; Don't Cry Alone, 1992; Vagabonds, 1993; Jessica's Girl, 1993; Nobody's Darling, 1993; More Than Riches, 1994; Born to Serve, 1994; Little Badness, 1995; Living a Lie, 1995; A Time For Us, 1996; The Devil You Know, 1996; Miss You Forever, 1997; Cradle of Thorns, 1997; Love Me or Leave Me, 1998; Tomorrow the World, 1998; Gilded Cage, 1999; Somewhere, Someday, 1999; Rainbow Days, 2000; Looking Back, 2000; Let It Shine, 2001; The Woman Who Left, 2001; Child of the North: memories of a northern childhood (autobiog.), 2001; Jinnie, 2002; Bad Boy Jack, 2002; The Beachcomber, 2003; Lovers and Liars, 2004; Live the Dream, 2004; The Journey, 2005; Journey's End, 2006; The Loner, 2007; Songbird, 2008; Born Bad, 2009; Divorced and Deadly, 2009; Blood Brothers, 2010; Midnight, 2011; Three Letters, 2012; The Broken Man, 2013; The Runaway Woman, 2014; Lonely Girl, 2015; A Mother's Gift, 2016; as Jane Brindle: Scarlet, 1991; No Mercy, 1992; The Tallow Image, 1994; No Heaven, No Hell, 1995; The Seeker, 1997; Hiding Game, 1998. *Address*: c/o LBA, 91 Great Russell Street, WC1B 3PS.

COX, Hon. Dame Laura (Mary), DBE 2002; a Judge of the High Court of Justice, Queen's Bench Division, 2002–16; *b* 8 Nov. 1951; *d* of John Arthur Bryant and Mary Eileen Bryant (*née* Clarke); *m* 1970, David Cox; three *s*. *Educ*: Queen Mary Coll., Univ. of London (LLB 1973; LLM 1975). Called to the Bar, Inner Temple, 1975, Bencher, 1999; in practice at the Bar, 1976–2002; QC 1994; Head of Chambers, 1996–2002; Associate Mem., Cloisters Chambers, 2016–. A Recorder, 1995–2002. Chairman: Equal Opportunities Cttee, Bar Council, 2000–02; Equal Treatment Adv. Cttee, Judicial Studies Bd, 2003–10; Mem., Justice, 1997–; Mem., Exec. Cttee, Justice Diversity Initiative, 2016–. British Mem., ILO Cttee of Experts, 1998–2013. Chm. Bd, Interights, 2002–05. Pres., Assoc. of Women Barristers, 2005–17; Vice-Pres., UK Assoc. of Women Judges, 2013–16. Hon. Life Pres., Univ. of Essex Law Soc. Hon. Fellow, Queen Mary, Univ. of London, 2005. *Recreations*: music, theatre, cinema, watching football, cooking, novels, walking, arguing with sons!

COX, Nigel John; HM Diplomatic Service, retired; Sensitivity Reviewer, Archives Management, Foreign and Commonwealth Office, since 2015; *b* 23 April 1954; *s* of late Basil Cox, DFC and Anne (*née* Webber); *m* 1992, Olivia Jane, *d* of Lt-Col Sir Julian Tolver Paget, 4th Bt, CVO. *Educ*: The High Sch., Dublin; Trinity Coll., Dublin (BA, LLB); Ecole Nat. d'Administration, Paris. FCO 1975; Chinese lang trng, Cambridge and Hong Kong, 1976–78; Second Sec., Peking, 1978–81; Second, later First, Sec., FCO, 1981–84; Asst Political Advr, Hong Kong, 1984; First Sec., Paris, 1985–90; Assistant Head: Western European Dept, FCO, 1990–91; Hong Kong Dept, FCO, 1991–92; Counsellor, Peking, 1992–96; Hd of SE Asian Dept, FCO, 1996–99; Minister, Peking, 2000–02; Dir, Asia-Pacific, FCO, 2003–05; Sen. Advr to Chief Exec., P&O Gp, 2005–06 (on secondment). Sen. Advr, E Asia, International Power plc, 2007–08; Mem. Adv. Panel, PricewaterhouseCoopers LLP, 2007–09. Clerk, Fishmongers' Co., 2009–13. Gov., Gresham's Sch., 2009–13. *Recreations*: trees, travel, cruise lecturing. *Club*: Travellers.

COX, Patricia Anne, (Mrs Roger Cox); *see* Edwards, P. A.

COX, Patrick; President: International European Movement, 2005–11; Jean Monnet Foundation for Europe, since 2015; Member (ELDR), Munster, 1989–2004, and President, 2002–04, European Parliament; *b* 29 Nov. 1952; *m* 1974, Kathleen Tighe; two *s* four *d*. *Educ*: Trinity Coll., Dublin (BA Mod. Econs 1974). Lecturer in Economics: Inst. of Public Admin, Dublin, 1974–76; Nat. Inst. for Higher Educn, Limerick, 1976–82; TV current affairs reporter and presenter, Today Tonight, Dublin, 1982–86. TD (Progressive Democrats), Cork S Central, 1992–94; Leader, Liberal Gp, European Parlt, 1998–2002. Gen. Sec., Progressive Democrat Party, 1986–89. Dir, Tiger Develts Europe; Member: Eur. Adv. Council, Microsoft; Eur. Adv. Council, Pfizer; Conseil de Surveillance, Michelin. Comr Gen., Europalia, Brussels, 2006, 2008. Pres., European Parlt Former Members' Assoc., 2010–14. EU Project Coordinator: Priority Project No. 1, TEN-T policy, 2010–13; Scandinavian-Mediterranean TEN-T Core Network Corridor, 2014–. Chm., Limerick City of Culture, 2014. Member: Bd, Michael Smurfit Grad. Sch. of Business, UCD; Pres.'s Adv. Bd, Univ. Coll. Cork. Member, Board of Trustees: Crisis Gp; Friends of Europe; Edmund Rice Schs Trust; Mem. Bd, Third Age Foundn. Patron: Blue Box Creative Learning Centre, Limerick; Fedn for Victim Assistance. Hon. Life Mem., Irish Inst. of Trng and Develt, 2002. Hon. Fellow, Irish Auctioneers and Valuers Instn, 2002. Freeman, Limerick City, 2002. Hon. LLD NUI, 2002; Hon. DHL American Coll., Dublin/Lynn Univ., Florida, 2002; Hon. Dr: TCD; Limerick; Open. President's Medal, Univ. of Limerick, 2002; European Movt/Aer Rianta European of Year Award, 2002; Charlemagne Prize, 2004. *Address*: Foundation Jean Monnet pour l'Europe, Ferme de Dorigny, 1015 Lausanne, Switzerland.

COX, Paul William; freelance artist and illustrator, since 1982; *b* 31 July 1957; *s* of late Oliver Jasper Cox, CBE, RIBA and Jean Cox; *m* 1987, Julia Claire Nichol; one *s* one *d*. *Educ*: Port Regis and Stanbridge Earls School; Camberwell Sch. of Art and Crafts (BA Hons); Royal Coll. of Art (MA). Contributor to: The Times, Daily Telegraph, Independent, Express, Spectator, Punch, Sunday Times, Observer, Guardian, New Yorker,

Vanity Fair, Town and Country, Wall St Journal, Traditional Home, Chatelaine, Business Week, House Beautiful, Country Life, Elle Decor Britain; founder contributor to Blueprint, 1984; designed: PO stamps for Lord Mayor's Show, 1989; mural for Eleanor Davies Colley Lect. Th., RCS, 2004; sets for 50th anniv. prodn of Salad Days, 2005; 15 paintings for St Charles Hosp., 2007; exhibns of watercolour drawings: Workshop Gallery, 1984; Illustrators' Gallery, 1985; Chris Beetles Gallery, 1989, 1993, 2001, 2006, 2009, 2010, 2011, major retrospective 2013, 2020; Molesworth Gall., Dublin, 2001; Durrell Wildlife Conservation Trusts, 2006; historical illustrations for Drama and Debate exhibn, Hampton Ct Palace, 2004; 65 covers for International Living, 2010–15; 15 illustrations, Anderson & Sheppard, 2011; illustrated Today Prog. for opening of House of Illustration, 2014. Vis. Lectr in Illustration, Camberwell Sch. of Art and Crafts, 1982–90; Sen. Tutor, West Dean Coll., 2009–11. *Publications:* illustrated books: Low Tech, 1982; Experiences of an Irish RM, 1984; The Common Years, 1984; A Varied Life, 1984; The Outing, 1985; The Character of Cricket, 1986; Romantic Gardens, 1988; Evacuee, 1988; Rebuilding the Globe, 1989; Dear Boy, 1989; Leave it to Psmith, 1989; Three Men in a Boat, 1989; The Cricket Match, 1991; Honourable Estates, 1992; The Darling Buds of May, 1992; The Russian Tea Room, 1993; The Wind in the Willows, 1993; Rumpole, 1994; Look out London, 1995; Jeeves & Wooster, 1996; The Plumbs of P. G. Wodehouse, 1997; Three Men on the Bummel, 1998, rev. edn 2018; Tinkerbill, 1999; Jeeves & Wooster II, 2000; Best After-Dinner Stories, 2003; The Giver, 2003; The Train To Glasgow, 2003; The Best of Blandings, 2004; The Folio Book of Comic Short Stories, 2005; My Family and Other Animals, 2006; The Elevator Man, 2008; Absolute Corkers, 2008; Jeeves & Wooster III, 2010; Gay and Lesbian Etiquette, 2011; Running is Flying, 2012; Did I Mention the Free Wine, 2012; Lord Peter Views the Body, 2016; Hangman's Holiday; 2018; In Search of Art, 2018; The Clicking of Cuthbert, 2019; The Long, The Short and The Tall, 2020. *Address:* 23 Bromwich Avenue, Highgate, N6 6QH. *T:* (020) 8347 9515. *E:* paulwcox@gmail.com. *Club:* Chelsea Arts.

**COX, Pauline Victoria,** MA; Head Teacher, The Tiffin Girls' School, 1994–2010; *b* 9 Oct. 1948; *d* of Harold and Lily Greenwood; *m* 1970, Stephen James Cox, *qv*; one *s* one *d*. *Educ:* High Storrs Girls' Grammar Sch., Sheffield; Birmingham Univ. (BA Hons Geography 1970); Inst. of Education, London Univ. (PGCE 1973); W London Inst. of HE (RSA Dip. TEFL 1981; MA London 1983. Asst Editor, Polish News Bulletin of British and American Embassies, Warsaw, 1971–72; Teacher, subseq. also Head of Geography, Wandsworth Boys' Sch., 1973–75; Teacher of Geography, Lady Eleanor Holles Sch., Hampton, 1976–77; Lectr in ESL, Univ. of Legon, Accra, Ghana, 1978–80; Teacher of Geography: Tiffin Girls' Sch., 1981–83; Teddington Sch., 1983–84; Head of Geography, Waldegrave Sch. for Girls, Twickenham, 1984–87; Dep. Head, Cranford Community Sch., Hounslow, 1987–94; Exec. Hd Teacher, Tiffin Boys' Sch., Jan.–Aug. 2009. Mem. Council, London South LSC, 2001–04. Judge, Teaching Awards, 2005–06. Trustee: Smallpeice Trust, 2007– (Chm., 2014–18); Arkwright Scholarships Trust, 2007– (Chm., 2014–18); Mus. of Richmond, 2010–. FRGS 1988. *Recreations:* reading crime fiction, watching sport.

**COX, Peter Frederick;** Head of Information & Archives (formerly Libraries), BBC, 1993–98; *b* 1 Dec. 1945; *s* of George William and Edna May Cox; *m* 1968, Gillian Mary Stevens; two *d*. *Educ:* Bedford Sch.; University Coll. London (BA); Univ. of Herts (MSc 1999). MCLIP (ALA 1968; MIInfSc). Chartered Librarian, 1968; Sen. Asst County Librarian, Herts, 1979–88; City of Westminster: City Librarian, 1989–92; Asst Dir (Leisure and Libraries), 1992–93. Member: Library and Information Services Council for England and Wales, 1992–95; Cttee on Public Library Objectives, 1992; Adv. Cttee, Nat. Sound Archive, 1996–98. FRSA 1991. JP Stevenage, 1980–88. *Publications:* professional articles and symposia papers. *Recreations:* sailing, painting. *Address:* 14 Ellis Grove, Norton Fitzwarren, Taunton, Somerset TA2 6SY. *T:* (01823) 284780.

**COX, Prof. Peter Michael,** PhD; Professor of Climate System Dynamics, University of Exeter, since 2006; *b* London, 4 March 1964; *s* of Thomas James Charles Cox and June Patricia Cox; *m* 2019, Hazel Ann Jeffery; three *s* one *d*. *Educ:* Hassenbrook Sch., Stanford-le-Hope; Palmer's Coll., Grays; Univ. of Warwick (BSc); King's Coll., Cambridge (MPhil); Imperial Coll. London (PhD 1990). Scientific Officer, UKAEA Culham Lab., 1988–90; Hd, Climate, Chemistry and Ecosystems, Met Office, 1990–2004; Sci. Dir, Climate Change, Centre for Ecol. and Hydrol., 2004–06. *Recreations:* cricket, walking. *Address:* The Stables, Hoppins, Southerton, Ottery St Mary, Devon EX11 1SD. *T:* 07827 412572. *E:* p.m.cox@exeter.ac.uk.

**COX, Philip Ardagh R.;** *see* Roxbee Cox.

**COX, Philip Christopher;** Chief Executive, Cheshire and Warrington Local Enterprise Partnership, since 2014; *b* Hertford, 30 Dec. 1963; *s* of Leonard and Jean Cox; *m* 1988, Gillian Plews; two *s* one *d*. *Educ:* Univ. of Durham (BA Hons Econs); Queen Mary Coll., Univ. of London (MSc Econ.). Economist, DSS, 1985–93; Economist, 1993–96, Hd, Railways Econs and Finance, 1996–98, Dept of Transport; Head: Housing and Urban Econs, DETR, 1998–2001; Millennium Dome Sale Unit, 2001–02, Regl Econ. Performance, 2003–05, ODPM; Principal Private Sec. to Dep. Prime Minister, 2005–07; Department for Communities and Local Government: Director: Homes and Communities Agency Implementation, 2007–08; Thames Gateway and Olympics, 2009–10; Olympics, Thames Gateway and Regeneration, 2010; Local Economies, Regeneration and European Progs, 2011–14. *Recreations:* walking, Member of Scout Association. *Address:* Cheshire and Warrington Local Enterprise Partnership, Wyvern House, The Drumber, Winsford CW7 1AH.

**COX, Philip Gotsall,** CBE 2013; Chairman, Drax Group plc, since 2015; *b* 22 Sept. 1951; *m* 1976, Brenda Sadler; one *s* one *d*. *Educ:* Queens' Coll., Cambridge (BA 1973; MA). FCA. Gp Controller, 1989–98, Chief Financial Officer, 1998–99, Siebe plc; Sen. Vice-Pres., Ops Invensys plc, 1999–2000; Chief Financial Officer, 2000–03, CEO, 2003–13, International Power plc, later GDF SUEZ Energy Internat. Chairman: Global Power Generation, 2015–17; Kier plc, 2017–19; Sen. Ind. Dir, Wm Morrison Supermarkets, 2009–15 (Chm., Audit Cttee, 2009–15); non-executive Director: Meggit plc, 2012–15; PPL, 2013–15; Talen, 2015–16. Mem., CBI President's Cttee, 2010–13. *Recreations:* golf, football. *T:* 07712 279757. *E:* philipgcox51@gmail.com.

**COX, Raymond Edwin;** QC 2002; *b* 6 May 1959; *s* of Edwin David Cox and Catherine (*née* Mook Lan, now Deverill-West); *m* 1990, Alexandra Clare Howell; two *s* two *d*. *Educ:* Mansfield Coll., Oxford (BA Hons Jurisprudence (1st cl.); Eldon Schol.). Called to the Bar, Gray's Inn (Arden Schol.), 1982, Bencher, 2008. Consultant Editor, Civil Procedure Reports, 2005–. *Publications:* (ed jtly) Commercial Court Procedure, 2000; (ed jtly) Law of Bank Payments, 4th edn, 2010; Private International Law of Reinsurance and Insurance, 2006. *Recreations:* music, ski-ing. *Address:* Fountain Court Chambers, Temple, EC4Y 9DH. *T:* (020) 7583 3335, *Fax:* (020) 7353 0329. *E:* rc@fountaincourt.co.uk.

**COX, Richard T.;** *see* Temple Cox.

**COX, Dr Roger;** Director, Centre for Radiation, Chemical and Environmental Hazards, Health Protection Agency, 2005–09; *b* 26 May 1947; *s* of Thomas and Leonora Cox; *m* 1971, Susan Whisstock; one *s* one *d*. *Educ:* Univ. of Reading (BSc Hons Microbiol. 1968; PhD Microbial Genetics 1973). With MRC, 1971–90; Hd of Dept, and Div. Hd, 1990–2003, Dir, 2003–05, NRPB. Hon. Prof., Brunel Univ., 1999–. Delegate to UN Scientific Cttee on Effects of Atomic Radiation, 2001–09. Member: Internat. Commn on Radiological Protection, 1996–2009 (Vice Chm., 2003–09); Biol Effects of Ionizing Radiation VII Cttee, NAS, 1999–2005. Hon. Mem., ARR, 2011. FMedSci 2006. Hon. Fellow, Soc. for Radiological Protection, 2007. (Jtly) Weiss Medal, ARR, 1992. *Publications:* (jtly) Health Risks from Exposure to Low Levels of Ionizing Radiation, 2005; numerous contribs to radiation sci. and cell/molecular biol. jls and reports. *Recreations:* family life, boats, fishing, cinema. *E:* rogercoxis@btinternet.com.

**COX, Roy Arthur,** CBE 1987; JDipMA; FCA, FCMA, FCBSI; Chief General Manager, 1970–85, Director, 1976–89, Alliance and Leicester (formerly Alliance) Building Society; *b* 30 Nov. 1925; *s* of J. W. Arthur Cox; *m* 1st, 1951, Joy (*née* Dunsford); one *s* one *d*, 2nd, 1980, Audrey (*née* Brayham); 3rd, 2007, Audrey (*née* Smith). *Educ:* Isleworth Grammar Sch. FCA 1953; FCMA 1957; FCBSI (FBS 1971). War Service, 1944–47. Wells & Partners, Chartered Accountants, 1942–49; Colombo Commercial Co. Ltd, 1950–61; Urwick, Orr & Partners, Management Consultants, 1961–65; Alliance Building Society: Sec., 1965; Gen. Man., 1967. Dir, Southern Bd, Legal & General Assce Soc. Ltd, 1972–86. Building Societies Association: Chm., S Eastern Assoc., 1972–74; Mem. Council, 1975–87; Chm., Gen. Purposes and Public Relations Cttee, 1975–77; Dep. Chm., Council, 1983–85; Chm., Council, 1985–87; Vice-Pres., 1987–2002. Mem., Royal Commn on Distribution of Income and Wealth, 1974–78; Dir, SE Electricity Bd, 1983–90; Dep. Chm., Seeboard plc, 1990–96; Chairman: PO Staff Superannuation Scheme, 1986–95; PO Pension Scheme, 1987–95; Siebe Pension Trustee Ltd, 1992–2000; Dir, Hermes Pensions Management Ltd, 1995–98. CCMI (CBIM 1980). *Recreations:* golf, snooker, bridge.

**COX, Sarah Elizabeth;** Chief Operating Officer, Office of Gas and Electricity Markets, since 2016; *b* 19 May 1967; *d* of Dr Joseph Cox and Dr Barbara Cox (*née* Smith). *Educ:* Arnold Sch., Blackpool; Univ. of Birmingham (BCom Hons 1988). APMI 1991. Commercial Union Assce Co., later CGU and Aviva, 1991–2001: operational mgt, 1991–95; Prog. Dir, 1995–98; IT Service Centre Manager, 1996–98; Sen. Consultant, 1998–2000; Business Develt Manager, Norwich Union Internat., Aviva plc, 2000–01; Partner, Business Change and Delivery, Barclays Solutions, Barclays plc, 2001–04; Dir, Business Change and Delivery, ODPM, 2004–06; a Dir, Capability Rev. Team, Prime Minister's Delivery Unit, 2006–07, Dir, Strategy, Planning and Performance, 2007–10, Cabinet Office; Hd, Business Planning and Prog. Mgt, London 2012 Olympic Games, 2010–12; Department for Work and Pensions: Dir, Universal Credit Prog., 2013; Sr Responsible Owner, State Pensions Reform; Dir, Deliver in Business Transformation Gp, 2016. DUniv Birmingham, 2012. *Recreations:* golf, season ticket holder at Chelsea FC. *Club:* Woodcote Park Golf (Lady Captain, 2013).

**COX, Sebert Leslie,** OBE 1994; Partner, Kingston Reid Consulting, since 2001; Chairman, Key Real Estate Ltd, since 2004; *b* 27 Dec. 1950; *s* of late Maunsell Newton Cox and Anna Louise Cox (*née* Reid); *m* 1974, Christine Lesley Hall; two *d*. *Educ:* Univ. of Lancaster (MSc). Granada Gp Ltd, 1967–70; Ford Motor Co. Ltd, 1970–72; Easton House Trust, 1972–73; Springboard Trust, 1973–76; Northumbria Probation Service, 1976–90; Develt Advr, Home Office, 1990–2001; Chairman: Thames Gateway Ltd Partnership, 2003–05; NNTLIFTCo Ltd, 2004–09. Chairman: N British Housing Assoc., subseq. Places for People Gp, 1997–2004; Co. Durham Probation Bd, 2007–10; Durham Tees Valley Probation Trust, 2010–14; Probation Assoc., 2010–15; Derwentside Homes Ltd, 2013–17; Karbon Homes, 2017–. Non-exec. Dir, Nat. Housing Fedn, 2018–. Mem., Inst. of Dirs, 1996. *Recreations:* cooking and entertaining, gardening, walking, visiting historic buildings. *Address:* Spurtop House, Whitehall Lane, Iveston, Co. Durham DH8 7TA.

**COX, Stella Anne;** *see* Burgess, S. A.

**COX, Stephen James,** CVO 1997; Executive Director (formerly Executive Secretary), Royal Society, 1997–2011; *b* 5 Dec. 1946; *s* of late Harold James West Cox and Norah Cox (*née* Wilkinson); *m* 1970, Pauline Victoria Greenwood (*see* P. V. Cox); one *s* one *d*. *Educ:* Queen Elizabeth Grammar Sch., Blackburn; Atlantic Coll.; Birmingham Univ. (BA Hons Geography 1969); Leeds Univ. (Postgrad. Dip. ESL 1970); Sussex Univ. (MA Educn 1977). VSO, Bolivia, 1965–66. British Council: Warsaw, 1970; Western Europe Dept, London, 1974; Accra, 1977; Staff Training Dept, 1981; Chm., British Council Whitley Council, Trade Union Side, 1981–84; Educn Attaché, Washington DC, 1984–85; Asst Sec., Royal Society, 1985–91; Dir Gen., Commonwealth Inst., 1991–97; Chief Exec., Westminster Foundn for Democracy, 1995–97. Member: Jt Commonwealth Socs Council, 1992–97; Court, RCA, 1993–99; Council, Parly and Scientific Cttee, 1997–2011 (Vice-Pres., 2004–08); Council, British Sci. Assoc. (formerly BAAS), 1997–2010; Crown Estate Paving Commn, 2002–14. Trustee: Council for Assisting Refugee Academics, 1997–2010; Internat. Polar Foundn, 2006–18. Chm., Richmond Duke of Edinburgh Awards Forum, 2003–07. Mem. Bd of Govs, 2002–09, and Chair, Audit Cttee, 2004–08, Kingston Univ.; Chm. of Govs, Atlantic Coll., 2010–15; Chm. Council, Royal Holloway, Univ. of London, 2011–18. FRGS (Member: Sci. and Public Affairs Cttee, 1994–96; Educn Cttee, 1996–98; Expedn and Field Work Cttee, 1998–2004). Mem., 1994–, Chm., 2002–06, Editl Bd, Commonwealth Round Table. Hon. DSc Lancaster, 2003. *Recreations:* cricket, travel, visiting galleries, architecture. *Address:* 25 Trowlock Avenue, Teddington, Middx TW11 9QT. *Clubs:* Royal Over-Seas League, Geographical; Middlesex County Cricket.

**COX, Stephen Joseph,** RA 1970; artist; *b* Bristol, 16 Sept. 1946; *s* of late Leonard John Cox and Ethel Minnie May Cox (*née* McGill); *m* 1996, Judith Atkins; two *d*. *Educ:* St Mary Redcliffe, Bristol; W of England Coll. of Art; Loughborough Coll. of Art; Central Sch. of Art and Design (DipAD Hons). Lectr, Brighton Poly., 1980–81; part-time Lectr, Coventry Coll. of Art, 1968–72; Stourbridge Coll. of Art, 1973–75; Newport Coll. of Art, 1975–77; Birmingham Poly., 1977–79, 1980–81. Sen. Res. Fellow, Wimbledon Sch. of Art, 1995–96. First Vis. Montgomery Fellow in Sculpture, Lincoln Coll., Oxford, 2009. Hon. Fellow, Hereford Coll. of Art, 2010. Solo exhibitions include: Lisson Gall., 1976, 1977, 1980; Gallerie Swart, Amsterdam, 1978; Bonomo Gall., Bari, 1981; Gallerie La Salita, Rome, 1982; 25th Festivale dei Due Mondi, Spoleto, 1982; Greenwood Gall., 1982; Villa Romana, Florence, 1983; Casa di Masacchio, San Giovanni Valdarno, 1984; Arnolfini Gall., Bristol, MOMA Oxford, Midland Gp Gall., Nottingham, 1985; Tate Gall., 1986; UK Rep., Indian Triennale, 1986; Gallerie Carini, Florence, 1987, 1989; Bath Fest. Artsite Gall., 1988; Art Now, Gothenberg, 1991; Mus. of Egyptian Modern Art, Cairo, 1995; Henry Moore Inst., 1995; Michael Hue-Williams Fine Art, 1995, 1996, 1998–99; Royal Botanic Gdns, Kew, 1995–96; An Indian Decade, three exhibitions, Art Today Gall., Ajanta Gall. and Jamali Kamali Gdns, 1996; Dulwich Picture Gall., 1997; Glyndebourne Opera Hse, 1998; Santa Maria Della Scala, Piazza del Duomo, Siena, 1999; Mus. Archeologico, Aosta, Italy, 2000; Culture Gall., NY, 2001; Eyestorm Gall., London, 2004; Mappa Mundi, Hereford Cathedral and Meadow Gall., Burford, 2004; San Francesco Della Scarpa, Bari, 2005; Bristol City Mus. and Art Gall., 2006; Lincoln Coll., Oxford, 2009; The Meaning of Stone, Ludlow Castle, 2011; Meaning in Drawing, Drawing Gall., Walford, 2011; Yogini Drawings, Chelsea Arts Club, 2012; Gemini, Canterbury Cathedral, 2016–17; *group exhibitions* include: Paris Biennale, 1977; Hayward Gall., 1978, 1983; Whitechapel Art Gall., 1981; Venice Biennale, 1982, 1984; Kunstmuseum, Lucerne, 1982; Tate Gall., 1983, 1985,

1992, 1994, 1997; Internat. Garden Fest., Liverpool, 1984; MOMA, NY, 1984; Twentieth Century Watercolours, V&A, 1984; Summer Exhibn, RA 1985, 1988 (Goldhill Prize for Sculpture); Kunstverein, Frankfurt, Sydney Biennale, 1986; Serpentine, 19th Biennale Antwerp, 1987; Musee d'Art Moderne, Brussels, 1987–88; Lincoln Cathedral, 1990; MOMA, Brussels, 1992; BM and Museo Egizio Torino, 1994–95; Hathill Foundn, Goodwood, 1997; Schloss Ambrass, Innsbruck, Jesus Coll., Cambridge, 1999; Gori Collection, Japan, Nat. Gall., Winchester Cathedral, 2000; Guggenheim, Venice, Cass Sculpture Foundn, 2002; Summer Exhibn, Burghley Hse, Lincs, 2003; Beyond Limits, Chatsworth, 2015; Sculpture Park, Madhavendra Palace, Nahagarth Fort, Jaipur, 2017–18; *work in collections* includes: Tate Gall., V&A, BM, British Council, Arts Council, Walker Art Gall., Liverpool, Henry Moore Centre for Sculpture, Hunterian Art Gall., Groningen Mus., Netherlands, Comune di Spoleto, Fogg Mus., USA, Hakone Open Air Mus., Japan; *commissions* include: Atyeo, Baltic Wharf, Bristol, 1987; 'Song', Cairo Opera Hse, 1989; Ganapathi and Devi, Broadgate, 1989; Osirisisis, Stockley Park, nr Heathrow, 1991; Hymn, Univ. of Kent at Canterbury, 1991; Mantra, British Council bldg, New Delhi, 1992; Echo, Fleet Place, Ludgate Hill, 1993; Reredos, altar, font and stations of the cross, Ch of St Paul Haringey, 1995; Rajiv Gandhi Samadi, New Delhi (Lotus Field), 1997; Adam and Eve vessels, St Luke's, Chelsea, 1996; Eucharist, Cathedral Ch of St Nicholas, Newcastle upon Tyne, 1997; Tribute sculpture, British High Commn, Canberra, 1997; Faceted Column, Finsbury Pavement, 1999; altar, St Anselm's Chapel, Canterbury Cathedral, consecrated 2006 (Art and Christianity Enquiry Award for Art in a Religious Context, 2007); Tribute to St Anselm, Aosta Cathedral, 2009; Peregrine and other sculpture, Goodwood, 2009; Virgin Mary and St Mildred, Tower Gateway, Lincoln Coll., Oxford, 2009; Holy Water Stoup, Canterbury Cathedral, 2010; Willoughby Meml, St Michael and All Angels Church, Edenham, Lincs, 2011; Elemental Head, St James' Gateway, London, 2013; 'Relief: Figure Emerging' and 'Commemorative Wall to Lutyens', Apple Tree Yard, 8 St James's Sq., 2015. *Relevant Publication*: The Sculpture of Stephen Cox, by Stephen Bann, 1995. *Address*: Lower House Farm, Coreley, Ludlow, Shropshire SY8 3AS. *T*: (01584) 891532. *E*: stephen@stephencoxra.com. *W*: www.stephencoxra.com. *Clubs*: Arts, Chelsea Arts.

*See also J. Cox.*

**COX, Prof. Susan Jean**, OBE 2011; Professor of Safety and Risk Management, Lancaster University, since 2001 (Dean, Lancaster University Management School, 2001–15, now Dean Emeritus); *b* 17 Oct. 1947; *d* of late Derric and Jean Minshall; *m* 1969, Thomas Rodford Cox, CBE; two *d*. *Educ*: Univ. of Nottingham (BSc (Chemistry and Psychol.) 1969; MPhil (Psychol.) 1988). Loughborough University: Director: Centre for Extension Studies, 1993–94; Centre for Hazard and Risk Mgt, 1994–97; Loughborough Business Sch., 1997–2001. Chm., Assoc. of Business Schs, 2002–04; Mem., Res. Priorities Bd, ESRC, 2003–07; Dir, Inspire Learning, 2003–06. *Publications*: (with Robin Tait) Reliability, Safety and Risk Management: an integrated approach, 1991, 2nd edn 1998; (with Tom Cox) Safety, Systems and People, 1996. *Recreations*: gardening, theatre, walking, football (Stoke City supporter), reading, travel. *Address*: Walnut Lodge, Rose Grove, Keyworth, Notts NG12 5HE. *T*: (0115) 937 5947, *Fax*: (office) (01524) 594720. *E*: s.cox@lancaster.ac.uk.

**COX, Timothy Blakiston**; Lord-Lieutenant of Warwickshire, since 2013; *b* Shrewsbury, 8 Sept. 1955; *s* of William Peter Cox and June Eleanor Cox; *m* 1984, Penny Roudoubous; one *s* one *d*. *Educ*: Shrewsbury Sch. MRICS 1980. With Chesshire Gibson & Co., 1974–86; founder, Tim Cox Associates, chartered surveyors, 1986–. High Sheriff, Warwicks, 2011–12. *Recreations*: sport, golf and tennis. *Address*: Tim Cox Associates, 37 Guild Street, Stratford-upon-Avon, Warks CV37 6QY.

**COX, Prof. Timothy Martin**, MD; FRCP, FMedSci; Professor of Medicine, 1989–2015, now Emeritus, and Director of Research, Department of Medicine, since 2015, University of Cambridge; Fellow of Sidney Sussex College, Cambridge, 1990–2015, now Life Fellow; *b* 10 May 1948; *s* of late William Neville Cox, Leicester and Joan Désirée Cox (*née* Ward); *m* 1975, Susan Ruth Mason; three *s* one *d*. *Educ*: Oundle Sch.; London Hosp. Med. Coll., Univ. of London (Price Entrance Scholar; James Anderson Prize; MB 1971, MSc 1978, MD 1979); MA Cantab 1990, MD Cantab (published works) 1991. FRCP 1984. Junior posts, Med. Unit, Royal London Hosp., 1971; Dept of Morbid Anatomy, Bernard Baron Inst., Hammersmith and United Oxford Hosps, 1972–77; Royal Postgraduate Medical School, London University: MRC Training Fellow, Cell Biology Unit, 1977–79; Wellcome Sen. Clinical Fellow and Sen. Lectr, Dept of Medicine, 1979–87; Sen. Lectr, Depts of Haematology and Medicine, 1987–89. Hon. Consultant Physician, Addenbrooke's Hosp., 1989–. Vis. Scientist, Dept of Biology, MIT, 1983–84. Vis. Prof., Weizmann Inst. of Sci., Rehovot, Israel, 2012. Pres., Translational Medicine Cttee, L'Agence nationale de la recherche, Paris, 2013–15. Lectures: A. J. S. McFadzean, Univ. of Hong Kong, 1990; Schorstein Meml, London Hosp. Med. Coll., 1994; Bradshaw, RCP, 1996; Flynn, RCPath, 2001 and 2009; Opening Lect., Gordon Res. Conf. on Lysosomal Diseases, Galveston, 2011; Hunterian Oration, Hunterian Soc., 2012; Benoziyo, Weizmann Inst. 2012; 17th McFadzean Oration, Hong Kong Coll. of Physicians, 2012 (Gold Medal); Cambridge Philosophical Soc., 2016. External examiner in Medicine: Univ. of Hong Kong, 1990; Univ. of London, 1993–97; RCSI, 1995–97; Chinese Univ. of HK, 2001; Univ. of Oxford, 2001–05. Member: MRC Grants Cttee, 1990–94; MRC Clin. Trng Career Develt Panel, 2000–03. Mem., Vet. Panel, Wellcome Trust, 1996–98. Trustee, Croucher Foundn, HK, 2001– (Vice-Chm., 2013–). Mem., Assoc. of Physicians of GB and Ire., 1984– (Mem., Exec. Cttee, 1995–97); Cambridge Philosophical Society: Mem. Council, 1994–; Vice Pres., 1999–2002, 2005–; Pres., 2002–03; Sen. Vice Pres., 2003–05. Fellow and Mem. Council, Galton Inst., 2007–15. Founder FMedSci 1998; FRSocMed 2009. FRSA 2000. Syndic, 1998–2014, Co-optee, Academic Publishing Cttee, 2014–18, CUP; Mem., Editl Bd, Qly Jl of Medicine; Ed.-in-Chief, Expert Reviews in Molecular Medicine, 2013–. *Publications*: Oxford Textbook of Medicine, (contrib.) 3rd edn, 1995, (ed jtly) 6th edn, 2019; (ed jtly) Molecular Biology in Medicine, 1997 (trans. Spanish 1998, Serbo-Croat 2000); over 280 contribs to sci. and med. jls on inborn errors metabolism, incl. Cell, New England Jl of Medicine, Lancet, Jl of Clin. Investigation, Jl Biol. Chem., Nature Reviews Genetics, Proc. Nat. Acad. Sci. (USA), Medicine (Baltimore), Nature Medicine, Jl of Pathology. *Recreations*: natural history, piano, making cider. *Address*: Department of Medicine, University of Cambridge School of Clinical Medicine, Hills Road, Cambridge CB2 0QQ. *T*: (01223) 336866, (assistant) (01223) 762007.

**COX, Vivienne**, CBE 2016; Executive Vice President, and Chief Executive Officer, Alternative Energy, BP plc, 2008–09; *b* 29 May 1959; *d* of Ewart Arthur Cox and Doreen Olive Cox (*née* Merchant); *m* 2007, Eric Vischer; two *d*. *Educ*: St Catherine's Coll., Oxford (BSc 1981, MA); INSEAD (MBA 1989). Joined BP, 1981; Chief Exec., Air BP, 1997–99; Group Vice President: Refining and Mkting, 1999–2001; Integrated Supply and Trading, 2001–05; Exec. Vice Pres., Gas Power and Renewables, 2005–08. Non-executive Director: Rio Tinto, 2005–14; Climate Change Capital, 2008–12 (Chm., 2009–12); Vallourec, 2010–14; DFID, 2010–; Pearson plc, 2012–; BG Gp, 2012–16. Mem., Internat. Council and Bd, INSEAD, 2009–13; Adjunct Prof., Imperial Coll. London. Patron, St Francis Hospice, 2006–. Hon. DSc Hull, 2009. *Recreations*: sailing, swimming, gardening.

**COX, Hon. William John Ellis**, AC 1999; RFD 1985; ED 1968; Governor, Tasmania, 2004–08; *b* 1 April 1936; *s* of Hon. William Ellis Cox, CBE, MC, and Alice May Cox; *m* 1970, Jocelyn Fay Wallace; two *s* one *d*. *Educ*: Xavier Coll., Melbourne; Univ. of Tasmania (BA, LLB). Called to the Bar, Tasmania, 1960; Partner, Dobson, Mitchell & Allport, 1961–76; Magistrate, Hobart, 1976–77; Crown Advocate, Tasmania, 1977–82; QC 1978; Judge, Supreme Court of Tasmania, 1982–95; Chief Justice, Tasmania, 1995–2004; Lieut Gov., Tasmania, 1996–2004. Dep. Pres., Defence Force Discipline Appeal Tribunal, 1988–95. Pres., Bar Assoc. of Tasmania, 1973–75. Lt Col, Army Reserve; CO, 6 Field Regt, RAA, 1972–75; Hon. Col Comdt, RAA (Tas), 1993–97. Dir, Winston Churchill Meml Trust, 1988– (Nat. Chm., 2000–04). Pres., St John Ambulance, Australia (Tas), 2002–04. Hon. LLD Tasmania, 2005. KStJ 2002. *Recreations*: bush walking, gardening. *Address*: 214 Davey Street, Hobart, Tas 7004, Australia. *Club*: Tasmanian.

**COYLE, Prof. Andrew Gerard**, CMG 2003; PhD; Professor of Prison Studies, King's College London, 2003–10, now Emeritus (Director, International Centre for Prison Studies, 1997–2005); *b* 17 June 1944; *m* 1st, Joyce Hamilton (marr. diss.); one *s* three *d*; 2nd, Vivien Stern (*see* Baroness Stern). *Educ*: Real Colegio Escocés, Valladolid; Open Univ. (BA); Univ. of Edinburgh (PhD 1986). Scottish Prison Service and HM Prison Service, 1973–97: Assistant Governor: Edinburgh Prison, 1973–76; Polmont Borstal, 1976–78; Dep. Gov., Shotts Prison, 1978–81; Head of Ops, Scottish Prison Service HQ, 1981–86; Governor: Greenock Prison, 1986–88; Peterhead Prison, 1988–90; Shotts Prison, 1990–91; Brixton Prison, 1991–97. Expert consultant on prison matters: to Office of UN High Comr for Human Rights, 1992–; to Council of Europe, 1992–. Member: Foreign Sec.'s Panel on Torture, 2003–15; Nat. Adv. Body on Offender Mgt, 2006–10; Judicial Appts Bd for Scotland, 2009–14; Administrative Justice and Tribunals Council, 2009–13; Adv. Bd, UN Global Study on Children Deprived of their Liberty, 2016–; Adv. Bd, Inst. for Criminal Policy Res., Birkbeck, Univ. of London, 2018–; undertook Review of Ind. Prison Monitoring for Scottish Govt, 2012–13. Chairman: Scottish Assoc. for Study of Delinquency, 1989–91; Inst. for Study and Treatment of Delinquency, 1993–97; Vice Pres., Nat. Assoc. of Prison Visitors, 1999–. Mem. Editl Bd, Punishment & Society, 1997–. Winston Churchill Travelling Fellow, 1984; University of Edinburgh: Associate Mem., Centre for Law and Society, 1988; Mem., Centre for Theol. and Public Issues, 1993–; Vis. Prof., Univ. of Essex, 2011–14; Hon. Prof., Min. of Justice Acad. of Law and Mgt, Russia, 2000–. Pres., Howard League Scotland, 2013–; Patron: Unlock, Assoc. of Former Prisoners, 1997–; Prisoners Abroad, 2013–18 (Trustee, 1999–2007). Trustee: Unit for Arts and Offenders, 2000–05; Royal London Aid Soc., 2002–05; Internat. Centre for Prison Studies, 2010–14; Inst. for Criminal Policy Res., 2014–17. Bd Mem., Eisenhower Foundn, Washington, 2004–08. FRSA 1993; FKC 2004. Medal: Russian Penitentiary Service, 2001; Min. of Justice, Russian Fedn, 2002. *Publications*: Inside: rethinking Scotland's prisons, 1991; The Prisons We Deserve, 1994; Managing Prisons in a Time of Change, 2002; Human Rights Approach to Prison Management: handbook for prison staff, 2002, 3rd edn 2018; (ed) Capitalist Punishment: prison privatisation and human rights, 2003; Humanity in Prison, 2003; Understanding Prisons, 2005; Imprisonment Worldwide: the current situation and an alternative future, 2016; contrib. numerous articles to learned jls on human rights, prisons, prison mgt and alternatives to prison. *Address*: c/o Institute for Criminal Policy Research, Birkbeck, University of London, 42 Store Street, WC1E 7DB. *E*: andrew.coyle@prisonstudies.org.

**COYLE, Prof. Diane**, CBE 2018 (OBE 2009); PhD; Bennett Professor of Public Policy, University of Cambridge, since 2018; Director, Enlightenment Economics, since 2001; *b* Feb. 1961; *d* of Joseph and Kathleen Coyle; *m* 1990, (Nicholas) Rory Cellan-Jones, *qv*; two *s*. *Educ*: Brasenose Coll., Oxford (BA Hons PPE 1981); Harvard Univ. (PhD Econs 1985). Sen. Econ. Asst, HM Treasury, 1985–86; Sen. Economist, DRI Europe, 1986–89; Eur. Ed. and features writer, Investors' Chronicle, 1989–93; Econs Ed., The Independent, 1993–2001; Prof. of Econs, Univ. of Manchester, 2014–18. Member: Competition Commn, 2001–09; Migration Adv. Cttee, UK Border Agency, 2007–12; BBC Trust, 2007–15 (Vice Chair, 2011–15); Browne Rev. of Higher Educn Funding, 2009–10; Natural Capital Cttee, DEFRA, 2016–; Econ. Experts Working Gp, ONS, 2016–; ESRC, 2018–; Industrial Strategy Council, 2019–. *Publications*: The Weightless World, 1996 (US edn 1997); Governing the World Economy, 2000; Paradoxes of Prosperity, 2001; Sex, Drugs and Economics, 2002; New Wealth for Old Nations, 2005; The Soulful Science, 2007; The Economics of Enough, 2011; GDP: a brief but affectionate history, 2014; contrib. chapters in books and articles to jls. *Recreations*: classical ballet, reading. *Address*: Bennett Institute for Public Policy, University of Cambridge, Alison Richard Building, 7 West Road, Cambridge CB3 9DT. *E*: dc700@cam.ac.uk.

**COYLE, Eurfron Gwynne, (Mrs Michael Coyle)**; *see* Jones, E. G.

**COYLE, Neil**; MP (Lab) Bermondsey and Old Southwark, since 2015; *b* Luton, Dec. 1978; *s* of Alan Coyle and Mary Coyle (*née* Wesson); *m* 2014, Sarah Lindars. *Educ*: Hull Univ. (BA Hons). Lived in China, 2001–03; Disability Rights Commn, 2003–07, latterly as Policy Manager for health and social care; Hd of Policy, Nat. Centre for Ind. Living, 2007–09; Dir of Policy, Disability Alliance, 2009–12; Dir of Policy and Campaigns, DRUK, 2012–13. Mem. (Lab), Southwark LBC, 2010–16; Dep. Mayor of Southwark, 2014–15. Vice Chm., Walworth Community Council, 2010–11. Trustee, N Southwark Envmt Trust. *Address*: House of Commons, SW1A 0AA.

**COYNE, Prof. John**, CBE 2016; Vice-Chancellor, University of Derby, 2004–15; *b* Barnsley, 27 Sept. 1951; *m* Julie; two *d*. *Educ*: Univ. of Nottingham (BA). University of Nottingham, 1975–90: Lectr, then Sen. Lectr, Dept of Industrial Econs, subseq. Dept of Industrial Econs, Accountancy and Insurance; Warden of Cripps Hall; Co-Dir, Centre for Mgt Buy-out Res.; De Montfort University: Prof. of Business, 1990–2000 (Bass Prof., 1990–93); Hd, Leicester Sch. of Business, 1990–97; Dean, Faculty of Business and Law, 1997–2000; Pro-Vice-Chancellor, 2000–04. Mem., UK Commn for Employment and Skills, 2011–15. Chair, British Canoeing, 2016–; CFE Ltd, 2017–. Hon. LLD Nottingham, 2014; DUniv Derby, 2016.

**COZENS, Andrew Geoffrey**, CBE 2005; Director, Acainn Ltd, since 2012; independent social care and health policy and improvement specialist, since 2012; *b* 3 June 1955; *s* of late Geoffrey Cozens and Iris Cozens (*née* Hammett). *Educ*: Peter Symonds Sch., Winchester; Magdalene Coll., Cambridge (BA 1977); Green Coll., Oxford (MSc, CQSW 1981). Social Worker, N Yorks CC, 1981–84; Develt Officer, N Yorks Forum for Vol. Orgns, 1984–88; North Yorkshire County Council: Principal Officer, 1988–90; Asst Dir, 1990–94; Sen. Asst Dir, 1994–96; Dir of Social Services, Glos CC, 1996–2000; Dir of Social Services, then of Social Care and Health, and Dep. Chief Exec., Leicester CC, 2000–06; Strategic Advr, Children, Adults and Health Services, Improvement and Develt Agency, subseq. Local Govt Improvement and Develt, 2006–12. Pres., Assoc. of Dirs of Social Services, 2003–04. Chm., 2012–15, Vice Pres., 2015–, Carers Trust; Member, Board: MHA, 2015–; Nat. Develt Team for Inclusion, 2015– (Chair, 2018–). Publishing Editor: Platform Mag., 1972–77; Green Horse Pubns, 1974–77; Avalon Editions, 1978–82. Hon. Fellow, Cheltenham and Gloucester Coll. of Higher Educn, 1998. *Recreations*: hill walking, the arts, reading, watching sport, travel. *Address*: 67 Knighton Drive, Leicester LE2 3HD.

**CRABB, Rt Hon. Stephen;** PC 2014; MP (C) Preseli Pembrokeshire, since 2005; *b* 20 Jan. 1973; *m* 1996, Béatrice Alice Claude Odile Monnier; one *s* one *d. Educ:* Bristol Univ. (BSc Hons 1995); London Business Sch. (MBA 2004). Res. Asst to Andrew Rowe, MP, 1995–96; Parly Officer, Nat. Council for Voluntary Youth Services, 1996–98; Policy and Campaigns Manager, LCCI, 1998–2002; mktg consultant, 2003–05. An Opposition Whip, 2009–10; an Asst Govt Whip, 2010–12; a Lord Comr of HM Treasury (Govt Whip), 2012–14; Parly Under-Sec. of State, Wales Office, 2012–14; Sec. of State for Wales, 2014–16, for Work and Pensions, 2016. Mem., Select Cttee on Exiting the EU, 2017–. *Recreations:* Rugby, cooking, spending time with family. *Address:* House of Commons, SW1A 0AA. *T:* (020) 7219 3000. *E:* crabbs@parliament.uk. *Clubs:* Balfour, Haverfordwest Co. Assoc. Football (Haverfordwest).

**CRABB, Tony William;** *b* 27 June 1933; *s* of William Harold Crabb and Ellen Emily Crabb; *m* 1957, Brenda Margaret (*née* Sullman) (*d* 2013); one *s* one *d. Educ:* Chiswick Grammar School; London School of Economics (BScEcon); Intelligence Corps Russian Interpreters Course, Cambridge, 1952–54. BBC, 1957–88; seconded as news adviser to Govt of Libya, 1968–69; Managing Editor: BBC TV News, 1979–82; BBC Breakfast Time, 1982–84; Controller, Corporate News Services, BBC, 1984–87; Special Asst, News and Current Affairs, BBC, 1987–88; Dep. Dir of Broadcasting, Radio TV Hong Kong, 1988–92; Gen. Manager, CCT Productions Ltd, 1995–97. Mem. (Lib Dem) Spelthorne BC, 1999–2003 and 2008–11. FRTS (Mem. Council, 2002–06). *Address:* 26 Meadows House, New Zealand Avenue, Walton-on-Thames KT12 1PG.

**CRABBIE, Christopher Donald,** CMG 1995; HM Diplomatic Service, retired; UK Permanent Representative to OECD, Paris, (with rank of Ambassador), 1999–2003; *b* 17 Jan. 1946; *s* of late William George Crabbie and of Jane (*née* Coe). *Educ:* Rugby Sch.; Newcastle Univ.; Liverpool Univ.; Corpus Christi Coll., Oxford. Second Sec., FCO, 1973–75; First Secretary: Nairobi, 1975–79; Washington, 1979–83; FCO, 1983–85; Counsellor and Hd of European Communities Div., HM Treasury, 1985–87; Counsellor, FCO, 1987–90; Dep. UK Perm. Rep., OECD, Paris, 1990; Counsellor, British Embassy, Paris, 1990–94; Ambassador: to Algeria, 1994–95; to Romania, 1996–99; to Moldova, 1999. *Recreations:* ski-ing, bridge, sailing, gardening.

**CRABTREE, Maj.-Gen. Derek Thomas,** CB 1983; *b* 21 Jan. 1930; *s* of late William Edward Crabtree and Winifred Hilda Burton; *m* 1960, Daphne Christine Mason; one *s* one *d. Educ:* St Brendan's Coll., Bristol. Commissioned, 1953; Regimental Service: 13th/18th Royal Hussars (QMO), 1953–56; Royal Berkshire Regt, 1956–59 (despatches, Cyprus, 1958); Technical Staff Course, RMCS, 1960–62; sc Camberley, 1964; BM 11 Inf. Bde, BAOR, 1965–67; CO 1st Bn Duke of Edinburgh's Royal Regt, UK and Berlin, 1970–72; Col GS, MGO Secretariat, MoD, 1974–76; Dep. Comdr and Chief of Staff Headquarters British Forces Hong Kong, 1976–79; Dep. Comdt RMCS, 1979–80; Dir Gen of Weapons (Army), MoD, 1980–84. Sen. Mil. Advr, Short Bros, 1984–86; Gen. Manager, Regular Forces Employment Assoc., 1987–94. Col, Duke of Edinburgh's Royal Regt, 1982–87, 1988–89. *Recreations:* amateur dramatics, Rugby, tennis, golf, computing, gardening, apiary. *Address:* 53 High Street, Shrivenham, Swindon SN6 8AW. *Club:* Army and Navy.

**CRABTREE, Harriet Mary,** OBE 2008; ThD; Director, Inter Faith Network for the UK, since 2007; *b* London, 25 Nov. 1958; *d* of His Honour Jonathan Crabtree and of Caroline Ruth Keigwin Crabtree (*née* Oliver, now Baden-Powell); *m* 1984, James Stewart (marr. diss. 1990). *Educ:* Mill Mount Grammar Sch. for Girls, York; Lewes Priory Comp. Sch.; King's Coll. London (BD); Harvard Divinity Sch. (ThM; ThD 1989). Coordinator, Progs and Develt, Center for Study of World Religions, Harvard Divinity Sch., 1988–89; Lectr in Study of Religion, Faculty of Arts and Scis, Harvard Univ., 1989–90; Asst Dir, Inter Faith Network, 1991–94; Dep. Dir, Inter Faith Network for UK, 1994–2007. Vis. Lectr, Univ. of Massachusetts, Boston, 1986–87. Mem., Commn on Integration and Cohesion, 2006–07; Trustee, UNICEF UK, 2007–13. *Publications:* The Christian Life: traditional metaphors and contemporary theologies, 1991; Inter Faith Activity in the UK: a survey, 2003; pubns for Inter Faith Network; contribs to jls. *Recreations:* time with family and other good company, music, history, woods and their preservation, railways. *Address:* Inter Faith Network for the UK, 2 Grosvenor Gardens, SW1W 0DH. *T:* (020) 7730 0410. *E:* harriet.crabtree@interfaith.org.uk. *Club:* Athenæum.

**CRABTREE, John Rawcliffe Airey,** OBE 2007; Lord-Lieutenant of West Midlands, since 2017; *b* Birmingham, 5 Aug. 1949; *s* of Norman Lloyd and Joyce Mary Crabtree; *m* 1998, Diana Charlotte; three *s* three *d. Educ:* Downs Sch., Colwall; Radley Coll.; Birmingham Univ. (LLB 1970). Admitted solicitor, 1973; Wragge & Co.: Partner, 1976–2004; Hd of Corporate, 1983–91; Man. Partner, 1991–93; Sen. Partner, 1993–2003. Chairman: Glen Howells Architects, 2010–; Real Estate Investors plc, 2010–; Staffline Gp plc, 2011–19; White & Black Ltd; Brandauer Hldgs Ltd; non-exec. Dir, Tara Develts, 2015–. Dir, Advantage W Midlands, 2005–12. Chm., Birmingham Ind. Improvement Panel, 2014–; Chair, Birmingham 2022 Commonwealth Games Organising Cttee, 2018–. Former Pres., Birmingham Chamber of Commerce. Chair, Birmingham Hippodrome Th., 2001–17. Chair, Sense, 2008–17. Hon. Dr: Birmingham; Birmingham City. DL 2005, High Sheriff, 2006–07, W Midlands. *Recreations:* all sport, all theatre. *Address:* The White House, School Lane, Crowle, Worcs WR7 4AR. *T:* 07721 780229. *E:* lordlieutenant@lieutenancy.org.

**CRABTREE, Peter Dixon,** OBE 1997; **His Honour Judge Crabtree;** a Circuit Judge, since 2014; Resident Judge, Swindon Law Courts, since 2019; *b* 2 March 1956; *s* of Kenneth and Elizabeth Crabtree; *m* 1981, Ann Davina Cooper; three *d. Educ:* Liverpool Coll.; Manchester Poly. (BA Hons); Univ. of Bristol (LLM); Inns of Court Sch. of Law. ACIS. Royal Navy, 1979–2005: served HMSs Fearless, Minerva, Ark Royal, Invincible; Captain. Called to the Bar, Gray's Inn, 1985; a District Judge (Magistrates' Courts), 2005–14; a Recorder, 2009–14. *Recreations:* walking, climbing, reading, family. *Address:* The Law Courts, Islington Street, Swindon SN1 2HG. *Club:* Royal Scots (Edinburgh).

**CRABTREE, Prof. Robert Howard,** DPhil; FRS 2018; Conkey P. Whitehead Professor of Chemistry, Yale University, since 2010; *b* Ealing, London, 17 April 1948; *s* of Arthur Crabtree and Marguerite Crabtree; *m* 1977, Holly Darico. *Educ:* Brighton Coll.; New Coll., Oxford (BA 1970); Univ. of Sussex (DPhil 1973). Attaché de Recherche, CNRS, 1973–77; Yale University: Asst Prof., 1977–82; Associate Prof., 1982–85; Prof., 1985–. *Publications:* The Organometallic Chemistry of the Transition Metals, 1985, 7th edn 2019; 600 papers in learned jls. *Recreations:* travel, photography. *Address:* Department of Chemistry, Yale University, 225 Prospect Street, New Haven, CT 06511–8499, USA. *T:* (203) 4323925. *E:* robert.crabtree@yale.edu.

**CRACKETT, Maj. Gen. John,** CB 2015; TD 1993; DL; CEng, FIMechE, FIET; Director Reserves, Army, 2016–18; *b* Newcastle upon Tyne, 19 Dec. 1958; *s* of John Thomas Morton and Yvonne Crackett; *m* 1987, Claire Luckhurst; two *d. Educ:* Hymers Coll.; Churchill Coll., Cambridge (BA Engrg 1981). CEng 1988; FIET (FIEE 1998); FIMechE 2004. Power stn design and project mgt engr, CEGB, 1978–90; National Power plc: Stn Develt and Consents Manager, 1990–95; Engrg Manager, Ironbridge Power Stn, 1995–97; TXU Europe Ltd: Stn Manager, Ironbridge, Rugeley and Drakelow Power Stns, 1997–2000; Hd of Prodn, 2000–02; E.ON UK: Managing Director: Shared Services, 2002–05; Energy Services, 2005–07; Central Networks, 2007–11. Trustee, E.ON UK Pension Scheme, 2003–06. Ind. Bd Mem., Office of Nuclear Regulation, 2011–17; non-exec. Mem., Strategy Bd, Arqiva, 2011–13; non-exec. Dir, Ofgem, 2018–. Trustee, Marches Energy Agency, 1997–2015. Territorial Army: enlisted Cambridge Univ. OTC, 1978; commnd 1980; troop and sqdn officer, 37 Signals Regt, then o/c 57 Signals Sqdn, 1982–95; SO2 2 Signals Bde, 1995; o/c 55 Signals Sqdn, 1996–98; CO, 39 Signals Regt, 1998–2000; DS JSCSC, 2000–02; Dep. Comdr 143 Bde, 2002–06; TA Col Royal Signals, 2007–09; Asst Comdr 5 Div., 2009–12; AComd Army Recruiting and Trng Div., 2012–13; ACDS (Reserves and Cadets), 2013–15. Col Comdt Royal Corps of Signals, 2014–19. Mem., Engr and Logistic Staff Corps, 2003–; Hon. Col, 37 Signals Regt, 2011–18. Pres., SSAFA Shropshire, 2016–. Liveryman: Co. of Engrs, 2001–; and Trustee, Shrewsbury Co. of Drapers, 2003–. DL Shropshire, 2016. *Recreations:* flying, walking, riding, DIY. *Club:* Army and Navy.

**CRACKNELL, David John;** Founder and Director, Big Tent Communications, since 2008; *b* 5 June 1968; *s* of David Lewis and Norma Rose Cracknell; *m* 1998, Rachel Laurent; one *s* two *d. Educ:* Southampton Univ. (LLB); Pembroke Coll., Oxford (BCL). Reporter, Coventry Evening Telegraph, 1993–95; Lobby Corresp., Press Assoc., 1995–98; Political Ed., Sunday Business, 1998–99; Dep. Political Ed., Sunday Telegraph, 1999–2001; Political Ed., Sunday Times, 2001–08; Chm., FD-LLM, 2008. *E:* david@bigtentcommunications.com.

**CRACKNELL, James Edward,** OBE 2005 (MBE 2001); Olympic oarsman, retired 2006; adventurer, broadcaster and journalist; *b* 5 May 1972; *s* of John David and Jennifer Ann Cracknell; *m* 2002, Beverley Anne Turner (marr. diss. 2019); one *s* two *d. Educ:* Kingston Grammar Sch.; Reading Univ. (BSc Geog.); Inst. of Educn, London Univ. (PGCE); Brunel Univ. (MSc). Gold Medal, Jun. World Championships, 1990; Mem., British rowing team, 1991–2006; winner: World Championships: Gold Medal, coxless fours, 1997, 1998 and 1999; (with Matthew Pinsent) Gold Medal, coxed pairs, 2001; Gold Medal, coxless pairs, 2001 and 2002; Gold Medal, coxless fours, Olympic Games, Sydney, 2000 and Athens, 2004. Journalist and columnist, Daily Telegraph, 1998–; broadcaster, ITV and Channel 4, 2005–. Contested (C) SW England and Gibraltar, EP, 2014. Pres., London Road Safety Council, 2015–. *Publications:* James Cracknell's No-Gym Health Plan, 2006; (with Ben Fogle) The Crossing: conquering the Atlantic in the world's toughest rowing race, 2006; (with Ben Fogle) Race to the Pole, 2009; (with Beverley Turner) Touching Distance, 2012. *Recreations:* motorbikes, surfboards. *Address:* M&CSaatchiMerlin, 15 Golden Square, W1F 9JG. *Club:* Leander (Captain, 2000–05) (Henley-on-Thames).

**CRACKNELL, His Honour Malcolm Thomas;** a Circuit Judge, 1989–2009; *b* 12 Dec. 1943; *s* of late Percy Thomas Cracknell and Doris Louise Cracknell; *m* 1st, 1968, Ann Carrington (*née* Gooding) (marr. diss. 1980); one *s* one *d*; 2nd, 1988, Felicity Anne Davies; two *s* one *d. Educ:* Royal Liberty Sch., Romford; Hull Univ. (LLB); King's Coll., London (LLM (Dist.)). Called to Bar, Middle Temple, 1969. Lectr in Law, Univ. of Hull, 1968–74; Barrister, NE Circuit, 1970–89; a Recorder, 1988; Designated Family Judge, Hull Combined Court Centre, 1994–2007. Mem., Parole Bd for England and Wales, 2009–16. *Recreations:* watching golf and cricket, reading. *Club:* MCC.

**CRACROFT-BRENNAN, (Stephen) Patrick,** FCA; sole practitioner, Bambury & Co. Chartered Accountants, since 1989; *b* Kingston-upon-Hull, 29 April 1951; *s* of Harry Brennan and Mildred Zadie Brennan (*née* Cracroft); *m* 1974, Angela Jane (separated 1975, marr. diss. 1981), *d* of Kenneth Archer Easby, FCA and Joan Mary Easby (*née* Hudson). *Educ:* Hull Grammar Sch. ACA 1974, FCA 1984. Several articles, Hodgson Harris, 1969–72; Dutton Moore, 1972–74; Sen. Manager, Kenneth Easby & Co., 1974–75; Accountant, Alton Computer Services Ltd, 1975–81; Computer Manager, Finnies, 1981–84; Financial Controller, Baronsmead Associates Ltd, 1984–87; Gp Chief Internal Auditor, Taylor Woodrow plc, 1987–89; Finance Manager, Servite Housing, 1995–97; Hd of Finance, Threshold Tennant Trust, 1998–2001; Hd of Finance and Admin, Office of Immigration Services Comr, 2006–10. Sole practitioner, Patrick Cracroft-Brennan & Co., 1975–89. Exec. Dir and Sec., Magistrates' Assoc., 2010–12. Man. Editor, Cracroft's Peerage Online, 1998–; Founder and Trustee, Peerage Research Trust, 2004–. Director: Heraldic Media Ltd; Heraldic Graphics Ltd; Heraldic China Ltd; Heraldry.com Ltd; Cracroft Genealogy Ltd (formerly Heraldic Genealogy.com Ltd); Cracroft's Peerage Ltd; Complete Peerage Ltd; Bambury Secretary Ltd; Bambury Director Ltd; Bambury Nominees Ltd; London Will Co. Ltd; Peerage Research Trust. Heraldry Society: Hon. Treas., 1983–88, 2012–16; Mem. Council, 1988–97, 2001–10, 2012–16; Hon. FHS 1988. St John Ambulance: Pres., Wimbledon Div., 1987–91; Mem., 1988–2012, Hospitaller, 1988–93, 1998–2015, St John Council for London; Pres., Crystal Palace and Anerley Div., 2001–13; Mem., London Regl Priory Gp, 2012–15. Freeman, City of London, 1986; Liveryman, Scriveners' Co., 1988 (Court Asst, 2013). SBStJ 1991. *Recreations:* heraldry, genealogy, classical music, international travel, cooking, baking. *Address:* The Bungalow, Parsonage Farm, Upper Street, Tingewick, Bucks MK18 4QG. *Club:* Cheap Ward.

**CRADDOCK, Prof. Charles Frank,** CBE 2016; DPhil; FRCP, FRCPath; Professor of Haemato-Oncology, University of Birmingham, since 2004; Consultant Haematologist, since 1999, and Academic Director, Centre for Clinical Haematology, since 2006, Queen Elizabeth Hospital, Birmingham; *b* London, 20 Sept. 1957; *s* of Charles and Susanna Craddock; *m* 1993, Louise Kirk; two *d. Educ:* Dr Challoner's Grammar Sch., Amersham; Lincoln Coll., Oxford (BA Physical Scis 1979; BM BCh 1982; DPhil 1994). FRCP 2008; FRCPath 2008. Registrar in Haematol., Hammersmith Hosp., London, 1987–89; Wellcome Trust Clinical Fellow, Inst. of Molecular Medicine, Univ. of Oxford, 1990–94; Sen. Fellow, Fred Hutchinson Cancer Res. Center, Univ. of Washington, Seattle, 1994–96; Consultant Haematologist, Hammersmith Hosp., London, 1997–99. Med. Dir, Antony Nolan, 2010–14 (Chair, Sci. and Med. Adv. Cttee, 2014–). Transitional Dir, Birmingham Inst. of Translational Medicine, 2012–13; Dep. Dir, Cancer Res. UK Clinical Trials Unit, Univ. of Birmingham, 2012–. Chair: UK Stem Cell Strategic Oversight Cttee, 2010–; UK Nat. Cancer Res. Inst. Acute Myeloid Leukaemia Working Pty, 2018–. President: British Soc. of Blood and Marrow Transplantation, 2005–07; British Soc. of Haematology, 2017–18; Sec., European Sch. of Haematology, 2014–. Founding Trustee, Cure Leukaemia, 2003–. Associate Ed., Jl of Clinical Oncology, 2018–. *Publications:* over 200 articles and chapters in scientific jls on leukaemia and stem cell transplantation. *Recreations:* cricket, chamber music, walking. *Address:* Centre for Clinical Haematology, Queen Elizabeth Hospital, Birmingham B15 2TH. *T:* (0121) 627 2000. *E:* charles.craddock@uhb.nhs.uk.

**CRADDOCK, Timothy James;** HM Diplomatic Service, retired; a Director and Trustee, UK National Commission for UNESCO, 2008–10; *b* 27 June 1956; *s* of James Vincent Craddock and Kathleen Mary Craddock (*née* Twigg). *Educ:* King Edward's Sch., Birmingham; Gonville and Caius Coll., Cambridge (Exhibnr; MA); School of Oriental and African Studies, London Univ. Entered FCO, 1979; Third Sec. and Vice-Consul, Chad, 1979–80; Vice-Consul, Istanbul, 1981–82; Second Sec., Ankara, 1982–85; Hd of Section, South America Dept, FCO, 1985–87; Sec., FCO Bd of Mgt, 1988–90; First Sec., Paris, 1990–94; Dep. Hd, Aid Policy and Resources Dept, FCO, 1995–97; Ambassador to Estonia, 1997–2000; Hd, Africa Gt Lakes and Horn Dept, DFID (on secondment),

2000–03; UK Perm. Delegate to UNESCO, 2003–07. Exec. Mem. and Trustee, Norwich Soc., 2011–. *Recreations:* hill walking, opera, London, gardening in France. *Address:* Stonewall Cottage, Stonewall Hill, Presteigne, Powys LD8 2HB; 52 rue du Bourg Voisin, 21140 Semur-en-Auxois, France.

**CRAFT, Sir Alan (William),** Kt 2004; MD; FRCP, FRCPE, FRCPI, FRCPCH, FMedSci, FRCR, FRCA; Director, Northern Institute for Cancer Research, 2007–09, and Sir James Spence Professor of Child Health, 1993–2007, now Emeritus, University of Newcastle upon Tyne; *b* 6 July 1946; *s* of William and Yvonne Craft; *m* 1st, 1968, Dorothy Noble (decd); one *s*; 2nd, 1992, Anne Nicholson. *Educ:* Rutherford Grammar Sch., Newcastle upon Tyne; Univ. of Newcastle upon Tyne (MB, BS; MD). FRCP 1982; FRCPCH 1997; FFPH (FFPHM 2001); FRCPE 2003; FRCPI 2003; FAAP 2003; FIAP 2003; FAMM 2003; FACP 2005; FRCR 2006; FRCA 2006. House Officer, Royal Victoria Infirmary, Newcastle upon Tyne, 1969–70; Sen. House Officer, then Registrar and Sen. Registrar, Newcastle Hosps, 1970–77; MRC Trng Fellow, Royal Marsden Hosp., 1976–77; Consultant Paediatrician: N Tyneside Hosp., 1977–86; Royal Victoria Infirmary, 1977–; Prof. of Paediatric Oncology, Univ. of Newcastle upon Tyne, 1991–93. Chm., European Osteosarcoma Intergroup, 1994–97; Sec. Gen., 1993–99, Pres., 2002–05, Internat. Paediatric Oncology Soc.; President: RCPCH, 2003–06 (Vice-Pres., 1998–2002); Assoc. for Care of Terminally Ill Children, 2001–. Chm., Academy of Med. Royal Colls, 2004–06. Non-exec. Dir, Northumbria Health Care Trust, 2018–. Mem. Bd, Med. Defence Union, 2010–. FMedSci 2003. Chm., JGW Patterson Foundn, 2014–; Pres., Together for Short Lives, 2004–. Chm., Scout Assoc., 2009–15; Pres., 2011–. Chm., 2015–, Northumberland Scouts. Chm. of Govs, Embleton Primary Sch., Northumberland, 2015–. Hon. FRCN 2013. *Publications:* papers on childhood cancer and other childhood disorders in BMJ, Lancet, Archives of Disease in Childhood, etc. *Recreations:* marathon running, orienteering, crosswords, scouting. *Address:* 1 The Villas, Embleton, Northumberland NE66 3XG. *T:* (01665) 576619. *Club:* Athenæum.

**CRAFT, Prof. Maurice,** PhD, DLitt; Emeritus Professor of Education, University of Nottingham; *b* 4 May 1932; *er s* of Jack and Polly Craft, London; *m* 1957, Alma, *y d* of Elio and Dinah Sampson, Dublin; one *d* (and one *d* decd). *Educ:* LCC Elem. Sch. and Colfe's Grammar Sch., SE13; LSE, Univ. of London (BSc Econ); Sch. of Education, Trinity Coll., Univ. of Dublin (HDipEd); Inst. of Education, Univ. of London (AcadDipEd); Dept of Sociology, Univ. of Liverpool (PhD 1972); Sch. of Education, Univ. of Nottingham (DLitt 1990). 2/Lt RAOC (Nat. Service), 1953–55. Asst Master, Catford Secondary Sch., SE6, 1956–60; Princ. Lectr and Head of Dept of Sociology, Edge Hill Coll. of Education, Ormskirk, Lancs, 1960–67; Sen. Lectr in Education, i/c Advanced Courses, Univ. of Exeter, 1967–73; Sub-Dean, Faculty of Educn, 1969–73; Prof. of Education, and Chairman, Centre for the Study of Urban Education, La Trobe Univ., Melbourne, 1973–75; Goldsmiths' Prof. of Education, Inst. of Educn, Univ. of London, and Head of Dept of Advanced Studies in Education, Goldsmiths' Coll., 1976–80; University of Nottingham: Prof. of Educn, and Hd, Div. of Advanced Studies, 1980–89; Dean, Faculty of Educn, 1981–83; Chm., Sch. of Educn, 1983–85, 1988–89; Pro-Vice-Chancellor, 1983–87; Foundn Dean of Humanities and Social Science, Hong Kong Univ. of Science and Technol., 1989–92; Foundn Prof. of Educn, Open Univ. of Hong Kong, 1992–94; Res. Prof. in Educn, Univ. of Greenwich, 1994–97; Vis Prof. of Educn, Goldsmiths' Coll., Univ. of London, 1997–2002. Adviser: Devon CC, 1970–72; Aust. Federal Poverty Commn, 1974–75; ACU, 1976, 1979; CNAA, 1978–89; Centre for Advice and Inf. on Educn Disadvantage (Chm., Teacher Educn Working Gp, 1979–80); Schools Council, 1979; CRE (Chm., Teacher Educn Adv. Gp, 1980–84); H of C Home Affairs Cttee, 1981; Swann Cttee, 1982–84; Leverhulme Trust, 1982–90; Macquarie Univ., Aust., 1982; Council for Educn and Trng in Youth and Community Work (Chm., In-service Wkg Gp, 1983); UNESCO, 1985; QUB, 1986; Univ. of Kuwait, 1988; Peshawar Univ., Pakistan, 1988; Hong Kong Council for Academic Accreditation, 1991; Hong Kong Educn Commn, 1991; Lagos Univ., Nigeria, 1991; City Polytechnic of Hong Kong, 1992; Hong Kong Baptist Univ., 1994; Griffith Univ., Aust., 1996; Hong Kong Govt Res. Grants Council, 1996–; Commonwealth of Learning, Vancouver, 1996; ESRC, 1997; Hong Kong Inst. of Educn, 1997; Southampton Univ., 1999; Chester UC, 2000; Surrey Univ., 2000–04; Lewisham PCT, 2003–14. Mem., UK Delegn to EEC Colloquium on Ethnic Min. Educn, Brussels, 1979, 1982; UK delegate to: Council of Europe Seminars on Intercultural Trng of Teachers, Lisbon, 1981, Rome, 1982, Strasbourg, 1983; UNESCO Colloquium on Educnl Disadvantage, Thessalonika, 1984. Member: Council of Validating Univs, 1982–89 (Vice-Chm., 1987–89); E Midlands Reg. Consultative Gp on Teacher Educn, 1980–84 (Chm., 1980–84); Exec. Cttee, Univs Council for Educn of Teachers, 1984–88 (Chm., Standing Cttee on Validation, 1984–87); Cttee on Validation, CVCP, 1986–88; Hong Kong Govt Bd of Inquiry in Educn, 1992; Hong Kong Govt Adv. Cttee on Teacher Educn and Qualifications, 1993; Exec. Cttee, Soc. for Educnl Studies, 1996–2002 (Chm., Res. sub-cttee, 1999–2002); Froebel Trust Council, 2000–16 (Chm., Res. Cttee, 2004–06; Chm., Educn Cttee, 2009–16); Ext. Advr, Res. Degrees Bd, Univ. of Roehampton, 2000–04. Chm., Blackheath Cator Estate Community Assoc., 2003–06. Non-exec. Dir, Greenwich PCT, 2007–09; Mem., Exceptional Treatment Panel, 2003–14, Chm., Clin. Excellence Cttee, 2006–08, Chm., Cardiol. Clin. Panel, 2008–10, Lewisham PCT. Member, Editorial Board: Sociology of Educn Abstracts, 1965–; Jl of Multilingual and Multicultural Develt, 1979–96; Multicultural Educn Abstracts, 1981–; Internat. Studies in Sociology of Educn, 1991–; British Jl of Educnl Studies, 1996–2002. FRSA 1989. *Publications:* (ed jtly) Linking Home and School, 1967, 3rd edn 1980; (ed jtly) Guidance and Counselling in British Schools, 1969, 2nd edn 1974; (ed) Family, Class and Education: a Reader, 1970; Urban Education—a Dublin case study, 1974; School Welfare Provision in Australia, 1977; (ed) Teaching in a Multicultural Society: the Task for Teacher Education, 1981; (jtly) Training Teachers of Ethnic Minority Community Languages, 1983; (ed jtly) Change in Teacher Education, 1984; (ed) Education and Cultural Pluralism, 1984; The Democratisation of Education, 1985; Teacher Education in a Multicultural Society, 1986; (ed jtly) Ethnic Relations and Schooling, 1995; (ed) Teacher Education in Plural Societies, 1996; contrib. to numerous books and to the following jls: Educnl Research, Internat. Review of Educn, Internat. Jl of Educnl Develt, Educnl Review, Social and Econ. Admin, Cambridge Jl of Educn, Educn for Teaching, British Jl of In-Service Educn, Internat. Social Work, Aust. Jl of Social Work, Aust. Educnl Researcher, THES, Higher Educn Jl, New Society, Education, Administration, New Era, Studies. *Recreations:* music, walking. *T:* (020) 8852 7611. *E:* almacraft@hotmail.com. *Club:* Royal Over-Seas League.

**CRAFTS, Prof. Nicholas Francis Robert,** CBE 2014; FBA 1992; Professor of Economic History, since 2006, and Director of ESRC Research Centre on Competitive Advantage in the Global Economy, since 2010, University of Warwick; *b* 9 March 1949; *s* of Alfred Hedley Crafts and Flora Geraldine Mary Crafts; *m* 1969, Barbara Daynes; one *s* two *d*. *Educ:* Brunts Grammar Sch., Mansfield; Trinity Coll., Cambridge (BA Econs 1st cl., 1970). Lectr in Econ. Hist., Exeter Univ., 1971–72; Lectr in Econs, Univ. of Warwick, 1972–77; Fellow in Econs, University Coll., Oxford, 1977–86; Professor of Economic History: Leeds Univ., 1987–88; Univ. of Warwick, 1988–95 (Hon. Prof., 1995–2006); LSE, 1995–2005. Vis. Asst Prof. of Econs, Univ. of Calif., Berkeley, 1974–76; Vis. Prof. of Econs, Stanford Univ., 1982–83. *Publications:* British Economic Growth during the Industrial Revolution, 1985; contrib. to Economic Jl, Jl of Economic Hist., Economic Policy, Population Studies, etc. *Recreations:* betting on horses, drinking beer. *Address:* Department of Economics, University of Warwick, Coventry CV4 7AL. *T:* (024) 7652 3468. *E:* n.crafts@warwick.ac.uk.

**CRAGG, Sir Anthony Douglas, (Sir Tony),** Kt 2016; CBE 2002; RA 1994; sculptor; Hon. Member, Kunstakademie, Düsseldorf, since 2015 (Professor of Sculpture, 2006–14; Director, 2009–13); *b* 9 April 1949; *m* 1990, Tatjana (*née* Verhasselt); one *s* one *d*, and two *s* by former *m*. *Educ:* Wimbledon Sch. of Art (BA); Royal Coll. of Art (MA). Prof., l'Ecole des Beaux Arts de Metz, 1976; teacher, 1978–88, Prof., 1989–2001, Co-Dir, 1989–2001, Hon. Prof., 2014, Kunstakademie, Düsseldorf; Prof., Univ. der Künste, Berlin, 2001–06; Chaire de Création Artistique, Collège de France, 2013. *One-man exhibitions include:* Lisson Gall., 1979, 1980, 1985, 1991, 1992, 1997, 1998, 2001, 2010, 2016; Whitechapel Art Gall. 1981, 1997; Kanrasha Gall., Tokyo, 1982, 1984, 1989, 1990; Konrad Fischer, Düsseldorf, 1982, 1986, 1989, 1990; Marian Goodman, NY, 1982, 1983, 1986, 1987, 1989; Palais des Beaux-Arts, Brussels, 1985; Brooklyn Mus. of Art, NY, 1986; Venice Biennale, 1986, 1988, 1997; Hayward Gall., 1987; Tate Gall., Liverpool, 1988, 2000; Tate Gall., 1989; Stedelijk Van Abbemus., Eindhoven, 1989, 1991; Corcoran Gall. of Art, Washington, 1991; Wiener Secession, 1991; IVAM, Valencia, 1992; Kunst- und Ausstellungshalle BRD, Bonn, 2003; Goodwood Sculpture Park, 2005; Das Potential der Dinge, Berlin, 2006; Tony Cragg versus Franz Messerschmidt, Belvedere, Vienna, 2008; Second Nature, Karlsruhe, 2009; Louvre, Paris, 2011; Scottish Nat. Gall. of Modern Art, 2011; CAFAM, Beijing, 2011; Mus. of Contemp. Art, Chengdu, 2011; Himalayas Art Mus., Shanghai, 2012; Exhibition Road, London, 2012; Nat. Taiwan Mus. of Fine Arts, Llotja Palma de Mallorca, Musée d'Art Moderne, St Etienne, Lehmbruck Mus., Duisburg, 2013; Heydar Aliyev Centre, Baku, Madison Sq. Art, NY, Salzburg Foundn, Salzburg, 2014; Benaki Mus., Athens, 2015; Hermitage Mus., St Petersburg, Hessisches Landesmus., Darmstadt, Galerie Thaddeus Ropac Paris Pantin, Paris, Von der Heydt Mus., Wuppertal; Djurgården, Stockholm, 2016; Yorkshire Sculpture Park, Mudam Luxembourg, Nat. Fine Arts Mus., Havana, Tehran Mus. of Contemp. Art, 2017; *group exhibitions:* Documenta 7, Documenta 8, 1987, Kassel; Mus. van Hedendaagse Kunst, Ghent, 1980; Bienal de São Paulo, 1983; Tate Gall., 1983, 1985; Sydney Biennale, 1984, 1990; Hayward Gall., 1985, 1990; Expo, Milan, 2015; Gothenburg Internat. Sculpture Exhibn, Pilane, 2015; and many others throughout Europe, US, Japan and Australia. Hon. Dr Azerbaijan, 2014. Citizen of Honour, City of Wuppertal, 2014. Turner Prize, 1988; Shakespeare Prize, 2001; Praemium Imperiale for Sculpture, Japan Art Assoc., 2007. Chevalier des Arts et des Lettres (France), 1992; Order of Merit (1st cl.) (Germany), 2012. *Address:* Lise Meitner Strasse 33, 42119 Wuppertal, Germany.

**CRAGG, Anthony John,** CMG 2000; JP; Deputy Chief of Defence Intelligence, Ministry of Defence, and Member, Joint Intelligence Committee, 1999–2003; *b* 16 May 1943; *s* of late Leslie Cragg and Gwendolen Cragg (*née* Pevler); *m* 1971, Jeanette Ann Rix; two *d*. *Educ:* Hastings Grammar School; Lincoln College, Oxford (Open Schol.). Ministry of Defence, 1966–2003: Asst Private Sec. to Sec. of State for Defence, 1974; UK Delegn to NATO, 1977; Asst Sec., 1979; Chief Officer, Sovereign Base Areas, Cyprus, 1983–85; RCDS 1988; Asst Under Sec. of State, 1990; Chm., Defence Organisation Planning Team, 1991–92; Asst Sec. Gen. for Defence Planning and Policy, then Ops, NATO, 1993–99. Sen. Associate Res. Fellow, Centre for Defence Studies, KCL, 2003–10; Associate Fellow, RUSI, 2003. Visiting Lecturer: NATO Defence Coll., 2003–16; Geneva Centre for Security Policy, 2005–12. Chm., MoD Grievance Appeal Panel, 2004–10. Lay Mem., First-tier Tribunal (Immigration and Asylum Chamber) (formerly Immigration Appeal Tribunal, then Asylum and Immigration Tribunal), 2003–13. JP London, 2005. *Publications:* (contrib.) Global Monitoring for Security and Stability, 2008; (contrib.) Remote Sensing From Space, 2009; articles on internat. security issues in press and specialised jls. *Recreations:* theatre, opera, music, walking.

**CRAGG, Dr Martin Robert;** Chief Executive and Secretary, Institution of Highways and Transportation, 1990–2001; *b* 8 June 1941; *s* of Robert Brooks Cragg and Hilda Cragg (*née* Bateman); *m* 1966, Pamela Watts; one *s* two *d*. *Educ:* Dixie Grammar Sch., Market Bosworth; Sheffield Univ. (BSc Hons Chem.; PhD Fuel Technol. 1966); London Business Sch. (Sloan Fellow). Industrial Advr, NEDO, 1979–88; Dir, then Dir-Gen. and Chief Exec., Business Equipt and Information Technol. Assoc., 1988–89, then Sen. Exec., Electronic and Business Equipt Assoc., 1989–90. *Recreations:* golf, fly fishing. *Address:* 10 Woodside Road, New Malden, Surrey KT3 3AH. *T:* (020) 8942 8008.

**CRAGG, Stephen James;** QC 2013; *b* Wisbech, 16 Dec. 1961; *s* of John Maurice Cragg and Audrey Anne Cragg; *m* 2000, Deborah Tripley; two *d*. *Educ:* King's Coll. London (LLB 1984); Brunel Univ. (MA Sociol. and Law 1986). Articled clerk, Christian Fisher & Co., 1987–89; admitted solicitor, 1989; solicitor: Hackney Law Centre, 1989–93; Public Law Project, 1993–96; called to the Bar, Middle Temple, 1996; in practice as barrister, 1996–. Chair, Public Law Project, 2007–15. Pt-time Judge, Mental Health Tribunals, 2007–. Mem., Ind. Adv. Panel on Deaths in Custody, 2014–; Jt Vice-Chm., Bar Human Rights Cttee, 2019– (Sec., 2016–18). *Publications:* (jtly) Police Misconduct: legal remedies, 2nd edn 1987 to 5th edn 2017. *Recreations:* walking, cycling and running in London, cinema, theatre, Proust, parenting, part-time student of Art History at Birkbeck, University of London. *Address:* Doughty Street Chambers, 54 Doughty Street, WC1N 2LS. *E:* s.cragg@doughtystreet.co.uk.

**CRAGGS, Madeleine Jennifer;** Chief Executive and Registrar, General Osteopathic Council, 1997–2007; *b* 28 Dec. 1945; *d* of René Beaumont-Craggs and Muriel (*née* Robinson). *Educ:* Couvent des Ursulines, Brussels; Alexandra Grammar Sch., Singapore; WRAC Coll., Camberley. MCMI. Commnd WRAC, 1965; served in UK and Germany, incl. staff appts, MoD and HQ BAOR; Maj., 1970; WRAC Advr, 16th Signal Regt, 1973–75; Battery Comdr, Royal Sch. Artillery, 1975–77; SO2(A), HQ York Dist, 1977–79; Chief Instructor, WRAC Trng Centre, 1979–81; Detachment Comdr, Manning and Records Office, Chester, 1981–82; SO2 (Manpower & Planning), WRAC Directorate, MoD, 1982–84; Develt Dir, St Bartholomew's Hosp. Med. Coll., 1984–90; Sec., ICRF, 1991–97. *Recreations:* travel, good wine, good food, good company. *Address:* 131 Cedar Drive, Chichester, W Sussex PO19 3EL.

**CRAIG,** family name of **Viscount Craigavon** and of **Baron Craig of Radley**.

**CRAIG OF RADLEY,** Baron *cr* 1991 (Life Peer), of Helhoughton in the County of Norfolk; **Marshal of the Royal Air Force David Brownrigg Craig,** GCB 1984 (KCB 1981; CB 1978); OBE 1967; Chief of the Defence Staff, 1988–91; *b* 17 Sept. 1929; *s* of Major Francis Brownrigg Craig and Mrs Olive Craig; *m* 1955, Elisabeth June Derenburg (*d* 2016); one *s* one *d*. *Educ:* Radley Coll.; Lincoln Coll., Oxford (MA; Hon. Fellow 1984). FRAeS 1986. Commnd in RAF, 1951; OC RAF Cranwell, 1968–70; ADC to the Queen, 1969–71; Dir, Plans and Ops, HQ Far East Comd, 1970–71; OC RAF Akrotiri, 1972–73; ACAS (Ops), MoD, 1975–78; AOC No 1 Group, RAF Strike Command, 1978–80; Vice-Chief of Air Staff, 1980–82; AOC-in-C, RAF Strike Command and C-in-C, UK Air Forces, 1982–85; CAS, 1985–88. Air ADC to the Queen, 1985–88. Dir, M. L. Holdings plc, 1991–92. Mem., H of L Select Cttee for Sci. and Technology, 1993–99; Convenor, Cross Bench Peers, 1999–2004. Chm. Council, King Edward VII's Hosp. (Sister Agnes) (formerly King Edward VII's Hosp. for Officers), 1998–2004. Dep. Chm. Council, RAF

Benevolent Fund, 1996–2013. Pres., Not Forgotten Assoc., 1996–2014. Hon. DSc Cranfield, 1988. *Recreations:* fishing, shooting. *Address:* House of Lords, SW1A 0PW. *Club:* Royal Air Force (Pres., 2002–13).

**CRAIG, Rev. Canon Alan Stuart;** Chaplain to the Bishop of Newcastle and Diocesan Director of Ordinands, 1999–2002; Chaplain to the Queen, 1995–2008; *b* 7 Feb. 1938; *s* of Dr John Gray Craig and Grace Craig (*née* Kay); *m* 1962, Marjorie (*née* Bell); one *s* two *d. Educ:* Uppingham Sch.; Leeds Univ. (BA (Hons)); Cranmer Hall, Durham Univ. (DipTh). Ordained deacon, Lichfield, 1961, priest, 1962; Assistant Curate: St Giles, Newcastle under Lyme, 1961–65; St Mary's, Scarborough, 1965–67; Vicar, Werrington, Stoke-on-Trent, 1967–72; Asst Chaplain, Manchester Prison, 1972–73; Chaplain: Hindley Borstal, 1973–78; Acklington Prison, 1978–84; Vicar, Longhirst and Hebron, Newcastle, 1984–90; Rector of Morpeth, 1990–99; Rural Dean of Morpeth, 1984–95. Hon. Canon, Newcastle Cathedral, 1990–2002. Chm., Newcastle Diocesan Pastoral Cttee, 1994–99. *Recreations:* music, classical guitar, theatre, fell-walking, visual arts. *Address:* 5 Springfield Meadow, Alnwick, Northumberland NE66 2NY. *T:* (01665) 602806. *E:* as.m.craig@talktalk.net.

**CRAIG, Surgeon Rear-Admiral Alexander;** Member, Criminal Injuries Compensation Appeal Panel, 1997–2007; *b* 22 Nov. 1943; *s* of Rev. Dr Albert Craig and Agnes Nicol (*née* Wards); *m* 1968, Kate Margaret Elliott; one *s* two *d. Educ:* George Watson's Boys' Coll., Edinburgh; Edinburgh Univ. (MB ChB 1967). Royal Infirmary, Edinburgh, 1968; Regimental MO, 45 Commando, RM, 1969–72; Jt Services Families Clinic, Malta, 1972–74; OC Med. Sqn, CDO LOG Regt, 1974–78; MoD, 1978–80, NDC 1981; UK Support Unit, Naples, 1981–83; CSO to Surgeon Cdre (NMT), 1983–86; PMO, HMS Sultan, 1986–87; CSO to SRA (OMS), 1987–89; MO i/c, Inst. of Naval Medicine, 1989–90; Dir, Med. Organisation, MoD, 1990–93; Surg. Rear-Adm. Support Med. Services, 1993–94; Med. Dir Gen. (Naval), 1994–97. Non-exec. Dir, IoW Healthcare NHS Trust, 1997–99. QHP, 1992–97. CStJ 1996. *Recreation:* travel. *Address:* Home Cottage, Seven Sisters Road, St Lawrence, Isle of Wight PO38 1UY.

**CRAIG, Anne Gwendoline, (Wendy);** actress; *b* 20 June 1934; *d* of late George Dixon Craig and Anne Lindsay; *m* 1955, John Alexander, Jack, Bentley (*d* 1994); two *s. Educ:* Durham High Sch. for Girls; Darlington High Sch.; Yarm Grammar Sch.; Central Sch. of Speech and Drama. *Theatre includes:* Ipswich Rep. Theatre, 1953; Royal Court season, 1957; The Wrong Side of the Park, 1960; The Ginger Man, Royal Court, 1964; Ride a Cock Horse, Piccadilly, 1965; I Love You Mrs Patterson; Finishing Touches; Peter Pan; Beyond Reasonable Doubt, Queen's, 1987; Easy Virtue, Chichester Fest., 1999; The Rivals, RSC, 2000; The Circle, Queen's, 2002; The Importance of Being Earnest, nat. tour, 2003; *television includes:* Not in Front of the Children, 1967–70; And Mother Makes Three, 1971–74; And Mother Makes Five, 1974–76; Butterflies, 1978–82; Nanny, 1981–83; Brighton Belles, 1993; The Forsyte Saga, Midsomer Murders, 2002; The Royal, 2002–06; Reggie Perrin, 2010; The Worst Witch, Unforgotten, 2016; Girlfriends, Emmerdale, 2018; *films include:* The Servant, The Mind Benders, 1963; The Nanny, 1965; Just Like a Woman, 1966; I'll Never Forget Whatsisname, 1967; Joseph Andrews, 1977. Awards incl. BAFTA award for best actress, 1968; BBC Personality of the Year, 1969. Hon. MA Teesside 1994; Hon. BA Sunderland, 2009. *Publications:* Happy Endings, 1972; The Busy Mums Cook Book, 1983; The Busy Mums Baking Book, 1986; Show Me the Way, 2006. *Recreations:* music, walking, reading, gardening.

**CRAIG, Cairns;** see Craig, R. C.

**CRAIG, Christopher John Sinclair,** CB 1991; DSC 1982; RN retired; *b* 18 May 1941; *s* of Richard Michael Craig and Barbara Mary Craig; *m* 1973, Daphne Joan Underwood; two *s. Educ:* Portchester Secondary Modern Sch.; Bournemouth. Joined RN, 1959; BRNC Dartmouth, 1959–62; qualified as anti-submarine helicopter pilot, 1963; HMS Eagle, 1964–66; HMS Dido, 1967–69; in command: HMS Monkton, 1970–72; naval air sqdns, 705, 1973–74, and 826, 1975; HMS London, 1976–77; Asst Sec. to Chiefs of Staff, 1978–79; in command: HMS Alacrity, 1980–82 (incl. Falklands War); HMS Avenger and Fourth Frigate Sqdn, 1985–86; RNAS Portland/HMS Osprey, 1986–87; HMS Drake, 1987–89; Cdre in command, RN Task Gp (Gulf War), 1990–91 (HMS London and HMS Brave); COS to FONA, 1991–93; retd 1994. Chm., Brooke, Evelyn and Thistlethwaite Trust, 2011–. US Bronze Star, 1991. *Publications:* Call for Fire: sea combat in the Falklands and the Gulf War, 1995. *Recreations:* watercolour painting, classical music, reading. *Address:* Greencroft, East Grinstead, near Salisbury, Wilts SP5 3SA.

**CRAIG, Dr Claire Harvey,** CBE 2006; Provost, Queen's College, Oxford, since 2019; *b* Scunthorpe, 8 Feb. 1961; *d* of Richard Harvey Craig and Yvonne Doris Craig-Inskip; *m* 1999, Christopher Robert Peter Diacopoulos. *Educ:* Redland High Sch.; Newnham Coll., Cambridge (BA Natural Scis (Physics) 1982); St John's Coll., Cambridge (PhD Geophysics 1986). Postdoctoral Res. Fellow, Univ. of Texas at Austin, 1986–87; Associate, McKinsey & Co., 1997–99; Commercial Dir, At-Bristol Sci. Centre, 1999–2002; Dir, UK Foresight prog., 2002–06; Rev. Manager, Prime Minister's Delivery Unit, 2006–08; Director of Strategy: OFT, 2008–10; BIS, 2010–11; Dir, Govt Office for Sci., 2011–16; Chief Scientific Policy Officer, Royal Soc., 2016–19. Associate Fellow, Newnham Coll., Cambridge, 2003. Mem., Faculty, World Economic Forum, 2006. UK Rep., EC Jt Res. Centre, 2015; Member: Governing Body, UWE, 2001–07; Council, KCL, 2013–16 (Dep. Chm., Maths Sch., 2013–16). *Publications:* How Does Government Listen to Scientists?, 2018; contribs to jls incl. Nature, Royal Soc. Open Sci., Futures, Harvard Business Rev. *Recreations:* Aikido (Mem., Open Aikido Assoc.), horse-riding, theatre, poetry. *Address:* Queen's College, Oxford OX1 4AW.

**CRAIG, Daniel;** actor. *Theatre* includes: Angels in America, A Number, RNT; Hurly Burly, Old Vic; A Steady Rain, Gerald Schoenfeld Th., NY, 2009; Betrayal, Ethel Barrymore Th., NY, 2013; Othello, New York Th. Workshop, 2016; *films* include: The Power of One, 1992; Obsession, 1997; Love and Rage, Elizabeth, Love is the Devil, 1998; The Trench, 1999; I Dreamed of Africa, Some Voices, Hotel Splendide, 2000; Lara Croft: Tomb Raider, 2001; Road to Perdition, Ten Minutes Older: The Cello, Occasional, Strong, 2002; The Mother, Sylvia, 2003; Enduring Love, Layer Cake, 2004; The Jacket, Sorstalanság, Munich, 2005; Casino Royale, 2006; The Golden Compass, Infamous, 2007; Flashbacks of a Fool, Quantum of Solace, 2008; Defiance, 2009; Cowboys and Aliens, Dream House, The Girl with the Dragon Tattoo, 2011; Skyfall, 2012; Spectre, 2015; Logan Lucky, 2017; Knives Out, 2019; *television* includes: Our Friends in the North, 1996; Sword of Honour, 2001; Copenhagen, 2002; Archangel, 2005.

**CRAIG, (David) Jonathan;** Member (DemU) Lagan Valley, Northern Ireland Assembly, 2007–16; *b* 2 Feb. 1965; *s* of David and Deborah Craig; *m* 1991, S. G. Yvonne; one *s* one *d. Educ:* Univ. of Ulster (HND with Dist. Mech. Engrg). Tool design engr, Shorts Bombardier, 1987–2007. Mem. Educn Cttee, NI Assembly, 2011–16. Mem., Policing Bd, NI, 2011–16. Member: (DemU) Lisburn CC, 2001–13 (Mayor, 2005–06); (DemU) Lisburn and Castlereagh CC, 2016–. Contested (DemU) Lagan Valley, NI Assembly, 2016. *Recreations:* following motorbike racing, building computers, home DIY.

**CRAIG, David Mark;** QC 2015; a Recorder, since 2018; *b* London, 24 July 1972; *s* of Graham Craig and Rosalind Craig (*née* Montague, now Simmons); *m* 2000, Ruth Elana Jonas; one *s* three *d. Educ:* University Coll. Sch., London; Manchester Univ. (BSc 1st Cl. Hons Psychol.); Queens' Coll., Cambridge (MPhil Criminol. 1995); City Univ. (CPE). Called to the Bar, Inner Temple, 1997; in practice as barrister, 1997–. *Publications:* (contrib.) Violence, Culture and Censure, 1997; (jtly) The Law of Reinsurance, 2004. *Recreations:* family, sport, theatre. *Address:* Essex Court Chambers, 24 Lincoln's Inn Fields, WC2A 3EG. *T:* (020) 7813 8000, *Fax:* (020) 7813 8080. *E:* dcraig@essexcourt.com.

**CRAIG, Prof. Edward John,** FBA 1993; Knightbridge Professor of Philosophy, University of Cambridge, 1998–2005; Fellow, Churchill College, Cambridge, since 1966; *b* 26 March 1942; *s* of Charles William Craig and Annie (*née* Taylor); *m* 1st, 1973, Isabel Nina Barnard (marr. diss. 1986); two *d*; 2nd, 1987, Gillian Helen Elizabeth Edwards. *Educ:* Charterhouse; Trinity Coll., Cambridge (MA 1966; PhD 1970). Cricket for Cambridge Univ. and Lancs CCC, 1961–63; Cambridge University: Asst Lectr and Univ. Lectr in Philosophy, 1966–92; Reader in Modern Philosophy, 1992–98. Visiting University appointments: Melbourne, 1974; Hamburg, 1977–78; Heidelberg, 1981; Indian Inst. of Advanced Studies, 1996. General Editor: Routledge Encyclopedia of Philosophy, 1991–2011; Routledge Encyclopedia of Philosophy Online, 2000–11 Editor, Ratio, 1988–92. *Publications:* David Hume: eine Einführung in seine Philosophie, 1979; The Mind of God and the Works of Man, 1987; Knowledge and the State of Nature, 1990; Pragmatische Untersuchungen zum Wissensbegriff, 1993; Hume on Religion, 1997; Philosophy: a very short introduction, 2002. *Recreations:* music, golf. *Address:* Churchill College, Cambridge CB3 0DS. *T:* (01223) 336000.

**CRAIG, George Charles Graham;** Senior Director, Social Affairs (formerly Social Policy and Land Affairs), Welsh Assembly Government, 1999–2003; *b* 8 May 1946; *s* of late George Craig and of E. S. Craig (*née* Milne); *m* 1968, (Ethne) Marian, er *d* of late H. H. A. Gallagher and of E. F. Gallagher; two *s* one *d. Educ:* Brockley County Grammar Sch.; Nottingham Univ. (BA). Asst Principal, Min. of Transport, 1967; Welsh Office: Private Sec. to Minister of State, 1970–72; Principal, 1972; Private Sec. to Sec. of State for Wales, 1978–80; Asst Sec., 1980; Under Sec., 1986; Dep. Sec., 1999. *Address:* c/o PO Box 2, RSS 545-549, Wallisdown Road, Bournemouth BH12 5ED.

**CRAIG, Gloria Linda,** CB 2010; Director (formerly Director-General), International Security Policy, Ministry of Defence, 2007–11 (Director General, Security Policy Jan.–June 2011, Special Studies, July–Aug. 2011); *b* 23 Nov. 1948; *née* Kristler; adopted *d* of late George Edward Franklin and of Victoria Franklin; *m* 1st, 1987, Gordon Montgomery Craig (marr. diss. 2001); 2nd, 2012, Robert Lee Ayers. *Educ:* St Martin-in-the-Fields High Sch. for Girls; Lady Margaret Hall, Oxford (MA). GB–USSR Assoc., 1970–71; joined MoD, 1971; Private Sec. to Parly Under Sec. of State (Navy), 1975–76; Planning Staff, FCO, 1979–81; Asst Sec., 1984; RCDS 1988; Dep. Dir, Cabinet Office, 1989–92, 1995–99; Ministry of Defence: Director General: Security and Safety, 1999–2003; Defence Export Services, 2003–07. Non-executive Member Board: Family Housing Assoc., 1999–2004; CS Healthcare, 2011–; Trustee, Somerset Army Cadet Force, 2013–. Mentor, RCDS, 2013–. Ehrenkreuz der Bundeswehr in Gold, Germany, 2011. *Publications:* papers and lectures on defence and public service issues, white papers and best practice guides. *Recreations:* antiques, music, travel, animals, gardening.

**CRAIG, Rev. Gordon Thomas,** QHC 2007; Chaplain, UK Oil and Gas Industry (formerly Offshore Oil and Gas Industry Association), since 2012; *b* Glasgow, 1959; *s* of John Craig and Elizabeth Craig; *m* 1984, Rhona; three *c. Educ:* Paisley Grammar Sch.; Univ. of Glasgow (BD 1985). RAF Chaplain: RAF Marham, 1988–91; RAF St Athan, 1991–93; RAF Lossiemouth, 1993–96; RAF Laarbruch, 1996–99; Senior Chaplain: RAF Coll. Cranwell, 1999–2002; RAF Cosford, 2002–04; RAF Cottesmore, 2004–06; Air Command, 2006–11; Principal Chaplain, Church of Scotland and Free Churches, RAF, 2009–12; Principal, Armed Forces Chaplaincy Centre, 2011–12. Hon. Chaplain: to RAF Widows' Assoc., 1991–2011; to War Widows' Assoc. of GB, 2007–09. *Recreation:* playing very loud bass guitar. *Club:* Royal Air Force.

**CRAIG, Dr (James) Oscar (Max Clark),** FRCS, FRCP, FRCSI, FRCR, FRCGP; Consultant Radiologist since 1963, and Hon. Senior Clinical Lecturer, since 1987, St Mary's Hospital, London; President, Royal College of Radiologists, 1989–92; *b* 7 May 1927; *s* of James Oscar Max Clark Craig and Olivia Craig; *m* 1st, 1950, Louise Burleigh (*d* 2008); four *d*; 2nd, 2009, Mary Gillian Sprange. *Educ:* Royal College of Surgeons in Ireland. LRCP&SI 1950; FRCSI 1956; DMRD 1959; FRCR (FFR 1962); FRCS 1982; MRCP 1989, FRCP 1993; FRCGP 1991. Asst GP, 1950–51; Ho. Surg., St Helier Hosp., Carshalton, 1951–52; Gen. practice, Sutton, 1952–54. Surg., RAF, 1954–56. Sen. Ho. Officer, Surgery, Hammersmith Hosp., 1956–57; Registrar and Sen. Registrar, Dept of Radiology, St Mary's Hosp., London, 1957–63; Lectr in Radiology, London Univ., 1963–87; Dir of Clinical Studies, 1969–75, Dir of Post Grad. Studies, 1979–81, St Mary's Hosp. Med. Sch. Visiting Professor: UBC, Canada, 1977; Univ. of Queensland, 1984; Concord Hosp., Sydney, 1988. Chm., Cases Cttee, Med. Protection Soc., 1986–92. Pres., Harveian Soc. of London, 2002. Hon. Pres., British Med. Students Assoc. Fellow, Med. Soc. of London, 2001. Hon. Member: Radiological Soc. of N America, 1993; British Soc. Interventional Radiologists. Hon. FFR RCSI 1985; Hon. Fellow, Hong Kong Coll. of Radiologists, 1995. Lifetime Achievement Award, Imperial Coll. London, 2012. *Publications:* A Life in Medicine (autobiog.), 2000; Medical Memoirs (autobiog.), 2006; Doctors at War, 2007; Can't You See the Seagulls?, 2008; Come Sit with Me Awhile, 2011; Reflections: the collected poems of Dr Oscar Craig, 2012; numerous papers and chapters in books on clinical radiology, phlebography, lymphangiography, gastro-intestinal radiology, medico-legal medicine and the develt of digital radiology. *Recreation:* country-walking. *Address:* 62 Burdon Lane, Cheam, Surrey SM2 7BY. *T:* (020) 8642 2696. *Clubs:* Royal Society of Medicine, MCC.

**CRAIG, John Frazer,** CB 1994; Director, Economic Affairs (formerly Head of Economic and Industrial Affairs), Welsh Office, 1990–97; *b* 8 Nov. 1943; *s* of late John Frazer Craig and Margaret Jane Gibson Craig; *m* 1st, 1963, Ann Bardo (marr. diss. 1972); two *s* one *d*; 2nd, 1973, Janet Elizabeth. *Educ:* Robert Richardson Grammar Sch., Sunderland. Customs and Excise, 1961–69; Nat. Bd for Prices and Incomes, 1969–70; Welsh Office, 1977–97: Private Sec. to Perm. Sec., 1972–74; Private Sec. to Sec. of State for Wales, 1980–82; Asst Sec., 1982–85, Under Sec. (Dir), 1985–87, Industry Dept; Under Sec. (Principal Finance Officer), Welsh Office, 1987–90; Dep. Sec., 1990–97.

**CRAIG, Jonathan;** see Craig, D. J.

**CRAIG, Jonathan Laurie;** Chief Political Correspondent, Sky News, since 2006; *b* Eastham, Cheshire, 9 Aug. 1957; *s* of late James Royan Craig and Muriel Craig (*née* Webb); *m* 1st, 1980, Jane Isobel Simons (marr. diss. 1987); 2nd, 1987, Fiona Mary Walsh (marr. diss. 1998); 3rd, 2013, Caroline Audrey Rachel Edmondson. *Educ:* King's Sch., Macclesfield; Wetherby High Sch.; Tadcaster Grammar Sch.; Southampton Univ. (LLB Hons). Pres., Students' Union, Southampton Univ., 1978–79. Trainee journalist, N Eastern Evening Gazette, 1979–81; Parly corresp., 1982–85, Sen. Political corresp., 1985–86, Thomson Regl Newspapers; Home Affairs corresp., Sunday Times, 1986–89; Political corresp.,

Today, 1989–92; Political Ed., Daily Express, 1992–96; Dep. Political Ed., The Express, 1996–98; Political Editor: Sunday Express, 1998–2001; BBC London, 2001–03; Political corresp., Sky News, 2003–06. Columnist, Public Affairs News, 2008–. *Publications:* contrib. articles to Tribune. *Recreations:* films, theatre, music, country walks, watching sport. *Address:* Sky News, 2nd Floor, 4 Millbank, SW1P 3JA. *T:* (020) 7032 2805, *Fax:* (020) 7032 2801. *E:* jon.craig@sky.uk. *Clubs:* Le Beaujolais, Phoenix Artist; Surrey County Cricket.

**CRAIG, Kenneth Allen;** a Judge of the Upper Tribunal (Asylum and Immigration Chamber), since 2011; Member, Special Immigration Appeals Commission, since 2015; *b* 19 Aug. 1950; *yr s* of Seymour Craig and Nancie Craig (*née* Livingstone); *m* 1971, Linda Lambert; two *s*. *Educ:* Haberdashers' Aske's Sch., Elstree; Sussex Univ. (BA Hons American Studies); Council of Legal Educn (Prize for obtaining only 1st in Bar Pt 1 Exams 1974). Called to the Bar, Lincoln's Inn, 1975, Bencher, 1999; in private practice as barrister, 1975–2011; Founder Mem., Hardwicke Bldg, 1990. Legal Mem. (and pt-time Chm.), Immigration and Asylum Tribunal, 2004–06; fee-paid Immigration Judge, 2006–11; Dep. Judge, Upper Tribunal (Asylum and Immigration Chamber), 2010–11. Mem., Bar Council, 1994–2011. *Recreations:* spending time with his grandchildren, theatre, travel, telling good jokes badly. *Address:* Asylum and Immigration Chamber, Field House, 15–25 Breams Buildings, EC4A 1DZ. *E:* uppertribunaljudge.craig@ejudiciary.net. *Clubs:* Athenæum, MCC; Tottenham Hotspur.

**CRAIG, (Mae) Rosalie;** actor; *b* Nottingham; 30 May, *d* of Ray Craig and Jane Craig; *m* 2014, Robert Hugh Fraser, (Hadley Fraser); one *d*. *Educ:* Arnold Hill Sch., Nottingham; Bilborough Coll., Nottingham; Rose Bruford Coll. of Speech and Drama. *Theatre:* début, Alice in Wonderland, RSC, 2001; National Theatre: London Road, 2011; The Light Princess (Evening Standard Th. Award for Best Musical Performance), 2013; As You Like It, 2015; The Threepenny Opera, 2016; Donmar Warehouse: City of Angels, 2014; The Vote, 2015; Becoming (also co-writer), 2017; Miss Julie/Black Comedy, Chichester Festival, 2014; The Ferryman, Company (Evening Standard Th. Award for Best Musical Performance), Gielgud, 2018. Fellow, Rose Bruford Coll. of Speech and Drama, 2015. *Recreations:* theatre, cinema, yoga, motherhood, design, fashion, architecture, music, composing.

**CRAIG, Nicholas;** QC 2019; *b* Edinburgh, 1972; *s* of John and Hilary Craig; *m* 1998, Karen Louise McAdam; two *s*. *Educ:* King's Coll. London (BA Hons); Linacre Coll., Oxford (MPhil); City Univ., London (DipLaw). Called to the Bar, Inner Temple, 1998. *Address:* 3 Verulam Buildings, Gray's Inn, WC1R 5NT. *T:* (020) 7831 8441. *E:* ncraig@3vb.com.

**CRAIG, Oscar;** *see* Craig, J. O. M. C.

**CRAIG, Prof. Paul Philip,** FBA 1998; Professor of English Law, University of Oxford, 1998–2019, now Emeritus (Professor of Law, 1996–98); Fellow of St John's College, Oxford, since 1998; *b* 27 Sept. 1951; *s* of Maurice and Beatrice Craig; *m* 1991, Dr Anita Cooper; one *s*. *Educ:* Worcester Coll., Oxford (MA, BCL). University of Oxford: Fellow, Worcester Coll., 1976–98, now Emeritus; Reader in Law, 1990–96. Vis. Prof. in Univs of Virginia, Cornell, Connecticut, York (Osgoode Hall) Canada, Indiana, Queensland. Hon. QC 2000. Hon. DLaws Maastricht, 2014. *Publications:* Administrative Law, 1983, 8th edn 2016; Public Law and Democracy in the United Kingdom and the United States of America, 1990; Text, Cases and Materials on Community Law, 1995, 6th edn 2015; Law Making in the European Union, 1998; The Evolution of EU Law, 1999, 2nd edn 2011; EU Administrative Law, 2006, 2nd edn 2012; The Lisbon Treaty: law, politics and treaty reform, 2010; UK, EU and Global Administrative Law: foundations and challenges, 2015; articles in jls. *Recreations:* riding, ski-ing, theatre, acting, ballet. *Address:* St John's College, Oxford OX1 3JP. *T:* (01865) 277340.

**CRAIG, Maj.-Gen. Peter;** *see* Craig, Maj.-Gen. R. P.

**CRAIG, Prof. R. Cairns,** OBE 2007; PhD; FBA 2005; FRSE; Glucksman Professor of Irish and Scottish Studies and Director, Research Institute of Irish and Scottish Studies, since 2005, and Director of AHRC Centre for Irish and Scottish Studies, 2006–10, University of Aberdeen; *b* 16 Feb. 1949. Lectr, Dept of English, Univ. of Aberdeen; Department of English Literature, University of Edinburgh: Lectr; Sen. Lectr; Reader; Prof. of Scottish and Modern Literature; Hd of Dept, 1997–2003; Dir, Centre for History of Ideas in Scotland. Hon. Prof. and Chm., Academic Adv. Bd, AHRC Centre for Irish and Scottish Studies, Univ. of Aberdeen, 2001–06. FRSE 2003. *Publications:* Yeats, Eliot, Pound and the Politics of Poetry: richest to the richest, 1982; Out of History: narrative paradigms in Scottish and English Culture, 1996; The Modern Scottish Novel: narrative and the national imagination, 1999; Iain Banks's Complicity: a reader's guide, 2002; Intending Scotland, 2009; Associationism and the Literary Imagination: from the phantasmal chaos, 2007. *Address:* Research Institute of Irish and Scottish Studies, Humanity Manse, 19 College Bounds, Aberdeen AB24 3UG.

**CRAIG, Maj.-Gen. (Robert) Peter,** MD; FRCS, FRCEM; expert medical witness, since 2001; Chairman, Queen Mary's Roehampton Trust, 2002–12; *b* 24 June 1940; *s* of late Dr Robert Theodore Gilpin Craig, TD, MB BS, MRCGP and Jessie Craig (*née* McKinstry); *m* 1971, Jean Toft, MA; one *s* two *d*. *Educ:* George Watson's Boys' Coll.; Durham Univ. Med. Sch. (MB BS 1964); MD Newcastle upon Tyne 1987; FRCS 1972; FRCEM (FFAEM 1994). Commissioned RA (TA) 1958; RAMC 1963; Royal Victoria Infirmary, Newcastle, 1964–65; RMO 1/2 Gurkha Rifles, 1966–68; Queen Alexandra Mil. Hosp.; Birmingham Accident Hosp.; Dept of Surgery, Univ. of Newcastle upon Tyne; BMH Rinteln; Guy's Hosp., 1974–78; Consultant Surgeon: BMH Hong Kong, 1979–81; Queen Elizabeth Mil. Hosp., 1981–86; Sen. Lectr in Mil. Surgery, Royal Army Med. Coll., 1981–86; BMH Rinteln, 1986–89, CO, 1987–89; Comd Med., 4th Armoured Div., 1989–90; Comd Surgeon, HQ BAOR, 1990–92; Dir of Army Surgery, 1992–93; Comd Medical, UKLF, 1993–94; Consultant in A & E Medicine, Wansbeck Gen. Hosp., 1994–96. Medical Member: War Pensions and Armed Forces Compensation Chamber, Pensions Appeals Tribunals, then First-tier Tribunal, 1997–2010 (Med. Chm., 2000–01); The Appeals Service, 1998–2008. QHS 1992–94. Liveryman, Soc. of Apothecaries, 2003–. Montefiore Meml Medal, 1979; Leishman Meml Medal, 1987. OStJ 1993. GSM Oman 1973, NI 1979. *Publications:* contribs to surgical jls. *Recreations:* golf, bridge, military history. *Address:* 162 New Kent Road, SE1 4YS. *T:* (020) 7701 6553. *E:* rpetercraig12@gmail.com. *Clubs:* Athenæum, Royal Society of Medicine; Northumberland Golf; Wilderness (Sevenoaks).

**CRAIG, Rosalie;** *see* Craig, M. R.

**CRAIG, Sheenagh;** *see* Adams, Sheenagh.

**CRAIG, Stuart (Norman),** OBE 2003; RDI 2004; film production designer; *b* 14 April 1942; *s* of Norman and Kate Craig; *m* 1965, Patricia Stangroom; two *d*. *Educ:* Royal Coll. of Art. *Films:* The Elephant Man, 1980 (BAFTA Award); Gandhi, 1982 (Acad. Award); Greystoke, 1984; Cal, 1984; The Mission, 1986; Cry Freedom, 1987; Dangerous Liaisons, 1988 (Acad. Award); Memphis Belle, 1990; Chaplin, 1992; The Secret Garden, 1993; Shadowlands, 1993; Mary Reilly, 1996; The English Patient, 1996 (Acad. Award); In Love and War, 1996; The Avengers, 1998; Notting Hill, 1999; The Legend of Bagger Vance, 2000; Harry Potter I–VIII, 2001–11; Gambit, 2012; The Legend of Tarzan, 2016; Fantastic Beasts and Where to Find Them, 2016 (BAFTA Award (jtly), 2017); Fantastic Beasts: the crimes of Grindelwald, 2018. *Address:* c/o Murtha Skouras Agency, 1025 Colorado Avenue, Santa Monica, CA 90401, USA.

**CRAIG, Susan Ann;** Sheriff of Lothian and Borders at Livingston, since 2013; Deputy Director, Judicial Institute for Scotland, since 2017; *b* Stirling, Scotland; *d* of Alasdair and Tove Fraser; four *s*. *Educ:* Univ. of Aberdeen (LLB; DipLP 1984). NP, 1986; Solicitor Advocate (Civil), 1994; WS, 1997; admitted to Faculty of Advocates, 2015; an Employment Judge, 2003–13; Sheriff (pt-time), 2011–13. *Recreations:* running, music, travel. *Address:* Livingston Sheriff Court, Howden South Road, Livingston, W Lothian EH54 6FF.

**CRAIG, Wendy;** *see* Craig, A. G.

**CRAIG-COOPER, Sir (Frederick Howard) Michael,** Kt 1991; CBE 1982; TD 1968 (3 bars); Director, Craig-Lloyd, since 1968; Vice Lord-Lieutenant of Greater London, 2005–11; *b* 28 Jan. 1936; *s* of late Frederick William Valentine Craig-Cooper and Elizabeth Oliver-Thompson Craig-Cooper (*née* Macdonald) (she *m* 1978, Col J. H. Carroll-Leahy, MC (decd)); *m* 1968, Elizabeth Snagge, MVO; one *s*. *Educ:* Horris Hill; Stowe; College of Law. Solicitor, 1961. National Service, RA, 1954–56; TA, 1956–88; Comdr, Naval Gunfire Liaison Unit, 29 Commando Regt, RA, 1972–75; Mem., Greater London TAVRA (Chm., Employers Support Cttee, 1987–90). Jaques & Co., 1956–61; Allen & Overy, 1962–64; Inco, 1964–85; Director: Paul Ray Internat., 1984–92 (merged with Carre Orban & Partners, 1989); Tichborne Enterprises Ltd, 1993–; Nat. Bank of Kuwait (Internat.) plc, 1993–2017 (Advr to Bd, 2017–); non-executive Director: Ely Place Holdings Ltd, 1994–2010; Craigmyle & Co. Ltd, 1995–2009; Westminster Forum (formerly WIB Publications) Ltd, 1996–2016; Advr, Weorclic Ltd, 2018–. Royal Borough of Kensington & Chelsea: Councillor, 1968–74; Chief Whip, 1971–74; Chm. Finance Cttee, 1972–74; Alderman, 1974–78; Mem. Investment Cttee, 1973–. Contested (C) Houghton-le-Spring, 1966, 1970; Chm., Cons. Nat. Property Adv. Cttee, 1986–93 (Mem., 1993–); Pres., Kensington and Chelsea (formerly Chelsea), Cons. Assoc., 1983–2005 (Chm., 1974–77). Trustee: Copper Develt Trust Fund, 1974–85; Order of Malta Homes Trust, 1980–2003; Orders of St John Trust, 1988–2003; Thames Diamond Jubilee Pageant Foundn, 2011–14; Founding Trustee, Mansion House Scholarship Scheme, 1998–. Mem. Council, Mining Assoc., 1977–82; Chm. Disciplinary Appeal Cttee, CIMA, 1994–2005. Mem. Adv. Bd, CANZUK Internat., 2017–. Comr, Royal Hosp. Chelsea, 1998–2005 (Pres., Friends of Royal Hosp. Chelsea, 2009–). Pres., Boys' Brigade (London Dist), 2002–05. Vice Pres., RFCA, Greater London, 2005–. Freeman, City of London, 1964; Liveryman, Drapers' Co., 1970– (Mem. Court of Assistants, 1987–; Master, 1997–98); Hon. Freeman, Royal Bor. of Kensington and Chelsea, 2011. DL Greater London, 1986; Rep. DL Kensington & Chelsea, 1987–2006. FCIArb 1992. KStJ 1990 (Chm., Council for London, 1990–94; Mem., Chapter-Gen., 1993–). Comdr, SMO Malta, 2001. *Publications:* (with Philippe De Backer) Management Audit: how to create an effective management team, 1993; (jtly) Maw on Corporate Governance, 1994; (jtly) Maximum Leadership, 1995, revd edn as Maximum Leadership 2000, 1997; (with Field Marshal Sir John Chapple *et al.*) Stepping Forward, 2014. *Recreations:* admiring wife's gardening, hill walking in the Scilly Isles. *Clubs:* Beefsteak, Pratt's, White's.

**CRAIG-McFEELY, Comdt Elizabeth Sarah Ann, (Mrs C. C. H. Dunlop),** CB 1982; DL; Director, Women's Royal Naval Service, 1979–82; *b* 28 April 1927; *d* of late Lt-Col Cecil Michael Craig McFeely, DSO, OBE, MC, and Nancy Sarah (*née* Mann, later Roberts); *m* 1995, Rear-Adm. Colin Charles Harrison Dunlop, CB, CBE (*d* 2009). *Educ:* St Rose's Convent, Stroud, Glos; Anstey College of Physical Educn, Birmingham. DipPE London. Taught PE at St Angela's Ursuline Convent Sch., 1948–52; joined WRNS, 1952; Third Officer, 1953; served in various Royal Naval, Royal Marines and Royal Naval Reserve Estabts, 1952–67; in charge, WRNS, Far Eastern Fleet, 1967–69; various appts, MoD (Navy), 1969–74; HMS Centurion, 1974–76; Supt WRNS, 1977. Naval member, NAAFI Bd of Management, 1977–79; Hon. ADC to the Queen, 1979–82; retired 1982. DL Kent, 1996–2005. *Recreations:* gardening and country pursuits. *Address:* 1 The Gatehouse, Elliscombe Park, Holton, Wincanton, Somerset BA9 8EA. *T:* (01963) 31534.

**CRAIG-MARTIN, Sir Michael,** Kt 2016; CBE 2001; RA 2006; artist; *b* 28 Aug. 1941; *s* of Paul and Rhona Craig-Martin; *m* 1963, Janice Lucia Hashey (separated); one *d*. *Educ:* Priory Sch., Washington; Yale Univ. Artist in Residence, King's Coll., Cambridge, 1970–72; Sen. Lectr, 1974–79, Prin. Lectr, 1979–88, Millard Prof. of Fine Art, 1994–2000, Goldsmiths' Coll., London (Hon. Fellow, 2001). Trustee, Tate Gall., 1989–99. *Exhibitions* include: Hayward Gall., 1972; Tate Gall., 1972; IX Biennale des Jeunes Artistes, Paris, 1975; Sydney Biennale, 1976, 1990; Whitechapel Art Gall., 1995; MOMA, NY, 1999; *one-man exhibitions* include: Whitechapel Art Gall., 1989 (retrospective); MOMA, NY, 1991; Centre Pompidou, Paris, 1994; Hannover Kunstverein, 1998; São Paulo Bienal, 1998; Stuttgart Kunstverein, 1999; Peter Blum, NY, 1999; Waddington Galls, 2000, 2002; IVAM, Valencia, Spain, 2000; Irish Mus. of Modern Art, 2006 (retrospective); Nat. Art Centre, Tokyo, 2007; Alan Cristea Gall., London, 2008, 2014; New Paintings and Sculptures, New Art Centre, Roche Court, Wilts, 2011; Sculptures, Chatsworth House, Derbys, 2014; Transience, Serpentine Gall., 2015; *curated:* Master Works, Alan Cristea Gall., London, 2014. *Publications:* On Being An Artist, 2015.

**CRAIGAVON,** 3rd Viscount *cr* 1927, of Stormont, Co. Down; **Janric Fraser Craig;** Bt 1918; *b* 9 June 1944; *s* of 2nd Viscount Craigavon; *S* father, 1974. *Educ:* Eton; London Univ. (BA, BSc). FCA. Elected Mem., H of L, 1999. *Heir:* none.

**CRAIGEN, James Mark;** Director and Secretary, Scottish Federation of Housing Associations, 1988–90; freelance writer; *b* 2 Aug. 1938; *e s* of James Craigen, MA and Isabel Craigen; *m* 1971, Sheena Millar. *Educ:* Shawlands Academy, Glasgow; Strathclyde University; MLitt Heriot-Watt 1974. Compositor, 1954–61. Industrial Relations Asst, Scottish Gas Bd, 1963–64; Head of Organisation and Social Services at Scottish TUC, 1964–68; Asst Sec., and Industrial Liaison Officer, Scottish Business Educn Council, 1968–74. Glasgow City Councillor, 1965–68, Magistrate, 1966–68. Member: Scottish Ambulance Service Bd, 1966–71; Race Relations Bd, Scottish Conciliation Cttee, 1967–70; Police Adv. Bd for Scotland, 1970–74; ITC Viewer Consultative Council for Scotland, 1990–93; S Scotland Electricity Consumers' Cttee, 1994–97. Contested Ayr constituency, 1970. MP (Lab and Co-op) Glasgow Maryhill, Feb. 1974–1987 (retired on grounds of experience, not age); PPS to Rt Hon. William Ross, MBE, MP, Sec. of State for Scotland, 1974–76; Opposition Spokesman on Scottish Affairs, 1983–85. Member: Select Cttee on Employment, 1979–83 (Chm., 1982–83); Select Cttee on Scottish Affairs, 1987; Chairman: Co-op. Party Parly Group, 1978–79; Scottish Group, Labour MPs, 1978–79; PLP Employment Gp, 1981–83. Member: UK Delegn to Council of Europe Assembly, 1976–80; Extra Parly Panel, Private Legislation Procedure (Scotland) Act 1936, 1996–2005. Trustee, Industry and Parliament Trust, 1983–88 (Fellow, 1978–79). Mem., Bd of Trustees, Nat. Museums of Scotland, 1985–91. Hon. Vice-Pres., Building Societies Assoc., 1985–88. Hon. Lectr, Strathclyde Univ., 1980–85; Fellow, Inst. of Advanced Studies in Humanities, Edinburgh Univ., 1990–91. JP: Glasgow, 1966; Edinburgh,

1975–2007. CCMI. *Publications*: (contrib.) Forward! Labour Politics in Scotland 1888–1988, 1989; contribs to Co-operative News. *Address*: 38 Downie Grove, Edinburgh EH12 7AX.

**CRAIGIE, Cathie**; Member (Lab) Cumbernauld and Kilsyth, Scottish Parliament, 1999–2011; *b* Stirling, 14 April 1954; *d* of George Mitchell and Marion (*née* Mandelkau); *m* 1978, Arthur Craigie; one *s* one *d*. *Educ*: Kilsyth Acad. Mem., Ext. Audit Team for Chartered Accountants, 1970–80. Parly Asst to MP, 1992–97. Member (Lab): Cumbernauld and Kilsyth DC, 1984–96; Council Leader, 1994–96; Chm., Planning, Housing, Policy & Resources and Equal Opportunities Cttees, 1984–96; N Lanarks Council, 1995–99: Vice-Chm., Housing, 1995–98; Chairman: Envmtl Services, 1998–99; Kilsyth Local Area Cttee, 1998–99; Cumbernauld Housing Partnership, 1997–98. Scottish Parliament: Member: Audit Cttee, 1999–2000; Social Inclusion, Housing and Voluntary Sector Cttee, 1999–2000; Social Justice Cttee, 2001. Contested (Lab) Cumbernauld and Kilsyth, Scottish Parlt, 2011. Labour Party: Mem., 1974–; Constituency Party Sec., 1992–99; Mem., Nat. Policy Forum, 1998–. *Recreations*: cycling, reading, family holidays.

**CRAIGMYLE**, 4th Baron *cr* 1929, of Craigmyle, co. Aberdeen; **Thomas Columba Shaw**; *b* 19 Oct. 1960; *s* of 3rd Baron Craigmyle and Anthea Esther Christine (*née* Rich); *S* father, 1998; *m* 1987, (Katherine) Alice (*née* Floyd); four *s*. *Heir*: *e s* Hon. Alexander Francis Shaw, *b* 1 July 1988.

**CRAIK, Prof. Fergus Ian Muirden**, PhD; FRS 2008; FRSC; psychologist; University Professor, University of Toronto, 1997–2000, now Emeritus; Senior Scientist, Rotman Research Institute, Baycrest Centre, Toronto, 1989, now Senior Scientist Emeritus; *b* Edinburgh, 17 April 1935; *s* of late George Craik and of Frances Craik; *m* 1961, Anne, *d* of Jack and Rita Catherall; one *s* one *d*. *Educ*: George Watson's Boys' Coll., Edinburgh; Univ. of Edinburgh (BSc 1960); Univ. of Liverpool (PhD 1965). Lectr in Psychol., Birkbeck Coll., Univ. of London, 1965–71; University of Toronto: Associate Prof. of Psychol., 1971–75; Prof. of Psychol., 1975–97; Chm. of Psychol., 1985–90; Glassman Prof. of Neuropsychol., 1996–2000. Fellow, Center for Advanced Study in Behavioral Scis, Stanford Univ., 1982–83; Killam Res. Fellow, 1982–84; Guggenheim Fellow, 1982–83. Ed., Jl of Verbal Learning and Verbal Behavior, 1980–84. Mem., Soc. of Experimental Psychologists; Foreign Hon. Mem., Amer. Acad. of Arts and Scis, 2016. Fellow: Canadian Psychol. Assoc. (Hon. Pres., 1997–98); Amer. Psychol. Assoc. FRSC 1985. Hon. Dr Bordeaux 2, 2006; Hon. DSocSc Edinburgh, 2012; Hon. Dr Saarland, 2013. Dist. Scientific Contribution Award, Canadian Psychol. Assoc., 1987; William James Fellow Award, Amer. Psychol. Soc., 1993; Hebb Award, Canadian Soc. for Brain, Behaviour and Cognitive Sci., 1998; Killam Prize, 2000; Anderson Lifetime Achievement Award, Soc. of Experimental Psychologists, 2009. *Publications*: Memory, Attention, and Aging: selected works of Fergus I. M. Craik, 2017; *edited jointly*: Levels of Processing in Human Memory, 1979; Aging and Cognitive Processes, 1982; Varieties of Memory and Consciousness, 1989; The Handbook of Aging and Cognition, 1992, 3rd edn 2008; The Oxford Handbook of Memory, 2000; Lifespan Cognition: mechanisms of change, 2006; Mind and the Frontal Lobes: cognition, behavior, and brain imaging, 2012. *Recreations*: reading, walking, music, tennis. *Address*: Rotman Research Institute of Baycrest, 3560 Bathurst Street, Toronto, ON M6A 2E1, Canada.
*See also* R. G. Craik.

**CRAIK, Roger George**; QC (Scot.) 1981; Sheriff of Lothian and Borders, 1984–2005; *b* 22 Nov. 1940; *s* of late George and of Frances Craik; *m* 1964, Helen Sinclair Sutherland; one *s* one *d*. *Educ*: Lockerbie Academy; Breadalbane Academy, Aberfeldy; George Watson's Boys' Coll.; Edinburgh Univ. (MA 1960, LLB 1962). Qualified as solicitor, 1962; worked for Orr Dignam & Co., Solicitors, Pakistan, 1963–65; called to Scottish Bar, 1966. Standing junior counsel to Min. of Defence (Army), 1974–80; Advocate Depute, 1980–83. Temp. Court of Session Judge, 2004–10. Mem., Sheriff Court Rules Council, 1990–95. *Publications*: The Advocates' Library 1689–1989, 1989; James Boswell: the Scottish perspective, 1994; Parliament House Portraits: the art collection of the Faculty of Advocates, 2000. *Recreations*: Scottish antiquities, modern jazz. *Address*: 9 York Road, Trinity, Edinburgh EH5 3EJ.
*See also* F. I. M. Craik.

**CRAM, Stephen**, CBE 2015 (MBE 1986); former middle distance runner; athletics presenter and commentator, BBC TV, since 1999; Chairman, English Institute of Sport, 2002–13; *b* 14 Oct. 1960; *s* of William Frank Cram and Maria Helene (*née* Korte); *m* 1983, Karen Anne Waters (marr. diss. 2005); one *s* one *d*. *Educ*: Jarrow Grammar Sch.; Newcastle Poly. (BA). Commonwealth Games: Gold Medal for 1500m, 1982, 1986; Gold Medal for 800m, 1986; European Championships: Gold Medal for 1500m, 1982, 1986; Bronze Medal for 800m, 1986; Gold Medal for 1500m, World Championships, 1983; Silver Medal for 1500m, Olympic Games, 1984; Member, British Olympic Squad, 1980, 1984, 1988; former world record for mile, 1500m and 2000m, 1985. Regular contributor, BBC Radio 5 Live, 1995–; athletics columnist, Guardian; motivational speaker and sports consultant. Chm. and Trustee, Northumberland Sport. Chm. and Dir, Comrades of Children Overseas, 1998–. Patron, Macmillan Cancer Relief. Chancellor, Sunderland Univ., 2008– (Hon. Fellow 1986). DUniv: Staffordshire, 2001; Sheffield Hallam, 2001. BBC Sports Personality of the Year, 1983. *Recreations*: golf, football, snooker. *Address*: Extra Mile Media and Events, Kiln Rigg, Wall, Hexham, Northumberland NE46 4EQ. *T*: 07900 223563. *E*: steve@extramileme.com. *Clubs*: Jarrow and Hebburn Athletic; Sunderland Association Football (Pres. London and Southern England Br., Supporters' Assoc.).

**CRAMER, Shirley Christine**, CBE 2009; Chief Executive, Royal Society for Public Health, since 2013; *b* Whitehaven, 11 April 1955; *d* of Joseph and Jean Tyson; *m* 1979, Carl Cramer; two *d*. *Educ*: Cockermouth Grammar Sch.; Univ. of Bradford (BA CQSW 1978); Columbia Univ., NY (MSc Social Admin 1985). Exec. Dir, Nat. Center for Learning Disabilities, NY, 1992–95; Dir, Coordinated Campaign for Learning Disabilities, USA, 1995–99; Chief Exec., Dyslexia Action, 2000–11; Interim CEO, Alzheimer's Res. UK, 2012. Chairman: Equality and Diversity Ext. Adv. Gp, 2009–13; British Future Think Tank, 2013–. Mem., Nat. Council, LSC, 2002–08. *Publications*: Learning Disabilities: lifelong issues, 1996. *Recreations*: ski-ing, walking, opera, theatre, art, singing in a choir. *Address*: 2 Little Dormers, 15 South Park Crescent, Gerrards Cross, Bucks SL9 8HJ. *T*: (01753) 899189, 07841 672081. *E*: scramer@rsph.org.uk, scramer0@gmail.com.

**CRAMP, Leslie Thomas**, CBE 2011; Deputy Chief Executive, Insolvency Service, 2010–13; *b* 25 Oct. 1949; *s* of Noel Clifford Cramp and Doris Nellie Irene Cramp; *m* 1974, Linda Ann Lipscomb; one *s* one *d*. *Educ*: Maidstone Grammar Sch. Local govt post, 1968–70; Insolvency Service, Department of Trade and Industry, later Department for Business, Enterprise and Regulatory Reform, then Department for Business, Innovation and Skills, 1970–2013: Companies Winding-up, London, 1970–82; Principal Examr, Policy Unit, 1982–88; Official Receiver, High Court, London, 1988–96; Manager, Anglia Reg., 1996–98; Dep. Inspector Gen. and Sen. Official Receiver, 1998–2010. *Recreations*: music, football, reading, gardening.

**CRAMP, Dame Rosemary Jean**, DBE 2011 (CBE 1987); FBA 2006; Professor of Archaeology, University of Durham, 1971–90, now Emeritus; *b* 6 May 1929; *er d* of Robert Kingston and Vera Cramp, Cranoe Grange, Leics. *Educ*: Market Harborough Grammar Sch.; St Anne's Coll., Oxford (MA, BLitt). Lectr, St Anne's Coll., Oxford, 1950–55; Lectr, Durham Univ., 1955, Sen. Lectr, 1966. Vis. Fellow, All Souls Coll., Oxford, 1992. Commissioner: Royal Commn on Ancient and Historical Monuments of Scotland, 1975–99; Historic Bldgs and Monuments Commn, 1984–89 (Mem., Adv. Cttee (Archaeology), 1984–89). Trustee, BM, 1978–88. Member: Adv. Bd for Redundant Churches, 1984–98; Validation Panel, Museums' Trng Inst., 1993–97; Reviewing Cttee on Export of Works of Art, 1994–2003. Chm., Archaeology Data Service, 1996–2001. President: Council for British Archaeology, 1989–92 (Hon. Vice-Pres., 1992–); Cumberland and Westmorland Antiquarian and Archaeol Soc., 1984–87; Soc. for Church Archaeology, 1996–2001; Soc. of Antiquaries of London, 2001–04 (Hon. Vice-Pres., 2004–); Vice-Pres., Royal Archaeol Inst., 1992–97; Hon. Vice Pres., Soc. for Medieval Archaeol., 2004–. Gen. Editor, Corpus of Anglo-Saxon Stone Sculpture, 1974–. Hon. DSc: Durham, 1995; Bradford, 2002; Cambridge, 2019; Hon. DLitt: NUI, 2003; Leicester, 2004; UCD, 2015. *Publications*: Corpus of Anglo-Saxon Stone Sculpture, vol. I, Durham and Northumberland, 1984, vol. 2, (with R. N. Bailey) Cumberland and Westmorland, 1986, vol. 7, South West England, 2006; Wearmouth and Jarrow Monastic Sites, vol. 1, 2005, vol. 2, 2006; The Hirsel Excavations, 2014; contribs in the field of early monasticism, early medieval sculpture and glass, and northern archaeology. *Address*: 5 Leazes Place, Durham DH1 1RE.

**CRAMPIN, Peter**; QC 1993; *b* 7 July 1946; *s* of late John Hames Crampin and of Gwendoline Edith (*née* Richardson); *m* 1975, Frida Yvonne Schoemann; one *s*. *Educ*: St Albans Sch.; University Coll., Oxford (Open Exhibnr; MA). Admitted Solicitor, 1973; called to the Bar, Middle Temple, 1976; in practice at Chancery Bar, 1978–; an Asst Recorder, 1990–95; a Recorder, 1995; 2nd Jun. Counsel to Attorney General in Charity Matters, 1988–93. *Address*: Radcliffe Chambers, 11 New Square, Lincoln's Inn, WC2A 3QB. *T*: (020) 7831 0081.

**CRAMPTON, Prof. Richard John**, PhD; Professor of East European History, University of Oxford, 1996–2006; Fellow of St Edmund Hall, Oxford, 1990–2006, now Emeritus; *b* 23 Nov. 1940; *s* of John Donald Crampton and Norah Crampton (*née* Haden); *m* 1965, Celia Harriss; two *s*. *Educ*: Univ. of Dublin (MA); MA Oxon; SSEES, Univ. of London (PhD). University of Kent at Canterbury: Lectr, 1967–78; Sen. Lectr, 1978–88; Prof. of East European History, 1988–90; Lectr in History, Univ. of Oxford, 1990–96. Fellow, Woodrow Wilson Internat. Center for Scholars, Washington, 1998–99. Dr *hc* Sofia, 2000. *Publications*: The Hollow Détente, 1981; Bulgaria 1878–1918: a history, 1984; Short History of Modern Bulgaria, 1987; Eastern Europe in the Twentieth Century, 1994; (with Ben Crampton) Atlas of Eastern Europe in the 20th Century, 1996; Concise History of Bulgaria, 1997; The Balkans since the Second World War, 2002; Bulgaria: Oxford History of Modern Europe, 2007; Aleksandŭr Stambolĭski: Bulgaria, 2009. *Recreations*: pure mathematics, trying to avoid pop music and mobile phones. *Address*: St Edmund Hall, Oxford OX1 4AR. *T*: (01865) 279000.

**CRAN, James Douglas**; *b* 28 Jan. 1944; *s* of James Cran and Jane McDonald Cran, Aberdeenshire; *m* 1973, Penelope Barbara Wilson; one *d*. *Educ*: Ruthrieston Sch., Aberdeen; Aberdeen Coll. of Commerce; King's Coll., Univ. of Aberdeen (MA Hons). Researcher, Cons. Res. Dept, 1970–71; Sec., 1971–73, Chief. Exec., 1973–79, Nat. Assoc. of Pension Funds; Northern Dir, 1979–84, West Midlands Dir, 1984–87, CBI. Councillor (C), London Borough of Sutton, 1974–79 (Chm., Health and Housing Cttee). MP (C) Beverley, 1987–97, Beverley and Holderness, 1997–2005. PPS to Sec. of State for NI, 1995–96; an Opposition Whip, 1997–2001 (Pairing Whip, 1998–2000); Opposition Asst Chief Whip, 2001. Member: Select Cttee on Trade and Industry, 1987–92, on NI, 1994–95, on Administration, 1997–98, on Selection, 1998–2001, on Defence, 2001–05; Chairmen's Panel, 2001–05; Vice Chairman: Cons. Backbench NI Cttee, 1992–95; All-Party Anglo-Mongolian Gp, 1993–94; Order of St John All-Party Gp, 1994–95; Secretary: Cons. Backbench Cttee on Constitutional Affairs, 1989–91, on European Affairs, 1989–91; All-Party Anglo-Malta Gp, 1992–94; Co-Founder, Parly Gp on Occupational Pensions, 1992. Mem., Council of Europe and WEU, 2001–02. Mem., NI Grand Cttee, 1996–2001. Fellow: Armed Forces Parly Scheme, attached to RM, 1992; Parlt and Industry Trust, 1994. Parly consultant, Lincoln Nat. (UK) plc, 1994–98. Treas., European Res. Gp, 1994–97; Mem., 92 Gp Steering Cttee, 2001–04. Vice-Pres., Beverley Combined Div., St John Ambulance. Council Mem., Pension Trustees Forum, 1992–95. Member of Court: Univ. of Birmingham, 1984–87; Univ. of Hull, 1987–2005. Dux Medallion, City of Aberdeen, 1959; Daily Mirror Nat. Speaking Trophy, 1969. OStJ. *Recreations*: travelling, reading biographies, autobiographies and military history. *Address*: The Mill House, Ashkirk, Selkirkshire TD7 4NY; Apartment 11, The Waterfront, Triq Stella Maris, San Pawl Il-Bahar, Malta.

**CRAN, Mark Dyson Gordon**; QC 1988; a Recorder, since 2000; *b* 18 May 1948; *s* of William Broadbent Gordon Cran and Diana Rosemary Cran (*née* Mallinson); *m* 1983, Prudence Elizabeth Binning (marr. diss.). *Educ*: Gordonstoun; Millfield; Bristol Univ. (LLB). Called to the Bar, Gray's Inn, 1973, Bencher, 2009; in practice as barrister, London, 1974–2013, Bermuda (ASW Law Ltd), 2013–17. *Recreations*: country sports, long walks, convivial disputation, wine and food, performing arts. *Address*: Brick Court Chambers, 7–8 Essex Street, WC2R 3LD. *T*: (020) 7379 3550; Crawford House, 50 Cedar Avenue, PO Box HM2879, Hamilton HMLX, Bermuda. *T*: 2956500. *Clubs*: Brooks's, MCC.

**CRANBORNE, Viscount; Robert Edward William Gascoyne-Cecil**; *b* 18 Dec. 1970; *s* and *heir* of Marquess of Salisbury, *qv*; one *d* by Camilla Mary Davidson.

**CRANBROOK**, 5th Earl of, *cr* 1892; **Gathorne Gathorne-Hardy**; Viscount Cranbrook, 1878; Baron Medway, 1892; Honorary Research Fellow, Micropathology Ltd, University of Warwick Science Park, since 2015; International Collaborative Partner, TunkuAbdul Rahman University Global Network, since 2016; *b* 20 June 1933; *er s* of 4th Earl of Cranbrook, CBE, and the Dowager Countess of Cranbrook (Fidelity, OBE 1972, *o d* of late Hugh E. Seebohm) (*d* 2009); *S* father, 1978; *m* 1967, Caroline (OBE 2006), *o d* of Col Ralph G. E. Jarvis, Doddington Hall, Lincoln; two *s* one *d*. *Educ*: Eton; Corpus Christi Coll., Cambridge (MA); University of Birmingham (PhD). Asst, Sarawak Museum, 1956–58; Fellow, Yayasan Siswa Lokantara (Indonesia), 1960–61; Asst Lectr, subseq. Lectr then Sen. Lectr in Zoology, Univ. of Malaya, 1961–70. Editor of Ibis, 1973–80. Mem., H of L Select Cttee on EC, then EU, three terms, 1979–99 (Mem., Envmt Sub-Cttee, 1979–85, 1987–90 (Chm., 1980–83, 1987–90), Chm., Envmt, Public Health and Consumer Protection Sub-Cttee, 1998–99). Bd Mem., Anglian Water Authy, 1987–89; non-exec. Dir, Anglian Water, 1989–98. Chairman: English Nature, 1990–98; Inst. for Eur. Envmtl Policy, 1990–2005; ENTRUST, Envmtl Trusts Scheme Regulatory Body, 1996–2002; Internat. Trust for Zool Nomenclature, 2001–08; Member: Royal Commn on Environmental Pollution, 1981–92; NERC, 1982–88; Foundn for Eur. Envmtl Policy, 1987–98 (Chm., 1998); UK Round Table on Sustainable Develt, 1994–98; Broads Authy, 1988–99; Harwich Haven Authy, 1989–97 (Vice Chm., 1995–97); NCC, 1990–91; Suffolk Coastal DC, 1974–83; Pres., Suffolk Wildlife Trust (formerly Suffolk Trust for

Nature Conservation), 1979–2014; Chm. Adv. Cttee, NERC Centre for Ecology and Hydrology, 1998–2005; Pres., Haven Gateway Partnership, 2001–08. Adjunct Sen. Res. Fellow, Sch. of Geog. and Envmtl Sci., Monash Univ., 2014–17. Advr, Ironwood Foundn (Yayasan Ulin), Indonesia, 2009–. Chm., Long Shop Project Trust, 1981–; Trustee, BM (Natural History), 1982–86. Skinner and Freeman of the City of London. DL Suffolk, 1984. FZS; FRGS; FRSB; MBOU. Hon. FCIWEM; Hon. FIWM; Hon. FLS 2006. Hon. DSc: Aberdeen, 1989; Cranfield, 1996. Founder's Medal, RGS, 1995. OStJ. Hon. Johan Bintang Sarawak, 1997; Hon. Panglima Negara Bintang Sarawak, 2005; WWF Internat. Duke of Edinburgh Gold Medal, 2014; Merdeka Award (Malaysia), 2014. *Publications:* Mammals of Borneo, 1965, 2nd edn 1977; Mammals of Malaya, 1969, 2nd edn 1978; (with D. R. Wells) Birds of the Malay Peninsula, 1976; Riches of the Wild: mammals of South East Asia, 1987, 2nd edn 1991; (ed) Key Environments: Malaysia, 1988; (with D. S. Edwards) Belalong: a tropical rain forest, 1994; Wonders of Nature in South-East Asia, 1997; (trans.) The Ballad of Jerjezang, 2001; (with C. K. Lim) Swiftlets of Borneo: builders of edible nests, 2002, 2nd edn 2014. *Heir:* s Lord Medway, *qv. Fax:* (home) (01728) 663339.

**CRANE, Nicholas Peter**; geographer, writer and broadcaster, since 1979; *b* 9 May 1954; *s* of Harold and Naomi Crane; *m* 1991, Annabel Huxley; one *s* two *d. Educ:* St Cedd's Primary Sch., Chelmsford; Ketteringham Hall Prep. Sch.; Town Close House Prep. Sch., Norwich; Wymondham Coll.; Cambridgeshire Coll. of Arts & Technol., Cambridge (BA Hons Geog., Univ. of London). Information Officer, Cyclists Touring Club, 1976–78. Presenter: documentaries, BBC Radio 4: Journey to the Centre of the Earth, 1987; Forbidden Journey, 1989; From Ancient Sparta to the Gates of Hell, 1990; BBC television: Blazing Pedals, 1990; The Pyrenees (for Wilderness Walks series), 1998; Map Man, Series 1, 2004, Series 2, 2005; Coast, Series 1 (BAFTA Award for Interactivity, 2005), Christmas Special, 2005, Series 2, 2006, Series 3, 2007, Series 4, 2009, Series 5, 2010, Series 6, 2011, Series 7, 2012, Series 8, 2013, Series 9, 2014, Series 10, 2015; Great British Journeys, 2007; Down the Line, 2008; Nicholas Crane's Britannia, 2009; In Search of England's Green and Pleasant Land, 2009; Munro: mountain man, 2009; Town with Nicholas Crane, 2011, 2013; producer, High Trails to Istanbul, 1995. Pres., Globetrotters Club, 1990–93; Mem. Mgt Cttee, Soc. of Authors, 2000–03; Mem. RSL 1998; Vice-Pres., CPRE, 2008–13. FRGS 1987 (Chm., Ind. Travellers' Seminar, 1989–90; Mem. Council, 2004–07; Pres., 2015–18). Editl Adv. Gp, Geographical magazine, 1999–. Come to Britain Trophy, BTA, 1977; Mungo Park Medal, RSGS, 1993; journalism award, British Guild of Travel Writers, 1996; Ness Award, RGS, 2014. *Publications:* (with Christa Gausden) The CTC Route Guide to Cycling in Britain & Ireland, 1980; Cycling in Europe, 1984; (with Richard Crane) Bicycles up Kilimanjaro, 1985; (with Richard Crane) Journey to the Centre of the Earth, 1987; The Great Bicycle Adventure, 1987; Nick Crane's Action Sports, 1989; Atlas Biker, 1990; Clear Waters Rising: a mountain walk across Europe, 1996 (Thomas Cook/Daily Telegraph Travel Book Award, 1997); Two Degrees West: a walk along England's Meridian, 1999; Mercator: the man who mapped the planet, 2002; Great British Journeys, 2007; Coast, 2010; World Atlas, 2011; The Making of the British Landscape: from the Ice Age to the present, 2016; You Are Here: a brief guide to the world, 2018. *Recreations:* walking, cycling, boating. *Address:* c/o United Agents, 12–26 Lexington Street, W1F 0LE.

**CRANE, Sir Peter (Robert)**, Kt 2004; PhD; FRS 1998; President, Oak Spring Garden Foundation, since 2016; *b* 18 July 1954; *s* of Walter Robert Crane and Dorothy Mary Crane; *m* 1986, Elinor Margaret Hamer; one *s* one *d. Educ:* Univ. of Reading (BSc 1975; PhD 1981). Lectr, Dept of Botany, Univ. of Reading, 1978–81; Post-doctoral Res. Schol., Indiana Univ., 1981–82; Field Museum, Chicago: Curator, Dept of Geology, 1982–92; Vice Pres., Acad. Affairs, 1992–99; Dir, 1995–99; Dir, Royal Botanic Gardens, Kew, 1999–2006; John and Marion Sullivan Prof., Dept of Geophys. Scis, Univ. of Chicago, 2006–09; Carl W. Knobloch Jr Dean, Sch. of Forestry and Envmtl Studies, Yale Univ., 2009–16. Visiting Professor: Univ. of Zürich, 1987; Univ. of Massachusetts, 1989; Univ. of Reading, 1999–2006; Royal Holloway, Univ. of London, 2000–06; ICSTM, 2003–06. President: Paleontol Soc., 1998–2000; Palaeontol Assoc., 2004–06. Foreign Associate, Nat. Acad. of Scis, USA, 2001; Foreign Member: Royal Swedish Acad. of Scis, 2002; Acad. Leopoldina, 2004; Royal Soc. of Arts and Sci., Göteborg, 2005; Amer. Acad. of Arts and Scis, 2008. Hon. DSc: Cambridge, 2009; Connecticut, 2011; Sewanee, 2017. Internat. Prize for Biology, Japan Soc. for Promotion of Sci., 2014. *Publications:* (ed jtly) The Origins of Angiosperms and their Biological Consequences, 1987; (ed jtly) The Evolution, Systematics and Fossil History of the Hamamelidae, vols 1 and 2, 1989; (jtly) The Origin and Diversification of Land Plants, 1997; (jtly) Early Flowers and Angiosperm Evolution, 2011; Ginkgo: the tree that time forgot, 2013. *Address:* Oak Spring Garden Foundation, 1776 Loughborough Lane, Upperville, VA 20184, USA.

**CRANE, Prof. Timothy Martin**, PhD; Professor of Philosophy, Central European University, since 2017; *b* Oxford, 17 Oct. 1962; *s* of Walter and Ann Crane; *m* 2000, Katalin Farkas. *Educ:* Durham Univ. (BA Hons Phil. 1984); York Univ. (MA Phil. 1985); Peterhouse, Cambridge (PhD 1989). University College London: Lectr in Philosophy, 1990–96; Reader, 1996–2002; Prof. of Philosophy, 2002–09; Dir, Inst. of Philosophy, Univ. of London, 2005–08; Knightbridge Prof. of Philosophy, Univ. of Cambridge, 2009–17; Fellow, Peterhouse, Cambridge, 2009–17. MAE 2008. *Publications:* The Contents of Experience, 1992; The Mechanical Mind, 1995, 2nd edn 2004; A Debate on Dispositions, 1996; History of the Mind-Body Problem, 2000; Elements of Mind, 2001; Metaphysics, 2004; Intentionalität als Merkmal des Geistigen, 2007; The Objects of Thought, 2013; Aspects of Psychologism, 2014; The Meaning of Belief, 2017. *Recreations:* music, wine. *Address:* Department of Philosophy, Central European University, Nádor u. 13, 1051 Budapest, Hungary. *W:* www.timcrane.com.

**CRANSTON, David Alan**, CBE 1993; Director General, National Association of Pension Funds, 2000–01; *b* 20 Oct. 1945; *s* of Stanley Cranston and Mary Cranston (*née* Fitzherbert); *m* 1968, Pippa Ann Reynolds; three *d. Educ:* Strathallan Sch., Perthshire; RMA, Sandhurst. Commnd RA, 1966; Army Staff Course, 1979–80; transf. to AAC, 1981; COS HQ, British Forces, Belize, 1983; DS, RMCS Shrivenham, 1984–86; Comd, 4th Regt, AAC, 1986–88; COS, 2nd Inf. Div., 1988–90; Higher Comd and Staff Course, 1990; Comd, British Army Aviation, Germany, 1990–92; Dep. Head of Mission, EC Monitor Mission to former Yugoslavia, 1992; rcds, 1993; Dep. Comdr, Multinational Airmobile Div., 1994–95. Head of Mem. Relns, PIA, 1995–97; Head of Gp Compliance, Royal Bank of Scotland, 1997–2000. Non-exec. Dir, National Olympic Cttee, 2001–10, Mem., Exec. Bd, 2007–10, British Olympic Assoc. Non-executive Director: Skandia UK, 2002–08 (Chm. Pension Trustee Bd, Skandia UK, then Old Mutual Wealth, 2002–16); Forces Pension Soc. Investment Co., 2002–13; Bankhall Investment Mgt, 2003–08; Voller Energy, 2005–09; Chairman, Pension Trustee Board: Austin Reed, 2002–16; Sibelco UK, 2007–17; MRC, 2010–16. Chm., British Biathlon Union, 1996–2011. *Recreations:* gardening, reading, tennis, ski-ing. *Club:* Army and Navy.

**CRANSTON, Sir Ross (Frederick)**, Kt 2007; FBA 2007; a Judge of the High Court of Justice, Queen's Bench Division, 2007–17; Judge in Charge of Administrative Court, 2016; Professor of Law, London School of Economics and Political Science, since 2017; *b* 23 July 1948; *s* of late Frederick Hugh Cranston and Edna Elizabeth Cranston (*née* Davies); *m* 1st, 1976, Prof. (Barbara) Jane Stapleton, *qv* (marr. diss. 1985); 2nd, 1988, Anna Whyatt (marr. diss. 1998); one *d*; 3rd, 2007, Hazel Phillips. *Educ:* Univ. of Queensland (BA 1970; LLB 1971); Harvard Law Sch. (LLM 1973); Oxford (DPhil 1976; DCL 1998). Called to the Bar, Gray's Inn, 1976, Bencher, 1998; Asst Recorder, 1991–97; Recorder, 1997–2007; QC 1998. Lectr, Univ. of Warwick, 1975–77; Res. Fellow, 1978–81, Sen. Lectr, then Reader, 1981–86, Assoc. Dean, 1984–86, Faculty of Law, ANU Canberra; W. G. Hart Sen. Fellow, QMC, 1983–84; Queen Mary and Westfield College, London University: Sir John Lubbock Prof. of Banking Law, 1986–92; Dean, Faculty of Laws, 1988–91; Dir, Centre for Commercial Law Studies, 1989–92; London School of Economics and Political Science: Cassel Prof. of Commercial Law, 1993–97; Vis. Prof., 1997–2005, 2007–17; Centennial Prof. of Law, 2005–07. Acad. Consultant, Woolf Inquiry into Access to Justice, 1994–96; Assessor, Jackson Rev. of Civil Litigation Costs, 2009; Consultant to various international bodies including World Bank, IMF, UN Conf. on Trade and Develt, Commonwealth Secretariat, 1988–96. Contested (Lab) Richmond, Yorks, 1992. MP (Lab) Dudley North, 1997–2005. Solicitor-Gen., 1998–2001. Chairman: All-Party Parly Gp on Alcohol Misuse, 2002–05; All-Party Parly Gp for the Bar, 2002–05. Judiciary Assessment Mission, Turkey, 2005, Justice and Home Affairs Peer Rev. Mission, Bulgaria, 2006, Croatia, 2007, Romania, 2012, 2013, 2014, 2016, Eur. Commn. Vice Pres., 1991–92, Pres., 1992–93, SPTL. Dep. Chm., 1993–96, Chm., 1996–97, Bd of Trustees, Public Concern at Work. Trustee: Build IT Internat., 2006–13; NOFAS-UK, 2006–12. Chair: Soc. of Labour Lawyers, 2003–06; Bd of Trustees, British and Irish Legal Info Inst., 2017–; Wkg Pty, Immigration and Asylum (Determination Reform), JUSTICE, 2017–18; Pres., Internat. Acad. of Commercial and Consumer Law, 2004–06. Mem., American Law Inst., 1999. Fellow, Australian Acad. of Law, 2015. FCIArb 2006. Hon. LLD: Queensland, 2015; Greenwich, 2016; ANU, 2018. *Publications:* Consumers and the Law, 1978, 3rd edn, as Cranston's Consumers and the Law, 2000; Regulating Business, 1979; Legal Foundations of the Welfare State, 1985; Law, Government and Public Policy, 1987; (ed) Banks, Liability and Risk, 1990, 2nd edn 1995; (ed) The Single Market and the Law of Banking, 1991, 2nd edn 1995; (ed with R. M. Goode) Contemporary Issues in International Commercial Law, 1993; (ed) European Banking Law, 1993, 2nd edn 1999; (ed) Legal Ethics and Professional Responsibility, 1995; (ed with A. Zuckerman) Reform of the Administration of Civil Justice, 1995; (ed) Making Commercial Law, 1997; Principles of Banking Law, 1997, 3rd edn 2017; How Law Works, 2006. *Address:* Law Department, London School of Economics and Political Science, Houghton Street, WC2A 2AE.

**CRANWORTH, 3rd Baron** *cr* 1899; **Philip Bertram Gurdon**; Lieutenant, Royal Wiltshire Yeomanry; *b* 24 May 1940; *s* of Hon. Robin Gurdon (killed in action, 1942) and Hon. Yoskyl Pearson (she *m* 2nd, 1944, as his 2nd wife, Lieut-Col Alistair Gibb, and 3rd, 1962, as his 2nd wife, 1st Baron McCorquodale of Newton, PC, KCVO; she *d* 1979), *d* of 2nd Viscount Cowdray; *S* grandfather, 1964; *m* 1st, 1968, Frances Henrietta Montagu Douglas Scott (*d* 2000), *d* of late Lord William Scott and Lady William Scott; two *s* one *d*; 2nd, 2006, Cameron Vail Noble. *Educ:* Eton; Magdalene Coll., Cambridge. *Heir:* s Hon. Sacha William Robin Gurdon, [*b* 12 Aug. 1970; *m* 2001, Susannah, *d* of Martin Bates; one *s*]. *Address:* Boulge House, Woodbridge IP13 6BW.
*See also Marquess of Huntly.*

**CRASNOW, Rachel**; QC 2015; a Recorder, since 2019; *b* Cambridge, 24 May 1970; *d* of E. and J. A. Crasnow; partner, Matthew Dodd; one *s* two *d. Educ:* Pembroke Coll., Oxford (BA Hons); City Univ., London (DipLaw 1993). Called to the Bar, Middle Temple, 1994, Bencher, 2019. Part-time Judge, Police Appeals Tribunal, 2015–. Legal Advr to UK Bd for Health Care Chaplaincy, 2015–. Mem., Equality and Diversity Cttee, 2010–, Chm., Legislation and Guidance Cttee, 2013–, Bar Council. Mem. Cttee, Employment Law Bar Assoc., 2013–. Co-ordinator, Employment Lawyers Appeals Advice Scheme; Member: Employment Lawyers Assoc.; Discrimination Law Assoc.; Industrial Law Soc.; Human Rights Lawyers' Assoc. Editor, Case Commentaries, Educnl Law Jl, 2002–05. Qualified Mediator. *Publications:* (jtly) Employment Law and Human Rights, 2005, 3rd edn 2018; (contrib. and ed) Human Rights and ECJ sections in Bullen and Leake and Jacob's Precedents of Pleadings, 2006; (jtly) Blackstone's Guide to the Equality Act, 2010; (jtly and ed) Family Rights in Employment Law, 2012. *Recreations:* travel, walking, cooking, reading. *Address:* Cloisters Chambers, 1 Pump Court, Temple, EC4Y 7AA. *T:* (020) 7827 4000.

**CRATHORNE, 2nd Baron** *cr* 1959; **(Charles) James Dugdale**; KCVO 2013; FSA; Bt 1945; Lord-Lieutenant of North Yorkshire, 1999–2014; *b* 12 Sept. 1939; *s* of 1st Baron Crathorne, PC, TD, and Nancy, OBE (*d* 1969), *d* of Sir Charles Tennant, 1st Bt; *S* father, 1977; *m* 1970, Sylvia Mary (*d* 2009), *yr d* of Brig. Arthur Herbert Montgomery, OBE, TD; one *s* two *d. Educ:* Eton College; Trinity Coll., Cambridge. MA Cantab (Fine Arts). FSA 2009. Impressionist and Modern Painting Dept, Sotheby & Co., 1963–66; Assistant to the President, Parke-Bernet, New York, 1966–69; James Dugdale & Associates, London, Independent Fine Art Consultancy Service, 1969–77; James Crathorne & Associates, 1977–; Director: Woodhouse Securities, 1989–99; Cliveden Ltd, 1999–2002; Hand Picked Hotels Ltd, 2001–02. Member: Yorks Regl Cttee, NT, 1978–84 and 1988–94; Council, RSA, 1982–88; Exec. Cttee, Georgian Gp, 1985–99 (Chm., 1990–99; Pres., 1999–2015); Cons. Adv. Gp on Arts and Heritage, 1988–98; Chm., Jt Cttee, Nat. Amenity Socs, 1996–99 (Dep. Chm., 1993–96); President: Cleveland Assoc., NT, 1982–96; Hambledon Dist, CPRE, 1988–; Cleveland Family History Soc., 1988–; Middlesbrough Sea Cadets, 1988–2014; Cleveland and N Yorks Br., 1997–2003, Cleveland and S Durham Br., 2003–14, Magistrates' Assoc.; Cleveland Search and Rescue Team, 1998–2015; Yorks and Humberside RFCA, 2005–08 (Vice Pres., 1999–2005); Yorks Agricultural Soc., 2014–15; Vice President: Cleveland Wildlife Trust, 1990–; Public Monuments and Sculpture Assoc., 1997–; N Yorks County Scouts, 1998–2014; N of England RFCA, 2001–14; Patron, Cleveland Community Foundn, 1990–. Member: Works of Art Sub-Cttee, H of L, 1983–2001 (Chm., 2004–07); Editorial Bd, House Magazine, 1983–; Lord Speaker's Adv. Cttee on Works of Art, 2017–; Hon. Secretary: All-Party Parly Arts and Heritage Gp, 1981– (Co-Chm., 2010–); All-Party Photography Gp, 1997–; elected Mem., H of L, 1999. Trustee: Captain Cook Trust, 1978– (Chm., 1993–2015); Georgian Theatre Royal, Richmond, Yorks, 1970–; Nat. Heritage Meml Fund, 1992–95; Patron: Attingham Trust for Study of the British Country House, 1991–; Middlesbrough Inst. of Modern Art, 2012–; Stokesley Agricl Soc., 2017–; Hon. Patron, Friends of Yorks Sculpture Park, 1992–2009. Church Warden, All Saints, Crathorne, 1977–. Annual lecture tours to America, 1970–90; lecture series, Metropolitan Mus., NY, 1981; Australian Bicentennial Lecture Tour, 1988. Member Court: Univ. of Leeds, 1985–97; Univ. of York, 1999–; Univ. of Hull, 1999–2014; Governor: Queen Margaret's Sch. York Ltd, 1986–99; Royal Humane Soc., 2008–. FRSA 1972. DL Cleveland, 1983, N Yorks, 1996; JP N Yorks, 1999. Freeman, Town of Richmond, N Yorks, 2014; Freedom: City of York, 2015; City of London, 2017. Mayor, Co. of Merchants of the Staple of England, 2017–18. Hon. LLD Teesside, 2013; DUniv York, 2015. KStJ 1999. Golden Jubilee Medal, 2002; Diamond Jubilee Medal, 2012. *Exhibitions:* Photographs: Middlesbrough Art Gall., 1980; Georgian Th. Royal, Richmond, N Yorks, 2005; All Party Photography Gp annual exhibn, Westminster and touring, 1992–. *Publications:* Edouard Vuillard, 1967; (co-author) Tennant's Stalk, 1973; (co-author) A Present from Crathorne, 1989; Cliveden: the place and the people, 1995; The Royal Crescent Book of Bath, 1998; (co-photographer) Parliament in Pictures, 1999; contribs to Apollo and The Connoisseur. *Recreations:* photography, travel, collecting, country pursuits, jazz. *Heir:* s Hon. Thomas Arthur John

Dugdale, b 30 Sept. 1977. *Address*: Crathorne House, Yarm, N Yorks TS15 0AT. *T*: (01642) 700431; House of Lords, SW1A 0PW. *T*: (020) 7219 5224. *E*: crathornej@parliament.uk, james.crathorne@btconnect.com. *Clubs*: Garrick, Pratt's.

**CRAUFURD, Sir Robert (James)**, 9th Bt *cr* 1781; *b* 18 March 1937; *s* of Sir James Gregan Craufurd, 8th Bt and Ruth Marjorie (*d* 1998), *d* of Frederic Corder; *S* father, 1970; *m* 1st, 1964, Catherine Penelope (marr. diss. 1987; she *d* 2017), *yr d* of late Captain Horatio Westmacott, Torquay; three *d*; 2nd, 1987, Georgina Anne, *d* of late John D. Russell, Lymington. *Educ*: Harrow; University College, Oxford. Elected Member of the London Stock Exchange, 1969. *Address*: East Grove, Grove Road, Lymington, Hants SO41 3RF.

**CRAUSBY, Sir David (Anthony)**, Kt 2017; MP (Lab) Bolton North East, since 1997; *b* 17 June 1946; *s* of Thomas Crausby and Kathleen Lavin; *m* 1965, Enid Anne Noon; two *s*. *Educ*: Derby Grammar Sch., Bury. Apprentice centre lathe turner, 1962, skilled turner, 1967; Works Convenor, AEEU (formerly AEU), 1978–97. Mem (Lab) Bury MDC, 1979–92. Contested (Lab): Bury N, 1987; Bolton NE, 1992. *Recreations*: football, walking, cinema. *Address*: (office) 140 Chorley Old Road, Bolton BL1 3AT. *T*: (01204) 391909.

**CRAVEN**, family name of **Earl of Craven**.

**CRAVEN**, 9th Earl of, *cr* 1801; **Benjamin Robert Joseph Craven**; Baron Craven, 1665; Viscount Uffington, 1801; *b* 13 June 1989; *s* of 8th Earl and of Teresa Maria Bernadette Craven; *S* father, 1990. *Heir: cousin* Rupert José Evelyn Craven, Lt-Comdr RN [*b* 22 March 1926; *m* 1st, 1985, Margaret Campbell (*d* 1985), *d* of Alexander Smith, MBE; 2nd, 2000, Susan Lilian Margaret Eaton].

**CRAVEN, Janet**; *see* Morrison, J. R.

**CRAVEN, Sir John (Anthony)**, Kt 1996; Member, Board of Managing Directors, Deutsche Bank AG, Frankfurt, 1990–96; Chairman, Morgan Grenfell, later Deutsche Morgan Grenfell, Group PLC, 1989–97 (Chief Executive, 1987–89); *b* 23 Oct. 1940; *s* of William Herbert Craven and Hilda Lucy Craven; *m* 1st, 1961, Gillian Margaret (*née* Murray); one *s* one *d*; 2nd, 1970, Jane Frances (*née* Stiles-Allen); three *s*; 3rd, 2005, Ning Chang (*d* 2009). *Educ*: Michaelhouse, S Africa; Jesus Coll., Cambridge (BA Hons Law); Queen's Univ., Kingston, Ont. Clarkson Gordon & Co., Toronto, Chartered Accountants, 1961–64; Wood Gundy, Investment Bankers, 1964–67; S. G. Warburg & Co., 1967–73, Dir 1969–73; Gp Chief Exec., White Weld & Co. Ltd, 1973–78; Vice Chm., S. G. Warburg & Co., 1979; Founder and Chm., Phoenix Securities Ltd, 1981–89; Dir, Mercury Securities Ltd, 1979. Non-executive Chairman: Tootal Group PLC, 1985–91; Lonmin plc (formerly Lonrho), 1997–2009; GEMS Funds, HK, 1998–; Fleming Family & Partners, 2003–07 (non-exec. Dir, 2000); Patagonia Gold plc, 2004–13; Director: Rothmans Internat. NV, 1993–95; Rothmans Internat. BV, 1995–99; non-executive Director: Reuters plc, 1997–2004; Robert Fleming Hldgs Ltd, 1999–2000; Ducati Motor Hldgs SpA, 1999–2000. Mem., Conseil d'Administration, Société Générale de Surveillance, Switzerland, 1989–98; Dir, SIB, 1990–93. Mem. Bd, Royal Marsden NHS Trust, 2008–15. Former Member: Ontario Inst. of Chartered Accts; Canadian Inst. of Chartered Accountants. *Recreation*: ski-ing. *Club*: White's.

**CRAVEN, Prof. John Anthony George**, CBE 2013; Vice-Chancellor, University of Portsmouth, 1997–2013; *b* 17 June 1949; *s* of late George Marriott Craven and Dorothy Maude Craven (*née* Walford); *m* 1974, Laura Elizabeth Loftis; one *s* one *d*. *Educ*: Pinner GS; King's Coll., Cambridge (BA 1970; MA 1974); King's Coll. London (MA 2015). Kennedy Meml Schol., MIT, 1970–71; University of Kent at Canterbury: Lectr in Econs, 1971–76; Sen. Lectr, 1976–80; Reader, 1980–86; Prof., 1986–96; Dean of Faculty, Social Scis, 1987–91; Pro Vice-Chancellor, 1991–93; Dep. Vice-Chancellor, 1993–96. Vis. Associate Prof., Univ. of Guelph, 1982–83. Chm., University Alliance, 2006–09; Mem. Bd, UUK, 2006–12. Mem., Archbishops' Council, 2006–13. Chair, St Martin's Trust for the Homeless, 1987–96. Governor: South Kent Coll., 1991–96; Highbury Coll., 1997–2003; St Luke's Sch., Portsmouth, 2002–09; Mem. Bd, UWE, 2014–. Dir, New Th. Royal, Portsmouth, 1999–2010; Member, Board: Nat. Mus. of the Royal Navy, 2008–18; E. C. Roberts Centre, Portsmouth, 2013–. FRSA. Hon. DSc: Univ. Teknologi, Malaysia; Southampton, 2013; Hon. DLaws Portsmouth, 2013. *Publications*: The Distribution of the Product, 1979; Introduction to Economics, 1984, 2nd edn 1990; Social Choice, 1992; articles in learned jls. *Recreations*: gardening, choral singing, house restoration. *Address*: Fyning Cross, Rogate, Petersfield GU31 5EF. *T*: (01730) 821392. *E*: jagcraven@yahoo.com.

**CRAVEN, Sir Philip (Lee)**, Kt 2005; MBE 1991; President, International Paralympic Committee, 2001–17; *b* 4 July 1950; *s* of Herbert and Hilda Craven; *m* 1974, Jocelyne Halgand; one *s* one *d*. *Educ*: Manchester Univ. (BA Hons (Geog.) 1972). Hd of Secretariat, British Coal Corp., 1986–91; Pres., 1989–2002, CEO, 1994–98, Internat. Wheelchair Basketball Fedn; Performance Dir, GB Men's Wheelchair Basketball Team, 1998–2001. Played wheelchair basketball for GB, 1969–93: Team Captain, 1982–88; Gold Medal, Commonwealth Games, 1970; European Championships: Bronze Medal, 1970; Gold Medal, 1971, 1973, 1974; Silver Medal, 1993; 4th Place, Paralympic Games, 1974; Bronze Medal, World Championship, 1975; Silver Medal, Internat. Stoke Mandeville Games, 1986; Gold Medal, European Champions Cup, 1994; Nat. Table Tennis Champion, 1977. Chm., GB Wheelchair Basketball Assoc., 1977–80, 1984–87 and 1989–94. International Olympic Committee: Mem., 2003–17; Chm., Olympic Educn Commn, 2015–17; Member: Sport and Envmt Commn, 2002–05; 2008 Beijing Co-ordination Commn, 2002–08; Culture and Olympic Educn Commn, 2005–15; Olympic Channel Commn, 2015–17; Bd, LOCOG, 2005–13. Foundn Bd Mem., World Anti-Doping Agency, 2002–12. Non-exec. Dir, Toyota Motor Corp., 2018–. Hon. Fellow, Liverpool John Moores Univ., 2009. Hon. DSc: Manchester Metropolitan, 2006; Stirling, 2010; Hon. LLD: Nottingham, 2007; York St John, 2013; DUniv: Staffordshire, 2008; Manchester, 2012; Bolton, 2013; Chester, 2015; Hon. Dr: Worcester, 2012; Azerbaijan State Acad. of Physical Trng and Sport, 2016. Sports Industry Awards—Lifetime Achievement, 2012. Medaille d'argent de la Jeunesse et des Sports (France), 1973; Gold Medal: City of Athens, 2004; City of Turin, 2006; Key to City of Beijing, 2008. Grande Ufficiale, Order of Merit (Italy), 2006; Chevalier, Ordre Ducal de la Croix de Bourgogne (France), 2007; Order of Friendship (Russia), 2012; Order of Honour (Russia), 2014; Officier de la Légion d'Honneur (France), 2014; Order of Friendship (Azerbaijan), 2016; Cross of Merit 1st cl. (Germany), 2016. *Recreations*: cricket, wheelchair basketball, gardening, the culture of wine.

**CRAWFORD**, 29th Earl of, *cr* 1398, **AND BALCARRES**, 12th Earl of, *cr* 1651; **Robert Alexander Lindsay**, KT 1996; GCVO 2002; PC 1972; Lord Lindsay of Crawford, before 1143; Lord Lindsay of Balcarres, 1633; Lord Balniel, 1651; Baron Wigan (UK), 1826; Baron Balniel (Life Peer), 1974; Premier Earl of Scotland; Head of House of Lindsay; Lord Chamberlain to the Queen Mother, 1992–2002; *b* 5 March 1927; *er s* of 28th Earl of Crawford and 11th of Balcarres, KT, GBE, and Mary (*d* 1994), 3rd *d* of late Lord Richard Cavendish, PC, CB, CMG; *S* father, 1975; *m* 1949, Ruth Beatrice, *d* of Leo Meyer-Bechtler, Zürich; two *s* two *d*. *Educ*: Eton; Trinity College, Cambridge. Served with Grenadier Guards, 1945–49. MP (C) Hertford, 1955–74, Welwyn and Hatfield, Feb.–Sept. 1974; Parliamentary Private Secretary: to Financial Secretary of Treasury, 1955–57; to Minister of Housing and Local Government, 1957–60; Opposition front-bench spokesman on health and social security, 1967–70; Minister of State for Defence, 1970–72; Minister of State for Foreign and Commonwealth Affairs, 1972–74. First Crown Estate Comr, 1980–85. Chairman: Lombard North Central Bank, 1976–80; Abela Hldgs (UK), 1983–95; Director: Nat. Westminster Bank, 1975–88; Scottish American Investment Co., 1978–88; a Vice-Chm., Sun Alliance & London Insurance Gp, 1975–91. President, Rural District Councils Assoc., 1959–65; Chairman: National Association for Mental Health, 1963–70; Historic Buildings Council for Scotland, 1976–83; Royal Commn on Ancient and Historical Monuments of Scotland, 1985–95; Bd of Trustees, Nat. Library of Scotland, 1990–2000. Hon. FRIAS; Hon. Fellow, Nat. Library of Scotland, 2012. DL Fife, 1976–2003. *Heir: s* Lord Balniel, *qv*. *Address*: House of Lords, SW1A 0PW.
*See also* C. G. Mackworth-Young.

**CRAWFORD, Alex Christine**, OBE 2012; Special Correspondent, based in Africa, Sky TV News, since 2011; *b* UK, 15 April 1962; *d* of Max Crawford and Emma Crawford (*née* Hale); *m* 1988, Richard Edmondson; one *s* three *d*. *Educ*: St John's Convent, Kitwe, Zambia; Chisipite Sch., Harare, Zimbabwe; Cobham Hall Sch., Kent; Open Univ.; Thomson Regl Newspapers Trng, Newcastle; Nat. Council for Trng of Journalists; BBC TV and Radio Trng, London. Reporter: Wokingham Times, 1981–83; BBC Radio Nottingham, 1983–85; BBC Radio News, London, 1985–86; sub-editor, BBC TV, London, 1986–88; producer, TV-am, 1988–89; Sky News: news producer, 1989–91; news corresp., 1991–2004; news corresp., Channel 5, 2004–05; Asia corresp., based in India, Sky News, 2005–10; Special corresp., based in UAE, Sky TV News, 2010–11. Hon. Dr Univ. of Arts London, 2012. Journalist of Year, RTS, 2007, 2009, 2010, 2011; Golden Nymph Award, Monte Carlo, 2010, 2011, 2012; News and Factual Award, 2010, Achievement of the Year, 2011, Women in Film and TV; Internat. Emmy Award for News Coverage, 2010; Story of the Year, For. Press Assoc., 2011; James Cameron Award, 2011; Broadcasting Journalist of Year, London Press Club, 2011; Bayeux War Corresp. Winner, 2011; Red's Hot Women Award, Red Mag., 2011. *Publications*: Colonel Gaddafi's Hat, 2012. *Recreations*: scuba diving, swimming, tennis, horse riding, running, parachuting, ski-ing, trekking, cycling, exploring, painting, writing, obsessively checking Blackberry. *Address*: c/o Sky TV News, 6 Centaurs Business Park, Grant Way, Osterley, Isleworth, Middx TW7 5QD. *T*: (020) 7705 3000. *E*: alex.crawford@sky.uk.

**CRAWFORD, Alistair Stephen**; Chairman, Access IS, since 2013; *b* 4 Jan. 1953; *s* of late Daniel Clark Crawford and Joan Crawford; *m* 1981, Susan Potter; two *d*. *Educ*: Oriel Coll., Oxford (MA Jurisprudence). Pres. and CEO, Computer Sciences Corp. (UK), 1989–94; Sen. Vice Pres., Oracle Corp., 1995–2000; Chief Operating Officer, CMG plc, 2001; CEO, Logica CMG plc, 2002–03; Chief Exec., Psion, 2003–06; Chairman: Lysanda Ltd, 2008–11; FutureGov Ltd, 2014–15. *Club*: Reform.

**CRAWFORD, Prof. Andrew Charles**, FRS 1990; Professor of Neurophysiology, Cambridge University, 1992–2016, now Emeritus; Fellow of Trinity College, Cambridge, since 1974; *b* 12 Jan. 1949; *s* of Charles and Vera Crawford; *m* 1974, Catherine Jones (*d* 2015); one *s* one *d*. *Educ*: King Edward VI Camp Hill Sch., Birmingham; Downing Coll., Cambridge (BA 1970); Emmanuel Coll., Cambridge (MA, PhD 1974). Cambridge University: Research Fellow, Emmanuel Coll., 1972; Univ. Demonstrator, 1974; Lectr, 1977; Reader in Sensory Physiology, 1987. *Publications*: contribs on physiology of hearing, in learned jls. *Address*: Department of Physiology, Development and Neuroscience, Physiological Laboratory, Downing Street, Cambridge CB2 3EG. *T*: (01223) 333879.

**CRAWFORD, Bruce**; *see* Crawford, R. H. B.

**CRAWFORD, Prof. Carolin Susan**, PhD; Public Astronomer (formerly Outreach Officer), Institute of Astronomy, University of Cambridge, since 2005; Fellow and College Lecturer, Emmanuel College, Cambridge, since 2004; Gresham Professor of Astronomy, since 2011; *b* Guildford, 10 Dec. 1963; *d* of Laurence and Elsie Crawford; *m* 1991, Prof. Andrew Christopher Fabian, *qv*; two *s*. *Educ*: Newnham Coll., Cambridge (BA Hons 1985; PhD 1988). Skynner-Radcliffe Res. Fellow, Balliol Coll., Oxford, 1988–91; Res. Fellow, Trinity Hall, Cambridge, 1991–94; University of Cambridge: SERC Postdoctoral Fellow, 1991–93, PPARC Advanced Fellow, 1994–96, Inst. of Astronomy; Royal Soc. Res. Fellow, 1996–2007; Associate Lectr in Astronomy, Newnham Coll., Cambridge, 2002–04. *Recreations*: weaving, reading, gardening. *Address*: Emmanuel College, St Andrews Street, Cambridge CB2 3AP; Institute of Astronomy, Madingley Road, Cambridge CB3 0HA. *T*: (01223) 337510. *E*: csc@ast.cam.ac.uk.

**CRAWFORD, Charles Graham**, CMG 1998; HM Diplomatic Service, retired; professional mediator, since 2008; speechwriter, negotiations expert and communication skills consultant, since 2008; *b* 22 May 1954; *s* of Graham Wellington James Crawford and Edith Ellen Crawford; *m* 1990, Helen Margaret Walsh; two *s* one *d*. *Educ*: St John's Coll., Oxford (BA Hons Jurisprudence 1976); Lincoln's Inn (part II Bar exams 1977); Fletcher Sch. of Law and Diplomacy, Boston, USA (MA 1979). Entered FCO, 1979; Second, later First Sec., Belgrade, 1981–84; FCO (air services then speechwriter), 1984–87; First Sec., Pretoria/Cape Town, 1987–91; FCO, 1991–93; Political Counsellor, Moscow, 1993–96; Ambassador to Bosnia and Herzegovina, 1996–98; Weatherhead Center for Internat. Affairs, Harvard Univ., 1998–99; Dep. Political Dir, FCO, 1999–2000; Dir, SE Europe, FCO, 2000; Ambassador to Federal Republic of Yugoslavia, subseq. Serbia and Montenegro, 2001–03; Ambassador to Poland, 2003–07. Qualified Mediator, 2007. Founder Partner, Ambassador Partnership (formerly ADRg Ambassadors), 2010–. Cicero Speechwriting Award, 2016, 2017. *Publications*: Speeches for Leaders, 2016. *Recreations*: chess, music, writing/website. *E*: charlescrawf@gmail.com. *W*: www.charlescrawford.biz.

**CRAWFORD, Sir Frederick (William)**, Kt 1986; DL; FREng; Chairman, Criminal Cases Review Commission, 1996–2003; Vice-Chancellor, Aston University, 1980–96; *b* 28 July 1931; *s* of William and Victoria Maud Crawford; *m* 1963, Béatrice M. J. Hutter, LèsL, MA, PhD; one *d* (one *s* decd). *Educ*: George Dixon Grammar Sch., Birmingham; Univ. of London (BSc Eng (1st cl. hons) 1952; MSc 1958; DSc 1975); Univ. of Liverpool (DipEd 1956; PhD 1955; DEng 1965); Open Univ. (DipStat 2006); BA Maths (1st cl. hons) 2007; MSc Maths 2015). Pres., Guild of Undergraduates, 1955–56, Mem. Court, 1955–62 and 1981–2013, Univ. of Liverpool; Treas., NUS, 1957–59; Winner, NUS-Observer Fifth Nat. Student Debating Tourn., 1958, followed by ESU debating tour of USA. FInstP 1964; FAPS 1965; FIET (FIEE 1965); FIEEE 1972; FIMA 1978; FREng (FEng 1985). Research Trainee, J. Lucas Ltd, 1948–52; Scientist, NCB Mining Res. Estabt, 1956–57; Sen. Lectr in Elec. Engrg, CAT Birmingham, 1958–59; Stanford University, California, 1959–82: Res. Associate, W. W. Hansen Labs of Physics, 1959–64; Institute for Plasma Research: Prof. (Research), 1964–67; Associate Prof., 1967–69; Prof., 1969–82; Consulting Prof., 1983–84; Chm., 1974–80; Dir, Centre for Interdisciplinary Res., 1973–77. Vis. Scientist, French Atomic Energy Commn, and Cons. to Comp. Française Thomson-Houston, 1961–62; Visiting Professor: Japan, 1969; Univ. of Paris, 1971; Australia, 1972; Mathematical Inst., Oxford Univ., 1977–78; Vis. Fellow, St Catherine's Coll., Oxford, 1977–78, 1996–97. Union Radio-Scientifique Internationale: Mem., US Nat. Cttee, 1975–81, UK Nat. Cttee, 1980–84; Commn H (Waves in Plasmas): US Chm., 1975–78; Internat. Chm., 1978–81; UK Rep., 1982–84; Chm. Internat. Sci. Cttee, Internat. Conf. on Phenomena in Ionised Gases, 1979–81; Universities Space Research Association: Member: Council, 1973–81

(Chm. 1977–78); Bd of Trustees, 1975–81 (Chm. 1976–77). Dir, Sigma Xi, 1976–78; Mem. Council, Amer. Assoc. of Univ. Profs, 1980–82; Vice-Chm., CVCP, 1993–95; Dir, HEQC, 1994–96; Vice-Pres., Parly and Scientific Cttee, 1992–95 (Vice-Chm., 1989–92). Member: Council, IEE, 1985–88, 1989–92 and 1993–96; Smeatonian Soc. of Civil Engrs, 1995– (Pres., 2017). Director: Birmingham Technology Ltd, 1982–96; West Midlands Technology Transfer Centre, 1985–93; Legal & General Gp plc, 1988–97; Rexam (formerly Bowater) plc, 1989–97; PowerGen plc, 1990–2002. Member: US-UK Educnl (Fulbright) Commn, 1981–84; British-North American Cttee, 1987–2013; Franco-British Council, 1987–98; Pilgrims, 2007–; Vice-President: Birmingham Civic Soc., 1990– (Chm., 1983–88). Founder Mem., Lunar Soc., Birmingham, 1991–. Freeman, City of London, 1986; Master: Co. of Engineers, 1996; Co. of Information Technologists, 2000. High Sheriff, W Midlands, 1995, DL W Midlands, 1995. Hon. Bencher, Inner Temple, 1996. CCMI (CBIM 1986; Special Award for Univ. Mgt, 1992). FAAAS 1971. Hon. FCIL (Hon. FIL 1987). Hon. DSc Buckingham, 1996. *Publications:* numerous papers on plasma physics and higher educn. *Address:* 47 Charlbury Road, Oxford OX2 6UX. *T:* (01865) 554 707. *Club:* Athenæum.

**CRAWFORD, Iain;** Director, Veterinary Field Service, Ministry of Agriculture, Fisheries and Food, 1988–98; *b* 8 April 1938; *s* of James and Agnes Crawford, Baillieston, Glasgow; *m* 1962, Janette Mary Allan; two *s* one *d*. *Educ:* Coatbridge High Sch., Lanarks; Glasgow Univ. (BVMS). MRCVS 1961. Entered private vet. practice, 1961; joined MAFF as a Vet. Officer, 1968; Dep. Regl Vet. Officer, Bristol, 1981; Vet. Head of Sect. (Regl Vet. Officer), 1983; Asst Chief Vet. Officer, 1986. *Recreations:* sailing, walking.

**CRAWFORD, Prof. Ian Andrew,** PhD; FRAS; Professor of Planetary Science and Astrobiology, Birkbeck, University of London, since 2012; *b* Warrington, Cheshire, 13 Aug. 1961; *s* of Anthony Crawford and Joan Crawford (*née* Heighway); *m* 1988, Naoko Yamagata; one *s*. *Educ:* North Cestrian Grammar Sch., Altrincham; University Coll. London (BSc 1982; PhD 1988); Univ. of Newcastle upon Tyne (MSc 1983). FRAS 1984. Royal Soc. Overseas Res. Fellow, Mt Stromlo Observatory, Canberra, 1989; Res. Fellow, UCL, 1990–92; Royal Soc. Overseas Fellow, Anglo-Australian Observatory, Sydney, 1993; Sen. Res. Fellow, UCL, 1994–2002; Lectr, 2003–07, Sen. Lectr, 2007–09, Reader, 2009–12, Birkbeck, Univ. of London. Pres., Soc. for Popular Astronomy, 2006–08; Geophysical Sec., 2007–11, Sen. Sec., 2011–17, Vice-Pres., 2017–19, RAS. Member: Eur. Space Scis Cttee, 2008–14; Human Spaceflight and Exploration Sci. Adv. Cttee, ESA, 2014–17. *Publications:* contrib. approx. 200 papers to scientific and professional jls on astronomy, planetary sci., astrobiol. and space exploration. *Recreations:* reading, classical music. *Address:* Department of Earth and Planetary Sciences, Birkbeck, University of London, Malet Street, WC1E 7HX. *T:* (020) 3073 8026. *E:* i.crawford@bbk.ac.uk.

**CRAWFORD, Ian James;** Director, Scottish Enterprise, 2008–12; *b* Peterborough, 27 July 1954; *s* of Henderson Crawford and Jane Crawford; *m* 1977, Sheila McNicol. *Educ:* John Neilson High Sch., Paisley; Glasgow Univ. (BAcc 1975). Joined IBM UK Ltd, 1972; Site Dir, IBM Greenock, 1994–98; Vice Pres. Procurement, IBM Corp., 1998–2007. Mem., Mgt Cttee, Kilmarnock FC, 2009–13; Dir, Riverside Inverclyde, 2009–13. *Publications:* Clyde Shipwrecks, 1988, 3rd edn 2004; Argyll Shipwrecks, 1994, 2nd edn 2003. *Recreations:* golf, music, shipwreck research. *E:* ianjcrawfordvp@btinternet.com. *Clubs:* Loch Lomond Golf, Kilmacolm Golf; Los Flamingos Golf (Spain).

**CRAWFORD, Prof. James Richard,** AC 2013; DPhil, LLD; FBA 2000; a Judge, International Court of Justice, since 2015; Whewell Professor of International Law, University of Cambridge, 1992–2015; Fellow of Jesus College, Cambridge, 1992–2015, now Emeritus; *b* 14 Nov. 1948; *s* of James Allens and Josephine Margaret Crawford; *m* 1st, 1971, Marisa Luigina (marr. diss. 1991); two *d*; 2nd, 1992, Patricia Hyndman (marr. diss. 1998); two *d*; 3rd, 1998, Joanna Gomula (marr. diss. 2014); one *s*; 4th, 2014, Freya Baetens; one *s* one *d*. *Educ:* Adelaide Univ. (LLB Hons; BA 1971); Oxford Univ. (DPhil 1977); LLD Cantab 2004. Called to the Bar, High Court of Australia, 1979; SC, NSW, 1997. University of Adelaide: Lectr, 1974; Sen. Lectr, 1977; Reader, 1982; Prof. of Law, 1983; Challis Prof. of Internat. Law, 1986–92, Dean, Faculty of Law, 1990–92, Univ. of Sydney. Chm., Faculty Bd of Law, Univ. of Cambridge, 2003–06. Res. Prof. (pt-time), La Trobe Univ., 2011–14. Comr, Australian Law Reform Commn, 1982–90; Mem., UN Internat. Law Commn, 1992–2001. *Publications:* The Creation of States in International Law, 1979, 2nd edn 2006; Australian Courts of Law, 1982, 4th edn 2003; (ed) The Rights of Peoples, 1988; The International Law Commission's Articles on State Responsibility, 2002; International Law as an Open System, 2002; (ed) The Law of International Responsibility, 2010; (ed jtly) Cambridge Companion to International Law, 2012; Brownlie's Principles of International Law, 8th edn 2012, 9th edn 2019; State Responsibility: the general part, 2013; Chance, Order, Change: the course of international law, 2014. *Recreations:* cricket, reading. *Address:* International Court of Justice, Peace Palace, Carnegieplein 2, 2517 KJ The Hague, Netherlands. *E:* j.crawford@icj-cij.org.

**CRAWFORD, (Jeremy) Patrick (Stewart),** CB 2013; Chief Executive, The Charity Bank Ltd, 2012–18; *b* 16 Sept. 1952; *s* of Sir (Robert) Stewart Crawford, GCMG, CVO and Mary Katharine (*née* Corbett); *m* 1980, Charlotte Elizabeth Cecily Burnaby-Atkins; one *s* three *d*. *Educ:* Worcester Coll., Oxford (BA Juris.). Called to the Bar, Middle Temple, 1975; Morgan Grenfell & Co. Ltd, then Deutsche Morgan Grenfell, subseq. Deutsche Bank AG, 1976–2002: Man. Dir and Global Hd, Project and Export Finance, 1998–2001; Global Hd, Project Finance, 2001–02; Man. Dir, Emerging Africa Advisers, fund manager of Emerging Africa Infrastructure Fund, 2002–04; Chief Exec., ECGD, 2004–12. Non-executive Director: Crossrail Ltd, 2008–11; UK Trade and Investment, 2011–12; Caxton Trust, 2014– (Chair, 2018–); Community Develt Finance Assoc., 2015–18; Emerging Africa Infrastructure Fund Ltd, 2015–; Private Infrastructure Develt Gp Ltd, 2018–.
*See also M. J. Crawford.*

**CRAWFORD, Lesley Jane;** *see* Anderson, L. J.

**CRAWFORD, Lionel Vivian,** FRS 1988; Principal Scientist, Imperial Cancer Research Fund Tumour Virus Group, Department of Pathology, Cambridge University, 1988–95; *b* 30 April 1932; *s* of John Mitchell Crawford and Fanny May Crawford (*née* Barnett); *m* 1957, Elizabeth Minnie (*née* Green); one *d*. *Educ:* Rendcomb College, Cirencester; Emmanuel College, Cambridge (BA, MA, PhD). Virus Lab., Berkeley, Calif., 1958–59; Calif. Inst. of Technology, 1959–60; Inst. of Virology, Glasgow, 1960–68; Molecular Virology Lab., Imperial Cancer Res. Fund, 1968–88. Mem., EMBO. FRSE 1970. Gabor Medal, Royal Soc., 2005. *Publications:* numerous scientific articles. *Recreation:* wood-turning.

**CRAWFORD, Prof. Michael Hewson,** FBA 1980; Professor of Ancient History, University College London, 1986–2005, now Emeritus (Honorary Fellow, 2009–10); *b* 7 Dec. 1939; *s* of late Brian Hewson Crawford and Margarethe Bettina (*née* Nagel). *Educ:* St Paul's School; Oriel College, Oxford (BA, MA). Scholar, British School at Rome, 1962–64; Jane Eliza Procter Visiting Fellow, Princeton Univ., 1964–65; Cambridge University: Research Fellow, 1964–69, Fellow, 1969–86, Christ's Coll.; Lectr, 1969–86. Visiting Professor: Univ. of Pavia, 1983, 1992; Ecole Normale Supérieure, Paris, 1984; Univ. of Padua, 1986; Sorbonne, Paris, 1989; San Marino, 1989; Milan, 1990; L'Aquila, 1990; Ecole des Hautes Etudes, Paris, 1997; Ecole des Hautes Etudes en Sciences Sociales, Paris, 1999; Trento, 2007; Naples, 2009; Joseph Crabtree Orator, UCL, 2000. Joint Director: Excavations of Fregellae, 1980–86; Valpolcevera Project, 1987–93; Velleia Project, 1994–95; San Martino Project, 1996–99. Mem. Bd, UK Research Reserve, 2010–16. Chm., JACT, 1992–95 (Chm., Ancient History Cttee, 1978–84); Vice-Pres., Roman Soc., 1981–. Membro Straniero, Istituto Lombardo, 1990; MAE 1995; Mem., Reial Acadèmia de Bones Lletres, 1998; Corresp. Member: Accademia Petrarca, 2004; Académie des Inscriptions et Belles Lettres, 2006. Editor: Papers of the British Sch. at Rome, 1975–79; Jl of Roman Studies, 1980–84. Derek Allen Prize, British Acad., 2017. Officier, Ordre des Palmes Académiques (France), 2001. *Publications:* Roman Republican Coin Hoards, 1969; Roman Republican Coinage, 1974; The Roman Republic, 1978; La Moneta in Grecia e a Roma, 1981; (with D. Whitehead) Archaic and Classical Greece, 1982; Sources for Ancient History, 1983; Coinage and Money under the Roman Republic, 1985; (with M. Beard) Rome in the Late Republic, 1985; L'impero romano e la struttura economica e sociale delle province, 1986; (with A. M. Burnett) The Coinage of the Roman World in the Late Republic, 1987; (with C. Ligota and J. B. Trapp) Medals and Coins from Budé to Mommsen, 1990; (ed) Antonio Agustín between Renaissance and Counter-reform, 1993; (ed) Roman Statutes, 1995; (jtly) The Customs Law of Asia, 2008; Imagines Italicae, 2012; contribs to Annales, Athenaeum, Economic History Rev., Jl of Roman Studies, etc. *Address:* Department of History, University College London, Gower Street, WC1E 6BT.

**CRAWFORD, Michael James,** CMG 2008; HM Diplomatic Service, retired; independent consultant and writer; *b* London, 3 Feb. 1954; *s* of Sir (Robert) Stewart Crawford, GCMG, CVO and Mary Katharine Crawford (*née* Corbett); *m* 1984, Georgia Anne Moylan; two *s* one *d* (of whom one *s* one *d* are twins). *Educ:* University Coll., Oxford (BA Juris. 1975); St Antony's Coll., Oxford (MPhil Mid. Eastern Studies 1980). Called to the Bar, Inner Temple, 1978; joined FCO, 1981; Second, then First Sec., Cairo, 1983–84; First Secretary: Sana'a, 1985–86; Riyadh, 1986–90; FCO, 1990–92; Warsaw, 1992–95; FCO, 1995–99; Counsellor: Islamabad, 1999–2001; FCO, 2001–09. Vis. Fellow, Near East Dept, Princeton Univ., 2009; Consulting Sen. Fellow, IISS, 2010–11. *Recreations:* travel, reading and writing on Middle East and Islam, second-hand bookshops.
*See also J. P. S. Crawford.*

**CRAWFORD, Michael Patrick,** CBE 2014 (OBE 1987); actor, since 1955; *b* 19 Jan. 1942. *Educ:* St Michael's Coll., Bexley; Oakfield Sch., Dulwich. In orig. prodn of Britten's Noyes Fludde and of Let's Make an Opera; *stage appearances include:* Come Blow Your Horn, Prince of Wales, 1961; Travelling Light, 1965; The Anniversary, 1966; No Sex Please, We're British, Strand, 1971; Billy, Drury Lane, 1974; Same Time, Next Year, Prince of Wales, 1976; Flowers for Algernon, Queen's, 1979; Barnum, Palladium, 1981, 1983, Victoria Palace, 1985–86 (Olivier Award; Show Business Personality of the Year, Variety Club of GB); The Phantom of the Opera, Her Majesty's, 1986 (Olivier Award, Best Actor in a Musical), NY, 1988 (Tony Award, Best Actor in a Musical), Los Angeles, 1989; The Music of Andrew Lloyd Webber (concert tour), USA, Australia and UK, 1991–92; EFX, Las Vegas, 1995–96; Dance of the Vampires, NY, 2002–03; The Woman in White, Palace, 2004; The Wizard of Oz, London Palladium, 2011; The Go-Between, Apollo Th., 2016. *Films include:* Soap Box Derby; Blow Your Own Trumpet; Two Left Feet; The War Lover; Two Living, One Dead; The Knack, 1964 (Variety Club Award for Most Promising Newcomer); A Funny Thing Happened on the Way to the Forum, 1965; The Jokers, How I Won the War, 1966; Hello Dolly, 1968; The Games, 1969; Hello and Goodbye, 1970; Alice in Wonderland, 1972; The Condorman, 1980. Numerous radio broadcasts and TV appearances; *TV series include:* Some Mothers Do 'Ave 'Em; Chalk and Cheese. *Publications:* Parcel Arrived Safely: tied with string (autobiog.), 1999. *Address:* c/o Knight Ayton Management, 29 Gloucester Place, W1U 8HX. *T:* (020) 3795 1806.

**CRAWFORD, Patrick;** *see* Crawford, J. P. S.

**CRAWFORD, His Honour Peter John;** QC 1976; a Senior Circuit Judge, 1992–2002 (a Circuit Judge, 1988–92); *b* 23 June 1930; *s* of William Gordon Robertson and Doris Victoria Robertson (*née* Mann, subseq. Crawford); *m* 1st, 1953, Jocelyn Lavender (marr. diss.; she *d* 2004); two *s* two *d*; 2nd, 1979, Ann Allen Travis. *Educ:* Berkhamsted Sch.; Brasenose Coll., Oxford (MA). Intelligence Corps (Field Security, Hong Kong), 1948–49. Called to Bar, Lincoln's Inn, 1953; Bencher, 1984; a Recorder, 1974–88; Resident Judge, Oxford Crown Court, 1991–92; Recorder of Birmingham, 1992–2001; Additional Judge, Court of Appeal (Criminal Div.), 1995–2002; Hon. Recorder of Oxford, 2001–02. Pres., Trent Region, Mental Health Review Tribunal, 1986–2002; Vice Chm., Appeal Cttee, ICA, 1987–88; Member: Council of Justice, 1986–88; Parole Bd, 1992–96. Chm., Disciplinary Ct, Univ. of Oxford, 2004–10. Associate, Kathryn Redway Associates, 2004–. Mem., Paddington Borough Council, 1962–65; Chm., W London Family Service Unit, 1972–79; Mem., Family Service Units Nat. Council, 1975–81. Hon. Pres., English Nat. Sect., Internat. Assoc. of Penal Law, 1998–2002. *Recreation:* gardening. *Address:* Wheatsheaf House, The Green, Culworth, Banbury OX17 2BB. *E:* petercrawfordqc@gmail.com. *Club:* Royal Over-Seas League.

**CRAWFORD, Prof. Robert,** DPhil; FBA 2011; FRSE, FEA; Professor of Modern Scottish Literature, since 1995, and Bishop Wardlaw Professor of Poetry, since 2011, School of English, University of St Andrews; *b* 23 Feb. 1959; *s* of Robert Alexander Nelson Crawford and Elizabeth Menzies Crawford; *m* 1988, Alice Wales; one *s* one *d*. *Educ:* Hutchesons' Grammar Sch., Glasgow; Univ. of Glasgow (MA Hons 1981); Balliol Coll., Oxford (DPhil 1985). Elizabeth Wordsworth Jun. Res. Fellow, St Hugh's Coll., Oxford, 1984–87; British Acad. Postdoctoral Res. Fellow, Univ. of Glasgow, 1987–89; University of St Andrews: Lectr in Modern Scottish Lit., 1989–95; Hd, Sch. of English, 2002–05. Ed., Verse mag., 1984–95; Poetry Ed., Polygon, 1991–99. FRSE 1999; FEA 1999. *Publications:* The Savage and the City in the Works of T. S. Eliot, 1987; A Scottish Assembly, 1990; (with W. N. Herbert) Sharawaggi, 1990; (ed) Other Tongues, 1990; (ed jtly) About Edwin Morgan, 1990; The Arts of Alasdair Gray, 1991; Talkies, 1992; Devolving English Literature, 1992, 2nd edn 2000; (ed jtly) Reading Douglas Dunn, 1992; Identifying Poets, 1993; (ed jtly) Liz Lochhead's Voices, 1993; (ed jtly) Talking Verse, 1995; Literature in Twentieth-Century Scotland, 1995; Masculinity, 1996; (ed) Robert Burns and Cultural Authority, 1997; (ed) The Scottish Invention of English Literature, 1998; (ed jtly) The Penguin Book of Poetry from Britain and Ireland since 1945, 1998; Spirit Machines, 1999; (ed jtly) The New Penguin Book of Scottish Verse, 2000; (ed jtly) Scottish Religious Poetry, 2000; The Modern Poet, 2001; The Tip of My Tongue, 2003; (ed) Heaven-Taught Fergusson, 2003; Selected Poems, 2005; (ed) The Book of St Andrews, 2005; (ed) Apollos of the North, 2006; (ed) Contemporary Poetry and Contemporary Science, 2006; Scotland's Books: the Penguin history of Scottish literature, 2007; Full Volume, 2008; The Bard, Robert Burns, a Biography, 2009; (ed jtly) The Best Laid Schemes, 2009; (ed) New Poems, Chiefly in the Scottish Dialect, 2009; The Beginning and the End of the World, 2011; Simonides, 2011; On Glasgow and Edinburgh, 2013; Bannockburns, 2014; Testament, 2014; Young Eliot: from St Louis to 'The Waste Land', 2015; Chinese Makars, 2016; (ed) The Book of Iona, 2016; Fire, 2017; The Scottish Ambassador, 2018; Strath, 2019. *Recreations:* walking, Scottish nationalism, internationalism, Anglophilia. *Address:* School of English, University of St Andrews, St Andrews, Fife KY16 9AL. *T:* (01334) 462666, *Fax:* (01334) 462655.

**CRAWFORD, (Robert Hardie) Bruce;** JP; Member (SNP) Stirling, Scottish Parliament, since 2007 (Scotland Mid and Fife, 1999–2007); *b* 16 Feb. 1955; *s* of Robert and Wilma Crawford; *m* 1980, Jacqueline Hamilton Scott; three *s. Educ:* Kinross High Sch.; Perth High Sch. Personnel Officer, then Equal Opportunities Officer, later Develt Advr, Scottish Office, 1974–99. Member (SNP): Perth and Kinross DC, 1988–96; Perth and Kinross Council, 1995–99 (Leader, 1995–99). Scottish Parliament: Opposition Chief Whip, 1999; Opposition frontbench spokesman on transport and the envmt, 2000–01, on envmt and energy, 2001–03, on Parliament, 2003–07; Minister for Parly Business, 2007–11; Cabinet Sec. for Parly Business and Govt Strategy, 2011–12. Business Convenor, 2005–, Gp Convenor, 2016–, Convenor, Finance and Constitution Cttee, 2017–, SNP. Member Board: Scottish Enterprise Tayside, 1996–99; Perthshire Tourist Bd, 1996–99; Perth Coll., 1996–99. Chairman: Perth and Kinross Recreational Facilities Ltd, 1996–99; Kinross-shire Partnership Ltd, 1998–99. JP Perth, Kinross, 1993. *Recreations:* politics, golf, football. *Address:* Scottish Parliament, Edinburgh EH99 1SP. *T:* (0131) 348 5686.

**CRAWFORD, Dr Robert McKay,** CBE 2004; Chairman, Economic Development Association Scotland, 2014–15; *b* 14 June 1951; *s* of Robert and Catherine Crawford; *m* 1975, Linda Acheson; one *s* one *d. Educ:* Strathclyde Univ. (BA Hons Politics); Harvard Univ. (John F. Kennedy Schol.); Glasgow Univ. (PhD Govt 1982). Leverhulme Fellow, Fraser of Allander Inst., Strathclyde Univ., 1983–85; Develt Exec., 1985–87, Manager of US Desk, 1987–89, SDA; Dir, N America, 1989–91, Dir, 1991–94, Locate in Scotland; Man. Dir, Scottish Enterprise Ops, 1994–96; Sen. Specialist in Investment, World Bank, 1996–98; Partner, Ernst & Young, 1998–2000; Chief Exec., Scottish Enterprise, 2000–04; Hd of Strategy and Special Projects, Wood Gp, 2004–05; Chief Exec., Mersey Partnership, 2005–06; Exec. Dir, Business Develt and Commercialisation, Glasgow Caledonian Univ., 2006–08; Gp Exec. Dir, Ops, SEEDA, 2008; Dir, Orgnl Develt, States of Jersey, 2012–14. Chm., Invest Thames Gateway, 2010. FRSA 1995. *Recreations:* running, reading, modern history, economics, biography.

**CRAWFORD, Sir Robert (William Kenneth),** Kt 2007; CBE 2002; Director-General, Imperial War Museum, 1995–2008 (Deputy Director-General, 1982–95); *b* 3 July 1945; *s* of late Hugh Merrall Crawford, FCA, and Mary Crawford (*née* Percival); *m* 1975, Vivienne Sylvia Polakowski; one *d* one *s. Educ:* Culford Sch.; Pembroke Coll., Oxford (Cleoburey Schol.; BA). Joined Imperial War Museum as Research Asst, 1968: Head of Research and Information Office, 1971–89; Keeper, Dept of Photographs, 1975–83; Asst Director, 1979–82. Chairman: UK Nat. Inventory of War Memorials, 1995–2008; Nat. Mus. Dirs' Conf., 2000–06; Member: British Nat. Cttee for History of Second World War, 1995–2008; Bd, Museum Documentation Assoc., 1998–2006; Nat. Historic Ships Cttee, 2000–06. Trustee: Imperial War Mus. Trust, 1982–2008; Sir Winston Churchill Archives Trust, 1995–2006; Florence Nightingale Mus. Trust, 1999–2011; Royal Logistic Corps Mus. Trust, 2000–13; Fleet Air Arm Mus., 2000–10; Horniman Mus. and Public Park Trust, 2001–13; Greenwich Foundn for Old Royal Naval Coll., 2007–14 (Chm., 2011–14); Chatham Historic Dockyard Trust, 2008–18; Nat. Maritime Mus., 2008–16; Nat. Mus. of the Royal Navy, 2008–18; Nat. Museums Liverpool, 2009–15; British Empire and Commonwealth Mus., 2010–13. Vice-Pres., Fedn of Merchant Mariners, 2005–18. Vice-Patron, Army Museums Ogilby Trust, 2009–; Patron, Evacuees Reunion Assoc., 1997–. Freeman, City of London, 1998; Liveryman, Glovers' Co., 1998–. *Clubs:* Special Forces, Royal Over-Seas League.

**CRAWFORD, Ruth;** QC (Scot.) 2008; *b* Glasgow, 17 July 1965; *d* of George Douglas Crawford and Joan Burnie. *Educ:* Cranley Sch. for Girls, Edinburgh; George Heriot's Sch., Edinburgh; Aberdeen Univ. (LLB Hons 1986; DipLP 1987). Called to Scottish Bar, 1993; Second Standing Jun. Counsel to Scottish Exec., 2000–08; ad hoc Advocate Depute, 2006–. Mem., Bd of Trustees, Nat. Library of Scotland, 2016–. *Recreation:* relaxing in France. *Address:* Advocates' Library, Parliament House, Edinburgh EH1 1RF. *T:* (0131) 226 5071. *E:* ruth.crawford@axiomadvocates.com.

**CRAWFORD, Prof. Vincent Paul,** PhD; FBA 2012; Drummond Professor of Political Economy, University of Oxford, since 2010; Fellow, All Souls College, Oxford, since 2010; *b* Springfield, Ohio, 6 April 1950; *s* of David James Crawford, III and Marjorie Piga Crain, and adopted *s* of Bennett Crain; *m* 1985, Zoë Marie Clark. *Educ:* Princeton Univ. (AB *summa cum laude* Econs 1972); Massachusetts Inst. of Technol. (PhD Econs 1976). University of California, San Diego: Asst Prof., 1976–81; Associate Prof., 1981–85; Prof., 1985–97; Dist. Prof. of Econs, 1997–2009, now Emeritus. Vis. Prof. of Econs and Vis. Res. Associate, Industrial Relns Section, Princeton Univ., 1985–86. Guggenheim Fellow, 1997–98. Associate Editor: Jl of Econ. Theory, 1986–96, 1998–2004; Econometrica, 2004–07; Co-Ed., Amer. Econ. Rev., 2005–09; Ed., Games and Econ. Behavior, 2011– (Mem. Editl Bd, 1988–); Member: Editl Adv. Bd, NZ Econ. Papers, 2007–; Editl Bd, Jl of Econ. Literature, 2010–12. MAE 2016. Fellow: Econometric Soc., 1990; Amer. Acad. of Arts and Scis, 2003. *Publications:* Essays in Economic Theory, 1983; International Lending, Long-Term Credit Relationships and Dynamic Contract Theory, 1987; contrib. articles to professional jls. *Recreations:* hiking, bicycling, sailing. *Address:* All Souls College, Oxford OX1 4AL. *T:* (01865) 279339; Department of Economics, Manor Road Building, Manor Road, Oxford OX1 3UQ. *E:* vincent.crawford@economics.ox.ac.uk.

**CRAWFORD, His Honour William Hamilton Raymund;** QC 1980; a Circuit Judge, 1986–2001; *b* 10 Nov. 1936; *s* of late Col Mervyn Crawford, DSO, DL, JP, and Martha Hamilton Crawford; *m* 1965, Marilyn Jean Colville; one *s* two *d. Educ:* West Downs, Winchester; Winchester Coll.; Emmanuel Coll., Cambridge (BA). Commnd 2nd Lt, Royal Scots Greys, 1955–57. Called to the Bar, Inner Temple, 1964; Dep. Chm., Agricultural Land Tribunal, 1978; a Recorder, 1979–86. Pres., Royal Scottish Forestry Soc., 2013–15 (Vice Pres., 2010–13). Chm., Dunscore Community Council, 2009–12. *Recreations:* hill farming, fishing, shooting (shot for GB in Kolapore Match, and for Scotland in Elcho and Twenty Matches on several occasions; mem., Scottish Rifle Team, Commonwealth Games, Jamaica, 1966). *Club:* Northern Counties (Newcastle).
*See also Earl of Kinnoull.*

**CRAWFORD COLLINS, Simon;** Managing Director, Slim Film and Television, since 2011; *b* London, 5 April 1967; *s* of David and Ann Crawford Collins; *m*; one *s* one *d. Educ:* Oriel Coll., Oxford (BA Mod. Hist. 1989). Kudos Film and Television Ltd: joined, 2001; Dir, Drama, 2005–08; Jt Man. Dir, 2008. *Address:* Slim Film and Television, Henry Wood House, 2 Riding House Street, W1W 7FA.

**CRAWLEY,** family name of **Baroness Crawley**.

**CRAWLEY, Baroness** *cr* 1998 (Life Peer), of Edgbaston in the co. of West Midlands; **Christine Mary Crawley;** *b* 9 Jan. 1950; *d* of Thomas Louis Quinn and Joan Ryan; *m*; one *s* two *d* (incl. twins). *Educ:* Notre Dame Catholic Secondary Girls' School, Plymouth; Digby Stuart Training College, Roehampton. Formerly teacher; S Oxfordshire District Council; contested (Lab) Staffordshire SE, gen. election, 1983. MEP (Lab) Birmingham E, 1984–99; Dep. Leader, Eur. PLP, 1994–99. Govt spokesman, H of L, on foreign affairs, 2002–05, defence, 2003–04 and 2008–10, transport, 2004–05 and 2007–08, N Ireland, 2007–08. A Baroness in Waiting (Govt Whip), 2002–08 and 2009–10. Chm., European Parlt Women's Rights Cttee, 1989–94. Chm., Women's Nat. Commn, 1999–2002. Dir, Northfield Regeneration Forum; Chm., W Midlands Regl Cultural Consortium, 1999–2002. Pres., Chartered Trading Standards Inst., 2009–. Patron: Orgn for Sickle Cell Anaemia Relief; Women's Returners Network. FRSA. *Address:* House of Lords, SW1A 0PW.

**CRAWLEY, Angela;** MP (SNP) Lanark and Hamilton East, since 2015; *b* Hamilton, 3 June 1987. *Educ:* John Ogilvie High Sch.; Stirling Univ. (BA Hons Politics 2009); Univ. of Glasgow (LLB 2015). Parly Asst, Scottish Parlt, 2007–09; Tour Co-ordinator and Sen. Gp Leader, Educn Travel Gp, 2009–11; Parly Asst and Researcher, Scottish Parlt, 2011–13; Legal Asst, Aamer Anwar & Co., Solicitors, 2014. Mem. (SNP), S Lanarkshire Council, 2012–15. SNP spokesperson for Equalities, Women and Children, 2015–, Disabilities, Child Maintenance, Housing, and Family Support, 2017–. Nat. Convenor, Young Scots for Independence, 2014–15. *Address:* House of Commons, SW1A 0AA.

**CRAWLEY, David Jonathan;** Director, Scottish Executive European Union Office, Brussels, 2005–06; *b* 6 May 1951; *s* of Frederick John Crawley and Olive Elizabeth Crawley (*née* Bunce); *m* 1983, Anne Anderson; one *s* two *d. Educ:* Chichester High Sch.; Christ Church, Oxford (BA Modern Hist. 1972; MA 1973). Scottish Office, 1972–81; Dept of Energy, 1981–84; Asst Sec., Scottish Educn Dept, 1984–87; Principal Private Sec. to Sec. of State for Scotland, 1987–89; Counsellor, UK Representation to EU, Brussels, 1990–94; Asst Dir, Finance, and Hd, Private Finance Unit, 1994–97, Hd, Powers and Functions, Constitution Gp, 1997–98, Scottish Office; Hd of Schs Gp, Scottish Office, then Scottish Exec., Educn Dept, 1998–99; Hd of Agriculture, Rural Affairs, then Envmt and Rural Affairs, Dept, Scottish Exec., 1999–2002; Hd of Dept, Scotland Office, 2002–05. Chm., Audit Cttee, Wales Office, 2005–15. Member: Bd, Scottish Natural Heritage, 2006–12; Jt Nature Conservation Cttee, 2007–12; Chm., Central Scotland Forest Trust, 2008–13. Treas., St Fillan's Episcopal Ch, 1998–99. Comr, Queen Victoria Sch., Dunblane, 2006–11. *Recreations:* gardening, music, travel to warm places.

**CRAWLEY, Most Rev. David Perry;** Archbishop of Kootenay and Metropolitan of British Columbia and Yukon, 1994–2004; *b* 26 July 1937; *s* of Rev. Canon George Antony Crawley, LTh and Lucy Lillian Crawley (née Ball); *m* 1st, 1959, Frances Mary Louise Wilmot; two *d*; 2nd, 1986, Joan Alice Bubbs; one *d* (and one *d* decd). *Educ:* Univ. of Manitoba (BA 1958); St John's Coll., Winnipeg (LTh 1961; DD 1990); Univ. of Kent at Canterbury (MA 1967). Ordained Deacon 1961, Priest 1962. Incumbent, St Thomas', Sherwood Park, Edmonton, 1961–66; Canon Missioner, All Saints Cathedral, Edmonton, 1967–70; Rector, St Matthew's, Winnipeg, 1971–77; Archdeacon of Winnipeg, 1974–77; Archdeacon of Rupert's Land, 1977–81; Lectr, St John's College, Winnipeg, 1981–82; Rector, St Michael and All Angels, Regina, 1982–85; Rector, St Paul's, Vancouver, 1985–90; Bishop of Kootenay, 1990–2004. *Recreations:* ski-ing, hiking. *Address:* c/o Diocese of Kootenay, 1876 Richter Street, Kelowna, BC V1Y 2M9, Canada.

**CRAWLEY, John Maurice,** CB 1992; Under Secretary, Inland Revenue, 1979–93; *b* 27 Sept. 1933; *s* of late Charles William and Kathleen Elizabeth Crawley; *m* 1978, Jane Meadows Rendel; three *s. Educ:* Rugby Sch.; New Coll., Oxford (MA). Assistant Principal, Inland Revenue, 1959; Principal, 1963; Asst Secretary, 1969; Under Sec., 1979; seconded to Cabinet Office (Central Policy Review Staff), 1973–76 and 1979–81. *Recreations:* music (piano and viola), travel, book-binding.

**CRAWLEY, Prof. Michael John,** PhD; FRS 2002; Professor of Plant Ecology, Imperial College London (formerly Imperial College, London University), since 1994; *b* 9 March 1949; *s* of John and Isabel Crawley; *m* 1971, Greer Anne Williams. *Educ:* Dukes Grammar Sch., Alnwick; Edinburgh Univ. (BSc Hons 1st Cl. 1970); Imperial Coll., London (DIC, PhD 1973). Lectr, Univ. of Bradford, 1973–79; Lectr, 1979–89, Reader, 1989–94, Imperial Coll., London. Mem. Council, RHS, 2015–; Trustee: Royal Botanic Gardens, Kew, 1996–2002, 2011–14; Botanical Soc. of Britain and Ireland, 2014–. *Publications:* Herbivory, 1983; Plant Ecology, 1986; Colonization, Succession and Stability, 1987; Natural Enemies, 1992; GLIM for Ecologists, 1993; Statistical Computing, 2002; The Flora of Berkshire, 2005; The R Book, 2007; Alien Plants, 2015; The Flora of St Kilda, 2017; papers on plant-herbivore interactions and biological invasions. *Recreations:* BSBI plant recorder for Berkshire and East Sutherland, mountains, croquet, Newcastle United. *Address:* Department of Biological Sciences, Silwood Park, Ascot, Berks SL5 7PY. *T:* (020) 7594 2216, *Fax:* (020) 7594 2339. *E:* m.crawley@imperial.ac.uk.

**CRAWLEY-BOEVEY, Sir Thomas (Michael Blake),** 8th Bt *cr* 1784; *b* 29 Sept. 1928; *er s* of Sir Launcelot Valentine Hyde Crawley-Boevey, 7th Bt, and Elizabeth Goodeth (*d* 1976), *d* of Herbert d'Auvergne Innes, late Indian Police; *S* father, 1968; *m* 1st, 1957, Laura Coelingh (*d* 1979); two *s*; 2nd, 2003, Judith Tillotson. *Educ:* Wellington Coll.; St John's Coll., Cambridge (BA 1952, MA 1956). 2nd Lieut, Durham Light Infantry, 1948. With Shipping Agents, 1952–61; with Consumers' Association, 1961–82; Editor: Money Which?, 1968–76; Which?, 1976–82; Editor-in-Chief, Which? magazines, 1980–82. Master, Girdlers' Co., 1992–93. *Heir: er s* Thomas Hyde Crawley-Boevey [*b* 26 June 1958; *m* 1992, Lynette Claire Gilbert; two *s*]. *Address:* 47 Belvoir Road, Cambridge CB4 1JH. *T:* (01223) 368698.

**CRAWSHAW, 5th Baron** *cr* 1892, of Crawshaw, co. Lancaster and of Whatton, co. Leics; **David Gerald Brooks;** Bt 1891; *b* 14 Sept. 1934; *s* of 3rd Baron Crawshaw and Sheila (*d* 1964), *o d* of Lt-Col P. R. Clifton, CMG, DSO; *S* brother, 1997; *m* 1970, Belinda Mary, *d* of George Burgess; four *d. Educ:* Eton; RAC, Cirencester. President: NW Leics Cons. Assoc., 2000–16; Leics Agricl Soc., 2009–13. High Sheriff, Leics, 1984–85. *Heir: b* Hon. John Patrick Brooks [*b* 17 March 1938; *m* 1967, Rosemary Vans Agnew, *o d* of C. Vans Agnew Frank; one *s* one *d*].

**CRAWSHAW, Steven John;** Group Chief Executive, Bradford & Bingley plc, 2004–08; *b* 15 April 1961; *s* of John Crawshaw and Serena Gillean Crawshaw; *m* 1991, Brigid Rushmore; two *s. Educ:* Eastbourne Coll.; Univ. of Leicester (LLB); Cranfield Univ. (MBA). Articled clerk and Asst Solicitor, Hewitson Becke & Shaw, 1984–88; Partner, Froggatt & Co., 1988–89; Manager, Legal Dept, 1990–95, Strategic Planner, 1995–96, Hd of Strategy, 1996–97, Cheltenham & Gloucester plc; PA to Gp Dir, Customer Finance, Lloyds TSB plc, 1998; Bradford & Bingley plc, 1999–2008, Gp Strategy, HR and IT Dir, 2002–04. *Recreations:* family, hill walking, cooking.

**CRAXTON, Christine Elizabeth;** *see* Gamble, C. E.

**CRAXTON, (Katharine) Jane;** *see* Carmichael, K. J.

**CRAY, Rt Rev. Graham Alan;** Archbishops' Missioner, and Team Leader, Fresh Expressions, 2009–14; an Honorary Assistant Bishop: Diocese of York, since 2009; Diocese of Rochester, 2011–14; *b* 21 April 1947; *s* of late Alan Cray and Doris Mary Kathleen Cray; *m* 1973, Jacqueline Webster; two *d. Educ:* Leeds Univ. (BA 1968); St John's Coll., Nottingham. Ordained deacon, 1971, priest, 1972; Asst Curate, St Mark, Gillingham, 1971–75; N Area Co-ordinator, Youth Dept, CPAS, 1975–78; Asst Curate, 1978–82, Vicar, 1982–92, St Michael-le-Belfrey, York; Principal, Ridley Hall Theol Coll., 1992–2001; Bishop Suffragan of Maidstone, 2001–09; an Hon. Asst Bishop, Dio. of Canterbury, 2009–14. Vis. Fellow, St John's Coll., Univ. of Durham, 2016–. *Publications:*

The Post Evangelical Debate, 1997; Postmodern Culture and Youth Discipleship, 1998; (with Paul Simmonds) Being Culturally Relevant, 2000; Youth Congregations and the Emerging Church, 2002; (ed) Mission-Shaped Church, 2004, rev. edn 2009; (jtly) Making Sense of Generation Y, 2006; (with Tim Sudworth and Chris Russell) Mission-shaped Youth, 2007; Disciples and Citizens, 2007; Discerning Leadership, 2010; Who's Shaping You?, 2010; (ed jtly) New Monasticism as Fresh Expression of Church, 2011; (ed jtly and contrib.) Fresh Expressions and the Kingdom of God, 2012; Making Disciples in Fresh Expression of Church, 2013; contributor: Mass Culture, 1999; Mission as Transformation, 1999; Christ and Consumerism, 2000; Beholding the Glory, 2000; Fanning the Flame, 2003; The Future of the Parish System, 2006; The Heart of Faith, 2008; Faith in the Future, 2008; The Art of Compassion, 2008; The Holy Spirit in the World Today, 2011; The Gospel after Christendom, 2012; (contrib.) Doorways to the Sacred: developing sacramentality in fresh expressions of Church, 2017. *Recreations:* listening to rock music, following sport, reading theology.

**CRAY, Timothy James**; QC 2019; Senior Treasury Counsel (Criminal), Central Criminal Court, since 2014; *b* Belfast, 1966; *s* of John and Florence Cray; *m* (marr. diss.); one *s* one *d*. *Educ:* Down High Sch., Downpatrick; Univ. of Durham (BA Hons Law). Called to the Bar, Inner Temple, 1989; in practice as barrister, 1989–. *Recreations:* golf, shooting. *Address:* 6KBW College Hill, 21 College Hill, EC4R 2RP. *T:* (020) 3301 0910. *E:* timothy.cray@6kbw.com.

**CREAGH, Mary Helen**; MP (Lab) Wakefield, since 2005; *b* 2 Dec. 1967; *d* of Thomas and Elizabeth Creagh; *m* 2001, Adrian Pulham; one *s* one *d*. *Educ:* Pembroke Coll., Oxford (BA Jt Hons Modern Langs (French and Italian)); London Sch. of Econs (MSc Eur. Studies). Press Officer: Youth Forum of EU, 1991–95; London Enterprise Agency, 1995–97; Lectr in Entrepreneurship, Cranfield Sch. of Mgt, 1997–2005. Mem. (Lab) Islington BC, 1998–2005 (Leader, Labour Gp, 2000–04). An Asst Govt Whip, 2009–10; Shadow Sec. of State for Envmt, Food and Rural Affairs, 2010–13, for Transport, 2013–14, for Internat. Develt, 2014–15. Trustee, Rathbone Trng, 1997–2004. *Recreations:* cycling, cooking, theatre, friends and family, pop music. *Address:* House of Commons, SW1A 0AA. *T:* (020) 7219 6984. *E:* mary@marycreagh.co.uk. *Club:* Red Shed (Wakefield).

**CREALLY, Eugene Patrick**, PhD; QC (Scot.) 2011; *b* Dungannon, Co. Tyrone, 3 Feb. 1961; *s* of Joseph Creally and Annie Creally (*née* Quinn); *m* 2004, Ailsa Mhairi Wilson; one step *s*. *Educ:* Queen's Univ. Belfast (LLB Hons 1983); Edinburgh Univ. (DipLP 1988; PhD 1991). Admitted as solicitor, 1990; Solicitor, Bird Semple Fyfe Ireland, 1990–92; Advocate, 1993–; Standing Counsel: to Lord Advocate, 1998–2005; to Advocate Gen. for Scotland, 2009–11. Clerk to Faculty of Advocates, 1999–2003. Vice Convenor, Free Legal Services Unit, 2003–. *Publications:* Judicial Review of Anti Dumping and Other Safeguard Measures in the European Community, 1992. *Recreations:* golf, tennis, hill walking. *Address:* Advocates Library, Parliament House, Edinburgh EH1 1RF. *T:* (0131) 226 5071. *E:* eugene.creally@advocates.org.uk.

**CREAN, Anthony Joseph Daniel**; QC 2006; *b* 9 June 1962; *s* of Michael and Patricia Crean; *m* 2003, Angela Roberts; two *s* three *d*. *Educ:* Univ. of Essex (BA); Univ. of Manchester (MPhil). Called to the Bar, Gray's Inn, 1987; in practice as barrister, 1987–, specialising in planning law. FRGS 2003. *Recreations:* hanging out with Alice, Laura, Francis, Lawrence and Hilary, scuba-diving, poetry, ski-ing, swimming, chess. *Address:* Kings Chambers, Embassy House, 60 Church Street, Birmingham B3 2DJ.

**CREAN, Hon. Simon (Findlay)**; Director, Ashley Services Group Ltd, 2014–15; *b* 26 Feb. 1949; *s* of late Hon. Francis Daniel Crean and of Mary Isobel Crean, AM; *m* 1973, Carole (*née* Lamb); two *d*. *Educ:* Middle Park Central, Melbourne; Melbourne High Sch.; Monash Univ. (BEc, LLB). Trade Union Official, Federated Storemen and Packers Union of Australia, 1970–85; Pres., ACTU, 1985–90. MP (ALP) Hotham, Vic, 1990–2013. Federal Minister for: Science and Technology, 1990; Primary Industries and Energy, 1991–93; Employment, Educn and Training, 1993–96; Dep. Leader of the Opposition, 1998–2001; Leader of the Opposition, 2001–03; Shadow Treasurer, 1998–2001, 2003–04; Shadow Trade Minister, 2004–07; Minister for Trade, 2007–10; Minister for Regl Australia, Regl Develt and Local Govt, and Minister for the Arts, 2010–13. Patron, North Melbourne FC. *Recreations:* bushwalking, tennis. *Club:* North Melbourne Football.

**CREASY, Dr Stella Judith**; MP (Lab Co-op) Walthamstow, since 2010; *b* 1977. *Educ:* Colchester High Sch.; Magdalene Coll., Cambridge; London Sch. of Econs (PhD Social Psychol.). Formerly: researcher to Douglas Alexander, MP, Charles Clarke, MP and Ross Cranston, MP; Dep. Dir, Involve think tank; Hd, Public Affairs and Campaigns, Scout Assoc. Formerly Mem. (Lab Co-op) Waltham Forest LBC (Dep. Mayor, then Mayor). Shadow Minister: for Home Affairs, 2011–13; BIS, 2013–15. *Address:* House of Commons, SW1A 0AA.

**CREDITON, Bishop Suffragan of**, since 2018; Rt Rev. Jacqueline Ann Searle; *b* Redhill, 26 Sept. 1960; *d* of Alan John Searle and Joan Mary Searle; *m* 1992, David Charles Runcorn; two *s*. *Educ:* Talbot Heath, Bournemouth; Whitelands Coll., Roehampton (BEd); Trinity Coll., Bristol (DipTh; MA Applied Theol.). Teacher: Gt Walstead, Sussex, 1982–85; Sheen Mt Primary Sch., E Sheen, 1985–89; ordained deacon, 1992, priest, 1994; Assistant Curate: Roxeth Team, Harrow, 1992–94; St Stephen's, Ealing, 1994–96; Tutor in Applied Theology, and Dean of Women, Trinity Coll., Bristol, 1996–2003; Vicar, St Peter's, Littleover, 2003–12; Dean of Women's Ministry, Dio. of Derby, 2006–10; Rural Dean, Derby South, 2010–12; Archdeacon of Glos, and Canon Res., Glos Cathedral, 2012–18. Hon. Canon, Derby Cath., 2011–12. Trustee, SPCK, 2009–13. Training Partner (formerly Associate Trainer), Bridge Builders, 2010–18. *Address:* 32 The Avenue, Tiverton, Devon EX16 4HW. *T:* (01884) 250002. *E:* bishop.of.crediton@exeter.anglican.org.

**CREECH, Rt Hon. Wyatt (Beetham)**, CNZM 2003; PC 1999; Deputy Prime Minister of New Zealand, 1998–99; *b* Oceanside, Calif, 13 Oct. 1946; *s* of Jesse Wyatt Creech and Ellanora Sophia (*née* Beetham); arrived in NZ, 1947; *m* 1981, Diana, (Danny), Marie Rose; three *s*. *Educ:* Hadlow Prep. Sch., Masterton; Wanganui Collegiate Sch.; Massey Univ. (Dip. Sheep Farming); Victoria Univ. (BA Pol Sci. and Internat. Politics). Farmer, Wairarapa, 1974–79; horticulturalist (vineyard developer), 1979–88; Accountant, Masterton, 1983–87. MP (Nat.) Wairarapa, NZ, 1988–99, List Seat, 1999–2002; Minister: of Revenue, 1990–95; of Customs, i/c Public Trust Office and responsible for Govt Superannuation Fund, 1990–91; for Sen. Citizens, and Associate Minister of Finance and of Social Welfare, 1991–93; for State Owned Enterprises, 1993; of Employment, 1993–96; of Revenue and Dep. Minister of Finance, 1993–96; Leader of the House, 1996–98; Minister of Educn, 1996–99; Minister of Courts and of Ministerial Services, 1997–98. Dep. Leader, Nat. Party, 1997–2001; Ind. Dir, Blue Chip NZ, 2004–06. Mem., Parly Services Commn; Chm., NZ Fire Service Commn, 2011–16. Chairman: NZ Windfarms Ltd; HHL Gp; Heritage NZ; Director: Kaimai Cheese Co. Ltd; Seales Ltd. Dir, Cognition Educn Trust. *Recreations:* outdoor pursuits, wine-tasting, gardening, traditional acoustic music. *Address:* 43 Kandy Crescent, Khandallah, Wellington 6035, New Zealand.

**CREED, Prof. Francis Hunter**, MD; FRCP, FRCPsych, FMedSci; Professor of Psychological Medicine, University of Manchester, 1997–2012, now Emeritus; *b* 22 Feb. 1947; *s* of late Albert Lowry Creed and Joyce Marian Creed; *m* 1st, 1972, Ruth Alison Kaye (*d* 2013); two *s* two *d*; 2nd, 2016, Eileen May Cann. *Educ:* Kingswood Sch., Bath; Downing Coll., Cambridge (Pilley Schol.; MB BChir 1971; MA; MD 1985); St Thomas' Hosp. Med. Sch., London. FRCP 1991; FRCPsych 1991. Registrar, Maudsley Hosp., 1974–76; Sen. Registrar, Maudsley and London Hosps, 1976–78; Mental Health Leverhulme Res. Fellow, 1978–80; Sen. Lectr, Univ. of Manchester and Consultant Psychiatrist, Manchester Royal Infirmary, 1980–92; Prof. of Community Psychiatry, 1992–97, Res. Dean, Faculty of Medicine, Dentistry, Nursing and Pharmacy, 1997–2001, Univ. of Manchester; Hon. Consultant Psychiatrist, Manchester Royal Infirmary, subseq. Central Manchester Healthcare Trust, then Central Manchester and Manchester Children's Univ. Hosps NHS Trust, 1981–2012. Co-chair, Psychosocial Cttee, Rome Working Team Report on Functional Bowel Disorders, 2000, 2006. Treas., Eur. Assoc. of Consultation-Liaison Psychiatry and Psychosomatics, 2004–11 (Pres., 2000–04). Churchill Travelling Fellow, 1993. FRSocMed 1980; FMedSci 2000. Ed., Jl of Psychosomatic Res., 1999–2011. Hackett Award, Acad. Psychosomatic Medicine, 2009; Frits Huyse Award, Eur. Assoc. of Psychosomatic Medicine, 2015. *Publications:* Medicine and Psychiatry, 1981; Psychiatry in Medical Practice, 1989, 2nd edn 1994; (ed jtly) Medically Unexplained Symptoms, Somatisation and Bodily Distress: developing better clinical services, 2011; over 250 articles in learned jls on psychological aspects of medicine and Community Psychiatry. *Recreations:* hill walking, swimming, travelling. *Address:* Neuroscience and Mental Health, University of Manchester, Rawnsley Building, Manchester Royal Infirmary, Oxford Road, Manchester M13 9WL. *T:* (0161) 276 5331.

**CREED, Martin**; artist; *b* 21 Oct. 1968; *s* of John Creed and Gisela Grosscurth. *Educ:* Slade Sch. of Fine Art, London (BA Hons Fine Art 1990). Exhibitions include: Martin Creed Works (organised by Southampton City Art Gall.), Leeds City Art Gall., Bluecoat Gall., Liverpool, Camden Arts Centre, London, 2000; Art Now: Martin Creed, Tate Britain, London, 2000; Martin Creed: Down Over Up, Fruitmarket Gall., Edinburgh, 2010; Mothers, Hauser & Wirth, London, 2011; Martin Creed: What's the point of it?, Hayward Gall., 2014; What You Find, Hauser & Wirth, Som, 2016; Martin Creed: toast, Hauser & Wirth, London, 2018. Works include: Work#227: The lights going on and off (Turner Prize, 2001); Work#1197: All the bells in a country rung as quickly and loudly as possible for three minutes, 2012. *Publications:* the whole world + the work = the whole world, 1996; Martin Creed Works, 2010. *E:* mail@martincreed.com.

**CREED, Murray Laurence; His Honour Judge Creed**; a Circuit Judge, since 2010; *b* Solihull, 21 Jan. 1955; *s* of Brian Creed and Pamela Creed; *m* 1982, Jacqueline Burbridge; one *s* two *d*. *Educ:* Tudor Grange Grammar Sch., Solihull; University Coll. London (LLB). Called to the Bar, Lincoln's Inn, 1978; in private practice as a barrister, 1978–95; a Chm., Employment Tribunals, 1992–95; an Employment Judge, 1995–2010; an Asst Recorder, 2000; a Recorder, 2000–10. *Recreations:* music, family, walking, hockey, ski-ing, gardening.

**CREEDON, Michael Francis**, QPM 2011; Chief Constable, Derbyshire Constabulary, 2007–17; *b* London, 14 June 1958; *s* of Raymond and Elizabeth Creedon; *m* 1994, Sally Deans; two *s* one *d*. *Educ:* City of Leicester Boys' Sch.; Univ. of Manchester (BA Hons Hist. and Econs); Univ. of Leicester (MA Criminol.). Leicestershire Constabulary, 1980–2003: served as detective in every rank; Basic Comd Unit Comdr, S Area, 2001–03; Derbyshire Constabulary: Asst Chief Constable (Ops), 2003–06; Dep. Chief Constable for ACPO, Nat. Co-ordinator for Serious and Organised Crime, 2006–07. Holder, ACPO portfolio for asset recovery and policy lead for serious and organised crime, financial investigation and proceeds of crime, investigative interviewing and for kidnap and extortion, 2005–17. *Recreations:* Middlesbrough Football Club, family, cookery (oriental especially), painting and decorating, running.

**CREEDON, Roger**, CBE 2005; Chief Executive, Electoral Commission, 2000–04; *b* 31 Dec. 1946; *s* of late Patrick Michael Creedon and Norah Creedon (*née* Rice); *m* 1969, Shirley Ann Clay; two *s*. Joined Home Office, 1964; Police Directorate, 1969–77; Asst Sec., Cttee on Obscenity and Film Censorship, 1977–80; Forensic Sci. Service, 1980–83; Gaming Bd, 1983–87; Home Office Finance Directorate, 1987–90; Police Sci. and Technology Gp, 1990–93; Dir, Nat. Criminal Intelligence Service, 1993–96; Corporate Resources and Constitutional Directorates, Home Office 1996–2000. Election Observer for Commonwealth Secretariat, 2005. Lay Member: First-tier Tribunal (Information Rights) (formerly Information Tribunal), 2006–; GMC Fitness to Practise Panel, 2006–13; Rules and Ethics/Standards Cttee, SRA, 2007–12; Standards Cttee, Bar Standards Bd, 2008–10; Fitness to Practise Panel, NMC, 2008–16; General Chiropractic Council, 2009–16; Fitness to Practise Panel, GDC, 2011–. Mem., Kentish Opera Council, 2005–11. *Recreations:* oil painting, reading. *E:* rcreedon@ntlworld.com.

**CREELMAN, Graham Murray**, OBE 2006; Managing Director, Anglia Television, 1996–2006; Director, Regional Programming, ITV, 2003–06; *b* 20 May 1947; *s* of late Robert Kelly Creelman and Jean Murray Creelman; *m* 1st, 1969, Eleanor McCulloch McAuslan (marr. diss. 1984); two *d*; 2nd, 1984, Sarah Katharine Bruce-Lockhart (marr. diss. 1996); two *d*; 3rd, 1997, Francesca Vivica Parsons; one step *s* one step *d*. *Educ:* Greenock Acad.; Univ. of Sussex (BA Hons). Journalist, Scotsman, 1969–70; journalist and producer, BBC Scotland, 1970–78; producer and dir documentaries, Anglia TV, 1978–89; Exec. Dir, Survival Anglia Ltd, 1989–94; Dir of Programmes, Anglia TV, 1994–96; Chm., Anglia Multimedia, 1999–2001. Founder, Creelman Associates Ltd, 2006. Dir, Eastern Arts Bd, 1995–2002; Chairman: Eastern Screen Commn, 1997–2002; East of England Cultural Consortium, 1999–2009; Screen East, 2001–06; Council Mem., Arts Council England, East, 2002–08; (and Founder) East of England Prodn Innovation Centre, 2010–12. Mem., Ofcom Adv. Cttee for England, 2009–. Mem., E of England Regl Assembly, 2001–09. Bd Associate, Govt Office for E of England, 2006–09. Trustee/Dir, Wildscreen Trustees, 1993–2001; Director: Writers' Centre Norwich (formerly New Writing Partnership), 2004–16 (Dep. Chm., 2008–12; Chm., 2012–16); Norwich Heritage Economic and Regeneration Trust, 2004–16; Chairman: Norwich Partnership, 2006–10; Norfolk Strategic Partnership for Older People's Services, (Dep. Chm., 2014–16); Norwich Creative Partnership, 2016–; Sen. Ind. Dir/Dep. Chair, Norfolk and Suffolk Foundn Trust, 2008–15. Dep. Chm., United Wildlife, 1997–2001. Norwich University of the Arts (formerly School of Art and Design, then Norwich University College of the Arts): Gov., 2004–16 (Vice-Chm., 2006; Chm., 2007–13; Pro-Chancellor, 2013–18); Vis. Prof. of Media, 2012–18. Sheriff of Norwich, 2013–14. DUniv Univ. of the Arts London, 2015. *Publications:* contribs to New Statesman, The Listener. *Recreations:* walking in Scotland, fly fishing, Schubert, the books of John Buchan, playing the ukelele. *Address:* 22 Christchurch Road, Norwich NR2 2AE. *Club:* Norfolk (Norwich).

**CREESE, Prof. Sadie**, DPhil; Professor of Cybersecurity, University of Oxford, since 2011; Fellow, Worcester College, Oxford, since 2011; *b* Gloucester, 6 Dec. 1973; *d* of Peter Creese and Vicky Creese; one *d*. *Educ:* Univ. of North London (BSc Hons 1st Cl. Maths and Philos. 1996); Worcester Coll., Oxford (MSc Computation 1997; DPhil Computer Sci. 2001). Sen. Res. Scientist, 2000–05, Dir, Strategic Progs, Trusted Information Systems Div., 2005–07, QinetiQ; Prof. and Dir of e-Security, Univ. of Warwick, 2007–11; Dir,

Cyber Security Centre, 2012–15, Global Capacity Centre, 2013–, Univ. of Oxford. *Address:* Department of Computer Science, University of Oxford, Robert Hooke Building, Parks Road, Oxford OX1 3PR. *T:* (01865) 273616. *E:* sadie.creese@cs.ox.ac.uk.

**CREIGHTON, Alan Joseph,** CEng, FRINA; RCNC; Chief Underwater Systems Executive, Ministry of Defence, 1989–91, retired; *b* 21 Nov. 1936; *s* of Joseph Kenneth and Iris Mary Creighton; *m* 1959, Judith Bayford; two *d*. *Educ:* Gillingham County Grammar School; Royal Naval College, Greenwich. Joined Admiralty, 1953; Cadetship to Royal Corps of Naval Constructors, 1957; pass out, RNC Greenwich, 1961; RCDS 1980; Technical Dir, Yarrow Shipbuilders, 1981 (on secondment); resumed MoD (PE) career, 1984; Dir Gen., Surface Ships, 1986–89. *Recreations:* music, golf, computers, website design, cabinet making. *Address:* Rose Cottage, West Littleton, Chippenham SN14 8JE. *T:* (01225) 891021.

**CREIGHTON, Robert Mandell;** Managing Director, Creighton Consulting and Management Services, 2013–18; *b* 18 Feb. 1950; *s* of Hugh Creighton and Christian Creighton (*née* Barclay); *m* 1st, 1977, Sok-Chzeng Ong (marr. diss. 1983); 2nd, 1985, Rosanne Jelley; two *d*. *Educ:* Marlborough Coll.; King's Coll., Cambridge (MA Hist.); King's Coll. London (PGCE). Teacher, King's Coll. Sch., Wimbledon, 1974–78; Internat. Sec., United World Colls, 1978–88; Department of Health: Principal, 1988–91; Asst Sec., 1991–95; Principal Private Sec. to Sec. of State for Health, 1992–94; Chief Exec., Great Ormond Street Hosp. for Children NHS Trust, 1995–2000; Chief Executive: Ealing PCT, 2002–10; Ealing, Hillingdon and Hounslow PCT, 2010–11; Dir, London Public Health Transition, later London Health Transition and Legacy Prog., NHS London, 2011–13. Chairman: London Primary Care Trusts Gp, 2006–11; Family Mediation Standards Bd, 2015–. Hon. Sen. Lectr, LSHTM, 2012–. Trustee: Waterford Sch. Trust, 1988–; Imperial Coll. Healthcare Charity, 2013–. *Recreations:* tennis, opera, art, walking, croquet. *Address:* 50 Thurleigh Road, SW12 8UD. *Clubs:* Hurlingham; Wimbledon Tennis.

**CRELLIN, Adrian Mark,** CBE 2019; FRCR, FRCP; Consultant Clinical Oncologist, St James's University Hospital, Leeds, since 1990; National Clinical Lead for Proton Beam Therapy programme, Department of Health and Social Care (formerly Department of Health) and NHS England, since 2012; *b* London, 11 Nov. 1954; *s* of Vivian Henry Crellin and Eileen Maud Crellin; *m* 1981, Dr Sarah Anne Humphreys; one *s* one *d*. *Educ:* Hitchin Grammar Sch.; Christ's Coll., Cambridge (MB 1979, BChir 1980; MA); St Bartholomew's Hosp. Med. Sch. FRCR 1988; FRCP 1997. Hse Officer and SHO, 1980–85; Registrar and Sen. Registrar, Middx Hosp. and Mt Vernon Hosp., 1985–90. Chair: Proton Nat. Clin. Reference Panel, 2008–; NHS England Radiotherapy Clinical Reference Gp, 2014–; Co-Chair, Nat. Radiotherapy Implementation Gp, 2012–13. Dean, Faculty of Clin. Oncol. and Vice Pres., RCR, 2010–12. Hon. Clinical Associate Prof., Univ. of Leeds, 2017. Member: Council, Bd of Trustees, CRUK, 2012–; Ind. Cancer Taskforce, 2015. *Recreations:* country sports, photography. *Address:* Institute of Oncology, Level 4 Bexley Wing, St James's University Hospital, Beckett Street, Leeds LS9 7TF. *T:* (0113) 206 8602. *E:* adrian.crellin@nhs.net.

**CREMONA, Hon. John Joseph;** Judge, 1965–92, Vice-President, 1986–92, European Court of Human Rights; Judge, 1985–92, Vice-President, 1987–92, European Tribunal in matters of State immunity; Emeritus Professor, University of Malta, since 1965; Chief Justice of Malta and President of the Constitutional Court, Court of Appeal and Court of Criminal Appeal, 1971–81; *b* 6 Jan. 1918; *s* of late Dr Antonio Cremona, KM, MD and Anne (*née* Camilleri); *m* 1949, Marchioness Beatrice Barbaro of St George (*d* 2001); one *s* two *d*. *Educ:* Malta Univ. (BA 1936, LLD *cum laude* 1942); Rome Univ. (DLitt 1939); London Univ. (BA 1st Cl. Hons 1946, PhD in Laws 1951). DJur Trieste, 1972. Crown Counsel, 1947; Lectr in Constitutional Law, Malta Univ., 1947–65, Prof. of Criminal Law, 1959–65; Attorney-Gen., 1957–64 (drafted Malta's Constitution); Vice-Pres., Constitutional Court and Court of Appeal, 1965–71; sometime Actg Governor General and Actg Pres., Republic of Malta. Chm., UN Cttee on Elimination of Racial Discrimination (CERD), 1986–88 (Mem., 1984–88). Chairman: Human Rights Section, World Assoc. of Lawyers; Planning Council, Foundn for Internat. Studies, Malta Univ.; Malta Human Rights Assoc.; Vice-Pres., Internat. Inst. of Studies, Documentation and Info. for the Protection of Envmt, Italy; Member: Cttee of Experts on Human Rights and Cttee of Experts on State immunity, Council of Europe, Strasbourg; Inst Internat. de Droits de l'Homme, Strasbourg; Scientific Council, Revue des Droits de l'Homme, Paris; Scientific Council, Centro Internazionale per la Protezione dei Diritti dell'Uomo, Pesaro, Italy; Scientific Council, Faculty of Law, Université de Saint Esprit, Lebanon; Editorial Adv. Board: Checklist of Human Rights Documents, NY; Rivista Internazionale dei diritti dell'Uomo, Milan; delegate and rapporteur, internat. confs. FRHistS; Fellow *ex titulo*, Internat. Acad. of Legal Medicine and Social Medicine; Hon. Fellow, LSE; Hon. Mem., Real Acad. de Jurisprudencia y Legislación, Madrid. Academic Excellence Award, Faculty of Law, Malta Univ., 2013. KStJ 1984 (Chm., St John Council, Malta, 1983–2014). KSG 1972. Kt, 1966, Commendatore al Merito Melitense, 2004, Sovereign Military Order of Malta; Companion, Order of Merit (Malta), 1994. Kt Comdr, 1968, Grand Officier, 1989, Kt Grand Cross, 1995, Order of Merit (Italy); Kt Comdr, 1971, Grand Cross of Merit, 1981, Constantinian Order of St George; Chevalier de la Légion d'Honneur (France), 1990. *Publications:* The Treatment of Young Offenders in Malta, 1956; The Malta Constitution of 1835, 1959; The Doctrine of Entrapment in Theft, 1959; The Legal Consequences of a Conviction, 1962; The Constitutional Development of Malta, 1963; From the Declaration of Rights to Independence, 1965; Human Rights Documentation in Malta, 1966; Selected Papers 1946–1989, 1990, vol. II, 1990–2000, 2002; The Maltese Constitution and Constitutional History, 1994; Malta and Britain: the early constitutions, 1996; six poetry books; articles in French, German, Italian, Portuguese and American law jls. *Recreation:* gardening. *Address:* Villa Barbaro, Zejtun Road, Tarxien, Malta. *T:* 21826414.

**CRERAR, Prof. Lorne Donald,** CBE 2019; Founding Partner and Chairman, Harper Macleod LLP, since 1987; Professor of Banking Law, University of Glasgow, 1997–2017, now Emeritus; *b* Renfrew, 29 July 1954; *s* of Ronald Crerar and Isobel Scott (*née* Pollock); *m* 2013, Taroub Zahran. *Educ:* Kelvinside Acad., Glasgow; Univ. of Glasgow (LLB Hons). NP 1980; FCIBS 1999. Partner, Mackenzie Robertson & Co., 1979–87. Chairman, Discipline for Scottish Rugby Union, 1995–; for European Rugby Cup Ltd, 1999–2018; for 6 Nations Ltd, 1999–2018; Judicial Officer, Internat. Rugby Bd, 1995–2018. Dep. Chm., Scottish Enterprise Glasgow, 2000–03; Chairman: Sub-Gp, Housing Improvement Task Force, 2001–03; Ind. Review of Audit, Inspection, Regulation and Complaints Handling in the Public Sector (Crerar Review), 2006–08; Highlands and Islands Enterprise, 2011– (Mem. Bd, 2007–11); Highlands and Islands Audit Cttee, 2011–12; Convener, Standards Commn for Scotland, 2003–07; non-exec. Dir, Scottish Govt Justice Dept, 2004–11; Mem., Scottish Strategic Bd for Economy, 2016–; Ind. Mem., Purchasers Information Adv. Gp, 2005–08; Ind. Reviewer, Lending Code, 2010–11. Mem., Adv. Bd, Scottish Investment Bank, 2011–. Lifetime Achievement Award, Scottish Legal Awards, 2019. *Publications:* The Law of Banking in Scotland, 1999, 2nd edn 2007; (contrib.) Stair Memorial Encyclopaedia, 2000. *Recreations:* West Highlands of Scotland and its history, hillwalking, fishing, sailing. *Address:* Harper Macleod LLP, Ca'd'oro Building, 45 Gordon Street, Glasgow G1 3PE. *T:* (0141) 227 9377. *E:* lorne.crerar@harpermacleod.co.uk; Tigh-na-mara, Fasaich, Lonemore, Gairloch, Wester Ross IV21 2DB.

**CRESSON, Edith;** Commandeur du Mérite Agricole, 1983; Chevalier de la Légion d'Honneur; Grand Croix de l'Ordre National du Mérite, 1991; Member, European Commission, 1995–99; *b* 27 Jan. 1934; *née* Campion; *m* Jacques Cresson (*d* 2001); two *d*. *Educ:* Diplômée de l'Ecole des Hautes Etudes Commerciales; Dr en démographie (doctoral thesis: the life of women in a rural district of Guéméné-Penfao, Loire-Atlantique). Mem., Convention des Institutions Républicaines (responsible for agricl problems), 1966; Dir of Studies, Bureau des Etudes Economiques privés (dealing especially with industrial investment); National Secretary, Parti Socialiste (in charge of youth organisation), 1974; Mem. Directing Cttee, Parti Socialiste; contested (for Parti Socialiste) Châtellerault, 1975; Mem., Eur. Parlt, 1979–81 (Mem., Cttee on Agriculture); elected Deputy, Vienne, 1981–93; Minister: of Agriculture, France, 1981–83; of For. Trade and Tourism, 1983–84; for Industrial Redeployment and Foreign Trade, 1984–86; for European Affairs, 1988–90; Pres.-Dir Gen., Schneider Industries Services Internat., 1990–91; Prime Minister of France, 1991–92; Pres. Dir Gen., Services Industries Strategies Internat. et Envmt, 1993–94. Consultant, Agence pour le Développement de l'Innovation et de la Technologie, 2008–. President: Inst d'Etudes Européennes de Paris 8, 2000–; Fondation des Ecoles de la Deuxième Chance, 2002–; Commission Scientifique de la Fondation France Israël, 2007–. Pres., Assoc. Démocratique des Français à l'Etranger, 1986–91. Member, Conseil Général of Vienne, 1978–98; Mayor of Châtellerault, Vienne, 1983–97 (Dep. Mayor, 1997–2008). Dr *hc* Weizmann Inst., Israel, 1999; DUniv Open, 1999. *Publications:* Avec le soleil, 1976; Innover ou subir, 1998; Histoires Françaises, 2007.

**CRESSWELL, John Harold;** Chief Executive Officer, Bibby Line Group Ltd, since 2018. *Educ:* Peter Symonds Sch., Winchester; Univ. of Keele (BA Hons Econs and Pols 1983). Practice Dept, KPMG, 1983–87; Gp Financial Accountant, latterly Financial Controller, TVS, 1987–92; United Broadcasting and Entertainment Ltd: Financial Dir, Meridian Broadcasting, 1992–95; Financial Dir, 1996–98; Chief Op. Officer, 1998–2000; Granada Content: Dir of Ops, 2000–01; Chief Op. Officer, 2001–05; ITV plc: Chief Op. Officer, 2005–06, 2007–10; Interim CEO, 2006–07, 2010; Finance Dir, 2006–08; CEO, Arqiva, 2011–15. Non-executive Director: Liverpool FC and Athletics Ground plc, 2003–07; Ambassador Theatre Gp, 2004–06; Capita plc, 2015–. *Recreations:* tennis, sport, family.

**CRESSWELL, Michael John,** CBE 2010; PhD; Director General, Assessment and Qualifications Alliance, 2003–10; consultant in educational assessment, since 2010; *b* 11 Dec. 1950; *s* of Sidney Walter Cresswell and Marjorie Mary Cresswell; *m* 1980, Lowena Orchard; one *s* one *d*. *Educ:* Chelsea Coll., London (BSc 1972; PGCE 1973); Inst. of Educn, London (PhD 1997). Various res. posts, NFER, 1973–80; Res. Officer, then Hd of Res., Associated Examining Bd, 1980–2000; Assessment and Qualifications Alliance: Hd of Res., 2000–02; Dir of Exams, 2002–03. Special Advr, Select Cttee on Educn, 2011–12. Visiting Professor of Educn, Inst. of Educn, London, 2000–09; Bristol Univ., 2010–13. Member, Board: TDA, 2010–12; Ofqual, 2013–19. *Publications:* (with D. Vincent) Reading Tests in the Classroom, 1976; (with J. Gubb) The Second International Mathematics Study in England and Wales, 1987; (with F. Good) Grading the GCSE, 1988; Research Studies in Public Examining, 2000; over 50 other articles and papers in learned jls and other pubns. *Recreations:* birding, philosophy, theatre, music, board and computer games.

**CRESSWELL, Prof. Peter,** PhD; FRS 2000; Eugene Higgins Professor of Immunobiology, Yale University, since 2009 (Professor of Immunobiology, 1991; Investigator at Howard Hughes Medical Institute, 1991–2016); *b* 6 March 1945; *s* of Maurice and Mary Cresswell; *m* 1969, Ann K. Cooney (*d* 2014); two *s*. *Educ:* Univ. of Newcastle upon Tyne (BSc, MSc); Guy's Hosp. Med. Sch., Univ. of London (PhD 1971). Post-doctoral Fellow, Harvard Univ., 1971–73; Duke University: Asst Prof., 1973–78; Associate Prof., 1978–85; Prof., 1985–91. Member: NAS, 2001; US Nat. Acad. of Medicine, 2010; Fellow, Amer. Acad. of Arts and Scis, 2010. Buchanan Medal, Royal Soc., 2010. *Address:* Department of Immunobiology, Yale University School of Medicine, PO Box 208011, New Haven, CT 06520–8011, USA. *T:* (203) 7855176.

**CRESSWELL, Hon. Sir Peter (John),** Kt 1991; a Judge of the High Court of Justice, Queen's Bench Division, 1991–2008; arbitrator and mediator, since 2008; Supplementary Judge, Qatar International Court, since 2012; *b* 24 April 1944; *s* of late Jack Joseph Cresswell and Madeleine Cresswell; *m* 1972, Caroline Ward (*d* 2003); one *s* (and one *s* decd). *Educ:* St John's Sch., Leatherhead; Queens' Coll., Cambridge (MA, LLM). Called to the Bar, Gray's Inn, 1966 (Malcolm Hilbery Award), Bencher, 1989; QC 1983; a Recorder, 1986–91; Nominated Commercial List Judge, 1991–2008 (Judge in Charge, 1993–94). Mem., Senate of Inns of Court and Bar, 1981–84, 1985–86; Chm., Common Law and Commercial Bar Assoc., 1985–87; Mem., 1987–88, Vice Chm., 1989, Chm., 1990, Gen. Council of the Bar. Mem., Civil Justice Council, 1999–2003. Trustee and Mem. Bd, Cystic Fibrosis Trust, 2002–13. Patron, Soc. of Mediators, 2014–; Companion, Acad. of Experts, 2014. Hon. Mem., Canadian Bar Assoc., 1990. DL Hants, 2008. *Publications:* Encyclopaedia of Banking Law, 1982, and subseq. service issues continuing until the present day. *Recreations:* fly-fishing, river management, the Outer Hebrides. *Club:* Flyfishers' (Pres., 2003–05).

**CREW, Sir Edward (Michael),** Kt 2001; QPM 1991; DL; Chairman, Surrey Health NHS Clinical Commissioning Group, 2013–14; *b* 13 Jan. 1946; *s* of Joseph Edwin Crew and Cecilia May Crew (*née* Davis); *m* 1967, Gillian Glover; one *s* one *d*. *Educ:* Haberdashers' Aske's Hatcham Sch. for Boys; Police Staff Coll. Joined Metropolitan Police from Cadet Corps, 1965; Inspector, 1970; Mem., investigation team into breach of security at Buckingham Palace, 1982; Chief Supt, comdg SE London Traffic Div., 1982–84; Asst Chief Constable, 1984–89, Dep. Chief Constable, 1989–93, Kent County Constabulary; rcds, 1988; Chief Constable: Northants, 1993–96; W Midlands Police, 1996–2002. Advr to Ind. Rev. of Police Service Pay and Conditions, 2011. DL West Midlands, 1999. CCMI 2001. Hon. LLD Birmingham, 2001. OStJ 1989. *Recreations:* good food, walking, gardening, travel.

**CREWE, Sir Ivor (Martin),** Kt 2006; DL; Master, University College, Oxford, 2008–Aug. 2020; *b* 15 Dec. 1945; *s* of Francis and Lilly Crewe; *m* 1968, Jill Barbara (*née* Gadian); two *s* one *d*. *Educ:* Manchester Grammar Sch.; Exeter Coll., Oxford (MA; Hon. Fellow, 1998); London School of Economics (MScEcon). Assistant Lecturer, Univ. of Lancaster, 1967–69; Junior Research Fellow, Nuffield Coll., Oxford, 1969–71; Lectr, Dept of Govt, Univ. of Essex, 1971–74; Dir SSRC Data Archive, 1974–82; University of Essex: Prof. of Govt, 1982–2007; Pro-Vice-Chancellor (Academic), 1992–95; Vice-Chancellor, 1995–2007; Res. Prof., 2007–09; Vis. Prof., 2009–. Member: Exec. Cttee and UK Council, UUK, 2000–07 (Chm., England and NI Bd, 2001–03; Pres., 2003–05); Bd, Univ. and Colls Employers Assoc., 2001–07; Bd, Leadership Foundn, 2003–09; Adv. Bd, Office of Fair Access, 2013–18; Governing Body: SOAS, 2007–15; Univ. of the Arts, London, 2008–15; Ind. Panel, Govt Rev. of Post-18 Educn and Funding, 2018–19; Trustee, Higher Educn Policy Inst., 2007– (Chair, 2015–). Pres., Acad. of Social Scis, 2014–Jan. 2020. Member: High Council, Eur. Univ. Inst., Florence, 1998–; Internat. Adv. Bd, Freie Universität Berlin, 2008–. Dir, USS Ltd, 2006–07. Co-Dir, Feb. 1974, Oct. 1974, 1979 British Election Studies; elections analyst for: BBC TV, 1982–89; The Times, 1990–92; BBC World TV, 1997, 2001, 2005. High Steward, Colchester, 2003–09. Editor, 1977–82, Co-editor, 1984–92, British Journal of Political Science. DL Essex, 2002. Hon. Fellow, Nuffield

Coll., Oxford, 2008. Hon. DLitt Salford, 1999; DUniv Essex, 2009. *Publications:* (with A. H. Halsey) Social Survey of the Civil Service (HMSO), 1969; ed, British Political Sociology Yearbook, vol. 1 1974, vol. 2 1975; (with Bo Sarlvik) Decade of Dealignment, 1983; (with Anthony Fox) British Parliamentary Constituencies, 1984; (ed jtly) Electoral Change in Western Democracies, 1985; (ed jtly) Political Communications: the general election campaign of 1983, 1986, of 1987, 1989, of 1992, 1995, of 1997, 1998; (with Anthony Fox and Neil Day) The British Electorate 1963–87, 1991, 2nd edn as The British Electorate 1963–92, 1992; (with Anthony King) SDP: the birth, life and death of the Social Democratic Party, 1995; (jtly) The New British Politics, 1998, 3rd edn 2004; (with Anthony King) The Blunders of Our Governments, 2013; (with David Sanders) Liberal Democracy and Authoritarian Populism, 2019; articles in various academic jls on public opinion, parties and elections in Britain. *Recreations:* music, mountain walking, ski-ing, friends, family. *Address:* University College, Oxford OX1 4BH.

**CREWE, Susan Anne;** Editor, House and Garden, 1994–2014; *b* 31 Aug. 1949; *d* of late Richard Cavendish and Pamela Cavendish; *m* 1st, 1970, Quentin Crewe (marr. diss.; he *d* 1998); one *s* one *d*; 2nd, 1984, (Christopher) Nigel (John) Ryan, CBE (marr. diss.; he *d* 2014). *Educ:* St Mary's Sch., Wantage; Cheshire Coll. of Agriculture. Harpers & Queen magazine, 1986–92: shopping editor, 1987; consultant editor, 1990; social editor, 1991–92; subseq. freelance writer, broadcaster, journalist; contribs to The Times, Daily Telegraph, Daily Mail, Evening Standard and Literary Review. *Recreations:* gardening, sea-swimming, music. *Address:* Ladysyke House, Haverthwaite, Ulverston, Cumbria LA12 8PQ. *Club:* Academy.
*See also Baron Cavendish of Furness.*

**CRIBB, Derek Wayne,** FCA; FRSM; Chief Executive, Institute and Faculty of Actuaries, since 2011; *b* Swansea, 5 July 1966; *s* of Albert John Cribb and Rita Cribb; *m* 1993, Tessa Julie Stone; one *s* one *d*. *Educ:* Ringwood Comp.; Canford Sch.; Imperial Coll. London (BSc Hons Chem.). ACA 1992, FCA 2012. Audit Manager, Touche Ross & Co., 1989–93; Internal Audit, Saudi Internat. Bank, 1993–94; Projects, Central Transport Rental Gp, 1994–96; Business Support Manager, EMI Records, 1996–97; Gp Hd of Corporate Planning and Investor Relns, Booker plc, 1997–2000; Consultant, Cisco Systems Europe, 2000–01; Chief Financial Officer, Customers and Products, Barclays plc, 2001–04; Gp Finance Consultant, Serco plc, 2004–05; Chief Financial Officer, Public Sector, Liberata plc, 2005; Finance and Ops Dir, Navigant Consulting Europe, 2006–07; Chief Operating Officer, Pension Protection Fund, 2007–09. Trustee, Hockering Residents' Assoc., 2011–. FRSocMed 2012. *Recreations:* good food, good wine, bad golf. *Address:* Institute and Faculty of Actuaries, 7th Floor, Holborn Gate, 326–330 High Holborn, WC1V 7PP. *T:* (020) 7632 2190. *E:* derek.cribb@actuaries.org.uk. *Club:* Wisley Golf.

**CRIBB, Joseph Edmond;** Keeper of Coins and Medals, British Museum, 2003–10; *b* 30 Oct. 1947; *s* of Peter William Cribb and Rewa Annie Cribb (*née* Bloor); *m* 1971, Margaret Morrison Moore (*d* 2013); two *s* two *d*; partner, Linda Crook. *Educ:* Queen Mary Coll., London (BA Hons Latin). British Museum: Curator of Asian coins, Dept of Coins and Medals, 1970–2003; Curator, HSBC Money Gall., 1997. Hon. Sec., 1983–94, Pres., 2004–09, RNS; Sec. Gen., Oriental Numismatic Soc., 2011–18. Trustee: Ditchling Mus., 2000–16; Living Archive, Milton Keynes, 2014–16; Milton Keynes Mus., 2015–16; Ancient India and Iran Trust, 2016–. Hon. Res. Associate, Ashmolean Mus., Oxford, 2011–. Hirayama Inst. of Silk Road Studies (Kamakura) Award, 1997; Silver Medal, RNS, 1999; Archer M. Huntington Medal, Amer. Numismatic Soc., 2009; Nelson Wright Medal, Indian Numismatic Soc., 2010. *Publications:* Money, from Cowrie Shells to Credit Cards, 1986; Money Fun Book, 1986; Money in the Bank, 1987; The Coin Atlas, 1990, 2nd edn 2003; Eyewitness Guide: Money, 1990, 2nd edn 1999; Collected Papers of Nicholas Lowick, vol. I, 1990, vol. II, 1991; Crossroads of Asia, 1992; A Catalogue of Sycee in the British Museum, Chinese Silver Currency Ingots *c.*1750–1933, 1992; Studies in Silk Road Coins and Culture, 1997; Magic Coins of Java, Bali and the Malay Peninsula, 1999; The Order of Industrial Heroism - Eric Gill's Medal for the Daily Herald, 2000; The Chand Collection - Ancient Indian Coins, 2003; The Indian Coinage Tradition, 2005; After Alexander: Central Asia before Islam, 2007; Eric Gill and Ditchling: the workshop tradition, 2007; Coins from Kashmir Smast, 2008; Eric Gill: lust for letter and line, 2011; Kushan, Kushano-Sasanian and Kidarite Coins from the Collection of the American Numismatic Society, 2015. *Recreations:* history of the Guild of St Joseph and St Dominic, Ditchling, numismatic research, grandchildren. *E:* joecribb@btinternet.com.
*See also P. J. W. Cribb.*

**CRIBB, Phillip James William,** PhD; botanist; Deputy Keeper of Herbarium, 1989–2006, Hon. Research Fellow, since 2006, Royal Botanic Gardens, Kew; *b* 12 March 1946; *s* of Peter William Cribb and Rewa Annie, (Nancy), Cribb (*née* Bloor); *m* 1984, Marianne Gafafer. *Educ:* Christ's Coll., Cambridge (BA 1968); Univ. of Birmingham (PhD 1972). Joined Royal Botanic Gardens, Kew, as Higher Scientific Officer, 1974. Hon. Research Associate: Harvard Univ., 1979–90; Royal Holloway and Bedford New Coll., Univ. of London, 2006–. Trustee: Gilbert White & Oates Mus., Selborne, 1993–2006; Jany Renz Foundn, Univ. of Basel, 2003–. Pres., Ray Soc., 2016–. Veitch Meml Medal, RHS, 2006; Linnean Medal for Botany, 2007. *Publications:* The Genus Paphiopedilum, 1987; The Genus Cypripedium, 1997; (jtly) Slipper Orchids of Vietnam, 2003; (with M. Tibbs) A Very Victorian Passion, 2004; (with C. Grey-Wilson) Guide to the Flowers of Western China, 2011; (contrib. and ed jtly) Genera Orchidacearum, 6 Vols, 1999–2014; (with Werner Frosch) Hardy Cypripedium, 2012. *Recreations:* natural history, travel. *Address:* The Herbarium, Royal Botanic Gardens, Kew, Richmond, Surrey TW9 3AE. *Fax:* (020) 8332 5278. *E:* p.cribb@kew.org.
*See also J. E. Cribb.*

**CRICH, Michael Arthur,** FCMA; independent consultant, since 2016; Corporate Director, Economy, Enterprise and Environment, Cornwall Council, 2014–16 (Corporate Director, Resources, 2010–14, Environment, Planning and Economy, 2013); *b* 9 Jan. 1957; *s* of Arthur Crich and Elizabeth Crich; *m* 1980, Gillian Anne Chamberlain; three *s* one *d*. *Educ:* Slough Grammar Sch.; Univ. of Hull; Emile Woolf Coll.; Warwick Business Sch., Univ. of Warwick (MBA 2002). FCMA 1991; CGMA. Financial Controller, Wendy Restaurants (UK) Ltd, 1981–84; Sketchley Dry Cleaning: Finance Manager, 1984–86; Financial Controller, 1986–87; Financial Dir, 1987–91; London Borough of Brent: Gen. Manager, Contract Services, 1992–93; Dir, Brent Business Support, 1993–96; Exec. Dir, Finance and Corporate Services, London Borough of Lambeth, 1996–2001; Dir of Resources, English Heritage, 2002–07; Corporate Dir, Resources, Advantage W Midlands, 2008–09; Dir, Michael Crich Associates Ltd, 2009–10. *Publications:* (contrib.) Local Government Governance, 2001. *Recreations:* food and wine, live music, motor racing, le parkour. *Address:* 17 Chessel Avenue, Bournemouth, Dorset BH5 1LQ.

**CRICHTON,** family name of **Earl of Erne**.

**CRICHTON-STUART,** family name of **Marquess of Bute**.

**CRICK, Michael Lawrence;** broadcaster and writer; Political Correspondent, Channel 4 News, 2011–19; *b* 21 May 1958; *s* of John Fairhurst Crick and late Patricia Margaret Crick (*née* Wright); *m* 1985, Beatrice Margaret Sarah Hounsell (marr. diss. 2008); one *d*; partner, Lucy Katharine Anna Hetherington; one *d*. *Educ:* Manchester Grammar Sch. (Foundn Schol.); New Coll., Oxford (BA 1st Cl. Hons PPE 1979). Pres., Oxford Union, 1979. Trainee journalist, ITN, 1980–82; Channel 4 News: producer, 1982–84; reporter, 1984–88; Washington Corresp., 1988–90; BBC: reporter, Panorama, 1990–92; reporter, 1992–2007, Political Editor, 2007–11, Newsnight. Chm., Young Fabian Gp, 1980–81. Organiser, Shareholders United, 1998–99 (Vice-Chm., 1999–2001). Associate Mem., Nuffield Coll., Oxford, 2015–. Lay Gov., Univ. of Manchester, 2012–; Bd Mem., Manchester University Press, 2013–. Mem., Manchester United Fans' Forum, 2000–02. Specialist Journalist of the Year Award, RTS, 2014, 2018; Journalist of the Year, Political Studies Assoc., 2014; Charles Wheeler Award for Broadcast Journalism, British Journalism Rev., 2018. *Publications:* (Founder Ed.) Oxford Handbook, 1978; (Founder Ed.) Oxbridge Careers Handbook, 1979; Militant, 1984; Scargill and the Miners, 1985; (with D. Smith) Manchester United: the betrayal of a legend, 1989; Jeffrey Archer: stranger than fiction, 1995; The Complete Manchester United Trivia Factbook, 1996; Michael Heseltine: a biography, 1997; The Boss: the many sides of Alex Ferguson, 2002; In Search of Michael Howard, 2005; Sultan of Swing: the life of David Butler, 2018. *Recreations:* following Manchester United, swimming, hill-walking, theatre, collecting political and football books and memorabilia. *Address:* 1 Sumburgh Road, SW12 8AJ. *E:* CrickML@aol.com. *W:* www.twitter.com/MichaelLCrick.

**CRICK, Prof. Thomas,** MBE 2017; PhD; Professor of Digital Education and Policy, Swansea University, since 2018; *b* Oxford, 8 Jan. 1981; *s* of Hedley Neil Crick and Judy Jean Marion Crick; *m* 2016, Dominique Kia Haynes; two *s*. *Educ:* Univ. of Bath (BSc Hons Computer Sci. 2004; PhD Computer Sci. 2009). CEng 2015; CSci 2015. Lectr in Computing, 2009–11, Sen. Lectr in Computing, 2011–15, Prof. of Computer Sci. and Public Policy, 2016–18, Cardiff Metropolitan Univ. Non-executive Director: Dŵr Cymru (Welsh Water), 2017–; Swansea Bay Univ. Health Bd, 2017–. Comr, Nat. Infrastructure Commn for Wales, 2018–. Liveryman, Livery Co. of Wales, 2014–. *Recreations:* cycling, Rugby, karate (full blue, Univ. of Bath, 2009). *E:* tcrick@bcs.org.uk. *W:* www.proftomcrick.com.

**CRICKMAY, Anthony John;** photographer, since 1961; *b* 20 May 1937; *s* of Jack and Peggy Crickmay. *Educ:* Belmont Sch., Dorking. Photographer, specialising in theatre, portraits, fashion, reportage; work has appeared in many publications throughout the world; has photographed personalities and stars incl. the Queen, the Queen Mother, the Prime Minister and family, etc. Solo exhibn, 60 Years of Photography, V&A, 2018. *Publications:* The Principles of Classical Dance, 1979; Lynn Seymour, 1980; Dancers, 1982. *Recreations:* swimming, but most of all, photography. *Address:* c/o Camera Press, 21 Queen Elizabeth Street, SE1 2PD. *T:* (020) 7378 1300.

**CRIDLAND, John Robert,** CBE 2006; Chairman: Transport for the North, since 2015; Home Group, since 2018; *b* 3 Feb. 1961; *s* of Walter and Doreen Cridland; *m* 1987, Denise Yates; one *s* one *d*. *Educ:* Christ's Coll., Cambridge (MA). Confederation of British Industry, 1982–2015: Director: Envmtl Affairs, 1991–95; Human Resources Policy, 1995–2000; Dep. Dir-Gen., 2000–11; Dir-Gen., 2011–15. Member: Low Pay Commn, 1997–2007; UK Commn for Employment and Skills, 2011–15; Bd, Ofsted, 2016–; Vice Chair, LSC, 2007–10; Councillor, ACAS, 1998–2007; Dir, Business in the Community, 2011–15. Ind. Reviewer, State Pension Age, 2016–17. Vis. Prof., UCL, 2015–. Mem. Council, Cranfield Univ., 2008–14; Pro-Chancellor, Brunel Univ., 2017–. Trustee, Comino Foundn, 2015–. *Recreations:* history, cinema, castles. *Address:* Transport for the North, 2nd Floor, 4 Piccadilly Place, Manchester M1 3BN.

**CRIGMAN, David Ian;** QC 1989; *b* 16 Aug. 1945; *s* of late Jack Crigman and of Sylvia Crigman; *m* 1980, Judith Ann Penny; one *s*. *Educ:* King Edward's Sch., Birmingham; Univ. of Leeds (LLB Hons). Called to the Bar, Gray's Inn, 1969; a Recorder, 1985. *Publications: novels:* What's Truth Got To Do With It?, 2006; The Molecule Man, 2008; In Death We Trust, 2009; The Hangman's Fracture, 2011. *Recreations:* tennis, ski-ing, writing, travel. *Address:* St Philips Chambers, 55 Temple Row, Birmingham B2 5LS. *T:* (0121) 246 7000.

**CRINE, Simon John Geoffrey;** Chief Operating Officer, Economic and Social Research Council, UK Research and Innovation, since 2018; *b* Weston-super-Mare, 30 Nov. 1955; *s* of Geoffrey V. Crine and Ruby E. Crine; *m* Alison Blom-Cooper; one *s* one *d*. *Educ:* Weston-super-Mare Grammar Sch.; Univ. of York (BA Hons Hist.). Various political and public policy appts, 1979–84; Dir, Nat. Campaign for the Arts, 1985–90; Gen. Sec., Fabian Soc., 1990–96; Dir, Public Affairs, APCO UK, 1997–2004; Dir, England and Industry, Ofcom, 2004–06; Dir of Corporate Affairs, Digital UK, 2006–12; Sen. Advr, UK Statistics Authy, 2013–17; Dir of Communications, Ofgem, 2014–17; Interim Dir, Money and Mental Health Policy Inst., 2017–18. Trustee, Money Advice Trust, 2013–. Mem., Adv. Bd, Social Market Foundn, 2000–09. Harkness Fellow, Washington, DC, 1993–94. *Publications:* various Fabian, WEA and Low Pay Unit reports; occasional journalism. *Recreation:* reading the papers - when not thinking about Vicarage Road and ball games. *T:* 07711 066378. *E:* simonjgcrine@gmail.com.

**CRIPPS,** family name of **Baron Parmoor**.

**CRIPPS, Prof. Martin William,** PhD; FBA 2011; Professor of Economics, University College London, since 2006; *b* London, 25 April 1960; *s* of Leonard Albert Cripps and Shirley Anne Cripps; *m* 1989, Louise Pincombe; two *s* two *d*. *Educ:* London Sch. of Econs and Pol Sci. (BSc Econs; MSc Econs; PhD Econs). Lectr, 1987–97, Prof. of Econs, 1997–2000, Univ. of Warwick; Wallace Dist. Prof. of Econs, Washington Univ., St Louis, 2000–06. Mem. Council, Game Theory Soc., 2007. Fellow, Econometric Soc., 2008. *Recreations:* squash, cycling, walking. *Address:* Department of Economics, University College London, Gower Street, WC1E 6BT. *E:* m.cripps@ucl.ac.uk.

**CRIPWELL, Lt Gen. Richard John,** CB 2016; CBE 2013; Deputy Commander, NATO Allied Land Command, Izmir, since 2019; *b* Newry, NI, 1962; *s* of John Cripwell and Ann Cripwell; *m* 1996, Louise Van Heyningen; one *s* one *d*. *Educ:* St Conleth's Coll., Dublin; Welbeck Coll.; RMA Sandhurst; Cranfield Univ. (BEng, MSc). Commnd Corps of RE, 1982; CO 26 Engr Regt, 2002–04; Comdr Engrs ARRC, 2008–10; Comdr British Forces Cyprus, 2013–14; Defence Attaché, Washington, 2015–17; Dep. Comdr, Resolute Support, Afghanistan, 2017–18. FRGS. *Recreations:* ballet, theatre, cricket, baseball, ceramics. *Address:* c/o Institution of Royal Engineers, Ravelin Building, Chatham, Kent ME4 4GU. *Club:* Naval and Military.

**CRISHAM, Catherine Ann;** lawyer, Treasury Solicitor's Department, 2003–07; *b* 29 April 1950; *d* of Air Vice-Marshal William Joseph Crisham, CB, CBE and Maureen Theresa Crisham (*née* Bergin). *Educ:* St Anne's Coll., Oxford (BA); Exeter Univ. (LLM). Lecturer in European Community Law: Leiden Univ., 1977–80; London Univ., 1980–82; called to the Bar, Gray's Inn, 1981; private practice, 1982–84; lawyer, MAFF, 1984–88 and 1991–94; Legal Sec., European Court of Justice, 1988–90; Dep. Hd, Legal Directorate, MAFF, subseq. DEFRA, 1994–2003. *Recreations:* classical studies, theatre, walking.

**CRISP,** family name of **Baron Crisp**.

**CRISP**, Baron *cr* 2006 (Life Peer), of Eaglescliffe in the County of Durham; **Edmund Nigel Ramsay Crisp**, KCB 2003; author on global health and international development; *b* 8 Jan. 1952; *s* of late Edmund Theodore Crisp and Dorothy Sheppard Crisp (*née* Ramsay); *m* 1976, Siân Elaine Jenkins; one *s* one *d*. *Educ*: Uppingham Sch.; St John's Coll., Cambridge (BA Hons 1973; MA 1976; Hon. Fellow 2008). Dep. Dir, Halewood Community Council, 1973; Production Manager, Trebor, 1978; Dir, Cambs Community Council, 1981; Unit Gen. Manager, E Berks HA, 1986; Chief Executive: Heatherwood and Wexham Park Hosps, 1988; Oxford Radcliffe Hosp. NHS Trust, 1993–97; Regl Dir, S Thames, 1997–98, London, 1999–2000, NHS Exec., DoH; Permanent Sec. and Chief Exec., DoH and NHS, 2000–06. Co-Chm., All Party Parly Global Health, 2011–. Hon. Prof., LSHTM, 2007–; Sen. Fellow, Inst. of Healthcare Improvement, Cambridge, Mass, 2007–; Dist. Vis. Fellow, Harvard Sch. of Public Health, 2010–15; Regents' Lectr, Univ. of Calif, Berkeley, 2014. Chairman: Sightsavers Internat., 2008–15; Nursing Now, 2018–; Mem. Council, BHF, 2008–10. Advr, HLM Architects, 2007–15. Trustee: Florence Nightingale Mus., 2007–10; Rand Europe, 2008–15. Co-Chair: Zambia UK Health Alliance, 2009–; Uganda UK Health Alliance, 2013–15. For. Associate, Nat. Acad. of Medicine (formerly Inst. of Medicine), USA, 2012. CCMI 2002; Companion, Inst. of Healthcare Mgt, 2003. FRSA 2015. Hon. FRCP, 2020; Hon. FRCPath 2010; Hon. FRCOG 2011; Hon. FRCPsych 2016; Hon. FFPH 2016. Hon. DSc City, 2001. *Publications*: Global Health Partnerships, 2007; Scaling Up, Saving Lives, 2008; Turning the World Upside Down: the search for global health in the 21st century, 2010; 24 Hours to Save the NHS: the Chief Executive's account of reform 2000 to 2006, 2011; (ed with Francis Omaswa) African Health Leaders: making change and claiming the future, 2014; One World Health: an overview of global health, 2016; articles in various jls incl. Lancet, BMJ and New England Jl of Medicine. *Recreation*: the countryside. *Address*: House of Lords, SW1A 0PW. *Club*: Reform.

**CRISP, Clement Andrew**, OBE 2005; contributor, since 1956, and Dance Critic, since 1970, Financial Times; *b* 21 Sept. 1931; *s* of Charles Evelyn Gifford Crisp and Bertha Dorothy (*née* Dean). *Educ*: Oxted Sch.; Bordeaux Univ.; Keble Coll., Oxford Univ. (BA). Critic and dance writer to various jls, 1956–; Ballet Critic, The Spectator, 1966–70. Lectr, Librarian and Archivist to Royal Acad. of Dancing, 1963–85, Archivist, 1985–2001. Associate Prof., Univ. of Notre Dame (London Faculty), 1997–2008. Queen Elizabeth II Coronation Award, Royal Acad. of Dancing, 1992; Vaslav Nijinsky Medal, Poland, 1995. Knight, Order of Dannebrog (Denmark), 1992. *Publications*: (with Peter Brinson) Ballet for All, 1971, rev. edn 1980; with Mary Clarke: Ballet: an illustrated history, 1973, rev. edn 1992; Making a Ballet, 1974; Ballet in Art, 1976; Design for Ballet, 1978; Introducing Ballet, 1978; Ballet-goer's Guide, 1981; History of Dance, 1981; How to Enjoy Ballet, 1983, 2nd edn 1987; Dancer, 1984; Ballerina, 1987; London Contemporary Dance, 1989. *Recreations*: avoiding noise, gardening, despair about dancing. *Address*: 82 Marsham Court, Marsham Street, SW1P 4LA.

**CRISP, Sir John Charles**, 5th Bt *cr* 1913, of Bungay, Suffolk; *b* 10 Dec. 1955; *s* of Sir (John) Peter Crisp, 4th Bt and Judith Mary Crisp (*née* Gillett); *S* father, 2005; *m* 1992, Mary Jo, *e d* of Dr and Mrs D. MacAuley; (one *s* decd). *Educ*: Radley; Birmingham Univ. *Heir*: *b* Michael Peter Crisp [*b* 1957; *m* 1988, Pauline Sarah Gold; two *s*].

**CRISP, June Frances**; *see* de Moller, J. F.

**CRISPIN, Prof. Sheila Margaret**, PhD; FRCVS; independent consultant, since 2010; Visiting Professorial Fellow, University of Bristol, 2004–17; *b* 21 Jan. 1944; *d* of William George Crispin and Winifred Margaret Crispin. *Educ*: Ulverston Grammar Sch.; University Coll. of N Wales (Bangor) (BSc Hons Zool. 1967); Girton Coll., Cambridge (ARC Vet. Trng Schol.; MA, VetMB 1972 (Dist.); Grad. Schol.); Univ. of Edinburgh (PhD 1984). DVA 1976; DVOphthal 1985; DipECVO 1993; FRCVS 1999. In private practice, Cumbria, 1972; Clin. Schol., then Univ. House Surgeon, Univ. of Cambridge, 1972–75; Bye-Fellow and Dir of Studies in Vet. Medicine, Girton Coll., Cambridge, 1974–75; Lectr, Univ. of Edinburgh, 1975–83; University of Bristol: Lectr, 1983–91; Sen. Lectr, 1991–2000; Reader, 2000–02; Prof. of Comparative Ophthalmol., 2002–04; Res. Fellow, 2003–04. Share-Jones Lectr, RCVS, 1991. Bull Fellow, Univ. of Guelph, Canada, 2000. Co-Chm., Quinquennial Sci. Audit, DEFRA Lab. Sci. Agencies, 2005–07; Mem., Sci. Adv. Council, DEFRA, 2005–09. Chief Panellist, BVA/Kennel Club/Internat. Sheep Dog Soc. Eye Scheme, 1992–96, 1998–99, 2008–09, 2016–18. Chm., Dog Welfare Rev. Bd, 2010; Founding Chm., Adv. Council on Welfare Issues of Dog Breeding, 2010–14. Member: Vet. Services Adv. Cttee, BVA, 1995–98; Council, RCVS, 1997–2015 (Univ. Rep., 1997–2003; Chm. of various cttees; Pres., 2006–07); Sci. Adv. Cttee, Animal Health Trust, 1998–; Adv. Gp, Ind. Inquiry into Dog Breeding, 2009–10; Companion Animal Welfare Council, 2009–; Envmtl Ethics Gp, 2018–. Chm., British Assoc. for Vet. Ophthalmol., 1983–86. Trustee, Wildlife Information Network, 2007–09. Affiliate MRCOphth (Associate MRCOphth 1990). Simon Award, 1989, Life Mem., 2014, British Small Animal Vet. Assoc.; Lifetime Achievement Award, British Assoc. of Vet. Ophthalmologists, 2013; J. A. Wight Meml Award, British Small Animal Vet. Assoc., 2015; Lifetime Achievement Award for res. in field of canine health, Kennel Club Charitable Trust, 2015. *Publications*: (ed and contrib. with S. M. Petersen-Jones) Manual of Small Animal Ophthalmology, 1993, 2nd edn 2002; (ed jtly and contrib.) A Colour Atlas and Text of Equine Ophthalmology, 1995, 2nd edn 2004; (ed and contrib. with K. C. Barnett) Feline Ophthalmology: an atlas and text, 1998; Notes on Veterinary Ophthalmology, 2005; contribs mainly in the field of comparative ophthalmology; peer-reviewed papers and book chapters. *Recreations*: sport (Univ. of Wales gold (Captain, athletics and hockey); Univ. of Cambridge blue (Captain, hockey and cricket); Captain, Combined Univs hockey team; Mem., British Univs Sports Fedn hockey team; Wales sen. hockey squad), mountaineering, sailing, classical music, environmental stewardship, moral philosophy. *Address*: Cold Harbour Farm, Underbarrow, Kendal, Cumbria LA8 8HD. *T: and Fax*: (01539) 568637. *E*: sheilacrispin6@gmail.com. *Clubs*: Farmers, Kennel; Pinnacle.

**CRITCHETT, Sir Charles George Montague**, 4th Bt *cr* 1908, of Harley Street, St Marylebone; engineer, W. S. Atkins, since 1998; *b* 2 April 1965; *s* of Sir Ian George Lorraine Critchett, 3rd Bt and of Jocelyn Daphne Margret Critchett (*née* Hall); *S* father, 2004; *m* 2004, Joanna Jane Sugden, *d* of late Dr H. J. S. Sugden and of Mrs Pamela Morrow; two *s*. *Educ*: Harrow; Univ. of Bristol (BEng 1st Cl. Aeronautical Engrg); Wolfson Coll., Cambridge (PGCE Design, Mfr and Mgt). Aerodynamicist and Project Mgr, British Aerospace, 1990–97. *Heir*: *s* Ralph Henry Anderson Critchett, *b* 22 Jan. 2006.

**CRITCHLEY, Philip**, CB 1990; consultant, Martin Jack & Co., 1991–2005; *b* 31 Jan. 1931; *s* of Henry Stephen and Edith Adela Critchley; *m* 1962, Stella Ann Barnes; two *s* one *d*. *Educ*: Manchester Grammar Sch.; Balliol Coll., Oxford (MA, 2nd Classical Mods and Greats). National Service, Intelligence Corps, 1953–55. Joined Min. of Housing and Local Govt, later Dept of Environment, 1955: Principal, 1960; Asst Sec., 1969; Under Sec., 1980; Dir of Waste Disposal, 1983; Dir of Contracts, Highways Administration and Maintenance, 1985–90; Dir of Network Mgt and Maintenance, 1990–91, Dept of Transport. Volunteer, Ulverston Br., MIND, 1996–2013. Mem., Cttee, S Cumbria Mental Health User and Carer Forum, 2004–09; Advr, Cumbria Mental Health Gp, 2009–13. FRSA 1990. *Recreations*: philosophy, writing poetry. *Address*: Singleton Nursing and Residential Home, Hoxton Close, Ashford, Kent TN23 5LB. *T*: ((01233) 632808. *Clubs*: Blackheath Harriers; Oxford Union Society.

**CRITCHLOW, His Honour Christopher Allan**; DL; a Circuit Judge, 2000–16; a Deputy Circuit Judge, since 2016; *b* 8 July 1951; *s* of late Charles Brandon Critchlow and Eileen Margerie (*née* Bowers); *m* 1974, Wendy Anne Lucey; one *s* two *d*. *Educ*: Royal Grammar Sch., Lancaster; Exeter Univ. (LLB). FCIArb 1994. Called to the Bar, Inner Temple, 1973, Bencher, 2003; Mem., Western Circuit; Asst Recorder, 1987–91; a Recorder, 1991–2000; Resident Judge, Guildford Crown Ct, 2008–16. Hon. Recorder of Guildford, 2010–17. Gov., RGS Guildford, 2004– (Vice-Chm., 2013–). DL Surrey, 2009. Pres., Old Lancastrians, 2018–19 (Vice-Pres., 2017–18). *Recreations*: golf, bridge, listening to music, reading history, five grandsons. *Clubs*: Reform; County (Guildford); Clandon Regis Golf.

**CRITCHLOW, Julian Richard**; Director General, Energy Transformation and Clean Growth, Department for Business, Energy and Industrial Strategy, since 2018; *b* Cambridge, 12 Jan. 1965; *s* of Nicholas Critchlow and Elizabeth Critchlow; *m* 1988, Sarah Blackburn; two *s* two *d*. *Educ*: Christ's Coll., Cambridge (BA 1986; MEng Chem. Engrg 1992); Wharton Sch., Univ. of Pennsylvania (MBA). Bain & Co.: Consultant, 1987–95; Mgr, 1995–98; Partner, 1998–2008; Dir, 2008–18. Mem., Channel Swimming and Piloting Fedn (Vice Chm., 2011–15). *Recreations*: English Channel swimming, sailing, Arsenal Football Club, technology. *Address*: Department for Business, Energy and Industrial Strategy, 1 Victoria Street, SW1H 0ET. *E*: julian.critchlow@beis.gov.uk.

**CROALL, Simon Martin**, QC 2008; *b* Bramhall, Cheshire, 12 Feb. 1963; *s* of Alan and Jean Croall; 1st, 1989 (marr. diss. 2010); two *s*; 2nd, 2013, Davina Richardson. *Educ*: Stockport Grammar Sch.; Emmanuel Coll., Cambridge (BA Law 1985; MA). Called to the Bar, Middle Temple, 1986; in practice as barrister, 1986–; Hd, Quadrant Chambers, 2018–. Mem., Professional Conduct and Complaints Cttee, Bar Council of England and Wales, 2001–04. Gov., Stanley Infant Sch., 1997–2001. *Publications*: (contrib.) Butterworth's Commercial Court & Arbitration Pleadings, 2005. *Recreations*: travel, golf, walking, tennis. *Address*: Quadrant Chambers, 10 Fleet Street, EC4Y 1AU. *T*: (020) 7583 4444, *Fax*: (020) 7583 4455. *E*: simon.croall@quadrantchambers.com.

**CROCKARD, Prof. (Hugh) Alan**, DSc; FRCS, FRCP; FDS RCS; National Director for Modernising Medical Careers, Department of Health, 2004–07; Professor of Surgical Neurology, Institute of Neurology, University College London, 2001–06, now Professor Emeritus; Consultant Neurosurgeon, National Hospital for Neurology and Neurosurgery, 1978–2006, now Hon. Consultant; *b* 24 Jan. 1943; *s* of Hugh and Mary Crockard; *m* 1977, Dr Caroline Orr; two *s*. *Educ*: Royal Belfast Academical Instn; Queen's Univ., Belfast (MB BCh, BAO 1966; DSc 2000). FRCSEd 1970; FRCS 1971; FDS RCS 2001; FRCP 2003. Wellcome Surgical Fellow, 1973; Hunterian Prof., RCS, 1974; Fogarty Internat. Fellow, 1974, Asst Prof., 1975, Univ. of Chicago; Sen. Lectr, QUB, 1975–78. Dir, Raven Dept of Educn, RCS, 1998–2003. Vis. Prof. of Surgical Neurology, Univ. of WA, 2000. Co-Founder, Hill Surgical Workshops, 1990. Chm., Global Spinal Tumour Study Gp, 2011–. President: British Cervical Spine Soc., 1997–99 (Co-Founder, 1986); Eur. Cervical Spine Res. Soc., 1999–2001; Member: British Soc. of Neurological Surgeons; Amer. Acad. of Neurological Surgeons. Sinclair Medal for Surgery, QUB, 1966; Olivecrona Lectr, Karolinska Inst., Stockholm, 1995; Harrington Medal, Scoliosis Res. Soc., USA, 1995; Arnott Demonstr, RCS, 1995. *Publications*: (jtly) Trauma Care, 1981; (jtly) Neurosurgery: scientific basis of clinical practice, 1985, 3rd edn 2000; more than 300 papers. *Recreations*: sailing, photography, birdwatching, travel, music. *Address*: Victor Horsley Department of Neurosurgery, National Hospital for Neurology and Neurosurgery, Queen Square, WC1N 3BG. *Clubs*: Athenæum, Royal Ocean Racing; Ocean Cruising.

**CROCKART, Michael**; Transformation Lead, Scottish Government, since 2016; *b* Perth, 19 March 1966; *m*; two *s*. *Educ*: Perth High Sch.; Edinburgh Univ. (BSc Social Scis 1987). Police Constable, Lothians and Borders Police, 1990–98; Standard Life Assurance Co.: systems developer, 1998–2005; Lead Business Service Developer, 2006–07; IT Project Manager, 2007–10. Contested (Lib Dem): Edinburgh N and Leith, 2005; Edinburgh N and Leith, Scottish Parlt, 2007. MP (Lib Dem) Edinburgh W, 2010–15; contested (Lib Dem) same seat, 2015. PPS to Sec. of State for Scotland, 2010. Convenor, Edinburgh W Lib Dems, 2009. Public Affairs Consultant, InsightScotland, 2015–16.

**CROCKER, His Honour John Fraser**; a Circuit Judge, 1995–2010; *b* 27 May 1943; *o s* of late Noel John Fraser Crocker and Marjorie Jean Crocker (*née* Heaton); *m* 1969, Janet Butteriss; one *s* twin *d*. *Educ*: The Leys, Cambridge; Christ's Coll., Cambridge (MA). Admitted Solicitor, 1969; called to the Bar, Inner Temple, 1973; a Recorder, 1991–95. Resident Judge: Isleworth Crown Court, 1999–2003; Guildford Crown Court, 2004–08. *Recreations*: reading thrillers, avoiding gardening.

**CROCKER, Steven James**, OBE 2018; Director, Children's Services, Hampshire County Council and Isle of Wight Council, since 2015; *b* Slough, 25 Dec. 1963; *s* of G. H. J. Crocker and Sylvia Crocker; *m* 2000, Clare Middleton; two *d*. *Educ*: Slough Grammar Sch.; Ruskin Coll., Oxford (CQSW 1991); Open Univ. (BA Hons Politics and Lit. 2000). Social Worker, Oxfordshire and Berkshire, 1989–2000; Manager, Youth Offending Team, Oxfordshire, 2000; Hd, Youth Offending Service, Wessex, 2005; Dep. Dir, Children's Services, Hampshire CC, 2009–15. *Publications*: contrib. to Centre for Social Justice reports. *Recreations*: AFC Wimbledon, birdwatching, modern literature, 1970s punk rock and reggae, running, pretentious European new wave cinema, Italian food and culture, New Order completist.

**CROFT**, family name of **Baron Croft**.

**CROFT**, 3rd Baron *cr* 1940, of Bournemouth, co. Southampton; **Bernard William Henry Page Croft**; Bt 1924; publisher; *b* 28 Aug. 1949; *s* of 2nd Baron Croft and Lady Antoinette Conyngham (*d* 1959), *o d* of 6th Marquess Conyngham; *S* father, 1997; *m* 1993, Elizabeth Mary Richardson, *o d* of late James Richardson, Co. Tyrone. *Educ*: Stowe; UCW, Cardiff (BScEcon). *Recreations*: shooting, fishing, ski-ing. *Address*: Croft Castle, Yarpole, near Leominster, Herefordshire HR6 9PW. *Clubs*: Naval and Military, Hurlingham.

**CROFT, Charles Beresford**, FRCS, FRCSE; Consultant Surgeon, Royal National Throat, Nose and Ear Hospital, and Royal Free Hospital, 1979–2004, now Emeritus; *b* 14 Jan. 1943; *s* of Arthur James Croft and Margaret Bays Croft (later Conyers); *m* 1968, Hilary Louise Whitaker; one *d*. *Educ*: Worksop Coll.; Leeds Univ. Med. Sch. (MB BCh Hons 1965). FRCS 1970; FRCSE 1972; Dip. Amer. Bd Otolaryngology, 1979. House Surg., then Physician, Leeds Gen. Infirmary, 1966–68; Demonstrator in Anatomy, Leeds Med. Sch., 1968–69; Surgical Registrar, 1969–73, Sen. Registrar, Otolaryngology, 1971–73, Leeds Gen. Infirmary; Fellow in Head and Neck Surgery, Albert Einstein Med. Sch., NY, 1973–76; Associate Prof. in Otolaryngology, Albert Einstein Med. Sch. and Montefiore Hosp., NY, 1976–79. Civil Consultant Laryngologist, RAF, 1984–2004; Consultant Otolaryngologist, Metropolitan Police Service, 2004–16. FRSocMed. Arnott Demonstrator and Medal, RCS, 1988. *Publications*: chapters and papers on mgt of head and neck tumours, surgery of sleep breathing disorders and sleep apnoea in textbooks on tumour mgt and otolaryngology. *Recreations:* golf, fly fishing, bridge. *Address:* Westward Barn, Woodcock Hill, Rickmansworth, Herts WD3 1PX. *T:* (01923) 897187. *Clubs:* MCC; Moor Park Golf.

**CROFT, David Michael Bruce;** Founder and Director, Andreas Wine Trading Ltd, since 2015; *b* 2 April 1955; *s* of late Eric David Croft and Catherine Margaret Croft (*née* Kelly); *m* 2001, Angela Jane Murray; two *s. Educ:* Epsom Coll.; Magdalen Coll., Oxford (MA Hons Modern Hist.). Ocean Transport & Trading; NFC; Thames TV; Channel Four TV; Dir, 1998–2009, Man. Dir, 2002–09, Yorkshire TV Ltd; Director: Tyne Tees TV, 1998–2007; Granada TV, 1998–2007; Meridian Broadcasting, 2001–07; Border TV, 2001–07; Anglia TV, 2001–07; Central Independent TV, 2004–07; HTV Gp, 2004–07; Westcountry TV, 2004–07; Dir, Regl Sales, ITV plc, 2009–11; Founder and Man. Partner, David Croft and Associates Ltd, 2011–12. Hon. Consul for S Africa in Yorks, 2006–. *Recreations:* golf, horse-racing, travel, wine. *Address:* Shamrock Cottage, Foxcovert Lane, Lower Peover, Knutsford, Cheshire WA16 9QP. *E:* Dmbcroft@hotmail.com. *Club:* Royal Liverpool Golf.

**CROFT, Giles Laurance;** director and writer; *b* 20 June 1957; *s* of John Rothschild Croft and Myrtle Maud Croft (*née* Geal). *Educ:* Monkton Combe Sch. Artistic Director: Bath Young People's Th. Co., 1978–80; Gate Th., London, 1985–89; Literary Manager, Nat. Th., 1989–95; Artistic Director: Palace Th., Watford, 1995–99; Nottingham Playhouse, 1999–2017. Director of plays including: Hinkemann, 1983; Naomi, 1987; (and adaptor) Kind Hearts and Coronets, 1997; Polygraph, 2001; Rat Pack Confidential, 2002; The Man Who, 2003; The White Album, 2006; Garage Band, 2009; (and adaptor) Forever Young, 2009; Private Lives, 2011; The Kite Runner, 2013, 2016; Any Means Necessary, 2016; Tony's Last Tape, 2016; The Cherry Orchard, 2017; The Rockford File, 2018; adapted: The Ladykillers, 1999; Loving April, 2010; writer (also actor), Channeling Jabez, 2017. Chair, Th. Writing Panel, Arts Council, 2000–03; Vice Pres., Eur. Th. Convention, 2003–12. FRSA 1993. *Recreations:* reading, music, guitar. *Club:* Blacks.

**CROFT, (Ivor) John,** CBE 1982; criminologist and artist; Head of Home Office Research and Planning Unit, 1981–83 (Head, Home Office Research Unit, 1972–81); *b* 6 Jan. 1923; *s* of Oswald Croft and Doris (*née* Phillips). *Educ:* Westminster Sch.; Christ Church, Oxford (Hinchcliffe Scholar in Mod. Hist.; MA); Inst. of Education, Univ. of London; LSE (MA, PGCE). Temp. jun. admin. officer, FO, 1942–45 (at GCHQ (Bletchley Park) and Govt Communications Bureau, London); asst teacher, LCC, 1949–51; Inspector, Home Office Children's Dept, 1952–66; Sen. Research Officer, Home Office Research Unit, 1966–72. Member: Criminological Scientific Council, Council of Europe, 1978–83, Chm., 1981–83; Conservative Study Gp on Crime, 1983–87; Kensington Crime Prevention Panel, 1984–87; Tribunal under I of M Interception of Communications Act, 1989–94. Mem., Crime Policy Gp, Centre for Policy Studies, 2001–04. Governor, ILEA Secondary Schs, 1959–68. Mem. Exec. Cttee, English Assoc., 1966–77 (Hon. Treas. 1972–75); Chairman: Pembridge Assoc., 1985–87; Peel Heritage Trust, 1991–93 (Mem. Cttee, 1989–93); Circus Area Residents' Assoc., 1997–99 (Mem. Cttee, 1996–99); Commn on Community Safety, Bath and NE Somerset Council, 1996–97; Working Gp on Evening Economy, Bath, 2004–05. Group shows, 1958, 1963, 1967, 1968, 1969, 1973, 1992, 1993, 2002, 2010, 2014, 2018; one-man shows, 1970, 1971, 2007, 2017. *Publications:* booklets, pamphlets and articles, and various studies of crime, criminological research and the administration of justice. *Address:* 15 Circus Mews, Bath BA1 2PW. *Clubs:* Athenæum, Reform.

**CROFT, Sir Owen (Glendower),** 14th Bt *cr* 1671; grazier; *b* 26 April 1932; *s* of Sir Bernard Hugh Denman Croft, 13th Bt, and of Helen Margaret (*née* Weaver); *S* father, 1984; *m* 1959, Sally Patricia (*d* 2015), *d* of Dr T. M. Mansfield, Brisbane; one *s* two *d. Educ:* Armidale School, NSW. Mem., State Council of Advice to Rural Lands Protection Bds of NSW, 1983–96; Member: NSW Feral Animal Control Council, 1983–96; NSW Footrot Strategic Plan Steering Cttee, 1986–96; NSW Non-Indigenous Species Adv. Cttee; Armidale Rural Lands Protection Bd, 1978–2001; NSW National Parks and Wildlife Service: Chm., Armidale Dist Adv. Cttee, 1988–2000; Chm., Northern Tablelands Region Adv. Cttee, 2000–04. *Recreations:* tennis; National Trust activities. *Heir: s* Thomas Jasper Croft [*b* 3 Nov. 1962; *m* 1989, Catherine Fiona, *d* of Graham William White; two *d*]. *Address:* Australia.

**CROFT, Rt Rev. Dr Steven John Lindsey;** *see* Oxford, Bishop of.

**CROFT, Prof. Stuart John,** PhD; Professor of International Security, since 2007, and Vice-Chancellor and President, since 2016, University of Warwick; *b* Leicester, 7 March 1963; *s* of John Croft and Margaret Croft; *m* 1994, Jane Usherwood; one *s. Educ:* Univ. of Southampton (BSc, MSc; PhD 1989). Prof. of Internat. Relns, 1996–2007, Hd, Sch. of Social Scis, 2000–03, Univ. of Birmingham; Pro Vice Chancellor for Res. (Arts and Soc. Scis), 2011–13, Provost, 2013–16, Univ. of Warwick. Mem., ESRC, 2011–14. Series Ed., New Security Challenges, 2009–. *Publications:* (ed) British Security Policy, 1991; (ed jtly) European Security without the Soviet Union, 1992; (ed) The Treaty on Conventional Armed Forces in Europe: the Cold War endgame, 1994; The End of British Superpower: Foreign Office conceptions of a changing world, 1945–51, 1994; Strategies of Arms Control: a history and typology, 1996; (jtly) The Enlargement of Europe, 1999; (jtly) Security Studies Today, 1999; (jtly) Britain and Defence, 1945–2000: a policy re-evaluation, 2001; (ed jtly) Critical Reflections on Security and Change, 2001; Culture, Crisis and America's War on Terror, 2006; (ed jtly) Comparative Regional Security Governance, 2012; Securitizing Islam, 2013. *Recreations:* football, walking. *Address:* Office of the Vice-Chancellor and President, University of Warwick, Coventry CV4 8UW. *T:* (024) 7657 4951, *Fax:* (024) 7652 4578. *E:* s.croft@warwick.ac.uk.

**CROFT, Sir Thomas (Stephen Hutton),** 6th Bt *cr* 1818, of Cowling Hall, Yorkshire; Principal, Thomas Croft, Architects, since 1988; *b* 12 June 1959; *o s* of Major Sir John Croft, 5th Bt and Lucy Elizabeth, *d* of late Major William Dallas Loney Jupp, OBE; *S* father, 1990; *m* 2001, Maxine Julia, *d* of Antonio Benato and Mrs Jean Sichel; one *d. Educ:* King's Sch., Canterbury; University Coll., London (BSc); Royal Coll. of Art, London (MA). Architect, Richard Meier & Partners, Architects, New York, 1985–86; Project Architect, Rick Mather, Architects, London, 1986–88. Completed buildings include Royal Yacht Squadron Pavilion, Cowes, 2000. *Address:* (office) 9 Ivebury Court, 325 Latimer Road, W10 6RA. *T:* (020) 8962 0066, *Fax:* (020) 8962 0088. *E:* email@thomascroft.com.

**CROFT, Trevor Anthony;** Inquiry Reporter, Scottish Government Planning and Environmental Appeals Division (formerly Scottish Executive Inquiry Reporters Unit), since 2002; *b* 9 June 1948; *s* of late Kenneth Edward Croft and Gladys (*née* Bartle); *m* 1980, Janet Frances Halley; two *d. Educ:* Belle Vue Boys' GS, Bradford; Hull Univ. (BSc 1969); Sheffield Univ. (DipTRP 1971). MRTPI 1974. Sen. Asst Planning Officer, Min. of Develt, NI, 1971–72; Asst Planning Officer, Countryside Commn for Scotland, 1972–75; Physical Planning Officer, Office of the President, Malawi, 1976–78; Parks Planning Officer, Dept of Nat. Parks and Wildlife, Malawi, 1978–82; National Trust for Scotland: Planning Officer, 1982–84; Head of Policy Res., 1984–88; Regl Dir, 1988–95; Dep. Dir and Dir of Countryside, 1995–97; Dir, 1997–2001; Consultant, 2001–03. Mem., Regl Adv. Cttee, S Scotland, Forestry Commn, 1987–90. Member Council: RSGS, 1998–2001, 2003–05 (Mem., Finance Cttee, 2003–08; Chm., Dunfermline Br., 1993–96); Europa Nostra, 1999–2001. Chm., British Equestrian Vaulting Ltd, 2002–03; Mem. Bd, BEF, 2002–03. Chm. Awards Panel, Kinross Civic Trust, 2005–09. Associate, RSGS, 1995; FRSA 1997. *Recreations:* travel, motorcycling, grandchildren. *Address:* Glenside, Tillyrie, Kinross KY13 0RW. *T:* (01577) 864105. *Club:* Royal Scots (Edinburgh).

**CROFTON,** family name of **Baron Crofton.**

**CROFTON,** 8th Baron *cr* 1797 (Ire.); **Edward Harry Piers Crofton;** Bt 1758; civil and structural engineer; *b* 23 Jan. 1988; *er* twin *s* of 7th Baron Crofton and of Gillian Crofton (*née* Bass); *S* father, 2007. *Educ:* Sandroyd Sch.; Stowe Sch.; Univ. of Bristol. *Recreations:* travel, popular music, outdoor sports. *Heir: yr* twin *b* Hon. Charles Marcus George Crofton, *b* 23 Jan. 1988. *E:* hcrofton@gmail.com.

**CROFTON, Major Sir Edward Morgan,** 9th Bt *cr* 1801, of Mohill, Leitrim; *b* Lyndhurst, Hants, 26 July 1945; *s* of Lt-Col Sir Morgan George Crofton, 6th Bt, DSO (*d* 1958) and his 3rd wife, Margaret Amelia Crofton (*née* Dallett) (*d* 2001); *S* brother, 2016; *m* 1977, Emma Victoria Mildred, *o d* of Sir Henry Dashwood, 8th Bt; two *s. Educ:* Eton; RMA Sandhurst. Regular Officer, Coldstream Guards, 1965–86, Regimental Adjt, 1986; stockbroker, Brewin Dolphin, 1987–95; Mem., RARO, 1987–95, Regimental Adjt, Coldstream Guards, 1995–2012. Mem., HM Body Guard, Hon. Corps of Gentlemen-at-Arms, 1996–2014 (Harbinger, 2012–14). Chm., Friends of St George's Meml Ch, Ypres, 2014–. *Recreations:* cricket, golf. *Heir: s* Henry Morgan Crofton [*b* 12 March 1979; *m* 1st, 2013, Charlotte (marr. diss. 2016), *d* of Robin Faber; 2nd, 2018, Sophie, *d* of Baron Imre von Maltzahn]. *Address:* Marchwood Lodge, Rake, Liss, Hants GU33 7PG. *T:* (01730) 893357. *E:* e.crofton@btinternet.com. *Clubs:* White's, Cavalry and Guards.

**CROFTON, Sir William Robert Malby,** 8th Bt *cr* 1838, of Longford House, Sligo; *b* 5 Jan. 1996; *s* of Sir Julian Malby Crofton, 7th Bt and of Hilary Crofton (*née* Twort); *S* father, 2018.

**CROFTS, Dr Carole Mary;** HM Diplomatic Service, retired; Ambassador to the Republic of Azerbaijan, 2016–19; *b* Nantwich, 24 June 1959; *d* of Gordon and Margaret Crofts; one *s* one *d. Educ:* Northwich Co. Grammar Sch. for Girls; Glasgow Univ. (MA; PhD Arabic and Latin 1985); Tübingen Univ. Entered FCO, 1987; Second Sec. (Pol), Bonn and Berlin, 1988–91; HR Manager, FCO, 1991–92; Multilateral Negotiator, FCO, 1992–94; Hd, Public Diplomacy, Bonn, 1994–97; Hd, Econ. and Commercial Section, Oslo, 1997–99; Dep. Hd, then Actg Hd, Public Diplomacy Dept, FCO, 2000–03; Asst Dir, HR Directorate, 2003–07; Hd, Internat. Educn, DWP and BIS (on secondment), 2008–10; Dir, Policy Skills, Nat. Sch. of Govt (on secondment), 2010–11; Dir, Energy, Transport and Construction, UKTI, 2012–15. *Recreations:* horse riding, ski-ing, walking, running, keep fit, gardening, crosswords, cycling, driving family mad.

**CROFTS, Max Osborn,** FRICS; Consultant, JLL (Jones Lang LaSalle) (formerly J. P. Sturge & Sons, then King Sturge LLP), since 2011 (Partner, 1981–2011); President, Royal Institution of Chartered Surveyors, 2009–10; *b* Northampton, 3 June 1950; *s* of Geoffrey Albert Crofts and Daphne Beryl Crofts; *m* 1973, Angela Clare Heazle; one *s* two *d. Educ:* King Edward VI Camp Hill, Birmingham; Keynsham Grammar Sch., Bristol; Coll. of Estate Mgt, Reading Univ. (BSc). FRICS 1983. Joined J. P. Sturge & Sons, Bristol, 1970. Royal Institution of Chartered Surveyors: Mem., Nat. Cttee, 1972–83, Nat. Chm., 1981, RICS Jun. Orgn; Mem. Council, 1977–83 and 1997–2010; Member: Pres.'s Panel of Arbitrators, 1990–2011; Standards and Practice Cttee, 1995–2000; Chairman: Compulsory Professional Indemnity Insce Wkg Party, 1995–2000; Public Affairs Policy Cttee, 2000–03; Members' Support Service Mgt Bd, 2003–09; Vice Chm., Ethics, Conduct and Consumer Policy Cttee, 2003–08; Mem., Commn on Major Disaster Mgt, 2005–08; Vice-Pres., 2006–09. Chm., Standards Setting Cttee, Internat. Property Measurement Standards Coalition, 2013–. Chm., Somerset Fedn of Young Farmers Clubs, 1976 (Pres., 1996–97); Pres., Bath Chamber of Commerce, 2008. Liveryman, Chartered Surveyors' Co., 1992. Hon. MA UWE, 2010. *Recreations:* supporting Bath Rugby, National Hunt Racing, village and family activities, reading newspapers, canal boating and restoration of Wilts and Berks Canal. *Address:* Glenacre, Dunkerton, Bath BA2 8BG. *T:* (01761) 436723. *E:* max.crofts@eu.jll.com. *Clubs:* Carlton; Bath Rugby.

**CROFTS, Roger Stanley,** CBE 1999; FRSE; independent environment and management adviser; Chief Executive, Scottish Natural Heritage, 1991–2002; *b* 17 Jan. 1944; *s* of Stanley Crofts and Violet May Crofts (*née* Dawson); *m* 1996, Lindsay Manson; one *s* one *d* by previous marriage. *Educ:* Hinckley Grammar Sch.; Liverpool Univ. (BA); Leicester Univ. (PGCE); Aberdeen Univ. (MLitt). Res. Asst to Prof. K. Walton, Aberdeen Univ., 1966–72; British Geomorphological Res. Gp, UCL, 1972–74; Central Res. Unit, Scottish Office, 1974–84; Scottish Office: Head of Highlands and Tourism, 1984–88; Head of Rural Affairs, 1988–91. Visiting Professor: of Geography, 1992–95, of Envmtl Mgt, 1997–2004, Royal Holloway, Univ. of London; of Geoscience, Univ. of Edinburgh, 2004–08; of Geog. and Envmt, Univ. of Aberdeen, 2008–12; Hon. Professor: of Geography and Environment, Univ. of Aberdeen, 1997–2008; of Geoscience, Univ. of Edinburgh, 2008–12, 2016–; of Geography, Univ. of Dundee, 2016–. Dir, Fieldfare Internat. Ecol Develt plc, 2005–. Chairman: UK Cttee, IUCN, 1999–2002; Europe Cttee, IUCN World Commn on Protected Areas, 2001–08, Emeritus, 2010; Southern Ayrshire and Galloway Biosphere Partnership Bd, 2011–14; National Trust for Scotland: Member: Council, 1992–2004 and 2005–10; Exec. Cttee, 2003–04; Bd, 2004–09; Convener, Conservation Cttee, 2004–09. Chm. Dalry Bird Town Steering Gp, 2010–; Dir, Esk Valley Trust, 2015–. Member: Council, Scottish Wildlife Trust, 1992–97; Scottish Assoc. for Marine Science, 1995–2005; Board Member and Trustee: Plantlife Internat., 2001–10 (Chm., 2007–10); Scottish Agricl Coll., 2002–10; Bd, Crichton Carbon Centre, 2009–14 (Fellow, 2014); Chairman: Sibthorp Trust, 2003–13; RSGS, 2014– (Mem., 1994–2000). Hon. Pres., Scottish Assoc. of Geography Teachers, 1994–95 (Patron, 2002–). FRSA 1997; FRSE 2001; FRSGS 2001; FRGS 2002; FCIEEM (FIEEM 2008); Fellow, Royal Canadian Geographical Soc. Hon. DSc: St Andrews, 2004; Glasgow, 2013. Chartered Inst. of Ecol. and Envmtl Mgt Medal, 2016; IUCN World Commn on Protected Areas Fred Packard Award, 2016. Knight's Cross, Order of the Falcon (Iceland), 2014. *Publications:* (with A. McKirdy) Scotland: the creation of its natural landscape, 1999; (ed) Scotland's Environment: the future, 2000; (ed) Conserving Nature: Scotland and the wider world, 2005; (with A. McKirdy and J. Gordon) Land of Mountain and Flood: the geology and landforms of Scotland, 2007; (ed jtly) Ecosystems and Health: a UK perspective, 2009; (ed) Climate Change Action After Copenhagen and Cancun: what next?, 2011; Healing the Land: the story of land reclamation and soil conservation in Iceland (Icelandic Soil Conservation Medal, Icelandic Soil Conservation Service), 2011; contribs to books on marginal regions, geomorph. mapping, second homes, field studies, conservation, envmtl policy; numerous articles. *Recreations:* designing gardens, choral singing, flower photography, cooking, hill walking. *Address:* 6 Eskside West, Musselburgh EH21 6HZ. *T:* (0131) 665 0788. *W:* www.rogercrofts.net.

**CROISDALE-APPLEBY, Lindsay;** HM Diplomatic Service; Director General, EU Exit, Foreign and Commonwealth Office, since 2017; *b* Amersham, 12 May 1973; *s* of David and Carolyn Croisdale-Appleby; *m* Barbara Maria; one *s* one *d. Educ:* Univ. of Oxford (BA Hons Modern Hist.); Univ. of Lancaster (MA Hons Internat. Relns and Internat. Law);

Univ. of Kingston (Postgrad. Dip. HR Mgt). Entered FCO, 1996; Desk Officer for Nigeria, FCO, 1996–97; ME Section, UK Mission to UN, 1997–98; Second Sec., Caracas, 1998–2001; Desk Officer, Afghanistan Emergency Unit, FCO, 2001–02; DEFRA, 2002; First Sec., UK Perm. Repn to EU, 2002–08; Asst Dir for Recruitment and Develt, Human Resources Directorate, FCO, 2008–10; Principal Private Sec. to Sec. of State for Foreign and Commonwealth Affairs, 2010–12; Ambassador to Colombia, 2012–15; Europe Dir, FCO, 2015–17. *Recreations:* reading, swimming, art, history. *Address:* c/o Foreign and Commonwealth Office, King Charles Street, SW1A 2AH.

**CROLL, Prof. James George Arthur,** FREng; Professor of Civil Engineering, University College London, 2003–09, now Emeritus; *b* 16 Oct. 1943; *s* of late Keith Waghorn Croll and Jean Croll; *m* 1st, 1966, Elisabeth Joan (*née* Sprackett) (marr. diss. 1997; she *d* 2007); one *s* one *d*; 2nd, 2005, Patricia Jean Hepker (*née* Hindmarsh); three step *d*. *Educ:* Palmerston North Boys' High Sch., NZ; Univ. of Canterbury, NZ (BE 1st cl. Hons, PhD). FIStructE, FICE, FIMA; CEng 1970, FREng (FEng 1990); CMath. Asst Engineer, Min. of Works, NZ, 1962–67; University College London: Res. Fellow, 1967–70; Lectr, 1970–81; Reader in Structural Engrg, 1981–85; Prof. of Structural Engrg, 1985–92; Chadwick Prof. of Civil Engrg, and Hd, Dept of Civil and Envmtl Engrg, 1992–2003. Director: Syncromesh Systems Ltd, 2008–14; Kapiti Engrg Ltd, 2012–; Kapiti Engrg Services Ltd, 2015–; Trinity Composites Ltd, 2015–. Vis. Fellow, Princeton, 1979; Visiting Professor: Univ. of Cordoba, Argentina, 1973; Fed. Univ. of Rio de Janeiro, 1973, 1981, 1984; Univ. of Hong Kong, 1985, 2000; Tohoku Univ., Japan, 1988; Toyohashi Univ., Japan, 2002, 2009. Chairman: British Soc. for Social Responsibility in Sci., 1978–82 (Mem., Nat. Cttee, 1974–82); Jt Bd of Moderators, 2000–03 (Mem., 1994–2004; Mem., Internat. Cttee, 1997–99). Chm., NZ Univs Graduates Assoc. FRSA. Hon. Fellow, Oxford Centre for Collaborative Applied Maths, Univ. of Oxford, 2011–. *Publications:* Elements of Structural Stability, 1972; Force Systems and Equilibrium, 1974; contrib. approx. 300 jl and conf. papers. *Recreations:* singing, piano, painting, drawing, sailing, ski-ing, travel. *Address:* 53 Mount View Road, Crouch Hill, N4 4SS. *T:* (020) 8341 7994. *Club:* Natural Science (UCL).

**CROLL, (Mary) Louise,** CBE 1995; HM Diplomatic Service, retired; Ambassador to Costa Rica, 1992–95; *b* 10 Sept. 1935. Joined FO, subseq. FCO, 1953; Bahrain, 1957; Addis Ababa, 1959; UK Mission, NY, 1961; FO, 1964; S America floater, 1967; Bilbao, 1969; Lusaka, 1972; First Sec., Madrid, 1979, FCO, 1984; Consul, Florence, 1988.

**CROMARTIE, 5th Earl of,** *cr* 1861; **John Ruaridh Grant Mackenzie,** MIExpE; Viscount Tarbat, Baron Castlehaven, Baron MacLeod, 1861; Chief of the Clan Mackenzie; explosives engineer; *b* 12 June 1948; *s* of 4th Earl of Cromartie, MC, TD and Olga (*d* 1996), *d* of late Stuart Laurance; *S* father, 1989; *m* 1973, Helen, *d* of John Murray; (one *s* decd); *m* 1985, Janet Clare, *d* of Christopher J. Harley; two *s*. *Educ:* Rannoch School, Perthshire; Strathclyde University. Pres., Mountaineering Council of Scotland, 2003–07 (Mem. Council, 1995–2007); Trustee, John Muir Trust, 2001–07. *Publications:* Selected Climbs in Skye, 1982; articles in Classic Rock Climbs and Cold Climbs. *Recreations:* mountaineering, art, astronomy, geology. *Heir: s* Viscount Tarbat, *qv*. *Address:* Castle Leod, Strathpeffer, Ross-shire IV14 9AA. *Clubs:* Army and Navy; Scottish Mountaineering (Pres., 2013–).

**CROMBIE, Sir Alexander Maxwell, (Sir Sandy),** Kt 2009; FFA; FRSE; Senior Independent Director, Royal Bank of Scotland, 2009–18; Chairman, Creative Scotland, 2010–14. *Educ:* Buckhaven High Sch., Fife. FFA 1973; FRSE 2018. Joined Standard Life as trainee actuary, 1966; Chief Investment Manager, 1994; Chief Exec., Standard Life Investments Ltd, 1998–2004; Dep. Gp Chief Exec., Standard Life Assurance Co., 2002–04; Gp Chief Exec., Standard Life Assurance Co., later Standard Life plc, 2004–09. Chm., Amiqus Resolution Ltd, 2017–. Chm., Edinburgh UNESCO City of Literature Trust, 2006–10; Vice-Chm., Bd of Govs, RSAMD, later Royal Conservatoire of Scotland, 2007; Pres., Cockburn Assoc., 2009–.

**CROME, Prof. Ilana Belle,** MD; FRCPsych; Professor of Addiction Psychiatry, 2002–11, now Emeritus, and Academic Director of Psychiatry, 2002–11, University of Keele; Hon. Consultant Addiction Psychiatrist, South Staffordshire and Shropshire NHS Foundation Trust, since 2009; *b* 2 Feb. 1951; *d* of late Solomon Glass and Yette Glass (*née* Golombick); *m* 1989, Prof. Peter Crome, *qv*; one *s*, and one step *s* one step *d*. *Educ:* Redhill Sch., Johannesburg; Lauriston Sch., Melbourne; Damelin Coll., Johannesburg; Univ. of Witwatersrand; New Hall, Cambridge (BA 1972, MA 1974); Univ. of Birmingham (MB ChB 1975; MD 1996). FRCPsych 1997. Sen. Lectr, Inst. of Psychiatry and Hon. Consultant, Maudsley and Bethlem Royal Hosp. and KCH, 1989–93; Sen. Lectr and Consultant Psychiatrist, St Bartholomew's Hosp. Med. Coll. and Barts NHS Trust, 1994; Consultant in Gen. Hosp. Liaison Psychiatry, City Gen. Hosp., Stoke-on-Trent, 1994–97; Prof. of Addiction Studies, 1997–98, Prof. and Hd, Dept of Psychiatry, 1998–2002, Univ. of Wolverhampton; Consultant Addiction Psychiatrist: Wolverhampton Healthcare Trust, 1997–2002; N Staffs Combined Healthcare Trust, Stoke-on-Trent, 2002–09. Associate, Drug and Alcohol Centre, Middx Univ., 2014–; Hon. Sen. Res. Fellow, Imperial Coll. London, 2011–14; Honorary Professor: St George's, Univ. of London, 2013–; QMUL, 2014–17. Member: Exec. Cttee, Soc. for the Study of Addiction, 1994–2010; Scientific Cttee on Tobacco and Health, DoH, 2000–07; Alcohol Educn and Res. Council, 2000–08; Adv. Council on Misuse of Drugs, 2002–10. Chair of Trustees, Drugscience (formerly Ind. Scientific Cttee on Drugs), 2016– (Trustee, 2012–). Chair, Faculty of Substance Misuse, RCPsych, 1998–2002. Pres., Drug and Alcohol Section, Assoc. of European Psychiatrists, 2006–08 (Pres.-elect, 2004–06); Vice-Pres., Profs of Psychiatry Club, 2012–18 (Hon. Sec., 2003–12). Internat. Ed., American Jl of Addictions, 2002–12; Ed., Drugs Educn, Prevention & Policy, 2002–11; Member: Internat. Adv. Bd, Addiction, 1994–2011; Jl Psychopharmacol., 2012–; British Jl Psychiatry, 2012–18. *Publications:* International Handbook of Addiction Behaviour, 1991, repr. 2016; Young People and Substance Misuse, 2004; Psychological Disorders in Obstetrics and Gynaecology, 2006; (Lead Ed.), Substance Misuse and Older People, 2015; (contrib. and Section Ed.) Textbook of Addiction Treatment: international perspectives, 2015; (ed jtly) Young People and Substance Misuse, 2019; contrib. book chapters; contrib. papers to Addiction, Drug & Alcohol Dependence, Anaesthesia, Psychiatric Bull., Alcohol & Alcoholism, Acta Psychiatrica Scandinavica, British Jl Psychiatry, Psychol Medicine, Neuropharmacol., Lancet, Psychoneuroendocrinol. Reviews in Gerontology, BMJ, Eur. Jl of Psychiatry, Canadian Jl of Addiction, Advances in Psychiatric Treatment, Yale Jl of Biology and Medicine, Age and Ageing; contrib. Oxford DNB. *Recreations:* painting and paintings (solo exhibition, One World, Peggy Jay Gallery, Hampstead, 2019), plays and playing, pots and pottering, but not pot! *E:* ilana.crome@btinternet.com, i.crome@keele.ac.uk.

**CROME, Prof. Peter,** MD, PhD, DSc; FRCPE, FRCP, FRCPGlas; FFPM; FBPhS; Professor of Geriatric Medicine, Keele University, 1994–2012, now Emeritus; *b* 4 Feb. 1947; *s* of Leonard Crome, MC, FRCPE, FRCPath and Helena Crome (*née* Huttner); *m* 1989, Ilana Belle Glass (*see* I. B. Crome); one *s*, and one *s* one *d* from a former marr. *Educ:* Dulwich Coll.; King's Coll. London; King's Coll. Hosp. Med. Sch. (MB BS 1970; MD 1980; PhD 1995); Keele Univ. (DSc 2009). LRCP 1970, MRCP 1974, FRCP 1990; MRCS 1970; DObstRCOG 1973; FRCPE 1988; FFPM 1992; FRCPGlas 1995; FBPhS (FBPharmacolS 2012). Consultant Geriatrician, Orpington Hosp., 1981–91; Sen. Lectr, King's Coll. Sch. of Medicine and Dentistry, 1991–94; Keele University: Dep. Head, 2001–05, Head, 2005, Med. Sch.; Head of Postgrad. Medicine, 2001–08. Hon. Consultant: Guy's and St Thomas' Hosp., 1988–2003; King's Healthcare NHS Trust, 1991–94. Dir, Shropshire and Staffs Strategic HA, 2003–06. President: Section of Geriatrics and Gerontol., RSocMed, 2001–03; British Geriatrics Soc., 2006–08 (Pres.-elect, 2004–06); Mem. Council, RCP, 2006–08; Sec.-Gen., Clinical Sect., Internat. Assoc. of Gerontol. and Geriatrics, 2007–15. Hon. Prof., Dept of Primary Care and Population Health, UCL, 2012. *Publications:* (with G. A. Ford) Drugs and the Older Population, 2001; (jtly) Pain in Older People, 2006; Substance Use and Older People, 2015; contrib. papers on geriatric medicine, stroke and clinical pharmacol. *Recreations:* travel, food, especially cheese. *Address:* 62 Redington Road, NW3 7RS. *T:* (020) 7209 4219. *E:* p.crome@ucl.ac.uk, p.crome@keele.ac.uk. *Club:* Royal Society of Medicine.

**CROMER, 4th Earl of,** *cr* 1901; **Evelyn Rowland Esmond Baring;** Baron Cromer, 1892; Viscount Cromer, 1899; Viscount Errington, 1901; Chief Executive, Cromer Associates Ltd, since 1994; *b* 3 June 1946; *e s* of 3rd Earl of Cromer, KG, GCMG, MBE, PC and Hon. Esmé Harmsworth, CVO, *d* of 2nd Viscount Rothermere; *S* father, 1991; *m* 1971, Plern Isarangkun Na Ayudhya (marr. diss. 1993); 2nd, 1993, Shelley Hu Cheng-Yu, *e d* of Hu Guoquin, Shanghai; one *s* one *d*. *Educ:* Eton; INSEAD. Managing Director: Inchcape (China) Ltd, 1979–94; Inchcape Vietnam Ltd, 1987–94; Inchcape Special Markets Ltd, 1990–94; Dir, Inchcape Pacific Ltd, 1985–94. Chairman: Lloyd George Standard Chartered China Fund Ltd (Hong Kong), 1994–2006; JP Morgan China Region Fund Inc. (USA), 1994–2018; Korea Asia Fund Ltd, 1996–2000; Philippine Discovery Investment Co. Ltd, 1997–2006; Cambridge Asia Fund Ltd, 2001–08; Western Provident Assoc., 2004–; China IPO Gp Ltd, 2005–09; Pedder St Asia Absolute Return Fund Ltd, 2006–; London Asia Capital plc, 2008–10; LG Asia Plus Fund Ltd, 2009–; LG India Plus Fund, 2010–; Director: Cluff Oil China Ltd (Hong Kong), 1990–99; China & Eastern Investments Ltd, 1991–96; Schroder AsiaPacific Fund Ltd, 1995–2011; Pacific Basin Shipping Ltd, 2004–08; Japan High Yield Property Fund Ltd, 2005–09; Cheetah Korea Value Fund, 2010–. Dir, Somerset TEC, 1999–2001; Chm., Business Link Somerset, 1999–2008. Chm., Cromer Foundn for Chinese Contemp. Art, 2009–18. Mem. St John's Council (Hong Kong), 1980–85. *Publications:* The Son from the West, 2007. *Recreations:* mountain climbing, deep sea diving. *Heir: s* Viscount Errington, *qv*. *Address:* 6 Sloane Terrace Mansions, SW1X 9DG; Kinnaree, 9/32 Katamanda, Katanoi Road, Karon, Phuket 83100, Thailand; Dragoneye, CPO Box 3187, Central Post Office, Muscat 111, Sultanate of Oman. *Clubs:* White's, Oriental; Hong Kong (Hong Kong), Royal Yacht Squadron.

**CROMIE, Sharon Nadine;** Headteacher, Wycombe High School, since 2009; *b* Carlisle, 6 Oct. 1965; *s* of Norman Mulholland and Daphne Mulholland; *m* 1990, Alistair Cromie; one *s* one *d*. *Educ:* Victoria Coll., Belfast; Queen's Univ., Belfast (LLB Hons 1988); Reading Univ. (CertEd 1994). IT Mgt Consultant, Arthur Andersen, 1988–90; Quality Assurance Manager, EPG Computer Services, 1990–93; Lectr and Curriculum Manager, Reading Coll., 1993–97; Lectr and Business Develt Manager, Henley Coll., 1997–2000; Asst Headteacher and Business Manager, Wycombe High Sch., 2003–07; Dep. Hd, John Hampden Grammar Sch., 2007–09. *Recreations:* family, reading, travelling. *Address:* Wycombe High School, Marlow Road, High Wycombe HP11 1TB. *T:* (01494) 523961, *Fax:* (01494) 510354. *E:* office@whs.bucks.sch.uk.

**CROMPTON, Adrian John Leonard;** Auditor General for Wales, since 2018; *b* Gloucester, 28 Aug. 1965; *s* of late John Richard de Jordan Crompton and of Kathleen Anne Crompton (*née* Hart); *m* 1996, Nicola Ruth Donlon; one *s* one *d*. *Educ:* Univ. of Bath (BSc Econ). Res. Clerk, Liby Res. Div., H of C, 1988–98; Welsh Office, subseq. National Assembly for Wales: Govt Statistician, 1998–99; Cttee Clerk, 1999–2004; Head: Members' Res. Service, 2004–06; Members' Res. and Cttee Service, 2006–07; Dir, Assembly Business, 2007–18. Advr to Constitution Unit, Univ. of London, 2002–03; Associate, Global Partners Governance, 2014–. Member: Study of Parlt Gp; Political Studies Assoc. *Recreations:* Rugby, cricket, running, golf, tennis, supporting my children's sporting commitments, writing and performing pantomime (Member, Westbury Players). *Address:* Wales Audit Office, 24 Cathedral Road, Cardiff CF11 9LJ. *E:* adrian.crompton@audit.wales. *Clubs:* Aston Ingham Tennis; Newnham Alpine.

**CROMPTON, Sir Dan,** Kt 2003; CBE 1996; QPM 1990; HM Inspector of Constabulary, North of England and Northern Ireland, 1995–2002; *b* 15 Feb. 1941; *s* of Arthur and Elizabeth Crompton; *m* 1962, Olive Ramsden; one *s*. *Educ:* Didsbury Technical Sch., Manchester. Manchester City Police, 1960–68; Manchester and Salford Police, 1968–74; Greater Manchester Police, 1974–87; Nottinghamshire Constabulary, 1987–95 (Chief Constable, 1990–95). *Recreations:* reading, popular classics, gardening, cricket, Rugby. *Address:* 1 Half Acre Lane, Rochdale, Lancs OL11 4BY.

**CROMPTON, Prof. Gareth,** FRCP, FFPH; Professor of Public Health Medicine, University of Wales College of Medicine, 1989–97, now Emeritus; Hon. Fellow, Cardiff Metropolitan University (formerly University of Wales Institute, Cardiff), since 1997; *b* 9 Jan. 1937; *s* of late Edward and Annie Jane Crompton, Drefach-Felindre, Carmarthenshire; *m* 1965; one *d*. *Educ:* Llandysul Grammar Sch.; Welsh Nat. Sch. of Medicine. MB, BCh Wales, 1960; DObstRCOG 1962; DPH Wales, 1964; FFPH (FFCM 1976); FRCP 1986 (MRCP 1980). County Med. Officer, County Welfare Officer and Principal Sch. Med. Officer, Anglesey CC, 1966–73; Area Med. Officer, Gwynedd Health Authority, 1974–77; CMO, Welsh Office, 1978–89; Chief Admin. MO and Dir of Public Health Medicine, S Glam HA, 1989–96. Specialty Advr, Health Service Comr for England and Wales, 1974–77; Advr in Wales, Faculty of Community Medicine, 1974–77. Chm., Anglesey Disablement Adv. Cttee, 1969–77; Sec., Fluoridation Study Gp, Soc. of Med. Officers of Health, 1969–73; Mem., Welsh Hosp. Bd, 1970–74. Member: GMC, 1981–83 and 1987–89; Bd, PHLS, 1990–97; Exec. Bd, FPHM, 1990–95. Med. Fellow, Council of Europe, 1971. Jt Life Pres., Bargod Rangers AFC, 2014–. QHP 1984–87. Hon. MD Wales, 1999. Alwyn Smith Prize Medal, Faculty of Public Health, RCP, 2000. *Publications:* papers on the effects of fluoridated water supplies on dental caries, and the epidemiology and management of chronic sickness and disablement. *Recreations:* bowls, watching Rugby football and cricket, reading contemporary Welsh verse. *Address:* 19 Kenilworth House, Castle Court, Westgate Street, Cardiff CF10 1DJ.

**CROMPTON, Kenneth Charles;** Chief Executive, General Sir John Monash Foundation, 2002–09; solicitor, now retired; *b* 19 July 1948; *s* of late Charles Frederic Crompton and of Margaret Joan Crompton; *m* 1971, Elizabeth Anne Meek; one *s* two *d*. *Educ:* Melbourne Univ. (LLB). Solicitor, Morris Komesaroff, Aarons & Co., 1971–75; Seton Williams & Smyth, 1975–79; Gen. Manager, Legal and Technical Services, Victorian Chamber of Manufactures, 1979–87; Dir, Industrial Relations, 1987–88, Chief Exec. (Vic.), 1988–92, Aust. Chamber of Manufactures; Agent-Gen. for Victoria in London, 1993–96. Dir, Corporate Counsel Pty Ltd. *Recreations:* golf, photography. *Address:* 104 Scenic Crescent, Eltham, Vic 3095, Australia. *Clubs:* Athenæum (Melbourne); Melbourne Cricket.

**CROMWELL, 7th Baron** *cr* 1375 (called out of abeyance, 1923); **Godfrey John Bewicke-Copley;** *b* 4 March 1960; *s* of 6th Baron Cromwell and of Vivian, *y d* of late Hugh de Lisle Penfold, Isle of Man; *S* father, 1982; *m* 1990, Elizabeth, *d* of John Hawksley; three *s* (incl. twins) one *d*. *Educ*: Eton; Selwyn Coll., Cambridge (BA 1982; MA 1986). Elected Mem., H of L, 2014. *Heir: s* Hon. David Godfrey Bewicke-Copley, *b* 21 Sept. 1997.

**CROMWELL, Tamsin Jane;** *see* Ford, T. J.

**CRONEY, Alan Malcolm,** FRICS; Director, Enbornewood Consulting Ltd, 2012–17; *b* Stoke Newington, London, 4 March 1955; *s* of Charles Frederick Croney and Joan Croney; one *s*. *Educ*: Latymer Sch., Edmonton, London; Coll. of Estate Mgt. FRICS 1985. Estates Manager, London Docklands Develt Corp., 1981–86; Gp Property Manager, Thames Water, 1986–90; Gen. Manager Estates, WH Smith plc, 1990–96; Exec. Dir, London First, 1997–2000; Dir, i-Scraper UK, 2000–02; Dir, Property Services, Metropolitan Police Service, 2002–09; Global Dir, Estates and Security, FCO, 2009–11; Interim Dir, Serco UK and Europe Ltd, 2012–14. Advr to MoJ, 2016–17. Sen. Civil Mem., ACPO, 2004–09. Former specialist panel mem. on water industry and town centre mgt, RICS. Mem., Enborne Parish Council, 2014– (Chair, 2017–). FRSA 2006. *Recreation:* country walking. *Address:* Enborne Wood Cottage, Newbury, Berks RG20 0HA. *T:* 07771 817519.

**CRONEY, Prof. Paul;** Vice-Chancellor and Chief Executive, Teesside University, since 2015; *b* Newcastle upon Tyne, 29 June 1963; *s* of William Turner Croney and Georgina Gibson Croney; *m* 1988, Pamela Pallister; one *s* one *d*. *Educ*: Manor Park Comp. Sch.; Sheffield City Poly. (BA Hons Business Studies 1986); Univ. of Warwick (MA Industrial Relns 1988). Chartered MCIPD 2003. Officer, Barclays Bank plc, 1979–82; researcher, AUT, 1986–87; Academic Staff: Leeds Poly., 1988–90; Sheffield City Poly., subseq. Sheffield Hallam Univ., 1990–99; Northumbria University: Academic Staff, 1999–2003; Dean, Newcastle Business Sch., 2003–10; Pro-Vice-Chancellor (Learning and Teaching), 2010–13; Dep. Vice-Chancellor, 2013–15. Honorary Professor: State Univ. of Management, Moscow, 2003–; Sinerghia Econs and Finance Inst., 2007–. FRSA 2016. *Recreations:* cycling, swimming, walking. *Address:* Teesside University, Middlesbrough TS1 3BX.

**CRONIN, Prof. Leroy, (Lee),** DPhil; FRSE; Regius Professor of Chemistry, University of Glasgow, since 2013; *b* Ipswich, 1 June 1973; *s* of Liam and Jill Cronin; *m* 1999, Deborah Aitken Porter; two *s*. *Educ*: Copleston High Sch., Ipswich; Northgate Sixth Form, Ipswich; York Univ. (BSc 1st Cl. Chem. 1994; DPhil Chem. 1997). Res. Fellow, Univ. of Edinburgh, 1997–99; Alexander von Humboldt Res. Fellow, Univ. of Bielefeld, Germany, 1999–2000; Lectr, Univ. of Birmingham, 2000–02; University of Glasgow: Lectr, 2002–05; Reader, 2005–06; Prof., 2006–09; Gardiner Prof., 2009–13. FRSE 2009. Tilden Prize, RSC, 2016; Interdisciplinary Prize, RSC, 2018; Inorganic Chemistry Lectureship, ACS, 2018. *Publications:* contrib. over 390 articles to peer-reviewed jls. *Recreations:* running, walking, sailing, science history, philosophy. *Address:* School of Chemistry, University of Glasgow, University Avenue, Glasgow G12 8QQ. *T:* (0141) 330 6650. *E:* lee.cronin@glasgow.ac.uk.

**CRONIN, Tacey Marguerite; Her Honour Judge Cronin;** a Circuit Judge, since 2018; *b* Forres, Scotland, 28 June 1959; *d* of Anthony Arthur Cronin and Margaret Elizabeth Cronin (*née* Roberts); *m* 1987, David Bain; three *d*. *Educ*: Stamford High Sch.; Univ. of Bristol (LLB Hons). Called to the Bar, Middle Temple, 1982; barrister, Albion Chambers, Bristol, 1984–2010; a District Judge, 2010–18. *Recreations:* theatre, motorsport.

**CROOK,** family name of **Baron Crook**.

**CROOK, 3rd Baron** *cr* 1947, of Carshalton, Surrey; **Robert Douglas Edwin Crook;** *b* 19 May 1955; *s* of 2nd Baron Crook and Ellenor Crook (*née* Rouse) (*d* 1998); *S* father, 2001; *m* 1981, Suzanne Jane Robinson, BA, LLB; two *s*. *Educ*: Sir William Borlase's Sch., Marlow; Newcastle Univ. (BSc Mining Engrg); Queensland Univ. (MBA). MIE (Aust); CPEng. CEO, Exoma Energy Ltd, Brisbane, until 2015. *Heir: s* Hon. Matthew Robert Crook, *b* 28 May 1990.

**CROOK, (Alan) Peter,** MA; Head of Music, Repton Senior School Dubai, 2012–17; *b* 1954; *s* of Donald Hartley Crook and Constance Crook (*née* Llewellyn); *m* 1981, Elaine Joyce Scragg; two *s*. *Educ*: Rydal Sch.; Charterhouse; Royal Acad. Music (BMus Hons; ARCO, ARAM); Univ. of London Inst. of Educn (PGCE); Univ. of Durham (MA). Asst Dir of Music, 1979–83, Dir of Music, 1983–85, Loretto Sch.; Dir of Music, 1985–2003, Co-ordinator of Performing Arts, 2003–07, Rugby Sch.; Headmaster, Purcell Sch., 2007–11. Conductor: Loretto Choral Soc., 1983–85; Rugby Philharmonic Choir and Orch., 1985–2007; Dubai Singers and Orch., 2015–17. FRSA 2007. *Publications:* hymn tunes and arrangements in various hymnals. *Recreations:* family, fiction, fly fishing, over-seas travel. *E:* crookp@gmail.com. *Club:* Royal Over-Seas League.

**CROOK, Colin,** FREng; special advisor to business, academia, governments and non-governmental organisations on advanced thinking for complex problems; Senior Fellow, Wharton School, University of Pennsylvania, since 1997; *b* 1 June 1942; *s* of Richard and Ruth Crook; *m* 1965, Dorothy Jean Taylor; two *d*. *Educ*: Harris Coll., Preston; Liverpool Polytechnic (ACT Hons; Dip. Elec. Engrg). CEng 1977, FREng (FEng 1981); MIET (MIEE 1976); MIERE 1976; MIEEE 1976; MACM 1977. Electronics Engr, Canadian Marconi, 1962–64; Computer Designer, The Plessey Co., 1964–68; Systems Engr, Eli Lilly Co., 1968–69; sen. appts, Motorola Semiconductor Div., Switzerland and USA, 1969–79; sen. appts, The Rank Organisation, 1979–83, including: Man. Dir, RPI, 1979–81; Man. Dir, Zynar, CEO Nestar Systems, USA, 1981–83; Mem. of Bd, British Telecom, and Man. Dir, BT Enterprises, 1983–84; Sen. Vice Pres., Data General Corp., 1984–89; Sen. Technol. Officer (formerly Chm., Corporate Technol. Cttee), Citicorp, 1990–97. Mem., various NAS adv. cttees, USA; advr to various global cos; Member: Bd, Onsett Internat., Boston, 1998–; Adv. Bd, Rein Capital, NJ, 1999–; Advr, IDAnalytics, San Diego, 1999–. Mem. Editl Bd, Emergence Jl, NY. *Publications:* The Power of Impossible Thinking, 2004; articles and learned papers on electronics and computers. *Recreations:* photography, walking, reading, wine, sailing. *Address:* Penberen House, Seifton, Shropshire SY7 9BY.

**CROOK, Frances Rachel,** OBE 2010; Chief Executive (formerly Director), Howard League for Penal Reform, since 1986; *b* 18 Dec. 1952; *d* of Sheila Sibson-Turnbull and Maurice Crook; one *d*. *Educ*: Camden School; Liverpool University (BA Hons History). Historical Researcher, Liverpool, 1977–78; Teacher, 1978–79; Campaign Co-ordinator, Amnesty International, 1980–85. Sen. Vis. Fellow, LSE, 2010–; Vis. Fellow, Leicester Univ., 2014–. Councillor (Lab) Barnet, 1982–90. Mem. Court, Greenwich Univ., 1996–2002 (Chm., Staffing and Gen. Cttee, 1997–2002). Mem., Sch. Food Trust, 2005–08. Non-exec. Dir, NHS Barnet, 2009–. Chm., Old Barn Youth and Community Centre, Finchley, 1996–97. Freeman, City of London, 1997. Hon. DLaws: Liverpool, 2016; Leeds Beckett, 2017. Perrie Award, Perrie Lectures Cttee, 2005. *Recreation:* demonstrations. *Address:* The Howard League, 1 Ardleigh Road, N1 4HS. *T:* (020) 7249 7373.

**CROOK, Maj.-Gen. James Cooper,** MD, FRCPath; late RAMC, retired 1981; Civilian Medical Practitioner, Army Blood Supply Depot, Aldershot, 1982–88; *b* 19 March 1923; *s* of late Francis William Crook and late Mary Catherine Perry, *d* of late Sir Edwin Cooper Perry, GCVO, MD, Superintendent of Guy's Hospital and Vice-Chancellor of London Univ.; *m* 1950, Ruth (*d* 2015), *d* of late W. A. Bellamy of Santa Cruz, Tenerife; one *s* two *d*. *Educ*: Worksop Coll.; Guy's Hosp. Med. Sch., Univ. of London. MB BS 1946, MD 1953; DTM&H 1952; FRCPath 1968. Guy's and Pembury Hosps, 1946; Commnd RAMC 1946; served Egypt and N Africa, 1946–49; Pathologist, Queen Alexandra's Mil. Hosp., 1950; David Bruce Laboratories, 1953; med. liaison officer to MRC Radiobiology Unit, AERE, Harwell, 1954; Asst Dir of Pathology, Middle East, 1957; Cons. in Pathology, 1958; RAMC Specialist, Chem. Defence Estab., Porton, 1960; Asst Dir of Pathology, Eastern Comd, 1963; ADGMS, 1966; Comd Cons. in Pathology, BAOR, 1969; Prof. of Pathology, Royal Army Med. Coll., 1974; Dir of Army Pathology and Consulting Pathologist to the Army, 1976–81; Hon. Physician to HM The Queen, 1978–81. Hon. Col, 380 Blood Supply Unit RAMC, TAVR, 1982–86. *Publications:* articles in Jl of Clinical Path., Nature, Med. Sci. and the Law, Jl of RAMC, British Jl of Radiology. *Recreations:* gardening, beekeeping. *Address:* Roseland, Newport Street, Millbrook, Torpoint, Cornwall PL10 1BW. *T:* (01752) 823697.

**CROOK, Rt Rev. John Michael;** Bishop of Moray, Ross and Caithness, 1999–2006; *b* 11 June 1940; *s* of late John Hadley Crook and Ada Crook; *m* 1965, Judith Christine, *d* of late Rev. John Angles Barber and Dorothy Barber; one *s* three *d*. *Educ*: Argyle Hse Sch., Sunderland; Dame Allan's Sch., Newcastle upon Tyne; William Hulme's GS, Manchester; St David's Coll., Lampeter (BA 1962); Coll. of the Resurrection, Mirfield. Ordained deacon, 1964, priest, 1965; Curate: Horninglow, 1964–66; Bloxwich, 1966–70; Rector: St Michael, Inverness, 1970–78; St John, Inverness, 1974–78; Aberfoyle, and Callander, and Doune, 1978–87; Bridge of Allan, 1987–99; Canon, St Ninian's Cathedral, Perth, 1985–99. Diocesan Synod Clerk, St Andrews, 1997–99. *Recreations:* bird-watching, music, history. *Address:* 163 Lothian Crescent, Stirling FK9 5SG.

**CROOK, Prof. Joseph Mordaunt,** CBE 2003; DPhil; FBA 1988; FSA; Professor of Architectural History, University of London at Royal Holloway and Bedford New College (formerly at Bedford College), 1981–99, now Emeritus; *b* 27 Feb. 1937; *e s* of Austin Mordaunt Crook and Irene Woolfenden; *m* 1st, 1964, Margaret, *o d* of James Mulholland; 2nd, 1975, Susan, *o d* of F. H. Mayor. *Educ*: Wimbledon Coll.; Brasenose Coll., Oxford (BA (1st cl. Mod. Hist.) 1958; DPhil 1961, MA 1962; Hon. Fellow, 2010). FSA 1972. Research Fellow: Inst. of Historical Res., 1961–62; Bedford Coll., London, 1962–63; Warburg Inst., London, 1970–71; Asst Lectr, Univ. of Leicester, 1963–65; Lectr, Bedford Coll., London, 1965–75; Reader in Architectural Hist., 1975–81; Dir, Victorian Studies Centre, RHBNC, 1990–99. Slade Prof. of Fine Art, Oxford Univ., 1979–80; Vis. Fellow: Brasenose Coll., Oxford, 1979–80; Humanities Res. Centre, ANU, Canberra, 1985; Waynflete Lectr and Vis. Fellow, Magdalen Coll., Oxford, 1984–85; Vis. Fellow, Gonville and Caius Coll., Cambridge, 1986; Humanities Fellow, Princeton Univ., 1990; Supernumerary Fellow, Brasenose Coll., Oxford, 2002–10. Public Orator, Univ. of London, 1988–90. Member: Exec. Cttee, Soc. Architect. Historians of Gt Britain, 1964–77 (Pres., 1980–84); RIBA Drawings Cttee, 1969–75; Exec. Cttee, Georgian Gp, 1970–77; Exec. Cttee, Victorian Soc., 1970–77, Council, 1978–88; Historic Buildings Council for England, 1974–80; Council, Soc. of Antiquaries, 1980–82; Adv. Council, Paul Mellon Centre for Studies in British Art, 1985–90; Gen. Cttee, Incorp. Church Building Soc., 1987–99; Council, British Acad., 1989–92; Adv. Bd for Redundant Churches, 1991–99; Westminster Abbey Architectural Adv. Panel, 1993–99 and Fabric Commn, 2000–18 (Vice-Chm., 2002–10). Freeman, 1979, Liveryman, 1984, Worshipful Co. of Goldsmiths. Hon. DLit London, 2004. Editor, Architectural History, 1967–75. *Publications:* The Greek Revival, 1968; Victorian Architecture: a visual anthology, 1971; The British Museum, 1972, 2nd edn 1973; The Greek Revival: Neo-Classical attitudes in British architecture 1760–1870, 1972, 2nd edn 1995; The Reform Club, 1973; (jtly) The History of the King's Works, Vol. VI, 1782–1851, 1973 (Hitchcock Medallion, 1974), Vol. V, 1660–1782, 1976; William Burges and the High Victorian Dream, 1981, rev. edn 2013; (jtly) Axel Haig and The Victorian Vision of the Middle Ages, 1984; The Dilemma of Style: architectural ideas from the picturesque to the post-modern, 1987, 2nd edn 1989; John Carter and the Mind of the Gothic Revival, 1995; The Rise of the Nouveaux Riches: style and status in Victorian and Edwardian architecture, 1999, 2nd edn 2000; London's Arcadia: John Nash and the planning of Regent's Park, 2001; The Architect's Secret: Victorian critics and the image of gravity, 2003; Brasenose: the biography of an Oxford college, 2008, 2nd edn 2010; *edited:* Eastlake, A History of the Gothic Revival, 1970, rev. edn, 1978; Emmet, Six Essays, 1972; Kerr, The Gentleman's House, 1972; The Strange Genius of William Burges, 1981; Clark, The Gothic Revival, 1995; Bedford College: memories of 150 years, 2001; *contrib. to:* Concerning Architecture, 1967; The Country Seat, 1970; The Age of Neo-Classicism, 1972; The Building of Early America, 1976; Seven Victorian Architects, 1976; The Ruskin Polygon, 1982; In Search of Modern Architecture, 1983; Rediscovering Hellenism, 1989; The University of London and the World of Learning 1836–1986, 1990; Brooks's: a social history, 1991; London: world city 1800–1840, 1992; Scottish Country Houses, 1995; The Question of Style in Philosophy and the Arts, 1995; Armchair Athenians, 2001; The Impact of the Railway on Society in Britain, 2003; All Souls and the Wider World, 2011; Brooks's, 1764–2014: the story of a Whig club, 2013; John Nash: architect of the picturesque, 2013; Architectural History After Colvin, 2014; Oxford Freemasons, 2018; Westminster Abbey, 2019; numerous articles in Architect. History, Architect. Review, Country Life, History Today, Jl Royal Soc. Arts, RIBA Jl, Antiquaries Jl, TLS, Architect Design, etc. *Recreation:* strolling. *Address:* D4, Albany, Piccadilly, W1J 0AP; West Wing, Maristow, near Roborough, Devon PL6 7BZ. *T:* (01752) 696648. *Clubs:* Athenæum, Brooks's.

**CROOK, Pamela June, (PJ Crook),** MBE 2011; RWA 1987; artist (painter and sculptor); *b* Cheltenham, 28 June 1945; *d* of John, (Jack), Albert Hagland and Jessie Edith Hagland (*née* Birch); *m* 1969, Dr Geoff Crook (marr. diss. 1980); one *s* one *d*; partner, 1983, *m* 2019, Richard Parker. *Educ*: Gloucestershire Coll. of Art and Design (NDD 1965). *Major solo exhibitions*: Portal Gall., London, 1980–94; Cheltenham Art Gall. and Mus., 1986, 1996, 2006; Lee Drexler, NY, 1989; Galerie Alain Blondel, Paris, 1991, 1993, 1995, 1997, 2002, 2008, 2011; Montpelier Sandelson, London, 1994–96; Musée Paul Valery, Sète, 1996; RWA, 1997; Brian Sinfield Gall., 1997, 1999, 2004, 2007, 2009, 2011; Nancy Poole Gall., Toronto, 1998; Theo Waddington Fine Art, London, 1998, Florida, 2000; Barry Friedman, NY at ArtChicago, 1998–99; Morohashi MOMA, Japan, 2001, 2006, 2012, 2016, 2018; Gloucester City Mus., 2002, 2006, 2012, 2016; Robert Sandelson Gall., London, 2003; Draakon Galerii, Tallinn, 2006; Loch Gall., Toronto, 2007, 2010; Vaal Galerii, Tallinn, 2010; Hay Hill Gall., London, 2010; Alpha Gall., London, 2012, 2013; Panter & Hall, London, 2014, 2015, 2016, 2019; RWA, Bristol, 2017; Trinity House, Broadway, 2018; *major group exhibitions*: RWA, 1978– (First Prize, 1984); RA Summer Exhibn, 1978– (World of Newspapers, RA/Sotheby's Prize, 1982); Salisbury Fest., 1986; British Council tour of Far East, 1988; Contemporary Icons, Royal Albert Meml Mus., Exeter, 1992; Lincoln Mus. and Art Gall. tour, 1993–94; contemp. paintings from perm. collection, Imperial War Mus., 1995; Mairie de Paris, 1995; Realismus der gegenwart, Berlin, 1996; Holbourne Mus. of Art, Bath, 2010; works in major museums, corporate and private collections, incl. Imperial War Mus., Morohashi MOMA, Japan, Cheltenham Art Gall. and

Mus., ALJ, Jeddah, Gloucester City Mus., Standard Chartered Bank, Open Mus., Leics, crucifixion for St Michael and All Angels, Bishop's Cleeve, Gloucester Royal Hosp., RWA, Ralli Mus., Caesarea, JP Morgan Inc., Longleat House. Dir, Artists' Collecting Soc., 2007–13. Pres., Friends of Cheltenham Art Gall. and Mus., 2007–; Hon. Vice Pres., Gloucester Coll., 2012. Trustee: Forest of Dean Sculpture Trail, 2011–13; Aston Project, 2015–. Patron: Nat. Star Coll., 1992–; Cheltenham Open Studios, 2011–; Linc, 2013–; Artshape, 2013–. Mem., Manchester Acad. of Fine Art, 1992. Hon. DArt Glos, 2010. FRSA 2010. *Relevant Publications*: P. J. Crook, ed Raymond Daussy, 1993; P. J. Crook, ed Jon Bennington, 1996; P. J. Crook, by Martin Bailey, 2003. *Recreations*: painting is all-embracing, entwined around my family and everything that I do; hatching schemes and ideas in the early hours. *Address*: The Old Police Station, 39 Priory Lane, Bishop's Cleeve, Cheltenham, Glos GL52 8JL. *T*: (01242) 675963; Panter & Hall, 11–12 Pall Mall, SW1Y 5LU. *E*: pj@pjcrook.com. *W*: www.pjcrook.com. *Club*: Chelsea Arts.

**CROOK, Peter;** *see* Crook, A. P.

**CROOKALL, Ian;** Chief Executive, Buckinghamshire County Council, 1995–2001; *b* 28 Dec. 1944; *s* of F. Harold Crookall and M. Ida Crookall (*née* Stubbs); *m* 1974, Georgina; one *s*. *Educ*: Arnold Sch., Blackpool; University Coll. London (LLB Hons). Admitted Solicitor, 1969; Asst Solicitor, N Yorks CC, 1974–82; Asst Clerk, Norfolk CC, 1982–85; Dep. County Solicitor, Dorset CC, 1985–89; Buckinghamshire County Council: County Secretary and Solicitor, 1989–95. *Recreations*: tennis, swimming, walking, theatre. *Address*: Flemings House, Old School, High Street, Wendover HP22 6DU. *T*: (01296) 696410.

**CROOKE, Alastair Warren,** CMG 2004; Founder, 2004, and Director, since 2005, Conflicts Forum; *b* 30 June 1949; *s* of Frederick Montague Warren and Shona Ann Crooke (*née* Thomson); *m* 1st, 1976, Carole Cecilia (*née* Flaxman) (marr. diss.); three *s*; 2nd, 2012, Aisling Byrne; one *s* one *d*. *Educ*: Aiglon Coll., Switzerland; St Andrews Univ. (MA Hons Pol Economy and Philos.). Contrib. to mediation, mgt and resolution of conflict in Ireland, Namibia, Afghanistan, Cambodia and Colombia; co-ordinated hostage negotiations in four overseas locations; Security Adviser: to EU Special Rep. for ME peace process, 1997–2003; to EU High Rep., Javier Solana, 1999–2003; Mem., US Senator George Mitchell's Fact Finding Cttee into causes of Palestinian Intifada, 2000–01; facilitated Israeli/Palestinian ceasefires, 2002, 2003; mediated negotiations that led to ending of siege of Church of Nativity, Bethlehem, 2002; instrumental in negotiations that led to ceasefire declared by Hamas and Islamic Jihad, 2003; initiated bringing together Islamist movts with European and US non-official participants, 2005–. Has made TV documentaries and broadcasts. *Publications*: Resistance: the essence of the Islamist Revolution, 2009; various articles in jls and newspapers on ME and Islamic affairs. *Recreations*: scuba diving instructing, climbing, ski-ing, study of 18th century art, architecture and furniture. *E*: exchange@conflictsforum.com.

**CROOKENDEN, Simon Robert;** QC 1996; a Recorder, 1998–2016; a Deputy High Court Judge, 2010–16; *b* 27 Sept. 1946; *s* of late Spencer Crookenden and Jean Phyllis (formerly Carter, *née* Dewing); *m* 1983, Sarah Anne Georgina Margaret Pragnell; one *s* two *d*. *Educ*: Winchester Coll.; Corpus Christi Coll., Cambridge (MA Mech. Scis). Management trainee, Westland Aircraft, 1968–69; various posts, incl. Brand Manager, Unilever, 1969–72; Brand Manager, Express Dairies, 1972–74; called to the Bar, Gray's Inn, 1975, Bencher, 2003; in practice as barrister, 1975–; Asst Recorder, 1994–98. *Recreations*: ski-ing, rowing, sailing. *Address*: Essex Court Chambers, 24 Lincoln's Inn Fields, WC2A 3EG. *T*: (020) 7813 8000.

**CROOKHAM, Ian;** Chief Executive, Kingston upon Hull City Council, 1995–2002; *b* 7 Oct. 1952; *s* of George Edward Crookham and Jean Crookham; *m* 1977, Shirley Ann Green; four *s*. *Educ*: St Margaret's Sch., Liverpool (BA Hons). CPFA 1979. Graduate trainee, Liverpool CC, 1974–77; various finance posts, Gtr Manchester Council, 1977–86; Chief Accountant, Trafford MBC, 1986–88; Asst Dir of Finance, 1988, Sen. Asst Dir of Finance, 1988–94, Humberside CC; Dir of Finance, Hull CC, 1994–95. Clerk to: Hull and Goole Port HA, 1995–2002; Humber Bridge Bd, 1996–2002; Humberside Police Authy, 1997–2002. Co. Sec., Hull City Vision, 1995–2002. Audit Cttee, Univ. of Hull Council, 2003–08. Commnd 2nd Lt, 1974, 5/8 Bn Kings Regt T&AVR, 1975–79. Chm. Governors, South Cave Sch., 1993–2005. *Recreations*: aviation, military history, reading.

**CROOKS, Colin James,** LVO 1999; HM Diplomatic Service; Ambassador to the Democratic People's Republic of Korea, since 2018; *b* Dungannon, Co. Tyrone, 18 Feb. 1969; *s* of James Crooks and Elizabeth Crooks; *m* 1996, Young-kee Kim; two *s*. *Educ*: Royal Sch., Dungannon; Fitzwilliam Coll., Cambridge (BA Hons 1992). Desk Officer, FCO, 1992–94; Second, later First Sec., Seoul, 1994–99; Hd of Section, FCO, 1999–2000; Principal Speechwriter to Foreign Sec., 2000–02; First Sec., Washington, 2002–06; Dep. Prog. Dir, FCO, 2006–08; Chargé d'Affaires, Pyongyang, 2008; Dep. Hd of Dept, FCO, 2009–11; Minister-Counsellor, later Chargé d'Affaires, EU Delegn, Jakarta, 2011–15 (on loan to Eur. External Action Service); Minister-Counsellor, Beijing, 2015–18. *Recreations*: reading, history, walking, running, languages. *Address*: British Embassy, Munsu-dong, Pyongyang, Democratic People's Republic of Korea. *T*: 23817980/2/4, ext. 2211. *E*: colin.crooks@fco.gov.uk.

**CROOKS, Air Marshal David Manson,** CB 1985; OBE 1969; FRAeS; Chief of Defence Staff, New Zealand Armed Forces, 1986–87, retired; aviation and defence industry consultant, 1988–99; *b* 8 Dec. 1931; *s* of James and Gladys Meta Crooks; *m* 1954, Barbara Naismith McDougall; four *d*. *Educ*: Rangiora, NZ. Joined RNZAF, 1951; Head, NZ Defence Liaison Staff, Singapore, 1967–70; Commanding Officer: RNZAF Base: Ohakea, 1971–72; Wigram, 1973–74; RCDS, UK, 1974–75; AOC RNZAF Ops Gp, 1978–80; DCAS, 1980–83; CAS, RNZAF, 1983–86. President: RNZAF Assoc., 1990–2000; Air Cadet League; Chairman: Patriotic Fund Bd; RNZAF Mus. Trust Bd. *Recreations*: gardening, reading, vintage motoring, sailing. *Address*: 269b Karori Road, Karori, Wellington 6012, New Zealand. *T*: (4) 4764588. *Club*: Wellington (Wellington, NZ).

**CROOKS, Emily Jane;** *see* Bell, E. J.

**CROPPER, Sir James (Anthony),** KCVO 2011; FCA; Director, James Cropper PLC, 1967–2013, now Honorary President (Chairman, 1971–2010); Lord-Lieutenant of Cumbria, 1994–2012 (Vice Lord-Lieutenant, 1991–94); *b* 22 Dec. 1938; *s* of Anthony Charles Cropper and Philippa Mary Gloria (*née* Clutterbuck); *m* 1967, Susan Rosemary, *y d* of Col F. J. N. Davis; one *s* one *d* (and one *s* decd). *Educ*: Eton; Magdalene Coll., Cambridge (BA). FCA 1966. James Cropper, 1966–; Dir, East Lancashire Paper Group, 1982–84. Member: Lancs River Authority, 1968–74; NW Water Authority, 1973–80, 1983–89; Dir, NW Water Group, 1989–90. Dir, Cumbria Rural Enterprise Agency, 1986–2010; Mem., NW Business Leadership Team, 1991–98. Pres., British Paper and Bd Fedn, 1988–90. Chm., Frieda Scott Charitable Trust, 1981–94; Trustee, Lakeland Arts Trust (formerly Abbot Hall Art Gall. and Mus.), 1992–2010 (Chm. Govs, 1983–88). Member (Indep.): S Westmorland RDC, 1967–74; S Lakeland DC, 1974–77. High Sheriff of Westmorland, 1971; DL Cumbria, 1985. KStJ 1997; CMLJ 2005. Commander, Order of the Lion (Finland), 1991. *Recreations*: shooting, golf. *Address*: Cunswick Hall, Kendal, Cumbria LA8 8JS. *T*: (01539) 722011.

**CROPPER, Peter John,** CBE 1988; Special Adviser: to Chief Secretary to the Treasury, 1979–82; to Chancellor of the Exchequer, 1984–88; *b* 18 June 1927; *s* of late Walter Cecil Cropper and Kathleen Cropper; *m* 1965, Rosemary Winning (*d* 2014); one *s*. *Educ*: Hitchin Grammar Sch.; Gonville and Caius Coll., Cambridge (MA). Served Royal Artillery, 1945–48. Conservative Research Dept, 1951–53, 1975–79, Dir, 1982–84. *Club*: Reform.

**CRORKIN, Colin Wynn,** OBE 2018 (MBE 1993); HM Diplomatic Service, retired; Deputy High Commissioner, Freetown, Sierra Leone, 2017–19; *b* Edinburgh, 31 Jan. 1957; *s* of Daniel and Elizabeth Crorkin; *m* 1991, Joanne Lynn Finnamore; two *s* one *d*. *Educ*: Rowlinson Sch., Sheffield. Entered FCO, 1975; Finance Dept, FCO, 1975–77; Chancery Officer, Rome, 1977–79; Visa Officer, Beirut, 1980–82; Asst Press Officer, UK Representation to EU, Brussels, 1983–84; Personnel Dept, FCO, 1984–87; Mgt Officer, then Dep. Hd of Mission, Kinshasa, 1987–91; British Trade and Investment Office, NY, 1992–94; Near East and N Africa Dept and HR, FCO, 1994–97; Sen. Mgt Officer, Lagos, 1997–2002; Dep. Hd of Mission, Tripoli, 2002–04; Sen. Mgt Officer, Baghdad, 2004–05; Consul Gen., Kirkuk, 2005–06; Dep. Hd of Mission, Manila, 2006–11; Consul Gen., Kabul, 2012–14; Ambassador to The Gambia, 2014–17. *Recreations*: sport, walking.

**CROSBIE, Annette,** OBE 1998; actress; *b* 12 Feb. 1934; *m* Michael Griffiths; one *s* one *d*. *Educ*: Bristol Old Vic Theatre Sch. *Stage* includes: Citizens' Theatre, Glasgow: A View from the Bridge; The Crucible; The Cherry Orchard; Bristol Old Vic: Romeo and Juliet; The Tempest; A Taste of Honey; Comedy Theatre: Tinker; A Singular Man; The Winslow Boy, New, 1970; Mr Bolfry, Aldwych; The Changeling, Royal Court; The Family Dance, Criterion, 1976; The Trojan War Will Not Take Place, NT, 1983; Curtains, Whitehall, 1988; I Thought I Heard a Rustling, Theatre Royal Stratford, 1991; A Delicate Balance, Haymarket, 1997; The Night Season, NT, 2004; *television* includes: *series and serials*: The Six Wives of Henry VIII, 1970 (BAFTA Award for best actress); Edward VII, 1975 (BAFTA Award for best actress); Lillie, 1978; Paradise Postponed, 1986; Take Me Home, 1989; Summer's Lease, 1989; One Foot in the Grave, 1989–2000; Dr Finlay (Scottish TV Award for best actress), 1993; An Unsuitable Job for a Woman, 1997; Little Dorrit, 2008; Hope Springs, 2009; Henry IX, 2017; Call the Midwife, 2019; *plays*: The Seagull; Waste, 1977; Richard III; Beyond the Pale, 1989; *TV film*: Cider with Rosie, 2015; radio plays and serials; *films* include: The Slipper and the Rose (Ev. News British Film Award for best actress), 1975; Ordeal by Innocence; The Pope Must Die, 1990; Calendar Girls, 2003; What We Did on Our Holiday, Into the Woods, 2014; Dad's Army, 2016. Founding Mem., Greyhounds UK, 1998; Vice Pres., League Against Cruel Sports (Pres., 2002–11). Hon. DVMS Glasgow, 2000. *Address*: c/o Independent Talent Group Ltd, 40 Whitfield Street, W1T 2RH.

**CROSBIE, Hon. John Carnell;** PC (Canada) 1979; OC 1998; QC; Counsel, Cox and Palmer (formerly Patterson Palmer Hunt Murphy, then Patterson Palmer), Atlantic Canada lawyers, 1994–2008; Lieutenant Governor of Newfoundland and Labrador, 2008–13; *b* 30 Jan. 1931; *s* of Chesley Arthur Crosbie and Jessie Carnell; *m* 1952, Jane Furneaux; two *s* one *d*. *Educ*: Bishop Feild Coll., St John's, Nfld; St Andrew's Coll., Aurora, Ont.; Queen's Univ., Kingston, Ont. (Top of Pol Sci. and Econs); Dalhousie Univ., Halifax, NS (Law); LSE, London, Eng. Joined Newfoundland Law Soc. and Newfoundland Bar; entered law practice, St John's, 1957; Mem. City Council, St John's, 1965; Dep. Mayor, 1966; Minister of Municipal Affairs and Housing, Province of Newfoundland, (Lib. Admin), July 1966; MHA, Prov. of Newfoundland, Sept. 1966; Minister of Health, 1967; resigned from Govt, 1968; re-elected Member for St John's West (Progressive Conservative), Provincial election, 1971; Minister of Finance, Pres. of Treasury Bd and Minister of Econ. Develt, 1972–74; Minister of Fisheries, Min. for Intergovtl Affairs and Govt House Leader, 1974–75; Minister of Mines and Energy and Minister for Intergovtl Affairs, 1975–76; resigned from Newfoundland Govt, Sept. 1976; elected to House of Commons, Oct. 1976; MP (PC) St John's West, Newfoundland, 1976–93; Chm. of Progressive Conservative Caucus Cttee on Energy, 1977; PC parly critic for Industry, Trade and Commerce, 1977–79; Minister of Finance, 1979–80; Party Finance Critic, 1980; Party External Affairs Critic, 1981–83; Minister of Justice and Attorney General, 1984–86; Minister of Transport, 1986–88; Minister for International Trade, 1988–91; Minister for Fisheries and Oceans and for Atlantic Canada Opportunities Agency, 1991–93. Dir, Atlantic Inst. of Market Studies, 1996–2008. Hon. Consul of Mexico in Newfoundland and Labrador, 1996–2008. Chancellor, Meml Univ. of Newfoundland, 1994–2008. *Publications*: No Holds Barred (memoirs), 1997.

**CROSBY, James Robert;** Senior Independent Director, Compass Group plc, 2007–13; *b* 14 March 1956; *m*; four *d*. *Educ*: Lancaster Royal Grammar Sch.; Brasenose Coll., Oxford (BA Maths). FFA 1980. With Scottish Amicable, 1977–94: posts incl. Investment Dir, 1983, and Hd of Marketing and Planning; Man. Dir, Halifax Life, Halifax Bldg Soc., 1994–96; Dir, Financial Services and Insurance, 1996–99, Chief Exec., 1999–2001, Halifax plc; Gp Chief Exec., HBOS plc, 2001–06. Sen. Ind. Dir, ITV (formerly Granada) plc, 2008–09 (non-exec. Dir, 2002–09); Chm., Misys plc, 2009–12. Member: Eur. Adv. Bd, Bridgepoint Capital, 2006–13; Finance Cttee of the Delegacy, OUP, 2006. Dep. Chm., FSA, 2007–09 (non-exec. Dir, 2004–09). Chairman: Public Private Forum on Identity Mgt, 2006–08 (report, Opportunities and Challenges in Identity Assurance, 2008); Private Investment Commn, North Way, 2008–09; Wkg Gp, Housing Finance Rev., HM Treasury, 2008–09. Trustee, CRUK, 2008–13.

**CROSBY, Sir Lynton (Keith),** Kt 2016; AO 2005; Chief Executive Officer, Crosby/Textor Group, since 2016 (Managing Director, 2002); Co-Founder, CTF Partners (UK), since 2010; Campaign Consultant, Conservative Party, 2013–15; *b* 23 Aug. 1956; *s* of Dudley Keith and Sheila Evelyn Crosby; *m* 1978, Dawn Heinrich; two *d*. *Educ*: Kadina Meml High Sch.; Univ. of Adelaide (BEc). Mkt analyst, Golden Fleece Petroleum, 1976–78; Executive Assistant: to Minister for Educn and Aboriginal Affairs, SA, 1980–82; to Leader of Opposition in Legislative Council, SA, 1982–86; Sen. Planning Officer, Santos Ltd, 1986–89; Manager, PR and Mktg Support, Elders Ltd, 1989–91; Liberal Party of Australia: State Dir, Qld Div., 1991–93; Dep. Federal Dir, 1994–97; Federal Dir, 1997–2002; Campaign Director: for Prime Minister of Australia, John Howard, 1998 and 2001 Gen. Elections; for Cons. Party, UK, 2005 Gen. Election and 2008 and 2012 London Mayoral Elections. *Recreations*: reading, tennis, hockey, politics. *Address*: CTF Partners, Fourth Floor, 6 Chesterfield Gardens, W1J 5BQ.

**CROSLAND, Neisha, (Mrs S. Perche),** RDI 2006; wallpaper and fabric designer with own business, since 1994; *b* 11 Dec. 1960; *d* of C. R. H. Crosland and Felicity Crosland (*née* d'Abreu); *m* 2002, Stephane Perche; two *s*. *Educ*: Camberwell Sch. of Arts and Crafts (BA 1st Cl. Hons Textile Design); Royal Coll. of Art (MA Printed Textiles). Freelance designer and teaching appointments: Glasgow Sch. of Art, 1989–90; Winchester Sch. of Art, 1991–92; Northbrooke Coll., 1992; freelance designer: designed: Romagna collection for Osborne & Little, 1988; Carnaval collection of wallpaper and fabrics for Harlequin Wall Coverings Ltd, 1990–94; contrib. First Eleven Portfolio, textile agency, 1991; launched: Neisha Crosland Scarves, 1994; Neisha at Debenhams, 1998; Ginka Ready to Wear and own Neisha Crosland Wallpaper Collection, 1999; home decorative and stationery collection and opened first retail outlet, London, 2000–01; licensed collection of scarves and fashion accessories for Hankyu, Japan, 2002–; first collection of home furnishing fabrics,

2003; collaboration with Rug Co., 2005–; designed: scarves and ties for Reed Employment, 2007; tiles for De Ferranti, 2008–; range of home furnishings for John Lewis, 2009; hand embroidered fabrics for Chelsea Textiles, 2010–; hand crafted stationery for Harris & Jones, 2011–; vinyl flooring collection for Harvey Maria, 2011–; Japan wallpaper collection for George Spencer Designs, 2015; range of home furnishings for Crate and Barrel, 2015–; secured UK distribn, 2009, worldwide fabric and wallpaper distribn, 2011, with Turnell & Gigon; tiles for Fired Earth, 2015–; tiles for Artisans of Devizes, 2018–; wallpaper collection for Christopher Farr, 2019. Ext. Examr, RCA, 2007. Mem. Panel, RSA Design Bursary Award, 2006–. Hon. Fellow, UAL, 2017. *Publications:* Neisha Crosland: life of a pattern, 2016. *Recreations:* food, wine, films, arts, music. *Address:* 29 Oberstein Road, SW11 2AE. *T:* (020) 7657 1150, *Fax:* (020) 7288 0346. *E:* info@neishacrosland.com. *Club:* Chelsea Arts.

**CROSS, Alistair Robert Sinclair B.;** *see* Bassett Cross.

**CROSS, Prof. Anthony Glenn,** FBA 1989; Professor of Slavonic Studies, 1985–2004, now Emeritus, and Fellow of Fitzwilliam College, 1986–2004, Cambridge University; *b* 21 Oct. 1936; *s* of Walter Sidney Cross and Ada Cross; *m* 1960, Margaret (*née* Elson); two *d*. *Educ:* High Pavement Sch., Nottingham; Trinity Hall, Cambridge (BA 1960, MA 1964, PhD 1966); Harvard Univ. (AM 1961); DLitt East Anglia 1981; LittD Cambridge 1997. Frank Knox Fellow, Harvard Univ., 1960–61; Univ. of East Anglia: Lectr in Russian, 1964–69; Sen. Lectr in Russian, 1969–72; Reader, 1972–81; Roberts Prof. of Russian, Univ. of Leeds, 1981–85. Vis. Fellow: Univ. of Illinois, 1969–70; All Souls Coll., Oxford, 1977–78. Leverhulme Emeritus Fellow, 2008. Pres., British Univs Assoc. of Slavists, 1982–84; Chm., British Academic Cttee for Liaison with Soviet Archives, 1983–95. Mem., Russian Acad. of Humanities, 1996. General Editor: Russia through European Eyes, 1966–68; Anglo-Russian Affinities, 1992–95; Reviews Editor, Jl of European Studies, 1971–; Editor, Study Group on Eighteenth-Century Russia Newsletter, 1973–2009. Hon. Dr, Inst. of Russian Lit., St Petersburg, 2008. Nove Prize, 1997; Antsiferov Prize, St Petersburg, 1998; Dashkova medal, Moscow, 2003. *Publications:* N. M. Karamzin, 1971; Russia Under Western Eyes 1517–1825, 1971; (ed) Russian Literature in the Age of Catherine the Great, 1976; Anglo-Russian Relations in the Eighteenth Century, 1977; (ed) Great Britain and Russia in the Eighteenth Century, 1979; By the Banks of the Thames, 1980; (ed) Russia and the West in the Eighteenth Century, 1981; The Tale of the Russian Daughter and her Suffocated Lover, 1982; (ed jtly) Eighteenth Century Russian Literature, Culture and Thought: a bibliography, 1984; (The Russian Theme in English Literature, 1985; (ed jtly) Russia and the World of the Eighteenth Century, 1988; (ed) An English Lady at the Court of Catherine the Great, 1989; Anglophilia on the Throne: the British and the Russians in the age of Catherine II, 1992; (ed) Engraved in the Memory: James Walker, engraver to Catherine the Great and his Russian anecdotes, 1993; Anglo-Russica: aspects of Anglo-Russian cultural relations in the eighteenth and early nineteenth centuries, 1993; (ed jtly) Literature, Lives and Legality in Catherine's Russia, 1994; By the Banks of the Neva: chapters from the lives of the British in eighteenth-century Russia, 1996; (ed) Russia in the Reign of Peter the Great: old and new perspectives, 1998; (ed jtly) Britain and Russia in the Age of Peter the Great: historical documents, 1998; Peter the Great through British Eyes: perceptions and representations of the tsar since 1698, 2000; Catherine the Great and the British, 2001; (ed) St Petersburg 1703–1825: a collection of essays, 2003; (ed) Anglo-Russian Cultural Encounters and Collisions in the Nineteenth and Early Twentieth Centuries, 2005; (ed) Days from the Reigns of Eighteenth-Century Russian Rulers, 2007; St Petersburg and the British: the city through the eyes of British visitors and residents, 2008; (ed) A People Passing Rude: British responses to Russian culture, 2012; In the Lands of the Romanovs: an annotated bibliography of first-hand English-language accounts of the Russian empire 1613–1907, 2014. *Recreations:* book collecting, cricket watching. *Address:* Fitzwilliam College, Storey's Way, Cambridge CB3 0DG. *T:* (01223) 332000. *E:* agc28@cam.ac.uk.

**CROSS, Anthony Maurice; His Honour Judge Cross;** QC 2006; a Circuit Judge, since 2016; *b* 16 June 1958; *s* of Maurice and Mia Cross; *m* 1982, Joanne Corrin; one *s* two *d*. *Educ:* St Mary's Marist Coll., Blackburn; Univ. of Manchester (LLB Hons 1980). Called to the Bar, Middle Temple, 1982, Bencher, 2016; in practice as a barrister, Manchester; a Recorder of the Crown Court, 2002–16; a Deemster, I of M, 2012–16. Chm., Criminal Bar Assoc., 2014–15 (Vice Chm., 2013–14). Registered Lawyer, FA. *Recreations:* travel, fashion, theatre, film, football, golf, cricket, physical fitness, Northern Soul. *Address:* Manchester Crown Court, Crown Square M3 3FL. *Club:* Burnley Football.

**CROSS, Prof. George Alan Martin,** FRS 1984; André and Bella Meyer Professor of Molecular Parasitology, 1982–2013, now Emeritus, and Dean of Graduate and Postgraduate Studies, 1995–99, Rockefeller University, New York; *b* 27 Sept. 1942; *s* of George Bernard and Beatrice Mary Cross; one *s*. *Educ:* Cheadle Hulme Sch.; Downing Coll., Univ. of Cambridge (BA, PhD). ICI Postdoctoral Fellow, Biochemistry, Cambridge, 1967–69; Research Fellow, Fitzwilliam Coll., Cambridge, 1967–70; Scientist, MRC Biochemical Parasitology Unit, Molteno Inst., Cambridge, 1969–77; Head, Dept of Immunochemistry, Wellcome Research Laboratories, 1977–82. Fleming Lectr, Soc. for General Microbiology, 1978; Leeuwenhoek Lectr, Royal Soc., 1998. Chalmers Medal, Royal Soc. for Tropical Medicine and Hygiene, 1983; (jtly) Paul Ehrlich and Ludwig Darmstaedter Prize, 1984. *Publications:* in journals of parasitology, biochemistry, microbiology and molecular biology. *Recreations:* tennis, building projects, observing people. *Address:* Rockefeller University, 1230 York Avenue, New York, NY 10065-6399, USA. *T:* (212) 3277571. *E:* george.cross@rockefeller.edu.

**CROSS, Gillian Clare,** DPhil; author; *b* 1945; *d* of James Eric Arnold and Joan Emma (*née* Manton); *m* 1967, Martin Francis Cross; two *s* two *d*. *Educ:* North London Collegiate Sch. for Girls; Somerville Coll., Oxford (MA); Univ. of Sussex (DPhil). Mem., Adv. Council on Libraries, 1995–2000. Mem., Soc. of Authors, 1978–. Member: Octavian Droobers, 1990–2009; Wimborne Orienteering Club, 2010–. Freeman, 2007–13, Liveryman, 2013–, Educators' Co. (formerly Guild of Educators). Hon. DLitt Glamorgan, 2008. *Publications:* The Runaway, 1979; The Iron Way, 1979; Revolt at Ratcliffe's Rags, 1980; Save Our School, 1981; A Whisper of Lace, 1981; The Dark Behind the Curtain, 1982; The Demon Headmaster, 1982; Born of the Sun, 1983; The Mintyglo Kid, 1983; On the Edge, 1984; The Prime Minister's Brain, 1985; Chartbreak, 1986 (USA as Chartbreaker, 1987); Swimathon, 1986; Roscoe's Leap, 1987; A Map of Nowhere, 1988; Rescuing Gloria, 1989; Wolf, 1990 (Carnegie Medal, LA, 1990); The Monster from Underground, 1990; Twin and Super-Twin, 1990; Gobbo The Great, 1991; Rent-A-Genius, 1991; The Great Elephant Chase, 1992 (Smarties Book Prize and Whitbread Children's Novel Award, 1992); Beware Olga!, 1993; Furry Maccaloo, 1993; The Tree House, 1993; Hunky Parker is Watching You, 1994; What will Emily Do?, 1994; New World, 1994; The Crazy Shoe Shuffle, 1995; Posh Watson, 1995; The Roman Beanfeast, 1996; Pictures in the Dark, 1996; The Demon Headmaster Strikes Again, 1996; The Demon Headmaster Takes Over, 1997; The Goose Girl, 1998; Tightrope, 1999; Down with the Dirty Danes, 2000; The Treasure in the Mud, 2001; Calling a Dead Man, 2001, US edn as Phoning a Dead Man, 2002; Beware of the Demon Headmaster, 2002; Facing the Demon Headmaster, 2002; The Dark Ground, 2004; The Black Room, 2005; The Nightmare Game, 2006; Brother Aelred's Feet, 2007; Where I Belong, 2010; The Odyssey (retold), 2012; The Monster Snowman, 2012; After Tomorrow, 2013; The Cupcake Wedding, 2013; The Mystery of the Man with the Black Beard, 2014; Mozart's Banana, 2014; Shadow Cat, 2015; The Iliad (retold), 2015; Changing Shape, 2016; Amber's Song, 2016; Film Crew, 2017; The Demon Headmaster: total control, 2017; Jason Banks and the Pumpkin of Doom, 2018; The Demon Headmaster: mortal danger, 2019; The Ghost Tower, 2019. *Recreations:* playing the piano, orienteering. *Address:* c/o Oxford Children's Books, Oxford University Press, Great Clarendon Street, Oxford OX2 6DP.

**CROSS, Hilary Janet;** Associate, Change & Transformation, since 2019; *b* Oxford, 28 Oct. 1960; *d* of Donald Alfred Edgar Cross and Janet Dorothy Cross (*née* Blackman); *m* 2003, Michael John Wrightson; one *s* two *d*. *Educ:* Sidcot Sch., Winscombe, Som; Univ. of Kent at Canterbury (BA Hons English and American Lit.). Bookseller, ICA, 1983–88; Ed., Well Red, Red Wedge, 1987–89; journalist, Time Out, 1990–92; Press Officer, World Soc. for Protection of Animals, 1993–96; Sen. Press Officer, NSPCC, 1996–2001; Macmillan Cancer Support (formerly Relief): Hd of Media, 2001–05; Dep. Dir of Communications, 2005–07; Dir, Ext. Affairs, 2007–12, Mktg and Communications, 2012–15; Mem., Exec. Bd, 2007–15; British Council: Dir, Strategy and Engagement, 2016–18; Global Mktg Dir, 2016–18; Mem., Exec. Bd, 2016–18. Member, Board of Trustees: Encompass, Daniel Braden Reconciliation Trust, 2014–; Prisoners' Educn Trust, 2015–. *Recreations:* social justice, the arts, Tottenham Hotspur Football Club.

**CROSS, James Edward Michael;** QC 2006; *b* 18 March 1962; *s* of Michael Cross and Mary (*née* Wright); *m* 1994, Victoria, *d* of Sir John Henry Lambert, KCVO, CMG; two *s*. *Educ:* Shrewsbury Sch.; Magdalen Coll., Oxford (MA Juris; Academical Clerk). Called to the Bar, Gray's Inn, 1985, Bencher, 2010; in practice specialising in construction and engrg law, professional negligence and liability, insurance, property damage and product liability. Member: Monitoring of Pupillage Review Panel, Bar Council, 1999–2002; Cttee, London Common Law and Commercial Bar Assoc., 2002–08; Cttee, Professional Negligence Bar Assoc., 2008–12; Chm., Pupillage Cttee, 4 Pump Ct, 2003–06. Lectr in Law, Magdalen Coll., Oxford, 1985–88. Mem. Cttee, Adjudication Soc., 2016–. Trustee, Shrewsbury Foundn, 2011–. *Publications:* (contrib.) The Architect's Legal Handbook, 9th edn 2010, 10th edn 2019. *Recreations:* singing (Mem., Vasari Singers, since 1992, Chm., 2004–07), hill walking, gardening. *Address:* 4 Pump Court, Temple, EC4Y 7AN. *Club:* Roehampton.

**CROSS, James Michael;** Founding Chief Executive Officer, Newcastle Parks and Allotments Trust, since 2018; Chairman, Newcastle Parks Enterprises Ltd, since 2019; Partner, Westgate Consultancy, since 2018; *b* Stockton on Tees, 7 Nov. 1974; *s* of Michael Arthur Cross and Winifred Cross (*née* Brown); *m* Karen Purvis; one *s* one *d* (and one *s* decd). *Educ:* Univ. of Teesside (BA Hons Business Econs); Inst. of Dirs (Dip. Company Direction). CMgr 2013; CDir 2016. Asst Chief Inspector of Court Admin in England and Wales, HM Inspectorate of Court Admin, 2005–10; Chief Executive Officer: Marine Mgt Orgn, 2010–14; Natural England, 2014–18 (Mem. Bd, 2015–18). Member: Exec. Cttee, DEFRA, 2014–; Heritage Council, 2018–19. Mem., Assoc. of Chief Execs, 2010–. Trustee, Univ. of Teesside, 2015–. FCMI 2013; FInstD 2015. *Recreations:* being with my family, being outdoors. *E:* james.cross@newcastleparksandallotments.org.uk.

**CROSS, James Richard, (Jasper),** CMG 1971; Under-Secretary, Principal Establishment Officer, Department of Energy, 1978–80; *b* 29 Sept. 1921; *s* of J. P. Cross and Dinah Cross (*née* Hodgins); *m* 1945, Barbara Dagg (decd); (one *d* decd). *Educ:* King's Hosp., Dublin; Trinity Coll., Dublin. Scholar, First Cl. Moderatorship Economics and Pol Science. RE (Lieut). Asst Principal, Bd of Trade, 1947; Private Sec. to Parly Sec., 1947–49; Principal, 1950; Trade Commissioner: New Delhi, 1953–56; Halifax, 1957–60; Winnipeg, 1960–62; Asst Sec., 1962; Sen. Trade Comr, Kuala Lumpur, 1962–66; Bd of Trade, 1966–67; Under Sec., 1968; Sen. British Trade Comr, Montreal, 1968–70 (kidnapped by terrorists and held for 59 days, Oct.–Dec. 1970); Under-Sec., Export Planning and Develt Div., DTI, 1971–73; Coal Div., DTI, later Dept of Energy, 1973–78. *Address:* 4 Crouchfield Close, Crooked Lane, Seaford, East Sussex BN25 1QE.

**CROSS, Jane Elizabeth;** QC 2010; *b* Sussex, 13 Nov. 1958; *d* of Ernest Leonard Cross and Patricia Mary Cross (*née* Baldwin); *m* 1986, Charles Garth McDonald; two *d* (and one *d* decd). *Educ:* Liverpool Univ. (LLB). Called to the Bar, Middle Temple, 1982; in practice as barrister, specialising in family law, Northern Circuit, 1982–. *Recreations:* art, opera, the outdoors. *Address:* Deans Court Chambers, 24 St John Street, Manchester M3 4DF. *T:* (0161) 214 6000, *Fax:* (0161) 214 6001. *E:* cross@deanscourt.co.uk.

**CROSS, Jasper;** *see* Cross, J. R.

**CROSS, Prof. Jonathan Guy Evrill,** PhD, DLitt; Professor of Musicology, University of Oxford, since 2003; Official Student in Music, Christ Church, Oxford, since 2003; *b* Cardiff, 4 Dec. 1961; *s* of late John Cross and of Margaret Cross; *m* 1991, Emma Slade; two *d*. *Educ:* Bishop of Llandaff High Sch., Cardiff; Univ. of Bristol (BA Music 1983); King's Coll. London (PhD 1994); DLitt Oxon 2013. Lectr, Univ. of Sussex, 1986–95; Lectr, 1996–2000, Reader, 2000–03, Univ. of Bristol. Brettschneider Vis. Prof., Cornell Univ., 2009; Prof. invité, Conservatoire de Paris, 2016; Chercheur associé, Inst. de Recherche et Coordination Acoustique/Musique, Paris, 2015–. Ed., Music Analysis, 2000–04. Series Consultant, Philharmonia Orch. (Stravinsky: Myths and Rituals), 2016. Trustee: Hinrichsen Foundn, 1998–2015; Wilts Music Centre, 2011–. MAE 2015. FRSA 2019. *Publications:* The Stravinsky Legacy, 1998; Harrison Birtwistle: man, mind, music, 2000; (ed) The Cambridge Companion to Stravinsky, 2003; Harrison Birtwistle: The Mask of Orpheus, 2009; Igor Stravinsky (Critical Lives), 2015. *Recreation:* cycling up ridiculously high European mountains. *Address:* Christ Church, Oxford OX1 1DP. *T:* (01865) 276186. *E:* jonathan.cross@music.ox.ac.uk.

**CROSS, Julia;** *see* Black, J.

**CROSS, Linda Mary,** MBE 2004; HM Diplomatic Service, retired; Fee Paid Officer, Home Office, since 2016; *b* Dundee, 15 March 1956; *d* of late W. Gordon Guild and Elizabeth Mary Guild; *m* 1989, Michael Cross. *Educ:* Leeds Metropolitan Univ. (BA Hons 1st Cl. Hospitality and Business Mgt). Entered FCO, 1978; Rabat, 1978–81; Prague, 1981–82; Quito, 1983–85; Paris, 1985–88; FCO, 1988–91; Third Sec., Chancery, and Vice-Consul, Vienna, 1992–94; Third Sec., UK Mission to UN, NY, 1995–97; Dep. Hd of Mission, Azerbaijan, 1998–2001; Consul Gen., Yekaterinburg, 2001–05; FCO, 2005–08; Ambassador: to Ecuador, 2008–12; to El Salvador, 2012–14; Exec. Officer to Ct of Aldermen, City of London Corp., 2014–16. *Recreations:* music, reading, swimming, learning languages.

**CROSS, Dame Margaret Natalie;** *see* Smith, Dame Maggie.

**CROSS, Dr Nigel;** consultant in international development; *b* 9 March 1953; *s* of Sir Barry Albert Cross, CBE, FRS and of Audrey Lilian Cross; *m* 1st, 1980, Dr Caroline Dakers (marr. diss. 2010); two *d*; 2nd, 2014, Josephine Namusisi. *Educ:* Univ. of Sussex (BA English 1974); University Coll. London (PhD 1980). Archivist, Royal Literary Fund, 1975–80; Leverhulme Res. Fellow, 1980–81; tutor-counsellor and tutor, third world studies, Open Univ., 1981–87; Sec., British Cttee, SOS Sahel-Internat., 1983–85; Director: SOS Sahel UK, 1985–95; Panos Inst., 1995–99; Dir, 1999–2003, Consultant, 2003–04, Internat. Inst.

for Envmt and Develt; Professorial Res. Fellow, Dept of Develt Studies, SOAS, Univ. of London, 2005–08; Dir, Netherlands Develt Orgn, S Sudan, 2008–11; Dir, Windle Trust Internat., S Sudan, 2012. Consultant: IDL Gp, 2004–07; Creative Exchange, 2006–08. Board Member: FARM Africa, 1989–94; Inst. for Develt Policy and Mgt, Univ. of Manchester, 1992–95; Agency for Co-op. and Res. in Develt (ACORD Africa), 1996–2002 (Chm., 1998–2000); Inst. for Global Envmtl Strategies, Japan, 1999–2003. Ext. collaborator, ILO, Geneva, 1984–86; Member: NGO Consultative Gp, IFAD, Rome, 1991–96 (Co-Chm., 1991–92); Adv. Bd, Grid Arendal, Norway, 2000–02. *Publications:* The Common Writer, 1985; (with N. Ardill) Undocumented Lives, 1987; The Sahel: the people's right to development, 1990; (with R. Barker) At The Desert's Edge: oral histories from the Sahel, 1991; (contributing ed.) Listening for a Change, 1993; (ed) Evidence for Hope: the search for sustainable development, 2003; contribs on literature and develt to various newspapers and specialist jls. *E:* nigelcross@ncross.plus.com.

**CROSS, Peter H.;** *see* Hulme Cross.

**CROSS, Philippa Jane, (Mrs Graham Lee);** Director, CrossDay Productions, since 2002; *b* Ipswich, 13 May 1956; *d* of Robert and Jill Cross; *m* 1982, Graham Lee; one *s* one *d*. *Educ:* Ipswich High Sch.; St Anne's Coll., Oxford (BA 1st Cl. English Lang. and Lit. 1977). Asst Entertainments Manager, Wembley Conf. Centre, 1978–80; Manager: Granada TV, 1980–85; TVS, 1985–88; Hd of Develt, 1988–93, Hd, 1993–2002, Granada Film; credits incl. My Left Foot, The Field, Jack and Sarah, Rogue Trader, House of Mirth, Longitude, Bloody Sunday; CrossDay Prodns credits incl. Shooting Dogs, Heartless, Chalet Girl, Summer in February, Desert Dancer, 100 Streets, Starfish. Member: Screen South, 2003–12; UK Film Council, 2009–10. *Recreations:* family, theatre, winter sports. *Address:* CrossDay Productions, 195 Wardour Street, W1F 8ZG. *T:* (020) 7292 3002. *E:* pippacro@aol.com.

**CROSS, Stefan Tylney;** Senior Partner, Stefan Cross Solicitors, 2002–13; *b* Chiswick, 5 Oct. 1960; *s* of Brian Cross and Jacqueline Ann Pilling; *m* 1986, Dr Alison Mary Steele; two *s* two *d*. *Educ:* Univ. of Southampton (LLB 1982); Univ. of Leicester (LLM 1990). Admitted solicitor, 1985; trainee solicitor, GA Mooring Aldridge and Brownlee, 1983–86; Partner: Brian Thompson and Partners, 1986–90; Thompsons Solicitors, 1990–2002. Part-time Chm., Employment Tribunal, subseq. Employment Judge, 2005–08. Director: Action4Equality Scotland Ltd, 2005–; Fox Cross Solicitors, 2009–11. Mem. (Lab) Newcastle CC, 1990–98. Hon. QC 2013. Campaigner for equal pay for women. *Recreations:* Newcastle United Football Club, trashy crime novels, indie rock music, travel, politics. *Address:* 23 Montagu Avenue, Newcastle upon Tyne NE3 4HY. *T:* (0191) 285 6110. *E:* Stc@stefancross.co.uk.

**CROSS, Maj.-Gen. Timothy,** CBE 2000; Chief Executive Officer, CROSSTC Ltd, since 2007 (Director, since 2006); *b* 19 April 1951; *s* of Sidney George and Patricia Mary Cross; *m* 1972, Christine Mary Pelly; two *s* one *d*. *Educ:* Welbeck; RMA, Sandhurst; RMCS Shrivenham (BSc Hons, MSc); ato. NI, 1978; Adjt 1 Ordnance Bn, 1979–80; UN, Cyprus, 1981; Army Staff Coll., 1982–83 (psc); British Liaison Bureaux, Paris, 1984–85; Co. Comdr, 1 Ordnance Bn, 1986–87; Directing Staff, Army Staff Coll., 1988–90; CO, 1 Ordnance Bn, 1990–92; deployed to Kuwait/Iraq, 1990–91; Comdr, Logistic Support 3 (UK) Div., 1992–96; deployed to Balkans (IFOR), 1995–96; HCSC, 1995; Dir, Materiel Support (Army), 1996–97; Comdr, 101 Logistic Bde, 1998–2000; deployed to Balkans/Kosovo, 1998 (SFOR), 2000 (KFOR); rcds 2000; Dir Gen., Defence Supply Chain (formerly Defence Logistic Support), 2000–03; deployed to Kuwait/Iraq as UK Deputy in ORHA/CPA, 2003; GOC Theatre Troops, 2004–06. Col Comdt RLC, 2003–11; Hon. Col 168 Pioneer Regt, RLC (V), 2007–13. Army Advr, Defence Cttee, H of C, 2007–11, 2013–14. Pres., Inst. of Civil Protection and Emergency Mgt, 2009–. Defence Advisor: Fujitsu, 2007–11; Harmonic, 2007–; Senior Military Adviser: Coker Logistic Solutions, 2007–14; Husons, 2008–12; SC Skills, 2012–17; Advr, Imeon Logistics, 2014–17. Mem., Ethics Cttee, Ultra Electronics, 2011–; non-exec. Bd Mem., Solent Stevedores, 2011–. Has lectured in UK and abroad; Visiting/Honorary Professor: Nottingham Univ., 2007–; Cranfield Univ., 2007–; Reading Univ., 2008–. Director: Centre for Internat. Humanitarian Co-operation, 2004–11; Humanitarian Internat. Services Gp, 2008–13; Caring for Ex-Offenders, 2011–12; William Wilberforce Trust, 2013–15; Agility Defence and Govt Services Bd, 2014–; Mem., Mgt Bd, Theos, 2007– (Chm., 2012–); Trustee, Leadership Trust Foundn, 2003–14. Local Lay Minister (formerly Lay Reader), C of E. Trustee: British and Foreign Bible Soc., 2007–12; Accts Mil. Ministries Internat., 2007–12. *Publications:* contribs chapters and articles to books and jls. *Recreations:* golf, walking, reading, writing.

**CROSS BROWN, Tom;** Deputy Chairman, JRP Group plc, 2016–18 (Chairman, Just Retirement Group plc, 2006–16); *b* Oxford, 22 Dec. 1947; *s* of Christopher James and Georgina Cross Brown; *m* 1972, Susan Rosemary Jackson; three *d* (one *s* decd). *Educ:* Uppingham Sch.; Brasenose Coll., Oxford (MA); INSEAD (MBA). Nat. and Grindlays Bank Ltd, 1970–75; Lazard Brothers & Co. Ltd, 1976–97: Dir. 1985–97, Man. Dir, 1994–97; Chief Exec., Lazard Brothers Asset Mgt Ltd, 1994–97; Chm., 1997–2003, Global Chief Exec., 2000–03, ABN AMRO Asset Mgt Ltd. Non-executive Chairman: Pearl Assce plc, 2005–09; National Provident Life Ltd, 2005–09; NPI Ltd, 2005–09; London Life Ltd, 2005–09; Ignis Asset Mgt Ltd, 2008–10; Xafinity plc, 2017–; non-executive Director: Whitegate Leisure plc, 1987–91; Artemis Investment Mgt Ltd, 2002–06; Quintain Estates and Develt plc, 2005–06; BlueBay Asset Mgt plc, 2006–10; Artemis Alpha Trust plc, 2006–; Phoenix Gp Hldgs, 2009–16; Artemis Investment Mgt LLP, 2011–. Dir, P. A. T. Pensions Ltd, 2005–08. Dir, Financial Planning Standards Bd, 2011–15. Chm., Heathfield Sch., 2005–14 and 2016– (Gov., 1999–2015 and 2016–). Trustee: Cancer Care and Haematol. Fund, Stoke Mandeville Hosp., 2004–14; Lazard Dirs' Pension Scheme, 2007–14. Mem., Finance and Gen. Purposes Cttee, VSO, 1979–82. Pres., INSEAD Alumni Assoc. UK, 1977–82. Hon. Sec., Benedict Soc., 2005–12 (Mem., 2001). *Recreations:* opera, shooting, gardening. *Address:* Shipton Old Farm, Winslow, Buckingham MK18 3JL. *Club:* Boodle's.

**CROSSE, Gordon;** composer; *b* 1 Dec. 1937; *s* of Percy and Marie Crosse; *m* 1965, Elizabeth Bunch (*d* 2011). *Educ:* Cheadle Hulme Sch.; St Edmund Hall, Oxford; Accademia di S Cecilia, Rome. Music Fellow, Essex Univ., 1969–74; Composer in residence, King's Coll., Cambridge, 1974–76; Vis. Lectr, Univ. of Calif at Santa Barbara, 1977–78. Hon. RAM 1980. *Operas:* Purgatory, 1966; The Grace of Todd, 1967; The Story of Vasco, 1970; Potter Thompson, 1973; *ballets:* Playground, 1979; Wildboy, 1981; *other compositions:* Concerto da Camera, 1962; Meet My Folks, 1963; "Symphonies", 1964; Second Violin Concerto, 1970; Memories of Morning: Night, 1972; Ariadne, 1973; Symphony 2, 1975; Wildboy (clarinet concerto), 1977; Play Ground, 1977; Dreamsongs, 1978; Cello Concerto, 1979; String Quartet, 1980; Trio for clarinet, cello and piano, 1980; Dreamcanon (chorus), 1981; Trio for piano, violin and cello, 1986; Trumpet Concerto, 1986; Rhyming with Everything for oboe, violin and cello, 2009; Fantasia on Ca' The Yowes for flute, harp (or clarsach) and strings, 2009; Brief Encounter for oboe d'amore, recorder and strings, 2009; Ad Patrem, 3rd elegy for small orchestra, 2009; Spring Awakening for 5 male voices and speaker, 2009; String Quartet No 2, Good to be Here, 2010; Sabbath Rest, anthem for TrATB and organ, 2010; Hey the Gift, Ho the Gift for SATB a capella, 2010; much other orchestral, vocal and chamber music. *Address:* Brant's Cottage, Blackheath, Wenhaston, Halesworth, Suffolk IP19 9EX.

**CROSSETT, Robert Nelson, (Tom),** DPhil; Chairman: National Flood Forum, 2004–06 (Director, 2003–06); Thames Flood Forum, 2005–08; *b* 27 May 1938; *s* of Robert Crossett and Mary Nelson; *m* 1966, Susan Marjorie Legg; two *s*. *Educ:* British School, Hamburg; Campbell College, Belfast; Queen's Univ., Belfast (BSc, BAgr); Lincoln College, Oxford (DPhil); Univ. of East Anglia. Group Leader Environmental Studies, Aust. Atomic Energy Commn, 1966; Sen. Sci. Officer, ARC Letcombe Lab., 1969; Develt Officer (Crops), Scottish Agricl Develt Council, 1972; PSO, Dept of Agric. and Fisheries for Scotland, 1975; Ministry of Agriculture, Fisheries and Food: Sci. Liaison Officer (Horticulture and Soils), 1978; Head, Food Sci. Div., 1984; Chief Scientist (Fisheries and Food), 1985–89; Head of Envmtl Policy, 1989–90, Envmt Dir, 1990–91, National Power; Sec. Gen., Nat. Soc. for Clean Air and Envmtl Protection, 1992–96; Dir-Gen., Internat. Union of Air Pollution Prevention Assocs, 1996–98. Chairman: Southern Regional Envmtl Protection Adv. Cttee, EA, 1996–2002; SE Water Resources Forum, 2005–08. Consultant, SE Inst. of Public Health, 1998–2000. Member: NERC, 1985–89; AFRC, 1985–89; UK Delegn, Tripartite Meetings on Food and Drugs, 1985–88; Cttee on Med. Aspects of Food Policy, 1985–89; Adv. Gp to Sec. of State for Envmt on Eco-Management and Audit, 1994–96; UK Round Table on Sustainable Develt, 1995–97. Vis. Fellow, Sci. Policy Res. Unit, Univ. of Sussex, 1997–2000; Sen. Vis. Fellow, Sch. of Health and Life Scis, KCL, 2000–05. *Publications:* papers in plant physiology, marine biology, food science and envmtl management. *Recreations:* walking, gardening, orienteering, boats.

**CROSSICK, Prof. Geoffrey Joel,** PhD; FRHistS; Distinguished Professor of the Humanities, School of Advanced Study, University of London, since 2013; *b* 13 June 1946; *s* of Louis Crossick and Rebecca Naomi (*née* Backen); *m* 1973, Rita Geraldine Vaudrey, JP; two *s*. *Educ:* Haberdashers' Aske's Sch., Elstree; Gonville and Caius Coll., Cambridge (BA Hist. 1967); Birkbeck Coll., London (PhD Hist. 1976). FRHistS 1993. Res. Fellow in Hist., Emmanuel Coll., Cambridge, 1970–73; Lectr in Social Hist., Univ. of Hull, 1973–78; University of Essex: Lectr in Hist., 1979–83; Sen. Lectr, 1983–86; Reader, 1986–91; Prof. of Hist., 1991–2002; Dean: Comparative Studies, 1992–95; Grad. Sch., 1996–97; Pro-Vice-Chancellor, 1997–2002; Chief Exec., AHRB, 2002–05; Warden, Goldsmiths Coll., later Goldsmiths, Univ. of London, 2005–10 (Hon. Fellow, 2012); Vice-Chancellor, Univ. of London, 2010–12. Vis. Prof., Univ. of Lyon 2, 1990–91. Member: Business and Community Strategy Cttee, then Enterprise and Skills Strategy Cttee, HEFCE, 2005–12; Bd, UUK, 2006–12; Sci. Adv. Council, DCMS, 2015–. Dir, AHRC Cultural Value Project, 2012–16. Member: British Library Adv. Council, 2004–14; Council, Royal Coll. Music, 2005–10; Bd, UCEA, 2007–09; Governing Body, Courtauld Inst., 2007–17 (Hon. Fellow, 2017); Council, Agence d'évaluation de la recherche et de l'enseignement supérieur, 2012–13; Bd of Govs, GSMD, 2016–; Bd of Govs, Nat. Film and Television Sch., 2017–; Chairman: Financial Sustainability Strategy Gp, 2008–12; Bd of Governance, Trinity Long Room Hub, TCD, 2010–18; Crafts Council, 2014–. Trustee: Nat. Maritime Mus., 2010–14; Samuel Courtauld Trust, 2010–17; Horniman Mus. and Gardens, 2013–; Goldsmiths Centre, 2014–17. Hon. Fellow, Emmanuel Coll., Cambridge, 2004. FRSA 2009. *Publications:* (ed) The Lower Middle Class in Britain, 1976; An Artisan Elite in Victorian Society, 1978; (ed jtly) Shopkeepers and Master Artisans in 19th Century Europe, 1984; (ed jtly) The Power of the Past: essays for Eric Hobsbawm, 1984; (with H. G. Haupt) The Petite Bourgeoisie in Europe 1780–1914, 1995; (ed) The Artisan and the European Town, 1997; (ed jtly) Cathedrals of Consumption: the European department store 1850–1939, 1998; Knowledge Transfer without Widgets: the challenge of the creative economy, 2006; (with P. Kaszynska) Understanding the Value of Arts and Culture: the AHRC Cultural Value Project, 2016; contrib. articles to learned jls. *Recreations:* Tottenham Hotspur, music, contemporary craft. *E:* geoffrey.crossick@london.ac.uk.

**CROSSLAND, Anthony;** Organist and Master of the Choristers, Wells Cathedral, 1971–96; *b* 4 Aug. 1931; *s* of Ernest Thomas and Frances Elizabeth Crossland; *m* 1960, Barbara Helen Pullar-Strecker; one *s* two *d*. *Educ:* Christ Church, Oxford. MA, BMus (Oxon), FRCO (CHM), ARCM. Asst Organist: Christ Church Cathedral, Oxford, 1957–61; Wells Cathedral, 1961–71. Conductor: Wells Cathedral Oratorio Soc., 1966–96; Wells Sinfonietta, 1985–96; Organs Advr to dio. of Bath and Wells, 1971–96. Pres., Cathedral Organists' Assoc., 1983–85. Chief Theory Moderator, Associated Bd of Royal Schs of Music, 2009–13. DMus Lambeth, 1994. *Recreations:* reading, photography, armchair travelling. *Address:* Barton End, 10b Newtown, Bradford-on-Avon, Wilts BA15 1NE. *T:* (01225) 864496.

**CROSSLEY,** family name of **Baron Somerleyton**.

**CROSSLEY, Prof. (Bernard) Paul,** PhD; FBA 2016; Professor of the History of Art, Courtauld Institute of Art, University of London, 1990–2012, now Emeritus; *b* Oxford, 19 July 1945; *s* of Goulbourne Crossley and Nancy Crossley; *m* 1993, Rev. Dr Joan Hichberger; one *s* one *d*. *Educ:* Worth Priory; Downside Abbey; Trinity Coll., Cambridge (BA 1967; PhD 1973). Reader in Hist. of Art, Univ. of Manchester, 1972–90. Slade Prof. in Hist. of Art, Univ. of Cambridge, 2012. Vis. Fellow, Leipzig Univ., 2002. Fellow, Polish Acad. of Arts and Scis, 2002. Pres., Cambridge Union. 1966. Editor, Jl of Warburg and Courtauld Insts, 1995–2012. *Publications:* Gothic Architecture in the Reign of Kasimir the Great: church architecture in Lesser Poland 1320–1380, 1985; (with Paul Frankl) Gothic Architecture, 2000; (contrib.) Rhetoric Beyond Words, 2010; (contrib.) Meditations on a Heritage, 2014. *Recreations:* classical music, playing piano, watercolouring, Wagner and Schopenhauer (to cheer me up). *Address:* Courtauld Institute of Art, Somerset House, Strand, WC2R 0RN. *T:* (020) 7848 2777.

**CROSSLEY, Prof. Gary;** Principal, Central School of Speech and Drama, 2000–07; *b* 11 Jan. 1946; *s* of John and Patricia Crossley; *m* 1981, Yvonne Stapleton-Henthorne; one *d*. *Educ:* Portsmouth Coll. of Art (BA Hons); Hornsey Sch. of Art (PG Dip.). Hd of Dept, E Ham Coll., 1979–85; Vice Principal, W Surrey Coll. of Art and Design, 1985–89; Dep. Dir, Surrey Inst. of Art and Design, 1989–98; Founding Chm., Consortium of Arts and Design Instns in Southern England, 1998–2000. Mem. Bd, 2000–05, Exec. Council, 2005–07, Standing Conf. of Principals. Mem., Univ. Choice TV Adv. Bd, 2004. *Recreations:* theatre, film, flyfishing. *Club:* Savile.

**CROSSLEY, Paul;** *see* Crossley, B. P.

**CROSSLEY, Paul Christopher Richard,** CBE 1993; concert pianist; Artistic Director, London Sinfonietta, 1988–94; *b* 17 May 1944; *s* of late Frank Crossley and Myra Crossley (*née* Barrowcliffe). *Educ:* Silcoates Sch., Wakefield; Mansfield Coll., Oxford (BA, MA; Hon. Fellow, 1992). International concert pianist; recitals and concerts with all major orchestras; numerous recordings and films for TV. *Recreations:* Mah-Jongg, reading, crosswords. *Address:* 39 Henry Tate Mews, SW16 3HA. *T:* (020) 8769 4471. *E:* pcr.crossley@btinternet.com. *W:* www.paulcrossleypianist.com.

**CROSSLEY, Sir Sloan (Nicholas),** 6th Bt *cr* 1909, of Glenfield, Dunham Massey, Chester; Managing Director, Pull Scar Estates (Pty) Ltd, White River, South Africa, until 2019; *b* 20 March 1958; *s* of late Wing Comdr Michael Nicholson Crossley, RAF, DSO, OBE, DFC and Sylvia Constance Crossley; *S* cousin, 2003; *m* 1999, Jane Elizabeth, *d* of late Henry Cecil Twycross and Katherine Elizabeth Twycross. *Educ*: St Alban's Coll., Pretoria; Kingston Polytech., London; Central Sch. of Art and Design, London (BSc Hons Industrial Design (Eng)). *Address*: Pull Scar Estate, PO Box 121, White River, 1240 Mpumalanga, South Africa.

**CROSSLEY-HOLLAND, Kevin John William,** FRSL; author; President, School Library Association, 2012–17; *b* 7 Feb. 1941; *s* of late Prof. Peter Charles Crossley-Holland and Joan Mary Crossley-Holland (*née* Cowper), MBE; *m* 1st, 1963, Caroline Fendall, *er d* of Prof. L. M. Thompson; two *s*; 2nd, 1972, Ruth, *er d* of John Marris; 3rd, 1982, Gillian Paula, *er d* of Peter Cook; two *d*; 4th, 1999, Linda Marie, *d* of Abner Jones. *Educ*: Bryanston Sch.; St Edmund Hall, Oxford (MA Hons; Hon. Fellow, 2001). FRSL 1998. Editor, Macmillan & Co., 1962–69; Gregory Fellow in Poetry, Univ. of Leeds, 1969–71; Talks Producer, BBC, 1972; Editl Dir, Victor Gollancz, 1972–77; Lectr in English: Tufts-in-London Program, 1967–78; Regensburg Univ., 1978–80; Arts Council Fellow in Writing, Winchester Sch. of Art, 1983 and 1984; Vis. Prof. of English and Fulbright Scholar, St Olaf Coll., Minnesota, 1987–90; Prof. and Endowed Chair in Humanities and Fine Arts, Univ. of St Thomas, Minnesota, 1991–95; Vis. Lectr for British Council in Germany, Iceland, India, Malawi, Yugoslavia, Slovakia. Editl Consultant, Boydell & Brewer, 1983–90. Chm., Literature Panel, Eastern Arts Assoc., 1986–89; Trustee, Wingfield Coll., 1989–99 (Chm., Friends, 1989–91). Dir, American Composers Forum, 1993–97. Chm., Poetry-next-the-Sea, 1999–2006. Patron: Thomas Lovell Beddoes Soc., 1999–2011; Soc. for Storytelling, 2002–; Publishing House Me, 2008–; European Storytelling Archive, 2009–; Story Mus., 2013–. Contribs to radio (incl. drama), TV (incl. educnl series); musical works: (with Sir Arthur Bliss) A Knot of Riddles, 1964; (with W. Mathias) Riddles, 1992; (with S. Paulus) Pilgrim Jesus, 1996; (with J. Wheeler), Sea Changes, 2004; (with B. Hughes) The Death of Balder, 2008, A Medieval Bestiary, 2011; (with R. Chilcott) Four Carols, 2010, My Perfect Stranger, 2016; (with C. McDowall) A Time for All Seasons, 2016, As Each Leaf Dances, 2016; Everyday Wonders: the girl from Aleppo, 2018. Hon. DLitt: Anglia Ruskin, 2011; Worcester, 2013. *Publications*: *poetry*: The Rain-Giver, 1972; The Dream-House, 1976; Time's Oriel, 1983; Waterslain, 1986; The Painting-Room, 1988; New and Selected Poems, 1991; The Language of Yes, 1996; Poems from East Anglia, 1997; Selected Poems, 2001; (with Norman Ackroyd) Moored Man, 2006; The Mountains of Norfolk: new and selected poems, 2011; Attraction Water, 2012; The Breaking Hour, 2015; (with Gillian Crossley-Holland) Veering North-Easterly, 2016; (with Andrew Rafferty) Seahenge: a journey, 2019; *for children*: Havelok the Dane, 1964; King Horn, 1965; The Green Children, 1966 (Arts Council Award); The Callow Pit Coffer, 1968; (with Jill Paton Walsh) Wordhoard, 1969; Storm and Other Old English Riddles, 1970; The Pedlar of Swaffham, 1971; The Sea Stranger, 1973; The Fire-Brother, 1974; Green Blades Rising, 1975; The Earth-Father, 1976; The Wildman, 1976; The Dead Moon, 1982; (with Charles Keeping) Beowulf, 1982; (with Gwyn Thomas) The Mabinogion, 1984; Axe-Age, Wolf-Age, 1985; Storm, 1985 (Carnegie Medal); (with Susanne Lugert) The Fox and the Cat, 1985; British Folk Tales, 1987, reissued as The Magic Lands, 2001; Wulf, 1988; (with Gwyn Thomas) The Quest for Olwen, 1988; Piper and Pooka, 1988; Small Tooth Dog, 1988; Boo!, 1988; Dathera Dad, 1989; (with Ian Penney) Under the Sun and Over the Moon, 1989; Sleeping Nanna, 1989; Sea Tongue, 1991; Tales from Europe, 1991; Long Tom and The Dead Hand, 1992; (with Gwyn Thomas) Taliesin, 1992; The Labours of Herakles, 1993; Norse Myths, 1993; The Green Children, 1994; The Dark Horseman, 1995; The Old Stories, 1997; Short!, 1998; The King Who Was and Will Be, 1998; Enchantment, 2000; The Seeing Stone, 2000 (Guardian Children's Fiction Prize; Tir na n-Og Award); At the Crossing-Places, 2001; (with Meilo So) The Ugly Duckling, 2001; Viking!, 2002; King of the Middle March, 2003; (with Peter Malone) How Many Miles to Bethlehem?, 2004; King Arthur's World, 2004; Outsiders, 2005; Gatty's Tale, 2006; Thor and the Master of Magic, 2007; Waterslain Angels, 2008; Short Too!, 2011; Bracelet of Bones, 2011; Scramasax, 2012; (with Jane Ray) Heartsong, 2015; (with Stéphane Jorisch) The Riddlemaster, 2016; Norse Myths: tales of Odin, Thor and Loki, 2017; Between Worlds: British and Irish folktales, 2018; *play*: (with Ivan Cutting) The Wuffings, 1999; *travel*: Pieces of Land, 1972; *mythology*: The Norse Myths, 1980; *history*: (with Andrew Rafferty) The Stones Remain, 1989; *translations from Old English*: (with Bruce Mitchell) The Battle of Maldon, 1965; (with Bruce Mitchell) Beowulf, 1968; The Exeter Book Riddles, 1978; The Illustrated Beowulf, 1987; The Anglo-Saxon Elegies, 1988; *edited*: Running to Paradise, 1967; Winter's Tales for Children 3, 1967; Winter's Tales 14, 1968; (with Patricia Beer) New Poetry 2, 1976; The Faber Book of Northern Legends, 1977; The Faber Book of Northern Folk-Tales, 1980; The Anglo-Saxon World, 1982; The Riddle Book, 1982; Folk-Tales of the British Isles, 1985; The Oxford Book of Travel Verse, 1986; Northern Lights, 1987; Medieval Lovers, 1988; Medieval Gardens, 1990; Peter Grimes by George Crabbe, 1990; The Young Oxford Book of Folk-Tales, 1998; (with Lawrence Sail) The New Exeter Book of Riddles, 1999; (with Lawrence Sail) Light Unlocked: Christmas card poems, 2005; *operas*: (with Nicola LeFanu): The Green Children, 1990; The Wildman, 1995; (with Rupert Bawden) The Sailor's Tale, 2002; *memoir*: The Hidden Roads, 2009. *Recreations*: walks, wine, opera, the company of friends, appreciating East Anglia. *Address*: Chalk Hill, Burnham Market, Norfolk PE31 8JR; c/o The Agency, 24 Pottery Lane, Holland Park, W11 4LZ. *Club*: Garrick.

**CROSSMAN, Prof. David Christopher,** MD; FRCP, FRCPE; Dean of Medicine, University of St Andrews, since 2014; Chief Scientist (Health), Scottish Government, since 2017; *b* Gravesend, 20 July 1957; *s* of William George Crossman and Charmian Jeanette Crossman; *m* 1988, Moira Katherine Brigid Whyte, *qv*; two *s*. *Educ*: Sedbergh Sch.; St Bartholomew's Med. Sch., London (BSc Physiol. 1979; MB BS 1982; MD 1991). MRCP 1985, FRCP 1998; FACC 1999; FESC 2000; FRCPE 2015. MRC Clin. Trng Fellow, 1988–91; Sen. Registrar, Cardiol., Hammersmith and St Mary's Hosps, 1991–94; Prof. of Cardiol., Univ. of Sheffield, 1994–2010; Dean of Medicine, Norwich Med. Sch., UEA, 2011–14. *Recreations*: running, classical music, motor bikes, fishing. *Address*: School of Medicine, University of St Andrews, North Haugh, St Andrews, Fife KY16 9TF. *T*: (01334) 463502, *Fax*: (01334) 463482. *E*: medical.dean@st-andrews.ac.uk.

**CROSSMAN, Moira Katherine Brigid;** *see* Whyte, M. K. B.

**CROTHERS, William,** CB 2014; Board Member and Senior Adviser, Cabinet Office, since 2015; Vice-Chair, Greensill Capital, since 2019 (Senior Advisor to Board, 2015); *b* Thirsk, Yorks, 9 Nov. 1960; *s* of Morland Crothers and Violet Crothers; *m* 2009, Lucy Bloem; four *d*. *Educ*: Belfast Royal Acad.; Univ. of Manchester (BSc 1st Cl. Hons Computer Sci. and Accounting 1982). FCA 1985; FBCS 2009; FCIPS 2012. Chartered Accountant, Peat Marwick, 1982–85; Mgt Consultant, Andersen Consulting, subseq. Accenture, 1985–2006, Partner and Mem. UK Bd, 1995–2006; Exec. Dir, Identity and Passport Service, 2007–10; Commercial Dir, Home Office, 2010–12; Crown Rep., 2010–12; Chm., Crown Commercial Service, 2014; Govt Chief Commercial (formerly Procurement) Officer, and Dir Gen., Commercial, Cabinet Office, 2012–15. Mem. Bd, Nat. Citizen Service, 2015–. Trustee, UK Youth, 2005–13 (Chm., 2010–13). Governor: Woldingham Sch. for Girls, 2010–; Hazelwood Sch., 2014–. *Recreations*: spending time with family and friends, enjoying sun, sea and sand of the south coast of England (West Sussex).

**CROUCH, Anne Elisabeth;** *see* Osbourn, A. E.

**CROUCH, Prof. Colin John,** DPhil; FBA 2005; FAcSS; Professor of Governance and Public Management, Warwick Business School, University of Warwick, 2005–11, now Emeritus; *b* 1 March 1944; *s* of Charles and Doris Crouch; *m* 1970, Joan Ann Freedman; two *s*. *Educ*: Latymer Upper Sch.; London School of Economics (BASoc; Pres., Students Union, 1968; Hobhouse Prize, 1969); Nuffield Coll., Oxford (MA; DPhil 1975). Lecturer in Sociology: LSE, 1969–70; Univ. of Bath, 1972–73; Lectr, 1973–79, Sen. Lectr 1979–80, Reader 1980–85, in Sociology, LSE; University of Oxford: Fellow and Tutor in Politics, Trinity Coll., Oxford, 1985–98; Prof. of Sociol., 1996–98; Curator, Bodleian Liby, 1991–95; Jun. Proctor, 1990–91; Deleg., OUP, 1992–98; European University Institute, Florence: Prof. of Comparative Social Instns, 1995–2004; Chm., Dept of Social and Political Scis, 2001–04. External Scientific Mem., Max-Planck Institut für Gesellschaftsforschung, Cologne, 1997–. Mem., Exec. Cttee, Fabian Soc., 1969–78 (Chm., 1976); Dir, Andrew Shonfield Soc., 1989–95. Vice Pres., British Acad., 2012–16. Member: Standing Cttee, Court of Govs, LSE, 1980–84; Scientific Adv. Bd, Univ. of Vienna, 2007–14. Fellow, Sunningdale Inst., 2005–09. Chm. Editl Bd, The Political Qly, 1999–2009 (Joint Editor, 1985–95). FAcSS (AcSS 2008). *Publications*: The Student Revolt, 1970; (ed jtly) Stress and Contradiction in Modern Capitalism, 1975; (ed) British Political Sociology Year Book, vol. III, 1977; Class Conflict and the Industrial Relations Crisis, 1977; (ed jtly) The Resurgence of Class Conflict in Western Europe since 1968, 2 vols, 1978; (ed) State and Economy in Contemporary Capitalism, 1979; The Politics of Industrial Relations, 1979, 2nd edn 1982; Trade Unions: the logic of collective action, 1982; (ed jtly) International Yearbook of Organizational Democracy, vol. I, 1983; (ed jtly) The New Centralism: Britain out of step in Europe?, 1989; (ed jtly) European Industrial Relations: the challenge of flexibility, 1990; (ed jtly) Corporatism and Accountability: organised interests in British public life, 1990; (ed jtly) The Politics of 1992: beyond the single European market, 1990; (ed jtly) Towards Greater Europe?, 1992; Industrial Relations and European State Traditions, 1993 (Political Studies Assoc. Book Prize, 1993); (ed jtly) Ethics and Markets: co-operation and competition in capitalist economies, 1993; (ed jtly) Reinventing Collective Action: the global and the local, 1995; (ed jtly) Organized Industrial Relations in Europe: what future?, 1995; (ed jtly) Les capitalismes en Europe, 1996; (ed jtly) Political Economy of Modern Capitalism, 1997; (jtly) Are Skills the Answer?, 1999; Social Change in Western Europe, 1999; (ed jtly) After the Euro, 2000; (ed jtly) Citizenship, Markets and the State, 2001; (ed) Coping with Post-Democracy, 2001; (jtly) Local Production Systems in Europe: rise or demise?, 2001; Commercialisation or Citizenship, 2003; Postdemocrazia, 2003, trans. English as Postdemocracy, 2004; (jtly) Changing Governance of Local Economies: responses of European local production systems, 2004; Capitalist Diversity and Change, 2005; (jtly) Innovation in Local Economies: Germany in comparative text, 2009; The Strange Non-Death of Neoliberalism, 2011; (ed jtly) The Responsible Corporation, 2011; Making Capitalism Fit for Society, 2013; Governing Social Risks in Post-Crisis Europe, 2015; The Knowledge Corrupters: hidden consequences of the financial takeover of public life, 2015; Society and Social Change in 21st Century Europe, 2016; Can Neoliberalism be Saved from Itself?, 2017; The Globalization Backlash, 2018; Will the Gig Economy Prevail?, 2019; numerous articles on industrial relns, politics, economic sociology and social structure in Britain and Western Europe. *Recreations*: playing violin, music, gardening, watching and refereeing football matches. *Address*: Warwick Business School, University of Warwick, Coventry CV4 7AL.

**CROUCH, Prof. David Bruce,** PhD; FBA 2014; FRHistS; Professor of Medieval History, University of Hull, 2000; *b* Cardiff, 31 Oct. 1953; *s* of Ronald Desmond Crouch and Elsie Mary Crouch (*née* Skipper); *m* 1987, Linda Helen Smith (marr. diss.); two *s*. *Educ*: Cantonian High Sch., Cardiff; University Coll., Cardiff (BA Hist. 1975); Univ. of Wales, Cardiff (PhD 1983). Secondary sch. teacher, Mountain Ash Comprehensive Sch., 1976–82; researcher, Inst. of Histl Res., 1983–89; Sen. Lectr, N Riding Coll., 1990–93; Prof. of Hist., University Coll., Scarborough, 1993–2000. FRHistS 1986. *Publications*: The Beaumont Twins, 1986; William Marshal, 1990, 3rd edn 2016; The Image of Aristocracy in Britain, 1992; The Reign of King Stephen, 2002; The Birth of Nobility, 2005; Tournament, 2005; The English Aristocracy, 1070–1272, 2011; Lost Letters of Medieval Life, 2013; The Newburgh Earldom of Warwick, 2015; The Acts and Letters of the Marshal Family, 2015.

**CROUCH, Sybil Edith;** Director, Taliesin Arts Centre, Swansea University (formerly University College of Swansea, then University of Wales, Swansea), 1990–2019; *b* 9 Aug. 1953; *d* of David George and Lilian Crouch; *m* 2010, David Phillips. *Educ*: Birkenhead High Sch. for Girls; Swansea Coll. of Art. Specialist Art Teacher. Dep. Dir, W Wales Assoc. for the Arts, 1979–90. Chm., Arts Council of Wales, 1999–2003. Mem. (Lab) Swansea CC, 2012– (Cabinet Mem. for Sustainability, 2012–14). *Recreation*: the company of friends.

**CROUCH, Tracey Elizabeth Anne;** MP (C) Chatham and Aylesford, since 2010; *b* Ashford, Kent, 24 July 1975; *d* of Kenneth Allen Crouch and Sallyanne Crouch (*née* French); one *s*. *Educ*: Folkestone Sch. for Girls; Hull Univ. (BA Jt Hons Law and Pols 1996). Parly Researcher, 1996–98; Sen. Public Affairs Manager, Harcourt Public Affairs, 1999–2000; Westminster Strategy, 2000–03; COS to Shadow Educn Sec., then Shadow Transport Sec., 2003; COS to Shadow Home Sec., 2003–05; Hd, Public Affairs, Aviva, 2005–10. Parly Under-Sec. of State for Sport and Tourism, then for Sport and Civil Society, DCMS, 2015–18. Mem., Culture, Media and Sport Select Cttee, 2012–15. Chm., All Party Parly Gp on Alcohol Misuse, 2011–14 (Vice Chm., 2010–11); Vice Chm., All Party Parly Gp on Athletics, 2010, on Dementia, 2010; Sec., All Party Parly Gp on Inscn and Financial Services, 2010–11. Mem., British delegn, OSCE, 2010; Parly Ambassador, Us Girls, 2011–. Mem., Exec., 1922 Cttee, 2010–12. Mem., Foundn Bd, World Anti-Doping Agency, 2016–. Trustee, Women's Sport and Fitness Foundn, 2013. Pres., RSPCA Medway, 2010–; Chm., Pet Adv. Cttee, 2011–; Patron: Chatham Town FC, 2011–; Nat. Osteoporosis Soc. Hon. MInstRE 2011. *Recreations*: sport, travel, manager of Meridian Girls FC. *Address*: House of Commons, SW1A 0AA. *E*: tracey.crouch.mp@parliament.uk.

**CROW, Jonathan Rupert;** QC 2006; Attorney General to the Prince of Wales, since 2006; a Judge of the Courts of Appeal of Jersey and Guernsey, since 2011; *b* 25 June 1958; *s* of Michael Frederick Crow and Edith Mae Crow; *m* 1998, Claudia Jane Turner; three *s* one *d*. *Educ*: St Paul's Sch.; Magdalen Coll., Oxford (BA Modern Hist.). Called to the Bar, Lincoln's Inn, 1981; Treasury Counsel (Chancery), 1994–98; First Treasury Counsel (Chancery), 1998–2006; Dep. High Court Judge, 2007–; Dep. Deemster, IoM, 2017–. *Address*: 4 Stone Buildings, Lincoln's Inn, WC2A 3XT. *T*: (020) 7242 5524, *Fax*: (020) 7831 7907. *E*: clerks@4stonebuildings.com. *Club*: Athenæum.

**CROW, Prof. Timothy John,** OBE 2018; PhD; FRCP, FRCPsych, FMedSci; Hon. Scientific Director, SANE Prince of Wales Centre for Research into Schizophrenia and Depression, University Department of Psychiatry, Warneford Hospital, Oxford, 1995; Titular Professor of Psychiatry, University of Oxford, 1998–2007, now Emeritus; *b* 7 June 1938; *s* of late Percy Arthur Crow and Barbara Bonner Davies; *m* 1966, Julie Carol Carter; one *s* one *d*. *Educ*: Shrewsbury Sch.; London Hosp. Med. Coll. MB BS, PhD, DPM.

Maudsley Hosp., 1966; University of Aberdeen: Lectr in Physiology, 1966–70; Lectr in Mental Health, 1970–72; Sen. Lectr in Psychiatry, Univ. of Manchester, 1972–73; Head, Div. of Psychiatry, Clinical Res. Centre, Northwick Park Hosp., 1974–94. Part-time Mem., Sci. Staff, Div. Neurophysiology and Neuropharmacology, Nat. Inst. for Med. Res., 1974–83; Dep. Dir, Clinical Res. Centre, 1984–89. Member: MRC Neuroscis Projects Grants Cttee, 1978–80; Neuroscis Bd, 1986–90; Chm., Biol. Psych. Gp, RCPsych, 1983–88 (Sec., 1980–83). Andrew W. Woods Vis. Prof., Univ. of Iowa, 1980; Lectures: St George's Hosp., 1980; St Louis, 1981; Univ. of Minnesota, 1981; Univ. of Ohio, 1986; RSocMed, 1988; Roche, RCPsych, Dublin, 1988; Stockholm, 1988; Maudsley, RCPsych, 1989; APA Internat. Scholars, 1990; Univ. of Oregon, 1991. Founder FMedSci 1998. A. P. Noyes Award, 1988; US Nat. Alliance Lieber Award, 1989; Res. Prize, World Fedn of Socs of Biol Psychiatry, 1991; Alexander Gralnick Award, Amer. Psych. Foundn, 2000; Kurt Schneider Award, 2006; Lifetime Achievement Award, British Assoc. Psychopharmacol., 2011. *Publications:* (ed) Disorders of Neurohumoral Transmission, 1982; (ed) Recurrent and Chronic Psychoses, 1987; (ed) The Speciation of Modern Homo Sapiens, 2002; papers on brain reward mechanisms, learning, evolution of language, speciation of Homo Sapiens, and schizophrenia in sci. and med. jls. *Recreations:* sciolistic archaeology, anthropology. *Address:* 16 Northwick Circle, Kenton, Middx HA3 0EJ. *T:* (020) 8907 6124. *Club:* Royal Society of Medicine.

**CROWCROFT, Prof. Jonathan Andrew,** PhD; FRS 2013; FREng, FIET, FBCS; Marconi Professor of Communications Systems, since 2001, and Associate Fellow, Centre for Science and Policy, University of Cambridge; Fellow, Wolfson College, Cambridge, since 2003; *b* 23 Nov. 1957; *s* of late Dr Andrew Crowcroft and of Prof. Kyla Crowcroft (*née* Greenbaum); *m* 1988, Noreen McKeever; two *s* one *d. Educ:* Trinity Coll., Cambridge (BA 1979); University Coll. London (PhD 1997). FREng 1999; FIET (FIEE 1999); FBCS 2000. Sen. Lectr, 1996–97, Prof. of Networked Systems, 1997–2001, UCL. FIEEE 2003 (SMIEE 1992); FACM 2004 (MACM 1988). *Publications:* WWW: beneath the surf, 1994; Open Distributed Systems, 1997; Internet Multimedia, 2000; Linux Internet Protocols, 2001. *Recreation:* classical guitar. *Address:* The Computer Laboratory, William Gates Building, 15 J. J. Thomson Avenue, Cambridge CB3 0FD. *T:* (01223) 763633, *Fax:* (01223) 334678. *E:* jon.crowcroft@cl.cam.ac.uk.

**CROWE, Sir Brian (Lee),** KCMG 2002 (CMG 1985); Director General for External and Defence Affairs, Council of the European Union, 1994–2002; *b* 5 Jan. 1938; *s* of Eric Crowe and Virginia Crowe; *m* 1969, Virginia Willis; two *s. Educ:* Sherborne; Magdalen Coll., Oxford (1st Cl. Hons PPE). Joined FO 1961; served: Moscow, 1962–64; London, 1965–67; Aden, 1967; Washington, 1968–73; Bonn, 1973–76; Counsellor and Hd of Policy Planning Staff, FCO, 1976–78; Hd of Chancery, UK Perm. Representation to EEC, Brussels, 1979–81; Counsellor and Hd of EEC Dept (External), FCO, 1982–84; Minister, Commercial, Washington, 1985–89; Ambassador to Austria, 1989–92; Dep. Under-Sec. of State (Dir Gen.) for Econ. Affairs, FCO, 1992–94. Dir, ITT Defence Ltd, 2006–12. Mem. Council, Chatham House, 2003–09 (Dep. Chm., 2005–09); Eur. Dir, Centre for Political and Diplomatic Studies, Oxford, 2003–. *Recreations:* family, international affairs, history, walking, cycling, travel. *Address:* 55 Ashley Gardens, Ambrosden Avenue, SW1P 1QF. *E:* blcrowe@gmail.com.

**CROWE, Frank Richard;** Sheriff of Lothian and Borders at Edinburgh, since 2009; *b* 15 March 1952; *s* of James Crowe and Helen Mary Harle or Crowe; *m* 1975, Alison Margaret Purdom or Crowe (separated 1997); two *d*; partner, Margaret Elizabeth Scott (*see* Hon. Lady Scott); one *s. Educ:* Valley and West Primary Schs, Kirkcaldy; Kirkcaldy High Sch.; Royal High Sch., Edinburgh; Dundee Univ. (LLB). Admitted solicitor, 1975, NP 1991, Solicitor Advocate, 1995; law apprentice, N of Scotland Hydro-Electric Bd, 1973–75; Procurator Fiscal Depute: Dundee, 1975–78; Glasgow, 1978–81; Sen. Legal Asst, Crown Office, 1981–83; Sen. Depute Procurator Fiscal, Edinburgh, 1983–87; Crown Office: Sen. Depute i/c Fraud Unit, 1987–88; Asst Solicitor i/c High Court Unit, 1988–91; Procurator Fiscal, Kirkcaldy, 1991–96; Regl Procurator Fiscal, Hamilton, 1996–99; Deputy Crown Agent, Crown Office, 1999–2001; Sheriff of Tayside Central and Fife, at Dundee, 2001–04; Dir of Judicial Studies in Scotland, 2004–08. Mem., Stephen Lawrence Steering Gp, Scottish Exec., 1999–2001; Chm., Adv. Gp to Zone Trng for New Futures, Dundee, 2002–04; consultant to Criminal Justice Oversight Comr, NI, 2003–07; Mem., Criminal Rules Council, 2012–; Mem., Res. Adv. Gp on Breach of Community Orders, Univ. of Strathclyde for Scottish Govt, 2013–. Mem. Council, Law Soc. of Scotland, 1996–99. Mem. and Vice Chm., Lothian Victim Support Scheme, 1983–89; Mem. Bd, Apex Scotland, 2014–. Chm. Bd, Stockbridge Primary Sch., 2006–08. Pres., Royal High Sch. Former Pupils Club, 2013–16. *Publications:* (jtly) Criminal Procedure, 1989, 2nd edn, as part of Stair Memorial Encyclopaedia of the Laws of Scotland, 2002; Justices of the Peace Bench Book and Legal Advisors' Manual, 2008. *Recreations:* golf, music, walking, racing, analysis. *Address:* Sheriff's Chambers, Sheriff Court House, 27 Chambers Street, Edinburgh EH1 1LB. *T:* (0131) 225 2525, *Fax:* (0131) 225 2288. *E:* sheriff.frcrowe@scotcourts.gov.uk.

**CROWE, Lucy Mary Elizabeth;** opera singer (soprano); *b* Burton upon Trent, 24 Dec. 1978; *d* of Charles John Crowe and Jeannie Crowe; *m* 2008, Joseph Nicholas Sidney Walters; one *s* one *d. Educ:* Denstone Coll.; Royal Acad. of Music (BMus 1st Cl. Hons; Dip. RAM; LRAM; ARAM; FRAM). Opera debuts: ENO, 2007; Royal Opera House, Covent Garden, 2009; Glyndebourne, 2010; Deutsche Oper Berlin, 2010; Chicago Lyric Opera, 2011; Bayerische Staatsoper, 2011; Metropolitan Opera, NY, 2012; major rôles include: Sophie in Der Rosenkavalier; Susanna in Le Nozze di Figaro; Poppea in Agrippine; Dorinda in Orlando; Iole in Hercules; Servilia in Clemenza di Tito; Rosina in Barber of Seville; Gilda in Rigoletto; Adina in L'Elisir d'amore; Eurydice in Orphée et Eurydice; Pamina in The Magic Flute; Adele in Die Fledermaus; Micaela in Carmen, Merab in Saul. Gov., Royal Acad. of Music, 2015–. *Recreations:* charity work (Songbound), cooking, baking, reading, tennis, festival going. *Address:* c/o Askonas Holt, 15 Fetter Lane, EC4A 1BW. *T:* (020) 7400 1715. *E:* lucycrowe@hotmail.com.

**CROWE, Dr Michael John,** DM; FRCP, FRCPsych; Consultant Psychiatrist, Bethlem Royal and Maudsley Hospital, London, 1978–2002; psychiatrist in private practice, 1978–2012; *b* 16 Oct. 1937; *s* of Robert James Crowe and Olive (*née* Kingston-Jones); *m* 1968, Diane Jordan; one *s* one *d. Educ:* St Paul's Sch., London; Exeter Coll., Oxford (MA, BM 1963); London Hosp. Med. Coll. MPhil London, 1970; DM Oxon, 1977. MRCP 1967; MRCPsych 1973; FRCPsych 1984; FRCP 1992. House Officer: London Hosp., 1964; Chelmsford and Essex Hosp., 1964; Senior House Officer: Addenbrooke's Hosp., 1965–66; London Hosp., 1966–67; Maudsley Hospital: Registrar, 1967–69; Sen. Registrar, Res. Worker and Lectr, 1970–74; Sen. Lectr, Inst. of Psychiatry, 1974–77 (Course Leader, Couple Therapy Dip. Course, 1989–2002). Vis. Fellow, Univ. of Vermont, USA, 1969. Lectr on behavioural and couple therapy, USA, Trinidad, Denmark, Italy, etc. Founder Mem., Inst. of Family Therapy, London, 1976–2002. Chm., Assoc. of Sexual and Marital Therapists, 1986–88. Gaskell Gold Medal, RCPsych, 1972. *Publications:* (with J. Ridley) Therapy with Couples, 1990, 2nd edn 2000; Overcoming Relationship Problems, 2005, 2nd edn (with K. Wylie) 2017; papers in med. and psychol. jls on behaviour therapy, couple therapy and sexual dysfunctions. *Recreations:* music (performing and listening), poetry, literature, languages, walking. *Address:* 66 Palace View, Shirley, Croydon CR0 8QN. *T:* (020) 8777 4823.

**CROWE, Rev. Philip Anthony;** Director, St Asaph Ministry Training Scheme, 1995–2001; *b* 16 Aug. 1936; *s* of late Frederick Francis Crowe and of Hilda Crowe; *m* 1963, Freda Maureen Gill; two *s* one *d. Educ:* Repton School; Selwyn Coll., Cambridge; Ridley Hall, Cambridge. National service, RA, 1955–57. Tutor in NT Greek and Mission, Oak Hill, 1962–67; Curate at Christchurch, Cockfosters, 1962–65; Editor, Church of England Newspaper, 1967–70; Sec., Bursary Scheme for Overseas Students, 1967–70; Senior Staff Member, St Martin in the Bull Ring, Birmingham, 1970–76; Rector of Breadsall, Derby 1977–88; Derby Diocesan Missioner, 1977–83; Tutor in Ethics, St John's Coll., Nottingham, 1986–88; Principal, Salisbury and Wells Theol Coll., 1988–94; Rector, Overton, Penley and Erbistock, 1995–97; Hon. Canon, Salisbury Cathedral, 1991–95. Mem., Gen. Synod, C of E, 1992–95. *Publications:* (contrib.) Mission in the Modern World, Church and Sacraments, 1977; Pastoral Reorganisation, 1978; Christian Baptism, 1980; The Use and Abuse of Alcohol, 1980; A Whisper will be Heard, 1994; Strange Design, 1999. *Recreations:* gardening, music, swimming, walking, study. *Address:* Alderlea, Babbinswood, Whittington, Shropshire SY11 4PQ. *T:* and *Fax:* (01691) 671698.

**CROWE, Stuart Davison;** Corporate Director, Resources, Durham County Council, 2008–10; *b* Blackhill, Consett, 28 March 1950; *s* of late Andrew Braid Crowe and Margaret Crowe; *m* 1980, Mary Jane Armstrong; one *s* one *d. Educ:* Blackfyne Secondary Sch., Consett; New Coll., Durham (CIPFA). Dep. County Treas., 1989–2002, County Treas., 2002–08, Durham CC. Treasurer: Durham and Darlington Fire and Rescue Authy, 2002–10; Durham Police Authy, 2002–09; Durham Charter Trustees, 2009–10. Consultant, 2011–13. *Recreations:* walking, photography, ornithology, gardening, stick making, Member of National Trust, Durham Wildlife Trust, Border Stick Dressers Association, British Stickmakers Guild.

**CROWLEY, Graham Neil;** Professor of Painting, and Head, Department of Painting, Royal College of Art, 1998–2006; *b* 3 May 1950; *s* of Victor Matthew Crowley and Violet Mary Crowley (*née* Lee); *m* 1978, Sally Ann Townshend; two *s. Educ:* St Martin's Sch. of Art (DipAD); Royal Coll. of Art (MA). Vis. Lectr, Painting, Royal Coll. of Art, 1978–85; Artist-in-Residence, Oxford Univ. and Fellow, St Edmund Hall, Oxford, 1982–83; Vis. Lectr, Goldsmiths' Coll., London, 1984–86; Sen. Fellow in Painting, S Glamorgan Inst. of Higher Educn, Cardiff, 1986–89; Artist-in-Residence: Riverscape Project, Cleveland, 1991–92; Dulwich Picture Gall., London, 1994–95; Hd of Fine Art, C&G, 1996–98. One-man exhibitions include: In Living Memory, Orchard Gall., Derry, and touring, 1987; Millfield Gall., Som, 1993; The Last Decade, Lamont Gall., London, 1995; A Drift, RCA, 1999; Familiar Ground, Beaux Arts, London, 2001; Are you serious?, Wolsey Art Gall., Ipswich, 2002; Graham Crowley, Beaux Arts, 2005; W Cork Arts Centre, Skibbereen, 2008; Churchill Coll., Cambridge, Atkinson Gall., Millfield, 2011; Mandells Gall., Norwich, Cross Gall., Dublin, 2016; Stubbs's Kongouro, Greystone Industries, Suffolk, 2018; A Love of Many Things, Peterborough Mus. and Art Gall., The Highlanes Gall., Drogheda, 2019; group exhibitions include: Arnolfini Gall., Bristol, 1977; Open Attitudes, MOMA, Oxford, 1979; South Bank Show, Hayward Gall. and Paris Biennale, 1982; Venice Biennale, 1984; Artists Against Apartheid, RFH, 1985; Edward Totah Gall., London, 1986, 1987; New British Painting, Queens Mus., NY, 1990; Royal Acad. Summer Exhibn, 1990, 1991, 1992; British Libry, 1994; Flowers E Gall., London, annually 1994–98, 2001, 2002; Summer Shows, 2000–02, Art 2001, Art 2002, Beaux Arts; The Discerning Eye, Mall Galls, London, 2000, 2001; British Art Fair, Beaux Arts, RCA, 2001, Commonwealth Inst., 2002; Govt Art Collection, Whitechapel Gall., 2011; Reality, Sainsbury Centre for Visual Arts and Walker Art Gall., Liverpool, 2014–15; John Moores Painting Competition, Liverpool, Various Species, Greystone Industries, Suffolk, 2016; A Table of Elements, Greystone Industries, Suffolk, 2017; Indoor Voices, Greystone Industries, Suffolk, 2019; *work in public collections* includes: Imperial War Mus.; V&A Mus.; Contemporary Arts Soc.; Kettles Yard, Cambridge; Castle Mus., Nottingham; Mus. of Auckland, NZ; Nat. Gall. of Poland, Gdansk. Mem. Adv. Cttee, The Prince's Trust, 2019. Selector, John Moores 24 Painting Competition, 2008. Prizewinner, John Moores 24 Painting Competition, 2006. *Publications:* De Sade for Beginners (with S. Hood), 1995; 'I don't like art', 2015; A Love of Many Things (with D. Bloomfield), 2019; *relevant publication:* Graham Crowley, by Martin Holman, 2009. *Recreations:* painting, classic motorcycles, writing, reading, learning piano and music theory, social philately. *W:* www.grahamcrowley.com.

**CROWLEY, Jane Elizabeth Rosser;** QC 1998; a Recorder, since 1995; *b* 5 Aug. 1953; *d* of Robert Jenkyn Rosser and Marion Rosser (*née* Davies); *m* 1986, (Jonathan) Mark Crowley; one *s* one *d. Educ:* Howell's Sch., Llandaff, Cardiff; King's Coll. London (LLB 1975). Called to the Bar, Gray's Inn, 1976; Bencher, 2004; in practice at the Bar, 1976–. Dep. High Ct Judge, Family Div., 1999–. Legal Mem., Mental Health Tribunal Restricted Order Panel, 2000–. *Recreations:* family, music, Pembrokeshire coast, supporting Wales Rugby, Glamorgan County Cricket Club, good friends, good wine. *Address:* 30 Park Place, Cardiff CF10 3BA. *T:* (029) 2039 8421; 1GC, 10 Lincoln's Inn Fields, WC2A 3BP. *T:* (020) 7797 7900.

**CROWLEY, Rt Rev. John;** Bishop of Middlesbrough, (R.C.), 1993–2007; *b* Newbury, 23 June 1941. Ordained priest, 1965; Holy Trinity Parish, Brook Green, W6, 1965–68; Catholic Missionary Soc., 1968–74; Private Sec. to Cardinal Hume, 1974–82; Vicar Gen. for Westminster dio., 1982–86; Auxiliary Bishop of Westminster (Bishop in Central London), and Titular Bishop of Tala, 1986–92. Chairman, Catholic Fund for Overseas Development, 1988–2000. Rep. of Bishops' Conf. of England and Wales to Conf. of European Bishops within EU, 2001. *Address:* Flat 2, Francis Court, Caddington Road, NW2 1RP.

**CROWLEY, John Desmond;** QC 1982; a Recorder of the Crown Court, 1980–2004; a Deputy Judge of the High Court, 1991–2004; *b* 25 June 1938; *s* of late John Joseph Crowley and Anne Marie (*née* Fallon); *m* 1977, Sarah Maria, er *d* of late Christopher Gage Jacobs and Joan Zara (*née* Atkinson); two *d. Educ:* St Edmund's College, Ware; Christ's College, Cambridge (BA 1961, LLB 1962). National Service, 2/Lieut 6th Royal Tank Regt, 1957–58. Called to the Bar, Inner Temple, 1962, Bencher, 1989. Member: Criminal Injuries Compensation Bd, 1985–2000; Criminal Injuries Compensation Appeal Panel, 2000–02. Chm., Appeal Cttee, ICAEW, 2000–04. *Recreations:* music, the turf, wine. *Address:* 37 Viceroy Road, SW8 2HA.

**CROWLEY, Robert,** RDI 1997; set and costume designer for theatre, opera, ballet and film; *b* Cork, 1952. *Educ:* Crawford Municipal Sch. of Fine Art; Bristol Old Vic Theatre Sch. *Productions* include: *theatre:* Royal Shakespeare Company: Love's Labour's Lost, 1984; As You Like It, 1985; Les Liaisons Dangereuses, 1986, transf. Ambassadors, NY, LA, Tokyo; Macbeth, A Penny for a Song, Principia Scriptoriae, 1986; The Plantagenets, 1988; Othello, 1989; Hamlet, 1992; National Theatre, later Royal National Theatre: Ghetto (Laurence Olivier Award for Designer of the Year, 1990), Hedda Gabler, Ma Rainey's Black Bottom, 1989; White Chameleon, Murmuring Judges, 1991; Carousel, 1992, transf. Shaftesbury, 1993, NY (Tony Award, 1994); Mourning Becomes Electra, 2003; The History Boys, 2004, NY (Tony Award, 2006); The Coast of Utopia, 2007, NY (Tony Award, 2007); Gethsemane, Fram, 2008; The Year of Magical Thinking, 2008, NY 2007; Every Boy Deserves Favour, Phèdre, 2009; Power of Yes, 2009; The Habit of Art, 2009;

Collaborators, 2011; Travelling Light, People, 2012; The Hard Problem, 2015; Pinocchio, 2017; Bristol Old Vic: Timon of Athens; A View from the Bridge; Destiny; Women All Over, King's, Edinburgh, 1985; Two Way Mirror, Young Vic, 1989; The Three Sisters, Gate, Dublin, 1990; The Cure at Troy, Guildhall, Derry, then Lyric, Belfast, 1990 (also Jt Dir); Saint Oscar, Field Day Theatre Co., Derry (Dir); Madame de Sade, Tokyo; No Man's Land, Almeida, 1992; When She Danced, Globe; Cunning Little Vixen, Châtelet, Paris; The Judas Kiss, Playhouse, then NY, 1998; The Capeman, NY, 1998; Twelfth Night, NY, 1998; Into the Woods, Donmar Warehouse, 1998; The Seagull, NY, 2001; Sweet Smell of Success, NY, 2002; Mary Poppins, Prince Edward, 2004 (Best Designer, Evening Standard Theatre Awards, 2005; Tony Award, 2007), Bristol Hippodrome, 2015; Moon for the Misbegotten, Old Vic, 2006, transf. NY, 2007; Love Never Dies, Adelphi, 2010; Juno and the Paycock, Abbey Th., Dublin, 2011; Once (musical), NY (Tony Award), 2012, transf. Phoenix Th., 2013; The Dark Earth and the Light Sky, Almeida, 2012; The Audience, Gielgud Th., 2013, transf. NY, 2015; The Glass Menagerie, NY, 2013, Edinburgh Fest., 2016; An American in Paris (musical), Châtelet, Paris, 2014, transf. NY (Tony Award), 2015, transf. Dominion Th., 2017 (Blue-I Th. Technol. Award for Best Set Design, Olivier Awards, 2018); Skylight, Wyndham's, 2014, transf. NY, 2015; The Inheritance, Young Vic, 2018; The Moderate Soprano, Duke of York's Th., 2018; My Name is Lucy Barton, Bridge Th., 2018; *opera:* Don Giovanni, Kent Opera; The Magic Flute, ENO, 1988, 1997, 2012; Aida, NY (Tony Award), 2001, Japan, 2009; Don Carlos, NY, 2010; Great Scott, Dallas Opera, 2015; Royal Opera: costumes, The King Goes Forth to France, 1987; The Knot Garden, 1988; La Traviata, 1994; Don Carlo, 2008, 2013; *ballet:* Anastasia, Pavane, Royal Ballet; Naked, Sadler's Wells, 2005; Alice's Adventures in Wonderland, Royal Ballet and Nat. Ballet of Canada, 2011; The Winter's Tale, Royal Ballet, 2014, Nat. Ballet of Canada, 2015; Strapless, Royal Ballet, 2016; *films:* Othello; Tales of Hollywood; Suddenly Last Summer, 1993; The Crucible, 1997. Robert L. B. Tobin Award for Lifetime Achievement, Th. Develt Fund/Irene Sharaff Awards, NY, 2009. *Address:* c/o Judy Daish Associates Ltd, 2 St Charles Place, W10 6EG.

**CROWN, Dr June Madge,** CBE 1998; FRCP, FFPH; President, Faculty of Public Health Medicine, Royal College of Physicians, 1995–98; *b* 5 June 1938; *d* of late Edward Downes and Madge Edith Downes; *m* 1964, Sidney Crown (*d* 2009); two *s* one *d*. *Educ:* Pate's Grammar Sch. for Girls, Cheltenham; Newnham Coll., Cambridge (MA); Middlesex Hosp. Med. Sch. (MB, BChir); London Sch. of Hygiene and Tropical Medicine (MSc). FFPH (FFPHM 1986); FRCP 1991. Area MO, Brent and Harrow AHA, 1980–82; Dir of Public Health, Bloomsbury HA, 1982–91. Dir, SE Inst. of Public Health, UMDS, 1991–99. Chairman: DoH Adv. Gp on Nurse Prescribing, 1988–89; DoH Rev. of Prescribing, 1996–98; Member: Standing Med. Adv. Cttee, DoH, 1984–88 and 1995–98; Clinical Standards Adv. Gp, DoH, 1995–99. Advr to WHO, 1984– (Special Advr on Ageing and Health, 2004–; Mem., Adv. Gp on Age Friendly Envmts in Europe, 2013–15); Consultant on Health Sector Mgt Develt to Czech Republic and Slovakia, 1992–93; Advr to NZ Govt and Health Bds on Health Care Reforms, 1992; Chm., UK Inquiry into Mental Health and Well-Being in Later Life, 2005–07. Vis. Lectr, Poly. Univ. Hong Kong, 2008–16. President: Sect. of Epidemiology and Public Health, RSocMed, 1994–96; Medical Action for Global Security (MEDACT), 1993–. Chm., 1998–2002, Vice Pres., 2002–09, Age Concern, England; Vice-Pres., Chartered Inst. of Envmtl Health, 2001. Chm., Queen's Nursing Inst., 2002–03 (Mem. Council, 1982–; Vice Pres., 2003–); Member: Bd of Govs, Royal Nat. Orthopaedic Hosp., 1976–82 (Vice-Chm., 1980–82); Inst. of Orthopaedics, Univ. of London, 1978–88 (Chm., 1982–88); Bd of Mgt and Court of Govs, LSHTM, 1983–94; Dep. Chm., Bd of Govs, Univ. of Brighton, 2002–10 (Mem., 2000–02). Trustee, Help the Aged, 2004–09. Chm., 2000–15, Pres., 2015–, Fitzrovia Youth in Action. Associate, Newnham Coll., Cambridge, 1992– (Associate Fellow, 1997–99; Chm., Associates, 1998–2000). Hon. Fellow: Soc. of Chiropodists, 1986; Australasian Faculty of Public Health Medicine, 1996; Faculty of Public Health Med., RCPI, 1997; RCPE, 1998; Hon. FDSRCS 2005; Hon. MCSP 2011. Hon. DSc Brighton, 2009. *Publications:* Health for All: revised targets, 1993; (with J. Connelly) Homelessness and Ill Health, 1995; Epidemiologically Based Needs Assessment: child and adolescent mental health, 1995. *Recreations:* family, opera, fine art, theatre, travel. *Address:* 118 Whitfield Street, W1T 5EG. *T:* (020) 7387 6787.

**CROWNE, Stephen Thomas;** Chief Executive, The Bar Council, 2013–17; *b* 9 Aug. 1957; *s* of late Charles and Beatrice Crowne; *m* 1979, Elizabeth; three *s*. *Educ:* Queens' Coll., Cambridge (BA (Hist.) 1978). Principal Private Sec. to Sec. of State for Educn, 1989–91; Hd, 16–19 Policy, DFEE, 1991–94; Chief Exec., Further Educn Develt Agency, 1994–98; Department for Education and Skills: Hd, Special Educnl Needs Div., 1998–2000; Dep. Dir, then Actg Dir, Standards and Effectiveness Unit, 2001–02; Dir, Sch. Resources, 2002–06; Chief Exec., British Educnl Commns and Technol. Agency, 2006–11; Dir, Global Education, Cisco Systems Inc., 2011–13. Dir, Partnership for Schs, 2004–06.

**CROWSON, Howard Keith; His Honour Judge Crowson;** a Circuit Judge, since 2010; *b* Belper, Derbys, 30 Dec. 1964; *s* of David John Crowson and Kathleen Cooper Crowson; *m* 1st, 1988, Alison Dawn Morritt (*d* 2012); one *s* one *d*; 2nd, 2016, Denise Breen-Lawton; one step *d*. *Educ:* Ecclesbourne Sch., Duffield; Leeds Univ. (LLB Hons). Called to the Bar, Inner Temple, 1987; in practice at the Bar, St Paul's Chambers, Leeds, specialising in crime and fraud, 1987–2010; Recorder, 2002–10. *Recreations:* Rugby Union, walking. *Address:* c/o Teesside Combined Court Centre, Russell Street, Middlesbrough TS1 2AE.

**CROWTHER, (David) Bruce,** MBE 2009; Executive Director, The FIG Tree, International Fair Trade Centre, since 2011; Field Interviewer, Office for National Statistics, since 2018; *b* 19 Oct. 1959; *s* of late John and Florence Crowther; *m* 1992, (Nancy) Jane Bamber; two *s* one *d*. *Educ:* Queen's Park High Sch., Chester; Liverpool Univ. Vet. Coll. (BVSc 1985). Dep. Vet. Officer, Min. of Agric., Dungannon, NI, 1985; Vet. Surgeon, 1986–2003; Vet. Surgeon (pt-time), 2003–12. Started campaigning for Oxfam, 1984; founded Garstang Oxfam Gp, 1992 (Chm., 1992–2002); led campaign to make Garstang the world's first Fairtrade Town, 2000; instigated twinning of Garstang with New Koforidua (a cocoa farming community) in Ghana, 2002; Fairtrade Towns Advr (formerly Co-ordinator) for Fairtrade Foundn (pt-time), 2003–12; Internat. Fair Trade Towns Ambassador (pt-time), 2013–15. Assoc. Mem., Oxfam 2011–06. Mem., Calder Bridge Meeting of Religious Soc. of Friends. Hon. Citizen and Sub-Chief (Nana Kwado Osafo I) of New Koforidua, 2004. Beacon Fellow for Creative Giving, 2004. *Recreations:* persuading people to buy, sell or use Fair Trade products, travelling, watching Manchester United FC live or on TV, archery. *T:* (01995) 602637. *E:* brucecrowther300@gmail.com.

**CROWTHER, Prof. Derek,** PhD; FRCP; Professor and Director, Cancer Research Campaign Department of Medical Oncology, Christie Hospital and Manchester University, 1974–97, now Professor Emeritus; *b* 1 July 1937; *s* of Robinson Westgarth Crowther and Gladys Hannah Crowther; *m* 1959, Margaret Frances Dickinson; two *d* (one *s* decd). *Educ:* City of London Sch. (John Carpenter Schol.); Clare Coll., Cambridge (MB, BChir (Natural Scis)); MA 1963); Baylor Univ., Texas (Fulbright Scholar, 1959–60); St Bartholomew's Hosp., Royal Postgraduate Medical Sch. and Chester Beatty Res. Lab., London (PhD 1968). FRCP 1976; FRCR 1993, Hon. FRCR. Sen. Registrar and Dep. Dir of Med. Oncology, St Bartholomew's Hosp., 1972–74. CMO, Friends Provident, 1995–2006.

Chairman: Leukaemia Res. Fund, Clinical Trials Adv. Panel, 2000–06; London Cancer Res. Mapping Working Gp, 2000–01; Co-Chm., CRUK (formerly CRC) Central Instnl Review Bd, 2001–04; Mem., Statutory Gene Therapy Adv. Cttee, 1994–97. Pres., Assoc. of Cancer Physicians, 1999–2007. Mem. Council, Manchester Lit. & Phil. Soc., 2002–. Hon. MRSocMed. Prizes in medicine, paediatrics, and pathology, incl. Gold Medal in Obstetrics and Gynaecology, St Bartholomew's Hosp.; Glyn Evans Gold Medal, RCR, 1980; Award of Distinction, CRC, 1997; Lifetime Achievement in Cancer award, Cancer BACUP, 1999. *Publications:* edited: Manual of Cancer Chemotherapy, 1978 (trans. several langs); Interferons, 1991; more than 300 publications in the field of anti-cancer therapy. *Recreations:* gardening, travel, cosmology, oriental and modern art.

**CROWTHER, Diane, (Dyan);** Chief Executive Officer, HS1, since 2017; *b* Bath, 4 Sept. 1963; *d* of Horace Wood and Elizabeth Clara Wood (*née* Owen); *m* 1994, Martin Crowther; one *s* two *d*. *Educ:* Corsham Sch., Wilts; Middlesex Univ. (BA Hons Geog. 1985); Salford Univ. (MSc Transport and Logistics 1996). MCIM 2002. Various mgt roles, British Rail, 1989–2000; Commercial Dir, 2000–01, Man. Dir, 2001–03, Arriva Trains Northern; Network Rail: Route Dir, 2004–10; Dir, Operational Services, 2010–12; Dir, Ops, 2013; Route Man. Dir, W Coast Mainline, 2013–14; Chief Operating Officer, Govia Thameslink Rlwy, 2014–16. Non-exec. Dir, E and N Herts NHS Trust, 2011–15. Mem., British Transport Police Authy, 2015–. Mem., ILM, 2016. *Recreations:* extreme walking, running, family. *Address:* HS1, Kings Place, York Way, N1 9AG. *E:* dyan.crowther@highspeed1.co.uk.

**CROWTHER, John Anthony;** Chief Executive, Vickers Defence Systems, 1994–96; Chief Executive, 1997–2006, Consultant, 2006–08, Lawn Tennis Association; *b* 16 Oct. 1951; *s* of Charles Alec Crowther and Joan Sylvia (*née* Boddam-Whetham); *m* 1975, Lorraine Ann Chadwick; three *s*. *Educ:* Malvern Coll.; Imperial Coll., London (BSc Eng). ACGI. British Aerospace PLC, 1970–77; Delta Neu Ltd, 1977–78; Panavia Aircraft GmbH, 1978–79; British Aerospace PLC, 1979–90; Vickers Defence Systems: Commercial Dir, 1990–92; Man. Dir, 1992–94. Confederation of British Industry: Chm., Contracts Panel, 1990–92; Regl Council Mem., Yorks & Humberside, 1994–96. Chm., Leeds Career Guidance, 1995–96. Dir, 2002–03, Chm., Major Spectator Sports Div., 2001–03 (Dep. Chm., 1999–2001), Treas., 2007–11, CCPR. Non-executive Director: Sports Leaders UK, 2002–09; N Yorks Sport, 2007– (Chm., 2009–16); Yorks Culture, 2007–08; Chairman: Sports Leaders Foundn, 2009; Amateur Swimming Assoc., 2009–13; Yorks Tennis, 2015–. Mem., Major Match Gp, 2006–17, Host Venue Panel, 2017–, ECB. *Recreations:* piano, tennis, golf, bridge, walking.

**CROWTHER, Paul Geoffrey,** OBE 2014; Chief Constable, British Transport Police, since 2014; *b* Woolwich, London, 7 Feb. 1961; *s* of Laurence Geoffrey Crowther and Daisy Elvina Crowther; *m* 1984, Louise Davies; two *d*. *Educ:* Eltham Green Comprehensive Sch. Police Officer, British Transport Police, 1980–; Area Comdr, resp. for London Underground, 2004–07; Asst Chief Constable, 2007–09; Dep. Chief Constable, 2009–14. Trustee, Cross Sector Safety and Security Communications, 2013–. Freeman, City of London, 2015. FInstD 2016. *Recreations:* travel, game and sea fishing, international cuisine sampling. *Address:* British Transport Police, 25 Camden Road, NW1 9LN. *T:* (020) 7830 8811. *E:* Paul.Crowther@btp.pnn.police.uk.

**CROWTHER, Prof. Richard,** PhD; CEng; FRAeS; Chief Engineer, UK Space Agency, since 2011; *b* Salisbury, Wilts, 5 Dec. 1960; *s* of William James Crowther and Shirley Gladys Crowther; partner, Dr Wendy Alison Holden; two *s*. *Educ:* Bishop Wordsworth's Sch., Salisbury; Univ. of Southampton (BSc Hons 1983; PhD 1989). CEng 1993; FRAeS 1998. PSO, RAE, 1991–98; Sen. Principal Consultant, DERA, 1998–2003; Head: Space Technol. Div., STFC, 2003–07; Internat. Relns, BNSC, 2007–11. Vis. Prof., Univ. of Southampton, 2005–. Hd, UK Delegn to UN Cttee on Peaceful Uses of Outer Space, 2007–. Member: Internat. Inst. of Space Law, 2008–; Adv. Bd, London Inst. of Space Policy and Law, 2010–; Internat. Inst. for Strategic Studies, 2013–; Mem. Council, RAeS, 2013–. Associate Ed., Aerospace Jl, 2004–08; Mem., Editl Bd, Encyclopedia Aerospace Engrg, 2010–. Expert, UN Gp of Govtl Experts on Transparency and Confidence Bldg Measures in Outer Space, 2012–13. Academician, Internat. Acad. of Astronautics, 2012–. *Publications:* contrib. papers to peer reviewed jls, incl. Philosophical Trans Royal Soc. *Recreations:* family, sailing, walking, gardening. *Address:* UK Space Agency, Polaris House, North Star Avenue, Swindon SN2 1SZ. *T:* (01793) 418071. *E:* richard.crowther@ukspaceagency.bis.gsi.gov.uk. *Club:* Royal Air Force.

**CROWTHER, Dr Richard Anthony,** FRS 1993; Member of Scientific Staff, 1969–2007, Visiting Scientist, since 2007, Medical Research Council Laboratory of Molecular Biology, Cambridge; Fellow of Peterhouse, Cambridge, 1981–2009, now Emeritus; *b* 26 July 1942; *s* of Albert Crowther and Joyce Edith Crowther (*née* Anthony); *m* 1964, Susan Elizabeth Hope; two *s*. *Educ:* Manchester Grammar Sch.; Jesus Coll., Cambridge (BA); PhD Cantab. Res. Fellow, Edinburgh Univ., 1968. FMedSci 2007. *Publications:* research papers and reviews in sci. jls. *Recreations:* walking, bird watching. *Address:* MRC Laboratory of Molecular Biology, Francis Crick Avenue, Cambridge CB2 0QH. *T:* (01223) 267815.

**CROWTHER, Sarah Helen;** QC 2018; *b* Blackburn, 3 June 1976; *d* of David Crowther and Eileen Crowther; *m* 2005, Arthur Alexander Crichton Cooke; one *s* one *d*. *Educ:* Runshaw Coll.; St John's Coll., Cambridge (BA Law 1998). Called to the Bar, 1999. Mem., Bar Council, 2014–. Chair of Govs, Bridge Sch., Islington, 2008–16. *Publications:* Accidents Abroad: a guide to the law, 2013, 2nd edn 2018; Jl of Personal Injury Law. *Recreations:* hockey (Cambridge blue, 1995, 1996, 1998); Blackburn Rovers FC supporter, family. *Address:* Outer Temple Chambers, 222 Strand, WC2R 1BA. *E:* sarah.crowtherqc@outertemple.com. *Club:* Richmond Hockey.

**CROWTHER, Thomas Edward;** QC 2013; *b* Newport, Mon, 25 May 1970; *s* of His Honour Thomas Rowland Crowther, *qv*; *m* 2003, Molly Ratna Das; two *d*. *Educ:* Croesyceiliog Comprehensive Sch.; Exeter Univ. (BSc; BA). Called to the Bar, Inner Temple, 1993; in practice at the Bar, 1993–2013, 2018–; Founder Mem., Apex Chambers, 2007, Hd of Chambers, 2012–13; a Recorder, 2009–13; a Circuit Judge, 2013–18. An Immigration Judge, 2006–13. Associate Judge, Sovereign Base Areas of Cyprus, 2015–. Mem., Bar Council, 2006–08 and 2010–12. Mem., Ethics Cttee, Sch. of Psychol., Univ. of Cardiff, 2016–. Chair, Ind. Inquiry, Telford Child Sexual Exploitation, 2019–. *Address:* Serjeants' Inn Chambers, 85 Fleet Street, EC4Y 1AE.

**CROWTHER, His Honour Thomas Rowland;** QC 1981; a Circuit Judge, 1985–2010; a Senior Circuit Judge, 2001–10; *b* 11 Sept. 1937; *s* of late Kenneth Vincent Crowther, MB, BCh, and Winifred Anita Crowther, MPS; *m* 1969, Gillian Jane (*née* Prince); one *s* one *d*. *Educ:* Newport High Sch.; Keble Coll., Oxford (MA). President, Oxford Univ. Liberal Club, 1957; Editor, Oxford Guardian, 1957. Called to the Bar, Inner Temple, 1961, Bencher, 2005; Junior and Wine Steward, Wales and Chester Circuit, 1974. A Recorder, 1980–85. Hon. Recorder, Bristol, 2001. Contested (L) General Elections: Oswestry, 1964 and 1966; Hereford, 1970. Founder Mem., Gwent Area Broadcasting, 1981. *Recreation:* garden. *Address:* Little Falcon, Melbourne Way, Newport NP20 3RH. *T:* (01633) 212640.
*See also* T. E. Crowther.

**CROWTHER, William Ronald Hilton;** QC 1980; a Recorder, 1984–96; *b* 7 May 1941; *s* of Ronald Crowther and Ann Bourne Crowther; *m* 1964, Valerie Meredith (*née* Richards); one *s*. *Educ*: Oundle Sch.; Univ. of Oxford (BA Jurisprudence). Called to the Bar, Inner Temple, 1963, Bencher, 1985–96. *Recreation*: bird-watching and all aspects of natural history.

**CROXALL, Prof. John Patrick,** CBE 2004; PhD; FRS 2005; Chair, BirdLife International Marine Programme (formerly Global Seabird Programme), since 2006; *b* 19 Jan. 1946; *s* of Harold Eli Croxall and Marjorie (*née* Jones); partner, Alison Jane Stattersfield. *Educ*: King Edward's Sch., Birmingham; Queen's Coll., Oxford (Open Schol.; BA 1st Cl. Hons Zool. 1968; MA 1987); Univ. of Auckland, NZ (Commonwealth Schol.; PhD 1971). Dir, Oiled Seabird Res. Unit and Sen. Res. Associate in Zool., Univ. of Newcastle upon Tyne, 1972–75; British Antarctic Survey: Hd, Birds and Mammals Section, 1976–85; SPSO, 1985; Hd, Higher Predator Section, 1986–2001; DCSO, 1992; Hd of Conservation Biology, 2001–06. Hon. Professor: Univ. of Birmingham, 1998–; Univ. of Durham, 1998–. Mem., Royal Soc. Interdisciplinary Cttee on Antarctic Res., 1997–2001 and 2005–. Scientific Committee for Antarctic Research: Member, Group of Specialists: on Seals, 1984–90; on Southern Ocean Ecol., 1986–96; Mem., Wkg Gp on Biol., 1986–2000; Mem., 1978–, Sec., 1980–85, Chm., 1986–94, Bird Biol Sub Cttee. Chm., Seabird Gp, 1984–87; Mem., 1990–, Mem. Perm. Exec., 1998–2006, Internat. Ornithol Cttee; British Ornithologists' Union: Mem. Council, 1974–78; Vice-Pres., 1987–91; Pres., 1995–99; Royal Society for the Protection of Birds: Mem. Council, 1989–2003 (Chm., 1998–2003); Chm., Conservation Cttee, 1993–98; Falklands Conservation: Trustee, 1987–; Chm., 1993–98; Trustee, S Georgia Heritage Trust, 2005– (Vice Chm., 2008–10). Vice-Chair, World Seabird Union, 2010–12. Scientific Medal, 1984, Marsh Award for Conservation, 2002, Zool Soc. of London; Polar Medal, 1992, clasp, 2004; President's Medal, British Ecol Soc., 1995; Robert Cushman and Murphy Prize and Medal, Internat. Waterbird Soc., 1997; Godman-Salvin Medal, 2004, Union Medal, 2015, BOU; Lifetime Achievement Award, Pacific Seabird Gp, 2008; Premio José Orensanz, 2015. *Publications*: (ed jtly) Status and Conservation of the World's Seabirds, 1984; (ed) Seabirds: feeding ecology and role in marine ecosystems, 1987; (ed with R. L. Gentry) Status, Biology and Ecology of Fur Seals, 1987; Seabird Status and Conservation: a supplement, 1991; contrib. numerous scientific papers and reports. *Recreations*: birdwatching, conservation, pteridology, French wines and countryside. *Address*: BirdLife International, David Attenborough Building, Pembroke Street, Cambridge CB2 3QZ. *T*: (01223) 234287, *Fax*: (01223) 277200. *E*: john.croxall@birdlife.org.

**CROXFORD, Ian Lionel;** QC 1993; *b* 23 July 1953; *s* of Peter Patrick Croxford, BEM, and Mary Helen Croxford (*née* Richardson); *m* 1976, Sandra McCord; one *s* one *d*. *Educ*: Westcliff High Sch. for Boys; Univ. of Leicester (LLB 1st Cl. Hons). Called to the Bar, Gray's Inn, 1976 (Bacon Schol.), Bencher, 2001; Lincoln's Inn, *ad eundem*, 1977. Mem. Council, Medical Protection Soc., 2007–16. Gov., Westcliff High Sch. for Boys, 1990–2016 (Chm. Govs, 1995). *Recreation*: watching sport. *Address*: Wilberforce Chambers, 8 New Square, Lincoln's Inn, WC2A 3QP. *T*: (020) 7306 0102.

**CROYDON, Area Bishop of,** since 2012; **Rt Rev. Jonathan Clark;** *b* Southend, 13 Feb. 1961; *s* of George and Elizabeth Clark; *m* 1984, Alison Walker; one *s* one *d*. *Educ*: Alleyn's Sch., Dulwich; Univ. of Exeter (BA Eng. Lit. 1983); Univ. of Bristol (MLitt Theol. 1990); Univ. of Southampton (MA Adult Educn 1999). Ordained deacon, 1988, priest, 1989; Curate, Stanwix, Carlisle, 1988–92; Chaplain, Univ. of Bristol, 1992–93; Dir of Studies, Southern Dioceses Ministerial Trng Scheme, 1994–97; Chaplain, London Metropolitan Univ., 1997–2003; Area Dean, Islington, 1999–2003; Rector, St Mary's, Stoke Newington, 2003–12. *Publications*: The Republic of Heaven, 2008; (contrib.) Ancient Faith Future Mission: fresh expressions in the sacramental tradition, 2009; (contrib.) Generous Ecclesiology, 2013; (contrib.) Doorways to the Sacred: developing sacramentality in fresh expressions of church, 2017. *Recreations*: visiting Westray, contemporary art and dance, poetry. *Address*: 6 St Peter's Road, Croydon CR0 1HD. *T*: (020) 8256 9630. *E*: bishop.jonathan@southwark.anglican.org.

**CROYDON, Archdeacon of;** *see* Skilton, Ven. C. J.

**CROYDON, Rear-Adm. John Edward Kenneth;** JP; DL; CEng, FIET; *b* 25 Feb. 1929; *s* of late Kenneth P. Croydon and Elizabeth V. Croydon; *m* 1953, Brenda Joyce Buss, MA (*d* 2015); one *s* two *d*. *Educ*: King Edward's Sch., Birmingham; Selwyn Coll., Cambridge (MA). BA London; CEng, FIET (FIEE 1975); jssc 1969. RN Special Entry Cadet (L), 1947; HMS Verulam and HMS Undine, 1954–55; Royal Naval Coll., Dartmouth, 1959–61; HMS Devonshire, 1961–64; HMS London, 1970–72; MoD, 1972–74; Captain Weapon Trials, 1974–77; Dir, Underwater Weapon Projects (Naval), 1978–80; Dir Gen. Weapons (Naval), 1981–83; Dep. Controller, Warships Equipment, MoD (Navy), 1983–84, retd. Rear Cdre (Dinghies), Royal Naval Sailing Assoc., 1980. Gov., Milton Abbey Sch., 1985–2002. Chm. Bd of Visitors, HMP Weare, 1997–2000. Trustee, Weldmar Cancercare Dorset, 2002–06. County Comr for Scouts, Dorset, 1986–93. JP Weymouth, 1985; DL Dorset, 1993. *Recreations*: cooking, music. *Address*: Hillside, Plaisters Lane, Sutton Poyntz, Weymouth, Dorset DT3 6LQ. *Clubs*: Royal Naval Sailing Association; Weymouth Sailing.

**CROZIER, Adam Alexander;** non-executive Chairman: Whitbread plc, since 2018; Asos plc, since 2018; Vue International, since 2017; Stage Entertainment, since 2017; *b* 26 Jan. 1964; *s* of Robert and Elinor Crozier; *m* 1994, Annette Edwards; two *d*. *Educ*: Heriot-Watt Univ. (BA Business Orgn). Pedigree Petfoods, Mars (UK) Ltd, 1984–86; Daily Telegraph, 1986–88; Saatchi & Saatchi, 1988–99: Dir, 1990; Media Dir, 1992; Vice Chm., 1994; Chief Exec., 1995; Chief Executive: FA, 2000–02; Royal Mail Group plc, 2003–10; Chief Exec., ITV plc, 2010–17. *Recreations*: football, golf, my children.

**CRUDDAS, Jon,** PhD; MP (Lab) Dagenham and Rainham, since 2010 (Dagenham, 2001–10); *b* 7 April 1962; *s* of John and Pat Cruddas; *m* 1992, Anna Mary Healy (*see* Baroness Healy of Primrose Hill); one *s*. *Educ*: Oaklands RC Comprehensive Sch., Waterlooville; Warwick Univ. (BSc, MA; PhD 1991). Labour Party: Policy Officer, 1989–94; Chief Asst to Gen. Sec., 1994–97; Dep. Political Sec., Prime Minister's Office, 1997–2001. Policy Rev. Co-ordinator, Labour Party, 2012–15. Mem., White Hart Angling Soc., 2000–. Mem., Dagenham Royal Naval Assoc., 2009–. *Publications*: Blue Labour: forging a new politics, 2015. *Recreations*: golf, angling. *Address*: House of Commons, SW1A 0AA. *Club*: Dagenham Working Men's.

**CRUICKSHANK, Alistair Ronald;** Trustee, since 2001, and Chair, since 2007, EcoLocal (formerly Centre for Environmental Initiatives); *b* 2 Oct. 1944; *s* of late Francis John Cruickshank and Kate Cameron Cruickshank (*née* Brittain); *m* 1967, Sandra Mary Noble; three *d*. *Educ*: Aberdeen Grammar School; Aberdeen University (MA). Joined MAFF as Assistant Principal, 1966; Principal, 1970; Asst Secretary, 1978; Under Sec. (Animal Health), 1986–88; Principal Finance Officer, 1989–94; Under Sec. (Agricl Inputs), 1995–96. Chairman: Surrey Organic Gardening Gp, 1997–2012; Sutton Future Network, subseq. Sutton Envmt Network, 2000–13; Director: EcoLocal Services Ltd, 2003–; Carshalton Lavender, then Carshalton Lavender CIC, 2003– (Chm., 2004–15); EcoLocal Lodge Develt Ltd, 2016–; Mem., Standards Bd, Soil Assoc., 2008–13. Vice Pres., London, CPRE, 2004–06. *Recreations*: gardening, looking at old buildings, various church activities. *Club*: Royal Over-Seas League.

**CRUICKSHANK, David Charles,** CA, CPFA; independent management consultant; *b* Christchurch, NZ, 22 April 1954; *s* of Clarence Albert Shepperd and Eunice Caroline Cruickshank (formerly Shepperd, *née* Wilson); *m* 1974, Linda Friel; one *d*. *Educ*: Queen Charlotte Coll., Picton, NZ; Victoria Univ. of Wellington (BCA 1979). Audit Dir, Audit NZ, 1977–98; Chief Financial Officer, Wellington CC, 1998–2002; Dir of Finance, Islington LBC, 2002–05. Mem., Inst. of Chartered Accountants of NZ, 1980– (Chm., Public Sector Cttee, 1997–2002); CPFA 2003. *Publications*: contrib. auditing and accounting articles to Accountants Jl. *Recreations*: cycling, family, golf, mountain biking. *Clubs*: Wellington; Manor Park Golf.

**CRUICKSHANK, David John Ogilvie,** CA; Chairman, Deloitte Global, since 2015 (Chairman, Deloitte UK, 2007–15); *b* Ellon, Aberdeenshire, 20 Feb. 1959; *s* of Ogilvie and Rosemary Cruickshank; *m* 1984, Rona; two *d*. *Educ*: Univ. of Edinburgh (BCom 1979). CA 1982. With Deloitte, 1979–: trainee, Edinburgh, 1979–82; Tax Manager, London, 1982–88; Tax Partner, London, 1988; partner i/c Tax, London office, 1995–98; Man. Partner, Tax, 1998–2006. Chair, Educn and Employer Taskforce, 2012– (Jt Chair, 2011). Mem. Bd, Social Progress Imperative, 2015–; Co-Chair, WEF Partnership Against Corruption Initiative, 2016–. *Recreations*: work, family, golf, tennis, watching sport, reading, charity support. *Address*: Deloitte, 2 New Street Square, EC4A 3BZ. *T*: (020) 7007 1826. *E*: dcruickshank@deloitte.co.uk. *Clubs*: Caledonian; Newtonmore Golf, Coombe Hill Golf.

**CRUICKSHANK, Sir Donald Gordon, (Sir Don),** Kt 2006; Chairman, 7 digital Group plc, since 2014; Director, Bureau of Investigative Journalism, since 2016; *b* 17 Sept. 1942; *s* of Donald Campbell Cruickshank and Margaret Buchan Cruickshank (*née* Morrison); *m* 1964, Elizabeth Buchan Taylor; one *s* one *d*. *Educ*: Univ. of Aberdeen (MA); Inst. of Chartered Accountants of Scotland (CA); Manchester Business School (MBA). McKinsey & Co., 1972–77; Times Newspapers, 1977–80; Pearson, 1980–84; Man. Dir, Virgin Group, 1984–89; Chief Exec., NHS in Scotland, 1989–93; Dir Gen., Oftel, 1993–98; Chairman: Scottish Media Gp, subseq. SMG plc, 1999–2004; London Stock Exchange, 2000–03; Formscape Gp Ltd, 2003–06; Taylor & Francis plc, 2004–05; Clinovia Gp Ltd, 2004–06; Audioboo Ltd, 2010–14. Non-exec. Dir, Christian Salvesen, 1994–95. Dir, Qualcomm Inc., 2005–16. Chairman: Wandsworth HA, 1986–89; Action 2000, 1997–2000; UK Banking Review, 1998–2000. Mem. Court, Univ. of Aberdeen, 2005–11. Hon. LLD Aberdeen, 2001. *Recreations*: education, sport, golf, opera. *E*: dgc_135@live.com.

**CRUICKSHANK, Prof. Garth Stuart,** PhD; FRCS, FRCSE; Professor of Neurosurgery, University of Birmingham and Queen Elizabeth Hospital, since 1997; *b* 24 Jan. 1951; *s* of Lt Col Alfred, (Jimmy), Cruickshank and Peggy Lillian Cruickshank (*née* Rushton); *m* 1979, Ros Fitzgerald; two *s* two *d*. *Educ*: Wellington Coll., Berks; Univ. of London (BSc Hons 1974); Royal Free Hosp. (PhD 1979; MB BS 1984). FRCS 1989; FRCSE 1989; FRCS (Surgical Neurol.) 1993. Institute of Neurological Sciences, Glasgow: Registrar, 1989–93; Sen. Lectr in Neurosurgery, 1993–97. Member: NCRI Brain Tumour Gp, 1998–; DVLA Adv. Panel, 2001– (Chair, Neurol. Panel, 2010); Cancer Services Cttee, RCS, 2009–; Council, British Assoc. for Surgical Oncol., 2015–. Clin. Lead, NICE Clin. Guidelines Primary Brain Tumours and Cerebral Metastases, 2016–17. *Publications*: publications in the area of brain tumour res., gene therapy and imaging. *Recreation*: sailing. *Address*: Queen Elizabeth Hospital, Edgbaston, Birmingham B15 2TH. *T*: (0121) 697 8225, *Fax*: (0121) 697 8248. *E*: garth.cruickshank@uhb.nhs.uk.

**CRUICKSHANK, Ian Hay;** Sheriff of Grampian, Highland and Islands at Lerwick, since 2018; *b* Aberdeen, 11 March 1966; *s* of William and Jane Cruickshank; *m* 1993, Helen Oates; two *d*. *Educ*: Keith Grammar Sch.; Aberdeen Univ. (LLB Hons; DipLP). Admitted as solicitor, 1990; Solicitor: Messrs Grigor and Young, 1990–97; Messrs Wink and Mackenzie, 1997–99; Cruickshank Law Practice, 1999–2018; Solicitor Advocate, 1998–2018. Convener, Criminal Law Cttee, Law Soc. of Scotland, 2013–18. *Publications*: contrib. articles to Jl Law Soc. of Scotland. *Recreations*: walking, fly fishing, traditional Scottish music. *Address*: Sheriff Court House, King Erik Street, Lerwick ZE1 0HD.

**CRUICKSHANK, Flight-Lieut John Alexander,** VC 1944; ED 1947; late RAF; with Grindlay's Bank Ltd, London, 1952–76; retired; Administrator, Northern Division, North West Securities Ltd, 1977–85; *b* 20 May 1920; *s* of James C. Cruickshank, Aberdeen, and Alice Bow, Macduff, Banffshire; *m* 1955, Marion R. Beverley (*d* 1985), Toronto, Canada. *Educ*: Aberdeen Grammar Sch.; Daniel Stewart's Coll., Edinburgh. Entered Commercial Bank of Scotland, 1938; returned to banking, 1946. Mem. of Territorial Army and called for service, Aug. 1939, in RA; transferred to RAF 1941 and commissioned in 1942; all RAF service was with Coastal Command. ADC to Lord High Commissioner to the Gen. Assembly of the Church of Scotland, 1946–48. *Clubs*: Naval and Military; Royal Northern and University (Aberdeen); Royal Scots (Edinburgh); Merchants of Edinburgh Golf.

**CRUICKSHANK, Sheena Carlin,** CVO 2011; JP; Lord-Lieutenant of Clackmannanshire, 2001–11; *b* 26 March 1936; *d* of David Irons Brown and Janet Cameron Carlin Brown; *m* 1957, Alistair Booth Cruickshank; two *s* one *d*. *Educ*: High Sch. of Stirling. Hon. Sheriff, Alloa Sheriff Court, 1996. JP Clackmannan, 1989. *Recreations*: quilting, travel.

**CRUISE, Prof. Adrian Michael, (Mike),** PhD; Professor of Astrophysics and Space Research, University of Birmingham, 1995–2012, now Emeritus; President, Royal Astronomical Society, 2018–May 2020; *b* Rhwbina, Glamorgan, 12 May 1947; *s* of Ambrose John Cruise and Ellen Florence Cruise (*née* Fox); *m* 1971, Elizabeth Jennifer Marks; two *d*. *Educ*: Dorking Co. Grammar Sch.; University Coll. London (BSc Hons 1st Cl. Physics 1968); Univ. of London (PhD 1973). FInstP 1999. Lectr, Dept of Physics, UCL, 1979–86; Dep. Dir, Mullard Space Sci. Lab., 1985–86; Div. Hd, Astrophysics and Geophysics, 1983–93, Associate Dir, Space Sci., 1993–95, Rutherford Appleton Lab.; Hd, Sch. of Physics and Astronomy, 1997–2002, Pro-Vice-Chancellor for Res. and Knowledge Transfer, 2001–08, University of Birmingham. Visiting Professor: UCL, 1986–89; Univ. of Leicester, 1992–95; Cranfield Univ., 1993–95. Chairman: PPARC/BNSC Space Sci. Adv. Cttee, 1999–2002; Major Projects Rev. Panel, PPARC, 2001–04; Cospar Commn H (Fundamental Physics), 2004–12; Astronomy Grants Panel, STFC, 2007–10; Physical Sci. Wkg Gp, 2010–14, Human Exploration Sci. Adv. Cttee, 2013–18, ESA; Sci. Prog. Adv. Cttee, UK Space Agency, 2017–19. Special Advr (Space Issues), Select Cttee on Trade and Industry, 2000, on Sci. and Technol., 2006–07, H of C. Mem. Council, Eur. Physical Soc., 2003–08; Treas., RAS, 2011–16. FRAS 1974. Mem., IAU, 1984. *Publications*: (jtly) Principles of Space Instrument Design, 1998; 130 papers in jls on space instrumentation, relativistic physics and gravitational waves. *Recreations*: portrait painting, military history, amateur radio. *Address*: Badgers Holt, Park Grove, Chalfont St Giles, Bucks HP8 4BG. *E*: cruiseam1@gmail.com.

**CRUISE MAPOTHER, Thomas, IV, (Tom Cruise);** actor and producer; *b* 3 July 1962; *s* of late Thomas Cruise Mapother, III and of Mary Lee Cruise Mapother (*née* Pfeiffer); *m* 1st, 1987, Mimi Rogers (marr. diss. 1990); 2nd, 1990, Nicole Mary Kidman, *qv* (marr. diss.

2001); one adopted *s* one adopted *d*; 3rd, 2006, Katie Holmes (marr. diss. 2012); one *d*. *Educ*: Glen Ridge High Sch., NJ. *Films*: actor: Endless Love, Taps, 1981; Losin' It, The Outsiders, Risky Business, All the Right Moves, 1983; Legend, 1985; Top Gun, The Color of Money, 1986; Rain Man, 1988; Cocktail, Born on the Fourth of July, 1989; Days of Thunder, 1990; Far and Away, A Few Good Men, 1992; The Firm, 1993; Interview with the Vampire, 1994; Jerry Maguire, 1996; Eyes Wide Shut, 1999; Magnolia, 2000; Vanilla Sky, Minority Report, 2002; Collateral, 2004; War of the Worlds, 2005; Rock of Ages, 2012; Oblivion, 2013; Edge of Tomorrow, 2014; The Mummy, American Made, 2017; actor and producer: Mission Impossible, 1996; Mission Impossible 2, 2000; The Last Samurai, 2003; Mission Impossible 3, 2006; Lions for Lambs, 2007; Valkyrie, 2009; Knight and Day, 2010; Mission: Impossible - Ghost Protocol, 2011; Jack Reacher, 2012; Mission Impossible: Rogue Nation, 2015; Jack Reacher: Never Go Back, 2016; Mission Impossible: Fallout, 2018; producer: Without Limits, 1998; The Others, 2001; co-producer: Ask the Dust, 2006. *Address*: c/o CAA, 2000 Avenue of the Stars, Los Angeles, CA 90067, USA.

**CRUMP, Bernard John**, FRCP, FFPH; Director, BC Healthcare Solutions Ltd, since 2011; Chief Executive Officer, NHS Institute for Innovation and Improvement, 2005–11; *b* 10 Nov. 1956; *s* of Vincent and Bridget Crump; *m* 1990, Izabela Kuncewicz; one *s* one *d*. *Educ*: Burton Grammar Sch.; Univ. of Birmingham (MB ChB). FFPH 1999; FRCP 2005. Engaged in clin. medicine, res. and public health trng, W Midlands and London, 1980–91; Director of Public Health: South Birmingham HA, 1991–95; Leicestershire HA, 1995–2002; CEO, Shropshire and Staffs Strategic HA, 2002–05. Vis. Prof., Public Health and Epidemiology, Univ. of Leicester, 2000; Hon. Prof., Medical Leadership Univ. of Warwick, 2012–. Sen. Associate, Nuffield Trust. MInstD. *Publications*: (with M. Drummond) Evaluating Clinical Evidence: a handbook for managers, 1993; articles in health and social care jls. *Recreations*: ski-ing, golf. *Club*: Leicestershire Golf (Leicester).

**CRUMP, Douglas Woodward**; fee-paid Employment Judge, Birmingham, 2011–15; fee-paid Tribunal Judge, Stoke, 2011–15; *b* W Bromwich, 26 May 1944; *s* of W. R. A. Crump and E. M. Crump; *m* 1971, Jennifer Ann Snape; two *d*. Legal practice, 1968–93; Chm., Employment Tribunals, 1993–2007; Regl Employment Judge (formerly Regl Chm., Employment Tribunals), Birmingham, 2007–11. *Recreations*: music, fly fishing.

**CRUMPTON, Michael Joseph**, CBE 1992; PhD; FRS 1979; Director of Research (Laboratories), Imperial Cancer Research Fund Laboratories, London, 1991–93, retired (Deputy Director of Research, 1979–91); *b* 7 June 1929; *s* of Charles E. and Edith Crumpton; *m* 1960, Janet Elizabeth Dean; one *s* two *d*. *Educ*: Poole Grammar Sch., Poole; University Coll., Southampton; Lister Inst. of Preventive Medicine, London. BSc, PhD, London. National Service, RAMC, 1953–55. Member, scientific staff, Microbiological Research Establt, Porton, Wilts, 1955–60; Visiting Scientist Fellowship, Nat. Insts of Health, Bethesda, Maryland, USA, 1959–60; Research Fellow, Dept of Immunology, St Mary's Hosp. Med. Sch., London, 1960–66; Mem., scientific staff, Nat. Inst. for Med. Research, Mill Hill, 1966–79, Head of Biochemistry Div., 1976–79. Visiting Fellow, John Curtin Sch. of Med. Research, ANU, Canberra, 1973–74. Non-exec. Dir, Imperial Cancer Research Technology Ltd, 1989–99 (Chief Operating Officer, 1993–94). Member: WHO Steering Cttee for Encapsulated Bacteria, 1984–91 (Chm., 1988–91); Cell Board, MRC, 1979–83; Scientific Adv. Cttee, Lister Inst., 1986–91; Sloan Cttee, General Motors Res. Foundn, 1986–88 (Chm., 1988); MRC AIDS Directed Prog. Steering Cttee, 1987–91; Scientific Cttee, Swiss Inst. for Experimental Cancer Res., 1989–96; DTI/SERC Biotech. Jt Adv. Bd, 1989–93. Member Council: Royal Instn, 1990–94 (Mem., Davy Faraday Lab. Cttee, 1985–90, Chm. of Cttee, 1988–90); MRC, 1986–90; Royal Soc., 1990–92; Mem. Sci. Council, Celltech Ltd, 1980–90; Chairman: Sci. Adv. Bd, Biomed. Res. Centre, Univ. of British Columbia, Vancouver, 1987–91; DoH/HSE Adv. Cttee on Dangerous Pathogens, 1991–98; Mem. Sci. Adv. Bd, Ciba Foundn, 1990–94. Chm., InferMed Ltd, 1998–2000; non-executive Director: Amersham Internat., 1990–97; Amersham Pharmacia Biotech Ltd, 1997–2001; Amersham Pharmacia Biotech Inc., 2001–02. Mem. Council, Inst. of Cancer Res., 1994–2001; Member, Governing Body: Imperial Coll. of Sci., Technol. and Medicine, 1994–98; BPMF, 1987–95; Gov., Strangeways Res. Lab., 1993–2000. Mem., EMBO, 1982; MAE, 1996; Hon. Mem., Amer. Assoc. of Immunologists, 1995. Trustee: EMF Biol Res. Trust, 1995–2007 (Chm., 2005–07; Chm., Sci. Adv. Cttee, 1995–2005); Breakthrough Breast Cancer, 1997–2004 (Hon. Fellow, 2009). Fellow, Inst. of Cancer Res., 2001. Bernal Lectr, Royal Soc., 2004. Founder FMedSci 1998. Hon. FRCPath 2000. Mem. Editorial Board: Biochemical Jl, 1966–73 (Dep. Chm., 1969–72); Eur. Jl of Immunology, 1972–86; Immunochemistry, 1975–79; Immunogenetics, 1979–85; Biochemistry Internat., 1980–86; Molecular Biol. and Medicine, 1983–86; Human Immunology, 1985–96; Regional Editor, Molecular Immunology, 1982–86. Biochem. Soc. Vis. Lectr, Australia, 1983. Sen. Treas., Royal Soc. Club, 1988–89. *Publications*: contribs to learned scientific jls. *Recreations*: gardening, reading. *Address*: 8 Ticknell Piece Road, Charlbury, Chipping Norton OX7 3TW. *T*: (01608) 811845.

**CRUTCHLOW, John Adrian**; Director of Finance, Metropolitan Police, 1986–96, retired; *b* 30 March 1946; *s* of James William Crutchlow and Elsie Nellie Crutchlow (*née* King); *m* 1971, Valerie Elizabeth Farage. *Educ*: Finchley County Grammar Sch.; HNC (with dist.) in Business Studies; BA Open; postgraduate Dip. Management Studies. Paymaster General's Office, 1962–65; Metropolitan Police Civil Staff, 1965–96; Principal, 1974–81; Dep. Dir of Finance, 1981–84; Dep. Establt Officer, 1984–86; Asst Sec., 1986–92; Asst Under-Sec. of State, 1992–96; Dep. to Receiver, Metropolitan Police Dist, 1994–96. President: New Scotland Yard Civil Staff Assoc., 1994–96; Metropolitan Police Former (formerly Metropolitan Police Retired) Civil Staff Assoc., 1996–. FCMI (FBIM 1992); FInstAM 1995. *Recreations*: reading, gardening, golf, renovating old houses. *Address*: 16 Edward Square, Surrey Quays, SE16 5EE.

**CRUTE, Prof. Ian Richard**, CBE 2010; PhD; non-executive Director, Agriculture and Horticulture Development Board, 2015–18 (Chief Scientist, 2009–14); *b* 3 June 1949; *s* of Walter and Rose Crute; *m* 1973, J. Elizabeth Harden; two *d*. *Educ*: Univ. of Newcastle upon Tyne (BSc Hons Botany 1970; PhD 1973). Research Leader, Nat. Vegetable Res. Station, Wellesbourne, Warwick, 1973–86; Horticulture Research International: Head, Crop and Envmt Protection Dept, E Malling, Kent, 1987–93; Head, Plant Pathology Dept, 1993–95, Dir, 1995–99, Wellesbourne; Dir, Rothamsted Research (formerly Inst. of Arable Crops Research), 1999–2009. Fulbright Fellow, Univ. of Wisconsin, 1986; Vis. Prof. in Plant Pathol., Faculty of Biol Scis, Univ. of Oxford, 1997–. Trustee Director: E Malling Trust, 2010–18; John Innes Foundn, 2012–19. FRSB (FIBiol 2000). Hon. Fellow, RASE 2010; ARAgS 2015, FRAgS 2018. Hon. DSc Harper Adams UC, 2010. *Publications*: numerous papers on plant pathol. genetics and sustainable agriculture in scientific jls. *Recreations*: gardening, golf, walking, theatre.

**CRUTZEN, Prof. Dr Paul**; Director, Atmospheric Chemistry Division, Max-Planck Institute for Chemistry, Germany, 1980–2000; *b* Amsterdam, 3 Dec. 1933; *m* 1958, Terttu Crutzen (*née* Soininen); two *d*. *Educ*: Stockholm Univ. (PhD 1968; DSc 1973). Member: Royal Swedish Acad. of Scis; Royal Swedish Acad. of Engrg Scis; Academia Europaea. Foreign Mem., Royal Soc., 2006. (Jtly) Nobel Prize for Chemistry, 1995. *Address*: c/o Max-Planck Institute for Chemistry, PO Box 3060, 55020 Mainz, Germany.

**CRWYS-WILLIAMS, Air Vice-Marshal David Owen**, CB 1990; Managing Director, Services Sound and Vision Corporation (SSVC), 1994–2005 (Deputy Managing Director, 1993–94); *b* 24 Dec. 1940; *s* of Gareth Crwys-Williams and Frances Ellen Crwys-Williams (*née* Strange); *m* 1st, 1964, Jennifer Jean (*née* Pearce) (marr. diss. 1971); one *s* one *d*; 2nd, 1973, Irene Thompson (Suzie) (*née* Whan); one *s* two *d*. *Educ*: Oakham Sch.; RAF Coll. Cranwell. Commnd as pilot, RAF, 1961; served No 30 Sqn, Kenya, 1962–64, No 47 Sqn, Abingdon, 1964–66; ADC to C-in-C RAF Trng Comd, 1966–68; OC 46 Sqn, 1969; RAF Masirah, 1972; Army Staff Coll., 1973; Personal Staff Officer to C-in-C NEAF, 1974–75; OC No 230 Sqn, 1976–77; Air Sec. Dept, MoD, 1977–78; Dep. Dir Air Plans, MoD, 1979–82; Dep. Dir Intelligence (Air), MoD, 1982; OC RAF Shawbury, 1983–84; RCDS 1985; Dir of Air Support and Dir of Air Staff Duties, MoD, 1986–88; Comdr, British Forces Falkland Is, 1988–89; Dir Gen., RAF Personal Services, MoD, 1989–92. Gp Captain 1979; Air Cdre 1985; Air Vice-Marshal 1988. Executive Chairman: SSVC Services Ltd, 1994–99; Columbia Communications Europe, 1994–98; VISUA Ltd, 1996–99; Man. Dir, Teleport London Internat., 1994–98; Director: Forces Events Ltd, 1999–2015; Amersham Business Centre, 2001–09; RAF Museum Enterprises Ltd, 2008–10; RAF Museum Investments Ltd, 2008–10; HDFDP Trading Ltd, 2008–18. Council Mem., Cinema and Television Benevolent Fund, 1994–2005. Chm., New Island South Conservation Trust, 1995–. Trustee: British Forces Foundn, 1999–2015; RAF Museum, 2002–10 (Chm., Finance Cttee, 2003–10); Hearing Dogs for Deaf People, 2006–18 (Hon. Treas., 2008–18); Patron, RAF Masirah and RAF Salalah Veterans' Assoc., 2015–. Gov., Amersham and Wycombe Coll., 1997–2009 (Vice-Chm., 1998–2000; Chm., 2000–03). Freeman, City of London, 2002; Liveryman, Hon. Co. of Air Pilots (formerly GAPAN), 2001–16. MInstD; FICPD (FIPM 1991); FCMI (FIMgt 1993). *Recreations*: walking, travelling the world, building, fishing. *Address*: Ashendon, Bucks HP18 0HB. *Club*: Royal Air Force.

**CRYAN, His Honour Donald Michael**; a Circuit Judge, 1996–2018; authorised to sit as a Judge of the High Court, Family Division, 1996–2018; a Deputy Circuit Judge (Family and Civil), since 2018; *b* 18 Jan. 1948; *s* of late Thomas Joseph Cryan and Helen McBeath Cryan (*née* Munro); *m* 1973, Pamela; two *s*. *Educ*: Salvatorian Coll.; UCL (LLB (Hons)). Called to the Bar, Inner Temple, 1970 (Bencher, 1992; Master of the House, 1993–98; Master of Marshals, 2002–14; Master of Silver, 2013–14; Reader, 2015; Treas., 2016); a Recorder, 1993–96; SE Circuit. Designated Family Judge, Medway, 2001–04, Kent, 2004–08. Chm., Working Party on Delay in Family Proceedings Courts, LCD, 2002; Member: Lord Chancellor's Children Act Judicial Case Mgt Adv. Cttee, 2002–04; Unified Admin Judicial Cttee, 2003–05; various cttees/sub-cttees, Judicial Studies Bd, 2003–07 (Vice Chm., 2005, Chm., 2005–07; Magisterial and Family sub-cttee); Working Party on Authorisation of Magistrates, DCA, 2004–05; Judicial Mem., Courts Bd for Kent, 2005–08; Chm., Family Justice Council for Kent, 2005–08. Vis. Prof., Goldsmiths, Univ. of London, 2018–. Freeman, City of London, 1978; Liveryman, Fruiterers' Co., 1978 (Master, 1999–2000); Freeman, Arbitrators' Co., 2019. Member, Committee: Marshall Hall Trust, 1991–2005; Centre for Child and Family Law Reform, City Univ., 1999– (Chm., 2010–14); Chm., Adv. Bd, Law Sch., City Univ., 2010–15. Mem., founding Cttee, IFLA, 2010–12 (Chm., Adv. Cttee, 2012–). Mem. Council, Selden Soc., 2017–. Hon. LLD City, 2012. *Recreations*: walking, three granddaughters. *Address*: 4 Paper Buildings, Temple, EC4Y 7EX. *T*: (020) 7583 0816. *E*: Donald@cryan.org.uk. *Clubs*: Garrick, Royal Over-Seas League.

**CRYER, (Constance) Ann**; JP; *b* 14 Dec. 1939; *d* of Allen Place and Margaret Ann Place; *m* 1st, 1963, George Robert, (Bob), Cryer, MP (*d* 1994); one *s* one *d*; 2nd, 2003, Rev. John Hammersley (*d* 2004); one step *s* one step *d*. *Educ*: St John's Primary Sch.; Spring Bank Secondary Mod. Sch., Darwen; Bolton Tech. Coll.; Keighley Tech. Coll. Clerk, ICI, 1955–60; telephonist, GPO, 1960–64; researcher, Social Hist. Dept, Essex Univ., 1969; PA to Bob Cryer, MP and MEP, 1974–94. MP (Lab) Keighley, 1997–2010. Member: Home Affairs Select Cttee, 2004–10; Parly Cttee, PLP, 2005–10; Jt Ecclesiastical Cttee, 2008–10; Speaker's Conf. on Diversity in H of C, 2008–10; Chair, All Party Parly Gp on Gardening and Horticulture, 2009–10; Vice Chair, PLP, 2008–10. Rep. of UK on Council of Europe, 1997–2003. Mem., Exec. Cttee, Assoc. of Former MPs, 2016–. Chm., Nat. Policy Forum, Labour Party, 2016–. Mem. (Lab), Darwen BC, 1962–65. Mem., Cathedral Council, 1999–. Hon. Lay Canon, 2005–12, Bradford Cathedral. President: Keighley and Worth Valley Railway Preservation Soc., 2003–; Friends of Cliffe Castle, Keighley, 2017–; Vice President: Friends of Settle to Carlisle Line, 2001–; Yorks Dales Soc., 2006–; Women and the Church; Cruse Bereavement Care. JP Bradford, 1996. DUniv Bradford, 2009. *Publications*: (contrib.) Boldness be My Friend: remembering Bob Cryer, 1997. *Recreations*: gardening, cinema, theatre, time with my 7 grandchildren and 3 step grandchildren. *Address*: 32 Kendall Avenue, Shipley, W Yorks BD18 4DY. *T*: (01274) 584701.
*See also J. R. Cryer*.

**CRYER, John Robert**; MP (Lab) Leyton and Wanstead, since 2010; *b* 11 April 1964; *s* of late (George) Robert Cryer, MP and of Ann Cryer, *qv*; *m* 1994, Narinder Bains (marr. diss. 2012), *d* of Shiv Singh Bains and Bakhshish Bains; two *s* one *d*; *m* 2012, Ellie Reeves, *qv*; one *s*. *Educ*: Oakbank Sch., Keighley; Hatfield Poly. (BA). Underwriter, 1986–88; Journalist, Morning Star, 1989–92; Editor, Labour Briefing, 1992–93; Journalist: GPMU Jl, 1992–93; Tribune, 1993–96; Lloyd's of London Pubns, 1996–97; Pol Officer, ASLEF, 2005–06; Nat. Pol Officer, T&G section of Unite – the union (formerly TGWU), 2006–10. MP (Lab) Hornchurch, 1997–2005; contested (Lab) same seat, 2005. Member: Treasury Select Cttee, 2010–11; Justice Cttee, 2014–15; Admin Cttee, 2015–17. Chm., Parly Labour Party, 2015–. Chm., Labour Against the Superstate. Trustee, Thames Chase Community Forest. Mem., Editl Bd, Tribune. *Publications*: (jtly) Boldness be My Friend: remembering Bob Cryer, 1997. *Recreations*: most sports, reading, cinema, old cars. *Address*: House of Commons, SW1A 0AA.

**CRYNE, Christine**; Chief Executive, Brainwave, 2008–11; *b* 5 March 1955; *d* of William George and Irene Ethel Austin; *m* 1978, John Michael Cryne. *Educ*: Univ. of Reading (BSc Hons Chem. Physics with Maths). Researcher, Unilever Res., 1977–82; Product Develt Exec., Schweppes, 1982–85; commercial and new product develt roles, RHM Foods, 1985–90; Gp Product Manager, Sharwoods, 1990–92; Marketing Manager, IPC Mags, 1992–94; Hd, Corporate, Trading and Develt, 1994–97, Mktg Dir, 1997–2001, Help the Aged; Exec. Dir, Muscular Dystrophy Campaign, 2001–04; Chief Exec., CIM, 2005–06; Sen. Dir, Consumer Direct, OFT, 2006–08. Non-exec. Dir, Dimensions, 2013–. A Dir, CAMRA, 1987–98 and 2011–15; Mem., British Guild of Beer Writers, 1998–. Chm., Mencap Trust, 2017–. Master Trainer, People 1st, 2016–. MInstD 2000. *Recreations*: swimming, tutored beer tastings, cooking. *Address*: 10 Sneyd Road, NW2 6AN. *E*: c.cryne@btinternet.com.

**CRYSTAL, Prof. David**, OBE 1995; FBA 2000; author, lecturer, broadcaster on language and linguistics, and reference books editor; Hon. Professorial Fellow, Bangor University (formerly University College of North Wales, then University of Wales, Bangor), since 1985; *b* 6 July 1941; *s* of late Samuel Cyril Crystal, OBE and Mary Agnes Morris; *m* 1st, 1964, Molly Irene Stack (*d* 1976); one *s* two *d* (and one *s* decd); 2nd, 1976, Hilary Frances Norman; one *s*. *Educ*: St Mary's Coll., Liverpool; University Coll. London (BA 1962; Hon. Fellow, 1998); London Univ. (PhD 1966). Res. Asst, UCL, 1962–63; Asst Lectr, UCNW, 1963–65; University of Reading: Lectr, 1965–69; Reader, 1969–75; Prof., 1975–85. Vis.

Prof., Bowling Green State Univ., 1969. Dir, Ucheldre Centre, Holyhead, 1991–. Member Board: British Council, 1996–2001; ESU, 2001–06. Chm., 2001–06, Hd, R&D, 2006–09, Crystal Reference Systems. Sec., Linguistics Assoc. of GB, 1965–70; Chm., Nat. Literacy Assoc., 1995–2003 (Patron, 2004–); Vice-Pres., Chartered Inst. of Linguists (formerly Inst. of Linguistics), 1998–; President: Johnson Soc., 2005–06; Soc. for Eds and Proofreaders, 2016– (Vice-Pres., 2004–16). Hon. Vice-Pres., Royal Coll. of Speech and Lang. Therapists, 1995– (Mem., Academic Bd, Coll. of Speech Therapists, 1972–79); FRCSLT (FCST 1983). Hon. President: Nat. Assoc. of Professionals concerned with Lang. Impaired Children, 1985–2002; English Project (Winchester), 2014–; Centre for Literacy in Primary Educn, 2016–. Sam Wanamaker Fellow, Shakespeare's Globe, 2003. FRSA 1983; FLSW 2010. Hon. FTCL 2003; Hon. Fellow, Wolfson Coll., Cambridge, 2005. Hon. DSc Queen Margaret UC, Edinburgh, 1997; Hon. DLitt: Cambridge, 2005; Winchester, 2010; Memorial Univ., Newfoundland, 2011; Lancaster, 2013; DUniv: Open, 2007; Huddersfield, 2014. Editor: Language Res. in Progress, 1966–70; Jl of Child Language, 1973–85; The Language Library, 1978–2008; Applied Language Studies, 1980–84; Child Language Teaching and Therapy, 1985–96; Linguistics Abstracts, 1985–96; Blackwells Applied Language Studies, 1986–95; Consultant Editor, English Today, 1985–94; Adv. Editor, Penguin Linguistics, 1968–75; Associate Editor, Jl of Linguistics, 1970–73; Co-Editor, Studies in Language Disability, 1974–2006. Regular BBC broadcasts on English language and linguistics. DVD, Introduction to Language, 2011. *Publications:* Systems of prosodic and paralinguistic features in English (with R. Quirk), 1964; Linguistics, language and religion, 1965; (ed jtly) Proceedings, Modern approaches to language teaching at university level, 1967; What is linguistics?, 1968, 5th edn 1985; Prosodic systems and intonation in English, 1969; (with D. Davy) Investigating English style, 1969; (ed with W. Bolton) The English language, vol. 2, 1969; Linguistics, 1971, 2nd edn 1985; Basic linguistics, 1973; Language acquisition, 1973; The English tone of voice, 1975; (with D. Davy) Advanced conversational English, 1975; (with J. Bevington) Skylarks, 1975; (jtly) The grammatical analysis of language disability, 1976, 2nd edn 1989; Child language, learning and linguistics, 1976, 2nd edn 1987; Working with LARSP, 1979; Introduction to language pathology, 1980, 4th edn (with R. Varley) 1998; A first dictionary of linguistics and phonetics, 1980, 6th edn 2008; (ed) Eric Partridge: in his own words, 1980; Clinical linguistics, 1981; Directions in applied linguistics, 1981; Profiling linguistic disability, 1982, 2nd edn 1992; (ed) Linguistic controversies, 1982; Who cares about English usage?, 1984, 2nd edn 2000; Language handicap in children, 1984; Linguistic encounters with language handicap, 1984; Listen to your child, 1986, 2nd edn 2018; (ed with W. Bolton) The English language, 1987; Cambridge Encyclopedia of Language, 1987, 3rd edn 2010; Rediscover grammar, 1988, 3rd edn 2004; The English Language, 1988, 2nd edn 2002; Pilgrimage, 1988; (with J. C. Davies) Convent, 1989; (ed) Cambridge Encyclopedia, 1990, 4th edn 2000; Language A to Z, 1991; Making Sense of English Usage, 1991; Nineties Knowledge, 1992; Introducing Linguistics, 1992; An Encyclopedic Dictionary of Language and Languages, 1992, 2nd edn, as The Penguin Dictionary of Language, 1999; (ed) Cambridge Concise Encyclopedia, 1992, 2nd edn 1995; (ed) Cambridge Paperback Encyclopedia, 1993, 3rd edn 1999; (ed) Cambridge Factfinder, 1993, 4th edn 2000; (ed) Cambridge Biographical Encyclopedia, 1994, 2nd edn 1998; Cambridge Encyclopedia of the English Language, 1995, 3rd edn 2018; Discover Grammar, 1996; (ed) John Bradburne, Songs of the Vagabond, 1996; Cambridge Biographical Dictionary, 1996; English as a Global Language, 1997, 2nd edn 2003; Language Play, 1998; (with H. Crystal) Words on Words, 2000 (Wheatley Medal, LA, 2001); Language Death, 2000; (with H. Crystal) John Bradburne's Mutemwa, 2000; Happenings, 2000; Language and the Internet, 2001, 2nd edn 2006; (with Ben Crystal) Shakespeare's Words, 2002; (ed) The New Penguin Encyclopedia, 2002, 3rd edn, as The Penguin Encyclopedia, 2006; (ed) The New Penguin Factfinder, 2003, 3rd edn, as The Penguin Factfinder, 2007; (ed) The Concise Penguin Encyclopedia, 2003, 3rd edn 2007; The Stories of English, 2004; Making Sense of Grammar, 2004; The Language Revolution, 2004; A Glossary of Netspeak and Textspeak, 2004; John Bradburne's Book of Days, 2004; Pronouncing Shakespeare, 2005; (with Ben Crystal) The Shakespeare Miscellany, 2005; Johnson's Dictionary: an anthology, 2005; Words, Words, Words, 2006; How Language Works, 2006; The Fight for English, 2006; As They Say in Zanzibar, 2006; By Hook or by Crook, 2007; (ed) John Bradburne's Birds, Bees and Beasts, 2007; The Ucheldre Story, 2007; Think on my Words: exploring Shakespeare's language, 2008; Txtng: the Gr8 Db8, 2008; Just a Phrase I'm Going Through: my life in language, 2009; The Future of Language, 2009; (ed) Fowler's Dictionary of Modern English Usage, 2009; (ed) John Bradburne on Love, 2009; A Little Book of Language, 2010; Begat: the King James Bible and the English language, 2010; Evolving English, 2010; (ed jtly) From International to Local English - and Back Again, 2010; Internet Linguistics, 2011; The Story of English in 100 Words, 2011; (ed jtly) Assessing Grammar: the languages of LARSP, 2012; Spell it Out: the singular story of English spelling, 2012; (with Hilary Crystal) Wordsmiths and Warriors: the English language tourist's guide to Britain, 2013; Words in Time and Place: exploring the historical thesaurus of the Oxford English Dictionary, 2014; (with Ben Crystal) You Say Potato, 2014; (with Ben Crystal) The Oxford Illustrated Shakespeare Dictionary, 2015; The Disappearing Dictionary, 2015; Making a Point: the pernickety story of English punctuation, 2015; The Unbelievable Hamlet Discovery, 2016; The Oxford Dictionary of Original Shakespearean Pronunciation, 2016; The Gift of the Gab: how eloquence works, 2016; (ed jtly) Profiling Grammar: more languages of LARSP, 2016; Making Sense: the glamorous story of English grammar, 2017; The Story of Be: a verb's eye view of the English language, 2017; We Are Not Amused: Victorian views on pronunciation as told in the pages of Punch, 2017; A Life Made of Words: the poetry and thought of John Bradburne, 2017; Sounds Appealing: the passionate story of English pronunciation, 2018; (with J. L. Foster) Databank series: Heat, Light, Sound, Roads, Railways, Canals, Manors, Castles, Money, Monasteries, Parliament, Newspapers, 1979; The Romans, The Greeks, The Ancient Egyptians, 1981; Air, Food, Volcanoes, 1982; Deserts, Dinosaurs and Electricity, 1983; Motorcycles, Computers, Horses and Ponies, Normans, Vikings, Anglo-Saxons, Celts, 1984; The Stone Age, Fishing, 1985; (with J. L. Foster) Datasearch series: Air and Breathing, Heating and Cooling, Light and Seeing, Sound and Hearing, 1991; contributions to: The Library of Modern Knowledge, 1978; A Dictionary of Modern Thought, 1978, 2nd edn 1987; Reader's Digest Great Illustrated Dictionary, 1984; Reader's Digest Book of Facts, 1985; A Comprehensive Grammar of the English Language, 1985; International Encyclopedia of Linguistics, 1992; William Shakespeare: the Complete Works (ed Wells and Taylor), 2005; and to numerous volumes on language, style, prosody, communication, religion, handicap, teaching and reading; symposia and proceedings of learned socs; articles and reviews in jls on linguistics, English language, Shakespeare, speech pathology and education. *Recreations:* cinema, music, bibliophily, development of the arts. *Address:* Akaroa, Gors Avenue, Holyhead, Anglesey LL65 1PB. *T:* (01407) 762764. *E:* davidcrystal1@icloud.com. *W:* www.davidcrystal.com, http://david-crystal.blogspot.com, www.originalpronunciation.com.

**CRYSTAL, Michael;** QC 1984; a Deputy High Court Judge, 1995–2018; Senior Visiting Fellow, Centre for Commercial Law Studies, Queen Mary (formerly Queen Mary College, then Queen Mary and Westfield College), University of London, since 1996 (Hon. Senior Visiting Fellow, 1987–96); *b* 5 March 1948; *s* of late Dr Samuel Cyril Crystal, OBE, and Rachel Ettel Crystal; *m* 1972, Susan Felicia Sniderman; one *s* one *d*. *Educ:* Leeds Grammar Sch.; Queen Mary Coll., Univ. of London (LLB Hons; Hon. Fellow, QMW, 1996); Magdalen Coll., Oxford (BCL). Called to the Bar, Middle Temple, 1970, Bencher, 1993 (Autumn Reader, 2012); called to the Bar *ad eundem,* Gray's Inn, 1989; Lecturer in Law, Pembroke Coll., Oxford, 1971–76. Vis. Prof., Dept of Laws, UCL, 2002–15. DTI Inspector into County NatWest Ltd and County NatWest Securities Ltd, 1988–89, and into National Westminster Bank plc, 1992. Member: Insolvency Rules Adv. Cttee, 1993–97; Financial Law Panel, 1996–2002; FA Premier League Panel, 2004–; Internat. Insolvency Inst., 2005– (Outstanding Contribn Award, 2017). Mem., Adv. Council, Centre for Commercial Law Studies, QMUL (formerly QMC, then QMW), 1996–. Gov., 1988–2006, Hon. Gov., 2007–, RSC. Trustee: British Friends of Haifa Univ., 2007–10; Israel Philharmonic Orchestra Foundn, 2009–. Fellow, Amer. Coll. of Bankruptcy, 2006–. Hon. Fellow, Soc. for Advanced Legal Studies, 1997. *Publications:* various legal text books. *Recreations:* travel, music, theatre. *Clubs:* Royal Automobile, MCC.

**CSÁK, János;** Director, Gedeon Richter plc, since 2014; Ambassador of Hungary to the Court of St James's, 2011–14; *b* Budapest, 15 Oct. 1962; *s* of János Csák and Erzsébet Holozsi; *m* 1986, Júlia Márton; three *s* one *d*. *Educ:* Corvinus Univ. (MSc Finance and Sociol. 1987). Finance Dir, MATÁV Hungarian Telecom, 1993–2000; Chairman: MOL Hungarian Oil and Gas Co., 1999–2000; T-Mobile Hungary, 1999–2001; Mem., Gp Exec. Bd, CreditAnstalt Investment Bank, 2001–03; CEO, Mobilnet, Finance and Strategy Advisory, 2003–10; Owner, Helikon Book Publishing, 2003–10. Treasury Advr, Ameritech Corp., Chicago, 1996; Advr to Pres. of Hungary, 2007–10. Vis. Fellow, Heritage Foundn, 2009–10. Founder, Széll Kálmán Club, 2003; Trustee, Saint Francis Children's Foundn, 2004–. Comdr's Cross, Order of Merit (Hungary), 2010. *Recreations:* family and friends, reading, football, travelling, walking. *Clubs:* Athenæum; Széll Kálmán (Budapest).

**CSOKA, Simon;** QC 2011; *b* Blackburn, 12 April 1968; *s* of Béla Csoka and Kathleen Csoka; *m* 1996, Elizabeth Baker; three *s*. *Educ:* Stonyhurst; Fitzwilliam Coll., Cambridge (BA 1990). Called to the Bar, Gray's Inn, 1991. *Recreations:* live music, hill walking. *Address:* Lincoln House Chambers, Tower 12, The Avenue North, Spinningfields, 18–22 Bridge Street, Manchester M3 3BZ. *T:* (0161) 832 5701, *Fax:* (0161) 832 0839. *E:* simon.csoka@lincolnhousechambers.com.

**CUBIE, Sir Andrew,** Kt 2009; CBE 2001; FRSE; Senior Partner, Fyfe Ireland LLP, 1994–2003; *b* 24 Aug. 1946; *s* of late Dr Alexander Cubie and Elsie B. C. Cubie (*née* Thorburn); *m* 1968, Heather Ann Muir (*see* H. A. Cubie); one *s* two *d*. *Educ:* Dollar Acad.; Edinburgh Univ. (LLB Hons). WS. Admitted solicitor, 1969; NP; Partner: Fyfe Ireland & Co., WS, 1971–87; Bird Semple Fyfe Ireland, WS, 1987–94 (Chm., 1991–94). Non-exec. Chm., Kinloch Anderson Ltd. Advr, World Bank, Washington. Chairman: CBI Scotland, 1995–97; Regl Chairmen of CBI, 1996–97; Scotland's Health at Work, 1996–2005; Independent Cttee of Inquiry into Student Finance, 1999–2000; Quality Scotland Foundn, 1999–2016; Scottish Credit and Qualification Framework, 2001–16; British Council, Scotland, 2002–08; Centre for Healthy Working Lives, 2005–; Jt Negotiating Cttee, USS, 2008–. Member, Board: HM Inspectorate of Educn and Education Scotland, 2004–13; Scotland's Futures Forum; Scottish Cancer Foundation; Chairman: Scotland's Garden Trust; Campaign Bd, Edinburgh Napier Univ.; Student Partnerships in Quality Scotland. Member: Consultative Steering Gp, Scottish Parliament, 1997–98; McIntosh Commn in respect of Scottish Local Govt, 1998–99. Fulbright Comr, 2005–08; Chm., Cttee of Univ. Chairmen, 2007–08. Chm., Northern Lighthouse Bd, 2009–12 (Vice Chm., 2007–09). Vice-Pres., 2000–, Dep. Chm., 2009–16, RNLI (Chm., Scottish Council, 1997–2017); Chm., UK Cttee, VSO, 2006–14 (Vice-Pres., 2001–04, Chm., 2004–05, BESO); Trustee, Common Purpose, 2003–11. Chairman: Governing Council, George Watson's Coll., 1994–99; Court, Napier Univ., 2001–08. FRSE 2001; FCGI 2012; FRSA. Hon. FRCPSGlas 2006. Hon. DBA Queen Margaret UC, Edinburgh, 2000; Hon. LLD: Edinburgh, 2001; Glasgow, 2001; Glasgow Caledonian, 2001; DUniv Edinburgh Napier, 2009. *Recreations:* sailing, gardening, reading more and contemplating. *Address:* Flat 4, 4 The Cedars, Colinton Road, Edinburgh EH13 0PL. *T:* (0131) 441 9079. *E:* andrew@cubie-edinburgh.com. *Clubs:* New (Edinburgh); Royal Highland Yacht.
*See also* G. Cubie.

**CUBIE, Andrew MacInnes;** Sheriff of Glasgow and Strathkelvin at Glasgow, since 2010; Appeal Sheriff, Sheriff Appeal Court, since 2017; *b* 12 Feb. 1963; *s* of John Pattison Cubie and Mary Moira Keir Cubie; *m* 1987, Joan Crockett; two *s* one *d*. *Educ:* Univ. of Glasgow (LLB 1st Cl. Hons; DLP). Admitted solicitor, 1986; Partner, Maxwell MacLaurin (Solicitors), Glasgow, until 2003. Temp. Sheriff, 1997–99; Floating Sheriff, 2003–04; Sheriff of Tayside, Central and Fife at Stirling, 2004–10. Dep. Dir, Judicial Inst. for Scotland, 2014–18. Lectr (pt-time), Centre for Professional Legal Studies, Univ. of Strathclyde, 1993–2003; external examiner: Univ. of Edinburgh, 2014–; Univ. of Strathclyde, 2014–. *Publications:* (contrib. ed.) Butterworth's Family Law Service; (contrib.) MacPhail, Sheriff Court Practice, 2006; Scots Criminal Law, rev. 3rd edn, 2010 to 4th edn 2016; contrib. articles to Scots Law Time, Green's Family Law Bulletin and Jl Law Soc. of Scotland. *Recreations:* family, sports, music, travel, the M8s. *Address:* Glasgow Sheriff Court, 1 Carlton Place, Glasgow G5 9DA. *T:* (0141) 429 8888.

**CUBIE, George,** CB 2003; Clerk of Committees, House of Commons, 2001–05; *b* 30 Aug. 1943; *s* of late Dr Alexander Cubie and Elsie B. C. Cubie (*née* Thorburn); *m* 1966, Kathleen S. Mullan; one *s*. *Educ:* Dollar Acad.; Edinburgh Univ. (MA Hons). Clerk in H of C, 1966; Clerk of Financial Cttees, H of C, 1987–89; Sec. to Public Accounts Commn, 1987–89; Clerk of Select Cttees, H of C, 1989–91; Clerk of the Overseas Office, 1991–95; Principal Clerk, Table Office, 1995–97; Clerk Asst, H of C, 1998–2001. *Publications:* (contrib.) Erskine May's Parliamentary Practice, 22nd edn, 1997; (contrib.) Halsbury's Laws of England, 5th edn. *Recreation:* walking. *Address:* 10 Lower Westport, Wareham, Dorset BH20 4FE. *T:* (01929) 554246.
*See also* Sir A. Cubie.

**CUBIE, Prof. Heather Ann, (Lady Cubie),** MBE 2012; PhD; FRCPath; FRSE; Senior Advisor, Global Health Academy, University of Edinburgh, since 2014; *b* Dunfermline, 8 Dec. 1946; *d* of William Muir and Freida Muir; *m* 1968, Sir Andrew Cubie, *qv*; one *s* two *d*. *Educ:* Dunfermline High Sch.; Univ. of Edinburgh (BSc 1st Cl. Hons 1968; MSc by thesis 1972; PhD 1989); Moray House (PGTCSE). FRCPath (MRCPath 1991). NHS Lothian: Consultant Clinical Scientist in Virology, 1993–2008; Dir, R&D, 1995–2008; Dir, Scottish HPV Reference Lab., 2008–12; University of Edinburgh: Hon. Prof., 2008–; Hd, HPV Res. Gp and Scottish HPV Archive, 2012–14. Trustee, Girl Guiding Scotland, 2009–14; Elder and Trustee, Mayfield Salisbury Parish Ch, 1990–. FRSE 2012. *Publications:* (jtly) Viral Warts, 2nd edn 1992; (contrib.) Medical Microbiology: a guide to microbial infections, 15th edn 1997 to 18th edn 2011; over 90 articles in academic jls. *Recreations:* gardening, walking. *Address:* Flat 4, 4 The Cedars, Colinton Road, Edinburgh EH13 0PL. *T:* (0131) 441 9079. *E:* heather.cubie@ed.ac.uk.

**CUBITT,** family name of **Baron Ashcombe**.

**CUBITT, Sir Hugh (Guy),** Kt 1983; CBE 1977; JP; DL; FRICS; Chairman, Peabody Trust, 1998–2003 (Governor, 1991–2003); Director, PSIT PLC (formerly Property Security Investment Trust PLC), 1962–97; b 2 July 1928; s of late Col Hon. (Charles) Guy Cubitt, CBE, DSO, TD, and Rosamond Mary Edith, d of Sir Montagu Cholmeley, 4th Bt; m 1958, Linda Ishbel, d of late Hon. Angus Campbell, CBE; one s two d. Educ: RNC Dartmouth and Greenwich. Lieut RN, 1949; served in Korea, HMS Charity, 1949–51; Flag Lieut to Adm., BJSM Washington, 1952 and to C-in-C Nore, 1953; retd 1953. Qual. Chartered Auctioneer and Estate Agent, 1958; Chartered Surveyor (FRICS) 1970. Partner: Rogers Chapman & Thomas, 1958–67; Cubitt & West, 1962–79. Regl Dir, 1970–77, Dir, 1977–90, Mem., UK Adv. Bd, 1990–91, National Westminster Bank; Chairman: Lombard North Central PLC, 1980–91; The Housing Corp., 1990–96; Rea Brothers Group PLC, 1996–98. Comr, and Chm., London Adv. Cttee, English Heritage, 1988–94. Mem. Westminster City Council, 1963–78; Leader of Council, 1972–76; Alderman, 1974–78; Lord Mayor and Dep. High Steward of Westminster, 1977–78. Pres., London Chamber of Commerce, 1988–91. Chairman: Anchor Trust (formerly Anchor Gp of Housing Assocs), 1991–98; Housing Assocs' Charitable Trust, 1991–97; Chairman of Governors: West Heath Sch., 1978–91; Cranleigh Sch., 1981–95; Dir and Mem. Governing Body, RAM, 1978–98. Hon. Steward, Westminster Abbey, 1978–2002 (Chief Steward, 1997–2002). Mem., Bd of Green Cloth Verge of Palaces, 1980–98. Trustee, Titsey Foundn, 1983–2016. FRSA; Hon. FRAM 1985. JP Surrey, 1964; Chairman: Dorking PSD, 1991–93; SE Surrey PSD, 1993–95. High Sheriff of Surrey, 1983–84; DL Greater London, 1978. Address: Chapel House, Westhumble, Dorking, Surrey RH5 6AY. T: (01306) 882994. Club: Boodle's.

**CUBITT, Maj. Gen. Sir William (George),** KCVO 2011; CBE 2005 (OBE 2000); DL; farmer and landowner; General Officer Commanding, London District, and Major General Commanding Household Division, 2007–11; b 19 Feb. 1959; m 1990, Lucy Jane Brooking (née Pym); two s one d. Educ: Beechwood Park, Herts; Stowe Sch., Bucks; Univ. of Edinburgh (BSc Hons Agric.). Served Coldstream Guards, 1977–98; regtl appts in 1st Bn in London, New Zealand (attached 2/1 RNZIR), N Ireland, Cyprus, Falkland Is and Hong Kong; Trng Officer, Mozambique Trng Team, Zimbabwe, 1989; acsc 1991–92; Military Asst 2 to Chief of GS, 1992–94; commanded No 2 Co. in Germany, Bosnia and Canada, 1994–96; Lt Col 1996; seconded to Cabinet Office 1996–98; transf. to Irish Guards, 1998–2011; commanded 1st Bn in Germany, Macedonia, Kosovo and Poland, 1998–2001; Col 2001; commanded Land Warfare School; hcsc 2002; commanded 8th Infantry Bde, N Ireland, 2002–04; Dir of Gen. Staff, 2004–07. Regtl Lt Col, Irish Guards and Chm Trustees, Irish Guards Charities, 2008–12. Member: Norfolk Cttee, CLA, 2011– (Vice Chm., 2013–15; Chm., 2015–17); Norfolk Churches Trust Cttee, 2012–16; Gallipoli Assoc., 2012–; Pres., Norfolk Br., RBL, 2014–. Trustee, E Anglian Air Ambulance, 2015– (Chm., 2015–). Member: Royal Forestry Soc.; Nat. Trust; British Assoc. of Shooting and Conservation; British Deer Soc.; Woodland Heritage; Game and Wildlife Conservation Trust; Inst. of Advanced Motorists. Freeman, City of London, 2012. High Sheriff, 2016–17, DL, 2018, Norfolk. Class IV, Order of St Olav (Norway), 1988. Clubs: Cavalry and Guards, Norfolk.

**CUCKNEY, Lady;** see Newell, Dame P. J.

**CUDDIGAN, Hugo Jonathan Patrick;** QC 2015; b London, 22 Feb. 1971; s of Dr Jeremy Cuddigan and Jacqueline Cuddigan; m 2007, Jemma Louise Whicheloe; one s two d. Educ: Ampleforth Coll.; Trinity Coll., Cambridge (BA Engrg 1993; MA); Univ. of Westminster (DipLaw). Called to the Bar, Middle Temple, 1995; in practice as a barrister, specialising in intellectual property, 1997–. Recreations: sailing, ski-ing, Arsenal Football Club. Address: 11 South Square, Gray's Inn, WC1R 5EY. T: (020) 7405 1222. E: clerks@11southsquare.com. Clubs: Soho House; Hawks' (Cambridge); Royal Yacht Squadron, Bembridge Sailing; Worthless Athletic Football.

**CUDMORE, Harold;** yachtsman/businessman; b 21 April 1944; s of late Harold Cudmore, LLD and Sheila Coleman; m 1993, Lauren E. Dagge; two d. Skipper, White Crusader, British challenger, America's Cup, 1986; Manager and sailor, British Admiral's Cup winning team, 1989; Adviser and Coach, America 3, America's Cup winning team, 1992; racing, worldwide, Maxi Yachts, 1979–, Internat. Twelve Metres, 1981–, Heritage/Classic Yachts, 1991–, and superyachts, 2006–. Winner of many world championships, internat. match-racing regattas and major events. Recreations: other sports, walking, travelling, socialising. Address: 4 Queen's Road, Cowes, Isle of Wight PO31 8BQ. T: (01983) 291376, 07710 270952. E: haroldcudmore@aol.com. Clubs: Royal Thames Yacht, Royal Ocean Racing; Royal Cork Yacht, Irish Cruising, Fort Worth Boat.

**CUI, Prof. Zhanfeng,** PhD, DSc; CEng, FREng; Donald Pollock Professor of Chemical Engineering, and Fellow of Hertford College, Oxford University, since 2000; b 16 Nov. 1962; s of Chun-Ting Cui and Su-e Li; m 1985, Dr Jing Yu; one s one d. Educ: Inner Mongolia Poly. Univ., China (BSc 1982); Dalian Univ. of Technol., China (MSc 1984; PhD 1987); MA 1994, DSc 2009, Oxon. CEng 1997; FREng 2013. Res. Fellow, Univ. of Strathclyde, 1988–91; Lectr in Chemical Engrg, Edinburgh Univ., 1991–94; Oxford University: Lectr in Engrg Sci., 1994–99; Reader, 1999–2000; Fellow, Keble Coll., 1994–2000. Visiting Professor: Georgia Inst. of Technol., Atlanta, 1999; Univ. of Minnesota, 2004; (also Chang Jiang Scholar) Dalian Univ. of Technol., China, 2005. Publications: contrib. numerous res. articles to professional jls, as sole or jt author. Recreations: bridge, basketball. Address: Department of Engineering Science, Oxford University, Parks Road, Oxford OX1 3PJ. T: (01865) 617693.

**CUIN-WOOD, Alexandra Frances Sara;** see Wood, A. F. S.

**CULHAM, Michael John,** CB 1992; Assistant Under Secretary of State (Civilian Management (Administrators)), Ministry of Defence, 1987–92, retired; b 24 June 1933; s of Cecil and Constance Culham; m 1963, Christine Mary Daish; one s two d. Educ: Reading Sch.; Lincoln Coll., Oxford (MA); Open Univ. (Dip. French, 1997). National Service, Queen's Own Royal West Kent Regt, RAEC, 1952–54. Exec. Officer, WO, 1957–61; Asst Principal, Air Min., 1962; Private Sec. to Under-Sec. of State for Air, 1962–64; Principal, MoD, 1964–72; Jt Services Staff Coll., 1969; 1st Sec. (Defence), UK Delegn to NATO, Brussels, 1972–74; Asst Sec., MoD, 1974–82; Asst Under-Sec. of State (Adjt-Gen.), MoD, 1982–87. Member: Royal Patriotic Fund Corp., 1983–87; Adv. Council, RMCS, Shrivenham, 1983–87. Commissioner: Duke of York's Royal Mil. Sch., 1982–87; Queen Victoria Sch., 1982–87; Welbeck Coll., 1985–87; Royal Hosp. Chelsea, 1985–88. Chm., Defence Sports and Recreation (formerly MoD Recreation) Assoc., 1985–92; Vice President: CS RFU, 1992–; Farnham Town Boys' FC, 1987– (Chm., 1983–85). Trustee, Nat. Army Mus., 1985–88. Recreations: music, sailing, walking, watching cricket. Address: 39 Waverley Lane, Farnham, Surrey GU9 8BH. Clubs: Civil Service; Surrey County Cricket; Hampshire County Cricket.

**CULHANE, Prof. (John) Leonard,** FRS 1985; Professor of Physics, 1981–2005, now Emeritus, Director, Mullard Space Science Laboratory, 1983–2003, and Head of Department of Space and Climate Physics, 1993–2003, University College London; Director, International Space Science Institute, Bern, 2010–13; b 14 Oct. 1937; s of late John Thomas Culhane and Mary Agnes Culhane; m 1961, Mary Brigid, d of James Smith; two s. Educ: Clongowes Wood College, Co. Kildare; University College Dublin (BSc Phys 1959; MSc Phys 1960); UCL (PhD Phys 1966). FRAS 1970; FInstP 1991. Physics Department, University College London: Res. Asst, 1963; Lectr, 1967; Reader, 1976; Prof., 1981. Sen. Scientist, Lockheed Palo Alto Res. Lab., 1969–70; Vis. Prof., Inst. of Space and Astronautical Sci., Tokyo, 1997. Chairman: SERC/BNSC Space Sci. Prog. Bd, 1989–92 (Vice-Pres., and UK Delegn, ESA Sci. Prog. Cttee, 1990–94); Royal Soc. Space Res. Cttee, 1990–93; COSPAR Commn E, 1994–2002; Eur. Space Sci. Cttee, ESF, 1997–2002; Member: Council, RAS, 1975–78; Space Sci. Adv. Cttee, ESA, 1985–89 (Chm., Astrophysics Working Group, 1985–89); SERC/BNSC Earth Obs. Prog. Bd, 1986–88; SERC Astronomy and Planetary Sci. Bd, 1989–92; Adv. Panel, ESA Space Sci. Dept, 1995–2000; PPARC, 1996–2000; Sci. Oversight Cttee, Internat. Space Sci. Inst., Bern, 2004–09. Mem. Council, Surrey Univ., 1985–90. MAE 2001; Member: IAU; Amer. Astronomical Soc.; Amer. Geophys. Union; Internat. Acad. of Astronautics; For. Mem., Norwegian Acad. of Scis and Letters, 1966. Fellow, UCL, 2008. Hon. DSc Wroclaw, 1993. Silver Award and Pardoe Space Prize, RAeS, 2005; Gold Medal in Astronomy, Royal Astronomical Soc., 2007. Publications: X-ray Astronomy (with P. W. Sanford), 1981; over 400 papers on solar physics, X-ray astronomy, X-ray instrumentation and plasma spectroscopy. Recreations: music, racing cars. Address: Mullard Space Science Laboratory, Holmbury St Mary, Dorking RH5 6NT. T: (01483) 204100. E: j.culhane@ucl.ac.uk.

**CULHANE, Simon Hugh Desmond,** Chartered FCSI; Chief Executive, Chartered Institute for Securities & Investment (formerly Securities Institute, then Securities & Investment Institute), since 2004; b 15 Feb. 1960; m 1985, Sarah; three s one d. Educ: St Paul's Sch.; Univ. of Surrey (BSc Hons Econs and Stats). ACIB 1984; Chartered FCSI 2010 (FSI 2005). Lloyds TSB Bank, 1981–95; Dep. Dir, Prime Minister's Efficiency Unit, Cabinet Office, 1995–98; Dir, Chairman's Office, Deutsche Bank AG, London, 1998–2002; Foundn Trust Project Dir, UCLH, 2003–04. Non-exec. Dir, Efficiency Project Prog. Bd, Office of Govt Commerce, 2004–07. MInstD 2004–09. Recreations: sailing, badminton, following AFC Wimbledon. Address: Chartered Institute for Securities & Investment, 20 Fenchurch Street, EC3M 3BY. E: simon.culhane@cisi.org. Club: Cornhill.

**CULL-CANDY, Prof. Stuart Graham,** PhD; FMedSci, FBPhS; FRS 2002; Gaddum Chair of Pharmacology and Professor of Neuroscience, University College London, since 2006; b 2 Nov. 1946; s of late Stanley William Cull-Candy and Margaret Cull-Candy; m Dr Barbara Paterson Fulton; one d. Educ: Royal Holloway Coll., Univ. of London (BSc Hons Biology 1969); UCL (MSc Physiology and Biophysics 1971); Univ. of Glasgow (PhD Synaptic Physiology 1974). FBPhS (FBPharmacolS 2005). Postdoctoral research: Royal Society European Exchange Prog. Fellow, Inst. of Pharmacology, Univ. of Lund, Sweden, 1974–75; University College London: Beit Meml Res. Fellow, and MRC Associate Res. Staff, Dept of Biophysics, 1975–82; Wellcome Trust Reader in Pharmacology, Dept of Pharmacology, 1982–90; Prof. of Pharmacology, 1990–2003; Royal Soc.—Wolfson Res. post, 2002–08; Prof. of Neuroscience, 2003–06. Japan Soc. for Promotion of Sci. Vis. Prof., Dept of Physiol., Kyoto Univ. Med. Sch., 1990; Internat. Res. Scholar, Howard Hughes Medical Inst., 1993–98. Mem., Neurosci. Cttee, MRC, 1987–91; Founder Mem., Wellcome Trust Internat. Interest Gp, 1991–97; Expert Advr, Scientific Bd, INSERM, France, 2007–. Member: Royal Soc. Univ. Res. Fellowships Grants Cttee, 2003–, Res. Grants Bd, 2005–; Panel, Leverhulme Trust Sen. Res. Fellowships, 2006–; Panel, REF 2014 sub-panel 5: Biol Scis, 2011–; Panel, Newton Internat. Fellowship Cttee, Royal Soc., 2016–. Mem., Faculty of 1000, 2006–. External Editl Advr in Neuroscience, Nature, 1993–97; Editor: Jl of Physiology, 1987–95; European Jl of Neuroscience, 1988–; Neuron, 1994–98; Reviewing Ed., Jl of Neuroscience, 2000–; Associate Ed., Molecular Pharmacology, 2012–; Guest Ed., Current Opinions in Neurobiology, 2007–; Mem., Adv. Bd for F1000 Medicine Reports, 2009–. FMedSci 2004. Hon. Fellow, Physiological Soc., 2015. G. L. Brown Prize, Physiological Soc., 1996; Wolfson Res. Award, Royal Soc., 2003. Publications: various book chapters; numerous basic research articles on fast excitatory synaptic transmission mediated by glutamate, the most important excitatory transmitter between nerve cells in the brain; research articles on glutamate receptors involved in nerve cell signalling in the brain and spinal cord, and role of NMDA receptors, AMPA receptors and associated proteins that underlie normal nerve cell signalling and certain important neurol disorders, in scientific jls Nature, Neuron, Jl of Neuroscience, Jl of Physiology, Nature Neuroscience and Science. Recreations: the Arts and Crafts movement, architecture, jazz and blues music, natural history, history of neurosciences and medicine. Address: Department of Neuroscience, Physiology and Pharmacology, University College London, Medical Sciences Building, University College London, Gower Street, WC1E 6BT. T: (020) 7679 3766. E: s.cull-candy@ucl.ac.uk.

**CULLEN,** family name of **Baron Cullen of Whitekirk**.

**CULLEN OF ASHBOURNE,** 4th Baron cr 1920, of Roehampton, co. Surrey; **Michael John Cokayne;** b 28 Nov. 1950; s of late John O'Brien Marsham Cokayne, y s of 1st Baron Cullen of Ashbourne, and Anne Frances (née Clayton); S uncle, 2016; m 1st, 1976, Baudilia Medina Negrin (marr. diss. 1985); one d; 2nd, 1986, Yvette Santana (marr. diss. 1994); 3rd, 2001, Ljubov Gruntal. Educ: City of Oxford High Sch. Heir: none.

**CULLEN OF WHITEKIRK,** Baron cr 2003 (Life Peer), of Whitekirk in East Lothian; **William Douglas Cullen,** KT 2007; PC 1997; Lord Justice-General of Scotland and Lord President of the Court of Session, 2001–05; b 18 Nov. 1935; s of late Sheriff K. D. Cullen and Mrs G. M. Cullen; m 1961, Rosamond Mary Downer (MBE 2007); two s two d. Educ: Dundee High Sch.; St Andrews Univ. (MA); Edinburgh Univ. (LLB). FRSE 1993. Called to the Scottish Bar, 1960. Standing Jun. Counsel to HM Customs and Excise, 1970–73; QC (Scot.) 1973; Advocate-depute, 1978–81; a Senator of the Coll. of Justice in Scotland, 1986–2005; Lord Justice-Clerk and Pres. of the Second Div. of the Court of Session, 1997–2001. A Justice, Qatar Financial Centre Civil and Commercial Court, 2007–15. Chairman: Medical Appeal Tribunal, 1977–86; Inquiry into the Piper Alpha disaster, 1988–90; Review of Business of the Outer House of the Court of Session, 1995; Tribunal of Inquiry into the shootings at Dunblane Primary Sch., 1996; Ladbroke Grove Rail Inquiry, 1999–2001; Rev. of fatal accident legislation, 2008–09. Chm., Bd of Dirs, The Signet Accreditation Ltd, 2007–15. Member: Scottish Valuation Adv. Council, 1980–86; Royal Commn on Ancient and Historical Monuments of Scotland, 1987–97. Mem., H of L, 2003–19. Mem., Constitution Select Cttee, H of L, 2013–16. President: SACRO, 2000–15; Saltire Soc., 2005–11. Chancellor, Abertay Univ. (formerly Univ. of Abertay, Dundee), 2009–19. Chairman: Council, Cockburn Assoc. (Edinburgh Civic Trust), 1984–86; Govs, St Margaret's Sch., Edinburgh, 1994–2001; Mem. Court, Napier Univ., 1996–2005. Hon. Bencher: Inner Temple, 2001; Inn of Court of NI, 2002. Hon. FREng (Hon. FEng 1995); Hon. FSaRS 2002; Hon. FRCSEd 2006; FRCPEd 2010. Hon. LLD: Aberdeen, 1992; St Andrews, 1997; Dundee, Edinburgh, Glasgow Caledonian, 2000; DUniv Heriot-Watt, 2005. Publications: The Faculty Digest Supplement 1951–60, 1965; non-legal booklets on buildings in Edinburgh. Recreations: gardening, natural history. Address: c/o Lord President's Private Office, Court of Session, Parliament House, Edinburgh EH1 1RQ.

**CULLEN, Donna-Maria;** Executive Director, Tottenham Hotspur Football Club, since 2006; *b* London; *d* of Richard and Joyce Cullen; *m* 1992, Gary Assim; two *s*. *Educ:* Collegiate High Sch., Port Elizabeth, SA; Univ. of Cape Town (MA Political Sci. and English). Good Relations, 1985–91; Lowe Bell and Chime Communications, 1991–2006; Consultant, Tottenham Hotspur FC, 1991–2006. *Recreations:* swimming, food and wine. *Address:* Tottenham Hotspur Football Club, Lilywhite House, 782 High Road, N17 0BX.

**CULLEN, Edmund William Hector;** QC 2012; *b* 29 Sept. 1966; *s* of Terence Lindsay Graham Cullen, QC and Muriel Elisabeth Cullen; *m* 1994, Emma; three *d*. *Educ:* Winchester Coll.; Bristol Univ. (BA Philosophy). Called to the Bar, Lincoln's Inn, 1990; in practice as barrister, 1991–. *Recreations:* horse racing, opera, weeding. *Address:* Maitland Chambers, 7 Stone Buildings, Lincoln's Inn, WC2A 3SZ. *T:* (020) 7406 1200.

**CULLEN, Felicity Ann;** QC 2008; *b* Talgarth, 5 March 1962; *d* of John Milton and Mary Christine London; *m* 1986, Christopher Cullen; two *s*. *Educ:* Holy Trinity Convent, Kidderminster; St David's Ursuline Convent, Brecon; Brecon High Sch.; Univ. of Birmingham (LLB 1983); Queens' Coll., Cambridge (LLM 1984). Called to the Bar, Lincoln's Inn, 1985; in practice as barrister, specialising in revenue law; Mem., Gray's Inn Tax Chambers, 1986–2014, Devereux Chambers, 2014–; CEDR Accredited Mediator, 2012. *Recreations:* arts, entertaining, architecture and design, adventure travel, sport. *Address:* Devereux Chambers, Queen Elizabeth Building, Temple, EC4Y 9BS.

**CULLEN, Hon. Sir Michael (John),** KNZM 2012; PhD; Chairman: New Zealand Post, 2010–16 (Deputy Chairman, 2009–10); Earthquake Commission, since 2018; *b* London, 5 Feb. 1945; adopted NZ citizenship, 1975; *s* of John Joseph Thomas Cullen and Ivy May Cullen; *m* 1st, 1967, Rowena Joy Knight (marr. diss. 1987); two *d*; 2nd, 1989, Lowson Anne Collins. *Educ:* Christ's Coll., Christchurch; Canterbury Univ. (BA 1965; MA Hist. 1967); Edinburgh Univ. (PhD Social and Economic Hist.). Asst Lectr, Univ. of Canterbury; Tutor, Univ. of Stirling; Sen. Lectr, Univ. of Otago. MP (Lab) St Kilda, 1981–96, Dunedin S, 1996–99, List MP (Lab), 1999–2009. Sen. Govt Whip, 1984–87; Associate Minister of Finance, 1987–90; Minister of Social Welfare, 1987–90; Associate Minister of Health, 1988–90; Associate Minister of Labour, 1989–90; opposition spokesperson on social welfare, war pensions and Accident Compensation Corp., 1990–91, on finance, 1991; Minister of Revenue, 1999–2005; Treasurer, Minister of Finance and Leader of the House, 1999–2008; Dep. Prime Minister, 2002–08; Minister for Tertiary Education, 2005–08; Attorney General, 2005–08. Dep. Leader, NZ Labour Party, 1996. Vis. Fellow, ANU. Hon. LLD Otago, 2010. *Publications:* The Statistical Movement in Early Victorian Britain, 1974; Lawfully Occupied, 1979; articles in jls. *Recreations:* music, reading, golf, house renovation. *Address:* 17 Manuera Place, Ohope 3121, New Zealand.

**CULLEN, Paul Benedict;** *see* Pentland, Hon. Lord.

**CULLEY, Carol Ann;** City Treasurer, Manchester City Council, since 2016; *b* Taunton, 26 Aug. 1968; *d* of Dean Rodney Hill and Ann Webber; *m* (separated); one *s*. *Educ:* Vyne Comprehensive Sch., Basingstoke; Queen Mary's Sixth Form Coll.; Hull Univ. (BA Social and Econ Hist.). CIPFA; Dip. Mgt Studies. Grad. trainee, then Principal Finance Manager, Oxfordshire CC, 1986–2001; Manchester City Council: Asst Dir of Finance (Social Services), 2001–08; Asst Chief Exec., 2008–14; Dep. City Treas., 2014–16. Director: Northern Gateway Ops Ltd; Destination Manchester Ltd; Manchester Creative Digital Assets Ltd; Sports City Mgt Co. Ltd; Manchester Knowledge Capital Ltd; Matrix Homes Ltd; Manchester Central Conventions Ltd; Manchester Working Ltd; Manchester Professional Services Ltd. Dir, Gtr Manchester Working Trust. *Recreations:* running, walking, Southampton FC season ticket holder. *Address:* Manchester City Council, Level 3, Town Hall Extension, Manchester M60 2LA. *T:* (0161) 234 3406. *E:* carol.culley@manchester.gov.uk.

**CULLEY, Ron;** author; Director: Liberabit UK, since 2010; Liberabit International, since 2013; *b* 2 Feb. 1950; *s* of Ronald Frank Culley and Mary McTavish Culley (*née* McLeod); *m* 1st, 1973, Margaret Ferguson (marr. diss. 1985); two *s*; 2nd, 1994, Jean Pollock; two *s*. *Educ:* Craigbank Comprehensive Sch.; Jordanhill Coll. of Educn (Dip. YCS); Moray House Coll. of Educn (CQSW, CSW); Univ. of Glasgow (Cert. Supervisory Mgt); Univ. of Strathclyde (MSc); Univ. of St Andrews (CTS). Various social work and social policy posts, Strathclyde Regl Council, 1975–87; Chief Executive: Govan Initiative Ltd, 1987–2000; Scottish Enterprise Glasgow, 2000–06; Strathclyde Partnership for Transport, 2006–10. Mem. Bd, Police Adv. Bd for Scotland, 1999–2005. Member Board: Scottish Urban Regeneration Foundn, 1992–2006; Quality Scotland, 1999–2000; Glasgow Alliance, 2000–06; Glasgow Economic Forum, 2001–06; Prince's Trust Glasgow, 2002–06; Wise Gp, 2003–10; Glasgow Community Planning Partnership, 2004–10; Clyde Valley Community Planning Partnership, 2004–10; Glasgow Sci. Centre, 2004–06. Sec., Ibrox Community Trust, 1990–99. Panel Mem., Investors in People, 1999–2002. Mem., British Transport Police Authy, 2008–10. Dir, 2011–, Trustee, 2013–, Harmony Row Developments Ltd (Hon. Mem., Harmony Row Youth Club, 2000–). Dir, Bd of Trustees, Humanist Soc. of Scotland, 2014–15. Contested (SLP) Scotland W, Scottish Parly elecns, 1999. Gov., Scottish Police Trng Coll., 1999–2004. *Publications:* The New Guards, 1999; I Belong to Glasgow, 2009, 2nd edn 2010; The Kaibab Resolution, 2010; Glasgow Belongs To Me, 2011; A Confusion of Mandarins, 2011; The Patriot Game, 2013; Shoeshine Man, 2014; One Year, 2015; Alba: who killed Willie McRae?, 2017; Odyssey, 2018; (ed) The Never Ending Story, 2018; The Butcher's Apron, 2019; The Last Colony, 2019. *Recreations:* family and friends, music, Association football (particularly Manchester United), socialising, reading biographies, Scottish, American and Irish politics, irreverence, song-writing, Glasgow memorabilia, convivial temulence, contumacy, public speaking, Humanism, Robert Burns, laughing out loud, travel, writing. *Address:* Liberabit UK, Garret Studios, Sutherland Drive, Glasgow G46 6PL. *T:* 07860 530972. *E:* author@ronculley.com, weegieron@hotmail.com. *W:* www.ronculley.com, www.twitter.com/lblogtoglasgow. *Clubs:* Pot Still, Rab Ha's (Glasgow).

**CULLIMORE, Charles Augustine Kaye,** CMG 1993; HM Diplomatic Service, retired; *b* 2 Oct. 1933; *s* of Rev. Canon Charles Cullimore and Constance Alicia Kaye Cullimore (*née* Grimshaw); *m* 1956, Val Elizabeth Margot (*née* Willemsen); one *s* one *d*. *Educ:* Portora Royal Sch., Enniskillen; Trinity Coll., Oxford (MA). N Ireland Short Service Commn, 1955–57. HMOCS, Tanganyika, 1958–61; ICI Ltd, 1961–71; joined HM Diplomatic Service, 1971; FCO, 1971–73; Bonn, 1973–77; FCO, 1977–79; Counsellor, New Delhi, 1979–82; Dep. High Comr, Canberra, 1982–86; FCO, 1986–89; High Comr, Uganda, 1989–93. Chief Exec., Southern Africa Business Assoc., 1995–2001; Chm., British African Business Assoc., 2001–09. Dir, Transparency Internat. (UK), 1996–99. External Lectr, SOAS, 1998–2010. Council Member: Royal African Soc., 2000–10; Overseas Service Pensioners' Assoc., 2004–17 (Vice Chm., 2011; Chm., 2013–17). Hon. Pres., Business Council for Africa UK, 2009–16. Member: Britain-Australia Soc., 1986–; The Pilgrims, 1993–; RIIA, 1996–. *Publications:* (contrib.) Portora - The School on the Hill: a quatercentenary history 1608–2008, 2009; contrib. Jl of Mod. African Studies, Jl Overseas Service Pensioners' Assoc. *Recreations:* theatre, walking, travel. *Address:* Deacon House, Bidborough, Kent TN3 0UP. *Club:* Royal Over-Seas League.

**CULLINAN, Edward Horder,** CBE 1987; RA 1991; RDI 2010; Chairman, Cullinan Studio (formerly Edward Cullinan Architects Ltd), since 1989 (Founder, 1965, and Senior Partner, 1965–89, Edward Cullinan Architects); *b* 17 July 1931; *s* of Dr Edward Cullinan and Joy (*née* Horder); *m* 1961, Rosalind Yeates; one *s* two *d*. *Educ:* Ampleforth Coll.; Cambridge Univ. (Anderson and Webb Schol., 1951; BA); Univ. of California at Berkeley (George VI Meml Fellow, 1956). AADip; RIBA. With Denys Lasdun, 1958–65. Bannister Fletcher Prof., UCL, 1978–79; Graham Willis Prof., Univ. of Sheffield, 1985–87; George Simpson Prof., Univ. of Edinburgh, 1987–90; Special Prof., Univ. of Nottingham, 2004–09. Mem., Royal Fine Art Commn, 1996–99. Designed and built: Horder House, Hampshire, 1959–60; Minster Lovell Mill, 1969–72; Parish Ch. of St Mary, Barnes, 1978–84; Lambeth Community Care Centre, 1979–84; RMC Internat. HQ, 1985–90; Fountains Abbey visitor centre and landscape, 1987–92; Archeolink Visitor Centre, Oyne, Aberdeenshire, 1994–97; Faculty of Divinity, 1995–2000, Centre for Mathematical Scis, 1996–2002, Cambridge Univ.; Univ. of East London, 1997–99; Downland Gridshell, Weald and Downland Open Air Mus., 1997–2002; Greenwich Millennium Sch. and Health Centre, 1998–2001; Singapore Mgt Univ., 2000–; Clink St, Southwark, 2000–09; Stonebridge Hillside Hub, W London, 2005–09; Maggie's Centre, Freeman Hospital, Newcastle upon Tyne, 2010. Masterplans: Univ. of N Carolina, 1996; Bristol Harbourside, 2000–; Masshouse, Birmingham, 2002–; Chinese Univ., Hong Kong, 2007–09; Shahat Garden City, Libya, 2009–11; all have received awards and been published internationally. FRSA 1984; Hon. FRIAS 1995; Hon. RIAI 2011; Hon. RAIC 2012. Royal Gold Medal, RIBA, 2008. *Publications:* Edward Cullinan, Architects, 1984; (with K. Powell) Edward Cullinan, Architect, 1995; *relevant publication:* Ends Middles Beginnings: Edward Cullinan Architects, by Jonathan Hale, 2005; contribs to many architectural jls. *Recreations:* horticulture, travel, building, history, geography. *Address:* 5 Baldwin Terrace, N1 7RU. *T:* (020) 7704 1975.

**CULLINAN, Nicholas Robert,** PhD; Director, National Portrait Gallery, since 2015; *b* New Haven, Conn, 29 Dec. 1977; *s* of Brian Cullinan and Valerie Cullinan. *Educ:* Courtauld Inst. of Art, Univ. of London (BA Hist. of Art 2002; MA Hist. of Art 2003; PhD 2010). Curator: Internat. Modern Art, Tate Modern, London, 2007–13; Modern and Contemp. Art, Metropolitan Mus. of Art, NY, 2013–15. Thaw Sen. Fellow, Morgan Liby and Mus., NY, 2013. *Publications:* 100 Portraits: National Portrait Gallery, 2017. *Recreations:* travel, reading, opera. *Address:* National Portrait Gallery, St Martin's Place, WC2H 0HE. *E:* director@npg.org.uk.

**CULLINGFORD, Martin James;** Editor, since 2011, and Publisher, since 2014, Gramophone; Editorial Director, MA Music, Leisure & Travel, since 2016; *b* Frimley, 3 Aug. 1978; *s* of Rodney and Jacqueline Cullingford; *m* 2001, Jasmine Wan; one *d*. *Educ:* Kirkley High Sch., Lowestoft; Girton Coll., Cambridge (BA Hist. 2000). Staff writer, Pensions Mgt, 2000–02; Gramophone: News and Online Ed., 2002–04; Features Ed., 2005–06; Dep. Ed., 2006–10; Ed., Gramophone Online, 2010–11. *Recreations:* classical guitar, museums and galleries, cycling, church music and architecture, Sunday school leader. *Address:* Gramophone, Mark Allen Group, St Jude's Church, Dulwich Road, SE24 0PB. *T:* (020) 7501 6361. *E:* martin.cullingford@markallengroup.com.

**CULLIS, Prof. Anthony George,** DPhil, DSc; FRS 2004; Professor of Semiconductor Nanocharacterisation (formerly of Electronic and Electrical Engineering), University of Sheffield, 1995–2009, now Emeritus; *b* 16 Jan. 1946; *s* of late George Thomas Cullis and Doris Mary Cullis; *m* 1979, Ruth Edith Allen; one *s* one *d*. *Educ:* Royal Grammar Sch., Worcester; Wadham Coll., Oxford (MA, DPhil, DSc). Mem. Tech. Staff, Bell Labs, Murray Hill, USA, 1972–75; posts to SPSO (Individual Merit), DERA/QinetiQ, Malvern, 1975–95. Chairman: Electron Microscopy and Analysis Gp, Inst. of Physics, 1980–82; Wkg Party on Transient Annealing, DoI, 1981–84; SERC MSEC Instrumentation Panel, 1988–93; Mem., Functional Materials Coll., EPSRC, 1997–. Pres., Scientific Council, TASC Italian Nat. Lab., Trieste, 2001–03. Ed., Procs vols for Microscopy of Semiconducting Materials internat. conf. series, 1979–; Co-ordinating Ed., Materials Sci. and Engrg Reports, 1994–. Holliday Award, IMMM, 1984. *Publications:* numerous refereed scientific papers in learned jls and other media. *Recreations:* philately, armchair archaeology, motoring. *Address:* Department of Electronic and Electrical Engineering, University of Sheffield, 3 Solly Street, Level 1, Sheffield S1 4DE. *T:* (0114) 222 5355. *E:* a.g.cullis@sheffield.ac.uk.

**CULLODEN, Lord;** Xan Richard Anders Windsor; *b* 12 March 2007; *o s* of and heir of Earl of Ulster, *qv*. Page of Honour to the Queen, 2017–.

**CULLOTY, James Hugh;** racehorse trainer, since 2006; breeder, farmer; *b* 18 Dec. 1973; *s* of Donal and Maureen Culloty; *m* 2004, Susannah Samworth; two *s* one *d*. *Educ:* St Brendan's Coll., Killarney. Stable jockey to Miss Henrietta Knight, 1996–2005; winner: Grand National, on Bindaree, 2002; Cheltenham Gold Cup, on Best Mate, 2002, 2003, 2004; Irish Grand National, on Timbera, 2003; wins as trainer include: with Lord Windermere, RSC Chase, 2013, Cheltenham Gold Cup, 2014; with Spring Heeled, Fulke Walwyn Kim Muir Challenge Cup Handicap Chase, 2013. *Recreations:* golf, farming. *Address:* Mount Corbitt, Churchtown, Mallow, Co. Cork, P51 Y727, Ireland. *T:* (22) 49776. *W:* www.jimculloty.com.

**CULLUM, Prof. Dame Nicola Anne, (Prof. Dame Nicky),** DBE 2013; PhD; FAAN, FMedSci; Professor of Nursing, University of Manchester, since 2011 (Head, Division of Nursing, Midwifery and Social Care, 2015–19); *b* Leeds, 6 June 1962; *d* of Ian and Brenda Cullum; *m* 1998, Deepak Popli; one *s* one *d*. *Educ:* Univ. of Liverpool (BSc Hons Pharmacol. 1984; PhD Pharmacol. 1990). RGN 1985. Res. Fellow, Nursing Practice Res. Unit, Univ. of Surrey, 1988–90; Lectr, Dept of Nursing, Univ. of Liverpool, 1990–94; University of York: Res. Fellow, Centre for Health Econs, 1994–96; Reader, 1996–2001, Prof., 2001–11, Dept of Health Scis. Prof., Sch. of Nursing and Midwifery, Griffith Univ., Qld, 2011–18; Hon. Vis. Prof., Dept of Health Scis, Univ. of York, 2011–16; Hon. Prof., Sch. of Nursing, Midwifery and Social Work, Univ. of Queensland, 2014–17; Hon. Professorial Fellow, Univ. of Melbourne, 2019–. NIHR Sen. Investigator, 2008–. FMedSci 2012; FAAN 2014. *Publications:* contrib. articles to jls on wounds, wound care and evidence-based nursing. *Recreations:* family, friends, laughter, music, art. *Address:* Division of Nursing, Midwifery and Social Work, University of Manchester, Jean McFarlane Building, Oxford Road, Manchester M13 9PL. *T:* (0161) 306 7779. *E:* nicky.cullum@manchester.ac.uk.

**CULLUM, Peter Geoffrey,** CBE 2011; FCII; Founding Executive Chairman, 1997–2011, non-executive Deputy Chairman, 2011–15, Towergate Partnership Ltd; *b* Norwich; *s* of Geoffrey and Doreen Cullum; *m* 2000, Ann Fulton; one *s* two *d*. *Educ:* City of Norwich Grammar Sch. for Boys; Cass Business Sch., City Univ., London (MSc, DSc); PhD Business Admin 2008); City Business Sch. (MBA 1975). FCII 1971; ACIM 2002. Inspector, Royal Insce, 1969–74; Commercial Union: Mktg Exec., 1975–82; Mktg Dir, London and Edinburgh, 1987–91; CEO, Economic Insce, 1991–96; Mktg Dir, Hiscox plc, 1996–97. Chairman: Global Risk Partners Ltd, 2013–; Minority Venture Partners Ltd, 2013–. Vice Pres., Nat. Autistic Soc., 2012–. FRSA. *Publications:* Panic, Passion and Power, 2007; contrib. articles to insce sector jls. *Recreations:* golf, tennis, reading, spectator at most sports.

**CULME-SEYMOUR, Sir Michael Patrick**; see Seymour.

**CULPIN, Sir Robert (Paul)**, Kt 2001; Managing Director, Budget and Public Finances, HM Treasury, 1998–2003. *Educ:* Christ's Coll., Cambridge (BA 1968); Harvard Univ.; California Univ. HM Treasury, 1965–2003; Press Sec. and Hd of Information, 1984–87; Under-Sec., Fiscal Policy Div., 1987–93; Dep. Sec., Public Finance, 1993–94; Second Permanent Sec., 1994; Dir, Public Expenditure, then Public Spending, 1994–98. *Address:* c/o HM Treasury, 1 Horse Guards Road, SW1A 2HQ.

**CULSHAW, Robert Nicholas**, MVO 1979; Deputy Director, British Antarctic Survey, 2006–12; HM Diplomatic Service, retired; *b* 22 Dec. 1952; *s* of late Ivan Culshaw and Edith Marjorie Jose Barnard; *m* 1977, Elaine Ritchie Clegg; one *s*. *Educ:* University Coll. Sch., Hampstead; King's Coll., Cambridge (BA 1st Cl. Hons Classics 1974; Major Univ. Scholarship for Classics, 1974; MA 1977). FCO, 1974–75; MECAS, Lebanon and Jordan, 1975–77; 3rd Sec., Muscat, 1977–79; 2nd Sec., Khartoum, 1979–80; 1st Sec., Rome, 1980–84; FCO, 1984–88; Head of Chancery, 1988–90, Dep. Hd of Mission and Consul-Gen., 1991–93, Athens; FCO Spokesman and Hd of News Dept, 1993–95; Minister-Counsellor, Washington, 1995–99; Consul Gen., Chicago, 1999–2003; Dir, Americas and Overseas Territories, FCO, 2003–05. Churchill Fellow, Westminster Coll., Fulton, 2001. Mem. Bd, US Friends of Leonard Cheshire, 1998–2005; Trustee, Lady Ryder of Warsaw Foundn (formerly Bouverie Foundn), 2007–10. Mem. Bd, Cambridge Leisure and Ice Centre, 2013–. Vice Chm., Cambridge Univ. Music Soc., 2008–10 (Singing Mem., 2005–17); Mem., Madrigal Soc., 2015–. FRSA 1995; FRGS 2007. *Recreations:* ski-ing, singing, poetry, languages, hiking. *Address:* Piney Lodge, 66 Cow Lane, Fulbourn, Cambridge CB21 5HB. *E:* robert.culshaw@me.com.

**CULVER, John Howard**, LVO 2000; HM Diplomatic Service, retired; *b* 17 July 1947; *s* of late Frank and Peggy Culver; *m* 1973, Margaret Ann Davis; two *s* one *d*. Entered FO, 1968; Moscow, 1974–76; La Paz, 1977–80; FCO, 1980–83; Rome, 1983–87; Head of Chancery, Dhaka, 1987–90; FCO, 1990–92; Ambassador to Nicaragua, 1992–97; Consul-General, Naples, 1997–99; Rome, 2000; Ambassador to Iceland, 2001–04; Hd of Resources, Europe Directorate-Gen., FCO, 2004–05; Chargé d'Affaires *ai*, Holy See, 2005. *E:* john@theculvers.com.

**CULYER, Prof. Anthony John**, CBE 1999; FMedSci; Professor of Economics, University of York, 1979–2014, on leave of absence, 2003–06, now Emeritus (Director of Health Development, 1997–2001); Chief Scientist, Institute for Work and Health, Toronto, 2003–06; Adjunct Professor, Institute of Health Policy Management and Evaluation, University of Toronto, since 2014 (Ontario Research Chair in Health Policy and Program Design, 2007–14); *b* 1 July 1942; *s* of late Thomas Reginald Culyer and Betty Ely (*née* Headland); *m* 1966, Sieglinde Birgit (*d* 2011); one *s* one *d*. *Educ:* Sir William Borlase's Sch., Marlow; King's Sch., Worcester; Exeter Univ. (BA Hons). Univ. of California at Los Angeles. Tutor and Asst Lectr, Exeter Univ., 1965–69; York University: Lectr, Sen. Lectr and Reader, 1969–79; Dep. Dir, Inst. of Social and Economic Research, 1971–82; Hd, Dept of Econs and Related Studies, 1986–2001; Pro-Vice-Chancellor, 1991–94; Dep. Vice-Chancellor, 1994–97. University of Toronto: Status-only Prof., 1989–2001 and Adjunct Prof., 2003–07. Sen. Research Associate, Ontario Economic Council, 1976, Vis. Professorial Lectr, Queen's Univ., Kingston, 1976; William Evans Vis. Professor, Otago Univ., 1979; Vis. Fellow, Australian National Univ., 1979; Visiting Professor: Trent Univ., 1985–86; Inst. für Med. Informatik und Systemforschung, Munich, 1990–91; Toronto Univ., 1991; Central Inst. of Technology, NZ, 1996; Imperial Coll. London, 2016–; Adjunct Scientist, Inst. for Work & Health, Toronto, 2007–15 (Sen. Scientist, 2006–07); Dist. Vis. Scholar, Univ. of Witwatersrand, 2015–16. Lectures: Woodward, Univ. of BC, 1986; Perey, McMaster Univ., and Champlain, Trent Univ., Canada, 1990; Francis Fraser, BPMF, 1994; Sinclair, Queen's Univ., Kingston, 2005; Emmett Hall Meml, 2015. Member: Value Focus Gp on cost and benefit perspective of NICE, DoH, 2008; Policy Res. Units Commng Panel, DoH, 2009–11. Member: Standing Cttee, Conf. of Heads of Univ. Depts of Econs, 1988–2001; Coll. Cttee, King's Fund Coll., London, 1989–92; Res. Adv. Cttee, 1990–2002, Sci. Adv. Cttee, 2002–03, Inst. for Work and Health, Toronto; Adv. Cttee for Centre for Health and Society, UCL, 1992–99; Rev. Adv. Cttee on London SHAs, 1992–93; Adv. Cttee, Canadian Inst. for Advanced Res., 1992–2002; Future Health Care Options Wkg Pty, IHSM, 1992–93; British Council Health Adv. Cttee, 1995–97; Academic Adv. Council, Univ. of Buckingham, 1996–2004. Royal School of Church Music: Chm., York Dist, 1984–95, NE Yorks Area, 1995–2003; Mem. Adv. Bd, 2002–; Mem. Council, and Trustee, 2003–10. Mem., 1982–90, non-exec. Mem., 1990–92, Northallerton HA; Dep. Chm., N Yorks HA, 1995–99 (non-exec. Mem., 1994–99); Member: Yorks RHA R&D Cttee, 1992–94; Northern and Yorks Regl R&D Adv. Cttee, 1995–99; Central R&D Cttee, NHS, 1991–2001; NHS Standing Gp on Health Technol., 1992–97; R&D Cttee of High Security Psychiatric Hosps Commissioning Bd, 1995–99; Chair: Methodology Panel, NHS Standing Gp on Health Technol., 1993–97; NHS Task Force on Supporting R&D in NHS, 1994; Advr to NHS Dir of R&D, 1997–99. NICE: Vice Chm., 1999–2003; Chm., R&D Cttee, 2007–10; Mem. Adv. Gp, NICE Internat., 2009–16 (Chair, 2012–16). Chm., Office of Health Econs, 2001–13 (Chm., Editl Bd, 1997–); Mem., Economics Adv. Panel, Home Office, 2005–08; Team Leader, Mid-term Evaluation of DFID Health Res. Prog. Consortia, 2015. Ontario Ministry of Health and Long Term Care: Member: Equity Editl Bd, 2006; Career Scientist Relevance Rev. Panel, 2007–08; Health Res. Adv. Council, 2007–09; Ext. Adv. Gp, Health System Strategy Div., 2009–11; Adv. Gp on Productivity, 2009–11; Steering Cttee for Partnerships for Health System Improvement, 2009–11; Bd, Canadian Agency for Drugs and Technologies in Health, 2013–14; Special Advr, Canada Health Council, 2005–07; Sen. Economic Advr, 2006–07, Chm., Pharmacoecons Unit Adv. Cttee, 2008–14, Cancer Care Ontario; Chair, Res. Adv. Council, Workplace Safety and Insce Bd (Ontario), 2006–10. Trustee, Canadian Health Services Res. Foundn, 2000–03. Mem., Health Sci. Policy Council, Internat. Soc. for Pharmacoecons and Outcomes Res., 2005–. Pres., Econs Section, BAAS, 1994. Founder FMedSci 1998. Ed.-in-Chief, Elsevier online Encyclopedia of Health Econs, 2009–; Co-Editor, Jl of Health Econs, 1982–2013; Member, Editorial Board: Econ. Rev., 1983–95; Med. Law Internat., 1992–95; BMJ, 1995–2000; Mem. Managing Cttee, Jl of Med. Ethics, 1994–2001. Hon. FRCP 2003. Hon. DEc Stockholm Sch. of Econs, 1999. (Jtly) William B. Graham Prize, Baxter Foundn, 2015; Avedis Donabedian Outcomes Res. Lifetime Achievement Award, Internat. Soc. for Pharmacoecons and Outcomes Res., 2015. *Publications:* The Economics of Social Policy, 1973; (ed with M. H. Cooper) Health Economics, 1973; (ed) Economic Policies and Social Goals, 1974; Need and the National Health Service, 1976; (with J. Wiseman and A. Walker) Annotated Bibliography of Health Economics, 1977; (ed with V. Halberstadt) Human Resources and Public Finance, 1977; Measuring Health: Lessons for Ontario, 1978; (ed with K. G. Wright) Economic Aspects of Health Services, 1978; The Political Economy of Social Policy, 1980; (ed) Health Indicators, 1983; (ed with B. Horisberger) Economic and Medical Evaluation of Health Care Technologies, 1983; Economics, 1985; (ed with G. Terny) Public Finance and Social Policy, 1985; (ed with B. Jonsson) Public and Private Health Services: complementarities and conflicts, 1986; (jtly) The International Bibliography of Health Economics: a comprehensive annotated guide to English language sources since 1914, 1986; Canadian Health Care Expenditures: myth and reality, past and future, 1988; (ed) Standards for the Socio-economic Evaluation of Health Care Products and Services, 1990; (ed jtly) Competition in Health Care: reforming the NHS, 1990; (ed) The Economics of Health, 1991; (ed jtly) Some Recent Developments in Health Economics, 1992; (ed jtly) Swedish Health Care: the best in the world?, 1993; (ed jtly) Reforming Health Care Systems: experiments with the NHS, 1996; (ed jtly) Being Reasonable about the Economics of Health: selected essays by Alan Williams, 1997; (ed jtly) Handbook of Health Economics, 2001; The Dictionary of Health Economics, 2005, 3rd edn 2014; Health Economics: critical perspectives on the world economy, 4 vols, 2006; (jtly) Economic Evaluation of Interventions for Occupational Health and Safety, 2008; The Humble Economist: Tony Culyer on health, health care and social decision making, 2012; (ed jtly) Portrait of a Health Economist: festschrift in honour of Bengt Jönsson, 2014; (jtly) A Star in the East: a short history of HITAP, Bangkok, 2016; articles in Oxford Econ. Papers, Economica, Scottish Jl of Political Economy, Public Finance, Jl of Public Economics, Kyklos, Qly Jl of Economics, Jl Royal Statistical Soc., Jl of Health Economics, Health Econs, BMJ, Jl Med. Ethics, and others. *Recreations:* church music (Organist and Choir Director, St Catherine's, Barmby Moor, 1971–2003), music generally. *Address:* Centre for Health Economics, University of York, York YO10 5DD. *E:* tony.culyer@york.ac.uk.

**CUMANI, Luca Matteo**; racehorse trainer; *b* 7 April 1949; *s* of Sergio Cumani and Elena Cardini Cumani; *m* 1979, Sara Doon Plunket; one *s* one *d*. *Educ:* Milan. Riding career: 85 winners in Italy, France and UK; champion amateur, Italy, 1972; won Moët and Chandon on Meissen, 1972; Prix Paul Noël de la Houtre on Harland, 1970, 1972, 1973; Asst to Sergio Cumani and to H. R. A. Cecil, 1974–75; first held licence, 1976; numerous major races won, incl. St Leger (Commanche Run), 1984; Derby and Irish Sweeps Derby, 1988 (Kahyasi); Breeders Cup Mile, 1994 (Barathea); Derby, 1998 (High Rise); Coral Eclipse Stakes, Sandown, 2003 (Falbrav); Juddmonte Internat. Stakes, 2003 (Falbrav); Queen Elizabeth II Stakes, Ascot, 2003 (Falbrav); Prix du Moulin, Longchamp, 2005 (Starcraft); Japan Cup, 2005 (Alkaased); Queen Elizabeth Cup, Hong Kong, 2009 (Presvis); Dubai Duty Free, 2011 (Presvis); King George VI and Queen Elizabeth Stakes, Ascot, 2015 (Postponed); Qatar Prix Foy, Longchamp, 2015 (Postponed). *Address:* Bedford House Stables, Bury Road, Newmarket, Suffolk CB8 7BX. *T:* (01638) 665432.

**CUMBERLEGE**, family name of **Baroness Cumberlege**.

**CUMBERLEGE, Baroness** *cr* 1990 (Life Peer), of Newick in the County of East Sussex; **Julia Frances Cumberlege**, CBE 1985; FRCP, FRCGP; Founder and Director: Cumberlege Connections Ltd, since 2001; Cumberlege Eden and Partners, since 2013; Director, Assuring Better Practice (UK) Ltd, 2004–07; Associate, Quo Health, 2001–05; *b* 27 Jan. 1943; *d* of late Dr L. U. Camm and M. G. G. Camm; *m* 1961, Patrick Francis Howard Cumberlege; three *s*. *Educ:* Convent of the Sacred Heart, Tunbridge Wells. FRCP 2007; FRCGP 2007; FRCOG 2013. Mem., East Sussex AHA, 1977–81; Chairman: Brighton HA, 1981–88; SW Thames RHA, 1988–92; Mem. Council, NAHA, 1982–88 (Vice-Chm., 1984–87; Chm., 1987–88). Member (C): Lewes DC, 1966–79 (Leader, 1977–78); East Sussex CC, 1974–85 (Chm., Social Services Cttee, 1979–82). Chairman: Review of Community Nursing for England, 1985 (report, Neighbourhood Nursing—a focus for care, 1986); Expert Maternity Gp, 1993 (report, Changing Childbirth, 1993); Nat. Review of Maternity Services in England, 2015–16 (report, Better Births, 2016); Ind. Medicines and Medical Devices Safety Review, 2018–. Member: Social Security Adv. Cttee, 1980–82; DHSS Expert Adv. Gp on AIDS, 1987–89; Council, UK Central Council for Nursing, Midwifery and Health Visiting, 1989–92; NHS Policy Bd, 1989–97. Parly Under-Sec. of State, DoH, 1992–97; Co-Chm., Associate Parly Health Gp, 2001–; Jt Chm., All Party Parly Osteoporosis Gp, 2000–; Jt Chm., All Party Parly Gp on Maternity, 2000–. Exec. Dir, MJM Healthcare Solutions, 1997–2001; Dir, Huntsworth plc, 2001–03. Chairman: AMRC, 2007–12; Adv. Bd, Humana Europe, 2008–09. Lay Mem., 1977–83, Mem. Appts Commn, 1984–90, Press Council. Vice Pres., RCN, 1989– (Hon. FRCN 2010); Life Vice Pres., Royal Coll. of Midwives, 2001–; Pres., Age UK (formerly Age Concern), E Sussex, 1995–; Mem. Council, ICRF, subseq. Cancer Res. UK, 1998–2007; Trustee: Princess Royal Trust for Carers, 1992–93; Life Education Centres, 1997–99; Patron: Nat. Childbirth Trust; Assoc. for Nurse Prescribing. Sen. Associate, King's Fund (Gen. Adv. Council, until 2012). Member Council: Brighton Poly., 1987–89; Univ. of Sussex, 2001–09; Chm. Trustees, Chailey Heritage Sch., 1997–2015 (Governor, 1982–88); Chm. Council, St George's, Univ. of London (formerly St George's Hosp. Med. Sch.), 2000–07; Trustee, Leeds Castle Foundn, 2005–15. Governor: Chailey Comprehensive Sch., 1972–86; Ringmer Comprehensive Sch., 1979–85; Newick Primary Sch., 1977–85; Lancing Coll., 2013–. Founder: Newick Playgp; Newick Youth Club. Fellow, Royal Coll. of Chiropractors, 2013. FRSA 1989. DL 1986, Vice Lord-Lieut, 1992, E Sussex; JP East Sussex, 1973–85. DUniv: Surrey, 1990; Brighton, 1994; Northampton, 2009; Hon. DSc (Med.) London, 2006. *Recreations:* bicycling, other people's gardens. *Address:* Snells Cottage, The Green, Newick, Lewes, East Sussex BN8 4LA. *T:* (01825) 722154, *Fax:* (01825) 723873. *Club:* Royal Society of Medicine.

**CUMING, Frederick George Rees**, RA 1974 (ARA 1969); ARCA 1954; NDD 1948; NEAC 1960; painter; *b* 16 Feb. 1930; *m* 1962, Audrey Lee Cuming; one *s* one *d*. *Educ:* University School, Bexley Heath; Sidcup Art School; Royal College of Art; travelling schol., Italy. Exhibns in Redfern, Walker, New Grafton, Thackeray, Fieldborne Galleries; Group shows at NEAC, RA, Schools' Exhibn, John Moores London Group; One Man exhibns at Thackeray Gall., galls in Chichester, Lewes, Eastbourne, Guildford, Durham, Chester, Folkestone, Canterbury, New York; featured artist, RA Summer Exhibn, 2001; artist in residence, Christchurch Coll., Canterbury, 2015–; works in collections: DoE; Treasury; Chantrey Bequest; RA; Kendal Mus.; Scunthorpe Mus.; Bradford; Carlisle; Nat. Mus. of Wales; Brighton and Hove Mus.; Maidstone Mus.; Towner Gall., Eastbourne; Monte Carlo Mus.; St John's Coll., Oxford; Worcester Coll., Oxford; Faringdon Trust, Oxon; ITV collection; Southend Mus.; Preston Mus.; Nat. Trust collection; Barings Bank; Lloyd's; Guinness collection: W. H. Smith; Nat. Portrait Gall.; City private collections; portrait of Prof. Stephen Hawking, NPG; works in galls in America, Argentina, Canada, Chile, France, Germany, Greece, Holland, Hong Kong and S Africa. Hon. ROI 1992; Hon. RBA. Hon. DLitt Kent, 2005. Grand Prix, Art Contemporaine, Monte Carlo. *Publications:* Figure in a Landscape, 2000; Another Figure in the Landscape, 2014. *Address:* The Gables, Wittersham Road, Iden, near Rye, E Sussex TN31 7UY. *T:* (01797) 280882.

**CUMMINES, Robert**, OBE 2011; Chief Executive, Unlock, 2002–12 (Deputy Chief Executive, 1999–2002); Founder and Chief Executive, MIDAS Association for Disadvantaged People; *b* Islington, 23 Nov. 1951; *s* of Frederick George Francis Cummines and Mary Cummines (*née* Passmore); *m* 2009, Ayumi Yokozéki; one step *s*; one *d* (and one *d* decd) from previous marriage. Criminal and prisoner, 1969–88; volunteer, SOVA: Supporting Others through Volunteer Action, 1989–90; Purchasing Manager, Van Gell Systems, Holland, 1991–93; Mem., On-call Critical Response Team, Stonham Housing Assoc., 1993–99. Sessional Lectr, Kent Univ. Formerly: Mem., Adv. Gp, ODPM; Specialist Advr, Zahid Mubarek Public Inquiry; Mem., H of C Home Affairs Select Cttee Inquiry on Rehabilitation of Offenders Act; Expert Witness to H of C Home Affairs Select Cttee on Prisoner Educn. Mem., SE Regl Reducing Re-offending Delivery Bd, Nat. Offender Mgt Service, MoJ; former Mem., Mgt Bd, Exodus: Ex-Offenders Discharged Under

Supervision. Contrib. to BBC, ITV and Sky TV, radio and nat. newspapers. FRSA. MUniv Open, 2012. *Publications:* I Am Not a Gangster (autobiog.), 2014; The Parkhurst Years: my time locked up with Britain's most notorious criminals, 2017. *Club:* National Liberal.

**CUMMING, Alexander James;** Chief Executive (formerly Project Director), IMMPACT (Initiative for Maternal Mortality Project), since 2004; *b* 7 March 1947; *s* of Alexander George Cumming and Jean Campbell (*née* McWilliam); *m* 1973, Margaret Ada Callan; one *s* two *d*. *Educ:* Fordyce Acad., Banffshire; Robert Gordon's Coll., Aberdeen; Univ. of Aberdeen (MA). Mem., CIMA; IPFA. Volunteer teacher, VSO, India, 1968–70; Trainee Accountant, Wiggins Teape, Papermakers, 1970–72; Company Sec., Glen Gordon Ltd, Aberdeen, 1972–74; Chief Accountant, BOC Offshore, 1974–75; Accountant, then Dir of Finance, Grampian Health Bd, 1975–93; Actg Dir of Finance, Mgt Exec., Scottish Health Service, 1994; Chief Exec., Acute Services Div., NHS Grampian (formerly Aberdeen Royal Hosps, later Grampian Univ. Hosps NHS Trust), 1994–2004. Chm., Langstane Housing Assoc., 1997–2002 (Hon. Treas., 1984–97). *Recreations:* music, literature, history, the outdoors. *Address:* (office) IMMPACT, University of Aberdeen, Health Sciences Building, Foresterhill, Aberdeen AB25 2ZD.

**CUMMING, Sir Alexander Penrose G.;** *see* Gordon Cumming.

**CUMMING, Maj. Gen. Andrew Alexander John Rennie,** CBE 1993; Controller, Soldiers, Sailors, Airmen and Families Association—Forces Help, 2004–12; *b* 12 March 1948; *s* of Donald Alexander Cumming and Evelyn Julia (*née* Rennie); *m* 1979, Gilly Thompson; three *d*. *Educ:* Hawtreys Prep. Sch.; Bradfield Coll.; Army Staff Coll. In command 17th/21st Lancers, 1988–90; hcsc 1992; Commander: 20 Armd Bde, 1992; 11 Armd Bde/British Forces, Croatia and Bosnia-Herzegovina, 1992–93; ACOS Ops, HQ LAND, 1993–95; Chief Jt Ops Centre, Intervention Force (IFOR), 1995–96; Comdr, Initial Trng Gp, 1996–99; Comdr, Land Warfare Centre, 1999–2002; UK Co-ordinator, Kosovo Protection Corps, 2002–04. Col, Queen's Royal Lancers, 2006–11. Dir, Wincanton Race Course, 2004–11. Trustee, Southern Spinal Injuries Trust, 2014–. *Recreations:* field sports, racing, walking, sailing, ski-ing, reading. *Club:* Cavalry and Guards.

**CUMMING, Edward Charles;** QC 2018; *b* Worcester, 27 Nov. 1982; *s* of Paul Jonathan Cumming and Pamela Lucy Cumming; *m* 2012, Emma Margaret Hilliard; one *s*. *Educ:* Hagley Sch.; King's Sch., Worcester; Downing Coll., Cambridge (BA Law); Univ. of Pennsylvania (LLM; Thouron Fellow). Called to the Bar, Middle Temple, 2006; in practice as a barrister, specialising in chancery and commercial, XXIV Old Bldgs, 2006–. Pres., Cambridge Union, 2003. *Publications:* (ed jtly) International Trust Laws, 2009–. *Recreations:* football (playing and supporting Bromsgrove Sporting and Birmingham City), travel, walking, family, real ale. *Address:* XXIV Old Buildings, Lincoln's Inn, WC2A 3UP. *T:* (020) 7691 2424. *E:* edward.cumming@xxiv.co.uk.

**CUMMING, Rima;** *see* Makarem, R.

**CUMMING, Valerie Lynn,** FMA; writer and lecturer; Deputy Director, Museum of London, 1988–97; *b* 11 Oct. 1946; *d* of late John Gunson Carter and Edna Ruth Carter (*née* Willis); *m* 1972, John Lawrence Cumming. *Educ:* Abbey Sch., Reading; Univ. of Leicester (BA); Courtauld Inst. of Art (Courtauld Cert. in History of Dress). Admin. trainee, Univ. of Surrey, 1968–69; Asst, Chertsey Mus., 1971–73; Res. Asst, 1973–75, Sen. Asst Keeper, 1975–78, Mus. of London; Curator, Court Dress Collection, Kensington Palace, 1978–81; Asst Dir, Mus. of London, 1981–88. Trustee: Olive Matthews Collection, Chertsey Mus., Surrey, 1983–2016 (Chm., 2003–16); Costume Soc., 2001–04 (Chm., 2004–09); Bullard and Callow Trusts, Museums Assoc., 1992–2015; Daphne Bullard, Kathy Callow and Elizabeth Hammond Assoc., 2016–. Curatorial advr, Chartered Insurance Inst., 1991–98. Vis. Lectr, 1997 and 2007, External Examr, 2003–06, Courtauld Inst. of Art. Editor, Costume, jl of Costume Soc., 2014–18. *Publications:* Exploring Costume History 1500–1900, 1981; Gloves, 1982; A Visual History of Costume: the Seventeenth Century, 1984; (with Aileen Ribeiro) The Visual History of Costume, 1989; Royal Dress, 1989; The Visual History of Accessories, 1998; Understanding Fashion History, 2004; (consulting ed.) Berg Encyclopedia of World Dress and Fashion, vol. 8: West Europe, 2010; (revising ed.) The Dictionary of Fashion History, 2010, 2nd edn 2017; (ed) The Streatham Sketchbook, 2017; contributed to: Tradescant's Rarities, 1983; The Late King's Goods, 1989; London—World City 1800–1840, 1992; The Oxford Companion to the Body, 2001; The Oxford Encyclopedia of Theatre and Performance, 2003; City Merchants and the Arts 1670–1720, 2004. *Recreations:* gardening, watching cricket. *Address:* 7 Frere Street, SW11 2JA. *T:* (020) 7223 1380.

**CUMMINGS, Prof. Alan John,** FRCA; higher education consultant and lecturer, since 2011; Pro-Rector and Director of Academic Development, Royal College of Art, 2000–11, now Emeritus Professor; *b* South Shields, 17 April 1950; *s* of Alan and Elizabeth Cummings; *m* 2002, Sarah Cove; two *s* two *d*. *Educ:* S Shields Grammar Tech. Sch. for Boys; Imperial Coll. London (BSc Hons 1971; ARCS); Courtauld Inst. of Art, London (Postgrad. Dip. Conservation of Paintings 1974). FRCA 1991. Freelance conservator of paintings for NPG, NT, English Heritage and others, 1975–98; Lectr in Conservation of Paintings, Courtauld Inst. of Art, 1984–85; Royal College of Art: Hd of Dept, RCA/V&A Conservation, 1988–2001; Hd, Sch. of Humanities, 1998–2001. Vis. Prof., Faculty of Engrg, Imperial Coll. London, 2011–16. Dir and Trustee, Creative Mentors Foundn, 2009–; Gov., Nat. Film and TV Sch., 2011–16. FHEA 2000; FCGI 2010. FRSA 2004. *Publications:* contribs to conservation and higher educn jls. *Recreations:* playing guitar, songwriting and recording, tennis, swimming, cycling, scuba-diving. *E:* alan.cummings@network.rca.ac.uk.

**CUMMINGS, Brian;** QC 2008; **His Honour Judge Cummings;** a Circuit Judge, since 2015; *b* Belfast, 10 April 1965; *s* of late Wilbur Cummings and Shirley Cummings (*née* Drum). *Educ:* Christ's Hosp., Horsham; Trinity Coll., Cambridge (BA 1987). Called to the Bar, Lincoln's Inn, 1988; in practice at the Bar, Liverpool, 1989–2015; a Recorder, 2005–15. *Recreations:* cycling, hill-walking/mountaineering, Rugby, cricket, foreign travel, foreign languages, reading. *Address:* Queen Elizabeth II Law Courts, Derby Square, Liverpool L2 1XA.

**CUMMINGS, Prof. Brian Allen,** PhD; FBA 2016; FSA; Anniversary Professor of English and Related Literature, University of York, since 2012; *b* Abergavenny, 18 July 1960; *s* of Dr Wesley Cummings and Sheila Cummings (*née* Scott); *m* 1st (marr. diss.); two *s*; 2nd, Dr Freya Sierhuis. *Educ:* King Edward's Sch., Birmingham; Trinity Coll., Cambridge (BA 1982; PhD 1988). Fellow, Trinity Coll., Cambridge, 1985–88; University of Sussex: Lectr, Sch. of Eur. Studies, 1988–2003; Reader, 2003–04; Prof. of English, 2004–12. Visiting Fellow: Ludwig-Maximilians-Universität Munich, 2010–11; Christ Church, Oxford, 2012; Univ. of Toronto, 2014; Folger Shakespeare Liby, Washington DC, 2017. FSA 2012. *Publications:* The Literary Culture of the Reformation: grammar and grace, 2002; (ed) The Book of Common Prayer: the texts of 1549, 1559 and 1662, 2011; Mortal Thoughts, 2013; The Book of Common Prayer: a very short introduction, 2018. *Recreations:* theatre, art, music, walking, cooking, gelato. *Address:* Department of English and Related Literature, University of York, Heslington, York YO10 5DD. *T:* (01904) 323068. *E:* brian.cummings@york.ac.uk.

**CUMMINGS, Prof. Keith Richard;** Professor of Glass Studies, School of Art and Design, University of Wolverhampton, 1991–2014, now Emeritus; *b* 15 July 1940; *s* of Henry Gordon Cummings and Kathleen Cummings; *m* 1963, Pamela Anne Cornall; two *s*. *Educ:* Univ. of Durham (BA Hons Fine Art). Sen. Lectr in Glass, Stourbridge Coll. of Art, 1967–85; Tutor, Sch. of Ceramics and Glass, RCA, 1986–89; Principal Lectr, Sch. of Art and Design, Univ. of Wolverhampton, 1989–94. Work exhibited in nat. and internat. collections, incl. V&A, Mus. of Decorative Art, Paris. *Publications:* Techniques of Glassforming, 1980; Techniques of Kiln-Formed Glass, 1997, 3rd edn 2007; A History of Glassforming, 2002; Contemporary Kiln-formed Glass, 2009. *Recreations:* reading, gardening, table-tennis. *Address:* The Granary, Thicknall Lane, Clent, Stourbridge, W Midlands DY9 0HP. *E:* kr.cummings@tiscali.co.uk.

**CUMMINGS, Laurence Alexander,** FRCO, FRCM; harpsichordist and conductor; William Crotch Professor of Historical Performance, Royal Academy of Music, since 2012 (Head of Historical Performance, 1997–2012); Musical Director: London Handel Society, since 2002; Casa da Música Baroque Orchestra, since 2004; Göttingen Handel Society, since 2012; *b* 25 May 1968; *s* of Geoffrey Victor and Maureen Cummings; civil partnership 2012, Martin Parr. *Educ:* Christ Church, Oxford (MA); Royal Coll. of Music (ARCM). FRCO 1985. Freelance harpsichordist, 1989–. Guest Conductor: ENO (Semele, 2004; Orfeo, 2006; Poppea, 2007; Messiah, 2009; Radamisto, 2010; The Indian Queen, 2015); Glyndebourne Fest. Opera (Giulio Cesare, 2005 and 2009; The Fairy Queen, 2009 and 2012; Saul, 2015 and 2018); Gothenburg Opera (Giulio Cesare, 2008; Alcina, 2011; Orfeo ed Euridice, 2014); Opera de Lyon (Messiah, 2012); Opernhaus Zurich (Sale, 2012, 2013); Opera North (Poppea, 2014); Buxton Opera (Tamerlano, 2016); OperaGlass Works (The Rake's Progress, 2017). Co-director: London Handel Fest., 1999–2002; Tilford Bach Fest., 1999–2002. Trustee, Handel House Mus., London, 2002–. Has made recordings. Hon. RAM (Hon. ARAM 2001). *Recreations:* travelling, reading, walking.

**CUMMINGS, Peter Joseph;** Chief Executive, Corporate, HBOS plc, 2006–09 (Director, 2005–09); *b* Dumbarton, 19 July 1955; *m* 1978, Margaret Mary Docherty. *Educ:* St Patrick's High Sch., Dumbarton; Glasgow Coll. of Technol.; Univ. of Strathclyde (MBA). Joined Bank of Scotland, 1973; worked in branches in W of Scotland; Chief Manager, Glasgow Chief Office, 1982–85; Advances Manager, Corporate Div., 1985–90; Hd, Corporate Recovery, 1990–93; Regl Manager, N of England, 1993–95; Dir, Corporate Banking, Bank of Scotland, subseq. HBOS plc, 1995–2005; Dep. Chief Exec., Corporate, HBOS plc, 2005–06. Mem., Adv. Cttee, Edinburgh Univ. Business Sch., 2008. Dir, Maggie's Cancer Care Centres, 2005. FCIBS 2000. *Recreations:* scuba-diving, swimming, football, music. *Clubs:* Mark's, George.

**CUMMINS, Gus,** RA 1992; artist; *b* 28 Jan. 1943; *s* of Harold George Cummins and Honor Cecilia (*née* Bird); *m* 1968, Angela Braven; two *s* one *d*. *Educ:* Sutton and Wimbledon Schs of Art; RCA (NDD, MA). Part-time teacher at nine art schs and colls, 1969–; currently at RA schs. Exhibns, mainly in UK, also Norway, Holland, UAE and USA, 1980–; 8 solo exhibns, 1991–, incl. Jerwood Gall., Hastings, 2018. Henry Moore Prize, London Gp, 1982; Spirit of London 2nd Prize, 1983; Daler-Rowney Prize, RA, 1987; Hunting Gp 1st Prize, Mall Gall., 1990, RCA, 1999; House & Garden Prize and Blackstone Award, RA Summer Show, 1992; RWS Prize, 2001; Jack Goldhill Sculpture Award, RA, 2005. *Recreations:* music, poetry, literature, swimming, cycling, pubs, snooker. *Address:* Harpsichord House, Cobourg Place, Hastings, Sussex TN34 3HY. *T:* (01424) 426429. *W:* www.guscummins.com.

**CUMMINS, Judith;** MP (Lab) Bradford South, since 2015; *b* W Yorks; one *s* one *d*. *Educ:* Ruskin Coll.; Univ. of Leeds. Former Mem. (Lab) Bradford MDC; Mem. (Lab), Leeds CC, 2012–16. An Opposition Whip, 2015–18; Shadow Minister for Internat. Trade, 2018–. *Address:* House of Commons, SW1A 0AA. *T:* (020) 7219 8607. *E:* judith.cummins.mp@parliament.uk.

**CUMMINS, Sir Michael (John Austin),** Kt 2003; Serjeant at Arms, House of Commons, 2000–04; *b* 26 Nov. 1939; *s* of Harold Leslie Cummins and Florence Gladys Cummins (*née* Austin); *m* 1st, 1964, Mary Isobel Farman (marr. diss. 1995); two *s*; 2nd, 1995, Catherine Ellen Lamb; one step *d*. *Educ:* Queen Mary Sch.; RMA Sandhurst; psc. Commnd 3rd Carabiniers (POW DG), 1959; Royal Scots Dragoon Guards, 1971–81. Serjeant at Arms Dept, H of C, 1981–2004; Dep. Serjeant at Arms, 1995–99. Trustee, Selwood Foundn, 1986–. *Publications:* (with Sir Peter Thorne) Serjeant for the Commons, 1994, 2nd edn 1999. *Address:* 140A Ashley Gardens, Westminster, SW1P 1HN.

**CUMMINS, Paul,** MBE 2015; ceramic artist; *b* Chesterfield, 26 Sept. 1977; *s* of David Edward and Glenys Cummins. *Educ:* Chesterfield Coll. of Arts (BSc Envmtl Architecture; Part II Architecture); Derby Univ. (BA Crafts; MA Arts). Installations include: Derby Royal Hosp., 2010; ceramic tulips, Chatsworth House, 2010; 200 ceramic bowls, Spitalfields Mkt, 2011; Tregoning Contemp. Exhibn, 2011; 600 hand-made roses, Hardwick Hall Exhibn, 2011; English Country Gdn Commn for Cultural Olympiad, Sandwich, Chiswick Hse, Castle Howard, Houses of Parlt, Blenheim Palace, Althorp Estate, Southbank Centre, 2012; (jtly) First World War Centenary poppies, Blood Swept Lands and Seas of Red, Tower of London, 2014; Tulipmania, 2015. Hon. PhD London Metropolitan, 2015. *Recreations:* gardening, the arts. *E:* paul@paulcumminsceramics.com.

**CUMPER, Patricia Clare,** MBE 2013; playwright, since 1978; *b* Kingston, Jamaica, 28 Nov. 1954; *d* of George Cumper and Gloria Cumper; one *s*. *Educ:* Girton Coll., Cambridge (BA Archaeol. and Anthropol. 1976). Information Attaché, Jamaican High Commn, 1996–2001; Artistic Dir and CEO, Talawa Th. Co., 2006–12; Co-Artistic Dir, Strongback Prodns, 2013–18. *Stage plays:* The Fallen Angel and the Devil's Concubine, 1990; The Key Game, 1999; Chigger Foot Boys, 2017; *radio plays:* The Darkest Eye, 1995; One Bright Child, 1997; Mr Trollope and the Labours of Hercules, 2017; Pardna, 2018; adaptations: Darker Face of the Earth, 2003; Small Island, 2005; The Color Purple, 2010; Three Strong Women, 2016; Beloved, 2017; I Know Why the Caged Bird Sings, 2018; Gather Together in My Name, 2018; All God's Children Need Travelling Shoes, 2019; A Song Flung Up to Heaven, 2019; *producer:* The Colored Museum, V&A, 2011; Rum and Coca Cola, 2010, Waiting for Godot, 2012, West Yorks Playhouse and English Touring Th.; director, Jab Molassie, Little Carib Th., Trinidad, 2014. Trustee: BM, 2013–; George Bernard Shaw Trust; English Touring Th. Co., until 2014; Standing on the Shoulders of Giants Th. Co., 2011–16; Spare Tyre Th. Co., 2013–15; Utopia Th. Co., Sheffield, 2018–. Freelancer, BBC Radio 4 Drama, 1994–; contrib., BBC World Service Current Affairs. *Publications: plays:* Champions of the Gayelle, 1995; Three Jamaican Plays, 2010; Inner Yardie (3 plays), 2016; Chigger Foot Boys, 2017; (novel) One Bright Child, 1997; (contrib.) Shakespeare, Race and Performance: the diverse bard, 2016; (contrib.) New Daughters of Africa Anthology, 2019. *Recreations:* family, reading, sport, cooking. *Address:* Flat 610, 7 St George Wharf, SW8 2JA. *E:* patriciaccumper@gmail.com, voxnobiscum2012@aol.com.

**CUMPSTY, Prof. Nicholas Alexander,** PhD, FREng; Professor of Mechanical Engineering, Imperial College, London, 2005–08, now Emeritus; *b* 13 Jan. 1943; *s* of Norman and Edith Cumpsty; *m* 1st, 1966, Annette Tischler (*d* 1982); one *s* one *d*; 2nd, 1983, Mary Cecily Hamer (*née* Turner); two step *d*. *Educ:* Haberdashers' Aske's Sch., Hampstead; Imperial Coll., London (BScEng 1964); Trinity Coll. and Peterhouse,

Cambridge (PhD 1967; MA 1968). Post Office Student Apprentice, 1960–64; Peterhouse Research Fellow, 1966–69; Rolls-Royce, 1969–71; Cambridge University: Sen. Asst in Research, Lectr, then Reader, Dept of Engineering, 1972–89; Prof. of Aerothermal Technology, 1989–99; Fellow of Peterhouse, 1972–99, now Emeritus; Chief Technologist, Rolls-Royce plc, 2000–05. Hunsaker Vis. Prof., Dept of Aeronautics and Astronautics, MIT, 1991–92. Mem., Royal Commn on Envmtl Pollution, 2005–09. Mem., Defence Scientific Adv. Council, 2005–11. FREng (FEng 1995). *Publications*: Compressor Aerodynamics, 1989; Jet Propulsion, 1997; numerous papers on aerodynamics, esp. relating to jet engines. *Recreations*: reading, music, walking. *Address*: Imperial College, London, SW7 2AZ. *T*: (020) 7594 2099. *E*: n.cumpsty@imperial.ac.uk.

**CUNINGHAME, Sir John Christopher Foggo M.**; *see* Montgomery Cuninghame.

**CUNINGHAME, Sir Robert Henry F.**; *see* Fairlie-Cuninghame.

**CUNLIFFE**, family name of **Baron Cunliffe**.

**CUNLIFFE, 3rd Baron** *cr* 1914, of Headley; **Roger Cunliffe**, RIBA; MCMI; farmer; writer; *b* 12 Jan. 1932; *s* of 2nd Baron and Joan Catherine Lubbock (*d* 1980); *S* father, 1963; *m* 1957, Clemency Ann Hoare; two *s* one *d*. *Educ*: Eton; Loughborough Tech. Coll.; Trinity Coll., Cambridge (MA); Architectural Association (AA Dipl.); Open Univ. With various architectural firms in UK and USA, 1957–65; Associate, Robert Matthew, Johnson-Marshall & Partners, 1966–69; Dir, Architectural Assoc., 1969–71; Partner, SCP, 1973–78; own practice as architectural, planning and management consultant, 1977–2002; Dir, Exhibition Consultants Ltd, 1981–2004. Member: Urban Motorways Cttee, 1969–72; Council, British Consultants Bureau, 1986–90. Member: Council, Lancing Coll., 1967–85; Delegacy, Goldsmiths' Coll., 1972–78; Bd, Coll. of Estate Management, 1992–2006 (Hon. Fellow, 2007); Vis. Sen. Fellow, Univ. of Suffolk (formerly Univ. Campus Suffolk), 2011–. Chm., Suffolk Craft Soc., 1994–97. Mem. Ct, Goldsmiths' Co., 1986–2012 (Prime Warden, 1997). DUniv UEA and Essex, 2008. *Publications*: (with Leonard Manasseh) Office Buildings, 1962; (with Santa Raymond) Tomorrow's Office, 1996; contrib. various professional jls. *Recreations*: chance encounters, old friends, metalwork. *Heir*: *s* Hon. Henry Cunliffe [*b* 9 March 1962; *m* (marr. diss.)]. *Address*: The Broadhurst, Brandeston, Woodbridge, Suffolk IP13 7AG. *Club*: Oriental.

**CUNLIFFE, Sir Barrington Windsor, (Sir Barry)**, Kt 2006; CBE 1994; FBA 1979; FSA; Professor of European Archaeology, Oxford University, 1972–2007, now Emeritus; Fellow of Keble College, Oxford, 1972–2007; *b* 10 Dec. 1939. *Educ*: Portsmouth; St John's Coll., Cambridge (MA, PhD, LittD). Lecturer, Univ. of Bristol, 1963–66; Prof. of Archæology, Univ. of Southampton, 1966–72. O'Donnell Lectr in Celtic Studies, Oxford Univ., 1983–84. Member: Ancient Monuments Bd for England, 1976–84; Historic Bldgs and Monuments Commn for England, 1987–92 (Mem., Ancient Monuments Adv. Cttee, 1984–); Comr, English Heritage, 2006–14 (Interim Chm., 2008–09). President: Council for British Archaeology, 1976–79; Soc. of Antiquaries, 1991–95 (Vice-Pres., 1982–86). Gov., Mus. of London, 1995–99; Trustee: British Mus., 2000–09; BM Trust, 2011–; English Heritage Foundn, 2011–15. Hon. DLitt: Sussex, 1983; Southampton, 2009; Kent, 2010; Hon. DSc Bath, 1984; DUniv Open, 1995; Bradford, 2014; Hon. Dr Celtic Studies Dublin, 2016. *Publications*: Fishbourne, a Roman Palace and its Garden, 1971; Roman Bath Discovered, 1971, rev. edn 1984; The Cradle of England, 1972; The Making of the English, 1973; The Regni, 1973; Iron Age Communities in Britain, 1974, 4th edn 2005; Rome and the Barbarians, 1975; Hengistbury Head, 1978; Rome and her Empire, 1978; The Celtic World, 1979; Danebury: the anatomy of an Iron Age hillfort, 1984; The City of Bath, 1986; Greeks, Romans and Barbarians, 1988; Wessex before AD 1000, 1991; (ed) The Oxford Illustrated Prehistory of Europe, 1994; Iron Age Britain, 1995; The Ancient Celts, 1997; Facing the Ocean: the Atlantic and its peoples, 2001 (Wolfson History Prize, 2002); The Extraordinary Voyage of Pytheas the Greek, 2001; The Celts: a very short introduction, 2003; (ed) England's Landscape: the west, 2006; Europe Between the Oceans: 9000 BC to AD 1000, 2008; The Druids: a very short introduction, 2010; Britain Begins, 2013; By Steppe, Desert and Ocean, 2017; On the Ocean, 2017; contribs to several major excavation reports and articles to Soc. of Antiquaries, and in other learned jls. *Recreation*: mild self-indulgence. *Address*: Institute of Archaeology, 36 Beaumont Street, Oxford OX1 2PG.

**CUNLIFFE, Ven. Christopher John**, DPhil; Archdeacon of Derby, since 2006; *b* 25 Sept. 1955; *s* of Joseph and Margaret Cunliffe; *m* 1979, Helen Margaret Ketley (*see* Ven. H. M. Cunliffe); two *s*. *Educ*: Charterhouse; Christ Church, Oxford (MA, DPhil 1981); Trinity Coll., Cambridge (MA 1986); Westcott House, Cambridge. ARHistS 1993. Ordained deacon, 1983, priest, 1984; Asst Curate, Chesterfield, 1983–85; Chaplain and Jun. Res. Fellow, Lincoln Coll., Oxford, 1985–89; Chaplain, City Univ. and Guildhall Sch. of Music and Drama, 1989–91; Selection Sec. and Vocations Officer, Adv. Bd of Ministry, 1991–96; Bp of London's Advr for Ordained Ministry, 1997–2003; Chaplain to Bp of Bradwell, 2004–06; Canon Residentiary, Derby Cathedral, 2006–08. Commissary of the Bishop of Angola, 2013–. Clerk, All Saints Educnl Trust, 2004. Chm., Mozambique and Angola Anglican Assoc., 2007–19. Vis. Fellow, Harris Manchester Coll., Oxford, 2017. *Publications*: (ed) Joseph Butler's Moral and Religious Thought, 1992. *Recreations*: walking, reading, listening to music, watching sport, fly-fishing. *Address*: Derby Church House, Full Street, Derby DE1 3DR. *T*: (01332) 388676, *Fax*: (01332) 292969. *E*: archderby@derby.anglican.org.

**CUNLIFFE, Sir David Ellis**, 9th Bt *cr* 1759; business development manager; *b* 29 Oct. 1957; *s* of Sir Cyril Henley Cunliffe, 8th Bt and of Eileen Lady Cunliffe, *d* of Frederick William and Nora Anne Parkins; *S* father, 1969; *m* 1983, Linda Carol, *d* of John Sidney and Ella Mary Batchelor; three *d*. *Educ*: St Albans Grammar School. *Heir*: *b* Andrew Mark Cunliffe [*b* 17 April 1959; *m* 1980, Janice Elizabeth, *d* of Ronald William Kyle; one *s* three *d*].

**CUNLIFFE, Ven. Helen Margaret**; Archdeacon of St Albans, 2003–07, now Emeritus; *b* 1954; *m* 1979, Ven. Christopher John Cunliffe, *qv*; two *s*. *Educ*: Homelands Sch., Derby; St Hilda's Coll., Oxford (BA 1977, MA 1978); Westcott House, Cambridge. Ordained deaconess, 1983, deacon, 1987, priest, 1994; Curate, St Mary and All Saints, Chesterfield, 1983–85; Dss, 1986–87, Parish Deacon, 1987–89, St Mary the Virgin with St Cross and St Peter, Oxford; Chaplain, Nuffield Coll., Oxford, 1986–89; Team Deacon, 1989–94, Team Vicar, 1994–96, Clapham Team Ministry; Residentiary Canon, Southwark Cathedral, 1996–2002; Diocesan Advr for Women in Ministry, Southwark, 1996–2002. Chaplain, Welcare, 1996–2002. Chair, USPG, 1997–2000. *Recreations*: walking, gardening, dogs. *Address*: 1 Thatch Close, Derby DE22 1EA.

**CUNLIFFE, Sir Jonathan (Stephen)**, Kt 2010; CB 2001; Deputy Governor for Financial Stability, and Member, Monetary Policy Committee, Bank of England, since 2013 (Deputy Chair: Financial Policy Committee, since 2013; Prudential Regulation Committee, since 2013); *b* 2 June 1953; *s* of Ralph and Cynthia Cunliffe; *m* 1984, Naomi Brandler; two *d*. *Educ*: St Marylebone GS, London; Manchester Univ. (BA Eng. 1975; MA 1976). Lectr in English and Drama, Univ. of Western Ontario, 1976–79; res. student, 1979–80; joined Civil Service, 1980; DoE, 1980–85; Department of Transport: Principal, 1985; Pvte Sec. to Sec. of State, 1985–88; Transport Industry Finance, 1988–90; HM Treasury: Asst Sec., Pay Gp, 1990–93; Internat. Financial Instns, and UK Alternate Dir, EBRD (on secondment), 1993–95; Debt and Reserves Mgt, 1995–97; Dep. Dir, Macroeconomic Policy and Prospects, 1997–98; Dep. Dir, then Dir, Internat. Finance, later Macroeconomic Policy and Internat. Finance, 1998–2001; Managing Director: Financial Regulation and Industry, 2001–02; Macroecon. Policy and Internat. Finance, 2002–05; Perm. Sec., Macroecon. Policy and Internat. Finance, subseq. Internat. and Finance, 2005–07; Prime Minister's Advr on Europe and global issues, G8 and G20 Sherpa, and Hd, Europe and Global Issues Secretariat, 2007–11; UK Perm. Rep. to EU, Brussels, 2012–13. UK Alternate Mem., EU Monetary Cttee, 1996–98; UK Mem., EU Economic and Financial Cttee and G7 Treaty, 2002–. *Address*: Bank of England, Threadneedle Street, EC2R 8AH.

**CUNLIFFE, Lawrence Francis**; *b* 25 March 1929; *m* 1950, Winifred (marr. diss. 1985), *d* of William Haslem; three *s* two *d*. *Educ*: St Edmund's RC Sch., Worsley, Manchester. Engr, NCB, 1949–79. Member (Lab): Farnworth BC, 1964–74 (Mayor 1968–69); Bolton MDC, 1974–79. Contested (Lab) Rochdale, Oct. 1972 and Feb. 1974. MP (Lab) Leigh, 1979–2001. An Opposition Whip, 1985–87. Hon. Alderman, Bolton, 1996. JP 1967–79.

**CUNLIFFE-LISTER**, family name of **Earl of Swinton** and **Baroness Masham of Ilton**.

**CUNLIFFE-LISTER, Hon. Dame (Elizabeth) Susan**, DCVO 2019; Lord-Lieutenant, East Riding of Yorkshire, 2005–19; *b* 2 Nov. 1944; *d* of 1st Viscount Whitelaw, KT, CH, MC, PC and Cecilia Doriel Whitelaw (*née* Sprot); *m* 1966, Nicholas John Cunliffe-Lister (*see* Earl of Swinton) (marr. diss. 1996); two *s* one *d*. Managed Burton Agnes Hall Estate, 1989–2008. High Sheriff, E Riding of Yorks, 2004–05. Gardener of Year, Country Life Mag., 2001. *Address*: c/o Burton Agnes Hall, Driffield, E Riding of Yorks YO25 4NB.
*See also* Lord Masham.

**CUNLIFFE-OWEN, Sir Hugo Dudley**, 3rd Bt *cr* 1920, of Bray; *b* 16 May 1966; *s* of Sir Dudley Herbert Cunliffe-Owen, 2nd Bt, and Jean (*d* 2015), *o d* of late Surg.-Comdr A. N. Forsyth, RN; *S* father, 1983; *m* 2005, Leanda Jane, *d* of Malcolm Harris. *Heir*: none.

**CUNNAH, Michael Graeme**; Co-Founder and Director, 2020 Seating Ltd, since 2016; Chairman: iSPORTCONNECT, since 2011; Mobsventures Ltd, since 2011; Chief Executive Officer, Stadium Management Systems Ltd, since 2012; *b* 26 Feb. 1958; *s* of Alan and Irene Cunnah; *m* 1984, Julie Kendrew; one *s* one *d*. *Educ*: Univ. of Aston in Birmingham (BSc Managerial and Admin. Studies). FCMA 1997. Guinness Plc, 1987–96: Financial Controller, Guinness GB, 1987–91; Dir, Corporate Finance, GBW, 1991–92; Finance Dir, Africa/Americas Region, 1992–93; Vice Pres., Finance, Desnoes & Geddes Ltd, Jamaica, 1993–95; Hd, Internal Audit, 1996; Corporate Finance Dir, Coca-Cola Schweppes, 1996–98; Finance Dir, FA, 1998–2002; CEO, Wembley Stadium, 2002–06; Director: Aston Villa FC, 2007–08; Internat. Media Content, 2011–14. Fellow, Aston Univ. Business Sch., 2006. *Recreations*: football, music, cricket, golf, reading. *E*: michaelcunnah@me.com.

**CUNNINGHAM**, family name of **Baron Cunningham of Felling**.

**CUNNINGHAM OF FELLING**, Baron *cr* 2005 (Life Peer), of Felling, in the county of Tyne and Wear; **John Anderson, (Jack), Cunningham**; PC 1993; DL; PhD; *b* 4 Aug. 1939; *s* of late Andrew and May Freda Cunningham; *m* 1964, Maureen; one *s* two *d*. *Educ*: Jarrow Grammar Sch.; Bede Coll., Durham Univ. Hons Chemistry, 1962; PhD Chemistry, 1966. Formerly: Research Fellow in Chemistry, Durham Univ.; School Teacher; Trades Union Officer. MP (Lab) Whitehaven, Cumbria, 1970–83, Copeland, 1983–2005. PPS to Rt Hon. James Callaghan, 1972–76; Parly Under-Sec. of State, Dept of Energy, 1976–79; opposition spokesman on industry, 1979–83; Mem., Shadow Cabinet, 1983–95 and 1996–97; spokesman on the environment, 1983–89; Shadow Leader, H of C, 1989–92; opposition front bench spokesman on foreign and Commonwealth affairs, 1992–94; on trade and industry, 1994–95; on national heritage, 1995–97; Minister of Agriculture, Fisheries and Food, 1997–98; Minister for the Cabinet Office and Chancellor of the Duchy of Lancaster, 1998–99. Mem., H of L Select Cttee on Sci. and Technol., 2008–13, Finance Cttee, 2016–; Chm., Secondary Legislation Scrutiny Cttee B, 2018–. DL Cumbria, 1991. Gold and Silver Star, Order of the Rising Sun (Japan), 2016. *Recreations*: fell walking, fly-fishing, gardening, shooting, classical and folk music, reading, listening to other people's opinions. *Address*: House of Lords, SW1A 0PW.

**CUNNINGHAM, Alex**; MP (Lab) Stockton North, since 2010; *b* 1 May 1955; *s* of John and Jean Cunningham; *m* 1977, Evaline; two *s*. *Educ*: Branksome Comprehensive Sch., Darlington; Queen Elizabeth Sixth Form Coll., Darlington; Darlington Coll. of Technol. (Cert. Journalism 1976). Journalist: Darlington and Stockton Times, 1974–76; The Mail, Hartlepool, 1976–77; Radio Tees, 1977–79; Radio Clyde, 1979; Evening Gazette, 1979–84; PR officer, British Gas, 1984–89; Transco: communications advr, 1995–2000; Hd of Communications, 2000–02; Man. Dir, Tees Valley Communicators, 2002–10. Chm., NE Mus. and Libraries Council, 1993–99; Member: NE Regl Bd, Arts Council England, 1992–2000; Bd, One North East, 2008–10; non-exec. Dir, N Tees and Hartlepool NHS Foundn Trust, 2008–10. PPS to Shadow Lord Chancellor and Sec. of State for Justice, 2010–15; Shadow Minister: for Envmt, Food and Rural Affairs, 2015–16; for Pensions, 2016–18. Mem., Envmtl Audit Cttee, H of C. Member (Lab): Cleveland CC, 1989–96; Stockton on Tees BC, 1999–2010. Mem. Council, MLA, 2008–09. *Address*: House of Commons, SW1A 0AA; Unit 142, Stockton Business Centre, 70–74 Brunswick Street, Stockton on Tees TS18 1DW.

**CUNNINGHAM, Carey Louise**; *see* Bennet, C. L.

**CUNNINGHAM, James Dolan**; MP (Lab) Coventry South, since 1997 (Coventry South East, 1992–97); *b* Coatbridge, 4 Feb. 1941; *s* of Adam and Elizabeth Cunningham; *m* 1985, Marion Douglas; one *s* one *d* and one step *s* one step *d*. *Educ*: St Mary's Primary Sch., Coatbridge; St Columba High Sch., Coatbridge. Trade Union Diplomas in Industrial Law and Social Sciences. Engineer, 1964–88. Mem. (Lab) Coventry CC, 1972–92 (Leader, 1988–92; formerly Dep. Leader, Chief Whip, Chm. and Vice Chm. of Cttees). Chm., W Midlands Jt Cttee of Local Authority, 1990–92; Sec., AMA, 1991–92. PPS to Solicitor Gen., 2005–07, to Minister of State, DWP, 2007–10. Chm., HM Treasury Back Bench Cttee, 1997–2010. Chm., W Midland Gp of MPs, 2005–10. Mem., UNITE. *Address*: House of Commons, SW1A 0AA.

**CUNNINGHAM, Prof. John**, KCVO 2014 (CVO 2008); DM, FRCP; Professor of Nephrology, University College London, and Consultant Nephrologist, Royal Free Hospital and University College London Hospitals, since 2003; Physician to the Queen and Head of HM Medical Household, 2005–14 (Physician to the Royal Household, 1993–2005); Physician, King Edward VII's Hospital Sister Agnes (formerly King Edward VII's Hospital for Officers), since 1993; *b* 27 June 1949; *s* of late Daniel John Chapman Cunningham and of Judith (*née* Hill); *m* 1st, 1970, Deborah Alison Yeates (marr. diss. 1996); three *s*; 2nd, 2001, Caroline Ann Hughes Hewitt; one *d*. *Educ*: Magdalen Coll. Sch., Oxford; Trinity Hall, Cambridge (BA 1970; Hon. Fellow, 2013); St John's Coll., Oxford (BM, BCh 1973; DM 1988). FRCP 1988. Junior appointments, 1973–77: Radcliffe Infirmary, Oxford; Whittington Hosp., London; Brompton Hosp., London; Central Middx Hosp., London; Lectr in Medicine, London Hosp. Med. Coll., 1977–80; Res. Fellow,

Washington Univ. Sch. of Medicine, St Louis, USA, 1980–82; Consultant Physician, London, subseq. Royal London, Hosp., 1982–2003; Sub-Dean for Med. Student Admissions, London Hosp. Med. Coll., 1990–97; Prof. of Renal and Metabolic Medicine, Queen Mary, Univ. of London, 2001–03. Special Trustee, Royal London Hosp., 1985–. Jan Brod Meml Lecture, Prague, 1993, and other invited lectures. *Publications:* contrib. chapters in books, reviews and numerous articles in scientific jls. *Recreations:* music, sport, walking. *Address:* 31A King Henry's Road, NW3 3QR. *T:* (020) 7722 3883. *Club:* MCC.

**CUNNINGHAM, Rt Rev. John,** JCD; Bishop of Galloway, (RC), 2004–14, now Bishop Emeritus; *b* 22 Feb. 1938. *Educ:* Blairs Coll.; St Peter's Coll., Cardross; Pontifical Scots Coll., Rome; Pontifical Gregorian Univ. (JCD). Ordained priest, 1961; Asst, Our Lady of Lourdes, Bishopton, 1964–69; Chaplain, Moredun Convent, 1969–74; Asst Priest, St Columba's, Renfrew, 1974–86; Officialis, Scottish Nat. Tribunal, 1986–92; Parish Priest, St Patrick's, Greenock, 1992–2004; VG Paisley, 1997. Prelate of Honour, 1999. *Address:* 24 Johnstone Terrace, Greenock PA16 8BD.

**CUNNINGHAM, Mark James;** QC 2001; *b* 6 June 1956; *s* of late James Arthur Cunningham and Carole Kathleen Cunningham; *m* 1980 (marr. diss. 1995); two *s* two *d*. *Educ:* Stonyhurst Coll.; Magdalen Coll., Oxford (BA Hons Modern Hist.); Poly. of Central London (Dip. Law). Called to the Bar: Inner Temple, 1980; E Caribbean, 2005; Junior Counsel to the Crown: Chancery, 1991–99; A Panel, 1999–2001; DTI Inspector, 1998–99. *Recreations:* cricket, tennis, horses, food, travel. *Address:* Maitland Chambers, 7 Stone Buildings, Lincoln's Inn, WC2A 3SZ. *T:* (020) 7406 1200, *Fax:* (020) 7406 1300. *E:* mcunningham@maitlandchambers.com. *Clubs:* Pegasus, Drayton Parslow Cricket, Stewkley Tennis.

**CUNNINGHAM, Michael Bernard,** QPM 2013; Chief Executive Officer, College of Policing, since 2018; *b* Crosby, 14 July 1961; *s* of Terence and Shirley Cunningham; *m* 1986, Felicity Carroll; two *s*. *Educ:* St Mary's Coll., Crosby; Univ. of Durham (BA Hons Theol.). Joined Lancs Police, 1987; held a variety of uniform and CID posts across the force, 1987–2002; Chief Superintendent and Divl Comdr, Western Div., 2002–05; Asst Chief Constable, 2005–07; Dep. Chief Constable, 2007–09; Chief Constable, Staffordshire Police, 2009–14; HM Inspector of Constabulary, 2014–18. *Recreations:* hill walking, cycling. *Address:* College of Policing, Riverside House, 2a Southwark Bridge Road, SE1 9HA.

**CUNNINGHAM, Phyllis Margaret,** CBE 1997; Chief Executive, Royal Marsden NHS Trust, 1994–98 (Chief Executive, Royal Marsden Hospital Special Health Authority, 1980–94); *b* 15 Sept. 1931; *d* of late Andrew Cunningham and of Minnie Cunningham (*née* Rees). *Educ:* Chorlton Central Sch., Manchester; Loreburn Coll., Manchester (Dip. in Business Studies, 1956). Trainee Adminr, Withington Hosp., Manchester, 1956–59; PA/Res. Asst to Med. Dir, Geigy Pharmaceutical Co., 1959–62; Unit Adminr, Roosevelt Hosp., NY, 1962–64; Planning Officer, Royal Free Hosp., London, 1964–74; Dep. House Gov./Sec. to Board, Royal Marsden Hosp., 1974–80. Mem., Ministerial Adv. Bd, Med. Devices Agency, 2001–03. Trustee and Mem. Council, St Christopher's Hospice, Sydenham, 1999–2013; Trustee: Headley Court Trust, 2001–13; Lady Capel's Charity, 2003–; Trustee/Chm., Abbeyfield Richmond, Thames and Dist Soc. Ltd, 2002–04; Trustee/Bd Mem., Abbeyfield UK, 2004–07. Governor: Christ's Sch., Richmond, 1996–99; Queen's Sch., Richmond, 2002–16. FRSA 1992. *Recreations:* current affairs, travel, theatre, music, gardening. *Address:* 12 Augustus Close, Brentford Dock, Brentford, Middx TW8 8QE. *T:* (020) 8847 1067.

**CUNNINGHAM, Roseanna;** Member (SNP) Perthshire South and Kinross-shire, Scottish Parliament, since 2011 (Perth, 1999–2011); Cabinet Secretary for Environment, Climate Change and Land Reform, since 2016; *b* 27 July 1951; *d* of Hugh and Catherine Cunningham. *Educ:* Univ. of Western Australia (BA Hons Politics 1975); Edinburgh Univ. (LLB 1982); Aberdeen Univ. (Dip. Legal Practice 1983). SNP Research Asst, 1977–79; Solicitor, 1983–90; admitted Faculty of Advocates, 1990; in practice, 1990–95. MP (SNP) Perth and Kinross, May 1995–1997, Perth, 1997–2001. Scottish Government: Minister for Envmt, 2009–11, for Envmt and Climate Change, 2010–11, for Community Safety and Legal Affairs, 2011–14; Cabinet Sec. for Fair Work, Skills and Trng, 2014–16; Convener, Health and Community Care Cttee, 2004–07, Rural Affairs and Envmt Cttee, 2007–09, Scottish Parlt. Dep. Leader, SNP, 2000–04. *Recreations:* hill walking, music, reading, stirring up trouble. *Address:* Scottish Parliament, Edinburgh EH99 1SP.

**CUNNINGHAM, Rt Rev. Seamus;** Bishop of Hexham and Newcastle, (RC), 2009–19; *b* Castlebar, Co. Mayo, 7 July 1942. *Educ:* St Nathy's Coll., Ballaghaderreen; St John's Coll., Waterford; Corpus Christi Coll., London. Ordained priest, 1966; Asst Priest, Our Lady and St Joseph's, Brooms, NW Durham, 1966–71; English Martyrs, Newcastle upon Tyne, 1971–72; Archdiocese of Hexham and Newcastle: Religious Educn and Catechetics Advr; Dir of Religious Educn; Spiritual Dir, Upshaw Coll., Durham, 1984–87; Administrator and Parish Priest, St Mary's Cathedral, 1987–97; Priest, Parish of St Oswin's, Tynemouth and St Mary's, Cullercoats; Vicar Gen., 2004–08.

**CUNNINGHAM, Sir Thomas Anthony, (Sir Tony),** Kt 2012; DL; *b* 16 Sept. 1952; *s* of late Daniel Cunningham and of Bessie Cunningham; *m* 1985, Anne Gilmore; one *s* one *d*, and one step *s* one step *d*. *Educ:* Workington GS; Liverpool Univ. (BA Hons). Mem., Allerdale DC, then BC, 1987–94 (Leader, 1992–94); Mayor of Workington, 1990–91. MEP (Lab) Cumbria and Lancs N, 1994–99; contested (Lab) NW Reg., 1999. MP (Lab) Workington, 2001–15. An Asst Govt Whip, 2005–08; a Lord Comr of HM Treasury (Govt Whip), 2008–10; Shadow Minister for Internat. Develt, 2011–13. DL Cumbria, 2015. *Address:* 17 Carlton Road, Workington, Cumbria CA14 4BX. *T:* (01900) 605799.

**CUNNINGHAM, Prof. Valentine David,** OBE 2017; DPhil; Professor of English Language and Literature, University of Oxford, 1996–2015; Fellow, and Tutor in English, Corpus Christi College, Oxford, 1972–2012, Emeritus Fellow, 2015 (Senior Research Fellow, 2012–14; Lecturer in English, 2014–15); *b* 28 Oct. 1944; *s* of Rev. Valentine Cunningham and Alma Lilian Cunningham (*née* Alexander); *m* 1966, Carol Ann Shaw; two *s*. *Educ:* Lawrence Sheriff Sch., Rugby; Keble Coll., Oxford (BA); St John's Coll., Oxford (MA, DPhil 1972). University of Oxford: Jun. Res. Fellow, St John's Coll., 1969–72; Dean, 1980–91, Sen. Tutor, 1991–94, Vice-Pres., 2008–12, Corpus Christi Coll.; Special Lectr, English Faculty, 1996–97. Visiting Professor: Univ. of Massachusetts, 1979–80; Konstanz Univ., 1980, 1983, 1989–90, 1992–93; Freiburg Univ., 2005; Goettingen Univ., 2005; Scholar-in-Residence, Univ. of Western Australia, 1985; Ständigergastprof., Konstanz Univ., 1994–2001; Fellow, Centre for British Studies, Humboldt Univ., Berlin, 2012–; Hon. Prof., Univ. of Bucharest, 2013–. *Publications:* Everywhere Spoken Against: dissent in the Victorian novel, 1975, 2nd edn 1977; (ed) The Penguin Book of Spanish Civil War Verse, 1979; (ed) Spanish Front: writers on the Civil War, 1986; British Writers of the Thirties, 1988; (ed) Cinco Escritores Britannicos/Five British Writers (bilingual text), 1990; In the Reading Gaol: postmodernity, texts and history, 1994; (ed) Adam Bede, 1996; (ed) The Victorians: an anthology of poetry and poetics, 2000; Reading After Theory, 2002; Victorian Poetry Now: poets, poems, poetics, 2011; The Connell Guide to Shakespeare's King Lear, 2012; (ed) Victorian Poets: a critical reader, 2014. *Recreations:* playing piano and trumpet (Leader, Dark Blues Jazz Band), listening to jazz, haunting bookshops, going to the cinema, reading bad novels, going to church. *Address:* 26 Frenchay Road, Oxford OX2 6TG. *T:* (01865) 556128. *E:* valentine.cunninghamn@ccc.ox.ac.uk. *Club:* Oxford and Cambridge.

**CUNO, James,** PhD; President and Chief Executive Officer, J. Paul Getty Trust, since 2011; *b* St Louis, Mo, 4 April 1951. *Educ:* Willamette Univ. (BA Hist. 1973); Univ. of Oregon (MA Hist. of Art 1978); Harvard Univ. (AM Fine Arts 1980; PhD Fine Arts 1985). Asst Curator of Prints, Fogg Art Mus., Harvard Univ., 1980–83; Asst Prof., Dept of Art, Vassar Coll., 1983–86; Adjunct Asst Prof., Dept of Art Hist., and Dir, Grunwald Center for Graphic Arts, UCLA, 1986–89; Adjunct Prof. of Art Hist., and Dir, Hood Mus. of Art, Dartmouth Coll., 1989–91; Prof. of Hist. of Art, Harvard Univ., and Elizabeth and John Moors Cabot Dir, Harvard Univ. Art Mus., 1991–2002; Dir and Märit Rausing Prof., Courtauld Inst. of Art, 2003–04; Pres. and Dir, Art Inst. of Chicago, 2004–11. Mem., Nat. Cttee for Hist. of Art, 1998. Association of Art Museum Directors: Mem., 1990; Trustee, 1999; Treas., 1999–2000; Vice-Pres., 2000–01; Pres., 2001–02. Trustee: Mus. of Fine Arts, Boston, 1991–2000; Wadsworth Atheneum Mus. of Art, Hartford, 2000. Fellow, Amer. Acad. Arts and Scis, 2001. *Publications:* (ed and contrib.) Foirades/Fizzles: echo and allusion in the art of Jasper Johns, 1987; (ed and contrib.) Politics and Polemics: French caricature and the Revolution 1789–1799, 1988; Who Owns Antiquity?: museums and the battle over our ancient heritage, 2008; contrib. numerous articles, reviews and papers to learned jls. *Address:* J. Paul Getty Trust, 1200 Getty Center Drive, Los Angeles, CA 90049–1679, USA.

**CUNY, Jean-Pierre;** Président Directeur Général, Bigot Mécanique Sopram, since 2011; *b* 8 April 1940; *s* of Robert Cuny and Marie Louise Marchal; *m* 1968, Anne-Marie Fousse; two *d*. *Educ:* Ecole Centrale de Paris (Ingénieur); Massachusetts Inst. of Technol. (MSc). Ingénieur, Serete, 1965–68; Director: Firmin Didot, 1968–73; DAFSA, 1973–76; Project Manager, CGA, 1976–78; joined Placoplatre, France, 1978: Prodn Dir, 1978–82; Commercial Dir, 1982–86; Pres. Dir Gen., BPB France, 1986–92; Dir, 1988–99, Chief Exec., 1994–99, BPB plc; Chm., St Eloi Finance, 2000–05; President-Director General: Bigot Mécanique, 2002–11; Sopram, 2003–11. Chevalier de la Légion d'Honneur, 1994. *Recreations:* ski-ing, photography.

**CUNYNGHAME, Sir Andrew (David Francis),** 12th Bt cr 1702; FCA; *b* 25 Dec. 1942; *s* of Sir (Henry) David St Leger Brooke Selwyn Cunynghame, 11th Bt, and of Hon. Pamela Margaret Stanley (*d* 1991), *d* of 5th Lord Stanley of Alderley; *S* father, 1978; *m* 1st, 1972, Harriet Ann, *d* of late C. T. Dupont, Montreal; two *d*; 2nd, 1989, Isabella King, *d* of late Edward Everett Watts, Jr and of Isabella Hardy Watts. *Educ:* Eton. *Heir: b* John Philip Henry Michael Selwyn Cunynghame [*b* 9 Sept. 1944; *m* 1981, Marjatta, *d* of Martti Markus; one *s* one *d*]. *Address:* 12 Vicarage Gardens, W8 4AH. *Club:* Brooks's.

**CUPITT, Rev. Don;** Fellow of Emmanuel College, 1965–96, now Life Fellow (Dean, 1966–91) and University Lecturer in Divinity, 1973–96, Cambridge; *b* 22 May 1934; *s* of late Robert and Norah Cupitt; *m* 1963, Susan Marianne (*née* Day); one *s* two *d*. *Educ:* Charterhouse; Trinity Hall, Cambridge; Westcott House, Cambridge. Curate, St Philip's Church, Salford, 1959–62; Vice-Principal, Westcott House, Cambridge, 1962–65. Writer and presenter, BBC TV series: The Big Question, 1973; Who Was Jesus?, 1976; The Sea of Faith, 1984. Hon. DLitt Bristol, 1985. *Publications:* Christ and the Hiddenness of God, 1971; Crisis of Moral Authority, 1972; The Leap of Reason, 1976; The Worlds of Science and Religion, 1976; (with Peter Armstrong) Who Was Jesus?, 1977; Jesus and the Gospel of God, 1979; The Nature of Man, 1979; The Debate about Christ, 1979; Explorations in Theology, 1979; Taking Leave of God, 1980; The World to Come, 1982; The Sea of Faith, 1984; Only Human, 1985; Life Lines, 1986; The Long-Legged Fly, 1987; The New Christian Ethics, 1988; Radicals and the Future of the Church, 1989; Creation Out of Nothing, 1990; What is a Story?, 1991; Rethinking Religion, 1992; The Time Being, 1992; After All, 1994; The Last Philosophy, 1995; Solar Ethics, 1995; After God, 1997; Mysticism After Modernity, 1998; The Religion of Being, 1998; The Revelation of Being, 1998; The New Religion of Life in Everyday Speech, 1999; The Meaning of It All in Everyday Speech, 1999; Kingdom Come in Everyday Speech, 2000; Philosophy's Own Religion, 2000; Reforming Christianity, 2001; Emptiness and Brightness, 2002; Is Nothing Sacred?, 2002; Life, Life, 2003; The Way to Happiness, 2005; The Great Questions of Life, 2006; Radical Theology, 2006; The Old Creed and the New, 2006; Impossible Loves, 2007; Above Us Only Sky, 2008; The Meaning of the West, 2008; The Method of Religious Studies (in Chinese), 2008; Jesus and Philosophy, 2009; Theology's Strange Return, 2010; A New Great Story, 2010; The Fountain, 2010; Turns of Phrase, 2011; The Last Testament, 2012; Creative Faith, 2015; Ethics in the Last Days of Humanity, 2016. *Address:* Emmanuel College, Cambridge CB2 3AP. *T:* (01223) 334200.

**CURA, José;** singer, composer, conductor and stage director; *b* Rosario, Argentina, 5 Dec. 1962; *m* 1985, Silvia Ibarra; two *s* one *d*. *Educ:* Nat. Univ. of Rosario; Sch. of Arts, Teatro Colon, Buenos Aires. Artist in Residence, Prague SO, 2015–. Débuts: Father, in Pollicino, Verona, 1992; Stiffelio (title rôle), Royal Opera, Covent Garden, 1995; La Gioconda, La Scala, Milan, 1997; Otello (title rôle), Teatro Regio, Torino, 1997; other rôles include: Cavaradossi, in Tosca; Samson, in Samson et Dalila; Don José, in Carmen; Rhadames, in Aida; Don Carlo; Alfredo, in La Traviata; Manrico, in Il Trovatore; Calaf, in Turandot; Dick Johnson, in La Fanciulla del West. Début as Stage Dir, Samson et Dalila, Badisches Staatstheater, Karlsruhe, 2010. Principal Guest Conductor, Sinfonia Varsovia, 2001–04. Founder and Pres., Cuibar Productions, 2001–. Recordings include: all tenor arias from Puccini's operas; Annelo, Argentine songs; Verismo Arias; Samson et Dalila. *W:* www.josecura.com.

**CURDS, Prof. Colin Robert,** DSc, PhD; Keeper of Zoology, 1991–97, Research Associate, since 1997, Natural History Museum; *b* 16 Sept. 1937; *s* of Robert Redvers Curds and Daisy Violet Curds (*née* Howsam); *m* 1961, Pauline (Polly) Armitage; one *s* one *d*. *Educ:* East Ham Grammar Sch.; Univ. of London (BSc 1960; PhD 1963; DSc 1978). FRSB (FIBiol 1979), CBiol 1982. Jun. Res. Fellow, Water Pollution Res. Lab., 1963–65; Min. of Technology, 1965–71; British Museum (Natural History), 1971–: Dep. Keeper of Zoology, 1976–89; Acting Keeper of Zoology, 1989–91. Visiting Lecturer: Chelsea Coll., 1965–73; Aston Univ., 1967–75; Surrey Univ., 1971–85; Vis. Prof., Mexico Univ., 1989–. Former mem., biol. and microbiol. cttees, 1972–; Member: Publications Policy Cttee, Inst. Biol., 1979–85; Council of Management, Project Urquhart, 1991–. Hon. Mem., Soc. of Protozoology, 1999–. Gov., Powell-Cotton Mus., 1992–97. *Publications:* (ed jtly) Ecological Aspects of Used-water Treatment Processes, vol. 1, 1979, vols 2 and 3, 1983; British and other freshwater ciliated protozoa, Pt 1, 1982, Pt 2 (jtly), 1983; Protozoa in the Water Industry, 1992; contribs to professional jls. *Recreations:* family life, furniture design, cabinet-making, France, cats, snorkelling, genealogy. *Address:* Department of Life Sciences, Natural History Museum, Cromwell Road, SW7 5BD. *T:* (home) (01825) 791796. *E:* colin.curds@googlemail.com.

**CURL, His Honour Philip;** DL; a Circuit Judge, 1996–2015; *b* 31 Oct. 1947; *s* of Dr Oliver Curl and Joan Curl; *m* 1983, Nicola Ruth Gurney; two *d*. *Educ:* Radley Coll.; Southampton Univ. (LLB). Called to the Bar, Gray's Inn, 1970; Asst Recorder, 1991–95; Recorder, 1995–96; Designated Family Judge, Norwich, 1998–2007. Legal Mem., Mental Health Review Tribunal (Restricted Patients Panel), 2002–. Mem., Disciplinary Panel, BHA, 2011–. Mem. Council, Norwich Cathedral, 2002–12. Local Steward: Gt Yarmouth and Fakenham Racecourses, 2004–17; Newmarket Racecourse, 2007–17. Patron, Childhood First, 2014–; Chm., Norfolk Boat, 2017–. DL Norfolk, 2016. *Recreations:* playing and watching sport, art, travel. *Clubs:* Boodle's, MCC; Norfolk (Norwich).

**CURL, Prof. Robert Floyd**, PhD; Kenneth S. Pitzer-Schlumberger Professor of Natural Sciences and University Professor, Rice University, Houston, 2003–05, now Emeritus; *b* Alice, Texas, 23 Aug. 1933; *s* of Robert Floyd Curl and Lessie Waldeen Curl; *m* 1955, Jonel Whipple; two *s*. *Educ:* Rice Inst. (BA 1954); Univ. of Calif, Berkeley (PhD 1957). Res. Fellow, Harvard, 1957–58; Rice Institute, then Rice University: Asst Prof., 1958–63; Associate Prof., 1963–67; Prof. of Chemistry, 1967–96; Chm., Chemistry Dept, 1992–96; Harry C. and Olga K. Wiess Prof. of Natural Scis, 1996–2003; Master, Lovett Coll., 1968–72. Honorary Professor: Univ. of Sci. and Technol. of China, 2002; Univ. of Xiamen, 2006; East China Univ. of Sci. and Technol., 2007; Nankai Univ., 2012. Member: NAS; ACS; Eur. Acad. of Scis and Arts; Fellow: Amer. Acad. of Arts and Scis; Optical Soc. of Amer. Hon. FRSNZ. Dr (*hc*): Buenos Aires, 1997; Littoral, 2003; Bar Ilan, 2010. (Jtly) Clayton Prize, IMechE, 1958; (jtly) APS Prize for New Materials, 1992; (jtly) Nobel Prize for Chemistry, 1996; (jtly) Texas Distinguished Scientist, Texas Acad. of Sci., 1997; (jtly) Achievement in Carbon Science, Amer. Carbon Soc., 1997; (jtly) Order of the Golden Plate, Amer. Acad. of Achievement, 1997. *Publications:* numerous contribs to scientific jls. *Recreation:* contract bridge. *Address:* Chemistry Department, Rice University, Houston, TX 77005, USA. *T:* (713) 3484816; 4141 South Braeswood Boulevard, Houston, TX 77025, USA.

**CURLE, James Leonard**; Member and Managing Director, Civil Aviation Authority, 1984–87; *b* 14 Nov. 1925; *s* of Leonard and Mary Curle; *m* 1952, Gloria Madeleine Roch (*d* 2016); one *s* one *d*. *Educ:* St Joseph's Academy, Blackheath; SE London Technical College; Borough Polytechnic. CEng, MIET. Royal Signals, 1944–48; joined Telecommunications Div., MTCA, 1957; Dir Telecommunications, ATS, 1976–79; Dir Gen. Telecommunications, NATS, 1979–84. *Address:* 6 Nightingale Lane, Bickley, Kent BR1 2QH. *T:* (020) 8460 8023.

**CURNOCK COOK, Jeremy Laurence**; Chairman: AmpliPhi Bioscience Corporation (formerly Targeted Genetics inc.), since 1998; International Bioscience Managers Ltd, since 2001; Chairman, Rex Bionics Pty Ltd, since 2017; Managing Director: Bioscience Managers Pty Ltd, since 2007; Bioscience Managers (UK) Ltd, since 2018; *b* 3 Sept. 1949; *s* of Colin Curnock Cook and Doris (*née* Wolsey); *m* 1st, 1975, Elizabeth Joanna Badgett (marr. diss. 1981); 2nd, 1987, Mary Elizabeth Thomasson (*see* M. E. Curnock Cook) (marr. diss. 1997); one *s* two *d*; 3rd, 2007, Sara Jane Stickland. *Educ:* Lycée Français de Londres; Westminster Sch.; Trinity Coll., Dublin (MA Natural Scis). Res. Scientist, Inst. Cancer Res., London, 1972–73; Managing Director: Badgett-Cook Biochems Ltd, London, 1973–75; Internat. Biochems Ltd, Dublin, London, 1975–87; Rothschild Asset Mgt (Biosci. Unit), 1987–2000. Non-executive Director: Cantab Pharmaceuticals plc, 1990–2001; Biocompatibles Internat. plc, 1992–2011; Vernalis, 1995–2001; Angiotech Pharmaceuticals Inc., 1995–2001; Amrad Corp., 1995–2002; Sirna Therapeutics Inc., 2003–06; Q chip, 2004–06; Silence Therapeutics (formerly S. R. Pharma) plc, 2005–10; Excalibur Group Holdings Ltd, 2005–16; Osteologix Inc., 2006–10; Eacom Timber Corp. Inc. (formerly Inflazyme Pharmaceuticals Inc.), 2006–13 (Chm., 2006–10); Aegera Therapeutics Inc., 2008–11; Topigen Pharmaceuticals Inc., 2008–10; Bioxyne Ltd (formerly Hunter Immunology Ltd), 2010–14; Virgin Health Bank QSTP LLC, 2011–13; Phylogica Ltd, 2012–17; Avita Medical Ltd, Perth, Aust., 2012–; Sea Dragon Ltd, Nelson, NZ, 2012–; Adherium (formerly Nexus6) Ltd, Auckland, NZ, 2013–; Arthurian Life Sciences Ltd, 2013–16; Smart Matrix Ltd, 2013–; Avena Therapeutics Ltd, 2013–18 (Chm., 2013–18); SummatiX Pty Ltd, 2017–; Arecor Ltd, 2018–; CEO, 2012–14, Dep. Chm., 2014–17, Rex Bionics plc (formerly Union MedTech plc). Mem., Biosci. Futures Forum, 2005–08. Mem., Soc. for Gen. Microbiol., 1971–. FInstD 1988; FRSA 1994. *Recreations:* keeping fit, music, ski-ing, hanging out in France. *Address:* 56 Chiswick Green Studios, Evershed Walk, Chiswick, W4 5BW. *Clubs:* Kildare Street and University (Dublin); Royal Automobile of Victoria (Melbourne).

**CURNOCK COOK, Mary Elizabeth**, OBE 2000; Chief Executive, Universities and Colleges Admissions Service, 2010–17; *b* London, 10 Oct. 1958; *d* of Christopher Thomasson and Bryony Thomasson; *m* 1987, Jeremy Laurence Curnock Cook, *qv* (marr. diss. 1997); one *s* two *d*. *Educ:* Convent of the Sacred Heart, Woldingham; London Business Sch. (MSc Gen. Mgt). Sales and Mktg Dir, International Biochemicals, 1980–88; Mktg Dir, Food from Britain, 1989–93; Chief Exec., BII, 1994–2001; Dir, Qualifications and Skills, QCA, 2003–09. Mem., FEFC, 1997–2001. Non-executive Director: Creative Learning Media, 2002–05; Laurel Pub Co., 2002–05; Student Loans Co., 2017–. Governor: Swindon Acad., 2006–18; Magdalen College Sch., 2016–17; Chair, Bd of Govs, Kensington and Chelsea Coll., 2017–18. Mem. Council, Open Univ., 2017–. Chair of Trustees: Access Proj., 2013–; National Star Coll., 2013–17; Trustee: Founders4Schools, 2018–; United Learning, 2018–. Fellow: Birkbeck, Univ. of London, 2015; Goldsmiths, Univ. of London, 2018. Hon. Dr Gloucestershire, 2017. *Recreations:* fine food and wine, tennis, sailing. *Address:* West Manor, Church Enstone, Oxon OX7 4NL. *T:* 07774 901982. *E:* mary@curnockcook.com. *Club:* Blacks.

**CURNOW, Rt Rev. Andrew William**, AM 2013; Bishop of Bendigo, 2003–18; *b* 26 Feb. 1950; *s* of Thomas William Curnow and Esma Jean Curnow (*née* Cook); *m* 1978, Jan Christina Jenkins; two *s* one *d*. *Educ:* Univ. of Melbourne (BComm); Melbourne Coll. of Divinity (BD); Presbyterian Sch. of Christian Educn, Richmond, VA, USA, (MA). Asst Curate, St Alban's, West Coburg, 1973–75; Rector, Parish of Milloo, 1975–79; on leave, USA, dios New York and Virginia, 1979–80; Rector of Elmore, 1980–83; Dir, Council for Christian Educn in Schools, Prov. of Victoria, 1983–89; Vicar of St George's, Malvern, 1989–94; Archdeacon of Kew, 1991–94; Asst Bishop, 1994–2003, Registrar, 2001–03, Dio. Melbourne. Mem., Standing Cttee, Gen. Synod, 1998–2017. Chairman: Anglicare Australia, 1997–2001; Anglican Superannuation Australia, 2003–06; Dir, Benetas, 2006–11; Pres., Bd, St Luke's Anglicare, 2007–14; Mem. Bd, Anglicare Victoria, 2014–. Exec. Chm., Trinity Coll. Theol Sch., 1997–2012 (Mem. Bd, 2003–11); Pres., Melbourne Coll. of Divinity, 2001–02. Life Mem., Oxford Business Alumni, 2002–; Mem., Australian Inst. of Co. Dirs, 2012–16. *Recreations:* reading, theatre, travel. *Address:* 5202 Calder Highway, Ravenswood, Vic 3453, Australia. *T:* 417390188. *Club:* Royal Automobile of Victoria (Melbourne).

**CURNYN, Christian**; music director and conductor; *b* 2 April 1971. *Educ:* Univ. of York; Guildhall Sch. of Music and Drama. Founder, Early Opera Co., 1994; has conducted productions for: Scottish Opera; ENO; Royal Opera Hse, Covent Gdn; Opera North; Opera Th. Co., Dublin; Halle Handel Fest.; Aldeburgh Fest.; Sam Wanamaker Playhouse; NY City Opera; Chicago Opera Th.; Opera Australia; Landestheater, Salzburg; Frankfurt Opera; Komische Oper, Berlin; Stuttgart Opera; Garsington Opera. Has made recordings. Stanley Sadie Handel Prize, 2008; Opera Award, BBC Music Mag. Awards, 2013. *Address:* c/o Maxine Robertson Management, Shakespeare House, 168 Lavender Hill, SW11 5TG.

**CURR, Surgeon Rear Adm. Ralph Donaldson**, FRCGP; Medical Director General (Naval), Ministry of Defence, 2002–03; *b* 25 Sept. 1943; *s* of George and Florence Curr; *m* 1972, Susan Brereton; two *s* three *d*. *Educ:* Dulwich Coll.; King's Coll. Hosp. (MB BS, AKC). LRCP, MRCS 1969; DRCOG 1975; FRCGP 1992. Joined RN 1969; HMS Mohawk, 1969; HMS Cleopatra, 1971; Malta, 1972–74; GP, NHS and RNR, HMS Vivid, 1975–76; Clyde Submarine Base, 1976–79; Gibraltar, 1979–81; PMO, HMS Raleigh, 1981–84; HK, 1984–86; HMS Intrepid, 1986–88; Dean of Naval Medicine, 1988–90; PMO, HMS Drake, 1990–95; Dir of Naval Personnel, MoD, 1995–97; COS to Med. Dir Gen. (Naval), MoD, 1997–2000; Dir, Med. Ops, CINCFLEET, 2000–02. QHP 2000–03. Civilian Med. Practitioner, HMS Raleigh, Torpoint, 2004–12. Founder Mem., DefenceSynergia, 2010–. Chm., Kosovo Mammography Project, 2007–08; Provost, Tamar Faculty, RCGP, 2011–14 (Sec., 2005–11). Director: Lord Caradon Trust, 2007–; UK Nat. Defence Assoc., 2008–10. Member: Britannia Assoc., 2004–; St Austell Bay Rotary Club, 2006– (Pres., 2009–11; Gov., Rotary District 1290, 2014–15, and Med. Dir, Overseas Project Team); ESU, 2015–; Pres., St Austell Sea Cadets, 2014–. Dir, Clergy Cottage Trust, 2004–. Mem., Parish Council, 2009–, and Churchwarden, All Saints, Pentewan. OStJ 2001. *Recreations:* walking, church, tennis, medical and defence politics. *Address:* Sea Garth, Pentewan Hill, Pentewan, St Austell, Cornwall PL26 6DD. *T:* (01726) 843106. *E:* rdcurr@hotmail.com.

**CURRAN, Edmund Russell**, OBE 2006; Editor-in-Chief, Independent News and Media (Northern Ireland), 2005–09; Columnist, Belfast Telegraph, since 2009; *b* 29 Sept. 1944; *s* of William John Curran and Elizabeth (*née* Russell); *m* 1st, 1968, Romaine Carmichael (marr. diss. 1991); two *s* two *d*; 2nd, 1994, Pauline Hall. *Educ:* Royal Sch., Dungannon; Queen's Univ., Belfast (BSc, DipEd). Dep. Editor, Belfast Telegraph, 1974–88; Editor, Sunday Life (NI), 1988–92; Actg Editor, Wales on Sunday, 1991; Editor, Belfast Telegraph, 1993–2005. Dir, Alpha Newspapers Ltd, 1983–. Mem. Bd, NCTJ, 2005–12. Mem., Press Complaints Commn, 2002–06. Fellow, Soc. of Editors, 2011 (Pres., 2001). Newspaper Focus UK Regl Newspaper Editor of Year, 1991. Hon. DLitt Ulster, 2012. *Recreations:* golf, tennis, travel. *Address:* c/o Belfast Telegraph, 33 Clarendon Road, Belfast BT1 3BG. *E:* Edmund.Curran@belfasttelegraph.co.uk. *Clubs:* Ulster Reform; Belvoir Park Golf, Belfast Boat (Belfast); Royal County Down Golf (Newcastle).

**CURRAN, Frances**; Member (Scot. Socialist) Scotland West, Scottish Parliament, 2003–07; *b* 21 May 1961. *Educ:* St Brendan's Sch., Linwood; St Andrew's Secondary Sch., Carntyne, Glasgow. Mem., NEC, Labour Party, 1984–86; worked for campaigns incl. red wedge, anti-poll tax, youth against racism in Europe; involved in launching Scottish Socialist Alliance, 1995, Scottish Socialist Party, 1998. Contested (Scot. Socialist) Glasgow E, July 2008, 2010. *Recreations:* reading, bingo, caravanning, socialising.

**CURRAN, Dr James Crowe**, MBE 2007; CPhys, CMet, FRMetS, CEng; Chair, James Hutton Institute, since 2017; *b* Glasgow, 1 Nov. 1951; *s* of Sir Samuel Crowe Curran, FRS and Joan Elizabeth Curran (*née* Strothers); *m* 1984, Artemis Pappa; one *s*. *Educ:* Glasgow Acad.; Aberdeen Univ. (BSc); Moray House Coll. (Cert Ed); London Univ. (BA ext.); Edinburgh Univ. (PhD 1975). FRMetS 1976; MInstP 1979; CPhys 1985; CEng 1989; CMet 1994. Sen. Consultant, Scottish Office, 1995–96; Scottish Environment Protection Agency: Hd of Sci., 1996–2001; Hd of Envmtl Strategy, 2001–06; Dir of Sci. and Strategy, 2009–11; Chief Exec. and Mem. Bd, 2012–15; Man. Dir, Encorp Ltd, 2006–08. Hon. Prof., Univ. of Stirling, 2015–. Dir, Green Purposes Co. Ltd, 2017–. Chair, Rev. Panel, 2004, Strategic Planning Cttee, 2004–06, UK Envmtl Res. Funders' Forum; Chair, Scottish Sustainable Develt Forum, 2007–09; Mem., Scottish Ministerial Resilience Adv. Bd, 2012–15, Climate Change Delivery Bd, 2012–17, Zero Waste Task Team, 2013–15; Chair, Climate Ready Clyde, 2017–. Hon. Fellow, Scottish Envmt Link, 2015. *Publications:* (ed) The State of Scotland's Environment and Natural Heritage, 2002; contrib. res. papers to envmtl jls on oceanography, pollution, ecology, envmtl mgt and climate change. *Recreation:* rewilding. *Address:* 15 Brooklands Avenue, Uddington, Glasgow G71 7AT. *T:* (01698) 812441. *E:* jamescurran@hotmail.co.uk.

**CURRAN, His Honour John Terence**; a Circuit Judge, 1996–2012; Resident Judge, Merthyr Tydfil Combined Court Centre, 1998–2012; acting Resident Judge, Cardiff Crown Court, 2012; *b* 31 Oct. 1941; *s* of Eugene Curran, OBE and Joan Curran; *m* 1971, Elizabeth Ann Bowcott; one *s* one *d*. *Educ:* Ratcliffe; Jesus Coll., Cambridge (MA). Hallinans, solicitors, Cardiff: articled clerk, 1963–68; admitted solicitor, 1968; Partner, 1968–83; called to the Bar, Gray's Inn, 1983; Asst Recorder, 1989–93; Actg Stipendiary Magistrate, 1989; Provincial Stipendiary Magistrate (Mid-Glam), 1990–96; a Recorder, 1993–96. *Recreations:* walking, gardening, history, supporting Cardiff RFC, looking for my spectacles. *Address:* Law Courts, Cathays Park, Cardiff CF10 3PG. *Club:* Cardiff and County.

**CURRAN, Kevin Barry**; Chair, Central London Hotel Workers, Unite, since 2008; *b* 20 Aug. 1954; *s* of John and Maureen Curran; *m* 1977, June Bartholomew; one *s* one *d*. GMB (formerly General, Municipal, Boilermakers and Allied Trades Union): joined 1975; Health and Safety Officer, London Region, 1988; Regl Organiser, 1990; Regl Industrial Organiser, 1996, Southern Region; Regl Sec., Northern Region, 1997; Gen. Sec., 2003–05; Internat. Co-ordinator, IUF, 2005–07. Living Wage Advr, London Citizens, 2007–. Tree surgeon, 2007–. *Recreations:* football, running, blacksmithing, woodlands, reading, allotment gardening, keeping fit, keeping the foes of working people on their toes. *Club:* Crystal Palace Football.

**CURRAN, Maj. Gen. Liam Diarmuid**, CB 2001; independent consultant, 2001–06; Engineering Adviser to Defence Procurement Agency and President of the Ordnance Board, 1998–2001; *b* 31 March 1946; *s* of late William James Curran and Genevieve Curran (*née* Lavery); *m* 1971, Evelyn Mary Elizabeth Strang; two *d*. *Educ:* Presentation Coll., Reading; Welbeck Coll.; Royal Military Acad., Sandhurst; Fitzwilliam Coll., Cambridge (MA 1970). CEng 1980; FIEE 1990. CO, 7 Armd Workshop, REME and Comdr, Fallingbostel Station, 1986–89; Equipt Support Manager on staff of QMG, 1989–91; Project Manager for Light Armd Vehicles, 1991–93; Equipt Support Dir on staff of QMG, 1993–96; Vice-Pres., Ordnance Bd, 1996–98. Col Comdt, REME, 2000–05. *Recreations:* walking, gardening, National Trust. *Address:* c/o Lloyds Bank, 38 Market Place, East Dereham, Norfolk NR19 2AT.

**CURRAN, Margaret Patricia**; *b* 24 Nov. 1958; *d* of James Curran and Rose McConnellogue; *m* Robert Murray; two *s*. *Educ:* Glasgow Univ. (MA Hons Hist. and Econ. Hist.); Cert. Community Educn. Welfare rights officer, 1982–83; community worker, 1983–87, sen. community worker, 1987–89, Strathclyde Regl Council; Lectr, Dept of Community Educn, Univ. of Strathclyde, 1989–99. Mem. (Lab) Glasgow Baillieston, Scottish Parlt, 1999–2011; Dep. Minister for Social Justice, 2001–02; Minister: for Social Justice, 2002–03; for Communities, 2003–04; for Parly Business, 2004–07. Contested (Lab) Glasgow E, July 2008. MP (Lab) Glasgow E, 2010–15; contested (Lab) same seat, 2015. Shadow Sec. of State for Scotland, 2011–15. *Recreations:* reading, theatre, American politics, spending time with my sons.

**CURRAN, His Honour Patrick David**; QC 1995; a Circuit Judge, 2007–18; a Deputy Judge of the High Court, Queen's Bench Division, 2008–18; *s* of late David Curran and Noreen Curran; *m* 1976; two *s* two *d*. *Educ:* Ratcliffe; Queen's Coll., Oxford (MA). Called to the Bar, Gray's Inn, 1972, Bencher, 2005; Asst Recorder, 1988–92; Recorder, 1992–2007; admitted to Bar of Ireland, 1993. Asst Comr, Parly Boundary Commn for

Wales, 1994–2007. Legal Mem., Mental Health Review Tribunal for Wales, 1995–2008. Legal Assessor, GMC, 2002–07. Governor, Westminster Cathedral Choir Sch., 2000–09. FRSocMed 2007–10. Editor, 1992–2004, Consultant Editor, 2004–, Personal Injuries and Quantum Reports. *Publications:* Personal Injury Pleadings, 1994, 5th edn 2014; (contrib.) Criminal Law and Forensic Psychiatry, 1995; (ed and contrib.) Personal Injury Handbook, 1997. *Club:* Athenæum.
*See also Dame D. J. Hine.*

**CURRAN, Prof. Sir Paul (James),** Kt 2016; PhD, DSc; CGeog, FRGS; President (formerly Vice-Chancellor), and Professor of Physical Geography, City, University of London (formerly City University London), since 2010; *b* 17 May 1955; *s* of late James Patrick Curran and Betty Doreen (*née* Bott); *m* 1978, Helen Patricia Palin; one *d. Educ:* Longslade Upper Sch., Birstall, Leics; Univ. of Sheffield (BSc Hons Geog. 1976); Univ. of Bristol (PhD 1979, DSc 1991); Univ. of Southampton (MBA Dist. 1998). FRGS 1979; CGeog 2002. Lectr, Univ. of Reading, 1979–81; Lectr, then Sen. Lectr, Univ. of Sheffield, 1981–89; Sen. Res. Associate, NASA Ames Res. Center, Calif, 1988–89; Prof. of Physical Geog., UC of Swansea, 1990–93; University of Southampton: Prof. of Physical Geog., 1993–2005; Hd, Dept of Geog., 1995–99; Dean of Sci., 2000–03; Hd, Winchester Sch. of Art, 2003–04; Dep. Vice Chancellor, 2004–05; Vis. Prof., 2005–; Vice-Chancellor, and Prof. of Physical Geog., Bournemouth Univ., 2005–10. Vis. Res. Fellow, Univ. of NSW, 1986. Member: NERC, 2006–14 (Mem., Terrestrial Life Scis Cttee, 1989–92; Mem., 2007–11, Chm., 2011–14; Audit and Risk Assurance Cttee; Mem., Remuneration Cttee, 2012–14); Bd, QAA, 2006–11 (Mem., Audit Cttee, 2007–11, Remuneration Cttee, 2007–11); Bd, UCEA, 2010–16 (Chm., 2011–16; Chm. employers' negotiating team in nat. pay negotiations, 2011–16); Chm., Nat. Review Body on Doctors' and Dentists' Remuneration, 2013–. Member: Sci. Adv. Gp, ESA, 1990–2009; Earth Observation Prog. Bd, BNSC, 1995–98; Sci. Adv. Cttee, ISPRS, 1999–2015; Wkg Party on Terrestrial Carbon Sinks, Royal Soc., 2000–01; Geog. Panel, 2001 RAE, HEFCE; Innovation, Growth and Skills Policy Cttee, 2005–, Research Policy Cttee, 2006–, UUK; Chairman: Wkg Gp on Global Ecosystem Monitoring, ISPRS, 1992–2000; Higher Educn Workforce Steering Gp (formerly High Level Academic Workforce), HEFCE, 2007–10; Pres., Remote Sensing and Photogrammetry Soc., 2009–. Mem. Trustee Bd, London Higher, 2018–. Patron, The Conversation UK, 2019– (Chm. Trustee Bd, 2013–19). Hon. Dr: ESCP Europe, 2017; Peter the Great Univ., St Petersburg, 2019. FRSPS 1995; FCIM 1999. Otto van Gruber Medal, ISPRS, 1988; Cuthbert Peek Award (1883), RGS, 1998; Gold Medal, Remote Sensing Soc., 2000; Patron's Medal, RGS, 2007. *Publications:* Principles of Remote Sensing, 1985; (jtly) Remote Sensing of Soils and Vegetation in the USSR, 1990; (ed) Environmental Remote Sensing from Regional to Global Scales, 1994; Remote Sensing in Biosphere Studies, 1994; Remote Sensing in Action, 1995; Scaling-up from Cell to Landscape, 1997; contrib. chapters in books and articles to conf. proc. and learned jls. *Recreations:* running, travel, family, art, sea. *Address:* City, University of London, Northampton Square, EC1V 0HB. *T:* (020) 7040 8002, *Fax:* (020) 7040 8596. *E:* president@city.ac.uk. *Clubs:* Athenæum, Geographical; Royal Motor Yacht.

**CURRAN, Terence Dominic;** HM Diplomatic Service, retired; Consul-General, Toronto, and Director-General of Trade and Investment in Canada, 1996–2000; *b* 14 June 1940; *m* 1969, Penelope Anne Ford; two *s* one *d.* Joined HM Diplomatic Service, 1966; DSAO, 1966–68; Peking, 1968–69; Consul, Dakar, 1970–73; Asst Trade Comr, then Consul (Commercial), Edmonton, 1973–78; FCO, 1978–80; First Sec., Pretoria, 1980–84; FCO, 1984–87; Counsellor (Commercial and Economic), Singapore, 1987–90; Head of Training, FCO, 1990–93; Dep. High Comr, Bombay, 1993–96. *Address:* Rother House, Nyewood, Petersfield, Hants GU31 5HY.

**CURRAN, Prof. Thomas,** PhD; FRS 2005; Chief Scientific Officer and Executive Director, Children's Research Institute, Children's Mercy Kansas City, since 2016; *b* 14 Feb. 1956; *s* of Thomas and Jane Curran; *m* (marr. diss.); one *s* one *d. Educ:* Univ. of Edinburgh (BS 1st cl. Hons Biol Sci. 1978; Ashworth Prize in Zool., 1978); ICRF Labs and University Coll. London (PhD 1982). Postdoctoral Damon Runyon Fellow, Salk Inst., San Diego, Calif, 1982–84; Sen. Scientist, Hoffman-La Roche, Inc., NJ, 1984–85; Asst Mem., 1985–86, Associate Mem., 1986–88, Full Mem., 1988–95, Associate Dir, 1991–95, Roche Inst., Molecular Biol., NJ; Prof. of Anatomy and Neurobiol., Univ. of Tennessee, 1995–2006; Mem. and Chm., Dept of Develtl Neurobiol., St Jude Children's Res. Hosp., Tenn, 1995–2006; Prof. of Pathol. and Lab. Medicine, 2006–16, Prof. of Cell and Develtl Biol., 2008–16, Perelman Sch. of Medicine, Univ. of Pennsylvania; Dep. Scientific Dir, 2006–16, Dir, Basic Scientific Res., Center for Childhood Cancer Res., 2007–16, Children's Hosp. of Philadelphia Res. Inst. (formerly Joseph Stokes Jr Res. Inst. at Children's Hosp. of Philadelphia). Adjunct Prof., Columbia Univ., NY, 1989–95. Mem., Bd of Scientific Advrs, Nat. Cancer Inst., Washington, 2000–05. Litchfield Lectr, Oxford Univ., 1993; W. W. Sutow Vis. Lectr in Pediatric Oncology, Univ. of Texas MD Anderson Cancer Centre, Houston, 2009. Lectures: Marguerite Vogt, Salk Inst., San Diego, 2006; Colleen Giblin Meml, Columbia Univ., NY, 2006. Pres., Amer. Assoc. for Cancer Res., Philadelphia, 2002. Mem., Inst. Medicine, 2009. Fellow, Amer. Acad. of Microbiol., 1994; FAAAS 1994; Fellow, Amer. Acad. of Arts and Scis, 2012; FAACR 2013. Tenovus-Scotland Medal, Glasgow, 1991; Rita Levi Montalcini Award in Neuroscis, 1992; Passano Foundn Young Scientist Award, Baltimore, 1992; Outstanding Achievement in Cancer Res. Award, Amer. Assoc. for Cancer Res., 1993; Golgi Award, Italian Acad. Neurosci., Brescia, 1994; Javitz Neurosci. Investigator Award, Nat. Inst. of Neurol Disorder and Stroke, NIH, 2001; Peter M. Steck Meml Award and Lecture, Houston, Texas, 2002; LIMA Internat. Award for Excellence in Pediatric Brain Tumour Res., PBT Foundn, NY, 2004. *Publications:* (as Tom Curran): (ed) The Oncogene Handbook, 1988; Origins of Human Cancer, 1991; (ed jtly) Two Faces of Evil: cancer and neurodegeneration, 2011; contrib. to books and over 270 articles in scientific jls. *Address:* Children's Research Institute, Children's Mercy Kansas City, 2401 Gillham Road, Kansas City, MO 64108, USA.

**CURRIE,** family name of **Baron Currie of Marylebone.**

**CURRIE OF MARYLEBONE,** Baron *cr* 1996 (Life Peer), of Marylebone in the City of Westminster; **David Anthony Currie;** Chairman, Advertising Standards Authority, since 2017; *b* 9 Dec. 1946; *s* of Kennedy Moir Currie and Marjorie Currie (*née* Thompson); *m* 1st, 1975, Shaziye Gazioglu Currie (marr. diss. 1992); two *s*; 2nd, 1995, Angela Mary Piers Dumas; one step *s. Educ:* Battersea Grammar Sch.; Univ. of Manchester (BSc 1st cl. Maths); Univ. of Birmingham (MSocSci Econs); PhD Econs London. Economist: Hoare Govett, 1971–72; Economic Models, 1972; Lectr, Reader and Prof. of Economics, Queen Mary College, Univ. of London, 1972–88; London Business School: Prof. of Econs, 1988–2000; Res. Dean, 1989–92; Gov., 1989–95; Dep. Principal, 1992–95; Dep. Dean for External Relations, 1999–2000; Dir, Centre for Econ. Forecasting, 1988–95; Dean, City Univ. Business Sch., subseq. Cass Business Sch., City of London, 2001–07. Res. Fellow, Centre for Economic Policy Research, 1983–. Houblon-Norman Res. Fellow, Bank of England, 1985–86; Vis. Scholar, IMF, 1987. Vis. Prof., UEA, 2019–. Member: Treasury's Panel of Independent Forecasters, 1992–95; Gas and Electricity Mkts Authy, 2000–02; Bd, Dubai FSA, 2004–; Chairman: Office of Communications, 2002–09; Ind. Audit, 2003–07; ICFR, 2009–12; Competition and Markets Authy, 2012–18. Assessor, Leveson Inquiry into culture, practice and ethics of the press, 2011–12. Dir and Chm. Exec. Cttee, Charter 88, 1993–97; Dir, Abbey National plc, 2001–02. Non-executive Director: BDO (formerly BDO Stoy Hayward), 2008–12; Royal Mail, 2009–12; IG Group, 2010–12; 4G Capital, 2019–. Chm., Semperian PPP Investment Partners, 2008–12. Chm. Council, Univ. of Essex, 2011–13, 2016–18. Mem., Bd, LPO, 2007–12. Trustee: Joseph Rowntree Reform Trust, 1989–2002; Alzheimer's Soc., 2019–. Hon. Fellow, QMW, 1997. Hon. DLitt Glasgow, 1998; Hon. DSc City, 2012; DU Essex, 2014; DSc London, 2017. *Publications:* Advances in Monetary Economics, 1985; (with Charles Goodhart and David Llewellyn) The Operation and Regulation of Financial Markets, 1986; (with David Vines) Macroeconomic Interactions Between North and South, 1988; (with Paul Levine) Rules, Reputation and Macroeconomic Policy Co-ordination, 1993; (with David Vines) North-South Linkages and International Macroeconomic Policy, 1995; The Pros and Cons of EMU, 1997; Will the Euro Work?: the ins and outs of EMU, 1998; articles in jls. *Recreations:* music, literature, swimming. *Address:* House of Lords, SW1A 0PW.

**CURRIE,** Btcy *cr* 1847; succession to this Baronetcy has not yet been established following the death of the 7th Bt in 2014; no name has yet been entered on the Official Roll of the Baronetage.

**CURRIE, Maj. Gen. Archibald Peter Neil,** CB 2001; CBE 2014; Lieutenant Governor, Royal Hospital, Chelsea, 2005–14; *b* Dar es Salaam, 30 June 1948; *s* of Donald and Ysobel Currie; *m* 1974, Angela Margaret Howell; two *s. Educ:* Sao Hill Sch., Tanzania; Monkton Combe Sch.; RMA, Sandhurst; Nottingham Univ. (BA Hons Hist. 1973). 2nd Regt, RA, 1970–75; 22 Regt, RA, 1975–79; RMCS, Shrivenham, 1980; psc, 1981; Operational Requirements, MoD, 1982–83; Batt. Comdr, 22 Regt, RA, 1984–86; Army Staff Duties, MoD, 1986–87; CO, 12 Regt RA, 1987–90; Instr, Staff Coll., Camberley, 1990–91; Col, Mil. Ops 1, MoD, 1991–93; HCSC, 1993; Comdr Artillery, HQ ARRC, 1994; Dep. Comdr, Multinat. Div. Central (Airmobile), 1995; DPS (Army), MoD, 1996–98; Mil. Advr to High Rep. in Bosnia Herzegovina, 1998–99; COS to Adjt Gen., 1999–2001; Dep. Adjt Gen., MoD, 2001–02. Has served in NI, Falkland Is and Bosnia. Advr to Sunday Mirror, 2003–05. Dir, Blue Force Gp, 2003–06. Non-exec. Dir, Close Brothers Mil. Services, 2004–06. Member: Bd, Services Sound and Vision Corp., 2003–09; Council, Forces Pension Soc., 2003–17; Trustee: Combat Stress, 2006–13 (Chm., 2007–13); Vice Pres., 2013–); St John's Charity, 2016–17; Family Counselling Trust, 2017–; Patron and Trustee, ICARUS, 2018–. *Recreations:* ski-ing, tennis, opera, walking in wild places, Persian rugs.

**CURRIE, Austin;** *see* Currie, J. A.

**CURRIE, Brian Murdoch;** President, Institute of Chartered Accountants in England and Wales, 1996–97 (Vice-President, 1994–95; Deputy President, 1995–96); *b* 20 Dec. 1934; *s* of William Murdoch Currie and Dorothy (*née* Holloway); *m* 1961, Patricia Maria, *d* of Capt. Frederick Eaton-Farr; three *s* one *d. Educ:* Blundell's Sch. (Scholar); Oriel Coll., Oxford (Open Scholar; MA). ACA 1963, FCA 1973; MIMC 1968, FIMC 1990; FCILT 2016. Commnd RTR, 1957–59; Arthur Andersen Chartered Accountants and Andersen Consulting, 1959–90: Partner, 1970–90; Man. Partner, London, 1977–82; Chm., Partnership Council, 1983–85. Dist Auditor, 1982–87. Dept of Trade Inspector, Fourth City and other cos, 1978; Mem., Foster Cttee of Inquiry into Road Haulage Licensing, 1977. Member: Management Bd, HMSO, 1972–74; Restrictive Practices Court, 1979–2004; Takeover Panel, 1989–97; Lay Mem., GDC, 1994–99; Dep. Chm., Financial Reporting Council, 1996–98. Institute of Chartered Accountants in England and Wales: Mem. Council, 1988–99; Chm., Practice Regulation, 1993; Chm., Chartered Accountants Jt Ethics Cttee, 1994–95; Mem., IFAC Compliance Cttee, 2000–02. Trustee, Oriel Coll. Develt Trust, 1980–94. Chm., Peter Blundell Soc., 1997–2002; Member, Committee: Exmoor Soc., 1993–2002 (Founder's Award, 2002); Glass Assoc., 1998–2003. Gov., Blundell's Sch., 2000–02. Jt Ed., Glass Cone, 1999–2005. *Publications:* A Principle-based Framework for Professional Independence, 1992; official public reports; papers and articles in professional and technical pubns. *Recreations:* natural history, Exmoor, church (lay assisting). *Address:* Westbrook House, Bampton, Tiverton, Devon EX16 9HU. *T:* (01398) 331418.

**CURRIE, Dr Christopher Richard John,** FRHistS, FSA; Senior Research Fellow, Institute of Historical Research, 2002–08 and since 2008; Gazette Editor, Church Times, 2002–18 (Deputy Web Editor, 2002–09); *b* 3 March 1948; *s* of George Samson Currie, MC and Norah Currie (*née* Kennedy); *m* 1981, Katherine Ruth Gommon; one *s* one *d. Educ:* Winchester; Balliol Coll., Oxford (MA 1976, DPhil 1976). FRHistS 1979; FSA 1984. Victoria County History: Asst Editor, Staffs, 1972–78; Dep. Editor, 1978–94; Gen. Editor, 1994–2000; Consultant Editor, 2000–02. Mem. Council, RHistS, 1996–2000. Pres., 2007–11, Vice Pres., 2011–14, Vernacular Architecture Gp; Hon. Editor, Vernacular Architecture, 1980–82. *Publications:* (ed with C. P. Lewis) English County Histories: a guide, 1994; articles in Victoria County Hist. and learned jls. *Recreations:* sleep, travel. *Address:* 14 Keston Road, N17 6PN. *T:* (020) 8801 2185.

**CURRIE, Edwina, (Edwina Currie Jones);** *b* 13 Oct. 1946; *m* 1st, 1972, Raymond F. Currie, BA, FCA (marr. diss. 2001); two *d*; 2nd, 2001, John Benjamin Paul Jones, former Det. Supt, Met. Police; four step *s. Educ:* Liverpool Inst. for Girls; St Anne's Coll., Oxford (scholar; MA 1972); London Sch. of Econs and Pol Science (MSc 1972). Teaching and lecturing posts in econs, econ. history and business studies, 1972–81. Birmingham City Council: Mem., 1975–86; Chm., Social Services Cttee, 1979–80; Chm., Housing Cttee, 1982–83. Chm., Central Birmingham HA, 1981–83. MP (C) Derbyshire South, 1983–97; contested (C) same seat, 1997. PPS to Sec. of State for Educn and Science, 1985–86; Parly Under-Sec. of State (Health), DHSS, later Dept of Health, 1986–88. Member: European Movement, 1992–2018 (Vice Pres., 1995–98); Cons. Gp for Europe, 1992– (Chm., 1995–97); Dir, Future of Europe Trust, 1992–97 (Jt Chm., 1994–97). Contested (C) Bedfordshire and Milton Keynes, Eur. Parly elecns, 1994. Regular contributor to nat. newspapers and magazines; presenter: Sunday Supplement, TV, 1993; Espresso, TV, 1997; various radio progs, incl. Late Night Currie, 1998–2003, BBC Radio Five Live. Trustee: Marie Curie Cancer Care, 1992–94; VOICE (UK) (Chm., 1994–97); The Patients Assoc., 2006–08; Patron: Reigate and Banstead Women's Aid, 2005–11; MRSA Action UK, 2007–; Partners in Educn Swaziland, 2015–. Pres., Tideswell Male Voice Choir, 2012–. Dir, Future of Europe Trust (Jt Chm., 1994–97). Pres., High Peak Cons. Assoc., 2015–17, 2018–; Founder and Chm., High Peak Business Club, 2014–. Speaker of the Year, Assoc. of Speakers' Clubs, 1990; Campaigner of the Year, Spectator Awards, 1994. *Publications:* Financing our Cities (Bow Group pamphlet), 1976; Life Lines, 1989; What Women Want, 1990; (jtly) Three-Line Quips, 1992; Edwina Currie Diaries: 1987–92, 2002, vol. II, 1992–97, 2012; *novels:* A Parliamentary Affair, 1994; A Woman's Place, 1996; She's Leaving Home, 1997; The Ambassador, 1999; Chasing Men, 2000; This Honourable House, 2001. *Recreations:* earning a living, theatre, reading other people's books, keeping up with nine grandchildren and three great-grandchildren. *Address:* c/o CJA Ltd, Whaley Bridge, Derbys SK23 7BA.

**CURRIE, Heriot Whitson;** QC (Scot.) 1992; *b* 23 June 1952; *s* of Heriot Clunas Currie and Evelyn Whitson; *m* 1st, 1975, Susan Carolyn Hodge (marr. diss. 2001); three *d*; 2nd, 2003, Paula Maria Christian. *Educ:* Edinburgh Academy; Wadham Coll., Oxford (MA); Edinburgh Univ. (LLB). Admitted to Faculty of Advocates, 1979; practice as Advocate,

1979–; called to the Bar, Gray's Inn, 1991; Mem., Monckton Chambers, 2005–14. Chm. (pt-time), Competition Appeal Tribunal, 2013–. *Recreations:* chamber music, cinema, golf, foreign languages. *Address:* 2 Doune Terrace, Edinburgh EH3 6DY. *Clubs:* New (Edinburgh); Honourable Company of Edinburgh Golfers, Royal Burgess Golfing Society (Edinburgh).

**CURRIE, James McGill;** Director-General (Environment, Climate and Nuclear Safety), European Commission, 1997–2001; *b* 17 Nov. 1941; *s* of late David Currie and of Mary (*née* Smith); *m* 1968, Evelyn Barbara MacIntyre; one *s* one *d*. *Educ:* St Joseph's High Sch., Kilmarnock; Blairs Coll., Aberdeen; Royal Scots Coll., Valladolid; Univ. of Glasgow (MA). Asst Principal, Scottish Home and Health Dept, 1968–72; Principal, Scottish Educn Dept, 1972–75; Secretary, Management Gp, Scottish Office, 1975–77; Scottish Development Dept: Principal, 1977–79; Asst Sec., 1979–81; Asst Sec., Scottish Economic Planning Dept, 1981–82; Counsellor, UK Perm. Representation to EEC, 1982–87; Dir of Regional Policy, EEC, 1987–89; Chef de Cabinet to Leon Brittan, EEC, 1989–92; Dep. Head, EC Delegn to USA, 1993–96; Dir-Gen. (Customs and Indirect Taxation), EC, 1996–97. Vis. Prof. of Law, Georgetown Law Center, Washington, 1997–2005. Chm., Davaar Associates, 2002–13; Chm. and Sen. Advr, Burson-Marsteller Brussels, 2007–. Non-executive Director: Royal Bank of Scotland, 2001–09; Total UK, 2004–15; Vimetco NV, 2007–; Met Office, 2007–11. FRSA 2007. Hon. DLitt Glasgow, 2001. *Recreations:* tennis, golf, guitar, good food. *Club:* New (Edinburgh).

**CURRIE, (Joseph) Austin;** retired politician and author; Minister of State, Departments of Health, Education and Justice, Irish Parliament, 1994–97; only person to have been elected to both Irish Parliaments and to have served as a Minister in both; *b* 11 Oct. 1939; *s* of John Currie and Mary (*née* O'Donnell); *m* 1968, Anne Ita Lynch; two *s* three *d*. *Educ:* Edendork Sch.; St Patrick's Academy, Dungannon; Queen's Univ., Belfast (BA). MP (Nat) Tyrone, Parlt of N Ireland, 1964–72; Founder Mem., SDLP, 1970; Mem. (SDLP), Fermanagh and S Tyrone, NI Assembly, 1973–75; NI Constitutional Convention, 1975–76, NI Assembly, 1982–86; Minister of Housing, Planning and Local Govt, 1974. Contested (FG) Presidency of Ireland, 1990. Irish Parliament: TD (FG), Dublin W, Dail Eireann, 1989–2002. Mem., Anglo-Irish Parly tier; frontbench spokesperson: on communications, 1991–93; on equality and law reform, 1993–94; spokesperson on energy, 1997–2001; dep. spokesperson on foreign affairs, 2001–02. Mem., Forum for Peace and Reconciliation, 1995–. Mem. Bd, Caranua, 2013–17. Advr to Eur. Commn, 1984–87. *Publications:* All Hell Will Break Loose (autobiog.), 2004. *Recreations:* Gaelic football, golf, snooker, reading. *Address:* Tullydraw, Derrymullen, Robertstown, Naas, Co. Kildare, W91 WP9V, Ireland.

**CURRIE, Rachel Alexandra Louise;** *see* Wang, R. A. L.

**CURRIE JONES, Edwina;** *see* Currie, E.

**CURRIMBHOY, Sir Mohamed;** *see* Ebrahim, Sir M. C.

**CURRY,** family name of **Baron Curry of Kirkharle.**

**CURRY OF KIRKHARLE,** Baron *cr* 2011 (Life Peer), of Kirkharle in the County of Northumberland; **Donald Thomas Younger Curry**, Kt 2001; CBE 1997; Chairman: Royal Veterinary College, since 2012; Cawood Scientific, since 2014; *b* 4 April 1944; *s* of Robert Thomas Younger Curry and Barbara Ramsey Curry; *m* 1966, Rhoda Mary Murdie; two *s* one *d*. *Educ:* Northumberland Coll. of Agric. Estabd farming business, 1971–2018; farmed 450 acres in Northumberland (C&G Farm Mgt and Orgn). Comr, MLC, 1986–2001 (Dep. Chm., 1992–93; Chm., 1993–2001); Crown Estate Comr, 2000–07; Chm., NFU Mutual Insurance Soc., 2003–11 (non-exec. Dir, 1997–2011; Vice-Chm., 2000–03). Chairman: Commn on the Future of Farming and Food, 2001–02; Better Regulation Exec., BIS, 2009–15; Cawood Scientific, 2015–. Founder/Chm., At Home in the Community (provides residential homes for people with a learning disability), 1992–2013; Chm., Leckford Estate, Waitrose, 2009–16. Chm., Prince's Countryside Fund, 2016–. Trustee: Clinton Devon Estate, 2009–; Lawes Trust (Rothamsted Research) 2009–17; Anglican Internat. Develt, 2010–; Prospects, 2013–16; National Land Based Coll., 2015–18 (Chm., 2015–18). Hon. BSc Cranfield, 2004; Hon. Dr Gloucester, 2005; Hon. DCL Newcastle, 2008. *Recreations:* church responsibilities, photography, travel, gardening. *Address:* Corchester Towers, Corbridge, Northumberland NE45 5NP. *Club:* Farmers.

**CURRY, Prof. Anne Elizabeth, (Mrs J. G. Painter),** PhD; FRHistS, FSA, FHA; Professor of Medieval History, University of Southampton, since 2004 (Dean, Faculty of Humanities, 2010–18); *b* Chester-le-Street, Co. Durham, 27 May 1954; *d* of Ralph Curry and Jean Mary Curry (*née* Whittaker); *m* 1979, John Geoffrey Painter; one *s*. *Educ:* Deanery Secondary Sch., Chester-le-Street; Univ. of Manchester (BA 1st Cl. Hist. 1975; MA 1977); CNAA (Teesside Poly.) (PhD 1985). FRHistS 1986. Res. Asst, Teesside Poly., 1976–78; University of Reading: Lectr in Hist., 1978–94; Sen. Lectr, 1994–2001; Prof., 2001–04. Ed., Jl Medieval Hist., 2001–08. Dep. Chair, Hist. Sub-panel, REF 2014. Mem., Battlefields Panel, English Heritage, 2012–. Co-Chair, Agincourt 600, 2012–. Pres., Histl Assoc., 2008–11; Vice-Pres., RHistS, 2006–09. Trustee, Royal Armouries, 2014–. Member: Soc. de l'Histoire de France, 1980; Soc. des Antiquaires de Normandie, 2014. FSA 1996; FHA 2006. Liveryman, Fletchers' Co., 2013. *Publications:* The Hundred Years War, 1993, 2nd edn 2003; The Battle of Agincourt: sources and interpretations, 2000, 2nd edn 2009; Essential Histories: the Hundred Years War, 2002; Agincourt: a new history, 2005, 2nd edn 2006; The Parliament Rolls of Medieval England, X, XI and XII (1422–1453), 2005; (with G. Foard) Bosworth: a battlefield rediscovered, 2013; (jtly) The Soldier in Later Medieval England, 2013; Great Battles: Agincourt, 2015; Henry V: playboy prince to warrior king, 2015; (ed with M. Mercer) The Battle of Agincourt, 2015; (ed with V. Gazeau) La guerre en Normandie xie-xve siècles, 2018. *Recreations:* classical music, singing, escaping to the fifteenth century. *Address:* Faculty of Humanities, University of Southampton, Southampton SO17 1BF. *T:* (023) 8059 5419, *Fax:* (023) 8059 3868. *E:* a.e.curry@soton.ac.uk. *Club:* Athenæum.

**CURRY, Rt Hon. David (Maurice);** PC 1996; *b* 13 June 1944; *s* of late Thomas Harold Curry and Florence Joan (*née* Tyerman); *m* 1971, Anne Helene Maud Roullet; one *s* two *d*. *Educ:* Ripon Grammar Sch.; Corpus Christi Coll., Oxford (MA Hons); Kennedy Sch. of Govt, Harvard (Kennedy Scholar, 1966–67). Reporter, Newcastle Jl, 1967–70; Financial Times: Trade Editor, Internat. Cos Editor, Brussels Corresp., Paris Corresp., and European News Editor, 1970–79. Sec., Anglo-American Press Assoc. of Paris, 1978; Founder, Paris Conservative Assoc., 1977. MEP (C) Essex NE, 1979–89; Chm., Agriculture Cttee, 1982–84; Vice-Chm., Budgets Cttee, 1984–85; spokesman on budgetary matters for European Democratic Gp, 1985–89; Gen. Rapporteur for EEC's 1987 budget. MP (C) Skipton and Ripon, 1987–2010. Parly Sec., 1989–92, Minister of State, 1992–93, MAFF; Minister of State, DoE, 1993–97; Shadow Sec. of State for Local and Devolved Govt Affairs, 2003–04. Chairman, Select Committee: on agriculture, 1999–2001; on envmt, food and rural affairs, 2001–03; Member: Public Accounts Cttee, 2004–10; Cttee on Standards & Privileges, 2007–10. Chm., Dairy UK, 2005–08. Chm., Internat. Develt Enterprises, subsistence farming charity, 2013–16 (Vice Chm., 2010–13). Editor in Chief, Westminster Publications, 2013–. *Publications:* The Food War: the EEC, the US and the battle for world food markets, 1982; (ed) The Conservative Tradition in Europe, 1998; Lobbying Government, 1999. *Recreations:* digging, windsurfing. *Address:* Newland End, Arkesden, Essex CB11 4HF. *T:* (01799) 550368.

**CURRY, Prof. Gordon Barrett,** PhD; Professor of Geoscience, University of Glasgow, 2017–18, now Emeritus; *b* 27 June 1954; *s* of Robert and Violet Curry; *m* 1983, Gillian. *Educ:* Masonic Sch., Dublin; Trinity Coll., Dublin (BA Mod.); Imperial Coll. London (PhD, DIC). University of Glasgow: Research Asst to Sir Alwyn Williams, 1980–84; Royal Soc. Res. Fellow, 1984–92; Reader, 1992–2013, Sen. Lectr, 2013–17, Dept of Geol. and Applied Geol., then Div. of Earth Scis, subseq. Sch. of Geographical and Earth Scis; Dep. Dir, Human Identification Centre, 1995–98; Project Manager, Taxonomy Prog., 1996–99; Chief Advr for Sci., Coll. of Sci. and Engrg, 2011–13. Mem., Exec. Cttee, 2015–, Exec. Sec., 2016–, University Geoscience UK (formerly Heads of UK Geol. Depts); Mem., Cttee on Educn, European Geoscis Union, 2018–. Treas., Systematics Assoc., 1996–2004. SFHEA 2015; Sen. Fellow, Recognising Excellence in Teaching, Univ. of Glasgow, 2015. President's Award, Geol Soc., 1985; Clough Award, Edinburgh Geol Soc., 1985–86; Wollaston Fund, Geol Soc., 1989; Teaching Excellence Award, Univ. of Glasgow, 2009; Teaching Excellence Award, Student Rep. Council, Univ. of Glasgow, 2015. *Publications:* (jtly) British Brachiopods, 1979; (ed) Allochthonous Terranes, 1991; (jtly) Molecules through Time: fossil molecules and biochemical systematics, 1991; Biology of Living Brachiopods, 1992; (ed) Biodiversity Databases, 2007; (ed) Evolution and Development of the Brachiopod Shell, 2010; numerous contribs to learned jls. *Recreations:* music, walking, swimming, cricket, golf, travel. *Address:* School of Geographical and Earth Sciences, Gregory Building, University of Glasgow, Lilybank Gardens, Glasgow G12 8QQ. *T:* (0141) 330 5444. *E:* Gordon.Curry@glasgow.ac.uk.

**CURRY, John Arthur Hugh,** CBE 1997; Chairman, All England Lawn Tennis Ground plc, 1990–2011; *b* 7 June 1938; *s* of Alfred Robert and Mercia Beatrice Curry; *m* 1962, Anne Rosemary Lewis; three *s* one *d*. *Educ:* King's College School, Wimbledon; St Edmund Hall, Oxford (MA); Harvard Univ. Graduate College (MBA). FCA. Arthur Andersen, 1962–64; Man. Dir, Unitech, 1966–86 (non-exec. Dir, 1986–96); Exec. Chm., 1986–2001, non-exec. Chm., 2001–05, ACAL plc. Dir and Chm. of private cos, 1976–. Non-executive Director: Dixons, 1993–2001; Foreign & Colonial Smaller Cos PLC, 1996–2004 (Chm., 2002–04); Terence Chapman Group plc, 1999–2003; Chm., Invicta Leisure Gp, 1999–2002. *Publications:* Partners for Profit, 1966. *Recreations:* tennis, Rugby. *Address:* Stokewood Park House, Sheardley Lane, Droxford, Hants SO32 3QY. *Clubs:* Farmers, Institute of Directors; All England Lawn Tennis and Croquet (Chm., 1989–99, Mem. Cttee, 1979–99, Vice Pres., 2000–); International Lawn Tennis of GB (Hon. Treas., 1977–86); Oxford University Lawn Tennis (Pres., 2003–10).

**CURRY, Judith Penelope;** Director, Curry Consultants, since 2016; Chief Executive, Commonwealth Book Publishers Association, since 2018; *b* Cambridge, 7 Aug. 1952; *d* of Sir Denys Haigh Wilkinson, FRS and Dr Christiane Andrée Wilkinson (*née* Clavier); *m* 1981, Philip Curry; two *d*. *Educ:* Oxford High Sch.; Somerville Coll., Oxford (BA Maths 1973); Laban Art of Movement Studio (Dip. Dance Th. 1975); Cass Business Sch. (MSc Math. Trading and Finance 2001). ACA 1982. Scientific Sub-Editor, Academic Press, 1977–78; Computer Audit Senior and Trainee Accountant, Hill Vellacott, 1979–82; Mem., Micro Computer Adv. Service, Peat Marwick, 1982–83; Finance and Inf. Manager, Univ. Centre, Cambridge, 1996; Supervisor, 1997, Manager, 1998, Sen. Manager, 1999–2000, Global Risk Mgt Solutions, Coopers & Lybrand, later PricewaterhouseCoopers; Finance Dir, 2000–02, Finance Dir and Sec., 2003–07, Commonwealth Inst.; Chief Exec., Commonwealth Educn Trust, 2007–16. Chair, Thirty Bird Prodns, 1998–2011. Member: Adv. Bd, Caribbean Poetry Project, 2010–15, Southern African Poetry Project, 2013–15, Cambridge Univ.; Cttee, Oxford Educn Soc., 2012–17 (Treas., 2013–17). Mem., Clavering Players, 2008– (Mem., Cttee, 2012–; Treas., 2014–). Mem., 100 Women in Hedge Funds, 2010–16. *Recreations:* travel, hiking, dance, drama. *T:* 07796 177908. *E:* judith@curryconsultants.com.

**CURRYER, Ian;** Chief Executive, Nottingham City Council, since 2013; *b* Stevenage, Herts, 19 Sept. 1962; *s* of Dennis and Barbara Curryer; *m* 1991, Margaret Figures; two *s*. *Educ:* Nobel Sch., Stevenage; Nottingham Trent Univ. (BEd Hons Primary Generalist). Accredited OFSTED Inspector, 2002. Teacher: Crossdale Drive Primary Sch., 1986–88; Claremont Primary and Nursery Sch., 1988–91; Head Teacher, Forest Fields Primary Sch., 1991–99; Nottingham City Council: Primary Sch. Advr, 1999–2002; Asst Dir, Equalities, Regeneration and Partnerships, 2002–04; Asst Dir, Economic and Social Regeneration, 2004; Asst Dir, Inclusion and Family Services, 2004–06; Dir, Schs Services, 2006–07; Dir, Targeted Services for Children and Young People, 2007–08; Corporate Dir for Children and Families, 2008–11. *Publications:* Strategies for Building School Improvement, 2002; Grasping the Nettle: early intervention for children and families, 2011. *Recreations:* ski-ing, cycling, cookery, travel, football. *Address:* Nottingham City Council, Loxley House, Station Street, Nottingham NG2 3NG. *T:* (0115) 876 3600. *E:* ian.curryer@nottinghamcity.gov.uk.

**CURTEIS, Ian Bayley,** FSA; dramatist; *b* 1 May 1935; *m* 1st, 1964, Mrs (Dorothy) Joan Macdonald (marr. diss.; she *d* 2009); two *s*; 2nd, 1985, Joanna Trollope, *qv* (marr. diss. 2001); two step *d*; 3rd, 2001, Lady Deirdre Freda Mary Hare, *e d* of 5th Earl of Listowel, GCMG, PC and *widow* of 7th Baron Grantley, MC; two step *s*. *Educ:* Iver Council Sch.; Slough Grammar Sch.; Slough Trading Estate; London Univ. FSA 2011. Director and actor in theatres all over Great Britain, and BBC-tv script reader, 1956–63; BBC and ATV staff director (drama), directing plays by John Betjeman, John Hopkins, William Trevor and others, 1963–67. Pres., Writers' Guild of GB, 1998–2001 (Mem. Exec. Council and Chm. various cttees, 1979–2001). Founder and Trustee, Joanna Trollope Charitable Trust, 1995–2003. *Television plays:* Beethoven, Sir Alexander Fleming (BBC's entry at 1973 Prague Fest.), Mr Rolls and Mr Royce, Long Voyage out of War (trilogy), The Folly, The Haunting, Second Time Round, A Distinct Chill, The Portland Millions, Philby, Burgess and Maclean (British entry 1978 Monte Carlo Fest., BAFTA nomination), Hess, The Atom Spies, Churchill and the Generals (BAFTA nomination; Grand Prize, Best Programme of 1980, NY Internat. Film and TV Fest.), Suez 1956 (BAFTA nomination), Miss Morison's Ghosts (British entry 1982 Monte Carlo Fest.), The Mitford Girls, BB and Joe (trilogy), Lost Empires (adapted from J. B. Priestley), The Trials of Lady Sackville, Eureka (1st Euroserial simultaneously shown in UK, West Germany, Austria, Switzerland, Italy and France), The Nightmare Years, The Zimmerman Telegram, The Choir (dramatisation of Joanna Trollope novel), The Falklands Play; also originated and wrote numerous popular television drama series; *film screenplays:* Andre Malraux's La Condition humaine, 1982; Graham Greene's The Man Within, 1983; Tom Paine (for Sir Richard Attenborough), 1983; *plays:* A Personal Affair, Globe, 1982; The Bargain, Bath and nat. tour, 2007; Lafayette, NY, 2015; *radio plays:* Eroica, 2000; Love, 2001; The Falklands Play, 2002; After the Break, 2002; More Love, 2003; Yet More Love, 2004; Miss Morison's Ghosts, 2004; Boscobel, 2008; Last Tsar, 2009; The Road to Yalta, 2014; The Bargain, 2016. *Publications: plays:* Long Voyage out of War (trilogy), 1971; Churchill and the Generals, 1979; Suez 1956, 1980; The Falklands Play, 1987; numerous articles and speeches on the ethics and politics of broadcasting. *Recreations:* history of art, history of architecture, country pursuits. *Address:*

Markenfield Hall, Ripon, N Yorks HG4 3AD. *T*: (01765) 603411; 2 Warwick Square, SW1V 2AA. *T*: (020) 7821 8606. *Clubs*: Beefsteak, Garrick.
*See also T. A. Curteis.*

**CURTEIS, Tobit Armstrong,** FIIC; FSA; architectural conservator, Tobit Curteis Associates LLP, since 1996; *b* 2 March 1966; *s* of Ian Bayley Curteis, *qv* and late Dorothy Joan Curteis; *m* 1996, Victoria Ellen Kaye; one *s* one *d*. *Educ*: King's Sch., Canterbury; Univ. of Warwick (BA Hons Hist. of Art 1988); Courtauld Inst. of Art, Univ. of London (Dip. Conservation of Wall Paintings 1991). Research and treatment projects include: Winchester Cathedral, 1995, 2012–; Hill Hall (English Heritage), 1995–2005; Chartwell (NT), 1998–2005; Fitzwilliam Mus., Cambridge, 1999–2001; Peterborough Cathedral, 1999–2005; Cormac's Chapel, Cashel, Ireland, 2001–; St John's Coll., Cambridge, 2002; Golden Temple, Amritsar, 2003; Worcester Cathedral, 2003–06, 2017–; Hampton Court Palace, 2004–; Chinese Palace, St Petersburg, Russia (World Monument Fund), 2004–08; Blickling Hall, Norfolk (NT), 2005; Lincoln Cathedral, 2006; Canterbury Cathedral, 2008–; Windsor Castle, 2009–10; King's Coll. Chapel, Cambridge, 2010–; Westminster Cathedral, 2011–15; Hypogeum Hal Saflieni, Malta, 2011–13; Knole, Kent (NT), 2011–; York Minster, 2011–; Rochester Cathedral, 2011–; Westminster Abbey, 2013–; Exeter Cathedral, 2013–; Durham Cathedral, 2013–; St Paul's Cathedral, 2013–; Coventry Cathedral, 2014–; Liverpool Metropolitan Cathedral, 2016–; Carlisle Cathedral, 2016–17; Eton Coll., 2016; Palace of Westminster, 2018–; St Patrick's Cathedral, Dublin, 2018–. Mem., Fabric Adv. Cttee, Rochester Cathedral, 2015–. Consultant to Historic England (formerly English Heritage) on conservation of wall paintings, 2002–; Wall Paintings Advr to NT, 2005–. FIIC 2003; FSA 2015. *Publications*: (ed jtly) Building Environment, 2014; contrib. numerous articles and published lectures to conf. proc. and professional jls. *Recreations*: paragliding, hill walking, cooking. *Address*: Tobit Curteis Associates LLP, 33 Cavendish Avenue, Cambridge CB1 7UR. *T*: (01223) 501958, *Fax*: (01223) 790225. *E*: tc@tcassociates.co.uk.

**CURTICE, Prof. Sir John (Kevin),** Kt 2018; FBA 2014; FRSE; FAcSS; Professor of Politics, University of Strathclyde, since 1998; *b* Redruth, Cornwall, 10 Dec. 1953; *s* of Thomas John and Mildred Winifred Curtice; *m* 1978, Dr Lisa Joan Riding; one *d*. *Educ*: Truro Sch.; Magdalen Coll., Oxford (MA). Gwilym Gibbon Prize Res. Fellow, Nuffield Coll., Oxford, 1981–83; Lectr in Politics, Univ. of Liverpool, 1983–88; University of Strathclyde: Lectr in Politics, 1988–89; Sen. Lectr in Politics, 1989–96; Reader in Politics, 1997; Dir, Social Stats Lab., 1989–2009. Fellow in Residence, Netherlands Inst. for Advanced Study, 1988–89. Co-Dir, British Election Study, 1983–98. Res. Consultant, 2001–15, Sen. Res. Fellow, 2015–, NatCen/ScotCen Social Res. Freelance broadcaster and newspaper commentator, 1979–. President: British Polling Council, 2008–; British Politics Gp, 2012–14. FRSA 1992; FRSE 2004; FAcSS (AcSS 2013). Hon. FSS 2017. *Publications*: (jtly) How Britain Votes, 1985; (jtly) Understanding Political Change, 1991; (ed jtly) British Social Attitudes Reports, annually, 1994–; (ed jtly) Labour's Last Chance, 1994; (jtly) On Message, 1999; (jtly) The Rise of New Labour, 2001; (jtly) New Scotland, New Politics, 2001; (jtly) New Scotland, New Society?, 2002; (ed jtly) Devolution: Scottish answers to Scottish questions?, 2003; (ed jtly) Has Devolution Delivered?, 2006; (ed jtly) Has Devolution Worked?, 2009; (jtly) Revolution or Evolution? The 2007 Scottish Elections, 2009; contribs to ed books and contrib. papers to academic jls. *Recreations*: music, theatre, gardening, walking. *Address*: School of Government and Public Policy, University of Strathclyde, 16 Richmond Street, Glasgow G1 1XQ. *T*: 07710 348755. *E*: J.Curtice@strath.ac.uk. *Club*: National Liberal.

**CURTIS, Anne-Marie;** Editor-in-Chief, Elle UK, 2017–19; *b* Chelmsford, 29 July 1964; *d* of Sydney Colin Curtis and Margaret Mary Curtis; *m* 2009, Tony Matthew Collins; one *s* one *d*. *Educ*: Ursuline Convent High Sch., Brentwood; Univ. of Nottingham (BA Hons Fashion). Fashion Director: Sky Mag., 1990–95; Wallpaper, 1996–2003; freelance consultant, 2003–04; Fashion Dir, Elle UK, 2004–17. *Recreations*: walking on Hampstead Heath with our mini Schnauzer Edward aged 7, corralling our 2 teenage children Cecilia and Luca, fan of musicals, yoga attempter, lover of husband's cooking, amateur baker, film buff, avid reader.

**CURTIS, Sir Barry (John),** Kt 1992; Mayor of Manukau, New Zealand, 1983–2007; *b* 27 Feb. 1939; *s* of John Dixon Cory Curtis, Donaghadee, NI, and Vera Gladys Curtis (*née* Johnson); *m* 1961, Miriam Ann Brooke (marr. diss. 1991); three *d*. *Educ*: Otahuhu College; Univ. of Auckland (Dip. TP). MRICS, MNZIS, MNZPI. Town Planner, Chartered and Registered Surveyor. Manukau City Councillor, 1968–83; Member: Auckland Regl Authy, 1971–84 (Chm., Regl Planning Cttee, 1977–83); Prime Minister's Safer Communities Council, 1990–96; Chairman: Hillary Commn Task Force on Recreation, 1988; Jean Batten Meml Trust, 1989; Manukau Healthy City Cttee, 1989–93; Manukau Safer Community Council, 1990–93; Auckland Mayors' Forum, 1990–96, 2004–05; Electoral Coll., Infrastructure Auckland, 1998–2004; Auckland Regl Econ. Develt Strategy Establishment Gp, 2002–04; Nat. Taskforce for Community Violence Reduction Leaders Gp, 2005–07; Dep. Chm., Auckland Regl Growth Strategy Forum, 1996–2007; Dir, NZ Food Innovation (Auckland) Ltd, 2010–13. Past Pres., NZ Sister Cities Cttee. A Dir, XIVth Commonwealth Games Ltd, 1989–92 (Mem. Exec. Bd, 1989–90). Pres., Auckland Football Fedn, 2010–. Patron, Auckland Hockey Assoc. Valedictory Award, NZ Pacific Business Council, 2007. Seiuli (High Chief Matai title) conferred by HE Malietoa Tanumafili II, Western Samoa, 1993; Kaumatua conferred by Tuhoe and Te Arawa tribes, Aotearoa, 2007; Hon. Residence, Cook Islands, 2005. *Recreations*: jogging, surfing, gardening, follower of Rugby, hockey, cricket, tennis, yachting. *Address*: 1/1A The Esplanade, Eastern Beach, Manukau 2012, Auckland, New Zealand. *T*: (9) 5348153, *Fax*: (9) 5349153.

**CURTIS, Bronwen Mary,** CBE 2008; Director of Human Resources and Organisation Development, Northamptonshire Healthcare NHS Foundation Trust, 2011–15; *b* 17 May 1955; *d* of Hywel Arwyn Hughes and Doris Winifred Hughes (*née* Billingham); *m* 1990, Alan Curtis (marr. diss. 2002); one *s* (one *d* decd). *Educ*: Sheffield Poly. (HND Business Studies (Dist.)); University Coll., Cardiff (Postgrad. Dip. Personnel Mgt). Avon Cosmetics: Dir, UK Manufg, 1988–90; Vice President: Manufg, 1990–92; Planning and Develt, 1993–95; HR, 1995–2001. Chairman: Two Shires Ambulance Trust, 1995–98; Northampton Gen. Hosp. NHS Trust, 1998–2007. Home Sec.'s Rep., Northants Police Authy Selection Panel, 1997–2003; a Civil Service Comr, 2001–07; Ind. Mem., Sen. Salaries Rev. Bd, DCMS, 2005–08; Member: Prison Service Pay Rev. Body, 2007–12; NHS Pay Rev. Body, 2015–; Speaker's Cttee, Ind. Parly Standards Authy, 2016–; Disciplinary Panel, Judicial Conduct Investigations Office, 2016–; Regulatory Appts Panel, ICAEW, 2016–. Chairman: Appts Cttee, GDC, 2010–12; Sen. Remuneration Cttee, H of C, 2016–; Remuneration Cttee, Inst. and Faculty of Actuaries, 2017–. Non-executive Director: Nat. Archives, 2007–12; Northants Healthcare Trust, 2007–12; Service Personnel and Veterans Agency, 2009–12. Mem., Forum UK, 1990–. Midlands Businesswoman of Year, Winged Fellowship Trust, 1990. *Recreations*: playing and watching sport, learning from others, solving complex problems and making life easier for others.

**CURTIS, Bronwyn Nanette,** OBE 2008; Head of Global Research, HSBC Bank plc, 2008–13; *b* Bendigo, Australia; *d* of Edward J. and Loris M. Schlotterlein; *m* Paul G. Curtis (*d* 2011); one *s* one *d*. *Educ*: La Trobe Univ., Australia (BEc Hons); London Sch. of Econs (MSc Econ.). Sen. Manager, Mars Confectionery, 1977–82; Chief Economist, Gill and Duffus plc, 1982–84; Res. Dir, Landell Mills Commodities Studies, 1984–87; Global Hd, Currency and Fixed Income Strategy, Deutsche Bank, 1987–97; Chief Economist, Nomura Internat., 1997–99; Managing Ed. and Hd, Eur. Broadcasting, Bloomberg LP, 1999–2006; Econ. Advr, Arch Financial Products, LLP, 2006–08. Non-executive Director: JP Morgan Asian Investment Trust plc, 2013– (Chm., 2017–); Scottish Amer. Investment Trust plc, 2014–; Mercator Media Ltd, 2015–; Sen. Ind. Dir, Pershing Sq. Hldgs Ltd, 2018–. Chm., 2006–13, Vice Chm., 2013–16, Soc. of Business Economists. Chief Econ. Advr, Official Monetary and Financial Instns Forum, 2014–15. Consultant: UN, 1984–87; World Bank, 1984–87. Vis. Prof., Cass Business Sch., 1997–2005. Non-exec. Dir, OFT, 2007–08. Member: ESRC, 1998–2003; Bd of Mgt, NIESR, 2005–. Non-exec. Mem., Office for Budget Responsibility, 2018–. Gov., 2002–18, Mem. Council, 2009–12, LSE. Hon. DLitt La Trobe, 2017. *Publications*: Cocoa, A Trader's Guide, 1987. *Recreations*: yacht racing and cruising, ballet. *Clubs*: Royal Thames Yacht, Royal Southern Yacht.

**CURTIS, Cathleen, (Kate);** *see* Purkiss, C.

**CURTIS, Prof. Charles David,** OBE 2001; Independent Member, Repository Development Management Board, Nuclear Decommissioning Authority, 2008–16; *b* 11 Nov. 1939; *s* of Charles Frederick Curtis and Kate Margaret Curtis (*née* Jackson); *m* 1963, Dr Diana Joy Saxty; two *d*. *Educ*: Imperial College London, Univ. of Sheffield (BSc, PhD). University of Sheffield: Lectr, Sen. Lectr, Reader, 1965–83; Personal Chair in Geochem., 1983–88; University of Manchester: Professor of Geochemistry, 1988–2004, now Emeritus; Hd, Dept of Geology, 1989–92; Res. Dean, Faculty of Science and Engrg, 1994–2000. Hd of Res. and Develt Strategy, UK Nirex Ltd, 2004–07; Hd of Res. and Develt Strategy, Radioactive Waste Mgt Directorate, Nuclear Decommng Authy, 2007–08. Ind. non-exec. Mem. Bd, Dounreay Site Restoration Ltd, 2008–12; Ind. non-exec. Dir, Radioactive Waste Mgt Ltd, 2014–. Vis. Prof., Dept of Geology and Geophys., UCLA, 1970–71; Res. Associate, British Petroleum Res. Centre, 1987–88; Hon. Res. Fellow, Natural Hist. Mus., 1999–. Member: Council, NERC, 1990–93; Radioactive Waste Mgt Adv. Cttee, 1994–2004 (Chm., 1999–2004); Radioactivity Res. and Envmtl Monitoring Cttee, 1995–2004; Bd Assurance Cttee, UKAEA, 2002–. Pres., Geological Soc., 1992–94. Murchison Medal, Geological Soc., 1987. *Publications*: numerous articles in learned jls. *Recreations*: mountaineering, gardening, photography. *Address*: Lodestone, 55 Eccles Close, Hope, Hope Valley, Derbyshire S33 6RG.

**CURTIS, Colin Hinton Thomson,** CVO 1970; ISO 1970; retired; Chairman, Metropolitan Public Abattoir Board, 1971–81; Member, Queensland Meat Industry Authority, 1972–78; *b* 25 June 1920; *s* of A. Curtis, Brisbane; *m* 1943, Anne Catherine Drevesen; one *s*. *Educ*: Brisbane Grammar School. RANR Overseas Service, 1940–45. Sec. and Investigation Officer to Chm., Sugar Cane Prices Board, 1948–49; Asst Sec. to Central Sugar Cane Prices Board, 1949; Sec. to Premier of Queensland, 1950–64; Mem., Qld Trade Missions to SE Asia, 1963 and 1964; Asst Under-Sec., Premier's Dept, 1961–64; Assoc. Dir and Dir of Industrial Development, 1964–66; Under-Sec., Premier's Dept and Clerk of Exec. Council, 1966–70; State Dir, Royal Visit, 1970; Agent-General for Queensland in London, 1970–71. *Address*: 57 Daru Avenue, Runaway Bay, Gold Coast, Qld 4216, Australia. *Club*: RSL Memorial (Queensland).

**CURTIS, Daniel Nicholas Mansfield;** a District Judge (Magistrates' Courts), since 2005; *b* 15 May 1963; *s* of late Cyril Frank Paul Curtis and of Joyce Mary Curtis (*née* Bailey); two *s* two *d*. *Educ*: Boston Spa Comp. Sch.; King's Coll., London (LLB Hons). Partner, Tates, solicitors, 1992–2005; a Dep. District Judge, 2003–05. *Recreations*: travel, running (almost as slowly as District Judge Browne), golf, playing the drums. *Address*: Grimsby Magistrates' Court, Victoria Street, Grimsby, Lincs DN31 1PE. *T*: (01472) 320444, *Fax*: (01472) 320440. *E*: DJMC.Daniel.Curtis@ejudiciary.net.

**CURTIS, Major Sir Edward (Philip),** 8th Bt *cr* 1802, of Cullands Grove, Middlesex; *b* Livingstone, Northern Rhodesia, 25 June 1940; *s* of late Gerald Edward Curtis and Philippa Curtis (*née* Alcock); *S* cousin, 2014; *m* 1978, Catherine Mary (*née* Armstrong) (*d* 2015); two *s* two *d*. *Educ*: Bradfield Coll.; RMA Sandhurst. Commnd 16th/5th Queen's Royal Lancers, 1961; Adjt, 1970–71; Sqn Ldr, 1971–73; Co. Comdr, RMA Sandhurst, 1973–75; retired from Army, 1977. Stockbroker, 1981–2002. *Recreations*: cricket, fishing, shooting. *Heir*: *s* George Edward Curtis, *b* 31 Oct. 1980. *Clubs*: I Zingari, Free Foresters.

**CURTIS, Frank;** *see* Curtis, R. F.

**CURTIS, James William Ockford;** QC 1993; a Recorder, since 1991; *b* 2 Sept. 1946; *s* of late Eric William Curtis, MC, TD and Margaret Joan Curtis (*née* Blunt); *m* 1985, Genevra Fiona Penelope Victoria Caws, QC (*d* 1997); one *d*. *Educ*: Bedford Sch.; Worcester Coll., Oxford (MA Jurisp). Called to the Bar, Inner Temple, 1970. *Recreations*: farming, field sports, ski-ing, classics. *Address*: 21 College Hill, EC4R 2RP. *T*: (020) 3301 0910. *Club*: Flyfishers'.

**CURTIS, Most Rev. John Barry;** Honorary Assistant, St Matthew's Anglican Church, Ottawa, since 2008; Archbishop of Calgary, 1994–99; Metropolitan of Rupert's Land, 1994–99; *b* 19 June 1933; *s* of Harold Boyd Curtis and Eva B. Curtis (*née* Saunders); *m* 1959, Patricia Emily (*née* Simpson) (decd); two *s* two *d*. *Educ*: Trinity Coll., Univ. of Toronto (BA 1955, LTh 1958); Theological Coll., Chichester, Sussex. Deacon 1958, priest 1959; Asst Curate, Holy Trinity, Pembroke, Ont, 1958–61; Rector: Parish of March, Kanata, Ont, 1961–65; St Stephen's Church, Buckingham, Que, 1965–69; Church Schools Consultant, Diocese of Ottawa, 1969; Rector, All Saints (Westboro), Ottawa, 1969–78; Director of Programme, Diocese of Ottawa, 1978–80; Rector, Christ Church, Elbow Park, Calgary, Alta, 1980–83; Bishop of Calgary, 1983–99. Member, Governing Board: Canadian Council of Churches, 1994 (Pres., 1999); Habitat for Humanity Canada, 1994. Hon. DD Trinity Coll., Toronto, 1985. *Recreations*: reading, hiking, ski-ing, cycling. *Address*: Apartment 2527, 200 Clearview Avenue, Ottawa, ON K1Z 8M2, Canada. *T*: (613) 6801703. *Club*: Ranchmen's (Calgary, Alta).

**CURTIS, John Edward,** OBE 2006; PhD; FBA 2003; FSA; Keeper, Department of Middle East (formerly Department of Western Asiatic Antiquities, then of Ancient Near East), British Museum, 1989–2011; Chief Executive Officer, Iran Heritage Foundation, since 2014; *b* 23 June 1946; *yr s* of late Arthur Norman Curtis and of Laura Letitia Ladd (*née* Thomas); *m* 1977, Vesta Sarkhosh; one *s* one *d*. *Educ*: Collyer's Grammar Sch., Horsham; Univ. of Bristol (BA). Inst. of Archaeology, Univ. of London (Postgrad. Diploma in Western Asiatic Archaeology; PhD 1979). FSA 1984. Fellow, British Sch. of Archaeology in Iraq, 1969–71; Res. Asst, Dept of Western Asiatic Antiquities, British Museum, 1971–74, Asst Keeper, 1974–89. Chm., British Assoc. for Near Eastern Archaeol., 1996–2001; Member, Governing Council: British Sch. of Archaeol. in Iraq, 1980–2001 and 2002–08; British Inst. of Persian Studies, 1991–2001, 2002–05 and 2012–18; Pres., British Inst. for Study of Iraq, 2012–. Corresponding Member: German Archaeol Inst., 2010; Archaeol Inst. of America, 2013. Trustee: Ancient Persia Fund, 1987–; Honor Frost Foundn, 2012–; Chm., Friends of Basrah Mus., 2019– (Hon. Sec., 2010–19). Iran Heritage Foundn Award, 2005 and 2013; Persian Golden Lioness Award for Outstanding Research, 2008. *Publications*: (ed) Fifty Years of Mesopotamian Discovery, 1982; Nush-i Jan III: the Small

Finds, 1984; (ed) Bronzeworking Centres of Western Asia *c* 1000–539 BC, 1988; Excavations at Qasrij Cliff and Khirbet Qasrij, 1989; Ancient Persia, 1989, 2nd edn 2000; (ed) Early Mesopotamia and Iran: Contact and Conflict 3500–1600 BC, 1993; (ed with J. E. Reade) Art and Empire: treasures from Assyria in the British Museum, 1995; (ed) Later Mesopotamia and Iran: tribes and empires 1600–539 BC, 1995; (ed) Mesopotamia and Iran in the Persian period: conquest and imperialism 539–331 BC, 1997; (with A. R. Green) Excavations at Khirbet Khatuniyeh, 1997; (ed) Mesopotamia and Iran in the Parthian and Sasanian periods: rejection and revival *c* 238 BC–AD 642, 2000; (with M. Kruszyński) Ancient Caucasian and Related Material in the British Museum, 2002; (ed with N. Tallis) Forgotten Empire: the world of Ancient Persia, 2005 (Book of the Yr Prize, Islamic Republic of Iran, 2009); (ed with N. Tallis) The Balawat Gates of Ashurnasirpal II, 2008; (ed jtly) New Light on Nimrud, 2008; (ed with St John Simpson) The World of Achaemenid Persia: history, art and society in Iran and the Ancient Near East, 2010; (with N. Tallis) The Horse: from Arabia to Royal Ascot, 2012; (ed with R. Matthews) Proceedings of the 7th International Congress on the Archaeology of the Ancient Near East, 3 vols, 2012; An Examination of Late Assyrian Metalwork, 2013; The Cyrus Cylinder and Ancient Persia, 2013; articles in learned jls. *Address:* 4 Hillfield Road, NW6 1QE. *T:* (020) 7435 6153; 1 Francis Cottage, Sandy Hill Road, Saundersfoot, Dyfed SA69 9HW. *Club:* Athenaeum.

**CURTIS, Michael Alexander;** QC 2008; *b* Birmingham, 4 July 1959; *s* of Frank and Ann Curtis; *m* 1992, Cathleen Purkiss, *qv*; one *s* two *d*. *Educ:* King Henry VIII Sch., Coventry; Brasenose Coll., Oxford (MA); King's Coll. London (MSc). Called to the Bar, Middle Temple, 1982; in practice as barrister, specialising in construction, commercial and public law, 1982–. *Publications:* (ed) Emden's Construction Law. *Recreation:* watching football. *Address:* Crown Office Chambers, 2 Crown Office Row, Temple, EC4Y 7HJ. *T:* (020) 7797 8100, *Fax:* (020) 7797 8101. *E:* curtis@crownofficechambers.com. *Club:* Arsenal Football.

**CURTIS, Michael John;** Executive Director of Resources and Assets, Royal Borough of Kensington and Chelsea, since 2018; *b* 2 Aug. 1961; *s* of John and Sylvia Curtis; *m* 1992, Julie Thompson; two *s*. *Educ:* Portsmouth Poly. (BA Hons 1982); Miami Univ., Ohio (MA 1984); St Antony's Coll., Oxford. CPFA 1989. Trainee Accountant, 1986–89, Finance Manager, 1989–90, Kent CC; Projects Consultant, Berks CC, 1990–93; Manager, CSL Managed Services, 1993–95; Head of Financial Services, 1996–98, Dir of Finance, 1998–2001, Broxbourne BC; Asst Dir, Adult Care Services, Herts CC, 2001–06; Dir of Finance, then Corporate Dir of Finance and Resources, Islington Council, 2006–18. Bd Mem., B3Living (formerly Broxbourne Housing Assoc.), 2005–15 (Chm., Audit Cttee). Trustee and Treas., One World Action, 2006–12; Treasurer: Highfield Park Trust, 2011–; Old Albanians RFC, 2012–16. *Recreations:* travel, walking, reading, cricket, football, Rugby, theatre, music. *Address:* Royal Borough of Kensington and Chelsea, Town Hall, Hornton Street, W8 7NX.

**CURTIS, Monica Anne;** Head, Chelmsford County High School for Girls, 1997–2006; *b* 26 May 1946; *d* of H. L. Seale; *m* 1968, Timothy Chaytor Curtis (*d* 1986), former Dep. Dir, Lancashire Poly.; two *s*. *Educ:* Manchester Univ. (BA English and History of Art 1968). Teacher: Urmston Grammar Sch. for Girls, 1968–70; various schs in Newcastle upon Tyne, 1970–80; Lancaster Girls' Grammar Sch., 1980–89; Kesteven and Grantham Girls' Sch., 1989–97. Gov., Felsted Sch., Essex, 2003–13 (Chm., Govs' Academic Cttee, 2009–13). *Address:* 12 Rivington Road, Hale, Altrincham, Cheshire WA15 9PH.

**CURTIS, Prof. Paul Tyrrel,** PhD; FREng; FRAS; Senior Fellow, Defence Science and Technology Laboratory (formerly Defence Evaluation and Research Agency), Ministry of Defence, 1997–2017; *b* London; *s* of Noel Curtis and Constance Curtis; *m* 1977, Anne Denise Clark; one *s* three *d*. *Educ:* Christ's Coll., Cambridge (BA Hons Nat. Scis 1973); Univ. of Surrey (PhD 1976). FIMMM 1998; FRAeS 2004; FREng 2013; FRAS 2013. Joined Royal Aircraft Establishment, Farnborough, 1978; Principal Scientific Officer, DRA, Farnborough, 1991; Res. Fellow, Surrey Univ., 1997. Vis. Prof., 1997–, Sen. Res. Investigator (pt time), 2011–, Imperial Coll. London; Vis. Prof., Univ. of Bristol, 2004–. *Publications:* over 150 articles in learned jls. *Recreations:* Andover Astronomical Society, Andover Radio Amateur Society (callsign M0PTZ), family, walking, radio control model aircraft. *Address:* Aeronautics Department, Imperial College London, Prince Consort Road, SW7 2AZ. *T:* (020) 7594 5040. *E:* p.curtis@imperial.ac.uk. *W:* www.amateurastronomy.co.uk.

**CURTIS, Dr Penelope;** Director, Museu Calouste Gulbenkian, Lisbon, since 2015; *b* London, 24 Aug. 1961; *d* of late Prof. Adam Sebastian Genevieve Curtis and of Ann Curtis. *Educ:* Westbourne Sch., Glasgow; Corpus Christi Coll., Oxford (BA Mod. Hist. 1982); Courtauld Inst. of Art, London (MA Art Hist. 1985; PhD 1989). Exhibns Curator, Tate Gall., Liverpool, 1988–94; Hd, 1994–99, Curator, 1999–2010, Henry Moore Centre for the Study of Sculpture, later Henry Moore Inst., Leeds; Dir, Tate Britain, 2010–15. *Publications:* Barbara Hepworth, 1998, 5th edn 2010; Sculpture 1900–1945: after Rodin, 1999; Patio and Pavilion: the place of sculpture in modern architecture, 2007; Modern British Sculpture, 2011; Barbara Hepworth: sculpture for a modern world, 2015; Sculpture Vertical, Horizontal, Closed, Open, 2017. *Recreations:* the Hebrides, modern architecture, 19th-century novels. *Address:* Museu Calouste Gulbenkian, Avenida de Berna 45A, 1067–001 Lisbon, Portugal. *T:* (21) 7823417.

**CURTIS, Hon. Sir Richard Herbert,** Kt 1992; a Judge of the High Court of Justice, Queen's Bench Division, 1992–2005; Presiding Judge, Wales and Chester Circuit, 1994–97. *Educ:* Oxford Univ. (MA). Called to Bar, Inner Temple, 1958, Bencher, 1985; QC 1977; a Recorder, 1974–89; Recorder of Birmingham, 1989–92; Hon. Recorder, City of Hereford, 1981–92; Sen. Circuit Judge, Oxford and Midland Circuit, 1989–92. *Address:* c/o Royal Courts of Justice, Strand, WC2A 2LL.

**CURTIS, Richard Whalley Anthony,** CBE 2000 (MBE 1995); freelance writer; *b* 8 Nov. 1956; *s* of late Anthony J. Curtis and Glynness S. Curtis; partner, Emma Vallencey Freud, *qv*; three *s* one *d*. *Educ:* Papplewick Sch.; Harrow Sch.; Christ Church, Oxford (BA). Freelance writer: *television:* Not the Nine O'clock News (four series), 1979–83; Blackadder (four series), 1984–89; Mr Bean, 1989–95; Bernard and the Genie, 1993; The Vicar of Dibley, 1994–2000; The Girl in the Café, 2005 (Emmy Award, 2006); Mary and Martha, 2013; Esio Trot, 2015; *films:* The Tall Guy, 1988; Four Weddings and a Funeral, 1994; Bean, 1997; Notting Hill, 1999; (jtly) Bridget Jones's Diary, 2001 ((jtly) Best Screenplay, Evening Standard British Film Awards, 2002); (also dir) Love Actually, 2003; (jtly) Bridget Jones: The Edge of Reason, 2004; (also dir) The Boat that Rocked, 2009; (jtly) War Horse, 2012; (also dir) About Time, 2013; Mamma Mia! Here We Go Again, 2018; Yesterday, 2019; producer, Comic Relief, 1985–2003. Campaigner, Make Poverty History and Live 8, 2005. Fellow, BAFTA, 2007. Outstanding Contribn to British Film and TV Award, Dirs' Guild of GB, 2004. *Recreations:* too much TV, too many films, too much pop music. *Address:* c/o United Agents, 12–26 Lexington Street, W1F 0LE.

**CURTIS, Prof. (Robert) Frank,** CBE 1985; PhD, DSc; Chairman, Norfolk Mental Health Care NHS Trust, 1994–98; Professor, University of East Anglia, 1977–88, Hon. Professor, 1988–2001; *b* 8 Oct. 1926; *s* of late William John Curtis, Somerset, and Ethel Irene Curtis, Bath; *m* 1954, Sheila Rose, *y d* of Bruce Rose, Huddersfield; two *s* one *d*. *Educ:* City of Bath Sch.; Univ. of Bristol (BSc 1949, PhD 1952, DSc 1972). FRIC 1966; FIFST 1977. Johns Hopkins University: W. H. Grafflin Fellow, 1952; Instr in Chemistry, 1953; Technical Officer, ICI Ltd, Manchester, 1954–56; Res. Fellow, Univ. of WI, 1956–57; Lectr in Chem., University Coll., Swansea, 1957–62, Sen. Lectr, 1962–69; Reader, Univ. of Wales, 1969–70; Head, Chem. Div., 1970–77, Dir, 1977–85, ARC Food Res. Inst.; Dir, AFRC Inst. of Food Res., Reading, 1985–88. Chm., Food Adv. Cttee, MAFF, 1983–88 (Chm., Food Standards Cttee, 1979–83); Mem. Management Bd, AFRC, 1987–88. Mem., Norwich HA, 1989–94 (Vice-Chm., 1993–94); Mem. Council, RVC, 1991–2000. Hon. ScD UEA, 1988. *Publications:* res. papers on chemistry and food science in jls of learned socs. *Address:* Manor Barn, Colton, Norwich NR9 5BZ. *T:* (01603) 880379.

**CURTIS, Prof. Sarah Elizabeth,** DPhil; FBA 2014; FRSE; FAcSS; FRGS; Professor of Health and Risk, 2006–16, now Emeritus, and Executive Director, Institute of Hazard Risk and Resilience, 2012–16, Durham University; *d* of Dr Leonard Curtis and Diana Curtis; *m* Brian Blundell. *Educ:* Redland High Sch. for Girls, Bristol; St Hilda's Coll., Oxford (BA Geog.); Univ. of Kent at Canterbury (DPhil Urban and Regl Studies 1981). Res. Associate, Personal Social Services Res. Unit, Univ. of Kent, 1979–81; Department of Geography, Queen Mary College, subseq. Queen Mary and Westfield College, then Queen Mary, University of London: Res. Fellow, 1981–84; Sen. Res. Fellow, 1984–88; Lectr, 1988–91; Sen. Lectr, 1991–95; Reader in Geog., 1995–99; Prof. of Geog., 1999–2006. Hon. Prof., Univ. of Edinburgh, 2017–. MRSocMed; Mem., Soc. of Social Medicine. FHEA; FRSE 2018. *Publications:* Health and Inequality: geographical perspectives, 2004; Space, Place and Mental Health, 2010; contribs to learned jls incl. Social Sci. and Medicine, Health and Place, Envmt and Planning. *Recreations:* music, gardening. *E:* s.e.curtis@durham.ac.uk.

**CURTIS, Stephen Russell;** Chairman, Association of Company Registration Agents Ltd, 2009–18; *b* 27 Feb. 1948; *s* of Barry Russell and Joyce Muriel (*née* Smith); *m* 1972, Gillian Mary Pitkin; three *s* one *d*. *Educ:* Forest Sch., E17; Exeter Univ. (BA Econs and Stats). Asst Statistician, Business Stats Office, 1970–72; DTI, 1972–78, Statistician, Export Stats, 1975–78; Statistician, 1978–83, Chief Statistician, 1983–85, Business Stats Office; Registrar of Companies, 1985–90, and Chief Exec., 1988–90, Companies House; Chief Exec., DVLA, 1990–95; Man. Dir, Professional Services Div., Jordans Ltd, 1997–2003; Statistician, 2004–. *Recreations:* travel, photography, walking.

**CURTIS-RALEIGH, Dr Jean Margaret Macdonald,** FRCPsych; Consultant Psychiatrist, Queen Mary's University Hospital, Roehampton, 1979–98; *b* 12 July 1933; *d* of late Dr Harry Hubert Steadman and Janet Gilchrist Steadman (*née* Macdonald); *m* 1964, His Honour Judge Nigel Hugh Curtis-Raleigh (*d* 1986); five *s*. *Educ:* Convent of the Sacred Heart, Epsom, Surrey; Sutton High Sch. for Girls; Guy's Hospital Med. Sch. (MB BS). DPM 1965; MRCPsych 1973, FRCPsych 1996. Psychiatric trng, Maudsley and Bethlem Royal Hosps, 1963–66. Med. Mem., Mental Health Review Tribunal, 1994–2006. Mem., Broadcasting Standards Council, 1988–95. *Recreations:* opera, gardening, walking.

*See also* J. H. Steadman.

**CURTIS-THOMAS, Claire;** Chief Executive, British Board of Agrément, since 2013; *b* 30 April 1958; *d* of late Joyce Curtis; *m* Michael Louis Jakub; one *s* two *d*. *Educ:* Mynyddbach Comp. Sch. for Girls, Swansea; UC Cardiff (BSc); Aston Univ. (MBA). CEng; FIMechE 1995; FIET (FIEE 2000). Shell Chemicals, 1990–92; Hd, Strategic Planning, 1992–93, Hd R&D Lab., 1993–95, Birmingham CC; Dean, Faculty of Business and Engrg, Univ. of Wales Coll. Newport (formerly Gwent Coll. of Higher Educn), 1996–97. MP (Lab) Crosby, 1997–2010. Member: Home Affairs Select Cttee, 2003–05; Sci. and Technology Select Cttee, 1997–2002. CEO, Instn of Gas Engineers and Managers, 2011–13. Senator, Engrg Council, 1996–2002; Mem., Engrg Technol. Bd, 2002–08. Chair: Waterloo Partnership, 2006–08; Construction and Develt Partnership, 2008–. Pres., Instn of Engrg Designers, 2003–06 (Hon. FIED). Pres., SETup (Promotion of Science Engrg and Technol.), 1997–2005; Patron Trustee, Severn Bridges Trust; Trustee, IMechE, 2005–10. FICES 2000; FCGI 2001. Hon. PhD Staffordshire Univ., 1999. *Address:* British Board of Agrément, Bucknalls Lane, Watford, Herts WD25 9BA. *E:* curtisthomasc@gmail.com.

**CURTISS, Jonathan;** Executive Director for Human Resources (job-share), Bank of England, since 2017; *b* Warminster, Wilts, 8 April 1966; *s* of Dennis Curtiss and Irene Curtiss; *m* 1991, Allison Jane Horton; two *d*. *Educ:* Kingdown Comp. Sch., Warminster. FCIPD 2013. Bank of England: Manager, Statistics, 1983–89; Manager, IT Mgt, 1990–2006; on secondment to FSA, 2007; Hd, Human Resources, 2008–13; Project Dir, 2014–17. Mem., Audit and Risk Cttee, Univ. of Nottingham, 2016–18. *Recreations:* gym, walking, theatre, dog.

**CURWEN, Peter Stewart;** Director, Economics and Financial Affairs, UK Representation to the European Union, Brussels, since 2015; *b* 25 Oct. 1963; *s* of late Brian Stewart Curwen and Pamela Westgarth Curwen (*née* Jones); *m* 1996, Helene Radcliffe; one *s* one *d*. *Educ:* King Edward VI Grammar Sch. for Boys, Aston; Manchester Univ. (BA Econ Hons); Warwick Univ. (MA Econs). Economist, MSC, 1985–87; HM Treasury: Macroeconomist, 1987–90; World economy forecaster, Econ. Advr, 1991–94; EU coordination and strategy, 1994–96; Dep. Hd, Communications, 1996–97; Head: Communications, 1997–99; EU and Internat. Tax Team, 1999–2002; on secondment to FCO, as Counsellor, Econs, Finance and Tax, UK Perm. Repn to EU, 2002–06; Dir, Budget and Tax Policy, 2006–08; Dir, Europe, 2008–15. *Recreations:* golf, tennis, ski-ing, campanology. *Club:* Sandy Lodge Golf (Northwood, Middx).

**CURZON;** see Roper-Curzon, family name of Baron Teynham.

**CURZON,** family name of **Earl Howe** and **Viscount Scarsdale**.

**CURZON, Viscount; Thomas Edward Penn Curzon;** *b* 22 Oct. 1994; *s* and *heir* of Earl Howe, *qv*.

**CUSACK, Niamh;** actress; *b* 20 Oct. 1959; *d* of late Cyril James Cusack and Mary Margaret, (Maureen), Cusack (*née* Kiely); *m* 2001, Finbar Lynch; one *s*. *Educ:* Scoil Lorcáin; Coláiste Iosagáin; Royal Acad. of Music; Guildhall Sch. of Music and Drama. Actress in theatre, television, film and radio; *theatre* includes: Royal Shakespeare Company: Othello, 1985; Romeo and Juliet, 1986; As You Like It, 1996; Macbeth, 2018; National Theatre: His Dark Materials, 2003–04; The Enchantment, 2007; The Curious Incident of the Dog in the Night-Time, 2012, transf. West End, 2013; other productions: Three Sisters, Gate, Dublin, then Royal Court, 1990; Playboy of the Western World, Old Vic, 1991; A Doll's House, 1993; Ghosts, 2007, Gate, Dublin; Dancing at Lughnasa, 2009, Cause Célèbre, 2011, Old Vic; Juno and the Paycock, Bristol Old Vic, then Liverpool Playhouse, 2014; Afterplay, Crucible, Sheffield, 2014; The Rehearsal, Minerva, Chichester, 2015; Ticking, Trafalgar Studios, 2015; The Winter's Tale, Sam Wanamaker Playhouse, 2016; Unfaithful, Found 111, 2016; Ghosts, Home Th., Manchester, 2016; My Brilliant Friend, Rose Th., 2017, transf. NT, 2019; The Remains of the Day, Royal Th., Northampton, and UK tour, 2019; *television* series: Heartbeat, 1992–95; Always and Everyone, 1999–2002; The Hollow Crown, 2012; The Virtues, 2019; *films:* Fools of Fortune, 1990; The Playboys, 1992; The Closer You Get, 2000; Hereafter, 2011; Departure, 2015. *Recreations:* walking, reading, people watching. *Address:* c/o Independent Talent Group, 40 Whitfield Street, W1T 2RH.

**CUSACK, Dr Stephen Anthony,** PhD; FRS 2015; Group Leader, Senior Scientist and Head, Grenoble Outstation, European Molecular Biology Laboratory, since 1989; *b* 1952. *Educ:* Caius Coll., Cambridge (BSc Physics and Theoretical Physics 1973); Imperial Coll., London (PhD Theoretical Solid State Physics 1976). Postdoctoral work, 1976–80, staff scientist, 1980–89, EMBL Grenoble. Eur. Res. Council Advanced Investigator. Mem., EMBO, 1998. *Publications:* contribs to scientific jls. *Address:* European Molecular Biology Laboratory, 71 avenue des Martyrs, CS 90181, 38042 Grenoble Cedex 9, France.

**CUSCHIERI, Prof. Sir Alfred,** Kt 1998; MD; FRCS, FRCSE; FRSE; Professor of Surgery, Scuola Superiore S'Anna di Studi Universitari, Pisa, since 2003; Chief Scientific Advisor, Institute for Medical Science and Technology, University of Dundee, since 2008; *b* 30 Sept. 1938; *s* of Saviour and Angela Cuschieri; *m* 1966, Marguerite Holley; three *d*. *Educ:* Univ. of Malta (MD 1961); Univ. of Liverpool (ChM 1968). FRCSE 1965; FRCS 1967; FRSE 1998. University of Liverpool: Sen. Lectr in Surgery, 1970–74; Reader, 1974–76; Prof., and Hd of Dept of Surgery, Univ. of Dundee, 1976–2003. Dir, Minimal Access Therapy Unit for Scotland, 1992–2000. Mem. Council, RCSE, 1980–; President: Internat. Hepatobiliary Pancreatic Assoc., 1992–93; European Assoc. Endoscopic Surgeons, 1995–97. Founder FMedSci 1998. Hon. FRCSGlas 1996; Hon. FRCSI 1996. Hon. MD Liverpool, 1997; Hon. DSc: Abertay, 2002; St Andrews, 2007; Hon. LLD Dundee, 2007. Gold Medal, Scandinavian Soc. Gastroenterology, 1990; Society Prize for pioneering work in minimal access surgery, Internat. Soc. of Surgery, 1993. *Publications:* Essential Surgical Practice, 1986, 4th edn 2001; contrib. to learned jls incl. Brit. Jl Surgery, Surgical Endoscopy, Lancet, Annals of Surgery, Archives of Surgery. *Recreations:* music, fly-fishing, carving. *Address:* Denbrae Mill, Strathkinness Low Road, St Andrews, Fife KY16 9TY. *T:* (01334) 475046. *Club:* Athenæum.

**CUSENS, Prof. Anthony Ralph,** OBE 1989; PhD; FRSE; FREng; FICE, FIStructE; Professor of Civil Engineering, University of Leeds, 1979–92, now Emeritus (Dean, Faculty of Engineering, 1989–91); *b* 24 Sept. 1927; *s* of James Henry Cusens and May Edith (*née* Thomas); *m* 1953, Pauline Shirin German; three *d*. *Educ:* St John's Coll., Southsea; Portsmouth Municipal Coll.; University Coll. London (BSc Eng; PhD 1955). FICE 1966; FIStructE 1972; FASCE 1972; FREng (FEng 1988). FRSE 1974. Res. Engr, British Cast Concrete Fedn, 1952–54; Sen. Lectr, RMCS, Shrivenham, 1954–56; Sen. Lectr, Univ. of Khartoum, Sudan, 1956–60; Prof. of Structl Engrg, Asian Inst. of Technol., Bangkok, 1960–65; Prof. of Civil Engineering: Univ. of St Andrews, 1965–67; Univ. of Dundee, 1967–78. Visitor, Transport and Road Res. Lab., 1982–88; President: Concrete Soc., 1983–84; IStructE, 1991–92; Chairman: Jt Bd of Moderators of ICE, IStructE and CIBSE, 1986–89; UK Certifying Authy for Reinforcing Steels, 1994–2001. Hon. DSc Aston, 1993. *Publications:* (jtly) Bridge Deck Analysis, 1975; Finite Strip Method in Bridge Engineering, 1978; res. papers on concrete technol. and structures. *Recreations:* golf, gardening, family history. *Address:* c/o Holly Lodge, Fulbeck, Morpeth NE61 3JT.

**CUSHING, Her Honour Penny;** a Circuit Judge, 2013–16; *b* 10 April 1950; *d* of George Norman Cushing and Doris Cushing. *Educ:* Birkenhead High Sch. (GPDST); University Coll., London (LLB Hons 1971). Admitted solicitor, 1974; Solicitor: London Bor. of Harrow, 1974–75; Camden Community Law Centre, 1975–80; Trng Officer, Law Centres Fedn, 1980–83; Partner, Cushing & Kelly, subseq. Clinton Davis Cushing & Kelly, solicitors, 1983–90; Mem., Mental Health Act Commn, 1991–94; District Judge, Principal Registry, Family Div., 1994–2013. Performed in: Medea, Edinburgh Fringe, 2008; Blue Remembered Hills, 2012; dir, The Tempest, 2012. *Recreations:* theatre, reading, gardening, walking, singing.

**CUSHING, Philip Edward;** Chairman, Loyalty Street, since 2014; *b* 9 Sept. 1950; *s* of Cyril Edward Willis Cushing and Marguerite Ellen Cushing (*née* Whaite); *m* 1st, 1972, Margareta Barbro Westin (marr. diss.); one *s* one *d*; 2nd, 2000, Ruth Christine Clarke. *Educ:* Highgate Sch.; Christ's Coll., Cambridge (BA 1st Cl. Hons Econs). Marketing Manager, Norprint Ltd, 1972–78; Man. Dir, Modulex Systems, 1978–84; Norton Opax plc: Marketing Dir, 1984–86; Chief Exec., Internat. Ops, 1986–89; Inchcape plc: Chief Exec., Inchcape Berhad, 1990–92; Dir, Services, 1992–95; Gp Man. Dir, 1995–96; Gp Chief Exec., 1996–99; Chief Exec., Vitec, 2000–01. Chairman: Paragon Print and Packaging Ltd, 2002–13; DCI Biologicals Inc., 2002–11; Strix Investments Ltd, 2007–08; Wrapfilm Systems Ltd, 2008–13; American Golf Ltd, 2010–12; Dir, Ikon Office Solutions, 1998–2008. *Recreations:* golf, reading, bridge, cricket, travel, music.

**CUSHING, Sir Selwyn (John),** KNZM 1999; CMG 1994; FCA; Chairman: Skellerup Holdings Ltd, 2007–17; New Zealand Rural Property Trust Management Ltd; Director, Rural Equities Ltd (Chairman, 2004–11); *b* 1 Sept. 1936; *s* of Cyril John Cushing and Henrietta Marjory Belle Cushing; *m* 1964, Kaye Dorothy Anderson; two *s*. *Educ:* Hastings High Sch.; Univ. of NZ. FCA 1957; ACIS 1958; CMA 1959. Dir, Esam Cushing & Co., later Forsyth Barr Esam Cushing, sharebrokers, Hastings, 1960–2011 (Partner, 1960–86); Brierley Investments Ltd: Exec. Dir, 1986–93; Chm. and Chief Exec., 1999–2001; Chairman: Carter Holt Harvey Ltd, 1991–93; Electricity Corp. of NZ, 1993–99; Director: Air New Zealand (Dep. Chm., 1988–98; Chm., 1998–2001); PGG Wrightson, 2005–12. Chm., NZ Symphony Orch. Ltd, 1996–2002. *Recreations:* cricket, music. *Address:* 1 Beatson Road, Hastings 4122, New Zealand. *T:* (6) 8786160. *Clubs:* Wellington; Auckland; Dunedin.

**CUSHLEY, Most Rev. Leo;** *see* St Andrews and Edinburgh, Archbishop of, (RC).

**CUSINE, Douglas James;** Sheriff of Grampian, Highland and Islands at Aberdeen, 2001–11 (at Peterhead, 2000–01); *b* 2 Sept. 1946; *s* of James Fechnie Cusine and Catherine Cusine (*née* McLean); *m* 1973, Marilyn Calvert Ramsay; one *s* one *d*. *Educ:* Hutchesons' Boys' Grammar Sch.; Univ. of Glasgow (LLB (Hons)). Admitted Solicitor, 1971; in private practice, 1971–74; Lectr in Private Law, Univ. of Glasgow, 1974–76; University of Aberdeen: Lectr in Private Law, 1976–82; Sen. Lectr in Conveyancing and Professional Practice of Law, 1982–90; Prof. (personal), 1990–92; Hugh McLennan Prof. of Conveyancing, 1990–2000. Temp. Sheriff, 1998–99; Hon. Sheriff: Aberdeen; Stonehaven. Member: Council, Law Soc. of Scotland, 1988–2000; Lord President's Adv. Council on Messengers-at-Arms and Sheriff Officers, 1989–2000; Legal Practice Course Bd, Law Soc. (England and Wales), 1993–97; Adv. Cttee on Feudal System, 1997–2000, Adv. Cttee on Real Burdens, 1998–2000, Scottish Law Commn; UK Mem., CCBE, 1997–2000; Rep., Internat. Union of Latin Notaries, 1989–97. Examiner, Messengers-at-Arms and Sheriff Officers, 1989–92; Examiner in Conveyancing, Faculty of Advocates, 1992–2011. Mem., AID sub-cttee, RCOG, 1976–79. Hon. Researcher in Law, Univ. of Glasgow. Mem., 1978, Fellow, 1981, Galton Inst. (formerly Eugenics Soc.). Review Ed., Jl Law Soc. of Scotland, 1988–98. *Publications:* (ed jtly) The Impact of Marine Pollution: law and practice, 1980; (ed jtly) Scottish Cases and Materials in Commercial Law, 1987, 2nd edn 2002; (ed) A Scots Conveyancing Miscellany: essays in honour of Professor Halliday, 1988; New Reproductive Techniques: a legal perspective, 1988; (jtly) The Law and Practice of Diligence, 1990; (ed jtly) Reproductive Medicine and the Law, 1990; (ed) The Conveyancing Opinions of Professor Halliday, 1992; Standard Securities, 1991, 2nd edn (jtly) 2002; (jtly) Missives, 1993, 2nd edn 1999; (jtly) The Requirements of Writing, 1995; (ed) Green's Practice Styles, vol. 1, 1996; (ed jtly) McDonald's Conveyancing Manual, 6th edn 1997; (jtly) Servitudes and Rights of Way, 1998; articles in legal journals. *Recreations:* golf, swimming, walking, bird watching, photography. *Address:* The Brae, Gurney Street, Stonehaven, Kincardineshire AB39 2EB.

**CUSK, Rachel Emma;** novelist and writer; *b* Saskatchewan, 8 Feb. 1967; *d* of Peter Cusk and Carolyn Cusk (*née* Woods); *m* 2001, Adrian Clarke (marr. diss.); two *d*, and one step *d*; *m* Siemon Scamell-Katz. *Educ:* St Mary's Convent, Cambridge; New Coll., Oxford (BA). Reader in Creative Writing, Kingston Univ. FRSL 2012. *Publications:* novels: Saving Agnes, 1992 (Whitbread First Novel Award, 1993); The Temporary, 1995; The Country Life (Somerset Maugham Award), 1997; The Lucky Ones, 2003; In the Fold, 2005; Arlington Park, 2006; The Bradshaw Variations, 2009; Outline, 2014; Transit, 2016; Kudos, 2018; non-fiction: A Life's Work: on becoming a mother (autobiog.), 2001; Aftermath: on marriage and separation (autobiog.), 2012; The Last Supper: a summer in Italy, 2009; Coventry, 2019; numerous articles and short stories; contrib. The Times, The Guardian, Daily Telegraph, Evening Standard, etc. *Address:* c/o The Wylie Agency, 17 Bedford Square, WC1B 3JA. *T:* (020) 7908 5900.

**CUST,** family name of **Baron Brownlow.**

**CUSTARD, Rakhi G.;** *see* Goss-Custard.

**CUSTIS, Ronald Alfred;** Director General, Energy Industries Council, 1981–92; *b* 28 Feb. 1931; *yr s* of late Alfred and Amy Custis, Dublin; *m* 1st, 1957, Enid Rowe (*d* 1984); one *s* one *d*; 2nd, 1986, Valerie Mackett (*née* Holbrook). *Educ:* The High Sch., Dublin. Joined HM Treasury, 1947; DES, 1964; Min. of Technology, 1964–70: Private Sec. to Permanent Under Sec., 1964–66; Principal, 1967; Sec. to Cttee of Inquiry into the Brain Drain, 1967–68; Min. of Aviation Supply, later MoD (Procurement Exec.), 1970–74: Private Sec. to Sec. of State for Defence, 1971–73; Asst Sec., 1973; Dept of Energy, 1974–81: Private Sec. to successive Secs of State for Energy, 1974–75; Under Sec., 1978; Dir Gen., Offshore Supplies Office, 1980–81. *Recreations:* reading, walking public footpaths, listening to music, gardening. *Address:* 11 Chantry Hall, Foxbury Lane, Westbourne, W Sussex PO10 8FG. *T:* (01243) 371450.

**CUSWORTH, Nicholas Neville Grylls;** QC 2009; a Recorder, since 2006; a Deputy High Court Judge, since 2011; *b* Barnes, London, 20 March 1964; *s* of Neville Cusworth and Susan Cusworth; *m* 1994, Rachel Platts; one *s* one *d*. *Educ:* St Paul's Sch., London; Christ Church, Oxford (BA Juris. 1985; MA). Called to the Bar, Lincoln's Inn, 1986, Bencher, 2018; barrister specialising in matrimonial finance. Hd of Chambers, 1 Hare Ct, 2011–17. Mem. Cttee, Family Law Bar Assoc., 1998– (Vice Chair, 2010–11; Chair, 2012–13); Member: Training for the Bar Cttee, Bar Council, 2006–11 (Chm., Recruitment and Entry Sub-Cttee, 2009–11); Money and Property Sub-Cttee, Family Justice Council, 2007–11. Liveryman, Stationers' Co., 1994. *Publications:* (contrib.) Essential Family Practice, 2000–02; (contrib.) Financial Provision in Family Matters, 2003–. *Recreations:* Queens Park Rangers FC, works of Bob Dylan. *Address:* 1 Hare Court, Temple, EC4Y 7BE. *T:* (020) 7797 7070. *E:* cusworth@1hc.com. *Club:* Garrick.

**CUTHBERT, Ceri Jayne;** *see* Jones, C. J.

**CUTHBERT, Sir Ian Holm;** *see* Holm, Sir Ian.

**CUTHBERT, Jeffrey Hambley;** Police and Crime Commissioner for Gwent, since 2016; *b* 4 June 1948; *s* of William and Jennie Cuthbert; *m* 1985, Catherine (marr. diss.); one *s* four *d*. *Educ:* University Coll., Cardiff (BSc Hons; Pres., Students' Union, 1974–75). Mining surveyor, Saudi Arabia, 1978–81, Libya, 1981–82, NCB. Sen. Consultant, Welsh Jt Educn Cttee; Principal (pt-time), Aberbargoed Adult Educn Centre. Mem. (Lab) Caerphilly, Nat. Assembly for Wales, 2003–16. Dep. Minister for Skills, 2011–13, for Skills and Technol., 2013; Minister for Communities and Tackling Poverty, 2013–14. Lead Police and Crime Comr in Wales for Combatting People Trafficking and Modern Slavery; Mem. Bd, Assoc. of Police and Crime Comrs. *Recreations:* reading, politics and trade union studies, walking, travel. *Address:* Police Headquarters, Cwmbran, Torfaen NP44 2XJ.

**CUTHBERT, Stephen Colin,** CBE 2005; FCA; Chief Executive, Port of London Authority, 1999–2004; *b* 27 Oct. 1942; *s* of Colin Samuel Cuthbert and Helen Mary Cuthbert (*née* Scott); *m* 1st, 1969, Jane Elizabeth Bluett (marr. diss. 1984); two *s* one *d*; 2nd, 1987, Susan Melanie Shepherd; one step *s* two step *d*. *Educ:* Trinity Sch. of John Whitgift; Bristol Univ. (BScEng). FCA 1968. Voluntary Service, UNRWA, Jordan, 1964–65; Price Waterhouse, London, 1965–76; Finance Dir, 1976–79, Chief Exec., 1980–93, Brent International plc; Dir Gen., Chartered Inst. of Marketing, 1994–99. Chm., UK Major Ports Gp, 2002–04. Dir, London Chamber of Commerce and Industry, 2000–02. Mem. Council, 1989–99, Chm. Southern Reg., 1992–93, CBI. Chm., Iain Rennie Grove House Hospice Care (formerly Iain Rennie Hospice at Home), 2006–13. Freeman: City of London, 1998; Co. of Watermen and Lightermen, 2000; Liveryman: Co. of Marketors, 1998–2006; Co. of Shipwrights, 2003–. *Recreations:* opera, gardening, family pursuits.

**CUTHBERT-BROWN, Col Mark,** CBE 2010; Vice Lord-Lieutenant of Shropshire, since 2017; *b* Hampton Court, 1957; *s* of John Cuthbert Cuthbert-Brown and Pauline Sheila Cuthbert-Brown (*née* Wade); *m* 1st, 1979, Rosamund Wood (marr. diss. 2007); one *s* one *d*; 2nd, 2018, Jayne Day. *Educ:* Chigwell Sch.; West Hatch Tech. High Sch.; RMA Sandhurst; Army Staff Coll., Camberley; Cranfield Univ. (MBA 1994). Commnd Corps of RMP, 1977, early service incl. NI with RMP and 1st Bn Argyll and Sutherland Highlanders, Berlin, US Army MP Sch., Ala and instructional tour, RMA Sandhurst; Command RMP Companies: Catterick, 1988; London, 1992–93; BAOR, Hohne, 1994; MoD, 1990–92; jsdc 1994; Provost Marshal: UN Assistance Mission, Rwanda, 1994–95; HQ 3 (UK) Div., 1995–98, incl. comd 3 Regt RMP, Balkans, 1995–96; MoD, 1998–2000; HQ ARRC, Rheindahlen, 2000–02; Dep. COS (Personnel and Logistics), HQ 5 Div., Shrewsbury, 2003–05; SO within US mil. team, Iraqi Min. of Interior, 2005–06; Dep. Comdr, then Comdr, Osnabrück Garrison, 2006–09, managing redeployment of Bde and closure of Garrison, 2009; Comdt, Royal Mil. Sch. of Music and Dir, Corps of Army Music, Kneller Hall, Twickenham, 2009–12. Dir, Daimler and Lanchester Owners' Club, 2012–; Member: Mil. Vehicle Trust; Shropshire Hortl Soc. (Mem. Cttee, 2013–); Shropshire Soc. in London (Pres., 2018–); Shropshire Gundog Soc. (Pres., 2018–). Hon. Mem., Kneller Hall Club, 2012. DL Shropshire. Queen's Commendation for Bravery, 1995; Bronze Star Medal (USA), 2006. *Recreations:* unsporting and un-new cars, Shropshire beers, spaniels, pheasant keeping, more spaniels, shooting, demise of grey squirrels, maintenance of footpaths (chairing parish voluntary group in partnership with Shropshire Council), spaniels. *Address:* c/o Assistant Clerk to the Lieutenancy, Shropshire Council, The Shirehall, Shrewsbury SY2 6ND. *T:* (01743) 742186. *E:* markcuthbertbrown@mac.com. *Club:* Victory Services.

**CUTHBERTSON, Lauren Louise;** Principal Dancer, Royal Ballet, since 2008; *b* Torquay, 11 June 1984. *Educ:* Royal Ballet Sch. Joined Royal Ballet, 2002; soloist, 2003, first soloist, 2006. Awards include: Lynn Seymour Award, 2000, Phyllis Bedell Prize, 2000, Royal Ballet Sch.; Young British Dancer of Year, Ricki Gail Conway, 2001; Critics Circle Award, 2004; Silver Medal, Varna Internat. Competition, 2006; Arts and Culture Woman of Future Award, Woman of the Future Awards, 2007. Patron: London Children's Ballet, 2007–; Nat. Youth Ballet, 2012–. *Recreations:* theatre, music, cinema, art galleries. *Clubs:* Ivy, h.

**CUTIFANI, Mark;** Chief Executive, Anglo American plc, since 2013; *b* Wollongong, Australia, 2 May 1958; *m* 1994, Luana Morgante; two *s* two *d*; one *s* two *d* from previous marriage. *Educ:* Wollongong Univ., NSW (BSc 1st Cl. Hons Engrg). FREng 2017. Trainee engr to Manager, Ops, CRA (Rio Tinto), Kembla Coal and Coke, 1976–88; Gen. Manager, Ops, Kalgoorlie Consolidated Gold Mines, 1988–93; Gen. Manager, Ops and CEO, Liddell Jt Venture Savage Resources, 1993–94; Ops Manager, Nickel Div., then Gp Manager, Project Mgt, Western Mining Corp., 1994–98; Gp Exec., Normandy Mining, 1998–2000; Man. Dir, Sons of Gwalia, 2000–03; Vice Pres., CanUK Div., then Pres., N America/Europe, later Chief Operating Officer, INCO, 2003–06; Chief Operating Officer, CVRD-INCO, 2006–07; CEO, Anglo Gold Ashanti, 2007–13. Chm., Internat. Council on Mining and Metals, 2013–15; Pres., SA Chamber of Mines; Dir, World Gold Council. Member: Internat. Adv. Council, Fundação Dom Cabral Brasil Univ.; Internat. Adv. Cttee, Kellogg Innovation Network, Northwestern Univ.; Adv. Bd, Grad. Sch. of Business, Univ. of Cape Town; Advr on global trends in sustainable business practices, Columbia Univ. Hon. Chair, World Mining Congress, 2013. Fellow, Australasian Inst. of Mining and Metallurgy, 2000. Rotary Paul Harris Fellowship Award, 2006. *Recreations:* Rugby, cricket, family. *Address:* Anglo American plc, 20 Carlton House Terrace, SW1Y 5AN. *T:* (020) 7968 8542.

**CUTLER, Prof. (Elizabeth) Anne,** PhD; FRS 2015; Research Professor, 2006–18 (part time, 2006–13, full time, 2013–18), Distinguished Professor, since 2018, MARCS Institute, Western Sydney University (formerly University of Western Sydney); Director, Max Planck Institute of Psycholinguistics, Nijmegen, 1993–2013, now Emeritus Director; Program Leader, ARC Centre of Excellence in the Dynamics of Language, since 2014; *b* Melbourne, 17 Jan. 1945; *d* of Clifford Ian Cutler and Betty Cutler (*née* O'Loghlen); *m* 1979, Anthony William Sloman. *Educ:* Univ. of Melbourne (BA 1964; DipEd 1966; MA 1971); Univ. of Texas, Austin (PhD 1975). Research Assistant: Univ. of Melbourne, 1966–67; Univ. of Bonn, 1968–69; Teaching Fellow, then Sen. Teaching Fellow, Monash Univ., 1969–71; Res. Asst and Teaching Asst, Univ. of Texas, Austin, 1972–75; Postdoctoral Fellow, MIT, 1975–76; Res. Fellow, Univ. of Sussex, 1976–82; Res. Scientist, MRC Applied Psychol. Unit, Cambridge, 1982–93; Prof. of Comparative Psycholinguistics, Radboud Univ. Nijmegen, 1995–2013. MAE 1999; Mem., Netherlands Royal Acad. of Scis, 2000; MNAS 2008. FAHA 2005; FASSA 2009. *Publications:* Native Listening, 2012; approx. 400 articles. *Recreation:* learning more (especially about food and wine). *Address:* MARCS Institute, Western Sydney University, Locked Bag 1797, Penrith South DC, NSW 2751, Australia.

**CUTLER, Keith Charles,** CBE 2010; **His Honour Judge Cutler;** a Senior Circuit Judge, since 2009; Resident Judge of Winchester and Salisbury, since 2009; Hon. Recorder of Salisbury, 2007–10 and of Winchester, since 2009; *b* 14 Aug. 1950; *s* of Henry Walter Cutler and Evelyn Constance Cutler; *m* 1975, Judith Mary Haddy; one *s* one *d*. *Educ:* Bristol Univ. (LLB Hons). Called to the Bar, Lincoln's Inn, 1972 (Bencher, 2005); Asst Recorder, 1989; Recorder, 1993–96; Circuit Judge, 1996–2009; Resident Judge, Salisbury, 2003–09; Additional Judge, Court of Appeal Criminal Div., 2013–. Asst Dep. Coroner for Inquest into death of Mark Duggan, 2013–14. Dep. Chancellor, dio. of Portsmouth, 2003–13; Wilts Magistrates Liaison Judge, 2006–09. Judicial Member: Parole Bd, 2001–04; Wilts Courts Bd, 2004–07; Chm., Salisbury and Dist, Mediation, 2001–09. Mem., Judges' Council, 2005–09 and 2012– (Chm., Standing Cttee on Communications and Media, 2009–); Pres., Council of HM Circuit Judges, 2012 (Asst Sec., 2003–04, 2009–10; Hon. Sec., 2005–09; Jun. Vice-Pres., 2010; Sen. Vice-Pres., 2011). Lay Canon, Salisbury Cathedral, 2009–14, now Lay Canon Emeritus. Mem. Council, Salisbury Cathedral, 2014–. *Recreations:* church music, history, maps, travel. *Address:* Winchester Combined Court Centre, Winchester SO23 9EL. *T:* (01962) 814100.

**CUTLER, Most Rev. Ronald Wayne;** *see* Nova Scotia and Prince Edward Island, Archbishop of.

**CUTLER, Timothy Robert, (Robin),** CBE 1995; Director-General and Deputy Chairman, Forestry Commission, 1990–95; *b* 24 July 1934; *s* of Frank Raymond Cutler and Jeannie Evelyn Cutler (*née* Badenoch); *m* 1958, Ishbel Primrose; one *s* one *d*. *Educ:* Banff Academy; Aberdeen Univ. (BSc Forestry 1956). National Service, Royal Engineers, 1956–58. Colonial Forest Service, Kenya, 1958–64; New Zealand Forest Service: joined 1964; Dir of Forest Management, 1978; Dep. Dir-Gen., 1986; Chief Exec., Min. of Forestry, 1988–90. Hon. DSc Aberdeen, 1992. *Recreations:* golf, gardening, stamps. *Address:* 14 Swanston Road, Fairmilehead, Edinburgh EH10 7BB.

**CUTRESS, James Stuart;** QC 2018; *b* Yemen, 26 March 1976; *s* of Ivan Cutress and Bahijeh Cutress; *m* 2009, Charlotte Warren-Gash; two *s*. *Educ:* Bedford Sch.; Worcester Coll., Oxford (BA 1997; BCL 1998); Harvard Univ. (Kennedy Schol.; LLM 1999). Called to the Bar, Lincoln's Inn, 2000 (Eldon Schol.); in practice as a barrister specialising in commercial law, Fountain Court Chambers, 2001–. *Publications:* (jtly) The Law of Privilege, 2006, 3rd edn 2018. *Recreations:* squash, hockey (blue, 1997, 1998), walking, ski-ing, reading. *Address:* Fountain Court, Temple, EC4Y 9DH. *T:* (020) 7583 3335.

**CUTTELL, Very Rev. Dr Jeffrey Charles;** Dean of Derby, 2008–10; Chaplain, HM Young Offender Institution, Werrington, 2010–15 and since 2019; *b* Giltbrook, Notts, 1959; *s* of late Vernon Howard Cuttell and Joan Cuttell (*née* Brown); *m* 1981, Dr Elizabeth Jane Beton; two *d*. *Educ:* Broadoak Comp. Sch., Weston-super-Mare; Birmingham Univ. (BSc 1980; PhD 1983); Trinity Theol Coll., Bristol (DipHE 1986); Sheffield Univ. (MA 1991). Res. Student, AERE Harwell, Oxon, 1980–83; ordained deacon, 1987, priest, 1988; Asst Curate, 1987–91, Vicar, 1991–95, Normanton; producer and presenter, BBC Religious Progs, 1995–99; Rector, Astbury with Smallwood, 1999–2008, 2015–19. Associate Lectr, Cardiff Univ., 2001–06; Tutor, St Michael's Theol Coll., Cardiff, 2001–06. Chaplain, 4th Bn Parachute Regt Res., 1997–2006. *Recreations:* spending time with my family, motorcycling, day dreaming, meeting interesting people, encountering serendipity. *Address:* Corner Cottage, Pools Lane, Smallwood, Sandbach, Cheshire CW11 2XD. *E:* jeffrey.cuttell@btinternet.com.

**CUTTER, David John;** Group Chief Executive, Skipton Building Society, since 2009; Chairman, Building Societies Association, 2013–15; *b* Bradford, 1 Jan. 1962; *s* of Geoffrey and Valerie Cutter; *m* 1987, Carol Ingham; three *s*. *Educ:* Malsis Sch.; Rugby Sch.; Durham Univ. (BA). ACA 1987. Grad. trainee to Sen. Audit Manager, KPMG, 1983–93; Skipton Building Society: Hd, Internal Audit, 1993–96; Gen. Manager, 1996–99; Exec. Dir, 2000–. *Recreations:* hockey, golf, piano. *Address:* Skipton Building Society, The Bailey, Skipton, N Yorks BD23 1DN. *T:* (01756) 705509. *E:* David.Cutter@skipton.co.uk. *Clubs:* Ben Rhydding Hockey, Ilkley Golf.

**CUTTING, Ven. Alastair Murray;** Archdeacon of Lewisham and Greenwich, since 2013; *b* Birmingham, 29 May 1960; *s* of William Alexander Murray Cutting and Margaret, (Margot), McLean Cutting (*née* Manderson); *m* 1984, Kay Elizabeth Greenhalgh; two *d*. *Educ:* George Watson's Coll., Edinburgh; Lushington Boys Sch., Ootacamund, S India; Watford Grammar Sch. for Boys; Westhill Coll., Birmingham (BEd 1983); St John's Coll., Nottingham (LTh; DPS 1987); Heythrop Coll., Univ. of London (MA 2003). Ordained deacon, 1987, priest, 1988; Curate: Woodlands, Doncaster, 1987–88; Wadsley, Sheffield, 1989–91; Chaplain to The Nave and Town Centre, Uxbridge, 1991–96; Vicar: Copthorne, W Sussex, 1996–2010; Henfield with Shermanbury and Woodmancote, W Sussex, 2010–13. *Recreations:* family and friends, South Indian food, Kiwiana. *Address:* Trinity House, 4 Chapel Court, Borough High Street, SE1 1HW. *T:* (020) 7939 9408, 07736 676106. *E:* Alastair.Cutting@southwark.anglican.org.

**CUTTS, Hon. Dame Johannah,** DBE 2018; **Hon. Mrs Justice Cutts;** a Judge of the High Court, Queen's Bench Division, since 2018; *b* Taplow, 13 Jan. 1964; *d* of Anthony and Jacqueline Cutts. *Educ:* Sch. of St Helen and St Katharine, Abingdon; Chelmer Inst. of Higher Educn (LLB Hons). Called to the Bar, Inner Temple, 1986; in practice as barrister, specialising in criminal law, particularly in cases involving vulnerable witnesses, 1986–2011; a Recorder, 2002–11; QC 2008; a Circuit Judge, 2011–18. *Publications:* (contrib.) Rook and Ward on Sexual Offences, 2003, 5th edn 2016. *Recreations:* walking my dogs in Somerset, travelling with my niece, relaxing and eating with friends. *Address:* Royal Courts of Justice, Rolls Building, Fetter Lane, EC4A 1NL.

**CYPRUS, Archdeacon in;** *see* Futcher, Ven. C. D.

**CYPRUS AND THE GULF, Bishop in,** since 2007; **Most Rev. Michael Augustine Owen Lewis;** President Bishop and Primate, Province of Jerusalem and the Middle East, since 2019; *b* 8 June 1953; *er s* of John Lewis, Swaythling, Hants, and Jean Lewis (*née* Pope); *m* 1979, Julia Donneky (*née* Lennox); one *s* one *d* (and one *s* decd). *Educ:* King Edward VI Sch., Southampton; Merton Coll., Oxford (Postmaster; BA Oriental Studies 1975; MA 1979); Cuddesdon Coll. (BA Theology, Oxon 1977). Ordained deacon, 1978, priest, 1979; Curate, Salfords, 1978–80; Chaplain, Thames Poly., 1980–84; Vicar, Welling, 1984–91; Team Rector, Worcester SE Team Ministry, 1991–99; Rural Dean, Worcester E, 1993–99; Canon, Worcester Cathedral, 1998–99; Bishop of Middleton, 1999–2007. Chairman: House of Clergy, Worcester Diocesan Synod, 1997–99; Diocesan Adv. Cttee, Worcester, 1998–99; Manchester Diocesan Bd of Educn, 2000–07; Jt Adv. Cttee, Church Colls and Univs, 2005–07; C of E Bd of Educn HE Panel, 2006–07; Member: Bd, Al-Amana Interfaith Centre, Muscat, Oman, 2008–; Internat. Commn for Anglican-Orthodox Theol Dialogue, 2009–; Anglican Consultative Council, 2012–19. Warden of Readers and Lay Assts, dio. of Manchester, 2001–07. Visitor, Community of the Sisters of the Love of God, Fairacres, Oxford, 2006–; Governing Trustee, St Michael's Coll., Llandaff, 2006–07. *Recreations:* enjoying architecture, food and drink, Middle Eastern and Caucasian travel. *Address:* Bishop's Office, St Paul's Cathedral, 2 Grigori Afxentiou, PO Box 22075, Nicosia 1517, Cyprus. *T:* (22) 671220, *Fax:* (22) 674553. *E:* bishop@spidernet.com.cy.

**CYRUS, Sir (Arthur) Cecil,** KCMG 2019 (CMG 2002); OBE 1985; Consultant Surgeon, Botanic Hospital, St Vincent, 1976–2001; Curator, Dr Cecil Cyrus Medical and Non Medical Museums of Memorabilia, since 2002; *b* Layou, St Vincent, WI, 6 Jan. 1929; *s* of Abraham Cyril Cyrus and Dorothy Ambrose Cyrus; *m* 1963, Kathryn Sinclair McTurk; two *s* two *d*. *Educ:* Layou Primary Sch., St Vincent; St Vincent Boys' Grammar Sch.; Queen's Univ. Belfast (BSc, MB BCH, BAO, MCh). DO; DObstRCOG; FRCS; FRCSE; FACS; DSc. Houseman, Royal Victoria Hosp., Belfast, 1957–58; Sen. Registrar, York County Hosp., 1961–63; Consultant Surgeon, Colonial Hosp., St Vincent, 1963–75. *Publications:* A Clinical and Pathological Atlas: the records of a surgeon in St Vincent, the West Indies, 1989; Dr Grandad: a Caribbean doctor and his little patients and family, 2012; A Dream Come True: the autobiography of a Caribbean surgeon, 2015; A Harvest Richer than Gold: an odyssey of a Caribbean surgeon, 2017. *Recreations:* squash, listening to classical music, writing, gardening. *Address:* Lismore, Government House Road, New Montrose, VC0100–359, St Vincent and the Grenadines. *T:* 4579781. *E:* cyrusclinic@gmail.com.

**CZAKÓ, Borbála;** Global Partner and Global Director, Ernst & Young Global Ltd, since 2010; *b* Budapest, 22 Nov. 1953; *d* of Jozsef Serfozo and Ilona Bock; two *d*. *Educ:* Budapest Tech. Coll. (BA 1975); Univ. of Econs, Budapest (MA 1987); Tulane Univ., New Orleans (MBA 1991). CDir 2011. Sen. Manager, Ernst & Young Hungary, 1989–91; Chief of Mission and Investment Officer, World Bank and IFC, 1991–2002; Man. Partner and Hd of Corporate Finance, Ernst & Young Hungary, 2002–07; Dep. Man. Partner, Central Europe and South, Ernst & Young, 2003–07; Ambassador of Hungary to the UK, 2007–10. Pres., Hungarian Business Leaders Forum, 2003–. Mem., Bd of Dirs, Central European Univ., 2003–06. Pro-Europe Award, 2005. *Recreations:* reading, theatre, gardening, cooking. *Address:* Ernst & Young Global Ltd, 1 More London Place, SE1 2AF.

**CZERNIN,** family name of **Baroness Howard de Walden.**

**CZERNIN, Hon. Peter John Joseph;** Co-Founder and Producer, Blueprint Pictures Ltd, since 2005; *b* London, 1 Jan. 1966; *s* of late Count Joseph Czernin and of Baroness Howard de Walden, *qv*; *m* 1994, Lucinda Wright; one *s* one *d*. *Educ:* Eton Coll.; Univ. of Bristol (BA Hons 1988). Producer of films including: In Bruges, 2008; The Best Exotic Marigold Hotel, 2011; Seven Psychopaths, 2012; The Riot Club, 2014; The Second Best Marigold Hotel, 2015; Three Billboards Outside Ebbing, Missouri, 2018; TV series, A Very English Scandal, 2018. Gov., BFI, 2014–. *Recreations:* Liverpool FC, the Turf, fishing, shooting, travel, literature, pop music. *Address:* Avington Manor, Hungerford, Newbury, Berks RG17 0UL.

**CZYZAK-DANNENBAUM, Peggy Scott;** Chairman, Maison Madeleine Ltd, 2013–16 (Director, since 2011); President, British Friends of Verbier Festival, since 2009; Member, Board, American Friends of Covent Garden, since 2007; *b* Cleveland, Ohio, 29 March 1947; *d* of John Joseph Czyzak and Marjorie Czyzak (*née* Kemp); *m* 1973, Karl Hermann Dannenbaum; four *s*. *Educ:* Wellesley Coll. (BA Hist. of Art 1969); London Business Sch. (MSc 1976); Alumni Achievement Award 1993; Alumni Service Award, 2011). Man. Dir, La Fornaia Ltd, 1985–95. Director: Thornton's plc, 1994–2002 (Chm., Audit Cttee, 1996–2002); Cavaghan & Grey Ltd, 1997–98; Village du Pain, 2002–09; Member Advisory Board: Sapphire Partners, 2006–; Hubbub Online Ltd, 2009–. Vice Chm., Wellhouse NHS Trust, 1991–94; Mem., Assessment Panel, 1993–96, Adv. Bd, 1996–99, Business Link. London Business School: Chm., UK Regl Adv. Bd, 1999–2009; Gov., 2001–07; Chm., Capital Soc., 2006–09; Mem., Global Adv. Council, 2009–. Vice Chm., Brogdale Horticl Trust, 2002–09. Member, Board of Trustees: Royal Opera House, 2006–10 (Chm., Friends Adv. Council, 2007–11); Florida Grand Opera, 2010–13. Mem., Develt Bd, World Wide Web Foundn, 2013–. FRSA. *Recreations:* opera, ballet, theatre, travelling, mountain hiking, reading, cooking (plus London Marathon, 2007). *Address:* Albany, I6, Piccadilly, W1J 0AZ. *T:* 07831 527755. *E:* peggy@czyzak.com; 6899 Collins Avenue, Miami Beach, FL 33141, USA. *Club:* Reform.

# D

**DABBOUS, Oliver Elie;** Chef and Owner, Hide, since 2018; *b* Kuwait City, 5 Oct. 1980; *s* of Gilbert Dabbous and Jan Dabbous. *Educ:* Cranleigh Sch. Commis to Sen. Chef de Partie, Le Manoir aux Quat'Saisons, Oxon, 2000–04; Sous Chef, Hibiscus, Ludlow, 2005; Chef de Partie, Mugaritz, San Sebastian, 2006; Hd Chef, Texture, 2007–09; freelance chef, 2009–11; Chef and Owner, Dabbous, 2012–17. *Publications:* Dabbous: the cookbook, 2014. *Address:* Hide, 85 Piccadilly, W1J 7NB.

**DABER, Timothy Mark;** a District Judge (Magistrates' Courts), since 2007; *b* Manchester, 24 Feb. 1958; *s* of Dr Keith Daber and Patricia Daber; *m* 2005, Karen Sonja Vanterpool; one *d*. *Educ:* William Hulme's Grammar Sch., Manchester; Sch. of Oriental and African Studies, Univ. of London (LLB Hons); Univ. of Portsmouth (Dip. Mgt Studies with dist.). Called to the Bar, Gray's Inn, 1981; Principal Court Clerk, SE Hants Magistrates' Courts, 1982–87; Principal Asst, S Hants Magistrates' Courts, 1987–98; Dep. Clerk to Justices, N Hants Magistrates' Courts, 1989–96; Clerk to N Cambs Justices, 1996–2000, to Cambs Justices, 2000–07; Dep. Dist Judge (Magistrates' Courts), 2000–07. *Recreations:* golf, tennis. *Address:* Northampton Magistrates' Court, Campbell Square, Northampton NN1 3EB.

**DABY, Janet Jessica;** MP (Lab) Lewisham East, since June 2018; *b* 15 Dec. 1970; *m* 2003, Donald Daby; one *s* one *d*. Mem. (Lab) Lewisham Council, 2010– (Cabinet Mem. for Community Safety, 2012–18). Founder and Dir, Whitefoot and Downham Community Food + Project, 2013–. *Address:* House of Commons, SW1A 0AA.

**DACOMBE, William John Armstrong;** *b* 21 Sept. 1934; *s* of late John Christian Dacombe and of Eileen Elizabeth Dacombe; *m* 1962, Margaretta Joanna (*née* Barrington); two *d*. *Educ:* Felsted School; Corpus Christi College, Oxford (MA). Kleinwort Benson, 1961–65; N. M. Rothschild & Sons, 1965–73 (Dir, 1970–73); Dir, 1973–84, Asst Chief Exec., 1979–82, Williams & Glyn's Bank; Group Exec. Dir, Royal Bank of Scotland Group, 1982–84; Chief Exec. Dir, Rea Brothers Group, 1984–88. Co-founder and Partner, Campbell Lutyens and Co., 1988–96; Chairman: Brown Shipley Holdings, 1991–2005; Postern Ltd, 1996–2002; Albert E. Sharp Hldgs, 1997–98. Mem., Export Guarantees Adv. Council, 1982–86 (Dep. Chm., 1985–86). *Recreations:* art, historic buildings, reading. *Address:* Mullion Cottage, Well Lane, SW14 7AJ. *T:* (020) 8876 4336. *Club:* Brooks's.

**DACRE, Baroness** (29th in line) *cr* 1321; **Emily Douglas-Home;** *b* Oxford, 7 Feb. 1983; *o d* of 28th Baron Dacre and Christine Douglas-Home (*née* Stephenson) (*d* 2008); *S* father, 2014; *m* 2015, Charles William Beamish. *Educ:* St Mary's Sch., Calne; Univ. of Edinburgh (MA Hist. of Art). Impressionist and Modern Art Dept, Sotheby's, 2007–10; Gall. Asst, Portland Gall., 2010–. *Heir:* co-heiresses: aunts Hon. Sarah [*b* 4 July 1954; *m* 1977, Nicholas Charles Dent; two *s* two *d*]; Hon. Gian Leila [*b* 23 June 1958; one *s*]; Hon. Dinah Lilian [*b* 22 Jan. 1964; *m* 1989, Harry Marriott; three *s* one *d*]. *Address:* Easter Society House, Hopetoun, South Queensferry EH30 9SL.

**DACRE, James;** Artistic Director, Royal & Derngate Theatre, Northampton, since 2013; *b* London, 21 May 1984; *s* of Paul Michael Dacre, *qv*. *Educ:* Jesus Coll., Cambridge (Scholar); Columbia Univ. Sch. of the Arts (Fulbright Scholar Th. Directing). Trainee, Channel 4 Th. Dirs Scheme; Associate Director: New Vic Th., 2009–12; Theatre503, 2009–13. Stage productions include: The Mountaintop, Theatre503, 2009, transf. West End, 2010; Precious Little Talent, West End, 2011; The Accrington Pals, Royal Exchange, Manchester, 2013; Royal & Derngate: Cat on a Hot Tin Roof, A Tale of Two Cities, 2014; The Hook, Brave New World, 2015; The Herbal Bed, 2016; The Pope, Our Lady of Kibeho, 2019. Trustee, Talawa Th. Co., 2017–. Dir, Bd, Spirit of 2012, 2018–. Franco-British Young Leader, 2017–18. FRSA. *Address:* Royal & Derngate Theatre, 17–21 Guildhall Road, Northampton NN1 1DP.

**DACRE, Dame Jane (Elizabeth),** DBE 2018; MD; FRCP; Professor of Medical Education, since 2001, Vice Dean, since 2005, and Director, UCL Medical School (formerly Division of Medical Education), since 2008, University College London; President: Royal College of Physicians, 2014–18; Medical Protection Society, since 2018; *b* 11 Nov. 1955; *d* of late Peter Verrill and Christine Verrill; *m* 1979, Nigel Dacre, *qv*; one *s* two *d*. *Educ:* Univ. Coll. Hosp. Med. Sch. (BSc 1977; MB BS 1980; MD 1992). MRCP 1983, FRCP 1994; FRCPGlas 1999. Sen. Lectr in Clin. Skills and Consultant Physician and Rheumatologist, St Bartholomew's Med. Coll., 1980–95. Academic Vice-Pres., RCP, 2006–08. Mem., GMC, 2009–13. Mem., Med. Women's Fedn, 2015–. FHEA 2006. Hon. FRCPI 2014; Hon. FAcadMed 2015; Hon. FACP 2015; Hon. FRCGP 2016; Hon. FRACP 2016; Hon. FFPH 2019. Woman of Achievement Award for Medicine and Healthcare, Women in the City, 2012. *Publications:* (with M. Nicol) Clinical Skills: the learning matrix for students of medicine and nursing, 1996; (with P. Kopelman) Handbook of Clinical Skills, 2002; articles on med. educn, assessment, fitness to practice and women in medicine. *Recreations:* family life, all things French. *Address:* University College London Medical School, 134 Medical School Building, 74 Huntley Street, WC1E 6AU. *T:* (020) 7679 0894. *E:* j.dacre@ucl.ac.uk.

**DACRE, Nigel;** Chief Executive, Inclusive Digital Ltd, since 2008; *b* 3 Sept. 1956; *s* of late Peter and of Joan Dacre; *m* 1979, Jane Elizabeth Verrill (*see* Dame J. E. Dacre); one *s* two *d*. *Educ:* St John's Coll., Oxford (MA, PPE). BBC News Trainee, 1978; Regl Journalist, BBC Bristol, 1980; ITN, 1982–2002: ITN Scriptwriter, 1982; Programme Editor, Super Channel News, 1986; Editor, World News, 1987; Editor, News at One, 1989; Head of Programme Output and Exec. Producer, News at Ten, 1992; Dep. Editor, News Programmes, 1993–95; Editor, ITN News on ITV, subseq. ITV News, 1995–2002; Chief Exec., Teachers' TV, 2003–06; Man. Dir, Ten Alps Digital, 2007. Chm., Local TV Network, 2013–15.
*See also* P. M. Dacre.

**DACRE, Paul Michael;** Editor in Chief, since 1998, and Chairman, since 2018, Associated Newspapers; Editor, Daily Mail, 1992–2018; *b* 14 Nov. 1948; *s* of Joan and late Peter Dacre; *m* 1973, Kathleen Thomson; two *s*. *Educ:* University College Sch.; Leeds Univ. (Hons English). Reporter, feature writer, Associate Features Editor, Daily Express, 1970–76; Washington and NY corresp., Daily Express, 1976–79; Daily Mail: NY Bureau Chief, 1980; News Editor, 1981–85; Asst Editor (News and Foreign), 1986; Exec. Editor (Features), 1987; Associate Editor, 1989–91; Editor, Evening Standard, 1991–92. Director: Associated Newspaper Holdings, 1991–; Daily Mail & General Trust plc, 1998–2018; Teletext Hldgs Ltd, 2000–02; Press Assoc., 2018–; Chairman: Bd, Mail Newspapers, 2010–; Mail Online Adv. Bd, 2013–. Member: Press Complaints Commn, 1998–2008; Press Bd of Finance, 2004–16; Chairman: Editors' Code of Practice Cttee, 2008–16; Govt Rev. into Reform of 30 year Rule, 2008. Ambassador for Alzheimer's Soc., 2007–. Cudlipp Lect., London Coll. of Communication, 2007. FRSA 2007. Hon. Mem., NSPCC, 2009. Journalist Laureate, London Press Club, 2018; Lifetime Achievement Award, Soc. of Editors, 2018. *Address:* Associated Newspapers, Northcliffe House, 2 Derry Street, W8 5TT. *T:* (020) 7938 6000. *Club:* Garrick.
*See also* J. Dacre, N. Dacre.

**DADSON, Prof. Trevor John,** PhD; FBA 2008; Professor of Hispanic Studies, Queen Mary University of London, 2004–17, now Emeritus (Vice-Principal, 2006–10); *b* 7 Oct. 1947; *s* of Leonard John Dadson and Chrissie Vera (*née* Black); *m* 1975, Maria Angeles Gimeno; two *s*. *Educ:* Borden Grammar Sch., Sittingbourne; Univ. of Leeds (BA Hons); Univ. of Durham (PGCE); Emmanuel Coll., Cambridge (PhD 1974). Queen's University, Belfast: Lectr, 1978–86; Reader, 1986–88; Prof., 1988–90; University of Birmingham: Prof. of Hispanic Studies, 1990–2004; Head, Sch. of Modern Langs, 1993–97; Dir, Centre for European Langs and Culture, 2001–02. Pres., Assoc. of Hispanists of GB and Ire., 2011–15. Corresponding Fellow: Real Acad. Española, Spain, 2016; Real Acad. de la Historia, Spain, 2016. Encomienda, Orden de Isabel la Católica (Spain), 2015. *Publications:* The Genoese in Spain, 1983; Avisos a un Cortesano, 1985; (ed) G. Bocángel, La Lira de las Musas, 1985; (ed) D. Silva y Mendoza, Antología Poética, 1985; (ed) A. Barros, Filosofía Cortesana, 1987; (ed) Una Familia Hispano-Genovesa, 1991; Libros, lectores y lecturas: bibliotecas particulares españolas del Siglo de Oro, 1998; (gen. ed) Actas del XII Congreso de la AIH, 1998; (ed) Ludisimo e intertextualidad en la lírica española moderna, 1998; (ed) Voces subversivas: poesía bajo el Régimen, 2000; (ed) G. Bocángel, Obra Completa, 2001; (ed) La poesía española del siglo XX y la tradición literaria, 2003; Estudios sobre poesía española contemporánea, 2005; Los moriscos de Villarrubia de los Ojos, siglos XV–XVIII, 2007, 2nd edn 2015; Historia de la impresión de las Rimas de Lupercio y Bartolomé Leonardo de Argensola, 2010; Diego de Silva y Mendoza: poeta y político en la corte de Felipe III, 2011; (ed) La España del siglo XIX vista por dos inglesas: Lady Holland y la novelista George Eliot (1802–1804 y 1867), 2012; (ed) Epistolario e historia documental de Ana de Mendoza y de la Cerda, princesa de Éboli, 2013; Tolerance and Co-existence in Early Modern Spain: Old Christians and Moriscos in the Campo de Calatrava, 2014; (ed) Britain, Spain and the Treaty of Utrecht 1713–2013, 2014; (ed) Diego de Silva y Mendoza, Conde de Salinas y Marqués de Alenquer: cartas y memoriales (1584–1630), 2015; Cautiva del rey: Vida de Ana de Mendoza y de la Cerda, princesa de Éboli, 2015; (ed) Conde de Salinas. Obra completa: La poesía desconocida, 2016; Tolerancia y convivencia en la España de los Austrias: Cristianos y moriscos en el Campo de Calatrava, 2017; (ed) L. P. Harvey, Islamic Culture in Spain to 1614: essays and studies, 2019; numerous articles. *Recreations:* ski-ing, walking, tennis, reading.

**DAFFERN, Paul George;** Chief Financial Officer, Greengate Holdings (formerly Greengate Management Services) Ltd, 2008–12; *b* 5 May 1953; *s* of late George Thomas Daffern and Kathleen Esther Daffern; *m* 1984, Hilary Margaret Jenkins; one *s* one *d*. *Educ:* Foxford School, Coventry. Unbrako Ltd, 1969–73; Massey-Ferguson UK, 1973–75; Chrysler UK, 1975–77; Lucas Service UK, 1978–79; National Freight Co., 1980–88; Autoglass, 1988–91; Exec. Dir, Finance, AEA Technology, 1991–95; Chief Financial Officer, X/Open Co. Ltd, 1995–97; Finance Dir, Autoglass Ltd, 1998–2000; Dir, IMS, 2000–02; Gp Finance Dir, PD Ports, Logistics and Shipping Gp, then PD Ports Gp Ltd, subseq. PD Ports plc, 2002–06; Finance Dir, Infinis Ltd, 2006–07. Gov., St Hugh's Sch., Faringdon, 2005–. *Recreations:* golf, reading.

**DAFIS, Cynog Glyndwr;** Member (Plaid Cymru) Mid and West Wales, National Assembly for Wales, 1999–2003; *b* 1 April 1938; *s* of Annie and George Davies; *m* 1963, Llinos Iorwerth Jones; two *s* one *d*. *Educ:* Aberaeron County Secondary Sch.; Neath Boys' Grammar Sch.; UCW Aberystwyth (BA Hons English, MEd). Teacher of English: Coll. of Further Educn, Pontardawe, 1960–62; Newcastle Emlyn Secondary Modern Sch., 1962–80; Aberaeron Comprehensive Sch., 1980–84; Dyffryn Teifi Comprehensive Sch., Llandysul, 1984–91; Research Officer, Dept of Adult Continuing Educn, UC Swansea, 1991–92. Contested (Plaid Cymru) Ceredigion and Pembroke North, 1983 and 1987. MP (Plaid Cymru) Ceredigion and Pembroke N, 1992–97, Ceredigion, 1997–Jan. 2000. Member: Select Cttee, Welsh Affairs, 1995–97; Envmtl Audit Cttee, 1997–2000. National Assembly for Wales: Chair: Post-16 Educn and Culture Cttee, 1999–2000; Educn and Lifelong Learning Cttee, 2000–02. Dir of Policy, Plaid Cymru, 1997–2003. Vice Chm., Cymru Yfory/Tomorrow's Wales. Fellow: Univ. of Aberystwyth; Univ. of Wales Trinity St David. *Publications:* Mab y Pregethwr (autobiog.), 2005; (with A. Jones Williams) Duw Yw'r Broblem (God is the Problem), 2016; pamphlets and articles on bilingualism, Welsh and Green politics, religion and devolved govt. *Recreations:* walking, jogging, reading, listening to music, singing, theatre. *Address:* Cedrwydd, Llandre, Bow Street, Ceredigion SY24 5AB. *T:* (01970) 828262.

**DAGLISH, Simon Edward De Guingand;** Group Commercial Director, ITV plc, since 2011; *b* London, 29 Aug. 1965; *s* of Richard and Sarah Daglish; *m* 1998, Emma Charlotte Suter; two *s*. *Educ:* Holmwood House Prep. Sch.; Duke of York's Royal Mil. Sch.; RMA Sandhurst. Asst, Daily Express, 1988–90; Gp Hd, Telegraph Gp, 1990–95; Sales Dir, Independent Magazines, 1995–99; Sales Dir, Classic FM, 1999–2002; Commercial Dir, GCAP Media, 2002–09; Vice Pres., Commercial, Fox Internat., 2009–11. Chm., Nat. Advertising Benevolent Soc., 2016–. Jt Founder, Walking with the Wounded charity, 2010. *Publications:* Walking with the Wounded, 2011. *Recreations:* polar travel, adventure, Rugby, cricket, polar history. *Address:* 40 Westbridge Road, Battersea, SW11 3PW. *T:* (020) 7350 2247, 07833 234069. *E:* simon.daglish@me.com.

**DAGWORTHY, Prof. Wendy**, OBE 2011; Professor, 1998–2014, and Dean, School of Material, 2011–14, Royal College of Art (Head, Department of Fashion, 1998–2000; Head, School of Fashion and Textiles, 2000–11); *b* Gravesend, 4 March 1950. *Educ:* Medway Coll. of Art (Foundn and Pre-Dip. 1968); Middx Poly. (Hornsey Coll. of Art) (DipAD 1st Cl. Hons 1971). Designer, Radley (Quorum), 1971–72; designer and Dir, Wendy Dagworthy Ltd, 1972–88; Dir, London Design Collections, 1982–90; Central St Martins College of Art and Design: Course Dir, BA Hons Fashion, 1989–98; Fashion Prof., 1998; Actg Dean, Sch. of Fashion and Textiles, 1998. Consultant: fashion course, Temask Poly., Singapore, 1992; Export Promotion Bd, Pakistan, 1993–94; Crown Paints Fashion for Walls range, 2006–; Designer/Consultant: Laura Ashley, 1992; Liberty Retail and Internat., 1997–99; Design Consultant, Betty Jackson, 1996–2011. Guest Ed., Good Housekeeping, 2002–. Member: Adv. Bd, British Fashion Council, 1991–; Assoc. of Degree Courses in Fashion and Textile Design, 1999–. Has lectured at colls of art and design; external assessor for Foundn, BA Hons and MA Hons Fashion courses at univs and colls, 1982–, including: Domus Acad., Milan, 2004–; UCE, Birmingham, 2005–; Univ. of Westminster, 2006–; judge of art and design projects, awards and competitions. Outfits on display: exhibn at V&A Mus., 1997–; Cutting Edge Exhibn, V&A Mus., 1997; Matter in Hand Exhibn, London Inst. Gall., 1999–2000; outfits archived at V&A Mus., Brighton Mus., Manchester City Galls, Mus. of London, Bath Mus. of Fashion. Curated Club to Catwalk Exhibn, V&A Mus., 2013. *Publications:* contrib. articles to newspapers and mags, incl. Woman & Home, Good Housekeeping, Wall St Jl, The Times, Mail on Sunday, Guardian, Independent.

**DAIN, Sir David (John Michael)**, KCVO 1997; CMG 1991; HM Diplomatic Service, retired; High Commissioner to Pakistan, 1997–2000; *b* 30 Oct. 1940; *s* of late John Gordon Dain and Joan (*née* Connop); *m* 1969, Susan Kathleen Moss; one *s* four *d*. *Educ:* Merchant Taylors' Sch.; St John's Coll., Oxford (MA Lit.Hum.). Entered HM Diplomatic Service, 1963; Third, later Second Sec., Tehran and Kabul, 1964–68; seconded to Cabinet Office, 1969–72; First Sec., Bonn, 1972–75; FCO, 1975–78; Head of Chancery, Athens, 1978–81; Counsellor and Dep. High Comr, Nicosia, 1981–85; Head of Western European Dept, FCO, 1985–89; on attachment to CSSB, 1989–90; High Comr, Cyprus, 1990–94; Asst Under-Sec. of State, then Dir, S Asian and SE Asian Depts, FCO, 1994–97. Chm., Anglo-Hellenic League, 2007–15. FCIL (FIL 1986). Royal Order of Merit, Norway, 1988. *Recreations:* tennis, bridge, flying, walking, natural history. *Address:* Manor Cottage, Frant, Tunbridge Wells, Kent TN3 9DR. *Clubs:* Oxford and Cambridge; Oxford Union Society.

**DAINTITH, Prof. Terence Charles**; Professor of Law: University of London, 1988–2002, now Professor Emeritus; University of Western Australia, 2002–04 (Visiting Professor, 2005–19); *b* 8 May 1942; *s* of Edward Terence and Irene May Daintith; *m* 1965, Christine Anne Bulport; one *s* one *d*. *Educ:* Wimbledon Coll.; St Edmund Hall, Oxford (BA Jurisp., MA); Univ. of Nancy (Leverhulme European Schol.). Called to the Bar, Lincoln's Inn, 1966; Bencher, 2000. Associate in Law, Univ. of California, Berkeley, 1963–64; Lectr in Constitutional and Admin. Law, Univ. of Edinburgh, 1964–72; University of Dundee: Prof. and Head of Dept of Public Law, 1972–83; Dir, Centre for Petroleum and Mineral Law Studies, 1977–83; Prof. of Law, European Univ. Inst., Florence, 1981–87; Dir, Inst. of Advanced Legal Studies, Univ. of London, 1988–95; Dean, Univ. of London Sch. of Advanced Study, 1994–2001. Sen. Fellow (formerly Vis. Fellow), Sch. of Law, Univ. of Melbourne, 2004–; Hon. Prof., Univ. of Dundee, 2014–. MAE 1989 (Chm., Law Cttee, 1993–96; Chm., Social Scis Section, 1996–98). Editor, Jl Energy and Natural Resources Law, 1983–92. Hon. LLD: De Montfort, 2001; Aberdeen, 2013. *Publications:* The Economic Law of the United Kingdom, 1974; (with G. Willoughby) United Kingdom Oil and Gas Law, 1977, 3rd edn (with A. D. G. Hill) 2000; (with L. Hancher) European Energy Strategy: the legal framework, 1986; (with S. Williams) The Legal Integration of Energy Markets, 1987; Law as an Instrument of Economic Policy, 1988; (with G. R. Baldwin) Harmonisation and Hazard, 1992; Implementing EC Law in the United Kingdom, 1995; (with A. C. Page) The Executive in the Constitution, 1999; Discretion in the Administration of Offshore Oil and Gas, 2006; Finders Keepers? How the Law of Capture Shaped the World Oil Industry, 2010; contribs to UK and foreign law jls. *Recreations:* cycling, carpentry. *Address:* Institute of Advanced Legal Studies, 17 Russell Square, WC1B 5DR. *Club:* New (Edinburgh).

**DAINTON, Prof. John Bourke**, DPhil; FRS 2002; CPhys, FInstP; Sir James Chadwick Professor of Physics, 2002–16, now Professor Emeritus, and Hon. Senior Research Fellow, since 2016, University of Liverpool; Founding Director, Cockcroft Institute of Accelerator Science and Technology, 2005–07; *b* 10 Sept. 1947; *s* of Lord Dainton, FRS and Dr Barbara Hazlitt Dainton (*née* Wright); *m* 2008, Josephine Zilberkweit (*d* 2010); *m* 2018, Dorothy Robinson. *Educ:* Merton Coll., Oxford (BA Hons 1969; MA, DPhil 1973). CPhys, FInstP, 1982. Lectr in Physics, Merton Coll., Oxford, 1972–73; Res. Associate, SRC Daresbury Lab., 1973–77; Lectr in Physics, Univ. of Glasgow, 1978–85; University of Liverpool: Lectr in Physics, 1986–88; Sen. Lectr in Physics, 1988–91; Reader in Physics, 1991–94; SERC Sen. Fellow, 1992–97; Prof. of Physics, 1994–2002. Vis. Prof., Lancaster Univ., 2017–. Vis. Scientist, DESY, Hamburg, 1980–82, 1997–99; Fellow, Alexander von Humboldt Stiftung, Germany, 2003. Chm., Super Proton Synchrotron and PS Cttee, CERN, 2003–09. Gov., Stockport Grammar Sch., 2008–18. Freeman, City of London, 1982; Liveryman, Goldsmiths' Co., 1982–. FRSA 2003. Max Born Medal, Inst. of Physics and German Physical Soc., 1999. Ed. in Chief, Phil. Trans of the Royal Soc. A, 2018–. *Publications:* more than 300 articles in Zeitschrift für Physik C, European Jl of Physics, Nuclear Physics B, Physics Letters B, Jl of High Energy Physics, Jl of Physics G, Nuclear Instruments and Methods, Phil. Trans of the Royal Soc. A, Physics World, conf. proceedings, reports for SERC, PPARC and STFC, written evaluations for internat. sci. reviews. *Recreations:* music, travel when in control of the means, taking time to think and understand. *Address:* Cockcroft Institute of Accelerator Science and Technology, Daresbury Science and Innovation Campus, Warrington WA4 4AD. *T:* (01925) 603820. *E:* John.Dainton@cockcroft.ac.uk; Oliver Lodge Laboratory, Department of Physics, University of Liverpool L69 7ZE. *T:* (0151) 794 7769, 07973 247769; Department of Physics, Lancaster University, Lancaster LA1 4YW.

**DAINTY, Prof. (John) Christopher**, PhD; MRIA; Pilkington Professor of Applied Optics, Imperial College London, 1984–2012, Distinguished (formerly Senior) Research Fellow, since 2012; Professorial Research Associate, University College London, 2013–18, now Emeritus Professor; *b* 22 Jan. 1947; *s* of late Jack Dainty and of Mary Elizabeth (*née* Elbeck); *m* 1978, Janice Hancock; one *s* one *d*. *Educ:* George Heriot's, Edinburgh; City of Norwich Sch.; Polytechnic of Central London (Diploma); Imperial Coll. of Science and Technol. (MSc; PhD 1972). Lectr, Queen Elizabeth Coll., Univ. of London, 1974–78; Associate Prof., Inst. of Optics, Univ. of Rochester, NY, USA, 1978–83. Sen. Res. Fellow, SERC, 1987–92; PPARC Sen. Res. Fellow, Imperial Coll., Univ. of London, 2001–02; Sci. Foundn Ireland Prof. of Experimental Phys, subseq. Prof. of Applied Phys, NUI, 2002–12, now Emeritus. President: Internat. Commn for Optics, 1993–96; European Optical Soc., 2002–04; Pres., Optical Soc. of America, 2011. MRIA 2008. Internat. Commn of Optics Prize, 1984; Thomas Young Medal and Prize, Inst. of Physics, 1993; Mees Medal and Prize, Optical Soc. of America, 2003; Robert E. Hopkins Leader Award, Optical Soc., 2017. *Publications:* (with R. Shaw) Image Science, 1974; (ed) Laser Speckle and Related Phenomena, 1975, 2nd edn 1984; (ed with M. Nieto-Vesperinas) Scattering in Volumes and Surfaces, 1989; scientific papers. *Address:* UCL Institute of Ophthalmology, 11–43 Bath Street, EC1V 9EL. *T:* (020) 7608 4057.

**DAKIN, Nicholas**; MP (Lab) Scunthorpe, since 2010; *b* 10 July 1955; *m* Audrey; three *c*. *Educ:* Longslade Upper Sch., Birstall, Leics; Hull Univ.; King's Coll. London. English teacher: Greatfield High Sch., Hull; Gävle, Sweden; trainee accountant, Arthur Young & Co., 1981–82; John Leggott College, Scunthorpe: English teacher, then Vice Principal, 1982–2007; Principal, 2007–10. Mem. (Lab) N Lincs Council, 1996–2007 (Leader, 1997–2003; Leader, Lab Gp, 2003–07). An Opposition Whip, 2011–15, 2016–; Shadow Schools Minister, 2015–16. Mem., Select Cttee on Educn, 2010–11, on Procedure, 2011–. *Address:* House of Commons, SW1A 0AA.

**DAKIN, Rt Rev. Timothy**; *see* Winchester, Bishop of.

**DALAI LAMA**; *see* Tenzin Gyatso.

**DALBY, Dr (Terry) David (Pereira)**; Reader in West African Languages, School of Oriental and African Studies, University of London, 1967–83, now Emeritus; Director, Linguasphere Observatory (Observatoire linguistique), since 1997; *b* 7 Jan. 1933; *s* of Ernest Edwin Dalby and Rose Cecilia Dalby; one *s* four *d*. *Educ:* Cardiff High Sch.; Queen Mary Coll., London (BA 1954, PhD 1961; Hon. Life Mem., Queen Mary Coll. Union Soc., 1954). Served to Lieut, Intell. Corps, 1954–56. United Africa Co. Ltd, London and W Africa, 1957–60; Lectr in Mod. Languages, University Coll. of Sierra Leone, 1961–62; Lectr in W African Langs, SOAS, Univ. of London, 1962–67; Hon. Res. Fellow, Adran y Gymraeg, Univ. of Wales, Cardiff, 1996–2005. Hanns Wolff Vis. Prof., Indiana Univ., 1969. Chm., Centre for Afr. Studies, Univ. of London, 1971–74; Dir, Internat. African Inst., 1974–80; Chairman: Internat. Conf. on Manding Studies, 1972, and Drought in Africa Conf., 1973; UK Standing Cttee on Univ. Studies of Africa, 1978–82 (Dep. Chm., 1975–78). Vice-Pres., Unesco Meeting on Cultural Specificity in Africa, Accra, 1980. Member: Governing Body, SOAS, 1969–70; Council, African Studies Assoc. of UK, 1970–73; Cttee of Management, British Inst. in Paris, 1975–82; Conseil Internat. de Recherche et d'Etude en Linguistique Fondamentale et Appliquée, 1980–86 (Président, 1984); Centre Internat. de Recherche sur le Bilinguisme, Laval Univ., Que, 1981–89; Eur. Council on African Studies, 1985–87; Centre Internat. des Industries de la Langue, Univ. Paris X, 1993–95; Comité Français des Etudes Africaines, 1993–94; BSI Cttee TS/1, 2001–06; ISO Cttee TC37, 2002–05; Carmarthen Family Centres Mgt Cttee, 2005–11; ISO 639 Jt Adv. Cttee, 2012–14. Hon. Mem., SOAS, 1983. Editor, African Language Review, 1962–72; Co-editor, Africa, 1976–80. Endowed Rhoswen Enfys awards, Nat. Eisteddfod Wales, 2002–08. *Publications:* Lexicon of the Mediaeval German Hunt, 1965; Black through White: patterns of communication in Africa and the New World, 1970; (ed) Language and History in Africa, 1970; (ed jtly) Drought in Africa, 1st vol. 1973, 2nd vol. 1978; Language Map of Africa and the adjacent islands, 1977; Clavier international de Niamey, 1984; (jtly) Les langues et l'espace du français, 1985; Afrique et la lettre, 1986; (jtly) Thesaurus of African Languages, 1987; Linguasphere Register of the World's Languages and Speech Communities, 2 vols, 2000; articles in linguistic and other jls. *Recreations:* keeping fit, campaigning for women's and children's rights.

**DALDRY, Stephen David**, CBE 2004; Director, Stephen Daldry Pictures, since 1998; Associate Director, Royal Court Theatre, since 1999; *b* 2 May 1961; *s* of late Patrick Daldry and Cherry (*née* Thompson); *m* 2001, Lucy Sexton; one *d*. *Educ:* Huish GS, Taunton; Univ. of Sheffield (BA). Trained with Il Circo di Nando Orfei, Italy; Artistic Dir, Metro Theatre, 1984–86; Associate Artist, Crucible Theatre, Sheffield, 1986–88; Artistic Director: Gate Theatre, Notting Hill, 1989–92; English Stage Co., Royal Court Theatre, 1992–99. Exec. Prod., Creative, London 2012 Ceremonies, 2010–12. Cameron Mackintosh Vis. Prof. of Contemp. Theatre, St Catherine's Coll., Oxford, 2002. Major productions include: Damned for Despair, Gate, 1991; An Inspector Calls, RNT, 1992, Aldwych, 1994, Garrick, 1995, NY, 1995, Playhouse, 2001; Machinal, RNT, 1993; The Audience, Gielgud Th., 2013, NY, 2015; Skylight, Wyndham's, 2014; Royal Court: The Kitchen, 1995; Via Dolorosa, 1998, NY, 1999, filmed 1999; Far Away, 2000, transf. Albery, 2001; A Number, 2002; Wall, 2009; Billy Elliot - the Musical, Victoria Palace, 2005, NY, 2008; The Jungle (co-dir), Young Vic, 2017, transf. Playhouse Th., 2018; The Inheritance, Young Vic, transf. Noël Coward, 2018 (Best Dir, Olivier Awards, 2019). *Films:* Eight (short), 1998; Billy Elliot, 2000; The Hours, 2003; The Reader, 2009; Extremely Loud and Incredibly Close, 2012; Trash, 2015. *Television series:* The Crown (exec. prod.), 2016–. *Address:* c/o Stephen Daldry Pictures Ltd, 71 Queen Victoria Street, EC4V 4BE.

**DALE, Barry Gordon**, FCA; Partner, Baird Partners, and International Corporate Finance Group, since 2003; *b* 31 July 1938; *s* of Francis and Catherine Dale; *m* 1963, Margaret (*née* Fairbrother); one *s* one *d*. *Educ:* Queen Elizabeth Grammar Sch., Blackburn. Coopers Lybrand, Montreal, 1960–62; Pilkington Brothers Glass, St Helens, 1962–65; ICI, 1965–85: Mond Div., Cheshire, 1966–68; Head Office, 1968–72; Dep. Chief Acct, Mond Div., 1972–78; Finance Dir, ICI Latin America (Wilmington, USA), 1978–80; Chief Acct, Organics Div., Manchester, 1980–84; Bd Mem. for Finance, LRT, 1985–88; Gp Finance Dir, 1988–92, Gp Chief Exec., 1993–95, Littlewoods Orgn. Director: Ellis & Everard, 1978–81; Magadi Soda Co. (Kenya), 1980–82; Triplex Lloyd, 1994–98; London Buses Ltd, 1985–88; London Underground Ltd, 1985–88; LRT Bus Engineering Ltd, 1985–88; Greenalls, then De Vere, Gp, 1992–2000; Chairman: London Transport Trustee Co., 1985–88; London Transport Pension Fund Trustees, 1985–88; Datanetworks, 1987–88; Creightons, 1997–99. *Recreations:* golf, fell walking, other sports. *Address:* Tanglewood, Spinney Lane, Knutsford WA16 0NQ. *Clubs:* Carlton; Tatton (Knutsford); Knutsford Golf.

**DALE, Iain Campbell**; Presenter: LBC Radio, since 2010; CNN Talk, since 2017; *b* Cambridge, 15 July 1962; *s* of late Garry Dale and Jane Dale; civil partnership 2008, *m* 2015, John Simmons. *Educ:* Saffron Walden County High Sch.; Univ. of East Anglia (BA Hons German 1985). Researcher, H of C, 1985–87; Public Affairs Mgr, British Ports Fedn, 1987–89; Insce Corresp., Lloyd's List, 1990; Public Affairs Mgr, Waterfront Partnership, 1990–96; Founder and Man. Dir, Politico's Bookstore, 1996–2006; Man. Dir, Politico's Publishing, 1998–2003; COS to Rt Hon. David Davis, MP, 2005; Presenter, 18 Doughty Street TV, 2006–07; Publisher, Total Politics Magazine, 2008–12; Founder and Man. Dir, Biteback Publishing, 2009–18. Ed., Iain Dale's Diary, 2003–10; columnist, Daily Telegraph, 2007–09. Contested (C) N Norfolk, 2005. *Publications:* (edited): The End of the Dock Labour Scheme, 1991; Unofficial Book of Political Lists, 1997; As I Said to Denis: the Margaret Thatcher book of quotations, 1997; The Blair Necessities, 1998; Bill Clinton Joke Book, 1998; Tony Blair New Labour Joke Book, 1998; Dictionary of Conservative Quotations, 1999, 2nd edn 2013; Wit and Wisdom of Tony Banks, 1999; Labour Party General Election Manifestos 1900–97, 1999; Liberal Party General Election Manifestos 1990–97, 1999; Conservative Party General Election Manifestos 1990–97, 1999; Memories of Maggie, 2000; Directory of Political Websites, 2001; Directory of Think Tank Publications, 2001; Memories of the Falklands, 2002, 2nd edn 2012; Directory of Political Lobbying, 2003; (jtly) Prime Minister Portillo and Other Things That Never Happened, 2003; Times Guides to the House of Commons 1906–10, 2003; Times Guides to the House of Commons 1929–35, 2003; Politico's Book of the Dead, 2003; Margaret Thatcher: a tribute in words and pictures, 2005; Little Red Book of New Labour Sleaze, 2006; Big Red

Book of New Labour Sleaze, 2007; 500 of the Most Witty, Acerbic and Erudite Things Ever Said About Politics, 2007; Guide to Political Blogging in the UK, 2007; Little Book of Boris, 2007; Total Politics Guide to the General Election, 2009; Total Politics Guide to Political Blogging 2010–11, 2010; Margaret Thatcher: in her own words, 2010; Talking Politics: political conversations with Iain Dale, 2010; West Ham United: when football was football, 2011; (jtly) Prime Minister Boris and Other Things That Never Happened, 2011; The Bigger Book of Boris, 2011; Norwich City: when football was football, 2012; Memories of Margaret Thatcher, 2013; Great Parliamentary Speeches 1978–2013, 2014; The Honourable Ladies Vol. 1: profiles of women MPs 1918–1996, 2018; The Honourable Ladies Vol. 2: profiles of women MPs 1997–2019, 2019; (author): The Blogfather, 2012; The NHS: things that need to be said, 2015. *Recreations:* politics, books, Jack Russells, Europop, golf, debating, radio, travel, Audis. *T:* (020) 7091 1260. *E:* iain@iaindale.com. *Clubs:* Two Brydges; West Ham United.

**DALE, Maj.-Gen. Ian Conway**, CBE 2007; CEng; Director and Principal Consultant, SELIX Ltd, since 2012; *b* Leicester, 8 Sept. 1957; *s* of Eric Dale and Gwendolen Dale (*née* Mann); *m* 1983, Karen Moore; two *d. Educ:* Gateway Grammar Sch., Leicester; Army Apprentices Coll., Arborfield; RMA, Sandhurst; Royal Mil. Coll. of Sci., Shrivenham (BSc Eng Hons 1983; MSc 1988). CEng 1987; FIET 2011 (MIET 1986). REME Apprenticeship, 1974–76; Lance-Corp., REME Wing, Royal Sch. of Artillery 1977; Troop Comd, 14/20 King's Hussars, Germany and Canada, 1979; 2IC Light Aid Detachment REME, 14/20 King's Hussars, Germany, 1980; Trng Officer, 20 Electronics Workshop REME, Germany, 1984; OC, 32 Regt RA Workshop REME, Germany, 1985–86; Adjt, Logistic Bn, Falkland Is, 1987; psc† 1989; Gen. Staff, Directorate of CIS (Army), MoD, 1990–91; Co. Comd, 20 Electronics Workshop REME, Germany, 1992–93; Gen. Staff, HQ ARRC, Germany and Denmark, 1994–95; CO, 6 Bn REME, UK and Bosnia, 1996–97; COS Inspector REME, UK, 1998; Comdr Equipment Support, Germany, 1999–2000, DCS, Germany and Oman, 2001, 1 (UK) Armoured Div.; hcsc 2001; Commander: 101 Logistic Bde, UK, 2002–03; UK Jt Force Logistics Component, Kuwait and Iraq, 2003; Deputy Chief of Staff: ARRC, Germany, 2004–05; Internat. Security Assistance Force, Afghanistan, 2006; rcds 2007; Mil. Team Leader, Service Personnel Command Paper, MoD, 2008; Dir (formerly Dir Gen.) Land Equipment, Defence Equipment and Support, 2008–11. Global Mkt Advr, Inmarsat Global Govt, 2012–; Eur. Advr, Portafloor UK, 2012–16; Sen. Defence Advr, Glue Reply Ltd, 2013–16; Sen. Defence Consultant, CMI Defence, 2016–17. President: Army Rugby League, 2007–11; REME Winter Sports, 2008–12; Dep. Pres., Army Winter Sports, 2009–11. Chm., Trustees, REME Central Charitable Trust, 2012–14; Chm., Council for Cadet Rifle Shooting, 2012–. FCIM 2010. *Recreations:* mountain sports, ski-ing, deer management. *Address:* RHQ REME, MoD Lyneham, Lyneham, Chippenham SN15 9HB.

**DALE, Jim**, MBE 2003; actor, director, singer, composer, lyricist; *b* 15 Aug. 1935; *m;* three *s* one *d. Educ:* Kettering Grammar School. Music Hall comedian, 1951; singing, compèring, directing, 1951–61; *films,* 1965–, include: Lock Up Your Daughters, The Winter's Tale, The Biggest Dog in the World, National Health, Adolf Hitler—My Part in his Downfall, Joseph Andrews, Pete's Dragon, Hot Lead Cold Feet, Bloodshy, The Spaceman and King Arthur, Scandalous, Carry On films: Carry On Cabby, Carry On Cleo, Carry On Jack, Carry On Cowboy, Carry On Screaming, Carry On Spying, Carry On Constable, Carry On Doctor, Carry On Again Doctor, Carry On Don't Lose Your Head, Carry On Follow that Camel, Carry On Columbus. *Stage:* joined Frank Dunlop's Pop Theatre for Edinburgh Festival, 1967–68; National Theatre, 1969–71: main roles in National Health, Love's Labour's Lost, Merchant of Venice, Good-natured Man, Captain of Köpenick, The Architect and the Emperor of Assyria; also appeared at Young Vic in Taming of the Shrew, Scapino (title rôle and wrote music); title rôle in musical The Card, 1973; Compère of Sunday Night at the London Palladium, 1973–74; Scapino (title rôle), Broadway, 1974–75 (Drama Critics' and Outer Circle Awards for best actor; Tony award nomination for best actor); Privates on Parade, Long Wharf Theatre, New Haven, Conn, 1979; Barnum (title rôle), Broadway, 1980 (Tony award for best actor in a musical, Drama Desk Award); A Day in the Death of Joe Egg, NY, 1985 (Tony nomination for best actor; Outer Circle Award for best actor); Me and My Girl, NY, 1987–88; Privates on Parade, NY, 1989; Oliver!, London Palladium, 1995; The Music Man, Travels With My Aunt, NY (Drama Desk Award, Outer Circle Award and Critics Award, 1995); Comedians, NY, 2003; A Christmas Carol, NY, 2003–04; Address Unknown, NY, 2004; The Threepenny Opera, NY, 2006; Busker Alley, NY, 2006; The Oak Tree, NY, 2007; Don Juan in Hell, Williamstown, 2007; The Road to Mecca, NY, 2012; one-man show, Just Jim Dale, NY, transf. Vaudeville Th., 2015. *Television* includes: host of Ringling Brothers Barnum and Bailey Circus (TV special), 1985; Adventures of Huckleberry Finn, 1985; Pushing Daisies, 2007–08. Composed film music for: The Winter's Tale, Shalako, Twinky, Georgy Girl (nominated for Academy Award), Joseph Andrews. Audio recordings incl. Harry Potter series (Grammy Award, best children's audio recording: 2001, for Harry Potter and the Goblet of Fire; 2008, for Harry Potter and the Deathly Hallows), A Christmas Carol, 2004; Peter and the Wolf, The Shoe Bird, 2008. 10 Audie Awards, Audio Publishers Assoc.; 2 Earphones Awards, AudioFile Mag. *Address:* c/o Tom Celia, CED, 257 Park Avenue South, New York, NY 10010, USA; c/o Janet Glass, Eric Glass Ltd, 25 Ladbroke Crescent, W11 1PS.

**DALE, John;** Editor: Brentford Today and TV social media; Take a Break, 1991–2011; *b* Cleethorpes, Lincs, 1 May 1946; *s* of Ken Dale and Eileen Dale. *Educ:* Wintringham Grammar Sch., Grimsby. Reporter: Daily Mail, 1968–78; The Observer, 1978–79; Now!, 1979–81; London Ed., Sunday Standard (Scotland), 1981–83; freelance journalist, 1983–91. Editor of the Year, weekly women's mags, 1992, 1994, 1995, 1996, 1997, 2001, 2003, 2007, 2009, Innovation of the Year, 1998, 2002, BSME. *Publications:* The World Beneath My Wheels, 1976; The Prince and the Paranormal, 1986; 24 Hours in Journalism, 2012. *Recreation:* making videos. *Address:* Brentford, Middx. *T:* 07720 054626. *E:* johnkdale@msn.com.

**DALE, Peter David;** television executive producer, since 2016; Head of Documentaries, National Film and Television School, since 2018; *b* 25 July 1955; *s* of late David Howard Dale and Betty Marguerite Dale (*née* Rosser); *m* 1988, Victoria Francesca Pennington; one *s* two *d. Educ:* King Henry VIII Grammar Sch., Coventry; Liverpool Univ. (BA Hons English Lit. and Lang.). BBC Television: research asst trainee, 1980–82; Dir and Producer, 1982–98; Channel 4: Commissioning Ed., Documentaries, 1998–2000; Head of Documentaries, 2000–05; Head of More4, 2005–08; Founder, Rare Day Ltd, 2008–17. Non-exec. Dir, Fresh One Prodns, 2009–12. Dir, Sheffield Internat. Documentary Fest., 2002–04. Mem. Exec. Cttee, Guardian Edinburgh TV Fest., 2002–05. Associate Fellow, IPPR, 2009–. Trustee, Grierson Trust, 2007–11. Journalism Prize, Anglo-German Foundn, 1992; Best Documentary Award, 1994, Best Documentary Series, 1996, RTS; Producer of Year Award, Broadcast Mag., 1997; Grierson Award for Best British Documentary, BFI, 1997. *Recreations:* family, sailing.

**DALE, Robert Alan;** business consultant, retired; Director, Business Development, Lucas Industries plc, 1992–93; *b* 31 Oct. 1938; *s* of Horace and Alice Dale; *m* 1963, Sheila Mary Dursley; one *s* one *d. Educ:* West Bromwich Grammar Sch.; Birmingham Univ. (BA Hons). Joined Lucas Industries as graduate apprentice, 1960; first management appt, 1965; first Bd appt, 1971; Dir, Lucas CAV, 1972–77; Dir and Gen. Man., Lucas Batteries, 1978–81; joined Exec. Cttee of Lucas (Joseph Lucas Ltd), 1980; Managing Director: Lucas World Service, 1981–85; Lucas Electrical, 1985–87; Lucas Automotive, 1987–92; Dir, Lucas Industries, 1987–93. Vice-Pres., SMMT, 1989–92. *Recreations:* sport, photography, travel.

**DALE, Spencer;** Chief Economist, BP plc, since 2014; *b* London, 12 Jan. 1967; *s* of John James Dale and B Dale; *m* Natasha Cavill; one *s* one *d. Educ:* Exeter Coll.; University Coll. Cardiff (BSc Econs 1988); Univ. of Warwick (MSc Econs 1989). Bank of England, 1989–2014: Private Sec. to Mervyn King, 1997–99; Hd, Monetary Assessment and Strategy Div., 1999–2000; Hd, Conjunctural Assessment and Projects Div., 2000–06; on secondment as Vis. Sen. Advr, Bd of Govs, Federal Reserve System, USA, 2006–08; Chief Economist, and Mem., Monetary Policy Cttee, 2008–14; Exec. Dir, Financial Stability Strategy and Risk, 2014. Mem. Council, REconS, 2008–11. Mem., Soc. of Professional (formerly Business) Economists, 2008–. *Publications:* numerous res. articles in acad. jls and central bank pubns. *Recreations:* running, theatre, tennis. *Address:* BP plc, 1 St James's Square, SW1Y 4PD.

**DALES, Sir Richard (Nigel)**, KCVO 2001; CMG 1993; HM Diplomatic Service, retired; Ambassador to Norway, 1998–2002; *b* 26 Aug. 1942; *s* of late Kenneth Richard Frank Dales and Olwen Mary (*née* Preedy); *m* 1966, Elizabeth Margaret Martin; one *s* one *d. Educ:* Chigwell Sch.; St Catharine's Coll., Cambridge (BA 1964). Entered FO, 1964; Third Sec., Yaoundé, Cameroon, 1965–67; FCO, 1968–70; Second Sec., later First Sec., Copenhagen, 1970–73; FCO, 1973; Asst Private Sec. to Foreign and Commonwealth Sec., 1974–77; First Sec., Head of Chancery and Consul, Sofia, Bulgaria, 1977–81; FCO, 1981; Counsellor and Head of Chancery, Copenhagen, 1982–86; Dep. High Comr, Harare, 1986–89; Head of Southern Africa, later Central and Southern Africa, Dept, FCO, 1989–91; Resident Chm. (FCO), CSSB, 1991–92; High Comr, Zimbabwe, 1992–95; Asst Under-Sec. of State, later Dir, Africa and Commonwealth, FCO, 1995–98. Chm., Anglo-Norse Soc., 2003–19; Trustee, Internat. Alert, 2005–10 (Chm., 2006–10). Mem. Bd, Norfolk and Norwich Fest., 2003–06. Mem. Council, UEA, 2004–13. *Recreations:* music, walking, cross-country ski-ing, grandchildren. *Club:* Oxford and Cambridge.

**DALEY, Her Honour Judith Mary Philomena;** a Circuit Judge, 1994–2013; *b* 12 Aug. 1948; *d* of James Patrick Daley and Mary Elizabeth Daley (*née* Rawcliffe), BA. *Educ:* Seafield Convent Grammar Sch., Crosby; King's Coll. London (LLB Hons). Called to the Bar, Gray's Inn, 1970; Asst Recorder, 1984; Recorder, 1989–94 (Northern Circuit). *Recreations:* opera, music, theatre, travel, gardening. *Club:* Athenæum (Liverpool).

**DALGETY OF SIKOTILANI TONGA, Rt Hon. Lord,** Life Peer of Tonga (*cr* 2008); **Rt Hon. Ramsay Robertson Dalgety;** PC (Tonga) 2008; a Law Lord, Tonga, since 2008; *b* 2 July 1945; *s* of James Robertson Dalgety and Georgia Dalgety (*née* Whyte); *m* 1971, Margaret Bernard (*d* 2012); one *s* one *d. Educ:* High School of Dundee; Univ. of St Andrews (LLB Hons). Advocate, 1972; Temp. Sheriff, 1987–91; QC (Scot.) 1986. Dep. Traffic Comr for Scotland, 1988–93. Councillor, City of Edinburgh, 1974–80. Director/Chairman: Archer Transport Ltd and Archer Transport (London) Ltd, 1982–85; Venture Shipping Ltd, 1983–85. Director: Scottish Opera Ltd, 1980–90; Scottish Opera Theatre Trust Ltd, 1987–90; Chm., Opera Singers Pension Fund, 1990–92 (Dep. Chm., 1989–90; Trustee, 1983–92); Dep. Chm., Edinburgh Hibernian Shareholders Assoc., 1990–92. Judge of the Supreme Court, Tonga, 1991–95, and sometime Acting Chief Justice; Sec. Gen., Tonga Chamber of Commerce, 1998–2001. Chm., Electoral Commn of Tonga, 2016–. Chairman: Tonga Electric Power Bd, 2003–08; Electricity Commn, 2008–17; Judicial Cttee, Privy Council, 2008–; Mem. Defence Bd, Tonga, 2011–. Vice-Pres. and Treas., Tonga Internat. Gamefishing Assoc., 1994–98; Pres., Tonga Archery Fedn, 1998–2010; Dep. Chef de Mission, Kingdom of Tonga team, Olympic Games, Athens, 2004. Grand Cross, Order of Queen Salote (Tonga), 2008; Coronation Medal (Tonga), 2008. *Recreations:* heraldry, opera, travel, cricket, football, archery. *Address:* PO Box 38 Nuku'alofa, Kingdom of Tonga, South Pacific. *T:* 8723400. *E:* lawlord.tonga@gmail.com. *Club:* Royal Nuku'alofa (Tonga) (Mem. Cttee, 2003–13; Pres., 2014–).

**DALGLEISH, Andrew Stuart;** HM Diplomatic Service; Ambassador to Croatia, since 2016; *b* Wakefield, W Yorks, 17 Dec. 1975; *s* of Bruce Dalgleish and late Hilary Dalgleish (*née* Brentnall); *m* 2002, Aline Therese Vandenbussche; two *s. Educ:* King's High Sch., Pontefract; New Coll., Pontefract; Warwick Univ. (LLB 1st Cl. Hons Eur. Law). Entered FCO, 1999; Second Sec., Social Affairs, 1999–2001, First Sec., Envmtl Affairs, 2001–04, UK Perm. Representation to EU, Brussels; Dep. Hd, Internat. Climate Change, 2004–06, Dep. Hd, Envmtl Land Mgt, 2006–08, DEFRA; Hd, Europe Strategy Gp, FCO, 2008–11; Dep. Hd of Mission and Dir, UKTI, Seoul, 2011–15; lang. trng (Croatian), 2015–16. *Recreations:* family (playing, walking, telling stories together, watching old and new films), reading, cooking, writing. *Address:* British Embassy, Ivana Lučića 4, 10000 Zagreb, Croatia. *T:* (1) 6009100, *Fax:* (1) 6009111. *E:* andrew.dalgleish@fco.gov.uk.

**DALGLISH, Sir Kenneth Mathieson,** Kt 2018; MBE 1985; Manager, Liverpool Football Club, 2011–12 (Carling Cup winners, 2012); *b* Glasgow, 4 March 1951; *m* 1974, Marina (MBE 2009); one *s* three *d.* Professional football player, 1968–89: Celtic FC, 1970–77; Liverpool FC, 1977–89 (also Manager, 1985–91) (winner, Eur. Cup, 1978, 1981, 1984, FA Cup, 1986, 1989); Scotland, 1971–86 (102 caps); Manager, 1991–95, Dir of Football, 1995–96, Blackburn Rovers FC; New Business Develt Manager, Carnegie Sports Internat., 1996; Manager, Newcastle Utd FC, 1997–98; Dir of Football Ops and Bd Mem., Celtic FC, 1999–2000; with Liverpool FC Acad., 2009–11. Non-exec. Dir, Liverpool FC, 2013–. Founder, Marina Dalglish Appeal, 2004. Football Writers' Footballer of Year, 1979, 1983; Player of Year, PFA, 1983; Manager of Year, 1986, 1988, 1990, 1995. Freeman: City of Glasgow, 1986; City of Liverpool, 2016. *Publications:* Kenny Dalglish (autobiog.), 1996; My Liverpool Home (autobiog.), 2010.

**DALHOUSIE, 17th Earl of,** *cr* 1633; **James Hubert Ramsay;** Baron Ramsay 1618; Lord Ramsay 1633; Baron Ramsay (UK) 1875; Vice Lord-Lieutenant, Angus, since 2002; Lord Steward of HM Household, since 2009; Director, Jamestown Investments Ltd, since 1987; *b* 17 Jan. 1948; *er s* of 16th Earl of Dalhousie, KT, GCVO, GBE, MC; *S* father, 1999; *m* 1973, Marilyn, *yr d* of Major Sir David Henry Butter, KCVO, MC; one *s* two *d. Educ:* Ampleforth. 2nd Bn Coldstream Guards, commnd 1968–71, RARO 1971. Director: Hambros Bank Ltd, 1981–82; (exec.) Enskilda Securities, 1982–87; Capel-Cure Myers Capital Management Ltd, 1988–91; Dunedin Smaller Cos Investment Trust, 1993–2015 (Chm., 1998–2015); Scottish Woodlands Ltd, 1993–2005 (Chm., 1998–2005). Chm., (Scotland) Mental Health Foundn, 2000–02. Capt., 2010–, Pres. Council and Silver Stick for Scotland, 2013, Royal Co. of Archers (The Queen's Body Guard for Scotland). Vice Chm., Game Conservancy Trust, 1994–2009; President: British Deer Soc., 1987–2010; Dundee and Angus Br., Scots Guards Assoc., 2008. DL Angus, 1993. CStJ 2012 (OStJ 2001). *Heir: s* Lord Ramsay, *qv. Address:* Brechin Castle, Brechin, Angus DD9 6SG. *Clubs:* White's, Pratt's, Caledonian (Pres., 1990–), Turf.

**DALKEITH, Earl of;** Walter John Francis Montagu Douglas Scott; *b* 2 Aug. 1984; *s* and *heir* of Duke of Buccleuch, *qv* and of Duchess of Buccleuch, *qv;* *m* 2014, Elizabeth Honor Cobbe. A Page of Honour to HM The Queen, 1996–99.

**DALLAGLIO, Lawrence Bruno Nero,** OBE 2008 (MBE 2004); professional Rugby Union player, 1995–2008; Founding Partner, BBH Sport, since 2014; *b* 10 Aug. 1972; *s* of Vincenzo Dallaglio and late Eileen Dallaglio; *m* 2006, Alice Corbett; one *s* two *d. Educ:* Ampleforth Coll.; Kingston Univ. Debut, Wasps Rugby Union team, 1992, Capt., 1995–2008; Mem., British Lions touring teams, 1997, 2001, 2005; England team: debut, 1995; 85 caps, 1995–2007; Capt., 1997–99 and 2004; Mem., World Cup winning team, Australia, 2003. Dir, 2008–12, non-exec. Dir, 2015–, Wasps. Rugby Ambassador for: World Cup England 2015; Amlin. Lead Rugby expert, BT Sport, 2013–; columnist, Sunday Times. Sales Dir, Serco Global Services (formerly The Listening Company), 2006–13. Founder, Dallaglio RugbyWorks (formerly Dallaglio Foundn), 2009. *Publications:* Diary of a Season, 1997; Know the Modern Game, 1999; It's in the Blood: my life (autobiog.), 2007; Rugby Tales, 2009; World Cup Rugby Tales, 2011. *Recreations:* golf, cycling, Chelsea supporter.

**DALLAS, James;** Partner, Dentons (formerly Denton Wilde Sapte, then SNR Denton), since 1985; Executive Director, Energy and Natural Resources Law Institute, Centre for Commercial Law Studies, since 2014, and Professor of Energy Law, since 2017, Queen Mary University of London; *b* 21 April 1955; *m* 1979, Annabel Hope; one *s* two *d. Educ:* Eton Coll.; St Edmund Hall, Oxford (BA, MA Jurisprudence). Trainee and asst solicitor, 1976–81; Sen. Legal Advr, Internat. Energy Develt Corp., 1981–84; Denton Hall, subseq. Denton Wilde Sapte, later SNR Denton: Solicitor, 1984–; Chm., 1996–2009; Sen. Partner, ME and Africa, 2009–12. Non-exec. Dir, AMEC plc, 1999–2007. Mem., Legal Cttee, Red Tape Initiative, 2017–. Mem., Action for the River Kennet, 2003–. *Recreations:* fishing, birdwatching, cricket. *Address:* Dentons, One Fleet Place, EC4M 7WS.

**DALLAT, John James;** Member (SDLP) East Londonderry, Northern Ireland Assembly, 1998–2016 and since 2017; *b* 24 March 1947; *s* of Daniel and Ellen Dallat; *m* 1975, Anne Philomena Long; two *s* one *d. Educ:* Coleraine Coll. of Further Educn (qual. teacher, commercial subjects, 1968); North West Inst., Derry (Business Studies Teacher's Dip., 1975); Univ. of Ulster (Dip. in Advanced Studies in Educn, 1979); UC, Galway (Dip. in Rural Studies, 1997). Teacher: Technical Coll., Carndonagh, 1968–74; St Paul's Coll., Kilrea, 1975–98. Mem. (SDLP) Coleraine BC, 1977–98; Mayor of Coleraine, 2001–02. Contested (SDLP) Londonderry East, 2001. Dep. Speaker, NI Assembly, 2007–16. Chm., District Policing Partnership, 2007–08. *Recreations:* attending meetings!, walking, reading. *Address:* Northern Ireland Assembly, Parliament Buildings, Stormont, Belfast BT4 3XX.

**DALLISTON, Very Rev. Christopher Charles;** Dean of Peterborough, since 2018; *b* 2 April 1956; *s* of Gerald and Rosemary Dalliston; *m* 1989, Michelle Aleysha Caron; two *s* two *d. Educ:* Diss Grammar Sch.; Peterhouse, Cambridge (MA 1980); St Stephen's House, Oxford (BA 1984). Ford Motor Co., 1978–81. Ordained deacon, 1984, priest, 1985; Curate, Halstead, 1984–87; Domestic Chaplain to Bp of Chelmsford, 1987–91; Vicar, St Edmund, Forest Gate, 1991–95; St Botolph, Boston, 1995–2003; Dean of Newcastle, 2003–18. *Recreations:* choral music, folksong, theatre, Norwich City FC, walking. *Address:* The Deanery, 14 Minster Precincts, Peterborough PE1 1XX. *E:* Dean.PA@peterborough-cathedral.org.uk.

**DALLMAN, Prof. Margaret Jane,** OBE 2016; DPhil; FRSB; FCGI; Professor of Immunology, since 1999, Associate Provost (Academic Partnerships), since 2015, and Vice President (International), since 2018, Imperial College London; *b* Farnborough, Kent, 14 May 1957; *d* of James Philip Dallman and Margaret Florence Dallman (*née* Ware); *m* 1997, Andrew Christopher George Porter; one *s. Educ:* Ravensbourne Sch. for Girls; Univ. of Bristol (BSc Hons Cellular Pathol. 1978); Linacre Coll., Oxford (DPhil 1982; MA 1985). Res. scientist, Wellcome Res. Labs, 1978–79; Post-doctoral Res. Fellow, Stanford Univ., 1982–84; Nuffield Foundn Jun. Res. Fellow, Hertford Coll., Oxford, 1984–87 (Emeritus Fellow, 1994); MRC Sen. Res. Fellow, Univ. of Oxford, 1987–94; Imperial College London: Lectr in Immunol., 1994–96; Reader in Immunoregulation, 1996–99; Dean, Faculty of Natural Scis, 2008–14. Chair, Basic Scis Underpinning Health Bd, BBSRC, 2011–14. Non-exec. Dir, Imperial Coll. Healthcare NHS Trust, 2010–11. Mem. Bd, Francis Crick Inst. (formerly UK Centre for Med. Res. and Innovation), 2011–. Member: Scientific Adv. Bd, Pirbright Inst. (formerly Inst. for Animal Health), 2010–15; Bd, NC3Rs, 2010–15; Res. and Innovation Strategic Adv. Cttee, HEFC, 2011–12; Strategic Adv. Cttee for Res. and Knowledge Exchange, HEFCE, 2012–16; BBSRC, 2014–18. Trustee and Chm., Wye Coll. Foundn Trust, 2009–14. Gov., Westminster Sch., 2017–. FRSB (FSB 2011); FCGI 2011. *Publications:* contrib. papers, book chapters and reviews to scientific lit. in fields of immunol. and transplantation biol. *Recreations:* painting, reading, ski-ing, walking. *Address:* L2 Faculty Building, Imperial College London, SW7 2AZ. *T:* (020) 7594 5406. *E:* m.dallman@imperial.ac.uk.

**DALLAWAY, Simeilia H.;** *see* Hodge-Dalloway.

**DALMENY, Lord; Harry Ronald Neil Primrose;** DL; Chairman, Sotheby's United Kingdom and Ireland, since 2017 (Director, Sotheby's, since 2001; Chairman, Sotheby's Private Clients, 2013–17); *b* 20 Nov. 1967; *s* and *heir* of 7th Earl of Rosebery, *qv*; *m* 1994, Caroline (marr. diss. 2014), *e d* of Ronald Daglish and Mrs William Wyatt-Lowe; one *s* four *d* (incl. triplets). *Educ:* Dragon Sch., Oxford; Eton Coll.; Trinity Coll., Cambridge (BA Hons). Mem., Royal Co. of Archers, The Queen's Body Guard for Scotland, 2002–. DL Midlothian, 2006. *Heir: s* Hon. Caspian Albert Harry Primrose, *b* 8 Sept. 2005. *Address:* Dalmeny House, South Queensferry, West Lothian EH30 9TQ. *T:* (0131) 331 1784. *Clubs:* White's; University Pitt (Cambridge); Midlothian (Edinburgh); Royal Caledonian Hunt; St Moritz Tobogganing.

**DALRYMPLE,** family name of **Earl of Stair**.

**DALRYMPLE, Viscount; John James Thomas Dalrymple;** *b* 3 Jan. 2008; *s* and *heir* of Earl of Stair, *qv*.

**DALRYMPLE, Sir Hew (Richard) Hamilton,** 11th Bt *cr* 1697; *b* 3 Sept. 1955; *e s* of Sir Hew Fleetwood Hamilton-Dalrymple, 10th Bt, GCVO; *S* father, 2018, but his name does not appear on the Official Roll of the Baronetage; *m* 1987, Jane Elizabeth, *yr d* of Lt-Col John Morris; one *s* three *d. Educ:* Ampleforth; Corpus Christi Coll., Oxford (MA); Clare Hall, Cambridge (MPhil); Birkbeck Coll., Univ. of London (MSc). ODI Fellow, Swaziland, 1982–84; KPMG Mgt Consultants, 1984–92; Scottish & Newcastle Breweries, 1993–2005. Dir, Broadland Wineries, 2017–. Trustee: Scottish Seabird Centre, 1998–2017; Inst. for Turnaround, 2010–18. Sloan Fellow, London Business Sch., 1987–88. *Heir: s* Hew John Lucian Hamilton Dalrymple, *b* 25 Aug. 1990. *Address:* Blackdykes, North Berwick, E Lothian EH39 5PQ.

**DALRYMPLE, Prof. Mary Elizabeth,** PhD; FBA 2013; Professor of Syntax, University of Oxford, since 2006; *b* Missouri, 9 March 1954; *d* of Thomas W. and Mary E. Dalrymple; *m* 1999, Kenneth M. Kahn; one step *s. Educ:* Cornell Coll. (BA Hons English 1976); Univ. of Texas at Austin (MA Linguistics 1984); Stanford Univ. (PhD Linguistics 1990). Mem., Res. Staff, 1990–2001, Sen. Mem., Res. Staff, 2001–02, Palo Alto Res. Center, Calif; Sen. Lectr, Dept of Computer Sci., KCL, 2003–04; Lectr in Gen. Linguistics, Univ. of Oxford, 2004–06. MAE 2018. *Publications:* The Syntax of Anaphoric Binding, 1993; Lexical Functional Grammar, 2001; (with I. Nikolaeva) Objects and Information Structure, 2011; (with S. Mofu) Dusner, 2012. *Recreations:* cinema, theatre, swimming, travelling. *Address:* Centre for Linguistics and Philology, Walton Street, Oxford OX1 2HG. *T:* (01865) 280412, *Fax:* (01865) 280412. *E:* mary.dalrymple@ling-phil.ox.ac.uk.

**DALRYMPLE, William Benedict Hamilton;** writer; Co-Director, Jaipur Literature Festival, since 2005; *b* 20 March 1965; *s* of Sir Hew Fleetwood Hamilton-Dalrymple, 10th Bt, GCVO and Lady Anne-Louise Mary Hamilton-Dalrymple; *m* 1991, Olivia Fraser; two *s* one *d. Educ:* Ampleforth Coll.; Trinity Coll., Cambridge (Exhibr; Sen. Hist. Schol.; MA Hons 1992). Television series: Stones of the Raj, 1997; Indian Journeys, 2000 (Grierson Award, Best Documentary Series, 2001); Sufi Soul, 2005; radio series: Three Miles an Hour, 2002; The Long Search, 2002 (Sandford St Martin Prize for Religious Broadcasting), 2003. Exhibn, Princes and Painters in Mughal Delhi, 1707–1857, Asia Soc., NY, 2012. Whitney J. Oates Fellow in S Asian Studies, Princeton Univ., 2012. FRSL 1993; FRGS 1993; FRAS 1998. Corresp. FRSE 2018. Hon. DLitt: St Andrews, 2006; Lucknow, 2007; Aberdeen, 2008; Bradford, 2012. Mungo Park Medal, RSGS, 2002; Sir Percy Sykes Meml Medal, RSAA, 2005; Col James Todd Award, Mewar Foundn, 2008. *Publications:* In Xanadu, 1989 (Yorks Post Best First Work Award, Scottish Arts Council Spring Book Award, 1990); City of Djinns, 1993 (Thomas Cook Travel Book Award, Sunday Times Young British Writer of Year Award, 1994); From the Holy Mountain (Scottish Arts Council Autumn Book Award), 1997; The Age of Kali (collected journalism), 1998 (Prix d'Astrolabe, 2005); White Mughals, 2002 (Wolfson Hist. Prize, 2003; Scottish Book of the Year Prize, 2003); The Last Mughal, 2006 (Duff Cooper Memorial Prize, 2007); Nine Lives: in search of the sacred in modern India, 2009 (Asia House Literary Award, 2010); (with Yuthika Sharma) Princes and Painters in Mughal Delhi, 1707–1857, 2012; Return of a King: the battle for Afghanistan 1835–42, 2012; (with Anita Anand) Koh-i-Noor: the history of the world's most infamous diamond, 2017; The Anarchy: the relentless rise of the East India Company, 2019; contribs to jls incl. TLS, Granta, New Yorker, NY Review of Books, Guardian. *Address:* 1 & 2 Pages' Yard, Church Street, Old Chiswick, W4 2PA. *T:* (020) 8994 4500. *E:* williamdalrymple@gmail.com.

**DALRYMPLE HAMILTON, (North) John (Frederick),** OBE 1992; TD 1989; farmer, since 1982; Vice Lord-Lieutenant, Ayrshire and Arran, since 1998; *b* 7 May 1950; *s* of late Captain North Edward Frederick Dalrymple-Hamilton, CVO, MBE, DSC, RN and Hon. Mary Colville; *m* 1980, Sally Anne How; two *s* one *d. Educ:* Aberdeen Univ. (MA Hons 1972); E of Scotland Coll. of Agriculture (Cert. Agric. 1983). Sales Manager, Scottish & Newcastle Breweries, 1973–82; Bargany estate, 1982–; Chm., Gardening Leave, 2008–12. Commnd TA, 1970; CO, QOY, 1989–92; Dep. Comdr (Col), 52 Bde, 1993–94. Chm., Lowlands RFCA, 2003–07. DL Ayrshire and Arran, 1995–98. *Address:* Lovestone House, Bargany, Girvan, Ayrshire KA26 9RF. *T:* (01465) 871227. *Club:* New (Edinburgh).

**DALRYMPLE-HAY, Sir Malcolm (John Robert),** 8th Bt *cr* 1798, of Park Place, Wigtownshire; FRCS; Consultant Cardiac Surgeon, since 2001; *b* Epsom, 1 April 1966; *o s* of Sir John Hugh Dalrymple-Hay, 7th Bt and of Jennifer Phyllis, *d* of Brig. Robert Johnston, OBE; *S* father, 2009; *m* 1998, Vanessa Long; three *d. Educ:* Univ. of London (MB BS 1990; PhD 1997). FRCS 1999; FECTS 1999. *Recreations:* golf, ski-ing, running. *Heir: uncle* Ronald George Inglis Dalrymple-Hay [*b* 3 March 1933; *m* 1973, Anne Valerie, *d* of Bernard James Dawson; one *s*]. *E:* malcolm@dalrymple-hay.com.

**DALRYMPLE-WHITE, Sir Jan Hew,** 3rd Bt *cr* 1926, of High Mark, Wigtownshire; Director, Mia Online Ltd, since 2003; *b* 26 Nov. 1950; *o s* of Sir Henry Arthur Dalrymple-White, 2nd Bt and Mary (*née* Thomas); *S* father, 2006, but his name does not appear on the Official Roll of the Baronetage; *m* 1st, 1979, Elizabeth Wallis (marr. diss); 2nd, 1984, Angela Stevenson (marr. diss.); one *s*; 3rd, 1990, Elizabeth Smith. *Educ:* Stowe.

**DALTON, Carol;** *see* Monaghan, C.

**DALTON, Daniel Anthony Thomas;** Member (C) West Midlands Region, European Parliament, 2015–19; *b* Oxford, 31 Jan. 1974; *s* of Anthony Thomas Dalton and Anita Jirina Dalton; *m* 2010, Silke Hermannsdörfer; one *s* one *d. Educ:* Warwick Sch.; Coventry Univ. (BA Hons Internat. Relns and Politics); Warwick Univ. (MA Internat. Politics of E Asia). Professional cricketer, Warwickshire CCC and cricket coach, 1996–2005. Hd of Office, Neil Parish, MEP, 2005–09; Policy Advr, Eur. Conservatives and Reformists Gp, EP, 2009–15. Contested (C) W Midlands, EP, 2019.

**DALTON, Duncan Edward S.;** *see* Shipley Dalton.

**DALTON, Vice-Adm. Sir Geoffrey (Thomas James Oliver),** KCB 1986; Secretary-General of Mencap, 1987–90; *b* 14 April 1931; *s* of late Jack Rowland Thomas Dalton and Margaret Kathleen Dalton; *m* 1957, Jane Hamilton (*née* Baynes); four *s. Educ:* Parkfield, Sussex; Reigate Grammar Sch.; RNC Dartmouth. Midshipman 1950; served in HM Ships Illustrious, Loch Alvie, Cockade, Virago, Flag Lieut to C-in-C The Nore, and HMS Maryton (in comd), 1950–61; served HMS Murray, RN Staff Course and HMS Dido, 1961–66; served HMS Relentless (in Comd), RN Sch. of PT, HMS Nubian (in Comd), Staff of Flag Officer Second in Comd Far East Fleet and Second Flotilla, 1966–72; Asst Dir of Naval Plans, 1972–74; RCDS, 1975; Captain RN Presentation Team, 1976–77; in Comd HMS Jupiter, 1977–79 and HMS Dryad, 1979–81; Asst Chief of Naval Staff (Policy), MoD, 1981–84; Dep. SACLANT, 1984–87. Commander, 1966; Captain, 1972; Rear-Adm. 1981; Vice-Adm. 1984. President: RBL, 1993–97; Regular Forces Employment Assoc., 1999–2002; Chm., Ex-Services Fellowship Centres, 1991–2006. Hon. Col 71st (Yeomanry) Signal Regt (Volunteers), 1998–2001. Gov., QMW, 1992–2002. Mem. Ct of Assts, Drapers' Co., 1989– (Master, 1996). FCMI (FBIM 1987). *Address:* 28 Valley Park Drive, Waterlooville, Hants PO8 0PD.

**DALTON, Graham Edward,** CEng, FREng, FICE, FCIHT; Chief Executive, Defence Infrastructure Organisation, since 2016; *b* 24 Sept. 1960; *s* of John and Jocelyn Dalton; *m* 1985, Fiona Jane Iles; three *d. Educ:* Gillotts Sch., Henley-on-Thames; Imperial Coll., London (BSc 1st Cl. Civil Engrg 1983); Henley Mgt Coll. (MBA 2000). CEng 1989; FICE 2003; FCIHT 2013; FREng 2016. Mgt trainee, BR, 1979–88; civil engr, L. G. Mouchel & Partners, 1988–95; Project Manager, Bovis Construction, 1995–2001; Project Dir, Strategic Rail Authy, 2001–05; Dir, Rail Projects, DfT, 2005–08; Chief Exec., Highways Agency, 2008–15. Mem. Council, ICE, 2004–07. *Recreations:* sailing, walking. *E:* grahamdalton@icloud.com. *Clubs:* Royal Air Force; Dell Quay Sailing (Chichester).

**DALTON, Ian Mark Marshall,** CBE 2011; Executive Chair, Government Automation Taskforce, since 2019; *b* Welwyn Garden City, 14 Jan. 1964; *s* of Douglas Vivian Marshall Dalton and Helgard Dalton (*née* Herzog); *m* 1992, Juliet Kearsley; one *s* one *d. Educ:* Verulam Sch., St Albans; Univ. of York (BA Hons Econs); MA Mental Handicap Services); Univ. of Durham (MBA). Residential Care Officer, N Yorks CC, 1985–86; Project, 1986–88, Dist Officer, 1988–90, RSMHCA; Develt Manager, Community Mental Health, Durham CC, 1990–91; Policy Officer, Community Care, then Hd of Primary and Community Care, Northern and Yorks (formerly Northern) RHA, 1991–95; Hd, Primary and Community Care, 1995–96, Purchaser Perf. Develt, 1996–97, Northern & Yorks Regl Office, NHS Exec.; Dir, Planning and Develt, Hartlepool and E Durham NHS Trust, 1997–99; Dir, Acute Services, Planning and Develt, N Tees and Hartlepool NHS Trust, 1999–2000; Department of Health: Regl Dir of Perf. Mgt (Northern and Yorks), 2000–02;

Dir of Perf. (N), 2002–03; Chief Executive: N Cheshire Hosps NHS Trust, 2003–05; N Tees and Hartlepool NHS Trust, 2005–07; NE Strategic HA, 2007–11 (on secondment as Nat. Dir for NHS Flu Resilience, DoH, 2009–10; on assignment as Man. Dir, Provider Develt, DoH, 2010–11); NHS North of England, 2011–12; Chief Operating Officer and Dep. Chief Exec., NHS Commissioning Bd, 2012–13; Pres., Global Health, 2013–14, Global Govt and Health, 2014–16, BT Global Services; CEO, Imperial Coll. Healthcare NHS Trust, 2017; Chief Exec., NHS Improvement, 2017–19. Non-exec. Dir, Crown Agents Ltd, 2016–. Hon. Col, (250) Med. Sqdn (V), 3 Med. Regt (formerly B (250) Med. Sqdn (V), 5 Gen. Med. Support Regt), RAMC, 2007–12.

**DALTON, Maurice Leonard**, LVO 1986 (MVO 1981); OBE 1996; HM Diplomatic Service, retired; former protocol consultant, 2000–17; *b* 18 May 1944; *s* of Albert William Dalton and Mildred Eliza (*née* Wraight); *m* 1982, Cathy Lee Parker. Joined FO, 1965; Enugu and Lagos, 1967–68; FCO, 1968–70; Attaché, Ankara, 1970–72; Third Secretary: E Berlin, 1973–74; Abu Dhabi, 1974–76; Second Sec., FCO, 1977–79; Second, later First Sec., Oslo, 1979–83; First Secretary: Kuala Lumpur, 1983–86; Peking, 1986; FCO, 1987–92; Asst Head of Protocol Dept, FCO, and HM Asst Marshal of Diplomatic Corps, 1992–96; Counsellor and Head of Conference Dept, FCO, 1996–98; Head of Protocol Dept, FCO, 1998–99; HM First Asst Marshal of Diplomatic Corps, 1998–2000; Protocol Consultant, FCO, 2001–05. Protocol Adviser: Jamaican Govt, 2010–12; St Lucia Gov.-Gen.'s Office, 2013–14. Chm., Tenterden and Dist Nat. Trust Assoc., 2012–16 (Mem. Cttee, 2010–12); Chm. (formerly Sec.) Smallhythe 500 Commemoration Cttee, 2013–. Royal Norwegian Order: of St Olav, 1981; of Merit, 1994. *Publications*: (jtly) From Ships to Sheep: the story of Smallhythe, 2015. *Recreations*: National Trust volunteer, genealogy. *Address*: Brookside, Hope's Grove Lane, Smallhythe Road, Tenterden, Kent TN30 7LT.

**DALTON, Sir Richard (John)**, KCMG 2005 (CMG 1996); HM Diplomatic Service, retired; consultant; *b* 10 Oct. 1948; *s* of Maj.-Gen. John Cecil D'Arcy Dalton, CB, CBE and Pamela Frances (*née* Segrave); *m* 1972, Elisabeth Mary Keays; two *s* two *d* (and one *s* decd). *Educ*: Winchester Coll.; Magdalene Coll., Cambridge (BA). Joined HM Diplomatic Service, 1970: FCO, 1971; MECAS, 1971–73; 2nd Sec., Amman, 1973–75; 2nd, later 1st, Sec., Mission to UN, NY, 1975–79; FCO, 1979–83; Dep. Head of Mission, Muscat, 1983–87; Dep. Head, Southern African Dept, FCO, 1987–88; Head, Tropical Foods Div. and Ext. Relns and Trade Div., MAFF, 1988–91; Vis. Fellow, RIIA, 1991–92; Head, CSCE Unit, FCO, 1992–93; Consul Gen., Jerusalem, 1993–97; Dir (Personnel), FCO, 1998–99; Ambassador to: Libya, 1999–2002; Iran, 2003–06. Dir Gen., Libyan British Business Council, 2006–09. President: Iran Soc., 2009–; British Iranian Chamber of Commerce, 2015–. *Publications*: Peace in the Gulf: a long term view, 1992; (ed) Iran: breaking the nuclear deadlock, 2009; Iran's Nuclear Future, 2014. *Recreation*: land and woodland management. *Address*: Hauxwell Hall, Leyburn, N Yorks DL8 5LR.

**DALTON, Air Chief Marshal Sir Stephen (Gary George)**, GCB 2012 (KCB 2009; CB 2006); FRAeS; Lieutenant-Governor and Commander-in-Chief, Jersey, since 2017; Bath King of Arms, since 2018; *b* 23 April 1954. *Educ*: Univ. of Bath (BSc). Royal Air Force: exercises in Europe, USA and Canada; psc; qwi 1983; RAF Brockwell, 1990; Comdr, RAF Coltishall and Jaguar Force, 1997–99; Dir, Eurofighter Prog. Assurance Gp, MoD, 2000; hcsc, 2002; Dir Air Ops, MoD, 2002–03; Capability Manager (Information Superiority), 2003–04; Controller Aircraft, 2004–07; Dir Gen. Typhoon, 2006–07; Dep. C-in-C Personnel and Air Mem. for Personnel, HQ Air Comd, 2007–09; CAS, 2009–13; Air ADC to the Queen, 2009–13. Pres., RAeS, 2017–18. Hon. LLD Leicester. CCMI.

**DALTON, William Robert Patrick**, FCIB, FICB; Chief Executive, HSBC (formerly Midland) Bank plc, 1998–2004; *b* 8 Dec. 1943; *s* of Albert and Emily Dalton; *m* 1993, Starr Underhill; one *s* one *d*. *Educ*: Univ. of British Columbia (BComm 1971). FICB 1971; FCIB 1998. Joined Bank of Montreal, 1961; Wardley Canada Ltd, later HSBC Bank, Canada, 1980, Pres. and CEO, 1992–97; Director: HSBC Holdings, 1998–2004; HSBC Private Banking Hldgs (Suisse) SA, 2001–04; Crédit Commercial de France SA, 2000–04; AEGIS Insce Services Inc. (formerly AEGIS Ltd), 2004–15. Non-executive Director: Mastercard Internat., 1998–2004; HSBC Finance Inc. (formerly Household Internat. Inc.), 2003–08; AEGIS London, 2004– (Chm., 2015–); First Choice Holidays plc, 2004–07; Swiss Re GB, 2005–08; Talisman Energy Inc., 2005–14; TUI Travel plc, 2007–12; United States Cold Storage Ltd, 2007–; HSBC Hldgs USA Inc., 2008–15. Vice-Pres., CIB, 2001–. Pres., BBA, 2003–04. Chm., Young Enterprise UK, 1998–2004; Trustee: Crimestoppers Trust, 2000–04; Duke of Edinburgh's Commonwealth Study Confs (UK Fund), 2002–10; Centre for Study of Financial Innovation, 2003–13. Hon. Dr UCE, 2001.

**DALTREY, Roger Harry**, CBE 2005; singer; *b* Hammersmith, 1 March 1944; *s* of Harry and Irene Daltrey; *m* 1971, Heather Taylor; two *s* two *d*; one *s* by a previous marriage. *Educ*: Acton Co. Grammar Sch. Lead singer, The Detours, later The Who, 1964–84; solo singer, 1984–. Albums with The Who: My Generation, 1965; A Quick One, 1966; Happy Jack, 1967; The Who Sell Out, 1967; Magic Bus, 1968; Tommy, 1969; Who's Next, 1971; Meaty Beefy Big And Bouncy, 1971; Quadrophenia, 1973; The Who By Numbers, 1975; The Story of the Who, 1976; Who Are You, 1978; Face Dances, 1981; Hooligans, 1982; It's Hard, 1982; Once Upon A Time, 1983; Two's Missing, 1987; Endless Wire, 2006; Who, 2019; solo albums: Daltrey, 1973; Ride A Rock Horse, 1975; One of the Boys, 1977; Parting Should Be Painless, 1984; Under a Raging Moon, 1985; Can't Wait to See the Movie, 1987; Rocks in the Head, 1992; As Long As I Have You, 2018; (with Wilko Johnson) Going Back Home, 2014. Actor in films including: Tommy, 1974; Lisztomania, 1975; The Legacy, 1978; McVicar (also prod.), 1980; Mack the Knife, 1990; Buddy's Song (also prod.), 1991. *Publications*: Thanks a Lot Mr Kibblewhite (memoir), 2018. *Address*: c/o Trinifold Management Ltd, 12 Oval Road, NW1 7DH.

**DALY, Angela Josepha**; see Garvey, A. J.

**DALY, Hon. Francis Lenton**; Judge of District Courts, Queensland, Australia, 1989–99; Judge of Planning and Environment Court, Queensland, 1994–99; *b* 23 June 1938; *s* of late Sydney Richard Daly and Lilian May Daly (*née* Lindholm); *m* 1964, Joyce Brenda (*née* Nicholls). *Educ*: Forest School; London School of Economics (LLB). Called to Bar, Gray's Inn, 1961 (Lord Justice Holker Exhibn). English Bar, 1961–66; Legal Secretary, Lord Chancellor's Office, 1966; Bermudian Bar, 1966–72; Asst Judge Advocate General to the Forces, UK, 1972–78; Principal Magistrate, Malaita, Solomon Islands, 1978; Attorney General, 1979, Chief Justice, 1980–84, Solomon Islands; Chief Justice, Nauru, 1983; admitted, Qld Bar, 1984. *Publications*: contribs to International and Comparative Law Qly, Commonwealth Judicial Jl. *Recreations*: yachting, rowing, reading. *Address*: 22 Booth Street, Balmain, NSW 2041, Australia.
*See also* O. L. Aikin.

**DALY, James**, CVO 1994; HM Diplomatic Service, retired; re-employed, Foreign and Commonwealth Office, since 2001; *b* 8 Sept. 1940; *s* of late Maurice Daly and Christina Daly; *m* 1970, Dorothy Lillian Powell; one *s* (and one *s* decd). *Educ*: St Thomas More, Chelsea; University College London (BSc Hons Econ). Served RM, 1958–67. Joined Foreign Office, 1968: Third Secretary: Accra, 1971–73; Moscow, 1973–76; Second Sec., Karachi, 1976–78; First Secretary: FCO, 1978–79; Sofia, 1979–86; Consul-Gen., Paris, 1986–92; Counsellor and Consul-Gen., Moscow, 1992–95; High Commissioner: Vanuatu, 1995–97; Mauritius, 1997–2000. Mem., Special Immigration Appeals Commn, 2002–12. *Recreations*: reading, music, walking. *Address*: 44 Ashley Court, Morpeth Terrace, SW1P 1EN. *Club*: Naval and Military.

**DALY, Rev. Mgr John Anthony**; Parish Priest, St Mary's Horwich, since 2018; Vicar General, Diocese of Salford, since 2016; Principal Roman Catholic Chaplain, Royal Air Force, 2004–07; *b* 23 Sept. 1952; *s* of Richard and Mary Daly. *Educ*: St Anne's RC Primary Sch., Stretford; St Mary's Secondary Sch., Stretford; Ushaw Coll., Durham. Ordained, 1977; Priest: St Osmund's, Breightmet, Bolton, 1977–83; St Mary's, Radcliffe, Bury, 1983–84; joined RAF, 1985; Gp Captain, 2004. QHC, 2004–07; Vicar General, 2004–07; Parish Priest, St Mary's Oswaldtwistle, 2008–18. *Recreations*: supporting Manchester United, ski-ing, golf, music, cooking. *Address*: St Mary's Presbytery, 86 Chorley New Road, Horwich, Bolton BL6 5QJ. *E*: John.Daly@dioceseofsalford.org.uk.

**DALY, Margaret Elizabeth**; *b* 26 Jan. 1938; *d* of Robert and Elizabeth Bell; *m* 1964, Kenneth Anthony Edward Daly; one *d*. *Educ*: Methodist Coll., Belfast. Departmental Head, Phoenix Assurance Co., 1956–60; Trade Union Official, Guild of Insurance Officials, later Union of Insurance Staffs, and subseq. merged with ASTMS, 1960–71; Consultant, Cons. Party, 1976–79; Nat. Dir of Cons. Trade Unionists, 1979–84. MEP (C) Somerset and Dorset W, 1984–94; contested (C) Somerset and N Devon, Eur. Parly elecns, 1994; Mem., Develt Cttee, Eur. Parlt, 1984–94 (Vice Chm., 1987–89; Cons. spokesman, 1989–94); Vice-Pres., Jt EEC/African Caribbean Pacific Lomé Assembly, 1988–94. Contested (C), Weston-super-Mare, 1997. Mem. Bd, Traidcraft PLC, 1995–98. Mem. Bd, South West in Europe, 2000–01; European Movement: Mem. Mgt Bd, 1999–2006; Vice-Pres., Somerset Br., 2002– (Chair, 1999–2001); Pres., Devon Br., 2005–. Direct Mem., EPP, 1990–. Vice Chm., Britain Stronger in Europe South West, 2016. *Recreations*: swimming, music, travel, positive actions regarding the EU. *Address*: The Old School House, Aisholt, Bridgwater, Somerset TA5 1AR.

**DALY, Michael Francis**, CMG 1989; HM Diplomatic Service, retired; *b* 7 April 1931; *s* of late William Thomas Daly and Hilda Frances Daly; *m* 1st, 1963, Sally Malcolm Angwin (*d* 1966); one *d*; 2nd, 1971, Juliet Mary Siragusa (*née* Arning); one step *d*. *Educ*: Downside; Gonville and Caius Coll., Cambridge (Scholar; MA). Mil. Service, 1952–54: 2nd Lieut, Intell. Corps. E. D. Sassoon Banking Co., London, 1954; Transreef Industrial & Investment Co., Johannesburg, 1955–66; General Electric Co., London, 1966; HM Diplomatic Service: 1st Sec., FCO, 1967; 1st Sec. (Commercial), Rio de Janeiro, 1969; 1st Sec. (Inf.) and Head of Chancery, Dublin, 1973; Asst, Cultural Relations Dept, FCO, 1976; Counsellor, Consul-Gen. and Head of Chancery, Brasilia, 1977–78; Ambassador to Ivory Coast, Upper Volta and Niger, 1978–83; Head of West African Dept, FCO, and Ambassador (non-resident) to Chad, 1983–86; Ambassador: to Costa Rica and (non-resident) to Nicaragua, 1986–89; to Bolivia, 1989–91. Sec., Margaret Mee Fellowship Programme, 1993–. Kew Medal, 2002. *Recreations*: sailing, theatre, golf, watching cricket, am-dram. *Address*: 45 Priory Road, Kew, Surrey TW9 3DQ. *T*: (020) 8940 1272. *Club*: Canning.

**DALY, Michael Vincent**; Director, Corporate Services Transformation Programme, Department for Children, Schools and Families (formerly Efficiency and Reform Unit, Department for Education and Skills), 2006–09; *b* 23 July 1958; *s* of Michael Joseph Daly and Mary Anne Daly. *Educ*: St Philip's Grammar Sch., Edgbaston; Birmingham Univ. (DMS 1989). HEO (D), HSE, 1989; Second Sec. for Social Affairs, UK Repn to EC, 1990; Private Sec. to Parly Under Sec. of State, Dept of Employment, 1990–93; UK Rep. on Social Affairs to Council of Europe, Strasbourg, 1993–95; Divl Manager, DFEE, 1999–2001; Project Dir, No 10 Forward Strategy Unit, 2001–02; Hd, Learning Acad., 2002–04, Dir of Change, 2004–06, DFES. *Recreations*: pickleball, golf, film, early science fiction.

**DALY, Nigel Jonathan; His Honour Judge Daly**; a Circuit Judge, since 2018; *b* Chard, Somerset; *s* of John Daly and Joan Daly; *m* 1980, Joanne Lorraine; two *s* one *d*. *Educ*: Skegness Grammar Sch.; King's Coll. London (LLB). Called to the Bar, Gray's Inn, 1979; a Recorder, 2002–18. *Recreations*: food, wine, family, dog.

**DALYELL, Kathleen Mary Agnes**, OBE 2005; National Trust for Scotland Administrator at The Binns, since 1972; Chairman, Royal Commission on Ancient and Historical Monuments of Scotland, 2000–05; *b* 17 Nov. 1937; *o d* of Rt Hon. Lord Wheatley and Agnes (Nancy) Lady Wheatley (*née* Nichol); *m* 1963, Tam Dalyell (*d* 2017); one *s* one *d*. *Educ*: Convent of the Sacred Heart, Aberdeen; Edinburgh Univ. (MA Hons History 1960); Craiglochart Teacher Trng Coll., Edinburgh. Teacher of History: St Augustine's Secondary Sch., Glasgow, 1961–62; James Gillespie's High Sch. for Girls, Edinburgh, 1962–63. Member: Historic Buildings Council for Scotland, 1975–87; Lady Provost of Edinburgh's Delegn to China, 1987; Nat. Cttee of Architectural Heritage Soc. for Scotland, 1983–89 (Vice-Chm., 1986–89); Ancient Monuments Bd for Scotland, 1989–99; Royal Fine Art Commn for Scotland, 1992–2001. Chm., Bo'ness Heritage Trust, 1988–93; Director: Heritage Educn Trust, 1987–2005; Weslo Housing Assoc., 1994–2003; Trustee: Paxton Trust, 1988–92; Carmont Settlement Trust, 1997–2013; Hopetoun Preservation Trust, 2005–16; Mus. of Scotland Charitable Trust, 2005–. DL W Lothian, 2001. Mem. Ct, Stirling Univ., 2003–08. Hon. Dr: Edinburgh, 2006; Stirling, 2008. *Publications*: House of The Binns, 1973. *Recreations*: reading, travel, chess, hill walking. *Address*: The Binns, Blackness, Linlithgow, Scotland EH49 7NA. *T*: (01506) 834255.

**DALZIEL, Ian Martin**; Head of Global Private Wealth, Threadneedle Asset Management Ltd, 2009–12; Member, Advisory Board, Cerno Capital, 2010–12; *b* 21 June 1947; *s* of late John Calvin Dalziel and of Elizabeth Roy Dalziel, *e d* of Rev. Ian Bain, FRSE and Mrs Christian Stuart Fisher Bain, Gairloch; *m* 1972, Nadia Maria Iacovazzi; four *s*. *Educ*: Daniel Stewart's Coll., Edinburgh; St John's Coll., Cambridge; Université Libre de Bruxelles (Weiner Anspach Foundation Scholarship, 1970). Mullens & Co., 1970–72; Manufacturers Hanover Ltd, 1972–83. Mem., Richmond upon Thames Council, 1978–79. Mem. (C) Lothian, European Parlt, 1979–84. Chairman: Continental Assets Trust plc, 1989–98; Invesco Smaller Continental Cos Trust plc, 1998–2005; Director: Adam & Co. plc, 1983–92; Lepercq-Amcur Fund NV, 1989–2005; Gen. Man., Devin SA, 1992–2008; Consultant, Primwest Hldg NV, 1992–2008. Mem., Queen's Body Guard for Scotland (Royal Company of Archers). *Recreations*: golf, stalking, ski-ing. *Address*: Stable House, Maxton, St Boswells, Roxburghshire TD6 0EX. *T*: (01835) 824262. *E*: imd4@mac.com. *Clubs*: Brooks's; Hawks (Cambridge); Royal and Ancient Golf (St Andrews); Hon. Company of Edinburgh Golfers; Royal St George's Golf (Sandwich).

**DALZIEL, Maureen**, MD; FFPH; Director, MD health consultancy Ltd, since 2004; *b* 7 April 1952; *d* of late Peter and of Eileen Farrell; *m* 1974, Ian Dalziel. *Educ*: Notre Dame High Sch., Glasgow; Univ. of Glasgow (MB ChB); MD London 2004. MFCM 1985, FFPH (FFPHM 1990). Jun. hosp. posts, Glasgow and Lanarkshire Hosps, 1976–79; GP, E Kilbride, 1979–81; Registrar, then Sen. Registrar in Public Health Medicine: SW Herts HA, 1981–83; Brent HA, 1983–85; Consultant in Public Health Medicine, 1985–89, Associate Dir, 1989, NW Thames RHA; Chief Executive: SW Herts DHA, 1990–93 (Dir, Public Health, 1989–90); Hillingdon Health Agency, 1993–95; Regl Dir of Public Health and Med. Dir, N Thames Regl HA, then N Thames Regl Office, NHS Exec., DoH,

1995–99; Dir, Nat. Co-ordinating Centre for NHS Service Delivery and Orgn, LSHTM, 1999–2001; Med. Dir, NHS Litigation Authy, 1999–2000; Chief Exec., HFEA, 2001–02. Associate: Zenon Consulting, 2009–13; Hill Coates, 2009–13. Chair, Barking, Havering and Redbridge Univ. Hosps NHS Trust, 2014–17 (non-exec. Dir, Barking, Havering and Redbridge NHS Hosps Foundn Trust, 2012–14). Sec., Contract Skill Ltd, 2002–05; Sen. Consultant, Hoggett Bowers, 2008–09; Director: Solena Solutions, 2010–12; COC, 2010–13. Lectr in Public Health Medicine, 1981–85, Sen. Lectr, 1989–90, Hon. Sen. Lectr, 1999–, LSHTM. Mem., European Steering Gp, Mégapoles, 1997–2001; Chairman: Sub-network on Social Disadvantage, Mégapoles, 1997–2001; Migration Foundn, 2010–11; Mem., Health and Social Care Adv. Cttee, Centre for Progressive Policy, 2018–. Member Board: Housing 21, 1995–2002; Intensive Care Nat. Audit and Res. Centre, 1997–2017; Refugee Housing Assoc., 2005–07; Metropolitan Support Trust, 2007–11 (Trustee, 2007–11; Vice Chair, 2010–11, Chair, 2010–11); Trustee, British Pregnancy Adv. Service, 2007–13 (Chair, Clinical Governance Cttee, 2010–13). *Publications:* numerous articles in learned jls and papers presented at nat. confs. *Recreations:* ski-ing, reading novels and biographies, golf (par 3), watching old films. *E:* dalziel@btinternet.com.

**DAMANAKI, Maria;** Global Managing Director for Oceans, Nature Conservancy, since 2014; *b* Crete, 1952; one *s* two *d. Educ:* Nat. Tech. Univ. of Athens (MSc Hons Chem. Engrg 1975); Lancaster Univ. Active in underground student opposition to dictatorship in Greece, 1970–74; leading role in coordination of activities and as speaker on clandestine radio transmitter, Nov. 1973; imprisoned, 1973–74. Engr, Pechiney Aluminium Industries, 1974; Adminr, Dept of Import-export Planning, Min. of Finance, Greece, 1975–76; Sect. Manager, Dept of Energy and Waste Mgt, Helector SA, 2003–04. MP 1977–93, 2000–03 and 2004–09; Vice Pres., Greek Parlt, 1986–90; Pres., Coalition of Left and Progress, 1991–93; Head, PASOK Group in Select Cttees on Educn and Culture, on Social Affairs, on Environment; Chm., Select Cttee on Foreign Affairs and Defence, 2009. Member, Parliamentary Assembly: Council of Europe; WEU; NATO. Member, Political Council, PASOK for educn, 2004–06, for social affairs, 2006–07, for culture, 2008–09. Mem., Inter-parly Union. Hd of Opposition, Athens CC. Mem., EC, 2010–14.

**DAMATO, Bertil,** PhD, MD; FRCOphth; Professor of Ophthalmology and Radiation Oncology, University of California, San Francisco, 2013–18, now Emeritus; Hon. Consultant Ophthalmologist, Oxford Eye Hospital, since 2018; Locum Consultant Ocular Oncologist, Moorfields Eye Hospital, London, since 2018; *b* Malta, 8 Nov. 1953; *s* of Pierre Damato and Margareta Damato; *m* 1978, Frankanne Fenech; one *s* one *d. Educ:* St Edward's Coll., Malta; Univ. of Glasgow (PhD 1988; Univ. of Malta (MD 1989). MRCS, LRCP 1977; FRCSEd 1982; FRCOphth 1989; FRCSGlas 1990. Resident House Surgeon and Physician, 1978–79, Sen. House Officer in Pathol., 1979–80, Glasgow Royal Infirmary; Registrar in Ophthalmol., Glasgow Western Infirmary, 1980–83; Sen. Registrar in Ophthalmol., Glasgow Teaching Hosps, 1983–84; Lectr, 1984–87, Sen. Lectr, 1987–91, Reader, 1991–92, in Ophthalmol., Univ. of Glasgow; Consultant Ophthalmic Surgeon, Royal Liverpool Univ. Hosp., 1993–2013. Hon. Prof., Univ. of Liverpool, 2000–. Member: Eur. Ophthalmic Oncology Gp, 1992– (Pres., 1995–97); Club Jules Gonin, 1995–; President: Eur. Vision and Eye Res. Assoc., 2001; Internat. Soc. of Ocular Oncology, 2011–13 (Vice-Pres., 2007–11; Pres., 2012–13). Bjerrum Medal, Danish Ophthalmol. Soc., 2008; Dora Gold Medal, Univ. of Witwatersrand, 2008; Platinum Award, NHS, 2009; Ashton Medal, Royal Coll. of Ophthalmologists, 2012; Watson Medal, Cambridge Ophthalmol. Symposium, 2012; Shields Award, Asia-Pacific Soc. of Ocular Oncology and Pathology, 2012; Paul Harris Award, Rotary Club of Mid-Wirral, 2013; Vision of Hope Award, Cure Ocular Melanoma, 2016; Rhett Buckler Film Fest. Award, Amer. Soc. of Retina Specialists, 2016. *Publications:* Ocular Tumours: diagnosis and treatment, 2000; over 50 chapters in textbooks; approx. 275 articles in learned jls. *Recreations:* sailing, travelling, writing, music. *Address:* Nuffield Department of Clinical Neurosciences, University of Oxford, West Wing, John Radcliffe Hospital, Oxford OX3 9DU.

**DAMAZER, Mark David,** CBE 2011; Master, St Peter's College, Oxford, since 2010; *b* 15 April 1955; *s* of Stanislaw and Suzanne Damazer; *m* 1981, Rosemary Jane Morgan; one *s* one *d. Educ:* Gonville & Caius Coll., Cambridge (BA History); Harvard Univ. Harkness Fellow, 1977–79; American Political Sci. Fellow, 1978–79. Trainee, ITN, 1979–81; Producer: BBC World Service, 1981–83; TV-AM, 1983–84; BBC: Six O'Clock News, 1984–86; Output Editor, Newsnight, 1986–88; Dep. Editor, 1988–89, Editor, 1989–94, Nine O'Clock News; Editor, TV News, 1994–96; Head: Current Affairs, 1996–98; Political Progs, 1998–2000; Asst Chief Exec. (Dir of Journalism), BBC News, 2000–01; Dep. Dir of News, BBC, 2001–04; Controller, BBC Radio 4 and BBC Radio 7 (formerly BBC7), 2004–10. Dep. Chm., Internat. Press Inst., 2005–10. Mem. Bd, Centre for Contemporary British Hist., Univ. of London, 2005–11. Trustee: Victoria and Albert Mus., 2011–18; BBC Trust, 2015–17. *Publications:* articles in various newspapers and periodicals. *Recreations:* opera, Tottenham Hotspur, Boston Red Sox, cycling, gardening, Italian painting, church architecture.

**DAMER;** *see* Dawson-Damer, family name of Earl of Portarlington.

**DAMMERS, Dianna Patricia;** *see* Melrose, D. P.

**DANCE, Charles Walter,** OBE 2006; actor; *b* 10 Oct. 1946; *s* of late Walter Dance and Eleanor Dance (*née* Perks); *m* 1970, Joanna Haythorn (marr. diss.); one *s* one *d. Educ:* Widey Tech. Sch.; Plymouth Sch. of Art; Leicester Poly. Rep. theatre at Nottingham, Leeds, Greenwich and Chichester Fest.; joined RSC, 1975; appeared in Henry IV, Hamlet, Richard III, Perkin Warbeck, As You Like It, The Changeling, Henry VI, title rôles in Henry V and Coriolanus; other *theatre* includes: Irma La Douce, 1978; The Heiress, 1980; Turning Over, 1982; Good, Donmar Warehouse, 1999; Long Day's Journey Into Night, Lyric, 2000; Shadowlands, Wyndham's, 2007; *television*: Edward VII, 1973; The Fatal Spring, 1978; Little Eyolf, 1980; Frost in May, Nancy Astor, 1981; Saigon, the Last Day, The Jewel in the Crown, 1982; Rainy Day Women, The Secret Servant, 1984; Thunder Rock, The McGuffin, 1985; Out on a Limb, 1986; Out of the Shadows, First Born, 1988; Goldeneye, The Phantom of the Opera, 1989; Undertow, 1993; In the Presence of Mine Enemies, 1995; Rebecca, 1996; Randall & Hopkirk Deceased, Bloodlines, 1999; Justice in Wonderland, 2000; Nicholas Nickleby, 2001; Trial and Retribution, Henry VIII, Looking for Victoria, 2003; To the Ends of the Earth, Don Bosco, Last Rights, 2004; Bleak House, 2005; Fallen Angel, Consenting Adults, 2007; Trinity, 2008; Neverland, 2010; Game of Thrones, 2011, 2012, 2013, 2014; This September, 2010, 2011; Strike Back 3, Secret State, 2012; Common Ground, 2013; The Great Fire, 2014; And Then There Were None, 2015; Deadline Gallipoli, 2016; Childhood's End, 2016; Who Do You Think You Are?, 2017; The Woman in White, 2018; Hang Ups, 2018; The Little Drummer Girl, 2018; The Widow, 2019; The Crown, 2019; *films:* For Your Eyes Only, 1979; Plenty, 1984; The Golden Child, Good Morning Babylon, 1985; White Mischief, Hidden City, 1986; Pascali's Island, Kalkstein, 1989; China Moon, 1990; Alien 3, 1991; Century, Last Action Hero, Exquisite Tenderness, 1992; Kabloonak (Best Actor, Paris Film Fest., 1994), Shortcut to Paradise, 1993; Michael Collins, Space Truckers, 1995; The Blood Oranges, Don't Go Breaking My Heart, What Rats Won't Do, 1997; Hilary and Jackie, 1998; Jurij, 1999; Dark Blue World, Gosford Park, Ali G Indahouse, 2002; Swimming Pool, 2003; Black and White, (writer and dir) Ladies in Lavender, 2004; Remake, Funny Farm, 2005; Starter for Ten, 2006; Going Postal, Your Highness, There Be Dragons, Ironclad, 2009; Winds of Change, 2011; Underworld 4: Awakening, Midnight's Children, St George's Day, 2012; Patrick, 2013; Dracula Untold, The Imitation Game, 2014; Woman in Gold, 2015; Despite the Falling Snow, Pride and Prejudice and the Zombies, Me Before You, Ghostbusters, 2016; Underworld Blood Wars, That Good Night, 2017; Johnny English Strikes Again, 2018; Godzilla: king of the monsters, 2019. *Recreations:* tennis, swimming. *Address:* c/o Tavistock Wood, 45 Conduit Street, W1S 2YN. *T:* (020) 7494 4767. *Club:* Groucho.

**DANCE, Sebastian;** Member (Lab) London Region, European Parliament, since 2014; *b* London, 1 Dec. 1981; partner, Baron Livermore, *qv. Educ:* Univ. of Manchester. Communications Officer, Univ. of Manchester Students' Union; advr on campaigns in public, private and voluntary sector; Advr to Sec. of State for NI, 2007–09; campaigner, ActionAid UK. *Address:* European Parliament, 60 Rue Wiertz, 1047 Brussels, Belgium; (office) 149–151 Jamaica Road, SE16 4SH.

**DANCER, Sir Eric,** KCVO 2013; CBE 1991; JP; Lord-Lieutenant of Devon, 1998–2015; Managing Director, Dartington Crystal Ltd, 1986–2000; *b* 17 April 1940; *s* of Joseph Cyril Dancer and Mabel Dancer; *m* 1980, Carole Anne Moxon. *Educ:* King Edward VII Sch., Sheffield; Sheffield Poly. Buyer: Moorwood-Vulcan Ltd, 1959–63; Balfour-Darwins Ltd, 1963–67; Purchasing Officer, Brightside Foundry and Engineering Co. Ltd, 1965–67; Dep. Chief Buyer, Metro-Cammell Ltd, 1967–68; Chief Buyer, Chrysler Parts Div., 1968–69; Supplies Manager, Jensen Motors Ltd, 1969–72; Dir, Anglo Nordic Hldgs plc, 1972–80; Man. Dir, Dartington Hall Corp., 1980–87; Chm., English Country Crystal, 1983–87. Trustee, Dartington Hall Trust, 1984–87; Member: SW Regl IDB, 1984–91; Council, CBI, 1997–2000; Chairman: Devon Cttee, Rural Develt Commn, 1981–86; Devon and Cornwall TEC, 1989–93; Gp of 10, 1990–92; West Country Develt Corp., 1993–99; Nat. Assessor, TEC, 1993–98. Gov., Univ. of Plymouth, 1992–96. CCMI (CIMgt 1987); FCIPS 1990 (President's Prize, 1964); FInstD 1981 (Dip. 1989); FRSA 1984 (Mem. Council, 1994–98). Freeman, City of London, 1992; Liveryman, Co. of Glass Sellers, 1992–2017. JP Devon, 1998. Hon. Captain RNR, 2001. DUniv Sheffield Hallam, 1999; Hon. LLD Exeter, 2010; Hon. DBus Plymouth, 2010. KStJ 1998. *Recreations:* travel, reading, music. *Clubs:* Army and Navy; Royal Dart Yacht (Dartmouth).

**DANCEY, Martin Alan Gordon; His Honour Judge Dancey;** a Circuit Judge, since 2015; Designated Family Judge, Dorset, since 2018; *b* Bournemouth, 21 March 1957; *s* of Alan and Sonia Dancey; *m* 1982, Hilary Davies; two *d. Educ:* Westminster Abbey Choir Sch.; Poole Grammar Sch.; Brunel Univ. (LLB Hons). Admitted as solicitor, 1981; Partner, 1985–93, Man. Partner, 1993–99, Ellis Jones Solicitors, Bournemouth; Dep. Dist Judge, 1993–99; Dist Judge, 1999–2015; Regl Costs Judge, 2005–15. Course Dir, Judicial Coll., 2013–17. *Recreations:* sailing, singing, music, painting. *Address:* Bournemouth and Poole County Court, Courts of Justice, Deansleigh Road, Bournemouth BH8 9RU. *T:* (01202) 502800. *Club:* Christchurch Sailing.

**DANCEY, Roger Michael,** MA; Chief Master, King Edward's School, Birmingham, and Educational Adviser, King Edward VI Foundation, 1998–2005; *b* 24 Nov. 1945; *s* of Michael and Rosalind Dancey; *m* 1988, Elizabeth Jane Shadbolt; one step *s* one step *d. Educ:* Lancing Coll.; Exeter Univ. (MA). Careers Master, Whitgift Sch., 1972–76; Head of Sixth Form, Greenshaw High Sch., 1976–81; Sen. Master, Royal Grammar Sch., Worcester, 1982–86; Headmaster: King Edward VI Camp Hill Sch. for Boys, 1986–95; City of London Sch., 1995–98. Mem. Council, 1999–2005, Dep. Pro Chancellor, 2005–09, Birmingham Univ. Vice Chm., Warwick Ind. Schools Foundn, 2007–09; Chm., Warwick Sch. Cttee, 2009–15. Gov., Lancing Coll., 2015–17. DUniv Birmingham, 2008. *Recreations:* cricket, golf, theatre, cinema. *Address:* 7 Austen Place, Edgbaston, Birmingham B15 1NJ. *Club:* Edgbaston Golf.

**d'ANCONA, Matthew Robert Ralph;** political commentator and writer; Editor-in-Chief, Finch Publishing, since 2018; *b* 27 Jan. 1968; *e s* of John Edward William d'Ancona, CB and Mary Helen d'Ancona; *m* 2002, Sarah Schaefer (marr. diss.); two *s. Educ:* St Dunstan's Coll.; Magdalen Coll., Oxford (Demy; H. W. C. Davis Prize in Hist. 1987; BA 1st Cl. Hons Hist. 1989). Fellow, All Souls Coll., Oxford, 1989–96; The Times, 1991–95 (Asst Ed., 1994–95); Sunday Telegraph: Dep. Ed. (Comment), 1996–98; Dep. Ed., 1998–2006; Ed., The Spectator, 2006–09; Contributing Ed. and Political Columnist, GQ magazine, 2006–; Columnist: Evening Standard, 2009–; Internat. New York Times, 2013–; Guardian, 2015–. Res. Fellow, Sch. of Politics and Internat. Relns, QMUL, 2013–. Member: Bd of Dirs, Centre for Policy Studies, 1998–2006; Adv. Council, Demos, 1998–2006; Millennium Commn, 2001–06; Puttnam Commn on Parliament in the Public Eye, 2004–05; Steering Bd, Digital Britain, 2008–09; Mem. Bd, Social Market Foundn, 2015–18 (Mem., Policy Adv. Bd, 2002–06); Chm., Bright Blue, 2014– (Mem., Adv. Bd, 2013). Mem., British Exec., IPI, 1998–2006. Trustee, Sci. Mus. Gp, 2015– (Mem., Adv. Bd, 2015–). Philip Geddes Meml Lectr, St Edmund Hall, Oxford, 2006. FRSA 2004. Judge, Man Booker Prize, 2011. Charles Douglas-Home Meml Trust Prize, 1995; Political Journalist of the Year: British Press Awards, 2004; Political Studies Assoc. Awards, 2006; Ed. of the Year, Current Affairs Magazines, BSME, 2007; UK Commentator of the Year, Comment Awards, 2011. *Publications:* (with C. P. Thiede) The Jesus Papyrus, 1996; The Ties That Bind Us, 1996; (with C. P. Thiede) The Quest for the True Cross, 2000; Going East (novel), 2003; Tabatha's Code (novel), 2006; Confessions of a Hawkish Hack, 2006; Nothing to Fear (novel), 2008; (contrib.) Magdalen College Oxford: a history, 2008; (ed) Being British, 2009; (contrib.) Tory Modernisation 2.0, 2013; In It Together: the inside story of the coalition government, 2013; Post Truth: the new war on truth and how to fight back, 2017. *Recreations:* cinema, opera. *Address:* 33 Culverley Road, SE6 2LD. *W:* www.twitter.com/MatthewdAncona. *Clubs:* Ivy, Newspeak House.

**DANCY, Prof. John Christopher,** MA; Professor of Education, University of Exeter, 1978–84, now Emeritus; *b* 13 Nov. 1920; *e s* of late Dr J. H. Dancy and Dr N. Dancy; *m* 1944, Angela Bryant (*d* 2013); two *s* one *d. Educ:* Winchester (Scholar); New Coll., Oxford (Scholar, MA). 1st Class, Classical Hon. Mods, 1940; Craven Scholar, 1946; Gaisford Greek Prose Prize, 1947; Hertford Scholar, 1947; Arnold Historical Essay Prize, 1949. Served in Rifle Brigade, 1941–46; Capt. GSO(3)I, 30 Corps, 1945; Major, GSO(2)I, 1 Airborne Corps, 1945–46. Lecturer in Classics, Wadham Coll., 1946–48; Asst Master, Winchester Coll., 1948–53; Headmaster of Lancing Coll., 1953–61; Master, Marlborough Coll., 1961–72; Principal, St Luke's Coll. of Educn, Exeter, 1972–78. Dir, St Luke's Coll. Foundn, 1978–86. Member, Public Schools' Commission, 1966–68. Chm., Higher Educn Foundn, 1981–86. Chm., British Accreditation Council for Independent Further and Higher Educn, 1984–93. Chevalier, Légion d'Honneur (France), 2015. *Publications:* Commentary on 1 Maccabees, 1954; The Public Schools and the Future, 1963; Commentary on Shorter Books of Apocrypha, 1972; Walter Oakeshott: a diversity of gifts, 1995; The Divine Drama: the Old Testament as literature, 2001. *Address:* Wharf House, Mousehole, Penzance, Cornwall TR19 6RX. *T:* (01736) 731137.
*See also J. P. Dancy.*

**DANCY, Prof. Jonathan Peter,** FBA 2016; Professor of Philosophy (part-time), University of Texas at Austin, since 2005; *b* Oxford, 8 May 1946; *s* of Prof. John Christopher Dancy, *qv*; *m* 1973, Sarah Birley; two *s* one *d. Educ:* Winchester Coll.;

Corpus Christi Coll., Oxford (BA 1st Cl. Hons Classical Hons Mods and Lit. Hum. 1969; BPhil Philosophy 1971; Hon. Fellow, 2014). University of Keele: Lectr, 1971–87; Sen. Lectr, 1987–89; Reader, 1989–91; Prof. of Philosophy, 1991–96; Prof. of Philosophy, Univ. of Reading, 1996–2011. *Publications:* Introduction to Contemporary Epistemology, 1985; Berkeley: an introduction, 1987; Moral Reasons, 1993; Practical Reality, 2000; Ethics Without Principles, 2004; Practical Shape: a theory of practical reasoning, 2018; contrib. articles on moral philosophy, philosophy of action. *Recreations:* double bass, woodwork. *Address:* 40 Lonsdale Road, Oxford OX2 7EW. *T:* (01865) 514998. *E:* jdancy@austin.utexas.edu.

**DANCZUK, Simon Christopher;** *b* 24 Oct. 1966; *m* 1st (marr. diss.); one *s* one *d*; 2nd, 2012, Karen Burke; two *s*. *Educ:* Gawthorpe Comprehensive Sch., Padiham; Lancaster Univ. (BA Econs and Sociol. 1991). Prodn worker, Main Gas, Padiham, 1982–86; labourer, ICI factory, Darwen, 1986–88; barman, ICI Sports and Social Club, Darwen, 1988–91; res. asst, Sociol. Dept, Lancaster Univ., 1991–93; Res. Officer, Bolton Bury TEC, 1993–95; res. consultant, Opinion Res. Corp. Internat., 1995–97; Res. Co-ordinator, 1997–98, Media and PR Officer, 1998–99, Big Issue in N Trust; Co-founder and Dir, Vision Twentyone, 1999–2011. Mem. (Lab) Blackburn with Darwen BC, 1993–2001. MP (Lab) Rochdale, 2010–17; contested (Ind) same seat, 2017. *Publications:* (jtly) Smile for the Camera: the double life of Cyril Smith, 2014.

**DANDEKER, Prof. Christopher,** PhD; FAcSS; Professor of Military Sociology, King's College London, 1997–2015, now Emeritus; *b* 12 July 1950; *s* of late Arjun Dandeker and Yvonne Florentina Margerat (*née* Bogaert); *m* 2011, Anna Felicity Alexander-Williams. *Educ:* Worthing High Sch. for Boys; Univ. of Leicester (BSc (Sociol.) 1971; PhD 1978). Lecturer: in Applied Social Studies, Hallam Univ., 1973–74; in Sociol., Univ. of Leicester, 1974–90; King's College London: Sen. Lectr in War Studies, 1990–97; Head, Dept of War Studies, 1997–2001; Co-Dir, King's Centre for Military Health Res., 2004–; Head, Sch. of Social Sci. and Public Policy, 2005–08; Fellow 2012. FAcSS (AcSS 2011). Morris Janowitz Career Achievement Award, Inter-Univ. Seminar on Armed Forces and Society, 2011. *Publications:* The Structure of Social Theory (jtly), 1984; Surveillance, Power and Modernity, 1990; (with B. Boene) Les Armées en Europe, 1998; Nationalism and Violence, 1998; Facing Uncertainty: Sweden in international perspective, 2000; (contrib.) Israel's Armed Forces in Comparative Perspective: the new citizen armies, 2009; (contrib.) Modern Warfare and the Utility of Force, 2010; contribs to jls inc. Armed Forces and Society, Political Quarterly, British Jl of Sociol., Sociol Rev., The Lancet, Commonwealth & Comparative Politics. *Recreations:* wine, food, walking, gardening, travel, classical music, being near the sea! *Address:* Department of War Studies, King's College London, Strand, WC2R 2LS. *T:* (020) 7848 2673, 07751 604918, *Fax:* (020) 7848 2026. *E:* christophe.dandeker@kcl.ac.uk, chrisdandeker@gmail.com. *Club:* Travellers.

**DANDO, Stephen Gordon;** Managing Director, Bain Capital, since 2013; *b* 13 Feb. 1962; *s* of Douglas and Anne Dando; *m* 1985, Catherine Macquarrie Fraser; one *s* one *d*. *Educ:* Univ. of Strathclyde (BA Hons 1984); Univ. of Edinburgh (MBA 1990). Mgt Develt Dir, United Distillers, 1995–97; Gp Mgt Develt Dir, Diageo plc, 1997–99; Human Resources Director: (Europe), United Distillers & Vintners, 1999–2000; Guinness Ltd, 2000–01; Dir, Human Resources and Internal Communications, BBC, subseq. BBC People, 2001–06; Gp Human Resources Dir, Reuters, 2006–08; Exec. Vice-Pres. and Chief Human Resources Officer, Thomson Reuters, 2008–12. Chartered CCIPD 2004; FRSA. *Recreations:* family, keeping fit, golf, current affairs. *E:* stephen@dandomail.co.uk. *Clubs:* Roehampton; Elie Golf House.

**DANDRIDGE, Nicola,** CBE 2015; Chief Executive, Office for Students, since 2017; *d* of Lawrence and Dorothy Dandridge; *m* 1995, Andrew Nairne, *qv*; two *s*. *Educ:* Chichester High Sch. for Girls; Univ. of Oxford (BA Lit. Hum.); City of London Poly.; Glasgow Univ. Admitted Solicitor: England, 1987; Scotland, 1991; Partner, Thompsons Solicitors, 1989–2006; Chief Executive: Equality Challenge Unit, 2006–09; UUK, 2009–17. Trustee, Cara, 2016–.

**DANDY, David James,** MD; FRCS; Consultant Orthopaedic Surgeon: Addenbrooke's Hospital, Cambridge, 1975–2002; Newmarket General Hospital, 1975–2002; *b* 30 May 1940; *s* of late James Dandy, Great Shelford, Cambs, and Margaret Dandy (*née* Coe); *m* 1966, (Stephanie) Jane Essex; one *s* one *d*. *Educ:* Forest Sch.; Emmanuel Coll., Cambridge (Windsor Student, 1965; BA 1961, MA 1963; BChir 1964; MB 1965; MD 1990; MChir 1994); London Hosp. Med. Coll. (Robert Milne Prize for Surgery, 1995). LRCP, MRCS 1964, FRCS 1969. Surg. Registrar, St Andrew's Hosp., Bow, 1966–67; Surg., then Orthopaedic Registrar, London Hosp., 1967–69; Orthopaedic Registrar: Royal Nat. Orthopaedic Hosp., 1969–71; St Bartholomew's Hosp., 1971; Princess Alexandra Hosp., Harlow, 1971–72; Norfolk and Norwich Hosp., 1972–73; Sen. Registrar: St Bartholomew's Hosp., 1973–75; Hosp. for Sick Children, Gt Ormond St, 1974; Sen. Fellow, Toronto Gen. Hosp., 1973–74; Associate Lectr, Univ. of Cambridge, 1975–2007; Civilian Advr in Knee Surgery, RN and RAF, 1980–2006. Lectures: Mackenzie Crooks, RAF Hosp., Ely, 1980; Munsif Meml Orator, Bombay, 1987; Sir Ernest Finch Meml, Sheffield, 1990; William Gissane, Inst. of Accident Surgery, 1998; Bradshaw, 2004, Vicary, 2005, RCS. Director: Internat. Soc. of the Knee, 1989–93; European Soc. for Sports Traumatology, Knee Surgery, Sports Medicine and Arthroscopy, 1992–96; President: Internat. Arthroscopy Assoc., 1989–91; British Orthopaedic Sports Trauma Assoc., 1993–95; British Orthopaedic Assoc., 1998–99 (Robert Jones Prize and Assoc. Medal, 1991; Naughton Dunn Lectr, 1991; Mem. Council, 1992–95); Combined Services Orthopaedic Soc., 2001–04; Mem. Council, RCS, 1994–2006 (James Berry Prize, 1985; Hunterian Prof., 1994; Treas., 2003–06; Vice-Pres., 2005–06; Cheselden Medal, 2009). Chm., Granta Decorative and Fine Arts Soc., 2007–11. Trustee, Gretton Court Ltd (formerly Barton Housing Assoc.), 2009–. Hon. FRCSE 1998; Hon. FFGDP(UK) 2007; Hon. Fellow, British Orthopaedic Assoc., 2011. *Publications:* Arthroscopy of the Knee, 1973; Arthroscopic Surgery of the Knee, 1981, rev. edn 1987; Arthroscopy of the Knee: a diagnostic atlas, 1984; Essentials of Orthopaedics and Trauma, 1989, rev. edn 2009; articles on surgery of the knee and arthroscopic surgery. *Recreation:* travel. *Clubs:* East India, Royal Society of Medicine.

**DANESH, Prof. John Navid,** DPhil; FRCP; FFPH; FMedSci; Professor of Epidemiology and Medicine, and Head, Department of Public Health and Primary Care, University of Cambridge, since 2001; *b* 21 April 1968; *s* of Dr Ali Danesh and Dr Mahtaban Danesh (*née* Safapour); *m* 2005, Nathalie Jacoby. *Educ:* Univ. of Otago Med. Sch., NZ (MB ChB Dist. 1992); London Sch. of Hygiene and Trop. Medicine (MSc Epidemiol. Dist. 1995); DPhil Epidemiol. Oxon 2000. MRCP (Dist.) 2005. House Officer, Royal Melbourne Hosp., 1993; Rhodes Schol., New Coll. and Balliol Coll., Oxford, 1994–97; Jun. Res. Fellow, Merton Coll., Oxford, 1997–99; Clin. Res. Fellow, Univ. of Oxford, 1999–2001. FMedSci 2015. *Publications:* (jtly) Reason and Revelation, 2002; Search for Values, 2004; (jtly) The Baha'i Faith in Words and Images, 2008; contrib. articles to scientific jls on epidemiology of chronic diseases, particularly molecular risk factors in heart disease. *Recreations:* food, conversation. *Address:* Department of Public Health and Primary Care, University of Cambridge, Strangeways Research Laboratory, Wort's Causeway, Cambridge CB1 8RN. *T:* (01223) 748655, *Fax:* (01223) 748658. *E:* john.danesh@phpc.cam.ac.uk.

**DANGAN, Viscount; Henry Arthur Peter Wellesley;** *b* 3 Dec. 1991; *s* and *heir* of Earl Cowley, *qv*.

**DANIEL, Brother;** *see* Matthews, Brother D. F.

**DANIEL, Caroline Frances;** Partner, Brunswick Group, since 2016; *b* Aldershot, 10 March 1971; *d* of late Peter Edward Burgoyne Daniel, OBE and of Alison Daniel (*née* Taylor). *Educ:* St Helen's Sch., Northwood, Middx; St John's Ravenscourt Sch., Winnipeg; St John's Coll., Cambridge (BA 1st Cl. Hist. 1993). Non-exec. Dir Dip., FT, 2014. Researcher, Gordon Brown, MP, 1994–96; reporter, New Statesman, 1996–99; tech. corresp., 1999–2002; Financial Times: Chicago corresp., 2002–05; White House corresp., 2005–09; comment and analysis ed., 2009; Asst Ed., 2009; Ed., Weekend FT, 2010–16; Consulting Ed., FT Events and Conferences, 2014–16. Mem., Trilateral Commn. Trustee: IPPR, 2013–; Samuel Johnson Prize, 2015–; The Trampery, 2017–. *Recreations:* photography, swimming, reading, films. *Address:* Brunswick Group, 16 Lincoln's Inn Fields, WC2A 3ED. *T:* (020) 7404 5959. *E:* cdaniel@brunswickgroup.com.

**DANIEL, Gareth John;** Director, GDA Ltd, since 2013; consultant on public policy, partnerships and governance, since 2013; *b* 30 March 1954; *s* of late Evan John Daniel and Eileen Marie Daniel; partner, Margaret Wilson; three *s*. *Educ:* St Edward's Coll., Liverpool; Jesus Coll., Oxford (BA Hons); South Bank Poly. (DASS, CQSW). Pres., Oxford Univ. Students' Union, 1974–75. Social worker, London Borough of Ealing, 1976–83; London Borough of Brent, 1986–2012: Principal Develt Officer; Divl Manager, Strategy; Head, Central Policy Unit; Dir, Partnership and Res.; Chief Exec., 1998–2012. Member (Lab): Ealing LBC (Chm., Planning and Econ. Develt, 1986–90); Ealing North, GLC, 1981–86. Contested (Lab): Worcs S, 1979; Ealing, Acton, 1983. *Recreations:* family, hill-walking, foreign travel. *T:* 07774 738009.

**DANIEL, His Honour (Gruffydd) Huw Morgan,** CVO 2014; a Circuit Judge, 1986–2006; Lord-Lieutenant of Gwynedd, 2006–14; *b* 16 April 1939; *s* of Prof. John Edward Daniel, MA, and Catherine Megan Daniel (*née* Parry Hughes); *m* 1968, Phyllis Margaret (*née* Bermingham); one *d*. *Educ:* Ampleforth; University College of Wales (LLB; Pres., Students' Law Soc., 1962–63); Inns of Court School of Law. Commissioned 2nd Lieut First Bn Royal Welch Fusiliers, 1959; Captain 6/7 Bn Royal Welch Fusiliers (TA), 1965; served MELF, Cyprus. Called to the Bar, Gray's Inn, 1967; Wales and Chester Circuit (Circuit Junior, 1975); Hd of Chambers, Stanley Place, Chester, 1975–86; Recorder, 1980–86; Asst Liaison Judge, 1983–87, Liaison Judge, 1988–2006, Gwynedd; Liaison Judge for N Wales, 1998–2006; Dep. Sen. Judge, 1995–2002, Sen. Judge, 2002–06, Sovereign Base Area, Cyprus. Asst Parly Boundary Comr for Wales, 1981–82, 1985–86; Pres., Mental Health Appeals Tribunal, 2002–06. Chairman: N Wales Judicial Forum, 2005–06; Lord Chancellor's Adv. Cttee on JPs for N Wales, 2012–16. President: Caerns Br., SSAFA, 1995–2006; St John's Council in Gwynedd, Anglesey and Conwy Co. Borough, 2006–16; Custos rotulorum of Gwynedd, 2006–16; Gwynedd Magistrates' Assoc., 2006–16; Gwynedd SSAFA, 2013–16; Vice President: RFCA Wales, 2006–16; Snowdonia Soc., 2016–; Trustee, St John Wales, 2006–16. Member of Court: Bangor Univ., 2006–16; Cardiff Univ., 2006–16. Hon. Col, 6th Cadet Bn, Royal Welch Fusiliers, 1997–2003. DL Gwynedd, 1993. KStJ 2012 (CStJ 2006). *Recreation:* gardening. *Address:* (residence) Rhiwgoch, Pont y Pandy, Bangor, Gwynedd LL57 3AX. *Club:* Reform.

**DANIEL, Hamish St Clair,** CMG 2008; OBE 2004 (MBE 1992); HM Diplomatic Service, retired; Deputy High Commissioner, Karachi and UK Director of Trade and Investment, Pakistan, 2004–08; *b* 22 Aug. 1953; *s* of James Anderson Daniel and Charlotte Daniel; *m* 2002, Heather Ann Bull; one *s* one *d* from previous marriage. *Educ:* Lerwick Central Public Sch., Scotland. Joined FCO, 1973: Algiers, 1975–77; Prague, 1977; Lisbon, 1978–80; Islamabad, 1980–82; FCO, 1982–85; San Francisco, 1985–88; Second Secretary: Khartoum, 1989–92; FCO, 1992–94; Dep. Hd of Mission, Sana'a, 1994–96; Pol and Econ. Sec., Jakarta, 1997–2001; British Rep., Dili, 2001–02; Ambassador to E Timor, 2002–03. *Recreations:* sailing, golf, walking.

**DANIEL, Huw Morgan;** *see* Daniel, His Honour G. H. M.

**DANIEL, Joan;** *see* Rodgers, J.

**DANIEL, John,** MA; Headmaster, Royal Grammar School, Guildford, 1977–92; *b* 7 March 1932; *s* of John Daniel and Mary (*née* Young); *m* 1st, 1956, Heather Joy Retey (marr. diss. 2001); two *d*; 2nd, 2001, Beatrice Miller McTighe. *Educ:* Truro Sch.; New Coll., Oxford (Hons Modern Langs 1955). Thomas Hedley & Son, 1955–57; Linton Lodge Hotel, Oxford, 1957–59; Hartford Motors, Oxford, 1959–62; Royal Grammar Sch., Worcester, 1963–65; Malvern Coll., 1965–72; Royal Grammar School, Guildford: Dep. Headmaster, 1972–75; Acting Headmaster, 1975–77. Chm. of Govs, Tormead Sch., Guildford, 1981–97. Asst Dir, Gap Activity Projects Ltd, 1994–2002. Chm., Guildford Symphony Orch., 1995–2002. *Recreations:* watching Rugby football, playing the piano, writing memoirs. *Address:* 800 Truman Street NE, Albuquerque, NM 87110, USA. *E:* upalong32@gmail.com.

**DANIEL, Sir John (Sagar),** Kt 1994; OC 2013; DSc; Chancellor, Acsenda School of Management, Vancouver, since 2017; *b* 31 May 1942; *s* of John Edward Daniel and Winifred (*née* Sagar); *m* 1966, Kristin Anne Swanson (*d* 2011); one *s* two *d*. *Educ:* Christ's Hosp.; St Edmund Hall, Oxford (BA Metallurgy, MA; Hon. Fellow, 1990); Univ. of Paris (DSc Metallurgy); Thorneloe Univ., Ont (Associate 1992); Concordia Univ., Quebec (MA Educnl Technol. 1995). Asst Prof., then Associate Prof., Ecole Polytechnique, Montreal, 1969–73; Dir, Etudes Télé-Univ., Univ. of Quebec, 1973–77; Vice Pres., Learning Services, Athabasca Univ., Alberta, 1977–80; Vice-Rector, Academic Affairs, Concordia Univ., Montreal, 1980–84; Pres., Laurentian Univ., Sudbury, Ont, 1984–90; Vice-Chancellor, Open Univ., 1990–2001 (Hon. Fellow, 2002); Pres., US Open Univ., 1998–2001; Asst Dir-Gen. for Educn, UNESCO, 2001–04; Pres. and CEO, Commonwealth of Learning, 2004–12. Chairman: UNESCO-CEPES Adv. Council, 1990–92; Adv. Council for Develt of RN Personnel, 1996–2001; Member: HEQC, 1992–94; Council of Foundn, Internat. Baccalaureate, 1992–99; Council for Industry and Higher Educn, 1994–2001; British N American Cttee, 1995–2001, 2006–08; Council, CBI, 1996–98; Steering Cttee, Defence Trng Rev., 1999–2001; Adv. Bd, Internat. Quality Gp, Council for Higher Educn Accreditation, USA, 2012–18. Member: Bd of Govs, Commonwealth of Learning, 1988–90; Council, Univ. of Buckingham, 1994–2001; Council, Open Univ. of Hong Kong, 1996–2001; Bd, Univ. for Industry, 1999–2001 (Mem. Transition Bd, 1998–99); Canadian Council on Learning, 2005–09; Member, Advisory Board: Whitney Internat. Univ. System, 2008–16; Taylor's Univ., Malaysia, 2011–17; Hamdan bin Mohammed e-Univ., Dubai, 2011–13; Educn Master, De Tao Masters Acad., China, 2011–18; Chm., Internat. Bd, United World Colls, 2013–18; Sen. Advr, Academic Partnerships Internat., USA, 2013–17; Trustee, Carnegie Foundn for Advancement of Teaching, 1993–2001. Mem., Adv. Bd, Xerox, Canada, 1998–99; Dir, Blackwells Publishing, 1998–2001. Hon. Chair, Canadian Soc. for Trng and Develt,

2006–08. Licensed Reader: Montreal, 1980–84, Algoma, 1984–90, Anglican Ch of Canada; St Albans, 1990–2001, Europe, 2003–04, C of E. Forum Fellow, World Econ. Forum, 1998. Hon. Fellow, Commonwealth of Learning, 2002. CCMI (CIMgt 1997; Pres., Milton Keynes Br., 1998–2001). Hon. FCP 1997. Hon. DLitt: Deakin, Aust., 1985; Lincolnshire and Humberside, 1996; Athabasca, Canada, 1998; Indira Gandhi Nat. Open Univ., India, 2003; Thompson Rivers, Canada, 2005; Netaji Subhas Open Univ., India, 2005; Kota Open Univ., India, 2007; McGill, Canada, 2007; Hon. DHumLitt: Thomas Edison State Coll., USA, 1997; Richmond Coll., London, 1997; Hon. DSc: Royal Mil. Coll., St Jean, Canada, 1988; Open Univ., Sri Lanka, 1994; Paris VI, 2001; Univ. of Education, Winneba, Ghana, 2006; Hon. DEd: CNAA, 1992; Sukhothai Thammathirat Open Univ., Thailand, 1999; Open Univ. Malaysia, 2009; Hon. LLD: Univ. of Waterloo, Canada, 1993; Wales, 2002; Laurentian, Canada, 2006; Canada West, 2008; Univ. of Ghana, 2013; DUniv: Aberta, Portugal, 1996; Anadolu, Turkey, 1998; Québec, Derby, and New Bulgarian, 2000; Open Univ., Hong Kong, 2001; Stirling, 2002; de Montreal, 2008; Hon. DLitt and DPhil South Africa, 2010; Hon. LittD State Univ. NY, 2011. Individual Excellence Award, Commonwealth of Learning, 1995; Morris T. Keeton Award, Council for Adult and Experiential Learning, USA, 1999; Symons Medal, Assoc. of Commonwealth Univs, 2008; Res. Excellence Prize, China TVU System, 2011. Officier, Ordre des Palmes Académiques (France), 1991 (Chevalier, 1987); Golden Jubilee Medal, Canada, 2002; 50th Anniversary Pioneer Medal, Univ. du Québec, 2018. *Publications:* Learning at a Distance: a world perspective, 1982; Mega-universities and Knowledge Media, 1996; Mega-Schools, Technology and Teachers: achieving education for all, 2010; more than 385 articles to professional pubns. *E:* ODLSirJohn@gmail.com.

**DANIEL, Nicholas;** oboe soloist; conductor; *b* 9 Jan. 1962; *s* of late Jeremy Daniel and Margaret Louise Daniel; *m* 1986, Joy Farrall, clarinettist (marr. diss. 2011); two *s*; *m* 2012, Piotr Rudkowski. *Educ:* Salisbury Cathedral Sch.; Purcell Sch.; Royal Acad. of Music. ARAM 1986, FRAM 1987; FGS (FGSM 1996). Prof., GSMD, 1986–97; Oboe Prof., Indiana Univ., 1997–99; Prince Consort Lectr, RCM, 1999–2002; Prof., Trossingen Musikhochschule, 2004–. Artistic Director: Osnabrück Chamber Music Fest., 2001–04; Leicester Internat. Music Fest., 2004–; Barbirolli-Isle of Man Internat. Oboe Fest. and Competition, 2005–; Founder Mem., Artistic Associate and Principal Oboe, Britten Sinfonia, 1992–. Mem., Royal Philharmonic Soc., 2016. Dedicatee and first performer of many new works; more than 30 recordings and many broadcasts. Internat. appearances in USA, Japan, Europe, Australasia. Competition prize winner: BBC Young Musician of Year, 1980; Munich, 1983; Graz, 1984; Duino, Italy, 1986. The Queen's Medal for Music, 2012. *Recreations:* childbirth studies (home birth), music, literature, Star Trek, travel, cinema. *E:* NDanielmusic@gmail.com. *Club:* Royal Over-Seas League.

**DANIEL, Paul Wilson,** CBE 2000; conductor; Chief Conductor and Artistic Advisor, Royal Philharmonic Orchestra of Galicia, since 2013; Music Director, Orchestre National Bordeaux Aquitaine, since 2013; *b* 5 July 1958; *s* of Alfred Daniel and Margaret Daniel (*née* Poole); *m* 1st, 1988, Joan Rodgers, *qv* (marr. diss. 2005); two *d*; 2nd, 2008, Sarah Walley. *Educ:* King Henry VIII Sch., Coventry; King's Coll., Cambridge; Guildhall Sch. of Music and Drama. Music Dir, Opera Factory, London, 1987–90; Artistic Dir, Opera North, 1990–97; Principal Conductor, English Northern Philharmonia, 1990–97; Music Dir, ENO, 1997–2005; Principal Conductor and Artistic Advr, West Australian SO, 2009–13. Has worked with ENO, Royal Opera House, Metropolitan Opera, New York, Bayerische Staatsoper, Munich, La Monnaie, Brussels, Geneva Opera and Teatro Real Madrid; has conducted many orchestras incl. Philharmonia, LSO, LPO, RPO, BBC SO, London Sinfonietta, CBSO, Scottish Chamber Orch., and ABC orchestras, Australia; has conducted many BBC Proms, including Last Night of the Proms 2005, and has also conducted in Germany, Holland, France and USA. Conductor: Gloriana (filmed), 2000; Lucrecia Borgia (filmed), 2011. Co-presenter, Harry Enfield's Guide to Opera, TV series, 1993. Has made numerous recordings. *Address:* c/o Groves Artists, 7 St George's Court, 131 Putney Bridge Road, SW15 2PA. *T:* (020) 8874 3222.

**DANIELS, David;** countertenor; *b* S Carolina, 12 March 1966. *Educ:* Cincinnati Conservatoire; Univ. of Michigan. Singing début, 1992; début with Metropolitan Opera, as Sesto in Giulio Cesare, 1999; *rôles* include: Rinaldo, Nerone in L'Incoronazione di Poppea, Didymus in Theodora, Hamor in Jeptha, Arsamenes in Xerxes, Oberon in A Midsummer Night's Dream; title rôles in Tamerlano, Giulio Cesare, Orfeo ed Euridice, Orlando, Radamisto; has performed with San Francisco SO, St Louis SO, New World SO, Philharmonia Baroque, San Francisco Opera, Florida Grand Opera, Bavarian State Opera, Glimmerglass Opera Fest., Brooklyn Acad. of Music, Royal Opera, Covent Gdn, Glyndebourne Fest., Salzburg Fest., Bayerische Staatsoper, NY City Opera, Canadian Opera Co., Lyric Opera of Chicago, Netherlands Opera, and Paris Opera; extensive recital and concert repertoire performed in US and Europe, incl. Promenade Concerts. Has made numerous recordings. Richard Tucker Award, 1997; Vocalist of Year Award, Musical America, 1999; Opera News Award, 2013. *Recreations:* theatre, sports, especially baseball. *Address:* c/o Askonas Holt Ltd, 15 Fetter Lane, EC4A 1BW. *T:* (020) 7400 1700.

**DANIELS, Edward David,** FREng, FIChemE; Executive Vice President, Strategy and Portfolio, Royal Dutch Shell plc, since 2014; *b* Haverfordwest, 26 Jan. 1966; *s* of Glyn Daniels and Meriel Daniels; *m* 1994, Laura Jane Stephens; three *d*. *Educ:* Sir Thomas Picton Sch., Haverfordwest; Imperial Coll. London (MEng 1988); Henley Management Coll. (MBA 1995). FIChemE 2010. Shell Europe Oil Products: Technologist, Project Mgt and Implementation, 1988–93; Refinery Technical Auditor and Economist, 1993–95; Mktg Co-ordination, Commercial Markets, 1995–96; Sales and Mktg Manager, Commercial Road Transport, 1996–97; Mktg Consultant, 1997; Mktg Manager, Eur. Fleet Business, 1998–2000; Shell International Oil Products: Consultancy Manager, Business Develt Consultancy, Singapore, 2000–03; Global Base Oil Business Gen. Manager, Shell Lubricants, 2003–06; Vice Pres. Commercial, Shell Global Solutions, 2006–09; Exec. Vice Pres., Global Solutions Downstream, Shell Projects and Technol., 2009–14; Chm., Shell UK Ltd, 2013–14. FREng 2014; FCGI 2015. Hon. DSc Imperial Coll. London, 2018. *Recreations:* gardening, travel, fitness. *Address:* Shell International Exploration and Production BV, Carel van Bylandtlaan 23, 2596 HP The Hague, Netherlands. *T:* (office) (70) 3775535. *E:* e.daniels@shell.com.

**DANIELS, Eric;** *see* Daniels, J. E.

**DANIELS, Prof. Harry Richard John,** PhD; Professor of Education, University of Oxford, since 2013; Fellow, Green Templeton College, since 2013; *b* S Molton, Devon, 6 June 1951; *s* of Alfred Hart Daniels and Wendy Irene Daniels; *m* (marr. diss.); two *d*, partner, Jill Porter. *Educ:* King's Sch., Ottery St Mary, Devon; Univ. of Liverpool (BSc Computational and Statistical Sci. 1972; BSc Hons Genetics 1973); Univ. of Leicester (PGCE); Inst. of Educn, Univ. of London (Dip. Psychol. and Educn of Children with Special Needs 1982; PhD 1986). Asst teacher, Leysland High Sch., Countesthorpe, Leics, 1975–76; Hd, Disruptive Unit, Wreake Valley Coll., Syston, Leics, 1977–80; Dep. Hd, Gp 7(S), Temple Court Special (MLD) Sch., Guildford, 1980–84; Sen. Lectr in Special Educn, W London Inst. Higher Educn, 1984–87; Sen. Lectr, Dept of Educnl Psychol. and Special Educnl Needs, Univ. of London, Inst. of Educn, 1988–95; Prof. of Special Educn and Educnl Psychol., Dep. Hd of Sch., Dir of Res. and Dir, Centre for Sociocultural and Activity Theory Res., Sch. of Educn, Univ. of Birmingham, 1995–2004; Prof. of Educn, Culture and Pedagogy, and Dir, Centre for Sociocultural and Activity Theory Res. (Bath), Dept of Educn, Univ. of Bath, 2004–13. Adjunct Prof., Centre for Learning Res., Griffith Univ., Brisbane, 2006–; Research Professor: Centre for Human Activity Theory, Kansai Univ., Osaka, 2006–; in Cultural Histl Psychol., Moscow State Univ. of Psychol. and Educn, 2006–. *Publications:* (with S. Sandow) Child Study in Special Education: the teacher-researcher in action, 1985; (with J. Anghileri) Secondary School Mathematics and Special Educational Needs, 1995; (jtly) Teacher Support Teams in Primary and Secondary Schools, 1997; (jtly) Educational Support for Children with Mental Health Issues including the Emotionally Vulnerable, 1999; (jtly) Emotional and Behavioural Difficulty in Mainstream Schools, 1999; (jtly) The Framework for Intervention: identifying and promoting effective practice (Second Evaluation Report), 2000; Vygotsky and Pedagogy, 2001 (Spanish edn 2003; Brazilian edn 2003; Japanese edn 2006); (jtly) The Mental Health Needs of Young People with Emotional and Behavioural Difficulties - Bright Futures: working with vulnerable people, 2002; Study of Young People Permanently Excluded from School, 2003; (with A. Parrilla) Criação e desenvolvimento de grupos de apoio entre professores, 2004; (jtly) Disability Data Collection for Children's Services, 2008; Vygotsky and Research, 2008 (Brazilian edn 2011); (jtly) Improving Inter-professional Collaborations: multi-agency working for children's well being, 2009; (with A. Edwards) Leading for Learning: how the intelligent leader builds capacity, 2012; *edited:* Charting the Agenda: educational activity after Vygotsky, 1993 (Brazilian edns 1994, 2007); An Introduction to Vygotsky, 1996, 2nd edn 2005 (Brazilian edn 2002); (with P. Garner) Inclusive Education: World Yearbook of Education 1999, 1999; Special Education Re-formed: beyond rhetoric?, 2000; (jtly) Effecting Change for the Child with Special Educational Needs: a celebration of the contribution of Professor Ron Gulliford, 2000; (jtly) Towards a Sociology of Pedagogy: the contribution of Basil Bernstein to research, 2001; (jtly) Emotional and Behavioural Difficulty in Mainstream Schools, 2001; (with A. Edwards) The Routledge Falmer Reader in the Psychology of Education, 2004; (jtly) New Learning Challenges: going beyond the industrial age system of school and work, 2005; (with P. Garner) Inclusive Education: world yearbook of education (in Japanese), 2006; (jtly) Knowledge, Power and Educational Reform: applying the sociology of Basil Bernstein, 2006; (jtly) Cambridge Companion to Vygotsky, 2007; (jtly) Knowledge, Values and Educational Policy: a critical perspective, 2009; (jtly) Educational Theories, Cultures and Learning: a critical perspective, 2009; (jtly) Learning and Expanding with Activity Theory, 2009; (jtly) Activity Theory in Practice: promoting learning across boundaries and agencies, 2009; (with M. Hedegaard) Vygotsky and Special Needs Education: rethinking support for children and schools, 2011; Vygotsky and Sociology, 2012; (jtly) Transforming Troubled Lives: strategies and interventions for children with social, emotional and behavioural difficulties, 2012; (jtly) The Routledge International Companion to Emotional and Behavioural Difficulties, 2012. *Recreations:* cooking, walking, music. *Address:* Department of Education, University of Oxford, 15 Norham Gardens, Oxford OX2 6PY. *T:* (01865) 274041. *E:* harry.daniels@education.ox.ac.uk.

**DANIELS, Hilary;** Lay Member for Finance and Primary Care, South Lincolnshire Clinical Commissioning Group, since 2017 (Independent Member, Audit and Risk Committee, since 2014); Lay Member for Finance, South West Lincolnshire Clinical Commissioning Group, since 2018; *b* Horsham, 1954; *m* 1995. *Educ:* High Sch. for Girls, Horsham; Southampton Univ. (BSc Hons Maths). CPFA 1981. Various posts, London Bor. of Barnet, 1975–86; Chief Accountant, London Fire and Civil Defence Auth., 1986–89; Dep. Treas., S Somerset DC, 1989–91; Dir of Finance, Cambridge CC; Dir of Finance and Inf., NW Anglia HA; Chief Exec., W Norfolk PCG, later PCT, 2000–06. Pres., CIPFA, 2003–04. Chm., Hinchingbrooke Healthcare NHS Trust, 2017– (non-exec. Dir, 2015–; Chm., Audit and Risk Cttee, 2015–17). Mem., Professional Oversight Bd, 2005–12, Conduct Cttee, Financial Reporting Council, 2012–15; Member Board: Olympic Lottery Distributor, 2006–13 (Chm., Audit Cttee); ILEX Professional Standards Ltd, 2008–14; Vice Chm., E Northants Standards Bd, 2009–12 (Mem., 2007–12); Indep. Mem., Audit and Risk Cttee, Gen. Pharmaceutical Council, 2010–17; Chm., Audit Cttee, 2014– (Ind. Mem., 2012–14), Trustee, 2014–, Peterborough Diocesan Bd of Finance; Dep. Chm., Audit and Risk Mgt Cttee, City of London, 2018– (Ext. Mem., 2012–); Ext. Mem., Audit Cttee, Law Soc., 2018–. Churchwarden, Nassington Church, 2011–18; Ringing Master, Peterborough Br., Peterborough Dio. Guild of Bellringers. *Recreations:* watching athletics, bellringing. *E:* hilarydaniels@btinternet.com.

**DANIELS, (John) Eric;** Chief Executive, Lloyds Banking Group (formerly Lloyds TSB Group) plc, 2003–11; Principal and Senior Adviser, StormHarbour, since 2012; *b* Montana, USA, 1951; *m*; one *s*. *Educ:* Cornell Univ. (BA 1973); Massachusetts Inst. of Technol. (MSc 1975). Joined Citibank, USA, 1975; Regl Hd, Citigroup Consumer Bank Europe, 1996; Chief Operating Officer, Citigroup Consumer Bank, 1998; Chm. and CEO, Travelers Life & Annuity, 1998–2000; Chm. and CEO, Zona Financiera, 2000–01; Exec. Dir, UK Retail Banking, Lloyds TSB Gp plc, 2001–03. Non-executive Director: BT, 2008–12; Funding Circle, 2016–. Trustee, Career Academies UK.

**DANIELS, Ruth Sarah;** *see* Farwell, R. S.

**DANIELS, Prof. Stephen J.,** PhD; FBA 2010; Professor of Cultural Geography, University of Nottingham, now Emeritus. *Educ:* Univ. of St Andrews (MA); Univ. of Wisconsin (MSc); Univ. of London (PhD). Joined Univ. of Nottingham, 1980, Dir, AHRC Landscape and Envmt Prog., Sch. of Geog., 2005–12. Vice Chancellor's Achievement Award, Univ. of Nottingham, 2010. *Publications:* Joseph Wright: art and enlightenment, 1999; Humphry Repton and the Geography of Georgian England, 1999; (jtly) Art of the Garden: the garden in British art, 1800 to the present day, 2004; (jtly) Landscapes of the National Trust, 2015; contribs to jls incl. British Art Jl, Jl Histl Geog., Cultural Geographies, Jl Garden Hist. *Address:* School of Geography, University of Nottingham, University Park, Nottingham NG7 2RD.

**DANIELSON, Tana Marie Therese;** *see* Adkin, T. M. T.

**DANKWORTH, Lady;** *see* Laine, Dame C. D.

**DANN, Mrs Jill;** *b* 10 Sept. 1929; *d* of Harold Norman Cartwright and Marjorie Alice Thornton; *m* 1952, Anthony John Dann (*d* 2000); two *s* two *d* (and one *s* decd). *Educ:* Solihull High Sch. for Girls, Malvern Hall; Birmingham Univ. (LLB); St Hilda's Coll., Oxford (BCL). Called to the Bar, Inner Temple, 1952. Mayoress of Chippenham, 1964–65. Church Commissioner, 1968–93; Member: General Synod of Church of England, 1965–95 (Mem., Standing Cttee, 1971–90; Vice-Chm. House of Laity, 1985–90); Crown Appointments Commn, 1977–87; Chairman: House of Laity, Bristol Diocesan Synod, 1982–88; C of E Evangelical Council, 1985–89; Trustee, Church Urban Fund, 1987–95. Vice Chm., Trinity Coll., Bristol, 1990–2006; Pres. of Fellows, Cheltenham and Gloucester Coll. of Higher Educn, subseq. Univ. of Gloucestershire, 1988–2003. Director: Wiltshire Radio, 1981–88; ARK 2 TV Ltd, 1995–97. Pres., Inner Wheel, 1978–79. *Recreations:* reading, enjoying being a grandmother, listening. *Address:* 47 The Cloisters, Pegasus Grange, Whitehouse Road, Oxford OX1 4QQ. *T:* (01865) 608009.

**DANNATT,** family name of **Baron Dannatt**.

**DANNATT**, Baron cr 2011 (Life Peer), of Keswick in the County of Norfolk; **Gen. (Francis) Richard Dannatt**, GCB 2009 (KCB 2004); CBE 1996; MC 1973; DL; Constable, HM Tower of London, 2009–16; b 23 Dec. 1950; s of late Anthony Richard Dannatt and of Mary Juliet Dannatt (née Chilvers); m 1977, Philippa Margaret Gurney (MBE 2013); three s one d. Educ: Felsted Jun. Sch.; St Lawrence Coll.; RMA, Sandhurst; Univ. of Durham (BA Hons Econ. Hist. 1976). Commnd Green Howards, 1971; Army Comd and Staff Coll., Camberley, 1982; COS, 20th Armd Bde, 1983–84; MA to Minister of State for Armed Forces, 1986–89; CO, 1 Green Howards, 1989–91; Col Higher Comd and Staff Course, Staff Coll., Camberley, 1992–94; Comdr, 4th Armd Bde, 1994–96; Dir, Defence Progs, MoD, 1996–98; GOC 3rd UK Div., 1999–2000; Dep. Comdr Ops, HQ SFOR, 2000–01; ACGS, 2001–02; Comdr, Allied RRC, 2003–05; C-in-C Land Comd, 2005–06; Chief of Gen. Staff, 2006–09; ADC Gen. to the Queen, 2006–09. Col, Green Howards, 1994–2003; Dep. Col Comdt, AGC (RMP), 1999–2005; Colonel Commandant: King's Div., 2001–05; AAC, 2004–09. Chm., Strategic Adv. Bd, Durham Global Security Inst., 2010–15; Chm., Cadence Consultancy, 2017–. Vice Pres., Officers Christian Union, 1998–2012; President: Soldiers' and Airmen's Scripture Readers Assoc., 1999–; Army Rifle Assoc., 2000–08; Royal Norfolk Agricl Assoc., 2008; YMCA Norfolk, 2010; Norfolk Churches Trust, 2011; Trustee: Windsor Leadership Trust, 2005–12; Royal Armouries, 2009–18 (Chm., 2015–18); Normandy Meml Trust, 2017–; Patron: Hope and Homes for Children, 2006–; There But Not There, 2017–; Veterans Covenant Hospital Alliance, 2017–; Founder Patron, Help for Heroes, 2007– (Pres., 2011–); Vice Patron, Blind Veterans UK (formerly St Dunstan's), 2010–15. DL: Gtr London, 2010; Norfolk 2012. Hon. DCL: Durham, 2009; Kent, 2009; Hon. DTech Anglia Ruskin, 2010; Hon. DLitt Buckingham, 2012. Publications: Leading from the Front, 2010; Boots on the Ground, 2016. Recreations: cricket, tennis, fishing, shooting, golf. Address: House of Lords, SW1A 0PW. T: (020) 7219 8949. Clubs: Army and Navy, Cavalry and Guards; Royal West Norfolk Golf.

**DANNATT, Prof. (James) Trevor**, OBE 2016; MA; RA 1983 (ARA 1977); FRIBA; Consultant, since 2003, Partner, 1975–2003, Dannatt, Johnson Architects (formerly Trevor Dannatt & Partners); Professor of Architecture: Manchester University, 1975–86; Royal Academy, 1988–2005; b 15 Jan. 1920; s of George Herbert and Jane Ellen Dannatt; m 1st, 1953, Joan Howell Davies (marr. diss. 1991); one s one d; 2nd, 1994, Dr Ann Crawshaw (née Critchley). Educ: Colfe's Sch.; Sch. of Architecture, Regent Street Polytechnic (Dip. Arch.). Professional experience in office of Jane B. Drew and E. Maxwell Fry, 1943–48; Architects Dept, LCC (Royal Festival Hall Gp), 1948–52; commenced private practice, 1952. Vis. Prof., Washington Univ., St Louis, 1976 and 1987. Assessor for national and international architectural competitions. Member: Cathedrals Adv. Commn, 1986–91; Historic Bldgs Adv. Cttee, English Heritage, 1988–91 (Mem., Post War Listing Adv. Cttee, 1986–2003); Fabric Cttees of Cathedrals: Lichfield, 1985–97; Portsmouth, 1990–96; St Paul's, 1991–2006. Pres., 20th Century Soc., 2003–11. Editor, Architects' Year Book, 1945–62. Exhibn of paintings and architecture, Whitworth Art Gall., 2006. Architectural work includes: private houses, housing, school buildings; university buildings (residences, Leicester, Hull; Trinity Hall Combination Room, Cambridge; Vaughan Coll. and Jewry Wall Mus., Leicester; devlt plan and extensive works for Univ. of Greenwich, formerly Thames Polytechnic, incl. studies for occupation of Wren and Hawksmoor at RNC Greenwich, comprising conversion and refurbishment of Queen Anne Quarters and Dreadnought Seamen's Hosp., 1999, Queen Mary's Quarters, 2000 and King William's Quarters, 2001); works for Univ. of Westminster; welfare buildings and schools for London boroughs; conservation and restoration, interiors for private, corporate and public clients; Architects for British Embassy and Diplomatic Staff housing, Riyadh, 1985; Consultant Architects, Royal Botanic Gardens, Kew, 1989–2005; Victoria Gate visitor reception and facilities building; various restorations and new buildings; houses for Morden Coll., Blackheath, 2004; Walker House, W Sussex, 2010. Won internat. competition for Conference complex in Riyadh, Saudi Arabia, completed 1974. Hon. FAIA 1988. Hon. DDes Greenwich, 2002. Publications: Modern Architecture in Britain, 1959; Trevor Dannatt: Buildings and Interiors 1951–72, 1972; (Editorial Adviser, and foreword) Buildings and Ideas 1933–83 from the Studio of Leslie Martin, 1983; (with P. Carolin) Sir Leslie Martin: architecture, education, research, 1996; Maritime Greenwich Campus, 2002; contribs to Architectural Rev., Architects' Jl, and various foreign journals; relevant publication: Trevor Dannatt: works and words, by R. Stonehouse, 2008. Recreations: the arts, including architecture. Address: (office) 77 Great Suffolk Street, SE1 0BU. T: (020) 7357 7100. E: trevordannatt@djarchitects.co.uk. W: www.trevordannatt.co.uk. Club: Travellers.

**DANNENBAUM, Peggy Scott C.**; see Czyzak-Dannenbaum.

**d'ANSEMBOURG, Count Jan Mark Vladimir Anton de Marchant et**; see de Marchant et d'Ansembourg.

**DANTON, Joanna Ruth**; see Place, J. R.

**DANTZIC, Roy Matthew**, MBE 2017; CA; Chairman, ISG (formerly Interior Services Group) plc, 2004–16; b 4 July 1944; s of David and Renee Dantzic; m 1969, Diane Clapham; one s one d. Educ: Brighton Coll., Sussex. CA 1968. Coopers & Lybrand, 1962–69; Kleinwort, Benson Ltd, 1970–72; Drayton Corporation Ltd, 1972–74; Samuel Montagu & Co. Ltd, 1974–80 (Exec. Dir, 1975); Mem. for Finance, BNOC, subseq. Finance Dir, Britoil plc, 1980–84; Dir, Pallas SA, 1984–85; Dir, Wood Mackenzie & Co., 1985–89; Finance Dir, Stanhope Properties, 1989–95; Dir, Merrill Lynch Internat., 1995–96; Man. Dir, British Gas Properties, then BG Property Hldgs, subseq. SecondSite Property Hldgs, 1996–2003 (non-exec. Dir, 2003–04). Chairman: Premier Portfolio Ltd, 1985–92; Associated British Cinemas Ltd, 1998–2000; Development Securities plc, 2003–07; Dep. Chm., Spazio Investment NV, 2007–09; non-executive Director: Moor Park (1958) Ltd, 1980–90; Saxon Oil plc, 1984–85; Total Oil Holdings, 1995–96; Airplanes Ltd, 1996–2018; Blenheim Bishop Ltd, 2003–07. pt-time Mem., CEGB, 1984–87; Pt-time Dir, BNFL, 1987–91. Mem., Council of Mgt, Architectural Heritage Fund, 2001–16 (Dep. Chm., 2014–16). Trustee, Portman Estate, 2005–. Governor, Brighton Coll., 1990–98. Recreations: cinema, theatre, playing golf, watching cricket. Clubs: MCC; Moor Park Golf.

**DARBISHIRE, Adrian Munro**; QC 2012; b Guildford, 11 Nov. 1966; s of David Hamilton Darbishire and Gaynor Darbishire. Educ: Charterhouse; Balliol Coll., Oxford (MA Hons 1988); City Univ. London (DipLaw 1993); King's Coll. London (LLM 1994). Called to the Bar, Lincoln's Inn, 1993; in practice as barrister, specialising in criminal law, 1995–. Treasury Counsel, Central Criminal Court, 2007–12. Address: QEB Hollis Whiteman, 1–2 Laurence Pountney Hill, EC4R 0EU. T: (020) 7933 8855. E: barristers@qebhw.co.uk. Club: Groucho.

**DARBY, John Oliver Robertson**; Chairman, Arthur Young, Chartered Accountants, 1974–87; b 5 Jan. 1930; s of Ralph Darby and Margaret Darby (née Robertson); m 1955, Valerie Leyland Cole; three s. Educ: Charterhouse. FCA 1953. Pilot Officer, RAF, 1953–55; Arthur Young, Chartered Accts, 1955–87, Partner, 1959–87. Chairman: Nat. Home Loans Hldgs PLC, 1985–92; Property Lending Trust, later Property Lending Bank, PLC, 1987–92; Ultramar, 1988–91; BREL Gp, later ABB Transportation (Hldgs) Ltd, 1989–94; Director: British Rail Engineering Ltd, 1986–89; Lightgraphix Ltd, 1996–2009. Recreations: racing, golf. Address: The Tithe Barn, Headley, Bordon, Hants GU35 8PW. Clubs: Garrick, Royal Thames Yacht; Royal & Ancient Golf (St Andrews); Liphook Golf.

**DARBY, Dr Michael Douglas**, FRES; taxonomic entomologist; Managing Director, Malthouse Books, since 2009; Scientific Associate, Department of Life Sciences, Natural History Museum, since 2015; b 2 Sept. 1944; s of Arthur Douglas Darby and Ilene Doris Darby (née Eatwell); m 1977, Elisabeth Susan Done; two s. Educ: Rugby School; Reading Univ. (PhD). FRES 1977; FRGS 1984; AMA 1990. Asst to Barbara Jones, 1963; Victoria and Albert Museum: Textiles Dept, 1964–72; Prints and Drawings Dept, 1973–76; Exhibitions Officer, 1977–83; Dep. Dir, 1983–87; Hd of Publications, Exhibitions and Design, 1988–89; Surveyor Gen., Carroll Art Collection, 1990–94. Member: Crafts Council, 1984–88; IoW Adv. Cttee, English Heritage, 1986–; Council, Royal Entomol Soc., 1988–90; Council, National Trust, 1989–93; Council, Wilts Archaeol and Natural Hist. Soc., 1996–2001; Council, British Entomol and Natural Hist. Soc., 2009–; Chm., Wilts Natural Hist. Pubns Trust, 2000–. Has described over 200 new species of beetle from across the world and has several named after him. FRSA 1989. Ed., Recording Wiltshire's Biodiversity, 1996–2004; Natural Hist. Ed., Wiltshire Studies, 2000–. Compiler, Biographical Dictionary of British Coleopterists at www.coleopterist.org.uk. Publications: Marble Halls, 1973; Early Railway Prints, 1974, 2nd edn 1979; British Art in the Victoria and Albert Museum, 1983; John Pollard Seddon, 1983; The Islamic Perspective, 1983; (as Nic Ryman) Bye Bye Pests, 2008; Wiltshire Beetles, 2009; New Species and Records of Featherwing Beetles (Coleoptera: Ptiliidae), 2017; articles in art, architectural and entomological periodicals. Recreations: beetles, books. Address: 33 Bedwin Street, Salisbury, Wilts SP1 3UT.

**DARBY, Prof. Sarah Caroline**, PhD; FMedSci; FRS 2019; Professor of Medical Statistics, University of Oxford, since 1997; Fellow of Green Templeton College, Oxford, since 1987; b London, 27 Dec. 1951; d of Henry Clifford Darby and Eva Constance Darby (née Thomson); m 1996, Tom Fearn. Educ: Berkhamsted Sch. for Girls; Perse Sch. for Girls; Imperial Coll., London (BSc Hons Maths 1973); Univ. of Birmingham (MSc Math. Stats 1974); London Sch. of Hygiene and Tropical Medicine (PhD Med. Stats 1977). Lectr in Med. Stats, Dept of Community Medicine, St Thomas's Hosp. Med. Sch., London, 1976–78; SSO, 1978–81, PSO and Gp Leader, 1981–84, Epidemiol. and Statistical Studies Gp, NRPB; University of Oxford: Res. Scientist, 1984–87, Sen. Scientist, 1987–92, Principal Scientist, 1992–99, Imperial Cancer Res. Fund Cancer Epidemiol. Unit; Cancer Res. UK Principal Scientist and Sen. Gp Leader, Clin. Trial Service Unit and Epidemiol Studies Unit, Nuffield Dept of Clin. Medicine, 1999–2007. Vis. Scientist, Radiation Effects Res. Foundn, Hiroshima, 1982–83 (on sabbatical from NRPB). Hon. Prof. in Radiotherapy, Univ. of Southern Denmark, 2012–17. FMedSci 2019. Guy Medal in Bronze, Royal Statistical Soc., 1988. Publications: articles in med. and scientific jls. Recreations: food, conversation, reading novels. Address: 37 St John Street, Oxford OX1 2LH.

**DARBYSHIRE, Jane Helen, (Mrs Jane Darbyshire-Walker)**, OBE 1994; Consultant, Jane Darbyshire and David Kendall Ltd, since 2000 (Director, 1995–2000); b 5 June 1948; d of Gordon Desmond Wroe and Patricia Keough; m 1st, 1973, David Darbyshire (marr. diss. 1987); one d; 2nd, 1993, Michael Walker. Educ: Univ. of Newcastle upon Tyne (BA Hons, BArch Hons). RIBA. Architect: Ryder and Yates, Newcastle upon Tyne, 1972–75; Barnett Winskell, 1975–79; Partner, Jane and David Darbyshire, 1979–87; Dir, Jane Darbyshire Associates, 1987–95. Ext. Examnr, Newcastle upon Tyne Univ., 1993–95. Mem., RIBA Nat. Council, 1998–2001; Board Member: Tyne and Wear Develt Corp., 1992–98; NE Regl Cultural Consortium, 1999–2001. Recreations: classical music, horse riding, art, textiles, English and French literature. Address: Jane Darbyshire and David Kendall Ltd, Millmount, Ponteland Road, Newcastle upon Tyne NE5 3AL.

**DARBYSHIRE, Prof. Janet Howard, (Mrs G. M. Scott)**, CBE 2010 (OBE 1996); FRCP, FFPH, FMedSci; Director, MRC Clinical Trials Unit, 1998–2010; Professor of Epidemiology, University College London, 1997–2010, now Emeritus; Joint Director, NIHR Clinical Research Network (formerly UK Clinical Research Network), 2005–10; b 16 Nov. 1947; d of Philip and Jean Darbyshire; m 1976, Dr Geoffrey M. Scott, FRCP, FRCPath. Educ: Manchester Univ. (MB ChB 1970); London Sch. of Hygiene and Tropical Medicine (MSc 1990). MRCP 1973, FRCP 1988; FFPH 2001; FMedSci 2005. Mem., Scientific Staff, MRC, 1974–2010. Hon. Professor: Dept of Pharmacol. and Therapeutics, Univ. of Liverpool, 1999–; LSHTM, 1999–; Univ. of Leeds, 2007–. Hon. Consultant Physician: Royal Brompton Hosp., 1982–2010; Camden PCT, 1997–2010. Publications: contribs on clinical trials and epidemiol studies in tuberculosis, HIV infection and other diseases. Recreations: music, horse-riding, walking, reading, cooking, flying. Address: Flat 64, County Hall North Block, 5 Chicheley Street, SE1 7PN.

**DARBYSHIRE, Martin Richard**; Founder and Chief Executive Officer, tangerine, since 1989; b Preston, 30 May 1961; s of Stanley Alexander Darbyshire and Barbara Helen Darbyshire; m 1986, Melinda Ann Ross; four s. Educ: Ongar Comp. Sch.; Central Sch. of Art and Design (BA Hons Industrial Design). Product Designer: Moggridge Associates, London, 1983–86; ID Two, San Francisco, 1986–87; Sen. Product Designer, Moggridge Associates, London, 1987–89. Course Tutor, 1990–97, Vis. Prof., 2000–10, Central St Martins Coll. of Art and Design, subseq. Central St Martins, UAL; Ext. Examnr, Product Design BA, Ravensbourne Sch. of Design and Communication, 2000–04. Design Council: Mem., Millennium Products Selection Panel, London, 1998–99; Mem., Bd of Trustees, 2015–. Advr to Design Council on behalf of Design Business Assoc., 2005. Mem. Bd, ICSID, 2008–12 (Mem. Steering Cttee, World Design Capital proj., 2012). Member, Jury: Red Dot Design awards, Essen, 2005–; China Good Design, 2015–. Mem., China-Britain Business Council, 2013–. FRSA; FCSD 1995. Mem., Design Business Assoc., 1998–. Publications: (contrib.) tangerine: 25 insights into extraordinary innovation and design, 2014. Recreations: dog walking, camping, travel, sailing, family, cinema, theatre. Address: tangerine, Unit 9, Blue Lion Place, 237 Long Lane, SE1 4PU. T: (020) 7357 0966. E: mail@tangerine.net.

**DARCEY, Michael William**; Managing Partner, Tide End Consulting Ltd, since 2015; b Oxford, 10 June 1965; s of Dr Warwick Darcey and Yvonne Darcey; m 1994, Julie Bishop; one s one d. Educ: St Patrick's Coll., Wellington, NZ; Victoria Univ., Wellington (BSc Hons Maths); London Sch. of Econs and Pol Sci. (MSc Econs). Mgt Consultant, KPMG, Wellington, NZ and London, 1987–89; Res. Associate, Putnam, Hayes & Bartlett, 1989–91; Partner, Lexecon Ltd, 1991–98; Dir of Strategy, 1998–2006, Chief Operating Officer, 2006–12, BSkyB; CEO, News UK, 2013–15. Chairman: Dennis Publishing, 2017–18; M247, 2017–. Non-exec. Dir, Home Retail Gp, 2010–16 (Sen. Ind. Dir, 2012–16); Director: Arqiva, 2017–; Sky TV NZ, 2017–. Chm., Bd of Trustees, RTS, 2010–12. Chm., British Gymnastics, 2019–. Recreations: mountains and water.

**DARCY DE KNAYTH**, 19th Baron cr 1332; **Caspar David Ingrams**; consultant engineer, since 2005; b 5 Jan. 1962; s of late Rupert George Ingrams and Baroness Darcy de Knayth (18th in line); S mother, 2008; m 1996, Catherine Ann Baker (marr. diss. 2013); three s. Educ: Eton Coll.; Reading Univ. (BSc (Hons) Mech. Engrg). Ops Mgr, Howden

Wade, 1987–98; Engrg Mgr, Airscrew Ltd, 1998–2004. *Recreations:* walking, opera, family. *Heir: s* Hon. Thomas Rupert Ingrams, *b* 23 Oct. 1999. *Address:* The Orchard, Rookery Lane, Broughton, Stockbridge SO20 8AZ. *T:* (01794) 301628. *Club:* Brooks's.

**DARDIS, Patrick;** Chief Executive Officer, Young & Co.'s Brewery plc, since 2015; *b* Kells, Co. Meath, Eire, 6 April 1959; *s* of Pat Dardis and Marcella Dardis; *m* 1991, Heather; two *s. Educ:* Christian Brothers Sch., Ireland. Whitbread plc/Courage Ltd, 1976–91; Guinness, 1991–93; Dir, Retail, Wolverhampton & Dudley Breweries plc, 1993–2001; Retail Dir, Young & Co.'s Brewery plc, 2002–15. Exec., Ind. Family Brewers of Britain. Mem., Council, British Beer and Pub Assoc. Freeman, City of London. *Recreations:* Rugby, golf. *T:* 07971 148237. *E:* pdardis@btinternet.com.

**DARE, Thomas Charles M.;** *see* Macey-Dare.

**DARELL, Sir Guy Jeffrey Adair,** 9th Bt *cr* 1795, of Richmond Hill, Surrey; Director, Tysers Insurance Brokers, since 1999; *b* London, 8 June 1961; *o s* of Brig. Sir Jeffrey Lionel Darell, 8th Bt, MC and Bridget Mary Darell (née Adair); *S* father, 2013; *m* 1988, (Justine) Samantha Reynolds; one *s* two *d. Educ:* Eton Coll.; RMA Sandhurst. Coldstream Guards, 1980–83. J. H. Minet, 1984–90; Fenchurch Insce Brokers, 1994–97; Windsor Insce Brokers, 1997–99. *Recreations:* tennis, ski-ing, shooting. *Heir: s* Harry Thomas Adair Darell, *b* 10 May 1995. *Address:* 5 Norland Square, W11 4PX. *T:* (020) 7229 9036. *E:* guy.darell@tysers.com. *Clubs:* Lansdowne, MCC.

**DARESBURY,** 4th Baron *cr* 1927, of Walton, co. Chester; **Peter Gilbert Greenall;** DL; Bt 1876; Chairman, Nasstar plc, since 2005; *b* 18 July 1953; *e s* of 3rd Baron Daresbury and his 1st wife, Margaret Ada, *y d* of C. J. Crawford; *S* father, 1996; *m* 1982, Clare Alison, *d* of late Christopher Nicholas Weatherby; four *s. Educ:* Eton; Magdalene Coll., Cambridge (MA); London Business Sch. (Sloan Fellowship). Dir, 1982–2006, Man. Dir, 1992–97, Chief Exec., 1997–2000, Chm., 2000–06, Greenalls Gp, later The De Vere Gp; Chairman: Aintree Racecourse Co. Ltd, 1988–2014; Highland Gold Mining Ltd, 2002–04; Kazakh Gold, 2005–07; Tewlint Services Ltd, 2005–11; Mallett plc, 2008–14; Stellar Diamonds plc, 2008–; Haydock Park Racecourse, 2013–; Timico Technology Gp Ltd, 2014–17; non-executive Director: Evraz, 2005–06; Sumatra Copper & Gold Ltd, 2007–11; RusAnt, 2007–; Bespoke Hotels, 2011–17; Auriant Mining AB, 2012–; Pesto Restaurants, 2012–. Steward, Jockey Club, 2013–18. DL Cheshire, 1993. *Heir: s* Hon. Thomas Edward Greenall [*b* 6 Nov. 1984; *m* 2014, Annabelle L. V. Sheppard; two *s*]. *Address:* Manor Farm, Wychough, Malpas, Cheshire SY14 7NQ. *T:* (home) (01948) 860963, (office) (01948) 861900, *Fax:* (01948) 861483. *E:* peter.daresbury@daresburyltd.co.uk. *Clubs:* Jockey, MCC; Royal & Ancient Golf (St Andrews).
*See also* J. R. *Weatherby*, R. N. *Weatherby*.

**DARKE, Christopher;** Director, Member Relations (formerly Regional Services), British Medical Association, since 2010; *b* 5 Aug. 1949; *s* of late Derek Herbert Darke and Helen Navina Darke (née Davies); *m* 1st, 1976, Marian Dyson (marr. diss. 1982); one *s* one *d*; 2nd, 1992, Lorraine Julie Hinchliffe; two *d. Educ:* Handsworth Secondary Sch., Birmingham. Engrg apprentice, GEC, 1967–70; Engrg Draughtsman, Lucas Industries, 1970–77; TU Officer, AUEW-TASS, 1977–82; Nat. Officer, AUEW-TASS, later MSF, 1982–92; Gen. Sec., BALPA, 1992–2002; Hd, Regl Services (England), BMA, 2002–10. Mem., Competition (formerly Monopolies and Mergers) Commn, 1998–2005. *Recreations:* flying, travel, reading, gardening. *Address:* (office) BMA House, Tavistock Square, WC1H 9JP.

**DARKE, Dr Wendy;** Founder and Chief Executive Officer, True to Nature Ltd, since 2016; *b* Gloucester, 29 May 1965; *d* of Robert William Darke and Janet Mary Darke; *m* 1996, Stephen Anthony Batty; two *d. Educ:* Univ. of Bristol (BSc Jt Hons Geol. and Zool. 1986); James Cook Univ., N Qld (PhD Marine Biol. 1991). BBC Natural History Unit: Researcher and Asst Producer, 1991–95; Producer and Dir, 1995–2000; Series Producer, 2000–06; Exec. Producer, 2006–12; Head, 2012–16. Hon. DSc Bristol, 2015; Hon. DArt UWE, 2015. Cherry Kearton Medal and Award for Cinematography of the Natural World, RGS, 2016. *Recreations:* family, friends, coral reefs, tennis, ski-ing, travel, Cornwall. *Address:* True To Nature Ltd, Films@59, 59 Cotham Hill, Bristol BS6 6JR. *E:* wendy.darke@truetonature.co.uk.

**DARLEY, Gillian Mary,** OBE 2015; FSA; architectural writer and biographer; *b* 28 Nov. 1947; *d* of Lt Col Robert Darley, MC and Caroline (née Swanston Ward); *m* 1986, Michael Horowitz, QC; one *d* (one *s* decd). *Educ:* Courtauld Inst. of Art, London Univ. (BA Hons 1969); Birkbeck Coll., London (MSc Politics and Admin 1986). Journalist and broadcaster; contributor to daily and Sunday newspapers, magazines and professional press, 1975–; Architectural correspondent, Observer, 1991–93. Dir, Landscape Foundn, 1994–98. Trustee, SPAB (Chm., 1997–2000); Member: Lottery Architecture Adv. Cttee, Arts Council of England, 1996–2001; Council, 2008–15, Architecture Panel, 2014–15, NT; London Diocesan Adv. Cttee, 2008–13; English Heritage Blue Plaques Panel, 2012–14. Pres., Twentieth Century Soc., 2014–. FSA 2007. Esher Award, SPAB, 2014. *Publications:* Villages of Vision, 1975, 2nd edn 2007; The National Trust Book of the Farm, 1981; Built in Britain, 1984; (with P. Lewis) Dictionary of Ornament, 1986; Octavia Hill: a life, 1990, 2nd edn 2010; (with A. Saint) The Chronicles of London, 1994; John Soane: an accidental romantic, 1999; Factory, 2003; John Evelyn: living for ingenuity, 2006; Vesuvius: the most famous volcano in the world, 2011; (with D. McKie) Ian Nairn: words in place, 2013; Excellent Essex, 2019. *Recreations:* gardening in a small space, Jack Russell, spending time in the desert.

**DARLEY, Kevin Paul;** freelance flat race jockey, retired 2007; Chief Executive, Professional Jockeys Association, 2009–12; racing adviser, Qatar and Pearl Racing Ltd, since 2014; Coaching Development Manager, Jockeys Education and Training Scheme, since 2018; *b* 5 Aug. 1960; *s* of Clifford Darley and Dorothy Thelma Darley (née Newby); *m* 1983, Debby Ford; two *d. Educ:* Colton Hills Comprehensive Sch., Wolverhampton. Apprentice Jockey to Reg Hollinshead, 1976–78 (Champion apprentice, 1978, with 70 winners); has ridden over 2,400 winners, incl. 71 Group winners (24 in Gp 1) in Britain and Europe, and 158 in one season, 2001; winner: French Derby, 1995, on Celtic Swing; St Leger, 2002, on Bollin Eric; English and Irish 1,000 Guineas, on Attraction, 2004; Champion Jockey, 2000. Jt Pres., Jockeys' Assoc. of GB, 2003–07. *Recreations:* shooting, golf, hunting, ski-ing. *Address:* The Old Granary, Gale Road, Alne, York, N Yorks YO61 1TH. *T:* (01347) 833015.

**DARLING,** family name of **Barons Darling** and **Darling of Roulanish**.

**DARLING,** 3rd Baron *cr* 1924; **Robert Julian Henry Darling;** chartered surveyor in private practice, since 1990; *b* 29 April 1944; *s* of 2nd Baron Darling and Bridget Rosemary Whishaw Darling (née Dickson); *S* father, 2003; *m* 1970, Janet Rachel (née Mallinson); two *s* one *d. Educ:* Wellington Coll.; RAC Cirencester. FRICS. Nuffield Scholar, Australia and NZ, 1984. Partner, Smith-Woolley, Chartered Surveyors, 1970–89. Vice-Chairman: Norfolk Mental Healthcare NHS Trust, 1993–97; Nat. Assoc. of Prison Visitors, 2000. Chairman: Gt Yarmouth and Waveney, Mind, 2001–08; Rural Enterprise (formerly Land Use and Access) Panel, NT, 2007–13. Chm., Nuffield Farming Scholarships Trust, 2016–18 (Vice-Chm., 2014–16); Ind. Monitoring Bd, MoJ, 2018–. *Recreations:* fishing, gardening.

*Heir: s* Hon. (Robert) James (Cyprian) Darling [*b* 6 March 1972; *m* 2007, Suzanne Claire Gwynder-Lewis; two *s* one *d* (incl. twin *s* and *d*)]. *Address:* Wood, Bishopsteignton, S Devon TQ14 9TN. *T:* (01626) 774446, *Fax:* (01626) 776187. *E:* jdarling@paston.co.uk. *Club:* Norfolk.

**DARLING OF ROULANISH,** Baron *cr* 2015 (Life Peer), of Great Bernera in the County of Ross and Cromarty; **Alistair Maclean Darling;** PC 1997; *b* 28 Nov. 1953; *m* 1986, Margaret McQueen Vaughan; one *s* one *d. Educ:* Aberdeen Univ. Mem., Faculty of Advocates, 1984–2010. Member: Lothian Regl Council, 1982–87; Lothian and Borders Police Bd, 1982–86. MP (Lab) Edinburgh Central, 1987–2005, Edinburgh SW, 2005–15. Shadow Chief Sec. to HM Treasury, 1996–97; Chief Sec. to HM Treasury, 1997–98; Secretary of State: for Social Security, 1998–2001; for Work and Pensions, 2001–02; for Transport, 2002–06; for Scotland, 2003–06; for Trade and Industry, 2006–07; Chancellor of the Exchequer, 2007–10; Shadow Chancellor of the Exchequer, 2010. Chm., Better Together, 2012–14. Non-exec. Dir, Morgan Stanley, 2016–. Trustee, Standard Life Foundn, 2016– (Chm., 2017–). Gov., Napier Coll., Edinburgh, 1982–87. Hon. Pres., Chatham House, 2016–. Hon. LLD Aberdeen, 2018. *Publications:* Back from the Brink: 1,000 days at Number 11, 2011.

**DARLING, Rt Rev. Edward Flewett;** Bishop of Limerick and Killaloe, 1985–2000; *b* 24 July 1933; *s* of late Ven. Vivian W. Darling and Honor F. G. Darling; *m* 1958, E. E. Patricia Mann; three *s* two *d. Educ:* Cork Grammar School; Midleton Coll., Co. Cork; St John's School, Leatherhead, Surrey; Trinity Coll., Dublin (MA). Curate: St Luke's, Belfast, 1956–59; St John's, Orangefield, Belfast, 1959–62; Incumbent, St Gall's, Carnalea, Co. Down, 1962–72; Chaplain, Bangor Hosp., Co. Down, 1963–72; Rector, St John's, Malone, Belfast, 1972–85; Minor Canon, Belfast Cathedral, 1974–85; Chaplain, Ulster Independent Clinic, Belfast, 1981–85. ARSCM 2010. Hon. FGCM 2006. *Publications:* Choosing the Hymns, 1984; (ed) Irish Church Praise, 1990; Sing to the Word, 2000, rev. edn 2015; (ed) Church Hymnal, 5th edn 2000; (jtly) Companion to Church Hymnal, 2005; Understanding Hymns, 2007. *Recreations:* music, gardening. *Address:* 17 Queensfort Court, Carryduff, Belfast BT8 8NF. *T:* (028) 9081 7949.

**DARLING, Ian Galen; His Honour Judge Darling;** a Circuit Judge, since 2009; *b* Sunderland, 27 Oct. 1962; *s* of late William Martindale Darling, CBE and of Ann Edith Darling, OBE; *m* 1st, 1990, Tessa Ross (née Thompson) (marr. diss. 1999); 2nd, 2002, Emma Charlotte Sillars (marr. diss. 2012); one *s* one *d. Educ:* Winchester Coll.; King's Coll., London (LLB 1984). Called to the Bar, Middle Temple, 1985; a Recorder, 2003–09. *Recreations:* Newcastle United Football Club, Harlequins Rugby Club. *Address:* Inner London Crown Court, Newington Causeway, SE1 6AZ. *Club:* Westoe Rugby Football.
*See also* P. A. *Darling*.

**DARLING, Ian Marshall,** OBE 2015; FRICS; a Vice President, Royal Society for the Protection of Birds, since 2013 (Chairman of Council, 2008–12); *b* Perth, Scotland, 16 April 1945; *s* of John Darling and Nora Darling; *m* 1971, Kathryn Pearman; one *s* one *d. Educ:* Perth Acad.; Coll. of Estate Mgt; Wye Coll., London (Dip. Farm Business Admin 1969). ARICS 1966, FRICS 1978. Partner, Bell Ingram Chartered Surveyors, 1974–96 (Man. Dir, 1987–96); Dir, Chesterton (Scotland), 1996–2001. Chm., RICS Scotland, 1997–98. Non-exec. Dir, British Waterways, 2000–06. Mem., Lands Tribunal for Scotland, 2004–13. Mem. Council, British Trust for Ornithology, 1994–99; Pres., Scottish Ornithologist Club, 1996–99; Chm., Isle of May Bird Observatory, 1999–2019. Mem. Court, Univ. of Edinburgh, 2004–09. Master, Edinburgh Merchant Co., 2000–01. *Recreations:* travel, natural history, birding. *Club:* New (Edinburgh).

**DARLING, Judith K.;** *see* Kirton-Darling.

**DARLING, Paul Antony,** OBE 2015; QC 1999; *b* 15 March 1960; *s* of late William Martindale Darling, CBE and of Ann Edith Darling; *m* 1st, 1983 (marr. diss.); 2nd, 1994 (marr. diss.); 3rd, 2013, Anne Camilla Frances, *d* of Brian John Barker, *qv* and Anne Barker (*see* Rt Hon. Dame A. J. Rafferty). *Educ:* Tonstall Sch., Sunderland; Winchester Coll. (Schol.); St Edmund Hall, Oxford (BA Jurisp. 1981; BCL 1982). Treas., Oxford Union, 1980. Called to the Bar, Middle Temple, 1983, Bencher, 2004; in practice, 1985–; Hd, Keating Chambers, 2010–15. Chairman: Technol. and Construction Bar Assoc., 2003–07; Access to the Bar Cttee, Bar Council, 2007–09; Mem., Gen. Council of the Bar, 2007–08. Dir, J. M. & W. Darling Ltd (pharmaceutical chemists), 1978–. Non-exec. Dir, Horserace Totalisator Bd, 2006–08; Mem., Horse Racing Betting Levy Bd, 2008–14; Chairman: Football Licensing Authy, 2009–11; Sports Grounds Safety Authy, 2011–15; Assoc. of British Bookmakers, 2014–19. Ed., Construction Industry Law Letter, 1990–94; Mem., editl team, Keating on Building Contracts, 5th edn 1991 to 8th edn 2016. Trustee, Free Repn Unit, 2004–12. *Recreations:* horse racing, Newcastle United, Apostrophe Chambers. *Address:* 39 Essex Chambers, 81 Chancery Lane, WC2A 1DD. *T:* (020) 7832 1111. *E:* paul.darling@39essex.com. *Clubs:* Garrick, Arts; South Shields and Westoe (South Shields).
*See also* I. G. *Darling*.

**DARLING, Peter S.;** *see* Stormonth Darling.

**DARLING, Susan;** writer; *b* 1942; *d* of Eric Francis Justice Darling and Monica Darling. *Educ:* Nonsuch County Grammar Sch. for Girls, Cheam; King's Coll., London (BA Hons). Joined BoT as Asst Principal, 1963; transf. to FCO, 1965; Nairobi, 1967–69; Second, later First Sec., Econ. and Social Affairs, UK Mission to UN, 1969–73; FCO, 1973–74; resigned, 1974; reinstated, 1975; FCO, 1975–78; Dep. High Comr and Head of Chancery, Suva, 1981–84; FCO, 1984–87; Consul-Gen., Perth, WA, 1987–88; resigned FCO, 1988; Dept of Chief Minister, NT, Australia, 1989–90; Quaker Service Australia, 1991–93; Aboriginal and Torres Strait Islander Commn, 1994–96; Law Soc. of England and Wales, 2000–02. *Recreations:* countryside, working horse. *Address:* Mayor House Farm Cottages, Farley Heath, Surrey GU5 9EW.

**DARLINGTON, Joyce B.;** *see* Blow Darlington.

**DARLINGTON, Stephen Mark,** MBE 2019; FRCO; Organist and Official Student in Music, Christ Church, Oxford, 1985–2018, now Emeritus Professor of Music, University of Oxford, and Emeritus Student, Christ Church; *b* 21 Sept. 1952; *s* of John Oliver Darlington and Bernice Constance Elizabeth (née Murphy); *m* 1975, Moira Ellen (née Hill); three *d. Educ:* King's Sch., Worcester; Christ Church, Oxford (Organ Schol.; MA). Asst Organist, Canterbury Cathedral, 1974–78; Master of the Music, St Albans Abbey, 1978–85. Artistic Dir, Internat. Organ Fest., 1979–85. Choragus, Oxford Univ., 2001–. Pres., RCO, 1998–2000. Chm., Ouseley Trust, 2007–. Hon. Lay Canon, Christ Church Cathedral, Oxford, 2016, now Emeritus. Hon. FRSCM 2014; Hon. RAM 2016. DMus Lambeth, 2001. *Publications:* (ed jtly) Composing Music for Worship, 2003. *Recreations:* travel, walking, punting, Italian food.

**DARLOW, Annabel Charlotte;** QC 2015; a Recorder, since 2010; *b* London, 19 March 1970; *d* of Clive Darlow and Rita Darlow. *Educ:* St Paul's Girls' Sch.; Westminster Sch.; St John's Coll., Cambridge (BA Eng. Lit. 1991); City Univ., London (DipLaw). Called to the Bar, Middle Temple, 1993; in practice as a barrister, 6KBW College Hill (formerly 6 King's

Bench Walk), 1993–. Standing Counsel to BIS, 2012–16. Mem., Glyndebourne Festival Soc. *Publications:* (ed and contrib.) EU Law in Criminal Practice, 2013. *Recreations:* family, opera and theatre, travel. *Address:* 6KBW College Hill, 21 College Hill, EC4R 2RP.

**DARLOW, Paul Manning; His Honour Judge Darlow;** a Circuit Judge, since 1997; Resident Judge, Plymouth, since 2012; *b* 7 Feb. 1951; *s* of late Brig. Eric William Townsend Darlow, OBE and Elsie Joan Darlow, JP (*née* Ring); *m* 1985, Barbara Joan Speirs; one *d*. *Educ:* Audley House Prep. Sch.; St Edward's Sch., Oxford; Mount Hermon Sch., Massachusetts; King's Coll., London (LLB). Called to the Bar, Middle Temple, 1973; in practice as barrister, London, 1974–78, Bristol, 1978–97; Asst Recorder, 1991–94; a Recorder, 1994–97. *Recreations:* sailing, tennis, bridge, walking, ski-ing. *Address:* Plymouth Combined Court Centre, 10 Armada Way, Plymouth, Devon PL1 2ER.

**DARNBROUGH, Monica Anne,** CBE 2003; PhD; Head of Bioscience Unit, Department of Trade and Industry, 1998–2005; independent consultant, writer and speaker on science policy; *b* 14 Aug. 1951; *d* of Cecil Charles Webb and Marjorie Edyth (*née* Perring); *m* 1974, Geoffrey Darnbrough (marr. diss.; he *d* 2015). *Educ:* Univ. of Nottingham (BSc Jt Hons (Physiol. and Psychol.) 1972; PhD (Develtl Biol.) 1979). Police Scientific Develt Br., Home Office, 1975–79; Department of Industry: Res. and Technol. and Space Div., 1979–80; Rayner study of res. estabts, 1980; Office of Chief Engr and Scientist, 1980–81; Office of Govt Chief Scientific Advr, Cabinet Office, 1981–83; Sec. to ACARD, 1981–83; IT Div., 1984–88, Personnel Div., 1989–93, DTI; Counsellor for Sci. and Technol., FCO, Paris, 1994–98. Member: Council, BBSRC, 2002–04; Commonwealth Scholarship Commn, 2006–12. Founder Mem., and Mem. Bd, Newton's Apple Foundn (formerly Newton's Apple Science Think Tank), 2006–. Hon. Sec., Twickenham Choral Soc., 2010–17. Mem., PCC, 2001–05, 2009–13, Church Warden, 2005–09, St Bartholomew the Great. *Publications:* (contrib.) Handbook of Medicinal Chemistry, 2006. *Recreations:* choral singing, photography (exhibitions in Hampstead, 2010, 2011, and Dore Abbey, annually, 2007–14), exploring the South Downs, weaving. *E:* mondarn@gmail.com.

**DARNLEY,** 12th Earl of, *cr* 1725; **Ivo Donald Stuart Bligh;** Baron Clifton of Leighton Bromswold, 1608; Baron Clifton of Rathmore, 1721; Viscount Darnley, 1723; *b* 17 April 1968; *s* of 11th Earl of Darnley and Countess of Darnley, *qv*; *S* father, 2017; *m* 1997, Peta, *d* of A. R. Beard; three *s*. *Educ:* Marlborough Coll.; Edinburgh Univ. *Heir:* *s* Lord Clifton, *qv*.

**DARNLEY, Dowager Countess of; Susan Elaine Bligh,** CVO 2019; Lord-Lieutenant of Herefordshire, since 2008; *b* 4 Sept. 1945; *d* of Sir Donald Forsyth Anderson and Margaret Elaine Anderson (*née* Llewellyn); *m* 1965, Hon. Adam Ivo Stuart Bligh, 11th Earl of Darnley (*d* 2017); one *s* one *d*. Member: Hereford Diocesan Synod; Bishop of Hereford's Council; Council, Hereford Cathedral; formerly: Mem., Hereford and Worcs Probation Cttee; Mem., Council for Social Responsibility; Vice Chm., Worcs Ethics and Standards Cttee. JP 1977–2005; DL Worcs, 2000–08. *Address:* Horndean, 22 Broomy Hill, Hereford, Herefordshire HR4 0LH.
*See also Earl of Darnley.*

**DARRINGTON, Sir Michael (John),** Kt 2004; FCA; Group Managing Director, Greggs plc, 1984–2008 (non-executive Director, 2008–09); Founder and Lead Campaigner, Pro Business Against Greed, since 2011; *b* 8 March 1942; *s* of George and Kathleen Darrington; *m* 1965, Paula Setterington; one *s* two *d*. *Educ:* Lancing Coll.; Harvard Business Sch. (PMD 1974). FCA 1965. Josolyne Miles and Co., 1960–66; United Biscuits, 1966–83: posts incl. Gp Export Acct; Commercial Dir, Foods Div.; Man. Dir, Sayers Confectioners Ltd, 1978–83. Prince of Wales Regl Ambassador, NE, BITC, 2003–04; Regional Councillor: NE, CBI, 1990–2009; Princes Trust, 2007–15. Founder and Owner, Common Sense Soc., 2009–. Director: Ragleth Ltd, 2012–18; Slaley Community Assets Ltd, 2013–; Northumberland Community Bank, 2017–. Mem. Ct, Newcastle Univ., 2007–16. Hon. DBA Sunderland, 2011; Hon. DCL Northumbria, 2011. *Recreations:* sailing, golf, reading, pyrotechnics.

**DARROCH, His Honour Alasdair Malcolm;** a Circuit Judge, 2000–12; *b* 18 Feb. 1947; *s* of Ronald George Darroch and Diana Graburn Darroch; *m* 1972, Elizabeth Lesley Humphrey; one *s*. *Educ:* Harrow Sch.; Trinity Coll., Cambridge. Articled Mills & Reeve, Solicitors, Norwich, 1969; admitted as solicitor, 1971; Partner, Mills & Reeve, 1974–2000; a Recorder, 1996–2000. Pres., Norfolk and Norwich Incorporated Law Soc., 1996–97. *Publications:* contrib. articles to legal press. *Recreations:* gardening, European travel, real ale.

**DARROCH, Sir (Nigel) Kim,** KCMG 2008 (CMG 1998); HM Diplomatic Service, retired; Ambassador to United States of America, 2016–19; *b* 30 April 1954; *s* of Alastair Macphee Darroch and Enid Darroch (*née* Thompson); *m* 1978, Vanessa Claire Jackson; one *s* one *d*. *Educ:* Abingdon Sch.; Durham Univ. (BSc Zool 1975). Joined FCO, 1976; First Secretary: Tokyo, 1980–84; FCO, 1985–86; Private Sec. to Minister of State, FCO, 1987–89; First Sec., Rome, 1989–92; Dep. Head, European Integration Dept, FCO, 1993–95; Head, Eastern Adriatic Dept, FCO, 1995–97; Counsellor (External Affairs), UK Perm. Rep. to EU, Brussels, 1997–98; Foreign and Commonwealth Office: Head, News Dept, 1998–2000; Dir, EU Comd, 2000–03; Dir Gen., EU Directorate, 2003–04; EU Advr to the PM and Hd, European Secretariat, 2004–07; UK Permanent Rep. to the EU, Brussels, 2007–11; Nat. Security Advr, 2012–15. *Recreations:* squash, ski-ing, sailing, cinema.
*[Created a Baron (Life Peer), 2019 but title not gazetted at time of going to press.]*

**DART, Dr Edward Charles,** CBE 1997; CBiol, FRSB; Chairman, Plant Bioscience Ltd (formerly John Innes Centre Innovations), since 1999 (non-executive Director, 1997–99); *b* 8 March 1941; *s* of late Arthur and Alice Dart; *m* 1964, Jean Ellen Long; one *s* two *d*. *Educ:* Univ. of Manchester Inst. of Science and Technol. (BSc 1962; PhD 1965); Univ. of Calif, LA; Univ. of Calif, Berkeley. Imperial Chemical Industries: Sen. Res. Scientist, Petrochemical and Polymer Lab. (and Lectr in Org. Chem., Univ. of Liverpool), 1968–71; Sen. Res. Scientist, Corporate Lab., 1971–73; Jt Gp Head, Bioscience Gp, 1973–75; Gp Head, Bioscience, 1975–78; Jt Lab. Manager, Corporate Lab. Policy Gp, 1981–83; Head, Corporate Bioscience and Colloids Lab., 1983–85; Associate Res. Dir, Plant Protection Div., 1985–86; Res. Dir, ZENECA (formerly ICI) Seeds, 1986–97; Chief Executive Officer: Norwich Res. Park, 1997–98; AdProTech plc, 1997–99. Chm., Novacta Biosystems Ltd, 2004–05; Board Member: Poalis AS, 2004–05; Rainbow Seed Fund, 2004–10. Science and Engineering Research Council: Mem., Biotechnol. Directorate, 1981–84, Chm., 1984–89; Member: Molecular Biology Sub Cttee, 1980–82; Science Bd, 1985–88. Member: BBSRC, 1994–98 (Chm., Technol. Interaction Bd, 1994–97; Mem., Appointments Cttee, 1998–; Mem., Strategy Bd, 2005–08); BBSRC/Science Mus. Consensus Conf. Steering Cttee, 1994. Chairman: Biotechnol. Jt Adv. Bd, 1992–94; Agric., Horticulture and Forestry Foresight Panel, 1997–99; Member: Adv. Cttee on Genetic Manipulation, 1984–96; DTI/MAFF Agro Food Quality Link Cttee, 1991–98; John Innes Council, 1986–94; MAFF/AFRC Arable Crops Sectoral Gp, 1991–93; Agric. and Envmt Biotechnology Commn, 2000–05; Mem., Internat. Adv. Bd, 2001–07, Exec. Advr, 2008–09, Kansai Res. Inst. Pres., Berks and Oxfordshire Assoc. for Science Educn, 1989–92. *Publications:* review articles in scientific books; papers in chemical and bioscience jls. *Recreations:* travel, books, music, golf, gardening.

**DART, Geoffrey Stanley;** Director, Office of Manpower Economics, 2010–14; *b* 2 Oct. 1952; *s* of Wilfrid Stanley Dart and Irene Jean Dart; *m* 1974, Rosemary Penelope Hinton; one *s* one *d*. *Educ:* Torquay Boys' Grammar Sch.; St Peter's Coll., Oxford (BA and MA Mod. Hist.). Researcher, Electricity Council, 1974–77; Department of Energy: Energy Policy, Offshore Supplies, Oil Policy, Gas, Asst Private Sec. to Sec. of State, to 1984; Cabinet Secretariat, 1984–85; Principal Private Sec. to Sec. of State for Energy, 1985–87; Asst Sec., Electricity Div., 1987–89; Offshore Safety Div., 1989–91; Estabt and Finance Div., 1991–92; Department of Trade and Industry, later Department for Business, Enterprise and Regulatory Reform, then Department for Business, Innovation and Skills: Competitiveness Div., 1992–94; Under Sec., 1994–2014; Dir, Deregulation Unit, 1994; Hd, Regl Develt Div., 1995–96; Shell UK (on secondment), 1996; Dir, Insurance, 1997–98; Dir, Oil and Gas, 1998–2002; Dir, Strategy, 2003–05; Dir of Corporate Law and Governance, 2005–09; Dir, Advanced Manufacturing Industries, 2009–10. Director: Laing Engineering, 1991–96; European Investment Bank, 1994–96. Trustee, Public Concern at Work, 2013– (Dep. Chair, 2015–). Gov., Gwyn Jones Sch., 1996–99. FRSA 2001. *Recreations:* gardening, reading, music, films. *E:* geoffrey.dart@sky.com.

**DART, Peter;** Global Client Leader, WPP plc, since 2001; *b* Torbay, 8 Sept. 1953; *s* of Edmund Dart and Doreen Dart; *m* 1997, Annette Mary; three *c*. *Educ:* Teignmouth Grammar Sch.; Hertford Coll., Oxford (Organ Scholar; BA Physics 1975). LRAM 1974; ATCL 1974. Mktg Dir, Unilever, UK, Germany, Philippines, 1975–88; Founder and Chm., Added Value Consultancy, 1988–2001. Trustee: Educn and Employers Taskforce, 2010–; United Westminster Schs, 2011–; Prince's Foundn, 2012–17. Trustee: Acad. of St Martin in the Fields, 2010–15; Voces Cantabilis Music, 2016–. Mem. Council, RCM, 2015–; Chm., Royal Choral Soc., 2017–. Dir, Music, St Mary's Ch, Wargrave, 2012–. FRSA. *Recreations:* music, opera, museums, wine, travel. *Address:* WPP plc, Sea Containers, 18 Upper Ground, SE1 9GL. *T:* (020) 3193 2817. *E:* peter.dart@wpp.com.

**DARTMOUTH,** 10th Earl of, *cr* 1711; **William Legge;** Baron Dartmouth 1682; Viscount Lewisham 1711; Member for South West Region, European Parliament, 2009–19 (UK Ind, 2009–18; Ind, 2018–19); Chartered Accountant; *b* 23 Sept. 1949; *e s* of 9th Earl of Dartmouth and Countess of Dartmouth (later Raine, Countess Spencer); *S* father, 1997; *m* 2009, Mrs Fiona Handbury (*née* Campbell). *Educ:* Eton; Christ Church, Oxford; Harvard Business Sch. Secretary, Oxford Union Soc., 1969. Contested (C): Leigh, Lancs, Feb. 1974; Stockport South, Oct. 1974; contested (C) Yorkshire and the Humber Region, Eur. Parly elecns, 1999. Mem., UKIP (Dep. Chm., 2016–18). Founder, Kirklees Cable. *Recreation:* tennis. *Heir:* *b* Hon. Rupert Legge [*b* 1 Jan. 1951; *m* 1984, Victoria, *d* of L. E. B. Ottley; one *s* one *d*]. *Address:* Blakelea House, Marsden, near Huddersfield, W Yorks HD7 5AU. *Clubs:* Buck's; Travellers (Paris).

**DARTON, Prof. Richard Charles,** OBE 2011; PhD; FREng, FIChemE; Professor of Engineering Science, University of Oxford, 2000–14, now Emeritus; Fellow, Keble College, Oxford, 1992–2014 (by special election, 1992–2001), now Emeritus; *b* 1 July 1948; *s* of Allan John Darton and Beryl Clare Darton (*née* Davies); *m* 1974, Diana Mildred Warrell; two *s* one *d*. *Educ:* King's Sch., Rochester; Univ. of Birmingham (BSc 1970); Downing Coll., Cambridge (PhD 1973). FIChemE 1987. ICI Post-doctoral Res. Fellow, Univ. of Cambridge, 1973–75; various appts, Shell Internat. Petroleum, Netherlands, 1975–91; on secondment to Univ. of Oxford, from Shell UK, 1991–99; Reader in Chem. Engrg, 2001–14, Head, Dept of Engrg Sci., 2004–09, Univ. of Oxford; Sen. Res. Fellow and Tutor, Keble Coll., Oxford, 2001–14. President: IChemE, 2008–09 (Council Medal, 2005; Dep. Pres., 2007–08); EFCE, 2010–13. FREng 2000. *Publications:* (ed jtly) Chemical Engineering: visions of the world, 2003. *Recreation:* reading history. *Address:* Department of Engineering Science, University of Oxford, Parks Road, Oxford OX1 3PJ. *E:* richard.darton@eng.ox.ac.uk.

**DARVILL, Keith Ernest;** Partner, Kenneth Elliott & Rowe, Solicitors, since 1999; *b* 28 May 1948; *s* of Ernest Arthur James Darvill and Ellen May (*née* Clarke); *m* 1971, Julia Betina de Saran; two *s* one *d*. *Educ:* Coll. of Law, Chester. Admitted solicitor, 1981. Port of London Authority: clerical posts, 1967–73; Asst Solicitor, 1973–84; Partner, Duthie Hart and Duthie, Solicitors, 1984–93; sole practitioner, 1993–97. MP (Lab) Upminster, 1997–2001; contested (Lab) same seat, 2001 and 2005. Mem. (Lab), Havering LBC, 2002– (Leader, Labour Gp, 2006–). Chm., Havering Fabian Soc. Chm. Govs, Havering Sixth Form Coll., 2002–. *Recreations:* tennis, gardening. *Address:* Kenneth Elliott & Rowe, Enterprise House, 18 Eastern Road, Romford RM1 3PJ. *Club:* Cranston Park Lawn Tennis (Upminster).

**DARVILL, Prof. Timothy Charles,** OBE 2010; PhD, DSc; Professor of Archaeology, and Head, Centre for Archaeology and Anthropology, Bournemouth University, since 1994; *b* Cheltenham, 22 Dec. 1957; *s* of Michael George Darvill and Winifred Rose Darvill. *Educ:* All Saints' Sch., Cheltenham; North Gloucestershire Coll. of Technol.; Univ. of Southampton (BA Archaeol. 1979; PhD 1983; DSc 2005). MCIfA 1984; FSA 1988; FSAScot 1990; RPA 2001. Field Officer, Western Archaeol Trust, 1983–84; Proj. Officer, Council for British Archaeol., 1984–85; Dir, Timothy Darvill Archaeol Consultants, 1985–91; Prof. of Archaeol. and Property Develt, Bournemouth Poly., subseq. Bournemouth Univ., 1991–94. Sec., Cttee for Archaeol. in Glos, 1978–91; Co-ordinator, Neolithic Studies Gp, 1983–; Sec., Regl Gp 13, 1984–88, Mem. Exec. Bd, 1987–88, Council for British Archaeol.; Mem., 1988–90, Chm., 1989–91, Inst. of Field Archaeologists; Mem. Council, NT, 1988–97; Chairman: Bd of Dirs, Cotswold Archaeol Trust, 1992–; Poole Harbour Heritage Proj., 1998–; Archaeol. Wkg Party, Dorset Coastal Forum, 1999–2001; Subject Cttee for Archaeol., 2001–04; Archaeol. Adv. Panel, Subject Hist., Classics and Archaeol. Centre, 2004–09; Mgt Cttee, Archaeol. Data Service, 2007–13; Vice-President: Soc. of Antiquaries of London, 2007–11; Royal Archaeol Inst., 2010–16; Pres., Bristol and Glos Archaeol Soc., 2013–14; Member: Adv. Cttee, Historic England, 2013–19; Nomination Cttee, Eur. Assoc. of Archaeologists, 2013–16. Corresp. Member, German Archaeol Inst., 2009. Nat. Award for protection of archaeol heritage of Russia, Russian Archaeol Heritage Foundn, 2006. *Publications:* Megalithic Chambered Tombs of the Cotswold-Severn Regions, 1982; The Archaeology of the Uplands, 1986; Prehistoric Britain, 1987, 2nd edn 2010; Ancient Monuments in the Countryside, 1987; Prehistoric Gloucestershire, 1987, 2nd edn 2010; (ed with Julian Thomas) Neolithic Houses in Northwest Europe and Beyond, 1996; Prehistoric Britain from the Air, 1996; (jtly) The Cerne Giant: an antiquity on trial, 1999; (jtly) Prehistory: a teacher's guide, 2000; (ed with Julian Thomas) Neolithic Enclosures in Atlantic Northwest Europe, 2001; (ed with Martin Gojda) One Land, Many Landscapes, 2001; (jtly) Oxford Guide to Archaeological Sites in England, 2002; Concise Oxford Dictionary of Archaeology, 2002, 2nd edn 2011; Long Barrows of the Cotswolds and Surrounding Areas, 2004; (ed jtly) Archaeology of Value, Heritage and Renown, 2005; Stonehenge: the biography of a landscape, 2006; (ed jtly) Round Mounds and Monumentality in the British Neolithic and Beyond, 2010; (ed with B. Dyer) The Book of Poole Harbour, 2010; (ed with Antonio Fernandes) Open-air Rock Art Conservation and Management: state of the art and future perspectives, 2014; over 150 papers, chapters and reports in learned jls and edited vols. *Recreations:* walking, reading, music, playing guitar with band The Standing Stones. *Address:* Department of Archaeology, Anthropology and Forensic Science, Bournemouth University, Fern Barrow, Poole, Dorset BH12 5BB. *T:* (01202) 965536. *E:* tdarvill@bournemouth.ac.uk.

**DARWALL SMITH, His Honour Simon Crompton;** a Circuit Judge, 1992–2012; *b* 13 April 1946; *s* of late Randle Darwall Smith and Barbara Darwall Smith (*née* Crompton); *m* 1968, Susan Patricia Moss (*see* S. P. Darwall Smith); two *d. Educ:* Charterhouse. Called to the Bar, Gray's Inn, 1968; in practice on Western Circuit, 1968–92; a Recorder, 1986–92. *Recreations:* opera, travel, ballet, theatre, concerts. *Club:* Army and Navy.

**DARWALL SMITH, Her Honour Susan Patricia;** DL; a Circuit Judge, 1992–2012; *b* 27 Oct. 1946; *d* of late George Kenneth Moss, JP and Jean Margaret Moss (*née* Johnston); *m* 1968, Simon Crompton Darwall Smith, *qv;* two *d. Educ:* Howell's Sch., Denbigh. Called to the Bar, Gray's Inn, 1968; in practice on Western Circuit, 1968–92; a Recorder, 1986–92. Pres., Grateful Soc., 2012–13. Chm., Bristol NSPCC, 2014–. Trustee, St Monica Trust, 2016–. Gov., Red Maids' Sch., Bristol, 1990–2010. Maître, Bristol Commanderie de Bordeaux, 2015–. DL Bristol, 2024. *Recreations:* travel, opera, ballet, theatre, gardening. *E:* su.darwallsm@gmail.com. *Club:* Army and Navy.

**DARWEN, 4th Baron** *cr* 1946, *of Heys-in-Bowland;* **(David) Paul (Cedric) Davies;** Design Consultant, Green Factory Ltd, since 2008; *b* London, 20 Feb. 1962; *er s* of 3rd Baron Darwen and of Gillian Irene (*née* Hardy); *S* father, 2011; one *s*; *m* 1996, Leilani N. Kamen; two *s* one *d*, and one step *d. Educ:* Oxford Brookes Univ. (BSc (Hons) Construction Mgt). Designer, Reed Educational Books, 1986–91; freelance book designer, 1992–2007. *Heir:* *s* Hon. Oscar Kamen Davies, *b* 24 April 1996. *Address:* Oxford. *E:* paulkdavies@yahoo.co.uk.

**DARWENT, Rt Rev. Frederick Charles;** JP; Bishop of Aberdeen and Orkney, 1978–92; *b* Liverpool, 20 April 1927; *y s* of Samuel Darwent and Edith Emily Darwent (*née* Malcolm); *m* 1st, 1949, Edna Lilian (*d* 1981), *oc* of David Waugh and Lily Elizabeth Waugh (*née* McIndoe); twin *d;* 2nd, 1983, Roma Evelyn, *er d* of John Michie and Evelyn Michie (*née* Stephen). *Educ:* Warbreck Sch., Liverpool; Ormskirk Grammar Sch., Lancs; Wells Theological Coll., Somerset. Followed a banking career, 1943–61; War service in Far East with Royal Inniskilling Fusiliers, 1945–48. Deacon 1963; priest 1964, Diocese of Liverpool; Curate of Pemberton, Wigan, 1963–65 (in charge of St Francis, Kitt Green, 1964–65); Rector of Strichen, 1965–71; New Pitsligo, 1965–78; Fraserburgh, 1971–78; Canon of St Andrew's Cathedral, Aberdeen, 1971; Dean of Aberdeen and Orkney, 1973–78. JP Aberdeen City, 1988. Hon. LTh St Mark's Inst. of Theology, 1974. *Recreations:* amateur stage (acting and production), music (especially jazz), calligraphy. *Address:* 107 Osborne Place, Aberdeen AB25 2DD. *T:* (01224) 646497. *Clubs:* Rotary International; Club of Deir (Aberdeens).

**DARWIN, Prof. John Gareth,** FBA 2012; DPhil; Professor of Global and Imperial History, 2014–17, and Director, Oxford Centre for Global History, until 2016, University of Oxford; Senior Research Fellow, Nuffield College, Oxford, since 2017 (Fellow, 1984–2017); *b* Exeter, 29 June 1948; *s* of Gerald Meredith Darwin and Maud Phyllis Darwin; *m* 1973, Caroline Atkinson; three *d. Educ:* Brockenhurst Grammar Sch.; St John's Coll., Oxford (BA; MA); Nuffield Coll., Oxford (DPhil 1978). Lectr in Hist., Univ. of Reading, 1972–84; Beit Lectr in Commonwealth Hist., Univ. of Oxford, 1984–2014. *Publications:* Britain, Egypt and the Middle East, 1981; Britain and Decolonization, 1988; The End of the British Empire, 1991; After Tamerlane, 2007; The Empire Project, 2009; Unfinished Empire, 2012; contrib. articles to learned jls. *Recreations:* walking, unskilled gardening. *Address:* Nuffield College, Oxford OX1 1NF. *T:* (01865) 278500. *E:* john.darwin@nuffield.ox.ac.uk.

**DARWIN, Kelyn Meher B.;** *see* Bacon Darwin.

**DARZI,** family name of **Baron Darzi of Denham.**

**DARZI OF DENHAM, Baron** *cr* 2007 (Life Peer), *of Gerrards Cross in the county of Buckinghamshire;* **Ara Warkes Darzi,** OM 2015; KBE 2002; PC 2009; FRS 2013; Professor of Surgery, since 1996, Paul Hamlyn Professor of Surgery, since 2005, and Director, Institute of Global Health Innovation, since 2010, Imperial College London; Consultant Surgeon: St Mary's Hospital, Paddington, since 1994; Royal Marsden Hospital, since 2005; Executive Chair, World Innovation Summit for Health, Qatar Foundation, since 2013; *b* 7 May 1960; adopted British citizenship, 2002; *m* 1991, Wendy Hutchinson; one *s* one *d. Educ:* RCSI (MB BCh, BAO 1984); TCD (MD 1992). FRCSI 1992; FRCS 1995; FACS 1998; FRCPSGlas 2003; FMedSci 2003. Consultant Surgeon/Sen. Lectr, Central Middx Hosp., 1993–94; Hd, Div. of Surgery, Anaesthetics and Intensive Care, Imperial Coll., London, 2004–07. Parly Under-Sec. of State, DoH, 2007–09. UK Business Ambassador, 2009–12; Exec. Chair, Global Health Policy Summit, 2012; Chm., Imperial Coll. Healthcare NHS Trust-Academic Health Science Partnership, 2012–13; non-executive Director: Monitor, then NHS Improvement, 2015–; NHS Trust Develt Authy, 2016. Director: CRUK Imperial Centre, 2016–; NIHR Patient Safety Translational Res. Centre, 2017–; Co-Dir, NHS Digital Acad., 2018–; Chm., Accelerated Access Collaborative, Mem., EPSRC, 2013–18. Foreign Associate, Inst. of Medicine, NAS, USA, 2013. FCGI 2004. Hon. FREng 2006; Hon. FRCSE 2005. Sash of Independence, Qatar, 2014; Order of Honour (Armenia), 2017. *Publications:* Laparoscopic Inguinal Hernia Repair, 1994; Laparoscopic Colorectal Surgery, 1995; Clinical Surgery, 1996, 2nd edn 2003; Atlas of Operative Laparoscopy, 1997; Key Topics in Surgical Research and Methodology, 2010; Evidence Synthesis in Healthcare: a practical handbook for clinicians, 2011; Metabolic Phenotyping in Personalized and Public Healthcare, 2016; over 1000 articles in learned jls. *Address:* Imperial College London, St Mary's Hospital Campus, 10th Floor, QEQM Building, Praed Street, W2 1NY. *T:* (020) 3312 1310, *Fax:* (020) 3312 6309. *E:* a.darzi@imperial.ac.uk. *Clubs:* Athenæum; Mosimann's.

**DASGUPTA, Partha;** Chairman, Pensions Advisory Service, 2010–14; *b* 23 Jan. 1969; *s* of Purnendu Dasgupta and Chandana Dasgupta; *m* 2000, Uttara Moorthy. *Educ:* Links Primary Sch., Edinburgh; Leith Acad.; Heriot-Watt Univ. (BSc 1st Cl. Maths 1990); Birkbeck, Univ. of London (Grad. Dip. Econs with Dist. 2011); King's College London (Grad. Dip. in Maths with Dist. 2016; MSc Theoretical Physics with Dist. 2018). Valuation Analyst, Prudential, 1991–94; Barclays Global Investors: Associate, 1994–98; Principal, 1998–2003; Man. Dir, 2003–05; Dir of Investment and Finance, 2005–06, CEO, 2006–09, Pension Protection Fund. Non-executive Member: Statistics Authy, 2008–14; Superannuation Arrangements of Univ. of London, 2010–14; Investment Cttee, Save the Children (UK), 2009–14. Hon. LittD Heriot-Watt, 2008. *Recreations:* reading, yoga, hill walking in Scotland.

**DASGUPTA, Sir Partha (Sarathi),** Kt 2002; PhD; FRS 2004; FBA 1989; Frank Ramsey Professor of Economics, Cambridge University, 1994–2010, now Emeritus (Professor of Economics, 1985–94); Fellow of St John's College, Cambridge, since 1985; *b* 17 Nov. 1942; *s* of late Prof. Amiya Dasgupta and Shanti Dasgupta, Santiniketan, India; *m* 1968, Carol Margaret, *d* of Prof. James Meade, CB, FBA; one *s* two *d. Educ:* Univ. of Delhi (BSc Hons 1962); Trinity Coll., Cambridge (BA 1965; PhD 1968; Stevenson Prize, 1967; Hon. Fellow, 2010). Res. Fellow, Trinity Hall, Cambridge, 1968–71, Supernumerary Fellow, 1971–74; Lectr, 1971–75, Reader, 1975–78, Prof. of Econs, 1978–84, LSE (Hon. Fellow, 1994); Prof. of Econs and Philosophy, Stanford Univ., 1989–92. Sen. Res. Fellow, Inst. for Policy Reform, 1992–94. Visiting Professor: Stanford Univ., 1974–75 and 1983–84; Delhi Univ., 1978; Harvard Univ., 1987; Princeton Univ., 1989; New Coll. of Humanities, London, 2012–; Andrew D. White Prof.-at-Large, Cornell Univ., 2007–13; Prof. of Envmtl and Develt Econs, later Professorial Res. Fellow, Sustainable Consumption Inst., Manchester Univ., 2008–13. Res. Advr, WIDER (UN Univ., 1989–94); Univ. Fellow, Resources for the Future, Washington, 1998–. Chairman: Beijer Internat. Inst. of Ecological Econs, Stockholm, 1991–97; Internat. Scientific Adv. Bd, Wittgenstein Centre, Vienna, 2011–15; Scientific Bd, Internat. Human Dimensions Prog. on Global Envmtl Change, Bonn, 2011–14; Govt of India Commn on Greening India's Nat. Accounts, 2011–13; Member: Science Cttee, Santa Fe Inst., 1992–96; External Adv. Council, World Bank Inst., 1999–2005; Millennium Ecosystem Assessment Panel, 2000–05; External Adv. Bd, Earth Inst., Columbia Univ., 2002–15; Annual Meeting Scientific Prog. Cttee, AAAS, 2006–09; Adv. Bd on Econ. Develt to Chief Economist, World Bank, 2009–13. President: European Econ. Assoc., 1999; REconS, 1998–2001; Sect. F, BAAS, 2006; European Assoc. of Environmental and Resource Economists, 2010–11. For. Hon. Mem., Amer. Acad. of Arts and Scis, 1991; For. Mem., Royal Swedish Acad. of Scis, 1991; Hon. Mem., Amer. Econ. Assoc., 1997; Mem., Pontifical Acad. of Social Scis, 1998; MAE 2009; For. Associate, US Nat. Acad. of Scis, 2001; Foreign Member: Amer. Phil Soc., 2005; Istituto Veneto di Scienze, Lettere ed Arti, 2009. Fellow: Econometric Soc., 1975; Third World Acad. of Sci., 2002; Soc. for Advancement of Econ. Theory, 2013; Assoc. of Envmtl and Resource Economists, 2017; Dist. Fellow, Ludwig-Maximilians Univ., Munich, 2011. Dr *hc:* Wageningen, 2000; Catholic Univ. of Louvain, 2007; Faculté Univ. Saint-Louis, 2009; Bologna, 2010; Tillberg, 2012; Harvard, 2013; York, 2017. Jt winner, Volvo Envmt Prize, 2002; John Kenneth Galbraith Award, Amer. Agricl Econs Assoc., 2007; Zayed Internat. Envmtl Prize, Dubai, 2011; Eur. Lifetime Achievement Award in Envmtl Econs, Eur. Assoc. Envmtl and Resource Econs, 2014; Blue Planet Prize, Asahi Glass Foundn, Tokyo, 2015; Tyler Prize, USC, 2016. *Publications:* (with S. Marglin and A. K. Sen) Guidelines for Project Evaluation, 1972; (with G. Heal) Economic Theory and Exhaustible Resources, 1979; The Control of Resources, 1982; (with K. Binmore) Economic Organizations as Games, 1986; (with K. Binmore) The Economics of Bargaining, 1987; (with P. Stoneman) Economic Policy and Technological Performance, 1987; An Inquiry into Well-Being and Destitution, 1993; (with K. G. Mäler) The Environment and Emerging Development Issues, vols 1 and 2, 1997; (with I. Serageldin) Social Capital: a multifaceted perspective, 1999; Human Well-Being and the Natural Environment, 2001; Economics: a very short introduction, 2007; Selected Papers: vol. 1, Institutions, Innovations and Human Values, 2010, vol. 2, Poverty, Population and Natural Resources, 2010; Time and the Generations: population ethics for a diminishing planet, 2019; (ed jtly) Biological Extinctions: new perspectives, 2019; articles on develt planning, optimum population, taxation and trade, welfare and justice, nat. resources, game theory, indust. org. and technical progress, poverty and unemployment, in Econ. Jl, Econometrica, Rev. of Econ. Stud., etc; *festschrift:* (ed S. Barrett, K-G Mäler and E. Maskin) Environment and Development Economics: essays in honour of Sir Partha Dasgupta, 2014; (ed D. Southerton and A. Ulph) Sustainable Consumption: multi-disciplinary perspectives, in honour of Sir Partha Dasgupta, 2014. *Address:* 1 Dean Drive, Holbrook Road, Cambridge CB1 7SW. *T:* (01223) 212179. *Club:* MCC.

**DASH, Penelope Jane;** Senior Partner, McKinsey & Co., since 2013 (Healthcare Expert, 2002; Partner, 2008–13); *b* 27 Jan. 1963; *d* of Hugo and Margaret Dash; *m* 1998, Guy Palmer; three *s. Educ:* Robinson Coll., Cambridge (BA Hons 1984); Middlesex Hosp. Med. Sch., London Univ. (MB BS 1987); LSHTM (MSc 1992); Stanford Univ. (MBA 1994). MRCP 1990. Jun. hosp. posts, UCH and Middlesex Hosps, 1987–88; Barnet Gen. Hosp., 1988; Northwich P Hosp., 1988–90; Registrar in Public Health Medicine, NW Thames RHA, 1990–92; Mgt Consultant, Boston Consulting Gp, 1994–99; Hd of Strategy and Planning, DoH, 2000–01; Founder and Dir, Palladium Consulting, 2002–08.

**DASHWOOD, Sir (Arthur) Alan,** KCMG 2013; CBE 2004; QC 2010; Professor of European Law, University of Cambridge, 1995–2009, now Emeritus; Fellow, Sidney Sussex College, Cambridge, 1995–2009, now Emeritus (Vice-Master, 1997–2000); Professor of Law, City, University of London (formerly City University), since 2012; *b* 18 Oct. 1941; *s* of late Alan Stanley Dashwood and of Dorothy Mary Dashwood (*née* Childe); *m* 1971, Julie Rosalind Pashley. *Educ:* Michaelhouse, Natal, SA; Rhodes Univ., Grahamstown, SA (BA Hons 1962); Oriel Coll., Oxford (MA). Called to the Bar, Inner Temple, 1969, Bencher, 2001. Asst Lectr, Dept of Civil Law, Univ. of Glasgow, 1966–67; Lecturer: Dept of Law, UCW, Aberystwyth, 1968–73; Centre of European Governmental Studies, Univ. of Edinburgh, 1973–75; Reader, Univ. of Sussex, 1975–78; Legal Sec. to Advocate General, Court of Justice of ECs, 1978–80; Prof. of Law, Univ. of Leicester, 1980–87; Dir, Legal Service, Council of EU, 1987–94. Editor: European Law Rev., 1975–91; Common Market Law Rev., 1995–2009. *Publications:* The Substantive Law of the EEC, 1980, 6th edn (with D. Wyatt *et al*) as Wyatt and Dashwood's European Union Law, 2011; contrib. to legal jls. *Recreation:* salmon and trout fishing. *Address:* Sidney Sussex College, Cambridge CB2 3HU. *T:* (01223) 338874; Henderson Chambers, 2 Harcourt Buildings, Temple, EC4Y 9DB. *T:* (020) 7583 9020. *Clubs:* Athenæum; Porcupines.

**DASHWOOD, Sir Edward (John Francis),** 12th Bt *cr* 1707, *of West Wycombe, Buckinghamshire;* Premier Baronet of Great Britain; *b* 25 Sept. 1964; *o s* of Sir Francis Dashwood, 11th Bt and Victoria Ann Elizabeth Gwynne (*née* de Rutzen); *S* father, 2000; *m* 1989, Lucinda Nell (*née* Miesegaes); two *s* one *d. Educ:* Eton; Reading Univ. (BSc Estate Mgt). MRICS. Land Agent. *Recreations:* shooting, fishing, tennis, bridge. *Heir:* *s* George Francis Dashwood, *b* 17 June 1992. *Address:* West Wycombe Park, High Wycombe, Bucks HP14 3AJ. *T:* (01494) 524411/2. *Clubs:* White's, Pitt, Daniel's; Shikar; Eton Ramblers.

**DASHWOOD, Sir Frederick George Mahon,** 10th Bt *cr* 1684, *of Kirtlington Park, Oxfordshire;* *b* 29 Jan. 1988; *s* of Sir Richard James Dashwood, 9th Bt, TD and Kathryn Ann Dashwood (*née* Mahon); *S* father, 2013.

**da SILVA, Joanna Gabrielle,** OBE 2011; FREng; Director, International Development, Arup, since 2006; *b* Washington, DC; *d* of John Burke da Silva, CMG and Jennifer Jane da Silva. *Educ:* Trinity Coll., Cambridge (BA Engrg 1988; MA). CEng; MIStructE 1994; MICE 1995; FICE 2014; FREng 2008. Associate Dir, Buildings, Arup, 2000–04; Sen. Shelter Co-ordinator, UNHCR, Colombo, 2005. Vis. Sen. Fellow, Centre for Sustainable Develt, Univ. of Cambridge, 2003–. Hon. DTech Coventry, 2014. Gold Medal, Institution of Structural Engineers, 2017. *Recreation:* mountaineering. *Address:* 116 Grosvenor Road, N10 2DT. *T:* (020) 8341 7057. *E:* jodasilva01@gmail.com.

**DAUBENY DE MOLEYNS,** family name of **Baron Ventry.**

**DAUNT, Katherine Mary;** *see* Steward, K. M.

**DAUNT, Sir Timothy Lewis Achilles,** KCMG 1989 (CMG 1982); HM Diplomatic Service, retired; Lieutenant-Governor of the Isle of Man, 1995–2000; *b* 11 Oct. 1935; *s* of L. H. G. Daunt and Margery (*née* Lewis Jones); *m* 1962, Patricia Susan Knight; one *s* two

d. *Educ:* Sherborne; St Catharine's Coll., Cambridge. 8th KRI Hussars, 1954–56. Entered Foreign Office, 1959; Ankara, 1960; FO, 1964; Nicosia, 1967; Private Sec. to Permanent Under-Sec. of State, FCO, 1970; Bank of England, 1972; UK Mission, NY, 1973; Counsellor, OECD, Paris, 1975; Head of South European Dept, FCO, 1978–81; Associate at Centre d'études et de recherches internationales, Paris, 1982; Minister and Dep. UK Perm. Rep. to NATO, Brussels, 1982–85; Asst Under-Sec. of State (Defence), FCO, 1985–86; Ambassador to Turkey, 1986–92; Dep. Under-Sec. of State (Defence), FCO, 1992–95. Chm., British Inst. (formerly British Inst. of Archaeology) at Ankara, 1995–2006. Chairman: Anglo-Turkish Soc., 2001–09; Ottoman Fund Ltd, 2005–09. *Address:* 20 Ripplevale Grove, N1 1HU.
*See also* K. M. Steward.

**DAUNTON, Prof. Martin James,** PhD, LittD; FBA 1997; Professor of Economic History, 1997–2015, and Head, School of Humanities and Social Sciences, 2012–15, University of Cambridge; Master of Trinity Hall, Cambridge, 2004–14 (Hon. Fellow, 2015); *b* 7 Feb. 1949; *s* of Ronald James Daunton and Dorothy May Daunton (*née* Bellett); *m* 1984, Claire Hilda Gabriel Gobbi. *Educ:* Barry Grammar Sch.; Univ. of Nottingham (BA 1970); Univ. of Kent (PhD 1974); LittD Cambridge, 2005. Lectr in Economic History, Univ. of Durham, 1973–79; University College London: Lectr in Economic History, 1979–85; Reader, 1985–89; Prof. of Modern History, 1989–92; Astor Prof. of British History, 1992–97; University of Cambridge: Fellow, Churchill Coll., Cambridge, 1997–2004, 2014–15; Chm., Faculty of History, 2001–03, Sch. of Humanities and Soc. Scis, 2003–05; Chm., Colls' Cttee, 2009–11. Vis. Fellow, ANU, 1985, 1994; Vis. Prof., Nihon Univ., Tokyo, 2000. Trustee: Nat. Maritime Mus., 2002–10; Barings Archive, 2007–14; Chm., Fitzwilliam Mus., 2008–14 (Syndic, 2006–08). Pres., RHistS, 2004–08 (Hon. Treas., 1986–91; Vice-Pres., 1996–2000; Convener, Studies in History, 1994–2000). Chair: Inst. of Historical Res., 1994–98; Res. Awards Adv. Cttee, Leverhulme Trust, 2012–18 (Mem., 2009–12); Mem., Adv. Bd, Inst. of Advanced Studies, Univ. of Durham, 2006–11. Consultant Ed., Oxford DNB, 1993–98; Member: Editorial Board: Historical Jl, 2000–15; English Historical Rev., 2001–13. Comr, Historic England (formerly English Heritage), 2014–. Hon. DLitt: UCL, 2006; Nottingham, 2010; Kent, 2011. *Publications:* Coal Metropolis: Cardiff 1870–1914, 1977; House and Home in the Victorian City, 1983; Royal Mail: the Post Office since 1840, 1985; A Property Owning Democracy?, 1987; Progress and Poverty: an economic and social history of Britain 1700–1850, 1995; Cambridge Urban History of Britain, 2000; Trusting Leviathan: the politics of taxation in Britain 1799–1914, 2001; Just Taxes: the politics of taxation in Britain 1914–79, 2002; Organisation of Knowledge in Victorian Britain, 2005; Wealth and Welfare: an economic and social history of Britain 1851–1951, 2007; State and Market in Victorian Britain, 2008; The Politics of State Finance, 2017; articles in learned jls. *Recreations:* collecting modern ceramics, opera, architectural tourism. *Address:* Primrose Farm, Primrose Farm Road, Little Wilbraham, Cambridge CB21 5JZ. *E:* mjd42@cam.ac.uk. *Club:* Oxford and Cambridge.

**DAURIS, James Edward;** HM Diplomatic Service; Foreign and Commonwealth Office, since 2019; *b* Harlow, Essex, 15 Jan. 1966; *s* of Colin James Dauris and Prudence Ann Dauris (*née* Butterworth); *m* 1995, Helen Claire Parker; three d. *Educ:* Haileybury; Downing Coll., Cambridge (MA); Coll. of Law, London. Admitted as solicitor, 1991; Solicitor, Ashurst Morris Crisp, 1991–95; entered FCO, 1995; FCO, 1995–98; First Sec. (Commercial), Moscow, 1998–2002; Dep. Hd, EU Dept, FCO, 2002–03; Dep. Hd, 2003–04, Hd, 2004–05, S Asia Dept, FCO; Dep. Hd of Mission, Bogota, 2005–09; Finance Directorate, FCO, 2009–10; Ambassador to Peru, 2010–14; High Comr to Sri Lanka and (non-resident) Ambassador (formerly High Comr) to Maldives, 2015–19. *Recreations:* travel, bird watching, choral singing. *Address:* c/o Foreign and Commonwealth Office, King Charles Street, SW1A 2AH.

**DAUSGAARD, Thomas;** Chief Conductor, BBC Scottish Symphony Orchestra, since 2016; Music Director, Swedish Chamber Orchestra, 1997–2019, now Conductor Laureate; Principal Guest Conductor, 2014–19, Music Director, since 2019, Seattle Symphony; *b* 4 July 1963; *s* of Erik Dausgaard and Bente Dausgaard; *m* 1993, Helle Ann Hentzer; three s. *Educ:* Royal Danish Acad. of Music (Master Conducting 1986); Royal Coll. of Music (Postgrad. Conducting 1988). Asst Conductor, Boston SO, 1993–95; Danish National Symphony Orchestra: Principal Guest Conductor, 2001–04; Principal Conductor, 2004–11; Hon. Conductor, 2011–. Hon. Conductor, Orch. della Toscana, 2014–. Over 70 CDs, including complete symphonic cycles by Beethoven, Schubert, Schumann and Rued Langgaard. Mem., Swedish Acad. of Music, 2004. Hon. DPhil Örebro, 2018. Cross of Chivalry (Denmark), 2009. *Recreations:* architecture, landscape, life and culture of remote communities. *Address:* c/o Alexander Monsey, IMG Artists, Capital Tower, 91 Waterloo Road, Lambeth, SE1 8RT. *T:* (020) 7957 5851. *E:* amonsey@imgartists.com.

**DAUTH, John Cecil,** AO 2011; LVO 1980; High Commissioner of Australia in the United Kingdom, 2008–12; *b* Brisbane, 9 April 1947; *s* of Cecil Neville Dauth and Olga Maud Dauth (*née* Acworth). *Educ:* Gosford High Sch.; Wesley Coll.; Univ. of Sydney (BA Hons; Hon. Fellow 1996). Joined Dept of Ext. Affairs, Australia, 1969; External Affairs Office, then Foreign Affairs Office: Third, later Second Sec., Lagos, 1970–72; First Sec. and Dep. Hd of Mission, Islamabad, 1974–77; on secondment as Asst Press Sec. to the Queen and Press Sec. to the Prince of Wales, 1977–80; Hd, Commonwealth and Multilateral Orgns Section, 1980–82; Chargé d'Affaires, Tehran, 1983–85; Consul-Gen., New Caledonia, 1986–87; Department of Foreign Affairs and Trade: Asst Sec., Public Affairs, 1987–89; Principal Private Sec. to Minister for Foreign Affairs, 1989–91; First Asst Sec., Internat. Security Div., 1991–93; High Comr in Malaysia, 1993–96; First Asst Sec., S and SE Asia Div., 1996–98; Dep. Sec., 1998–2001; Ambassador and Perm. Rep. to UN, NY, 2001–06; High Comr in NZ, 2006–08. Chm., Menzies Centre for Australian Studies, KCL, 2014–. Trustee, British Red Cross, 2014– (Vice Chm., 2014–). *Recreations:* sport (golf, cricket), music. *Club:* Royal Automobile.

**DAVAN WETTON, Hilary John;** Principal Conductor, City of London Choir, since 1989; Associate Conductor, London Mozart Players, since 2010; Musical Director, Jersey Symphony Orchestra, since 2019; Artistic Director, Military Wives Choirs, since 2019; freelance conductor and broadcaster; *b* 23 Dec. 1943; *s* of late Eric Davan Wetton, CBE and (Kathleen) Valerie Davan Wetton (*née* Edwards); *m* 1st, 1964, Elizabeth Jane Tayler; three d; 2nd, 1989, Alison Mary Moncrieff Kelly; one s one d; 3rd, 2003, Dr Antonia Louise Vincent; one d. *Educ:* Westminster Sch.; Royal Coll. of Music (ARCM); Brasenose Coll., Oxford (BA, MA, DipEd). Director of Music: St Alban's Sch., 1965–67; Cranleigh Sch., 1967–74; Stantonbury Music Centre, 1974–78; St Paul's Girls' Sch., 1978–93; Tonbridge Sch., 1993–2006; Conductor-in-residence, Wellington Coll., 2007–14; Artistic Dir, Leicester Philharmonic Choir, 2013–18. Conductor: Guildford Choral Soc., 1968–2008; Milton Keynes City Orch., 1974–2007; Holst Singers, 1978–91; Wren Orch., 1990–; Scottish Schools Orch., 1984–95; Edinburgh Youth Orch., 1994–97; Hastings Phil. Choir, 2008–12; Surrey Fest. Choir, 2009–13; guest conducting and recording with Philharmonia, LPO, Royal Phil. Orch., BBC Concert Orch., Ulster Orch., orchestras in Bulgaria, Iceland, USA, Australia. Prof. of Conducting, Guildhall Sch. of Music, 2012–15; Sen. Music Associate, Somerville Coll., Oxford, 2015–18. Presenter, Classic FM Masterclass. Member: RSA; Pepys Soc. Hon. Fellow, Birmingham Conservatoire, 2011. Hon. MA Open, 1984; Hon. DMus De Montfort, 1994. Diapason d'Or for Holst recording, 1994. *Publications:*
contrib. musical jls, The Lady, Guardian and Daily Telegraph. *Recreations:* tennis, table tennis. *Address:* 25 North End Road, Steeple Claydon, Bucks MK18 2PG. *Club:* Garrick.
*See also* P. H. D. Wetton.

**DAVE, Azra Catherine Hilary;** *see* Ghani, A. C. H.

**DAVENPORT;** *see* Bromley-Davenport.

**DAVENPORT, Major (retd) David John Cecil,** CBE 1989; DL; Member, Rural Development Commission, 1982–90 (Deputy Chairman, April–Oct. 1988); *b* 28 Oct. 1934; *s* of late Major John Lewes Davenport, DL, JP, and Louise Aline Davenport; *m* 1st, 1959, Jennifer Burness (marr. diss. 1969); two d; 2nd, 1971, Lindy Jane Baker; one s. *Educ:* Eton College; Royal Military Academy, Sandhurst. Commnd into Grenadier Guards, 1954, retired 1967. RAC, Cirencester, 1968–69. Chairman, Leominster District Council, 1975–76. Chm., CoSIRA, 1982–88. Chm., Regional Adv. Cttee of the Forestry Commn (SW), 1974–87; Pres., Royal Forestry Soc., 1991–93. DL, 1974, High Sheriff, 1989–90, Hereford and Worcester. *Address:* Mansel Court, Mansel Lacy, Hereford HR4 7HQ. *T:* (01981) 590624. *Clubs:* Boodle's, MCC.

**DAVENPORT, Hugo Benedick;** editorial consultant, writer, journalist, critic, broadcaster, since 2001; *b* 6 June 1953; *s* of late (Arthur) Nigel Davenport and Helena Davenport (*née* White); *m* 1988, Sarah Mollison; one s one d. *Educ:* Westminster Sch.; Univ. of Sussex (BA 1st Cl.). Trainee journalist, Liverpool Daily Post & Echo, 1977–80; reporter/diarist, Observer, 1981–84; feature writer, Mail on Sunday, 1985–87; op-ed news feature writer, then film critic, Daily Telegraph, 1987–96; contributor, BBC World Service, 1992–96; editor: FT New Media Markets, 1997–2000; Broadband Media, 2000–01; Sen. Communications Consultant, Caseworks Customer Interaction, 2005–. FRSA 2003. *Publications:* Days that Shook the World, 2003. *E:* hugodavenport1@gmail.com.
*See also* J. A. Davenport.

**DAVENPORT, Rev. Canon Ian Arthan;** a Chaplain to the Queen, since 2015; Rector, Malpas and Threapwood, since 2010, and Bickerton, since 2011; *b* Stockport, Cheshire, 30 Dec. 1954; *s* of Norman and Margaret Lyndon Davenport. *Educ:* Aston Trng Scheme; Lincoln Theol Coll. Ordained deacon, 1987, priest, 1988; Curate, Holy Trinity, Blacon, Chester, 1987–91; Vicar: St Michael and All Angels, Newton, W Kirby, 1991–97; St Saviour, Oxton, Birkenhead, 1997–2010; Chaplain, Birkenhead Sch., 2003–10; Rural Dean: of Birkenhead, 2005–10; of Malpas, 2014–. Hon. Canon, Chester Cathedral, 2006–. Former Wing Chaplain, Merseyside Wing, ATC; former Regl Chaplain, Wales and W Reg., ATC. *Recreations:* classical music, opera, walking, reading, the countryside. *Address:* The Rectory, Church Street, Malpas, Cheshire SY14 8PP. *T:* (01948) 860922. *E:* malpas.iandavenport@live.co.uk. *Club:* Army and Navy.

**DAVENPORT, Jack Arthur;** actor, since 1991; *b* Wimbledon, 1 March 1973; *s* of late (Arthur) Nigel Davenport and Maria Aitken, qv; *m* 2000, Michelle Gomez; one s. *Educ:* Dragon Sch.; Cheltenham Coll.; Univ. of East Anglia (BA Hons). *Theatre* includes: Hamlet, 1991; Enemies, Almeida, 2006; *films* include: The Talented Mr Ripley, 2000; Pirates of the Caribbean: The Curse of the Black Pearl, 2003, Dead Man's Chest, 2006, At World's End, 2007; Kingsman: The Secret Service, 2014; A United Kingdom, 2016; *television series:* This Life, 1995–97; Coupling, 2000–04; Swingtown, 2008; FlashForward, 2010; Smash, 2012; Breathless, 2013; The Good Wife, 2014; Next of Kin, 2018. Hon. LittD UEA, 2013. *Address:* c/o Hamilton Hodell Ltd, 20 Golden Square, W1F 9JL. *Club:* Stage Golfing Society.

**DAVENPORT, Maurice Hopwood,** FCIB; Director, First National Finance Corporation plc, 1985–95; *b* 19 March 1925; *s* of Richard and Elizabeth Davenport; *m* 1954, Sheila Timms (d 2008); one s two d. *Educ:* Rivington and Blackrod Grammar Sch. FIB 1982. Served RN, 1943–46. Joined Williams Deacon's Bank, 1940; Sec., 1960; Asst Gen. Man., 1969; Dir, 1978–85, Man. Dir, 1982–85, Williams & Glyn's Bank; Dir, Royal Bank of Scotland Gp and Royal Bank of Scotland, 1982–85. *Recreations:* walking, gardening, reading. *Address:* Pines, Dormans Park, East Grinstead, West Sussex RH19 2LX. *T:* (01342) 870439.

**DAVENPORT, Michael Hayward,** MBE 1994; HM Diplomatic Service; Ambassador to Kuwait, since 2017; *b* 25 Sept. 1961; *s* of late Montague Davenport and Olive Margaret Davenport (*née* Brabner); *m* 1992, Lavinia Sophia Braun; one s two d. *Educ:* Gonville and Caius Coll., Cambridge (BA 1983, MA 1985); Coll. of Law, London. Lectr, Graz Univ., Austria, 1983–84; with Macfarlanes, Solicitors, 1986–88; admitted solicitor, 1988; joined FCO, 1988: est. British Know-How Fund for Poland, Warsaw, 1990–93; Hd, Peacekeeping Section, FCO, 1993–95; First Sec. (Political), Moscow, 1996–99; Dir of Trade Promotion and Consul-Gen., Warsaw, 2000–03; Dep. Hd of Mission, Cairo, 2004–07; Dir for Russia, Central Asia and S Caucasus, FCO, 2007–10; Ambassador to Serbia, 2010–13; EU Ambassador to Serbia, 2013–17. *Recreations:* tennis, squash, German literature, cooking. *Address:* c/o Foreign and Commonwealth Office, King Charles Street, SW1A 2AH.

**DAVENPORT, Sara Jane;** Founder, The Haven (formerly Haven Trust, then Breast Cancer Haven), 1997 (Trustee, 1997–2014); Founder, Reboot Health, since 2017; *b* 11 March 1962; *d* of David Davenport and late Jennifer Davenport (*née* Burness, later Zuridis); *m* 1988, Adrian Kyriazi (marr. diss. 2002); two d; *m* 2016, Alnur Dhanani. *Educ:* N Foreland Lodge, Fitzwilliam Coll., Cambridge (BA 1983; MA). Publicity Dept, Hodder & Stoughton, 1983–84; Manager, Cadogan Gall., 1985–87; Sara Davenport Gall., Walton St, London, 1987–97; founded Haven Trust (breast cancer charity), 1997; opened London Haven, 2000, Hereford Haven 2004, Leeds Haven, 2008, Wessex Haven, 2015, Worcester Haven, 2016, Solihull Haven, 2017. *Publications:* Reboot Your Health, 2018. *Recreations:* travel, friends, complementary medicine. *Address:* 76 Chelsea Park Gardens, SW3 6AE. *T:* (020) 7352 4032. *E:* saradavenport@hotmail.com.

**DAVENPORT, Hon. Simon Nicholas;** QC 2009; *b* Plymouth, 10 Oct. 1963; *s* of late Keith Robin Davenport and of Baroness Wilcox, qv; *m* 2001, Angelika Brozler; two s two d. *Educ:* Blundell's Sch., Devon; Leeds Univ. (LLB Hons); Birkbeck Coll., London (BA Hons). Called to the Bar, Inner Temple, 1987, Bencher, 2015; in practice as barrister specialising in commercial and corporate recovery. *Recreations:* history of art, sailing, cricket, cooking. *Address:* 3 Hare Court, Temple, EC4Y 7BJ. *T:* (020) 7415 7800, *Fax:* (020) 7415 7811. *E:* sdavenport@3harecourt.com. *Clubs:* Lansdowne, Royal Automobile; Royal London Yacht, St Mawes Sailing.

**DAVENPORT-HINES, Richard Peter Treadwell,** FRSL, FRHistS; historian and biographer; *b* London, 21 June 1953; *m* 1978, Frances Jane Davenport; one s (and one d decd). *Educ:* St Paul's; Selwyn Coll., Cambridge (Corfield Exhibnr; BA 1975; PhD 1980). FRHistS 1984. Res. Fellow, LSE, 1982–86; slush-pile reader, Macmillan Publishers, 1987–89; Res. Associate, Oxford DNB, 1995–2018. Vis. Fellow, All Souls Coll., Oxford, 2016. Trustee: London Liby, 1996–2005; Royal Literary Fund, 2008–18. Judge: KCL Cosmo Davenport-Hines Prize for Poetry, 2008–18; Tony Lothian Prize, Biographer's Club, 2008; PEN-Hessell Tiltman Prize, 2010; PEN Ackerley Prize, 2011–16; RSL Jerwood Prizes, 2012; Authors' Found Awards, 2015; Slightly Foxed Prize, 2016; Elizabeth

Longford Prize, 2016–. FRSL 2003. *Publications:* Dudley Docker, 1984 (Wolfson Prize for Hist. and Biog., 1985; Wadsworth Prize, 1986); (ed) Speculators and Patriots, 1986; (ed) Markets and Bagmen, 1986; (ed) British Business in Asia since 1860, 1989; Sex, Death and Punishment, 1990; The Macmillans, 1992; Glaxo, 1992; Vice, 1993; Auden, 1995; Gothic, 1998; The Pursuit of Oblivion, 2001; A Night at the Majestic: Proust and the great modernist dinner party of 1922, 2006; (ed) Letters from Oxford: Hugh Trevor-Roper to Bernard Berenson, 2006; Ettie: the intimate life of Lady Desborough, 2008; (ed) Hugh Trevor-Roper's Wartime Journals, 2011; Titanic Lives, 2012; An English Affair: sex, class and power in the age of Profumo, 2013; (ed jtly) One Hundred Letters from Hugh Trevor-Roper, 2014; Universal Man: the seven lives of Maynard Keynes, 2015; Edward VII: the cosmopolitan king, 2016; Enemies Within: communists, the Cambridge spies and the making of modern Britain, 2018; John Meade Falkner: abnormal romantic, 2018; (ed) Hugh Trevor-Roper's China Journals, 2020; *contributor:* Appleyard and Schedvin, Australian Financiers, 1988; Levy-Leboyer and Teichova, Historical Studies in International Corporate Business, 1989; Porter and Teich, Sexual Knowledge, Sexual Science, 1994; Bucknell and Jenkins, Auden Studies, 1994; Chen and Skidelsky, High Time for Reform, 2001; Parini, British Writers, 2002; Parini, World Writers in English, 2004; Stanford, The Death of a Child, 2011; Louis, Irrepressible Adventures with Britannia, 2013; Louis, Resplendent Adventures with Britannia, 2015; contrib. reviews to Art Newspaper, Guardian, Literary Rev., London Rev. of Books, New Statesman, Oldie, Spectator, Sunday Times, The Times, TLS, Wall Street Jl and other periodicals. *Recreations:* abominating Brexit, quelling Torschlusspanik, loving the little Oxford platoons. *Address:* 315 chemin du Meygris, 07200 Ailhon, France. *E:* davenporthines@eclipso.eu. *Clubs:* Athenæum, Brooks's, Cranium.

**DAVENTRY**, 4th Viscount *cr* 1943; **James Edward FitzRoy Newdegate**; R. K. Harrison Insurance Group Ltd, since 1998; *b* 27 July 1960; *s* of 3rd Viscount Daventry and Hon. Rosemary, *e d* of 1st Baron Norrie, GCMG, GCVO, CB, DSO, MC; *S* father, 2000; *m* 1994, Georgia, *yr d* of John Stuart Lodge; one *s* two *d*. *Educ:* Milton Abbey; RAC Cirencester (MRAC). Surveyor, Shakespear, McTurk and Graham, 1980–83; Bain Dawes plc, 1983–87; Penrose Forbes Ltd, 1987–98. Mem. Cttee, Warwicks County and Land Assoc., 2000–. Gov., The Lady Katherine Leveson Charity. Patron: Mary Ann Evans Hospice; George Eliot Fellowship. Mem., Woodmen of Arden. *Recreations:* shooting, fishing, racing, golf, farming, occasional gardening. *Heir: s* Hon. Humphrey John FitzRoy Newdegate, *b* 23 Nov. 1995. *Address:* Arbury, Nuneaton, Warwickshire CV10 7PT. *Clubs:* White's, Saints and Sinners, Turf, MCC; Bean; Sunningdale, Trevose, Blackwell.

**DAVEY, Alan**, CBE 2015; Controller, BBC Radio 3, BBC Proms and BBC Orchestras and Choirs, since 2015; *b* 12 Nov. 1960; *s* of late William Patrick Davey and Alwyn Davey (*née* Dorrington); partner, Patrick Feeny, *qv. Educ:* Univ. of Birmingham (BA Hons (English Lang. and Lit.) 1982); Merton Coll., Oxford (MLitt (English) 1985); Birkbeck Coll., London (MA Hist. 1998). Admin. Trainee, DHSS, 1985; Sec. to Inquiry into Child Abuse in Cleveland, 1987; Private Sec. to Minister of State for Health, 1988–90; Hd, AIDS Treatment and Care, DoH, 1990–92; Hd, Nat. Lottery Bill Team, DNH, 1992–93; Principal Private Sec. to Sec. of State for Nat. Heritage, 1993–94; Hd, European Business, Medicines Control Agency, 1995–97; Sec., Royal Commn on Long Term Care, 1997–99; Fulbright/Helen Hamlyn Scholar, 1999; Hd, Arts Div., 2001–03, Dir of Arts and Culture, subseq. of Culture, 2003–08, DCMS; Chief Exec., Arts Council England, 2008–15. Chm., Internat. Fedn of Arts Councils and Cultural Agencies, 2009–14; Member: Access to the Professions Working Forum, 2010–14; Creative Industries Council, 2011–14; Council, Univ. of Birmingham, 2014–. Vice Chm., English Folk Dance and Song Soc., 2017–; Hon. DLitt Birmingham, 2011; Hon. DArt Teesside, 2012. *Recreations:* music, football, medieval Scandinavian literature, ancient history, cultural theory, Apple Macintosh computers. *Address:* BBC, Broadcasting House, W1A 1AA. *T:* (020) 7765 4928. *E:* alan.davey@bbc.co.uk. *Club:* Two Brydges.

**DAVEY, Rt Hon. Sir Edward (Jonathan),** Kt 2016; PC 2012; MP (Lib Dem) Kingston and Surbiton, 1997–2015 and since 2017; *b* 25 Dec. 1965; *s* of late John George Davey and Nina Joan (*née* Stanbrook); *m* 2005, Emily Jane Gasson; one *s* one *d*. *Educ:* Nottingham High Sch.; Jesus Coll., Oxford (BA 1st Cl. Hons PPE); Birkbeck Coll., London (MSc Econs). Sen. Econs Advr to Lib Dem MPs, 1989–93; Mgt Consultant, Omega Partners, 1993–97. Contested (Lib Dem) Kingston and Surbiton, 2015. Lib Dem spokesman: on econ. affairs, 1997–2001; for London, 2000–01; on Treasury affairs, 2001–02; on ODPM affairs, 2002–05; for education and skills, 2005–06; for trade and industry, 2006; on foreign affairs, 2007–10; on Home Affairs, 2017–; Parly Under-Sec. of State, BIS, 2010–12; Sec. of State for Energy and Climate Change, 2012–15; Chm., Lib Dem Campaigns and Communications, 2006–08; Chief of Staff to Lib Dem Leader, 2006–07; Dep. Leader, Lib Dems, 2019–. Mem., Treasury Select Cttee, 1999–2001. Chairman: Mongoose Energy, 2015–19; Fit for the Future, 2016–. Sen. Advr, MHP Communications, 2016–17; Mem., Adv. Bd, Next Energy Capital, 2016–. Trustee, Tourism for All, 2016–; Patron, Disability Law Service, 2017–. FRSA 2001. Hon. Testimonial, RHS, and Cert. of Commendation from Chief Constable of Brit. Transport Police (for rescuing a woman who had fallen on the track at Clapham Junction), 1995. *Recreations:* walking, music. *Address:* House of Commons, SW1A 0AA.

**DAVEY, Eric;** Chairman, Sea Fish Industry Authority, 1996–2002 (Deputy Chairman, 1990–96); *b* 16 Jan. 1933; *s* of William James Davey and Doris Evelynne Davey; *m* 1955, Janet Nicholson; two *d*. *Educ:* Woodbridge Sch.; Ilminster Sch. With Bank of England, 1953–88, Agent, Newcastle Br., 1980–88; Newcastle Building Society: Dir, 1988–2001; Dep. Chm., 1992–98; Chm., 1998–2001; Pres., 2001–04. *Recreations:* foreign travel, motoring, reading, theatre.

**DAVEY, Francis**, MA; Headmaster of Merchant Taylors' School, 1974–82; *b* 23 March 1932; *er s* of Wilfred Henry Davey, BSc and Olive (*née* Geeson); *m* 1st, 1960, Margaret Filby Lake, MA Oxon, AMA (marr. diss. 2004), *o d* of Harold Lake, DMus Oxon, FRCO; one *s* one *d*; 2nd, 2005, Patricia Quaife, *er d* of late Alfred Grover Quaife. *Educ:* Plymouth Coll.; New Coll., Oxford (Hon. Exhibr); Corpus Christi Coll., Cambridge (Schoolmaster Fellow Commoner). 1st cl. Class. Hon. Mods 1953, 2nd cl. Lit. Hum. 1955, BA 1955, MA 1958. RAF, 1950–51; Classical Upper Sixth Form Master, Dulwich Coll., 1955–60; Head of Classics Dept, Warwick Sch., 1960–66; Headmaster, Dr Morgan's Grammar Sch., Bridgwater, 1966–73. *Publications:* (with R. Pascoe) The Camino Português, 1997; William Wey, 2000; (with P. Quaife) The Camino Inglés, 2000; The Itineraries of William Wey, 2010; Richard of Lincoln: a medieval doctor travels to Jerusalem, 2013; Heart of Oak: the lost letters of Admiral Gardner, 2015; Priests, Paupers and Lepers: a mirror of medieval Exeter, 2018; articles in Enciclopedia dello Spettacolo, Classical Review, Jl of Royal Instn of Cornwall, Devon and Cornwall Notes and Queries. *Recreations:* Rugby, swimming, gardening, travel. *Address:* 1 North Street, Topsham, Exeter, Devon EX3 0AP. *T:* (01392) 873251. *Clubs:* East India, Devonshire, Sports and Public Schools; Union (Oxford).

**DAVEY, Grenville;** artist; Visiting Professor, University of the Arts, London (formerly London Institute), since 1997; Artist in Residence, Isaac Newton Institute for Mathematical Sciences, University of Cambridge, 2012; *b* 28 April 1961; *s* of Clifford Henry and Lillian Joyce Davey. *Educ:* Goldsmiths' Coll., London. Artist in Residence, Dept of Theoretical Physics, QMUL, 2010–11. Exhibitions: Lisson Gall., London, 1987; Stichting De Appel Foundn, Amsterdam, 1990; Kunsthalle, Berne, 1991; Kunstverein für die Rheinlande und Westfalen, Dusseldorf, 1992; Le Crypte Jules-Noriac, Limoges, 1993; Württembergischer Kunstverein, Stuttgart, 1994; Henry Moore Foundn, Dean Clough Foundn, 1994; Mus. of Modern Art, Vienna, Kunstverein, Hanover, 1996; Odense, Denmark, and Yorks Sculpture Park, 1999; Peggy Guggenheim, Venice, 2002; LSHTM, 2004; Tate Modern, 2005; William Morris Gall., London, 2006; No 1 Canada Square, London, 2007; Olympic Park, London, 2011; 'Chelsea Space', UAL, 2014. Turner Prize, 1992. *Recreation:* work.

**DAVEY, Jonathan Michael;** QC 2016; *b* Herts, 15 Sept. 1975; *s* of Michael Carveth Davey and Diana Sylvia Davey; *m* 2006, Naomi Clare Muller; one *s* three *d*. *Educ:* St Clement Danes Sch., Herts; Univ. of Nottingham (BA, MA); Downing Coll., Cambridge (MPhil); City Univ., London (CPE). Andersen Consulting, 1998–2000. Called to the Bar, Lincoln's Inn, 2003; in practice as a barrister, Wilberforce Chambers, 2003–; Attorney Gen.'s Panel of Counsel, 2007–16. Trustee: Holborn Estate Charity, 2011–; Hampstead Parish Ch, 2013–. *Publications:* (ed jtly) Butterworths Property Law Handbook, 7th edn 2007 to 11th edn 2018. *Recreations:* bringing up four children, spending as much time at Lord's as possible, running on Hampstead Heath, foreign travel, spicy food. *Address:* Wilberforce Chambers, 8 New Square, Lincoln's Inn, WC2A 3QP. *T:* (020) 7306 0102, *Fax:* (020) 7306 0095. *E:* jdavey@wilberforce.co.uk. *Club:* MCC.

**DAVEY, Julian;** mountain leader, since 1988; *b* 24 July 1946; *s* of Frederick Victor Davey and Dorothy Davey (*née* Stokes); *m* 1971, Prof. Katherine O'Donovan (marr. diss. 2004); one *d*; *m* 2007, Dr Kate Keohane. *Educ:* Kingston Grammar Sch.; Selwyn Coll., Cambridge; Inst. of Education, London Univ. (MA 1973). British Council: Ethiopia, 1969–72; E Africa Dept, 1973–75; Mgt Accountant, 1975–78; Malaysia, 1978–81; Dep. Controller, Finance, 1981–85; Dir, Hong Kong, 1985–90; Regl Dir, Asia-Pacific, 1992–94; Internat. Advr, Anglia Polytechnic Univ., 1994–97. Chm., Hesket Newmarket Brewery, 2000–10. Advr, CAB, 2012–17. Trustee, Friends of Theatre by the Lake, 2011– (Hon. Treas., 2016–). *Recreations:* climbing, ski-ing, caving, running, furniture making, performing arts, choir member of Cockermouth Harmonic Society 2016–. *Address:* Potts Gill, Hesket Newmarket, Wigton, Cumbria CA7 8LB. *T:* (016974) 78773. *Clubs:* Alpine; Eden Valley Mountaineering, Keswick Mountaineering; Kendal Caving; Hong Kong (Hong Kong).

**DAVEY, Marcus Ian T.;** see Tregilgas-Davey.

**DAVEY, Marcus John,** CBE 2019 (OBE 2012); Artistic Director and Chief Executive Officer, The Roundhouse, since 1999; *b* Malvern, 5 July 1967; *s* of Robin and Ruth Davey; *m* 1997, Tatty Theo; two *s*. *Educ:* Dartington Coll. of Arts (BA Hons). Administrator, Dartington Internat. Summer Sch., 1989–95; Dir, Dartington Arts Centre, 1992–95; Artistic Dir, Norfolk and Norwich Fest., 1995–99. Chairman: Hackney Youth Orchestras Trust, 1991–97; PRS Foundn, 1999–2006; Dartington Internat. Summer Sch. Foundn, 2010–15; Co-Chm., Adv. Council, Creative Industries Fedn, 2015–; Member: Adv. Bd, Clore Leadership Foundn, 2004–10; Bd, Arts Council, 2011–17; Barclays Life Skills Adv. Bd, 2014–16. Trustee, Longplayer Trust, 2010–17. Gov., Nat. Coll. of Creative Industries, 2017–. FRSA. *Recreations:* cooking, music, walking. *Address:* The Roundhouse, Chalk Farm Road, NW1 8EH. *T:* (020) 7424 9991, *Fax:* (020) 7424 9992. *E:* marcus.davey@roundhouse.org.uk. *Clubs:* Savile, Soho House.

**DAVEY, Dr (Ronald) William,** LVO 2001; Physician to the Queen, 1986–2001; *b* 25 Oct. 1943; *s* of Frederick George Davey and Cissy Beatrice Davey (*née* Lawday); *m* 1966; one *s* one *d*. *Educ:* Trinity School of John Whitgift; King's College London; King's College Hosp. (MB BS; FFHom; AKC); MD Imperial Coll., London, 1997. Gen. med. practice, 1970–77; research into electro-acupuncture, 1978–79; private med. and homoeopathic practice, 1980–2001; nutrition and counselling practice, 2001–. Under auspices of Blackie Foundation Trust, research into antibiotic properties of propolis, Nat. Heart and Lung Inst., Univ. of London, 1984–94; Hon. Med. Res. Dir, 1980–98, Vice Pres., 1998–, Blackie Foundation Trust. Vis. Schol., Green Coll., Oxford, 1998. Freeman, City of London, 1997; Liveryman, Barbers' Co., 2001– (Freeman, 1997). *Publications:* medical papers. *Recreations:* Scottish reeling, opera, reading, writing, art, Chinese armorial porcelain. *Address:* 27 Old Gloucester Street, WC1N 3AX.

**DAVEY, Valerie;** *b* 16 April 1940; *m* 1966, Graham Davey; twin *d* one *s*. *Educ:* Birmingham Univ. (MA); London Univ. Inst. of Educn (PGCE). Teacher: Wolverhampton; Tanzania; FE Coll. Mem. (Lab) Avon CC, 1981–96. MP (Lab) Bristol West, 1997–2005; contested (Lab) same seat, 2005. Mem., Educn and Employment Select Cttee, 1997–2005. Exec. Chair, Council for Educn in the Commonwealth, 2005–10. Mem., Amnesty International. Hon. DEd UWE, 2008. *Recreations:* gardens, cooking esp. marmalade.

**DAVEY, Dr William;** see Davey, R. W.

**DAVEY SMITH, Prof. George,** MD, DSc; FRS 2019; FRSE; Professor of Clinical Epidemiology, University of Bristol, since 1994; *b* 9 May 1959; *s* of George Davey Smith and Irmgaard Davey Smith (*née* Beckmann). *Educ:* Stockton Heath Primary Sch.; Lymm Grammar Sch.; Queen's Coll., Oxford (BA 1981; DSc 2000); Jesus Coll., Cambridge (MB BChir 1984; MD 1991); London Sch. of Hygiene and Tropical Medicine (MSc 1988). Clinical Res. Fellow (Hon. Clinical Med. Officer), Welsh Heart Prog., Cardiff, 1985–86; Wellcome Res. Fellow in Clinical Epidemiol., Dept of Community Medicine, UCL and Middlesex Sch. of Medicine, 1986–89; Lectr in Epidemiol., LSHTM, 1989–92; Sen. Lectr in Public Health and Epidemiol., and Hon. Sen. Registrar, 1992–93, Consultant in Public Health Medicine, 1993–94, Univ. of Glasgow. Hon. Prof., Dept of Public Health, Univ. of Glasgow, 1996–. Vis. Prof., Dept of Epidemiol. and Popn Health, LSHTM, 1999–. FMedSci 2006; FRSE 2014. Foreign Associate, Inst. of Medicine, 2008. *Publications:* (ed jtly) The Sociology of Health Inequalities, 1998; (jtly) The Widening Gap: health inequalities and policy in Britain, 1999; (ed jtly) Inequalities in Health: the evidence presented to the independent inquiry into inequalities in health, 1999; (ed jtly) Systematic Reviews in Health Care: meta-analysis in context, 2nd edn, 2001; (ed jtly) Poverty, Inequality and Health in Britain, 1800–2000: a reader, 2001; Health Inequalities: lifecourse approaches, 2003; (with M. Shaw) Cultures of Health, Cultures of Illness, 2004; (jtly) The Handbook of Inequality and Socioeconomic Position: concepts and measures, 2007; over 1000 articles in jls. *Recreations:* poor squash, bad tennis and abysmal badminton. *Address:* MRC Integrative Epidemiology Unit, University of Bristol, Oakfield House, Oakfield Grove, Bristol BS8 2BN. *T:* (0117) 928 7329.

**DAVID, Prof. Anthony Sion,** MD; FRCP, FRCPGlas, FRCPsych, FMedSci; Director and Sackler Chair, UCL Institute of Mental Health, University College London, since 2018; *b* 27 Sept. 1958. *Educ:* Univ. of Glasgow (MB ChB 1980; MD 1993); MSc Cognitive Neuropsychol. London 1990. FRCP 1994; FRCPGlas 1994; FRCPsych 1998; FMedSci 2002. Registrar: in Neurol., Southern Gen. Hosp., Glasgow, 1982–84; in Psychiatry, Maudsley Hosp., London, 1984–87; Institute of Psychiatry, University of London: Lectr, 1987–90; Sen. Lectr, 1990–94; Reader, 1994–96; King's College London: Prof. of Cognitive Neuropsychiatry, 1996–2018; Vice Dean, Academic Psychiatry, 2014–18. *Publications:* (ed with X. Amador) Insight and Psychosis, 1998, 2nd edn 2004; (with T. Kircher) Self in Neuroscience and Psychiatry, 2003; (ed jtly) Lishman's Organic Psychiatry,

2009; contrib. scientific articles on schizophrenia and neuropsychol. *Recreations:* football, jazz piano. *Address:* UCL Institute of Mental Health, University College London, Gower Street, WC1E 6BT.

**DAVID, George Alkiviades,** OBE 2009; Chairman, Coca-Cola HBC AG, 1981–2016, now Chairman Emeritus; *b* Petra, Cyprus, 1937; *s* of Alkiviades David and Kalliope David (*née* Leventis); *m* 1964, Kaity Hordovatzi; two *s* one *d*. *Educ:* English Sch., Nicosia; Lindisfarne Coll., Wales; Univ. of Edinburgh (BCom 1959). Gp Dir, A. G. Leventis Orgn, Nigeria, 1959–80. Chm., EFG Eurobank, 2013–14; Mem. Bd, Titan, 2001–13. Co-founder, Hellenic Initiative, 2012–. Mem., Bilderberg Gp, 1997–2010. Regent, Univ. of Edinburgh, 2012–. Chm. Bd, Centre for Asia Minor Studies, 2009–; Chm. Council, Univ. of Cyprus, 2019– (Vice Chm., 2015–19). Chm., Greek Cttee, A. G. Leventis Foundn, 1981–; Mem. Bd, Hellenic Foundn for Eur. and Foreign Policy, 1999–2013 (Mem., Hon. Cttee, 2013–). Chm., Bd of Trustees, Campion Sch., 2000–07, now Chm. Emeritus. Hon. Dr: Nat. and Kapodistrian, Athens, 2013; Cyprus Inst. of Neurology and Genetics, Nicosia, 2016. Archon Maistor, Ecumenical Patriarchate of Constantinople, 2003. Mem., Order of Federal Republic (Nigeria), 2008. *Recreations:* golf, gardening, reading. *Address:* 40 Gladstone Street, 1095 Nicosia, Cyprus. *T:* 22667706, *Fax:* 22675002. *E:* george.david@leventis.net. *Club:* Loch Lomond Golf.

**DAVID, Dr Hefin Wyn;** Member (Lab) Caerphilly, National Assembly for Wales, since 2016; *b* Caerphilly, 13 Aug. 1977; *s* of Wynne and Christine David; two *d*. *Educ:* Heolddu Comprehensive Sch., Bargoed; Cardiff Univ. (BSc Econ 1998; MSc Econ 1999); Univ. of Wales, Newport (PGCE 2002); Univ. of Gloucestershire (PhD 2014). Lectr, Univ. of Wales, Newport, 2000–07; Sen. Lectr, Cardiff Metropolitan Univ., 2007–16. Mem. (Lab), Caerphilly BC, 2007–16. Chm., Tiryberth Village Hall Mgt Cttee, 2009–16. Governor: Glyngaer Primary Sch., 2009–; Trinity Fields Sch., 2009–. *Recreations:* theatre, Rugby. *Address:* National Assembly for Wales, Cardiff Bay, Cardiff CF99 1NA. *T:* 0300 200 7154. *E:* hefin.david@assembly.wales.

**DAVID, Prof. (Julian) Saul Markham,** PhD; writer, since 1991; Professor of Military History, University of Buckingham, since 2014 (Professor of War Studies, 2009–14); *b* Monmouth, 27 March 1966; *s* of Robin David and Cherry David (*née* Quinn); *m* 1995, Louise Harper; three *d*. *Educ:* Ampleforth Coll.; Univ. of Edinburgh (MA Hons); Univ. of Glasgow (PhD 2001). Staff writer, Haymarket Publishing, 1989–91; broadcaster, 1999– (TV series incl. Escape From…, Boots, Bullets and Bandages). Vis. Prof. of Mil. Hist., Hull Univ., 2007–08. Judge, Guggenheim-Lehrman Mil. Book Award, 2012–14. Mem., Acad. Adv. Cttee, Nat. Army Mus., 2013–18. Trustee, RA Mus., 2014–18. *Publications:* Churchill's Sacrifice of the Highland Division, 1994; Mutiny at Salerno, 1995; The Homicidal Earl, 1997; Military Blunders, 1997; Prince of Pleasure, 1998; The Indian Mutiny, 2002; Zulu, 2004; Victoria's Wars, 2006; The Bengal Army and the Outbreak of the Indian Mutiny, 2009; Zulu Hart, 2009; Hart of Empire, 2010; All the King's Men, 2012; Mud and Bodies, 2013; 100 Days to Victory, 2013; Operation Thunderbolt, 2015; The Prince and the Whitechapel Murders, 2018; The Force, 2019; Okinawa, 2020. *Recreations:* tennis, ski-ing, sailing, Arsenal FC, poker. *Address:* c/o Caroline Michel, Peters Fraser & Dunlop, 55 New Oxford Street, WC1A 1BS. *T:* (020) 7344 1000. *W:* www.sauldavid.co.uk. *Clubs:* Soho House, Frontline.

**DAVID, Prof. Miriam Elizabeth,** PhD; FAcSS; Professor of Sociology of Education, Institute of Education, University of London, 2006–10, now Emerita; Visiting Professor of Education, Centre for Higher Education Equity Research, University of Sussex, since 2010; *b* Keighley, Yorks, 9 Aug. 1945; *d* of Curt L. David and Esther L. David; *m* 1st, 1974, Prof. Robert Reiner (marr. diss. 1994); one *s* one *d*; 2nd, 2002, Prof. Jeffrey Duckett. *Educ:* Univ. of Leeds (BA Hons Sociol. 1966); Queen Mary Coll., Univ. of London (PhD 1975). Researcher: Univ. of London, at Inst. of Psychiatry, LSE and QMC, 1966–73; Harvard Univ. Grad. Sch. of Educn, 1972–73; Lectr in Social Admin, 1973–85, Grad. Studies Officer, 1982–85, Univ. of Bristol; Hd, Dept of Social Scis, 1986–92 (Prof., 1989), Prof. of Social Scis and Dir, Social Scis Res. Centre, 1992–97, South Bank Poly., later London South Bank Univ.; Dean of Res. and Prof., London Inst., 1997–99; University of Keele: Prof. of Policy Studies in Educn, 1999–2005; Dir, Grad. Sch. of Social Scis, 2002–04; Res. Dean, Faculty of Humanities and Social Scis, 2004–05; Associate Dir (Higher Educn), ESRC's Teaching and Learning Res. Prog., on secondment to Dept of Educn, Cambridge Univ., 2004–05, then Inst. of Educn, Univ. of London, 2005–09, Dir, 2009. Vis. Prof. of Policy Studies in Educn, Univ. of Keele, 2005–10; Vis. Res. Consultant, Centre for Med. Educn, St George's, Univ. of London, 2010–12. International Research Consultant: Acad. of Finland, 2010–; Eur. Res. Foundn, 2010–; Res. Council of Norway, 2010–; Univ. of Helsinki, 2010–. Mem., Exec. Editl Bd, British Jl Sociol. of Educn, 1990–2012; Co-Editor: Jl Social Policy, 1993–98; 21st Century Society, 2005–09. Member: Gender and Education Assoc., 2002– (Policy Officer, 2010–14; Policy Consultant, 2018–); Governing Council, SRHE, 2005–11; Res. Grants Bd, ESRC, 2006–09. Trustee: British Shalom-Salaam Trust, 2004–12; Women's Therapy Centre, 2010–18 (Chair, 2010–18). FAcSS (AcSS 1999) (Chair of Council, 2005–09). FRSA 1994. Hon. DEd Bedfordshire, 2009. *Publications:* School Rule in the USA, 1975; (jtly) Gambling Work and Leisure, 1976, re-issued 2013; Reform, Reaction and Resources, 1977; Half the Sky: an introduction to women's studies, 1979; The State, the Family and Education, 1980, re-issued 2015; (with C. New) For the Children's Sake, 1985; (jtly) Mothers and Education: inside out?, 1993; (jtly) Choosing a Secondary School, 1993; Parents, Gender and Education Reform, 1993; (jtly) Mother's Intuition? Choosing Secondary Schools, 1994; (ed) The Fragmenting Family: does it matter?, 1998; (ed with D. Woodward) Negotiating the Glass Ceiling: senior women in the academic world, 1998; (jtly) Closing the Gender Gap, 1999; Personal and Political: feminisms, sociology and family lives, 2003; (jtly) Degrees of Choice: social class, race and gender in higher education, 2005; (with P. Alldred) Get Real About Sex, 2007; (jtly) Improving Learning Through Widening Participation to Higher Education, 2010; Feminism, Gender and Universities: politics, passion and pedagogies, 2014; A Feminist Manifesto for Education, 2016; Reclaiming Feminism: challenging everyday misogyny, 2016; Sage Encyclopedia of Higher Education, 5 vols, 2020. *Recreations:* travel, film, theatre, walking, feminist psychotherapy and analysis, politics. *Address:* (office) 20 Bedford Way, WC1H 0AL. *T:* 07711 959765. *E:* miriam.david@ucl.ac.uk; 29 Cholmeley Lodge, Cholmeley Park, N6 5EN. *E:* miriamedavid3@gmail.com.

**DAVID, Prof. Paul Allan,** PhD; FBA 1995; Professor of Economics, 1969–2005, now Emeritus, and Senior Fellow, Stanford Institute for Economic Policy Research, since 1983, Stanford University, California; Professor of Economics and Economic History, University of Oxford, 1993–2002, now Emeritus; Senior Research Fellow, All Souls College, Oxford, 1993–2002, now Emeritus Fellow; *b* 24 May 1935; *s* of Henry David and Evelyn (*née* Levinson); *m* 1st, 1958, Janet Williamson (marr. diss. 1982); one *s* one *d*; 2nd, 1982, Sheila Ryan Johansson; one step *s* one step *d*. *Educ:* High Sch. of Music and Art, NYC; Harvard Coll. (AB *summa cum laude* 1956); Pembroke Coll., Cambridge (Fulbright Schol.); Harvard Univ. (PhD 1973); MA Oxon. Stanford University, California: Asst Prof. of Econs, 1961–66; Associate Prof., 1966–69; William Robertson Coe Prof. of American Econ. Hist., 1978–94; Chair, Dept of Economics, 1979–82; Sen. Fellow, Oxford Internet Inst., 2002–08; Prof. Titulaire, Chaire Innovation et Régulation des Services Numérique, École Polytechnique and Telecom ParisTech, France, 2008–11. Vis. Fellow, All Souls Coll., Oxford, 1967–68 and 1992–93; Vis. Prof. of Econs, Harvard Univ., 1972–73; Pitt Prof. of American Hist. and Institutions, Univ. of Cambridge, 1967–68; Vis. Res. Prof. in Econs of Sci. and Technol., Rijksuniversiteit Limburg, 1993–95; Marshall Lectr, Univ. of Cambridge, 1992. Guggenheim Fellow, 1975–76; Fellow, Center for Advanced Study in the Behavioral Scis, 1978–79; Professorial Fellow, UN Univ. MERIT, 2004–. Dir, Cie Saint-Gobain, 2002–07. Pres.-Elect and Pres., Econ. Hist. Assoc., 1987–89 (Vice Pres., 1986); Past Pres., Western Econ. Assoc. Internat., 2011 (Vice Pres., 2009; Pres., 2010). Mem. Council, REconS, 1996–2002. Fellow: Internat. Econometrics Soc., 1975; Amer. Acad. Arts and Scis, 1979; Amer. Philos. Soc., 2003. Phi Beta Kappa, Harvard, 1956. Hon. Dr Inf. and Commns Scis, Torino, 2003. *Publications:* (ed) Households and Nations in Economic Growth, 1974; Technical Choice, Innovation and Economic Growth, 1975, 2nd edn 2003; Reckoning with Slavery, 1976; The Economic Future in Historical Perspective, 2003; (with C. Antonelli) The Economics of Knowledge and the Knowledge Driven Economy, 2016; over 200 articles, contribs to edited books and govt and internat. orgn reports and policy briefs. *Recreations:* photography, Chinese cooking, tennis, walking. *Address:* Department of Economics, Stanford University, Stanford, CA 94305–6072, USA. *Fax:* (650) 7255702. *E:* pad@stanford.edu.

**DAVID, Robert Allan,** MBE 2011; Head of International and Tourism Division, Department of Employment, 1989–91; *b* 27 April 1937; *s* of George David and Mabel Edith David; *m* 1961, Brenda Marshall; three *d*. *Educ:* Cathays High Sch., Cardiff. BoT, 1955–71; Dept of Employment, 1971–91. Mem. (Ind.), Tandridge DC, 2003–15. *Recreations:* badminton, gardening. *Address:* The Briars, Ninehams Road, Tatsfield, Westerham, Kent TN16 2AN. *T:* (01959) 577357.

**DAVID, Saul;** *see* David, J. S. M.

**DAVID, Prof. Timothy Joseph,** PhD, MD; FRCP, FRCPCH; Professor of Child Health and Paediatrics, University of Manchester, 1991, now Emeritus; Hon. Consultant Paediatrician, Royal Manchester (formerly Booth Hall) Children's Hospital, Manchester, since 1991; two *s*. *Educ:* Clifton Coll., Bristol; Univ. of Bristol (MB ChB 1970; PhD 1975; MD 1981); DCH 1976 (RCP). MRCP 1976, FRCP 1986; FRCPCH 1997. Posts in Bristol, Taunton and Plymouth, 1970–78; Tutor/Lectr in Child Health, 1978–81, Sen. Lectr, Dept of Child Health, 1981–91, Univ. of Manchester. *Publications:* (jtly) Applied Paediatric Nursing, 1982; (ed) Cystic Fibrosis in Children, 1986; (ed) Recent Advances in Paediatrics, vol. 9, 1991–vol. 23, 2006; (ed) Role of the Cystic Fibrosis Nurse Specialist, 1992; Food and Food Additive Intolerance in Childhood, 1993; Symptoms of Disease in Childhood, 1995 (Dutch edn, 1999); (jtly) Eczema in Children, 1995; (ed) Major Controversies in Infant Nutrition, 1996; (jtly) Problem-based Learning in Medicine, 1999; author or editor of over 400 scientific and med. pubns, inc. conf. procs. *Recreations:* classical music, opera. *Address:* The Medical School, University of Manchester, Manchester M13 9PT.

**DAVID, Wayne;** MP (Lab) Caerphilly, since 2001; *b* 1 July 1957; *s* of late D. Haydn David and of Edna A. David; *m* 1991, Catherine Thomas (marr. diss. 2008); *m* 2016, Jayne Edwards. *Educ:* Cynffig Comprehensive Sch.; University Coll., Cardiff (BA Hons History; PGCE); University Coll., Swansea. History teacher, Brynteg Comprehensive Sch., Bridgend, 1983–85; Mid Glam Tutor Organiser, S Wales Dist, WEA, 1985–89. Policy Advr, Wales Youth Agency, 1999–2001. MEP (Lab) S Wales, 1989–94, S Wales Central, 1994–99. Treas., 1989–91, Leader, 1994–98, European Parly Labour Party (formerly British Labour Gp); 1st Vice-Pres., Regl Policy and Planning Cttee, Eur. Parlt, 1992–94; Sec., Tribune Gp of MEPs, 1992–94. Mem., Labour Party NEC, 1994–98. PPS to Minister of State for Armed Forces, 2005–06; an Asst Govt Whip, 2007–08; Parly Under-Sec. of State, Wales Office, 2008–10; Shadow Minister: for Europe, 2010–11; for Political and Constitutional Reform, 2011–13; for Justice, 2015–16; for Cabinet Office, 2015–16; for Scotland, 2015–16; for Armed Forces and Defence Procurement, 2016–; PPS to Leader of the Opposition, 2013–15. Mem., European Scrutiny Select Cttee, 2001–07; Chair: All Party Parly Gp on EU, 2006–07; All Party Parly Gp on Vietnam, 2016–. Sec., DWP Gp, 2002–07, Wales Gp, 2003–07, PLP; Sec., Labour Movt for Europe, 2003–07. Bd Mem., European Movt, 2002–07; Pres., Wales Council, European Movt, 2006–. Pres., Council for Wales of Voluntary Youth Services, 2001–; Vice-Pres., City of Cardiff Br., UNA, 1989–; Mem., Cefn Cribwr Community Council, 1985–91. President: Aber Valley Male Voice Choir, 2001–; Caerphilly Local Hist. Soc., 2006–; Lab Heritage, 2015–. Fellow, Univ. of Wales Coll. of Cardiff, 1995. *Publications:* (contrib.) Oxford Companion to the Literature of Wales, 1986; Remaining True: a biography of Ness Edwards, 2006; Morgan Jones: man of conscience, 2019; three pamphlets; contrib. Llafur—Jl of Welsh Labour History, Gelligaer Hist. Soc. Jl. *Recreations:* music, reading. *Address:* c/o House of Commons, SW1A 0AA. *T:* (020) 7219 8152. *Club:* Bargoed Bowls (Pres., 2005–).

**DAVID-WEILL, Michel Alexandre;** Chairman, Lazard Frères & Co., LLC, New York, 1977–2005; Partner, Lazard Frères et Cie, Paris, 1965–2005; *b* 23 Nov. 1932; *s* of Berthe Haardt and Pierre David-Weill; *m* 1956, Hélène Lehideux; four *d*. *Educ:* Institut de Sciences Politiques, Paris; Lycée Français de New York. Brown Brothers Harriman, 1954–55; Lehman Brothers, NY, 1955–56; Lazard Frères & Co., NY, 1956–2005, Partner, 1961, Sen. Partner, 1977; Lazard Brothers & Co., London, Dir, 1965–2005; Chm., Lazard Partners, 1984–2005. Chm., Supervisory Bd, Eurazeo, 2003–. Dir, French Amer. Foundn, NY; Member Council: Musée de la Légion d'Honneur, Paris, 1975; Cité Internat. des Arts, Paris, 1976; Mem., Acad. des Beaux-Arts, 1983; Pres., Conseil Artistique de la Réunion des Musées Nationaux, Paris. Gov., NY Hosp. Officier, Legion of Honour (France), 1990. *Publications:* A Taste for Happiness, 2015. *Address:* c/o Eurazeo, 1 rue Georges Berger, 75017 Paris, France.

**DAVIDSON,** family name of **Viscount Davidson**.

**DAVIDSON,** 3rd Viscount *cr* 1937, of Little Gaddesden; **Malcolm William Mackenzie Davidson;** *b* 28 Aug. 1934; *yr s* of 1st Viscount Davidson, GCVO, CH, CB, PC and Hon. Frances Joan Dickinson, (Baroness Northchurch (Life Peer), DBE), *yr d* of 1st Baron Dickinson, KBE, PC; *S* brother, 2012; *m* 1970, Mrs Evelyn Ann Carew Perfect (*d* 2011), *yr d* of William Blackmore Storey; one *s* one *d*. *Educ:* Westminster; Pembroke Coll., Cambridge (BA 1958; MA 1962). *Heir: s* Hon. John Nicolas Alexander Davidson [*b* 1971; *m* 2002, Venetia Sophie Maunsell; four *d*]. *Address:* Berwick Place, Hatfield Peverel, Essex CM3 2EY. *T:* (01245) 380321.

**DAVIDSON OF GLEN CLOVA,** Baron *cr* 2006 (Life Peer), of Glen Clova in Angus; **Neil Forbes Davidson;** QC (Scot.) 1993; *b* 13 Sept. 1950; *s* of John and Flora Davidson; *m* 1980, Regina Anne Sprissler, Philadelphia. *Educ:* Univs of Stirling (BA), Bradford (MSc), Edinburgh (LLB, LLM). Admitted Faculty of Advocates, 1979; called to the Bar, Inner Temple, 1990; Standing Jun. Counsel to Registrar Gen., 1982, to Depts of Health and Social Security, 1988; Solicitor Gen. for Scotland, 2000–01; Advocate Gen. for Scotland, 2006–10. Opposition Spokesman on Law and Treasury, H of L, 2010–. Dir, City Disputes Panel, 1993–2000. ICJ missions to Egypt, 1997, 1998. Reviewer, Davidson Review on UK Implementation of EU Legislation, 2005–06. Mem., Adv. Council, Internat. Monetary

Inst., Renmin Univ., 2017–. Pres., Clan Davidson Assoc., 2004–. DUniv Stirling, 2012. Hon. 5th Dan, Internat. Taekwon-Do Fedn, 2015. *Publications:* (jtly) Judicial Review in Scotland, 1986; (contrib.) ADR in Scotland, 1995. *Address:* House of Lords, SW1A 0PW.

**DAVIDSON, Amanda;** Director, Baigrie Davies, 2005–15; *b* London, 1 April 1955; *d* of His Honour Ian Thomas Rollo Davidson, QC and Gyöngyi Magdolna Davidson (*née* Anghi). *Educ:* Channing Sch.; Queen Elizabeth Coll., London Univ. (BSc). Dir, Chase de Vere, 1982–84; sole trader, 1986–88; Director: Holden Matthews Financial Services, 1988–92; Holden Meehan, 1992–2005. Personal Investment Authority: Mem., Membership and Disciplinary Cttee, 1994–2001; Mem. Bd, 1998–2001; Financial Services Authority: Mem., Regulatory Decisions Cttee, 2001–06, Financial Capability Steering Gp, 2008–10; Mem. Bd, 2010–13; non-exec. Dir, Financial Conduct Authy, 2013–16 (Chair, Remuneration Cttee, 2013–16). Non-exec. Dir, Saunderson House, 2017– (Chm., Risk, Audit and Compliance Cttee, 2017–). Mem. Council, Assoc. of Ind. Financial Advrs, 2000–10 (Dep. Chm., 2007–10). Certified Financial Planner, 2003. Gov., Channing Sch., 1997–2013. *Recreations:* violin, theatre, ballet, opera, travel, scuba diving. *E:* amandamdavidson@icloud.com.

**DAVIDSON, Brian John;** HM Diplomatic Service; Ambassador to Thailand, since 2016; *b* Kingston, Jamaica, 28 April 1964; *s* of John Burton Davidson and Joan Margaret Davidson (*née* Stevenson); *m* 2015, Scott Kelly Chang; two *s* one *d*. *Educ:* Sullivan Upper Grammar Sch., Holywood, Co. Down, NI; Trinity Coll., Cambridge (BA Hons 1985). Entered FCO, 1985; lang. trng (Mandarin Chinese), 1986–88; Second Sec., Beijing, 1988–92; Cabinet Office, 1992–94; Hd, China Section, FCO, 1994–96; First Sec., Canberra, 1996–2000; Dep. Hd of Mission, Vilnius, 2001–04; Dep. Chief Exec., Internat. Financial Services London (on secondment), 2005–06; Consul General: Guangzhou, 2006–10; Shanghai, 2011–15. *Recreations:* badminton, tennis, photography, travel, art, science fiction. *Address:* c/o Foreign and Commonwealth Office, King Charles Street, SW1A 2AH.

**DAVIDSON, Carolyn Jayne;** HM Diplomatic Service; Ambassador to Guatemala, 2017–19; *b* Manchester, 18 April 1964; *d* of late Derek Davidson and Barbara Wild (*née* Morris); *m* 1997, Thomas Henry Carter, *qv*; two *s*. *Educ:* Manchester High Sch. for Girls; Univ. of Bristol (BA Hons French and German); Sch. of Oriental and African Studies, Univ. of London (Japanese); Open Univ. (MBA). Entered FCO, 1986; Third Secretary: Tokyo, 1989–92; on secondment to EC Commn, 1993; Bonn, 1993–95; FCO, 1995–99; Jt Dep. Hd of Mission, Bratislava, 2004–08; Jt High Comr to Zambia, 2008–12; FCO, 2012–15; Ambassador (non-resident) to Honduras, 2015–17. *Recreations:* sport (doing rather than watching), travel, family and friends. *Address:* c/o Foreign and Commonwealth Office, King Charles Street, SW1A 2AH.

**DAVIDSON, Charles Peter Morton;** a District Judge (Magistrates' Courts) (formerly Metropolitan Stipendiary Magistrate), 1984–2004; a Deputy District Judge (Magistrates' Courts), 2004–10; *b* 29 July 1938; *s* of William Philip Morton Davidson, MD, and Muriel Maud Davidson (*née* Alderson); *m* 1966, Pamela Louise Campbell-Rose. *Educ:* Harrow; Trinity Coll., Dublin (MA, LLB). Called to the Bar, Inner Temple, 1963; employed by Legal and General Assurance Soc., 1963–65; in practice at Bar, 1966–84; a Recorder, 1991–99. Chairman, London Rent Assessment Panel, 1973–84; part-time Immigration Appeals Adjudicator, 1976–84; a Chairman: Inner London Juvenile Courts, 1985–88; Family Court, 1991–2004. Contested (C) North Battersea, 1966. Member: Wandsworth BC, 1964–68; Merton BC, 1968–71. *Recreations:* music, gardening. *Club:* Hurlingham.

**DAVIDSON, Christopher Kenneth,** CBE 2008; Director, Tax Management Consulting, KPMG UK, since 2014; *b* Leeds, 15 June 1957; *s* of Joseph Hector Davidson and Elinor Margery Kathleen Davidson (*née* Dibbs); *m* 1989, Ann Elizabeth Buckland; two *s*. *Educ:* Leeds Modern Sch.; Bradford Univ. Board of Inland Revenue, later HM Revenue and Customs: Tax Officer (Higher Grade), 1976–80; qualified as Tax Inspector, 1983; Tax Inspector, 1980–85; Inspector (P), 1985–92; Inspector (SP), 1992–97; Sen. Civil Servant, 1997–2014; Disclosure of Tax Avoidance Schemes, 2004–06; Dep. Dir, Tax Intermediaries Study, 2006–08; Nat. Business Dir, Large Business Service, 2008–11; Hd, Anti-Avoidance Group, 2011–14. Trustee, IFS, 2009–. Governor: Chelmer Valley High Sch., 2001–; Columbus Sch. and Coll., 2015–. Personality of Year, Taxation Awards, 2009. *Recreations:* local politics, listening to music, cricket, family and friends, Spain. *Address:* KPMG UK, 15 Canada Square, E14 5GL.

**DAVIDSON, David;** independent consultant in organisational strategy, governance and audit, since 2010; *b* 25 Jan. 1943; *s* of John and Marjory Davidson; *m* 1968, Christine Hunter; three *s* two *d*. *Educ:* Heriot-Watt Univ. (Pharmacy); Manchester Business Sch. (DipBA). MRPharmS. Manager, 1966–69, Proprietor, 1969–74, community pharmacy, Kent; developed gp of community pharmacies in Scotland and Northern England, 1974–93; Dir, Unichem Ltd, 1977–90; Regl Chm., Unichem plc, 1990–93. Managing Director: Earlston Ltd, 1984–2008; Carse Ltd, 1996–2008; Associate Dir, Caledonia Consulting, 2007–10. Non-exec. Dir, NHS Borders, 2010–18 (Vice Chm., 2018); Director: Bill McLaren Park Ltd, 2013– (Chair, 2015–); Home Basics Ltd, 2013–. Mem., Scottish Borders Jt Integration Bd for Health and Social Care, 2014–18. Mem. (C) Stirling Council, 1995–99. MSP (C) Scotland NE, 1999–2007. Founder Chm., Assoc. Scottish Community Councils, 1993–95. Chair, Hawick Sports Initiative, 2010–17. *Recreations:* travel, Rugby football development, reading, local history research. *Address:* Ravenslea, Sunnyhill Road, Hawick, Roxburghshire TD9 7HS. *T:* (01450) 590288.

**DAVIDSON, Dennis Arthur;** Principal, DDA Consulting, since 2013; *b* Chester, 11 March 1947; *s* of Arthur Davidson and Elizabeth Joan Morgan; *m* 1991, Janette Graydon Dickson; three *s* one *d*. *Educ:* Helsby Grammar Sch.; Ellesmere Port Grammar Sch. Associated British Picture Corp., 1964–70; Chm., DDA Public Relations Ltd, 1970–2013. Member: BAFTA, 1975; Acad. of Motion Picture Arts and Scis, 1980. FCIPR 1991, FRSA 2007; FInstD 2008. *Recreations:* tennis, cinema, food and wine consumption, Rugby Union. *Address:* Barrihurst House, Cranleigh, Surrey GU6 8LQ. *T:* (01483) 279779. *E:* dennis.davidson@ddaconsulting.co.uk. *Clubs:* Hurlingham, Groucho, Soho House.

**DAVIDSON, Duncan Henry;** Chairman, 1972–2006, Life President, since 2006, Persimmon plc; *b* 29 March 1941; *s* of late Col Colin Keppel Davidson, CIE, OBE, RA (killed in action 1943) and late Lady (Mary) Rachel Davidson (later Lady (Mary) Rachel Pepys, DCVO); *m* 1965, Sarah Wilson; four *d*. *Educ:* Ampleforth Coll. Lieut, Royal Scots Greys, 1959–63; Manager, George Wimpey plc, 1963–65; Founder and Chm., Ryedale Homes Ltd, 1965–72. *Recreation:* country pursuits. *Address:* Lilburn Tower, Alnwick, Northumberland NE66 4PQ. *T:* (01668) 217291. *Clubs:* White's, Turf; Northern Counties.

**DAVIDSON, Edward Alan;** QC 1994; *b* 12 July 1943; *o s* of late Alan T. Davidson and H. Muriel Davidson, Sheffield; *m* 1973, Hilary Jill, *er d* of late Major N. S. Fairman, MBE; two *s*. *Educ:* King's Sch., Canterbury; Gonville and Caius Coll., Cambridge (schol., Tapp Postgrad. Schol.; MA, LLB). Called to the Bar, Gray's Inn, 1966 (Atkin and Birkenhead Schol.), Bencher, 2002. Chm., Summer Fields Sch. Trust, 2007–13 (Gov., 1998–2018). *Recreations:* tennis, bridge, gardening. *Address:* Thatch End, Furneux Pelham, Buntingford, Herts SG9 0LW.

**DAVIDSON, Ian Graham;** *b* 8 Sept. 1950; *s* of Graham Davidson and Elizabeth Crowe; *m* 1978, Morag Mackinnon; one *s* one *d*. *Educ:* Jedburgh Grammar Sch.; Galashiels Acad.; Edinburgh Univ. (MA Hons); Jordanhill Coll. (Teacher Cert.). Chm., Nat. Orgn of Labour Students, 1973–74; Pres., Jordanhill Coll. Students' Assoc., 1975–76; PA/Researcher, Janey Buchan, MEP, 1978–85; Community Service Volunteers, 1985–92. Councillor, Strathclyde Region, 1978–92 (Chm., Educn Cttees, 1986–92). MP (Lab and Co-op) Glasgow, Govan, 1992–97; Glasgow Pollok, 1997–2005, Glasgow SW, 2005–15; contested (Lab and Co-op) same seat, 2015. Member: Public Accounts Select Cttee, 1997–2010; Select Cttee on Scottish Affairs, 2005–15 (Chm., 2010–15); Liaison Select Cttee, 2010–15; Chairman: MSF Parly Gp, 1996–97; Co-op Gp, 1998–99; Bermuda Gp, 1998–2015; Secretary: New Europe Parly Gp, 2001–15; British/German All Party Parly Gp, 1998–2002; British/Japanese All Party Parly Gp, 1998–2015; Aerospace All Party Parly Gp, 1998–2001; Ship Building and Repair All Party Parly Gp, 2000–15; Parly Rugby Union team, 1996–2015. Secretary: Tribune Gp of MPs, 1997–2015; Trade Union Gp of Lab MPs, 1998–2015; Vice Chm., Scotland Lab Gp; Chm., Lab Against the Euro. *Recreations:* running, swimming, family.

**DAVIDSON, Jane Barbara;** see Stevenson, J. B.

**DAVIDSON, Jane Elizabeth;** Director of Sustainability, since 2011, and Pro Vice Chancellor for External Engagement and Sustainability, since 2016, University of Wales Trinity Saint David (Associate Pro Vice Chancellor for External Engagement, 2014–16); *b* 19 March 1957; *d* of Dr Lindsay Alexander Gordon Davidson and Dr Joyce Mary Davidson; *m* 1994, Guy Roger George Stoate; one *d*, and two step *s*. *Educ:* Malvern Girls' Coll.; Birmingham Univ. (BA 2nd Cl. Hons English); UCW, Aberystwyth (PGCE). Teacher, Cardigan and Pontypridd, 1981–83; Develt Officer, YHA, 1983–86; youth and community worker, Dinas Powys Youth Centre, 1986–89; researcher to Rhodri Morgan, MP, 1989–94; Welsh Co-ordinator, Nat. Local Govt Forum Against Poverty, 1994–96; Hd, Social Affairs, Welsh Local Govt Assoc., 1996–99. National Assembly for Wales: Mem. (Lab) Pontypridd, 1999–2011; Dep. Presiding Officer, 1999–2000; Sec., then Minister, for Educn and Lifelong Learning, subseq. Minister for Educn, Lifelong Learning and Skills, 2000–07; Minister for Sustainability and Rural Develt, 2007; Minister for Envmt, Sustainability and Housing, 2007–11. Hon. Dr Glamorgan, 2011. *Publications:* The Anti Poverty Implications of Local Government Reorganisation, 1990; (jtly) Freeing the Dragon, 1998; (contrib.) The One Planet Life, 2014; (contrib.) The Sustainable University, 2014; contrib. to social policy jls. *Recreations:* theatre, walking, cycling, sea kayaking.

**DAVIDSON, Prof. John Frank,** FRS 1974; FREng; Shell Professor of Chemical Engineering, University of Cambridge, 1978–93 (Professor of Chemical Engineering, 1975–78); Vice-Master, Trinity College, Cambridge, 1992–96; Adjunct Professor, Monash University, Australia, 1996–99; *b* 7 Feb. 1926; *s* of John and Katie Davidson; *m* 1948, Susanne Hedwig Ostberg (*d* 2011); one *s* one *d*. *Educ:* Heaton Grammar Sch., Newcastle upon Tyne; Trinity Coll., Cambridge. MA, PhD, ScD; FIChemE, MIMechE. 1st cl. Mech. Scis Tripos, Cantab, 1946, BA 1947. Engrg work at Rolls Royce, Derby, 1947–50; Cambridge Univ.: Research Fellow, Trinity Coll., 1949; research, 1950–52; Univ. Demonstrator, 1952; Univ. Lectr, 1954; Steward of Trinity Coll., 1957–64; Reader in Chem. Engrg, Univ. of Cambridge, 1964–75. Visiting Professor: Univ. of Delaware, 1960; Univ. of Sydney, 1967. Member: Flixborough Ct of Inquiry, 1974–75; Adv. Cttee on Safety of Nuclear Installations, HSC, 1977–87. Pres., IChemE, 1970–71; Vice Pres. and Mem. Council, Royal Soc., 1988. FREng (Founder FEng, 1976). For. Associate, Nat. Acad. of Engrg, US, 1976; For. Fellow, Indian National Science Acad., 1990; For. Mem., Russian Engrg Acad., 1998. Dr *hc* Institut Nat. Polytech. de Toulouse, 1979; Hon. DSc Aston, 1989. Leverhulme Medal, Royal Soc., 1984; Messel Medal, Soc. of Chemical Industry, 1986; Royal Medal, Royal Soc., 1999; Prince Philip Medal, RAEng, 2010. *Publications:* (with D. Harrison): Fluidised Particles, 1963; Fluidization, 1971, 2nd edn (with R. Clift and D. Harrison), 1985; (with D. L. Keairns) Fluidization (Conference Procs), 1978. *Recreations:* gardening, upholstery, mending domestic artefacts. *Address:* 5 Luard Close, Cambridge CB2 8PL. *T:* (01223) 246104.

See also I. G. Letwin.

**DAVIDSON, John Roderick,** OBE 2004; Director of Administration, 1991–2004, Clerk of the Council, 1994–2004, University of London; *b* 29 Jan. 1937; *yr s* of late Alexander Ross Davidson and Jessie Maud (*née* Oakley). *Educ:* Portsmouth Northern Grammar Sch.; Univ. of Manchester (BA). Advr to students, Chelsea Sch. of Art, 1966–68; Asst Sch. Sec., RPMS, 1968–74; Imperial College of Science, Technology and Medicine: Asst Sec., 1974–77; Personnel Sec., 1977–85; Admin. Sec., 1985–89; London University: Clerk of Senate, 1989–94; Member: Exams and Assessment Council, 1991–2000; Bd, British Inst. in Paris, 1993–2004. Director: London E Anglian Gp, 1990–96; Superannuation Arrangements of Univ. of London Trustee Co., 1993–98; London and S Eastern Library Region, 1995–2001; Senate House Services Ltd, 1996–2004; Digital Preservation Coalition Ltd, 2002–04. Chm., Lansdowne (Putney) Ltd, 1999–2018. Trustee: Univ. of London Convocation Trust, 1997–2004; St Stephen's AIDS Trust, 2003–19 (Chm., Finance and Gen. Purposes Cttee, 2014–19). Governor: Charterhouse Sch., 1994–2003; More House Sch., 2000–15 (Chm., 2005–14). Mem., More House Assoc., 2000–); Wimbledon High Sch., 2001–09. *Recreations:* theatre, opera, genealogy. *Address:* 10 Lansdowne, Carlton Drive, SW15 2BY. *T:* (020) 8789 0021. *Club:* Athenæum.

**DAVIDSON, Katharine Mary, (Mrs Christopher Baylis);** QC 2011; *b* Edinburgh, 19 June 1962; *d* of late Andrew Davidson and of Dorothy Davidson; *m* 2007, Christopher Baylis; two *s* one *d*. *Educ:* Epsom Coll.; Lincoln Coll., Oxford (BA Juris.; MA). Called to the Bar, Lincoln's Inn, 1987; in practice as a barrister, specialising in family law, 1 Mitre Court, then 1 Hare Court, 1988–. *Recreations:* family, ski-ing, art. *Address:* 1 Hare Court, Temple, EC4Y 7BE. *T:* (020) 7797 7070. *E:* clerks@1hc.com.

**DAVIDSON, Lisa Margaret;** see Henderson, L. M.

**DAVIDSON, Sir Martin (Stuart),** KCMG 2014 (CMG 2007); Chairman, Great Britain China Centre, since 2015 (Member of Board, since 2009); *b* 14 Oct. 1955; *s* of Westland Davidson and Freda (*née* Hill); *m* 1980, Elizabeth Fanner; two *s* one *d*. *Educ:* Royal Grammar Sch., Guildford; St Andrews Univ. (MA). Admin. Officer, Hong Kong Govt, 1979–83; British Council: Peking, 1984–87; Regl Officer, China, 1987–89; Dir, S China, 1989–93; Asst Regl Dir, E and S Europe, 1993–95; Cultural Counsellor and Dir, British Council, Peking, 1995–2000; Dir, E Asia and Americas, 2000–03; Dir, Europe, Americas and Middle East, 2003–05; Dep. Dir-Gen., 2006–07; Chief Exec., 2007–14. Non-exec. Dir, House of Fraser Gp, 2015–18. Vice Chm., Leonard Cheshire Disability, 2012–; Trustee, United Purpose, 2017–. FRSA. *Recreations:* hill walking, reading, gliding, beekeeping, Rugby. *Address:* c/o Great Britain China Centre, 15 Belgrave Square, SW1X 8PS. *Club:* Athenæum.

**DAVIDSON, Nicholas Ranking;** QC 1993; a Deputy High Court Judge, since 2000; *b* 2 March 1951; *s* of late Brian Davidson, CBE and Priscilla Margaret (*née* Chilver); *m* 1978, Gillian Frances Watts; two *d*. *Educ:* Winchester (Schol.); Trinity Coll., Cambridge (Exhibnr; BA; MA). Called to the Bar, Inner Temple, 1974 (Treas.'s Prize, Hughes Parry Prize and Inner Temple Scholarship, 1974); Bencher, 1998. Chm., Professional Negligence

Bar Assoc., 1997–99. MCIArb 2004, FCIArb 2018. Mem. Council (formerly Trustee), St Mary's Sch., Ascot, 2012– (Gov., 1996–2006). *Publications:* (contrib.) Now and Then, 1999; (contrib.) Professional Negligence and Liability, 2000. *Recreations:* bridge, music, ski-ing. *Address:* 4 New Square, Lincoln's Inn, WC2A 3RJ. *T:* (020) 7822 2000.

**DAVIDSON, Prof. Peter Robert Keith Andrew,** PhD; Senior Research Fellow and Archivist, Campion Hall, Oxford, since 2015; *b* 14 May 1957; *s* of Robert Ritchie Davidson and Daphne Davidson (*née* Sanderson); *m* 1989, Jane Barbara Stevenson, *qv. Educ:* Clare Coll., Cambridge (BA 1979; PhD 1986); Univ. of York (MA 1980). Lectr, Univ. of St Andrews, 1989–90; Docent in Lit. and Book Studies, Universiteit Leiden, Netherlands, 1990–92; University of Warwick: Lectr in English, 1992–97; Sen. Lectr, 1997–99; Reader, 1999–2000; Aberdeen University: Chalmers Regius Prof. of English, 2000–05; Prof. of Renaissance Studies and Scholar-Keeper of University Renaissance Collections, 2005–15. Dir, St Omers Press, 2013–. Academic Advr, Stonyhurst Coll. Christian Heritage Centre Trust, 2014–. Trustee, Scottish Catholic Heritage Trust, 2012–19. *Publications:* (with A. H. van der Weel) Poems of Sir Constantijn Huygens, 1996; The Vocall Forest, 1996; The Poems and Translations of Sir Richard Fanshawe, vol. I, 1998, vol. II, 1999; Poetry and Revolution, 1998; (with Jane Stevenson) Early Modern Women's Verse, 2000; The Idea of North, 2005; (with Anne Sweeney) Collected Poems of St Robert Southwell, SJ, 2007; The Universal Baroque, 2007; (with Jill Bepler) The Triumphs of the Defeated, 2007; The Palace of Oblivion, 2008; (with Jane Stevenson) The Lost City, 2008; Winter Light, 2010; (with Iain Beavan and Jane Stevenson) The Library and Archive Collections of the University of Aberdeen, 2011; Distance and Memory, 2013; (ed) The Celebrated Museum of the Roman College, 2015; The Last of the Light, 2015; (with Kate Bennett and Kelsey Jackson Williams) Aubrey's Villa, 2018. *Recreation:* casuistry. *Address:* Campion Hall, Brewer Street, Oxford OX1 1QS.

**DAVIDSON, Prof. Robin,** DPhil; Chairman, UK SMART Recovery, since 2014; *b* Belfast, 4 July 1950; *s* of James and May Davidson; *m* 1975, Patricia Anderson; three *s*. *Educ:* Queen's Univ., Belfast (BSc, MSc); Univ. of Ulster (DPhil 1989). Consultant Clinical Psychologist: Leeds Addiction Service, 1980–84; NI DHSS, 1984–2008; Chm., Alcohol Res. UK (formerly Alcohol Educn and Res. Council), 2007–14. Lectr, Greenwich and S Bank Univs. Hon. Prof., Univ. of Ulster, 2002–; Hon. Lectr, Faculty of Medicine, QUB, 1992–. *Publications:* Alcoholism and Drug Addiction, 1985; Counselling Problem Drinkers, 1990. *Recreation:* motor cycling. *Address:* UK SMART Recovery, Dresden House, The Strand, Stoke on Trent, Staffs ST3 2QH. *T:* 07783 729709.

**DAVIDSON, Rt Hon. Ruth;** PC 2016; Member (C) Edinburgh Central, Scottish Parliament, since 2016 (Glasgow, 2011–16); Leader, Scottish Conservative and Unionist Party, 2011–19; *b* 10 Nov. 1978; *d* of Douglas and Elizabeth Davidson; partner, Jen Wilson; one *s*. *Educ:* Buckhaven High Sch.; Univ. of Edinburgh (MA English Lit.); Glasgow Univ. (Internat. Develt). Trainee reporter, Glenrothes Gazette; reporter: Kingdom FM; Real Radio; reporter, radio journalist, producer and presenter, BBC Scotland, 2002–09; Aide to Leader, Scottish Conservatives, 2009–11. Served TA, Signal Regt, 2003–06; Hon. Col, 32 Signal Regt Army Reserve, 2017–. Contested (C) Glasgow NE, 2009, 2010. *Publications:* Yes She Can: why women own the future, 2018. *Address:* Scottish Parliament, Edinburgh EH99 1SP.

**DAVIDSON, Shearer Carroll;** *see* West, S. C.

**DAVIDSON, Stephen Robert;** DL; Headmaster, Bradford Grammar School, 1996–2011; *b* 20 Oct. 1950; *er s* of late Robert Davidson and Joan Davidson, Tynemouth; *m* 1983, Carol, *d* of Ralston and Dorothy Smith, St Bees; one *s*. *Educ:* Univ. of Manchester Inst. of Sci. and Technol. (BSc Hons Engrg 1972); Univ. of Newcastle (PGCE 1974). Teacher, Lord Wandsworth Coll., 1974–83; Middle Sch. Master, Manchester Grammar Sch., 1983–96. DL 2001, High Sheriff 2012–13, W Yorks. *Recreations:* travel (especially USA), sport, civil aviation.

**DAVIE, Jonathan Richard;** Chairman, First Avenue Partners, since 2007; *b* Esher, 21 Sept. 1946; *s* of Richard Davie and Anne Davie; *m* 1986, Belinda Mary Blake; two *d*. *Educ:* Tonbridge Sch.; École de Commerce, Neuchatel. FCA 1969. Wedd Durlacher Mordaunt, 1969–86, Partner, 1975–86; Man. Dir, Barclays de Zoete Wedd, 1986–98; Vice Chm., Credit Suisse First Boston, 1998–2007; Chm., IG Gp Hldgs, 2004–14. Non-executive Director: Infrastata plc (formerly Portland Gas), 2008–10; Persimmon, 2010–17; Hansa Trust plc, 2013–; Gabelli Value Plus Investment Trust plc, 2016–. Gov., Heathfield Sch., 2006–13. *Recreations:* golf, ski-ing, tennis, antiques. *Address:* c/o First Avenue Partners LLP, Swan House, 17–19 Stratford Place, W1C 1BQ. *T:* (020) 7016 6600, *Fax:* (020) 7016 6699. *E:* jdavie@firstavenue.com.

**DAVIE, Sir Michael F.;** *see* Ferguson Davie.

**DAVIE, Rex;** *see* Davie, S. R.

**DAVIE, Ronald,** PhD; FBPsS; Director, National Children's Bureau, 1981–90; *b* 25 Nov. 1929; *s* of late Thomas Edgar Davie and Gladys (*née* Powell); *m* 1957, Kathleen, *d* of William Wilkinson, Westhoughton, Lancs; one *s* one *d*. *Educ:* King Edward VI Grammar Sch., Aston, Birmingham; Univ. of Reading (BA 1954); Univ. of Manchester (PGCE and Dip. Deaf Educn 1955); Univ. of Birmingham (Dip. Educnl Psych. 1961); Univ. of London (PhD 1970). FBPsS 1973. Teacher, schs for mainstream and disabled children, 1955–60; Co. Educnl Psychologist, IoW, 1961–64; Nat. Children's Bureau, London: Sen. Res. Officer, 1964; Dep. Dir, 1968; Dir of Res., 1972; Prof. of Educnl Psychology, Dept of Educn, UC Cardiff, 1974–81. Expert Witness for Official Solicitor, Family Courts, 1990–2000. Mem., Special Educnl Needs Tribunal, 1994–2003. Visiting Professor: Oxford Poly., later Oxford Brookes Univ., 1991–97; Cheltenham and Gloucester Coll. of Higher Educn, later Univ. of Gloucestershire, 1997–2006; Visiting Fellow: Inst. of Educn, Univ. of London, 1985–93; Univ. of Newcastle, 1995–2006; Hon. Res. Fellow, UCL, 1991–2006. Co-Dir, Nat. Child Develt Study, 1968–73; Scientific Adviser: Local Authority Social Services Res. Liaison Gp, DHSS, 1975–77; Mental Handicap Res. Liaison Gp, DHSS, 1977–81; Prof. Advr, All Party Parly Gp for Children, 1983–91. President: Links Assoc., 1977–90; Child Develt Soc., 1990–91; Nat. Assoc. for Special Educnl Needs, 1992–94; Vice-Pres., British Assoc. for Early Childhood Educn, 1984–95, Young Minds, 1991–2007; Chairman: Trng and Educn Cttee, Nat. Assoc. Mental Health, 1969–72; Assoc. for Child Psychol. and Psychiatry, 1972–73 (Hon. Sec. 1965–70); Working Party, Children Appearing Before Juvenile Courts, Children's Reg. Planning Cttee for Wales, 1975–77; Wales Standing Conf. for Internat. Year of the Child, 1978–79; Steering Cttee, Child Health and Educn Study, 1979–84; Bd of Trustees, Eden Valley Hospice, 2000 (Trustee, 1998–2006; Vice Chm., 2001). Mem., Nat. Curriculum Council, 1988–90. Chm. Govs, 1998–2001. Church Warden, St Kentigern's, Caldbeck, 2004–11. FRSA 1991. Hon. FRCPCH 1996. Hon. DEd: CNAA, 1991; UWE, 1998; Hon. DLitt Birmingham, 1999. *Publications:* (co-author) 11,000 Seven-Year Olds, 1966; Directory of Voluntary Organisations concerned with Children, 1969; Living with Handicap, 1970; From Birth to Seven, 1972; Child Sexual Abuse: the way forward after Cleveland, 1989; Listening to Children in Education, 1996; The Voice of the Child, 1996; chapters in books and papers in sci. and other jls on special educn, psychol., child care health, effects of TV on children, and children's ownership and use of mobile phones. *Recreations:* photography, antiques, good music of all kinds. *Address:* Beck Rise, Upton, Caldbeck, Cumbria CA7 8EU.

**DAVIE, (Stephen) Rex,** CB 1993; Member: Council on Tribunals, 1995–2001; Civil Service Appeal Board, 1995–2001; Principal Establishment and Finance Officer (Under Secretary), Cabinet Office, 1989–93; *b* 11 June 1933; *s* of late Sydney and Dorothy Davie; *m* 1955, Christine Stockwell; one *s* one *d*. *Educ:* Ilfracombe Grammar Sch. Executive Officer, Inland Revenue, 1951. National Service, RAF, 1952–54. Office of Minister for Science, 1962; NEDO, 1967; CSD, 1970; Asst Sec. 1979; Cabinet Office, 1983; Sen. Sec., Security Commn, 1979–89. Mem. Council, Inst. of Cancer Res., 1993– (Vice Chm., then Dep. Chm., 1995–2003). *Recreations:* reading, family, travel, gardening. *Address:* 2 Linnet Close, Basingstoke, Hants RG22 5PD. *Clubs:* Athenæum, Civil Service.

**DAVIE, Timothy Douglas,** CBE 2018; Chief Executive, BBC Studios (formerly BBC Worldwide), since 2013; *b* 25 April 1967; *s* of Douglas John Davie and Alicia Margaret Davie; *m* 1997, Anne Claire Shotbolt; three *s*. *Educ:* Selwyn Coll., Cambridge (BA 1989). Brand Manager, Procter and Gamble, 1989–93; Vice Pres., Pepsico, 1993–2005; Dir, Marketing, Communications and Audiences, BBC, 2005–08; Dir, BBC Audio and Music, 2008–12; Acting Dir-Gen., BBC, 2012–13. Mem., Mktg Gp of GB, 2001– (Chm., 2009–10). Chm., Comic Relief, 2013–. Trustee: Tate, 2015–; Royal Television Soc., 2016– (Vice Chair, 2013–16); Co-Chm., Creative Industries Council, 2018–. *Recreations:* my family, running, reading, ski-ing, live music, fresh air, strong coffee. *Address:* BBC Studios, 1 Television Centre, 101 Wood Lane, W12 7FA. *T:* (020) 8433 3533. *E:* tim.davie@bbc.com. *Club:* Soho House.

**DAVIES,** family name of **Barons Darwen, Davies, Davies of Abersoch, Davies of Oldham** and **Davies of Stamford**.

**DAVIES,** 3rd Baron *cr* 1932, of Llandinam; **David Davies,** CEng, MICE; Vice Lord-Lieutenant of Powys, 2004–15; Chairman, Welsh National Opera Company, 1975–2000; *b* 2 Oct. 1940; *s* of 2nd Baron and Ruth Eldrydd (*d* 1966), 3rd *d* of Major W. M. Dugdale, CB, DSO; *S* father (killed in action), 1944; *m* 1972, Beryl, *d* of W. J. Oliver; two *s* two *d*. *Educ:* Eton; King's Coll., Cambridge (MA); MBA. DL Powys, 1997. *Heir: s* Hon. David Daniel Davies [*b* 23 Oct. 1975; *m* 2001, Leyla Natasha, *d* of Martin and Elaine Pope]. *Address:* Maethfa, Llandinam, Powys SY17 5AB.

**DAVIES OF ABERSOCH,** Baron *cr* 2009 (Life Peer), of Abersoch in the County of Gwynedd; **(Evan) Mervyn Davies,** CBE 2002; FCIB; Chairman and Partner, Corsair Capital, since 2014 (Member, Advisory Board, 2007–09; Vice Chairman and Partner, 2010–14); Chairman, Advisory Board, and Senior Advisor to Chief Executive Officer, Moelis & Co., 2010–14; *b* 21 Nov. 1952; *s* of Richard Aled Davies and Margaret Davies; *m* 1979, Jeanne Marie (*née* Gammie); one *s* one *d*. *Educ:* Rydal Sch., N Wales; Harvard Business Sch. (PMD). FCIB 1990. Joined Midland Bank, 1973; Man. Dir, UK Banking and Sen. Credit Officer, Citibank, 1983–93; Standard Chartered plc, 1993–2009: Dir, 1997–2009; Gp Chief Exec., 2001–06; Chm., 2006–09; Dir, Standard Chartered Bank, Hong Kong, 1997–2001. Minister of State, BIS (formerly BERR), and FCO, 2009–10. Chairman: Fleming Family and Partners, 2008–09; Nordic Windpower Ltd, 2008–09; PineBridge Investments, 2010–14; Chime Communications plc, 2012–15; NoteMachine Gp Hldgs Ltd, 2012–; Jack Wills, 2013–16; LetterOne Holdings SA (Dep. Chm., 2015); Dir, FF&P Private Equity Ltd, 2007–09. Non-executive Director: Tesco plc, 2003–08; Tottenham Hotspur FC, 2004–09; Breakingviews Ltd, 2007–09; Bharti Airtel, 2010–12; Diageo plc, 2010–; J Rothschild Capital Mgt, 2012–13; Mem., Adv. Cttee, Native Land, 2010–; Adviser: Ridgeway Partners, 2010–16; Teneo Hldgs, 2013–. Chair, public review of role of women on boards, 2010–11. Past Member: Singapore Business Council; UK-India Forum; UK-China Forum; Asia House Internat. Adv. Council; Mem. Bd, Hong Kong Monetary Authy, 1997–2002; Dir, Hong Kong Assoc., 2006–; Chairman: Prime Minister's Business Council for Britain, 2007–08; Interim Exec. Cttee, ICFR, 2007–09; UK-ASEAN Business Council, 2011–14; UK-India Business Council, 2017–. Former Chairman: British Chamber of Commerce, HK; HK Assoc. of Banks; HK Youth Arts Fest.; Asia Youth Orch.; Generations Appeal, Breakthrough Breast Cancer. Pres., Royal Soc. of Asian Affairs, 2013–. Mem., Roundhouse, 2008–09. Chm., Council, Bangor Univ., 2008–14. Chm., Garden Bridge Trust, 2013–18. Chm., LTA, 2018–; Mem., Exec. Cttee, World Rugby, 2016–; Trustee: Sir Kyffin Williams Trust, 2007–09; RA, 2008–18 (Chm., RA Trust, 2012–18); Dir, Glyndebourne Prodns Ltd, 2012–. JP Hong Kong, 2000. *Recreations:* soccer, cricket, tennis, golf, Rugby, art, opera. *Address:* House of Lords, SW1A 0PW. *T:* (020) 7152 6536. *Clubs:* Arts, Mark's, Oswald's, Soho House; Shek O (Hong Kong).

**DAVIES OF OLDHAM,** Baron *cr* 1997 (Life Peer), of Broxbourne in the co. of Hertfordshire; **Bryan Davies;** PC 2006; *b* 9 Nov. 1939; *s* of George William and Beryl Davies; *m* 1963, Monica Rosemary Mildred Shearing; two *s* one *d*. *Educ:* Redditch High Sch.; University Coll. London (BA Hons History); Inst. of Education (CertEd); London Sch. of Economics (BScEcons). Teacher, Latymer Sch., 1962–65; Lectr, Middlesex Polytechnic at Enfield, 1965–74. Sec., Parly Labour Party, 1979–92. Contested (Lab): Norfolk Central, 1966; Newport W, 1983. MP (Lab): Enfield North, Feb. 1974–1979; Oldham Central and Royton, 1992–97. An Asst Govt Whip, 1978–79; front bench spokesman on Further and Higher Educn, 1993–97. Member: Select Cttee on Public Expenditure, 1975–79; Select Cttee on Overseas Develt, 1975–79; Select Cttee on Nat. Heritage, 1992–93. A Lord in Waiting (Govt Whip), 2000–03; Captain of the Yeomen of the Guard (Dep. Govt Chief Whip), 2003–10; Parly Under-Sec. of State, DEFRA, 2009–10; Shadow Minister for Transport, 2010–15; Opposition Treasury Spokesman, 2010–. Chm., FEFCE, 1998–2000. Mem., MRC, 1977–79. Pres., RoSPA, 1998–2000. *Recreations:* sport, literature. *Address:* 28 Churchfields, Broxbourne, Herts EN10 7JS. *T:* (01992) 410418.

**DAVIES OF STAMFORD,** Baron *cr* 2010 (Life Peer), of Stamford in the County of Lincolnshire; **(John) Quentin Davies;** *b* 29 May 1944; *e s* of late Dr Michael Ivor Davies and Thelma Davies (*née* Butler), Oxford; *m* 1983, Chantal, *e d* of late Lt-Col R. L. C. Tamplin, 17/21 Lancers, Military Kt of Windsor, and Claudine Tamplin (*née* Pleis); two *s*. *Educ:* Dragon Sch.; Leighton Park (exhibnr); Gonville and Caius Coll., Cambridge (Open Scholar; BA Hist. Tripos 1st cl. Hons 1966; MA); Harvard Univ. (Frank Knox Fellow, 1966–67). HM Diplomatic Service, 1967; 3rd Sec., FCO, 1967–69; 2nd Sec., Moscow, 1969–72; 1st Sec., FCO, 1973–74. Morgan Grenfell & Co.: Manager, later Asst Dir, 1974–78; Rep. in France, later Dir-Gen. and Pres., Morgan Grenfell France SA, 1978–81; Director (main bd), and Hd of Eur. Corporate Finance, 1981–87; Consultant, 1987–93. Director: Dewe Rogerson International, 1987–95; SGE, later Vinci SA, 1999–2001, 2003–08; Vinci UK (formerly Norwest Holst), 2001–08. Adviser: NatWest Securities, then NatWest Markets, 1993–99; Royal Bank of Scotland, 1999–2003. Mem. Council, Lloyds of London, 2004–07. Parly Advr, Chartered Inst. of Taxation, 1993–2008. Contested (C) Birmingham, Ladywood, Aug. 1977. MP Stamford and Spalding, 1987–97, Grantham and Stamford, 1997–2010 (C, 1987–2007, Lab, 2007–10). Parliamentary Private Secretary: to Minister of State for Educn, 1988–90; to Minister of State, Home Office, 1990–91; Opposition spokesman on social security and pensions, 1998–99; Shadow Paymaster-Gen.,

1999–2000; Opposition spokesman on defence, 2000–01; Shadow NI Sec., 2001–03; Parly Under-Sec. of State (Minister for Defence Equipment and Support), MoD, 2008–10. Member: Treasury Select Cttee, 1992–98; Cttee on Standards and Privileges, 1995–98; Eur. Standing Cttee, 1991–97; Eur. Legislation Cttee, 1997–98; Internat. Develt Cttee, 2003–07; Chairman: British-German Parly Gp, 2005–08 (Jt Chm., 1997–2005); British-Romanian Parly Gp, 2011–; Vice Chairman: Anglo-French Parly Gp, 1997–2008; British-Netherlands Parly Gp, 1999–2008; British-Italian Parly Gp, 2005–08; Chm., Conservative Gp for Europe, 2006–07. Chm., Inquiry into Nat. Recognition of our Armed Forces, 2007 (report publd 2008). Mem., European Select Cttee, H of L, 2013–16. Chm., City in Europe Cttee, 1975. Parly Fellow, RCDS, 2012–13. Freeman, City of London; Liveryman, Goldsmiths' Co. Trustee and Mem. Council, Centre for Econ. Policy Res., 1996–2008. Freedom of Information Award, 1996; Guardian Backbencher of the Year Award, 1996; Spectator Parliamentarian of the Year Award, 1997. *Publications:* Britain and Europe: a Conservative view, 1996. *Recreations:* reading, walking, riding, ski-ing, travel, playing (bad) tennis, looking at art and architecture. *Address:* House of Lords, SW1A 0PW. *Clubs:* Brooks's, Beefsteak, Travellers.

**DAVIES, Adele, (Mrs R. O. Davies);** see Biss, A.

**DAVIES, Alan Roger;** comedian, actor and presenter; *b* 6 March 1966; *s* of Roy and Shirley Davies; *m* 2007, Katie Maskell; two *s* one *d*. *Educ:* Bancroft's Sch.; Loughton Coll. of Further Educn; Univ. of Kent (BA Hons 1988). Stand-up comedian, 1988–; Live at the Lyric (one-man show), 1994; Urban Trauma (one-man show), Duchess Th., 1998; Life is Pain (one-man show), Criterion Th., 2012; Little Victories (one-man show), UK tour, 2016; *television* series include: Jonathan Creek, 1997–2016; Bob and Rose, 2001; QI, 2003–; The Brief, 2004, 2005; Alan Davies' Teenage Revolution, 2010; Whites, 2010; Show Me The Funny, 2011; Alan Davies: As Yet Untitled, 2014–17; The Dog Rescuers with Alan Davies, 2014–; Damned, 2016, 2018; *radio* series include: The Alan Davies Show, Radio 4, 1998; *films* include: Angus, Thongs and Perfect Snogging, 2008. Contributor: The Times, 2003–06; Wisden Cricket Monthly. Hon. DLitt Kent, 2003. *Publications:* My Favourite People and Me, 2009. *Recreations:* Arsenal FC, motor cycling, scuba diving. *Address:* c/o United Agents, 12–26 Lexington Street, W1F 0LE.

**DAVIES, Alan Seymour;** JP; Headmaster, Copland Community School and Technology Centre Foundation, 1988–2009; *b* 21 Feb. 1947; *s* of Seymour George Davies and Sarah Louise Davies; *m* 1972, Frances Patricia Williamson; one *s* two *d*. *Educ:* Inst. of Educn, London Univ. (BEd, CertEd); NE London Poly. (MEd). Teacher, E Barnet Sch., 1972–75; Teacher, 1975–80, Dep. Head, 1980–86, McEntee Sen. High Sch.; Headteacher, Sidney Chaplin Sch., 1986–88; Acting Headteacher, Harlesden Primary Sch., 2000. Consultant Headteacher, London Leadership Challenge, 2003. Chm. of Govs, Chalkhill Primary Sch., 2003–09; Governor: Park Lane Primary Sch., 1998; Mitchell Brook Primary Sch., 1999; Harlesden Primary Sch., 2000. JP Barnet, 1984. Hon. DSc Westminster, 2007. *Recreation:* sport. *Address:* 39 Grants Close, Mill Hill, NW7 1DD. *T:* (020) 8349 9731.

**DAVIES, Alun;** Member (Lab) Blaenau Gwent, National Assembly for Wales, since 2011 (for Wales Mid and West, 2007–11); *b* Tredegar, 12 Feb. 1964; *s* of Thomas Rhys Davies and Mair Davies; one *s* one *d*. *Educ:* Tredegar Comprehensive Sch.; University Coll. of Wales, Aberystwyth (BSc Hons Econs). Campaigner on envmtl issues, WWF; poverty campaigner, Oxfam; Public and Corporate Affairs Manager, Hyder; Hd, Public Affairs, UKAEA; Dir, Corporate Affairs, S4C; founded Bute Communications, 2004. Dep. Minister for Agric., Fisheries and Eur. Progs, 2011–13, Minister for Natural Resources and Food, 2013–14, Minister for Lifelong Learning and Welsh Lang., 2016–17, Cabinet Sec. for Local Govt and Public Services, 2017–18, Welsh Govt. Contested: (Plaid Cymru-Green Alliance) Blaenau Gwent, 1992; (Plaid Cymru) Cynon Valley, 1997; (Lab) Ceredigion, 2005. *Address:* National Assembly for Wales, Cardiff Bay, Cardiff CF99 1NA.

**DAVIES, Prof. Alun Millward,** PhD; FMedSci; FRS 2011; FRSE, FLSW; Distinguished Research Professor, School of Biosciences, Cardiff University, since 2004; Wellcome Trust Senior Investigator, since 2014; *b* Newport, Gwent, 2 Aug. 1955; *s* of Gwynfryn Millward Davies and Nancy Eva Davies; partner, Christina Burch; two *s*. *Educ:* Pontllanfraith Grammar Tech. Sch.; Univ. of Liverpool Med. Sch. (MB ChB 1978); Univ. of Liverpool (BSc Cell Biol. and Biochem. 1979); Guy's Hosp. Med. Sch., Univ. of London (PhD Develtl Neurobiol. 1984). Lectr, Middlesex Hosp. Med. Sch., Univ. of London, 1982–83; Lectr, 1983–88, Sen. Lectr, 1988–89, Reader in Neurobiol., 1989–93, St George's Hosp. Med. Sch., Univ. of London; Prof. of Develtl Neurobiol., Sch. of Biol Scis, St Andrews Univ., 1993–2000; Prof. of Physiol., Royal (Dick) Sch. of Veterinary Studies, Edinburgh Univ., 2000–04. Exec. Vice Pres. of Res., Rinat Neuroscience Corp., Palo Alto, Calif, 2001–03. Mem., EMBO, 2000; MAE 2011. FRSE 2000; FMedSci 2010; FLSW 2011. *Publications:* articles in learned jls. *Recreations:* playing piano and harpsichord, portraiture, carpentry, single-handed sailing, scuba diving. *Address:* Life Sciences Building, School of Biosciences, Cardiff University, Museum Avenue, Cardiff CF10 3AT. *T:* (029) 2087 4303. *E:* daviesalun@cf.ac.uk.

**DAVIES, Prof. Alwyn George,** FRS 1989; Professor of Chemistry, University College London, 1969–91, now Emeritus; *b* 13 May 1926; *s* of John Lewis and Victoria May Davies; *m* 1956, Margaret Drake; one *s* one *d*. *Educ:* Hamond's Grammar Sch., Swaffham; University College London (BSc, PhD, DSc; Fellow 1991). CChem, FRSC. Lectr, Battersea Polytechnic, 1949; Lectr, 1953, Reader, 1964, UCL. Ingold Lectr, RSC, 1992–93. Medal for Organic Reaction Mechanism, RSC, 1989; Humboldt Prize, Freiburg Univ., 1994. *Publications:* Organic Peroxides, 1959; Organotin Chemistry, 1997, 2nd edn 2004; (ed jtly) Tin Chemistry, 2008; (with P. J. Garratt) UCL Chemistry Department 1828–1974, 2013; scientific papers on physical organic chemistry and organometallic chemistry in learned jls. *Address:* Chemistry Department, University College London, 20 Gordon Street, WC1H 0AJ. *T:* (020) 7679 4701. *E:* a.g.davies@ucl.ac.uk.

**DAVIES, Andrew;** see Davies, D. A.

**DAVIES, Andrew L.;** see Lloyd-Davies.

**DAVIES, Andrew Oswell Bede;** Chief Executive Officer, Kier Group, since 2019; *b* Wantage, 12 Oct. 1963; *m* Catherine Louise Hendry; two *s* one *d*. *Educ:* King Edward VI Sch., Norwich; Univ. of Sheffield (BA Hons Business Studies). With BAE Systems plc, 1985–2013 (Man. Dir, Land Systems Div.; Gp Strategy Dir and Mem., Exec. Cttee; Man. Dir, Maritime); CEO, Wates Gp, 2014–18. Non-exec. Dir, Chemring plc, 2016–.

**DAVIES, Andrew Robert Tudor;** Member (C) South Wales Central, National Assembly for Wales, since 2007; *b* 8 April 1968; *s* of Tudor John Davies and Margaret Elizabeth Rees Davies; *m* 1991, Julia Mary; two *s* two *d*. *Educ:* Balfour House Sch., St Athan; Wycliffe Coll., Stonehouse. Partner, family farming and agricl business. National Farmers Union: Chm., 2001, Pres., 2002, Glamorgan; Mem., Welsh Council, 2002–07; Mem., Nat. Combinable Crops Bd, 2004–07. Chm., Creative Rural Communities, 2003–04. Various positions in Cons. Party; Leader, Welsh Conservative Gp, 2011–18; Leader of Opposition, Nat. Assembly for Wales, 2011–16, 2017–18. Mem. (C), Vale of Glamorgan Council, 2019–. Gov., Llanfair Primary Sch., 2001–07. Chm., Llantrisant Young Farmers' Club,

1988. *Recreations:* work, travel, family. *Address:* Tudor Barn, The Garn Farm, St Hilary, Vale of Glamorgan CF71 7DP. *T:* 0300 200 7227. *E:* andrewrt.davies@assembly.wales. *Club:* Farmers (Glamorgan).

**DAVIES, Andrew Wynford;** writer; *b* Rhiwbina, Cardiff, 20 Sept. 1936; *e s* of Wynford and Hilda Davies; *m* 1960, Diana Lennox Huntley; one *s* one *d*. *Educ:* Whitchurch Grammar Sch., Cardiff; University College London. Teacher: St Clement Danes Grammar Sch., 1958–61; Woodberry Down Comprehensive Sch., 1961–63; Lecturer: Coventry Coll. of Educn, 1963–71; Univ. of Warwick, 1971–87. Hon. Fellow, Univ. of Wales, Cardiff, 1997. Hon. DLitt: Coventry, 1994; Warwick, 2004; UCL, 2006; Hon. DArts De Montfort, 2003; DUniv Open, 2004. Guardian Children's Fiction Award, 1979; Boston Globe Horn Award, 1979; BPG Award, 1980, 1990, 1995, 1997, 2000, 2006; Pye Colour TV Award, best children's writer, 1981; writer's awards: RTS, 1986–87, 2006; BAFTA, 1989, 1993, 1998, 2006 (Fellow 2002); Writers' Guild, 1991, 1992, 1996; Primetime Emmy, 1991. *Television includes:* To Serve Them All My Days, 1979; A Very Peculiar Practice, 1986–87; Mother Love, 1989; House of Cards, 1990; Filipina Dreamers, 1991; The Old Devils, Anglo-Saxon Attitudes, A Very Polish Practice, 1992; Anna Lee, Harnessing Peacocks, To Play the King, 1993; Middlemarch, 1994; Game On, Pride and Prejudice, The Final Cut, 1995; Emma, Moll Flanders, Wilderness, 1996; A Few Short Journeys of the Heart, Bill's New Frock, 1997; Getting Hurt, Vanity Fair, A Rather English Marriage, 1998; Wives and Daughters, 1999; Take a Girl Like You, 2000; Othello, The Way We Live Now, 2001; Tipping the Velvet, Dr Zhivago, Daniel Deronda, 2002; Boudica, 2003; He Knew He Was Right, 2004; Falling, Bleak House, 2005; The Chatterley Affair, The Line of Beauty, 2006; Northanger Abbey, The Diary of a Nobody, Fanny Hill, A Room With A View, 2007; Sense and Sensibility, Affinity, Sleep With Me, Little Dorrit (Emmy Award, 2009), 2008; South Riding, 2011; Mr Selfridge, 2013–15; Quirke, A Poet in New York, 2014; War and Peace, 2016; Les Misérables, 2018; Sanditon, 2019; *stage plays:* Rose, 1981; Prin, 1990; *film screenplays:* Circle of Friends, 1995; B. Monkey, 1996; Bridget Jones's Diary, The Tailor of Panama, 2001; Bridget Jones: The Edge of Reason, 2004; The Three Musketeers, 2011; *radio:* The Purple Land, 2011. *Publications: for children:* The Fantastic Feats of Dr Boox, 1972; Conrad's War, 1978; Marmalade and Rufus, 1980; Marmalade Atkins in Space, 1981; Educating Marmalade, 1982; Danger Marmalade at Work, 1983; Marmalade Hits the Big Time, 1984; Alfonso Bonzo, 1987; Marmalade on the Ball, 1995; (with Diana Davies): Poonam's Pets, 1990; Raj in Charge, 1994; *fiction:* A Very Peculiar Practice, 1986; The New Frontier, 1987; Getting Hurt, 1989; Dirty Faxes, 1990; B. Monkey, 1992. *Recreation:* lunch. *Address:* c/o The Agency, 24 Pottery Lane, W11 4LZ.

**DAVIES, Ven. Anthony;** see Davies, Ven. V. A.

**DAVIES, (Anthony) Roger;** a District Judge (Magistrates' Courts) (formerly Metropolitan Stipendiary Magistrate), 1985–2005; Chairman, Family Courts, 1989–2005; a Recorder, 1993–2005; *b* 1 Sept. 1940; *er s* of late R. George Davies and Megan Davies, Penarth, Glam; *m* 1967, Clare, *e d* of Comdr W. A. Walters, RN; twin *s* one *d*. *Educ:* Bridgend; King's Coll., London. LLB (Hons); AKC. Called to the Bar, Gray's Inn, 1965 (Lord Justice Holker Sen. Schol.). Practised at Bar, London and SE Circuit, 1965–85. *Recreations:* reading (history, biography), music (especially opera), travel, family life. *Club:* Travellers.

**DAVIES, Barry George,** MBE 2005; broadcaster, BBC Television sport and events; *b* 24 Oct. 1937; *s* of Roy Charles Davies and Dorothy Davies; *m* 1968, Edna (Penny) Pegna; one *s* one *d*. *Educ:* Cranbrook Sch., Kent; London Univ. (King's Coll. Royal Dental Hosp.). Commnd RASC, 1960. Sub-editor/reporter, The Times, 1963–66; Independent Television, 1966–69; commentator, World Cup 1966, Olympic Games 1968; joined BBC Television, 1969; commentator, Match of the Day, 1969–2004; commentator and presenter covering variety of sports, including: World Cup, 1970–2002; Olympic Games, 1972–2012; Winter Olympics, 1978–2006; Commonwealth Games, 1978–; Wimbledon, 1983–2018; University Boat Race, 1993–2004; commentator, LBC, University Boat Race, 2008–09; Pres. Boat Race World prog., 2010–; commentator, The Jump, Channel 4, 2014–17; guest commentator, Match of the Day 50th anniv., 2014. Commentator: Lord Mayor's Show, 1996–2003; (last) Royal Tournament, 1999; All the Queen's Horses, 2003. Presenter, Maestro Series, 1985–87. *Publications:* Interesting, Very Interesting: the autobiography, 2007. *Recreations:* family, theatre, political biographies, all sports (enthusiasm way ahead of talent), classical music. *Clubs:* Lord's Taverners; Hawks (Cambridge).

**DAVIES, (Beverley) Jane,** OBE 2010; self-employed management consultant in science parks and innovation, since 2012; Chief Executive, Manchester Science Parks Ltd, 2000–12; *b* Leeds, 3 June 1952; *d* of Peter Baxendale and Patricia Baxendale; *m* 1975, Wyn Davies. *Educ:* Lawnswood High Sch., Leeds; St Anne's Coll., Oxford (MA Chem.). Plant Chemist, BP Chemicals, 1974–81; Section Leader, Supply, BP Oil Internat., 1981–84; Crude Oil Trader, BP N America, 1984–86; Policy Planner, FCO, 1986–88 (on secondment); Sen. Consultant, BP Corp. Inf. Systems, 1988–91; Regl Manager, Air BP, 1991–92; self-employed mgt consultant, 1992–94; Gen. Manager, Buxton Fest., 1994–98. Non-exec. Dir, NI Sci. Park, 2013–. Mem., Project Adv. Bd, Sci. Park Graz, Austria, 2014–. Pres., Adv. Council, Internat. Assoc. of Sci. Parks, 2009–13. Cavaliere, Ordine al Merito (Italy), 2006. *Recreations:* Italy, theatre, opera, music, travel, eating good food with good friends. *E:* jane.davies@polidori.co.uk.

**DAVIES, Brian;** see Davies, E. B.

**DAVIES, Prof. Brian Lawrence,** PhD, DSc; FREng, FIMechE; Professor of Medical Robotics, Imperial College, London, since 2000; *b* 18 July 1939; *s* of William and Elizabeth Davies; *m* 1975, Marcia Mills; one *d*. *Educ:* Harrow Grammar Sch.; UCL (MPhil 1970); Imperial Coll., London (PhD 1995; DSc 2001). CEng 1973, FREng 2005; FIMechE 1990. GEC Ltd: indentured apprenticeship, 1955–60; design engr, 1960–63; Res. Asst in Mech. Engrg, 1963–69, Lectr, 1969–83, UCL; Lectr, 1983–89, Sen. Lectr, 1989–93, Reader, 1993–2000, in Mech. Engrg, Imperial Coll., London. Founder and Tech. Dir, Acrobot Co. Ltd, 1999–2010; Founder and Res. Dir, Signature Robot Ltd, 2018–. Institute of Mechanical Engineering: Mem. Bd, 1990–, Chm., 1998–2001, Med. Engrg Div.; Mem. Council, 1998–2001. Chm., Strategic Acad. Bd, Swiss Nat. Computer Aided Med. Engrg, 2001–13. *Publications:* Engineering Drawing and Computer Graphics, 1986; (jtly) Computer-aided Drawing and Design, 1991; Computer Integrated Surgery, 1995; over 200 refereed papers mainly on computer-aided surgery and med. robotics. *Recreations:* painting, walking. *Address:* Department of Mechanical Engineering, Imperial College, London, SW7 2AZ. *T:* (020) 7594 7054.

**DAVIES, Bryn,** CBE 1987 (MBE 1978); DL; Member, General Council, Wales Trades Union Congress, 1974–91 (Vice-Chairman, 1983–84, Chairman, 1984–85); *b* 22 Jan. 1932; *s* of Gomer and Ann Davies; *m* 1st, 1956, Esme Irene Gould (*d* 1988); two *s*; 2nd, 1991, Katherine Lewis. *Educ:* Cwmlai School, Tonyrefail. Served HM Forces (RAMC), 1949–51; Forestry Commn, 1951–56; South Wales and Hereford Organiser, Nat. Union of Agricultural and Allied Workers, subseq. TGWU (following merger), 1956–91. Chm., Mid Glamorgan AHA, 1978–94; Member: Welsh Council, 1965–81; Development Commn, 1975–81; Nat. Cttee (Wales), Forestry Commn, 1978–86; Nat. Water Council, 1982–85; Council, British Heart Foundn, 1986–. Trustee, Sir Geraint Evans Wales Heart Res. Inst. Patron, Mencap Jubilee Festival. DL Mid Glamorgan, 1992. *Recreations:* cricket, Rugby football. *Address:* 3 Lias Cottages, Porthcawl, Mid Glamorgan CF36 3AD. *T:* (01656) 785851. *Clubs:* Tonyrefail Rugby (Pres., 1985–88); Pyle and Kenfig Golf; Pyle Rugby; Pirates (Porthcawl).

**DAVIES, Byron,** OBE 2008; DL; CEng, FICE; FCMI; Managing Director, BD Consulting (UK) Ltd, since 2010; Welsh Government Commissioner, 2011; *b* 23 April 1947; *s* of Cecil and Elizabeth Gwendoline Davies; *m* 1972, Sarah Kay Lott; one *s* one *d*. *Educ:* Swansea Univ. (BSc Hons); Univ. of Glamorgan (MPhil). CEng 1976; FICE 1992. Work in private sector orgns, 1968–72; with Swansea CC and Devon CC, 1972–77; South Glamorgan County Council, 1977–90: various sen. civil engrg, property develt and gen. mgt posts; Dir, Property Services, 1990–92, Chief Exec., 1992–96; Chief Exec., Cardiff CC, 1996–2009. Director: Cardiff-Wales Airport, 1992–2009; Millennium Stadium plc, 1996–2009; Cardiff Chamber of Trade and Commerce, 1999–2009; Cardiff Marketing, 1999–2009; Cardiff Initiative, 1999–2009. Chm., Wales Internat. Business Council (formerly Wales N America Business Chamber), 2010–16. Clerk to Lieutenancy of S Glam, 1992–2009; Sec. to Lord Chancellor's Adv. Cttee for S Glam, 1992–2009. Sec., Soc. of Local Authority Chief Execs and Sen. Managers in Wales, 2004–09; Pres., Solace UK, 2007–08 (Jun. Vice-Pres., 2005–07); Pres., Union des Dirigeants Territoriaux de l'Europe, 2008–10 (Vice Pres., 2006–08). Ex-Officio Mem., Council and Court, Univ. of Wales, Cardiff, 1992. FCMI (FIMgt 1992); Pres., Cardiff Inst. of Mgt, 1999–2000. DL S Glamorgan, 2011. *Publications:* contrib. on engrg and mgt to professional jls. *Recreations:* walking, sport, cinema, photography. *Address:* The Cottage, Ystradowen, Cowbridge CF71 7SZ.

**DAVIES, Byron;** *see* Davies, H. B.

**DAVIES, Prof. Christine Tullis Hunter,** OBE 2006; PhD; FInstP; FRSE; Professor of Physics, University of Glasgow, since 1999; *b* Clacton, 19 Nov. 1959; *d* of Crawford Stewart and Elizabeth Stewart (*née* Clachan); *m* 1982, John Davies; two *d*. *Educ:* Colchester Co. High Sch. for Girls; Churchill Coll., Cambridge (BA 1981; PhD 1984). FInstP 1988. Postdoctoral res. associate, Cornell Univ., NY, 1984–86; SERC Advanced Fellow, 1987–93; Lectr, 1993–96, Reader, 1996–99, Univ. of Glasgow. Fulbright Schol. and Leverhulme Trust Fellow, Univ. of Calif at Santa Barbara, 1997–98. Science and Technology Facilities Council: Mem., Particle Physics Grants Panel (theory), 2006–09; Mem., Educn, Trng and Careers Cttee, 2006–09; Chair, Project Mgt Bd, Distributed Res. utilising Adv. Computing, High Performance Computing Facility, 2011–16; Mem., Sci. Bd, 2015–18; Mem., Physics Rev. Panel, Res. Council UK, 2008. Mem. Council, Inst. of Physics, 2007–11 (Chm., Diversity Cttee, 2007–11). FRSE 2001; Fellow, American Physical Soc., 2016. Rosalind Franklin Award, Royal Soc., 2005; Nuclear and Particle Physics Div. Prize, Inst. of Physics, 2011; Wolfson Res. Merit Award, Royal Soc., 2012–17. *Publications:* contrib. jls on theoretical particle physics. *Recreations:* walking, photography. *Address:* Department of Physics and Astronomy, University of Glasgow, Glasgow G12 8QQ. *T:* (0141) 330 4710.

**DAVIES, Christopher Graham, (Chris);** Member (Lib Dem) North West Region, England, European Parliament, 1999–2014 and since 2019; Director, CCS Alliance, since 2018; *b* 7 July 1954; *s* of Caryl St John Davies and Margaret (*née* McLeod); *m* 1979, Carol Hancox; one *d*. *Educ:* Cheadle Hulme Sch.; Gonville and Caius Coll., Cambridge (BA 1975, MA 1978); Univ. of Kent. Member: Liverpool City Council, 1980–84 (Chm., Housing Cttee, 1982–83); Oldham MBC, 1994–98. Manager: Public Affairs Div., Extel, 1983–85; Northern PR, Liverpool, 1985–87; Dir, Abercromby Consultancy Ltd, 1988–91; marketing and communications consultant, 1991–95; Sen. Consultant, Concept Communications, 1997–99. Contested (Lib Dem) Littleborough and Saddleworth, 1987, 1992. MP (Lib Dem) Littleborough and Saddleworth, July 1995–1997; contested (Lib Dem) Oldham East and Saddleworth, 1997. Leader, British Lib Dem MEPs, 2004–06; Lib Dem spokesman on envmt and climate change, 1999–2014; EP rapporteur on carbon capture and storage, 2008–14; Alliance of Liberals and Democrats for Europe co-ordinator, Cttee for Envmt, Food Safety and Public Health, 2008–14; Mem., Cttee for Fisheries, 2012–14; Secretary: All-Party Fish for the Future Gp, 2011–14; Carbon Capture and Storage Gp, 2013–14; Mem., delegn to Palestinian Legislative Council, 2004–14; Sub-Mem., delegn to Israel, 2009–14. Mem., UK Parly Adv. Gp on Carbon Capture and Storage, 2016. Sen. Advr, FleishmanHillard, Brussels, 2015–. Chm., NW Liberal Democrats, 2015. Contested (Lib Dem) NW England, EP, 2014. MEP of Year (Envmt), Parlt Mag., 2014; Parliamentarian of Year (MEP), Green Ribbon Pol Awards, 2015. *Recreations:* fell running, ultra distance running. *Address:* 4 Higher Kinders, Greenfield, Oldham OL3 7BH. *E:* chrisdavies@greenfield.org.uk.

**DAVIES, Christopher Paul;** *b* Swansea, 18 Aug. 1967; *s* of T. V. S. Davies and late M. G. Davies (*née* Morgan); *m* 2006, Elizabeth Mary Dwyer; two *d*. *Educ:* Morriston Sch., Swansea. Rural auctioneer and estate agent; Manager, Hay Vet. Gp, Hay-on-Wye, 2008–14. Mem., Brecon Beacons Nat. Park Authy, 2012–15. Asst Hon. Dir, Royal Welsh Show, 2014–. Mem. (C) Powys CC, 2012–15. MP (C) Brecon and Radnorshire, 2015–June 2019. PPS, Wales Office, 2018. Member: Envmt, Food and Rural Affairs Select Cttee, 2015–17; Welsh Affairs Cttee, 2015–19; Public Accounts Cttee, 2018–19; Chm., DEFRA Backbench Cttee, 2016–19; Chm., All Party Parly Gp on Forestry, 2015–19, on Soft Drinks Industry, 2016–19. Contested (C) Brecon and Radnorshire, Welsh Assembly, 2011. Gov., Gwernyfed High Sch., 2012–. *Recreation:* countryside activities. *Club:* Carlton.

**DAVIES, Prof. Colin;** architect and architectural writer; Professor of Architectural Theory, London Metropolitan University (formerly University of North London), 2005–12 (Professor, 2000–05); Arts Society Lecturer, since 2015; *b* 24 March 1948; *s* of John and Hazel Davies; *m* 1st, 1973, Diana Lamont (marr. diss.); one *s*; 2nd, 1992, Susan Wallington (marr. diss.). *Educ:* King Henry VIII Sch., Coventry; Oxford Polytechnic; Architectural Assoc.; University College London (MSc). AADip, RIBA. Asst Editor, Building Magazine, 1975–77; Associate Partner, Derek Stow and Partners, 1977–81; freelance journalist, 1981–88; Editor, Architects' Jl, 1989–90. Lecturer: Bartlett, Canterbury and Brighton Schs of Architecture, 1983–91; Univ. of North London, 1992–2000. *Publications:* High Tech Architecture, 1988; Century Tower, 1992; Hopkins, 1993; Commerzbank, Frankfurt, 1997; Hopkins 2, 2001; The Prefabricated Home, 2005; Key Houses of the Twentieth Century, 2006; Thinking About Architecture, 2010; A New History of Modern Architecture, 2017; contribs to arch. jls. *Recreation:* choral singing.

**DAVIES, Colin Godfrey,** CEng, FIET, FRAeS; Director (formerly Director General, Projects and Engineering), National Air Traffic Services, 1991–97; *b* 9 Nov. 1934; *s* of Thomas William Godfrey Davies and Kathleen Mabel Davies; *m* 1966, Enid Beryl Packham; two *s*. *Educ:* King's Sch., Bruton; Loughborough Univ. (BSc Hons 1964; BA Hons 2009). FIET (FIEE 1986); FRAeS 1995. RAF Flying Officer (Aircrew), 1952–54. Cable and Wireless, 1955–90: Radio Technician, 1955–59; student, 1960–64; Special Projects Engr, Engr-in-Chief's Dept, 1964–68; Project Manager, 1968–75; Manager Transmission, Omantel, 1975–76; Manager Engrg, Fintel, 1976–77; Chief Engr Long Distance Services, Emirtel, 1978–79; Manager Internat. Services, 1980–82, Gen. Manager, 1983–87, Qatar; Dir of Corporate Technology and of two associated cos, 1987–90; Dep. Dir, Communications, NATS, 1990–91. Sen. Advr, Frequentis, Vienna, 1998–2003. *Recreations:* sport (badminton, sailing, ski-ing), gardening, photography. *Address:* Ibex House, Church Lane, Worplesdon, Guildford, Surrey GU3 3RU. *T:* (01483) 233214.

**DAVIES, Cynog Glyndwr;** *see* Dafis, C. G.

**DAVIES, Dai;** *see* Davies, David Clifford.

**DAVIES, Dr David;** Director: Elmhirst Trust, 1987–2002; Open College of the Arts, 1989–99 (Administrative Director, 1988–89); *b* 11 Aug. 1939; *s* of late Trefor Alun and Kathleen Elsie Davies; *m* 1968, Joanna Rachel, *d* of late David Brian Peace, MBE; one *s* three *d*. *Educ:* Nottingham High Sch.; Peterhouse, Cambridge. MA, PhD. Res. Scientist, Dept of Geophysics, Cambridge, 1961–69; Leader, Seismic Discrimination Gp, MIT Lincoln Laboratory, 1970–73; Editor of Nature, 1973–79; Dir, Dartington N Devon Trust, 1980–87. Rapporteur, Seismic Study Gp of Stockholm Internat. Peace Res. Inst. (SIPRI), 1968–73; Chm., British Seismic Verification Res. Project, 1987–91. Member: Warnock Cttee on artificial human fertilisation, 1982–84; BMA Working Party on Surrogacy, 1988–89. Chm., Ivanhoe Trust, 1986–2001. Member Council: Internat. Disaster Inst., 1979; Beaford Arts Centre, 1980–87; Voluntary Arts Network, 1992–95; Trustee: Bristol Exploratory, 1983–90; Cooper Art Gall., Barnsley, 1994–2001; Yorks Organiser, Open Coll. of the Arts, 1987–89. Musical Director: Blackheath Opera Workshop, 1977–79; Winterbourne Opera, 2006–12; Conductor: Exmoor Chamber Orch., 1980–87; Cross Keys Orch., 2014–; Member: Musica Rustica, 2002–; Cross Keys Ensemble, 2006–13; Salisbury Baroque, 2010–; Producer: Ebblesway Opera, 2004–05; Opera at Chilmark, 2006–. Hon. Lectr, Bretton Hall Coll., 1987–2001. Hon. Fellow: Univ. of Leicester, 1988; Univ. of Leeds, 1989. *Publications:* Seismic Methods for Monitoring Underground Explosions, 1968; numerous scientific papers. *Recreation:* keyboard playing.

**DAVIES, (David) Andrew;** Chairman, Abertawe Bro Morgannwg University Health Board, 2013–19; *b* 5 May 1952; *s* of Wallace Morton Davies and Elizabeth Muriel Jane Davies (*née* Baldwin); *m* 1978, Deborah Frost (marr. diss. 1991). *Educ:* UC, Swansea (BSc Econ 1979; PGCE 1981); Gwent Coll. of Higher Educn (Dip. Counselling). Lectr in Adult and Further Educn, Swansea Univ., WEA and Swansea Coll., 1980–84; Regl Official, Wales Labour Party, 1984–91; Head of Employee Develt and Assistance Prog., Ford Motor Co., 1991–96; Lectr, Swansea Coll., 1994–97; Special Projects Officer (Referendum), Wales Labour Party, 1997–98; Associate Dir, Welsh Context, 1998–99. National Assembly for Wales: Mem. (Lab) Swansea West, 1999–2011; Chief Whip, Labour Gp, 1999–2000; Business Manager, then Minister for Assembly Business, 1999–2002; Minister: for Econ. Develt, 2002–06; for Transport, 2003–06; for Enterprise, Innovation and Networks, 2006–07; for Social Justice and Public Service Delivery, 2007; for Finance and Public Service Delivery, 2007–09. Strategic Advr, Swansea Univ., 2012. Chairman: National Dance Co. Wales, 2010–16; Welsh Commn on Co-operatives and Mutuals, 2012–15. Trustee, Charity Bank, 2010–13. *Recreations:* bird watching, cooking, gardening, the arts (especially contemporary dance and film).

**DAVIES, David Clifford, (Dai);** community worker in training and education, Blaenau Gwent; *b* 26 Nov. 1959; *m* 1996, Amanda Gearing; one *s*. *Educ:* secondary sch.; served electrical apprenticeship. Steelworker, British Steel, subseq. Corus, Blaenau Gwent, 1976–2002; work with trade unions, 2002–05. Researcher for Peter Law, MP, 2005–06. MP (Ind) Blaenau Gwent, June 2006–2010; contested (People's Voice) same seat, 2010. Mem. (Ind), Blaenau Gwent CBC, 2017–.

**DAVIES, Sir David (Evan Naunton),** Kt 1994; CBE 1986; PhD, DSc; FRS 1984; FREng; Chairman, Hazard Forum, 2003–10; President, Royal Academy of Engineering, 1996–2001; *b* 28 Oct. 1935; *s* of David Evan Davies and Sarah (*née* Samuel); *m* 1st, 1962, Enid Patilla (*d* 1990); two *s*; 2nd, 1992, Jennifer E., (Jenna), Rayner. *Educ:* Univ. of Birmingham (MSc 1958; PhD 1960; DSc 1968). FIET (FIEE 1969); FIERE 1975; FREng (FEng 1979). Lectr and Sen. Lectr in Elec. Engrg, Univ. of Birmingham, 1961–67 (also Hon. SPSO, RRE, Malvern, 1966–67); Asst Dir of Elec. Res., BR Bd, Derby, 1967–71; Vis. Industrial Prof. of Elec. Engrg, Loughborough Univ. of Technol., 1969–71; University College London: Prof. of Elec. Engrg, 1971–88; Pender Prof. and Hd of Dept of Electronic and Electrical Engrg, 1985–88; Vice-Provost, 1986–88; Vice-Chancellor, Loughborough Univ. of Technology, 1988–93; Chief Scientific Advr, MoD, 1993–99. Chm., Railway Safety, 2001–03; Safety Advr, Nat. Grid plc (formerly Nat. Grid Transco), 2002–08. Non-executive Director: Gaydon Technology (Rover Group), 1986–88; Loughborough Consultants, 1988–93; Inst. Consumer Ergonomics, 1988–93; ERA Technology, 1996–2003; Lattice plc, 2000–02; ERA Foundn, 2002–07. Member: SERC, 1985–89; IT Adv. Bd, DTI, 1988–91; EPSRC, 1994–99; Bd, POST, 2006–; Chm., Defence Scientific Adv. Council, 1992–93. Mem. Council, Imperial Soc. Kts Bachelor, 2013–16. Pres., IEE, 1994–95; Vice Pres., Royal Acad. of Engrg, 1995–96. Pro Chancellor, Univ. of Sussex, 1998–2001. Liveryman, Engineers' Co., 1995 (Master Engineer, 2003–04). Hon. FIChemE 1997; Hon. FIMechE 1998; Hon. FIStructE 2001; Hon. FIEE 2002; Hon. Fellow UCL, 2006. Hon DSc: Birmingham, Loughborough, South Bank, 1994; Bradford, 1995; Surrey, 1996; Bath, Warwick, 1997; Heriot-Watt, 1999; Wales, 2002; Hon. DEng UMIST 2000. Rank Prize for Optoelectronics, 1984; Callendar Medal, Inst. of Measurement & Control, 1984; Faraday Medal, IEE, 1987; President's Medal, RAEng, 2006. *Publications:* technical papers and articles on radar, antennae and aspects of fibre optics. *Address:* Church Hill House, Church Lane, Danehill, Haywards Heath, W Sussex RH17 7EY. *T:* (01825) 790321.

**DAVIES, (David) Ian,** MA; Headmaster, Brentwood School, since 2004; *b* 17 May 1959; *s* of Dillwyn and Morfydd Davies; *m* 1989, Sara Stern. *Educ:* St John's Coll., Oxford (MA 1980); Fitzwilliam Coll., Cambridge (PGCE 1981). Hd, Lower Sch., Latymer Upper Sch., 1992–98; Headmaster, St Dunstan's Coll., 1998–2004. Boarding Headmaster, Admiralty Bd, 2000–04; Ind. Schs Advr to Duke of Edinburgh's Award Scheme, 2004–13. Chm., London Div. (S), HMC, 2002, 2017. Chm., Brentwood Th. Trust, 2009–19. Gov., St Aubyn's Prep. Sch., Woodford Green, 2006–18. Liveryman, Co. of Wax Chandlers. *Recreations:* golf, tennis, cricket, reading, France. *Address:* Brentwood School, Brentwood, Essex CM15 8EE. *T:* (01277) 243243, *Fax:* (01277) 243299. *E:* headmaster@brentwood.essex.sch.uk. *Clubs:* East India, National Liberal, Lansdowne.

**DAVIES, Sir David (John),** Kt 1999; *b* 1 April 1940; *s* of late Stanley Kenneth Davies, CBE and Stephanie Davies; *m* 1st, 1967, Deborah Frances Loeb (marr. diss.); one *s*; 2nd, 1985, Linda Wong Lin-Tye (marr. diss.); one *s* two *d*. *Educ:* Winchester Coll., Winchester; New Coll., Oxford (MA; Hon. Fellow 2015); Harvard Business Sch. (AMP). Chase Manhattan Bank, 1963–67; Hill Samuel Group, 1967–73: Dir, Hill Samuel Inc., New York, 1970–73; Dir, Hill Samuel Ltd, London, 1973; Finance Dir, 1973–83, and Vice-Chm., 1977–83, MEPC Ltd; Man. Dir, The Hongkong Land Co. Ltd, 1983–86; Director: Jardine Matheson Gp, 1983–86; Hong Kong Electric Co., 1983–86; Chairman: Hong Kong Land Property Co. Ltd, 1983–86; Mandarin Oriental Hotel Gp, 1983–86; Dairy Farm Ltd, 1983–86; Dir, 1986–88, Chief Exec. and Exec. Vice Chm., 1987–88, Hill Samuel Gp; Jt Chm., Hill Samuel & Co., 1987–88. Chm., 1990–98, Chief Exec., 1994–98, Johnson Matthey plc. Chairman: Wire Ropes Ltd, Wicklow, 1979–; Imry Merchant Developers (formerly Imry Internat.), 1987–89; Imry Holdings, 1992–98; MBO Partners Ltd, HK, 1992–2000; Semara (formerly Sketchley) PLC, 1990–2000; EFG Private Bank Ltd, 199–2006; Dep. Chm., Charter Consolidated, 1988–89; Director: American Barrick Resources Corp., Toronto, 1986–94; Delaware North Cos Inc., Buffalo, NY, 1986–2017; Singapore Land Ltd, 1986–90; Fitzwilton PLC, Dublin, 1987–90; Asia Securities, Hong

Kong, 1987–89; Hardwicke Ltd, Dublin, 1987–2007; TSB Group, 1987–89; First Pacific Co., Hong Kong, 1988–91; Irish Life Assce, 1991–97; The Wharf (Holdings) Ltd, Hong Kong, 1992–99; Wheelock NatWest, 1994–97; Glyndebourne Productions Ltd, 1990–2000; Hilton Gp (formerly Ladbroke Gp) plc, 1997–2001; General Enterprise Mgt Services Ltd, 1998–2001; European Financial Gp, EFG (Luxembourg) SA, 2006–12; Gluskin Sheff and Associates, Toronto, 2007–08. Chm., Adv. Cttee on Business and the Envmt, 1995–98 (Mem., 1993–98); Dep. Chm., Prince of Wales' Business Leaders Forum, 1997–98 (Dir, 1991–96); Mem., Prince of Wales Business and the Envmt Prog., 1993–99. Member: Council, Ireland Fund of GB, 1988–2002; Bd, Wales Millennium Centre, 2004–10; Governing Council, Centre for Study of Financial Innovation, 2004–13; Chm., Global Leadership Foundn, UK, 2008–. Director: Irish Georgian Soc., 2002–09 (Pres., 2015); Everard Read Gall., 2005–14. Chm., Wexford Fest. UK Trust, 1997–; Pres., Wexford Fest. Trust, 2014–; Chm., Grange Park Opera, 1998–2005 (Chm., Adv. Council, 2005–; Trustee and Jt Chm. of Appeal, 2015–); Vice-Pres., Leeds Internat. Piano Comp., 2004–12. Chairman: Irish Heritage Trust, 2006–12; Develt Bd, Saïd Business Sch., Univ. of Oxford, 2007–10; Member: Adv. Cttee for Fund Raising, Ashmolean Mus., 1991–96; New Coll. Develt Fund, 1995–2016 (Chm., 2007–16; Mem., New Coll. Endowment Cttee, 1994–2007); Winchester Coll. Develt Council, 2002–08; Dep. Chm., Campaign for Oxford, 2008–10; Trustee: Anglo-Hong Kong Trust, 1989–2004; Monteverdi Trust, 1991–97; Royal Opera House Trust, 1997–2001 (Mem., Appeal Cttee, 1997–2001); St Catherine Foundn, 2001–17; World Monuments Fund in Britain, 2002–07; Cape Town Opera, 2004–11. *Recreations:* trees, reading, opera. *Address:* 1712 Tower One Times Square, 1 Matheson Street, Hong Kong. *Clubs:* Beefsteak, Garrick; All England Lawn Tennis; Kildare Street and University (Dublin); Hong Kong, China (Hong Kong).

**DAVIES, His Honour David Theodore Alban;** a Circuit Judge, 1994–2007; *b* 8 June 1940; *s* of late John Rhys Davies, Archdeacon of Merioneth, and Mabel Aeronwy Davies; *m* 1966, Janet Mary, *er d* of late Frank and Barbara Welburn, Cheadle Hulme, Cheshire; one *s* one *d*. *Educ:* Rossall School (Scholar); Magdalen College, Oxford (Exhibnr, 2nd cl. Mods 1960, 1st cl. Lit.Hum., 1962, BA 1962; Eldon Law Schol., 1963; MA 1967). Called to the Bar, Gray's Inn, 1964 (Entrance Schol., Arden Atkin and Mould Prize, Lord Justice Holker Sen. Schol.). Practised SE Circuit, 1965–83; Registrar, then a Dist Judge, Family Div., High Court, 1983–94; a Recorder, 1989–94; Designated Family Judge, Rhyl County Court, 1994–2007. Chancellor, dio. of Bangor, 1995–2012. Sec., Family Law Bar Assoc., 1976–80, Treasurer, 1980–83; Member: Senate Law Reform Cttee, 1979–83; Civil and Family Cttee, 1988–93, Main Bd, 1991–93, Judicial Studies Bd. *Publications:* (ed jtly) Jackson's Matrimonial Finance and Taxation, 2nd edn 1975, 5th edn 1992. *Recreations:* reading, walking, history. *Address:* c/o Prestatyn Justice Centre, Victoria Road, Prestatyn, Denbighshire LL19 7TE.

**DAVIES, David Thomas Charles;** MP (C) Monmouth, since 2005; *b* 26 June 1970; *s* of Peter Hugh Charles Davies and Kathleen Diane Davies (*née* Elton); *m* 2003, Aliz Harnisföger; one *s* two *d*. *Educ:* Clytha Sch., Newport; Bassaleg Sch., Newport. MInstTA; MILog; MIFF. BSC, 1988–89; Australia, 1989–91; Gen. Manager, Tea Importing and Shipping Co. (family business), 1991–99. Chm., Welsh Affairs Select Cttee, 2010–. Mem. (C) Monmouth, Nat. Assembly for Wales, 1999–2007. Contested (C) Bridgend, 1997. *Recreations:* running, surfing, white collar boxing (incl. charity bouts as 'The Tory Tornado'), salsa dancing, debunking climate change alarmism. *Address:* (constituency office) The Grange, 16 Maryport Street, Usk, Monmouthshire NP15 1AB; House of Commons, SW1A 0AA. *Clubs:* Abergavenny Conservative; Chepstow Conservative; Monmouth Conservative; Usk Conservative.

**DAVIES, Deborah;** see Arnott, D.

**DAVIES, Dickie;** television sports presenter, since 1964; *s* of Owen John Davies and Ellen Davies; *m* 1962, Elisabeth Ann Hastings Mann; twin *s*. *Educ:* William Ellis Sch., Highgate; Oldershaw Grammar Sch., Wallasey, Cheshire. Purser, Cunard Line, 1953–60; Television Announcer, Southern TV, 1960–63; World of Sport Presenter, 1964–85, Presenter: ITV Sport, 1985–89; Sportsmasters, 1988–92; The World of Golf, 1990; Classic FM, 1995–; Bobby Charlton's Football Scrapbook, Sky Sports TV, 1995–; Dickie Davies's Sporting Heroes, 1998–; World Cup Classics, 1999. *Recreations:* golf, walking our dogs.

**DAVIES, Donald,** CBE 1978 (OBE 1973); consultant; *b* 13 Feb. 1924; *s* of late Wilfred Lawson Davies and Alwyne Davies; *m* 1948, Mabel (*née* Hellyar) (*d* 2010); two *d*. *Educ:* Ebbw Vale Grammar Sch.; UC Cardiff (BSc). CEng, FIMinE. National Coal Board: Colliery Man., 1951–55; Gp Man., 1955–58; Dep. Prodn Man., 1958–60; Prodn Man., 1960–61; Area Gen. Man., 1961–67; Area Dir, 1967–73; Bd Mem., 1973–84; Chairman: Nat. Fuel Distributors, 1973–89; Southern Depot Co., 1973–89; NCB (Ancillaries), 1979–89; Horizon Exploration, 1981–89. *Recreations:* golf, walking. *Address:* Wendy Cottage, Dukes Wood Avenue, Gerrards Cross, Bucks SL9 7LA. *T:* (01753) 885083.

**DAVIES, Rev. Prof. Douglas James,** PhD, DLitt; FBA 2017; Professor in the Study of Religion, since 2000, and Director, Centre for Death and Life Studies, since 2007, University of Durham (Head, Department of Theology, 2002–05); *b* 11 Feb. 1947; *s* of Llewelyn James Davies and Gladys Evelyn Davies (*née* Morgan). *Educ:* Lewis Sch., Pengam; St John's Coll., Durham (BA Anthropology 1969; BA Theology 1973); St Peter's Coll., Oxford (MLitt 1972); PhD Nottingham 1980; DLitt Oxon 2004. Ordained deacon 1975; priest 1976; University of Nottingham: Lectr in Theology, 1974–90; Sen. Lectr, 1990–93; Prof. of Religious Studies, 1993–97; Principal, Coll. of St Hild and St Bede, and Prof. of Theol., Univ. of Durham, 1997–2000. Vis. Res. Fellow, Rothermere American Inst., Oxford Univ., 2006; Mayers Fellow, Huntington Library, Calif, 2007; Res. Fellow, Collegium for Advanced Studies, Helsinki Univ., 2011; Vis. Fellow, Harris Manchester Coll., Oxford, 2014. Pres., British Assoc. for Study of Religion, 2009–12; Hon. Vice-Pres., Cremation Soc. of GB, 2017–. FAcSS (AcSS 2009). FLSW 2012. Hon. DTheol Uppsala, 1998. SBStJ 2011. *Publications:* Meaning and Salvation in Religious Studies, 1984; Mormon Spirituality, 1987; (jtly) Church and Religion in Rural England, 1991; Frank Byron Jevons: an evolutionary realist, 1991; (jtly) Reusing Old Graves, 1995; (ed) Mormon Identities in Transition, 1996; Death, Ritual and Belief, 1997, 3rd edn 2017; The Mormon Culture of Salvation, 2000; Private Passions, 2000; Anthropology and Theology, 2002; Introduction to Mormonism, 2003; A Brief History of Death, 2004; (ed jtly) Encyclopedia of Cremation, 2005; (jtly) Studying Local Churches, 2005; (jtly) Bishops, Wives and Children: spiritual capital across the generations, 2007; The Theology of Death, 2008; Joseph Smith, Jesus and Satanic Opposition: atonement, evil and the Mormon vision, 2010; Emotion, Identity and Religion: hope, reciprocity and otherness, 2011; (ed jtly) Emotion, Identity and Death: mortality across disciplines, 2012; (jtly) Natural Burial: traditional-secular spiritualities and funeral innovation, 2012; (ed) Emotions and Religious Dynamics, 2013; (ed jtly) Sacred Selves, Sacred Settings: reflecting Hans Mol, 2015; Mors Britannica: lifestyle and death-style in Britain today, 2015; (jtly) Cremation in Modern Scotland, History, Architecture and the Law, 2017. *Recreations:* squash, cacti, gardening. *Address:* Department of Theology and Religion, Abbey House, Palace Green, Durham DH1 3RS. *Club:* Royal Over-Seas League.

**DAVIES, Edward;** QC 2017; *b* Dorking, 24 Aug. 1974; *s* of John Hamilton Davies, *qv*; *m* 2000, Lucy Palmer; two *d*. *Educ:* Felsted Sch.; Peterhouse, Cambridge (BA); St Edmund Hall, Oxford (BCL). Called to the Bar, Inner Temple, 1998. Chm., Nat. Eczema Soc. *Recreations:* running, cycling, swimming, birdwatching. *Address:* Erskine Chambers, 33 Chancery Lane, WC2A 1EN. *T:* (020) 7242 5532. *E:* clerks@erskinechambers.com.

**DAVIES, Prof. (Edward) Brian,** DPhil; FRS 1995; Professor of Mathematics, King's College London, 1981–2010, now Emeritus; *b* 13 June 1944; *s* of Arthur Granville Davies and Mary Davies (*née* Scudamore); *m* 1968, Jane Christine Phillips; one *s* one *d*. *Educ:* Jesus Coll., Oxford (BA 1965; MA); Merton Coll., Oxford; Brasenose Coll., Oxford (DPhil Maths 1968). Tutorial Fellow, St John's Coll., Oxford, 1970–81; Univ. Lectr, Oxford Univ., 1973–81; Head, Dept of Maths, KCL, 1990–93; FKC 1996. Pres., London Mathematical Soc., 2007–09. Editor, Qly Jl of Mathematics, 1973–81; Founding Editor: London Mathematical Soc. Student Text Series, 1983–90; Jl of Spectral Theory, 2011–14. *Publications:* Quantum Theory of Open Systems, 1976; One-Parameter Semigroups, 1980; Heat Kernels and Spectral Theory, 1989; Spectral Theory and Differential Operators, 1995; Science in the Looking Glass, 2003; Linear Operators and Their Spectra, 2007; Why Beliefs Matter, 2010. *Recreations:* family, scientific reading, archaeology. *E:* brian@users.org.uk.

**DAVIES, (Edward) Hunter,** OBE 2014; author, journalist; *b* Renfrew, Scotland, 7 Jan. 1936; *s* of late John Hunter Davies and Marion (*née* Brechin); *m* 1960, Margaret Forster, author (*d* 2016); one *s* two *d*. *Educ:* Creighton Sch., Carlisle; Carlisle Grammar Sch.; University Coll., Durham (BA 1957, DipEd 1958; Hon. Fellow 2007; Editor of Palatinate). Reporter: Manchester Evening Chronicle, 1958–59; Sunday Graphic, London, 1959–60; Sunday Times, 1960–84: Atticus, 1965–67; Chief Feature Writer, 1967; Editor, Sunday Times Magazine, 1975–77; Columnist: Punch, 1979–89; Stamp News, 1981–86; London Evening Standard, 1987; The Independent, 1989–93; New Statesman & Society, 1996–; Money section, Sunday Times, 1999–; Cumbria Life, 2008–. Presenter, Bookshelf, Radio 4, 1983–86. Mem., British Library Consultative Gp on Newspapers, 1987–89; Dir, Edinburgh Book Festival Bd, 1990–95; Chm., Cumbria Wildlife Trust, 1995–2008. Dep. Pro-Chancellor, Lancaster Univ., 1996–97. *Television:* The Playground (play), 1967; The Living Wall, 1974; George Stephenson, 1975; A Walk in the Lakes, 1979. Outstanding Achievement Award, Carnegie Sporting Words Awards, 2008. *Publications: fiction:* Here We Go, Round the Mulberry Bush, 1965 (filmed, 1968); The Rise and Fall of Jake Sullivan, 1970; (ed) I Knew Daisy Smuten, 1970; A Very Loving Couple, 1971; Body Charge, 1972; Flossie Teacake's Fur Coat, 1982; Flossie Teacake—Again!, 1983; Flossie Teacake Strikes Back, 1984; Come on Ossie!, 1985; Ossie Goes Supersonic, 1986; Ossie the Millionaire, 1987; Saturday Night, 1989; S.T.A.R.S (12 books in Penguin series), 1989–90; Snotty Bumstead, 1991; Striker, 1992; Snotty Bumstead and the Rent-a-Mum, 1993; Snotty the Hostage, 1995; Flossie Wins the Lottery, 1996; Flossie Teacake's Holiday, 2000; *non-fiction:* The Other Half, 1966; (ed) The New London Spy, 1966; The Beatles, 1968, illus. edn 2002, 3rd edn 2009; The Glory Game, 1972, 4th edn 2000; A Walk Along the Wall, 1974, 2nd edn 1984; George Stephenson, 1975, 2nd edn 2004; The Creighton Report, 1976; (ed) Sunday Times Book of Jubilee Year, 1977; A Walk Around the Lakes, 1979, 2nd edn 2000; William Wordsworth, 1980, 3rd edn 2009; The British Book of Lists, 1980; The Grades, 1981; Father's Day, 1981 (television series, 1983); Beaver Book of Lists, 1981; A Walk Along the Tracks, 1982, 2nd edn 2002; England!, 1982; (with Frank Herrmann) Great Britain: a celebration, 1982; A Walk Round London Parks, 1983; The Joy of Stamps, 1983; London at its Best, 1984; (also publisher) The Good Guide to the Lakes, 1984, 6th edn 2003; The Grand Tour, 1986; The Good Quiz Book to the Lakes, 1987; Back in the USSR, 1987; Beatrix Potter's Lakeland, 1988; My Life in Football, 1990; In Search of Columbus, 1991; Teller of Tales: in search of Robert Louis Stevenson, 1994; Hunting People: thirty years of interviews with the famous, 1994; Wainwright: the biography, 1995; Living on the Lottery, 1996; Born 1900, 1998; London to Loweswater, 1999; Dwight Yorke, 1999; A Walk Around the West Indies, 2000; Joe Kinnear: still crazy, 2000; The Quarrymen, 2001; The Eddie Stobart Story, 2001; Hurry, Hurry While Stocks Last, 2001; The Best of Lakeland, 2002; Relative Strangers, 2003; Boots, Balls and Haircuts, 2003; The Fan (anthol.), 2003; (jtly) Gazza—My Story, 2004; The Best of Wainwright, 2004; Strong Lad Wanted for Strong Lass, 2004; Mean With Money (anthol.), 2005; (jtly) Being Gazza, 2006; I Love Football, 2006; The Beatles, Football and Me: a memoir, 2006; The Second Half (anthol.), 2006; (jtly) Wayne Rooney, 2006; The Bumper Book of Football, 2007; (jtly) Prezza: my story - pulling no punches, 2008; Cold Meat and How to Disguise It, 2009; Confessions of a Collector, 2009; Behind the Scenes at the Museum of Baked Beans, 2010; Postcards from the Edge of Football, 2010; (ed) The Wainwright Letters, 2011; (ed) Sellafield Stories: life with Britain's first nuclear plant, 2012; (ed) The John Lennon Letters, 2012; The Biscuit Girls, 2014; The Beatles Lyrics, 2014; The Co-op's Got Bananas, 2016; The Beatles Book, 2016; Lakeland: a personal journey, 2016; A Life in the Day, 2017; (ed) Diary of an Unknown Schoolgirl, 2017; My Cumbria Life, 2018; Happy Old Me, 2019. *Recreation:* breathing. *Address:* 11 Boscastle Road, NW5 1EE.

**DAVIES, Emrys Thomas,** CMG 1988; HM Diplomatic Service, retired; *b* 8 Oct. 1934; *s* of Evan William Davies and Dinah Davies (*née* Jones); *m* 1960, Angela Audrey, *er d* of late Paul Robert Buchan May, ICS and of Esme May; one *s* two *d*. *Educ:* Parmiters Foundation Sch. RAF, 1953–55; commnd RAFVR, 1955. Sch. of Slavonic Studies, Cambridge Univ., 1954; Sch. of Oriental and African Studies, London Univ., 1955–56. Served Peking, 1956–59; FO, 1959–60; Bahrain, 1960–62; FO, 1962–63; Asst Political Adviser to Hong Kong Govt, 1963–68; First Sec., British High Commn, Ottawa, 1968–71; FCO, 1972–76; Commercial Counsellor, Peking, 1976–78 (Chargé, 1976 and 1978); Oxford Univ. Business Summer Sch., 1977; NATO Defense Coll., Rome, 1979; Dep. High Comr, Ottawa, 1979–82; Overseas Inspector, FCO, 1982–84; Dep. UK Perm. Rep. to OECD, and Counsellor (Econ. and Financial) to UK Delegn, Paris, 1984–87; Ambassador to Hanoi, 1987–90; High Comr, Barbados, Grenada, St Lucia, Dominica, Antigua and Barbuda, St Vincent and the Grenadines, and St Kitts and Nevis, 1990–94; Hd, UK Delegn to EC Monitoring Mission to former Yugoslavia, 1995 and 1998–99. Sec. Gen., Tripartite Commn for Restitution of Monetary Gold, Brussels, 1995–98. Appointments Advr to Welsh Office, 1997–2002; Pol Advr, EU Police Mission to Bosnia and Herzegovina, 2003. *Club:* Royal Air Force.

**DAVIES, Dr Ernest Arthur;** JP; management consultant and lecturer, retired 1987; *b* 25 Oct. 1926; *s* of Dan Davies and Ada (*née* Smith), Nuneaton; *m* 1st, 1956, Margaret Stephen Tait Gatt (marr. diss. 1967), *d* of H. Gatt, Gamesley, near Glossop; no *c*; 2nd, 1972, Patricia (marr. diss. 1980), *d* of S. Bates, Radford, Coventry; no *c*. *Educ:* Coventry Jun. Techn. Coll.; Westminster Trng Coll., London; St Salvator's Coll., University of St Andrews; St John's Coll., Cambridge. PhD Cantab 1959; MInstP 1959, CPhys 1986. RAF Aircraft Apprentice, 1942–43 (discharged on med. grounds). Westminster Trng Coll., 1946–48; Teacher, Foxford Sch., Coventry, 1948–50; University of St Andrews, 1950–54 (1st cl. hons Physics, Neil Arnott Prize, Carnegie Schol.); subseq. research in superconductivity, Royal Society Mond Lab., Cambridge; AEI Research Scientist, 1957–63; Lectr in Physics, Faculty of Technology, University of Manchester, 1963–66; Management Selection Consultant, MSL, 1970–81; Lectr in Business Studies, Hammersmith and West London Coll., 1981–87. MP (Lab) Stretford, 1966–70; Parliamentary Private Secretary to: PMG (Mr Edward Short), Nov.–Dec. 1967; Foreign Secretary (Mr George Brown), Jan.–March 1968; Foreign and

Commonwealth Sec. (Mr Michael Stewart), 1968–69; Jt Parly Sec., Min. of Technology, 1969–70. Co-Vice-Chm., Parly Labour Party's Defence and Services Group; Mem., Select Cttee on Science and Technology, 1966–67, 1967–68, 1968–69; Parly Deleg. to 24th Gen. Assembly of UN (UK Rep. on 4th Cttee). Councillor: Borough of Stretford, 1961–67; Borough of Southwark, 1974–82. JP Lancs, 1962, Inner London, 1972. *Publications*: contribs to Proc. Royal Society, Jl of Physics and Chem. of Solids. *Recreations*: reading, art and design practice, writing family history. *Address*: 43 Frensham Drive, Nuneaton, Warwickshire CV10 9QH.

DAVIES, Prof. (Eurfil) Rhys, CBE 1990; FRCR, FRCPE; FFR (RCSI); FDSRCS; Professor of Clinical Radiology (formerly Radiodiagnosis), University of Bristol, 1981–93; *b* 18 April 1929; *s* of late Daniel Haydn Davies and Mary Davies; *m* 1962, Zoë Doreen Chamberlain (*d* 2019); three *s*. *Educ*: Rhondda Grammar Sch.; Llandovery Coll.; Clare Coll., Cambridge (MB, BChir 1953; MA); St Mary's Hosp., London. FRCR (FFR 1964); FRCPE 1971; FFR (RCSI) 1978; FDSRCS 1989. Served RAMC, 1954–56 (Regtl MO 24 Regt). Sen. Registrar, St Mary's Hosp., 1963–66; Consultant Radiologist, United Bristol Hosps, 1966–81; Clinical Lectr, 1972–81, Hd, Clinical Sch., 1992–93, Univ. of Bristol. Vis. Sen. Lectr, Lagos Univ., 1971; Mayne-Guest Vis. Prof., Queensland Univ., 1982. Civilian Cons. Advr to RN, 1989–94. Mem., Bristol and Weston DHA, 1983–86. Member: Admin of Radio Active Substances Adv. Cttee, DHSS, 1978–83; Clin. Standards Adv. Cttee, 1991–93; GMC, 1989–93; Ionising Radiation Adv. Cttee, HSC, 1995–97 (Mem., Working Gp, 1987–95). Royal Coll. of Radiologists: Sen. Examr, 1973–74; Mem., Fellowship Bd, 1974–76; Registrar, 1976–81; Chm., Examining Bd, 1981–84; Warden of the Fellowship, 1984–86; Pres., 1986–89; Chm., Nuclear Medicine Cttee, 1972–78; Knox Lectr, 1990. Pres., Nuclear Medicine Soc., 1974–76 (Sec., 1972–74); Chm., Inter Collegiate Standing Cttee for Nuclear Medicine, 1982–84 (Sec., 1980–82). *Publications*: (contrib.) Textbook of Radiology, ed Sutton, 1969, Associate Editor, 6th edn 1998; (contrib.) Textbook of Urology, ed J. P. Blandy, 1974; (jtly) Radioisotopes in Radiodiagnosis, 1976; (contrib.) Radiological Atlas of Biliary and Pancreatic Disease, 1978; Textbook of Radiology by British Authors, 1984; (ed with W. E. G. Thomas) Nuclear Medicine for Surgeons, 1988; papers in Clin. Radiology, British Jl of Radiology, Lancet. *Recreations*: theatre, cooking, wine, travel. *Address*: 19 Hyland Grove, Bristol BS9 3NR.

DAVIES, (Evan) Huw; QC 2006; *b* 22 Jan. 1962; *s* of John and Joan Davies; *m* 1988, Alison Susan Keen; one *s* one *d*. *Educ*: Carr Lane Primary Sch., Hull; Wolfreton Comprehensive Sch., Hull; Imberhorne Comprehensive Sch., E Grinstead; University Coll., Cardiff (LLB 1st Cl. Hons). Called to the Bar, Gray's Inn, 1985; in practice, specialising in commercial litigation and arbitration. CEDR accredited mediator. *Recreations*: Rugby, ski-ing, mountaineering, cycling, golf (still learning), travel, food. *Address*: Essex Court Chambers, 24 Lincoln's Inn Fields, WC2A 3EG. *T*: (020) 7813 8000. *E*: hdavies@essexcourt.net.

DAVIES, Sir Frank (John), Kt 1999; CBE 1993; Chairman, Health and Safety Commission, 1993–99; *b* 24 Sept. 1931; *s* of late Lt-Col F. H. Davies and Veronica Josephine Davies; *m* 1956, Sheila Margaret Bailey (*d* 2015); three *s*; *m* 2016, Olga Parsons. *Educ*: Monmouth Sch.; UMIST. BPB Industries plc, 1953–63; RTZ Pillar Ltd, 1964–67; Alcan Aluminium (UK) Ltd, 1967–83: Div. Man. Dir, 1971–83; Dir, 1977–83; Dir, Alcan Booth, 1972–82; Gp Chief Exec., Rockware Gp, 1983–93. Chairman: Dartington Crystal, 1989–94; ACI Europe Ltd, 1991–93; Bardon Gp plc, 1994–97; Mediwatch plc, 2003–05; non-executive Director: Ian Proctor M. Masts, 1974–83; Ardagh plc, 1985–2003; BTR Nylex, 1991–94; Saltire (formerly Cannon St Investments), 1993–99; Aggregate Industries plc, 1997–2002; Investor Champions plc, 2000–04; Ardagh Glass Gp, 2003–10. Mem., Oxfordshire HA, 1981–90; Chm., Nuffield Orthopaedic Centre NHS Trust, 1990–98. Dep. Chm., Railway Safety, 2001–03; non-exec. Dir, Railway Safety and Standards Board, 2003–08. President: Glass Manufrs Fedn, 1985, 1986; Fédn Européene du Verre d'Emballage, 1987–88; Member: Council, Cttee Permanent Industrie du Verre, Brussels, 1984–86; Council, Aluminium Fedn, 1980–82; Council, CBI, 1985–93; Council, Industry Council for Packaging and the Envmt, 1986–93; Packaging Standards Council, 1992–93; Vice-President: Inst. of Packaging, 1992; Inst. of Occupational Safety & Health, 1995. Trustee, British Occupnl Health Res. Foundn, 1993–99; Chm. of Trustees, Back Care, 1998–2004. Governor: Inst. of Occupl Medicine, 2000–15; British Safety Council, 2000–06 (Chm., 2001–06). CCMI (CBIM 1986); FRSA 1986. Freeman, City of London, 1986; Liveryman: Basketmakers' Co., 1987; Glass-Sellers' Co., 1990. OStJ 1977 (Mem., Council of St John, Oxfordshire, 1973–2000); Vice-Pres., Oxfordshire St John Ambulance, 1973–2000. *Recreations*: gardening, theatre, travel. *Address*: Stonewalls, Castle Street, Deddington, Banbury, Oxon OX15 0TE. *Club*: Carlton.

DAVIES, Col (Frederic) Nicolas (John), LVO 2002; JP; DL; Independent Member: Standards Committee, Surrey County Council, 2001–10 (Chairman, 2007–08); Standards Committee, Waverley Borough Council, 2001–11 (Chairman, 2002–09); Secretary for Appointments and Chief Clerk, Duchy of Lancaster, 1992–2002; *b* 11 May 1939; *s* of late Rev. William John Davies and Winifred Mary Davies (*née* Lewis); *m* 1970, Caroline Tweedie; one step *s* one step *d*, and one *s* one *d* by previous *m*. *Educ*: King's Coll., Taunton; RMA Sandhurst. Nat. Service, Queen's Royal Regt, 1957; commnd Royal Regt of Artillery, 1959; served in UK, Cyprus, Hong Kong and Germany; COS, Catterick Garrison, N Yorks, 1982–85; Defence and Military Attaché, Hungary, 1986–91; retd 1992. Non-exec. Dir, Guildford and Waverley PCT, 2003–06. Trustee, Queen's Royal Surrey Regtl Mus., 2003–11 (Chm., 2006–11). Member: Surrey County Priory Gp (formerly St John Council for Surrey), 1995– (Pres., Haslemere Div., 2000; OStJ 2010); Court, Univ. of Surrey, 1997–. Mem., Ex-Services Mental Welfare Soc. (Combat Stress), 2007–. Mem., Pilgrims Soc., 1996–. Governor: St Ives Sch., Haslemere, 1994–96; Corp. of Sons of the Clergy, 1997– (Mem., Court of Assts, 1999–2005). Surrey Magistrates Soc., 2002–09 (Cttee, 2007–09). JP Inner London 1997–2002, SW Surrey 2002 (supplemental list, 2009); DL Surrey, 1997. Hon. Mem., Order of Vitéz (Hungary), 1994. *Recreations*: walking, gardening, reading. *Club*: Army and Navy.

DAVIES, Gareth, CBE 1992; FCA; Group Chief Executive, 1984–93, Chairman, 1986–98, Glynwed International plc; *b* 13 Feb. 1930; *s* of Lewis and Margaret Ann Davies; *m* 1953, Joan Patricia Prosser; one *s*. *Educ*: King Edward's Grammar School, Aston, Birmingham. Joined Glynwed Group, 1957; Computer Manager, 1964; Financial Dir, 1969; Man. Dir, 1981. Non-executive Director: Midlands Electricity Plc, 1989–96; Midlands Ind. Newspapers plc, 1994–97; Lloyds Chemists plc, 1995–97. *Recreations*: music, gardening. *Address*: Berkley House, Barton-on-the-Heath, Morton-in-Marsh, Glos GL56 0PJ. *T*: (01608) 674043.

DAVIES, Gareth; *see* Davies, W. G.

DAVIES, His Honour Gareth Lewis; a Circuit Judge, 1990–2002; *b* 8 Sept. 1936; *s* of David Edward Davies and Glynwen Davies; *m* 1st, 1962; two *s* two *d*; 2nd, 2001, Emma Messenger. *Educ*: Brecon County Grammar Sch.; Univ. of Wales (LLB). National Service, RAF, 1954–56. Articled 1959, qualified Solicitor, 1962; Partner, Ottaways', Solicitors, St Albans, 1965–90; a Recorder, 1987. *Recreations*: sailing instructor, ski guide, classic cars, cycling. *Address*: Bronllys Castle, Bronllys, Brecon, Powys LD3 0HL. *T*: (01874) 711930.

DAVIES, Gareth Neil; Director General for Business and Science (formerly Director General of Knowledge and Innovation), Department for Business, Energy and Industrial Strategy (formerly Department for Business, Innovation and Skills), since 2015; *b* Liverpool, 13 July 1973; *s* of Peter and Laraine Davies; *m* 2013, Emma Loxton. *Educ*: Wallasey Comprehensive Sch.; Christ Church, Oxford (BA PPE 1994; MA); London Sch. of Econs and Pol Sci. (MSc Econs 1999). Mgt consultant, Coopers and Lybrand, subseq. PriceWaterhouseCoopers, 1994–2002; Dep. Dir, Prime Minister's Strategy Unit, 2002–03; Sen. Advr, Downing St Policy Unit, 2003–07; Prog. Dir, DIUS, 2007–09; Exec. Dir, Cabinet Office, 2009–13; Dir, Gp Strategy, AIA Insce, 2013–15. Chm. Govs, Bolingbroke Acad., 2012–. *Recreations*: running, cycle touring, theatre, Liverpool Football Club. *Address*: Department for Business, Energy and Industrial Strategy, 1 Victoria Street, SW1H 0ET. *T*: (020) 7215 1219. *E*: gareth.davies@beis.gov.uk.

DAVIES, Gareth Thomas; Comptroller and Auditor General, National Audit Office, since 2019; *b* Middlesbrough, 6 Oct. 1965; *s* of Peter Davies and Anne Davies; *m* 1990, Alison; two *d*. *Educ*: Sidney Sussex Coll., Cambridge (BA Maths 1987). Fellow, CIPFA, 1992; Mem., ICAEW, 2012. Audit Commission: trainee auditor, 1987–91; Audit Manager, 1991–95; Dist Auditor, 1995–2000; Regl Dir, 2000–06; Man. Dir, 2006–12; Partner and Hd, Public Services, Mazars LLP, 2012–19. Hon. Treasurer: Oxfam GB, 2005–11; Save the Children UK, 2014–19. Trustee, Inst. of Develt Studies, 2015–19. *Recreations*: progressive rock music, playing piano, football, cricket, reading. *Address*: National Audit Office, 157–197 Buckingham Palace Road, SW1W 9SP. *T*: (020) 7798 7000. *E*: gareth.davies@nao.org.uk.

DAVIES, Gavyn, OBE 1979; Chairman, Fulcrum Asset Management; Principal, KKR Prisma (formerly Prisma Capital Partners), since 2005; *b* 27 Nov. 1950; *s* of W. J. F. Davies and M. G. Davies; *m* 1989, Susan Jane Nye (*see* Baroness Nye); two *s* one *d*. *Educ*: St John's Coll., Cambridge (BA); Balliol Coll., Oxford. Economic Advr, Policy Unit, 10 Downing Street, 1974–79; Economist, Phillips and Drew, 1979–81; Chief UK Economist, Simon & Coates, 1981–86; Goldman Sachs: Chief UK Economist, 1986–93; Partner, 1988–2001; Hd of Investment Res. (London), 1991–93; Head, later Co-Head, Eur. Investment Res., 1993–99; Chief Internat. Economist, 1993–2001; Chm., Investment Res. Dept, 1999–2001; Adv. Dir, 2001. Vis. Prof. of Economics, LSE, 1988–98. Principal Econs Commentator, The Independent, 1991–99. Mem., HM Treasury's Ind. Forecasting Panel, 1993–97. Chairman: Future Funding of the BBC (govt inquiry), 1999; Bd of Govs, BBC, 2001–04 (Vice-Chm., 2001). Fellow, Univ. of Wales, Aberystwyth, 2002. Hon. DSc (Social Sci.) Southampton, 1998; Hon. LLD Nottingham, 2002; Hon. Dr Middlesex, 2004. *Recreation*: Southampton FC.

DAVIES, George William; Chairman, FG4 Childrenswear and Ladieswear, since 2011; *b* 29 Oct. 1941; *s* of George Davies and late Mary Davies; *m* 1st, 1964, Anne; three *d*; 2nd, 1985, Liz; two *d*; 3rd, 1992, Fiona; two *s*; 4th, 2016, Arlene. *Educ*: Netherton Moss Primary Sch.; Bootle Grammar Sch.; Birmingham Univ. Littlewoods, 1967–72; School Care (own business), 1972–75; Pippa Dee (subsid. of Rosgill Hldgs)—Party Plan/Lingerie, 1975–81; J. Hepworth & Son plc (responsible for launch of Next), 1981; Jt Gp Man. Dir, J. Hepworth & Son, 1984; Chief Exec., 1985–88, Chm., 1987–88, Next (name changed from J. Hepworth & Son); Managing Director: George Davies Partnership plc, 1989–2000; George Clothing, 1995–2000; Pres., Asda Gp, 1995–2000; Chm., Per Una clothing for Marks and Spencer plc, 2001–08 (Chief Exec., 2004–05). Chairman: S. Porter, 1995–2009; S'Porter Internat. Ltd, 2009–; FG4 Middle East, 2011–. Sen. Fellow, RCA, 1988. FRSA 1987; Hon. FSDC 2004. Patron, Circulation Foundn, 2016. Hon. DBA Liverpool Polytechnic, 1989; Hon. DDes: Nottingham Trent, 1996; Middlesex, 2002; De Montfort, 2006; Hon. DLitt Heriot-Watt, 2003; Hon. DCL Northumbria, 2005; Hon. DBA Edge Hill, 2012. Guardian Young Businessman of the Year, 1985; Wood Mackenzie Retailer of the Year, 1987; Marketing Personality of the Year, 1988; Lifetime Achievement Award, Drapers' Co., 2003; Designer of the Decade, Prima mag., 2004; Forum Award, Textil Wirtschaft mag., 2004. *Publications*: What Next? (autobiog.), 1989. *Recreations*: tennis, golf, cycling. *Clubs*: Formby Golf; Liverpool Ramblers; Blackwell Golf.

DAVIES, Geraint Rhys; Member (Plaid Cymru), Rhondda Cynon Taff County Borough Council, since 2012; *b* 1 Dec. 1948; *s* of John Davies and Sarah Olwen Davies; *m* 1973, Merril Margaret Williams; three *s* one *d*. *Educ*: Pentre Grammar Sch.; Chelsea Coll., London (BPharm). MRPharmS. Community pharmacist: Boots, Treorci, Rhondda, 1972–75; self-employed, 1975–. Member (Plaid Cymru): Rhondda CBC, 1983–95; Rhondda Cynon Taff CBC, 1995. Mem (Plaid Cymru), Nat. Assembly for Wales, 1999–2003. Contested (Plaid Cymru): Rhondda, Nat. Assembly for Wales, 2003; Rhondda, 2010. *Recreations*: playing tennis, listening to music, reading.

DAVIES, Geraint Richard; MP (Lab and Co-op) Swansea West, since 2010; *b* 3 May 1960; *s* of David Thomas Morgan Davies and Betty Ferrer Davies; *m* 1991, Dr Vanessa Catherine Fry; three *d*. *Educ*: Llanishen Comp. Sch., Cardiff; Jesus Coll., Oxford (JCR Pres.; Maths mods; BA Hons PPE, MA). Joined Brooke Bond Oxo as sales and mkting trainee, 1982; subseq. Gp Product Manager, Unilever; Marketing Manager, Colgate Palmolive Ltd; Founder, and Director: Pure Crete, 1989–2010; Pure Aviation, 1996–2010; Dir, Equity Creative Ltd, 1989–2001. Chair, Flood Risk Mgt Wales, 2005–10. Mem., Croydon BC, 1986–97 (Chm. of Housing, 1994–96; Leader of Council, 1996–97); Chm., London Boroughs Housing Cttee, 1994–96. Contested (Lab): Croydon S, 1987; Croydon Central, 1992. MP (Lab) Croydon Central, 1997–2005; contested (Lab) same seat, 2005. Team PPS, Dept of Constitutional Affairs, 2003–05. Member: Public Accounts Select Cttee, 1997–2003; Welsh Affairs Select Cttee, 2010–15, 2017–; European Scrutiny Select Cttee, 2013–; Envmtl Audit Select Cttee, 2015–; Chairmen's Panel, 2015–. Sec., Parly Gp on Domestic Violence, 2003–05; Parly Ambassador, NSPCC, 2003–05. Chair: Lab. Finance and Industry Gp, 1998–2003 (Mem. Exec., 1994–; Vice Pres., 2003–); Deptl Cttee, Envmt, Transport and Regions, 1997–2003. Mem., Parly Assembly of the Council for Europe, 2010–18 (rapporteur on trade agreements, fracking, air quality). Published parliamentary bills: Physical Punishment of Children (Prohibition) Bill, 2003; Regulation of Child Care Providers Bill, 2003; Regulation of Hormone Disrupting Chemicals Bill, 2004; School Meals and Nutrition Bill, 2005; Credit Card Regulation (Child Pornography) Bill, 2010; Multinational Motor Companies (duty of care to former employees) Bill, 2012; Regulation of Psychotherapists and Counsellors Bill, 2013, 2019; Sugar in Food and Drinks Bill, 2014, 2019; Bill criminalising Revenge Pornography, 2014 (incorporated into Criminal Justice and Courts Act, 2015); Electronic Cigarettes Bill, 2014; Internat. Trade Agreements (Security) Bill, 2014; Fracking Bill, 2015; Urban Centres Air Quality Bill (Diesel Emissions), 2016; Terms of Withdrawal from the EU (Referendum) Bill, 2016, 2017 (to delay Article 50 until after a popular vote on EU Exit Package); EU Environmental Protection Safeguards Bill; Clean Air Bill, 2016, 2018; Plastics Bill, 2018; EU (Revocation of Notification of Withdrawal) Bill, 2018. *Recreations*: spending time with the family, singing and song writing, stand-up comedy, political and comedy writing, painting, film making. *Address*: House of Commons, SW1A 0AA.

DAVIES, Geraint Talfan, OBE 2014; DL; Chairman: Institute of Welsh Affairs, 1992–2014; Welsh National Opera, 2000–03 and 2006–16; *b* 30 Dec. 1943; *s* of late Aneirin Talfan Davies, OBE and Mary Anne (*née* Evans); *m* 1967, Elizabeth Shân Vaughan (*née*

Yorath); three s. *Educ:* Cardiff High Sch.; Jesus Coll., Oxford (MA; Hon. Fellow, 2013). Western Mail, Cardiff, 1966–71; The Journal, Newcastle upon Tyne, 1971–73; The Times, 1973; Asst Editor, Western Mail, Cardiff, 1974–78; HTV Wales: Head, News and Current Affairs, 1978–82; Asst Controller of Progs, 1982–87; Dir of Progs, Tyne Tees TV, 1987–90; Controller, BBC Wales, 1990–2000. Non-executive Director: Glas Cymru Cyf, 2000–11; Wales Millennium Centre, 2000–03, 2006–09; Shakespeare Schs Fest., 2014–; Mem., BT Wales Adv. Forum, 2001–09. Chairman: Newydd Housing Assoc., 1975–78; Cardiff Bay Arts Trust, 1997–2003; Wales Internat. Film Festival, 1998–2001; Arts Council of Wales, 2003–06; Wales for Europe, 2016–. Mem., Prince of Wales' Cttee, 1993–95; Trustee: Tenovus Cancer Appeal, 1984–87; British Bone Marrow Donor Appeal, 1987–95; Media Standards Trust, 2006–16. Member: Management Cttee, Northern Sinfonia, 1989–90; Radio Authy, 2001–04; UK Cttee, Eur. Cultural Foundn, 2005–09. Governor: Welsh Coll. of Music and Drama, 1993–97; UWIC, 2000–06. DL S Glamorgan, 2007. Hon. Fellow: UWIC, 2000; RIBA, 2000; Swansea Univ., 2011; Bangor Univ., 2013; Coleg Cymraeg Cenedlaethol, 2015. Hon. Dr, Glamorgan, 1996. *Publications:* At Arm's Length, 2008; (ed) English is a Welsh Language, 2009; Unfinished Business: journal of an embattled European, 2018. *Recreations:* theatre, music, architecture. *Address:* 15 The Parade, Whitchurch, Cardiff CF14 2EF. *T:* (029) 2062 6571. *E:* geraint.talfan@btopenworld.com.
*See also* R. T. Davies.

**DAVIES, Geraldine Mary**; educational consultant, since 2017; Principal, 2011–16, Lead Co-Principal, 2016–17, UCL Academy; *b* London, 11 Sept. 1954; *d* of Charles and Mary Bayley; *m* 1978, Michael Davies; one *s*. *Educ:* St Victoire's Convent Grammar Sch.; St Mary's Coll., Twickenham (BSc Hons Botany and Chem.; Cert Ed); Inst. of Educn, Univ. of London (MBA Higher Educn Mgt). Teacher of chem. and sci., Holy Cross Convent, New Malden, 1977–87; Hd of Sci. and Sen. Teacher, Coombe Girls Sch., 1987–90; Dep. Headteacher, Bishop Thomas Grant, Streatham, 1990–2000; Headteacher, Douay Martyrs Sch., Ickenham, 2000–07; Hd, Sch. of Educn, St Mary's UC, Twickenham, 2007–11. Hon. Fellow, UCL, 2017. *Recreations:* art, choir, ski-ing, sailing, Italian.

**DAVIES, Prof. Gideon John**, PhD; FRS 2010; FRSC; FMedSci; Professor of Chemistry, University of York, since 2001; *b* Great Sutton, Cheshire, 6 July 1964; *s* of Robert Edward Davies and Phyllis Dinah Davies (*née* Parker); *m* 1999, Dr Valérie Marie-Andrée Ducros; two *d*. *Educ:* Univ. of Bristol (BSc Hons Biochem. 1985; PhD 1990; DSc 2007). FRSC 2002. EMBO Res. Fellow, EMBL, Hamburg, 1990; Postdoctoral Fellow, Univ. of York, 1991–95; Royal Soc. Univ. Res. Fellow, 1996–2005. Peter Wall Catalytic Visitor, Univ. of BC, 2000. Mem., EMBO, 2010. FMedSci 2014. Carbohydrate Chem. Medal, 1998, Corday Morgan Medal, 2001, Proteins and Peptides Award, 2008, Khorana Prize, 2014, RSC; Whistler Prize, Internat. Carbohydrate Orgn, 2006; Wolfson Res. Merit Award, 2007, Gabor Medal, 2010, Davy Medal, 2015, Royal Soc.; GlaxoSmithKline Award, Biochem. Soc., 2010; Global Energy Award, IChemE, 2016; Haworth Meml Award, RSC, 2018. *Publications:* contrib. scientific papers. *Recreations:* music, sailing, fishing, hockey. *Address:* Department of Chemistry, York Structural Biology Laboratory, University of York, Heslington, York YO10 5DD. *T:* (01904) 328260, *Fax:* (01904) 328266. *E:* gideon.davies@york.ac.uk.

**DAVIES, Prof. Gillian**, PhD; DL; barrister; Professor of International and EU Intellectual Property Law, Centre for Commercial Law Studies, Queen Mary University of London, since 2015 (Visiting Professor, 2007–14); *b* 5 April 1940; *d* of late Ninian Rhys Davies and Gweneth Elizabeth Davies (*née* Griffith). *Educ:* Cheltenham Ladies' Coll.; Grenoble Univ.; Univ. of Wales, Aberystwyth (PhD 1997). Called to the Bar, Lincoln's Inn, 1961; in practice at the Bar, 1961–63, and 2005–. Legal Assistant: De La Rue Co., 1963–65; United Internat. Bureaux for Protection of Intellectual Property, Geneva, 1965–70; Legal Advr, 1970–73, Asst Dir Gen., 1973–80, Associate Dir Gen. and Chief Legal Advr, 1980–91, IFPI. Res. Fellow, Max Planck Inst. for Foreign and Internat. Patent, Copyright, and Competition Law, Munich, 1990; Hon. Prof., Aberystwyth Univ. (formerly Univ. of Wales, Aberystwyth), 1994–2015; Vis. Prof., Centre for Commercial Law Studies, QMUL, 2007–14. Bangor University: Member: Adv. Bd, Centre for Internat. Law, 2012–; Council, 2015–19; Finance and Resources Cttee, 2015–19. Mem., Wkg Gp on the Rôle of the State vis-à-vis the Cultural Industries, Council of Europe, 1980–86; Legal Mem., Bds of Appeal, 1991, Mem., Enlarged Bd of Appeal, 1996, Chm., Tech. Bd of Appeal, 1997–2005, European Patent Office. Chm., British Literary and Artistic Copyright Assoc., 2013–17 (Vice-Pres., 2010–13; Mem., Exec. Cttee, 2017–). DL Gwynedd, 2001. Liveryman, Livery Co. of Wales (formerly Welsh Livery Guild), 2007 (Master, 2017–18; Dep. Master, 2018–19; Mem., N Wales Cttee, 2008– (Chm., 2009–13)). *Publications:* Piracy of Phonograms, 1981, 2nd edn 1986; Private Copying of Sound and Audiovisual Recordings, 1984; (jtly) Challenges to Copyright and Related Rights in the European Community, 1983; (jtly) Music and Video Private Copying, 1993; Copyright and the Public Interest, 1994, 2nd edn 2002; Copinger and Skone James on Copyright, suppl. (jtly) 1994, 14th edn (ed jtly) 1999 to 17th edn (ed jtly) 2016, suppls (jtly), 2017, 2018, 2019; Clerk and Lindsell on Torts, suppl. (jtly) 2009, 20th edn (ed jtly) 2010, suppls (jtly) 2011, 2012, 2013, 21st edn (ed jtly) 2014, suppl. (jtly) 2015, 2016; (jtly) Moral Rights, 2010, 2nd edn (jtly) 2016; many articles in intellectual property law jls. *Recreations:* gardening, art, travel. *Address:* Hogarth Chambers, 1 New Square, Lincoln's Inn, WC2A 3RJ; Trefaes, Abersoch, Gwynedd LL53 7AD. *T:* (01758) 712426. *Clubs:* Athenæum, Hurlingham; Cardiff and County.

**DAVIES, Most Rev. Glenn Naunton**; *see* Sydney, Archbishop of.

**DAVIES, Glyn**; *see* Davies, R. H. G.

**DAVIES, Glyn**; MP (C) Montgomeryshire, since 2010; *b* 16 Feb. 1944; *m* 1969, Bobbie; three *s* one *d*. *Educ:* Caereinion High Sch.; UCW, Aberystwyth. Mem. (C) Montgomeryshire DC, 1985–88 (Chm.). Chm., Develt Bd for Rural Wales, 1989–94; Member: WDA, 1989–94; Wales Tourist Bd, 1989–94. Mem. (C) Mid & W Wales, Nat. Assembly for Wales, 1999–2007. Contested (C) Montgomeryshire, 1997. PPS to Sec. of State for Wales, 2016–. *Recreations:* countryside, sport. *Address:* Cil Farm, Berriew, Welshpool, Montgomeryshire, Mid Wales SY21 8AZ. *T:* 07968 082891.

**DAVIES, Prof. Glyn Arthur Owen**, FRAeS; FCGI; Professor of Aeronautical Structures, 1985–99, and Senior Research Fellow and Senior Research Investigator in Aerostructures, 1999–2013, Imperial College London (formerly Imperial College of Science, Technology and Medicine, London) (Head of Department of Aeronautics, 1982–89; Pro-Rector (Resources), 1997–99); *b* 11 Feb. 1933; *s* of Arthur and Florence Davies; *m* 1959, Helen Rosemary (*née* Boot); two *d*. *Educ:* Liverpool Inst., Univ. of Liverpool (BEng); Cranfield Inst. of Technology (DCAe); PhD Sydney, 1966. Res. Asst, MIT, 1956; Advanced Project Engr, Brit. Aerospace, 1957–59; Lectr, Sen. Lectr, Dept of Aeronautics, Univ. of Sydney, 1959–66; Lectr, Sen. Lectr, Dept of Aeronautics, Imperial Coll. of Sci., Technol. and Medicine (formerly Imperial Coll. of Sci. and Technol.), 1966–85. Consultant to: ARC, 1975–81; MoD, 1980–2005; Nat. Agency for Finite Element Methods and Standards, 1983–95; SERC, 1986–90 (Supercomputing, 1991–93); The Computer Bd, 1989–91; ABRC (Supercomputing), 1991–94; UFC (IT), 1991–93; DTI (Aviation), 1991–2005; RAeS, 1994–2013; EPSRC, 1994–2005; OST (Foresight) Defence & Aerospace, 1994–2002. FRAeS 1987; FCGI 2000. Consultant Ed. (Aero Engrg), McGraw-Hill, 2009–13. *Publications:* Virtual Work in Structural Analysis, 1982; Mathematical Methods in Engineering, 1984; Finite Element Primer, 1986; Background to Benchmarks, 1993; Finite Element Modelling of Composite Materials and Structures, 2002; The Standard Handbook for Aeronautical and Astronautical Engineers, 2003; From Lysander to Lightning: Teddy Petter, aircraft designer, 2014. *Recreations:* photography, archaeology, painting and drawing life and portraits, theatre, music, allotment. *Address:* Hedsor School House, Bourne End, Bucks SL8 5JJ.

**DAVIES, Sir Graeme (John)**, Kt 1996; FREng; FRSE; Vice-Chancellor, University of London, 2003–10; *b* 7 April 1937; *s* of Harry John Davies and Gladys Edna Davies (*née* Pratt); *m* 1st, 1959, Florence Isabelle Martin (*d* 2014); one *s* one *d*; 2nd, 2015, Svava Bjarnason. *Educ:* Mount Albert Grammar School, Auckland, NZ; Univ. of Auckland (BE, PhD); St Catharine's College, Cambridge (MA, ScD). FREng (FEng 1988). Junior Lectr, Univ. of Auckland, 1960–62; University of Cambridge: TI Research Fellow, 1962–64; Univ. Demonstrator in Metallurgy, 1964–66; Lectr, 1966–76; Fellow of St Catharine's Coll., 1967–77 (Hon. Fellow 1989); Prof. of Metallurgy, Univ. of Sheffield, 1978–86; Vice Chancellor, Univ. of Liverpool, 1986–91; Chief Executive: UFC, 1991–93; PCFC, 1992–93; HEFCE, 1992–95; Principal and Vice-Chancellor, Univ. of Glasgow, 1995–2003. Visiting Professor: Brazil, 1976–77; Israel, 1978; Argentina, 1980; China, 1981; Hon. Professor: Zhejiang Univ., China, 1985; Yantai Univ., China, 1996; Chm. and Pres., 2009–, Chancellor, 2018–, British Univ., Vietnam; Chairman: Apollo Educn Gp, Vietnam, 2015–18; European Univ. of Business, 2016–. Chm., Univs Superannuation Scheme, 1996–2006. Mem., ACOST, 1991–93. Member: Merseyside Enterprise Forum, 1986–90; London Economic Panel, 2004–10; Chairman: Scottish Educn and Trng, 1996–2001; Observatory on Borderless Higher Educn, 2001–10; Higher Educn Policy Inst., 2004–15 (Trustee, 2002–15). Guardian, Sheffield Assay Office, 1983–86; Chairman: CCLRC, 2001–07; Glasgow Sci. Centre, 2002–06, 2007–10; NZ-UK Link Foundn, 2011–17; Member Council: Inst. Metals, 1981–86; Sheffield Metallurgical and Engineering Assoc., 1977–86 (Pres., 1984–85); ACU, 1987–91, 1998–2002, 2007–10; UUK (formerly CVCP), 1996–2010; Pres., Council of Military Educn Cttees, 2006–10. Trustee: Bluecoat Soc. of Arts, 1986–91; Museums and Galls on Merseyside, 1987–92; Iona Trust, 1995–2003; Carnegie Trust for the Univs of Scotland, 1995–2003; Scottish Science Trust, 1996–2003; Internat. Students House, 2005–16; Cumberland Lodge, 2005–13; Foundn for Liver Research, 2009– (Chair, 2012–). Governor: Shrewsbury Sch., 1989–95; Glasgow Sch. of Art, 2004–08; Univ. of Seychelles, 2010–17; Univ. of Herts, 2011–17; Taylors Univ., Malaysia, 2012–; Univ. of Lincoln, 2013–; Regent's Univ., 2016–. FRSA 1989; FRSE 1996; CCMI (CBIM 1991). Freeman, City of London, 1987; Liveryman, Co. of Ironmongers, 1989 (Mem., Court, 1992–; Master, 2005–06); Freeman and Burgess Holder, City of Glasgow, 1996. DL Merseyside, 1989–92. Hon. FRSNZ 1993; Hon. FTCL 1995; FRCPSGlas 1999; Hon. FCIPS 2003; Hon. FIPENZ 2007; Hon. FRVC 2011; Hon. Fellow, Sch. of Pharmacy, UCL, 2012. Hon. LLD: Liverpool, 1991; Strathclyde, 2000; Edinburgh, 2003; London, 2012; Hon. DSc: Nottingham, 1995; Ulster, 2004; Hon. DMet Sheffield, 1995; Hon. DEng: Manchester Metropolitan, 1996; Auckland, 2002; DUniv: Glasgow, 2004; Paisley, 2004; London South Bank, 2006; Hon. DLitt Bath Spa, 2010. Rosenhain Medal, Inst. of Metals, 1982. *Publications:* Solidification and Casting, 1973; Texture and Properties of Materials, 1976; Solidificação e Fundição de Metais e Suas Ligas, 1978; Hot Working and Forming Processes, 1980; Superplasticity, 1981; Essential Metallurgy for Engineers, 1985; Herding Cats, 2010; Herding Professional Cats, 2013; papers to learned jls. *Recreations:* cricket, birdwatching, golf, The Times crossword. *Address:* The Coach House, Fosse Road, Farndon, Newark NG24 3SF. *E:* graeme.davies@lon.ac.uk. *Club:* Athenæum.

**DAVIES, Prof. Graham Ivor**, PhD, DD; FBA 2003; Professor of Old Testament Studies, University of Cambridge, 2001–11, Fellow, Fitzwilliam College, Cambridge, since 1983; *b* 26 Sept. 1944; *s* of late Ivor Samuel Davies and Pauline Beryl Davies (*née* Serjeant); *m* 1971, Nicola Rina Galeski; three *s* one *d*. *Educ:* King's Coll. Sch., Wimbledon; Merton Coll., Oxford (Postmaster in Classics; BA 1st cl. hons Lit. Hum. 1967; 1st cl. hons Theol. 1969; MA 1970; DD 1998); Peterhouse, Cambridge (PhD 1975). FSA 1987–2015. Asst Lectr, then Lectr, in Theol., Univ. of Nottingham, 1971–78; University of Cambridge: Lectr in Divinity, 1979–93; Reader in OT Studies, 1993–2001; Chm., Faculty Bd of Divinity, 1995–97. Director of Studies in Theology: Pembroke Coll., 1979–87; Peterhouse, 1979–88; Fitzwilliam Coll., 1983–2008; Director: Hebrew Inscriptions Project, 1987–2003; Cambridge Centre, Semantics of Ancient Hebrew Database, 1995–2018 (Sec., ESF Network Co-ordinating Cttee, 1991–95). Mem., Exec. Cttee, Palestine Exploration Fund, 1981–2001, 2009–13; Sec., Fifteenth Congress, Internat. Orgn for Study of OT, Cambridge, 1995. Chm., Theol. and Religious Studies Section, British Acad., 2006–09. Macbride Sermon, Oxford, 1986; Schweich Centenary Lect., British Acad., 2008. Editor: Cities of the Biblical World series, 1981–96; Palestine Exploration Qly, 1990–2000; Internat. Critical Commentary (OT), 2004–; Mem. Editl Bd, Zeitschrift für die Alttestamentliche Wissenschaft, 2007–. *Publications:* The Way of the Wilderness, 1979; Megiddo (Cities of the Biblical World), 1986; Ancient Hebrew Inscriptions: corpus and concordance, vol. 1, 1991, vol. 2, 2004; Hosea (New Century Bible Commentary), 1992; Hosea (Old Testament Guide), 1993; (with A. N. S. Lane) John Calvin's The Bondage and Liberation of the Will, 1996; The Schweich Lectures and Biblical Archaeology, 2011; Exodus 1–18: a critical and exegetical commentary, 2019; contrib. Vetus Testamentum, Palestine Exploration Qly, Jl of Semitic Studies and other learned jls and collections of essays. *Recreations:* steam trains, Rugby football, hill-walking, gardening, religious poetry. *Address:* Fitzwilliam College, Cambridge CB3 0DG. *T:* (01223) 763002, *Fax:* (01223) 763003. *E:* gid10@cam.ac.uk.

**DAVIES, Prof. Graham James**, PhD, DSc; CEng, FREng, FIET, FInstP, FIEAust, FIMMM, FTSE; FLSW; Dean of Engineering, UNSW Australia (formerly University of New South Wales), 2008–15, now Emeritus Professor; *b* 2 July 1946; *s* of William Thomas and Amy Davies; *m* 1975, Frances Vivienne Martin (marr. diss. 2010); two *s*. *Educ:* UCW Aberystwyth (BSc 1968; PhD 1971; DSc 1986). MRSC 1969; CEng, FIET (FIEE 1998); FInstP 1990; FREng 1999; FIMMM 2002; FIEAust 2009; FTSE 2014. Res. Officer, KCL, 1971–72; Post Office Research: Jun. Res. Fellow, 1972–75; Hd of Gp, 1975–84; British Telecom Research Laboratories: Head: Advanced Materials and Devices Section, 1984–90; Competitor Analysis Section, 1990–93; Director: Corporate Res., 1993–98; Technol. Acquisition, 1998–2001; Sir James Timmins Chance Prof. of Engrg and Hd, Sch. of Engrg, Univ. of Birmingham, 2001–08. Chm., Foresight Materials Panel, DTI, 2000–04. Chm., Mining Educn Australia, 2012–15. Director: Inst. of Physics Publishing, 2001–03; Birmingham R&D, 2001–08; Diamond Light Source, 2003–08; NSi Innovations (formerly New South Innovations), 2009–15; Advanced Manufacturing, 2010–15, CO2, 2010–15, Collaborative Res. Centre. Chm., TRex, 2018–; Dir, Oxford Scientific Consultants, 2019–. Member: Council, CCLRC, 2003–07; Bd, Collaborate Res. Centre for Carbon Capture and Storage, 2010–15; Chief Scientist of Wales Cttee, 2015–; RAEng Educn Cttee and Fellowship Cttee, 2015–; Awards Cttee, Inst. of Materials, Minerals and Mining, 2018–. Trustee: Daphne Jackson Trust, 2015–; UNSW Foundn UK, 2015– (Mem. Bd, 2014–); Wheatley Playing Fields Assoc., 2016–. FLSW 2015. Liveryman, Co. of Engrs, 2003; Freeman, City of London, 2003. Associate Ed., Nature Microsystems and Nanoengineering, 2015–. *Publications:* (with R. H. Williams) Semiconductor Growth, Surfaces and Interfaces, 1994; (jtly) Chemical Beam Epitaxy and Related Techniques, 1997;

over 170 refereed pubns; contrib. papers to peer-reviewed learned jls. *Recreations:* walking, music, golf, reading. *Address:* 1 St Mary's Close, Wheatley, Oxon OX33 1YP. *E:* g.davies@unsw.edu.au.

**DAVIES, Prof. Graham Michael;** Professor of Psychology, University of Leicester, 1989–2006, now Emeritus; Honorary Professor: University of Birmingham, since 2007; University of Coventry, since 2007; *b* 19 Feb. 1943; *s* of Harold Cecil Davies and Mona Florence Daisy Wisbey; *m* 1st, 1966, Heather Jane Neale; one *s* one *d*; 2nd, 1987, Noelle Robertson; two *d*. *Educ:* Bodmin Grammar Sch.; Univ. of Hull (BA, PhD, DSc). CPsychol, FBPsS. Lectr in Psychology, 1967–77, Sen. Lectr, 1977–87, Univ. of Aberdeen; Prof. of Psychology, NE London Poly., 1987–89. Hon. Prof., Univ. of Nottingham, 2013–16. Chm., Soc. for Applied Res. in Memory and Cognition, 1998–99; Pres., Eur. Assoc. for Psychology and Law, 2003–06. Fellow, Assoc. for Psychol Sci., USA, 2010. Founding Editor, Applied Cognitive Psychology, 1987. JP: Melton, Belvoir and Rutland, 2000; Loughborough, Melton, Belvoir and Rutland, 2011–13. Sen. Academic Award in Forensic Psychol., BPsS, 2012. *Publications:* edited jointly: Perceiving and Remembering Faces, 1981; Identification Evidence: a psychological evaluation, 1982; Memory in Context, 1988; Memory in Everyday life, 1993; Psychology, Law and Criminal Justice: international developments in research and practice, 1995; Recovered Memories: seeking the middle ground, 2001; Children's Testimony: a handbook of psychological research and forensic practice, 2002; Practical Psychology for Forensic Investigations and Prosecutions, 2006; Forensic Psychology, 2008, 3rd edn as Forensic Psychology: crime, justice, law, interventions, 2017; Current Issues in Applied Memory Research, 2010; reports for the Home Office: (jtly) An evaluation of the live link for child witnesses, 1991; (jtly) Videotaping of Children's Evidence: an evaluation, 1995; (jtly) The training needs of officers investigating child sexual abuse, 1998; (jtly) Interviewing child witnesses under the 'Memorandum of Good Practice': a research review, 1999. *Recreations:* reading, walking, collecting modern first editions. *Address:* Department of Neuroscience, Psychology and Behaviour, Centre of Life Sciences, University of Leicester, University Road, Leicester LE1 7RH. *T:* (home) (01664) 474708.

**DAVIES, Grahame Brian;** entrepreneur; Chairman, London Internet Exchange, 2000–14; *b* 6 May 1961; *s* of Brian and Joyce Davies; *m* 1990, Karen Uridge; two *s*. *Educ:* Haberdashers' Aske's Boys' Sch., Elstree. Computer operator, Unilever Computer Services Ltd, 1979–81; computer programmer, Impetus Computer Services, 1981–83; Dir, Demon Systems Ltd, 1983–95; Founder, Demon Internet, 1992; Gp Man. Dir, Easynet Gp plc, 1995–2001; Dir, Internet Watch Foundn, 1997–2002; Dir, Great Scores, digital sheet music, 2005–, and other internet start-ups; non-exec. Dir, Bytemark Hosting, 2012–17; Dir, Agile Spice Ltd, 2012–; Chm., Simwood eSMS Ltd, 2013–; Chief Technology Officer: Boardroom Excellence, 2014–; PayDashboard Ltd, 2015–16. *Recreations:* piano, running, tennis, golf, kart racing. *E:* grahame@tptb.co.uk.

**DAVIES, Helen Louise;** QC 2008; *b* Hampshire, 24 May 1969; *d* of Terence Alan Davies and Joan Davies; one *s* one *d*. *Educ:* Emmanuel Coll., Cambridge (BA 1st Cl. Law 1990). Called to the Bar, Inner Temple, 1991, Bencher, 2010; in practice at the Bar, 1992–; Jt Hd, Brick Court Chambers, 2014–. Mem., B Panel to the Crown, 1999–2008. Stage, Competition Directorate, EC, 1993. Trustee, Council of Inns of Court, 2017–. *Recreations:* opera, theatre, ski-ing. *Address:* Brick Court Chambers, 7/8 Essex Street, WC2R 3LD. *T:* (020) 7379 3550.

**DAVIES, (Henry) Byron;** Chairman, Welsh Conservative Party, since 2017; *b* Swansea, 4 Sept. 1952; *s* of William John Davies and Gladys Mary Davies; *m* 1978, Gill; one *s*. *Educ:* Gowerton Boys' Grammar Sch., Swansea; Univ. of West London (LLB Hons). Officer, Metropolitan Police, 1971–2003; owner and dir of consultancy co. advising foreign govts on organised crime, 2003–11. Mem. (C) S Wales W, Nat. Assembly for Wales, 2011–May 2015. MP (C) Gower, 2015–17; contested (C) same seat, 2017. Member: Welsh Affairs Select Cttee, 2015–17; Home Affairs Select Cttee, 2016–17. *Recreations:* general aviation, private pilot, cycling, Rugby. *Address:* Welsh Conservative Party, Unit 5, Pro Copy Business Centre, Parc Ty Glas, Cardiff CF14 5DU. *E:* chairman@welshconservatives.com. *Clubs:* Carlton, Royal Air Force; Gowerton Conservative and Unionist.

*[Created a Baron (Life Peer), 2019 but title not gazetted at time of going to press.]*

**DAVIES, Dame Hilary Margaret, (Dame Til);** *see* Wykes, Dame H. M.

**DAVIES, Howard Colin,** FRGS; Chief Executive, National Association for Areas of Outstanding Natural Beauty, since 2010; *b* London, 5 May 1966; *s* of Colin and Barbara Davies; *m* 1991, Nicole Gibbs; three *s*. *Educ:* Open Univ. (Dip. Biol Scis 1999; BSc Hons Natural Sci. with Biol. 2002). FRGS 2004. Sen. Warden, Clwydian Range Area of Outstanding Natural Beauty, 1991–2002; Protected Landscape Policy Officer, Countryside Council for Wales, 2002–08; Dir, Wildlife Trusts Wales, 2008–10. Mem. Bd, Natural Resources Wales, 2015–. Hon. Vice Pres., N Wales Wildlife Trust, 2009–. Chm. Govs, Fedn of Schs in Ceiriog Valley, 2006–15. *Recreations:* my family, music, fly fishing, dogs and grouse (Member, Pointer Club), leaving faintly positive evidence of my existence. *Address:* Rosehill, Glyn Ceiriog, Llangollen LL20 7NG. *T:* (01691) 718177. *E:* howard.c.davies@gmail.com.

**DAVIES, (Sir) Howard (John),** Kt 2000; Chairman, Royal Bank of Scotland, since 2015; *b* 12 Feb. 1951; *s* of late Leslie Powell Davies and Marjorie Davies; *m* 1984, Prudence Mary Keely; two *s*. *Educ:* Manchester Grammar Sch.; Memorial Univ., Newfoundland; Merton Coll., Oxford (MA History and Mod. Langs); Stanford Graduate Sch. of Business, USA (MS Management Science). Foreign Office, 1973–74; Private Sec. to HM Ambassador, Paris, 1974–76; HM Treasury, 1976–82; McKinsey & Co. Inc., 1982–87 (Special Adviser to Chancellor of the Exchequer, 1985–86); Controller, Audit Commn, 1987–92; Dir Gen., CBI, 1992–95; Dep. Gov., 1995–97, Dir, 1998–2003, Bank of England; Chm., FSA, 1997–2003; Dir, London Sch. of Econs and Pol Sci., 2003–11. Chm., Phoenix Gp plc, 2012–15; Director: GKN plc, 1990–95; Morgan Stanley Inc., 2004–15; Paternoster Ltd, 2006–10; Prudential plc, 2010–; Chair, Internat. Adv. Council, China Securities Regulatory Commn, 2013–; Mem., NatWest Internat. Adv. Bd, 1992–95. Director: BOTB, 1992–95; BITC, 1992–95. Chm., Airports Commn, 2012–15. Vis. Prof., Institut d'Etudes Politiques, Paris, 2011–. Trustee, Tate Gall., 2002–10; Dir, Nat. Theatre, 2011–15; Chm., London Liby, 2015–. Pres., Age Concern England, 1994–98. Governor: De Montfort Univ. (formerly Leicester Polytechnic), 1988–95; Royal Acad. of Music, 2005–13. Chm. Judges, Man Booker Prize for Fiction, 2007. *Publications:* The Chancellors' Tales, 2006; Global Financial Regulation: the essential guide, 2008; Banking on the Future: the fall and rise of central banking, 2010; The Financial Crisis: who's to blame?, 2010; Can Financial Markets be Controlled?, 2015. *Recreation:* cricket. *Clubs:* Barnes Common Cricket; Manchester City Supporters.

**DAVIES, Hugh Curry,** OBE 2011; QC 2013; *b* Pembury, 11 Jan. 1967; *s* of Roy and Ann Ursula Davies; *m* 1999, Claire Ellis; one *s* two *d*. *Educ:* Reading Sch.; Pembroke Coll., Oxford (BA Hons Juris.; Domus Schol.; Winter Williams Prize for Law 1988). Called to the Bar, Lincoln's Inn, 1990 (Walter Wigglesworth Maj. Schol. 1990); in practice as a barrister, specialising in criminal law, police misconduct and regulation, inquests, and child exploitation. Legal Advr to Child Exploitation and Online Protection Centre, 2006–. *Publications:* (with J. Beggs) Police Misconduct, Complaints and Public Regulation, 2009, 2nd edn 2018. *Recreations:* hill-walking, running. *Address:* 3 Raymond Buildings, Gray's Inn, WC1R 5BH. *T:* (020) 7400 6400. *Club:* MCC.

**DAVIES, Hugh Llewelyn,** CMG 1994; HM Diplomatic Service, retired; Senior Partner, Orient Asian Partners, since 2005; *b* 8 Nov. 1941; *s* of late Vincent Davies (formerly ICS), OBE, and Rose (*née* Temple); *m* 1968, Virginia Ann Lucius; one *d* one *s*. *Educ:* Rugby School; Churchill College, Cambridge (Hons History degree). HM Diplomatic Service, 1965–99: Chinese Language Studies, Hong Kong, 1966–68; Second Sec., Office of British Chargé d'Affaires, Peking, 1969–71; Far Eastern Dept, FCO, 1971–74; First Sec. (Econ.), Bonn, 1974–77; Head of Chancery, Singapore, 1977–79; Asst Head, Far Eastern Dept, FCO, 1979–82; on secondment, Barclays Bank International, 1982–83; Commercial Counsellor, Peking, 1984–87; Dep. British Permanent Rep., OECD, Paris, 1987–90; Hd, Far Eastern Dept, FCO, 1990–93; Sen. British Trade Comr, Hong Kong, June–Sept. 1993; British Sen. Rep., (Ambassador), Sino-British Jt Liaison Gp, Hong Kong, 1993–97; Special Enquiry on China Trade and Special Co-ordinator, China, Taiwan and Hong Kong, FCO, 1997–98; Exec. Dir, Prudential Corp. Asia, 1999–2005; Sen. Advr, China, Old Mutual, 2005–06. Chm., China Assoc., 2002–14; Mem. Bd, China Britain Trade Council, 1999–2013; Vice Chm., GB China Centre, 2003–16. Mem., Adv. Bd, China Policy Inst., Univ. of Nottingham, 2008–15. Hon. Chm., Sinophi Healthcare, 2013–. Gov., Bruton Sch. for Girls, 2009–. Chm., Cucklington Village Meeting, 2016–. *Recreations:* writing and researching family history, watersports, sketching, travel, gardens, walking. *Address:* Church Farm, Cucklington, Wincanton, Somerset BA9 9PT.
*See also Sir J. M. Davies.*

**DAVIES, Hunter;** *see* Davies, Edward H.

**DAVIES, His Honour Huw;** QC 2001; a Circuit Judge, 2008–16; *b* 25 Oct. 1955; *s* of Walter Stephen Davies and May Davies. *Educ:* UCW, Aberystwyth (LLB); Sidney Sussex Coll., Cambridge (MPhil). Called to the Bar, Gray's Inn, 1978; Asst Recorder, 1994–98; Recorder, 1998–2008; Standing Counsel to HM Customs and Excise, Wales and Chester Circuit, 1996–2001.

**DAVIES, Huw;** *see* Davies, Evan H.

**DAVIES, Huw Humphreys;** Chief Executive, Channel Television, 2000–06; *b* Aug. 1940; *s* of William Davies and Sian Davies; *m* 1966, Elizabeth Shân Harries; two *d*. *Educ:* Llangynog Primary School; Llandovery College; Pembroke College, Oxford. MA (Lit.Hum.). Director/Producer: Television Wales and West, 1964; HTV, 1968; HTV Cymru/Wales: Asst Controller of Programmes, 1978; Controller of Programmes, 1979–81; Dir of Programmes, 1981–87; Chief Exec., 1987–91; Gp Dir of Television, HTV, 1989–94; Pres., HTV Internat., 1994–96; Chairman: Square Circle Prodns Ltd, 1996–2002; Content Media Corp., 2010–14 (Dir, Content Film, 2004–10); Dir, 1996–2003, Chm., 2003–04, Winchester Entertainment (formerly Winchester Multimedia). Produced and directed many programmes and series in English and Welsh; latterly numerous plays and drama-documentaries. Chm., Regional Controllers, ITV, 1987–88. Mem., Gorsedd of Bards. *Recreation:* driving around America. *Address:* Penarth, S Glamorgan CF64 3HY.

**DAVIES, Lt-Col Hywel William;** *b* 28 June 1945; *s* of late William Lewis Davies, JP and Barbara Beatrice Eleanor Davies, JP, MFH, Pantyderi, Boncath, Pembs; *m* 1969, Patricia (*d* 2017), *d* of late Lt-Col E. B. Thornhill, MC; one *s* one *d*. *Educ:* Harrow; Magdalene Coll., Cambridge (MA). Commnd RHG (The Blues, later Blues & Royals), 1965; Staff Coll., 1977; Operational Requirements, MoD, 1978–80; Defence Intelligence, MoD, 1982–84; CO, Blues & Royals, 1985–87; with Pilkington Optronics, 1989–91; Chief Executive: RHASS, 1991–98; BHS, 1998–2000. Chm., Peatland Gp, 2000–07; Man. Dir, Peatland Smokehouse Ltd, 2002–07; Director: G. D. Golding & Son Ltd, 1988–2015; Challenger Consultancy Ltd, 1987–91; Ingliston Hotels Ltd, 1997–98; Scottish Farming and Educnl Trust, 1991–98; Scottish Agricl & Rural Develt Centre Ltd, 1992–98; The Countryside Movt, 1995–97; Ingliston Develt Trust, 1996–98; British Horse Soc. Trading Co. Ltd, 1998–2000. Mem., Countryside Cttee, Countryside Alliance, 1997–99. Chairman: Assoc. of Show and Agricl Orgns, 1998–99 (Hon. Life Mem., 2000); Draught Horse Trng Cttee, 1998–2000; Royal Internat. Horse Show, 1998–2000. Mem. (C) S Ayrshire Council, 2003–17 (Convenor, Rural Affairs Cttee and HR Cttee, 2005–07; Sen. Councillor, Leadership Panel, Lifelong Learning portfolio, 2007–12). Chairman: Central Region, 1998, Ayr and Arran, 2004–12, Assoc. of Order of St John; W Lowland Cadet Force League, 2001–09; Vice Pres., Ayrshire and Arran Red Cross, 2002–04; Mem., Strathclyde Police Authy, 2012–13. Treasurer: St Brynach's Ch, Nevern, 2014–19; Pembrokeshire br., Welsh Historic Gardens Trust, 2017–. ARAgS 1996. CStJ 2009 (OStJ 1997). *Recreations:* equestrian pursuits (Mem., Coaching Club; represented UK at Four-in-Hand Carriage Driving, 1984–87), shooting, fishing, gardening. *Address:* Shieldaig, Nevern, Newport, Pembrokeshire SA42 0NQ.

**DAVIES, Ian;** HM Diplomatic Service; One HMG Liaison and Communications Manager, Estates Department, Foreign and Commonwealth Office, since 2016; *b* 1 Aug. 1956; *s* of late John Davies and of Freda Mary Davies; *m* 1979, Purificación Bautista Hervias; two *d*. *Educ:* Queen Mary Coll., London (BSc Econs 1983); Birkbeck Coll., London (MSc Econs 1985); Open Univ. (MBA 2011). Joined FCO, 1976; Moscow, 1978–80; Protocol Dept, FCO, 1983–85; Paris, 1985–88; Moscow, 1988–90; Far Eastern Dept, FCO, 1990–93; Dep. Head of Mission, Bolivia, 1993–96; Consul Gen., Marseille, 1997–2001; Dep. Head of Mission, Peru, 2002–05; FCO Response Centre, FCO, 2005–08; project work, FCO, 2008–09; Hd, Chem. and Biol Weapons Conventions Team, 2010–13; Hd, Home Estate Team, Estates and Security Dept, 2013–16. *Recreations:* walking, classical music, cinema, theatre. *Address:* c/o Foreign and Commonwealth Office, King Charles Street, SW1A 2AH.

**DAVIES, Ian;** *see* Davies, D. I.

**DAVIES, Iestyn Ioan,** MBE 2017; FRAM; countertenor singer; *b* York, 16 Sept. 1979; *s* of Dr Ioan Charles Davies and Diana Davies (*née* Wood); *m* 2016, Gemma Lawley. *Educ:* Wells Cathedral Sch.; St John's Coll., Cambridge (BA Archaeol. and Anthropol. 2002; MA); Royal Acad. of Music (PGDip; ARAM). FRAM 2012. Operatic début, Zurich, 2005; roles in operas by Handel, Britten, Adès and Benjamin; Farinelli in Farinelli and the King, Shakespeare's Globe, 2015; first British countertenor to appear at Metropolitan Opera, NY, 2011. Residency at Wigmore Hall, 2012–13. Music Award for Young Artist, Royal Philharmonic Soc., 2009; Gramophone Award for Recital Disc, 2012, 2014, 2017; Critics' Circle Award for Best Singer, 2013. *Recreations:* archaeology, Georgian architecture, football (Liverpool FC), wine collecting, baroque music, dogs, impersonations. *Address:* c/o Askonas Holt Ltd, 15 Fetter Lane, EC4A 1BW. *T:* (020) 7400 1700. *E:* sue.spence@askonasholt.co.uk. *Clubs:* Savile, Garrick.

**DAVIES, (Ifor) Huw I.;** *see* Irranca-Davies.

**DAVIES, Isobel Mary M.;** *see* Macdonald-Davies.

**DAVIES, Prof. (Ivor) Norman (Richard),** CMG 2001; PhD; FBA 1997; historian; Senior Research Associate, Oxford University, since 1997; Fellow, St Antony's College, Oxford, 2007–10, now Honorary; Supernumerary Fellow, Wolfson College, Oxford,

1998–2005; Professor of Polish History, School of Slavonic and East European Studies, University of London, 1985–96, now Emeritus; *b* Bolton, 8 June 1939; *s* of Richard Davies and Elizabeth Bolton; *m* 1st, 1966, Maria Zielińska; one *s*; 2nd, 1984, Maria Korzeniewicz; one *s*. *Educ*: Bolton Sch.; Grenoble Univ.; Magdalen Coll., Oxford (MA); Sussex Univ. (MA); Jagiellonian Univ., Cracow (PhD). Asst Master, St Paul's Sch., London, 1963–65; Alistair Horne Res. Fellow, St Antony's Coll., Oxford, 1969–71; Lectr, 1971–84, Reader, 1984–85, SSEES, London Univ. Visiting Professor: Columbia Univ., 1974; McGill Univ., 1977–78; Hokkaido Univ., 1982–83; Stanford Univ., 1985–86; Harvard Univ., 1991; Univ. of Adelaide, 1998; ANU, Canberra, 1999; Visiting Fellow: Clare Hall, Cambridge, 2006–07; Peterhouse, Cambridge, 2008–09. FRHistS 1974. Dr *hc*: Marie Curie-Skłodowska Univ., Lublin, 1993; Univ. of Gdańsk, 2000; Jagiellonian Univ., 2003; Sussex, 2006; Warsaw, 2007; Hon. DLit UCL, 2015. Hon. Citizen: Cracow, 1999; Lublin, 2000; Wrocław, 2002; Warsaw, 2004. Kt Cross, Order of Polonia Restituta (Poland), 1984; Commander Cross, 1992, Grand Cross, 1998, Order of Merit (Poland); Medal of Bene Merito (Poland), 2010; Mem., Order of White Eagle (Poland), 2012. *Publications*: White Eagle, Red Star: the Polish-Soviet war of 1919–20, 1972; Poland Past and Present: a bibliography of works in English on Polish history, 1976; God's Playground: a history of Poland, 2 vols, 1981; Heart of Europe: a short history of Poland, 1984; (ed with A. Polonsky) The Jews in Eastern Poland and the Soviet Union 1939–45, 1991; Europe: a history, 1996; The Isles: a history, 1999; (with Roger Moorhouse) Microcosm: portrait of a central European city, 2002; Rising '44: the battle for Warsaw, 2003; Europe East & West, 2006; Europe at War 1939–1945: no simple victory, 2006; Vanished Kingdoms: the history of half-forgotten Europe, 2011; Trail of Hope, 2015; Beneath Another Sky: a global journey into history, 2017; books trans. into most European langs and others, incl. Chinese and Japanese. *Recreation*: not writing. *Address*: St Antony's College, Oxford OX2 6JF.

**DAVIES, James Michael**; general practitioner, North East Wales and West Cheshire, since 2017; *b* St Asaph, 27 Feb. 1980; *s* of Michael Davies and Belinda Davies; *m* 2012, Nina Jones; two *s*. *Educ*: King's Sch., Chester; Christ's Coll., Cambridge (BA; MB BChir 2004; MA 2005). MRCGP 2008. Pre-registration House Officer, Glan Clwyd Hosp., 2004–05; Sen. House Officer, Countess of Chester Hosp., 2005–07; GP Registrar, City Walls Med. Centre, Chester, 2007–08; GP, Boughton Med. Gp, Chester, 2008–15, Partner, 2010–15. Mem. (C), Denbighshire CC, 2004–15. MP (C) Vale of Clwyd, 2015–17; contested (C) same seat, 2017. *Recreations*: travelling, walking, languages, local community regeneration, cinema, real ale and dining out, DIY. *Address*: c/o Vale of Clwyd Conservatives, Hanover House, The Roe, St Asaph, Denbighshire LL17 0LT. *E*: mail@jamesdavies.org.uk. *W*: www.twitter.com/jamesdavies, www.facebook.com/jamesdaviesofficial. *Club*: Carlton.

**DAVIES, James Selwyn, (Joe)**; Master of Haileybury, 2009–17; *b* Harlech, 29 June 1956; *s* of John Selwyn Davies and Joan Davies; *m* 1981, Virginia Felicity Graham; three *s* one *d*. *Educ*: Christ Coll., Brecon; St John's Coll., Cambridge (BA 1977); University Coll., Cardiff (PGCE 1980). Housemaster, Tonbridge Sch., 1980–94, exchange teacher, Anglican Church Grammar Sch., Brisbane, 1988; Dep. Hd, St John's Sch., Leatherhead, 1994–2000; Headmaster, Sutton Valence Sch., 2001–09. Chm., Ind. Schs Teacher Induction Panel, 2014–17. *Recreations*: Rugby football (Cambridge blue, London Welsh, Penarth), cricket, squash, marathon running, reading, cycling, camping. *Clubs*: East India, Lansdowne, Oriental; Hawks (Cambridge).

**DAVIES, Jane**; *see* Davies, B. J.

**DAVIES, Janet**; Member (Plaid Cymru) South Wales West, National Assembly for Wales, 1999–2007; *b* 29 May 1938; *d* of late David Rees and Jean Wardlaw Rees; *m* 1965, Basil Peter Ridley Davies (*d* 2000); one *s* one *d*. *Educ*: Howell's Sch., Llandaff; Trinity Coll., Carmarthen (BA); Open Univ. (BA Hons Social Scis). Mem. (Plaid Cymru) Taff Ely BC, 1983–96 (Leader, 1991–96); Mayor, Taff Ely, 1995–96. National Assembly for Wales: Plaid Cymru spokesperson on local govt, 1993–99, on housing, 1999–2002, for envmt, planning and transport, 2002, for transport, 2003–07; Plaid Cymru Chief Whip, 2003–07; Chm., Audit Cttee, 1999–2002, 2003–07. Dir of Elections, Plaid Cymru, 1996–2001. Contested (Plaid Cymru) Brecon and Radnorshire, 2010.

**DAVIES, Janet Mary H.**; *see* Hewlett-Davies.

**DAVIES, Jill Adrian**; *see* Kraye, J. A.

**DAVIES, Jocelyn Ann**; Member (Plaid Cymru) South East Wales, National Assembly for Wales, 1999–2016; *b* 18 June 1959; *d* of Edward and Marjorie Davies; one *s* two *d* by Michael Davies. *Educ*: Harris Manchester Coll., Oxford. Work in local govt, Islwyn BC and Newport BC, 1976–80. Mem. (Plaid Cymru) Islwyn BC, 1987–91. Dep. Minister for Housing, 2007–09, for Housing and Regeneration, 2009–11, Nat. Assembly for Wales. *Recreations*: walking, people watching.

**DAVIES, Joe**; *see* Davies, James S.

**DAVIES, Prof. John Brian**, FREng; Professor of Electrical Engineering, University College London, 1985–97, now Emeritus Professor; *b* 2 May 1932; *s* of John Kendrick Davies and Agnes Ada Davies; *m* 1956, Shirley June (*née* Abrahart); one *s* two *d*. *Educ*: Jesus Coll., Cambridge (MA); Univ. of London (MSc, PhD, DSc Eng). Research Engineer, Mullard Res. Labs, Redhill, 1955–63; Lectr, Dept of Electrical Engineering, Univ. of Sheffield, 1963; Sen. Lectr 1967, Reader 1970–85, Dean of Engrg, 1989–91, University College London. Vis. Scientist, Nat. Bureau of Standards, Boulder, Colo, 1971–72; Visitor, Univ. of Oxford, 1983; Vis. Prof., Univ. of Colorado, 1988–89. FREng (FEng 1988). *Publications*: Electromagnetic Theory, vol. 2, 1972; (contrib.) Numerical Techniques for Microwave and Millimeter Wave Passive Structures, 1989. *Recreations*: fell walking, music.

**DAVIES, Rt Rev. John David Edward**; *see* Wales, Archbishop of.

**DAVIES, Rt Rev. John Dudley**; Hon. Assistant Bishop: diocese of Lichfield, 1995–2005; diocese of St Asaph, since 2009; Bishop Suffragan, then Area Bishop, of Shrewsbury, 1987–94; *b* 12 Aug. 1927; *s* of Charles Edward Steedman Davies and Minnie Paton Davies; *m* 1956, Shirley Dorothy Gough; one *s* two *d*. *Educ*: Trinity Coll., Cambridge (BA 1951, MA 1963); Lincoln Theol Coll. Deacon 1953, priest 1954, dio. Ripon; Curate: Halton, Leeds, 1953–56; Yeoville, Johannesburg, 1957; Priest-in-Charge, Evander, dio. Johannesburg, 1957–61; Rector and Dir of Missions, Empangeni, dio. Zululand and Swaziland, 1961–63; Anglican Chaplain, Univ. of Witwatersrand and Johannesburg Coll. of Educn, 1963–70; Chm., Div. of Christian Educn, S African Council of Churches, 1964–70; Mem. Exec., Univ. Christian Movement of Southern Africa, 1966–69; Sec. for Chaplaincies of Higher Educn, C of E Bd of Educn, 1970–74; Vicar of Keele and Chaplain, Univ. of Keele, 1974–76; Principal, Coll. of Ascension, Selly Oak, 1976–81; Preb. of Sandiacre, Lichfield Cathedral, 1976–87; Diocesan Missioner, St Asaph, 1982–87; Canon Res. and Hellins Lectr, St Asaph, 1982–85; Vicar/Rector, Llanrhaeadr-ym-Mochnant, Llanarmon-Mynydd-Mawr, Pennant, Hirnant and Llangynog, 1985–87. *Publications*: Free to Be, 1970; Beginning Now, 1971; Good News in Galatians, 1975; Creed and Conflict, 1979; The Faith Abroad, 1983; (with John J. Vincent) Mark at Work, 1986; World on Loan, 1992; The Crisis of the Cross, 1997; Be Born in us Today, 1999; God at Work, 2001; Only Say the Word, 2002; A Song for Every Morning, 2008; (jtly) Stilling the Storm, 2011; Acts in Practice, 2012; Leviticus in Practice, 2014; Three Mountains to Freedom: practice interpretation of Paul's Letter to the Galatians, 2016; contribs to jls. *Address*: Nyddfa, By Pass Road, Gobowen, Oswestry SY11 3NG. *T*: (01691) 653434.

**DAVIES, John Hamilton**, OBE 2005; Chairman, Civil Service Appeal Board, 1999–2011; *b* 24 Nov. 1943; *s* of Albert Victor Davies and Betty Davies; *m* 1971, Helen Ruth Thomas; three *s*. *Educ*: Lewis Sch., Pengam, S Wales; Selwyn Coll., Cambridge (MA). ACIB 1970, FCIB 1991; FCIPD (FIPD 1991). With Barclays Bank, 1966–98: Local Dir, Chelmsford Reg., 1983–86; Hd, Career Planning, Gp Personnel, 1986–90; Dep. Dir, Gp Personnel, 1991–95; Dir, Personnel, Barclays UK Banking Services, 1995–98. Non-exec. Dir, ILX Gp (formerly Intellexis plc), 2001–06. Vis. Fellow, Cranfield Univ. Sch. of Mgt, 1998–2002. Board Member: Employers' Forum on Disability, 1991–96; BESO, 1991–98; Member: CBI Employment Policy Cttee, 1996–98; Armed Forces Pay Review Body, 1999–2005; Prison Service Pay Review Body, 2007–13. Treas. and Mem., Exec. Bd, CIB, 1998–99. Gov., Felsted Sch., 1990–95 and 1998– (Chm., 2007–). Freeman, City of London, 2002; Liveryman, Curriers' Co., 2002– (Master, 2016–17). *Recreations*: walking, Church of England, music, travel. *Address*: Denbies, Bardfield Saling, Essex CM7 5EG. *T*: (01371) 850735. *Clubs*: Oxford and Cambridge; Essex.

*See also* E. Davies.

**DAVIES, Very Rev. Dr John Harverd**; DL; Dean of Wells, since 2016; *b* Bolton, Lancs, 29 Nov. 1957. *Educ*: Brentwood Sch.; Keble Coll., Oxford (MA 1984); Corpus Christi Coll., Cambridge (MPhil 1984); Lancaster Univ. (PhD); Westcott House, Cambridge. Ordained deacon, 1984, priest, 1985; Assistant Curate: Our Lady and St Nicholas with St Anne, Liverpool, 1984–87; St John the Baptist, Peterborough, 1987–90; Minor Canon, Peterborough Cathedral, 1988–90; Vicar, St Margaret's, Anfield, 1990–94; Chaplain, Fellow and Lectr, Keble Coll., Oxford, 1994–99; Vicar, St Michael, Melbourne, 1999–2010; Dir of Ordinands, Dio. of Derby, 2000–09; Dean of Derby, 2010–16. Hon. Canon, Derby Cathedral, 2010. Chm., Industrial Mission in Derbys, 2009–16. DL: Derbys, 2011; Somerset, 2017. *Recreations*: reading, walking, musing. *Address*: Wells Cathedral Office, Chain Gate, Cathedral Green, Wells, Som BA5 2UE. *T*: (01749) 677888. *E*: thedeanofwells@gmail.com.

**DAVIES, Rev. Canon John Howard**; Director of Theological and Religious Studies, University of Southampton, 1981–94; *b* 19 Feb. 1929; *s* of Jabez Howard and Sarah Violet Davies; *m* 1956, Ina Mary (*d* 1985), *d* of Stanley William and Olive Mary Bubb; two *s* (and two *s* decd). *Educ*: Southall Grammar Sch.; St John's Coll., Cambridge (MA); Westcott House, Cambridge; Univ. of Nottingham (BD); FRCO 1952. Ordained deacon, 1955, priest 1956. Succentor of Derby Cathedral, 1955; Chaplain of Westcott House, 1958; Lectr in Theology, Univ. of Southampton, 1963, Sen. Lectr 1974. Canon Theologian of Winchester, 1981–91. *Publications*: A Letter to Hebrews, 1967; (contrib.) Walter Frere, 2011. *Recreations*: music, architecture, the countryside. *Address*: 13 Glen Eyre Road, Southampton SO16 3GA. *T*: (023) 8067 9359.

**DAVIES, John Irfon**, CBE 1998 (MBE (mil.) 1963); Under Secretary, Welsh Office, 1985–90, retired; Chairman, Health Promotion Authority for Wales, 1992–99; *b* 8 June 1930; *s* of late Thomas M. Davies and Mary M. Davies (*née* Harris); *m* 1950, Jean Marion Anderson (*d* 2000); one *d*. *Educ*: Stanley School; Croydon Polytechnic. Joined RAF, 1948, commissioned 1950, Specialist Navigator 1957; psc 1963; MoD, 1964–66; Chief Navigation Instructor, Cranwell, 1967; OC Flying, Muharraq, 1967–69; aws 1970; MoD, 1970–72; Cabinet Office, 1972–74; retd from RAF, 1974 (Wing Comdr); Principal, 1974–78, Asst Sec., 1978–85, Welsh Office; Private Sec. to Sec. of State for Wales, 1977–78. Mem., GMC, 1990–99. *Recreations*: golf, piano, fishing, books. *Address*: 7 Danybryn Close, Radyr, Cardiff CF15 8DJ. *Clubs*: Royal Air Force; Cardiff and County; Radyr Golf.

**DAVIES, Prof. John Kenyon**, MA, DPhil; FSA; FBA 1985; Rathbone Professor of Ancient History and Classical Archaeology, University of Liverpool, 1977–2003; *b* 19 Sept. 1937; *s* of Harold Edward Davies and Clarice Theresa (*née* Woodburn); *m* 1st, 1962, Anna Elbina Morpurgo (Prof. Anna Morpurgo Davies, Hon. DBE, FBA) (marr. diss. 1978; she *d* 2014); 2nd, 1978, Nicola Jane, *d* of Dr and Mrs R. M. S. Perrin; one *s* one *d*. *Educ*: Manchester Grammar Sch.; Wadham Coll., Oxford (BA 1959; MA 1962; DPhil 1966). FSA 1986. Harmsworth Sen. Scholar, Merton Coll., Oxford, 1960–61 and 1962–63; Jun. Fellow, Center for Hellenic Studies, Washington, DC, 1961–62; Dyson Jun. Res. Fellow, Balliol Coll., Oxford, 1963–65; Lectr in Ancient History, Univ. of St Andrews, 1965–68; Fellow and Tutor in Ancient History, Oriel Coll., Oxford, 1968–77; Pro-Vice-Chancellor, Univ. of Liverpool, 1986–90. Leverhulme Res. Prof., 1995–2000. Vis. Lectr, Univ. of Pennsylvania, 1971; Teaching Fellow, and Dir, Postgraduate residential course, British Sch. of Archaeology, Athens, 2004, 2006, 2008; Sen. Fellow, Istituto di Studi Avanzati, Univ. di Bologna, 2006; Onassis Foundn Vis. Fellow, Inst. of Greek and Roman Antiquity, Athens, 2010. Chairman: St Patrick's Isle (IOM) Archaeological Trust Ltd, 1982–86; NW Archaeol Trust, 1982–91. Chm., Adv. Cttee, Inst. of Classical Studies, Univ. of London, 2005–13; Expert Advr, Eur. Sci. Foundn, 2006–. Corresp. Mem., Deutsche Archäologische Institut, 2000. Editor: Jl of Hellenic Studies, 1972–77; Archaeol Reports, 1972–74. *Publications*: Athenian Propertied Families 600–300 BC, 1971; Democracy and Classical Greece, 1978, 2nd edn 1993 (Spanish trans. 1981, German and Italian trans. 1983, Polish trans. 2003, Russian trans. 2004, Greek trans. 2014); Wealth and the Power of Wealth in Classical Athens, 1981; (ed with L. Foxhall) The Trojan War: its historicity and context, 1984; (ed jtly) Cambridge Ancient History vol. 5, 2nd edn, 1992; (ed jtly) Hellenistic Economies, 2001; (ed jtly) Making, Moving, and Managing, 2005; (ed jtly) The Economies of Hellenistic Societies, Third to First Centuries BC, 2011; (ed jtly) Epigraphy and the Historical Sciences, 2012; articles and reviews in learned jls. *Recreations*: canal walking, choral music, mainland European railways. *Address*: 20 North Road, Grassendale Park, Liverpool L19 0LR. *T*: (0151) 427 2126.

**DAVIES, Sir (John) Michael**, KCB 2002; Clerk of the Parliaments, House of Lords, 1997–2003; *b* 2 Aug. 1940; *s* of late Vincent Ellis Davies, OBE and Rose Trench (*née* Temple); *m* 1971, Amanda Mary Atkinson; two *s* one *d*. *Educ*: The King's Sch., Canterbury; Peterhouse, Cambridge. Joined Parliament Office, House of Lords, 1964; seconded to Civil Service Dept as Private Sec. to Leader of House of Lords and Govt Chief Whip, 1971–74; Establishment Officer and Sec. to Chm. of Cttees, 1974–83; Principal Clerk, Overseas and European Office, 1983–85; Principal Clerk, Private Bill and Overseas Offices and Examiner of Petitions for Private Bills, 1985–88; Reading Clerk, 1988–90, and Clerk of Public Bills, 1988–94; Clerk Asst, 1991–97, and Principal Finance Officer, 1994–97. Secretary: Soc. of Clerks-at-the-Table in Commonwealth Parlts, and Jt Editor, The Table, 1967–83; Statute Law Cttee, 1974–83. Pres., Assoc. of Secs-General of Parlts, 1997–2000. Chm., BACSA, 2008–19. *Address*: 26 Northchurch Terrace, N1 4EG. *Club*: Garrick.

*See also* H. L. Davies.

**DAVIES, Rt Rev. John Stewart**; Bishop of St Asaph, 1999–2008; *b* 28 Feb. 1943; *s* of John Edward Davies and Dorothy Stewart Davies (*née* Jones); *m* 1965, Joan Patricia Lovatt; two *s*. *Educ*: St John's Sch., Leatherhead; UCNW, Bangor (BA Hebrew); Westcott House,

Cambridge; Queens' Coll., Cambridge (MLitt 1974). Journalism, 1960–68; ordained deacon, 1974, priest, 1975; Curate, Hawarden, 1974–78; Vicar: Rhosymedre, 1978–87; Mold, 1987–92; Archdeacon of St Asaph, 1991–99. *Recreations:* hill walking, cycling.

**DAVIES, Jonathan,** OBE 2015 (MBE 1995); writer and commentator on Rugby Union and League football; *b* 24 Oct. 1962; *s* of late Len and of Diana Davies; *m* 1984, Karen Hopkins (*d* 1997); one *s* two *d*; *m* 2002, Helen Jones (marr. diss.); *m* 2016, Jay Thorburn. *Educ:* Gwendraeth Grammar Sch. Rugby Union footballer to 1989; played for Neath and Llanelli; 37 Wales caps, 4 as Captain; transferred to Rugby League, 1989; with Widnes, 1989–93, Warrington, 1993–95; returned to Rugby Union, 1995; with Cardiff, 1995–97, retired. Player of the Year Award, 1991, 1994; Stones Bitter Man of Steel, 1994. Pres., Velindre Cancer Centre, 2009–. *Publications:* with Peter Corrigan: Jonathan (autobiog.), 1989; Codebreaker, 1996. *Recreations:* golf, football.

**DAVIES, Jonathan Norval; His Honour Judge Jonathan Davies;** a Circuit Judge, since 2019; *b* Birmingham, 21 July 1959; *s* of Robert Davies and Doreen Davies; *m* 1991, Bridget Williams; one *s* one *d*. *Educ:* Netherstowe Comp. Sch., Lichfield; Queen Mary Coll., Univ. of London (LLB). Called to the Bar, Inner Temple, 1981; barrister, Guildford Chambers, 1984–99, 9–12 Bell Yard, 1999–2017, Foundry Chambers, 2017–19; a Recorder, 2009–19. *Recreations:* ski-ing, mountain biking, windsurfing. *Address:* Kingston Crown Court, 6–8 Penrhyn Road, Kingston upon Thames KT1 2BB.

**DAVIES, Prof. Julian Edmund,** PhD; FRS 1994; FRSC 1996; Professor and Head of Department of Microbiology and Immunology, University of British Columbia, 1992–97, now Professor Emeritus; *b* 9 Jan. 1932; *s* of Norman Alfred Davies and Lilian Constance (*née* Clarke); *m* 1957, Dorothy Jean Olney; two *s* one *d*. *Educ:* Univ. of Nottingham (BSc Hons Chem., Maths and Phys.; PhD 1956). Lectr in Chem., Univ. of Manchester, 1959–62; Associate in Bacteriol., Harvard Univ., 1962–67; University of Wisconsin: Associate Prof. of Biochem., 1967–70; Prof., 1970–80; Biogen: Res. Dir, 1980–83; Pres., 1983–85; Prof., Inst. Pasteur, Paris, 1986–91; Dir, West-East Center, Univ. of BC, 1993–96; Chief Scientific Officer, and Vice-Pres. of Res., TerraGen Diversity Inc., 1996–2000; Exec. Vice-Pres. for Technology Develt, Cubist Pharmaceuticals, Vancouver, 2000–04; Dir, Life Scis Inst., Univ. of British Columbia, 2005–06. President: Amer. Soc. for Microbiol., 1999–2000; Internat. Union Microbiol. Soc., 2002–05. Foreign Associate, US NAS, 2014. Hon. DSc: UBC 2003; Nottingham, 2009; McGill, 2011; Guelph; McMaster, 2015. Hoechst-Roussel Award, 1986, Lifetime Achievement Award, 2012, Amer. Soc. for Microbiol.; Thom Award, Soc. for Industrial Microbiol., 1993; Scheele Prize, Swedish Acad. of Pharmaceutical Scis, 1997; Bristol Myers Squibb Award, 1999; Soc. for Gen. Microbiol. Medal, 2012. *Publications:* (jtly) Elementary Biochemistry, 1980; (jtly) Milestones in Biotechnology, 1992; (ed jtly) Manual of Industrial Microbiology and Biotechnology, 2nd edn 1999, 3rd edn 2010; articles and contribs to books, symposia and commentaries. *Recreations:* cycling, wine, gym. *Address:* 202/5760 Hampton Place, Vancouver, BC V6T 2G1, Canada. *T:* (604) 2228235.

**DAVIES, Julienne Elizabeth;** *see* Meyer, J. E.

**DAVIES, Karl;** *see* Davies, R. K.

**DAVIES, Dame Kay (Elizabeth),** DBE 2008 (CBE 1995); DPhil; FMedSci; FRS 2003; Professor of Genetics, since 2018, Deputy Director, MDUK Oxford Neuromuscular Centre, since 2018, and Associate Head (Development, Impact and Equality), Medical Sciences Division, since 2011, University of Oxford; Fellow of Hertford College, Oxford, since 1998; *b* 1 April 1951; *d* of Harry Partridge and Florence Partridge (*née* Farmer); *m* 1973, Stephen Graham Davies (marr. diss. 2000); one *s*. *Educ:* Stourbridge Girls' High Sch.; Somerville Coll., Oxford (BA, MA, DPhil; Hon. Fellow, 1995). MRCPath 1990, FRCPath 1997. Guy Newton Jun. Res. Fellow, Wolfson Coll., Oxford, 1976–78; Royal Soc. European Post-doctoral Fellow, Service de Biochimie, Centre d'Etudes, Gif-sur-Yvette, France, 1978–80; St Mary's Hospital Medical School: Cystic Fibrosis Res. Fellow, 1980–82; MRC Sen. Res. Fellow, 1982–84; Nuffield Department of Clinical Medicine, John Radcliffe Hospital, Oxford: MRC Sen. Res. Fellow, 1984–86; MRC Ext. Staff, 1986–92; Univ. Res. Lectr, 1990; MRC Ext. Staff, Inst. of Molecular Medicine, Oxford, 1989–95; Fellow of Green Coll., Oxford, 1990–95; MRC Res. Dir, MRC Clin. Scis Centre, Hammersmith Hosp., 1992–94; Oxford University: Prof. of Genetics, and Fellow, Keble Coll., 1995–98; Dr Lee's Prof. of Anatomy, 1998–2018; Hon. Dir, MRC Functional Genetics Unit, 1999–2017; Co-Dir, Henry Wellcome Centre for Gene Function, 2001–11; Hd, Dept of Physiol., Anatomy and Genetics, Med. Scis Div., 2008–11. Mem., MRC, 2002–. Dep. Chm., Wellcome Trust, 2013–17. Mem., Royal Commn for Exhibn of 1851, 2011–. Editor (with S. Tilghman), Genome Analysis Reviews, 1990–. Bristol-Myers Prof., USA, 1986; 7th Annual Colleen Giblin Dist. Lectr, Columbia Univ., 1992; Dist. Lectr, Mayo Clinic, USA, 1994. Founder FMedSci 1998. Hon. FRCP 1994. Hon. DSc Victoria, Canada, 1990; DUniv Open, 1999. Wellcome Trust Award, 1996; SCI Medal, 1999; Allan Award, Amer. Soc. of Human Genetics, 2015. *Publications:* (with A. P. Read) Molecular Analysis of Inherited Diseases, 1988, rev. edn 1992; (ed) Human Genetics Diseases: a practical approach, 1988, rev. edn 1993; (ed) Genome Analysis: a practical approach, 1988; (ed) The Fragile X Syndrome, 1989; (ed) Application of Molecular Genetics to the Diagnosis of Inherited Diseases, 1989; numerous reviews and 400 peer-reviewed pubns. *Recreations:* music, gardening, walking. *Address:* Department of Physiology, Anatomy and Genetics, University of Oxford, Parks Road, Oxford OX1 3PT.

**DAVIES, Keith Laurence M.;** *see* Maitland Davies.

**DAVIES, Keith Price;** Member (Lab) Llanelli, National Assembly for Wales, 2011–16; *b* Gwaun-Cae-Gurwen, 25 May 1940; *s* of James Glyn Davies and Elizabeth Iris Davies; *m* 1st, 1963, Margaret Legge (marr. diss. 1991); two *s* one *d*; 2nd, 1992, Heddyr Gregory; two *s*. *Educ:* Ystalyfera Grammar Sch.; University Coll. Swansea (BSc 1st Cl.; MSc); University Coll. of South Wales and Monmouthshire (PGCE). Hd of Maths, Maesteg Grammar Tech. Sch., 1963–65; Sen. Lectr, Cardiff Coll. of Educn, 1965–72; Advr in Maths, Glamorgan LEA, 1972–74; Mid Glamorgan County Council: Sen. Advr, Secondary, 1974–79; Chief Advr, 1979–94; Dir of Educn, 1994–96; Dir of Educn, Carmarthenshire CC, 1996–2000; Chief Exec. (pt-time), Birmingham Careers and Educn Business Partnership, 2000; Dir (pt-time), Welsh Baccalaureate Qualification, WJEC, 2003–08. *Recreations:* sport in general, reading. *Address:* Caedelyn, 2 Pen-y-Fai Lane, Llanelli SA15 4EN. *T:* 07540 964669.

**DAVIES, Keith Robert,** OBE 2009; Manager, Legal Change Programme, British Council, 2017–18; independent consultant, since 2018; *b* Frodsham, Cheshire, 9 May 1954; *s* of Robert Charles Davies and Mary Davies (*née* Briscoe); *m* 1994, Christine Loh (*d* 2018); one *d*. *Educ:* Helsby Co. Grammar Sch. for Boys; Univ. of Hull (BA Hons Drama and English 1975); Poly. of Central London (Postgrad. Dip. Film Studies 1983). Joined British Council, 1976; Club Sec., British Council Students Centre, London, 1976–80; Acquisitions Officer, Film Dept, 1980–84; Asst Rep., Bahrain, 1985–88; Promotions Officer, Educn Counselling Service, London, 1988–90; Educn Counsellor, Malaysia, 1990–95; Dep. Dir, Thailand, 1995–99; Hd, Ops, China, 1999–2004; Director: Vietnam, 2004–08; Indonesia, 2009–13; Sri Lanka, 2013–17. Trustee and Co. Sec., No. 1 Community Trust, 2019–. *Recreations:* assiduously following the trials and tribulations and occasional triumphs of Everton Football Club, travel, cinema, exploring, reading, food, Asian cultures. *Address:* 3 Stuart Close, Tunbridge Wells, Kent TN2 5PJ. *E:* keithdaviesvn@yahoo.co.uk.

**DAVIES, Dame Laura (Jane),** DBE 2014 (CBE 2000; MBE 1988); professional golfer; *b* 5 Oct. 1963; *d* of David Thomas Davies and Rita Ann Davies (*née* Foskett). *Educ:* Fullbrook County Secondary Sch. Mem., Curtis Cup team, 1984; professional début, 1985; Mem., Solheim Cup team, 1990, 1992, 1994, 1996, 1998, 2000, 2002, 2003, 2005, 2007, 2009, 2011; Winner: Belgian Ladies' Open, 1985; Ladies' British Open, 1986; US Ladies' Open, 1987; Italian Open, 1987, 1988, 1996; Ford Classic, Woburn, 1988; Biarritz Ladies' Open, 1988; Itoki Classic, Japan, 1988; European Open, 1992; Thailand Ladies' Open, 1993, 1994; English Open, 1993, 1995; Australian Ladies' Masters, 1993, 1994, 2003; LPGA Championship, 1994, 1996; Irish Open, 1994, 1995; Scottish Open, 1994; French Masters, 1995; Danish Open, 1997; Championship of Europe, 1999; Norwegian Masters, 2002, 2006; Australian Open, 2004, 2009; Pegasus NZ Women's Open, 2010; German Open, 2010; Austrian Open, 2010; Spanish Open, 2010; Indian Open, 2010. Mem., Golf Foundn. *Publications:* Carefree Golf, 1991. *Address:* c/o IMG Golf, Building 6, Chiswick Park, 566 Chiswick High Road, W4 5HR.

**DAVIES, Leighton;** *see* Davies, Robert L.

**DAVIES, Her Honour Linda Hillary;** a Circuit Judge, 1992–2009; *b* 31 May 1945; *d* of Lt-Col Robert Blowers and Doris Rhoda (*née* Hillary); *m* 1966, Michael Llewelyn Lifton Davies; two *d*. *Educ:* Folkestone Grammar Sch. for Girls; King's Coll., London (LLB Hons); Chichester Univ. (BA Hons Fine Arts 2017). Called to the Bar, Gray's Inn, 1969; Barrister, 1972–92, a Recorder, 1990–92, Western Circuit. Part-time Chm., Industrial Tribunals, 1986–92. Trustee, Roberts Centre, 2006–19.

**DAVIES, Lindsay Jane; Her Honour Judge Lindsay Davies;** a Circuit Judge, since 2012; *b* Swansea, 9 Aug. 1952; *d* of Raymond Peter and Finvola Clifford Davies. *Educ:* Llwyn-y-bryn Sch., Swansea; University Coll. of Wales, Aberystwyth (LLB Hons). Called to the Bar, Gray's Inn, 1975. Mem., Fenners Chambers, Cambridge, 1977–2012. Mem., RSAA, 1984. *Recreation:* travel in Central Asia. *Address:* Cambridge County Court, 197 East Road, Cambridge CB1 1BA.

**DAVIES, Dr Lindsey Margaret,** CBE 2004; FFPH; independent public health consultant, since 2013; President, Faculty of Public Health, Royal Colleges of Physicians of the UK, 2010–13; *b* 21 May 1953; *d* of Dr Frank Newby and Margaret Newby; *m* 1974, Peter Davies (marr. diss. 1994); two *s*. *Educ:* Univ. of Nottingham (BMedSci, BM, BS). MHSM 1987; FFPH (FFPHM 1991); FRCP 2002; FRCPE 2013. Community paediatrics, 1976–82; trainee in public health medicine, 1982–85; Director of Public Health: Southern Derbys HA, 1985–89; Nottingham HA, 1989–92; Hd, Public Health Div., NHS Exec., DoH, 1992–94; Dir of Public Health, Trent RHA, 1994–96; Dir of Public Health and Med. Dir, Trent Regl Office, NHS Exec., DoH, 1996–2002; Regl Dir of Public Health, E Midlands, DoH, 2002–06; Nat. Dir of Pandemic Influenza Preparedness, DoH, 2006–10; Dir of Olympics and Paralympics Prog., DoH, 2008–10; Interim Regl Dir of Public Health, NHS London, 2009–10. Hon. Prof. (formerly Special Prof.), Nottingham Univ. Med. Sch., 2001–. British Medical Association: Mem. Council, 1989–92; Chm., Cttee for Public Health Medicine and Community Health, 1990–92. Hon. FRCPI 2013. Hon. MD Sheffield, 2013. *Publications:* contribs to learned jls. *Recreations:* family life, gardening, walking.

**DAVIES, Ven. Lorys Martin;** Archdeacon of Bolton, 1992–2001, now Emeritus; *b* 14 June 1936; *s* of Evan Tudor Davies and Eigen Morfydd Davies; *m* 1960, Barbara Ethel (*née* Walkley); two *s*. *Educ:* Whitland Grammar Sch.; St David's Coll., Lampeter, Univ. of Wales (BA Hons); Philips Hist. Schol.; Organ Exhibnr. Wells Theol Coll. ALCM 1952. Ordained: deacon, 1959; priest, 1960; Curate, St Mary's, Tenby, 1959–61; Asst Chaplain, Brentwood Sch., 1962–66; Chaplain and Head of Dept, Solihull Sch., 1966–68; Vicar, St Mary's, Moseley, 1968–81; Residentiary Canon, Birmingham Cathedral, 1981–92; Diocesan Dir of Ordinands, Birmingham, 1982–90; Advr to Bishop of Manchester on Hosp. Chaplaincies, 1992–2001, Warden of Readers, 1994–2000, dio. of Manchester. Chm., House of Clergy, Birmingham Diocesan Synod, 1990–91; Proctor in Convocation, 1998–2001. Member: Nat. Stewardship Cttee, 2000–05; Hosp. Chaplaincies Council, 2000–05 (Vice-Chm., 2003–05). Reviewer: Community Health Improvement, 2001–04; Healthcare Commn, 2004–07. Midland Rep., Retired Clergy Assoc., 2009–12. JP Birmingham, 1978–92. *Recreations:* sport, theatre, music, reading. *Address:* 18 Bilberry Place, Recreation Road, Bromsgrove, Worcestershire B61 8DT.

**DAVIES, Lucy Alexandra;** Executive Producer, Royal Court Theatre, since 2013; *b* Birmingham, 24 July 1970; *d* of Prof. Llewellyn, (Tony), Davies and Hon. Teresa Davies; *m* 2005, Jonathan Glynn; two *s*. *Educ:* Swanshurst Sch., Birmingham; Cadbury Coll., Birmingham; Univ. of Exeter (BA Hons 1st Cl. Drama); University Coll. London (MA Philos.). Asst Dir and Asst Administrator, Kneehigh Th., 1992–94; Donmar Warehouse: Carlton Donmar Trainee Dir, 1994–95; Literary Manager and Producer, New Writing Seasons, 1995–99; Asst to Jez Butterworth, Miramax/Film 4, 1999–2001; Hd of Develt, Fox Phillips, 2001–04; Hd of Studio, RNT, 2004–07; Exec Producer, Donmar Warehouse, 2007–09; Founding Exec. Producer, National Theatre Wales, 2009–13. FRSA. *Recreations:* politics, visual arts, literature, travel, cooking, cycling, swimming, yoga. *Address:* Royal Court Theatre, Sloane Square, SW1W 8AS.

**DAVIES, Lynn,** CBE 2006 (MBE 1967); President, UK Athletics, 2002–15; *b* Nantymoel, Wales, 20 May 1942; *s* of Tegfryn Davies and Gwladys Davies; *m* 1966, Meriel Griffiths; one *d*. *Educ:* Cardiff Coll. of Educn (DipPE; Cert Ed). Teacher, Bridgend Grammar Sch., 1964–66; Lectr in Sport and PE, Cardiff Coll. of Educn, 1966–72; Tech. Dir, Canadian athletics, 1972–76; Team Manager, British Athletics Team, 1978–84, incl. Moscow and LA Olympic Games; Sen. Lectr in Sport and PE, UWIC, 1996–2007. Mem., Sports Council Wales, 2000–06; Vice Pres., British Olympic Assoc., 2001–12. Athlete: gold medal for long jump: Tokyo Olympics, 1964; European Championships, 1966; Commonwealth Games, 1966, 1970; European Indoor Championships, 1967; silver medal for long jump: European Championships, 1969; European Indoor Championships, 1969. Hon. MA: Open 1992; Wales 2008; Hon. Dr Cardiff Metropolitan, 2015. *Recreations:* gardening, golf, tennis, fitness, reading, cinema. *Address:* 1 Orchard Close, Marshfield, Cardiff CF3 2UA. *T:* (01633) 681672.

**DAVIES, Rt Rev. Mark;** *see* Middleton, Bishop Suffragan of.

**DAVIES, Rt Rev. Mark;** *see* Shrewsbury, Bishop of, (RC).

**DAVIES, Mark Edward Trehearne,** CVO 2017; DL; Chairman, Stonehage Fleming (UK) Ltd, since 2015 (Chief Executive, 2008–14, Director, 2003–14, Fleming Family & Partners Ltd); Director, Stonehage Fleming Family & Partners, since 2015; *b* 20 May 1948; *s* of late Denis Norman Davies and Patricia Helen (*née* Trehearne); *m* 1987, Antonia Catharine Chittenden; two *s* two *d*. *Educ:* Stowe. Chief Executive: Intercommodities Ltd, 1971–85; GNI Ltd, 1985–95; Gerrard Gp plc, 1995–2001 (Dir, 1986–2001); Chairman: Townhouse Hotel Investments Ltd, 1994–2006; Thornhill Nominees (formerly Thornhill

Hldgs) Ltd, 2001–10; Director: Thornhill Investment Mgt Ltd, 2001–10; Thornhill Hldgs (formerly Thornhill Acquisitions) Ltd, 2001–10; Thornhill Unit Trust Managers Ltd, 2001–10; Ascot Authority (Hldgs) Ltd, 2002–17; Caledonia Investments plc, 2002–12; FF&P Capital Mgt Ltd, 2004–10; Chairman: FF&P Asset Mgt Ltd, 2003–10; Stonehage Fleming Advisory Ltd, 2015–; Stonehage Fleming Private Equity, 2015–; Stonehage Fleming Wealth Planning Ltd, 2015–; FPE Capital Ltd, 2017–. Director: Rank Foundn Ltd, 1991–2018; Admington Hall Farms Ltd, 1995–; Racing Welfare, 2001–10; Racing Welfare (Enterprises) Ltd, 2006–10; Safeline, 2018–. High Sheriff, 2017–18, DL 2018, Warwickshire. *Publications:* (jtly) Trading in Commodities, 1974. *Recreations:* hunting, racing. *Address:* 26 Chester Street, SW1X 7BL; Stonehage Fleming Family & Partners Ltd, 15 Suffolk Street, SW1Y 4HG. *Club:* White's.

**DAVIES, Prof. Melanie Jane,** CBE 2016; MD; FRCGP; Professor of Diabetes Medicine, University of Leicester, since 2007; *b* Portsmouth, 8 July 1961; *d* of David Davies and Gillian Davies; *m* 1992, Dr Andrew Hall; two *s* one *d*. *Educ:* Henry Beaufort Sch., Winchester; Peter Symonds Coll., Winchester; Univ. of Sheffield (MB ChB; MD). MRCP. Consultant Physician, 1996–2006, Hon. Consultant Physician, 2006–, University Hosps of Leicester NHS Trust. Clin. Lead, Diabetes East Midlands Strategic Clin. Network, 2010–; Director: NIHR Leicester-Loughborough Biomedical Res. Unit in Diet, Lifestyle and Nutrition, 2011–17; Leicester Clin. Trials Unit, 2012–; NIHR Leicester Biomedical Res. Centre, 2017–; Div. 2 Clin. Lead, East Midlands Clin. Res. Network, 2014– (Speciality Lead for Diabetes and Endocrinol.). Member: Diabetes UK; British Show Jumping Assoc. FMedSci 2018. *Recreations:* smallholder, equestrianism, gardening, ski-ing, horse breeding, show jumping. *Address:* Wayside Drive, Covert Lane, Scraptoft, Leicester LE7 9SP. *T:* (0116) 243 3495. *E:* melanie.davies@uhl-tr.nhs.uk.

**DAVIES, Prof. Michael,** PhD; Professor of Building Physics and Environment, University College London, since 2007; *b* Dartford, 2 May 1965; *s* of Derek Davies and Beatrice Davies (*née* Prince); partner, Lynda Webb; two *s* one *d*. *Educ:* Univ. of Manchester (BSc Phys 1986); Univ. of York (PGCE 1990); Univ. of Westminster (PhD Computational Phys 1994). Lecturer: Univ. of Westminster, 1994–98; Brunel Univ., 1998–2000; Open Univ., 2000–04; Sen. Lectr, 2004–07, Dir, UCL Inst. for Envmtl Design and Engrg, 2014–17, University Coll. London. Mem., Adaptation Sub-Cttee, Cttee on Climate Change, 2018–. *Publications:* res. papers relating to design, construction and mgt of built envmts with regards to sustainability and health. *Recreations:* sailing, walking. *Address:* UCL Institute for Environmental Design and Engineering, Central House, 14 Upper Woburn Place, WC1H 0NN. *T:* (020) 3108 9008. *E:* michael.davies@ucl.ac.uk.

**DAVIES, Sir Michael;** *see* Davies, Sir J. M.

**DAVIES, Michael Jeremy Pugh,** CBE 2000; RIBA; FICPD; Founder Director, 1977–2011, Senior Partner, since 2011, Rogers Stirk Harbour & Partners (formerly Richard Rogers Partnership), Architects; *b* 23 Jan. 1942; *er s* of late Leonard Gwerfyl Davies and of Nancy Hannah Davies; *m* 1st, 1967, Isabel Christina Hogg (marr. diss. 1977); 2nd, 1977, Elizabeth Renee Yvonne Escalmel; one *s* one *d*. *Educ:* Highgate Sch.; Architectural Assoc. (AA Dip.); UCLA (Charles Scott Fellow; MArch Urban Design). Dir, Airstructures Design, 1966–68; Partner, Chrysalis USA, 1969–72; Project architect, Piano and Rogers, 1972–77 (projects incl. Centre Pompidou and IRCAM, Paris, 1971–77); Partner, Chrysalis Architects (London), 1978–83. Richard Rogers Partnership projects incl. Lloyd's of London, 1978–86; Project Director: Masterplan Royal Albert Docks, 1983–85; INMOS, 1984; Greenwich Peninsula Masterplan, 1996–2000; Millennium Dome, London, 1996–2000; Terminal 5, Heathrow Airport, 1989–2008; Wood Wharf Masterplan, London, 2004–08; Grand Paris Masterplan, 2008–10; Masterplan Bercy Charenton, Paris, 2010–; Masterplan Charolais Rambouillet, Paris, 2012–. Dir, MustRD, 2010–14. Trustee, Useful Simple Trust, 2010–. Has lectured at univs, confs and schools of architecture worldwide. FRGS; FICPD 1998; FRSA; FRAS. Hon. Fellow, Goldsmiths, Univ. of London, 2007. Chevalier, Legion d'Honneur, 2010. *Publications:* contrib. articles and papers to professional jls. *Recreations:* astronomy, sailing. *Address:* Rogers Stirk Harbour & Partners, The Leadenhall Building, 122 Leadenhall Street, EC3V 4AB. *T:* (020) 7385 1235.

**DAVIES, Mims;** MP (C) Eastleigh, since 2015; Parliamentary Under-Secretary of State, Department for Work and Pensions, since 2019; *b* Crawley, 2 June 1975; *m* Mark Davies; two *d*. *Educ:* Forest Grange Sch., Horsham; Royal Russell Sch., Croydon; Univ. of Swansea (BA Hons Politics with Internat. Relns). Radio presenter and events asst, The Wave, Swansea; radio presenter, Heartbeat FM, Knebworth; reporter and producer, BBC Southern Counties Radio; Communications Officer, Sussex Safer Roads Partnership. An Asst Govt Whip, 2018; Parly Under-Sec. of State, Wales Office, 2018, DCMS, 2018–19. Member: Mid Sussex DC; Haywards Heath Town Council. *Recreations:* running, pop music, family time, sport. *Address:* House of Commons, SW1A 0AA. *T:* (020) 7219 6853. *E:* mims.davies.mp@parliament.uk. *W:* www.mimsdavies.org.uk. *Club:* Haywards Heath Harriers.

**DAVIES, Neal Antony;** opera and concert singer, since 1991; *b* Newport, Monmouthshire, 13 June 1966; *s* of late Don Brynmor Davies and of Margaret Davies. *Educ:* St Julians Sch., Newport; King's Coll. London (BMus 1987); Royal Acad. of Music (Dip 1990); Internat. Opera Studio, Zurich. ARAM; FRAM 2003. Principal Bass, Landestheater, Coburg, 1991–94; performances with WNO, ROH, ENO, Chicago Lyric Opera, Deutsche Staatsoper, Berlin, Aix-en-Provence Fest., BBC Proms and Edinburgh Fest. Lieder Prize, Cardiff Singer of the World Competition, 1991. *Recreations:* art, architecture, church crawling. *Address:* c/o Askonas Holt Ltd, 15 Fetter Lane, EC4A 1BW. *T:* (020) 7400 1700. *E:* info@askonasholt.com. *Club:* Lansdowne.

**DAVIES, Prof. Nicholas Barry,** DPhil; FRS 1994; Professor of Behavioural Ecology, University of Cambridge, since 1995, and Fellow of Pembroke College, Cambridge, since 1979; *b* 23 May 1952; *s* of Anthony Barry Davies and Joyce Margaret Davies; *m* 1979, Jan Parr; two *d*. *Educ:* Merchant Taylors' Sch., Crosby; Pembroke Coll., Cambridge (BA 1973, MA 1977); Edward Grey Inst., Oxford Univ. (DPhil 1976). Demonstrator, Dept of Zoology (Edward Grey Inst. of Field Ornithology), Oxford Univ., 1976–79, and Jun. Res. Fellow, Wolfson Coll., Oxford, 1977–79; Demonstrator and Lectr in Zoology, 1979–92, Reader in Behavioural Ecology, 1992–95, Univ. of Cambridge. Pres., Internat. Soc. for Behavioural Ecology, 2000–02 (Hamilton Prize Lect., 2010). Hon Dr Bielefeld, 2011. Scientific Medal, Zool Soc., 1987; Cambridge Foundn Teaching Prize, 1995; William Bate Hardy Prize, Cambridge Phil Soc., 1995; Medal, Assoc. Study Animal Behaviour, 1996; Frink Medal, Zool Soc. of London, 2001; Elliott Coues Award, Amer. Ornithologists' Union, 2005; Croonian Medal and Lect., Royal Soc., 2015. *Publications:* (ed with J. R. Krebs) Behavioural Ecology, 1978, 4th edn 1997; (with J. R. Krebs) An Introduction to Behavioural Ecology, 1981, 4th edn (with J. R. Krebs and S. A. West) 2012; Dunnock Behaviour and Social Evolution, 1992; Cuckoos, Cowbirds and other Cheats, 2000; Cuckoo: cheating by nature, 2015; contribs to learned jls. *Recreations:* bird watching, cricket. *Address:* Department of Zoology, Downing Street, Cambridge CB2 3EJ. *T:* (01223) 336600.

**DAVIES, Rt Hon. Dame Nicola (Velfor),** DBE 2010; PC 2018; **Rt Hon. Lady Justice Davies;** a Lady Justice of the Appeal, since 2018; *b* 13 March 1953. *Educ:* Bridgend Girls' Grammar School; Birmingham Univ. (LLB). Called to the Bar, Gray's Inn, 1976, Bencher, 2001; QC 1992; Recorder, 1998–2010; Dep. High Ct Judge, 2003–10; a Judge of the High Court of Justice, QBD, 2010–18; Presiding Judge, Wales Circuit, 2014–17. Hon. Fellow, Cardiff Univ., 2012. Hon. LLD: S Wales, 2014; Wales, 2017. *Address:* Royal Courts of Justice, Strand, WC2A 2LL.

**DAVIES, Col Nicolas;** *see* Davies, Col F. N. J.

**DAVIES, Rev. Noel Anthony,** OBE 2003; PhD; Co-ordinator of Training, College of Welsh Independents, 2005–09; *b* 26 Dec. 1942; *s* of late Rev. Ronald Anthony Davies and Anne Davies; *m* 1968, Patricia Barter. *Educ:* UCNW, Bangor (BSc Chem. and Biochem.); Mansfield College, Oxford (BA Theol.); PhD Wales 1998; Open Univ. (BSc 2013). Ordained, 1968; Minister, Bryn Seion Welsh Congregational Church, Glanaman, 1968–77; General Secretary: Council of Churches for Wales and Commn of Covenanted Churches in Wales, 1977–90; Cytûn: Churches Together in Wales, 1990–98; Minister: Ebeneser Newydd Congregational Ch, Swansea, 1996–2013; Swansea and Clydach Ecumenical Pastorate, 2000–05. Pres., Union of Welsh Independents (Congregational), 1998–99 (Chm. Council, 1990–93); Moderator, Churches' Commn on Mission, CCBI, 1991–95. Associate Lectr, Cardiff Univ. (formerly Univ. of Wales, Cardiff), 2000–04; Dir, Welsh Nat. Centre for Ecumenical Studies, University of Wales Trinity Saint David (formerly Trinity Coll., then Trinity Univ. Coll., Carmarthen), 2001–09. Trustee, 1998–2009, Vice-Chm., 2006–09, Christian Aid. *Publications:* Wales: language, nation, faith and witness, 1996; (ed jtly) Wales: a moral society?, 1996; Un er mwyn y byd (A History of Welsh Ecumenism), 1998; God in the Centre, 1999; Religion and Ethics, 2003; (with Martin Conway) World Christianity in the 20th Century, 2 vols, 2008; A History of Welsh Ecumenism, 2008; Moeseg Gristnogol Gyfoes: dylanwadau ecwmenaidd (Contemporary Christian Ethics: ecumenical influences), 2013; (with T. Hefin Jones) Cristnogaeth a Gwyddoniaeth (Christianity and Science), 2017; articles in ecumenical jls and Welsh language items. *Recreations:* classical music and hi-fi, gardening, West Highland White terriers, oriental cookery. *Address:* 16 Maple Crescent, Uplands, Swansea SA2 0QD.

**DAVIES, (Norah) Olwen,** MA; Headmistress, St Swithun's School, Winchester, 1973–86; *b* 21 March 1926; *d* of late Rev. and Mrs E. A. Davies. *Educ:* Tregaron County Sch.; Walthamstow Hall, Sevenoaks; Edinburgh Univ. (MA). DipEd Oxon. Staff of Girls' Remand Home, Essex, 1948–50; Russell Hill Sch., Purley, 1950–53; Woodford House, NZ, 1953–57 (Dep. Headmistress); Westonbirt Sch., 1957–65; Headmistress, St Mary's Hall, Brighton, 1965–73. Pres., Girls' Schools Association, 1981–82. *Address:* 28 Arle Gardens, Alresford, Hants SO24 9BA.

**DAVIES, Norman;** *see* Davies, I. N. R.

**DAVIES, Col Norman Thomas,** OBE 1996 (MBE (mil.) 1970); Registrar, General Dental Council, 1981–96; *b* 2 May 1933; *s* of late Edward Ernest Davies and Elsie Davies (*née* Scott); *m* 1961, Penelope Mary, *e d* of late Peter Graeme Agnew, MBE and (Mary) Diana Agnew; one *s* one *d*. *Educ:* Holywell; RMA, Sandhurst; Open Univ. (BA 1979). Commnd RA, 1954; Regtl and Staff Appts, Malaya, Germany and UK, 1954–64; ptsc 1966; psc 1967; Mil. Asst to C of S Northern Army Gp, 1968–69; Commanded C Bty RHA and 2IC 3RHA, 1970–72; GSO I (DS), Staff Coll., Camberley, and Canadian Land Forces Comd and Staff Coll., 1972–74; Commanded 4 Field Regt, RA, 1975–77; Mil. Dir of Studies, RMCS, Shrivenham, 1977–80. Mem., EEC Adv. Cttee on the Training of Dental Practitioners, 1983–96. Vice Pres., British Dental Hygienists Assoc., 1996–99. Hon. Mem., BDA, 1990; Hon. FDSRCS 1997. JP Hants, 1984–2003. *Recreations:* Rugby football (Treas., RARFC, 1984–2000), Welsh Rugby football, fly fishing, wine, travel, keeping up with four grandchildren, battling with the computer. *Address:* 6 Weatherby Gardens, Hartley Wintney, Hook, Hants RG27 8PA. *T:* (01252) 843303.

**DAVIES, Olwen;** *see* Davies, N. O.

**DAVIES, His Honour Owen Handel;** QC 1999; a Circuit Judge, 2011–19; *b* 22 Sept. 1949; *s* of Trevor Davies and Mary Davies (*née* Jacobs); *m* 1971, Dr Caroline Jane Smith; one *s* one *d*. *Educ:* Hazelwick Sch.; Magdalene Coll., Cambridge (MA). Called to the Bar, Inner Temple, 1973, Bencher, 2001; in practice at the Bar, 1974–2011; a Recorder, 2000–11; Jt Head of Chambers, 1980–2011. Chm., Admin. Law Bar Assoc., 2002–05; Mem., Bar Council, 1998–2002. *Publications:* numerous contribs on humanitarian laws of conflict, extradition, information technol. and legal practice. *Recreations:* silversmithing, stained glass windows, narrowboating. *Address:* 57–60 Lincoln's Inn Fields, WC2A 3LS. *Club:* India.

**DAVIES, Patrick Taylor,** CMG 1978; OBE 1967; HM Overseas Civil Service, retired; *b* 10 Aug. 1927; *s* of Andrew Taylor Davies and Olive Kathleen Mary Davies; *m* 1959, Marjorie Eileen (*née* Wilkinson); two *d*. *Educ:* Shrewsbury Sch.; St John's Coll., Cambridge (MA); Trinity Coll., Oxford. Lieut, RA, Nigeria, 1945–48. Colonial Admin. Service, Nigeria, 1952; Permanent Sec., Kano State, 1970; Chief Inspector, Area Courts, Kano State, 1972–79. *Address:* 1 Millfield Drive, Market Drayton, Shropshire TF9 1HS. *T:* (01630) 653408.

**DAVIES, Ven. Paul;** *see* Davies, Ven. R. P.

**DAVIES, Dr Paul Charles,** CB 2006; JP; CEng, FRSC; Chief Scientist and Director, Corporate Science and Analytical Services Directorate, Health and Safety Executive, 1999–2006; *b* 25 April 1948; *s* of Philip Davies and Edith Mary Davies (*née* Johnson); *m* 1970, Sheila Tatham; one *s* one *d*. *Educ:* James Watt Tech. High Sch., Smethwick; Leicester Poly. (BSc 1st Cl. Hons Applied Chem.); Univ. of Leicester (PhD 1974). FRSC 1990; CEng 1996. With Unilever, 1968–69; Health and Safety Executive, 1975–2006: Factory Inspector, 1975–83; Major Hazards Assessment Unit, 1983–86; Hazardous Installations Policy Unit, 1986–89; Area Dir, London, 1989–93; Hd, Occupational Health Br., 1993–96; Mem. Bd, and Hd, Chemical and Hazardous Installations Div., 1996–99; Dir, Hazardous Installations Directorate, 1999–2002. Mem., Internat. Adv. Cttee on Health & Safety, Govt of Singapore, 2006–09. Dir, Crosby Housing Assoc., 2005–15. JP Ormskirk, 2004–16, Lancs, 2016–18. *Publications:* contrib. papers on risk management. *Recreations:* walking, music, gardening, Aston Villa FC. *Address:* 5 Chartwell Road, Southport, Merseyside PR8 2QP.

**DAVIES, Prof. Paul Charles William,** AM 2007; PhD; Regents' Professor, since 2012, and Director, Beyond: Center for Fundamental Concepts in Science, since 2006, Arizona State University (College Professor, 2006–11); *b* London, 22 April 1946; *s* of Hugh Augustus Robert Davies and Pearl Vera Davies; *m* 2003, Pauline. *Educ:* University Coll. London (BSc 1st Cl. 1967; PhD 1970). Res. Fellow, Inst. of Theoretical Astronomy, Univ. of Cambridge, 1970–72; Lectr in Maths, KCL, 1972–80; Prof. of Theoretical Physics, Univ. of Newcastle upon Tyne, 1980–90; Prof. of Mathematical Physics, 1990–93, Prof. of Natural Philos., 1993–97, Univ. of Adelaide; Prof. of Natural Philos., Macquarie Univ., Sydney, 2001–06. Vis. Prof., Imperial Coll., London, 1998–2003; Adjunct Prof., Univ. of Queensland, 1998–. Hon. Fellow, UCL, 2011. Hon. DSc: Macquarie, 2006; Chapman,

2009. *Publications:* The Physics of Time Asymmetry, 1974; Space and Time in the Modern Universe, 1977; The Runaway Universe, 1978; The Forces of Nature, 1979, 2nd edn 1986; Other Worlds, 1980; The Search for Gravity Waves, 1980; The Edge of Infinity, 1981; The Accidental Universe, 1982; (with N. D. Birrell) Quantum Fields in Curved Space, 1982; God and the New Physics, 1983; Superforce, 1983; Quantum Mechanics, 1984, 2nd edn (with D. Betts) 1994; (with J. R. Brown) The Ghost in the Atom, 1986; Fireball, 1987; The Cosmic Blueprint, 1987, rev. edn 2004; (with J. R. Brown) Superstrings: a theory of everything?, 1988; (ed) The New Physics, 1989; (with J. Gribbin) The Matter Myth, 1991; The Mind of God, 1992; The Last Three Minutes, 1994; About Time: Einstein's unfinished revolution, 1995; Are We Alone?: the philosophical basis of the search for extraterrestrial life, 1995; (with Phillip Adams) The Big Questions, 1996; One Universe or Many Universes?, 1998; (with Phillip Adams) More Big Questions, 1998; The Fifth Miracle: the search for the origin of life, 1998, rev. edn as The Origin of Life, 2003; How to Build a Time Machine, 2001; (ed jtly) Science and Ultimate Reality, 2004; The Goldilocks Enigma: why is the universe just right for life?, 2006 (US title, Cosmic Jackpot, 2007); (ed with Philip Clayton) The Re-Emergence of Emergence, 2006; (ed jtly) Instruments, Methods and Missions for Astrobiology, 2007; The Eerie Silence: are we alone in the universe?, 2010; (ed jtly) Information and the Nature of Reality: from physics to metaphysics, 2010; (ed jtly) A One Way Mission to Mars: colonizing the Red Planet, 2011; (ed jtly) Complexity and the Arrow of Time, 2013; The Demon in the Machine: how hidden webs of information are finally solving the mystery of life, 2019. *Recreation:* keeping fit. *Address:* PO Box 870506, Tempe, Arizona 85287–0506, USA. *T:* (480) 9653240. *E:* deepthought@asu.edu. *Club:* Victory Services.

**DAVIES, Prof. Paul Lyndon,** FBA 2000; Allen and Overy Professor of Corporate Law, University of Oxford, 2009–14, now Emeritus; Fellow of Jesus College, Oxford, 2009–14, now Emeritus; Senior Research Fellow, Commercial Law Centre, Harris Manchester College, Oxford, since 2014; *b* 24 Sept. 1944; *s* of John Clifford Davies and Kathleen Gertrude Davies (*née* Webber); *m* 1973, Saphié Ashtiany, *qv*; two *d*. *Educ:* Cardiff High Sch.; Balliol Coll., Oxford (BA, MA); London Sch. of Econs and Pol Sci. (LLM); Yale Univ. (LLM). Lectr, Univ. of Warwick, 1969–73; University of Oxford: CUF Lectr, 1973–91; Reader in Law of Enterprise, 1991–96, Prof., 1996–98; Chm. Bd, Faculty of Law, 1992–95; Balliol College: Fellow and Tutor in Law, 1973–98, Emeritus Fellow, 1998; Estates Bursar, 1983–86; Cassel Prof. of Commercial Law, LSE, 1998–2009. Mem., Steering Gp, Co. Law Rev., 1999–2001. Dep. Chm., Central Arbitration Cttee, 2001–15. Vice-Pres., Industrial Law Soc., 2001. Hon. QC 2006; Hon. Bencher, Gray's Inn, 2008. *Publications:* (with K. W. Wedderburn) Employment Grievances and Disputes Procedures in Britain, 1969; Takeovers and Mergers, 1976; (with M. R. Freedland) Labour Law: text and materials, 1979, 2nd edn 1984; (with M. R. Freedland) Labour Legislation and Public Policy, 1993; (ed) Gower's Principles of Modern Company Law, 6th edn 1997, 10th edn 2016; Introduction to Company Law, 2002, 2nd edn 2010; (ed) Palmer's Company Law, 23rd edn 1982 to 25th edn 1992; (jtly) Anatomy of Corporate Law, 2004, 3rd edn 2017; (with M. R. Freedland) Towards a Flexible Labour Market, 2007; (jtly) Principles of Financial Regulation, 2016. *Recreation:* walking. *Address:* Harris Manchester College, Mansfield Road, Oxford OX1 3TD.

**DAVIES, Paul Windsor;** Member (C) Preseli Pembrokeshire, National Assembly for Wales, since 2007; *b* 2 Jan. 1969; *s* of Timothy Iorwerth Davies and Mair Elizabeth Davies; *m* 2006, Julie Wheeler. *Educ:* Tregroes Primary Sch.; Llandysul Grammar Sch.; Newcastle Emlyn Comp. Sch. Lloyds Bank, subseq. Lloyds TSB, 1987–2007, Business Manager, Haverfordwest, 1994–2007. *Recreations:* reading, visiting historical attractions, Rugby. *Address:* National Assembly for Wales, Cardiff Bay, Cardiff CF99 1NA. *T:* 0300 200 7216. *E:* Paul.Davies@assembly.wales.

**DAVIES, Pauline Elizabeth,** MEd; Headmistress, Wycombe Abbey School, 1998–2008; *b* 8 April 1950; *d* of Gordon White and Petroula White (*née* Theohari); *m* 1970, Alan Henry Davies; two *s*. *Educ:* Univ. of Manchester (BSc Jt Hons 1971; PGCE 1972; MEd 1978). Teacher of Biology, 1972–77, Head of Dept, 1974–77, Urmston Girls' Grammar Sch.; various posts, incl. Dep. Head and Head of Middle Sch., King Edward VI Grammar Sch. for Boys, Chelmsford, 1979–90; Headmistress, Croydon High Sch., 1990–98. Pres., GSA, 2003. Gov., St Paul's Girls' Sch., 2007–15; Mem. Court, Whitgift Foundn, 2009–. *Recreations:* reading, theatre, music, travel.

**DAVIES, Peter Douglas Royston,** CMG 1994; HM Diplomatic Service, retired; *b* 29 Nov. 1936; *e s* of Douglas and Edna Davies; *m* 1967, Elizabeth Mary Lovett Williams; one *s* two *d*. *Educ:* Brockenhurst County High Sch.; LSE (BSc(Econ)). Joined HM Diplomatic Service, 1964; FO, 1964–66; Second Sec., Nicosia, 1966–67; FO, 1967–68; First Sec., Budapest, 1968–71; FCO, 1971–74; Consul (Commercial), Rio de Janeiro, 1974–78; Counsellor (Commercial): The Hague, 1978–82; Kuala Lumpur, 1982–83; Dep. High Comr, Kuala Lumpur, 1983–85; RCDS 1986; Head of Arms Control and Disarmament Dept, FCO, 1987–91; Consul-Gen., Toronto, and Dir-Gen. of Trade and Investment in Canada, 1991–96. Pres., Peter Davies Associates, 1997–2000. Mem. (C), S Northants DC, 2011–. Mem., British Malaysian Soc., 2006–. *Recreations:* golf, ski-ing, biography, travel. *Address:* South Wing, The Manor, Moreton Pinkney, Northants NN11 3SJ.

**DAVIES, Rear-Adm. Peter Roland,** CB 2005; CBE 1996 (MBE 1984); Chair of Governors, Morley College, London, 2015; *b* 2 April 1950; *s* of Roland and Winifred Davies; *m* 1974, Dianne Whittaker; one *s* one *d*. *Educ:* Thornleigh Grammar Sch., Bolton; King's Coll. London (BSc Elec. Engrg 1971); RMCS Shrivenham (MSc Guided Weapons Systems 1977). Naval service, 1973–89: Weapon Engineer Officer: HMS Opportune, 1973–75; HMS Narwhal, 1975–77; Submarine Harpoon Project, 1978–80; Weapon Engineer Officer: 3rd Submarine Sqn, 1980–82; HMS Courageous, 1982–84; 2nd Submarine Sqn, 1984–87; Submarine Senser's Commns Office Flag Officer Submarine Staff, 1987–89; Ministry of Defence: Future Projects, 1991–92; Res. Requirements, 1992–93; Project Manager: Sonar, 1993–95, Tomahawk, 1995–97, Procurement Exec.; Asst Dir, (Command, Control, Computers, Commns, Intel) Directorate of Communication & Inf. Systems (Navy), 1997–98; CO, HMS Collingwood, 1998–2001; FO Trng and Recruiting and Chief Exec., Naval Recruiting and Trng Agency, 2001–04. Principal and Chief Exec., City Literary Inst., 2004–11; Interim CEO, Educn and Trng Foundn, 2013–14. *Recreations:* music, sailing, swimming. *Clubs:* Royal Naval Sailing Assoc.; Royal Naval Swimming Assoc.

**DAVIES, Maj.-Gen. Peter Ronald,** CB 1992; Chairman, Marjan Centre for the Study of Conflict and Conservation, Department of War Studies, King's College London, since 2010; *b* 10 May 1938; *e s* of Lt-Col Charles Henry Davies and Joy Davies (*née* Moore); *m* 1960, (Rosemary) Julia, *er d* of late David Felice of Douglas, IoM; one *s* one *d*. *Educ:* Llandovery College; Welbeck College; RMA Sandhurst; RMCS 1969; Army Staff Coll., 1970; RCDS, 1985. Commissioned Royal Corps of Signals, 1958; service in BAOR, Berlin, Borneo, Cyprus and UK, 1958–68; OC Artillery Bde Sig. Sqn, 1971–72; Bde Maj., 20 Armd Bde, 1973–75; Directing Staff, Staff Coll., Camberley, 1975–76; CO 1 Armd Div. HQ and Signal Regt, 1976–79; Col GS SD, HQ UKLF, 1979–82; Brigade Comdr, 12 Armd Brigade, 1982–84; Dep. Comdt and Dir of Studies, Staff College, Camberley, 1985–86; Comdr Communications, BAOR, 1987–90; GOC Wales, 1990–91. Director-General: RSPCA, 1991–2002; WSPA, 2002–09 (Dir, 1992–2002; Vice-Pres., 1998–2000; Pres., 2000–02); Dir, 1992–2002, Pres., 2012–15, Eurogroup for Animals (formerly Animal Welfare), Brussels. Mem., Internat. Strategic Planning and Adv. Bd, Andrew Corp., USA, 1991–92. Consultant, NESS, 2011–12. Chairman: Brooke, 2009–13; Freedom Food Ltd, 1994–2002; Animals in War Meml Fund, 1996–2009; Trustee: Flora for Fauna Soc., 2000–10; Wildlife Inf. Network, 2002–04; Vier Pfoten (Four Paws), Vienna, 2012–. Regtl Colonel, King's Regt, 1986–94; Chm., Regtl Council and King's and Manchester Regts' Assoc., 1986–94; Col Comdt, RCS, 1990–96; Life Pres., Jullunder Bde Assoc., 1990. Member, Executive Committee: Lord Roberts Workshops and Forces Help Soc., 1994–96; Addaction (Drug and Alcohol Abuse), 1997–2000; Nat. Equine Forum, 2009–13. Patron, Sikhs 1914, 2014–. Gov., Welbeck Coll., 1980–81; Trustee, Llandovery Coll., 1992–2003. CCMI (CIMgt 1994); FIPD 1991; FRSA 2002. Queen Victoria Silver Medal, RSPCA, 2003; Angell Humanitarian Award, Mass Soc. for Prevention Cruelty to Animals, USA, 2003; Assisi Medal, NZ Soc. for Prevention of Cruelty to Animals, 2007; Eurogroup for Animals Award, 2008. *Recreations:* Italy, wine, jazz music. *E:* pdavies@fastmail.fm. *Clubs:* Army and Navy; Fadeaways (Founder and Chm., 1992–).
*See also* T. D. H. Davies.

**DAVIES, Peter Wilton,** MBE 2009; Vice Lord-Lieutenant for Cornwall, since 2017; Chief Executive, Cornwall County Council, 1999–2002; *b* 7 March 1945; *s* of late John Finden Davies and Mary (*née* Harrison); *m* 1971, Ann Mary Dawn Jones; two *d*. *Educ:* Blundell's Sch.; Southampton Inst. FCIPD (FIPD 1979). Grad. trainee, Devon CC, 1964–67; Personnel Officer, Berkshire CC, 1967–69; Sen. Personnel Officer, Camden LBC, 1969–70; Industrial Relations Officer, Hampshire CC, 1970–74; Dep. County Personnel Officer, 1974–81, Dir of Personnel, 1981–99, Cornwall CC. Chairman: Central Cornwall PCT, 2002–06; Royal Cornwall Hosps NHS Trust, 2007–08; Mem., Exec. Bd, SW Strategic HA (NHS SW), 2006–09. Mem., Lord Chancellor's Adv. Cttee for Cornwall on JPs, 1998–2008. Chairman: Common Purpose Cornwall, 2001–06; Hall for Cornwall, 2002–11; Vice Chm., SW Regl Adv. Bd (formerly Devon and Cornwall Regl Cttee), NT, 2004–; Chm., Nat. Maritime Mus., 2014– (Trustee, 2013–). FCMI (FIMgt 1988); FRSA 1994. DL Cornwall, 2002. *Recreations:* walking, shooting, the arts, Rotary. *Address:* Arundell, 1 Moresk Gardens, Truro, Cornwall TR1 1BJ. *T:* (01872) 274764.

**DAVIES, Philip Andrew;** MP (C) Shipley, since 2005; *b* 5 Jan. 1972; *s* of Peter Davies and Marilyn (*née* Johnson, now Lifsey); *m* 1994, Debbie Hemsley (marr. diss. 2012); two *s*. *Educ:* Univ. of Huddersfield (BA Hons Histl and Pol Studies). Asda: various positions, 1993–2000; Customer Service Project Manager, 2000–04; Mktg Manager, 2004–05. Contested (C) Colne Valley, 2001. Member: Culture, Media and Sport Select Cttee, 2006–15; Justice Select Cttee, 2015–17; Women and Equalities Cttee, 2016–; Backbench Business Cttee, 2010–12; Chairmen's Panel, 2010–. Mem. Exec. Cttee, 1922 Cttee, 2006–12. *Recreation:* horse racing. *Address:* House of Commons, SW1A 0AA. *E:* philip.davies.mp@parliament.uk.

**DAVIES, Philip John,** CB 2001; Deputy Counsel, House of Commons, since 2011; consultant legislative drafter, since 2011; *b* 19 Sept. 1954; *s* of late Glynn Davies and Mary Davies (*née* Adams); *m* 1981, Jacqueline Sara Boutcher; one *d*. *Educ:* St Julian's High Sch., Newport, S Wales; Hertford Coll., Oxford (MA, BCL). Called to the Bar, Middle Temple, 1981; Lectr in Law, Univ. of Manchester, 1977–82; Asst and Sen. Asst Parly Counsel, 1982–90; Dep. Parly Counsel, 1990–94 (seconded to Law Commn, 1992–94); Parly Counsel, 1994–2011. *Publications:* articles and notes in Law Qly Rev., Modern Law Rev. and other legal jls. *Recreations:* family, Welsh terriers, the garden. *Address:* Pinecroft, The Downs, Givons Grove, Leatherhead, Surrey KT22 8JY. *T:* (01372) 373915; 5 Glendower House, The Norton, Tenby, Pembrokeshire SA70 8AH. *T:* (01834) 842840. *E:* davies.pinecroft@hotmail.co.uk. *Club:* Crawshay's Rugby.

**DAVIES, Maj.-Gen. Philip Middleton,** OBE 1975; *b* 27 Oct. 1932; *s* of late Hugh Davies and Miriam Allen (*née* Tickler); *m* 1956, Mona Wallace; two *d*. *Educ:* Charterhouse; RMA, Sandhurst. Commnd Royal Scots, 1953; served Korea, Canal Zone, Cyprus, Suez, Berlin, Libya 1st Bn Royal Scots, 1953–63; Staff Coll., 1963; National Defence Coll., 1971; commanded 1st Bn Royal Scots, Norway, Cyprus, N Ireland (despatches), 1973–76; DS, Staff Coll., 1976–77; comd 19 Bde/7 Fd Force, 1977–79; RCDS, 1980; Comd Land Forces, Cyprus, 1981–83; GOC NW Dist, 1983–86; retired. *Recreations:* fishing, gardening.

**DAVIES, Rhiannon Laura; Her Honour Judge Rhiannon Davies;** a Circuit Judge, since 2019; *b* Leicester, 9 June 1979; *d* of Michael John Davies and Carol Ann Davies; *m* 2016, Dr Paul Michael Ingley. *Educ:* Univ. of Birmingham (LLB 2000); Nottingham Law Sch. (BVC 2001); Univ. of Northumbria (LLM Child Law 2009). Called to the Bar, Gray's Inn, 2001; a Dep. District Judge, 2010–16; a District Judge, 2016–19; a Recorder, 2016–19. *Publications:* (jtly) How to Represent Yourself in the Family Court, 2015; (jtly) A Child's Journey Through Contemporary Issues in Child Protection, 2017. *Recreations:* cave, mine and wreck diving.

**DAVIES, Rhodri;** *see* Davies, W. R.

**DAVIES, Rhodri Talfan;** Director, BBC Cymru Wales, since 2011; *b* Cardiff, 9 Feb. 1971; *s* of Geraint Talfan Davies, *qv*; two *s* one *d*. *Educ:* Ysgol Gyfun Gymraeg Glantaf, Cardiff; Royal Grammar Sch., Newcastle upon Tyne; Jesus Coll., Oxford (BA Hons); Cardiff Univ. (Post Grad. Dip. Journalism). Sub-editor, Western Mail, 1993; news trainee, BBC, 1993; news reporter and producer, BBC, 1994–99; Hd, Regl Progs, BBC West, 1999–2001; Dir, TV, Video Networks/Home Choice, 2001–05; Hd, TV Mktg, ntl, 2005–06; Hd, Strategy and Communications, BBC Cymru Wales, 2006–11. *Recreations:* Rugby, ski-ing, US politics, useless gadgets. *Address:* BBC Cymru Wales, Broadcasting House, Llandaff, Cardiff CF5 2YQ. *T:* (029) 2032 2001. *E:* rhodri.talfan.davies.pa@bbc.co.uk.

**DAVIES, Rhys;** *see* Davies, E. R.

**DAVIES, His Honour Sir Rhys (Everson),** Kt 2000; QC 1981; a Senior Circuit Judge, 1990–2003; retired; *b* 13 Jan. 1941; *s* of late Evan Davies and Nancy Caroline Davies; *m* 1963, Katharine Anne Yeates; one *s* one *d*. *Educ:* Cowbridge Grammar School; Neath Grammar School; Victoria University of Manchester. LLB (Hons). Called to the Bar, Gray's Inn, 1964, Bencher, 1993. Northern Circuit, 1964–90; a Recorder, 1980–90; Hon. Recorder of Manchester, 1990–2003. Mem., Sentencing Adv. Panel, 2000–05. Pres., Manchester and District Medico-Legal Soc., 2002–04 (Patron, 2004–). Ind. Monitor, Criminal Records Bureau, 2004–08. Mem. Court and Council, Victoria Univ. of Manchester, 1993–2004 (Dep. Chm. Council, 2000–04); Visitor, Univ. of Manchester, 2004–. *Recreations:* music, conversation.

**DAVIES, Prof. Richard Bees,** PhD; Vice-Chancellor, Swansea University (formerly University of Wales, Swansea), 2003–19; *m*; three *c*. *Educ:* Milford Haven Grammar Sch.; Sidney Sussex Coll., Cambridge (MA); Univ. of Birmingham (MSc); Univ. of Bristol (PhD). Lectr, then Sen. Lectr, Dept of Town Planning, UWIST, subseq. UWCC; Univ. of Lancaster, 1989–2003: Prof. and Dir, Centre for Applied Statistics; Dean, Faculty of Engrg, Computing and Math. Scis; Pro-Vice-Chancellor.

**DAVIES, Richard John**; Management Board Director and Head, Department for Public Services and Performance, Welsh Assembly Government, 2006–09; *s* of Sydney John Davies and Valerie Reynolds Davies; *m* 1971, Margaret Mary Goddard; one *s* one *d*. *Educ*: King's Coll., Taunton; Univ. of Liverpool (BA Hons 1971; MA 1976). Teaching Asst, Dept of Political Theory and Instns, Liverpool Univ., 1972–73; entered Civil Service, 1973; MoD, FCO, MPO, etc, 1973–84; Welsh Office: Asst Sec., 1985; Head of Division: Health Mgt, Systems and Personnel, 1985–87; Health and Social Services Policy, 1987–89; Housing, 1989–94; School Performance, 1994–97; Gp Dir, Educn Dept, Welsh Office, subseq. Dept for Trng and Educn, Nat. Assembly for Wales, 1997–2006. Registered Comr, Infrastructure Planning Commn, 2010–12; Chair: Fitness to Practise Cttees, NMC, 2012–; Health Cttee, 2013–17, Professional Conduct Cttee, 2017–, Gen. Osteopathic Council; non-exec. Mem., Knowledge and Membership Bds, 2009–18, and Ind. Appeals Panel, 2014–17, Chm., Membership/Global Qualifications Gp, 2013–, RICS; Mem., Internat. Ethics Standards Coalition Trustees' Standards Setting Cttee, 2015–; Adjudicator, SRA, 2008–13; Lay Mem., Educn and Trng Cttee, Bar Standards Bd, 2012–15; Lay Mem., Adv./Statutory Cttee, MPTS, 2014–17; Associate: GMC, 2006–16; Gen. Pharmaceutical Council, 2010–19. Trustee: Nationwide Foundn, 2008–13; Carnegie (UK), 2009–17; Regent's Coll., London, 2009–10. Vis. Prof., Univ. of Glamorgan, 2006–11; Practitioner Doctorate Ethics Chair, Univ. of Buckingham, 2017–. Nuffield-Leverhulme Fellow, 1990. Doctoral FCollT, 2016. *Recreations*: family, walking, swimming, music.

**DAVIES, Ven. (Richard) Paul**; Archdeacon of Surrey, since 2017; *b* Carmarthen, 15 March 1973; *s* of David Alan Davies and Margaret Novello Davies (née Roche); *m* 1999, Louise Elizabeth Cummins; one *s* one *d*. *Educ*: Pembroke Sch., Pembrokeshire; Univ. of Wales, Lampeter (BA Hons Theology 1994); Regent's Park Coll., Oxford (MTh 1997); Ripon Coll., Cuddesdon. Ordained deacon, 1997, priest, 1998; Minor Canon, 1997–2001, Succentor, 2001–06, St Davids Cathedral; Vicar: Whitchurch, Solva, Brawdy and Llandeloy, 2001–06; Burry Port with Pwll, 2006–11; Rector, Llanfairmathafarneithaf with Llanbedrgoch and Pentraeth, 2012–14; Archdeacon of Bangor and Anglesey, 2012–17. Ecumenical Officer, 2002–07, Dir of Ordinands, 2010–11, Diocese of St Davids. Officiating Chaplain to the Military: 14th Signal Regt, 2003–07; RAF Valley, Anglesey, 2015–17. *Recreations*: all things maritime (former RNLI crew member), most music, messing around with wood. *Address*: Archdeacon's House, Lime Grove, West Clandon, Guildford, Surrey GU4 7UT. *T*: (01483) 212663. *E*: archdeacon.surrey@cofeguildford.org.uk.

**DAVIES, (Robert Harold) Glyn**; HM Diplomatic Service, retired; Ambassador to Panama, 1999–2002; Records and Archive Management, Foreign and Commonwealth Office (part-time), since 2008; *b* 23 March 1942; *s* of late Robert Leach Davies and Edith Greenwood Davies (née Burgoyne); *m* 1968, Maria Del Carmen Diaz; one *s*. *Educ*: Hulme Grammar Sch., Oldham; St John's Coll., Cambridge. Joined FO, 1963; Havana, 1964; FO, 1964; Third, later Second Sec., Mexico, 1968; FCO, 1972; Consul (Commercial), Zagreb, 1980; First Sec., on loan to Cabinet Office, 1983; First Sec., Consul and Head of Chancery, Luanda, 1986; FCO, 1989; High Commissioner to Namibia, 1996–98. *Address*: c/o Global Digital Technology, FCO Services, Foreign and Commonwealth Office, SW1A 2AH.

**DAVIES, Dr Robert James**; Partner, Masters-in-Science LLP, since 2011 (Partner, Masters-in-Science.com, then Managing Director, Masters-in-Science, 2004–11); *b* 24 Feb. 1943; *s* of late Rev. Canon Dilwyn Morgan Davies and Kate Davies (née Maltby); *m* 1st, 1969 (marr. diss. 1980); two *s*; 2nd, 1981, Karen, *d* of Dennis Henley. *Educ*: St Catharine's Coll., Cambridge (BA 1964); St Thomas's Hosp. Med. Sch. (BChir 1967; MB BS, MA 1968); Univ. of Cambridge (MD 1977); Univ. of Greenwich (MSc Computing and Info. Systems (Distinction) 2003; PGCE 2003); Goldsmiths, Univ. of London (MA Art and Politics (Merit) 2016). FRCP 1982. Res. Fellow, Brompton Hosp., 1971–73; Lectr in Medicine, St Thomas's Hosp., 1973–76; MRC Res. Fellow, Univ. of Tulane, New Orleans, 1976–77; St Bartholomew's Hospital: Consultant Physician, 1977–82; Dir, Asthma & Allergy Res. Dept, 1981–99; Reader in Respiratory Medicine, 1982–90; Dir, General and Emergency Medicine, 1994–96; Prof. of Respiratory Medicine, St Bartholomew's and Royal London Sch. of Medicine and Dentistry, QMW, London Univ., 1991–99; Cons. Physician, 1994–99, Dir of R&D, 1995–97, Royal Hosps NHS Trust. British Allergy Foundn: Founder and Chm., 1991–97; Pres., 1997–2002; Dir of Tech. and Educn, Allergy UK, 2000–02; Scientific Dir, Allergy Res. Ltd, 2000–02; Lectr in Computing, NW Kent Coll., 2003–11. Ed., Respiratory Medicine, 1988–95. Pres., Brit. Soc. for Allergy and Clin. Immunology, 1987–90; 2nd Vice Pres., Internat. Assoc. of Allergology and Clin. Immunology, 1997–99 (Treas., 1985–94); Chm., World Allergy Forum, 1996–99; Mem., Collegium Internationale Allergologicum, 1998–2000. Hon. Mem., Argentinian Assoc. of Allergy and Immunology, 1997. Fellow, Amer. Acad. Allergy, Asthma and Immunology, 1984. Medal, Faculty of Medicine, Univ. of Montpellier, 1981. *Publications*: Allergy The Facts, 1989; (ed) Formoterol: clinical profile of a new long acting inhaled B2-Agonist, 1990; Hay Fever and Other Allergies, 1995; contrib. Allergy. *Recreations*: hill-walking, mountain and moorland ponies. *Address*: Upper Penlan, Llanfilo, Brecon, Powys LD3 0RE.

**DAVIES, Robert John**; Chairman, Home Group, 2012–18; *b* 12 Oct. 1948; *s* of William Davies and Janet Davies (née Robinson); *m* 1971, Eileen Susan Littlefield; one *s*. *Educ*: Univ. of Edinburgh (LLB Law and Econs). FCMA 1976. With Ford Motor Co., in UK, USA and latterly as Finance Dir, Ford Spain, 1970–85; Coopers & Lybrand, 1985–87; Finance Director: Waterford Wedgwood plc, 1987–91; Ferranti Internat. plc, 1991–93; Finance Dir, 1994–97, Chief Exec., 1997–98, E Midlands Electricity plc; Chief Exec., Arriva plc, 1998–2006. Non-executive Director: T & S Stores plc, 1998–2003; Geest plc, 1998–2004; Barratt Developments plc, 2004–12; British Energy, 2006–09; Northern Rock plc, 2008–09; Northern Rock (Asset Mgt) plc, 2010; Kelda Hldgs Ltd, 2012–16; Chairman: Biffa plc, 2006–08; Euroports Hldgs, SARL, 2010–13; Countrywide PLC, 2013. Chm., NE Regl Council, CBI, 2007–08. Chm. Bd Govs, Sunderland Univ., 2003–09. *Recreations*: golf, vintage cars.

**DAVIES, (Robert) Karl**; broadcaster and commentator, since 1986; Chief Adviser Wales (formerly Head, Governance and Accountability), BBC Trust, 2007–17; English Language Teacher, Education First, Foshan, China, since 2018; *b* 26 July 1963; *s* of late R. Keith Davies and of Dilys Catherine Davies (née Hughes). *Educ*: Ysgol Glan Clwyd, St Asaph; University Coll. of Wales, Aberystwyth (BA). Editor, Tafod Y Ddraig, 1983–84; Chm., Welsh Lang. Soc., 1984–85; Res. Dir, Plaid Cymru, 1985–89; BBC Wales: Producer, Radio, 1989–90; Parly Editor, 1990–93; Chief Exec., Plaid Cymru, 1993–2002; Dir for Wales, NAHT, 2002–03; Sec., BBC Wales, 2003–06. Mem. Council, UCW, Aberystwyth, 1988–91. Fellow, British American Proj., 1996–. Trustee, Voices from Care, 2013–18. Warden, Eglwys Dewi Sant, 2017–18. *Publications*: Beth am Gynnau Tân?, 1988. *Recreations*: travel, cinema, gossip, Italy. *Address*: Flat 25, Clive Court, Cardiff CF5 1HW. *T*: 07894 966228. *E*: Robertkarld@aol.com.

**DAVIES, (Robert) Leighton**; QC 1994; a Recorder, 1994–2014; a Deputy High Court Judge, 2001–14; *b* 7 Sept. 1949; *s* of Robert Brinley Davies and Elizabeth Nesta Davies (née Jones); *m* 1979, Linda Fox; two *s* one *d*. *Educ*: Rhondda Co. Grammar Sch., Porth, Rhondda; Corpus Christi Coll., Oxford (MA, BCL; boxing blue, 1971–72); Inns of Court Sch. of Law. Called to the Bar, Gray's Inn, 1975, Bencher, 2002; practising on Wales and Chester Circuit, 1975–2014; Asst Recorder, 1990–94. *Recreations*: fly-fishing, gardening, military history. *Address*: Bryn Corun, Glyncoli Road, Treorchy, Rhondda CF42 6SB. *T*: (01443) 774559. *Club*: Vincent's (Oxford).

**DAVIES, (Robert) Russell**; freelance writer and broadcaster, since 1970; *b* 5 April 1946; *s* of late John Gwilym Davies and of Gladys Davies (née Davies); *m* 1972, Judith Anne Slater (marr. diss.); one *s*; *m* 2003, Emma Jane Kingsley; three *s*. *Educ*: Manchester Grammar Sch.; St John's Coll., Cambridge (Scholar; BA Mod. Langs). Comedy actor and TV presenter, 1970–71; literary reviewer and caricaturist, 1972–; football reporter, 1973–76, film critic, 1973–78, Observer; TV critic, Sunday Times, 1979–83; Dep. Editor and acting Editor, Punch, 1988; sports columnist, Sunday Telegraph, 1989–94. Presenter and feature-maker, 1979–: radio includes: When Housewives had the Choice; Turns of the Century; Word of Mouth (Premio Ondas, 1997); Jazz Century; Russell Davies Song Show, 1998–2013 (Gold Badge of Merit, BACS, 2001); Russell Davies with…, 2013; Chm., Brain of Britain, 2009–; television includes: What the Papers Say (also Annual Awards, 1989–97); jazz weeks and weekends; Saturday Review. *Publications*: (with Liz Ottaway) Vicky, 1987; Ronald Searle, 1990; (ed) The Kenneth Williams Diaries, 1993; (ed) The Kenneth Williams Letters, 1994; Foreign Body: secret life of Robert Maxwell, 1996; (with Wes Butters) Kenneth Williams Unseen, 2008. *Recreations*: playing trombone, bass saxophone, American crosswords, painting, visiting Wales. *Address*: c/o United Agents, 12–26 Lexington Street, W1F 0LE.

**DAVIES, Roger**; see Davies, Anthony R.

**DAVIES, Roger John**; Assisted Living Director, Castleoak, 2015; *b* Altrincham, 29 Oct. 1959; *m* Helen; one *s* one *d*. *Educ*: Altrincham Grammar Sch.; Cheltenham Grammar Sch.; Leeds Poly. (HND Hotel Mgt). Chief Exec., Methodist Homes, 2001–14. Former non-executive Director: English Community Care Assoc.; Associated Retirement Community Operators; non-executive Director: Your Care Rating; Somerset Care Gp, 2016–; Chm., Rangeford Retirement Living, 2018–. FCMA. *Recreations*: yoga, wildlife, church.

**DAVIES, Prof. Roger Llewelyn**, PhD; FRAS; FInstP; Philip Wetton Professor of Astrophysics, since 2002, and Director, Hintze Centre for Astrophysical Surveys, since 2014, Oxford University; Student, since 2002, Dr Lee's Reader in Physics, since 2006, Christ Church, Oxford; *b* 13 Jan. 1954; *s* of Albert Edward Davies and late Gwendoline Mary Davies; *m* 1982, Ioana Christina Westwater; one *s* one *d*. *Educ*: John Leggott Grammar Sch., Scunthorpe; University Coll. London (BSc Physics 1975); Inst. of Astronomy and Churchill Coll., Cambridge (PhD 1979). FRAS 1979; FInstP 2009. Lindemann Fellow, Lick Observatory, Calif, 1979–80; Res. Fellow, Christ's Coll., Cambridge, 1979–82; Staff Mem., US Nat. Optical Astronomy Observatories, Tucson, Arizona, 1982–88; Scientist, UK Gemini Project, 1988–96; Lectr in Physics, Oxford Univ. and Fellow, St Peter's Coll., Oxford, 1992–94; Prof. of Astronomy, Dept of Physics, Univ. of Durham, 1994–2002; Hd, Sub-Dept of Astrophysics, 2004–05, 2011–14, Chm. of Physics, 2005–10, Oxford Univ. PPARC Senior Res. Fellow, 2001–04 (Mem. Council, PPARC, 1999–2001, 2006–07). Vis. Prof., Beihang Univ., Beijing, 2006. Chairman: Anglo-Australian Telescope Bd, 1997–99 (Mem., 1996–99); Eur. Space Telescope Co-ordinating Facility Users Cttee, 2001–03; Gemini Telescopes Bd, 2002–03 (Mem., 2001–04; Chm., UK Gemini Telescopes Steering Cttee, 1996–99); Extremely Large Telescope Standing Review Cttee, ESO, 2006–12; Chair, Working Gp on Future Large Scale Facilities, 2011–15, Co-chair, Working Gp on Global Co-ordination of Ground and Space Astrophysics, 2016–, IAU. Member: VISTA Telescope Bd, 1999–2001; Adv. Cttee, Australian Astronomical Observatory, 2011–18; Council, Space Telescope Sci. Inst., 2011–17; Pres., Commn 28, Galaxies, IAU, 2009–12. President: RAS, 2010–12 (Mem. Council, 2005–08; Vice Pres., 2006–08); Eur. Astronomical Soc., 2017– (Mem. Council, 2012–; Vice Pres., 2012–17). Member: IAU, 1980; AAS, 1980. Fellow, UCL, 2009. Chm., Bd of Visitors, History of Sci. Mus., Oxford, 2018–. Dr hc Univ. Claude Bernard Lyon 1, 2006. Daiwa-Adrian Prize, Daiwa Anglo Japanese Foundn, 2001; Royal Soc. Wolfson Merit Award, 2006; RAS Gp Achievement Award for SAURON survey, 2013. *Publications*: contrib. papers to Astrophysical Jl, Monthly Notices of RAS, Astronomical Jl and conf. procs. *Recreations*: hiking, swimming, photography, films, listening to music, pilates. *Address*: Denys Wilkinson Building, Keble Road, Oxford OX1 3RH. *T*: (01865) 273305.

**DAVIES, Roger Oliver**; *b* 4 Jan. 1945; *s* of Griffith William Davies and Dorothy Anne Davies; *m* 1973, Adele Biss, *qv*; one *s*. *Educ*: Reading Sch.; Devonport High Sch.; London School of Economics (BScEcon). Marketing Dir, 1972, Man. Dir, 1977, Thomson Holidays; Man. Dir, 1982, Chm., 1984–90, Thomson Travel Gp; Chairman: Going Places, 1994–97; Sunway Travel, 1997–2000; Travel Chest.com, 2000; Dir, Airtours PLC, 1994–2000. Mem., Monopolies and Mergers Commn 1989–98. Governor, LSE, 1995–99. Commandeur de la République (Tunisia), 1987. *Recreations*: walking, ski-ing, reading. *Address*: 7 Elsworthy Road, NW3 3DS.

**DAVIES, Rt Hon. Ronald**; PC 1997; Commercial Manager, Bedwas Rugby Football Club, 2012; *b* 6 Aug. 1946; *s* of late Ronald Davies; *m* 1981, Christina Elizabeth Rees, *qv* (marr. diss. 2000); one *d*; *m* 2002, Lynne Hughes; one *s* two *d*. *Educ*: Bassaleg Grammar Sch.; Portsmouth Polytechnic; University Coll. of Wales, Cardiff. Schoolteacher, 1968–70; WEA Tutor/Organiser, 1970–74; Further Educn Adviser, Mid-Glamorgan LEA, 1974–83. Councillor, Rhymney Valley DC (formerly Bedwas and Machen UDC), 1969–84 (Vice-Chm.). MP (Lab) Caerphilly, 1983–2001. Opposition Whip, 1985–87; Opposition spokesman on agriculture and rural affairs, 1987–92, front bench spokesman on Wales, 1992–97; Sec. of State for Wales, May 1997–Oct. 1998. National Assembly for Wales: Mem. (Lab) Caerphilly, 1999–2003; Mem., Econ. Develt Cttee, 1999–2003 (Chm., 1999). Contested (Plaid Cymru) Caerphilly, Nat. Assembly for Wales, 2011. Mem. (Ind), Caerphilly CBC, 2008–12. Dir, Valleys Race Equality Council, 2003–. Highest Order, Gorsedd of the Bards, 1998. *Publications*: paper on devolution. *Address*: Wernddu House, Wernddu, Caerphilly CF83 3DA.

**DAVIES, Rt Rev. Ross Owen**; Bishop of The Murray, 2002–10; *b* 4 Feb. 1955; *s* of Rex John Davies and Margaret June Cooper; *m* 1983, Christine Fyfield; two *s* twin *d*. *Educ*: Melbourne Univ. (BA 1977, LLB 1979); St Barnabas Coll., ACT (ThL 1981). Ordained deacon, 1981, priest, 1982; Assistant Curate: St Peter's, Ballarat, 1981–83; St Lucia, Brisbane, 1984–85; Rector, Camperdown, Vic, 1985–91; Parish Priest, England: Mundford, 1991–93; Kingsdon, 1993–97; Rector, Hindmarsh, Vic, 1997–2000; Archdeacon of The Murray, 2000–02. *Recreations*: singing, gardening, reading.

**DAVIES, Russell**; see Davies, R. R.

**DAVIES, Ryland**; opera singer; tenor; Head of Vocal Department, Escuela Superior de Música Reina Sofía, Madrid, since 2014; *b* 9 Feb. 1943; *s* of Gethin and Joan Davies; *m* 1st, 1966, Anna Elizabeth Howells, *qv* (marr. diss. 1981); 2nd, 1983, Deborah Rees; one *d*. *Educ*: Royal Manchester College of Music (Fellow, 1971) (studied with Frederic R. Cox, OBE). Voice teacher: RNCM, 1987–94; RCM 1989–2009; RAM, 2008–; teaches privately and gives masterclasses at home and abroad. Début as Almaviva in The Barber of Seville, WNO, 1964; Glyndebourne Fest. Chorus, 1964–66; has since sung with Royal Opera, Sadler's Wells Opera, WNO, Scottish Opera, at Glyndebourne, and in Brussels, Chicago, NY, San Francisco, Houston, Paris, Salzburg, Buenos Aires, Hong Kong, Berlin, Hamburg,

Stuttgart, Munich and Milan; solo rôles include: Belmonte in Il Seraglio; Fenton, and Dr Caius, in Falstaff; Ferrando in Così Fan Tutte; Flamand in Capriccio; Tamino in The Magic Flute; Essex in Britten's Gloriana; Hylas in The Trojans; Don Ottavio in Don Giovanni; Cassio in Otello; Ernesto in Don Pasquale; Lysander in A Midsummer Night's Dream; title rôle in Werther; Prince in L'Amour des Trois Oranges; Nemorino in L'Elisir d'amore; Don Basilio in Le Nozze di Figaro; Rector in Peter Grimes; Triquet in Eugene Onegin; Alfredo in La Traviata, Pelléas in Pelléas et Melisande; Eneas in Esclarmonde; Jack in The Midsummer Marriage; Chaplin in Dialogues des Carmelites; Remendado in Carmen; Sellem in The Rake's Progress; Albazar in The Turk in Italy; Gaudenzio in Leoncavallo's La Bohème; Hauk Šendorf in The Makropulos Case; Francis Flute in A Midsummer Night's Dream; Ein Hirt in Tristan and Isolde; Monsieur Taupe in Capriccio. Many concerts at home with all major British orchestras, and abroad with such orchestras as: Boston Symphony, Cleveland Symphony, Chicago Symphony, Philadelphia, San Francisco, Los Angeles, Bavarian Radio and Vienna Symphony. Principal oratorio rôles include: Bach, B minor Mass; Beethoven: Mass in C; Berlioz, narrator in L'Enfance du Christ; Elgar, St John, in The Kingdom; Handel: Acis, in Acis and Galatea; title rôle, Judas Maccabaeus; Messiah; Jonathan, in Saul; Haydn: Nelson Mass; The Seasons; Mendelssohn: Obadiah, in Elijah; Hymn of Praise; Rossini, Messe Solennelle; Schubert, Lazarus; Tippett, Child of Our Time. Has sung in all major religious works including: Missa Solemnis, Verdi's Requiem, Dream of Gerontius, St Matthew Passion, The Creation. Many recordings incl. Il Seraglio, The Trojans, Saul, Così Fan Tutte, Thérèse, Monteverdi Madrigals, Idomeneo, Haydn's The Seasons, Messiah, L'Oracolo (Leone), Judas Maccabaeus, Il Matrimonio Segreto (Cimarosa), L'Amore dei Tre Re (Montemezzi), La Navarraise (Massenet), Lucia di Lammermoor (Donizetti). Hon. RAM, 2012. FRMCM; FRWCMD (FWCMD 1996). John Christie Award, 1965. *Recreations:* antiques, art, cinema, sport. *Address:* c/o Hazard Chase Ltd, 25 City Road, Cambridge CB1 1DP; Escuela Superior de Música Reina Sofia, Calle Requena 1, 28013 Madrid, Spain.

**DAVIES, Sally Alexandra;** Senior Partner, Mayer Brown, London, since 2017; *b* Wellington, Shropshire, 8 Oct. 1969; *d* of Edmund John Davies and Maria Bessie Charlotte Davies; *m* 2010, Richard Caleb Shepherd; two step *s* two step *d. Educ:* Shrewsbury High Sch. GDST; Shrewsbury 6th Form Coll.; University Coll. London (LLB Hons). Admitted solicitor, 1994, solicitor advocate with Higher Rights of Audience (Civil), 2000; Rowe & Maw: trainee solicitor, 1992–94; Associate, 1994–2001; Partner, Mayer Brown, 2001–. *Address:* Mayer Brown, 201 Bishopsgate, EC2M 3AF. *T:* (020) 3130 3757. *E:* sdavies@mayerbrown.com.

**DAVIES, Dame Sally (Claire),** DBE 2009; FRS 2014; Master, Trinity College, Cambridge, since 2019; Emeritus Professor, Imperial College London, since 2011; *b* 24 Nov. 1949; *d* of John Gordon Davies and Emily Mary Davies (*née* Tordoff); *m* 1st, 1974, R. F. W. Skilbeck (marr. diss. 1982); 2nd, 1982, P. R. A. Vulliamy (*d* 1982); 3rd, 1989, W. H. Ouwehand; two *d. Educ:* Manchester Univ. (MB ChB); London Univ. (MSc). FRCP 1992; FRCPath 1997; FRCPCH 1997; FFPH (FFPHM 1999). House Phys. and Surg., and SHO, Manchester, 1972–74; clin. assistant in cardiology, Clínica la Concepción, Fundación Jimenez Díaz, Madrid, 1974–77; SHO in Paediatrics, Middlesex Hosp., 1978–79; Lectr, 1979–83, MRC Fellow in Recombinant DNA Technology, 1983–85, Middlesex Hosp. Med. Sch.; Consultant Haematologist, Central Middlesex Hosp., 1985–2011; Dep. Dir, 1997–2004, Dir Gen. (formerly Dir), Res. and Develt, DoH, 2004–11; Chief Scientific Adviser, DoH, 2004–15; Chief Medical Officer, DoH, subseq. DHSC, 2011–19. Mem., MRC, 2009–17. Wkg Gp on Haemoglobinopathies, European Haematology Assoc., 1999–. Non-exec. Dir, Genomics England Ltd, 2013–. Mem., Exec. Bd, WHO, 2014–17. FMedSci 2002. Ed. for haemoglobinopathies, Internat. Cochrane Collaboration. Author, Annual Report of the CMO, 2011, 2012, 2013, 2014, 2015, 2016, 2017, 2018, 2019. Hon. Fellow: Imperial Coll. London Faculty of Medicine, 2009; Harris Manchester Coll., Oxford, 2012; QMUL, 2015; Assoc. of Anaesthetists of GB and Ireland, 2015; Homerton Coll., Cambridge, 2016; SCI, 2017; FMLM, 2018; C&G, 2018; RSTM&H, 2019; Hon. Vis. Fellow, Trinity Coll., Oxford, 2013–. Hon. FRCOG 2013; Hon. FRSM 2014. Hon. DM: Southampton, 2007; Birmingham, 2008; Leeds, 2011; KCL, 2011; Hon. DSc: Sheffield, 2008; Cranfield, 2008; Liverpool, 2009; Lincoln, 2010; Exeter, 2010; Keele, 2011; Lancaster, 2011; Aston, 2012; Manchester, 2012; Brunel, 2013; Leicester, 2014; Loughborough, 2014; Nottingham Trent, 2014; Surrey, 2014; Warwick, 2015; UCL, 2016; Bradford, 2017; Imperial Coll. London, 2018; Glasgow, 2019; Canterbury Christ Church, 2019; DUniv York, 2012; Hon. DCL Newcastle, 2013; Hon. DL Melbourne, 2018; Hon. Dr RCSI, 2019. *Publications:* The Drugs Don't Work: a global threat, 2013; contribs to med. jls, mainly relating to research strategy and sickle cell disease and to antimicrobial resistance. *Recreations:* travel, opera, music, cooking, art, architecture. *Address:* Trinity College, Cambridge CB2 1TQ.

**DAVIES, Saphié, (Sue);** *see* Ashtiany, S.

**DAVIES, Sarah Alice Ruth;** Clerk Assistant and Managing Director, Chamber and Committees Team, House of Commons, since 2019; *b* Bournemouth, 29 Sept. 1971; *d* of Peter Adams and Ruth Adams; *m* 1996, James Davies; one *s* one *d* (and one *s* decd). *Educ:* Arnewood Comp. Sch.; Brockenhurst Further Educn Coll.; King's Coll., Cambridge (BA Hons 1993); Open Univ. (MBA). Clerk, H of C, 1993–. *Recreations:* bodyboarding, Marvel films, cycling, explaining why we can't have a family dog. *Address:* House of Commons, SW1A 0AA. *E:* daviess@parliament.uk. *Club:* Haringey Aquatics.

**DAVIES, Sarah Jeannette; Her Honour Judge Sarah Davies;** a Circuit Judge, since 2016; *b* London, 20 May 1959; *d* of Frank Davies and Jeannette Davies; *m* Richard; one *s* one *d*, and two step *s* one step *d. Educ:* Felixstowe Coll.; Norwich High Sch.; Univ. of Kent at Canterbury (BA Hons Law). Called to the Bar, Gray's Inn, 1984; barrister, 1 Pump Court, Temple, 1991–2013; a Fee-paid Judge, First-tier Tribunal, 2011–13; a District Judge, 2013–16. *Recreations:* boxing training, fly-fishing, running, gardening, reading. *Club:* Sloane.

**DAVIES, Siân;** Co-founder, The Behavioural Architects, since 2011; *b* Long Eaton, 1 Aug. 1966; *d* of Alyn and Margaret Davies; *m* 2002, Chad Wollen; one *d. Educ:* Hertford Coll., Oxford (BA PPE). Mercer Mgt Consulting, 1988–96; Henley Centre: Associate Dir, 1996–97; Dir, 1998–2000; Man. Dir, 2000–01; Chief Exec., Henley Centre, then Henley Centre HeadlightVision, later The Futures Co., 2001–10. Mem., Mktg Soc. *Recreations:* contemporary art, photography. *E:* sian@thebearchitects.com.

**DAVIES, Simon James;** Chief People, Legal and Strategy Officer, Lloyds Banking Group, 2016–17; *b* London, 29 May 1967; *s* of T. D. Davies and late M. J. Davies; *m* 2007, Minori Mano; two *d. Educ:* Emmanuel Coll., Cambridge (BA Law 1989). Admitted Solicitor, 1992; Linklaters: Solicitor, 1992–99; Partner, 1999–2003; Man. Partner, Asia, 2003–07; Firmwide Man. Partner, 2008–15. Comr, Commn on Justice in Wales, 2018–. *Recreations:* theatre, Rugby, running.

**DAVIES, Simon Philip;** Headmaster, Eastbourne College, 2005–16; *b* 27 July 1964; *s* of late Ven. Philip Bertram Davies and of Jane Davies (*née* Richardson); *m* 1991, Robina Pelham Burn; two *s* one *d. Educ:* Radley Coll.; Lady Margaret Hall, Oxford (MA); Inst. of Educn, Univ. of London (PGCE 1994). Grad. trainee, Chase Manhattan Bank, 1986–87; Futures and Options Broker, James Capel, London and Goodbody James Capel, Dublin, 1987–92; Form Teacher, Hereward House Prep. Sch., 1992–93; Hd of Biol. and Sen. Housemaster, Abingdon Sch., 1994–2002; Vice Master and Usher, Bedford Sch., 2002–05. *Recreations:* cycling, fly fishing, cryptic crosswords.

**DAVIES, Siobhan;** *see* Davies, Susan.

**DAVIES, Col Stephen,** MBE 1998; Managing Director, International Railway Heritage Consultancy Ltd, since 2016; motivational and organisational speaker, Inspired Exchange and Raise the Bar, since 2015; *b* Darwen, Lancs, 22 April 1959; *s* of Thomas Davies and Elsie Davies; *m* 1985, Ruth Lomax; one *s* one *d. Educ:* Bishop Rawstorne Sch., Croston; Royal Mil. Acad. Sandhurst; Army Staff Coll. Camberley. Joined Army, 1975; commnd, 1978; ADC to Quartermaster Gen., 1988–90; various appts, 1991–99; CO 1st Bn Queen's Lancashire Regt, 1999–2002; Chief G3 HQ 3rd Div., 2002–03; SO1 Comd and Staff Trainer (N), 2003–04; MoD Advr Sierra Leone, 2004–05; COS HQ 2nd Div., 2005–08. Man. Dir, Conwy Adventure Leisure Ltd, 2012–15. Director: Mus. of Sci. and Industry, Manchester, 2008–10; Nat. Railway Mus., 2010–12; Wensleydale Railway plc, 2016–; Hoverbridge Ltd, 2019–. Dep. Col, Duke of Lancaster's Regt, 2006–14; Trustee: Lancashire Infantry Mus. (formerly Mus. of Queen's Lancashire Regt), 2006–; Bala Lake Railway Trust, 2017–; Army Museums Ogilby Trust, 2018–. Pres. and Dir, 76084 Locomotive Co. Ltd, 2010–18; Pres., Friends of Sierra Leone Nat. Railway Mus. Charity, 2014– (Chm., Sierra Leone Nat. Railway Mus. Supporters Fund, 2010–14). Mem., Leaders Club. Pres., Friends of Darwen Cemetery, 2013–. QCVS 2002. *Recreations:* railways, military history, industrial archaeology, running to stave off old age. *T:* 07880 382638. *E:* info@internationalrailheritage.com. *Club:* Grand Junction.

**DAVIES, Stephen Rees;** QC 2000; *b* 2 May 1960; *s* of John Stephen Davies and Auriol (*née* Huber, now Barriball); *m* 2010, Daisy Leticia Brown. *Educ:* Stanwell Comprehensive Sch.; Cowbridge Comprehensive Sch.; London Sch. of Economics (LLB 1981); Trinity Hall, Cambridge (LLB 1982). Called to the Bar, Gray's Inn, 1983, Bencher 2006; in practice at the Bar, 1983–. Trustee: CLIC, subseq. CLIC Sargent, 2003–06; Jessie May Trust, 2006–13. *Recreations:* music, poetry, Welsh Rugby. *Address:* 9 Old Square, Lincoln's Inn, WC2A 3SR. *E:* stephendavies@enterprisechambers.com.

**DAVIES, Stephen Richard; His Honour Judge Stephen Davies;** a Specialist Circuit Judge, Business and Property Courts, Manchester Civil Justice Centre, since 2007; *b* 7 Feb. 1963; *s* of Robert Davies and Merle Davies; *m* 1996, April Marland; two *d. Educ:* Baines Sch., Poulton-le-Fylde, Lancs; Downing Coll., Cambridge (BA Law 1984). Called to the Bar, Middle Temple, 1985; in practice as barrister in Manchester, 1986–2007; a Recorder of the Crown Court, 2002–07. *Recreations:* my dog, family and friends, cooking. *Address:* Manchester Civil Justice Centre, 1 Bridge Street West, Manchester M60 9DJ. *E:* HHJ.Stephen.Davies@ejudiciary.net.

**DAVIES, Susan, (Siobhan),** CBE 2002 (MBE 1995); choreographer; Artistic Director, Siobhan Davies Dance Company, since 1988; *b* 18 Sept. 1950; *d* of Grahame Henry Wyatt Davies and Tempé Mary Davies (*née* Wallich); one *s* one *d* with David John Buckland, *qv. Educ:* several schools, ending with Queensgate School for Girls; Hammersmith College of Art and Building. With London Contemporary Dance Theatre, 1967–87: first choreography, 1972; Associate Choreographer, 1971; Associate Dir, 1983. Formed Siobhan Davies and Dancers, 1980; Jt Dir, with Ian Spink and Richard Alston, Second Stride, 1981–86; Associate Choreographer, Rambert Dance Co., 1988–93. Choreographed works include: White Man Sleeps, 1988; Art of Touch, 1995; Eighty-Eight, 1998; 13 Different Keys, 1999; Wild Air, 1999; Of Oil and Water, 2000; Plants and Ghosts, 2002; Bird Song, 2004; In Plain Clothes, 2006; Two Quartets, 2007; (with Victoria Miro) The Collection, 2009; Rotor, 2010; (with Matthias Sperling) To hand, 2011; (with Helka Kaski) Manual, 2013; (jtly) Table of Contents, 2014; material/rearranged/to/be, 2017; film work (with David Hinton): All This Can Happen, 2012; The Running Tongue, 2015. Artist Researcher, Faculty of Arts and Humanities, Coventry Univ., 2016–. Hon. FTCL 1996. DUniv: Surrey, 1999; Leicester, 2003. Arts Award, Fulbright Commn, 1987, to travel and study in America; Digital Dance Award, 1988, 1989, 1990, 1992; Laurence Olivier Award for Outstanding Achievement in Dance, 1993, 1996; Prudential Award for Dance, Evening Standard Dance Award, 1996; Time Out Award, 1997; South Bank Show Award for Dance, Prudential Creative Britons Award, 2000. *Address:* Siobhan Davies Studios, 85 St George's Road, SE1 6ER.

**DAVIES, Susan Elizabeth, (Mrs John Davies),** OBE 1988; Founder and Director, Photographers' Gallery, 1971–91; freelance consultant; *b* 14 April 1933; *d* of Stanworth Wills Adey and Joan Mary Margaret Adey (*née* Charlesworth); *m* 1954, John Ross Twiston Davies (*d* 2004); two *d* (and one *d* decd). *Educ:* Nightingale Bamford Sch., NY; Eothen Sch., Caterham. Municipal Journal, 1952–54; local and voluntary work, 1960–67; Artists Placement Group, 1967–68; ICA, 1968–71. Curator, Istanbul Photo-Biennial, 1995–96. Mem. (Ind) S Bucks DC, 1995–99; Parish Councillor, Burnham, Bucks, 1995–2003. Hon. FRPS (President's Medal, 1982). Photokina Award, 1986; National Artist Karel Plicka Medal, Czechoslovakia, 1989. *Recreations:* jazz live and recorded, reading, gardening. *Address:* 57 Sandilands Road, Fulham, SW6 2BD. *Club:* Chelsea Arts.

**DAVIES, Dr Susan Jane;** Lecturer in Palaeography, Aberystwyth University (formerly University of Wales, Aberystwyth), 1979–2008; *b* 4 April 1941; *d* of Iorwerth Howells and Megan Howells; *m* 1966, Brian Harold Davies; one *s* one *d. Educ:* Queen Elizabeth Grammar Sch. for Girls, Carmarthen; University Coll. of Wales, Aberystwyth (BA Hist., Dip. in Palaeography and Archive Admin, PhD in Medieval Ecclesiastical History). Trustee: Nat. Mus. Wales (formerly Mem., Council and Court of Govs, Nat. Museums and Galls of Wales), 1994–2007 (Vice-Pres., 2002–07); Nat. Library of Wales, 2015–18; Member: Royal Commn on Historical Manuscripts, 1995–2003; Lord Chancellor's Adv. Council on Nat. Records and Archives, 2002–03; Adv. Council, CyMAL: Museums Archives and Libraries Wales, 2004–10; AHRC's Peer Review College, 2004–13; Expert Advr, 2008–11, Monitor, 2011–15, HLF. Trustee and Chm., Friends Assoc., Ceredigion Mus., 2018–. Ellis Prize, Archives and Records Assoc., 2014.

**DAVIES, Tansy Abigail Helder,** PhD; composer; *b* Bristol, 29 May 1973; *d* of Nicholas Davies and Jacqueline Davies; partner, Rolf Wallin. *Educ:* Mascalls Sch., Paddock Wood, Kent; Invicta Girls' Grammar Sch., Maidstone; Colchester Inst. (BA Hons Anglia Poly. Univ. 1994); Guildhall Sch. of Music (MMus with distinction 1998); Royal Holloway, Univ. of London (PhD 2004). Freelance horn player, incl. work with Royal Philharmonic Concert Orch.; dep. horn, Les Misérables, W End, London. Composer in Residence, Royal Holloway, Univ. of London, 2004–07; Composition Prof., RAM, 2012–16, now Hon. Prof. DUniv Essex, 2011. Composer in Residence, Concertgebouw, Amsterdam, 2018–19. *Compositions* include: Loure, 2000; Loopholes and Lynchpins, 2001; inside out 2, 2003; make black white, 2004; Residuum, 2004; Iris, 2004; neon, 2004; Spiral House, 2004; Tilting, 2005; Dark Ground, 2005; salt box, 2005; Spine, 2005; Falling Angel, 2006; grind show (electric), 2007; grind show (unplugged), 2008; Adorned, 2008; Destroying Beauty, 2008; Forgotten Game 2, 2009; Static, 2009; This Love, 2009; Wild Card, 2010; As With Voices and Tears, 2010; Greenhouses, 2010; Troubairitz, 2010; Aquatic, 2011; Christmas Eve, 2011; Nature, 2012; Delphic Bee, 2012; The Beginning of the World,

2013; Song of Pure Nothingness, 2013; Between Worlds, 2014; Re-greening, 2015; concerto for horn and orchestra, 2016; Forest, 2017; Cave, 2018. *Recreations:* high intensity interval training (HIIT), koi keeping, reiki healing, astrology. *Address:* 163 High Street, Rochester, Kent ME1 1EH. *T:* (01634) 404954. *E:* tahdavies@gmail.com.

**DAVIES, Prof. Trevor David,** PhD; FRMetS; Professor of Environmental Sciences, 1993, now Emeritus, and Deputy Director, Tyndall Centre for Climate Change Research, University of East Anglia; Special Professor and Director, Fudan Tyndall Centre, Fudan University, Shanghai, since 2011; *b* 29 March 1946; *s* of David Vincent Davies and Alice Beatrice Davies (*née* Savage); *m* 1970, Sandra Patricia Rowles (marr. diss. 2007); one *s* one *d*. *Educ:* Saltley Grammar Sch., Birmingham; Univ. of Sheffield (BSc 1967, PhD 1970). FRMetS 1974. Res. Asst, Univ. of New England, Australia, 1967; University of East Anglia: Lectr in Meteorol., 1970–88; Reader in Atmospheric Scis, 1988–93; Dir, Climatic Res. Unit, 1993–98; Dean, Sch. of Envmtl Scis, 1998–2004; Pro Vice-Chancellor, Res., Enterprise and Engagement, 2004–11; Pro Vice-Chancellor, 2011. Mem., NERC, 2001–08. *Publications:* contrib. numerous scientific papers to specialist jls. *Recreation:* many things. *Address:* Tyndall Centre for Climate Change Research, University of East Anglia, Norwich NR4 7TJ. *T:* (01603) 592836. *E:* t.d.davies@uea.ac.uk.

**DAVIES, Tristan David Henry;** Co-Deputy Editor, Mail on Sunday, since 2016 (Assistant Editor, 2012–16); *b* 26 Oct. 1961; *s* of Maj.-Gen. Peter Ronald Davies, *qv*; *m* 2006, Shane, *d* of Maj.-Gen. Andrew Linton Watson, *qv*; two *s* one *d* from a former marriage. *Educ:* Douai; Bristol Univ. (English and Hist. (failed)). Editor: Covent Gdn Courier, 1983–86; Piazza Mag., 1986–87; joined The Independent, 1987: Listings Ed., 1988–90; Arts and Weekend Ed., 1990–93; Dep. Features Ed., 1993–96; Asst Ed., Mail on Sunday, Night and Day Mag., 1996–98; Exec. Ed., The Independent, 1998–2001; Ed., Independent on Sunday, 2001–07; Exec. Ed., Sunday Times, 2008–12. *Recreations:* football, singing. *Address:* Mail on Sunday, Northcliffe House, 2 Derry Street, W8 5TT. *Club:* Groucho.

**DAVIES, Ven. (Vincent) Anthony;** Archdeacon of Croydon, 1994–2011, now Archdeacon Emeritus; *b* 15 Sept. 1946; *s* of Vincent Davies and Maud Mary Cecilia Davies (*née* Hackett); unmarried. *Educ:* Brasted Place Theol Coll.; St Michael and All Angels Theol Coll., Llandaff. Curate: St James, Owton Manor, dio. Durham, 1973–76; St Faith, Wandsworth, dio. Southwark, 1976–78; Parish Priest: St Faith, Wandsworth, 1978–81; St John, Walworth, 1981–94; RD of Southwark and Newington, 1988–93. Bishop's Advr for Healthcare Chaplaincy, dio. Southwark, 2000–11. FRSA. *Recreations:* walking, reading, country pubs, all things Italian. *Club:* National Liberal.

**DAVIES, Vivian;** *see* Davies, W. V.

**DAVIES, Prof. Wendy Elizabeth,** OBE 2008; FSA, FRHistS, FLSW; FBA 1992; Professor of History, 1985–2007, now Emerita, and Pro-Provost, 1995–2007, University College London; *b* 28 Aug. 1942; *d* of Douglas Charles Davies and Lucy (*née* Evans). *Educ:* University Coll. London (BA, PhD). Temporary Lectr 1970, Res. Fellow 1971, Lectr 1972, Univ. of Birmingham; University College London: Lectr 1977; Reader 1981; Hd, Dept of Hist., 1987–92; Dean of Arts, 1991–94; Dean of Social and Historical Scis, 1994–95; Fellow, 1997. Dist. Vis. Prof., Univ. of Calif, Berkeley, 2001. Member: Ancient Monuments Bd for Wales, 1993–2003; Humanities Res. Bd, 1996–98. Vice-Pres., British Acad., 2003–05. UK Team Mem., Bologna Experts (formerly Promoters), 2004–08. Gov., Mus. of London, 1995–2001. FLSW 2010. Hon. DLit UCL, 2014. *Publications:* An Early Welsh Microcosm, 1978; The Llandaff Charters, 1979; Wales in the Early Middle Ages, 1982; (ed with P. Fouracre) Settlement of Disputes in Early Medieval Europe, 1986; Small Worlds: the village community in early medieval Brittany, 1988; Patterns of Power, 1990; (with G. Astill) The East Brittany Survey, Field Work and Field Data, 1994; (ed with P. Fouracre) Property and Power, 1995; (with G. Astill) A Breton Landscape, 1997; Inscriptions of Early Medieval Brittany, 2000; (ed) From the Vikings to the Normans, 2003; (ed jtly) People and Space, 2006; Acts of Giving: individual, community and church in tenth-century Christian Spain, 2007; Welsh History in the Early Middle Ages: texts and societies, 2009; Brittany in the Early Middle Ages: texts and societies, 2009; (ed with P. Fouracre) The Languages of Gift in the Early Middle Ages, 2010; Windows on Justice in Northern Iberia 800–1000, 2016; papers in Eng. Historical Rev., Past and Present, Francia, Bull. of Bd of Celtic Studies, Etudes Celtiques, Hist. and Anthropology, Oxford Jl of Archaeology, etc. *Recreations:* walking, gardening, friends, early music, cello.

**DAVIES, Dame Wendy (Patricia),** DBE 2001; Head Teacher, Selly Park Technology College (formerly Selly Park School), 1986–2003; *b* 19 Dec. 1942; *d* of Cecil and Mary Trotter; *m* 1967, Mansel John Davies; one *s* (one *d* decd). *Educ:* Portsmouth High Sch., GPDST; UCNW (BSc Hons); DipEd Oxford Univ. Teacher, Birmingham LEA, 1966; Dep. Hd, 1969–74, Hd, 1974–80, Dept of Maths; Dep. Head Teacher, 1980–86. Associate Dir, Specialist Schs and Academies Trust (formerly Specialist Schs Trust), 2005–; Trustee, e-Learning Foundn. *Recreations:* maths, travelling, reading, ICT. *Address:* 82 Lugtrout Lane, Solihull, W Midlands B91 2SN. *T:* (0121) 624 2693. *Club:* Selly Park Technol. Coll. Saturday.

**DAVIES, (William) Gareth;** Chairman, Welsh Rugby Union Ltd, since 2014; *b* 29 Sept. 1955; *s* of late David Elvet Davies and Sarah Davies; *m* 1st, 1979, Helen (marr. diss. 2003); two *d*; 2nd, 2012, Fiona Neivandt. *Educ:* UWIST, Cardiff (BSc); Oxford Univ. Manager, Burnley Bldg Soc. (Nat. and Provincial Bldg Soc.), 1979–87; Asst Dir, CBI, Wales, 1987–89; Hd of Sport, BBC Wales, 1989–94; Chief Exec., Cardiff Rugby Club, 1994–99; Commissioning Ed., Sports and Events (formerly Sports Advr), S4C, 1999–2006; Dir for Welsh Affairs, Royal Mail Gp, 2003–06; Hd, Australia and NZ, Internat. Business Wales, 2006–09; Dean, Carnegie Faculty of Sport and Educn, later Carnegie Faculty, Leeds Metropolitan Univ., 2009–13; Chief Exec., Newport Gwent Dragons and Newport RFC, 2013–14. Chm., Sports Council for Wales, 1999–2003. Rugby journalist: Independent on Sunday, 1999; Sunday Times, 2002–06. Member, Board: Leeds Carnegie Rugby, 2009–13; Yorks CCC, 2011–13. Hon. Fellow, Cardiff Univ., 1995. *Publications:* Standing Off, 1985. *Recreations:* golf, wine (Burgundy and Bordeaux). *Address:* Welsh Rugby Union, Principality Stadium, Westgate Street, Cardiff CF10 1NS. *Clubs:* MCC; Royal Porthcawl Golf, Moortown Golf.

**DAVIES, William Llewellyn M.;** *see* Monro Davies.

**DAVIES, (William) Rhodri;** QC 1999; a Recorder, since 2004; *b* 29 Jan. 1957; *s* of His Honour (Lewis) John Davies, QC; *m* 1984, Vicky Platt; three *d*. *Educ:* Winchester Coll.; Downing Coll., Cambridge (BA Hons Law). Called to the Bar, Middle Temple, 1979; Bencher, 2011; practising barrister, 1980–. *Recreations:* running, sailing, swimming. *Address:* 1 Essex Court, Temple, EC4Y 9AR. *T:* (020) 7583 2000. *Club:* Thames Hare and Hounds.

**DAVIES, Rev. Dr William Rhys;** Principal of Cliff College, Sheffield, 1983–94; Moderator of the Free Church Federal Council, 1991–92; *b* Blackpool, 31 May 1932; *m* 1955, Barbara; one *s* one *d*. *Educ:* Junior, Central Selective and Grammar schools, Blackpool; Hartley Victoria Methodist Coll., Manchester; Univ. of Manchester. BD London 1955; MA 1959, PhD 1965, Manchester. Junior Rating and Valuation Officer (Clerical), Blackpool Corp., 1950–51. Methodist Circuit Minister: Middleton, Manchester, 1955–60; Fleetwood, 1960–65; Stockton-on-Tees, 1965–66; Sen. Lectr in Religious Studies, Padgate Coll. of Higher Education, and Methodist Minister without pastoral charge on Warrington Circuit, 1966–79; Superintendent Minister, Bradford Methodist Mission, 1979–83. Nat. Advr, Aglow Internat. (GB), 1983–. Pres., Methodist Conf., 1987–88. Methodist Committees: Chairman: Cttee for Relations with People of Other Faiths, 1988–98; Ministerial Candidates Appeals Cttee, 1994–2004. Member: Cliff Coll. Gen. Cttee, 1974–77 and 1981–94; Faith and Order Cttee, 1975–82; Doctrinal Cttee, 1979–82; Divl Bd for Social Responsibility, 1982–85; Home Mission Bd, 1983–94. Mem. Council, Garden Tomb (Jerusalem) Assoc., 1992–95. Patron: Pen-y-Rhondda Trust, 2003–; Philippi Trust, 2007–. Co-Editor, Dunamis (renewal magazine for Methodists), 1972–94. *Publications:* (with Ross Peart) The Charismatic Movement and Methodism, 1973; Spirit Baptism and Spiritual Gifts in Early Methodism, (USA) 1974; Gathered into One (Archbishop of Canterbury's Lent Book), 1975; (with Ross Peart) What about the Charismatic Movement?, 1980; (contrib.) A Dictionary of Christian Spirituality, 1983; Rocking the Boat, 1986; Spirit without Measure, 1996; (contrib.) An Encyclopedia: Jesus in history, thought and culture, 2003; contribs to jls. *Recreations:* reading, sport (soccer). *Address:* 25 Grange Avenue, Thornton Cleveleys, Lancs FY5 4PA. *T:* (01253) 864678.

**DAVIES, (William) Vivian,** FSA 1980; Keeper, Ancient Egypt and Sudan (formerly Egyptian Antiquities), British Museum, 1988–2011; *b* 14 Oct. 1947; *s* of late Walter Percival Davies and Gwenllian Davies (*née* Evans); *m* 1970, Janet Olwen May Foat (marr. diss. 1994); one *s* one *d*; *m* 1996, Renée Frances Friedman. *Educ:* Llanelli Grammar Sch.; Jesus Coll., Oxford (BA, MA). Randall-MacIver Student in Archaeology, Queen's Coll., Oxford, 1973–74; Asst Keeper, 1974–81, Dep. Keeper, 1981–88, Dept of Egyptian Antiquities, BM. Vis. Prof. of Egyptology, Univ. of Heidelberg, 1984–85. Hon. Librarian, 1975–85, Gen. Ed. of Pubns, 1990–99, Egypt Exploration Soc.; Chm., Sudan Archaeol Res. Soc., 1991–2012; Member: Governing Council, British Inst. in Eastern Africa, 1989–2005; German Archaeol Inst., 1992–. Hon. Sen. Res. Associate, Griffith Inst., Univ. of Oxford, 2015–. Reviews Editor, Jl of Egyptian Archaeology, 1975–85. *Publications:* A Royal Statue Reattributed, 1981; (with T. G. H. James) Egyptian Sculpture, 1983; The statuette of Queen Tetisheri: a reconsideration, 1984; (with A. el-Khouli, A. B. Lloyd, A. J. Spencer) Saqqara Tombs, I: The Mastabas of Mereri and Wernu, 1984; (ed with J. Assmann and G. Burkard) Problems and Priorities in Egyptian Archaeology, 1987; Egyptian Hieroglyphs, 1987; Catalogue of Egyptian Antiquities in the British Museum, VII: Tools and Weapons—1: Axes, 1987; (ed) Egypt and Africa: Nubia from prehistory to Islam, 1991; (ed with R. Walker) Biological Anthropology and the Study of Ancient Egypt, 1993; (ed with J. Putnam) Time Machine: Ancient Egypt and contemporary art, 1994; (ed with L. Schofield) Egypt, the Aegean and the Levant: interconnections in the second millennium BC, 1995; (with R. Friedman) Egypt, 1998; (ed) Studies in Egyptian Antiquities: a tribute to T. G. H. James, 1999; (ed) Colour and Painting in Ancient Egypt, 2001; (ed with D. Welsby) Uncovering Ancient Sudan: a decade of discovery by the Sudan Archaeological Research Society, 2002; contribs to: Egypt's Golden Age: the art of living in the New Kingdom, 1982; Excavating in Egypt: The Egypt Exploration Society 1882–1982, 1982; Tanis: l'or des pharaons, 1987; Africa: the art of a continent, 1996; Sudan: ancient treasures, 2004; Hatshepsut, from Queen to Pharaoh, 2005; reviews and articles in learned jls.

**DAVIES-JONES, Jonathan;** QC 2013; *b* Sheffield, 10 June 1967; *s* of Dr Aelwyn Davies-Jones and Geraldine Davies-Jones; *m* 1997, Annette King; three *s*. *Educ:* Winchester Coll.; St John's Coll., Cambridge (BA 1988). Called to the Bar, Middle Temple, 1994; in practice as a barrister, specialising in commercial law. Chm. Govs, Balham Nursery Sch. and Children's Centre, 2010–. *Recreations:* family, walking, cycling, laughter. *Address:* 3 Verulam Buildings, Gray's Inn, WC1R 5NT. *T:* (020) 7831 8441, *Fax:* (020) 7831 8447. *E:* jdj@3vb.com.

**DAVIGNON, Count Etienne;** Minister of State and Ambassador of HM the King of the Belgians; Chairman: Foundation P. H. Spaak, since 1983; Institut Egmont (formerly Royal Institute for International Relations), since 1987; *b* Budapest, 4 Oct. 1932; *m* 1959, Françoise de Cumont; one *s* two *d*. *Educ:* University of Louvain (LLD). Diplomat; Head of Office of Minister for Foreign Affairs, Belgium, 1963; Political Director, Ministry for Foreign Affairs, Belgium, 1969; Chm., Gov. Board, Internat. Energy Agency, 1974. Mem., 1977–84 (with responsibility for internal mkt, customs, union and indust. affairs), and Vice-Pres., 1981–84 (with responsibility for industry, energy and research policies), EEC. Chairman: CMB (Belgium), 2002; Recticel (Belgium), 2004–15; Brussels Airlines, Belgium, 2005–; Genfina, 2010–; Vice-Chairman: Fortis, 1989–2004; ACCOR, 2000–09 (Dir, 1990–2000); Société Gén. de Belgique, 2001–03 (Chm., 1989–2001); Suez-Tractebel, 2003–10; Director: Umicore, 1989–92 and 2000–05 (Chm., 1992–2000); Suez, 1989–2010; Gilead (USA), 1990–. *Recreations:* tennis, golf. *Address:* 35 Avenue d'Italie, 1050 Brussels, Belgium.

**DAVIS;** *see* Clinton-Davis.

**DAVIS;** *see* Hart-Davis.

**DAVIS, Adam David;** QC 2012; *b* London, 6 May 1963; *s* of Edgar Davis and Leila Davis; *m* 1994, Cheryl Fellerman; one *s* two *d*. *Educ:* Mill Hill Sch.; Queen Mary Coll., Univ. of London (LLB Hons). Called to the Bar, Inner Temple, 1985; in practice as barrister, specialising in crime and sports. Very High Cost Cases Appeals Cttee, 2003–; Sports Disputes Resolution Panel, 2005–09. *Recreations:* football (Tottenham Hotspur FC), golf, cricket, cinema. *Address:* 3 Temple Gardens, EC4Y 9AU. *T:* (020) 7353 3120. *E:* adqc@3TG.co.uk. *Clubs:* MCC; Hampstead Golf.

**DAVIS, Prof. Adrian Charles,** OBE 2007; PhD; Professor of Hearing and Communication, and Director, MRC Hearing and Communication Group, University of Manchester, 2004; *b* 21 March 1950; *s* of Albert H. W. Davis and G. H., (Trudy), Davis; *m* 1978, Kathryn Southworth; two *s* one *d*. *Educ:* Douai Sch.; University Coll. London (Dip. Theol. 1970; PhD Psychol. 1984); Univ. of Exeter (BSc Mathematical Stats and Psychol. 1973); Stirling Univ. (MSc Mathematical Psychol. 1974). Lectr in Community Medicine, St Thomas's Hosp. Med. Sch., 1977–78; SRC Res. Fellow (Psychol.), Lancaster Poly., 1978; Sen. Scientific Epidemiologist, MRC Inst. of Hearing Res., 1978–2004. Special Prof., Dept of Surgery, Univ. of Nottingham, 1996; Hon. Consultant Clinical Scientist, Queens Med. Centre, Nottingham, 1996; Hon. Consultant, Central Manchester and Manchester Children's Univ. NHS Trust, 2005. Director: NHS Newborn Hearing Screening Prog., 2001; NHS Clinical Audiology Res. Network, 2005; DoH Advr, Audiology, 2005; DoH Clinical/Scientific Audiology Champion for Physiol Measurement Strategy Gp, 2005. Vice Pres., Action on Hearing Loss, 2017–. Medal, Swedish Med. Assoc., 1992; Amer. Auditory Soc. Award, 1998; Thomas Simm Littler Prize, British Soc. of Audiology, 1999; Internat. Award for Hearing, Amer. Acad. of Audiol., 2010; Lifetime Achievement Award, British Acad. of Audiol., 2015. *Publications:* Hearing in Adults, 1995; over 100 books, conf. papers and over 100 articles in scientific jls. *Recreations:* badminton, running.

**DAVIS, Adrian Derek;** Governor, Montserrat, 2011–15 (on secondment from Department for International Development); *b* London, 22 July 1950; *s* of Bernard and Betty Davis; *m* 1975, Sujue Sattayipiwat; two *s*. *Educ:* University Coll., London (BSc (Econ) 1971); London Sch. of Econs (MSc (Econ) 1974). Department for International Development,

1974–2015; First Secretary: (Econ.), Dhaka, 1977–79; Econ. Advr, SE Asia Develt Div., Bangkok, 1980–83; (Aid/Econ.), Cairo, 1984–87; Dep. Hd, FCO/DFID Know-How Fund for Eastern Europe, 1987–91; UK Exec. Dir, Asia Develt Bank, Manila, 1991–94 (on secondment); Hd, E Asia and Pacific Dept, 1994–96; Hd, Information and Services Dept, 1996–99; Hd, Envmt Dept, 1999–2003; Country Rep. for Cambodia, China, Indonesia, N Korea and Vietnam, 2003–11. *Recreations:* ten-pin bowling, table tennis, word games, reading, music.

**DAVIS, Alan Henry;** strategy consultant; Director of Neighbourhood Renewal Strategy, Department for Communities and Local Government (formerly Office of the Deputy Prime Minister), 2004–07; *b* 1 May 1948; *s of* Arthur Wallace Davis and Phyllis Marjorie Davis (*née* Grudgings); *m* 1st, 1972, Angela Joy Wells (marr. diss. 2003); two *s* one *d*; 2nd, 2012, Theresa Mary Crossley (*née* Short). *Educ:* Wyggeston Boys' Sch., Leicester; University Coll., Oxford (MA Chem. 1973). Joined DoE, 1973; on secondment to GLC, 1979–80; Private Sec. to successive Secs of State, 1983–85; Asst Sec., 1986; Head of Divs in Local Govt, Housing, Global Atmosphere; Principal Private Sec. to Sec. of State, 1994–97; Under-Sec., 1997; Director: Water and Land, DETR, 1997–2001; Integrated and Local Transport, DfT (formerly DETR, then DTLR), 2001–04. Churchwarden, St Paul's Ch, Winchmore Hill, 2015–. *Recreations:* gardening, walking, watching sport. *Address:* 11 Old Park View, Enfield, Middx EN2 7EG. *T:* (020) 8364 4043.

**DAVIS, Ven. Alan Norman;** Archdeacon of West Cumberland, 1996–2004; *b* 27 July 1938; *s of* Arthur William and Bertha Eileen Davis; *m* 1966, Françoise Marguerite Blondet; one *s* two *d*. *Educ:* King Edward's Sch., Birmingham; Durham Univ.; Lichfield Theol Coll.; Open Univ. (BA). Ordained deacon, 1965, priest, 1966; Asst Curate, St Luke's Birmingham, 1965–68; Priest-in-charge, 1968–73, Vicar, 1973–75, St Paul, Wordsworth Avenue, Sheffield; Vicar, St James and St Christopher, Shiregreen, Sheffield, 1975–80; Team Rector, Maltby, Sheffield, 1980–89; Archbishop's Officer for Urban Priority Areas, 1990–92; Priest-in-charge, St Cuthbert, Carlisle, and Diocesan Communications Officer, 1992–96; Area Dean, Sparkenhoe W, Dio. Leicester, 2007–09. *Recreations:* French holidays, RSC Theatre Stratford, Aston Villa Football Club. *Address:* 71 North Street, Atherstone, Warwicks CV9 1JW. *T:* (01827) 718210.

**DAVIS, Alan Roger M.;** *see* Maryon Davis.

**DAVIS, Andrew;** Founder and Executive Chairman, von Essen group of companies, 1997–2011; Executive Chairman, PremiAir Aviation Services Ltd, 2007–12; *b* 22 Feb. 1964; *s of* Brendon G. F. Davis and Catharine Agnes Davis (*née* Smyth); one *s*. Farmer; property develt and investment; art consulting. *E:* andrew.davis@andrew-davis.co.uk.

**DAVIS, Sir Andrew (Frank),** Kt 1999; CBE 1992; conductor; Musical Director, Chicago Lyric Opera, since 2000; Chief Conductor, Melbourne Symphony Orchestra, 2012–19, now Conductor Laureate; *b* 2 Feb. 1944; *m* 1989, Gianna Rolandi; one *s*. *Educ:* Watford Grammar Sch.; King's Coll., Cambridge (MA, BMus); Accademia di S Cecilia, Rome. Assistant Conductor, BBC Scottish Symphony Orchestra, 1970–72; Asst Conductor, New Philharmonia Orchestra, 1973–77; Artistic Dir and Chief Conductor, Toronto Symphony, 1975–88, now Conductor Laureate; Musical Dir, Glyndebourne Fest. Opera, 1988–2000; Chief Conductor, BBC SO, 1989–2000, now Conductor Laureate. Principal Guest Conductor: Royal Liverpool Philharmonic Orchestra, 1974–77; Royal Stockholm Philharmonic, 1995–2000. Has conducted major US orchestras: New York, Boston, Chicago, Cleveland, Philadelphia and LA. Particularly noted for interpretations of Strauss operas; conducts at: La Scala, Milan; Metropolitan Opera, NY; Chicago Lyric; San Francisco; Glyndebourne; Royal Opera House, Covent Gdn; Bayreuth Fest. Toronto Symphony Orchestra tours: US Centres, China, Japan, 1978; Europe, 1983, 1986, incl. London, Helsinki, Bonn, Paris and Edinburgh Fest.; BBC SO tours: Far East, 1990; Europe, 1992 and 1996; Japan, 1993; N America, 1995 and 1998; Korea and Japan, 1997; Salzburg Fest., 1997; other tours include: Australia, 2002; LSO, 2002, 2004. Many commercial recordings include: complete Dvorak Symphonies, Philharmonia Orch.; Mendelssohn Symphonies, Bavarian Radio Symphony; Borodin Cycle, Holst's The Planets and Handel's Messiah, Toronto Symphony; Tippett's The Mask of Time, BBC SO and Chorus (Record of the Year, Gramophone Awards, 1987); The British Line (British Orchestral Series), BBC SO; world première of Elgar/Payne Symphony No 3. *Recreation:* the study of mediaeval stained glass. *Address:* c/o Opus 3 Artists, 470 Park Avenue South, 9th Floor North, New York, NY 10016, USA.

**DAVIS, Ann-Louise;** *see* Kinmonth, A.-L.

**DAVIS, Prof. Anne Christine,** PhD; FInstP; Professor of Mathematical Physics (1967), University of Cambridge, 2013–18, now Emeritus; Fellow, King's College, Cambridge, since 1986; *b* Bristol, 5 Feb. 1951; *d of* Albert and Esmé Davis; *m* (marr. diss.) one *d*. *Educ:* Ashton Park Sch., Bristol; Royal Holloway Coll., Univ. of London (BSc); Bristol Univ. (PhD 1975). FInstP 2001. Postdoctoral Res. Associate in Theoretical Physics: Durham Univ., 1976–78; Blackett Physics Lab., Imperial Coll. London, 1978–80; Fellow, Theory Div., CERN, Geneva, 1980–82; Mem., Inst. for Advanced Study, Princeton, USA, 1982–83; University of Cambridge: Res. Council Advanced Fellow, Dept of Applied Maths and Theoretical Physics, 1983–88; Coll. Teaching Officer, King's Coll., 1988–95; Department of Applied Mathematics and Theoretical Physics: Asst Dir of Res., 1995–96; Reader in Theoretical Physics, 1996–2002; Prof. of Theoretical Physics, 2002–13. Vis. Prof., Brown Univ., USA, 1989; CNRS Vis. Prof., Paris, 1996. MAE 2009. *Publications:* Formation and Interactions of Topological Defeats, 1995; contrib. papers on theoretical physics, incl. theoretical cosmol. and high energy physics. *Recreations:* walking and trekking, opera, theatre, ballet, time with my family, reading, travelling. *Address:* Department of Applied Mathematics and Theoretical Physics, Centre for Mathematical Sciences, University of Cambridge, Wilberforce Road, Cambridge CB3 0WA. *T:* (01223) 337878. *E:* a.c.davis@damtp.cam.ac.uk.

**DAVIS, Anthony Ronald William James;** media consultant, since 1990; *b* 26 July 1931; *e s of* Donald William Davis, Barnes and Mary Josephine Davis (*née* Nolan-Byrne), Templeogue Mill, Co. Dublin; *m* 1960, Yolande Mary June, *o d of* Patrick Leonard, retd civil engr; one *s* two *d* (and one *d* decd). *Educ:* Hamlet of Ratcliffe and Oratory; Regent Street Polytechnic. Joint Services School for Linguists on Russian course as National Serviceman (Army), 1953–55; Architectural Asst, Housing Dept, Middx County Architect's Dept, 1956–58; Sub-Editor, The Builder, 1959; Editor: Official Architecture and Planning, 1964–70; Building, 1970–74; Director, Building, 1972–77; Editor-in-Chief, New World Publishers Ltd, 1978–83; Editl Dir, New World Publishers Ltd, Middle East Construction and Saudi Arabian Construction, 1983–86; Editor, World Property, 1986–90. Member Board: Architecture and Planning Publications Ltd, 1966; Building (Publishers) Ltd, 1972. Mem. Council, Modular Soc., 1970–71. JP Berkshire, 1973–81. *Publications:* contribs to various, architectural and technical. *Recreations:* collecting porcelain, music and dreaming.

**DAVIS, Barbara Ann;** *see* Cassani, B. A.

**DAVIS, Prof. Benjamin Guy,** DPhil; FRS 2015; Professor of Chemistry, University of Oxford, since 2005; Fellow, Pembroke College, Oxford, since 2001; *b* Hatfield, 8 Aug. 1970; *s of* Stanley Stewart Davis and Jennifer Margaret Morley. *Educ:* Nottingham High Sch.; Keble Coll., Oxford (BA Chem. 1st Cl. with Chem. Pharmacol. (Dist.) 1993; DPhil Chemistry 1997); Univ. of Durham (PGCHE 2001). Postdoctoral Researcher, Dept of Chem., Univ. of Toronto, 1997–98; Demonstrator and Lectr, Dept of Chem., Univ. of Durham, 1998–2001; Lectr, Univ. of Oxford, 2001–05. Vis. Prof., Pierre and Marie Curie Univ., Paris, 2011. *Publications:* Carbohydrate Chemistry, Oxford Chemistry Primer No. 99 (with A. J. Fairbanks), 2002; over 30 book chapters; over 200 scientific jl articles; over 30 patents. *Recreations:* rowing (Mem., Stewards' Enclosure, Henley Royal Regatta), open-water swimming, art. *Address:* Pembroke College, Oxford OX1 1DW. *Clubs:* City of Oxford Rowing, Pembroke College Boat (Sen. Mem.), Oxford University Lightweight Rowing (Sen. Mem.).

**DAVIS, Dr Brian Elliott,** CBE 2000; Chief Executive, Nationwide Building Society, 1994–2001; *b* 22 Sept. 1944; *s of* William and Bessie Davis; *m* 1972, Elizabeth Rose; one *s* two *d*. *Educ:* St John's Coll., Southsea; Sussex Univ. (BSc); Sheffield Univ. (PhD). FCIB 2000. With Esso Petroleum Co., 1969–86; joined Nationwide Building Soc., 1986; Gen. Manager (Technology), 1987; Resource Dir, 1989; Ops Dir, 1992. Chm., BSA, 1996–98. *Recreations:* sport, computing.

**DAVIS, Maj.-Gen. Brian William,** CB 1985; CBE 1980 (OBE 1974); Head of Public Affairs, Royal Ordnance plc, 1987–94 (Director, Product Support Group, 1985–87); *b* 28 Aug. 1930; *s of* late Edward William Davis, MBE, and Louise Jane Davis (*née* Webber); *m* 1954, Margaret Isobel Jenkins; one *s* one *d*. *Educ:* Weston-super-Mare Grammar Sch.; Mons OCS, Aldershot. Commissioned Royal Artillery, 1949; Regtl Duty, 1949–56 and 1960–61, UK/BAOR; Instr-in-Gunnery, 1956–59; Staff Coll. Camberley, 1962; DAA and QMG HQ 7 Armd Bde BAOR, 1963–66; GSO2 SD UN Force, Cyprus, 1966; Regtl Duty, 1967–69; Lt-Col 1969, Directing Staff, Staff Coll. Camberley, 1969–71; CO 32 Lt Regt RA BAOR/England/N Ireland, 1971–74; Col AQ Ops HQ BAOR, 1975; Brig. 1975; CRA 3 Div., 1976–77; RCDS 1978; Chief of Staff N Ireland, 1979–80; Chief of Comdrs-in-Chief Mission to Soviet Forces in Germany, 1981–82; Maj. Gen., 1982; C of S, Logistic Exec. (Army), 1982–83; DGLP (A) (formerly VQMG), MoD, 1983–85, retired. Col Comdt RA, 1987–93. Mem., HAC, 1987–95. *Recreations:* Rugby (President, RARFC, 1975–78; Dep. Pres., Army Rugby Union, 1984–89), cricket, fishing, ornithology. *Clubs:* Special Forces, MCC; Army Rugby Union; Fadeaways; Piscatorial Society (Pres., 2003–07).

**DAVIS, Carl,** Hon. CBE 2005; composer; *b* 28 Oct. 1936; *s of* Isadore and Sara Davis; *m* 1971, Jean Boht; two *d*. *Educ:* New England Conservatory of Music; Bard Coll. (BA). Associate Conductor, London Philharmonic Orchestra, 1987–88; Principal Conductor, Bournemouth Pops, 1984–87; Principal Guest Conductor, Munich SO, 1990–93; Artistic Dir, Liverpool Philharmonic Summer Pops, 1993–2000; *major TV credits:* The Snow Goose, 1971; World at War (Emmy Award), 1972; The Naked Civil Servant, 1975; Marie Curie, 1977; Our Mutual Friend, 1978; Prince Regent, The Old Curiosity Shop, 1979; Hollywood, Oppenheimer, The Sailor's Return, Fair Stood the Wind for France, 1980; The Commanding Sea, Private Schulz, 1981; The Last Night of the Poms, Home Sweet Home, La Ronde, 1982; The Unknown Chaplin, The Tale of Beatrix Potter, The Far Pavilions, 1983; The Day the Universe Changed, 1985; Hotel du Lac, 1986; The Accountant (BAFTA Award), The Pied Piper, 1989; Flight Terminal, Secret Life of Ian Fleming, 1990; The Black Velvet Gown, Buried Mirror, Yellow Wallpaper, The Last of the Romantics, Ashenden, Separate But Equal, 1991; The Royal Collection, A Very Polish Practice, A Sense of History, Fame in the 20th Century, 1992; A Year in Provence, Genghis Cohen, Thatcher: the Downing Street Years, 1993; Red Eagle, Hope in the Year 2, 1994; Pride and Prejudice, 1995; A Dance to the Music of Time, 1997; Cold War, Good Night Mr Tom, Seesaw, Coming Home, 1998; The Great Gatsby, 2000; Christopher Columbus, 2002; Promoted by Glory, 2003; Upstairs Downstairs, 2012; *radio:* presenter, Carl Davis Classics, R2, 1997–2000; *scores:* for RSC, National Theatre and Birmingham Royal Ballet; *musicals:* The Projector, 1971; Pilgrim, 1975; Cranford, 1976; Alice in Wonderland, 1978; The Wind in the Willows, 1985; Kip's War, 1987; *opera:* Peace, 1978; *TV operas:* The Arrangement, 1967; Orpheus in the Underground, 1976; *West End:* Forty Years On, 1969; Habeas Corpus, 1973; *films:* The French Lieutenant's Woman (BAFTA Original Film Score Award), 1981; Champions, 1984; King David, 1985; Girl in a Swing, Scandal, The Rainbow, 1988; Frankenstein Unbound, Fragments of Isabella, 1989; Crucifer of Blood, Raft of the Medusa, 1991; The Voyage, 1992; The Trial, 1993; Widows Peak, 1994; Topsy-Turvy, 1999; Book of Eve, 2002; Ethel and Ernest, 2016; *silent films:* Napoleon, 1980, newly adapted, 2000, US premiere, San Francisco Silent Film Fest., 2012; The Crowd, 1981; Flesh and the Devil, Show People, How to Make Movies, 1982; Broken Blossoms, The Wind, The Musketeers of Pig Alley, An Unseen Enemy, 1983; Thief of Bagdad, 1984; The Big Parade, Greed, 1985; The General, Ben Hur, 1987; Mysterious Lady, Intolerance, City Lights (re-creation of Chaplin score), 1988; Safety Last, Kid Brother, 1989; The Immigrant, 1991; IT, The Four Horsemen of the Apocalypse, 1992; Wings; The Gold Rush (re-creation of Chaplin score), 1993; The Wedding March, 1998; Old Heidelberg, 1999; The Iron Mask, 1999; The Adventurer, 2000; The Rink, Behind the Screen (Chaplain short films), 2003; The Freshman (Harold Lloyd film), 2013; Steamboat Bill Jr, The Playhouse, Why Worry?, 2014; *ballets:* Dances of Love and Death, 1981; Fire and Ice (ice ballet for Torvill and Dean), 1986; The Portrait of Dorian Gray (for SWRB), 1987; A Simple Man (based on L. S. Lowry, for Northern Ballet Theatre), 1987; Liaisons Amoureuses, 1988; Lipizzaner (Northern Ballet Theatre), 1988; A Christmas Carol (Northern Ballet Theatre), 1992; Savoy Suite (English Nat. Ballet), 1993; Alice in Wonderland (English Nat. Ballet), 1995; Aladdin (Scottish Ballet), 2000; Cyrano (Birmingham Royal Ballet), 2007; The Lady of the Camellias (Ballet HNK, Croatia), 2008; Nijinsky (Slovak Nat. Ballet), 2015; The Great Gatsby (Pittsburgh Ballet Theatre), 2019; Chaplin, The Tramp (Slovak Nat. Ballet), 2019; *orchestral compositions:* Lines on London (symphony), 1984 (commnd by Capital Radio); Clarinet Concerto, 1984; Fantasy for flute, 1985 (commnd by Acad. of St Martin in the Fields); Glenlivet Firework Music, 1987; Beginners Please!, 1987; (with Paul McCartney) Paul McCartney's Liverpool Oratorio, 1991; On the Beach at Night Alone, 1999; Ballade for Cello and Orchestra, 2011 (commnd by Royal Liverpool Philharmonic Orch.); *choral:* The Last Train to Tomorrow, 2012. Has made numerous recordings. Formed Carl Davis Collection (with Jean Davis and Charles Padley) for promotion of recordings of own music, 2009. Mem. BAFTA, 1979–. First winner, BAFTA Award for Original TV Music, 1981; BAFTA Lifetime Achievement Award for Contribution to Film and TV, 2003. Chevalier de L'Ordre des Arts et des Lettres, 1983. *Publications:* sheet music of television themes. *Recreations:* reading, gardening, playing chamber music, cooking. *Address:* c/o Peter Hall, Musichall, Oast House, Crouch's Farm, Hollow Lane, E Hoathly, E Sussex BN8 6QX. *E:* peter@musichall.uk.com.

**DAVIS, Christopher John;** Headmaster, Sherborne School, 2010–14; *b* Middx, 27 April 1961; *s of* John Priddis Davis and Juliet Myfanwy Davis (*née* Stearns); *m* 1994, Innes Flora McLeod Fraser; two *d*. *Educ:* Eton Coll.; Corpus Christi Coll., Cambridge (BA 1984; MA). Asst Master, St Edmund's Sch., Canterbury, 1984–85; Bank of England: Internat. Div.,

1986–90; on secondment to Cabinet Office, 1990–92; Editor, Qly Bulletin, 1992–94; Eton College: Asst Master, 1994–2001; House Master, 2001–10. *Recreations:* music, reading, sport, theatre, English literature.

**DAVIS, Prof. (Conrad) Glyn,** AC 2002; PhD; Chief Executive Officer, Paul Ramsay Foundation, since 2019. *Educ:* Univ. of NSW (BA 1st Cl. Hons Pol Sci. 1981); ANU (PhD 1985). FIPAA 1995; FASSA 2003. Lectr in Politics and Public Policy, Griffith Univ., 1985; Harkness Fellow, Univ. of Calif, Berkeley, Brookings Instn, Washington and John F. Kennedy Sch. of Govt, Harvard, 1987–88; Griffith University: Aust. Res. Council QE II Res. Fellow, 1992–95, 1996–98; Prof., 1998; Vice-Chancellor and Pres., 2002–05; on secondment to Queensland Government: as Comr for Public Sector Equity, Qld Public Sector Mgt Commn, 1990–93; as Dir Gen., Office of the Cabinet, 1995–96; as Dir Gen., Qld Dept of the Premier and Cabinet, 1998–2002; Vice-Chancellor and Pres., Univ. of Melbourne, 2005–18. Chm., Aust. and NZ Sch. of Govt, Univ. of Melbourne, 2002–06; Mem. Bd, Menzies Centre, KCL, 2007–. Chairman: Universities Australia, 2011–13; Educn and Curriculum Wkg Gp, Anzac Centenary Adv. Bd, 2012–. Director: South Bank Corp., 1998–2001; Qld Theatre Co., 2002–05; Melbourne Theatre Co., 2005–; Asialink, 2005–. DUniv Griffith, 2006. *Publications:* Breaking Up the ABC, 1988; A Government of Routines, 1995; (with P. Bridgman) The Australian Policy Handbook, 1998, 5th edn (with P. Bridgman and C. Althaus) 2012; (ed with M. Keating) The Future of Australian Governance: policy choices, 2000; (ed with P. Weller) Are You Being Served?: state, citizens and governance, 2001; The Republic of Learning: higher education transforms Australia, 2010.

**DAVIS, Sir Crispin Henry Lamert,** Kt 2004; Chief Executive Officer, Reed Elsevier, 1999–2009; Chairman, StarBev B.V., 2010–12; *b* 19 March 1949; *s* of late Walter Patrick Carless Davis and Jane (*née* Lamert); *m* 1970, Anne Richardson; three *d*. *Educ:* Charterhouse; Oriel Coll., Oxford (MA Mod. Hist.). Joined Procter & Gamble, 1970: Man. Dir, Procter & Gamble Germany, 1981–84; Vice-Pres., Food Div., Procter & Gamble USA, 1984–90; European Man. Dir, 1990–92, Gp Man. Dir, 1992–94, United Distillers; CEO, Aegis plc, 1994–99. Non-executive Director: GlaxoSmithKline plc, 2003–13; Vodafone, 2014–; Rentokil Initial plc, 2017–; Ind. Dir, Hasbro Inc., 2016–. Trustee, Nat. Trust, 2005–12. Mem. Council, Oxford Univ., 2009–. *Recreations:* sport: tennis, squash, golf, ski-ing; gardening, art, antique furniture. *Clubs:* Royal Automobile, MCC; Sunningdale Golf.
See also Sir I. E. L. Davis, Rt Hon. Sir N. A. L. Davis.

**DAVIS, Prof. Daniel Michael,** PhD; Professor of Immunology and Director of Research, Manchester Collaborative Centre for Inflammation Research, University of Manchester, since 2013; *b* London, 2 Aug. 1970; *s* of Gerald and Marilyn Davis; *m* 2000, Katie Nicholls; one *s* one *d*. *Educ:* Univ. of Manchester (BSc 1st Cl. Physics 1992); Strathclyde Univ. (PhD 1995). Postdoctoral Res. Fellow, Dept of Molecular and Cell Biol., Harvard Univ., 1996–99; Imperial College London: Lectr, Dept of Biol., 1999–2005; Prof. of Molecular Immunology, 2005–13; Hd, Immunology Sec., 2008–13. *Publications:* The Compatibility Gene, 2013; The Beautiful Cure: harnessing your body's natural defences, 2018; contrib. papers to scientific jls. *Recreation:* reading and collecting American super-hero comic books. *Address:* University of Manchester, CTF Building, 2nd Floor, 46 Grafton Street, Manchester M13 9NT. *T:* (0161) 275 5019. *E:* daniel.davis@manchester.ac.uk.

**DAVIS, Rt Hon. David (Michael);** PC 1997; MP (C) Haltemprice and Howden, 1997–June 2008 and since July 2008 (Boothferry, 1987–97); *b* 23 Dec. 1948; *s* of Ronald and Elizabeth Davis; *m* 1973, Doreen Margery Cook; one *s* two *d*. *Educ:* Warwick Univ. (BSc); London Business Sch. (MSc); Harvard (AMP). Joined Tate & Lyle, 1974: Strategic Planning Dir, 1984–87; Dir, 1987–89. PPS to Parly Under-Sec. of State, DTI, 1989–90; an Asst Govt Whip, 1990–93; Parly Sec., Office of Public Service and Science, Cabinet Office, 1993–94; Minister of State, FCO, 1994–97; Chm., Cons. Party, 2001–02; Shadow Sec. of State, ODPM, 2002–03; Shadow Home Sec., 2003–08; Sec. of State for Exiting the EU, 2016–18. Chm., H of C Public Accounts Cttee, 1997–2001. Resigned seat June 2008 to contest by-election on civil liberties issue; re-elected July 2008. Non-exec. Dir, New City Agenda, 2014–16. Mem., Financial Policy Cttee, CBI, 1977–79; Exec. Mem., Industrial Soc., 1985–87. Chm., Fedn of Cons. Students, 1973–74. *Recreations:* writing, flying, mountaineering. *Address:* House of Commons, SW1A 0AA.

**DAVIS, Dennis Tyrone,** CBE 2004 (OBE 1996); QFSM 1991; CEng, FIFireE; independent fire adviser, since 2004; HM Chief Inspector of Fire Services for Scotland, 1999–2004; *b* 10 Feb. 1947; *s* of Dennis and Winifred Davis; *m* 1968, Maureen; two *s*. *Educ:* Queen Mary's Grammar Sch., Walsall; MPhil Univ. of Central Lancs 2005. Joined Fire Bde, 1965; Walsall, 1965–71; Cheshire, 1971–99, Chief Fire Officer, 1986–99. Chm., Fire Confs and Exhibitions Ltd, 1990–2005 (Dir, 1990–2011). Chm., Fedn of British Fire Orgns, 2006–11 (Vice Chm., 2004–06); Vice Chm., Fire Sector Fedn, 2011–; Vice Pres., Internat. Assoc. Fire and Rescue Services, 2007–. FIFireE 1981 (Chm., 1988–2006; Life Fellow, 1999); CEng 1998; CCMI (CIMgt 1995). OStJ 1996. *Recreation:* old cars. *Address:* 11 Private Walk, Chester CH3 5XB.

**DAVIS, Derek Richard;** Chairman, British Geological Survey, 2005–10 (Chairman, Commercialisation Strategy Group, 2009–10; Board Member, 2004); *b* 3 May 1945; *s* of late Stanley Lewis Davis, OBE and Rita Beatrice Rachel Davis (*née* Rosenheim), MBE; *m* 1987, Diana Levinson; one *s* one *d*. *Educ:* Clifton Coll., Bristol; Balliol Coll., Oxford (BA 1967; MA 2009). Asst Master, Scindia Sch., Gwalior, 1962–63. Asst Principal, BoT, 1967; Pvte Sec. to Perm. Sec., DTI, 1971–72; Principal, 1972; Asst Sec., Dept of Energy, 1977; Secretary: Energy Commn, 1977–79; NEDC Energy Task Force, 1981; seconded to NCB, 1982–83; Under Sec., Gas Div., 1985–87, Oil and Gas Div., 1987–93, Dept of Energy, subseq. DTI; Dir Gen., BNSC, 1993–99; Dir, Chemicals, Biotechnology, Consumer Goods and Posts, 1999–2002, Nuclear and Coal Liabilities, 2002–04, DTI. Member: BBSRC, 2000–02. Trustee: Nat. Space Sci. Centre, 1998–99; Royal Asiatic Soc., 2014–18 (Mem. Council, 2019–). *Publications:* contribs to Jl RAS, Trans Jewish Histl Soc. of England. *Address:* 6 Roman Road, Bedford Park, W4 1NA. *T:* (020) 8747 3931.

**DAVIS, Lt Gen. Edward Grant Martin,** CB 2014; CBE 2012 (OBE 2005; MBE 1996); Governor and Commander-in-Chief of Gibraltar, since 2016; *b* Hereford, 13 Feb. 1963; *s* of Robert and Heather Davis; *m* 1987, Lorraine Francine Ezra. *Educ:* Coleraine Academical Instn; King's Coll. London (MA Defence Studies). Joined Royal Marines, 1981; ACSC 1996; CO Commando Unit, 2002–04; Hd, Dept of Acquisition and Ops, MoD, 2005–09; HCSC 2009; Comdr 3 Commando Bde (incl. Task Force Helmand, Afghanistan), 2010–11; Comdt Gen., RM and Comdr, UK Amphibious Forces, 2011–14; Dep. Comdr Land Comd, Izmir, Turkey, 2014–16. KStJ 2016. Legion of Merit (USA), 2011. *Recreations:* gardening, enjoying the countryside.

**DAVIS, Evan Harold;** Presenter, PM, BBC Radio 4, since 2018; *b* 8 April 1962; *s* of Quintin Visser Davis and Hazel Noreen Davis. *Educ:* Ashcombe Sch., Dorking; St John's Coll., Oxford (PPE Hons 1984); Kennedy Sch. of Government, Harvard Univ. (MPA 1988). Res. Officer, Inst. for Fiscal Studies, 1984–86; Res. Fellow, London Business Sch., 1988–92; Res. Co-ordinator, Inst. for Fiscal Studies, 1992–93; Econs Correspondent, 1993–2001, Econs Ed., 2001–08, Presenter, Today prog., Radio 4, 2008–14, Newsnight, 2014–18, BBC. *Publications:* Public Spending, 1998; (jtly) Penguin Dictionary of Economics, 4th edn 1987 to 7th edn 2003; (jtly) New Penguin Dictionary of Business, 2003; Made in Britain: how the nation earns its living, 2011; Post-Truth: why we have reached peak bullshit and what we can do about it, 2017. *Address:* BBC New Broadcasting House, 3rd floor, Portland Place, W1A 1AA. *E:* evan.davis@bbc.co.uk.

**DAVIS, Gareth;** Chairman: Ferguson (formerly Wolseley) plc, 2011–19 (non-executive Director, 2003–Jan. 2020); DS Smith plc, since 2012 (non-executive Director, since 2010); *b* 13 May 1950; *m* 1973, Andrea Allan; one *d* (and one *d* decd). *Educ:* Beal Grammar Sch., Ilford; Univ. of Sheffield (BA Hons Econ.). Mgt trainee, Imperial Tobacco, 1972; W. D. & H. O. Wills: Prodn Manager, Newcastle, 1973–79; Prodn Control Manager, Bristol, 1979–83; Factory Manager, Players, Nottingham, 1983–89; Mfg Dir, Imperial, 1987–95, and Man. Dir, Imperial Internat., 1988–95; CEO, Imperial Tobacco Gp plc, 1996–2010. Chm., William Hill plc, 2010–18. *Recreations:* most sports, especially cricket, golf, soccer.

**DAVIS, Glen Milton;** QC 2011; *b* London, 11 Sept. 1956; *s* of David and June Davis; *m* 1st, 1986 (marr. diss.); 2nd, 2002, Mary Jane Aladren; two *s* two *d*. *Educ:* University Coll. Sch., Hampstead; Balliol Coll., Oxford (Goldsmith Schol.; BA 1st Cl. Hons English Lang. and Lit. 1979); City Univ., London (DipLaw 1991); London Business Sch. (Dip. Investment Mgt 1991); Inns of Court Sch. of Law (BVC 1992). CEDR Accredited Mediator, 1998; MCIArb 2011. Playwright (with Martin Bergman), Brown Rice with Everything, performed by Cambridge Footlights at Edinburgh Fest., 1979; researcher on TV prog., Police, and asst producer and studio dir, Newsnight and other progs, BBC TV, 1979–84; Brook Productions Ltd: Associate Producer, A Week in Politics, Channel 4, 1984–86; special asst to Jt Chief Execs, later Hd of Publicity and Dep. Hd of Marketing, ITV Superchannel Ltd, 1987–88. Called to the Bar: Middle Temple, 1992; Gibraltar (for specific cases); Eastern Caribbean Supreme Court (BVI), 2014; Cayman Is (for specific case), 2016; in practice at the Bar, specialising in insolvency, financial services and asset recovery, 1993–; licensed to practice in Courts of Dubai Internat. Financial Centre, 2014. Member: Users Cttee, Bankruptcy and Companies Courts (formerly Insolvency Courts), 2001–16; Insolvency Rules Cttee, 2002–12; Panel of Sen. Decision Makers, Guernsey Financial Services Commn, 2014–; Panel of Mediators, INSOL Internat. Coll. of Mediation, 2015–. Society for Computers and Law: Chair, Media Bd, 2001–06; Trustee/Dir, 2002–06; Fellow, 2007. Chair, Africa Cttee, Commercial Bar Assoc., 2006–; Trustee, Africa Commercial Law Foundn, 2019–. Fellow, Assoc. of Business Recovery Professionals, 2010–16. *Publications:* Insolvent Partnerships, 1996; (ed) Butterworth's Insolvency Law Handbook, 4th edn 1997 to 21st edn 2019; (contrib.) Company Directors: duties, liabilities and remedies, ed Simon Mortimore, QC, 2009, 3rd edn 2017. *Recreations:* contemporary art, African music, football (Arsenal), photography. *Address:* South Square, 3–4 South Square, Gray's Inn, WC1R 5HP. *T:* (020) 7696 9900, *Fax:* (020) 7696 9911. *E:* glendavis@southsquare.com. *W:* www.twitter.com/GDQC.

**DAVIS, Prof. Glyn;** see Davis, C. G.

**DAVIS, Godfrey Pawle;** non-executive Chairman, Mulberry Group plc, 2012–14 and since 2015 (Chairman and Chief Executive, 2002–12; Executive Chairman, 2014–15); *b* Bristol, 27 Feb. 1949; *s* of late Granville Davis and of Pauline Davis; *m* 1971, Sally Anne; one *s* one *d*. *Educ:* Clifton Coll. FCA 1972. Arthur Andersen, 1974–88, Partner, 1986–88; Dir, Mulberry Gp plc, 1989–2012. *Recreations:* fishing, shooting, travel. *Address:* Mulberry Group plc, The Rookery, Chilcompton, Somerset BA3 4EH. *T:* (01761) 234501. *E:* godfreyd@mulberry.com.

**DAVIS, Gray;** see Davis, Joseph G.

**DAVIS, Rt Hon. Helen Elizabeth;** see Clark, Rt Hon. H. E.

**DAVIS, Sir Ian (Edward Lamert),** Kt 2019; Chairman, Rolls-Royce plc, since 2013; *b* 10 March 1951; *s* of late Walter Patrick Carless Davis and Jane Davis (*née* Lamert); *m* 1st, 1977, Sally J. Fuller; one *s* one *d*; 2nd, 1994, Penny A. Thring. *Educ:* Charterhouse; Balliol Coll., Oxford (MA). Bowater, 1972–79; McKinsey & Company: Associate, 1979–85; Principal, 1985–90; Dir, 1990–2010; Man. Dir, UK, 1996–2003; Worldwide Man. Dir, 2003–09; Sen. Partner, 2009–10; Man. Dir Emeritus, 2010. Non-executive Director: BP plc, 2010–; Johnson & Johnson Inc., 2010–; Teach for All, 2010–. Non-exec. Mem. Bd, Cabinet Office, 2011–16. Patron, Eton Fives Assoc. *Recreations:* the Alps, watching cricket, golf, biographies. *Clubs:* Hurlingham, Queen's; Berkshire Golf.
See also Sir C. H. L. Davis, Rt Hon. Sir N. A. L. Davis.

**DAVIS, Ian Paul,** CEng; Operations Director, National House-Building Council, 2006–17; *s* of George Davis and Margaret Davis; *m* 1978, Jane Fidell; two *d*. *Educ:* Grove Sch., Newark; Univ. of Liverpool (BEng 1976); Open Univ. (MBA 1999). CEng, MICE 1982. Site Engr, Head Wrightson Process Engrg, 1976–78; Design Engr, Simpson Coulson & Partners, 1978–80; Project Engr, Davy International, 1980–83; Regl Engr, 1983–90, Dir of Standards, 1990–94, Dep. Chief Exec., 1994–97, NHBC; Dir Gen., Fedn of Master Builders, 1997–2006. Chm., Soha Housing (formerly S Oxfordshire Housing Assoc.), 2000–03 (Dir, 1996–2005). *E:* idavis2121@btinternet.com.

**DAVIS, Ivan,** OBE 2005; Member (UU) Lagan Valley, Northern Ireland Assembly, 1998–2003; *b* 16 April 1937; *s* of late James and Susan Davis; *m* 1960, Hannah Elizabeth (Betty), Murphy; three *s* one *d*. *Educ:* Lisburn Public Elementary Sch. Lisburn Borough Council: Mem., 1973–2002; Chairman: Police Liaison Cttee, 1977–81; Recreation and Allied Services, 1977–79, 1993–95; Housing Liaison Cttee, 1984–2002; Planning Cttee, 1987–89; Leisure Services Cttee, 1997–99; Capital Develt Cttee, 1997–99; Member: Health Cttee, 1994–96; Strategic Policy Cttee, 1997–99; Dep. Mayor of Lisburn, 1989–91, Mayor, 1991–93; Mem. (UU) Lisburn CC, 2002–10. Member: NI Assembly, 1982–86; NI Forum (Dep. Chm.), 1996–98. Northern Ireland Assembly: Dep. Whip, 1998–2002; Chief Whip, 2002; Member: Culture, Arts and Leisure Cttee; Business Cttee, 1998–2002; Cttee on Procedures, 2001–02. Member: UUP, 1987– (Mem. Exec. Cttee, 1993–99, 2000–); UU Council, 1993– (Mem., Exec. Cttee, 1993–99). Member: Sport Lisburn (formerly Lisburn Sports Adv. Council), 1989–2014; SE Educn and Liby Bd, 1993–95; Lisburn CAB, 1997–. Vice President: Lisburn Amateur Boxing Club, 1985–; Lisburn Swimming Club, 1989–. Freeman of Lisburn, 2010. *Address:* 29 Roseville Park, Lisburn BT27 4XT. *T:* (028) 9267 8164. *Club:* Lambeg Golf (Pres., 1998–2000).

**DAVIS, James Gresham,** CBE 1988; FCILT; FICS; Chairman, International Maritime Industries Forum, 1981–2015, now Life President; *b* 20 July 1928; *s* of Col Robert Davis, OBE, JP and Josephine Davis (*née* Edwards); *m* 1973, Adriana Johanna Verhoef, Utrecht, Holland; three *d*. *Educ:* Bradfield Coll.; Clare Coll., Cambridge (MA). FCILT (FCIT 1969, FILT); FIEx; FInstLM (FISM 1989); FNI. Served RN, 1946–49. P&OSN Co., 1952–72: Calcutta, 1953; Kobe, Japan, 1954–56; Hong Kong, 1956–57; Director: P&O Lines, 1967–72; Kleinwort Benson Ltd, 1973–88; DFDS Ltd, 1975–97 (Chm., 1984–95); Advr, 1995–97); Pearl Cruises of Scandinavia Inc., 1982–86; Rodskog Shipbrokers (Hong Kong) Ltd, 1983–88; Associated British Ports Holdings plc, 1983–97; Transport Develt Gp plc, 1984–91; TIP Europe Plc, 1987–93 (Chm., 1990–93); Global Ocean Carriers Ltd, 1988– (Chm., 1996–); Sedgwick Energy & Marine Ltd, 1988–99; Sedgwick Gp Develt Ltd, 1991–99; Hempel Paints Ltd, 1992–2000; Tsavliris Salvage (International) Ltd, 1994–2000;

2M Invest AS (Copenhagen), 1996–2000; Catenas Ltd, 2000–02; Foresight Ltd, 2002–16; Shipserve Ltd, 2002–; Chairman: Bromley Shipping, 1989–94; Trinitas Services Ltd, 1993–2006; Marine Risk Mgt Services, 1995–99; Liberia Maritime Adv. Bd, 1998–2001; Wigham Richardson Shipbrokers Ltd, 2003–08; Caterham Leasing Ltd, 2003–06; Dep. Chm., Hanjin Eurobulk Ltd, 2003–07; Member Advisory Board: J. Lauritzen A/S, Copenhagen, 1981–85; DFDS A/S, Copenhagen, 1981–85; Adviser, Tjaerborg (UK) Ltd, 1985–87. Mem. (part-time), British Transport Docks Bd, 1981–83; Chm., SITPRO, 1987–98; Dir, British Internat. Freight Assoc., 1989–; Chm., Danish-UK Chamber of Commerce, 1992–2001 (Pres., 2001–). Chairman: Friends of the World Maritime Univ., 1985–; Marine Soc., 1987–93 (Vice-Pres., 1993); Anglian Bd, BR, 1988–92; Trinitas Management Services Ltd (Trinity House), 1999–2006; Mem. Council, Missions to Seamen, subseq. Mission to Seafarers, 1981–2008 (Trustee, 2008–). President: World Ship Soc., 1969, 1971, 1984–86, 2003–08 (Vice Pres., 2008–); CIT, 1981–82; Inst. of Freight Forwarders, 1984–86; National Waterways Transport Assoc., 1986–91; Inst. of Supervisory Management, 1989–92; Inst. of Chartered Shipbrokers, 1990–92 (Vice-Pres., 1988–90); Inst. of Export, 1995–2001, 2008–16 (Vice Pres., 1991–95); Harwich Lifeboat, RNLI, 1984–; Vice-President: British Maritime League, 1984–88; British Maritime Charitable Foundn, 1992–; Member: Baltic Exchange, 1973–; Greenwich Forum, 1982–2016; Internat. and UK Cttees, Bureau Veritas, 1989–2017; Gen. Cttee, Lloyds Register, 1998–2006; Lloyds Register, 2008– (Trustee, Lloyds Register Hldgs, 2006–08). Trustee, Nat. Maritime Mus., 1993–98. UK Ambassador, Women's Internat. Shipping and Trading Assoc., 2008–. Lectures: Grout, CIT, 1975; Wakeford Meml, Southampton Univ., 1993; Thomas Gray Meml, RSA, 1990. FRSA 1986. Hon. FNI 1985; Hon. FIFF 1986. Hon. RSMA, 2006. Freeman, City of London, 1972; Liveryman and Mem., Court of Assts, Shipwrights' Co.; Master, World Traders' Co., 1996–97; Associate Mem., Master Mariners' Co., 1998. Younger Brother, Trinity House, 1989. Seatrade Personality of the Year, Seatrade Orgn, 2002; Lifetime Achievement Award, Lloyd's List, 2011. Knight Commander, Order of Dannebrog (Denmark), 1996. *Publications:* You and Your Ships (autobiog.), 2007. *Recreations:* golf, family, ships. *Clubs:* Brooks's, Hurlingham, Golfers; Fanlingerers (Hong Kong); Harwich & Dovercourt Golf, Royal Calcutta Golf; Holland Park Lawn Tennis.

**DAVIS, Col Jane Elizabeth,** OBE 2012; QVRM 2001; TD 1994; Vice Lord-Lieutenant, Greater London, since 2018; *b* Brighton, 22 March 1955; *d* of John Murphy and Doris Murphy. *Educ:* Fitzherbert RC Sch., Brighton; St Stephen's Hosp., Chelsea. RGN 1976. Staff Nurse: St Stephen's Hosp., Chelsea, 1976–77; Ear Nose and Throat Hosp., Brighton, 1977; Staff Nurse, 1977–78, Sister, Coronary Care Unit, 1978–79, Sister, Trauma Unit, 1979–81, Royal Sussex Co. Hosp., Brighton; Night Sister: King's Coll. Hosp., 1981–83; St Stephen's Hosp. Chelsea, 1983–84; Sen. Nurse Night Duty, UCH, 1984–85; Sen. Nurse Mgr A&E, Royal Free Hosp., 1985–93; Master Scheduler, Royal Brompton Hosp., 1994–95; Service Mgr A&E, 1995–98, Clin. Ops Mgr and Hd of Nursing, Emergency Services Directorate, 1998–2001, W Middx Univ. Hosp.; Operational and Service Develt Mgr A&E, Barking, Havering and Redbridge Hosps NHS Trust, 2001–04; Network Mgr, NE London Cardiovascular and Stroke Network, 2005–12; Matron, Role 3 Hosp. Camp Bastion, Afghanistan, MoD Mobilised Service, 2011; Secondary care nurse, Govg Body, NHS Camden CCG, 2013–; Registrant Chair, Fitness to Practise, NMC, 2013–. Officer, T&AVR, subseq. Army Reserve, 1981–2015. Col Comdt, QARANC, 2014–. DL Gtr London, 2008. *Recreations:* gardening, family, ski-ing. *Address:* Greater London Lieutenancy Office, Gwydyr House, Whitehall, SW1A 2NP. *T:* (020) 7270 0412. *E:* info@greaterlondonlieutenancy.com.

**DAVIS, Prof. John Allen,** MD, FRCP; Professor of Paediatrics, and Fellow of Peterhouse, University of Cambridge, 1979–88, now Professor Emeritus and Fellow Emeritus; *b* 6 Aug. 1923; *s* of Major H. E. Davis, MC, and Mrs M. W. Davis; *m* 1st, 1957, Madeleine Elizabeth Vinicombe Ashlin (author with D. Wallbridge of Boundary and Space: introduction to the work of D. W. Winnicott, 1981) (*d* 1991); three *s* two *d*; 2nd, 2004, Prof. Ann-Louise Kinmonth, *qv*. *Educ:* Blundell's Sch., Tiverton (Scholar); St Mary's Hosp. Med. Sch. (Scholar; MB, BS 1946; London Univ. Gold Medal); MSc Manchester 1967; MA Cantab 1979, MD 1988. FRCP 1967. Army Service, BAOR, 1947–49. House Physician: St Mary's Hosp., 1947; Gt Ormond St Hosp. for Sick Children, 1950; Registrar/Sen. Registrar, St Mary's Paediatric Unit and Home Care Scheme, 1951–57; Sen. Asst Resident, Children's Med. Centre, Boston, Mass, and Harvard Teaching Fellow, 1953; Nuffield Res. Fellowship, Oxford, 1958–59; Sen. Lectr, Inst. of Child Health, and Reader, Hammersmith Hosp., 1960–67; Prof. of Paediatrics and Child Health, Victoria Univ. of Manchester, 1967–79. Second Vice Pres., RCP, 1986; Member: Assoc. of Physicians; Société française de pédiatrie; Hon. Member: BPA (former Chm., Academic Bd); Hungarian Acad. Paediatrics; Neonatal Soc.; Pres., Eur. Soc. for Pediatric Research, 1984–85; Patron: Arts for Health, 1989–; Squiggle Foundn, 1993–. Greenwood Lectr, Univ. of Exeter, 1981; Teale Lectr, RCP, 1990. Hon. FRSocMed 2006. Dawson Williams Prize, BMA, 1986; James Spence Medal, BPA, 1991; Hunterian Medal, Hunterian Soc., 1995. *Publications:* Scientific Foundations of Paediatrics (ed and contrib.), 1974 (2nd edn 2003); Place of Birth, 1978; (ed jtly) Parent-Baby Attachment in Premature Infants, 1984, repr. 2015; Mortalia and Other Things (verse), 2003, 2nd edn 2016; Historiae et Fabulae (short stories), 2008; papers in various medical and scientific jls. *Recreations:* collecting and painting watercolours, gardening, reading, music. *Address:* Four Mile House, 1 Cambridge Road, Great Shelford, Cambridge CB22 5JE.

**DAVIS, Sir John (Gilbert),** 3rd Bt *cr* 1946; *b* 17 Aug. 1936; *s* of Sir Gilbert Davis, 2nd Bt, and of Kathleen, *d* of Sidney Deacon Ford; *S* father, 1973; *m* 1960, Elizabeth Margaret, *d* of Robert Smith Turnbull; one *s* two *d*. *Educ:* Oundle School; Britannia RNC, Dartmouth. RN, 1955–56. Joined Spicers Ltd, 1956; emigrated to Montreal, Canada, 1957; joined Inter City Papers and progressed through the company until becoming Pres., 1967; transf. to parent co., Abitibi-Price Inc., 1976 and held several exec. positions before retiring as Exec. Vice-Pres., 1989; co-developer, Greenfield de-inked pulp business, Château Thierry, France. *Recreations:* retirement living, music, reading. *Heir:* s Richard Charles Davis, *b* 11 April 1970. *Address:* 19 Rean Drive, Apt 1016, Toronto, ON M2K 0A4, Canada. *T:* (416) 2224916. *Clubs:* Donalda, Rosedale Golf (Toronto).

**DAVIS, Jonathan;** author, columnist and investment professional, since 1991; founder and Managing Director, Jonathan Davis & Associates, since 1991; *b* RAF Halton, Bucks, 17 Feb. 1954; *s* of Air Cdre John Frank Davis and Elaine Davis (*née* Smorthwaite); *m* 1st, 1982, Janet Prior (marr. diss. 1996); one *s* one *d*; 2nd, 2008, Kristin van Santen. *Educ:* Winchester Coll. (Schol.); Gonville and Caius Coll., Cambridge (BA Hist. 1975; MA); Sloan Sch. of Mgt, Massachusetts Inst. of Technol. (MSc Mgt 1991). Grad. trainee, Westminster Press (editl staff, Durham Advertiser, Oxford Mail), 1975–78; City office, Sunday Telegraph, 1978–82; Energy, then Business Corresp., The Times, 1982–85; Energy Ed., The Economist, 1985–86; Dep. Business Ed., Independent, 1986–88; Hd of Public Affairs, Enterprise Oil plc, 1988–90; City Ed., The Week, 1995–98; columnist: Independent, 1995–2007; FT, 2007–15; Editl Dir, Money Makers JV, 2015–; Ed., The Investment Reader, 2015–. Founder and Chm., JDA Independent Investor LLP, 2006–12; Director: Genagro Services Ltd, 2008–; Smith & Williamson Investment Mgt, 2012–14; non-executive Director: Hargreaves Lansdown plc, 2008–10; Jupiter Primadona Growth Trust, 2011–; Senior Adviser: Saunderson House, 2014–. Founder, Andrew Robson Bridge in Oxford. MCSI 2013. *Publications:* Learn Bridge in a Weekend, 1992; Money Makers, 1998, 2nd edn 2013; Investing with Anthony Botton, 2006, 2nd edn 2008; (with Dr S. Nairn) Templeton's Way with Money, 2012; The Investment Trusts Handbook (annually), 2017, 2018, 2019. *Recreations:* bridge, Real tennis, golf. *E:* jd@independent-investor.com. *W:* www.independent-investor.com. *Clubs:* Savile (Chm., 2002–08), Portland; Huntercombe Golf.

**DAVIS, Joseph Graham, (Gray),** Jr; Counsel, Loeb & Loeb LLP, Los Angeles, since 2004; Governor of California, 1999–2003; *b* New York City, 26 Dec. 1942; *s* of Joseph G. and Doris Davis; *m* 1983, Sharon Ryer. *Educ:* Stanford Univ. (BA Hist. *cum laude*); Columbia Univ. Law Sch. (JD). Served US Army, 1967–69 (Bronze Star for Meritorious Service, Vietnam War). Chief of Staff to Gov. of Calif., Edmund G. Brown Jr, 1975–81; Mem. for Los Angeles, Calif. State Assembly, 1983–87; Controller, State of Calif., 1987–95; Lt Gov., Calif., 1995–99. Mem., Calif. State Bar, 1969–. Dist. Fellow, Sch. of Public Affairs, UCLA. *Recreations:* golf, reading.

**DAVIS, Dame Karlene (Cecile),** DBE 2001; General Secretary and Chief Executive, Royal College of Midwives, 1997–2008; *b* 10 Oct. 1946; *d* of late Herman Leiba and Inez Leiba; *m* 1975, Victor Davis; one *s*. *Educ:* Titchfield Secondary Sch., Port Antonio, Jamaica; BEd Hons South Bank Poly. 1986; MA Inst. of Educn, London Univ. 1989. RN 1970; RM 1974; MTD 1980. SRN, 1967–70; SCM, 1973–74; Midwife Clinician, 1974–80; Midwife Tutor, Pembury Hosp., 1980–84; Sen. Midwife Teacher, Mayday Hosp., Croydon, 1984–87; Dir, Midwifery Educn, Olive Hayden Sch. of Midwifery, Guy's, St Thomas' and Lewisham Hosps, 1987–91; Regl Nurse, Midwifery Practice and Educn, SE Thames RHA, 1991–94; Dep. Gen. Sec., Royal Coll. of Midwives, 1994–97. Member: Modernisation Bd overseeing implementation of NHS plan, 2000–04; SOS Stakeholder Gp, 2005–08; Bevan Commn, 2010–. Dir, WHO Collaborating Centre for Midwifery, 1997–2008. Pres., 2005–08, Consultant, Sierra Leone, 2009–12, Internat. Confedn of Midwives. Vis. Prof. of Midwifery, London South Bank Univ., 2008–11. Non-exec. Dir, NUS, 2010–13. Consultant, Bounty, 2013–. FRSocMed 1998. FRSA 2010. Hon. Fellow, London South Bank Univ., 2011. Hon. DSc: Brighton, 2001; Kingston, 2002; Greenwich, 2002; Nottingham, 2004; City, 2005; Wolverhampton, 2006; West Indies, 2008; Anglia Ruskin, 2009. *Recreations:* politics, reading political biographies, travel to experience different cultures. *T:* (020) 8239 0611.

**DAVIS, Kenneth Joseph;** Director of Children and Young People Services, London Borough of Bromley, 2006; *b* 19 March 1948; *s* of late Kenneth Sydney Joseph Davis and Dorothy May Davis (later Addison); *m* 1970, Susan Mary Thompson; one *s*. *Educ:* Mark Hall Sch., Harlow; City of Portsmouth Coll. of Education (BEd Hons 1971); Wolverhampton Poly. (DMS 1978); Inst. of Education, London Univ. (MA 1981). Computer operator, London & Manchester Assce Co., 1966–67; Asst Teacher, Brune Pk Comp. Sch., Gosport, 1971–73; Head of Physics, Darlaston Comp. Sch., Walsall, 1973–78; Professional Asst, E Sussex CC, 1978–80; Kent County Council: Asst Educn Officer, 1980–83; Divl Educn Officer, 1983–86; Area Educn Officer, 1986–89; Area Dir of Educn Services, 1989–96; Dir of Educn, 1996–2004, of Educn and Libraries, 2004–06; Bromley LBC. FCMI. *Recreations:* sailing, ski-ing, golf. *Address:* Walmer, Deal, Kent. *Clubs:* Downs Sailing; Walmer and Kingsdown Golf.

**DAVIS, Dom Leo M.;** *see* Maidlow Davis.

**DAVIS, Leonard Andrew, (Leon),** AO 2004; Chairman, Westpac Banking Corporation, 2000–07; *b* 3 April 1939; *s* of Leonard Harold Davis and Gladys Davis; *m* 1963, Annette Brakenridge; two *d*. *Educ:* S Australian Inst. of Technol. (Dip. in Primary Metallurgy). Man. Dir, Pacific Coal, 1984–89; Gp Exec., CRA Ltd, 1989–91; Mining Dir, RTZ Corp., 1991–94; Man. Dir and Chief Exec., CRA Ltd, 1994–95; Chief Operating Officer, RTZ-CRA, 1996; Chief Exec., 1997–2000, Dep. Chm., 2000–05, Rio Tinto. Dir, Codan Ltd, 2000–04. Bd Mem., Walter and Eliza Hall Inst. of Med. Res., 2001–13 (Pres., 2003–13); Gov., Ian Potter Foundn, 2007–. Hon. DSc: Curtin Univ., 1998; Qld Univ., 2004; DUniv S Australia, 2005. Centenary Medal, Australia, 2003. *Address:* 150 Clarendon Street, East Melbourne, Vic 3002, Australia. *Clubs:* Melbourne; Melbourne Cricket.

**DAVIS, Margaret Elaine;** *see* Gardner, M. E.

**DAVIS, Prof. Mark Herbert Ainsworth;** Professor of Mathematics, Imperial College London, 2000–09 and 2011–12, now Emeritus; *b* 1 May 1945; *s* of Christopher A. Davis and Frances E. Davis (*née* Marsden); *m* 1988, Jessica I. C. Smith. *Educ:* Oundle Sch.; Clare College, Cambridge (BA 1966, MA 1970, ScD 1983); Univ. of California, Berkeley (PhD 1971). FSS 1985; FIMS 1994. Research Asst, Electronics Res. Lab., Univ. of California, Berkeley, 1969–71; Lectr, 1971–79, Reader, 1979–84, Prof. of System Theory, 1984–95, Imperial College, London; Hd of Res. and Product Develt, Tokyo-Mitsubishi Internat., 1995–99. Visiting appointments: Polish Acad. of Sciences, 1973; Harvard, 1974; MIT, 1978; Washington Univ., St Louis, 1979; ETH Zurich, 1984; Oslo Univ., 1991; Technical Univ., Vienna, 2000. Hon. FIA 2001. Editor, Stochastics and Stochastics Reports, 1978–95; Founding Co-Editor, Mathematical Finance, 1990–93. *Publications:* Linear Estimation and Stochastic Control, 1977, Russian edn 1984; (with R. B. Vinter) Stochastic Modelling and Control, 1985; Markov Models and Optimization, 1993; (with A. Etheridge) Louis Bachelier's Theory of Speculation: the origins of modern finance, 2006; (with S. Lleo) Risk-Sensitive Investment Management, 2014; Mathematical Finance a very short introduction, 2019; jl articles on stochastic analysis, control theory, maths of finance. *Recreation:* classical music (violin and viola). *Address:* 11 Chartfield Avenue, SW15 6DT. *T:* (020) 8789 7677; Department of Mathematics, Imperial College London, SW7 2AZ. *T:* (020) 7594 8486.

**DAVIS, Nicholas L.;** *see* Lester-Davis.

**DAVIS, Rt Hon. Sir Nigel (Anthony Lamert),** Kt 2001; PC 2011; **Rt Hon. Lord Justice Davis;** a Lord Justice of Appeal, since 2011; *b* 10 March 1951; *s* of late Walter Patrick Carless Davis and Jane (*née* Lamert); *m* 1st, 1977, Sheila Ann Gillies Nickel (marr. diss. 1992); three *d*; 2nd, 2001, Emma Douglas. *Educ:* Charterhouse; University Coll., Oxford (BA 1973; MA 1983). Called to the Bar, Lincoln's Inn, 1975 (Hardwicke Schol., Kennedy Schol.; Bencher, 2000). Jun. Counsel to Crown (Chancery), 1985–92; QC 1992; an Asst Recorder, 1995–98; a Recorder, 1998–2001; a Judge of the High Court, QBD, 2001–11; a Presiding Judge of Wales (formerly Wales and Chester) Circuit, 2006–09; Vice-Pres., QBD, 2014–16. Counsel to inquiry of Bd of Banking Supervision into collapse of Barings Bank, 1995. *Address:* Royal Courts of Justice, Strand, WC2A 2LL. *Clubs:* MCC; Vincent's (Oxford).
*See also* Sir C. H. L. Davis, Sir I. E. L. Davis.

**DAVIS, Nira Y.;** *see* Yuval-Davis, N.

**DAVIS, Peter Anthony;** Director General, National Lottery, 1993–98; *b* 10 Oct. 1941; *s* of late Stanley H. S. Davis and Betty H. Davis (*née* Back); *m* 1971, Vanessa C. E. Beale; two *s*. *Educ:* Winchester Coll.; Lincoln Coll., Oxford (MA Law). CA 1967. With Price Waterhouse, 1963–80, Gen. Audit Partner, 1974–80; Exec. Dep. Chm., Harris Queensway

PLC, 1980–87; Sturge Holdings PLC: Gp Finance Dir, 1988–93; Dep. Chm., 1991–93; Abbey National PLC: non-exec. Dir, 1982–94; Dep. Chm., 1988–94; Chm., Audit Cttee, 1988–93, and Scottish Adv. Bd, 1989–92. Non-executive Director: Horne Bros, 1984–87; Symphony Gp, 1984–87; Avis Europe, 1987–89; Provident Financial, 1994–2000; Proned Holdings, 1992–94; Equitable Life Assurance Soc., 1995–2001; Boosey & Hawkes, 1998–2003; non-exec. Chm., Ascent Gp, 2001–17. Institute of Chartered Accountants in England and Wales: Council Mem., 1989–95; Chm., Bd for Chartered Accountants in Business, 1991–94; Mem., Senate, 1989–99. MInstD 1993. *Recreations:* fishing, football, theatre. *Address:* 29 Arthur Road, SW19 7DN. *Club:* Hurlingham.

**DAVIS, Sir Peter (John),** Kt 1997; Chairman, Marie Curie Cancer Care, 2006–11, now Life Vice President; *b* 23 Dec. 1941; *s* of John Stephen Davis and Adriaantje de Baat; *m* 1968, Susan Hillman; two *s* one *d*. *Educ:* Shrewsbury Sch.; Grad. Inst. of Marketing (Drexler Travelling Schol., 1961). Management trainee and sales, Ditchburn Orgn, 1959–65; marketing and sales posts, General Foods Ltd, Banbury, 1965–72; Fitch Lovell Ltd, 1973–76: Marketing Dir, Key Markets; Man. Dir, Key Markets and David Greig; J. Sainsbury, 1976–86: Marketing Dir, 1977; Asst Man. Dir, 1979; Dep. Chief Exec., 1986, Chief Exec., 1986–92, Chm., 1990–94, Reed Internat.; Chief Exec., 1993, Chm., 1993–94, Reed Elsevier; Gp Chief Exec., Prudential Corp., 1995–2000; Chief Exec., 2000–04, Chm., 2004, J. Sainsbury plc. Director: Boots Co. PLC, 1991–2000; UBS AG, 2001–07; Mem., Adv. Bd, Permira Advisers Ltd, 2005–09; non-exec. Dir, Kind Consumer Ltd, 2014– (Strategic Advr, 2009–14); Investment Partner, Vestra Wealth LLP, 2008–16. Chairman: Basic Skills Agency (formerly Adult Literacy and Basic Skills Unit), 1989–97; Nat. Adv. Council for Educn and Training Targets, 1993–97; BITC, 1997–2002 (Dep. Chm., 1991–97); Welfare to Work New Deal Task Force, 1997–2000. Vice Pres., Chartered Inst. of Marketing, 1991–2010. Dir, Royal Opera House, 1999–2005 (Trustee, 1994–2005); Trustee, V&A Mus., 1994–97; Chm., Adv. (formerly Internat. Adv.) Bd, 2011–15, Mem. Bd, 2013–16, WNO. Mem. Council, Bangor Univ., 2007–16 (Dep. Chm., 2012–16; Vice-Pres., then Pro-Chancellor, 2007–12). Governor: Duncombe Sch., Hertford, 1976–2000; Queenswood Sch., 1993–95; Shrewsbury Sch., 2017–. FRSA. Hon. LLD Exon, 2000. Gold Medal, BIM, 2003. *Recreations:* sailing, reading, opera, wine. *Club:* Trearddur Bay Sailing (Cdre, 1982–84).

See also C. V. Gipps.

**DAVIS, Peter John;** Senior Vice President and European Competition Practice Head, since 2016, Director and Head, London Office, since 2018, Cornerstone Research; *b* Lincoln, 4 Aug. 1970; *s* of John and Joyce Davis; *m* 2006, Lara Sevanot; two *s* one *d*. *Educ:* London Sch. of Econs (BSc Stats); St Peter's Coll., Oxford (MPhil Econs); Yale Univ. (PhD Econs 1999). Asst Prof. of Applied Econs, MIT, 1998–2002; Leverhulme Lectr in Econs, LSE, 2002–06. Dir, Applied Economics Ltd, 2004–18; Sen. Vice Pres., 2011–13, Exec. Vice Pres., 2013–16, Compass Lexecon. Dep. Chm., Competition Commn, 2006–11. Vis. Prof., Faculty of Laws, UCL, 2012–15. Pres., Assoc. of Competition Economists, 2009–11. *Publications:* Quantitative Techniques for Competition and Antitrust Analysis, 2010; (jtly) Damages Claims for the Infringement of EU Competition Law, 2015; contrib. articles to Jl Econometrics, Rand Jl Econs, Eur. Econ. Rev., Jl Industrial Econs, Jl Law and Econs, Internat. Jl Industrial Econs, Agricl Econs, Econ. Jl, Scandinavian Jl of Econs, Eur. Competition Law Rev., Concurrences. *Recreations:* keeping up with three young children, piano, French. *E:* peter_john_davis@yahoo.com.

**DAVIS, Philip Michael;** *b* 15 May 1954; *o s* of late Ronald Davis and Joan Davis (*née* Williams); *m* 1977, Susan Jean Wolton; one *s* two *d*. *Educ:* Holly Lodge High Sch.; Southampton Univ. (BA Jt Hons Mod. Hist./Politics) Warwick Univ. (Master Ind. Relns). Full-time Officer, GMB, 1979–2000. Member (Lab): Wrekin DC, 1979–97 (Chm., Planning and Envmt Cttee, 1991–97); Telford and Wrekin Council, 1997–2006 (Leader, 2000–04); Birmingham CC, 2012– (City Heritage Lead and Chm., Heritage Strategy Gp, 2012–; Chm., Trusts and Charities Cttee, 2014–16). Mem., Nat. Exec., Assoc. of Labour Councillors, 2013–15. Chm., W Midlands Regl Assembly, 2001–03; Sen. Vice-Chm., W Midlands LGA, 2003–05 (Vice-Chm., 2000–01); Mem., LGA Regeneration Bd, 2004–06. Chairman: W Midlands Low Pay Unit, 1989–2000; W Midlands Regl Mus Council, 1995–2000; Midlands Rail Passengers' Cttee, 1999–2005; Campaign for English Regions, 2003–; Founder Chair, TravelWatch Midlands West, 2005–07; Vice Chm., Transport Delivery, 2016–18, Air Quality Lead, 2018–, Transport for W Midlands; Founder Mem., W Midlands Civil Society Forum, 2015–. Mem., Nat. Rail Passengers' Council, 1999–2010 (Mem., Passenger Focus Bd, 2005–10); Public Mem., Network Rail, 2002–06; Network Dir, Regl Action W Midlands, 2006–07; Mem. Bd, Commn for Integrated Transport, 2007–10. Chair: NHS S Birmingham Community Health Pilot, 2008–10; Birmingham Community Healthcare NHS Trust, 2010–11. Mem. Bd, Chamberlain Highbury Trust, 2016–; non-exec. Chm., Birmingham Jewellery Quarter Develt Trust, 2017–; Pres., Birmingham Pen Mus., 2018–; City Guardian, Birmingham Proof House, 2018–. Lay Mem., Employment Tribunal, 2000–. Comr, English Heritage, 1999–2002. Pres., Eurotowns, 2001–04. Founder Chm., UK World Heritage Forum, 1995–2005 (Hon. Pres., 2005–07); Trustee, Ironbridge Mus. Trust, 1982– (Mem. Bd, 1982–2005). Contested (Lab): Ludlow, 1983; W Midlands, EP, 1999. *Address:* Bach Mill Drive, Birmingham B28 0XN.

**DAVIS, Richard Cuthbert Tolley M., (Dom Leo M.);** see Maidlow Davis.

**DAVIS, Maj. Gen. Richard Roderick,** CB 2015; CBE 2004 (MBE 1996); Managing Director, Nant Enterprises Ltd, since 2015; *b* Hampshire, 2 Aug. 1962; *s* of Peter and Cynthia Davis; *m* 1985, Martina Stewart; two *s*. *Educ:* Bloxham Sch.; RMCS Shrivenham (BSc Civil Engrg 1983); Cranfield Univ. (MSc Defence Technol. 2004). Joined Army, 1983; Staff Coll., 1993–94; OC 51 Field Sqn, 1995–96; DCOS 1 Mech. Bde, 1997–99; Instructor, RMCS Shrivenham, 1999–2001; CO, 22 Engr Regt, 2001–03; Comdr, UK Provincial Reconstruction Team, Mazar-e-Sharif, 2003; Col Strategy, HQ Army Recruiting and Trng Agency, 2004–05; Chief Engr, HQ ARRC, 2005–07; Dir Plans, Land Forces, 2007–09; COS Regl Comd (South), 2009–10; Dir Gen. Army Recruiting and Trng, 2011–13; Dir Gen. Personnel, Army HQ, 2013–14. Chairman: RE Mus., 2012–; RE Officers' Widows Soc., 2012–16; Army Sports Control Bd, 2013–14; Vice Pres., Army Winter Sports Assoc., 2013–14. Non-exec. Chm., Water to Go Ltd, 2018–. Special Advr, Brenthurst Foundn, 2015–. FCMI 2015. Hon. Col, Royal Monmouthshire RE (Militia), 2014–. QCVS 2000, 2003, 2007, 2011. Bronze Star (USA), 2010. *Publications:* (jtly) A Great Perhaps?: Colombia: conflict and convergence, 2015; (jtly) Making Africa Work: a handbook for economic success, 2017. *Recreations:* mountaineering, mountain biking, cycling, ski-ing, following my sons up rock climbs.

**DAVIS, (Richard) Simon; His Honour Judge Simon Davis;** a Circuit Judge, since 2004; *b* 29 July 1956; *s* of Peter Richard Davis and Evelyn Davis; *m* 1980, Caroline Jane Neal; two *s* one *d*. *Educ:* Wellington Sch.; Somerset; Univ. of Leicester (LLB Hons). Called to the Bar, Inner Temple, 1978, Bencher, 2007; a Recorder, 1998–2004. Judicial Mem., Parole Bd, 2009–15; Jt Course Dir, Judicial Coll. Criminal Induction Course, 2013–14. Freeman, Haberdashers' Co., 2010 (Liveryman, 2013). *Recreations:* sport, theatre, travel. *Address:* Isleworth Crown Court, 36 Ridgeway Road, Isleworth TW7 5LP. *T:* (020) 8380 4500. *Clubs:* Roehampton; Rye Golf.

**DAVIS, Robert Jonathan,** MBE 2015; DL; Partner, 1985–2015, Consultant, since 2015, Freeman Box Solicitors; *b* London, 27 Sept. 1957; *s* of late Gerald and Pamela Davis; civil partnership 2007, Sir Simon Henry Milton (*d* 2011). *Educ:* Brooklands Primary Sch., Finchley; Christ's Coll., Finchley; Gonville and Caius Coll., Cambridge (MA 1982); Wolfson Coll., Cambridge; Coll. of Law, London. Research Assistant: to Rt Hon. Peter Walker, MP, 1977–79; to John Watson, MP, 1979–80; admitted solicitor, 1983; Asst Solicitor, Freeman Box Solicitors, 1983–85. Westminster City Council: Mem. (C), 1982–2018; Chairman: Traffic and Works Cttee, 1987–90; Envmt Cttee, 1990–93; Planning and Transportation Cttee, 1993–95; Planning Sub-Cttee, 2000–17; Customer Services Cttee, 2000–01; Gen. Purposes Cttee, 2000–08; Leader of Opposition, Parking Cttee for London, 1994–95; Cabinet Member: for Customer Services, 2001–06; for Planning, 2006–08; for Built Envmt, 2008–17; for Business, Culture and Heritage, 2017–18; Chief Whip, 2000–08; Dep. Leader, 2008–18; Lord Mayor of Westminster, 1996–97; Lord Mayor of Westminster Locum Tenens, 2003–18. Chm., Regent's Park (formerly New Shakespeare) Theatre Ltd, 2009– (Dir, 1986–); Director: Soho Theatre Ltd, 1986–2004; Film and Video Develt Agency, 1992–93; London Film Commn, 1997–2002. Chm., Amusement Arcade Action Gp, 1983–96. Chm., Cambridge Univ. Tory Reform Gp, 1977–78; Nat. Sec., Tory Reform Gp, 1979–82. Exec. Producer and creator, West End Live, 2005–18; Chief Curator, City of Westminster City of Sculpture Fest., 2010–18; Chairman: Westminster Partnership Public Realm Bd, 2013–18; Oxford Street Steering Bd, 2017–18. Chm., London Mayors' Assoc., 1998–2016. Pres., Westminster Guild Lectrs' Assoc., 2008–17. Trustee: Savoy Educnl Trust, 2000–; Heritage of London Trust, 2005–14 (Vice Pres., 2014–); Founding Trustee, Sir Simon Milton Foundn, 2013–. Dir, Mousetrap Foundn for the Arts, 2011–. Internat. Goodwill Ambassador, London Parade, 1997–. Freeman: City of London, 1991; Watermen and Lightermen's Co., 1997; Liveryman, Fan Makers' Co., 1997. Mem., Guild of Freemen of City of London, 1993–. DL Gtr London, 2006. Cons. Councillor of the Year, Asian Voice, 2014. *Publications:* The Law of Amusement Arcades, 1979; Civic Ceremonial for Mayors of the London Boroughs, 2009. *Recreations:* the theatre, collecting miniature mayors. *E:* rjd432@aol.com.

**DAVIS, Air Vice-Marshal Robert Leslie,** CB 1984; RAF, retired 1983; *b* 22 March 1930; *s* of Sidney and Florence Davis; *m* 1956, Diana, *d* of Edward William Bryant; one *s* one *d*. *Educ:* Wolsingham Grammar Sch., Co. Durham; Bede Collegiate Sch., Sunderland, Co. Durham; RAF Coll., Cranwell. Nat. Service, Corporal, Phys. Trng Instructor, 1948–49. Commnd, 1952; served fighter units, exchange posting, USAF, Staff Coll., OR and Ops appts, MoD, DS Staff Coll., 1953–69; comd No 19 Sqdn, 1970–72; Dep. Dir Ops Air Defence, MoD, 1972–75; comd RAF Leuchars, 1975–77; Comdr RAF Staff, and Air Attaché, British Defence Staff, Washington, DC, 1977–80; Comdr, British Forces Cyprus, and Administrator, Sovereign Base Areas, Cyprus, 1980–83, retired. Man. Dir, Bodenseewerk Geratetechnik/British Aerospace GmbH, 1983–86, retd. Chm. Durham Br., SSAFA Forces Help, 1993–2002. QCVSA 1966. *Recreations:* golf, antiques, music. *Address:* High Garth Farm, Witton-le-Wear, Bishop Auckland, Co. Durham DL14 0BL.

**DAVIS, Prof. Roger John,** PhD; FRS 2002; Professor of Molecular Medicine and H. Arthur Smith Professor of Cancer Research, University of Massachusetts Medical School; Investigator, Howard Hughes Medical Institute, since 1990. *Educ:* Queens' Coll., Cambridge (BA 1979; MPhil Biochem.; PhD 1983). Damon Runyon-Walter Winchell Cancer Fund Fellow, Dept of Biochem. and Molecular Biol., Univ. of Massachusetts Med. Sch. Fellow, Amer. Acad. Microbiol. 2012. MNAS 2018. Steven C. Beering Award, Indiana Univ., 2013. *Address:* Program in Molecular Medicine, University of Massachusetts Medical School, 373 Plantation Street, Suite 309, Worcester, MA 01605, USA.

**DAVIS, Simon;** *see* Davis, R. S.

**DAVIS, Simon Ward;** Litigation Partner, Clifford Chance, since 1994; President, Law Society of England and Wales, 2019–July 2020; *b* Mauritius, 26 June 1959; *s* of Tony and Sue Davis; *m* 1997, Jane Ray; one *s* one *d*. *Educ:* Wellington Coll.; Magdalen Coll., Oxford (Underhill Exhibnr; MA Juris.). Admitted as solicitor, 1984; Clifford Chance, 1982–: Partner, 1994; Partner i/c Grad. Recruitment, 1995–2000; Mem., Partnership Council, 2010–16. Pres., London Solicitors' Litigation Assoc., 2007–09; Mem. Bd, Law Soc. of England and Wales, 2018–. Gov., Birkbeck, Univ. of London, 2016–. *Recreation:* sorting out problems. *Address:* Law Society, 113 Chancery Lane, WC2A 1PL. *E:* simon.davis@lawsociety.org.uk.

**DAVIS, Prof. Stanley Stewart,** CChem, FRSC; Lord Trent Professor of Pharmacy, Nottingham University, 1975–2003, now Emeritus Professor; *b* 17 Dec. 1942; *s* of William Stanley and Joan Davis; *m* 1984, Lisbeth Illum; three *s*. *Educ:* Warwick Sch.; London Univ. (BPharm, PhD, DSc). FRPharmS. Lecturer, London Univ., 1966–70; Sen. Lectr, Aston Univ., 1970–75. Fulbright Scholar, Univ. of Kansas, 1967–68; various periods as visiting scientist to pharmaceutical industry. Founder: Danbiosyst (UK) Ltd; Pharmaceutical Profiles Ltd. Mem., Medicines Commn, 1994–97. *Publications:* (co-ed) Radionuclide Imaging in Drug Research, 1982; (co-ed) Microspheres and Drug Therapy, 1984; (co-ed) Site Specific Drug Delivery, 1986; (co-ed) Polymers in Controlled Drug Delivery, 1988; (co-ed) Drug Delivery to the Gastrointestinal Tract, 1989; (co-ed) Pharmaceutical Application of Cell and Tissue Culture to Drug Transport, 1991; ed jtly over 700 research pubns in various scientific jls. *Recreations:* ski-ing, horse riding, painting, travel. *Address:* 19 Cavendish Crescent North, The Park, Nottingham NG7 1BA. *T:* (0115) 948 1866.

**DAVIS, Steve,** OBE 2000 (MBE 1988); snooker player and commentator; *b* 22 Aug. 1957; *s* of Harry George Davis and Jean Catherine Davis; *m* 1990, Judy Greig; two *s*. *Educ:* Alexander McLeod Primary School and Abbey Wood School, London. Became professional snooker player, 1978; has won numerous championships in UK and abroad; major titles include: UK Professional Champion, 1980, 1981, 1984, 1985, 1986, 1987; Masters Champion, 1981, 1982, 1988, 1997; International Champion, 1981, 1983, 1984, 1987, 1988, 1989; World Professional Champion, 1981, 1983, 1984, 1987, 1988, 1989. BBC Sports Personality of the Year, 1988. Mem. Bd, World Professional Billiards and Snooker Assoc., 1993–. *Publications:* Steve Davis, World Champion, 1981; Frame and Fortune, 1982; Successful Snooker, 1982; How to be Really Interesting, 1988. *Recreations:* chess, keep fit, listening to records (jazz/soul), Tom Sharpe books. *Address:* Mascalls, Mascalls Lane, Brentwood, Essex CM14 5LJ. *T:* (01277) 359900. *Club:* Matchroom (Romford).

**DAVIS, Susan;** *see* Gubbay, S.

**DAVIS, Rt Hon. Terence Anthony Gordon, (Terry),** CMG 2010; PC 1999; Secretary General, Council of Europe, 2004–09; *b* 5 Jan. 1938; *s* of Gordon Davis and Gladys (*née* Avery), Stourbridge, West Midlands; *m* 1963, Anne, *d* of F. B. Cooper, Newton-le-Willows, Lancs; one *s* one *d*. *Educ:* King Edward VI Grammar Sch., Stourbridge, Worcestershire; University Coll. London (LLB; Fellow 2007); Univ. of Michigan, USA (MBA). Company Executive, 1962–71. Motor Industry Manager, 1974–79. Joined Labour Party, 1965; contested (Lab): Bromsgrove, 1970, Feb. and Oct. 1974; Birmingham, Stechford, March 1977. MP (Lab): Bromsgrove, May 1971–Feb. 1974; Birmingham, Stechford, 1979–83; Birmingham, Hodge Hill, 1983–2004. Opposition Whip, 1979–80; opposition spokesman: on the health service and social services, 1980–83; on Treasury and economic affairs, 1983–86; on industry, 1986–87. Member: Public Accounts Cttee, 1987–94; Adv. Council on Public Records, 1989–94. Chm., Birmingham Lab. MPs, 1992–97. Leader: British delegn to WEU Assembly, 1997–2002 (Mem., 1992–2004; Leader, Lab. delegn, 1995–97; Pres., Socialist Gp, 1996–99; Vice Pres. Assembly, 1997–2001); British delegn to Council of Europe Assembly, 1997–2002 (Mem., 1992–2004; Leader, Labour delegn, 1995–97; Chairman: Econ. Affairs and Develt Cttee, 1995–98; Pol Affairs Cttee, 2000–02; Vice Pres. Assembly, 1997–2002; Pres., Socialist Gp, 2002–04); British Delegn to OSCE Assembly, 2002–04 (Mem., 1997–2004). Mem., MSF. Member, Yeovil Rural District Council, 1967–68. *Address:* Hermitage, The Green, Adderbury, Oxon OX17 3ND. *T:* (01295) 810813. *E:* rthonterrydavis@gmail.com.

**DAVIS, Trevor Fraser C.;** *see* Campbell Davis.

**DAVIS, Hon. Sir William (Easthope),** Kt 2014; **Hon. Mr Justice Davis;** a Judge of the High Court of Justice, Queen's Bench Division, since 2014; *b* 20 June 1954; *s* of Prof. Ralph Davis, FBA and Dorothy Davis (*née* Easthope); *m* 1990, Susan Virginia Smith; one *s* one *d*. *Educ:* Wyggeston Boys' Sch., Leicester; Queen Mary Coll., London (LLB 1974). Called to the Bar, Inner Temple, 1975, Bencher, 2007; Recorder, 1995–2008; QC 1998; a Circuit Judge, 2008–14; a Sen. Circuit Judge and Resident Judge, Birmingham Crown Court, 2009–14; Presiding Judge, N Circuit, 2016–19. Judicial Lead for Youth Justice in England and Wales, 2014–. Mem., Sentencing Council, 2012–15. Dir of Trng, Judicial Coll., 2014–. *Recreations:* Rosie and Ralph, writing and performing in sketches, wine. *Address:* Royal Courts of Justice, Strand, WC2A 2LL.

**DAVIS, Hon. William Grenville;** PC (Can.) 1982; CC (Canada) 1986; QC (Can.); barrister and solicitor; Counsel to Davis Webb LLP, Ontario, since 2010; Member of the Provincial Parliament, Ontario, 1959–85; Premier of Ontario, Canada, and President of the Council, Ontario, 1971–85; Leader, Progressive Conservative Party, 1971–85; *b* Brampton, Ont, 30 July 1929; *s* of Albert Grenville Davis and Vera M. Davis (*née* Hewetson); *m* 1st, 1953, Helen MacPhee (*d* 1962), *d* of Neil MacPhee, Windsor, Ontario; 2nd, 1963, Kathleen Louise, *d* of Dr R. P. Mackay, California; two *s* three *d*. *Educ:* Brampton High Sch.; University Coll., Univ. of Toronto (BA); Osgoode Hall Law Sch. (grad. 1955). Called to Bar of Ontario, 1955; practised gen. law, Brampton, 1955–59. Elected Mem. (C) Provincial Parlt (MPP) for Peel Riding, 1959, 1963, Peel North Riding, 1967, 1971, Brampton Riding, 1975, 1977, 1981. Minister of Educn, 1962–71; also Minister of Univ. Affairs, 1964–71; Special Envoy on Acid Rain, apptd by Prime Minister of Canada, 1985–86. Counsel, Torys LLP, 1985–2010. Dir, Magellan Aerospace Corp. A Freemason. Chevalier, Légion d'Honneur. Holds hon. doctorates in Law from eight Ontario Univs: Waterloo Lutheran, W Ontario, Toronto, McMaster, Queen's, Windsor; Hon. Graduate: Albert Einstein Coll. of Med.; Yeshiva Univ. of NY; NUI; Ottawa; Tel Aviv. Amer. Transit Assoc. Man of the Year, 1973. *Publications:* Education in Ontario, 1965; The Government of Ontario and the Universities of the Province (Frank Gerstein Lectures, York Univ.), 1966; Building an Educated Society 1816–1966, 1966; Education for New Times, 1967. *Address:* 61 Main Street South, Brampton, ON L6Y 1M9, Canada; Davis Webb LLP, 24 Queen Street East, Suite 800, Brampton, ON L6V 1A4, Canada. *Clubs:* Kiwanis, Shriners, Masons, Albany (Ont.).

**DAVIS-GOFF, Sir Robert William;** *see* Goff.

**DAVIS SMITH, Dr Justin,** CBE 2011; Senior Lecturer, Centre for Charity Effectiveness, Cass Business School, City, University of London (formerly City University London), since 2016; *b* Ilford, Essex, 3 Aug. 1961; *s* of Christopher and Barbara Smith; *m* 1986, Julia Davis. *Educ:* Ashlyns Sch., Berkhamsted; Loughborough Univ. (BA 1st Cl. Hons Modern Social Hist. 1982; PhD 1986). Pol Asst to Rt Hon. Sir James Callaghan, MP, 1986–87; Hd of Res., Nat. Centre for Volunteering, 1988–97; Founding Dir, Inst. for Volunteering Res., 1997–2008; Chief Exec., Volunteering England, 2008–13; Exec. Dir for Volunteering, NCVO, 2013–16. Vis. Prof., Birkbeck, Univ. of London, 2005–13. Mem., Russell Commn on Youth Volunteering, 2004–05. Mem., ESRC, 2011–14. Chair, Nationwide Foundn, 2005–08. Assessor, Queen's Anniversary Awards Cttee for Further and Higher Educn, 2005–16; Mem., Queen's Awards for Voluntary Service Cttee, 2005–17. Chair, Volunteering Adv. Gp, Canal and River Trust, 2012–16; Member, Advisory Committee: Step up to Serve, 2013–16; Mayor of London's Volunteering Prog., 2016–; Trustee: v (youth volunteering charity), 2005–09; Join-In Trust, 2012–16; Watford FC Community, Sport and Educn Trust, 2013–; Global's Make Some Noise, 2016–. *Publications:* The Attlee and Churchill Administrations and Industrial Unrest, 1945–55, 1991; (ed jtly) Volunteering and Society: principles and practice, 1992; (ed jtly) An Introduction to the Voluntary Sector, 1994; (ed jtly) Volunteering and the Test of Time, 2007; 100 Years of NCVO and Voluntary Action: idealists and realists, 2019. *Recreations:* football, cricket, reading, walking, supporting Watford Football Club. *Address:* Cass Business School, City, University London, 106 Bunhill Row, EC1Y 8TZ.

**DAVIS-WHITE, Malcolm;** QC 2003; **His Honour Judge Davis-White;** a Specialist Civil Circuit Judge, since 2016; *b* 18 Sept. 1960; *m* 1989, Sarah O'Hara; two *s* one *d*. *Educ:* Hertford Coll., Oxford (BCL; MA). Called to the Bar, Middle Temple, 1984; Bencher, Lincoln's Inn, 2009; JC to the Crown (A Panel), 1994; a Recorder, 2009–16; a Dep. Judge of the High Court, Chancery Div., 2013–16; Acting Judge of Eastern Caribbean Supreme Court, Commercial Div., Territory of Virgin Is, 2016. Vice Chm., 2008–10, Chm., 2010–12, Chancery Bar Assoc. Mem., Panel of Sen. Decision Makers, Guernsey Financial Services Commn, 2014–. *Publications:* (with Adrian Walters) Directors' Disqualification and Bankruptcy Restrictions: law and practice, 1999, 3rd edn 2010; (contrib.) Atkin's Court Forms, vol. 9 Companies General, 1999, 2004, 2009, vol. 9 (2)-(4) Companies (Insolvency), 2000, 2006; (with Sandra Frisby) Kerr & Hunter on Receivers and Administrators, 19th edn, 2009. *Recreations:* walking, gardening, sailing, opera. *Address:* Leeds Combined Court Centre, The Courthouse, 1 Oxford Row, Leeds LS1 3BG.

**DAVISON, Alan John,** EdD; Headteacher, Dame Alice Owen's School, 2005–16; *b* 9 April 1956; *s* of Sydney and Margaret Davison; *m* 2002, Prof. Kholoud Porter; one *s* one *d*, and two step *s*. *Educ:* Durham Inst. of Educn (Cert Ed 1977); Univ. of Leicester (MBA 1994; EdD 1998). Headteacher: Notley High Sch., 1993–97; Mill Hill County High Sch., 1997–2003; Strategic Dir, London Leadership Strategy, London Challenge, 2003–05. Lectr (pt-time), Univ. of Leicester, 1999–2002. Advisor to Department for Education and Skills: Educn Action Zones, 1999; Teacher Threshold, 2000–02; Transforming Sch. Workforce Pathfinder Proj., 2002–04. *Publications:* (contrib.) Raising Boys' Achievement in Schools, 1998. *Recreations:* ski-ing, theatre, cinema, travel.

**DAVISON, Andrew Michael;** a District Judge (Magistrates' Courts), since 2011; *b* Leeds, 26 July 1956; *s* of late Charles Raymond Davison and of Prudence Mary Davison; *m* 1977, Carol Ann Johnson; one *s* one *d*. *Educ:* Prince Henry's Grammar Sch., Otley; Bristol Poly. (DipLaw for Magistrates' Court Clerks with Dist. 1979); Manchester Metropolitan Univ. (CPE 1982). Called to the Bar, Middle Temple, 1986; Legal Advr, then Sen. Legal Advr, Leeds Magistrates' Court, 1979–87; Principal Legal Advr, Batley and Dewsbury Magistrates' Court, 1987–91; Dep. Justices' Clerk, Manchester City Magistrates' Court, 1991–95; Justices' Clerk and Justices' Chief Exec., Rotherham Magistrates' Court, 1995–2001; Justices' Clerk: Doncaster and Rotherham Magistrates' Courts, 2001–04; S Yorks, 2004–11; Dep. Dist Judge (Magistrates' Courts), 2000–11. Chm., S Yorks Criminal Justice Bd, 2007–11. Pres., Yorks and Humber Justices' Clerks' Soc., 1999–2000. *Recreations:* crown green bowling (over 100 caps for Yorks and S Yorks county sides), supporting Bradford City AFC, reading, cruising the world P&O style. *Address:* Chesterfield Magistrates' Court, The Courthouse, Tapton Lane, Chesterfield S41 7TW. *T:* (01246) 246505, *Fax:* (01246) 246510. *E:* djmc.andrew.davison@ejudiciary.net.

**DAVISON, Air Vice Marshal Christopher,** MBE 1978; *b* 26 Sept. 1947; *s* of Dixon and Kathleen Lillian Davison; *m* 1971, Rosemary Stamper; one *s* one *d*. *Educ:* Tynemouth Grammar Technical Sch.; Borough Road Coll., London. Joined RAF Phys. Educn Br., 1970; RAF Halton, Inst. of Aviation Medicine, Farnborough and RAF Hereford, 1970–76; Comd, RAF Outdoor Activity Centre, Scotland, 1976–78; Sqn Leader, 1978; HQ Strike Comd, 1979–80; Chief Instr, RAF Sch. of Physical Trng, RAF Cosford, 1981–82; RAF Staff Coll., Bracknell, 1983; PSO to Controller Aircraft, MoD, 1984–85; Wing Comdr, 1985; OC Admin Wing, RAF Wattisham, 1985–87; Dep. Comdr, Support Gp, HQ AFCENT, 1987–89; Gp Capt., 1989; Admin. Trng, HQ Support Comd, 1989–91; OC RAF Swinderby, 1991–93; Head of Physical Educn Specialisation, RAF, 1994; Air Cdre, 1994; AOA and AOC Directly Administered Units, RAF HQ PTC, 1994–96 and 2000–01; Dir Personnel (Airmen) and Controller Reserve Forces, RAF, 1997–99; retd 2001. Dir, RAF Sports Bd, 2001–09. *Recreations:* golf, watching all sport. *Address:* c/o National Westminster Bank plc, 225 High Street, Lincoln LN2 1AZ. *Club:* Royal Air Force.

**DAVISON, Ian Frederic Hay,** CBE 2003; Managing Partner, Arthur Andersen & Co., 1966–82; Deputy Chairman and Chief Executive, Lloyd's of London, 1983–86; *b* 30 June 1931; *s* of late Eric Hay Davison, FCA, and Inez Davison; *m* 1955, Maureen Patricia Blacker; one *s* two *d*. *Educ:* Dulwich Coll. (Fellow 2014); London Sch. of Econs and Pol Sci. (BScEcon; Hon. Fellow, 2004); Univ. of Michigan. ACA 1956, FCA 1966. Chairman: Crédit Lyonnais Capital Markets, 1988–91; Storehouse plc, 1990–96; NMB Group plc, 1992–2000; McDonnell Information Systems, later Northgate plc, 1993–99; Director: Midland Bank, 1986–88; Newspaper Publishing, 1986–94 (Chm., 1993–94); Chloride plc, 1988–98; Cadbury-Schweppes plc, 1990–2000; CIBA plc, 1991–96. Chm., Ruffer LLP, 2002–11. Mem. Council, ICA, 1975–99; Chm., Accounting Standards Cttee, 1982–84. Mem., NEDC for Bldg Industry, 1971–77; Member: Price Commn, 1977–79; Audit Commn, 1983–85; Chairman: NEDC for Food and Drink Manufg Industry, 1981–83; Securities Review Cttee, Hong Kong, 1987–88. Dept of Trade Inspector, London Capital Securities, 1975–77; Inspector, Grays Building Soc., 1978–79. Chm., Regulatory Council, Dubai FSA, 2002–04. Trustee: V&A Museum, 1984–93 (Chm., V&A Enterprises Ltd, 1993–2002); Holburne Mus., Bath, 2005–09; Mus. of E Asian Art, 2009–19; Dir, Royal Opera House, 1984–86; Chm., 1979–84, Dir, 2013–15, Pres., 2015–, Monteverdi Trust; Chm., Sadler's Wells Foundation, 1995–2003. Pres., Nat. Council for One-Parent Families, 1991–2004; Chairman: SANE, 2000–02; Railway Heritage Cttee, 2000–04. Council Mem., Nat. Trust, 1992–94. Governor, LSE, 1982–2007; Pro-Provost and Chm. Council, RCA, 1996–2007 (Sen. Fellow, 2007). Chairman: Wells Cathedral Trust, 1997–2009; Council, Exeter Cathedral, 2002–08. Councillor and Alderman, London Bor. of Greenwich, 1961–73. Hon. DSc Aston, 1985; Hon. LLD Bath, 1998. *Publications:* A View of the Room: Lloyd's change and disclosure, 1987. *Recreations:* opera, theatre, music, bell-ringing. *Address:* 13 Catharine Place, Bath BA1 2PR. *Clubs:* Athenæum, Beefsteak, MCC; Bath and County.

**DAVISON, (John) Stanley,** OBE 1981; Secretary General, World Federation of Scientific Workers, 1987–2001; *b* 26 Sept. 1922; *s* of George Davison and Rosie Davison (*née* Segger); *m* 1959, Margaret Smith; two *s* one *d*. *Educ:* Timothy Hackworth Sch., Shildon, Co. Durham; Shildon Senior Boys' Sch.; St Helens Tech. Coll. RAF, 1941–46. Civil Servant (Technical), 1946–52; Regional Organiser, 1953–60, Dep. Gen. Sec., 1960–68, Assoc. of Scientific Workers; Dep. Gen. Sec., ASTMS, 1968–87. Member: Engineering Council, 1986–94; Heavy Electrical NEDO, 1976–87; Exec. Council, CSEU, 1981–88; Exec. Council, Internat. Metalworkers' Fedn, 1986–87; All Party Energy Cttee, 1982–88; Chm., Trade Union Side, GEC NJC, 1965–87; Governor, Aston CAT, 1955–60; Mem. Council, Brunel Univ., 1989–2000. Mem., Henlow Amateur Theatre Soc. (RAF). MUniv Brunel, 2001. *Recreations:* science policy, amateur dramatics, bridge, caravanning. *Address:* 1 Hazel Close, Shefford, Beds SG17 5YE. *Clubs:* Players' Theatre; Addington Theatre Group (Hon. Mem.); Caravan.

**DAVISON, Peter;** *see* Moffett, P.

**DAVISON, Richard Harold;** Master, Queen's Bench Division, Royal Courts of Justice, since 2016; *b* Tynemouth, 25 Feb. 1959; *s* of Eric and Elizabeth Davison; *m* 1988, Vanessa Lines; one *s* three *d*. *Educ:* Sedbergh Sch., Cumbria; Corpus Christi Coll., Oxford (BA Juris). Called to the Bar, Gray's Inn, 1982; Fee-paid Employment Judge, 2000–16; Recorder, 2004–. *Recreations:* sea kayaking, choral music, visiting art galleries. *Address:* Royal Courts of Justice, Strand, WC2A 2LL. *E:* QBEnquiries@hmcts.gsi.gov.uk.

**DAVISON, Stanley;** *see* Davison, J. S.

**DAVISON, Timothy Paul;** Chief Executive, NHS Lothian, since 2012; *b* 4 June 1961; *s* of late John Paul Davison and of Patricia Davison; *m* 1st, 1984, Hilary Williamson Gillick (marr. diss. 2009); one *s*; 2nd, 2012, Fiona Jane Maguire. *Educ:* Univ. of Stirling (BA Hons Hist.); Univ. of Glasgow (MBA, MPH); DipHSM. NHS nat. mgt trainee, 1983–84; Gen. Services Manager, Stirling Royal Infirmary, 1984–86; Asst Unit Administrator, Royal Edinburgh Hosp., 1986–87; Patient Services Manager, Lothian Mental Health Unit, 1987–88; Hosp. Administrator, Glasgow Royal Infirmary, 1988–90; Sector Gen. Manager, Gartnavel Royal Hosp., 1990–91; Unit Gen. Manager, Gtr Glasgow Community and Mental Health Unit (formerly Gtr Glasgow Mental Health Unit), 1991–94; Chief Executive: Gtr Glasgow Community and Mental Health Services NHS Trust, 1994–99; Gtr Glasgow Primary Care NHS Trust, 1999–2002; NHS Gtr Glasgow, N Glasgow Univ. Hosps NHS Trust, subseq. N Glasgow Univ. Hosps Div., 2002–05; Chief Exec., NHS Lanarkshire, 2005–12. Non-exec. Dir, Clinical Standards Bd for Scotland, 1999–2002. Mem. Ct, UWS, 2007–09. *Recreations:* tennis, military and political history, motor-cycling. *Address:* Lothian NHS Board, Waverley Gate, 2–4 Waterloo Place, Edinburgh EH1 3EG.

**d'AVRAY, Prof. David Levesley,** DPhil; FBA 2005; Professor of History, University College London, since 1996; *b* 3 Feb. 1952; *s* of Hector Anthony d'Avray and Audrey Sabina d'Avray (*née* Atkinson); *m* 1985, Julia Caroline Walworth. *Educ:* St John's Coll., Cambridge (BA 1973, MA 1977); DPhil Oxon 1977. Lectr, 1977–93, Reader, 1993–96, UCL. Corresp. Fellow, Medieval Acad. of America, 2016. *Publications:* The Preaching of the Friars, 1985; Death and the Prince, 1994; Medieval Marriage Sermons, 2001; Medieval Marriage, 2005; Medieval Religious Rationalities, 2010; Rationalities in History, 2010; Dissolving Royal Marriages, 2014; Papacy, Monarchy and Marriage, 2015. *Recreations:* alpine walking, domestic discussion of television. *Address:* Department of History, University College London, Gower Street, WC1E 6BJ. *E:* ucradav@ucl.ac.uk.

**DAVSON, Sir George Trenchard Simon,** 4th Bt *cr* 1927, of Berbice, British Guiana; *b* 5 June 1964; *s* of Sir Christopher Davson, 3rd Bt and Evelyn Mary Davson (née Wardrop); *S* father, 2004; *m* 1985, Joanna (marr. diss. 1996), *e d* of Rev. Dr James Bentley; one *s* one *d*. *Educ*: Eton; Magdalen Coll., Oxford. *Heir: s* James Davson, *b* 23 Dec. 1990.

**DAVY, Diana Margaret;** *see* Green, D. M.

**DAVY, Margaret Ruth;** *see* Bowron, M. R.

**DAW, Christopher;** QC 2013; *b* Milton Keynes, 21 Jan. 1970; *s* of Alan Charles Daw and Sandra Daw; *m* 2002, Ruth Hannah; two *s* two *d*. *Educ*: Univ. of Manchester (LLB Hons 1992); Inns of Court Sch. of Law. Called to the Bar, Gray's Inn, 1993; in practice as barrister, 1993–. *Recreations:* food, wine, travel. *Address:* Serjeants' Inn Chambers, 85 Fleet Street, EC4Y 1AE. *E:* uklawyer@aol.com.

**DAW, Roger Keith;** Principal Policy Advisor to the Director of Public Prosecutions, Crown Prosecution Service, 2009–10; *b* 10 March 1959; *s* of Owen William Albert Daw and late Mavis Hilda Daw (née Elson); partner, Courtney David Spence. *Educ*: Tiffin Sch., Kingston-upon-Thames; Birmingham Univ. (LLB). Called to the Bar, Middle Temple, 1982. Chief Crown Prosecutor, Hants and IoW, 1999–2003; Speaker's Sec., H of C, 2003–04; Prog. Dir, Police Reform, 2005–07, Dir, Policy, 2007–10, CPS. *Recreations:* genealogy, theatre.

**DAWANINCURA, Sir John (Norbert),** Kt 1999; OBE 1992; President, Papua New Guinea Sports Federation and Olympic Committee, since 2012 (Vice President, 1983; Secretary General, 1984–2010); *b* 25 May 1945; *s* of Stephen Joe Frank Dawanincura and Giro Paulo; *m* Lenah; one *s* two *d*. *Educ*: Chevalier Coll., NSW. Dist Valuer, W Highlands Province, Valuer Gen.'s Office; Manager, E Highlands Province, Bureau of Mgt Services; Graemme Dunnage Real Estate, 1977–78; Partner, Property Mgt and Maintenance, 1979–85. Rugby Football Union Player, Papua New Guinea team, 1965–70; Gen. Team Manager, PNG Contingents, 1981–86; Chief of PNG Delegation: Olympic Games, LA, 1984, Seoul, 1988, Barcelona, 1992; Commonwealth Games, 1982–97, 1999; S Pacific Games, 1983–98 (Chm. of Sports, Organising Cttee, Port Moresby, 1991); Mini S Pacific Games, 1981, 1993; Mem., 1984–97, Vice Pres., 1993–97, 2001–04, Oceania Nat. Olympic Cttee (Chm., Develt Commn, 1993–97); Alternate Mem., PNG Sports Commn, 1992; Schol. Mem., Mgt Cttee, Oceania Olympic Trng Coll., 1993–97; Mem. Mgt Cttee, Australia S Pacific 2000 Prog., 1995–97; Mem., Assoc. of Nat. Olympic Cttees, 1993–97; Deleg., 1981–86, Bd Mem., 1987–91, Pres. and Chm., 1995–99, S Pacific Games Council; Mem., Nat. Coaching Council, 1988. Sir Buri Kidu Heart Inst., 1996. *Recreations:* golf, circuit training, fishing. *Clubs:* Carbine, Golf, Yacht (Papua New Guinea).

**DAWE, Howard Carlton;** Chairman, Bellway plc, 1999–2013; *b* 7 April 1944; *s* of Sydney Carlton Dawe and Dorothy Dawe (née Cooke); *m* 1968, Kathryn Jennifer Adcock; one *s* two *d*. *Educ*: Newlands Sch., Newcastle; Durham Cathedral Choir Sch.; Newcastle Royal Grammar Sch.; various tech. colls. Joined Bellway, 1961; Man. Dir, 1984–99. *Recreations:* country pursuits, photography, environmental travel (particularly rainforests and Africa). *Address:* Fenham Grange, Fenham le Moor, Belford, Northumberland NE70 7PN.

**DAWE, Roger James,** CB 1988; OBE 1970; education advisor; *b* 26 Feb. 1941; *s* of late Harry James and Edith Mary Dawe; *m* 1965, Ruth Day Jolliffe; one *s* one *d*. *Educ*: Hardyes Sch., Dorchester; Fitzwilliam House, Cambridge (MA; Hon. Fellow, Fitzwilliam Coll., 1996). Entered Min. of Labour, 1962; Dept of Economic Affairs, 1964–65; Private Sec. to Prime Minister, 1966–70; Principal, Dept of Employment, 1970; Private Sec. to Secretary of State for Employment, 1972–74; Asst Sec., Dept of Employment, 1974–81; Under Sec., MSC, 1981; Chief Exec., Trng Div., MSC, 1982–84; Dep. Sec., Dept of Employment, 1985–87; Dir Gen., MSC, then Training Commn, subseq. Training Agency, 1988–90; Dir Gen., Training, Enterprise and Educn Directorate, Dept of Employment, 1990–92; Dep. Sec., Further and Higher Educn, DFE, 1992–95; Dir Gen. for Further and Higher Educn and Youth Trng, DFEE, 1995–2000. Educn Advr, KPMG, 2001–14. Mem., Exec. Cttee, Better Govt Initiative, 2007–. Chm., Strategy and Resources Cttee, Methodist Church, 2000–06. Dep. Chm., Council, Open Univ., 2003–09 (Mem., 2001–09); Mem., Council, Roehampton Univ., 2010–19; Chair: Bromley Coll. Corporation, 2012–16; London SE Colleges, 2016–17; Careers Coll. Trust, 2017–. FRSA. Hon. DEd UWE, 2000; DUniv Open, 2010. *Recreations:* tennis, Plymouth Argyle supporter, music, theatre, cinema.

**DAWE, Sandra, (Sandie),** CBE 2015 (MBE 2008); Chief Executive, VisitBritain, 2009–14; *b* Colombo, Ceylon, 29 Sept. 1955; *d* of Peter Vincent Dawe and Mary Hood Dawe; *m* 1987, John Reid Meikle. *Educ*: St Margaret's Sch., Edinburgh; Univ. of Edinburgh (MA Hons German 1977); Univ. of Freiburg; Napier Coll. of Commerce, Edinburgh (Business Dip.); INSEAD (AMP 2009). MCIPR 1990. Sec. to Hd of German Lang. Service and Announcer/Translator, BBC World Service, 1978–80; Officer Manager, W S Wotherspoon, 1980–82; travelling and working, USA, Australia and Far East, 1982–83; Publicity Exec., Book Mktg Council, Publishers' Assoc., 1983–85; Press Officer, 1985–86, PR Manager, 1986–88, BTA and England Tourist Bd; Hd of PR, London Tourist Bd, 1988–91; Hd of PR, 1991–96, Press and PR Dir, 1997, BTA and England Tourist Bd; Mktg Communications Dir, BTA, 1999–2003; Strategy and Communications Dir, VisitBritain, 2003–08. Member, Board: Visit London, 2009–11; Visit England, 2009–14; Dir, London & Partners, 2014–. Trustee: Nat. Heritage Meml Fund, 2014–18; Heritage Lottery Fund, 2014–18; Culture Perth and Kinross, 2017–; Chm., Bd of Trustees, Kids in Museums, 2014–17. FTS 1988. *Recreations:* yoga, swimming, sailing. *Address:* 58 Sussex Street, SW1V 4RG.

**DAWES, Prof. Edwin Alfred,** CBiol, FRSB, CChem, FRSC; Reckitt Professor of Biochemistry, University of Hull, 1963–90, now Emeritus; *b* 6 July 1925; *s* of late Harold Dawes and Maude Dawes (née Barker); *m* 1950, Amy Rogerson (*d* 2014); two *s*. *Educ*: Goole Grammar Sch.; Univ. of Leeds. (BSc, PhD, DSc). Asst Lectr, later Lectr, in Biochemistry, Univ. of Leeds, 1947–50; Lectr, later Sen. Lectr, Univ. of Glasgow, 1951–63; Hull University: Head of Biochemistry Dept, 1963–86; Dean of Science, 1968–70; Pro-Vice-Chancellor, 1977–80; Dir, Biomed. Res. Unit, 1981–92. Visiting Lecturer: Meml Univ., Newfoundland, Dalhousie Univ., 1959; Univ. of Brazil, 1960, 1972; Univ. of S California, 1962; Univ. of Rabat, 1967; Univ. of Göttingen, 1972; Osmania Univ., Hyderabad, 1986; Univ. of Massachusetts, Amherst, 1989; Univ. of Padua, 1991; Lectures: Biochemical Soc., Australia and NZ, 1975; Amer. Medical Alumni, Univ. of St Andrews, 1980–81; Biodegradable Plastics Soc., Japan, 1991. Editor, Biochemical Jl, 1958–65; Editor-in-Chief, Jl of Gen. Microbiol., 1976–81; Man. Editor, Fedn of European Microbiol Socs, and Editor-in-Chief, FEMS Microbiology Letters, 1982–90. Vice Chm., 1987–2009, Chm., Scientific Adv. Cttee, 1978–2006, Yorks Cancer Res. Campaign; Member: Scientific Adv. Cttee, Whyte-Watson-Turner Cancer Res. Trust, 1984–91; Adv. Gp for Cancer Res., Sheffield Univ., 1991–96. President: Hull Lit. Philosophical Soc., 1976–77; British Ring of Internat. Brotherhood of Magicians, 1972–73; Hon. President: Scottish Conjurers' Assoc., 1973–; Scottish Assoc. Magical Socs, 1996–; Hon. Vice-Pres., Magic Circle (Official Historian, 1987–; Mem., 1959–; Maskelyne Trophy, 1998; David Devant Internat. Award, 2002); Chm., Centre for the Magic Arts Ltd, 2005–09. Chm., Philip Larkin Soc., 1995–. Governor, Pocklington Sch., 1965–74; Member, Court: Leeds Univ., 1974–2002; Bradford Univ., 1985–2002. Mem., Hall of Fame and H. A. Smith Literary Award, Soc. Amer. Magicians, 1984, 1997; Literary Fellowship and Hon. Life Mem., 1985, Special Fellowship, 2017, Acad. Magical Arts, USA; Hon. Mem. Bd, Houdini Historical Center, Wisconsin, 1990–. Consultant, The Mysteries of Magic, Learning Channel, 1998. Hon DSc Hull, 1992. Maskelyne Literary Award, 1988, 2009; Literary Award, Milbourne Christopher Foundn, USA, 1999; Special Award for Hist. and Res., Fédn Internat. des Sociétés Magiques, 2006; Gold Medal, Magic Circle, 2017; Lifetime Achievement Award, Allan Slaight Foundn, 2018. *Publications:* Quantitative Problems in Biochemistry, 1956, 6th edn 1980; (jtly) Biochemistry of Bacterial Growth, 1968, 3rd edn 1982; The Great Illusionists, 1979; Isaac Fawkes: fame and fable, 1979; The Biochemist in a Microbial Wonderland, 1982; Vonetta, 1982; The Barrister in the Circle, 1983; (ed) Environmental Regulation of Microbial Metabolism, 1985; (ed) Enterobacterial Surface Antigens, 1985; Microbial Energetics, 1985; (jtly) The Book of Magic, 1986, re-issued as Making Magic, 1992; The Wizard Exposed, 1987; (ed) Continuous Culture in Biotechnology and Environment Conservation, 1988; (contrib.) Philip Larkin: the man and his work, 1989; Henri Robin: expositor of science and magic, 1990; (ed) Molecular Biology of Membrane-Bound Complexes in Photosynthetic Bacteria, 1990; (ed) Novel Biodegradable Microbial Polymers, 1990; The Magic of Britain, 1994; Charles Bertram: the court conjurer, 1997; Stodare: the Enigma variations, 1998; (ed jtly) The Annals of Conjuring, 2001; Stanley Collins: conjuror and iconoclast, 2002; Harry Leat, 2003; The Great Lyle, 2005; (ed jtly and contrib.) Circle Without End, 2005; (jtly) David Nixon: entertainer with the magic touch, 2009; (jtly) John Henry Anderson the Great Wizard of the North and his Magical Family: a revisionary biography, 2014; Dr Ormonde: the Orcadian magician and his talented family, 2016; Willane: a creative performer, 2018; A Rich Cabinet of Magical Curiosities, vol. 1, 2019; (jtly) Jon Gresham: the life and adventures of a sideshowman, fire-eater and magician, 2019; numerous papers in scientific jls. *Recreations:* conjuring, book-collecting, genealogy. *Address:* Dane Hill, 393 Beverley Road, Anlaby, E Yorkshire HU10 7BQ. *T:* (01482) 657998.

**DAWES, Rev. Dr Helen Elizabeth;** Team Rector, Shaftesbury, Dorset, since 2015; Dean of Women's Ministry, Diocese of Salisbury, since 2016; *b* 5 Jan. 1974; *d* of John Bridger and Carolyn Bridger; *m* 1997, Jonathan Dawes; one *s* two *d*. *Educ*: S Wilts Grammar Sch., Salisbury; Trinity Coll., Cambridge (MA); Westcott House, Cambridge; Anglia Ruskin Univ. (MA); King's Coll. London (PhD). Analyst, Roland Berger and Partners, 1996–98; Res. Associate, Caminus Energy Ltd, 1998–99; ordained deacon, 2002, priest, 2003; Asst Curate, St Andrew's, Chesterton, Cambridge, 2002–05; Priest-in-charge, United Benefice of Sandon, Wallington and Rushden with Clothall, Herts, 2005–09; Archbishop of Canterbury's Dep. Sec. for Public Affairs, 2009–13; Archbishop of Canterbury's Social and Public Affairs Advr, 2013–15. *Recreations:* gardening, singing, cycling, reading. *Address:* Shaftesbury Team Office, 5 Gold Hill, Shaftesbury, Dorset SP7 8JW.

**DAWES, James Christopher;** QC 2018; *b* Kent, 11 July 1968; *s* of Charles and Valerie Dawes; *m* 1996, Victoria Mary Clough; three *d*. *Educ*: Hamstreet Primary Sch.; Wellesley House Sch.; Charterhouse Sch.; Durham Univ. (BSc Physics 1990). Called to the Bar, Inner Temple, 1993; in practice as barrister, specialising in criminal law, 1993–. *Recreations:* astrophysics, conversational Kikamba. *Address:* 2 Harcourt Buildings, Temple, EC4Y 9DB. *T:* (020) 7353 2112. *E:* clerks@2hb.co.uk.

**DAWES, Melanie Henrietta,** CB 2013; Permanent Secretary, Ministry of Housing, Communities and Local Government (formerly Department for Communities and Local Government), since 2015; *b* 9 March 1966; *d* of Nigel G. K. Dawes and Rosalie J. Dawes (née Wood); *m* 1992, Benedict Brogan; one *d*. *Educ*: Malvern Girls' Coll.; New Coll., Oxford (BA Hons); Birkbeck Coll., London (MSc Econ.). Econ. Asst, Dept of Transport, 1989–91; joined HM Treasury, 1991: Econ. Advr, then Team Leader, Econ. and Monetary Union, 1996–98; Head: Work Incentives and Poverty Analysis, 1998–2001; Educn and Culture, 2001–02; Dir (Europe), 2002–06; HM Revenue and Customs: Dir, Large Business Service, 2006–07; Dir Gen., Business Tax, and Commissioner, 2007–11; Dir Gen., Econ. and Domestic Secretariat, Cabinet Office, 2011–15. Chair, Civil Service People Bd, 2016–. Chair, Alcohol Recovery Project, 2003–05. Mem. Council, Which?, 2011–15. Trustee, Patchwork Foundn, 2018–. *Recreation:* gardening. *Address:* Ministry of Housing, Communities and Local Government, 2 Marsham Street, SW1P 4DF.

**DAWES, Rt Rev. Peter Spencer;** Bishop of Derby, 1988–95; *b* 5 Feb. 1928; *s* of Jason Spencer Dawes and Janet Dawes; *m* 1954, Ethel Marrin; two *s* two *d*. *Educ*: Bickley Hall School; Aldenham School; Hatfield Coll., Durham (BA); Tyndale Hall, Bristol. Assistant Curate: St Andrew's, Whitehall Park, 1954–57; St Ebbe's, Oxford, 1957–60; Tutor, Clifton Theological Coll., 1960–65; Vicar, Good Shepherd, Romford, 1965–80; Archdeacon of West Ham, 1980–88. Examining Chaplain to Bishop of Chelmsford, 1970–88. Member, General Synod, 1970–95. *Address:* 45 Arundell, Ely, Cambs CB6 1BQ. *T:* (01353) 661241.

**DAWES, Prof. William Nicholas,** PhD; FREng, FRAeS; Francis Mond Professor of Aeronautical Engineering, Cambridge University, since 1996; Fellow of Churchill College, Cambridge, since 1984; *b* 5 Sept. 1955; *s* of Kenneth Frederick Dawes and Doris Jacyntha Hulm; *m* 1980, Luigia Cuomo; two *d*. *Educ*: Churchill Coll., Cambridge (BA, MA, PhD). CEng; FRAeS 1997; FREng 2000. Res. Officer, CEGB, 1980–84; Sen. Res. Asst, 1984–86, Lectr, 1986–96, Engrg Dept, Cambridge Univ. Mem., Amer. Inst. Aeronautics and Astronautics, 1990. *Publications:* articles in professional jls. *Recreations:* Italy, good food and good wine. *Address:* Church Farm, 7 Church Lane, Little Eversden CB23 1HQ. *T:* (01223) 263318.

**DAWID, Prof. (Alexander) Philip,** ScD; FRS 2018; Professor of Statistics, University of Cambridge, 2007–13, now Emeritus; Fellow, Darwin College, Cambridge, 2007–13, now Emeritus; *b* 1 Feb. 1946; *s* of Israel Dawid and Rita Dawid; *m* 1974, Fatemeh Elahe Madjd; one *s* one *d*. *Educ*: Trinity Hall and Darwin Coll., Cambridge (BA 1966; Dip. Math. Statistics 1967; ScD 1982). CStat 1993. Lectr, UCL, 1969–78; Prof. of Statistics, City Univ., 1978–81; University College London: Reader, 1981–82; Prof. of Statistics, 1982–2007; Hon. Prof., 2007–. Hon. Prof., Univ. of Hong Kong, 2009–18; Vis. Fellow, Inst. of Criminology, Univ. of Cambridge, 2013–15. Editor: Jl of Royal Stat. Soc. Series B, 1992; Biometrika, 1992–96; Bayesian Analysis, 2005–09; Jl of Causal Inference, 2011–. *Publications:* (ed jtly) Bayesian Statistics 4, 1992, 5, 1996, 6, 1999, 7, 2003, 8, 2007; (jtly) Probabilistic Networks and Expert Systems, 1999; (ed jtly) Simplicity, Complexity and Modelling, 2011; (ed jtly) Evidence, Inference and Enquiry, 2011; (ed jtly) Beauty, 2013. *Recreation:* music. *Address:* Darwin College, Silver Street, Cambridge CB3 9EU. *E:* apd25@cam.ac.uk.

**DAWKINS, Prof. (Clinton) Richard,** FRS 2001; Charles Simonyi Professor of the Public Understanding of Science, University of Oxford, 1995–2008; Fellow, New College, Oxford, 1970–2008, now Emeritus; *b* 26 March 1941; *s* of late Clinton John Dawkins and of Jean Mary Vyvyan (née Ladner); *m*; one *d*. *Educ*: Oundle Sch.; Balliol Coll., Oxford (MA, DPhil, DSc; Hon. Fellow 2004). Asst Prof. of Zoology, Univ. of California, Berkeley, 1967–69; Oxford University: Lectr, 1970–89; Reader in Zoology, 1989–95. Gifford Lectr, Glasgow Univ., 1988; Sidgwick Meml Lectr, Newnham Coll., Cambridge, 1988; Kovler Vis. Fellow, Univ. of Chicago, 1990; Nelson Lectr, Univ. of California, Davis, 1990; Royal Instn Christmas Lects for Young People, 1991. Presenter, BBC TV Horizon progs, 1985,

1986. Chm., Richard Dawkins Foundn for Reason and Sci., 2006–19; Mem. Bd, Center for Inquiry, 2019–. Editor: Animal Behaviour, 1974–78; Oxford Surveys in Evolutionary Biology, 1983–86. FRSL 1997. Hon. Fellow, Regent's Coll., London, 1988. Hon. DLitt: St Andrews, 1995; ANU, 1996; Hon. DSc: Westminster, 1997; Hull, 2001; DUniv Open, 2003. Silver Medal, Zool Soc., 1989; Michael Faraday Award, Royal Soc., 1990; Nakayama Prize, Nakayama Foundn for Human Scis, 1994; Internat. Cosmos Prize, 1997; Kistler Prize, Foundn for the Future, 2001; Shakespeare Prize, 2005; Lewis Thomas Prize, Rockefeller Univ., NY, 2007; Deschner Prize, Johann-Wolfgang-Goethe Univ., Frankfurt, 2007. *Publications*: The Selfish Gene, 1976, 2nd edn 1989; The Extended Phenotype, 1982; The Blind Watchmaker, 1986 (RSL Prize 1987; LA Times Lit. Prize 1987); River Out of Eden, 1995; Climbing Mount Improbable, 1996; Unweaving the Rainbow: science, delusion and the appetite for wonder, 1998; A Devil's Chaplain and Other Selected Essays, 2003; The Ancestor's Tale, 2004; The God Delusion, 2006 (Book of Year, Galaxy Book Awards, 2007); (ed) The Oxford Book of Modern Science Writing, 2008; The Greatest Show on Earth, 2009; The Magic of Reality, 2011; An Appetite for Wonder: the making of a scientist, 2013; Brief Candle in the Dark: my life in science, 2015; Science in the Soul, 2017; Outgrowing God: a beginner's guide, 2019. *Recreation:* the Apple Macintosh. *Address:* New College, Holywell Street, Oxford OX1 3BN.

**DAWKINS, Hon. John Sydney,** AO 2000; economist, consultant, company director; Chairman, John Dawkins & Co., since 1994; *b* 2 March 1947; *s* of Dr A. L. Dawkins and M. Dawkins (née Lee Steere); *m* 1987, Maggie Maruff; one *d*, one step *s*, and one *s* one *d* by previous marr. *Educ:* Roseworthy Agricl Coll., SA (RDA); Univ. of WA (BEc). MHR, Tangney, 1974–75; Press Officer, WA Trades and Labor Council, 1976–77; MP (ALP) Fremantle, WA, 1977–94; Shadow Minister for Educn, 1980–83; Minister: for Finance and assisting Prime Minister for Public Service Matters, 1983–84; for Trade and assisting Prime Minister for Youth Affairs, 1984–87; for Employment, Educn and Trng, 1987–91; Treasurer of Australia, 1991–93. Presiding Mem., Educn and Early Childhood Services Registration and Standards Bd of SA, 2015–. Special investment rep., 1994–95; Chairman: Innisfree Australia Pty, 1994–; Elders Rural Ltd, 1998–2006; Med. Corp. of Australasia, 1997–2000; Law Central, 2000–06; Integrated Legal Hldgs Ltd, 2000–14; Retail Energy Market Co., 2003–09; Australian Qualifications Council, 2008–14; TVET Australia Pty, 2010–11; Sovereign Gold Ltd, 2010–15; Australian Bauxite Ltd, 2011–14; Nat. Skills Standards Council, 2011–13; Precious Metal Resources Ltd, 2012–14; Vocation Ltd, 2013–14; Co-Chm., GRACosway, 2014–; (Dir, Govt Relns Australia, 2000); Ind. Dir, Cbus Super Fund, 2012–17; Director: Sealcorp Hldgs, 1994–2004; Genetic Technologies, 2004–07; MGM Wireless, 2007–10; M & C Saatchi Direct Ltd, 2009–14; Archer Exploration Ltd, 2010–12. Chairman: Botanic Gardens of Adelaide, 2003–05; Inst. of Trade, 2005–13 (Mem., Bd Govs). Bd Mem., Fred Hollows Foundn, 1995–2004. Hon. Dr: Univ. of S Australia, 1996; Queensland Univ. of Technol., 1997; Ballarat, 2009. Centenary Medal, Australia, 2003. *Address:* PO Box 376, Walkerville, SA 5081, Australia.

**DAWKINS, Prof. Marian Ellina Stamp,** CBE 2014; DPhil; FRS 2014; Professor of Animal Behaviour, University of Oxford, since 1998; *b* Hereford, 13 Feb. 1945; *d* of Arthur Maxwell Stamp and (Alice) Mary Stamp (née Richards); *m* 1967, (Clinton) Richard Dawkins, *qv* (marr. diss. 1984). *Educ:* Queen's Coll., Harley St, London; Somerville Coll., Oxford (BA 1966; DPhil 1971). Pt-time res. asst to Prof. Niko Tinbergen, 1971–74; Deptl Demonstrator in Animal Behaviour, Dept of Zool., Oxford Univ., 1974–80; Mary Snow Fellow in Biol Scis, Somerville Coll., Oxford, 1980–2012, now Fellow Emeritus. *Publications*: Animal Suffering: the science of animal welfare, 1980; Unravelling Animal Behaviour, 1986, 2nd edn 1995; Through Our Eyes Only?: the search for animal consciousness, 1993; Observing Animal Behaviour, 2007; Why Animals Matter: animal consciousness and human well-being, 2012; (with A. Manning) An Introduction to Animal Behaviour, 2012. *Recreations:* photography, wind-surfing, walking, playing the piano. *Address:* Department of Zoology, University of Oxford, South Parks Road, Oxford OX1 3PS. *T:* (01865) 271215. *E:* marian.dawkins@zoo.ox.ac.uk.

**DAWKINS, Mark;** Partner, Akin Gump Strauss Hauer & Feld LLP, since 2014; *b* 2 May 1960; *s* of late Douglas Alfred Dawkins and of Diana Pauline Dawkins; *m* 2002, Kim (née Taylor); two *s* two *d*. *Educ:* Exeter Univ. (LLB). Admitted solicitor, 1985; Simmons & Simmons: Partner, 1990–2011; Hd of Litigation, 1997–2000; Hd, Financial Mkts, 2000–05; Man. Partner, 2005–11; Partner, Bingham McCutchen, 2011–14. *Recreations:* family, running, motorcycling, Southern African history, photography. *Address:* Akin Gump Strauss Hauer & Feld LLP, Ten Bishop Square, Eighth Floor, E1 6EG. *T:* (020) 7661 5330.

**DAWKINS, Richard;** *see* Dawkins, C. R.

**DAWKINS, Simon John Robert,** MA; Headmaster, Merchant Taylors' School, Crosby, 1986–2005; *b* 9 July 1945; *s* of Col William John Dawkins, TD and Mary Doreen Dawkins (née King); *m* 1968, Janet Mary Stevens; one *s* one *d*. *Educ:* Solihull Sch.; Univ. of Nottingham (BA); Queens' Coll., Cambridge (PGCE); Birkbeck Coll. London (MA distn). Head of Economics: Eltham Coll., 1968–71; Dulwich Coll., 1971–86 (Housemaster, 1979–86). Headmasters' Conference: Chm. NW Div., 1996 (Sec., 1995); Member: Memship Cttee, 1996–99; Academic Policy Cttee, 2000–04. Gov., Arnold Sch., Blackpool, 2005–10. Freeman, Merchant Taylors' Co., 2005–. *Recreations:* physical exercise, tennis, golf, ski-ing, reading. *Address:* Brackenwood, St George's Road, Hightown, Liverpool L38 3RT. *T:* (0151) 929 3546. *Clubs:* Hightown (Lancs); Formby Golf.

**DAWNAY,** family name of **Viscount Downe**.

**DAWNAY, Caroline Margaret;** Partner, United Agents LLP, since 2012; *b* Reading, 22 Jan. 1950; *d* of late Captain Oliver Payan Dawnay, CVO and of Lady Margaret Dawnay (née Boyle); one *s*. *Educ:* St Mary's Sch., Wantage; Università per Stranieri, Florence. Noel Gay Artists, 1968–70; Michael Joseph, 1971–77; A. D. Peters, subseq. Peters Fraser and Dunlop, 1977–2007; United Agents, 2008–. Treas., then Pres., Assoc. of Authors' Agents, 1994–97. Literary Agent of the Year, Bookseller Industry Awards, 2014. *Publications:* (with Mungo McCosh) An Alphabet of Aunts, 2007. *Address:* United Agents LLP, 12–26 Lexington Street, W1F 0LE. *T:* (020) 3214 0800. *E:* cdawnay@unitedagents.co.uk. *Club:* Academy.

**DAWNAY, (Charles) James (Payan);** DL; Chairman, CCLA Investment Management Ltd, 2004–17; *b* 7 Nov. 1946; *s* of late Captain Oliver Payan Dawnay, CVO and of Lady Margaret Dawnay (née Boyle, now Lady Margaret Stirling-Aird); *m* 1978, Sarah Stogdon; one *s* three *d*. *Educ:* Trinity Hall, Cambridge (BA 1968). Investment Manager, M & G Gp Ltd, 1969–78; Export Sales Dir, Alginate Industries Ltd, 1979–81; Man. Dir, Vannick Products Ltd, 1981–83; S G Warburg & Co. Ltd, 1983–87 (Dir, 1984–87); Dir, Mercury Asset Mgt Gp plc, 1987–92; Chm., Mercury Fund Managers Ltd, 1987–92; Business Develt Dir, 1992–99, Dep. Chm., 1999–2000, Martin Currie Ltd; Chairman: China Heartland Fund Ltd, 1997–2006; Northern Aim VCT plc, 2000–11; Gurr Johns Ltd, 2000–06; Investec High Income Trust plc, 2001–09; Resources Investment Trust plc, 2001–08; New Opportunities Investment Trust plc, 2002–06; Director: Govett Strategic Trust plc, 2000–03; Taiwan Opportunities Trust Ltd, 2001–. Mem. Bd of Trustees, Nat. Galls of Scotland, 2003–11. Mem., Finance Cttee, NT, 1991–2005; Mem. Finance Cttee, 1993–2005, Dir NTS Enterprises, 2001–05 and Chm. Commercial Develt Cttee, 2001–05, Nat. Trust for Scotland, 1993–2005. Chairman: Biggar Mus. Trust, 1993–; Penicuik House Preservation Trust, 2001–14; Hermitage Foundn UK, 2015–. DL Lanarks, 2012. *Recreations:* collecting, conservation. *Address:* Symington House, by Biggar, Lanarkshire ML12 6LW. *T:* (01899) 308211, *Fax:* (01899) 308727. *E:* cjdawnay@gmail.com. *Clubs:* Brooks's, Pratt's; Biggar.
*See also* C. M. Dawnay, R. S. Johnson.

**DAWNAY, Lady Jane Meriel;** Member of Board, Historic Buildings Council for Scotland, 1996–99; *b* 8 Feb. 1953; *yr d* of 5th Duke of Westminster, TD and Hon. Viola Maud Lyttelton (*d* 1987); *m* 1st, 1977, 10th Duke of Roxburghe (marr. diss. 1990); two *s* one *d*; 2nd, 1996, Edward William Dawnay. *Educ:* Collegiate Sch., Enniskillen; Sherborne Hill; Switzerland; Bedgebury Park; Paris. Macmillan Cancer Relief (formerly Cancer Relief Macmillan Fund): Vice Pres., Scotland, 1994– (Dir and Bd Mem., 1990–94); Chm., Scotland and NI, 1989–94. Mem. Bd, Ancient Monuments Scotland, 1993–96; Member: Adv. Cttee, Royal Parks, 1994–99; Royal Highland & Agricultural Soc. of Scotland, 1998 (Pres., 1998–). Trustee, Atlantic Salmon Trust Scotland, 1995–2014. Dir, Radio Borders, 1992–98. Mem., Racehorse Owners' Assoc.; Partner, Hillington Hall Bloodstock Partnership, 2006–. Vice Pres., NW Norfolk Cons. Assoc. (Pres., 1999–2002). Pres., W Norfolk, King's Lynn and Wisbech Br., NSPCC, 2007–; Chm., FirstLight Trust, 2016–. Life Patron, George Thomas Soc. MInstD 1997. Freeman: City of Chester, 1997; City of London, 2012; Farriers' Co., 2009 (Liveryman, 2012). Queen Elizabeth the Queen Mother's Award for Envmt, Scotland, 1996. *Address:* Hillington Hall, Hillington, King's Lynn, Norfolk PE31 6BW; 48f Eaton Square, SW1W 9BD.
*See also* Viscount Grimston, Duke of Roxburghe.

**DAWNAY, Rachel Sabiha;** *see* Johnson, R. S.

**DAWSON, (Archibald) Keith;** educational consultant, since 1996; Headmaster, Haberdashers' Aske's School, Elstree, 1987–96; *b* 12 Jan. 1937; *s* of Wilfred Joseph and Alice Marjorie Dawson; *m* 1961, Marjorie Blakeson; two *d*. *Educ:* Nunthorpe Grammar School for Boys, York; The Queen's College, Oxford. MA, Dip Ed distinction. Ilford County High School for Boys, 1961–63; Haberdashers' Aske's Sch., 1963–71 (Head of History, 1965–71); Headmaster, John Mason Sch., Abingdon, 1971–79; Principal, Scarborough Sixth Form Coll., 1979–84; Principal, King James's College of Henley, 1984–87. Liveryman, Haberdashers' Co., 1996–. *Publications:* Society and Industry in 19th Century England (with Peter Wall), 1968; The Industrial Revolution, 1971. *Recreations:* theatre, 'cello, cricket, tending my fruit and vegetables, seeing Europe by rail. *Address:* Puffins, 77 Chapel Street, Sidbury, Sidmouth EX10 0RQ.

**DAWSON, Celia Anne, (Mrs D. Charlton); Her Honour Judge Dawson;** a Circuit Judge, since 2018; *b* 25 Sept. 1959; *d* of David and Jean Dawson; *m* 1983, Dr David Charlton; one *s* two *d*. *Educ:* Essex Univ. (BA Hons (Lit.) 1981); Coll. of Law. Admitted solicitor, 1983; Partner, Thompson Smith and Puxon, Solicitors, Colchester, 1987–91; Sen. Legal Advr, Essex Magistrates' Courts, 1991–98; Partner, Birkett Long, Solicitors, Colchester, 1998–2004; Dep. Dist Judge, Sussex, 2001–04; Dist Judge (Magistrates' Courts), 2004–18; Recorder, 2016–18. Mem. Bd, and Chm., Mgt Cttee, Colne Housing Soc., 1999–2004. Trustee: Coram Children's Legal Centre (formerly Children's Legal Centre), Univ. of Essex, 2007–16; Coram Cambridge Adopt, 2014–; Coram, 2017– (Mem. Bd, 2017–). *Recreations:* obsessive sailing, unsuccessful garden taming, making a mess in the kitchen. *Address:* Norwich Combined Court Centre, The Law Courts, Bishopgate, Norwich, Norfolk NR3 1UR. *Clubs:* Brightlingsea Sailing, Colne Yacht.

**DAWSON, Hon. Sir Daryl (Michael),** AC 1988; KBE 1982; CB 1980; Justice of the High Court of Australia, 1982–97; Non-permanent Member, Hong Kong Court of Final Appeal, 1997–2003; Professorial Fellow, University of Melbourne, since 1998; *b* 12 Dec. 1933; *s* of Claude Charles Dawson and Elizabeth May Dawson; *m* 1971, Mary Louise Thomas. *Educ:* Canberra High Sch.; Ormond Coll., Univ. of Melbourne (LLB Hons); LLM Yale. Sterling Fellow, Yale Univ., 1955–56. QC 1971; Solicitor-General for Victoria, 1974–82. Mem. Council, Univ. of Melbourne, 1976–86; Chm. Council, Ormond Coll., Univ. of Melbourne, 1991–92. Adjunct Prof. of Law, Monash Univ., 1997–2006. Chairman: Australian Motor Sport Appeal Court, 1986–88 (Mem., 1970–86); Longford Royal Commn, 1998–99; Trade Practices Act Review Cttee, 2002–03. Chm., Menzies Foundn, 1998–2008; Gov., Ian Potter Foundn, 1998–. Hon. LLD: Monash, 2006; Melbourne, 2008. *Recreation:* gardening. *Address:* PO Box 147, East Melbourne, Vic 8002, Australia. *Clubs:* Melbourne, Savage, RACV (Melbourne).

**DAWSON, David;** international freelance choreographer, since 2002; Associate Artist, Dutch National Ballet, since 2015; *b* London, 4 March 1972; *s* of John William Dawson and Jacqueline Ann Dawson; *m* 2015, Joachim Fürst. *Educ:* Fleet Prim. Sch., London; Rona Hart Sch. of Dance, London; Arts Educational Schs, London; Royal Ballet Sch., London. Leading soloist dancer: Birmingham Royal Ballet, 1991–94; English Nat. Ballet, 1994–95; Dutch Nat. Ballet, 1995–2000; Principal Dancer, Ballett Frankfurt, 2000–02; House Choreographer: Dutch Nat. Ballet, 2004–06; Dresden Semperoper Ballet, 2006–09; Royal Ballet of Flanders, 2009–12. Choreographed and staged works, 2002–, for: Berlin Staatsballett, Boston Ballet, Ballet Nat. de Marseilles, Dutch Nat. Ballet and Jun. Co., Semperoper Ballet, English Nat. Ballet, Aalto Ballet Th. Essen, Finnish Nat. Ballet, Hungarian Nat. Ballet, Norwegian Nat. Ballet, Mariinsky Ballet, Pacific Northwest Ballet, Royal Ballet of Flanders, Royal New Zealand Ballet, Royal Ballet, Saarbrücken Staatstheater Ballet, San Francisco Ballet, Scottish Ballet, Royal Swedish Ballet, Singapore Dance Th., West Australian Ballet, Slovenian Nat. Ballet, Ballet du Capitole Toulouse, Tulsa Ballet, Vienna State Opera Ballet. Professional Level Prize, Prix de Lausanne, 1991; Benois de la Danse award for choreography, 2003; Golden Mask Award for Best Choreographer, 2005. *W:* www.dawsonarts.net.

**DAWSON, Dee;** *see* Dawson, J. D.

**DAWSON, Prof. Donald Andrew,** PhD; FRS 2010; FRSC; FIMS; Professor Emeritus and Distinguished Research Professor, School of Mathematics and Statistics, Carleton University, Ottawa, since 1999; *b* Montreal, Canada, 4 June 1937. *Educ:* McGill Univ. (BSc Hons Maths and Physics 1958; MSc Maths 1959); Massachusetts Inst. of Technol. (PhD 1963). Sen. Res. Engr, Space Div., Raytheon Corp., Mass, 1962–63; Asst Prof., 1963–66, Associate Prof., 1967–70, Dept of Maths, McGill Univ.; Associate Prof., 1970–71, Prof. of Maths and Statistics, 1971–96, Carleton Univ.; Dir, Fields Inst. for Res. in Mathematical Scis, Toronto, 1996–2000; Adjunct Professor: Depts of Maths and Statistics, Univ. of Toronto, 1996–2000; Dept of Maths and Statistics, McGill Univ., 2000–10. Pres., Bernoulli Soc., 2003–05. FIMS 1977; FRSC 1987; FAMS 2012. Gold Medal, Statistical Soc. of Canada, 1991. *Publications:* over 100 articles in jls. *Address:* School of Mathematics and Statistics, Carleton University, 1125 Colonel By Drive, Ottawa, ON K1S 5B6, Canada.

**DAWSON, Ven. Hilary Joan;** Archdeacon of Gloucester and Residentiary Canon, Gloucester Cathedral, since 2019; *b* Shebbear, Devon, 3 Oct. 1964; *d* of Dick and Joan Birch; *m* 1990, Richard Dawson; one *s* one *d*. *Educ:* Edgehill Coll., Bideford; St David's Univ. Coll., Lampeter (BA Hons Theol. 1985); Univ. of the West of England (PGCE 1989); Univ. of Exeter (MA Biblical Studies 2008); SW Ministry Trng Course. Residential social worker, RNID, 1985–88; Primary School Teacher, 1989–2003; Lay Sch. Chaplain,

Exeter Cathedral Sch., 2003–08; ordained deacon, 2008, priest, 2009; Curate, Netherexe Parishes, 2008–11; Rector, Branscombe and Colyton with Colford, Musbury and Southleigh, 2011–19. Tutor, 2012–17, Trustee, 2015–18, SW Ministry Trng Course. Governor: Blundells Sch., 2009–12; Jubilee Fedn, 2011–18; Colyton Grammar Sch., 2012–18. *Recreations:* music, reading, theatre, walking, quilting, travel. *Address:* 2 College Green, Gloucester GL1 2LY. *T:* (01452) 835555. *E:* archdglos@glosdioc.org.uk.

**DAWSON, Hilton;** see Dawson, T. H.

**DAWSON, James Grant Forbes,** CEng, FICE; Strategic Development Director, BST Consultants, 2002; Chairman, Vilnius Consult, 2002; Associate, First Class Partnerships, 2003; *b* 6 Sept. 1940; *s* of William Maxwell Hume Dawson and Caroline Margaret Storey Dawson; *m* 2nd, 1993, Joan Margaret Davison. *Educ:* Edinburgh Univ. (BSc). FIPENZ (FNZIE); Eur Ing. GIBB Ltd: Chief Engr, 1975–78; Associate, 1978–80; Head of Transport, 1980–82; Partner, 1982; Director, 1989; Chm., 1995–2001; Chm. Emeritus, Jacobs GIBB Ltd, 2001–. Consultant: RSM Robson Rhodes, 2002–03; MVA, 2005–06. Member: DTI Cttee for S Africa Trade, 1998–2001; E Europe Trade Council, 1999–2001; Mem., ME and African Gp, 2001–03, Chm., Ports and Logistics Gp, British Trade Investments. Chm., ACE, 1999–2000. Liveryman, Engineers' Co., 2001–. *Recreations:* golf, gardening. *Address:* Woodpeckers, Pangbourne Hill, Pangbourne, Berks RG8 8JS. *Club:* East India.

**DAWSON, Joan Denise, (Dee);** Medical Director, Rhodes Farm Clinic, 1991–2011; *b* 17 Jan. 1947; *d* of Horace and Joan Webb; *m* 1st, 1969, Stephen Dawson (marr diss.); 2nd, 1979, Ian Dear (marr. diss.); one *s* four *d*; 3rd, 2002, Eberhard von Wick. *Educ:* Chelsea Coll., London Univ. (BSc); London Business Sch.; Royal Free Hosp. Sch. of Medicine (MB BS 1989). Voluntary Teacher, VSO, Madagascar, 1969–71; Mkt Res. Manager, Parker Ltd, 1974–75; Man. Dir, Dee Dawson Fashion Ltd, 1977–84; House Physician, 1989–90, House Surgeon, 1990–91, North Middx Hosp.; set up Rhodes Farm Clinic, first residential unit, incl. full-time school, dedicated solely to treatment of anorexic children, 1991. *Publications:* A Quick Guide to Eating Disorders, 1995; Anorexia and Bulimia - a parents' guide, 2001. *Recreations:* tennis, water ski-ing. *Address:* The Old House, Totteridge Green, N20 8PA.

**DAWSON, Prof. John Alan,** FRSE; Professor of Marketing, University of Edinburgh, 1990–2009, now Emeritus; Professor of Retail Studies, University of Stirling, 2005–09, now Emeritus; *b* 19 Aug. 1944; *s* of Alan and Gladys Dawson; *m* 1967, Jocelyn M. P. Barker (marr. diss. 2007); one *s* one *d*. *Educ:* University College London (BSc, MPhil); University of Nottingham (PhD). Lectr, Univ. of Nottingham, 1967–71; Lectr, 1971, Sen. Lectr, 1974, Reader, 1981–83, Univ. of Wales, Lampeter; Fraser of Allander Prof. of Distributive Studies, and Dir, Inst. for Retail Studies, Univ. of Stirling, 1983–90. Vis. Lectr, Univ. of Western Australia, 1973; Vis. Res. Fellow, ANU, 1978; Vis. Prof., 2000–, Dist. Prof., 2003–11, Univ. of Mktg and Distribn Sci., Kobe; Visiting Professor: Florida State Univ., 1982; Chuo Univ., 1986; Univ. of S Africa, 1999; Sch. for Higher Mgt and Business Strategy, Barcelona, 2000–07; Bocconi Univ., Milan, 2000; Saitama Univ., 2002; Kobe Univ., 2010; Valencia Univ., 2010. Chm., Nat. Museums of Scotland Retailing Co., 1992–2003. Member: Distributive Trades EDC, 1984–87; Board, Cumbernauld Develt Corp., 1987–96. Hon. Sec., Inst. of British Geographers, 1985–88. FRSE 2003. Hon. DBA Abertay Dundee, 2010. *Publications:* Evaluating the Human Environment, 1973; Man and His World, 1975; Computing for Geographers, 1976; Small Scale Retailing in UK, 1979; Marketing Environment, 1979; Retail Geography, 1980; Commercial Distribution in Europe, 1982; Teach Yourself Geography, 1983; Shopping Centre Development, 1983; Computer Programming for Geographers, 1985; Shopping Centres Policies and Prospects, 1985; Evolution of European Retailing, 1989; Competition and Markets, 1991; Retail Environments in Developing Countries, 1991; Distribution Statistics, 1992; Internationalisation of Retailing in Asia, 2003; International Retailing Plans and Strategies in Asia, 2005; Strategic Issues in International Retailing, 2006; The Retail Reader, 2008; Global Strategies in Retailing, 2013; articles in geographical, management and marketing jls. *Recreations:* sport, travel. *Address:* University of Edinburgh Business School, Edinburgh EH8 9JS. *T:* (0131) 651 3220.

**DAWSON, John Anthony Lawrence,** FICE, FCIHT; Chairman: European Road Assessment Association, 2002–16 (Director, European Road Assessment Programme, since 2002); International Road Assessment Programme, 2005–17; *m* 1980, Frances Anne Elizabeth Whelan; two *d*. *Educ:* Mill Hill Sch.; Southampton Univ. British Rail Engineering Scholar, 1968–72; Depts of Envmt and Transport, 1972–81; Overseas Transport Consultant, 1981–85; Dir (Transport), London Regl Office, Dept of Transport, 1985–88; Chief Road Engineer, Scottish Develt Dept, 1988; Dir of Roads and Chief Road Engr, Scottish Office, 1989–95; Automobile Association: Policy Dir, 1995–2004; Internat. Dir, 2003–04; Mem. Cttee, 1996–99; Man. Dir, AA Foundn for Road Safety Research, 1995–2004; Dir, AA Motoring Trust, 2003–04; Chm., Mgt Cttee, Road Safety Foundn, 2005–. Mem. Bd, Ertico, 1995–97, 1999–2002; Trustee, Air Ambulance Assoc., 1999–2002; Vice-Chm., FIA Foundn for Automobile and Soc., 2012–16 (Sec., 2001–12). *Recreations:* touring, music. *Address:* EuroRAP AISBL, Worting House, Basingstoke, Hants RG23 8PX. *T:* (01256) 345598.

**DAWSON, John Kelvin,** AM 2008; Agent-General for Queensland in London, and Commissioner, Europe, 2001–07; Adviser to: Russell Reynolds Associates, since 2008; iCarehealth, since 2008; Corporate Value Associates, since 2008; *b* Melbourne, 15 Sept. 1943; *s* of John Inglis Dawson and Marie Victoria Dawson; one *s* one *d*. *Educ:* Ivanhoe Grammar Sch.; Univ. of Melbourne (BA). National Australia Bank Ltd: Gen. Manager, Strategic Develt, 1991–93; Man. Dir, UK and Europe, 1993–95; Gp Gen. Manager, Asian and Internat. Banking, 1995; CEO, Bank of Queensland Ltd, 1996–2001. Director: Clydesdale Bank, 1993–95; Nat. Irish Bank, 1993–95; Northern Bank, Belfast, 1993–95; Yorkshire Bank, 1993–95; Bank of Hawaii Internat., 1999–2001; Queensland Treasury Corp., 2008–11. Chm., Exec. Cttee, Aust. Bankers' Assoc., 1992–93. Dir, British-Aust. Soc., 2001–07. Freeman, City of London, 2004. *Recreations:* all sports, wine, reading. *Address:* Villa 2, Stradbroke Apartments, 2 Goodwin Street, Kangaroo Point, Qld 4169, Australia. *Clubs:* East India; Australian, Melbourne Cricket (Melbourne); Brisbane, Tattersalls (Qld); Hong Kong Foreign Correspondents'.

**DAWSON, Keith;** see Dawson, A. K.

**DAWSON, Lorna Anne,** PhD; CBE 2018; FRSE; Head, Forensic Soil Science, since 2005, and Senior Principal Scientist, since 2015, James Hutton Institute (formerly Macaulay Land Use Research Institute); *b* Forfar, 13 Nov. 1957; *d* of David Gordon Mackie and Moira Grant Mackie (née Baird); *m* 1987, Dr Robert Dawson; one *s* two *d*. *Educ:* Forfar Acad. Primary; Forfar Acad.; Univ. of Edinburgh (BSc Hons Geog. 1979); Univ. of Aberdeen (PhD Soil Sci. 1984). HSO, 1984–2005, PSO, 2005–11, Macaulay Inst. for Soil Res., then Macaulay Land Use Research Inst. Vis. Prof., Robert Gordon Univ., 2011–. Scottish Govt Prog. Advr, 2011–, Knowledge Exchange Lead for Envmt, 2016–, Scottish Envmt Food and Agric. Res. Insts. Fellow, British Soc. of Soil Sci., 2015; FRSA 2016; FRSE 2019. *Publications:* (ed jtly) Criminal and Environmental Soil Forensics, 2009; (jtly) Soils of the Crofts, 2011, 2nd edn 2016; (ed jtly) Environmental and Criminal Geoforensics, 2013; contrib. book chapters; over 100 refereed papers in jls. *Recreations:* art, family, walking, crime fiction, drama, theatre. *Address:* James Hutton Institute, Aberdeen AB15 8QH. *T:* (01224) 395044. *E:* lorna.dawson@hutton.ac.uk.

**DAWSON, Malcolm Edward,** OBE 2008; Director, Yewdale Consulting Ltd, since 2014; *b* Harrogate, N Yorks, 8 April 1961; *s* of late Thomas Edward Dawson and of Ruth Dawson; *m* 1985, Tracey Anne Brewin; one *s*. *Educ:* Ashville Coll., Harrogate; Kingston Univ. (MA Human Resource Mgt). Procurement Officer, MoD, 1982–85; HM Customs and Excise: VAT Inspector, 1985–89; various HR rôles, 1989–94; Personnel Manager, Office of Nat. Lottery, 1994–97; Cabinet Office: Mgt Develt Advr, 1997–99; Project Advr, Prime Minister's Strategy Unit, 1999; Hd, Sen. Pay, 2000–02; Prog. Dir, Centre for Mgt and Policy Studies, 2002–03; Department for Constitutional Affairs, later Ministry of Justice: Hd, HR Strategy, 2003–06; Actg HR Dir, 2006–07; Dir, Workforce Reform, 2007–08; HM Land Registry: Dir, HR, 2008–11; Chief Land Registrar and Chief Exec., 2011–13; Interim Chief Exec., DVLA, 2013; Dir, BIS, 2014. Chm. Govs, Boroughbridge High Sch., 2015–; Chm. Govs, Graham Sch., 2017–. Mem., Bewerley Parish Council, 2016–. FCIPD 2010. FRSA. Hon. RICS 2012. *Publications:* (contrib.) Public Sector Leadership for the 21st Century, 2001. *Recreations:* badminton, golf, walking, family.

**DAWSON, Sir Nicholas Antony Trevor,** 5th Bt *cr* 1920, of Edgewarebury, co. Middlesex; *b* 17 Aug. 1957; *yr s* of Sir (Hugh Halliday) Trevor Dawson, 3rd Bt and Caroline Jane, *d* of William Antony Acton; *S* brother, 2007; *m* 1995, Gisela Bücherl.

**DAWSON, Rev. Peter,** OBE 1986; education consultant, since 1985; employment law consultant, since 2002; *b* 19 May 1933; *s* of Richard Dawson and Henrietta Kate Dawson (née Trueman); *m* 1957, Shirley Margaret Pentland Johnson; two *d*. *Educ:* Beckenham Technical Sch.; Beckenham Grammar Sch.; London School of Economics (BScEcon); Westminster Coll. (Postgrad. CertEd). Schoolmaster Fellow Commoner, Keble Coll., Oxford, 1969, and Corpus Christi Coll., Cambridge, 1979. Asst Master, Roan Grammar School for Boys, London, 1957–62; Head of Upper School, Sedgehill Sch., London, 1962–67; Second Master, Gateacre Comprehensive Sch., Liverpool, 1967–70; Headmaster, Eltham Green Sch., London, 1970–80; Gen. Sec., Professional Assoc. of Teachers, 1980–92; OFSTED Registered Inspector of Schs, 1993–2000. Methodist Minister, ordained 1985; Asst Minister, Queen's Hall Methodist Mission, Derby, 1984–87; Minister, Spondon Methodist Church, Derby, 1989–90; Free Church Minister, Church on Oakwood, Derby, 1990–94; Minister, Mayfield Rd Methodist Church, Derby, 1994–98. Member: Burnham Cttee, 1981–87; Council of Managerial and Professional Staffs, 1989–92 (Pres.); Econ. and Social Cttee, EC, 1990–94; Employment Appeal Tribunal, 1992–2004. Chairman: East Midlands RSA, 2004–06; Church Wilne Probus Club, 2003 (Sec., 2009–11). *Publications:* Making a Comprehensive Work, 1981; Teachers and Teaching, 1984; Why Preach?, 2000; A Short History of the Employment Appeal Tribunal, 2002, rev. and updated edn 2004; Messages and Other Short Stories, 2011; Never Was There Tale of Brighter Hue and Other Short Stories, 2013; The Grey Lady and Other Stories and Stuff, 2015; Easter, 2017. *Recreations:* reading, theatre, cinema, grandparenthood. *Address:* 30 Elm Street, Borrowash, Derby DE72 3HP. *T:* (01332) 672669. *E:* ockery@ntlworld.com.

**DAWSON, Prof. Peter,** PhD; FRCP, FRCR, FBIR, FInstP; Professor of Radiology and Consultant Radiologist, 1999–2009, Chairman and Clinical Director of Radiology, 2002–09, University College London Hospitals; *b* 17 May 1945; *s* of Frederick and May Dawson; *m* 1968, Hilary Sturley; one *s* one *d*. *Educ:* Firth Park Sch., Sheffield; King's Coll. London (BSc 1st Cl. Hons 1966; PhD 1970); Westminster Med. Sch. (MB BS 1978). FRCR 1984; FRCP 1994; FInstP 2005; FBIR 2007. Sen. Lectr and Reader in Radiology, 1985–96, Prof. of Med. Imaging, 1996–99, RPMS. Pres., BIR, 1994–95; Royal College of Radiologists: Roentgen Prof., 2002; Registrar, 2002–06. Mem., Internat. Commn on Radiation Units and Measurements, 1999–; Special Asst to IAEA, 2003–. Bd Mem., Internat. Soc. of Radiology, 2002–07; Mem. Res. Cttee, European Assoc. of Radiology, 2005–07. Barclay Prize, 1984, Barclay Medal, 1998, BIR; (jtly) Finzi Prize, RSM, 1991, 1993. *Publications:* Contrast Media in Practice, 1993; Functional CT, 1997; A Textbook of Contrast Media, 1999; Protocols for Multi-slice Computed Tomography, 2006; some 250 papers on physics and medical imaging in learned jls. *Recreations:* music, mathematics, wine, scuba diving. *Address:* Beechers, Green Lane, Chesham Bois, Bucks HP6 5LQ. *T:* (01494) 728222. *E:* peterxdawson@gmail.com. *Club:* Royal Society of Medicine.

**DAWSON, Peter,** OBE 2015; Secretary, Royal and Ancient Golf Club of St Andrews, 1999–2015; *b* 28 May 1948; *s* of George Dawson and Violet Dawson (née Smith); *m* 1969, Juliet Ann Bartlett; one *s* one *d*. *Educ:* Westcliff High Sch.; Corpus Christi Coll., Cambridge (MA). Managing Director: Grove Cranes, 1977–83; Blackwood Hodge (UK), 1983–89; Grove Europe, 1989–93; Thos Storey, 1994–97. Pres., Internat. Golf Fedn, 2011– (Jt Sec., 1999–2011). *Address:* Royal and Ancient Golf Club, St Andrews, Fife KY16 9JD. *T:* (01334) 460000. *Clubs:* Northumberland Golf; Royal Worlington and Newmarket Golf.

**DAWSON, Rex Malcolm Chaplin,** FRS 1981; PhD, DSc; Deputy Director and Head of Biochemistry Department, Institute of Animal Physiology, Babraham, Cambridge, 1969–84, retired (Deputy Chief Scientific Officer, 1969–84); *b* 3 June 1924; *s* of late James Dawson and Ethel Mary Dawson (née Chaplin); *m* 1st, 1946, Emily Elizabeth Hodder (*d* 2005); one *s* one *d*; 2nd, 2009, June Margaret Buschman. *Educ:* Hinckley Grammar Sch.; University Coll., London (BSc 1946, DSc 1960). Univ. of Wales (PhD 1951). MRC Fellowship followed by Beit Meml Fellowship, Neuropsychiatric Res. Centre, Whitchurch Hosp., Cardiff, 1947–52; Betty Brookes Fellow, Dept of Biochemistry, Univ. of Oxford, 1952–55. Vis. Res. Fellow, Harvard Univ., 1959; Vis. Prof., Northwestern Univ., Chicago, 1974. International Lipid Prize, Amer. Oil Chemists' Assoc., 1981. *Publications:* Metabolism and Physiological Significance of Lipids, 1964; Data for Biochemical Research, 1959, 3rd edn 1986; Form and Function of Phospholipids, 1973; numerous papers on structure, turnover and role of phospholipids in cell membranes in various scientific jls. *Recreations:* mercantile marine history, sailing, gardening. *Address:* Kirn House, Holt Road, Langham, Norfolk NR25 7BX. *T:* (01328) 830396.

**DAWSON, Ruth Mitchell;** see McKernan, R. M.

**DAWSON, Dame Sandra (June Noble),** DBE 2004; KPMG Professor of Management Studies, University of Cambridge, 1995–2013, now Emeritus (Director, Judge Business School (formerly Judge Institute of Management Studies), 1995–2006; Deputy Vice Chancellor, 2008–12); Fellow, Sidney Sussex College, Cambridge, since 2009 (Master, 1999–2009); *b* 4 June 1946; *d* of late Wilfred Denyer and Joy (née Noble); *m* 1969, Henry R. C. Dawson; one *s* two *d*. *Educ:* Dr Challoner's Grammar Sch., Amersham; Univ. of Keele (BA 1st Cl. Hons Hist. and Sociol. 1968). Research Officer, Govt Social Survey, 1968–69; Imperial College of Science, Technology and Medicine: Res. Officer, Lectr, then Sen. Lectr, Industrial Sociol. Unit, Dept of Social and Econ. Studies, 1969–90; Prof. of Organisational Behaviour, Mgt Sch., 1990–95; Fellow, Jesus Coll., Cambridge, 1995–99. Non-exec. Dir, Riverside HA, 1990–92; Chm., Riverside Mental Health Trust, 1992–95. Member: Res. Strategy Bd, Offshore Safety Div., HSE, 1991–95; Strategic Review Gp, PHLS, 1994; Sen. Salaries Review Body, 1997–2003; Futures and Innovation Bd, DTI, 1998–2002; Res. Priorities Bd, ESRC, 2000–03; Task Force on Accounting for People, 2003; Fire and Rescue Service Ministerial Adv. Gp, 2004–07; Council for Sci. and

Technol., 2011–14. Chm., Exec. Steering Cttee, ESRC Advanced Inst. of Mgt, 2007–11. Non-executive Director: Cambridge Econometrics, 1996–2007; Fleming Claverhouse Investment Trust, 1996–2003; PHLS, 1997–99; Soc. for Advancement of Mgt Studies, 1999–2003; Barclays plc, 2003–09; Oxfam, 2006–12; FSA, 2010–13; DRS plc, 2012–16; Inst. for Govt, 2012–18 (Trustee, 2012–18); Winton Capital Gp, 2013–17; TSB, 2014–. Mem. Adv. Bd, Alchemy Partners, 2000–04. Member: UK-India Roundtable, 2006–16; Adv. Bd, UK India Business Council, 2007–10; Social Sci. Res. Council, USA, 2009–19, Mem., Ind. Adv. Gp, Windrush Lessons Learned Review, 2018–19. Trustee, RANDEurope (UK), 2001–04. Companion, Assoc. of Business Schs, 2007. Internat. Women's Forum Hall of Fame, 2007. *Publications:* Analysing Organisations, 1986, 3rd edn 1996; Safety at Work: the limits of self regulation, 1988; Managing in the NHS, 1995; (ed) Future Health Organisations and Systems, 2005; (ed) Policy Futures for UK Health, 2006; Engaging with Care: a vision for the health and care workforce of England, 2007; (ed) Future Public Health: burdens, challenges and opportunities, 2009; contribs to mgt learned jls. *Recreations:* music, walking, family. *Address:* Sidney Sussex College, Cambridge CB2 3HU.

**DAWSON, His Honour Stephen Eric;** a Circuit Judge, 2010–17; *b* 16 Feb. 1952. Admitted Solicitor, 1977. Articled and subseq. Partner, Victor Lissack, solicitors, 1978–82; Partner, Reynolds Dawson, 1982–94; Metropolitan Stipendiary Magistrate, later District Judge (Magistrates' Courts), 1994–2010; Recorder, 2000–10.

**DAWSON, (Thomas) Hilton;** Director, Northumbria People, since 2013; *b* 30 Sept. 1953; *s* of late Harry Dawson and Sally Dawson; *m* 1973, Susan, *d* of Ellis and Alice Williams; two *d*. *Educ:* Warwick Univ. (BA Hons Philos. and Pols 1975); Lancaster Univ. (Dip. in Social Work 1982); Reg. Social Worker, 2004; Dip. Funeral Celebrancy 2013. Brickworks labourer, 1975; clerk, 1976; kibbutz volunteer, 1976; community worker, 1977; social worker, 1979; Lancs Social Services, 1982–97; youth justice worker, 1983; social work manager, 1989. Mem. (Lab) Lancaster CC, 1987–97. MP (Lab) Lancaster and Wyre, 1997–2005. Chief Exec., Shaftesbury Homes and Arethusa, subseq. Shaftesbury Young People, 2005–08; Develt Consultant, Serco Educn and Children's Services, 2008–09; Chm., Nat. Acad. for Parenting Practitioners, 2007–09; Chief Exec., BASW, 2009–13; Gen. Sec., Social Workers Union, 2011–13. Founding Chm., North East Party, 2014–. Columnist, The Journal, Newcastle, 2013–. Founding Chm., Northumberland County of Sanctuary, 2016–. Civil Celebrant. *Publications:* Frank Renner's Bairns: looking at the world through the lives of a Northumbrian family, 2013; (jtly) Newbiggin Resilient, 2014; Eddie, 2015; Pride of Newbiggin by the Sea: 12 lifeboat coxswains and their families 1851–1981, 2017. *Recreations:* family, four grandchildren, the arts, politics, Chair of Newbiggin by the Sea Genealogy Project. *Address:* 36 Morwick Road, Warkworth, Northumberland NE65 0TD. *T:* (01665) 711817.

**DAWSON-DAMER,** family name of **Earl of Portarlington.**

**DAWTRY, Ven. Dr Anne Frances;** Archdeacon of Halifax, since 2011; *b* Grantham, 25 Oct. 1957; *d* of Frederick Ewart Dawtry and Mary Josephine Dawtry. *Educ:* Westfield Coll., Univ. of London (BA Hons 1979; PhD 1985). Sen. Lectr, Univ. of Chester, 1983; ordained deacon, 1993, priest, 1994; Curate: St Hubert's, Corfe Mullen, 1993–96; St Peter's, Parkstone with Branksea, 1996–97; Sen. Chaplain, Bournemouth Univ., 1997–99; Principal, Ordained Local Ministry, Dio. of Salisbury, 1999–2003; Dir of Ministry Trng, Dio. of Manchester, 2003–06; Dir, Southern NW Trng Partnership, 2006–08; Rector, St Werburgh's, Chorlton cum Hardy, 2008–11; Warden of Readers, Dio. of Wakefield, 2012–16, Dio. of Leeds, 2016–. Hon. Canon: Wakefield Cath., 2011–; Bradford Cath., 2015–; Ripon Cath., 2015–. Member: Gen. Synod, 2015–; Church Buildings Council, 2016–; Consultant, 2000–05, Mem., 2005–15, Liturgical Commn. *Publications:* (contrib.) They Shaped our Worship, 1998; (contrib.) Companion to Common Worship, vol. 1, 2001, vol. 2, 2006; (jtly) Art and Worship, 2000, 2nd edn 2002; (contrib.) New Dictionary of Liturgy and Worship, 2002. *Recreations:* architecture, photography, stained glass design, gardening. *Address:* 2 Vicarage Gardens, Brighouse, W Yorks HD6 3HD. *T:* (01484) 714553. *E:* archdeacon.halifax@leeds.anglican.org. *Club:* Army and Navy.

**DAY, Anneliese Mary;** QC 2012; *b* Edinburgh, 6 March 1973; *d* of Alan and Katherine Day; one *s* one *d*. *Educ:* Edinburgh Acad.; Clare Coll., Cambridge (BA 1994); Harvard Univ. (Kennedy Schol.; MA Law). Called to the Bar, Inner Temple, 1996, Bencher, 2015; in practice as barrister, specialising in commercial, construction, insurance and professional liability, 1996–. Mem., Legal Services Bd, 2013–16. *Publications:* (ed) Jackson & Powell on Professional Negligence, 1982, 7th edn 2012. *Recreations:* my children, travel, hot yoga. *Address:* Fountain Court Chambers, Fountain Court, Temple, EC4Y 9DH.

**DAY, Sir Barry (Stuart),** Kt 2014; OBE 2007; Chief Executive, Greenwood Academies Trust, 2009–15; *b* Stevenage, 12 June 1953; *s* of Sidney William Day and Peggy Joyce Day; *m* 1991, Brenda Partridge; two *d*. *Educ:* Alleyne's Grammar Sch., Stevenage; Loughborough Univ. (MSc). Teacher of Maths, Stonehill High Sch., Leicester, 1974–75; 2nd i/c Maths, Wreake Valley Coll., Leicester, 1975–81; Hd of Maths, Hamilton Community Coll. Leicester, 1981–85; Vice Principal, Mundella Community Coll., Leicester, 1985–91; Head Teacher, Greenwood Dale Sch., Nottingham, 1992–2008; Exec. Principal, Nottingham Acad., 2008–09. Hon. DEd Nottingham Trent, 2008. *Recreations:* walking, swimming, travel. *T:* 07733 227244. *E:* barryday5@btinternet.com.

**DAY, Bernard Maurice,** CB 1987; Chairman, The Riverside (East Molesey) Management Co., 1996–99, 2004–05 (Director, 1999–2004); *b* 7 May 1928; *s* of M. J. Day and Mrs M. H. Day; *m* 1956, Ruth Elizabeth Stansfield (*d* 2010); two *s* one *d*. *Educ:* Bancroft's Sch.; London School of Economics (BScEcon). Army service, commnd RA, 1946–48. British Electric Traction Fedn, 1950–51; Asst Principal, Air Ministry, 1951; Private Sec. to Air Mem. for Supply and Organisation, 1954–56; Principal, 1956; Cabinet Secretariat, 1959–61; Asst Sec., 1965; Sec., Meteorological Office, 1965–69; Estabt Officer, Cabinet Office, 1969–72; Head of Air Staff Secretariat, MoD, 1972–74; Asst Under Sec. of State, MoD, 1974; Civilian Staff Management, 1974–76; Operational Requirements, 1976–80; Programmes and Budget, 1980–82; Supply and Orgn, Air, 1982–84; Resident Chm., CSSB, 1984–85; Asst Under-Sec. of State (Fleet Support), MoD, 1985–88. Panel Chm., CSSB, 1988–96. Chairman: MoD Branch, First Div. Assoc., 1983–84; MoD Liaison Cttee with CS Benevolent Fund, 1975–84. Mem., Residents' Panel, Elmbridge BC, 2015–. Pres., Fellowship Club, Weybridge, 2008–10 (Immediate Past Pres., 2010–11). *Recreations:* local church, arts and family. *Address:* 26 The Riverside, Graburn Way, East Molesey, Surrey KT8 9BF. *T:* (020) 8941 4520.

**DAY, Prof. Christopher,** DPhil, DLitt; FAcSS; Professor, School of Education, University of Nottingham, 1993–2010, now Emeritus; Professor of Educational Leadership, University of Sydney; *b* 3 May 1943; *s* of Walter Day and Patricia Jane Day; *m* 1984, Alison Jane Stewart; two *s*. *Educ:* St Luke's Coll., Exeter (Cert Ed 1964); Univ. of Sussex (MA 1976; DPhil 1979); Univ. of Nottingham (DLitt 2008). LRAM 1966. School teacher, 1964–68; Lectr, 1968–71; LEA Advr, London Borough of Barking and Dagenham, 1972–76; Associate Prof., Univ. of Calgary, Alberta, 1979–81; Lectr, Sen. Lectr and Reader, Univ. of Nottingham, 1981–93. Editor, Developing Teachers and Schools series, 1991–94; Founding Editor, Teachers and Teaching, 1995–; Co-Editor: Jl of In-Service Teacher Educn, 1975–2002; Educational Action Res. Jl, 1993–2011. FRSA 1972; FAcSS (AcSS 2013). Hon. PhD Linköping, Sweden, 1993. *Publications:* Developing Teachers: the challenges of lifelong learning, 1999; A Passion for Teaching, 2004; New Understandings of Teachers' Work: emotions and educational change, 2011; *jointly:* Managing Primary Schools, 1985; Appraisal and Professional Development in Primary Schools, 1987; Reconceptualising School-Based Curriculum Development, 1990; Managing Primary Schools in the 1990s, 1990; Leadership and Curriculum in Primary Schools, 1993; Developing Leadership in Primary Schools, 1998; Leading Schools in Times of Change, 2001; Effective Leadership for School Improvement, 2003; Teachers Matter: connecting work, lives and effectiveness, 2007; The New Lives of Teachers, 2010; School Leadership on Pupil Outcomes: building and sustaining success, 2011; Resilient Leaders, Resilient Schools, 2013; Leading Schools Successfully: stories from the field, 2014; *edited jointly:* Staff Development in Secondary Schools, 1986; Partnership in Educational Management, 1988; Insights into Teachers' Thinking and Practice, 1990; Managing the Professional Development of Teachers, 1991; Research on Teacher Thinking, 1993; Children and Youth at Risk and Urban Education, 1997; Teachers and Teaching: international perspectives on school reform and teacher education, 1997; The Life and Work of Teachers in Changing Times: international perspectives, 1999; Developing Teachers and Teaching Practice, 2002; Theory and Practice in Action Research, 2002; (and contrib.) International Handbook of the Continuing Professional Development of Teachers, 2004; Successful Principal Leadership in Times of Change: an international perspective, 2007; International Handbook on Teacher and School Development, 2012; A Decade of Research on School Principals, 2016. *Recreations:* walking, tennis, reading, swimming. *Address:* School of Education, University of Nottingham, Jubilee Campus, Wollaton Road, Nottingham NG8 1BB. *T:* (0115) 951 4423.

**DAY, Prof. Christopher Paul,** MD, PhD; DL; FRCP, FRCPE, FMedSci; Vice Chancellor and President, Newcastle University, since 2017; *b* Darlington, 2 Feb. 1960; *s* of Raymond Day and June Day; *m*; one *s*; two *s* one *d* by former marriage. *Educ:* Churchill Coll., Cambridge (BA 1981; MB BChir 1983); Univ. of Newcastle upon Tyne (MD (with commendation) 1994; PhD 1994). MRCP 1986, FRCP 1998; FRCPE 2005. University of Newcastle upon Tyne, later Newcastle University: MRC Trng Fellow and Clinician Scientist, 1990–97; Prof. of Liver Medicine, 2000–16; Hd, Sch. of Clinical Med. Scis, 2004–08; Pro Vice-Chancellor, Faculty of Med. Scis, 2008–16; Hon. Consultant Hepatologist, Freeman Hosp., then Newcastle upon Tyne Hosps NHS Foundn Trust, 1995–2016. Mem., MRC, 2010–18. Vice Pres. (Clin.), Acad. of Med. Scis, 2014–17. Chair, OSCHR, 2018–. FMedSci 2008. DL Tyne and Wear, 2014. *Publications:* over 200 articles on all aspects of liver disease in jls incl. Lancet, New England Jl of Medicine, Nature Genetics; approx. 200 review articles. *Recreations:* playing guitar, tennis, golf. *Address:* Newcastle University, Newcastle upon Tyne NE1 7RU. *T:* (0191) 208 6064. *E:* chris.day@ncl.ac.uk. *Clubs:* Athenæum; Medical Pilgrims, 1942.

**DAY, Rev. David Vivian;** Principal, St John's College, University of Durham, 1993–99; non-stipendiary Curate, St Nicholas, Durham, since 1999; *b* 11 Aug. 1936; *s* of Frederick Vivian Day and Enid Blodwen (*née* Evans); *m* 1959, Lorna Rosemary Taylor; two *s* one *d*. *Educ:* The Grammar Sch., Tottenham; QMC, Univ. of London (BA Classics); Univ. of Nottingham (MEd, MTheol). Classics Master, Southgate County Sch., 1958–64; Head of Religious Education: Southgate Sch., 1964–66; Bilborough Sch., 1966–73; Sen. Lectr in Theol., Bishop Lonsdale Coll., Derby, 1973–79; Sen. Lectr in Educn, Univ. of Durham, 1979–97. Ordained deacon, 1999, priest, 2000. Lanfranc Award for Educn and Scholarship, 2016. *Publications:* This Jesus, 1980, 2nd edn 1981; Jeremiah: speaking for God in a time of crisis, 1987; Teenage Beliefs, 1991; (ed jtly) The Contours of Christian Education, 1992; Beyond the Here and Now, 1996; A Preaching Workbook, 1998, 4th edn 2004; Pearl beyond Price, 2002; Christ Our Life, 2003; (ed jtly) A Reader on Preaching, 2005; Embodying the Word, 2005. *Recreations:* watching Rugby and soccer, opera. *Address:* 35 Orchard Drive, The Sands, Durham DH1 1LA. *T:* (0191) 386 6909.

**DAY, Douglas Henry;** QC 1989; a Recorder, 1987–2015; *b* 11 Oct. 1943; *s* of James Henry Day and Nancy Day; *m* 1970, Elizabeth Margaret (*née* Jarman); two *s* one *d*. *Educ:* Bec Sch.; Selwyn Coll., Cambridge (MA). Called to the Bar, Lincoln's Inn, 1967, Bencher, 1996. Asst Parly Boundary Comr, 1994–. Treas., Gen. Council of the Bar, 1999–2001. *Address:* Farrar's Building, Temple, EC4Y 7BD. *T:* (020) 7583 9241. *Clubs:* Garrick; Bec Old Boys Rugby.

**DAY, Sir Graham;** see Day, Sir J. G.

**DAY, Dame (Henrietta Miriam) Ottoline;** see Leyser, Dame H. M. O.

**DAY, John Leigh,** MD; FRCP; Consultant Physician, Ipswich Hospital, 1972–2002, now Emeritus; *b* 30 Nov. 1939; *s* of Peter Leigh Day and Jean Metcalfe Bailey; *m* 1972, Anne Pamela Northcote; two *s* one *d*. *Educ:* King's Coll., London (MD 1973). FRCP 1979. Medical Registrar: Ipswich and E Suffolk Hosp., 1966; KCH, 1967; Lectr in Medicine, KCL; Clinical Dir of Medicine, Ipswich Hosp., 1998–2002; Prof. of Internal Medicine, Catholic Univ. of Mozambique, 2002–14. Advr on Educn, WHO, 1990–95. Chm., Educn Adv. Cttee, Diabetes UK, 1985–92; Pres., Diabetes Educn Study Gp, European Assoc. of Diabetes, 1985–92. Dir, Ipswich-Beira Health Initiative, 2003–. Hon. DSc UEA, 2000. *Publications:* Learning Diabetes Type 1, and Type 2 Diabetic, 1986, 3rd edn 2001; res. articles in Diabetes Educn and Care, Diabetes Medicine, Patient Educn and Counselling, BMJ. *Recreations:* golf, canal boating. *E:* days_bealings@hotmail.com.

**DAY, Air Chief Marshal Sir John (Romney),** KCB 1999; OBE 1985; FCGI; Senior Military Adviser, BAE Systems, 2003–10; *b* 15 July 1947; *er s* of John George Day and Daphne Myrtle Day (*née* Kelly); *m* 1969, Jane Richards; two *s*. *Educ:* King's Sch., Canterbury; Imperial Coll., Univ. of London (BSc Aer. Eng.). No 72 Sqn, 1970–73; Flying Instructor, RAF Linton-on-Ouse, 1973–76; OC Oxford Univ. Air Sqn, 1976–79; RAF Staff Coll., 1981; PSO to Air Mem. for Personnel, 1982–83; OC No 72 Sqn, 1983–85; OC RAF Odiham, 1987–89; RCDS, 1990; Dir, Air Force Plans and Progs, MoD, 1991–94; AOC No 1 Gp, 1994–97; DCDS (Commitments), MoD, 1997–2000; AMP and C-in-C, RAF PTC, 2000–01; C-in-C Strike Comd, 2001–03; Air ADC to the Queen, 2001–03. Chm. Trustees, Hants and Isle of Wight Air Ambulance Charity, 2017–. FCGI 2002. *Address:* c/o Lloyds Bank, Ashford, Kent TN24 8SS. *Club:* Royal Air Force.
*See also Air Vice Marshal N. J. Day.*

**DAY, Sir Jonathan Stephen, (Sir Jon),** Kt 2016; CBE 1999; Chairman, Joint Intelligence Committee, Cabinet Office, 2012–15; Director, Centre for Security Studies, University of Southampton, since 2017; *b* 23 April 1954; *s* of late Peter Alan John Day and Josephine Day; *m* 1980, Sandra Ayres; one *d*. *Educ:* Marling Sch., Stroud; Univ. of Nottingham (LLB Hons 1976). Ministry of Defence: admin trainee, 1979; early posts included Naval, out-of-area and policy studies secretariats, and Asst Private Sec. to Armed Forces Minister; seconded: to FCO in UK Delegn to NATO, Brussels, 1988–92; to NATO as Hd, Force Planning, 1992–95; Dep. Comd Sec., Land Comd, 1995–97; Dir, Defence Policy, 1997–99; sabbatical, Harvard Univ., 1999–2000; seconded: to Cabinet Office as Chief, Jt Intelligence Cttee Assessments Staff, 2000–01; to NATO as Dir, Sec. Gen.'s Private Office, 2001–03; Comd Sec., Fleet Comd, 2004–06; Dir, Operational Policy, 2007–08, Dir Gen., then Dir,

Security Policy, 2008–11, Second Permanent Sec., 2011–12; MoD. Hon. Prof., Strategy and Security Inst., Univ. of Exeter, 2012–. *Publications*: Gloucester and Newbury 1643, Turning Point of the Civil War, 2007. *Recreations*: history, reading, theatre and cinema, cricket, walking, unsuitably juvenile loud music. *E*: dayjands54@yahoo.com.

**DAY, Sir (Judson) Graham**, Kt 1989; OC 2014; Chairman, PowerGen, 1990–93 (Director, 1990–93); *b* 3 May 1933; *s* of Frank Charles Day and Edythe Grace (*née* Baker); *m* 1958, Leda Ann (*née* Creighton); one *s* two *d*. *Educ*: Queen Elizabeth High Sch., Halifax, NS; Dalhousie Univ., Halifax, NS (LLB). Private practice of Law, Windsor, Nova Scotia, 1956–64; Canadian Pacific Ltd, Montreal and Toronto, 1964–71; Chief Exec., Cammell Laird Shipbuilders Ltd, Birkenhead, Eng., 1971–75; Dep. Chm., Organising Cttee for British Shipbuilders and Dep. Chm. and Chief Exec. designate, British Shipbuilders, 1975–76; Prof. of Business Admin and Dir, Canadian Marine Transportation Centre, Dalhousie Univ., NS, 1977–81; Vice-Pres., Shipyards & Marine Develt, Dome Petroleum Ltd, 1981–83; Chm. and Chief Exec., British Shipbuilders, 1983–86; Chief Exec., 1986–88, Chm., 1986–91, BL, subseq. The Rover Gp Hldgs. Chm., Cadbury Schweppes, 1989–93 (Dir, 1988–93); Deputy Chairman: MAI plc, 1989–93 (Dir, 1988–93); Ugland Internat. Hldgs plc, 1997; Director: The Laird Gp plc, 1985; British Aerospace, 1986–92 (Chairman, 1991–92); Extendicare (formerly Crownx) Inc. (Canada), 1989; Bank of Nova Scotia (Canada), 1989–2004; NOVA Corp. of Alberta, 1990; EMI Gp, 1991; Empire Co. Ltd, 1991–2006; Sobeys Inc., 1998–2005. Counsel, Stewart McKelvey (formerly Stewart McKelvey Stirling Scales), 1991. Pres., ISBA, 1991–93. Member: Nova Scotia Barristers' Soc.; Law Soc. of Upper Canada; Canadian Bar Assoc. Freeman, City of London. ARINA. Hon. Fellow, Univ. of Wales Coll. of Cardiff, 1990. Hon. doctorates: Dalhousie; City; CNAA; Cranfield; Aston; Warwick; Humberside; South Bank. Order of Nova Scotia, 2011. *Recreation*: reading. *Address*: 162 Avon Street, PO Box 422, Hantsport, NS B0P 1P0, Canada.

**DAY, Martyn**; MP (SNP) Linlithgow and East Falkirk, since 2015; *b* Falkirk, 26 March 1971. Former bank worker. Mem. (SNP), W Lothian Council, 1999–2015. Member: Public Accounts Cttee, 2016–; Petitions Cttee, 2017–. *Address*: House of Commons, SW1A 0AA.

**DAY, Sir Michael (John)**, Kt 1992; OBE 1981; Chairman, Commission for Racial Equality, 1988–93; *b* 4 Sept. 1933; *s* of Albert Day and Ellen Florence (*née* Itter); *m* 1960, June Marjorie (*d* 2018), *d* of late Dr John William and Edith Mackay; one *s* one *d*. *Educ*: University College Sch., Hampstead; Selwyn Coll., Cambridge (MA); London School of Economics (Cert. Social Work and Social Admin). Probation Officer, Surrey, 1960–64; Sen. Probation Officer, W Sussex, 1964–67; Asst Prin. Probation Officer, 1967–68, Chief Probation Officer, 1968–76, Surrey; Chief Probation Officer, W Midlands, 1976–88. Chm., Chief Probation Officers' Conf., 1974–77; First Chm., Assoc. Chief Officers of Probation, 1982–84. Member: Probation Adv. and Trng Bd, Home Office, 1970–73; Adv. Council for Probation and Aftercare, 1973–78. Member Council: Howard League for Penal Reform, 1966–73; Volunteer Centre, 1977–81; Grubb Inst., 1980–93. Dir, Shropshire and Mid Wales Hospice, 1998–2003. *Publications*: contribs to professional jls and others. *Recreations*: family and friends, gardening, the countryside, turning wood and pages. *Address*: 30 Broad Street, Ludlow, Shropshire SY8 1NJ.
*See also R. M. Gordon Clark.*

**DAY, Michael Patrick**, CVO 2015; Chief Executive, Historic Royal Palaces, 2003–17; *b* 20 Feb. 1953; *s* of Harry and Anne Day; *m* 1998, Anne Murch; one *s* one *d*. *Educ*: Nottingham High Sch.; Univ. of Leeds (BA Hons (English) 1974). Graduate trainee, Mus. Asst, then Asst Keeper of Social Hist., Norfolk Mus Service, 1974–83; Curator of Social Hist., Ironbridge Gorge Mus. Trust, 1983–86; Dir, Jersey Heritage Trust, 1987–2003. Mem. Faculty, Mus. Leadership Prog., UEA, 1994–2011; Co-Dir, Nordic Mus. Leadership Prog., Copenhagen, 2001–08; Mem. Bd, Cultural Leadership Prog., 2009–11. Vice Pres., Assoc. of Ind. Museums, 2016–. Vis. Prof., Univ. of Illinois, 2017. Trustee: Alnwick Garden Trust, 2010–13; Nat. Trust, 2016–; Chm., Battersea Arts Centre, 2012–18. FMA 1994; FRSA 1995; FCMI (FIMgt 1999); CCMI 2007. Hon. DArts Kingston, 2010. *Recreations*: family and friends, ski-ing, Real tennis, mountain walking, cycling, sailing (Mem., National 12 Owners' Association), cinema. *Address*: 1 Tudor Avenue, Hampton, Middx TW12 2ND. *T*: 07717 581632. *Clubs*: Ski Club of Great Britain; Royal Tennis Court (Chm., 2017–).

**DAY, Prof. Nicholas Edward**, CBE 2001; PhD; FRS 2004; FRCPath, FMedSci; MRC Research Professor in Epidemiology, 1999–2004, and Fellow of Hughes Hall, since 1992, University of Cambridge; *b* 24 Sept. 1939; *s* of late John King Day, TD and Mary Elizabeth (*née* Stinton); *m* 1961, Jocelyn Deanne Broughton; one *s* one *d*. *Educ*: Magdalen Coll., Oxford (BA Maths); Aberdeen Univ. (PhD Med. Stats). FRCPath 1997. Res. Fellow, Aberdeen Univ., 1962–66; Fellow, ANU, 1966–69; Statistician, 1969–78, Head, Unit of Biostats and Field Studies, 1979–86, Internat. Agency for Res. on Cancer, Lyon; Cancer Expert, Nat. Cancer Inst., USA, 1978–79; Dir, 1986–89, Hon. Dir, 1989–99, MRC Biostats Unit; Prof. of Public Health, Cambridge Univ., 1989–99; Fellow, Churchill Coll., Cambridge, 1986–92. Founder FMedSci 1998. *Publications*: Statistical Methods in Cancer Research, vol. 1 1980, vol. 2 1988; Screening for Cancer of the Uterine Cervix, 1986; Screening for Breast Cancer, 1988; over 300 articles in scientific jls. *Recreations*: sea fishing, fruit growing. *Address*: Seawinds Les Jardins, Rue de la Lague, St Pierre du Bois, Guernsey GY7 9BU. *T*: (01481) 267257.

**DAY, Air Vice Marshal Nigel James**, CBE 2000; Senior Defence Adviser, MBDA Missile Systems, 2004–13; *b* 13 Feb. 1949; *s* of John George Day and Daphne Myrtle Day (*née* Kelly); *m* 1971, Gillian Cronk; one *s* one *d*. *Educ*: King's Sch., Canterbury; Imperial Coll., Univ. of London (BSc). No 45 Sqn, 1974; No 17 Sqn, 1975–76; No 31 Sqn, 1976–78; No 725 Sqn, Royal Danish Air Force, 1979–81; Flight Comdr, No 226 (Jaguar) OCU, 1982–83; RAF Staff Coll., 1984; Operational Requirements Staff, MoD, 1985–87; OC No 617 (DamBusters) Sqn, 1987–90; Air Offensive Staff, MoD, 1990–93; OC RAF Lossiemouth, 1993–95; rcds, 1996; OC Brit. Forces, Gulf Region, 1997; Dir, Air Ops, Strike Command, 1997–99; Dep. UK Mil. Rep. to NATO, 1999–2001; Capability Manager (Strike), MoD, 2001–04. *Recreations*: dog walking, sailing, painting. *Club*: Royal Air Force.
*See also Air Chief Marshal Sir J. R. Day.*

**DAY, Penelope Jane, (Penny)**; *see* Dyer, P. J.

**DAY, Prof. Peter**, DPhil; FRS 1986; FRSC, FInstP; Fullerian Professor of Chemistry, Royal Institution, 1994–2008, now Emeritus; Emeritus Professor of Chemistry, University of London, since 2008; Royal Institution Professorial Research Fellow, University College London, since 1995 (Honorary Fellow, 2003); *b* 20 Aug. 1938; *s* of Edgar Day and Ethel Hilda Day (*née* Russell); *m* 1964, Frances Mary Elizabeth Anderson (*d* 2018); one *s* one *d*. *Educ*: Maidstone Grammar School; Wadham College, Oxford (BA 1961; MA, DPhil 1965; Hon. Fellow, 1991). FInstP 1996. Cyanamid European Research Institute, Geneva, 1962; Jun. Res. Fellow, 1963–65, Official Fellow, 1965–91, Hon. Fellow, 1994, St John's College, Oxford; Departmental Demonstrator, 1965–67, Lectr in Inorganic Chemistry, 1967–89, *ad hominem* Prof. of Solid State Chemistry, 1989–91, Oxford Univ. Dir, Inst. Laue-Langevin, Grenoble, 1988–91 (on secondment); Royal Institution: Dir, 1991–98; Resident Prof. of Chemistry, 1991–94; Dir, Davy Faraday Res. Lab., 1991–98. Prof. Associé, Univ. de Paris-Sud, 1975; Prof. Invité, Univ. Rennes, 1997; Guest Prof., Univ. of Copenhagen, 1978; Iberdrola Prof., Univ. of Valencia, 2001. Vis. Fellow, ANU, 1980; Senior Research Fellow, SRC, 1977–82. Lectures: Du Pont, Indiana Univ., 1988; Royal Soc. Blackett Meml, 1994; Bakerian, 1999; ACL, Chinese Univ. Hong Kong, 1997; Birch, ANU, 1997; Humphry Davy, Royal Soc., 2002; Stefan, Stefan Inst., Ljubjana, 2010; Coochbehaar, Indian Assoc. for Cultivation of Sci., Kolkata, 2010. Science and Engineering Research Council: Member: Neutron Beam Res. Cttee, 1983–88; Chemistry Cttee, 1985–88; Molecular Electronics Cttee, 1987–88; Nat. Cttee on Superconductivity, 1987–88; Materials Commn, 1988–90. British Council: Mem., Sci. and Engrg Cttee, 1991–98; Chm., Anglo-French Res. Grants Cttee, 1995–98; Member: COPUS, 1991–98; EC DG Res. Infrastructures Panel, 1992–98; Phys. and Engrg Sci. Cttee, ESF, 1994–2000; Medicines Commn, 1998–2005; Adv. Council, RIKEN Advanced Sci. Inst., Tokyo, 2009–12; Council Member: Inst. for Molecular Scis, Okazaki, Japan, 1991–95; Parly and Scientific Cttee, 1992–98; Internat. Advr, Tohoku Univ., Sendai, 2008–10. Royal Society of Chemistry: Vice-Pres., Dalton Div., 1986–88; Sci. Adv. Ed., Jl of Material Chemistry, 1996–2004; Corday-Morgan Medal, 1971; Solid State Chem. Award, 1986; Daiwa Adrian Prize, Daiwa Foundn, 1998. Governor: Sevenoaks Sch., 1977–88; Birkbeck Coll., London, 1993–2001. Vice Pres., Jury, LABEX, Agence Nationale de Recherche, France, 2011. Mem., Academia Europaea, 1992 (Mem. Council, 2000–09; Treas., 2000–09; Trustee, 2002–09). Fellow, Internat. Union of Pure and Applied Chem., 2009. Hon. Foreign Mem., Indian Soc. of Materials Res., 1994. Hon. Fellow, Indian Acad. of Sci., 1995. Hon. DSc: Newcastle, 1994; Kent, 1999. *Publications*: Physical Methods in Advanced Inorganic Chemistry (ed with H. A. O. Hill), 1968; Electronic States of Inorganic Compounds, 1974; Emission and Scattering Techniques, 1980; Electronic Structure and Magnetism of Inorganic Compounds, vols 1–7, 1972–82; (ed with A. K. Cheetham) Solid State Chemistry, vol. 1 1987, vol. 2 1992; The Philosopher's Tree, 1999; Nature Not Mocked, 2006; Molecules into Materials, 2007; On the Cucumber Tree, 2012; papers in Jl Chem. Soc.; Inorg. Chem. *Recreation*: cultivating gardens (horticultural and Voltairean). *Address*: Department of Chemistry, University College London, 20 Gordon Street, WC1H 0AJ; Field House, Marsh Baldon, Oxford OX44 9LL.

**DAY, Peter Rodney**, PhD; Founding Director, Biotechnology Center for Agriculture and the Environment (formerly Center for Agricultural Molecular Biology), Rutgers University, New Jersey, 1987–2001; *b* 27 Dec. 1928; *s* of Roland Percy Day and Florence Kate (*née* Dixon); *m* 1950, Lois Elizabeth Rhodes (*d* 2018); two *s* one *d*. *Educ*: Birkbeck Coll., Univ. of London (BSc); John Innes Inst. and Univ. of London (PhD). John Innes Institute, 1946–63; Associate Prof. of Botany, Ohio State Univ., 1963–64; Chief, Dept of Genetics, Connecticut Agricl Experiment Station, 1964–79; Dir, Plant Breeding Inst., Cambridge, 1979–87. Sec., Internat. Genetics Fedn, 1984–93. Special Prof. of Botany, Nottingham Univ., 1982–88. Commonwealth Fund Fellow, 1954; John Simon Guggenheim Meml Fellow, 1973. *Publications*: Fungal Genetics (with J. R. S. Fincham), 1963, 4th edn 1979; Genetics of Host-Parasite Interaction, 1974; (with H. H. Prell) Plant-Fungal Pathogen Interaction, 2001; contrib. Genetical Research, Genetics, Heredity, Nature, Proc. Nat. Acad. Sci., Phytopathology, etc. *Recreations*: Scottish country dancing, bird watching. *Address*: 8200 Tarsier Avenue, New Port Richey, FL 34653–6559, USA. *E*: p1rd@verizon.net.

**DAY, Richard D.**; *see* Digby Day.

**DAY, Rosemary**; Trustee: Chiswick House and Grounds Trust, since 2005; Plant Heritage, since 2017; I Fagiolini Charitable Trust, since 2018; *b* 20 Sept. 1942; *d* of Albert Rich and Alice Rich (*née* Wren); *m* (marr. diss.). *Educ*: Bedford Coll., Univ. of London (BA Hons 1964); Birkbeck, Univ. of London (MA 2011). ATII 1978. Asst Dir Gen., GLC, 1964–83; Admin. Dir, London Transport, 1983–88; Ops Dir, Allied Dunbar, 1988–94; Chm., London Ambulance Service, 1995–99. Non-executive Director: Nationwide Building Soc., 1984–88; Milk Mktg Bd, 1993–95; London Transport, 1994–99; Govt Offices Mgt Bd, 1996–98; NATS, 1997–2001; UKAEA, 1999–2006; Picker Inst. Europe, 2002–05; NI Dept of Regl Develt, 2007–08. Member: Legal Aid Adv. Bd, 1992–94; Sen. Salaries Review Body, 1994–2000. Chm., Joyful Company of Singers, 1988–2001. Trustee, Railway Children, 1999–2015. Chm. Govs, Hounslow Town Primary Sch., 2001–10. CCMI (CBIM 1984); FRSA. *Recreations*: economic and architectural research, the arts, gardening, books. *Address*: 63a Barrowgate Road, W4 4QT.

**DAY, Sir Simon (James)**, Kt 1997; farmer; *b* 22 Jan. 1935; *s* of late John Adam Day and Kathleen Day (*née* Hebditch); *m* 1959, Hilary Maureen Greenslade Gomm; two *s* (and one *s* decd). *Educ*: S Devon Tech. Coll.; Emmanuel Coll., Cambridge (MA Hist.). Nat. Service, RN, 1954–56. Devon County Council: Councillor, Modbury Div., 1964–74, Modbury and Salcombe Div., 1974–2005, Thurlestone, Salcombe and Allington Div., 2005–13; Whip, 1981–89; Dep. Leader, 1989, Leader, 1991–93; Opposition Leader, 1993–99; Chm., 2001–02. Non-exec. Dir, SW Water, 1989–98; Regl Dir, Portman Building Soc., 1989–91; Director: Plymouth Sound Radio, 1966–80; Plymouth Develt Corp., 1993–96; Exeter Internat. Airport, 1997–2006; Chm., West of England Newspapers Gp, 1981–86. Mem., Exec. Council, ACC, 1981–85, 1990–96 (Chm., Police Cttee, 1991–93; Dep. Leader, 1992; Vice Chm., 1993–95; Cons. Leader, 1993–95); Chm., Devon and Cornwall Police Authy, 1990–93; Member: Police Adv. Bd, Home Office, 1989–93; Police Negotiating Bd, 1989–93; Chairman: Devon Sea Fisheries Cttee, 1986–95; Assoc. of Sea Fisheries Cttees, England and Wales, 1993–96 (Vice-Chm., 1991–93); Mem., Govt Salmon Adv. Cttee, 1987–90; Chm., Devon and Cornwall Develt Bureau, 1989–91; Vice Chairman: Nat. Parks Cttee for England and Wales, 1981–83; Local Govt Finance Cttee, 1983–85; Member: Consultative Council, Local Govt Finance, 1983–85 and 1993; Standing Conf. of Local and Regl Authies, Council of Europe, 1990–97; Cttee of Regions, EU, 1994–97, 1998–2001, 2002–05, 2006–13 (Vice-Chm., UK Delegn, 2006–13); Chm., Cons. Nat. Local Govt Adv. Cttee, 1994–95; Cons. Leader, 2004, Vice Chm., 2004–08, Chm., 2008–09, SW Regl Assembly. President: S Devon Herd Book Soc., 1986; Devon Co. Show, 2006–07. Chm. Govs, Bicton Coll. of Agric., 1983–2000. Trustee, West Country Rivers Trust, 1997–. Mem. Count, Exeter Univ., 1964–2009. Pres., Devon County LTA, 2002–. Contested (C): Carmarthen, 1966, by-election 1966; N Cornwall, 1970. High Sheriff, Devon, 1999–2000. Hereditary Freeman, City of Norwich. *Recreations*: shooting, sailing, fishing. *Address*: Keaton House, near Ivybridge, Devon PL21 0LB. *T*: (01752) 691212. *Clubs*: Buck's, Beefsteak, Royal Thames Yacht; Royal Yacht Squadron; Hawks (Cambridge) (Hon. Mem., 1995).

**DAY, Stephen Nicholas**; a District Judge (Magistrates' Courts) (formerly Stipendiary Magistrate), Middlesex, 1991–2017; a Deputy District Judge, since 2017; *b* 17 Aug. 1947; *s* of late Robert Weatherston Day and Margaret Diana (*née* McKenzie); *m* 1973, Shama (*née* Tak); one *s* one *d*. *Educ*: St Mary's Coll., Southampton; King Edward VI Sch., Southampton; Brasenose Coll., Oxford (MA). Called to the Bar, Middle Temple, 1972. Trainee, Berks Magistrates' Courts Cttee, 1969–73; Sen. Court Clerk, Nottingham, 1973–77; Justices Clerk, Abingdon, Didcot and Wantage, 1977–91. Member: Gtr London Magistrates' Courts Authy, 2002–05; Sentencing Adv. Panel, Sentencing Guidelines Council, 2006–08. *Club*: Oxford and Cambridge.

**DAY, Stephen Peter,** CMG 1989; HM Diplomatic Service, retired; consultant, Middle East affairs; *b* 19 Jan. 1938; *s* of Frank William and Mary Elizabeth Day; *m* 1965, Angela Doreen (*née* Waudby); one *s* two *d*. *Educ*: Bancroft's School; Corpus Christi Coll., Cambridge. MA. Entered HMOCS as Political Officer, Western Aden Protectorate, 1961, transf. to FO, 1965; Senior Political Officer, South Arabian Federation, 1964–67; FO, 1967–70; First Sec., Office of C-in-C, Far East, Singapore, 1970–71; First Sec. (Press), UK Mission to UN, NY, 1971–75; FCO, 1976–77; Counsellor, Beirut, 1977–78; Consul-Gen., Edmonton, 1979–81; Ambassador to Qatar, 1981–84; Head of ME Dept, FCO, 1984–87; attached to Household of the Prince of Wales, 1986; Ambassador to Tunisia, 1987–92; Sen. British Trade Comr, Hong Kong, 1992–93; Dir, Council for Advancement of Arab-British Understanding, 1993–94. Dir, Claremont Associates, 1995–. Mem., Exec. Cttee, Soc. for Arabian Studies, 1995–2000. Chairman: British-Tunisian Soc., 1993–2008; Palestine Exploration Fund, 1995–2000; British-Yemeni Soc., 1998–99; MBI Trust, SOAS, 2000–03; MBI Foundn, 2002–07. Governor, Qatar Academy, 1996–2002. Comdr, Order of the Republic (Tunisia), 2002. *Publications*: At Home in Carthage, 1991. *Recreations*: walking, family. *Address*: Stedham Lodge, The Highlands, East Horsley, Surrey KT24 5BG. *T*: (01483) 281880, 07971 806677. *E*: s.day@claremontassociates.net. *Club*: Hong Kong.

**DAY, Stephen Richard;** political columnist, Cyprus Today, since 2006; *b* 30 Oct. 1948; *s* of late Francis and of Anne Day; one *s* by former marriage. *Educ*: Otley Secondary Modern Sch.; Park Lane Coll., Leeds; Leeds Polytechnic. MIEx 1972. Sales Clerk, William Sinclair & Sons, stationery manufrs, Otley, W Yorks, 1965–70, Asst Sales Manager (working in Home and Export Depts), 1970–77; Sales Representative: Larkfield Printing Co. Ltd (part of Hunting Group), Brighouse, W Yorks, 1977–80; A. H. Leach & Co. (part of Hunting Gp), photographic processing lab., Brighouse, 1980–84; Sales Executive: PPL Chromacopy, photographic labs, Leeds and Manchester, 1984–86; Chromogene, photographic lab., Leeds, 1986–87; self-employed public affairs consultant, 2001–06. Vice-President: Stockport Chamber of Commerce, 1987–2001; Stockport and Dist Heart Foundn, 1985–2001. Chm., Yorks Area Cons. Political Centre, 1983–86; Vice-Chm., NW Leeds Constituency, 1983–86. Town Councillor, Otley, 1975–76 and 1979–83; City Councillor, Leeds, 1975–80. Contested (C): Bradford West, 1983; Cheadle, 2001; Prospective Parly Cand. (C) Cheadle, 2002–05. MP (C) Cheadle, 1987–2001. An Opposition Whip, 1997–2001. Member: Select Cttee on Social Security, 1990–97; Select Cttee on Envmt, Transport and Regions, 1997; Co-Chm., Parly Adv. Council for Transport Safety, 1989–97; Vice-Chm., All-Party Non-Profit-Making Clubs Gp, 1995–2001; Co-Chm., All-Party West Coast Main Line Gp, 1993–2001. Sponsor, Private Member's Bill to introduce compulsory wearing of rear car seat belts by children, enacted into law 1988. Mem., Cheadle Hulme Cons. Club, 1987–2006; Vice-Chm., CPA (UK), 1996–97; Nat. Chm., Assoc. of Cons. Clubs, 1997–2006 (Vice-Chm., 1995–97). Pres., Council of Registered Club Assocs, 2002–06. Mem., Bramhall and Woodford Rotary Club, 2001–06; Pres., Cheadle Hulme Br., RBL, 2001–06. Mem. Chm., British Residents Soc. (N Cyprus), 2014–17 (Vice Chm., 2009–10; Actg Chm., 2010–11; Chm., 2011–12). *Publications*: pamphlets on Otley and on rate reform. *Recreations*: movies, music, history (particularly Roman).

**DAY, William,** PhD; CPhys; Editor-in-Chief, Biosystems Engineering, since 2007; *b* 11 June 1949; *s* of late Arthur Thomas Day and Barbara Nan Day; *m* 1973, Virginia Lesley Elisabeth Playford; two *s* one *d*. *Educ*: Norwich Sch.; Gonville and Caius Coll., Cambridge (MA Natural Scis (Physics)); PhD Physics Cantab 1974. CPhys 1980. Higher Scientific Officer, SSO, then PSO, Physics Dept, Rothamsted Exptl Stn, 1974–81 Head: Envmtl Physiol. Gp, Long Ashton Res. Stn, 1982–83; Physiology and Envmtl Physics Dept, Rothamsted Exptl Stn, 1983–88; Process Engrg Div., Silsoe Res. Inst., 1988–99; Dir, Silsoe Res. Inst., BBSRC, 1999–2006. Special Prof. of Agricl Engrg, Univ. of Nottingham, 1993–2002; Vis. Prof., Cranfield Univ. at Silsoe, 2003–07. *Publications*: contribs relating to interaction between biological systems and envmt in numerous jls, include. Jl Agricl Sci., Agricl and Forest Meteorol. and Phytopathol. *Recreations*: bird watching, choral singing, tandem-ing.

**DAY, William Michael;** Fellow, Cambridge Institute for Sustainability Leadership (formerly University of Cambridge Programme for Industry, then Cambridge Programme for Sustainability Leadership), since 2013 (Senior Associate, 2003–13); Sustainability Advisor, PricewaterhouseCoopers, since 2008; Chair, Sainsbury's Foundation Advisory Board, since 2017; *b* 26 June 1956; *s* of Sir Derek Malcolm Day, KCMG and Sheila Margaret Day (*née* Nott); *m* 1986, Kate Gardener; one *s* two *d*. *Educ*: Univ. of Exeter (BA). Save the Children Fund: Uganda, 1983; Ethiopia, 1983–84; Sudan, 1984–86; BBC World Service for Africa, 1986–87; Oxfam, Ethiopia, 1987–88; Grants Dir for Africa, Charity Projects/Comic Relief, 1988–94; Dir, Opportunity Trust, 1994–96; Chief Exec., CARE International UK, 1996–2004. Non-exec. Dir, S Kent Hosps NHS Trust, 1994–96. Public Appts Ind. Assessor, DCMS, 1999–2008; Member: Corporate Responsibility Adv. Gp, ICAEW, 2011–14; Corporate Responsibility Panel, British Land, 2012–14; Council, ODI, 2000–12 (Chm., 2012); Adv. Bd, SEE Change Net, 2012–; Bd, SDGLead, 2016–; Sustainability Adv. Bd, Procter & Gamble, 2016–17; Special Advr, UNDP, 2004–11; Chairman: Sustainable Develt Commn, 2009–11; Water and Sanitation for the Urban Poor, 2006–18. Member: BBC Central Appeals Cttee, 1992–2003 (Chm., 1997–2003); Grants Council, Charities Aid Foundn, 1990–94; Globalisation and Global Poverty Commn, 2006; Ramphal Centre Commn on Migration and Develt, 2010–11; Council of Ambassadors, WWF (UK), 2011–. Chm., On Purpose, 2016–; Co-Chair, Kent Local Nature Partnership, 2014–17; Trustee: BBC Children in Need, 1998–2008 (Chm., 2006–08); Disasters Emergency Cttee, 1998–2004. *Address*: Pilgrims, Hastingleigh, Ashford, Kent TN25 5HP. *T*: (01233) 750196. *E*: william.day@phonecoop.coop.

**DAY-LEWIS, Sir Daniel,** Kt 2014; actor; *s* of late Cecil Day-Lewis, CBE, CLit and Jill Angela Henriette Balcon; *m* 1996, Rebecca, *d* of Arthur Miller, playwright; two *s*. *Educ*: Bedales; Bristol Old Vic Theatre Sch. *Stage*: The Recruiting Officer, Troilus and Cressida, Funny Peculiar, Old King Cole, A Midsummer Night's Dream, Class Enemy, Edward II, Oh! What a Lovely War, Look Back in Anger, Dracula, Another Country, Romeo and Juliet, The Futurists, Hamlet; *films*: Gandhi, 1981; The Saga of HMS Bounty, 1983; My Beautiful Laundrette, 1985; A Room With a View, 1985; Nanou, 1985; The Unbearable Lightness of Being, 1986; Stars and Bars, 1987; My Left Foot, 1988 (Oscar best actor and numerous other awards); Ever Smile New Jersey, 1988; Last of the Mohicans, 1991 (Variety Club best actor); Age of Innocence, 1992; In the Name of the Father, 1993; The Crucible, 1997; The Boxer, 1998; Gangs of New York, 2002; The Ballad of Jack and Rose, 2006; There Will Be Blood, 2008 (Oscar and BAFTA for best actor); Nine, 2009; Lincoln, 2013 (Oscar, BAFTA and Golden Globe for best actor); Phantom Thread, 2018; principal roles in TV. *Address*: c/o Julian Belfrage Associates, 3rd Floor, 9 Argyll Street, W1F 7TG.

**DAY-LEWIS, Séan;** journalist and author; *b* 3 Aug. 1931; *s* of late Cecil Day-Lewis, CBE, CLit and Mary Day-Lewis; *m* 1960, Anna Mott; one *s* one *d*. *Educ*: Allhallows Sch., Rousdon, Devon. National Service, RAF, 1949–51. Bridport News, 1952–53; Southern Times, Weymouth, 1953–54; Herts Advertiser, St Albans, 1954–56; Express and Star, Wolverhampton, 1956–60; The Daily Telegraph, 1960–86 (first nat. newspaper Arts Reporter, 1965–70; TV and Radio Editor, 1970–86); TV Editor, London Daily News, 1987; TV Critic, Country Life, 1989–2003. Arts Editor, Socialist Commentary, 1966–71; Founder-Chm., 1975, Chm., 1990–92, BPG; Vice Pres., Bulleid Soc., 1970; Member, BAFTA, 1976. *Publications*: Bulleid: last giant of steam, 1964; C. Day-Lewis: an English literary life, 1980; (ed) One Day in the Life of Television, 1989; TV Heaven: a review of British television from the 1930s to the 1990s, 1992; Talk of Drama: views of the television dramatist now and then, 1998. *Recreations*: music (J. S. Bach preferred), reading the Guardian and books, giving in to temptation. *Address*: Restorick Row, Rosemary Lane, Colyton, Devon EX24 6LW. *T*: (01297) 553039. *E*: seandaylewis@gmail.com.

**DAYAN, Edouard;** Director General, International Bureau, Universal Postal Union, 2005–12. La Poste, France: Hd, Air Transport Bureau, 1984–86; Manager, Dept of Internat. Mail Mgt and Internat. Accounting, then Internat. Partnership Strategy Dept, 1986–92; European Commission: expert, 1992–93; Dep. Dir, 1993–97, Dir, 1998–2005, Eur. and Internat. Affairs. Chm., Eur. Social Dialogue Cttee for postal sector, 1994–; former Mem., Mgt Bd, PostEurop; Universal Postal Union: Chm., Tech. Co-operation Action Gp; Chm., Bd of Trustees, Quality Service Fund. Chevalier: Ordre national du Mérite (France), 1995; Légion d'Honneur (France), 2001. *Address*: c/o Universal Postal Union, Weltpoststrasse 4, 3000 Bern 15, Switzerland.

**DAYKIN, Christopher David,** CB 1993; FIA; Government Actuary, 1989–2007; *b* 18 July 1948; *s* of John Francis Daykin and Mona Daykin; *m* 1977, Kathryn Ruth (*née* Tingey); two *s* one *d*. *Educ*: Merchant Taylors' Sch., Northwood; Pembroke Coll., Cambridge (BA 1970, MA 1973). FIA 1973. Government Actuary's Department, 1970; VSO, Brunei, 1971; Govt Actuary's Dept, 1972–78; Principal (Health and Social Services), HM Treasury, 1978–80; Govt Actuary's Dept, 1980–2007, Principal Actuary, 1982–84, Directing Actuary (Social Security), 1985–89. Mem., Council, Inst. of Actuaries, 1985–99 (Hon. Sec., 1988–90; Vice Pres., 1993–94; Pres., 1994–96); Chm., Internat. Forum of Actuarial Assocs, 1996–97; Chm., Perm. Cttee for Statistical, Actuarial and Financial Studies, ISSA, 1992–2007; Vice Chm., 2008–10, Chm., 2010–11, Groupe Consultatif Actuariel Européen (Chm., Educn Cttee, 1992–2007). Mem. Pensions Observatory, EC Commn, 1992–96. Chm., CS Insce Soc., 1991–. Visiting Professor: City Univ., 1997–; Shanghai Univ. of Finance and Econs, 1998–. Treasurer, Emmanuel Church, Northwood, 1982–87 and 1998–; Chm., VSO Harrow and Hillingdon, 1976–91. Hon. DSc City, 1995. *Publications*: Practical Risk Theory, 1993; articles and papers on pensions, demography, consumer credit, social security and insurance. *Recreations*: travel, photography, languages. *Address*: c/o Institute and Faculty of Actuaries, 7th Floor, Holborn Gate, 326–330 High Holborn, WC1V 7PP.

**DAYMAN, Stephen John,** MBE 2011; Executive Founder, Meningitis Now, since 2013; *b* Dursley, Glos, 17 April 1948; *s* of Fredrick and Patricia Dayman; *m* 1968, Gloria Clements; three *s* two *d* (and one *s* decd). *Educ*: Wotton under Edge Secondary Modern Sch. Founding Chm., Meningitis Trust, 1986–89; Founder: Meningitis Res. Foundn, 1989–97; Spencer Dayman Meningitis UK, 1999–2013. Hon LLD Bristol, 2014. *Recreation*: football (Manchester United and Bristol Rovers). *Address*: Homeside, Old Gloucester Road, Alveston, Bristol BS35 3LQ. *T*: (01454) 413344. *E*: Steve.Dayman@btinternet.com.

**DAYMOND, Nicholas Joseph;** Headmaster, Parmiter's School, 2010–17; *b* London, 3 Jan. 1962; *s* of Mark and Margot Daymond; *m* 1992, Kate Randall; one *s* one *d*. *Educ*: St Paul's Sch., Barnes; Queens' Coll., Cambridge (BA Hons Langs and Theol. 1983); Homerton Coll., Cambridge (PGCE 1985). NPQH 2003. Teacher of Modern Foreign Langs, Goffs Sch., Cheshunt, 1985–98; Dep. Headteacher, Beaumont Sch., St Albans, 1999–2003; Headteacher, Roundwood Park Sch., Harpenden, 2004–10. Nat. Leader of Educn, 2012–. *Publications*: (contrib.) The Parentalk Guide to Secondary School, 2005. *Recreations*: theatre, cinema, reading, travel, watching cricket. *E*: n.daymond1@ntlworld.com.

**DE, Ina;** Managing Director, since 2001, and Head, Financial Sponsor Group, Europe, Middle East and Africa, since 2019, J.P. Morgan; *b* London, 9 July 1965; *d* of Amit and Ingrid De; *m* 1991, Prof. James Spicer; one *s* one *d*. *Educ*: City of London Sch. for Girls; Westminster Sch.; Univ. of Bristol (BSc Econs and Stats 1987). Joined J.P. Morgan, 1987; Hd, Equity Capital Mkts, EMEA, 2008–13; Hd, J.P. Morgan Cazenove UK, 2013–19. Gov., Westminster Sch., 2014–. Mem., ESU. *Recreations*: theatre, opera, singing. *Address*: J.P. Morgan, 25 Bank Street, E14 5JP. *T*: (020) 7742 9075. *E*: ina.de@jpmorgan.com. *Club*: Conduit.

**DEACON, Emma Rebecca;** QC 2016; a Recorder, since 2016; *b* Bolton, 11 June 1970; *d* of Stuart Deacon and late Glenda Deacon; *m* 2002, Fatos Kastrati; two *s*. *Educ*: Bolton Sch.; King's Coll. London (LLB). Called to the Bar, Inner Temple, 1993; in practice as barrister, specialising in criminal law, 1994–. *Recreations*: family, food, music, reading, yoga. *Address*: 5 Paper Buildings, Temple, EC4Y 7HB. *T*: (020) 7583 6117, *Fax*: (020) 7353 0075. *E*: clerks@5pb.co.uk.

**DEACON, Richard,** CBE 1999; RA 1998; sculptor; *b* Bangor, 15 Aug. 1949; *s* of late Gp Capt. Edward William Deacon, RAF (retd) and Dr Joan Bullivant Winstanley; *m* 1977, Jacqueline Poncelet (marr. diss. 2000); one *s* one *d*. *Educ*: Somerset Coll. of Art; St Martin's Sch. of Art; RCA; Chelsea Sch. of Art. *Solo exhibitions* include: Orchard Gall., Londonderry, 1983; Lisson Gall., 1983, 1985, 1987, 1992, 1995, 1999, 2002, 2012; Riverside Studios, Chapter Arts Centre, Cardiff, and Fruitmarket Gall., Edinburgh, 1984; Tate Gall., 1985; Marian Goodman Gall., NY, 1986, 1988, 1990, 1992, 1997, 2004, 2012, 2019; Whitechapel Art Gall., Musée Nat. d'Art Moderne, Paris, 1989; Kunstnernes Hus, Oslo, and Mala Galerija, Slovenia, 1990; Kunstverein Hanover, 1993; LA Louver, 1995, 2001, 2004, 2007; tour of South America, 1996–97; Musée de Rochechouart, 1997; Tate Gall., Liverpool, 1999; Dundee Contemp. Arts, 2001; PSI Center for Art and Urban Resources, NY, 2001; Museum Ludwig, Cologne, 2003; Atelier Brancusi, CNAC, Paris, 2003; Tate St Ives, 2005; Museo Artium, Vitoria-Gasteiz, Spain, 2005; Sara Hilden Art Mus., Tampere, Finland, 2005–06; Arp Mus., Remagen, Germany, 2006; Ikon Gall., Birmingham, 2007; New Art Centre, Salisbury, 2007, 2010; rep. Wales at the Venice Biennale, 2007; Gall. Thaddaeus Ropac, Paris, 2007, 2010, Salzburg, 2010; Fondation Maeght, France, 2008; Madison Square Park, NY, 2008; Stedelijk Mus., s'Hertogenbosch, 2008; Gall. Thomas Schulte, Berlin, 2009; Musée d'Art Moderne et Contemporaine, Strasbourg, 2010; Sprengel Mus., Hannover, 2011; Univ. of New Mexico, 2011; Tyler Print Inst., Singapore, 2012; Centro de Arte Contemporáneo, Malaga, 2012; Tate Britain, 2014; (jtly with B. Woodrow) New Art Centre, Salisbury, 2014; Kunstmus. Winterthur, 2015; Wolfson Coll., Cambridge, 2015; Heydar Aliyev Centre, Baku, 2016; Langen Foundn, Thomas Schütte Skulpturenhalle, Neuss, Germany, 2016; Folkwang Mus., Essen, 2016; San Diego Mus. of Art, 2017; Municipal Liby, Prague, 2017; Middelheim Mus., Antwerp, 2017; Kunsthalle Vogelmann, Heilbronn, 2017; MOMA Machynlleth, 2017; Gall. Thaddaeus Ropac, Paris, 2017; Beijing Commune Gall., 2018; École des Beaux Arts, Paris, 2018; LA Louver, 2018; represented in collections in: Tate Gall.; Mus. of Modern Art, NY; Art Gall. of NSW, Sydney; Musée Beaubourg, Paris; Bonnefanten Mus., Maastricht; Kunstmus. Winterthur; V&A Mus. Vis. Prof., Chelsea Sch. of Art, 1992–; Professor: Ecole Nat. Supérieure des Beaux-Arts, Paris, 1999–2009; Kunstakademie, Dusseldorf, 2009–15. Member: Grants to Artists Sub Cttee, 1986–92, Visual Arts Adv. Gp, 1990–93, British Council; Architecture Adv. Gp, Arts Council of England, 1996–2000; Trustee: Tate Gall., 1991–96; Art Fund, 2015–; Vice Chm. Trustees, Baltic Flour Mills

Centre for Contemporary Art, 1999–2004. Member: Akademie der Kunst, Berlin, 2010; Eur. Acad. of Scis and Arts, 2015. Hon. Fellow, Univ. of the Arts London, 2013. Turner Prize, 1987; Robert Jakobsen Prize, Mus. Wurth, Germany, 1995; Ernst Franz Vogelmann Prize, Heilbronn, Germany, 2017. Chevalier des Arts et des Lettres (France), 1997. *Publications*: Stuff Box Object, 1972, 1984; For Those Who Have Ears #2, 1985; Atlas: Gondwanaland & Laurasia, 1990; In Praise of Television, 1997; About the Size of It, 2005; Water Under The Bridge, 2008; I Met Paul, Out of the Woods, Judd-Like, 2009; In the Garden, 2010; Por Escrito 1970–2010, 2012; So, And, If, But: Richard Deacon writings 1970–2012, 2014; Transmission, Reception, Noise: abstract drawing, 2014. *Address*: c/o Lisson Gallery, 67 Lisson Street, NW1 5DA. *W*: www.richarddeacon.net.

**DEACON, Prof. Susan Catherine,** CBE 2017; Chair, Scottish Police Authority, since 2017; *b* 2 Feb. 1964; *d* of James Deacon and Barbara Deacon (*née* Timmins); *m* John Boothman; one *s* one *d*. *Educ*: Edinburgh Univ. (MA Hons Social Policy and Politics 1987; MBA 1992). Local Govt officer, 1987–94; sen. mgt consultant, 1994; Dir of MBA Programmes, Edinburgh Business Sch., Heriot-Watt Univ., 1994–98; business consultant, 1998–99. Mem. (Lab) Edinburgh E and Musselburgh, Scottish Parlt, 1999–2007; Minister for Health and Community Care, Scottish Exec., 1999–2001. Prof. of Social Change, Queen Margaret Univ., 2007–10; Asst Principal Corp. Engagement, then Asst Principal Ext. Relns, Univ. of Edinburgh, 2012–18. Mem., UK Adv. Bd, ScottishPower, 2007–09; non-executive Director: ScottishPower Renewables Ltd, 2009– (Chm., 2010–12); Scottish Power Ltd, 2012–17; Lothian Buses, 2015–. Chm., Inst. of Dirs Scotland, 2015–18. Chm., Edinburgh Festivals Forum, 2016–; Mem. Bd, Traverse Th. Co., 2007–10. Chm., Hibernian Community Foundn, 2008–12; Mem. Bd, Pfizer UK Foundn, 2007–13; Trustee, Iberdrola Foundn, 2009–14. Early Years Champion, Scottish Govt, 2010–11. Gov., Inst. of Occupational Medicine, 2013–18. Hon. Prof., Sch. of Social and Political Sci., Univ. of Edinburgh, 2010–12. CCMI 2017.

**DEAKIN, Maj. Gen. Gary Colin,** CBE 2015 (OBE 2009); Deputy Chief of Staff Plans, NATO Joint Force Command Naples, since 2018; *b* Arbroath, 18 June 1966; *s* of Colin Deakin and Jean Deakin; *m* 2006, Carolyn Collins; one *s*. *Educ*: Royal Hospital Sch., Holbrook; Cranfield Univ. (MA Defence Studies); King's Coll. London (MA Defence Studies). Commnd King's Regt, 2004; commanded: 1st Bn Duke of Lancaster's Regt, 2006–08; 51 (Inf.) Bde and HQ Scotland, 2012–14. Hon. Vice Pres., Royal Caledonian Educn Trust, 2016–. *Recreations*: offshore sailing, hill running, mountain marathons, reading, family. *Address*: Plans Division, Allied Joint Force Command Naples, BFPO 8 BF1 2AG. *T*: 07872 493220. *E*: deakingc@aol.com, gary.deakin@jfcnp.nato.int.

**DEAKIN, Prof. (John Francis) William,** PhD; FRCPsych; Professor of Psychiatry, since 1990, and Director, Neuroscience and Psychiatry Unit, since 2000, Manchester University; *b* 5 July 1949; *s* of John Deakin and Kathleen Brown; *m* 1973, Hildur Jakobsdottir; three *d*. *Educ*: Eltham Coll., Kent; Leeds Univ. (BSc 1st Cl. Physiol. 1970; MB Hons, ChB dist. and prize 1973); PhD London 1982. MRCPsych 1984, FRCPsych 1990. MRC Trng Fellow, NIMR, Mill Hill, and Clin. Res. Centre, Harrow, 1974–83; Sen. Lectr, Manchester Univ., 1983–90. FMedSci 2000. *Publications*: contrib. numerous articles to learned jls on neuroscientific basis of mental illness and novel ways of imaging the action of drugs on the brain, especially the rôle of serotonin in neuroses. *Recreations*: jazz, playing classical guitar, the game of Go, astronomy, cycling. *Address*: 3 Chesham Place, Bowdon, Cheshire WA14 2JL. *T*: (0161) 941 6385.

**DEAKIN, Michael;** writer, documentary and film maker; Director, Gryphon Productions Ltd, 1985–2005; *b* 21 Feb. 1939; *s* of Sir William Deakin, DSO, and Margaret Hodson (*née* Beatson-Bell); civil partnership 2006, David Steele. *Educ*: Bryanston; Univ. d'Aix-Marseille; Emmanuel Coll., Cambridge (MA Hons). Founding Partner, Editions Alecto, Fine Art Publishers, 1960–64; Producer, BBC Radio Current Affairs Dept, 1964–68; Producer, then Editor, Yorkshire Television Documentary Unit, 1968–81; Sen. Vice-Pres., Paramount/Revcom, 1987–93. Documentary film productions include: Out of the Shadow into the Sun—The Eiger; Struggle for China; The Children on the Hill; Whicker's World—Way Out West; The Japanese Experience; The Good, the Bad and the Indifferent; Johnny Go Home (British Academy Award, 1976); David Frost's Global Village; The Frost Interview—The Shah; Rampton—The Secret Hospital; Painting With Light (co-prodn with BBC); other films: Act of Betrayal, 1987; Not a Penny More, Not a Penny Less, 1990 (TV mini series); Secret Weapon, 1990; The Supergun, 1994; Good King Wenceslas, 1994; The Human Bomb, 1996; The Place of Lions, 1997; Varian's War, 2001; also many others. Founding Mem., TV-am Breakfast Television Consortium, 1980; Consultant, TV-am, 1984–87 (Dir of Programmes, 1982–84; Bd Mem., 1984–85). *Publications*: Restif de la Bretonne—Les Nuits de Paris (critical edn and trans. with Nicholas Deakin), 1968; Gaetano Donizetti—a biography, 1968; (for children) Tom Grattan's War, 1970, 2nd edn 1971; The Children on the Hill, 1972, 9th edn 1982; (with John Willis) Johnny Go Home, 1976; (with Antony Thomas) The Arab Experience, 1975, 2nd edn 1976; Flame in the Desert, 1976; (with David Frost) I Could Have Kicked Myself, 1982, 2nd US edn 1983; (with David Frost) Who Wants to be a Millionaire, 1983; (with David Frost) If You'll Believe That You'll Believe Anything…, 1986. *Recreations*: travel, music, books, pictures. *Address*: 6 Glenhurst Avenue, NW5 1PS; La Marsaulaie, Saint Mathurin 49250, France. *Club*: Hat.
*See also* N. D. Deakin.

**DEAKIN, Prof. Nicholas Dampier,** CBE 1997; Professor of Social Policy and Administration, University of Birmingham, 1980–98, now Emeritus Professor (Dean, Faculty of Commerce and Social Science, 1986–89; Foundation Fellow, 2006); Visiting Professor: London School of Economics, 1998–2004; Warwick Business School, 1998–2001; *b* 5 June 1936; *s* of Sir (Frederick) William Deakin, DSO and Margaret Ogilvy Hodson; *m* 1st, 1961, Rose Albinia Donaldson (marr. diss. 1988), *d* of Baron Donaldson of Kingsbridge, OBE and Frances Donaldson; one *s* two *d*; 2nd, 1988, Lucy Moira, *d* of Jack and Moira Gaster. *Educ*: Westminster Sch.; Christ Church Coll., Oxford (BA (1st cl. Hons) 1959, MA 1963); DPhil Sussex 1972. Asst Principal, Home Office, 1959–63, Private Sec. to Minister of State, 1962–63; Asst Dir, Nuffield Foundn Survey of Race Relations in Britain, 1963–68; Res. Fellow, subseq. Lectr, Univ. of Sussex, 1968–72; Head of Social Studies, subseq. Head of Central Policy Unit, GLC, 1972–80. Scientific Advr, DHSS, later Dept of Health, 1986–91. Chm., Ind. Commn on Future of Voluntary Sector in England, 1995–96. Vice-Chm., Social Affairs Cttee, ESRC, 1984–86. Chair, Social Policy Assoc., 1989–92; Member: Exec. Cttee, NCVO, 1988–90; Council, RIPA, 1984–88; Governing Council, Family Policy Studies Centre, 1987–2001. Trustee: Nationwide Foundn, 1999–2005; Baring Foundn, 2005–10 (Vice Chm., 2008–10). Chair, Birmingham City Pride, 1998–2001. FAcSS 2015; FRSA 1996. *Publications*: (ed and trans.) Memoirs of the Comte de Gramont, 1965; Colour and the British Electorate 1964, 1965; Colour, Citizenship and British Society, 1969; (with Clare Ungerson) Leaving London, 1977; (jtly) Government and Urban Poverty, 1983; (ed) Policy Change in Government, 1986; The Politics of Welfare, 1987, 2nd edn 1994; (ed jtly) Consuming Public Services, 1990; (jtly) The Enterprise Culture and the Inner Cities, 1992; (ed jtly) The Costs of Welfare, 1993; (jtly) Public Welfare Services and Social Exclusion, 1995; (jtly) Contracting for Change, 1997; (with Richard Parry) The Treasury and Social Policy, 2000; In Search of Civil Society, 2001; (ed jtly) Welfare and the State, 2003; (contrib.) Angleterre ou Albion, entre fascination et répulsion, ed by G. Millat, 2006; (ed jtly and contrib.) Beveridge and Voluntary Action in Britain and the Wider British World, 2011; (ed and contrib.) Radiant Illusion?, 2015; contribs to other vols and learned jls. *Recreations*: reading fiction, music. *Address*: Chedington, Lynmouth Road, N2 9LR.
*See also* M. Deakin.

**DEAKIN, Richard Simon,** CEng, FRAeS; consultant, aerospace and HiTec industries; Chief Executive Officer, NATS, 2010–15; Chairman, Europe, Middle East and Africa, AirMap, since 2016; *b* Ipswich, 25 Feb. 1964; *s* of Comdr David Deakin, RN and Mary Deakin; *m* 1997, Marian Whitelock; one *s* one *d*. *Educ*: Kingston Poly. (BSc Hons Aero Engrg 1987); Cranfield Univ. (MBA 1991). CEng 1990; FRAeS 1996. British Aerospace, 1982–91; TRW, 1999–2001; Gp Dir, Progs, GKN Aerospace, 2001–03; Man. Dir, Thales Aerospace, 2004–08; Sen. Vice-Pres., Thales Air Systems, 2008–10. Hon. DEng Kingston, 2008. *Publications*: Battlespace Technologies: network enabled information dominance, 2010. *Recreations*: sailing, clay pigeon shooting, photography.

**DEAKIN, Prof. Simon Francis,** PhD; FBA 2005; Professor of Law, University of Cambridge, since 2006; Fellow, Peterhouse, Cambridge, since 1990; *b* 26 March 1961; *s* of Anthony Francis and Elizabeth Mary Deakin; *m* 1989, Elaine Skidmore; one *s*. *Educ*: Netherthorpe Grammar Sch., Staveley; Peterhouse, Cambridge (BA 1983, MA 1985, PhD 1990). Res. Fellow, Peterhouse, Cambridge, 1985–88; Lectr in Law, QMC, 1987–90; Cambridge University: Asst Lectr, Lectr, then Reader in Law, 1990–2001; Asst Dir, 1994–2014, Dir, 2014–, Centre for Business Res.; Robert Monks Prof. of Corporate Governance, Judge Inst. of Mgt, subseq. Judge Business Sch., 2001–06. Bigelow Fellow, Univ. of Chicago Law Sch., 1986–87; Visiting Fellow: Univ. of Nantes, 1993, 1995; Univ. of Melbourne, 1996; European Univ. Inst., Florence, 2004; Doshisha Univ., Kyoto, 2004–; Vis. Prof., Columbia Univ., 2003, 2008; Francqui Vis. Prof., Univ. of Antwerp, 2013–14. Mem. Exec. Cttee, Inst. of Employment Rights, 1990–2002. Mem., Ind. Commn of Inquiry into Drug Testing at Work, 2003–05. Tanner Lectures, Oxford Univ., 2008; Mike Larkin Meml Lect., Univ. of Cape Town, 2009; V. V. Giri Meml Lect., Jawaharlal Nehru Univ., New Delhi, 2013. Hon. Dr Univ. Catholique de Louvain, 2012. *Publications*: (with B. S. Markesinis) Tort Law, 3rd edn 1994, 4th edn 1999, 5th edn 2003, 6th edn (with A. Johnston) 2007; (with G. S. Morris) Labour Law, 1995, 5th edn 2009; (ed with J. Michie) Contracts, Co-operation and Competition, 1997; (ed with A. Hughes) Enterprise and Community, 1997; (with F. Wilkinson) The Law of the Labour Market: industrialization, employment and legal evolution, 2005; (ed with A. Supiot) Capacitas: contract law and the institutional preconditions of a market economy, 2009; (ed with D. H. Whittaker) Corporate Governance and Managerial Reform in Japan, 2009; (jtly) Hedge Fund Activism in Japan: the limits of shareholder primacy, 2012; contribs to jls in law, econs, corporate governance and industrial relns. *Recreation*: fell walking. *Address*: Peterhouse, Cambridge CB2 1RD. *T*: (01223) 338200, *Fax*: (01223) 337578. *E*: s.deakin@cbr.cam.ac.uk.

**DEAKIN, William;** *see* Deakin, J. F. W.

**DEAKINS, Eric Petro;** international public affairs consultant; *b* 7 Oct. 1932; *er s* of late Edward Deakins and Gladys Deakins; *m* 1990, Sandra Weaver; one *s* two *d*. *Educ*: Tottenham Grammar Sch.; London Sch. of Economics. BA (Hons) in History, 1953. Nat. Service (commn), 1953–55. Executive with FMC (Meat) Ltd, 1956; General Manager, Pigs Div., FMC (Meat) Ltd, 1969. Contested (Lab): Finchley, 1959; Chigwell, 1966; Walthamstow W, 1967. MP (Lab): Walthamstow W, 1970–74; Walthamstow, 1974–87. Parly Under-Sec. of State, Dept of Trade, 1974–76, DHSS, 1976–79. Member: Select Cttee on Educn, 1971–74; Select Cttee on Foreign Affairs, 1979–82; Public Accts Cttee, 1983–87. *Publications*: A Faith to Fight For, 1964; You and your MP, 1987; What Future for Labour?, 1988. *Recreations*: writing, cinema, yoga, football. *Address*: 36 Murray Mews, NW1 9RJ.

**DEAL, Hon. Timothy Edward;** Senior Vice President, United States Council for International Business, Washington, 1996–2010; *b* 17 Sept. 1940; *s* of Edward Deal and Loretta (*née* Fuemuller); *m* 1964, Jill Brady; two *s*. *Educ*: Univ. of California at Berkeley (AB Pol Sci.). First Lieut, US Army, 1963–65. Joined Foreign Service, US Dept of State, 1965; served Tegucigalpa, Honduras, Warsaw, Poland, and Washington, 1965–76; Sen. Staff Mem., Nat. Security Council, 1976–79 and 1980–81; Special Asst to Asst Sec. of State for European Affairs, 1979–80; Counsellor for Econ. Affairs, London, 1981–85; Dep. US Rep., OECD, Paris, 1985–88; Dir, Office of Eastern European Affairs, Washington, 1988–89; Special Asst to President and Sen. Dir for Internat. Econ. Affairs, Nat. Security Council, 1989–92; Minister and Dep. Chief of Mission, US Embassy, London, 1992–96. Presidential Awards for: Meritorious Service, 1991; Distinguished Service, 1993. *Recreations*: theatre, cinema, horse racing.

**DEALTRY, Prof. (Thomas) Richard;** Managing Director: Intellectual Partnerships Consultancy Ltd, since 1999; Global Association of Corporate Universities and Academies, since 2004; independent real-time business development process designer; *b* 24 Nov. 1936; *s* of George Raymond Dealtry and Edith (*née* Gardner); *m* 1962, Pauline (*née* Sedgwick) (marr. diss. 1982); one *s* one *d*. *Educ*: Cranfield Inst. of Advanced Technol., MBA. CEng, MIMechE; MInstM; FIMCB. National Service Commn, 1959–61: Temp. Captain 1960. Divl Exec., Tube Investments Ltd, 1967–71; Sen. Exec., Guest, Keen & Nettlefold Gp Corporate Staff, 1971–74; Dir, Simpson-Lawrence Ltd, and Man. Dir, BUKO BV, Holland, 1974–77; Under Sec./Industrial Adviser, Scottish Econ. Planning Dept, 1977–78; Director, Gulf Regional Planning, Gulf Org. for Industrial Consulting, 1978–82; Man. Dir, RBS Management Services Ltd, London and Kuwait, 1982–85; Regl Dir, Diverco Ltd, 1985–; Prof. of Strategic Mgt, Internat. Mgt Centres, Buckingham, 1989–93; Programmes Director: BAA plc, 1993–99; Univ. of Surrey Mgt Learning Partnership, 1993–99. Vis. Prof., Birmingham City Univ., 2008–13. *Publications*: From Learning to Earning: in the age of knowledge innovation, 2007; Achieving Competitive Edge with Quantum Sports Management, 2013; Quantum Management: meeting the need for a dynamic system of performance management, 2013; The Corporate University Blueprint, 2013; Corporate Universities, 2015. *Recreations*: golf, squash. *Address*: 43 Hunstanton Avenue, Harborne, Birmingham B17 8SX.

**DEAN, (Barbara) Helen, (Mrs G. M. Mundy);** Chief Executive Officer, National Employment Savings Trust Corporation, since 2015; *b* Newcastle upon Tyne, 31 Dec. 1959; *d* of James Gordon Dean and Jean Dean (*née* Dowdy); *m* 2003, George Micheal Mundy. *Educ*: West Denton High Sch., Newcastle upon Tyne; North East London Poly. (BSc Hons Psychol.); Univ. of Birmingham (MBA). Civil Servant, DWP, 1984–2014. Mem. Bd, Personal Accounts Delivery Authy, 2007–10; Exec. Dir, Nat. Employment Savings Trust Corp., 2010–15. Mem., Council of Scholar Advrs, Centre for Retirement Initiatives, Georgetown Univ., 2015–. Gov., Pensions Policy Inst. Trustee and Dir, Foundn for Credit Counselling. *Recreations*: spending time with my husband, genealogy, eating out and writing the odd restaurant review. *Address*: National Employment Savings Trust Corporation, Riverside House, 2a Southwark Bridge Road, SE1 9HA. *T*: (020) 3056 3773.

**DEAN, Dame Caroline,** DBE 2016 (OBE 2004); DPhil; FRS 2004; Project Leader, John Innes Centre, Norwich, since 1988; *b* 2 April 1957; *d* of late D. H. Dean and Alice Joy Dean; *m* 1991, Jonathan Dallas George Jones, *qv*; one *s* one *d*. *Educ*: Univ. of York (BA Hons (Biol.); DPhil (Biol.) 1982). Res. Scientist, Advanced Genetic Sciences, Oakland,

Calif, 1983–88; Associate Res. Dir, John Innes Centre, Norwich, 1999–2008. Hon. Chair, UEA, 2000–. Royal Soc. Res. Prof., 2018. Foreign Mem., US NAS, 2008. Medal, Genetics Soc., 2007; FEBS/EMBO Women in Sci. Award, 2015; Darwin Medal, Royal Soc., 2016; L'Oréal/UNESCO European Laureate, Women in Sci., 2018; Novartis Award, Biochem. Soc., 2019. *Publications:* numerous articles in learned jls, incl. Science, Cell, Plant Cell, Plant Jl, EMBO Jl, Nature, Nature Genetics. *Recreation:* sailing. *Address:* John Innes Centre, Norwich Research Park, Norwich, Norfolk NR4 7UH. *T:* (01603) 450526, *Fax:* (01603) 450045. *E:* caroline.dean@jic.ac.uk.

**DEAN, (Catherine) Margaret,** CVO 2013; HM Lord Lieutenant of Fife, 1999–2014; *b* 16 Nov. 1939; *d* of Thomas Day McNeil Scrimgeour and Catherine Forbes Scrimgeour (née Sunderland); *m* 1962, Brian Dean; three *d. Educ:* George Watson's Ladies' Coll., Edinburgh; Univ. of Edinburgh (MA). *Address:* Viewforth, 121 Rose Street, Dunfermline, Fife KY12 0QT. *T:* (01383) 722488.

**DEAN, Christopher Colin,** OBE 2000 (MBE 1981); professional ice skater; *b* 27 July 1958; *s* of Colin Gordon Dean and Mavis (née Pearson) and step *s* of Mary Betty (née Chambers); *m* 1st, 1991, Isabelle Duchesnay (marr. diss. 1993); 2nd, 1994, Jill Trenary; two *s. Educ:* Calverton Manor Sch., Nottingham; Sir John Sherbrooke Sch., Nottingham; Col Frank Seely Sch., Nottingham. Police constable, 1974–80. Ice dancer, with Jayne Torvill, *qv*: British Champions, 1978, 1979, 1980, 1981, 1982, 1983, 1994; European Champions, 1981, 1982, 1984, 1994; World Champions, 1981, 1982, 1983, 1984; World Professional Champions, 1984, 1985, 1990, 1995 and 1996; Olympic Champions, 1984; Olympic Bronze Medallists, 1994. Choreographer, Encounters, English Nat. Ballet, 1996; trainer, choreographer and performer: Stars on Ice, USA, 1998–99, 1999–2000; Dancing on Ice, ITV, 2006–14; trainer, Ice Rink on the Estate, ITV, 2015; judge: Dancing on Ice, ITV, 2018. Hon. MA Nottingham Trent, 1993. With Jayne Torvill: BBC Sportsview Personality of the Year, 1983–84; Figure Skating Hall of Fame, 1989. *Publications:* (with Jayne Torvill) Facing the Music, 1995; (with Jayne Torvill) Our Life on Ice, 2014. *Recreations:* motor racing, films, dance. *Address:* PO Box 32, Heathfield, E Sussex TN21 0BW. *T:* (01435) 867825. *Club:* Groucho.

**DEAN, Gillian Margaret;** *see* Weeks, G. M.

**DEAN, Helen;** *see* Dean, B. H.

**DEAN, Janet Elizabeth Ann;** *b* 28 Jan. 1949; *d* of late Harry Gibson and Mary Gibson (née Walley); *m* 1968, Alan Dean (*d* 1994); two *d. Educ:* Winsford Verdin County Grammar Sch., Cheshire. Clerk: Barclays Bank, 1965–69; Bass Charrington, 1969–70. Member (Lab): Staffordshire County Council, 1981–97; E Staffordshire BC, 1991–97; Uttoxeter Town Council, 1995–97. MP (Lab) Burton, 1997–2010. *Recreations:* dressmaking, reading.

**DEAN, Margaret;** *see* Dean, C. M.

**DEAN, His Honour Michael;** QC 1981; a Circuit Judge, 1991–2009; *b* 2 Feb. 1938; *m* 1st, 1967, Diane Ruth Griffiths; 2nd, 1992, Jane Isabel Glaister; one *s. Educ:* Altrincham Co. Grammar Sch.; Univ. of Nottingham (LLB 1st Cl. Hons 1959). Lectr in Law, Univ. of Manchester, 1959–62; called to the Bar, Gray's Inn, 1962 (Arden Scholar and Holker Sen. Scholarship, 1962); Northern Circuit, Manchester, 1962–65; Lectr in Law, LSE, 1965–67; practice at the Bar, London, 1968–91; an Asst Recorder, 1986–89; a Recorder, 1989–91. *Publications:* articles in various legal periodicals. *Recreations:* conversation, music, theatre, sailing, family life.

**DEAN, Nicholas Arthur;** QC 2003; **His Honour Judge Dean;** a Circuit Judge, since 2013; *b* 11 July 1960; *s* of John and Alwyne Dean; *m* 1987, Nicola Anne Kay Carslaw; one *s* one *d. Educ:* Wyggeston Boys' Sch.; Univ. of Leeds (LLB Hons). Called to the Bar, Lincoln's Inn, 1982; in practice specialising in crime, clinical negligence and commercial competition law; Recorder, 2001–13. *Recreations:* cycling, reading, keeping chickens, listening to the Archers.

**DEAN, Nigel Francis;** a District Judge (Magistrates' Courts), since 2011; *b* Epping, 17 March 1956; *s* of Roger Dean and Paula Holmes (née Waller); *m* 1993, Megan Galliet; one *s* two *d. Educ:* Wellington Coll.; Univ. of Westminster (BA Hons). Admitted as solicitor, 1982; Asst Solicitor, Sowman Pinks & Co., 1982–84; Edward Fail Bradshaw & Waterson: Asst Solicitor, 1984–87; Partner, 1987–2011; a Dep. Dist Judge (Magistrates' Courts), 2005–11. *Recreations:* sports, classic cars, cinema, history, family. *Address:* Westminster Magistrates' Court, 181 Marylebone Road, NW1 5BR.

**DEAN, Dr Paul,** CB 1981; Director, National Physical Laboratory, 1977–90 (Deputy Director, 1974–76); *b* 23 Jan. 1933; *s* of late Sydney and Rachel Dean; *m* 1961, Sheila Valerie Gamse; one *s* one *d. Educ:* Hackney Downs Grammar Sch.; Queen Mary Coll., Univ. of London (Fellow, 1984). BSc (1st cl. Hons Physics), PhD; CPhys; FInstP, FIMA, CMath. National Physical Laboratory: Sen. Sci. Officer, Math. Div., 1957; Principal Sci. Officer, 1963; Sen. Principal Sci. Officer (Individual Merit), 1967; Head of Central Computer Unit, 1967; Supt, Div. of Quantum Metrology, 1969; Under-Sec., DoI (Head of Space and Air Res. and R&D Contractors Divs), 1976–77; initiated testing lab. accreditation in UK, leading to NAMAS, 1985 and UKAS, 1995. Part-time Head, Res. Estabts Management Div., DoI, 1979–82; Exec. Dep. Chm., Council of Res. Estabts, 1979–82. Mem., Internat. Cttee of Weights and Measures, 1985–90; Pres., Comité Consultatif pour les Etalons de Mesure des Rayonnements Ionisants, 1987–90; Founder Pres., British Measurement and Testing Assoc., 1990–95; First Chm., EUROMET, 1988–90. *Publications:* papers and articles in learned, professional and popular jls. *Recreations:* scientific interests, piano, bridge, table tennis. *Address:* Dorset.

**DEAN, Peter Henry,** CBE 1993; Chairman, Gambling Commission, 2005–07 (Chairman, Gaming Board for Great Britain, 1998–2005); *b* 24 July 1939; *s* of late Alan Walduck Dean and Gertrude (née Bürger); *m* 1965, Linda Louise Keating; one *d. Educ:* Rugby Sch.; London Univ. (LLB). Admitted Solicitor, 1962. Joined Rio Tinto-Zinc Corp., 1967; Sec., 1972–74; Dir, 1974–85; freelance business consultant, 1985–96. Director: Associated British Ports Holdings, 1982–2001 (Mem., British Transport Docks Bd, 1980–82); Liberty Life Assce Co., 1986–95; Seeboard, 1993–96. Chm., G. H. Dean & Co., 2001–14 (Dir, 1999–2014). Dep. Chm., Monopolies and Mergers Commn, 1990–97 (Mem., 1982–97); Investment Ombudsman, 1996–2001. Chm., Council of Management, Highgate Counselling Centre, 1991–2002 (Mem., 1985–2002); Chairman: English Baroque Choir, 1985–89, 1999–2000; City Chamber Choir, 2003–07. Trustee, Responsible Gambling Fund, 2009–11. *Recreations:* choral singing, ski-ing, tennis. *Address:* 11 Mawson Mansions, 4 Marwood Square, N10 3EW. *T:* (020) 8883 5417. *E:* deanpeterh@gmail.com.

**DEAN, Robert John,** CMG 2012; President, Kennet and Avon Canal Trust, since 2019 (Chairman of Trustees, 2012–18); *b* Portsmouth, 21 May 1959; *s* of Albert and Margaret Dean; *m* 1981, Julie Margaret Stott; two *d. Educ:* Southern Grammar Sch., Portsmouth. ACMA 1996. Entered FCO, 1978; various roles incl. mgt services, personnel ops and IT devlt, 1978–86; Second Sec., Copenhagen, 1987–92; Mgt Accountant and Hd of Finance, FCO, 1992–99; First Sec., Wellington, NZ, 1999–2004; Co-ordinator, Intelligence and Security Secretariat, Cabinet Office (on secondment), 2004–06; Dir, FCO, 2007–12. *Recreations:* inland waterways cruising, heritage restoration and management, conservation and woodland management, passenger boat master and trainer. *Address:* c/o Kennet and Avon Canal Trust, Couch Lane, Devizes, Wilts SN10 1EB. *T:* 07795 116223. *E:* robdeancmg@gmail.com.

**DEAN, Prof. Roger Thornton,** DSc, DLitt, PhD; FAHA; Research Professor of Sonic Communication, MARCS Institute for Brain, Behaviour and Development (formerly Macarthur Auditory Research Centre Sydney, then MARCS Auditory Laboratories), Western Sydney University (formerly University of Western Sydney), since 2007; *b* UK, 6 Sept. 1948; *s* of Cyril Thornton Dean and Kathleen Ida Dean (née Harrington); *m* 1973, Dr Hazel Anne Smith. *Educ:* Corpus Christi Coll., Cambridge (BA 1970; PhD 1974); Brunel Univ. (DSc 1984, DLitt 2002). Post-Doctoral Fellow, Dept of Exptl Pathol., UCH Med. Sch., 1973–76; MRC Scientist, Div. of Cell Pathol., Clinical Res. Centre, London, 1976–79; Brunel University: Hd, Cell Biol. Res. Gp, and Reader in Applied Biol., 1979–84; Hd, Cell Biol. Res. Gp, and Prof. of Cell Biol., 1984–88; Hon. Prof., Faculty of Medicine, Sydney Univ., 1988–2002; Foundn Exec. Dir, Heart Res. Inst. Ltd, Sydney, Australia, 1988–2002; University of Canberra: Vice-Chancellor and Pres., and Prof., 2002–07; Founder, Sonic Communications Res. Gp, 2004. Founder and Artistic Dir, LYSIS and austraLYSIS, internat. sound and intermedia creative and perf. gp, 1970–. Hon. FAHA 2004. Musical and multimedia compositions, many included in compact disc pubns as creator and performer. Centenary Medal, Australia, 2003. *Publications:* include: (with Dr M. Davies) Protein Oxidation (monograph), 1997; Hyperimprovisation, 2003; (ed jtly) The Oxford Handbook of Algorithmic Music, 2018; contrib. learned jls in cell biol., music cognition and humanities res. *Recreations:* film, visual arts. *Address:* MARCS Institute, Western Sydney University, Locked Bag 1797, Penrith South, NSW 2751, Australia. *T:* (2) 97726902. *E:* roger.dean@westernsydney.edu.au.

**DEAN, Rosa Mary; Her Honour Judge Dean;** a Circuit Judge, since 2011; Resident Judge, Harrow Crown Court, since 2017; *b* Cuckfield; *d* of late Geoffrey and of Una Dean; *m* 2000, Edward; four *s. Educ:* Brighton and Hove High Sch.; Westminster Sch.; Magdalen Coll., Oxford (BA). Called to the Bar, Gray's Inn, 1993, Bencher, 2015; a Dep. Dist Judge (Magistrates' Court), 2006–11; a Recorder, 2009–11. Mem., Sentencing Council for England and Wales, 2018–. *Recreations:* cooking, gardening, football. *Address:* Harrow Crown Court, Hailsham Drive, off Headstone Drive, Harrow HA1 4TU.

**DEAN, Simon Dominic;** Deputy Chief Executive, NHS Wales, since 2014; *b* Cheltenham, 28 March 1958; *s* of Denis and Margaret Dean; *m* 1988, Alison Downes; one *s* one *d. Educ:* Univ. of Warwick (BA Hons English and American Lit. 1980). MIHM 1986. Admin. Asst, NE Thames RHA, 1983; Hosp. Manager, Southend HA, 1984–90; Dir, Avon FHSA, 1990–94; Avon Health Authority: Dep. Dir, Contracting, 1994–96; Dir of Commng, 1996–2000; Dir, Planning and Organisational Develt, 2000–01; Chief Exec., 2001–02; Dir, Business Mgt, Avon, Glos and Wilts SHA, 2002–03; mgt consultant, 2004–05; Chief Exec., Health Comm Wales, 2006–07; Dir, Service Delivery, Dept of Health and Social Services, Welsh Govt, 2007–08; Transition Dir, Gwent (on secondment), 2008–09; Dir, Strategy, Dept of Health and Social Services, Welsh Govt, 2009–10; Chief Exec., Velindre NHS Trust, 2010–14; Interim Chief Exec., Betsi Cadwaladr Univ. Health Bd, 2015–16. *Recreations:* scuba diving, underwater photography, music, watching Rugby, walking. *Address:* Department of Health and Social Services, Welsh Government, Cathays Park, Cardiff CF10 3NQ. *T:* (029) 2080 6305. *E:* Simon.Dean2@gov.wales.

**DEAN, Tacita Charlotte,** CBE 2019 (OBE 2013); RA 2008; artist; *b* Canterbury, 12 Nov. 1965; *d* of His Honour Joseph Jolyon Dean and of Hon. Jenefer Dean, yr *d* of 5th Baron Hillingdon, MC, TD; partner, Mathew Hale; one *s. Educ:* Kent Coll., Canterbury; Canterbury Coll. of Art (Art Foundn); Falmouth Sch. of Art (BA Hons Fine Art); Slade Sch. of Fine Arts (Higher Dip.). *Solo exhibitions*: Mus. für Gegenwartskunst, Basel, Museo de Arte Contemporáneo, Barcelona, Tate Britain, 2001; Kunstverein für die Rheinlande und Westfalen, Düsseldorf, 2002; ARC/Musée d'art moderne de la ville de Paris, 2003; De Pont, Tilburg, 2004; Tate St Ives, 2005; Nat. Mus. of Art, Architecture and Design, Oslo, Schaulager, Basel, 2006; Guggenheim, NY, Hugh Lane, Dublin, Miami Art Central, Miami, 2007; Frith St Gall., 1997, 2001, 2004, 2007, 2010, 2013, 2016; Dia:Beacon, NY, Fondazione Nicola Trussardi, Milan, Australian Centre for Contemporary Art, Melbourne, Sprengel Mus., Hanover, 2009; Marian Goodman Gall., NY, 2000, 2003, 2009, 2013, 2016, 2018, Paris, 1999, 2001, 2007, 2008, 2010, 2012, 2014; Museo Nacional Centre de Arte Reina Sofia, Madrid, 2010; MUMOK, Vienna, 2011; FILM, Tate Modern, 2011; Norton Mus. of Art, Florida, New Mus., NY, 2012; JG, Arcadia Univ. Art Gall., Philadelphia, 2013; De Mar en Mar, Fundación Botín, Santander, The Measure of Things, Instituto Moreira Salles, Rio de Janeiro, Studio di Giorgio Morandi, MAMbo, Bologna; Statens Mus. for Kunst, Copenhagen, 2014; Museo Tamayo, Mexico City, 2016; Portrait, NPG, Still Life, Nat. Gall., and Landscape, RA, 2018; Woman with a Red Hat, Fruitmarket Gall., Edinburgh, 2018; Kunsthaus Bregenz, 2018; Museo Serralves, 2019. Mem., Akademie der Künste, 2007. *Publications:* Book with Leaves, 1995; Disappearance at Sea, 1997; Tacita Dean: missing narratives, 1997; Teignmouth Electron, 1999, 2nd edn 2009; (with Martyn Ridgewell) FLOH, 2001; Tacita Dean: 12.10.02–21.12.02, 2002; Tacita Dean: the Green Ray, 2003; Die Regimentstochter, 2005; Darmstädter Werkblock, 2008; Fontainebleau is in France, 2008; Clover Book, 2013; c/o Jolyon, 2013; Buon Fresco, 2016. *Recreation:* various collections. *Club:* Chelsea Arts.

**DEAN, Victoria Glynis;** HM Diplomatic Service; Partner, Portland Communications, since 2016; *b* Chichester, W Sussex; *d* of Peter and Glynis Courtney; *m* 2006, Marcus Scott Dean; one *s* one *d. Educ:* Internat. Sch. of Geneva, Switzerland; Univ. of Kent (BSc Clin. Psychol. 1999). Entered FCO, 2000; Second, then First Sec., Paris, 2001–04; Head of: Communications, UK Perm. Repn, Brussels, 2004–08; Political Team, Washington, 2009–10; of Strategic Finance, FCO, 2010–11; Dep. Dir, Europe, FCO, 2011–13; High Comr to Barbados and (non-resident) to Dominica, Grenada, Antigua, Barbuda, St Vincent and the Grenadines, St Lucia and St Christopher and Nevis, 2013–16. *Recreations:* travelling and exploring, reading, family, yoga, France, politics. *Address:* Portland Communications, 85 Strand, WC2R 0DW.

**DEANE,** family name of **Baron Muskerry**.

**DEANE, Derek,** OBE 2000; choreographer; Artistic Director, English National Ballet, 1993–2001; *b* 18 June 1953; *s* of William Gordon Shepherd and Margaret Shepherd; adopted Deane as stage name. *Educ:* Royal Ballet School. With Royal Ballet Co., 1972–89; Asst Dir, Rome Opera, 1990–92. Productions for English Nat. Ballet include: Alice in Wonderland, 1995; Swan Lake, 1997 and 2011; Strictly Gershwin, 2008 and 2011; Romeo and Juliet, 2014. *Recreations:* theatre, all performing arts, travelling, tennis.

**DEANE, Julie Patricia,** OBE 2014; Founder and Chief Executive Officer, Cambridge Satchel Company, since 2008; *b* Swansea, Dec. 1966; *d* of Donald Gerald Thomas and Freda Thomas; *m* 1991, Kevin Peter Deane (marr. diss. 2016); one *s* one *d. Educ:* St Michael's Sch., Bryn, Llanelli; Gonville and Caius Coll., Cambridge (BA Hons 1987; Hon. Fellow 2017). ACA 1994. Audit Senior, Deloitte, Haskins and Sells, 1987–90; Coopers and Lybrand USA, 1990; Fellow for Develt, 1994–99, Registrary, 1997–99, Gonville and Caius Coll.,

Cambridge. Entrepreneur in Residence, BL, 2016. RSM Internat. Entrepreneur of the Year, Eur. Business Awards, 2013. *Recreations:* photography, riding, gardening. *E:* julie@cambridgesatchel.com. *Club:* Soho House.

**DEANE, Robert Edward;** HM Diplomatic Service; Head of Department, Foreign and Commonwealth Office, since 2013; *b* 28 Sept. 1962; *s* of Edward Stuart Deane and Jennifer Mary Deane; *m* 1993, Corinna Osmann; one *s* two *d*. *Educ:* London Sch. of Economics (BSc 1984); Univ. of Southampton (MSc 1985). HM Treasury, 1985–94; Bonn, 1994–99; First Sec., FCO, 1999–2005; Dep. Hd of Mission, Abu Dhabi, 2005–07; Counsellor, 2007–09, Dep. Hd of Mission, 2009–11, Rome; Counsellor, FCO, 2011–12; Dep. Hd of Mission, Baghdad, 2012–13. *Recreations:* photography, diving, travel, sailing. *Address:* c/o Foreign and Commonwealth Office, SW1A 2AH.

**DEANE, Sir Roderick (Sheldon),** KNZM 2012; PhD; Chairman: IHC Foundation (NZ), 2006–18 (Vice President, 1982–88; President, 1988–94); Pataka Foundation, 2014–17; *b* Devonport, Auckland, 8 April 1941; *s* of Reginald Roderick Deane and Jessie Margaret Deane; *m* 1964, Gillian Gibson; (one *d* decd). *Educ:* Pukekohe Primary and Mauku Primary Schs; Opunake and New Plymouth Boys High Schs; Victoria Univ. of Wellington (BCom 1st Cl. Hons; PhD). Union Steamship Co. of NZ Ltd, 1960–63; Reserve Bank of NZ, 1963–74; Alt. Exec. Dir, IMF, 1974–76; Dep. Governor, Reserve Bank of NZ, 1982–86; Chm., State Services Commn, 1986–87; Chief Executive Officer: Electricity Corp. of NZ, 1987–92; Telecom Corp. of NZ, 1992–99 (Chm., 1999–2006); Chairman: TransPower Ltd, 1987–2002; PowerDesignBuild Ltd, 1987–2002; Fletcher Bldg Ltd, 1999–2010; Pacific Road Gp, 2010–13; Director: Woolworths Ltd (Australia), 2000–13; ANZ Bank, 1994–2006; TransAlta Corpn, 2000–03. Part-time Lectr, 1964–78, Prof. of Econs, 2000–03, Victoria Univ. of Wellington. Chairman: Mus. of NZ (Te Papa), 2000–06; NZ Seed Fund, 2000–15. Trustee, Deane Endowment Trust, 1995–. FCIS 1987; FNZIM 1992. Fellow Associate Chartered Accountant, 1988. Hon. LLD Victoria Wellington, 1999. NZ Commemoration Medal, 1990. *Publications:* Foreign Investment in New Zealand Manufacturing, 1970; (ed with P. W. Nicholls and contrib.) Monetary Policy and the New Zealand Financial System, 1979, (ed jtly) 2nd edn 1983; (ed jtly and contrib.) External Economic Structure and Policy, 1981; (ed) Financial Policy Reform, 1986; research papers; contribs to jls incl. New Data for Econ. Res., Reserve Bank of NZ Bulletin, NZ Econ. Papers, NZ Economist. *Recreations:* being with friends, travelling, photography, wetland restoration. *Address:* Box 28049, Wellington 6150, New Zealand. *E:* roderick.deane@independenteconomics.com. *Club:* Wellington.

**DEANE, Hon. Sir William (Patrick),** AC 1988; KBE 1982; Governor-General of the Commonwealth of Australia, 1996–2001; *b* 4 Jan. 1931; *s* of C. A. Deane, MC and Lillian Hussey; *m* 1965, Helen, *d* of Dr Gerald and Kathleen Russell; one *s* one *d*. *Educ:* St Christopher's Convent, Canberra; St Joseph's College, Sydney; Univ. of Sydney (BA, LLB); Trinity Coll., Dublin; Dip. Internat. Law, The Hague. Called to the Bar of NSW, 1957. Teaching Fellow in Equity, Univ. of Sydney, 1956–61 (Actg Lectr in Public Internat. Law, 1956–57); QC 1966; Judge, Supreme Court of NSW, 1977; Judge, Fed. Court of Australia, 1977–82; Pres., Trade Practices Tribunal, 1977–82; Justice of the High Court of Australia, 1982–95. Hon. LLD: Sydney, NSW, Griffith, Notre Dame, TCD, UTS, Melbourne, Queensland; DUniv: Southern Cross, Aust. Cath., Western Sydney, Qld Univ. of Technol.; Hon. Dr Sac. Theol. Melbourne Coll. of Divinity. KStJ 1996. *Address:* PO Box 4168, Manuka, ACT 2603, Australia.

**DEANFIELD, Prof. John Eric,** FRCP; Professor of Cardiology, since 1996, and Director, National Centre for Cardiovascular Disease Prevention and Outcomes, since 2012, University College London (British Heart Foundation Vandervell Professor of Cardiology, 2003–17); Director, National Institute for Cardiovascular Outcomes Research, since 2012; Consultant Cardiologist, since 1984, and Academic Head, 1996–2012, Cardiothoracic Unit, Great Ormond Street Hospital; Consultant Cardiologist, Barts Heart Centre (formerly The Heart Hospital), since 1988; *b* 28 April 1952; *s* of Sigmund and Tina Deanfield; *m* 1983, Melanie Fulford; one *s* one *d*. *Educ:* Churchill Coll., Cambridge (BA 1972); Middlesex Hosp. Med. Sch. (MB BChir 1975). FRCP 1993. MRC Trng Fellow, RPMS, 1980–83; Sen. Registrar in Cardiol., Gt Ormond St Hosp., 1983–84. FACC; FESC. *Publications:* numerous peer reviewed contribs to med. jls. *Recreations:* fencing (represented GB in Fencing at Olympics, 1972, 1976, 1980), wine tasting, antique collecting (English porcelain lectr). *Address:* National Centre for Cardiovascular Disease Prevention and Outcomes, Level 2 East, 1 St Martin's Le Grand, EC1A 4NP. *T:* (020) 7679 9411. *E:* j.deanfield@ucl.ac.uk.

**DEANS, Mungo Effingham;** a Judge of the Upper Tribunal and Resident Judge, Immigration and Asylum Chamber, First-tier Tribunal, Glasgow, 2010–17 (Resident Senior Immigration Judge, Glasgow, 2005–10); Deputy Judge of the Upper Tribunal, since 2017; *b* Lytham St Anne's, Lancs, 25 May 1956; *s* of Effingham Fairrington Deans and (Agnes) Beryl (Hutchison) Deans (*née* Ramsey); *m* 1983, Kathryn Atkinson; three *s*. *Educ:* Fettes Coll., Edinburgh; London Sch. of Econs and Pol Sci. (BSc Econ 1977); Univ. of Edinburgh (LLB 1979). Admitted as solicitor, 1981; Lectr in Law, Univ. of Dundee, 1983–95; Regl Adjudicator, Immigration Appellate Authy, Glasgow, 1996–2005; Legal Mem., Immigration Appeal Tribunal, 2000–05. *Publications:* Scots Public Law, 1995. *Recreation:* tree planting. *Club:* Royal Over-Seas League.

**DEAR,** family name of **Baron Dear**.

**DEAR, Baron** *cr* 2006 (Life Peer), of Willersey in the County of Gloucestershire; **Geoffrey James Dear,** Kt 1997; QPM 1982; Vice Lord-Lieutenant, Worcestershire, 1998–2001; HM Inspector of Constabulary, 1990–97; *b* 20 Sept. 1937; *er s* of Cecil William Dear and Violet Mildred (*née* Mackney); *m* 1st, 1958, Judith Ann Stocker (*d* 1996); one *s* two *d*; 2nd, 1998, Alison Jean Martin Jones. *Educ:* Fletton Grammar Sch., Hunts; University Coll., London (LLB). Joined Peterborough Combined Police after cadet service, 1956; Mid-Anglia (now Cambridgeshire) Constab., 1965; Bramshill Scholarship, UCL, 1965–68 (Fellow, 1990); Asst Chief Constable (Ops), Notts (City and County), 1972–80; seconded as Dir of Comd Training, Bramshill, 1975–77; Metropolitan Police: Dep. Asst Comr, 1980–81; Asst Comr, 1981–85 (Personnel and Trng, 1981–84; Ops, 1984–85); Chief Constable, W Midlands Police, 1985–90. Member: Govt Adv. Cttee on Alcoholism, 1975–78; Glidewell Rev. into CPS, 1997–98; Council, RUSI, 1982–89 (Mem. Cttee, 1976–94). Lecture tour of Eastern USA univs, 1978; visited Memphis, Tenn, USA to advise on reorganisation of Police Dept, 1979. Dep. Speaker and Dep. Chm. of Cttees, H of L, 2015–. Non-executive Chairman: Image Metrics plc, 2001–03; Skyguard Technologies Ltd, 2001–11; Omniperception plc, 2005–12; Key Forensic Services Ltd, 2005–11; Forensic DNA Services Ltd, 2006–11; Blue Star Capital plc, 2008–13; Assoc. of Business Crime Partnerships Ltd, 2010–12; Blaythorne Gp Ltd, 2014–; non-executive Director: Reliance Security Services Ltd, 1997–2005; Reliance Custodial Services, subseq. Reliance Secure Task Management Ltd, 1999–2005; Mem. Adv. Bd, Pegasus Bridge Fund Mgt Ltd, 2006–08. Chm., Action against Business Crime, 2004–10. Vice Chm., London and SE Reg., Sports Council, 1984–85. Vice President: Warwickshire CCC, 1985–; W Midlands and Hereford & Worcester Grenadier Guards Assocs, 1992–2010. Trustee: Police Rehabilitation Trust, 1987–2018; World Horse Welfare, 2010–15. Hon. Fellow, Birmingham City Univ. (formerly Univ. of Central England in Birmingham), 1991. Hon. Bencher, Gray's Inn, 2008. FRSA 1990. DL W Midlands, 1985, Hereford and Worcester, 1995. Freeman, City of London, 2003. CStJ 1996. Queen's Commendation for Bravery, 1979. *Publications:* (contrib.) The Police and the Community, 1975; articles in Police Jl and other pubns. *Recreations:* field sports, Rugby football (Pres., Met. Police RFC, 1983–85), fell-walking, literature, gardening, music, fine arts. *Address:* House of Lords, SW1A 0PW. *Clubs:* East India, Special Forces.

**DEAR, Jeremy;** Deputy General Secretary, International Federation of Journalists, since 2016; *b* 6 Dec. 1966; *s* of John and Jan Dear; *m* 1999, Paula Jolly. *Educ:* Coventry Polytech. (BA Hons Mod. Studies); UC Cardiff (Postgrad. Dip. Journalism). Journalist, freelance, and on staff of Essex Chronicle Series, and The Big Issue, 1989–94; Ed., Big Issue in the Midlands, 1994–97; Nat. Organiser, Newspapers, NUJ, 1997–2001; Gen. Sec., NUJ, 2002–11.

**DEARLOVE, Sir Richard (Billing),** KCMG 2001; OBE 1984; Master of Pembroke College, Cambridge, 2004–15; Deputy Vice-Chancellor, University of Cambridge, 2005–10; *b* 23 Jan. 1945; *m* 1968, Rosalind McKenzie; two *s* one *d*. *Educ:* Monkton Combe Sch.; Kent Sch., Conn, USA; Queens' Coll., Cambridge (MA; Hon. Fellow, 2004). Entered FO, 1966; Nairobi, 1968–71; Prague, 1973–76, FCO, 1976–80; First Secretary: Paris, 1980–84; FCO, 1984–87; Counsellor: UKMIS Geneva, 1987–91; Washington, 1991–93; Secret Intelligence Service: Dir, Personnel and Admin, 1993–94; Dir, Ops, 1994–99; Asst Chief, 1998–99; Chief, 1999–2004. Chairman: Ascot Underwriting Ltd, 2006–; Crossword Cybersecurity, 2016–; Director: Kosmos Energy, 2013–; Ascot Gp, 2017–. Vis. Lectr, Fletcher Sch., Tufts Univ., Boston, USA, 2005–10. Advr, Monitor Gp, 2005–11; Mem. Adv. Bd, AIG, 2005–10. Chairman of Trustees: Cambridge Union Soc., 2007–15; Univ. of London, 2014–; Trustee, Kent Sch., Conn, USA, 2001–. Gov., ESU, 2008–10. Hon. LLD Exeter, 2007. *Address:* Pembroke College, Cambridge CB2 1RF.

**DEARNLEY, Mark William,** CEng; FIET, FBCS; Senior Adviser, Bain & Co., since 2018; *b* Huddersfield, 12 April 1969; *s* of William and Margaret Dearnley; *m* 1991, Lorraine Michelle; two *c*. *Educ:* Dauntsey's Sch.; Brunel Univ. (BEng Hons Electrical and Electronic Engrg 1991). Prog. Dir, Boots Gp plc, 2002–04; Chief Information Officer: Cable & Wireless Internat. Gp, 2004–10; Vodafone UK, 2010–13; Dir Gen. and Chief Digital and Inf. Officer, HM Revenue and Customs, 2013–16; Chief Inf. Officer, Premium Credit Ltd, 2016–17. *Recreation:* tennis. *Club:* Morgan Sports Car.

**DEARY, Prof. Ian John,** OBE 2019; PhD; FRCPE; FRCPsych; FBA 2003; FRSE; FMedSci; Professor of Differential Psychology, University of Edinburgh, since 1995; Director, University of Edinburgh Centre for Cognitive Ageing and Cognitive Epidemiology, 2008–19; *b* 17 May 1954; *s* of Hugh McCulloch Deary and Isobelle Ferguson Deary; *m* 1978, Ann Marie Barclay; one *s* two *d*. *Educ:* Hamilton Acad.; Univ. of Edinburgh (BSc; MB ChB; PhD 1992). MRCPsych 1991, FRCPsych 2008; FRCPE 1996; FRSE 2003. Med. House Officer, 1983–84, Surgical House Officer, 1984, Royal Infirmary of Edinburgh; Sen. House Officer, Psychiatry, Bethlem Royal and Maudsley Hosps, 1984–85; Lectr, 1985–90, Sen. Lectr, 1990–92, Reader, 1992–95, in Psychology, Univ. of Edinburgh; Registrar, Psychiatry, Royal Edinburgh Hosp., 1989–90. FMedSci 2007; James McKeen Cattell Fellow, Assoc. for Psychol Sci., 2015. Lifetime Achievement Award, Internat. Soc. for Intelligence Res., 2014. *Publications:* (with G. Matthews) Personality Traits, 1998, 3rd edn 2009; Looking Down on Human Intelligence: from psychometrics to the brain, 2000; Intelligence: a very short introduction, 2001; (with L. J. Whalley and J. M. Starr) A Lifetime of Intelligence, 2009; over 800 articles in learned jls on human mental abilities, personality, cognitive ageing and cognitive epidemiology. *Recreations:* cycling, lyric writing, saxophone, Motherwell FC, English Romantic composers, late Victorian English novelists. *Address:* Department of Psychology, University of Edinburgh, 7 George Square, Edinburgh EH8 9JZ. *T:* (0131) 650 3452. *E:* i.deary@ed.ac.uk.

**DEATHRIDGE, Prof. John William,** DPhil; FRCO; King Edward Professor of Music, King's College London, 1996–2013, now Emeritus; *b* 21 Oct. 1944; *s* of Leslie and Iris Deathridge; *m* 1985, Victoria L. Cooper; one *d*. *Educ:* King Edward's Sch., Birmingham; Lincoln Coll., Oxford (MA; DPhil 1974). FRCO 1967. Organist and Choirmaster, St Wolfgang, Munich, 1971–81; Ed., Richard Wagner-Gesamtausgabe, Munich, 1981–83; University of Cambridge: Fellow, and Dir, Studies in Music, King's Coll., 1983–96; Lectr in Music, 1983–95; Reader in Music, 1995–96. Pres., Royal Musical Assoc., 2005–08 (Vice-Pres., 2002–05). Mem. Bd, European Acad. of Music Theatre, 2011–. Corresp. Mem., Amer. Musicological Soc., 2002. *Publications:* Wagner's Rienzi: a reappraisal based on a study of the sketches and drafts, 1977; (with C. Dahlhaus) The New Grove Wagner, 1984; (jtly) Verzeichnis der musikalischen Werke Richard Wagners und ihrer Quellen, 1986; (ed) Family Letters of Richard Wagner, 1991; (ed jtly) Wagner Handbook, 1992; Wagner Beyond Good and Evil, 2008; (trans.) Wagner's Ring, 2018; edited with K. Döge: Richard Wagner: Lohengrin, 3 vols, 1996–2000; Dokumente und Texte zu "Lohengrin", 2003; contribs to Musical Times, 19th Century Music, Cambridge Opera Jl, Jl Royal Musical Assoc., Opera Quarterly. *Recreations:* keep fit, films, pond care. *Address:* 12 Cook Close, Cambridge CB4 1PH; Music Department, King's College London, Strand, WC2R 2LS. *E:* john.deathridge@kcl.ac.uk. *Club:* Athenæum.

**DEAVE, John James;** former barrister-at-law; *b* 1 April 1928; *s* of Charles John Deave and Gertrude Debrit Deave; *m* 1958, Gillian Mary, *d* of Adm. Sir Manley Power, KCB, CBE, DSO; one *s* one *d*. *Educ:* Charterhouse; Pembroke Coll., Oxford (MA). Served RA, 2nd Lieut, 1946–48; Pembroke Coll., 1948–51; called to the Bar, Gray's Inn, 1952; in practice at Nottingham, 1957–98; a Recorder, 1980–98. *Recreations:* history, gardening. *Address:* Greensmith Cottage, Stathern, Melton Mowbray, Leics LE14 4HE. *T:* (01949) 860340. *Club:* Nottinghamshire United Services.

**DEAYTON, (Gordon) Angus;** writer and presenter; *b* 6 Jan. 1956; *s* of Roger Davall Deayton and Susan Agnes Deayton (*née* Weir). *Educ:* Caterham Sch.; New Coll., Oxford (BA Modern Langs (French and German)). Dir, Oxford Revue, 1979. Writer and performer: *radio:* Radio Active, 1980–87 (Mem., Hee Bee Gee Bees pop parody band); It's Your Round, 2011–12; Alone, 2018–19; *stage:* Rowan Atkinson's Stage Show, 1986–90; Radio Active Stage Show, 2016–19; *television:* Alexei Sayle's Stuff, 1987–90; KYTV, 1990–93; One Foot in the Grave, 1990–2000; Have I Got News For You?, 1990–2002; TV Hell, 1992; End of the Year Show, 1995–2000; Before They Were Famous, 1997–2004; Not Another Awards Show, 1999; Not Another Game Show, News Bulletin, Eurovision, 2002; University Challenge (for Comic Relief), 2002, 2004; Nighty Night, 2003; Absolute Power, 2004–07; Hell's Kitchen, 2004–07; Bognor or Bust, 2004; Heartless, New Year's Honours List, Stick to What You Know, 2005; Help Yourself, Only Fools On Horses, 2006; Would I Lie to You?, 2007–08; Comedy Sketchbook, British Comedy Awards, 2008; Pete 'n Dud—The Lost Sketches, 2010; Pramface, 2011–14; Waterloo Road, 2013–15; World Cup Epic Fails, Christmas Epic Fails, 2014; Benidorm, 2015; Drive, 2016; Bake Off: Creme de la Creme, 2017; Death in Paradise, 2019; *documentaries:* In Search of Happiness, 1995; The Lying Game, 1997; The Temptation Game, 1998; The History of Alternative Comedy, 1999; Posh 'n Becks: the Reign in Spain, 2003; *films:* Elizabeth, 1998; Swinging with the Finkels, 2011; The Great European Disaster Movie, 2015. *Publications:* Radio Active Times, 1986; The Uncyclopaedia of Rock, 1987; Have I Got News For

You?, 1994; In Search of Happiness, 1995; Have I Got 1997 For You?, 1997. *Recreations:* soccer, tennis, ski-ing. *Address:* c/o Independent Talent Group Ltd, 40 Whitfield Street, W1T 2RH. *Clubs:* Garrick, Groucho, Soho House, Home House.

**DEBBONAIRE, Thangam Rachel;** MP (Lab) Bristol West, since 2015; *b* 3 Aug. 1966; *née* Singh. *Educ:* Bradford Girls' Grammar Sch.; Chetham's Music Sch.; ARCM 1986; Univ. of Oxford; St John's City Coll. of Technol., Manchester; Bristol Univ. (MSc 1995). Professional cellist in string quartets, chamber music and soloist, 1977–2006; cellist, Royal Liverpool Philharmonic Orch., 1990–91; House-parent, girls boarding, Chetham's Sch. of Music, Manchester, 1989–91; Nat. Children's Officer, Women's Aid Fedn, 1991–98; Dir and lead indep. practitioner, Domestic Violence Responses, 1997–; Accreditation Officer, 2006–08, Res. and Fundraising Manager, 2008–15, Respect. An Opposition Whip, 2016–. *Publications:* (contrib.) Children Living with Domestic Violence, 1994; (jtly) Health Professionals Responding to Men for Safety, 2014; Responding to Domestic Violence in Diverse Communities, 2015. *Address:* House of Commons, SW1A 0AA. *W:* www.debbonaire.co.uk.

**DEBEN, Baron** *cr* 2010 (Life Peer), of Winston in the County of Suffolk; **John Selwyn Gummer;** PC 1985; Chairman: Sancroft International Ltd, since 1997; Committee on Climate Change, since 2012; *b* 26 Nov. 1939; *s* of late Canon Selwyn Gummer and Sybille (*née* Mason); *m* 1977, Penelope Jane, *yr d* of John P. Gardner; two *s* two *d*. *Educ:* King's Sch., Rochester; Selwyn Coll., Cambridge (Exhibr). BA Hons History 1961; MA 1971; Chm., Cambridge Univ. Conservative Assoc., 1961; Pres., Cambridge Union, 1962; Chm., Fedn of Conservative Students, 1962. Editor, Business Publications, 1962–64; Editor-in-Chief, Max Parrish & Oldbourne Press, 1964–66; BPC Publishing: Special Asst to Chm., 1967; Publisher, Special Projects, 1967–69; Editorial Coordinator, 1969–70. Mem., ILEA Educn Cttee, 1967–70; Dir, Shandwick Publishing Co., 1966–81; Man. Dir, EP Gp of Cos, 1975–81; Chairman: Selwyn Shandwick Internat., 1976–81, Siemssen Hunter Ltd, 1979–80 (Dir, 1973–80). Contested (C) Greenwich, 1964 and 1966; MP (C) Lewisham W, 1970–Feb. 1974, Eye, Suffolk, 1979–83, Suffolk Coastal, 1983–2010. PPS to Minister of Agriculture, 1972; an additional Vice-Chm., Conservative Party, 1972–74; an Asst Govt Whip, 1981; a Lord Comr of HM Treasury, 1981–83; Parly Under-Sec. of State for Employment, Jan.–Oct. 1983; Minister of State, Dept of Employment, 1983–84; Paymaster-Gen., 1984–85; Chm., Cons. Party, 1983–85; Minister of State: MAFF, 1985–88; DoE, 1988–89; Minister of Agric., Fisheries and Food, 1989–93; Sec. of State for the Envmt, 1993–97. Chairman: Cons. Gp for Europe, 1997–2000; Marine Stewardship Council, 1998–2005; Quality of Life Commn, 2007–08. Chairman: Valpak Ltd, 1998–; Assoc. of Professional (formerly Ind.) Financial Advrs, 2003–17; Veolia Water UK (formerly General Utilities Ltd), 2004–13 (Dir, 1997–2013); Personal Investment Mgt and Financial Advice Assoc., 2017–; non-executive Director: Sovereign Reversions plc, 2004–10; Castle Trust Mgt Ltd, 2011–; Castle Trust Capital Mgt Ltd, 2011–; Sistema-Hals, 2007–09. Mem., Gen. Synod of the Church of England, 1979–92; joined Roman Catholic Church, 1993. *Publications:* (jtly) When the Coloured People Come, 1966; The Permissive Society, 1971; (with L. W. Cowie) The Christian Calendar, 1974; (contrib.) To Church with Enthusiasm, 1969; (contrib.) Faith In Politics, 1987; Christianity and Conservatism, 1990. *Address:* Sancroft International Ltd, 46 Queen Anne's Gate, SW1H 9AP.
*See also Baron Chadlington, Rt Hon. B. M. Gummer.*

**DE BENEDETTI, Carlo;** Cavaliere del Lavoro, Italy, 1983; Chairman: Compagnie Industriali Riunite, 1995–2009, now Hon. Chairman (Vice-Chairman and Chief Executive, 1976–95); Compagnia Finanziaria De Benedetti, 1995–2009, now Hon. President (Chief Executive, 1991–95); Sogefi, 1981–2005, now Hon. Chairman; *b* 14 Nov. 1934; *m*; three *s*. *Educ:* Turin Polytechnic (degree in electrotech. engrg). Chm./Chief Exec., Gilardini, 1972–76; Chief Exec., Fiat, 1976; Olivetti SpA: Chief Exec., 1978–96; Chm., 1983–96; Hon. Chm., 1996–99. Director: Pirelli SpA; Valeo; l'Espresso SpA; Mem., European Adv. Cttee, NY Stock Exchange, 1985–2005; Chm., Cerus, 1986–99. Dir, Center for Strategic and Internat. Studies, Washington, 1978; Mem. Bd of Trustees, Solomon R. Guggenheim Foundn, NY, 1984; Vice Chm., Eur. Roundtable of Industrialists, Brussels, 1999–2004. Foreign Mem., Royal Swedish Acad. of Engrg Scis, Stockholm, 1987. Officier, Légion d'Honneur (France), 1987; Silver Medal of Merit (Austria), 2006. *Publications:* lectures and articles in business jls. *Address:* CIR SpA, Via Ciovassino 1, 20121 Milano, Italy. *T:* (2) 722701.

**DEBENHAM, Sir Thomas Adam,** 4th Bt *cr* 1931, of Bladen, co. Dorset; *b* 28 Feb. 1971; *s* of George Andrew Debenham and of Penelope Jane (*née* Carter); *S* grandfather, 2001, but his name does not appear on the Official Roll of the Baronetage; *m* 1998, Melanie Bargh.
*Heir: cousin* Oliver William Debenham, *b* 1976.

**de BERNIÈRE-SMART, Louis Henry Piers;** author, poet and musician as Louis de Bernières; *b* 8 Dec. 1954; *s* of Major Reginald Piers Alexander de Bernière-Smart, *qv*; one *s* one *d*. *Educ:* Grenham House; Bradfield Coll.; Manchester Univ. (BA Hons Philosophy 1977); Leicester Poly. (PGCE 1981); Inst. of Educn, London Univ. (MA 1985). Landscape gardener, 1972–73; teacher and rancher, Colombia, 1974; philosophy tutor, 1977–79; car mechanic, 1980; English teacher, 1981–84; bookshop asst, 1985–86; supply teacher, 1986–93. Chancellor, Norfolk Children's Univ., 2010–. Patron: Families House, Norwich; Banjo, Mandolin and Guitar Fedn; Norfolk Youth Orch., 2009–; Families Need Fathers, 2010–15. Mem., Antonius Players, 2002–10. FTCL 1999. Recording: The Songs of Louis de Bernières, Vol. 1, 2018. *Publications:* The War of Don Emmanuel's Nether Parts, 1990; Señor Vivo and the Coca Lord, 1991; The Troublesome Offspring of Cardinal Guzman, 1992; Captain Corelli's Mandolin, 1994 (filmed, 2001; adapted for stage, 2019); Red Dog, 2001 (filmed, 2012); Sunday Morning at the Centre of the World, 2001; Birds Without Wings, 2004; A Partisan's Daughter, 2008; Notwithstanding, 2009; Imagining Alexandria (poems in honour of Constantin Cavafis), 2013; The Dust That Falls From Dreams, 2015; Of Love and Desire (poems), 2016; Blue Dog, 2016; So Much Life Left Over, 2018; The Cat in the Treble Clef (poems), 2018; Labels and Other Stories, 2019; Station Jim, 2019. *Recreations:* music, literature, golf, fishing, carpentry, gardening, cats, restoring and making musical instruments. *Address:* c/o Caroline Wood, Felicity Bryan Literary Agency, 2a North Parade Avenue, Oxford OX2 6LX. *T:* (01865) 513816.

**de BERNIÈRE-SMART, Major Reginald Piers Alexander;** Director, The Shaftesbury Homes and Arethusa, 1988–89, retired (General Secretary, 1971–88); general duties, Chichester Division, SSAFA/FHS, 1995–2000 (caseworker, 1990–94); *b* 3 March 1924; *s* of Kenneth de Bernière-Smart and Audrey (*née* Brown); *m* 1951, Jean Ashton Smithells (*d* 2010); one *s* one *d*. *Educ:* Bowden House, Seaford; Bradfield Coll. Commnd The Queen's Bays (2nd Dragoon Guards), 1943; Italian Campaign, 1944–45 (despatches); Staff, RAC OCTU and Mons OCS, 1948–49; GSO 3 7th Armd Bde, 1951; Adjt, The Queen's Bays, 1952–54; Adjt, RAC Centre, Bovington, 1956–58; retired from 1st The Queen's Dragoon Guards, 1959. Exec. Sec., British Diabetic Assoc., 1960–65; joined Shaftesbury Homes and Arethusa exec. staff, 1966. Dir, Wad (West Wittering) Management Co., 1992–94. Chm., Management Cttee, Bradfield Club, Peckham, 1990–92 (Mem. Council, 1992–2000). Member: IAM, 1959–; NCVCCO, 1971–89. West Wittering PCC, 1991–97; Foundn Gov., W Wittering Parochial C of E Sch., 1997–2000 (Chm. of Govs, 1998–2000). Hon. Fellow, Cancer Res. UK, 2003. *Publications:* (as Piers Alexander) Golden Apples (poetry), 2006; Windfall: Golden Apples, Vol. II, 2015. *Recreations:* open air activities, photography, steam and model railways, theatre, poetry, militaria. *Address:* 9 The Wad, West Wittering, Chichester, W Sussex PO20 8AH. *T:* (01243) 511072. *Clubs:* Cavalry and Guards, Victoria League for Commonwealth Friendship.
*See also L. H. P. de Bernière-Smart.*

**de BERNIÈRES, Louis;** *see* de Bernière-Smart, L. H. P.

**de BERTODANO, Sylvia Philippa Theresa; Her Honour Judge de Bertodano;** a Circuit Judge, since 2009; *b* Cirencester, 16 Oct. 1969; *d* of Martin de Bertodano and Tessa de Bertodano (*née* Avery); *m* 1995, Stuart Robert Alford, *qv*; two *s* two *d*. *Educ:* St Mary's Convent, Ascot; Marlborough Coll.; Christ Church, Oxford (BA Hons PPE). Called to the Bar, Middle Temple, 1993; in practice as a barrister specialising in internat. criminal law, 1994–2009. *Publications:* (contrib.) Internationalized Criminal Courts, 2004; (contrib.) Defense in International Criminal Proceedings, 2006; (contrib.) The Oxford Companion to International Criminal Justice, 2009; (jtly) Closing the Gap: the role of non-judicial mechanisms in addressing impunity, 2010. *Recreations:* opera, poetry, scuba diving, playing violin. *Address:* Warwickshire Justice Centre, 3 Newbold Terrace, Leamington Spa, Warwicks CV32 4EL. *T:* (01926) 682100.

**de BLOCQ van KUFFELER, John Philip;** Group Chief Executive, Non-Standard Finance plc, since 2017 (Chairman, 2014–17); Chairman, Paratus AMC Ltd, since 2015; *b* 9 Jan. 1949; *s* of late Captain Frans de Blocq van Kuffeler and Stella de Blocq van Kuffeler (*née* Hall); *m* 1st, 1971, Lesley Callander (marr. diss. 2014); two *s* one *d*; 2nd, 2015, Eva Nijhof; one *d*. *Educ:* Atlantic Coll.; Clare Coll., Cambridge (MA). FCA 1975. Peat Marwick & Mitchell, 1970–77; Grindlays Bank: Manager, 1977–80; Head of Corporate Finance, 1980–82; Brown Shipley & Co.: Head: Corporate Finance, 1983–88; Investment Banking, UK and USA, 1986–88; Gp Chief Exec., 1988–91; Chief Exec., 1991–97, Chm., 1997–2014, Provident Financial plc; Chairman: Hyperion Insurance Gp Ltd, 2009–13; Marlin Financial Gp Ltd, 2010–14. Council Mem., CBI, 1997–99. Executive Chairman: Finsbury Smaller Quoted Companies Trust plc, 1992–2003; J. P. Morgan Fleming Technology Trust plc, 1998–2003; Huveaux plc, 2001–08; non-exec. Chm., Eidos plc, 2002–05; non-exec. Dir, Medical Defence Union, 2001–04. Mem. Council, Prince's Trust, 2001–08. *Recreations:* contemporary dance, opera, history, countryside. *Address:* 2 St James's Street, SW1A 1EF. *Club:* Walbrook.

**de BOIS, Geoffrey Nicholas, (Nick);** author, broadcaster and political commentator; *b* Ely, 23 Feb. 1959; *s* of Wing Comdr John de Bois and Paula de Bois; *m* Vanessa Coleman; one *s* three *d*; *m* 2009, Helen Seaman. *Educ:* Culford Sch.; Cambridge Coll. of Arts and Technol. (HND Business Studies 1981). Public Relations Exec., Advertising Standards Authy, 1982–84; Rapiergroup: Client Proj. Manager, 1984–86; Client Proj. Dir, 1986–88; Chm. and Man. Dir, 1989–2010. Contested (C): Stalybridge and Hyde, 1997; Enfield N, 2001, 2005. MP (C) Enfield N, 2010–15; contested (C) same seat, 2015, 2017. Mem., Justice Select Cttee, 2011–; Chm., All Party Parly Gp on UK Events Industry, 2011–15; Vice Chm., All Party Parly Gp on Trade and Investment, 2012–15; Co-Chair, All Party Parly Gp on Public Health and Primary Care, 2012–15; Mem., Public Admin Cttee, 2010–11; Sec., 1922 Cttee, 2012–15. COS to Sec. of State for Exiting the EU, 2018. Member: Crossrail 2 Growth Commn, 2015–16; Serious Violence Task Force, Home Office, 2018. Chm., UK Events Industry Bd, 2016–18. Chm., BackZac2016, 2015–16. Mem., Adv. Bd, Kids Count, 2016–19. Guest broadcaster and political commentator, LBC and talkRADIO, 2015–17; Broadcast Host, talkRADIO, 2018–. *Publications:* Confessions of a Recovering MP, 2018. *Recreations:* travel, writing, theatre, gym, armchair sports fan, dining out and entertaining. *E:* nickdebois@gmail.com.

**de BOISSIEU, Pierre;** Secretary-General of the Council of the European Union, 2009–11 (Deputy Secretary-General, 1999–2009); *b* Paris, 14 June 1945; *s* of Michel and Françoise de Boissieu; *m* 1968, Béatrice; three *s* two *d*. *Educ:* École Nationale d'Administration. First Sec., French Embassy, Bonn, 1973–78; Hd, Cabinet of Vice-Pres., Eur. Commn, 1978–84; Dir for Econ. Affairs, Foreign Ministry, 1984–93; Perm. Rep. to EU, 1993–99. Commandeur de la Légion d'Honneur (France), 2010. *Address:* 29 avenue Bosquet, 75007 Paris, France.

**DE BOLLE, Catherine;** Executive Director, Europol, since 2018; *b* Aalst, Belgium, 17 Feb. 1970; *d* of Antoine De Bolle and Christiane De Muyter; *m* 1998, Anton Segers; three *s*. *Educ:* Sint Aloysiuscollege, Ninove; Ghent Univ. (Law degree 1993); Sch. for Officers, Royal Gendarmerie Acad. Officer, Gendarmerie, 1994–97; Chief of Police, Ninove, 2001–12; Comr Gen., Belgian Federal Police, 2012–18. Member: Police Reform Commn, 2011; Standing Cttee on Operational Cooperation on Internal Security, EU, 2012–18; Federal Police Council, 2012–18; Exec. Cttee, INTERPOL, 2015–18. Pres., Coordination Cttee for Intelligence and Security, 2015–18. Vice Pres., Bd of Chiefs of Local Police, 2007–12. Mem., Pearls in Policing (Pres., The Future of Policing internat. wkg gp). Hon. Citizen, Ninove, 2018. Public Manager of the Year, 2015. Officer, Ordre National de la Légion d'Honneur (France), 2017. *Recreations:* hiking, reading. *Address:* Europol, Eisenhowerlaan 73, 2517 KK, The Hague, The Netherlands. *T:* (70) 3025000. *E:* G1@europol.europa.eu.

**DE BONO, Dr Anne Mary;** Consultant Occupational Physician, University Hospitals of Leicester NHS Trust, since 2000; President, Faculty of Occupational Medicine, Royal College of Physicians, 2017–Dec. 2020; *b* Preston, 26 Nov. 1947; *d* of John Fingleton and Constance Fingleton; *m* 1971, David de Bono (*d* 1999); two *s*. *Educ:* Holy Child Convent, Preston; Girton Coll., Cambridge (BA 1968); St Mary's Hosp. Med. Sch. (MA MB). FRCGP 2004; FFOM 2005; FRCP 2015. Fellow, and Dir of Studies in Medicine, Girton Coll., Cambridge, 1973–78; Principal in Gen. Practice, Oxford, Edinburgh and Leicester, 1978–91; Registrar in Occupational Medicine, Leicester Royal Infirmary, 1991–96; Consultant Occupational Physician, Leicester Gen. Hosp., 1996–2000. *Publications:* papers in occupational medicine. *Recreations:* reeling, surfing, talking. *Address:* Occupational Health Department, University Hospitals of Leicester NHS Trust, Leicester LE1 5WW. *T:* (0116) 258 7683. *E:* anne.debono@uhl-tr.nhs.uk.
*See also J. H. de Bono.*

**de BONO, Dr Edward Francis Charles Publius;** Lecturer in Medicine, Department of Medicine, University of Cambridge, 1976–83; Director of The Cognitive Research Trust, Cambridge, since 1971; Secretary-General, Supranational Independent Thinking Organisation (SITO), since 1983; *b* 19 May 1933; *s* of late Prof. Joseph de Bono, CBE and of Josephine de Bono (*née* O'Byrne); *m* 1971, Josephine (marr. diss.), *d* of Maj. Francis Hall-White, MBE; two *s*. *Educ:* St Edward's Coll., Malta; Royal Univ. of Malta; Christ Church, Oxford (Rhodes Scholar). BSc, MD Malta; DPhil Oxon; PhD Cantab. Research Asst, Dept of Regius Prof. of Medicine, Univ. of Oxford, 1958–60; Jun. Lectr in Med., Oxford, 1960–61; Asst Dir of Res., Dept of Investigative Medicine, Cambridge Univ., 1963–76. Research Associate: also Hon. Registrar, St Thomas' Hosp. Med. Sch., Univ. of London; Harvard Med. Sch., and Hon. Consultant, Boston City Hosp., 1965–66. Hon. Prof. of Thinking, Univ. of Pretoria, 2003; Da Vinci Prof. of Thinking, Univ. of Advancing Technol., Arizona, 2005–; Prof. of Constructive Thinking, Dublin City Univ., 2005–. EU Ambassador for Thinking, Year of Creativity, 2009. Chm. Council, Young Enterprise

Europe, 1998–. Established World Centre for New Thinking, Malta, 2004. TV series: The Greatest Thinkers, 1981; de Bono's Thinking Course, 1982. Hon. LLD Dundee, 2005; Hon. DDes RMIT, 2003. Planet DE73 named edebono after him, 1997. Carl Sloans Award, Internat. Assoc. Mgt Consulting Firms, 2006. *Publications:* The Use of Lateral Thinking, 1967; The Five-Day Course in Thinking, 1968; The Mechanism of Mind, 1969; Lateral Thinking: a textbook of creativity, 1970; The Dog Exercising Machine, 1970; Technology Today, 1971; Practical Thinking, 1971; Lateral Thinking for Management, 1971; Beyond Yes and No, 1972; Children Solve Problems, 1972; Eureka!: an illustrated history of inventions from the wheel to the computer, 1974; Teaching Thinking, 1976; The Greatest Thinkers, 1976; Wordpower, 1977; The Happiness Purpose, 1977; The Case of the Disappearing Elephant, 1977; Opportunities: a handbook of business opportunity search, 1978; Future Positive, 1979; Atlas of Management Thinking, 1981; de Bono's Thinking Course, 1982; Tactics: the art and science of success, 1984; Conflicts: a better way to resolve them, 1985; Six Thinking Hats, 1985; Masterthinker's Handbook, 1985; Letters to Thinkers, 1987; I am Right, You are Wrong, 1990; Positive Revolution for Brazil, 1990; Handbook for a Positive Revolution, 1990; Six Action Shoes, 1992; Sur/Petition, 1992; Serious Creativity, 1992; Teach Your Child to Think, 1992; Water Logic, 1993; Parallel Thinking, 1994; Teach Yourself to Think, 1995; Mind Pack, 1995; Edward de Bono's Textbook of Wisdom, 1996; How To Be More Interesting, 1997; Simplicity, 1998; New Thinking for the New Millennium, 1999; Why I want to be King of Australia, 1999; The de Bono Code Book, 2000; Why So Stupid: how the human race has never really learned to think, 2003; How to have a Beautiful Mind, 2004; Six Value Medals, 2005; H+, 2006; How to have Creative Ideas, 2007; Free or Unfree?: are Americans really free?, 2007; Six Frames for Looking at Information, 2008; Think!: before it's too late, 2009; The Love of Two Cockroaches, 2009; contribs to Nature, Lancet, Clinical Science, Amer. Jl of Physiology, etc. *Recreations:* travel, toys, thinking. *Address:* L2 Albany, Piccadilly, W1J 0AZ. *Club:* Athenæum.

**de BONO, John Hugh;** QC 2014; *b* Cambridge, 6 Nov. 1972; *s* of late Prof. David de Bono and of Dr Anne Mary de Bono, *qv*; *m* 1998, Caroline Marshall; three *s* one *d*. *Educ:* Edinburgh Acad.; Downside Sch.; Oriel Coll., Oxford (MA 1st Cl. Philosophy and Theol. 1993); De Montfort Univ. (CPE 1994). Called to the Bar, Gray's Inn, 1995; in practice as barrister, specialising in clinical negligence and police law. *Recreations:* sailing, walking. *Address:* Serjeants' Inn Chambers, 85 Fleet Street, EC4Y 1AE. *E:* jdebonoqc@ serjeantsinn.com.

**de BOTTON, Alain;** author, since 1993; Creative Director, Living Architecture; *b* 20 Dec. 1969; *s* of late Gilbert de Botton and of Jacqueline (*née* Burgauer); *m* 2003, Charlotte Neser; two *s*. *Educ:* Gonville and Caius Coll., Cambridge (BA Hist. 1st Cl. Hons). Hon. FRIBA 2009. *Publications:* Essays in Love, 1993; The Romantic Movement, 1994; Kiss and Tell, 1995; How Proust Can Change Your Life, 1997; The Consolations of Philosophy, 2000; The Art of Travel, 2002; Status Anxiety, 2004; The Architecture of Happiness, 2006; The Pleasures and Sorrows of Work, 2009; A Week at the Airport: a Heathrow diary, 2009; Religion for Atheists: a non-believer's guide to the uses of religion, 2012; (jtly) Art as Therapy, 2013; The News: a user's manual, 2014; The Course of Love, 2016. *Recreations:* French Cinema 1960–1970, nature, art. *Address:* c/o Caroline Dawnay, United Agents, 12–26 Lexington Street, W1F 0LE.

**de BOTTON, Hon. Dame Janet (Frances Wolfson),** DBE 2013 (CBE 2006); Trustee, since 1987, and Chairman, since 2010, Wolfson Foundation; *b* 31 March 1952; *d* of Baron Wolfson and Ruth, Lady Wolfson; *m* 1st, 1972, Michael Philip Green, *qv* (marr. diss. 1989); two *d*; 2nd, 1990, Gilbert de Botton (*d* 2000). *Educ:* St Paul's Girls' Sch. Dir, Christie's International, 1994–98. Trustee, Tate Gall., 1992–2002. *Recreation:* bridge. *Address:* c/o Wolfson Foundation, 8 Queen Anne Street, W1G 9LD. *T:* (020) 7323 5730.

**DEBRÉ, Jean Louis;** President, Constitutional Council, France, 2007–16; *b* Toulouse, 30 Sept. 1944; *s* of late Michel Jean-Pierre Debré; *m* 1971, Anne-Marie Engel; two *s* one *d*. *Educ:* Lycée Janson-de-Sailly; Institut d'Etudes Politiques, Paris; Faculté de Droit, Paris (DenD); Ecole Nationale de la Magistrature. Asst, Faculté de Droit, Paris, 1972–75; Technical Counsellor, then Chargé de Mission, office of Jacques Chirac, as Minister of Agric., 1973–74, Minister of the Interior, 1974, and Prime Minister, 1974–76; Dep. Public Prosecutor, High Court of Evry, 1976–78; Magistrate, Central Admin, Ministry of Justice, 1978; Chef de Cabinet to Minister of the Budget, 1978; Examng Magistrate, High Court of Paris, 1979. Dep. (RPR) for Eure, Nat. Assembly, 1986–95 and 1997–2007; Minister of the Interior, France, 1995–97; Pres., Nat. Assembly, 2002–07; Vice-Pres., 1990–95, Pres., 1997–2007, RPR Gp in Nat. Assembly. Councillor: Evreux, 1989–95; Paris, 1995–97; Conseiller Général, Canton de Nonancourt, 1992–2004; Mayor of Evreux, 2001–07. Pres., Conseil supérieur des Archives, 2016. *Publications:* Les Idées constitutionnelles du Général de Gaulle, 1974; La Constitution de la V$^e$ République, 1974; Le Pouvoir politique, 1977; Le Gaullisme, 1978; La Justice au XIX$^e$, 1981; Les Républiques des Avocats, 1984; Le Curieux, 1986; En mon for intérieur, 1997; Pièges, 1998; Le Gaullisme n'est pas une nostalgie, 1999; Qu'est ce que l'Assemblée Nationale?, 2006; Quand les brochets font courir les carpes, 2008; Les oubliés de la République, 2008; Meurtre à l'Assemblée, 2010; En tête-à-tête avec Charles de Gaulle, 2010; Regard de femme, 2010; Jeux de haine, 2011; En tête à tête avec les présidents de la République, 2012; Ces femmes qui ont réveillé la France, 2013. *Recreations:* horse-riding, tennis.

**de BROKE;** see Willoughby de Broke.

**de BRÚN, Bairbre;** Member (SF) Northern Ireland, European Parliament, 2004–May 2012. *Educ:* University Coll., Dublin (BA Hons 1974); Queen's Univ., Belfast (PGCE 1980). Teacher, specialised in Irish Medium Educn, 1991–97. Mem. (SF) W Belfast, NI Assembly, 1998–2004; Minister of Health, Social Services and Public Safety, NI, 1999–2002. *Recreations:* hill-walking, theatre, cinema.

**DEBY, John Bedford;** QC 1980; a Recorder of the Crown Court, 1977–95; *b* 19 Dec. 1931; *s* of Reginald Bedford Deby and Irene (*née* Slater). *Educ:* Winchester Coll.; Trinity Coll., Cambridge (MA). Called to the Bar, Inner Temple, 1954, Bencher, 1986. *Address:* 11 Britannia Road, Fulham, SW6 2HJ. *T:* (020) 7736 4976. *Club:* Athenæum.

**de CARMOY, Hervé Pierre;** Comte de Carmoy; Chairman, Supervisory Board, Meridiam, since 2013; *b* 4 Jan. 1937; *s* of Guy de Carmoy and Marie de Gourcuff; *m* Roseline de Rohan Chabot; two *c*. *Educ:* Institut d'Etudes Politiques, Paris; Cornell Univ. Gen. Man., Western Europe, Chase Manhattan Bank, 1963–78; Chm., Exec. Bd, Midland Bank, Paris, 1978–79; Gen. Man., Europe, Midland Bank, London, 1979–84; Chief Exec., Internat. Midland Bank, London, 1984–86; Dir and Chief Exec., Global Banking Sector, Midland Bank, 1986–88; Chief Exec. Officer, Société Générale de Belgique, 1988–91; Chairman and Chief Executive: Union Minière, 1989–91; Banque Industrielle et Mobilière Privée, 1992–98; Man. Dir, Rhône Group LLC, New York, 1999–2003. Chairman: Cimenteries Belges Réunies, 1989–; Gechem, 1989–; Parvalind Gérance, 1991–; Almatis, 2003–07; Etam, 2009–13; Vice Chm., Générale de Banque, 1989–. Prof. of Internat. Strategy, Institut d'Etudes Politiques, Paris, 1996–2002. Chm., France, 1989–2004, Vice-Chm., Europe, 2004–, Trilateral Commn. Commander de la Légion d'Honneur (Côte d'Ivoire), 1978; Chevalier de l'Ordre du Mérite (France), 1987; Chevalier de la Légion d'Honneur (France), 1992. *Publications:* Third World Debt, 1987; Stratégie Bancaire: le refus de la dérive, 1988; La Banque du XXI$^e$ Siècle, 1996; L'entreprise, l'individu, l'Etat: conduire le changement, 1999; Euramérique, 2007; Où va l'Amérique d'Obama?, 2011. *Recreations:* tennis, music. *Address:* 64 avenue Raymond Pioncasé, 75116 Paris, France. *E:* herve@decarmoy.be.

**de CHARETTE, Hervé;** barrister; Deputy for Maine-et-Loire, 1988–93 and 1997–2012 (UDF, 1988–93 and 1997–2002; UMP, 2002–09; Nouveau Centre, 2009–12); Deputy President, Union pour la Démocratie Française, 1998–2002; *b* 30 July 1938; *s* of Hélion de Charette; *m* 1980, Michelle Delor; one *d*, and one *s* three *d* by former marriage. *Educ:* Institut d'Etudes Politiques; HEC; Ecole Nationale de l'Administration. Conseil d'Etat: Mem., 1966–; Auditor, 1966–73; Dep. Sec. Gen., 1969–73; Maître des Requêtes, 1973–; tech. advr to Minister of Social Affairs, 1973–74; Cabinet Director for: Sec. of State for Immigration, 1974–76; Minister of Employment, 1976–78; Chargé de Mission for Minister of Commerce, 1978–81; Conseil d'Etat, 1982–86; Asst to Prime Minister and Minister of Public Service, Planning and Social Econs, 1986–88; Minister of Housing, 1988–95; Minister for Foreign Affairs, 1995–97. Vice-Pres., UDF, 1989; Delegate-Gen., 1995–97, Pres., 1995–2002, PPDF. Vice-Pres., Pays-de-Loire Regl Council, 1992–2010; Mayor, St Florent-le-Vieil, 1989–2014. Pres., Franco-Arab Chamber of Commerce, 2008–16. Pres., St Florent-le-Vieil Music and Dance Fest., 1989–2014. *Publications:* Whirlwind over the Republic, 1995; Lyautey, 1997. *Address:* 6 Avenue Emile Acollas, 75007 Paris, France. *E:* h.decharette@orange.fr.

**de CHASTELAIN, Gen. (Alfred) John (Gardyne Drummond),** CC 2014 (OC 1993); CMM 1984; CH 1999; Chairman, Independent International Commission on Decommissioning, Northern Ireland, 1997–2011; *b* Bucharest, 30 July 1937; *s* of late Alfred George Gardyne de Chastelain, DSO, OBE, and Marion Elizabeth de Chastelain (*née* Walsh); *m* 1961, MaryAnn Laverty; one *s* one *d*. *Educ:* Fettes Coll., Edinburgh; Mount Royal Coll., Calgary, Alberta; Royal Mil. Coll. of Canada (BA Hons Hist. 1960). Army Staff Coll., Camberley. Commnd 2nd Lieut, 2nd Bn, PPCLI, 1960; Capt. 1962; Maj. 1967; Lt-Col 1970; CO, 2nd Bn, PPCLI 1970–72; Col 1974; Commander: Canadian Forces Base, Montreal, 1974–76; Canadian Contingent, UN Forces, Cyprus, 1976–77; Brig. Gen. 1977; Comdt, RMC of Canada, 1977–80; Comdr, 4th Canadian Mechanized Bde Gp, Germany, 1980–82; Dir Gen., Land Doctrine and Ops, Nat. Defence HQ, 1982–83; Maj.-Gen. 1983; Dep. Comdr, Mobile Comd, Quebec, 1983–86; Lt-Gen. 1986; Asst Dep. Minister (Personnel), NDHQ, 1986–88; Vice Chief, Defence Staff, 1988–89; Gen. 1989; Chief of Defence Staff, 1989–92; Ambassador for Canada to USA, 1993; Chief of Defence Staff, 1994–95; Mem., Internat. Body on Decommissioning of Arms in NI, 1995–96; Chm., Business Cttee and Co. Chm., Strand Two Talks, NI Peace Process, 1996–98. Col of Regt, PPCLI, 2000–03. Hon. Fellow, LMH, Oxford, 2006. Hon. DScMil RMC, Canada, 1996; Hon. LLD: Royal Roads, Canada, 2001; Carleton, Ontario, 2006; Queen's, Kingston, 2007; St Mary's, Halifax, NS, 2008; Brock, St Catharines, Ont, 2011; Concordia Univ., Montreal, 2012; Mt Allison, NB, 2014; Hon. DPhil (Educn) Nipissing, Ontario, 2006; Dr *hc* Edinburgh, 2014. CStJ 1991. Pres. of Ireland's Distinguished Service Award for the Irish Abroad, 2017. CD (Canada), 1968; Medal of Merit and Honour (Greece), 1992; Comdr, Legion of Merit (USA), 1995. *Publications:* (contrib.) Canada on the Threshold of the 21st Century, 1992; (contrib.) Herding Cats: multiparty mediation in a complex world, 1999; (contrib.) From Political Violence to Negotiated Settlement, 2004; contrib. to Canadian Defence Qly. *Recreations:* painting, fishing, bagpipes. *Address:* 1008–111 Wurtemburg Street, Ottawa, ON K1N 8M1, Canada. *T:* (613) 7447300.

**DECIE, Elizabeth Anne Scott P.;** see Prescott-Decie.

**DECIES,** 7th Baron *cr* 1812 (Ire.); **Marcus Hugh Tristram de la Poer Beresford;** *b* 5 Aug. 1948; *o s* of 6th Baron Decies and of his 2nd wife, Diana, *d* of Wing Comdr George Turner-Cain and widow of Major David Galsworthy; *S* father, 1992; *m* 1st, 1970, Sarah Jane Gunnell (marr. diss. 1974); 2nd, 1981, Edel Jeannette, *d* of late Vincent Hendron; two *s* two *d*. *Educ:* St Columba's Coll.; Dublin Univ. (MLitt). FCIArb. *Heir:* s Hon. Robert Marcus Duncan de la Poer Beresford, *b* 14 July 1988.

**de CLIFFORD,** 28th Baron *cr* 1299; **Miles Edward Southwell Russell;** *b* 7 Aug. 1966; *s* of late Hon. William Southwell Russell and Jean Brodie (*née* Henderson); *S* uncle, 2018; *m* 1995, Marion Elaine, *yr d* of D. W. Arkley; one *s* one *d*. *Heir: s* Hon. Edward Southwell Russell, *b* 18 Nov. 1998.

**DE CORDOVA, Marsha Chantol;** MP (Lab) Battersea, since 2017. Action for Blind People: Welfare Rights Officer, 2005–07; Service Develt Manager, 2007–10; Policy and Develt Manager, 2010–12; Welfare Benefit Specialist, Turn2us, 2013–14; Develt Manager, Thomas Pocklington Trust, 2014–15; Chief Exec., South East London Vision, 2015–16; Engagement and Advocacy Dir, Thomas Pocklington Trust, 2016–17. Mem. (Lab), Lambeth LBC, 2014–. Mem., Work and Pensions Select Cttee, 2017–. *Address:* House of Commons, SW1A 0AA.

**de COSSART, Linda Mary,** CBE 2010; FRCS; Consultant Vascular and General Surgeon, 1988–2009, now Emeritus Consultant, and Director of Medical Education, 2010–14, Countess of Chester Hospital NHS Foundation Trust (formerly Countess of Chester Hospital); Director, Ed4MedPrac Ltd, since 2005; *b* Swansea, 9 Nov. 1947; *d* of Leonard and Elizabeth Jones; *m* 1977, Michael de Cossart (*d* 1989). *Educ:* Univ. of Liverpool Med. Sch. (MB ChB 1972; ChM 1983). FRCS 1977. Mersey Deanery: Associate Postgrad. Dean, 1993–2006; Prog. Dir, Gen. Surgery, 1993–2004. Jt Vice Pres., RCS, 2008–10 (Mem. Council, 1999–2010). Hon. Sec., Vascular Soc. of GB and Ire., 1994–98. Member: Liverpool Medical Instn, 1977– (Pres., 2013–14); Travelling Surgical Soc., 1995–. Hon. Prof., Univ. of Chester, 2010–. FRSocMed 1985; FAcadMed 2012. *Publications:* Cultivating a Thinking Surgeon, 2005; Developing the Wise Doctor, 2007; articles in vascular and general surgery jls. *Recreations:* cooking, poetry, writing. *Address:* The Lodge, Cranham Corner, Cranham, Glos GL4 8HB. *T:* 07778 215801. *E:* decossart@btinternet.com. *Clubs:* Athenæum; Lister; Needles.

**de COURCY,** family name of **Baron Kingsale**.

**de COURCY-IRELAND, Patrick Gault,** CVO 1980; HM Diplomatic Service, retired; Director of Marketing, 1987–2013, Consultant, 2013–19, Rezayat Group (formerly Alireza Group of Companies); Director, Rezayat Europe Ltd, 1988–2013; *b* 19 Aug. 1933; *e s* of late Lawrence Kilmaine de Courcy-Ireland and Elizabeth Pentland Gault; *m* 1957, Margaret Gallop (*d* 2017); one *s* three *d*; *m* 2018, Marie-Antoinette Engelhard. *Educ:* St Paul's Sch.; Jesus Coll., Cambridge (MA). HM Forces (2nd Lieut), 1952–54. Joined Foreign Service, 1957; Student, ME Centre for Arab Studies, 1957–59; Third, later Second Sec., Baghdad, 1959–62; Private Sec. to HM Ambassador, Washington, 1963; Consul (Commercial), New York, 1963–67; UN (Polit.) Dept, 1967–69; Asst Head of Amer. Dept, 1969–71; First Sec. and Hd of Chancery, Kuwait, 1971–73; Asst Hd of SW Pacific Dept, 1973–76; Hd of Trng Dept and Dir, Diplomatic Serv. Language Centre, FCO, 1976–80; Consul-Gen., Casablanca, 1980–84; Consul-Gen., Jerusalem, 1984–87. Chm., British Sch. of Archaeology in Jerusalem, 1990–99; Member: Exec. Cttee, Palestine Exploration Fund, 1991–95; Council, Soc. for Moroccan Studies, 1992–99; Sec., MECAS Assoc., 2002–18.

Director: Napier Court Freehold Ltd, 2003–11; Napier Court Management Ltd, 2005–10. MEI (MInstPet 1992). Great Comdr, Order of KHS, 1985. *Recreations:* book collecting, opera. *Address:* 49 Napier Court, Ranelagh Gardens, SW6 3UU. *T:* (020) 7736 0622.

**DECTOT, Xavier Pierre André,** PhD; FSA, FSA (Scot.); Keeper of Art and Design, National Museums Scotland, since 2016; *b* Pithiviers, France, 8 June 1973; *s* of Hervé Dectot and Françoise Fortin; *m* 2001, Agnès Bos; one *s* one *d*. *Educ:* Lycée Henri IV, Paris; École nationale des Chartes (Archiviste-Paléographe); École pratique des Hautes Études (PhD Art Hist. 2001); École nationale du Patrimoine (Curator Diploma). Scientific Mem., Casa de Velázquez, 1998–2001; Curator, in charge of sculptures, ivories and maiolicas, 2001–11; Dir, Louvre-Lens, 2011–16. Lecturer: École de Chaillot, 2001–11; École du Louvre, 2001–07; Paris IV - Sorbonne, 2002–11. Chm., Mgt Bd, Corpus of Romanesque Sculpture in Britain and Ireland, 2018–. Hon. Reader, Univ. of St Andrews, 2019–. Chevalier, Ordre des Arts et Lettres (France), 2013. *Publications:* L'Art Roman en France, 2004; Sculptures des XI$^e$–XII$^e$ siècles: roman et premier art gothique, 2005; Pierres tombales médiévales: sculptures de l'au-delà, 2006; Les tombeaux des familles royales de la péninsule ibérique au Moyen Âge, 2009; (jtly) À la table de l'histoire, 2011; (jtly) l'Histoire passe à table, 2016. *Recreations:* ski-ing, sailing, cooking. *Address:* National Museums Scotland, Chambers Street, Edinburgh EH1 1JF. *T:* (0131) 247 4410. *E:* x.dectot@nms.ac.uk.

**DEDMAN, His Honour Peter George;** Designated Civil Judge for Chelmsford South, 2007–10; a Circuit Judge, 2000–10; a Deputy Circuit Judge, 2010–12; *b* 22 May 1940; *s* of late George Stephen Henry Dedman and Jessie Maud Dedman (*née* Hanson); *m* 1965, Patricia Mary Gordon, JP, RGN, RHV; one *d*. *Educ:* Tottenham Grammar Sch. Magistrates' Courts Service, Brentford, Tottenham and Newham; Principal Asst to Clerk to the Justices, Newham, 1965–69; called to the Bar, Gray's Inn, 1968 (amongst first to qualify following removal of embargo on Justices' Clerks and their assts from reading for the Bar); in practice at the Bar, specialising in personal injury litigation; a Recorder, 1992–2000; South Eastern Circuit. Pres., Mental Health Tribunals, 2010–12. *Recreations:* music - playing the piano and trombone, plays in a number of jazz, dance and concert bands, theatre, film, attending concerts. *Address:* Adelaide House, 308 Roman Road, Mountnessing, Brentwood, Essex CM15 0TZ.

**DEDRING, Isabel Margaret,** JD; Global Transport Leader, Arup, since 2016; *b* Boston, Mass, 10 Aug. 1971; *d* of Jürgen and Elisabeth Dedring; *m* 2005, James Roland Sinker; two *s*. *Educ:* Hunter College High Sch., NY; Harvard Univ. (AB 1993 *magna cum laude*; JD 1998 *cum laude*). Mem., NY Bar. Mkt Entry Dir, Almaty, Kazakhstan, Ernst & Young, 1993–95; McKinsey & Co., London, 1998–2003; COS and Dir, Policy Unit, TfL, 2003–08; Mayor of London's Envmt Advr, GLA, 2008–11; Dep. Mayor of London, Transport, 2011–16. Mem. Bd, Inst. for Sustainability, 2009–15. *Address:* 3 Agincourt Road, NW3 2PB.

**DEE, Christopher;** *see* Evans, D. C.

**DEE, Janie, (Mrs R. S. M. Wickham);** actress; *b* 20 June 1962; *d* of John Henry Leonard Lewis and Ruth Winifred Lewis (*née* Miller); adopted stage name Janie Dee; *m* 1995, Rupert Stewart Makepeace Wickham; one *s* one *d*. *Educ:* Arts Educational Schs, London. *Theatre* includes: Carousel, RNT, 1992 (Best Supporting Performance in a Musical, Olivier awards, 1993); Comic Potential, Lyric, 1999, transf. NY, 2000 (Best Actress, Evening Standard, Critics' Circle, Olivier awards, 2000; Obie award, and Best Newcomer, Theater World Award, 2001); My One and Only, Chichester Fest. Th., 2001, transf. Piccadilly, 2002; Three Sisters, Chichester Fest. Th., 2001; Paradise Moscow, Opera North, UK tour, Convoy; Women of Troy, NT, 2001; Divas at the Donmar, Donmar Warehouse, 2002; Much Ado About Nothing, Peter Hall Co., Bath, 2003; Mack and Mabel, Criterion, 2006; Old Times, UK tour, 2007; Shadowlands, Wyndham's, 2007; Woman in Mind, Vaudeville, 2009; The Apple Cart, Th. Royal, Bath, 2009; Calendar Girls, Noël Coward, 2009; The Little Hut, Yvonne Arnaud Th., 2010; A Month in the Country, Chichester, 2010; The King and I, The Curve, Leicester, 2010; All's Well That Ends Well, Shakespeare's Globe 2011; Private Lives, Nottingham Playhouse, 2011; Noises Off, Old Vic, 2011, transf. Novello Th., 2012; Janie Dee Show, Hippodrome, 2012; NSFW, Royal Court, 2012; Hello, Dolly!, Curve, Leicester, 2012 (Best Perf. in a Musical, UK Theatre Awards, 2013); Putting it Together, St James Th., 2014; Blithe Spirit, Gielgud Th., 2014; A Midsummer Night's Dream, Shakespeare's Globe on tour, Asia and Russia, 2014; 84 Charing Cross Road, Salisbury Playhouse, 2015; Ah, Wilderness!, Young Vic, 2015; The Seagull, Open Air Th., 2015; Hand to God, Vaudeville Th., 2016; Shakespeare at the Bowl, Hollywood Bowl and Barbican, 2016; Linda, Manhattan Th Club, NYC, 2017; Follies, NT, 2017, 2019; Monogamy, Park Th., 2018; Pinter Four, Harold Pinter Th., 2018; *television* includes: Death in Holy Orders, 2003; The Murder Room, 2004; Celebration, 2007; Crashing, 2016; *films* include: Me and Orson Welles, 2009; Dare to Be Wild, 2009. Dir, Royal Theatrical Fund, 2002–. Trustee, Arts Educnl Schs, 2001–. *Recreations:* sailing, ballet, bell ringing.

**DEE, Maurice Patrick, (Moz);** Co-Founder and Director, Contented Digital Media, since 2013; *b* Coventry, 13 Sept. 1966; *s* of Maurice and Moira Dee; partner, Liane Charldwood; one *s* one *d*. *Educ:* Cardinal Newman Comprehensive Sch., Coventry. Actor and writer, 1983–91; presenter, BBC Coventry and Warwicks Radio, 1991–95; presenter, 1995–97, Hd of Sport, 1997–2000, Talk Radio; Editl Exec., Sports Rights and Programming, 2000–02; Commng Ed., 2002–05, Man. Ed., 2005–08, BBC Radio Five Live; Dir of Progs, talksport, 2008–13. Mem. Cttee, Radio Acad., 2005–. Radio Programmer of Year, Sony Radio Acad., 2011. *Recreations:* writing, cinema, fishing, golf. *Address:* Contented Digital Media, Elsey Court, 20–22, Great Titchfield Street, W1W 8BE.

**DEECH,** family name of **Baroness Deech**.

**DEECH,** Baroness *cr* 2005 (Life Peer), of Cumnor in the County of Oxfordshire; **Ruth Lynn Deech,** DBE 2002; Chairman, Bar Standards Board, 2009–14; *b* 29 April 1943; *d* of Josef Fraenkel and Dora (*née* Rosenfeld); *m* 1967, Dr John Stewart Deech; one *d*. *Educ:* Christ's Hosp., Hertford; St Anne's Coll., Oxford (BA 1st Cl. 1965; MA 1969; Hon. Fellow, 2004); Brandeis Univ., USA (MA 1966). Called to the Bar, Inner Temple, 1967, Hon. Bencher, 1996. Legal Asst, Law Commn, 1966–67; Asst Prof., Faculty of Law, Univ. of Windsor, Canada, 1968–70; Oxford University: Fellow and Tutor in Law, 1970–91, Vice-Principal, 1988–91, Principal, 1991–2004, St Anne's Coll.; CUF Lectr in Law, 1971–91; Sen. Proctor, 1985–86; Mem., Hebdomadal Council, 1986–2000; Chm., Jt Undergrad. Admissions Cttee, 1993–97, Admissions Exec., 2000–03; Pro-Vice-Chancellor, 2001–04. Ind. Adjudicator for Higher Educn, 2004–08. Chm., HFEA, 1994–2002. Member: Cttee of Inquiry into Equal Opportunities on Bar Vocational Course, 1993–94; Human Genetics Commn, 2000–02; Chairman: Nat. Working Gp on Women in Medicine, 2008–09; Equality Act 2010 and Disability Cttee, H of L, 2015–16. A Governor, BBC, 2002–06. Non-exec. Dir, Oxon HA, 1993–94. Mem., Exec. Council, Internat. Soc. on Family Law, 1988–2012. Visiting Professor: Osgoode Hall Law Sch., York Univ., Canada, 1978; Univ. of Florida, 2004; Santa Clara Univ., 2006; Gresham Prof. of Law, Gresham Coll., 2008–12. Governor: Carmel Coll., 1980–90; Oxford Centre for Hebrew and Jewish Studies, 1994–2000; UCS, 1997–2002. Rhodes Trustee, 1997–2006; Mandela Rhodes Foundn Trustee, 2003–06. Gov., United Jewish Israel Appeal, 1997–99. Freeman, City of London, 2003; Liveryman, Drapers' Co., 2008. FRSocMed 2001. Hon. Fellow,

Soc. for Advanced Legal Studies, 1997. Hon. QC 2013. Hon. Mem., SLS, 2018. Hon. LLD: Strathclyde, 2003; Richmond American Internat. Univ. in London, 2006; Hon. PhD Ben Gurion, 2012. *Publications:* From IVF to Immortality, 2007; articles on family law and property law. *Recreations:* after-dinner speaking, music, entertaining. *Address:* House of Lords, SW1A 0PW. *E:* deechr@parliament.uk.

**DEEDES, Hon. Jeremy (Wyndham);** non-executive Chairman, Pelham Public Relations, 2007–10; *b* 24 Nov. 1943; *s* of Baron Deedes, KBE, MC, PC; *m* 1973, Anna Gray, *d* of late Maj. Elwin Gray; two *s*. *Educ:* Eton Coll. Reporter: Kent and Sussex Courier, 1963–66; Daily Sketch, 1966–69; Londoner's Diary, Evening Standard, 1969–76; Dep. Editor, Daily Express, 1976–79; Managing Editor: Evening Standard, 1979–85; Today, 1985–86; Editorial Dir, Daily Telegraph and Sunday Telegraph, 1986–96; Man. Dir, 1996–2003, Dep. Chm. and Chief Exec., 2004–05, Telegraph Gp Ltd; Chm., The Sportsman, 2005–06. Chm., Trafford Park Printers, 1998–2000; Dep. Chm., West Ferry Printers, 1998–2005; Director: Millbourne Productions (Watermill Theatre), 1985–; Horserace Totalisator Bd, 1992–98; Warwick Racecourse, 2005–14 (Chm., 2002–05). Chm., Nat. Publishers Assoc., 1998–99. *Recreations:* racing, cricket, golf, cabinet making. *Address:* Hamilton House, Compton, Newbury, Berks RG20 6QJ. *T:* (01635) 578695. *Clubs:* Boodle's, MCC; Sunningdale Golf, Huntercombe Golf; Royal Cape (Cape Town).

**DEEGAN, Sir Michael,** CBE 2003; Kt 2014; Chief Executive, Manchester University NHS Foundation Trust, since 2017. *Educ:* Univ. of Warwick (LLB; MA Industrial Relns). Dep. Dir, then Dir, HR, NHS Exec., DoH, until 1998; Chief Executive: Warrington Hosp.; N Cheshire Hosps NHS Trust; on secondment to DoH as Project Dir for develt of NHS Plan, 2000; Chief Exec., Central Manchester Univ. Hosps NHS Foundn Trust (formerly Central Manchester and Manchester Children's Univ. Hosps NHS Trust), 2001–17. Trustee: Central Manchester Foundn Trust Charity; Nuffield Trust. *Address:* Manchester University NHS Foundation Trust, Manchester Royal Infirmary, Cobbett House, Oxford Road, Manchester M13 9WL.

**DEEKS, Rev. David Gerald;** General Secretary of the Methodist Church, 2003–08; *b* 5 July 1942; *s* of Horace J. Deeks and Irene Deeks; *m* 1967, Jennifer Wakefield; one *s* two *d*. *Educ:* Downing Coll., Cambridge (MA); Wesley House, Cambridge. Asst Tutor, Richmond Coll., Surrey, 1966–70; Ecumenical Lectr, Lincoln Theol Coll., 1970–74; Minister, Maidstone Circuit, 1974–80; Tutor, Wesley House, Cambridge, 1980–88; Minister, Bristol (Clifton and Redland) Circuit, and Methodist Chaplain, Univ. of Bristol, 1988–92; Gen. Sec., Div. of Social Responsibility, 1992–96, Co-ordinating Sec., Church and Society, 1996–2003, Methodist Church. *Publications:* Calling, God?, 1976; Pastoral Theology: an inquiry, 1987. *Recreations:* walking, art, music. *Address:* 1 Shields Avenue, Bristol BS7 0RR. *E:* david.deeks@gmail.com.

**DEELEY, Michael;** film producer; *b* 6 Aug. 1932; *s* of John Hamilton-Deeley and Anne Deeley; *m* 1955, Teresa Harrison; one *s* two *d*; *m* 1970, Ruth Stone-Spencer. *Educ:* Stowe. Entered film industry as film editor, 1952; Distributor, MCA TV, 1958–60; independent producer, 1961–63; Gen. Man., Woodfall Films, 1964–67; indep. prod., 1967–72; Man. Director: British Lion Films Ltd, 1973–76; EMI Films Ltd, 1976–77; Pres., EMI Films Inc., 1977–79; Chief Exec. Officer, Consolidated Television Inc., 1984–90. Dep. Chm., British Screen Adv. Council, 1985–2015 (Hon. Pres., 2017–). Member: Prime Minister's Film Industry Working Party, 1975–76; Film Industry Interim Action Cttee, 1977–84. *Films* include: Robbery; The Italian Job; The Knack; Murphy's War; Conduct Unbecoming; The Man who fell to Earth; The Deer Hunter (Academy Award, Best Picture Producer, 1978); Convoy; Blade Runner; many TV films and series. Hon. Pres., British Screen Adv. Council, 2018. *Publications:* Blade Runners, Deer Hunters and Blowing the Bloody Doors Off, 2008. *Address:* 36 Elizabeth Court, SW10 0DA; 300 Hot Springs Road, Montecito, CA 93108, USA. *Club:* Santa Barbara Polo and Racquet.

**DEELY, Neil Matthew,** RIBA; Director, Metropolitan Workshop, since 2005; *b* Harrow, 2 Aug. 1972; *s* of Michael and Deirdre Deely; *m* 2005, Line Lund; two *s*. *Educ:* St Dominic's Coll., Harrow on the Hill; Univ. of Brighton (BA Hons; DipArch (Dist.)); Univ. of Arkansas. RIBA 1998. Associate, 2000–02, Dir, 2002–05, MacCormac Jamieson Prichard Architects. Built envmt expert, 2011–. Enabler, 2005–11, Mem., Nat. Design Rev. Panel, 2007–11, CABE; Member: Planning Cttee, London Thames Gateway Develt Corp., 2009–12; Design Panel, American Embassy, London, 2010–12; Design Review Panel, London Bor. of Newham, 2011– (Chm., 2013–); London Legacy Quality Review Panel, 2012– (Vice Chm., 2016–); Cabe at Design Council Design Rev. Panel, London Bor. of Greenwich, 2014–; a Design Advr, Urban Design London, 2009–. Major projects include: Jersey Archive, 2000; redevelt of BBC Broadcasting House, 2001–03; housing for Univ. of Cambridge, West Cambridge, 2004; Adamstown Dist Centre, Ireland, 2005–07; Mus. of Conflict, Libya, 2009; Somerleyton Rd housing, 2014–; Blackwall Reach Regeneration Project. Mem., Editl Panel, RIBA Jl, 2015–. Mem., Inst. of Norwegian Architects, 2007–. FRSA; FRGS 2012. *Recreations:* hill walking, expeditions to High Arctic, alpine sport, painting. *Address:* Metropolitan Workshop, Architecture & Urbanism, 14–16 Cowcross Street, EC1M 6DG. *T:* (020) 7566 0450. *E:* info@metwork.co.uk.

**DEEM, Prof. Rosemary,** OBE 2013; PhD; Vice Principal (Teaching Innovation, Equality and Diversity), since 2017, and Dean, Doctoral School, since 2014, Royal Holloway, University of London (Vice Principal (Education), 2011–17); *b* 18 Jan. 1949; *d* of Leslie Thomas George Deem and Peggy Deem (*née* Stoyle); *m* 1985, Kevin Joseph Brehony (*d* 2013). *Educ:* Univ. of Leicester (BA Hons Social Scis (Sociol.) 1970; MPhil Sociol. 1973); Open Univ. (PhD Sociol. of Leisure 1990). Lectr in Sociol., N Staffs Poly., 1975–79; Lectr in Sociol. of Educn, 1980–87, Sen Lectr in Educn, 1987–91, Open Univ.; Prof. of Educnl Res., 1991–2000, Dean of Social Scis, 1994–97, Univ. of Lancaster; Founding Dir, Univ. of Lancaster Grad. Sch., 1998–2000; Prof. of Educn, 2001–09, Res. Dir, Faculty of Social Scis and Law, 2007–09, Univ. of Bristol; Dean of Hist. and Social Scis, Royal Holloway, Univ. of London, 2009–11. Jt Man. Ed., Sociol. Rev., 2001–04; Co-editor, Higher Educn, 2013–. Dir, UK Subject Centre for Educn (ESCalate), Learning and Teaching Support Network, 2001–04. Chairman: British Sociol Assoc., 1986–87 and 1994–96; Publications Cttee, SRHE, 2004–07; Develt Cttee, SRHE, 2007–09; Mem., UK Council for Graduate Educn, 2012–15 (Chair, 2015–18); Mem., European Sci. Foundn Peer Review Coll., 2016–18. FAcSS (AcSS 2006); FSRHE 2010. Hon. DLitt Leicester, 2014. *Publications:* Women and Schooling, 1978; (ed) Schooling for Women's Work, 1980; (ed) Co-education Reconsidered, 1984; All Work and No Play, 1986; Work, Unemployment and Leisure, 1988; (with K. J. Brehony and S. J. Heath) Active Citizenship and the Governing of Schools, 1995; (with S. Hillyard and M. Reed) Knowledge, Higher Education and the New Managerialism: the changing management of UK universities, 2007; (ed jtly) The University as a Critical Institution?, 2017; contrib. numerous articles and chapters in social sci. jls and academic books. *Recreations:* walking, cycling (Mem., Cyclists Touring Club), photography, camping and caravanning (Mem., Camping and Caravanning Club), reading. *Address:* Principal's Office, Founders East, Royal Holloway, University of London, Egham Hill, Egham TW20 0EX. *T:* (01784) 443994. *E:* R.Deem@rhul.ac.uk.

**DEENY, Rt Hon. Sir Donnell (Justin Patrick),** Kt 2004; PC 2017; **Rt Hon. Lord Justice Deeny;** DL; a Lord Justice of Appeal, Supreme Court of Judicature, Northern Ireland, since 2017; *b* 25 April 1950; *y s* of late Dr Donnell McLarnon Deeny, JP and Annie

(*née* McGinley); *m* 1998, Alison Jane, *y d* of late Ian Scott and of Tressan Scott; one *s* two *d*, and two *d* by a previous marriage. *Educ:* Clongowes Wood Coll.; TCD (Auditor, The Hist.; MA); QUB. Called to the Bar: NI, 1974 (Bencher, 2001); Ireland, 1986; Middle Temple, 1987 (Bencher, 2006); one of Attorney Gen.'s Counsel, NI, 1985–2003; QC (NI) 1989; SC (Ireland) 1996; a Judge of the High Court of Justice, NI, 2004–17. Mem., UK Spoliation Adv. Panel, 2001– (Chm., 2012–). Dir, Hearth Social Housing, 1999–2003. Mem. (APNI), Belfast CC, 1981–85. Mem., 1991–93, Chm., 1993–98, Arts Council of NI; Vice Chm., 1984–88, Chm., 1988–93, Opera NI. Trustee: Ulster Mus., 1983–85; Ireland Chair of Poetry Trust, 1997– (Chm., 1997–2008); Dir, Tyrone Guthrie Centre, 2001–06; President: Ulster Architectural Heritage Soc., 2006–17; Irish Legal Hist. Soc., 2015–18. Pro Chancellor, Univ. of Dublin, 2014–. Hon. MRTPI 2012. High Sheriff 1983, DL 2003, Belfast; JP Co. Down, 1988. *Publications:* (ed) To the Millennium: a strategy for the arts in Northern Ireland, 1995. *Recreations:* books, the arts, ski-ing. *Address:* Royal Courts of Justice, Chichester Street, Belfast BT1 3JF.
See also M. F. A. Cook, M. E. McL. Deeny.

**DEENY, Michael Eunan McLarnon**, FCA; Chairman, Equitas Trust, since 2014 (Deputy Chairman, 1996–2014); *b* 12 Nov. 1944; *s* of late Dr Donnell McLarnon Deeny and Annie Deeny (*née* McGinley); *m* 1975, Dr Margaret Irene Vereker, *d* of late Dr Richard Vereker and Judy Vereker; one *s* two *d*. *Educ:* Clongowes Wood Coll., Ireland; Magdalen Coll., Oxford (MA). FCA 1974. Articled Clerk, Chalmers Impey, 1966–70; Chief Accountant, Peter Kennedy Ltd, 1970–71; Manager (Murray Head, Horslips, Noosha Fox, Barry McGuigan, etc), 1971–91; Concert Promoter (U2, Bruce Springsteen, Nirvana, Prince, The Eagles, Aerosmith, Luciano Pavarotti, etc), 1984–2015. Chairman: Gooda Walker Action Gp (obtained compensation for Lloyd's names), 1993–2008; Litigating Names' Cttee, 1994–2010; Assoc. of Lloyd's Members, 1998–2009 (Dir, 1995–). Director: GW Run-Off, 1995–97; Equitas Ltd, 1996–; non-exec. Dir, Randall and Quilter Underwriting Ltd, 2012–15. Mem. Council, Lloyd's, 1996–97, 2009–16. *Recreation:* taking risks and living to tell the tale. *Address:* Shepherds Close House, Upper Woodford, Salisbury SP4 6PA.
See also M. F. A. Cook, Rt Hon. Sir D. J. P. Deeny.

**DEER, Clare;** *see* Connor, C.

**DEFFEE, Leslie Ann;** *see* Morphy, L. A.

**de FONBLANQUE, John Robert**, CMG 1993; HM Diplomatic Service, retired; Director, Office of High Commissioner on National Minorities, Organisation for Security and Co-operation in Europe, 2004–07; *b* 20 Dec. 1943; *s* of late Maj.-Gen. E. B. de Fonblanque, CB, CBE, DSO and of Elizabeth de Fonblanque; *m* 1984, Margaret Prest; one *s*. *Educ:* Ampleforth; King's College, Cambridge (MA); London School of Economics (MSc); Sch. of Oriental and African Studies, London Univ. (Dip. Asian Art 2009; MA 2012). FCO, 1968; Second Sec., Jakarta, 1969; Second, later First Sec., UK Representation to European Community, Brussels, 1972; Principal, HM Treasury, 1977; FCO, 1980; Asst Sec., Cabinet Office, 1983; Head of Chancery, New Delhi, 1986; Counsellor (Pol and Instnl), UK Repn to EC, Brussels, 1988; Vis. Fellow, RIIA, 1993; Asst Under-Sec. of State, Internat. Orgns, then Dir, Global Issues, FCO, 1994–98; Dir (Europe), FCO, 1998–99; Hd, UK Delegn to OSCE, Vienna (with rank of Ambassador), 1999–2003. Mem., PPARC, 1994–98. *Recreation:* mountain walking.

**DE FREYNE**, 8th Baron *cr* 1851, of Coolavin; **Fulke Charles Arthur John French;** development and construction surveyor; *b* Dublin, 21 April 1957; *s* of 7th Baron De Freyne and of Shirley Ann, *d* of late D. R. Pobjoy; *S* father, 2009; *m* 1986, Julia Mary, *o d* of Dr James H. Wellard; two *s*. *Educ:* Downside; Poly. of South Bank (BA Hons 1986); London South Bank Univ. (MSc 2008). MRAC 1981. FRGS 1988. *Recreations:* photography, travel, tennis, sailing. *Heir: s* Hon. Alexander James Charles French, *b* 22 Sept. 1988. *Club:* Roehampton.

**DEFRIEZ, Alistair Norman Campbell**, FCA; financial consultant; Managing Director, UBS Investment Bank (formerly Warburg Dillon Read, then UBS Warburg), 1999–2007; *b* 2 Nov. 1951; *s* of late Norman William Defriez and Helen Catherine Defriez (*née* Maclean); *m* 1978, Linda Mavis Phillips, BSc, PGCE, ACA; two *s* one *d*. *Educ:* Dulwich Coll.; University Coll., Oxford (Open Gladstone Schol., MA). FCA 1981. With Coopers & Lybrand, 1973–78; joined S. G. Warburg & Co. Ltd, 1978, Dir, 1987; Dir-Gen., Panel on Takeovers and Mergers, 1996–99 (on secondment) (Mem., 2008–17). *Recreations:* golf, Rugby, music, reading. *Clubs:* London Scottish; Royal Wimbledon Golf; Rye Golf; St George's Hill Golf.

**DE FRUTOS, Javier;** choreographer, director; *b* Caracas, 15 May 1963; *s* of Esteban De Frutos and Angela Fernandez. *Educ:* Caracas Sch. of Contemporary Dance; Merce Cunningham Sch., NY; London Sch. of Contemporary Dance. Dancer, Laura Dean Dancers and Musicians, NY, 1988–92; Choreographer in Residence, Movement Res., NYC, 1993; Founder and Artistic Dir, Javier De Frutos Dance Co., 1994–2000; Artistic Dir, Phoenix Dance Th., 2006–09. Fellow, Arts Council of England, 2000–02. *Choreographed:* for De Frutos Dance Co.: D, 1990; The Montana Affair, J, Trilogy + Country, Consecration, 1991; Almost Montana, Meeting, Hemisphere, Jota Dolce, 1993; Simone and the Jacaranda Tree, Dialogue Between Hemispheres, Frasquita, The Palace Does Not Forgive, Gota a Gota, 1994; Sweetie J, Meeting J, 1995; Carnal Glory, Out of J, Transatlantic, 1996; Grass, Weed, The Golden Impossibility, 1997; The Hypochondriac Bird, 1998; Mazatlan, 1999; Affliction of Loneliness, 2000; for Phoenix Dance Theatre: Nopalitos, 2006; Los Picadores, Paseillo, Blue Roses, 2007; Cattle Call, 2008; for Ricochet Dance Co.: E Muoio Disperato, 1995 (Bagnolet Prix d'Auteur, France, 1996); All visitors bring happiness, some by coming, some by going, 1995 (S Bank Award, 1997); for Rambert Dance Co.: The Celebrated Soubrette, 2000 (re-staged for Royal NZ Ballet, 2004); Elsa Canesta, 2003; Elysian Fields, 2011; for Royal NZ Ballet: Milagros, 2003; Banderillero, 2006; The Anatomy of a Passing Cloud, 2015; for Royal Ballet: The Misty Frontier, 2001; Les Enfants Terrible, 2017; for Sadler's Wells: The Most Incredible Thing (also dir), 2011 (London Evening Standard Beyond Th. award (jtly), 2011); for BalletBoyz: Fiction, 2016; *theatre:* Carousel, Chichester Fest., 2006; Cabaret, Lyric, 2006 (Olivier Award for Best Th. Choreographer, 2007); Macbeth, Shakespeare's Globe, 2010; London Road, NT, 2011; From Here to Eternity, Shaftesbury Th., 2013; Everyman, NT, 2015. Paul Hamlyn Foundn Award, 1995; Critics' Circle Nat. Dance Award for Best Choreog. (Contemp.), 2005. *Address:* 153 Brettenham Road, E17 5AX. *T:* 07582 841167. *E:* javierdefru@hotmail.com, (agent) klewis@themorganagency.com.

**de GARR ROBINSON, Anthony John;** QC 2006; *b* 4 July 1963; *s* of Peter de Garr Robinson and Audrey Robinson; *m* 1997, Miranda Wilson; one *s* one *d*. *Educ:* Brighton Coll.; University Coll., Oxford; Grad. Sch. of Arts and Scis, Harvard Univ.; Inns of Court Sch. of Law. Called to the Bar, Lincoln's Inn, 1987; in practice as barrister specialising in commercial, company and chancery law. *Address:* One Essex Court, Middle Temple, EC4Y 9AR. *T:* (020) 7583 2000.

**de GREY**, family name of **Baron Walsingham**.

**de GREY, Spencer Thomas**, CBE 1997; RA 2008; RIBA; Senior Partner, since 1991, and Head of Design, since 2007, Foster + Partners; *b* 7 June 1944; *s* of Sir Roger de Grey, KCVO, PPRA, and Flavia de Grey, RA; *m* 1977, Hon. (Amanda) Lucy, *d* of Baron Annan, OBE; one *s* one *d*. *Educ:* Eton Coll.; Churchill Coll., Cambridge (BA 1966; MA 1970; DipArch 1969; Hon. Fellow 2018). ARCUK 1969; RIBA 1993. Architect, Merton LBC, 1969–73; joined Foster Associates, later Foster & Partners, 1973–: estabd Hong Kong office, 1979; Dir, 1981– (responsible for Third London Airport, Stansted, 1991, and Sackler Galls, Royal Acad., 1991); *projects* include: Lycée Albert Camus, Fréjus, 1995; Law Faculty, Univ. of Cambridge, 1995; Commerzbank HQ, Frankfurt, 1997; Sir Alexander Fleming Med. Bldg, Imperial Coll., London, 1998; Nat. Botanical Gdns for Wales, 1999; Great Court, BM, 2000; Dresden Stn, 2002; World Squares for All, London, 2003; eight City Academies, 2003–08; HM Treasury, Whitehall, 2004; Sage Music Centre, Gateshead, 2005; Kogod Courtyard, Nat. Portrait Gall., Smithsonian Instn, 2007; Elephant House, Copenhagen, 2008; masterplan, Slussen, Stockholm, 2008–; Winspear Opera House, Dallas, 2009; Vieux Port, Marseille, 2010–; Mus. of Fine Art, Boston, USA, 2010; Mus. of Roman Antiquities, Narbonne, 2011–; masterplan, West Kowloon Cultural Dist, 2011; Norton Mus., Palm Beach, USA, 2019. Vis. Prof. of Design, Univ. of Cambridge, 2009–. Pres., Bldg Centre Trust, 2017–. FRSA 2006. *Recreations:* music, theatre, travel. *Address:* (office) Riverside Three, 22 Hester Road, SW11 4AN. *T:* (020) 7738 0455, *Fax:* (020) 7738 1107.

**DE GROOT, Prof. Gerard Jan**, PhD; Professor of History, University of St Andrews, since 2000; *b* 22 June 1955; *s* of Jan De Groot and Johanna Hendrika De Groot (*née* Jansen); *m* 1991, Sharon Lynn Roe; one *s* one *d*. *Educ:* Whitman Coll., USA (BA 1977); Edinburgh Univ. (PhD 1983). Beach lifeguard, San Diego, Calif, 1973–77; insce adjuster, Portland, Oregon, 1977–80; lollipop man, Edinburgh, 1980–81; pt-time Tutor, WEA and Edinburgh Univ., 1983–85; Lectr, Univ. of St Andrews, 1985–2000. Freelance journalist, 1988–. RUSI Westminster Medal for Mil. Lit., 2001; Ray and Pat Brown Award, Popular Culture Assoc./Amer. Culture Assoc., 2009. *Publications:* Douglas Haig 1861–1928, 1988; Liberal Crusader, 1993; Blighty, 1996; Military Miscellany, 1997; Student Protest, 1998; A Noble Cause, 1999; A Soldier and a Woman, 2000; The First World War, 2001; The Bomb: a life, 2004; Dark Side of the Moon, 2006; Sixties Unplugged, 2008; Seventies Unplugged, 2010; Back in Blighty, 2014; Selling Ronald Reagan, 2015. *Recreations:* cooking, carpentry, following baseball on the internet. *Address:* 11 Walker Place, St Andrews, Fife KY16 9NY. *T:* (01334) 473107. *E:* gjdg@st-andrews.ac.uk.

**de GROOT, Lucy Manuela**, CBE 2009; Chief Executive, Community Service Volunteers, 2011–14; *b* 7 June 1951. *Educ:* St Anne's Coll., Oxford (BA 1973); LSE (Dip Social Admin 1974). Community worker, Islington, Manchester and Hackney, 1974–85; Prin. Employment Officer, Hackney BC, 1985–87; Employment Policy Advr, ALA, 1987–89; Hd of Policy, Lewisham BC, 1989–93; Hd of Policy, 1993–94, Acting Chief Exec., 1994–95, Chief Exec., 1995–2000, Bristol CC; Dir of Public Services, HM Treasury, 2000–03; Exec. Dir, Improvement and Develt Agency, 2003–09. Independent Chair: Surrey Children's Services Improvement Bd, 2008–10; Cornwall Children's Services Improvement Bd, 2009–13. Lay Mem., and Chm., Audit Cttee, NHS Islington CCG, 2015–. Vis. Prof., UWE, 2002–09. Trustee: Common Purpose UK, 2000–09; Campaign for Learning, 2002–06; Coram (formerly Coram Family), 2005–12 (Gov., 2004–05); Join In Trust, 2012–16; Baring Foundn Charitable Trust, 2013–; Community Links, 2015–17; New Philanthropy Capital, 2017–. Chm. Govs, Tower Hamlets/Hackney Community Coll., subseq. New City Coll., 2016–17; Gov., Working Men's Coll., 2007–17. FRSA. *Address:* 8 Southcote Road, N19 5BJ.

**de GRUBEN, Baron Thierry;** Ambassador of Belgium to the Court of St James's, 2002–06, now Hon. Ambassador; *b* 17 Nov. 1941; *s* of Baron Guy de Gruben and Baroness Guy de Gruben (*née* Monique Dierckx de Casterlé); *m* 1980, Françoise Francq; one *s*. *Educ:* Namur; Univ. of Leuven (law degree). Joined diplomatic service, 1969; diplomatic trainee, NATO, Brussels, 1969–70; Press Service, Min. of Foreign Affairs, Brussels, 1970–71; Attaché, then Sec., Moscow, 1971–76; Sec., then First Sec., London, 1976–80; Consul General, Bombay, 1980–82; Private Office, Minister of External Relns, Brussels, 1982–85; Ambassador: Warsaw, 1985–90; Moscow, 1990–95; Dep. Pol Dir, Brussels, and Special Envoy for E Slavonia, Croatia, 1995–97; Ambassador and Perm. Rep. of Belgium to NATO, Brussels, 1997–2002. Commandeur, Ordre de Léopold (Belgium), 1996; Grand Officier: Ordre de Léopold II (Belgium), 2000; Ordre de la Couronne (Belgium), 2003. *Address:* 4 rue Descartes, 75005 Paris, France. *E:* dgrubt@hotmail.com.

**de GRUCHY, Nigel Ronald Anthony;** General Secretary, National Association of Schoolmasters Union of Women Teachers, 1990–2002; *b* 28 Jan. 1943; *s* of Robert Philip de Gruchy and Dorothy Louise de Gruchy (*née* Cullinane); *m* 1970, Judith Ann Berglund, USA; one *s*. *Educ:* De La Salle Coll., Jersey; Univ. of Reading (BA Hons (Econs and Philosophy) 1965); PGCE London Univ. 1969; Cert. Pratique de Langue Française, Paris Univ., 1968; Cert. de Français Parlé et du Diplôme de Langue Française, L'Alliance Française, 1968. TEFL, Berlitz Schs, Santander, 1965–66, Versailles, 1966–67; student of French/Tutor in English, Paris, 1967–68; Head of Econs Dept, St Joseph's Acad., ILEA, 1968–78; Asst Sec., 1978–82, Dep. Gen. Sec., 1982–89, NAS UWT. Sec., London Assoc., 1975–78, Mem., Nat. Exec., 1975–78, NAS UWT. Member: Gen. Council, TUC, 1989–2003 (Pres., 2002–03); Exec., The Educn Internat., 1993–2004; Accountancy Foundn, 2000–04. Sec., Orpington Lab. Party, 2007–17. Contested (Lab) Orpington, 2015, 2017. *Publications:* History of the NASUWT 1919–2002: the story of a battling minority, 2013; contribs to Career Teacher. *Recreations:* sport, golf, literature, music, politics. *Address:* 26 Glentrammon Road, Green Street Green, Orpington, Kent BR6 6DE. *E:* nigel.degruchy1943@gmail.com.

**DE GUCHT, Karel;** Member, European Commission, 2009–14; President, Institute of European Studies, since 2015; *b* Overmere, Belgium, 27 Jan. 1954; *m* Mireille Schreurs; two *s*. *Educ:* Vrije Univ. Brussels (law degree). Lawyer, Dendermonde, 1976–99; Partner, TEG Holding NV, 1990–96; Prof. in Eur. Law, Vrije Univ. Brussels, 1991–. MEP, 1980–94; Alderman responsible for Finance, Lebbeke, 1983–88; Municipal Councillor, Berlare, 1989– (Chm., 2006–09, 2012–); Mayor, Berlare, 2006–12; Senator, 1994–95; Mem., Flemish Parlt, 1995–2003; Mem., House of Representatives, Belgium, 2003–09; Minister for Internat. Trade, 2007–09, for Foreign Affairs and Eur. Affairs, 2004–09; Dep. Prime Minister, 2008–09; Minister of State (for life), 2002. Flemish Party for Freedom and Progress, later Flemish Liberal and Democratic Party: Mem., Bureau, 1977–; Vice Pres., 1985–88; Pres., 1999–2004. Pres., Brussels, 1974–75, Nat. Pres., 1975–77, Flemish Assoc. of Liberal Students; Pres., Young Flemish Liberal Movt, 1977–79. Owner and CEO, La Macinaia SS, Tuscany. Director: Dexia Hldg NV, and Mem., Strategic Cttee, 1996–2004; Port of Antwerp, 2001–07; Merit Capital NV, 2015–18; Proximus Gp, 2015– (Mem., Transformation and Innovation Cttee (formerly Strategic Cttee), 2015–); ArcelorMittal, 2016– (Mem., Audit and Risk Cttee, 2016–). Mem. Adv. Bd, CVC Capital Partners, 2015–. Columnist, Het Laatste Nieuws, 2015–17. Resident Fellow, Kennedy Sch. of Govt, Harvard Univ., 2015. Knight, Order of Leopold, 1995. *Publications:* Time and Tide Wait for No Man: the changing European geopolitical landscape, 1991; (with Dirk Sterckx) Er zijn geen eilanden meer: over de democratie, vrijheid en de mensrechten, 1999; (with Johan

Van Hecke) Het einde der pilaren: een Toscaans gesprek, 2001; De toekomst is vrij: over het liberalisme in de 21ste eeuw, 2002; Pluche—Over de banalisering van extreem rechts, 2007; Vrijheid: liberalisme in tijden van cholera, 2012; Ketterijen, 2017.

de HAAN, Kevin Charles; QC 2000; a Recorder, since 2002; *b* 30 Oct. 1952; *s* of Michael James de Haan and Barbara Ada de Haan; *m* 1983, Katy Monica Foster. *Educ:* Davenant Foundn Grammar Sch.; Queen Mary Coll., Univ. of London (LLB); Vrije Univ., Brussels (LLM Internat. and Comparative Law). Called to the Bar, Inner Temple, 1976, Bencher, 1997; Jt Hd of Chambers, 2019–. *Publications:* Food Safety Law and Practice, 1994; Pollution in the United Kingdom, 1994; (contrib.) Smith & Monkcom, The Law of Betting, Gaming and Lotteries, 2nd edn 2000. *Recreations:* ski-ing, flying light aircraft, mountain bicycling, cooking. *Address:* Gough Square Chambers, 6–7 Gough Square, EC4A 3DE. *Club:* Ski of GB.

DE HAAN, Sir Roger Michael, Kt 2014; CBE 2004; DL; philanthropist; Chairman, Saga Group, until 2004; *b* 1948; *s* of late Sidney De Haan. Co-Founder and Chm., Roger De Haan Charitable Trust, 1978– (incl. redevelt of Folkestone Harbour and Old Town); Chm., Creative Foundn. Trustee, NHMF, 2014–17. DL Kent, 2003. Hon. DCL Kent, 2005.

de HAAS, Margaret Ruth, (Mrs I. S. Goldrein); QC 1998; **Her Honour Judge de Haas;** a Circuit Judge, since 2004; Designated Family Judge for Liverpool, since 2005, and for Cheshire and Merseyside, since 2010; a Senior Circuit Judge, since 2010; *b* 21 May 1954; *d* of Josef and Lilo de Haas; *m* 1980, Iain Saville Goldrein, *qv*; one *s* one *d*. *Educ:* Townsend Sch., Zimbabwe; Bristol Univ. (LLB Hons 1976). Called to the Bar, Middle Temple, 1977; in practice at the Bar, 1977–2004; a Recorder, 1999–2004. Mem., Criminal Injuries Compensation Bd, 1999–. *Publications:* (jtly) Butterworths Personal Injury Litigation Service, 1988–; (jtly) Property Distribution on Divorce, 1989; (jtly) Domestic Injunctions, 1997; (jtly) Medical Negligence: cost effective case management, 1997; (jtly) Structured Settlements, 1997. *Recreations:* family, swimming, reading, theatre. *Address:* c/o Liverpool Family and Civil Courts, 35 Vernon Street, Liverpool L2 2BX.

de HALPERT, Rear-Adm. Sir Jeremy (Michael), KCVO 2009; CB 2001; Deputy Master, Trinity House, 2002–11; *b* 9 July 1947; *s* of late Lt Comdr Michael Frances de Halpert and Eleanor Anne Love de Halpert; *m* 1972, Jane Fattorini, *d* of late Joseph Fattorini; two *s* one *d*. *Educ:* Canford Sch., Wimborne. Joined Royal Navy, 1966. BRNC, Dartmouth; served HM Ships Aurora, Chilcompton, London, Phoebe, Lowestoft, 1967–75; CO, HMS Sheraton, 1975–76; Specialised Principal Warfare Officer (Navigation): HMS Ajax and HMS Ariadne, 1978–80; HMS Bristol and Falklands Campaign, 1982–84; Comdr, 1984; CO, HMS Apollo, 1985–86; jsdc 1987; Directorate of Naval Staff Duties, MoD, 1987–89; USN War Coll., Newport, RI, 1989–90; Capt., 1990; CO, HMS Campbeltown, 1990–92; COS, Flag Officer Surface Flotilla, 1992–94; Dep. UK Mil. Rep., SHAPE, 1994–96; Cdre, 1996; Dir, Overseas Mil. Activity, MoD, 1996–98; Rear-Adm., 1998; Naval Sec., and Chief Exec., Naval Manning Agency, 1998–2002. Dir, Standard (London) P & I Club, 2002–11. Gov., Canford Sch., 2002–19. Younger Brother, 1993, Elder Brother, 2001, Trinity House. Dir, IALA World Wide Acad., 2012–; Trustee: Marine Soc. & Sea Cadets (formerly Marine Soc.), 2002–10; Royal Nat. Mission to Deep Sea Fishermen, 2012–; Rosemary Foundn, 2013–; Vice Patron, Gallantry Medallists' League, 2002–19; Patron, Nat. Maritime Mus., 2012–. Pres., Veterans Outreach Support, 2014–. HM Lieut, City of London, 2006–. Liveryman, Shipwrights' Co., 2003– (Mem., Ct of Assts, 2008–; Prime Warden, 2016–17). Mem., Tennis & Racquets Assoc. MRIN 1980, FRIN 2002, Hon. FRIN 2011; Hon. FNI 2011. Commandeur de Bordeaux à Londres, 2005. *Recreations:* Royal tennis, ski-ing, cricket, military history. *Address:* Carpenters Cottage, Froxfield Green, Petersfield, Hants GU32 1DH. *Clubs:* Boodle's, Royal Navy of 1765 and 1785, MCC.

de HAMEL, Christopher Francis Rivers, DPhil, PhD; FSA; FRHistS; Donnelley Librarian, 2000–16, and Fellow, since 2000, Corpus Christi College, Cambridge; *b* 20 Nov. 1950; *s* of Dr Francis Alexander de Hamel and Joan Littledale de Hamel (née Pollock); *m* 1st, 1974 (marr. diss. 1989); two *s*; 2nd, 1993, Mette Tang Simpson (née Svendsen) (d 2019). *Educ:* Otago Univ., NZ (BA Hons); Oxford Univ. (DPhil); PhD Cambridge 2005. FSA 1981; FRHistS 1986. Sotheby's: cataloguer of medieval manuscripts, 1975; Asst Dir, 1977; Dir, Western and Oriental, later Western, Manuscripts, 1982–2000. Vis. Fellow, All Souls Coll., Oxford, 1999–2000; Sandars Reader in Bibliography, Univ. of Cambridge, 2003–04; Lyell Reader in Bibliography, Univ. of Oxford, 2008–09. Chm., Assoc. for Manuscripts and Archives in Res. Collections, 2000–15. Hon. LittD St John's, Minn, 1994; Hon. DLitt Otago, 2002. *Publications:* include: Glossed Books of the Bible and the Origins of the Paris Booktrade, 1984; A History of Illuminated Manuscripts, 1986, 2nd edn 1994; (with M. Manion and V. Vines) Medieval and Renaissance Manuscripts in New Zealand Collections, 1989; Syon Abbey, The Library of the Bridgettine Nuns and their Peregrinations after the Reformation, 1991; Scribes and Illuminators, 1992; The British Library Guide to Manuscript Illumination, 2001; The Book: a history of the Bible, 2001; The Rothschilds and their Collections of Illuminated Manuscripts, 2004; Liber Bestiarum, 2008; Gilding the Lilly, 2010; Bibles: an illustrated history from papyrus to print, 2011; Meetings with Remarkable Manuscripts, 2016 (Duff Cooper Prize, 2016; Wolfson History Prize, 2017). *Address:* Corpus Christi College, Trumpington Street, Cambridge CB2 1RH. *Clubs:* Athenæum; Roxburghe (Arundel); Grolier (New York); Association Internationale de Bibliophilie (Paris).

de HAVILLAND, Dame Olivia (Mary), DBE 2017; actress; *b* Tokyo, Japan, 1 July 1916; *d* of Walter Augustus de Havilland and Lilian Augusta (née Ruse) (parents British subjects); *m* 1st, 1946, Marcus Aurelius Goodrich (marr. diss., 1953); one *s* decd; 2nd, 1955, Pierre Paul Galante (marr. diss. 1979; he *d* 1998); one *d*. *Educ:* in California; won scholarship to Mills Coll., 1934, but career prevented acceptance. *Theatre* (USA): Hermia in Max Reinhardt's stage production of Midsummer Night's Dream, 1934 (and in film version, 1935); Juliet in Romeo and Juliet, 1951; Candida, 1951 and 1952; A Gift of Time, 1962. *Films include:* The Adventures of Robin Hood, 1938; Gone With the Wind, 1939 (Acad. Award nomination); Hold Back the Dawn, 1941 (Acad. Award nomination); Princess O'Rourke, 1943; To Each His Own, 1946 (Acad. Award); The Dark Mirror, 1946; The Snake Pit, 1948 (Acad. Award nomination; NY and San Francisco Critics' Awards); The Heiress, 1949 (Acad. Award; NY and San Francisco Critics' Awards; Golden Globe Award; Venice Fest. Award); My Cousin Rachel, 1952; Not as a Stranger, 1955; The Ambassador's Daughter, 1956 (Belgian Prix Femina, 1957); Proud Rebel, 1958; Light in the Piazza, 1962; Lady in a Cage, 1964 (Films and Filming Award, UK, 1967); Hush … Hush, Sweet Charlotte, 1965; Airport '77, 1977. *Television includes:* Noon Wine, 1966; The Screaming Woman, 1972; Roots, The Next Generations, 1979; 3 ABC Cable-TV Cultural Documentaries, 1981; Murder is Easy, 1982; Charles & Diana, a Royal Romance, 1982; North and South, Book II, 1986; Anastasia, 1986 (Golden Globe Award); The Woman He Loved, 1988. US Lecture tours, 1971, 1972, 1973, 1974, 1975, 1976, 1978, 1979, 1980. First woman Pres. of Jury, Cannes Film Festival, 1965. Took part in narration of France's BiCentennial Gift to US, Son et Lumière, A Salute to George Washington, Mount Vernon, 19 May 1976; read excerpts from Thomas Jefferson at BiCentennial Service, American Cathedral in Paris, 4 July 1976. Special appearance, Acad. Awards, 2003, introducing 59 former winners; participated in Acad. tribute to Bette Davis, 2008. Hon. DHL Amer. Univ. of Paris, 1994; Hon. Dr Letters Univ. of Hertfordshire, 1998. Women's National Press Club Award, 1950; French Winged Victory Award, 1950; Filmex Tribute, 1978; Amer. Acad. of Achievement Award, 1978; Gold Medal, John F. Kennedy Center for Performing Arts, 2005; Amer. Acad. and Viennale Tributes, 2006. Amer. Legion Humanitarian Medal, 1967; Freedom Foundn American Exemplar Medal, 1980; Nat. Medal of Arts (USA), 2008. *Publications:* Every Frenchman Has One, 1961, new edn 2016; (contrib.) Mother and Child, 1975.

DEHENNIN, Baron Herman; Hon. Grand Marshal of Belgian Royal Court; Hon. Belgian Ambassador; *b* 20 July 1929; created Baron, 1990; *s* of Alexander Dehennin and Flora Brehmen; *m* 1954, Margareta-Maria Donvil; two *s*. *Educ:* Catholic Univ. of Leuven. Dr in Law 1951. Lieut, Royal Belgian Artillery, 1951–53; entered Belgian Diplomatic Service, 1954; served The Hague, New Delhi, Madrid, the Congo; Ambassador to Rwanda, 1966–70; Economic Minister, Washington, 1970–74; Dir-Gen., Foreign Econ. Relations, Brussels, 1974–77; Ambassador to Japan, 1978–81; Grand Marshal, Belgian Royal Court, 1981–85; Ambassador to USA, 1985–91; to UK, 1991–94. Pres., Special Olympics, Belgium, 1995. Chm., Club Chateau Ste Anne, Brussels, 1997, now Hon. Pres. Grand Cross, Order of Leopold, 1985; Grand Cross, Order of the Crown, 1983; foreign Orders: Comoros, France, Greece, Japan, Luxembourg, Mexico, Netherlands, Portugal, Rwanda, Sweden, Zaire. *Recreations:* hiking, reading (history, philosophy). *Clubs:* Royal Anglo-Belgian; Cercle Gaulois.

DEHN, Conrad Francis; QC 1968; Barrister; a Recorder of the Crown Court, 1974–98; a Deputy High Court Judge, 1988–96; *b* London, 24 Nov. 1926; *s* of late C. G. Dehn, Solicitor and Cynthia Dehn (née Fuller) painter, musician and poet, as Francyn; *m* 1st, 1954, Sheila (née Magan) (marr. diss. 1978); two *s* one *d*; 2nd, 1978, Marilyn, *d* of late Peter and Constance Collyer. *Educ:* Charterhouse (Sen. Exhibnr); Christ Church, Oxford (Holford Schol. 1944; Slade Exhibnr 1948). Served RA, 1945–48, Best Cadet Mons Basic OCTU, 1946, 2nd Lieut 1947. 1st cl. hons PPE Oxon. 1950, MA 1952; Holt Schol. and Lord Justice Holker Sen. Exhibnr, Gray's Inn, 1951; Pres., Inns of Court Students Union, 1951–52. WEA Tutor, 1951–55. Called to Bar, Gray's Inn, 1952; Bencher, 1977; Chm., Management Cttee, 1987; Vice-Treas., 1995; Treas., 1996. Head, Fountain Court Chambers, 1984–89. Chairman: Bar Council Working Party on Liability for Defective Products, 1975–77; Planning Cttee, Senate of Inns of Court and Bar, 1980–83; London Univ. Disciplinary Appeals Cttee, 1986–90; Adv. Cttee, Gen. Comrs of Income Tax, Gray's Inn, 1994–2003. Dir, Bar Mutual Indemnity Fund Ltd, 1988–2010. Mem., Foster Cttee of Inquiry into Operators' Licensing, Dept of Transport, 1978. Member: Council of Legal Educn, 1981–86; London Legal Aid Cttee, 1965–92 (Vice-Chm., 1987–92); Hon. Advr, S London Psychotherapy Centre, 1982–2001; Hon. Legal Adviser: Age Concern London, 1987–2002 (Vice-Pres., 2001–02); Southwark Action for Voluntary Orgns, 2003–08. Pres., Camberwell Soc., 1996–2007. Member: Governing Body, United Westminster Schs, 1953–57; Adv. Bd, Inst. of Law, City Univ., 2002; Govs, Inns of Court Sch. of Law, 1996–2002. Appeared in film, The History Boys, 2007. Hon. Liberty, Camberwell, 2006. *Publications:* (contrib.) Ideas, 1954; (contrib.) Reform of Civil Procedure, 1996; (ed) Commercial Court Practice, 1999, 2nd edn 2000. *Recreations:* theatre, living in France. *Club:* Reform.

De HOCHEPIED LARPENT, Lt Col Andrew Lionel Dudley, OBE 1992; Chairman, Commonwealth Association for the Ageing - CommonAge, since 2012; *b* 10 Feb. 1951; *s* of Douglas De Hochepied Larpent and Patience (née Johnson); *m* 1974, Anne Marion Knights; two *s* one *d*. *Educ:* Bradfield Coll.; RMA Sandhurst; Reading Univ. (BSc Hons Estate Mgt 1976). Royal Regt of Fusiliers, 1969–94, CO, 3rd Bn, 1990–92; Dir, Rehau Ltd, 1994–96; construction industry consultant, 1996–97; Chief Executive Officer: Cancer and Leukaemia in Childhood, 1997–2001; Somerset Care Gp, 2001–11; Southern Cross Care (S Australia and Northern Territory), 2011–16. Chairman: Care Focus Somerset, 2005–07; Nat. Care Forum, 2006–11; Dignity in Care Australia, 2014–16; Mem. Bd, Internat. Assoc. of Homes and Services for the Ageing, 2006–12. *Recreations:* cycling, croquet.

de HOGHTON, Sir (Richard) Bernard (Cuthbert), 14th Bt *cr* 1611; KM; DL; landowner and investment manager; *b* 26 Jan. 1945; 3rd *s* of Sir Cuthbert de Hoghton, 12th Bt, and Philomena, *d* of late Herbert Simmons; *S* half-brother, 1978; *m* 1974, Rosanna Stella Virginia (née Buratti); one *s* one *d*. *Educ:* Ampleforth College, York; McGill Univ., Montreal (BA Hons); Birmingham Univ. (MA). Turner & Newall Ltd, 1967–70; international fund management, Vickers Da Costa & Co. Ltd, 1970–77; international institutional brokerage, de Zoete & Bevan & Co., 1977–86 (Partner, 1984–86); Dir, BZW Ltd (Europe), 1986–89; Asst Dir, Brown Shipley, 1989–94; Associate Dir, Teather & Greenwood, 1994–98; Dir, Tutton & Saunders Ltd, 1998–99. Pres., Royal Lancs Agricl Soc., 1995; Pres., Friends of Real Lancs, 2009–14; Nat. Vice-Pres., Internat. Tree Foundn, 1983–2013; Vice-Pres., Nat. Assoc. of Almshouses, 2012–17. UN Special Ambassador, 1985. Patron: ACU (NW), 1980–2014; Internat. Spinal Res. Trust, 1984–2014. Chm., Hoghton Tower Preservation Trust, 1978–2015; Chm. and Dir, Hoghton Tower Ltd, 1981–2015. Founder Mem., HHA, 1973 (Mem., NW Reg. Exec. Cttee, 2006–17). Hon. Lay Rector, The Minster, Preston, 1972–2018. FCSI. DL Lancs, 1988. Constantinian Order of S George (Naples), 1984; Kt SMO, Malta, 1980. *Recreations:* tennis, shooting, ski-ing, travelling, local historical research. *Heir:* *s* Thomas James Daniel Adam de Hoghton, *b* 11 April 1980. *Address:* 22 St Maur Road, Fulham, SW6 4DP.

de HOOP SCHEFFER, Jakob Gijsbert, (Jaap), Hon. KCMG 2009; Secretary-General, NATO, 2004–09; Professor of International Relations and Diplomatic Practice, Leiden University; *b* 3 April 1948; *m* Jeannine van Oorschot; two *d*. *Educ:* Leiden Univ. (law degree 1974). Joined Foreign Service, Netherlands, 1976; Accra, 1976–78; Perm. Delegn, NATO, Brussels, 1978–80; i/c pvte office, Minister of Foreign Affairs, Netherlands, 1980–86. MP (Christian Democratic Alliance), Netherlands, 1986–2003; Minister of Foreign Affairs, 2002–03. Dep. Leader 1995–97, Leader, 1997–2001, Christian Democratic Alliance. Pieter Kooijmans Prof. for Peace, Law and Security, Leiden Univ., 2009. Co-Pres., Security and Defence Agenda, 2010. *Address:* c/o NATO, Boulevard Leopold III, 1110 Brussels, Belgium.

**DEIGHTON,** family name of **Baron Deighton**.

DEIGHTON, Baron *cr* 2012 (Life Peer), of Carshalton in the County of Surrey; **Paul Clive Deighton**, KBE 2013; Chairman, Heathrow Ltd, since 2016; *b* 18 Jan. 1956; *s* of Walter Francis and Mabel Alice Deighton; *m* 1985, Alison Zoe Klebanoff; two *s*. *Educ:* Trinity Coll., Cambridge (BA 1978). Goldman Sachs International, 1983–2006: Investment Banking Div., 1983–93; Head of Controllers Dept, NY, 1993–96; Partner and Man. Dir, 1996–2000; Chief Operating Officer, Europe, 2000–06; Chief Exec., LOCOG, 2006–12. Commercial Sec., HM Treasury, 2013–15. Non-executive Director: Holdingham Gp Ltd, 2016– (Chm., 2018–); Square Inc., 2016–; Economist Gp, 2018– (Chm., 2018–); Chm. Govs, King's Coll. Sch., 2017–. *Address:* House of Lords, SW1 0PW.

DEIGHTON, Jane Elizabeth; Senior Consultant, Deighton Pierce Glynn, since 2014 (Partner, 2012–14); *b* 18 March 1952; *d* of late Herbert Stanley Deighton and of Mary Elizabeth Anne Deighton (née Duncan). *Educ:* Univ. of Sussex (BA); Coll. of Law.

Admitted as solicitor, 1985; Solicitor, Seifert Sedley Williams, 1983–90; Partner, Deighton Guedella, 1990–2012. Mem., Law Soc. *Publications:* Human Rights in Malawi, 1992; Emergency Powers in Northern Ireland, 1998. *Address:* Deighton Pierce Glynn, 382 City Road, EC1V 2QA. *T:* (020) 7407 0007, *Fax:* (020) 7837 7473. *E:* jdeighton@dpglaw.co.uk.

**DEIGNAN, Elizabeth Mary;** professional cyclist: Boels-Dolmans Cycling Team, since 2013; British Cycling, since 2003; *b* Otley, 18 Dec. 1988; *d* of John Armitstead and Carol Armitstead; *m* 2016, Philip Deignan; one *d*. *Educ:* The Whartons Prim. Sch., Otley; Prince Henry's Grammar Sch., Otley. Gold Medal, team pursuit, Silver Medal, scratch, Bronze Medal, points race, UCI World Track Cycling Championships, 2009; British Nat. Road Champion, 2011, 2013, 2015; Silver Medal, Olympic Games, London, 2012; Gold Medal, road race, Commonwealth Games, 2014; winner, UCI Women's World Cup Series, 2014, 2015; UCI World Road Race Champion, 2015; winner: Tour of Flanders, 2016; Aviva Women's Tour of Britain, 2016; UCI World Team Trial Champion, 2016; British Nat. Road Champion, 2017. Rider of the Year, Cycling Weekly, 2014. *Publications:* Steadfast: my autobiography, 2016. *Address:* c/o bespoke M Ltd, Sanderum House, Oakley Road, Chinnor, Oxon OX39 4TW. *T:* (01844) 345914. *E:* emma@bespoke-m.com. *Club:* Otley Cycling.

**DEIN, David Barry,** MBE 2019; Vice Chairman, Arsenal Football Club, 1984–2007; former Vice Chairman, Football Association; *b* 7 Sept. 1943; *s* of Isidore and Sybil Dein; *m* 1972, Barbara Einhorn; two *s* one *d*. *Educ:* Orange Hill Grammar Sch., Edgware. Proprietor, sugar and commodity trading business, 1961–88; Dir, 1983–2007, full-time exec. role, 1988–2007, Arsenal FC. Founding Mem., Kick It Out campaign, 1993; Pres., G-14 Gp of clubs, 2006–07. Internat. Pres., England 2018 FIFA World Cup Bid, 2009–10. Ambassador, Premier League. Chm., Stage One (formerly Theatre Investment Fund), 2001–09. Motivational speaker in schools and prisons, 2012–. *Recreations:* theatre, films, golf, tennis, scrabble.

**DEISENHOFER, Prof. Johann,** PhD; Regental Professor and Professor in Biophysics (formerly Biochemistry), University of Texas Southwestern Medical Center at Dallas, 1988–2019, now Emeritus; Investigator, Howard Hughes Medical Institute, 1988–2010; *b* 30 Sept. 1943; *s* of Johann and Thekla Deisenhofer; *m* 1989, Kirsten Fischer-Lindahl, PhD. *Educ:* Technische Universität München (Physics Diploma 1971; PhD 1974). Max-Planck-Institut für Biochemie: graduate student, 1971–74; Postdoctoral Fellow, 1974–76; Staff Scientist, 1976–88. (Jtly) Biological Physics Prize, Amer. Physical Soc., 1986; (jtly) Otto Bayer Preis, 1988; (jtly) Nobel Prize in Chemistry, 1988. *Publications:* contribs to Acta Crystallographica, Biochemistry, Jl of Molecular Biology, Nature, Science, etc. *Recreations:* ski-ing, hiking, classical music. *Address:* University of Texas Southwestern Medical Center, 6001 Forest Park Road, Dallas, TX 75390–8816, USA. *T:* (214) 6455941.

**DEJARDIN, Ian Alan Charles;** Chief Executive, McMichael Canadian Art Collection, since 2017; *b* 26 Aug. 1955; *s* of Alan A. Dejardin and Pamela B. Dejardin (*née* Wilcock); civil partnership 2007, *m* 2015, Eric Pearson. *Educ:* Daniel Stewart's Coll., Edinburgh; Univ. of Edinburgh (MA 1st Cl. Hons Hist. of Art 1977); Univ. of Manchester (Dip. Art Gall. and Mus. Studies 1987). Curatorial Asst, Royal Acad. of Arts, 1988–90; English Heritage: Curator of Paintings, London Historic Houses, 1990–94; Sen. Curator of Collections, 1994–96, Hd, Historic Team, 1996–97, Historic Properties, London Reg.; Curator, 1998–2005, Dir, then Sackler Dir, 2005–17, Dulwich Picture Gall. *Publications:* exhibition catalogues: Paintings from the Chantrey Bequest, 1989; Henry Moore at Dulwich Picture Gallery, 2004; Director's Choice, 2005; The Dutch Italianates: 17th Century masterpieces from Dulwich Picture Gallery, 2008; Painting Canada: Tom Thomson and the Group of Seven, 2011; From the Forest to the Sea: Emily Carr in British Columbia, 2014. *Recreations:* piano, knitting. *Address:* McMichael Canadian Art Collection, 10365 Islington Avenue, Kleinburg, ON L0J 1C0, Canada.

**de JERSEY, Hon. Paul,** AC 2000; Governor of Queensland, since 2014; *b* 21 Sept. 1948; *s* of Ronald Claude and Moya Clarice de Jersey; *m* 1971, Kaye Brown; one *s* two *d*. *Educ:* C of E Grammar Sch., Brisbane; Univ. of Qld (BA, LLB Hons). Admitted to Qld Bar, 1971; QC (Qld) 1981; a Judge of the Supreme Court, Qld, 1985–2014; Chief Justice of Qld, 1998–2014. Chm., Qld Law Reform Commn, 1996–98; Pres., Industrial Court of Qld, 1996–98. Chm. Judicial Section, Law Assoc. for Asia and Pacific, 2006–14. Chancellor, Anglican Dio. Brisbane, 1991–2014. Chm., Qld Cancer Fund, 1994–2001; Pres., Australian Cancer Soc., 1998–2001. Visitor, Univ. of South Pacific, 2006–09. Hon. LLD Qld, 2000; DUniv: Southern Qld, 2008; Griffith, 2014. *Recreations:* reading, music. *Address:* Government House, GPO Box 434, Brisbane, Qld 4001, Australia. *Clubs:* Queensland, United Service (Brisbane).

**de JONGH, Nicholas Raymond;** theatre critic, writer; Dramaturg, Bill Kenwright Ltd, 2013–14; *b* London; *s* of late Louis de Jongh and Vivian (*née* Creditor). *Educ:* Hall Sch., Hampstead; St Paul's Sch.; University Coll. London (BA Hons, MPhil 1983). Secker & Warburg, 1967; Scriptwriter, BBC External Services, 1968; The Guardian: Reporter, 1968; Theatre Reviewer, 1969; Dep. Theatre Critic, 1972–91; Arts Reporter, 1973–78; Arts Corresp., 1978–90; Theatre Critic: Mail on Sunday, 1983; Evening Standard, 1991–2009. Chm., Drama Section, Critics' Circle, 1984–86. Writer of plays: Plague Over England, Finborough Th., 2008, Duchess Th., 2009; To Keep the Ghost Awake, Finborough Th., 2010; There Goes My Future, Finborough Th., 2011; The Unquiet Grave of Garcia Lorca, Drayton Arms, 2014; Pricked Out, King's Head, 2017. *Publications:* (ed) Bedside Guardian, 1989, 1990; Not in Front of the Audience, 1992; (contrib.) Approaching the Millennium: essays on Angels in America, 2000; Politics, Prudery and Perversions (Theatre Book Prize, Soc. of Theatre Res.), 2000; (contrib.) British Theatre of the 1990s, 2007; Plague over England, 2009. *Recreation:* trying to make my dreams come true. *E:* nicholasdejongh@hotmail.co.uk. *W:* nicholasdejongh.co.uk. *Club:* Holborn Athletic.

**DEJONGHE, Willem Michel Georges Clara;** Senior Partner, Allen & Overy LLP, since 2016; *b* Belgium, 27 Feb. 1961; *s* of Guido Dejonghe and Roza Bonte; *m* 2012, Caroline Pill; five *s*. *Educ:* Katholieke Univ., Leuven (Licentiaat in de rechten 1984). Stagiaire, Belgium, 1986–89; admitted as advocate, Belgium, 1989; Asst, Internat. and Eur. Law Dept, Univ. of Leuven; Partner, 1993–2001, Man. Partner, 1996–2001, Loeff Claeys Verbeke; Man. Partner, Belgian offices, 2001–08, Global Man. Partner, 2008–16, Allen & Overy. Registered Eur. Lawyer, England and Wales, 2008. Member: Internat. Business and Diplomatic Exchange, 1984; Vlaams Rechtsgenootschap (Flemish Law Soc.), 1984. *Publications:* (contrib.) European Counsel Mergers and Acquisitions Handbook, 2000; (with W. Van de Voorde) Mergers and Acquisitions in Belgium, 2001; contrib. to Vennootschapsrecht en Fiscaliteit. *Recreations:* ski-ing, cycling, sailing. *Address:* Allen & Overy LLP, One Bishops Square, E1 6AD. *T:* (020) 3088 0000. *E:* wim.dejonghe@allenovery.com. *Club:* De Warande (Brussels).

**de KLERK, Frederik Willem;** Leader of the Opposition, National Assembly of South Africa, 1996–97; Chairman Emeritus, F W de Klerk Foundation; Chairman, Global Leadership Foundation; *b* 18 March 1936; *s* of Jan and Corrie de Klerk; *m* 1st, 1959, Marike Willemse (marr. diss. 1998; she *d* 2001); two *s* one *d*; 2nd, 1998, Elita Georgiadis. *Educ:* Monument High School, Krugersdorp; Potchefstroom Univ. Law practice, 1961–72; MP (Nat. Party) Vereeniging, 1972–89; Information Officer, Transvaal, Nat. Party, 1975; Minister: of Posts and Telecommunications and Social Welfare and Pensions, 1978; of Posts and Telecommunications and of Sport and Recreation, 1978–79; of Mines, Energy and Environmental Planning, 1979–80; of Mineral and Energy Affairs, 1980–82; of Internal Affairs, 1982–85; of Nat. Educn and Planning, 1984–89; Leader, Nat. Party, 1989–97 (Transvaal Leader, 1982–89); Chm., Council of Ministers, 1985–89; State President, 1989–94, Dep. President, 1994–96, S Africa. Hon. LLD: Potchefstroom, 1990; Bar-Ilan, Tel Aviv, 1991; S Africa, 1995; Zululand, 1995; Salisbury, USA, 2007; Hon. DPhil: Stellenbosch, 1990; Nat. Chengchi, Taipei, Taiwan, 1991; Haifa, Israel, 2014; Hon. Dr Vrije, Brussels, 1994. Newsmaker of the Year: Johannesburg Press Club, 1989, (with N. R. Mandela) 1994; Pretoria Press Club, 1989, 1990; Man of the Year, Inst. of Mgt Consultants, 1991; Marketing Man of the Year, Federated Hospitality Assoc. of S Africa, 1991; Houphouët-Boigny Prize for Peace, UNESCO, 1991; Prix du Courage Politique Internationale, 1992; Prince of Asturias Prize, 1992; Philadelphia Liberty Medal, 1993; Nobel Peace Prize, 1993 (with N. R. Mandela); Hon. Fellowship Award, Coll. of Medicine of S Africa, 1994. Decoration for Meritorious Service (S Africa), 1981; Gold Order of Mapungubwe (S Africa), 2002. *Publications:* The Last Trek: a new beginning (autobiog.), 1999. *Address:* PO Box 15785, Panorama, 7506, Western Cape, South Africa. *T:* (21) 930 0966.

**de KRETSER, Prof. David Morritz,** AC 2006 (AO 2000); MD; FRACP, FAA, FTSE; Emeritus Sir John Monash Distinguished Professor, Monash University, since 2011; Governor of Victoria, Australia, 2006–11; *b* Colombo, Sri Lanka, 27 April 1939; *s* of Percival Shirley de Kretser and Iris Aileen de Kretser; *m* 1962, Janice Margaret Warren; four *s*. *Educ:* Camberwell Grammar Sch.; Univ. of Melbourne (MS BS 1962); Monash Univ. (MD 1969). FRACP 1994; FAA 1996; FTSE 2001. Lectr, 1966–68, Sen. Lectr, 1968, Dept of Anatomy, Monash Univ.; Sen. Fellow in Endocrinol., Dept of Medicine, Univ. of Washington, and USPHS Postdoctoral Fellow, 1969–71; Monash University: Sen. Lectr, Depts of Medicine and Anatomy, 1971–75; Reader in Anatomy, 1976–78; Prof. of Anatomy, 1978–2006, Emeritus Prof., 2006–11; Hd, Dept of Anatomy, 1978–91; Dir, Centre for Reproductive Biol., 1989–91; Dir, Inst. of Reproduction and Develt, subseq. Monash Inst. of Med. Res., 1991–2005; Associate Dean, Biotechnol. Develt, 2002–06; Prince Henry's Hospital: Asst Endocrinologist, 1971–85; Physician, 1973–74; Sen. Res. Fellow, 1974–78, Associate Dir, 1977–78, Med. Res. Centre; Consultant, Reproductive Medicine Clinic, Inst. of Med. Res., 1976–2006. Fellow, Aust. Acad. of Health and Med. Scis, 2013. Hon. LLD: Monash, 2011; Melbourne, 2012. Centenary Medal, Aust., 2003. *Publications:* The Pituitary and Testis: clinical and experimental studies, 1983; (Section Ed.) Jameson & De Groot Endocrinology: adult and paediatric, 7th edn 2015; 504 papers in jls and 170 chapters in texts on endocrinology and infertility. *Recreations:* bushwalking, fishing, tennis, jazz. *Address:* Hudson Institute, Monash University, 27–31 Wright Street, Clayton, Vic 3168, Australia. *Clubs:* Athenæum, Royal Automobile (Melbourne); West Brighton (Vic).

**de la BILLIÈRE, Gen. Sir Peter (Edgar de la Cour),** KCB 1988; KBE 1991 (CBE 1983); DSO 1976; MC 1959 and Bar 1966; DL; Commander British Forces Middle East, 1990–91; *b* 29 April 1934; *s* of Surgeon Lieut Comdr Claude Dennis Delacour de Labillière (killed in action, HMS Fiji, 1941) and of Frances Christine Wright Lawley; *m* 1965, Bridget Constance Muriel Goode; one *s* two *d*. *Educ:* Harrow School; Staff College. Joined KSLI 1952; commissioned DLI; served Japan, Korea, Malaya (despatches 1958), Jordan, Borneo, Egypt, Aden, Gulf States, Sudan, Oman, Falkland Is; CO 22 SAS Regt, 1972–74; GSO1 (DS) Staff Coll., 1974–77; Comd British Army Training Team, Sudan, 1977–78; Dir SAS and Comd, SAS Group, 1978–82; rcds 1983; Comd, British Forces Falkland Is and Mil. Comr, 1984–85; GOC Wales, 1985–87; GOC SE Dist, and Perm. Peace Time Comdr, Jt Forces Operations Staff, 1987–90; ME Advr to MOD, 1991–92, retd. Col Comdt, Light Div., 1986–89. Chairman: ME Div., Robert Fleming Hldgs, 1998–99 (non-exec. Dir, 1992–98); Meadowland Meats Ltd, 1994–2002. Mem. Council, RUSI, 1975–77. Chm., FARM Africa, 1998–2001 (Mem. Bd, 1992–2001; Vice-Chm., 1995–98). Chm., Jt Services Hang Gliding, 1986–89; Cdre, Army Sailing Assoc., 1989–91. President: SAS Assoc., 1991–96; ACF, 1992–99. Vice-Pres., UK Falkland Is Assoc., 1993–. Comr, Duke of York's Mil. Sch., 1988–90. Trustee, Imperial War Mus., 1992–99; President: Imperial War Mus. Friends, 2001–08; Harrow Sch. Assoc., 2001–05; Herefordshire LI Mus. Friends, 2004–14. Special Advr to Vice Chancellor, Durham Univ., 2008–. Patron: Jt Educnl Trust, 1998–2009; Farm Africa, 2001–; Gallantry Medallists' League, 2005–07; Blind Veterans UK (formerly St Dunstan's), 2007–. Freeman, City of London, 1991; Hon. Freeman, Fishmongers' Co., 1991. Stowaway Mem., Southampton Master Mariners Assoc., 1992. Lord of the Manor of Garway, 1966–2010. DL Hereford and Worcester, 1993. Hon. DSc Cranfield Inst. of Technol., 1992; Hon. DCL Durham, 1993. Order of Bahrain, 1st Cl., 1991; Officer, 1991, Chief Comdr, 1992, Legion of Merit (USA); Meritorious Service Cross, (Canada), 1992; Order of Abdul Aziz, 2nd Cl. (Saudi Arabia), 1992; Kuwait Decoration, 1st Cl., 1992; Qatar Sash of Merit, 1992. *Publications:* Storm Command: a personal story, 1992; (autobiog.) Looking for Trouble, 1994; Supreme Courage: 150 years of the Victoria Cross, 2004. *Recreations:* family, squash, down market apiculture, tennis, farming, sailing. *Clubs:* Farmers, Naval and Military (Trustee, 1999–2003), Victory Services.

**DELAHUNTY, Johanne Erica;** QC 2006; barrister; a Recorder, since 2009; *b* 15 Sept. 1963; *d* of Pauline Delahunty; *m* 1990, Jonathan Light; one *s* two *d*. *Educ:* Copthall Comp. Sch., Mill Hill; St Anne's Coll., Oxford (BA Law Juris. 1983, MA). Called to the Bar, Middle Temple, 1986, Bencher, 2011; in practice, 1986–, specialist child abuse and family law practitioner; accredited specialist in family law and child protection. Accredited Family Mediator, 2011. Prof. of Law, Gresham Coll., 2016–. Member: Family Law Bar Assoc.; Assoc. of Lawyers for Children; Assoc. of Women Barristers; Steering Cttee, Member Women's Temple Forum; Steering Cttee, Centre for Child Law Reform. Member: Amnesty; NSPCC; Barnardo's; Save the Children; Help the Aged. Patron, Assoc. for Multiple Endocrine Neoplasia Disorders. Freeman, City of London, 2019. *Publications:* contribs to specialist child care and family law publications. *Recreations:* mother, feminist, married, loves the seaside, a dab hand at dry capsizing a dinghy, drives classic cars (1963 Vauxhall VX490, 1967 Moggie, 1964 Jaguar Mark 2 and a battered 15-year-old Zaphira!), distracts herself from work and politics with silversmithing. *Address:* 4 Paper Buildings, Temple, EC4Y 7EX. *T:* (020) 7427 5200. *E:* jd@4pb.com. *W:* www.twitter.com/jodqc.

**DELAMERE, 5th Baron** *cr* 1821; **Hugh George Cholmondeley;** *b* 18 Jan. 1934; *s* of 4th Baron Delamere, and Phyllis Anne (*d* 1978), *e d* of late Lord George Scott, OBE; *S* father, 1979; *m* 1964, Mrs Ann Willoughby Tinne, *o d* of late Sir Patrick Renison, GCMG and Lady Renison, Mayfield, Sussex; one *s*. *Educ:* Eton; Magdalene Coll., Cambridge. MA Agric. *Publications:* Not in the History Books, 2019. *Heir: g s* Hugh Derrick Cholmondeley, *b* 9 Nov. 1998. *Address:* Soysambu, Elmenteita, Kenya.

**de la MORENA, Felipe,** Hon. CBE 2001; Ambassador of Spain; President, British Hispanic Foundation, Madrid, 1993–2013, now Hon. President; *b* 22 Oct. 1927; *s* of Felipe de la Morena and Luisa Calvet; *m* 1958, María Teresa Casado Bach; two *s* two *d*. *Educ:* Univ. Complutense de Madrid; Univs of Grenoble and Oxford; Diplomatic Sch., Madrid. Entered diplomatic service 1957; served Beirut, Berne, Washington and Min. of Foreign Affairs, Madrid; Dir, Technical Office, later Dir-Gen., Territorial Planning, Min. of Develt

Planning, 1974–76; Minister Counsellor, Lisbon, 1976; Ambassador to People's Republic of China, 1978; Dir-Gen., Foreign Policy for Latin America, 1982; Ambassador to Syria and Cyprus (residence Damascus), 1983, to Tunisia, 1987, to UK, 1990–93; Permanent Rep. to WEU, 1990–93. Spanish Orders: Alfonso X el Sabio, 1965; Mérito Civil, 1973; Isabel la Católica, 1970; Carlos III, 1980; Gran Cruz del Mérito Naval, 1992; Sacra y Militar Orden Constantiniana de San Jorge, 1993; holds foreign decorations. *Recreation:* golf. *Address:* Fundación Hispano-Británica, Avda. Pío XII 92, 28036 Madrid, Spain. *Clubs:* Travellers; Puerta de Hierro, Real Automóvil de España, Gran Peña (Madrid).

**DELANEY, Ven. Peter Anthony,** MBE 2001; Archdeacon of London, 1999–2009, now Emeritus; Priest-in-charge, St Stephen's Walbrook and St Swithun, City of London, 2005–14; Associate Priest, St Bartholomew the Great, Smithfield; *b* 20 June 1939; *s* of Anthony Mario Delaney and Ena Margaret Delaney. *Educ:* King's Coll., London (AKC); St Boniface Coll., Warminster. Ordained deacon, 1966, priest, 1967; Curate, St Marylebone Parish Church, 1966–70; Chaplain, London University Church of Christ the King, 1970–74; Canon Residentiary and Precentor, Southwark Cathedral, 1974–77; Vicar, All Hallows by the Tower, 1977–2004; Guild Vicar, St Katharine Cree, 1997–2002. Hon. Canon, St Paul's Cathedral, Nicosia, Dio. Cyprus and the Gulf, 1984–; Prebendary, St Paul's Cathedral, London, 1995–99. Director: City Churches Develt Gp, 1997–2000; London Internet Church, 2006. Trustee, Trust for London (formerly City Parochial Foundn), 2001–. Chm., Ind. Adv. Gp, City of London Police, 2006–. Gov., St Dunstan's Coll., Catford, 1977–2000; Master: Co. of World Traders of City of London, 1994–95; Gardeners' Co., 1999–2000. Kt Comdr, SMO of Knights Templars. *Publications:* The Artist and his Exploration into God, 1981; (contrib.) The Canon Law of the Church of England, 1975. *Recreations:* painting, theatre, gardening.

**de LANGE, Prof. Nicholas Robert Michael,** DPhil, PhD, DD; FBA 2011; Professor of Hebrew and Jewish Studies, University of Cambridge, 2001–11, now Emeritus; Fellow, Wolfson College, Cambridge, since 1985; *b* Nottingham, 7 Aug. 1944; *s* of late (George) David de Lange and Elaine de Lange (née Jacobus); *m* 1990, Patricia Touton-Victor (marr. diss. 1998); two *s* one d. *Educ:* Harrow Co. Sch.; Christ Church, Oxford (MA; DPhil 1970); Leo Baeck Coll. (Rabbinical Dip.); Univ. of Cambridge (PhD 1971; DD 2001). University of Cambridge: Lectr in Rabbinics, 1971–95; Reader in Hebrew and Jewish Studies, 1995–2001. MAE 2013. *Publications:* Origen and the Jews, 1976; Apocrypha: Jewish literature of the Hellenistic age, 1978; Atlas of the Jewish World, 1984; Judaism, 1986, 2nd edn 2003; Greek Jewish Texts from the Cairo Genizah, 1996; (ed) An Illustrated History of the Jewish People, 1997; An Introduction to Judaism, 2000, 2nd edn 2010; The Penguin Dictionary of Judaism, 2008; Japheth in the Tents of Shem, 2015; many articles and literary translations. *Recreations:* reading, conversation. *Address:* Wolfson College, Cambridge CB3 9BB. *T:* (01223) 740561. *E:* nrml1@cam.ac.uk.

**DÉLANO ORTÚZAR, Juan Carlos;** farmer; Director: Compañía de Seguros Generales Penta Security SA; Agrícola Gildemeister SA; *b* Santiago, 14 June 1941; *m* Maria Paz Valenzuela; three *s* one d. *Educ:* St George's Coll., Catholic Univ., Chile; OCD, Belgium. Private enterprise: Distribuidora Audicol SA, Commercial Magara Ltd; Pres., Trading Assoc. of Chile, Dir, Chamber of Commerce of Santiago, 1979–83; Pres., Chilean Nat. Chamber of Commerce and Advr to Confedn of Trade and Industry, 1983–85; Minister of Economy, Promotion and Reconstruction, 1985–87; Ambassador to UK, 1987–90. Chief Exec. Officer, Equs SA, 1990; Dir, Icare, 1990. Dir, Universidad Adolfo Ibáñez, 1998–2004. *Address:* Americo Vespucio Norte 1776, Dept 31, Vitacura, Santiago, Chile. *E:* juancdelano@yahoo.com. *Club:* Polo.

**de la PEÑA VELASCO, Jaime;** Partner, Skene Catling de la Peña, since 2003; *b* Murcia, Spain, 9 Feb. 1964; *s* of Gaspar de la Peña and Carmen Velasco; civil partnership 2006, Ronald Worrall. *Educ:* Univ. of Westminster (BA Arch 1992; DipArch 1995). Architectural asst, Geoffrey Bawa Architects, 1993; jun. architect, Walters and Cohen, 1995–98; private practice, 1998–2003. *Address:* 7 Trevor Place, SW7 1LA. *T:* (020) 7584 3261. *E:* jaimedelapena@hotmail.com.

**DE LA PUENTE RIBEYRO, Claudio Julio;** Permanent Representative of Peru to the United Nations, since 2017; *b* Cuzco, Peru, 30 April 1955; *s* of Jorge De la Puente Raygada and Mercedes Ribeyro Zúñiga; *m* Diana Cunliffe; two *s* one d. *Educ:* Peruvian Diplomatic Acad., Lima (Internat. Affairs and Diplomacy 1977); Pontifical Catholic Univ. and San Martin de Porres Univ., Lima (BA Law 1980); Ecole de Commerce Solvay, Univ. Libre de Bruxelles (Postgrad. Internat. Trade 1983). Entered diplomatic service, Peru, 1978; Third Sec., Econ. Div., 1978; Asst to Cabinet of Minister of Foreign Affairs, 1979–80; Third, then Second Sec., Washington, 1981–84; Chargé d'Affaires, Copenhagen, 1985–86; Desk Officer, S American Div., Min. of Foreign Affairs, 1987–88; COS, Prime Minister's Office, 1988; Counsellor, and Hd, Peruvian Trade Office, Brussels, and Mission of EU, 1990–94; Diplomatic Advr to Foreign Affairs Cttee, Peruvian Parlt, 1995; Dir for N America, Min. of Foreign Affairs, 1996; Deputy Head of Mission: Bogota, 1997–99; Washington, 1999–2001; Dir-Gen. for Security Affairs, and Dir for S America, Min. of Foreign Affairs, 2003; Ambassador to Australia, 2005–10; Dir-Gen. for Americas, Min. of Foreign Affairs, 2010–14; Vice Minister of Foreign Affairs, 2014–15; Ambassador of Peru to the Court of St James's, 2015–17, and (concurrently) to Republic of Ireland, 2016–17. Order José Gregario Paz Soldan, Diplomatic Service, Peru, 2014. Order of Merit: for Dist. Services (Peru), 1980 and 2005; Ecuador, 2006; Order of the Crown (Belgium), 1995; Order Rio Branco (Brazil), 2004; Order Bernardo O'Higgins (Chile), 2005. *Clubs:* Travellers', Naval and Military.

**de LAROSIÈRE de CHAMPFEU, Jacques (Martin Henri Marie),** Hon. KBE 1998; Grand Officier, Legion of Honour, 2013 (Commander, 1996); Chevalier, National Order of Merit, 1970; Inspector General of Finance, since 1981; Chairman, Eurofi, 2011–16 (Co-Chairman, 2000–11); *b* 12 Nov. 1929; *s* of Robert de Larosière and Hugayte de Champfeu; *m* 1960, France du Bos; one *s* one d. *Educ:* Institut d'Etudes Politiques, Paris (L ès L, licencié en droit); Nat. Sch. of Administration, Paris. Inspecteur des Finances, 1958; appointments at: Inspectorate-General of Finance, 1961; External Finance Office, 1963; Treasury 1965; Asst Dir, Treasury, 1967; Dep. Dir then Head of Dept, Min. of Economics and Finance, 1971; Principal Private Sec. to Minister of Economics and Finance, 1974; Dir, Treasury, 1974–78; Man. Dir, IMF, 1978–87; Gov., Banque de France, 1987–93; Pres., EBRD, 1993–98. Prof., Sciences Po, Paris, 2013–. Advr, BNP Paribas, 1998–2008. Director: Renault, 1971–74; Banque Nat. de Paris, 1973–78; Air France and French Railways, 1974–78; Société nat. industrielle aérospatiale, 1976–78; Power Corp., 1998–2001; Alstom, 1998–2000; France Telecom, 1998–2009; Trustee, Reuters, 1999–2004. Director appointed by Treasury, General Council, Bank of France, 1974–78; Auditor: Crédit national, 1974–78; Comptoir des entrepreneurs, 1973–75; Crédit foncier de France, 1975–78. Vice Pres., Caisse nat. des télécommunications, 1974–78; Pres., Observatoire de l'Epargne Européenne, 1999–; Chm., Strategic Cttee, Agence France Trésor, 2000–; Mem., Conseil de Régulation Financière et du Risque Systematique, 2011–12. Member: Internat. Adv. Bd, AIG, 2002–09; Adv. Bd, China Develt Bank, 2005–08; Chm. Adv. Bd, Mid Europa Fund, 2006–. Chairman: OECD Econ. and Develt Review Cttee, 1967–71; Deputies Gp of Ten, 1976–78; Cttee of Gp of Ten, 1990–93. Institute of International Finance: Co-Chairman: Cttee on Crisis Mgt and Crisis Resolution in Emerging Markets, 2003–09; Mkt Monitoring Gp, 2009–; Principles for Stable Capital Flows, 2006–. Chm., Stichting NYSE Euronext (Dutch Foundn), 2007–14; Trustee, NYSE Gp Trust I (US Trust), 2007–14; Prés., Assoc. Internat. Cardinal Henri de Lubac, 1994–. Mem., Acad. of Moral and Pol Scis, 1993; Hon. Mem., Société des Cincinnati de France, 1992. Grand Cordon: Order of Sacred Treasure (Japan), 1993; Order of the Brilliant Star (Taipei), 1998; Grand Cross, Order of Merit: Argentina, 1992; Italy, 1993; Stana Platina (Bulgaria), 1993; Order of Aztec Eagle (Mexico), 1994; Cross, Order of Merit (Germany), 1996; Comdr, Order of Merit (Poland), 1997; Order of Friendship (Russia), 1997; Order of Merit (Hungary), 1998; Comdr, Order of Southern Cross (Brazil), 1999; Order of Cross of Terra Mariana (Estonia), 2001. *Address:* Eurofi, 66 Rue de Miromesnil, 75008 Paris, France.

**de la RUE, Sir Andrew (George Ilay),** 4th Bt *cr* 1898, of Cadogan Square; company director; farmer; *b* 3 Feb. 1946; *s* of Sir Eric Vincent de la Rue, 3rd Bt and Cecilia (*d* 1963), *d* of late Maj. Walter Waring and Lady Clementine Waring, *d* of 10th Marquess of Tweedale; *S* father, 1989; *m* 1984, Tessa Ann, *er d* of David Dobson; two *s*. *Educ:* Millfield. With Lloyd's (Insurance), 1966; Dir, Private Company, 1976–. *Recreations:* shooting, coursing, tennis. *Heir: s* Edward Walter de la Rue, *b* 25 Nov. 1986. *Address:* Stragglethorpe Grange, Brant Broughton, Lincolnshire LN5 0RA. *T:* (01636) 626505.

**de la TOUR, Frances;** actress; *b* 30 July 1944; *d* of Charles de la Tour and Moyra (née Fessas); one *s* one d. *Educ:* Lycée français de Londres; Drama Centre, London. Royal Shakespeare Company, 1965–71: rôles include Audrey in As You Like It, 1967; Hoyden in The Relapse, 1969; Helena in A Midsummer Night's Dream (Peter Brooks's production), 1971 (also USA tour); Belinda in The Man of Mode, 1971; Violet in Small Craft Warnings, Comedy, 1973 (Best Supporting Actress, Plays and Players Award); Ruth Jones in The Banana Box, Apollo, 1973; Isabella in The White Devil, Old Vic, 1976; appearances at Hampstead Theatre, and Half Moon Theatre incl. title rôle in Hamlet, 1979; Stephanie in Duet for One, Bush Theatre and Duke of York's, 1980 (Best New Play, and Best Perf. by Actress, Drama Awards, Best Perf. by Actress in New Play, SWET Award, Best Actress, New Standard Award); Jean in Skirmishes, Hampstead, 1982 (also television, 1982); Sonya in Uncle Vanya, Haymarket, 1982; Josie in A Moon for the Misbegotten, Riverside, 1983 (SWET Best Actress award); title rôle in St Joan, NT, 1984; Dance of Death, Riverside, 1985; Sonya and Masha in Chekhov's Women, Lyric, 1985; Brighton Beach Memoirs, NT, 1986; Lillian, Lyric, 1986, Fortune, 1987; Façades, Lyric, Hammersmith, 1988; Regan in King Lear, Old Vic, 1989; Arkadina, Ranyevskaya and Olga Knipper in Chekhov's Women, Moscow Art Theatre, 1990; Miss Belzer in When She Danced, Globe, 1991 (Olivier Award); Witch in The Pope and the Witch, Comedy, 1992; Yoko Sitsuki in Greasepaint, Lyric, Hammersmith, 1993; Leonie in Les Parents Terribles, RNT, 1994; Three Tall Women, Wyndham's, 1994; Elinor in Blinded by the Sun, RNT, 1996; the woman in The Play about the Baby, Almeida, 1998; Raisa in The Forest, RNT, 1999; Cleopatra in Antony and Cleopatra, RSC, 1999; Jane in Fallen Angels, Apollo, 2000 (Variety Club Best Actress award); The Good Hope, 2001, Pinter Sketches, 2002, NT; Alice in Dance of Death, Lyric, 2003; Mrs Lintott in The History Boys, NT, 2004, NY, 2006 (Tony Award); Bertha in Boeing-Boeing, Comedy, 2007; The Habit of Art, NT, 2009–10; People, NT, 2012. *Films* include: Rising Damp, 1979 (Best Actress, New Standard British Film Award, 1980); The Cherry Orchard, 1998; Harry Potter and the Goblet of Fire, 2005; The History Boys, 2006; The Nutcracker, 2008; Book of Eli, Alice in Wonderland, Harry Potter and the Deathly Hallows, Pt 1, 2010; Hugo, 2011; Private Peaceful, 2012; Trap for Cinderella, Suspension of Disbelief, 2013; Into the Woods, Mr Holmes, Lady in the Van, Survivor, Miss You Already, 2015; Alice Through the Looking Glass, 2016. *Television* includes: Play for Today (twice), 1973–75; Rising Damp (series), 1974, 1976; Flickers, 1980; Duet for One, 1985; Cold Lazarus, 1995; Tom Jones, 1997; The Egg, 2002; Death on the Nile, 2003; Waking the Dead, 2004; Sensitive Skin, 2005; Vicious (series), 2013, 2015, 2016; Big School (series), 2013, 2014; Outlander, 2015; The Collection, 2016; Vanity Fair, 2018. *Address:* c/o Claire Maroussas, Independent Talent Group Ltd, 40 Whitfield Street, W1T 2RH. *T:* (020) 7636 6565; c/o Barry McPherson, APA Agency, 135 West 50th Street, 17th Floor, New York, NY 10020. *T:* (212) 205 4335.

**DE LA WARR,** 11th Earl *cr* 1761; **William Herbrand Sackville;** DL; Baron De La Warr, 1299 and 1572; Viscount Cantelupe 1761; Baron Buckhurst 1864; Partner, Toscafund Asset Management, since 2016; farmer; *b* 10 April 1948; *s* of 10th Earl De La Warr and Anne Rachel, *d* of Geoffrey Devas, MC; *S* father, 1988; *m* 1978, Anne, Countess of Hopetoun, *e d* of Arthur Leveson; two *s* and two step *s*. *Educ:* Eton. Stockbroker, Credit Lyonnais Securities (formerly Laing & Cruickshank), 1980–2004. Dir, Shore Capital Stockbrokers Ltd, 2004–16. Non-exec. Dir, Cluff Natural Resources, 2012–17. DL E Sussex, 2016. *Heir: s* Lord Buckhurst, *qv*. *Address:* Buckhurst Park, Withyham, E Sussex TN7 4BL; 21 Bourne Street, SW1W 8JR. *Clubs:* White's, Turf.
See also Hon. T. G. Sackville.

**DELAY, Thomas Auguste Read,** CBE 2018; CEng; Chief Executive, Carbon Trust, since 2001; *b* London, 15 April 1959; *s* of late Francis and Jill Delay; *m* 1990, Valerie; two *s*. *Educ:* Univ. of Southampton (BSc Mech. Engrg 1981); INSEAD, Fontainebleau (MBA 1988). CEng, MIMechE 1985. Engrg/Ops Manager, Shell Djibouti, 1982–85; Project Engr, Shell UK, 1985–87; Sales/Mktg Manager, Shell Lubricants, 1988–90; Planning Manager, Shell UK, 1990–92; Gen. Manager, Pizo Shell, Gabon, 1992–96; Mgt Consultant, McKinsey & Co., 1996–98; Principal, A. T. Kearney, 1999–2001. *Recreations:* looking for powder snow, Surrey walks in my 1977 Fiat Spyder, cooking pasta, playing a reasonable game of tennis. *Address:* c/o The Carbon Trust, 4th Floor, Dorset House, 27–45 Stamford Street, SE1 9NT. *T:* (020) 7170 7000. *E:* tom.delay@carbontrust.com.

**DELGADO, Ana Irene;** Partner, since 2006, and Manager, London office, Solis, Endara, Delgado and Guevara; *b* Panama, 18 April; *d* of Hernán Delgado and Irene de Delgado. *Educ:* French Inst., Panama; French Inst. Alliance Française, Paris; Colegio Las Esclavas del Sagrado Corazón de Jesus; Beaver Coll., Pennsylvania; S Bend, Indiana Lang. Inst.; Univ. of Delaware; Florida State Univ. (BSc Internat. Affairs 2004); Santa Maria La Antigua Univ., Panama (BSc Law and Political Scis *summa cum laude* 2004); New York Univ. (Advanced Professional Cert. Law and Business 2006; Graduate of Yr, 2012); New York Univ. Sch. of Law (LLM 2006). Ed., Internat. Law and Policy Jl, Univ. of NY, 2005–06. Gen. Manager, Radio Emporium, Radio Gp integrated by Fabulosa Estero, Tropi Q, Power92 and Radio Ancon, 2003–05; Ambassador of Panama to UK, and concurrently Ambassador to Iceland and Republic of Ireland, 2011–14; Perm. Rep. of Panama to IMO, 2011–14. Member, Board of Directors: Latin America and Caribbean Friendship with People's Republic of China Fedn, 2009–; Panamanian Assoc. of Friendship with China, 2007–09 (Sec.); Vice Pres., 2011–); Panamanian Bar Assoc., 2007–09; (Counsel) Panama Chamber of Commerce and Industries, 2009–. Advr, Legal Affairs Cttee, Panamanian Assoc. of Business Execs, 2009–. Second Vice-Pres., IMO Assembly; Dir, Nat. and internat. cos related to trade and industry. Mem., Bd of Govs, World Maritime Univ., 2012–. *Publications:* contribs to Univ. mag., Cocuyo Child Mag., Panama. *Recreations:* golf, running, equestrian (jumping and cross-country; Equestrian Invitational Champion, Harroway, 2013; 6th in Europe, Coupe d'Europe, Naples, 2013), fencing (épée), flamenco dance (Grupo Alandaluz, City of Panama, 2001–), classical ballet (Ruffo Cholewa Acad., 1986–89, Teresa Mann Acad.,

1990–97, City of Panama). *Address:* Calle 50 Edificio Solendeg, Panama. *T:* 81600828. *E:* anaidelgado@solendeg.com, anairene.delgado@gmail.com. *Clubs:* Royal Automobile, 5 Hertford Street, Lansdowne, HAC Saddle; Los Andes.

**DELGADO, Prof. Maria Milagros,** PhD; Professor and Director of Research, Royal Central School of Speech and Drama, University of London, since 2015; *b* London, 18 June 1965; *d* of Alfonso Delgado Alava and Severina Delgado (*née* González Pérez); *m* 1997, Henry Little; one *s*. *Educ:* St Peter's Comprehensive Sch., Huntingdon; University Coll. of Swansea (BA Spanish and Drama 1987); Univ. of Leeds (MA Theatre Studies 1988); Univ. of Newcastle upon Tyne (PhD 1994). Special Lectr in Drama, Univ. of Hull, 1988–89; Lectr, 1993–96, Sen. Lectr, 1996–97, in Drama, Manchester Metropolitan Univ.; Lectr, 1997–2000, Sen. Lectr, 2000–01, Reader, 2002–04, in Theatre Arts, Prof. of Theatre and Screen Arts, 2003–15, QMUL. George Watson Fellow, Univ. of Qld, 2013; Vis. Prof., Univ. of Santiago de Compostela, 2016. Ed., Contemp. Th. Rev., 2003–; Member, Editorial Board: Theatre Forum, 1999–2018; Western Eur. Stages, 2004–12; Stychomythia, 2008–12; Don Galán, 2010–; Episkenion, 2012–; Eur. Stages, 2013–. Prog. Advr, BFI London Film Fest., 1997–; film programming and curatorial work for London Spanish Film Fest. Chair, Sub-panel 35 Music, Drama, Dance and Performing Arts, REF 2014, 2010–14; Chair, Sub-panel 33, Music, Drama, Dance, Performing Arts, Film and Screen Studies, 2018–; Dep. Chair, Main Panel D, REF 2021, 2018–. Arts and Humanities Research Council: Chm., Fellowships Panel, 2013; Member: Strategic Reviewers' Gp, 2011–13, 2017–; Peer Rev. Coll., 2004–05, 2009–13, 2017–; Res. Panel 7 (Music and Performing Arts), 2005–08); Block Grant Partnerships 2 Expressions of Interest Panel, 2012; BGP2 Panel, 2013; DTP2 Moderating Panel, 2018; Council, Res. England, 2018–; Higher Education Funding Council for England: Mem., Expert Adv. Gp for REF 2009; Res. and Knowledge Exchange Strategic Adv. Cttee, 2015–18; Knowledge Exchange Framework Steering Gp, 2017–18; Envmt Working Group REF 2021, 2017–18; Mem., Res. Strategy Forum, JISC, 2019–. Artistic and Quality Assessor, Arts Council England, 2010–. Mem., Adv. Panel, Leverhulme Trust, 2010–. Chm. Bd, Actors Touring Co., 2009–19 (Mem., 2006–09, 2019–); Mem., Bd of Dirs, People's Palace Projects, 1999–2004; Mem., Bd of Govs, GSMD, 2019–. Member: Res. Grants Panel, Portuguese Foundn for Sci. and Technol., 2010–11; Mem., Train 2 Move Panel, ESF, 2015. Freelance critic and cultural commentator, BBC, Sight & Sound, The Theatre Times and other nat. and internat. media. Member, Jury: Nominating Panel, Rolex Mentor and Protegée Scheme, 2002; Buenos Aires Internat. Fest. of Ind. Cinema Comp., 2011; Birmingham Eur. Fest., 2015; Lukas: UK Latin Awards Best Film, 2017. Founder Mem., Theatre and Performance Res. Assoc., 2003 (Life Mem. 2013). MAE 2015. FRSA. Hon. Life Mem., Standing Conf. of Univ. Drama Depts, 2015; Hon. Fellow, Inst. of Modern Languages, Univ. of London, 2016. Premi Joan B. Cendrós, 2008; Excellence in Editing Award, Assoc. for Theatre in Higher Educn, 2013; TaPRA Research Prize for Editing, 2017. Encomienda, Orden de Isabel la Católica (Spain), 2003; Cruz, Orden Civil de Alfonso X el Sabio (Spain), 2016; Premi Fundació Ramon Llull, Promoció Internacional de la Creació Catalana, 2018. *Publications:* (trans.) Valle-Inclán: Plays One, 1993, rev. edn 1997; Other Spanish Theatres: erasure and inscription on the Twentieth-Century Spanish stage, 2003; Federico García Lorca, 2008; Otro teatro español: supresión e inscripción en la escena española de los siglos XX y XXI, 2017; edited jointly: In Contact with the Gods?: directors talk theatre, 1996; Teatro Contemporaneo d'autore: Peter Sellars, 1999; Diálogos no Palco: 26 diretores falam sobre Teatro, 1999; Conducting a Life: reflections on the theatre of Maria Irene Fornes, 1999; The Paris Jigsaw: internationalism and the city's stages, 2002; Theatre in Crisis?: performance manifestos for a new century, 2002; Bernard-Marie Koltès: Plays Two, 2004; Contemporary European Theatre Directors, 2010; A History of Theatre in Spain, 2010; Spanish Cinema 1973–2010: auteurism, politics, landscape and memory, 2013; The Wiley-Blackwell Companion to Latin American Cinema, 2017; contrib. articles to learned jls. *Recreations:* theatre, cinema, reading, watching football (especially Liverpool FC), cooking, travel, Scandinavian crime drama, dinner table discussions, the family cat, music. *Address:* Royal Central School of Speech and Drama, University of London, Eton Avenue, NW3 3HY. *E:* maria.delgado@cssd.ac.uk. *Club:* House of St Barnabas.

**DELIBEGOVIĆ-BROOME, Almira;** QC (Scot.) 2017; *b* Tuzla, Bosnia-Herzegovina, 21 March 1971; *d* of Col Enver Delibegović and Izabeta Delibegović (*née* Rešidbegović); *m* 1996, Jonathan Broome; two *s*. *Educ:* Meša Selimović Grammar Sch., Tuzla; Univ. of Edinburgh (LLB Hons 1995; DipLP 1996); Harvard Univ. (Fulbright Schol.; LLM 2002). Trainee solicitor, McGrigor Donald, 1996–98; Legal and Transactions Manager, Hodgson Martin Ltd, 1998; admitted solicitor, 1998; solicitor, Dundas & Wilson CS, 1999–2002; admitted to Faculty of Advocates, 2003; Standing Jun. Counsel to HMRC, Scot., 2012–15. Vis. Scholar, Harvard Law Sch., 2018–19. *Recreations:* travel, reading, cross-country ski-ing. *Address:* Advocates Library, Parliament House, Edinburgh EH1 1RF. *E:* almira.db@axiomadvocates.com.

**DE L'ISLE,** 2nd Viscount *cr* 1956; **Philip John Algernon Sidney,** CVO 2019; MBE 1977; Baron De L'Isle and Dudley 1835; Bt of Castle Goring, 1806; Bt of Penshurst Place, 1818; Lord-Lieutenant of Kent, since 2011 (Vice Lord-Lieutenant, 2002–11); *b* 21 April 1945; *s* of 1st Viscount De L'Isle, VC, KG, GCMG, GCVO, PC and Hon. Jacqueline Vereker (*d* 1962), *o d* of Field-Marshal 6th Viscount Gort, VC, GCB, CBE, DSO, MVO, MC; *S* father, 1991; *m* 1980, Isobel Tresyllian, *y d* of Sir Edmund Compton, GCB, KBE; one *s* one *d*. *Educ:* Tabley House; Mons OCS; RMA Sandhurst. Commnd Grenadier Guards, 1966. Served BAOR, UKLF, NI, Belize and Sudan at Regtl Duty; GSO3 Ops/SD HQ 3 Inf. Bde, 1974–76; retired 1979. Landowner, 1979–. Member: H of L Adv. Panel on Works of Art, 1994–97; Lord Chancellor's Adv. Council on Nat. Records and Archives, 2004–09. Chm., Kent County Cttee, CLA, 1983–85. Pres., Canterbury Cathedral Trust Fund, 2014– (Chm., 2007–14). Vice-Pres., SE RFCA, 2011–; President: RBL Industries, 2011–; Assoc. of Men of Kent and Kentish Men, 2012–; St John's Kent Priory Gp, 2012–; Patron: Action with Communities in Rural Kent, 2011–; Kent Br., Army Benevolent Fund, 2011–; City of Canterbury Shrievalty Assoc., 2011–; Friends of Kent Churches, 2011–; Kent Community Foundn, 2011–; Safer Kent (formerly Kent People's Trust), 2011–; RBL Kent, 2011–; St John's Ambulance Kent, 2011–; SSAFA (formerly SSAFA Forces Help) Kent, 2011–; RE Mus. Foundn, 2011–13; Vice Patron, South of England Agricl Soc., 2007–; Trustee: Rochester Cathedral Trust, 2011–; Nat. Army Mus. Foundn, 2013–. Hon. Colonel: 5th (V) Bn, Princess of Wales's Royal Regt, 1992–99; Kent ACF, 2006–12. Freeman, City of London; Liveryman, Goldsmiths' Co. DL Kent, 1996. Hon. Dr: Hampden-Sydney Coll., Va, 2012; Greenwich, 2016. *Heir: s* Hon. Philip William Edmund Sidney, PhD, *b* 2 April 1985. *Address:* Penshurst Place, Penshurst, Tonbridge, Kent TN11 8DG. *T:* (01892) 870307. *E:* KentLL343@penshurstplace.com. *Clubs:* White's, Pratt's.

**de LISLE, Timothy John March Phillipps;** journalist, since 1979; *b* 25 June 1962; *s* of late Everard de Lisle and of Hon. Mary Rose de Lisle (*née* Peake); *m* 1991, Amanda Barford; one *s* one *d*. *Educ:* Sunningdale; Eton; Worcester Coll., Oxford (BA Hons). Freelance journalist, 1979–86, revs and features for LAM, Smash Hits, Harpers & Queen and The Observer; Founder, Undergraduate Tutors, 1982–86; The Daily Telegraph: diary reporter, 1986–87; chief rock critic, 1986–89; news reporter, 1987; feature writer, 1987–89; arts editor, The Times, 1989; Weekend editor, The Daily Telegraph, 1989–90; Independent on Sunday: cricket correspondent, 1990–91; arts editor, 1991–95; freelance, 1995–: features: Independent on Sunday and Daily Telegraph, 1995–98; The Guardian G2, 2004–07; cricket column: Independent, 1995–96; 1999–2003; Evening Standard, 1997–98; The Times, 2004–06; rock column, Mail on Sunday, 1999–; cricket writer, The Guardian, 2016–; sen. consultant, Innovation Media, 2016–; Wisden, 1996–2003: Editor: Wisden Cricket Monthly, 1996–2000 (Editor of the Year, Special Interest Mags, British Soc. of Mag. Editors, 1999); Wisden Online, 1999–2002; Wisden Cricketers' Almanack, 2003; Intelligent Life, 2008–15 (Dep. Ed., 2007–08) (Editor of the Year, Lifestyle Mags, British Soc. of Mag. Editors, 2010); founder and consultant editor, Wisden Asia Cricket mag., 2001–05; columnist, Cricinfo.com, 2006–09. *Publications:* (ed) Lives of the Great Songs, 1994, rev. edn 1995; Young Wisden, 2007, 2nd edn 2011; How to Write Well, 2017. *Recreations:* watching football, opening emails. *Address:* c/o Mail on Sunday, 2 Derry Street, W8 5TS. *E:* tim.delisle@gmail.com. *Club:* Eton Ramblers.

**DELL, Prof. Anne,** CBE 2009; PhD; FRS 2002; FMedSci; Professor of Carbohydrate Biochemistry, since 1991, and Head, Department of Life Sciences, since 2017, Imperial College London; *b* 11 Sept. 1950; *d* of Edgar Dell and Elneth Dell; one *d*. *Educ:* Univ. of Western Australia (BSc); King's Coll., Cambridge (PhD 1975). Imperial College: Lectr, 1979–86; Reader, 1986–91; Hd, Dept of Biochemistry, 1999–2001. BBSRC Professorial Fellow, 2002–07. FMedSci 2008. *Recreations:* theatre, gardening, reading, walking. *Address:* Department of Life Sciences, Imperial College London, SW7 2AZ. *T:* (020) 7594 5219, *Fax:* (020) 7225 0458. *E:* a.dell@imperial.ac.uk.

**DELL, David Michael,** CB 1986; Deputy Secretary, Department of Trade and Industry, 1983–91; *b* 30 April 1931; *s* of late Montague Roger Dell and Aimée Gabrielle Dell; partner, 1971, Eliseo Cabrejos (*d* 1995), Lima, Peru. *Educ:* Rugby Sch.; Balliol Coll., Oxford (MA). 2nd Lieut Royal Signals, Egypt and Cyprus, 1954–55. Admiralty, 1955; MoD, 1960; Min. of Technol., 1965; DTI, 1970; DoI, 1974, Under Sec., 1976; Regl Dir, Yorks and Humberside, DTI, 1976–78; Dir, EIB, 1984–87; Chief Exec., BOTB, 1987–91. Chm., Internat. Rubber Study Gp, 1975. Dir, Nesbit Evans Gp, 1991–93. Mem., British-Peruvian Trade & Investment Gp, 1997–2001. Mem., London Diocesan Conf., 1968–69. Chm., Christ Church Bentinck Sch., 1979–92. Sec., London Numismatic Club, 1995–97; Mem. Council, Oxford Soc., 1995–2001; Dep. Chm., Anglo-Peruvian Soc., 2005–07. *Clubs:* Oriental, Royal Automobile.

**DELL, Michael S.;** Chairman, since 1984, Chief Executive Officer, 1984–2004 and since 2007, Dell Inc. (formerly PCs Ltd, then Dell Computer Corporation); *b* Houston, Texas, 23 Feb. 1965; *s* of Alexander and Lorraine Dell; *m* 1989, Susan Lieberman; four *c* (incl. twins). *Educ:* Univ. of Texas. Founder, PCs Ltd, 1984; co. renamed Dell Computer Corp., 1987. Member: Computer Systems Policy Proj.; The Business Council; Member Board: US Chamber of Commerce; World Econ. Forum. *Publications:* Direct From Dell: strategies that revolutionized an industry, 1999. *Address:* Dell Inc., 1 Dell Way, Round Rock, TX 78682, USA.

**DELL, Dame Miriam (Patricia),** ONZ 1993; DBE 1980 (CBE 1975); JP (NZ); Hon. President, International Council of Women, 1986–88 (President, 1979–86; Vice-President, 1976–79); *b* 14 June 1924; *d* of Gerald Wilfred Matthews and Ruby Miriam Crawford; *m* 1946, Richard Kenneth Dell; four *d*. *Educ:* Epsom Girls Grammar Sch.; Univ. of Auckland (BA); Auckland Teachers' Coll. (Teachers' Cert. (Secondary Sch.)). Teaching, 1945–47, 1957–58 and 1961–71. Nat. Pres., Nat. Council of Women, 1970–74 (Vice-Pres., 1967–70); Chm., Cttee on Women, NZ, 1974–81; Chm., Envmt and Conservation Orgns of NZ, 1989–94; Chm., 1993 Suffrage Centennial Year Trust, 1991–94; Chair, Landmarks Project - Celebrating Women Trust, 1999–2010. Member: Nat. Develt Council, 1969–74; Cttee of Inquiry into Equal Pay, 1971–72; Nat. Commn for UNESCO, 1974–83; Social Security Appeal Authority, 1974–99; Anglican Provincial Commn on Ordination of Women, 1991; Project Develt Bd, Mus. of NZ, 1988–92; Dep. Chm., Wellington Conservation Bd, 1990–98; Nat. Convener, Internat. Women's Year, 1975; Co-ordinator, Internat. Council of Women Develt Prog., 1988–91; Sec., Inter-Church Council on Public Affairs, 1986–89 (Chm., 1982–86); Convener, Public Affairs Unit, Anglican Church of NZ, 1988–92. JP NZ 1975. Jubilee Medal, 1977; NZ Commemoration Medal, 1990; NZ Suffrage Centennial Medal, 1993. *Publications:* Role of Women in National Development, 1970; numerous articles in popular and house magazines, on role and status of women. *Recreations:* gardening, reading, handcrafts, beachcombing. *Address:* 137 Te Maire Road, Kahutara, Featherston 5771, New Zealand.

**DELLA DORA, Prof. Veronica,** PhD; FBA 2018; Professor of Human Geography, Royal Holloway, University of London, since 2013; *b* Venice, 10 Dec. 1976; *d* of Riccardo Della Dora and Luisa Zennaro. *Educ:* Univ. of Ca' Foscari, Venice (BA Oriental Studies 2000); Univ. of Calif, Los Angeles (PhD Geog. 2005). Postdoctoral Fellow, Getty Res. Inst., 2005–06; Sen. Associate Researcher, UCLA, 2006–07; Lectr, 2007–11, Sen. Lectr, 2011–13, Univ. of Bristol. *Publications:* Imagining Mount Athos: visions of a holy place from Homer to World War II, 2011; Landscape, Nature and the Sacred in Byzantium, 2016; Mountain: nature and culture, 2016. *Recreation:* amateur radio. *Address:* Department of Geography, Royal Holloway, University of London, Egham TW20 0EX.

**DELLER, Jeremy;** artist; *b* London, 1966. *Educ:* Dulwich Coll.; Courtauld Inst. of Art (BA Art Hist. 1988); Sussex Univ. (MA Art Hist. 1992). Curator, producer and dir of projects, incl. orchestrated events, films and pubns. *Works include:* Acid Brass (collaboration with Williams Fairey Brass Band), 1997; (with A. Kane) Folk Archive, 2000; The Battle of Orgreave (filmed re-enactment), 2001; Social Parade (video), Five Memorials, This is US (CD), 2003; Memory Bucket (mixed-media installation), 2003 (Turner Prize, 2004); group exhibn, New British Art 2000: Intelligence, Tate Britain, 2000; Joy in People (retrospective), Hayward Gall., 2012; Sacrilege (inflatable Stonehenge), Glasgow, then UK tour, 2012; English Magic, Turner Contemporary, Margate, 2014; group exhibn, From Life, Royal Acad., 2017. Trustee: Artangel, 2005 (Chm., 2015); Tate Gall., 2007–11 (Mem., Collection Cttee); Mem. Council, Tate Liverpool. *Address:* The Modern Institute, 14–20 Osborne Street, Glasgow G1 5QN.

**DELLOW, Sir John (Albert),** Kt 1990; CBE 1985 (OBE 1979); DL; Deputy Commissioner, Metropolitan Police, 1987–91; *b* 5 June 1931; *s* of Albert Reginald and Lily Dellow; *m* 1952, Heather Josephine Rowe; one *s* one *d*. *Educ:* William Ellis Sch., Highgate; Royal Grammar Sch., High Wycombe. Joined City of London Police, 1951; seconded Manchester City Police, 1966; Superintendent, Kent County Constabulary, 1966, Chief Supt, 1968; jssc 1969; Asst Chief Constable, Kent Co. Constabulary, 1969; Metropolitan Police: Deputy Assistant Commissioner: Traffic Planning, 1973; Personnel, 1975; No 2 Area, 1978; 'A' Dept Operations, 1979; Inspectorate, 1980; Assistant Commissioner: 'B' Dept, 1982; Crime, 1984; Asst Comr (Specialist Ops), 1985–87. Pres., ACPO, 1989–90 (Vice-Pres., 1988–89). Former Chairman: Metropolitan Police History Soc.; Metropolitan Police Climbing, Canoe, Rowing and Heavy Boat Sections; Cdre, Metropolitan Police Sailing Club. Member Council: London Dist, Order of St John of Jerusalem, 1988–96; RUSI, 1991–95. DL Greater London, 1991. *Publications:* contrib. RUSI Defence Studies series and other jls. *Recreations:* walking, history, listening to wireless, water colour painting.

**DELORS, Jacques Lucien Jean;** President, Council for Employment, Income and Social Cohesion, 2000–09; President, Commission of the European Economic Community, 1985–95; *b* Paris, 20 July 1925; *s* of Louis Delors and Jeanne (*née* Rigal); *m* 1948, Marie Lephaille; one *d* (one *s* decd). *Educ:* Paris Univ.; Dip., Centre for Higher Studies of Banking. Joined Banque de France, 1945; in office of Chief of Securities Dept, 1950–62, and in Sect. for the Plan and Investments, Conseil Economique et Social, 1959–61; Chief of Social Affairs, Gen. Commissariat of Plan Monnet, 1962–68; Gen. Sec. for Perm. Trng and Social Promotion, 1968; Gen. Sec., Interministerial Cttee for Professional Educn, 1969–73; Mem., Gen. Council, Banque de France, 1973–79, and Dir, on leave of absence, 1973. Special Advr on Social and Cultural Affairs to Prime Minister, 1969–72. Socialist Party Spokesman on internat. econ. matters, 1976–81; Minister of the Economy and Finance, 1981–83; Minister of Economy, Finance and Budget, 1983–84. Mem., European Parlt, 1979–81 (Pres., Econ. and Financial Cttee, 1979–81). Mayor of Clichy, 1983–84. Pres., Internat. Commn on Educn for the Twenty First Century, UNESCO, 1993–96. Associate Prof., Univ. of Paris-Dauphine, 1973–79. Dir, Work and Society Res. Centre, 1975–79; Pres., Bd of Admin, College of Europe, Bruges, 1996–2000; Founding Pres., Jacques Delors Inst. (formerly Notre Europe), 1996. Founder, Club Echange et Projets, 1974–79. Hon. doctorates from 29 univs. Awards and honours from 15 countries. *Publications:* Les indicateurs sociaux, 1971; Changer, 1975; (jtly) En sortir ou pas, 1985; La France par L'Europe, 1988 (Our Europe: the community and national development, 1992); Le Nouveau Concert Européen, 1992; L'unité d'un homme, 1994; Combats pour l'Europe, 1996; Mémoires, 2004; L'Europe tragique et magnifique, 2006; Investir dans le social, 2009; essays and articles.

**DELPY, Prof. David Thomas,** CBE 2014; DSc; FMedSci; FRS 1999; FREng; Emeritus Professor of Biomedical Optics, University College London, 2014; Chair, Strategic Advisory Board, UK National Quantum Technologies Programme, since 2014; *b* 11 Aug. 1948; *s* of R. M. Delpy and M. H. Delpy; *m* 1972, Margaret E. Kimber; two *s*. *Educ:* Heaton Grammar Sch., Newcastle upon Tyne; Brunel Univ. (BSc 1st Cl. Hons Applied Phys); UCL (DSc Med. Phys London). Technical Mgt Services, Darchem Ltd, Darlington, 1970–71; Non-clinical Lectr, UCL Med. Sch., 1971–76; University College Hospital, London: Sen. Physicist, 1976–82; Principal Physicist, 1982–86; University College London: Sen. Lectr, 1986–91; Hd, Dept of Med. Phys and Bioengrg, 1992–99; Hamamatsu Prof. of Med. Photonics, 1991–2007; Vice Provost, 1999–2007; Chief Exec., EPSRC, 2007–14. Chm., Defence Sci. Expert Cttee (formerly DSAC), MoD, 2014–17. Mem., BBSRC, 2004–07. FMedSci 2000; FREng 2002. *Publications:* numerous scientific papers. *Recreations:* work, classical music, gardening.

**DELVIN, Lord;** title borne by eldest son of Earl of Westmeath, *qv;* not at present used.

**DEMACK, (James) David;** a Judge of the Upper Tribunal (Tax and Chancery Chamber), 2009–14 (a Special Commissioner of Income Tax, 2000–09; Vice-President for England and Wales, VAT and Duties Tribunals, 2001–09); *b* 1 March 1942; *s* of James and Edith Annie Demack; *m* 1969, Ruth Cicely Hosker. *Educ:* Balshaw's Grammar Sch., Leyland, Lancs; Manchester Univ.; Manchester Poly.; Salford Poly. CTA (FTII 1982). Admitted solicitor, 1965; solicitor, private practice, 1965–93. Mem., 1986–92, pt-time Chm., 1990–93, full-time Chm., 1993–2001, VAT Tribunals, subseq. VAT and Duties Tribunals. Mem. UK Panel, Adv. Commn under EU Arbitration Convention, EU Jt Transfer Pricing Forum, 2002–14. Steward, 1978–, Sec., Fabric Adv. Cttee, 2016–, York Minster. Trustee, Cuerden Valley Park Trust, 1998–2007. *Recreations:* rehabilitation of injured and disabled wild birds of prey, walking, golf, classical music, railways, all things Swiss, medieval church architecture. *E:* jddemack@icloud.com. *Clubs:* Royal Over-Seas League; Leyland Golf.

**de MAIZIÈRE, Dr Thomas;** Member (CDU/CSU), Bundestag, since 2009; *b* Bonn, 21 Jan. 1954; *s* of Ulrich de Maizière and Eva de Maizière; *m* 1985, Martina Willeke; two *s* one *d*. *Educ:* Bonn; studied law and history, Albert-Ludwigs Univ., Freiburg and Wilhelms Univ., Münster (Dr Law 1986). Chief of Policy Br., Berlin Senate Chancellery, 1985–89; State Sec. of Educn, Mecklenburg-Western Pomerania, 1990–94; Hd, Mecklenburg-Western Pomerania State Chancellery, 1994–98; State Minister and Hd, Saxon State Chancellery, 1999; State of Saxony: Minister of Finance, 2001–02, of Justice, 2002–04, of the Interior, 2004–05; Federal Minister and Hd, Federal Chancellery, 2005–09; Federal Minister of the Interior, 2009–11, 2013–18; Federal Minister of Defence, 2011–13. Chm., Deutsche Telekom Stiftung, 2018–. Hon. Prof., Univ. of Leipzig, 2018. *Address:* Deutscher Bundestag, Platz der Republik 1, 11011 Berlin, Germany. *T:* (30) 22773625. *E:* thomas.demaiziere@bundestag.de.

**de MARCHANT et d'ANSEMBOURG, Count Jan Mark Vladimir Anton;** Ambassador of the Netherlands to the Court of St James's, 2003–06; *b* 9 Oct. 1941; *s* of Count François de Marchant et d'Ansembourg and Fernandine, Countess de Bombelles; *m* 1979, Countess Nicole de Marchant et d'Ansembourg-Rougé; (one *s* decd). *Educ:* Leyden Univ. (MA Law). Lieut, military service, 1961–63; diplomatic postings, Damascus, NY, The Hague, 1970–82; Counsellor, Paris, 1982; Dep. Hd of Delegation, CSCE Meeting, Vienna, 1986; Dir, UN Dept, Min. of Foreign Affairs, 1989; Dep. Permanent Rep., Permanent Mission to NY, 1990–94; Dir European Dept, Min. of Foreign Affairs, 1994–96; Ambassador at large, 1996; Dep. Political Dir, 1997; Ambassador to Spain, 1998–2003. Officer, Order of Orange Nassau (Netherlands), 1994; Commander: Cross of St Olav (Norway), 1996; Ordre du Mérite (France), 1997; Grand Cross, Isabella la Católica (Spain), 2001. *Address:* 9 rue Colbert, 7800 Versailles, France. *Club:* Haagsche (The Hague).

**DE MARCO, Nick, (Nicholas Peter);** QC 2018; *b* Walton-on-Thames, 22 Feb. 1967; *s* of Agostino Francesco De Marco and Pauline Elizabeth De Marco (*née* Dean); partner, Ripon Ray. *Educ:* University Coll. London (LLB 1st cl. Law). Worked as film and video editor, 1990–97, nightclub doorman, 1996–2001; called to the Bar, Middle Temple, 2001; barrister specialising in sports law, 2001–. Director: Queens Park Rangers FC, 1997; Brit. Assoc. of Sport and the Law, 2018–; Chair, Judicial Bd, British Wrestling, 2012–; Legal Chair Panel Mem., FA County Anti-Discrimination Panels, 2013–; Specialist Sports Arbitrator, Asian Regl Arbitration Centre, 2016–; Mem., Sports Resolutions Arbitration Panel, 2018–. *Publications:* (ed and contrib.) Challenging Sports Governing Bodies, 2016; (ed) Football and the Law, 2018. *Recreations:* photographer, blogger, wine maker, Italophile, QPR fan, progressive; love to grow, cook, photograph, eat and share good food, ideally sitting on terrace of my house in Italy, by my vineyard, sipping local wine. *Address:* Blackstone Chambers, Blackstone House, Temple, EC4Y 9BW. *T:* (020) 7583 1770. *E:* nickdemarco@blackstonechambers.com.

**DEMARCO, Prof. Richard,** CBE 2007 (OBE 1985); RSW; Professor of European Cultural Studies, Kingston University, 1993–2000, now Professor Emeritus; *b* 9 July 1930; *s* of Carmine Demarco and Elizabeth (*née* Fusco); *m* 1957, Anne Muckle. *Educ:* Holy Cross Academy, Edinburgh; Edinburgh College of Art. National Service, KOSB and RAEC, 1954–56. Art Master, Duns Scotus Academy, Edinburgh, 1956–67; Co-Founder, Traverse Theatre Club; Vice-Chm. and Director, Traverse Art Gall., 1963–67; Dir, Richard Demarco Gall., Melville Crescent, Edinburgh, 1966–92, appointed by co-founders John Martin, Andrew Elliott and James Walker; introduced contemporary visual arts into official Edinburgh Festival programme with Edinburgh Open 100 Exhibn, 1967; introduced works of 330 internat. artists to UK, mainly through Edinburgh Fest. exhibns, from Canada, 1968, W Germany, 1970, Romania, 1971, Poland, 1972 and 1979, France, 1973, Austria, 1973, Yugoslavia, 1975, Aust. and NZ, 1984, Netherlands, 1990; incl. Joseph Beuys, 1970, Gunther Uecker, 1991, and Tadeusz Kantor's Cricot Theatre, with prodns of The Water Hen, 1972, Lovelies and Dowdies, 1973, The Dead Class, 1976. Has presented, 1969–, annual programmes of theatre, music and dance prodns, incl. the Freehold Company's Antigone, 1970; Dublin Project Company's On Baille Strand, 1977; Mladen Materic's Obala Theatre from Sarajevo, 1988 and 1989; Teatro Settimo from Turin, and Grupa Chwilowa from Lublin, 1991; Yvette Bozsik Theatre from Budapest, 1993; prod Macbeth for Edinburgh Fest., on Inchcolm Is, 1988 and 1989. Director: Sean Connery's Scottish Internat. Educn Trust, 1972–74; Edinburgh Arts annual summer sch. and expedns, 1972–92; Artistic Advr, Eur. Youth Parlt, 1992–. Has directed annual exhibn prog. with Special Unit, HM Prison, Barlinnie, with partic. reference to sculpture of James Boyle, 1974–80; directed Edinburgh Fest. Internat. Confs, Towards the Housing of Art in the 21st Century, 1983, Art and the Human Environment, 1984 (also at Dublin Fest.). Was subject of film, Walkabout Edinburgh, dir. by Edward McConnell, 1970; acted in feature films: Long Shot, 1978; That Sinking Feeling, 1980; subject of TV film, The Demarco Dimension, 1987. Has broadcast regularly on television and radio, 1966–; has lectured in over 150 univs, art colls, schools, art galls; as water-colour painter and printmaker is represented in over 1600 public and private collections, incl. Nat. Gall. of Modern Art of Scotland, V&A Museum, Scottish Arts Council; retrospective exhibn, Richard Demarco at 80: a life in pictures, Royal Scottish Acad., 2010; Richard Demarco and Joseph Beuys: A Unique Partnership, Scottish Nat. Gall. of Modern Art, 2017. Hon. Vis. Prof. of Fine Art, Dundee Univ., 2007. Trustee: Kingston Demarco European Art Foundn, 1993–; Green Cross (UK), 1999–; Edinburgh Coll. Develt Trust, 2014–; Vice-Pres., Kingston Th. Trust, 2001. Contributing Editor, Studio International, 1982–. SSA 1964; RWSScot 1966. Mem., AICA, 1992; FRSA 1998. Hon. FRIAS 1991; HRSA 2001; Hon. Fellow, Inst. of Contemp. Scotland, 2002; Hon. RWS 2006. Hon. Fellow: Edinburgh Coll. of Art, 2008; Rose Bruford Coll. of Th. and Performance, 2010; Southampton Solent Univ., 2011. Hon. DFA: Atlanta Coll. of Art, 1993; Wroclaw Acad. of Fine Art, 2006; DUniv Stirling, 2007; Hon. DArts Leeds Beckett, 2016. Gold Order of Merit, Polish People's Republic, 1976; Order of the Cavaliere della Repubblica d'Italia, 1987; Chevalier de l'Ordre des Arts et des Lettres (France), 1991; Gloria Artis Medal (Poland), 2007; Grand Cross, Order of Merit (Germany), 2010; Bene Merito Medal (Poland), 2010; Gloria Artis Medal (Poland), 2012; Order of Cultural Merit (Romania), 2012; Eur. Citizen of the Year, EP, 2013; Edinburgh Award, City of Edinburgh, 2013. *Publications:* The Artist as Explorer, 1978; The Road to Meikle Seggie, 1978; A Life in Pictures, 1994; (jtly) The Demarco Collection and Archive: an introduction, 2009; The Road to Meikle Seggie, 2015; Richard Demarco and Joseph Beuys: a unique partnership, 2016. *Recreations:* exploring: the small and secret spaces in townscape; cathedrals, abbeys, parish churches; coastlines and islands and The Road to Meikle Seggie. *Address:* Demarco European Art Foundation, 1 Milkhall Cottages, Howgate, Penicuik, Midlothian EH16 8PX; 23A Lennox Street EH4 1PY. *T:* (0131) 343 2124. *Club:* Scottish Arts (Hon. Mem.) (Edinburgh).

**de MAULEY, 7th Baron** *cr* 1838; **Rupert Charles Ponsonby,** TD 1988; Master of the Horse, since 2019; *b* 30 June 1957; *s* of Hon. Thomas Maurice Ponsonby, TD and of Maxine Henrietta Ponsonby (*née* Thellusson); *S* uncle, 2002; *m* 2002, Hon. Lucinda Katherine Fanshawe Royle, *d* of Baron Fanshawe of Richmond, KCMG. *Educ:* Eton. FCA 1990 (ACA 1980). Director: Samuel Montagu & Co. Ltd, 1990–93; Standard Chartered Merchant Bank Asia Ltd, Singapore, 1994–99 (Man. Dir, 1996–99); FixIT Worldwide Ltd, 1999–2006. CO, The Royal Wessex Yeomanry (TA), 2003–04 (commnd, 1976). Elected Mem., H of L, March 2005; Opposition Whip and Opposition BERR (formerly DTI) spokesman, 2005–09; Opposition spokesman for Cabinet Office, 2006–08, DIUS, 2008–09; a Lord in Waiting (Govt Whip), 2010–12; govt spokesman for Home Office, 2010, for HM Treasury, BIS and DEFRA, 2010–12, for DWP, 2011–12; Parly Under-Sec. of State, DEFRA, 2012–15. Pres., Council, RFCA, 2010–. Chairman: LAPADA, 2017–; London Cremation Co., 2018–. Col Comdt, Yeomanry, TA, 2011–; Hon. Col, Royal Wessex Yeomanry, 2015. *Heir: b* Hon. (Ashley) George Ponsonby [*b* 17 Nov. 1959; *m* 2006, Mrs Camilla Gordon Lennox (*née* Pilkington)].

**DEMBRI, Mohamed-Salah;** Ambassador of Algeria to the Court of St James's, and also to Ireland, 2005–10; *b* 30 Jan. 1938; *s* of Hardjem Dembri and Zelikha Dembri (*née* Bendaoud); *m* 1960, Monique Paule Alleaume; one *s* one *d*. *Educ:* Sorbonne Univ. (BA; Higher Educn Dip.). Secretary General: Min. of Higher Educn and Scientific Res., 1973–79; Min. of Foreign Affairs, 1979–82; Ambassador to Canada, 1982–84; Sec. Gen., Min. of Labour and Social Affairs, 1988–89; Official Rep. (Special Advr) to Hd of Govt on political and diplomatic issues, 1989–91; Ambassador to Hellenic Republic, 1991–93; Minister of Foreign Affairs, 1993–96; Ambassador to UN, Geneva, 1996–2004 and (non-resident), to Holy See, 1997–2004. Jubilee Medal (Bulgaria), 1979; Kt, Nat. Order of Chad, 1994; Gt Cross, Order of St Gregory the Gt (Vatican), 1999; Grand Officer, Nat. Order of Mono (Togo), 2002. *Publications:* contribs to Algerian Arts and Human Scis Rev., Algerian Notebooks of Comparative Lit., and publications of Algerian Inst. of Global Strategy and UN; papers on Euro-Mediterranean relations and on St Augustine. *Recreations:* reading, cinema, theatre, sight-seeing, tourism. *Address:* 9, 17[d] Ihabbène Street, El-Biar, Algiers, Algeria.

**de MESTRE, Andrew Etienne,** QC 2019; *b* Winchester, 21 Aug. 1974; *s* of Peter de Mestre and Lynette de Mestre; *m* 2003, Lyndsey Claire Mein (*see* L. C. de Mestre); one *s* one *d*. *Educ:* Sherborne Sch.; Magdalene Coll., Cambridge (BA Hons 1996). Called to the Bar, Middle Temple, 1998; in practice as a barrister, 4 Stone Bldgs, 1998–. *Publications:* (contrib.) Annotated Companies Legislation, 2010. *Recreations:* cricket, football, travel, walking. *Address:* 4 Stone Buildings, Lincoln's Inn, WC2A 3XT. *T:* (020) 7242 5524. *E:* a.demestre@4stonebuildings.com.

**de MESTRE, Lyndsey Claire;** QC 2018; *b* Ashington, 3 June 1976; *d* of Paul Mein and Angela Mein; *m* 2003, Andrew Etienne de Mestre, *qv*; one *s* one *d*. *Educ:* Downing Coll., Cambridge (BA 1st Cl. 1998). Called to the Bar, Lincoln's Inn, 1999; in practice as a barrister, specialising in company and insolvency law, and as a mediator and arbitrator, XXIV Old Bldgs, 2000–. Chancellor, Dio. of St Albans, 2018– (Dep. Chancellor, 2015–18). *Recreations:* reading, walking, swimming, choral singing, friends and family. *Address:* XXIV Old Buildings, Lincoln's Inn, WC2A 3UP. *T:* (020) 7691 2424. *E:* clerks@xxiv.co.uk.

**DEMETRIOU, Marie-Eleni Eliza;** QC 2012; *b* Brighton, 13 Feb. 1972; *d* of George and Doreen Demetriou; *m* 2009, Neil Richard Calver, *qv*; one *s* one *d*. *Educ:* St Hilda's Coll., Oxford (BA 1993; BCL 1994). Called to the Bar, Middle Temple, 1995, Bencher, 2013; in practice as barrister, 1995–; Référendaire, Eur. Court of Justice, 1999–2002. Mem., Attorney Gen.'s A Panel, 2009–12. Vis. Fellow, KCL, 2008–. *Publications:* (jtly) Sports Law, 1999, 2nd edn 2012; (with D. Anderson) References to the European Court, 2nd edn 2002. *Recreations:* family, wine, reading novels, opera, Tottenham Hotspur Football Club. *Address:* Brick Court Chambers, 7–8 Essex Street, WC2R 3LD. *T:* (020) 7379 3550.

**De MEYER, Prof. Arnoud Cyriel Leo,** PhD; President, Singapore Management University, 2010–18; *b* 12 April 1954; *s* of Eugeen De Meyer and Emma (*née* De Winter). *Educ*: Univ. of Ghent (MSc Electrical Engrg; PhD Mgt 1983). Institut Européen d'Administration des Affaires (INSEAD): Prof. of Technol. Mgt, 1983–2006; Associate Dean for Exec. Educn, 1992–99; Dir Gen., Euro-Asia Centre, 1995–99; Akzo Nobel Fellow in Strategic Mgt, 1997–2006; Dean, Campus in Asia, 1999–2002; Dep. Dean, then Dean of Admin and Ext. Relns, 2001–06; Dir, Judge Business Sch., Univ. of Cambridge, 2006–10. Pt-time Prof., De Vlerick Leuven Gent Mgt Sch., Univ. of Ghent, 1988–2004. Vis. Prof., Grad. Sch. of Business Admin, Waseda Univ., Tokyo, 1999–2000. Board Member: Option Internat., NV, 1997; Dassault Systèmes, 2005–; Temasek Mgt Services Pte Ltd, 2010–; Viva Energy Pty Ltd. Gold Public Service Medal (Singapore); Comdr, Order of Leopold (Belgium). *Publications*: (jtly) Benchmarking for Global Manufacturing, 1992; Creating Product Value: a strategic manufacturing perspective, 1992; (jtly) The Bright Stuff, 2001; Belgique On Line: 30 propositions pour la e-Belgique de demain, 2002; (jtly) Global Future, The Next Challenge for Asian Business, 2005; (with S. Garg) Inspire to Innovate, Management of Innovation in Asia, 2005; (jtly) Managing the Unknown: a new approach to managing high uncertainty and risk in projects, 2006; (jtly) The Information Society in an Enlarged Europe, 2006; (jtly) Process Theory, 2018; contrib. articles to jls incl. R&D Mgt, IEEE Trans on Engrg Mgt, Sloan Mgt Rev., Strategic Mgt Jl, Mgt Sci., Manufg and Service Ops Mgt, Jl of Ops Mgt. *Address*: Singapore Management University, Administration Building, 81 Victoria Street, Singapore 188065.

**DEMIDENKO, Nikolai Anatolyevich;** concert pianist; *b* 1 July 1955; *s* of Anatoli Antonovich Demidenko and Olga Mikhailovna Demidenko; granted British citizenship, 1995; *m* 1994, Julia B. Dovgiallo; one *s* by a previous marriage. *Educ*: Gnessin Music Sch., Moscow; Moscow State Conservatoire. Professional début, Saratov, 1974; British début, 1985; NY début, 2001. Teacher: Moscow State Conservatoire, 1979–84; Yehudi Menuhin Sch. of Music, 1990–95; Vis. Prof., Univ. of Surrey. 2nd prize, Montreal Piano Competition, 1976; 3rd prize, Moscow Tchaikovsky Competition, 1978. Has made numerous recordings. Hon. Dr Surrey, 2014. Gramophone Award, 1992; Classic CD Award, 1995; Deutsche Schallplatten Prize; MIDEM Classical Award, 2010. *Recreations*: photography, computing.

**de MILLE, His Honour Peter Noël;** a Circuit Judge, 1992–2010 (Midland and Oxford Circuit, 1992–2002; South Eastern Circuit, 2002–10); *b* 19 Nov. 1944; *s* of late Noël James de Mille and Ailsa Christine de Mille (*née* Ogilvie); *m* 1977, Angela Mary Cooper; one *d*. *Educ*: Fettes Coll.; Trinity Coll., Dublin (BA, LLB). Called to the Bar, Inner Temple, 1968; a Recorder, 1987–92. *Recreations*: sailing, music, theatre. *Club*: Aldeburgh Yacht.

**de MOL, John H.;** Owner and Chief Creative Director, Talpa Media Group, since 2004; *b* The Hague, 24 April 1955; one *s*. Founder: John de Mol Produkties, 1978; Endemol Entertainment, 1994; Talpa Media Gp, 2004; developed progs incl. Big Brother, Deal or No Deal and The Voice. *Recreation*: golf. *Address*: Talpa Media Group, PO Box 154, 1250 AD Laren, Netherlands. *T*: (35) 5333333.

**de MOLEYNS;** see Daubeny de Moleyns, family name of Baron Ventry.

**de MOLLER, June Frances;** DL; Managing Director, Carlton Communications plc, 1993–99; *b* 25 June 1947; *m* 1st, 1967 (marr. diss. 1980); 2nd, 1996, John Robert Giles Crisp. *Educ*: Roedean; Hastings Coll.; Sorbonne Univ., Paris. Exec. Dir, Carlton Communications, 1983–99. Non-executive Director: Anglian Water plc, 1992–2000; Riverside Mental Health NHS Trust, 1992–96; Lynx Gp plc, 1999–2002; Cookson Gp plc, 1999–2004; British Telecommunications plc, 1999–2002; J. Sainsbury plc, 1999–2005; Archant (formerly Eastern Counties Newspapers Gp) Ltd, 1999–2011; London Merchant Securities plc, subseq. Derwent London plc, 2002–15; Temple Bar Investment Trust plc, 2006–. Mem., Listed Cos Adv. Cttee, Stock Exchange, 1998–99. Mem., Adv. Bd, Judge Inst. for Management Studies, Cambridge, 1996–2004. Member Council: Aldeburgh Music (formerly Productions), 2000–10; UEA, 2002–11. Mem. Cttee, Home of Rest for Horses, 1999–2005. DL Suffolk, 2009. *Recreations*: reading, travelling, breeding Red Poll cows.

**de MONTEBELLO, (Guy) Philippe (Lannes);** Director, 1978–2008, and Chief Executive Officer, 1999–2008, Metropolitan Museum of Art, now Director Emeritus; Fiske Kimball Professor in the History and Culture of Museums, Institute of Fine Arts, New York University, since 2009; *b* 16 May 1936; *s* of Roger Lannes de Montebello and Germaine (*née* Croisset); *m* 1961, Edith Bradford Myles; two *s* one *d*. *Educ*: Harvard Coll. (BA *magna cum laude*); New York Univ., Inst. of Fine Arts (MA). Curatorial Asst, European Paintings, Metropolitan Mus. of Art, 1963; Asst Curator, Associate Curator, MMA, until 1969; Director, Museum of Fine Arts, Houston, Texas, 1969–74; Vice-Director: for Curatorial Affairs, MMA, Jan.–June 1974; for Curatorial and Educnl Affairs, 1977–78; Actg Dir, MMA, 1977–78. Gallatin Fellow, New York Univ., 1981. Schol. in Residence, Prado Mus., Madrid, 2009. Mem., Bd of Trustees, Musée d'Orsay, 2009–13. Hon. LLD: Lafayette Coll., East Pa, 1979; Bard Coll., Annandale-on-Hudson, NY, 1981; Dartmouth Coll., 2004; Hon. DFA Iona Coll., New Rochelle, NY, 1982; Hon. DArts: Harvard, 2006; New York, 2007. Alumni Achievement Award, New York Univ., 1978; Nat. Medal of Arts (USA), 2003; Amigos del Museo del Prado Prize, 2004. Officier, Ordre Nat. de la Légion d'Honneur (France), 2005. *Publications*: Peter Paul Rubens, 1968; (with Martin Gayford) Rendez-vous with Art, 2014. *Club*: Knickerbocker (New York).

**DEMPSEY, Andrew;** see Dempsey, J. A.

**DEMPSEY, Dr Anthony Michael;** Headmaster, Tiffin School, 1988–2004; *b* 12 June 1944; *s* of Michael and Bertha Laura Dempsey; *m* 1970, Sandra Lynn Atkins; one *s*. *Educ*: Tiffin Sch.; Bristol Univ. (BSc, PhD). Chemistry Teacher, King's College Sch., 1969–73; Heathland School, Hounslow: Head of Sci., 1973–75; Head, Maths and Sci. Faculty, 1975–79; Feltham Community School: Dep. Head, 1979–82; Sen. Dep. Head, 1982–88. *Publications*: Visual Chemistry, 1983; Science Master Pack, 1985; contrib. to Nuffield Chemistry books; papers in carbohydrate res. *Recreations*: walking, travel, sport, church, industrial archaeology. *Address*: 63 Gilpin Crescent, Twickenham TW2 7BP. *T*: (020) 8898 2860.

**DEMPSEY, (James) Andrew;** independent exhibition curator and organiser, since 1996; *b* 17 Nov. 1942; *s* of James Dempsey, Glasgow; *m* 1st, 1966, Grace (marr. diss. 1998), *d* of Dr Ian MacPhail, Dumbarton; one *s* one *d*; 2nd, 2006, Catherine Emily Lampert, *qv*. *Educ*: Ampleforth Coll.; Glasgow Univ. Whistler Research Asst, Fine Art Dept, Univ. of Glasgow, 1963–65; exhibn work for art dept of Arts Council, 1966–71; Keeper, Dept of Public Relations, V&A, 1971–75; Asst Dir of Exhibitions, Arts Council of GB, 1975–87; Asst Dir, 1987–94, Associate Curator, 1994–96, Hayward Gall., S Bank Centre.

**DEMPSEY, Lisa;** see Markwell, L.

**DEMPSEY, Michael Bernard,** RDI 1994; Founder, Studio Dempsey, since 2008; *b* 25 July 1944; *s* of John Patrick Dempsey and Britannia May (*née* Thompson); *m* 1st, 1967, Sonja Green (marr. diss. 1988); two *s* one *d*; 2nd, 1989, Charlotte Antonia Richardson (marr. diss. 2008); three *d*. *Educ*: St Vincent RC Primary Sch., Dagenham; Bishop Ward RC Secondary Mod. Sch., Dagenham. Asst designer, Cheveron Studio, 1963–64; in-house designer, Bryan Colmer Artist Agent, 1964–65; freelance designer, 1965–66; Designer, Cato Peters O'Brien, 1966–68; Art Director: William Heinemann Publishers, 1968–74; William Collins Publishers, 1974–79; Founder Partner, Carroll & Dempsey Ltd, 1979–85; Partner, 1985–2007, Chm. and Creative Dir, 1993–2007, Carroll, Dempsey Thirkell Ltd, later CDT Design Ltd. Feature film title designer: The Duellists, 1977; Wetherby, 1985; Comrades, 1986; Blackeyes, 1987; Paris By Night, 1989; Strapless, 1990; Call it Night, 1990; Heading Home, 1991; The Secret Rapture, 1994; Look Me in the Eye, 1994; Beg, 1994; Blue Juice, 1995; Last Dance, 1996; The Designated Mourner, 1997; Consultant Art Dir to Royal Mail for 1999 Millennium stamps, 1997–99, designer: Mind and Matter stamps, 2000; Definitive stamps, 2006; Sounds of Britain stamps, 2006; Endangered Plants, 2009; Classic Album Covers stamps, 2010; identity and communications consultant, DCMS, 1997–99; Ext. Design Advr to Design Council, 2009–15. Presenter and producer, RDInsights, RSA, 2006–. Art Dir and Mem., Editl Bd, RSA Jl, 1997–2002; feature writer: Design Week, 2001–; Blueprint, 2006–; Eye mag. Pres., British Design and Art Dirs Assoc., 1997–98. Master of Faculty, RDI, 2005–07. Member: AGI, 1998–2002, 2011–; BAFTA, 2003–. FRSA. Silver award, 1981, 1984, 1985, 1989, 1992, 2000, 2001, Gold award, 1985, Special Award for most awarded designer, 2012, D&AD (formerly Design and Art Dirs Assoc.); CSD Minerva Award, 1996; Reginald M. Phillips Medal, Royal Mail, 2010; Silver Cube, Art Director's Club, 2011. *Publications*: Bubbles: early advertising art from A. & F. Pears, 1978; The Magical Paintings of Justin Todd, 1978; Pipe Dreams: early advertising art from the Imperial Tobacco Company, 1982. *Recreations*: living, looking, blogging, being. *Address*: The Hayloft, Church Lane, Osmington, Dorset DT3 6EZ. *T*: (01305) 832520. *E*: mike@studiodempsey.co.uk. *W*: www.studiodempsey.co.uk, http://mikedempsey.typepad.com.

**DEMPSTER, Jennifer Margaret Pert;** QC 2018; a Recorder, since 2018; *b* Edinburgh, 3 Nov. 1970; *d* of George Dempster and Gloria Dempster; one *s*. *Educ*: Broughton High Sch., Edinburgh; London Sch. of Econs and Political Sci. (LLB Hons). Called to the Bar, Lincoln's Inn, 1993. *Address*: Red Lion Chambers, 18 Red Lion Court, EC4A 3EB. *T*: (020) 7520 6000. *E*: jenni.dempster@18rlc.co.uk.

**DEMPSTER, John William Scott,** CB 1994; Director, United Kingdom Major Ports Group Ltd, 1999–2007; *b* 10 May 1938; *m* 1965, Ailsa Newman (marr. diss. 1972). *Educ*: Plymouth Coll.; Oriel Coll., Oxford (MA PPE). HM Inspector of Taxes, Inland Revenue, 1961–65; Ministry of Transport: Asst Principal, 1965–67; Principal, 1967–73; Asst Sec., Property Services Agency, 1973–76; Principal Private Sec. to Sec. of State for the Environment, 1976–77; Asst Sec., Dept of Transport, 1977–80; Principal Estabt and Finance Officer, Lord Chancellor's Dept, 1980–84; Department of Transport: Head of Marine Directorate, 1984–89; Principal Establishment Officer, 1989–90; Principal Establishment and Finance Officer, 1990–91; Dir Gen. of Highways, 1991–94; Dep. Sec., Aviation and Shipping, 1994–96; Dir, Bahamas Maritime Authy, 1996–99. Chm., St John Ambulance Devon, 2008–12. *Publications*: The Rise and Fall of the Dock Labour Scheme, 2010; James Common in Antarctica, 2016. *Recreations*: mountaineering, sailing, bridge, Munro collecting. *Address*: 7 Willow Bridge Road, N1 2LB. *T*: (020) 7226 7553. *Clubs*: Alpine (Hon. Treas., 2014–17), Fell and Rock; Swiss Alpine (Pres., Association of British Members, 2006–09).

**DEMPSTER, Prof. Michael Alan Howarth,** PhD; Professor Emeritus, Statistical Laboratory, Centre for Mathematical Sciences, since 2007, Professor of Management, Judge Institute of Management, 1996–2005, Emeritus, 2006, and Director, Centre for Financial Research, 1997–2008, University of Cambridge (Director of Research, 1997–2001; Director, PhD Programme, 1997–2002); Fellow, Hughes Hall, Cambridge, 2002–07, now Quondam Fellow; *b* 10 April 1938; *s* of Cedric William Dempster and Honor Fitz Simmons Dempster (*née* Gowan); *m* 1st, 1963, Ann Laura Lazier (marr. diss. 1980); one *d*; 2nd, 1981, Elena Anatolievna Medova; one *d*. *Educ*: Univ. of Toronto (BA 1961); Carnegie Mellon Univ. (MS 1963; PhD 1965); Oxford Univ. (MA 1967); Cambridge Univ. (MA 2005). IBM Res. Fellow, Math. Inst., Oxford, 1965–66; Jun. Res. Fellow, Nuffield Coll., Oxford, 1966; Fellow, Tutor and Univ. Lectr in Maths, 1967–81, Lectr in Maths, 1982–87, Balliol Coll., Oxford; R. A. Jodrey Res. Prof. of Mgt and Inf. Scis, Sch. of Business Admin, and Prof. of Maths, Stats and Computing Science, Dalhousie Univ., 1981–93; Prof. of Maths, 1990–95, and Dir, Inst. for Studies in Finance, 1993–95, Univ. of Essex. Fellow, Center for Advanced Study in Behavioral Scis, Stanford, 1974–75; Sen. Res. Scholar, Internat. Inst. for Applied Systems Analysis, Laxenburg, Austria, 1979–81; Vis. Prof., Univ. of Rome, La Sapienza, 1988–89; Vis. Fellow, Princeton Univ., 1995. Chm., Oxford Systems Associates Ltd, 1974–79; Man. Dir, Cambridge Systems Associates Ltd, 1996–. Cons. to numerous cos and govts, 1965–. Mem., Res. Adv. Bd, Canadian Inst. for Advanced Res., 1986–2002. Foreign Mem., Academia Nazionale dei Lincei, 2013. FIMA 1974. Hon. FIA 2000. Editor: Quantitative Finance, 2000–; Oxford Handbooks in Finance, 2006–. *Publications*: (jtly) Introduction to Optimization Methods, 1974; (ed) Stochastic Programming, 1980; (ed jtly) Analysis and Optimization of Stochastic Systems, 1980; (ed jtly) Large-Scale Linear Programming, 1981; (ed jtly) Deterministic and Stochastic Scheduling, 1982; (ed jtly) Mathematical Models in Economics, 1994; (ed jtly) Mathematics of Derivative Securities, 1997; (ed jtly) Risk Management: value at risk and beyond, 2002; (ed jtly) Quantitative Fund Management, 2009; (ed jtly) Stochastic Optimization Methods in Finance and Energy, 2011; (jtly) The Euro in Danger: reform and reset, 2012; (ed jtly) Commodities, 2015; (ed jtly) High-Performance Computing in Finance, 2018; *translations* from Russian: (jtly) Stochastic Models of Control and Economic Dynamics, 1987; (jtly) Sequential Control and Incomplete Information, 1990. *Recreations*: reading, gardening, tennis, sailing, ski-ing. *Address*: 1 Earl Street, Cambridge CB1 1JR; Statistical Laboratory, Centre for Mathematical Sciences, University of Cambridge, Wilberforce Road, Cambridge CB3 0WA.

**DENARO, Maj.-Gen. Arthur George,** CBE 1996 (OBE 1991); DL; Extra Equerry to the Prince of Wales, since 2000; *b* 23 March 1948; *s* of late Brig. George Tancred Denaro, CBE, DSO and of Francesca Violet Denaro (*née* Garnett); *m* 1980, Margaret Roney Acworth, *widow* of Major Michael Kealy, DSO; one *s* one *d*, and one step *s* two step *d*. *Educ*: Downside Sch.; RMA Sandhurst. Commissioned Queen's Royal Irish Hussars, 1968; Staff Coll., 1979–80; CO QRIH, 1989–91; Comdr 33 (later 20) Armd Bde, 1992–94; RCDS 1994; COS HQ UNPROFOR, former Yugoslavia, 1994–95; COS HQ British Forces, Cyprus, 1995–96; Chief, Combat Support, HQ ARRC, 1996–97; Comdt, RMA Sandhurst, 1997–2000; GOC 5th Div., 2000–03. Middle East Adviser: to Sec. of State for Defence, 1997–2002; to JCB, 2003–09; Advr to Ct of Crown Prince of Bahrain, 2003–07; Special Advr, Inspirational Develt Gp, 2007–19; Sen. Advr to Qatar Nat. Food Security Prog., 2011–13; Advr to Conservative Middle East Council, 2011–18; Advr to Royal Hashemite Court, 2015–18; Sen. Advr on Middle East to Serco, 2016–17; Advr to Min. of Defence, Qatar, 2017–. Col, Queen's Royal Hussars (Queen's Own and Royal Irish), 2004–09; Hon. Colonel: Royal Glos Hussars, 2003–13; Royal Wessex Yeomanry, 2003–09. Pres., Combined Irish Regts Assoc., 2003–. Chairman: Prince's Trust Team Prog., 2000–08; Army Benevolent Fund (Hereford), 2003–13. President: Army Rugby Union, 2001–03; Army Polo Assoc., 2002–09; Herefordshire Sector, St John Ambulance, 2011–16. Chm. Govs, Moor Park Sch., 2011–17. Trustee, Plant for Peace, 2012–. DL Herefordshire, 2008. *Recreations*: fieldsports, ski-ing. *Clubs*: Cavalry and Guards, Pratt's.

**de NAVARRO, Michael Antony;** QC 1990; a Recorder, 1990–2014; *b* 1 May 1944; *s* of A. J. M. (Toty) de Navarro and Dorothy M. de Navarro; *m* 1975, Jill Margaret Walker (*d* 2013); one *s* two *d*. *Educ*: Downside School; Trinity College, Cambridge (BA Hons). Called to the Bar, Inner Temple, 1968, Bencher, 2000; pupil of Hon. Mr Justice Cazalet and Hon. Mr Justice Turner; Mem., Western Circuit. Chm., Personal Injuries Bar Assoc., 1997–99. Trustee: Longborough Fest. Opera, 2000–13; Broadway Arts Fest., 2010–16. *Recreations*: opera, cricket, gardening, cooking. *Address*: 2 Temple Gardens, Temple, EC4Y 9AY. *T*: (020) 7822 1200.

**DENBIGH,** 12th Earl of, *cr* 1622, **AND DESMOND,** 11th Earl of, *cr* 1622; **Alexander Stephen Rudolph Feilding;** Baron Feilding 1620; Viscount Feilding 1620; Viscount Callan 1622; Baron St Liz 1663; *b* 4 Nov. 1970; *o s* of 11th Earl of Denbigh and Caroline Judith Vivienne, *o d* of Lt-Col Geoffrey Cooke; *S* father, 1995; *m* 1996, Suzanne Jane, *d* of Gregory R. Allen; two *s* one *d*. *Heir*: *s* Viscount Feilding, *qv*. *Address*: Newnham Paddox, Monks Kirby, Rugby CV23 0RX; 34 Keildon Road, Battersea, SW11 1XH.

**DENCH, Dame Judith Olivia, (Dame Judi Dench),** CH 2005; DBE 1988 (OBE 1970); actress (theatre, films and television); *b* 9 Dec. 1934; *d* of Reginald Arthur Dench and Eleanora Olave Dench (*née* Jones); *m* 1971, Michael Leonard Williams, actor (*d* 2001); one *d*. *Educ*: The Mount Sch., York; Central Sch. of Speech and Drama. *Theatre*: Old Vic seasons, 1957–61: parts incl.: Ophelia in Hamlet; Katherine in Henry V; Cecily in The Importance of Being Earnest; Juliet in Romeo and Juliet; also 1957–61: two Edinburgh Festivals; Paris-Belgium-Yugoslavia tour; America-Canada tour; Venice (all with Old Vic Co.). Subseq. appearances incl.: Royal Shakespeare Co., 1961–62: Anya in The Cherry Orchard; Titania in A Midsummer Night's Dream; Dorcas Bellboys in A Penny for a Song; Isabella in Measure for Measure; Nottingham Playhouse tour of W Africa, 1963; Oxford Playhouse, 1964–65: Irina in The Three Sisters; Doll Common in The Alchemist; Nottingham Playhouse, 1965: Saint Joan; The Astrakhan Coat (world première); Amanda in Private Lives; Variety London Critics' Best Actress of the Year Award for perf. as Lika in The Promise, Fortune, 1967; Sally Bowles in Cabaret, Palace, 1968; Associate Mem., RSC, 1969–; London Assurance, Aldwych, 1970, and New, 1972; Major Barbara, Aldwych, 1970; Bianca in Women Beware Women, Viola in Twelfth Night, doubling Hermione and Perdita in The Winter's Tale, Portia in The Merchant of Venice, the Duchess in The Duchess of Malfi, Beatrice in Much Ado About Nothing, Lady Macbeth in Macbeth, Adriana in The Comedy of Errors, Regan in King Lear, Imogen in Cymbeline; The Wolf, Oxford and London, 1973; The Good Companions, Her Majesty's, 1974; The Gay Lord Quex, Albery, 1975; Too True to be Good, Aldwych, 1975, Globe, 1976; Macbeth, RSC, 1976 (SWET award, 1977); Pillars of the Community, The Comedy of Errors, Aldwych, 1977; The Way of the World, 1978; Juno and the Paycock, Aldwych, 1980 (Best Actress award, SWET, Evening Standard, Variety Club, and Plays and Players); The Importance of Being Earnest, A Kind of Alaska, Nat. Theatre, 1982; Pack of Lies, Lyric, 1983 (SWET award); Mother Courage, Barbican, 1984; Waste, Barbican and Lyric, 1985; Mr and Mrs Nobody, Garrick, 1986; Antony and Cleopatra (Best Actress award, Evening Standard, Olivier award), Entertaining Strangers, Nat. Theatre, 1987; Hamlet, Royal Nat. Theatre, and Dubrovnik Theatre Fest., 1989; The Cherry Orchard, Aldwych, 1989; The Plough and the Stars, Young Vic, 1991; The Sea, Nat. Theatre, 1991; Coriolanus, Chichester, 1992; The Gift of the Gorgon, Barbican, 1992, transf. Wyndham's, 1993; The Seagull, RNT, 1994; Absolute Hell, RNT, 1995 (Best Actress, Olivier award, 1996); A Little Night Music, RNT, 1995 (Best Actress in a Musical, Olivier award, 1996); Amy's View, RNT, 1997, transf. Aldwych (Critics' Circle Drama Award), 1998, NY (Tony Award), 1999; Filumena, Piccadilly, 1998; The Royal Family, 2001, The Breath of Life, 2002, Theatre Royal, Haymarket; All's Well That Ends Well, RSC Stratford, transf. Gielgud, 2004; Hay Fever, Th. Royal, Haymarket, 2006; Merry Wives - The Musical, RSC Stratford, 2006; Madame de Sade, Wyndham's, 2009; Titania in A Midsummer Night's Dream, Rose Th., Kingston, 2010; Peter and Alice, Noël Coward Th., 2013; The Winter's Tale, Garrick Th., 2015 (Best Supporting Actress, Olivier Awards, 2016); Director, for Renaissance Theatre Co.: Much Ado About Nothing, 1988; Look Back in Anger, 1989; Director: The Boys from Syracuse, Regent's Park, 1991; Romeo and Juliet, Regent's Park, 1993. Recital tour of W Africa, 1969; RSC tours: Japan and Australia, 1970; Japan, 1972. *Films*: He Who Rides a Tiger; A Study in Terror; Four in the Morning (Brit. Film Acad. Award for Most Promising Newcomer, 1965); A Midsummer Night's Dream, 1968; The Third Secret; Dead Cert; Saigon: Year of the Cat; Wetherby, 1984; A Room with a View, 1985 (Best Supporting Actress, BAFTA award, 1987); 84 Charing Cross Road, 1986; A Handful of Dust (Best Supporting Actress, BAFTA award), 1988; Henry V, 1990; Goldeneye, 1995; Mrs Brown (Best Actress awards: BAFTA Scotland, 1997; Golden Globe, London Film Critics, BAFTA, and Screen Actors' Guild, NY, 1998); Tomorrow Never Dies, 1997; Shakespeare in Love (Oscar and BAFTA Award for Best Supporting Actress), Tea with Mussolini, The World is Not Enough, 1999; Chocolat, 2001; Iris (Best Actress, BAFTA award), The Shipping News, The Importance of Being Earnest, Die Another Day, 2002; Ladies in Lavender, The Chronicles of Riddick, 2004; Pride and Prejudice, Mrs Henderson Presents, 2005; Casino Royale, 2006; Notes on a Scandal, 2007; Quantum of Solace, 2008; Nine, Rage, 2009; Jane Eyre, My Week with Marilyn, 2011; J. Edgar, The Best Exotic Marigold Hotel, Skyfall, 2012; Philomena, 2013; The Second Best Exotic Marigold Hotel, 2015; Miss Peregrine's Home for Peculiar Children, 2016; Victoria and Abdul, Murder on the Orient Express, 2017; Nothing Like a Dame, Tulip Fever, 2018; All is True, Red Joan, Cats, 2019. *Television* appearances include, 1957–: Talking to a Stranger (Best Actress of Year award, Guild of Television Dirs, 1967); Major Barbara; Hilda Lessways; Langrishe, Go Down; Macbeth; Comedy of Errors; On Giant's Shoulders; A Village Wooing; Love in a Cold Climate; Saigon; A Fine Romance (BAFTA Award, 1985); The Cherry Orchard; Going Gently; Mr and Mrs Edgehill (Best Actress, Amer. Cable Award, 1988); The Browning Version; Make or Break; Ghosts; Behaving Badly; Absolute Hell; Can You Hear Me Thinking?; As Time Goes By (8 series); Last of the Blonde Bombshells, 2000 (Best Actress, BAFTA TV Award, 2001); Cranford, 2007, 2009; Esio Trot, 2015; The Hollow Crown: The War of the Roses, 2016; Judi Dench's Wild Borneo Adventure, 2019. Member: Bd, Royal Nat. Theatre, 1988–; Council, Royal Theatrical Support (formerly Royal Shakespeare Theatre) Trust. Awards incl. British and foreign, for theatre, films and TV, incl. BAFTA award for best television actress, 1981, Rothermere Award for Lifetime Achievement, 1997, and Critics' Circle Award for Outstanding Achievement, 1998; William Shakespeare Award, Washington, DC, 2004; Evening Standard Lifetime Achievement Award, 2004; Special Award, Olivier Awards, 2004; Sky Arts Award for Lifetime Achievement, 2011; Praemium Imperiale, 2011; Moscow Art Theatre's Golden Seagull, London Evening Standard Theatre Awards, 2012. Fellow BAFTA, 2001; Fellow BFI 2011. Hon. Fellow, Lucy Cavendish Coll., Cambridge, 2005. Hon. DLitt: Warwick, 1978; Birmingham, 1989; Loughborough, 1991; London, 1994; Oxford, 2000; Queen Margaret Univ. Coll., Edinburgh, 2000; UEA, 2000; Leeds, 2002; St Andrews, 2008; Nottingham Trent, 2010; DUniv: York, 1983; Open, 1992; RSAMD, 1995; Surrey, 1996; Hon. Dr: Wales, 2001; Mary Baldwin Coll., Staunton, 2004; Hull; Hon. Dr Fine Arts Juilliard Acad., 2004; Hon. Dr Arts, Harvard, 2017. *Publications*: Scenes from My Life, 2005; And Furthermore, 2010. *Recreations*: sewing, drawing, catching up with letters.

**DENDY, Prof. Richard Otwell,** DPhil; FInstP; Professor of Physics, and Joint Director, Centre for Fusion, Space and Astrophysics, Warwick University, since 2006; Senior Research Staff, UK Atomic Energy Authority, since 2001; *b* Surrey, 31 May 1958; *s* of Dr Paul Dendy and Patricia Dendy; *m* 1989, Felicity Carr; one *s* one *d*. *Educ*: Magdalen Coll. Sch., Oxford; Merton Coll., Oxford (BA 1st Cl. Physics 1979); Peterhouse, Cambridge (Part III Mathematical Tripos 1980); Oxford Univ. (DPhil 1983). FInstP 1996. Physics res., Euratom/UKAEA, 1983– (Gp Leader for Theoretical Physics, 1995–2011); Jun. Res. Fellow, Wolfson Coll., Oxford, 1987–94. Hon. Professor: of Physics, Warwick Univ., 1997–2006; Res. Inst. for Applied Mechanics, Kyushu Univ., Japan, 2010–. Comr, Marshall Aid Commemoration Commn, 2010–16 (Chm., Educn Cttee, 2014–16). Mem., Nuclear Res. Adv. Council, MoD, 2005–15. Mem., Physical Scis Strategy Adv. Team, EPSRC, 2007–14. Mem., Physics Sub-Panel, REF 2014, 2012–14, REF 2021, 2018–. Mem., Sci. Bd, Inst. of Physics, 2005–10. Chm. Bd, Plasma Physics Div., Eur. Physical Soc., 2016– (Vice Chm., 2012–16). Ed.-in-Chief, Plasma Physics and Controlled Fusion, 2005–. *Publications*: Plasma Dynamics, 1990; Plasma Physics: an introductory course, 1993; contrib. articles to jls on plasma physics and its applications. *Recreations*: running, gardening, cultivating my general knowledge (University Challenge, 1977). *Address*: Culham Science Centre, Abingdon, Oxon OX14 3DB. *T*: (01235) 466377. *E*: r.dendy@warwick.ac.uk.

**DENEGRI, Simon,** OBE 2018; National Director for Patients, Carers and the Public (formerly Public Participation and Engagement in Research), National Institute for Health Research, since 2012; *b* 17 March 1967; *s* of Donald and Annie Denegri; *m* 2006, Nicola Margaret Bain; three *s* from former marr. *Educ*: Dean Row Jun. Sch., Handforth; New Beacon Sch., Sevenoaks; Judd Grammar Sch., Tonbridge; Univ. of Hull (BA Hons Politics and Legislative Studies). Hd, Public Affairs, Alzheimer's Soc., 1992–97; Corporate and Financial Media Relns Manager, Procter and Gamble, USA, 1997–2000; Dir, Communications, Sainsbury Centre for Mental Health, 2001–03; Asst Chief Exec., Alzheimer's Soc., 2003; Dir, Corporate Communications, RCP, 2003–06; Chief Executive: Assoc. of Medical Res. Charities, 2006–11; Ovarian Cancer Action, 2011. Chm., INVOLVE, 2011–17. *Recreations*: poetry, cinema, live music, gardening, supporting Crystal Palace Football Club. *Address*: c/o UCL School of Life and Medical Sciences, University College London, Gower Street, WC1E 6BT. *E*: simon.denegri@nihr.ac.uk. *W*: http://simondenegri.com.

**DENEUVE, Catherine;** French film actress; *b* 22 Oct. 1943; *d* of Maurice Dorléac and Renée (*née* Deneuve); one *s* by Roger Vadim (*d* 2000); *m* 1967, David Bailey, *qv* (marr. diss.); one *d* by Marcello Mastroianni (*d* 1996). *Educ*: Lycée La Fontaine, Paris. Pres.-Dir Gen., Films de la Citrouille, 1971–79. Chm. Jury, Cannes Film Fest., 1994. *Films include*: Les petits chats, 1959; Les portes claquent, 1960; Le vice et la vertu, 1962; Les parapluies de Cherbourg, 1963; La Constanza della Ragione, 1964; Repulsion, 1964; Liebes Karusell, 1965; Belle de jour, 1967; Folies d'avril, 1969; Un flic, 1972; Le sauvage, 1975; Âmes perdues, 1976; Hustle, 1976; A nous deux, 1978; Le dernier métro, 1980 (César for best actress, 1981); Le choc, 1982; The Hunger, 1982; Le bon plaisir, 1984; Let's Hope It's A Girl, 1987; Drôle d'endroit pour une rencontre (Strange Place to Meet), 1989; Indochine, 1992; Ma Saison préférée, 1994; The Convent, 1995; Les voleurs, 1996; Généalogie d'un Crime, 1997; Place Vendôme, 1998; Pola X, Time Regained, Dancer in the Dark, East-West, 2000; The Musketeer, 8 Women, 2002; Les temps qui changent, 2005; Rois et Reine, 2005; Persepolis, 2008; Un Conte de Noël, 2009; Potiche, 2011; Beloved, 2012; Lines of Wellington, 2012; Astérix and Obélix: God Save Britannia, 2012; On My Way, 2013; In the Courtyard, 2014; In the Name of My Daughter, 2014; 3 Hearts, 2014; Standing Tall, 2015; The Brand New Testament, 2015; The Midwife, 2017; Bonne pomme, 2017; Tout nous sépare, 2017; La dernière folie de Claire Darling, 2018; Mauvaises herbes, 2018. *Publications*: A l'ombre de moi-même, 2004 (Close Up and Personal, 2005). *Address*: c/o Artmédia, 8 rue Danielle Casanova, 75002 Paris, France.

**DENHAM,** 2nd Baron *cr* 1937, of Weston Underwood; **Bertram Stanley Mitford Bowyer,** KBE 1991; PC 1981; Bt 1660, of Denham; Bt 1933, of Weston Underwood; Captain of the Gentlemen at Arms (Government Chief Whip in the House of Lords), 1979–91; an Extra Lord-in-Waiting to the Queen, since 1998; *b* 3 Oct. 1927; *s* of 1st Baron and Hon. Daphne Freeman-Mitford (*d* 1996), 4th *d* of 1st Baron Redesdale; *S* father, 1948; *m* 1956, Jean, *o d* of Kenneth McCorquodale, Fambridge Hall, White Notley, Essex; three *s* one *d*. *Educ*: Eton; King's Coll., Cambridge. Mem. Westminster CC, 1959–61. A Lord-in-Waiting to the Queen, 1961–64 and 1970–71; Opposition Jun. Whip, 1964–70; Captain of the Yeomen of the Guard, 1971–74; Opposition Dep. Chief Whip, 1974–78; Opposition Chief Whip, 1978–79; elected Mem., H of L, 1999–. Countryside Comr, 1993–99. Dep. Pres., British Field Sports Soc., 1992–98. *Publications*: The Man who Lost his Shadow, 1979; Two Thyrdes, 1983; Foxhunt, 1988; Black Rod, 1997. *Recreation*: field sports. *Heir*: *s* Hon. Richard Grenville George Bowyer [*b* 8 Feb. 1959; *m* 1st, 1988, Eleanor (marr. diss. 1993), *o d* of A. Sharpe; 2nd, 1996, Dagmar, *o d* of Karel and Jaroslava Božek, Břeslaw, Czech Republic]. *Address*: The Laundry Cottage, Weston Underwood, Olney, Bucks MK46 5JZ. *T*: (020) 7219 6056. *Clubs*: Pratt's, Garrick.

**DENHAM, Ashten R.;** *see* Regan-Denham.

**DENHAM, Grey;** Chairman, Young Enterprise, 2015–19 (Trustee, 2006–19); *b* Coleshill, Warwickshire, 11 Feb. 1949; *s* of Sydney Charles Denham and Ivy Denham; *m* 1976, Janet Miranda Lea; one *s*. *Educ*: Handsworth Grammar Sch.; Brooklyn Tech. Coll.; Bristol Coll. of Commerce; Dept of Internat. Progs, Univ. of London (LLB Hons 1971); Inns of Court Sch. of Law; Grad. Sch. of Business, Columbia Univ. (Sen. Exec. Prog. 1995). Called to the Bar, Inner Temple, 1972; Lectr in Law, Leicester Poly., 1972–74; Sen. Lectr in Law, Nottingham Law Sch., 1974–76 and 1977–78; Co. Legal Officer, Alfred Herbert Ltd, 1978–80; GKN plc: Co. Lawyer, 1980–83; Dep. Hd, 1983–86, Hd, 1986–95, Legal Dept; Sec. and Gp Dir, Legal and Compliance, 1996–2009; Dir, GKN Gp Services Ltd, 1995–2009 (Chm., 1995–97); Director: GKN (UK) plc, 1996–2009; GKN Hldgs plc, 2001–09; President: GKN N America Inc., 1996–2001; GKN America Corp., 2001–09; Dir, Westland Gp, 2001–09. Chm., Primary Mkts Gp, London Stock Exchange, 2000–04 (Member: Regl Adv. Gp, 1996–2000; Exchange Mkts Gp, 2000–04). Non-exec. Dir, Competition Commn, 2009–14. Non-executive Director: Charter plc, 2005–08; Charter Internat. Plc, 2008–12 (Sen. Ind. Dir, 2009–12). Confederation of British Industry: Chm., W Midlands and Oxon, 2005–07 (Vice Chm., 2004–05 and 2007–08); Member: W Midlands Regl Council, 1996–2009; Chm.'s Cttee, 2005–07. Member: Legal Cttee, SMMT, 1985–95; Council, Birmingham Chamber of Commerce, 1996–2009. Chm., GKN Charitable Appeals Cttee, 1998–2009. Trustee, Univ. of London Convocation Trust, 2017–. Gov. Mem., RNLI, 1988–. FRSA 1992. *Recreations*: Warwickshire County Cricket Club, ornithology, wildlife photography, ballet. *E*: greydenham@aol.com.

**DENHAM, (John Martin) Giles,** CBE 2004; Director of Strategic Relationships, Health Education England, since 2016; *b* 13 Feb. 1959; *s* of late Ernest William Denham and Penelope Agatha Denham; *m* 1986, Heather Gillian Yarker; three *d*. *Educ*: Merchant Taylors' Sch., Northwood; Christ Church, Oxford (MA 1981). Various Civil Service appts, DHSS, HM Treasury and DoH, 1981–90; Gen. Manager, Eastman Dental Hosp., 1990–95; Branch Head, Dentistry, Community Pharmacy, Optometry and Community Care, 1995–2001, Hd of Policy, Children, Older People and Social Care, 2001–03, DoH; Dir,

Civil Affairs, Coalition Provl Authy, Iraq, 2004; Dir of Policy, HSE, 2005–09; Dir of Medicines, Pharmacy and Industry Gp, 2009–14, Dir of Workforce, 2014–16, DoH. Trustee: Marie Curie Cancer Care, 1991–2000; Kepplewray Trust, 2001–19. Churchwarden, Emmanuel Church, Northwood, 2018–. *Recreations:* tennis, playing squash with friends. *Address:* Health Education England, Stewart House, 32 Russell Square, WC1B 5DN. *T:* (020) 7125 7265. *Clubs:* Athenæum; Eastcote Lawn Tennis.

**DENHAM, Rt Hon. John (Yorke);** PC 2000; Visiting Professor, and Director, Centre for English Identity and Politics, University of Winchester, since 2015; *b* 15 July 1953; *s* of Albert Edward Denham and Beryl Frances Ada Denham; *m* 1979, Ruth Eleanore Dixon (marr. diss.); one *s* one *d*; *m* 2015, Susan Jane Littlemore; one *s*. *Educ:* Woodroffe Comprehensive Sch., Lyme Regis; Univ. of Southampton (BSc Hons Chemistry; Pres., Students' Union, 1976–77). Advr, Energy Advice Service, Durham, 1977; Transport Campaigner, Friends of the Earth, 1977–79; Head, Youth Affairs, British Youth Council, 1979–82; Publications Sec., Clause IV Publications, 1982–84; Campaigns Officer, War on Want, 1984–88; Consultant to develt NGOs, 1988–92. Member (Lab): Hants CC, 1981–89; Southampton CC, 1989–93 (Chm., Housing Cttee, 1990–92). Contested (Lab) Southampton, Itchen, 1983, 1987. MP (Lab) Southampton, Itchen, 1992–2015. Parly Under-Sec. of State, DSS, 1997–98; Minister of State, 1998; Dept of Health, 1998–2001; Home Office, 2001–03; Secretary of State: for Innovation, Univs and Skills, 2007–09; for Communities and Local Govt, 2009–10; Shadow Sec. of State for Communities and Local Govt, 2010, for Business, Innovation and Skills, 2010–11; PPS to Leader of Opposition, 2011–13. Chm., Select Cttee on Home Affairs, 2003–07. Chm., Culture Southampton, 2015–16. Vis. Prof., LSE, 2016–. *Address:* Centre for English Identity and Politics, University of Winchester, Sparkford Road, Winchester SO22 4NR.

**DENHAM, Pamela Anne,** CB 1997; DL; PhD; management consultant, since 1998; Regional Director, Government Office for the North East, 1994–98; *b* 1 May 1943; *d* of late Matthew Gray Dobson and Jane (*née* Carter); *m* 1965, Paul Denham (marr. diss. 1980); partner, Brian Murray (*d* 1993). *Educ:* Central Newcastle High Sch.; King's Coll., Univ. of London (BSc 1964; PhD 1969). Asst Principal, Ministry of Technol., 1967–72; Department of Trade and Industry: Principal, 1972–79; Asst Sec., 1979–85; Under Sec., 1985–89; Under Sec., Cabinet Office (Office of Minister for CS), 1989–90; Regl Dir, DTI NE, 1990–94. Non-executive Director: Mono Pumps and Saunders Valve, 1982–85; Newcastle Primary Care Trust, 2001–13. Member: Governing Body, Sunderland Univ., 1993, 1998–2007; Local Governing Body, Central Newcastle High Sch., 1992–2006 (Chair, 2001–06); Trustee, Univ. of Sunderland Develt Trust, 1999–2008. Chair, Project North East, 1998–2009; Mem. Bd, Community Foundn serving Tyne & Wear and Northumberland, 2001–07. Trustee: Age UK (formerly Age Concern), Newcastle, 2000–16 (Chm., 2011–16); Age Concern England, 2002–05. FRSA. DL Tyne and Wear, 2000. Hon. LLD Sunderland, 1994. *Publications:* papers in scientific jls. *Recreations:* travel, reading, walking, cooking. *Address:* 43 Lindisfarne Close, Jesmond, Newcastle upon Tyne NE2 2HT. *T:* (0191) 212 0390.

**DENHAM, Susan Gageby;** Chief Justice of Ireland, 2011–17; *b* 22 Aug. 1945; *d* of late Douglas Gageby and Dorothy Mary Gageby (*née* Lester); *m* 1970, Brian Denham; three *s* one *d* (and one *s* decd). *Educ:* Trinity Coll. Dublin (BA (Mod.), LLB); Columbia Univ., NY (LLM); King's Inns, Dublin. Called to the Irish Bar, 1971, Bencher, King's Inns, 1991; in practice on Midland Circuit, 1971–87; SC, called to Inner Bar, 1987; Judge of High Court, 1991–92; Judge, Supreme Court of Ireland, 1992–2011. Chair: Working Gp on Courts Commn, 1995–98; Family Law Develt Cttee, 1999–2001; Finance Cttee, 2001–04; Cttee on Court Practice and Procedure, 2000–17; Courts Service Bd, 2001–04, 2011–17 (Mem., Interim Bd and Courts Service Bd, 1999–2001; Chair, Interim Judicial Council, 2011–17); Wkg Gp on a Court of Appeal, 2007–09; ISC Steering Cttee to plan for system of inf. on sentencing, 2005–17. Founding Mem., Eur. Network of Councils for the Judiciary, 2004 (Mem., Steering Cttee, 2004–07); Pres., Network of Presidents of Supreme Judicial Courts of EU, 2015–16 (Vice-Pres., 2011–15). Chair, Courts Centenary Commemoration Cttee, 2013–17. Trustee, Holocaust Educn Trust Ireland, 2011–17. MRIA 2013. Hon. Sec., Cttee on Judicial Conduct and Ethics, 1999–2002. Pro-Chancellor, Dublin Univ., 1995–2010. Gov., Marsh's Liby, Dublin, 2017–. Dist. Fellow, Griffith Coll. Dublin, 2013. Hon. Bencher, Middle Temple, 2005. Hon. LLD: QUB, 2002; Ulster, 2013; UCD, 2014; Hon. DPhil Dublin City, 2014. Hon. Fellow and James Joyce Award, Literary and Historical Soc., UCD, 2017. The Denham Fellowship, 2017–. *Recreations:* gardens, horses, reading.

**DENING, Geraldine Rachel;** Co-Director, Architects for Social Housing, since 2015; *b* Winchester, 1975; *d* of Richard and Penelope Dening. *Educ:* Newnham Coll., Cambridge (BA Hons Arch. (Pt 1) 1997); University Coll. London (Grad. DipArch (Pt 2) 2001); Westminster Univ. (Postgrad. Dip. Professional Practice in Arch. (Pt 3) (Dist.) 2009). Mem., ARB, 2009; Architect, Geraldine Dening Architects, 2010–. Sen. Lectr, Leicester Sch. of Architecture, De Montfort Univ., 2009–. Mem., Bd of Trustees, SPID Th., 2013–18. *Publications:* contrib. articles to City, Architecture and Culture. *Recreations:* walking, wild swimming, drawing, skateboarding, geopoetry. *Address:* 40 Fairford House, Cotton Gardens Estate, Kennington Lane, Kennington, SE11 4HW. *T:* (020) 7735 5000. *E:* info@architectsforsocialhousing.co.uk.

**DE NIRO, Robert;** actor and producer; *b* NYC, 17 Aug. 1943; *s* of late Robert De Niro and of Virginia Admiral; *m* 1st, 1976, Diahnne Abbott (marr. diss. 1988); one *s*, and one adopted *d*; 2nd, 1997, Grace Hightower (marr. diss. 1999; remarried 2004); one *s* one *d*; twin *s* by Toukie Smith. *Educ:* Rhodes Sch., NY; High Sch. of Music and Art, NY. Co-founder and Pres., Tribeca Prodns 1989–. Chm. Jury, Cannes Film Fest., 2011. Co-creator, We Will Rock You (musical), 2002. *Films include:* The Wedding Party, 1969; Jennifer on my Mind, Bloody Mama, Born to Win, The Gang That Couldn't Shoot Straight, 1971; Bang the Drum Slowly, Mean Streets, 1973; The Godfather Part II, 1974 (Acad. Award for best supporting actor, 1975); The Last Tycoon, Taxi Driver, 1976; 1900, New York, New York, 1977; The Deer Hunter, 1978; Raging Bull (Acad. Award for best actor), 1980; True Confessions, 1981; The King of Comedy, 1983; Once Upon a Time in America, Falling in Love, 1984; Brazil, 1985; The Mission, 1986; Angel Heart, The Untouchables, 1987; Midnight Run, Letters Home from Vietnam, 1988; Jacknife, We're No Angels (also prod.), 1989; Stanley and Iris, Goodfellas, Awakenings, Fear No Evil, 1990; Guilty by Suspicion, Backdraft, Cape Fear, 1991; Mad Dog and Glory, Night and the City, Mistress (also co-prod.), 1992; This Boy's Life, A Bronx Tale (also dir and co-prod.), 1993; Mary Shelley's Frankenstein, 1994; Casino, Heat, 1995; The Fan, Sleepers, Marvin's Room (also prod.), 1996; Cop Land, Jackie Brown, Wag the Dog (also prod.), 1997; Great Expectations, Ronin, 1998; Analyse This, 1999; Flawless (also prod.), Meet the Parents (also prod.), 2000; The Adventures of Rocky and Bullwinkle (also prod.), Men of Honour, 15 Minutes (also prod.), The Score, 2001; Showtime, City By the Sea, 2002; Analyse That, Godsend, 2003; Meet the Fockers (also prod.), Hide and Seek, 2005; The Good Shepherd (also dir), Stardust, 2007; What Just Happened?, Righteous Kill, 2008; Everybody's Fine, Machete, Little Fockers (also prod.), 2010; Silver Linings Playbook, 2012; The Big Wedding, The Family, 2013; Grudge Match, 2014; The Intern, Joy, 2015; Dirty Grandpa, 2016; The Wizard of Lies (also prod.), 2017; The Irishman (also prod.), Joker, 2019; *producer:* Thunderheart, 1992; Entropy, 1999; Conjugating Niki, 2000; Prison Song, About a Boy, 2001; Stage Beauty, 2004. Appearance in TV documentary, Remembering the Artist: Robert De Niro, Sr, 2014. Cecil B. DeMille Award for Lifetime Achievement, Golden Globe Awards, 2011; Presidential Medal of Freedom (USA), 2016. *Address:* c/o CAA, 2000 Avenue of the Stars, Los Angeles, CA 90067, USA; Tribeca Productions, 375 Greenwich Street, New York, NY 10013, USA.

**DENISON,** family name of **Baron Londesborough**.

**DENISON, Prof. David Michael Benjamin,** DPhil; FBA 2014; Smith Professor of English Language and Medieval Literature, University of Manchester, 2008–15, now Emeritus; *b* London, 6 Sept. 1950; *s* of William David Denison (formerly Wilhelm David Deutsch) and Celia Denison (*née* Cissie Shusman); *m* 1975, Elizabeth Ann Price; two *d*. *Educ:* Highgate Sch., London; St John's Coll., Cambridge (BA 1973); Lincoln Coll., Oxford (DPhil 1981). University of Manchester: Lectr, 1976–93; Sen. Lectr in English Lang., 1993–95; Prof. of English Linguistics, 1995–2008, now Emeritus. Vis. Lectr, Univ. of Amsterdam, 1985–86; Visiting Professor: Univ. of BC, 1992; Univ. of Santiago de Compostela, 1998; Univ. Sorbonne Nouvelle, Paris, 2006; Aichi Prefectural Univ., 2016–17. Hon. PhD Uppsala, 2014. *Publications:* English Historical Syntax, 1993; Syntax 1776–1997, 1998; (ed jtly) Generative Theory and Corpus Studies, 2000; (ed jtly) Fuzzy Grammar, 2004; (ed jtly) A History of the English Language, 2006; (ed jtly) Analysing Older English, 2012; (ed jtly) Morphosyntactic Categories and the Expression of Possession, 2013; contrib. book chapters, jl articles and linguistic corpora. *Recreations:* cinema, music, being abroad. *Address:* School of Languages, Linguistics and Cultures, University of Manchester, Samuel Alexander Building, Oxford Road, Manchester M13 9PL. *E:* david.denison@manchester.ac.uk.

**DENISON, Simon Neil;** QC 2009; a Recorder, since 2018; *b* Dar-es-Salaam, 28 Dec. 1961; *s* of His Honour (William) Neil Denison, QC and Philippa Jean Denison (*née* Wilkinson; later Napier); *m* 1991, Victoria Mary Wright; two *s* one *d*. *Educ:* St Catharine's Coll., Cambridge (BA Hons Law 1983). Called to the Bar, Lincoln's Inn, 1984; in practice as barrister, 1984– ; Jun. Treasury Counsel, 2001–07; Sen. Treasury Counsel, 2007–14. *Recreations:* football, Rugby, ski-ing, golf, boating. *Address:* 6KBW, 21 College Hill, EC4R 2RP. *T:* (020) 3310 0910, *Fax:* (020) 3310 0911. *E:* simon.denison@6kbw.com. *Club:* Garrick.

**DENISON-PENDER,** family name of **Baron Pender**.

**DENISON-SMITH, Lt-Gen. Sir Anthony (Arthur),** KBE 1995 (MBE 1973); DL; Lieutenant, HM Tower of London, 1998–2001; *b* 24 Jan. 1942; *s* of late George Denison-Smith and Dorothy Gwendolin Phillips; *m* 1966, Julia Henrietta Scott; three *s*. *Educ:* Harrow; RMA, Sandhurst. Commissioned Grenadier Guards, 1962; Staff Coll., 1974; Brigade Major, 7th Armoured Brigade, 1977–79; Directing Staff, Staff Coll., 1979–81; CO 2nd Bn Grenadier Guards, 1981–83; Chief of Staff, 4th Armoured Div., 1983–85; Comdr, 22nd Armoured Brigade, 1985–87; Chief of Staff, 1 (BR) Corps, 1987–89; Dir Gen. Trng and Doctrine (Army), 1990–91; Comdr, 4th Armoured Div., 1991–93; Comdr, 1st (UK) Armoured Div., 1993–94; GOC Southern Dist, 1994–95; GOC 4th Div., 1995–96. Col, Princess of Wales's Royal Regt (Queen's and Royal Hampshires), 1992–99. Chm., ACFA, 1996–2001; President: Essex Br., Grenadier Guards Assoc., 1998–; Essex ABF The Soldiers' Charity (formerly Army Benevolent Fund), 2008–14. Hon. Col, Essex ACF, 2002–07. Consultant, Rave Technologies Ltd (formerly Karnataka Gp Ltd), 1996–. DL Essex, 2001. Comdr (1st cl.), Order of the Dannebrog (Denmark), 1996. *Recreation:* family and friends. *Address:* Cranford, Bran End, Stebbing, Dunmow, Essex CM6 3RX. *Clubs:* Cavalry and Guards; MCC; I Zingari, Free Foresters, Essex.

**DENMAN,** family name of **Baron Denman**.

**DENMAN, 6th Baron** *cr* 1834; **Richard Thomas Stewart Denman;** Bt 1945; *b* 4 Oct. 1946; *e s* of 5th Baron Denman, CBE, MC, TD and Sheila Anne (*née* Stewart); *S* father, 2012; *m* 1984, (Lesley) Jane, *d* of John Stevens; one *s* three *d*. *Educ:* Milton Abbey. *Heir: s* Hon. Robert Joseph Denman, *b* 19 Dec. 1995.

**DENNAY, Charles William,** CEng; Consultant, Quantel Ltd, 1993–2001; *b* 13 May 1935; *s* of Charles Dennay and Elsie May Smith; *m* 1955, Shirley Patricia Johnston; one *s*. *Educ:* Humberston Foundation Sch.; Borough Polytechnic. DipEE, MIERE. Scientific Asst (Govt), 1953; Technician, BBC, 1956; Transmitter Engineer, 1958; Asst Lectr/Lectr, 1961; Head of Ops Transmitters, 1973; Head of Engrg Transmitter Ops, 1976; Asst Chief Engineer, Transmitters, 1978; Chief Engineer, External Broadcasting, 1979; Controller, Ops and Engineering Radio, 1984; Asst Dir of Engineering, 1985; Dir of Engineering, 1987; Man. Dir, Resources Engrg and Services, 1993, retd. Director: Brighton Fest. Soc. Ltd, 1996–2000; Brighton Dome & Museum Develt Co. Ltd, 1999–2005. Mem., Steering Bd, Radio Communication Agency, 1996–2003. Vis. Prof., Internat. Acad. of Broadcasting, Montreux, 1994–98. President: IEEIE, 1994–98 (Vice-Pres., 1990–94); IIE, 2001–03. FRTS 1997 (a Vice-Pres., 1989–94); FIIE 1998, Hon. FIIE 2003. FRSA 1993. Hon. FIET; Hon. FBKS 1990. *Recreations:* photography, music, civil aviation. *Address:* Montmore Cottage, 1 Orchard Dean, Alresford, Hants SO24 9DE. *T:* (01962) 735103.

**DENNEN, Ven. Lyle;** Archdeacon of Hackney, 1999–2010; Vicar, St Andrew, Holborn, 1999–2014; *b* 8 Jan. 1942; *s* of Ernest and Rose Dennen; *m* 1977, Xenia Howard-Johnston, *d* of Rear Adm. C. D. Howard-Johnston, CB, DSO, DSC, and Lady Alexandra Haig (who *m* 1954, Hugh Trevor-Roper (later Lord Dacre of Glanton)); two *s*. *Educ:* Trinity Coll., Cambridge (BA 1970, MA 1975); Harvard Law Sch. (DJur); Harvard Univ. (PhD); Cuddesdon Coll., Oxford. Ordained deacon, 1972, priest, 1973; Curate, St Anne, S Lambeth, Southwark, 1972–75; Curate in charge, St Matthias, Richmond, 1975–78; Vicar, St John the Divine, Kennington, 1978–99; RD of Brixton, 1988–99; Permission to Officiate, Dio. London, 2014–. Hon. Canon, Southwark Cathedral, 1999. Chairman of Governors: St John the Divine Primary Sch., 1978–99; Charles Edward Brooke Secondary Sch., 1978–99; Chm., Lambeth WelCare, 1978–99. Chairman: London Cttee, Southwark & London Diocesan Housing Assoc., 1999–; Alexander Stafford Trust, 1999–; Trustee: St Gabriel's Coll. Trust, 1978–99; Bromfield Educnl Charity, 1999–2014; Lady Elizabeth Hatton Charity, 1999–2014; Lady Neville Charity, 1999–2014; St Andrew Holborn Ch Foundn, 1999–2014; St Andrew Holborn Parish Estates Charity, 1999–2014; St Andrew Holborn Charity, 2002–14. *Recreation:* sailing. *Address:* Flat 1, Victoria Wharf, 46 Narrow Street, E14 8DD. *T:* (020) 7353 3544, *Fax:* (020) 7583 2750. *Clubs:* Athenæum; Harlequins Supporters.

**DENNER, Dr (William) Howard (Butler);** freelance photographer, especially of pop, blues and jazz musicians, since 1996; *b* 14 May 1944; *s* of late William Ormonde Ralph Denner and Violet Evelyn Arscott; *m* 1st, 1966, Gwenda Williams (*d* 2008); two *d*; 2nd, 2014, Judith Dynes. *Educ:* Cyfarthfa Castle Grammar School, Merthyr Tydfil; UCW Cardiff (BSc, PhD Biochem.). Research Associate: Miami Univ., 1968; Cardiff Univ., 1969; Ministry of Agriculture, Fisheries and Food, 1972–96: Secretary: Food Additives and Contaminants Cttee, 1974–84; Cttee on Toxicity of Chemicals in Food, Consumer Products and the Environment, 1978–84; Mem., Jt FAO/WHO Expert Cttee on Food Additives, 1978–85; Head of Food Composition and Information Unit, 1984; Chm., Codex Cttee on Fats and Oils, 1987–92; Assessor, Adv. Cttees on Novel Foods and Processes and on Genetic Modification, 1985–92; Head of Food Sci. Div. II, 1989; Chief

Scientist (Food), 1992–96. Lectr and Judge, E Anglia Fedn of Photographic Alliance of GB, 1978–88; Judge, Essex Internat. Salon of Photography, 1987–88. One-man exhibition of photographs: Half Moon Gall., 1974; Anteros Gall., Norwich, 2018; individual photographs in internat. exhibns, newspapers, jls and books. AFIAP 1972. *Publications:* papers on food safety in learned jls. *Recreations:* photography, golf. *Address:* 29 Pineheath Road, High Kelling, Holt, Norfolk NR25 6QF. *T:* (01263) 713495. *E:* howard@howarddenner.com.

**DENNEY, Anna Louise;** *see* Bancroft, A. L.

**DENNEY, Stuart Henry MacDonald;** QC 2008; *b* Welwyn, Herts, 15 June 1959; *s* of late Robert Waterson Denney and of Jane Denney (*née* Kemp); *m* 1988, Anna Louise Bancroft, *qv;* one *s. Educ:* Gonville & Caius Coll., Cambridge (BA 1980). Called to the Bar, Inner Temple, 1982, Bencher, 2015; in practice as a barrister, specialising in criminal and regulatory law. *Recreation:* Rugby Union. *Address:* Deans Court Chambers, 24 St John Street, Manchester M3 4DF. *T:* (0161) 214 6000, *Fax:* (0161) 214 6001. *E:* clerks@deanscourt.co.uk; Thomas More Chambers, 7 Lincoln's Inn Fields, WC2A 3BP. *T:* (020) 7404 7000. *Club:* London Scottish Football.

**DENNING, Prof. David Wemyss,** FRCP, FRCPath; FMedSci; Professor of Infectious Disease in Global Health, University of Manchester, since 2013; *b* Gosport, 18 May 1957; *s* of Basil Wemyss Denning and Antoinette Carter Denning (*née* Gossett); *m* 1984, Merian Llewelyn Roberts; three *s. Educ:* St Paul's Sch., London; Guy's Hosp. Med. Sch., Univ. of London (LMSSA 1980; MB BS 1980; DCH 1984). FRCP 1995; FRCPath 1997. Postgrad. trng, London, Glasgow and Stanford Univ.; Clin. Res. Fellow, Infectious Diseases and Microbiol., Stanford Univ., 1987–90; Sen. Lectr in Infectious Disease, 1990–2005, Prof. of Medicine and Med. Mycology, 2005–13, Univ. of Manchester. Founder and Director: F2G Ltd, 1998, Consultant, 2004–12; Myconostica Ltd, 2006–11. Director: Nat. Aspergillosis Centre, 2009–; Leading Internat. Fungal Education, 2012–; Founder and Pres., Global Action Fund for Fungal Infections, 2013–. Ed., Aspergillus website, 1998–. Consultant to pharmaceutical cos incl. Pfizer, Merck, Gilead and Astellas. Scientific Advr, Fungal Infection Trust (formerly Fungal Res. Trust), 1991–. FMedSci 2010. Fellow, Eur. Confedn of Med. Mycology, 2017. *Publications:* (jtly) Medicine, 1997, 3rd edn 2008; (contrib.) Harrison's Principles of Internal Medicine, 18th edn 2011, 20th edn 2018; (contrib.) Goldman-Cecil Medicine, 26th edn 2019; contribs to over 500 learned jls on infectious diseases, AIDS, fungal infections, asthma, fungal diagnostics and treatment of fungal disease. *Recreations:* ski-ing, socialising with friends, hill-walking. *Address:* Education and Research Centre, Wythenshawe Hospital, Southmoor Road, Manchester M23 9LT. *T:* (0161) 291 5353, *Fax:* (0161) 291 5806. *E:* ddenning@manchester.ac.uk.

**DENNIS, Maj.-Gen. Alastair Wesley,** CB 1985; OBE 1973; *b* 30 Aug. 1931; *s* of late Ralph Dennis and of Helen (*née* Henderson); *m* 1st, 1957, Susan Lindy Elgar (*d* 1998); one *s* two *d;* 2nd, 2000, Caroline Brenda Dowdall. *Educ:* Malvern Coll.; RMA, Sandhurst. Commanded 16th/5th The Queen's Royal Lancers, 1971–74; Col GS, Cabinet Office, 1974–75; Comd 20 Armoured Bde, 1976–77; Dep. Comdt, Staff Coll., 1978–80; Director of Defence Policy (B), MoD, Whitehall, 1980–82; Dir, Military Assistance Overseas, MoD, 1982–85. Sec., Imperial Cancer Res. Fund, 1985–91; Chm., Assoc. of Med. Res. Charities, 1987–91. Mem., Malvern Coll. Council, 1988–92. Col, 16th/5th The Queen's Royal Lancers, 1990–93, The Queen's Royal Lancers, 1993–95. *Recreations:* fishing, golf, gardening. *Address:* St Maur, Long Street, Sherborne, Dorset DT9 3BS.

**DENNIS, Colin,** CBE 2009; PhD; DL; Director-General, Campden BRI (formerly Campden Food and Drink Research Association, then Campden & Chorleywood Food Research Association), 1988–2009, now Hon. Member; adviser to UK government and food industry, since 2009; *b* Boston, Lincs, 10 May 1946; *s* of George Henry Dennis and Jane Dennis (*née* Simpson); *m* 1968, Susan Day; one *s* one *d. Educ:* Sheffield Univ. (BSc 1st Cl. Hons 1967; Boswell Meml Prize, Lindsey Educn Prize; PhD 1970). FIFST 1982; CSci 2004. Certified Food Scientist, 2013. Hd, Mycology Section, ARC Food Res. Inst., 1970–81; Hd, Food Technol. Div., Campden Food and Drink Res. Assoc., 1981–88. Hon. Lectr, UEA, 1971–76; Vis. Scientist, Norwegian Food Res. Inst., 1981; Unilever Vis. Prof., QUB, 1991–2006; Hon. Prof., Univ. of Birmingham, 1993–2009; Royal Agricultural University (formerly College): Vis. Prof., 2007–16; Shareholder, 2009–; Gov. (formerly Mem. Bd), 2009–16; Pension Trustee, 2011–13; Mem., Audit and Risk Cttee (formerly Audit Cttee), 2015–. Non-exec. Dir, UK Accreditation Service, 1998–2009. Assessor, Knowledge Transfer Partnerships, Innovate UK (formerly Technol. Strategy Bd), 2001–; Member: Food Directorate Mgt Cttee, BBSRC, 1994–96; Food and Drink Foresight Panel, OST, 1994–98; Sustainable Food and Farming Res. Priorities Gp, DEFRA, 2003–06; Bioscis for Industry Panel, 2005–08, Modular Trng for Industry Panel, 2006–08, BBSRC; Gen. Adv. Cttee on Sci., Food Standards Agency, 2012–17; Chairman: Agric. Sector Adv. Gp, UK Trade and Investment, 2005–08; Industry Adv. Gp, Internat. Agri-Technology Centre, 2009–11; English Food and Drink Alliance, 2010–13; Exec. Bd, Agrifood Trng Partnership, 2017–. Member Board: Glos Develt Agency, 2001–11 (Vice Chm., 2007–11); SW Food and Drink, 2002–10; Countryside and Community Res. Inst., 2007–; Nat. Skills Acad. for Food and Drink, 2008–; Internat. Food Information Service, 2009– (Chm., Bd of Trustees, 2013–); Inst. of Food Technologists, 2010–17; British Nutrition Foundn, 2012– (Vice Chm., Bd of Trustees, 2016–18; Chm., 2018–); Pres., Inst. of Food Sci. and Technol., 2011–13 (Mem., Membership Assessment Panel, 2017–). Member: World Food Prize Selection Cttee, 1996–2002; Food Safety Adv. Council, Maple Leaf Foods Inc., 2010–14; Adv. Bd, Internat. Food Network Inc., 2011–15; Scientific Adv. Bd, Flanders Food, 2011– (Chm., 2012–17); S African Assoc. of Food Sci. and Technol., 2015–. Mem. Bd, Friends of the Cotswolds, 2007–10. Mem. Court, Hon. Co. of Glos., 2012– (Warden, 2014–15). Fellow: Inst. of Food Sci. and Technol., 1982; Inst. of Food Technologists, 2001 (Pres., 2015–16); Internat. Acad. of Food Sci. and Technol., 2001; Hon. Mem., Soc. of Applied Microbiol., 2006 (Denver Meml Lectr, 2014); Life Mem., Phi Tau Sigma Honor Soc., 2015. Hon. FRAgS 2010. FRSA 2000. DL Glos 2005. Myron Solberg Award, Inst. of Food Technol., USA, 2011; Hon. Fellowship Award, Inst. of Food Sci. and Technol., 2017. *Publications:* (ed jtly) Opportunities for Improving Crop Yields, 1980; (ed) Post-Harvest Pathology of Fruits and Vegetables, 1983; (ed jtly) Vegetable Processing, 1990; (ed jtly) Chilled Foods: a comprehensive guide, 1992, 2nd edn 2000. *Recreations:* gardening, golf, volunteer work, travel. *Address:* The Hill Farm, Hurdlers Lane, Ilmington, Warwickshire CV36 4PT. *T:* (01608) 682585, 07976 956468. *E:* cnsdennis@btinternet.com.

**DENNIS, Geoffrey Adrian;** Chief Executive Officer, Society for the Protection of Animals Abroad, since 2017; *b* 15 Aug. 1951; *s* of Clive Gardner Dennis and Audrey Joan Dennis; *m* 1998, Joanna Mary Snook; one *s. Educ:* Enfield Coll. (BA Hons); Univ. of Sussex (MA 1976). Main Bd Dir, Ewbank Preece Consultants, 1979–90; Man. Dir, Travers Morgan Consultants (Environmental), 1990–92; Internat. Dir, British Red Cross, and Hd of Delegn, Dem. People's Rep. of Korea, Internat. Fedn of the Red Cross, 1992–98; Hd of Regl Delegn, S Asia, Internat. Fedn of the Red Cross, 1998–2000; Chief Executive Officer: Friends of the Elderly, 2000–04; CARE Internat. UK, 2004–14; Royal Nat. Children's Foundn, 2014–16. Mem. Global Bd, and Mem. Exec. Cttee, CARE Internat. Worldwide, 2006–14. Chm., Rocking Horse Appeal (volunteer), 2004–09. Badge of Honour, British Red Cross, 1998. *Recreations:* hockey (Sussex County 1st Eleven, Brighton Hockey Club), squash, travel. *Address:* Cuckfield, Sussex.

**DENNIS, Hugh;** *see* Dennis, P. H.

**DENNIS, Rt Rev. John;** Bishop of St Edmundsbury and Ipswich, 1986–96; an Hon. Assistant Bishop, Diocese of Winchester, since 1999; *b* 19 June 1931; *s* of late Hubert Ronald and Evelyn Dennis; *m* 1956, Dorothy Mary (*née* Hinnels); two *s. Educ:* Rutlish School, Merton; St Catharine's Coll., Cambridge (BA 1954; MA 1959); Cuddesdon Coll., Oxford (1954–56). RAF, 1950–51. Curate, St Bartholomew's, Armley, Leeds, 1956–60; Curate of Kettering, 1960–62; Vicar of the Isle of Dogs, 1962–71; Vicar of John Keble, Mill Hill, 1971–79; Area Dean of West Barnet, 1973–79; Prebendary of St Paul's Cathedral, 1977–79; Bishop Suffragan of Knaresborough, 1979–86; Diocesan Dir of Ordinands, Dio. Ripon, 1980–86; Asst Bp, Ely, 1996–99. Episcopal Guardian of Anglican Focolarini, 1981–96; Chaplain to Franciscan Third Order, 1988–94. Co-Chairman: English ARC, 1988–92; Anglican-Oriental Orthodox Dialogue, 1989–95. *Recreations:* walking, wood working, family. *Address:* 7 Conifer Close, Winchester, Hants SO22 6SH. *E:* 7johndennis@gmail.com.
*See also* J. D. Dennis, P. H. Dennis.

**DENNIS, John David;** HM Diplomatic Service; Ambassador to Angola and concurrently to São Tomé and Príncipe, 2014–18; *b* 6 Aug. 1959; *s* of Rt Rev. John Dennis, *qv;* m 1989, Jillian Kemp; two *s. Educ:* Haberdashers' Aske's Sch., Elstree; St Catharine's Coll., Cambridge (BA Hons 1981). Entered FCO, 1981; Hong Kong, 1983–85; Peking, 1985–87; Hd, Political Section, Kuala Lumpur, 1992–96; on secondment to Standard Chartered Bank, 1997–98; Dir, Automotive, DTI, 1998–2001; Dir, Trade and Investment Promotion, New Delhi, 2001–03; Minister, Consul-Gen. and Dep. Head of Mission, Beijing, 2003–06; Additional Dir, Asia, FCO, 2006–08; Hd of Zimbabwe Unit, FCO, 2009–10; Hd of Africa Dept (South Central and Western), FCO, 2010–13. *Recreations:* my children, reading, creative writing. *Address:* Foreign and Commonwealth Office, King Charles Street, SW1A 2AH. *E:* jjdennis@btinternet.com.
*See also* P. H. Dennis.

**DENNIS, Mark Jonathan;** QC 2006; **His Honour Judge Mark Dennis;** a Circuit Judge, since 2016; a Senior Circuit Judge, since 2018; *b* 15 March 1955; *s* of Edward John Dennis and Patricia Edna Dennis; *m* 1985, Christabel Birbeck; one *s* one *d. Educ:* Battersea Grammar Sch.; Peterhouse, Cambridge (BA Hons Law; MA). Called to the Bar, Middle Temple, 1977; Jun. Treasury Counsel, Central Criminal Court, 1993–98; Sen. Treasury Counsel, Central Criminal Court, 1998–2006; a Recorder, 2000–16. *Club:* Reform.

**DENNIS, (Peter) Hugh;** actor, comedian and writer; *b* Kettering, 13 Feb. 1962; *s* of Rt Rev. John Dennis, *qv;* m 1996, Kate Abbot Anderson (marr. diss. 2018); one *s* one *d. Educ:* University Coll. Sch., Hampstead; St John's Coll., Cambridge (BA 1984). Actor and comedian: *television:* Carrott Confidential, 1987–89; Canned Carrott, 1990–92; The Mary Whitehouse Experience, 1991–92; The Imaginatively Titled Punt & Dennis Show, 1994–95; My Hero, 2000–06; Mock the Week, 2005–; Outnumbered, 2007–14; The Great British Countryside, 2012; Ballot Monkeys, 2015; Not Going Out, 2015–; Fleabag, 2016, 2019; *radio:* The Now Show, 1998–; It's Been a Bad Week, 1999–2006; Quiz Nite! (also co-writer), 2019; *theatre:* The Messiah, Richmond Th., The Other Palace, 2018. Punt and Dennis UK tour, 2011; Punt and Dennis: Ploughing on Regardless (UK tour), 2014. Mem., BAFTA. FRGS 2010. *Publications:* (jtly) The Mary Whitehouse Experience Encyclopedia, 1991; (with S. Punt) The Punt & Dennis Instant Library, 1993; The Now Show Book, 2010; Britty Britty Bang Bang, 2013. *Recreations:* running, cycling, reading, watching, being nice to my family. *Address:* c/o Independent Talent, 40 Whitfield Street, W1T 2RH. *T:* (020) 7636 6565.
*See also* J. D. Dennis.

**DENNIS, Brig. Richard William,** OBE 2004; Managing Director, Richard Dennis Consultancy Ltd, since 2013; Chief of Staff, Defence People, Ministry of Defence, since 2019; *b* Chelmsford, 18 Aug. 1959; *s* of William Dennis and Elsie Dennis; *m* 1982, Suzannah Mott; four *s. Educ:* Portsmouth Grammar Sch.; RMA Sandhurst; Open Univ. (MBA 1997); Cranfield Univ. Commnd Royal Hampshire Regt, 1978; COS 20 Armoured Bde, 1992–94; CO, 2nd Bn The Princess of Wales's Royal Regt, 1997–99; COS, HQ Theatre Troops, 2001–03; rcds 2004; Comdr 15 (NE) Bde, 2004–08; Dir, Infantry, 2008–11; Dep. Comdr (Army), NATO Trng Mission to Afghanistan, 2012–13. Chair, Service Complaints Panel, 2013–16; STRIKE Experiment Lead, Niteworks Partnership, 2016–17. Chief Operating Officer, Estari Gp, 2019–. Col, The Princess of Wales's Royal Regt, 2010–16. Comdr, 1st Cl., Order of the Dannebrog (Denmark), 2011; Officer, US Legion of Merit, 2017. *Recreations:* family, ski-ing, sailing, golf, shooting, military history, cooking. *Address:* Regimental Headquarters, The Princess of Wales's Royal Regiment, HM Tower of London, EC3N 4AB. *T:* (020) 3166 6917. *E:* rhq@123pwrr.co.uk. *Club:* Naval and Military.

**DENNIS, Ronald,** CBE 2000; Chairman and Chief Executive, McLaren Technology Group Ltd (formerly McLaren Group), 1984–2017; Chairman, McLaren Automotive, 2009–17; British Business Ambassador for the UK, since 2010; Global Consultant, Minsheng Investment Corporation, since 2015; *b* 1 June 1947; *s* of late Norman Stanley Dennis and of Evelyn (*née* Reader); *m* 1985, Lisa Ann Shelton (marr. diss. 2011); one *s* two *d. Educ:* Guildford Technical Coll. (vehicle technology course). Mechanic, Cooper Racing Car Co.; Chief Mechanic, Brabham Racing Orgn; Founder, Rondel Racing; Owner/Manager, Project Four Racing, 1976–80 (winners: Procar Championship, 1979; Formula 3 Championship, 1979–80); merged with McLaren, 1980; McLaren Formula 1 Racing Team (winners: 8 Constructors' Championships; 11 Drivers' Championships). Co-Chair, Defence Innovation Adv. Panel, MoD, 2017–. Founder, Dreamchasing Foundn, 2007. Patron, Tommy's Campaign, 2016–. Gov., Wellington Coll., 2011–. Hon. DTech De Montfort, 1996; Hon. DSc City, 1997; DUniv Surrey, 2000; Hon. DEng Bath, 2013. Gold Medal, British Racing Drivers' Club, 2001; Prince Philip Medal, RAEng 2008; Golden Plate, Acad. of Achievement, 2017. *Recreations:* golf, snow and water ski-ing, diving, shooting. *Club:* British Racing Drivers'.

**DENNIS, Toby Edward Drake;** Lord-Lieutenant of Lincolnshire, since 2015; *b* Lincoln, 18 Sept. 1954; *s* of Richard and Mary Dennis; *m* 1982, Sarah Haggas; twin *s* one *d. Educ:* Heatherdown Prep. Sch.; Harrow Sch.; Royal Agricl Coll., Cirencester. Agriculture, 1976–. High Sheriff, Lincs, 2013–14. Hon. Col, Lincs ACF, 2014–16. CStJ 2018. *Recreations:* shooting, conservation, oenology, Rugby, football, Elton John. *Address:* Rowston Manor, Lincoln LN4 3LT. *T:* 07730487901. *E:* toby.dennis@dennisestates.co.uk. *Clubs:* White's; Lincolnshire; Royal West Norfolk Club, Brancaster.

**DENNISS, John Annear; His Honour Judge Denniss;** a Circuit Judge, since 2009; *b* London, 7 Oct. 1951; *s* of Colin Denniss and Sheila Denniss; *m* 1980, Angela Frances Raisman; one *s* two *d. Educ:* Winchester Coll.; Bristol Univ. (LLB). Called to the Bar, Inner

Temple, 1974; a Recorder, 2002–09. *Recreations:* music, reading, fishing, ski-ing, sailing, gardening. *Address:* Isleworth Crown Court, 36 Ridgeway Road, Isleworth TW7 5LP. *Clubs:* Lansdowne; Royal Cornwall Yacht.

**DENNY, Sir Charles Alistair Maurice,** 4th Bt *cr* 1913, of Dumbarton, co. Dunbarton; Associate Director, HSBC Global Markets, 2006–11 (Associate Director, HSBC Bank, 2004–06); *b* 7 Oct. 1950; *e s* of Sir Alistair Maurice Archibald Denny, 3rd Bt and Elizabeth Hunt, *y d* of Major Sir Guy Lloyd, 1st Bt, DSO; *S* father, 1995; *m* 1st, 1981, Belinda (marr. diss. 2002), *yr d* of J. P. McDonald; one *s* one *d*; 2nd, 2011, Carolyn Hilton, *o d* of late Derek Davis and of Mrs Kathleen Redpath. *Educ:* Wellington Coll.; Edinburgh Univ. *Heir: s* Patrick Charles Alistair Denny, *b* 2 Jan. 1985. *Address:* Winston House, Standish Court, Stonehouse, Glos GL10 3DW. *E:* charlesdenny1950@msn.com.

**DENNY, John Ingram,** CMG 1997; RIBA; Managing Director, Property Consulting Ltd, 2001–05; *b* 28 May 1941; *s* of Thomas Ingram Denny, Macclesfield and Claire Dorothy Denny (*née* Lewis); *m* 1967, Carol Ann Frances, *d* of Walter James Hughes, St Leonards, Bournemouth; one *s* two *d*. *Educ:* Normain Coll., Chester; Northern Poly. (Dip. Arch. (Hons)); Univ. of Reading (MSc). RIBA 1967. Partner, 1970–90, Sen. Partner, 1990–95, Man. Dir, 1995–2001, Cecil Denny Highton, architects and project managers; Jt Man. Dir, HOK Internat., 1995–2001; Sen. Vice Pres., Hellmuth, Obata + Kassabaum Inc., 1995–2001. Involved in architecture, conservation and mgt; Consultant to FCO, Home Office, MoD, Parly Works Office, Royal Household, HM Treasury, Cabinet Office, PACE and Natural Hist. Mus. *Recreations:* golf, photography.

**DENNY, Sir Piers Anthony de Waltham,** 9th Bt *cr* 1782, of Tralee Castle, Co. Kerry, Ireland; *b* 14 March 1954; *s* of Sir Anthony Coningham de Waltham Denny, 8th Bt and Anne Catherine, *e d* of Samuel Beverley, FRIBA; *S* father, 2013; *m* 1987, Ella Jane, *o d* of Peter P. Huhne; two *d*. *Educ:* King Alfred Sch.; Westfield Coll., Univ. of London. *Heir: b* Thomas Francis Coningham Denny [*b* 12 May 1956; *m* 1985, Benita Jane Kevill-Davies; one *d*, and one adopted *s*].

**DENNY, Ross Patrick;** HM Diplomatic Service; Ambassador to Costa Rica and (non-resident) to Nicaragua, since 2015; *b* Southampton, 13 Sept. 1955; *s* of Clifford Charles and Doreen Agnes Denny; *m* 2000, Claudenise De Lima; two *s* two *d*. *Educ:* Eyre Tech. High Sch. Whyalla, SA; Bitterne Park Sch., Southampton. Served RN, 1972–79. Entered FCO, 1979; WI and Atlantic Dept, FCO, 1979–80; Santiago, 1980–83; Doha, 1983–85; Vice Consul, Warsaw, 1985–88; Personnel Dept, 1988–89, S Pacific Dept, 1989–92, FCO; Second Sec., Political and EU Affairs, The Hague, 1992–97; Vice Consul Commercial, São Paulo, 1998–2001; Dep. Hd of Mission, Luanda (and non-resident accredited to São Tomé e Príncipe), 2002–05; Res. Analysts Dept, FCO, 2005–08; Adminr, Ascension Is, 2008–11; Ambassador to Bolivia, 2011–15. *Recreations:* aviation, travel, languages. *Address:* c/o Foreign and Commonwealth Office, King Charles Street, SW1A 2AH; British Embassy, Edificio Centro Colón, Paseo Colón y Calles 38/40, San José, Costa Rica.

**DENNY, William Eric,** CBE 1984; QC 1975; barrister; a Recorder of the Crown Court, 1974–93; *b* 2 Nov. 1927; *s* of William John Denny and Elsie Denny; *m* 1960, Daphne Rose Southern-Reddin; one *s* two *d*. *Educ:* Ormskirk Grammar Sch.; Liverpool Univ. (Pres., Guild of Undergraduates, 1951–52; LLB). Served RAF, 1946–48. Called to the Bar, Gray's Inn, 1953, Bencher, 1985. Lectured at LSE, 1953–58. Chm., Home Secretary's Adv. Bd on Restricted Patients, 1980–85 (Mem., 1979). *Recreations:* music, gardening.

**DENNYS, Nicholas Charles Jonathan;** QC 1991; a Recorder, 2000–12; *b* 14 July 1951; *m* 1977, Frances Winifred Markham (marr. diss. 2001); four *d*. *Educ:* Eton; Brasenose Coll., Oxford (BA 1973). Admitted Middle Temple, 1973; called to the Bar, 1975, Bencher, 2001; Asst Recorder, 1996–2000. Chm. Trustees, China Oxford Scholarship Fund. *Publications:* (ed) Hudson's Building and Engineering Contracts, 12th edn 2011, 13th edn 2015. *Recreations:* windsurfing, golf, music. *Address:* First Floor Ground, 26 Ansdell Terrace, W8 5BY.

**DeNORA, Prof. (Lisabette) Tia,** PhD; FBA 2018; Professor of Sociology of Music, University of Exeter, since 2003; *b* New Jersey, USA, 19 May 1958; *d* of John DeNora and Shirley S. DeNora; *m* 1982, Douglas S. Tudhope. *Educ:* West Chester Univ. (BA); Univ. of Calif, San Diego (MA; PhD 1989). Univ. of Wales Fellow, Univ. of Wales, Cardiff, 1989–91; Univ. of Exeter: Lectr, 1992–95; Sen. Lectr, 1995–2000; Reader, 2000–03. Associate, Nordoff Robbins Music Therapy Centre, London, 2018–. Prof. II (Music Therapy), Univ. of Bergen, 2018–. *Publications:* Beethoven and the Construction of Genius, 1995; Music in Everyday Life, 2000; After Adorno, 2003; Music Asylums, 2013; Making Sense of Reality, 2014; (with G. Ansdell) Musical Pathways in Recovery, 2016. *Recreations:* cold water swimming, walking, formal poetry, music, astronomy (amateur) with reference to Jupiter and Saturn. *Address:* Department of Sociology, Philosophy and Anthropology, College of Social Sciences and International Studies, University of Exeter, Amory Building, Rennes Drive, Exeter EX4 4RJ. *E:* tdenora@exeter.ac.uk.

**DENT, Helen Anne,** CBE 2010; Chief Executive, Family Action (formerly Family Welfare Association), 1996–2013; *b* 29 June 1951; *d* of Frederick and Muriel Dent. *Educ:* Lancaster Univ. (BEd 1977); South Bank Poly. (MSc 1987). London Bor. of Enfield, 1981–86; Cambs CC, 1986–90; NCH, 1990–96. Mem., ESRC, 2003–07. Non-exec. Dir, Gt Ormond St Hosp. for Children NHS Trust, 1998–2008. Trustee, Internet Watch Foundn, 2015–. *Recreations:* music: choral and opera, theatre, cinema, reading, gardening.

**DENT, Kevin Joseph;** QC 2019; *b* Swanley, Kent; *s* of Malcolm Dent and Sheila Dent; *m* 2006, Serife Deveci; one *s* two *d*. *Educ:* Swanley Sch.; Univ. of Sussex (BA Hons Law with Eng. and Amer. Studies). Called to the Bar, Inner Temple, 1991; in practice as a barrister, 2 Paper Bldgs, later 2 Dr Johnson's Bldgs, 1993–2013, 5 St Andrew's Hill, 2013–. *Recreations:* running, photography, poetry, catching the moment. *Address:* 5 St Andrew's Hill, EC4V 5BZ. *T:* (020) 7332 5400, *Fax:* (020) 7489 7847. *E:* kevindent@5sah.co.uk.

**DENT, Teresa Ogilvy,** CBE 2015; Chief Executive Officer, Game and Wildlife Conservation Trust, since 2001; *b* London, 22 April 1959; *d* of Christopher John Neil Stanford and Jean Ethel Ogilvie Stanford; *m* 1991, Richard Goodwill Onslow Dent; one *d*. *Educ:* Salisbury Grammar Sch.; Reading Univ. (BSc Hons Agric.). FRAgS. Partner, Strutt & Parker, 1981–2001. Non-exec. Bd Mem., National England, 2014–. Director: Game and Wildlife Trading Ltd, 2007–; Langholm Moor Demonstration Project, 2008–18; Chm., Marlborough Downs Nature Enhancement Project, 2012–15. Member: NFU; Countryside Alliance; CLA; British Assoc. of Shooting and Conservation; NT; Hon. Mem., Gamekeepers' Assoc. *Recreations:* downhill ski-ing, dressmaking. *Clubs:* Ski of GB; Grasshoppers Farmers (Hon. Mem.).

**DENT COAD, Emma;** MP (Lab) Kensington, since 2017. *Educ:* Royal Coll. of Art (MA Design Hist. 1992). Worked on Designer mag., 1980–86; features ed., Unique mag., 1987; freelance work, 1988–. Ed., Docomomo UK Newsletter, 2000–. Mem. (Lab), Kensington and Chelsea LBC, 2006–. *Publications:* Spanish Design and Architecture, 1990; Javier Mariscal: designing the new Spain, 1992; (contrib.) The Oxford Companion to Architecture, 2009; articles in Design mag. *Address:* House of Commons, SW1A 0AA.

**DENTON, Charles;** Head of Drama, BBC Television, 1993–96; *b* 20 Dec. 1937; *s* of Alan Charles Denton and Mary Frances Royle; *m* 1961, Eleanor Mary Player; one *s* two *d*. *Educ:* Reading Sch.; Bristol Univ. BA History (Hons). Deckhand, 1960; advertising trainee, 1961–63; BBC TV, 1963–68; freelance television producer with Granada, ATV and Yorkshire TV, 1969–72; Dir, Tempest Films Ltd, 1969–71; Man. Dir, Black Lion Films, 1979–81; ATV: Head of Documentaries, 1974–77; Controller of Programmes, 1977–81; Dir of Progs, Central Ind. TV, 1981–84; Dir, Central Ind. Television plc, 1981–87; Chief Exec., Zenith Prodns, 1984–93. Chairman: Zenith North Ltd, 1988–93; Action Time Ltd, 1988–93; Producers Alliance for Cinema and TV, 1991–93; Cornwall Film, 2001–03. Mem., Arts Council of England, 1996–98. Chm., British Film and TV Producers Assoc., 1988–91. Governor, BFI, 1992–99; Mem. Bd, Film Council, 1999–2002; Chm., Nat. Film Trustee Co., 2001–08. FRSA 1988; FRTS 1988. *Recreations:* walking, music.

**DENTON, Prof. Derek Ashworth, (Dick),** AC 2005; FRACP, FRCP; FRS 1999; Founding Director, Howard Florey Institute of Experimental Physiology and Medicine, Melbourne, 1971–89, Emeritus Director and Consultant Scientist, since 1990; Honorary Professorial Fellow, Florey Neuroscience and Mental Health Institute, University of Melbourne, since 2004; *b* 27 May 1924; *s* of Arthur A. and Catherine Denton; *m* 1953, Catherine Margaret Mary Scott (Dame Margaret Scott, AC, DBE) (*d* 2019); two *s*. *Educ:* Launceston Grammar Sch.; Univ. of Melbourne (MB BS). FAA 1979; FRACP 1986; FRCP 1988. Haley Res. Fellow, Walter & Eliza Hall Inst., Melbourne, 1948; Med. Res. Fellow, then Sen. Med. Res. Fellow, 1948–62, Principal Res. Fellow, 1962–70, NH&MRC. Adjunct Scientist, Texas Biomed. Res. Inst. (formerly SW Foundn for Biomed. Res.), San Antonio, Texas, 1991–; Pres., Howard Florey Biomed. Foundn, Melbourne, 1997–2009. Dir, David Syme Ltd, 1984–93. First Vice-Pres., Internat. Union of Physiol. Sci., 1983–89 (Chm., Nominating Cttee, and Cttee on Commns, 1986–93). Mem. Jury, Albert and Mary Lasker Foundn Awards in Med. Sci., 1979–90. For. Med. Mem., Royal Swedish Acad. of Sci., 1974; Mem., Amer. Acad. Arts & Sci., 1986; Foreign Associate: NAS, 1995; French Acad. of Scis, 2000. Excellence in Hypertension Prevention through Dietary Salt Reduction at Popn Level Award, World Hypertension League, 2014. *Publications:* The Hunger for Salt, 1982; The Pinnacle of Life, 1994 (trans. French 1997, Japanese 1998); Les emotions primordiales et l'éveil de la conscience, 2005 (The Primordial Emotions: the dawning of consciousness, 2006). *Recreations:* wine, tennis, fly-fishing. *Address:* Office of the Dean, Faculty of Medicine, University of Melbourne, Parkville, Vic 3010, Australia; 816 Orrong Road, Toorak, Vic 3142, Australia. *Club:* Melbourne (Melbourne).

**DENTON, Jane,** CBE 2007; Director, Multiple Births Foundation, since 1999; Co-Lead, Elizabeth Bryan Multiple Births Centre, since 2017; *b* 30 June 1953; *d* of Ronald and Joan Gulliver; *m* 1987, Nigel Denton. *Educ:* Nottingham Bluecoat Sch.; St Bartholomew's Hosp., London (RGN 1974); Mill Rd Maternity Hosp., Cambridge (RM 1976). Staff Nurse, St Bartholomew's Hosp., 1974–76; Midwife, Mill Road Maternity Hosp., 1977–78; Nursing Director: Hallam Med. Centre, 1978–91; Multiple Births Foundn, 1991–99. Mem., HFEA, 1992–2004 (Dep. Chm., 1997–2000). Pres., British Fertility Soc., 2018–. FRCN 2006. Hon. Mem., British Fertility Soc., 2008. *Publications:* (ed jtly) Infertility: nursing and caring, 1995; (jtly) Expecting Twins?: a complete guide to pregnancy, birth and your twins' first year, 2013; contrib. articles on multiple births. *Recreations:* music, walking. *Address:* Multiple Births Foundation, Queen Charlotte's and Chelsea Hospital, W12 0HS. *T:* (020) 3313 3519. *E:* jane.denton@bcu.ac.uk.

**DENTON, Prof. John Douglas,** PhD; FRS 2000; FREng; Professor of Turbomachinery Aerodynamics, Cambridge University, 1991–2005; Fellow of Trinity Hall, Cambridge, 1977–2005, now Emeritus (Vice-Master, 2002–05); *b* 1 Dec. 1939; *s* of Donald and Mary Denton; *m* 1966, Maureen Hunt; three *d*. *Educ:* Trinity Hall, Cambridge (BA, PhD); Univ. of British Columbia (MASc). MIMechE, CEng, FREng (FEng 1993). Lectr, Univ. of East Africa, 1967–69; Res. Officer, later Section Head, CEGB, 1969–77; Lectr, Dept of Engrg, Cambridge, 1977–91. *Recreations:* travel, mountain walking, bee keeping.

**DENTON, John Grant,** AM 2005; OBE 1977; General Secretary, General Synod of Anglican Church of Australia, 1969–94 (part time until 1977); *b* 16 July 1929; *s* of Ernest Bengrey Denton and Gladys Leonard Stevenson; *m* 1956, Shirley Joan Wise; two *s* two *d*. *Educ:* Camberwell C of E Grammar School, Melbourne. Personnel and Industrial Relations Dept, Mobil Oil (Aust.), 1950–54; Administrative Sec., Dio. of Central Tanganyika, as CMS missionary, 1954–64; Dir of Information, Dio. of Sydney, 1964–69; Registrar, Dio. of Sydney, 1969–77. Mem., ACC, 1976–84 (Chm., 1980–84); Chm., Aust. Churches' Cttee for Seventh Assembly of WCC, Canberra, 1991. Mem., Central Coast Regl Council, Dio. of Newcastle, 1997–2005. Chm., Sydney Bethel Union Trust, 1986–2002. *Recreations:* model railway, photography.

**DENTON, Prof. Richard Michael,** PhD, DSc; FMedSci; FRS 1998; Professor of Biochemistry, University of Bristol, 1987–2011, now Emeritus, and Senior Research Fellow, 2010–15; *b* 16 Oct. 1941; *s* of Arthur Benjamin Denton and Eileen Mary Denton (*née* Evans); *m* 1965, Janet Mary Jones; one *s* two *d*. *Educ:* Wycliffe Coll.; Christ's Coll., Cambridge (MA, PhD 1967); Univ. of Bristol (DSc 1976). University of Bristol: Lectr in Biochemistry, 1967–78; Reader in Biochemistry, 1978–87; Hd, Dept of Biochemistry, 1995–2000; Chm., Med. Scis, 2000–04; Founder Dean, Med. and Vet. Scis, 2003–04. MRC Sen. Res. Leave Fellow, 1984–88. Mem., MRC, 1999–2004; Founder FMedSci 1998. *Publications:* more than 240 res. papers, mainly on molecular basis of effects of insulin on metabolism, and role of calcium ions in mitochondria, in internat. res. jls. *Recreations:* family, walking, keeping fit, cooking. *Address:* School of Biochemistry, Biomedical Sciences Building, University of Bristol, Bristol BS8 1TD.

**DENTON, Zane William;** Head, Commercial Litigation Team, since 2014, and Training Principal, since 2012, Government Legal Department (formerly Treasury Solicitor's Department); *b* Pembury, 20 Jan. 1967; *s* of William and Valerie; two *s* one *d*. *Educ:* Univ. of East Anglia (LLB Hons). Engr, 1983–93; admitted as solicitor, 1999; lawyer, Treasury Solicitor's Dept, then Govt Legal Dept, 1997–; Hd, Gen. Private Law and Tribunals Team, 2004–06; Asst Queen's Proctor, 2004–06; Hd, Gen. Public Law Team, 2006–09; Dir, Bona Vacantia Div., 2009–14. *Recreations:* cycling, motorcycling, photography, climbing, music, practical application. *Address:* Government Legal Department, 102 Petty France, SW1H 9AJ.

**DENYER, Caryn Dawn;** *see* Franklin, C. D.

**DENYER, His Honour Roderick Lawrence;** QC 1990; a Circuit Judge, 2002–17; Designated Civil Judge for Bristol, 2010–17; *b* 1 March 1948; *s* of Oliver James Denyer and Olive Mabel Jones; *m* 1st, 1973, Pauline (*née* Vann) (marr. diss.); two *d*; 2nd, Yoko Ujile; two step *d*. *Educ:* Grove Park Grammar School for Boys, Wrexham; London School of Economics (LLM). Called to the Bar, Inner Temple, 1970, Bencher, 1996; Lectr in Law, Bristol Univ., 1971–73; in practice at Bar, 1973–2002; a Recorder, 1990–2002. Vis. Fellow, UWE, 1994–. Mem., Bar Council, 1992–95. *Publications:* Children and Personal Injury Litigation, 1993, 2nd edn 2002; Case Management in Criminal Trials, 2010, 2nd edn 2012; contrib. legal jls. *Recreations:* cricket, 19th century history, theatre, restaurants.

**DENZA, Mrs Eileen,** CMG 1984; Visiting Professor, University College London, 1997–2008 (Senior Research Fellow, 1996–97); Second Counsel to Chairman of Committees and Counsel to European Communities Committee, House of Lords, 1987–95; *b* 23 July 1937; *d* of Alexander L. Young and Mrs Young; *m* 1966, John Denza (*d* 2016); two *s* one *d*. *Educ:* Aberdeen Univ. (MA); Somerville Coll., Oxford (MA); Harvard Univ. (LLM). Called to the Bar, Lincoln's Inn, 1963. Asst Lectr in Law, Bristol Univ., 1961–63; Asst Legal Adviser, FCO (formerly FO), 1963–74; Legal Counsellor, FCO, 1974–80; Counsellor (Legal Adviser), Office of UK Perm. Rep. to European Communities, 1980–83; Legal Counsellor, FCO, 1983–86. Pupillage and practice at the Bar, 1986–87. Member: EC Law Section of Adv. Bd, British Inst. of Internat. and Comparative Law, 1988–95; Adv. Bd, Inst. of European Public Law, 1992–96; Justice Expert Panel on Human Rights in the EU, 1997–2002. Vis. Lectr, QMUL, 2007–08, 2009–10. FRSA 1995. *Publications:* Diplomatic Law, 1976, 4th edn 2016; The Intergovernmental Pillars of the European Union, 2002; contribs to: Satow's Guide to Diplomatic Practice, 5th edn 1976 to 7th edn 2017; Essays in Air Law; Airline Mergers and Cooperation in the European Community; Lee's Consular Law and Practice, 2nd edn; Institutional Dynamics of European Integration; The European Union and World Trade Law; Legislative Drafting: a modern approach, 1998; Evans' International Law, 2003, 5th edn 2018; EU Law for the 21st Century; The Harvard Research in Internat. Law; 1951 Convention Relating to the Status of Refugees and its 1967 Protocol: a commentary, 2010; The European Union after Lisbon, 2011; The International Responsibility of the European Union, 2013; Judging Europe's Judges, 2013; The Treaty on European Union, 2013; The EU Charter of Fundamental Rights, 2014; The Treaty on the Functioning of the European Union, 2017; (contrib.) Research Handbook on the EU's Common Foreign and Security Policy, 2018; articles in British Yearbook of Internat. Law, Yearbook of European Law, Revue du Marché Commun, Internat. and Comparative Law Quarterly, Statute Law Rev., Common Market Law Rev., European Foreign Affairs Rev., European Law Rev., Netherlands Internat. Law Rev., Cambridge Handbook of Immunities and Internat. Law.

**DEPARDIEU, Gérard;** actor; *b* 27 Dec. 1948; *m* 1970, Elisabeth Guignot (marr. diss. 1996); one *d* (one *s* decd). *Educ:* Ecole d'art dramatique de Jean Laurent Cochet. Pres., Cannes Film Fest. Jury, 1992. Fellow BFI, 1989. Chevalier, Ordre Nat. du Mérite (France), 1985; Chevalier, Légion d'Honneur (France), 1996. *Stage:* Les Garçons de la Bande, Th. Edouard VII, 1968; Une fille dans ma soupe, 1970, Galapagos, 1971, Th. de la Madeleine; Saved, Th. Nat. de Chaillot, 1972; Home, 1972, Isme, Isaac, 1973, La Chevauchée sur le Lac de Constance, 1974, Espace Pierre Cardin; Les Gens deraisonnables sont en voie de disparition, Nanterre, 1977; Tartuffe, Strasbourg, 1983; Lily Passion (musical), Zénith, 1986. *Films:* Le Tueur, 1971; L'affaire Dominici, Un peu de soleil dans l'eau froide, Au rendez-vous de la mort joyeuse, La Scoumoune, Deux hommes dans la ville, Le viager, 1972; Rude journée pour la reine, Stavisky, Les Gaspards, Les Valseuses, 1973; Vincent, François, Paul et les autres, Pas si méchant que ça, 1974; 1900, La dernière femme, Sept morts sur ordonnance, Maîtresse, 1975; Barocco, René la Canne, Baxter, Vera Baxter, 1976; Dites-lui que je l'aime, Le Camion, La nuit tous les chats sont gris, Préparez vos mouchoirs, Rêve de singe, 1977; Le Sucre, Les chiens, Le Grand embouteillage, 1978; Buffet froid, Rosy la bourrasque, Loulou, Mon oncle d'Amérique, 1979; Le dernier métro (Caesar best actor award, 1980), Inspecteur la Bavure, Je vous aime, 1980; Le Choix des armes, La Femme d'à côté, La Chèvre, Le Retour de Martin Guerre, Danton, 1981; Le Grand frère, La Lune dans le caniveau, 1982; Les Compères, Fort Saganne, 1983; Tartuffe (also dir), Rive droite, rive gauche, Police, 1984; Une femme ou deux, Tenue de soirée, Jean de Florette, 1985; Les Fugitifs, Sous le soleil de Satan, 1986; Camille Claudel, 1987; Drôle d'endroit pour une rencontre, Deux, Trop belle pour toi, I Want to go Home, 1988; Cyrano de Bergerac, 1989 (Best Actor, Cannes, 1990; Caesar and de Donatello best actor awards, 1991); Green Card (Golden Globe award, 1991), Uranus, Merci la vie, 1990; Mon Père ce héros, 1492: Columbus, Tous les matins du monde, 1991; Hélas pour moi, Germinal, 1992; Une pure formalité, Le Colonel Chabert, 1993; La Machine, Elisa, Les Cents et une nuits, Les anges gardiens, 1994; Unhook the Stars, 1995; Hamlet, 1997; The Man in the Iron Mask, 1998; Astérix et Obelix contre César, Un pont entre deux rives (dir), 1999; 102 Dalmatians, 2000; Astérix et Obelix: Mission Cléopatre, The Closet, 2002; Bon voyage, Nathalie, 2004; Les temps qui changent, 2005; Last Holiday, 36 Quai des Orfèvres, 2006; La Môme, La vie en rose, The Singer, 2007; Astérix aux Jeux Olympiques, Babylon A. D., 2008; Mesrine: Killer Instinct, 2009; My Afternoons with Margueritte, Potiche, Mammuth, 2011; Welcome to New York, 2014; Valley of Love, 2016; Let the Sunshine In, 2018; has also appeared on TV. *Publications:* Lettres volées, 1988; Ca s'est fait comme ça (autobiog.), 2014. *Address:* c/o VMA, 20 avenue Rapp, 75007 Paris, France.

**de PEAR, Ben;** Editor, Channel 4 News, since 2012; *b* Hammersmith, 5 Dec. 1970; *s* of John Andrew de Pear and Susan Elizabeth Kerr de Pear; *m* 2003, Leila Amanpour; two *s* one *d*. *Educ:* St Gabriel's Sch., Bridgetown, Barbados; Oakham Sch., Oakham; Univ. of Leeds (BA Hons English Lit.). Trainee reporter, Staines & Ashford News, 1994; Sky News: runner, 1994–95; foreign producer (Kosovo, Turkey, Israel), 1996–2000; Africa Ed. (incl. fall of Baghdad, Afghanistan), 2000–05; Sen. Foreign Producer, 2005–08, Foreign Ed., 2008–12, Channel 4 News. *Recreations:* football, cricket, open water swimming, cycling, literature, theatre, film, TV drama. *Address:* c/o ITN, 200 Gray's Inn Road, WC1X 8XZ. *T:* (020) 7430 4601. *E:* Ben.depear@itn.co.uk. *Clubs:* Frontline, Serpentine Swimming; Queens Park Rangers Football, Wolverhampton Wanderers Football.

**de PENCIER, Theo;** Chief Executive, Freight Transport Association, 2007–15; *b* Carlisle, 16 Feb. 1952; *s* of Edwin and Maria de Pencier; *m* 1976, Fiona Margaret Lyall; one *s* two *d*. *Educ:* Taunton Sch., Som; Univ. of Newcastle upon Tyne (BA Hons Econ 1974). Grad. trainee, Tube Investments Ltd, 1970–74; Mktg Exec., H. J. Heinz Ltd, 1974–79; Senior Manager: Grand Metropolitan plc, 1980–85; NFC plc, 1985–95; Managing Director: Danzas Ltd, 1995–99; Bibby Line Gp, 1999–2007. Non-exec. Dir, London Ambulance Service, 2014– (Sen. Ind. Dir, 2014–17; Dep. Chm., 2017–); Mem. Bd, Transport Focus (formerly Passenger Focus), 2015–. MInstD 2006–14. FCILT 2001. Liveryman, Co. of Carmen. *Recreations:* travel, Rugby, theatre. *Address:* Aysgarth House, 9 Moreton Avenue, Harpenden, Herts AL5 2EU. *T:* (01582) 712170. *E:* depenciertheo@gmail.com.

**de PEYER, David Charles;** Director General, Cancer Research Campaign, 1984–96; *b* 25 April 1934; *s* of late Charles de Peyer, CMG and Flora (*née* Collins); *m* 1959, Ann Harbord. *Educ:* Rendcomb Coll., Cirencester; Magdalen Coll., Oxford (BA PPE). Asst Principal, Min. of Health, 1960; Sec., Royal Commn on NHS, 1976–79; Under Sec., DHSS, 1979–84. Vice-Chm., Suffolk HA, 1996–98. Mem., Criminal Injuries Compensation Appeals Panel, 1997–2006. Trustee: Disabled Living Foundn, 1988–2004; Res. into Ageing, 1996–2001. Chm., Friends of All Saints, Middleton, 2007–14. *Address:* Mayfield, Rectory Road, Middleton, Suffolk CO10 7LN.

**DE PIERO, Gloria;** MP (Lab) Ashfield, since 2010; *b* Bradford, 21 Dec. 1972; *d* of Giorgio and Maddalena De Piero; *m* 2012, James Robinson. *Educ:* Yorkshire Martyrs Sch., Bradford; Bradford and Ilkley Coll.; Univ. of Westminster (BA Social Sci. 1996); Birkbeck Coll., Univ. of London (MSc Social and Political Theory 2001). Researcher, Jonathan Dimbleby prog., ITV, 1997–98; Producer/Reporter: On The Record, 1998–2002, Politics Show, 2002–03, BBC; Political Corresp., GMTV, 2003–10. Shadow Minister for Women and Equalities, 2013–15, for Young People and Voter Registration, 2015–16, for Justice, 2017–19. *Recreations:* karaoke, swimming. *Address:* House of Commons, SW1A 0AA. *T:* (01623) 720399. *E:* gloria.depiero.mp@parliament.uk.

**DEPLEDGE, Alexandra Helen,** MBE 2016; Chief Executive, Resi (formerly BuildPath), since 2016; *b* Bradford, 9 Feb. 1981; *d* of Michael Depledge and Judith Depledge; *m* 2010, David Cockle; one *d*. *Educ:* Univ. of Nottingham (BA Hist. and Amer. Studies 2003); Univ. of Chicago (MA Internat. Relns 2005). Consultant, Accenture, 2006–12; CEO, Hassle.com, 2012–15. Chair, Coalition for Digital Economy, 2015–17; Mem. Bd, London Economic Action Partnership, 2017–. *Recreations:* horse riding, painting.

**DEPLEDGE, Prof. Michael Harold,** CBE 2017; PhD, DSc; FRSB; Professor of Environment and Human Health, 2007–19, now Emeritus, and Chairman, European Centre for Environment and Human Health, 2010–19, University of Exeter Medical School (formerly Peninsula Medical School); *b* 8 Jan. 1954; *s* of Clifford and Edna Depledge; *m* 1977, Juliana Eileen Dearden; two *s*. *Educ:* Leeds Modern Grammar Sch.; Westfield Coll., Univ. of London (BSc 1st Cl. Hons Biol Scis 1975; PhD 1982; DSc 1996). Res. Fellow, Brompton Hosp., London, 1979; Clinical Scientist, Royal Marsden Hosp., Sutton, 1979–82; Lectr in Physiol., Med. Sch., Univ. of Hong Kong, 1983–87; Prof. of Ecotoxicol., Odense Univ., Denmark, 1987–94; Prof. of Ecotoxicol. and Dir, Plymouth Envmtl Res. Centre, Univ. of Plymouth, 1994–2002; Hd of Sci., 2002–05, Chief Scientific Advr, 2005–06, Envmt Agency. Sen. Scientific Advr, Plymouth Marine Lab., 2005–07. Keeley Vis. Fellow, Wadham Coll., Oxford, 2006; Vis. Prof. in Zool., Univ. of Oxford, 2008–; Hon. Prof. of Public Policy, UCL, 2012–; Hon. Vis. Prof., Chiba Univ., Japan, 2013–. Member: NERC, 2003–06; Natural England, 2006–09; Royal Commn on Envmtl Pollution, 2006–11; Bd, Climate and Health Council, 2009–; Adv. Cttee on Hazardous Substances, 2012–; Global Health Cttee, Public Health England, 2014–; Sci. Adv. Cttee, UNEP, 2015–; Vice-Chm., 2006–08, Chm., 2009–13, Sci. Adv. Cttee, DG Research, EC. Royal Soc. rep., Eur. Academies Sci. Adv. Council, 2008–15. Special Advr, Eden Project, Cornwall, 2017– (Chief Scientific Advr, 2018–). Advr to various UN bodies, 1990–. Prod. and Narrator, The Blue Gym, 2010 (RTS award for best non-broadcast film, 2010). FRSA. Hon. FRCP 2015. Hon. DSc Westminster, 2011. Poulssen Medal of Honour, Norwegian Soc. of Pharmacology and Toxicology, 2009. *Publications:* contrib. numerous peer-reviewed scientific papers, book chapters and abstracts to internat. scientific literature and learned jls, incl. Lancet, Thorax, Envmtl Sci. and Technol., Envmtl Health Perspectives, Marine Biol., Aquatic Toxicol., Science, Nature Climate Change, Jl of the Amer. Medical Assoc. *Recreations:* travel, guitar, football, sailing, reading. *Address:* European Centre for Environment and Human Health, University of Exeter, Medical School, Knowledge Spa, Royal Cornwall Hospital, Truro, Cornwall TR1 3HD. *E:* m.depledge@exeter.ac.uk.

**DEPP, John Christopher, (Johnny);** actor; *b* 9 June 1963; *s* of John Christopher Depp and late Betty Sue Depp (*née* Palmer); *m* 1983, Lori Anne Allison (marr. diss. 1985); one *s* one *d* by Vanessa Chantal Paradis; *m* 2015, Amber Heard (marr. diss. 2017). *Television series:* 21 Jump Street, 1987–90; United States of Poetry, 1995. *Films include:* A Nightmare on Elm Street, 1984; Private Resort, 1985; Platoon, 1986; Cry Baby, Edward Scissorhands, 1990; Freddy's Dead: The Final Nightmare, 1991; Benny and Joon, What's Eating Gilbert Grape, Arizona Dream, 1993; Ed Wood, Don Juan DeMarco, 1994; Dead Man, Nick of Time, 1995; The Brave (also writer and dir), Donnie Brasco, 1997; Fear and Loathing in Las Vegas, 1998; The Astronaut's Wife, The Ninth Gate, Sleepy Hollow, 1999; The Man Who Cried, Before Night Falls, Chocolat, 2000; Blow, From Hell, 2001; Pirates of the Caribbean: The Curse of the Black Pearl, Once Upon a Time in Mexico, 2003; Secret Window, Finding Neverland, The Libertine, 2004; Charlie and the Chocolate Factory, 2005; Pirates of the Caribbean: Dead Man's Chest, 2006; Pirates of the Caribbean: At World's End, 2007; Sweeney Todd: The Demon Barber of Fleet Street, 2008 (Golden Globe for Best Actor in a Musical); Public Enemies, The Imaginarium of Dr Parnassus, 2009; Alice in Wonderland, When You're Strange, The Tourist, 2010; Pirates of the Caribbean: On Stranger Tides, The Rum Diary, 2011; Dark Shadows (also prod.), 2012; The Lone Ranger, 2013; Transcendence, 2014; Into the Woods, Mortdecai, Black Mass, 2015; Alice Through the Looking Glass, Fantastic Beasts and Where to Find Them, 2016; Pirates of the Caribbean: Salazar's Revenge, Murder on the Orient Express, 2017; Fantastic Beasts: the crimes of Grindelwald, 2018; Waiting for the Barbarians, 2019. *Address:* c/o Creative Artists Agency, 2000 Avenue of the Stars, Los Angeles, CA 90067, USA.

**de PURY, Christopher Mark;** Partner, since 2008, and Head of Real Estate, since 2013, Bryan Cave Leighton Paisner (formerly Berwin Leighton Paisner) LLP; *b* London, 11 Feb. 1968; *s* of Andrew and Lois de Pury; *m* 2000, Carolyn Sara Rice-Oxley; two *s* one *d*. *Educ:* Christ Church, Oxford (MA Hons Juris.). Admitted solicitor, 1992; Solicitor, Herbert Smith LLP, Partner, 1998–2008. Mem., Develt Bd, Old Vic. Chm., Sedos. Ind. Gov., Conservatoire of Drama and Dance. Ambassador, Children's Soc. *Recreations:* theatre, drama, the arts, family. *E:* chris.depury@bclplaw.com.

**de QUINCEY, Paul Morrison;** Director, Russia, British Council, 2011–15; *b* 23 June 1954; *s* of Ronald Anthony and Margaret Claire de Quincey; *m* 1976, Theresa Elizabeth Patricia Casabayo; one *s* one *d*. *Educ:* Univ. of Leeds (BA Hons English 1975; PGCE English/Drama 1976; MA Linguistics 1979). Teacher: of English, Ubiaja, Nigeria, 1976–78; of English and Drama, Wakefield, 1979–81; British Council, 1981–2015: Asst Rep., S Korea, 1981–84; Consultant, ELSD, London, 1984–87; Deputy Director: Algeria, 1987–91; Czechoslovakia, 1991–93; Director: Venezuela, 1993–98; Americas, 1998–2000; UK, 2000–02; Grant Funded Services, 2002–04; Dir and Cultural Counsellor, France, 2004–09; Regl Dir, Russia and N Europe, 2009–11. Trustee, Akram Khan Co., 2018–. FRSA. *Recreations:* fishing, shooting, the arts. *Address:* 167 Kennington Road, SE11 6SF.

**DE RAMSEY,** 4th Baron *cr* 1887, of Ramsey Abbey, Huntingdon; **John Ailwyn Fellowes;** DL; Chairman, Environment Agency, 1995–2000; *b* 27 Feb. 1942; *s* of 3rd Baron De Ramsey, KBE and Lilah Helen Suzanne (*d* 1987), *d* of Frank Labouchere; *S* father, 1993; *m* 1st, 1973, Phyllida Mary Forsyth; one *s*; 2nd, 1984, Alison Mary Birkmyre; one *s* two *d*. *Educ:* Winchester Coll.; Writtle Inst. of Agriculture. Dir, Cambridge Water Co., 1974–94 (Chm., 1983–89). Crown Estate Comr, 1994–2002. President: CLA, 1991–93; Assoc. of Drainage Authorities, 1993–94 and 2004–. FRAgS 1993 (Pres., 2001–02). DL Cambs, 1993. Hon. DSc Cranfield, 1997. *Recreations:* golf, fishing, fine arts. *Heir: s* Hon. Freddie John Fellowes [*b* 31 May 1978; *m* 2010, Joanna Bernadette Brough; one *s* one *d*]. *Address:* Abbots Ripton Hall, Huntingdon PE28 2PQ. *T:* (01487) 773555. *Club:* Boodle's.

**DERBY,** 19th Earl of, *cr* 1485; **Edward Richard William Stanley;** DL; Bt 1627; Baron Stanley 1832; Baron Stanley of Preston 1886; Chairman, FF&P Trustee Co. Ltd, since 2004; *b* 10 Oct. 1962; *er s* of Hon. Hugh Henry Montagu Stanley (*d* 1971), *g s* of 17th Earl, and of Mary Rose Stanley (*née* Birch); *S* uncle, 1994; *m* 1995, Hon. Caroline Emma Neville, *d* of 10th Baron Braybrooke; two *s* one *d*. *Educ:* Ludgrove; Eton Coll.; RAC Cirencester. Commnd Grenadier Guards, 1982, resigned 1985. Merchant banker with Robert Fleming Hldgs Ltd, 1987–2001. Director: Fleming Private Fund Management Ltd, 1991–96; Fleming Private Asset Management Ltd, 1992–2000; The Haydock Park Racecourse Co. Ltd, 1994–; Robert Fleming & Co. Ltd, 1996–98; Robert Fleming Internat. Ltd, 1998–2001; Stonehage Fleming (formerly Fleming Family & Partners),

2001–. Trustee, Nat. Mus Liverpool (formerly Nat. Mus and Galls on Merseyside), 1995–2006 (Mem., Finance Cttee, 2006–). President: Liverpool Chamber of Commerce and Industry, 1995–; Knowsley Chamber of Commerce and Industry, 1995–; Sefton Chamber of Commerce and Industry, 1998; Liverpool Council of Social Service, 1996–. Trustee, Aintree Racecourse Charitable Appeal Trust, 1995– (Chm., 2017–). Chm., Aintree Racecourse Develts Ltd, 2017. President: Royal Liverpool Philharmonic Soc., 1995–; Rugby Football League Assoc., 1997–; Vice Pres., PGA, 2001–. Mem. Council, Univ. of Liverpool, 1998–2004 and 2011– (Vice Pres., 2012–14; Pres., 2015–). Patron, Liverpool Veterans, 2017–. Hon. Comdr, RNR, 2015. Hon. LLD Liverpool, 2008; Hon. DBA Chester, 2009. DL Merseyside, 1999. *Publications:* Ouija Board: a mare in a million, 2007. *Recreations:* diving, shooting, ski-ing, food and wine. *Heir: s* Lord Stanley, *qv*. *Address:* Knowsley, Prescot, Merseyside L34 4AF. *T:* (0151) 489 6148. *E:* private.office@knowsley.com. *Clubs:* White's, Jockey Club Rooms (Newmarket).
   See also Hon. P. H. C. Stanley.

**DERBY, Bishop of,** since 2019; **Rt Rev. Elizabeth Jane Holden Lane;** *b* High Wycombe, 8 Dec. 1966; *d* of Dennis and Helen Holden; *m* 1990, Rev. George Lane; one *s* one *d*. *Educ:* Manchester High Sch. for Girls; St Peter's Coll., Oxford (MA; Hon. Fellow, 2015); St John's Coll., Cranmer Hall, Durham (DipMin). Ordained deacon, 1993, priest, 1994; Curate, St James, Blackburn, 1993–96; Permission to officiate, Dio. of York, 1996–99; Hosp. Chaplain, Hull, 1998–99; Social Responsibility Officer, Dio. of Chester, 2000–02; Team Vicar, St George's Stockport, 2002–07; Asst Dir of Ordinands, Dio. of Chester, 2005–07; Vicar, St Peter's, Hale and St Elizabeth's, Ashley, 2007–14; Dean of Women in Ministry, Dio. of Chester, 2010–14; Bishop Suffragan of Stockport, 2015–19. Participant Observer, House of Bishops, 2013. Vice-Chair, Children's Soc., 2016–. Chair, Council, Cranmer Hall, Durham, 2016–. Hon. DD: Univ. of Wales Trinity St David, 2015; Chester, 2017; Hon. LLD Bath, 2017. *Recreations:* reading, performing arts, sport, music, cryptic crosswords. *Address:* Bishop's House, 6 King Street, Duffield, Belper, Derbyshire DE56 4EU.

**DERBY, Dean of;** *no new appointment at time of going to press.*

**DERBY, Archdeacon of;** *see* Cunliffe, Ven. C. J.

**DERBYSHIRE, Benjamin Charles Edward;** Chair, HTA Design LLP, since 2016; President, Royal Institute of British Architects, 2017–19; *b* Leeds, 15 May 1953; *s* of Sir Andrew George Derbyshire and of Lily Derbyshire; *m* 2011, Dr Jane McNeill; one *s* one *d*, and two step *s* one step *d*. *Educ:* Bryanston Sch.; Hatfield Grammar Sch.; Birmingham Sch. of Architecture; Dept of Architecture, Univ. of Cambridge (DipArch). Hunt Thompson Associates, then HTA Ltd, later HTA Design LLP: Partner, 1986; Dir, 2000; Man. Dir, 2005–13; Man. Partner, 2013–16. *Recreations:* music, opera, architecture, cycling, seaside. *Address:* 69 Corsica Street, N5 1JT. *T:* 07850 375373. *E:* ben.derbyshire@hta.co.uk.

**DERCON, Prof. Stefan Nicolaas Alfons Anna,** Hon. CMG 2018; DPhil; Professor of Economic Policy, University of Oxford, since 2015; Fellow, Jesus College, Oxford, since 2015; *b* Ekeren, Belgium, 4 Dec. 1964; *s* of René Dercon and Maria Nelen; *m* 1996, Pramila Krishnan; one *s*. *Educ:* Katholieke Univ. Leuven, Belgium (BA Phil. 1985; License in Econs 1986); Queen's Coll., Oxford (MPhil Econs 1988; DPhil Econs 1993). Post-doctoral Res. Fellow, Nuffield Coll., Oxford, 1993–97; Prof. of Develt Econs, Katholieke Univ. Leuven, 1993–2000; University of Oxford: Lectr, 2001–04; Fellow and Tutor in Econs, Jesus Coll., 2001–04; Prof. of Develt Econs, 2004–15; Fellow, Wolfson Coll., 2004–15; Chief Economist, DFID, 2011–17. Vis. Prof., Econs Dept, Addis Ababa Univ., 1992–93. *Publications:* Insurance Against Poverty, 2004; Dull Disasters? How planning ahead will make a difference, 2016; contribs to learned jls incl. Jl of Pol Econ., Rev. of Econs and Stats, Econ. Jl, Jl of Develt Econs, Demography. *Address:* Blavatnik School of Government, University of Oxford, Woodstock Road, Oxford OX2 6GG.

**DERHAM, Catherine Beatrice Margaret, (Katie), (Mrs J. Vincent);** Presenter: BBC2 Proms, since 2010, and Proms Extra, since 2013; BBC Radio 3, since 2010; Managing Director, Peanut and Crumb Ltd, since 2015; *b* 18 June 1970; *d* of John and Margaret Derham; *m* 1999, John Vincent; two *d*. *Educ:* Cheadle Hulme Sch.; Magdalene Coll., Cambridge (BA Econ). Joined BBC, 1993: researcher, Money Box, Radio 4, 1993–94; Producer, Radio Business Progs, 1994–95; Presenter, Money Check, Radio 5 Live, 1995–96; Consumer Affairs Corresp., TV business progs, 1996–97; reporter, Film '96, '97; Media and Arts Corresp., 1998–2001, Media and Arts Editor, 2001–03, ITN; newscaster, ITV News, 1999–2010, and ITV Evening News, 2001–10; presenter: London Tonight, ITV, 2004–10; ITV lunchtime news, 2005–10; All Together Now: The Great Amateur Orchestra Challenge, BBC, 2016; The Girl from Ipanema, BBC, 2016; Dame Vera Lynn: Happy 100th Birthday, BBC, 2017; series for BBC Radio 4: Traveller's Tree, 2008–10; The Global Reach, 2012; Discovering, 2019; documentaries for BBC Radio 4 include: Inside Fortress Bill, 2012; One Man's War, 2012; The Synchro Girls, 2012. Presenter: Classical Brit Awards, annually, 2001–04; Classic FM, 2002–09; LBC, 2003. Judge: Lost Booker Prize, 2010; Costa Book Prize, 2013; Bailey's Women's Prize for Fiction, 2017. Contestant, Maestro, BBC TV, 2008; First Love, Sky Arts, 2010; Finalist, 2015, Christmas Champion, 2017, Strictly Come Dancing. *Recreations:* reading, travel, music - listening and playing, film, sailing. *Address:* c/o BBC Radio 3, Broadcasting House, W1A 1AA.

**DERHAM, Patrick Sibley Jan,** OBE 2018; MA; Head Master, Westminster School, since 2014; *b* 23 Aug. 1959; *s* of John Joseph Sibley Derham and Helena Petronella Trimby (*née* Verhagen); *m* 1982, Alison Jane Sheardown; one *s* one *d*. *Educ:* Training Ship Arethusa; Pangbourne Coll. (Hd of Sch.); Pembroke Coll., Cambridge (Foundn Schol., 1st Cl. Hons Hist. 1982, MA 1985). Assistant Master: Cheam, 1982–84; Radley Coll., 1984–96 (Hd of Hist. and Tutor, 1990–96); Headmaster, Solihull Sch., 1996–2001; Head Master, Rugby Sch., 2001–14. Trustee: Solihull Community Foundn, 1998–2001; IntoUniversity, 2006– (Dep. Chm., 2008–); Gladstone Library, 2012–; Springboard Bursary Foundn, 2013–; Founding Trustee, Arnold Foundn, 2003. *Publications:* The Irish Question 1868–1886: a collection of documents, 1988; (ed jtly) Liberating Learning: widening participation, 2010; Cultural Olympians, 2013 (ed) Loyal Dissent, 2016; contrib. articles and reviews. *Recreations:* quizzes, collecting Tom Merry political cartoons, reading contemporary fiction, family. *Address:* Westminster School, Little Dean's Yard, Westminster, SW1P 3PF.

**de RIVAZ, (Philippe) Vincent (Jacques Léon Marie),** Hon. CBE 2012; Chief Executive, EDF Energy plc, 2003–17; *b* Paris, 4 Oct. 1953; *s* of François de Rivaz and Isabelle de Rivaz (*née* de Buttet); *m* 1980, Anne de Valence de Minardière; three *s*. *Educ:* Ecole Nat. Supérieure d'hydraulique, Grenoble. Hydraulic engineer; Electricité de France: joined External Engrg Centre, 1977; Manager, Far East Div., 1985–91; Man. Dir, Hydropower Dept, 1991–94; Dep. Hd, Internat. Develt, i/c New Projects Develt, 1995–98; Corporate Finance and Treasury Dir, 1999–2001; Chief Exec., London Electricity, 2002–03; Mem., Exec. Cttee, EDF Gp, 2004–17. FREng 2015. Melchett Medal, Energy Inst., 2006. Chevalier de la Légion d'honneur (France), 2010. *Recreations:* photography, cycling.

**DERMODY, Paul Bernard,** OBE 2004; Director, 1997–2003, Chief Executive, 2000–03, De Vere Group plc (formerly Greenalls Group plc); *b* 1 Oct. 1945; *s* of Bernard and Jessie Dermody; *m* 1967, Margaret Eileen Horsfield; one *s* one *d*. *Educ:* De La Salle Coll., Salford; Salford Tech. Coll. ACMA 1971. Mgt accounting trainee, 1963–68, Asst Accountant, 1968–72, Groves & Whitnall; Mgt Accountant, Greenalls Brewery, 1972–77; Financial Controller, Greenalls Retail Div., 1977–84; Finance Dir and Dep. Man. Dir, 1984–89, Dep. Chm., 1989–95, De Vere Hotels; Chief Exec., Premier House & Village Leisure Hotels, 1995–97; Man. Dir, Greenalls Hotels & Leisure Ltd, 1997–2000. Non-exec. Chm., Conferma Ltd, 2008–; non-executive Director: Majestic Wine, 2004–13; Aga Rangemaster (formerly Foodservice) Gp plc, 2004–14. Chm., Nat. Football Mus., 2005–17. Mem., Adv. Bd, Univ. of Salford Business Sch., 2013–. School Governor. FIH (FHCIMA 1997); FBAHA 1985; FRSA 2000; CCMI 2001. *Recreations:* singing, swimming, reading, travel. *Address:* 6 Roe Green, Worsley, Manchester M28 2RF.

**DERNIE, Prof. David James;** Principal, David Dernie Studio, since 2000; Professor of Architecture, Chinese University of Hong Kong, since 2018; *b* 16 Dec. 1962; *s* of B. S. Broughton and M. J. Dernie; one *s*. *Educ:* Lancaster Royal Grammar Sch.; Fitzwilliam Coll., Cambridge (BA 1985; DipArch 1988). RIBA 1990; ARB 1990. Rome Scholar, British Sch. at Rome, 1991–93; Lectr in Architecture, Univ. of Cambridge, and Fellow, Fitzwilliam Coll., Cambridge, 1998–2005; Reader in Architecture, Univ. of Nottingham, 2005; Hd, Manchester Sch. of Architecture, 2005–09; Prof. of Architecture, Manchester Metropolitan Univ., 2005–09; Head, Leicester Sch. of Architecture, De Montfort Univ., 2009–12; Dean, Faculty of Architecture and Built Envmt, Univ. of Westminster, 2012–17. *Publications:* Victor Horta, 1995; Villa D'Este at Tivoli, 1996; New Stone Architecture, 2003; Material Imagination, 2005; Exhibition Design, 2006; Architectural Drawings, 2010; Material Imagination in Architecture, 2016; Shipwreck, 2016; Victor Horta: the architect of Art Nouveau, 2018. *Recreations:* drawing, painting, music, travel. *Address:* 77 Highsett, Cambridge CB2 1NZ. *T:* 07866 602574. *E:* daviddernie@icloud.com.

**de ROS,** 28th Baron *cr* 1264 (Premier Barony of England); **Peter Trevor Maxwell;** *b* 23 Dec. 1958; *s* of Comdr John David Maxwell, RN, and late Georgiana Angela Maxwell, 27th Baroness de Ros; *S* mother, 1983; *m* 1987, Siân Ross; one *s* two *d*. *Educ:* Headfort School, Kells, Co. Meath; Stowe School, Bucks; Down High School, Co. Down. Upholstered furniture maker. *Recreations:* gardening, travel and sailing. *Heir: s* Hon. Finbar James Maxwell, *b* 14 Nov. 1988.

**de ROTHSCHILD;** *see* Rothschild.

**DERRICK, Peter;** Chamberlain, City of London Corporation (formerly Corporation of London), 1999–2007; *b* 2 April 1948; *s* of John Moorhead Derrick and Lucy (*née* Norman); *m* 1972, Joyce Bainbridge; two *d*. *Educ:* Univ. of Lancaster (BA Hons Politics 1974). CPFA 1971. Gateshead CBC, 1965–71; Principal Accountant, Carlisle CC, 1974–77; Chief Tech. Asst, Knowsley MBC, 1977–79; Principal Accountant, Lothian Regl Council, 1979–81; Under Sec. (Finance), ADC, 1981–85; Director of Finance: London Bor. of Hounslow, 1985–88; London Bor. of Camden, 1988–91; Chief Exec., London Bor. of Hammersmith and Fulham, 1991–93; Dir, Finance and Corporate Services, Surrey CC, 1993–98. Actg Prin., GSMD, 2003–04. Chm., London Financial Adv. Cttee, CIPFA, 2000–06; Chm., Officer Adv. Gp, Local Govt Pension Scheme, Local Govt Employers Orgn, 1997–2006; Mem., Employer Task Force on Pensions, DWP, 2003–04. Council Mem., Nat. Assoc. of Pension Funds, 1997–2002; Pres., Soc. of London Treasurers, 2003–04. Order of the Dannebrog (Denmark), 2000. *Recreations:* football, golf, squash, film, opera. *Address:* 352 Wimbledon Central, Wimbledon, SW19 4BJ. *Clubs:* Wimbledon Racquets and Fitness; Wimbledon Park Golf; Sunderland AFC Supporters.

**DERRY, Bishop of, (RC),** since 2014; **Most Rev. Donal McKeown;** *b* Belfast, 12 April 1950; *s* of James McKeown and Rose McKeown (*née* McMeel). *Educ:* Mount St Michael's Primary Sch.; St MacNissi's Coll., Garron Tower; Pontifical Gregorian Univ., Rome (LTh); Univ. of Leicester (MBA 2000). Teacher of English, Dieburg, Germany, 1970–71; NI Correspondent, Katholiche Nachrichten Agentur, 1971–73; Teacher: St Patrick's Coll., Knock, 1978–83; St MacNissi's Coll., Garron Tower, 1983–87; Teacher, Dean of Seminary and Pres., St Malachy's Coll., Belfast; Titular Bishop of Cell Ausaille, and Auxiliary Bishop of Down and Connor, 2001–14. *Address:* Diocesan Offices, St Eugene's Cathedral, Francis Street, Derry BT48 9AP.

**DERRY, Kim Daniel B.;** *see* Bromley-Derry.

**DERWENT, 5th Baron** *cr* 1881; **Robin Evelyn Leo Vanden-Bempde-Johnstone,** LVO 1957; Bt 1795; DL; Deputy Chairman, Hutchison Whampoa (Europe) Ltd, 1998–2007 (Managing Director, 1985–97); *b* 30 Oct. 1930; *s* of 4th Baron Derwent, CBE and Marie-Louise (*d* 1985), *d* of Albert Picard, Paris; *S* father, 1986; *m* 1957, Sybille, *d* of late Vicomte de Simard de Pitray and Madame Jeanine Hennessy; one *s* three *d*. *Educ:* Winchester College; Clare Coll., Cambridge (Scholar, MA 1953). 2nd Lieut 1949, 60th Rifles; Lieut 1950, Queen Victoria's Rifles (TA). HM Diplomatic Service, 1954–69; served FO, Paris, Mexico City, Washington. Director, NM Rothschild & Sons, Merchant Bankers, 1969–85. Director: F&C (Pacific) Investment Trust Ltd, 1989–2001; Scarborough Building Soc., 1991–2001. Chm., London & Provincial Antique Dealers' Assoc., 1989–95. Mem., N York Moors Nat. Park Authy, 1997–99. Chm., Scarborough Mus Trust, 2004–08 (Patron, 2008–). Patron, Derwent Trng Assoc., 2000–. DL N Yorks, 1991. Hon. Freeman, Bor. of Scarborough, 2008. Chevalier de la Légion d'Honneur (France), 1957; Officier de l'Ordre National du Mérite (France), 1978. *Recreations:* shooting, fishing. *Heir: s* Hon. Francis Patrick Harcourt Vanden-Bempde-Johnstone [*b* 23 Sept. 1965; *m* 1990, Cressida, *o d* of late Christopher John Bourke; one *d*]. *Address:* Low Hall, Hackness, Scarborough YO13 0JN; Penthouse 6, Sovereign Court, 29 Wrights Lane, W8 5SH. *Club:* Boodle's.

**DERWENT, Henry Clifford Sydney,** CB 2006; climate change policy consultant, retired; Chief Executive Officer and Senior Advisor, Climate Strategies, 2011–18; *b* 19 Nov. 1951; *s* of late Clifford Sydney Derwent and Joan Kathleen (*née* Craft); *m* 1988, Rosemary Patricia Jesse Meaker; three *d*. *Educ:* Berkhamsted Sch.; Worcester Coll., Oxford. Department of the Environment, 1974–86: planning policy; PSA; London housing; commercial property; Rayner scrutiny; seconded to Midland Bank; inner cities; Department of Transport, subseq. DETR, now DEFRA, 1986–2008: private office; local finance; vehicle licensing; central finance; highways; Under Sec., then Dir, Nat. Roads Policy, 1992–97; (on secondment) Corporate Finance Div., SBC Warburg, later UBS Warburg, 1997–99; Dir, Envmt: Risks and Atmosphere, subseq. Climate, Energy and Envmtl Risk, then Internat. Climate Change Air and Analysis, 1999–2008; Pres. and CEO, Internat. Emissions Trading Assoc., 2008–12 (Hon. Vice Pres., 2012–18). Chm., Renewable Energy and Energy Efficiency Partnership, Vienna, 2014–18; Dep. Chm., Verified Carbon Standard, Washington DC, 2013–18. *Recreations:* flutes, trombone, accordions, saxophones, riding, drawing, watercolours.

**DERX, Donald John,** CB 1975; non-executive Director, Glaxo Holdings, later Glaxo Wellcome plc, 1991–97; *b* 25 June 1928; *s* of John Derx and Violet Ivy Stroud; *m* 1956, Luisa Donzelli (*d* 2016); two *s* two *d*. *Educ:* Tiffin Boys' Sch., Kingston-on-Thames; St Edmund Hall, Oxford (BA). Asst Principal, BoT, 1951; seconded to Cabinet Office, 1954–55; Principal, Colonial Office, 1957; Asst Sec., Industrial Policy Gp, DEA, 1965; Dir,

Treasury Centre for Admin. Studies, 1968; Head of London Centre, Civil Service Coll., 1970; Under Sec., 1971–72, Dep. Sec., 1972–84, Dept of Employment; Dir, Policy Studies Inst., 1985–86; with Glaxo Holdings plc, 1986–90.

**DESAI**, family name of **Baron Desai**.

**DESAI**, Baron *cr* 1991 (Life Peer), of St Clement Danes in the City of Westminster; **Meghnad Jagdishchandra Desai**, PhD; Professor of Economics, 1983–2003, now Emeritus, Director, Centre for the Study of Global Governance, 1992–2003, and Hon. Fellow, 2005, London School of Economics and Political Science; *b* 10 July 1940; *s* of late Jagdishchandra and of Mandakini Desai; *m* 1st, 1970, Gail Graham Wilson (marr. diss. 2004); one *s* two *d*; 2nd, 2004, Kishwar Ahluwalia. *Educ*: Univ. of Bombay (BA Hons, MA); Univ. of Pennsylvania (PhD 1964). Associate Specialist, Dept of Agricultural Econs, Univ. of Calif, Berkeley, 1963–65; London School of Economics: Lectr, 1965–77, Sen. Lectr, 1977–80, Reader, 1980–83, Dept of Econs; Head, Develt Studies Inst., 1990–95. Pres., Assoc. of Univ. Teachers in Econs, 1987–90; Mem. Council, REconS, 1988. Life Pres., Islington South and Finsbury Constituency Labour Pty, 1993– (Chm., 1986–92). Hon. DSc Kingston, 1992; Hon. DSc (Econ) E London, 1994; DUniv Middlesex, 1993; Hon. DPhil London Guildhall, 1996; Hon. LLD Monash, 2005. Jewel of Ruia, Ruia Coll. Alumni Assoc., 2011. Pravasi Bharatiya Puraskar (India), 2004; Padma Bhushan (India) 2008. *Publications*: Marxian Economic Theory, 1974; Applied Econometrics, 1976; Marxian Economics, 1979; Testing Monetarism, 1981; (Asst Editor to Prof. Dharma Kumar) The Cambridge Economic History of India 1757–1970, 1983; (ed jtly) Agrarian Power and Agricultural Productivity in South Asia, 1984; (ed) Lenin on Economics, 1987; Macroeconomics and Monetary Theory: selected essays, vol. 1, 1995; Poverty, Famine and Economic Development: selected essays, vol. 2, 1995; (ed jtly) Global Governance, 1995; (ed) On Inequality, 1995; Marx's Revenge, 2002; Nehru's Hero: Dilip Kumar in the life of India, 2004; Development and Nationhood, 2005; Rethinking Islamism, 2006; The Route to All Evil: political economy of Ezra Pound, 2006; The Rediscovery of India, 2009; Dead on Time, 2009; Pakeeza: ode to a bygone age, 2013; Who Wrote the Bhagavad Gita?: a secular inquiry into a sacred text, 2014; Hubris: why economists failed to predict the crisis and how to avoid the next one, 2015; Politicshock: Trump, Modi, Brexit and the prospects for the Liberal order, 2017; The Raisina Model: Indian democracy at seventy, 2017; contrib. Econometrica, Econ. Jl, Rev. of Econ. Studies, Economica, Econ. Hist. Rev. *Address*: House of Lords, SW1A 0PW.

**DESAI, Anita**, FRSL; novelist; *b* 24 June 1937; *d* of Toni Nimé and D. N. Mazumbar; *m* 1958, Ashvin Desai; two *s* two *d*. *Educ*: Queen Mary's Sch., Delhi; Miranda House, Univ. of Delhi (BA Hons). FRSL 1963. First story published 1946; novelist and book reviewer (freelance), 1963–. Helen Cam Vis. Fellow, 1986–87, Hon. Fellow, 1988, Girton Coll., Univ. of Cambridge; Elizabeth Drew Prof., Smith Coll., USA, 1987–88; Purington Prof. of English, Mount Holyoke Coll., USA, 1988–92; Prof. of Writing, 1993, John E. Burchard Emeritus Prof., 2003, MIT; Ashby Fellow, 1989, Hon. Fellow, 1991, Clare Hall, Univ. of Cambridge. Hon. Mem., Amer. Acad. of Arts and Letters, 1993. Neil Gunn Prize for Internat. Writers, Scotland, 1993; Alberto Moravia Prize for Internat. Writers, Italy, 1999. Padma Sri, 1990; Ca' Foscari Prize, Univ. of Venice, 2006; Giuseppe di Lampedusa Prize, Sicily, 2006. *Publications*: Cry, The Peacock, 1963; Voices in the City, 1965; Bye-Bye Blackbird, 1971; Where Shall We Go This Summer?, 1973; Fire on the Mountain, 1978 (Winifred Holtby Award, RSL, 1978); Games at Twilight, 1979; Clear Light of Day, 1980; The Village by the Sea, 1983 (Guardian Prize for Children's Fiction, 1983; filmed, 1992); In Custody, 1984 (screenplay, filmed 1994); Baumgartner's Bombay, 1988 (Hadassah Prize, Hadassah Magazine, NY, 1989); Journey to Ithaca, 1995; Fasting, Feasting, 1999; Diamond Dust and Other Stories, 2000; The Zigzag Way, 2004; The Artist of Disappearance, 2011. *Address*: c/o Rogers, Coleridge & White Ltd, 20 Powis Mews, W11 1JN.

**de SAUMAREZ, 7th Baron** *cr* 1831; **Eric Douglas Saumarez;** Bt 1801; farmer; *b* 13 Aug. 1956; *s* of 6th Baron de Saumarez and Joan Beryl, (Julia) (*d* 2004), *d* of late Douglas Raymond Charlton; *S* father, 1991; *m* 1st, 1982, Christine Elizabeth (marr. diss. 1990), *yr d* of B. N. Halliday; two *d*; 2nd, 1991, Susan M. Hearn. *Educ*: Milton Abbey; Nottingham Univ.; RAC, Cirencester. *Recreations*: flying, shooting, ski-ing, fishing. *Heir*: *twin b* Hon. Victor Thomas Saumarez, *b* 13 Aug. 1956. *Address*: Les Beaucamps de Bas, Castel, Guernsey GY5 7PE.

**de SAVARY, Peter John**; international entrepreneur; *b* 11 July 1944; *m* Marcia (marr. diss., she *m* Maj. Hon. Sir John (Jacob) Astor, MBE, ERD); two *d*; *m* 1986, (Lucille) Lana Paton; three *d*. *Educ*: Charterhouse. Activities in the energy, property, finance, maritime and hospitality fields. Chm., Victory Syndicate, Admiral's Cup, 1981 and 1983 British Challenge for America's Cup. Founder of Clubs: Carnegie (Chm., 1994–2003); Carnegie Abbey; Cherokee Plantation; Abaco; London Outpost; St James's, NY, Antigua, London, Paris, LA. Diplomatic Ambassador for Inward Investment, Grenada, 2012–. Contested (Referendum) Falmouth and Camborne, 1997. Patron, Teenage Cancer Trust, 1995–. Tourism Personality of the Year, English Tourist Bd, 1988. *Recreations*: sailing, riding, carriage driving, landscape gardening. *Clubs*: St James's, 5 Hertford Street, Royal Thames Yacht; Royal Burnham Yacht, Royal Torbay Yacht, Royal Corinthian Yacht, Royal Cornwall Yacht; New York Yacht.

**de SILGUY, Count Yves-Thibault Christian Marie**; Vice Chairman and Lead Director, VINCI, since 2010 (Chairman, 2006–10); Chairman, YTSeuropaconsultants, since 2010; *b* Rennes, 22 July 1948; *s* of Raymond de Silguy and Claude de Pompery; *m* 1976, Jacqueline de Montillet de Grenaud (decd); one *s* one *d*. *Educ*: Collège Saint-Martin; Univ. of Rennes (Law and Econ Scis); Sch. of Public Service, Institut d'Etudes Politiques, Paris (Dip.); Ecole Nationale d'Administration. Sec. for Foreign Affairs to Dir for Econ. and Financial Affairs, 1976–80; Advr, then Dep. Staff Dir for Vice-Pres. Ortoli, Comr for Econ. and Monetary Affairs, 1981–84; Advr i/c Econ. Affairs, French Embassy in Washington, 1985–86; Tech. Advr to Prime Minister i/c European Affairs and Internat. Econ. and Financial Affairs, 1986–88; Manager, Internat. Business Div. and Gp Internat. Business Dir, Usinor Sacilor, 1988–93; Sec. Gen., Interministerial Cttee for European Econ. Co-operation and Advr for European Affairs to Prime Minister, 1993–95; Mem., European Commn, i/c economic, monetary and financial affairs, 1995–99. Bd Mem., 2000–02, Sen. Exec. Vice-Pres., 2002–06, SUEZ. Gen. Deleg. of French Steel Fedn, 1990–93; Chm. Bd, Professional Center for Steel Stats, 1990–93; Chm., Finance Cttee, Eurofer, 1990–93; Trustee, Internat. Accounting Standards Cttee Foundn, 2010–13. Commandeur: Ordre des Arts et des Lettres (France), 2007 (Officier, 1994); du Mérite Agricole (France), 2010 (Officier, 1995); Légion d'Honneur (France), 2011; Officier, Ordre Nat. du Mérite (France), 2000. *Recreations*: tennis, yachting, hunting. *Address*: c/o VINCI, 1 cours Ferdinand de Lesseps, 92851 Rueil-Malmaison Cedex, France. *Clubs*: Polo, Cercle de l'Union Interalliée (Paris).

**de SILVA, Harendra (Aneurin Domingo)**; QC 1995; a Recorder, since 1991; *b* 29 Sept. 1945; *s* of Annesley de Silva and Maharani of Porbandar; *m* 1972, Indira Raj; one *s* one *d*. *Educ*: Doon Sch., Dehra Dun, India; Millfield Sch.; Queens' Coll., Cambridge (MA, LLM). Called to the Bar, Middle Temple, 1970, Bencher, 2003. *Recreations*: golf, bridge. *Address*: Goldsmith Chambers, Goldsmith Building, Temple, EC4Y 7BL. *T*: (020) 7353 6802. *Clubs*: Roehampton; Ooty (Ootacamund, S India).

**DESLANDES, Ian Anthony**; Chief Executive, Construction Confederation, 1997–99; *b* 17 July 1941; *s* of Albert Deslandes and Christine Veronica Deslandes (*née* Hale); *m* 1965, Mary Catherine Bowler; two *s*. *Educ*: Stonyhurst Coll.; St Catherine's Coll., Oxford. Conservative Res. Dept, 1965–70; PA to Conservative Party Chm., 1970–72; Dir, Housebuilders' Fedn, 1973–78; Dir, Manpower Services, 1978–86, Dep. Dir Gen., 1985–92, Dir Gen., 1992–97, Building Employers' Confedn. CBI: Chm., Trade Assoc. Council, 1999; Mem., Council and President's Cttee, 1999. *Recreations*: reading, jazz, gardening, walking. *Address*: Greystones, Downhouse Lane, Higher Eype, Bridport, Dorset DT6 6AH. *T*: (01308) 424498.

**DESLONGCHAMPS, Prof. Pierre**, OC 1989; OQ 1997; PhD; FRS 1983; FRSC 1974; FCIC; Professor of Organic Chemistry, Université de Sherbrooke, Canada, 1972–2006, now Emeritus; Associate Professor, Laval University, Quebec, since 2008; *b* 8 May 1938; *s* of Rodolphe Deslongchamps and Madeleine Magnan; *m* 1st, 1960, Micheline Renaud (marr. diss. 1975); two *s*; 2nd, 1976, Shirley E. Thomas (marr. diss. 1983); 3rd, 1987, Marie-Marthe Leroux. *Educ*: Univ. de Montréal (BSc Chem., 1959); Univ. of New Brunswick (PhD Chem., 1964). FCIC 1980; FAAAS 1988. Post-doctoral Student with Dr R. B. Woodward, Harvard Univ., USA, 1965; Asst Prof., Univ. de Montréal, 1966; Asst Prof. 1967, Associate Prof. 1968, Univ. de Sherbrooke. A. P. Sloan Fellow, 1970–72; E. W. R. Steacie Fellow, 1971–74. Founder, NeoKimia, later Tranzyme Pharma Inc., 1998–2005. Member: Amer. Chem. Soc.; Ordre des Chemistes du Québec; Assoc. Canadienne-Française pour l'Avancement des Sciences; Fellow, World Innovation Foundn (UK), 2002; For. Asst Mem., Acad. des Scis de Paris, 1995. Dr *hc*: Univ. Pierre et Marie Curie, Paris, 1983; Bishop's Univ. and Univ. de Montréal, 1984; New Brunswick Univ., 1985; Univ. of Moncton, 1995. Scientific Prize of Québec, 1971; E. W. R. Steacie Prize (Nat. Scis), NRCC, 1974; Médaille Vincent, ACFAS, 1975; Merck, Sharp and Dohme Lectures Award, CIC, 1976; Canada Council Izaak Walton Killam Meml Scholarship, 1976–77; John Simon Guggenheim Meml Foundn Fellow, 1979; Médaille Pariseau, ACFAS, 1979; Marie-Victorin Médaille, Province of Quebec, 1987; Alfred Bader Award in Organic Chemistry, 1991, Lemieux Award, 1994, Bernard Belleau Award, 2011, Canadian Soc. for Chemistry; Canada Gold Medal for Science and Engrg, NSERCC, 1993. Holder of 21 patents. *Publications*: Stereoelectronic Effects in Organic Chemistry, 1983; over 240 contribs on organic chemistry in Tetrahedron, Jl Amer. Chem. Soc., Canadian Jl of Chem., Pure Applied Chem., Synth. Commun., Nouv. Jl Chim., Heterocycles, Jl Molecular Struct., Interface, Aldrichimica Acta, Angewandte Chemie, Internat. Edn, Jl Organic Chem., Organic Letters, Chem. - an Asian Jl, Bioorganic and Medical Chem. Letters, Eur. Jl of Chem., Bull. Soc. Chim., France, and Organic & Biomolecular Chem. *Recreations*: fishing, reading, walking. *Address*: 5607 St Louis Street, Apt 403, Lévis, QC G6V 4G2, Canada. *T*: (418) 6033753. *E*: pierre.deslongchamps@chm.ulaval.ca.

**DESMET, Anne Julie**, RA 2011; RWA 2008; RE 1988; artist-printmaker, since 1987; Editor, Printmaking Today magazine, 1998–2013; *b* Liverpool, 14 June 1964; *d* of late Louis Desmet and of Irene Desmet (*née* Irving); *m* 1994, Roy Willingham; one *s* one *d*. *Educ*: Seafield Grammar Sch., later Sacred Heart High Sch., Crosby, Liverpool; Worcester Coll./Ruskin Sch. of Drawing, Oxford (BFA 1986; Hon. Fellow, 2018); Central Sch. of Art and Design (Postgrad. Dip. Printmaking 1988); British Sch. at Rome (Scholarship in Printmaking 1990); MA Fine Art Oxon 1991. Specialist in wood engraved prints and collages of architectural/metamorphosing subjects; *solo exhibitions* include: Duncan Campbell Fine Art, London, 1991, 1992, 1994, 1996, 1998, 2000, 2002; Royal Over-Seas League, 1992, 2016; Godfrey and Watt Gall., Harrogate, 1993, 1995, 2009; Ex Libris Mus., Moscow, 1995; Hart Gall., London, 2004, 2006, 2008, 2010, 2011, 2012; Long and Ryle Gall., London, 2015, 2018; *retrospective exhibitions*: Towers and Transformations, Ashmolean Mus., Oxford and UK tour, 1998–99; Urban Evolution, Whitworth Art Gall., Manchester and UK tour, 2008–10; Under Changing Skies, Holburne Mus., Bath, 2017; An Italian Journey, Gainsborough's House, Sudbury, Suffolk, 2018; *group exhibitions* include: Royal Acad. Summer Exhibns, 1990–; Manhattan Graphics Centre, NY, 2001; Grafisch Mus., Groningen, 2001; Center for Contemp. Print, Connecticut, 2003; Nat. Art Club, New York, 2010; *work in public and private collections*, including: The Queen; V&A; RA; Nat. Art Liby; BM; BL; Ashmolean Mus.; Whitworth Art Gall.; Fitzwilliam Mus.; Bradford Mus. and Art Galls; Harrogate Mus.; Pallant House Gall.; Aberystwyth Univ. Mus.; Kent Univ.; UWE; Ex Libris Mus., Moscow; Contemp. Art Mus., Chamalières, France; Ostrobothnian Mus. and Lahti Art Mus., Finland; Mus. de Arte do Espirito Santo, Vitoria, Brazil; Lodz Mus., Poland, Mus. Civico, Cremona, Italy; Franciscan Mus., Gorica, Livno, Bosnia and Herzegovina; Gov. Art Collection, Gibraltar; Whangarei Art Mus., NZ; Guanlan Print Mus., Nanjing Art Gall., Heilongjiang Provincial Mus. of Art and Yinchuan Mus. of Art, China; *commissions* include: engravings for V&A, BM, Nat. Gall., BL, Sotheby's. Vis. lectr/tutor at instns incl. RA Schs, Middx Univ., Ruskin Sch. of Art, Oxford, 1989–. Arts Council funded artist-in-residence, Lauriston Primary Sch., Hackney, 2007–08; Artist-in-residence, Eton Coll., 2016. External examiner: Kingston Coll. of Art, 2010–13; Sch. of Art, Aberystwyth Univ., 2003–07. Hon. Fellow, Sch. of Art, Aberystwyth Univ., 2010–. Awards include: Pollock-Krasner Foundn Award, NY, 1998; Elizabeth Greenshields Foundn Award, Canada, 1989, 1996, 2007; RA Summer Exhibn Print Prize, 2010; V&A Purchase Prize, 2011. *Publications*: Anne Desmet: towers and transformations, 1998; (jtly) Handmade Prints, 2000, 4th edn 2012; (ed jtly) Printmakers: the directory, 2006; Primary Prints, 2010; Anne Desmet: an Italian journey, 2016; Anne Desmet: a Greek journey, 2019. *Recreations*: juggling work and family, vegetarian cuisine, Scandinavian and Italian TV dramas, sketching in Italy, book group. *Address*: Royal Academy of Arts, Burlington House, Piccadilly, W1J 0BD. *T*: (020) 7300 8000, *Fax*: (020) 7300 8001. *E*: anne.desmet@btinternet.com. *W*: www.annedesmet.com.

**DE SMET, Prof. Ingrid A. R.**, PhD; FBA 2014; Professor of French and Neo-Latin Studies, University of Warwick (Director, Centre for Study of the Renaissance, 2007–10 and 2014–18). *Educ*: Univ. of Leuven (PGDip); St John's Coll., Cambridge (PhD 1993); Univ. of Warwick (DLitt). Magdalen College, Oxford: Prize Fellow, 1993–96; British Acad. Postdoctoral Fellow, 1995–97; University of Warwick: Lectr, 1997; Leverhulme Maj. Res. Fellow, 2011–14; Academic Dir, Warwick in Venice, 2015–18. Member, Editorial Board: Lias; Jl Early Modern Intellectual Culture and its Sources; Renaissance Studies. Pres., Internat. Assoc. for Neo-Latin Studies, 2015–18 (Vice-Pres., 2013–15). *Publications*: Menippean Satire in the Republic of Letters, 1581–1655, 1996; (ed jtly and contrib.) Eros et Priapus: érotisme et obscénité dans la littérature néo-latine, 1997; Thuanus: the making of Jacques-Auguste de Thou (1553–1617), 2006; (contrib.) The Classical Tradition, 2010; La Fauconnerie à la Renaissance: le Hieracosophion (1582–1584) de Jacques Auguste de Thou, 2013; (contrib.) The Oxford Handbook of Neo-Latin, 2015; contribs to jls. *Address*: School of Modern Languages and Cultures, Humanities Building, University Road, University of Warwick, Coventry CV4 7AL.

**DESMOND, Sir Denis (Fitzgerald)**, KCVO 2018; CBE 1989; Lord-Lieutenant of Co. Londonderry, 2000–18; Chairman, Desmond & Sons Ltd, 1970–95; *b* 11 May 1943; *s* of late Major James Fitzgerald Desmond, DL, JP and Harriet Ivy Desmond (*née* Evans); *m* 1965, Annick Marie Françoise Marguerite Faussemagne; one *d*. *Educ*: Trinity Coll., Glenalmond. 2nd Lieut, then Lieut RCT (TA), 1964–69. ADC to Governor of NI, 1967–69. Dir, Ulster Bank, 1990–97. Chm., Altnagelvin Hosps Health Trust, 1996–2004.

Dir, Ulster Orchestra Soc. Ltd, 2008–12. Mem. Council, Prince's Trust, NI, 2008–12. Chm., Ulster Historical Foundn, 2008–. Pres., RFCA (NI), 2013–18. Hon. Colonel: 1 Bn ACF (NI), 2005–10; 152 Transport Regt RLC (TA), 2010–13. High Sheriff 1973, DL 1992–2000, Co. Londonderry. Hon. DSc: QUB, 1987; Ulster, 1991. *Address*: Bellarena, Limavady, Co. Londonderry BT49 0HZ.

**DESMOND, Michael John**; Commercial Director, All England Lawn Tennis and Croquet Club, since 2010; Co-founder and Executive Chairman, IPCN, since 2007; *b* 10 March 1959; *s* of Frank and Eileen Desmond; *m* 1984, Christine; one *s* two *d*. *Educ*: Leeds Univ. Gp Sales Manager, Anglia TV, 1982–86; Sales Controller, HTV, London, 1986–88; Sales Controller, 1988–92, Sales Dir, 1992–94, Granada; Chief Executive Officer: Laser, 1994–98; Granada Media Sales, 1998; Granada Broadcasting and Enterprises; Jt Man. Dir, ITV, 2002–04; Chief Exec., ITV Broadcast, 2004–05; Internat. Advr, Hunan Broadcasting Co., 2006. *Recreations*: golf, tennis, watching most sports. *Address*: 5 Copse Hill, SW20 0NB. *Club*: Solus.

**DESMOND, Richard Clive**; Chairman, Northern & Shell Network, since 1974; Proprietor, Express Newspapers, 2000–18; Owner, Channel 5 (formerly Five), 2010–14; Health Lottery, since 2011; *b* 8 Dec. 1951; *s* of late Cyril Desmond and of Millie Desmond; *m* 1983, Janet Robertson (marr. diss. 2010); one *s*; *m* 2012, Joy Canfield; one *s* one *d*. *Educ*: Christ's Coll., Finchley. Musician, 1967; Advertisement Exec., Thomson Gp, 1967–68; Group Advertisement Manager, Beat Pubns Ltd, 1968–74; launched International Musician, 1974 (separate editions in US, Europe, Australia and Japan); publr of numerous magazines in areas incl. leisure, music, hi tech, fitness, cooking, envmt, business, automotive, and men's and women's lifestyle; De Monde Advertising Ltd, 1976–89; OK! magazine, 1993– (separate editions in 20 countries); Fantasy Channel, 1995–; OK! TV, 1999–2011; owner: Portland TV, 1995–; Westferry Printers Ltd; Broughton Printers Ltd, 2000–; launched: Daily Star Sunday, 2002; New! mag., and Star mag., 2003. Pres., Norwood, 2006–; owner, Richard Desmond Crusaders Foundn, charitable trust. *Publications*: The Real Deal: the autobiography of Britain's most controversial media mogul, 2015. *Recreations*: music and drumming, fitness, family, philanthropy. *Address*: Northern & Shell Building, Number 10 Lower Thames Street, EC3R 6EN. *T*: (020) 8612 7000.

**de SOUZA, Christopher Edward**; freelance composer; broadcaster; Music Director, Cranford Choral Society, since 2015; *b* 6 June 1943; *s* of Denis Walter de Souza and Dorothy Edna (*née* Woodman); *m* 1971, Robyn Ann Williams (marr. diss. 1981); partner, Elinor Anne Kelly; two *s*. *Educ*: Prior Park Coll., Bath; Univ. of Bristol (BA Music 1966); Old Vic Theatre Sch. Head of Music, St Bernadette's RC Comp. Sch., Bristol, 1966–70; Producer, Sadlers Wells/ENO, 1971–75; Arts Producer, BBC Radio London, 1975–79; Producer, BBC Radio 3, 1980–95. Founder Dir, Liszt Fest. of London, 1977; (with J. Piper) music organiser, HM Silver Jubilee Fireworks, 1977. Director: UK stage premières: Don Sanche (Liszt), 1977; The Mother of Us All (Virgil Thompson), 1979; The Duenna (Prokofiev), 1980; Palestrina (Pfitzner), 1981; William Tell (Gretry), 1984; USA première: Don Sanche (Liszt), 1986. Founder (with Tristan de Souza and Sebastian de Souza), Artsplay.co.uk, 2009. *Compositions include*: music for TV, incl. Maharajahs, 1987; orch., chamber and choral works including The Ides of March, 1995, Bottom's Dream, 2009, Trombone Concerto, 2010, Loved and Unloved, 2011; (with Adrian Morris) Children of the Light (musical), 2001; Missa Douensis, 2003. *Publications*: A Child's Guide to Looking at Music, 1979; (ed jtly) Liszt: Don Sanche, 1985; Kingfisher Book of Music, 1996; contrib. to The Listener, Music and Musicians, Musical Times, Radio Times, Strad, The Times, BBC Music Mag., British Music Year Book. *Recreations*: reading, travel, swimming, drawing. *Address*: 61 Westbrook, Boxford, Berks RG20 8DL. *Club*: Royal Over-Seas League.

**DE SOUZA, Dame Rachel (Mary)**, DBE 2014; Chief Executive, Inspiration Trust, since 2012; *b* Scunthorpe, 12 Jan. 1968; *d* of David Kenny and Roselle Kenny (*née* Fekete); *m* 1991, Christopher de Souza; one *s*. *Educ*: St Bede's RC Sch., Lincs; Heythrop Coll., Univ. of London (BA Hons Philosophy and Theol. 1989); King's Coll. London (PGCE; MA Educn). Teacher: Kidlington Sch., Oxford, 1991–93; Sir John Cass Sch., Tower Hamlets, 1993–96; Hd of Dept, Luton Sixth Form Coll., 1996–2003; Dep. Headteacher, Denbigh High Sch., Luton, 2004–06; Founding Principal, Barnfield W Acad., 2006–10; Exec. Principal, Ormiston Victory Acad., 2010–13. Trustee, Shakespeare's Globe Th., 2014–. *Address*: Inspiration Trust, Weights and Measures Building, Old Fire Station, Bethel Street, Norwich, Norfolk NR2 1NR. *T*: (01603) 280931. *E*: chiefexecutive@inspirationtrust.org.

**DESPONTIN, Dr Brenda**; Principal, British School of Brussels, 2008–11; *b* 22 Oct. 1950; *d* of Telford and Nancy Betty Griffiths; *m* 1975, Robert Despontin; one *s*. *Educ*: University Coll., Cardiff (BA Hons Psychol.; MA English; PhD English - Children's Lit. 1996); Univ. of Bath (PGCE (Dist.)); Univ. of Hull (MBA); Cardiff Law Sch. (LLM Dist. 2013). Teacher, British Sch. of Brussels, 1973–77; residential social worker, 1977–78; teacher: Willlows Sch., Cardiff, 1978–85; New Coll., Cardiff, 1985–92; Principal, Girls' Div., King's Sch., Macclesfield, 1992–97; Headmistress, Haberdashers' Monmouth Sch. for Girls, 1997–2008. Pres., GSA, 2006; Associate Mem., HMC, 2016–. MCMI (MBIM 1995). FRSA. Teachers' Award for Sch. Leadership in Wales, 2003. *Publications*: (contrib. and ed jtly) Leading Schools in the 21st Century, 3 vols, 2008; contrib. Cardiff Law Sch. Jl, The Times, Daily Telegraph, FT, Independent, TES. *Recreations*: writing, reading, people-watching, following Fox's advice to 'walk cheerfully', travel, playing the piano (badly), learning Italian (slowly!).

**DESSAU, Hon. Linda Marion**, AC 2017 (AM 2010); Governor of Victoria, Australia, since 2015; *b* Melbourne, 1953. *Educ*: St Catherine's Girls' Sch., Melbourne; Univ. of Melbourne (LLB Hons). Admitted a solicitor, 1975; solicitor, Wisewoulds, 1975–78; barrister, Vic, 1978–82; Sen. Crown Counsel, Hong Kong, 1982–85; Referee, Small Claims and Residential Tenancies Tribunals, 1986; Magistrate, Vic, 1986–95; a Judge, Family Court of Australia, 1995–2013. Pres., Melbourne Fest., 2014. Comr, Aust. Football League, 2007–14; Chair, AFL SportsReady and ArtsReady, 2012–14. Trustee, Nat. Gall. of Vic, 2013–15; Dir, Winston Churchill Meml Trust, until 2015. Peter Baxter Churchill Fellow, 1994. *Address*: Government House, Government House Drive, Melbourne, Vic 3004, Australia.

**de SWIET, Eleanor Jane**, MA; Headteacher, The Henrietta Barnett School, 1989–99, retired; *b* 18 Aug. 1942; *d* of Richard and Joan Hawkins; *m* 1964, Prof. Michael de Swiet; two *s* one *d*. *Educ*: Girton Coll., Cambridge (MA Classics); Inst. of Education (PGCE). Teacher of Classics: Francis Holland Sch., 1965–67; St Paul's Girls' Sch., 1967–70; Queen's Coll., London, 1975–84; City of London Sch., 1984–89. Pres., JACT, 1995–97; Chm., Assoc. of Maintained Girls' Schs, 1997–98. Mem. Council, Cheltenham Ladies' Coll., 1999–2008; Governor: Asmount Primary Sch., 2007–17; Channing Sch., 2010–18; Hornsey Girls' Sch., 2014–. Trustee: Open Door, 2000–09 (Chm., 2007–09); Toynbee Hall, 2001–08. *Recreations*: walking, reading, Yorkshire, travelling, opera. *Address*: 15 Wren View, 75 Hornsey Lane, N6 5LH. *T*: (020) 8347 9014. *E*: jdeswiet@gmail.com.

**DETHRIDGE, Dame Kathleen, (Dame Kate)**, DBE 2015; Deputy Director, North West London and South Central London Regional Schools Commissioner's Office, since 2016; *b* Barking, Essex, 1962; *d* of Frederick Caldon and Patricia Caldon; *m* 1986, Rod Dethridge; two *s*. *Educ*: Brentwood Ursuline Convent; Durham Univ. (BA Hons; PGCE). Class teacher, 1985–88; Dep. Headteacher, 1988–98; Headteacher, 1998–2016, Exec. Headteacher, 2005–16, Churchend Primary Sch., Reading. Ofsted Inspector, 2000–14; Mem., Headteacher Ref. Gp, Ofsted, 2011–14; Vice Chm., Bureaucracy Ref. Gp, DfE, 2011–; Mem., Headteacher Bd, Regl Schs Comr for S Central England and NW London, 2014–16. Sch. Improvement Advr, 2005–10. Associate Dir, Nat. Educn Trust, 2011–; Mem. Bd, Freedom and Autonomy for Schs - Nat. Assoc., 2014–. Nat. Leader of Educn, 2008. *Publications*: (contrib.) Taking Forward the National Curriculum, 2013; A Practical Guide to the Early Years Foundation Stage, 2016. *Recreations*: cooking, riding, family, school governor, walking, cinema. *Address*: Heartwood, Water Street, Hampstead Norreys, Berks RG18 0RU. *T*: (01635) 886253. *E*: kate.dethridge@hotmail.co.uk.

**DETMER, Prof. Don Eugene**, MD; Professor of Medical Education, University of Virginia, since 1999; *b* 3 Feb. 1939; *s* of Lawrence D. Detmer and Esther B. Detmer (*née* McCormick); *m* 1961, Mary Helen McFerson (*d* 2018); two *d*. *Educ*: Univ. of Kansas (MD 1965); MA Cantab 2002. Asst Prof., 1973–77, Associate Prof., 1977–80, Prof., 1980–84, of Surgery and Preventive Medicine, Univ. of Wisconsin-Madison; Vice Pres. for Health Sci., and Prof. of Surgery and Med. Informatics, Univ. of Utah, 1984–88; University of Virginia: Vice Pres. for Health Sci., and Prof. of Surgery and Business Admin, 1988–92; Co-Dir, Virginia Health Policy Center, 1992–99; Vice Pres. and Provost for Health Sci., and Prof. of Health Policy and Surgery, 1993–96; Louis Nerancy Prof. of Health Scis Policy, Univ. Prof. and Sen. Vice Pres., 1996–99; Prof. Emeritus, 1999; Dennis Gillings Prof. of Health Mgt, Cambridge Univ., 1999–2003; Life Fellow, Clare Hall, Cambridge, 2000; Sen. Associate, Judge Inst. of Mgt, subseq. Judge Business Sch., Univ. of Cambridge, 2004–06; American Medical Informatics Association: Pres. and CEO, 2004–09; Sen. Advr, 2009–11; Dir, Advanced Interprofessional Informatics Certification, 2014; Med. Dir, Advocacy and Health Policy, Amer. Coll. of Surgeons, 2011–13; Founding Mem., Internat. Acad. of Health Scis and Informatics, 2017–. Vis. Prof., Centre for Health Informatics and Multiprofessional Educn, UCL, 2005–14. Sen. Ed., Applied Clinical Informatics Jl, 2015–. Vice-Pres., N Amer. Truffle Growers Assoc., 2019–. *Publications*: (ed jtly and contrib.) The Computer-Based Patient Record: an essential technology for health care, 1991, rev. edn 1997; articles in jls and contribs to books. *Recreations*: tree farming, journal writing, handcrafts. *Address*: Branch Point Farm, 5245 Brown's Gap Turnpike, Crozet, VA 22932, USA. *Club*: Colonnade (Charlottesville, Va) (Mem. Bd of Govs, 2014–).

**de TRAFFORD, Sir John (Humphrey)**, 7th Bt *cr* 1841, of Trafford Park, Lancashire; MBE 2010; Chairman, National Savings and Investments, 2012–16 (non-executive Director, 2010–16); *b* London, 12 Sept. 1950; *e s* of Sir Dermot Humphrey de Trafford, 6th Bt and Patricia Mary Beeley; *S* father, 2010; *m* 1975, Anne, *d* of J. Faure de Pebeyre; one *s* one *d*. *Educ*: Ampleforth; Univ. of Bristol (BSc). Sales and Mktg Dir, Thistle Hotels, 1982–87; with American Express, 1987–2005 (Regl Pres., Northern Europe, 2000–04). Chm., Pension, Disability and Carers Service, 2008–10. Chair, St Barbe Mus. and Art Gall., 2018–. *Recreation*: sailing. *Heir*: *s* Alexander Humphrey de Trafford [*b* 28 June 1978; *m* 2008, Imogen King; one *s* one *d*]. *Address*: Ground Floor, 17 Bolton Gardens, SW5 0AJ. *T*: (020) 7373 2669. *Clubs*: Royal Ocean Racing, Royal Cruising.

**DETTMER, Ven. Douglas James**; Archdeacon of Totnes, since 2015; *b* Kansas City, Missouri, 5 March 1964; *s* of Arlen and Peggy Dettmer; *m* 1998, Chloë Archer. *Educ*: Univ. of Kansas (BA 1986); Yale Univ. (MDiv 1990). Ordained deacon, 1990, priest, 1991; Asst Curate, Ilfracombe Team Ministry, 1990–94; Domestic Chaplain to Bishop of Exeter, 1994–98; Priest-in-charge: Raddon Team Ministry, 1998–2010; Stoke Canon Benefice, 2006–10; Rector, Netherexe Parishes, 2010–15. Member: Gen. Synod, 2012–; Rural Affairs Gp, Mission and Public Affairs Div., 2013–; Legal Adv. Commn, 2016–. Chm., Exeter Diocesan Bd of Educn, 2016–. *Recreations*: reading, walking, gardening, music, museums. *Address*: Blue Hills, Bradley Road, Bovey Tracey, Newton Abbot, Devon TQ13 9EU. *T*: (01626) 832064. *E*: archdeacon.of.totnes@exeter.anglican.org.

**DETTORI, Lanfranco, (Frankie)**, Hon. MBE 2000; flat race jockey; *b* Italy, 15 Dec. 1970; *s* of Gianfranco Dettori and Maria Dettori (*née* Nieman); *m* 1997, Catherine, *d* of W. R. Allen, *qv*; two *s* three *d*. Winner: Fillies' Mile, on Shamshir, 1990, on Glorosia, 1997, on Teggiano, 1999, on Crystal Music, 2000, on White Moonstone, 2010; World Young Jockey Championship, Japan, 1992, 1993; Ascot Gold Cup, on Drum Taps, 1992, 1993, on Papineau, 2004, on Colour Vision, 2012, on Stradivarius, 2018, 2019; French Derby; German Derby; Nonthorpe; Sussex Stakes; Prix de l'Abbaye, Longchamp, on Lochsong, 1993, 1994, on Var, 2004; Irish Derby, on Balanchine, 1994; Oaks, on Balanchine, 1994, on Moonshell, 1995, on Kazzia, 2002, on Enable, 2017; Queen Elizabeth II, on Lammtarra, 1995, on Poet's Voice, 2010; St Leger, on Classic Cliché, 1995, on Shantou, 1996, on Scorpion, 2005, on Sixties Icon, 2006, on Conduit, 2008; Prix de l'Arc de Triomphe, on Lammtarra, 1995, on Sakhee, 2001, on Marienbard, 2002, on Golden Horn, 2015, on Enable, 2017, 2018; Two Thousand Guineas, on Mark of Esteem, 1996, on Island Sands, 1999, on Galileo Gold, 2016; Irish Champion Stakes, on Swain, 1998, on Daylami, 1999, on Fantastic Light, 2001, on Grandera, 2002, on Snow Fairy, 2012; on Galileo Gold, 2016; One Thousand Guineas, on Cape Verdi, 1998; on Kazzia, 2002, on Blue Bunting, 2011; Breeders' Cup Turf, NY, on Daylami, 1999, on Fantastic Light, 2001, on Red Rocks, 2006, on Dangerous Midge, 2010; French Two Thousand Guineas, on Bachir, 2000, on Noverre, 2001, on Shamardal, 2005; Prix de Diane, on West Wind, 2007, on Star of Seville, 2015; Irish Oaks, on Lailani, 2001, on Vintage Tipple, 2003, on Blue Bunting, 2011, on Enable, 2017; Epsom Derby, on Authorized, 2007, on Golden Horn, 2015; Goodwood Cup, on Schiaparelli, 2009, on Opinion Poll, 2011; Eclipse Stakes, on Golden Horn, 2015; St James's Palace Stakes, on Galileo Gold, 2016, on Without Parole, 2018; King George and Queen Elizabeth Diamond Stakes, on Enable, 2017; Yorkshire Oaks, on Enable, 2017; Champion Stakes, on Cracksman, 2017; all seven winners, Ascot, 28 Sept. 1996. Champion Jockey, 1994, 1995, 2004. Presenter, Channel 4 Racing, 2014. Jt Proprietor, Frankie's Italian Bar and Grill, London, Dublin and Dubai, 2004–. *Publications*: A Year in the Life of Frankie Dettori, 1996; (with Jonathan Powell) Frankie: the autobiography of Frankie Dettori, 2004. *Address*: c/o Peter Burrell, 5 Jubilee Place, SW3 3TD. *T*: (020) 7352 8899.

**DEUCHAR, Rev. Andrew Gilchrist**; independent consultant on international relations, sport and community development, since 2012; Director: BUILD, 2011–12; Football Clubs in Global Partnerships, since 2013; *b* 3 June 1955; *s* of late David and (Lucretia) Marian Deuchar; *m* 1977, Francesca Fowler; three *s* two *d*. *Educ*: Royal Hospital Sch., Ipswich; Southampton Univ. (BTh); Salisbury and Wells Theol Coll. HM Diplomatic Service, 1974–81; ordained deacon, 1984, priest, 1985; Asst Curate, Alnwick, Northumberland, 1984–88; Team Vicar, S Wye Team Ministry, Hereford, 1988–90; Social Responsibility Advr, Canterbury and Rochester dios, 1990–94; Archbp of Canterbury's Sec. for Anglican Communion Affairs, 1994–2000; Rector of St Peter and All Saints (formerly St Peter with St James), Nottingham, 2000–08; Priest-in-charge, St Mary the Virgin, Nottingham, 2004–08; a Chaplain to the Queen, 2004–08; Diocesan Audit Officer, Dio. of Moray, Ross and Caithness, 2008–10. Hon. Canon, Canterbury Cathedral, 1995–2000. Chaplain to High Sheriff of Notts, 2007–08. Mem., Bd of Trustees, USPG, 2003–06; Trustee: Swindon Town Football in the Community Trust, 2012–15; Hay2Timbuktu Partnership, 2014–16. Consultant: Handa Foundn, 2016; Anglican Alliance, 2016. Mem., Exec. Cttee, Brecon and Radnor Lib Dems, 2015– (Chair, 2016). Patron, Bishop Mubarak Scholarship Fund,

2004–08. *Publications:* (contrib.) Anglicanism: a global communion, 1998; (contrib.) An Introduction to the Anglican Communion, 1998; (ed) A Last Embrace: essays in honour of Nadir Dinshaw, 2003; (contrib.) Faith in Action: Njongonkulu Ndungane, Archbishop for the Church and the world, 2008. *Recreations:* music, travel, walking, football, the Isle of Skye, genealogy.
*See also P. L. Deuchar.*

**DEUCHAR, Patrick Lindsay;** *b* 27 March 1949; *s* of late David and of Marian Deuchar; *m* Gwyneth Miles (marr. diss.); one *s* one *d*; *m* 1997, Liz Robertson; one *d*. *Educ:* Christ's Hospital; Lackham Coll. of Agriculture. Farming, 1967–72; IPC Business Press, 1972–74; PR Manager, RASE, 1974–77; PR Manager, Earls Court and Olympia, 1977–80; European Dir, World Championship Tennis, 1981–89; Chief Exec., Royal Albert Hall, 1989–98; Chm., London Centre Mgt Co., 1998–99; Chief Exec., Rugby Hospitality for Rugby World Cup, 1998–99; Events Consultant to Somerset House Trust Ltd, 1998–99; 7th Regt Armory Conservancy, NY, 1998–99. Director: London First, 1996–99; TS2K (Trng and Skills 2000) (formerly Trafalgar Square 2000), 1996– (Dep. Chm.); Covent Gdn Fest., 1998–2001; (non-exec.) Cavendish Consultancy, 2000–. Chm., Sparks Charity, 1992–96; Member: Nat. Fundraising Cttee, Muscular Dystrophy Group, 1989–92; Nat. Music Day Cttee, 1993–97; London Visitor Council, 1994–97; Royal Concert Cttee, 1994–97; Mem. Council, 1995, Chm. Develt Cttee, 2000, RCM. Trustee: Albert Meml Trust, 1994–99; Cardiff Bay Opera House, 1994–96. Barker, Variety Club of GB, 1992; Mem., Inst. of Dirs. FRSA 1992. *Recreations:* music, theatre, art, cooking, wines, family life. *Address:* Flat 1, 27 Sloane Gardens, SW1W 8EB.
*See also Rev. A. G. Deuchar.*

**DEUCHAR, Dr Stephen John,** CBE 2010; Director, Art Fund, since 2010; *b* 11 March 1957; *s* of late Rev. John Deuchar and Nancy Dorothea Deuchar (*née* Jenkyns); *m* 1982, Prof. Katie Scott; one *s* three *d*. *Educ:* Dulwich Coll. (Schol.); Univ. of Southampton (BA 1st Cl. Hons Hist.); Westfield Coll., London (PhD Hist. of Art 1986). Andrew W. Mellon Fellow in British Art, Yale Univ., 1981–82. Curator of Paintings, then Exhibns Dir, National Maritime Museum, 1985–98; Dir, Tate Britain, 1998–2010. Trustee: Creative Foundn, 2008–; British Council, 2019–. Chair, Jury, Turner Prize, 2008–09; Chair, Judging Panel, Mus. of the Year, 2013–19. *Publications:* Noble Exercise: the sporting ideal in 18th-century British art, 1982; Paintings, Politics and Porter: Samuel Whitbread and British art, 1984; (jtly) Concise Catalogue of Oil Paintings in the National Maritime Museum, 1988; Sporting Art in 18th-Century England: a social and political history, 1988; (jtly) Nelson: an illustrated history, 1995; contrib. articles on British art and museums. *Recreation:* motor sport. *Address:* Art Fund, 2 Granary Square, King's Cross, N1C 4BH. *T:* (020) 7225 4800.

**DEUTSCH, Anthony Frederick;** Sheriff of Glasgow and Strathkelvin, 2005–18; *b* 9 June 1952; *s* of Robert and Elizabeth Deutsch; *m* 1977, Barbara MacDonald; two *s* one *d*. *Educ:* Univ. of Edinburgh (MA, LLB). Admitted solicitor, 1978; Partner, Macdonalds Solicitors, Glasgow, 1980–2005. *Recreations:* reading (mostly history), walking (mostly Isle of Arran), cooking, wine.

**DEUTSCH, Prof. David Elieser,** DPhil; FRS 2008; Visiting Professor, Centre for Quantum Computation, Clarendon Laboratory, University of Oxford, since 1999; *b* Haifa, 18 May 1953; *s* of Oskar Deutsch and Tikva Deutsch. *Educ:* William Ellis Sch., London; Clare Coll., Cambridge (BA Natural Scis, Math. Tripos Pt III 1974); Wolfson Coll., Oxford (DPhil Theoretical Physics); Hon. Fellow 2016). *Publications:* The Fabric of Reality, 1997; The Beginning of Infinity, 2011. *Address:* Centre for Quantum Computation, Clarendon Laboratory, Parks Road, Oxford OX1 3PU. *E:* david.deutsch@qubit.org.

**DEUTSCH, James Chobot,** PhD; Director of Wildlife Conservation, Vulcan Philanthropy, Vulcan Inc., since 2015; Director of Biodiversity, Paul G. Allen Philanthropies, since 2015; *b* 28 Nov. 1963; *s* of late Harold Kauffman Deutsch and Barbara Chobot Deutsch. *Educ:* St George's Sch., Newport, RI; Harvard Coll. (AB 1987); King's Coll., Cambridge (MPhil 1988, PhD 1992). Temp. Lectr, UEA, 1992–93; Res. Fellow, Churchill Coll., Cambridge, 1993–95; Lectr, Imperial Coll., London, 1995–97; Chief Exec., Crusaid, 1997–2002; Africa Dir, 2002–14, Vice Pres., Conservation Strategy, 2014–15, Wildlife Conservation Soc. Chairman: Aidspan, 2002–11 (Bd Mem., 2002–); COMACO, 2010–; Member: Bd, AIDS Treatment Project, 1996–2000; Exec. Cttee, British HIV Assoc., 1999–2001; Council, Crusaid, 2002–10. *Publications:* (ed) Wild Rangelands, 2010; contrib. articles to Nature, Proc. Royal Soc., Evolution, HIV Medicine, Animal Behaviour, Conservation Biol., African Jl Ecol., and other jls. *Address:* Vulcan Inc., 505 5th Avenue South, Seattle, WA 98104, USA. *T:* (206) 4505153.

**DEVA, Niranjan Joseph Aditya, (Nirj);** DL; Member (C) South East Region, England, European Parliament, 1999–2019; *b* Colombo, 11 May 1948; *s* of late Thakur Dr Kingsley de Silva Deva Aditya and of Zita Virginia Deva; *m* Indra Lavinia, *d* of Romy Govindia; one step *s*. *Educ:* St Joseph's Coll., Colombo; Loughborough Univ. of Technol. (BTech Hons Aero. Eng.). Company dir and adviser; Chm., Symphony Environmental Plastics Ltd; Director: Ceylon and Foreign Trades (Sri Lanka) Ltd; Distilleries Co. of Sri Lanka Ltd, 2006–; Aitken Spence Ltd, Sri Lanka, 2006–; Hotel Services (Sri Lanka) Ltd, 2009–; Sri Lankan Airlines, 2015–. Pol Officer, 1979, Chm., 1981, Bow Gp. Organiser, Conf. on Overseas Develt and Brandt Report, 1979. Member: Governing Council, Royal Commonwealth Soc., 1979–83; Nat. Consumer Council, 1982–88; Dept of Employment Adv. Cttee, 1988–91; Chairman: DTI/NCC Cttee on De-regulation of European Air Transport, 1985–86; One Nation Forum Political Cttee, 1986–91. Pres., Bow Group Trade and Industry Cttee, 1996. Contested (C) Hammersmith, 1987; MP (C) Brentford and Isleworth, 1992–97; contested (C) same seat, 1997. PPS to Minister of State, Scottish Office, 1996–97. Mem., Select Cttee on Parly Admin (Ombudsman), 1992–96, on Educn, 1995–96; Vice-Chm., Cons. back bench Aviation Cttee, 1994–97 (Jt Sec., 1992); Member: Asylum Bill Cttee, 1992; Deregulation Bill Cttee, 1994–97; Caravans Rating Bill Cttee, 1996–97; Asylum and Immigration Bill Cttee, 1996–97; European Standing Cttee B, 1992–97; All-Party Manufacturing Gp, 1993–97; Hon. Sec., All-Party Uganda Gp, 1994–97. European Parliament: spokesman on overseas develt and co-operation, 1999, on internat. develt, 2009–19; Member: Envmt Cttee, 1999–2019; EU-ACP Delegn, 1999–2019; Delegn to ASEAN countries, 2002–19; Delegn to South Asian Assoc. for Regl Cooperation, 2004–19 (Vice Chm., 2007–19); Foreign Affairs Cttee, 2004–09; Chairman: Delegn to UN Commn on Sustainable Development, NY, 2005; Delegn to Korean Peninsular, 2014–19; Co-Leader, Delegn to World Summit and Gen. Assembly, 2006; Vice Pres., Internat. Develt Cttee, 2009–19; Co-ordinator, Eur. Conservatives and Reformists Gp, 2009–19; Rapporteur: WTO and Develt Issues of World Trade, 2000–19; Aid to Uprooted People in Asia and Latin America, 2000–19; Pacific Strategy, 2007–19; Nation Building in Post-Conflict Situations, 2008–19; Private Sector Develt, 2016–19; Mem., Clinton Global Initiative, 2008. Co-Chm., Burke's Club for Transatlantic Relns, 2009–. Chairman: Indonesia Gp, 2000–19; Afghan Gp, 2000–19; EU-India Chamber of Commerce, 2005–19; EU-China Friendship Gp, 2006–19; Wkg Gp 'B', Develt Cttee, 2006–19; Vice Pres., India Gp, 2001–19; EPP-ED Coordinator, Develt Commn, 2004–19; Co-Chairman: Wkg Gp on Colombia, 2004–19; Delegn to UN World Summit and Gen.

Assembly, 2005; Tsunami Co-ordinator, 2005–19; budget draftsman, Develt Budget, 2006. Contested (C) SE Reg., EP, 2019. Pres., Internat. Cttee on Human Dignity. Hon. Advr to Prime Minister of Sri Lanka, 2002–. Mem., Organising Cttee, World Culture Fest., 2006–. Editor, Crossbow, 1983–85. Presenter, Deva's Hour, Sunrise Radio, 1995, 1998–99. FRSA 1997. DL Greater London, 1986. Hon. Ambassador-at-Large for Sri Lanka, 2003–. Vishwa Kirthi Sri Lanka Ahbimani, 2007. Knight of Merit with Star, Sacred Military Constantinian Order of St George, 2011. MEP of the Year, Parlt Mag., 2012; Editor's Award, GG2, 2017. *Publications:* Wealth of Nations Part II: Adam Smith revisited, 1998; various pamphlets and memoranda for Bow Group, 1980–85. *Recreations:* riding, reading, tennis. *Clubs:* Carlton; Hounslow Conservative.

**de VALLERA, João;** Ambassador of Portugal to the Court of St James's, 2011–16; *b* Malange, Angola, 1 June 1950; *s* of Manuel and Nolga de Vallera; *m* 1982, Margarida Azevedo; one *s*. *Educ:* Univ. of Lisbon (Dr in Econs). Joined Portuguese Diplomatic Service, 1974; Bonn, 1977–79; Perm. Mission to EC, Brussels, 1979–84; Hd, Eur. Integration Dept, 1986–89; Asst Dir Gen. for Eur. Communities, 1988; Minister, Madrid, 1989; Perm. Repn to EC, Brussels, 1990–98, Dep. Perm. Rep., 1993–98; Ambassador to Ireland, 1998–2001; Dir Gen., Eur. Affairs, 2001; Delegate to Convention on Future of Europe, 2002; Ambassador: to Germany, 2002–07; to USA, 2007–11. Officer, Order of Infante D. Henrique (Portugal), 1978; Grand Cross: Order of Merit (Portugal), 2002; Military Order of Christ (Portugal), 2005; Cross, Order of Merit 1st Cl. (Germany), 2006. *Recreations:* classical music, painting, photography. *Clubs:* Royal Automobile; Royal Mid-Surrey Golf; Grémio Literário (Lisbon).

**DEVANE, Sir Ciarán (Gearóid),** Kt 2015; Chief Executive, British Council, since 2015; *b* 25 Oct. 1962; *s* of Micheal and Eibhlín Devane; *m* 1998, Katy Ashburner (*d* 2003). *Educ:* University Coll., Dublin (BEng); George Washington Univ. (Masters Internat. Policy and Practice). Process Engr, ICI, 1984–93; Mgt Consultant, Gemini Consulting, 1993–2003; Chm., Pavilion Housing Gp, 2004–05; Chief Exec., Macmillan Cancer Support, 2007–14. Trustee: Liver Gp, 2010–12; Makaton Charity, 2011–14; NCVO, 2012–15. Non-exec. Dir, NHS England, 2012–15. Chm., Health Service Exec., Ireland, 2018–. FRSA. *Recreations:* hill walking, theatre. *Address:* c/o British Council, 10 Spring Gardens, SW1A 2BN.

**DEVAUX, His Honour John Edward;** DL; a Circuit Judge, 1993–2019; *b* 1947; *s* of Henry Edward Devaux and Anne Elizabeth Devaux; *m* 1979, Fiona O'Conor; two *d*. *Educ:* Beaumont Coll.; Bristol Univ. (LLB). Called to the Bar, Lincoln's Inn, 1970; a Recorder, 1989–93; Resident Judge, Ipswich, 1998–2007. Hon. Recorder of Ipswich, 2000–18. DL Suffolk, 2013.

**DEVENISH, Anthony Stuart;** Member (C) West Central, London Assembly, Greater London Authority, since 2016; *b* London, 31 March 1968. Rolls-Royce, 1990–97; Kvaerner, 1998–99; Thames Water, 1999–2004; Veolia, 2004–12. Mem. (C), Westminster CC, 2006–. *Recreation:* travel (previously lived and worked in Gulf and Far East, 1990–99). *Address:* c/o Westminster City Council, 64 Victoria Street, SW1E 6QP. *E:* tdevenish@westminster.gov.uk.

**de VERE WHITE, Hon. Mrs;** *see* Glendinning, Hon. Victoria.

**DEVEREAU, (George) Michael,** CB 1997; Head of Government Information Service, 1990–97; Chief Executive (formerly Director General), Central Office of Information, 1989–96; *b* 10 Nov. 1937; *s* of George Alfred Devereau and Elspeth Mary Duff Devereau; *m* 1961, Sarah Poupart; four *s*. *Educ:* King William's Coll., Isle of Man; University Coll. London. Asst Ed., Architects' Jl, 1962; Information Officer, MPBW, BRE and DoE, 1967–75; Chief Information Officer: Price Commn, 1975; DoE, 1978; Dept of Transport, 1982; Gp Dir, 1985, Dep. Dir Gen., 1987, COI. Trustee, Manx Nat. Heritage, 2007–18. *Publications:* Architects Working Details, 1964. *Recreations:* house restoration, travel. *Address:* 24 Fairway Drive, Ramsey, Isle of Man IM8 2BB.

**DEVERELL, Gen. Sir Christopher (Michael),** KCB 2015; MBE; Commander, Joint Forces Command, 2016–19; Aide-de-Camp General to the Queen, 2016–19; *m* Alex; two *s*. *Educ:* Wellington Coll.; Mansfield Coll., Oxford (BA Hons PPE 1982). Commnd 2nd RTR, 1979; served NI, Germany, Belize and Cyprus; i/c Jt Nuclear Biol. and Chem. Regt (1st RTR), RAF Honington, Suffolk; DACOS for Land Ops, Perm. Jt HQ; COS to Sen. British MA, US Central Comd; DACOS (Ops Commitments), HQ Land Forces; Asst Private Sec. to Sec. of State for Defence; HCSC 2004; Comdr, 4th Armd Bde, Iraq and Germany, 2005–07; Dir, Equipt Capability (Ground Manoeuvre), MoD, 2007–08; Dir Gen., Logistics Support and Equipt, HQ Land Forces, 2008–11; Dir, Materiel Strategy, 2011–12, Chief of Materiel (Land) and Quartermaster Gen., 2012–16, Defence Equipt and Support, MoD. Colonel Commandant: RTR, 2010–15; REME, 2010–16.

**DEVERELL, Gen. Sir John Freegard, (Sir Jack),** KCB 1999; OBE 1986; DL; Commander-in-Chief, Allied Forces North, 2001–04; *b* 27 April 1945; *s* of Harold James Frank Deverell and Joan Beatrice Deverell (*née* Carter); *m* 1973, Jane Ellen Solomon; one *s* one *d*. *Educ:* King Edward's Sch., Bath; RMA Sandhurst. Commnd Somerset and Cornwall LI, 1965; RN Staff Coll., Greenwich, 1977; Comd 3rd Bn LI, 1984–86; Mil. Dir of Studies, RMCS, Shrivenham, 1988; Higher Command and Staff Course, Camberley, 1988; Comdr 1st Infantry Bde (UK Mobile Force), 1988–90; NDC, India, 1991; Dir, Army Recruiting, 1992–93; Dir Gen., Army Manning and Recruiting, 1993–95; Comdt, RMA Sandhurst, 1995–97; Dep. C-in-C, HQ Land Comd and Insp. Gen. TA, 1997–98 and 1999–2001; Dep. Comdr (Ops), HQ SFOR, Bosnia, 1998–99. Chm., Nat. Army Museum, 2005–14. Pres., ACFA, 2004–11. Pres., Free Foresters Cricket Club, 2013–. DL Wilts, 2015. *Recreations:* golf, cricket, horses. *Clubs:* Cavalry and Guards, Mounted Infantry.

**DEVERELL, Richard George;** Director, Royal Botanic Gardens, Kew, since 2012; *b* 4 Dec. 1965; *s* of Geoff and Pauline Deverell; *m* 1993, Sarah Ann Inigo-Jones; one *s* two *d*. *Educ:* St Mary's Coll., Southampton; Magdalene Coll., Cambridge (BA Nat. Scis 1987). Associate Consultant, LEK Partnership, 1990–92; joined BBC, 1992; Sen. Advr, Policy and Planning, 1992–96; Head: Strategy and Mktg, BBC News, 1996–2000; BBC News Interactive, 2000–05; Chief Operating Officer, 2005–06, Controller, 2006–09, BBC Children's; Chief Operating Officer, BBC North, 2009–11; Programme Dir, W12 Project, BBC, 2011–12; Dep. Gp Dir, Strategy, Ofcom, 2012. Trustee, Royal Botanic Gdns, Kew, 2003–09. *Recreations:* cooking, fly fishing. *Address:* Royal Botanic Gardens, Kew, Richmond, Surrey TW9 3AB.

**DEVEREUX,** family name of Viscount Hereford.

**DEVEREUX, Hon. Edward Mark de Breteuil;** QC 2017; *b* London, 8 June 1977; *yr s* of 18th Viscount Hereford and Susan Mary, *d* of Maj. Maurice Godley. *Educ:* Summer Fields, Oxford; Eton; Peterhouse, Cambridge (Exhibnr; BA Hist.); City Univ. (DipLaw); Coll. of Law. Called to the Bar, Middle Temple, 2001 (Schol.); in practice as barrister specialising in internat. family law, 2001–. Jun. Family Barrister of Year, Chambers and Partners, 2015. *Publications:* (Contrib. Ed.) Dicey, Morris and Collins on The Conflict of Laws, 2012; (contrib.) Child Case Management Practice, 2009, 3rd edn 2017; (contrib.)

Standard Family Orders Handbook, vol. 2, 2018. *Recreations:* history, international family law, collecting fine art, Italy. *Address:* Harcourt Chambers, 2 Harcourt Buildings, Temple, EC4Y 9DB. *Club:* White's.
*See also Viscount Hereford.*

**DEVEREUX, Prof. Michael Peter,** PhD; Director, Oxford University Centre for Business Taxation, since 2006; Fellow, Oriel College, Oxford, since 2006; *b* Dover, 9 May 1959; *s* of Roy Devereux and Mary Margaret Devereux; *m* 1983, Katherine Mary Ronan; two *s* one *d*. *Educ:* St John's Coll., Oxford (BA 1980); London Sch. of Econs (MSc 1982); University Coll. London (PhD 1990). Institute of Fiscal Studies: Res. Officer, 1982–85; Sen. Res. Officer, 1985–86; Dir of Corporate Sector Prog., 1987–90; Prof. of Econs and Finance, 1990–98, and Chair, Econs Dept, 1993–96, Univ. of Keele; Prof. of Econs, 1998–2006, and Chair, Econs Dept, 2002–05, Univ. of Warwick. Eur. Tax Policy Forum, 2004–; Hon. Pres., Internat. Inst. for Public Finance, 2015 (Vice Pres., 2009–12; Pres., 2012–15). Houblon-Norman Fellow, Bank of England, 1992–93; Research Fellow: IFS, 1990–2005; Centre for Econ. Policy Res., 2000–; CESifo, 2006–. *Publications:* (ed) The Economics of Tax Policy, 1996; (jtly) The Effective Levels of Company Taxation in the Member States of the EU, 2001; contrib. papers to jls incl. Econ. Jl, Econ. Policy, Jl Public Econs, Jl Econometrics, Internat. Tax and Public Finance, Jl Internat. Econs. *Recreations:* family, tennis, music. *Address:* Oxford University Centre for Business Taxation, Saïd Business School, Park End Street, Oxford OX1 1HP. *T:* (01865) 288507, *Fax:* (01865) 288805. *E:* michael.devereux@sbs.ox.ac.uk.
*See also Sir R. J. Devereux.*

**DEVEREUX, Robert Harold Ferrers;** Founder and Director, African Arts Trust, since 2012; Executive Chairman, The Conduit Ltd, since 2016; *b* Woking, 11 April 1955; *s* of Robert Humphrey Bouchier Devereux and Barbara Devereux (*née* Heywood); *m* 1983, Vanessa (marr. diss.), *d* of late Edward James Branson; three *s* one *d*. *Educ:* Marlborough Coll.; Downing Coll., Cambridge (BA Hons 1978). Founding shareholder and Chm., Virgin Communications and Entertainment Gp, 1979–96; Chairman: Soho House, 1998–2008; Frieze Events Ltd, 2010–15; Frieze Publishing Ltd, 2010–15. Dir, New Forest Co. Hldgs Ltd, 2007– (Chm., 2007–15). Mem., DCMS Creative Industries Task Force; Mem. Supervisory Panel, Catalyst Partners LLP, 2011–. Trustee and Chm., Portobello Trust, 1993–2003; Chm., Trustees, Save the Rhino Internat., 1997–2006; Trustee, Westside Sch., Westminster, 2008–. Gov., South Bank Centre, 1997–2009; Chm., Tate Africa Acquisitions Cttee, 2011–15; Mem. Adv. Bd, Cambridge Conservation Initiative, 2011–; Founder, African Arts Trust, 2012–; Dep. Chm., Workplace Foundn, 2017–; Mem. Council, ICA. *Recreations:* art, walking, tree planting, history, Africa, literature, theatre. *Address:* 148 Highlever Road, W10 6PJ. *T:* 07768 270416. *E:* robert.hfd@virgin.net. *Clubs:* Soho House, Conduit.
*See also Sir R. C. N. Branson.*

**DEVEREUX, Sir Robert (John),** KCB 2016; Permanent Secretary, Department for Work and Pensions, 2011–18; *b* 15 Jan. 1957; *s* of Roy Devereux and Mary Margaret Devereux; *m* 1980, Margaret Alexandra Johnson; two *d*. *Educ:* St John's Coll., Oxford (MA Maths; Hon. Fellow, 2017); Edinburgh Univ. (MSc Stats). ODA, 1979–83; HM Treasury, 1984–94 (Hd, Defence Expenditure, 1992–94); Guinness Brewing Worldwide, 1995–96 (on secondment); Department for Social Security: Hd, Family Policy, 1996–98; Director: Fraud Strategy, 1998–2000; Working Age Strategy, 2000–01; Dir, Planning and Performance, DWP, 2001–02; Dir Gen., Roads, Regl and Local Transport, subseq. Road Transport, Aviation and Shipping, DfT, 2003–07; Permanent Sec., DfT, 2007–10.
*See also M. P. Devereux.*

**de VESCI,** 7th Viscount *cr* 1766; **Thomas Eustace Vesey;** Bt 1698; Baron Knapton, 1750; Managing Director, Horticultural Coir Ltd, since 1999; *b* 8 Oct. 1955; *s* of 6th Viscount de Vesci and Susan Anne (*d* 1986), *d* of late Ronald (Owen Lloyd) Armstrong-Jones, MBE, QC, DL, and of the Countess of Rosse; *S* father, 1983; *m* 1987, Sita-Maria (marr. diss. 2011), *oc* of late Brian de Breffny; two *s* one *d*. *Educ:* Eton; St Benet's Hall, Oxford. *Address:* Knapton, Abbeyleix, Co. Laois, Ireland.

**DEVEY, Hilary Lorraine,** CBE 2013; Founder, Chief Executive Officer and Chairman, Pall-Ex Group, since 1996; *b* Bolton, Gtr Manchester, 10 March 1957; *d* of Arthur Brewster and Wyn Cross; one *s*. Vice Pres., Carers Trust. Patron, Stroke Assoc. Hon. Dr: Leicester, 2010; Bolton, 2012; Wolverhampton, 2014. Sir Robert Lawrence Award, CILT, 2009. *Publications:* Bold As Brass: my story, 2012. *Recreation:* campaigner for charities. *Address:* Pall-Ex, Pall-Ex House, Victoria Road, Ellistown, Leics LE67 1FH. *T:* (01530) 239000.

**DE VILLE, Sir Harold Godfrey, (Sir Oscar),** Kt 1990; CBE 1979; PhD; Chairman, Meyer International plc, 1987–91 (Deputy Chairman, 1985–87; Director, 1984–91); *b* Derbyshire, 11 April 1925; *s* of Harold De Ville and Anne De Ville (*née* Godfrey); *m* 1947, Pamela Fay Ellis; one *s*. *Educ:* Burton-on-Trent Grammar Sch.; Trinity Coll., Cambridge (MA); PhD London 1995. Served RNVR, 1943–46. Ford Motor Co. Ltd, 1949–65; BICC, 1965–84: Dir, 1971–84; Exec. Dep. Chm., 1978–84. Director: Balfour Beatty Ltd, 1971–78; Phillips Cables Ltd, Canada, 1982–84; Metal Manufacturers Ltd, Australia, 1983–84; Scottish Cables Ltd, S Africa, 1983–84. Mem., BRB, 1985–91. Chairman: Iron and Steel EDC, 1984–86; Govt Review of vocational qualifications, 1985–86; NCVQ, 1986–90; Nat. Jt Council for Engrg Construction Industry, 1985–87. Member: Commn on Industrial Relations, 1971–74; Central Arbitration Cttee, 1976–77; Council: ACAS, 1976–91; BIM, 1982–86; Confederation of British Industry, 1977–85 (Chm., Working Party on Employee Participation, 1975–78). Mem. Council, Reading Univ., 1985–91. *Recreation:* genealogy.

**de VILLEPIN, Dominique Marie François René Galouzeau;** Prime Minister of France, 2005–07; lawyer, since 2008; *b* Rabat, Morocco, 14 Nov. 1953; *s* of Xavier Galouzeau de Villepin and Yvonne (*née* Hétier); *m* 1985, Marie-Laure Le Guay; one *s* two *d*. *Educ:* Ecole Nat. d'Admin; Paris Inst. of Pol Scis (BA Arts and Law). Ministry of Foreign Affairs, France: Sec. of Foreign Affairs, Dept for African Affairs, 1980–81; Hd of Mission, Dept for African Affairs and Analysis and Forecasting Centre, 1981–84; First Sec., 1984–87, Press Officer and Spokesperson, 1987–89, Washington; Second Counsellor, 1989–90, First Counsellor, 1990–92, New Delhi; Dep. Hd, African Affairs, Min. of Foreign Affairs, 1992–93; COS to Minister of Foreign Affairs, 1993–95; Sec. Gen. of Presidency of Republic, 1995–2002; Minister of Foreign Affairs, 2002–04; Rep., Convention on Future of Europe, 2002; Minister of the Interior, Internal Security and Local Rights, 2004–05. Chm., Admin. Council, Nat. Forests Office, 1996–99. *Publications:* Les Cent Jours ou l'esprit de sacrifice, 2001; Le cri de la gargouille, 2002; Eloge des voleurs de feu, 2003; "Un autre monde": Cahiers de l'Herne, 2003; Le requin et la mouette, 2004; L'homme européen, 2005; Histoire de la diplomatie française, 2005; Le soleil noir de la puissance, 2007; Hôtel de l'insomnie, 2008; La chute ou l'Empire de la solitude, 2008; La cité des hommes, 2009; Le dernier témoin, 2009; De l'esprit de cour: la malédiction française, 2010; Notre vieux pays, 2011; Seul le devoir nous rendra libres, 2012; Mémoire de paix pour temps de guerre, 2016; *poetry:* Parole d'exil, 1986; Le droit d'aînesse, 1988; Sécession, 1996; Elégies barbares, 1996. *Address:* 84 Avenue Foch, 75116 Paris, France.

**de VILLIERS,** 4th Baron *cr* 1910; **Alexander Charles de Villiers;** *b* 29 Dec. 1940; *o s* of 3rd Baron de Villiers and Edna Alexis Lovett (*née* MacKinnon); *S* father, 2001; *m* 1966 (marr. diss.); *m* 1987, Christina Jacobsen.

**de VILLIERS, Dawid Jacobus,** DPhil; Advisor to the Secretary General of the United Nations World Tourism Organisation, 2006–15 (Chairman, Strategic Committee and World Committee for Ethics in Tourism, 2006–15); Deputy Secretary General, World Tourism Organisation, 1997–2005; *b* 10 July 1940; *m* 1964, Suzaan Mangold; one *s* three *d*. *Educ:* Univ. of Stellenbosch (BA Hons Philosophy; BTh, DPhil); Rand Afrikaans Univ. (MA Phil., 1972). Abe Bailey Scholar, 1963–64; Markotter Scholar, 1964. Part-time Lectr in Philosophy, Univ. of Western Cape, 1963–64; Minister of Dutch Reformed Church, Wellington, Cape, 1967–69; Lectr in Philosophy, 1969–72, and Pres. Convocation, 1973–96, Rand Afrikaans Univ.; MP for Johannesburg W, 1972–79, for Piketberg, 1981–94, list MP, 1994–97; Chm., Nat. Party's Foreign Affairs Cttee in Parlt; Ambassador of S Africa to London, 1979–80; Minister: of Trade and Industry (formerly Industries, Commerce and Tourism), SA, 1980–86; of Budget and Welfare, 1986–88; for Admin and Privatisation, 1988–90; for Public Enterprises, 1989–91; for Mineral and Energy Affairs, 1990–91; for Economic Co-ordination, 1991–92; for Public Enterprises, 1992–94; for the Envmt and Tourism, 1994–96; Leader, Houses of Parliament, 1989–92. Leader, Nat. Party, Cape Province, 1990–96. National Party Delegn Leader, Constitutional Conf., Convention for a Democratic S Africa, 1992. Visited: USA on US Leaders Exchange Prog., 1974; UK as guest of Brit. Govt, 1975; Israel as guest of Israeli Govt, 1977. Represented S Africa in internat. Rugby in S Africa, UK, Ireland, Australia, NZ, France and the Argentine, 1962–70 (Captain, 1965–70). State President's Award for Sport, 1968 and 1970; S African Sportsman of the Year, 1968; Jaycee's Outstanding Young Man of the Year Award, 1971; State President's Decoration for Meritorious Service, Gold, 1988. *Recreations:* sports, reading. *Address:* Koloniesland 8, Stellenbosch, 7600, South Africa.

**de VILLIERS, Etienne Marquard;** non-executive Chairman: BBC Worldwide, 2005–09; Virgin Racing, 2009–10; BrandsEye, since 2012; PinDrop, since 2015; *b* Pretoria, SA, 19 Aug. 1949; *s* of Dr J. T. Marquard and Anita R. L. de Villiers; *m* 1973, Anita Du Plooy; one *s* one *d*. *Educ:* Pretoria Boys High Sch.; Univ. of Pretoria (BSc (Eng-Civil) *cum laude*; Galion Gold Medal 1970); Trinity Coll., Oxford (MA PPE). Rhodes Schol., 1971. Associate, McKinsey & Co., London, 1979–81; Exec. Dir, Solaglas Internat., 1981–84; CEO, Satbel, 1984–86; Walt Disney Co.: Man. Dir, 1986–2000; President: Buena Vista Internat., 1986–94; Walt Disney TV Internat., 1994–99; Pres. and Man. Dir, Walt Disney Internat. EMEA, 1999–2000; Co-Founder, i-Gabriel, 2000–01; Mem. Bd, SLEC, 2001–02; Co-Founder, Englefield Capital, 2001–05; Exec. Chm. and Pres., ATP, 2005–08. Member, Board: Videonetworks, 2000–06; Carlton Communications, 2001–03; ITV plc, 2003–04; Jetix, 2005–07; non-exec. Dir, Pi Capital, 2002–16. *Recreations:* politics, news, sport, passionate cyclist and tennis player, avid off piste skier, despite the divorce threats; contemporary British figurative art collector thankfully curtailed by lack of wall space; music, film and TV fanatic; travelling with Anita and spending time in the Algarve; re-learning about life from my grandsons Leo, Elliot and Reuben who call me Oupie (the Afrikaans diminutive for Oupa (Grandpa)), similar to new 'handle' Opil (Old Person in Lycra). *Address:* c/o 22 Bolton Gardens, SW5 0AQ. *T:* (020) 7373 0758. *E:* paula@boltongardens.co.uk.

**de VILLIERS, Fleur Olive Lourens,** CMG 2011; Chairman of Trustees, International Institute for Strategic Studies, 2000–19; *b* Port Elizabeth, South Africa, 1 Dec. 1937; *d* of late Frederick, (Dick) and Edna de Villiers (*née* Walker). *Educ:* Loreto Convent, Hillcrest; Univ. of Pretoria (BA); Harvard Univ. (Nieman Fellow 1981). Theatre critic, Econs Corresp., Political Reporter, then Leader writer, Pretoria News, 1961–73; Sunday Times, Johannesburg: Political Corresp. and travelling corresp., 1973–80; Asst Ed. and Opinion Page Ed., 1981–86; Leader Writer and consultant on S Africa for The Times, 1986–93. Public Affairs Consultant to: De Beers, 1988–2003; Anglo American Corp., 1988–98. Vis. Fellow, 1986–87, Vice Chm. Council, 2000–19, IISS. Mem., Internat. Adv. Bd, 2004–, Global Ambassador, 2011–, SOAS. Mem., London Diocesan Synod, 2015–. Mem. Council, Chelsea Soc., 2014–. *Publications:* Professional Secrecy in South Africa, 1983; Bridge or Barricade: a guide to South Africa's new constitution, 1983; Apartheid: Capitalism or Socialism?, 1986; articles in Strategic Survey, National Interest, TES, The Times, etc. *Recreations:* gardening, reading, music, theatre, talking politics, theology. *Address:* 14 Caversham Street, SW3 4AH.

**DEVINE, Prof. Fiona,** CBE 2019 (OBE 2010); PhD; FAcSS; Professor of Sociology, since 2001, and Head, Alliance Manchester Business School (formerly Manchester Business School), since 2014 (Interim Head, 2013–14), University of Manchester; *b* 6 June 1962; *d* of Patrick Noel Devine and Martha (*née* Daly); *m* 2008, James B. Husband. *Educ:* Univ. of Essex (BA Sociol. and Govt 1983); MA Sociol.; PhD Sociol. 1990. Res. officer, PSI, 1988–89; Lectr in Sociol., Univ. of Liverpool, 1989–94; University of Manchester: Lectr, 1994–97; Sen. Lectr, 1997–99; Reader, 1999–2001; Hd of Sociol., 2004–07; Hd, Sch. of Social Scis, 2009–13. Mem. Council, ESRC, 2003–07 (Chm., Internat. Adv. Cttee, 2003–07). FAcSS (AcSS 2011); FRSA 2015. *Publications:* Affluent Workers Revisited, 1992; Social Class in America and Britain, 1997; (jtly) Sociological Research Methods in Context, 1999; Class Practices, 2004; (jtly) Doing Social Science, 2009; (jtly) Social Class in the 21st Century, 2015. *Recreations:* walking in Spain, bird-watching, classical and world music, swimming, badminton. *Address:* Alliance Manchester Business School, University of Manchester, Booth Street West, Manchester M15 6PB. *T:* (0161) 306 1322. *E:* Fiona.Devine@manchester.ac.uk.

**DEVINE, James;** *b* 24 May 1953; *s* of James and Rose Devine; *m* 1974, Elizabeth (marr. diss.); one *s* one *d*. *Educ:* St Mary's Acad., W Lothian; Moray House Coll. Sch. of Nursing. Student teacher, 1970–72; student nurse, 1972–75; Staff Nurse, Bangour Hosp., 1975–77; Charge Nurse, psychiatric nursing team, Blackburn Health Centre, 1977–82; union official, COHSE, then Unison (Head of Health, Scotland), 1982–2005. MP (Lab) Livingston, Sept. 2005–2010. Hon. Lectr in Industrial Relns, Stirling Univ., 1985–2005. Agent, Rt Hon. Robin Cook, MP, 1982–2005. Mem., Scottish Exec., Labour Party, 1983–95; Chm., Scottish Labour Party, 1996–95. *Recreations:* reading, chess, football, horse racing. *Club:* Loganlea Miners.

**DEVINE, Sir Thomas (Martin),** Kt 2014; OBE 2005; PhD, DLitt; FBA 1994; FRSE; FRHistS; FSAScot; Sir William Fraser Professor of Scottish History and Palaeography, University of Edinburgh, 2005–11, Emeritus, 2015 (Head, School of History, Classics and Archaeology, 2008–10; Founding Director, Scottish Centre for Diaspora Studies, 2008–14; Personal Senior Research Professor in History, 2012–14); *b* 30 July 1945; *s* of Michael Gerard Devine and Norah Martin; *m* 1971, Catherine Mary Lynas; one *s* three *d* (and one *s* decd). *Educ:* Strathclyde Univ. (BA; PhD 1972; DLitt 1992). FRHistS 1980; FRSE 1992. University of Strathclyde: Lectr in History, 1969–78; Sen. Lectr in History, 1978–83; Reader in Scottish History, 1983–88; Prof. of Scottish History, 1988–98; Dir, Res. Centre in Scottish History, 1993–98; Dean, Faculty of Arts and Social Studies, 1993–94; Dep. Principal, 1994–97; Aberdeen University: Univ. Res. Prof. in Scottish Hist. and Dir, Res. Inst. of Irish and Scottish Studies, 1998–2003; Dir, AHRB, subseq. AHRC Centre for Irish-Scottish Studies, 2001–06; Glucksman Res. Prof., 2004–06. Adjunct Professor in

History: Univ. of Guelph, Canada, 1989–; Univ. of N Carolina, 1997–. Member: Sec. of State for Scotland's Adv. Cttee, 2001–04; Res. Awards Adv. Cttee, Leverhulme Trust, 2002–09; Adv. Cttee, ESRC Prog. on Devolution, 2002–06. Chm., Econ. and Social History Soc. of Scotland, 1984–88; Convenor of Council, Scottish Catholic Historical Assoc., 1990–95; Convener, Irish-Scottish Academic Initiative, 1998–2001; UK Rep., Internat. Commn for Hist. of Towns, 2000–06. Mem. Council, British Acad., 1998–2001. Mem., Adv. Cttee, Eur. Assoc. of History Educators, 2001–. Trustee, 1995–2002, Chair, 1999–2002, European Ethnol Res. Centre, Nat. Museums of Scotland. Gov., St Andrew's Coll. of Educn, 1990–94. Prothero Lectr, RHistS, 2005. FSAScot 2014; FRSA 2015. Hon. MRIA 2001. Hon. Fellow, Bell Coll., 2005. Hon. DLitt: QUB; Abertay Dundee; DUniv Strathclyde, 2006. Sen. Hume Brown Prize in Scottish Hist., 1976; Saltire Prize, 1992; Henry Duncan Prize, RSE, 1994; Royal Medal, RSE, 2001; John Aitkenhead Award and Medal, Inst. of Contemp. Scotland, 2006; RSE/Beltane Sen. Prize for Excellence in Public Engagement, 2012; Inaugural Sir Walter Scott Senior Prize for Excellence in Humanities and Creative Arts, RSE, 2012; Wallace Award, Amer. Scottish Foundn, USA, 2016; Lifetime Achievement Award, All-Party Parly Gp on Hist. and Archives, 2018. *Publications:* The Tobacco Lords, 1975, 2nd edn 1990; (ed) Ireland and Scotland 1600–1850, 1983; (ed) Farm Servants and Labour in Lowland Scotland, 1984; A Scottish Firm in Virginia 1767–77, 1984; (ed) People and Society in Scotland, 1988; The Great Highland Famine, 1988; (ed) Improvement and Enlightenment, 1989; (ed) Conflict and Stability in Scottish Society 1700–1850, 1990; (ed) Irish Immigrants and Scottish Society in 18th and 19th Centuries, 1991; Scottish Emigration and Scottish Society, 1992; The Transformation of Rural Scotland 1660–1815, 1994; Clanship to Crofters' War, 1994; (ed) Scottish Elites, 1994; Glasgow, vol. I, 1995; Exploring The Scottish Past, 1995; (ed) Scotland in the Twentieth Century, 1996; (ed) Eighteenth Century Scotland: new perspectives, 1999; (ed) Celebrating Columba: Irish-Scottish connections 1597–1997, 1999; The Scottish Nation 1700–2000, 1999; (ed) Scotland's Shame?: bigotry and sectarianism in modern Scotland, 2000; (ed) Being Scottish: personal reflections on Scottish identity, 2002; Scotland's Empire 1600–1815, 2003; The Transformation of Scotland, 2005; Clearance and Improvement: land, power and people in Scotland, 1660–1860, 2006; The Scottish Nation 1700–2007, 2006; (ed) Scotland and the Union, 1707 to 2007, 2008; To the Ends of the Earth: Scotland's global diaspora 1750–2010, 2011; (ed jtly) Scotland and the British Empire, 2011; (ed jtly) The Oxford Handbook of Modern Scottish History 1500–2010, 2012; (ed) Recovering Scotland's Slavery Past: the Caribbean connection, 2015; Independence or Union: Scotland's past and Scotland's present, 2016; (ed jtly) Scots in Asia: settlers and sojourners 1700 to the present, 2016; (jtly) Tea and Empire, 2017; (ed jtly) New Scots: Scotland's Immigrant Communities since 1945, 2018; The Scottish Clearances: a history of the dispossessed, 1600–1900, 2018; numerous articles in learned jls and book collections. *Recreations:* grandchildren, walking and staying in the Hebrides, foreign travel, music, watching skilful soccer. *Address:* School of History, Classics and Archaeology, University of Edinburgh, William Robertson Wing, Teviot Place, Edinburgh EH8 9AG. *T:* (01698) 421057. *E:* Tmdevine1@aol.com.

**DEVITT, Sir James (Hugh Thomas),** 3rd Bt *cr* 1916, of Chelsea, Co. London; hotel and leisure consultant; Managing Director, Herald Hotels Ltd, since 2013; *b* 18 Sept. 1956; *o s* of Sir Thomas Gordon Devitt, 2nd Bt and of Janet Lilian, *o d* of Col H. S. Ellis, CBE, MC, *S father,* 1995; *m* 1985, Susan Carol (*née* Duffus); two *s* one *d. Educ:* Corpus Christi Coll., Cambridge (MA). MRICS. Dir, CB Richard Ellis Hotels, 2003–12; Chartered Surveyor, Wivenhoe House Hotel Ltd, 2012–13. *Recreations:* family, football. *Heir: s* Jack Thomas Michael Devitt, *b* 29 July 1988. *Address:* The Old Rectory, Ford Lane, Alresford, Colchester, Essex CO7 8AX. *T:* (01206) 827315.

**DEVLIN, Graham Thomas,** CBE 2010; theatre writer and director, since 1973; arts consultant, since 1999; *b* London, 11 Nov. 1948; *s* of Alan Devlin and Eileen Devlin; *m* 2005, Susan Linda Hoyle, *qv. Educ:* Tonbridge Sch.; University Coll., Oxford (MA). Artistic Dir and Chief Exec., Major Road Theatre Co., 1973–97; Dep. Sec. Gen. and Acting Chief Exec., Arts Council of England, 1997–99. Fellow in Theatre, Bradford Univ., 1978–82; Dir, Wakefield Fest., 1981–82. Chairman: Phoenix Dance, 1989–97; Tipping Point, 2007–17; Dep. Chm., Royal Court Th., 2005–; Exec. Chm., Dance Training and Accreditation Partnership, 2009–14. Vis. Prof., Queen Margaret University Coll., Edinburgh, 1998–2003. Dir of over 80 theatre and opera prodns. *Publications:* Stepping Forward, 1989; A Place to Think, 2010. *E:* graham_devlin@yahoo.co.uk.

**DEVLIN, Hugh Gerard;** Founding Partner, Delightful LLP, since 2008; *b* Lanark, 1 March 1962; *s* of Francis and Maureen Devlin; *m* 1998, Sarah Rebecca Polden. *Educ:* Our Lady's High Sch., Motherwell; Univ. of Glasgow (MA, LLB); Univ. of Edinburgh (DipLP). NP 1987. Solicitor, Drummond & Co., 1986–89; Manager, Corporate Finance, British Linen Bank, 1989–94; joined Withers LLP, 1994, Partner, 1995–2008, Consultant, 2008–. Mentor, Grad. Fashion Week, 2008–. Trustee, Design Mus., 2012–. *Recreations:* contemporary art and design, opera and ballet, Italy, fashion history, assisting creative talent. *Address:* 75 Aberdeen Park, N5 2AZ. *T:* (020) 7354 0233, 07879 465422. *E:* hugh@hughdevlin.com.

**DEVLIN, (Josephine) Bernadette;** *see* McAliskey, J. B.

**DEVLIN, Roger William;** Chairman: Persimmon plc, since 2018; William Hill plc, since 2018; *b* Bolton, 22 Aug. 1957; *s* of William and Edna Devlin; *m* 1983, Louise Alice Temlett; two *d. Educ:* Manchester Grammar Sch.; Wadham Coll., Oxford (MA Juris. 1978). Hd, Mergers and Acquisitions, Hill Samuel, 1978–92; Director: Hilton Internat., 1993–2007; Ladbrokes, 1993–2007. Chm., Marstons plc, 2013–18; non-exec. Dir, Nat. Express plc. Sen. Ind. Dir, FA, 2012–18. Writer and producer, ind. feature film, Breaking the Bank, 2016. *Recreations:* golf, horse racing. *Address:* c/o William Hill plc, 1 Bedford Avenue, WC1B 3AU. *Clubs:* Turf; Sunningdale Golf, Royal St George's Golf (Sandwich), Royal and Ancient Golf (St Andrews).

**DEVLIN, Tim;** Founder and Director, Tim Devlin Enterprises, public relations consultancy, 1989–2013; *b* 28 July 1944; 3rd *s* of Rt Hon. Lord Devlin, PC, FBA, and Madeleine, *yr d* of Sir Bernard Oppenheimer, 1st Bt; *m* 1967, Angela Denise, *d* of late A. J. G. and Mrs Laramy; two *s* two *d. Educ:* Winchester Coll.; University Coll., Oxford (Hons degree, History). Feature Writer, Aberdeen Press & Journal, 1966; Reporter, Scotsman, 1967; Educn Reporter, Evening Echo, Watford, 1968–69; Reporter, later News Editor, The Times Educnl Supplement, 1969–71; Reporter, The Times, 1971–73, Educn Corresp., 1973–77; Nat. Dir, ISIS, 1977–84; Public Relations Dir, Inst. of Dirs, 1984–86; Assoc. Dir, Charles Barker Traverse-Healy, 1986–89. *Publications:* (with Mary Warnock) What Must We Teach?, 1977; Good Communications Guide, 1980; Independent Schools—The Facts, 1981; Choosing Your Independent School, 1984; (with Brian Knight) Public Relations and Marketing for Schools, 1990; (with Hywel Williams) Old School Ties, 1992; (with Angela Devlin) Anybody's Nightmare, 1998; Public Relations Manual for Schools, 1998. *Recreations:* writing, art, crochet, Italian life, opera. *T:* (01424) 256352. *E:* tim.devlin.ostuni@gmail.com.

**DEVLIN, Timothy Robert;** barrister; *b* 13 June 1959; *e s* of late H. Brendan Devlin, CBE, FRCS and of Anne Elizabeth Devlin, MB BCh; *m* 1st, 1986 (marr. diss. 1989); 2nd, 1991 (marr. diss. 2002); 3rd, 2011, Donna Kusman. *Educ:* Dulwich Coll.; LSE; City Univ. Called to the Bar, Lincoln's Inn, 1985 (Hardwick and Thomas More Scholar; Mem., Finance Cttee, 2006–). Sen. Expert, Technical Assistance to CIS, EU, 1998–99; Consultant, Stanbrook & Hooper, Brussels, 1999–2000. Co. Sec., Furnival Ltd, 2008–. Dep. Chm., NHS Tribunal, 2001–. Mem., Cons. Research Dept, 1981; former Chm., LSE Conservatives; Chm., Islington North Cons. Assoc., 1986. MP (C) Stockton South, 1987–97; contested (C) same seat, 1997, 2001. PPS to Attorney Gen., 1992–94; PPS to Ministers of Trade and Industry, 1995–97. Mem., Select Cttee on Scottish Affairs, 1995–97; formerly Chm., Parly Panel on Charity Law; Chm., Northern Gp of Cons. MPs, 1992–97. Dep. Chm., Foreign Affairs Forum, 1990–92; Member: SE Circuit, Criminal Bar Assoc., 1998–; Bar Council, 2007–10, 2012– (Chair, EU Law Cttee, 2016–18). Member: Soc. of Cons. Lawyers; European Bar Assoc.; Friends of the RA. Trustee, NSPCC, 1993–95; Gov., Yarm Sch., 1988–98. *Recreations:* sailing, opera, travel. *Address:* 32 Furnival Street, EC4A 1JQ. *Clubs:* Royal Ocean Racing, Bar Yacht; Island Sailing.

**DEVON, 19th Earl of,** *cr* 1553; **Charles Peregrine Courtenay;** Bt 1644; *b* 14 Aug. 1975; *o s* of 18th Earl of Devon and Diana Frances Courtenay (*née* Watherston); *S father,* 2015; *m* 2004, Allison Joy Langer; one *s* one *d. Educ:* St John's Coll., Cambridge (BA Hons History of Art, 1997; MA 2001; Rugby half-Blue 1996). Called to the Bar, Inner Temple, 1999; admitted to California Bar, 2004. Latham & Watkins LLP: Associate, Los Angeles, 2005–13; Counsel, 2014–18, Hd of Intellectual Property Litigation, Europe, 2015–18; Partner, Michelmores LLP, 2019–. London Scottish 1st XV Rugby, 1998–2003; Santa Monica 1st XV Rugby, 2003–05. Elected Mem., H of L, 2018. Mem., Grocers' Co. *Heir: s* Lord Courtenay, *qv. Clubs:* Hawks'; St Moritz Tobogganing; Butterflies Cricket; Santa Monica Rugby.

**DEVONPORT,** 3rd Viscount *cr* 1917, of Wittington, Bucks; **Terence Kearley;** Bt 1908; Baron 1910; architect and landowner; Chairman: Peasmarsh Place (Country Care), since 1984; Millhouse Developments Ltd, since 1989; *b* 29 Aug. 1944; *s* of 2nd Viscount Devonport and Sheila Isabel, *e d* of Lt-Col C. Hope Murray; *S father,* 1973; *m* 1st, 1968, Elizabeth Rosemary (marr. diss. 1979), *d* of late John G. Hopton; two *d*; 2nd, 2000, Dr Meiyi Pu, *d* of Prof. Wan Jun Pu, Beijing; one *d. Educ:* Aiglon Coll., Switzerland; Selwyn Coll., Cambridge (BA, DipArch, MA); Newcastle Univ. (MPhil). Architect: Davis Brody, New York City, 1967–68; London Borough of Lambeth, 1971–72; Barnett Winskell, Newcastle-upon-Tyne, 1972–75; landscape architect, Ralph Erskine, Newcastle, 1977–78; in private practice, 1979–84 (RIBA, ALI), Forestry Manager, 1973–; farmer, 1978–. Chairman: Cape Acre Ltd; Devonport Farms Ltd; Devonport Estates; Man. Dir, Tweedswood Enterprises, 1979–2011, and dir various other cos, 1984–. Member: Lloyds, 1976–90; Internat. Dendrology Soc., 1978– (Council, 1995–); N Adv. Cttee, TGEW, 1978–94; N Adv. Cttee, CLA, 1980–85; Nat. Land Use and Envmt Cttee, TGUK, 1984–87. Pres., Arboricultural Assoc., 1995–2001; Forestry Commn Reference Panel, 1987–94. Patron, Golden Retriever Club, Northumbria. MInstD. FRSA; FLS. Order of Mark Twain (USA), 1977. *Recreations:* nature, travel and good food; interests: trees, the arts, country sports. *Heir: cousin* David Kearley, *b* 18 Jan. 1982. *Address:* Ray Estate Office, Lynnheads Barn, West Woodburn, Hexham, Northumberland NE48 2TE. *Clubs:* Royal Automobile, Beefsteak, Farmers, Royal Over-Seas League; Northern Counties (Newcastle upon Tyne).

**DEVONSHIRE,** 12th Duke of, *cr* 1694; **Peregrine Andrew Morny Cavendish,** KCVO 2009; CBE 1997; DL; Baron Cavendish, 1605; Earl of Devonshire, 1618; Marquess of Hartington, 1694; Earl of Burlington, 1831; Baron Cavendish (UK), 1831; Chairman, Chatsworth House Trust, since 2004; *b* 27 April 1944; *s* of 11th Duke of Devonshire, KG, MC, PC and Dowager Duchess of Devonshire, DCVO; *S father,* 2004; *m* 1967, Amanda Carmen, *d* of late Comdr E. G. Heywood-Lonsdale, RN, and of Mrs Heywood-Lonsdale; one *s* two *d. Educ:* Eton; Exeter Coll., Oxford. Sen. Steward, Jockey Club, 1989–94; Chm., British Horseracing Bd, 1993–96; HM's Rep., 1998–2011, and Chm., 1998–2008, Ascot Racecourse. Dep. Chm., Sotheby's Holdings Inc., 1996– (Dir, 1994–). Trustee: Wallace Collection, 2007–15; Storm King Art Centre, New York, 2007–; Mus Sheffield (formerly Sheffield Galls and Mus) Trust, 2007–12; Derby Museums, 2012–. Mem. Shadow Bd, Derby, Derbyshire, Nottingham and Nottinghamshire LEP, 2010–12. DL Derbys, 2008. *Heir: s* Earl of Burlington, *qv. Address:* Chatsworth, Bakewell, Derbyshire DE45 1PP.

**de VOS, Niels;** Founder and Chief Executive Officer, Fabric Group Ltd, since 2018; Creator and Chief Executive Officer, Athletics World Cup Ltd, since 2018; *b* 27 March 1967; *s* of Leendert and Christine de Vos; *m* 1990, Kirsten Macleod; two *s* one *d. Educ:* Dorridge Jun. Sch.; King Edward's Sch., Edgbaston; Keble Coll., Oxford (BA Hons Modern Hist.). Hd, Corporate Relns, Barnardo's, 1994–97; Commercial Gen. Manager, Millennium Dome, 1997–99; Commercial Dir, Manchester 2002 Commonwealth Games, 1999–2002; CEO, Sale Sharks Rugby Club, 2002–07; CEO, UK Athletics, 2007–18; CEO, 2017 World Athletics and Para Athletics Championships, 2013–17. Jt Chm., 2018 European Indoor Athletics Championships, 2015–18. Mem., Nat. Olympic Cttee, 2007–; Executive Director: British Olympic Assoc., 2009–15 (Chm., Audit Cttee, 2009–11); European Athletics Marketing AG, 2015–. Founder and Trustee, Children's Promise, 1999–2004; non-exec. Dir, Birmingham Children's Hosp., 2010–11; Chair, Birmingham St Mary's Hospice, 2017–. *Recreations:* football, running, films, family holidays.

**DEVOY, Dame Susan (Elizabeth Anne),** DNZM 1998; CBE 1993 (MBE 1986); professional squash rackets player, 1982–92, retired; formerly Chief Executive Officer, then Chairperson, Sport Bay of Plenty; *b* 4 Jan. 1964; *d* of John and Tui Devoy; *m* 1986, John Brandon Oakley; four *s. Educ:* McKillop Coll., Rotorua. Ranked no 1 internat. women's squash rackets player, 1984–92; winner: World Championships: Dublin, 1985; Auckland, 1987; Sydney, 1990; Vancouver, 1992; British Open Championships, 1984–90, 1992; 86 other internat. titles. Walked length of NZ in 53 days, raising NZ500,000 for Muscular Dystrophy, 1988. Trustee: Halberg Trust for Crippled Children (Chm., 1996–2005); Tauranga Energy Consumer Trust. Race Relations Comr, Human Rights Commn, NZ, 2013–18. NZ Sportsperson of Year, Halberg Trust, 1985–87, 1990, 1992. *Publications:* Susan Devoy on Squash, 1988; Out on Top, 1993. *Recreation:* yoga.

**DEW, John Anthony;** HM Diplomatic Service, retired; consultant; illustrator and printmaker; *b* 3 May 1952; *s* of late Roderick Dew and of Katharina (*née* Kohlmeyer); *m* 1975, Marion, *d* of late Prof. Kenneth Kirkwood; three *d. Educ:* Hastings Grammar Sch.; Lincoln Coll., Oxford (Schol.); Ruskin Sch. of Drawing, Oxford. Joined HM Diplomatic Service, 1973; Third Sec., Caracas, 1975–79; FCO, 1979–83; First Sec., UK Delegn to OECD, Paris, 1983–87; Asst Hd, Falkland Is and Resource Mgt Depts, FCO, 1987–92; Counsellor, Dublin, 1992–96; Minister, Madrid, 1996–2000; Hd of Latin America and Caribbean Dept, FCO, 2000–03; on secondment to Lehman Brothers Internat., 2003–04; Ambassador: to Cuba, 2004–08; to Colombia, 2008–12. Printmaker, Taller Experimental de la Gráfica, Havana, Taller Arte Dos, Bogotá and Print Makers' Co-op., Oxford. Solo exhibition, Galeria Arte Dos Bogotá, 2011; group exhibitions: RE, 2014, 2017; RWS, 2016. *Recreations:* books, pictures. *E:* johnanthonydew@gmail.com. *W:* www.johndew.uk. *Club:* Real Gran Pena (Madrid).

**DEW, His Eminence Cardinal John Atcherley;** *see* Wellington (NZ), Archbishop of, (RC).

**de WAAL, Edmund Arthur Lowndes,** OBE 2011; artist and writer; *b* 10 Sept. 1964; *s* of Rev. Victor Alexander de Waal, *qv*; *m* 1997, Susan Chandler; two *s* one *d*. *Educ*: Trinity Hall, Cambridge (BA 1st cl. Hons (English Lit.) 1986; Hon. Fellow 2009); Sheffield Univ. (Postgrad. Dip. Japanese Lang. 1992). Apprenticeship with Geoffrey Whiting, 1981–83; Cwm Pottery, 1986–88; studios in: Sheffield, 1988–92; London, 1993–. Daiwa Anglo-Japanese Foundn Schol., 1991–93; University of Westminster: Leverhulme Special Res. Fellow, 1999–2001; Sen. Res. Fellow in Ceramics, 2000–02; Prof. of Ceramics, 2004–11. Trustee, Victoria and Albert Mus., 2011–. Mem., Adv. Cttee, Royal Mint, 2012–. FRSA 1996; Sen. FRCA 2012. *Solo exhibitions* include: Galerie Besson, London, 1997; Garth Clark Gall., NY, 1998; Egg, London, 1998, 2002; High Cross House, Dartington Hall, 1999; Geffrye Mus., London, 2002; New Art Centre, Roche Court, Salisbury, 2004, 2007, 2010, 2018; Mus. of Wales, 2005; Blackwell House, Lake District, 2005; Kettle's Yard, Cambridge, 2007; Middlesbrough Inst. of Modern Art, 2007; Chatsworth House, Derbyshire, 2007; V&A Mus., 2009; Alan Cristea, London, 2010, 2012; Waddesdon Manor, 2012; Gagosian, NY, 2013, LA, 2016, San Francisco, 2018; Fitzwilliam Mus., 2013–14; Turner Contemp., 2014; Southwark Cathedral, 2014; Theseus Temple, Vienna, 2014; RA, 2015; Galerie Max Hetzler, Berlin, 2016; Kunsthaus Graz, 2016; Kunsthistorisches Mus., Vienna, 2016; Artipelag, Stockholm, 2017; Espace Muraille, Geneva, 2017; Museo de Arte Contemporáneo de Ibiza, 2018; Schindler House, LA, 2018; Frick Collection, NY, 2019; Ivorypress, Madrid, 2019; Jewish Mus. and Ateneo Veneto, Venice, 2019; Japanisches Palais, Dresden, 2019. Hon. DPhil: Arts London, 2013; Sheffield, 2013; Nottingham, 2014; Hon. Dr Canterbury Christ Church, 2014; DUniv York, 2016. Windham-Campbell Prize for Non-Fiction, Yale Univ., 2015. *Publications:* Bernard Leach, 1998, 3rd edn 2014; 20th Century Ceramics, 2003; The Hare with Amber Eyes, 2010 (Costa Biog. Award, Ondaatje Prize, RSL, 2011); The Pot Book, 2011; The White Road, 2015. *W:* www.edmunddewaal.com.
*See also* J. H. L. de Waal.

**de WAAL, John Henry Lowndes;** QC 2013; *b* Cambridge, 7 Jan. 1962; *s* of Rev. Victor Alexander de Waal, *qv*; *m* 1994, Mandy Teresa O'Loughlin (marr. diss. 2017); one *s* one *d*; *m* 2019, Julia Joana Weiss; one *d*. *Educ*: Pembroke Coll., Cambridge (BA 1983); Birmingham Univ. (Cert Ed); Birmingham Poly. (CPE); Inns of Court Sch. of Law. Teacher and lectr, 1983–90; called to the Bar, Middle Temple, 1992. *Recreations:* walking, camping. *Address*: Hardwicke Building, New Square, Lincoln's Inn, WC2A 3SB. *T*: (020) 7242 2523. *E:* john.dewaal@hardwicke.co.uk.
*See also* E. A. L. de Waal.

**de WAAL, Judith Mary;** *see* Slater, J. M.

**de WAAL, Rev. Victor Alexander;** Dean of Canterbury, 1976–86; *b* 2 Feb. 1929; *s* of late Hendrik de Waal and Elisabeth von Ephrussi; *m* 1960, Esther Aline Lowndes Moir, PhD; four *s*. *Educ*: Tonbridge School; Pembroke Coll., Cambridge (MA); Ely Theological College. With Phs van Ommeren (London) Ltd, 1949–50; Asst Curate, St Mary the Virgin, Isleworth, 1952–56; Chaplain, Ely Theological Coll., 1956–59; Chaplain and Succentor, King's Coll., Cambridge, 1959–63; Chaplain, Univ. of Nottingham, 1963–69; Chancellor of Lincoln Cathedral, 1969–76; Chaplain, SSC, Tymawr, 1990–2000. Hon. DD Nottingham, 1983. *Publications:* What is the Church?, 1969; The Politics of Reconciliation: Zimbabwe's first decade, 1990; Holy Wisdom: Father Augustine Baker (1575–1641), 2008; contrib.: Theology and Modern Education, 1965; Stages of Experience, 1965; The Committed Church, 1966; Liturgy Reshaped, 1982; Liturgie et Espace Liturgique, 1987; Vie Ecclesiale—communauté et communautés, 1989; Beyond Death, 1995; La Confession et les Confessions, 1995; Les Artisans de Paix, 1996; Travail et Repos, 2000; Loi et Transgression, 2002. *Address:* 6 St James Close, Bishop Street, N1 8PH. *T:* (020) 7354 2741.
*See also* E. A. L. de Waal, J. H. L. de Waal.

**DEWAR,** family name of **Baron Forteviot**.

**DEWAR, Dame Alison Fettes;** *see* Richard, Dame A. F.

**DEWAR, David Alexander;** an Assistant Auditor General, National Audit Office, 1984–94; *b* 28 Oct. 1934; *s* of James and Isabella Dewar; *m* 1959, Rosalind Mary Ellen Greenwood; one *s* one *d*. *Educ*: Leith Academy, Edinburgh. Entered Exchequer and Audit Dept, 1953; Chief Auditor, 1966; Deputy Director of Audit, 1973; Director of Audit, 1977; Dep. Sec. of Dept, 1981. *Publications:* (jtly) A History of British National Audit, 2017. *Recreations:* gardening, golf. *Address:* 14 Drovers Way, Barnham, Bognor Regis, W Sussex PO22 0DD. *T:* (01243) 553594.

**DEWAR, Ian Stewart;** JP; Member: South Glamorgan County Council, 1985–93 (Vice-Chairman, 1990–91; Finance Chairman, 1992–93); South Wales Valuation Tribunal, 1995–2001; *b* 29 Jan. 1929; *er s* of late William Stewart Dewar and Eileen Dewar (*née* Godfrey); *m* 1968, Nora Stephanie House (*d* 2017); one *s* one *d*. *Educ:* Penarth County Sch.; UC Cardiff; Jesus Coll., Oxford (MA). RAF, 1947–49. Asst Archivist, Glamorgan County Council, 1952–53. Entered Min. of Labour, 1953; Asst Private Sec. to Minister, 1956–58; Principal, Min. of Labour and Civil Service Commn, 1958–65; Asst Sec., Min. of Labour, Dept of Employment and Commn on Industrial Relations, 1965–70; Asst Sec., 1970–73, and Under-Sec., 1973–83, Welsh Office. Member, Governing Body: Univ. of Wales, 1985–93; Nat. Mus. of Wales, 1985–93; Chm., Museum Schs Service Cttee, 1989–93. Mayor of Penarth, 1998–99. JP S Glam, 1985.

**DEWAR, Robert Scott,** CMG 2006; HM Diplomatic Service, retired; High Commissioner to Nigeria, and Permanent Representative to Economic Community of West African States, 2007–11; *b* 10 June 1949; *s* of Robert James Dewar, CMG, CBE and Christina Marianne Dewar (*née* Ljungberger); *m* 1979, Jennifer Mary Ward; one *s* one *d*. *Educ:* Loretto; Brasenose Coll., Oxford; Open Univ. (MSc Envmtl Decision Making 2003). VSO, Port Sudan, 1971–72; Scottish Office, 1972–73; FCO, 1973; served Colombo and FCO, to 1981, Asst Sec. Gen. to Lancaster House Conf. on Southern Rhodesia, 1979; Head of Chancery, Luanda, 1981–84; FCO, 1984–88; Dep. Head of Mission, Dakar, 1988–92; Dep. High Comr, Harare, 1992–96; Ambassador to Republic of Madagascar, 1996–99; FCO, 1999–2000; High Comr to Mozambique, 2000–03; Ambassador to Ethiopia and Djibouti, and Permanent Rep. to the African Union, 2004–07. Associate Fellow, Africa Prog., RIIA, 2011–. Trustee, BRCS, 2013–19. *Recreations:* sport, esp. squash, tennis and fly fishing.

**DEWAR, Sally Marie;** Head, Strategy Group, Allen & Overy LLP, since 2018; *b* Farnham, 25 Dec. 1968. *Educ:* Univ. of Manchester Inst. of Sci. and Technol. (BSc 1st Cl. Jt Hons Pure Maths and French). Corporate Finance Manager: KPMG Manchester, 1991–97; BOC, 1997–98; Associate, 1998–99, Manager, 1999–2000, Equity Mkts, UK Listing Authy, London Stock Exchange; Chief Financial Officer, LeisureHunt.com, 2000–01; Hd, Corporate Actions and Projects, London Stock Exchange, 2001–02; Financial Services Authority: Hd, UK Listing Authy, 2002–05; Dir of Mkts, 2005–07; Man. Dir, Wholesale and Instnl Mkts, 2008–09; Man. Dir, Risk, 2009–11; Man. Dir, Internat. Office of Regulatory Affairs, JP Morgan Chase & Co., 2011–18. Mem., Business Develt Cttee, LPO, 2007–09. Mem., Bd of Trustees, Disability Challengers, 2007–. *Address:* Allen & Overy LLP, One Bishops Square, E1 6AD.

**DEWAR-DURIE, Andrew Maule,** CBE 1999; DL; Chairman, Seafish Industry Authority, 2002–07 (Deputy Chairman, 2000–02); *b* 13 Nov. 1939; *s* of late Lt Col Raymond Varley Dewar-Durie and Frances St John Dewar-Durie (*née* Maule); *m* 1972, Marguerite Maria Jarmila Kottulinsky; two *s* one *d*. *Educ:* Cheam Sch.; Wellington Coll. Nat. Service, Argyll and Sutherland Highlanders, 1958–68, retd with rank of Captain. Export Rep. to Sen. Export Dir, White Horse Distillers, 1968–83; Internat. Sales Dir, Long John Distillers, 1983–87; Internat. Sales Dir, Man. Dir, then CEO, James Burrough Ltd, 1987–92; Man. Dir, 1992–97, Chm., 1997–99, Allied Distillers. Dir, Britannic Asset Mgt, 2001–04. Vice-Chm., 1996–97, Chm., 1997–99, CBI Scotland. Dir, 2000–08, Vice Chm., 2008–10, Edinburgh Mil. Tattoo, later Royal Edinburgh Mil. Tattoo; Dir, St Andrews Links Ltd, 2012–17. Vice-Chm., Strathendrick Agricl Soc., 2018–. DL Dunbartonshire, 1996. Hon. Pipe Pres., Crossed Swords Pipes and Drums, 2018–. *Publications:* The Scottish Sheep Industry: a way forward, 2000. *Recreations:* ski-ing, rough shooting. *Address:* Finnich Malise, Croftamie, W Stirlingshire G63 0HA. *T:* (01360) 660257, *Fax:* (01360) 660101. *E:* andrewdewardurie@gmail.com. *Club:* New (Edinburgh).

**de WATERVLIET, Jean-Michel V.;** *see* Veranneman de Watervliet.

**DEWBERRY, David Albert;** HM Diplomatic Service, retired; Deputy Head of Mission, the Holy See, Rome, 1996–2001; *b* 27 Sept. 1941; *s* of Albert Dewberry and Grace Dewberry (*née* Tarsey); *m* 1974, Catherine Mary (*née* Stabback); three *s* one *d*. *Educ:* Cray Valley Sch., Foots Cray, Kent. Joined CRO, 1958; Karachi, 1963; Kingston, 1966; Warsaw, 1970; Brussels, 1971; Second Sec. (Aid), Dhaka, 1972; FCO, 1974; Consul: Mexico City, 1977; Buenos Aires, 1980; FCO, 1982; Dep. High Comr, Dar es Salaam, 1987; FCO, 1991–96. *Recreations:* reading, walking. *E:* dadewberry@hotmail.com.

**DEWEY, Prof. John Frederick,** FRS 1985; FGS; FAA; Professor of Geology, University of Oxford, 1986–2001, now Emeritus; Fellow, since 1986, Senior Research Fellow, since 2001 and Supernumerary Fellow, since 2004, University College, Oxford; Professor of Geology, University of California, Davis, 2001–06, now Distinguished Professor Emeritus; *b* 22 May 1937; *s* of John Edward and Florence Nellie Mary Dewey; *m* 1961, Frances Mary Blackhurst, MA, DSc; one *s* one *d*. *Educ:* Bancroft's School; Queen Mary Coll. and Imperial Coll., Univ. of London (BSc, PhD, DIC); MA 1965, ScD 1988, Cantab; DSc Oxon 1989. CGeol 1990. Lecturer: Univ. of Manchester, 1960–64; Univ. of Cambridge, 1964–70; Prof., State Univ. of New York at Albany, 1970–82; Prof. of Geology, Durham Univ., 1982–86. Vis. Res. Fellow, British Geol Survey, 2001–; Vis. Res. Prof., Imperial Coll., Univ. of London, 2001–. MAE 1990; MNAS 1995. FAA 2011. Hon. MRIA 2008. Hon. DSc: Meml Univ. of Newfoundland, 1996; Rennes, 2012; Hon. LLD: NUI, 1998, Dalhousie, 2018, St Francis Xavier, 2018; Hon. DEng Istanbul Tech. Univ., 2019. Numerous honours and awards, UK and overseas, incl. Penrose Medal, Geol Soc. of America, 1992; Arthur Holmes Medal, Eur. Union of Geoscis, 1993; Wollaston Medal, Geol Soc. of London, 1999; Fourmarier Medal, Royal Acad. of Scis, Belgium, 1999. *Publications:* 175 scientific papers; contribs to Geol Soc. of America Bulletin, Geol Soc. London Jl, Jl Geophysical Res. and other learned jls. *Recreations:* ski-ing, cricket, water colour and oil painting, British and Irish music 1850–1950, model railways. *Address:* Sherwood Lodge, 93 Bagley Wood Road, Kennington OX1 5NA. *T:* (01865) 735525.

**DEWEY, Sir Rupert (Grahame),** 4th Bt *cr* 1917, of South Hill Wood, Bromley, Kent; *b* Poole, Dorset, 29 March 1953; *s* of Sir Anthony Hugh Dewey, 3rd Bt and of Sylvia Dewey (*née* MacMahon); *S* father, 2016; *m* 1978, Suzanne Rosemary Lusk; two *s* one *d*. *Educ:* Wellington Coll.; Coll. of Law, Guildford. Admitted as Solicitor, 1978; with Warrens, 1977–81; Partner, Thrings, Bath, 1982–88; Owner and Partner, Dewey & Co., 1990–2004; company dir, 2004–15. *Recreations:* fly-fishing, shooting, tennis, golf. *Heir: s* Thomas Andrew Dewey [*b* 27 Jan. 1982; *m* 2015, Camilla Ruth Kelson, *d* of Alan Brierley; one *s* one *d*]. *Address:* Summer Field, Wellow, Bath BA2 8PU. *T:* (01225) 832051. *E:* rupertdewey2004@gmail.com.

**DEWEY, Timothy William;** Chief Executive, Timothy Taylor & Co. Ltd, since 2014; *b* Grand Rapids, Mich, USA, 8 Sept. 1958; *s* of Daniel George Dewey and Jean Marie Dewey; *m* 1982, Jane Caroline Alison Langdon; two *d*. *Educ:* Bates Coll., Lewiston, Maine (BA English Lit.). Graduate trainee and entry level posts, Unilever, 1984–88; sen. roles incl. Internat. Mktg Dir, Smirnoff Vodka, Grand Metropolitan plc, subseq. Diageo plc, 1988–2000; Internat. Mktg Dir, William Grant & Sons, 2001–03; Global Brands Dir, SABMiller, 2004–06; Divl Mktg Dir, British Bakeries, 2006–08; mktg consultancy, 2009–10; Global Mktg Dir, Drambuie Liqueur Co. Ltd, 2010–14. Chm., Yorks Beer and Pub Assoc., 2018–. *Recreations:* tennis, hillwalking, cinema, reading, gardening. *Address:* Timothy Taylor & Co. Ltd, Knowle Spring Brewery, Keighley, W Yorks BD21 1AW. *T:* (01535) 603139, *Fax:* (01535) 691167. *E:* timd@timtaylors.co.uk. *Club:* Ilkley Tennis.

**DEWHURST, Neil Gordon,** MD; FRCP, FRCPE, FRCPGlas; Consultant Cardiologist and General Physician, NHS Tayside, 1995–2013; President, Royal College of Physicians of Edinburgh, 2010–14; *b* Blackburn, Lancs, 8 Sept. 1952; *m* 1979, Elspeth Lucy Campbell. *Educ:* Hutton Grammar Sch.; Univ. of Edinburgh (BSc Hons 1st Cl. Bacteriol. 1974; MB ChB 1976; MD 1982). FRCPE 1991; FRCP 1995; FRCPGlas 2005. Lectr in Gen. Medicine, Univ. of Edinburgh, 1978–81; Registrar in Gen. Medicine with special interest in Cardiol., Edinburgh, 1981–83; Sen. Registrar in Gen. Medicine and Cardiol., Edinburgh, 1983–87; Consultant Cardiologist and GP, South Devon Healthcare Trust, 1987–95. Hon. Sen. Lectr in Medicine, Univ. of Dundee, 1995–2013. Hon. FACP 2010. *Recreations:* fishing, travel, music, gardening.

**de WILDE, (Alan) Robin;** QC 1993; *b* 12 July 1945; *s* of late Capt. Ronald Cedric de Wilde and of Dorothea Elizabeth Mary (*née* Fenningworth); *m* 1977, Patricia Teresa Bearcroft; three *s*. *Educ:* Dean Close Sch.; RAF Coll., Cranwell; Inns of Court Sch. of Law. Called to the Bar, Inner Temple, 1971, Bencher, 1996; a Recorder, 2000–04. Mem., Bar Council, 1985–90, 1998–99, 2002–04; Chm., Professional Negligence Bar Assoc., 1995–97 (Hon. Vice Pres., 1998–; Chm., Ogden Working Party, 2003–17; Gen. Editor, Facts & Figures - Tables for the Calculation of Damages, annually 1996–2017); Mem. Council, Bodily Injury Claims Mgt Assoc., 2003. FRSocMed 1997. Hon. FIA 2016. *Address:* 83 Woodstock Road, Chiswick, W4 1EF. *T:* (020) 8994 1949.

**DE WITT, Prof. Sir Ronald (Wayne),** Kt 2002; international consultant, justice and health, since 2008; Chief Executive, HM Courts Service, 2004–07; *b* 31 March 1948; *s* of James Goldwyn De Witt and Una Doreen De Witt (*née* Lane). *Educ:* Sch. of Advanced Nursing, Wellington, NZ (RN; Dip. N 1978); Univ. of Humberside (BA Hons Business Studies, MA Health Mgt 1992; Hon. Fellow 1998). Registered Comprehensive Nurse 1970, NZ 1975, Canada 1970; SRN; Cert. of Burns and Plastic Surgery, 1971; Cert. of Mgt, 1976. Chief Nurse, Auckland Health Bd, 1988–89; Dist Manager, Central Auckland Health Services, 1989–90; Chief Executive: Auckland Hosp., 1990–91; Hull Acute Services, Hull HA, later Royal Hull Hosps NHS Trust, 1991–96; Leeds HA, 1996–99; KCH NHS Trust, 1999–2002; NW London Strategic HA, 2002–04. Chm., English Nat. Bd for Nursing, Midwifery and Health Visiting, 1996–2002. Patron, Foundn for Nursing Studies, 2010– (Trustee, 2005–10); Regency Patron, Royal Pavilion Brighton, 2013–; Trustee: Cancer BACUP, subseq. Cancerbackup, 2005–08; Gen. Nursing Council, 2005– (Mem., 1996–; Chair, 2008–); Chm., Lepra, 2011–15 (Trustee, 2007–10). Associate Mem.

Bd, Bupa, 2011–18. Chair, Brunswick Town Assoc., 2017–. Hon. DCL Humberside, 2004. *Publications:* (contrib.) Public Health, 1999; Managing the Business of Health Care, 2001. *Recreations:* travel, reading, walking, books, antiques.

**DEWS, Vivienne Margaret, (Mrs Alan Cogbill);** Chief Executive, Office of Fair Trading, 2014 (Executive Director, 2008–14); *b* 29 Dec. 1952; *d* of late Albert Dews and of Eva Margaret Dews (*née* Hayman); *m* 1st, 1972, Stephen Ladner (marr. diss. 1977); 2nd, 1979, Alan Cogbill; one *s* one *d* (and two *d* decd). *Educ:* Northampton High Sch. for Girls; Newnham Coll., Cambridge (BA 1974). Joined Home Office, 1974, Private Sec. to Minister for Police and Prisons, 1979–80; Dep. Dir, Top Mgt Prog., Cabinet Office, 1987–89; Home Office: Head: Immigration Policy, 1989–91; After Entry Casework and Appeals, 1991–93; Consulting Efficiency and Market Testing, 1994–95; Dir, Finance and Services, Immigration and Nationality Directorate, 1995–99; Chief Exec., Police Inf. Technol. Orgn, 1999–2001; Dir, Modernising Corporate Support, Inland Revenue, 2002; Dir, Resources and Planning, HSE, 2002–08. Mem., CIPFA, 2007. Member: Audit Cttee, Mencap, 2011–15; Jt Audit Cttee, Kent Police, 2017–; Hon. Treas., Charity for Civil Servants, 2012–19; Trustee: Henry Smith Charity, 2014–; Young Epilepsy, 2015–; Independent Age, 2016–; Mathematics in Educn and Industry, 2019–. Chm., Educn Governing Body, St Piers Sch. and Coll., 2016–; Vice Chm., Governing Body, Fedn of St Elphege's and Regina Coeli Schs, 2014–16 (Mem., Interim Exec. Bd, Regina Coeli Catholic Prim. Sch., 2013–14); Mem., Governing Body, Winterbourne Nursery and Infants Sch., 2014–18 (Chm., 2015–18). *Recreations:* family, home, garden, Italy. *Club:* Oxford and Cambridge.

**DEXTER, Edward Ralph,** CBE 2001; Managing Director, Ted Dexter & Associates, 1978–2005; *b* 15 May 1935; *m* 1959, Susan Georgina Longfield; one *s* one *d*. *Educ:* Radley College; Jesus College, Cambridge (Captain of cricket and of golf). Served 11th Hussars, 1956–57 (Malaya Campaign Medal 1955). Cricketer, 1958–68; Captain of Sussex, 1960–65; Captain of England, 1962–65; freelance journalist, 1965–88; sports promotion consultant, 1978–. Chm., England (Cricket) Cttee, TCCB, 1989–93. Contested (C) Cardiff, 1965. *Publications:* Ted Dexter's Cricket Book, 1963; Ted Dexter Declares, 1966; (jtly) Test Kill, 1976; Deadly Putter, 1979; From Bradman to Boycott, 1981; My Golf, 1982; Ted Dexter's Little Cricket Book, 1996. *Recreations:* golf, reading. *Clubs:* MCC (Chm., Cricket Cttee, 1998–2003; Pres., 2001–02), Sussex CC (Pres., 2007); Sunningdale Golf, Royal and Ancient Golf.

**DEXTER, Prof. (Thomas) Michael,** PhD, DSc; FRS 1991; FMedSci; scientific consultant; Director, Wellcome Trust, 1998–2003; *b* 15 May 1945; *s* of Thomas Richard Dexter and Agnes Gertrude Deplege; *m* 1966, Frances Ann Sutton (marr. diss. 1978); one *s* one *d* (twins); one *s* one *d* by Dr Elaine Spooncer; *m* 2009, Dr Clare Heyworth. *Educ:* Salford Univ. (BSc 1st class Hons 1970; DSc 1982); Manchester Univ. (PhD 1973). MRCPath 1987, FRCPath 1997; CBiol, FRSB (FIBiol 1997). Lady Tata Meml Scholar, 1970–73; Paterson Institute for Cancer Research: Res. Scientist, 1973; Prof. of Haematology and Hd of Dept of Exptl Haematol., 1982–98; Dep. Dir, 1994–97; Dir, 1997–98. Chairman: Stem Cell Sciences Ltd, 2003–06 (non-exec. Dir, 2003–09); Centre for Life, Newcastle upon Tyne, 2003–07; Cockcroft Inst. for Accelerator Science, 2004–09. Internat. Scientific Advr, Rothschild Asset Mgt, 2003–08. Life Fellow, Cancer Res. Campaign, Manchester, 1978; Personal Chair, Univ. of Manchester, 1985–98, Emeritus Prof. of Hematol., 2013; Gibb Res. Fellow, CRC, 1992–97. Visiting Fellow: Sloan Kettering Inst., NY, 1976–77; Weizmann Inst., Israel, 1980. Lectures: Annual, Leukaemia Res. Fund, 1987; Michael Williams, RSM, 1990; Maximov, Leningrad, 1990; Almoth-Wright, St Mary's, London, 1992; Medawar, RPMS, 1994; Henry Hallett Dale, Nat. Inst. of Biol Standards of Control, 1997; Annual, British Soc. of Haematology, 1998; Inst. Distinguished, Inst. of Cancer Res., 1999; 5th Chamlong-Harinasuta, Bangkok, 1999; Lloyd Roberts, RCP, 2000. Member: MRC, 1993–96 (Chairman: Molecular and Cellular Medicine Bd, 1994–96; Human Genome Mapping Project Co-ordinating Cttee, 1996–98); Scientific Cttee, Leukaemia Res. Fund, 1983–86; Scientific Grants Cttee, CRC, 1987–93; Scientific Adv. Bd, Biomedical Res. Center, BC, 1987–91; Scientific Adv. Bd, Wellcome/ CRC Inst., Cambridge, 1992–98; AFRC Grants Cttee, 1992–94; Cttee on Med. Aspects of Radiation in Envmt, 1994–98; Adv. Bd, EMF Trust, 1995–; NW Sci. Council, 2003–09; Adv. Bd, First London plc, 2008–09. Pres., Internat. Soc. for Exptl Hematology, 1988. Founder FMedSci 1998. Hon. MRCP 1995, Hon. FRCP 1998. Hon. DSc: Salford, 1998; UMIST, 1999; London, 2002; Lancaster, 2006; Manchester Metropolitan, 2014. *Publications:* author of 360 articles in scientific jls; editor of four books. *Recreations:* folk singing, gardening, poetry, dominoes, messing around on my boat (Coris) in Dartmouth, Devon.

**DEY, Graeme James;** Member (SNP) Scottish Parliament, since 2011; Minister for Parliamentary Business and Veterans, since 2018; *b* Aberdeen, 29 Oct. 1962; *s* of Donald Dey and Marion Dey; *m* 1985, Linda Gatt; one *s* one *d*. *Educ:* Broomhill Primary Sch., Aberdeen; Springhill Primary Sch., Aberdeen; Harlaw Acad., Aberdeen. Sports Journalist, Aberdeen Office, DC Thomson, 1980–85; Sports Journalist, 1985–91, Sports Editor, 1991–2010, The Courier. Dep. Convenor, Rural Affairs Climate Change and Envmt Cttee, 2012–16, Convenor, Envmt Climate Change and Land Reform Cttee, 2016–, Scottish Parlt. *Recreations:* golf, gym, swimming, music, stand-up comedy. *Address:* Scottish Parliament, Holyrood, Edinburgh EH99 1SP. *T:* (0131) 348 6292. *E:* graeme.dey.msp@parliament.scot.

**DEY, Rajeeb,** MBE 2016; Founder and Chief Executive Officer, Learnerbly, since 2016; Founder, Enternships.com, since 2009 (Chief Executive Officer, 2009); Co-Founder, StartUp Britain, since 2011; *b* 6 Dec. 1985; *s* of Dr Krishna Ranjan Dey and Supriya Dey. *Educ:* King Edward VI Sch., Chelmsford; Jesus Coll., Oxford (BA 1st Cl. Hons Econs and Mgt; MA). Trustee: Phoenix Educn Trust, 2004–13; UnLtd, 2008–. Young Global Leader, WEF, 2012; Queen's Award for Enterprise Promotion, 2013. *Recreations:* travelling, fitness, ski-ing, eating out, cinema, theatres, voluntary work. *Address:* Learnerbly, 6th Floor, Aldgate Tower, E1 8FA.

**d'EYNCOURT, Sir Mark Gervais T.;** *see* Tennyson-d'Eyncourt, Sir M.

**DHAMIJA, Dinesh;** Member (Lib Dem) London Region, European Parliament, since 2019; *b* 28 March 1950; *s* of Jagan and Devika Dhamija; *m* 1977, Tani Malhotra; two *s*. *Educ:* King's Sch., Canterbury; Fitzwilliam Coll., Cambridge (BA 1974; MA). Founded first travel agency, Dabin Travel Ltd, 1980; estabd Flightbookers, 1983; Royal Nepal Airlines: Gen. Sales Agent, UK and Ireland, 1987–93; Regl Dir, Europe, 1992–94; Founder, Chm. and Chief Exec., ebookers plc, 1999–2005; Chm., Copper Beech Gp, 2006–. Pres., TiE (The Indus Entrepreneurs) London, 2014–. Advr on Enterprise to Tim Farron, MP, 2016. Dep. Treas., 2017–, Vice Chair, Federal Bd, 2018–, Liberal Democrats. *Recreations:* golf, tennis. *Address:* Cinnabar, Portnall Drive, Virginia Water, Surrey GU25 4NR. *Clubs:* Royal Automobile, Oxford and Cambridge; Wentworth, Queenwood; Delhi Golf, Delhi Gymkhana (Delhi).

**DHANDA, Parmjit Singh;** author; Executive Director, Back Heathrow, since 2017; *b* 17 Sept. 1971; *s* of Balbir Singh Dhanda and Mrs Balbir Singh Dhanda; *m* 2003, Rupi Rai; two *s*. *Educ:* Mellow Lane Comprehensive, Hayes, Middx; Univ. of Nottingham (BEng (Hons) Elec Eng; MSc IT 1995). Labour Party Organiser, W London, 1996–98; Asst Nat. Organiser, Connect, 1998–2001. Mem. (Lab), Hillingdon BC, 1998–2002. Contested (Lab) SE Reg., England, EP elecn, 1999. MP (Lab) Gloucester, 2001–10; contested (Lab) same seat, 2010. An Asst Govt Whip, 2005–06; Parly Under-Sec. of State, DES, then Dept for Children, Schools and Families, 2006–07; Parly Under-Sec. of State, DCLG, 2007–08. Parly and Campaigns Officer, 2010–17, Private Sector Negotiations Officer, 2017, Prospect. Founder Mem., Gloucester Urban Regeneration Co., 2005–10; Member, Board: Hanover Housing Assoc., 2010–16; Swan Housing Assoc., 2015–18; Longhurst Gp, 2016–; Milton Keynes Univ. Hosp. Foundn Trust, 2017–. Non-exec. Chm., Allied Health Professions Fedn, 2017–. Member: Fabian Society; Co-operative Society; USDAW. *Publications:* My Political Race, 2015. *Recreations:* football, cricket, writing. *E:* parmjitsdhanda@hotmail.com.

**DHANOWA, Charles Pritam Singh,** OBE 2007; Registrar, Competition Appeal Tribunal, since 2003; *b* Cardiff, 18 June 1961; *s* of Sumitar Singh Dhanowa and Eunice Dhanowa (*née* Lane); *m* 1990, Dara Ann Vexter; one *s* one *d*. *Educ:* Radyr Comp. Sch., Cardiff; Downing Coll., Cambridge (MA); Coll. of Law, Christleton (Law Final); King's Coll. London (Dip. Competition Law). Admitted solicitor, 1986; commercial litigation, Linklaters & Paines, 1986–92; Mckenna & Co., 1993; corporate litigation, Treasury Solicitor's Dept, 1994–96; Asst Legal Advr, Monopolies and Mergers Commn, 1996–98; Competition Commission: Hd, Secretariat, 1999–2001; Registrar, Competition Commn Appeal Tribunals, 2000–03; Sec.-Gen., Assoc. of Eur. Competition Law Judges, 2002–. Hon. QC 2012. *Recreations:* gardening, reading, walking, painting. *Address:* Competition Appeal Tribunal, Victoria House, WC1A 2EB. *T:* (020) 7979 7979. *Club:* Athenæum.

**DHARKER, Imtiaz;** poet; *b* Lahore, 31 Jan. 1954; *d* of Kausar and Sher Mohd Mobarik; *m* 2006, Simon Powell (*d* 2009); one *d* by a previous marriage. *Educ:* Hutchesons' Grammar Sch.; Univ. of Glasgow (MA Eng. Lit. and Philos.). Artist (11 solo exhibns). Owner and Dir, Solo Films, 1980–. Dir, Poetry Live!, 2008–; Trustee and Editor, Poems on the Underground; Trustee, Poetry Archive. Queen's Gold Medal for Poetry, 2014. *Publications:* Purdah, 1989; Postcards From God (including Purdah), 1997; I Speak for the Devil, 2001; The Terrorist at my Table, 2006; Leaving Fingerprints, 2009; Over the Moon, 2014; Luck is the Hook, 2018. *Address:* c/o Bloodaxe Books, UK, Eastburn, South Park, Hexham, Northumberland NE46 1BS. *T:* (01434) 611581. *E:* publicity@bloodaxebooks.com.

**DHESI, Tanmanjeet Singh;** MP (Lab) Slough, since 2017; *b* Slough, 17 Aug. 1978; *m* 2005, Manveen; two *s*. *Educ:* Sir Joseph Williamson's Mathematical Sch., Rochester; Gravesend Grammar Sch.; University Coll. London (Maths with Mgt Studies); Keble Coll., Oxford (Applied Stats); Fitzwilliam Coll., Cambridge (MPhil). Joined family business. Mem. (Lab), Gravesham BC, 2007–17 (Mayor, 2011–12; Mem. Cabinet, 2012). Contested (Lab) Gravesham, 2015. *Address:* House of Commons, SW1A 0AA.

**DHILLON, Jasbir Singh;** QC 2013; *b* Taplow, 23 Feb. 1969; *s* of Karnail and Surjit Dhillon; *m* 2000, Ajneet Jassey; two *s*. *Educ:* Desborough Sch.; Keble Coll., Oxford (BA 1st cl. Hons 1991); Harvard Law Sch. (LLM 1992). Associate, Cravath, Swaine & Moore, NY, 1992–95; admitted to US Dist Court, Southern Dist of NY Bar, 1993; Attorney-at-Law, New York, 1993; Lectr and Tutor in Law, Exeter Coll., Oxford, 1995–96; called to the Bar, Gray's Inn, 1996, Bencher, 2017; Pupil, Brick Court Chambers, 1996–97; in practice as barrister, specialising in commercial law, 1997–; admitted to US Supreme Court Bar, 1998. Mem., Attorney Gen.'s Panel on Counsel, 2002–11. Mem., Standards Cttee, Bar Standards Bd, 2006–11. Dir, Bar Mutual Indemnity Fund Ltd, 2013–. *Publications:* (contrib.) Paget's Law of Banking, 13th edn 2007; (contrib.) Competition Litigation, UK Practice and Procedure, 2010; (contrib.) SIAC Rules: an annotation, 2014. *Recreations:* basketball, history, music, football. *Address:* Brick Court Chambers, 7–8 Essex Street, WC2R 3LD. *T:* (020) 7379 3550. *E:* Jasbir.Dhillon@brickcourt.co.uk.

**DHIR, Anuja Ravindra;** QC 2010; **Her Honour Judge Dhir;** a Circuit Judge, since 2012; *b* Dundee, Scotland, 19 Jan. 1968; *d* of Prof. Ravindra Kumar Dhir, OBE and Bharti Dhir; *m* 2002, Nicholas Lavender (*see* Hon. Sir Nicholas Lavender); two *s* one *d*. *Educ:* Harris Acad.; Dundee Univ. (LLB Hons). Called to the Bar, Gray's Inn, 1989, Bencher, 2009; a Recorder, 2009–12. Circuit Judge Comr, Judicial Appts Commn, 2018–. Tutor Judge, Judicial Coll., 2016–. Hon. Dr Dundee, 2018. *Recreations:* walking, cooking. *Address:* Central Criminal Court, Old Bailey, EC4M 7EH.

**DHOLAKIA,** family name of **Baron Dholakia**.

**DHOLAKIA,** Baron *cr* 1997 (Life Peer), of Waltham Brooks in the co. of West Sussex; **Navnit Dholakia,** OBE 1994; PC 2010; JP, DL; *b* 4 March 1937; *s* of Permananddas Mulji Dholakia and Shantabai Permananddas Dholakia; *m* 1967, Ann McLuskie; two *d*. *Educ:* Home Sch. and Inst. of Science, Bhavnagar, Gujarat; Brighton Tech. Coll. Medical Lab. Technician, Southlands Hosp., Shoreham-by-Sea, 1960–66; Develt Officer, Nat. Cttee for Commonwealth Immigrants, 1966–68; Sen. Develt Officer, 1968–74, Principal Officer and Sec., 1974–76, Community Relns Commn; Commission for Racial Equality: Principal Fieldwork, Admin and Liaison Officer, 1976–78; Principal Officer, Management, 1978–81; Head of Admin, Justice Section, 1984–94. Lib Dem spokesman on home affairs, 1997–; an Asst Lib Dem Whip, 1997–99, Dep. Leader of Lib Dems, 2004–, H of L. Member: Hunt Cttee on Immigration and Youth Service, 1967–69; Bd of Visitors, HM Prison, Lewes, 1978–95; Home Office Inter-Deptl Cttee on Racial Attacks and Harassment, 1987–92; Carlisle Cttee on Parole Systems Review, 1987–88; Sussex Police Authority, 1991–94; Ethnic Minority Adv. Cttee, Judicial Studies Bd, 1992–96; Council, Howard League for Penal Reform, 1992–94 (Mem. Editl Bd, Howard Jl of Criminology, 1993–); Police Complaints Authy, 1994–97. Mem., H of L Appts Commn, 1999–2010. Pres., NACRO, 2003– (Mem. Council, 1984–; Chm., Race Issues Adv. Cttee, 1989–; Vice-Chm., 1995–98; Chm., 1998–2003); Vice-Chm., Policy Res. Inst. on Ageing and Ethnicity, 1999–2014. Vice Pres., Mental Health Foundn, 2002– (Trustee, 1997–2002); Trustee: British Empire and Commonwealth Mus., Bristol, 1999–2005; Pallant House Gall., Chichester, 2000–09; Police Foundn, 2002–. Gov., Commonwealth Inst., 1998–2005. Chairman: Brighton Young Liberals, 1959–62; Brighton Liberal Assoc., 1962–64; Sec., Race and Community Relns Panel, Liberal Party, 1969–74; Liberal Democrats: Mem., Federal Policy and Federal Exec. Cttee, 1996–97; Pres., Lib Dem Party, 1999–2004; Trustee, 2005–. Mem. (L) Brighton CBC, 1961–64. Mem. Council, SCF, 1992– (Chm., Programme Adv. Cttee, 1992–). JP Mid Sussex, 1978; DL West Sussex, 1999. Hon. LLD: Hertfordshire, 2009; York, 2010; East London, 2010. *Publications:* articles on criminal justice. *Recreations:* photography, travel, gardening, cooking exotic dishes. *Address:* House of Lords, SW1A 0PW.

**DIACK, Lamine;** President, International Association of Athletics Federations (formerly International Amateur Athletics Federation), 1999–2015, now Honorary Life President; *b* 7 June 1933; *s* of Ibrahima Diack and Aissatou Cisse; *m* 1st, 1962, Tondut Fatoumata Bintou; four *s* seven *d* (and one *s* decd); 2nd, 1964, Gaye Ngoné Diaba (*d* 1981); one *s* three *d*; 3rd, 1988, Sy Aissatou (*d* 1994). *Educ:* Dakar Univ. (MA); Ecole Nationale des Impôts de Paris (Inspecteur des Impôts et Domaines). French long jump Champion, 1958; French Univ. long jump Champion, 1959; holder, French/W African long jump record, 1957–60; Member: Senegalese Volleyball team, 1953–59; Senegalese Football team, 1954–61.

Football Coach, Foyer France Senegal, 1964–69; Tech. Dir, nat. football team, Senegal, 1966–69; Gen. Comr for State Sport, 1969–70; State Sec. for Youth and Sport, 1970–73; Pres., Assoc. Sportive et Culturelle Diarafs de Dakar, 1974–78 and 1994–; MP (Socialist Party) Senegal, 1978–93; Dep. Speaker, Nat. Assembly of Senegal, 1988–93; Chm., Nat. Water Co. of Senegal, 1995–2001. Member: Exec. Cttee, Supreme Council for Sport in Africa, 1973–87; Nat. Olympic Cttee of Senegal, 1974– (Pres., 1985–2002); IOC, 1999–2013 (Member: Olympic Games Study, 2002–03; Internat. Relns, 2004–09; Congress Commn, 2006–09; Hon. Mem., 2014–); Vice-Pres., 1976–91, Sen. Vice Pres., 1991–99, IAAF. Gen. Sec., 1963–64, Pres., 1974–78, Hon. Pres., 1978–, Senegalese Athletic Fedn; Pres., African Amateur Athletic Confedn, 1973–2003. Hon. Dr: Donetsk; Beijing Sports Univ.; Port Harcourt. Holds numerous decorations and orders, including: Olympic Order, 1994; Order of Merit, IAAF, 1997; Merit Award, Assoc. of Nat. Olympic Cttees, 2014; Chevalier: Ordre Nat. du Lion (Senegal), 1976; Légion d'Honneur (France), 1984; Ordre Nat. (Benin); Comdr, Order of Good Hope (RSA), 1999; Comdr of Distinction (Jamaica), 2002; Grand Cordon of Order of the Rising Sun (Japan), 2007; Order of Merit I Class (Ukraine), 2010; Order of Friendship (Russia); Officer, Nat. Order (Ivory Coast). *Recreations:* reading, family (grandchildren). *Address:* Route des Almadies, BP 16 641, Dakar-Yoff, Dakar-Fann, Senegal. *T:* 338202405, *Fax:* 338202406.

**DIAMANTOPOULOU, Anna;** President, Diktio Network for Reform in Greece and Europe, since 2013; *b* Kozani, 1959; *m* Yannis Savalanos; one *s. Educ:* Aristotle Univ. of Thessaloniki (Civil Engrg); Panteion Univ. of Athens (Postgrad. Studies in Regl Develt). Civil engr, 1981–85; Lectr, Insts of Higher Technol Educn, 1983–85; Prefect of Kastoria, 1985–86; Sec. Gen. for Adult Educn, 1987–88, for Youth, 1988–89; Man. Dir, regl develt co., 1989–93; Sec. Gen. for Industry, 1994–96; MP for Kozani, 1996–99; Dep. Minister for Develt, Greece, 1996–99; Mem., European Commn, 1999–2004; MP (PASOK), 2004; Minister of Educn, Lifelong Learning and Religious Affairs, 2009–12, of Develt, Competitiveness and Shipping, 2012. Mem. Central Cttee, Panhellenic Socialist Movt, 1991–99. *Address:* Ath. Diakou 20 and Syggrou 1, 11743 Athens, Greece.

**DIAMOND, His Honour Anthony Edward John;** QC 1974; a Circuit Judge, 1990–98; international and maritime arbitrator; *b* 4 Sept. 1929; *s* of late Arthur Sigismund Diamond, former Master of the Supreme Court, and of Gladys Elkah Diamond (*née* Mocatta); *m* 1965, Joan Margaret Gee; two *d. Educ:* Rugby; Corpus Christi Coll., Cambridge (MA). Served RA, 1947–49. Called to the Bar, Gray's Inn, 1953 (Bencher, 1985); practised at Bar as a specialist in commercial law, 1958–90; Head of Chambers at 4 Essex Court, EC4, 1984–90; Dep. High Court Judge, 1982–90; a Recorder, 1985–90; Judge i/c of Central London County Court Business List, 1994–98. Chm., Banking Act Appeals, 1980; Mem., indep. review body under colliery review procedure, 1985. *Publications:* papers on maritime law and arbitration. *Recreation:* the visual arts. *Club:* Athenæum.

**DIAMOND, Prof. Sir Ian (David),** Kt 2013; PhD; FBA 2005; FRSE; FAcSS; Chief Executive, UK Statistics Authority, National Statistician and Permanent Secretary, since 2019 (Member, Board, since 2018); *b* 14 March 1954; *s* of Harold and Sylvia Diamond; *m* 1997, Jane Harrison; one *s*, and one step *s* one step *d. Educ:* London Sch. of Econs and Pol Sci. (BSc (Econ.) 1975; MSc 1976); Univ. of St Andrews (PhD 1981). Lectr, Heriot-Watt Univ., 1979; University of Southampton: Lectr, 1980–88; Sen. Lectr, 1988–92; Prof. of Social Statistics, 1992–2002; Dep. Vice-Chancellor, 2001–02; Chief Exec., ESRC, 2003–10 (Mem., 2000–10); Principal and Vice Chancellor, Univ. of Aberdeen, 2010–18. Mem. Bd, UK Res. and Innovation, 2017–. Chair, SSAC, 2018–19. Chairman: Lloyds TSB Foundn for England and Wales, 2009–14; Plan Internat. UK, 2018–. Chair: British Univs and Colls Sport, 2014–; Council for Math. Scis, 2018–. Chair, Edinburgh Coll. of FE, 2018–; Mem. Council, Aberystwyth Univ., 2018–. Trustee, WWF UK, 2008–14. FAcSS (AcSS 2000); FRSE 2009. *Publications:* (with J. Jefferies) Beginning Statistics in the Social Sciences, 2001, 2nd edn (with L. Forster and J. Jefferies) 2012; over 100 articles in acad. jls, incl. Jl of Royal Statistical Soc., Demography and Popn Studies. *Recreations:* family, swimming, running, football. *Address:* 35 Cornish Cottages, Henley Lane, Butleigh, Somerset BA6 8UA. *Club:* Gordonians Cricket.

**DIAMOND, Jane;** *see* Hilsenrath, R. J.

**DIAMOND, Michael;** *see* Diamond, P. M.

**DIAMOND, Prof. Peter A.,** PhD; Institute Professor and Professor of Economics, Massachusetts Institute of Technology, 1997–2011, now Emeritus; *b* New York, 29 April 1940; *m* 1966, Priscilla, (Kate), Myrick; two *s. Educ:* Yale Univ. (BA Maths 1960); Mass Inst. of Technol. (PhD Econs 1963). Asst Prof., 1963–65, Actg Associate Prof., 1965–66, Univ. of Calif, Berkeley; Massachusetts Institute of Technology: Associate Prof., 1966–70; Prof., 1970–88; John and Jennie S. MacDonald Prof., 1989–91; Paul A. Samuelson Prof., 1992–97. Fellow: Econometric Soc., 1968 (Pres., 1991); Amer. Acad. of Arts and Scis, 1978; MNAS 1984; Founder Mem., Nat. Acad. of Social Insce, 1988 (Pres., 1994–97; Chm., 1996–98; Mem. Bd, 1998–2001); Pres., AEA, 2003. (Jtly) Nobel Prize in Econs, 2010. Associate Ed., Jl of Econ. Theory, 1969–71; Adv. Ed., Jl of Public Econs, 1996– (Associate Ed., 1971–86; Co-Ed., 1986–95). *Publications:* (ed with M. Rothschild) Uncertainty in Economics: readings and exercises, 1978, rev. edn 1989; A Search Equilibrium Approach to the Micro Foundations of Macro-economics, 1984; (ed) Growth, Productivity, Unemployment: essays to celebrate Bob Solow's birthday, 1990; On Time: lectures on models of equilibrium, 1994; (ed jtly) Social Security: what role for the future?, 1996; Social Security Reform, 2002; Taxation, Incomplete Markets and Social Security, 2002; (with Peter R. Orszag) Saving Social Security: a balanced approach, 2004, rev. edn 2005; (ed with Hannu Vartiainen) Behavioral Economics and its Applications, 2007; (with Nicholas Barr) Reforming Pensions: principles and policy choices, 2008; (with Nicholas Barr) Pension Reform: a short guide, 2010; papers in jls. *Address:* Department of Economics, Massachusetts Institute of Technology, 50 Memorial Drive, Building E52, Room 450, Cambridge, MA 02142-1347, USA.

**DIAMOND, (Peter) Michael,** OBE 1996; MA, FMA; arts and heritage consultant, 1995–2018; Director, Birmingham City Museums and Art Gallery, 1980–95; *b* 5 Aug. 1942; *s* of late William Howard and Dorothy Gladys Diamond; *m* 1968, Anne Marie; one *s* one *d. Educ:* Bristol Grammar Sch.; Queens' Coll., Cambridge (MA Fine Art 1964, MA 1966). Dip. of Museums Assoc. 1968, FMA 1980. Sheffield City Art Galleries: Art Asst, 1965; Keeper, Mappin Art Gall., 1967; Dep. Dir, 1969; City Arts and Museums Officer, Bradford, 1976. Chairman: Gp of Dirs of Museums, 1985–89; Public Art Commns Agency, 1987–88. Chm., Avoncroft Mus. of Historic Buildings, 2005–15; Member, Executive Committee: Yorks Arts Assoc., 1977–80; Yorks Sculpture Park, 1978–82 (Chm., 1978–82); Pres., Yorks Fedn of Museums, 1978–80; Member: Crafts Council, 1980–84; Council, Museums Assoc., 1987–90; Board, Museums Training Inst., 1990–93; Board, Worcester Porcelain Mus., 2001–. Mem., Fabric Adv. Cttee, 2001–, Lay Mem. of Chapter, 2015–, Lichfield Cathedral. Mem. Council, Aston Univ., 1983–92. Hon. DSc Aston, 1993. *Publications:* numerous exhibition catalogues incl. Victorian Paintings, 1968; Art and Industry in Sheffield 1850–75, 1975; Bike Art, 1994; (contrib.) Manual of Curatorship, 1984 and 1992; articles in Museums Jl and Internat. Jl of Arts Mgt. *Address:* 5 Anchorage Road, Sutton Coldfield, W Midlands B74 2PJ.

**DIAMOND, Prof. Philip John,** PhD; Director General, SKA Organisation, since 2012; *b* Bude, 18 Feb. 1958; *s* of John Diamond and Denise Diamond; *m* 1985, Jill Hamblett; one *s* one *d. Educ:* Leeds Univ. (BSc Hons Physics with Astrophysics 1979); Manchester Univ. (Dip. Advanced Studies in Sci. 1980; PhD Radio Astronomy 1982). Royal Soc. Post-doctoral Res. Fellow, Onsala Space Observatory, Sweden, 1982–84; Staff Scientist, Max-Planck Inst. für Radioastronomie, Bonn, 1984–86; Asst Scientist, Computer Div., NRAO, Charlottesville, 1987–91; National Radio Astronomy Observatory, Socorro, USA: Asst Scientist, 1991–92, Associate Scientist, 1992–93, Scientist, 1994–95, Very Long Baseline Array Operations; Dep. Asst Dir for Very Large Array/Very Long Baseline Array Ops and Computing, 1995–99; Dir, Multi-Element Radio-Linked Interferometer Network and Very Long Baseline Interferometry Nat. Facility, Jodrell Bank Observatory, 1999–2006; Prof. of Radio Astronomy, 2002–10, Hd of Astronomy and Astrophysics and Dir, Jodrell Bank Centre for Astrophysics, 2006–10, Univ. of Manchester; Chief, CSIRO Astronomy and Space Science, 2012–12. Coordinator: RadioNet (EC-funded Integrated Infrastructure Initiative), 2003–10; EC 7th Framework Prog. Preparatory Phase Proposal for Square Kilometre Array, 2007–10. *Publications:* contrib. numerous papers to jls incl. Nature and Science. *Recreations:* reading, playing squash, worldwide travel, Rugby Union, football. *Address:* SKA Organisation, Jodrell Bank Observatory, Lower Withington, Macclesfield, Cheshire SK11 9DL. *E:* p.diamond@skatelescope.org.

**DIAMOND, Yasmin,** CB 2011; Executive Vice President Global Corporate Affairs, InterContinental Hotels Group, since 2016 (Senior Vice President, 2012–16); *b* 27 Oct. 1967; *d* of Barkat Ali and Khurshid Begum; *m* 1999, Mark Diamond; one *s* one *d. Educ:* Univ. of Leeds (BA Hons Hist. with Business Mgt); Leeds Business Sch. (Postgrad. DipM). Sen. Communications Manager, NHS Exec., 1995–99; Publicity Comr, BBC Broadcast, 1999–2000; Head: Welfare to Work, DfEE, 2000–01; Strategic Mktg, DfES, 2001–05; Dir of Communications, DEFRA, 2005–07; Dir of Communication, Home Office, 2008–12. Mem., Bd of Trustees, British Council, 2017–. *Recreations:* spending leisure time with my family and friends, travelling, fashion and design. *Address:* c/o InterContinental Hotels Group, Broadwater Park, Denham, Bucks UB9 5HR. *Clubs:* Soho House, Ivy.

**DIAS, Julia Amanda, (Mrs S. J. Orford);** QC 2008; barrister; a Deputy High Court Judge, since 2018; *b* Cambridge, 31 Jan. 1959; *d* of late Reginald Walter Michael Dias and Norah Hunter Dias (*née* Crabb); *m* 1983, Stuart John Orford (*d* 2015); one *s* one *d. Educ:* Perse Sch. for Girls, Cambridge; Trinity Hall, Cambridge (BA 1981). MCIArb. Called to the Bar, Inner Temple, 1982, Bencher, 2012 (Chair, Finance Cttee, 2017–). Chm., Disciplinary Tribunals, Bar Tribunals and Adjudication Service, 2009–18. FRSA. Trustee, Magpie Dance, 2012–. *Recreations:* classical music, sport, cooking, gardening, reading. *Address:* 7 King's Bench Walk, Temple, EC4Y 7DS. *T:* (020) 7910 8300, *Fax:* (020) 7910 8400. *E:* jdias@7kbw.co.uk.

**DIBBEN, Michael Alan Charles;** HM Diplomatic Service, retired; High Commissioner, Fiji, also accredited to Tuvalu, Kiribati and Nauru, 1997–2000; *b* 19 Sept. 1943; *s* of Lt-Col Alan Frank Dibben and late Eileen Beatrice Dibben (*née* Donoghue). *Educ:* Dulwich College. With Ottoman Bank, London, 1961–64; CRO 1964; Min. of Overseas Develt, 1965; Protocol Dept, FCO, 1966; served Montreal, Nassau, Stuttgart, Port of Spain, St Georges, Douala; First Sec., 1981; Nuclear Energy Dept, FCO, 1981–83; Munich and Hamburg, 1983–87; Inf. Dept, FCO, 1987–90; Ambassador to Paraguay, 1991–95; Head of Contracts, Travel and Related Services Gp, FCO, 1995–96. Mem., Horners' Co. *Recreations:* reading, walking, golf, classical music. *Address:* 5 Broadhurst Road, Easthouses, Dalkeith EH22 4DW.

**DIBBLE, Prof. Jeremy Colin,** PhD; Professor of Music, Durham University, since 2002; *b* Epping, 17 Sept. 1958; *s* of Colin Morriss Dibble and Pamela Ann Elizabeth Dibble; *m* 1984, Alison Jane Manning. *Educ:* Buckhurst Hill Co. High Sch.; Trinity Coll., Cambridge (BA 1980); Univ. of Southampton (PhD 1986). Lectr, University Coll., Cork, 1987–93; Lectr, 1993–99, Reader, 1999–2002, Durham Univ. Pres., Stanford Soc., 2016– (Vice-Pres., 2006–16). Fellow, Bogliasco Foundn, 2007. FRSCM 2010; FGCM 2013. *Publications:* C. Hubert H. Parry: his life and music, 1992, rev. edn 1998; Charles Villiers Stanford: man and musician, 2002; (ed) Hubert Parry: sonatas for violin and pianoforte, Musica Britannica, vol. 80, 2003; John Stainer: a life in music, 2007; Michele Esposito, 2010; Hamilton Harty: musical polymath, 2013; (ed with Julian Horton) British Musical Criticism and Intellectual Thought 1850–1950, 2018; The Music of Frederick Delius: style, form and ethos, 2020. *Recreations:* wine, model railways, steam railways, church architecture, ornithology, cooking, European languages. *Address:* Music Department, Durham University, Palace Green, Durham DH1 3RL. *T:* (0191) 334 3158. *E:* jeremy.dibble@durham.ac.uk. *Club:* Oxford and Cambridge.

**DIBBLE, Roy Edwin,** CEng, FBCS; HM Diplomatic Service, retired; Chief Executive Services, Foreign and Commonwealth Office, 2000–01; *b* 16 Dec. 1940; *s* of Edwin Dibble and Gwendoline Vera Dibble (*née* Nicholls); *m* 1967, Valerie Jean Denham Smith. *Educ:* Maidstone Tech. High Sch. DipEE; MIET. Central Computer Telecommunications Agency: Head of Div., HM Treasury, 1985–91, Cabinet Office, 1991–94; Dir, OPS, Cabinet Office, 1994–96; Dir, Gen. Services, FCO, 1996–2000. *Recreation:* sailing.

**DICE, Brian Charles,** OBE 1997; Chief Executive, British Waterways Board, 1986–96; *b* 2 Sept. 1936; *s* of late Frederic Charles Dice and Eileen Dice (*née* Rich); *m* 1965, Gwendoline Tazeena Harrison; two *d. Educ:* Clare College, Cambridge; Middle Temple. Cadbury Schweppes, 1960–86, Director, 1979; Managing Director, Schweppes, 1983.

**DICK, Dame Cressida (Rose),** DBE 2019 (CBE 2015); QPM 2010; Commissioner, Metropolitan Police, since 2017; *b* 16 Oct. 1960. *Educ:* Dragon Sch., Oxford; Oxford High Sch.; Balliol Coll., Oxford; Fitzwilliam Coll., Cambridge (MPhil Criminol. 2001). Joined Metropolitan Police Force as constable, 1983; transferred to Thames Valley Police as Superintendent, 1995–2001; Metropolitan Police: Comdr, Diversity Directorate, 2002–03; Hd, Operation Trident, 2003; Dep. Asst Comr, 2009–11; Assistant Commissioner: i/c counter terrorism, incl. London Olympics, 2011–14; Specialist Crime Directorate, 2014; security role, FCO, 2015–17. *Address:* Metropolitan Police Service, New Scotland Yard, Victoria Embankment, SW1A 2JL.

**DICK, Sir Iain Charles M.;** *see* Mackay-Dick.

**DICK-LAUDER, Sir Piers Robert;** *see* Lauder.

**DICKENSON, Alastair John;** silver expert; Managing Director, Alastair Dickenson (formerly Alastair Dickenson Fine Silver) Ltd, since 1996; *b* Leatherhead, 27 Oct. 1950; *s* of Ronald William and Evelyn Marion Dickenson; *m* 1975, Julia Catherine Baguley (marr. diss. 2013); one *s* one *d. Educ:* Epsom Coll.; Guildford Poly. (HND Business Studies). Cataloguer, valuer and auctioneer, Phillips Auctioneers, 1971–82; Sen. Buyer, ADC Heritage, 1982–83; Hd, Antique Silver and Dir, Antiques Dept, Asprey, 1983–95; Dir, Tessier, 1995–96. Expert, Antiques Roadshow, BBC, 1991–; Expert Advr to MLA; Advr to Metalwork Dept, West Dean Coll. Liveryman, Goldsmiths' Co., 2007; Founding Mem. and Freeman, Art Scholars' Co., 2006 (Liveryman; Mem. Court, 2007–11).

*Recreations:* sailing, music, collecting guitars, golf, walking, art. *Address:* Alastair Dickenson Ltd, 128–130 High Street, Godalming, Surrey GU7 1AB. *T:* (01483) 425329. *E:* adickensonsilver@btconnect.com. *Clubs:* MCC; Bosham Sailing.

**DICKENSON, Prof. Anthony Henry,** PhD; Professor of Neuropharmacology, University College London, since 1995; *b* 5 Oct. 1952; *s* of Henry and Kathleen Dickenson; *m* 1975, Joanna Schepp; two *d. Educ:* St Mary's Coll., Southampton; Univ. of Reading (BSc 1974); PhD London 1977. MRC French Exchange Fellow, 1978–79; Scientific Staff, MRC, 1979–83; University College London: Lectr, 1983–90; Sen. Lectr, 1990–92; Reader, 1992–95. Mem. Council, Internat. Assoc. for Study of Pain, 1996–2002. Vis. Prof., Univ. of Calif, 1986; RSocMed Vis. Prof., USA, 1995; Medal and Lecture in Neuroscience, Univ. of Pavia, Italy, 1993. FMedSci 2007. Hon. Mem., British Pain Soc., 2009. *Publications:* (with M. M. Dale and D. G. Haylett) Companion to Pharmacology, 1993, 2nd edn 1995; (with J.-M. Besson) Pharmacology of Pain, 1997; contrib. chapters in books; numerous contribs to learned jls. *Recreations:* dubstep, friends, family, travel, tennis. *Address:* UCL Neuroscience, Physiology & Pharmacology, University College London, Gower Street, WC1E 6BT. *T:* (020) 7679 3742.

**DICKEY, Prof. Eleanor,** DPhil; FBA 2014; Professor of Classics, University of Reading, since 2013; *b* New Haven, Conn, 9 April 1967; *d* of Thomas Atherton Dickey and Barbara Dickey; civil partnership 2008, Philomen Probert. *Educ:* Bryn Mawr Coll., USA (AB 1989; MA 1989); Balliol Coll., Oxford (MPhil 1991); Merton Coll., Oxford (DPhil 1994). Asst Prof. of Classics, Univ. of Ottawa, Canada, 1995–99; Asst Prof., 1999–2005, Associate Prof. of Classics, 2005–07, Columbia Univ., NY; Associate Prof. of Classics, Univ. of Exeter, 2007–13. *Publications:* Greek Forms of Address, 1996; Latin Forms of Address, 2002; Ancient Greek Scholarship, 2007; The Colloquia of the Hermeneumata Pseudodositheana, vol. I, 2012, vol. II, 2015; Learning Latin the Ancient Way, 2016; An Introduction to the Composition and Analysis of Greek Prose, 2016; Stories of Daily Life from the Roman World, 2017; Learn Latin from the Romans, 2018. *Recreations:* music, walking, admiring architecture. *Address:* Department of Classics, School of Humanities, University of Reading, Whiteknights, Reading RG6 6AA. *E:* E.Dickey@reading.ac.uk.

**DICKIE, Brian James;** General Director, Chicago Opera Theater, 1999–2012; Director of Auditions, Bertelsmann Stiftung, since 1999; *b* 23 July 1941; *s* of late Robert Kelso Dickie, OBE and Harriet Elizabeth (*née* Riddell); *m* 1st, 1968, Victoria Teresa Sheldon (*née* Price); two *s* one *d;* 2nd, 1989, Nancy Gustafson; 3rd, 2002, Elinor Rhys Williams; one *d. Educ:* Haileybury; Trinity Coll., Dublin. Admin. Asst, Glyndebourne Opera, 1962–66; Administrator, Glyndebourne Touring Opera, 1967–81; Glyndebourne Festival Opera: Opera Manager, 1970–81; Gen. Administrator, 1981–89. Artistic Dir, Wexford Fest., 1967–73; Artistic Advr, Théâtre Musical de Paris, 1981–87; Gen. Dir, Canadian Opera Co., 1989–93; Artistic Counsellor, Opéra de Nice, 1994–97; Gen. Dir, EU Opera, 1997–99. Member: Bd, Opera America, 1991–93, 2005–11; Bd, Chicago Coll. of the Performing Arts, 2003–12; Music Vis. Cttee, Univ. of Chicago, 2006–11. Chm., London Choral Soc., 1978–85; Vice-Chm., TNC, 1980–85 (Chm., TNC Opera Cttee, 1976–85); Vice-Pres., Theatrical Management Assoc., 1983–85. *Address:* 23 Primrose Mansions, Prince of Wales Drive, SW11 4EE. *Club:* Garrick.

**DICKIE, Gordon Bruce;** Vice Lord-Lieutenant of Dumfries, since 2016; *b* Abernyte, 19 Feb. 1951; *s* of Bruce Dickie and Marjorie Dickie; *m* 1981, Charlotte Butterworth; three *d. Educ:* Glenalmond; Royal Agricultural Coll., Cirencester. Commnd 1st Queen's Dragoon Guards, 1972; served Germany and NI, 1972–75. Sheep farmer, Dumfriesshire, 1979–2005. Director: National Investment Co. Ltd, 1975–; Dundee Property and Reversionary Co. Ltd, 1975–. DL Dumfries, 2005. *Recreations:* tree planting, dry stone walling, country life. *Address:* Poundland, Moniaive, Thornhill, Dumfriesshire DG3 4EG. *E:* gbrucedickie@gmail.com. *Club:* Cavalry and Guards.

**DICKIE, John Kane;** Director of Strategy and Policy, London First, since 2008; *b* 31 Aug. 1965; *s* of John Dickie and Gladys Dickie (*née* O'Neil); *m* 1991, Susan Grunstein; one *s* one *d. Educ:* Morecambe High Sch.; Worcester Coll., Oxford (BA Mod. Hist.); London Business Sch. (MBA). Grad. trainee, Swiss Bank Corp. Internat., 1987–89; Prima Europe, 1989–98 (Man. Dir, 1997–98); GPC International: Man. Dir, GPC London, 1998–99; Hd, Internat. Regulatory Practice, 1999–2000; Dir, Regulatory Affairs, European Competitive Telecommunications Assoc., 2000–03; Hd, Political and Parly Affairs, 2003–04, Public Affairs, 2004–06, Corporate Affairs, 2006–08, BBC. Mem., Camden LBC, 1994–2003 (Dep. Leader, 2000–03). *Recreations:* film, opera, reading, gym. *Address:* c/o London First, Middlesex House, 34–42 Cleveland Street, W1T 4JE. *T:* (020) 7665 1500. *E:* jdickie@London-first.co.uk. *Club:* Reform.

**DICKINS, Janet Constance Elizabeth;** *see* Watson, J. C. E.

**DICKINS, Mark Frederick Hakon S.;** *see* Scrase-Dickins.

**DICKINS, Robert,** CBE 2002; Chairman: Instant Karma Ltd, 1999–2007; Pop Art Ltd, since 1999; *b* 24 July 1950; *s* of late Percy Charles Dickins and Sylvia Marjorie Dickins; *m* 2000, Cherry Ann Gillespie. *Educ:* Ilford Co. High Sch. for Boys; Loughborough Univ. (BSc Politics, Sociol. and Russian 1971). Man. Dir, Warner Bros Music Ltd, 1974–79; Sen. Vice Pres., Warner Brothers Music Corp., 1979–83; Chairman: Warner Music Gp UK, 1983–98; Dharma Music Ltd, 1999–2011. Visiting Professor: Univ. of the Arts, London, 2008–14; London Metropolitan Univ., 2009–. Chm., British Phonographic Industry, 1986–88 and 1997–2002. Chairman: Nat. Mus. of Childhood, Bethnal Green, 2002–07; Theatres Trust, 2009–15; Trustee: BRIT Trust, 1997–; Nat. Foundn for Youth Music, 1999–2006; V&A Mus., 2000–07; Watts Gall., 2004–; Dimbola House, IoW, 2012–13; Handel House Mus., 2012–; Nat. Portrait Gall., 2016–; Mem. Bd, V&A Enterprises, 2000–09. FRSA 2007. Hon. DLitt Loughborough, 2002; Hon. Dr Music Product Publishing Univ. of the Arts, London, 2014; Hon. Dr Business Mgt London Metropolitan, 2015. *Recreations:* art, film, theatre, photography, music, design, travel. *E:* karmarob1@me.com. *Clubs:* Groucho, Ivy.

**DICKINSON,** family name of **Baron Dickinson.**

**DICKINSON,** 2nd Baron *cr* 1930, of Painswick; **Richard Clavering Hyett Dickinson;** *b* 2 March 1926; *s* of late Hon. Richard Sebastian Willoughby Dickinson, DSO (*o s* of 1st Baron) and May Southey, *d* of late Charles Lovemore, Melsetter, Cape Province, S Africa; *S* grandfather, 1943; *m* 1st, 1957, Margaret Ann (marr. diss. 1980), *e d* of late Brig. G. R. McMeekan, CB, DSO, OBE; two *s;* 2nd, 1980, Rita Doreen Moir. *Heir: s* Hon. Martin Hyett Dickinson [*b* 30 Jan. 1961; *m* 1995, Caroline Sally Edwards]. *Address:* The Stables, Gloucester Road, Painswick, Glos GL6 6TH. *T:* (01452) 813646.
*See also Very Rev. H. G. Dickinson.*

**DICKINSON, Maj. Gen. Alastair Scott,** CBE 2015; FInstRE; construction industry, since 2017; Director General Army Basing and Infrastructure, Army Headquarters, 2014–17; *b* Knutsford, 3 Aug. 1963; *s* of Arnold Dickinson and Eunice Dickinson; *m* 1992, Alice Mary McGee; two *s. Educ:* Rishworth Sch., Ripponden; Royal Military Acad. Sandhurst. Commnd Corps of RE, 1981; served with: 36 Engr Regt, 1983–85; Jun. Leaders Regt, 1985–86; 21 Engr Regt, 1986–88; Second i/c, 59 Ind. Cdo Sqn RE, 1989–91; Platoon Comdr, Rowallan Co., RMA Sandhurst, 1991–93; Canadian Jt Service Staff Coll., Toronto, 1993–94; Officer Commanding: 59 Ind. Cdo Sqn RE, 1997–2000; 28 Engr Regt, Hameln, 2003–06; Col Army Plans, Army Resource and Plans, 2006–09; HCSC 2009; Comdr, 8 Force Engr Bde, 2009–11; Dir, Army Resource and Plans, 2011–13. Col Comdt, RE, 2014–. FInstRE 2010. *Recreations:* ex water polo player (Combined Services), current parental sport supporter.

**DICKINSON, Anne;** *see* Dickinson, V. A.

**DICKINSON, Prof. Anthony,** DPhil; FRS 2003; Professor of Comparative Psychology, University of Cambridge, 1999–2011, now Emeritus; Fellow of Hughes Hall, Cambridge, since 1999; *b* 17 Feb. 1944; *m* 1977, Susan Caroline Melhuish; one *s* two *d. Educ:* Univ. of Manchester (BSc 1967); Univ. of Sussex (DPhil 1971); MA Cantab 2001. Postdoctoral Res. Fellow, Sussex Univ., 1971–77; Cambridge University: Demonstrator, 1977–78, Lectr, 1978–94, Dept of Exptl Psychol.; Reader in Comparative Psychol., 1994–99. *Address:* Department of Psychology, University of Cambridge, Downing Street, Cambridge CB2 3EB.

**DICKINSON, David Roscoe;** Partner, Simmons & Simmons, 1988–2011 (Managing Partner, 1999–2005; Senior Partner, 2006–11); *b* 13 Dec. 1950; *s* of John Roscoe Dickinson and Barbara Fleetwood Dickinson (*née* Thomas); *m* 1975, Linda Susan Voneshen; two *s* one *d.* Admitted solicitor: England and Wales, 1974; Hong Kong, 1998; Dir, Legal Services, UBS (Securities) Ltd, 1984–88. Trustee, SkillForce, 2013–16. *Recreations:* family, garden, collecting, bridge. *Address:* Woldingham, Surrey.

**DICKINSON, Gregory David Mark;** QC 2002; **His Honour Judge Dickinson;** a Circuit Judge, since 2012; a Senior Circuit Judge and Resident Judge, Nottingham Crown Court, since 2016; *b* 26 Aug. 1959; *s* of late David Dickinson and Ethel Dickinson; *m* 1989, Frances Judith Betts. *Educ:* Poole Grammar Sch.; Univ. of Leicester (LLB Hons 1980). Called to the Bar, Gray's Inn, 1981, Bencher, 2008; in practice, specialising in criminal law; Midland Circuit, 1982–2012; Asst Recorder, 1998–2000; a Recorder, 2000–12. Hon. Recorder of Nottingham, 2016–. Midland Circuit Rep., Bar Council, 2004–08. Hon. Prof., Nottingham Law Sch., Nottingham Trent Univ., 2017–. Mem. Court, Univ. of Leicester, 2011–. Mem., Judicial Bd, Archbold: Criminal Pleading, Evidence and Practice, 2019–; Assisting Ed., Crown Court Compendium, 2017–. *Recreations:* gardening, walking, travelling, watching old movies with my wife. *Address:* Nottingham Crown Court, 60 Canal Street, Nottingham NG1 7EL.

**DICKINSON, Prof. Harry Thomas,** DLitt; FRHistS; FHA; FRSE; Richard Lodge Professor of British History, University of Edinburgh, 1980–2006, now Emeritus, and Hon. Professorial Fellow, since 2006; *b* 9 March 1939; *s* of Joseph Dickinson and Elizabeth Stearman Dickinson (*née* Warriner); *m* 1961, Jennifer Elizabeth Galtry; one *s* one *d. Educ:* Gateshead Grammar Sch.; Durham Univ. (BA 1960, DipEd 1961, MA 1963); Newcastle Univ. (PhD 1968); DLitt Edinburgh 1986. FRSE 1998. History Master, Washington Grammar Sch., 1961–64; Earl Grey Fellow, Newcastle Univ., 1964–66; Edinburgh University: Asst Lectr, Lectr and Reader, 1966–80; Associate Dean of Arts (Postgrad. Studies), 1992–95; Convener (Senatus, Postgrad. Studies), 1998–2001. Fulbright Award, 1973; Huntington Library Fellowship, 1973; Folger Shakespeare Library Sen. Fellowship, 1973; Winston Churchill Meml Trust Travelling Fellowship, 1980; Leverhulme Award, 1986–87; William Andrews Clark Library Fellow, 1987. Vis. Prof., Nanjing Univ., 1980, 1983, 1994, Concurrent Prof. of Hist., 1987–; Douglas Southall Freeman Prof., Univ. of Richmond, Va, 1997; Vis. Prof., Beijing Univ., 2004, 2011; Concurrent Prof., South East Univ., Nanjing, 2017–20. Anstey Meml Lectr, Kent Univ., 1989; Vis. Lectr to USA, Japan, Taiwan, Canada, France, Czech Republic, Italy, Poland, Norway, Sweden, Estonia, Germany and China; Dean, Scottish Universities Summer School, 1979–85. Acad. Sponsor, Scotland's Cultural Heritage, 1984–91; Mem., Marshall Aid Commemoration Commn, 1986–98; Specialist Advr, CNAA, 1987–93 (Mem., Cttee on Humanities, 1990–93); Auditor, Quality Assurance Gp, Higher Educn Quality Council, 1992–2001; Mem., Hist. Panel, UFC RAE, 1992; Team Assessor (Hist.), Teaching Quality Assessment, SHEFC, 1995–96; Hist. Benchmarking Panel, 1998–99, Academic Reviewer, 1999–2001, QAA; Chm., Hist. Panel, AHRC (formerly AHRB), 2002–06 (Mem., 1999–2002); Mem., Lord Chancellor's Adv. Council on Nat. Records and Archives, 2002–14. Vice-Pres., RHistS, 1991–95 and 2003–06 (Mem., Council, 1986–90); Historical Association: Mem. Council, 1982–; Vice-Pres., 1995–96, 2005–07; Dep. Pres., 1996–98; Pres., 2002–05; Chm. of Publications, 1991–95; FHA 2007. FHEA 2007. Editor, History, 1993–2000; Mem. Editl Bds, Nineteenth Century Short Title Catalogue and Nineteenth Century Microfiche Series. *Publications:* (ed) The Correspondence of Sir James Clavering, 1967; Bolingbroke, 1970; Walpole and the Whig Supremacy, 1973; (ed) Politics and Literature in the Eighteenth Century, 1974; Liberty and Property, 1977; (ed) The Political Works of Thomas Spence, 1982; British Radicalism and the French Revolution 1789–1815, 1985; Caricatures and the Constitution 1760–1832, 1986; (ed) Britain and the French Revolution 1789–1815, 1989; The Politics of the People in Eighteenth Century Britain, 1995; (ed) Britain and the American Revolution, 1998; (ed jtly) The Challenge to Westminster, 2000; (ed) A Companion to Eighteenth-Century Britain, 2002; (ed) Constitutional Documents of the United Kingdom 1776–1849, 2005; (ed jtly) Reactions to Revolutions, 2007; (ed) British Pamphlets on the American Revolution, 8 vols, 2007–08; (ed) Ireland in the Age of the American Revolution, 3 vols, 2013; (ed) Ireland in the Age of the French Revolution, 3 vols, 2013; (jtly) Les îles Britanniques face à la Révolution française (1789-1802), 2019; pubns trans. into French, German, Spanish, Polish, Romanian, Chinese and Japanese; pamphlets, essays, articles and reviews. *Recreations:* films, theatre, watching sports. *Address:* 44 Viewforth Terrace, Edinburgh EH10 4LJ. *T:* (0131) 229 1379, *T:* 07974 725568.

**DICKINSON, Very Rev. Hugh Geoffrey;** Dean of Salisbury, 1986–96, now Emeritus; *b* 17 Nov. 1929; *s* of late Hon. Richard Sebastian Willoughby Dickinson, DSO (*o s* of 1st Baron Dickinson) and of May Southey, *d* of late Charles Lovemore; *m* 1963, Jean Marjorie Storey; one *s* one *d. Educ:* Westminster School (KS); Trinity Coll., Oxford (MA, DipTh); Cuddesdon Theol Coll. Deacon 1956, priest 1957; Curate of Melksham, Wilts, 1956–58; Chaplain: Trinity Coll., Cambridge, 1958–63; Winchester College, 1963–67; Bishop's Adviser for Adult Education, Diocese of Coventry, 1969–77; Vicar of St Michael's, St Albans, 1977–86. *Recreations:* woodturning, fishing, gardening. *Address:* 5 St Peter's Road, Cirencester, Glos GL7 1RE. *T:* (01285) 657710.

**DICKINSON, Prof. Hugh Gordon;** Sherardian Professor of Botany, Oxford, 1991–2009, now Emeritus Professor; Fellow of Magdalen College, Oxford, since 1991; *b* 5 Aug. 1944; *s* of Reginald Gordon Dickinson and Joan Hartley Dickinson; *m* 1980, Alana Gillian Fairbrother; one *s* one *d. Educ:* St Lawrence Coll., Ramsgate; Univ. of Birmingham (BSc, PhD, DSc). Postdoctoral Fellow, UCL, 1969–72; University of Reading: Lectr, 1972–79; Reader, 1979–85; Prof. of Plant Cell Genetics, 1985–91. Trustee, Royal Botanic Gardens, Kew, 1996–2001; Council Mem., John Innes Centre, 1999–2015. Chm., Annals of Botany Co., 2008–. *Publications:* (ed with C. W. Evans) Controlling Events in Meiosis, 1984; (ed with P. Goodhew) Proceedings of IXth European Congress for Electron Microscopy, 1988; (ed jtly) Post-Translational Modification in Plants, 1992; contribs to books and internat. jls, 1967–. *Recreations:* owning and restoring Lancia cars of the '50s and '60s, rock music 1955–75, Mozart operas. *Address:* Magdalen College, Oxford OX1 4AU.

**DICKINSON, Mark**; see Dickinson, S. M.

**DICKINSON, Matthew John, (Matt)**; Chief Sports Writer, The Times, since 2015; b 16 Nov. 1968; s of Jimmy Gordon and Celia Dickinson; m 2000, Helen Willis; two s. Educ: Perse Sch., Cambridge; Robinson Coll., Cambridge (MA); NCTJ Postgrad. Dip in Journalism, Cardiff. Staff News Reporter, Cambridge Evening News, 1992–94; Sports Reporter: Daily Express, 1994–97; The Times, 1997–: Football Correspondent, 2000–02; Chief Football Correspondent, 2002–07; Chief Sports Writer, 2007–15. Young Sports Writer of the Year, Sports Council, 1992; Sports Journalist of the Year, British Press Awards, 2000; Specialist Correspondent of the Year, 2002, 2005, Columnist of the Year, 2016, British Sports Journalism Awards. Publications: assisted with: David Beckham: My World, 2000; Gary Neville: Red, 2011; Bobby Moore: the man in full, 2014. Recreations: playing football, golf, film, travel. Address: c/o The Times, 1 London Bridge Street, SE1 9GF. Club: Cambridge University Lightweight Rowing.

**DICKINSON, Patric Laurence**, LVO 2006; Clarenceux King of Arms, since 2010; Secretary, Order of the Garter, since 2004; b 24 Nov. 1950; s of late John Laurence Dickinson and April Katherine, d of Robert Forgan, MC, MD, sometime MP. Educ: Marling Sch.; Exeter Coll., Oxford (Stapeldon Schol.; MA). Pres., Oxford Union Soc., 1972. Called to the Bar, Middle Temple, 1979, Bencher, 2015. Res. Asst, College of Arms, 1968–78; Rouge Dragon Pursuivant, 1978–89; Richmond Herald of Arms, 1989–2010; Norroy and Ulster King of Arms, 2010; Earl Marshal's Sec., 1996–2012. Hon. Treasurer: English Genealogical Congress, 1975–91; Bar Theatrical Soc., 1978–; Treas., Coll. of Arms, 1995–. Vice-Pres., British Record Soc., 2019– (Hon. Sec. and Registrar, 1979–2010); Vice-Pres., 1988–2011, Pres., 2011–, Assoc. of Genealogists and Researchers in Archives (formerly Assoc. of Genealogists and Record Agents); Vice-Pres., 1997–2005, Pres., 2005–, Soc. of Genealogists; Pres., Bristol and Glos Archaeol Soc., 1998–99. Vice-Pres., Anthony Powell Soc., 2008– (Chm., 2003–07). FSG 2000. Recreation: retirement planning. Address: College of Arms, Queen Victoria Street, EC4V 4BT. T: (020) 7236 9612; 3 Stone Buildings, Lincoln's Inn, WC2A 3XL. Club: Brooks's.

**DICKINSON, Prof. Peter**, DMus; composer, writer, pianist; Head of Music, Institute of United States Studies, University of London, 1997–2004; Professor of Music, Goldsmiths College, London University, 1991–97, now Emeritus; b 15 Nov. 1934; s of late Frank Dickinson, FBOA (Hons), FAAO, DOS, FRSH, contact lens specialist, and Muriel Porter; m 1964, Bridget Jane Tomkinson, d of late Lt-Comdr E. P. Tomkinson, DSO, RN; two s. Educ: The Leys Sch.; Queens' Coll., Cambridge (organ schol., Stewart of Rannoch schol.; MA); Juilliard Sch. of Music, New York (Rotary Foundn Fellow). DMus London 1992; LRAM, ARCM; FRCO. Teaching and freelance work in New York, 1958–61, London and Birmingham, 1962–74; first Prof. of Music, Keele Univ., 1974–84, subseq. Prof. Emeritus; founded Centre for American Music, Keele. Broadcasts and records as pianist (mostly with sister Meriel Dickinson, mezzo soprano, 1966–94). Member, Board: Trinity Coll. of Music, 1984–98; Inst. of US Studies, London Univ., 1997–2004. Trustee: Berners Trust, 1988–; Rainbow Dickinson Trust (formerly Bernarr Rainbow Trust), 1996–. Hon. FTCL 1992. Hon. DMus Keele, 1999. Publications: compositions include: orchestral: Monologue for Strings, 1959; Five Diversions, 1969; Satie Transformations, 1970; Organ Concerto, 1971; Piano Concerto, 1984; Violin Concerto, 1986; Merseyside Echoes, 1988; chamber: String Quartet No 1, 1958; Juilliard Dances, 1959; Fanfares and Elegies, 1967; Translations, 1971; String Quartet No 2, 1975; American Trio, 1985; London Rags, 1986; Sonatas for piano and tape playback, 1987; Auden Studies, 1988; Swansongs, 1992; works for solo organ, piano, clavichord, recorder, flute, violin, guitar and baryton; vocal: song cycles to poems by: W. H. Auden, 1956, 1972; Dylan Thomas, 1959; E. E. Cummings, 1965; Alan Porter, 1968; Gregory Corso, 1969; Emily Dickinson, 1970; John Heath-Stubbs, 1982; Stevie Smith, 1984; Philip Larkin, 1989; John Betjeman, 1991; choral: Martin of Tours (Thomas Blackburn), 1966; The Dry Heart (Alan Porter), 1967; Outcry, 1969; Late Afternoon in November, 1975; A Mass of the Apocalypse, 1984; Tiananmen 1989, 1990; ballet: Vitalitas, 1959; musical drama: The Judas Tree (Thomas Blackburn), 1965; various church music; (ed) Twenty British Composers, 1975; (ed) Songs and Piano Music by Lord Berners, 1982, 2nd edn 2000; The Music of Lennox Berkeley, 1989, 2nd edn 2003; Marigold: the music of Billy Mayerl, 1999; (ed) Copland Connotations, 2002; (ed) Collected Works for Solo Piano by Lennox Berkeley, 2003; (ed) CageTalk: dialogues with and about John Cage, 2006; Lord Berners: composer, writer, painter, 2008; (ed) Complete Piano Duets by Lord Berners, 2010; Samuel Barber Remembered: a centenary tribute, 2010; (ed) Lennox Berkeley and Friends: writings, letters and interviews, 2012; (ed) Music Education in Crisis: the Bernarr Rainbow Lectures and other assessments, 2013; Peter Dickinson: words and music, 2016; contrib. to The New Grove, and various books and periodicals. Recreation: rare books. Address: c/o Novello & Co., 14–15 Berners Street, W1T 3LJ. W: www.foxborough.co.uk. Club: Garrick.

**DICKINSON, Robert Henry**, CBE 1998; DL; Senior Partner, Dickinson Dees, 1987–97; Chairman, Northern Rock PLC (formerly Northern Rock Building Society), 1992–99; b 12 May 1934; s of Robert Joicey Dickinson and Alice Penelope Dickinson (née Barnett); m 1963, Kyra Irina Boissevain; one s two d. Educ: Harrow; Christ Church, Oxford (MA). Admitted solicitor (Hons), 1960; Partner, Dickinson Dees, 1963–97. Chairman: Northern Investors PLC, 1984–2005; Grainger Trust PLC, 1992–2007; Director: Reg Vardy PLC, 1988–2002; Yorkshire Tyne Tees TV PLC, 1992–97. Chm., Univ. of Newcastle upon Tyne Develt Trust, 2000–05. DL Northumberland, 1992. Recreations: shooting, fishing. Address: Styford High Barns, Stocksfield, Northumberland NE43 7UA. T: (01434) 634452. Clubs: Boodle's, Pratt's; Northern Counties (Newcastle).

**DICKINSON, Sally Jane**; Policy Director, Magistrates' Association, 2010–12 (Secretary, 1994–2010); b 12 Sept. 1955; d of Colin James Rayner Godden and Margaret Godden (née Cowin); m 1987, James Anthony Dickinson. Educ: Chatham Grammar Sch. for Girls; Bristol Univ. (BA Theol); Bristol Poly. (BA Law). Clerical Officer, Inland Revenue Collection, 1978–81; Exec. Officer, Law Soc. (Legal Aid), 1981–85; Regl Dir, Apex Charitable Trust, 1985–92; Cttee Sec., Magistrates' Assoc., 1992–93. Trustee: Fair Trials Internat., 2011–14; Griffins Soc., 2013–. Sec., Friends of the Windmill Hill Windmill. Publications: (Asst Ed.) The Magistracy at the Crossroads, 2012. Recreations: walking my dog, archery, ukulele. Address: 8 Sussex Place, West End, Herstmonceux, E Sussex BN27 4NJ.

**DICKINSON, Simon Clervaux**; Chairman: Simon C. Dickinson Ltd, Agents and Dealers in Fine Art, since 1993; Dickinson Roundell Inc., since 1993; b 26 Oct. 1948; s of Peter Dickinson and Anne Dickinson (née Chayter); m 1983, Hon. Jessica, d of 2nd Baron Mancroft, KBE, TD; one s two d. Educ: Aysgarth Sch.; Harrow (art schol.). Mem., First cricket and football XIs. Christie's: joined 1968; Dir, 1974–93; Sen. Picture Dir, 1990–93. Recreations: gardening, shooting, fishing, golf, tennis. Address: Simon C. Dickinson Ltd, 58 Jermyn Street, SW1Y 6LX. T: (020) 7493 0340, Fax: (020) 7493 0796. E: simon@simondickinson.com. Club: White's.

**DICKINSON, (Stephen) Mark**; Chairman, Prolific North and Prolific London, since 2013; b 20 Jan. 1951; s of Stanley Park Dickinson and Beatrice Joan Dickinson; m 1981, Pauline Patricia Mills; two s two d. Educ: Dame Alice Owen's Sch.; Univ. of Manchester (BA 2nd Cl. Hons Psychol). Publicity asst, Macmillan Jls, 1975–76; sub-editor, Daily Telegraph, Manchester, 1976–87; author, 1988–89; Chief Sub Editor: Tonight, Chester, 1990–91; Aberdeen Evening Express, 1991–92; Asst Ed., The Journal, Newcastle, 1992–93; Dep. Ed. in Chief, Chronicle Newspapers, Chester, 1993–96; Editor: The Journal, Newcastle, 1996–2000; Liverpool Echo, 2000–05; Ed.-in-Chief, Trinity Mirror NW and N Wales, 2002–05; Editl Dir, Trinity Mirror Midlands, 2005–07; Business Development Director: Trinity Mirror NW and Wales, 2007–10; Trinity Mirror Regionals, 2011–12; Man. Dir, Dickinson Communications, 2012–16. Dir and Gov., W Kirby Residential Sch., 2014–. Publications: The Manchester Book, 1984; To Break a Union, 1986; Goodbye Piccadilly: the history of abolition of Greater Manchester Council, 1990. Recreations: reading, gardening, football, Rugby, entertaining, my family.

**DICKINSON, (Vivienne) Anne, (Mrs Basil Phillips)**; Chairman, Forexia UK, 1997–98; Director, Leedex Public Relations, 1993–96; b 27 Sept. 1931; d of F. Oswald Edward Dickinson and M. Ida Ismay Dickinson; m 1st, 1951, John Kerr Large (marr. diss.); one s decd; 2nd, 1979, David Hermas Phillips (d 1989); 3rd, 1993, Basil B. Phillips, OBE (d 2019). Educ: Nottingham Girls' High School. Account Executive, W. S. Crawford, 1960–64; Promotions Editor: Good Housekeeping, 1964–65; Harpers Bazaar, 1965–67; Dir in charge of Promotions, Nat. Magazine Co., 1967–68; Dir, Benson PR (later Kingsway), 1968–69; Chm. and Chief Exec., Kingsway Public Relations Ltd (later Kingsway Rowland), 1969–89; Chairman: The Rowland Co., 1989–90; Graduate Appointments Ltd, 1993–94; Dir, Birkdale Group plc, 1991–96. Chm., PR Consultants' Assoc., 1989 (Chm., Professional Practices Cttee 1989). Chm., Family Welfare Assoc., 1990–94. Member: Rye Town Council, 1995–99; Bd, Rye Health & Care Ltd, 1996–2004, 2009– (Vice Pres., 2004–08, Pres., 2008–). FCIPR (FIPR 1985); CCMI (CBIM 1986). PR Professional of the Year, PR Week, 1988–89. Recreations: friends, food, dogs. Address: St Mary's House, 62 Church Square, Rye TN31 7HF. Club: Sloane.

**DICKINSON, William George Heneage**; Global Head of Finance Audit, Global Internal Audit, HSBC Holdings plc, since 2013; b Bath, 11 Nov. 1966; s of Michael and Sonia Dickinson; m 1997, Nancy Zonana; one s one d. Educ: Marlborough Coll.; Durham Univ. (BSc Hons). FCA 1992. Accountant: KPMG Peat Marwick McLintock, subseq. KPMG Peat Marwick, Bristol, 1988–92; KPMG: Boston, 1992–94; London, 1994–99; Montvale, 1999–2001; Partner, 2001–09; Partner i/c UK Dept of Professional Practice for Audit, 2001–03; Audit Partner, Financial Services, 2003–09; UK Hd of Audit for Asset Mgt, 2007–08; on secondment as Dir Gen., Finance and Corporate Services, DIUS, later BIS, 2008–09; Financial Risk Dir, DWP, 2009–10; HM Treasury: Chief Financial and Operating Officer, 2010–11, Chief Exec., 2011–12, Asset Protection Agency; Dir, Financial Services Gp, 2012–13. Recreations: film, theatre, tennis, sailing, reading. Address: Top Maisonette, 6 Eccleston Square, SW1V 1NP. T: (020) 7931 7620. E: wghdickinson@gmail.com.

**DICKS, Terence Patrick, (Terry)**; b 17 March 1937; s of Frank and Winifred Dicks; m; one s two d; m 1985, Janet Cross; one d. Educ: London Sch. of Econs and Pol Science (BScEcon); Oxford Univ. (DipEcon). Clerk: Imperial Tobacco Co. Ltd, 1952–59; Min. of Labour, 1959–66; Admin. Officer, GLC, 1971–86. Contested (C) Bristol South, 1979. MP (C) Hayes and Harlington, 1983–97. Mem., Select Cttee on Transport, 1986–92. Member: Council of Europe, 1993–97; WEU, 1993–97. Member (C): Surrey CC, 1999–2009; Runnymede BC, 2011–18.

**DICKSON, Brice**; see Dickson, S. B.

**DICKSON, George**, CBE 1991 (OBE 1974); HM Diplomatic Service, retired; Consul General, Amsterdam, 1987–91; b 23 May 1931; s of late George James Stark Dickson and Isobel (née Brown). Educ: Aberdeen Acad. DSIR, 1952; CRO, 1952–54; Karachi, 1954–56; Penang, 1957–59; Nicosia, 1960–62; Kampala, 1962–66; FCO, 1966–68; Manila, 1968–71; Jakarta, 1971–75; Stuttgart, 1975–76; Beirut, 1976–79; Baghdad, 1979–81; Asst Dir, Internat. Affairs, Commonwealth Secretariat, 1981–85; Dep. High Comr, Kingston, Jamaica, 1985–87. Address: Flat 17, 12 Constitution Place, Edinburgh EH6 7DL. T: (0131) 237 2639. Club: Royal Northern and University (Aberdeen).

**DICKSON, Jennifer (Joan), (Mrs R. A. Sweetman)**, CM 1995; RA 1976 (ARA 1970); RE 1965; graphic artist, photographer and lecturer on the history of gardens; b 17 Sept. 1936; 2nd d of late John Liston Dickson and Margaret Joan Turner, S Africa; m 1962, Ronald Andrew Sweetman (d 2018); one s. Educ: Goldsmith's College Sch. of Art, Univ. of London; Atelier 17, Paris. Taught at Eastbourne Sch. of Art, 1959–62 (French Govt Schol., to work in Paris under S. W. Hayter). Directed and developed Printmaking Dept, Brighton Coll. of Art, 1962–68; developed and directed Graphics Atelier, Saidye Bronfman Centre, Montreal, 1970–72. Exhibitions: L'Ultimo Silenzio, Palazzo Te, Mantua, Italy, 1993; Romantic Idylls and Classical Dreams, Wallack Galls, Ottawa, 2011. Has held appointments of Vis. Artist at following Universities: Ball State Univ., Muncie, Indiana, 1967; Univ. of the West Indies, Kingston, Jamaica, 1968; Univ. of Wisconsin, Madison, 1972; Ohio State Univ., 1973; Western Illinois Univ., 1973; Haystack Mountain Sch. of Crafts, Maine, 1973; Vis. Artist, Queen's Univ., Kingston, Ont., 1977; part-time Instructor of Drawing, 1980–81, 1983, Sessional Instructor, 1980–85, Ottawa Univ.; Vis. Prof., 1987, Hon. LLD 1988, Univ. of Alberta. Founder Mem., Brit. Printmakers' Council. Prix des Jeunes Artistes (Gravure), Biennale de Paris, 1963; Major Prize, World Print Competition, San Francisco, 1974; Norwegian Print Biennale Prize, 1981. Publications: suites of original prints and photographs: Genesis, 1965; Alchemic Images, 1966; Aids to Meditation, 1967; Eclipse, 1968; Song of Songs, 1969; Out of Time, 1970; Fragments, 1971; Sweet Death and Other Pleasures, 1972; Homage to Don Juan, 1975; Body Perceptions, 1976; The Secret Garden, 1976; Openings, 1977; Three Mirrors to Narcissus, 1978; Il Paradiso Terrestre, 1980; Il Tempo Classico, 1981; Grecian Odes, 1983; Aphrodite Anadyomene, 1984; The Gardens of Paradise, part 1, 1984, part 2, 1985; Reflected Palaces, 1985; The Gilded Cage, 1986; Water Gardens, 1987; The Hospital for Wounded Angels, 1987; The Gardens of Desire, 1988; Pavane to Spring, 1989; Sonnet to Persephone, 1990; The Gardener's Journal, 1990; Cadence and Echo: the song of the garden, 1991; The Spirit of the Garden, 1992; The Haunted Heart, 1993; Sanctuaries and Paradeisos, 1994; Old and New Worlds, 1995; Quietude and Grace, 1996; Water Song, 1997; Sanctuary: a landscape of the mind, 2000; Nature and Artifice, 2003; Time is the Thief of Time, 2006; The Royal Academy Suites: passages and transitions, 2008; Romantic Idylls and Classical Dreams, 2011; Contemplative Moments, 2012; Water Games, 2013. Address: 20 Osborne Street, Ottawa, ON K1S 4Z9, Canada. T: (613) 7302083, Fax: (613) 7301818. E: jenniferdickson@kalixo.com.

**DICKSON, Martin Charles Gregor**; journalist; b London, 21 Aug. 1948; s of George and Stella Dickson; m 1973, Hilary Wilce; one s two d. Educ: Haileybury; Trinity Hall, Cambridge (BA Hist. 1970); Univ. of London (BSc Econ. ext.). VSO, Thailand, 1966–67; journalist, Reuters, UK, S Africa and Turkey, 1970–76; Financial Times: journalist, 1976–2014; Africa Ed., 1978–79; Energy Corresp., 1980–82; NY Bureau Chief, 1990–94; Financial Ed., 1994–2000; Lombard Columnist, 2001–05; Dep. Ed., 2005–12; US Man. Ed., 2012–14. Mem. Bd, British Library, 2015–19. Recreations: singing, running, travel, galleries, gardening. E: martincgdickson@hotmail.com.

**DICKSON, Niall Forbes Ross**, CBE 2017; Chief Executive, NHS Confederation, since 2017; b 5 Nov. 1953; s of late Sheriff Ian Anderson Dickson, WS and Margaret Forbes Ross or Dickson; m 1979, Elizabeth Selina Taggart, d of late James Mercer Taggart, Lisburn, Co.

Antrim; one s two d. *Educ:* Glasgow Acad.; Edinburgh Acad.; Edinburgh Univ. (MA Hons; DipEd); Moray House Coll. of Educn (Cert Ed). Teacher, Broughton High Sch., Edinburgh, 1976–78; Publicity Officer, Nat. Corp. for Care of Old People, 1978; Press Officer, 1978–79, Hd of Publishing, 1979–81, Age Concern England; Editor: Therapy Weekly, 1981–83; Nursing Times, 1983–88; BBC News: Health Corresp., 1988–90; Chief Social Affairs Corresp., 1990–95; Social Affairs Editor, 1995–2004; Chief Exec., The King's Fund, 2004–09; Chief Exec. and Registrar, GMC, 2010–16. Chairman: Direct Payments Steering Gp, DoH, 2004–06; Individual Budgets Reform Gp, 2006–08; Ind. Chair, Somerset Sustainability and Transformation Plan, 2017–18; Brexit Health Alliance, 2017–. Member: NHS Modernisation Bd, 2004–05; Nat. Leadership Network, DoH, 2005–07; CMO's Review of Med. Regulation and Related Matters, 2005–06; Wkg Party on Med. Professionalism, RCP, 2005–06; Health Honours Cttee, 2005–12; Ministerial Adv. Gp on social care reform, 2008–10; DoH Nat. Quality Bd, 2012–16; Bd of Govs, European Hosp. and Healthcare Assoc., 2017–; Adv. Bd, Healthcare UK, 2018–; NHS Assembly, 2019–. Chm., Health Commn, LGA, 2007–08. Chair, Internat. Assoc. of Med. Regulatory Authorities, 2014–16. Mem. Council, Which?, 2006–10. Mem. Ct of Govs, LSHTM, 2005–10. Trustee, Leeds Castle Foundn, 2008–12 (Chm., 2012–). UK Rep., Internat. Hosps Fedn, 2018–. Hon. Fellow: Univ. of Cardiff, 2006; Inst. of Educn, Univ. of London, 2007; Queen's Nursing Inst., 2009. Hon. MRCP 2007; Hon. MRCGP 2008. DUniv Oxford Brookes, 2007. Charles Fletcher Med. Broadcaster of Year, BMA, 1997; Healthcare Communications Advocate, Communiqué Awards, 2016; Award for Excellence in Editl Writing, Fedn of State Med. Bds, 2017. *Publications:* contribs to newspapers, jls and specialist pubns on health and social issues. *Recreations:* golf, tennis, history, current affairs. *Address:* NHS Confederation, Floor 15, Portland House, Bressenden Place, SW1E 5BH. *Clubs:* Reform; Golf House (Elie), Hever Castle Golf, Isle of Harris Golf.
*See also* R. H. Dickson.

**DICKSON, Prof. Peter George Muir,** DPhil, DLitt; FBA 1988; Professor of Early Modern History, University of Oxford, 1989–96; Fellow, St Catherine's College, Oxford, since 1960; b 26 April 1929; s of William Muir Dickson, and Regina Dowdall-Nicolls; m 1964, Ariane Faye; one d. *Educ:* St Paul's Sch.; Worcester Coll., Oxford (Schol.; BA (1st Cl. Hons), MA, DPhil); DLitt Oxon 1992. FRHistS. Research Fellow, Nuffield Coll., Oxford, 1954–56; Tutor, St Catherine's Soc., Oxford, 1956–60; Vice-Master, St Catherine's Coll., 1975–77; Reader in Modern Hist., Oxford Univ., 1978–89. *Publications:* The Sun Insurance Office 1710–1960, 1960; The Financial Revolution in England 1688–1756, 1967, rev. edn 1993; Finance and Government under Maria Theresia 1740–1780, 2 vols, 1987. *Recreations:* reading, art. *Address:* Taunton House, Freeland OX29 8AQ.

**DICKSON, Prof. Robert Andrew,** DSc; FRCS, FRCSE; Professor and Head of Department of Orthopaedic Surgery, University of Leeds, 1981–2009; Consultant Surgeon, St James's University Hospital, Leeds, and Leeds General Infirmary, 1981–2009; b 13 April 1943; s of Robert Campbell Miller Dickson and late Maude Evelyn Dickson; m 1980, Ingrid Irene Sandberg; one s. *Educ:* Edinburgh Academy; Edinburgh Univ. (MB, ChB 1967, ChM 1973); MA 1979, DSc 1992, Oxon. FRCSE 1972; Moynihan Medal (Assoc. of Surgeons of GB and Ire.), 1977; FRCS *ad eund*, 1982. Lecturer, Nuffield Dept of Orthopaedic Surgery, Univ. of Oxford, 1972–75; Fellow in Spinal Surgery, Univ. of Louisville, Kentucky, 1975–76; Reader, Nuffield Dept of Orthopaedic Surgery, Univ. of Oxford, 1976–81. Chm., Professional Conduct Cttee, GMC, 2003–. Arris and Gale Lectr, and Hunterian Prof., RCS. Fellow, Brit. Orthopaedic Assoc. (Chm., Res. and Scholarship Cttee, 1999–); Member: Brit. Soc. for Surgery of the Hand; Brit. Orthopaedic Research Soc.; Brit. Scoliosis Soc. Treas., Council of Mgt, Jl of Bone and Jt Surgery, 2002–. *Publications:* Surgery of the Rheumatoid Hand, 1979; Musculo-skeletal disease, 1984; Management of spinal deformities, 1984; Management of spinal deformities, 1988; papers on scoliosis and spinal surgery. *Recreations:* squash, music. *Address:* 14A Park Avenue, Leeds LS8 2JH.

**DICKSON, Robert Hamish,** DL; WS; Sheriff of South Strathclyde, Dumfries and Galloway, at Airdrie, 1988–2015; b 19 Oct. 1945; s of late Sheriff Ian Anderson Dickson, WS, and Mrs Margaret Forbes Ross or Dickson; m 1976, Janet Laird (d 2004), d of late Alexander Campbell, Port of Menteith; one s. *Educ:* Glasgow Acad.; Drumtochty Castle; Glenalmond; Glasgow Univ. (LLB). WS 1969. Solicitor: Edinburgh, 1969–71; Glasgow, 1971–86 (Partner, Brown Mair Mackintosh, 1973–86); Sheriff of South Strathclyde, Dumfries and Galloway, at Hamilton, 1986–88 (floating). Pres., Sheriffs' Assoc., 2006–09; Mem., Scottish Civil Justice Council (formerly Sheriff Court Rules Council), 2011–15. Pres., Scottish Medico Legal Soc., 2004–08. DL Lanarks, 2012. *Publications:* (jtly) Powers & Harris' Medical Negligence, 2nd edn 1994, 4th edn 2007; Medical and Dental Negligence, 1997; articles in medical legal jls. *Recreations:* golf, music, reading. *Clubs:* Royal and Ancient Golf, Elie Golf House (Capt., 1997–99), Harris Golf.
*See also* N. F. R. Dickson.

**DICKSON, Robert Maurice French C.;** *see* Chatterton Dickson.

**DICKSON, Sarah Margaret;** HM Diplomatic Service; High Commissioner to the Bahamas, since 2019; b London, 1972; d of Rowan Hill and Gabrielle Hill; m 2006, Philip Antony Dickson; two d. *Educ:* St John's Coll., Cambridge (BA Hons 1995). Joined FCO, 1995; Desk Officer, 1995–96; Third Sec., Belgrade, 1996–97; Second Sec. (Pol), Buenos Aires, 1997–2000; Hd, Internet. Security Section, Security Policy Dept, FCO, 2000–02; First Sec. (Pol/Mil.), Madrid, 2002–03; Hd, Migration and Justice and Home Affairs Section, EU-Internal, 2003–04, Hd, Consular and Africa Section, Press Office, 2004, FCO; Communications Dir and Internal Pol Officer, 2005–08, Manager for Embassy and Consulate Gen. relocation, 2008–09, COS, 2009–10, Madrid; Ambassador to Guatemala and (non-resident) to Honduras, 2012–15; Dir of Global Affairs, Scotch Whisky Assoc., 2015–19. *Address:* c/o Foreign and Commonwealth Office, King Charles Street, SW1A 2AH.

**DICKSON, Prof. (Sidney) Brice;** Professor of International and Comparative Law, Queen's University, Belfast, 2005–17, now Emeritus; b 5 Dec. 1953; s of Sidney Dickson and Mary Dickson (née Murray); m 1993, Patricia Mary Josephine Mallon; one step d (one step s decd). *Educ:* Wadham Coll., Oxford (BA, BCL); Univ. of Ulster (MPhil). Called to the Bar, NI, 1976; Lectr in Law, Univ. of Leicester, 1977–79; Lectr, 1979–89, Sen. Lectr, 1989–91, QUB; Prof. of Law, Univ. of Ulster, 1991–99; Chief Comr, NI Human Rights Commn, 1999–2005. Ind. Mem., Policing Bd of NI, 2012–March 2020. Leverhulme Eur. Student, 1976–77; Salzburg Fellow, 1985; Churchill Fellow, 1994; Leverhulme Res. Fellow, 1999, 2013–14. *Publications:* The Legal System of Northern Ireland, 1984, 5th edn 2005; Introduction to French Law, 1994; (ed) Human Rights and the European Convention, 1997; (ed) Civil Liberties in Northern Ireland: the CAJ handbook, 1990, 5th edn as Human Rights in Northern Ireland: the CAJ handbook, 2015; (ed with P. Carmichael) The House of Lords: its parliamentary and judicial roles, 1999; (ed) Judicial Activism in Common Law Supreme Courts, 2007; (ed jtly) The Judicial House of Lords 1876–2009, 2009; The European Convention on Human Rights and the Conflict in Northern Ireland, 2010; Law in Northern Ireland: an introduction, 2011, 3rd edn 2018; Human Rights and the UK Supreme Court, 2013; (ed with H. Hardman) Electoral Rights in Europe: advances and challenges, 2017; The Irish Supreme Court: historical and comparative perspectives, 2019. *Recreations:* fiction, classical music, philately, travel. *Address:* Maryville Park, Belfast BT9 6LP.

**DICKSON, Stewart Clyde;** Member (Alliance) East Antrim, Northern Ireland Assembly, since 2011; b Belfast, 8 Dec. 1950; s of Clyde Dickson and Evelyn Dickson; m 1978, Elizabeth Alexandra Millar. Sen. Employment Relns Officer, Labour Relations Agency, 1985–2011. Mem. (Alliance), Carrickfergus BC, 1977–81, 1985–2011. Chief Whip, Alliance Party (Chm., 2010–11). Contested (Alliance) E Antrim, 2015, 2017. Churchill Fellow, 1999. *Recreations:* reading, travel, Member of 1st Greenisland Boys' Brigade Company. *Address:* 6 Farm Lodge Park, Greenisland, Carrickfergus BT38 8YB. *E:* stewart.dickson@mla.niassembly.gov.uk. *Club:* Ulster Reform.

**DICKSON, Susan Jane;** HM Diplomatic Service; Legal Counsellor, UK Mission to the United Nations, New York, since 2017; b 30 July 1964; d of John Morton Dickson and Marlene Linek Dickson (née Allan). *Educ:* Mearns Castle High Sch.; Univ. of Strathclyde (LLB Hons 1986; DipLP 1988); Europa Inst., Univ. of Amsterdam (Postgrad. Dip. in European Law 1987). Admitted solicitor (Scotland), 1990; Asst, then Sen. Asst, Legal Advr, FCO, 1990–97; First Sec. (Legal), UK Mission to UN, NY, 1997–2000; First Sec. (Legal Advr British Overseas Territories), British High Commn, Bridgetown, 2000–03; Legal Counsellor, FCO, 2003–17. *Publications:* (with I. D. Hendry) British Overseas Territories Law, 2011, 2nd edn, 2018. *Recreations:* yoga, tennis, reading, interior design, Caribbean beaches. *Address:* Foreign and Commonwealth Office, King Charles Street, SW1A 2AH. *E:* susan.dickson@fco.gov.uk.

**DICKSON, William Andrew;** HM Diplomatic Service, retired; Ambassador to Mongolia, 2009–11; Chief Executive Officer, Independent (UK) Exports Ltd, 2012–18; Director of UK Operations, MongoliaNation, 2011; Managing Partner, International Export Partners, 2013; b Glasgow, 17 Dec. 1950; s of William Paul McBean Dickson and Isabella Dickson (née Goodwin); m 2007, Patricia Ann Daniels; two step s. *Educ:* Lenzie Acad.; Stirling Univ.; Willesden Coll.; Univ. of Northumbria (Law). Served RM; concrete engineer, construction industry; joined HM Diplomatic Service; Vice Consul, Cairo, 1976–80; Third Sec., Nairobi, 1980–82; Second Sec., Budapest, 1982–86; FCO spokesman, 1986–89; First Sec., Vienna, 1989–93; British Govt spokesman, Hong Kong, 1994–98; Administrator: Ascension, 2001; Tristan da Cunha, and Consul Gen., S Atlantic Ocean, 2001–04; Consul Gen., Erbil, Iraq, 2007–08. Director: Orgill-Dickson Associates, 2011–15; Independent Gorman LLC, 2014–. Member, Board: Broads Authy, 2016– (Member: Navigation Cttee, 2015–16; Planning Cttee, 2016–; Vice-Chm., 2018–); Marine Mgt Orgn, 2019–. Chm., Internat. Old Boys Assoc. UK, 2012–; President: Probus Club of Broadlands, 2014–; Hoveton and Coltishall Mountain Rescue Team, 2014–; Chm., Allotments Cttee, Coltishall Parish Council, 2017–. Gov., Stalham High Sch., 2012–13. *Recreations:* boating on the Norfolk Broads, ocean racing, wooden sailing ship modelling Nelson's Navy, gardening in small spaces, thinking about getting fit. *Address:* 12 Trail Quay Cottages, Marsh Road, Hoveton, Norfolk NR12 8UH. *E:* shipwreckbt@hotmail.com. *Clubs:* Cape Town; Montagu Golf (Montagu, Western Cape); Foreign Correspondents' (Hong Kong).

**DIEHL, His Honour John Bertram Stuart;** QC 1987; a Circuit Judge, 1990–2011; Hon. Recorder of Swansea, 2001–11; b 18 April 1944; s of late E. H. S. Diehl and C. P. Diehl; m 1967, Patricia L. Charman; two s. *Educ:* Bishop Gore Grammar Sch., Swansea; University Coll. of Wales, Aberystwyth (LLB 1965). Called to the Bar, Lincoln's Inn, 1968, Bencher (Additional Bencher, 2007). Asst Lectr and Lectr in Law, Univ. of Sheffield, 1965–69; barrister, in practice on Wales and Chester Circuit, 1969–90; Asst Recorder, 1980–84; Recorder, 1984–90. *Address:* c/o Crown Court, St Helen's Road, Swansea SA1 4PF.

**DIENES-WILLIAMS, Katherine Frances Maria,** FRCO; Organist and Master of the Choristers, Guildford Cathedral, since 2008; Director, Southern Voices, since 2012; b Wellington, NZ, 10 Jan. 1970; d of Julius Joseph Eugene Dienes and Frances Armstrong Dienes; m 1996, Patrick Williams; one d. *Educ:* St Mark's Ch Sch., Wellington, NZ; Samuel Marsden Collegiate Sch., Wellington; Victoria Univ., Wellington (BA, BMus); Leeds Univ. (MA Music and Liturgy). LTCL (Piano 1986, Organ 1987); ARCO 1992, FRCO 1993. Richard Prothero Organ Schol., 1988–89, Asst Organist, 1990–91, Wellington Cathedral; Organ Schol., Winchester Cathedral, and Asst Organist, Winchester Coll., 1991–94; Organist and Asst Master of Choristers, Liverpool Metropolitan Cathedral, 1994–97; Asst Organist and Dir of Girls' Choir, Norwich Cathedral, 1997–2001; Dir of Music, St Mary's Collegiate Ch, Warwick, 2001–07. Mem. Council, RSCM, 2008–. Hon. ARSCM 2006; Hon. FRSCM 2017; Hon. FGCM 2018. Knight: Order of Vitéz, 1994; Order of St László, 1995. *Recreations:* classical music, travel, reading, fitness. *Address:* Cathedral Office, Stag Hill, Guildford, Surrey GU2 7UP. *T:* (01483) 547866. *E:* Katherine@guildford-cathedral.org.

**DIEPPE, Prof. Paul Adrian,** MD; FRCP; Chair, Health and Wellbeing, University of Exeter Medical School (formerly Peninsula Medical School), since 2012; Hon. Professor of Musculoskeletal Sciences, University of Oxford, since 2007; b 20 May 1946; s of late Richard Willan Dieppe and Muriel Grace Dieppe (née Gascoigne); m 1970, Elizabeth Anne Stadward; two d. *Educ:* Caterham Sch.; St Bartholomew's Hosp. Med. Coll. (BSc 1967; MB BS 1970; MD 1985). FRCP 1985. General medical trng posts in London and Southend, 1970–74; Rheumatology Registrar, Guy's Hosp., London, 1974–75; Res. Fellow and Sen. Registrar in Medicine and Rheumatology, St Bartholomew's Hosp., London, 1975–78; University of Bristol: Consultant Sen. Lectr, 1978–87; ARC Prof. of Rheumatology, 1987–97; Res. Dir, Clinical Medicine and Dentistry, 1993–95; Dean, Faculty of Medicine, 1995–97; Hon. Prof. of Health Services Res., 1997–2007; Dir, MRC Health Services Res. Collaboration, 1997–2007; Hon. Consultant Rheumatologist: to Bristol and Bath hosps, 1978–2007; United Bristol Healthcare NHS Trust, 1992–2007; N Avon Hosp. Trust, 1997–2007; Chair, Clinical Educn Res., Peninsula Med. Sch., 2009–12. *Publications:* Crystals and Joint Disease, 1983; Rheumatological Medicine, 1985; Atlas of Clinical Rheumatology, 1986; Arthritis: BMA Family Doctor Guide, 1988; Rheumatology, 1993, 2nd edn 1997; contrib. chapters in books and numerous papers in jls. *Recreations:* sailing, cycling, carving, reading, writing, resting.

**DIFFLEY, Dr John Francis Xavier,** FRS 2005; Associate Research Director, Francis Crick Institute, since 2015; b 4 March 1958; s of John and Joan Diffley. *Educ:* New York Univ. (BA 1978; PhD 1985). Postdoctoral Fellow, Cold Spring Harbor Lab., 1984–90; Imperial Cancer Research Fund, Clare Hall Laboratories: res. scientist, 1990–95; Sen. Scientist, 1995–99; Principal Scientist, 1999–2002; Principal Scientist, Cancer Res. UK, London Res. Inst., 2002–15. Mem., Eur. Acad. of Cancer Scis, 2011. FMedSci 2011. (Jtly) Canada Gairdner Internat. Award, 2019. *Recreations:* playing the guitar, cycling. *Address:* Francis Crick Institute, 1 Midland Road, NW1 1AT.

**DIGBY,** family name of **Baron Digby.**

**DIGBY,** 13th Baron (Ire.) *cr* 1620, and 6th Baron (GB) *cr* 1765; **Henry Noel Kenelm Digby;** b 6 Jan. 1954; s of 12th and 5th Baron Digby, KCVO and of Dione Marian Sherbrooke (*see* Dame D. M. Digby); S father, 2018; m 1st, 1980, Susan (marr. diss. 2001), er d of Peter Watts; one s one d; 2nd, 2002, Sophie, d of Robin Malim; one s two d (of whom one s one d are twins). *Educ:* Eton. ACA. Dir, Chase Fleming Private Wealth Mgt Ltd. *Heir:* s Hon. Edward St Vincent Kenelm Digby [*b* 5 Sept. 1985; *m* 2016, Jessica Frances Smith; twin *s*].

**DIGBY, Dame Dione (Marian),** DBE 1991; DL; Founder Chairman, 1963–2005, Artistic Director and Hon. Secretary, 1963–2012, Summer Music Society of Dorset; *b* 23 Feb. 1934; *d* of Rear-Adm. Robert St Vincent Sherbrooke, VC, CB, DSO, and of Rosemary Neville Sherbrooke (*née* Buckley), Oxton, Notts; *m* 1952, 12th and 5th Baron Digby, KCVO; two *s* one *d. Educ:* Talindert State Sch., Victoria, Australia; Southover Manor Sch., Lewes, Sussex. Chairman: Dorset Assoc. of Youth Clubs, 1966–73; Dorset Community Council, 1977–79; Standing Conf. of Rural Community Councils and Councils of Voluntary Service SW Region, 1977–79. Councillor (Ind.) W Dorset DC, 1976–86; Mem. Dorset Small Industries Cttee, CoSIRA, 1977 (Chm. 1982–85); Mem., Wessex Water Authority, 1983–89; National Rivers Authority: Mem., 1989–96; Chm., Wessex Regl Adv. Bd, 1989–93; Co-Chm., S Western Adv. Bd, 1993–95; Chm., Southern Regl Adv. Bd, 1995–96. Dir, SW Regl Bd, then Western Adv. Bd, Nat. Westminster Bank, 1986–92. Member: BBC/IBA Central Appeals Adv. Cttee, 1975–80; Ethical Trust Adv. Bd, Scottish Widows Investment Partnership (formerly Abbey Life Investment Services), 1996–2003; Cttee of Reference, Premier Asset Mgt (formerly Credit Suisse Fellowship Trust), 1997–2011. Governor: Dorset Coll. of Agriculture, 1978–83; Sherborne Sch., 1986–2000; Chm. Adv. Bd, Jt Univ. Centre at Yeovil Coll., Bournemouth and Exeter Univs; Mem. Council, Exeter Univ., 1981–96; Chancellor, Bournemouth Univ., 2006–09 (Pro-Chancellor, 2001–06). Mem. Bath Festival Soc. Council of Management, 1971–81 (Chm. of the Society, 1976–81); Chm. Bath Fest. Friends Trust, 1982–87; Foundation Trustee, RAM, 1985–2000; Trustee, Tallis Scholars Trust, 1984–2004. Member: SW Arts Management Cttee, 1981–86; Arts Council of GB, 1982–86 (Chm., Trng Cttee; Vice-Chm., Dance Panel; Mem., Music Panel); South Bank Bd, 1985–88 (Gov., 1988–90); Bd of Mgt, Bournemouth Orchs, 1989–2000 (Mem. Bd of Mgt, Western Orchestral Soc., 1989–91); Chairman: S and W Concerts Bd, 1989–2001; Friends of Dorset Opera Trust, 2000–; President: Dorset Opera, 1975–2012, now Emeritus; Dorset Youth Assoc., 1994–2004. Mem., Council of Management, The Joseph Weld and Trimar (formerly Dorset Respite) Hospice Trust, 1990–2007 (Pres., 1993–2007). DL Dorset, 1983. Hon. DArts Bournemouth, 1997. *Recreations:* music and the arts, ski-ing; interest in local government, politics, history, people. *Address:* The West Wing, Minterne House, Dorchester, Dorset DT2 7AX. *T:* (01300) 341425.

*See also* Baron Digby.

**DIGBY DAY, Richard;** freelance director, since 1984; Director, London Dramatic Academy, 2003–12; *b* Wales, 27 Dec. 1940; *né* Richard Day; *s* of Donald Day and Doris Mary Day (*née* George). *Educ:* Rhiwbina Jun. Sch., Cardiff; Solihull Sch., Warks; Royal Acad. of Dramatic Art (Leverhulme Schol.; first student of direction). Thames TV trainee dir, Nottingham Playhouse, 1963–64; Artistic Director: Bournemouth Th. Co., 1966–68; New Shakespeare Co. Open Air Th., Regent's Park, 1967–85; Director: Welsh Th. Co., Cardiff, 1969–71; York Th. Royal, 1971–76; Northcott Th., Exeter, 1977–80; Nottingham Playhouse, 1980–84; freelance dir, prodns at Guildford, Colchester, Perth, West End and work in Canada, Denmark, Ireland and SA; Dir, National Th. Inst., O'Neill Centre, Waterford, Conn, 1990–98; Associate Prof., Connecticut Coll., 1993–; Founder, London Acad. of Theatre, Rutgers Univ., 1998–2003; teacher and lectr at univs in USA. Member: Regl Panel, Arts Council GB, 1980–83; Nat. Council for Drama Trng, 1981–90. Chm. of Associates, 2008–10, Mem. Council, 2008–13, RADA; Mem., Clarence Derwent Award Cttee, 1985–2018; Vice Pres., Shaw Soc., 1991–; Mem. Bd, Drama League of NY, 1991–99. *Recreations:* art (collecting watercolours and drawings), opera, ballet, sightseeing. *Address:* 14 Monkton House, Monkton Park, Chippenham, Wilts SN15 3PE. *E:* r.digbyday@btinternet.com.

**DIGGLE, Prof. James,** LittD; FBA 1985; Professor of Greek and Latin, University of Cambridge, 1995–2011, now Emeritus; Fellow of Queens' College, 1966–2011, now Life Fellow; *b* 29 March 1944; *m* 1973, Sedwell Mary Chapman (*d* 2018); three *s. Educ:* Rochdale Grammar School; St John's College, Cambridge (Major Scholar; Classical Tripos Pt I, first cl., 1964, Pt II, first cl. with dist., 1965; Pitt Scholar, Browne Scholar, Hallam Prize, Members' Latin Essay Prize, 1963; Montagu Butler Prize, Browne Medals for Greek Elegy and Latin Epigram, 1964; Porson Prize, Chancellor's Classical Medal, Craven Student, Allen Scholar, 1965; BA 1965; MA 1969; PhD 1969; LittD 1985). Queens' College, Cambridge: Research Fellow, 1966–67; Official Fellow, 1967–2011; Sen. Fellow, 2007–11; Director of Studies in Classics, 1967–2011; Librarian, 1969–77; Praelector, 1971–73, 1978–2015; Cambridge University: Asst Lectr in Classics, 1970–75; Lectr, 1975–89; Reader in Greek and Latin, 1989–95; Chm., Faculty Bd of Classics, 1989–90; Orator, 1982–93. Jt Editor, Cambridge Classical Texts and Commentaries, 1977–. Corresponding Mem., Acad. of Athens, 2001. *Publications:* The Phaethon of Euripides, 1970; (jtly) Flavii Cresconii Corippi Iohannidos, Libri VIII, 1970; (ed jtly) The Classical Papers of A. E. Housman, 1972; (ed jtly) Dionysiaca: nine studies in Greek poetry, presented to Sir Denys Page, 1978; Studies on the Text of Euripides, 1981; Euripidis Fabulae (Oxford Classical Texts), vol. ii 1981, vol. i 1984, vol. iii 1994; (ed jtly) Studies in Latin Literature and its Tradition, in honour of C. O. Brink, 1989; The textual tradition of Euripides' Orestes, 1991; (ed jtly) F. R. D. Goodyear, Papers on Latin Literature, 1992; Euripidea: collected essays, 1994; Cambridge Orations 1982–1993: a selection, 1994; Tragicorum Graecorum Fragmenta Selecta, 1998; Theophrastus: Characters, 2004; (with R. Bittlestone and J. Underhill) Odysseus Unbound: the search for Homer's Ithaca, 2005; (Ed. in Chief) The Cambridge Greek Lexicon, 2019. *Recreations:* family life, Cambridge United FC. *Address:* Queens' College, Cambridge CB3 9ET. *E:* jd10000@cam.ac.uk.

**DIGGLE, Judith Margaret, (Mrs P. J. Diggle);** *see* Brown, Judith M.

**DIGGORY, Dr Colin;** Headmaster, Alleyn's School, 2002–10; Senior Advisor, RSAcademics Ltd, 2013–17; *b* 22 July 1954; *s* of late John Harold Diggory and Olga (*née* Midcalf); *m* 1976, Susan Janet Robinson; one *s* two *d. Educ:* Sir William Turner's Sch., Redcar; Univ. of Durham (BSc 1st cl. Hons Maths, PGCE); Open Univ. (MA 1999; EdD 2005 (Sir John Daniel Award, 2005)). CMath, FIMA 1994. Assistant Master: Manchester Grammar Sch., 1976–83; St Paul's Sch., Barnes, 1983–87; Head of Maths, Merchant Taylors' Sch., 1987–90; Second Master, 1990–91, Headmaster, 1991–2002, Latymer Upper Sch. Chief Examr, A Level Maths, Univ. of London, 1989–91. Sen. Educn Consultant, CfA Exec. Search and Selection, 2011–13. Chm., London Div., 1999, Jun. Schs Sub-Cttee, 1999–2001, HMC. Trustee, Dulwich Picture Gall., 2005–08; Vice Pres., Soc. of Schoolmasters and Schoolmistresses, 2011–18 (Trustee, 2004–08). Gov., Highgate Sch., 2003–08; Chairman, Board of Directors: Radnor House Gp of Schs, Twickenham, 2010–; Mount House Sch. Ltd, 2017–. FRSA 1994. *Recreations:* walking, theatre. *Address:* c/o Radnor House, Pope's Villa, Cross Deep, Twickenham, Middx TW1 4QG. *Club:* East India, Devonshire, Sports and Public Schools.

**DIGHT, Marc David,** CBE 2017; **His Honour Judge Dight;** a Senior Circuit Judge (Chancery), since 2007; Designated Civil Judge, County Court at Central London and Mayor's and City of London Court, since 2016 (Resident Judge, 2014–16); *b* 27 Feb. 1961; *s* of Harvey Dight and Gillian Dight (*née* Strauss); civil partnership 2009, Pierre Göran Folke Fredrik Andersson. *Educ:* Bancroft's Sch.; Univ. of Bristol (LLB Hons 1983). Called to the Bar, Inner Temple, 1984; admitted Lincoln's Inn *ad eundem*, 1986, Bencher, 2010; Recorder, 2002–07. Dep. Adjudicator, HM Land Registry, 2004–07; Lead Diversity and Community Relns Judge for England and Wales, 2010–. Trustee: Counsel and Care for the Elderly, 2003–11 (former Hon. Treas.; Chm., Fundraising Cttee); Independent Age, 2013–17. Hon. Mem. Bd, UK Law Students' Assoc., 2011–. Freeman: City of London, 2009; Drapers' Co., 2009. *Recreations:* Swedish horticulture, Thai cuisine. *Address:* Royal Courts of Justice, Strand, WC2A 2LL. *Club:* Athenæum.

**DILHORNE,** 2nd Viscount *cr* 1964, of Green's Norton; **John Mervyn Manningham-Buller;** Bt 1866; Baron 1962; Barrister-at-Law; *b* 28 Feb. 1932; *s* of 1st Viscount Dilhorne, PC, and Lady Mary Lilian Lindsay, 4th *d* of 27th Earl of Crawford, KT, PC; S father, 1980; *m* 1st, 1955, Gillian Evelyn (marr. diss. 1973), *d* of former George Stockwell; two *s* one *d*; 2nd, 1981, Prof. Susannah Jane Eykyn, MB BS, FRCS, FRCP, FRCPath. *Educ:* Eton; RMA Sandhurst. Called to the Bar, Inner Temple, 1979. Formerly Lieut, Coldstream Guards. Managing Director, Stewart Smith (LP&M) Ltd, 1970–74. Mem., Wilts County Council, 1967–70. Chm., VAT Tribunal, 1988–95; Member, Joint Parliamentary Committee: on Statutory Instruments, 1981–88; on Consolidation Bills, 1994–99; Mem., EC Select Cttee (Law and Instns), 1989–92. FTII (Mem. Council, 1967–74). *Heir: s* Hon. James Edward Manningham-Buller, formerly Captain Welsh Guards [*b* 20 Aug. 1956; *m* 1985, Nicola Marion, *e d* of Sven Mackie; one *s* one *d. Educ:* Harrow; Sandhurst]. *Clubs:* Pratt's, Buck's, Beefsteak; Swinley Forest Golf.

*See also* Baroness Manningham-Buller.

**DILKE;** *see* Fetherston-Dilke.

**DILKE, Rev. Sir Charles (John Wentworth),** 6th Bt *cr* 1862, of Sloane Street; FRAS; priest of the London Oratory, since 1966; *b* 21 Feb. 1937; *er s* of Sir John Dilke, 5th Bt and Sheila (*née* Seeds, later Knapp); S father, 1998. *Educ:* Ashdown House, Sussex; Winchester Coll.; King's Coll., Cambridge (BA). Joined the London Oratory, 1961; ordained priest, 1966; elected Provost (Superior), 1981–87. FRAS 2004. *Recreations:* painting, study of architecture, astronomy. *Heir: b* Dr Timothy Fisher Wentworth Dilke [*b* 1 Aug. 1938; *m* 1965, Carolina Sophia Dilke; one *s* one *d*]. *Address:* The Oratory, SW7 2RP. *T:* (020) 7808 0900. *Club:* Athenæum.

**DILKE, Kairbaan Michael H.;** *see* Hodivala-Dilke.

**DILKS, Prof. David Neville,** FRHistS; FRSL; Vice-Chancellor, University of Hull, 1991–99; *b* Coventry, 17 March 1938; *s* of Neville Ernest Dilks and Phyllis Dilks; *m* 1963, Jill Medlicott; one *s. Educ:* Royal Grammar Sch., Worcester; Hertford Coll., Oxford (BA Modern Hist., Class II, 1959); St Antony's Coll., Oxford (Curzon Prizeman, 1960). Research Assistant to: Rt Hon. Sir Anthony Eden (later Earl of Avon), 1960–62; Marshal of the RAF Lord Tedder, 1963–65; Rt Hon. Harold Macmillan, 1964–67; Asst Lectr, then Lectr, in International History, LSE, 1962–70; University of Leeds: Prof. of Internat. History, 1970–91; Chm., Sch. of History, 1974–79; Dean, Faculty of Arts, 1975–77. Vis. Fellow, All Souls Coll., Oxford, 1973. Consultant, Sec.-Gen. of the Commonwealth, 1967–75; Chm., Commonwealth Youth Exchange Council, 1968–73. Member: Adv. Council on Public Records, 1977–85; Central Council, 1982–85, Library Cttee, 1982–91, Royal Commonwealth Soc.; British Nat. Cttee for History of Second World War, 1983–2006 (Pres., Internat. Cttee, 1992–2000); UFC, 1989–91; Adv. Council, Politeia, 1995–. Trustee: Edward Boyle Meml Trust, 1982–96 (Hon. Sec., 1981–82); Imperial War Museum, 1983–90; Lennox-Boyd Meml Trust, 1984–91; Nathaniel Trust, 1986–90. Pres., Worcester Old Elizabethans' Assoc., 1986–87. FRSL 1986; FCGI 1999. Liveryman, Goldsmiths' Co., 1984– (Freeman, 1979). Wrote and presented BBC TV series, The Loneliest Job, 1977; interviewer in BBC TV series, The Twentieth Century Remembered, 1982; historical consultant, TV films, The Gathering Storm, 2002, Winston Churchill at War, 2009. Hon. Dr of History, Russian Acad. of Scis, 1996. Médaille de Vermeil, Acad. Française, 1994. Emery Reves Award, Churchill Center, USA, 2006. *Publications:* Curzon in India, Vol. I, 1969, Vol. II, 1970; (ed) The Diaries of Sir Alexander Cadogan, 1971; (contrib.) The Conservatives (ed Lord Butler of Saffron Walden), 1977; (ed and contrib.) Retreat from Power, vol. 1, 1906–1939, Vol. 2, After 1939, 1981; (ed and contrib.) Britain and Canada (Commonwealth Foundn Paper), 1980; (ed and contrib.) The Missing Dimension: governments and intelligence communities in the twentieth century, 1984; Neville Chamberlain, Vol. I: Pioneering and Reform 1869–1929, 1984; (ed jtly and contrib.) Grossbritannien und der deutsche Widerstand, 1994; (ed jtly) Barbarossa: the axis and the allies, 1994; The Great Dominion: Winston Churchill in Canada 1900–1954, 2005; Churchill and Company, 2012; reviews and articles in English Historical Rev., Survey, History, Scandinavian Jl of History, etc. *Recreations:* ornithology, painting, railways, Bentley cars. *Address:* Wits End, Long Causeway, Leeds LS16 8EX. *T:* (0113) 267 3466. *Club:* Brooks's.

**DILKS, John Morris Whitworth;** Managing Director, Peribase Ltd, 1999–2017; Manager, Cranesbill Nursery, 2012–16; *b* 10 Feb. 1950; *s* of John Amos Whitworth Dilks and Margaret (*née* Thraves); *m*; one *s* one *d. Educ:* Oakham Sch.; Sheffield Univ. (BA Hons). ACMA. Audit Manager, British Gas E Midlands, 1985–86; Asst Dir of Finance, British Gas, 1985–86; Regl Dir of Finance, British Gas NE, 1986–91; Regl Chm., British Gas Eastern, 1991–93; Dir, Transco, 1994–98; Chm., Britannia Movers International plc, 2004–12. Trustee, Hardy Plant Soc., 2013–15 (Chm., 2014–15). *Recreations:* sailing, walking, gardening. *Address:* Little Claydon, Westmancote, Tewkesbury, Glos GL20 7ES.

**DILLAMORE, Ian Leslie,** PhD, DSc; FREng; FIMMM; Chairman and Chief Executive, Doncasters plc, 1996–2000; *b* 22 Nov. 1938; *s* of Arthur Leslie Dillamore and Louise Mary Dillamore; *m* 1962, Maureen Birch; two *s. Educ:* Birmingham Univ. (BSc, MSc, PhD, DSc). ICI Research Fellow, Birmingham Univ., 1962–63, Lectr in Physical Metallurgy, 1963–69; Head of Phys. Metallurgy, BISRA, 1969–72; Head of Metals Technology Unit, British Steel Corp., 1972–76; Head of Metallurgy Dept, Aston Univ., 1976–81, Dean of Engineering, 1980–81; Director of Research and Development, INCO Europe, 1981–82; Dir of Technology, 1982–87, Gp Man. Dir, 1987–96, INCO Engineered Products Ltd. Hon. Professor of Metallurgy, Birmingham Univ., 1981–. Mem. Council: Metals Soc., 1980–84; Instn of Metallurgists, 1981–84; Vice-Pres., Inst. of Metals, 1985–88; Mem. SRC Metallurgy Cttee, 1972–75, Materials Cttee, 1977–82; Chm., Processing Sub-Cttee, SRC, later SERC, 1979–82; Mem., DTI Non Ferrous Metals Exec. Cttee, 1982–85; Pres. Birmingham Metallurgical Assoc., 1980–81. FREng (FEng 1985). Hon. DEng Birmingham, 1999. Sir Robert Hadfield Medal and Prize, Metals Soc., 1976; Platinum Medal, Inst. of Materials, 1999; Bunge Award, Internat. Conf. on Textures of Materials, 2008. *Publications:* An Industrial Evolution, 2014; numerous contribs to metallurgical and engrg jls. *Recreation:* industrial archaeology.

**DILLEY, Sir Philip (Graham),** Kt 2014; FICE; Chairman, Woods Bagot, since 2015 (non-executive Director, since 2015); *b* Portsmouth, 16 Feb. 1955; *s* of William Henry and Dorothy May Dilley; *m* 2003, June Donaldson; three *s. Educ:* Imperial Coll. of Sci., Technol. and Medicine, Univ. of London (BSc (Eng)). MIStructE 1982; FICE 2008. Joined Arup as grad. engr, 1976; Dir, Ove Arup Partners, 1993; Dir, Building Engrg Bd, 1998–2004; Hd, EMEA Reg., Arup, 2004–09; Exec. Chm., Arup Gp, 2009–14. Chm.,

Envmt Agency, 2014–16. Non-exec. Dir, Grosvenor Gp Ltd, 2014–. Chm., London First, 2012–15. Mem. Council, Imperial Coll. London, 2011– (Chm., 2014–19). Trustee, Poppy Factory, 2013–15. ACGI 1976. Hon. FRIBA 2013. Hon. Fellow, UCL, 2015. *Recreations:* tennis, golf, opera, wine. *Address:* (office) 13 Fitzroy Street, W1T 4BQ. *T:* (020) 7755 2029. *E:* sirphilip.dilley@gmail.com.

**DILLON,** family name of **Viscount Dillon.**

**DILLON,** 22nd Viscount *cr* 1622, of Castello Gallen, Co. Mayo, Ireland; **Henry Benedict Charles Dillon;** Count in France, 1711; *b* 6 Jan. 1973; *s* of 21st Viscount Dillon and of Mary Jane, *d* of late John Young, Castle Hill House, Birtle, Lancs; *S* father, 1982; *m* 2007, Kristin Marsh; one *s. Heir: s* Francis Charlie Robert Dillon, *b* 2013.

**DILLON, Sir Andrew (Patrick),** Kt 2010; CBE 2003; Chief Executive, National Institute for Health and Care Excellence (formerly for Clinical Excellence, then for Health and Clinical Excellence), since 1999; *b* 9 May 1954; *m* two *d. Educ:* Univ. of Manchester (BSc Hons). Asst Sector Adminr, Bolton Royal Infirmary, 1978–81; Unit Adminr, Queen Elizabeth Hosp. for Children, London, 1981–83; Dep., then Actg Unit Adminr, Royal London Hosp., 1983–86; Unit Gen. Manager, Royal Free Hosp., 1986–91; Chief Exec., St George's Gp, then St George's Healthcare NHS Trust, 1991–99. Trustee, Centre for Mental Health, 2012–. Vis. Prof., Inst. for Global Health Innovation, Imperial Coll. London, 2017–. FMedSci 2015. *Recreation:* family. *Address:* National Institute for Health and Care Excellence, 10 Spring Gardens, SW1A 2BU. *T:* (020) 7045 2048.

**DILLON, Patrick George Hubert;** writer and architect; *b* London, 1 Nov. 1962; *s* of Rt Hon. Sir (George) Brian (Hugh) Dillon and Alison Dillon; *m* 1990, Nicola Thorold (*d* 2016); one *s* one *d. Educ:* University Coll. London (BSc; DipArch). RIBA 1989. Dir, Patrick Dillon Architects, 1989–2006; Architect, Haworth Tompkins, 2006–15. Director: Allies and Morrison, 2015–18; Paddy Dillon Architect, 2018–. Major projects include: Chelsea Th., 1999; Benjamin Franklin House, 2003; Regeneration of Snape Maltings, 2008; Dovecot Studio, 2008; The Shed Temporary Th., 2013; NT Future regeneration of Nat. Th., 2015. Trustee, Theatres Trust, 2015–. *Publications:* The Much Lamented Death of Madam Geneva, 2002; The Last Revolution, 2005; The Story of Britain, 2010; The Story of Buildings, 2014; Concrete Reality, 2015; A Moment of Grace, 2018; *novels:* Truth, 1996; Lies, 1997; Ithaca, 2016. *Recreations:* music, theatre.

**DILLON, His Honour Thomas Michael;** QC 1973; a Circuit Judge, 1985–2000; *b* 29 Nov. 1927; *yr s* of Thomas Bernard Joseph Dillon, Birmingham, and Ada Gladys Dillon (*née* Noyes); *m* 1956, Wendy Elizabeth Marshall Hurrell; two *s* one *d. Educ:* King Edward's Sch., Aston, Birmingham; Birmingham Univ. (LLB); Lincoln Coll., Oxford (BCL). Called to Bar, Middle Temple, 1952, Master of the Bench 1981. 2nd Lieut, RASC, 1953–54. In practice as barrister, 1954–85; a Recorder, 1972–85; Part-time Chm. of Industrial Tribunals, 1968–74. *Recreations:* reading, listening to music.

**DILLWYN-VENABLES-LLEWELYN, Sir John Michael;** *see* Venables-Llewelyn.

**DILNOT, Sir Andrew (William),** Kt 2013; CBE 2000; Warden, Nuffield College, Oxford, since 2012; *b* 19 June 1960; *s* of Anthony William John Dilnot and Patricia Josephine Dilnot; *m* 1984, Catherine Elizabeth Morrish; two *d. Educ:* Olchfa Comprehensive Sch.; St John's Coll., Oxford (BA Hons PPE; Hon. Fellow, 2002). Institute for Fiscal Studies: Res. Asst, 1981–83; Res. Officer, 1983–84; Sen. Res. Officer, 1984–86; Prog. Dir, 1986–90; Dep. Dir, 1990–91; Dir, 1991–2002; Principal, St Hugh's Coll., Oxford, 2002–12; Pro-Vice-Chancellor, Univ. of Oxford, 2005–12. Lectr (part-time) in Econs, Exeter Coll., Oxford, 1988–89. Vis. Fellow, ANU, 1986; Downing Meml Fellow, Melbourne Univ., 1989. Presenter, Radio 4: Analysis, 1994–2001; More or Less, 2001–07; A History of Britain in Numbers, 2013, 2015. Member: Social Security Adv. Cttee, 1992–2002; Retirement Income Inquiry, 1994–95; Foresight Panel on Aging Population, 1999–2001; Evidence Based Policy Panel, HM Treasury, 2001–03; Balance of Funding Inquiry, ODPM, 2002–04; Bd, NCC, 2003–08; OST Rev. of Use of Science in ODPM, 2005–06; Chairman: Commn on Funding of Care and Support, 2010–11 (report, Fairer Care Funding, 2011); UK Statistics Authy, 2012–17; Oversight Bd, Health and Social Care Sustainability Res. Centre, Health Foundn, 2019–; Geospatial Commn, 2019–. Member: Council, REconS, 1993–98; Chm., Statistics Users Forum, Royal Statistical Soc., 2009–12. Mem. Council, Westfield Coll., then QMW, Univ. of London, 1987–95. Mem. Bd, World Vision UK, 1991–97. Trustee: Relate, Oxon, 1999–2004; Our Right to Read, 2004–06; Nuffield Foundn, 2009–12; Chair, Nuffield Dominions Trust, 2015–. Patron: Oxford Youth Works, 2007–17; Oxford Youth Choirs, 2015–. FCGI 2014. Hon. FIA 2001; Hon. FBA 2018. Hon. Fellow: Queen Mary, Univ. of London, 2004; Swansea Inst. of HE, 2004; St Hugh's Coll., Oxford, 2012. Hon. DSc City, 2002; DUniv Open, 2015. *Publications:* The Reform of Social Security, 1984; The Economics of Social Security, 1989; Pensions Policy in the UK: an economic analysis, 1994; The Tiger That Isn't: seeing through a world of numbers, 2007; contrib. articles on taxation, public spending and economics of public policy. *Address:* Nuffield College, Oxford OX1 1NF.

**DILWORTH, Prof. Jonathan Robin,** DPhil, DSc; FRSC; Professor of Chemistry, University of Oxford, 1998–2009, now Emeritus; Fellow of St Anne's College, Oxford, 1997–2009; *b* 20 Aug. 1944; *s* of Robert Arnold Dilworth and Jean Marion Dilworth; *m* 1971, Nicola Jane Still; two *d. Educ:* Jesus Coll., Oxford (BA 1967, MA 1972); Univ. of Sussex (DPhil 1970; DSc 1983). FRSC 1984. AFRC Unit of Nitrogen Fixation, 1967–85; Prof. of Chemistry, Univ. of Essex, 1985–97. *Publications:* some 300 papers and review articles in internat. chemistry jls. *Recreations:* tennis, badminton, golf. *Address:* The Croft, Newland Close, Eynsham, Oxon OX29 4LE. *T:* (01865) 884102.

**di MAMBRO, Louise;** Registrar of the Supreme Court of the United Kingdom, since 2009, and of the Privy Council, since 2011; *b* Trowbridge, Wilts, 14 Sept. 1953; *d* of Rolland Gaer and Joan Gaer; *m* 1978, David di Mambro; one *s. Educ:* Trowbridge Girls High Sch.; King's Coll. London (LLB Hons). Called to the Bar, Middle Temple, 1976; Treasury Solicitor's Dept, 1977–80; Lord Chancellor's Dept, 1980–98; a Dep. Master, Court of Appeal, 1998–2008; Dep. Hd, Judicial Office, H of L, 2008–09. *Publications:* (Gen. Ed.) The Civil Court Practice, 1999–; (Gen. Ed.) Butterworths Civil Court Precedents, 1999–; (contrib. ed.) Atkin's Court Forms, 2004–; (consulting and contrib. ed.) The Caribbean Civil Court Practice, 2008–; (contrib. ed.) Butterworths Costs Service, 2009–. *Recreations:* opera, shopping, avoiding gardening. *Address:* Judicial Committee of the Privy Council, Parliament Square, SW1P 3PD. *T:* (020) 7960 1985, *Fax:* (020) 7960 1901. *E:* louise.dimambro@supremecourt.uk.

**DIMAS, Stavros;** a Vice President, New Democracy Party, Greece, 2010 (Secretary General, 1995–2000); *b* 30 April 1941. *Educ:* Univ. of Athens; NY Univ. (LLM). Sullivan & Cromwell, law firm, NY, 1969–70; lawyer, Internat. Finance Corp., World Bank, 1970–75; Dep. Gov., Hellenic Industrial Develt Bank, 1975–77. MP (New Democracy), Greece, 1977–2004; Dep. Minister of Econ. Co-ordination, 1977–80; Minister: of Trade, 1980–81; of Agriculture, 1989–90; of Industry, Energy and Technol., 1990–91; of Foreign Affairs, 2011–12. Mem., Eur. Commn, 2004–10.

**DIMBLEBY, David;** broadcaster; Chairman, Dimbleby & Sons Ltd, 1986–2001 (Managing Director, 1966–86); President, Dimbleby Cancer Care (formerly Richard Dimbleby Cancer Fund), since 2012 (Trustee and Chairman, 1966–2012); *b* 28 Oct. 1938; *e s* of (Frederick) Richard and Dilys Dimbleby; *m* 1st, 1967, Josceline Rose Gaskell (*see* J. R. Dimbleby) (marr. diss. 2000); one *s* two *d*; 2nd, 2000, Belinda Giles; one *s. Educ:* Glengorse Sch.; Charterhouse; Christ Church, Oxford (MA); Univs of Paris and Perugia. News Reporter, BBC Bristol, 1960–61; Presenter and Interviewer on network programmes on: religion (Quest), science for children (What's New?), politics (In My Opinion), Top of the Form, etc, 1961–63; Reporter, BBC2 (Enquiry), and Dir films, incl.: Ku-Klux-Klan, The Forgotten Million, Cyprus: Thin Blue Line, 1964–65; Special Correspondent CBS News, New York; documentary film (Texas-England) and film reports for '60 minutes', 1966–68; Reporter, BBC1 (Panorama), 1967–69; Presenter, BBC1 (24 Hours), 1969–72; Yesterday's Men, 1971; Chm., The Dimbleby Talk-In, 1971–74; films for Reporter at Large, 1973; Presenter: BBC 1 (Panorama), 1974–77, 1980–82, 1989–94; (People and Power), 1982–83; (This Week, Next Week), 1984–86; Chm., BBC Question Time, 1994–2018; Election Campaign Report, 1974; BBC Election and Results programmes, 1979, 1983, 1987, 1992, 1997, 2001, 2005, 2010, 2015, 2017; moderator for BBC Leaders' Debate, 2010 (Diamond Jubilee Broadcast Journalist Award, Political Studies Assoc.); for BBC Election Debate, 2015; Presenter: BBC 1 (US Presidential Elections), 1984, 1988, 1992, 1996, 2000, 2004, 2008, 2012; The People's Coronation, 2013; BBC Scotland Decides, The Dimbleby Interviews, 2014; BBC EU Referendum: the Great Debate, 2016; BBC EU Referendum Results, 2016; Chm., BBC The EU: In or Out?, 2016; Presenter, BBC World War One Remembered: The Battle of Jutland, 2016; Presenter, Panorama: Putin's Russia with David Dimbleby, BBC1, 2018; film series: The White Tribe of Africa, 1979 (RTS Supreme Documentary Award); An Ocean Apart, 1988; The Struggle for South Africa, 1990 (Emmy Award, 1991; Golden Nymph Award, 1991); David Dimbleby's India, 1997; Mandela: The Living Legend, 2003; A Picture of Britain, 2005 (TV Arts/Documentary Prog. Award, TRIC, 2006); How We Built Britain, 2007; Seven Ages of Britain, 2010; Britain and the Sea, 2013; live commentary on many public occasions including: State Opening of Parliament, Trooping the Colour, Remembrance Service at the Cenotaph; Lord Olivier Meml Service, 1989 (RTS Outside Broadcasts Award); funerals of Diana, Princess of Wales, 1997 (RTS Live Event Award) and of Her Majesty the Queen Mother, 2002; funeral of Baroness Thatcher, Coronation Anniv. Service, Westminster Abbey, funeral and meml progs in SA for Nelson Mandela, 2013; meml service for Nelson Mandela, Westminster Abbey, 2014. Chm., Bd of Trustees, Towner Art Gall., 2014–. Richard Dimbleby Award, BAFTA, 1998; TRIC Special Award, 2006; Media Soc. Award, 2006; Lifetime Achievement Award, RTS, 2011; Special Recognition Award, Nat. TV Awards, 2019. *Publications:* An Ocean Apart (with David Reynolds), 1988; A Picture of Britain, 2005; How We Built Britain, 2007; Seven Ages of Britain, 2010. *Address:* c/o United Agents, 12–26 Lexington Street, W1F 0LE.
*See also* J. Dimbleby.

**DIMBLEBY, Jonathan;** freelance broadcaster, journalist, historian and author; *b* 31 July 1944; *s* of Richard and Dilys Dimbleby; *m* 1st, 1968, Bel Mooney, *qv* (marr. diss. 2006); one *s* one *d*; 2nd, 2007, Jessica Ray; two *d. Educ:* University Coll. London (BA Hons Philosophy). TV and Radio Reporter, BBC Bristol, 1969–70; BBC Radio, World at One, 1970–71; for Thames TV: This Week, 1972–78, 1986–88; TV Eye, 1979; Jonathan Dimbleby in South America, 1979; documentary series, Witness (Editor), 1986–88; for Yorkshire TV: series, Jonathan Dimbleby in Evidence: The Police, 1980; The Bomb, 1980; The Eagle and the Bear, 1981; The Cold War Game, 1982; The American Dream, 1984; Four Years On—The Bomb, 1984; First Tuesday (Associate Editor/Presenter), 1982–86; for TV-am: Jonathan Dimbleby on Sunday (Presenter/Editor), 1985–86; for BBC TV: On the Record, 1988–93; Election Call, 1992; documentary series, The Last Governor (presenter/producer), 1997; series, Russia: A Journey with Jonathan Dimbleby (writer/presenter), 2008; An African Journey (writer/presenter), 2010; A South American Journey (writer/presenter), 2011; The Road to El Alamein—Churchill's Desert Campaign (writer/presenter), 2012; The BBC at War (writer/presenter), 2015; for Central TV: Charles: the private man, the public role (documentary), 1994; for LWT: Jonathan Dimbleby, 1995–2005; for ITV: anchor, Gen. Election coverage, 1997, 2001, 2005; An Ethiopian Journey (writer/producer/dir), 1998; A Kosovo Journey (writer/presenter), 2000; Heseltine—A Life in the Political Jungle (writer/presenter), 2000; for Teachers TV: The Big Debate (series), 2006–08; Presenter, BBC Radio 4: Any Questions?, 1987–2019; Any Answers, 1989–2012; The Candidate, 1998. Pres., Soil Assoc., 1997–2008; Pres., CPRE, 1992–97; President: VSO, 1999–2012; RSPB, 2001–03; Bath Fests Trust, 2003–06 (Chm., 1996–2003); Chairman: Susan Chilcott Scholarship, 2007–09; Index on Censorship, 2008–13; Trustee: Dimbleby Cancer Care (formerly Richard Dimbleby Cancer Fund), 1966– (Chair, 2013–); Forum for the Future, 1995–2005. SFTA Richard Dimbleby Award, for most outstanding contribution to factual TV, 1974. *Publications:* Richard Dimbleby, 1975; The Palestinians, 1979; The Prince of Wales: a biography, 1994; The Last Governor, 1997; Russia: a journey to the heart of a land and its people, 2008; Destiny in the Desert: the road to El Alamein - the battle that turned the tide, 2012; The Battle of the Atlantic: how the Allies won the war, 2015. *Recreations:* music, sailing, tennis. *Address:* c/o David Higham Associates Ltd, 7th Floor, Waverley House, 7–12 Noel Street, W1F 8GQ.

**DIMBLEBY, Josceline Rose;** writer; *b* 1 Feb. 1943; *d* of late Thomas Josceline Gaskell and Barbara Montagu-Pollock; *m* 1967, David Dimbleby, *qv* (marr. diss. 2000); one *s* two *d. Educ:* Cranborne Chase Sch., Dorset; Guildhall School of Music. Contributor, Daily Mail, 1976–78; cookery writer for Sainsbury's, 1978–98; Cookery Editor, Sunday Telegraph, 1982–97. Contributor: Food Prog., BBC Radio; MasterChef, BBC TV. André Simon Award, 1979; Glenfiddich Prize for Cookery Writer of Year, 1993. Talks at literary festivals and other events; travel writing. *Publications:* A Taste of Dreams, 1976, 3rd edn 1984; Party Pieces, 1977; Josceline Dimbleby's Book of Puddings, Desserts and Savouries, 1979, 2nd edn 1983; Favourite Food, 1983, 2nd edn 1984; Josceline Dimbleby's Complete Cookbook, 1997; Josceline Dimbleby's Cooking Course, 1999; Josceline Dimbleby's Almost Vegetarian Cookbook, 1999; A Profound Secret: May Gaskell, her daughter Amy, and Edward Burne-Jones, 2004, US edn as May and Amy, 2005; Orchards in the Oasis: travels, food and memories, 2010 (Kate Whiteman Award, Guild of Food Writers, 2011); (for Sainsbury's): Cooking for Christmas, 1978; Family Meat and Fish Cookery, 1979; Cooking with Herbs and Spices, 1979; Curries and Oriental Cookery, 1980; Salads for all Seasons, 1981; Marvellous Meals with Mince, 1982, rev. edn 2012; Festive Food, 1982; Sweet Dreams, 1983; First Impressions, 1984; The Josceline Dimbleby Collection, 1984; Main Attractions, 1985; A Traveller's Tastes, 1986; The Josceline Dimbleby Christmas Book, 1987; The Josceline Dimbleby Book of Entertaining, 1988; The Essential Josceline Dimbleby, 1989; The Cook's Companion, 1991; The Almost Vegetarian Cookbook, 1994; The Christmas Book, 1994; contribs to magazines and newspapers. *Recreations:* singing, travel, photography, drawing. *Address:* c/o Lucas Alexander Whitley, 14 Vernon Street, W14 0RJ. *W:* www.joscelinedimbleby.com.

**DIMERY, Bridget Maeve;** *see* Phillipson, B. M.

**DIMITROV, Konstantin Stefanov**; Ambassador of Bulgaria to the Court of St James's, 2012–19; *b* Sofia, Bulgaria, 28 Jan. 1957; *m* Nadya; one *d*. *Educ*: Univ. of Sofia (Masters degree in English and German Langs and Lit. 1984). Lectr in English Lang. and Anglo-American Studies, Technical Univ., Sofia, 1988–92; expert, Western Europe and N America Dept, Min. of Foreign Affairs, Bulgaria, 1992–94; Third Sec., Washington, 1994–95; expert, Information Dept, Min. of Foreign Affairs, 1995–97; Hd, Policy Planning and Coordination Dept, 1997, NATO, WEU and Security Issues Dept, 1997–98, Min. of Foreign Affairs; Dep. Minister of Foreign Affairs, 1998–2000; Hd, Mission to NATO and WEU and Ambassador to Belgium and Luxembourg, 2000–02; Dir, Inst. of Euro-Atlantic Security, Sofia, 2002–09. MP (Democrats for Strong Bulgaria), 2005–09; MEP, 2007; Dep. Foreign Minister for European Affairs, 2009–12. *Club*: Travellers.

**DIMOND, Paul Stephen**, CMG 2005; HM Diplomatic Service, retired; Managing Trustee, Daiwa Anglo-Japanese Foundation, since 2014; *b* 30 Dec. 1944; *yr s* of late Cyril James Dimond and Dorothy Mabel Louisa Hobbs (*née* Knight); *m* 1965, Carolyn Susan Davis-Mees, *er d* of late Dennis Charles Mees and of Eileen Lilian (*née* Barratt); two *s*. *Educ*: St Olave's and St Saviour's Grammar Sch. for Boys, Bermondsey. British Bakeries Ltd, 1962–63; FO, 1963–65; Diplomatic Service Admin, 1965–66; Japanese lang. student, Tokyo, 1966–68; Vice-Consul (Commercial), 1968–70, Consul (Commercial), 1970–72, Osaka; Second Sec. (Commercial), Tokyo, 1972–73; seconded to Dept of Trade as assistant to Special Advr on Japanese Mkt, BOTB, 1973–75; FCO, 1975–76; First Secretary: (Economic), Stockholm, 1977–80; FCO, 1980–81; (Commercial), Tokyo, 1981–86; FCO, 1986–88; seconded to Smiths Industries plc as Strategic Marketing Advr, Smiths Industries Med. Systems, 1988–89; Commercial Counsellor, Tokyo, 1989–93; Dep. Hd of Mission, The Hague, 1994–97; Consul-Gen., Los Angeles, 1997–2001; Ambassador to the Philippines, 2002–04; Outplacement Advr, FCO, 2004–06. Director: Intralink Ltd, 2005–15; Baillie Gifford Japan Trust plc, 2006–18; Westminster Gardens Ltd, 2006–18 (Chm., 2007–10); Dep. Chm., 2007–17, Sen. Advr, 2017–18, DAKS Simpson Gp plc and DAKS Ltd; Man. Dir, H. O. Kammann GmbH, 2009–13; Chm., Bond Street Mgt Gp, 2014–18. Fund Develt Officer, British Neurological Res. Trust, 2005–11; Sen. Advr, Think London, 2005–10. Sec., First Anglo-Mongolian Round Table, Ulaan Baatar, 1987; Chm., FriendsPhilippines, 2006–16. Member: BAFTA, 2002–; London Reg. Cttee, RSA, 2005–11; Central Council, ROSL, 2006–12. Mem. Council, Japan Soc., 2005–11 (Vice Chm., 2008–11); Dir, Anglo-Netherlands Soc., 2010–. Governor: British Sch. in the Netherlands, 1994–97; British Film Office, LA, 1998–2000. Chm., Torch Trophy Trust, 2013–19. FRSA 1980; FCIL (FIL 1988); FCIM 1989–2015. *Recreations*: the arts, vintage Batsfords, city walking. *Clubs*: Travellers, Royal Over-Seas League.

**di MONTEZEMOLO, Luca Cordero**; Chairman, Alitalia, since 2015; *b* Bologna, 1947. *Educ*: Univ. of Rome (Law degree); Columbia Univ., NY (Internat. Commercial Law). Worked with Chiomenti law firm, Rome; with Bergreen & Bergreen, NY, until 1973; Asst to Enzo Ferrari and Team Manager, Maranello racing team, 1973–77 (won 2 Formula 1 world drivers' championships, 1975 and 1977); Sen. Vice Pres., Ext. Relns, Fiat Gp, 1977–81; Chief Executive Officer: ITEDI SpA (holding co. for Fiat Gp publishing activities), 1981–83; Cinzano Internat. SpA, 1984–86; Dir, Organizing Cttee, 1990 Italian World Cup Football Championship, 1986–90; CEO, RCS Video and Mem. Bd of Dirs, TFI, 1990–91; CEO, 1991–2006, Chm., 1991–2014, Ferrari SpA; Chm. and CEO, Maserati SpA, 1997–2005; Chairman: Confindustria, 2004–08; Fiat SpA, 2004–10. Member Board: PPR; Tod's; Merloni Elettrodomestici; Le Monde. Chm., Telethon, 2009–. Former President: Industrialists of Modena; FIEG (Italian Newspaper Publishers Assoc.); President: Bologna Internat. Trade Fair; Libera Università Internazionale degli Studi Sociali, 2004–10; Vice Pres., UNICE. Hon. Dr Mech. Engrg Modena. Cavaliere del Lavoro (Italy); Legion d'Honneur (France), 2005. *Address*: Alitalia, Piazza Almerico da Schio 3, 00054 Fiumicino, Italy.

**DINEEN**; *see* Kerr-Dineen.

**DINENAGE, Caroline**; MP (C) Gosport, since 2010; Minister of State, Department of Health and Social Care, since 2018; *b* Portsmouth, 28 Oct. 1971; *d* of Fred Dinenage, MBE and Beverley Dinenage; *m* 2014, (John) Mark Lancaster (*see* Rt Hon. J. M. Lancaster); two *s* by a previous marriage. *Educ*: Univ. of Wales, Swansea (BA Hons English and Politics). Dir, Dinenage Ltd, 1996–. Mem. (C) Winchester CC, 1998–2003. Contested (C) Portsmouth S, 2005. PPS to Rt Hon. Nicola Morgan, 2014–15; Parly Under-Sec. of State, MoJ, 2015–16, DfE, 2015–17, DWP, 2017–18. Member: Sci. and Technol. Select Cttee, 2012–13; BIS Select Cttee, 2012–15; Vice Chairman: (RN), All-Party Parly Gp for Armed Forces, 2010–14; Associate Parly Gp for Manufg, 2012–; Chairman: All-Party Parly Gp on Local Growth, 2012–14; All-Party Parly Gp on Maths and Numeracy, 2014–. *Address*: House of Commons, SW1A 0AA. *T*: (020) 7219 7078. *E*: caroline.dinenage.mp@parliament.uk.

**DINES, Rev. Griff**; *see* Dines, Rev. P. J. G.

**DINES, Peter Munn**, CBE 1991; Secretary, School Examinations and Assessment Council, 1988–91; *b* 29 Aug. 1929; *e s* of Victor Edward Dines and Muriel Eleanor Dines (*née* Turner); *m* 1952, Kathleen Elisabeth Jones (*d* 2008); two *s* one *d*. *Educ*: Palmer's Sch., Grays, Essex; Imperial Coll. London (ARCS; BSc 1st cl. 1949); Inst. of Education, London (PGCE 1950); Bristol Univ. (MEd 1968). RAF, 1950–53. Teaching maths, 1953–69; Headmaster, Cramlington High Sch., 1969–76; Jt Sec., Schools Council, 1976–78; Headmaster, Sir John Leman High Sch., Beccles, 1978–80; Examinations Officer, Schools Council, 1980–83; Dep. Chief Exec., 1983–87, Chief Exec., 1988, Secondary Examinations Council. Educn Consultant, British Council, Swaziland, 1993 and Pakistan, 1994. Mem., Schools Broadcasting Council, later Educn Broadcasting Council, 1982–91; occasional broadcaster on radio and TV. *Recreations*: sailing, esp. on W coast of Scotland; walking. *Address*: Spring Cottage, Langton Road, Norton, Malton, N Yorks YO17 9PY.

*See also* Rev. P. J. G. Dines.

**DINES, Rev. (Philip Joseph) Griff**, PhD; Head, Office of the Bishop of Lincoln, since 2019; *b* 22 June 1959; *s* of Peter Munn Dines, *qv* and Kathleen Elisabeth Dines; *m* 1st, 1987, Dr Margaret Owen (marr. diss. 2006); two *d*; 2nd, 2009, Rev. Canon Sally-Anne McDougall. *Educ*: Royal Grammar Sch., Newcastle upon Tyne; University Coll. London (BScEng 1980); Clare Coll., Cambridge (PhD 1984); Westcott House, Cambridge; Univ. of Manchester (MA Theol 1993); City of Bath Coll. (Cert. English Lang. Teaching to Adults 2011); Bishop Grosseteste Univ. (PGCE 2013). Ordained deacon, 1986, priest, 1987; Curate: St Mary, Northolt, 1986–89; St Paul, Withington, 1989–91; Vicar, St Martin, Wythenshawe, 1991–98, and Priest-in-charge, St Francis, Newall Green, 1995–98; Provost and Rector, St Mary's Cathedral, Glasgow, 1998–2005. Business Manager and Associate, Macdonald Associates Consultancy, 2005–09; Partner, McDougall Dines LLP, 2005–15. Director: Barrio San Pedro Ltd, 2008–18; Systems Leadership Consulting Ltd, 2009–11. Teacher of Maths, Lincoln Univ. Technical Coll., 2013–19. Founder Mem., Unicorn Grocery Co-op., Manchester, 1996. Mem., Iona Community, 1999–2008. *Recreations*: vexillology, travelling hopefully, troglodytic living. *Address*: 12 Eastgate, Lincoln LN2 1QG. *E*: griff@dines.org. *Club*: Castle Hill (Lincoln).

**DINEVOR**; *see* Dynevor.

**DINGEMANS, Rt Hon. Sir James (Michael)**, Kt 2013; PC 2019; **Rt Hon. Lord Justice Dingemans**; a Lord Justice of Appeal, since 2019; *b* 25 July 1964; *s* of Rear-Adm. Peter George Valentin Dingemans, CB, DSO and of Faith Vivien Dingemans (*née* Bristow); *m* 1991, Janet Griffiths; one *s* two *d*. *Educ*: Mansfield Coll., Oxford (Rugby Union blue, 1985; BA Jurisprudence 1986). Called to the Bar, Inner Temple, 1987; QC 2002; a Recorder, 2002–13; a Dep. High Ct Judge, 2010–13; a Judge of the High Ct of Justice, QBD, 2013–19; Presiding Judge of Western Circuit, 2014–18. Leading Counsel to Hutton Inquiry, 2003. Mem., Exec. Cttee, Commonwealth Lawyers' Assoc., 2002–13; Chm., Internat. Cttee, Bar Council, 2009–11 (Vice-Chm., Internat. Relations Cttee, 2006–08). Judicial Mem., Adv. Panel, Rugby Football League, 2005–10; Judicial Officer, RFU, 2013–; Appeal Officer, World Rugby, 2015–. *Recreations*: Rugby, sailing, cricket. *Address*: Royal Courts of Justice, Strand, WC2A 2LL. *Clubs*: Broadhalfpenny Brigands Cricket; Bar Yacht.

**DINGEMANS, Simon Paul**; Executive Director and Chief Financial Officer, GlaxoSmithKline plc, 2011–19; *b* 26 April 1963; *s* of Norman Dingemans and Patricia Dingemans; *m* 1994, Elizabeth, (Liz), Hawkins; one *s* two *d*. *Educ*: Kent Coll., Canterbury; Christ Church, Oxford (BA Hons Geog.; MA). S. G. Warburg & Co. Ltd, 1985–95; Goldman Sachs, 1995–2010; a Man. Dir, 1998–2010, Partner, 2000–10, Goldman Sachs Internat. Chair, Financial Reporting Council, 2019–. *Recreations*: theatre, running, cycling. *Club*: Royal Automobile.

**DINGLE, David Keith**, CBE 2009; Chairman, Carnival UK, since 2014 (Chief Executive Officer, 2007–14); *b* Fareham, Hants, 11 Feb. 1957; *s* of Keith Dingle and Joy Dingle; *m* 1990, Lovie Tan; two *s*. *Educ*: Portsmouth Grammar Sch.; Jesus Coll., Cambridge (BA Classics 1978; MA 1981). Joined P&O, 1978; Mktg Dir, 1988–98, Commercial Dir, 1998–2000, P&O Cruises; Man. Dir, P&O Princess Cruises UK, later Carnival UK, 2000–07. Pres., UK Chamber of Shipping, 2007–08. Chairman: Eur. Cruise Council, 2007–10; Maritime UK, 2015–18; CLIA Europe, 2018. Younger Brother, Trinity House, 2008–. Hon. DBA Plymouth, 2012. *Recreations*: family, ski-ing, travel, opera, ballet, music, history. *Address*: Carnival UK, Carnival House, 100 Harbour Parade, Southampton, Hants SO15 1ST. *E*: david.dingle@carnivalukgroup.com. *Club*: Royal Automobile.

**DINGLE, Sir Graeme**, KNZM 2017 (ONZM 2001); MBE 1988; mountaineer, adventurer, artist, writer and humanitarian; Founder, 1972, and Patron, since 2018, Hillary Outdoors (formerly Sir Edmund Hillary Outdoor Pursuits Centre of New Zealand) (Chief Executive Officer, 1972–79; Trustee, 1973–85, now Life Trustee); Co-Founder, 1994, Fundraiser, since 1994, and Trustee, Endowment Board, Graeme Dingle Foundation (formerly Project K Trust) (Director, 1994–2000; Trustee, 1995–2013; Chair, 2003–06); *b* Gisborne, NZ, 30 Nov. 1945; *m* Jo-anne Wilkinson; one *d*. Former Tech. and Mktg Dir, Hallmark Internat., designed and marketed backpacks, tents and other equipment. Founder Chm., Outdoors NZ; former Chm., Foundn for Youth Develt. Mountaineering, rock climbing and adventuring achievements include: first ascents in Andes, Himalaya, Antarctica and NZ; first ascent in one season of all six classic European north faces, incl. Eiger and Matterhorn; first traverse of Southern Alps; first traverse of Himalaya from Kanchenjunga to K2; 400-day circumnavigation of Arctic in two stages, incl. mainly solo winter traverse of Northwest Passage; ran length of Tararua Range in 18.5 hours; led six convicted violent offenders on arduous 1200 km journey. Gov.-Gen.'s Young Adult Award; Award of NZ; Officer, NZ Order of Merit; Antarctic Service Medal (USA). Lifetime Achievement Award, Sport NZ; Supreme Award, Outdoor NZ. *Publications*: Dingle: discovering the sense in adventure (autobiog.) (Montana Book Award for biog., 2006); eleven books; numerous articles. *Club*: New Zealand Alpine (Life Mem.).

**DINGLE, John Thomas**, PhD, DSc; President, Hughes Hall, Cambridge, 1993–98 (Hon. Fellow, 1998); *b* 27 Oct. 1927; *s* of Thomas Henry and Violet Nora Dingle; *m* 1953, Dorothy Vernon Parsons; two *s*. *Educ*: King Edward Sch., Bath; London Univ. (BSc, DSc); Clare Coll., Cambridge (PhD). Royal National Hosp. for Rheumatic Diseases, Bath, 1951–59; Research Fellowship, Strangeways Research Laboratory, Cambridge, 1959–61; MRC External Staff, 1961–79; Strangeways Research Laboratory: Head of Tissue Physiology Dept, 1966; Dep. Dir, 1970–79; Dir, 1979–93; Fellow, Corpus Christi Coll., Cambridge, 1968–93 (Life Fellow, 1998); Bursar of Leckhampton, 1972–80, Warden, 1980–86. Co-Dir, Rheumatism Res. Unit, Addenbrooke's Hosp., 1997–2001. Visiting Professor: of Biochemistry, Royal Free Hosp. Med. Sch., 1975–78; of Rheumatology, New York Univ., 1977. Chm., British Connective Tissue Soc., 1980–87. Chm. Editorial Bd, Biochemical Jl, 1975–82. Pres., Cambridge Univ. RFC, 1990–2002 (Treas., 1982–90). Heberden Orator and Medalist, 1978; American Orthopaedic Assoc. Steindler Award, 1980. *Publications*: communications to learned jls. *Recreations*: Rugby football (playing member, Bath, Bristol, Somerset RFCs, 1943–57), sailing. *Address*: Hughes Hall, Cambridge CB1 2EW; Corpus Christi College, Cambridge CB2 1RH; Middle Watch, Mount Boone Hill, Dartmouth, Devon TQ6 9NZ. *Club*: Hawks (Cambridge).

*See also* T. T. Dingle.

**DINGLE, Timothy Thomas**; Chief Executive Officer: London School of Excellence, since 2011; Ghost Bus Tours, since 2017; Founder, Be Amazing Every Day Group, since 2015; *b* 9 June 1959; *s* of Dr John Thomas Dingle, *qv*. *Educ*: Perse Sch., Cambridge; UEA (BSc 1980; PGCE 1981); Univ. of Westminster (MBA 1998); London Sch. of Mediation (Mediator, 2007). Mill Hill School: Head of Biology Dept, 1985–90; Housemaster, 1990–95; Dep. Head, 1995–99; Headmaster, Royal Grammar Sch., High Wycombe, 1999–2006. Exec. Trng Consultant, Unitas Hospitality, 2013–; Sen. Trainer, American Consulting Experts (Middle East), 2018–. Member: Cttee, Nat. Grammar Schs Assoc., 1999–2006; Conservative Party Task Force on Grammar Schs, 2000–06. Nat. Selector (Rugby), 1998; Member: Middlesex RFU, 1985–2001; London and SE RFU, 1990; Cttee, England Schs RFU, 2002 (Chm., 16 Gp, 2003; Life Mem., 2015). Governor: Highcrest Community Sch., 2001; Davenies Prep. Sch., 2001. Winston Churchill Fellow, 2002. Mem., BNI (Central London). MInstD. *Publications*: Cartilage Disc Degeneration, 1981; European Dimension in Schools, 1994; Hidden By Order, 2010; Revision and Learning, 2011; Pitch and Grow Rich, 2012; Want More Clients, 2013; A Brief History of Tim, 2016; Social and Societal Marketing, 2018; multiple articles on digital learning, mobile learning and the highs of business. *Recreations*: Rugby, cricket, painting, sailing, travel, poetry, stand up comedy (comedy club owner, 2009–; Edinburgh Fest., 2015–), ski-ing. *Address*: c/o 178 High Holborn, WC1V 7AA. *Clubs*: MCC, National Liberal.

**DINGWALL**, Baron; *see* Lucas of Crudwell and Dingwall.

**DINHAM, Martin John**, CBE 1997; independent consultant, since 2010; Director General, International, Department for International Development, 2008–10; *b* 9 July 1950; *s* of late John A. Dinham and Gwenyth Dinham; *m* 1980, Jannie Sanderson; one *s* one *d*. *Educ*: Haberdashers' Aske's Sch., Elstree; Christ's Coll., Cambridge (BA Mod. Langs 1971). Joined ODM, later ODA, as exec. officer, 1974; Asst Private Sec. to successive Ministers for Overseas Develt, 1978–79; Desk Officer for Zambia and Malawi, ODA, 1979–81; on secondment to World Bank, Washington, as Asst to UK Exec. Dir, 1981–83; Hd, Personnel Br., ODA, 1983–85; Private Sec. to successive Ministers for Overseas Develt, 1985–87; Hd, SE Asia Develt Div., ODA, Bangkok, 1988–92; on secondment to Hong Kong Govt as Advr to Governor, 1992–97; Department for International Development: Hd of Personnel and Principal Estabt Officer, 1997–2000; Dir, Asia and the Pacific, then Asia, 2000–04; Dir, Europe, Middle E and Americas, subseq. Europe, Middle E, Americas, Central and E Asia, 2005–07; Dir, UN, Conflict and Humanitarian Div., 2007; Acting Dir Gen., Corporate Performance, 2007–08. Interim Chm. Bd, Global Fund to Fight AIDS, Tuberculosis and Malaria, 2011; Chair Bd, Frontline AIDS (formerly Internat. HIV/AIDS Alliance), 2015–19 (Trustee, 2010–19; Chair, Finance and Audit Cttee, 2010–15); Trustee, BBC Media Action, 2013–19 (Vice-Chair, 2016–19); Vice-Pres., Sightsavers Internat., 2019– (Trustee, 2010–19; Vice-Chair, 2012–15; Chair Bd, 2015–19). *Recreations:* theatre, cinema, planning holidays. *E:* martin.dinham@btinternet.com.

**DINKIN, Anthony David;** QC 1991; barrister; a Recorder of the Crown Court, 1989–2017; *b* 2 Aug. 1944; *s* of late Hyman Dinkin and Mary (*née* Hine); *m* 1968, Derina Tanya (*née* Green), MBE. *Educ:* Henry Thornton Grammar Sch., Clapham; Coll. of Estate Management, London (BSc (Est. Man.)). Called to the Bar, Lincoln's Inn, 1968, Bencher, 2003. Legal Mem., Lands Tribunal, 1998–2000; Tribunal Judge (formerly Mem., Mental Health Review Tribunal), 1998–. Examr in Law, Reading Univ., 1985–93; Ext. Examr, City Univ., 2003–14. Pres., Estate Mgt Club, 1998–99. *Recreations:* gardening, theatre, music, travel. *E:* ad.qc@hotmail.com. *Club:* Athenaeum.

**DINNAGE, Calista Jane;** *see* Probyn, C. J.

**DINNEEN, Sandra Caroline,** OBE 2019; Chief Executive, South Norfolk Council, 2008–19; Managing Director, Big Sky, 2013–19; Director, Build Insight, 2014–19; *b* Brentwood, 10 March 1964; *d* of William Dinneen and Irene Dinneen; *m* 1997, Andrew Hitchings; one *s* one *d* (and one *d* decd). *Educ:* Wymondham Coll.; University Coll. London (BSc Hons Econs 1986). City Coll., Norwich (Dip. Mgt Studies 1990); Neuro-Linguistic Programming Practitioner 2008; Cert. Coaching and Mentoring, CIPD. Mktg for a fashion co., London, managing a restaurant, Sydney, founded photo liby co., Sydney, then trainee underwriter, insce co., San Francisco, 1985–88; Econ. Develt Officer, Norwich CC, 1988–97; Hd, Econ. Develt, Norfolk CC, 1997–2008. Chm., Dist Councils Chief Execs Network, 2015–17. Comr, Historic England, 2017–. Gov., Easton and Otley Coll., 2009–; Mem., Sapienta Educn Trust, 2014–. *Recreations:* family, sailing, tennis, theatre.

**DINSMORE, David;** Chief Operating Officer, News UK, since 2015; *b* Glasgow, 2 Sept. 1968; *m* Jillian; one *s* one *d*. *Educ:* Strathallan Sch. Joined The Sun, 1990: Night Ed., 2004–06; Scottish Ed., 2006–10; Gen. Manager, News Internat. Scotland, 2010; Man. Ed., The Sun; Dir of Ops, News Internat., 2012–13; Ed., The Sun, 2013–15. *Recreation:* cycling. *Address:* News UK & Ireland Ltd, 1 London Bridge Street, SE1 9GF.

**DINWIDDY, Bruce Harry,** CMG 2003; HM Diplomatic Service, retired; Governor, Cayman Islands, 2002–05; *b* 1 Feb. 1946; *s* of late Thomas Lutwyche Dinwiddy and Ruth Dinwiddy (*née* Abbott); *m* 1974, Emma Victoria Llewellyn, *d* of Sir David Treharne Llewellyn and Joan Anne Llewellyn (*née* Williams), OBE; one *s* one *d*. *Educ:* Winchester Coll.; New Coll., Oxford (MA). Economist, Govt of Swaziland (ODI Nuffield Fellow), 1967–69; Res. Officer, ODI, 1970–73; HM Diplomatic Service, 1973; First Sec., UK Deleg. to MBFR talks, Vienna, 1975–77; FCO, 1977–81; Head of Chancery, Cairo, 1981–83; FCO, 1983–86; Asst Sec., Cabinet Office, 1986–88; Counsellor, Bonn, 1989–91; Dep. High Comr, Ottawa, 1992–95; Head of African Dept (Southern), FCO, 1995–98; Comr (non-resident), British Indian Ocean Territory, 1996–98; High Comr, Tanzania, 1998–2001; on secondment to Standard Chartered Bank, 2001–02. Mem. Council, and Chm., Wider Caribbean Wkg Gp, UK Overseas Territories Conservation Forum, 2006–15; Consultant, UK Trade and Investment, 2007–09. *Publications:* Promoting African Enterprise, 1974. *Recreations:* golf (captained Oxford *v* Cambridge, 1967), swimming, music, theatre, travel. *Address:* 8 Connaught Avenue, East Sheen, SW14 7RH. *Clubs:* Vincent's (Oxford); Royal Wimbledon Golf.

**DINWOODIE, Prof. Graeme Baxter,** JSD; Global Professor of Intellectual Property Law, and Co-Director, Chicago-Kent Centre for Design, Law and Technology, Chicago-Kent College of Law, since 2018 (University Professor, 2016–18); *b* Glasgow, 20 July 1966; *s* of David John Dinwoodie and Isabella Steele Dinwoodie (*née* Colgan). *Educ:* Univ. of Glasgow (LLB 1st Cl. Hons); Harvard Law Sch. (LLM); Columbia Law Sch. (JSD 2000). John F Kennedy Schol., Harvard Law Sch., 1987–88; Burton Fellow in Residence, Columbia Law Sch., 1988–89; Litigation Associate, Sullivan & Cromwell, NY, 1989–94; Asst Prof. of Law, then Prof. of Law, Coll. of Law, Univ. of Cincinnati, 1994–2000; Prof. of Law, and Dir, Prog. in IP Law, Chicago-Kent Coll. of Law, 2000–09; Prof. of IP Law, QMW, Univ. of London, 2005–09; Prof. of Intellectual Property and Information Technol. Law, and Dir, Oxford Intellectual Property Res. Centre, Univ. of Oxford, 2009–18; Fellow, St Peter's Coll., Oxford, 2009–18. Vis. Associate Prof. of Law, Sch. of Law, Univ. of Pennsylvania, 1999–2000; Hon. Prof. of Law, Univ. of Strasbourg; George P. Smith II Dist. Vis. Prof., Maurer Sch. of Law, Indiana Univ.; Global Prof. of Law, NY Univ. Sch. of Law; Yong Shook Lin Vis. Prof. of IP Law, Nat. Univ. of Singapore, 2016. Consultant: World IP Orgn; UN Conf. on Trade and Develt on Protection of Traditional Knowledge. Advr, Amer. Law Inst. Project: on Principles of Jurisdiction and Recognition of Judgements in IP Matters; on Restatement of Copyright. Chm., IP Section, Assoc. of Amer. Law Schs. Pres., Internat. Assoc. for Advancement of Teaching and Res. in IP, 2011–13. Mem., Amer. Law Inst., 2003. Pattishall Medal, Internat. Trademark Assoc., 2008. *Publications:* (with M. Janis) Trademarks and Unfair Competition Law and Policy, 2004, 4th edn 2014; (jtly) International Intellectual Property Law and Policy, 2001, 2nd edn 2008; Trade Dress and Design Law, 2010; (with R. C. Dreyfuss) A Neofederalist Vision of TRIPS, 2012; (jtly) Conflict of Laws in Intellectual Property, 2013; (ed with M. Janis) Trademark and Unfair Competition Law: themes and theories, vol. I, 2014; (ed with M. Janis) Trademark and Unfair Competition Law: doctrinal debates, 2014; (ed) Intellectual Property and General Legal Principles, 2015; contrib. chapters to books; contrib. to jls incl. Internat. Rev. of Industrial Property and Copyright Law, Univ. of Pennsylvania Law Rev., Iowa Law Rev., NC Law Rev., Columbia Jl Law and Arts, Lewis & Clark Law Rev., William and Mary Law Rev., Houston Law Rev., NY Univ. Jl Internat. Law and Politics. *Address:* Chicago-Kent College of Law, 565 West Adams Street, Chicago, IL 60661–3691, USA.

**DIOUF, Jacques,** PhD; Director-General, 1994–2011, Special Envoy for the Sahel and the Horn of Africa, 2014, United Nations Food and Agriculture Organization; Special Advisor to the President of the Republic of Guinea, since 2016; *b* St Louis, Senegal, 1 Aug. 1938; *m* 1963, Aïssatou Seye; one *s* four *d*. *Educ:* Ecole nationale d'agriculture, Grignon-Paris (BSc Agric.); Ecole nationale d'application d'agronomie tropicale, Nogent-Paris, (MSc Trop. Agronomy); Panthéon-Sorbonne, Paris (PhD Agricl Econs). Dir, European Office and Agricl Prog. of Mkting Bd, Dakar/Paris, 1963–64; Executive Secretary: African Groundnut Council, Lagos, 1965–71; W Africa Rice Develt Assoc., Liberia, 1971–77; Sec. of State for Sci. and Technol., Senegal, 1978–83; MP Senegambian Confedn, 1983–84: Chm. and Elected Sec., Foreign Relns Cttee, 1983–84; Chm., Friendship Parly Gp, Senegal-UK, 1983–84; Advr to Pres. and Regl Dir, Internat. Develt Res. Centre, Ottawa, 1984–85; Central Bank for W African States, Dakar: Sec.-Gen., 1985–90; Special Advr to Governor, 1990–91; Ambassador, Senegal Perm. Mission to UN, 1991–93. Commander: Legion of Honour (France), 1998 (Officer 1978); Order of Agricl Merit (Canada), 1995; Grand Comdr, Order of Star of Africa (Liberia), 1977; Grand Cross: Order of Merit in Agric., Fisheries and Food (Spain), 1996; Order of May for Merit (Argentina), 1998; Order of Solidarity (Cuba), 1998. *Publications:* contrib. to learned jls.

**DI ROLLO, Simon Ronald;** QC (Scot.) 2002; *b* 28 Oct. 1961; *s* of late Rino Di Rollo and of Teresa Di Rollo (*née* de Marco); *m* 1st, 1990, Alison Margaret Lafferty (marr. diss. 2012); one *s* one *d*; 2nd, 2013, Kim Louise Leslie; one *s*. *Educ:* Holy Cross Acad., Edinburgh; Scotus Acad., Edinburgh; Univ. of Edinburgh (LLB Hons 1983; DLP 1984). Admitted: solicitor, 1986; to Faculty of Advocates, 1987; Advocate Depute, 1997. Dir, Quality Assurance, Faculty of Advocates, 2016–. Lectr (pt-time) in Civil Procedure, Univ. of Edinburgh, 1999–2012. Mem., Sheriff Court Rules Council, 2002–11; Mem., Parole Bd for Scotland, 2018–. Curator, Advocates Liby, 2009–13. *Recreations:* Italian, walking, food and drink. *Address:* Advocates' Library, Parliament House, Edinburgh EH1 1RF. *E:* sdirollo@advocates.org.uk; 2 West Savile Road, Edinburgh EH16 5NG.

**DI RUPO, Elio;** Prime Minister of Belgium, 2011–14; Mayor of Mons, 2014–18; *b* Morlanwelz, Belgium, 18 July 1951. *Educ:* Univ. of Mons-Hainaut (DSc). Lectr, Univ. of Leeds. Mem., Mons Municipal Council, 1982–85, 1988–2000 (Alderman, 1986); Mayor of Mons, 2000–05, 2007. MP (Soc.) Mons-Borinage, 1987–89; MEP, 1989; Senator, 1991; Minister of Educn, 1992–94, of Audiovisual Policy, 1993–94; Dep. Prime Minister and Minister for Communications and Public Undertakings, 1994; Dep. Prime Minister and Minister for Economics and Telecommunications, and for Foreign Trade, 1998–99; Minister-Pres., Walloon Reg., 1999–2000, 2005–07; Minister of State, 2002–11; MP, 2003; Informateur, 2003; Préformateur, 2010–11; Formateur, 2011. Pres., Socialist Party, 1999–2011, 2014–; Vice Pres., Socialist Internat., 1999–. *Publications:* Le Progrès Partagé, 2003; Nouvelles conquêtes, 2017.

**DISMORE, Andrew;** Member (Lab) Barnet and Camden, London Assembly, Greater London Authority, since 2012; *b* 2 Sept. 1954; *s* of late Ian and of Brenda Dismore. *Educ:* Warwick Univ. (LLB 1972); LSE, London Univ. (LLM 1976). Educn Asst, GMWU, 1976–78; Partner: Robin Thompson & Partners, Solicitors, 1978–95; Russell Jones & Walker, Solicitors, 1995–2003, consultant, 2003–09. Mem. (Lab), Westminster CC, 1982–97 (Leader, Labour Gp, 1990–97). MP (Lab) Hendon, 1997–2010; contested (Lab) same seat, 2010, 2015. Chm., Jt Cttee on Human Rights, H of C, 2005–10; Mem., Standards and Privileges Cttee, 2001–10. London Assembly, Greater London Authority: Chair, Economy Cttee, 2012–13; Fire, Resilience and Emergency Planning Cttee, 2019–; Member: Econ., Envmt and Health Cttees, 2013–15; Regeneration, Econ. and Police Cttees, 2015–19; Police and Crime, Regeneration and Audit Cttees, 2019–. Mem., London Fire and Emergency Planning Authy, 2012–13 and 2014–18. *Recreations:* gardening, travel, Greece, Greek culture. *Address:* Greater London Authority, City Hall, Queen's Walk, SE1 2AA.

**DISS, Eileen, (Mrs Raymond Everett),** RDI 1978; freelance designer for theatre, film and television, since 1959; *b* 13 May 1931; *d* of Thomas and Winifred Diss; *m* 1953, Raymond Everett; two *s* one *d*. *Educ:* Ilford County High Sch. for Girls; Central Sch. of Art and Design. FRSA. BBC Television design, 1952–59. *Television* series and plays: Maigret, 1962–63; The Tea Party, 1964; Up the Junction, 1965; Somerset Maugham, 1969; Uncle Vanya, 1970; The Duchess of Malfi, and Candide, 1972; The Importance of Being Earnest, and Pygmalion, 1973; Caesar and Cleopatra, 1974; Moll Flanders, 1975; Ghosts, and The Winslow Boy, 1976; You Never Can Tell, 1977; The Rear Column, Hedda Gabler, 1980; The Potting Shed, 1981; Porterhouse Blue, 1987; Behaving Badly, 1989; Jeeves & Wooster, 1989, 1990, and 1992; Best of Friends, 1991; Head Over Heels, 1993; Love on a Branch Line, 1993; A Dance to the Music of Time, 1997; television opera: The Merry Widow, 1968; Tales of Hoffmann, 1969; Die Fledermaus, 1971; Falstaff, 1972; The Yeomen of the Guard, 1974; television films: Cider with Rosie, 1971; Robinson Crusoe, 1974; Longitude, 1999; Dead Gorgeous, 2002. *Theatre:* Exiles, 1969; Butley, 1971; The Caretaker, 1972, 1991, 2009 and 2010; Otherwise Engaged, 1975; The Apple-cart, 1977; The Rear Column, The Homecoming, 1978; The Hothouse, 1980; Translations, Quartermaine's Terms, Incident at Tulse Hill, 1981; Rocket to the Moon, 1982; The Communication Cord, 1983; The Common Pursuit, 1984; Other Places, The Seagull, Sweet Bird of Youth, 1985; Circe and Bravo, 1986; The Deep Blue Sea, 1988; Veterans Day, The Mikado, Steel Magnolias, 1989; Burn This, 1990; The Philanthropist, 1991; Private Lives, A Month in the Country, 1992; Oleanna, 1993; Pinter Fest., Dublin, 1994; Cell Mates, 1995; Taking Sides, The Hothouse, 1995; Twelve Angry Men, 1996; Ashes to Ashes, 1996; Life Support, 1997; A Letter of Resignation, 1997; The Heiress, 1997; Arcadia, 1999; The Late Middle Classes, 1999; The Room, and Celebration, 2000; Port Authority, and The Homecoming, 2001; The Dwarfs, 2002; The Old Masters, 2004; Endgame, 2006; National Theatre: Blithe Spirit, 1976; The Philanderer, 1978; Close of Play, When We Are Married, 1979; Watch on the Rhine, 1980; The Caretaker, 1980; Measure for Measure, 1981; The Trojan War Will Not Take Place, 1983; Landscape, 1994; No Man's Land, 2001. *Films:* Joseph Losey's A Doll's House, 1972; Sweet William, 1978; Harold Pinter's Betrayal, 1982; Secret Places, 1984; 84 Charing Cross Road, 1986; A Handful of Dust, 1988; August, 1994. Television Design Award, 1962, 1965, 1974, 1992 and 2000, Lifetime Achievement Award, 2006, BAFTA; RTS Lifetime Achievement award, 2002. *Recreations:* music, cinema. *Address:* 4 Gloucester Walk, W8 4HZ. *T:* (020) 7937 8794.

**DISSANAIKE, Prof. Gishan Romesh,** PhD; financial economist; Adam Smith Professor of Corporate Governance (formerly Robert Monks Professor of Corporate Governance), University of Cambridge, since 2010; Fellow, Hughes Hall, Cambridge, since 2016; *b* Colombo, Sri Lanka, 17 Feb. 1963; *s* of late Prof. George Alexander Dissanaike, PhD and of Vijayalakshmi Indranee Senanayake Atapattu; *m* 1988, Varnini Padmika; two *s*. *Educ:* Trinity Coll., Kandy; Univ. of Peradeniya (BA 1st Cl. Hons 1986); Trinity Coll., Cambridge (MPhil; PhD 1994). Exec. trainee, Banque Indosuez, 1987–88; Lectr in Econs, Univ. of Durham, 1993–94; University of Cambridge: Lectr in Financial Econs, 1994–99; Sen. Lectr in Finance, 1999–2004; Reader in Finance, 2004–09; Actg Dir, Studies for Mgt Studies, Queens' Coll., 1995–97, St John's Coll., 2006–07, Corpus Christi Coll., 2007–08, 2011; Director: Studies for Mgt Studies, Trinity Coll., 1996–; MPhil in Finance prog., 2001–12, 2016–19; Hd, Finance and Accounting Subject Gp, Judge Business Sch., 2010–11; Mem. Council, Sch. of Technol., 2014–18; Member: Faculty Bd of Business and Mgt, 2000–02, 2005–; Univ. Finance Cttee, 2006–10; Bd, Cambridge Endowment for Res. in Finance, 2011–; Cambridge Finance, 2011–; Manager: Sir Evelyn De Rothschild Fund for Finance, 2010–15; Pembroke Vis. Prof. of Internat. Finance Fund, 2010–15; Keynes, J. M. Fellowships in Financial Economics, 2011, 2018–. Mem., Investment Cttee, Comtrust Equity Fund, 2011–13; Member, Organising Committee: Corp. Governance: An Internat. Review Conf. on Nat. Governance Bundles, 2012; 40th Eur. Finance Assoc. Conf., 2013. Vis. Associate Prof., Cornell Univ., 2004. Mem., Governing Bd, Inst. of Policy Studies, Sri Lanka, 2015–. Ext. Res. Studentship, Trinity Coll., Cambridge, 1989–92; ORS Award, CVCP, 1989–92; ICAEW Acad. Fellow, 1995–2001; ESRC Res. Fellow, 1995–99; Finance Ed., Jl Asia Business Studies, 2007–10. Non-exec. Dir, Internat. Centre for Ethnic Studies, 2008–09. Co-chair, Eur. Financial Mgt Assoc. Symposium on Corporate Governance, 2009; Mem., Exec. Cttee, Emerging Mkts Finance and Econ. Conf., Istanbul, 2007. Ryde Gold Medal, Trinity Coll., Kandy, 1982; P. D. Khan Gold

Medal and Arts Faculty Schol., Univ. of Peradeniya, 1986; Iddo Sarnat Prize, Jl Banking and Finance and Eur. Finance Assoc., 1995; Pilkington Prize, Univ. of Cambridge, 2002. *Publications:* contribs to learned jls and books on finance and econs. *Recreations:* travel, Ceylon history, genealogy. *Address:* Judge Business School, University of Cambridge, Trumpington Street, Cambridge CB2 1AG.

**DITLHABI OLIPHANT, Tuelonyana Rosemary;** Managing Director, CotroHoldings Pty Ltd, since 2014; *b* 13 Sept. 1954; *d* of late Matlhape Ditlhabi and of Tsetsele Ditlhabi; *m* 1986, Clement S. Oliphant; one *s. Educ:* Univ. of Botswana (BA Admin 1977); Pennsylvania State Univ. (MPA 1981). Joined Public Service, Botswana, 1977: Asst, Sen. and Principal Admin. Officer, Min. of Mineral Resources and Water Affairs, 1977–85; transferred to Dept of Foreign Affairs, 1985: Counsellor: Washington, 1985–88; NY, 1988–90; High Comr, Namibia and Ambassador, Angola, 1990–96; Doyenne of Diplomatic Corps and African Gp, 1992–96; High Comr, UK, 1996–98; Dep. Perm. Sec., 1998–99, Perm. Sec. for Pol Affairs, 1999–2005; Dean of Diplomatic Corps and Africa Gp; Chair, Commonwealth Gp, Zambia; High Comr to Zambia, also accredited to Tanzania, Uganda and Democratic Republic of the Congo, 2005–14. *Recreations:* music, reading, swimming, squash, active in community development activities and youth empowerment, the elderly, horticulture, consultancy. *Address:* PO Box 70239, Gaborone, Botswana. *E:* tuelonyanaoliphant1@gmail.com, tuelonyana@yahoo.co.uk.

**DITTNER, Patricia Ann;** *see* Troop, P. A.

**DIVALL, Prof. Colin Michael,** PhD; Professor of Railway Studies, University of York, 1995–2015, now Emeritus; *b* 8 Nov. 1957; *s* of late (Ernest) Gordon Divall and Gwendoline Florence Divall; partner, Prof. Karen Hunt. *Educ:* Univ. of Bristol (BSc Physics and Phil. 1979); Victoria Univ. of Manchester (MSc Structure and Orgn of Sci. and Technol. 1980; PhD 1985). Ops mgt, BR, 1984–85; Res. Associate, Centre for Hist. of Sci., Technol. and Medicine, Univ. of Manchester, 1986–88; Sen. Lectr in Social Studies of Technol., Manchester Metropolitan Univ., 1989–94; Hd, Inst. Railway Studies and Transport Hist., Nat. Railway Mus. and Univ. of York, 1995–2014. Vice Pres., Internat. Assoc. for Hist. of Transport, Traffic and Mobility, 2008–13; Pres., Histl Model Railway Soc., 2015–19. *Publications:* (with S. F. Johnston) Scaling Up: the Institution of Chemical Engineers and the rise of a new profession, 2000; (with A. Scott) Making Histories in Transport Museums, 2001; (ed with W. Bond) Suburbanizing the Masses: public transport and urban development in historical perspective, 2003; (ed with R. Roth) From Rail to Road and Back Again?: a century of transport competition and interdependency, 2015; (ed) Cultural Histories of Sociabilities, Spaces and Mobilities, 2015; (ed jtly) Transport Policy: learning lessons from history, 2016. *Recreations:* observing the feline world, listening to jazz, building Wimborne Station at 1/76th scale. *Address:* Department of History, University of York, Heslington, York YO10 5DD. *T:* (01904) 322981. *E:* colin.divall@york.ac.uk.

**DIX, Prof. Gerald Bennett,** RIBA; Lever Professor of Civic Design, University of Liverpool, 1975–88; Professor Emeritus and Hon. Senior Fellow, Liverpool University, since 1988; Hon. Senior Research Fellow, Chinese Research Academy of Environmental Sciences, since 1989; *b* 12 Jan. 1926; *s* of late Cyril Dix and Mabel Winifred (*née* Bennett); *m* 1st, 1956 (marr. diss.); two *s*; 2nd, 1963, Lois Nichols, one *d. Educ:* Altrincham Grammar Sch.; Univ. of Manchester (BA (Hons Arch.), DipTP (dist.)); Harvard Univ. (MLA). Studio Asst, 1950–51, Asst Lectr in Town and Country Planning, 1951–53, Manchester Univ.; Asst Architect, 1954; Chief Architect-Planner, Addis Ababa, and chief asst to Sir Patrick Abercrombie, 1954–56; Planning Officer, Singapore, 1957–59; Acting Planning Adviser, 1959; Sen. Research Fellow, Univ. of Science and Technol., Ghana, 1959–63; UN Planning Mission to Ghana, 1962; Planner, later Sen. Planner, BRS/ODM, 1963–65 (adv. missions to W Indies, W Africa, Aden, Bechuanaland, Swaziland, Cyprus); Nottingham University: Lectr, 1966–68; Sen. Lectr, 1968–70; Prof. of Planning, and Dir, Inst. of Planning Studies, 1970–75; Liverpool University: Chm., Fac. of Social and Environmental Studies, 1983–84; Pro Vice-Chancellor, 1984–87. Dir, Cyprus Planning Project, 1967–71; adv. visits on planning educn, to Uganda 1971, Nigeria 1972, Sudan 1975, Mexico 1978, Egypt 1980; UK Mem., Adv. Panel on planning Canal towns, Egypt, 1974, and Western Desert, 1975; Jt Dir, Alexandria Comprehensive Master Plan Project, 1980–86. Member: Professional Literature Cttee, RIBA, 1966–80, 1981–88 (Chm. 1975–80); Library Management Cttee, 1969–72, 1975–80; Historic Areas Adv. Cttee, English Heritage, 1986–88. Vice-Pres., World Soc. for Ekistics, 1975–79, Pres., 1987–90. Mem., Editl Adv. Bd, Ekistics (journal), 1972–2014; Chm., Bd of Management, Town Planning Rev., 1976–88; (Founder) Editor, Third World Planning Rev., 1978–90. FRTPI (resigned 2001); FRSA 1977. Hon. DEng Dong-A Univ., Korea, 1995. *Publications:* ed, C. A. Doxiadis, Ecology and Ekistics, 1977, Boulder, Colo, 1978, Brisbane, 1978; numerous planning reports to govts in various parts of world; articles and reviews in Town Planning Rev., Third World Planning Rev., Ekistics, RIBA Jl, Arch. Rev. *Recreations:* photography, listening to music, reading. *Address:* 49 Gaveston Gardens, Deddington, Banbury, Oxon OX15 0NX. *T:* (01869) 336215. *Club:* Athenæum.

**DIX, Malcolm;** *see* Dix, W. M. H.

**DIX, Dr Michèle,** CBE 2015; *b* Lincs, 5 Feb. 1955; *d* of James Alan and Nancy Eileen Holland; *m* 1977, Clive James Dix; one *s* one *d. Educ:* Cleethorpes Girls' Grammar Sch.; Univ. of Leeds (BSc Hons Civil Engrg; PhD Transport Planning 1982). CEng 1983; MICE 1983, FICE 2015. Transport planner, GLC, 1979–85; Bd Dir, Urban Transport, Halcrow Fox, 1985–2000; Transport for London: Dir, Congestion Charging, 2000–07; Man. Dir, Planning, 2007–15. Chm., Prescom, UITP, 2008–. Vis. Prof., UCL, 2014–. Dir, Future of London, 2010–15. Dir, Major Projects Assoc., 2015–. Trustee, London Transport Mus., 2015–. FCILT 2013; FCIHT 2014. *Recreations:* dog walking, ski-ing, gardening. *E:* micheledix@tfl.gov.uk.

**DIX, (Walter) Malcolm (Hutton);** President, Sport Newcastle (formerly Newcastle Sports Development Trust), since 2014 (Secretary, since 2000); *b* 10 May 1942; *s* of Charles Walter Dix and Rita May Dix; *m* 1964, Mary Johanne Nilsen; one *s* four *d. Educ:* Ascham House Sch., Gosforth; St Bees Sch., Cumbria; Coll. of Commerce, Newcastle upon Tyne (Business Studies). Drawing office, Walter Dix & Co., Newcastle, 1958–62; tech. sales rep., William Dickinson, Newcastle, 1962–68; Sales Manager, British Rototherm Ltd, London and S Wales, 1968–77; Chm. and Jt Man. Dir, Walter Dix & Co., Newcastle, 1971–97; Jt Founder, Magpie Gp, 1988. Chairman: Newcastle Sports Council, 1977–92; Tyne & Wear Sports Council, 1980–86. Executive Member: NE Fedn of Sport and Recreation, 2000–08 (Dir, 2008–); NE Sport, 2000–08. Chm., Beamish Develt Trust, 1995–99; Dir, Friends of Beamish Mus., 1999–. Chm., Tyne Th. and Opera Hse Preservation Trust, 2002–14 (Hon. Vice Pres., 2014). Trustee: McCrory Foundn, 2005–10; Newcastle Eagles Community Foundn, 2005–; NE Circus Develt Trust, 2014–18. Chm., NE Br., St Beghian Soc., 1992–2008 (Pres., 2006–08). Mem. Council for Northumbria, OStJ, 2004–10. Consultant, Special Events Cttee, Variety Club of GB, 2000–14. Chairman: Newcastle Supporters Assoc., 1978–82; Newcastle Gosforth Rugby Club, 1989–92 (Sen. Vice-Pres., 1992–95). Outstanding Contribution to Sport award, Newcastle upon Tyne Sports Council, 1992. *Recreations:* walking, reading and writing, music, all types (managed pop groups in the 1960s), driving, practically all sport. *Address:* 74 Neptune Road, Dumpling Hall, Newcastle upon Tyne NE15 7QN. *T:* (0191) 267 6342. *E:* Dixysport5@aol.com. *Clubs:* Newcastle United Football (Hon. Life Vice-Pres., 1992); Newcastle Falcons Rugby; Jesmond Lawn Tennis.

**DIXEY, John,** OBE 1976; Development Co-ordinator, Evening Standard Company, 1987–91; *b* 29 March 1926; *s* of John Dixey and Muriel Doris Dixey; *m* 1948, Pauline Seaden; one *s* one *d. Educ:* Battersea Grammar Sch. Served Royal Marines and Royal Fusiliers, 1944–47. Press Telegraphist, Yorkshire Post and Glasgow Herald, 1948–59; Asst to Gen. Sec., Nat. Union of Press Telegraphists, 1959; Labour Officer, Newspaper Soc., 1959–63; Labour Adviser, Thomson Organisation Ltd, 1963–64; Asst Gen. Manager, Liverpool Daily Post & Echo, 1964–67; Executive Dir, Times Newspapers, 1967–74; Special Adviser to Man. Dir, Thomson Org., 1974; Dir, Newspaper Publishers Assoc. Ltd, 1975–76; Employment Affairs Advr, IPA, 1977–79; Sec., Assoc. of Midland Advertising Agencies, 1977–79; Production Dir and Bd Mem., The Guardian, 1979–84; Asst Man. Dir, Mirror Gp Newspapers, 1985; Newspaper Consultant, 1986. Chm., Advertising Assoc. Trade Union Liaison Group, 1975–84; Mem., TUC New Daily Newspaper Advisory Group, 1982–83. Ward-Perkins Vis. Fellow, Pembroke Coll., Oxford, 1978. Mem., Printing and Publishing Industry Trng Bd, 1975–76; Governor, London Coll. of Printing, 1975–76. *Recreations:* cooking, photography. *Address:* 1 Hornor Close, Norwich NR2 2LY. *T:* (01603) 505656.

**DIXIT, Prof. Avinash Kamalakar;** John J. F. Sherrerd '52 Professor of Economics, Princeton University, USA, 1989–2010, now Emeritus (Professor of Economics, 1981–89); *b* 8 June 1944; *s* of Kamalakar Ramchandra Dixit and Kusum Dixit. *Educ:* Bombay Univ. (BSc); Cambridge Univ. (BA, MA); Massachusetts Inst. of Technology (PhD). Acting Asst Professor, Univ. of California, Berkeley, 1968–69; Lord Thomson of Fleet Fellow and Tutor in Economics, Balliol Coll., Oxford, 1970–74; Professor of Economics, Univ. of Warwick, 1974–80. Guggenheim Fellowship, 1991–92. Pres., Amer. Economic Assoc., 2008 (Vice-Pres., 2002). Fellow: Econometric Society, 1977 (Pres., 2001); Amer. Acad. of Arts and Scis, 1992; US Nat. Acad. of Scis, 2005; Amer. Philosophical Soc., 2010. Corresp. FBA 2005. Co-Editor, Bell Journal of Economics, 1981–83. Padma Vibhushan (India), 2016. *Publications:* Optimization in Economic Theory, 1976; The Theory of Equilibrium Growth, 1976; (with Victor Norman) Theory of International Trade, 1980; (with Barry Nalebuff) Thinking Strategically, 1991; (with Robert S. Pindyck) Investment Under Uncertainty, 1994; The Making of Economic Policy: a transaction-cost politics perspective, 1996; (with Susan Skeath) Games of Strategy, 1999; Lawlessness and Economics, 2004; (with Barry Nalebuff) Art of Strategy, 2009; Microeconomics: a very short introduction, 2014; several articles in professional jls. *Recreations:* reading, listening to music, travel. *Address:* Department of Economics, Princeton University, Princeton, NJ 08544–1021, USA. *E:* dixitak@princeton.edu.

**DIXON,** family name of **Baron Glentoran.**

**DIXON, Prof. Adrian Kendal,** MD; FRCP, FRCR, FRCS, FMedSci; Professor of Radiology, University of Cambridge, 1994–2009, now Emeritus; Master of Peterhouse, Cambridge, 2008–16 (Fellow, 1986–2008; Hon. Fellow, 2016); Hon. Consultant Radiologist, Addenbrooke's Hospital, Cambridge, 1979–2014; *b* 5 Feb. 1948; *s* of late Kendal Cartwright Dixon and Anne Sybil (*née* Darley); *m* 1979, Anne Hazel Lucas; two *s* one *d. Educ:* Uppingham; King's Coll., Cambridge; St Bartholomew's Hosp. Med. Coll., London; MD Cantab 1988. FRCR 1978; FRCP 1991; FRCS 2003. Medical posts in: St Bartholomew's Hosp., 1972–79; Gen. Hosp., Nottingham, 1973–75; Hosp. for Sick Children, Gt Ormond St, 1978; Lectr, Dept of Radiology, Univ. of Cambridge, 1979–94. Visiting Professor: Md and Washington, 1988; Dublin, 1991; Univ. of Otago, NZ, 1992; Stanford, 2002; Edmonton, 2007. Member: Univ. Grants Cttee, Hong Kong, 2014–19; Governing Body, Univ. Coll. Cork, 2015–19. Arnott Demonstrator, RCS, 1995; Skinner Lectr, RCR, 1996. Warden, RCR, 2002–06. FMedSci 1998. Hon. Fellow, Faculty of Radiology, RCSI, 1999 (Houghton Medal, 1999); Hon. FRANZCR 2001; Hon. FACR 2009; Hon. Fellow, HK Coll. of Radiologists, 2016; Hon. Member: Swedish Soc. of Radiology, 2001; Hungarian Soc. of Radiologists, 2002; Soc. Française de Radiologie, 2003; Swiss Radiology Soc., 2009; Spanish Radiol Soc., 2010; Radiol Soc. of N America, 2011; German Radiol Soc., 2015; Austrian Soc. of Radiology, 2016. Pres., Cambridge Univ. Golf Club, 2009–17. Editor: Clinical Radiology, 1998–2002; European Radiology, 2007–13. Hon. MD: Cork, 2011; Ludwig Maximilians, Munich, 2013. Gold Medal, Eur. Soc. Radiol., 2014. *Publications:* Body CT, 1983; CT and MRI, Radiological Anatomy, 1991; Human Cross Sectional Anatomy, 1991, 2nd edn as Human Sectional Anatomy, 1999; (jtly) Diagnostic Radiology, 4th edn, 2002, 7th edn, 2019; papers on computed tomography, magnetic resonance imaging and radiological strategies. *Recreations:* family, golf. *Address:* Peterhouse, Cambridge CB2 1RD. *T:* (01223) 338200.

**DIXON, Andrew;** Director, Culture Creativity Place Ltd, since 2013; *b* Manchester; *s* of Geoff Dixon and Maureen Dixon; *m* 1988, Charlotte Kendall; one *s* one *d. Educ:* Univ. of Bradford (BSc Managerial Scis). Adminr and Youth Projects Dir, Major Road Theatre Co., 1981–84; County Arts Officer, Humberside CC, 1984–89; Northern Arts: Asst Dir, 1989–92; Dep. Dir, 1992–96; Chief Exec., 1997–2003; Exec. Dir, Arts Council England, 2003–05; Chief Executive: NewcastleGateshead Initiative, 2005–10; Creative Scotland, 2010–13. Prog. Dir, World Summit on Arts and Culture, 2006. Visiting Professor: Warwick Business Sch.; Coventry Univ. Hon. DCL Northumbria, 2008. *Recreations:* ski-ing, vegetarian cooking, rock musician. *Address:* Culture Creativity Place Ltd, 12a Great Stuart Street, Edinburgh EH3 7TN. *W:* www.andrewdixon.org.

**DIXON, Andrew Michael G.;** *see* Graham-Dixon.

**DIXON, Barry,** CBE 2007; QFSM 1999; DL; County Fire Officer and Chief Executive, Greater Manchester County Fire Service, 2002–09; *b* 5 Jan. 1951; *s* of Thomas Henry and Ruby Harriet Dixon; *m* 1976, Jill Ormrod; one *s* one *d. Educ:* Stand Grammar Sch. Joined Manchester City Fire Bde as jun. fireman, 1967; Gtr Manchester Fire Service, 1974; progressed through ranks; posts in Rochdale, Oldham and Bury; Asst Co. Fire Officer (Ops), 1995–2000; Dep. Co. Fire Officer, 2000–02. DL Gtr Manchester, 2008. *Recreations:* clay pigeon shooting, fishing, countryside in general.

**DIXON, Dr Bernard,** OBE 2000; science writer and consultant; *b* Darlington, 17 July 1938; *s* of late Ronald Dixon and Grace Peirson; *m* 1963, Margaret Helena Charlton (marr. diss. 1988); two *s* one *d*; partner, Kath Adams (*d* 2019). *Educ:* Queen Elizabeth Grammar Sch., Darlington; King's Coll., Univ. of Durham; Univ. of Newcastle upon Tyne. BSc, PhD. Luccock Res. Fellow, 1961–64, Frank Schon Fellow, 1964–65, Univ. of Newcastle; Asst Editor, 1965–66, Dep. Editor, 1966–69, World Medicine; Editor, New Scientist, 1969–79; European Editor: The Scientist, 1986–89; Bio Technology, 1989–97; Amer. Soc. for Microbiol., 1997–; Member, Editorial Board: Biologist, 1988–2005; World Jl of Microbiology and Biotechnology, 1988–2002. Chm., Cttee, Assoc. of British Science Writers, 1971–72; Member: CSS, 1982–91 (Vice-Chm., 1989–91); Soc. for Applied Microbiol. (formerly Applied Bacteriol.), 1989–; Amer. Soc. for Microbiol., 1995–; Council, BAAS, 1977–83 (Pres., Section X, 1979; Vice-Pres., Gen. Section, 1986–96); Bd, Edinburgh Internat. Science Fest., 1990–2003. Convenor, Eur. Fedn of Biotechnol. Task Gp on Public Perceptions of Biotechnol., 1996–. FRSB (FIBiol 1982); CBiol 1984. Hon.

DSc Edinburgh, 1996. Charter Award, Inst. of Biol., 1999; Biochemical Soc. Award, 2002. *Publications:* (ed) Journeys in Belief, 1968; What is Science For?, 1973; Magnificent Microbes, 1976; Invisible Allies, 1976; Beyond the Magic Bullet, 1978; (with G. Holister) Ideas of Science, 1984; Health and the Human Body, 1986; Engineered Organisms in the Environment, 1986; Recombinant DNA: what's it all about, 1987; The Science of Science: changing the way we think, 1989; The Science of Science: changing the way we live, 1989; (ed) From Creation to Chaos: classic writings in science, 1989; (with A. L. W. F. Eddleston) Interferons in the Treatment of Chronic Virus Infections of the Liver, 1989; (with E. Millstone) Our Genetic Future: the science and ethics of genetic technology, 1992; Genetics and the Understanding of Life, 1993; Power Unseen: how microbes rule the world, 1994; Enzymes Make the World Go Round, 1994; Animalcules: the activities, impacts and investigators of microbes, 2009; *contributor to:* Animal Rights—A Symposium, 1979; The Book of Predictions, 1980; Development of Science Publishing in Europe, 1980; Medicine and Care, 1981; From Biology to Biotechnology, 1982; Encyclopædia Britannica, 15th edn, 1984; Encyclopædia Britannica Yearbook, 1986–2001; Inquiry into Life, 1986; The Domesday Project, 1986; Industrial Biotechnology in Europe: issues for public policy, 1986; Biotechnology Information, 1987; Future Earth, 1989; Harrap's Illustrated Dictionary of Science, 1989; Biotechnology—A Brave New World?, 1989; Soundings from BMJ columnists, 1993; Taking Sides: clashing views on controversial issues in health and society, 1993; Wider Application and Diffusion of Bioremediation Technologies, 1996; Biotechnology for Clean Industrial Products and Processes, 1998; numerous articles in scientific and general press on microbiology, and other scientific topics. *Recreations:* listening to Elgar, Mahler and Scottish traditional music, collecting old books. *Address:* 130 Cornwall Road, Ruislip Manor, Middlesex HA4 6AW. *T:* (01895) 632390.

**DIXON, Catherine Helen;** Chief Executive, Askham Bryan College, 2017–19; *b* N Ferriby, 29 April 1966; *d* of late Kenneth Dixon and of Audrey Irene Dixon; *m* 2006, Sally Elizabeth Light, *qv. Educ:* Leeds Metropolitan Univ. (LLB Hons 1991); Coll. of Law; Open Univ. (MBA 2003). Admitted solicitor, 1994; Solicitor, Eversheds, 1997–99; Hd, Legal, 1999–2003, Commercial Dir, 2003–07, Bupa Care Services; Dir, Vancouver Coastal HA, 2007–08; Gen. Counsel and Co. Sec., NSPCC, 2009–12; Chief Executive: NHS Resolution Authy, 2012–15; Law Soc. of England and Wales, 2015–17. Trustee: PDSA, 2010–17; Stonewall, 2017–; CEDR, 2017–; York and N Yorks LEP, 2018–. Army Officer, Royal Signals (TA), 1989–96, 2010–12, now RARO. *Recreation:* cycling.

**DIXON, Sir (David) Jeremy,** Kt 2000; RIBA; architect in private practice; Principal, Dixon Jones Ltd (formerly Jeremy Dixon Edward Jones), since 1991; *b* 31 May 1939; *s* of late Joseph Lawrence Dixon and Beryl Margaret Dixon (*née* Braund); *m* 1964, Fenella Mary Anne Clemens (separated 1990); one *s* two *d*; partner, Julia Somerville, *qv. Educ:* Merchant Taylors' School; Architectural Assoc. Sch. of Architecture (AA Dip. (Hons)). Principal: Jeremy Dixon, 1975–90 (with Fenella Dixon); Jeremy Dixon BDP, 1983–90. Work includes: international competitions, first prize: Northampton County Offices, 1973; Royal Opera House, 1983; Piazzale Roma, Venice, 1990; Chelsea Barracks, 2009; other competitions won: Tate Gallery Coffee Shop and Restaurant, 1984; Study Centre, Darwin Coll., Cambridge, 1988; Robert Gordon Univ. Residence, Aberdeen, 1991; Portsmouth Univ. Science Bldg, 1993; Nat. Portrait Gallery extension, 1994; Saïd Business Sch., Oxford, 1996; Magna Carta Building, Salisbury Cathedral, 2001; Panopticon, UCL, 2001; St Peter's Arcade, Liverpool, 2001; Kings Place Develt, 2002; Exhibition Road Project, 2004; other works: reconstruction of Tatlin Tower, 1971 and at RA, 2012; London housing, St Mark's Road, 1975; Compass Point, Docklands, 1989; Henry Moore Sculpture Inst., Leeds, 1988; Sainsbury's superstore, Plymouth, 1991; Regent Palace Development, 2005. Tutor: Architectural Assoc., 1974–83; RCA, 1979–81. Chm., RIBA Regl Awards Gp, 1991–. Exhibitions: Venice Biennale, 1980, 1991; Paris, 1981; Bordeaux Chateau, Paris, 1988. Trustee, Midsummer Music, 2012–; Patron, London Chamber Music Soc., 2012–. *Recreations:* walking in English landscape, contemporary sculpture and painting, music. *Address:* (office) 2–3 Hanover Yard, Noel Road, N1 8YA. *T:* (020) 7483 8888. *E:* jeremydixon@dixonjones.co.uk.

**DIXON, David Steven; His Honour Judge Dixon;** a Circuit Judge, since 2016; *b* Sunderland, July 1970; *s* of Robert and Joan Dixon; *m* 2013, Cassie Williams. *Educ:* Billingham Campus Sch.; Bede Sixth Form Coll., Billingham; Univ. of Newcastle upon Tyne (LLB Law); Inns of Court Sch. of Law (BVC). Called to the Bar, Lincoln's Inn, 1992; a Recorder, 2012–16. *Recreations:* family, travel, good food and wine. *Address:* Sheffield Crown Court, 50 West Bar, Sheffield S3 8PH.

**DIXON, (Henry) Joly,** CMG 2004; Chairman: Fiscal Policy Panel, Jersey, 2007–16; Fiscal Policy Panel, Guernsey, 2010–11; Special Adviser to Vice President of European Commission, attached to Task Force for Greece, 2010–15; *b* 13 Jan. 1945; *s* of late Gervais Joly Dixon and Kay Dixon; *m* 1976, Mary Minch; three *s* two *d. Educ:* Shrewsbury Sch.; York Univ. Lecturer in: Econs and Stats, York Univ., 1970–72; Econs, Exeter Univ., 1972–74; European Commission, 1975–2003: Econ. Advr to Jacques Delors, 1987–92; Dir for Internat. Econ. and Financial Affairs, 1992–99; Dep. Special Rep. i/c econ. reconstruction and develt, UN Mission, Kosovo, on secondment, 1999–2001; Principal Advr, Directorate Gen. for Econ. and Financial Affairs, 2001–02; Special Advr to Pascal Lamy, EC, 2003–05; Statistics Comr, 2006–08; Sen. Advr, Office of Chief Economist, EBRD, 2007–. Associate, GPlus Europe, 2006–09. Chairman: Indirect Tax Policy Commn, Bosnia and Herzegovina, 2003–04; Governing Bd, Indirect Tax Policy Authority, Bosnia and Herzegovina, 2004–06; Strategic Adv. Bd for Intellectual Property Policy, 2008–10; Mem. Bd, Kosovo Pension Savings Trust, 2015–. Guest Scholar, Brookings Instn, Washington, 1980. Liveryman, Cordwainers' Co., 1969–. Fellow, Royal Statistical Soc., 2006. *Recreations:* gardening, photography. *Address:* 47 Clanricarde Gardens, W2 4JN. *E:* jdx@skynet.be.

**DIXON, Dr Jennifer,** CBE 2013; FFPH; Chief Executive, The Health Foundation, since 2013; *b* 25 April 1960; *m* 2002, John Simon Vorhaus; two *d. Educ:* Bristol Univ. (MB ChB); London Sch. of Hygiene and Tropical Medicine (MSc Public Health; PhD 2002). FFPH (FFPHM 1999). Harkness Fellow, Commonwealth Fund of NY, 1990–91; Sen. Registrar in Public Health and Hon. Lectr, LSHTM, 1991–95; Fellow, King's Fund Inst., 1995–98; Policy Advr to Chief Exec., NHS, 1998–2000; Dir of Policy, King's Fund, 2000–08; Chief Exec. (formerly Dir), Nuffield Trust, 2008–13. Member, Board: Audit Commn, 2004–12; Healthcare Commn, 2005–09; Care Quality Commn, 2013–16. Visiting Professor: LSE, 2009–12; Imperial Coll. Business Sch., 2009–12; LSHTM, 2010–15. Mem. Bd, Nat. Centre for Social Res., 2011–15. Hon. FRCP 2009. Hon. DSc Bristol, 2016. *Publications:* (with A. H. Harrison) The NHS: facing the future, 2000. *Recreations:* Russian literature, painting. *Address:* The Health Foundation, 8 Salisbury Square, EC4Y 8AP.

**DIXON, Sir Jeremy;** see Dixon, Sir D. J.

**DIXON, Joly;** see Dixon, H. J.

**DIXON, Sir Jonathan (Mark),** 4th Bt *cr* 1919, of Astle, Chelford, Co. Chester; *b* 1 Sept. 1949; *s* of Captain Nigel Dixon, OBE, RN (*d* 1978), and of Margaret Josephine Dixon; *S* uncle, 1990; *m* 1978, Patricia Margaret, *d* of James Baird Smith; two *s* one *d. Educ:* Winchester Coll.; University Coll., Oxford (MA). *Recreation:* fishing. *Heir: s* Mark Edward Dixon, *b* 29 June 1982.

**DIXON, Kenneth Herbert Morley,** CBE 1996; DL; Chairman: Joseph Rowntree Foundation, 2001–04; Rowntree (formerly Rowntree Mackintosh) plc, 1981–89, retired; Vice-Chairman, Legal & General Group, 1986–94 (Director, 1984–94); Deputy Chairman, Bass, 1990–96 (Director, 1988–96); *b* 19 Aug. 1929; *yr s* of Arnold Moore Dixon and Mary Jolly; *m* 1955, Patricia Oldbury Whalley; two *s. Educ:* Cathedral Sch., Shanghai; Cranbrook Sch., Sydney, Australia; Manchester Univ. (BA(Econ) 1952); Harvard Business Sch. (AMP 1969). Lieut Royal Signals, 1947–49. Calico Printers Assoc., 1952–56; joined Rowntree & Co. Ltd, 1956; Dir, 1970; Chm., UK Confectionery Div., 1973–78; Dep. Chm., 1978–81. Dir, Yorkshire-Tyne Tees (formerly Yorks) TV Hldgs, 1989–97; Mem., British Railways Bd, 1990–97. Member: Council, Incorporated Soc. of British Advertisers, 1971–79; Council, Cocoa, Chocolate and Confectionery Alliance, 1972–79; Council, Advertising Assoc., 1976–79; BIM Econ. and Social Affairs Cttee, 1980–84; Council, CBI, 1981–90 (Mem., Companies Cttee, 1979–84; Mem., Employment Policy Cttee, 1983–90); Governing Council, Business in the Community, 1983–90; Council, Food from Britain, 1986–89; Exec. Cttee, Food and Drink Fedn, 1986–89 (Mem. Council, 1986–87); Council for Industry and Higher Educn, 1986–97; Council, Nat. Forum for Management Educn & Develt, 1987–96; HEQC (Chm., Quality Audit Steering Council, 1993–97); Chm., Cttee of Univ. Chairmen, 1998–2000. Chm., Food Assoc., 1986. Trustee: York Civic Trust, 1996–2013; Joseph Rowntree Foundn, 1996–2004 (Dep. Chm., 1998); Nat. Centre for Early Music, 2010–. Treas., York Archaeol Trust, 1993–97. Mem. Council, York Univ., 1983–2001 (Chm., 1990–2001), Pro-Chancellor, 1987–2001; Mem. Adv. Gp, Business History Unit, LSE, 1981–2013 (Chm., 2000–10); Chm., Vis. Cttee, Open Univ., 1990–92. FRSA; CCMI. Member: Co. of Merchant Adventurers, 1981–; Co. of Merchant Taylors, 1981–. DL N Yorks, 1991. Morrell Fellow, Univ. of York, 2007. DUniv: York, 1993; Open, 1997. *Recreations:* reading, music, fell walking. *Address:* Joseph Rowntree Foundation, The Homestead, Water End, York YO30 6WP. *T:* (01904) 615901. *Club:* Reform.

**DIXON, Sir Michael,** Kt 2014; DPhil; DL; Director, The Natural History Museum, since 2004; *b* 16 March 1956; *s* of late Walter Dixon and Sonia Ivy Dixon (*née* Doidge); *m* 1st, 1988, Richenda Milton-Thompson (marr. diss. 1999); one *s* one *d*; 2nd, 2001, Deborah Mary Reece (*née* McMahon); one *s. Educ:* Tiffin Boys' Sch., Kingston-upon-Thames; Imperial Coll., London (BSc; ARCS); Univ. of York (DPhil 1984). Sponsoring Ed., Pitman Publishing Ltd, 1980–83; Publisher, then Publishing Dir, John Wiley & Sons Ltd, 1983–96; Man. Dir, Thomson Sci. Europe, 1996–98; Gp Man. Dir, Sweet & Maxwell Ltd, 1998–99; Dir Gen., Zool Soc. of London, 2000–04. Chief Scientific Advr, 2006–07, Chm., Sci. and Res. Adv. Cttee, 2009–14, DCMS. Non-exec. Dir, British Geological Survey, 2018–. Trustee: Internat. Trust for Zool Nomenclature, 2004–14 (Chm., 2008–14); WWF-UK, 2014–. Mem. Council, Royal Albert Hall, 2004–; Member of Court: Imperial Coll., London, 2005– (Chm., Res. Ethics Cttee, 2009–); Univ. of Reading, 2007–. Chm., Nat. Mus. Dirs Council (formerly Conf.), 2009–13; Co-Chair, Exhibition Road Cultural Gp, 2017–. Gov., Powell-Cotton Mus., 2008–12. DL Gtr London, 2017. FCGI 2012. Hon. DSc Imperial Coll. London 2015. *Recreations:* natural history, photography, music. *Address:* The Natural History Museum, Cromwell Road, SW7 5BD. *Club:* Chelsea Arts.

**DIXON, Michael David,** LVO 2015; OBE 2001; General Practitioner; Chairman, NHS Alliance, 1998–2015; *b* 12 May 1952; *s* of Anthony Neville Dixon and Hazel Dixon; *m* 1982, Joanna Withers-Lancashire; one *s* two *d. Educ:* Eton Coll.; Exeter Coll., Oxford (MA Hons 1973); Guy's Medical Sch. (MB BS 1979). LRCP 1979; DRCOG, MRCOG 1984; FRCGP 2001. House Surgeon, Royal Devon and Exeter Hosp., 1979; House Physician, Guy's Hosp., 1980; Exeter GP Vocational Trng Scheme, 1980–84; GP, College Surgery, Cullompton, 1984–. Chm. NHS Nat. Life Check Bd, 2007–10; Pres., 2012–14, Sen. Advr, 2014–, NHS Clinical Comrs; Nat. Clin. Champion for Social Prescription, NHS England, 2016–. Med. Advr to the Prince of Wales, 2008–. Hon. Sen. Fellow, Sch. of Public Policy, Univ. of Birmingham, 2004–; Sen. Associate, 2005–14, Sen. Advr, 2011–14, King's Fund; Hon. Sen. Lectr in Integrated Health, Peninsula Med. Sch., 2005–; Visiting Professor: Univ. of Westminster, 2006–; UCL, 2012–. Trustee, 2003–, Med. Dir, 2008–, Prince's Foundn for Integrated Health. Chm. Council, Coll. of Medicine, 2010–. Pres., Guild of Health Writers, 2010–13. *Publications:* (ed jtly) The Locality Commissioning Handbook, 1998; (ed with Kieran Sweeney) The Human Effect in Medicine, 2000; (ed with Kieran Sweeney) A Practical Guide to Primary Care Groups and Trusts, 2001; contrib. articles in all main med. jls. *Recreations:* fishing, gardening, writing, philosophy. *Address:* College Surgery Partnership, Culm Valley Integrated Centre for Health, Willand Road, Cullompton, Devon EX15 1FE. *T:* (01884) 831300. *Clubs:* Royal Society of Medicine, National Liberal.

**DIXON, Sir Peter (John Bellett),** Kt 2009; Chairman, Diabetes UK, since 2013; *b* 18 May 1945; *s* of Hugh and Mildred Dixon; *m* 1967, Judith Ann Duckworth (*d* 2019); one *s* one *d* (and one *d* decd). *Educ:* Caterham Sch., Surrey; Corpus Christi Coll., Cambridge (MA); London Business Sch. (MSc). Asst Dir, Edward Bates & Sons Ltd, 1975–77; Managing Director: Metal Pretreatments Ltd, 1977–86; Turner Curzon Ltd, 1979–86; British Pepper & Spice Co. Ltd, 1981–83; Hd, Capital Markets, Den norske Bank, 1986–90; Chairman: Ketlon Ltd, 1991–93; Welpac PLC, 1994–95; Union Discount Ltd, 1997–2001; Manifest Voting Agency Ltd, 1998–2005. Chairman: Enfield and Haringey HA, 1998–2001; UCL Hosps NHS Foundn Trust (formerly NHS Trust), 2001–10; Office of Public Mgt, 2007–12; Colchester Hospital Univ. NHS Foundn Trust, 2009–10; Basildon and Thurrock Univ. Hosps, 2011–12; Pharmaceutical Services Negotiating Cttee, 2011–15; Barking, Havering and Redbridge Univ. Hosps, 2012–14; Anglia Ruskin Health Partnership, 2012–17; Imperial Coll. Health Partners, 2014–18; SE Coast Ambulance Service NHS Foundn Trust, 2016–17. Lay Mem., Inf. Tribunal, 2003–12. Chairman: Housing Corp., 2003–08; Optivo Housing Assoc., 2017–; Dir, Quintain Estates and Develt plc, 2010–16; Board Member: New Islington and Hackney Housing Assoc., 1976–98 (Chm., 1995–98); Focus Housing Gp, 1996–97; English Churches Housing Gp, 2000–01; London & Quadrant Housing Trust, 2001–03; Mem. Council, NHS Confedn, 1998–2008 (Trustee, 2002–08); Pres., English Rural Housing Assoc., 2009–. Member: Broads Authy, 2010–18 (Vice-Chair, 2015–18); Nat. Parks Partnerships, 2016–18. *Recreations:* sailing, mountains, music, theatre. *Address:* The Smea, Hickling, Norfolk NR12 0YL. *T:* (office) (020) 7226 2011. *E:* peterjbdixon@hotmail.com.

**DIXON, Dr Philip Willis,** FSA, FRHistS; Director, Philip Dixon Associates, archaeological consultancy, since 2003; Reader in Archaeology, University of Nottingham, 1996–2003; *b* 2 Jan. 1945; *s* of Dr C. Willis Dixon and Marjorie Dixon (*née* Harbron); *m* 1st, 1968, Doris Janet Davenport Sisson (marr. diss. 1973); 2nd, 1979, Patricia Borne (*d* 1987); 3rd, 2001, Jan White (*née* Greenwood). *Educ:* Tiffin Sch.; New Coll., Oxford (MA 1971; DPhil 1976). FSA 1977; FRHistS 1995. Lectr, 1972–81, Sen. Lectr, 1981–96, Nottingham Univ. Vis. Prof., Univ. of Aarhus, Denmark, 1997, 2006. Comr, Cathedrals Fabric Commn, 1996–2006. Sec., 1981–95, Pres., 1995–98, Council for British Archaeol.; Vice Pres., Royal Archaeol Inst., 2008–11. Director of excavations: Crickley Hill, Glos,

1969–96; Greenwich Palace, 1970–71; Richmond Palace, 1972, and other sites. Archaeologist: for Cathedrals of Southwell and Leicester, and for Selby Abbey; Archaeologist Emeritus for Cathedrals of Ely and Lincoln. *Publications:* Excavations at Greenwich Palace, 1972; Barbarian Europe, 1976; Crickley Hill: the Defences, 1994, the Hillfort Settlement, 2004; Knights and Castles, 2007; Southwell Minster, 2009; Lincoln Cathedral: the Romanesque frieze, 2010; (with Jane Kennedy): Mont Orgueil Castle: a review, 2001; Mont Orgueil Castle, 2002; contrib. numerous articles to learned jls. *Recreations:* visiting places, photographing them and consuming their food and drink. *Address:* Castle End, Dunstanburgh Road, Craster, Alnwick, Northumberland NE66 3TT. *T:* (01665) 576064; 83 London Road, New Balderton, Newark, Notts NG24 3AA. *T:* (01636) 659464.

**DIXON, Prof. Raymond Alan,** DPhil; FRS 1999; Head, Department of Molecular Microbiology, John Innes Centre, 2010–12, Project Leader, since 2014 (Emeritus Fellow, 2012–13); Director, CAS-JIC Centre for Excellence in Plant and Microbial Sciences, Beijing, since 2015; *b* 1 Dec. 1947; *s* of late Henry George Dixon and Emily Dixon (*née* Emmins); *m* 1st, 1971, Ing-Britt Maj Wennerhag (marr. diss. 1980); one *d*; 2nd, 1985, Greta Margaret Dunne (marr. diss. 1995). *Educ:* Univ. of Reading (BSc 1st cl. Hons Microbiology 1969); Univ. of Sussex (DPhil Microbial Genetics 1972). University of Sussex: Postdoctoral Res. Fellow, 1973–75; Higher Scientific Officer, 1975–76, SSO, 1976–78, PSO, 1978–87, SPSO, 1987–95, Unit of Nitrogen Fixation; Res. Gp Leader, Nitrogen Fixation Lab. and Dept of Molecular Microbiol., John Innes Centre, 1995–2009. Hon. Prof., UEA, 1998–. Mem., EMBO, 1987. Fleming Medal, Soc. for Gen. Microbiology, 1984. *Publications:* numerous articles in learned jls. *Recreations:* music, various outdoor pursuits. *Address:* Department of Molecular Microbiology, John Innes Centre, Norwich NR4 7UH. *T:* (01603) 450747.

**DIXON, Prof. Richard Newland,** PhD, ScD; FRS 1986; CChem, FRSC; Senior Research Fellow, 1996–2016, and Alfred Capper Pass Professor of Chemistry, 1990–96, now Emeritus Professor, University of Bristol; *b* 25 Dec. 1930; *s* of late Robert Thomas Dixon and Lilian Dixon; *m* 1954, Alison Mary Birks; one *s* two *d*. *Educ:* The Judd Sch., Tonbridge; King's Coll., Univ. of London (BSc 1951); St Catharine's Coll., Univ. of Cambridge (PhD 1955; ScD 1976). FRSC 1976; CChem 1976. Scientific Officer, UKAEA, 1954–56; Res. Associate, Univ. of Western Ontario, 1956–57; Postdoctoral Fellow, NRCC, Ottawa, 1957–59; ICI Fellow, Univ. of Sheffield, 1959–60, Lectr in Chem., 1960–69; Bristol University: Prof. and Hd of Dept of Theoretical Chemistry, 1969–90; Dean, Faculty of Science, 1979–82; Pro-Vice-Chancellor, 1989–92. Sorby Res. Fellow, Royal Soc., 1964–69; Vis. Schol., Stanford Univ., 1982–83. Leverhulme Emeritus Fellow, 1996–99. Hallam Lectr, Univ. of Wales, 1988; Harkins Lectr, Univ. of Chicago, 1994. Mem. Council, Faraday Div., RSC, 1985–98, Vice-Pres., 1989–98; Mem., and Chm. sub-cttee, Laser Facility Cttee, 1987–90, and Mem., Physical Chem. Cttee, 1987–90, SERC. Non-exec. Dir, United Bristol Healthcare NHS Trust, 1994–2003 (Vice-Chm., 1995–2003). Trustee, Charitable Trusts for United Bristol Hosps, 2003–11 (Chm., 2006–11). Corday-Morgan Medal and Prize, Chemical Soc., 1968; Spectroscopy Medal, RSC, 1985; Liversidge Lectr and Medal, RSC, 1993–94; Rumford Medal, Royal Soc., 2004. *Publications:* Spectroscopy and Structure, 1965; Theoretical Chemistry: Vol. 1, 1974, Vol. 2, 1975, Vol. 3, 1978; numerous articles in res. jls of chemistry and physics. *Recreations:* mountain walking, travel, theatre, concerts. *Address:* 22 Westbury Lane, Bristol BS9 2PE. *T:* (0117) 968 1691; School of Chemistry, The University, Bristol BS8 1TS. *E:* r.n.dixon@bris.ac.uk.

**DIXON, Dr Sarah Elizabeth Ann;** Pro Vice-Chancellor International, University of Leicester, 2016–18; *b* Stafford, 21 Nov. 1953; *d* of Aubrey Lacey Parsons and Kathleen Helen Parsons; one *s*. *Educ:* Univ. of Bradford (BA Hons Russian and German 1976); Chartered Inst. of Marketing (DipM 1983); Kingston Univ. (MBA Dist. 2002; PGCert Teaching and Learning in HE 2003); Henley Management Coll. (DBA 2006). Royal Dutch Shell Group: product mgt, mktg asst, translator and interpreter, 1976–86; Petrochemicals Manager, Austria, 1986–89; Area Manager, Petrochemicals, USSR and Poland, 1989–92; Chemicals Manager, Russia, 1992–96; Business Strategist, 1996–97; Mergers and Acquisitions Manager, 1998–2000; Vice Pres., DeWitt & Co. Inc., 2000–03; Dir, Postgrad. Progs, Principal Lectr, Sen. Lectr in Strategy, Faculty of Business and Law, Kingston Univ., 2002–08; Hd, MSc Progs and Sen. Lectr in Strategy, Univ. of Bath, 2008–10; Dean, Bradford Univ. Sch. of Mgt, 2010–12; Prof. of Strategic Mgt and Dean, XJTLU Business Sch., Xi'an Jiaotong-Liverpool Univ., China, 2013–16. Director: Albany Dixon Ltd, 2000–03; Kingston Strategy Consulting, 2006–11. *Publications:* Organisational Transformation in the Russian Oil Industry, 2008; contrib. Jl of Mgt Studies, Human Relations, Jl of Change Mgt, Leadership and Organisational Develt Jl. *Recreations:* walking, jogging, cycling, theatre, reading, travel.

**DIXON-SMITH,** family name of **Baron Dixon-Smith.**

**DIXON-SMITH, Baron** *cr* 1993 (Life Peer), of Bocking in Essex; **Robert William Dixon-Smith;** DL; farmer, since 1958; *b* 30 Sept. 1934; 2nd *s* of Dixon Smith, Braintree, Essex and Winifred Smith (*née* Stratton); Dixon Smith adopted by Deed Poll as surname, 1961; *m* 1960, Georgina Janet, *d* of George Cook, Halstead, Essex and Kathleen Cook; one *s* one *d*. *Educ:* Oundle; Writtle Coll. Nat. Service, 2nd Lt, King's Dragoon Guards, 1955–57. Member: Essex CC, 1965–93 (Chm., 1986–89); Association of County Councils, 1983–93 (Chm., 1992–93). Member: H of L EC Cttee sub-cttee C (Envmt), 1994–96; H of L Select Cttee on Sci. and Technol., 1994–98. Opposition spokesman, House of Lords: on local govt, 1998–2001, on home affairs, 2001–02, on envmtl affairs, 2003–07, on communities and local govt, 2007–09. Member: Local Govt Management Bd, 1991–93; Council, Essex Univ., 1991–94; Chm., Anglia Polytechnic Univ., 1992–93. Governor, Writtle Coll., 1967–94 (Chm., 1973–85; Fellow, 1993). Hon. Dr Anglia Poly. Univ., 1995. Freeman, City of London, 1988; Liveryman, Farmers' Co., 1991. DL Essex, 1986. *Recreations:* shooting, fishing, golf. *Address:* Sun House, Long Melford, Suffolk CO10 9HZ.

**DIXON-WOODS, Prof. Mary,** DPhil; FMedSci; FAcSS; Health Foundation Professor of Healthcare Improvement Studies, University of Cambridge, since 2018 (RAND Professor of Health Services Research, 2016–18); Fellow, Homerton College, Cambridge, since 2016; *b* Athlone, Ireland, 11 Dec. 1966; *d* of Patrick Dixon and Maire Dixon; *m* 1996, William Woods; one *d*. *Educ:* Our Lady's Bower, Athlone; Nat. Inst. for Higher Educn, Dublin (BA Communications Studies 1988); Trinity Coll., Dublin (DipStat 1990); Linacre Coll., Oxford (MSc Soc. Res. and Soc. Policy 1991); Nuffield Coll., Oxford (DPhil Soc. Studies 1997). Civil servant, Dept of Energy, Ireland, 1985–89; proj. leader, Dublin City Univ., 1989–90; Res. Fellow, Oxford Regl Postgrad. Office, 1991–94; University of Leicester: Lectr, 1994–2002; Sen. Lectr, 2002–06; Reader, 2006–07; Prof. of Medical Sociology, 2007–16. Adjunct Professor: Johns Hopkins Univ., 2011–; Dartmouth Coll., 2015–16; Vis. Prof., Imperial Coll. London, 2012–15. Sen. Investigator, NIHR, 2018–. Dist. Vis. Fellow, QMUL, 2007. FAcSS 2011; FMedSci 2015; Hon. FRCP 2018; Hon. FRCGP 2018. Co-Editor-in-Chief, BMJ Quality and Safety, 2018– (Dep. Editor-in-Chief, 2012–18). *Publications:* contribs to learned jls on quality and safety in healthcare, ethics of care and res., and methodological innovations. *Recreations:* family, friends, books.

*Address:* Healthcare Improvement Studies Institute, University of Cambridge, Biomedical Campus, Clifford Allbutt Building, Cambridge CB2 0AH. *T:* (01223) 761556. *E:* md753@medschl.cam.ac.uk. *Club:* Royal Society of Medicine.

**DIXSON, Maurice Christopher Scott,** DPhil; FRAeS; Executive Chairman, Cranfield Aerospace Ltd, 2003–10; Chairman, Southside Thermal Sciences Ltd, 2004–12 (non-executive Director, since 2004); *b* 5 Nov. 1941; *s* of late Herbert George Muns Dixson and Elizabeth Eileen Dixson; *m* 1965, Anne Beverley Morris. *Educ:* Palmers Grammar Sch.; University Coll., Swansea (BA Jt Hons); Carleton Univ., Ottawa (MA); Pembroke Coll., Oxford (DPhil). Commercial Exec., Hawker Siddeley Aviation, 1969–74; Contracts Manager, Export, later Commercial Manager, Export, Mil. Aircraft Div., BAC, 1974–80; British Aerospace: Warton Division: Div. Commercial Manager, 1980–81; Exec. Dir, Contracts, 1981–83; Divl Commercial Dir, 1983–86; Military Aircraft Division: Dir-in-Charge, Saudi Arabian Ops, March–Aug. 1986; Commercial Dir and Dir-in-Charge, Saudi Arabian Ops, 1986–87; Chief Exec., Royal Ordnance PLC, 1987–88; Man. Dir, British Aerospace (Commercial Aircraft), 1988–90; Supervisory Man. Dir, Electronic Metrology and Components Groups, and Main Bd Dir, GEC, 1990–93; Chief Exec., Simon Engineering, then Simon Gp, 1993–2002; Dir, Higgs & Hill, then Swan Hill plc, 1994–2003. Chm., Kington Langley Parish Council, 2008–. Mem. Ct, Cranfield Univ., 2010–. *Recreations:* played representative soccer at school and university, supporter of Tottenham Hotspur Football Club, fishing, shooting, sport, fine arts, politics and current affairs. *Address:* The Poundhouse, Middle Common, Kington Langley, Chippenham, Wilts SN15 5NW. *Club:* Royal Automobile.

**DJANOGLY, Sir Harry Ari Simon,** Kt 1993; CBE 1983; Chairman, Coats plc (formerly Coats Viyella), 1999–2003; *b* 1 Aug. 1938. Former Man. Dir and Dep. Chm., Vantona Viyella; Dir, 1987–2003, Dep. Chm., 1999–2003, Singer & Friedlander; former Chm., Nottingham Manufacturing Co. Ltd. Non-exec. Dir, Carpetright plc, 1993–2005. Patron and Trustee, Djanogly City Acad., Nottingham; Patron, Djanogly Learning Resource Centre, Nottingham Univ.

**DJANOGLY, Jonathan Simon;** MP (C) Huntingdon, since 2001; *b* 3 June 1965; *s* of Sir Harry Djanogly, *qv* and Lady Djanogly; *m* 1991, Rebecca Silk; one *s* one *d*. *Educ:* University Coll. Sch.; Oxford Poly. (BA Hons); Guildford Law Sch. Admitted solicitor, 1990; Partner, S J Berwin LLP, 1998–2009. Chm., Pembroke VCT plc, 2012–. Mem. (C) Westminster LBC, 1994–2001. Contested (C) Oxford East, 1997. Shadow Minister, Constitutional, Legal and Home affairs, 2004–05; Shadow Solicitor Gen., and Shadow Trade and Industry Minister, 2005–10; Parly Under-Sec. of State, MoJ, 2010–12. Member: Trade and Industry Select Cttee, 2001–05; Cttee on Exiting the EU, 2017–; Chm., All-Party Parly Gp on Corporate Governance, 2015–, on Corporate Responsibility, 2015–, on Legal and Constitutional Affairs, 2017–. Chm., British Shooting Sports Council, 2017–. Trustee, Cromwell Mus. Trust, 2016–. *Recreations:* sports, arts. *Address:* House of Commons, SW1A 0AA. *T:* (020) 7219 2367.

**DLHOPOLČEK, František,** PhD; Ambassador of Slovakia to Kenya, since 2016; *b* 13 Sept. 1953; *s* of Jozef Dlhopolček and Anna Pončková; *m* 1977, Dagmar Izraelova; one *s* one *d*. *Educ:* Sch. of Econs, Banská Bystrica, Czechoslovakia; Diplomatic Acad., Moscow (PhD History and Politology 1989). Univ. Asst Lectr, Sch. of Econs, Banská Bystrica, 1977–79; joined Federal Ministry of Foreign Affairs, Czechoslovakia, 1979: Nairobi, 1979–83; African Dept, 1983–84; Office of Minister of Foreign Affairs, 1984–87; Dept of Arab and Africa Countries, 1989–90; Dir, African Dept, 1990–91; Consul-Gen., Pretoria, 1991–92; Ambassador of Czech and Slovak Fed. Republic (subseq. of Slovak Republic) to RSA, 1992–93; Dir-Gen., Political Affairs, Min. of Foreign Affairs, 1993–94; Ambassador to Israel, 1994–98; Political Dir Gen., Min. of Foreign Affairs, 1998–2000; Ambassador to UK, 2000–05; Deputy Sec. Gen. and Dir of Human Resources, 2005–07, Dir, Dept of Central and N Europe, 2007–10, Min. of Foreign Affairs; Ambassador to China, 2010–15. *Address:* c/o Ministry of Foreign Affairs, Hlboká 2, 83336 Bratislava, Slovak Republic.

**DOBBIE, Dr Robert Charles,** CB 1996; Regional Director, Government Office for the North East, 1998–2001; *b* 16 Jan. 1942; *s* of Scott U. Dobbie and Isobel M. Dobbie (*née* Jamieson); *m* 1st, 1964, Elizabeth Barbour (marr. diss. 2013); three *s*; 2nd, 2013, Susan Clayton (*née* Beale). *Educ:* Univ. of Edinburgh (BSc); Univ. of Cambridge (PhD). Res. Fellow, Univ. of Alberta, 1966–67; ICI Res. Fellow, Univ. of Bristol, 1967–68; Lectr in Inorganic Chemistry, Univ. of Newcastle upon Tyne, 1968–76; sabbatical, California State Univ., LA, 1974; Tutor, Open Univ., 1975–85; Principal, DTI, 1976–83; Asst Sec., Dept of Industry, 1983–90; Under Sec., DTI, 1990–97; Dir, Merseyside Task Force, 1990–92 (seconded to DoE); Head, Competitiveness Unit (formerly Industrial Competitiveness Div.), DTI, 1992–97. Vis. Prof., Univ. of Newcastle upon Tyne, 2002–04. *Publications:* on inorganic and organometallic chemistry. *Recreations:* theatre, hill walking, malt whisky. *Address:* 1 Oak Hill Park, NW3 7LB.

See also S. J. Dobbie.

**DOBBIE, Scott Jamieson,** CBE 1998; Senior Advisor, Deutsche Bank AG, London, since 1999; Chairman, Securities and Investment Institute (formerly Securities Institute), 2000–09; *b* 24 July 1939; *s* of Scott U. Dobbie and Isobel M. Dobbie (*née* Jamieson); *m* 1962, Brenda M. Condie; two *d*. *Educ:* Dollar Acad.; Univ. of Edinburgh (BSc). Industrial mktg, Unilever, 1961–66, and ICI, 1966–72; Wood Mackenzie & Co., stockbrokers, 1972–88: Partner, 1975–82; Man. Partner, 1982–88; acquired by NatWest Securities, 1988: Man. Dir, 1988–93; Chm., 1993–98; acquired by Bankers Trust Internat., 1998–99 (Vice-Chm.). Chairman: CRESTCo Ltd, 1996–2001; Standard Life European Private Equity Trust, 2001–13; Edinburgh Investment Trust PLC, 2003–11 (non-exec. Dir, 1998–2002); non-executive Director: Murray VCT4 plc, 2000–03; Premier Oil plc, 2000–08; Scottish Financial Enterprise, 2001–05; FRESCO SICAV, 2001–03; QCA, later QCDA, 2009–12. Director: SFA, 1993–2001; Financial Services NTO, 2001–04; Comr, Jersey Financial Services Commn, 1999–2008; Mem., Regulatory Decisions Cttee, FSA, 2001–05. Ind. Mem., Standards Cttee, Corp. of London, 2001–09 (Chm., 2007–09). Liveryman, Clockmakers' Co., 2010. Hon. DSc City, 2009. *Recreations:* mechanical objects, books. *Address:* Deutsche Bank AG London, Winchester House, 1 Great Winchester Street, EC2N 2DB. *E:* scott.dobbie@db.com.

See also R. C. Dobbie.

**DOBBIN, (Timothy) David,** CBE 2005; Group Chief Executive, United Dairy Farmers Ltd, 2000–16; Chairman, Belfast Harbour, since 2015 (Member, Board, since 2012); *b* 1 May 1955; *s* of George and Phoebe Dobbin; *m* 1977, Pauline Gregg; two *s*. *Educ:* Grosvenor Grammar Sch., Belfast; Queen's Univ., Belfast (BSc 1st cl. Hons Mech Engrg). Cert. of Professional Competence in Nat. Road Haulage Ops. CEng, MIMechE 1983. Manufg Manager, Rothmans Internat., 1977–83; Gen. Manager, Northern Publishing Office, 1983–85; Ops Dir, Cantrell & Cochrane, 1985–89; Regl Dir, Dalgety Agriculture, 1989–95; Gp Develt Dir, Boxmore Internat. plc, 1995–2000. Dir, Medevol, 2002–10. Non-executive Director: CBI, 2005–08 (Chm., CBI NI, 2003–05); Strategic Investment Bd, 2005–13 (Chm., 2009–13); Mem. Adv. Bd, BT Ireland, 2007–09; Mem. Bd, Invest NI, 2008–14; Mem., NI Adv. Bd, KPMG, 2016–. Vice Chm. and Dir, Belfast Port Employers Assoc., 1989–94; Pres. and Exec. Mem., NI Grain Trade Assoc., 1989–95; Director: Food and Drink Industry Trng Adv. Council NI, 1992–95; LEDU, 1998–2002; Investment

Belfast, 1998–2002; Dairy UK and NI Dairy Council, 2002– (Vice Chm., 2013–15; Chm., 2015–17); NI Food and Drink Assoc., 2002–17 (Chm., 2014–17); Chairman: NI Quality Centre, 1995–97; NI Agricl Res. Council, 1997–2000; Intertrade Ireland, 2007–11; UK Internat. Dairy Fedn, 2007–09; Member: NI Water Council, 1986–92; Food from Britain Council, 2003–09. Expert to Agricultural Markets Taskforce, EU Commn, 2015–16. Chm., Sentinus, 1995–2003; Trustee, Prince's Trust, 2005–09 (Chm., Prince's Trust NI, 2005–09). Mem., Senate, QUB, 2007–14. Vice Chm., Ire. and NI bid for 2023 Rugby World Cup, 2016–18. FInstD 2009. Hon. DScEcon QUB, 2005. Hon. Chinese Citizenship, Kunshan City, 1998. Lunn's Award for Excellence, 2008, Large NI Company Dir of the Year, 2012, IoD. *Recreations:* Ulster Rugby (Chm., 2010–17), golf, boating, gardening, music, Irish art. *Clubs:* Farmers; Ulster Reform; Knock Golf.

**DOBBIN, Rev. Dr Victor,** CB 2000; MBE 1980; Chaplain General to the Forces, 1995–2000; *b* 12 March 1943; *s* of late Vincent Dobbin and Annie Dobbin (*née* Doherty); *m* 1967, Rosemary Gault; one *s* one *d*. *Educ:* Trinity Coll., Dublin (MA 1967); Queen's Univ., Belfast (MTh 1979; PhD 1984). Asst Minister, Rosemary Presbyterian Ch, Belfast, 1970–72; joined RAChD, 1972; Dep. Warden, RAChD Centre, 1982–86; Sen. Chaplain, 3rd Armd Div., 1986–89; Staff Chaplain, HQ BAOR, 1989–91; Sen. Chaplain, SE Dist, 1991–93; Asst Chaplain Gen., Southern Dist, 1993–94. QHC 1993–2000. Mem., Council of Reference, Barnabas Fund, 1998–. Hon. DD Presbyterian Theol Faculty, Ireland, 1995. *Recreations:* golf, walking, cycling, reading. *Address:* Glenview, 20 Cushendall Road, Bonamargy, Ballycastle, Co. Antrim, N Ireland BT54 6QR.

**DOBBS,** family name of **Baron Dobbs.**

**DOBBS, Baron** *cr* 2010 (Life Peer), of Wylye in the County of Wiltshire; **Michael John Dobbs;** novelist, dramatist and parliamentarian; *b* Nov. 1948; *s* of Eric William Dobbs and Eileen Dobbs; *m*; four *s*. *Educ:* Christ Church, Oxford (MA); Fletcher School of Law and Diplomacy, USA (PhD, MALD, MA). Govt Special Adviser, 1981–87; Chief of Staff, Conservative Party, 1986–87; Dep. Chm., Saatchi & Saatchi, 1983–86, 1988–91; Jt Dep. Chm., Cons. Party, 1994–95. Non-exec. Dir, M&C Saatchi, 2015–. Vis. Prof. of Contemporary Politics, Fletcher Sch. of Law and Diplomacy, 2017. Presenter, Despatch Box, BBC, 1999–2001; Exec. Producer, TV series, House of Cards, 2013–18. Lifetime Achievement Award: Political Book Awards, 2014; Tufts Univ., 2014; P. T. Barnum Excellence in Entertainment Award, 2014; Blenheim Prize, Internat. Churchill Soc., 2017. *Publications:* House of Cards, 1989 (televised, 1990, US version, 2013–); Wall Games, 1990; Last Man to Die, 1991; To Play the King, 1992 (televised, 1993); The Touch of Innocents, 1994; The Final Cut, 1995 (televised, 1995); Goodfellowe MP, 1996; The Buddha of Brewer Street, 1998; Whispers of Betrayal, 2000; Winston's War, 2002; Never Surrender, 2003 (Benjamin Franklin Award, 2008); Churchill's Hour, 2004; Churchill's Triumph, 2005; First Lady, 2006; The Lord's Day, 2007; The Edge of Madness, 2008; The Turning Point (play), 2009; A Family Affair (play), 2009; The Reluctant Hero, 2010; Old Enemies, 2011; A Sentimental Traitor, 2012; A Ghost at the Door, 2013. *Recreations:* genealogy, walking. *Address:* House of Lords, SW1A 0PW. *W:* www.michaeldobbs.com. *Club:* Royal Automobile.

**DOBBS, Hon. Dame Linda (Penelope),** DBE 2004; legal consultant, since 2013; a Judge of the High Court of Justice, Queen's Bench Division, 2004–13; a Deputy High Court Judge, since 2013; *b* 3 Jan. 1951; *m* (marr. diss.). *Educ:* Univ. of Surrey (BSc 1976); London School of Economics and Political Science (LLM 1977; PhD 1980). Called to the Bar, Gray's Inn, 1981, Bencher, 2002; QC 1998; in practice at the Bar, 1982–2004. Acting Judge, Grand Cayman, 2013–; Mem., Panel of Appeal Ct Judges, Turks and Caicos, 2016–. Judicial Comr, Investigatory Powers Commn, 2017–. Chm., Criminal Bar Assoc., 2003–04. Pres., International Lawyers for Africa, 2014–18 (Mem., Adv. Bd, 2010–14); Member, Advisory Board: Protimos, 2011–; I-ProBono, 2014–. Ind. Assessor of Compensation for Miscarriages of Justice, 2016–; Bonavero Inst. of Human Rights, 2018–. Trustee: Oxford Sch. of Drama, 2006–16; Internat. Law Book Facility, 2009–14 (Patron, 2015–); Patron: African Prisons Proj., 2008–; Lotte Bette-Priddy Educn Trust, 2008–; Masiphumele Trust, 2010–; BLD Foundn, 2012–; Pinotage Youth Develt Acad., 2013–; Alison Wetherfield Foundn, 2013–14; Make it Happen in Sierra Leone, 2013–. Mem., Ct of Govs, 2006–15, Chm., Ethics Policy Cttee, 2012–15, LSE. Hon. Fellow, London South Bank Univ., 2017. DUniv: Sheffield Hallam, 2006; Surrey, 2010; Hon. LLD: City, 2008; Coll. of Law, 2009; BPP University Coll., 2010. *Publications:* (with M. Lucraft) Road Traffic Law and Practice, 1993, 3rd edn 1995; (Contrib. Ed.) Archbold, 1997–; (Consultant Ed.) Fraud: law, practice and procedure, 2004–15. *Recreations:* reading, music, theatre, travel, food and wine.

**DOBKIN, His Honour Ian James;** a Circuit Judge, 1995–2010; *b* 8 June 1948; *s* of Morris Dobkin, dental surgeon, Leeds, and Rhoda Dobkin; *m* 1980, Andrea, *d* of Jack and Rose Dante; two *s*. *Educ:* Leeds Grammar Sch.; Queen's Coll., Oxford (Hastings Exhibnr in Classics; BA Jurisp. 1970; MA 1974). Called to the Bar, Gray's Inn, 1971; barrister, North Eastern Circuit, 1971–95; Asst Recorder, 1986–90; Recorder, 1990–95; Liaison Judge, Leeds Area Magistrates' Courts, 2002–07. Judicial Mem., W Yorks Probation Bd, 2002–08. Mem., Adv. Cttee, Centre for Criminal Justice Studies, Univ. of Leeds, 1987–. United Hebrew Congregation, Leeds: Vice-Pres., 1981–84 and 1992–96; Pres., 1984–88, 1996–99 and 2005–06; Hon. Life Vice-Pres., 2003; Vice-Chm., Leeds Hillel Foundn, 1989–2009. Contested (C) Penistone, July 1978, gen. election, 1979. *Recreations:* crosswords, reading, music. *Clubs:* Moor Allerton Golf (Leeds); Yorkshire County Cricket.

**DOBLE, Denis Henry;** HM Diplomatic Service, retired; Consul-General, Amsterdam, 1991–96; *b* 2 Oct. 1936; *s* of Percy Claud Doble and Dorothy Grace (*née* Petley); *m* 1975, Patricia Ann Robinson; one *d* one *s*. *Educ:* Dover Grammar School; New College, Oxford (MA Modern Hist.). RAF, 1955–57. Colonial Office, 1960–64; HM Diplomatic Service, 1965; First Sec., Brussels, 1966–68, Lagos, 1968–72; S Asian and Defence Depts, FCO, 1972–75; First Sec. (Economic), Islamabad, 1975–78; Head of Chancery, Lima, 1978–82; E African Dept, FCO, 1982–84; Actg Dep. High Comr, Bombay, 1985; Deputy High Commissioner: Calcutta, 1985–87; Kingston, 1987–91. Mem. Council, Anglo-Netherlands Soc., 1996–; Member: London Br., Prayer Book Soc., 2001– (Mem. Cttee, 2002–11); Cttee, Oxford Mission, 2001–15; Cttee, London Br., Oxford Univ. Soc., 2002–; Life Mem., BACSA, 1998– (Mem. Cttee, 2002–15). Member: Battersea Pk Rotary Club, 1998– (Pres., 2003–04 and 2017–18); Anglo-Belgian Soc., 1999–; Britain-Nigeria Educnl Trust, 1999–; Pakistan Soc., 2000–; P. G. Woodehouse Soc., 2006–15; Life Member: RAFA 1990; Anglo-Peruvian Soc., 1998–. Mem., Royal Soc. for Asian Affairs, 1997–. Member: Friends of Georgian Soc. of Jamaica, 1999– (Trustee, 2007–11); Pilgrims Soc., 2010–. Freeman, City of London, 2009. SBstJ 1972. *Recreations:* cricket, tennis, long rail and road journeys, British colonial history, English cathedrals, quizzes. *Address:* 38 Eglantine Road, Wandsworth, SW18 2DD. *Club:* MCC (Life Mem.).

**DOBLE, John Frederick,** OBE 1981; HM Diplomatic Service, retired; High Commissioner to Swaziland, 1996–99; *b* 30 June 1941; *s* of Comdr Douglas Doble, RN and Marcella (*née* Cowan); *m* 1st, 1975, Isabella (marr. diss. 1992), *d* of late Col W. H. Whitbread, TD; one *d*; 2nd, 2009, Susan Maria, *d* of Sir Henry Francis Colden Farrington, 7th Bt. *Educ:* Sunningdale; Eton (Scholar); RMA Sandhurst; Hertford College, Oxford.

17th/21st Lancers, 1959–69 (Captain); attached Lord Strathcona's Horse (Royal Canadians), 1967–69; joined HM Diplomatic Service, 1969; Arabian Dept, FCO, 1969–72; Beirut, 1972–73; UK Delegn to NATO, Brussels, 1973–77; Commonwealth Dept, FCO, 1977–78; Maputo, 1978–81; Inf. Dept, FCO, 1981–83; attached Barclays Bank International, 1983–85; Consul General, Edmonton, 1985–89; Consul General, Johannesburg, 1990–94. *Recreations:* mountaineering, history, manual labour. *Address:* Hole Farm, Hockworthy, Devon TA21 0NQ.
*See also* Sir H. W. Farrington, Bt.

**DOBRIN, Josephine;** Co-Founder and Chief Executive Officer, Creative Access, since 2013; *b* London, 3 Nov. 1973; *d* of Michael Dobrin and Barbara Dobrin; *m* 2002, Jonathan Gordon; three *d*. *Educ:* South Hampstead High Sch. for Girls; Univ. of Manchester (BA Hons 1st Cl. Human Communication and Communication Disorders 1995). Consultant, Luther Pendragon, 1996–2000; Press Officer, GLA, 2001; Dir, Lexington Communications, 2001–06. Trustee, Myeloma UK, 2006–13. Gov., Coldfall Primary Sch., 2012–17. *Recreations:* reading, travelling, running, tennis, swimming, netball, painting and drawing, drinking coffee and eating chocolate. *Address:* Creative Access, 2 Waterhouse Square, 140 Holborn, EC1N 2AE. *T:* (020) 7157 6671. *E:* josie@creativeaccess.org.uk.

**DOBROSIELSKI, Marian,** PhD; Banner of Labour, 1st Class 1975 (2nd Class 1973); Knight Cross of the Order of Polonia Restituta, 1964; Professor of Philosophy, Warsaw University, 1974–88; Ambassador *ad personam*, since 1973; *b* 25 March 1923; *s* of Stanislaw and Stefania Dobrosielski; *m* 1950; one *d*. *Educ:* Univ. of Zürich (PhD); Univ. of Warsaw. Served in Polish Army in France, War of 1939–45. With Min. of Foreign Affairs, 1948–81; Polish Legation, Bern, 1948–50; Head of Section, Min. of Foreign Affairs, 1950–54; Asst Prof., Warsaw Univ. and Polish Acad. of Sciences, 1954–57; Mem. Polish delegn to UN Gen. Assembly, 1952, 1953, 1958, 1966, 1972, 1976. First Sec., Counsellor, Polish Embassy in Washington, 1958–64; Min. of Foreign Affairs: Counsellor to Minister, 1964–69; Acting Dir, Research Office, 1968–69; Polish Ambassador to London, 1969–71; Dir, Polish Inst. of Internat. Affairs, 1971–80; Dep. Minister of Foreign Affairs, 1978–81. Univ. of Warsaw: Associate Prof., 1966; Vice-Dean of Faculty of Philosophy, 1966–68; Dir, Inst. of Philosophy, 1971–73 (Chm. Scientific Council, 1969). Chair of Diplomacy, Private Coll. of Business and Admin, Warsaw, 1999–2008; Prof. of European Studies, Univ. of Ateneum, Gdansk, 2007–12. Chm., Editorial Bd of Studia Filozoficzne, 1968–69; Sec., Polish Philos. Soc., 1955–57 and 1965–69. Chm., Polish Cttee for European Security and Co-operation, 1973–79 (Vice-Chm., 1971–73); Vice-Chm., Cttee on Peace Research, Polish Acad. of Scis, 1984–91; Chm., Scientific Council, Inst. of Peace Res. and Security Policy, Univ. of Hamburg, 1987–97. Hon. Vice-Pres., Scottish-Polish Cultural Assoc., Glasgow, 1969–71; Chm., Polish delegn to: 2nd stage Conf. on Security and Co-operation in Europe, 1973–75; CSCE Belgrade Meeting, 1977–78; CSCE Meeting, Madrid, 1980–81. Chm., Polish Nat. Interest Club, 1991–98. Hon. Mem., World Innovation Foundn, 1999. *Publications:* A Basic Epistemological Principle of Logical Positivism, 1947; The Philosophical Pragmatism of C. S. Peirce, 1967; On some contemporary problems: Philosophy, Ideology, Politics, 1970; (trans. and introd) Selection of Aphorisms of G. C. Lichtenberg, Oscar Wilde, Karl Kraus, M. von Ebner-Eschenbach, Mark Twain, C. Norwid, 1970–85; On the Theory and Practice of Peaceful Coexistence, 1976; Belgrad 77, 1978; Chances and Dilemmas, 1980; The Crisis in Poland, 1984; On Politics and Philosophy, 1988; Philosophy of Reason, 1988; Karl R. Popper's Philosophy of History and Politics, 1991; (jtly) Next Europe, 1993; (jtly) Prominent Diplomats of the XX Century, 1996; Rationalism and Irrationalism, 1999; On History, Myths and Facts - Politico-philosophical Essays, 2004; Poland-Germany-Europe, 2007; numerous articles on philosophy and internat. problems in professional jls. *Address:* Kozia Street 9–14, 00–070 Warszawa, Poland.

**DOBRY, Rosemary Anne;** *see* Alexander, R. A.

**DOBSON, Vice-Adm. Sir David (Stuart),** KBE 1992; Secretary-General, Institute of Investment Management and Research, later Chief Executive, UK Society of Investment Professionals, 1995–2002; *b* 4 Dec. 1938; *s* of Walter and Ethel Dobson; *m* 1962, Joanna Mary Counter; two *s* one *d*. *Educ:* English School, Nicosia, Cyprus; RN College, Dartmouth. Joined RN 1956; qualified Observer, 1961; served HM Ships Ark Royal, Protector, Eagle; BRNC Dartmouth, 1968–70; Flight Comdr, HMS Norfolk, 1970–72; Staff of FO Naval Air Comd, 1972–74; CO HMS Amazon, 1975–76; Naval Sec's Dept, MoD, 1976–78; Naval and Air Attaché, Athens, 1980–82; Senior Naval Officer, Falklands, 1982–83; Captain 5th Destroyer Sqdn (HMS Southampton), 1983–85; Captain of the Fleet, 1985–88; Naval Sec., 1988–90; Chief of Staff to Comdr Allied Naval Forces Southern Europe, 1991–94. Chm. of Trustees, Hands Around the World, charity, 1995–2009. Vice-Pres., Royal Star and Garter Home, Richmond, 2004– (Gov., 1996–2003; Chm. Govs, 1999–2003). Pres., FAA Field Gun Assoc., 1998–. Pres., RN Bird Watching Soc., 1992– (Ed., Sea Swallow jl, 2012–); Ed., Steep and Stroud Newsletter, 1997–. *Recreations:* hill walking, bird watching, choral singing. *Address:* c/o Lloyds Bank, The Square, Petersfield, Hants GU32 3HL. *Clubs:* Royal Navy of 1765 and 1785 (Chm., 1995–98), Union Jack (Pres., 2001–11).

**DOBSON, Rt Hon. Frank (Gordon);** PC 1997; *b* 15 March 1940; *s* of late James William and Irene Shortland Dobson, York; *m* 1967, Janet Mary, *d* of Henry and Edith Alker; three *c*. *Educ:* Dunnington County Primary Sch., York; Archbishop Holgate's Grammar Sch., York; London School of Economics (BScEcon). Administrative jobs with Central Electricity Generating Bd, 1962–70, and Electricity Council, 1970–75; Asst Sec., Commn for Local Administration (local Ombudsman's office), 1975–79. Member, Camden Borough Council, 1971–76 (Leader of Council, 1973–75); Chm., Coram's Fields and Harmsworth Meml Playground, 1977–. MP (Lab) Holborn and St Pancras S, 1979–83, Holborn and St Pancras, 1983–2015. Front bench spokesman on educn, 1981–83, on health, 1983–87; Shadow Leader of the Commons and Party Campaign Co-ordinator, 1987–89; opposition front bench spokesman on energy, 1989–92, on employment, 1992–93, on transport, 1993–94, on London, 1993–97, and on the envmt, 1994–97; Sec. of State for Health, 1997–99. Chm., NHS Unlimited, 1981–89. Gov., Coram, 2008–12. Governor: LSE, 1986–2001; Inst. of Child Health, 1987–92; RVC, 2002–. Member, Court: Univ. of York, 2001–; LSHTM, 2008–. Fellow, Birkbeck, Univ. of London, 2010; Hon. FRCP 2010. *Club:* Covent Garden Community Centre.

**DOBSON, Jo-Anne Elizabeth;** Member (UU) Upper Bann, Northern Ireland Assembly, 2011–17; *b* Banbridge, Co. Down; *d* of Eric Elliott and Joan Elliott; *m* 1986, John Ernest Dobson; two *s*. *Educ:* Abercorn Prim. Sch., Banbridge; Banbridge Acad. Mem. (UU), Craigavon BC., 2010–15. Sec., All Party Parly Gp on Learning Disability, NI Assembly, 2011–16; Chm., All Party Parly Gp on Organ Donation, NI Assembly, 2013–16. Mem., NI Assembly Br., Commonwealth Parly Assoc., 2011–17 (Chair, 2016–17). Contested (UU): Upper Bann, 2015; Upper Bann, NI Assembly, 2011–17. Mem., NI Kidney Patients' Assoc., 2008–. NI Ambassador, Kidney Care UK, 2017–. *Recreations:* reading, gym. *Club:* Waringstown Cricket.

**DOBSON, Very Rev. John Richard;** DL; Dean of Ripon, since 2014; *b* Swillington, Leeds, 16 Nov. 1964; *s* of Sidney Dobson and Barbara Dobson; *m* 1989, Nicola Jane Hollinshead; one *s* one *d*. *Educ:* Garforth Comprehensive; Van Mildert Coll., Univ. of Durham (BA Hons Dunelm 1997); Ripon Coll., Cuddesdon (PGCTh Oxon 1989).

Ordained deacon, 1989, priest, 1990; Assistant Curate: Benfieldside, Durham, 1989–92; St Cuthbert, Darlington, 1989–92; Curate-in-charge, Blackwell Conventional District, 1996–98; Vicar of Blackwell, 1998–2014; Area Dean of Darlington, 2001–14; Priest-in-charge, Coniscliffe, 2004–14. Chair, Ripon Together Community Interest Co., 2015–. Member, Board: Darlington Strategic Partnership, 2003–14; Anglican Dio. of Leeds, 2014–. Trustee: Darlington Abbeyfield Soc., 2003–14; Darlington CVS, 2003–14. Patron: N Yorks Dementia Forward, 2017–; Jennyruth Workshop, Ripon, 2017–. Gov. of several Darlington schs, 2000–14. DL N Yorks, 2019. *Recreations:* walking, bell ringing, golf, music, wine tasting, rotarian, charities trustee. *Address:* The Minster House, Bedern Bank, Ripon, N Yorks HG4 1PE. *T:* (01765) 602609; The Cathedral Office, Liberty Court House, Minster Road, Ripon, N Yorks HG4 1QS. *T:* (01765) 603462. *E:* deanjohn@riponcathedral.org.uk.

**DOBSON, Keith;** *see* Dobson, W. K.

**DOBSON, Dr Mary Janet, (Lady Dobson);** author; Director, Wellcome Unit for History of Medicine, and Reader in the History of Medicine, University of Oxford, 1999–2001; Fellow, Green College, Oxford, 1997–2001; *b* 27 Dec. 1954; *d* of late Derek Justin Schove and Vera Florence Schove; *m* 1977, Sir Christopher Martin Dobson FRS (*d* 2019); two *s*. *Educ:* Sydenham High Sch. (GPDST); St Hugh's Coll., Oxford (BA 1st Cl. Hons Geog. 1976); Harvard Univ. (AM 1980); Nuffield Coll., Oxford (DPhil 1982). Harkness Fellow, Harvard Univ., 1978–80; University of Oxford: E. P. Abraham and Prize Res. Fellow, Nuffield Coll., 1981–84; Deptl Demonstrator, Sch. of Geog., 1983–89; Lectr in Human Geog., Keble Coll., 1985–88; Res. Fellow, Wolfson Coll., 1987–94; Wellcome Fellow in Health Services Res., Dept of Community Medicine and Gen. Practice, 1989–90; Wellcome Unit for History of Medicine: Wellcome Res. Fellow in Historical Epidemiol., 1990–93; Sen. Res. Officer, 1993–98; Actg Dir and Wellcome Trust Unit Fellow, 1998–99. Affiliated Res. Scholar, Dept of Hist. and Philos. of Sci., Univ. of Cambridge, 2005–11; Res. Associate, Wellcome Centre for Hist. of Medicine, UCL, 2005–11. Radcliffe Sen. Common Room Mem., Green Templeton Coll., Oxford, 2011–; Affiliated Scholar and Mem., St John's Coll., Cambridge, 2019–. FRSTM&H 1997. Member: Soc. of Authors, 1996–; Historical Novel Soc., 1997–. *Publications:* Contours of Death and Disease in Early Modern England, 1997; Tudor Odours, 1997; Roman Aromas, 1997; Victorian Vapours, 1997; Reeking Royals, 1998; Vile Vikings, 1998; Wartime Whiffs, 1998; Greek Grime, 1998; Mouldy Mummies, 1998; Medieval Muck, 1998; Messy Medicine, 1999; Disease: the extraordinary stories behind history's deadliest killers, 2007, US edn 2014 (trans. Japanese, Chinese, German); The Story of Medicine: from bloodletting to biotechnology, 2013 (trans. German, Chinese); Murderous Contagion: a human history of disease, 2015.

**DOBSON, Prof. Michael,** DPhil; FEA; Director, Shakespeare Institute, Stratford-upon-Avon, and Professor of Shakespeare Studies, University of Birmingham, since 2011; *b* Bournemouth, 28 Sept. 1960; *s* of Derek and June Dobson; *m* 1987, Prof. Nicola Watson; two *d*. *Educ:* Bournemouth Grammar Sch.; Christ Church, Oxford (BA English Lang. and Lit. 1982; MA 1984; DPhil 1990). Lectr in English, Christ Ch, Oxford, 1987; Vis. Fellow and Tutor, Harvard Univ., 1987–89; Asst Prof., Indiana Univ., Bloomington, 1989–93; Associate Prof., Univ. of Illinois at Chicago, 1993–95; Prof. of Renaissance Drama, Roehampton Inst., London, 1996–2005; Prof. of Shakespeare Studies, Birkbeck, Univ. of London, 2005–11. Vis. Asst Prof., Northwestern Univ., 1991–92; Vis. Fellow, Peking Univ., 1999; Vis. Prof., Lund Univ., 2010. Hon. Gov., RSC, 2011–; Exec. Trustee, Shakespeare Birthplace Trust, 2011–. Hon. Patron, Brownsea Open-Air Th., 2013–. FEA 2012. Hon. Dr: Craiova, 2014; Lund, 2016. *Publications:* The Making of the National Poet, 1992; (with S. Wells) The Oxford Companion to Shakespeare, 2001, 2nd edn 2015; (with N. Watson) England's Elizabeth: an afterlife in fame and fantasy, 2002; Performing Shakespeare's Tragedies Today, 2006; Great Shakespeareans: John Philip Kemble, 2010; Shakespeare and Amateur Performance, 2011; contrib. essays, reviews and articles to London Rev. of Books, Shakespeare Survey, Shakespeare Qly, Shakespeare Bull., Around the Globe, The Guardian. *Recreations:* theatre-going, writing programme notes at short notice, playing in rock 'n' roll bands, walking. *Address:* c/o Shakespeare Institute, Mason Croft, Church Street, Stratford-upon-Avon, Warks CV37 6HP. *T:* (0121) 414 9500. *E:* m.dobson@bham.ac.uk.

**DOBSON, Captain Michael F.;** *see* Fulford-Dobson.

**DOBSON, Michael William Romsey;** Chairman, Schroders plc, since 2016 (Chief Executive, 2001–16); *b* 13 May 1952; *s* of Sir Denis (William) Dobson, KCB, OBE, QC; *m* 1998, Frances, *d* of Count Charles de Salis; two *d*. *Educ:* Eton; Trinity Coll., Cambridge. Joined Morgan Grenfell, 1973: Morgan Grenfell NY, 1978–80, Man. Dir, 1984–85; Hd, Investment Div., 1987–88; Dep. Chief Exec., 1988–89; Gp Chief Exec., Morgan Grenfell, then Deutsche Morgan Grenfell, 1989–97; Mem., Bd of Man. Dirs, Deutsche Bank AG, 1996–2000; Chm., Beaumont Capital Mgt, 2001. *Address:* Schroders plc, 31 Gresham Street, EC2V 7QA.

**DOBSON, Prof. Peter James,** OBE 2013; PhD; FInstP; FRSC; Professor of Engineering Science, 1996–2013, now Emeritus, and Academic Director, Begbroke Science Park, 2002–13, University of Oxford; Fellow, Queen's College, Oxford, since 1988; *b* Liskeard, Cornwall, 24 Oct. 1942; *s* of Cyril and Mary Dobson; *m* 1965, Catherine Roberts; two *d*. *Educ:* Newquay Grammar Sch.; Southampton Univ. (BSc Physics 1965; PhD 1968). FInstP 2003; FRSC 2011. Lectr, Imperial Coll., London, 1968–84; Sen. Principal Scientist, Philips Res. Labs, 1984–88; Lectr in Engrg Sci., Univ. of Oxford, 1988–94. Co-founder: Oxonica, 1999; Oxford Biosensors, 2000; Oxford NanoSystems, 2012. Strategic Advr on Nanotechnol. to Res. Councils UK, 2009–13. Vis. Prof. in Physics, KCL, 2016–; Vis. Prof. in Chem. Engrg, UCL, 2017–. Mem., ACS, 1999. Principal Fellow, Warwick Manufg Gp, 2013. *Recreations:* gardening, cooking. *Address:* Queen's College, Oxford OX1 4AW. *T:* (01865) 515436. *E:* peter.dobson@queens.ox.ac.uk; 92 Lonsdale Road, Oxford OX2 7ER. *T:* (01865) 515436.

**DOBSON, Ronald James,** CBE 2011; QFSM 2005; Commissioner for Fire and Emergency Planning, London Fire Brigade, 2007–16; *b* Lambeth, 9 March 1959; *s* of Ronald and Patricia Dobson; *m* 1979, Jacqueline Joy Willson; two *s* one *d*. MIFireE 1996. Joined London Fire Bde, 1979; Asst Divl Officer, 1988–92, Divl Officer, 1992–96, Southwark Trng Centre; Divl Comdr, Ops, Eastern Comd, 1996–2000; Asst Comr, 2000–07. Dir, Chief Fire Officers Assoc., 2007–16. Pres., London Fire Bde Retd Mems' Assoc., 2008–16. *Recreations:* golf, music, walking. *Club:* Sunridge Park Golf (Bromley).

**DOBSON, Sue;** freelance travel writer and editor; Travel Editor, Choice, 2002–05 (Editor-in-Chief, 1994–2002); *m* 1966, Michael Dobson (marr. diss. 1974). *Educ:* convent schs; DipHE; BA Hons CNAA. From 1964, worked for a collection of women's magazines, including Femina and Fair Lady in S Africa, variously as fashion, cookery, beauty, home and contributing editor, editor at SA Institute of Race Relations and editor of Wedding Day and Successful Slimming in London, with breaks somewhere in between in PR and doing research into the language and learning of children; Editor, Woman and Home, 1982–94. Mem. Bd, Plan Internat., 1993–2004. *Publications:* The Wedding Day Book, 1981, 2nd edn 1989; Travellers Cape Verde, 2008, 2nd edn 2010; Travellers Namibia, 2008, 2nd edn 2010; The 50 Greatest Churches and Cathedrals in the World, 2017. *Recreations:* travelling, photography, reading, exploring.

**DOBSON, (William) Keith,** OBE 1988; Director, Interstate Programmes Ltd, 2005–11; *b* 20 Sept. 1945; *s* of Raymond Griffin Dobson and Margaret (*née* Wylie); *m* 1972, Valerie Guest; two *d*. *Educ:* King Edward's Grammar School, Camp Hill, Birmingham; Univ. of Keele (BA Internat. Relns 1968); Univ. of Essex (DipSoc 1972). With Clarks Ltd, Shoemakers, 1968–71; British Council, 1972–2000: Lagos, 1972–75; London, 1975–77; Ankara, 1977–80; Caracas, 1980–84; Budapest, 1984–87; London, 1987–90; Europe Div., 1990–93; Dir, Germany, 1993–2000; Sec.-Gen., Anglo-German Foundn, 2000–05. Gov., ESU, 2002–. *Recreations:* music, cinema, bridge, woodworking. *Address:* 18C Church Green, Witney, Oxon OX28 4AW. *E:* keithdobson20@googlemail.com.

**DOCHERTY, Dr David,** OBE 2018; Chairman, Digital Television Group, since 2009; *b* Glasgow, 10 Dec. 1956; *s* of David Docherty and Anna Docherty (*née* Graham); *m* 1992, Kate, *d* of Sir Murray Stuart-Smith, *qv*; two *d*. *Educ:* St Mungo's Acad.; Univ. of Strathclyde (BA 1st Cl. Hons 1979); London Sch. of Econs and Pol Sci. (PhD 1983; MSc 1985). Dir of Res., Broadcasting Standards Council, 1988–89; Head: Broadcasting Analysis, BBC TV, 1990–92; Television Planning and Strategy, BBC Network TV, 1992–96; Dir of Strategy and Channel Develt, 1996–97, Dep. Dir of Television, 1997–99, BBC Broadcast; former Dir, New Media, BBC; Chief Exec., YooMedia, 2003–05; CEO, Council for Industry and Higher Educn, then Nat. Centre for Univs and Business, 2009–18. Former Chm., Bd of Govs, Univ. of Bedfordshire. Former Chair, Broadcasting Cttee, Soc. of Authors. Hon. Fellow: Univ. of Bedfordshire; Sch. of Advanced Study, Univ. of London, 2018. *Publications:* non-fiction: The Last Picture Show?, 1987; Keeping Faith, Channel 4 and its Audience, 1988; Running the Show, 1990; Violence in Television Fiction, 1990; *fiction:* The Spirit Death, 2000; The Killing Jar, 2002; The Fifth Season, 2003. *Recreations:* writing, running. *Address:* Serge Hill, Serge Hill Lane, Bedmond, Herts WD5 0RY. *T:* (01923) 291167.

**DOCHERTY, Dame Jacqueline,** DBE 2004; Chief Executive, London North West University Healthcare NHS Trust, since 2015; *b* 19 Feb. 1950; *d* of William Docherty and Elizabeth Barrie Docherty. *Educ:* Hairmyres Hosp. (RGN; Gold Medallist); Caledonian Univ. (MBA Dist.; DMS Dist.). Sen. Sister, Royal Free Hosp., London, 1973–79; Nursing Officer, Inverclyde Royal Infirmary, Greenock, 1979–80; Sen. Nurse, Royal Infirmary, Glasgow, 1980–90; Dep. Dir of Nursing, St John's Hosp., W Lothian, 1990–92; Nursing Officer, Scottish Office, DoH, 1992–96; Exec. Dir of Nursing and Ops, 1996–2009, Dep. Chief Exec., 2000–09, King's Coll. Hosp.; Chief Exec., W Middlesex Univ. Hosp., 2009–15. Ind. Consultant, Evidence-based Medicine Prog., Mexican Dept of Health, 1997–2000. Visiting Prof., S Bank Univ., 2004–; KCL, 2006–. Trustee: GNC Trust, 2007– (Chm., 2010–13); King's Fund, 2007–13 (Mem., Commn on Leadership and Mgt in the NHS, 2010). *Publications:* (contrib.) A Critical Guide to the UKCC's Code of Conduct, 1999; contribs to DoH (Scotland) clinical pubns, and various articles in professional jls. *Recreations:* country walks, antiques, music, socialising with friends. *Address:* London North West University Healthcare NHS Trust, Northwick Park Hospital, Watford Road, Harrow HA1 3UJ.

**DOCHERTY, Joseph Paul;** Managing Director, Bede Homes Ltd, since 2018; *b* Helensburgh, 7 Sept. 1969; *s* of Patrick Docherty and Mary Docherty; *m* 2015, Marcelo Digap; one *s*. *Educ:* St Mary's Prim. Sch., Alexandria; St Joseph's Prim. Sch., Milngavie; St Ninians High Sch., Kirkintilloch; Univ. of Strathclyde (BEng Hons Civil Engrg 1992; MPhil Construction Mgt 1994); Harvard Business Sch. (Ralph James Scholar; AMP 2011). Barclays plc: Grad. Trainee, Business Analyst, 1994–96; Asst to Chm., 1996–97; Special Policy Advr, Northern Develt Co., 1997–98 (on secondment); Asst Dir, 1998–2000, Dir, 2000–02, Corporate Banking Div.; Chief Exec., Tees Valley Regeneration, 2002–09; Chief Exec., NCG (formerly Newcastle Coll. Gp), 2013–18. Mem., Commn on Public Services in N of England, IPPR, 2006. Arts Council England: Trustee and Mem. Council, 2011–17; Chm., NE Bd, 2011–14; Chm., Museums and Libraries Accreditation Scheme, 2011–15; Chm., Area Council North, 2014–. Chm., Govt Office London Objective 2 Implementation Cttee, 2000–02; Member: HM Govt Urban Sounding Bd, 1998–2004; London Develt Agency Private Investment Commn, 2000–01; British Urban Regeneration Assoc. Steering and Development Forum, 2004–10. Trustee: Baltic Centre for Contemporary Art, 1999–2007 (Chm., Finance and Gen. Purpose Cttee, 2001–07); Esmée Fairbairn Foundn, 2013–; Univ. Council, Univ. of Durham, 2018– (Mem. Council, 2007–16; Chm., George Stephenson Coll., 2007–12; Chm., Finance and Gen. Purposes Cttee, 2012–16). FRSA 2008. Mem., Edit Bd, Jl for Urban Regeneration and Renewal, 2007–13. *Recreations:* art, architecture, current affairs and history, travel. *Club:* Reform.

**DOCHERTY, Leo;** MP (C) Aldershot, since 2017; an Assistant Government Whip, since 2019; *m* Lucy; two *c*. *Educ:* Sch. of Oriental and African Studies, Univ. of London; Royal Mil. Acad. Sandhurst. Commnd 1st Bn Scots Guards, 2001–06. Dir, Cons. Middle East Council, 2010. Mem., Defence Select Cttee, 2017–. Contested (C) Caerphilly, 2015. *Publications:* Desert of Death, 2007. *Address:* House of Commons, SW1A 0AA.

**DOCHERTY, Martin John;** *see* Docherty-Hughes.

**DOCHERTY, Michael,** FCCA, CPFA; Chief Executive, South Lanarkshire Council, 1999–2006; *b* 12 Jan. 1952; *s* of Michael and Susan Docherty; *m* 1972, Linda Thorpe; two *s* one *d*. *Educ:* St Mungo's Acad., Glasgow. FCCA 1978; CPFA 1986. Accountancy trainee, S of Scotland Electricity Bd, 1970–74; Accounts Asst, Coatbridge Burgh Council, 1974–75; Accountant: Monklands DC, 1975–77; Stirling DC, 1977–79; Sen. Accountant, 1979–80, Principal Accountant, 1980–82, Monklands DC; Principal Accountant, Renfrew DC, 1982–84; Depute Dir of Finance, Motherwell DC, 1984–92; Dir of Finance, 1992–94, Chief Exec., 1994–95, Hamilton DC; Depute Chief Exec. and Exec. Dir, Corporate Resources, 1995–97, Depute Chief Exec. and Exec. Dir, Enterprise Resources, 1997–99, S Lanarkshire Council. *Recreations:* music, reading, running, golf.

**DOCHERTY, Paul Francis;** Director, France, British Council, 2013–18; *b* 17 Sept. 1951; *s* of Joseph Docherty and Elizabeth Eileen Docherty (*née* Waters); *m* 1987, Karen Leithead (marr. diss. 2007); three *s*. *Educ:* Queen Victoria Sch., Dunblane; Univ. of Strathclyde (BA Hons 1977; MLitt 1985). English teacher, Spain, 1977–83; Lectr in English, Moscow State Univ., 1983–84; joined British Council, 1985: Helsinki, 1986–89; English Language Div., 1989–93; Moscow, 1993–96; Corporate Affairs, 1996–97; Sec., 1997–2000; Dir, Czech Republic, and Cultural Counsellor, Prague, 2000–03; Director: Italy, 2003–09; Scotland, 2009–11; UK 2012, 2011–12; UK Major Events, 2013–14. Gov., British Inst., Florence, 2003–09. FRSA 2008. *Recreations:* music especially opera, playing blues/rock guitar, reading history and current affairs.

**DOCHERTY, Sadie;** Lord Provost and Lord Lieutenant of Glasgow, 2012–17; *b* Glasgow, 6 June 1956; *d* of Patrick and Margaret Boyle; *m* 1978, William Docherty; one *s* one *d*. *Educ:* Daisgie Terrace Primary Sch.; St Margaret Mary's Secondary Sch.; Strathclyde Univ. (Scottish Local Authy Mgt 1999). Neighbourhood Housing Manager, Glasgow CC, 1996–2007. Mem. (Lab) Glasgow CC, 2007–17. *Recreations:* reading, gardening.

**DOCHERTY, Thomas;** Head of Public Affairs (Nations and Regions), Which?, since 2018 (Head of Public Affairs (Scotland), 2017; Public Affairs Manager, 2017–18); *b* 28 Jan. 1975; *s* of Robert and Margarita Docherty; *m* 2004, Katie McCulloch; one *s* one *d*. *Educ:* Open Univ. Res. Asst to Scott Barrie, MSP, 1999–2002; Public Affairs Officer, BNFL, 2002–05; Communications Manager, Network Rail, 2006–07; Account Dir, communications consultancy, 2007–10. MP (Lab) Dunfermline and W Fife, 2010–15; contested (Lab) same seat, 2015. PPS: to Shadow Chief Sec. to the Treasury, 2010–11; to Shadow Leader of H of C, 2011–15. Member: Envmt, Food and Rural Affairs Select Cttee, 2010–15; Defence Select Cttee, 2010–15; Admin Select Cttee, 2010–15; Procedure Cttee, 2011–15. Contested (Lab): Tayside N, 2001; S of Scotland, Scottish Parlt, 2003.

**DOCHERTY-HUGHES, Martin John;** MP (SNP) West Dunbartonshire, since 2015; *b* 1971. *Educ:* Glasgow Coll. of Food Technol. (HND Business Admin 1997); Univ. of Essex (BA Politics); Glasgow Sch. of Art (MA 2004). W Dunbartonshire Community and Volunteering Services. Member (SNP): Clydebank DC, 1992; Glasgow CC, 2012–15. *Address:* House of Commons, SW1A 0AA.

**DOCKERILL, Julia Louise;** *see* Lopez, J. L.

**DOCKRAY, Prof. Graham John,** PhD; FRS 2004; FMedSci; Professor of Physiology, University of Liverpool, 1982–2013, now Emeritus; *b* 19 July 1946; *s* of Ben and Elsie Dockray; *m* 1985, Andrea Varro; one *s* one *d*. *Educ:* Univ. of Nottingham (BSc 1st cl. Hons (Zool.) 1967; PhD 1971). University of Liverpool: Lectr in Physiol., 1970–78; Sen. Lectr, 1978–80; Reader, 1980–82; Pro-Vice-Chancellor, 2004–06; Dep. Vice-Chancellor, 2006–08. Fogarty Internat. Fellow, UCLA/Veterans Hosp., LA, 1973–74. FMedSci 1998. Hon. FRCP 2001. *Publications:* Cholecystokinin (CCK) in the Nervous System: current developments in neuropeptide research, 1987; The Neuropeptide Cholecystokinin (CCK), 1989; Gut Peptides: physiology and biochemistry, 1994; numerous papers in peer-reviewed jls. *Recreation:* gardening. *Address:* Cell and Molecular Physiology, Institute of Translational Medicine, University of Liverpool, Crown Street, Liverpool L69 3BX. *T:* (0151) 794 5324, *Fax:* (0151) 794 5315. *E:* g.j.dockray@liverpool.ac.uk.

**DOCTOR, Brian Ernest;** QC 1999; *b* 8 Dec. 1949; *s* of Hans and Daphne Doctor; *m* 1973, Estelle Ann Lewin; three *s*. *Educ:* Balliol Coll., Oxford (BCL); Univ. of Witwatersrand (BA, LLB). Solicitor, 1978–80; Advocate, S Africa, 1980–92; SC S Africa 1990; called to the Bar, Lincoln's Inn, 1991, Bencher, 2009; in practice at the Bar, 1992–. *Recreations:* reading, theatre, opera, cycling. *Address:* Fountain Court Chambers, Temple, EC4Y 9DH. *T:* (020) 7583 3335.

**DOCTOROW, Cory Efram;** writer; *b* Toronto, 17 July 1971; *s* of Gordon and Roslyn Doctorow; *m* 2008, Alice Jane Taylor; one *d*. Canadian Fulbright Chair in Public Diplomacy, UCLA, 2006–07; Vis. Sen. Lectr, Open Univ., 2009; Schol. in Virtual Residence, Univ. of Waterloo, Ont, 2009. Res. Affiliate, Media Lab, MIT. Dir, Metabrainz Foundn; Special Advr, Electronic Frontier Foundn; Adv. Bd Mem., Participatory Culture Foundn; Mem., Adv. Council, Open Technol. Fund. Founder, UK Open Rights Gp (Adv. Bd Mem.). FRSA. *Publications:* Down and Out in the Magic Kingdom, 2003; Eastern Standard Tribe, 2003; A Place so Foreign and Eight More (short stories), 2003; Someone Comes to Town, Someone Leaves Town, 2004; Overclocked (short stories), 2007; Cory Doctorow's Futuristic Tales of the Here and Now, 2008; Content, 2008; Little Brother, 2008; Makers, 2009; With a Little Help, 2009; For the Win, 2010; Context: further selected essays on productivity, creativity, parenting and politics in 21st century, 2011; (with Charles Stross) The Rapture of the Nerds, 2012; Homeland, 2013; Pirate Cinema, 2013; Information Doesn't Want to be Free, 2014; (with Jen Wang) In Real Life, 2014; Walkaway, 2017. *E:* doctorow@craphound.com. *Club:* Shoreditch House.

**DODD, Dominic;** Chairman, Royal Free London NHS Foundation Trust, since 2010; Director, UCL Partners, since 2009; *b* Ely, 16 Aug. 1967; *s* of Charles Gordon Dodd and Jennifer Anne Dodd; *m* 1999, Catherine Apap Bologna; two *s*. *Educ:* Lincoln Coll., Oxford (BA Hons PPE). Marakon Associates: Consultant, 1989–97; Partner and UK Br. Manager, 1997–2000; Man. Partner, 2000–03; Sen. Advr, 2004–07; Exec. Dir, Children's Investment Fund Foundn, 2008–09. Non-exec. Dir, Royal Free Hampstead NHS Trust, 2006–09; Sen. Ind. Dir, Permanent TSB plc, 2012–16. Trustee, King's Fund, 2016–. *Publications:* (jtly) The Three Tensions, 2007; contrib. Harvard Business Rev. *Recreations:* sea, garden, guitar, walking, wood, magic. *Address:* Royal Free London NHS Foundation Trust, Royal Free Hospital, Pond Street, NW3 2QG.

**DODD, John Stanislaus;** QC 2006; **His Honour Judge Dodd;** a Circuit Judge, since 2012; *b* 3 April 1957; *s* of James and Mary Dodd; *m* 1990, Margaret Ann Roberts (*see* M. A. Dodd); two *s*. *Educ:* St Aloysius' Coll.; Univ. of Leicester (LLB Hons 1978); London Sch. of Economics. Called to the Bar, Gray's Inn, 1979, Bencher, 2011; barrister, specialist in criminal law; a Recorder, 2000–12. Standing Counsel to HM Customs and Excise, subseq. HMRC, 2002–06. Member: Cttee, SE Circuit, 1995–; Bar Council, 1998–2006; Magistrates' Courts Rules Cttee; Sec., Criminal Bar Assoc., 2002–03. *Recreations:* long-distance cycling, squash, playing violin. *Address:* Wood Green Crown Court, Lordship Lane, N22 5LF.

**DODD, Margaret Ann;** a District Judge (Magistrates' Courts), since 2018; *b* London, 2 June 1957; *d* of George Roberts and Peggy Roberts; *m* 1990, John Stanislaus Dodd, *qv*; two *s*. *Educ:* Lady Eleanor Holles Sch., Hampton; Univ. of Southampton (LLB Hons 1978). Called to the Bar, Middle Temple, 1979; Dep. Justices Clerk, London Magistrates' Court Service, 1980–89; a criminal barrister, 1990–2018; a Dep. Dist Judge (Magistrates' Courts), 1999–2018. *Recreations:* reading, music, theatre, ski-ing, cycling, wild swimming. *Address:* St Albans Magistrates' Court, 2 Civic Close, St Albans AL1 3LB.

**DODD, Nicholas Henry;** Director, National Coal Mining Museum for England, since 2017; *b* Broxbourne, Herts, 9 Dec. 1959; *s* of Mark Wilson Dodd and Shirley Mary Elizabeth Dodd; *m* 1984, Catherine Clare; one *s* one *d*. *Educ:* Univ. of Sussex (BA Hons 1981); Univ. of Leicester (Dip. Museums Studies 1983); Univ. of Warwick (MA Cultural Policy and Admin 1994). AMA 1987. Exhibn Officer, Nat. Postal Mus., 1982–84; Educn and Interpretation Officer, Kent CC, 1984–88; Sen. Curator and Proj. Dir, Coventry CC, 1988–94; Hd, Arts and Mus, Wolverhampton CC, 1994–2002; Chief Exec., Mus Sheffield, 2002–12; Exec. Dir, Derby Mus Trust, 2013; Dir, Wentworth Castle Gardens and Stainborough Park Trust, 2016–17. Trustee, NHMF and HLF, 2000–06; Mem. Bd, MLA, 2006–11. Mem. Bd, Craftspace Touring, 1994–2002. Mem. Court, Univ. of Sheffield, 2006–10. Guardian, Assay Office of Sheffield, 2011. FRSA. *Recreations:* making marmalade, gardening, taking busman's holidays, walking around. *Address:* The Old Hall, 2 Stoney Lane, Chapelthorpe, Wakefield WF4 3JN. *T:* (01924) 254387, 07711 400079. *E:* nick.dodd1@gmail.com.

**DODD, Philip;** Founder and Chairman, Made in China, consultancy, since 2004; *b* Grimethorpe, 25 Oct. 1949; *s* of Ernest and Mavis Dodd; two *s*; *m* 2017, Enrica Costamagna. *Educ:* UC, Swansea (BA Hons); Univ. of Leicester (MA). Lectr in English Literature, Univ. of Leicester, 1976–89; Dep. Editor, New Statesman and Society, 1989–90; Editor, Sight and Sound, BFI, 1990–97; Dir, ICA, 1997–2004. Visiting Professor: KCL, 2000–03; Univ. of the Arts London, 2004–. Consultant, Music and Arts: BBC, 1986–91; Wall to Wall TV, 1991–97. Presenter: Night Waves, 2000–12, Free Thinking, 2012–, BBC Radio 3. Chief Internat. Advr, Shanghai eArts Festival, 2007–; Advr, Beijing Internat. Cultural and Creative Industry Expo, 2008. Founder, Global Private Mus. Summit and Network, 2014. Mem. Adv. Bd, Christie's Educn. Hon. DLitt Leicester, 2012. Small Publisher of the Year, PPA, 1993; Sony Radio Award, 1996. *Publications:* (ed jtly) Englishness: politics and culture 1880–1920, 1986, 2nd edn 2014; (jtly) Relative Values: what's art worth, 1991; The Battle over Britain, 1995; (ed jtly) Spellbound, Art and Film, 1996.

**DODD, Philip Kevin,** OBE 1987; a District Judge (Magistrates' Courts) (formerly Stipendiary Magistrate), Cheshire, 1991–2004; *b* 2 April 1938; *s* of Thomas and Mary Dodd; *m* 1962, Kathleen Scott; one *s* one *d*. *Educ:* St Joseph's Coll., Dumfries; Leeds Univ. (BA, LLB). Admitted Solicitor, 1966. Articled Clerk, Ashton-under-Lyne Magistrates' Court, 1961–63; Dep. Justices' Clerk, 1963–67; Justices' Clerk: Houghton-le-Spring and Seaham, 1967–70; Wolverhampton, 1970–76; Manchester, 1976–91. Council Member: Justices' Clerks' Soc., 1974–89 (Pres., 1985–86); Manchester Law Soc., 1978–91 (Pres., 1987–88). Sec., Standing Conf., Clerks to Magistrates' Courts Cttees, 1974–82 (Chm., 1983–84). *Recreation:* planning holidays.

**DODD, Sara; Her Honour Judge Sara Dodd;** a Circuit Judge, since 2016; *b* Burnley, Lancs, 19 Nov. 1964; *d* of late William Dodd and Irene Dodd (*née* Hephrun). *Educ:* St Hilda's RC Girls' High Sch., Burnley; St Theodore's RC Sixth Form Coll.; City of Birmingham Poly. (LLB). Called to the Bar, Lincoln's Inn, 1987; a Recorder, 2012–16. *Recreations:* gardening, supporting Burnley Football Club, learning Portuguese. *Address:* Preston Combined Court Centre, The Law Courts, Openshaw Place, Ringway, Preston PR1 2LL.

**DODD, Thomas Erik;** HM Diplomatic Service; Ambassador to Finland, since 2018; *b* Weald, 11 April 1965; *s* of A. P. Dodd and Birte Dodd (*née* Qvørtrup); *m* 1997, Catharine Mary French; one *s* one *d*. *Educ:* Sevenoaks Sch.; Lawrenceville Sch. (USA-ESU Scholarship); Univ. of Bristol (BA Hist.); London Sch. of Econs and Political Sci. (MSc Internat. Relns). H of C Service, 1991–98; Jt Intelligence Orgn and Overseas Secretariat, Cabinet Office, 1998–2003; Dep. Consul Gen., Basra, 2004; Internat. Immigration Policy, Home Office, 2005–08; Dep. Ambassador, Kabul, 2009–10; Dep. Chief Assessments Staff, Cabinet Office, 2011–12; Head, SE Asia Dept, 2013–15, Counter Terrorism Dept, 2016–17, FCO. Iraq Reconstruction Service Medal; Civilian Service Medal, Afghanistan. *Publications:* defence articles. *Recreations:* travel, print collecting, pig scratching. *Address:* British Embassy Itäinen Puistotie 17, 00140 Helsinki, Finland.

**DODDS, Dr Anneliese Jane;** MP (Lab Co-op) Oxford East, since 2017; *b* Aberdeen, 16 March 1978; partner, Edward Turner; one *s* one *d*. *Educ:* St Hilda's Coll., Oxford (BA 1st Cl. Hons PPE 2001); Univ. of Edinburgh (MRes Dist. 2002); London Sch. of Econs and Pol Sci. (PhD Govt 2006). ESRC Postdoctoral Fellow, LSE, 2006; Lectr in Public Policy, 2007–10, and Actg Dir, NIHR Patient Safety and Service Quality Res. Centre, 2009–10, KCL; Sen. Lectr in Public Policy, Aston Univ., 2010–14. Vis. Prof., Univ. of Prishtina, 2010. Shadow Treasury Minister, 2017–18. Contested (Lab): Billericay, 2005; Reading E, 2010. MEP (Lab) SE Reg., 2014–17. *Publications:* Comparative Public Policy, 2013; contribs to books and peer-reviewed articles. *Address:* House of Commons, SW1A 0AA.

**DODDS, Diane Jean;** Member (DemU) Northern Ireland, European Parliament, since 2009; *b* 16 Aug. 1958; *m* 1985, Nigel Alexander Dodds (*see* Rt Hon. N. A. Dodds); two *s* one *d*. *Educ:* Banbridge Acad.; Queen's Univ., Belfast (BA Hist. and English); Stranmillis Coll. (PGCE). Teacher of History and English, Laurelhill High Sch., Lisburn. Mem. (DemU) W Belfast, NI Assembly, 2003–07. Mem. (DemU), Belfast CC, 2005–10. *Address:* European Parliament, Rue Wiertz, 1047 Brussels, Belgium.

**DODDS, Jane;** MP (Lib Dem) Brecon and Radnorshire, since Aug. 2019. *Address:* House of Commons, SW1A 0AA.

**DODDS, Rt Hon. Nigel (Alexander),** OBE 1997; PC 2010; MP (DemU) Belfast North, since 2001; barrister; *b* 20 Aug. 1958; *s* of Joseph Alexander and Doreen Elizabeth Dodds; *m* 1985, Diana Jean Harris (*see* D. J. Dodds); two *s* one *d*. *Educ:* Portora Royal Sch., Enniskillen; St John's Coll., Cambridge (MA); Inst. of Professional Legal Studies, Belfast (Cert. of Professional Legal Studies). Called to the Bar, NI, 1981. Mem., Belfast City Council, 1985–2010 (Chairman: F and GP Cttee, 1985–87; Develt Cttee, 1997–99); Lord Mayor of Belfast, 1988–89 and 1991–92; Alderman, Castle Area, 1989–97. Mem., NI Forum, 1996–98. Mem. (DemU) Belfast N, NI Assembly, 1998–2010; Minister: for Social Develt, NI, 1999–2000 and 2001–02; of Enterprise, Trade and Investment, NI, 2007–08; for Finance and Personnel, NI, 2008–09. Vice Pres., Assoc. of Local Authorities of NI, 1988–89. Mem., Senate, QUB, 1987–93. *Address:* House of Commons, SW1A 0AA.

**DODDS, His Honour (Robert) Stephen;** a Circuit Judge, 2007–19; *b* Blackburn, 6 Nov. 1952; *s* of George Dodds and Edith Mary Dodds; *m* 1980, Kathryn Hadley (separated 2010); one *s* one *d*. *Educ:* Queen Elizabeth's Grammar Sch., Blackburn; Leeds Poly. (LLB); Coll. of Law. Called to the Bar, Gray's Inn, 1976; Asst Recorder, 1995–99; Recorder, 1999–2007. Asst Parly Boundary Comr, 2003–07. Chm., Old Blackburnians' Assoc., Queen Elizabeth's Grammar Sch., Blackburn, 2011–14. *Recreations:* watching Blackburn Rovers FC, collecting football programmes, collecting malt whisky, reading, cricket (Lancashire CCC). *Club:* District and Union (Blackburn).

**DODGE, Ian James;** National Director, Strategy and Innovation (formerly Commissioning Strategy), NHS England, since 2014; *b* Tunbridge Wells, 20 Aug. 1971; *s* of Ron Dodge and Jean Dodge; *m* 2001, Elizabeth Woodeson (CBE 2012). *Educ:* Kent Coll., Canterbury; Lincoln Coll., Oxford (BA Hons Mod. Hist. 1993); Imperial Coll. London (MBA 2000). Department of Health, 1993–2014: Hd, Primary Care, 2001–04; Dep. Dir, NHS Performance, 2004–05; (on secondment) Sen. Policy Advr to the Prime Minister, 2005–06; Dir, Policy Unit, DoH, 2006–12; Hd, Policy Profession, 2010–14; Dir, NHS Policy and Outcomes Group, 2012–14. Adjunct Prof., Inst. of Global Health Innovation, Imperial Coll. London, 2012–. *Recreations:* Greek islands, new music, running, tennis, clematis. *Address:* 22 Alma Street, NW5 3DJ. *T:* (020) 7267 6008. *E:* iandodge@gmail.com.

**DODGSHON, Prof. Robert Andrew,** PhD; FBA 2002; FLSW; Gregynog Professor of Human Geography, 2001–07, now Emeritus Professor, and Director, 1998–2003, Institute of Geography and Earth Sciences, University of Wales, Aberystwyth; *b* 8 Dec. 1941; *s* of Robert and Dorothy Dodgshon; *m* 1969, Katherine Simmonds; two *d*. *Educ:* Liverpool Univ. (BA 1963, PhD 1969). Asst Keeper, Mus. of English Rural Life, Univ. of Reading, 1966–70; Lectr, 1970–80, Sen. Lectr, 1980–84, Reader, 1984–88, Prof., 1988–2001, UCW Aberystwyth, subseq. Univ. of Wales, Aberystwyth. Council Member: Countryside Council for Wales, 1997–2004; NT, 2001–08; Mem., JNCC, 2003–04. Pres., Soc. for Landscape Studies, 1997–2008. Founding FLSW 2010. Murchison Award, RGS, 1996; Scottish Geographical Medal, RSGS, 2003. *Publications:* (ed jtly) An Historical Geography of England and Wales, 1978, 2nd edn 1990; The Origin of British Field Systems, 1980; Land and Society in Early Scotland, 1980; The European Past, 1987; From Chiefs to Landlords, 1998; Society in Time and Space, 1998; (ed jtly) An Historical Geography of Europe, 1998; The Age of the Clans, 2002; No Stone Unturned, 2015; Farming Communities in the

Western Alps, 1500–1914, 2019. *Recreations:* travel, music, historic landscapes, arts and crafts movement. *Address:* 4 Stratton Audley Manor, Mill Road, Stratton Audley, Oxon OX27 9AR. *T:* (01869) 278258. *E:* rad@aber.ac.uk.

**DODGSON, Clare;** Director, CD Consulting, since 2009; *b* 10 Sept. 1962; *d* of William Baxter and Ann Baxter (*née* Mattimoe); *m* 1988, Gerard Dodgson. *Educ:* St Robert of Newminster Sch., Washington; Newcastle Business Sch. (MBA). Dir of Planning and Service Develt, S Tyneside FHSA, 1990–92; Chief Executive: Newcastle FHSA, 1992–93; Sunderland HA, 1993–99; Dir, Jobcentre Services, subseq. Chief Operating Officer, Employment Services Agency, DfEE, 1999–2002; Chief Operating Officer, DWP, Jobcentre Plus, 2002–03; Chief Exec., Legal Services Commn, 2003–06; Public Appts Ambassador, Govt Equalities Office, then Home Office, 2009–12. Chm., Strategic Adv. Bd, Bar Tribunals and Adjudication Service, 2014–. Non-executive Director: NW London Strategic HA, 2002–06; HMRC Prosecution Office, 2008–09; Ind. Dir, Agric. and Hort. Develt Bd, 2007–12; Seafish Authy, 2012–18, DEFRA; Ind. Panel Mem., Judicial Conduct Investigation Office (formerly Office for Judicial Complaints), 2012–15; Ind. Mem., Service Complaints Panels, MoD, 2013–. Mem., Healthcare Commn, 2007–09. Public Interest Mem., Regulation and Compliance Bd, ICAS, 2011–. *Recreations:* travel, great food with good friends.

**DODGSON, Paul; His Honour Judge Dodgson;** a Circuit Judge, since 2001; *b* 14 Aug. 1951; *s* of late Reginald Dodgson and Kathleen Dodgson; *m* 1982, Jan Hemingway; one *s* two *d*. *Educ:* Tiffin Sch.; Univ. of Birmingham (LLB Hons). Called to the Bar, Inner Temple, 1975; Asst Recorder, 1992–96; a Recorder, 1996–2001. Mem., Parole Bd of Eng. and Wales, 2003–15. Treas., Criminal Bar Assoc., 1992–94. *Recreations:* ski-ing, sailing, golf, socialising.

**DODSON,** family name of **Baron Monk Bretton.**

**DODSON, Prof. Eleanor Joy,** FRS 2003; Research Fellow, University of York, since 1976; *b* 6 Dec. 1936; *d* of Arthur McPherson and Alice Power; *m* 1965, (George) Guy Dodson, FRS (*d* 2012); three *s* one *d*. *Educ:* Univ. of Melbourne (BA Hons). Res. Asst, Lab. of Dorothy Hodgkin, Univ. of Oxford, 1961–76. *Recreations:* family, theatre, opera.

**DODSON, Joanna;** QC 1993; *b* 5 Sept. 1945; *d* of late Jack Herbert Dodson and Joan Muriel (*née* Webb); *m* 1974 (marr. diss. 1981). *Educ:* James Allen's Girls' Sch.; Newnham Coll., Cambridge (entrance exhibnr; BA 1967; MA 1971). Called to the Bar, Middle Temple, 1971, Bencher, 2000. Gov., James Allen's Girls' Sch., 1999–2009.

**DODSON, Robert North;** *see* North, R.

**DODSWORTH, Sir David John S.;** *see* Smith-Dodsworth.

**DODSWORTH, Prof. (James) Martin;** Professor of English, Royal Holloway (formerly Royal Holloway and Bedford New College), University of London, 1987–2001, now Emeritus; *b* 10 Nov. 1935; *s* of Walter Edward and Kathleen Ida Dodsworth; *m* 1967, Joanna Rybicka; one *s*. *Educ:* St George's Coll., Weybridge; Univ. of Fribourg, Switzerland; Wadham Coll., Oxford (MA). Asst Lectr and Lectr in English, Birkbeck Coll., London, 1961–67; Lectr and Sen. Lectr, Royal Holloway Coll., later Royal Holloway and Bedford New Coll., London, 1967–87. Vis. Lectr, Swarthmore Coll., Pa, 1966. Chairman: English Assoc., 1987–92 (Centenary Hon. Fellow, 2006); Cttee for University English, 1988–90; Mem., Common English Forum, 2001–05. Editor, English, 1976–87; Advr, Agenda, 2004–11. *Publications:* (ed) The Survival of Poetry, 1970; Hamlet Closely Observed, 1985; (ed) English Economis'd, 1989; (ed) The Penguin History of Literature, vol. 7: The Twentieth Century, 1994; (with J. B. Bamborough) Commentary to Robert Burton, the Anatomy of Melancholy, vol. 1, 1998, vols 2 and 3, 2000; Assessing Research Assessment in English, 2006; contribs to The Guardian, Essays in Criticism, The Review, Review of English Studies, etc. *Recreations:* reading, eating and drinking, short walks. *Address:* 59 Temple Street, Brill, Bucks HP18 9SU. *T:* (01844) 237106.

**DODWELL, Christina;** writer and explorer; Chairman, Dodwell Trust, since 1996; Senior Attaché, Madagascar Consulate, since 1990; *b* Nigeria, 1 Feb. 1951; *d* of Christopher Bradford Dodwell and Evelyn Dodwell (*née* Beddow); *m* 1991, Stephen Hobbs (*d* 2013). *Educ:* Southover Manor, Lewes; Beechlawn Coll., Oxford. Journeys through Africa by horse, 1975–78, and through Papua New Guinea by horse and canoe, 1980–81; presenter, BBC films: River Journey-Waghi, 1984 (BAFTA award); Black Pearls of Polynesia, 1991; African Footsteps—Madagascar, 1996; over 40 documentary progs for BBC Radio 4. FRGS 1982. Mungo Park Medal, RSGS, 1989; Internat. Medal, Spanish Geographical Soc., 2014. *Publications:* Travels with Fortune, 1979; In Papua New Guinea, 1982; An Explorer's Handbook, 1984; A Traveller in China, 1986; A Traveller on Horseback, 1987; Travels with Pegasus, 1989; Beyond Siberia, 1993; Madagascar Travels, 1995. *E:* dodwellandhobbs@gmail.com.

**DODWELL, William John Ignatius;** Tax Director, Office of Tax Simplification, since 2019; Editor in Chief, Tax Adviser magazine, since 2018; *b* Purley, Surrey, 31 July 1956; *s* of Oscar Dodwell and Jennifer Dodwell; two *d*. *Educ:* John Fisher Sch., Purley; King's Coll. London (LLB); Queens' Coll., Cambridge (LLB 1978; LLM 1985). CTA 1981, CTA (Fellow) 2008; ACA 1981. Arthur Andersen, 1978–2002, Tax Partner, 1989–2002; Partner, Deloitte LLP, 2002–18, Hd of Tax Policy, 2005–18. *Recreations:* bridge, cooking, travel, movies. *Address:* Office of Tax Simplification, 1 Horse Guards Road, SW1A 2HQ. *E:* bill.dodwell@ots.gov.uk.

**DODWORTH, Air Vice-Marshal Peter,** CB 1994; OBE 1982; AFC 1971; DL; Royal Air Force, retired; Military Adviser to Vosper Thornycroft (formerly Bombardier Aerospace Defence Services), 1996–2003; *b* 12 Sept. 1940; *e s* of Eric and Edna Dodworth; *m* 1963, Kay Parry (*d* 2016); three *s* (and one twin *s* decd). *Educ:* Southport Grammar Sch.; Leeds Univ. (BSc Physics, 1961). Served: 54 Sqn Hunters, 1963–65; 4 FTS Gnats, 1965–67; Central Flying Sch., 1967–68; Harrier Conversion Team, 1969–72; Air Staff RAF Germany, 1972–76; OC Ops, RAF Wittering, 1976–79; ndc 1980; Air Comdr, Belize, 1980–82; staff, RAF Staff Coll., 1982–83; Stn comdr, RAF Wittering, 1983–85; Command Group Exec., HQ AAFCE, Ramstein, 1985–87; RCDS, 1987; Dir of Personnel, MoD, 1988–91; Defence Attaché and Hd, British Defence Staff (Washington), 1991–94; Sen. DS (A), RCDS, 1995–96. FRAeS 1997–2011. DL Lincs, 2004. Vice Chm., Burma Star Assoc., 2006–12. Chm. of Govs, Stamford Endowed Sch., 2005–10. Liveryman, Hon. Co. of Air Pilots (formerly GAPAN), 2004–. *Recreations:* golf, DIY, reading. *Club:* Royal Air Force (Chm., 1994–96).

**DOE, Rt Rev. Michael David;** an Hon. Assistant Bishop, Diocese of Southwark, since 2004; Preacher to Gray's Inn, since 2011; *b* Lymington, Hants, 24 Dec. 1947; *s* of late Albert Henry Doe and Violet Nellie Doe (*née* Curtis). *Educ:* Brockenhurst Grammar Sch.; Durham Univ. (BA 1969); Ripon Hall Theol Coll., Oxford. Ordained deacon, 1972, priest, 1973; Asst Curate, 1972–76, Hon. Curate, 1976–81, St Peter, St Helier, Morden; Youth Sec., BCC, 1976–81; Priest-Missioner, 1981–88, Vicar, 1988–89, Blackbird Leys LEP, Oxford; RD, Cowley, 1986–89; Social Responsibility Advr, dio. of Portsmouth, and Canon Residentiary, Portsmouth Cathedral, 1989–94; Suffragan Bp of Swindon, 1994–2004; Gen. Sec., USPG: Anglicans in World Mission (formerly Utd Soc. for the Propagation of the Gospel), 2004–11. Hon. LLD Bath, 2002. *Publications:* Seeking the Truth in Love, 2000; Today! The Mission of Jesus in the Gospel of Luke, 2009; Saving Power: the mission of God and the Anglican Communion, 2011. *Recreations:* theatre, radio, English fiction. *Address:* 405 West Carriage House, Royal Carriage Mews, Royal Arsenal, Woolwich, SE18 6GA.

**DOE, Prof. William Fairbank,** FRCP, FRACP, FMedSci; Provost, Aga Khan University, 2008–11; Professor and Head of Medical School, University of Birmingham, 1998–2007, now Professor Emeritus of Medicine (Dean of Medicine, Dentistry and Health Sciences, 1998–2002; Dean of Medicine, 2002–07); *b* 6 May 1941; *s* of Asa Garfield Doe and Hazel Thelma Doe; *m* 1982, Dallas Elizabeth Edith Ariotti; two *s*. *Educ:* Newington Coll., Sydney; Univ. of Sydney (MB BS); Chelsea Coll., Univ. of London (MSc). FRACP 1978; FRCP 1982. MRC Fellow, 1970–71, Lectr, 1973–74, RPMS; Consultant, Hammersmith Hosp., 1973–74; Lilly Internat. Fellow, 1974–75, Postdoctoral Fellow, 1975–77, Scripps Clinic and Res. Foundn, Calif; Associate Prof., Univ. of Sydney, and Hon. Physician, Royal N Shore Hosp., 1978–81; Prof. of Medicine and Clin. Scis, 1982–88, Head of Div. of Molecular Medicine, 1988–98, John Curtin Sch. of Med. Res., ANU; Dir of Gastroenterology, Canberra Hosp., 1991–97; Prof. of Medicine, Univ. of Sydney, 1995–98. WHO Cons., Beijing, 1987; Dist. Vis. Fellow, Christ's Coll., Cambridge, 1988–89. Dep. Chm., Council of Hds of Med. Schs, 2002–06. Non-executive Director: Birmingham HA, 1998–2003; Birmingham and Black Country Strategic HA, 2003–06. Pres., Gastroenterological Soc. of Australia, 1989–91 (Dist. Res. Medal, 1997); Member: NH&MRC Social Psychiatry Adv. Cttee, 1982–92; Council, Nat. Centre for Epidemiology Population Health, 1987–98; Aust. Drug Evaluation Cttee, 1988–95; Council, RACP, 1993–98 (Censor, 1980–87); NH&MRC Res. Strategy Cttee, 1997–98; Workforce Develt Confedn, 2002–06; Wkg Party, Defining and Maintaining Professional Values in Medicine, RCP, 2004–07. Mem. Council, Univ. of Birmingham, 2004–06; Gov., Univ. of Worcester (formerly UC Worcester), 2004–07. Mem., Lunar Soc., 1999–2008. FMedSci 1999. Sen. Editor, Jl Gastroenterology and Hepatology, 1993–2001. *Publications:* numerous scientific papers on molecular cell biology of mucosal inflammation and colon cancer. *Recreations:* opera, reading, wine, tennis. *E:* williamfdoe@gmail.com. *Club:* Athenæum.

**DOEL, Air Cdre Prof. Martin Terry,** CBE 2016 (OBE 1998); FETL Professor for Further Education and Skills, and Co-Director, Centre for Post-14 Education, Institute of Education, University College London, since 2016; *b* Romsey, Hants, 21 Nov. 1956; *s* of Terry and Brenda Doel; *m* 1980, Angela; two *s*. *Educ:* Totton Grammar Sch.; Totton Sixth Form Coll.; King Alfred's Coll., Winchester (BEd 1st Cl. Hons); King's Coll. London (MA War Studies (Dist.)); RAF Staff Coll., Cranwell. FRAeS 2002. Served RAF, 1980–2008: RAF Staff Coll., 1994; Mem., Directing Staff, JSCSC, 1998–2000; Station Comdr, RAF Wyton, Brampton and Henlow, 2000–03; Director: RAF Div., JSCSC, 2003–04; Personnel and Trng Strategy, RAF, 2004–06; Trng and Educn, MoD, 2006–08. Chief Exec., Assoc. of Colls, 2008–16. Member: UK Council of Colls, 2010–16; Adv. Bd, Skills Funding Agency, 2010–17 (Mem., Audit Bd, 2013–17); Bd, Skills Show (UK), 2011–13; Adv. Bd, Career Academies UK, 2012–; Further Educn Learning Technol. Action Gp, 2013–16; Owners' Bd, JISC, 2014–16; Internat. Educn Adv. Forum, British Council, 2014–16; Adv. Bd, Step Up to Serve, 2014–16; Bd, UK/India Educn and Res. Initiative, 2015–; Audit and Risk Bd, Inst. for Apprenticeships, then Inst. for Apprenticeships and Tech. Educn, 2017–. Special Advr, Career Colls, 2014–. Treas., World Fedn of Colls and Polys, 2009–16. Trustee: Aspire and Achieve Foundn, 2008–14; Challenge Network, 2015–; Royal Soc. for Blind Children, 2016–; Cadet Vocational Qualifs Orgn, 2017–. Dir, Skilful Strategies Ltd, 2016–. Gov., Cambridge Regl Coll., 2017–. Liveryman, Educators' Co. FRSA 2008. *Publications:* (contrib.) International Frontiers in College Education, 2018; contrib. articles on military assistance in humanitarian aid ops, apprenticeships and enterprise educn. *Recreations:* soccer (Life Vice-Pres., RAF FA), cinema, modern art, military history and theory. *Address:* UCL Institute of Education, 20 Bedford Way, WC1H 0AL. *E:* m.doel@ioe.ac.uk. *Club:* Royal Air Force.

**DOERRIES, Chantal-Aimée Renée Amelia Annemarie;** QC 2008; *b* 26 Aug. 1968; *d* of Dr Reinhard R. Doerries and Elaine L. Doerries (*née* Sulli). *Educ:* Roedean Sch.; Univ. of Pennsylvania; New Hall, Cambridge (BA 1990). Pres., Cambridge Union Soc., 1989. Called to the Bar, Middle Temple, 1992 (Maj. Harmsworth Entrance Exhibn and Diplock Schol.), Bencher, 2010; Head, Atkin Chambers, 2017–. Chairman: Technol. and Construction Bar Assoc., 2010–13 (Vice-Chm., 2007–10); Bar Council of England and Wales, 2016 (Vice Chm., 2015); Chm., Internat. Cttee, 2011–14); Co-Chair, Forum for Barristers and Advocates, Internat. Bar Assoc., 2009–11. Fellow, Amer. Bar Foundn, 2010. Gertrude de Gallaix Achievement Award, Fedn of Amer. Women's Clubs Overseas, 1990. Jt Ed., Building Law Reports, 1999–; Co-Ed. in Chief, Internat. Construction Law Rev., 2015–. *Publications:* (contrib. ed) Hudson's Building and Engineering Contracts, 12th edn, 2010, 13th edn, 2015. *Address:* 1 Atkin Building, Gray's Inn, WC1R 5AT. *T:* (020) 7404 0102. *E:* clerks@atkinchambers.com.

**DOGANIS, Sally Elizabeth;** freelance executive television producer, broadcaster, journalist and media consultant; Executive Producer, Brook Lapping, since 2005; *b* London, 16 Jan. 1942; *d* of Joe and Freda Davis; *m* 1968, Prof. Rigas Doganis; one *s* one *d*. *Educ:* Woodhouse Grammar Sch.; Sorbonne, Paris (Dip. Civilisation Français); London Sch. of Econs (Leverhulme Schol.; BA Hons); Univ. of Calif, Berkeley (Fulbright Schol.; MA). W African corresp., BBC Africa Service and Sunday Times, 1967–68; Producer Director: Money Prog., 1968–71; Current Affairs Special Projects, BBC World Service, 1972–73; Dir, two films for English learners, BBC External Service, 1975–76; sen. producer and exec. producer, Nationwide, 1978–80, Money Prog., 1980 (Shell Award for best financial film, 1980), Newsnight, 1982, Panorama (Best Journalism Awards, RTS, 1982, 1983), Everyman and documentary series, BBC TV; producer, 1978–94: The Marketing of Margaret; The Falklands and the Media; Jasmine a Death too Many; A Bitter Pill; Family Secrets; TV and No. 10; Out of the Doll's House; The People's Century; Legendary Trails; On Trial; Just Deserts; Series Ed., Hard Luck Stories, 1981–82; Exec. Producer, Mentorn, 1995–96; Consultant, Channel One, on trng video journalists, 1995–97; Mental Health Manager: Tower Hamlets, 1997–99; Royal Free Hosp., 2000–04; Exec. Producer and Controller, Factual Progs, Carlton TV, 1998–2003: producer: Churchill's Secret Army; Ancient Greek Olympics; Britain at War in Colour; The Facts of Life; Kelly and her Sisters (BAFTA, RTS, Broadcast and Grierson Awards for Best Documentary, 2002); Hd of Documentaries, Target, 2004–05. Vis. Course Leader in Media Mgt, London Business Sch., 1985–88. Member: AHRC, 2007–13 (Chm., Stakeholders Cttee, 2012–13); Adv. Bds, Res. Councils UK, 2008–; Ethics Cttee, NHS, 2011–. Mem. Council, RTS, 1996–2003. Trustee: MA Media Mgt Course, LSE, 1997–2001; Catch 22 (charity), 2003–10; Fundraising Cttee, Central Ballet Sch., 2004–07; Mem. Council, Friends of Kenwood, 2004–; Chm., Corporate Benefactors Cttee, Kenwood, 2010–; Mem., Develt Cttee, Tricycle Th., 2010–. Member Board: Forum UK, 2010–; Internat. Women's Fedn UK, 2011–15. Jury mem. for awards from RTS, BAFTA, Grierson, One World Trust and Emmy Awards, 1997–. FRTS 1997. Golden Jury USA Award, Worldfest Houston, 1998; Gemini Canada Award, Canadian Acad. of Film and TV, 1998. *Publications:* (with Margaret Jay) Battered: the abuse of children, 1986; for children: Three Bags Full, 1976; The Milk Run, 1976; Bricks and

Mortar, 1977; Fish and Ships, 1977; contrib. articles to The Guardian, Sunday Times, The Listener, History Today. *Recreations:* tennis, swimming, ballet, learning Greek, relaxing in Antiparos, grandmothering. *E:* sally@doganisassociates.co.uk. *Club:* Globe Tennis.

**DOHERTY, Hon. Lord; (Joseph) Raymond Doherty;** a Senator of the College of Justice in Scotland, since 2010; *b* 1958; *s* of late James Doherty and of Mary Doherty; *m* 1994, Arlene Donaghy; one *s* two *d*. *Educ:* St Mungo's Primary Sch., Alloa; St Joseph's Coll., Dumfries; Univ. of Edinburgh (LLB 1st Cl. Hons 1980); Hertford Coll., Oxford (BCL 1982); Harvard Law Sch. (LLM 1983). Simpson & Marwick WS, 1980–81; Lord Reid Schol., 1983–85; admitted Faculty of Advocates, 1984; QC (Scot.) 1997. Standing Junior Counsel: MoD (Army), Scotland, 1990–91; Scottish Office Industry Dept, 1992–97; Advocate Depute, 1998–2001; Mem., Lands Valuation Appeal Court, 2011–; Judge, Upper Tribunal (Tax and Chancery Chamber), 2014–; Commercial Judge, 2014–19, Principal Commercial Judge, 2018–; Exchequer Judge, 2014–; Chm., Competition Appeal Tribunal, 2015–. Clerk of the Faculty of Advocates, 1990–95. *Publications:* (ed jtly) Armour on Valuation for Rating, 1990–; (contrib.) Stair Memorial Encyclopaedia of the Laws of Scotland. *Address:* Supreme Courts, Parliament House, Parliament Square, Edinburgh EH1 1RQ.

**DOHERTY, Andrew,** FREng, FIET, FIRSE; Chief Rail Technology Officer, Network Rail, since 2015; *b* Redhill, 1956; *s* of late Richard and Mary Doherty; *m* 1979, Jacqueline; three *s*. *Educ:* Brunel Univ. (BSc Electrical and Electronic Engrg 1979). FIET 1991; FREng 2014. Project Dir, Central and Northern Line Projects, London Underground, 1994; Dir, System Engrg, Network Rail, 2003–15. Visiting Professor: Newcastle upon Tyne Univ., 2009–14; Southampton Univ., 2011–; Cranfield Univ., 2013–. FIRSE 1992; FPWI 2017.

**DOHERTY, Berlie;** author, playwright and librettist, since 1982; *b* 6 Nov. 1943; *d* of Walter and Margaret Hollingsworth; *m* 1st, 1966, Gerard Doherty (marr. diss. 1996); one *s* two *d*; 2nd, 2013, Alan James Brown. *Educ:* Upton Hall Convent; Durham Univ. (BA Hons English); Liverpool Univ. (Postgrad. Cert. Social Studies); Sheffield Univ. (Postgrad. Cert Ed). Social worker, Leics Social Services, 1966–67; English teacher, Sheffield, 1979–82; on secondment to BBC Radio Sheffield Schools Progs, 1980–82. Various writing workshops for WEA, Sheffield Univ. and Arvon Foundn, 1978–90. Hon. Dr Derby, 2002. *Publications:* How Green You Are!, 1982; The Making of Fingers Finnigan, 1983; Tilly Mint Tales, 1984; White Peak Farm, 1984; Children of Winter, 1985; Granny Was a Buffer Girl, 1986; Tilly Mint and the Dodo, 1988; Tough Luck, 1988; Paddiwak and Cosy, 1988; Spellhorn, 1989; Dear Nobody, 1991; Requiem, 1991; Snowy, 1993; Walking on Air, 1993; Big Bulgy Fat Black Slugs, 1993; Old Father Christmas, 1993; Street Child, 1993; The Vinegar Jar, 1994; Willa and Old Miss Annie, 1994; The Magical Bicycle, 1995; The Golden Bird, 1995; The Snake-Stone, 1995; Our Field, 1996; Daughter of the Sea, 1996; Running on Ice (collected stories), 1997; Bella's Den, 1997, re-publd 2018; Tales of Wonder and Magic, 1997; Midnight Man, 1998; The Forsaken Merman, 1998; The Sailing Ship Tree, 1998; The Snow Queen, 1998; Fairy Tales, 2000; The Famous Adventures of Jack, 2000; Zzaap and the Wordmaster, 2000; Holly Starcross, 2001; The Nutcracker, 2002; Blue John, 2003, 2nd edn 2017; Coconut Comes to School, 2003; Deep Secret, 2003; Tricky Nelly's Birthday Treat, 2003; The Starburster, 2004; Jinnie Ghost, 2005; Jeannie of White Peak Farm, 2005; The Humming Machine, 2006; Abela: the girl who saw lions, 2007, 2nd edn as The Girl Who Saw Lions, 2018; The Oxford Book of Bible Stories, 2007; The Windspinner, 2008; A Beautiful Place for a Murder, 2008; A Calf called Valentine, 2009; Valentine's Day, 2009; Nightmare, 2009; Treason, 2011; The Three Princes, 2011; Wild Cat, 2012; The Company of Ghosts, 2013; The Starburster Stories, 2013; Snowy, 2014; Far From Home, 2015; Joe and the Dragonosaurus, 2015; *playscripts include:* Sacrifice, 1985; Return to the Ebro, 1986; Dear Nobody, 1995; Morgan's Field, 1995; Heidi, 1996; The Water Babies, 1998; Lorna Doone, 2001; Granny Was a Buffer Girl, 2002; Street Child, 2005; The Snake-stone, 2006; Thin Air, 2012; *operas include:* The Magician's Cat, 2004; Daughter of the Sea, 2004; Wild Cat, 2007. *Recreations:* walking, music, reading, theatre and opera going. *Address:* c/o David Higham Associates Ltd, 7th Floor, Waverley House, 7–12 Noel Street, W1F 8GQ.

**DOHERTY, (Christina) Claire,** MBE 2015; Associate Director, Situations, since 2019 (Founder Director, 2002–17); Associate, People Make It Work, since 2019; *b* Guildford, 29 Dec. 1969; *d* of Neil and Barbara Doherty; *m* 2001, Michael Prior; two *d*. *Educ:* Herts and Essex High Sch.; Felsted Sch.; Courtauld Inst. Art (BA Hist. of Art 1993); Royal Coll. of Art (MA Curating and Commng Contemp. Art 1995). Curator, Ikon Gall., Birmingham, 1995–2000; Associate Curator, Foundn for Art and Creative Technol., Liverpool, 2001–03; Curatorial Dir, One Day Sculpture, NZ, 2006–09; Dir, Arnolfini, 2017–19. Sen. Res. Fellow in Fine Art, UWE, 2002–17. Trustee: Common Guild, 2016–18; Artes Mundi, 2016–. Mem., Feminism Club. *Publications:* Contemporary Art: from studio to situation, 2004; Situation: documents of contemporary art, 2009; Public Art Now, 2015. *Recreations:* theatre, film, Radio 4, cheerleader of girls and young women.

**DOHERTY, Michael Eunan;** Chairman, Epsom and St Helier NHS Trust, 2002–07; *b* 21 Sept. 1939; *s* of Michael Joseph Doherty and Grace Doherty (*née* Gallagher); *m* 1st, 1965, Judy Battams (marr. diss 2008); two *s* two *d*; 2nd, 2009, Marion Eames. *Educ:* St Bernard's RC Sch., London. FCA 1977. Partner, Turquands Barton Mayhew, 1960–72; Man. Dir, Anglo-Thai Gp, 1973–82; Chief Exec., Cope Allman Internat. plc, 1982–88; Chairman: Henlys plc, 1985–88, 1991–97; Norcros plc, 1988–97. Chm., King's Healthcare, then King's Coll. Hosp., NHS Trust, 1996–2002; Trustee, KCH Charitable Trust, 1999–2004. Chm. Govs, St John's Sch., Leatherhead, 1997–2006. CCMI (CIMgt 1985). *Recreations:* golf, music, reading, politics. *Address:* Walnut Tree House, 10 Sycamore Close, Fetcham, Surrey KT22 9EX. *T:* (01372) 375212. *Club:* Royal Automobile.

**DOHERTY, Moira;** Deputy Secretary, Engaged Communities, Department for Communities, Northern Ireland, since 2019; *b* Newtownards, NI, 20 March 1974; *d* of Michael Doherty and Bernadette Doherty; *m* 2006, Chris Matthews; two *s*. *Educ:* Queen's Univ., Belfast (LLB, MPhil). Policy roles, NI Office, 1999–2010; Department of Justice: Director: Central Co-ordination Div., 2010–13; Strategy, Innovation and Res., 2013–14; Community Safety, 2014–15; Department for Infrastructure (formerly Department for Regional Development): Director: Strategy, Communication and Change, 2015–17; Public Transport Div., 2017–19. Trustee, Turnaround charity, 2018–. *Recreations:* theatre, cinema, reading. *Address:* Department for Communities, Level 9, Causeway Exchange, 1–7 Bedford Street, Belfast BT2 7EG. *T:* (028) 9082 3556. *E:* moira.doherty@communities-ni.gov.uk.

**DOHERTY, Pat;** *b* Glasgow, 18 July 1945; *m* Mary; two *s* three *d*. Sinn Féin: Dir of Elections, 1984–85; Nat. Organiser, 1985–88; Vice-Pres., 1988–2009; Leader of delegn to Forum for Peace and Reconciliation, Dublin, 1994–96. Northern Ireland Assembly: Mem. (SF) W Tyrone, 1998–June 2012; Chm., Enterprise, Trade and Investment Cttee, 1999–2002. Contested (SF) W Tyrone, 1997. MP (SF) W Tyrone, 2001–17.

**DOHERTY, Prof. Peter Charles,** AC 1997; FRS 1987; FAA 1983; Laureate Professor, Department of Microbiology and Immunology, University of Melbourne, since 2002; *b* 15 Oct. 1940; *s* of Eric C. and Linda M. Doherty; *m* 1965, Penelope Stephens; two *s*. *Educ:* Univ. of Queensland (BVSc, MVSc); Univ. of Edinburgh (PhD). Veterinary Officer, Queensland Dept of Primary Industries, 1962–67; Scientific Officer, Moredun Research Inst., Edinburgh, 1967–71; Research Fellow, Dept of Microbiology, John Curtin Sch. of Med. Research, Canberra, 1972–75; Associate Prof., later Prof., Wistar Inst., Philadelphia, 1975–82; Prof. of Experimental Pathology, John Curtin Sch. of Medical Res., ANU, 1982–88; Michael F. Tamer Chair of Biomed. Res., 1988–, Chm., Dept of Immunology, 1988–2002, St Jude Children's Res. Hosp., Memphis. Bd Mem., Internat. Lab. for Res. on Animal Disease, Nairobi, 1987–92. Mem., US Nat. Acad. of Sci., 1998. Hon. doctorates from 23 univs. Paul Ehrlich Prize and Medal for Immunology, 1983; Gairdner Internat. Award for Med. Research, 1987; Alumnus of Year, Univ. of Queensland, 1993; Lasker Award for Basic Med. Res., 1995; (jtly) Nobel Prize in Physiology or Medicine, 1996; Australian of the Year, Nat. Australia Day Council, 1997. *Publications:* The Beginner's Guide to Winning the Nobel Prize, 2005; A Light History of Hot Air, 2007; Sentinel Chickens: what birds tell us about our health and the world, 2012, 2nd edn as Their Fate is Our Fate: how birds foretell threats to our health and our world, 2013; Pandemics: what everyone needs to know, 2013; The Knowledge Wars, 2015; The Incidental Tourist, 2018; over 450 re. papers and review articles in scientific jls. *Recreations:* walking, reading, listening to music. *Address:* Department of Microbiology and Immunology, Peter Doherty Institute, University of Melbourne, Vic 3010, Australia. *T:* (3) 83447968.

**DOHERTY, Raymond;** *see* Doherty, Hon. Lord.

**DOHERTY, Una Frances;** QC (Scot.) 2018; *b* Stirling, 25 July 1963; *d* of James Doherty and Mary Doherty; *m* 2000, Douglas Fairley; one *s* one *d*. *Educ:* High Sch. of Stirling; Univ. of Edinburgh (LLB Hons; DipLP). Admitted solicitor, 1988; solicitor in private practice, 1988–98, Partner, Balfour & Manson, 1993–98; called as Advocate, Scottish Bar, 1999. *Recreations:* music, travel, family. *Address:* Advocates' Library, Parliament House, Edinburgh EH1 1RF. *T:* (0131) 226 5071.

**DOHMANN, Barbara;** QC 1987; *b* Berlin; *d* of Paul Dohmann and Dora Dohmann (*née* Thiele). *Educ:* schools in Germany and USA; Univs of Erlangen, Mainz and Paris. Called to the Bar, Gray's Inn, 1971, Bencher, 2007; a Recorder, 1990–2002; a Dep. High Court Judge, 1994–2003. Judge (part-time) of Civil and Commercial Court, Qatar Financial Centre, Doha, 2007–17; Chm., Internat. Arbitration Centre, Astana, Kazakhstan, 2018–. Arbitrator: ICC; London Court of Internat. Arbitration; Hong Kong Internat. Arbitration Centre; ICSID; Mediator, CEDR, 2010. Member: BVI Bar; Learned Soc. for Internat. Civil Procedure Law, 1991–; London Ct of Internat. Arbitration, 2012–; Chm., Commercial Bar Assoc., 1999–2001 (Treas., 1997–99; Mem. Cttee, 2001–); Member: Gen. Council of the Bar, 1999–2001, 2014–; Legal Services Cttee, 2000–01; German Bar Assoc., 2012–; Bar Eur. Gp, 2000– (Leader, Eur. Circuit, 2014–16); Lord Chancellor's Standing Cttee of Internat. Law, 2007–; London Metal Exchange: Special Cttee, 2007–; Appeal Panel; Arbitration Panel, 2014–. Member: Bd of Govs, London Inst. Higher Educn Corp., 1993–2000; Chancellor's Forum, Univ. of the Arts, London (formerly London Inst. Higher Educn Corp.), 2000–. *Recreations:* gardening, mountain walking, opera, art. *Address:* Blackstone Chambers, Blackstone House, Temple, EC4Y 9BW. *T:* (020) 7583 1770. *Club:* Athenæum.

**DOHNÁNYI, Christoph v.;** *see* von Dohnányi.

**DOIG, David William Neal;** Clerk of Bills, House of Commons, 2006–08; *b* 15 Jan. 1950; *s* of William Doig and Audrey Doig; *m* 1977, Alison Dorothy Farrar; one *s* three *d*. *Educ:* Perse Sch., Cambridge; Jesus Coll., Cambridge (BA Mod. and Mediaeval Langs 1972); City of London Poly. (Dip. Tech. and Specialist Translation 1973). House of Commons: Asst Clerk, 1973–77; Sen. Clerk, 1977–85; Dep. Principal Clerk, 1985–2000; Registrar of Members' Interests, 2000; Principal Clerk of Select Cttees, 2001–06. Advr, Inquiry into MPs' expenses, Cttee on Standards in Public Life, 2009. *Recreations:* gardening, cricket, meccano. *Address:* Quayham, Foots Lane, Burwash Weald, E Sussex TN19 7LE.

**DOIMI DE FRANKOPAN, Peter;** *see* Frankopan, P. D. de.

**DOLAN, Dorothy Elizabeth;** *see* Porter, D. E.

**DOLAN, Prof. Liam,** PhD; FRS 2014; Sherardian Professor of Botany, University of Oxford, since 2009; Fellow, Magdalen College, Oxford, since 2009. *Educ:* University Coll. Dublin (BSc, MSc); Univ. of Pennsylvania (PhD). Project Leader, Cell Patterning, Morphogenesis and Evolution in Plants, John Innes Centre, Norwich, until 2009. Hon. Prof. of Biol., UEA, until 2009. Mem., Bd of Trustees, Royal Botanic Gardens, Kew, 2016–. Mem. EMBO, 2009. *Publications:* (jtly) Plant Biology, 2009; articles in jls. *Address:* Department of Plant Sciences, University of Oxford, South Parks Road, Oxford OX1 3RB.

**DOLAN, Prof. Paul,** DPhil; Professor of Behavioural Science, since 2010 and Head, Department of Psychological and Behavioural Science, London School of Economics and Political Science. *Educ:* University Coll. of Swansea (BSc (Econ) 1989); Univ. of York (MSc (Econ) 1991; DPhil (Econ) 1997). Res. Fellow, Centre for Health Scis, Univ. of York, 1991–94; Lectr in Econs, Univs of Newcastle upon Tyne and York, 1994–98; University of Sheffield: Sen. Lectr in Health Econs, 1998–2000; Prof. of Health Econs, 2000–06; Dir, Centre for Well-being in Public Policy, 2004–06; Prof. of Econs, Imperial Coll. London, 2006–09; on secondment as Mem., Behavioural Insights Team, Cabinet Office, 2010–11. Vis. Res. Schol., Princeton Univ., 2004–05. Philip Leverhulme Prize for Econs, Leverhulme Trust, 2002. *Publications:* (with J. Olsen) Distributing Health Care: economic and ethical issues, 2002; Happiness by Design, 2014; Happy Ever After: escaping the myth of the perfect life, 2019. *Address:* Department of Psychological and Behavioural Science, London School of Economics and Political Science, Houghton Street, WC2A 2AE. *E:* p.h.dolan@lse.ac.uk.

**DOLAN, Prof. Raymond Joseph,** MD; FRCP, FRCPsych, FMedSci; FRS 2010; Kinross Professor of Neuropsychiatry, since 2001, Director, Wellcome Centre for Human Neuroimaging (formerly Wellcome Trust Centre for Neuroimaging), since 2006, and Director, Max Planck Centre for Computational Psychiatry and Ageing, since 2014, University College London; *b* 21 Jan. 1954; *s* of John Dolan and Julia Dolan (*née* Coppenger); *m* 1996, Sheela Kulaveerasingam; three *s*. *Educ:* St Jarlath's Coll., Tuam; University Coll. Galway Medical Sch. (MB BCh BAO Hons 1977; MD 1987). FRCPsych 1995; FRCP 2002. Psychiatry trng, Royal Free and Maudsley Hosps; Sen. Lectr, Royal Free Hosp. Sch. of Medicine, 1987–94; Reader, Inst. of Neurology, 1995–96; Prof., Inst. of Neurology, UCL, 1996–2001. Einstein Vis. Fellow, 2010. Ext. Scientific Mem., Max Planck Soc., 2012–. FMedSci 2000. Hon. MRIA 2011. Klaus Joachim Zülch Prize, Gertrud Reemtsma Foundn, 2013; (jtly) Brain Prize, Lundbeck Foundn, 2017. *Publications:* Human Brain Function, 1997, 2nd edn 2004; over 400 papers in jls incl. Nature, Science, Neuron, Jl of Neuroscience, Nature Neuroscience, Brain. *Recreations:* walking, reading, music, fly-fishing, midnight rambling. *Address:* Wellcome Centre for Human Neuroimaging, 12 Queen Square, WC1N 3BG. *T:* (020) 3448 4346. *E:* r.dolan@ucl.ac.uk. *Clubs:* Groucho, Soho House; Country Half-Life.

**DOLBY, Elizabeth Grace;** *see* Cassidy, E. G.

**DOLCE, Domenico**; Chief Executive Officer, Dolce & Gabbana; b 13 Sept. 1958; s of Saverio Dolce. Worked in father's clothing factory, Sicily; Asst in design studio, Milan; with Stefano Gabbana opened fashion consulting studio, 1982; Co-founder, Dolce & Gabbana, 1985; first major women's collection, 1986; knitwear, 1987; beachwear, lingerie, 1989; men's collection, 1990; women's fragrance, 1992; D&G line, men's fragrance, 1994; eyewear, 1995; opened boutiques in major cities in Europe, America and Asia. *Publications*: (with Stefano Gabbana): 10 Years Dolce & Gabbana, 1996; Wildness, 1997; Mémoires de la Mode, 1998; Animal, 1998; Calcio, 2004; Music, 2005; 20 Years Dolce & Gabbana, 2005; (with Eve Claxton and Stefano Gabbana) Hollywood, 2003. *Address*: Dolce & Gabbana, Via Goldoni 10, 20129 Milan, Italy.

**DOLE, Robert Joseph, (Bob)**; Purple Heart; Special Counsel, Alston & Bird, since 2003; Founder and President, Bob Dole Enterprises Inc.; b Russell, Kansas, 22 July 1923; s of Doran and Bina Dole; m 1975, Elizabeth Hanford; one d. *Educ*: Univ. of Kansas (AB); Washburn Municipal Univ. (LLB). Served US Army, 1943–48; Platoon Ldr, 10th Mountain Div., Italy; wounded and decorated twice for heroic achievement. Captain. Kansas Legislature, 1951–53; Russell County Attorney, Kansas, 1953–61; US House of Reps, 1960–68; US Senator, 1968–96; Republican Leader, 1985–96, Leader, 1995–96, US Senate; Leader, Republican Party, US, 1992–96; Republican Nominee for President, 1996. Special Counsel, Verner, Liipfert, Bernhard, McPherson and Hand, 1999–2003. Chairman: Internat. Commn on Missing Persons, 1997–; Nat. World War II Meml. US Presidential Medal of Freedom, 1997. *Publications*: (ed) Great Political Wit, 1998; (ed) Great Presidential Wit; One Soldier's Story (autobiog.), 2005. *Address*: c/o Alston & Bird LLP, 10th Floor, The Atlantic Building, 950 F Street NW, Washington, DC 20004–1404, USA.

**DOLLERY, Sir Colin (Terence)**, Kt 1987; FRCP, FMedSci; Dean, Royal Postgraduate Medical School, 1991–96, Pro-Vice-Chancellor for Medicine (formerly Medicine and Dentistry), 1992–96, University of London; b 14 March 1931; s of Cyril Robert and Thelma Mary Dollery; m 1958, Diana Myra (née Stedman); one s one d. *Educ*: Lincoln Sch.; Birmingham Univ. (BSc, MB, ChB); FRCP 1968. House officer: Queen Elizabeth Hosp., Birmingham; Hammersmith Hosp., and Brompton Hosp., 1956–58; Hammersmith Hospital: Med. Registrar, 1958–60; Sen. Registrar and Tutor in Medicine, 1960–62; Consultant Physician, 1962–; Lectr in Medicine, 1962–65, Prof. of Clinical Pharmacology, 1965–87, Prof. of Medicine, 1987–91, Royal Postgrad. Med. Sch. Sen. Consultant, R&D, Smithkline Beecham, later GlaxoSmithKline plc, 1996–2016. Member: MRC, 1982–84; UGC, subseq. UFC, 1984–91. Founder FMedSci 1998; FIC 2003. Hon. Mem., Assoc. of Amer. Physicians, 1982. Wellcome Gold Medal, British Pharmacol Soc., 2008; Oscar B. Hunter Award in Therapeutics, American Soc. of Clinical Pharmacol. and Therapeutics, 2009. Chevalier de l'Ordre National du Mérite (France), 1976. *Publications*: The Retinal Circulation, 1971 (New York); Therapeutic Drugs, 1991, 2nd edn 1998; numerous papers in scientific jls concerned with high blood pressure, drug action and importance of the secondary genome with project ENCODE. *Recreations*: travel, amateur radio G3GAF top of the honour roll, work on new targets for medicines. *Address*: 101 Corringham Road, NW11 7DL. *T*: (020) 8458 2616; Crossways, Spring Elms Lane, Little Baddow, Essex CM3 4SQ. *T*: (01245) 223326. *Club*: Athenæum.

**DOLMAN, Edward James**; Chief Executive Officer, Phillips, since 2014 (Chairman, 2014–17); b 24 Feb. 1960; s of James William Dolman and Jean Dolman; m 1st, 1987, Clare Callaghan (marr. diss.); one s one d; 2nd, 2015, Samantha Helen Gilbert. *Educ*: Dulwich Coll.; Southampton Univ. (BA Hons History). Joined Christie's, 1984; Dir and Head of Furniture Dept, Christie's S Kensington, 1990–95; Man. Dir, Christie's Amsterdam, 1995–97; Commercial Dir, 1997, Man. Dir, 1998–99, Christie's Europe; Dir, Christie, Manson & Woods Ltd, 1997; Man. Dir, Christie's America, 1999–2000; CEO, 2000–10, Chm., 2010–11, Christie's International plc; Exec. Dir, 2011–14, Acting Chief Exec., 2012–14, Qatar Museums Authy. Officier, Légion d'Honneur (France), 2012 (Chevalier, 2007). *Recreations*: art history, Rugby, cricket, sailing. *Clubs*: Royal Automobile, Old Alleynian (Vice Pres., 1998–); New York Yacht; Deepdale (NY).

**DOLMAN, Rev. Dr William Frederick Gerrit**; JP; HM Assistant Coroner (formerly Assistant Deputy Coroner), Inner West London, since 2007, South London, since 2008, and Inner North London, since 2012; b 14 Nov. 1942; s of Dr Gerrit Arnold Dolman and Madeline Joan Dolman. *Educ*: Whitgift Sch., Croydon; KCH Med. Sch., Univ. of London (MB BS 1965); LLB Hons London (ext.) 1987; SE Inst. of Theol Educn (DipTh (Merit) Univ. of Kent 2007). MRCS 1965; LRCP 1965; FFFLM 2005. Principal in Gen. Practice, 1967–74; Asst Dep. Coroner, 1974–86, Dep. Coroner, 1986–93, S London; Medical Referee, Croydon Crematorium, 1986–2017; Asst Dep. Coroner, 1988–89, Dep. Coroner, 1989–93, Inner W London; Coroner, N London, 1993–2007; Dep. Coroner, E London, 2007–12. Associate Dermatology Specialist, St Helier Hosp., Carshalton, 1992–2000. BBC Radio Doctor, Jimmy Young Show, Radio 2, 1977–2002. FRSocMed 1967 (Mem. Council, Forensic and Legal Medicine Section, 1996–2000); Pres., Croydon Medical Soc., 2002; Med. Sec., Coroners' Soc., 2004–08. Examiner, Soc. of Apothecaries, 2002–04 and 2007–10. Med. Editor, Modern Medicine, 1976–80; Editor: Coroner sect., Atkin's Court Forms, 2003–08; The Coroner, 2003–07. Founder and benefactor, Stanford-Dolman (formerly Dolman) Travel Book Award, 2006–. Ordained deacon, 2006, priest, 2007. JP Croydon, 1975 (Chm. Bench, 2007–08). *Publications*: Can I Speak to the Doctor?, 1981; Doctor on Call, 1987. *Recreations*: classical music, good food, fine wine, real ale, sitting in the garden looking at work that ought to be done. *Address*: Coroner's Court, 2nd Floor, Davis House, Robert Street, Croydon CR0 1QQ. *Clubs*: Authors' (Chm., 2000–04), Savile, National Liberal.

**DOLPHIN, Prof. Annette Catherine**, PhD; FMedSci; FRS 2015; Professor of Pharmacology, University College London, since 1997; b Maidenhead, 3 April 1951; d of Geoffrey William Dolphin and Yvonne Mary Dolphin (née Dowsett); m 2010, William James Frith. *Educ*: Alwyn Sch., Maidenhead; Hooker Sch., New Haven, Conn; Courthouse Sch., Maidenhead; Sch. of St Helen and St Katharine, Abingdon; St Hugh's Coll., Oxford (BA 1st Cl. Biochem. 1973); Inst. of Psychiatry, London (PhD 1977). MRC French Exchange Fellow, Collège de France, Paris, 1977–78; Fellowship, Yale Univ., 1978–80; Scientist, NIMR, 1980–83; Lectr, St George's Hosp. Med. Sch., 1983–89; Prof. of Pharmacol. and Chair of Dept, Royal Free Hosp. Sch. of Medicine, 1990–97. MAE 2018. FMedSci 1999. *Publications*: over 200 primary res. papers, reviews and book chapters. *Recreations*: extreme trekking, cross country ski-ing. *Address*: Department of Neuroscience, Physiology and Pharmacology, University College London, Gower Street, WC1E 6BT. *E*: a.dolphin@ucl.ac.uk.

**DOLPHIN, Prof. David Henry**, OC 2006; PhD; FRS 2002; FRS(Can); FRSC, FCIC; QLT/NSERC Industrial Research Professor of Photodynamic Technology, University of British Columbia, since 2005 (Professor of Chemistry, 1979–2005, now Emeritus). *Educ*: Univ. of Nottingham (BSc 1962; PhD 1965; DSc 1982). FRS(Can) 2001; FCIC 1981. Joined Harvard Univ. as Res. Fellow, 1965, subseq. Associate Prof. of Chemistry, until 1974; Associate Prof. of Chemistry, Univ. of BC, 1974. Vice-Pres., Technol. Develt, Quadra Logic Technologies, Vancouver, 1992. Guggenheim Fellow, 1980; Univ. Killam Prof., 2004. Gold Medal in Health Scis, Sci. Council of BC, 1990; Syntex Award, CIC, 1993; Bell Canada Forum Award, 1993; Izaak Walton Killam Res. Prize, Canada Council, 1996; Prix Galien Award, 2002; Friesen-Rygiel Prize, 2002; Award of Leadership in Canadian Pharmaceutical Scis, Canadian Soc. for Pharmaceutical Scis, 2002; Academic of the Year, Confedn of Univ. Faculty Assocs of BC, 2003; Hero of Chemistry, Amer. Chem. Soc., 2004; Award of Excellence, 2004, Herzberg Award, 2006, NSERC. *Publications*: (jtly) Tabulation of Infrared Spectral Data, 1977; (ed jtly) Biological Aspects of Inorganic Chemistry, 1977; (ed jtly) The Porphyrins, vol. I–VII, 1978–79; (ed jtly) Biomimetic Chemistry, 1980; Murakami and I. Tabushi, 1980; (ed) B12, 2 vols, 1982; (ed jtly) Biological Chemistry of Iron, 1982; (ed jtly) Coenzymes and Cofactors, vol. 1, 1986, vol. 2, 1987, vol. 3, 1989; articles in jls. *Address*: Department of Chemistry, University of British Columbia, 2036 Main Mall, Vancouver, BC V6T 1Z1, Canada.

**DOMBROVSKIS, Valdis**; Member and a Vice-President, European Commission, since 2014; b Riga, 5 Aug. 1971. *Educ*: Univ. of Latvia (BSc Physics 1993); Riga Tech. Univ. (BA Econs 1995; Professional Master's degree in customs and tax admin 2007); Univ. of Latvia and Univ. of Mainz (MSc Physics 1996); Univ. of Maryland (PhD 1998). Laboratory assistant: Inst. of Solid State Physics, Univ. of Latvia, 1991–93; Faculty of Physics and Maths, Dept of Semi-conductor Physics, Univ. of Latvia, 1993–95; Inst. of Physics, Meinz Univ., Germany, 1995–96; researcher, Inst. of Solid State Physics, Univ. of Latvia, 1997; lab. asst, Dept of Electrical Engrg, Univ. of Maryland, 1997–98; Monetary Policy Board, Bank of Latvia: specialist in macroecons, 1998–99; Sen. Economist, 1999–2001; Chief Economist, 2001–02; MP (New Era) Saeima, 2002–04; Minister for Finance, 2002–03; Advr to Minister of Econs, 2004–06; MEP (New Era) and Hd, Latvian delegn in ETP-ED gp, 2004–09; Minister for Children, Family and Integration Affairs, March–July 2009; Prime Minister of Latvia, 2009–13; MP (Unity), 2010–14. *Publications*: (jtly) Aufgelöste J2 Spektren mit Breitbandigen LasernÄ, 1997; (contrib.) The Role of Tax Administration and Customs in National Economy, 2003; contribs on econs and politics to periodicals, jls and electronic media. *Address*: European Commission, Rue de La Loi, 1049 Brussels, Belgium.

**DOMINGO, Placido**, Hon. KBE 2002; tenor singer, conductor; General Director: Washington Opera, 1996–2011; Los Angeles Opera, 2000–19; b Madrid, 21 Jan. 1941; s of Placido Domingo and Pepita (née Embil), professional singers; m 1962, Marta Ornelas, lyric soprano; two s (and one s by former marriage). *Educ*: Instituto, Mexico City; Nat. Conservatory of Music, Mexico City. Operatic début, Monterrey, as Alfredo in La Traviata, 1961; with opera houses at Dallas, Fort Worth, Israel, to 1965; débuts: NY City Opera, 1965; at NY Metropolitan Opera, as Maurizio in Adriana Lecouvreur, 1968; at La Scala, title rôle in Ernani, 1969; at Covent Garden, Cavaradossi in Tosca, 1971; has sung record 130 tenor rôles, 1961–2009; title rôle in Simon Boccanegra, State Opera, Berlin, 2009, Covent Garden, 2010. Has conducted in Vienna, Barcelona, NY and Frankfurt; début as conductor in UK, Covent Garden, 1983. *Films*: La Traviata, 1983; Carmen, 1984; Otello, 1986; appears on TV, makes recordings, throughout UK and Europe. Founder, Operalia competition, 1993. FRCM; FRNCM. Hon. doctorates include: RNCM, 1982; Philadelphia Coll. of Performing Arts, 1982; Complutense, Madrid, 1989; Anáhuac, Mexico, 2001; Hon. DMus Oxon, 2003. Birgit Nilsson Prize, Birgit Nilsson Foundn, 2009. Medal of City of Madrid; Orden de Isabel la Católica (Spain), 1986; Gran Cruz, Orden del Mérito Civil (Spain), 2002; foreign orders include: Chevalier, Legion of Honour (France), 2002 (Officer, 1983); US Medal of Freedom, 2002; Comdr, Ordre des Arts et des Lettres (France); Grande Ufficiale, Ordine al Merito della Repubblica Italiana; Grand Cross, Order of Infante Dom Henrique (Portugal); Order of Aztec Eagle (Mexico). *Publications*: My First Forty Years (autobiog.), 1983. *Recreations*: piano, swimming, football (Real Madrid), tennis, Formula 1. *W*: www.placidodomingo.com.

**DOMINICZAK, Prof. Dame Anna (Felicja)**, DBE 2016 (OBE 2005); MD; FRCPGlas; FRCPEd; FMedSci; FRSE; Regius Professor of Medicine, Vice Principal, and Head of College of Medical, Veterinary and Life Sciences, University of Glasgow, since 2010; b 26 Aug. 1954; d of Jacob Penson and Joanna Muszkowska; m 1976, Marek Dominiczak; one s. *Educ*: Medical Sch., Gdansk, Poland (MD Hons); Univ. of Glasgow (MD); MRCP 1986; FRCPGlas 1995; FRCPEd 2016. Jun. House Officer, Glasgow Royal Infirmary, 1982; Sen. House Officer and Registrar, Royal Alexandra Hosp., Paisley, 1983–86; MRC Clin. Scientist and Sen. Registrar, Western Infirmary, Glasgow, 1986–89; Res. Fellow, Univ. of Michigan, Ann Arbor, 1990–91; Clin. Lectr and Hon. Sen. Registrar, Univ. of Glasgow, 1992–93; University of Glasgow: BHF Sen. Res. Fellow, 1993–98; Sen. Lectr, Reader in Medicine, 1993–96; Prof. of Cardiovascular Medicine, 1997–; BHF Prof. of Cardiovascular Medicine, 1998–2010; Hon. Consultant Physician and Endocrinologist, 1993–, non-exec. Mem., 2011–, Gtr Glasgow and Clyde Health Bd. Pres., European Soc. of Hypertension, 2013–15. Ed.-in-Chief, Hypertension, 2012–. Vice Pres., Life Scis, RSE, 2012–15. Trustee, BHF, 2014–. FAHA 1996; FMedSci 2001; FRSE 2003. *Publications*: (ed) Genetics of Essential Hypertension, 1999; (ed) Genetics of Hypertension, 2007. *Recreation*: modern literature. *Address*: College of Medical, Veterinary and Life Sciences, University of Glasgow, Wolfson Medical School Building, University Avenue, Glasgow G12 8QQ. *T*: (0141) 330 2738, *Fax*: (0141) 330 5339. *E*: Anna.Dominiczak@glasgow.ac.uk.

**DOMOKOS, Dr Mátyás**; Ambassador, retired; General Director, CD Hungary (formerly Diplomatic Service Directorate, Ministry of Foreign Affairs, Hungary), 1989–95; b 28 Oct. 1930; m 1956, Irén Beretyán; one d. *Educ*: Karl Marx Univ. of Econs, Budapest. Foreign trading enterprises, 1954–57; Commercial Sec., Damascus and Trade Comr, Khartoum, 1958–61; various posts in Ministry for Foreign Trade, Hungary, 1961–74; Ambassador to UN, Geneva, 1974–79; Head of Dept of Internat. Organisations, Ministry of Foreign Affairs, 1979–84; Ambassador to UK, 1984–89. *Recreations*: gardening, chess. *Address*: 32 Str. Árnyas, 1121 Budapest, Hungary.

**DON, Montagu Denis Wyatt, (Monty)**, OBE 2018; writer and broadcaster; b 8 July 1955; s of late Denis Don and Janet Wyatt; m 1983, Sarah; two s one d. *Educ*: Magdalene Coll., Cambridge (MA Eng. 1979). Jt Founder, Monty Don Ltd (costume jewellery co.), 1981–91; freelance gardening journalist, 1988–; TV broadcaster, 1989–; presenter: Gardeners' World, 2002–08 and 2011–; Chelsea Flower Show, 2014–. Gardening Editor, The Observer, 1994–2006. Pres., Soil Assoc., 2008–. *Publications*: The Prickotty Bush, 1990; The Weekend Gardener, 1995; The Sensuous Garden, 1997; Gardening Mad, 1997; Urban Jungle, 1998; Fork to Fork, 1999; The Complete Gardener, 2003; (with Sarah Don) The Jewel Garden, 2004; Gardening from Berryfield, 2005; My Roots, 2005; Growing out of Trouble, 2006; Around the World in 80 Gardens, 2008; The Ivington Diaries, 2009; Gardening at Longmeadow, 2012; The Road to Tholonet: a French garden journey, 2013; (with Ann Dumas) Painting the Modern Garden: Monet to Matisse, 2015; Nigel: my family and other dogs, 2016; Down to Earth, 2017; (with Derry Moore) Paradise Gardens, 2018; (with Derry Moore) Japanese Gardens, 2019. *Recreations*: gardening, farming.

**DON, Nigel Anderson**; composer and music arranger, since 1989; b 16 April 1954; s of late Derek Don and Margaret Don; m 1977, Wendy Wrieden; one s one d. *Educ*: King's College Sch., Wimbledon; Pembroke Coll., Cambridge (BA 1975; MA 1979; MEng 2001); Univ. of London (LLB (ext.) 1982). CEng, MIChemE 1982. Chemical engr, Unilever plc, 1976–89; self-employed musician, 1989–2007. Mem. (SNP), Dundee CC, 2003–07. Mem. (SNP) Scotland NE, 2007–11, Angus N and Mearns, 2011–16, Scottish Parlt. *Recreations*: music, walking.

**DON-WAUCHOPE, Sir Roger (Hamilton),** 11th Bt *cr* 1667 (NS), of Newton Don and of Edmonstone; chartered accountant, retired, South Africa; Partner, Deloitte & Touche, 1972–98; *b* 16 Oct. 1938; *s* of Sir Patrick George Don-Wauchope, 10th Bt and Ismay Lilian Ursula (who later *m* George William Shipman), *d* of Sidney Richard Hodges; *S* father, 1989; *m* 1963, Sallee, *yr d* of Lt-Col Harold Mill-Colman, OBE, AMICE, Durban; two *s* one *d*. *Educ*: Hilton Coll., Natal; Univ. of Natal, Durban; Univ. of Natal, Pietermaritzburg (Higher Diploma in Taxation). Past Chm., Midlands Branch, KZN Inst. of Chartered Accountants. Gov., 1999–2012, and former Dep. Chm., Hiltonian Soc. Former Trustee, Tembaletu Educn Trust; Trustee, Emuseni Centre for the Aged. Mem. Cttee, Senior Golfers' Soc. of KwaZulu-Natal, 2005–13 (Capt., 2011; Pres., 2012–13). *Heir*: *s* Dr Andrew Craig Don-Wauchope [*b* 18 May 1966; *m* 1990, Louise Sylvia, *d* of John Crawford Johnstone-Dougall; one *s* two *d*]. *Address*: Newton, 53 Montrose Drive, Pietermaritzburg 3201, KwaZulu-Natal, South Africa. *T*: (033) 3471107. *E*: don-wauchope@intekom.co.za. *Clubs*: Victoria Country (Chm., 1993–95), Fleur-de-Lys (former Treas.) (Pietermaritzburg); Old Hiltonian (Chm., 1992–97; Vice Pres., 1998–); Prince's Grant Golf (Stanger).

**DONAGHY,** Baroness *cr* 2010 (Life Peer), of Peckham in the London Borough of Southwark; **Rita Margaret Donaghy,** CBE 2005 (OBE 1998); FCIPD; Chair, Advisory, Conciliation and Arbitration Service, 2000–07; *b* 9 Oct. 1944; *d* of late William Scott Willis and Margaret Brenda Willis (*née* Howard, later Bryan); *m* 1968, James Columba Donaghy (*d* 1986); *m* 2000, Ted Easen-Thomas. *Educ*: Leamington Coll. for Girls; Durham Univ. (BA 1967). FCIPD 2002. Tech. asst, NUT, 1967–68; Asst Registrar, 1968–84, Perm. Sec., Students' Union, 1984–2000, Inst. of Educn, Univ. of London. Member: Low Pay Commn, 1997–2000; Cttee on Standards in Public Life, 2001–07 (Interim Chm., 2007); Select Cttee on Personal Services, 2014; EU Sub-Cttee on Internal Mkts, H of L, 2015–; Statutory Instruments Cttee B, H of L, 2018–; Chair, H of L Inf. Cttee, 2014–16. Member: Nat. Exec. Council, NALGO/UNISON, 1973–2000; TUC Gen. Council, 1987–2000; President: NALGO, 1989–90; TUC, 2000; Mem. Exec., Eur. TUC, 1992–2000. Non-exec. Dir, KCH NHS Trust, 2005–09. Chm., DWP Inquiry into Fatal Construction Accidents, 2009. Member: Business Adv. Bd, Birmingham Univ., 2006–; Adv. Bd, Modern Records Centre, Warwick Univ., 2007–17. DUniv: Open, 2002; Keele, 2004; Hon. DBA Greenwich, 2005. *Recreations*: theatre, gardening, photography, watching cricket, eating out, reading. *Address*: House of Lords, SW1A 0PW. *Club*: Surrey County Cricket.

**DONAHOE, Arthur Richard;** QC (Can.) 1982; Secretary-General, Commonwealth Parliamentary Association, 1993–2001; *b* 7 April 1940; *s* of Richard A. Donahoe and Eileen (*née* Boyd); *m* 1972, Carolyn Elizabeth MacCormack. *Educ*: public schools in Halifax, NS; St Mary's Univ. (BComm 1959); Dalhousie Univ. (LLB 1965). Admitted to Bar of Nova Scotia, 1966; Exec. Asst to Leader of Opposition, Senate of Canada, 1967; barrister and solicitor, 1968–81; Lectr in Commercial Law, St Mary's Univ., 1972–75; MLA (PC), Nova Scotia, 1978–92, Speaker, 1981–91. Canadian Regl Rep., CPA Exec. Cttee, 1983–86. Hon. Mem., Exec. Council, Nova Scotia, 2015–. Hon. LLD St Mary's, 2008. *Publications*: contrib. articles to Parliamentarian, Canadian Parly Rev., and Round Table. *Recreations*: golf, reading, bridge. *Address*: Unit 13, 6770 Jubilee Road, Halifax, NS B3H 2H8, Canada. *T*: (902) 4227937. *Club*: Ashburn Golf (Pres., 1982–83).

**DONALD, Prof. Dame Athene Margaret,** DBE 2010; PhD; FRS 1999; Professor of Experimental Physics, University of Cambridge, since 1998; Master, Churchill College, Cambridge, since 2014; *b* 15 May 1953; *d* of Walter Griffith and Annette Marian (*née* Tylor); *m* 1976, Matthew J. Donald; one *s* one *d*. *Educ*: Camden Sch. for Girls; Girton Coll., Cambridge (BA, MA; PhD 1977; Hon. Fellow 2010). Postdoctoral research, Cornell Univ., 1977–81; University of Cambridge: SERC Res. Fellow, 1981–83; Royal Soc. Univ. Res. Fellow, 1983–85; Lectr, 1985–95; Reader, 1995–98; Dir, Women in Sci., Engrg and Technol. Initiative, 2007–14, and Gender Equality Champion, 2010–14; Fellow, Robinson Coll., Cambridge, 1981–2014 (Hon. Fellow, 2014). Member: Council, Royal Soc., 2004–06 and 2013–15; Scientific Council, Eur. Res. Council, 2013–18; Pres., British Sci. Assoc., 2015–16. Mem., Governing Council, Inst. Food Res., 1999–2003. Chairman: Sci. Adv. Council, DCMS, 2015–17; Interdisciplinary Adv. Panel, REF 2021, 2017–. Mem. Cttee, Longitude Prize, 2014–. Trustee, Nat. Mus. of Sci. and Industry, subseq. Sci. Mus. Gp, 2011–16. Hon. DSc: Exeter, 2012; UEA, 2012; Sheffield, 2013; Swansea, 2014; UCL, 2014; Liverpool, 2015; Manchester, 2015; Heriot-Watt, 2015; Leeds, 2016; Open, 2017; York, 2018; Brunel, 2018; Hon. LLB Bath 2017. Bakerian Prize Lect., Royal Soc., 2006; Samuel Locker Award in Physics, Birmingham Univ., 1989; Charles Vernon Boys Prize, 1989, Mott Prize, 2005, Faraday Medal, 2010, Inst. of Physics; Rosenhain Medal and Prize, Inst. Materials, 1995; William Hopkins Prize, Cambridge Philosophical Soc., 2003; For Women in Science Award, L'Oréal-UNESCO, 2009; Women of Outstanding Achievement Lifetime Achievement Award, UKRC, 2011. *Publications*: (with A. H. Windle) Liquid Crystalline Polymers, 1992, 2nd edn (with S. Hanna and A. H. Windle) 2006; (jtly) Starch: structure and function, 1997; Starch: advances in structure and function, 2001; articles on polymer, biopolymer, proteins, colloid and food physics and cellular biophysics in learned jls. *Address*: Cavendish Laboratory, University of Cambridge, J. J. Thomson Avenue, Cambridge CB3 0HE; Churchill College, Storey's Way, Cambridge CB3 0DS.

**DONALD, George Malcolm,** RSA 1992 (ARSA 1975); RSW 1976; SSA 1976; Keeper, Royal Scottish Academy, 2003–09 and 2013–18; *b* 12 Sept. 1943; *s* of George Donald and Margaret (*née* Tait); *m* 1966 (marr. diss.); one *s* one *d*. *Educ*: Edinburgh Coll. of Art (DA 1966; Post Grad. Dip. 1967); Hornsey Coll. of Art, London Univ. (ATC 1969); Edinburgh Univ. (MEd 1980). ILTM 2002. Edinburgh College of Art: Lectr, Sch. of Drawing and Painting, 1972–96; Tutor and Asst to Vice Principal (Art and Design), 1984–87; Director: Summer Sch., 1991–2004; Centre for Continuing Studies, 1996–2001. Printmaker in Residence, Soulisquoy Print Workshop, Orkney Is, 1988; Visiting Artist: Szechuan Fine Art Inst., China, 1989; Silpakorn Univ., Thailand, 1989; Chulalongkorn Univ., Thailand, 1989; Visiting Professor: Zhejiang Acad. Fine Art, China, 1994–; Univ. of Sharja, 2003–; British Council Vis. Prof., Kyoto, 1999, 2002, Korea, 2000; Adjunct Prof., Univ. of Central Florida, 2002–; Hon. Prof., Al Maktoum Inst., Dundee, 2009–; Vis. Lectr, Royal Drawing Sch. (formerly Prince's Drawing Sch.), London, 2008–. Solo exhibitions include: Art Dept Gall., Univ. of Central Florida, 1985, 2002, 2003, 2016; Dept of Fine Art, Univ. of Georgia, 1987; Open Eye Gall., Edinburgh, 1987, 1990, 1993, 1995, 1998, 2002, 2003, 2005, 2007, 2012, 2013, 2015, 2018; Galerija Fakulteta Likovnih Umetnosti, Belgrade, 1987; Bohun Gall., Henley-on-Thames, 2009, 2011, 2013; Scottish Arts Club, Edinburgh, 2012, 2015; touring exhibn, UK and France, 1990; Christopher Hull Gall., London, 1992; World Trade Centre, Dubai, 1994; Art Connection, Dubai, 2003, 2007, 2009; commissions: portrait, Glasgow Univ., Univ. of Edinburgh and Scottish Arts Council, 1985; window design, New Scottish Nat. Library, Edinburgh, 1986; portrait: Edinburgh Chamber of Commerce, 1986; St John's Hosp., Livingston, 1994; public collections include: Scottish Arts Council; Edinburgh, Aberdeen and Leeds CCs; Hunterian Mus., Glasgow Univ.; Heriot-Watt Univ.; Edinburgh Univ.; Victoria and Albert Mus.; IBM; BBC; Nat. Library of Scotland; Scottish Nat. Gall. of Modern Art; private collections in UK, Europe, Canada and USA, Asia and Australia. Latimer Award 1970, Guthrie Award 1973, Royal Scottish Acad.; Scottish Arts Council Bursary, 1973; Gillies Bequest Travel Award to India, Royal Scottish Acad., 1978, 2003. *Publications*: The New Maths, 1969; An Account of Travels in Turkey, Iran, Afghanistan, Pakistan, India, Kashmir and Nepal, 1969; An Indian Diary, 1980; Aims and Objectives in Teaching Drawing and Painting, 1980; The Day Book, 1987; Anatomia: an artists' book, 2004. *Recreations*: music, travelling. *Address*: c/o Royal Scottish Academy, Edinburgh EH2 2EL. *W*: www.georgedonald.com.

**DONALD, James Graham,** FRICS; Consultant, Strutt & Parker, since 2004 (Chairman 1996–2003); *b* 4 April 1944; *s* of William Graham Donald and Jean (Bubbles) Donald; *m* 1976, Jennifer Seaman; one *s* two *d*. *Educ*: Cranleigh Sch.; Coll. of Estate Mgt (BSc Estate Mgt). FRICS 1981. Savills, 1966–72; joined Strutt & Parker, 1972, Partner, 1978–2004. *Recreations*: cycling, travel, supporting the children, sport, reading. *Address*: c/o Strutt & Parker, 13 Hill Street, W1J 5LQ. *T*: (020) 7318 5020. *Clubs*: Richmond FC; Old Cranleighans.

**DONALD, Rob,** CEng, FCILT; Director General, Centro (West Midlands Passenger Transport Executive), 1995–2006; *b* 25 March 1949; *s* of John Donald and Mary Donald (*née* Gardiner); *m* 1st, 1972, Yvonne Dyer (marr. diss.); two *d*; 2nd, 1991, Marilyn Downie (*d* 2015); 3rd, 2019, Kathleen Binns. *Educ*: George Heriot's Sch., Edinburgh; Univ. of Edinburgh (BSc Hons); Imperial Coll., Univ. of London (MSc). MICE 1976; CEng 1976; FCILT (FCIT 1996). Graduate Asst, Brian Colquhoun and Partners, Consultants, London, 1971–73; Sen. Asst Officer, SIA Transport Consultants, London, 1973–75; Project Leader, County Surveyor's Dept, Kent CC, 1975–79; Chief Transportation Officer, Jt Transportation Unit, Merseyside CC, 1979–86; Merseytravel: Section Leader, then Manager, 1986–91; Passenger Services Dir, 1991–95. *Recreations*: travelling, reading, computing. *Address*: Norton Lodge, 32 Greyhound Lane, Stourbridge, W Midlands DY8 3AG. *T*: (01384) 838735.

**DONALDSON, Dr Alexander Ivan,** OBE 2003; Visiting Professor, Royal Veterinary College, University of London, since 2008; *b* 1 July 1942; *s* of Basil Ivan Donaldson and Dorothy Cunningham Donaldson; *m* 1966, Margaret Ruth Elizabeth Swan; one *d* one *s*. *Educ*: High Sch., Dublin; Trinity Coll., Univ. of Dublin (BA 1965; MVB 1965; MA 1968; ScD 1983); Ontario Veterinary Coll., Univ. of Guelph (PhD 1969). MRCVS 1965. Post-doctoral research, 1969–71, Vet. Res. Officer, 1973–76, Principal Vet. Res. Officer, 1976–89, Animal Virus Res. Inst., subseq. AFRC. Inst. for Animal Health, Pirbright Lab.; Head: World Ref. Lab. for Foot-and-Mouth Disease, 1985–89; Pirbright Lab., Inst. for Animal Health, 1989–2002. Vis. Prof., Ontario Vet. Coll., Univ. of Guelph, 1972–73. Hon. FRCVS 2003. Hon. DVM&S Edinburgh, 2002. Research Medal, RASE, 1988; Gold Medal, World Orgn for Animal Health, 2004. *Publications*: numerous articles on animal virology in learned jls. *Recreations*: reading, listening to music, travelling, walking, photography. *Address*: 290 London Road, Burpham, Guildford, Surrey GU4 7LB.

**DONALDSON, Brian;** HM Diplomatic Service, retired; Ambassador to Republic of Madagascar and concurrently to The Comoros, 2002–05; *b* 6 April 1946; *s* of late William Donaldson and Elsie Josephine Donaldson (*née* Longstaff); *m* 1st, 1969, Elizabeth Claire Sumner (marr. diss. 2011); three *s*; 2nd, 2012, Nicole Rasoamiaramanana. Assistant, Establishments Office, Min. of Civil Aviation, 1963–65; joined HM Diplomatic Service, 1965: Mgt Officer, Algiers, 1968–71; Archivist, La Paz, 1971–73; Communications Ops Dept, FCO, 1974–75; Entry Clearance Officer, Lagos, 1975–79; Vice Consul, Luxembourg, 1979–82; Second Sec., Trade Relns and Exports Dept, FCO, 1982–83; Asst Private Sec. to Minister of State, FCO, 1983–85; Second, later First Sec., Port Louis, Mauritius, 1985–89; Dep. Hd of Mission, Yaoundé, Cameroon, 1989–92; First Sec., Dhaka, 1992–96; Personnel Mgt Dept, FCO, 1996–97; Dep. Hd, Information Dept, FCO, 1997–99; High Comr, Republic of Namibia, 1999–2002. Dir Gen., President of Madagascar's Small Grants Scheme, 2005–08. Political Advisor: Fuelstock, 2008–11; Madagascar Development Partners, 2010–. Patron, Madagascar Development Fund, 2008–; Trustee, Equitrade Foundn, 2006–08. Council Mem., Assoc. of Business Execs, 2006–11; Mem., Adv. Bd, Africa Res. Inst., 2009–. Chm., Grants Cttee, Kitchen Table Charities Trust, 2006–. Chevalier de l'Ordre National (Madagascar), 2016. *Recreations*: family, work, people watching. *Address*: Lot II H 41 I, Ankerana, Boite Postale 13056 67 Ha, Antananarivo 101, Madagascar; 2 The Crescent, St Austell, Cornwall PL25 4TA.

**DONALDSON, Prof. (Charles) Ian (Edward),** FBA 1993; Foundation Director, 1974–90, Director, 2004–07, Humanities Research Centre, Australian National University, now Emeritus Professor; Hon. Professorial Fellow, School of Culture and Communication, University of Melbourne, since 2007; Fellow, Trinity College, Melbourne, since 2012; *b* 6 May 1935; *s* of Dr William Edward Donaldson and Elizabeth Donaldson (*née* Weigall); *m* 1st, 1962, Tamsin Jane Procter (marr. diss. 1990); one *s* one *d*; 2nd, 1991, Grazia Maria Therese Gunn. *Educ*: Melbourne Grammar Sch.; Melbourne Univ. (BA 1957); Magdalen Coll., Oxford (BA 1960; MA 1964). Sen. Tutor in English, Univ. of Melbourne, 1958; Oxford University: Harmsworth Sen. Scholar, Merton Coll., 1960–62; Fellow and Lectr in English, Wadham Coll., 1962–69; CUF Lectr in English, 1963–69; Prof. of English, ANU Canberra, 1969–91; Regius Prof. of Rhetoric and English Lit., Univ. of Edinburgh, 1991–95; University of Cambridge: Grace I Prof. of English, 1995–2002; Fellow, King's College, 1995–2005; Dir, Centre for Res. in the Arts, Social Scis and Humanities, 2001–03. Vis. appts, Univ. of California Santa Barbara, Gonville and Caius Coll., Cambridge, Cornell Univ., Melbourne Univ. Syndic, CUP, 1997–2001. President: Australian Acad. of Humanities, 2008–09; Nat. Academies Forum, 2009. FAHA 1975; Corresp. FBA 1987; FRSE 1993. Hon. DLitt Melbourne, 2014; DUniv ANU, 2016. *Publications*: The World Upside-Down: comedy from Jonson to Fielding, 1970; (ed) Ben Jonson Poems, 1975; The Rapes of Lucretia, 1982; (ed) Jonson and Shakespeare, 1983; (ed) Transformations in Modern European Drama, 1983; (ed with Tamsin Donaldson) Seeing the First Australians, 1985; (ed) Ben Jonson, 1985; (ed jtly) Shaping Lives: reflections on biography, 1992; (ed) Ben Jonson: Selected Poems, 1995; Jonson's Magic Houses, 1997; Ben Jonson: a life, 2011; (gen. ed. with David Bevington and Martin Butler) The Cambridge Edition of the Works of Ben Jonson, 7 vols, 2012; (ed jtly) Taking Stock: the humanities in Australian life since 1968, 2012. *Address*: School of Culture and Communication, University of Melbourne, Vic 3010, Australia.

**DONALDSON, David Torrance;** QC 1984; a Recorder, 1994; *b* 30 Sept. 1943; *s* of Alexander Walls Donaldson and Margaret Merry Bryce. *Educ*: Glasgow Academy; Gonville and Caius College, Cambridge (Maj. Schol.; MA); University of Freiburg i. Br., West Germany (Dr jur). Fellow, Gonville and Caius College, Cambridge, 1965–69. Called to the Bar, Gray's Inn, 1968, Bencher, 1995. *Address*: Blackstone Chambers, Blackstone House, Temple, EC4Y 9BW. *T*: (020) 7583 1770.

**DONALDSON, Prof. Graham Hunter Carley,** CB 2009; Honorary Professor, University of Glasgow (Professor, School of Education, 2014); *b* 11 Dec. 1946; *s* of Matthew and Margaret Donaldson; *m* 1972, Dilys Lloyd; two *s* one *d*. *Educ*: High Sch. of Glasgow; Univ. of Glasgow (MA, DipEd, MEd). Teacher, Glasgow, 1970–73; Hd of Dept, Dumbartonshire, 1973–75; Lectr, Jordanhill Coll. of Educn, 1975–83; Inspector of Schs, 1983–90; Chief Inspector, 1990–96; Depute Sen. Chief Inspector, 1996–2002; Sen. Chief Inspector of Educn in Scotland, 2002–10. Leader: Rev. of Teacher Educn in Scotland, 2010–11 (report published, 2011); Rev. of Curriculum and Assessment in Wales, 2014–15 (report, Successful Futures, 2015). President: Standing Internat. Conf. of Inspectorates, 2007–12; Internat. Professional Develt Assoc. Nat. Curriculum Evaluator, 1975–83. FRSA

2003. Hon. DLitt Wales, Trinity St David, 2015. *Publications:* James IV: a Renaissance King, 1975; Industry and Scottish Schools, 1981; Teaching Scotland's Future, 2011; (jtly) Work-Based Learning in Teacher Education, 2013; Successful Futures, 2015. *Recreations:* golf, supporting Motherwell FC, reading, particularly history and biographies. *Address:* School of Education, University of Glasgow, St Andrew's Building, 11 Eldon Street, Glasgow G3 6NH. *E:* Graham.Donaldson@glasgow.ac.uk.

**DONALDSON, Hamish**, MBE 2013; DL; Chairman, Haslemere Festival, since 2003; *b* 13 June 1936; *s* of late James Donaldson and Marie Christine Cormack; *m* 1965, Linda, *d* of late Dr Leslie Challis Bousfield; three *d*. *Educ:* Oundle School; Christ's College, Cambridge (MA). Nat. Service, 2nd Lieut, Seaforth Highlanders, 1955–57. De La Rue Bull, 1960–66; Urwick, Orr & Partners, 1966–73; Hill Samuel & Co., 1973–91; Man. Dir, Hill Samuel Merchant Bank (SA), 1985–86; Chief Exec., Hill Samuel Bank, 1987–91. Director: TSB Bank, 1988–91; TSB Group, 1990–91; Macquarie Bank, 1989–91; RSH Trading Ltd, 1994–2016. Chm., Guildford DAC for the Care of Churches and Churchyards, 1992–2011; Founder Chm., Surrey Churches Preservation Trust, 1997–. Lay Canon, Guildford Cathedral, 2012–17. Gov., Royal Sch., Haslemere, 1994–2016 (Chm., 2009–13). Freeman, City of London, 1988; Liveryman, Information Technologists' Co., 1992–. DL Surrey, 2004. *Publications:* A Guide to the Successful Management of Computer Projects, 1978; Mantrap: avoiding the pitfalls of project management, 2006. *Recreation:* amateur operatics. *Address:* Edgecombe, Hill Road, Haslemere, Surrey GU27 2JN. *T:* (01428) 644473.

**DONALDSON, Ian**; see Donaldson, C. I. E.

**DONALDSON, Rt Hon. Sir Jeffrey (Mark)**, Kt 2016; PC 2007; MP Lagan Valley, since 1997 (UU, 1997–2003, DUP, since 2004); *b* 7 Dec. 1962; *s* of James Alexander Donaldson and Sarah Anne Donaldson; *m* 1987, Eleanor Mary Elizabeth Cousins; two *d*. *Educ:* Castlereagh Coll. (DipEE); Chartered Insurance Inst. (Financial Planning Cert.). Agent to Rt Hon. J. Enoch Powell, MP, 1983–85; Mem., NI Assembly, 1985–86; Partner in financial services/estate agency practice, 1986–97. Mem., NI Forum, 1996–98. Mem., Lagan Valley, NI Assembly, 2003–10 (UU, 2003–04, DUP, 2004–10). Jun. Minister, Office of the First Minister and Dep. First Minister, NI, 2008–09. Prime Minister's Trade Envoy to Egypt, 2016–; Parly Ambassador for Motorsports, 2018–. Alderman, Lisburn CC, 2005–10. Hon. Sec., 1988–2000, Vice-Pres., 2000–03, UU Council. Chm., Causeway Inst. for Peace Building and Conflict Resolution, 2011–. *Recreations:* travelling, walking, reading, war graves and battlefield heritage, motorsports. *Address:* House of Commons, SW1A 0AA. *T:* (020) 7219 3407; Old Town Hall, 29 Castle Street, Lisburn, Co. Antrim BT27 4DH. *T:* (028) 9266 8001.

**DONALDSON, Joanna Mary**, FCIPD; Acting Director General, Corporate Effectiveness, 2012, and Director, Human Resources, 2010–13, Department for Business, Innovation and Skills; *d* of Norman Donaldson and Caryl Donaldson; *m* 1979, Crispin Southgate; two *s* one *d*. *Educ:* St Anne's Coll., Oxford (BA Hons PPE). Fast stream, DTI, 1977; Private Sec. to Minister for Industry, 1981–83; policy and HR roles: DTI; Oftel, 1985–87; OST, 1998–99; BERR, subseq. BIS; DoH (rev. of whistleblowing in NHS, Freedom to Speak Up), 2014–15. Exec. Coach and Mentor, Associate Hay KornFerry. Trustee: St Christopher's Hospice, 2013–; Brand Foundn, 2016–. *Recreations:* family, walking, travelling, reading, bridge.

**DONALDSON, Julia Catherine**, CBE 2019 (MBE 2011); FRSL; writer of books, songs and plays for children; Children's Laureate, 2011–13; *b* 16 Sept. 1948; *d* of James Shields and Elizabeth Shields (*née* Ede); *m* 1972, Malcolm Donaldson; two *s* (and one *s* decd). *Educ:* Camden Sch. for Girls; Univ. of Bristol (BA Drama and French 1970); Falmer Coll. of Educn (PGCE English 1976). Editl Asst, Michael Joseph, 1971–72; Short-Story Editor, BBC Radio Bristol, 1973–74; Editor, Robert Tyndall, 1974–75; English Teacher, St Mary's Hall, Brighton, 1976–78; freelance contrib. of songs to BBC television progs, 1974–. Writer in Residence, Easterhouse, Glasgow, 1998–2001. Chm., Assoc. of Children's Writers and Illustrators in Scotland, 2001–03. Volunteer, CAB, Glasgow, 1993–97. FRSL 2018. Hon. DLitt Bristol, 2011. *Publications:* A Squash and a Squeeze, 1993; The Gruffalo, 1999; Monkey Puzzle, Follow the Swallow, Tales from Acorn Wood: Fox's Socks, Rabbit's Nap, Postman Bear, Hide and Seek Pig, 2000; Room on the Broom, 2001; The Dinosaur's Diary, Night Monkey Day Monkey, 2002; The Smartest Giant in Town, Spinderella, The Head in the Sand, Bombs and Blackberries, The Magic Paintbrush, Conjuror Cow, Princess Mirror-Belle, The Snail and the Whale, Brick-A-Breck, 2003; The Wrong Kind of Bark, Wriggle and Roar, Sharing a Shell, The Giants and the Joneses, The Gruffalo's Child, One Ted Falls out of Bed, Crazy Mayonnaisy Mum, 2004; The Gruffalo Song and other Songs, Princess Mirror-Belle and the Magic Shoes, Chocolate Mousse for Greedy Goose, Rosie's Hat, The Jungle House, The Quick Brown Fox Cub, Charlie Cook's Favourite Book, 2005; Hippo Has a Hat, Princess Mirror-Belle and the Flying Horse, Play Time!, The Princess and the Wizard, (with John Henderson) Fly Pigeon Fly, 2006; Room on the Broom and other Songs, Tyrannosaurus Drip, Tiddler, 2007; One Mole Digging a Hole, Stick Man, 2008 (adapted for stage, 2017); Running on the Cracks, What the Ladybird Heard, Toddle Waddle, Tabby McTat, 2009; Cave Baby, Zog, Freddie and the Fairy, 2010; The Rhyming Rabbit, Jack and the Flumflum Tree, Zog (televised, 2018; adapted for stage, 2019), The Highway Rat, 2011 (televised, 2017); Sugarlump and the Unicorn, 2013; The Scarecrows' Wedding, Princess Mirror-belle and the Dragon Pox, 2014; The Cook and the King, The Girl, the Bear and the Magic Shoes, 2018; The Go-Away Bird, The Smeds and the Smoos, 2019; also various educnl pubns incl. Songbirds (series of 60 phonic reading books), part of Oxford Reading Tree, 2006–09. *Recreations:* piano playing, singing, walking, study of flowers and fungi. *Address:* c/o Macmillan Children's Books, 20 New Wharf Road, N1 9RR.

**DONALDSON, Sir Liam (Joseph)**, Kt 2002; MD; FRCP, FRCPE, FRCSE, FFPH, FRCGP, FMedSci; Professor of Public Health, London School of Hygiene and Tropical Medicine, since 2016; Honorary Distinguished Professor, Cardiff University, since 2015; Chief Medical Officer, Department of Health, 1998–2010; *b* 3 May 1949. *Educ:* Univ. of Bristol (MB, ChB 1972); Univ. of Birmingham (MSc 1976); Univ. of Leicester (MD 1982). FRCSE 1977; FFPH (FFCM 1987; FFPHM 1990); FRCP 1997; FRCGP 1999; FRCPE 1999. House Officer, United Bristol Hosps, 1972–73; Lectr in Anatomy, Univ. of Birmingham, 1973–75; Surgical Registrar, United Birmingham Hosps, 1975–77; Lectr in Anatomy, then Sen. Lectr in Epidemiol., Univ. of Leicester, 1977–86; Regl Med. Officer and Head of Clinical Policy, then Director of Public Health, Northern RHA, 1986–92; Regl Gen. Manager and Dir of Public Health, Northern and Yorks RHA, later Regl Dir and Dir of Public Health, Northern and Yorks NHS Exec., 1994–98. Prof. of Health Policy, Imperial Coll. London, 2011–15. Hon. Prof. of Applied Epidemiol., 1989–98, Chancellor, 2009–, Newcastle Univ. Patient Safety Envoy to Dir Gen. (formerly Chm., World Alliance for Patient Safety), WHO, 2010–; Chairman: Ind. Monitoring Bd on Global Polio Eradication, 2011–; Nat. Patient Safety Agency, 2010–12. Associate Fellow, Chatham House, 2015–. QHP 1996–99. FMedSci 1999. Hon. doctorates from univs of Bristol, Leicester, Cranfield, Huddersfield, Portsmouth, York, Sheffield, Teesside, Birmingham, De Montfort, Nottingham, Hull, East Anglia, Sunderland, Imperial Coll. London and Macquarie. Gold Medal, RCSE, 2000. *Publications:* (with R. J. Donaldson) Essential Community Medicine, 1983, 4th edn (with P. D. Rutter) as Donaldsons' Essential Public Health, 2018; (ed with B. R. McAvoy) Health Care for Asians, 1990; (with S. Sheard) The Nation's Doctor, 2005; over 200 papers on various aspects of health services research. *Address:* Faculty of Epidemiology and Population Health, London School of Hygiene and Tropical Medicine, Keppel Street, WC1E 7HT.

**DONALDSON, Maureen**; see Watt, M.

**DONALDSON, Air Vice-Marshal Michael Phillips**, MBE 1973; FRAeS; Chief Executive and Principal, Yorkshire Coast College, 1996–2003; *b* 22 July 1943; *s* of George Millar Donaldson and Mabel Donaldson (*née* Phillips); *m* 1970, Mavis Cornish; one *s* one *d*. *Educ:* Chislehurst and Sidcup Grammar Sch. for Boys. RAF Gen. Duties; Pilot and Weapons Instructor; No 23 Sqn (Lightning), 1965–68; No 226 OCU, 1969; USAF Florida (F106), 1970–73; No 29 Sqn (Phantom), 1974–76; No 228 OCU, 1977; Army Staff Coll., 1978; PSO to Dep. Comdr in Chief AFCENT, Brunssum, 1979–80; MoD, 1980–83; OC 19 Sqn, 1983–85; OC 23 Sqn (Falkland Is), 1985; Dep. PSO to CDS, 1986–87; OC RAF Wattisham, 1987–89; RCDS 1990; SASO, 11 Group, 1990–93; Comdt, RAF Staff Coll., 1993–96. Life Vice-Pres., RAF Squash Rackets Assoc., 1996. FRAeS 1997. *Recreations:* music, history, squash, tennis, golf. *Club:* Royal Air Force.

**DONALDSON, Dame Patricia Anne**; see Hodgson, Dame P. A.

**DONALDSON, Sir Simon (Kirwan)**, Kt 2012; DPhil; FRS 1986; Professor of Pure Mathematics, Imperial College London, since 1998; *b* 20 Aug. 1957; *m* 1986, Ana Nora Hurtado; two *s* one *d*. *Educ:* Sevenoaks Sch., Kent; Pembroke Coll., Cambridge (BA 1979; Hon. Fellow, 1992); Worcester Coll., Oxford (DPhil 1983; Hon. Fellow 2015). Jun. Res. Fellow, All Souls Coll., Oxford, 1983–85; Wallis Prof. of Maths, and Fellow, St Anne's Coll., Univ. of Oxford, 1985–98, Hon. Fellow, 1998. Mem., Simons Center for Geometry and Physics, Stony Brook Univ., 2014–. Fields Medal, IMU, 1986; Frederic Esser Nemmers Prize, Northwestern Univ., 2008; Shaw Prize in Math. Scis, 2009. *Publications:* (with P. B. Kronheimer) The Geometry of Four-manifolds, 1990; papers in mathematical jls. *Recreation:* sailing. *Address:* Department of Mathematics, South Kensington Campus, Imperial College London, SW7 2AZ.

**DONALDSON, Stuart Blair**; Senior Campaigns Manager, Campaign for Real Ale, since 2018; *s* of Bruce Donaldson and Maureen Donaldson (*see* Maureen Watt). *Educ:* Banchory Acad.; Univ. of Glasgow (MA 2013). Parly Asst to Christian Allard, MSP, 2013; Constituency Officer, 2013–15. MP (SNP) W Aberdeenshire and Kincardine, 2015–17; contested (SNP) same seat, 2017. Sec., European Beer Consumers Union, 2018–. Trustee, Stand Alone, 2018–.

**DONCASTER, Bishop Suffragan of**; *no new appointment at time of going to press*.

**DONCASTER, Archdeacon of**; *no new appointment at time of going to press*.

**DONE, Frances Winifred**, CBE 2003; FCA; Chair, Youth Justice Board, 2008–14; *b* 6 May 1950; *d* of Rt Hon. Lord Bishopston, PC and Winifred Mary (*née* Bryant); *m* 1981, James Hancock; two *s*. *Educ:* Manchester Univ. (BA Econ.). FCA 1976. Chm., Finance Cttee, Manchester CC, 1984–88; Treas., 1991–98, Chief Exec. and Treas., 1998–2000, Rochdale MBC; Chief Exec., Manchester 2002 Ltd, XVII Commonwealth Games Org. Cttee, 2000–03; Man. Dir, Local Govt, Housing and Criminal Justice, subseq. Local Govt and Housing, Audit Commn, 2003–06; Interim Dir Gen., RBL, 2007. Mem. Bd, Professional Standards Authy, 2017–. Trustee: Waterways Trust, 2003–12; Canal and River Trust, 2013–18. *Recreations:* canals, walking, family.

**DONEGALL**, 8th Marquess of, *cr* 1791 (Ire.); **Arthur Patrick Chichester**; Viscount Chichester and Baron Chichester of Belfast, 1625; Earl of Donegall, 1647; Earl of Belfast, 1791; Baron Fisherwick (GB), 1790; Baron Templemore (UK), 1831; Hereditary Lord High Admiral of Lough Neagh; Governor of Carrickfergus Castle; farmer and business owner; *b* 9 May 1952; *s* of 7th Marquess of Donegall, LVO and Lady Josceline Gabrielle Legge, *y d* of 7th Earl of Dartmouth, GCVO, TD; *S* father, 2007; *m* 1989, Caroline, *er d* of Major Christopher Philipson; one *s* one *d*. *Educ:* Harrow; Royal Agricl Coll., Cirencester. Coldstream Guards. *Recreations:* hunting, shooting, fishing. *Heir:* *s* Earl of Belfast, *qv*. *Address:* Dunbrody Park, Arthurstown, Co. Wexford, Eire; Hunthill, Jedburgh, Roxburghshire TD8 6QR.

**DONELAN, Michelle Emma May Elizabeth**; MP (C) Chippenham, since 2015; a Lord Commissioner of HM Treasury (Government Whip), since 2019; *b* Whitley, Cheshire, 8 April 1984; *d* of Michael and Kathryn Donelan. *Educ:* Univ. of York (BA Hons Hist. and Politics). Mktg asst on Marie Claire mag. and That's Life mag., Pacific Magazines, 2006–07; Mktg Exec., then Sen. Mktg Exec., Hist. Channel, AETN UK, 2007–10; Internat. Mktg Manager, World Wrestling Entertainment, 2010–14; mktg freelancer, Wilts, 2014–15. Contested (C) Wentworth and Dearne, 2010. PPS to Attorney Gen.'s Office, 2017–18; an Asst Govt Whip, 2018–19. Mem., Educn Cttee, 2015–18, Petitions Cttee, 2017–. *Recreations:* cycling, swimming, walking, cooking. *Address:* House of Commons, SW1A 0AA. *T:* 07794 040334. *E:* michelle.donelan.mp@parliament.uk.

**DONERAILE**, 10th Viscount *cr* 1785 (Ire.); **Richard Allen St Leger**; Baron Doneraile, 1776; *b* 17 Aug. 1946; *s* of 9th Viscount Doneraile and of Melva, Viscountess Doneraile; *S* father, 1983; *m* 1970, Kathleen Mary Simcox, Churchtown, Mallow, Co. Cork; one *s* one *d*. *Educ:* Orange Coast College, California; Mississippi Univ. Served US Army. Air Traffic Control specialist; antiquarian book appraiser, 1970–73; food marketing analyst, 1974. *Recreations:* outdoor sports, ski-ing, golf, sailing. *Heir:* *s* Hon. Nathaniel Warham Robert St John St Leger, *b* 13 Sept. 1971. *Club:* Yorba Linda Country (California).

**DONLEY, Dr Anita Jane**, OBE 2007; FRCP; Independent Chair, Mid and South Essex Sustainability and Transformation Partnership, 2016–19; Consultant Physician in Acute Medicine, Plymouth Hospitals NHS Trust, 1990–2019; Clinical Vice President, Royal College of Physicians, 2013–16; *b* Warwick, 13 Aug. 1952; *d* of Charles Edwin Robert Donley and Daisy Phyllis Grant Donley; *m* (marr. diss.); one *s* one *d*. *Educ:* King's High School for Girls, Warwick; Univ. of Bristol Med. Sch. (MB ChB; PhD 1991); Univ. of Wales Coll. of Medicine (DipMedEd 1992). FRCP 1992. MRC/AFRC Fellow in Nutrition, 1986–88; Sen. Lectr and Consultant Physician, Univ. of Southampton, 1988–90; BAAS Media Fellow, 1989. Head Assessor, Professional Performance Procedures, GMC, 2000–11; Nat. Clin. Dir, Venous Thromboembolism Prevention, 2007–10; Med. Dir, Revalidation, DoH, 2011–13. Member: Lowermoor Subgp, Cttee on Toxicity, 2001–11; Scientific Adv. Cttee on Nutrition, FSA, 2001–11; Postgrad. Med. Educn and Trng Bd, 2002–09 (Chair, Trng Cttee, 2002–09); UK Panel for Res. Integrity in Health and Biomedical Sci., 2005–08; Human Genetics Commn, 2007–12; Ind. Chair, Success Regime, Essex, 2016–. INSEAD Eur. Health Leadership Alumnus, 2010. Hon. MRCGP 2005; Hon. MFPH 2014. *Publications:* contrib. to learned publications on nutrition and care of older people; ind. reports on venous thromboembolism and medical care of suspected internal drugs traffickers. *Recreations:* theatre, literature, drama, trekking. *Address:* 1 Mill View Terrace, Glen Island, Taplow, Maidenhead SL6 0BN. *E:* anitadonley@me.com. *Club:* Royal Automobile.

**DONN, Mary Cecilia;** see Spinks, M. C.

**DONNACHIE, Prof. Alexander,** FInstP; Professor of Physics, 1969–2001, now Emeritus, and Hon. Professor of Physics and Astronomy, 2001, University of Manchester; *b* 25 May 1936; *s* of John Donnachie and Mary Ramsey Donnachie (*née* Adams); *m* 1960, Dorothy Paterson; two *d*. *Educ:* Kilmarnock Acad.; Glasgow Univ. (BSc, PhD). DSIR Res. Fellow 1961–63, Lectr 1963–65, UCL; Res. Associate, CERN, Geneva, 1965–67; Sen. Lectr, Univ. of Glasgow, 1967–69; University of Manchester: Hd of Theoretical Physics 1975–85; Dean of Faculty of Science, 1985–87; Chm., Dept of Physics, 1988–94; Dir of Physical Labs, 1989–94; Dean, Faculty of Science and Engrg, 1994–97. Mem., SERC, 1989–94 (Chm., Nuclear Phys Bd, 1989–93); CERN: Chairman: Super Proton Synchrotron Cttee, 1988–90; Super Proton Synchrotron and LEAR Cttee, 1991–93; Member: Res. Bd, 1988–95; Sci. Policy Cttee, 1988–93; Council, 1989–94; Particle, Space and Astronomy Bd, 1993–94; Sec., C11 Commn, IUPAP, 1989–91. Divl Associate Ed., Physical Rev. Letters, 2010–16. Glazebrook Medal, Inst. of Physics, 1997. *Publications:* Electromagnetic Interactions of Hadrons, vols I and II, 1978; Pomeron Physics and QCD, 2002; Electromagnetic Interactions and Hadronic Structure, 2007; nearly 200 articles in learned jls of Particle Physics. *Recreations:* golf, walking. *Address:* c/o School of Physics and Astronomy, University of Manchester, Manchester M13 9PL.

**DONNAI, Prof. Dian,** CBE 2005; FRCP, FRCOG, FMedSci; Professor of Medical Genetics, University of Manchester, 2001–10, now Emerita (Hon. Professor, 1994–2001); Consultant Clinical Geneticist, Manchester Centre for Genomic Medicine (formerly Regional Genetics Service), since 1980 and Strategic Clinical Director, since 2018, St Mary's Hospital, Manchester; *b* 15 Feb. 1945; *d* of Arnold Sydney Aughton and May Aughton; *m* 1968, Paul Donnai; one *s* one *d*. *Educ:* Whitchurch Girls' High Sch., Shropshire; St Mary's Hosp. Med. Sch., London Univ. (MB BS 1968). FRCP 1984; FRCOG *ad eundem* 1995; FMedSci 2001. Consultant Advr in Genetics to CMO, DoH, 1998–2003. President: Med. Scis Section, BAAS, 2007; European Soc. of Human Genetics, 2009–10. Arno Motulsky-Barton Childs Award for Excellence in Human Genetics Educn, Amer. Soc. of Human Genetics, 2017. *Publications:* (ed jtly) Congenital Malformation Syndromes, 1996; (ed jtly) Antenatal Diagnosis of Fetal Abnormalities, 1991; (ed jtly) Early Fetal Growth and Development, 1994; (with A. Read) New Clinical Genetics, 2007, 3rd edn 2015; numerous articles on genetic disorders and syndromes. *Recreation:* travelling in France. *Address:* Manchester Centre for Genomic Medicine, 6th Floor, Manchester Academic Health Sciences Centre, St Mary's Hospital, Manchester University NHS Foundation Trust, Oxford Road, Manchester M13 9WL. *T:* (0161) 276 6002, *Fax:* (0161) 276 6145. *E:* dian.donnai@mft.nhs.uk.

**DONNAN, Prof. Hastings Samuel Charles,** DPhil; FBA 2013; Professor of Anthropology, since 1997, Director, Institute for Study of Conflict Transformation and Social Justice, since 2012, and Director, Senator George J. Mitchell Institute for Global Peace, Security and Justice, since 2015, Queen's University Belfast; *b* Portadown, 12 March 1953; *s* of Robert J. and Noreen C. Donnan; *m* 1985, Katharine Marshall; three *d*. *Educ:* Bangor Grammar Sch.; Queen's Univ. Belfast (BA Hons 1975); Univ. of Sussex (DPhil 1981). Lectr in Anthropol., QUB, 1979–97. Panel Chair: RAE, 2005–08; REF, 2010–14. MRIA 2001. FAcSS (AcSS 1999). *Publications:* Marriage Among Muslims: preference and choice in Northern Pakistan, 1988; (ed with G. McFarlane) Social Anthropology and Public Policy in Northern Ireland, 1989; (ed with P. Werbner) Economy and Culture in Pakistan: migrants and cities in a Muslim society, 1991; (ed jtly) Irish Urban Cultures, 1993; (ed with A. S. Ahmed) Islam, Globalization and Postmodernity, 1994; (ed with F. Selier) Family and Gender in Pakistan: domestic organization in a Muslim society, 1997; (ed with G. McFarlane) Culture and Policy in Northern Ireland: anthropology in the public arena, 1997; (ed) Interpreting Islam, 2002; (ed with F. Magowan) Transgressive Sex: subversion and control in erotic encounters, 2009; (with F. Magowan) The Anthropology of Sex, 2010; (ed jtly) Migrating Borders and Moving Times: temporality and the crossing of borders in Europe, 2017; *with T. M. Wilson:* (ed) Border Approaches: anthropological perspectives on frontiers, 1994; (ed) Border Identities: nation and state at international frontiers, 1998; Borders: frontiers of identity, nation and state, 1999 (Turkish edn 2005; Polish edn 2007); (ed) Culture and Power at the Edges of the State: national support and subversion in European borderlands, 2005; The Anthropology of Ireland, 2006; (ed) Borderlands: ethnographic approaches to security, power and identity, 2010; (ed) A Companion to Border Studies, 2012. *Recreations:* equestrian. *Address:* Senator George J. Mitchell Institute for Global Peace, Security and Justice, Queen's University Belfast, Belfast, Northern Ireland BT7 1NN. *T:* (028) 9097 3284. *E:* h.donnan@qub.ac.uk.

**DONNE, Jeremy Nigel,** RD 1992; QC 2003; **His Honour Judge Donne;** a Circuit Judge, since 2012; *b* 22 Jan. 1954; *s* of Tom and Shirley Donne; *m* 1984, Caroline Susan O'Brien-Gore; two *d*. *Educ:* County Grammar Sch., Merthyr Tydfil; Cyfarthfa High Sch., Merthyr Tydfil; Inns of Court Sch. of Law. Called to the Bar, Middle Temple, 1978, Bencher, 2011; specialised in criminal, regulatory and disciplinary law; Asst Recorder, 1998–2000; Recorder, 2000–12. Mem., S Eastern Circuit. Chm., British Equestrian Fedn Disciplinary Appeals Panel, 2011–12; Member: Justice, 2005–; Exec. Council, British Acad. of Forensic Sci., 2013–17 (Treas., 2015–17); former Mem., Criminal Bar Assoc. Tutor judge, Judicial Coll., 2015–. RNR, 1977–94, Commnd 1978, retired Lt Comdr. Chm., Govs, All Saints C of E Sch., Putney, 2006–09. *Recreations:* sailing, ski-ing, cycling. *Address:* Inner London Crown Court, Sessions House, Newington Causeway, SE1 6AZ. *Clubs:* Royal Naval Volunteer Reserve Yacht (Cdre, 2007–08), Royal Thames Yacht, Bar Yacht.

**DONNELLAN, Declan Michael Martin,** OBE 2017; Joint Artistic Director, Cheek By Jowl, since 1981; Associate Director, Royal National Theatre, 1989–97; *b* 4 Aug. 1953; *s* of Thomas Patrick John Donnellan and Josephine Margaret Donnellan. *Educ:* Queens' Coll., Cambridge (MA). Called to the Bar, Middle Temple, 1978. Associate Dir, Russian Th. Confedn, 1999–. Productions: Cheek By Jowl: The Country Wife, 1981; Othello, 1982; Vanity Fair, 1983; Pericles, 1984; Andromache, 1985; A Midsummer Night's Dream, 1985; The Man of Mode, 1985; The Cid, 1986; Twelfth Night, 1986; Macbeth, 1987; A Family Affair, 1988; Philoctetes, 1988; The Tempest, 1988; Lady Betty, 1989; The Doctor of Honour, 1989; Sara, 1990; Hamlet, 1990; As You Like It, 1991, 1994; Don't Fool with Love, 1993; The Blind Men, 1993; Measure for Measure, 1994, 2014; The Duchess of Malfi, 1995; Out Cry, 1997; Much Ado About Nothing, 1998; Othello, 2004; The Changeling, 2006; Cymbeline, 2007; Troilus and Cressida, 2008; Macbeth, 2010; 'Tis Pity She's a Whore, 2011, 2012; Ubu Roi, 2013; The Winter's Tale, 2016; Périclès, Prince de Tyr, 2018; The Knight of the Burning Pestle, 2019; Royal National Theatre: Fuente Ovejuna, 1989; Peer Gynt, 1990; Angels in America: part 1, Millennium Approaches, 1992, part 2, Perestroika, 1993; Sweeney Todd, 1993; The Mandate, 2004; Royal Shakespeare Company: The School for Scandal, 1999; King Lear, 2002; Great Expectations, 2005; Russian Theatre Confederation: Boris Godunov, 2001; Twelfth Night, 2003; Three Sisters, 2005; The Tempest, 2011; The Winter's Tale, Maly Drama Theatre, St Petersburg, 1997; Le Cid, Avignon Fest., 1998; Homebody/Kabul, NY, 2001; Falstaff, Salzburg Fest., 2001; Romeo and Juliet, 2004, Hamlet, 2015, Bolshoi Ballet, Moscow; Shakespeare in Love, Noël Coward Th., 2014. Dir, Bel Ami (film), 2012. Olivier Awards for Dir of Yr, 1987, Best Dir of a Musical, 1994, Best Dir of a Play, 1995, Outstanding Achievement, 1990; Internat. Shakespeare Prize, Craiova, Romania, 2008; (jtly) Charlemagne Award, 2009; Lifetime Achievement Award, Golden Lion of Venice, 2016. Chevalier, Ordre des Arts et des Lettres (France), 2004. *Publications:* The Actor and the Target, 2002 (trans. 13 languages). *Address:* c/o Cheek By Jowl, Barbican Centre, Silk Street, EC2Y 8DS.

**DONNELLY, Alan John;** Executive Chairman: Sovereign Strategy, since 2000; International Management Partners, since 2012; Secretary, Co-operative Commission, since 2000; *b* 16 July 1957; *s* of John and Josephine Donnelly; *m* 1979 (marr. diss. 1982); one *s*. *Educ:* Valley View Primary School and Springfield Comprehensive School, Jarrow; Sunderland Poly. (Hon. Fellow, Sunderland Univ., 1993). GMBATU Northern Region: Health and Safety Officer, 1978–80; Education Officer, 1980–84; Finance and Admin Officer, 1984–87; GMB Central Finance Manager, 1987–89. European Parliament: Member (Lab): Tyne and Wear, 1989–99; NE Reg., England, 1999–Jan. 2000; Pres., Delegn, Relations with USA, 1992–98; Leader, Lab. Party, 1998–2000; a Vice Pres., Socialist Gp. Mem., S Tyneside MBC, 1979–82. B Director, Unity Trust Bank, 1987–89. Kt Comdr, Order of Merit (Germany), 1991. *Recreations:* tennis, swimming, reading.

**DONNELLY, Brendan Patrick;** Director, Federal Trust, since 2003; Secretary, Federal Union, since 2010 (Chairman, 2003–10); *b* 25 Aug. 1950; *s* of Patrick Aloysius Donnelly and late Mary Josephine Donnelly (*née* Barrett). *Educ:* Christ Church, Oxford (BA Classics 1972; MA 1976). Theodor Heuss Travelling Scholar, Munich, 1974–76; FCO, 1976–82; Private Sec. to Sir Henry Plumb, 1983–86; on staff of Lord Cockfield, a Vice-Pres. of CEC, 1986–87; Political Consultant on EC, 1987–90; Special Advr to Leader of Conservatives in EP, 1990–94. MEP (C) Sussex S and Crawley, 1994–99. Sen. Res. Fellow, Global Policy Inst., 2011–. Contested (4 Freedoms) London, EP, 2014. *Publications:* (jtly) Not in Our Name, 2005; (with Hugh Dykes) On the Edge: Britain and Europe, 2012; numerous articles on European Union. *Recreations:* watching cricket, modern languages, modern history. *Address:* 61 Leopold Road, N2 8BG. *T:* (020) 8444 0154.

**DONNELLY, Sir Brian;** see Donnelly, Sir J. B.

**DONNELLY, Prof. Christl Ann,** CBE 2018; ScD; FRS 2016; FMedSci; Professor of Statistical Epidemiology, Imperial College London, since 2002; Professor of Applied Statistics, University of Oxford, since 2018; Fellow, St Peter's College, Oxford, since 2018; *b* 19 June 1967; *d* of Rett F. Donnelly and Lou Ellen Donnelly (*née* Hartke); *m* 2000, Ben Hambly; two *s*. *Educ:* Oberlin Coll., Ohio (BA 1988); Harvard Univ. (MSc 1990; ScD 1992). Lectr, Univ. of Edinburgh, 1992–95; Hd, Statistics Unit, Wellcome Trust Centre for Epidemiol. of Infectious Disease, Univ. of Oxford, 1995–2000; Lectr, St Catherine's Coll., Oxford, 1998–2000; Reader, Imperial Coll., London, 2000–02. Dep. Chm., Ind. Scientific Gp on Cattle TB, 1998–2007; Member: Scientific Cttee on Health and Wellbeing in Changing Urban Envmt, ICSU, 2012–16; WHO Ebola Response Team, 2014–16. Mem. Council, Royal Statistical Soc., 2001–05, 2018–. Associate Editor: Applied Statistics, 2001–04; Jl of Applied Ecology, 2007–10; Member, Editorial Board: Internat. Jl of Biostatistics, 2004–12; Procs of Royal Soc. B, 2011–13; Philosophical Transactions of Royal Soc. B, 2017–; founding Co-Ed., Statistical Communications in Infectious Diseases, 2009–12. FMedSci 2015. Franco-British Prize, Acad. des Scis, Paris, 2002; Dist. Alum Award, Dept of Biostats, Harvard Univ., 2005; Suffrage Sci. Award for Maths, MRC Clinical Scis Centre, 2016. *Publications:* (with N. M. Ferguson) Statistical Aspects of BSE and vCJD: models for epidemics, 2000; (with D. R. Cox) Principles of Applied Statistics, 2011; many contribs to learned jls, incl. Nature, Science, New England Jl of Medicine and Lancet. *Recreations:* family board games, travel, theatre, pilates. *Address:* Department of Infectious Disease Epidemiology, Faculty of Medicine, Imperial College London, St Mary's Campus, Norfolk Place, W2 1PG. *T:* (020) 7594 3394. *E:* c.donnelly@imperial.ac.uk; Department of Statistics, University of Oxford, 24–29 St Giles', Oxford OX1 3LB. *T:* (01865) 281228. *E:* christl.donnelly@stats.ox.ac.uk.

**DONNELLY, Christopher Nigel,** CMG 2004; TD 1982; Director, Institute for Statecraft (formerly for Statecraft and Governance), since 2005; *b* 10 Nov. 1946; *s* of Anthony Donnelly and Dorothy Mary Donnelly (*née* Morris); *m* 1971, Jill Norris; one *s* one *d*. *Educ:* Cardinal Langley Sch., Middleton, Lancs; Manchester Univ. (BA Hons (Russian Studies) 1969). Royal Military Academy Sandhurst: Instructor, 1969–72; Sen. Lectr, 1972–79, Dir, 1979–89, Soviet Studies Res. Centre; Special Advr for Central and E European affairs to Sec. Gen. of NATO, 1989–2003; Sen. Fellow, Defence Acad. of UK, 2005–11; Dir, Atlantic Council of UK, 2008–11. Adjunct Professor: Carnegie Mellon Univ., 1985–89; Georgia Inst. of Technol., 1989–93. TA Officer (Intelligence Corps), 1970–93. Hon. Col, Specialist Gp Mil. Intelligence Army Reserve, 2015–. *Publications:* Red Banner, 1988, 2nd edn 1989; War and the Soviet Union, 1990; Gorbachev's Revolution, 1991; Nations, Alliances and Security, 2004; (jtly) Defence Acquisition for the Twenty-First Century, 2015. *Recreations:* shooting, fishing. *Address:* Institute for Statecraft, 2 Temple Place, WC2R 3BD. *T:* (020) 7836 5888, *Fax:* (01539) 722707. *E:* cdonnelly@statecraft.org.uk. *Club:* Army and Navy.

**DONNELLY, Declan Joseph Oliver,** OBE 2016; actor and presenter; *b* Newcastle upon Tyne, 25 Sept. 1975; *s* of Alphonsus and Anne Donnelly; *m* 2015, Alison Margaret Astall; one *d*. Music career, 1993–97 (14 Top 20 hits; UK, European and world tours); television: actor: Byker Grove, 1989–93; A Tribute to the Likely Lads, 2002; presenter of series with Anthony McPartlin, *qv* as Ant and Dec: The Ant and Dec Show, 1995; Ant and Dec Unzipped, 1997; SM:TV Live, 1998–2001 (British Comedy Award, 2000; RTS Award, 2001); CD:UK, 1998–2001; Ant and Dec's Secret Camera Show, 2000; Friends Like These, 2000; Slap Bang with Ant and Dec, 2001; Pop Idol, 2001–03; Ant and Dec's Saturday Night Takeaway, 2002– (British Comedy Awards, 2003, 2004, 2005; Nat. TV Awards, 2007, 2010; British Acad. TV Award, 2014; Best Entertainment Perf., BAFTA, 2014, 2015); I'm a Celebrity… Get Me Out of Here!, 2002– (British Comedy Award, 2004; Best Entertainment Perf., BAFTA, 2010; Nat. TV Awards, 2011–18; TRIC Special Award, 2013; RTS Award, 2013); Gameshow Marathon, 2005; Pokerface, 2006–07; Britain's Got Talent, 2007–; Wanna Bet? (USA), 2008; Push the Button, 2010–11; Red or Black?, 2011–12; When Ant and Dec Met the Prince, 2016; host (with Anthony McPartlin) Brit Awards, 2001, 2015, 2016; film: Alien Autopsy, 2006. Awards with Anthony McPartlin include: Most Popular Entertainment Presenter, annually, 2001–08 and 2010–15, Best TV Presenter, 2016–19, Landmark Award, 2014, Nat. TV Awards; Best Entertainment Personality, British Comedy Awards, 2003, 2004; Best Entertainment Performers, RTS Awards, 2011; Personality of the Year, Freesat Free TV Awards, 2014; TV Personality of the Year, TRIC Awards, 2013, 2014; UK TV Legends, Nickelodeon Kids' Choice Awards, 2015; TV Personality of the Year, TV and Radio Industry Club Awards, 2016, 2018; TV Times Favourite Presenter, 2017; Guinness World Record for Most Nat. TV Awards Won Consecutively, 2019. *Publications:* (with A. McPartlin) Ooh! What a Lovely Pair: our story, 2009. *Address:* c/o YMU Group, 4th Floor, 180 Great Portland Street, W1W 5QZ.

**DONNELLY, Jane Caroline;** see Owen, J. C.

**DONNELLY, Sir (Joseph) Brian,** KBE 2003; CMG 1998; HM Diplomatic Service, retired; Ambassador (formerly High Commissioner) to Zimbabwe, 2001–04; *b* 24 April 1945; *s* of Joseph Donnelly and Ada Agnes (*née* Bowness); *m* 1st, 1966, Susanne Gibb (marr. diss. 1994); one *d*; 2nd, 1997, Julia Mary Newsome; one step *s* one step *d*. *Educ:* Workington Grammar Sch.; Queen's Coll., Oxford (Wyndham Scholar, MA; Hon. Fellow, 2015);

Univ. of Wisconsin (MA). Admin. trainee, GCHQ, 1970; joined HM Diplomatic Service, 1973; 2nd Sec., FCO, 1973; 1st Sec., UK Mission to UN, NY, 1975–79; Head of Chancery, Singapore, 1979–82; Asst Head, Personnel Policy Dept, FCO, 1982–84; Dep. to Chief Scientific Adviser, Cabinet Office, 1984–87; Counsellor and Consul General, Athens, 1988–91; RCDS, 1991; Head of Non-Proliferation Dept, FCO, 1992–95; Minister and Dep. Perm. Rep., UK Delegn to NATO and WEU, Brussels, 1995–97; Ambassador to Yugoslavia, 1997–99; Dir and Special Rep. for SE Europe, FCO, 1999–2000, on secondment to BP Amoco, 2000–01. Special Advr to Sec. of State for Foreign and Commonwealth Affairs, 2005–06; Vis. Directing Staff, RCDS, 2007–09. Mem., Commonwealth Scholarships Commn, 2006–12; Lay Mem., Special Immigration Appeals Commn, 2012–15. Trustee: Senhouse Museum Trust, 2007–08; Cumbria Community Foundn, 2010–13; Dir, Roman Maryport Ltd, 2011–13. *Recreations:* MG cars, flying kites, reading, golf. *Clubs:* MG Owners'; Maryport Golf.

**DONNELLY, Kieran James,** CB 2019; Comptroller and Auditor General, Northern Ireland, since 2009; *b* 16 May 1958; *s* of late James Donnelly and Mary Donnelly (*née* Fegan); *m* 1989, Bernadette Hetherington; four *d*. *Educ:* Christian Brothers' Grammar Sch., Armagh; Queen's Univ., Belfast (BA 1st Cl. Hons Econ. and Soc. Hist. 1980). CIPFA 1988. Joined NI Civil Service, 1983; Dir, NI Audit Office, 1997–2007; Dep. Comptroller and Auditor Gen., NI, 2007–09. *Recreations:* gardening, hillwalking. *Address:* Northern Ireland Audit Office, 106 University Street, Belfast BT7 1EU. *T:* (028) 9025 1107. *E:* kieran.donnelly@niauditoffice.gov.uk.

**DONNELLY, Sir Martin (Eugene),** KCB 2016; CMG 2002; independent consultant, since 2017; President and Managing Director (UK and Ireland Division), Boeing Europe, since 2019; *b* 4 June 1958; *s* of Eugene Lawrence Donnelly and Mary Jane Ormsby; *m* 1985, Carol Jean Heald (*d* 1996); three *d*. *Educ:* Campion Hall, Oxford (MA); Coll. of Europe (Dip. European Studies 1980). Joined HM Treasury, 1980; Private Sec. to Financial Sec., 1982–83; École Nationale d'Admin, Paris, 1983–84; Principal, HM Treasury, 1984–87; Private Sec. to Sec. of State for NI, 1988; Mem., cabinet of Sir Leon Brittan, EC, 1989–92; Asst Sec., Defence Team, HM Treasury, 1993–95; chargé de mission, Direction du Trésor, Finance Min., France, 1995–96; Dep. Hd, European Secretariat, Cabinet Office, 1997–2003; Dep. Dir Gen., Immigration and Nationality Directorate, Home Office, 2003–04; Dir Gen. (Econ.), subseq. (Europe and Globalisation), FCO, 2004–08; Sen. Partner, Office of Communications, 2008–09 (on secondment); Leader, Smarter Govt Review, Cabinet Office, 2009; Acting Perm. Under-Sec., FCO, 2010; Perm. Sec., BIS, 2010–16; Jt Perm. Sec., BEIS, 2016; interim Perm. Sec., DIT, 2016–17. Academic Visitor, Hertford Coll., Oxford, 2017–19. Trustee, Gingerbread, 2017–; Mem. Council, RADA, 2017–. *Publications:* articles on UK trade, G-8, European Commission and cabinet system, and Civil Service neutrality. *Recreations:* reading, music, walking.

**DONNELLY, Prof. Peter Duncan,** MD; FRCP, FRCPE, FFPH; President and Chief Executive Officer, Public Health Ontario, since 2014; Professor: Dalla Lana School of Public Health, University of Toronto, since 2015; Faculty of Health Sciences, McMaster University (part-time), since 2017; Adjunct Professor, Queen's University, Toronto, since 2016; *b* 27 Jan. 1963; *s* of Dr James Donnelly and Gwyneth Donnelly; *m* 1988, Joan Dymock; three *s*. *Educ:* Univ. of Edinburgh (MB ChB 1985; MD 1999); Univ. of Stirling (MBA 1989); Univ. of Wales Coll. of Medicine (MPH); Harvard Univ. (PMD). FFPH 1997; FRCP 2000; FRCPE 2001. Junior hosp. doctor appts, 1985–88; South Glamorgan Health Authority: Registrar, 1989–90; Sen. Registrar, 1990–92; Consultant in Public Health Medicine, 1992–93; Actg Dir, Planning and Procurement, 1993–94; Dep. Chief Admin. MO/Dep. Dir of Public Health Medicine, 1994–96; Dir of Public Health and Exec. Mem. Bd, Morgannwg HA, 1996–2000; Dir, Public Health and Health Policy, Lothian Health Bd, 2000–04; Dep. Chief Medical Officer to Scottish Exec., later Scottish Govt, 2004–08; Prof. of Public Health Medicine, Bute Med. Sch., later Sch. of Med. and Biol Scis, Univ. of St Andrews, 2008–14 (Hon. Prof., 2014–). Lectr, 1989–92, Sen. Lectr, 1992–96, Hon. Sen. Lectr, 1996–2000, in Public Health Medicine, UWCM; Hon. Sen. Lectr in Public Health Medicine, Univ. of Wales, Swansea, 1996–2000; Hon. Prof. of Public Health, Univ. of Edinburgh, 2002–11. Pres., Assoc. of Dirs of Public Health, 1999–2001; Vice Pres., Faculty of Public Health Medicine, RCP, 2001–04 (Treas., 1999–2001). Hon. DSc Napier, 2003. *Publications:* articles in scientific and professional press on public health and resuscitation. *Address:* Public Health Ontario, Suite 300, 480 University Avenue, Toronto, ON M5G 1V2, Canada.

**DONNELLY, Sir Peter (James),** Kt 2019; DPhil; FRS 2006; FMedSci; Professor of Statistical Science, University of Oxford, since 1996 (Director, Wellcome Trust, subseq. Wellcome Centre for Human Genetics, 2007–18); Fellow of St Anne's College, Oxford, since 1996; Founder and Chief Executive Officer, Genomics plc, since 2017; *b* 15 May 1959; *s* of late Augustine Stanislaus Donnelly and Sheila Bernadette Donnelly (*née* O'Hagan); *m* 1986, Dr Sarah Helen Harper (marr. diss. 2006); one *s* two *d*; one *d* by Kerstin Sallows. *Educ:* St Joseph's Coll., Brisbane; Univ. of Queensland (BSc 1979; Univ. Medal 1980); Balliol Coll., Oxford (Rhodes Schol., DPhil 1983; Hon. Fellow, 2014). FMedSci 2008. Vis. Asst Prof., Michigan Univ., 1983–84; Res. Fellow, UC Swansea, 1984–85; Lectr, UCL, 1985–88; Prof. of Math. Stats and Operational Res., QMW, 1988–94; Prof. of Stats and Ecology and Evolution, Chicago Univ., 1994–96. Medallion Lectr, Inst. of Math. Stats, 2007. Mem., EMBO, 2014–. Hon. FIA 1999. Mitchell Prize, Amer. Statistical Soc., 2002; Guy Medal, Silver, Royal Statistical Soc., 2004; Weldon Meml Prize, Univ. of Oxford, 2008. *Publications:* (ed jtly) Progress in Population Genetics and Human Evolution, 1997; (ed jtly) Genes, Fossils and Behaviour, 2001; contrib. to learned jls. *Recreations:* sport, music, children. *Address:* Wellcome Centre for Human Genetics, Roosevelt Drive, Oxford OX3 7BN. *T:* (01865) 287725.

**DONOGHUE, Barbara Joan, (Mrs S. Vavalidis);** Partner, Manzanita Capital, since 2007; *b* 16 July 1951; *d* of Hubert Graham Donoghue and Marjorie Larlham Donoghue; *m* 1976, Stefanos Vavalidis (*d* 2016); two *s*. *Educ:* McGill Univ., Montreal (BCom 1972; Schol.; Transportation Develt Agency Fellow, 1974; MBA 1974). Canadian Pacific Ltd, 1973–77; Bank of Nova Scotia, 1977–79; Vice Pres., Bankers Trust Co., 1979–93; Man. Dir, NatWest Markets/Hawkpoint Partners, 1994–98; Teaching Fellow, London Business Sch., 2000–04; Dir, Noventus Partners, 2004–06. Non-exec. Dir, Eniro AB, 2003–11; Chm., Byredo AB, 2013–. Member: ITC, 1999–2003; Competition Commn, 2005–14. Trustee, Refuge, 2009–. *Recreation:* learning Greek. *E:* barbara.donoghue@btinternet.com. *Club:* Hurlingham.

**DONOGHUE, Bernard;** Director, Association of Leading Visitor Attractions, since 2011; *b* Aylesbury, Bucks, 22 March 1969; *s* of late Michael Donoghue and Carmel Donoghue; civil partnership 2007, Nigel Campbell. *Educ:* Aylesbury Grammar Sch.; Goldsmiths Coll., Univ. of London (BA Hons). Chm., British Youth Council, 1991–93; Parly and Campaigns Manager, SENSE, 1992–96; Sen. Parly and Policy Manager, Nat. Aids Trust, 1996–97; Hd of Govt and Public Affairs, VisitBritain, 1997–2010. Chm., Visit Manchester, 2008–10. Chairman: Young@Now UK and USA, 1996–2005; London Internat. Fest. of Theatre, 2010– (Trustee, 2005–); Council of Ambassadors, WWF-UK, 2012– (Trustee, 2004–10); Tourism Alliance, 2015– (Dep. Chm., 2014–15). Mem., Cathedral Council, St Paul's Cathedral, 2009–. Trustee: Centrepoint, 1995–2012; Tourism Soc., 2001–13; Kaleidoscope Trust, 2011–13; Geffrye Mus. of the Home, 2012–; Kids in Museums, 2012–18 (Dep. Chm., 2014–18); Heritage Alliance, 2012–18; Nat. Funding Scheme, 2013–17; Prince's Regeneration Trust Enterprise Bd, 2015–17; People's History Mus., Manchester, 2018–. Mem., Prog. Adv. Bd, Two Temple Place, 2018–. MCIPR 2002. FTS 2007; FRSA. *Recreations:* theatre, travel, collecting contemporary art, museums and galleries, indulgent uncle and godfather. *Address:* c/o Association of Leading Visitor Attractions, Somerset House, New Wing, WC2R 1LA. *E:* bernarddonoghue@alva.org.uk.

**DONOGHUE, Prof. Denis,** MA, PhD, LittD; literary critic; Henry James Professor of Letters, New York University, 1979, now Emeritus; *b* 1 Dec. 1928. *Educ:* University College, Dublin. BA 1949, MA 1952, PhD 1957; MA Cantab 1965. Admin. Office, Dept of Finance, Irish Civil Service, 1951–54. Asst Lectr, Univ. Coll., Dublin, 1954–57; Coll. Lectr, 1957–62; Visiting Schol., Univ. of Pennsylvania, 1962–63; Coll. Lectr, Univ. Coll., Dublin, 1963–64; University Lectr, Cambridge Univ., 1964–65; Fellow, King's Coll., Cambridge, 1964–65; Prof. of Modern English and American Literature, University Coll., Dublin, 1965–79. Mem. Internat. Cttee of Assoc. of University Profs of English. Mem. BBC Commn to monitor the quality of spoken English on BBC Radio, 1979. Reith Lectr, BBC, 1982. *Publications:* The Third Voice, 1959; Connoisseurs of Chaos, 1965; (ed jtly) An Honoured Guest, 1965; The Ordinary Universe, 1968; Emily Dickinson, 1968; Jonathan Swift, 1969; (ed) Swift, 1970; Yeats, 1971; Thieves of Fire, 1974; (ed) W. B. Yeats, Memoirs, 1973; Sovereign Ghost: studies in Imagination, 1978; Ferocious Alphabets, 1981; The Arts without Mystery, 1983; We Irish (selected essays), 1987; Pure Good of Theory, 1992; Walter Pater: lover of strange souls, 1995; The Practice of Reading, 1998; Words Alone: the poet T. S. Eliot, 2001; Adam's Curse, 2001; Speaking of Beauty, 2003; The American Classics: a personal essay, 2005; On Eloquence, 2008; Irish Essays, 2011; contribs to reviews and journals. *Address:* Department of English, New York University, 244 Greene Street, New York, NY 10003, USA; Gaybrook, North Avenue, Mount Merrion, Dublin, Ireland.

**DONOGHUE, Prof. Philip Conrad James,** PhD; FRS 2015; Professor of Palaeobiology, University of Bristol, since 2010; *b* Morriston, 5 April 1971; *s* of Terrence and Margaret Donoghue; *m* 1998, Mandy Howells; two *s*. *Educ:* Univ. of Leicester (BSc Geol. 1992; PhD Palaeontol. 1997); Univ. of Sheffield (MSc Palynology 1994). 1851 Res. Fellow, Univ. of Birmingham, 1997–98; NERC Res. Fellow, Univ. of Leicester, then Univ. of Birmingham, 1998–2002; Lectr in Palaeobiol., Univ. of Birmingham, 1999–2003; Lectr, 2003–07, Sen. Lectr, 2007–08, Reader in Geol., 2008–10, Univ. of Bristol. President's Award, 1996, Hodson Prize Fund, 2005, President's Medal, 2014, Palaeontol Assoc.; Murchison Prize, 2002, Bigsby Medal, 2007, Geol Soc.; Philip Leverhulme Prize, Leverhulme Trust, 2004; Charles Schuchert Award, Paleontol Soc., 2010; Wolfson Merit Award, Royal Soc., 2013. *Publications:* Telling the Evolutionary Time: molecular clocks and the fossil record, 2003; contrib. papers to internat. peer-reviewed jls, incl. Nature, Science, Proc. NAS. *Recreation:* running. *Address:* School of Earth Sciences, University of Bristol, Life Sciences Building, 24 Tyndall Avenue, Bristol BS8 1TQ. *T:* (0117) 394 1209. *E:* phil.donoghue@bristol.ac.uk.

**DONOHOE, Sir Brian (Harold),** Kt 2019; *b* 10 Sept. 1948; *s* of late George Joseph Donohoe and Catherine Sillars Donohoe (*née* Ashworth); *m* 1973, Christine Pawson; two *s*. *Educ:* Irvine Royal Academy; Kilmarnock Technical Coll. Apprentice fitter-turner, 1965–69; draughtsman, 1969–81; Trade Union Official, NALGO, 1981–92. MP (Lab) Cunninghame S, 1992–2005, Central Ayrshire, 2005–15; contested (Lab) same seat, 2015. PPS to Minister of Transport, 2008–09, to Sec. of State for Transport, 2009–10. Member, Select Committee: on transport, 1993–97 and 2002–05; on environment, transport and the regions, 1997–2001; on transport, local govt and the regions, 2001–02; Admin, 2005–10. Jt Chm., All Party Parly Gp against Fluoridation, 2005–15; Chm., All Party Aviation Gp, 2009–15; Secretary: All Party Parly Gardening and Horticl Gp, 1994–2015; All Party Parly Scotch Whisky and Spirits Gp (formerly Scotch Whisky Gp), 1996–2015; Jt Treas., 2002–09, Hon. Sec., 2009–15, British-American Parly Gp; Chm., PLP Transport Cttee, 2004–15. Chm., Parliamentary Contributory Pension Fund, 2011–. Trustee, Thrive, 2003– (Chm., 2011–14; Patron, 2014–); Dir, Rangers First, 2016. Chm., 2012–15, Dir, 2018–, Westminster Green Mgt Co. Ltd. *Recreations:* gardening, cycling, flying model helicopters, supporting Glasgow Rangers, watching my grandchildren grow.

**DONOHOE, Peter Howard,** CBE 2010; pianist; *b* 18 June 1953; *s* of Harold Donohoe and Marjorie Donohoe (*née* Travis); *m* 1980, Elaine Margaret Burns; one *d*. *Educ:* Chetham's School of Music, Manchester; Leeds Univ.; Royal Northern Coll. of Music; Paris Conservatoire. BMus; GRNCM, ARCM; Hon. FRNCM 1983. Professional solo pianist, 1974–; London début, 1978; concert tours in Europe, USA, Canada, Australia, Asia, USSR; regular appearances at Royal Festival Hall, Barbican Hall, Queen Elizabeth Hall, Henry Wood Promenade concerts, 1979–; numerous TV and radio broadcasts, UK and overseas; recordings include music by Rachmaninov, Stravinsky, Prokofiev, Britten, Messiaen, Muldowney, Tchaikovsky; British piano concertos. Competition finalist: British Liszt, London, 1976; Liszt-Bartok, Budapest, 1976; Leeds International Piano, 1981; winner, Internat. Tchaikovsky competition, Moscow, 1982. Concerto Recording Award, Gramophone, 1988; Grand Prix Internat. du Disque Liszt. *Recreations:* jazz, golf, helping young musicians, clock collecting. *Address:* c/o Ikon Arts-Edition Peters, 2–6 Baches Street, N1 6DN.

**DONOHOE, Prof. Timothy James,** DPhil; Professor of Chemistry, University of Oxford, since 2004; Fellow, Magdalen College, Oxford, since 2001; *b* Darwen, Lancs, 28 Jan. 1967; *s* of William Thomas and Christine Ruth Donohoe; *m* 1991, Ann Louise Budge; two *s*. *Educ:* Tarleton High Sch.; Hutton Grammar Sch.; Univ. of Bath (BSc Hons); Univ. of Oxford (DPhil 1992). Post-doctoral researcher, Univ. of Texas at Austin, 1993–94; Lectr in Chem., 1994–2000, Reader in Chem., 2000–01, Univ. of Manchester; University of Oxford: Lectr, 2001–04; Hd of Organic Chem., 2006–11. Established Career Fellow, EPSRC, 2014. Ed., Tetrahedron Letters, 2015–; Chm., Exec. Bd of Editors, Tetrahedron Pubns, 2018–. Corday Morgan Medal, RSC, 2006; Synthetic Organic Chemistry Award, RSC, 2011; UK Prize for Process Chemistry Res., SCI, 2012; Charles Rees Award, RSC, 2014. *Publications:* Oxidation and Reduction in Organic Synthesis, 2000; contrib. papers to learned jls. *Recreations:* squash, golf. *Address:* Chemistry Research Laboratory, Department of Chemistry, University of Oxford, Mansfield Road, Oxford OX1 3TA.

**DONOUGHMORE, 8th Earl of,** *cr* 1800; **Richard Michael John Hely-Hutchinson;** Baron Donoughmore, 1783; Viscount Hutchinson (UK), 1821; Chairman, Hodder Headline (formerly Headline Book Publishing) PLC, 1986–97; *b* 8 Aug. 1927; *er s* of 7th Earl of Donoughmore and Dorothy Jean (MBE 1947) (*d* 1995), *d* of late J. B. Hotham; *S* father, 1981; *m* 1st, 1951, Sheila (*d* 1999), *oc* of late Frank Frederick Parsons and Mrs Learmond Perkins; four *s*; 2nd, 2001, Margaret, *widow* of Comdr J. M. W. Morgan, RN and *d* of late E. C. Stonehouse. *Educ:* Winchester; Groton Sch., USA; New College, Oxford (MA; BM, BCh). *Heir: s* Viscount Suirdale, *qv*. *Address:* Frogwell, 14 Bushey Row, Bampton, Oxon OX18 2JU.
See also Hon. T. M. Hely Hutchinson.

**DONOUGHUE,** family name of **Baron Donoughue.**

**DONOUGHUE**, Baron *cr* 1985 (Life Peer), of Ashton in the County of Northamptonshire; **Bernard Donoughue;** *b* 8 Sept. 1934; *s* of late Thomas Joseph Donoughue and of Maud Violet Andrews; *m* 1st, 1959, Carol Ruth Goodman (marr. diss. 1989); two *s* two *d*; 2nd, 2009, Sarah Anne Berry, (Hon. Lady Berry). *Educ:* Secondary Modern Sch. and Grammar Sch., Northampton; Lincoln Coll. and Nuffield Coll., Oxford (BA (1st class hons), MA, DPhil). Henry Fellow, Harvard, USA. Mem., Editorial Staff: The Economist, Sunday Times, Sunday Telegraph. Sen. Res. Officer, PEP, 1960–63; Lectr, Sen. Lectr, Reader, LSE, 1963–74; Sen. Policy Advr to the Prime Minister, 1974–79; Development Dir, Economist Intelligence Unit, 1979–81; Asst Editor, The Times, 1981–82; Partner, 1983–86, Head of Res. and Investment Policy, 1984–86, Grieveson, Grant & Co.; Dir, 1986–88, Head of Res., 1986–87, of Internat. Res. and Investment Policy, 1987–88, Kleinwort Grieveson Securities; Exec. Vice-Chm., London and Bishopsgate Internat. Investment Holdings, 1988–91. Opposition spokesman on Treasury, 1991–92, on Energy, 1991–93, on Nat. Heritage, 1992–97; Parly Under-Sec. of State, MAFF, 1997–99; Mem., H of L Select Cttee on Stem Cell Res., 2001–02; Treas., All Party Parly Gp on Integrated Educn in NI; Sec., All Party Racing and Bloodstock Cttee, 2001–; Mem., All Party Jt Scrutiny Cttee on Gambling, 2003–04. British-Irish Parly Assembly, 2000–. Chairman: British Horseracing Bd Commn Inquiry into stable staff, 2003–04; Starting Price Regulatory Bd, 2003–; Future Funding of Racing Gp, 2005–06; Inquiry into Regulation of British Greyhound Industry, 2007–08. Dir, Towcester Racecourse Ltd, 1992–97. Vis. Prof., LSE, 2000–02. Member: Sports Council, 1965–71; Commn of Enquiry into Association Football, 1966–68; Ct of Governors, LSE, 1968–74, 1982–97; Civil Service Coll. Adv. Council, 1976–79; Adv. Bd, Wissenschaftzentrum, Berlin, 1978–91; Bd, Centre for European Policy Studies, Brussels, 1982–87; London Arts Bd, 1991–97. Trustee, Inst. for Policy Res., 1990–. Consultant, British Horse Industry Confedn, 1999–2005. Chm. Exec. Cttee, London Symphony Orch., 1978–93 (Patron, 1989–). Associate Mem., Nuffield Coll., Oxford, 1982–87; Mem., Sen. Common Room, Lincoln Coll., Oxford, 1985– (Hon. Fellow, 1986); Patron: Inst. of Contemporary British History, 1988–; Hansard Soc., 2001–; Vice Pres., Assoc. of Comprehensive Schs, 2000–08. Pres., Gambling Care, 1997; Trustee: Dorneywood Trust, 1997–2015; Internat. League for Protection of Horses, 2002–08; World Horse Welfare, 2008–10; Global Warming Policy Foundn, 2013–; Common Good Foundn, 2015–. Hon. Fellow: LSE, 1989; Northampton Univ., 2006. Hon. LLD Leicester, 1990. *Publications:* (ed jtly) Oxford Poetry, 1956; Wage Policies in the Public Sector, 1962; Trade Unions in a Changing Society, 1963; British Politics and the American Revolution, 1964; (with W. T. Rodgers) The People into Parliament, 1966; (with G. W. Jones) Herbert Morrison: portrait of a politician, 1973; Prime Minister, 1987; The Heat of the Kitchen (memoirs), 2003; Downing Street Diary: with Harold Wilson in Number 10, 2005; Downing Street Diary Volume Two: with James Callaghan in Number 10, 2008; Westminster Diaries: reluctant minister under Blair, 2015. *Recreations:* politics, sport, economics, music. *Address:* House of Lords, SW1A 0PW. *Clubs:* Pratt's, Beefsteak.

**DONOVAN, Prof. Desmond Thomas;** Yates-Goldsmid Professor of Geology and Head of Department of Geology, University College, London, 1966–82; Hon. Curator, Wells Museum, Somerset, 1982–85; *b* 16 June 1921; *s* of T. B. Donovan and M. A. Donovan (*née* Benker); *m* 1959, Shirley Louise Saward (*d* 2007); two *s* one *d*. *Educ:* Epsom Coll.; University of Bristol (BSc 1942; PhD 1951; DSc 1960). FGS 1942, CGeol 1991; FLS 1960. Asst Lectr in Geology, University of Bristol, 1947–50; Lectr in Geology, Bristol, 1950–62; Prof. of Geology, University of Hull, 1962–66. Geologist on Lauge Koch's Danish expeditions to E Greenland, 1947–57. Consultant to British Geol Survey, 1956–. Pres., Palaeontographical Soc., 1979–84. *Publications:* Stratigraphy: An Introduction to Principles, 1966; (ed) Geology of Shelf Seas, 1968; Wells Cathedral: conservation of figure sculpture 1977–1986, 2011; papers on fossil cephalopods, Jurassic stratigraphy, Quaternary deposits, marine geology. *Recreations:* opera, geology. *Address:* 4 North Grove, Wells, Somerset BA5 2TD. *T:* (01749) 677981.

**DONOVAN, Ian Edward,** FRAeS; FCMA; Director, Aeronautical Trusts Ltd, 2002–10; Chairman of Trustees, Royal Aeronautical Society Pension and Assurance Scheme, 2007–10; *b* 2 March 1940; *s* of late John Walter Donovan and Ethel Molyneux; *m* 1969, Susan Betty Harris; two *s*. *Educ:* Leighton Park, Reading. FCMA 1985. Gen. Factory Manager, Lucas CAV, 1969–72; Finance Man., Lucas Girling, 1972–78; Finance Director: Lucas Girling, Koblenz, 1978–81; Lucas Electrical Ltd, 1982–84; Mem., 1985–88, Gp Dir, Finance and Central Services, 1986–88, CAA; Dir and Gp Controller, 1988–98, Gp Dir, Aerospace, 1998–2000, Smiths Industries Aerospace & Defence Ltd; Chm., Chart Co. Ltd, 1998–2000; Dir, Cranfield Aerospace Ltd, 2002–07; Pres., Lambda Advanced Analog Inc., 2000. Dir, English Symphony Orch., 2000–02. Mem. Council, SBAC, 1994–97; Hon. Treasurer: Air League, 1995–2000 and 2002–05; Homeless Network, 1999–2002; Trustee, Air League Educnl Trust, 1995–2000 and 2002–05. FRAeS 2001. *Recreations:* music, fly fishing, photography, gardening. *Address:* Lawn Farm, Church Lane, Tibberton, Droitwich, Worcs WR9 7NW. *Club:* Royal Air Force.

**DONOVAN, Joël;** QC 2011; *b* Paris, 20 Sept. 1963; *s* of late John Donovan and of Françoise Donovan; *m* 2002, Clare Gambling; one *d*. *Educ:* Diss High Sch.; Norwich City Coll.; Durham Univ. (BA Law 1986); Coll. of Law, Chester. Admitted Solicitor, 1989; called to the Bar, Lincoln's Inn, 1991; in practice as a barrister, specialising in complex clinical negligence and personal injury, New Court Chambers, 1992–2000, Cloisters, 2000– (Jt Hd of Chambers, 2017–18). *Recreations:* visual arts, tennis, family. *Address:* Cloisters, 1 Pump Court, Temple, EC4Y 7AA. *T:* (020) 7827 4080. *E:* jd@cloisters.com. *Club:* Hartswood Lawn Tennis.

**DONOVAN, Judith,** CBE 1997; Chairman, DIY Direct Marketing, since 2000; *b* 5 July 1951; *d* of late Ernest and Joyce Nicholson; *m* 1977, John Patrick Donovan. *Educ:* Univ. of Hull (BA Hons English 1973); DipCAM 1979. Mktg Asst, Ford Motor Co., 1973–75; Account Handler, J. Walter Thomson, 1975–77; Advertising Manager, Grattan, 1977–82; Chm., JDA, 1982–2000. Dir, British Direct Marketing Assoc., 1987–91; Chm., Direct Marketing Assoc., 1999–2001 (Dir, 1991–2001); Pres., Bradford Chamber of Commerce, 1999–2001 (Dir, 1988–2003); Director: Bradford City Challenge, 1988–89; Business Link West Yorks, 2001–03; Dep. Chm., Bradford Breakthrough, 1988–90; Chairman: Bradford & Dist TEC, 1989–98; Postwatch, N of England (formerly Northern Region), 2000–08 (Vice Chair, Postwatch Nat. Council, 2007–08); Chair, Keep Me Posted Campaign, 2012–. Member: Millennium Commn, 2000–06; Health and Safety Commn, 2000–10; UK Bd, Big Lottery Fund, 2007–11; British Wool Marketing Bd, 2009–15; Lord Chancellor's Adv. Cttee, N Yorks, then N and W Yorks, 2009–18; DEFRA Task Force on Farming Regulation, 2009–10; Public Mem., Network Rail, 2012–15. Diversity in Public Appts Ambassador, Cabinet Office, 2010–11. Chairman: Yorks Tourist Bd, 2005–08; Ripon City Partnership, 2009–13; Eden Project Ltd, 2013–19; Director: Yorks Dales Nat. Park Authy, 2012–March 2020; York Mailing Gp, 2013–16. Mem. Adv. Bd, York Minster, 2008–09; Chm., Project Bd, York Minster Revealed, 2010–12; Chm., Council, Ripon Cathedral, 2016–. Dir, Northern Ballet Theatre, 1991–2008. Mem. Alumni Adv. Bd, 2013–, Trustee, Univ. Union, 2012–16, Hull Univ. Trustee: Nat. Army Mus., 2017–Oct. 2020; Sci. Mus. Gp, 2019–. Freeman: City of London, 1999; Guild of Entrepreneurs, 2014– (Mem. Court, 2014–); Liveryman: Co. of Woolmen, 2010; Co. of Marketors, 1999. Gov., Margaret McMillan Sch., 1985–87. Gov., Legacy Trust, 2007–13. FRSA 1996; FCAM 1996; FCIM 1998; FInstD 2000; CCMI (CIMgt 2000); FIDM 2001. Hon. Dr Leeds Metropolitan, 2003; Hon. DLitt Hull, 2009. *Recreations:* after dinner speaking, the Western Front, pets. *Address:* DIY Direct Marketing, Biggin Barns, Ringbeck, Kirkby Malzeard, Ripon, N Yorks HG4 3TT. *T:* (01765) 650000, *Fax:* (01765) 650153. *E:* judith@diydirectmarketing.co.uk. *Club:* Reform.

**DONOVAN, Justin;** Chief Education Officer (formerly Director of Education, Sport and Culture), States of Jersey, 2014–18; *b* Cardiff, 1 June 1957; *s* of John and Frances Donovan; *m* 1981, Yvette Chandler; two *s* two *d*. *Educ:* Shoreditch Coll., Univ. of London (BEd; CertEd); Univ. of E London (MEd Policy Studies). Teacher, Angering Sch., Littlehampton, W Sussex, 1979–81; Hd of Dept, Brentside High Sch., Ealing, 1981–83; Hd of Faculty, Grey Court Sch., Richmond, 1983–86; Sen. Advr and Ofsted Inspector, Barking and Dagenham, 1986–2004; Dep. Dir, 2004–10, Dir of Educn, 2010–11, Dir of Educn and Early Intervention, 2011–14, Herts CC. *Recreation:* wreck diving (BSAC advanced diver). *Address:* 1 Butts Paddock, Canewdon, Essex SS4 3QT. *T:* (01792) 258157. *E:* justin.donovan@hotmail.co.uk.

**DONOVAN, Dame Katharine Mary;** *see* Barker, Dame K. M.

**DONOVAN, Stephen Kenneth,** PhD, DSc; Researcher (formerly Curator) of Palaeozoic and Mesozoic Macroinvertebrates, Naturalis Biodiversity Center (formerly Nationaal Natuurhistorisch Museum, then Nederlands Centrum voor Biodiversiteit - Naturalis), Netherlands, since 2001; *b* 3 June 1954; *s* of Alfred Haig Donovan and Beatrice Georgina Donovan (*née* Nichols); *m* 1st, 1997, Catriona Margaret Isobel MacGillivray, PhD (*d* 2003); one *s* one *d*; 2nd, 2005, Fiona Elizabeth Fearnhead (marr. diss. 2009). *Educ:* Univ. of Manchester (BSc 1980); Univ. of Liverpool (PhD 1983; DSc 1994). Royal Soc. Res. Fellow, TCD, 1983–84; Higher Scientific Officer, NERC, 1985–86; University of West Indies, Jamaica: Lectr, 1986–89; Sen. Lectr, 1989–92; Reader in Palaeozoology, 1992–96; Prof. of Palaeozoology, 1996–98; Keeper of Palaeontology, Natural Hist. Mus., 1998–2001. Sen. Res. Fellow, Nat. Mus. of Natural History, Smithsonian Instn, Washington, 1994–95; Visiting Professor: Univ. of Portsmouth, 1996–2004; UCL, 2000–01; Univ. of Liverpool, 2001–02; Adjunct Prof., Univ. of New Brunswick, 2000–. Sec., 2011–17, Vice-Pres., 2017–18, Pres., 2018–, Palaeontographical Soc. Editor: Scripta Geologica, 2002–15; Procs of Yorks Geol Soc., 2017–18; Book Rev. Ed., Geological Jl, 2009–16; Exec. Ed., GeoResJ, 2013–15. FLS 2004–17; Fellow, Geol Soc. of America, 2013. Linnean Medal for Zoology, 2008. *Publications:* (ed) Mass Extinctions: processes and evidence, 1989; (ed) The Processes of Fossilization, 1991; (ed) The Palaeobiology of Trace Fossils, 1994; (ed jtly) Caribbean Geology: an introduction, 1994; (ed jtly) The Adequacy of the Fossil Record, 1998; (ed) The Pliocene Bowden Shell Bed, Southeast Jamaica, 1998; (ed) The Mid-Cainozoic White Limestone Group of Jamaica, 2004; (ed) Palaeontological Papers in Honour of Chris Paul, 2005; (ed) Trace Fossils in the Museum, 2006; (ed) Crustal and Biotic Evolution of the Caribbean Plate, 2008; (jtly) British Silurian Crinoidea, 3 vols, 2009–12; (ed) Jamaican Rock Stars 1823–1971: the geologists who discovered Jamaica, 2010; (ed jtly) Early Palaeozoic Ecosystems, Environments and Evolution, 2011; How Not to Alienate your Editor: some everyday aspects of academic publishing, 2014; (jtly) British Devonian Crinoidea, Pt 1, 2014; (ed jtly) Pleistocene on the Hoof, 2015; Writing for Earth Scientists, 2017; numerous res. papers and reviews, particularly on palaeontology and Caribbean geology. *Recreations:* reading, writing, walking, cricket, tramway and railway history. *Address:* Naturalis Biodiversity Center, Postbus 9517, 2300 RA Leiden, Netherlands. *T:* (71) 7519642.

**DOOCEY,** family name of **Baroness Doocey**.

**DOOCEY,** Baroness *cr* 2010 (Life Peer), of Hampton in the London Borough of Richmond upon Thames; **Elizabeth, (Dee), Doocey,** OBE 1993; Member (Lib Dem), 2004–12, and Deputy Chairman, 2011–12, London Assembly, Greater London Authority (Chair, 2010–11); *m* James Doocey; one *s*. Finance Dir, Liberal Party and Lib Dem Party; Financial Advr, Lib Dem Parly Party; Gp Man. Dir, Tricoville Gp; mgt consultant, DD Enterprises. Mem. (Lib Dem) Richmond-upon-Thames BC, 1986–94. Chm., Economy, Culture and Sport (formerly Econ. Develt, Culture, Sport and Tourism) Cttee, GLA. Mem., Metropolitan Police Authy, 2006–12; Govt Rep., Criminal Justice Bd, 2010–15. Lib Dem spokesperson without portfolio, H of L. Chm., Finance Cttee, H of L, 2016–. *Address:* House of Lords, SW1A 0PW.

**DOOLEY, Michael Matthew Patrick,** FRCOG; Consultant Gynaecologist, since 1992; Surgeon Gynaecologist to the Duchess of Cornwall, since 2007; *b* London, 30 March 1957; *s* of late Denis Dooley and of Eileen Dooley; *m* 1981, Barbara Thompson; two *s* one *d*. *Educ:* King's Coll. Sch., Wimbledon; Charing Cross Hosp., Univ. of London (MB BS 1980); Univ. of Galway (Master Med. Sci. 1985). FRCOG 1998. Res. Fellow, King's Coll. Hosp., 1988–89; Sen. Registrar, St Thomas' Hosp., 1989–91; Consultant Gynaecologist: Dorset Co. Hosp., 1992–; King Edward VII Hosp., London, 1998–; Lister Hosp., 2002–; Med. Dir, 1994–, Consultant Gynaecologist, 2004–, Poundbury Clinic. Dir, Sport Sci. and Medicine, BEF, 1995–2002; Sport Gynaecologist, Olympic Med. Inst., 1998–. Mem., Med. Soc. of London. Treas., Coll. of Medicine; Pres., Obstetrics and Gynaecology Sect., RSM, 2018–19. *Publications:* (ed jtly) Understanding Common Disorders in Reproductive Endocrinology, 1994; (jtly) DRCOG Practice Exams, 2004; (jtly) Your Change Your Choice, 2006; Fit for Fertility, 2007. *Recreations:* walking, gardening, opera, ballet. *Address:* King Edward VII Hospital, Beaumont Street, W1G 6AA. *T:* (020) 7486 4411; Poundbury Clinic, Middlemarsh Street, Poundbury, Dorchester, Dorset DT1 3FD. *T:* (01305) 262626. *E:* mdooley@mdooley.co.uk. *Clubs:* Royal Automobile; Royal Society of Medicine.

**DOPSON, Prof. Susan Elizabeth,** PhD; Rhodes Trust Professor of Organisational Behaviour, since 2010 and Deputy Dean, since 2018, Saïd Business School, University of Oxford; Fellow of Green Templeton College (formerly Templeton College), Oxford, since 1993; *b* Nuneaton, 28 March 1961; *d* of John Wyatt and Marlene Wyatt; *m* 1986, Julian Richard Dopson; one *s* three *d*. *Educ:* Nicholas Chamberlaine Comp. Sch., Bedworth; Univ. of Leicester (BSc; PhD); Bedford Coll., London (MSc); Univ. of Oxford (MA). Pt-time Lectr, Dept of Humanities and Gen. Studies, Coventry Tech. Coll., 1982–83; Personnel Manager, Nuneaton Hosps N Warks DHA, 1982–83; Res. Asst, Dept of Community Medicine, W Essex DHA, 1984–85; Templeton College, subseq. Green Templeton College, Oxford: Res. Associate, 1985–89; Res. Fellow in Orgnl Behaviour, 1990–93; Sen. Tutor, 1999–2003; Vice Pres., 2003–08; Dean, 2009–12; Saïd Business School, University of Oxford: Founding Mem., 1993; Lectr in Mgt Studies (Orgnl Behaviour), 1993–2004; DPhil Course Dir, 1994–98; Reader, 2004–10; Dir, Res. Degrees, 2006–09; Faculty Dean, 2010–13, 2014–17. Vis. Prof., Univ. of Alberta, 2007–. *Publications:* Managing Ambiguity and Change: the case of the NHS, 1997; (ed with N. Austin) Managing the Clinical Directorate, 1997; (ed with A. Mark) Organizational Behaviour in Healthcare: the research agenda, 1999; (ed with A. L. Mark) Leading Health Care Organizations, 2003; (with L. Fitzgerald) From Knowledge to Action?: evidence based medicine in context, 2005; (ed with M. Earl) When the Map Changes: forty years of change in management research, 2012; (jtly) The Modernisation of the Nursing Workforce: valuing the healthcare assistant, 2012; (jtly) Making Wicked Problems Governable?: the case of managed networks in health care, 2012; (with A. Athanasopoulou) Developing Leaders by Executive Coaching: the field, practices and empirical studies, 2015; (jtly) The Politics of

Management Knowledge in Turbulent Times, 2018; (ed with N. Meier) Context in Action and How to Study It: illustrations from healthcare, 2018. *Recreations:* gardening, walking. *Address:* Saïd Business School, University of Oxford, Park End Street, Oxford OX1 1HP.

**DORAN, Gregory;** Artistic Director, Royal Shakespeare Company, since 2012 (Associate Director, 1996–2005; Chief Associate Director, 2005–12); *b* 24 Nov. 1958; *s* of John Doran and Margaret Freeman; civil partnership 2005, *m* 2015, Sir Antony Sher, *qv. Educ:* Bristol Univ. (BA Hons); Bristol Old Vic Theatre Sch. Joined RSC 1987; *RSC productions include:* The Odyssey, 1992; Henry VIII, 1996; Cyrano de Bergerac, 1997; The Merchant of Venice, The Winter's Tale, 1998; Oroonoko, Timon of Athens, Macbeth, 1999; As You Like It, 2000; King John, Jubilee, 2001; Much Ado About Nothing, The Island Princess, 2002; The Taming of the Shrew, The Tamer Tamed, All's Well That Ends Well, 2003; Othello, Venus and Adonis, 2004; A Midsummer Night's Dream, Sejanus, Canterbury Tales, 2005; Antony and Cleopatra, Merry Wives (musical), 2006; Coriolanus, 2007; Hamlet, Love's Labour's Lost, A Midsummer Night's Dream, 2008; Twelfth Night, 2009; Morte D'Arthur, 2010; Cardenio (Shakespeare's 'lost play' re-imagined), 2011; Written on the Heart, 2011; Julius Caesar, The Orphan of Zhao, 2012; Richard II, 2013; Henry IV Parts I & II, The Witch of Edmonton, 2014; Death of a Salesman, Henry V, 2015; King Lear, The Tempest, 2016; Hamlet, Pt I, Conspirator, Pt II, Dictator, 2017; Troilus and Cressida (filmed), 2018; Measure for Measure (filmed), The Boy in the Dress, 2019; *other productions include:* Long Day's Journey into Night, Waiting for Godot, Nottingham Playhouse, 1982–83; Titus Andronicus, Market Th., Johannesburg, and RNT, 1995 (TMA Award for Best Production); Black Comedy, and The Real Inspector Hound, Comedy Th., 1998; York Millennium Mystery Plays, York Minster, 2000; Mahler's Conversion, Aldwych, 2001; The Merchant of Venice, Japan, 2007; The Giant, Hampstead Th., 2007; Anjin: The English Samurai, Tokyo, 2009, Sadler's Wells, 2013; *films:* Macbeth, 1999; Hamlet, 2009; Julius Caesar, 2012; Richard II, 2013; Henry IV, Parts I and II, 2014; Henry V, 2015; King Lear, The Tempest, 2016; *television:* Shakespeare Live! From the RSC, 2016. Humanitas Vis. Prof. in Drama, Oxford Univ., 2012–13. Richard Dimbleby Lect., 2016. Hon. Fellow, Shakespeare Birthplace Trust, 2010; Hon. Sen. Res. Fellow, Shakespeare Inst., 2013. Hon. DLitt: Huddersfield, 2004; Bristol, 2011; Nottingham, 2011; Warwick, 2013; Birmingham, 2015; Hull, 2017; York, 2018. Olivier Award for Outstanding Achievement of the Year, 2003; Sam Wanamaker Award, Globe Th., 2012. *Publications:* (with Sir Antony Sher) Woza Shakespeare!, 1996; The Shakespeare Almanac, 2009; Shakespeare's Lost Play: in search of Cardenio, 2012. *Address:* c/o Royal Shakespeare Theatre, Stratford-upon-Avon, Warwicks CV37 6BB.

**DORBER, Very Rev. Adrian John;** Dean of Lichfield, since 2005; *b* 23 Sept. 1952; *s* of John and Thelma Dorber; *m* 1984, Caroline Perry; three *s* two *d. Educ:* St John's Coll., Durham (BA 1974); King's Coll. London (MTh 1991); Westcott House, Cambridge. Ordained deacon, 1979, priest, 1980; Curate, St Michael and St Mary Magdalene, Easthampstead, 1979–85; Priest-in-charge, St Barnabas, Emmer Green, 1985–88; Chaplain, Portsmouth Poly., 1988–92; Lectr, 1991–97, Sen. Chaplain and Public Orator, 1992–97, Portsmouth Univ.; Priest-in-charge, Brancepeth, 1997–2000; Dir, Ministries and Trng, Dio. Durham, 1997–2005. Chair, Assoc. of English Cathedrals, 2016–. Hon. Chaplain, Portsmouth Cathedral, 1992–97; Hon. Canon, Durham Cathedral, 1997–2005. *Recreations:* gardening, modern fiction, cinema, good food. *Address:* The Deanery, 16 The Close, Lichfield, Staffs WS13 7LD. *T:* (01543) 306250. *E:* adrian.dorber@lichfield-cathedral.org.

**DORCHESTER, Area Bishop of,** since 2000; **Rt Rev. Colin William Fletcher,** OBE 2000; *b* 17 Nov. 1950; *s* of Alan Philip Fletcher, QC; *m* 1980, Sarah Elizabeth Webster; one *s* two *d. Educ:* Marlborough Coll.; Trinity Coll., Oxford (MA 1976). Ordained deacon, 1975, priest, 1976; Asst Curate, St Peter, Shipley, 1975–79; Tutor, Wycliffe Hall, Oxford and Asst Curate, St Andrew, N Oxford, 1979–84; Vicar, Holy Trinity, Margate, 1984–93; Rural Dean of Thanet, 1988–93; Chaplain to the Archbishop of Canterbury, 1993–2000. Cross of St Augustine, 2008. *Recreations:* ornithology, walking, sport. *Address:* Arran House, Sandy Lane, Yarnton, Oxford OX5 1PB. *T:* (01865) 208218.
See also P. J. Fletcher.

**DORCHESTER, Archdeacon of;** *see* French, Ven. J. K.

**DOREY, Gregory John,** CVO 1997; HM Diplomatic Service, retired; Sub-Treasurer (Chief Executive Officer), Inner Temple, since 2018; *b* 1 May 1956; *s* of Michael John Dorey and Avril Dorey (*née* Gregory); *m* 1981, Alison Patricia Taylor; two *s* one *d. Educ:* Painswick Co. Primary Sch.; Rendcomb Coll., Cirencester; Exeter Coll., Oxford (MA Modern Hist.); Open Univ. (Post Grad. Cert. in Business Admin). Nat. Westminster Bank, 1973–74; Supply and Transport Service, RN, 1977–78; Army Dept, 1978–79, Defence Secretariat, 1979–81, MoD; UK Delegn to NATO, 1982–84; MoD PE, 1984–86; Soviet Dept, FCO, 1986; Asst Hd, CSCE Dept, FCO, 1986–89; First Sec., Budapest, 1989–92; Private Sec., Minister of State, FCO, 1992–94; Asst Hd, ME Dept, FCO, 1994–96; Counsellor, then Dep. Head of Mission, Islamabad, 1996–99; on secondment to HSBC plc, 2000; Dep. Hd of Mission, Hong Kong, 2000–04; Asst Dir (Ops), HR Directorate, FCO, 2005–07; Ambassador to Republic of Hungary, 2007–11; to Fed. Democratic Rep. of Ethiopia, Djibouti and the African Union, 2011–15; Sen. Policy Coordinator, Africa Directorate, FCO, 2016. Associate, Ambassador Partnership, 2016–17. Non-executive Director: Project Odyssey, 2016–18; Blue Nile Hldg, 2017–. Mem. Exec. Cttee, Eastern Africa Assoc., 2016–18. *Recreations:* literature, theatre, cinema, tennis, gardening, travel, walking, history.

**DORFMAN, Prof. Ariel;** Walter Hines Page Professor of Literature and Latin American Studies, Duke University, 1984–2016, now Emeritus; author, poet, playwright, journalist, academic and human rights activist; *b* Buenos Aires, 6 May 1942; *s* of Adolfo Dorfman and Fanny Zelicovich; naturalized Chilean citizen; *m* 1966, Angélica Malinarich; two *s. Educ:* Univ. of Chile. Univ. of Chile, Santiago, 1963–73; Univ. of Calif, Berkeley, 1968–69; Friedrich Ebert Stiftung Res. Fellow, Bonn, 1974–76; Sorbonne, Paris IV, 1975–76; Univ. of Amsterdam, 1976–80; Woodrow Wilson Internat. Centre for Scholars at the Smithsonian, Washington, DC, 1980–81; Inst. for Policy Studies, Washington, DC, 1981–84; Univ. of Maryland, Coll. Park, 1983. Member: Acad. Adv. Bd, NPR Contemp. Latino-American Novel Series, 1981–82; American Stories Project, Radio Smithsonian, 1982–83; Adv. Cttee, Nat. Public Radio Latin-America Writers and Their Times Project, Annenburg, 1985–87; Acad. Universelle des Cultures, Paris, 1993–; Amer. Acad. Arts and Scis, 2001–; Internat. PEN; Nat. Writers' Union; Drama Guild; Sociedad de Escritores Chilenos; Academic Freedom Cttee, America Watch; Member, Editorial Advisory Board: Readers Internat.; New Press, New York; Revista de Crítica Literaria Latinoamericana; Editl Advr, Internat. Encyclopedia of Communications. Hon. DHL: Illinois Wesleyan Univ., 1989; Bradford Coll., 1993; American Univ., 2001; Franklin and Marshall Coll., 2011; Hon. LitD Wooster Coll., 1991. *Publications: fiction:* Hard Rain, 1973, 1991; My House is on Fire, 1979, 2nd edn 1991; Widows, 1983, 4th edn 2002; The Last Song of Manuel Sendero, 1987; Mascara, 1988, 3rd edn 2004; Konfidenz, 1995, 3rd edn 2003; The Nanny and the Iceberg, 1999, 2nd edn 2003; Blake's Therapy, 2001; The Rabbit's Rebellion, 2001; (with J. Dorfman) The Burning City, 2003, 2nd edn 2005; Allegro (Spanish), 2015; Darwin's Ghosts: a novel, 2018; *poetry:* Missing, 1982; Last Waltz in Santiago and Other Poems of Exile and Disappearance, 1988; In Case of Fire in a Foreign Land, 2002; *plays:* (adaptation, with Tony Kushner) Widows, 1988, 2008; Death and the Maiden, 1991, 2nd edn 1992; Reader, 1995, 2008; (with R. Dorfman) Who's Who, 1997; (adaptation, with R. Dorfman) Mascara, 1998; The Resistance Trilogy, 1998; Purgatorio, 1999, 3rd edn 2006; Speak Truth to Power: voices from beyond the dark, 2000; Manifesto for Another World: voices from beyond the dark, 2004; The Other Side, 2004, 2008; Picasso's Closet, 2006; Dancing Shadows, 2007; *non-fiction:* (with A. Mattelart) How to Read Donald Duck, 1971, 2nd edn 1975, republd 2018; The Empire's Old Clothes, 1983, 3rd edn 1996; Some Write to the Future, 1991, 2nd edn 1992; Heading South, Looking North: a bilingual journey (memoir, vol. 1), 1998, 3rd edn 2011; Exorcising Terror: the incredible unending trial of Gen. Augusto Pinochet, 2002; Desert Memories: journeys through the Chilean North, 2004; Other Septembers, Many Americas: selected provocations 1980–2004, 2004; Writing the Deep South: the Mandela lecture and other mirrors for South Africa, 2011; Feeding on Dreams: confessions of an unrepentant exile (memoir, vol. 2), 2011; Homeland Security Ate My Speech: messages from the end of the world, 2017. *Address:* 101 Friedl Building, PO Box 90670, 1316 Campus Drive, Duke University, Durham, NC 27708, USA.

**DORFMAN, Sir Lloyd (Marshall),** Kt 2018; CBE 2008; Founder, 1976, Chairman and Chief Executive, 1976–2005 and Chairman, 2005–15, Travelex Group; Chairman: Esselco, since 2007; Doddle, since 2014; Dorfman Media Holdings, since 2018; *b* 25 Aug. 1952; *s* of Harold and Anita Dorfman; *m* 1974, Sarah (*née* Matthews); one *s* two *d. Educ:* St Paul's Sch. Non-exec. Dir, M & C Saatchi plc, 2004–15; Chm., Office Gp, 2010–17. Shareholder and Dir, London Theatre Co., 2016–. Mem., Business Adv. Bd, Mayor of London, 2017–. Chairman: Roundhouse, 2007–10; Prince's Trust, 2015–18 (Trustee, 2007–18; Chm., Develt Cttee, 2007–18); Prince's Trust Internat., 2015–; Trustee: Community Security Trust, 1997– (Dep. Chm., 2005–); Royal Nat. Theatre, 2007–15; JW3, 2007–; Royal Acad. Trust, 2014–; Royal Opera House, 2015–; BAFTA, 2017–; UK Holocaust Meml Foundn, 2019–. Gov., St Paul's Sch., London, 2005–16. Hon. Col 3rd Bn, Princess of Wales's Royal Regt, 2013–. Hon. Fellow, St Peter's Coll., Oxford, 2003. Hon. Bencher, Lincoln's Inn, 2013. *Recreations:* travel, theatre, sailing. *Address:* 22 Manchester Square, W1U 3PT. *T:* (020) 7725 1234. *E:* chairman@esselco.org. *Clubs:* Garrick; Royal Yacht Squadron, Royal Southern Yacht.

**DORGAN, John Christopher,** FRCS; Consultant Orthopaedic and Spinal Surgeon, Royal Liverpool Children's Hospital Alder Hey, 1984–2009; *b* 26 Nov. 1948; *s* of William Leonard Dorgan and Mary Ellen Dorgan (*née* Gorringe); *m* 1978, Ann Mary Gargan (*d* 2003); three *d. Educ:* Thornleigh Salesian Coll., Bolton; Liverpool Univ. (MB ChB 1973; MChOrth 1979). FRCS 1977. House Officer, Walton Hosp., Liverpool, 1973–74; Sen. House Officer, Royal Southern Hosp., Liverpool, 1974–75; Registrar, Whiston and St Helens Hosps, 1975–77; Research Fellow, Univ. of Liverpool, 1977–78; Registrar, Broadgreen Hosp. and Royal Liverpool Children's Hosp., 1978–80; Lectr, Dept of Orthopaedic Surgery, Univ. of Liverpool, 1981–84; Consultant Orthopaedic Surgeon, Royal Liverpool Univ. Hosp., 1984–96. Ext. Examr, 2010–13, Invited Lectr and Examr, 2014–, MChOrth course, Univ. of Dundee. Pres., British Scoliosis Soc., 2005–06 (Hon. Sec. and Treas., 1999–2002; Mem., Exec. Cttee, 2002–03). *Publications:* articles on orthopaedic and spinal surgery in med. jls. *Recreations:* member of two trad jazz bands, watching Bolton Wanderers FC and Waterloo RUFC. *Address:* 23 Elton Avenue, Blundellsands, Liverpool L23 8UW. *T:* (0151) 924 1818. *Club:* Stamps (Crosby).

**DORGU, Rt Rev. (Woyin) Karowei;** *see* Woolwich, Area Bishop of.

**DORIS, Robert Joseph;** Member (SNP) Glasgow Maryhill and Springburn, Scottish Parliament, since 2016 (Glasgow, 2007–16); *b* 11 May 1973; *s* of Robert Doris and Mary Drummond Doris; *m* 2011, Janet Tyson; one *s. Educ:* Univ. of Glasgow (MA Soc. Sci. with Distn 1994); St Andrew's Coll. (PGCE (secondary) Hist. and Mod. Studies 1995). Teacher, Hist. and Mod. Studies, 1995–2007. Scottish Parliament: Mem., 2007–11, Convener, 2016–, Local Govt and Communities Cttee; Dep. Convener, Health and Sport Cttee. *Address:* Parliamentary Constituency Office, Maryhill Burgh Halls, 10–24 Gairbraid Avenue, Glasgow G20 8YE; Scottish Parliament, Edinburgh EH99 1SP. *E:* bob.doris.msp@parliament.scot.

**DORKEN, (Anthony) John;** Chief Executive, British Tyre Manufacturers' Association, 2006–09; Secretary, Tyre Industry Federation, 2005–09; *b* 24 April 1944; *s* of late Oscar Roy Dorken, OBE and Margaret Dorken; *m* 1972, Satanay Mufti; one *s* one *d. Educ:* Mill Hill Sch.; King's Coll., Cambridge (BA Classics 1965; MA 1969). VSO, Libya, 1965–66; Asst Principal, BoT, 1967–71; Private Sec. to Parly Under Sec. of State for Industry, 1971–72; Principal, DTI, later Dept of Energy, 1972–77; seconded to Cabinet Office, 1977–79; Asst Sec., Dept of Energy, 1980–86; seconded to Shell UK Exploration and Prodn, 1986–89; Dir of Resource Management, Dept of Energy, 1989–92; Dep. Dir Gen., Office of Gas Supply, 1992–93; Head of Consumer Affairs Div., DTI, 1993–96; Dep. Dir, 1996–97, Dir, 1997–2005, British Rubber Manufacturers' Assoc. Sec., British Rubber and Polyurethane Products Assoc., 2006–. Sec. and Treas., Medical Aid and Relief for Children of Chechnya, 2001–. *Publications:* articles on gas regulation and tyre issues in specialist jls. *Recreations:* reading, walking, music, squash. *Address:* 10 Connaught Gardens, N10 3LB. *T:* (020) 8372 6213.

**DORKING, Bishop Suffragan of,** since 2016; **Rt Rev. Dr Joanne Caladine Bailey Wells;** *b* 1965; *m* 1994, Rev. Dr Samuel Martin Bailey Wells, *qv;* one *s* one *d. Educ:* Corpus Christi Coll., Cambridge (BA 1987); Minnesota Univ. (MA 1990); St John's Coll., Durham (BA 1992; PhD 1997); Cranmer Hall, Durham. Ordained deacon, 1995, priest, 1996; permission to officiate: Dio. of Ely, 1995–2005; Dio. of Norwich, 1999–2004; Univ. Chaplain, 1995–98, Dean, 1998–2001, Clare Coll., Cambridge; Pastoral Tutor, Ridley Hall, Cambridge, 2001–05; Dir, Anglican Episcopal House of Studies, and Assoc. Prof. of Bible and Ministry, Duke Divinity Sch., N Carolina, 2005–12; Chaplain to the Archbishop of Canterbury, 2013–16. Canon Theologian, Liverpool Cathedral, 2015–16. *Address:* Dayspring, 13 Pilgrim's Way, Guildford GU4 8AD.

**DORKING, Archdeacon of;** *no new appointment at time of going to press.*

**DORLING, Prof. Danny,** PhD; Halford Mackinder Professor of Geography, University of Oxford, since 2013; Fellow, St Peter's College, Oxford, since 2013; *b* Oxford, 16 Jan. 1968; *s* of David and Bronwen Dorling; *m* 1999, Alison Briggs; two *s* one *d. Educ:* Cheney Comprehensive Secondary Sch.; Univ. of Newcastle upon Tyne (BSc 1st Cl. Jt Hons Geog., Maths and Stats 1989; PhD Visualization of Social Spatial Structure 1991). Teacher and pt-time researcher, 1987–91; University of Newcastle upon Tyne: Joseph Rowntree Foundn Fellow, 1991–93; British Acad. Res. Fellow, 1993–96; Lectr in Geographical Scis, 1996–99, Reader in Geog., 1999–2000, Univ. of Bristol; Professor: of Quantitative Human Geog., Univ. of Leeds, 2000–03; of Human Geog., 2003–12, for Public Understanding of Social Sci., 2013, Univ. of Sheffield. Visiting Professor: Dept of Social Medicine, Univ. of Bristol, 2002–; Dept of Sociol., Goldsmiths, Univ. of London, 2013–16; Adjunct Prof., Dept of Geog., Univ. of Canterbury, NZ, 2007–; Vis. Fellow, IPPR, 2012–. Advr, UN World Econ. and Social Survey, 2014. Comr, London Fairness Commn, 2015–. Mem., Editl Adv. Bd, 2002–, Graphics Ed., 2009–, Envmt and Planning A; Member, Editorial Board: Local Economy, 2008–; Jl Social and Cultural Geog., 2010–15. Hon. Pres., Soc. of

Cartographers, 2008–. Patron, RoadPeace, 2011–. Sen. Associate, RSocMed, 2015. FAcSS (AcSS 2003). FRSA 2010. Hon. FFPH 2014. Hon. Dr York, 2019. Award for Excellence in Leading Geography, Geographical Assoc., 2007, 2013; Back Award (1882), RGS, 2009; Political Studies Communicator Award for Explaining Complexity, Political Studies Assoc., 2013; Transmission Prize for communication of ideas, Salon London, 2017; Soc. Award, Soc. of Cartographers, 2017. *Publications:* A New Social Atlas of Britain, 1995; (jtly) The Population of Britain in the 1990s: a social and economic atlas, 1996; (with D. Fairbairn) Mapping Ways of Representing the World, 1997; (jtly) The Widening Gap: health inequalities and policy in Britain, 1999; (ed with S. Simpson) Statistics in Society: the arithmetic of politics, 1999 (trans. Japanese, 2003); (ed jtly) Inequalities in Health: the evidence, 1999; (jtly) Inequalities in Life and Death: what if Britain were more equal?, 2000; (ed jtly) Poverty, Inequality and Health: 1800–2000: a reader, 2001; (jtly) Health, Place and Society, 2002; (with B. Thomas) People and Places: a census atlas of the UK, 2004; (jtly) Geography Matters: simulating the local impacts of national social policies, 2004; Human Geography of the UK, 2005; (jtly) Life in Britain: using Millennial Census data to understand poverty, 2005; (jtly) The Great Divide: an analysis of housing inequality, 2005; (jtly) Poverty, Wealth and Place in Britain, 1968 to 2005, 2007; (with B. Thomas) Identity in Britain: a cradle-to-grave atlas, 2007; (jtly) The Real World Atlas, 2008, 2nd edn 2010 (Gold Prize, Geographical Assoc., 2009) (trans. German, Dutch, French, Italian, Japanese, Korean, 2010); (jtly) The Grim Reaper's Road Map: an atlas of mortality in Britain, 2008; (jtly) Criminal Obsessions: why harm matters more than crime, 2008; Injustice: why social inequality persists, 2010 (trans. Korean 2012); So You Think You Know About Britain?, 2011; (with B. Thomas) Bankrupt Britain: an atlas of social change, 2011; (jtly) Introduction to Maps and Cartographic Methods, 2011; The No-nonsense Guide to Equality, 2012; The Visualization of Social Spatial Structure, 2012; The Population of the UK, 2012; Fair Play: a reader on social justice, 2012; Unequal Health: the scandal of our times, 2013; The 32 Stops: lives on London's Central Line, 2013; Population 10 Billion: the coming demographic crisis and how to survive it, 2013; All That Is Solid: the great housing disaster, 2014; (jtly) The Social Atlas of Europe, 2014; Inequality and the 1%, 2014; Injustice: why social equality still persists, 2015; (jtly) Geography, 2016; A Better Politics: how government can make us happier, 2016; (jtly) People and Places: a twenty-first century atlas of the UK, 2016; (jtly) The Human Atlas of Europe: a continent united in diversity, 2017; The Equality Effect, 2017; (jtly) Why Demography Matters, 2017; Do We Need Economic Inequality?, 2017; Peak Inequality: Britain's ticking time bomb, 2018; (with S. Tomlinson) Rule Britannia: Brexit and the end of empire, 2019. *Recreation:* sandcastles and hydrological sand sculpture (dams) on beaches, preferably somewhere warm. *Address:* School of Geography and the Environment, University of Oxford, South Parks Road, Oxford OX1 3QY. *T:* (01865) 275986. *E:* danny.dorling@ouce.ox.ac.uk.

**DORMAN, Sir Philip (Henry Keppel),** 4th Bt *cr* 1923, of Nunthorpe, co. York; tax accountant; *b* 19 May 1954; *s* of Richard Dorman (*d* 1976) and of Diana Keppel (*née* Barrett); *S* cousin, 1996; *m* 1982 (marr. diss. 1992); one *d; m* 1996 (marr. diss. 2004); *m* 2011, Sally Crawford. *Educ:* Marlborough; Univ. of St Andrews. Life Protector, Dorman Mus., Middlesbrough, 1996–. *Recreations:* golf, tennis. *E:* pd@philipdorman.co.uk. *Clubs:* MCC; Wickwoods Country.

**DORMAN, Richard Bostock,** CBE 1984; HM Diplomatic Service, retired; High Commissioner to Vanuatu, 1982–85; Chairman, British Friends of Vanuatu, 1990–99 (Co-ordinator, 1986–90); *b* 8 Aug. 1925; *s* of late John Ehrenfried and Madeleine Louise Dorman; *m* 1950, Anna Illingworth; one *s* two *d. Educ:* Sedbergh Sch.; St John's Coll., Cambridge. Army Service (Lieut, S Staffs Regt), 1944–48; Asst Principal, War Office, 1951; Principal, 1955; transferred to Commonwealth Relations Office, 1958; First Sec., British High Commission, Nicosia, 1960–64; Dep. High Commissioner, Freetown, 1964–66; SE Asia Dept, FO, 1967–69; Counsellor, Addis Ababa, 1969–73; Commercial Counsellor, Bucharest, 1974–77; Counsellor, Pretoria, 1977–82. Order of Merit (Vanuatu), 1999. *Address:* 67 Beresford Road, Cheam, Surrey SM2 6ER. *T:* (020) 8642 9627.

**DORMANN, Jürgen;** Chairman, V-Zug AG, 2007; *b* Heidelberg, 12 Jan. 1940. *Educ:* Univ. of Heidelberg (MEc). Joined Hoechst AG as mgt trainee, 1963; Fiber Sales Dept, 1965–72; Corporate Staff Dept, 1973–84 (Head of Dept, 1980–84); Dep. Mem., Bd of Mgt, 1984–87; Chief Financial Officer, 1987–94; Chm., 1994–99; Hoechst merged with Rhône-Poulenc to form Aventis, 1999; Chm., Bd of Mgt, 1999–2002, Chm., Supervisory Bd, 2002–04, Aventis; Dir, 1998–2007, Chm., 2001–07, CEO, 2002–04, ABB; Vice-Chm., Sanofi-aventis, 2004–07; Dir, 2004–08, Chm., 2007–08, Adecco; Chairman: Sulzer AG, 2009–13; Metall Zug AG, 2008–13. Non-executive Director: IBM, 1999; Allianz AG, 1999; BG Gp, 2005–10. Sen. Advr, Internat. Adv. Bd, Blackstone Gp. Hon. Pres., ETH Zurich Foundn, 2008.

**DORMENT, Richard,** CBE 2014; FSA; PhD; Art Critic, Daily Telegraph, 1986–2015; *b* 15 Nov. 1946; *s* of James Dorment and Marguerite Dorment (*née* O'Callaghan); *m* 1st, 1970, Kate S. Ganz (marr. diss. 1981); one *s* one *d*; 2nd, 1985, Harriet Mary Waugh. *Educ:* Georgetown Prep. Sch.; Princeton Univ. (BA 1968); Columbia Univ. (MA 1969, MPhil, PhD 1975). Faculty Fellow, Columbia Univ., 1968–72; Asst Curator, European Painting, Philadelphia Mus. of Art, 1973–76; Curator, Alfred Gilbert: Sculptor and Goldsmith, RA, 1985–86; Art Critic, Country Life, 1986; Co-curator, James McNeill Whistler, Tate Gall., 1994–95. Member: Judging Panel, Turner Prize, 1989; Adv. Cttee, Govt Art Collection, 1996–2005; Reviewing Cttee on the Export of Works of Art, 1996–2002; British Council Visual Arts Adv. Cttee, 1997–2006. Trustee: Watts Gallery, 1996–2019 (Chm., Collections Cttee, 2006–); Wallace Collection, 2003–13 (Chm., Internat. Council, 2008–13); Wallace Collection Foundn, 2014–. Mem., Literary Soc. Hawthornden Prize for art criticism in Britain, 1992; Critic of the Year, British Press Awards, 2000. FSA 2014. *Publications:* Alfred Gilbert, 1985; British Painting 1750–1900: A Catalogue of the British Paintings in the Philadelphia Museum of Art, 1986; Alfred Gilbert Sculptor and Goldsmith, 1986; (with Margaret McDonald) James McNeill Whistler, 1994; (contrib.) Oscar Wilde in Context, 2013; Exhibitionist, 2016; contributor to exhibition catalogues: Victorian High Renaissance, 1978; Pre-Raphaelite and Other Masters: the Andrew Lloyd Webber Collection, 2003; Manet and the Sea, 2003; reviews for NY Rev. of Books; contrib. to Burlington Magazine, TLS, Literary Rev. *Address:* Flat 1, 63 Montagu Square, W1H 2LU. *Club:* Brooks's.

**DORMER,** family name of **Baron Dormer.**

**DORMER,** 18th Baron *cr* 1615, of Wynge, co. Buckingham; **William Robert Dormer;** Bt 1615; *b* 8 Nov. 1960; *er s* of 17th Baron Dormer and Pamela Dormer (*née* Simpson); *S* father, 2016; *m* 1st, 1985, Paula (marr. diss. 2011), *d* of Peter Robinson; one *s* one *d*; 2nd, 2013, Susan Viney (*née* Rivière). *Educ:* Southampton Univ. (BSc); Cranfield Univ. (MBA). Company dir. Yachtsman, photographer and Regatta commentator. *Heir: s* Hon. Hugo Edward Geoffrey Dormer, *b* 7 July 1995. *E:* thelorddormer@gmail.com.

**DORMER, Ian Gareth,** CBE 2016; Managing Director, Rosh Engineering Ltd, since 1989; *b* Loughborough, 30 March 1964; *s* of Roy Leonard and Sheila Ann Dormer; *m* 1996, Prof. Julia Lindsey Newton; one *s* one *d. Educ:* Essex Univ. (BA Hons Govt 1986); Georgetown Univ., Washington. Reporter, Flight Internat., 1986–89. Dir, ING Ltd, 2008–11. Chairman: Business Link Tyne & Wear, 2002–04; Enterprise Develt NE Ltd, 2008–11; Mem. Bd, One North East, 2007–12. Dir, NE Says No, 2004. Chairman: Newcastle Coll., 2017–19; Primary Science Teaching Trust, 2019–; Trustee, Herbert Dove Trust, 2018–. Dir, 1999–2010, Chm., 2012–15, Inst. of Dirs; CDir 2013. *Recreations:* skiing, family, travel. *Address:* Rosh Engineering Ltd, Riverside Court, Factory Road, Blaydon, Newcastle upon Tyne NE21 5SA. *T:* (0191) 414 1124. *E:* ian@rosh.co.uk.

**DORMER, Robin James;** Parliamentary Counsel, 2005–11; on secondment to Law Commission, 2006–11; *b* 30 May 1951; *s* of late Dudley James Dormer and Jean Mary (*née* Brimacombe). *Educ:* Internat. Sch. of Geneva, Switzerland; Univ. of St Andrews; University Coll. of Wales, Aberystwyth (LLB). Admitted solicitor, 1980; articled clerk and asst solicitor, Messrs Coward Chance, 1976–80; Mem. Staff, Law Commn, 1980–87; Asst Parly Counsel, Office of Parly Counsel, 1987–90; Solicitor's Office, DoH, 1990–99, Grade 5 (Sen. CS), 1992–99; Office of the Parliamentary Counsel, 1999–2011: Prin. Asst Parly Counsel, 1999–2000; Dep. Parly Counsel, 2000–05. Mem., Legal Services Gp, Terrence Higgins Trust, 1987–99 (Gp Leader, 1992–95). Co. Sec., Food Chain, 2003–06. Bd Sec., We Are Family, 2017–.

**DORNAN, Prof. James Connor,** MD; FRCOG, FRCPI; Consultant, Royal Maternity Hospital, Belfast, 1986–2013; Senior Vice President, Royal College of Obstetricians and Gynaecologists, 2004–07; *b* 5 Feb. 1948; *s* of James Dornan and Clare Elizabeth Dornan (*née* Dunn); *m* 1st, 1970, Lorna Jordan (*d* 1998); one *s* two *d*; 2nd, 2002, Samina Mahsud. *Educ:* Bangor Grammar Sch.; Queen's Univ. of Belfast (MB BCh, BAO; MD 1981). MRCOG 1978, FRCOG 1991; FRCPI 2003. Queen's University of Belfast: Sen. Lectr and Consultant, Sch. of Clinical Medicine, 1986–92; Hon. Clinical Lectr, 1993–98; Hon. Sen. Clinical Lectr, 1998–2002; Hon. Reader, 2002–06; Hon. Prof. of Fetal Medicine, 2006–12, now Emeritus. Hon. Prof. of Health and Life Scis, Univ. of Ulster, 2003–. Mem. Council, RCOG, 1999–2004 and 2008–14. Estab. (with Prof. N. Rooney) first Perinatal Psychology Service, Royal Maternity Hosp., Belfast, 1998. Founder: Tinylife (formerly NI Mother and Baby Action), 1989 (Chm., 1996–2006; Pres., 2006–); (with Dr Suresh Tharma) 3fivetwo Healthcare, 2002; AfterBook, 2017; Up & Up, 2013. Invented Circular Soccer with TriGoal. *Publications:* An Everyday Miracle, 2015; 159 pubns; contrib. chapters to med. textbooks; contrib. numerous papers to learned jls on biophysical assessment of fetal well-being and fetal behaviour; many contribs to med. jls. *Recreations:* tennis, golf, good conversation. *Address:* Shigar, Ballymullan Road, Crawfordsburn, Co. Down BT19 1JG. *T:* (028) 9185 3375. *E:* JimDornan@me.com. *Clubs:* Royal Society of Medicine; Gynaecological Travellers; Royal Belfast Golf; Royal Northern Ireland Yacht; Royal Portrush Golf.

**DORNAN, Prof. Peter John,** DSc; FRS 2003; FInstP; Professor of Physics, Imperial College London, 1991–2012, now Emeritus (Head, High Energy Physics Group, 1991–2007); *b* 5 Sept. 1939; *s* of Philip James and Edith Mary Dornan; *m* 1963, Mary Gwendoline Clarke; one *s* one *d. Educ:* Lancaster Royal Grammar Sch.; Emmanuel Coll., Cambridge (BA 1961; PhD 1965). FInstP 1992. Res. Associate, Brookhaven Nat. Lab., NY, 1965–68; Lectr, ICSTM, 1968–91. Scientific Associate, CERN, Geneva, 1989–91 and 1997–2000 (Spokesman, Aleph Experiment, 1997–2000). Hon. DSc Lancaster, 2000. Rutherford Medal and Prize, Inst. of Physics, 2002. *Publications:* contribs to Physics Letters, Physical Rev. Letters, Physics Reports, Jl European Physics, Nuclear Instruments and Methods, Jl Instrumentation, Jl High Energy Physics, Reports on Progress in Physics, Biographical Memoirs of Fellows of Royal Soc. *Recreations:* travel, photography, walking, food, wine. *Address:* Blackett Laboratory, Imperial College London, SW7 2BW. *T:* (020) 7594 7822, *Fax:* (020) 7823 8830. *E:* p.dornan@imperial.ac.uk.

**DORRANCE, Dr Richard Christopher;** Company Secretary, since 2000, and Finance Director, since 2014, Brilliant Publications Ltd (Partner, 1996–2013); *b* 25 Feb. 1948; *s* of Eric and Joan Dorrance; *m* 1996, Priscilla Hannaford; one *s* one *d. Educ:* Wolverhampton GS; Aylesbury GS; Univ. of East Anglia (BSc Chem. 1969; PhD 1973); London Univ. (PGCE 1974 ext.). FRSC. Res. into properties of detergents, Unilever and UEA, 1969–72; taught chemistry and geology, Royal GS, High Wycombe (and i/c stage lighting), 1972–80; Head of Science, Monks Walk Sch., Welwyn Garden City, 1980–83; Gen. Advr, Berks CC, 1983–88; Asst Chief Exec., Nat. Curriculum Council, 1989–91; Dep. Chief Exec., Sch. Exams and Assessment Council, 1991–93 (acting Chief Exec., 1991–92); Chief Exec., Early Years NTO, 1998–2005. Chief Exec., Council for Awards in Care, Health and Educn (formerly Children's Care and Educn), 1994–2013. Mem. UK Cttee, Organisation Mondiale pour l'Education Préscolaire, 1996–99 (Treas., 1998–99). Chm. Bd, Training Qualifications UK, 2014–; Member, Board: Fedn of Awarding Bodies, 2010–13; Open Schs Trust, 2013– (Chm. 2016–); Mem., Adv. Bd, Gordon Associates, 2013–. Gov., West Herts Coll., 1997–2001. Advr, Nursery World magazine, 1997–2007. Trustee, Northall Village Hall Mgt Cttee, 2007–. *Publications:* Eye (computer prog.), 1983; GAS 81, 1982; papers in professional jls. *Recreations:* walking, foreign travel, natural history, bowling, gardening, model making, photography. *Address:* The Old School Yard, Leighton Road, Northall, Dunstable, Beds LU6 2HA. *T:* (01525) 221273.

**DORRELL, Rt Hon. Stephen (James);** PC 1994; Chairman, NHS Confederation, since 2015; *b* 25 March 1952; *s* of Philip Dorrell; *m* 1980, Penelope Anne Wears, *y d* of Mr and Mrs James Taylor, Windsor; three *s* one *d. Educ:* Uppingham; Brasenose Coll., Oxford (BA 1973). Personal asst to Rt Hon. Peter Walker, MBE, MP, Feb. 1974; contested (C) Kingston-upon-Hull East, Oct. 1974. MP (C) Loughborough, 1979–97, Charnwood, 1997–2015. PPS to the Secretary of State for Energy, 1983–87; Asst Govt Whip, 1987–88; a Lord Comr of HM Treasury (Govt Whip), 1988–90; Parly Under-Sec. of State, DoH, 1990–92; Financial Sec. to HM Treasury, 1992–94; Secretary of State: for Nat. Heritage, 1994–95; for Health, 1995–97; Shadow Sec. of State for Educn, 1997–98. Chm., Health Select Cttee, H of C, 2010–14. Chm., European Movement, 2016–. Contested (Change UK) W Midlands, EP, 2019. *Recreations:* walking, reading.

**DORRIAN, Rt Hon. Lady; Leeona June Dorrian;** PC 2013; a Senator of the College of Justice in Scotland, since 2005; Lord Justice Clerk and President, Second Division, Court of Session, since 2016; *b* 16 June 1957; *d* of Thomas and June Dorrian. *Educ:* Cranley Sch.; Univ. of Aberdeen (LLB 1977). Admitted to Faculty of Advocates, 1981; QC (Scot.) 1994; Standing Jun. Counsel, Health and Safety Exec. and Commn, 1987–94; Advocate Depute, 1988–91; Standing Jun. Counsel, Dept of Energy, 1991–94; a Temp. Judge, Court of Session, 2002–05. Mem., English Bar, Inner Temple, 1991–. Mem., CICB, 1998–2002. Pres., Franco-British Lawyers Soc., 2008–11. Hon. LLD Aberdeen, 2012. *Address:* Court of Session, Parliament House, Parliament Square, Edinburgh EH1 1RF. *Clubs:* Royal Automobile; Scottish Arts (Edinburgh); Royal Forth Yacht; Royal Highland Yacht.

**DORRIES, Nadine;** MP (C) Mid Bedfordshire, since 2005; Parliamentary Under-Secretary of State, Department of Health and Social Care, since 2019; *b* 21 May 1957; *d* of George and Sylvia Bargery; *m* 1984, Paul Dorries (marr. diss.); three *d. Educ:* Halewood Grange Comprehensive Sch., Liverpool; Warrington Dist Sch. of Nursing. Former nurse and businesswoman. Dir, BUPA. Advr to Oliver Letwin, MP. Contested (C) Hazel Grove, 2001. Mem., Panel of Chairs, 2011–. *Publications:* novels: The Four Streets, 2014; Hide Her

Name, 2014; The Ballymara Road, 2015; Ruby Flynn, 2015; The Angels of Lovely Lane, 2016; The Children of Lovely Lane, 2016; The Mothers of Lovely Lane, 2017; Christmas Angels, 2017. *Address:* House of Commons, SW1A 0AA. *E:* dorriesn@parliament.uk. *Club:* Carlton.

**DORSET, Archdeacon of;** *see* MacRow-Wood, Ven. A. C.

**DORWARD, David Keay;** Chief Executive, Dundee City Council, 2009–14 (Director of Finance, 1995–2009); *b* 24 May 1954; *s* of David Dorward and Christina Dorward (*née* Keay); *m* 1977, Gail Elizabeth Bruce; three *d*. *Educ:* Kinross High Sch.; Perth High Sch.; Glasgow Coll. of Technology. CPFA 1982. Trainee Accountant, Perth and Kinross Jt CC, 1971–75; Tayside Regional Council: Trainee Accountant, 1975–82; Sen. Accountant, 1982–83; Principal Accountant, 1983–84; Financial Planning Officer, 1984–86; Chief Financial Planning Officer, 1986–93; Depute Dir of Finance, 1993–95. Associate Dir, Rank Foundn, 2015–. *Recreations:* golf, supporting Dundee United, going to the theatre. *Address:* 4 Norrie Street, Broughty Ferry, Dundee DD5 2SD. *T:* (01382) 739006. *Clubs:* Dundee United Football; Grange Golf.

**DOSANJH, Hon. Ujjal;** PC (Can.) 2004; QC (BC) 1995; *b* India, 9 Sept. 1947; *s* of Giani Pritam Singh Dosanjh and Surjit Kaur Dosanjh; *m* Raminder; three *s*. *Educ:* Simon Fraser Univ. (BA); Univ. of BC (LLB). Called to Canadian Bar, 1977; opened law practice, Dosanjh & Pirani, 1979, subseq. Dosanjh Woolley, then Vertlieb Dosanjh, now Dosanjh Law Gp. MLA (NDP) Vancouver-Kensington, 1991–2001; Attorney Gen., BC, 1995–2000; Premier, BC, 2000–01. Leader, NDP, 2000–01. MP (L) Vancouver S, 2004–11; contested (L) same seat, 2011. Minister of Health, Canada, 2004–06; Official Opposition Critic: for Nat. Defence, 2006–07, 2008–09; for Foreign Affairs, 2007; for Public Safety, 2007–08. Hon. LLD Guru Nanak Dev Univ., Amritsar, 2001. *Recreations:* walking, writing, blogging at www.ujjaldosanjh.org and www.commentindia.com. *Address:* 2520 SW Marine Drive, Vancouver, BC V6P 6C2, Canada.

**DOSS, Alan Claude,** CMG 2011; President, Kofi Annan Foundation, Geneva, since 2018 (Senior Political Adviser, 2011–14; Executive Director, 2014–18); *b* 7 Jan. 1945; *m* Soheir; three *d*. *Educ:* London Sch. of Econs and Pol Sci. UN Resident Coordinator and UNDP Resident Rep., Benin, Zaire and Vietnam, 1977–79; Dep. Resident Rep., UNDP, China, 1979; Resident Coordinator and UNDP Regl Rep., Bangkok and Dir, UN Border Relief Gp, Thai-Cambodian border; Director: UNDP Eur. Office, Geneva; UN Develt Gp; Dep. Special Rep. of UN Sec.-Gen. for Sierra Leone and UN Resident Coordinator, Humanitarian Coordinator and UNDP Resident Rep., until 2004; Principal Dep. Special Rep. of UN Sec.-Gen. for Côte d'Ivoire, 2004–05; Special Rep. for Liberia, 2005–07; Special Rep. and Hd, UN Mission in Democratic Republic of Congo, 2007–10. Vis. Fellow, Geneva Centre for Security Policy, 2010. *Address:* c/o Kofi Annan Foundation, PO Box 157, 1211 Geneva 20, Switzerland.

**dos SANTOS, Eduardo,** Hon. CVO 1997; Consul General of Brazil in Milan, since 2018; *b* Rio de Janeiro, 29 Dec. 1952; *s* of late Vitto Raphael dos Santos and Esther da Conceição dos Santos; *m* 1976, (Maria) Elisabeth Zamith (*d* 2014); two *d*. *Educ:* Federal Univ. of Rio de Janeiro (BA Legal and Social Studies 1975). Entered Diplomatic Service of Brazil, 1974; Advr to Office of Foreign Minister, 1986–89, 1992–93; served at embassies of Brazil in Moscow and Buenos Aires; Counsellor, 1989–94, Minister Counsellor, 1994–99, London; Special Advr to Office of Finance Minister, 1993; Diplomatic Advr to Pres. of Brazil, 1999–2002; Ambassador: to Uruguay, 2002–06; to Switzerland and Liechtenstein, 2006–08; to Paraguay, 2008–13; Sec.-Gen., Min. of Ext. Relns, 2013–15; Ambassador to UK, 2015–18. *Publications:* contrib. articles to specialised foreign affairs mags. *Recreations:* music, reading, walking, football.

**DOSSETT, David Patrick,** MBE 2011; Executive Chairman, BEAMA (formerly British Electrotechnical and Allied Manufacturers' Association) Ltd, 2008–10, Adviser to President and Chief Executive Officer, 2010–12 (Director General, 1998–2001; Chief Executive, 2001–08); Chief Executive, BEAMA Installation Ltd, 1999–2010; *b* 20 Oct. 1943; *s* of John Dossett and Elizabeth Dossett (*née* Walsh); *m* 1964, Teresa Richards; four *s* two *d*. *Educ:* City Univ., London (BSc (Electrical and Electronic Engrg)). MIET (MIEE 1990). Distribn engr, London Electricity Bd, 1967–71; Tech. Officer, BSI, 1971–77; Hd of Standards, Kala (Iranian oil co.), 1977–84; Sen. Tech. Officer, AMDEA, 1984–91; Dir, EIEMA, 1991–98. Director: ASTA BEAB (formerly Asta) Certification Services, 1991–2007; Electrical Safety Council (formerly NICEIC), 2001– (Vice-Chm., 2005–07, Chm., 2007–09); Pres., CENELEC, 2010–12 (Vice Pres., 2008–09), Chm., Orgalime, 2005–07, Gov., St Bede's Sch., Romford, 1978–88 (Chm., 1984–88). *Recreations:* West Ham United, real ale, 14 grandchildren. *Address:* 12A Marlborough Drive, Sudbury CO10 2PS. *T:* 07768 045211. *E:* dpd1@hotmail.co.uk.

**DOUBLE, Paul Robert Edgar,** LVO 2012; Remembrancer, since 2003, and Parliamentary Agent, since 2004, City of London; Parliamentary Agent, The Honourable The Irish Society, since 2004; *b* 4 Oct. 1951; *s* of Edgar Harold Double and Iris Joan Double; *m* 1986, Glynis Mycock (Dr Glynis Double, MB, ChB, MSc, FRCPath, FFPHM); one *s* three *d*. *Educ:* Univ. of Bristol (BSc); University Coll. London (LLM). MRSC 1984. Called to the Bar, Middle Temple, 1981; joined Civil Service, 1974; seconded to Univ. of Aston, 1975; Sec., Printing Industry Adv. Cttee, Dept of Employment, 1976; Mem., Legislation Review Unit, 1981; apptd Counsel to City Remembrancer, following pupillage in chambers of Hon. Sir Michael Turner and as prosecutor for HM Factory Inspectorate, 1985; Asst Remembrancer, 1994–98; Dir, 1998–2003. City Corporation's Patron, Financial Markets Law Cttee, 2009–. Dir, Lord Mayor's Show Ltd, 2004–; Hon. Sec., Lord Mayor and Sheriffs' Cttee, 2003–. Dir, Global Law Summit, 2013–; Mem., 2014–17, Trustee, 2015–17, Agincourt 600 Organising Cttee. Trustee, Magna Carta Trust, 2011–. Governor: Sutton's Hosp. in Charterhouse, 2004–17; Sion Coll., 2018–. Vis. Lectr in Law, Univ. of London, 1983–98. Freeman, City of London, 1985. Consulting Ed., London Govt, Halsbury's Laws of England, 2011–. Hon. Bencher, Middle Temple, 2017. Sponsor, City of London Corp. Multi-Faith Network, 2015–. *Recreations:* sailing, leisure cycling. *Address:* Guildhall, EC2P 2EJ. *T:* (020) 7332 1200, *Fax:* (020) 7710 8579. *Club:* Guildhall.

**DOUBLE, Stephen Daniel;** MP (C) St Austell and Newquay, since 2015; *b* St Austell, 19 Dec. 1966; *m* 1986, Anne Bird; two *s*. *Educ:* Poltair Sch., St Austell. Barclays Bank, 1983–92; church pastor, 1992–2002. Director: Bay Direct Media Ltd, 2001–15; Phoenix Corporate Ltd, 2011–15. Mem. (C), Cornwall Council, 2009–13. *Address:* House of Commons, SW1A 0AA.

**DOUBLEDAY, John Vincent;** sculptor, since 1968; *b* 9 Oct. 1947; *s* of late Gordon V. and Margaret E. V. Doubleday; *m* 1969, Isobel J. C. Durie; two *s* (and one *s* decd). *Educ:* Stowe; Goldsmiths' College School of Art. *Exhibitions include:* Waterhouse Gallery, 1968, 1969, 1970, 1971; Galerie Sothmann, Amsterdam, 1969, 1971, 1979; Richard Demarco Gallery, Edinburgh, 1973; Laing Art Gallery, Newcastle, Bowes Museum, Barnard Castle, 1974; Pandion Gallery, NY, Aldeburgh Festival, 1983; Ujjain Internat. Fest., 2010; retrospective, Minories Galls, Colchester, 2017; *works include:* Prince Philip, Duke of Edinburgh, Earl Mountbatten of Burma, Golda Meir, 1976; Charlie Chaplin (Leicester Square), 1982; Beatles (Liverpool), Dylan Thomas, 1984; Royal Marines Commando Meml, Lympstone, Devon, 1986; Sherlock Holmes (Meiringen), 1991; Dorothy L. Sayers (Witham), 1994; J. B. Pflug (Biberach), 1994; Nelson Mandela (Mbabane and London), 1997; Gerald Durrell (Jersey Zoo), Sherlock Holmes (Baker Street Stn, London), 1999; The Dorset Shepherd, Dorchester, 2000; Col Jabara (USAF ACAD., Colorado Springs), 2004; Nelson (Gibraltar), 2005; Battle of Maldon Monument (Blackwater Estuary, Essex), 2006; Guruji Chinchalkar (Indore), 2010; Municipal Mus., Meiringen, Switzerland, 2012; HM The Queen, Gibraltar, 2013; Herbert Columbine VC (Walton-on-the-Naze), 2014; HM The Queen, Southend-on-Sea, 2016; Nat. Police Dog Meml, Chelmsford, 2019; *works in public collections:* Ashmolean Mus., British Mus., Herbert F. Johnson Mus., USA, Tate Gall., V & A, Nat. Mus. of Wales. *Publications:* John Doubleday: work, 2016. *Recreation:* enthusiasm for the unnecessary. *Address:* Goat Lodge, Goat Lodge Road, Great Totham, Maldon, Essex CM9 8BX. *T:* (01621) 891329.

**DOUCE, Prof. John Leonard,** FREng; FIEE; Professor of Electrical Science, Warwick University, 1965–94 (part-time 1989–94), now Emeritus; *b* 15 Aug. 1932; *s* of John William and Florrie Douce; *m* 1959, Jean Shanks; one *s* one *d*. *Educ:* Manchester Grammar Sch.; Manchester Univ. (BSc, MSc, PhD, DSc). Lectr, Sen. Lectr, Reader, Queen's Univ., Belfast, 1958–65. Member: Technology Sub-Cttee, UGC, 1980–89; Engrg Bd, 1987–91, Science Bd, 1989–91, SERC; Contract Assessor, HEFCE, 1993–94. FIEE 1970; FREng 1991. Sir Harold Hartley Silver Medal, Inst. of Measurement and Control, 1989. *Publications:* Introduction to Mathematics of Servomechanisms, 1963, 2nd edn 1972; papers on control engineering. *Recreations:* bridge, boating, home-brewing. *Address:* 259 Station Road, Balsall Common, Coventry CV7 7EG. *T:* (01676) 532070. *E:* john.douce@btinternet.com.

**DOUCET, Lyse Marie,** OBE 2014; CM 2018; presenter and correspondent, since 1999, and Chief International Correspondent, since 2012, BBC World News TV and BBC World Service Radio; *b* Bathurst, NB, Canada, 24 Dec. 1958; *d* of Clarence and Norma Doucet. *Educ:* Queen's Univ., Kingston, Ont (BA Hons 1980); Univ. of Toronto (MA Internat. Relns 1982). Joined BBC, 1983; W Africa reporter, 1983–88; Kabul corresp., 1988–89; Pakistan corresp., 1989–94; Jordan corresp., 1994–95; ME corresp., 1995–99. Member, Council: Chatham House, 2004–10; Internat. Council on Human Rights Policy, 2005–12. Hon. Patron, Canadian Crossroads Internat., 2006. Mem., Friends of Aschiana, 2006–. Hon. DCL King's Coll., Halifax, 2003; Hon. DLitt: New Brunswick, 2006; Moncton, 2010; York St John, 2016; Hon. DLaws: Toronto, 2009; St Andrews, 2014; Hon. Dr: York, 2012; Queen's, Kingston, 2015; Cranfield, 2019; Hon. DHL Liverpool Hope, 2015; Hon. DArts Bedfordshire, 2017; DUniv: Sussex, 2018; QUB, 2019. Silver Sony Radio News Broadcaster of Year, 2003; TV Personality of Year, Assoc. for Internat. Broadcasting, 2007; News and Factual Award, Women in Film and TV, 2007; David Bloom Award for Excellence in Enterprise Reporting, Radio and Television Correspondents Assoc., 2010; Gold Sony News Journalist of the Year, 2010; Peabody Award, Univ. of Georgia, 2010, 2013; Edward R. Murrow Award, Radio TV Digital News Assoc., 2012; James Cameron Prize, 2013; Women in Film and TV - ITV Studios Achievement of the Year, 2014; Emmy News Award Syria, 2014; Sandford St Martin Trustees Award for religious broadcasting, 2015; Lifetime Achievement, Columbia Univ., 2016; Charles Wheeler Award, British Journalism Review, 2017; Global Trailblazer Award, Georgetown Inst. for Women, Peace and Security, 2018; Queen Soraya Award for Media Excellence, Embassy of Afghanistan, London, 2018; Best Individual Contributor to Radio, VLV Awards for Excellence, 2019. *E:* lyse.doucet@bbc.co.uk. *Club:* Frontline.

**DOUEK, Ellis Elliot,** FRCS; Consultant Otologist, 1970–99, now Emeritus, and Chairman, Hearing Research Group, 1974–99, Guy's Hospital; author; *b* 25 April 1934; *s* of Cesar Douek and Nelly Sassoon; *m* 1993, Gill Green; two *s* by former marriage. *Educ:* English School, Cairo; Westminster Medical School. MRCS, LRCP 1958; FRCS 1967. House appts, St Helier Hosp., 1959, and Whittington Hosp., 1963; nat. service, RAMC, 1960–62; ENT Registrar, Royal Free Hosp., 1966; Sen. Registrar, King's College Hosp., 1968. Mem., MRC working party on Hearing Research, 1975; MRC Rep. to Eur. Communities on Hearing Res., 1980; UK Rep. to Eur. Communities on Indust. Deafness, 1983; Mem., Scientific Cttee, Inst. de Recherche sur la surdité, Paris, 1989–. Littman Meml Lect., UCL, 2005. Dalby Prize for hearing research, RSM, 1978. *Publications:* Sense of Smell—Its Abnormalities, 1974; Eighth Nerve, in Peripheral Neuropathy, 1975; Olfaction, in Scientific Basis of Otolaryngology, 1976; Cochlear Implant, in Textbook of ENT, 1980; A Middle Eastern Affair (autobiog.), 2004; Overcoming Deafness; the story of hearing and language, 2014; papers on hearing and smell; contrib. online jl, The Fickle Grey Beast. *Recreations:* drawing and painting, studying history. *Address:* (home) 14 Heathcroft, Hampstead Way, NW11 7HH. *T:* (020) 8455 6427. *E:* elgildouek@aol.com. *Club:* Athenæum.

**DOUETIL, Dane Jonathan,** CBE 2007; Group Chief Executive Officer: Minova Insurance Holdings (formerly BMS Associates) Ltd, since 2013; Brit Insurance Holdings N.V. (formerly PLC), 2005–11 (Director, 1999–2011); Chief Executive, Brit Syndicates Ltd, 2002–11; Head, Brit Group Underwriting, 2002–11; *b* 28 July 1960; *s* of late Dane Peter Douetil and of Fleur Caroline Douetil; *m* 1986, Antonia Clare Williamson; three *d*. *Educ:* Birmingham Univ. (BA Hons Commerce 1982). Willis Faber Gp, 1982–89 (Dir, Political and Financial Risk Div., 1988–89); Founding Shareholder and Dir, Special Risk Services Ltd, 1989–94; Consultant, Benfield Gp, 1997; Dir and Chief Exec., Brit Insce Ltd, 1998–2011. Mem., and Chm., London Mkt Reform Gp, 2006–07; Dir, ABI, 2010–11. *Recreations:* fishing, shooting, wine, cricket. *Club:* Boodle's.

**DOUGAL, Andrew James Harrower;** non-executive Director, Victrex plc, 2015–18 (Chairman, Audit Committee, 2015–18); *b* 2 Sept. 1951; *s* of late Andrew James Harrower Dougal and Muriel Mary Dougal (*née* MacDonald); *m* 1978, Margaret Mairi MacDonald; two *s* one *d*. *Educ:* Greenock Acad.; Paisley GS; Glasgow Univ. (BAcc 1972). CA 1975. Articled Clerk, then Asst Manager, Arthur Young Glasgow, 1972–77; Gp Chief Accountant, Scottish & Universal Investments Ltd, 1977–86; Hanson plc, 1986–2002: Finance Comptroller, 1986–89; Finance Dir, ARC Ltd, 1989–92; Man. Dir, ARC Southern, 1992–93; Dep. Finance Dir, 1993–95; Finance Dir, 1995–97; Chief Exec., 1997–2002. Non-executive Director: Taylor Woodrow plc, 2002–07 (Chm., Audit Cttee, 2003–07); BPB, 2003–05; Celtel Internat. BV, 2004–05; Premier Farnell plc, 2006–15; Creston plc, 2006–15; Taylor Wimpey plc, 2007–11 (Chm., Audit Cttee, 2007–09); Carillion plc, 2011–18 (Chm., Audit Cttee, 2011–18). Institute of Chartered Accountants of Scotland: Mem. Council and Oversight Bd, 2012–18; Mem., Qualification Bd, 2000–05; Convenor, Business Policy Cttee, 2010–12; Mem., Tech. Policy Bd, 2010–17 (Chm., 2012–17). FRSA 2005. *Recreations:* family, sports, travel, history.

**DOUGAL, Malcolm Gordon;** HM Diplomatic Service, retired; *b* 20 Jan. 1938; *s* of late Eric Gordon Dougal and Marie (*née* Wildermuth); *m* 1st, 1964, Elke (marr. diss.); one *s*; 2nd, 1995, Brigid Pritchard (*née* Turner) (*d* 2000); two step *s*; 3rd, 2003, Diana Blade (*née* Price); two step *s*. *Educ:* Ampleforth Coll., Yorkshire; The Queen's Coll., Oxford (MA Mod. History). National Service in Korea and Gibraltar with Royal Sussex Regt, 1956–58; Oxford, 1958–61; Contracts Asst, De Havilland Aircraft, Hatfield, 1961–64; Asst to Export Manager, Ticket Equipment Ltd (Plessey), 1964–66; Export Manager, Harris Lebus Ltd, 1967–69; entered HM Diplomatic Service, 1969; Foreign Office, 1969–72; 1st Secretary

(Commercial): Paris, 1972–76; Cairo, 1976–79; Foreign Office, 1979–81; Consul Gen., Lille, 1981–85; Dep. High Comr and Head of Chancery, Canberra, 1986–89; RCDS, 1990; Dir, Jt FCO/DTI Directorate of Overseas Trade Services, FCO, 1991–94; Consul Gen., San Francisco, 1994–98. Warden, John Spedan Lewis Trust for the Advancement of the Natural Scis, 1998–2005. *Publications:* (contrib.) The Third Battle of Ypres (Seaford House Papers), 1990. *Recreations:* natural history, history, walking, books, sport, horse racing, wine. *Address:* The Old Paddock, Monk Sherborne, Tadley, Hants RG26 5HR.

**DOUGALL, Rebecca Jane;** Headmistress, St Helen and St Katharine, Abingdon, since 2015; *b* Epsom, 1 Aug. 1970; *d* of David Mallard and Tink Mallard; *m* 2005, Tim Dougall. *Educ:* Charlton Park Sch., Cheltenham; Bristol Univ. (BA Hons English Lit.); King's Coll. London (MA Nineteenth Century Lit.). Teacher of English, Wycombe Abbey Sch., 1994–99; Teacher of English, 1999–2006, Dep. Hd, 2003–06, Oxford High Sch., GDST; Dep. Hd, 2006–09, Hd, 2010–14, Royal High Sch., Bath, GDST. *Recreations:* reading, travel, gardening, music, sport. *Address:* St Helen and St Katharine, Faringdon Road, Abingdon, Oxon OX14 1BE. *T:* (01235) 520173. *E:* head@shsk.org.uk.

**DOUGAN, Dr David John;** County Arts Officer, Essex County Council, 1989–97; *b* 26 Sept. 1936; *s* of William John Dougan and Blanche May; *m* 1st, 1959, Eileen Ludbrook (marr. diss. 1985); one *s*; 2nd, 1986, Barbara Taylor; one *s* one *d. Educ:* Durham Univ. (BA, MA); City Univ. (PhD 1982) BA Open Univ. 2002. Reporter, Tyne Tees Television, 1963; presenter, BBC, 1966; Director, Northern Arts, 1970; Dir, Crafts Council, 1984–88. Chairman: Nat. Youth Dance Trust, 1985–91; Dance East, 1999–2003; Suffolk Univs of the Third Age, 2005–. Special Advr, H of C Educn, Sci. and Arts Cttee, 1981–82; Mem., Calouste Gulbenkian Foundn Enquiry into the Arts in Schs, 1982. *Publications:* History of North East Shipbuilding, 1966; Great Gunmaker, 1968; Shipwrights Trade Union, 1971; The Jarrow March, 1976; To Return a King, 2006. *Recreations:* theatre, music, tennis. *Address:* Grovelands, 1 Grove Road, Bury St Edmunds, Suffolk IP33 3BE. *T:* (01284) 752588.

**DOUGAN, Prof. Gordon,** PhD; FRS 2012; FMedSci; GlaxoSmithKline Professor of Microbial Pathogenesis, University of Cambridge, since 2015; Fellow, Wolfson College, Cambridge. *Educ:* Univ. of Sussex (BSc Biochem.; PhD). Postdoctoral studies, Univ. of Washington, Seattle; Lectr, Moyne Inst., TCD; Wellcome Foundn, until 1992; Rank Prof. of Physiological Biochem., and Dir, Centre for Molecular Microbiol. and Infection, Imperial Coll. London; Wellcome Trust Sanger Institute: Principal Res. Scientist and Hd of Pathogen Res., 2004; Sen. Gp Leader; Mem., Bd of Mgt, 2004–14. Hon. Prof., Veterinary Sch., Univ. of Cambridge; Visiting Professor: LSHTM; Univ. of Nottingham. Chm., New Vaccines Steering Cttee, WHO. Former Chair, Scientific Adv. Bd, Novartis Vaccines and Diagnostics; Mem., Scientific Adv. Bd, GlycoVaxyn, AG. Mem., EMBO. FMedSci 2002. *Publications:* contribs to jls.

**DOUGHERTY, Charles Egmont;** QC 2013; *b* Stockholm, 27 July 1972; *s* of Peter Dougherty and Wanja Dougherty (née Tornberg). *Educ:* Winchester Coll.; Magdalen Coll., Oxford (BA; BCL). Law tutor and researcher, Freie Univ., Berlin, 1994–95; Mgt Consultant, Arkwright Ltd, 1995–96; called to the Bar, Middle Temple, 1997; in practice as barrister, specialising in commercial law, 1997–. *Publications:* (asst ed.) European Civil Practice, 2nd edn 2004. *Recreations:* theatre, art, wine travel, walking. *Address:* 2 Temple Gardens, Temple, EC4Y 9AY. *T:* (020) 7822 1200, *Fax:* (020) 7822 1300. *E:* cd@2tg.co.uk.

**DOUGHERTY, Prof. Michele Karen,** CBE 2018; PhD; FRS 2012; FRAS; Professor of Space Physics, Blackett Laboratory, since 2004, Royal Society Research Professor, since 2014 and Head, Department of Physics, since 2018, Imperial College London; *b* 1962. *Educ:* Univ. of Natal (PhD 1988). Postdoctoral Fellow, Germany, 1989–90; Imperial College London: PPARC Advanced Fellow in Space Physics, 1995–2000; Lectr, 2000–02; Reader in Space Physics, 2002–04; Mem., Team for Jupiter analysis of Ulysses Mission, 1991–; Eur. Hd, NASA-ESA Europa Jupiter system mission to Jupiter; Guest Investigator, NASA Jupiter System Data Analysis Prog.; Principal Investigator, Internat. NASA-ESA-ASI Cassini Huygens mission to Saturn and its moons. Associate Ed., Jl Geophysical Res. - Space Physics. Chair, Scientific Prog. Adv. Cttee, UK Space Agency, 2013–. Fellow, Amer. Geophysical Union; FCGI 2014. Zeldovich Medal, Russian Acad. Scis and Cttee on Space Res., 1996; Hughes Medal, Royal Soc., 2008; Gold Medal, RAS, 2017. *Publications:* contribs to learned jls, incl. Jl Geophysical Res. - Space Physics, Planetary and Space Sci. *Address:* Department of Physics, Imperial College London, South Kensington Campus, SW7 2AZ.

**DOUGHERTY, Air Vice-Marshal Simon Robert Charles,** FRCP; FFOM; Director-General Medical Services, Royal Air Force, 2004–08, and Chief of Staff (Health) HQ Air Command, 2006–08; *b* 26 Feb. 1949; *s* of late Patrick Cecil George Dougherty and Valerie June Dougherty (née Appleby); *m* 1971, Margaret Snape; two *s* one *d. Educ:* Framlingham Coll.; London Hosp. Med. Coll. (MB BS 1971); LSHTM (MSc Occupational Medicine 1986). DObstRCOG 1976; DAvMed (Stewart Meml Prize) 1979; AFOM 1980, MFOM 1984, FFOM 1993; FRCP 2009. Commnd RAF Med. Br., 1969; MO, RAF Binbrook, 1974–75; UK Delegn & Support Unit HQ AFCENT, 1975–77; Sen. MO, UK Support Unit, HQ AAFCE, 1977–78; DAvMed course, RAF Inst. of Aviation Medicine, 1979; Chief Instructor, RAF Aviation Medicine Trng Centre, 1979–82; Sen. MO, TriNat. Tornado Trng Est., RAF Cottesmore, 1982–85; Deputy Principal Medical Officer: (Occupational Health and Safety) HQ RAF Support Comd, 1986–87; HQ RAF Germany, 1987–91; jsdc, Greenwich, 1991–92; Officer Commanding: RAF Inst. of Health and Med. Trng, 1992–94; Princess Mary's Hosp., RAF Halton, 1994; Dep. Dir, Med. Policy and Plans (RAF), HQ PTC, 1994–96; CO, The Princess Mary's Hosp., RAF Akrotiri and Comd Med. Advr, HQ British Forces Cyprus, 1996–99; Dir Health Services (RAF), HQ PTC, 1999–2001; Dir Med. Personnel, Policy and Plans (RAF), HQ PTC, 2001–02; Dir Med. Policy, Defence Med. Services Dept, MoD, 2002–04. QHP 2002–09. Taylor Prof. of Occupational Medicine, Jt RAF and RCP, 1990–96; Consultant Advr, Occupational Medicine, RAF, 1997–2002. Hon. Air Cdre, 4626 Aeronautical Evacuation Sqdn, RAuxAF, 2009–19. Member: Ct of Govs, LSHTM, 2004–10; Fellowship Cttee, Faculty of Occupational Medicine, 2006–08. Chm. of Trustees, Stewart Meml Trust, 2004–08; Trustee: Headley Court Charity, 2010–13; RAF Benevolent Fund, 2012– (Chm., Main Grants Cttee, 2012–; Chm., Welfare Cttee, 2012–); Governor: Royal Star and Garter Homes, 2004–; Framlingham Coll., 2008–. Mem. SOM, 1980; MRAeS 1982, FRAeS 2000; FRSocMed 1994 (United Services Section Council, 2002–08; Vice Pres., 2004–08); FCMI (FIMgt 1999). Freeman, City of London, 2008. Liveryman, Soc. of Apothecaries, 2006–; Freeman, Hon. Co. of Air Pilots (formerly GAPAN), 2007–. Pres., Soc. of Old Framlinghamians, 2011–13 and 2019– (Vice Pres., 2003–11). Parish Councillor, Abberton and Langenhoe, 2010–. OStJ 1991. *Recreations:* travelling, ski-ing, computers, gardening, cruising the East Coast. *Clubs:* Royal Air Force; West Mersea Yacht.

**DOUGHTY, Louise;** author, since 1990; *b* Melton Mowbray, 4 Sept. 1963; *d* of Kenneth Herbert George Doughty and Avis Doughty; two *c. Educ:* Leeds Univ. (BA Hons English Lit. 1984); Univ. of E Anglia (MA Creative Writing 1987). FRSL 2018. Ian St James Award, 1990; Radio Times Drama Award, 1990; K. Blundell Trust Award, 1999; Writers' Award, Arts Council, 2001. *Publications:* Crazy Paving, 1995; Dance With Me, 1996; Honey-Dew, 1998; Fires in the Dark, 2003; Stone Cradle, 2006; A Novel in a Year, 2007; Whatever You Love, 2010; Apple Tree Yard, 2013 (televised, 2017); Black Water, 2016; Platform Seven, 2019. *Recreations:* none. *Address:* c/o Antony Harwood, Antony Harwood Literary Agency Ltd, 103 Walton Street, Oxford OX2 6EB. *W:* www.louisedoughty.com.

**DOUGHTY, Stephen John;** MP (Lab) Cardiff South and Penarth, since Nov. 2012; *b* Cardiff, 1980; *s* of Barry and Eileen Doughty. *Educ:* Llantwit Major Comprehensive Sch.; Lester B. Pearson United World Coll.; Corpus Christi Coll., Oxford (BA Hons 2001); St Andrews Univ. (MLitt 2003). Campaigns Coordinator, World Vision UK, 2004–06; Hd, Govt Relns, Oxfam GB, 2006–09; Special Advr, DFID, 2009–10; Hd, Oxfam Cymru/ Wales, 2011–12. PPS to Shadow Chief Sec. to HM Treasury, 2013; an Opposition Whip, 2013–15; Shadow Minister for Trade and Industry, 2015, for Foreign Affairs, 2015–16. Member: Welsh Affairs Cttee, 2012–15; Internat. Develt Cttee, 2016–17; Cttee on Arms Export Controls, 2016–17; Home Affairs Cttee, 2017–. Associate, RCDS, 2017–18. *Recreations:* walking, music, travel, singing, outdoor pursuits. *Address:* House of Commons, SW1A 0AA. *T:* (020) 7219 5348. *E:* stephen.doughty.mp@parliament.uk.

**DOUGHTY, Stuart John,** CMG 2005; CEng, FICE, FCIHT; Chief Executive, Costain Group plc, 2001–05; *b* 13 Sept. 1943; *s* of late Henry John Doughty and of Marie Louise Doughty; *m* Penelope Ann; one *d* (one *s* decd). *Educ:* UC, Cardiff (BSc). John Laing Construction: grad. trainee, 1965; Regl Manager, 1974–84; Man. Dir, Civil Engrg Div., 1984–86; Exec. Dir, Tarmac Construction, 1986–91; Chm. and Man. Dir, Construction Div., Alfred McAlpine, 1991–94; Dir, Hyder Plc, 1994–97; Chm., Alstec Ltd, Beck & Pollitzer, and Kennedy Construction, 1997–2001. Non-executive Director: Viborant plc, 1997–2001; Balfour Beatty, 2015–; Sen. non-exec. Dir, Scott Wilson plc, 2005–11; non-exec. Chm., Somero plc, 2006–09. Chm., UK Trade Internat. (Sectors), DTI, 1997–2001. Mem. Council, ECGD, 1997–2001. Lt Col, Engr and Logistics Staff Corps, 1998–. Gov., King's Sch., Worcester, 1999–2012; Mem. Council, Aston Univ., 2012– (Chm., Finance and Major Projects Cttee, 2013–). Hon. DSc Aston, 2018. *Recreations:* classic and historic motor sport and houses. *Address:* Bradley Farm House, Kinlet, Bewdley, Worcs DY12 3BU. *T:* (01299) 841327.

**DOUGHTY, Susan Kathleen, (Mrs D. Orchard);** Director: Corporate Climate Ltd, 2006–10; Ashdown Inventory, since 2016; independent advisor on environment and government, since 2006; *b* 13 April 1948; *d* of Ronald and Olive Powell; *m* 1st, 1974, John Doughty (marr. diss.); two *s*; 2nd, 1995, David Orchard (*d* 2015); two step *d. Educ:* Northumberland Coll. of Educn (CertEd); holds various business qualifications. Primary sch. teacher, 1969–70; Work Study Analyst, Northern Gas Mgt Services, 1970–73; Work Study Officer, CEGB Mgt Services, 1974–75; Orgn and Method Analyst, Wilkinson Match Mgt Services, 1976–77; career break (charity work), 1977–83; Ind. Mgt Consultant, 1984–89, 1999–2001; Project Manager, Thames Water, 1989–98. MP (Lib Dem) Guildford, 2001–05; contested (Lib Dem) same seat, 2005, 2010. Lib Dem spokesman on envmt, 2001–03, front bench spokesman on envmt, 2003–05. Mem., Envmtl Audit Select Cttee, 2001–05. Mem., Federal Exec., Liberal Democrats, 2010–16. Chm., Thatcham Children's Centre, 1982–84. *Recreations:* gardening, cricket, walking, theatre, opera, Arsenal, the arts. *Address:* 3 Wharf Cottages, Stonebridge Wharf, Shalford, Surrey GU4 8EH.

**DOUGILL, John Wilson,** FREng, FICE, FIStructE, FASCE; Chief Executive and Secretary, Institution of Structural Engineers, 1994–99 (Director of Engineering, 1987–94); *b* 18 Nov. 1934; *s* of William John Dougill and Emily Firmstone Wilson; *m* 1959, Daphne Maude Weeks (*d* 2008); one *s* one *d. Educ:* Trinity Sch. of John Whitgift, Croydon; King's Coll., London; Imperial Coll. of Science and Technology. MScEng, DIC, PhD; FREng 1990. Engineer with George Wimpey, 1956–58 and 1960–61; Research Asst to Prof. A. L. L. Baker, Imperial Coll., 1961–64; King's College London: Lectr in Civil Engrg, 1964–73; Reader in Engrg Science, 1973–76; Prof. of Engrg Science, 1976–81; Prof. of Concrete Structures and Technology, Imperial Coll., 1981–87. Vis. Res. Engineer, Univ. of California, Berkeley, 1967–68; Visiting Professor: Dept of Civil Engrg, Imperial Coll., 1991–97; Sch. of Engrg, Univ. of Surrey, 2000–06; South China Univ. of Technol., 2001–. Chm., SERC Civil Engrg Sub-Cttee, 1982–83; Mem., NEDO Res. Strategy Cttee, 1983–85. Sec. Gen., Fedn Internat. de la Précontrainte, 1992–98. Mem. Court of Governors, Whitgift Foundn, 1981–2007. FCGI 1997. *Publications:* papers in jls of engrg mech., materials and struct. engrg. *Recreations:* coarse gardening, travel, good food, walking, continuing interest in structural mechanics and particularly human structure interaction. *Address:* Ashcroft, 4 Larch Close, Kingswood, Tadworth, Surrey KT20 6JF. *T:* (01737) 833283.

**DOUGLAS,** family name of **Marquess of Queensberry**, **Earl of Morton**, and **Viscount Chilston**.

**DOUGLAS AND CLYDESDALE, Marquess of; Douglas Charles Douglas-Hamilton;** *b* 9 July 2012; *s* and *heir* of Duke of Hamilton, *qv*.

**DOUGLAS, Anthony Gordon,** CBE 2008; Chief Executive, Children and Family Court Advisory and Support Service, 2004–19; *b* 4 July 1949; *s* of late Gordon Louis Albert Douglas and Lily Douglas (née Graves); *m* 1975, Margaret Olga Jean Friedlander; two *d. Educ:* St Nicholas Grammar Sch., Northwood; St Peter's Coll., Oxford (Pt I PPE); N London Poly. (CQSW 1980); Open Univ. (BSc 1984). Social worker, Hackney Social Services, 1976–83; various mgt posts in Southwark, Barnet and Newham Councils, London, 1983–91; Asst Dir of Social Services, Hackney, 1991–96; Havering Council: Dir, Social Services, 1996–98; Exec. Dir, Community Services, 1998–2002; Dir, Social Care and Health, Suffolk CC, 2002–04. Visiting Fellow: UEA, 2003–; Univ. of Plymouth, 2012–. Chair: London Assoc. of Dirs of Social Services, 1997–2000; British Assoc. for Adoption and Fostering, 2003–15; Cornerstone Partnership, 2017–. Hon. LLD UEA, 2018. *Publications:* (with T. Philpot) Caring and Coping, 1998; (with A. Weir) Child Protection and Adult Mental Health: conflicts of interest, 1999; Is Anyone Out There?, 2002; (with T. Philpot) Adoption: changing families, changing times, 2003; Partnership Working, 2009. *Recreations:* cricket, opera. *Clubs:* Groucho; Middlesex CC, Arsenal Football.

**DOUGLAS, Barry;** *see* Douglas, W. B.

**DOUGLAS, Boyd;** farmer; Member (TUV), Causeway Coast and Glens Borough Council, since 2015; *b* 13 July 1950; *s* of William Douglas and late May Douglas; *m* 1972, Kathleen Semple; two *s* two *d. Educ:* Burnfoot Primary Sch.; Dungiven Secondary Sch.; Strabane Agriculture Coll. Farmer, 1970–. Mem. (U) E Londonderry, NI Assembly, 1998–2003. Mem. (U, then TUV), Limavady BC, 1997–2015. *Address:* 279 Drumrane Road, Dungiven, Co. Londonderry BT47 4NL.

**DOUGLAS, Caroline;** Director, Contemporary Art Society, since 2013; *b* London, 25 June 1961; *d* of John and Elizabeth Douglas; *m* 2001, Guy Morey; one *s. Educ:* Leeds Univ. (BA Jt Hons French and Spanish 1983); Courtauld Inst. of Art (MA Hist. of Art 1994). Exhibns Coordinator, Momart Ltd, 1987–92; Asst Gall. Manager, Whitechapel Art Gall., 1993–94; Curator, Visual Arts Dept, British Council, 1994–2006; Hd, Arts Council Collection, 2006–13. Member: Fine Art Faculty, British Sch. at Rome, 2006–15; AICA (UK), 2007–. Trustee: Space Studios, London, 2006–15; Charles Wallace (India) Trust, 2006–. Hon. Dr

Norwich Univ. of Arts, 2014. *Recreations:* theatre, opera, reading, cinema, gardening. *Address:* Contemporary Art Society, 59 Central Street, EC1V 3AF. *T:* (020) 7017 8400. *E:* caroline@contemporaryartsociety.org.

**DOUGLAS, Colin Antony;** Director, Southside Communications Ltd, since 2013; *b* 10 Sept. 1963; *s* of Kendric Manasseh Douglas and Adassa Beatrice Douglas; *m* 1992, Petrina Hall; two *s*. *Educ:* Tulse Hill Comprehensive Sch., S London; Keble Coll., Oxford (BA Hons PPE); Oxford Brookes Univ. (MBA). Dip. Mktg, CIM. Dir, Citigate Public Relns, 1994–99; Dir of Communications, Sport England, 1999–2001; Dir of Public Affairs, Transport for London, 2001–02; Director of Communications: Audit Commn, 2002–04; HSE, 2004–08; Dir of NHS Communications, DoH, 2008–13. Non-exec. Dir, London Ambulance Service, 1996–2006. *Publications:* West Indian Women at War: British racism in World War II, 1991. *Recreations:* photography, family.

**DOUGLAS, Derek Jack,** CBE 2006; CA; Founder, Chairman and Chief Executive Officer, Adam Smith Ltd, since 1988; *b* 17 Oct. 1953. *Educ:* Heriot-Watt Univ. (BSc); Aberdeen Univ. CA 1982. Chartered accountant: Coopers & Lybrand, 1978–81; Arthur Young, 1981–83; Gen. Manager, NZ United Corp., 1983–85; Barclays de Zoete Wedd, 1985–88. Chairman: Digital Animations Gp plc, 1996–2001; Acuid Corp. Ltd, 2001–06; Carlton Bingo Plc, 2001–08; NGenTec Ltd, 2009–; Founder and Chairman: Kymata Ltd, 1998–99, Solve-It-Blocks Ltd, 2013–16; Plan-It-Cube Ltd, 2013–16; Dir, Bremner plc, 1990–91. Chm. and Trustee, Maggie Keswick Jencks Cancer Caring Centres Trust, 1996–2003; Dir and Trustee, Macmillan Cancer Support, 2006–12. FRSA 2003. Hon. DBA Abertay, 2003. *Publications:* contribs to Jl ICAS. *Recreations:* sailing, golf. *Address:* Adam Smith Ltd, Adam Smith House, Melville Castle Estate, Lasswade, Edinburgh EH18 1AW. *T:* 07791 1900626. *Clubs:* Bruntsfield Links Golfing Society; North Berwick Golf.

**DOUGLAS, Prof. (Felicity) Gillian,** LLD; FBA 2017; FLSW; FAcSS; Executive Dean, Dickson Poon School of Law, King's College London, since 2017; *b* London, 11 Nov. 1955; *d* of Jack and Doris Douglas; *m* 1981, Hugh Fenton Rawlings, *qv*; one *s* one *d*. *Educ:* City of London Sch. for Girls; Univ. of Manchester (LLB 1977); London Sch. of Econs and Pol Sci. (LLM 1978); Cardiff Univ. (LLD 2011). Lectr in Law, Univ. of Bristol, 1978–89; Cardiff University: Lectr in Law, 1989–92; Sen. Lectr, 1992–95; Reader, 1995–98; Prof. of Law, 1998–2017; Dep. Hd, 2000–05, Hd, 2005–10, Cardiff Law Sch. Vis. Teaching Fellow, NUS, 1983–84; Leverhulme Major Res. Fellow, 2015–17. Chair, Law Sub-panel, REF, 2010–14. Trustee, Family Mediation Cardiff, 2002–12. Hon. Bencher, Gray's Inn, 2018. FHEA 2007; FLSW 2012; FAcSS 2016. *Publications:* Law, Fertility and Reproduction, 1991; (with C. Barton) Law and Parenthood, 1995; (with N. Lowe) Bromley's Family Law, 9th edn 1998 to 11th edn 2015; An Introduction to Family Law, 2001, 2nd edn 2004; Obligation and Commitment in Family Law, 2018; (ed jtly) International and National Perspectives on Child and Family Law, 2018. *Recreations:* reading, theatre, cinema, following Arsenal FC. *Address:* Dickson Poon School of Law, King's College London, Strand, WC2R 2LS. *E:* gillian.douglas@kcl.ac.uk.

**DOUGLAS, Hilary Kay,** CB 2002; Executive Coach, Praesta Partners, since 2010; *b* 27 July 1950; *d* of late James Robert Keith Black and Joan Margaret Black (*née* Boxall); *m* 1972, Robert Harold Douglas, *qv*; two *s*. *Educ:* Wimbledon High Sch.; New Hall, Cambridge (BA Hons History 1971). Press Librarian, RIIA, 1971–73; joined DES, 1973: Sec. of State's Private Office, 1975–76; appts in teacher trng, educnl disadvantage and local authy finance, 1977–84; Head: Teacher Supply Div., 1985–87; School Govt Div., 1987–89; freelance consultancy and teaching, Netherlands, 1989–91; Sec., FEFC, 1991–92; set up SCAA, 1992–93; Hd of Personnel, DFE, 1993–94; Dir of Admin, Office for Standards in Educn, 1994–96; Dir, Civil Service Employer Gp, Cabinet Office, 1996–97; Dir, Personnel and Support Services, DfEE, 1997–2000; Man. Dir, Corporate Services and Develt, HM Treasury, 2000–04; Chief Operating Officer, ONS, 2004–06; Chief Operating Officer, later Dir Gen., Ops and Change, DTI, then BERR, later BIS, 2006–09. Trustee, British Red Cross, 2013–. *Recreations:* travel, European languages, singing. *Address:* Praesta Partners, 43 Berkeley Square, W1J 5AP.

**DOUGLAS, Janet Elizabeth,** CMG 2008; HM Diplomatic Service; High Commissioner to Barbados and (non-resident) to Dominica, Grenada, Antigua and Barbuda, St Vincent and the Grenadines, St Lucia and St Christopher and Nevis, since 2017; *b* Deal, Kent, 6 Jan. 1960; *d* of late Duncan and Mary Douglas; *m* 2012, George Anthony Furlong. *Educ:* Cheltenham Ladies' Coll.; St Catharine's Coll., Cambridge (BA Hons Archaeol. and Anthropol. 1982). Joined FCO, 1985; Second, later First Sec., Ankara, 1988–92; UN Dept, FCO, 1992–94; on secondment to ODA, 1994–96; First Sec. (EU), Stockholm, 1996–2000; Dep. Hd, Africa Dept (Southern), FCO, 2000–02; Head: Personnel Mgt Unit, HR Directorate, 2002–04; Consular Assistance Gp, Consular Directorate, 2004–07; Africa Dept (Southern, later Southern, Central and Western), FCO, 2007–10; Asst Dir, HR Directorate, FCO, 2010–11; Dep. Hd of Mission, Ankara, 2011–17. *Recreations:* ski-ing, sailing (fair weather only), visiting art galleries and museums, reading crime fiction. *Address:* c/o Foreign and Commonwealth Office, King Charles Street, SW1A 2AH.

**DOUGLAS, Jill Alison, (Mrs Carl Hogg);** broadcaster; Chief Executive Officer, My Name'5 Doddie Foundation, since 2018; *b* Hawick, Scotland, 23 Dec. 1969; *d* of Henry and Aileen Douglas; *m* 2000, Carl Hogg; one *s* one *d*. *Educ:* Jedburgh Grammar Sch.; Napier Univ., Edinburgh. Reporter, Southern Reporter, Selkirk, 1987–91; news reporter and presenter, Border TV, 1993–97; sports presenter: BBC Scotland, 1997–99; Sky Sports, 1999–2003; BBC Sport, 2003–08; freelance sports presenter, incl. for BBC and ITV, 2008–. *Recreations:* Rugby, cycling, reading, family, walking. *E:* mel@iwillknowsomeone.com. *T:* 07768 878975. *Clubs:* Soho House, Farmers; Cheltenham Rugby (Pres., Ladies Section, 2016–).

**DOUGLAS, Jonathan David;** Director, National Literacy Trust, since 2007; *b* Birmingham, 16 Jan. 1970; *s* of John and Margaret Douglas; partner, Gary Mack. *Educ:* Handsworth Grammar Sch.; Durham Univ. (BA Hons Theol. 1991); London Metropolitan Univ. (Postgrad. Dip. Inf. Studies 1996). MCLIP 1998. Librarian, Westminster Libraries, 1992–99; Professional Advr, Youth and Sch. Libraries, CILIP/Liby Assoc., 1999–2003; Hd, Policy Develt, Mus, Libraries and Archives Council, 2003–07. Non-exec. Dir, Money Advice Service, 2011–18. Mem., Adv. Gp, Man Booker Prize, 2009–. Trustee: Philosophy Foundn, 2017–; World Book Day, 2018–. Hon. Life Mem., Youth Libraries Gp, 2003. Chm., Govs, St William of York Primary Sch., 2012–. Hon. DLitt Oxford Brookes, 2014. *Publications:* The CILIP Guidelines for Secondary School Libraries, 2004; Read On Get On: a strategy to get England's children reading, 2016. *Recreations:* opera, concerts, food, wine and friends, contemporary fiction. *Address:* National Literacy Trust, 68 South Lambeth Road, SW8 1RL. *E:* jonathan.douglas@literacytrust.org.uk.

**DOUGLAS, Kenneth George,** ONZ 1999; President, New Zealand Council of Trade Unions, 1987–99; *b* 15 Nov. 1935; *s* of John Atholwood Douglas and Marjorie Alice (*née* Farrow); *m* 1956, Lesley Barbara Winter (marr. diss. 1986); two *s* two *d*; partner, Marilyn Gay Tucker. *Educ:* Wellington Coll. President: Wellington Section, Drivers Union, 1958–79; NZ Drivers Fedn, 1972–79; Treas., Nat. Sect., NZ Fedn of Labour, 1979–87. Mem., Exec. Bd, ICFTU, 1987–99; Pres., ICFTU-Asia Pacific Regl Orgn, 1990–99. Mem., Prime Minister's Enterprise Council, 1990–99. Mem. (Ind.), Porirua CC, 1998. JP Porirua, 1999. Hon. LLD Victoria Univ. of Wellington, 1999. *Publications:* contrib. articles on industrial relns and Labour movement to jls. *Recreation:* golf. *Clubs:* Porirua, Titahi Golf (NZ).

**DOUGLAS, Lesley;** Founder, Lonesome Pine Productions, since 2013; *b* 7 June 1963; *d* of William and Sarah Douglas; *m* Nick Scripps; one *s* one *d*. *Educ:* Manchester Univ. (BA English). Joined BBC, 1986: prodn asst, res. dept, then David Jacobs Show, 1986–87; Promotions Asst, 1987–88; Producer: Music Dept, 1988–90; Promotions, 1990–93; Ed., Presentation and Planning, Radio 2, 1993–97; Managing Ed., 1997–2000, Hd of Progs, 2000–04, Radio 2; Controller, Radio 2 and 6 Music, 2004–08; Dir of Programming and Business Develt, Universal Music UK, 2008–12; Chief Exec., Lime Pictures, 2012–13. Chm., Steering Cttee, Radio Fest. Fellow, Radio Acad. Hon. Fellow, Univ. of Sunderland. Woman of Year Award, Music Industry, 2004.

**DOUGLAS, Michael John;** QC 1997; a Recorder, since 2000; *b* 7 Aug. 1952; *s* of late James Murray Douglas, CBE. *Educ:* Westminster Sch.; Balliol Coll., Oxford (BA Hons Jurisprudence). Called to the Bar, Gray's Inn, 1974. *Recreations:* theatre, cinema, eating out, football, travel. *Address:* 4 Pump Court, Temple, EC4Y 7AN. *T:* (020) 7842 5555.

**DOUGLAS, Michael Kirk;** actor and producer; *b* 25 Sept. 1944; *s* of Kirk Douglas, actor and late Diana Douglas; *m* 1977, Diandra Morrell Luker (marr. diss.); one *s*; *m* 2000, Catherine Zeta-Jones (CBE 2010); one *s* one *d*. *Educ:* Univ. of Calif at Santa Barbara (BA 1967). Films include: *actor:* Hail Hero, 1969; Napoleon and Samantha, 1972; Star Chamber, 1983; A Chorus Line, 1985; Black Rain, 1990; The War of the Roses, 1990; Shining Through, 1992; Basic Instinct, 1992; Falling Down, 1993; Disclosure, 1994; The American President, 1995; The Game, 1997; Traffic, 2001; Don't Say a Word, 2002; The In-Laws, 2003; You, Me and Dupree, 2006; King of California, 2007; Beyond a Reasonable Doubt, 2009; Ghosts of Girlfriends Past, 2009; Solitary Man, 2009; Behind the Candelabra, 2013 (Best Actor in a Mini-Series or TV Movie, Golden Globe Awards, 2014); Last Vegas, 2014; And So It Goes, 2014; Ant-Man, 2015; Ant-Man and the Wasp, 2018; Animal World, 2018; Avengers: Endgame, 2019; *producer:* One Flew Over the Cuckoo's Nest, 1975; Flatliners, 1990; (jtly) Made in America, 1993; The Rainmaker, 1997; A Song for David, 2000; Flatliners, 2017; *actor and producer:* The China Syndrome, 1979; Romancing the Stone, 1984; The Jewel of the Nile, 1985; Fatal Attraction, 1987; Wall Street, 1988 (Academy Award for best actor); A Perfect Murder, 1998; Wonder Boys, 1999; Still Life, 1999; One Night at McCool's, 2001; It Runs in the Family, 2003; The Sentinel, 2006; narrator, One Day in September (documentary), 2000; Wall Street: Money Never Sleeps, 2010; Beyond the Reach, 2015; *television* includes: Streets of San Francisco, 1972–76; The Kominsky Method, 2018 (Golden Globe for Best Actor in a Comedy or Musical, 2019). UN Messenger of Peace, 1998; UN Ambassador for Nuclear Disarmament, 2000. Genesis Foundn Prize, Israel, 2015. *Address:* c/o United Talent Agency, 9336 Civic Center Drive, Beverly Hills, CA 90210, USA.

**DOUGLAS, Neil;** Sheriff of North Strathclyde at Paisley, 1996–2014; *b* 15 Oct. 1945; *s* of Dr Neil Douglas and Doreen Douglas; *m* 1971, Morag Isles; two *d*. *Educ:* Glasgow Acad.; Glasgow Univ. (LLB). Solicitor, 1968; Notary Public, 1972. Trainee solicitor, Brechin Welsh & Risk, Glasgow, 1968–70; Asst Solicitor, Ross Harper & Murphy, Glasgow, 1970–72; Partner, Brechin Robb, Glasgow, 1972–95; Floating Sheriff, All Scotland, 1995–96. *Recreations:* hill-walking, ski-ing, Scottish country dancing.

**DOUGLAS, Prof. Sir Neil (James),** Kt 2009; MD, DSc; FRCP, FRCPE; Professor of Respiratory and Sleep Medicine, University of Edinburgh, 1995–2012, now Emeritus; President, Royal College of Physicians of Edinburgh, 2004–10 (Dean, 1995–2000; Vice-President, 2000–03); Founding Chairman, Faculty of Medical Leadership and Management, 2011–17; *b* 28 May 1949; *s* of Sir Donald Macleod Douglas, MBE and of (Margaret) Diana Douglas; *m* 1977, Susan McLaren Galloway; one *s* one *d*. *Educ:* Glenalmond Coll.; St Andrews Univ. (Schol.); Univ. of Edinburgh (MB ChB 1973; MD 1983; DSc 2003). FRCPE 1985; FRCP 1998. University of Edinburgh: Lectr in Medicine, 1975–83; Sen. Lectr, 1983–91; Reader in Medicine, 1991–95. MRC Fellow, Univ. of Colorado, 1980–81; Dir, Scottish Nat. Sleep Centre, Royal Infirmary, Edinburgh, 1983–2004. Chm., Acad. of Med. Royal Colls, 2009–12. Hon. Sec., British Thoracic Soc., 1988–90. Ed.-in-Chief, Clinical Science, 1990–92. Hon. MD St Andrews, 2007. *Publications:* Clinicians' Guide to Sleep Medicine, 2002; over 300 papers in jls, mainly on breathing during sleep. *Recreations:* hill-walking, fishing, ski-ing, sailing. *E:* n.j.douglas@ed.ac.uk.

**DOUGLAS, Richard Philip,** CB 2006; Director General, Finance and NHS (formerly Director of Finance, then Director General Finance and Chief Operating Officer, later Director General, Policy, Strategy and Finance), Department of Health, 2001–15; *b* 20 Nov. 1956; *s* of William Ronald Douglas and Margery Alice Douglas; *m* 1978, Carole Elizabeth Hodgson; two *s* one *d*. *Educ:* Archbishop Holgate's Grammar Sch., York; Hull Univ. (BA Hons). HM Customs and Excise, 1978–80; Exchequer and Audit Dept, later Nat. Audit Office, 1980–96 (Dir, 1994–96); Dep. Dir of Finance, NHS Exec., 1996–99; Dir of Finance, Nat. Savings, 1999–2001; Hd, Govt Finance Profession, HM Treasury, 2011–14. Non-executive Director: NHS Improvement, 2016–; NHS England, 2018–. Mem., CIPFA, 1983. *Recreations:* reading, gardening, walking.

**DOUGLAS, Robert Harold,** CBE 2005; DL; Director, Douglas Associates Ltd, since 2000; *b* Gosforth, Northumberland, 27 July 1948; *s* of Robert Francis Douglas and Cecily Isabel Douglas (*née* Mills); *m* 1972, Hilary Kay Black (*see* H. K. Douglas); two *s*. *Educ:* Fettes Coll., Edinburgh; Churchill Coll., Cambridge (BA Anglo-Saxon and Old Norse 1971; MA); Univ. of Liverpool (Dip. Study of Records and Admin of Archives 1972). Assistant archivist: Hudson's Bay Co., 1972–73; Guildhall Liby, London, 1973–74; HM Inspector of Taxes, Inland Revenue, 1974–80; Royal Dutch Shell: Tax Advr, 1980–85; Shell UK Tax Manager, 1985–88; Hd, Internat. Tax, 1989–91; Area Co-ordinator, Far East, 1992–95; Chief Executive: Belgian Shell, 1995–96; Shell Italia, 1997; Vice-Pres., Mergers, Acquisitions and Competitive Intelligence, Global Exploration and Prodn, 1997–99. Chm., Iceni Oil and Gas Ltd, 2007. Member: Energy Gp Adv. Bd, DTI, 2004–06; Bd, Small Business Service, 2006–07; Fair Mkts Gp Adv. Bd, BERR, later BIS, 2007–10. Chm., Steering Bd, UK Space Agency, 2011–15. Chm., Surrey, 2000–07, Mem., SE Regl Council, 2007–10, LSC; Member: Bd, SEEDA, 2001–07 and 2009–12 (Dep. Chm., 2003–07; Chm., 2009–12); Bd, HEFCE, 2008–13. Gov. and Trustee, Nat. Centre for Langs, CILT, 2007–10. Chm., Queen Elizabeth's Foundn for Disabled People, 2011–17. Trustee: Walton Charity, 2011–; The Lightbox, Woking, 2012; Almshouse Assoc., 2016–; Leonard Hackett Meml Trust, 2016–. High Sheriff, 2010–11, DL, 2012, Surrey. FRSA. *Recreations:* walking, bird watching, opera, foreign travel, languages. *Address:* c/o Queen Elizabeth's Foundation for Disabled People, Leatherhead Court, Woodlands Road, Leatherhead, Surrey KT22 0BN. *Clubs:* Reform, Lansdowne.

**DOUGLAS, Hon. Sir Roger (Owen),** Kt 1991; MP (ACT NZ) New Zealand, 2008–11; *b* 5 Dec. 1937; *s* of Norman and Jennie Douglas; *m* 1961, Glennis June Anderson; one *s* one *d*. *Educ:* Auckland Grammar Sch.; Auckland Univ. (Accountancy Degree). Company Sec. and Acct. MP (Lab) Manurewa, 1969–90; Cabinet Minister, NZ, 1972–75; Minister in Charge of Inland Revenue Dept and Minister in Charge of Friendly Societies, 1984; Minister of Finance, 1984–88; Minister of Immigration and Minister of Police, 1989–90.

Director: Brierley Investments Ltd, 1990–99 (Chm., 1998); Aetna Health NZ Ltd, 1995–99; John Fairfax Hldgs, 1997–98. Finance Minister of the Year, Euromoney Mag., 1985; Freedom Prize, Max Schmidheiny Foundn, 1996; Ludwig Erhard Prize for Economic Journalism, 1997; Friedrich von Hayek Medal, 2001. *Publications:* There's Got to be a Better Way, 1981; papers on NZ economy: An Alternative Budget, 1980; Proposal for Taxation, 1981; Toward Prosperity, 1987; Unfinished Business, 1993; Completing the Circle, 1996. *Recreations:* cricket, Rugby League, reading. *Address:* 411 Redoubt Road, Totara Park, Auckland 2019, New Zealand. *T:* (9) 2639596.

**DOUGLAS, Rowan Malcolm,** CBE 2016; Chief Executive Officer, Capital, Science and Policy Practice, Willis Towers Watson plc (formerly Willis Group), since 2014; *b* Woking, 12 Dec. 1968; *s* of David and Marlene Douglas; *m* 2005, Dr Ana Gonzalez Pelaez; one *s* one *d*. *Educ:* Shebbear Coll., N Devon; Univ. of Durham (BA Hons Geog.); Bristol Univ. (MPhil Geog.). Asst underwriter, M. W. Petzold and others, Lloyd's, 1992–94; Founder and Man. Dir, WIRE Ltd, 1994–2000; with Willis Gp, subseq. Willis Towers Watson plc, 2000–; Chm., Willis Res. Network, 2006–; Chief Exec., Global Analytics, Willis Re, 2010–13. Member: Investment and Innovation Cttee, NESTA, 2005–06; NERC, 2008–15 (Mem., Audit Cttee, 2011–15). Member: External Adv. Cttee, Sch. of Engrg, Computing and Maths, Univ. of Exeter, 2008–11; Adv. Council, Inst. of Hazard, Risk and Resilience, Durham Univ., 2008–11; Adv. Cttee, Earth Systems Lab., Nat. Center for Atmospheric Res., Boulder, Colo, 2010–; Co-Chair, Willis Res. Network Capital Forum, Georgia State Univ., 2011–. Mem., Governing Bd, Global Earthquake Model Foundn, 2009–. Member: Private Sector Adv. Gp, UN Internat. Strategy for Disaster Reduction, Geneva, 2010–; Insce Commn, UN Envmt Prog. Finance Initiative, Geneva, 2010–; Prime Minister's Council for Sci. and Technol., 2011. Hon. Vis. Res. Fellow, Sci. and Technol. Policy Res. Unit, Univ. of Sussex, 1995–2000. *Recreations:* anything with Ana. *Address:* Willis Towers Watson, Willis Building, 51 Lime Street, EC3M 7DQ. *E:* rowan.douglas@willis.com. *Club:* Athenæum.

**DOUGLAS, Steven Franklyn,** CBE 2019; Group Chief Executive, Aquila Services (formerly General Industries) plc, since 2019 (Co-Chief Executive, 2015–19); Co-Chief Executive, Altair Consultancy & Advisory Services Ltd, since 2010; *b* Hackney, 1964; *s* of Baldwin Douglas and Pamela Douglas (*née* Rodney); four *s*. *Educ:* Sedgehill Comprehensive Sch.; Corpus Christi Coll., Oxford (BA PPE 1985). Sen. Valuation Surveyor, London & Quadrant Housing Trust, 1986–89; Hd of Develt, London & Quadrant Housing Trust, 1989–94; Chief Executive: Spitalfields Housing Assoc., 1994–96; ASRA Housing Assoc., 1996–2001; Housing Corporation: Dir, Investment and Regeneration, 2001–04; Dir (London), 2004–05; Dep. Chief Exec., 2005–06; Chief Exec., 2007–08; Dir, DouglasWood Ltd (housing, regeneration and development consultants), then Partner, Altair Consultancy & Advisory Services Ltd, 2009. Member: Callcutt rev. gp into house bldg delivery, 2006–07; Commn on Integration and Cohesion, 2006–07. Vice Chm., Williams Commn into Design and Quality in Thames Gateway, 2006–07. Chairman: London Housing Fedn Develt Gp, 1994–97; Greenwich Jt Commng Forum, 1994–99; London Develt Conf., 1997–99. Vice-Chm., AmicusHorizon Housing Gp, then Optivo, 2009–18; Chm., One Housing Gp, 2019–; Member: Housing Mgt and Maintenance Cttee, Nat. Housing Fedn, 1994–99; Bd, Hexagon Housing Assoc., 1994–99. Trustee: Richmix, 2010–18; Commonweal Social Justice Charity, 2010– (Chm., 2019–). *Recreations:* football, watching and playing, particularly with my boys, Aaron, Ethan, Freddie and Theo, Arsenal, R&B music, Mary J. Blige, dancing. *Address:* Altair Consultancy & Advisory Services Ltd, Tempus Wharf, 29a Bermondsey Wall West, SE16 4SA.

**DOUGLAS, Susan Margaret;** media consultant, since 2015; Co-founder, Brand News Ltd, 2017; Media Director, Learning Partnership, since 2018; *b* 29 Jan. 1957; *d* of Kenneth Frank Douglas and Vivienne Mary Douglas; *m* 1994, Niall Campbell Ferguson, *qv* (marr. diss. 2011); two *s* one *d*. *Educ:* Tiffin Girls' Sch., Kingston; Southampton Univ. (BSc Hons Biochem.). Management consultant, Arthur Andersen & Co., 1978–79; Haymarket Publishing, 1979; reporter, writer, Sunday Express, Johannesburg, 1979–80; Mail on Sunday: medical corresp., 1980–81; Features Editor and Associate Editor, 1981–86; Asst Editor, Daily Mail, 1986–91; Sunday Times: Associate Editor, 1991–94; Dep. Editor, 1995; Editor, Sunday Express, 1996; Consultant Editor, Scotsman, Scotland on Sunday, Edinburgh Evening News, Sunday Business, and Gear magazine (NY), 1997–2001; Exec. Consultant, Sunday Business, 1998–2001; Dir, 1999–2001, Pres., 2001–07, New Business, Condé Nast; New Business Dir, Peters Fraser and Dunlop, 2008–09; Publisher, Sunday brands, Trinity Mirror, 2013–14. Media consultant: HarperCollins, 2009; Future Publishing, 2009–10; LuxeTV, 2010–12; New Business Director: Barefoot Books, 2010–13; The Tab, 2014–15; Dir, Lingospot Media Software, 2010–14. Member: Develt Bd and Med. Develt Bd, Univ. of Oxford, 2008–; Develt Cttee, Globe Th., 2008–10; Media Bd, Prince's Foundn for Children and the Arts, 2008–13; K. T. Wong Foundn for Cultural Exchange with China, 2011. *Recreations:* riding, shooting. *Address:* Middle Park Farm, Beckley, Oxon OX3 9SX. *E:* susandouglas@aol.com. *Clubs:* Arts, Chelsea Arts, Ivy, Royal Automobile, Soho House.

**DOUGLAS, (William) Barry,** OBE 2002; concert pianist; *b* 23 April 1960; *m* Deirdre O'Hara; two *s* one *d*. *Educ:* Royal College of Music; private study with Maria Curcio. Gold Medal, Tchaikovsky International Piano Competition, Moscow, 1986; Berlin Philharmonic début, 1987; engagements incl. regular appearances in major European, US and Far East cities; European première, Penderecki piano concerto Resurrection, 2002. Artistic Founder Dir, Camerata Ireland, 1999– (first all-Ireland orch.; concerts in Ireland and abroad; début USA tour, 2001); Artistic Dir, Clandeboye Fest. Prince Consort Prof. of Piano, Royal Coll. of Music, 1998–. Recordings incl. Tchaikovsky Concerto No 1 and Sonata in G, Mussorgsky Pictures at an Exhibition, Brahms Piano Quintet in F minor and Piano Concerto No 1, Liszt Concertos Nos 1 and 2, Beethoven Sonata Op 106, Prokofiev Sonatas 2 and 7, Rachmaninov Concerto No 2, Reger Concerto, Strauss Burleske, Britten Concerto, Debussy Fantaisie, Brahms: works for solo piano vol. 1, vol. 2, vol. 3, Schubert: works for solo piano vol. 1, Celtic Reflections. Vis. Fellow, Oriel Coll., Oxford, 1992–93. Hon. DMus QUB, 1986. *Recreations:* driving, reading, food and wine. *Address:* c/o IMG Artists, Capital Tower, 91 Waterloo Road, SE1 8RT.

**DOUGLAS, Prof. Zachary;** QC 2015; PhD; Professor of International Law, Graduate Institute, Geneva, since 2016 (Associate Professor of International Law, 2011–16); *b* Melbourne, Australia, 23 Oct. 1974; *s* of Ronald and Susan Douglas; *m* 2007, Marion Colombani; one *s* two *d*. *Educ:* Univ. of Melbourne (BA, LLB Hons); Lincoln Coll., Oxford (BCL Hons); Jesus Coll., Cambridge (MA, PhD). Admitted solicitor, 2000; Solicitor-Advocate, Freshfields, Paris, 2001–05; called to the Bar, Gray's Inn, 2006; Lecturer: UCL, 2005–07; Univ. of Cambridge, 2007–11. *Publications:* The International Law of Investment Claims, 2009; contrib. British Yearbook of Internat. Law; contribs to jls incl. Internat. and Comparative Law Qly. *Recreations:* sailing, ski-ing, jazz. *Address:* Matrix Chambers, Griffin Building, Gray's Inn, WC1R 5LN. *T:* (020) 7407 3447. *E:* zacharydouglas@matrixlaw.co.uk. *Clubs:* Royal Ocean Racing; Société Nautique de Genève.

**DOUGLAS-FAIRHURST, Prof. Robert John,** PhD; FRSL; Professor of English, University of Oxford, since 2015; Fellow and Tutor, Magdalen College, Oxford, since 2002; *b* Bickley, Kent, 16 Sept. 1968; *s* of Colin and Ann Douglas-Fairhurst; partner, Mac Castro. *Educ:* Eltham Coll.; Pembroke Coll., Cambridge (BA 1990; PhD 1995). Jane Eliza Procter Vis. Fellow, Princeton Univ., 1991–92. Jun. Res. Fellow, Fitzwilliam Coll., Cambridge, 1995–96; Fellow and Tutor, Emmanuel Coll., Cambridge, 1996–2002. Histl consultant on TV adaptations of literary works, 2006–. Reviewer and literary judge, incl. Man Booker Prize, Biographers' Club, Baillie Gifford Prize, 2002–. FRSL 2015. *Publications:* Victorian Afterlives: the shaping of influence in nineteenth-century literature, 2002; (ed) Dickens, A Christmas Carol, and Other Christmas Books, 2006; (ed) Dickens, Great Expectations, 2008; (ed) Mayhew, London Labour and the London Poor: a selected edition, 2010; Becoming Dickens: the invention of a novelist, 2011; (ed) Kingsley, The Water-Babies, 2013; The Story of Alice: Lewis Carroll and the secret history of Wonderland, 2015; (ed) The Collected Peter Pan, 2019; (ed) A Tale of Two Cities, 2019; contrib. essays and reviews. *Recreations:* travel, cinema, ski-ing, food and wine, Liverpool FC, books. *Address:* Magdalen College, High Street, Oxford OX1 4AU. *T:* (01865) 276000. *E:* robert.douglas-fairhurst@magd.ox.ac.uk.

**DOUGLAS-HAMILTON,** family name of **Duke of Hamilton and Brandon, Earldom of Selkirk** and **Baron Selkirk of Douglas.**

**DOUGLAS-HOME,** family name of **Earl of Home** and **Baroness Dacre.**

**DOUGLAS-HOME, Jessica Violet, (Lady Leach of Fairford);** painter; freelance theatre set and costume designer, since 1968; *b* 7 Feb. 1944; *d* of John Gwynne and Patricia (*née* Morrison-Bell); *m* 1st, 1966, Charles Cospatrick Douglas-Home (*d* 1985), Editor, The Times; two *s*; 2nd, 1993, (Charles Guy) Rodney Leach, later Baron Leach of Fairford (*d* 2016). *Educ:* Cranborne Chase Sch.; Chelsea Sch. of Art; Slade Sch. of Fine Art. Productions include: When We Are Married, RNT, 1979; Watch on the Rhine, 1980; Anyone for Dennis, Whitehall, 1981; The Mikado, Savoy, 1989. Solo exhibns of paintings and etchings in London, Brussels, Washington and Princeton, USA, 1977–85. Worked with dissidents behind the Iron Curtain, 1983–90. Trustee: Jan Hus Foundn and Jagiellonian Trust, 1983–; Butrint Foundn, 2002–12; Founder and Chm., Mihai Eminescu Trust, 1987–. Europa Nostra Cultural Heritage Award, 2007. Officer, National Order for Faithful Service (Romania), 2007; Knight, Order of the Crown (Romania), 2014. *Publications:* Violet: the life and loves of Violet Gordon Woodhouse, 1996; Once Upon Another Time, 2000; A Glimpse of Empire, 2011; William Simmonds: the silent heart of the Arts and Crafts Movement, 2018; contributed drawings: Book on Dinosaurs, 1975; Love Life, 1979; The English Taste, 1991. *Recreations:* reading, riding. *Address:* Knights Mill, Quenington, Cirencester, Glos GL7 5BN.

**DOUGLAS HOME, Mark;** author; Editor, The Herald, 2000–05; *b* 31 Aug. 1951; *s* of late Edward Charles Douglas Home and Nancy Rose Douglas Home; *m* 1976, Colette O'Reilly; one *s* one *d*. *Educ:* Eton Coll.; Univ. of Witwatersrand. Scottish corresp., The Independent, 1986–90; News Ed., 1990–93, Asst Ed., 1993–94, The Scotsman; Deputy Editor: Scotland on Sunday, 1994–98; Sunday Times Scotland, 1998–99; Scotland Editor, Sunday Times, 1999–2000. *Publications:* The Sea Detective (novel), 2011; The Woman Who Walked into the Sea (novel), 2013; The Malice of Waves, 2016. *Recreation:* gardening.

**DOUGLAS-HUGHES, Jonathan Peter,** OBE 2008; Senior Partner, Gepp & Sons, Solicitors, Chelmsford, since 2002; Vice Lord-Lieutenant for Essex, 2012–19; *b* Great Henny, Essex, 30 March 1944; *s* of Douglas Arthur and Beryl Marcia Douglas-Hughes; *m* 1978, Lindsay Louise Grant; two *s* one *d*. *Educ:* Oundle Sch., Northants. Admitted solicitor, 1969; Solicitor, 1969–72, Partner, 1972–2002, Gepp & Sons. Country Land and Business Association: Chm., 2001–04, Pres., 2010, Essex Br.; Chm., Eastern Reg., 2003–05. Chairman: Essex Boys and Girls Clubs, 1989–; Stubbers Adventure Centre, 1998–. Chairman: Cirdan Sailing Trust, 2008–; Essex Heritage Trust, 2010–. Under Sheriff, 1988–2013, DL 1996, Essex. *Recreation:* farming. *Address:* The Old Rectory, Gestingthorpe, Halstead, Essex CO9 3BB. *T:* (01782) 460722. *E:* Douglas-hughesj@gepp.co.uk. *Clubs:* Cavalry and Guards; Essex (Pres., 2004), Beef Steak (Essex).

**DOUGLAS-JONES, Benjamin Timothy;** QC 2018; a Recorder, since 2018; *b* Swansea, 16 Aug. 1974; *s* of Timothy Nigel Douglas-Jones and Caroline Justina Douglas-Jones; *m* 2001, Jane Amanda Sandiford; one *s* one *d*. *Educ:* Taunton Sch.; Univ. of Reading (LLB Hons 1996); Cardiff Univ. (Bar Vocational Qual. 1998); Univ. of Wales (MPhil 1999). Called to the Bar: Gray's Inn, 1998; Grenada, 2011; in practice as a barrister, specialising in complex fraud, serious and appellate crime and regulatory law, 5 Paper Bldgs, 2005–; door tenant: Apex Chambers, 2008–; Linenhall Chambers, 2013–; St Ives Chambers, 2018–. Complex risk and compliance consultant, Altion Law Ltd, 2017–. Freeman, City of London, 2015–; Liveryman, Environmental Cleaners' Co., 2016–. *Publications:* The Rights of the Foetus in Medical Procedures Affecting Mother and Child, 1999; Blackstone's Guide to the Consumer Rights Act 2015, 2016; (jtly) Human Trafficking and Modern Slavery: law and practice, 2018. *Recreations:* harmonica, mandolin and guitar. *Address:* 5 Paper Buildings, First Floor, Temple, EC4Y 7HB. *T:* (020) 7583 6117, *Fax:* (020) 7353 0075. *E:* clerks@5pb.co.uk.

**DOUGLAS MILLER, Robert Alexander Gavin;** Director, Edinburgh Worldwide Investment Trust, 1988–2008; *b* 11 Feb. 1937; *s* of late F. G. Douglas Miller and Mora Kennedy; *m* 1963, Judith Madeleine Smith; three *s* one *d*. *Educ:* Harrow; Oxford Univ. (MA). 9th Lancers, 1955–57; Oxford, 1958–61. Treasurer, Queen's Body Guard for Scotland (Royal Company of Archers), 1977–88. Chm., Jenners (Princes St Edinburgh) Ltd, 1975–2005; Director: Kennington Leasing Ltd, 1977–2005; Dunedin Income Growth Trust, 1988–2006. Pres., Edinburgh Chamber of Commerce & Manufactures, 1985–87. Mem., Kyle & Sutherland Fishery Bd, 1980–2007; Member, Council: Assoc. of Scottish Salmon Fishery Bds, 1984–90; Atlantic Salmon Trust, 1989–90; Chm., Game Conservancy (Scotland), 1990–94. Chm., Outreach Trust, 1976–94. Pres., Royal Warrant Holders, 1987–88. *Recreations:* shooting, fishing. *Address:* Bavelaw Castle, Balerno, Midlothian EH14 7JS. *T:* (0131) 449 3972; Forneth Estate, Blairgowrie, Perthshire PH10 6SN. *T:* (01250) 884255. *Club:* New (Edinburgh).

**DOUGLAS-PENNANT,** family name of **Baron Penrhyn.**

**DOUGLAS-SCOTT, Prof. Sionaidh;** Anniversary Chair in Law and Co-Director, Centre for Law and Society in a Global Context, Queen Mary, University of London, since 2015; *b* Edinburgh, 1959; *m* 1st, 1984, Michael Douglas-Scott; two *s* one *d*; 2nd, 2009, Peter Winship. *Educ:* St Denis Sch., Edinburgh; Edinburgh Acad.; University Coll. London (BA Hons); London Sch. of Econs and Pol Sci. (LLM); City Univ. (DipLaw); MA Oxon. Called to the Bar, Gray's Inn; Lectr, Reader, then Prof., KCL, 1991–2007; Prof. of European and Human Rights Law, Univ. of Oxford, 2008–15; Fellow, Lady Margaret Hall, Oxford, until 2015, now Hon. Res. Fellow. Vis. Prof., Univ. of Bonn, 1994. *Publications:* Faith in Law, 2000; Constitutional Law of the European Union, 2002, Law After Modernity, 2013; contrib. articles on EU law, public law and legal theory, Scottish Independence Referendum and Britain's role in EU. *Address:* Department of Law, Queen Mary, University of London, Mile End Road, E1 4NS.

**DOUGLAS-SCOTT-MONTAGU**, family name of **Baron Montagu of Beaulieu**.

**DOULTON, John Hubert Farre**; Principal, Elizabeth College, Guernsey, 1988–98; *b* 2 Jan. 1942; *s* of late Alfred John Farre, CBE, TD; *m* 1986, Margaret Anne (*née* Ball); two step *d*. *Educ*: Rugby School; Keble College, Oxford (1st Mods, 2nd Greats). Teacher: Rugby, 1965–66; Radley, 1966–88. *Recreations*: music, walking, boats, foreign travel, carpentry. *Address*: 15 Hungerford Hill, Lambourn, Berks RG17 8NP.

**DOUNE, Lord**; Jack Alexander Stuart; *b* 30 Nov. 2002; *s* and *heir* of Earl of Moray, *qv*.

**DOURO, Marquess of**, courtesy title of Duke of Wellington, not used by current heir; see Earl of Mornington.

**DOVE, Claire**, OBE 2013 (MBE 1993); DL; Chief Executive, Blackburne House Group (formerly Women's Technology and Education Centre), since 1985; Crown Representative, Voluntary, Community and Social Enterprise sector, since 2018; *b* Liverpool, 29 Aug. 1952; *d* of B. L. Dove and Frances Murnane; *m* 2004, Colin V. F. Henfrey; three *s* one *d*. *Educ*: Univ. of Liverpool (BA Hons). Chairman: Social Enterprise UK (formerly Social Enterprise Coalition), 2007–17; Liverpool Fairness Commn. Mem. Bd, Charity Commn, 2013–16. Former Dep. Chm., Liverpool Community Coll.; former Mem. Bd, Liverpool John Moores Univ. DL Merseyside, 2005. FRSA. Queen's Lifetime Achievement Award for Enterprise Promotion, 2013. *Address*: Blackburne House Group, Blackburne House, Blackburne Place, off Hope Street, Liverpool L8 7PE. *T*: (0151) 708 3932. *E*: clairedove@blackburnehouse.co.uk.

**DOVE, Hon. Sir Ian William**, Kt 2014; **Hon. Mr Justice Dove**; a Judge of the High Court, Queen's Bench Division, since 2014; a Presiding Judge, Northern Circuit, since 2017; *b* 31 Dec. 1963; *s* of late Jack Richard Dove and of Janet Yvonne Dove; *m* 1988, Juliet Caroline Gladston; two *s*. *Educ*: Northampton Sch. for Boys; St Catherine's Coll., Oxford (MA; Hon. Fellow, 2017); Inns of Court Sch. of Law. Called to the Bar, Inner Temple, 1986, Bencher, 2010; QC 2003; a Recorder, 2003–14; a Dep. High Ct Judge, 2008–14. Immigration Adjudicator (pt-time), 2001–04; Mem., Immigration Appeal Tribunal, 2004–05; an Immigration Judge, 2005–14. *Recreations*: supporting Northampton Saints and Aston Villa FC, walking, poetry, the visual arts, good food, music, bell ringing. *Address*: Royal Courts of Justice, Strand, WC2A 2LL.

**DOVE, Jonathan**, CBE 2019; composer; National Theatre Associate, 2003–15; *b* 18 July 1959; *s* of Myles Harrison Dove and Deirdre Cecily Dove. *Educ*: St Joseph's Acad., Blackheath; ILEA Centre for Young Musicians; Trinity Coll., Cambridge (MA); Goldsmiths' Coll., London (MMus). Asst Chorus Master, Glyndebourne, 1987–88; Music Advr, Almeida Th., 1990–2009; Artistic Director, Spitalfields Fest., 2001–06. Composer of scores for 30 plays (Almeida, NT, RSC) and of music for film and television. Trustee: Stephen Oliver Trust, 1997–2006; Michael Tippett Foundn, 1999–. Patron: London Fest. of Contemp. Church Music, 2007–; Durham Opera Ensemble, 2007–. Hon. Pres., Soc. of Recorder Players, 2017–. Hon. RAM, 2013. Hon. DMus East London, 2006. *Compositions* include: Figures in the Garden, 1991; Seaside Postcards, Tuning In, 1995; The Ringing Isle, 1997; The Magic Flute Dances, 1999; The Passing of the Year, 2000; Stargazer, Out of Time, 2001; Moonlight Revels, Koethener Messe, 2002; The Middleham Jewel, The Far Theatricals of Day, Run to the Edge, The Crocodiamond, Out of Winter, 2003; Across the Walls, All the Future Days, On Spital Fields, Work in Progress: Fourteen Site-Visits for Piano and Orch. with Film, 2004; Airport Scenes, 2005; Hojoki, 2006; It sounded as if the Streets were running, Minterne, 2007; There Was a Child, 2008; Missa Brevis, Piano Quintet, 2009; River Songs, A Song of Joys, Innocence, 2010; Cut My Shadow, Three Tennyson Songs, Two Sonnets, The Pied Piper, 2011; The Immortal Ship, The Wells Service, A Portrait of Aung San Suu Kyi, Diana and Actaeon (ballet), 2012; The Portsmouth Service, Out of the Whirlwind, Who Wrote the Book of Love?, 2013; Gaia Theory, Psalms for Leo, For an Unknown Soldier, The Dancing Pipes, Te Deum, 2014; Vadam et circuibo civitatem, Arion and the Dolphin, Nights Not Spent Alone, A Brief History of Creation, In Damascus, 2015; Seasons and Charms, Catching Fire, On This Wondrous Sea, Sunshine, 2016; Under Alter'd Skies, 2017; Letters from Claude, They Will Rise, Sappho Sings, Northern Lights, 2018; Vertue, Vanishing Gold, Moon Songs, 2019; *operas*: Pig, 1992; L'Augellino Belverde, Siren Song, 1994; Flight, 1998; Tobias and the Angel, 1999; The Palace in the Sky, 2000; The Hackney Chronicles, L'Altra Euridice, 2001; When She Died: Death of a Princess, 2002; La Dama ed il Pulitore di Damasco, Le Porte di Bagdad, 2003; Kwasi & Kwame (formerly The Two Hearts of Kwasi Boachi), 2005; The Enchanted Pig, Man on the Moon, An Old Way to Pay New Debts, 2006; The Adventures of Pinocchio, 2007; Swanhunter, Seven Angels, 2009; Mansfield Park, 2010, (orchestral version) 2017; Life is a Dream, The Walk from the Garden, 2012; The Day After, The Monster in the Maze, 2015 (British Composer Award, 2016); Marx in London, 2017. *Recreation*: photography. *Address*: c/o Peters Edition Ltd, 2-6 Baches Street, N1 6DN. *T*: (020) 7553 4000. *W*: www.jonathandove.com.

**DOVER, Bishop Suffragan of**, since 2019; **Rt Rev. Rose Josephine Hudson-Wilkin**; *b* 19 Jan. 1961; *m* 1983, Rev. Kenneth Wilkin; one *s* two *d*. *Educ*: Montego Bay High Sch.; Church Army Coll.; Queen's Theol Coll. (W Midlands Ministerial Trng Course); Birmingham Univ. (BPhil Ed 2000). Lay Trng Officer, Anglican Dio. Jamaica, 1982; ordained deacon, 1991, priest, 1994; Curate, St Matthew, Wolverhampton, 1991–94; Priest, Good Shepherd, W Bromwich, 1995–98; Officer for Black Anglican Concerns, Lichfield Dio., 1995–98; Vicar, Holy Trinity, Dalston and All Saints, Haggerston, 1998–2014; a Chaplain to the Queen, 2008–19; Chaplain to the Speaker of the H of C, and Priest Vicar, Westminster Abbey, 2010–19; Preb., St Paul's Cathedral, 2013–19; Priest-in-charge, St Mary at Hill with St Andrew Hubbard, St George Botolph Lane, and St Botolph by Billingsgate, 2014–19. Mem., Broadcasting Standards Commn, 1998–2004. Member: Gen. Synod of C of E, 1995–98, 2005–10 (Chm., Cttee for Minority Ethnic Anglican Concerns, 1999–2009); Theol Bd, WCC, 1996–98; Chm., Worldwide Cttee, SPCK, 1998–2004. Trustee: Trusthouse Charitable Foundation, 2009–; Silverline, 2015–18; Patron, City YMCA, 2011–. Hon. LLD, 2017. *Recreations*: reading, travelling, entertaining, tennis, scrabble. *Address*: The Bishop's Office, Old Palace, The Precincts, Canterbury CT1 2EE.

**DOVER, Den**; Member, North West Region, England, European Parliament, 1999–2009 (C, 1999–2008; Ind, 2008–09); *b* 4 April 1938; *s* of Albert and Emmie Dover; *m* 1st, 1959, Anne Marina Wright (marr. diss. 1986); one *s* one *d*; 2nd, 1989, Kathleen Edna Fisher. *Educ*: Manchester Grammar Sch.; Manchester Univ. BSc Hons. CEng, MICE. John Laing & Son Ltd, 1959–68; National Building Agency: Dep. Chief Executive, 1969–70; Chief Exec., 1971–72; Projects Dir, Capital and Counties Property Co. Ltd, 1972–75; Contracts Manager, Wimpey Laing Iran, 1975–77. Director of Housing Construction, GLC, 1977–79. Member, London Borough of Barnet Council, 1968–71. MP (C) Chorley, 1979–97; contested (C) same seat, 1997. Mem., Commons Select Cttee on Transport, 1979–87, on Envmt, 1995–97. European Parliament: Budgets Spokesman, 2000–05; Regl Develt Spokesman, 2005; Chief Whip (C), 2007–08. *Recreations*: cricket, hockey, golf. Methodist. *Address*: 166 Furzehill Road, Boreham Wood, Herts WD6 2DS. *T*: (020) 8953 5945.

**DOW, Biba**; see Dow, E. C.

**DOW, Carol**, CMG 2003; Chief Medical Adviser, Foreign and Commonwealth Office, 1998–2003; Consultant in Occupational Health, Guy's and St Thomas' Hospital NHS Trust, London, 1989–2003; *b* 3 April 1951; *d* of John Dickson Dow and Catherine Dow (*née* Robertson). *Educ*: St Bartholomew's Hospital Medical Sch., London Univ. (MB BS 1976; DTM&H 1988); Univ. of Glasgow (Dip. Travel Medicine 1996). MRCP 1981; AFOM 1992. Registrar, St George's Hosp., 1982–86; Malaria Emergency Unit and Air Evacuation Service, African Med. and Res. Foundn, Nairobi, 1983–84; Registrar, Hosp. for Tropical Diseases, London, 1986–88; Med. Registrar, Middlesex Hosp., 1988–89; Principal Med. Advr, FCO, 1989–98. *Publications*: (contrib.) Health Information for Overseas Travel, 1995, 2nd edn 2001; (contrib.) Dawood's Travellers' Health: how to stay healthy abroad, 4th edn 2002. *Recreations*: travel, fishing, hill-walking, medicine. *Address*: Upper Camerory, Ballieward, Grantown-on-Spey, Moray PH26 3PR. *T*: (01479) 872548. *E*: carol.dow146@btinternet.com.

**DOW, Rear-Adm. Douglas Morrison**, CB 1991; DL; Director, National Trust for Scotland, 1992–97; *b* 1 July 1935; *s* of George Torrance Dow and Grace Morrison MacFarlane; *m* 1959, Felicity Margaret Mona Napier, *d* of John Watson Napier and Beatrix Mary Carson; two *s*. *Educ*: George Heriot's School; BRNC Dartmouth. Joined RN, 1952; served HMS Sheffield, 1957–59; Staff of C-in-C Plymouth, 1959–61; HMS Plymouth, 1961–63; RN Supply Sch., 1963–65; Staff of Comdr FEF, 1965–67; HMS Endurance, 1968–70; BRNC Dartmouth, 1970–72; Asst Dir, Officer Appointments (S), 1972–74; Sec. to Comdr British Navy Staff, Washington, 1974–76; HMS Tiger, 1977–78; NDC Latimer, 1978–79; CSO(A) to Flag Officer Portsmouth, 1979; Sec. to Controller of the Navy, 1981; Captain, HMS Cochrane, 1983; Commodore, HMS Centurion, 1985; RCDS 1988; Dir Gen., Naval Personal Services, 1989–92. Hon. ADC to the Queen, 1986–89. President: South Queensferry Sea Cadets, 1994–2009; Royal Naval Assoc., Edin., 1996–2017. Gov., George Heriot's Sch., 1993–2009 (Vice Chm., 1997–2009). DL Edinburgh, 1996. *Recreations*: Royal Navy Rugby Union (Chairman, 1985–91), fly fishing, golf, gardening.

**DOW, Elizabeth Clare, (Biba)**; Co-Founder and Director, Dow Jones Architects, since 2000; *b* London, 9 July 1969; *d* of John Christopher Roderick Dow and Clare Mary Keegan; *m* 1996, Alun Rhys Jones, *qv*; one *s* two *d*. *Educ*: Lycée Français de Londres; Francis Holland Sch., Graham Terrace; Westminster Sch.; Clare Coll., Cambridge (BA 1990; DipArch 1993). RIBA 1995. Architectural Asst, Powell Moya Partnership, 1995–98. Completed projects include: Christ Church Spitalfields, 2015; Garden Mus., 2017; St Mary Magdalene, Paddington, 2019; Maggie's Centre, Cardiff, 2019. Tutor, diploma unit, London Metropolitan Univ., 2011–13; external examr, Dept of Art and Arch., Kingston Sch. of Art, 2015–. Mem., Old Oak and Park Royal Design Rev. Panel, 2018–. Gov., Corpus Christi Sch., Brixton Hill, 2018–. *Recreations*: art, reading, opera, walking, sewing. *Address*: Dow Jones Architects, 10 Station Parade, Balham High Road, SW12 9AZ. *T*: (020) 8675 2544. *E*: biba@dowjonesarchitects.com.

**DOW, Rt Rev. Geoffrey Graham**; Bishop of Carlisle, 2000–09; an Honorary Assistant Bishop: Diocese of Chester, since 2009; Diocese of Manchester, since 2011; *b* 4 July 1942; *s* of Ronald Graham Dow and Dorothy May Dow (*née* Christie); *m* 1966, Molly Patricia (*née* Sturges); three *s* one *d*. *Educ*: St Albans Sch.; Queen's Coll., Oxford (BA 1963; BSc 1965; MA 1968; MSc 1981); Clifton Theol Coll.; Birmingham Univ. (Dip. Pastoral Studies 1974); Nottingham Univ. (MPhil 1982). Ordained deacon, 1967, priest, 1968; Asst Curate, Tonbridge Parish Church, 1967–72; Chaplain-Student, St John's Coll., Oxford, 1972–75; Lectr in Christian Doctrine, St John's Coll., Nottingham, 1975–81; Vicar, Holy Trinity, Coventry, 1981–92; Canon Theologian, Coventry Cathedral, 1988–92; Area Bp of Willesden, 1992–2000. Chairman: Govs, St Martin's Coll., 2002–08; Council, Ridley Hall, 2003–10; Mem., Gov. Body, Univ. of Cumbria, 2007–09. Trustee, Settle and Carlisle Railway Trust, 2009– (Chm., 2015–17). *Publications*: Dark Satanic Mills? Shaftesbury Project, 1979; The Local Church's Political Responsibility, 1980; St John's College Extension Studies B1—God and the World, 1980; Whose Hand on the Tiller?, 1983; Those Tiresome Intruders, 1990; Explaining Deliverance, 1991; Christian Renewal in Europe, 1992; A Christian Understanding of Daily Work, 1994; Pathways of Prayer, 1996; Reader Upbeat!, 2008; When He Comes, 2010; Leading Rural Churches for Growth, 2015. *Recreations*: steam and narrow gauge railways, model railways, travel, music, political biographies. *Address*: 34 Kimberley Avenue, Romiley, Stockport SK6 4AB.

**DOW, Simon Charles**, CBE 2016; Executive Chair, London Housing Foundation, since 2015; *b* 21 Sept. 1950; *s* of Alan Dow and Rosamund Dow; *m* 1984, Virginia Anne, *d* of late Arthur Charles William Crook; one *s* one *d*. *Educ*: King's Sch., Chester; United World Coll. of the Atlantic (Internat. Bacc.; RNLI coxswain); SOAS, London Univ. (BA Hons); Brunel Univ. (MA Public Admin). Notting Hill Housing Trust, 1974–78; Dep. Dir, New Islington and Hackney Housing Assoc., 1978–87; Sen. Regulation Manager, Housing Corp., 1985–87 (on secondment); Gp Chief Exec., Samuel Lewis Housing Trust, subseq. Southern Housing Gp, 1987–95; Housing Corporation: Dep. Chief Exec., 1995–97; Chief Ops Officer, 1997–2000; Actg Chief Exec. and Accounting Officer, 2000; Chief Exec., Guinness Trust Gp, later The Guinness Partnership, 2001–15. Dir, ARHAG Housing Assoc., 2006–08; Chairman: Dolphin Living Ltd, 2014–16; Dolphin Square Foundn, 2016– (Mem. Bd, 2016–). Chm., 1991–2006 and 2013, Mem. Bd, 1991–, London Housing Foundn; Dir, Housing Forum, 2000–02 (Chm., Off-site Manufg Gp, 2001–03); Member: Nat. Council, 2002–06, Bd of Dirs, 2003–06, Nat. Housing Fedn; Dep. Prime Minister's Home Ownership Task Force, 2003; Ministerial Adv. Gp on Planning Obligations, 2004–05; ODPM Ministerial Task Force on Planning Obligations, 2004–06; Cave Review of Social Housing Regulation, 2006–07; Bd, Homes and Communities Agency, 2017–18 (Member: Regulation Cttee; Audit Cttee); Interim Chair, Regulator of Social Housing (formerly Regulation Cttee, Homes and Communities Agency), 2017–; Ind. Ext. Mem., Audit Cttee, Ind. Police Complaints Commn, 2005–09; Chair, Reall (formerly Homeless Internat.), 2011–14 (Mem., Financial Services Gp, 2010–14; Mem. Council, 2010–); Mem. Bd, Deptford Reach, 2018. FRSA 2009. Nat. Private Pilot's Licence, 2009. *Recreations*: sailing, flying, being outdoors.

**DOWD, James Patrick**; *b* Germany, 5 March 1951; *s* of late James Patrick Dowd and Elfriede Anna Dowd (*née* Janocha); *m* 2016, Janet Anderson, *qv*. *Educ*: Dalmain JM&I Sch., London; Sedgehill Comprehensive, London; London Nautical School. Apprentice telephone engineer, GPO, 1967–72; Station Manager, Heron petrol stations, 1972–73; Telecomms Engineer, Plessey Co., later GPT, 1973–92. Group Rep. and Br. Cttee, PO Engrg Union, 1967–72; Sen. Negotiator, ASTMS, then MSF. Lewisham Council: Councillor, 1974–94: Chief Whip; Chm. of Cttees; Dep. Leader; Dep. Mayor, 1987, 1991; Mayor, 1992. Former Mem., Lewisham and Southwark DHA. Contested (Lab): Beckenham, 1983; Lewisham W, 1987. MP (Lab) Lewisham W, 1992–2010, Lewisham W and Penge, 2010–17. An Opposition Whip, 1993–95; opposition front-bench spokesman on Northern Ireland, 1995–97; a Lord Comr of HM Treasury (Govt Whip), 1997–2001. Member: Select Cttee on Health, 2001–10; Select Cttee on Sci. and Technol., 2012–17. Former school governor. *Recreations*: music, reading, theatre, Cornwall, being with friends.

**DOWD, Peter;** MP (Lab) Bootle, since 2015; *b* Bootle, 20 June 1957. *Educ:* Liverpool Univ.; Lancaster Univ. CQSW. Health and social care worker, Merseyside. Member (Lab): Merseyside CC, 1981–86; Sefton BC, 1991– (Leader, Labour Gp, 2008–15; Leader of Council, 2011–15). Shadow Chief Sec. to the Treasury, 2017–. *Address:* House of Commons, SW1A 0AA.

**DOWDALL, John Michael,** CB 2003; Comptroller and Auditor-General for Northern Ireland, 1994–2009; *b* 6 Sept. 1944; *s* of late Lt-Col W. Dowdall, MBE, and E. Dowdall; *m* 1964, Aylerie, (*née* Houston); three *s* one *d*. *Educ:* King Edward's Sch., Witley, Surrey; Queen's Univ., Belfast (BScEcon). CPFA 2001. Lectr in Economics, Royal Univ. of Malta, 1966–69; Lectr in Political Econ., King's Coll., Univ. of Aberdeen, 1969–72; Economic Advr, Dept of Commerce, N Ireland, 1972–78, Principal, Dept of Commerce, 1978–82; Asst Sec., Dept of Finance and Personnel, N Ireland, 1982–85; Dep. Chief Exec., Industrial Develt Bd, NI, 1986–89; Under Sec., Dept of Finance and Personnel, NI, 1989–94. Vis. Prof., Faculty of Business and Mgt, Univ. of Ulster, 2002–18.

**DOWDALLS, Catherine;** QC (Scot.) 2013; *b* Hamilton, Scotland, 18 Sept. 1962; *d* of Hugh Kentigern Dowdalls and Mary Dowdalls. *Educ:* Holy Cross High Sch., Hamilton; Univ. of Strathclyde (LLB Hons; DipLP). Admitted as solicitor, 1985; Solicitor, 1985–99; Called to the Bar, 2000; Advocate, specialising in family law, 2000–. Mem., Scottish Law Commn, 2018–. *Address:* Advocates Library, Parliament House, Edinburgh EH1 1RF. *T:* (0131) 226 5071. *E:* katedowdalls@amadvocates.co.uk.

**DOWDEN, Rt Hon. Oliver (James),** CBE 2015; PC 2019; MP (C) Hertsmere, since 2015; Minister for the Cabinet Office and Paymaster General, since 2019; *b* Park St, Herts; *m* Blythe; one *s* one *d*. *Educ:* Parmiter's Sch., Watford; Trinity Hall, Cambridge (BA). Teacher, Japan; lawyer, London; Account Dir, LLM; Dep. Campaigns Dir, Cons. Party; Man. Consultant, Hill and Knowlton Strategies, 2007; Dir, Political Ops, Cons. Party; Political Advr to Prime Minister, 2010–12; Dep. COS and Advr to Prime Minister, 2012–15. Parly Sec., Cabinet Office, 2018–19. *Address:* House of Commons, SW1A 0AA.

**DOWDEN, Penny;** *see* Mansfield, P.

**DOWDEN, Richard George;** Africa analyst, lecturer, film maker and writer; Executive Director, Royal African Society, 2002–16; *b* 20 March 1949; *s* of late Peter Dowden and Eleanor Dowden; *m* 1976, Penny Mansfield, *qv*; two *d*. *Educ:* St George's Coll., Weybridge, Surrey; London Univ. (BA History). Volunteer Teacher, Uganda, 1971–72; Asst Sec., Justice and Peace Commn, 1973–76; Editor, Catholic Herald, 1976–79; journalist, The Times, 1980–86; Africa Editor, 1986–94, Diplomatic Editor, 1994–95, The Independent; Africa Editor, The Economist, 1995–2001. Mem. Bd, Nation Media Gp, 2010–17. *Publications:* Africa: altered states, ordinary miracles, 2008. *Address:* 7 Highbury Grange, N5 2QB.

**DOWDESWELL, Prof. Julian Andrew,** PhD, ScD; Professor of Physical Geography, since 2001, and Director, Scott Polar Research Institute, since 2002, University of Cambridge; Fellow, Jesus College, Cambridge, since 2002; *b* 18 Nov. 1957; *s* of Robert Dowdeswell and Joan Marion Dowdeswell (*née* Longshaw); *m* 1983, Evelyn Kae Lind; one *s* one *d*. *Educ:* Magdalen Coll. Sch., Oxford; Jesus Coll., Cambridge (BA 1980; schol., 1980; PhD 1985; ScD 2016); Univ. of Colorado (MA 1982). Research Associate, Scott Polar Res. Inst., Univ. of Cambridge, 1985; Lectr, Univ. of Wales, Aberystwyth, 1986–89; University of Cambridge: Sen. Asst in Research, 1989–92; Asst Dir of Res., Scott Polar Res. Inst., 1992–94; Dir, Centre for Glaciology, 1994–98, and Dir, Inst. of Geog. and Earth Scis, 1997–98, Univ. of Wales, Aberystwyth; Prof. of Physical Geog. and Dir, Bristol Glaciology Centre, Bristol Univ., 1998–2001. Natural Environment Research Council: Member: Polar Science and Technol. Bd, 1995–97; Earth Scis Res. Grants and Training Awards Cttee, 1996–2000; Polar Scis Expert Gp, 1997–99; Earth Scis Bd, 1997–2000; Peer Review Coll., 2003–06, 2012–. Hd of Glaciers and Ice Sheets Div., Internat. Commn for Snow and Ice, 1999–2011. Chm., UK Nat. Cttee on Antarctic Res., 2002–06; UK Alternate Deleg. to Council, Scientific Cttee on Antarctic Res., 2002–06; UK Deleg. to Council, Internat. Arctic Science Cttee, 2002–10; UK Mem., Arctic Ocean Scis Bd, 2006–10. Mem. Council, Internat. Glaciol Soc., 1993–96. Trustee: Fuchs Foundn, 2008–; Oates Mus., 2010–; Royal Mus Greenwich, 2018–. Gov., Plascrug Sch., Aberystwyth, 1996–98. FRGS 1985; FLSW 2018; Fellow: British Soc. of Geomorphol., 2014; Royal Canadian Geographical Soc., 2017. Hon. Fellow, Aberystwyth Univ., 2016. Polar Medal, 1995; Gill Meml Award, 1998, Founder's Medal, 2008, RGS; Louis Agassiz Medal, Eur. Geoscis Union, 2011; IASC Medal, Internat. Arctic Sci. Cttee, 2014; Lyell Medal, Geol Soc., 2018. *Publications:* (ed jtly) Glacimarine Environments: processes and sediments, 1990; (ed jtly) The Arctic and Environmental Change, 1996; (ed jtly) Glacial and Oceanic History of the Polar North Atlantic Margins, 1998; Islands of the Arctic, 2002; (ed jtly) Glacier-influenced sedimentation on high-latitude continental margins, 2002; The Antarctic Paintings of Edward Seago, 2006; (ed jtly) Atlas of Submarine Glacial Landforms, 2016; The Continent of Antarctica, 2018; papers in learned jls on glaciology, glacier-marine interactions, cryosphere and climate change, and satellite remote sensing of ice. *Recreations:* hill-walking, ski-ing, watching Oxford United FC. *Address:* Jesus College, Cambridge CB5 8BL.

**DOWDING,** family name of **Baron Dowding.**

**DOWDING, 3rd Baron** *cr* 1943, of Bentley Priory, Middlesex; **Piers Hugh Tremenheere Dowding;** Professor of English, Okayama Shoka University, Japan, 1999–2013, now Emeritus (Associate Professor, 1977–99); *b* 18 Feb. 1948; *s* of 2nd Baron Dowding and of his 2nd wife, Alison Margaret, *d* of Dr James Bannerman and *widow* of Major R. W. H. Peebles; *S* father, 1992; *m* Noriko Shiho; two *d*. *Educ:* Fettes Coll.; Amherst Coll., Mass (BA 1971). LTCL. Patron, Assoc. of RAF Fighter Control Officers. Life Pres., Dumfries and Galloway Aircrew Assoc., 1996–. *Heir: b* Hon. Mark Denis James Dowding [*b* 11 July 1949; *m* 1982, Heather Arter; one *s*].

**DOWDING, Nicholas Alan Tatham;** QC 1997; *b* 24 Feb. 1956; *s* of Alan Lorimer Dowding and Jennifer Mary Dowding (*née* Hughes); *m*; three *d*. *Educ:* Radley Coll.; St Catharine's Coll., Cambridge (BA 1978; MA 1982). Called to the Bar, Inner Temple, 1979. Chm., Property Bar Assoc., 2006–08. Hon. RICS 2007. *Publications:* (ed jtly) Handbook of Rent Review, 1980–85; (ed jtly) Woodfall on Landlord and Tenant, 1994–; (jtly) Dilapidations: the modern law and practice, 1995, 6th edn 2018; (ed) Landlord and Tenant Reports, 1998–. *Recreations:* sailing, riding, music, juggling, limericks. *Address:* Malcolm Hollis LLP, 140 London Wall, EC2Y 5DN. *T:* (020) 7622 9555, *Fax:* (020) 7627 9850. *E:* nicholas.dowding@malcolmhollis.com.

**DOWDING, Hon. Peter M'Callum;** SC 2002; barrister; *b* 6 Oct. 1943; *m*; five *c*. *Educ:* Hale School, Perth; Univ. of Western Australia (LLB 1964). Churchill Fellowship, 1974, UK and Canada. In practice as solicitor and barrister until 1983 and as barrister, 1990–; Partner, Briggs Paul Dowding, 1992–94; Man. Partner, DCH Legal Gp, 1994–96. Dir, Biotech Internat. Ltd, 1998–2001. MLC North Province, WA, 1980–86; MLA (ALP) Maylands, 1986–90; Cabinet Member, 1983–90; Minister for: Mines, Fuel and Energy, 1983; Planning, and Employment and Training, 1983–84; Consumer Affairs, 1983–86; Minister assisting the Minister for Public Sector Management, 1984–88; Minister for Works and Services, Labour, Productivity and Employment, and assisting the Treasurer, 1987–88; Treasurer, and Minister for Productivity, 1988–89; Leader, WA Parly Lab. Party, 1987–90; Premier, WA, 1988–90; Minister, Public Sector Management, and Women's Interests, 1989–90. *Recreations:* sailing, bushwalking, reading. *Address:* PO Box 1262, Fremantle, WA 6959, Australia. *T:* (8) 94304411, *Fax:* (8) 94304417. *E:* pdowding@peterdowding.com.au.

**DOWDING, Sally; Her Honour Judge Dowding;** a Circuit Judge, since 2013; Designated Family Judge for Wolverhampton and Telford, since 2019; *b* Hereford; *d* of late Edward Charles Wisnom Dowding and Grace Evelyn Dowding (*née* Ridley); *m* 1976; two *d*. *Educ:* Stratford upon Avon Grammar Sch. for Girls; Univ. of Manchester (LLB); Keele Univ. (MA). Admitted as solicitor, 1979; Solicitor, Elwyn Jones and Co., Bangor, 1987–2007; Dep. Dist Judge, 2000–07; Dist Judge, 2007–13. Pres., Gwynedd Law Soc., 2005–06. *Address:* Wolverhampton Combined Court Centre, Pipers Row, Wolverhampton WV1 3LQ.

**DOWELL, Sir Anthony (James),** Kt 1995; CBE 1973; Senior Principal, 1967–2001, Director, 1986–2001, Royal Ballet, Covent Garden (Assistant to Director, 1984–85; Associate Director, 1985–86); *b* 16 Feb. 1943; *s* of late Catherine Ethel and Arthur Henry Dowell; unmarried. *Educ:* Hampshire Sch., St Saviour's Hall, Knightsbridge; Royal Ballet Sch., White Lodge, Richmond, Surrey; Royal Ballet Sch., Barons Court. Joined Opera Ballet, 1960, Royal Ballet, for Russian Tour, 1961; promoted Principal Dancer, 1966. *Principal roles with Royal Ballet include:* La Fête Etrange, 1963; Napoli, 1965; Romeo and Juliet, 1965; Song of the Earth, 1966; Card Game, Giselle, Swan Lake, 1967; The Nutcracker, Cinderella, Monotones, Symphonic Variations, new version of Sleeping Beauty, Enigma Variations, Lilac Garden, 1968; Raymonda Act III, Daphnis and Chloe, La Fille Mal Gardée, 1969; Dances at a Gathering, 1970; La Bayadère, Meditation from Thaïs, Afternoon of a Faun, Anastasia, 1971; Triad, Le Spectre de la Rose, Giselle, 1972; Agon, Firebird, 1973; Manon, 1974; Four Schumann Pieces, Les Sylphides, 1975; Four Seasons, 1975; Scarlet Pastorale, 1976; Rhapsody, 1981; A Month in the Country, The Tempest, Varii Capricci, 1983; Sons of Horus, Frankenstein: the modern Prometheus, 1986; Ondine, 1988. Guest Artist with Amer. Ballet Theater, 1977–79; *performed in:* The Nutcracker; Don Quixote; Other Dances; *created:* The Dream, 1964; Shadow Play, 1967; Pavane, 1973; Manon, 1974; Contredanses; Solor in Makarova's La Bayadère; Fisherman in Le Rossignol (Ashton's choreography), NY Metropolitan Opera, 1981; Winter Dreams, 1991. Narrator in A Wedding Bouquet (first speaking role), Joffrey Ballet, 1977; guest appearances with Nat. Ballet of Canada (The Dream, Four Schumann Pieces), 1979 and 1981; Anthony Dowell Ballet Gala, Palladium, 1980 (for charity); narrated Oedipus Rex, NY Metropolitan Opera, 1981. *Television performances:* La Bayadère (USA); Swan Lake, Cinderella, Sleeping Beauty, A Month in the Country, The Dream, Les Noces (all BBC); Winter Dreams; All the Superlatives (personal profile), Omnibus, BBC. Dance Magazine award, NY, 1972. *Recreations:* painting, paper sculpture, theatrical costume design. *Address:* c/o Royal Opera House, Covent Garden, WC2E 9DD.

**DOWELL, Ian Malcolm,** MBE 1999; Editor, Birmingham Evening Mail, 1987–2001; *b* 15 Nov. 1940; *s* of late James Mardlin and Lilian Dowell; *m* 1st, 1967, Maureen Kane; two *d*; 2nd, 1980, Pauline Bridget Haughian. *Educ:* Exmouth Grammar Sch., Devon. Reporter, Exmouth and East Devon Journal, 1958; Sub-Editor, Woodrow Wyatt Newspapers, 1960; Editor, Wallingford News, Berks, 1962; Dep. Editor, Birmingham Planet, 1964–66; Birmingham Evening Mail: Sub-Editor, 1966; Dep. Features Editor, 1972; Chief Sub-Editor, 1976; Asst Editor, 1981; Dep. Editor, 1985. Bd Mem., Birmingham Post & Mail Ltd, 1992–2001. Chm., W Midlands Reg. Guild of Editors, 1994; Mem., Code of Practice Cttee, Newspaper and Magazine Publishing in the UK, 1996–2001. Pres., Black Country Olympics Cttee, 1985–94; Mem. Foundn Bd, Solihull Coll., 1994–98. Chm., Birmingham Mail Christmas Tree Fund, 1992–2001; Member: Bd, Birmingham Jazz Festival, 1996–2001; Birmingham Town Hall Adv. Panel, 1999–2001. Fellow, RSPB, 1987. *Recreations:* the countryside, gardening.

**DOWELL, Prof. John Derek,** FRS 1986; CPhys, FInstP; Poynting Professor of Physics, University of Birmingham, 1997–2002, now Emeritus; *b* 6 Jan. 1935; *s* of William Ernest Dowell and Elsie Dorothy Dowell (*née* Jarvis); *m* 1959, Patricia Clarkson; one *s* one *d*. *Educ:* Coalville Grammar Sch., Leics; Univ. of Birmingham (BSc, PhD). CPhys, FInstP 1987. Research Fellow, Univ. of Birmingham, 1958–60; Res. Associate, CERN, Geneva, 1960–62; University of Birmingham: Lectr, 1962–70; Sen. Lectr, 1970–75; Reader, 1975–80; Prof. of Elementary Particle Physics, 1980–97. Vis. Scientist, Argonne Nat. Lab., USA, 1968–69. CERN, Geneva: Scientific Associate, 1973–74, 1985–87; Mem., Scientific Policy Cttee, 1982–90, 1993–96; Co-spokesman, UA1 Experiment (discovery of W and Z particles), 1985–88; Mem., Res. Bd, 1993–96; Chairman: Large Electron Positron Collider Cttee, 1993–96; Collaboration Bd, ATLAS experiment, 1995–97 (discovery of Higgs Boson, 2012); Mem., ATLAS Exec. Cttee, 1995–98. Mem., Nuclear Physics Bd, 1974–77, 1981–85, Chm., Particle Physics Cttee, 1981–85, SERC; Member: Eur. Cttee for Future Accelerators, 1989–93; BBC Science Consultative Gp, 1992–94; Deutsches Elektronen Synchrotron Extended Scientific Council, 1992–98; PPARC, 1994–97. Mem., Panel for Physics, 2001 RAE, HEFCE. Vice Pres. and Mem. Council, Royal Soc., 1997–98. Lay Chm., Birmingham Children's Hosp. NHS Trust, 2004–12. Mem. Court, Univ. of Warwick, 1992–2001. Fellow, APS, 2004. Rutherford Prize and Medal, InstP, 1988. *Publications:* numerous, in Phys. Letters, Nuovo Cimento, Nuclear Phys., Phys. Rev., Proc. Royal Soc., and related literature. *Recreations:* piano, amateur theatre, golf. *Address:* 57 Oxford Road, Moseley, Birmingham B13 9ES; School of Physics and Astronomy, University of Birmingham, Birmingham B15 2TT.

**DOWER, Michael Shillito Trevelyan,** CBE 1996; Director-General, Countryside Commission, 1992–96; *b* 15 Nov. 1933; *s* of late John Gordon Dower and Pauline Dower; *m* 1960, Agnes Done; three *s*. *Educ:* Leys Sch., Cambridge; St John's Coll., Cambridge (MA); University Coll. London (DipTP). MRTPI, MRICS. Town Planner: LCC, 1957–59; Civic Trust, 1960–65; Amenity and Tourism Planner, UN Develt Prog., Ireland, 1965–67; Dir, Dartington Amenity Res. Trust and Dartington Inst., Devon, 1967–85; Nat. Park Officer, Peak Park Jt Planning Bd, 1985–92. Vis. Prof., Univ. of Glos (formerly Cheltenham and Gloucester Coll. of HE), 1996–. Co-ordinator, PREPARE Partnership for Rural Europe, 2000–06, 2014–16; Jt Co-ordinator, Eur. Rural Parlt, 2014–16. Chm., Public Inquiry into Foot and Mouth Disease in Northumberland, 2002. Member: Sports Council, 1965–72; English Tourist Bd, 1969–76; Founder Chm., Rural Voice, 1980; European Council for Village and Small Town: Pres., 1986–90; Sec.-Gen., 1995–2000; Vice-Pres., 2000–04. Vice-President: YHA, 1996–2017 (Ambassador, 2017–); TCV (formerly BTCV), 1996–; Scottish Campaign for Nat. Parks, 2009–; Hon. Councillor, Rural Buildings Preservation Trust, 1996–2000; Patron: Landscape Design Trust, 1997–2018; Acad. for Sci. of Acting, 2004–; Dorset Nat. Park CIC, 2018–. Mem. Exec. Cttee, S Dorset (formerly Chalk and Cheese) Local Action Gp (Dorset), 2013–; Co-founder and Coordinator, Beaminster Area Eco Gp, 2018–. Ambassador: Nat. Forest Co., 2011–; Internat. Terraced Landscapes Alliance, 2016–. Trustee, Afghanaid, 2002–03. Gov., Beaminster Sch., 2019–. Hon. FLI 1995. Hon. DSc Plymouth, 1994. *Publications:* Fourth Wave, 1965; Hadrian's Wall, 1976; (jtly) Leisure Provision and People's Needs, 1981; (jtly) Community Spirit Wins, 2013; Rubbish! A history of refuse disposal in the Beaminster area,

2014; Empowering Rural Stakeholders in the Western Balkans, 2014; Wood you Know, 2017; research and consultancy reports. *Recreations:* walking, landscape painting, sculpture, travel, woodland management. *Address:* 6 Newtown, Beaminster, Dorset DT8 3EW.

**DOWLER, Ven. Dr (Robert) Edward (Mackenzie);** Archdeacon of Hastings, since 2016; *b* Highgate, 1967; *s* of Robert Dowler and Catherine Dowler; *m* 1999, Anna Tims; one *s* one *d*. *Educ:* Harrow Sch.; Christ Church, Oxford (BA 1989); Selwyn Coll., Cambridge (BA 1993); Westcott House, Cambridge; Durham Univ. (PhD 2007). Ordained deacon, 1994, priest, 1995; Assistant Curate: Christ Church, Southgate, 1994–97; St Mary, Somers Town, 1997–2001; Dir of Pastoral Theology, 2001–09, Vice Principal, 2003–09, St Stephen's House, Oxford; Vicar, St John and St Luke, Enfield, 2010–16. *Publications:* (with B. Clover) An Everlasting Gift, 2004; SCM Core Text in Theological Ethics, 2011; The Church and the Big Society, 2013; Inclusive Gospel, 2015. *Recreations:* cooking, reading, playing the piano. *Address:* Beechmount, Beacon Road, Crowborough, E Sussex TN6 1UQ. *T:* 07990 675242. *E:* archhastings@chichester.anglican.org.

**DOWLEY, Dominic Myles;** QC 2002; *b* 25 March 1958; *s* of late Laurence Edward Dowley and Audrey Virginia Dowley (*née* Jorgensen); *m* 1985, Emma Sian Elizabeth (*née* Lewis); five *d*. *Educ:* Ampleforth Coll., Yorks; New Coll., Oxford (MA Hons). Called to the Bar, Gray's Inn, 1983. *Address:* 6 New Square, Lincoln's Inn, WC2A 3QS. *Clubs:* Garrick, MCC; Royal West Norfolk Golf.
*See also* L. J. Dowley.

**DOWLEY, (Laurence) Justin,** FCA; Chairman, Melrose Industries (formerly Melrose) plc, since 2019 (non-executive Director, since 2011); *b* Leicester, 9 June 1955; *s* of late Laurence Edward Dowley and Audrey Virginia Dowley (*née* Jorgensen); *m* 1st, 1980, Sarah Hamilton-Fairley (marr. diss. 1984); 2nd, 1986, Emma Louise Lampard; two *s* two *d*. *Educ:* Ampleforth; Balliol Coll., Oxford (BA Mod. Hist.; MA). Price Waterhouse, 1977–80; Morgan Grenfell & Co., 1981–96, Dir, 1988–96; Merrill Lynch, 1996–2001, Co-Hd, Investment Banking, Europe, 1999–2001; Founder Partner, Tricorn Partners, 2003–09; Vice Chm., Nomura Internat. plc, 2010–11. Chm., Intermediate Capital Gp plc, 2010–16 (non-exec. Dir, 2006–10); non-executive Director: Wyevale Garden Centres plc, 2001–06; Bridgewell Gp plc, 2001–07; Sporting Exchange Ltd, 2005–06; Ascot Authy (Hldgs) Ltd, 2008–15; Ind. Port Handling Ltd, 2009–16; Scottish Mortgage Investment Trust plc, 2015–; Novae Gp plc, 2015–17; JP Boden & Co. Ltd, 2016–; Chm., Greenhouse Sports, 2014–15. Non-exec. Dir, Nat. Crime Agency, 2013–16. Dep. Chm., Takeover Panel, 2018–. Mem. Adv. Bd, Open Europe, 2008–. Chm., Lord Mayor of London's Appeal, 2011–12. Gov., St Francis of Assisi Sch., Notting Hill, 1986–2003; Mem., Develt Council, RNT, 1993–2006; Endowment Trustee, 2008–14, Mem., Investment Cttee, 2014–, Balliol Coll., Oxford; Trustee, New Schools Network, 2012–. Liveryman, Gunmakers' Co., 2015. *E:* justin@dowley.me. *Clubs:* Boodle's, Garrick, Jockey (Steward, 2017–), MCC (Treas., 2006–12); Royal West Norfolk Golf; Aldeburgh Golf; Royal St George's (Sandwich).
*See also* D. M. Dowley.

**DOWLING, Prof. Dame Ann Patricia, (Dame Ann Hynes),** OM 2015; DBE 2007 (CBE 2002); PhD, ScD; FRS 2003; FREng; FIMechE; FRAeS; Professor of Mechanical Engineering, 1993–2019, now Emeritus, and Deputy Vice-Chancellor, 2013–14 and 2015–19, University of Cambridge (Head, Department of Engineering, 2009–14); Fellow, Sidney Sussex College, Cambridge, since 1979; President, Royal Academy of Engineering, 2014–19; *b* 15 July 1952; *d* of Mortimer Joseph Patrick Dowling and Joyce Dowling (*née* Barnes); *m* 1974, Dr Thomas Paul Hynes. *Educ:* Ursuline Convent Sch., Westgate, Kent; Girton Coll., Cambridge (BA 1973; MA 1977; PhD 1978; ScD 2006). CEng, FIMechE 1990 (Hon. FIMechE 2011); FREng (FEng 1996); FRAeS 1997; Fellow, Inst. Acoustics, 1989. Cambridge University: Res. Fellow, 1977–78, Dir of Studies in Engrg, 1979–90, Sidney Sussex Coll.; Asst Lectr in Engrg, 1979–82; Lectr, 1982–86; Reader in Acoustics, 1986–93; Dep. Hd, Engrg Dept, 1990–93, 1996–99. Jerome C. Hunsaker Vis. Prof., MIT, 1999–2000; Moore Dist. Schol., CIT, 2001–02. Member: AIAA, 1990; Defence and Aerospace Technology Foresight Panel, 1994–97; Defence Sci. Adv. Council, 1998–2001; EPSRC, 2001–06 (Mem., 1998–2002, Chm., 2003–06, Technical Opportunities Panel). Non-executive Director: DRA, 1995–97; BP plc, 2012–; BIS, 2014–16; BEIS, 2016–18; Smiths Gp plc, 2018–. Mem. Scientific Adv. Bd, DERA, 1997–2001. Member, Council: Royal Acad. of Engrg, 1998–2002 (Vice-Pres., 1999–2002); Royal Soc., 2009–10. Trustee: Ford of Britain Trust, 1993–2002; Cambridge European Trust, 1994–2014; Nat. Mus. of Sci. and Industry, 1999–2008; Foundn of Queen Elizabeth II Prize for Engrg, 2014–19; Cambridge Commonwealth, European and Internat. Trust, 2016–; Trustee and Council Mem., Royal Foundn for Sci. and Technology, 2014–19. Gov., Felsted Sch., 1994–99. Foreign Associate: French Acad. of Scis, 2007; US NAE, 2008; MAE 2009; Fellow, AIAA, 2011; Foreign Mem., Chinese Acad. of Engrg, 2018. Honorary Fellow: Internat. Inst. of Acoustics and Vibration, 2017; Cambridge Philosophical Soc., 2018. Hon. ScD: TCD, 2008; Kent, 2013; KTH Royal Inst. of Technol., Stockholm, 2013; Oxford, 2015; Hon. DSc(Eng): QUB, 2015; Leeds, 2015; Hon. DEng: London South Bank, 2015; Heriot-Watt, 2015; Cranfield, 2016; Leicester, 2016; Strathclyde, 2016; Lincoln, 2018; Hon. DTech Loughborough 2016; DUniv Huddersfield 2016; Hon. DSc: Northumbria, 2016; Royal Holloway, London, 2018; McGill, 2019; Hon. Dr Tech. Univ. of Eindhoven, 2018. A. B. Wood Medal, Inst. of Acoustics, 1990; Sugden Prize, Combustion Inst., 2012; Kate Gleason Award, Amer. Soc. of Mech. Engrs, 2013; Inst. of Acoustics Engrg Medal, 2014; James Watt Internat. Gold Medal, IMechE, 2016; Royal Medal, Royal Soc., 2019. *Publications:* (with J. E. Ffowcs Williams) Sound and Sources of Sound, 1983; (with D. G. Crighton *et al.*) Modern Methods in Analytical Acoustics, 1992; contribs to scientific and engrg jls, mainly on fluid mechanics, combustion, vibration and acoustics. *Recreations:* opera, walking, travelling. *Address:* Engineering Department, Cambridge University, Trumpington Street, Cambridge CB2 1PZ. *T:* (01223) 332739.

**DOWLING, Prof. Patrick Joseph,** CBE 2001; DL; PhD; FRS 1996; FREng; Chairman, British Science Association (formerly British Association for the Advancement of Science), 2005–09; Vice President, Community Foundation for Surrey, since 2015 (Founder Chairman, 2005–14); *b* 23 March 1939; *s* of John Dowling and Margaret McKittrick, Dublin; *m* 1966, Grace Carmine Victoria Lobo, *d* of Palladius Lobo and Marcilia Moniz, Zanzibar; one *s* one *d*. *Educ:* Christian Brothers Sch., Dublin; University Coll., Dublin (BE NUI 1960); Imperial Coll. of Science and Technol., London (DIC 1961; PhD 1968; FIC 1997). FRINA 1985; FIStructE 1978; FICE 1979; FREng (FEng 1981); FCGI 1989; FIAE 2000. Demonstr in Civil Engrg, UC Dublin, 1960–61; Post-grad. studies, Imperial Coll., London, 1961–65; Bridge Engr, British Constructional Steelwork Assoc., 1965–68; Imperial Coll., London: Res. Fellow, 1968–74; Reader in Structural Steelwork, 1974–79; British Steel Prof. of Steel Structures, 1979–94; Hd of Civil Engrg Dept, 1985–94; Vice Chancellor and Chief Exec., Univ. of Surrey, 1994–2005. Partner, Chapman and Dowling, Consulting Engineers, 1981–94. Chm., Eurocode 3 (Steel Structures) Drafting Cttee, 1981–94. Mem. UK Bd, UUK, 2000–05. Member: Council, RHBNC, 1990–95; Governing Authy, University Coll., Dublin, 2009–13. Pres., IStructE, 1994–95; Chairman: Steel Construction Inst., 1998–2002; Engrg Council, 2002–03 (Senator, 1996–2002); Mem., Engrg Technology Bd, 2002–08. Chm., Govt Expert Adv. Panel on SS Montgomery, 2018–. Foreign Member: Nat. Acad. of Engrg, Korea, 1997; Serbian (formerly Yugoslav) Acad. of Engrg, 2003; Corresponding Member: Nat. Acad. of Engrg of Argentina, 2001; Nat. Acad. of Exact, Physical and Natural Scis, Argentina, 2001. Non-executive Director: DSTL, 2005–08; Ploughshare Innovations Ltd, 2006–08. Patron, Yvonne Arnaud Th., 2007– (Mem. Bd of Trustees, 2002–07). Editor, Jl of Constructional Steel Research, 1980–2005. DL Surrey, 1999. Hon. Mem., RIA, 2007. Hon. LLD: NUI, 1995; Roehampton, 2005; Hon. DSc: Vilnius Tech. Univ., 1996; Ulster, 1998; Hon. PhD Kuopio, 2005; DUniv Surrey, 2006. Institution of Structural Engineers: Oscar Faber Award, 1971; Henry Adams Medal, 1976; Guthrie Brown Medal, 1979; Oscar Faber Medal, 1985, 1996; Telford Premium, ICE, 1976; Gustave Trasenster Medal, Assoc. des Ingénieurs sortis de l'Univ. de Liège, 1984; Silver Medal, RINA, 1993; Curtin Medal, ICE, 1993; James Alfred Ewing Medal, ICE, 2006. *Publications:* Steel Plated Structures, 1977; Buckling of Shells in Offshore Structures, 1982; Structural Steel Design, 1988; Constructional Steel Design, 1992; technical papers on elastic and inelastic behaviour and design of steel and composite land-based and offshore structures. *Recreations:* travelling, theatre, reading, the enjoyment of good company. *Address:* A4 Trinity Gate, Epsom Road, Guildford, Surrey GU1 3PJ. *Clubs:* Athenæum, Chelsea Arts; Guildford County; National Yacht of Ireland.

**DOWLING, Sir Robert,** Kt 2002; Chairman, Board of Trustees and Education Committee, St George's School, Edgbaston, Birmingham, since 2015 (Headmaster, 2009–15); *s* of Nicholas and Elizabeth Dowling; *m* 1967, Helen Bernadette Ryan; two *s* one *d*. *Educ:* St Mary's Univ. Coll., Twickenham (qualified teacher, London Univ.); Cambridge Inst. of Educn (Dip Exp. Psychology); Univ. of Nottingham (MEd); University Coll. Northampton (Dip SPLD); Birmingham City Univ. (MA Writing). Headmaster: Collingwood Sch., Birmingham, 1976–90; Selly Oak Special Sch., Birmingham, 1990–96; Uffculme Sch., Birmingham, 1996–98; George Dixon Internat. Sch., Birmingham, 1998–2008. Chm., Bd of Trustees, George Dixon Acad., 2009–. Sen. Educn Advr, Birmingham LEA, 1988–92. Non-exec. Chm., Care Through the Millennium, 2010– (CEO, 2009). Member: Catenian Assoc.; Birmingham and Edgbaston Debating Soc. *Recreations:* golf, theatre, music, reading, debating. *Address:* St George's School, 31 Calthorpe Road, Edgbaston, Birmingham B15 1RX. *Club:* Edgbaston Golf.

**DOWN AND CONNOR, Bishop of, (RC),** since 2008; **Most Rev. Noel Treanor;** *b* Silverstream, Co. Monaghan, 25 Dec. 1950. *Educ:* St Patrick's Coll., Maynooth; Pontifical Gregorian Univ., Rome. Ordained priest, 1976; Asst Priest, Dio. of Clogher, 1980; Dir of Studies, Pontifical Irish Coll. in Rome, 1981–85; Sec. Gen., Commn of Bishops' Conferences of European Community, 1993–2008. *Address:* Lisbreen, 73 Somerton Road, Belfast BT15 4DE. *T:* (028) 9077 6185.

**DOWN, Ven. Philip Roy;** Archdeacon of Ashford, 2011–17; *b* 28 March 1953; *s* of Keith Phillip Down and Ivy Olive Down; *m* 1972, Christine Mary Oakley; one *s* three *d*. *Educ:* Royal Melbourne Inst. of Technol. (Dip. Applied Sci. 1976); Melbourne Coll. of Divinity (BTh 1982, MTh 1988); Hull Univ. (MA 1993). Medical scientist: Dept of Pathology, Austin Hosp., Melbourne, 1971–76; Macleod Pathology Services, Melbourne, 1976–78; Siddons Fellow (postgrad. teaching fellowship), Melbourne Coll. of Divinity, 1982; Minister, Brighton Parish, Uniting Ch in Aust., 1983–86; Associate Minister, British Methodist Conf., Scunthorpe Circuit and Westcliffe LEP, and Chaplain (part-time), Scunthorpe Gen. Hosp., 1986–89; ordained deacon and priest, 1989; Curate, 1989–91, Team Vicar, 1991–95, Grimsby; Rector, St Stephen's, Canterbury, 1995–2002; Area Dean of Canterbury, 1999–2002; Archdeacon of Maidstone, 2002–11. *Recreations:* opera, poetry, music, natural history, travel, theatre, cinema, dogs.

**DOWN, Rt Rev. William John Denbigh;** Assistant Bishop of Leicester and Priest-in-charge, St Mary, Humberstone, 1995–2001; Hon. Assistant Bishop, Diocese of Oxford, since 2001; *b* 15 July 1934; *s* of late William Leonard Frederick Down and Beryl Mary Down (*née* Collett); *m* 1960, Sylvia Mary Aves; two *s* two *d*. *Educ:* Farnham Grammar School; St John's Coll., Cambridge (BA 1957; MA 1961); Ridley Hall, Cambridge. Deacon 1959, priest 1960, Salisbury: Asst Curate, St Paul's Church, Salisbury, 1959–63; Chaplain, Missions to Seamen, 1963–74: South Shields, 1963–65; Hull, 1965–71; Fremantle, WA, 1971–74; Dep. Gen. Secretary, Missions to Seamen 1975, Gen. Sec. 1976–90; Chaplain, St Michael Paternoster Royal, 1976–90; Hon. Asst Curate, St John's, Stanmore, 1975–90; Bishop of Bermuda, 1990–95. Hon. Canon of Gibraltar, 1985–90, of Kobe, 1987–. Chaplain RANR, 1972–74. Hon. Chaplain, Worshipful Co. of Carmen, 1977–90 (Hon. Chaplain Emeritus, 1990), of Farriers, 1983–90 (Hon. Chaplain Emeritus, 1990), of Innholders, 1983–90. Freeman, City of London, 1981. Hon. FNI 1991. *Publications:* On Course Together, 1989; (contrib.) Chaplaincy, 1999; Down to the Sea (autobiog.), 2004; The Bishop's Bill of Fare, 2005; contrib. to Internat. Christian Maritime Assoc. Bulletin. *Recreations:* sport (keen follower of soccer, cricket, golf), ships and the sea, travel, walking. *Address:* 54 Dark Lane, Witney, Oxon OX28 6LX. *T:* (01993) 706615. *E:* Bishbill@aol.com. *Club:* MCC.

**DOWNE,** 12th Viscount *cr* 1680; **Richard Henry Dawnay;** Bt 1642; Baron Dawnay of Danby (UK) 1897; *b* 9 April 1967; *o s* of 11th Viscount Downe and of Alison Diana (*née* Sconce); *S* father, 2002. *Educ:* Eton; Durham Univ. FCA 1992. Chm., Dawnay Estates Ltd, 2002–. Bledisloe Gold Medal, RASE, 2018. *Heir: cousin* Thomas Payan Dawnay, *b* 24 July 1978.

**DOWNER, Hon. Alexander John Gosse,** AC 2013; Executive Chair, International School for Government, King's College London, since 2018; *b* 9 Sept. 1951; *s* of Hon. Sir Alexander Downer, KBE and of Mary Downer (*née* Gosse); *m* 1978, Nicola Robinson; one *s* three *d*. *Educ:* Geelong GS, Vic; Radley Coll., Oxford; Univ. of Newcastle upon Tyne (BA Hons Pol. and Econs). Economist, Bank of NSW, Sydney, 1975–76; Australian Diplomatic Service, 1976–82: Mission to EEC, Representation to NATO, and Belgium and Luxembourg, 1977–80; Sen. Foreign Affairs Rep., S Australia, 1981; political advr to Prime Minister and Federal Leader of Opposition, 1982–83; Exec. Dir, Australian Chamber of Commerce, 1983–84. MP (L) Mayo, SA, 1984–July 2008; Shadow Minister: for Arts, Heritage and Envmt, 1987; for Housing, Small Business and Customs, 1988–89; for Trade and Trade Negotiations, 1990–92; for Defence, 1992–93; Shadow Treas., 1993–94; Leader of Opposition, 1994–95; Shadow Minister for Foreign Affairs, 1995–96; Minister for Foreign Affairs, 1996–2007. UN Special Advr on Cyprus, 2008–14; High Comr for Australia in UK, 2014–18. Non-executive Director: CQS, 2018–; Yellowcake plc. Chm., Trustees, Policy Exchange, 2017–; Mem., Bd of Trustees, Internat. Crisis Gp, 2018–. Mem. Bd, Adelaide SO, 2009–10. Hon. DCL: Newcastle; Hon. Dr: Adelaide; S Australia. *Recreations:* reading, music, tennis, golf. *Clubs:* White's; Adelaide.

**DOWNER, Dame Jocelyn Anita;** *see* Barrow, Dame J. A.

**DOWNER, Prof. Martin Craig;** Emeritus Professor, University College London, since 2009 (Hon. Professor, University of London, 1996–2009); Hon. Professor, University of Manchester, since 1996; writer and independent oral health consultant; *b* 9 March 1931; *s* of Dr Reginald Lionel Ernest Downer and Mrs Eileen Maud Downer (*née* Craig); *m* 1961, Anne Catherine (*née* Evans); four *d*. *Educ:* Shrewsbury Sch.; Univ. of Liverpool; Univ. of Manchester (PhD 1974; DDS 1989); Univ. of London; Bath Spa Univ. (MA 2010). LDSRCS 1958; DDPH RCS 1969. Dental Officer, St Helens Local Authority, 1958–59; gen. dental practice, 1959–64; Dental Officer, Bor. of Haringey, 1964–67; Principal Dental

Officer, Royal Bor. of Kensington and Chelsea, 1967–70; Res. Fellow in Dental Health, Univ. of Manchester, 1970–74; Area Dental Officer, Salford HA (also Hon. Lectr, Univ. of Manchester), 1974–79; Chief Dental Officer, SHHD (also Hon. Sen. Lectr, Univs of Edinburgh and Dundee), 1979–83; Chief Dental Officer (Under Sec.), Dept of Health (formerly DHSS), 1983–90; Prof. and Head of Dept, Dental Health Policy, and Hon. Consultant in Dental Public Health, Eastman Dental Inst., London Univ., 1990–96; Dir, Oral Health Consultancy Services, 1996–2010. Distinguished Scientist Award for Behavioural, Epidemiological and Health Services Res., Internat. Assoc. for Dental Res., 2010. *Publications:* contribs to books and papers in learned jls in gen. field of dental public health, incl. epidemiology and biostatistics, clin. trials and trial methodology, inf. systems, health services res., and econs of dental care. *Recreations:* creative writing, music, reading, cookery, natural history, vintage aviation, walking. *Address:* 1 Middle Croft, Stapleton, Shrewsbury SY5 7EA. *T:* (01743) 719413.

**DOWNES, Sir (Charles) Peter,** Kt 2015; OBE 2004; PhD; FMedSci, FRSE, FRSB; Principal and Vice Chancellor, 2009–18, and Professor of Biochemistry, 1989–2018, University of Dundee, now Principal Emeritus and Professor Emeritus; *b* Manchester, 15 Oct. 1953; *s* of George Downes and Ada Downes; *m* 1983, Elizabeth Naomi Hodgson; one *d* (one *s* decd). *Educ:* King's Sch., Macclesfield; Stockport Coll. of Technol. (HNC Applied Biol. 1975; MIBiol 1978); Univ. of Birmingham (PhD 1981). Scientific Officer, ICI Pharmaceuticals, 1973–78; MRC Trng Fellow, Univ. of Cambridge, 1981–83; Biosci. Gp Leader, ICI Pharmaceuticals, 1983–85; Cellular Pharmacologist, Smith Kline and French, then SmithKline Beecham, 1985–89; University of Dundee: Dean, Life Scis, 2000–06; Hd, Coll. of Life Scis, 2006–09. FRSE 1990; FRSB (FSB 2009); FMedSci 2010. *Publications:* over 200 biochem. and cell biol. articles in jls. *Recreations:* football (past player, current supporter), golf, cycling, skiff rowing.

**DOWNES, Prof. David Malcolm;** Professor of Social Administration, London School of Economics, 1987–2003, now Emeritus; *b* 26 Aug. 1938; *s* of Bernice Marion Downes and Herman Leslie Downes; *m* 1961, Susan Onaway Correa-Hunt; one *s* two *d*. *Educ:* King Edward VII Grammar Sch., Sheffield; Keble Coll., Oxford (BA Hons Mod. Hist. 1959); LSE (PhD Criminology 1964). London School of Economics: Asst Lectr, Lectr, Sen. Lectr in Social Admin, 1963–82; Reader, 1982–87; Dir, Mannheim Centre for Criminology and Criminal Justice, 1998–2003; Vice-Chm., Academic Bd, 1996–99. Sen. Res. Fellow, Nuffield Coll., Oxford, 1970–72. Visiting Professor/Academic Visitor: Univ. of California at Berkeley, 1975; Univ. of Toronto, 1977; Free Univ. of Amsterdam, 1981; Univ. of Bologna, 1991. British Mem., Harvard Internat. Seminar, 1966. Member, Council: Centre for Crime and Justice Studies, KCL, 1998–2008; Liberty, 2003–09. Mem., Family Commn, Nat. Family and Parenting Inst., 2004–05. Mem., BFI. Editor, British Jl of Criminology, 1985–90. Jt Official Historian, Criminal Justice System, 2009–. *Publications:* The Delinquent Solution, 1966, 3rd edn 1973; Gambling, Work and Leisure, 1976; (ed with Paul Rock) Deviant Interpretations, 1979; (with Paul Rock) Understanding Deviance, 1982, 7th edn (with Eugene McLaughlin) 2016; Contrasts in Tolerance: postwar penal policy in the Netherlands and England and Wales, 1988; (ed) Crime and the City: essays in memory of John Mays, 1989; (ed) Unravelling Criminal Justice, 1992; (ed jtly) Crime, Social Control and Human Rights: from moral panics to states of denial - essays in honour of Stanley Cohen, 2007; (ed jtly) The Eternal Recurrence of Crime and Control: essays in honour of Paul Rock, 2010; Working Out of Crime, 2012. *Recreations:* modern literature, cinema, theatre. *Address:* 140 Poplar Road South, Merton Park, SW19 3JY. *T:* (020) 8715 2212.

**DOWNES, Giles Patrick Stretton,** CVO 1998; Partner, Sidell Gibson Partnership, 1988–2011, consultant architect and sculptor, since 2011; *b* 11 Nov. 1947; *s* of late George Stretton Downes, CBE; *m* 1989, Jessica Jane Harness; one *d*. *Educ:* Wimbledon Coll.; Kingston Coll. of Art (DipArch 1972). ARCUK 1973; RIBA 1989. Foster Associates, 1969–73; Farrell Grimshaw Partnership, 1973–74; joined Sidell Gibson Partnership, 1974: Associate in charge of Housing Projects, 1980; Equity Partner, 1988–2011. *Projects* include: Sheltered Housing Schemes for English Courtyard Assoc., 1978– (Housing Design Awards, 1983 (2), 1987 (3), 1989, 1991, 1993 (2)); Redevelt of Winchester Peninsula Barracks, 1988; Prince of Wales Sch., Dorchester, 1992; Thomas Hardye Sch., Dorchester, 1993; New Design Areas for Fire Restoration of Windsor Castle, 1994 (Bldg of the Year award, Royal Fine Art Commn, for Lantern Lobby, RIBA Award, RICS Conservation Award, 1998; Carpenters Special Award, 1999; Europa Nostra Conservation Award, 2000); 3 Sheldon Square, Paddington (British Council for Offices Award, 2003); 7–10 Old Bailey, 2009 ((jtly) Best New Global Design, Chicago Athenaeum Internat. Architecture Awards, 2010). Exhibitions of sculpture: Artshow, France, 2014, 2017; Parallax, London, 2014; RiberArt, France, 2017; (solo) The Gall., London, 2018. Mem., Fabric Cttee, Royal Albert Hall, 2007–16. Mem., IWSc: Wood Technol. Soc., Inst. of Materials, Minerals and Mining (formerly Inst. of Wood Science), 2008–. Gov., Building Crafts Coll., 2002– (Chm., 2011–). Liveryman, Carpenters' Co., 2001– (Master, 2010–11); Brother, Art Workers Guild, 2012. *Publications:* (jtly) Timber in Contemporary Architecture: a designer's guide, 2009. *Recreations:* sculpture, ceramics, building craft skills, sketching.
*See also Dame J. S. Higgins.*

**DOWNES, His Honour Paul Henry;** a Circuit Judge, 1995–2011; *b* 23 Nov. 1941; *s* of Eric and Lavinia Downes; *m* 1st; two *s* one *d*; 2nd, 1986, Beverley Jill Rogers; one *s*. *Educ:* Ducie High Sch., Manchester; Coll. of Commerce, UMIST; Coll. of Law, London (Bar degree 1967); Cardiff (LLM Canon Law 2003). Deputy Magistrates' Clerk: Manchester Co. Magistrates' Court, 1960–63; Sheffield City Magistrates' Court, 1963–67; Nottingham City Magistrates' Court, 1967; County Prosecuting Service, Suffolk, 1967–71; in private practice at Norwich Bar, 1971–95; Asst Recorder, 1991–94; Recorder, 1994–95. Pres., Mental Health Review Tribunals, 2008–. Vice Chancellor, Dio. St Edmundsbury and Ipswich, 2001–; Chancellor: Dio. of Wakefield, 2007–12; Dio. of Norwich, 2007–12. Chm., Norwich Cathedral Choir Endowment Trust, 2013–. Hon. LLD UEA, 2008. *Recreations:* music, singing, chamber choir, instrumental playing, reading, walking, solo baritone singing. *Address:* The Old Chapel, Chapel Road, Sea Spalling, N Norfolk NR12 0UQ.

**DOWNES, Sir Peter;** *see* Downes, Sir C. P.

**DOWNEY, Aileen Patricia; Her Honour Judge Downey;** a Circuit Judge, since 2014; *b* Ballycastle, NI, 26 Sept. 1969. *Educ:* Rye St Antony Sch., Oxford; King's Coll., London (LLB Hons). Called to the Bar, Lincoln's Inn, 1991; barrister, 1991–2014; a Recorder, 2009–14. *Address:* c/o West London Family Court, Gloucester House, Dukes Green Avenue TW14 0LR.

**DOWNEY, Sir Gordon (Stanley),** KCB 1984 (CB 1980); Parliamentary Commissioner for Standards, 1995–98; Comptroller and Auditor General, 1981–87; *b* 26 April 1928; *s* of Stanley William and Winifred Downey; *m* 1952, Jacqueline Goldsmith; two *d*. *Educ:* Tiffin Sch.; London Sch. of Economics (BSc(Econ)). Served RA, 1946–48. Ministry of Works, 1951; entered HM Treasury, 1952; Asst Private Sec. to successive Chancellors of the Exchequer, 1955–57; on loan to Ministry of Health, 1961–62; Asst Sec., 1965, Under-Sec., 1972, Head of Central Unit, 1975; Dep. Sec., 1976–81; on loan as Dep. Head, Central Policy Review Staff, Cabinet Office, 1978–81. Special Advr, Ernst & Young (formerly Ernst & Whinney), 1988–90; Complaints Comr, The Securities Assoc., 1989–90; Chairman: FIMBRA, 1990–93; PIA, 1993. Readers' Rep., The Independent, 1990–95.

Chm., Delegacy, King's College Med. and Dental Sch., 1989–91; Mem. Council, KCL, 1989–91; FKC 2002. *Recreations:* reading, visual arts. *Address:* 137 Whitehall Court, SW1A 2EP. *T:* (020) 7321 0914. *Club:* Athenæum.

**DOWNEY, Michael Shaun;** Chief Executive Officer, Tennis Canada, 2004–13 and since 2017; *b* Toronto, 12 June 1957; *s* of Ross and Ruth Downey; *m* 2013, Jinder Chalmers; two *s*. *Educ:* Univ. of Western Ontario (HBA). Molson Canada: Sen. Vice Pres., Mktg, 2000–02; Regl Pres., 2002–04; Pres., Molson Sports and Entertainment, 2001–03; Chief Exec., LTA, 2014–17. Pres., Toronto Humane Soc., 2010–11.

**DOWNIE, Caren;** Brand Director and Founder, Finery London, 2014–17; *b* Enfield, 24 Dec. 1960; *d* of Roger and Margaret Wheaton; *m* 1988, Charles Downie. *Educ:* London Sch. of Econs (BSc Hons Internat. Trade and Develt). Began career at Warehouse, 1983, subseq. progressed via many High St names incl. French Connection, Wallis, Framework and Pilot; Buying Dir, Topshop, 2003–08; Buying Dir, Womenswear, ASOS plc, 2008–12. Mem. Panel, New Generation, British Fashion Council, 2000–; Ext. Examr, Univ. of the Arts, London (formerly London Inst.), 2000–. *Publications:* articles in Elle mag. and Daily Telegraph. *Recreations:* shopping the world, collecting expensive shoes.

**DOWNIE, Prof. Robert Silcock, (Robin),** FRSE 1986; Professor of Moral Philosophy, 1969–2002, now Emeritus, Hon. and Professorial Research Fellow, since 2002, Glasgow University; *b* 19 April 1933; *s* of late Robert Mackie Downie and late Margaret Barlas Downie; *m* 1958, Eileen Dorothea Flynn (*d* 2018); three *d*. *Educ:* The High Sch. of Glasgow; Glasgow Univ. (MA, first cl. hons, Philosophy and Eng. Lit., 1955); The Queen's Coll., Oxford (Ferguson Schol., 1958; BPhil 1959). Russian linguist, Intelligence Corps, 1955–57; Glasgow University: Lectr in Moral Philosophy, 1959; Sen. Lectr in Moral Philosophy, 1968; Stevenson Lectr in Med. Ethics, 1985–88. Visiting Professor: Philosophy, Syracuse Univ., NY, USA, 1963–64; Univ. of BC, 1997; Univ. of Sydney, 1997; Hong Kong Health Authy, 1999; Univ. of Durham, 1999–2002. FRSA 1997. *Publications:* Government Action and Morality, 1964; (jtly) Respect for Persons, 1969; Roles and Values, 1971; (jtly) Education and Personal Relationships, 1974; (jtly) Values in Social Work, 1976; (jtly) Caring and Curing, 1980; Healthy Respect, 1987; (jtly) Health Promotion: models and values, 1990; (jtly) The Making of a Doctor, 1992; (ed) Francis Hutcheson: selected writings, 1994; (ed) The Healing Arts: an Oxford anthology, 1994; Palliative Care Ethics, 1996; (ed) Medical Ethics, 1996; Clinical Judgement: evidence in practice, 2000; (jtly) The Philosophy of Palliative Care, 2006; Bioethics and the Humanities, 2007; End of Life Choices: consensus and controversy, 2009; contribs to: Mind, Philosophy, Analysis, Aristotelian Society, Political Studies, Scottish Rev. *Recreations:* music (especially composition), assorted public performances. *Address:* Department of Moral Philosophy, University of Glasgow G12 8QQ. *T:* (0141) 339 1345.

**DOWNING, Anne Elizabeth;** *see* Fleming, A. E.

**DOWNING, Carolyn Louise;** freelance sound designer, since 2003; *b* Salford, 3 May 1980; *d* of Peter Downing and Angela Gabrielle Downing; partner, David Holmes; one *d*. *Educ:* Moorside High Sch., Salford; Eccles Coll., Salford; Royal Central Sch. of Speech and Drama, London (BA 1st Cl. Hons Theatre Practice (Sound Design)). Sound designer in theatre, museum and gallery exhibns, fashion shows and film (live action and animation); theatre includes: Royal Shakespeare Co.: The Winter's Tale, Pericles, 2007; The Gods Weep; King John, 2012; Donmar Warehouse: Absurdia, 2008; Dimetos, 2009; Fathers and Sons, 2014; Teddy Ferrara, Les Liaisons Dangereuses, 2015; Frantic Assembly: Beautiful Burnout, 2010; Lovesong, The Believers, 2014; National Theatre: Double Feature, 2011; As You Like It, Our Country's Good, The Mother F***er with the Hat, Dara, 2015; Royal Court: Choir Boy, 2012; The Low Road, 2013; The Pass, Hope, 2014; other productions: All My Sons, NY, 2007; Chimerica, Almeida and West End, 2013 (Olivier Award for Best Sound Design (jtly), 2014); exhibitions include: Collider, Sci. Mus., London, 2012; Exhibitionism: The Rolling Stones, Saatchi, London, 2016; You Say You Want A Revolution?, V&A, 2016. *Recreations:* books, friends, art installation and galleries, sound art, live performance, film, travelling and exploring, playing games with my daughter, enjoying the beauty both city and countryside bring to life. *W:* www.carolyndowning.co.uk.

**DOWNPATRICK, Lord; Edward Edmund Maximilian George Windsor;** Senior Associate, Estée Lauder Companies, since 2015; Founder and Creative Director, FIDIR, since 2016; *b* 2 Dec. 1988; *s* and *heir* of Earl of St Andrews, *qv*. *Educ:* King's Coll. Sch., Cambridge; Dragon Sch., Oxford; Eton Coll.; Keble Coll., Oxford. Analyst: J P Morgan Private Bank, 2012–14; First Point Equity, 2014–15. *Clubs:* Royal West Norfolk Golf (Jun. Captain, 2005–06), Old Etonian Racquets and Tennis.

**DOWNS, Carolyn Grace,** CB 2011; Chief Executive, Brent Council, since 2015; *b* 5 Feb. 1960; *d* of Eric and Mildred Downs; *m* 1988, Prof. Jonathan Michie, *qv*; two *s*. *Educ:* Kingston Univ. (BA Hons French and Politics); UCL (Postgrad. DipLib, MA Liby and Inf. Studies). Asst Dir of Leisure Services, Stevenage BC, 1994–96; Dir of Leisure Services, Calderdale MBC, 1996–99; Corporate Dir, 1999–2003, Chief Exec., 2003–09, Shropshire CC; Dep. Perm. Sec. and Dir Gen., Corporate Perf., MoJ, 2009–10; Chief Executive: Legal Services Commn, 2010–11; Local Govt Assoc., 2011–15. *Recreations:* tennis, ski-ing, watching Manchester United. *Address:* Brent Council, Brent Civic Centre, Engineers Way, Wembley HA9 0FJ. *E:* carolyn.downs@brent.gov.uk.

**DOWNSHIRE, 9th Marquess of,** *cr* 1789 (Ire.); **Arthur Francis Nicholas Wills Hill;** Viscount Hillsborough, Baron Hill, 1717; Earl of Hillsborough, Viscount Kilwarlin, 1751; Baron Harwich (GB), 1756; Earl of Hillsborough, Viscount Fairford (GB), 1772; Baron Sandys 1802; Hereditary Constable of Hillsborough Fort; company director and landowner; *b* 4 Feb. 1959; *e s* of 8th Marquess of Downshire and Hon. Juliet Mary (*d* 1986), *d* of 7th Baron Forester; *S* father, 2003; *m* 1990, Janey, *d* of Gerald Bunting; one *s* three *d*. *Educ:* Eton College; Royal Agricultural Coll., Cirencester; Central London Polytechnic. ACA 1985. Touche Ross & Co., 1981–87; Finance Controller, 1988–89, Finance Dir, 1989–2001, Scheduling Technol. Gp Ltd; Chm., Identify UK Ltd, 2001–12; Director: Animalcare Group plc (formerly Ritchey Tagg Ltd, then Ritchey plc), 1998–; base2stay (formerly Western Heritable Apartco) Ltd, 2004–12; Farmway Ltd, 2007–14; MFB Ltd, 2010–; STL Ltd, 2011–16. Chm., Moorland Assoc., 2018–; Mem. Bd, CLA, 2019– (Chm., Yorks Br., 2014–17). Trustee, Game and Wildlife Conservation Trust; Member: Council, Duchy of Lancaster, 2018–; Rural Cttee, Duchy of Cornwall, 2017–. *Recreations:* country pursuits, sport. *Heir:* *s* Earl of Hillsborough, *qv*.

**DOWNWARD, Prof. Julian,** PhD; FRS 2005; FMedSci; Associate Research Director, Francis Crick Institute, since 2015; *b* 25 Oct. 1960; *s* of Maj.-Gen. Sir Peter Aldcroft Downward, KCVO, CB, DSO, DFC; *m* 1997, Tanya Basu; three *d*. *Educ:* Eton Coll.; Clare Coll., Cambridge (BA 1982); ICRF/Imperial Coll. London (PhD 1986). Res. Fellow, MIT, 1986–89; ICRF Laboratory, subseq. CRUK, London Research Institute: Hd, Signal Transduction Lab., 1989–2015; Principal Scientist, 1996–2015; Associate Dir, 2005–15; Team Leader, Lung Cancer Gp, Inst. of Cancer Res., London, 2012–; Sen. Scientist, Oncogene Biol. Lab., Francis Crick Inst., 2015–. Hon. Professor: Biochem. Dept, UCL 1997–; Barts and the London, Queen Mary Sch. of Medicine and Dentistry, 2004–; Immunol. Dept, KCL, 2017–; Nat. Heart and Lung Inst., Imperial Coll. London, 2017–.

Chm., British Assoc. for Cancer Res., 2016–. FMedSci 2009. Hon. FRCP 2012. *Publications:* contrib. papers on molecular biol. of cancer to scientific jls. *Recreations:* ski-ing, theatre, scuba diving, music. *Address:* Francis Crick Institute, 1 Midland Road, NW1 1AT. *E:* julian.downward@crick.ac.uk.

**DOWSE, His Honour John;** a Circuit Judge, 2001–16; a Deputy Circuit Judge, since 2016; *b* 12 Nov. 1946; *s* of Douglas Richard Maurice Dowse and Lilian Maude Dowse (*née* Cade); *m* 2000, Elaine Winstanley (*née* McLean); two step *s* one step *d*, and one *s* two *d* from former marriage. *Educ:* Univ. of Leeds (LLB Hons 1972); Univ. of Wales, Cardiff (LLM 1996). Called to the Bar, Lincoln's Inn, 1973; Asst Recorder, 1990–94; Recorder, 1994–2001; Magistrates' Court Liaison Judge, N Bank of Humberside, 2002; Designated Family Judge, Humberside, 2007–16. Judicial Mem., Parole Bd, 2016–. *Recreations:* cooking, eating out, tennis, snooker, chess. *E:* judge99@btinternet.com.

**DOWSE, Vivien Frances;** *see* Life, V. F.

**DOWSON, Prof. Duncan,** CBE 1989; FRS 1987; FREng; Professor of Engineering Fluid Mechanics and Tribology, 1966–93, now Professor Emeritus, Hon. Fellow, since 1993, and Research Professor, since 1995, Leeds University; *b* 31 Aug. 1928; *o s* of Wilfrid and Hannah Dowson, Kirkbymoorside, York; *m* 1951, Mabel, *d* of Mary Jane and Herbert Strickland; one *s* (and one *s* decd). *Educ:* Lady Lumley's Grammar Sch., Pickering, Yorks; Leeds Univ. (BSc Mech Eng. 1950; PhD 1952; DSc 1971) FIMechE; Fellow ASME 1973 (Life Fellow); FREng (FEng 1982); Fellow ASLE 1983. Research Engineer, Sir W. G. Armstrong Whitworth Aircraft Co., 1953–54; Univ. of Leeds: Lecturer in Mechanical Engineering, 1954; Sen. Lecturer, 1963; Reader, 1965; Dir, Inst. of Tribology, Dept of Mech. Engrg, 1967–87; Pro-Vice-Chancellor, 1983–85; Head of Dept of Mech. Engrg, 1987–92; Dean for Internat. Relns, 1987–93. Hon. Professor: Hong Kong Univ., 1992–2004; Bradford Univ., 1996–2003; External Prof., Loughborough Univ., 2001–; Dist. Res. Prof., Univ. of Cardiff, 2004–13. Hinton Lectr, Royal Acad. of Engrg, 1990. Pres., IMechE, 1992–93 (Chm., Tribology Group Cttee, 1967–69). Chm., Yorks Region, RSA, 1992–97. Mem., EPSRC Peer Rev. Coll., 2003–05. Hon. Citizen, Kirkbymoorside, 2008. Editor: Pt H (Engrg in Medicine), 1981–90, Pt C, Jl Mech. Engrg Sci., 1990–2008, IMechE Proceedings; WEAR, 1983–98, now Emeritus; Engrg Res. Bk Series, 1999–2003. Foreign Mem., Royal Swedish Acad. of Engrg Sciences, 1986. FCGI 1997. Hon. FIPEM 1998; Hon. Fellow, Soc. of Tribologists and Lubrication Engrs; Hon. FIMechE 2001; Hon. FRSE 2011. Hon. DTech Chalmers Univ. of Technology, Göteborg, 1979; Hon. DSc: Institut Nat. des Sciences Appliquées de Lyon, 1991; Loughborough, 2005; Dr *hc* Liège, 1996; DEng *hc*: Waterloo, Canada, 2001; Bradford, 2003; Leeds, 2004. Institution of Mechanical Engineers: James Clayton Fund Prize (jtly), 1963; Thomas Hawksley Gold Medal, 1966; James Clayton Prize, 1978; Tribology Gold Medal, 1979; James Clayton Meml Lectr, 2000; James Watt Internat. Gold Medal, 2001; (jtly) Water Arbitration Prize, 2004; Gold Medal, British Soc. of Rheology, 1969; Nat. Award, ASLE, 1974; American Society of Mechanical Engineers: Lubrication Div. Best Paper Awards (jt), 1975, 1976, 1999; Melville Medal (jt), 1976; Mayo D. Hersey Award, 1979; Engr Historian Award, 1995; first Robert Henry Thurston Award, 2000; (jtly) Tribology Best Paper Award, 1999; Kelvin Medal, ICE, 1998; Sarton Medal, Univ. of Gent, 1998. *Publications:* Elastohydrodynamic Lubrication—the fundamentals of roller and gear lubrication (jtly), 1966, 2nd edn 1977; History of Tribology, 1979, 2nd edn 1998; (jtly) An Introduction to the Biomechanics of Joints and Joint Replacement, 1981; (jtly) Ball Bearing Lubrication: The Elastohydrodynamics of Elliptical Contacts, 1981; papers on tribology and bio-medical engrg, published by: Royal Society; Instn of Mech. Engineers; Amer. Soc. of Mech. Engineers; Amer. Soc. of Lubrication Engineers. *Recreations:* genealogy, calligraphy. *Address:* Ryedale, 23 Church Lane, Adel, Leeds LS16 8DQ. *T:* (0113) 267 8933.

**DOWTON, Prof. (Stephen) Bruce,** MD; FRACP; Vice-Chancellor and President, Macquarie University, Sydney, since 2012; *b* Ivanhoe, NSW, 23 April 1956; *s* of Cecil and Ailsa V. Dowton; two *s* one *d*. *Educ:* Dubbo High Sch., NSW; Univ. of Sydney (MB BS Hons 1980; MD 1994). FRACP 1999. Internship and residency in paediatrics and Fellow of Cell Biol., Children's Hosp., Boston and Harvard Med. Sch., 1985–86; Dir, Div. of Med. Genetics, St Louis Children's Hosp., 1986–97; Washington University School of Medicine: Associate Dean for Med. Educn, 1993–96; Associate Vice-Chancellor, 1996–98; Dean, Sch. of Medicine and Prof. of Paediatrics, Univ. of NSW, 1998–2005; Clin. Prof. of Paediatrics, Harvard Med. Sch., 2009–12; CEO, Dowton Consulting Internat., 2012–. Sen. Consultant, 2007, Sen. Vice-Pres., 2007–08, Exec. Vice-Pres., 2008, Vice-Pres. and Chief Operating Officer, 2008–11, Harvard Medical Internat.; Pediatrician, Mass Gen. Hosp., 2008–12. Chair: Med. Educn and Trng Council, Australia, 2001–04; Cttee of Deans of Australian Med. Schs, 2002–04; Bd, Open Univs Australia, 2014–. Mem. Bd, Maggie Beer Foundn, 2013–16. Trustee, Art Gall. of NSW, 2015–. FACMG 1994; FAICD 2016. *Publications:* contrib. articles to jls incl. Science, Med. Jl Australia, Blood, Scandinavian Jl Immunol., Biochem., Jl Biol Chem., Amer. Jl Genetics. *Recreations:* photography, cooking. *Address:* Office of the Vice-Chancellor, Macquarie University, NSW 2109, Australia. *T:* 98507440, *Fax:* 98509950. *E:* vc@mq.edu.au.

**DOYLE, Most Rev. Adrian Leo,** AM 2009; Archbishop of Hobart (Australia), (RC), 1999–2013; *b* 16 Nov. 1936; *s* of George Leo Doyle and Gertrude Mary (*née* O'Donnell). *Educ:* Urbaniana Univ., Rome (ThL, PhL); Gregorian Univ., Rome (DCL). Ordained priest, Rome, 1961; Parish Priest, Sandy Bay, Tasmania, 1974–90; VG, Archdio. of Hobart, 1997–99; apptd Coadjutor Archbishop of Hobart, 1997, ordained bishop, 1998. Judge: Regl Marriage Tribunal, Victoria and Tasmania, 1968; Nat. Appeal Tribunal, Aust. and NZ, 1974. *Recreations:* golf, walking, reading. *Club:* Athenæum (Hobart).

**DOYLE, Dr Amanda Mary,** OBE 2014; General Practitioner Partner, Bloomfield Medical Centre, Blackpool, since 1995; Chief Clinical Officer, since 2012, and Chief Officer, Lancashire and South Cumbria, since 2016, NHS Blackpool Clinical Commissioning Group, since 2012; Co-Chair, NHS Clinical Commissioners, since 2013; *b* Liverpool, 22 Sept. 1964; *d* of John Doyle and Mary Doyle; *m* 1992, William Morrison; four *s*. *Educ:* Notre Dame High Sch.; Univ. of Manchester (MB ChB 1988). Jun. med. posts, 1988–95; Med. Dir, Blackpool PCT, 2006–12. *Recreations:* reading, family, cooking. *Address:* NHS Clinical Commissioners, 50 Broadway, SW1H 0DB; NHS Blackpool Clinical Commissioning Group, The Stadium, Seasider's Way, Blackpool FY1 6JX. *T:* (01253) 951227. *E:* amanda.doyle@blackpool.nhs.uk.

**DOYLE, Bernard;** *see* Doyle, F. B.

**DOYLE, Dr Brian John;** President, Employment Tribunals (England and Wales), since 2014; *b* 12 Jan. 1955; *s* of late Jude Doyle and Mary Doyle (*née* Clancy); *m* 1st, 1986, Antoinette Cecile Chang (marr. diss. 2006); one *d*; 2nd, 2007, Helen Rippon Wile (*née* Glover); one *d*. *Educ:* St Joseph's Primary Sch., Crayford; St Joseph's Acad., Blackheath; Queen Mary Coll., Univ. of London (LLB Hons 1976, LLM 1978); Coll. of Law, London; PhD Salford 1993. Called to the Bar, Inner Temple, 1977; Res. Asst in Law, Poly. of N London, 1978–80; Lectr in Law, 1980–88, Sen. Lectr in Law, 1988–95, Univ. of Salford; Prof. of Law, and Dean, Faculty of Law, Univ. of Liverpool, 1995–2000; Chm., Employment Tribunals, 2000–03; Regl Employment Judge (formerly Regl Chm. of Employment Tribunals), Manchester and Liverpool, 2003–14. *Publications:* New Directions Towards Disabled Workers' Rights, 1994; Disability Discrimination and Equal Opportunities, 1994; Disability Discrimination: the new law, 1995; Disability Discrimination Law and Practice, 1996, 6th edn 2008; Employment Tribunals: the new law, 1998; Equality and Discrimination: the new law, 2010; (contrib.) Tolley's Employment Law, 1994–; (contrib.) Jordans Employment Law Service, 1998–; contrib. articles to Industrial Law Jl, Modern Law Rev. *Recreations:* walking, travel, literature, computing, theatre. *Address:* Employment Tribunals (England and Wales), Victory House, 30–34 Kingsway, WC2B 6EX.

**DOYLE, David Charles,** CBE 2019; advocate; HM First Deemster and Clerk of the Rolls, Isle of Man, 2010–18; a Judge of Appeal, Courts of Jersey and Guernsey, 2015–18; *b* 26 April 1960; *s* of late David Gordon Doyle and Beatrice Lilian Doyle (*née* Cain); *m* 1991, Barbara, *d* of late John Denton and Doreen Holgate; three *s*. *Educ:* King William's Coll., I of M; Univ. of Newcastle upon Tyne (LLB 1981). Called to the Bar, Gray's Inn, 1982, Bencher, 2011; admitted to the Manx Bar, 1984; partner, Dickinson Cruickshank & Co., Advocates, 1985–2003; HM Second Deemster, I of M, 2003–10. Sen. lawyer, Litigation Dept, Cains Advocates, 2018–. Deputy High Bailiff and Coroner of Inquests, 2002–03. Isle of Man Law Society: Mem. Council, 1997–2003; Chm., Educn Cttee, 1997–2003; Chm., Human Rights Cttee, 2001–03; Vice Pres., 2003. Mem. Council, I of M Chamber of Commerce, 1997–2003; Mem., Corporate Services Review Cttee, 2001–03. Parent Governor, Peel Clothworkers' Sch., 2001. *Publications:* Manx Criminal Law and Procedure, 2010; *contributions to:* Solly's Government and Law in the Isle of Man, 1994; Solly's Isle of Man Partnership Law, 1996; International Tracing of Assets, 1998; Offshore Cases and Materials, 1999; Offshore Financing: security and insolvency, 1998; various articles on legal topics in professional jls. *Recreations:* family, Manx law past, present and future, running, walking.

**DOYLE, Elaine Mary;** *see* Griffiths, E. M.

**DOYLE, (Frederick) Bernard;** Partner, Gatenby Sanderson, 2005–09; *b* 17 July 1940; *s* of James Hopkinson Doyle and Hilda Mary Doyle (*née* Spotsworth); *m* 1963, Ann Weston; two *s* one *d*. *Educ:* St Bede's Coll.; Univ. of Manchester (BSc Hons); Harvard Business Sch., 1965–67 (MBA). CEng 1965; FICE 1980; FIWEM (FIWES 1986). Resident Civil Engineer with British Rail, 1961–65; Management Consultant with Arthur D. Little Inc., 1967–72; Booker McConnell Ltd: Secretary to Executive Cttee, 1973; Director, Engineering Div., 1973–76; Chairman, General Engineering Div., 1976–78; Chm. and Chief Exec., Booker McConnell Engineering, and Director, Booker McConnell, 1978–81; Chief Executive: SDP, 1981–83; Welsh Water Authy, 1983–87; MSL International, then MSL Search and Selection: Dir, Public Sector Ops, 1988–90; Dir, 1994–97; Man. Dir, 1997–99; Man. Dir, Hamptons, 1990–92; Gen. Manager, Bristol & West Building Soc., 1992–94; Dir, MSL Gp, 1996–99; Hd of Public Sector Practice, Hoggett Bowers Exec. Search and Selection, 1999–2000; Dir, KPMG Search and Selection, 2001–05. Chairman: Sustainability W Midlands, 2003–07; Wolverhampton Sangat Educn Trust, 2013–16. Vice-Chm., NE Worcester Coll., 1998–2002, 2003–07; Gov., Warwicks Coll., 2009– (Chm., 2011–13). CCMI (CBIM 1987); FRSA 1987. *Recreations:* sailing (Times Clipper 2000 Round the World Yacht Race), theatre, reading, walking, bird watching. *Address:* 6 Westminster Court, 3 College Road, Bromsgrove B60 2NE. *T:* (01527) 873565.

**DOYLE, Gemma;** Senior Director, FTI Consulting, since 2017; *b* Vale of Leven, 1981. *Educ:* Our Lady and St Patrick's High Sch., Dumbarton; Univ. of Glasgow (MA Eur. Civilisation). Conf. Develt Manager, 2006–07; Conf. Producer, ICE, 2007–08; Political Officer, Parly Lab Party, 2008–10. MP (Lab) W Dunbartonshire, 2010–15; contested (Lab) same seat, 2015. Shadow Minister for Defence Personnel, Welfare and Veterans, 2010–15. Contested (Lab) Scotland, EP, 2004. Member: Community Union; Co-op Party. Interim Dir, Interel, 2016–17; Associate, Global Partners Governance, 2016–.

**DOYLE, John Howard,** MBE 1995; PPRWS (RWS 1968); landscape painter; President, Royal Watercolour Society, 1996–2000; *b* 15 Feb. 1928; *s* of Eric Howard Doyle and Frances Doyle (*née* Maclean); *m* 1st, 1956, Caroline Knapp-Fisher (marr. diss.); one *s* one *d*; 2nd, 1968, Elizabeth Rickatson-Hatt; one *s* one *d*. *Educ:* Sherborne Sch. Dir, C. F. Doyle Ltd, 1961–96; Chm., Thomas Seager Ltd, 1968–86. Mem., Canterbury DAC, 1975–85 (Advr, 1985–). Founder Mem. and Chm., Romney Marsh Historic Churches Trust, 1980–90 (Pres., 1986–). Exhibitions: Chapter House, Canterbury Cathedral, 1973–76, 1997, 2008 and 2009; Spink & Sons, 1981–84, 1991, 1997; Catto Gall., 1988; Sanders of Oxford, 1999; Chris Beetles Gall., 2002; Nat. Trust, Sissinghurst Castle, 2010; Paintings of Mount Athos, Hellenic Centre, Paddington, 2014; Osborne Studio Gall., 2016; exhibitor, RA, 1982–90. Hon. RE 1996; Hon. RI 1996. *Publications:* An Artist's Journey down the Thames, 1993. *Recreations:* golf, gardening. *Address:* Church Farm, Warehorne, Ashford, Kent TN26 2LP. *Club:* Garrick.

**DOYLE, Hon. John Jeremy,** AC 2002; Chief Justice, Supreme Court of South Australia, 1995–2012; *b* 4 Jan. 1945; *s* of John Malcolm Doyle and Mary Margaret Doyle; *m* 1969, Marie McLoughlin; two *s* three *d*. *Educ:* St Ignatius Coll., Norwood; Univ. of Adelaide (LLB); Magdalen Coll., Oxford (BCL). Partner, Kelly & Co., 1970–77; called to the Bar, SA, 1970; Barrister, Hanson Chambers, 1977–86; QC (SA) 1981; Solicitor-General for S Australia, 1986–95. Pro-Chancellor, Flinders Univ. of S Australia, 1988–2001. Chm., Nat. Judicial Coll. of Australia, 2002–07. Hon. LLD Flinders, 2002; DUniv Adelaide, 2008. *Address:* c/o Chief Justice's Chambers, Supreme Court, 1 Gouger Street, Adelaide, SA 5000, Australia. *T:* (8) 82040390, *Fax:* (8) 82040442.

**DOYLE, John Michael;** freelance theatre director and writer; Artistic Director, Classic Stage Company, New York, since 2016; *b* 9 Nov. 1952; *s* of John Martin Doyle and Mary Christina Doyle; one *d*; *m* Robert Wilson. *Educ:* RSAMD (DSD); Univ. of Glasgow (CertDS). Jun. Artist-in-Residence, Univ. of Georgia, 1973–74; Dir, Tie-up Th. Co., 1975–78; Dir of Prodns, Eden Court Th., Inverness, 1979–80; Artistic Director: Swan Th., Worcester, 1982–85; Everyman Th., Cheltenham, 1985–89; Everyman Th., Liverpool, 1989–93; Theatre Royal, Yorks, 1993–97; Associate Dir, Watermill Th., Newbury, 1997–2005. Productions in NY include: Sweeney Todd (Tony Award for Best Dir of a Musical, 2006); Company; A Catered Affair; Road Show; The Visit; The Color Purple; Carmen Jones; engagements with Scottish Opera, NY Metropolitan Opera, LA Opera, American Conservatory Th., Stratford Ontario, Houston Grand Opera, Cincinnati Playhouse in the Park, Opera Australia, Royal Danish Opera. Visiting Artist: Univ. of Western Kentucky, 1997, 2000, 2003; Oregon State Univ., 2002; Artist in Residence, Pace Univ., NY, 2013–14; Prof. in Theatre, Princeton Univ., 2013–. Fellow, Rose Bruford Coll., 2004. FRSA 2001. *Publications:* (with R. Lischner) Shakespeare for Dummies, 1999; contribs to acad. textbooks. *Recreations:* music, tennis, being in Italy. *Address:* Creative Artists Agency, 405 Lexington Avenue, 19th Floor, New York, NY 10174, USA.

**DOYLE, (Michael) Leo (Haygarth),** CB 2004; Director for Policy and Resources, Government Communications Headquarters, 2003–04; *b* 14 March 1944; *s* of late James Harold Doyle and Florence Doyle (*née* Brown); *m* 1967, Barbara Sillence; two *d*. *Educ:* St John's Coll., Cambridge (Maths Tripos; BA 1965, MA 1969). Joined GCHQ, 1965; on secondment to Diplomatic Service, Washington, 1986–89. Non-exec. Dir, Great Western Ambulance Service NHS Trust, 2006–13. *Recreations:* bell-ringing, gardening. *E:* Leo.Doyle@doylehome.org.uk.

**DOYLE, Patrick;** composer of film and television scores; *b* 6 April 1953; *s* of Patrick and Sarah Doyle; *m* 1978, Lesley Howard; two *s* two *d. Educ:* Royal Scottish Acad. of Music and Drama (FRSAMD 2004). Composer and musical dir, Renaissance Th. Co., 1987–92; *compositions* include: The Thistle and the Rose (song cycle for soprano and mixed choir) to commemorate 90th birthday of the Queen Mother, 1990; *TV scores include:* Look Back in Anger; Twelfth Night; *film scores* include: Henry V, 1989 (Ivor Novello Award for Best Film Theme); Shipwrecked, 1990; Dead Again, 1991; Indochine, Into the West, 1992; Much Ado About Nothing, Carlito's Way, 1993; Frankenstein, 1994; A Little Princess (LA Critics Best Film Score), Une Femme Française, Sense and Sensibility, 1995; Mrs Winterbourne, Hamlet, 1996; Donnie Brasco, 1997; (and songs) Great Expectations, 1998; East West, 1999; Love's Labour's Lost, 2000; Bridget Jones's Diary, Gosford Park, 2001; Killing Me Softly, 2002; Calendar Girls, 2003; Nouvelle France, 2004; Man to Man, Jekyll & Hyde, Nanny McPhee, Harry Potter and the Goblet of Fire, 2005; Wah Wah, 2006; As You Like It, Pars Vite et Reviens Tard, Eragon, The Last Legion, Sleuth, 2007; Nim's Island, Igor, 2008; Jig, La Ligne Droite, Thor, Rise of the Planet of the Apes, 2011; Brave, 2012; The Enchanted Kingdom, 2013; Jack Ryan, 2014; Cinderella, 2015; A United Kingdom, Whisky Galore, 2016; Murder on the Orient Express, 2017; Sgt. Stubby: An American Hero, 2018; All Is True, 2019. *Recreations:* swimming, tennis. *Address:* c/o Air-Edel, 18 Rodmarton Street, W1U 8BJ. *T:* (020) 7486 6466, *Fax:* (020) 7224 0344. *E:* air-edel@air-edel.co.uk. *Club:* Glasgow Arts.

**DOYLE, Dr Peter,** CBE 1992; FRSE; Chairman, Biotechnology and Biological Sciences Research Council, 1998–2003; *b* 6 Sept. 1938; *s* of late Peter and Joan Penman Doyle; *m* 1962, Anita McCulloch; one *s* one *d. Educ:* Univ. of Glasgow (BSc Hons 1st class 1960; PhD 1963). FRSE 1993. Research Chemist, ICI Pharmaceuticals, 1963; Manager, Quality Control Dept, 1973–75; Manager, Chemistry Dept, 1975–77; Research Dir, ICI Plant Protection, 1977–86; Business Dir, ICI Seeds, 1985–86; Dep. Chm. and Technical Dir, ICI Pharmaceuticals, 1986–88; Res. and Technol. Dir, ICI Gp, 1989–93; Dir, Zeneca Gp, 1993–99. Dir, AFRC Rothamsted Experimental Station, 1991–98; non-exec. Dir, Oxford Molecular Group PLC, 1997–2000. Member: ACOST, 1989–93; MRC, 1990–94; Royal Commn on Envmtl Pollution, 1994–98; Central R&D Cttee for NHS, 1995–98; UK Round Table on Sustainable Develt, 1998–2000. Trustee, Nuffield Foundn, 1998–2011. Foreign Mem., Royal Swedish Acad. of Engineering Scis, 1990. Liveryman, Salters' Co., 1983 (Master, 2003–04). Hon. DSc: Glasgow, 1992; Nottingham, 1993; Dundee, 1995; Sussex, 1996. *Publications:* contribs to Chemical Communications and Jl Chem. Soc. *Recreation:* golf.

**DOYLE, Peter John;** QC 2002; *b* 29 Dec. 1951; *s* of Kenneth Charles Doyle and Margaret Doyle (*née* Porter); *m* 1977, Gail Patricia Horspool; one *s* two *d. Educ:* Portchester Sch.; Southampton Univ. (LLB Hons). Called to the Bar, Middle Temple, 1975; in practice in criminal law, particularly in serious and complex fraud and related cases; appeared in Public Inquiries incl. Stephen Lawrence, Marchioness, Victoria Climbié. Instructed on behalf of mems of Sen. Police Officers' Assoc. (ACPO ranks). Member: Proceeds of Crime Regulatory Assoc.; Assoc. of Regulatory and Disciplinary Lawyers; Financial Services Lawyers Assoc. Founding Chair and Trustee, Kalisher Scholarship Trust. Volunteer speaker for Inspiring the Future, Educn and Employers Taskforce. *Recreations:* collecting books, music, gardening. *Address:* 25 Bedford Row, WC1R 4HD. *T:* (020) 7067 1500. *E:* clerks@25bedfordrow.com.

**DOYLE, Rt Rev. Peter John Haworth;** *see* Northampton, Bishop of, (R.C).

**DOYLE, Prof. William,** DPhil; FBA 1998; FRHistS; Professor of History, 1986–2008, now Emeritus, and Senior Research Fellow, since 2008, University of Bristol; *b* 4 March 1942; *s* of Stanley Joseph Doyle and Mary Alice Bielby; *m* 1968, Christine Thomas. *Educ:* Bridlington Sch.; Oriel Coll., Oxford (BA 1964; MA, DPhil 1968). FRHistS 1976. University of York: Asst Lectr, 1967; Lectr, 1969; Sen. Lectr, 1978; Prof. of Modern History, Univ. of Nottingham, 1981–85. Visiting Professor: Univ. of S Carolina, 1969–70; Univ. de Bordeaux III, 1976; Ecole des Hautes Etudes en Sciences Sociales, Paris, 1988; Vis. Fellow, All Souls Coll., Oxford, 1991–92; Hans Kohn Mem., IAS, Princeton, 2004; Douglas Southall Freeman Prof. of History, Univ. of Richmond, Va, 2010. Jubilee Fellow, Historical Assoc., 2016. Dr *hc* Bordeaux, 1978. Chevalier des Palmes Académiques (France), 2019. *Publications:* The Parlement of Bordeaux, 1974; The Old European Order 1660–1800, 1978; Origins of the French Revolution, 1980; The Ancien Régime, 1986; (ed jtly) The Blackwell Dictionary of Historians, 1988; The Oxford History of the French Revolution, 1989; Officers, Nobles and Revolutionaries, 1995; Venality: the sale of offices in eighteenth century France, 1996; (ed jtly) Robespierre, 1999; Jansenism, 1999; La Vénalité, 2000; (ed) Old Regime France, 2001; The French Revolution: a very short introduction, 2001; Aristocracy and its Enemies in the Age of Revolution, 2009; Aristocracy: a very short introduction, 2010; (ed) The Oxford Handbook of the Ancien Regime, 2011; France and the Age of Revolution: regimes old and new from Louis XIV to Napoleon Bonaparte, 2013; Napoleon Bonaparte, 2015; The Connell Guide to Louis XIV, 2017; contribs to Past and Present, Historical Jl, French Historical Studies, Studies on Voltaire, Trans RHistS, TLS. *Recreations:* books, decorating, travelling about, historical memorabilia. *Address:* (home) Linden House, College Road, Lansdown, Bath BA1 5RR. *T:* (01225) 314341. *Clubs:* Athenæum, Oxford and Cambridge.

**DOYLE, William Patrick,** PhD; President/Proprietor, Middle East-Asia Consultants, since 1997; President, Texaco Middle East/Far East, 1991–96; *b* 15 Feb. 1932; *s* of James W. Doyle and Lillian I. Doyle (*née* Kime); *m* 1957, Judith A. Gosha; two *s* one *d* (and one *s* decd). *Educ:* Seattle Univ. (BS 1955); Oregon State Univ. (PhD 1959). Texaco, USA: Chemist, 1959; Res. Supervisor, 1966; Asst to Vice Pres. of Petrochemicals, 1968; Asst to Sen. Vice Pres. of Supply and Distribn, 1971; Asst Manager, Producing, 1972; Asst Regional Man., Marketing, 1974; Texaco Ltd: Dep. Man. Dir, 1977; Man. Dir, Exploration and Production, 1981; Vice President: Texaco Europe, 1987; Texaco Latin America and Africa, 1989. Pres., UK Offshore Operators Assoc., 1985 (Vice Pres., 1984). Mem. Council, Amer. Geographic Soc., 1994–2002 (Chm., 2000–02); Vice Chm., Forum of World Affairs, 1998. CCMI (FBIM 1980); MInstD 1982. *Publications:* contrib. Jl of Amer. Chem. Soc. *Recreations:* tennis, music, theatre. *Address:* PO Box 246, Williamsburg, VA 23187–0246, USA.

**DOYLE, Dr Yvonne Gabrielle, (Mrs M. R. Fenlon),** CB 2016; MD; FRCPI; FFPHM; FFPHMI; Medical Director and Director for Health Protection, Public Health England, since 2019; *b* Dublin, 29 Sept. 1957; *d* of Terence and Maureen Doyle; *m* 1985, Michael Robert Fenlon; one *s* one *d. Educ:* St Louis High Sch., Dublin; University Coll., Dublin (MPH 1984; MD 2008). DCH 1983; FRCPI 1996; FFPHM 1998; FFPHMI 1993. Dir, Public Health, Merton, Sutton and Wandsworth HA, 1999–2002; Dir, Public Health, and Med. Dir, SW London SHA, 2002–03; SE London SHA, 2003–06; Regl Dir, Public Health, NHS SE Coast, DoH, 2006–12; Dir, Public Health, NHS S of England, DoH, 2012–13; Dir for London, PHE, 2013–19. Vis. Prof., LSHTM, 2013–. *Publications:* contribs to peer-reviewed scientific jls. *Address:* Public Health England, Fleetbank House, 2–6 Salisbury Square, EC4Y 8JX. *E:* yvonne.doyle@phe.gov.uk.

**DOYLE-PRICE, Jackie,** MP (C) Thurrock, since 2010; *b* Sheffield, 5 Aug. 1969; *d* of Brian and Kathleen Doyle-Price. *Educ:* Notre Dame RC Sch., Sheffield; Univ. of Durham (BA Hons Econs/Politics). Asst Parly Officer, City of London, 1993–2000; Asst Private Sec. to Lord Mayor of City of London, 2000–05; Associate, FSA, 2005–10. An Asst Govt Whip, 2015–17; Parly Under-Sec. of State, DoD, then DHSC, 2017–19. Mem., Grays RAFA. *Recreations:* reading, theatre, music. *Address:* House of Commons, SW1A 0AA. *T:* (020) 7219 7171. *E:* jackie.doyleprice.mp@parliament.uk. *Club:* Grays Conservative.

**D'OYLY, Sir Hadley Gregory,** 15th Bt *cr* 1663, of Shottisham, Norfolk; *b* 29 May 1956; *o s* of Sir Nigel D'Oyly, 14th Bt and Dolores, *d* of R. H. Gregory; *S* father, 2000; *m* 1st, 1978, Margaret May Dent (marr. diss. 1982); 2nd, 1991, Annette Frances Elizabeth (*née* White); two *d. Educ:* Milton Abbey.

**DRABBLE, Jane;** *see* Drabble, M. J.

**DRABBLE, Dame Margaret, (Dame Margaret Holroyd),** DBE 2008 (CBE 1980); author; *b* 5 June 1939; 2nd *d* of His Honour J. F. Drabble, QC and late Kathleen Marie Bloor; *m* 1st, 1960, Clive Walter Swift (marr. diss. 1975; he *d* 2019); two *s* (one *d* decd) 2nd, 1982, Michael (de Courcy Fraser) Holroyd (*see* Sir Michael Holroyd). *Educ:* The Mount Sch., York; Newnham Coll., Cambridge. Lives in London and W Somerset. Chm., Nat. Book League, 1980–82 (Dep. Chm., 1978–80). E. M. Forster Award, 1973, Hon. Mem., 2002, Amer. Acad. of Arts and Letters; Hon. Fellow, Sheffield City Polytechnic, 1989. Hon. DLitt: Sheffield, 1976; Manchester, 1987; Keele, 1988; Bradford, 1988; Hull, 1992; UEA, 1994; York, 1995; Cambridge, 2006. St Louis Literary Award, St Louis Univ. Liby Associates, 2003; Golden Pen Award, 2011. *Publications:* A Summer Birdcage, 1963; The Garrick Year, 1964; The Millstone (John Llewellyn Rhys Prize), 1966 (filmed, as A Touch of Love, 1969); Jerusalem the Golden (James Tait Black Meml Prize), 1967; The Waterfall, 1969; The Needle's Eye, 1972; (ed with B. S. Johnson) London Consequences, 1972; The Realms of Gold, 1975; The Ice Age, 1977; The Middle Ground, 1980; The Radiant Way, 1987; A Natural Curiosity, 1989; The Gates of Ivory, 1991; The Witch of Exmoor, 1996; The Peppered Moth, 2001; The Seven Sisters, 2002; The Red Queen, 2004; The Sea Lady, 2006; A Day in the Life of a Smiling Woman: complete short stories, 2011; The Pure Gold Baby, 2013; The Dark Flood Rises, 2016; *non-fiction:* Wordsworth, 1966; Arnold Bennett, a biography, 1974; (ed) The Genius of Thomas Hardy, 1976; (ed jtly) New Stories 1, 1976; For Queen and Country, 1978; A Writer's Britain, 1979; (ed) The Oxford Companion to English Literature, 5th edn, 1985, 6th edn 2000; (ed with Jenny Stringer) The Concise Oxford Companion to English Literature, 1987; Safe as Houses, 1989; Angus Wilson: a biography, 1995; The Pattern in the Carpet: a personal history with jigsaws, 2009. *Recreations:* walking, dreaming. *Address:* c/o United Agents Ltd, 12–26 Lexington Street, W1F 0LE.
*See also* R. J. B. Drabble.

**DRABBLE, (Mary) Jane,** OBE 2000; Director of Education, BBC, 1994–99; Chair, Bath Festivals, 2009–14; *b* 15 Jan. 1947; *d* of late Walter Drabble and of Molly (*née* Boreham). *Educ:* Bristol Univ. (BA Hons 1968). BBC: Studio Manager, 1968–72; Producer, Radio Current Affairs, 1972–75; Asst Producer, then Producer, TV Current Affairs, 1975–87; Editor, Everyman, 1987–91; Head of Factual Progs, 1993–94, Asst Man. Dir, 1991–94, Network TV. Comr for Judicial Appts, 2001–06; Mem., Capability Reviews Team, Cabinet Office, 2006–09. Mem., LSC, 2000–06; Vice-Chm., Basic Skills Agency, 2001–04. Chair: Mental Health Media, 2002–06; Nat. Skills Academies Panel, 2005–08; Arts Award Partnership Bd, 2005–10. Mem., SW Regl Arts Council, 2012–13. Director: Birmingham Royal Ballet, 2002–10; Bournemouth SO, 2013–. Gov., 2002–, Bd Mem., 2003–12, RSC.

**DRABBLE, Richard John Bloor;** QC 1995; *b* 23 May 1950; *s* of His Honour John Frederick Drabble, QC and late Kathleen Marie Drabble; *m* 1980, Sarah Madeleine Hope Lewis; two *s* (and one *s* decd). *Educ:* Leighton Park Sch., Reading; Downing Coll., Cambridge (BA Hons). Called to the Bar, Inner Temple, 1975, Bencher, 2002; Junior Counsel to the Crown, Common Law, 1992. Chm., Administrative Law Bar Assoc., 1999–2001; Mem., Law Reform Cttee, Bar Council. *Publications:* (contrib.) Judicial Review, ed Supperstone and Goudie, 1992, 5th edn 2006; (ed) Local Authorities and Human Rights, 2004; (consultant ed.) Halsbury's Law: welfare benefits and state pensions, 2014; various articles. *Recreations:* reading, walking. *Address:* Landmark Chambers, 180 Fleet Street, EC4A 2HG. *T:* (020) 7430 1221.
*See also* Dame A. S. Byatt, Dame M. Drabble.

**DRACE-FRANCIS, Charles David Stephen,** CMG 1987; *b* 15 March 1943; *m* 1967, Griselda Hyacinthe Waldegrave; two *s* one *d. Educ:* Magdalen Coll., Oxford. HM Diplomatic Service, 1965–2001: Third Sec., FO, 1965; Tehran, 1967; Second, later First Sec., FCO, 1971; Asst Political Advr, Hong Kong, 1974; First Sec., Office of UK Rep. to EEC, Brussels, 1978; FCO, 1980; All Souls Coll., Oxford, 1983; Chargé d'affaires, Kabul, 1984; Counsellor, Lisbon, 1987; Govt Affairs Dir, BAe, 1991 (on secondment); Head, West Indian and Atlantic Dept, FCO, 1994–97; High Comr, PNG, 1997–2000. Sales asst, Hugh Macpherson (Scotland) Ltd, 2001–03. Chm., Gwalior Children's Hosp., 2002–09; Mem. Bd, 2005–09, Chm., 2007–09, PNG Church Partnership. *Publications:* (contrib.) Blue Guide to Greece, 1966; contrib. Jl of Royal Soc. for Asian Affairs. *Recreation:* sailing. *Address:* 66 Marchmont Crescent, Edinburgh EH9 1HD. *T:* (0131) 237 1891. *Club:* Elie and Earlsferry Sailing.

**DRAGO RODRÍGUEZ, Rolando;** Ambassador of Chile to the Court of St James's, 2014–18; *b* Santiago, Chile, 27 May 1953; *s* of Angel Drago and Elsa Rodríguez; *m* 1979, Edith Gallardo; one *s* one *d. Educ:* Technol. Inst. of Chile (BA 1974); Univ. Católica de Chile (MA Internat. Relns 1977); Diplomatic Acad. of Chile. Ambassador and Dir of HR, Min. of Foreign Affairs, Chile, 2005; Ambassador to Indonesia and E Timor, 2006–07; to Venezuela, 2007–09; Ambassador and Dir of Protocol, Min. of Foreign Affairs, 2009–10; Ambassador to Cuba, 2010–14. Pres., Assembly, IMO, 2017–19. *Recreations:* scuba diving, squash. *Club:* Canning.

**DRAINEY, Rt Rev. Terence Patrick;** *see* Middlesbrough, Bishop of, (R.C.).

**DRAINVILLE, Rt Rev. Dennis Paul;** Bishop of Quebec, 2009–17; *b* Joliette, Quebec, 20 Feb. 1954; *s* of Gabriel Joseph Drainville and Dorothy May Drainville (*née* Griffin); *m* 1995, Cynthia Ann Patterson; one *d. Educ:* E York Collegiate Inst., Toronto; Trinity Coll., Univ. of Toronto (BA 1978; MDiv 1982). Ordained deacon, 1982; priest, 1983; Parish Priest, Land O' Lakes, Ontario, 1982–84; Exec. Dir, STOP 103 Ministry to the Poor, Toronto, 1984; Associate Priest, Christ Church Cathedral, Montreal, 1986; Incumbent, Fenelon Falls and Coboconk, Toronto, 1987–90; Regl Dean, Victoria-Haliburton, 1989; elected to Provincial Parlt, 1990–93; Teacher, CEGEP de la Gaspésie et des Isles, Gaspé, 1994–2006; Archdeacon of Gaspé and Incumbent, Greater Parish of Gaspé, 2002–06; Missioner to Dio. of Quebec, 2006–07; Coadjutor Bishop, 2007. Hon. DD: Montreal

Diocesan Theol. Coll., 2010; Trinity Coll., Univ. of Toronto, 2015. 125th Anniv. of Confedn of Canada Medal, 1992. *Publications:* Poverty in Canada, 1985. *Recreations:* medieval studies, music.

**DRAKE**, Baroness *cr* 2010 (Life Peer), of Shene in the County of Surrey; **Jeannie Lesley Patricia Drake**, CBE 2006 (OBE 2002); a Deputy Secretary General, Communication Workers Union, 1995–2008; *b* 16 Jan. 1948. *Educ:* Brunel Univ. (BSc); London Sch. of Econs and Pol Sci. (MSc). Res. Officer, NUPE; Gp Sec., CPSA Post and Telecom Gp, 1976–85; Dep. Gen. Sec., Nat. Communication Union, 1985–95. Pres., TUC, 2004–05. Comr, Equal Opportunities Commn, 2000–07; Member: Pensions Commn, 2002–06; Equality and Human Rights Commn, 2006–09; Chm., Rly Pensions Commn, 2006–08. Member: Employment Tribunal, 1988–2001; Employment Appeal Tribunal, 2001–; Bd, Sector Skills Develt Agency, 2001–08; Personal Accounts Delivery Authority, 2007–08 (actg Chm., 2008–10); Ind. Mem., Walker Guidelines Monitoring Gp (Private Equity), 2008–. Non-exec. Dir, Pension Protection Fund, 2004–10. Mem., Supervisory Bd, Union Moderation Fund, BIS (formerly BERR), 2005–11. Trustee: Santander (formerly Alliance & Leicester) Pension Scheme, 1992–; O2 (Telefónica) Pension Scheme, 2003–. Gov., Pensions Policy Inst. *Address:* House of Lords, SW1A 0PW.

**DRAKE, David Paul**, FRCS; Consultant Surgeon, 2012–15, Hon. Paediatric Surgeon, 2016–17, Evelina London Children's Hospital (formerly Evelina Children's Hospital); Visiting Anatomy Demonstrator, King's College London, Guy's Campus, since 2017; *b* 9 Feb. 1945; *s* of late Ronald Ingram Drake and Diana Louisa Drake (*née* Markham); *m* 1976, Linda Ann Callear; two *s*. *Educ:* Blundell's Sch., Tiverton; Clare Coll., Cambridge (MA; MB BChir). FRCS 1974; FRCPCH 1997. Consultant Paediatric Surgeon: Guy's Hosp., London, 1979–88; Gt Ormond St Hosp. for Children, 1988–2010 (Med. Dir, 2002–05). Hon. Sen. Lectr, Inst. of Child Health, Univ. of London, subseq. UCL, 1988–2012. Hon. Paediatric Surgeon, St Luke's Hosp. for the Clergy, 1989–2004; Vis. Paediatric Surgeon, Kilimanjaro Christian Med. Coll., Tanzania, 2011–12. Pres., British Assoc. of Paediatric Surgeons, 2008–10. Mem., Christian Med. Fellowship. *Publications:* contrib. chapter on neonatal surgery to The New Aird's Companion in Surgical Studies, ed K. Burnand and A. Young, 1992, 2nd edn 1998; contrib. papers to surgical and paediatric jls on neonatal surgical and paediatric surgical topics. *Recreations:* travelling, sailing, swimming. *Address:* 14 College Gardens, Dulwich, SE21 7BE. *T:* (020) 8693 3220. *Clubs:* Royal Society of Medicine; Weir Quay Sailing.

**DRAKE, Fergus John**; Chief Executive, Crown Agents, since 2017; *b* Carlisle, 13 Feb. 1974; *m* 2007, Tiffany; four *c*. *Educ:* Univ. of York (BA Hons Econs and Politics 1996); Cranfield Sch. of Mgt (MBA 2004). Regl Dir, E Africa Disaster Response Team, Tearfund, 2000–03; Sen. Manager, Deloitte, 2004–09; Exec. Dir, Global Progs, Save the Children UK, 2009–17. Policy Advr, HM Treasury, 2006–07; Governance and Delivery Advr, Office of Rt Hon. Tony Blair, SGI Rwanda, 2008–09. *Recreations:* travelling the world, arthouse cinema, losing at chess to my children. *Address:* Crown Agents, Blue Fin Building, 110 Southwark Street, SE1 0SU. *T:* 07747 473631. *E:* fergus.drake@crownagents.co.uk.

**DRAKE, Howard Ronald**, CMG 2017; OBE 2002; HM Diplomatic Service, retired; High Commissioner to Canada, 2013–17; *b* 13 Aug. 1956; *s* of late Ronald Henry Drake and Marie Kathleen Drake; *m* 1988, Gillian Summerfield; one *s* one *d*. *Educ:* Churcher's Coll., Petersfield. Joined Foreign and Commonwealth Office, 1975; Vice-Consul (Commercial), Los Angeles, 1981–83; Second Sec. (Political), Santiago, 1985–88; First Sec., FCO, 1988–92; First Sec. and Head of Chancery, Singapore, 1992–95; Dep. Head, Non-Proliferation Dept, FCO, 1995–97; Dir, Invest in Britain Bureau USA, subseq. Invest UK-USA, and Dep. Consul-Gen., NY, 1997–2002; Asst Dir, Human Resources, FCO, 2002–05; Ambassador to Chile, 2005–09; High Comr to Jamaica and the Commonwealth of the Bahamas, 2010–13. *Recreations:* popular music, military history, cricket, tennis.

**DRAKE, James Frederick**; QC 2011; barrister and arbitrator; *b* Adelaide, SA, 13 March 1959; *s* of Frederick George Drake and Palmira Rose Drake; *m* 1993, Karen Falcocchio; one *s* two *d*. *Educ:* Sacred Heart Coll., Adelaide; Univ. of South Australia (BA 1980); Univ. of Adelaide (LLB Hons 1985); Columbia Univ., NY (LLM 1992). Chartered Arbitrator 2004; FCIArb 2004; Fellow, Australian Centre for Internat. Commercial Arbitration, 2012. Admitted: Barrister and Solicitor, SA, 1985; Solicitor, NSW, 1987; Attorney, NY, 1991; called to the Bar, Lincoln's Inn, 1998. Accountant, KPMG Adelaide, 1980–81; solicitor, Reilly Ahern and Kerin, Adelaide, 1985–86; Sen. Associate, Baker & McKenzie, Sydney and NY, 1987–93; Attorney and Partner, Owen & Davis, NY, 1994–98; barrister, 7 King's Bench Walk, 1999–. Chair, Anglo-Australasian Lawyers Soc., 2012–16. *Recreations:* family, vineyard, travel, reading. *Address:* 7 King's Bench Walk, Temple, EC4Y 7DS. *T:* (020) 7910 8300, *Fax:* (020) 7910 8400. *E:* jdrake@7kbw.co.uk. *Clubs:* Roehampton, 67 Pall Mall; Wentworth.

**DRAKE, Julius Michael**; pianist; Artistic Director: Machynlleth Festival, since 2009; Temple Song, since 2010; *b* 5 April 1959; *s* of Michael Drake and late Jean Drake (known professionally as Jean Meikle); *m* 1987, Belinda, *d* of Gen. Sir (James) Michael Gow, GCB; two *d*. *Educ:* Purcell Sch.; Royal Coll. of Music (ARCM). Débuts: Wigmore Hall, with Nicholas Daniel, 1983; Paris, with Sally Burgess, 1990; New York, with Derek Lee Ragin, 1991; Tokyo, with Emma Johnson, 1993; since 1983 has appeared regularly at all major concert halls in Europe and USA, with Victoria de los Angeles, Simon Keenlyside, Sir Thomas Allen, Olaf Bär, Ian Bostridge, Wolfgang Holzmair, Thomas Quasthoff, Angelika Kirchschlager, Dorothea Röschman, Alice Coote, Gerald Finley, Christopher Maltman, etc; has also performed in vocal and instrumental recitals in Amsterdam, Cologne, Salzburg Fest., Edinburgh Fest., Frankfurt, London, NY, Chicago, Paris, San Francisco, Vienna and Zurich; has taken masterclasses in Amsterdam, Oxford, Vienna, Brussels, Porto, Toronto and Cleveland, Ohio. Director: Perth Internat. Chamber Music Fest., Australia, 2001–03; Leeds Lieder, 2009. Professor: Royal Acad. of Music, 1992–2015; Kunstuniversität, Graz, 2010–; Guildhall Sch. of Music, 2015–. Devised song recital series: Schumann, S Bank, 1990; Britten, 1995–96, Nineties, 1997–98, Vaughan Williams, 2008–09, Schumann, 2010; Wolf Songbooks 2011–12: Wigmore Hall; Brahms, Concertgebouw Amsterdam, 2002–03; Julius Drake and Friends, Middle Temple Hall, 2005–17. Broadcasts include: presenting and performing Complete Songs of Gabriel Fauré (radio), 1994; with Ian Bostridge, Schubert's Winterreise (TV film and documentary), 1997. Recordings with world's leading singers incl. Schumann Myrten op. 25, Howells Complete Songs, Schumann Dichterliebe, Schubert Lieder (2 vols), Schumann Lieder, The English Songbook, Sibelius Songs, Gurney Songs, Britten Canticles, Ives Songs, Spanish Songs, Barber Songs, Mahler Songs, Schumann Frauenliebe und Leben, Grieg Songs, Schumann Heine Songs, Tchaikovsky Songs, Ravel Songs, Britten Songs, French Sonatas (oboe and piano), Kodaly Sonata (cello and piano), Songs with Words (solo piano); Franz Liszt Complete Songs (8 vols). Hon. FRAM. Hon. Bencher, Middle Temple, 2013. Gramophone Award, 1998, 2007, 2009, 2011; Edison Award, 2002; BBC Music Mag. Award, 2010, 2012; Juno Award, 2015; Jahrespreis, Preis der deutschen Schallplattenkritik (German Record Critics' Award), 2016. *Recreations:* tennis, walking, novels. *Address:* c/o IMG Artists, Capital Tower, 91 Waterloo Road, SE1 8RT. *T:* (020) 7957 5800, *Fax:* (020) 7957 5801. *E:* aianni@imgartists.com. *W:* www.juliusdrake.com.

**DRAKE, Madeline Mary**; consultant and writer; Chief Executive, Richmond Fellowship, 1995–2001; *b* 5 Oct. 1945; *d* of Ernest and Olive Drake; *m* 1st, 1971, Anthony Gerald Biebuyck (marr. diss.); 2nd, 1983, Prof. Stephen Bernard Torrance; one *s* one *d*. *Educ:* Birmingham Univ. (BA Hons Russian/French; DipSocSc); Middlesex Univ. (BSc Herbal Medicine 2009). Home Office researcher, 1972–73; researcher, Centre for Envmtl Studies, 1973–80; Founder and Dir, Housing and Social Policy Res., 1980–95. Member, Board: Circle Thirty Three Gp, 1976–2005 (Vice-Chm., 1987–94); Shelter, 1987–2005 (Mem., Audit and Finance Cttee, 2007–); Dir, Turnstone Support, 2009–; Mem. Council, Internat. Year for Shelter for Homeless, 1987. Lectures, broadcasts. Mem., IPSM. FRSA. *Publications:* Single and Homeless, 1981; Homelessness: a capital problem, 1984; Managing Hostels, 1986; Housing Associations and 1992, 1992; Europe and 1992, 1992; numerous articles on housing, Europe and the Soviet Union in nat. and internat. jls. *Recreations:* violin, walking, riding, gardening. *Address:* 13 Quermore Road, N4 4QT.

**DRAKEFORD, Rt Hon. Mark**; PC 2019; Member (Lab) Cardiff West, National Assembly for Wales, since 2011; First Minister of Wales, since 2018; *m*; three *c*. Probation Officer, then Sen. Probation Officer, S Glam Probation Service, 1979–89; Project Leader, Ely Community Shop, Barnardo's, 1989–91; Lectr in Applied Social Studies, Univ. of Wales, Swansea, 1991–95; Cardiff University: Lectr, Sch. of Social and Admin. Studies, 1995–99; Sen. Lectr, 1999–2003; Prof. of Social Policy and Applied Social Scis, 2003–11. Health and Social Policy Advr and Hd, First Minister's Political Office, Welsh Assembly Govt, 2000–10. Mem. (Lab) S Glamorgan CC, 1985–93. Minister for Health and Social Services, 2013–16, Cabinet Sec. for Finance (formerly Finance and Local Govt), 2016–18, Nat. Assembly for Wales. *Publications:* (with Ian Butler) Scandal, Social Policy and Social Welfare, 2003, 2nd edn 2005; (with Ian Butler) Social Work on Trial: the Maria Colwell Inquiry and the state of welfare, 2011; (with Bill Jordan) Social Policy and Social Work, 2012; articles in jls and chapters in books. *Address:* National Assembly for Wales, Cardiff Bay, Cardiff CF99 1NA.

**DRAPER, Alan Gregory**; Director, Defence Procurement Management Group, Royal Military College of Science, 1988–91; *b* 11 June 1926; *e s* of late William Gregory Draper and Ada Gertrude (*née* Davies); *m* 1st, 1953, Muriel Sylvia Cuss, FRSA (marr. diss.); three *s*; 2nd, 1977, Jacqueline Gubel (*d* 2006); one step *d*. *Educ:* Leeds Grammar Sch.; The Queen's Coll., Oxford (Scholar 1944; MA 1951). RNVR, 1945; Sub-Lt, 1946–47. Admiralty: Asst Principal, 1950; Private Sec. to Civil Lord of the Admiralty, 1953–55; MoD, 1957–60; Head of Pol Sect., Admiralty, 1960–64; First Sec., UK Delegn to NATO, 1964–66; Asst Sec., MoD, 1966; Counsellor, UK Delegn to NATO, 1974–77; Chm., NATO Budget Cttees, 1977–81; Royal Ordnance Factories: Personnel Dir, 1982–84; Dir Gen., Personnel, 1984; Dir, Management/Career Develt, Royal Ordnance plc, 1985; Sen. Lectr, Defence Procurement, RMCS, 1986–91. MIPM 1985. *Publications:* British Involvement in Major European Collaborative Defence Projects 1957–87, 1990. *Recreations:* reading, music, watching international Rugby Union on television. *Address:* 63 Homelawn House, Bexhill on Sea, E Sussex TN40 1PN.

**DRAPER, Gerald Carter**, OBE 1974; Chairman: G. Draper Consultancy, 1988–92; Draper Associates Ltd, 1982–88; *b* 24 Nov. 1926; *s* of Alfred Henderson Draper and Mona Violanta (*née* Johnson); *m* 1951, Winifred Lilian Howe; one *s* three *d*. *Educ:* Univ. of Dublin, Trinity Coll. (MA). FCIM, FCIT. Joined Aer Lingus, 1947; Advertising and PR Manager, 1950; Commercial Man., Central Afr. Airways, 1959; British European Airways: Advertising Man., 1964; Asst Gen. Man. (Market Develt), 1966; Gen. Man. and Dir, Travel Sales Div., 1970; British Airways: Dir, Travel Div., 1973; Marketing Dir, 1977; Dir, Commercial Ops, 1978; Mem. Bd, 1978–82; Man. Dir, Intercontinental Services Div., 1982. Chairman: British Air Tours Ltd, 1978–82; Silver Wing Surface Arrangements Ltd, 1971–82; Deputy Chairman: Trust Houses Forte Travel Ltd, 1974–82; ALTA Ltd, 1977–82; Hoverspeed, 1984–87; Member Board: Internat. Aeradio Ltd, 1971–82; British Airways Associated Cos Ltd, 1972–82; British Intercontinental Hotels Ltd, 1976–82; Communications Strategy Ltd, 1984–86; AGB Travel Research Internat. Ltd, 1984–86; Centre for Airline and Travel Marketing Ltd, 1986–90; BR (Southern Region), 1990–92; British Travel Educnl Trust, 1990–2005. Chm., Outdoor Advertising Assoc., 1985–92. Master, Co. of Marketors, 1990; Mem., Guild of Freemen, 1991. FRSA 1979. Chevalier de l'Ordre du Tastevin, 1980; Chambellan de l'Ordre des Coteaux de Champagne, 1982. *Recreation:* shooting. *Address:* Old Chestnut, Onslow Road, Burwood Park, Walton-on-Thames, Surrey KT12 5AY. *Club:* National Clay Shooting Centre (Bisley).

**DRAPER, Very Rev. Dr Jonathan Lee**; General Secretary, Modern Church, since 2017; *b* Boston, Mass, 27 Feb. 1952; *s* of Robert and Lois Draper; *m* 1979, Maggie Barham; one *s* two *d*. *Educ:* Plainfield High Sch., NJ; Gordon Coll., USA (BA 1976); Univ. of Durham (BA Hons 1978; PhD 1984); Univ. of Oxford (CTh 1983). Ordained deacon, 1983, priest, 1984; Asst Curate, St John the Divine, Manchester, 1983–85; Lectr in Theology, and Dir of Studies, Ripon Coll., Cuddesdon, Oxford, 1985–92; Vicar of Putney, 1992–2000; Canon Theologian, York Minster, 2000–12; Dean of Exeter, 2012–17. *Publications:* (ed) Communion and Episcopacy, 1988; To Love and Serve, 2003; (ed jtly) Liberating Texts?, 2008; (ed jtly) Christianity and the renewal of Nature, 2011; articles and reviews in jls incl. Modern Believing, Cross Currents, Modern Theology, Jl of Theol. Studies, Jl of Coll. of Preachers. *Recreations:* walking in wild places, entertaining, cinema, sport, reading.

**DRAPER, Michael William**; Under Secretary, Department of Health and Social Security, 1976–78, retired; *b* 26 Sept. 1928; *s* of late John Godfrey Beresford Draper and Aileen Frances Agatha Draper (*née* Masefield); *m* 1952, Theodora Mary Frampton, *o d* of late Henry James Frampton, CSI, CIE; one *s* two *d*. *Educ:* St Edward's Sch., Oxford. FCA. Chartered Accountant, 1953; various posts in England, Ireland, Burma, Nigeria, Unilever Ltd, 1953–64; joined Civil Service, 1964; Principal, Min. of Power, 1964; Asst Sec., DHSS, 1972–76. Sec., Diocese of Bath and Wells, 1978–88; mem. of staff team, Lamplugh House, Christian Renewal Conf. Centre, 1988–89; working with Anglican Church in Zambia, 1991; associated with Sharing of Ministries Abroad, 1992–2000. *Recreations:* philately, church affairs. *Address:* 25 Clift House, 14 Langley Road, Chippenham, Wilts SN15 1DS.

**DRAPER, Prof. Paul Richard**, PhD; Professor of Finance, 2002–08, now Emeritus, and Head of School of Business and Economics, 2002–08, University of Exeter; Professor of Finance (part-time), University of Leeds, 2009–14; *b* 28 Dec. 1946; *s* of James Krishen Draper and Dorothy Jean Draper; *m* 1972, Janet Margaret Grant; one *s* one *d*. *Educ:* Univ. of Exeter (BA Econs 1968); Univ. of Reading (MA Econs 1969); Univ. of Stirling (PhD Finance 1973). Esmée Fairbairn Lectr, Univ. of St Andrews, 1973–75; Lectr, Univ. of Edinburgh, 1976–78; University of Strathclyde: Esmée Fairbairn Sen. Lectr, 1976–86, Prof., 1986–95; Hd, Dept of Accounting and Finance, 1990–95; Vice Dean, Business Sch., 1993–97; University of Edinburgh: Walter Scott and Partners Prof. of Finance, 1997–2001; Hd, Sch. of Business and Econs, 2000–01. Hon. Prof., Heriot-Watt Univ., 2011–16; Vis. Prof., Portsmouth Business Sch., Univ. of Portsmouth, 2013–16. Director: Thomas Hall Estates, 2005–08; China Eagle Hedge Fund, 2013– (Chm., 2016–). Member: Panel for Accounting and Finance, 2001 and 2008 RAEs; Acad. Bd, Inst. of Financial Services, 2005–08. *Publications:* The Scottish Financial Sector (jtly), 1988; Investment Trust Industry in the UK, 1989; articles in Jl of Derivatives, Jl of Futures Markets, Jl of Financial Res., Jl of Business Finance and Accounting, European Financial Mgt, Financial Analysts Jl, etc. *Recreations:* travel, urban walking, houses. *Address:* 58 Lynch Road, Farnham, Surrey GU9 8BX. *T:* (01252) 710175. *E:* P.R.Draper@ex.ac.uk.

**DRAPER, Peter Sydney,** CB 1994; Principal Establishment and Finance Officer, Property Services Agency, 1993–95; *b* 18 May 1935; *s* of late Sydney George Draper and Norah Draper; *m* 1959, Elizabeth Ann (*née* French); two *s* (and one *s* decd). *Educ:* Haberdashers' Aske's; Regent Polytechnic Sch. of Management (Dip. in Management Studies). Joined GCHQ, Cheltenham, 1953; Min. of Transport, 1956–70; Principal, 1969; Department of the Environment, 1970–95: Directorate of Estate Management Overseas, PSA, 1970; Asst Sec., 1975; Head of Staff Resources Div., 1975–78; Asst Dir, Home Regional Services, 1978–80; RCDS, 1981; Dir, Eastern Reg., 1982–84, Under Sec., Dir of Defence Services II, 1985–87, Principal Establishment Officer, 1987–93, PSA. Mem., CSAB, 1996–2002. *Recreations:* gardening, golf. *Address:* Langdale, 22 Brewery Road, Pampisford, Cambs CB22 3EN. *Club:* Saffron Walden Golf.

**DRAPER, Roger James;** Global Business Advisor, BCG, since 2018; *b* 19 Jan. 1970; *s* of Eric Draper and Marjorie Draper; *m* 1994, Nicola Entract (marr. diss. 2018); two *s*; partner, Lisa Edmunds. *Educ:* Bolton Sch.; Winstanley Coll.; Loughborough Univ. (BSc Hons (PE, Sports Sci. and Recreation Mgt)). Dir of Develt, LTA, 1998–2002; Sport England: Chief Operating Officer, 2002–03; Chief Exec., 2003–06; Chief Executive: LTA, 2006–13; Warrington Wolves, 2015–16; Chief Commercial Officer, RFL, and Exec. Dir, Super League, 2017–18. Non-exec. Dir, SportsCover Europe, 2015–. MInstD 1999; Mem., Inst. of Leisure and Amenity Mgt, 2000. *Recreations:* Rugby League (professional player, GB Students Rugby League, 1988–94), tennis (winner, British Univs Tennis Championship, 1989–92; senior county player; Captain, Lancs and Surrey, 1996–). *Club:* International Club of GB.

**DRAPER, Prof. Ronald Philip,** PhD; Regius Chalmers Professor of English, University of Aberdeen, 1986–94, now Professor Emeritus; *b* 3 Oct. 1928; *s* of Albert William and Elsie Draper; *m* 1950, Irene Margaret Aldridge; three *d*. *Educ:* Univ. of Nottingham (BA, PhD). Educn Officer, RAF, 1953–55. Lectr in English, Univ. of Adelaide, 1955–56; Lectr, Univ. of Leicester, 1957–68, Sen. Lectr, 1968–73; Prof., Univ. of Aberdeen, 1973–86. *Dramatic scripts:* (with P. A. W. Collins) The Canker and the Rose, Mermaid Theatre, 1964; (with Richard Hoggart) D. H. L., A Portrait of D. H. Lawrence, Nottingham Playhouse, 1967 (televised 1980). *Publications:* D. H. Lawrence, 1964, 3rd edn 1984; (ed) D. H. Lawrence, The Critical Heritage, 1970, 3rd edn 1986; (ed) Hardy, The Tragic Novels, 1975, rev. edn 1991; (ed) George Eliot, The Mill on the Floss and Silas Marner, 1977, 3rd edn 1984; (ed) Tragedy, Developments in Criticism, 1980; Lyric Tragedy, 1985; The Winter's Tale, Text and Performance, 1985; (ed) Hardy, Three Pastoral Novels, 1987; (ed) The Literature of Region and Nation, 1989; (with Martin Ray) An Annotated Critical Bibliography of Thomas Hardy, 1989; (ed) The Epic: developments in criticism, 1990; (ed with P. Mallett) A Spacious Vision: essays on Hardy, 1994; An Introduction to Twentieth-Century Poetry in English, 1999; Shakespeare: the comedies, 2000; contrib. Oxford DNB; articles and reviews in Archiv für das Studium der Neueren Sprachen und Literaturen, Critical Qly, Essays in Criticism, Etudes Anglaises, English Studies, Jl of D. H. Lawrence Soc., Lit. of Region and Nation, Longman Critical Essays, MLR, New Lit. Hist., Notes and Queries, Revue des Langues Vivantes, Rev. of English Studies, Shakespeare Qly, Studies in Short Fiction, THES, Thomas Hardy Annual, Thomas Hardy Jl. *Recreations:* reading, listening to music, verse writing. *Address:* Eldon House, Wootton Village, Boars Hill, Oxford OX1 5HP. *T:* (01865) 682158.
*See also* I. F. Hudson.

**DRAX, Richard Grosvenor;** MP (C) South Dorset, since 2010; farmer; *b* 29 Jan. 1958; *s* of late (Henry) Walter Plunkett-Ernle-Erle-Drax and of Hon. Pamela Rose (*née* Weeks); *m* 1st, 1985, Zara Victoria Legge-Bourke (marr. diss. 1997); two *s* two *d*; 2nd, 1998, Eliza Sarah Dugdale; 3rd, 2009, Elsebet Bodtker. *Educ:* Harrow Sch.; Royal Agricl Coll., Cirencester (Dip. Rural Land Mgt 1990); Dip. Journalism 1995. Served Coldstream Guards, 1978–87. Journalist: Yorks Evening Press, 1991–96; Tyne Tees TV, Daily Express and Daily Telegraph, 1996–97; and reporter, BBC Radio Solent and BBC South Today, 1997–2006. *Address:* House of Commons, SW1A 0AA.

**DRAYSON,** family name of **Baron Drayson.**

**DRAYSON, Baron** *cr* 2004 (Life Peer), of Kensington in the Royal Borough of Kensington and Chelsea; **Paul Rudd Drayson;** PC 2008; PhD; FMedSci; FREng; FIET; Chairman, Drayson Technologies Group, since 2015; Managing Director, Drayson Racing Technologies (formerly Drayson Motor Racing) LLP, since 2010; Chief Executive, Sensyne Health, since 2018; *b* 5 March 1960; *s* of Michael Rudd Drayson and Ruth Irene Drayson; *m* 1994, Elspeth Jane Bellhouse; three *s* two *d*. *Educ:* St Dunstan's Coll., London; Aston Univ. (BSc Hons; PhD); FREng 2011. Man. Dir, Lambourn Food Co., 1986–91; founder and Dir, Genysys Develt Ltd, 1991–95; co-founder, 1993 and Chief Exec., 1993–2003, PowderJect Pharmaceuticals; Entrepreneur in Residence, Saïd Business Sch., Oxford Univ., 2003–05. Parly Under-Sec. of State, MoD, 2005–07; Minister of State: MoD and BERR, 2007; DIUS, later BIS, 2008–10; MoD, 2009–10. Chm., BioIndustry Assoc., 2001–02. Non-executive Director: Royal Navy Bd, 2015–17; Airbus, 2017–. Mem. Council, Univ. of Oxford, 2014–17. Chm., Oxford Children's Hosp. Campaign, 2002–05. Hon. Pres., Motorsport Industry Assoc., 2010–15. FMedSci 2019. *Recreations:* sword fencing, motor racing. *Address:* House of Lords, SW1A 0PW. *Clubs:* British Racing Drivers, Royal Automobile.

**DRECHSLER, Paul Joseph,** Hon. CBE 2015; Chairman, Bibby Line Group, since 2015; President, Confederation of British Industry, 2015–18; *b* 16 April 1956; *s* of Frank Stephen Drechsler and Marie Winifred Drechsler (*née* Clancy); *m* 1981, Wendy Isobel Hackett; two *s* one *d*. *Educ:* Trinity Coll., Dublin (BA, BAI); INSEAD (IEP). Chief Executive Officer: ICI Brasil SA, 1992; ICI Acrylics Inc., 1993–96; ICI Polyester, 1996–98; Quest Internat., 1998–2003; Exec. Dir, ICI plc, 1998–2003; Chief Exec., 2004–13, Chm., 2006–13, Wates Gp Ltd. Sen. Ind. Dir, Essentra (formerly Filtrona) plc, 2005–15. Chairman: Teach First, 2013–; London First, 2018–. Dir, BITC, 2011–17; Mem., Main Bd, CBI, 2012– (Vice-Pres., 2018–19). Member: Adv. Bd, Business Sch., TCD, 2005–; Adv. Council, Step up to Serve, 2014–; Bd, ICC UK, 2016–. Chancellor, Teesside Univ., 2017–. Hon. LLD TCD, 2018. *Recreations:* Blues music, ski-ing, golf, family vacations, music of Eric Clapton.

**DREHER, Derek,** MBE 2018; Consultant, Northern Ireland Office, since 1997; *b* 12 Jan. 1938; *s* of Frederick Charles Dreher and Mary Emily Dreher (*née* Rutherford); *m* 1961, Patricia Audrey Dowsett; one *s* one *d*. *Educ:* Roan Grammar Sch., Greenwich. Joined War Office as Exec. Officer, 1956; Nat. Service, RAF, 1956–58 (trained as Russian linguist); with War Office, 1958–64, then MoD: postings include: Cyprus, 1962–65; NI, 1969–71; on secondment to Treasury, 1976–79; Asst Sec., 1980; Asst Under Sec. of State, 1992–97. *Recreations:* all forms of sport, but particularly tennis, theatre, foreign travel, reading, particularly political works. *Address:* Kantara, Church Road, Hartley, Kent DA3 8DL. *Club:* Hartley Country.

**DREW, Dr David Elliott;** MP (Lab and Co-op) Stroud, 1997–2010 and since 2017; *b* 13 April 1952; *s* of Ronald Montague Drew and late Maisie Joan Drew; *m* 1990, Anne Baker, *d* of Brian and Sheila Baker; two *s* two *d*. *Educ:* Kingsfield Sch., Glos; Nottingham Univ. (BA Hons 1974); Birmingham Univ. (PGCE 1976); Bristol Poly., later UWE (MA 1988; MEd 1994; PhD 2017). Teacher: Princethorpe Coll., Warwicks, 1976–78; St Michael's Sch., Stevenage, 1978–82; Maidenhill Sch., Glos, 1982–85; Dene Magna Sch., Glos, 1985–86; Sen. Lectr, Bristol Poly., later UWE, 1986–97. Member: Stevenage BC, 1981–82; Stroud DC, 1987–95; Stonehouse Town Council, 1987–2015; Glos CC, 1993–97. Shadow Minister for Envmt, Food and Rural Affairs, 2017–. Contested (Lab) Stroud, 1992. Contested (Lab and Co-op) Stroud, 2010, 2015. *Address:* House of Commons, SW1A 0AA.

**DREW, Joanna Louise;** *see* Roper, J. L.

**DREW, John Sydney Neville;** Chancellor, 2013–17, now Emeritus, Director, Institute of Contemporary European Studies, 2011–17, and Jean Monnet Visiting Professor of European Business and Government, European Business School, 2007–17, Regent's University London (formerly Regent's College, London); *b* 7 Oct. 1936; *s* of late John William Henry Drew and Kathleen Marjorie (*née* Wright); *m* 1962, Rebecca Margaret Amanda (*née* Usher); two *s* one *d*. *Educ:* King Edward's Sch., Birmingham; St John's Coll., Oxford (MA); Fletcher School of Law and Diplomacy, Tufts Univ. (AM). 2nd Lieut, Somerset LI, 1955–57. HM Diplomatic Service, 1960–73: Third Sec., Paris, 1962; MECAS, 1964; Second Sec., Kuwait, 1965; First Sec., Bucharest, 1968; FCO, 1970; Sloan Fellow, 1971, Dir of Marketing and Exec. Programmes, 1973–79, London Business Sch.; Dir of Internat. Corporate Affairs, Rank Xerox, 1979–84; Dir of European Affairs, Touche Ross Internat., 1984–86; Head of UK Offices, EEC, 1987–93; Dir, Europa Times, 1993–94; Dep. Chm., ESG, 1993–95; Dir, Change Gp Internat., 1996–2003. Associate Fellow, Templeton Coll., Oxford, 1982–86; Visiting Professor of European Management: Imperial Coll. of Science and Technology, 1987–91; Open Univ., 1993–99. Durham University: Special Advr, Howlands Trust, 1994–95; Dir, Res. Inst. for the Study of Change, subseq. Chm., Durham Res. Inst., later Durham Inst., 1996–2003; Vis. Prof. of European Business, 1995–2004. Chm., DSL Ltd, 1995–97. President: Inst. of Linguists, 1993–99 (Hon. FIL 1993); European Transpersonal Assoc., 1998–2003. Trustee, Thomson Foundn, 1996–2007. Hon. Editor, European Business Jl, 1987–2002. Hon. MBA Univ. of Northumbria, 1991. *Publications:* Doing Business in the European Community, 1979, 3rd edn 1991 (trans. Spanish and Portuguese 1987); Networking in Organisations, 1986; (ed) Readings in International Enterprise, 1995, 2nd edn 1999; (ed) Ways Through the Wall, 2005; (ed jtly) UK and Europe: costs, benefits, options, 2013; (ed jtly) The Regent's Report 2014: Transatlantic Relations: A European Perspective, 2014; (ed jtly) The Regent's Report 2015: Europe and its Neighbours, 2015; articles on European integration and management development. *Recreations:* writing, travelling, meditating, golf. *Address:* 49 The Ridgeway, NW11 8QP. *Club:* Oxford and Cambridge.

**DREW, Jonathan Iqbal,** MBE 2009; HM Diplomatic Service; Head, Trade Diplomacy Department, Foreign and Commonwealth Office, since 2017; *b* Toronto, 5 Feb. 1970; *s* of John and Rani Drew; civil partnership 2012, *m* 2016, Grant Suckling. *Educ:* Hills Rd Sixth Form Coll., Cambridge; London Sch. of Econs and Pol Sci. (BSc (Econ) 1991); Sch. of Oriental and African Studies, Univ. of London (MA 1993). Entered FCO, 1993; Producer, TV Unit, FCO, 1993–97; on secondment to British Antarctic Survey, 1997–98; Desk Officer (Australia), 1998–2000; Dep. Rep. to E Timor, 2000–01; Dep. High Comr, PNG, 2001–04; Consul (Commercial), Toronto, 2004; Dep. Hd, Counter Terrorist Assistance Section, FCO, 2004–06; Head: W Africa Team, FCO, 2007–09; Political-Mil. Team, Kabul, 2009–10; Dep. Hd, Africa Dept, FCO, 2012–14; High Comr to Mauritius, Ambassador to Union of Comoros and Hd, British Indian Ocean Network, 2014–17. Afghanistan Civilian Service Medal, 2011. *Recreations:* tennis, walking, sailing, diving. *Address:* c/o Foreign and Commonwealth Office, King Charles Street, SW1A 2AH. *E:* jonathan.drew@fco.gov.uk.

**DREW, Prof. Linda Sally,** PhD; Professor and Vice Chancellor (formerly Director and Chief Executive Officer), Ravensbourne University London (formerly Ravensbourne College), since 2015; *b* Billericay, Essex, 18 July 1958; *d* of Peter and Patricia Drew; one *d*; partner, Roger Marvin. *Educ:* St Martin's Sch. of Art (Art Foundn; BA Hons Fashion Design 1981); Garnett Coll., London (PGCE 1984); Middlesex Univ. (MA Hist. of Design 1993); Lancaster Univ. (PhD Educnl Res. 2003). Fashion designer, Courtaulds Design Studio, 1978–79; fashion buyer, Hobbs Retail, 1981–82; Lectr, Coll. for Distributive Trades, 1982–89; Sen. Lectr, London Coll. of Printing and Distributive Trades, 1989–96; Principal Lectr, London Coll. of Fashion, 1996–99; Co-Dir, Subject Centre for Art, Design and Media, Univ. of Brighton, 2000–03; Dean, Chelsea Coll. of Art and Design, 2003–11, Prof. of Art and Design Pedagogy in Higher Educn, 2007–11, Univ. of Arts London; Prof. and Dep. Dir, Glasgow Sch. of Art, 2011–14. Ed., Art, Design and Communication in Higher Educn (Intellect), 2001–14. Reviewer, Arts Quality Assce Framework, Min. of Educn, Singapore, 2008–10. UK Mem., Singapore British Business Council, 2005–12. Exec. Mem., GuildHE, 2017– (Vice Chm., 2019–). Gov., Stationers' Crown Woods Acad., 2015–. Trustee: London Higher, 2017–; Higher Educn Stats Agency, 2018–. Freeman, City of London, 2017; Liveryman, Stationers' and Newspaper Makers' Co., 2017–. *Publications:* The Business of Fashion, 1992; (ed) The Student Experience in Art and Design Higher Education: drivers for change, 2008. *Recreations:* cinema, theatre, art, design, fashion, architecture, family, cooking and wine, fancy dress (making and wearing). *Address:* Ravensbourne University London, 6 Penrose Way, SE10 0EW. *T:* (020) 3040 3562. *E:* l.drew@rave.ac.uk. *Club:* Chelsea Arts.

**DREW, Philippa Catherine,** CB 2001; Vice-Chairman, Coalition for International Court for the Environment, since 2011 (Trustee, since 2009); *b* 11 May 1946; *d* of Sir Arthur Charles Walter Drew, KCB and Rachel Anna Drew (*née* Lambert). *Educ:* St Paul's Girls' Sch.; St Anne's Coll., Oxford (MA Hons 1968 PPE); Univ. of Pennsylvania (MA Hons 1969 Internat. Relations). Foreign and Commonwealth Office: Central and Southern Africa Dept, 1969; New Delhi, 1970–74; First Sec., S Asia Dept, 1974–75; Home Office: EEC Referendum Count Unit, 1975; Criminal Dept, 1976–78; Police Dept, 1978–81; Gen. Dept, 1981–84; Prison Dept, 1984–85; Field Dir, SCF, Nepal, 1985–87; Head, Probation Service Div., 1987–91; Dir of Custody, HM Prison Service, 1992–95; Dir, Personnel and Office Services, then Corporate Resources, Home Office, 1995–99; Dir for Educn, Trng, Arts and Sport, DCMS, 1999–2002; Dir, Global Issues, FCO, 2002–06. Chm., Diplomatic Service Appeal Bd, 2006–11; Member: London Probation Bd, 2007–08; Bd, Oxford Research Gp, 2007–10. Trustee: Stakeholder Forum, 2011–15; Human Dignity Trust, 2014–; Kaleidoscope Trust, 2014–. *Recreations:* opera, travel, talk. *Address:* 12 Thorney Hedge Road, Chiswick, W4 5SD. *T:* (020) 8747 0836.
*See also* J. R. Bretherton.

**DREW, Simon Patrick;** QC 2011; **His Honour Judge Drew;** a Circuit Judge, since 2012. *Educ:* Leeds Univ. (LLB Hons). Called to the Bar, Lincoln's Inn, 1987; in practice as barrister, Birmingham, London and Bristol, specialising in criminal law and licensing law; Recorder, 2005–12. *Address:* Birmingham Crown Court, Queen Elizabeth II Law Courts, 1 Newton Street, Birmingham B4 7NA.

**DREW, Thomas,** CMG 2015; HM Diplomatic Service; High Commissioner to Pakistan, 2016–19; *b* Haslemere, Surrey, 26 Sept. 1970; *s* of Peter John Drew and Rosemary Jane Beverley Drew (*née* Sach); *m* 2016, Joanna Louise Roper, *qv*. *Educ*: Charterhouse; Trinity Coll., Oxford (BA Hons Lit.Hum. (Classics) 1993). McKinsey and Co., London, 1993–95; entered FCO, 1995; Second Sec., FCO, 1995–97; Russian lang. trng, 1997–98; Second, then First Sec., Moscow, 1998–2002; Head: EU Intergovtl Conf. Unit, FCO, 2002–04; EU Enlargement and SE Europe Gp, FCO, 2004–06; Political Counsellor, Islamabad, 2006–08; on loan to Home Office as Dir, Office for Security and Counter-Terrorism, 2008–11; Dir for Nat. Security, FCO, 2011–12; Principal Pte Sec. to Sec. of State for Foreign Affairs, 2012–14; Vis. Fellow, McKinsey Global Inst. (on secondment), 2015. *Recreations*: cycling, triathlon, opera, food. *Address*: c/o Foreign and Commonwealth Office, King Charles Street, SW1A 2AH.

**DREWRY, Prof. David John;** Vice-Chancellor, 1999–2009, and Professor, 1999–2009, now Emeritus, University of Hull; *b* 22 Sept. 1947; *s* of late Norman Tidman Drewry and Mary Edwina Drewry (*née* Wray); *m* 1971, Gillian Elizabeth (*née* Holbrook). *Educ*: Havelock School, Grimsby; Queen Mary Coll., Univ. of London (BSc 1st cl. hons 1969; Hon. Fellow, QMW, 1992); Emmanuel College, Cambridge (PhD 1973; Hon. Fellow, 2008). FRGS 1972, CGeog 2002. UK-US Antarctic Expdns, 1969–70 and 1971–72; Sir Henry Strakosh Fellow, 1974; UK-US Antarctic Expdns, 1974–75, 1977–78 (leader), 1978–79 (leader), Sen. Asst in Research, Univ. of Cambridge, 1978–83; leader, UK-Norwegian Svalbard Expdns, 1980, 1983, 1985, 1986; Asst Dir of Research, Univ. of Cambridge, 1983; Director: Scott Polar Res. Inst., Univ. of Cambridge, 1984–87; British Antarctic Survey, 1987–94 (Emeritus Fellow, 2009); Sci. and Technol., NERC, 1994–98; Dir Gen., British Council, 1998. Vice-Pres. and Bd Mem., Eur. Univ. Assoc., 2009–17. Non-exec. Dir (Natural Scis), UK Nat. Commn for UNESCO, 2017–. Vis. Fellow, Green Coll., Oxford, 1995; Vis. Prof., QMUL (formerly QMW), 1996–2001, 2008–; Vis. Scholar, Univ. of Cambridge, 1999; Guest Prof., Xiamen Univ., China, 2006–; Hon. Prof., Krakow Acad., 2010–. Vice-President: Council, RGS, 1990–93 (Mem., 1986–93 and 1995–96); Council, Internat. Glaciological Soc., 1990–96 (Mem., 1980–82); Member: Council of Managers, Nat. Antarctic Programmes, 1988–95 (Chm., 1988–91); Royal Soc. Interdisciplinary Scientific Cttee on Antarctic Res., 1990–98; Internat. Arctic Sci. Cttee, 1994–2002 (Pres., 1997–2002); Exec. Council, ESF, 1996–98 (Mem., Eur. Polar Bd); Trustee, Antarctic Heritage Trust, 1993–2005; UK alternate deleg., Sci. Cttee on Antarctic Res., 1985–97. Chm., S Georgia Assoc., 2010–. Trustee, Nat. History Mus., 2008–16; Chm., Univ. of Hull Maritime History Trust, 2014–. Chm., Yorkshire Univs, 2002–04; Mem., Yorkshire Innovation (formerly Yorkshire Science), 2005–09. Non-executive Director: Hull Urban Regeneration Co., 2003–09; The Deep, 2006–09. CCMI (Pres., Humberside Br., 2002–04). Hon. DSc: Robert Gordon, 1993; Humberside, 1994; Anglia Poly. Univ., 1998; Hull, 2010. US Antarctic Service Medal, 1979; Cuthbert Peek Award, 1979, Patron's Medal, 1998, RGS; Polar Medal, 1986; Prix de la Belgica Gold Medal, Royal Acad. of Belgium, 1995. *Publications*: Antarctica: glaciological and geophysical folio, 1983; Glacial Geologic Processes, 1986; papers on polar glaciology, geophysics, remote sensing, science policy in learned jls. *Recreations*: music, ski-ing, walking, gastronomy. *Address*: University of Hull, Hull HU6 7RX. *T*: (01482) 465131. *Clubs*: Athenæum, Geographical.

**DREYFUS, Prof. Laurence,** PhD, DLitt; FBA 2002; Professor of Music, University of Oxford, 2006–15, now Emeritus (Lecturer, 2005–06); Fellow of Magdalen College, Oxford, 2005–15, now Emeritus; *b* Boston, Mass, 28 July 1952; naturalised British citizen, 2002. *Educ*: studied 'cello with Leonard Rose, Juilliard Sch.; Yeshiva Univ. (BA Pol Sci. 1973); Columbia Univ. (MA 1975, MPhil 1976, PhD 1980, in Musicology); studied viola da gamba with Wieland Kuijken, Royal Conservatory, Brussels, 1979–81 (Premier Prix, 1980; Diplôme supérieur, 1981); DLitt Oxon 2013. Lectr, Univ. of Wisconsin-Madison, 1979; Mellon Fellow in Humanities, Columbia Univ., 1979–81; Asst Prof., Washington Univ. in St Louis, 1981–82; Asst Prof., 1982–88, Associate Prof. of History of Music and Sen. Faculty Fellow, 1988–89, Yale Univ.; Associate Professor of Music: Univ. of Chicago, 1989–90; Stanford Univ., 1990–93; King's College, London: Prof. of Perf. Studies in Music, with the RAM, 1992–96; Thurston Dart Prof. of Perf. Studies in Music, 1996–2005; Hd, Dept of Music, 1995–99. *Appearances include*: Bergen Fest., Norway, 1990; Early Music Network tour of GB, 1990; Utrecht Early Music Fest., 1991; San Francisco SO, 1992; Skálholt Music Fest., Iceland, 1992–95; London Bach Fest., 1993, 1994; Three Choirs Fest., 2006; Edinburgh Fest., 2007. Dir-at-Large, Amer. Musicol Soc., 1989–91 (Otto Kinkeldey Prize, 1997); Vice-Pres., Amer. Bach Soc., 1992–94; Mem. Council, RMA, 1994–98. Hon. RAM 1995. First Prize, Bodky Competition in Early Music, Boston, 1978. Several solo and chamber recordings, incl. Purcell's Complete Fantasies for Viols (Gramophone award for best baroque instrumental recording, 1997), Orlando Gibbons' Consorts for Viols (Gramophone award, 2004) and John Dowland's Lachrimae (Gramophone award, Diapason d'Or de l'Année, 2017). Jt Gen. Ed., Musical Performance and Reception (formerly Cambridge Musical Texts and Monographs), 1994–. *Publications*: Bach's Continuo Group: players and practices in his vocal works, 1987; Bach and the Patterns of Invention, 1996; (contrib.) The Cambridge Companion to Bach, 1997; Wagner and the Erotic Impulse, 2010; papers, and articles in jls. *E*: laurence.dreyfus@magd.ox.ac.uk.

**DRIELSMA, Sir Claude Dunbar H.;** *see* Hankes-Drielsma.

**DRIFE, Prof. James Owen,** MD; FRCOG, FRCSE, FRCPE; Professor of Obstetrics and Gynaecology, University of Leeds, 1990–2009, now Emeritus; *b* 8 Sept. 1947; *s* of late Thomas Drife and Rachel Drife (*née* Jones); *m* 1973, Diana Elizabeth, *d* of late Ronald Haxton Girdwood, CBE; one *s* one *d*. *Educ*: Cumnock Acad.; Univ. of Edinburgh (BSc Hons; MB ChB 1971; MD 1982). FRCPE 1998. Hosp. appts, Edinburgh, 1971–79; MRC Res. Fellow in Reproductive Biology, Edinburgh, 1974–76; Lectr in Obst. and Gyn., Univ. of Bristol, 1979–82; Dept of Surgery, Frenchay Hosp., Bristol, 1980–81; Sen. Lectr, Obst. and Gyn., Univ. of Leicester, 1982–90. Non-exec. Dir, United Leeds Teaching Hosps NHS Trust, 1991–98. Mem., Cases Cttee, Medical Protection Soc., 1985–94; Assessor for England, Enquiries into Maternal Deaths, 1992–2011; Mem., Midwifery Cttee, UKCC, 1993–99; Mem. Council, RCOG, 1993–2008 (Convenor of Study Gp, 1989–92; Chm., Liby Cttee, 1994–97; Jun. Vice-Pres., 1998–2001); Mem., GMC, 1994–2005; Chairman: Assoc. of Profs of Obstetrics and Gynaecology, 2002–06; Academic Assoc. of Obstetrics and Gynaecology, 2006–07; President: N of England Obstetric and Gynaecol Soc., 2007–08; Leeds Medico-Chirurgical Soc., 2014–16; York Med. Soc., 2019–20. FRSA 1997. Hon. FASPOG, 1988; Hon. Fellow, Amer. Gynecol and Obstetrical Soc., 1998; Hon. FCOG(SA) 2002; Hon. FFSRH 2009; Hon. Mem., Jordanian Soc. of Obstetricians and Gynaecologists, 2000. Editor or co-editor, obst. and gyn. jls, 1985–2014; Editor-in-Chief, Eur. Jl of Obstetrics and Gynaecology, 2010–14 (Co-Editor-in-Chief, 2003–09). *Publications*: Dysfunctional Uterine Bleeding and Menorrhagia, 1989; (jtly) Micturition, 1990; (with J. Studd) HRT and Osteoporosis, 1990; (with D. Donnai) Antenatal Diagnosis of Fetal Abnormalities, 1991; (with A. Calder) Prostaglandins and the Uterus, 1992; (with A. Templeton) Infertility, 1992; (with D. Baird) Contraception, 1993; The Benefits and Risks of Oral Contraceptives, 1994; (with J. J. Walker) Caesarean Section, 2001; (with B. Magowan) Clinical Obstetrics and Gynaecology, 2004, 3rd edn 2013; (jtly) Obstetrics and Gynaecology for the MRCOG, 2004, 3rd edn 2016; contribs to BMJ. *Recreations*: songwriting (founder Mem., Abracadabarets; perf. at Edinburgh Fringe Fest., 1974, 1979, 1982, 1989, 1997, 2000, 2002, 2007, 2009, 2010, 2012, Boswell Book Fest., 2015), theatre going, opera, walking. *Address*: School of Medicine, Worsley Building, University of Leeds, Leeds LS2 9JT. *T*: (0113) 343 1654. *Clubs*: Athenæum, National Liberal, Royal Society of Medicine.

**DRINKALL, (Christopher John) Julian;** Chief Executive Officer, Academies Enterprise Trust, since 2017; *b* London, 5 April 1964; *s* of John Drinkall and Patricia Drinkall; *m* 1996, Gillian Marshall; one *s* two *d*. *Educ*: Eton Coll.; Merton Coll., Oxford (BA PPE 1986); Harvard Business Sch. (MBA 1991); John F. Kennedy Sch. of Govt, Harvard Univ. (MPA 2006; Littauer Fellow). Associate Consultant, LEK Partnership, 1986–89; Business Develt Manager and Country Manager, Jamaica, Island Internat., 1991–96; Sen. Manager, Corporate Finance Adv. Services, Arthur D. Little, 1996–98; Hd, Financial and Commercial Strategy, BBC, 1998–2001; Gp Strategy Dir, IPC Media (Time Warner), 2001–03; Dir, Strategy and M&A, Boots Gp, 2003–05; Chief Operating Officer, Macmillan Publishers, 2006–07; CEO, Macmillan Educn, 2007–10; CEO and Pres., EMEA and India, Cengage Learning, 2012–14; CEO, Alpha Plus Gp, 2014–16. Chm., Dragons in Europe, 2012–17. MInstD; FRSA. *Recreations*: development, education, Real and lawn tennis, travel. *Address*: 39 Saltoun Road, SW2 1EN. *T*: 07738 752926. *E*: julian.drinkall@gmail.com.

**DRISCOLL, Daphne Jane;** *see* Todd, D. J.

**DRISCOLL, Fiona Elizabeth Lawrence;** Chair, Audit Committee and non-executive Director, UK Research and Innovation, since 2017; *b* London, 1958; *d* of Jim Driscoll and Jeanne Driscoll. *Educ*: Somerville Coll., Oxford (MA). Mem., Major Projects Rev. Gp, HM Treasury, 2016–. Gov., Nuffield Health, 2010–; Chair, Wessex Academic Health Sci. Network, 2015–. Non-exec. Dir, BotOptions (UK) plc, 2015–. Mem. Council, Univ. of Bradford, 2015–18. *E*: fiona@driscoll.org.uk.

**DRISCOLL, Dr James Philip,** CEng; independent management consultant; Partner, PricewaterhouseCoopers (formerly Coopers & Lybrand, then Coopers & Lybrand Deloitte), 1990–99, retired; *b* 29 March 1943; *s* of Reginald Driscoll and Janetta Bridget Driscoll; *m* 1969, Josephine Klapper, BA; two *s* two *d*. *Educ*: St Illtyd's Coll., Cardiff; Birmingham Univ. (BSc 1964; PhD 1972); Manchester Business Sch. MIChemE 1975; MIGEM (MIGasE 1975); MInstF 1975. Taught at St Illtyd's Coll., Cardiff, 1964; res. posts with Joseph Lucas, Solihull, 1968–69; British Steel Corporation: res. posts, 1969–70; commercial posts, 1971–79, incl. Manager, Divl Supplies, 1973; Reg. Manager, BSC (Industry), 1979–82; Dir, S Wales Workshops, 1980–82; Industrial Dir, Welsh Office, 1982–85; Associate Dir, 1985–87, Dir, 1987–90, Coopers & Lybrand Associates. Non-exec. Dir of a number of companies. Mem., Glas Cymru. *Publications*: various technical papers. *Recreations*: family, sport. *Address*: 6 Cory Crescent, Wyndham Park, Peterston-super-Ely, Cardiff CF5 6LS. *T*: (01446) 760372. *Club*: Peterston Football (Cardiff).

**DRISCOLL, Prof. Judith Louise,** PhD; FREng; Professor of Materials Science, University of Cambridge, since 2008; *b* Edgware, 25 May 1966; *d* of Paul MacManus and Elaine Marie MacManus (*née* Clews); *m* 1991, Dr Kelly John Driscoll; two *d*. *Educ*: St Michael's Convent Grammar Sch., Finchley; Imperial Coll., London (BSc Engrg); New Hall, Cambridge (PhD 1991). Lectr, 1995–99, Reader, 1999–2003, Imperial Coll. London; Lectr, 2003–05, Reader, 2005–08, Univ. of Cambridge. Vis. Staff Mem., Los Alamos Nat. Lab., 2003–. Gov., St Mary's Sch., Cambridge, 2010–19. FREng 2018. *Publications*: over 400 res. articles. *Recreations*: hiking, ski-ing, travel, wine, Catholic faith, women in science and engineering advocate. *Address*: Department of Materials Science and Metallurgy, University of Cambridge, 27 Charles Babbage Road, Cambridge CB3 0FS. *T*: (01223) 334468. *E*: jld35@cam.ac.uk.

**DRISCOLL, Lindsay Jane;** Consultant, Bates Wells & Braithwaite, 2008–19; *b* 17 April 1947; *d* of Clement Milligan Woodburn and Evelyn Miriam Woodburn; *m* 1978, Rev. Canon David Driscoll; two *s*. *Educ*: Queen's Sch., Chester; St Hugh's Coll., Oxford (MA Hons Jurisp.). Admitted Solicitor, 1971; Asst Solicitor, Biddle & Co., 1971–73; Asst Public Trustee of Kenya, 1973–78; Lectr, Kenya Sch. of Law, 1973–78; charity law consultant, 1982–87; Consultant, Bowling & Co., 1985; Asst Legal Advr, 1987–90, Legal Advr, 1990–95, NCVO; Partner, 1995–2000, Consultant, 2000–03, Sinclair Taylor & Martin. Chair, Bd, Internat. Center for Not for Profit Law, US, 2011–13 (non-exec. Dir, 1996–2003 and 2007–11); Mem., Supervisory Bd, Eur. Centre for Not for Profit Law, 2010–. Mem., Exec. Cttee, Charity Law Assoc., 1997–2003; Charity Comr, 2003–08. Chm., Steering Gp, Code of Governance for Voluntary and Community Sector, 2009–15; Adv. Council, NCVO, 2015–. Trustee: Newham Community Renewal Prog., 1981–87; Friends of Internat. Centre of Insect Physiology and Ecology Trust, 1997–2005; Assoc. of Church Accountants and Treasurers, 1998–2000; Womankind Worldwide, 1998–2006; ICNL Charitable Trust, 1998–2003; Widows Rights Internat. (formerly Empowering Widows in Develt), 2000–05; Balkans Community Initiatives Fund, 2002–06; Historia Theatre Co., 2003–; St Katherine and Shadwell Trust, 2005–10; Dance United, 2006–11; Journey of a Lifetime Trust, 2008–11; Rosa, 2010–15; Sangahta Global, 2011–12; W Wilts Multi Faith Forum, 2018–; Help Counselling Services, 2018–. Mem. Bd, Pemsel Case Foundn, 2012–. Governor: Davenant Foundn Sch., 1990–97; St Laurence Sch. Acad., Bradford on Avon, 2014–. *Publications*: (with Bridget Phelps) The Charities Act 1992: a guide for charities and other voluntary organisations, 1992, 2nd edn as The Charities Acts 1992 and 1993, 1993, 4th edn 1995; (contrib.) Modernising Charity Law, 2010; (contrib.) Regulating Charities: the inside story, 2017; articles on charity law in charity and legal press. *Recreations*: travel, walking, theatre. *Address*: 24 Baileys Barn, Bradford on Avon BA15 1BX.

**DRISCOLL, Michael John;** QC 1992; *b* 22 Feb. 1947; *s* of John and Gladys Mary Driscoll; *m* 1970, Heather Edyvean Nichols (marr. diss. 1986); one *s* two *d* (and one *s* decd); *m* 2010, Mary-Anne Cooke (*née* Bowles); two step *s* one step *d*. *Educ*: Rugby Sch.; St John's Coll., Cambridge (BA, LLB). Asst Lectr, Manchester Univ., 1969–70; called to the Bar, Middle Temple, 1970; Bencher, Lincoln's Inn, 2000. *Recreation*: family. *Address*: Maitland Chambers, 7 Stone Buildings, Lincoln's Inn, WC2A 3SZ.

**DRISCOLL, Prof. Michael John;** Vice-Chancellor and President, Taylor's University, Kuala Lumpur, since 2016; *b* 27 Oct. 1950; *s* of late Michael Driscoll and Catherine Driscoll; one *s* one *d*. *Educ*: Boteler GS, Warrington; Trent Poly. (BA 1973). Res. Asst, Sheffield Univ., 1973–77; Lectr, Birmingham Univ., 1977–89; Economist, OECD, Paris, 1986–89; Middlesex Polytechnic, later University: Prof. of Economics, 1989–2015; Hd of Sch. of Econs, 1989–91; Dean of Business Sch., 1991–95; Pro Vice-Chancellor, 1993–95; Dep. Vice-Chancellor, 1995–96; Vice-Chancellor, 1996–2015. Visiting Professor: Indian Statistics Inst., 1978; Centre for Econs and Maths Inst., Moscow, 1981; Limoges Univ. (annually), 1981–89; Univ. of the S Pacific, 1984. Chair, Lee Valley Business and Innovation Centre, 1996; Member: Ealing Tertiary Coll. Corp., 1995–96; Weald Coll. Corp., 1996–98; Coll. of NE London Corp., 1997–2005. Member: Council, London Playing Fields Soc., 1998–2000; Steering Cttee, London Higher (formerly London Higher Educn Consortium), 2000–06; N London LSC, 2001–04; Bd, UUK, 2001–07; Chairman: Higher Educn Partnership for Sustainability, 2000–04; CMU, 2003–07. Patron, N London

Hospice, 2002. MInstD 1997; CCMI (FIMgt 1995); FRSA 1995. *Publications:* (jtly) Risk and Uncertainty in Economics, 1994; (jtly) The Effects of Monetary Policy on the Real Sector, 1994; numerous articles in academic jls. *Recreations:* following Aston Villa FC, the arts, water sports, walking, mountain biking, food and wine.

**DRIVER, Alastair James;** conservationist and explorer; National Biodiversity Manager, Environment Agency, 2002–16; *b* Gloucester, 9 Oct. 1956; *s* of Dr Peter Driver and Margaret Driver; *m* 1980, Belinda Christina Anderson-Dixon; three *s. Educ:* Randwick Primary Sch.; Marling Grammar Sch., Stroud; Lancaster Univ. (BSc Hons Ecol.). Regl Conservation Officer, Thames Water Authy, 1984–89; Regional Conservation Manager, Thames Region: Nat. Rivers Authy, 1989–96; Envmt Agency, 1996–2002. Biodiversity Advr, Commonwealth Secretariat, 2005–; Specialist Advisor: Flow Partnership, 2016–; Arup, 2017–; Expert Panel Advr, Wild Trout Trust, 2018–; Dir, England and Wales, Rewilding Britain, 2017–. Member: Council, RSNC, 2000–02; Council, Wildfowl and Wetlands Trust, 2010–; Natural Envmt Adv. Panel, NT, 2010–16 (Volunteer specialist, 2016–); Council, Scientific Exploration Soc., 2019–. Hon. Prof. in Applied Envmtl Mgt, Univ. of Exeter, 2016–. Chm., Sonning Cricket Club, 2006–13 (Hon. Life Vice-Pres., 2014–); Dictator of Rugby, Reading Rhinos Rugby team, 2010–12; Vice-Pres., Reading Rugby Club, 2010–. Creator and voluntary warden, Ali's Pond Local Nature Reserve, Sonning, 1997–; Founder Mem., Sonning and Sonning Eye Soc., 2004–; Hon. Mem. and Expert Adviser, Vole Club, 2000–. FCIEEM (FIEEM 2012). Ambassador, Internat. RiverFoundation, 2007– (Co-founder and Judge, European River Prize, 2013–); Founder: SuDS for Schs, 2011; UK River Prize, 2014; Catchments in Trust, 2014. *Publications:* (contrib.) River Projects and Conservation, 1991; (contrib.) The New Rivers and Wildlife Handbook, 1994; scientific papers in Regulated Rivers: res. and mgt, Jl of Inst. of Water and Envmtl Mgt, British Wildlife. *Recreations:* former first class Rugby player and honours tie winner for London Irish, also played Rugby for Cainscross, Slough and Reading; club cricketer for Sonning Cricket Club; keen naturalist and moth botherer. *Address:* Wisteria, 2 Garde Road, Sonning, Berks RG4 6XJ. *T:* 07836 600868. *E:* ali@sonningdrivers.plus.com. *W:* www.twitter.com/AliDriverUK.

**DRIVER, Anne;** *see* Phillips, Anne.

**DRIVER, Bryan;** Chairman, Rail Access Disputes (formerly Rail Access Disputes Resolution) Committee, 1996–2002 (Vice Chairman, 2002–10); *b* 26 Aug. 1932; *s* of Fred and Edith Driver; *m* 1955, Pamela Anne (*née* Nelson); two *d. Educ:* Wath-upon-Dearne Grammar School. Joined British Railways (Junior Clerk), 1948; Royal Air Force, 1950–52; management training with BR, 1958–59; posts in London, Doncaster, Newcastle, 1959–69; Divisional Operating Manager, Norwich, 1969–71; Liverpool Street, 1971–72; Divisional Manager, West of England, 1972–75, South Wales, 1975–77; Dep. Gen. Manager, Eastern Region, 1977–82; Man. Dir, 1982–87, Chm., 1985–87, Freightliners Ltd; Bryan Driver Associates, 1987–96; Consultant Advr, 1987–88, Ops Dir, then Dir, Ops and Rolling Stock, 1988–93, Transmanche-Link (Channel Tunnel Contractors). *Recreations:* cricket, Rugby football. *Address:* Riverds Lea, 4 Shilton Garth Close, Earswick, York YO32 9SQ. *T:* (01904) 762848. *Clubs:* MCC; York Golf (Social Mem.).

**DRIVER, Charles Jonathan,** MPhil; writer; Master of Wellington College, 1989–2000; *b* 19 Aug. 1939; *s* of Rev. Kingsley Ernest Driver and Phyllis Edith Mary (*née* Gould); *m* 1967, Ann Elizabeth Hoogewerf; two *s* one *d. Educ:* St Andrew's Coll., Grahamstown; Univ. of Cape Town (BA Hons, BEd, STD); Trinity Coll., Oxford (MPhil). Pres., National Union of S African Students, 1963–64; Asst Teacher, Sevenoaks Sch., 1964–65 and 1967–68; Housemaster, Internat. Sixth Form Centre, Sevenoaks Sch., 1968–73; Dir of Sixth Form Studies, Matthew Humberstone Sch., 1973–78; Res. Fellow, Univ. of York, 1976; Principal, Island Sch., Hong Kong, 1978–83; Headmaster, Berkhamsted Sch., 1983–89. Hon. Sen. Lectr, Sch. of Lit. and Creative Writing, UEA, 2007–. Biogliasco Fellow, 2008; MacDowell Fellow, 2010; Hawthornden Fellow, 2012. FRSA. Trustee: Lomans Trust, 1986–; Beit Trust, 1998–; Governor: Benenden Sch., 1987–2005 (Advr, 2006–10); Eagle House Prep. Sch., 1989–2000; Milton Abbey Sch., 1998–2005 (Visitor, 2005–09); Farlington Sch., 1999–2004 (Chm. Governors, 2000–04); Millfield, 2001–10; Frewen Coll., 2002–16. Editor, Conference and Common Room, 1993–2000. *Publications: novels:* Elegy for a Revolutionary, 1968 (reissued, 2010); Send War in Our Time, O Lord, 1969 (reissued, 2010); Death of Fathers, 1972 (reissued, 2010); A Messiah of the Last Days, 1974 (reissued, 2010); Shades of Darkness, 2004; *poetry:* I Live Here Now, 1979; (with Jack Cope) Occasional Light, 1979; Hong Kong Portraits, 1986; In the Water-Margins, 1994; Holiday Haiku, 1997; Requiem, 1998; So Far: selected poems 1960–2004, 2005; Rhymes for the Grandchildren: Moose, Mouse and other rhymes, 2011; Citizen of Elsewhere: selected poems, 2013; Before: a sequence of poems, 2018; *biography:* Patrick Duncan, 1980, 2nd edn 2000; My Brother and I, 2013; The Man with the Suitcase: the life, execution and rehabilitation of John Harris, liberal terrorist, 2015; *memoir:* Some Schools, 2016. *Recreations:* keeping fit, reading, Rugby. *Address:* Apple Yard Cottage, Mill Lane, Mill Corner, Northiam, Rye, E Sussex TN31 6JU. *E:* jontydriver@hotmail.com. *W:* www.jontydriver.co.uk.

**DRIVER, Daniel Amir, (Danny);** concert pianist, since 2001; *b* London, 1977; *m* 1999, Rebecca Miller; one *s* one *d. Educ:* Clare Coll., Cambridge (BA Hons); Royal Coll. of Music (Postgrad. Dip.). Solo and chamber performances throughout N America, Europe and Far East, including Wigmore Hall and BBC Proms. Artistic Dir, Hampstead and Highgate Fest., 2010. Lectr in Performance, Goldsmiths Coll., Univ. of London, 2013–18; Prof. of Piano, RCM, 2016–. Many recordings. *Address:* c/o Royal College of Music, Prince Consort Road, SW7 2BS. *T:* (020) 7591 4300.

**DRIVER, Prof. Felix,** PhD; FBA 2011; Professor of Human Geography, Royal Holloway, University of London, since 1999; *b* Wednesbury, 23 Aug. 1961. *Educ:* Westminster City Sch., London; Emmanuel Coll., Cambridge (BA 1982; PhD 1987). FR.HistS 1999; FRGS. Lectr, Univ. of Exeter, 1986–88; Lectr, 1988–96, Reader, 1996–99, Royal Holloway, Univ. of London. FAcSS (AcSS 2007). *Publications:* Geography Militant, 2001; Imperial Cities, 2003; Tropical Visions, 2005; Power and Pauperism, 2004; Hidden Histories of Exploration, 2009. *Address:* Department of Geography, Royal Holloway, University of London, Egham, Surrey TW20 0EX.

**DRIVER, Rt Rev. Dr Jeffrey William;** Archbishop of Adelaide and Metropolitan of South Australia, 2005–16; *b* 6 Oct. 1951; *s* of Ernest Leslie Driver and Joyce Mary Driver; *m* 1978, Lindy Mary Muffet; one *s* one *d. Educ:* Aust. Coll. of Theol. (ThL 1977, ThSchol 1983); Sydney Coll. of Divinity (MTh 1991); Charles Sturt Univ. (PhD 2008). Newspaper journalist, 1970–74. Ordained deacon, 1977, priest, 1978; Asst Curate, dio. Bathurst, 1977–80; Rector: Mid-Richmond, 1980–84; Jamison, ACT, 1984–89; Archdeacon, Young, NSW, 1989–95; Exec. Dir. St Mark's Nat. Theol Centre, 1995–97; Head, Sch. of Theol., Charles Sturt Univ., 1996–97; Diocesan Archdeacon, Canberra, and Rector of Manuka, 1997–2001; Bishop of Gippsland, 2001–05. *Publications:* A Polity of Persuasion: gift and grief of Anglicanism, 2014; various articles and reviews in St Mark's Review. *Recreations:* fly-fishing, gardening. *Address:* 4 Patricia Street, Bairnsdale, Vic 3875, Australia.

**DRIVER, Nilli;** *see* Lavie, N.

**DRIVER, Olga Lindholm;** *see* Aikin, O. L.

**DRIVER, Paul William;** writer and critic; *b* 14 Aug. 1954; *s* of Thomas Driver and Thelma Driver (*née* Tavernor). *Educ:* Salford Grammar Sch.; St Edmund Hall, Oxford (MA Hons English Lit.). Contrib. music reviews, later book and theatre reviews to FT, 1979–95; Music Critic: Daily Telegraph, 1982–83; Boston Globe, 1983–84; Sunday Times, 1984–; contributor to: The Listener, Tempo, Musical Times, TLS, London Rev. of Books, Guardian, NY Times and numerous other pubns; frequent broadcasts on Radio 3, Radio 4, BBC 2, Channel 4, etc; has lectured on music in Britain and USA. Mem. Bd, Contemporary Music Rev., 1981–. Patron, Manchester Musical Heritage Trust, 2005–. *Publications:* (ed) A Diversity of Creatures, by Rudyard Kipling, 1987; (ed jtly) Music and Text, 1989; (ed) Penguin English Verse, 1995; (ed) Penguin Popular Poetry, 6 vols, 1996; Manchester Pieces, 1996; (contrib.) Sing, Ariel, 2003; Four Elegies (verse), 2009; A Metropolitan Recluse (novel), 2010; A Verlaine Dozen (verse), 2013. *Recreations:* walking, swimming, travel. *Address:* 15 Victoria Road, NW6 6SX. *T:* (020) 7624 4501.

**DRIVER, Ven. Penelope May;** Archdeacon of Westmorland and Furness, 2012–17; *b* 20 Feb. 1952; *d* of Arthur Anderson Glover and Bessie Glover. *Educ:* All Saints' Coll., London (Teaching Cert.); Northern Ordination Course (DipTh 1983); Manchester Univ. (MEd Adult Educn 1992). Ordained deacon, 1987, priest, 1994; Diocesan Youth Advr, dio. Newcastle, 1986–88; Curate of Cullercoats, Newcastle, 1987–88; Youth Chaplain, Ripon, 1988–96; Diocese of Ripon and Leeds: Asst Dir of Ordinands, 1996–98, Diocesan Dir of Ordinands, 1998–2006; Bishop's Advr in Women's Ministry, 1991–2006; Minor Canon, 1996–2006, Hon. Canon, 1998–2006, Ripon Cathedral; Archdeacon of Exeter, 2006–12. Mem., Gen. Synod, 2010–. *Recreations:* entertaining, singing, fell walking.

**DRIVER, Sheila Elizabeth;** a District Judge (Magistrates' Courts) (formerly Stipendiary Magistrate), South Yorkshire, 1995–2015; *b* 7 Oct. 1950; *d* of Alfred Derek Robinson and Joan Elizabeth Robinson; *m* 1974, John Graham Driver; one *s* two *d. Educ:* Bradford Girls' GS; Leeds Univ. (BA Hons Hist.); London School of Economics (MA Internat. Hist.). Admitted Solicitor, 1978; Solicitor: City of Bradford MDC, 1978–79; County Prosecuting Office, W Yorks, 1979–80; in private practice, 1981–95. *Recreations:* amateur dramatics, reading.

**DROGHEDA, 12th Earl of,** *cr* 1661 (Ireland); **Henry Dermot Ponsonby Moore;** Baron Moore of Mellifont, 1616; Viscount Moore, 1621; Baron Moore of Cobham (UK), 1954; photographer, professional name Derry Moore; *b* 14 Jan. 1937; *o s* of 11th Earl of Drogheda, KG, KBE and of Joan *o d* of late William Henry Carr; *S* father, 1989; *m* 1st, 1968, Eliza Lloyd (marr. diss. 1972), *d* of Stacy Barcroft Lloyd, Jr, and Mrs Paul Mellon; 2nd, 1978, Alexandra, *d* of Sir (John) Nicholas Henderson, GCMG, KCVO; two *s* one *d. Educ:* Eton; Trinity College, Cambridge. *Publications:* (as Derry Moore): (with Brendan Gill) The Dream Come True, Great Houses of Los Angeles, 1980; (with George Plumptre) Royal Gardens, 1981; (with Sybila Jane Flower) Stately Homes of Britain, 1982; (with Henry Mitchell) Washington, Houses of the Capital, 1982; (with Michael Pick) The English Room, 1984; (with Alvilde Lees-Milne) The Englishwoman's House, 1984; (with Alvilde Lees-Milne) The Englishman's Room, 1986; (with the Marchioness of Salisbury) The Gardens of Queen Elizabeth the Queen Mother, 1988; (with Sarah Hollis) The Shell Guide to the Gardens of England and Wales, 1989; Evening Ragas, 1997; (with Clive Aslet) The House of Lords, 1998; Rooms, 2006; Notting Hill, 2007; (with The Dowager Marchioness of Salisbury) A Gardener's Life, 2008; (with Tim Knox) Sir John Soane's Museum, London, 2009; In House, 2009; (with Monty Don) Great Gardens of Italy, 2011; An English Room, 2013; Horses: portraits by Derry Moore, 2016; In the Shadow of the Raj, 2017; (with David Mlinaric) Great English Interiors, 2018; (with Monty Don) Paradise Gardens, 2018; (with Monty Don) Japanese Gardens, 2019. *Heir: s* Viscount Moore, *qv. Address:* 40 Ledbury Road, W11 2AB. *E:* derry@derrymore.com. *Clubs:* Brooks's, Garrick.

**DROMEY, Jack;** MP (Lab) Birmingham Erdington, since 2010; *b* 29 Sept. 1948; *m* 1982, Harriet Harman (*see* Rt Hon. H. Harman); two *s* one *d. Educ:* Cardinal Vaughan Grammar Sch. Sec., Brent Trades Council, 1976–78; Transport and General Workers' Union, later Unite: various posts from dist officer to nat. organiser, 1978–2003; Dep. Gen. Sec., 2003–10. Treas., Labour Party, 2004–10. Shadow Minister for Housing, 2010–13, Home Affairs, 2013–16, Labour, 2016–18, Pensions, 2018–. Member, Select Committee: Business, Innovation and Skills, 2010; Regulatory Reform, 2010–15. *Address:* House of Commons, SW1A 0AA.

**DROMGOOLE, Dominic Charles Fleming;** Director, Open Palm Films, since 2016; Artistic Director, Classic Spring Theatre Company, since 2017; *b* 25 Oct. 1963; *s* of Patrick Shirley Brookes Fleming Dromgoole, *qv;* partner, Sasha Hails; three *d. Educ:* Millfield Sch.; St Catharine's Coll., Cambridge (BA (English Lit.) 1985). Artistic Dir, Bush Th., 1990–96; New Plays Dir, Old Vic Th., 1997; Artistic Director: Oxford Stage Co., 1999–2005; Shakespeare's Globe Th., 2006–16. Director: theatre: Shadow of a Gunman, Tricycle, 2004; Someone Who'll Watch Over Me, New Ambassadors, 2005; film: Making Noise Quietly, 2019. Producer, Saltwater (film), 2000. Essayist, Sunday Times and others, 2001–. *Publications:* The Full Room, 2001; Will and Me: how Shakespeare took over my life, 2006; Hamlet: Globe to Globe: taking Shakespeare to Every Country in the World, 2017. *Recreations:* walking, drinking. *Address:* 5 Newick Road, E5 0RP.

**DROMGOOLE, Patrick Shirley Brookes Fleming;** Chairman, PDP Ltd, since 1992; *b* 30 Aug. 1930; *s* of late Nicholas and Violet Dromgoole; *m* 1st, 1960, Jennifer Veronica Jill Davis (marr. diss. 1991); two *s* one *d*; 2nd, 1991, June Kell Morrow. *Educ:* Dulwich Coll.; University Coll., Oxford (MA). Actor and various employments in London and Paris, 1947–51; BBC Drama Producer/Dir, 1954–63; freelance theatre, film and television dir (directed first plays in West End of Orton, Wood, Welland, Halliwell and others), 1963–69; directed regularly Armchair Theatre for ABC TV and Thames TV; made number of films for cinema; joined HTV Ltd as Programme Controller, 1969; Asst Man. Dir, 1981; Man. Dir, HTV, 1987; Chief Exec., HTV Gp, 1988–91. Various awards incl. Pye Oscar, RTS, for Thick as Thieves, 1971; Best Play of the Year, for Machinegunner, 1973; Amer. Emmy, for D. P., 1985. FRTS 1978; FRSA 1989. *Recreations:* travel, œnophily, pre-Raphaelite art, reading. *Address:* Penkill Castle, Girvan, Ayrshire KA26 9TQ. *Clubs:* Garrick, Groucho.

*See also* D. C. F. Dromgoole.

**DROMORE, Bishop of, (RC),** since 1999; **Most Rev. John McAreavey;** *b* Banbridge, Ireland, 2 Feb. 1949. *Educ:* St Colman's Coll., Newry; Maynooth Coll.; Pontifical Univ., Maynooth; Pontifical Gregorian Univ., Rome. Ordained priest, 1973; Teacher, St Colman's Coll., Newry, 1978–79; Vice Judicial Vicar, 1979–83, Judicial Vicar, 1983–88, Armagh Regl Marriage Tribunal; Prof. of Canon Law, St Patrick's Coll., Maynooth, 1988–99. *Address:* Bishop's House, 44 Armagh Road, Newry, Co. Down BT35 6PN.

**DRONKE, Prof. (Ernst) Peter (Michael),** FBA 1984; Fellow of Clare Hall, 1964–2001, now Emeritus, and Professor of Medieval Latin Literature, 1989–2001, now Emeritus, University of Cambridge; *b* 30 May 1934; *s* of Senatspräsident A. H. R. Dronke and M. M. Dronke (*née* Kronfeld); *m* 1960, Ursula Miriam (*née* Brown) (*d* 2012); one *d. Educ:* Victoria University, NZ (MA 1st Cl. Hons 1954); Magdalen College, Oxford (BA 1st Cl. Hons 1957; MA 1961); MA Cantab 1961. Research Fellow, Merton Coll., Oxford, 1958–61;

Lectr in Medieval Latin, 1961–79, Reader, 1979–89, Univ. of Cambridge. Guest Lectr, Univ. of Munich, 1960; Guest Prof., Centre d'Etudes Médiévales, Poitiers, 1969; Leverhulme Fellow, 1973; Guest Prof., Univ. Autónoma, Barcelona, 1977; Vis. Fellow, Humanities Res. Centre, Canberra, 1978; Vis. Prof. of Medieval Studies, Westfield Coll., 1981–86. Lectures: W. P. Ker, Univ. of Glasgow, 1976; Matthews, Birkbeck Coll., 1983; Jackson, Harvard Univ., 1992; O'Donnell, Univ. of Toronto, 1993; Barlow, UCL, 1995. Corresp. Fellow: Real Academia de Buenas Letras, 1976; Royal Dutch Acad., 1997; Medieval Acad. of America, 1999; Austrian Acad. of Scis, 2001; Fondazione Lorenzo Valla, 2006; Istituto Lombardo Acad. of Scis and Letters, 2007. Hon. Pres., Internat. Courtly Literature Soc., 1974. Co-Editor, Mittellateinisches Jahrbuch, 1977–2002. Premio Internazionale Ascoli Piceno, 1988; Premio Bettarini, 2014. *Publications:* Medieval Latin and the Rise of European Love-Lyric, 2 vols, 1965–66; The Medieval Lyric, 1968; Poetic Individuality in the Middle Ages, 1970; Fabula, 1974; Abelard and Heloise in Medieval Testimonies, 1976; (with Ursula Dronke) Barbara et antiquissima carmina, 1977; (ed) Bernardus Silvestris, Cosmographia, 1978; Introduction to Francesco Colonna, Hypnerotomachia, 1981; Women Writers of the Middle Ages, 1984; The Medieval Poet and his World, 1984; Dante and Medieval Latin Traditions, 1986; Introduction to Rosvita, Dialoghi drammatici, 1986; (ed) A History of Twelfth-Century Western Philosophy, 1988; Hermes and the Sibyls, 1990; Latin and Vernacular Poets of the Middle Ages, 1991; Intellectuals and Poets in Medieval Europe, 1992; Verse with Prose: from Petronius to Dante, 1994; Nine Medieval Latin Plays, 1994; (ed with A. Derolez) Hildegard of Bingen, *Liber divinorum operum*, 1996; Sources of Inspiration, 1997; Dante's Second Love, 1997; Introduction to Alessandro nel medioevo occidentale, 1997; (with Ursula Dronke) Growth of Literature: the sea and the God of the sea, 1998; (ed) Etienne Gilson's Letters to Bruno Nardi, 1998; (ed with Charles Burnett) Hildegard of Bingen: the context of her thought and art, 1998; Imagination in the late Pagan and Early Christian World, 2003; Forms and Imaginings, 2007; The Spell of Calcidius, 2008; (ed) Giovanni Scoto Eriugena, Periphyseon I, 2012, II, 2013, III, 2014, IV, 2016, V, 2017; Sacred and Profane Thought in the Early Middle Ages, 2016; (with G. Ravasi) Su Dante, 2017; essays in learned jls and symposia. *Recreations:* music, film, Brittany. *Address:* 6 Parker Street, Cambridge CB1 1JL.

**DRORI, Tracy;** *see* Chevalier, T.

**DROWN, Julia Kate;** *b* 23 Aug. 1962; *d* of David Christopher Robert Drown and Audrey Marion Harris; *m* 1999, Bill Child; one *s* one *d* (and one *d* decd). *Educ:* Hampstead Comprehensive Sch.; University Coll., Oxford (BA); CIPFA Educn and Trng Coll., Croydon. Unit Accountant, Oxfordshire Unit for People with Learning Difficulties, 1988–90; Dir of Finance, Radcliffe Infirmary, Oxford, 1990–96. Mem. (Lab) Oxfordshire CC, 1989–96. MP (Lab) Swindon South, 1997–2005. Mem., Select Cttee on Health, 1997–99 and 2001–03; Chair, Select Sub-cttee on Maternity Services, 2003; All Party Groups: Chair: on Maternity, 2000–05; on Heavily Indebted Poor Countries (formerly Third World Debt), 2001–05; Co-Chair, on Illegal Camping and Traveller Mgt, 2002–05; Vice Chair: on Further Educn, 1998–99; Voice, 1998–2004. Hon. Secretary: on Osteoporosis, 1999–2005; on Rwanda, the Great Lakes Region and the Prevention of Genocide, 2001–05. Member: Health Professions Council, 2009–13; Appeals Cttee, HFEA, 2009–15; Chair, Veterinary Medicines Directorate Mgt Bd, 2014–; Nursing and Midwifery Council: Pension Trustee, 2009–19; Partner Mem., Business Planning and Governance Cttee, 2009–10; Mem., Audit Cttee, 2011–13 (Chair, 2011–12). Mem., Oxfordshire Music Educn Partnership, 2018–. Patron, Advocacy after Fatal Domestic Abuse, 2009–14. Mem., CIPFA, 1989–2005. *Recreations:* family, dance, music.

**DRU DRURY, Martin;** *see* Drury.

**DRUCKER, Prof. Daniel Joshua,** OC 2015; MD; FRCPC; FRSC 2012; FRS 2015; Professor of Medicine, University of Toronto, since 1987; Senior Scientist, Lunenfeld-Tanenbaum Research Institute (formerly Samuel Lunenfeld Research Institute), Mount Sinai Hospital, Toronto, since 2006; *b* Montreal, Quebec, 23 June 1956; *s* of Ernest Drucker and Cila Bernstein. *Educ:* Univ. of Toronto (MD 1980). FRCPC 1984. Intern in Medicine, Johns Hopkins Hosp., Baltimore, 1980–81; Toronto General Hospital: Resident in Medicine, 1981–82; Fellow in Endocrinol., 1982–83; Chief Med. Resident, 1983–84; Centennial Res. Fellow, Med. Res. Council of Canada, 1984–87; Res. Fellow in Medicine, Massachusetts Gen. Hosp., Harvard Univ., 1984–87; Staff Physician: Endocrinol., Toronto Gen. Hosp., 1987–2006; Mount Sinai Hosp., Toronto, 2006–; University of Toronto: Dir, Div. of Endocrinol., Dept of Medicine, 1992–2001; Dir, Banting and Best Diabetes Centre, until 2011. *Publications:* articles in learned jls. *Recreations:* golf, water sports, biking. *Address:* Mount Sinai Hospital, 600 University Avenue, TCP5-1004, Toronto, ON M5G 1X5, Canada. *T:* (416) 3612661, *Fax:* (416) 3612669.

**DRUCKMAN, Paul Bryan,** FCA; Chairman, UK Corporate Reporting Council, since 2017; Chairman, Clear Insurance Management, since 2005; *b* 23 Dec. 1954; *s* of Leonard and Phoebe Druckman; *m* 1983, Angela Samuel; one *s* one *d*. *Educ:* King's Coll. Sch., Wimbledon; Warwick Univ. (PGCE 1981); Dip. Envmtl Mgt, British Safety Council, 2002. FCA 1979. Sales Dir, Orchard Business Systems Ltd, 1986–90; Managing Director: Dit Ltd, 1990–99; Aston IT Gp, 1999–2001; Chairman: IT Faculty, 2001–02; SME Forum, 2001–03; Director: Business Link for London Ltd, 2004–06; Access UK (formerly Access Accounts, then Access Technol. Gp), 2004–11 (Chm., 2009–11); CEO, Internat. Integrated Reporting Council, 2010–16. Pres., ICAEW, 2004–05. Mem., Takeover Panel, 2004–05; Dir, Financial Reporting Council, 2004–07; Mem. Bd, UK Financial Reporting Council, 2017–19. Chairman: CCAB, 2004–05; M Institute, 2006–; Corporate Responsibility Adv. Gp, ICAEW, 2006–11; Sustainability Policy Gp, FEE, 2007–11; Prince of Wales's Accounting for Sustainability Forum (formerly Ext. Reporting Wkg Party), 2007–11; Mem., Eminent Persons Adv. Gp on Human Rights Standards, 2013–; Mem. Bd, Shift project, USA, 2018–. Freeman, City of London, 2003; Mem., Ct of Assts, Chartered Accountants' Co., 2004–05. *Recreations:* golf, tennis. *Address:* c/o Clear Insurance Management, 1 Great Tower Street, EC3R 5AA. *E:* paul.druckman@thecleargroup.com. *Clubs:* Royal Wimbledon Golf, Westside Lawn Tennis (Wimbledon).

**DRUICK, Dr Douglas;** President and Eloise W. Martin Director, Art Institute of Chicago, 2011–16. *Educ:* McGill Univ., Montreal (BA Hons English and Philosophy 1966); Univ. of Toronto (MA English 1967); Oberlin Coll., Ohio (MA Hist. of Art 1970); Yale Univ. (MPhil Hist. of Art 1972; PhD Hist. of Art 1979). Asst to Curator of Prints and Drawings, Yale Univ. Art Gall., 1971–72; Curator, Eur. and American Prints, Nat. Gall. of Canada, Ottawa, 1973–84; Art Institute of Chicago: Chair and Prince Trust Curator of Prints and Drawings, 1985–89; Searle Curator of Eur. Painting, 1989–2004; Searle Curator of Medieval through Modern Eur. Painting and Modern Eur. Sculpture, 2004–06; Chair and Searle Curator of Medieval to Modern Eur. Painting and Sculpture, 2006–11. Chm., Arts and Artifacts Indemnity Adv. Panel, Nat. Endowment for the Arts, 2002–04; Founding Bd Mem., Assoc. of Art Mus. Curators, 2002–08; Member: Nat. Cttee for the Hist. of Art, 2003–09; Bd of Dirs, After Sch. Matters, 2011; Assoc. of Art Mus. Dirs, 2011–; Internat. Gp of Organizers of Large-scale Exhibns (Bizot Gp), 2011. Mem., Editl Adv. Bd, Master Drawings, Master Drawings Assoc. Inc., 2002–.

**DRUMLANRIG, Viscount; Sholto Francis Guy Douglas;** *b* 1 June 1967; *s* and heir of 12th Marquess of Queensberry, *qv*.

**DRUMMOND,** family name of **Earl of Perth** and **Baron Strange**.

**DRUMMOND, Caroline Jane, (Mrs Philip Ward),** MBE 2009; CEnv; FRSB; Chief Executive, LEAF (Linking Environment and Farming), since 1991; Director, LEAF Marque, since 2004; *b* Hill Head, Fareham, Hants, 24 June 1963; *d* of late Lt Comdr (Geoffrey) Mortimer Heneage Drummond and of Sarah Drummond; *m* 1998, Philip Ward; one *d*. *Educ:* Rookesbury Park, Wickham; St Swithun's, Winchester; Seale Hayne Agricultural Coll. (BSc Hons Agric.). CEnv 2009. Agronomy Lectr, Shuttleworth Agric. Coll., 1989–91. Dir, Oxford Farming Conf., 2003–05 (Chm., 2005). Member: Bd, Crop Health and Protection (formerly Centre for Applied Crop Sci.), 2017–; Council, Inst. of Agricl Mgt, 2017–; Mem., Contemporary Agriculture Adv. Panel, Sci. Mus., 2016–. Governor: Inst. of Envmt and Grassland Res., 2005–08; Royal Agricultural Univ., 2006–14; Rothamsted Res. (formerly Rothamsted Experimental Station), 2007–15; British Nutrition Foundn, 2009–; Trustee, CPRE, 2008–11. Member: DEFRA Civil Soc. Adv. Bd, 2009–14; DEFRA Dame Glenys Stacey's Adv. Cttee, Farm Inspection and Regulation Report, 2019. Hon. DSc Harper Adams, 2013. FRAgS 1998; FIAgrM 2008; CEnv 2008; FRSA 2010; FRSB (FSB 2012). Hon. FSE 2014; Hon. FRAU 2018. Frank Arden Nuffield Scholarship, 2013. Pioneer to Life of the Nation, 2003; Ecological Engagement Award, British Ecol Soc., 2009; Contribn to Landbased Sector Award, Instn of Agricl Engrs, 2017; Outstanding Contribn to British Agric. Award, Brit. Farming Awards, 2017; Nat. Agric. Award, RASE, 2018; Women of the Decade in Sustainable Farming Award, Women Economic Forum, 2019. *Publications:* numerous scientific and farming articles, papers and comments. *Recreations:* singing, countryside matters, scientific kitchen experiments and art projects with my daughter. *Address:* LEAF, National Agricultural Centre, Stoneleigh, Warwicks CV8 2LG. *T:* (024) 7641 3911. *E:* caroline.drummond@leafuk.org; Butterwell, Tempellow Farm, Horningtops, Liskeard, Cornwall PL14 3QD. *Club:* Farmers.

**DRUMMOND, Caroline Stewart;** Commissioner, Scottish Law Commission, since 2015; *b* Dingwall, Scotland, 30 May 1959; *d* of James Macrae Skinner and Catherine Sutherland Skinner; *m* 1982, William Drummond; two *s* one *d*. *Educ:* Tain Royal Acad.; Univ. of Aberdeen (LLB); Univ. of Edinburgh (DipLP). Joined as trainee, 1981, Partner, 1988–2015, W & J Burness WS, subseq. Burness, then Burness Paull & Williamsons, later Burness Paull LLP. *Recreations:* ski-ing, golf, family. *Address:* Scottish Law Commission, 140 Causewayside, Edinburgh EH9 1PR. *T:* (0131) 668 2131. *E:* caroline.drummond@scotlawcom.gsi.gov.uk.

**DRUMMOND, Colin Irwin John Hamilton,** OBE 2012; DL; Chairman, Taunton and Somerset NHS Foundation Trust, since 2014; *b* 22 Feb. 1951; *s* of Rev. William Balfour Drummond, MA and Annie Rebecca Drummond (*née* Roy); *m* 1975, Georgina Lloyd; two *s*. *Educ:* Wadham Coll., Oxford (BA (double 1st Cl. Hons Classics), MA 1978); Harvard Graduate Sch. of Business Admin (Harkness Fellow; MBA 1977). LTCL 1969 (Colman Prize). Asst Superintendent, Economic Intelligence Dept, Bank of England, 1973–78; Consultant, Boston Consulting Gp, 1978–84; Dir for Corporate Develt, Renold plc, 1984–86; Chief Exec., Yarns Div., Coats Viyella plc, 1986–92; Exec. Dir, Pennon Gp plc, 1992–2013; Chief Executive: Viridor Ltd, 1998–2002; Viridor Waste Mgt Ltd, 2002–13; Chm., Viridor Ltd, 2013–14. Non-exec. Dir, Vymura plc, 1998–99. Member: Adv. Cttee on Business and the Envmt, 2001–03; Council, SW Reg., CBI, 1997–2003. Dir, Sustainability SW, 2005–12. Chairman: Envmt and Water Sector Adv. Gp (formerly Envmt Sector Adv. Gp), 2005–12; Envmtl Knowledge Transfer Network, 2007–09; Envmtl Sustainability Knowledge Transfer Network, 2009–13; Business Adv. Bd, Living with Envmtl Change, 2010–15. Vis. Sen. Fellow, Earth Scis, Oxford Univ., 2007–13. Pro-Chancellor and Chair of Govs, Univ. of Plymouth, 2016–. CCMI 2002. Hon. FSE 2013. Freeman, City of London, 1999; Liveryman, 1999–, Mem., Ct of Assts, and Master, 2007–08, Water Conservators' Co.; Chm., Water Related Livery Cos, 2009–13; Liveryman: Gardeners' Co., 2010–; Musicians' Co., 2011–. DL Somerset, 2016. Gov., Corp. of the Sons of the Clergy, 2008–. Organist and choirmaster, parish church of St John the Baptist, Wellington, Somerset, 1993–2006. Appearance in Undercover Boss, TV prog., 2010. Hon. DBA Edge Hill, 2012. *Recreations:* music, vegetable gardening. *Address:* Taunton and Somerset NHS Foundation Trust, Musgrove Park Hospital, Taunton, Somerset TA1 5DA. *T:* (01823) 342512. *Club:* Oxford and Cambridge.

**DRUMMOND, David Classon,** FRSB; Deputy Director, Research and Development Service, Agricultural Development Advisory Service, Ministry of Agriculture, Fisheries and Food, 1987–88, retired; *b* 25 July 1928; *s* of Roger Hamilton Drummond and Marjorie Holt Drummond; *m* 1952, Barbara Anne, *d* of late Prof. Alfred Cobban; three *d*. *Educ:* St Peter's Sch., York; University Coll., London (BSc 1952); Pennsylvania State Univ., USA (Kellogg Fellow; MS 1962). FRSB (FIBiol 1975). Project Manager, FAO, UN, Karachi, 1971–72; Agricultural Science Service, MAFF: Head of Rodent Res. Dept, and Officer i/c Tolworth Lab., 1974–82; Head of Biol. Div., and Officer i/c Slough Lab., 1982–85; Sen. Agricl Scientist with special responsibilities for R&D, 1985–87. Mem., WHO Expert Adv. Panel on Vector Biology and Control, 1980–97. *Publications:* William C. Hooker's Great American Mouse Trap, 2002, 2nd edn 2013; Nineteenth Century Mouse Traps Patented in the USA, 2004; Mouse Traps: a quick scamper through their long history, 2005; McGill Mouse Traps and the Stilson Brothers, 2006; Twentieth Century Mouse Traps Patented in the USA, 1900–1924, 2007; British Mouse Traps and their Makers, 2008; Twentieth Century Mouse Traps Patented in the USA, 1925–1949, 2008; Twentieth Century Mouse Traps Patented in the USA the Last Fifty Years, 2009; Norway Rat, Erie Canal and Little Giant, 2009; Neroth Mouse Traps and their Makers, 2010; German Mouse Traps and their Makers, 2011; French Mouse Traps and their Makers, 2012; Rats, Mice and Religion, 2012; A Book of Old Rat Catchers, 2012; Cat and Mouse, 2012; A Celebration of Mice, 2013; Twenty First Century Mouse Traps, 2013; Ceramic Mice, 2014; The Mouse Trap Guide, 2015; The History of the National Garden Scheme's Open Gardens in Mole Valley, 2016; Restaurants of Dorking and Some Thoughts on Food, 2016; The History of Religions and Places of Worship in Mole Valley, 2017; The Breweries and their Ales and the Pubs of Mole Valley, 2017; The Ancient and Medieval History of the Towns and Villages of Mole Valley, 2018; Mole Valley Wildlife and its Conservation, 2019; scientific papers and reviews mainly concerned with rodent biology and control and develt of agricl and urban rat control programmes. *Recreations:* travel, gardening, history of mouse traps and rat catching. *Address:* 36 Downs Way, Tadworth KT20 5DZ. *W:* www.mousetrapbooks.com.

**DRUMMOND, Felicia Jane Beatrix;** *b* 16 June 1962; *d* of (George) Anthony Shepherd, CMG and Sarah Shepherd; *m* 1987, Hereward John Heneage Drummond; two *s* two *d*. *Educ:* Hull Univ. (BA SE Asian Studies 1983); Southampton Univ. (MA Global Politics and Internat. Relns 2007). Insce broker, 1983–87; Ofsted lay sch. inspector, 1994–99; Dir, Corporate Affairs, Cons. Middle East Council, 2010–11; Dep. Chm., Political, Portsmouth S Cons. Assoc., 2011–13. Member: Healthwatch; Community Health Council. Mem. (C) Winchester CC, 1996–99. Contested (C): Southampton Itchen, 2005; Portsmouth S, 2010. MP (C) Portsmouth S, 2015–17; contested (C) same seat, 2017. Chair, SE Reg., Veterans Adv. and Pension Cttees, 2018–; Mem. Bd, Nat. Citizen Service Trust, 2018–. Trustee, Citizens Advice Portsmouth, 2010–. Mem. Bd, Salterns Academy Trust, 2017–.

**DRUMMOND, Gillian Vera,** OBE 2008; DL; Commissioner, English Heritage, 2002–10; *b* 15 Sept. 1939; *d* of Gavin and Vera Clark; *m* 1st, 1958, Graham Turner Laing (marr. diss. 1978; he *d* 2007); three *d* (and one *s* decd); 2nd, 1978, Maldwin Andrew Cyril Drummond, OBE (*d* 2017); one *s*. *Educ:* Roedean Sch.; Poggio Imperiale, Florence. Founder Chm., Hampshire Gardens Trust, 1984–96 (Pres., 2011–); Mem., Council of Mgt, 1989–2010, Adv. Cttee, 2011–, Sir Harold Hillier Gardens & Arboretum; Chairman: Wessex Region, Historic Houses Assoc., 2000–05; Historic Parks and Gardens Panel (formerly Adv. Cttee), English Heritage, 2001–06 (Mem., 1985–2001); Adv. Gp, Capability Brown Birthday Celebrations and Festival 2016, 2012–; Mem., Urban Green Spaces Taskforce, ODPM, 2001–03 (Chm., Wkg Gp); President: Waterside Charities, 1981–95; Blackfield Gardening Soc., 1993–; Assoc. of Gardens Trusts, 1995– (Founder Chm., 1992–95); Vice-Pres., Royal Southampton Soc., 1986–. Trustee: Solent Rescue, 1988–98; Learning Through Landscape Trust, 1991–2010; Gilbert White's House and The Oates Collection (formerly Oates Meml Mus.), 1992–2013; Chawton House Library, 1993–; Countryside Educn Trust, 1999–2013; Nat. Maritime Mus., 2005–13; Chiswick House and Gardens Trust (formerly Chiswick House and Park Trust), 2006–12; Llanthony Secunda Priory Trust, 2007–10. Patron: Folly Fellowship, 2001–; Green Space, 2002–. Sen. Judge, Southern Region In Bloom, 1986–2001. County Pres., St John Ambulance Bde, Hants, 1990–2003. Gov., Millbrook Sch., Southampton, 1988–2005. DL Hants, 1994. Gold Veitch Meml Medal, RHS, 1996. *Recreations:* gardening, sailing, art, architecture. *Address:* Stanswood Farm House, Fawley, Southampton SO45 1AB. *T:* (023) 8089 1543; Wester Kames Castle, Port Bannatyne, Isle of Bute PA20 0QW. *T:* (01700) 503983. *E:* gilly@cadland.co.uk. *Clubs:* Royal Cruising (Assoc. Mem.); Royal Yacht Squadron (Lady Assoc. Mem.).

*See also S. H. Turner Laing.*

**DRUMMOND, James Robert,** CBE 2009; international development consultant, since 2012; Senior Research Associate, Overseas Development Institute, since 2015; *b* 12 July 1953; *s* of Brian and Isobel Drummond; *m* 1988, Glynis Joan Fell; two *s* one *d*. *Educ:* Trinity Coll., Cambridge (MA Hist. 1979). Head: Develt Sect., British High Commn, New Delhi, 1989–92; Central and Southern Africa Dept, 1992–95, Personnel, 1995–97, ODA; Central Africa, Harare, DFID, 1997–2000; Asst Hd, Defence and Overseas Secretariat, Cabinet Office, 2000–03; Dir, Iraq, 2003–04, UN Conflict and Humanitarian Div., 2005–07, S Asia Div., 2007–10, Western and Southern Africa, 2010–12, DFID. Associate, Crown Agents, 2017–. Trustee, Orchid Project, Acid Survivors Trust Internat., 2012–16. FRGS 2012. *Recreations:* village cricket, birds, African history. *Club:* Shamley Green Cricket (Pres., 2009–).

**DRUMMOND, Jamie,** OBE 2016; Co-founder and Executive Director, ONE. *Educ:* Univ. of Bristol (BA Eng. and Philos. 1991); Sch. of Oriental and African Studies, London (MA Develt 1992). Christian Aid, 1992–98; Jubilee 2000 Drop the Debt, 1998–2001; Co-founder and Executive Director, Debt, AIDS, Trade, Africa, 2002, ONE: the Campaign to Make Poverty History, 2004, merged as ONE, 2008. *Recreation:* adventure.

**DRUMMOND, Kevin;** *see* Drummond, T. A. K.

**DRUMMOND, Lorna Allison;** QC (Scot.) 2011; Sheriff of Tayside, Central and Fife at Dundee, since 2014; Justice of the Appeal Court of St Helena, Ascension Island and Tristan Da Cunha, since 2015; *b* Edinburgh, 19 Dec. 1967; *d* of Iain P. Drummond and Dorothy J. Drummond; *m* 2001, Derrick Guild; two *d*. *Educ:* Hutchesons' Grammar Sch.; Glasgow Univ. (LLB Hons 1989); Sidney Sussex Coll., Cambridge (MPhil 1990); Edinburgh Univ. (DipLP 1991). Admitted to Faculty of Advocates, 1998; Asst Scottish Parly Counsel and Asst Legal Sec. to Scottish Law Officers, 1994–97; Standing Junior: to Home Office, 2002–07; to Scottish Govt, 2009–11; Crown Counsel, Ascension Is., 2007–09; pt-time Sheriff, 2009–14. Hon. Prof., Univ. of St Andrews, 2019–. *Recreations:* running, yoga, sailing, cycling. *E:* lornadrummond@aol.com.

**DRUMMOND, Rev. Norman Walker,** CBE 2014; MA, BD; FRSE; Founder and Chairman: Drummond International, since 1999; Columba 1400, Community and International Leadership Centre, Isle of Skye, 1997–2016, now Founder President; Visiting Professor of Leadership in Education, University of Edinburgh, since 2009; *b* 1 April 1952; *s* of late Edwin Payne Drummond and Jean (*née* Walker); *m* 1976, Lady Elizabeth Helen Kennedy, *d* of 7th Marquess of Ailsa, OBE; three *s* two *d*. *Educ:* Merchiston Castle Sch.; Fitzwilliam Coll., Cambridge (MA Law); New Coll., Univ. of Edinburgh (BD). FRSE 2008. Ordained as Minister of the Church of Scotland, and commnd to serve as Chaplain to HM Forces in the Army, 1976; Chaplain: Depot, Parachute Regt and Airborne Forces, 1977–78; 1st Bn The Black Watch (Royal Highland Regt), 1978–82; to the Moderator of the Gen. Assembly of the Church of Scotland, 1980; Fettes Coll., 1982–84; Headmaster, Loretto Sch., 1984–95; Minister of Kilmuir and Stenscholl, Isle of Skye, 1996–98. Chaplain to Gov. of Edinburgh Castle, 1991–93; Chaplain to the Queen in Scotland, 1993–. BBC Nat. Gov., and Chm., Broadcasting Council for Scotland, 1994–99; Mem., Scottish Broadcasting Commn, 2007–08. Chair, Scottish Commemorations Panel, 2012–; Special Rep. for Scotland, UK Adv. Gp, World War I Commemorations, 2012–. Chm., BBC Children in Need, 1997–99. Chairman: Musselburgh and Dist Council of Social Service, 1984–94; Community Action Network, Scotland, 2001–03; Lloyds TSB Foundn for Scotland, 2003–09; Founder and non-exec. Chm., The Change Partnership Scotland, 1999–2003. Non-exec. Dir, J. & J. Denholm Ltd, 2002–. Mem., Queen's Bodyguard for Scotland (Royal Co. of Archers), 1990–. Mem. Court, Heriot-Watt Univ., 1986–92; Gov., Gordonstoun Sch., 1995–2000; Chm. Govs, Aiglon Coll., Switzerland, 1999–2005. Former Trustee: Arthur Smith Meml Trust; Foundn for Skin Res. President: Edinburgh Bn, Boys' Bde, 1993–98; Victoria League in Scotland, 1995–98. Cambridge Univ. Rugby Blue, 1971; Captain: Scottish Univs XV, 1974; Army XV and Combined Services XV, 1976–77. Hon. Col, Black Watch Bn ACF, 2014–. DUniv Glasgow Caledonian, 2010. *Publications:* The First Twenty-five Years: official history of The Black Watch Kirk Session, 1979; Mother's Hands (collection of short stories for children, parents and teachers), 1992; The Spirit of Success: how to connect your heart to your head in work and life, 2004; The Power of Three: discovering what really matters in life, 2010; Step Back: finding the way forward in life, 2015. *Recreations:* Rugby football, cricket, golf, curling, traditional jazz, Isle of Skye. *Address:* 35 Drummond Place, Edinburgh EH3 6PW. *Clubs:* MCC; Hawks (Cambridge).

**DRUMMOND, Peter;** Director, 1991–2017, and Chairman, BDP South, 2014–17, Building Design Partnership (Chief Executive, 2004–13); *b* Essex, 12 Nov. 1953; *s* of Ian and Eileen Drummond; *m* 1977, Susan Jane Barrows; two *s*. *Educ:* Univ. of Manchester (BA Hons Town Planning). MRTPI 1978. Planner, Building Design Partnership, 1976–79; Sen. Planner, Bolton MBC, 1979–80; Building Design Partnership: Sen. Planner, 1980–84; Associate, 1984–87; Associate Dir, 1987–91. FRSA. Mem., Acad. of Urbanism, 2009–; Pres., BCSC, 2012. *Publications:* Urban Design for Retail Environments, 2002. *Recreations:* ski-ing, offshore ocean racing, Arsenal FC.

**DRUMMOND, Roderick Ian;** HM Diplomatic Service; Ambassador to the Kingdom of Bahrain, since 2019; *b* 7 Sept. 1962; *s* of Ian Drummond and Sarah (*née* Laird); *m* 2013, Yasmin; one *s* two *d* by former marriage. *Educ:* Edinburgh Univ. (MA Hons Hist.). Entered FCO, 1985; Arabic lang. trng, SOAS, 1986, Univ. of Jordan, 1987; Second Sec. (Pol/Econ.), Algiers, 1988–92; First Sec., FCO, 1992–96; Dep. Consul-Gen., Johannesburg, 1996–98; UK Rep. to EU, Brussels, 1998–2002; Deputy Head of Mission: Amman, 2002–04; Damascus, 2004–07; Hd of Mission, Doha, 2007–08; FCO, London, 2008–09; Dep. Hd of Mission, Riyadh, 2009–13; High Comr to Fiji, and Hd, S Pacific Network, 2013–16; Dir, Operational and Protective Security, FCO, 2016–19. *Recreations:* Rugby, golf, tennis, Scrabble, cuisine, wine, desert exploring, walking, scuba diving. *Address:* c/o Foreign and Commonwealth Office, King Charles Street, SW1A 2AH.

**DRUMMOND, (Thomas Anthony) Kevin;** QC (Scot.) 1987; Sheriff of Lothian and Borders at Jedburgh, Selkirk and Duns, 2000–13, and at Peebles, 2011–13; *b* 3 Nov. 1943; *s* of Thomas Drummond, BSc, and Mary (*née* Hughes); *m* 1966, Margaret Evelyn Broadley; one *d* (and one *d* decd). *Educ:* Blairs Coll., Aberdeen; St Mirin's Acad., Paisley; Edinburgh Univ. (LLB). Estate Duty Office, CS, 1963–70; Solicitor, 1970; admitted Faculty of Advocates, 1974; Advocate-Depute, 1985–90, Home Advocate-Depute, 1996–97, Crown Office, Edinburgh; Sheriff of Glasgow and Strathkelvin, 1997–2000. Member: Criminal Injuries Compensation Bd, 1990–96; Firearms Consultative Cttee, 1990–97; Criminal Injuries Compensation Authy, 1996. Chm., Discipline Tribunal, Inst. of Chartered Accts of Scotland, 1994–. Chm., Legislation, Regulation and Guidance Cttee, Partnership for Action against Wildlife Crime (Scotland), 2009–. Cartoonist, Scots Law Times, 1981–. Hon. US Dep. Marshal, 1998. *Publications:* legal cartoons under name of TAK: The Law at Work, 1982; The Law at Play, 1983; Great Defences of Our Time, 1995. *Recreations:* shooting, hill-walking, fishing, underwater hang-gliding. *Address:* Pomathorn House, Howgate, Midlothian EH26 8PJ. *T:* (01968) 74046.

**DRUMMOND YOUNG, Rt Hon. Lord;** James Edward Drummond Young; PC 2013; a Senator of the College of Justice in Scotland, since 2001; Chairman, Scottish Law Commission, 2007–12; *b* 17 Feb. 1950; *s* of late Duncan Drummond Young, MBE, DL, Edinburgh, and Annette (*née* Mackay); *m* 1991, Elizabeth Mary, *d* of John Campbell-Kease; one *d*. *Educ:* John Watson's Sch.; Sidney Sussex Coll., Cambridge (BA 1971); Harvard Univ. (Joseph Hodges Choate Meml Fellow, 1971–72; LLM 1972); Edinburgh Univ. (LLB 1974). Admitted to Faculty of Advocates, 1976. Standing Jun. Counsel in Scotland to Bd of Inland Revenue, 1986–88; QC (Scot.) 1988; Advocate-Depute, 1999–2001. *Publications:* (with J. B. St Clair) The Law of Corporate Insolvency in Scotland, 1988, 3rd edn 2004; (contrib.) Stair Memorial Encyclopaedia of Scots Law, 1989. *Recreations:* music, travel.

**DRURY, Caroline Mary;** *see* Elam, C. M.

**DRURY, Very Rev. John Henry;** Chaplain and Fellow, All Souls College, Oxford, since 2003; *b* 23 May 1936; *s* of Henry and Barbara Drury; *m* 1st, 1972, (Frances) Clare Nineham (*d* 2004), *d* of Rev. Prof. Dennis Eric Nineham; two *d*; 2nd, 2009, Caroline Mary Elam *qv*. *Educ:* Bradfield; Trinity Hall, Cambridge (MA (Hist. Pt 1, Cl. 1; Theol. Pt 2, Cl. 2/1); Hon. Fellow, 1997); Westcott House, Cambridge. Curate, St John's Wood Church, 1963; Chaplain of Downing Coll., Cambridge, 1966; Chaplain and Fellow of Exeter Coll., Oxford, 1969 (Hon. Fellow, 1991); Res. Canon of Norwich Cathedral and Examining Chaplain to Bp of Norwich, 1973–79; Vice-Dean of Norwich, 1978; Fleck Resident in Religion, Bryn Mawr Coll., USA, 1978; Lectr in Religious Studies, Sussex Univ., 1979–81; Dean, 1981–91, Fellow, 1982–91, King's College, Cambridge; Dean, Christ Church, Oxford, 1991–2003 (Hon. Student, 2003). Syndic, Fitzwilliam Museum, Cambridge, 1988–91. Examining Chaplain to Bp of Chichester, 1980–82. Mem., Doctrine Commn for C of E, 1978–82. Hussey Lectr, Univ. of Oxford, 1997. Jt Editor, Theology, 1976–86. *Publications:* Angels and Dirt, 1972; Luke, 1973; Tradition and Design in Luke's Gospel, 1976; The Pot and The Knife, 1979; The Parables in the Gospels, 1985; Critics of the Bible 1724–1873, 1989; The Burning Bush, 1990; Painting the Word, 1999; Music at Midnight: the life and poetry of George Herbert, 2013; (ed with Victoria Moul) George Herbert: the complete poetry, 2015; articles and reviews in Jl of Theol. Studies, Theology, Expository Times, TLS. *Recreations:* drawing, carpentry, reading. *Address:* All Souls College, Oxford OX1 4AL.

**DRURY, Martin Dru,** CBE 2001; FSA; Director-General, National Trust, 1996–2001 (Deputy Director-General, 1992–95); *b* 22 April 1938; *s* of late Walter Neville Dru Drury, TD; *m* 1971, Elizabeth Caroline, *d* of Hon. Sir Maurice Bridgeman, KBE; two *s* one *d*. *Educ:* Rugby. Commissioned, 3rd Hussars, 1957, Lieut, AER, 1958–67. Insurance Broker at Lloyd's, 1959–65; Mallett & Son Ltd, 1965–73; joined National Trust as Historic Buildings Rep., SE, and Furniture Advr, 1973; Historic Buildings Sec., 1981–95. Comr, Royal Hosp. Chelsea, 2002–08. Trustee: Attingham Trust, 1982– (Vice-Chm., 1982–2013); Landmark Trust, 1988–2011 (Chm., 1992–95, 2001–11); Heritage of London Trust, 1996–2008 (Chm., 2007–08; Vice-Pres., 2008–15; Pres., 2015–); Wallace Collection, 2001–11; Wentworth Woodhouse Preservation Trust, 2014–. Chairman: Stowe Adv. Panel, 2005–; Goldsmiths' Centre Trust, 2007–12; Strawberry Hill Conservation Steering Cttee, 2008–10; Project Hougoumont UK Appeal Cttee, 2011–15. Member: Council, Georgian Group, 1994–2017 (Mem. Exec. Cttee, 1976–94); Fabric Adv. Cttee, St Paul's Cathedral, 1991–; Exec. Cttee, SPAB, 2006–14. Mem. Council, UK Overseas Territories Conservation Forum, 2000–05. Vice-Pres., Arts Soc. (formerly Nat. Assoc. of Decorative and Fine Arts Socs), 2008–. FSA 1992. Mem., Court of Assts, Goldsmiths' Co., 1994– (Prime Warden, 2005–06). Hon. DArts Greenwich, 2000. Esher Award, for services to SPAB, 2002; EU Prize and Europa Nostra Award for Cultural Heritage, 2013. *Address:* 3 Victoria Rise, SW4 0PB; 18 The Street, Stedham, West Sussex GU29 0NQ. *Clubs:* Brooks's, Pratt's; Seaview Yacht.

**DRURY, Michael John,** CMG 2011; Partner, BCL Solicitors LLP (formerly BCL Burton Copeland), since 2010; *b* Camberwell, 22 May 1959; *s* of Kenneth and Joan Drury; *m* 1983, Elizabeth Greenhill; two *d*. *Educ:* Queen Mary Coll., Univ. of London (LLB Hons 1980; LLM 1981). Called to the Bar, Middle Temple, 1982; Legal Asst, HM Customs and Excise, 1985–88; Case Controller, Serious Fraud Office, 1988–96; admitted solicitor, 1996; Legal Advr, 1996–2002, Dir for Legal Affairs, 2002–10, GCHQ. *Recreations:* rowing, opera, Oxford United FC, remote places. *Address:* BCL Solicitors LLP, 51 Lincoln's Inn Fields, WC2A 3LZ. *T:* (020) 7430 2277. *E:* mdrury@bcl.com. *Clubs:* Garrick; Wallingford Rowing; Dummer.

**DRURY, Raymond Michael;** Under Secretary and Executive Director (Personnel), NHS Executive, Department of Health, 1993–95; *b* 28 Sept. 1935; *s* of late James Joseph Drury and Annie Drury (*née* Greenwood); *m* 1959, Joyce Mary (*née* Clare); two *s* two *d*. *Educ:* Manchester Grammar Sch.; University Coll. London (BA Hons Classics (Latin and Greek)). Exec. Officer, Nat. Assistance Bd, 1958–64; HEO and Manager, Legal Aid Assessment Office, N Western Reg., 1964–70; Principal, DHSS, 1970–77; Asst Sec. and Dir (Exports), DHSS, 1977–79; Sec. of State's Rep. on Mgt Sides of Whitley Councils for Health Services (GB) responsible for NHS pay and conditions of service, 1979–88; Hd, Industrial Relns and Negotiations, DoH, 1988–93. *Recreations:* family, gardening, walking, DIY. *Address:* Penlan, Main Street, Clopton, Kettering, Northants NN14 3DZ. *T:* (01832) 720129.

**DRY, Philip John Seaton;** Partner, Biggart Baillie, 1971–2007; President, Law Society of Scotland, 1998–99 (Vice-President, 1997–98); *b* 21 April 1945; *s* of William Good Dry and Georgina Wilson Macpherson or Dry; *m* 1970, Joyce Christine Hall; one *s* one *d*. *Educ:* George Watson's Coll.; Greenock Acad.; Glasgow Univ. (LLB). Apprenticeship, 1966–68, Asst Solicitor, 1968–70, with Biggart Lumsden & Co. Dir, Fyfe Chambers (Glasgow) Ltd,

1990–98. Mem., Disciplinary Appeal Bd, Faculty of Actuaries, 1999–2005. Dir, Westcot Homes plc and Westcot Homes II plc, 1989–2000. Mem., PO Users' Council for Scotland, 1994–98. Director: Scots Law Trust, 1998–99; Scottish Council of Law Reporting, 1998–99. Dir, Glasgow Renfrewshire Soc. *Recreations:* sailing, the garden, opera, swimming, travel. *Address:* 107 Octavia Terrace, Greenock, Renfrewshire PA16 7PY. *Club:* Royal Gourock Yacht.

**DRYDEN, Sir John (Stephen Gyles)**, 8th and 11th Bt *cr* 1795 and 1733; *b* 26 Sept. 1943; *s* of Sir Noel Percy Hugh Dryden, 7th and 10th Bt, and Rosamund Mary (*d* 1994), *e d* of late Stephen Scrope; *S* father, 1970; *m* 1970, Diana Constance, *o d* of late Cyril Tomlinson, Highland Park, Wellington, NZ; one *s* one *d. Educ:* Oratory School. *Heir: s* John Frederick Simon Dryden [*b* 26 May 1976; *m* 2005, Fiona Louise Marsh; one *s* one *d*]. *Address:* Spinners, Fairwarp, East Sussex TN22 3BE.

**DRYSDALE, Laura, (Mrs John Tipler);** Founder and Director, The Restoration Trust, since 2014; *b* 28 April 1958; *d* of late Andrew Drysdale and of Merida Drysdale; *m* 1989, John Tipler; one *s* one *d*, and one step *s* one step *d. Educ:* Charterhouse; St Andrews Univ. (MA 1979); City Univ. (C&G MA 1987). Textile Conservator: Dalmeny House, 1979–81; V&A Mus., 1981–83; Textile Conservation Studio, 1983–86; Conservation Projects, 1986–92; Partner, Drysdale and Halahan, 1992–96; Head of Collections Conservation, English Heritage, 1996–99; Head of Adv. Services, Mus and Galls Commn, 1999–2000; Dir, Sector and Professional Services, Resource: Council for Mus, Archives and Libraries, 2000. FIIC 1996. *Publications:* articles in learned jls, conf. proceedings. *Recreations:* treading grapes, walking with intent, culture therapy in historic landscapes. *Address:* Merchants Place, Church Street, Cromer, Norfolk NR27 9ES.

**DRYSDALE, Lynda;** *see* McMullan, L.

**DRYSDALE, Thomas Henry**, WS; solicitor, retired; *b* 23 Nov. 1942; *s* of late Ian Drysdale and Rosalind Marion Drysdale; *m* 1967, Caroline, *d* of late Dr Gavin Brown Shaw, CBE and Margaret Mabon Shaw; one *s* two *d. Educ:* Cargilfield; Glenalmond; Edinburgh Univ. (LLB). Partner, Shepherd & Wedderburn WS, 1967–99 (Man. Partner, 1988–94); Dep. Keeper of HM Signet, 1991–98; Partner, Olivers WS, 1999–2004. Dir, Edinburgh Solicitors' Property Centre, 1976–89 (Chm., 1981–88). Legal Chm., Tribunals Service, later part time First-tier Tribunal Judge, 2003–13. Mem., Gullane Area Community Council, 2012– (Vice Chm., 2013–18; Chm., 2018–). Hon. Consul in Scotland, Republic of Hungary, 2001–13. Chm. Council, Stair Soc., 2016–18 (Sec. and Treas., 1999–2016). *Publications:* (ed) Making Waves: Clive Freshwater's memoirs 1939–2015, 2018. *Recreations:* walking, gardening, reading, amateur photography. *Address:* 6 The Glebe, Manse Road, Dirleton, East Lothian EH39 5FB. *Club:* New (Edinburgh).

**D'SOUZA,** family name of **Baroness D'Souza**.

**D'SOUZA,** Baroness *cr* 2004 (Life Peer), of Wychwood in the County of Oxfordshire; **Frances Gertrude Claire D'Souza,** CMG 1999; PC 2009; DPhil; Lord Speaker, House of Lords, 2011–16; *b* 18 April 1944; *d* of Robert Anthony Gilbert Russell and Pauline Mary Russell (*née* Parmet); *m* 1st, 1959, Stanislaus Joseph D'Souza (marr. diss. 1974; remarried 2003; he *d* 2011); two *d*; 2nd, 1985, Martin Griffiths (marr. diss. 1994). *Educ:* St Mary's, Princethorpe; UCL (BSc 1970); Lady Margaret Hall, Oxford (DPhil 1976). Ford Foundn Res. Fellow in Comparative Physiology, Nuffield Inst. of Comparative Medicine, 1973–77; pt-time adult educn lectr, Morley Coll. and City Lit., 1973–78; pt-time Lectr on Race and Culture, LSE, 1974–80; Sen. Lectr, Dept of Humanities, Oxford Poly., 1977–80; Founder Dir and Res. Dir, Internat. Relief and Develt Inst., 1977–85; Ind. Res. Cons. for UN, SCF, Ford Foundn, carrying out field work in Africa, Asia, S Europe, Pacific Region, 1985–88; ODA Res. Fellow, 1988–89; Exec. Dir, Article 19, Internat. Centre against Censorship, 1989–98; Fellow, Open Soc. Inst. (Soros Inst.), 1998–99. Dir, 2002–04, Consultant, 2004–06, Redress Trust. Mem., RGS expedn to the Karakorums, 1980. Convenor of crossbench peers, 2007–11. Regular broadcasts, 1989–98. Editor, Internat. Jl of Disaster Studies and Practice, 1978–82. Hon. Dr Hull, 2016. *Publications:* (ed) Striking a Balance: hate speech, freedom of expression and non-discrimination, 1992; (jtly) The Right to Know: human rights and access to reproductive health information, 1995; numerous reports, scientific papers, contribs to books and articles in jls, incl. Nature, Scientific American, Third World Qly. *Recreations:* music (opera and string quartets), serious walking, gardening, reading. *Address:* House of Lords, SW1A 0PW.

**DUBE, Alfred Uyapo Majaye;** Office Director, Institute for Security Studies, since 2016; *b* 8 June 1949; *s* of Mbangwa Edison Majaye and Phakela Majaye (*née* Mongwa); *m* 1977, Elvyn Jones (*d* 2012); three *s. Educ:* Poly. of North London; Univ. of Essex (BA Hons Govt). Librarian, Nat. Liby Service, 1971–74; Foreign Service Officer, Dept of Ext. Affairs, Botswana, 1977–79; First Sec., Botswana Embassy and Mission to EC, Brussels, 1979–80; Counsellor, London, 1980–81; Under-Sec., Min. of Mineral Resources and Water Affairs, 1981–83; Minister Counsellor, Brussels, 1983–87; Under-Sec., Dept of Ext. Affairs, 1987–89; Ambassador to Sweden, all Nordic countries and USSR/Russia, 1989–93; High Comr, UK, 1993–96; Ambassador to Japan, 1996–98, to People's Republic of China, Republic of Korea, and Democratic People's Republic of Korea, and concurrently High Comr to Malaysia and Singapore, 1996–2002; Special Envoy on Diamonds, 2001–02; Perm. Rep. to UN, 2002–05; High Comr to Jamaica and Guyana, and Ambassador to Cuba, 2002–05. Man. Dir, Lazare Kaplan Botswana (Pty) Ltd, 2006–13. Non-exec. Dir, Barclays Bank Botswana, 2009–. Pres., American Chamber of Commerce, Botswana, 2012–15. *Recreations:* reading, jazz, wine, golf. *Address:* Private Bag #RW002, Riverwalk, Gabarone, Botswana.

**DUBENS, Peter Adam Daiches;** Co-founder and Managing Partner, Oakley Capital Ltd, since 1999; *b* London, 24 Sept. 1966; *s* of Stanley Maurice Dubens and Rachel Helen Dubens; *m* 1996, Joanna Penelope Cowan; three *d. Educ:* Sussex Hse Prep. Sch. Chairman: 365 Media plc, 2001–06; Pipex Communications plc, 2002–07; Daisy Gp plc, 2007–. Co-Founder and Director: KX Gym UK; Palmer Capital LLP; Global Licensing Ltd; Co-Founder: James Perse UK Ltd; Latitude Brands Ltd (Penfield); Humyo.com Ltd; Global Accessories Ltd (Vans & Eastpack). Entrepreneur of Year, Aim Market, London Stock Exchange, 2004. *Recreations:* golf, tennis, sailing, contemporary art, antiques. *Address:* Oakley Capital Ltd, 3 Cadogan Gate, SW1X 0AS. *T:* (020) 7766 6909. *E:* peter.dubens@oakleycapital.com. *Clubs:* Royal Automobile, Queen's; Royal Thames Yacht; Sunningdale Golf, Morfontaine Golf (France); Lyford Cay (Bahamas); Deepdale Golf (USA).

**DUBERLY, Sir (Archibald) Hugh,** KCVO 2015; CBE 1996; Lord-Lieutenant for Cambridgeshire, 2003–17; *b* 4 April 1942; *s* of late Commander Archibald Gray, DSO, RN, and Grey Cunliffe Gray (*née* Duberly); adopted surname Duberly, 1963; *m* 1967, Sarah Elizabeth Robertson; two *s* one *d. Educ:* Winchester Coll. Pres., Country Landowners' Assoc., 1993–95; Dir, Agricultural Mortgage Corp. Plc, 1995–2002. Crown Estate Comr, 2002–09. Chm., Ely Diocesan Bd of Finance, 1992–2017. Chairman: Papworth Trust, 1995–2012; Shuttleworth Trust, 2001–13. Chm., Kimbolton Sch., 1992–2000; Gov., Writtle Coll., 1997–2009. DL 1989, High Sheriff, 1991–92, Cambs. Hon. MA Cambridge, 2016. *Address:* The Cottage, Stonely, Cambs PE19 5EH. *T:* (01480) 860225. *Club:* Boodle's.

**DUBLIN, Archbishop of, and Primate of Ireland,** since 2011; **Most Rev. Michael Geoffrey St Aubyn Jackson,** PhD, DPhil; Bishop of Glendalough, since 2011; *b* 24 May 1956; *s* of late Robert Stewart Jackson and of Margaret Jane Frances Jackson (*née* Sloan); *m* 1987, Inez Elizabeth (*née* Cooke); one *d. Educ:* Trinity Coll. Dublin (BA Classics 1979, MA 1982); St John's Coll., Cambridge (BA Theol. and Religious Studies 1981, MA 1985; PhD 1986); C of I Theol Coll.; Christ Church, Oxford (MA, DPhil 1989, by incorporation). Ordained deacon, 1986, priest, 1987; Curate-asst, Zion Parish, Rathgar, 1986–89; Minor Canon, Treasurer's Vicar and Chancellor's Vicar, St Patrick's Cathedral, Dublin, 1987–89; Asst Lectr, Dept of Hebrew, Biblical and Theol Studies, TCD, and in C of I Theol Coll., 1987–89; Chaplain, Christ Church, Oxford, 1989–97; Asst Lectr, Theology Faculty, Oxford Univ., 1991–97; Dir of Studies in Theol., St Anne's Coll., Oxford, 1995–97; Incumbent, St Fin Barre's Union, Cork and Dean of Cork, 1997–2002; Chaplain to UC, Cork and Cork Inst. of Technol., and Asst Lectr, Sch. of Classics and Sch. of Educn, UC, Cork, 1997–2002; Bishop of Clogher, 2002–11. Examining Chaplain to Bp of Cork, Cloyne and Ross, 1999–2002. Chm., Network of Inter-Faith Concerns of Anglican Communion, 2004–; Mem., Anglican/Oriental Orthodox Internat. Commn, 2002–. Chm., St Fin Barre's Beyond 2000, 1998–2002. *Publications:* A History of the Vaughan Charity (with Claire Jackson), 1980; articles, papers and reviews. *Address:* Church of Ireland House, Church Avenue, Rathmines, Dublin 6, Republic of Ireland. *T:* (1) 4125663. *E:* archbishop@dublin.anglican.org.

**DUBLIN, Archbishop of, and Primate of Ireland, (RC),** since 2004; **Most Rev. Diarmuid Martin;** *b* Dublin, 8 April 1945. *Educ:* UC Dublin; Dublin Diocesan Seminary; Pontifical Univ. of St Thomas Aquinas (Angelicum), Rome. Ordained priest, 1969; Curate, St Brigid, Cabinteely, 1973–74; respons. for pastoral care of Dublin pilgrims in Rome, 1975; entered service of Holy See, 1976, Pontifical Council for the Family; Under-Sec., 1986, Sec., 1994, Pontifical Council for Justice and Peace; Titular Bp of Glendalough, 1999–2003; Archbishop, 2001, Permanent Observer of Holy See at UN, Geneva, 2001–03; Coadjutor Archbishop of Dublin, 2003–04. *Address:* Archbishop's House, Drumcondra, Dublin 9, Ireland.

**DUBLIN, (Christ Church), Dean of;** *see* Dunne, Very Rev. D. P. M.

**DUBLIN, (St Patrick's), Dean of;** *see* Morton, Very Rev. W. W.

**du BOULAY, Sir Roger William H.;** *see* Houssemayne du Boulay.

**DUBOW, Prof. Saul,** DPhil; Smuts Professor of Commonwealth History, University of Cambridge, since 2017; Fellow of Magdalene College, Cambridge, since 2017; *b* Cape Town, 28 Oct. 1959; *s* of Neville Dubow and Rhona Dubow; partner, Signe Gosmann; one *s* two *d. Educ:* Herzlia Sch., Cape Town; Univ. of Cape Town (BA Hons 1981); St Antony's Coll., Oxford (DPhil 1986). British Acad. Post-Doctoral Fellow, Inst. of Commonwealth Studies, 1987–89; Lectr, Sen. Lectr, then Reader, 1989–2001, Prof., 2001–12, Univ. of Sussex; Prof. of African Hist., QMUL, 2012–16. Chair, Mgt Cttee, Cambridge Centre for African Studies, 2019–. Hon. Prof., Centre for African Studies, Univ. of Cape Town, 2018–. *Publications:* Racial Segregation and the Origins of Apartheid in Twentieth Century South Africa, 1919–36, 1989; (rev. and ed) C. Bloomberg's Christian-Nationalism and the Development of the Afrikaner Broederbond, 1918–48, rev. edn 1990; Scientific Racism in Modern South Africa, 1995; (ed with William Beinart) Segregation and Apartheid in Twentieth-Century South Africa, 1995; (ed with Jacqueline Rose) W. Sachs' Black Hamlet, 1996; (ed) Science and Society in Southern Africa, 2000; The African National Congress, 2000 (trans. Arabic, 2010); (ed with Alan Jeeves) South Africa's 1940s: worlds of possibilities, 2005; A Commonwealth of Knowledge: science, sensibility and White South Africa 1820–2000, 2006; South Africa's Struggle for Human Rights, 2012; (ed) The Rise and Fall of Modern Empires, Vol. II, Colonial Knowledges, 2013; Apartheid: 1948–1994, 2014; articles in jls. *Recreations:* dinghy racing, tinkering with ipods. *Address:* Magdalene College, Cambridge CB3 0AG. *E:* shd28@cam.ac.uk. *Club:* Shoreham Sailing.

**DUBOWITZ, Prof. Victor,** MD, PhD; FRCP, FRCPCH; Professor of Paediatrics, University of London, at the Royal Postgraduate Medical School, 1972–96, now Emeritus; Consultant Paediatrician, Hammersmith Hospital, 1972–96; Director, Muscle Research Centre, Royal Postgraduate Medical School, 1975–96; *b* 6 Aug. 1931; *s* of late Charley and Olga Dubowitz (*née* Schattel); *m* 1960, Dr Lilly Magdalena Suzanne Sebok (*d* 2016); four *s. Educ:* Beaufort West Central High Sch., S Africa; Univ. of Cape Town (BSc, MB, ChB, 1954; MD 1960). PhD Sheffield, 1965; DCH 1958; FRCP 1972; FRCPCH 1997. Intern, Groote Schuur Hosp., Cape Town, 1955; Sen. House Officer, Queen Mary's Hosp. for Children, Carshalton, 1957–59; Res. Associate in Histochem., Royal Postgrad. Med. Sch., 1958–59; Lectr in Clin. Path., National Hosp. for Nervous Diseases, Queen Square, London, 1960; Lectr in Child Health, 1961–65, Sen. Lectr, 1965–67, and Reader, 1967–72, Univ. of Sheffield; Res. Associate, Inst. for Muscle Diseases, and Asst Paediatrician, Cornell Med. Coll., New York, 1965–66; Dir of Therapeutic Studies, European Neuro Muscular Centre, 1999–2003. Several lectureships and overseas vis. professorships. President: British Paediatric Neurol. Assoc., 1992–94; European Paediatric Neurology Soc., 1994–97; World Muscle Soc., 1995–2016; Medical Art Soc., 1996–2000. Curator of Art, RCPCH, 1997–. Founding Editor: Neuromuscular Disorders, 1990–; European Jl of Paediatric Neurology, 1996–2003. Hon. FRCPCH 1997. Arvo Ylppö Gold Medal, Finland, 1982; Baron ver Heyden de Lancey Prize, Med. Art Soc., 1980, 1982, 2002; Jean Hunter Prize, RCP, 1987; Gaetano Conte Medal, Italy, 1991; Cornelia de Lange Medal, Netherlands, 1997; Duchenne Erb Prize, German Speaking Muscular Dystrophy Assocs, 1999; James Spence Medal, RCPCH, 2007. Peter Emil Becker Prize, German-speaking Neuropediatric Soc., 2011. Comdr, Order of Constantine the Great, 1980. *Publications:* Developing and Diseased Muscle: a histochemical study, 1968; The Floppy Infant, 1969, 2nd edn 1980; (with M. H. Brooke) Muscle Biopsy: a modern approach, 1973, 4th edn (with C. Sewry and A. Oldfors) 2012; (with L. M. S. Dubowitz) Gestational Age of the Newborn: a clinical manual, 1977; Muscle Disorders in Childhood, 1978, 2nd edn 1995; (with L. M. S. Dubowitz) The Neurological Assessment of the Preterm and Full-term Newborn Infant, 1981, 2nd edn 2000; Colour Atlas of Muscle Disorders in Childhood, 1989; (jtly) A Colour Atlas of Brain Lesions in the Newborn, 1990; Ramblings of a Peripatetic Paediatrician, 2005; chapters in books and articles in learned jls on paediatric topics, partic. muscle disorders and newborn neurology. *Recreations:* sculpting, photography. *Address:* 25 Middleton Road, Golders Green, NW11 7NR. *T:* (020) 8455 9352.

**DUBS,** family name of **Baron Dubs**.

**DUBS,** Baron *cr* 1994 (Life Peer), of Battersea in the London Borough of Wandsworth; **Alfred Dubs;** Chairman, Broadcasting Standards Commission, 2001–03 (Joint Deputy Chairman, 1997); *b* Prague, Czechoslovakia, Dec. 1932; *m*; one *s* one *d. Educ:* LSE. BSc (Econs). Local govt officer. Mem., Westminster CC, 1971–78; Chm., Westminster Community Relns Council, 1972–77; Mem., Kensington, Chelsea and Westminster AHA, 1975–78. Dir, British Refugee Council, 1988–95. Member: TGWU; Co-operative Party. Contested (Lab): Cities of London and Westminster, 1970; Hertfordshire South, Feb. and Oct. 1974; Battersea, 1987 and 1992. MP (Lab): Wandsworth, Battersea S, 1979–83; Battersea, 1983–87. Mem., Home Affairs Select Cttee, 1981–83 (Mem., Race Relations and Immigration Sub-Cttee, 1981–83); opposition front bench spokesman on home affairs, 1983–87. House of Lords: an Opposition Whip, 1994–97; opposition front bench spokesman on energy, 1995–97, on health and safety, 1996–97; Parly Under-Sec. of State, NI Office, 1997–99; Member: Select Cttee on European Communities, 1995–97; Sub-Cttee F, European Select Cttee, 2003–07. Chairman: All Pty Parly Gp on Eur. Enlargement, 2000, on Moldova, 2006, on Portugal, 2008; Lab Party in H of L, 2000–06; Mem., Jt Cttee on Human Rights, 2007–12. Mem., 1988–94, Dep. Chm., 1995–97, Broadcasting Standards Council; Vice-Chm., ITC, 2000–01; Chairman: Road Safety Foundn, 2007; Eastern Alliance Safe and Sustainable Transport, 2009–. Chm., Ind. Code Panel, Assoc. of Energy Suppliers, 2004–. *Recreation:* walking in the Lake District. *Address:* c/o House of Lords, SW1A 0PW.

**duCHARME, Gillian Drusilla Brown;** educational consultant, since 2000; Headmistress, Benenden School, 1985–2000; *b* 23 Jan. 1938; *d* of Alfred Henry Brown and Alice Drusilla Grant; *m* 1969, Jean Louis duCharme (marr. diss.). *Educ:* Girton College, Cambridge. BA 1960, MA 1964. British Council, 1964–66; Chm., French Dept and Head of Upper Sch., Park Sch., Brookline, Mass, 1969–77; Registrar, Concord Acad., Concord, Mass, 1977–80; Headmistress, The Town Sch., New York City, 1980–85. Governor: Marlborough House Sch., 1987–; Wellington Coll., Crowthorne, 1996–2006; Blackheath Prep. (formerly Nursery and Prep.) Sch., 2009–. Mem., Adv. Bd, Westminster Acad., 2009–13. Member: Council, Friends of Nat. Maritime Mus., 2001–07 (Chm., 2004–07); Bd, Internat. Rescue Cttee, UK, 2004–11. Hon. DEd Greenwich, 2005. *Recreations:* hill-walking, art, design and architecture, film, birdwatching, travel, books, music. *Address:* 3 Saint Alfege Passage, Greenwich, SE10 9JS. *T:* (020) 8858 8186, 07758 355812. *E:* gillianducharme@hotmail.com.

**DUCIE, 7th Earl of,** *cr* 1837; **David Leslie Moreton;** Baron Ducie, 1763; Baron Moreton, 1837; *b* 20 Sept. 1951; *e s* of 6th Earl of Ducie and Alison May, *d* of L. A. Bates; *S* father, 1991; *m* 1975, Helen, *er d* of M. L. Duchesne; one *s* one *d*. *Educ:* Cheltenham College; Wye Coll., London Univ. (BSc 1973). *Heir: s* Lord Moreton, *qv*. *Address:* Talbots End Farm, Cromhall, Glos GL12 8AJ.

**DUCK, Michael Charles;** QC 2011; a Recorder, since 2016; *b* Solihull, 6 June 1965; *s* of Peter Duck and Valerie Duck; *m* 1990, Dawn Marie Job; two *d*. *Educ:* Solihull Sch.; Univ. of Warwick; Staffordshire Univ. (LLB Hons). Called to the Bar, Gray's Inn, 1988, Bencher, 2017; in practice as a barrister, specialising in crime; Leader, Midland Circuit, 2017–. Dir, Internat. Cttee, Criminal Bar Assoc., 2013–17. *Recreations:* golf, water ski-ing, cinema, travel. *Address:* No 5 Chambers, Steelhouse Lane, Birmingham B4 6DR. *T:* (0121) 606 0500. *E:* mcd@no5.com.

**DUCKETT, Prof. Jane,** PhD; FBA 2016; Edward Caird Chair of Politics, University of Glasgow, since 2012; *b* 20 Sept. 1964; *d* of Alan John Duckett and Lona Duckett (*née* Byram); two *s*. *Educ:* Univ. of Leeds (BA 1st Cl. Mod. Chinese Studies 1987); Sch. of Oriental and African Studies, Univ. of London (MSc 1991; PhD 1996). Lecturer: Univ. of Manchester, 1995–97; Univ. of York, 1997–99; University of Glasgow: Lectr, 1999–2002; Sen. Lectr, 2002–06; Reader, 2007–08; Prof., 2008–12. Guest Prof., Nankai Univ., Tianjin, 2013–. Pres., British Assoc. for Chinese Studies, 2014–17. Lord Provost of Glasgow Educn Award, 2012. *Publications:* The Entrepreneurial State in China, 1998; The Open Economy and its Enemies, 2006; (ed jtly) China's Changing Welfare Mix, 2011; The Chinese State's Retreat from Health, 2011. *Address:* School of Social and Political Sciences, University of Glasgow, Adam Smith Building, Bute Gardens, Glasgow G12 8RT. *T:* (0141) 330 2871. *E:* jane.duckett@glasgow.ac.uk.

**DUCKWORTH, Cecil,** CBE 2013 (OBE 2004); President: Worcester Warriors Rugby Club, since 2015 (Chairman, 1993–2015); Worcestershire County Cricket Club, since 2019; *b* Macclesfield, 1937; *s* of Charles Duckworth and Jean Duckworth; *m* 1962, Beatrice Elizabeth Lee; one *s* one *d*. *Educ:* Worcester and Cheltenham Coll. CEng 1967. Founder, CEO and Chm., Worcester Engineering Ltd, subseq. Worcester Heat Systems Ltd, 1962–92; co. sold to Bosch, 1992; Hd, Thermotechnol. Div., Bosch, 1992–96. Founder, Duckworth Worcestershire Trust, 1998. Mem., 2000–, High Master, 2009–, Clothiers' Co., Worcester. *Publications:* Worcester Warrior, 2012. *Recreations:* golf, following Rugby, live theatre. *Address:* Worcestershire.

**DUCKWORTH, Sir James (Edward Dyce),** 5th Bt *cr* 1909, of Grosvenor Place, City of Westminster; *b* 21 Dec. 1984; *s* of Sir Edward Richard Dyce Duckworth, 4th Bt and of Patricia, *o d* of Thomas Cahill; *S* father, 2005; *m* 2012, Suzanne, *d* of Nicholas Law. *Heir: uncle* Antony George Dyce Duckworth [*b* 20 Nov. 1946; *m* 1974, Geraldine Broderick; one *s*].

**DUCKWORTH, John Alan, (Joe);** independent adviser and consultant, since 2015; Chief Executive, League Against Cruel Sports, 2011–15; *b* St Helens, 18 May 1955; *s* of George and Alice Duckworth; *m* 1990, Julie Ratty; two *s* one *d*. *Educ:* Bristol Univ. (BSc Hons Econs); Manchester Univ. (MA Econs). National Research Officer: USDAW, 1980–83; Instn of Professionals, Managers and Specialists, 1983–91; Dir of Personnel, York CC, 1991–95; County Personnel Officer, Surrey CC, 1995–97; Exec. Dir, London Bor. of Hackney, 1997–2000; Dir, Envmt and Leisure, 2000–04, Dep. Chief Exec., 2004–06, Westminster CC; Chief Executive: Isle of Wight Council, 2006–08; Newham LBC, 2008–10. *Recreation:* cycling.

**DUCKWORTH, Rt Rev. Justin Charles Hopkins;** *see* Wellington (NZ), Bishop of.

**DUCKWORTH, Prof. Roy,** CBE 1987; MD; FRCS, FDSRCS, FRCPath; Emeritus Professor of Oral Medicine, University of London; Dean, The London Hospital Medical College, 1986–94; *b* Bolton, 19 July 1929; *s* of Stanley Duckworth and Hilda Evelyn Moores; *m* 1953, Marjorie Jean Bowness, Flimby; two *s* one *d*. *Educ:* King George V Sch., Southport; Univ. of Liverpool (BDS; MD 1964). FDSRCS 1957; FRCPath 1973; FRCS 1986. Served RAF Dental Br., 1953–55. Nuffield Fellow, RPMS and Guy's Hosp. Dental Sch., 1959–61; The London Hospital Medical College: Sen. Lectr in Oral Medicine, 1961; Reader in Oral Medicine, 1965; Dean of Dental Studies, 1969–75; Prof. and Head, Dept of Oral Medicine, 1968–90. Consultant in Oral Medicine, The London Hosp., 1965–90. Dean, Faculty of Dental Surgery, RCS, 1983–86. Civil Consultant: in Dental Surg., to Army, 1977–90; in Oral Medicine and Oral Path., to RN, 1982–90; Temp. Consultant, WHO, 1973; British Council Visitor, 1977. Vis. Prof. in many countries. President: British Soc. of Periodontology, 1972–73; British Soc. for Oral Medicine, 1986–87; BDA, 1990–91. Chm., Standing Dental Adv. Cttee, Dept of Health, 1988–92 (Mem., 1984–88); Member: Adv. Council on Misuse of Drugs, 1977–85; Medicines Commn, 1980–83; Council, Fédération Dentaire Internationale, 1981–90 (Mem., List of Honour, 1993); GDC, 1984–89. Hon. Fellow, QMW, 1997. Scientific Adviser, British Dental Jl 1975–82; Editor, Internat. Dental Jl, 1981–90. *Publications:* contrib. professional jls. *Recreation:* sailing.

**du CROS, Sir Julian Claude Arthur Mallet,** 4th Bt *cr* 1916, of Canons, Middlesex; *b* 23 April 1955; *o s* of Sir Claude Philip Arthur Mallet du Cros, 3rd Bt and Christine Nancy du Cros (*née* Bennett); *S* father, 2014; *m* 1984, Patricia Mary Wyatt (marr. diss. 2003); one *s* two *d*. *Educ:* Eton. *Heir: s* Alexander Julian Mallet du Cros, *b* 25 Aug. 1990.

**DUDDERIDGE, Philip Stephen;** Founder, 1989 and Executive Chairman, since 2012, Focusrite plc (formerly Focusrite Audio Engineering Ltd) (Managing Director, 1990–97 and 2007–12); *b* Herts, 6 Feb. 1949; *s* of John Dudderidge and Evelyn Dudderidge; *m* 1973, Jennifer; five *s* one *d*. *Educ:* Haberdashers' Aske's Sch., Elstree. Soundcraft Electronics Ltd: Founder and Man. Dir, 1973–84; Chm. and CEO, 1984–88. *Recreations:* music (listening to), reading, bus driving (own vintage bus). *Address:* Focusrite plc, Windsor House, Turnpike Road, High Wycombe, Bucks HP16 9BG. *T:* (01494) 462246. *E:* phil.dudderidge@focusrite.com.

**DUDDING, Richard Scarbrough;** freelance public policy consultant, since 2008; *b* 29 Nov. 1950; *s* of Sir John Scarbrough Dudding and Lady (Enid Grace) Dudding; *m* 1987, Priscilla Diana Russell; two *s*. *Educ:* Cheltenham Coll.; Jesus Coll., Cambridge (MA 1st Cl. Hons History). Joined DoE, 1972; Private Sec. to John Smith, MP, 1976–78; Principal, 1977; Asst Sec., 1984; Sec., Cttee of Inquiry into Conduct of Local Govt Business, 1985–86; Under Sec., 1990; Finance Dir, 1990–93; Director: Pollution Control and Wastes, 1993–96; Personnel and Central Support Services, 1996–97; Dir Gen., Strategy and Corporate Services, DETR, then DTLR, 1997–2002; Dir for Envmt and Economy, Oxfordshire CC, 2003–08. *Recreations:* gardening, local history, running, golf.

**DUDDRIDGE, James Philip;** MP (C) Rochford and Southend East, since 2005; Parliamentary Under-Secretary of State, Department for Exiting the European Union, since 2016; *b* 26 Aug. 1971; *s* of Philip and Jennifer Duddridge; *m* 2004, Kathryn Brigid Thompson; two *s* one *d*. *Educ:* Univ. of Essex (BA Politics). With Barclays Bank, 1993–2002: Sales Dir, Ivory Coast, 1997–98; Sales Manager for unit trust business, UK, 1998–2001; Service Delivery Dir, Botswana, 2001–02; Account Dir, YouGov, 2001–05; Dir, Okavango Ltd, 2002–05. An Opposition Whip, 2008–10; a Lord Comr of HM Treasury (Govt Whip), 2010–12; Parly Under-Sec. of State, FCO, 2014–16. Chairman: Regulatory Reform Select Cttee, 2012–14; High Speed 2 (W Midlands to Crewe) Bill Select Cttee, 2018–; Mem., Internat. Develt Cttee, 2006–08, 2017–. *Address:* House of Commons, SW1A 0AA. *T:* (020) 7219 4830. *E:* james@jamesduddridge.com. *Clubs:* Southend United Football, Southampton Football.

**DUDDY, Ian Richard;** HM Diplomatic Service; Ambassador to Uruguay, since 2016; *b* London, 23 Nov. 1972; *s* of Graham Duddy and Judith Duddy; partner, Neil Morrison. *Educ:* Loughborough Univ. (BSc Hons Econs 1996); Australia National Univ. (MA Envmtl Mgt and Develt 2007). English teacher, Japan, 1996–98; Res. Analyst, Meijiseimei Internat., London, 1998–99; entered FCO, 2000; Policy Officer, EU and Western Balkans, FCO, 2000–03; Pol and Commercial Officer, Buenos Aires, 2003–06; Hd, Afghanistan Progs Team, FCO, 2007–08; Dep. Dir, Intellectual Property Office (on secondment), 2008–11; Political Counsellor and Hd, Human Rights, UK Mission to the UN, Geneva, 2011–16. *Recreations:* running, swimming, theatre, cinema, music, travel. *E:* ianduddy@hotmail.com. *W:* www.twitter.com/ian_duddy

**DUDGEON, Alexander Stewart, (Sandy);** Director, Schroders Wealth Management, Hong Kong (formerly Cazenove Capital Management Asia Ltd), since 2013; *b* Edinburgh, 16 Oct. 1957; *s* of late John Dudgeon and Sheila Dudgeon (*née* Stein); *m* 1985, Jennifer Waddell; two *s* one *d*. *Educ:* Glenalmond Coll.; Univ. of Aberdeen (MA). CA 1982. Trainee, Arthur Young McClelland Moores & Co., 1979–83; Co. Sec., 1983–87, Dep. Man. Dir, 1991–94, Adam & Co. plc; Dir, Martin Currie Investment Mgt Ltd, 1994–2003; Man. Dir, Thornhill Hldgs Ltd, 2003–10; Dir, Private Wealth Mgt, Cazenove Capital Mgt Ltd, 2010–13. Director: Dunedin Investment Trust plc, 1998–2006; Man Alternative Investments Ltd, 2001–04. Steward, 2009–12, 2018–19, Sen. Steward, 2019–, Jockey Club. Mem., High Constables and Guard of Honour of Holyroodhouse, 1988–. *Recreations:* racing, golf, shooting, hiking. *Address:* Flat 1–01, 150 Kennedy Road, Hong Kong. *E:* sandy.dudgeon@schroders.com. *Clubs:* Jockey; New (Edinburgh); Hon. Company of Edinburgh Golfers; Hong Kong, Hong Kong Jockey, Shek O Country (Hong Kong).

**DUDGEON, Wing Comdr Michael Greville,** OBE 1996; Vice Lord-Lieutenant of Greater London, 2011–18; *b* Northampton, 6 Nov. 1943; *s* of Air Vice-Marshal Antony Greville Dudgeon, CBE, DFC and Phyllis Dudgeon; *m* 1973, Gillian Mary Kathrine de Chazal; two *s* one *d*. *Educ:* Eton; RAF Coll. Cranwell. RAF Officer and Pilot, 1966–2000: qualified Flying Instructor, 1971; sqdn service in various overseas and home appts; Chinook Proj. Pilot, Philadelphia, 1978–80; psc 1984; OC 78 Sqdn, Falklands, 1991; Staff HQ ARRC, 1993–95; Airpower Liaison Officer, Army Directorate of Land Warfare, 1996–2000. Chm., Action for Blind People, 2010–11. Vice Chm., Gresham Coll., 2009–12. Master, Mercers' Co., 2002–03. DL Gtr London, 2007, Hammersmith and Fulham, 2009–11. *Recreations:* my family, exploring the City of London, ringing my church bells. *Clubs:* Royal Air Force, Hurlingham.

**DUDLEY, 5th Earl of,** *cr* 1860; **William Humble David Jeremy Ward;** Baron Ward, 1644; Viscount Ednam, 1860; *b* 27 March 1947; *s* of 4th Earl of Dudley and Stella Viscountess Ednam, *d* of M. A. Carcano, KCMG, KBE; *S* father, 2013; *m* 1st, 1972, Sarah (marr. diss. 1976), *o d* of Sir Alastair Francis Stuart Coats, 4th Bt; 2nd, 1976, Debra Louise (marr. diss. 1980), *d* of George Robert and Marjorie Elvera Pinney; one *d*. *Educ:* Eton; Christ Church, Oxford. *Heir: half-b* Hon. Leander Grenville Dudley Ward, *b* 30 Oct. 1971.

**DUDLEY, 15th Baron** *cr* 1439 (called out of abeyance, 1916); **Jim Anthony Hill Wallace;** *b* 9 Nov. 1930; *e s* of Baroness Dudley (14th in line) and Guy Raymond Hill Wallace; *S* mother, 2002; *m* 1962, Nicola Jane, *d* of Lt-Col P. W. E. L. Dunsterville; two *s*. *Educ:* Lancing. *Recreations:* photography, listening to classical music, model engineering, restoring vintage vehicles and old machinery. *Heir: s* Hon. Jeremy William Guilford Wallace, *b* 12 Sept. 1964.

**DUDLEY, Bishop Suffragan of;** no new appointment at time of going to press.

**DUDLEY, Archdeacon of;** *see* Groarke, Ven. N. J.

**DUDLEY, Anthony Edward;** Hon. Mr Justice Dudley; Chief Justice, Gibraltar, since 2010; *b* Gibraltar, 18 Jan. 1967; *s* of George Dudley and Maria Dudley (*née* del Carmen Arrellano); *m* 1992, Lesley Curran; two *d*. *Educ:* Bayside Comp. Sch., Gibraltar; Univ. of Hull (LLB); Inns of Court Sch. of Law. Called to the Bar: England and Wales, 1989; Gibraltar, 1989; a Stipendiary Magistrate, 2004; Puisne Judge, Supreme Court, Gibraltar, 2010. *Recreations:* rowing, running, reading, eating. *Address:* Supreme Court, 277 Main Street, Gibraltar. *T:* 20078808, *Fax:* 20077118. *E:* jackiespiteri@supremecourt.gov.gi.

**DUDLEY, Martin Raymond,** PhD; Rector, Priory Church of St Bartholomew the Great, London, 1995–2016; Priest-in-charge, St Bartholomew the Less, Smithfield Gate, 2012–16; *b* 31 May 1953; *s* of Ronald Frank Dudley and Joyce Mary (*née* Gardiner); *m* 1976, Paula Jones (marr. diss. 2019); two *s*. *Educ:* King Edward's Sch., Birmingham; RMA Sandhurst; KCL (BD, AKC 1977, MTh 1978); St Michael's Coll., Llandaff; PhD London 1994; Cass Business Sch., City Univ. (MSc 2006); Univ. of Helsinki. Ordained deacon, 1979, priest, 1980; Curate, Whitchurch, 1979–83; Vicar, Weston, 1983–88; Priest i/c, Ardeley, 1986–88; Vicar, Smithmoor, 1988–95. Chaplain: Imperial Soc. of Kts Bach., 1995–2005; Butchers' Co., 1995–2009, 2013–14, 2015–18; Co. of Chartered Secretaries and Administrators, 1995–2000; Hackney Carriage Drivers' Co., 1998–2018; Master, Farmers'

Co., 1999–2000, 2002–03; Co. of Inf. Technologists, 2001–16; Master, Fletchers' Co., 2001–02, 2004–09, 2010–11, 2015–16; Tax Advisers' Co., 2002–16; Aldermanic Sheriff, City of London, 2003–04; City of London Br., Royal Soc. of St George, 2003– (Vice Chm., 2014–15; Chm., 2015–16; Vice Pres., 2016–); Public Relations Practitioners' Co., 2003–11, 2014–17. Mem., London Dio. Synod, 2003–06 (Mem., Bp's Council, 2003–06). Common Councilman (Aldersgate Ward), Corp. of London, 2002–17 (Master, Aldersgate Ward Club, 2015–16). Received into Orthodox Church, 2018. Member, Professional Conduct and Complaints Committee: Bar Council, 2000–07; CIArb, 2005–16; Mem., Professional Standards Panel, CIPR, 2014–18. Member: Hampstead Heath Mgt Cttee, 2003–04, 2010–17; Audit and Risk Mgt Cttee, City of London Corp., 2011–17; Court, Bridewell Royal Foundn, 2003–14; Licensing Cttee, 2004–16, Planning & Transportation Cttee, 2005–17, Community and Children's Services Cttee, 2006–16 (Chm., 2011–14), City Bridge Trust, 2007–11, Standards Cttee, 2007–11 and 2012–14, City of London Corp. (formerly Corp. of London); City of London Health and Well-Being Bd, 2012–17 (Chm., 2013–16). Chm., Resource Centre (London) Ltd, 2007–11. Governor: City Lit. Inst., 2001–03; City of London Sch. for Girls, 2002–14; City of London Acad., Southwark, 2003–13; Gatehouse Sch., 2009–12; Summerfield Primary Sch., 2017– (Chair, 2017–); Mus. of London, 2007–14 (Chm., Audit Cttee, 2009–14). Mem. Ct, City Univ., 2009–17; Mem. Bd, Assoc. of Governing Bodies of Ind. Schs, 2007–13; City of London Acad., Islington, 2014–16. Trustee: Butchers' and Drovers' Charitable Instn, 1996–2004; London Liby, 2003–07; Trust for London (formerly City Parochial Foundn), 2005–15. Hon. Res. Fellow, Queen's Foundn for Ecumenical Theological Educn, Birmingham, 2017–. Liveryman, Farriers' Co., 2000; Hon. Liveryman, Hackney Carriage Drivers' Co., 2014; Hon. Freeman: Farmers' Co., 2000; Guild of Public Relns Practitioners, 2005 (Master, 2012–13); Pres., Farringdon Ward Club, 2008–09 (Sen. Vice-Pres., 2007–08). Hon. MCGI 2011. FRHistS 1995; FSA 1997; FRSA 2006–14. SBStJ 1998. Hon. DArts City, 2014. *Publications:* The Collect in Anglican Liturgy, 1994; (ed) Like a Two-edged Sword, 1995; A Manual of Ministry to the Sick, 1997; Humanity and Healing, 1998; Ashes to Glory, 1999; A Herald Voice, 2000; Risen, Ascended, Glorified, 2001; Crowning the Year, 2003; with Virginia Rounding: Churchwardens: a survival guide, 2003, 2nd edn 2009; The Parish Survival Guide, 2004; Serving the Parish, 2006; Being Orthodox, 2019. *Recreations:* learning Finnish, Dudley genealogy. *Address:* The Workshop in the Jewellery Quarter, 13D Pitsford Street, Birmingham B18 6LJ. *T:* (0121) 523 5708. *E:* martin.dudley@btinternet.com. *Clubs:* Athenæum, Guildhall.

**DUDLEY, His Honour Michael John;** a Circuit Judge, 2003–15; *b* 24 Jan. 1947; *s* of John Kenneth and Ruby Marguerite Dudley; *m* 1968, Barbara; one *s* one *d*. *Educ:* Magdalen Coll. Sch., Brackley; Univ. of Birmingham (LLB); Univ. of Leeds (PGCE). Called to the Bar, Lincoln's Inn, 1972; specialised in crime and general common law; Dep. Stipendiary Magistrate, 1984–90; Asst Recorder, 1993–99, Recorder, 1999–2003. *Recreations:* walking, photography, music, watching Rugby. *Club:* Sutton Coldfield Rugby Football.

**DUDLEY, William Stuart,** RDI 1989; Associate Designer, Royal National Theatre, since 1981; *b* 4 March 1947; *s* of William Dudley and Dorothy Stacey. *Educ:* Highbury Sch., London; St Martin's School of Art; Slade School of Art. DipAD, BA Fine Art; UCL Postgrad. Dip. Fine Art. First production, Hamlet, Nottingham Playhouse, 1970; subseq. prodns include: The Duchess of Malfi and Man is Man, Royal Court, 1971; *National Theatre,* 1971–: Tyger, 1974; The Good-Natured Man, 1974; The Passion, 1977; Lavender Blue, 1977; The World Turned Upside Down, Has Washington Legs?, 1978; Dispatches, Lost Worlds, Lark Rise to Candleford, Undiscovered Country (SWET award, Designer of the Year, 1980), 1979; Good Soldier Schweyk, 1982; Cinderella, 1983; The Mysteries, Real Inspector Hound/The Critic, 1985 (Laurence Olivier (formerly SWET) Award, Designer of the Year, 1985); Futurists, 1986; Waiting for Godot, 1987; Cat on a Hot Tin Roof, The Shaughraun, and The Changeling, 1988; Bartholomew Fair, 1988; The Crucible, 1990; The Coup, 1991; Pygmalion, 1992; On the Ledge, 1993; Under Milk Wood, 1995; Mary Stuart, 1996; The Homecoming, 1997; The London Cuckolds, 1998; All My Sons, 2000 (Laurence Olivier Awards, Best Set Designer, 2001); The Coast of Utopia, 2002; Honour, 2003; The Permanent Way, Cyrano de Bergerac, 2004; *Royal Court:* Live Like Pigs, 1972; Merry-Go-Round, 1973; Magnificence, 1975; The Fool, 1975; Small Change, 1976; Hamlet, 1980; Kafka's Dick, 1986; Etta Jenks, 1990; I Licked a Slag's Deodorant, 1996; Hitchcock Blonde, 2003, transf. Lyric, 2003; *RSC:* Twelfth Night, 1974; Ivanov, 1976; That Good Between Us, 1977; Richard III, The Party, Today, 1984; Merry Wives of Windsor, 1985, 1992; A Midsummer Night's Dream, Richard II, 1986; Kiss Me Kate, 1987; The Winter's Tale, 2013; *West End:* Mutiny, Piccadilly, 1985; Heartbreak House, Haymarket, 1992; A Streetcar Named Desire, Haymarket, 1996; The Breath of Life, Haymarket, 2002; Woman in White, Palace, 2004; Carousel, Savoy, 2008; All My Sons, Apollo, 2010; *other productions:* The Ship, Glasgow, 1990; The Deep Blue Sea, Almeida, 1993; The Big Picnic, Glasgow, 1994; Some Sunny Day, Hampstead, 1996; The Alchemist, Birmingham, 1996; Titus Andronicus, Shakespeare's Globe, 2006 and 2014; Betrayal, Donmar Warehouse, 2007; Peter Pan, Kensington Gdns, 2009; The Beggar's Opera, Regent's Park, 2011; King Lear, Th. Royal, Bath, 2013; Fings Ain't Wot They Used T'be, Th. Royal, Stratford East, 2014; For Services Rendered, Minerva, Chichester, 2015; Gaslight, Royal Th., Northampton, 2015; Ross, Chichester, 2016; Comus, Sam Wanamaker Playhouse, 2016; Witness for the Prosecution, County Hall, 2017; Switzerland, Th. Royal, Bath, 2018, transf. Ambassadors, 2018; *opera:* WNO: Il barbiere di Siviglia, 1976; Idomeneo, 1991; Metropolitan, NY: Billy Budd, 1978; Glyndebourne: Die Entführung aus dem Serail, 1980; Il barbiere di Siviglia, 1981; Royal Opera: Les Contes d'Hoffman (sets), 1980; Don Giovanni, 1981; The Cunning Little Vixen, 1990, revived 2003; Bayreuth: Der Ring des Nibelungen, 1983; Der Rosenkavalier, 1984; Salzburg Festival: Un ballo in maschera, 1989; *television film:* Persuasion, 1994 (BAFTA and RTS Awards for set design). Designer of the Year, Laurence Olivier Awards, 1980, 1985, 1986, 1993. *Recreation:* playing the concertina. *Address:* 11 Halstow Road, SE10 0LD.

**DUDLEY-SMITH, Rt Rev. Timothy,** OBE 2003; Bishop Suffragan of Thetford, 1981–92; *b* 26 Dec. 1926; *o s* of Arthur and Phyllis Dudley Smith, Buxton, Derbyshire; *m* 1959, June Arlette MacDonald (*d* 2007); one *s* two *d*. *Educ:* Tonbridge Sch.; Pembroke Coll., and Ridley Hall, Cambridge. BA 1947, MA 1951; Certif. in Educn 1948. Deacon, 1950; priest, 1951; Asst Curate, St Paul, Northumberland Heath, 1950–53; Head of Cambridge Univ. Mission in Bermondsey, 1953–55, Hon. Chaplain, 1955–60; Hon. Chaplain to Bp of Rochester, 1960–67; Editor, Crusade, and Editorial Sec. of Evangelical Alliance, 1955–59; Asst Sec. of Church Pastoral-Aid Soc., 1959–65, Sec., 1965–73; Archdeacon of Norwich, 1973–81; Commissary to Archbp of Sydney, 1971–92; Exam. Chap. to Bp of Norwich, 1971–85. President: Evangelical Alliance, 1987–91; C of E Evangelical Council, 1990–93; Vice-Pres., UCCF, 1992–. Chm. of Govs, 1992–96, Patron, 1996–, Monkton Combe Sch. Fellow, Hymn Soc. in the US and Canada, 1997; Hon. Vice-Pres., Hymn Soc. of GB and Ireland, 2003. FRSCM 2011. Hon. FGCM 2019. MLitt Lambeth, 1991; Hon. DD Durham, 2009. *Publications:* Christian Literature and the Church Bookstall, 1963; What Makes a Man a Christian?, 1966; A Man Named Jesus, 1971; Someone who Beckons, 1978; Lift Every Heart, 1984; A Flame of Love, 1987; Songs of Deliverance, 1988; Praying with the English Hymn Writers, 1989; A Voice of Singing, 1992; John Stott: a comprehensive bibliography, 1995; (compiled) Authentic Christianity, 1995; Great is the Glory, 1997; John Stott: the making of a leader, 1999 (John C. Pollock Award for Christian Biog., Beeson Divinity Sch., Samford Univ., 2001); John Stott: a global ministry, 2001; (jtly) Beneath a Travelling Star, 2001, 2nd edn 2016; A House of Praise, 2003, Pt 2 2015, Pt 3 2019; A Door for the Word, 2006; (jtly) A Calendar of Praise, 2006; (jtly) High Days and Holy Days, 2007; (jtly) The Voice of Faith, 2008; (jtly) Above Every Name, 2009; Praise to the Name, 2009; (jtly) Draw Near to God, 2010; Beyond our Dreaming, 2012; (jtly) A Mirror to the Soul, 2013; A Functional Art, 2017; (jtly) One Big Family, 2018; (jtly) Light on the Way, 2019; contributor to hymn books. *Recreations:* reading, writing, verse, family and friends. *Address:* 38 Eights Marina, Mariners Ways, Cambridge CB4 1ZA.

**DUDLEY-WILLIAMS, Sir Alastair (Edgcumbe James),** 2nd Bt *cr* 1964, of Exeter; Director, Wildcat Consultants, 1986–2010; *b* 26 Nov. 1943; *s* of Sir Rolf Dudley Dudley-Williams, 1st Bt and Margaret Helen, *er d* of F. E. Robinson, OBE; *S* father, 1987; *m* 1972, Diana Elizabeth Jane, twin *d* of R. H. C. Duncan; three *d*. *Educ:* Pangbourne College. Hughes Tool Co. (Texas), 1962–64; Bay Drilling Corp. (Louisiana), 1964–65; Bristol Siddeley Whittle Tools Ltd, 1965–67; Santa Fe Drilling Co., 1967–72; Inchcape plc, 1972–86. *Recreations:* shooting, fishing, cultivating vegetables. *Heir: b* Malcolm Philip Edgcumbe Dudley-Williams [*b* 10 Aug. 1947; *m* 1973, Caroline Anne Colina, twin *d* of R. H. C. Duncan; two *s* one *d*]. *Address:* Fairfield House, 17 The Green, East Meon, Petersfield, Hants GU32 1QT.

**DUDSON, Ian James,** CBE 2002; Lord-Lieutenant of Staffordshire, since 2012; *b* Congleton, Cheshire, 15 July 1950; *s* of late Derek Hubert Dudson and Audrey Margaret Dudson (*née* Hamilton); *m* 1975, Jane, *d* of late Ralph and Marjorie Bassett; two *d*. *Educ:* Shrewsbury Sch.; Dundee Univ. (BSc); Staffordshire Univ. Dudson (Holdings) Ltd: Trainee Manager, 1973–75; Works Manager, 1975–82; Works Dir, 1982–88; Chief Exec., 1988–2009; non-exec. Chm., 2009–17. Dir, BPMF (Trustees) Ltd, 1997–. Pro-Chancellor and Chm. Council, Keele Univ., 2005–12. Chm., Staffs Magistrates' Adv. Cttee, 2012–. President: Eur. Fedn of Porcelaine and Faience, 2005–08; British Ceramic Confedn, 2007–09. Chm. Trustees, Dudson Centre, 1999–; Trustee, Beaudesert Trust, 2012–. Mem. Council, Lichfield Cath., 2013–. Pres., RFCA W Midlands, 2016– (Vice Pres., 2012–16). President: Tennis Staffs, 1999–; Staffs Co. Scouts, 2012–; St John (Priory Gp) Staffs, 2012–; CPRE Staffs, 2012–; Air Ambulance Staffs, 2012–; SSAFA Staffs, 2012–; Lichfield Fest., 2015–; Staffs Community Foundn, 2016–. Hon. President: Douglas Macmillan Hospice, 2005–; Staffs Historic Bldgs Trust, 2015–; Patron: Community Council Staffs, 2012–18; Lichfield Sci. and Engrg Soc., 2012–; Trent and Mersey Canal Soc., 2015–; Ministry at Work, 2015–; Kendall and Wall Charitable Trust, 2019–; Joint Patron: Friends of Lichfield Cathedral, 2012–; Peel Soc., 2012–; Shropshire and Staffs Blood Bikes, 2017–; Jt Hon. Patron, Pathway Proj., Lichfield, 2017–. DL, 2001, High Sheriff, 2010–11, Staffs. DUniv: Keele, 2013; Staffordshire, 2014. KStJ 2017 (CStJ 2013). *Recreations:* gardening, walking, travel, dining out. *Address:* Lieutenancy Office, Martin Street, Stafford ST16 2LH. *T:* (01785) 276805, *Fax:* (01785) 276115. *E:* officer.lieutenancy@staffordshire.gov.uk.

**DUERDEN, Prof. Brian Ion,** CBE 2008; MD; FRCPath, FRCPE; Inspector of Microbiology and Infection Control (formerly of Microbiology), Department of Health, 2004–10; Professor of Medical Microbiology, Cardiff University (formerly University of Wales College of Medicine), 1991–2008, now Emeritus; *b* 21 June 1948; *s* of Cyril Duerden and Mildred (*née* Ion); *m* 1972, Marjorie Hudson. *Educ:* Nelson Grammar Sch., Nelson, Lancs; Edinburgh Univ. (BSc Hons Med. Sci. Bacteriol. 1970; MB ChB 1972; MD 1979). MRCPath 1978, FRCPath 1990; FRCPE 2005. House Officer, Thoracic Surgery, 1972–73, and Infectious Diseases, 1973, City Hosp., Edinburgh; Lectr in Bacteriol., Univ. of Edinburgh Med. Sch., 1973–76; University of Sheffield Medical School: Lectr in Med. Microbiol., 1976–79; Sen. Lectr, 1979–83; Prof. of Med. Microbiol., 1983–90; Hon. Consultant in Med. Microbiol., Sheffield Children's Hosp., 1979–90; Dir, Cardiff Public Health Lab., and Hd, S Glamorgan Microbiol. Services, 1991–95; Dep. Dir, 1995–2002 and Med. Dir, 1999–2002, Dir, 2002–03, PHLS; Dir, Clinical Quality, HPA, 2003. Ed. in Chief, Jl Med. Microbiol., 1983–2002. *Publications:* (contrib. and vol. ed.) Topley and Wilson's Principles of Bacteriology, Virology and Immunology, 7th edn 1980 to 9th edn 1997; Textbook of Microbial and Parasitic Infection, 1987, 2nd edn 1993; Anaerobes in Human Disease, 1991; contrib. numerous scientific articles to professional jls. *Recreations:* travel, photography, music, cricket. *Address:* Pendle, Welsh Street, Chepstow, Monmouthshire NP16 5LU. *E:* bduerden@doctors.org.uk.

**DUFF, Andrew Nicholas,** OBE 1997; Member (Lib Dem) Eastern England, European Parliament, 1999–2014; *b* 25 Dec. 1950; *s* of late Norman Bruce Duff and Diana (*née* Wilcoxson). *Educ:* Sherborne Sch.; St John's Coll., Cambridge (MA; MLitt 1978); Université Libre de Bruxelles. Res. Officer, Hansard Soc. for Parly Govt, 1974–76; consultant and researcher on EC affairs, 1977–88; Res. Fellow, Joseph Rowntree Reform Trust, 1989–92; Dir, Federal Trust for Educn and Res., 1993–99. Mem. (L), 1982–87, (Lib Dem), 1987–90, Cambridge CC. Contested: (L) Cambridge and N Beds, 1984, (Lib Dem) Cambridgeshire, 1989, 1994, EP elecns; (Lib Dem) Huntingdon, Parly elecns, 1992; (Lib Dem) Eastern England, 2014. Vice Pres., Liberal Democrats, 1994–97. European Parliament: Constitutional Affairs spokesman, Alliance of Liberals and Democrats for Europe (formerly Eur. Lib Dem Gp), 1999–2014; Leader, UK Lib Dems, 2007–09; Vice-Pres., delegn to Convention on Future of Europe, 2002–03; President: Union of Eur. Federalists, 2008–13; Spinelli Gp, 2017–. Vis. Fellow, European Policy Centre, 2015–. *Publications:* include: (ed jtly) Maastricht and Beyond: building the European Union, 1994; Reforming the European Union, 1997; (ed) The Treaty of Amsterdam, 1997; The Struggle for Europe's Constitution, 2005; Saving the European Union: the logic of the Lisbon Treaty, 2009; (ed) Making the Difference, 2010; A Fundamental Law of the EU, 2013; Pandora, Penelope, Polity: how to change the European Union, 2015; The Protocol of Frankfurt: a new treaty for the eurozone, 2016; On Governing Europe: a federal experiment, 2018.

**DUFF, Anthony Michael;** communications strategist and executive coach, since 1999; *b* 7 Aug. 1946; *s* of Anthony Duff and Alice Mary Duff (*née* Conway); *m* 1997, Marisol de Lafuente. *Educ:* St Conleth's Coll., Dublin; University Coll., Dublin (BA Hons). LGSM (Drama) 1968; LRAM (Drama) 1970; RSA Dip. TEFLA 1972. Dir, Teacher Trng and Foundn Dir, Café Théâtre Anglais, Internat. House, Paris, 1971–74; Vis. Lectr in Drama, Thomond Coll., Co. Limerick, 1975–76; Pedagogic Advr to Longman Italia, 1977–79; International House, London: Dir of Educn, 1979–83; Dir, 1984–89; Dir-Gen., 1990–99. FRSA 1993. *Publications:* English For You, 2 vols, 1979, 1981; (ed) Explorations in Teacher Training, 1989. *Recreations:* music, reading, the theatre, walking, being solitary. *Address:* Villa della Luna, Località La Calandrina, 01015 Sutri (VT), Italy.

**DUFF, Antony;** *see* Duff, R. A.

**DUFF, Sir Gordon (William),** Kt 2007; PhD; FRCP, FRCPE, FMedSci, FRSE; Principal, St Hilda's College, Oxford, since 2014; Chairman, Biotechnology and Biological Sciences Research Council, 2015–18; *b* 27 Dec. 1947; *s* of William Munro Duff and Marion Gertrude Duff; *m* 1969, Naida Margaret, *d* of Air Cdre Charles Clarke, OBE and Eileen Clarke; two *d*. *Educ:* Perth Acad.; Hipperholme GS, Yorks; St Peter's Coll., Oxford (BA 1969, MA 1975; BM BCh 1975; Hon. Fellow, 2006); St Thomas's Hosp. Med. Sch., Univ. of London (PhD 1980); Saybrook Coll., Yale Univ. FRCPE 1989; FRCP 1998. House

Officer in Medicine, St Thomas's Hosp., London, and in Surgery, Stracathro Hosp., Brechin, 1975–76; Senior House Officer in Medicine: RAF Unit, King Edward VII Hosp., Midhurst, 1976–77; (Clinical Pharmacol.) Hammersmith Hosp. and RPMS, 1977–78; Med. Registrar posts, 1978–80; Yale University School of Medicine: Res. Associate, Internal Medicine (Infectious Diseases) and Pathol. (Immunol.), 1980–84; Associate Investigator, Howard Hughes Inst. of Cellular and Molecular Immunol., 1981–84; Clin. Lectr in Rheumatol., 1984–86, Clin. Sen. Lectr, Dept of Medicine, 1986–90, Univ. of Edinburgh; Hon. Consultant Physician, Lothian Health Bd, 1986–90; University of Sheffield: Lord Florey Prof. of Molecular Medicine, 1991–2014; Res. Dean, Sheffield Med. Sch., 1997–2002; Director: Div. of Molecular and Genetic Medicine, 1997–2000; of Res., Faculty of Medicine, 1999–2002; Div. of Genomic Medicine, 2000–06; Hon. Consultant Physician, Sheffield Teaching Hosps NHS Trust, 1991–. RSocMed Vis. Prof. to USA (Yale, NIH, Pfizer Res.), 1995; Lectures: Honyman-Gillespie, Univ. of Edinburgh, 1991; Harry Bostrom, Swedish Soc. Med., 1996; Faculty, Univ. of Geneva, 2001. Founding Ed., Cytokine, 1988–. Committee on Safety of Medicines: Mem., 1995–2005, Chm., 2003–05; Chairman: Biol Sub-cttee, 1998–2003 (Mem., 1995–2005); vCJD and Blood Products Expert Gp, 1998–2005; vCJD and Vaccines Expert Gp, 2000–05; Tissue Engrg Expert Gp, 2001–05; Mem., Safety and Efficacy Sub-cttee, 1992–95. Chairman: Foresight Internat. Health Gp, DTI (OST), 1998–2000; Nat. Biol Standards Bd, 2002–09; Gene Therapy Commissioning Gp, DoH, 2004; Commn on Human Medicines, 2005–12; Scientific Pandemic Influenza Adv. Cttee, 2008; Strategic Partnership Bd, Academic Health Sci. Centre, Imperial Coll. London, 2011–15; Strategic Bd, Academic Health Sci. Centre, Trinity Coll. Dublin, 2012–; Medicines and Healthcare Products Regulatory Agency, 2013–14; Member: Health and Life Scis Foresight Panel, DTI, 1997–99; Genomic Medicine Gp, Foresight Healthcare, 1999–2000; Adv. Gp on Genetics Res., DoH, 2003–07. Member: Adv. Bd, MRC, 1997–2005; Health Metrology Panel, EPSRC, 2000. Expert Advr (Biol Medicines), EMEA, 2001–. Clin. Trials Monitor, WHO, 1995–97. Member: R&D Exec., Central Sheffield Univ. Hosp. NHS Trust, 1996–99 (Chm., Res. Mgt Cttee, 1996–98); R&D Strategy Gp, Trent RHA, 2000–04. Mem., Internat. Scientific Adv. Bd, Medical Solutions plc, 1999–2005. Member: Council, Internat. Cytokine Soc., USA, 1992– (Pres., 1997–98); Council, Eur. Cytokine Soc., Paris, 1997–; International Scientific Advisory Board: Deutsches Rheuma-Forschungzentrum, Berlin, 1996–99; Dublin Molecular Medicine Centre, 2000–. Mem., Clin. Interest Gp, Wellcome Trust, 1994–97. Member: Res. Cttee, Arthritis and Rheumatism Council, 1993–97; Scientific Cttee, DEBRA (Fragile Skin Diseases), 1996–99; Scientific Cttee, GDBA, 1996–99; Mem. Council, Foundn for Sci. and Technol., 2015–. Mem. Council, Univ. of Sheffield, 2000–04. FMedSci 1999; FRSE 2008. Mem., Assoc. of Physicians of GB and Ireland, 1986–. MD (hc): Edinburgh, 2008; Sheffield, 2016. (Jtly) Sir Hiram Maxim Award for Res. in Immunol., 1987; Medal, Swedish Soc. Med., 1996; Clinical Res. Award, American Acad. of Periodontology, 2014; Sir Janus Black Award for Contribs to Drug Discovery, British Pharmacol Soc., 2016. *Publications:* contribs to res. jls in fields of inflammation, immunology and genetics; thirty patents in field of genetic diagnostics for common diseases. *Recreations:* hill-walking, botany, carpentry. *Address:* St Hilda's College, Cowley Place, Oxford OX4 1DY. *Clubs:* Athenæum, Lansdowne, Oxford and Cambridge.

**DUFF, Graham,** CB 1999; barrister; Consultant, Jacqueline Duff & Co., Solicitors, 2008–16; *b* 7 Jan. 1947; *s* of Norman Alexander Duff and Doris Duff; *m* 1987, Jacqueline Tremble; one *s* (one *d* decd). *Educ:* Newcastle Royal Grammar Sch.; Univ. of Durham (BA (Hons) Law); Univ. of Newcastle upon Tyne (Grad. Cert Ed). Called to the Bar, Lincoln's Inn, 1976. Asst Dir of Public Prosecutions, 1986; Br. Crown Prosecutor, Inner London, 1986; Chief Crown Prosecutor, Northumbria and Durham, 1987; a Dir, CPS, 1990–98; Mem., Trinity Chambers, Newcastle upon Tyne, 1999–2008. Mem., Cartington Parish Council, 2002–14. Chm., Rothbury and Dist Amenity Soc., 2001–03. *Recreations:* old Riley motor cars, Northumbrian countryside, ornithology. *Address:* Lynnholm, Northumberland NE65 7JE. *T:* (01669) 621779.

**DUFF, Rt Rev. Jillian Louise Calland;** *see* Lancaster, Bishop Suffragan of.

**DUFF, Prof. Michael James,** PhD; FRS 2009; FInstP; Abdus Salam Professor of Theoretical Physics, 2006–15, now Professor Emeritus, and Senior Research Investigator, since 2015, Imperial College London; *b* Manchester, 28 Jan. 1949; *s* of Edward Duff and Elizabeth Duff (*née* Kaylor); *m* 1984, Lesley Yearling; one *s* one *d*. *Educ:* De La Salle Coll., Salford; Queen Mary Coll., London (BSc 1969); Imperial Coll. London (DIC, PhD 1972). FInstP 2004. Post-doctoral Fellowships at Internat. Centre for Theoretical Physics, Trieste, Univ. of Oxford, KCL, QMC and Brandeis Univ., 1972–79; Faculty Mem., Imperial Coll. London, 1979–88; Sen. Physicist, CERN, Geneva, 1984–87; Prof. of Physics, 1988–92, Dist. Prof. of Physics, 1992–99, Faculty Fellow, Hagler Inst. for Advanced Study, 2018–19, Texas A & M Univ.; Oscar Klein Prof. of Physics, Univ. of Michigan, 1999–2005; Dir, Michigan Center for Theoretical Physics, 2000–05; Prof. of Physics and Principal, Faculty of Physical Scis, Imperial Coll. London, 2005–06. Leverhulme Emeritus Res. Fellow, 2016–18. Vis. Prof. of Maths, Univ. of Oxford, 2017–April 2020. Fellow, APS, 1994. FRSA. Meeting Gold Medal, El Colegio Nacional, Mexico, 2004; Paul Dirac Gold Medal and Prize, Inst. of Physics, 2017; Trotter Prize, Texas A & M Univ., 2018. *Publications:* The World in Eleven Dimensions, 1999; numerous articles on unified theory of elementary particles. *Recreations:* watercolours, scrabble. *Address:* Physics Department, Imperial College London, Prince Consort Road, SW7 2BZ. *T:* (020) 7594 8571, *Fax:* (020) 7594 7844. *E:* m.duff@imperial.ac.uk.

**DUFF, Prof. (Robin) Antony,** FBA 2004; FRSE; Professor, Department of Philosophy, University of Stirling, 1990–2009, now Emeritus; Professor, School of Law, University of Minnesota, 2010–15; *b* 9 March 1945; *s* of Rt Hon. Sir (Arthur) Antony Duff, GCMG, CVO, DSO, DSC, PC and of Pauline Marion Duff; partner, Sandra Marshall. *Educ:* St Peter's Sch., Seaford; Sedbergh Sch.; Christ Church, Oxford (BA). Vis. Lectr, Dept of Philos., Univ. of Washington, Seattle, 1968–69; University of Stirling: Lectr, Dept of Philos., 1970–80; Sen. Lectr, 1980–88; Reader, 1988–90. FRSE 1996. *Publications:* Trials and Punishments, 1986; Intention, Agency and Criminal Liability, 1990; Criminal Attempts, 1996; Punishment, Communication and Community, 2001; Answering for Crime, 2007; The Trial on Trial, 2007; The Realm of Criminal Law, 2018. *Address:* 9A Rutland Square, Edinburgh EH1 2AS. *E:* r.a.duff@stir.ac.uk.

**DUFF GORDON, Sir Andrew (Cosmo Lewis),** 8th Bt *cr* 1813; *b* 17 Oct. 1933; *o s* of Sir Douglas Duff Gordon, 7th Bt and Gladys Rosemary (*d* 1933), *e d* of late Col Vivien Henry, CB; *S* father, 1964; *m* 1st, 1967, Grania Mary (marr. diss. 1975; she *d* 2012), *d* of Fitzgerald Villiers-Stuart, Ireland; one *s*; 2nd, 1975, Eveline Virginia, BA, *d* of S. Soames, Newbury; three *s*. *Educ:* Repton. Served with Worcs Regiment and 1st Bn Ches Regt, 1952–54. Mem. of Lloyd's, 1962–91. Jt Hon. Pres., Nomadic Preservation Soc., 2006–. *Publications:* (with R. W. D. Fenn) The Life and Times of Sir George Cornewall Lewis, Bt, 2005; contrib. to Tarmac Papers. *Recreations:* golf, shooting, military history, family. *Heir:* *s* Cosmo Henry Villiers Duff Gordon [*b* 18 June 1968; *m* 2006, Araminta de Clermont; one *s* one *d*]. *Address:* Downton House, Walton, Presteigne, Powys LD8 2RD. *T:* (01544) 350223; 27 Cathcart Road, SW10 9JG. *T:* (020) 7351 1170. *Club:* Kington Golf.

**DUFFELL, Lt-Gen. Sir Peter Royson,** KCB 1992; CBE 1988 (OBE 1981); MC 1966; Director, Special Projects, Dechert LLP (formerly Titmuss Sainer Dechert), 2006–14 (Chief Executive, 1995–2006); *b* 19 June 1939; *s* of late Roy John Duffell, Lenham, Kent, and Ruth Doris (*née* Gustaffson); *m* 1982, Ann Murray, *d* of late Col Basil Bethune Neville Woodd, Rolvenden, Kent; one *s* one *d*. *Educ:* Dulwich Coll. psc, rcds. FRGS 1975; FRAS 1992. Commnd 2nd KEO Gurkha Rifles, 1960; Staff Coll., Camberley, 1971; Bde Major 5 Bde, 1972–74; MA to C-in-C UKLF, 1976–78; Comdt 1st Bn 2nd KEO Gurkha Rifles, 1978–81; Col GS Military Operations 3, MoD, 1981–83; Comdr Gurkha Field Force, 1984–85; COS 1 (BR) Corps, 1986–87; RCDS, 1988; Cabinet Office Efficiency Unit, 1989; Comdr, British Forces Hong Kong, and Maj.-Gen. Brigade of Gurkhas, 1989–92; Inspector Gen. Doctrine and Trng, MoD, 1992–95. Col, Royal Gurkha Rifles, 1994–99. Mem., Internat. Adv. Bd, SOAS, 2006–15. Trustee, Foyle Foundn, 2006–. Gov., Sandroyd Sch., 1995–2009. Pres., Sirmoor Rifles Assoc., 2006–15. Mem., Tripehounds. Freeman: City of London, 2001; Salters' Co., 2017. *Publications:* Gurkha Odyssey, 2019. *Recreations:* collecting beautiful things, watching cricket, my family, writing, lecturing. *Clubs:* Travellers, Pratt's, MCC.

**DUFFERIN AND CLANDEBOYE,** 11th Baron *cr* 1800 (Ire.); **John Francis Blackwood;** Bt (Ire.) 1763; Bt (UK) 1814; architect; *b* 18 Oct. 1944; *s* of 10th Baron and of Margaret Alice, *d* of Hector Kirkpatrick; *S* father, 1991 (claim to peerage not yet established); *m* 1971, Annette Kay, *d* of Harold Greenhill; one *s* one *d*. *Educ:* Barker Coll., Hornsby; Univ. of NSW (BArch). AAIA (ARAIA 1970). *Recreations:* organic farming, fishing. *Heir:* *s* Hon. Francis Senden Blackwood, *b* 6 Jan. 1979. *Address:* PO Box 1815, Orange, NSW 2800, Australia. *T:* (2) 63625608.

**DUFFETT, Roger Hugh Edward;** Secretary, Royal College of Surgeons of England, 1988–97; *b* 20 Jan. 1936; *s* of Dr Edward Cecil Duffett and Cicely Duffett (*née* Haw); *m* 1959, Angela Julie Olden; one *d* (one *s* decd). *Educ:* Sherborne Sch. (Scholar); Peterhouse, Cambridge (Scholar; MA). Commissioned RA (Nat. Service), 1954–56; British Petroleum Co.: joined 1956; refinery process foreman, 1959–60; research, molecular sieve properties of synthetic zeolites and reactions of frozen free radicals, 1960–64; creation of computerised manpower planning models, 1964–68; creation and operation of computerised linear programming models for integrated oil ops, 1968–71; application of mathematical models to corporate planning, 1971–73; planning, internat. ops for lubricants, 1973–78; negotiation and op., crude oil contracts, 1978–79; consultancy for analysis and resolution of orgnl problems: in shipping, research, engrg, marketing and personnel; for management of secondary schools, Cambs; Unicef (UK); employment of secondees to Enterprise Bds, 1979–87; orgn and systems consultant for BP Oil Internat., for Riding for Disabled, 1987–88. Gov., Basingstoke NHS Foundn Trust, 2006–08. Member, Management Committee, Clare Park, 1979–83; Riding for Disabled, 1990–2004 (Trustee, 1999–2004; Hon. Life Vice Pres., 2007); Dir, Quinta Nursing Home, Farnham, 1983–88. Freeman, Barbers' Co., 1998. Hon. FRCS 1997; Hon. DGDP 1998; Hon. FFGDP 1998. Mem., Editl Bd, Primary Dental Care, 2010–. *Publications:* contribs to learned jls. *Recreations:* golf, servicing golf club website magazine, coarse gardening, creating brain teasers, writing, reading. *Address:* Tavistock Cottage, Bentley, Farnham, Surrey GU10 5JA. *T:* and *Fax:* (01420) 520283. *E:* r.duffett@btinternet.com. *Club:* Liphook Golf.

**DUFFIELD, Christopher Paul;** Town Clerk and Chief Executive, City of London Corporation (formerly Corporation of London), 2003–12; *b* 20 May 1952; *s* of late Jack and Irene Duffield; *m* 1st, 1971 (marr. diss. 1979); one *s*; 2nd, 1987, Tricia Jackson; two *s*. *Educ:* St Albans Sch.; Univ. of Newcastle-upon-Tyne (BA Hons 1973). CPFA 1978. Asst Dir of Finance, GLC, 1983–85; Dep. Dir of Finance, London Bor. of Redbridge, 1985–87; Dep. County Treas., Essex CC, 1988–91; London Borough of Bexley: Dir of Finance, 1991–95; Chief Exec., 1995–2003. Mem., London Regl Risk and Audit Cttee, HM Courts Service, 2006–10. Member: London Resilience Partnership (formerly Regl Resilience Forum), 2004–12 (Chm., Local Authy Panel, 2008–12; Dep. Chm., 2011–12); Exec. Task Force, Film London, 2008–12; London Charter Bd, 2009–11; London Finance Commn, 2012–13; Crossrail 2 Growth Commn, 2015–16; Chm., Central London Resilience Forum, 2006–10. Dep. Chm., Bexley PCT, 2001–03. Trustee, Hackney Quest, 2009–12.

**DUFFIELD, Linda Joy,** CMG 2002; HM Diplomatic Service, retired; Chief Executive, Westminster Foundation for Democracy, 2009–14; *b* 18 April 1953; *d* of Bryan Charles Duffield and Joyce Eileen Duffield (*née* Barr). *Educ:* St Mary's Sch., Northwood, Middx; Exeter Univ. (BA Hons 1975). DHSS, 1976–85; Ecole Nat. d'Admin, Paris, 1985–86; joined FCO, 1987; First Sec., Moscow, 1989–92; First Sec., later Counsellor, FCO, 1993–95; Dep. High Comr, Ottawa, 1995–99; High Comr, Sri Lanka, 1999–2002; Dir, Wider Europe, FCO, 2002–04; Ambassador to the Czech Republic, 2004–09. *Recreations:* music, ski-ing, gardening.

**DUFFIELD, Rosemary Clare;** MP (Lab) Canterbury, since 2017; two *s*. Former teaching asst. Mem., Women and Equalities Cttee, H of C, 2017–. *Address:* House of Commons, SW1A 0AA.

**DUFFIELD, Dame Vivien (Louise),** DBE 2000 (CBE 1989); Chairman, Clore Duffield Foundation, since 2000; *b* 26 March 1946; *d* of Sir Charles Clore and Mrs Francine Clore (*née* Halphen); *m* 1969, John Duffield (marr. diss. 1976); one *s* one *d*. *Educ:* Cours Victor Hugo, Paris; Lycée Français de Londres; Heathfield Sch.; Lady Margaret Hall, Oxford (MA). Chairman: Clore Foundn, 1979–2000; Vivien Duffield Foundn, 1987–2000. Member: NSPCC Centenary Appeal Cttee, 1983; NSPCC Financial Develt Cttee, 1985; Vice-Chairman: Great Ormond Street Hosp. Wishing Well Appeal, 1987; Royal Marsden Hosp. Cancer Appeal, 1990; Campaign Chm., Univ. of Oxford, 2007–10; Director: Royal Opera House Trust, 1985–2001 (Dep. Chm., 1988–2001); Royal Opera House, 1990–2001 and 2014– (Chm., Royal Opera House Endowment Fund, 2005–); South Bank Bd, 2002–16; Mem., Royal Ballet Bd, 1990–2000; Gov., Royal Ballet, 2002–12; Trustee: Dulwich Coll. Picture Gall., 1993–2002; Jewish Community Centre for London, 2004–. Mem. Bd, Clore Leadership Prog., 2004–. Hon. FRIBA 2016. Hon. DLitt Buckingham, 1990; Hon. DPhil Weizmann Inst., 1985; Hon. RCM, 1987. *Recreations:* ski-ing, opera, ballet, shooting. *Address:* c/o Clore Duffield Foundation, 3 Chelsea Manor Studios, Flood Street, SW3 5SR; 79 Grubenstrasse, Gruben, Gstaad 3780, Switzerland.

**DUFFY, Sir (Albert Edward) Patrick,** Kt 1991; PhD; *b* 17 June 1920. *Educ:* London Sch. of Economics (BSc (Econ.), PhD); Columbia Univ., Morningside Heights, New York, USA. Served War of 1939–45, Royal Navy, incl. flying duties with FAA. Lecturer, University of Leeds, 1950–63, 1967–70. Visiting Professor: Drew Univ., Madison, NJ, 1966–70; Amer. Grad. Sch. of Internat. Business, 1982–93; Internat. Business Inst., Wheaton, Ill, 1992–; Associate, Centre of Defence Studies, Univs of Hull and Lancaster, 1997–. Contested (Lab) Tiverton Division of Devon, 1950, 1951, 1955. MP (Lab): Colne Valley Division of Yorks, 1963–66; Sheffield, Attercliffe, 1970–92. PPS to Sec. of State for Defence, 1974–76; Parly Under-Sec. of State for Defence (Navy), MoD, 1976–79; opposition spokesman on defence, 1979–80, 1983–84. Chairman: PLP Economic and Finance Gp, 1965–66, 1974–76; Trade and Industry Sub-Cttee of Select Cttee on Expenditure, 1972–74; PLP Defence Cttee, 1979–84; Vice-Chm., Anglo-Irish Gp, 1979–92. Pres., N Atlantic Assembly, 1988–90 (Mem., 1979–92; Chm., Defence Co-op. sub-cttee, 1983–87); Dep. Chm., Atlantic Council of UK, 1994–97. Co-Chm., Carrier

Conclave Gp, 1997–2012. President: Lower Don Valley Community Develt Trust, 1997–2005; The Labour Life Gp, 2001–; Doncaster Mayo Assoc., 2001–. Mem., Catholic Club, Doncaster. Hon. DHL Dominican Univ., Illinois, 1993. KCSG 2017. *Publications:* Growing up Irish in Britain and British in Ireland: and in Washington, Moscow, Rome and Sydney, 2013; contrib. to Economic History Review, Victorian Studies, Manchester School, Annals of Amer. Acad. of Pol. and Soc. Sci., etc. *Recreations:* annual pilgrimages on foot, incl. Walsingham, Croagh Patrick, Co. Mayo and Santiago de Compostela. *Address:* 153 Bennetthorpe, Doncaster, South Yorks DN2 6AH. *Club:* Naval.

**DUFFY, Dame Antonia Susan;** *see* Byatt, Dame A. S.

**DUFFY, Bernadette Marie,** OBE 2005; Head Teacher, Thomas Coram Centre, 1998–2016; *b* St Albans, 28 June 1958; *d* of James Edward Duffy and Mary Teresa Duffy; *m* (marr. diss.). *Educ:* Mater Dei Sch. for Girls, Welwyn Garden City; W London Inst. of Higher Educn (Cert Ed); Roehampton Inst. of Higher Educn (MA Primary and Early Educn). Teacher: Kilburn and Brondesbury High Sch., Brent, 1979; Wood End Lane Infants Sch., Hillingdon, 1980; St Mary's Infants Sch., Kensington and Chelsea, 1980–84; Rylston Day Nursery, Hammersmith, 1984–86; Dep. Hd, 1986–88, Head Teacher, 1988–98, Dorothy Gardner Centre; Foundn Stage Advr, QCA (on secondment), 2005–07. Member: Steering Gp for Effective Provision of Pre-sch. Educn Project, DFES, 1997–2003; Expert Gp for Early Years Foundn Stage, DFE, 2010–11. Member: Adv. Cttee for Cambridge Rev. of Primary Educn, 2007–09; Nat. Council for Educnl Excellence, 2008–10. Chm., British Assoc. for Early Childhood Educn, 2006–09. Trustee, Froebel Trust, 2009–. *Publications:* Supporting Creativity and Imagination in Early Years, 1998, 2nd edn 2006; Contemporary Issues in the Early Years, 2013. *Recreations:* drawing, painting, godchildren, family.

**DUFFY, Dame Carol Ann,** DBE 2015 (CBE 2002; OBE 1995); FRSL; poet and freelance writer; Poet Laureate, 2009–19; Professor of Contemporary Poetry, Manchester Metropolitan University, since 2004; *b* 23 Dec. 1955; *d* of Frank Duffy and May Black; one *d*. *Educ:* St Joseph's Convent, Stafford; Stafford Girls' High Sch.; Univ. of Liverpool (BA Hons Philosophy 1977). FRSL 1999; FRSA 2001. Hon. FBA 2015; Hon. FRSE 2015. Hon. DLitt: Hull, 2001; Warwick, 2001. *Awards:* Eric Gregory, 1983; Somerset Maugham, 1987; Dylan Thomas, 1990; Cholmondeley, 1992; Lannan, USA, 1995; Signal Poetry, 1997; PEN/Pinter, 2012. *Plays:* Take My Husband, 1982; Cavern of Dreams, 1984; Little Women, Big Boys, 1986; Loss (radio), 1986; Grimm Tales, 1994, More Grimm Tales, 1996, Young Vic; Beasts and Beauties, Bristol Old Vic, 2004; Casanova, W Yorks Playhouse, 2007; Rapunzel (ballet), Durham Gala Th., 2012; Rat's Tales, Royal Exchange, Manchester, 2012; Everyman, NT, 2015; My Country: A Work in Progress, NT, 2017. *Publications:* Standing Female Nude, 1985; Selling Manhattan, 1987, 4th edn 1994; (ed) Home and Away, 1988; The Other Country, 1990; (ed) I Wouldn't Thank You for a Valentine, 1992; Mean Time, 1993 (Whitbread Prize, Forward Prize, 1993); Selected Poems, 1994; (ed) Anvil New Poets, 1995; (ed) Stopping for Death, 1996; The Pamphlet, 1998; The World's Wife (poetry), 1999; Meeting Midnight (for children), 1999; Rumpelstiltskin and other Grimm Tales (for children), 1999; (ed) Time's Tidings (poetry), 1999; The Oldest Girl in the World (for children), 2000; (ed) Signal Poetry, 2000; (ed) E. M. Forster, 2001; (ed) Hand in Hand, 2001; Feminine Gospels (poetry), 2002; Underwater Farmyard (for children), 2002; Queen Munch and Queen Nibble (for children), 2002; (ed) Overheard on a Saltmarsh, 2003; (ed) Out of Fashion: an anthology of poems, 2004; Doris the Giant (for children), 2004; Rapture (poetry), 2005 (T. S. Eliot Prize, 2006); The Hat (poetry), 2007; New and Collected Poems for Children, 2009; To the Moon (anthology), 2009; Love Poems, 2010; The Gift (for children), 2010; The Bees (poetry), 2011 (Costa Poetry Award, 2011); (ed) Jubilee Lines (poetry), 2012; (ed) Sylvia Plath: poems, 2012; Collected Poems (poetry), 2015; Sincerity (poetry), 2018. *Address:* c/o Picador Books, 20 New Wharf Road, N1 9RR.

**DUFFY, Prof. Eamon,** PhD, DD; FBA 2004; FSA; Professor of the History of Christianity, University of Cambridge, 2003–14, now Emeritus; Fellow, Magdalene College, Cambridge, 1979–2014, now Emeritus (President (Senior Fellow and Vice-Master), 2001–06, 2008); *b* Dundalk, Eire, 9 Feb. 1947; *s* of Patrick Duffy and Lillian Frances Duffy (*née* Todd); *m* 1968, Jennifer Elizabeth Browning; one *s* two *d*. *Educ:* Univ. of Hull (BA 1968); Selwyn Coll., Cambridge (PhD 1972); Magdalene Coll., Cambridge (DD 1994). Res. Fellow in Arts, Dept of Hist., Univ. of Durham, 1971–74; Lectr in Ecclesiastical Hist., KCL, 1974–79; Lectr in Divinity, 1979–94, Reader in Church Hist., 1994–2003, Univ. of Cambridge. Hon. Prof., Univ. of Durham, 2011–. Mem., Pontifical Historical Commn, 2001–07. President: Ecclesiastical Hist. Soc., 2004–05 (Hon. Fellow 2011); Catholic Theol Assoc. of GB, 2004–06. Hon. (Etheldreda) Canon, Ely Cathedral, 2014–. Chm. Editl Bd, Calendar of Papal Registers, 1999–. FSA 2011. Hon. MRIA 2012. Hon. DD: Hull, 2014; Durham, 2013; Heythrop Coll., London, 2018; Hon. DLitt: KCL, 2009; Newman, 2015; Hon. Dr Medieval Studies, Pontifical Inst. for Medieval Studies, Toronto, 2013. Hawthornden Prize for Lit., 2002; Johannes Quasten Medal for Excellence in Scholarship and Leadership in Religious Studies, Catholic Univ. of America, 2016. Knight, Order of St Gregory the Great, 2017. *Publications:* (ed and contrib.) Challoner and His Church: a Catholic bishop in Georgian England, 1981; (ed and contrib. with B. Bradshaw) Humanism, Reform and Reformation: the career of Bishop John Fisher, 1988; The Stripping of the Altars, 1992; (jtly) A History of Magdalene College, Cambridge 1428–1988, 1994; The Creed in the Catechism: the life of God for us, 1996; Saints and Sinners: a history of the Popes, 1997, 2nd edn 2001 (trans. several langs); Catholicism and Its Pasts, 2000; The Voices of Morebath: Reformation and rebellion in an English village, 2001; Faith of Our Fathers: reflections on Catholic tradition, 2004; (ed jtly) The Church of Mary Tudor, 2006; Walking to Emmaus, 2006; Marking the Hours: English people and their prayers 1240–1570, 2006; Fires of Faith: Catholic England under Mary Tudor, 2009; Ten Popes who Shook the World, 2011; Saints, Sacrilege, Sedition: religion and conflict in the Tudor Reformations, 2012; The Heart in Pilgrimage: a prayerbook for Catholic Christians, 2014; Reformation Divided: Catholics, Protestants and the conversion of England, 2017; Royal Books and Holy Bones: essays in medieval religion, 2018. *Recreations:* early music, landscape painting, dog-walking. *Address:* Magdalene College, Cambridge CB3 0AG. *E:* ed10000@cam.ac.uk.

**DUFFY, Most Rev. Francis;** *see* Ardagh and Clonmacnoise, Bishop of, (RC).

**DUFFY, Dr Francis Cuthbert,** CBE 1997; PPRIBA; with DEGW, 1974–2011 (Founder, 1974); with DEGW North America, 2001–04; independent consultant, since 2012; *b* 3 Sept. 1940; *s* of late John Austin Duffy and Annie Margaret Duffy (*née* Reed); *m* 1965, Jessica Bear; three *d*. *Educ:* Architectural Assoc. Sch. (AA Dip Hons); Univ. of California at Berkeley (MArch); Princeton Univ. (MA, PhD). Asst Architect, Nat. Building Agency, 1964–67; Commonwealth Fund Harkness Fellow, Berkeley and Princeton, 1967–70; established London office, JFN Associates (of NY), 1971. Member: Council, RIBA, 1989–97 (Pres., 1993–95); Architects Registration Bd, 1997–2003; UKTI Construction Sector Adv. Gp, 2008–16; Pres., Architects' Council of Europe, 1994; Vice Pres., Archit Assoc., 2013–. Chairman: Architecture, Design and Workplace Cttee, BBC, 2006–09; Stratford City Design Rev. Panel, 2006–. Trustee, Architecture Foundn, 1999–2009. Visiting Professor: MIT, 2001–04; Reading Univ., 2007–; Univ. of Lancaster, 2009–. Mem., Adv. Council, Sch. of Architecture, Princeton Univ., 2009–11. Editor, AA Jl, 1965–67; founder Editor, Facilities, 1985–90. President's Award for Lifetime Achievement in Workplace Design, British Council of Offices, 2004; Lifetime Achievement Award, British Inst. of Facilities Mgt, 2013. *Publications:* Office Landscaping, 1966; (jtly) Planning Office Space, 1976; (jtly) The Changing City, 1989; The Changing Workplace, 1992; (jtly) The Responsible Workplace, 1993; The New Office, 1997; Architectural Knowledge, 1998; (jtly) New Environments for Working, 1998; Work and the City, 2008. *Recreations:* walking, talking, reading. *Address:* Threeways, The Street, Walberswick, Suffolk IP18 6UE. *T:* (01502) 723814. *Club:* Reform.

**DUFFY, Most Rev. Joseph,** DD; Bishop of Clogher, (RC), 1979–2010; *b* 3 Feb. 1934; *s* of Edward Duffy and Brigid MacEntee. *Educ:* St Macartan's College, Monaghan; Maynooth College. MA, BD, HDipEd. Ordained priest, 1958; Teacher, 1960–72; Curate, 1972–79. *Publications:* Patrick in his own words, 1972, 2nd edn 2000; Lough Derg Guide, 1980; Monaghan Cathedral, 1992; Tiarnach of Clones, 2018. *Recreations:* local history, travel. *Address:* Doire na gCraobh, Monaghan, Ireland. *T:* (47) 62725.

**DUFFY, Maureen Patricia,** FRSL 1985; FEA; author; *b* 1933; *oc* of Grace Rose Wright. *Educ:* Trowbridge High Sch. for Girls; Sarah Bonnell High Sch. for Girls; King's College, London (BA; FKC 2002). Chairman: Greater London Arts Literature Panel, 1979–81; Authors Lending and Copyright Soc., 1982–94 (Pres. of Honour, 2002–); British Copyright Council, 1989–98 (Vice Chm., 1981–86; Vice-Pres., 1998–2003; Hon. Pres., 2003); Copyright Licensing Agency, 1996–99 (Vice-Chm., 1994–96). Pres., Writers' Guild of GB, 1985–88 (Jt Chm., 1977–78); Co-founder, Writers' Action Group, 1972–79; Pres., European Writers Congress, 2003–05 (Vice-Pres., 1992–2003). FEA 2015. Hon. DLitt: Loughborough, 2011; Kent, 2013. Gold Medal for Lit., CISAC, 2002; Benson Silver Medal for Lit., RSL, 2004; Medal of Honour, Portuguese Soc. of Authors, 2009. *Publications:* That's How It Was, 1962; The Single Eye, 1964; The Microcosm, 1966; The Paradox Players, 1967; Lyrics for the Dog Hour (poetry), 1968; Wounds, 1969; Rites (play), 1969; Love Child, 1971; The Venus Touch, 1971; The Erotic World of Faery, 1972; I want to Go to Moscow, 1973; A Nightingale in Bloomsbury Square (play), 1974; Capital, 1975; Evesong (poetry), 1975; The Passionate Shepherdess, 1977; Housespy, 1978; Memorials of the Quick and the Dead (poetry), 1979; Inherit the Earth, 1980; Gorsaga, 1981 (televised as First Born, 1988); Londoners: an elegy, 1983; Men and Beasts, 1984; Collected Poems 1949–84, 1985; Change (novel), 1987; A Thousand Capricious Chances: Methuen 1889–1989, 1989; Illuminations (novel), 1991; Occam's Razor (novel), 1993; Henry Purcell (biog.), 1994; Restitution (novel), 1998; England: The Making of the Myth, 2001; Alchemy (novel), 2004; Family Values (poetry), 2008; The Orpheus Trail (novel), 2009; Sappho Singing (play), 2010; Environmental Studies (poetry), 2013; In Times Like These (novel), 2013; Pictures From An Exhibition (poetry), 2016; The Choice (play), 2017; Past and Present (poetry), 2017; *visual art:* Prop art exhibn (with Brigid Brophy), 1969. *Address:* 18 Fabian Road, SW6 7TZ. *T:* (020) 7385 3598.

**DUFFY, Sir Patrick;** *see* Duffy, Sir A. E. P.

**DUFFY, Philip James,** CBE 2017; Director, Enterprise and Growth, HM Treasury, since 2017; *b* Ascot, Berks, 5 May 1979; *s* of Henry Philip and Linda Gaye Duffy; partner, Robert Young. *Educ:* St Bernard's Convent Grammar Sch., Slough; Trinity Coll., Cambridge (MA Japanese Studies 2001); French Nat. Sch. of Govt. Dep. Dir, Strategy, 2007–08, Housing Mkts, 2008–09, DCLG; Hd, Strategy Team, UK Border Agency, 2009–11; Dir, Immigration and Border Policy, 2011–14; Chief Operating Officer, Border Force, 2014–17, Home Office. *Recreations:* playing the clarinet, gardening, running, complicated travel.

**DUFFY, Sean Richard Gerard,** MD; FRCSGlas, FRCOG; Senior Lecturer, University of Leeds, since 1994; Consultant Gynaecologist, St James's Hospital, Leeds, since 1994; National Clinical Director for Cancer, NHS England, 2013; *b* Limerick, Ireland, 10 April 1959; *s* of Peter and Peggie Duffy; *m* 1984, Wendy Peard; two *s*. *Educ:* St Clement's Coll., Limerick; University Coll., Cork (MB BCh BAO 1993; MD 1993). FRCSGlas 1987; FRCOG 2001. Res. Registrar and Registrar (Obstetrics and Gynaecol.), then Lectr and Sen. Registrar (Obstetrics and Gynaecol.), Northern Gen. Hosp., Sheffield, 1988–94; Clin. Dir, Leeds Teaching Hosps NHS Trust, 2000–05; Med. Dir, 2005–13, Dir, 2009–13, Yorks Cancer Network. *Publications:* contrib. book chapters and to peer reviewed jls. *Recreation:* gardening. *Address:* The Hawthorns, Milner Lane, Thorner, Leeds LS14 3AG. *E:* s.r.duffy@leeds.ac.uk.

**DUFFY, Simon Patrick;** Chairman, YouView TV Ltd, since 2014; *b* 27 Nov. 1949; *s* of Patrick and Eileen Duffy; *m* 1978, Katherine Haney; two *s*. *Educ:* Brasenose Coll., Oxford (BA (PPE)); Harvard Business Sch. (MBA; Harkness Fellow). Analyst: N. M. Rothschild & Sons, 1973–76; Shell, 1978–80; Consultant, Bain & Co., 1980–82; Gen. Manager, Planning and Treasury, Consolidated Gold Fields, 1982–86; Dir, Corporate Finance, Guinness, 1986–89; Ops Dir, United Distillers, 1989–92; Group Finance Director: Thorn EMI, 1992–96; EMI Gp, 1996–99 (also Dep. Chm.); Dep. Chm. and CEO, World Online Internat., 1999–2001; CEO, End2End, 2001–02; Chief Financial Officer, Orange SA, 2002–03; CEO, 2003–06, Exec. Vice-Chm., 2006–07, ntl; Exec. Chm., QXL Ricardo, later Tradus plc, 2007–08. Chairman: Cadogan Petroleum plc, 2008–11; mBlox Inc.; Symbiotic Technologies Pty Ltd; bwin.party digital entertainment plc, 2011–14; non-executive Director: Oger Telecom Ltd; Modern Times Gp AB, 2008–. FRSA 1995. *Recreations:* music, literature, science, politics. *Club:* Brooks's.

**DUFFY, Timothy David;** Chairman, M & C Saatchi UK, since 2010 (Chief Executive Officer, 2004–10); *b* 13 June 1963; *s* of Michael Duffy and Pauline Duffy; *m* 2006, Georgie Eyre; one *s* one *d*. *Educ:* Cheltenham Grammar Sch.; King's Coll., Cambridge (BA 1985). Saatchi & Saatchi: graduate trainee, 1986–87; Strategic Planner, 1987–92; Gp Account Dir, 1992–95; M & C Saatchi: Gp Account Dir, 1995–97; Man. Dir, 1997–2004. Mem., Mktg Gp of GB. Chm. Trustees, Free Word, 2012–. *Recreations:* history, ski-ing, freedom of expression, poetry. *Address:* c/o M & C Saatchi, 36 Golden Square, W1F 9EE. *T:* (020) 7544 3609. *E:* Timd@mcsaatchi.com. *Club:* Soho House.

**DUFTON, Robert;** Chief Executive, Moorfields Eye Charity, since 2017; *b* Nairobi, 20 March 1962; *s* of late Maj. Felix Dufton and of Rosemary Dufton. *Educ:* Sevenoaks Sch., Kent; Univ. of Bristol (LLB); Coll. of Law; City Univ. (Postgrad. Dip. Gen. Mgt). Articled clerk and solicitor, Lovells, 1984–90; admitted solicitor, 1986; Consultant, Adrian Ellis Associates, 1991; Prog. Dir, Arts & Business, 1992–94; Dep. Dir Ops, Heritage Lottery Fund, 1995–2002; Director: Rayne Foundn, 2002–04; Paul Hamlyn Foundn, 2004–13. Hon. Sen. Vis. Fellow, Cass Business Sch., 2013–; Dir of Campaigns, Univ. of Sheffield, 2014–16. Member: Bd, Arts Council London, 2012–14; AHRC, 2014–18. Trustee, 2012–14, Patron, 2014–, Nat. Funding Scheme. Mem. Council, 2002–08, Dep. Chm., Alumni, 2010–14, Univ. of Bristol. Gov., Mus. of London, 2004–13. Hon. LLD Bristol, 2014. *Recreations:* climbing, singing. *Address:* Moorfields Eye Charity, 162 City Road, EC1V 2PD. *E:* r.dufton@nhs.net.

**DUGDALE,** family name of **Baron Crathorne**.

**DUGDALE, Paul Damian Norwood;** His Honour Judge Dugdale; a Circuit Judge, since 2011; *b* W Sussex, 24 June 1967; *s* of late Peter Robin Dugdale, CBE and of (Esmé) Cyraine Dugdale (*née* Norwood Brown); *m* 1993, Alison, *d* of Frederick Elms and Rosemary Elms (*née* Groves); one *s. Educ:* Canford Sch.; King's Coll. London (LLB). Called to the Bar, Gray's Inn, 1990; barrister, 2 King's Bench Walk, 1991–2011; a Recorder, 2005–11. Mem., Western Circuit, 1991–. Chm. Govs, St Faith's Sch., Winchester, 1997–2011. *Recreations:* English choral music, music festivals and gigs, evenings spent with friends, Digby Dog. *Address:* Crown Court, The Old Shire Hall, The Forbury, Reading RG1 3EH. *Club:* Noblemen and Gentlemen's Catch.

**DUGDALE, Sir William (Matthew Stratford),** 3rd Bt *cr* 1936, of Merevale and Blyth, co. Warwick; DL; farmer and landowner; *b* Birmingham, 22 Feb. 1959; *s* of Sir William Stratford Dugdale, 2nd Bt, CBE, MC and Lady Belinda Dugdale, *d* of 6th Earl of Radnor; *S* father, 2014; *m* 1990, Paige Perkins Sullivan; two *s* two *d. Educ:* Eton Coll. Former Chm., Warwicks CLA. Governor: Foundn of Lady Katherine Leveson; Kingsbury Sch. High Sheriff 2002, DL 2012, Warwickshire. *Recreations:* golf, cycling. *Heir: s* William Stratford Dugdale, *b* 15 Aug. 1992. *Address:* Merevale Hall, Atherstone, Warwickshire CV9 2HG. *T:* (home) (01827) 711653, (office) (01827) 712181, 07768 520601, *Fax:* (01827) 718090. *E:* matthew9595@me.com. *Club:* White's.

**DUGGAN, Gregory Alan R.;** *see* Ripley-Duggan.

**DUGGAN, (James) Ross;** His Honour Judge Duggan; a Circuit Judge, since 2006; a Deputy High Court Judge, since 2007; a Family Court Judge, since 2014; *b* 14 July 1956; *s* of late Leonard Heaton Duggan and Dr Mona Leslie Duggan; *m* 1983, Fiona Elspeth Robb Fowlie. *Educ:* Merchant Taylors' Sch., Crosby; Univ. of Liverpool (LLB Hons 1977). Called to the Bar, Middle Temple, 1978; barrister, Northern Circuit (Liverpool), 1979–2006; Circuit Junior, 1981; Asst Recorder, 1993–97; Recorder, 1997–2006. Designated Family Judge, Stoke-on-Trent, 2007–14. Dir, Local Solutions (formerly Merseyside CVS), 1990–2008. Trustee: Lancs Wildlife Trust, 2015–; Lathom Park Trust, 2017–. *Recreations:* cricket, countryside, local history, music. *Address:* Sessions House, Lancaster Road, Preston PR1 2PD. *Club:* Lancashire County Cricket.

**DUGGAN, Michael;** QC 2014; Director, Duggan Press Ltd, since 2012; *b* Durham, 27 April 1960; *s* of Francis Sidney Duggan and Kathleen Duggan; *m* 1988, Michelle Jane; three *s. Educ:* Keele Univ. (BA); Durham Univ. (BCL); Sidney Sussex Coll., Cambridge (LLM 1985). Called to the Bar, Gray's Inn, 1984. Accredited Mediator, ADR, 2005. Mem., Bar Council, 2015– (Mem., Equality and Diversity Cttee, 2015–). *Publications:* The Modern Law of Strikes, 1987; Business Reorganisations and Employment Law, 1992; Unfair Dismissal, 2000, 2nd edn 2015; Wrongful Dismissal, 3rd edn 2015; Duggan on Employment Contracts, 4th edn 2014; (jtly) The Law of Industrial Action and Trade Union Recognition, 2nd edn 2011 to 3rd edn 2019; The Equality Act 2010, 2010. *Recreations:* guitar, guitarviol, violin, mandolin, driving my Morgan, music, walking, renovating waterwheel in Norfolk cottage, watching Chelsea FC.

**DUGGAN, Patrick Gerald;** actor (as **Patrick Malahide**) and writer; *b* 24 March 1945; *s* of John Cuthbert Duggan and Mary Clementine Duggan (*née* Andrews); *m* 1st, 1970, Rosemary Wright (marr. diss. 1990); one *s* one *d*; 2nd, 1993, Jo Ryan. *Educ:* Douai Sch.; Edinburgh Univ. Stage Manager, 1969, Dir of Prodns, 1970–72, Byre Th., St Andrews; joined Royal Lyceum Th., Edinburgh, as actor, 1972–76; *plays* include: The Android Circuit, Traverse and ICA, 1978; Judgement (one man show), Liverpool Playhouse, and subseq. at Edinburgh, Dublin and Amsterdam Fests, 1979; The Tempest, 1980, King Lear, 1981, Bristol Old Vic; Operation Bad Apple, Royal Court, 1982; Cock-ups, Manchester Royal Exchange, 1983; Bristol Old Vic: The Cherry Orchard, 1987; In The Ruins (one man show), transf. Royal Court, 1989–90; Clandestine Marriage, Uncle Vanya, 1990; Map of the Heart, Globe, 1991; Mutabilitie, RNT, 1998; Hinterland, RNT, 2002; Embers, Duke of York's, 2006; Hamlet, RNT, 2010; *television* series and serials include: Minder, 1979–87; Charlie, The Pickwick Papers, 1984; The Singing Detective, 1986; The One Game, The Franchise Affair, 1988; Children of the North, 1990; The Secret Agent, 1991; The Blackheath Poisonings, 1992; The Inspector Alleyn Mysteries, 1993–94; Middlemarch, 1994; In Search of the Brontës, 2003; Elizabeth I, 2005; Five Days, 2007; *plays* include: Miss Julie, 1987; A Doll's House, 1991; All the King's Men, 1999; Victoria and Albert, 2001; Goodbye Mr Chips, 2002; Friends and Crocodiles, 2005; A Short Stay in Switzerland, 2009; Game of Thrones, 2012–16; Hunted, 2012; The Paradise, 2012; Indian Summers, 2015–16; Luther, 2016–19; *films* include: The Killing Fields, Comfort and Joy, 1984; A Month in the Country, 1987; December Bride, 1990; A Man of No Importance, 1994; Two Deaths, Cutthroat Island, 1995; The Long Kiss Goodnight, 1996; US Marshals, 1998; The World is not Enough, 1999; Billy Elliot, Quills, 2000; Captain Corelli's Mandolin, 2001; Sahara, 2005; Brideshead Revisited, 2008; Mortal Engines, 2018. Dir, Bristol Old Vic Trust, 2008–14. *Publications:* screenplays as P. G. Duggan: Reasonable Force, 1988; The Writing on the Wall, 1996; Pleas and Directions, 2002. *Recreations:* sailing, walking. *Address:* c/o Independent Talent Group Ltd, 40 Whitfield Street, W1T 2RH. *Club:* Royal Fowey Yacht.

**DUGGAN, Ross;** *see* Duggan, J. R.

**DUGGIN, Sir Thomas (Joseph),** Kt 2004; HM Diplomatic Service, retired; Ambassador to Colombia, 2001–05; *b* 15 Sept. 1947; *s* of late Joseph Duggin and Alice Lilian Duggin (*née* Mansfield); *m* 1st, 1968 (marr. diss.); two *s*; 2nd, 1983 (marr. diss.); 3rd, 1999, Janette Mortimer (*née* David). *Educ:* Thornleigh Salesian Coll. Joined HM Diplomatic Service, 1967; Third Sec., Oslo, 1969–73; Third, later Second Sec. (Commercial), Bucharest, 1973–75; FCO, 1976–79; Second Sec., Bangkok, 1979–82; FCO, 1982–85; Head of Chancery and HM Consul, La Paz, 1985–88; Head of Chancery, Mexico City, 1989–91; High Comr, Vanuatu, 1992–95; Hd of Security Dept, then Asst Dir for Security, subseq. Hd of Security Comd, then Hd of Security Strategy Unit, FCO, 1995–2001. Bd Mem., British and Colombian Chamber of Commerce, 2005–. MSM, Order of Vanuatu, 1992. *Recreations:* walking, tennis, reading, music. *Address:* Oak Tree, 3 Woodside, North Walsham, Norfolk NR28 9XA.

**DUGGLEBY, (Charles) Vincent (Anstey),** MBE 2005; freelance broadcaster and financial journalist, since 1989; *b* 23 Jan. 1939; *s* of late Bernard Waldby Duggleby and Vivien Duggleby (*née* Hawkins); *m* 1964, Elizabeth Nora Frost; two *d. Educ:* Blundell's Sch.; Worcester Coll., Oxford (BA 1962, MA 2005). FRPSL 1979. Reporter, Bristol Evening Post, 1957–59; Sub-editor, Daily Express, 1960; BBC, 1963–89: sub-editor and sports presenter, 1963–67; Asst Sports Editor, 1967–70; Asst Editor, Current Affairs, 1970–80; Financial Editor, 1980–89. Mem., Royal Mint Adv. Cttee, 1987–94. Royal Philatelic Society: Mem. Council, 1979–2002; Hon. Treas., 1988–93; Vice-Pres., 1994–99. Numerous awards, including: Broadcasting Financial Journalist of Year, Harold Wincott Foundn, 1992; Best Personal Finance Broadcaster, ABI, 1997. *Publications:* Highlights from 21 Years of Sports Report, 1969; English Paper Money, 1975, 9th edn 2017; (with Louise Botting) Making the Most of Your Money, 1984, 2nd edn 1985; Days Beyond Recall: a brief history of the Duggleby family, 2005. *Recreations:* philately, genealogy, classic jazz.

**DUGHER, Michael Vincent;** Chief Executive, UK Music, since 2017; *b* Doncaster, 26 April 1975; *s* of Robert Dugher and Isobel Dugher (*née* Archer); *m* 2004, Joanna Nunney; one *s* two *d. Educ:* St Mary's RC Sch., Edlington; McAuley RC Sch., Doncaster; Univ. of Nottingham (BA Hons Politics). Convenor, Notts and Derbys NUS, 1995–96; Nat. Chair, Labour Students, Lab. Party, 1997–98; Res. Officer, 1998–2000, Hd of Policy, 2000–01, AEEU; Special Adviser: to Minister for Transport, 2001–02; to Sec. of State for Defence, 2002–05; to Leader of H of C, 2005–06; UK Dir, Govt Relns, EDS, 2006–07; Special Advr to Govt Chief Whip, 2007–08; Chief Political Spokesman to Prime Minister, 2008–10. MP (Lab) Barnsley East, 2010–17. Shadow Minister for Defence Equipment, Support and Technol., 2010–11; PPS to Leader of the Opposition, 2011; Shadow Minister without Portfolio, Cabinet Office, 2011–13; Shadow Minister for Cabinet Office, 2013–14; Shadow Sec. of State for Transport, 2014–15, for Culture, Media and Sport, 2015–16. Vice-Chair, Labour Party, 2012–14. Mem. Bd, Nottingham Forest Community Trust, 2017–. *Publications:* (with J. Spellar) Fools Gold: dispelling the myth of the Tory economic legacy, 1999; (contrib.) Dictionary of Labour Biography, 2001. *Recreations:* football (watching), cricket, horse racing, music (playing and listening), history. *Address:* UK Music, 4th Floor, Whitehall, SW1A 2BX.

**DUGUID, Andrew Alexander;** Integration, Marketing & Planning Executive, Global Aerospace, 2001–04; *b* 22 June 1944; *s* of Wing Comdr (retd) Alexander Gordon Duguid and Dorothy Duguid (*née* Duder); *m* 1967, Janet Hughes; two *s* one *d. Educ:* Whitby Dist High Sch.; Ashbury Coll., Ottawa; Sidcot Sch.; LSE (BSc Econs); Univ. of Lancaster (MA Marketing). Res. Assistant, Brunel Univ., 1967–69; Marketing Executive: Interscan Ltd, 1969–72; Ogilvy Benson and Mather, 1972–73; joined DTI as Principal, 1973; Prin. Pvte Sec. to Sec. of State for Industry, 1977–79; Asst Sec., seconded to Prime Minister's Policy Unit, 1979; returned to set up Policy Planning Unit, Dept of Industry, later DTI, 1982; Under Sec., DTI, 1985–86; Lloyd's of London: Head of Regulatory Services, 1986–88; Head of Market Services, 1988–92; Dir, Marketing Services, 1993–94; Dir, Policy and Planning, and Sec. to Council of Lloyd's, 1995–99; Dir, Develt, 1999–2000. Manager, SCI Barnski, 1993–. Non-executive Director: Kingsway Public Relations, 1982–85; Hammersmith and Fulham NHS PCT, 2005–11; Central London Community Healthcare, 2008–10 (Chm., 2008–09). Trustee, Sir John Cass Foundn, 2005–08; Chair of Trustees, London Sch. of Osteopathy, 2017–. *Publications:* (with Elliott Jaques) Case Studies in Export Organisation, 1971; On the Brink: how a crisis transformed Lloyd's of London, 2014. *Recreations:* tennis, ski-ing, walking, canoeing, photography. *Address:* 1 Binden Road, W12 9RJ. *T:* (020) 8743 7435. *Clubs:* Reform; Hartswood Lawn Tennis (Pres., 2006–).

**DUGUID, David James;** MP (C) Banff and Buchan, since 2017; *b* Turriff, 8 Oct. 1970; *m* 2010, Raziya Gasimova; one *s* one *d. Educ:* Banff Acad.; Robert Gordon Inst. of Technol. (HND Chemistry 1991). Chemical sales and service engr, Servo Oilfield Chemicals, 1992–93; Prodn Chemist, SGS, 1993–2001; BP: Prodn Efficiency Engr and Ops Excellence Coach, 2001–03; Integrity Mgt and Process Safety Engr, 2003–06; Common Process and Continuous Improvement Coach, 2006–11; Proj. Manager, Mgt Consulting and Change Mgt, Hitachi Consulting, 2011–16; Man. Dir, D&R Duguid Ltd, 2016–. Mem., Scottish Affairs Cttee, H of C, 2017–. *Recreation:* plays guitar. *Address:* House of Commons, SW1A 0AA. *T:* (020) 7219 2819. *E:* david.duguid.mp@parliament.uk.

**DUGUID, Air Vice-Marshal Ian,** OBE 2009; Chief of Staff Operations, Headquarters Air Command, and Air Officer Commanding Number 11 Group, since 2018; *b* Imtarfa, Malta, 1 Dec. 1966; *s* of Donald Duguid and Dorothy Duguid; *m* 1992, Anne McCoull; one *s* three *d. Educ:* Scarborough Sixth Form Coll.; King's Coll. London (MSc Defence Studies). Joined RAF, 1986; OC No. IV (Army Cooperation) Sqdn, 2005–08 (despatches 2008); Asst Hd Networked Capability, 2009–12; Hd Defence Operational Capability, MoD, 2013–15; Typhoon Force Comdr, 2015–18. Non-exec. Chair, Bd of Dirs, Marlow Educn Trust, 2013–. Gov., Sir William Borlase's Grammar Sch., Marlow, 2008–. *Recreations:* road cycling, long distance running, global strategic studies. *Address:* RAF High Wycombe, High Wycombe, Bucks HP14 4UE. *T:* (01494) 497311. *E:* ian.duguid823@mod.gov.uk.

**DUIGAN, Catherine Anne,** PhD; FLS, FRSB; Evidence Analysis Manager, Evidence, Policy and Permitting (formerly Evidence, Knowledge and Advice) Department, Natural Resources Wales, since 2014; *b* Dublin, 21 April 1962; *d* of Patrick Joseph Duigan and Christina Anne Duigan (*née* Phelan); *m* 1988, Dr Warren Kovach; one *s. Educ:* Sacred Heart Secondary Sch., Tullamore; University Coll. Dublin (BSc 1983; PhD 1989). FLS 1992; FRSB (FSB 2010). Vis. Res. Associate, Indiana Univ., Bloomington, 1984, 1986–87; Biologist (pt-time), Marine Studies Ltd, Aberdeen Univ., 1987–88; Scientific Officer, Freshwater Loch Survey - Isle of Skye and Kyle of Lochalsh, Nature Conservancy Council for Scotland, 1989; Post-doctoral Researcher, Inst. of Earth Studies, Univ. of Wales, Aberystwyth, 1989–91; Res. Fellow, Univ. of Wales, 1991–92; Countryside Council for Wales, later Natural Resources Wales: Freshwater Ecologist, 1992–2005; Head: Marine and Freshwater Scis, 2005–11; Marine and Freshwater Ecosystems Gp, Evidence, Knowledge and Advice Dept (formerly Evidence and Advice Directorate), Bangor, 2011–14. Mem., Editl Bd, The Biologist, Soc. of Biol., 2011–. Member: Fisheries, Ecol. and Recreation Adv. Cttee, Envmt Agency, 2001–04; Sci. and Innovation Strategy Bd, NERC, 2010–13. Mem., Council, Freshwater Biol Assoc., 2001–05. Hon. Lectr, Bangor Univ., 2011–. Contrib. to UK National Ecosystem Assessment, 2011. Trustee, Amgueddfa Cymru - Nat. Mus. of Wales, 2017–. *Publications:* (jtly) Vegetation Communities of British Lakes: a revised classification, 2006; (ed jtly) The Rivers of Wales: a natural resource of international and historical significance, 2009. *Recreations:* walking in nature, art and heritage, all things Irish, my garden. *Address:* Natural Resources Wales, Maes-Y-Ffynnon, Penrhosgarnedd, Bangor, Gwynedd LL57 2DW.

**DUKAKIS, Michael Stanley;** Distinguished Professor of Political Science, Northeastern University, since 1991; Governor, Commonwealth of Massachusetts, 1975–79, and 1983–90; *b* 3 Nov. 1933; *s* of Panos Dukakis and Euterpe Boukis-Dukakis; *m* 1963, Katharine Dickson; one *s* two *d. Educ:* Brookline High Sch. (Dip. 1951); Swarthmore Coll., Pa (BA 1955); Harvard Law Sch. (JD 1960). Attorney, Hill & Barlow, Boston, Mass, 1960–74; Lectr and Dir, Intergovtl Studies, John F. Kennedy Sch. of Govt, Harvard Univ., 1979–82. Visiting Professor: Univ. of Hawaii, 1991; UCLA, 1991–. Dir, Amtrack, 1998–2003. Moderator of public television's The Advocates, 1971–73. State Representative, Brookline, Mass, 1963–71; Democratic Candidate for the Presidency of the USA, 1988. *Publications:* (with Rosabeth Moss Kanter) Creating the Future: Massachusetts comeback and its promise for America, 1988; (jtly) How to Get Into Politics - And Why, 2000; (jtly) The Crisis Strikes, 2001; (jtly) Leader-Managers in the Public Sector, 2010. *Recreations:* walking, playing tennis, gardening. *Address:* 85 Perry Street, Brookline, MA 02446–6935, USA.

**DUKE,** family name of **Baron Merrivale**.

**DUKE, Guy Roderick John;** Director, GD NatCap Ltd, since 2016; Project Director, We Value Nature, Institute of Chartered Accountants in England and Wales, since 2018; *b* Claygate, Surrey, 13 Dec. 1962; *s* of John Duke and Diane Duke (*née* Marks); *m* 1994, Paola Movalli; one *d. Educ:* Dorking Grammar Sch.; Ashcombe Comp. Sch., Dorking; Collingwood Coll., Durham Univ. (BSc Hons Botany and Geog.); Wye Coll., Univ. of London (MSc Landscape Ecol., Design and Maintenance). Ind. ecologist and explorer,

1985–91; Coordinator and Chief Tech. Advr, Palas Conservation and Develt Project, NWFP, Pakistan, BirdLife Internat., 1991–97; Tech. Dir, Biodiversity and Natural Resources, Internat. Develt Services, Envmtl Resources Mgt Ltd, 1998–2002; Principal Administrator, Biodiversity Policy, Directorate Gen. Envmt, EC, 2002–07; ind. consultant, 2008–16; Dir, Europe, then Europe and Res., Envmt Bank Ltd, 2010–17. Ind. Mem., 2009–17, Dep. Chm., 2015–17, JNCC (Chm., Audit and Risk Mgt Cttee, 2012–15); Chair, Eur. Cooperation in Sci. and Technol. Action Eur. Raptor Biomonitoring Facility, 2017–. Hon. Res. Associate (formerly Sen. Vis. Res. Associate), Sch. of Geog. and Envmt, Envmtl Change Inst., Univ. of Oxford, 2011–; Fellow, Centre for Ecology and Hydrology, 2018–. FRGS 1986. *Publications:* white papers, consulting reports; contrib. articles in Ambio, Public Service Review EU, Geographical Mag., Ecosystem Services, Ecotoxicol., Envmt Internat., Acrocephalus, CSR Forum Internat., Bird Study. *Recreations:* being with family, our Welsh Springer, time in nature, playing piano, reading, cooking, enjoying the arts. *E:* guy.duke@skynet.be.

**DUKE, Timothy Hugh Stewart;** Norroy and Ulster King of Arms, since 2014; *b* 12 June 1953; *s* of William Falcon Duke and Mary Cecile Duke (*née* Jackson). *Educ:* Uppingham; Fitzwilliam Coll., Cambridge (MA). Peat, Marwick, Mitchell & Co., 1974–81; Research Asst, Coll. of Arms, 1981–89; Rouge Dragon Pursuivant, 1989–95; Chester Herald of Arms, 1995–2014; Registrar, Coll. of Arms, 2000–07. Hon. Sec., Harleian Soc., 1994–. FSA 2018. *Address:* College of Arms, Queen Victoria Street, EC4V 4BT. *T:* (020) 7236 7728. *Club:* Travellers.

**DUKES, Alan M.;** Public Affairs Consultant, Wilson Hartnell Public Relations, since 2003 (Director, 2008–12); Chairman, Irish Bank Resolution Corporation (formerly Anglo Irish Bank), 2010–13 (non-executive Director, 2008–13); *b* 22 April 1945; *s* of James and Rita Dukes; *m* 1968, Fionnuala Corcoran; two *d*. *Educ:* Coláiste Mhuire, Dublin; University College Dublin (MA). Chief Economist, Irish Farmers' Assoc., 1967–72; Dir, Irish Farmers' Assoc., Brussels, 1973–76; Personal Advr to Comr of European Communities, 1977–80. TD (FG) Kildare, 1981–2002; Minister for Agriculture, 1981–82; opposition spokesman on agric., March–Dec. 1982; Minister: for Finance, 1982–86; for Justice, 1986–87; for Transport, Energy and Communications, 1996–97; opposition spokesman on envmt and local govt, then on agriculture, marine and natural resources, 1977–2002. Leader, 1987–90, President, 1987–92, Fine Gael Party. Chm., Jt Oireachtas Cttee on Foreign Affairs, 1995–96. Vice-President: Internat. European Movt, 1991–96 (Pres., 1987–91, Chm., 1997–2000, Irish Council); European People's Party, 1987–96; Mem., Council of State, 1988–90. Adjunct Prof. of Public Admin/Management, Univ. of Limerick, 1991–2000. Dir Gen., Inst. of Eur. Affairs, Dublin, 2003–07. Governor: EIB, 1982–86; IMF. Officier, Légion d'Honneur (France), 2004; Comdr's Cross, OM (Poland), 2004. *Address:* Tully West, Kildare, Co. Kildare, Eire.

**DUKES, Philip Timothy,** FGS; international viola soloist and conductor; *b* 7 Jan. 1968; *s* of Ronald and Enid Dukes; *m* 2002, Caroline Lefilliatre; two *s*. *Educ:* Wells Cathedral Sch.; Guildhall Sch. of Music and Drama (FGS (FGSM 2006)). Artist-in-Residence, Queen's Univ., Belfast, 2000–09; Prof. of Viola, Royal Acad. of Music, 2003–; Hd of Strings, Wells Cathedral Sch., 2003–08; Artistic Director, Fest. International de Musique de la Hague, 2005–11; Marlborough Coll., 2008–; Vaughan Williams Fest., 2018–; Artistic Advr, Savannah Music Fest. 2020, USA, 2019–. Guest Prof. of Viola and Chamber Music, McGill Univ., 2009–11. Hon. ARAM 2007. *Recreations:* cricket, fine wines, food, obsession with Birmingham City Football Club, Jaguar cars. *Address:* Hamelin, Bath Road, Marlborough, Wilts SN8 1NN. *Club:* Royal Over-Seas League.

**DULEY, Giles Angus Guy;** freelance documentary photographer, specialising in photography of humanitarian issues and the consequences of conflict, since 1996; Founder and Chief Executive Officer, Legacy of War Foundation, since 2017; *b* Wimbledon, 15 Sept. 1971; *s* of Ray Duley and Flora Duley (*née* Stewart). *Educ:* Perrott Hill Sch.; Canford Sch. Photographer for Select, Q, Esquire, GQ, Elle, Vogue, Sunday Times, Observer, Sunday Telegraph; has worked with charities incl. Médecins sans Frontières, UNHCR. Trustee, Emergency UK, 2013–. Hon. FRPS 2013. *Publications:* Afghanistan: 2012, 2013; I Can Only Tell You What My Eyes See: photographs from the refugee crisis, 2017. *Recreations:* Yeovil Town supporter, bee keeping, gardening. *E:* info@gilesduley.com. *Clubs:* Chelsea Arts, Frontline.

**DULIEU, Nicola Joy;** Chairman, Notcutts Ltd, since 2015 (non-executive Director, 2014); *b* Chingford, 26 Dec. 1963; *d* of Ronald and Phyllis Dulieu; *m* Adam Brace. *Educ:* Chingford Sen. High Sch. FCCA; Order of Merit, Assoc. of Accounting Technicians. Joined Marks and Spencer plc, 1982, Property, Retail and HR Finance Dir, 2000–03, Food Gp Finance Dir, 2003–06; Hobbs Ltd: Finance Dir, 2006–08; Chief Exec., 2008–14; non-exec. Dir, 2014. Non-executive Director: Adnams plc, 2014–; Huntsworth plc, 2015–. *Recreation:* garden design and development. *Address:* Yaxham Park, Station Road, Yaxham, Norfolk NR19 1RD. *T:* 07795 664998.

**DULVERTON,** 3rd Baron *cr* 1929, of Batsford; **Gilbert Michael Hamilton Wills;** Bt 1897; farmer, forester and industrialist; *b* 2 May 1944; *s* of 2nd Baron and his 1st wife, Judith Betty (*d* 1983), *d* of Lt-Col Hon. Ian Leslie Melville, TD; *S* father, 1992; *m* 1st, 1980, Rosalind van der Velde-Oliver (marr. diss. 1999); one *s* one *d*; 2nd, 2000, Mrs Mary Vicary. *Educ:* Gordonstoun; RAC, Cirencester. Chm., Thwaites Ltd; Director: W Highland Woodlands Ltd; Batsford Estates (1983) Co. Ltd. Trustee, Dulverton Trust. *Heir:* *s* Hon. Robert Anthony Hamilton Wills, *b* 20 Oct. 1983.

**DUMAS, Roland;** Officier de la Légion d'Honneur; Croix de Guerre (1939–45); Croix du Combattant Volontaire; Minister of Foreign Affairs, France, 1988–93; *b* Limoges, Haute-Vienne, 23 Aug. 1922; *s* of Georges Dumas and Elisabeth (*née* Lecanuet); *m* 1964, Anne-Marie Lillet; two *s* one *d*. *Educ:* Lycée de Limoges; Faculté de Droit, Paris; Ecole des Sciences Politiques, Paris; Univ. of London; Ecole de langues orientales, Paris. LLL; Diplomas: in Advanced Studies in Laws; in Political Science, Paris, and London School of Economics. Counsel, Court of Appeal, Paris, 1950–; journalist; Sen. Political Dir, Journal Socialiste Limousin; Political Dir of weekly, La Corrèze Républicaine et Socialiste, 1967–; Deputy: UDSR, Haute Vienne, 1956–58; FGDS, Corrèze, 1967–68; Socialiste de la Dordogne, 1981–83, 1986–88; Minister for European Affairs, 1983–84; Govt spokesman, 1984; Minister for External Relations, 1984–86; Pres. Commn for Foreign Affairs, Nat. Assembly, 1986–87. Pres., Conseil Constitutionnel, 1995–99. Grand Cross, Order of Isabel (Spain), 1982. *Publications:* J'ai vu vivre la Chine, 1960; Les Avocats, 1970; Le Droit de l'Information et de la Presse, 1981; Plaidoyer pour Roger Gilbert Lecomte, 1985; Le droit de la propriété littéraire et artistique, 1986; Le Peuple Assemblé, 1989; Le Fil et la Pelote (memoirs), 1996; L'Epreuve, 2003; Diplomatie: les nœuds de l'histoire, 2007; (with J. Vergès) Crimes et fraudes en Côte d'Ivoire, 2011; (with J. Vergès) Sarko sous BHL, 2011; Coups et blessures, 2011. *Address:* 19 quai de Bourbon, 75004 Paris, France.

**DUMBRECK, Nicholas John,** FIA, FSA; Principal and Consulting Actuary, Milliman LLP, since 2009; *b* Woking, 12 Nov. 1954; *s* of late Alan Edwin Dumbreck and Sibyll Elisabeth Dumbreck; *m* 1978, Lesley Ann Devlin; one *s* two *d*. *Educ:* Royal Grammar Sch., Guildford; Jesus Coll., Cambridge (BA Maths 1976). FIA 1982; FSA 2008; CERA 2008. Various posts incl. Corporate Actuary, Imperial Life Assce Co. of Canada, 1976–86; Consulting Actuary, R. Watson & Sons, later Watson Wyatt Partners, then Watson Wyatt LLP, subseq. Watson Wyatt Ltd, 1986–2009 (Partner, 1987–2005). Actuarial Function: Omnilife Insce Co., 2005–; St James's Place UK, 2010–15; With-Profits Actuary: Ecclesiastical Life, 2005–09; Cooperative Insce Soc., 2010–14; Liverpool Victoria Friendly Soc., 2012–14; Ind. Expert for transfers of life assce business, 1995–; Member, With Profits Committee: Royal London Mutual, 2015–18; Legal & Gen., 2016–17. Director: Milliman Inc., 2014–18; CERA Global Assoc., 2015– (Chm., 2018–). Institute of Actuaries: Mem. Council, 1993–98 and 1999–2010; Hon. Sec., 1996–98; Vice Pres., 2003–05; Pres., 2006–08. Chm., Staple Inn Actuarial Soc., 2002–04; Mem. Council, 2008–10, Mem. Exec. Cttee, 2010–13, Internat. Actuarial Assoc.; Mem., Ct of Assts, Actuaries' Co., 2006–08 and 2009– (Master, 2017–18). FRSA. *Recreations:* opera, watching cricket, wine, travel, art, puzzles. *Address:* Meadow Barn, Priorsfield Road, Hurtmore, Godalming, Surrey GU7 2RQ. *T:* (01483) 415258. *E:* nick.dumbreck@btinternet.com.

**DUMFRIES, Earl of; John Bryson Crichton-Stuart;** *b* 21 Dec. 1989; *s* and *heir* of Marquess of Bute, *qv*.

**DUMONT, Dame Ivy (Leona),** DCMG 1995; DPA; Governor-General of the Bahamas, 2001–05; *b* 2 Oct. 1930; *d* of Alphonso Tennyson Turnquest and Cecilia Elizabeth Turnquest; *m* 1951, Reginald Deane Dumont (*d* 2011); one *s* one *d*. *Educ:* Univ. of Miami (BEd 1970); Nova Univ., USA (DPA 1978). Teacher, later Dir of Educn, Min. of Educn and Culture, Bahamas, 1945–75; Dep. Permanent Sec., Min. of Works and Utilities, 1975–78; Trng Officer, Personnel Manager then Gp Relations Manager, Natwest Trust Corp. (Bahamas) Ltd, then Coutts & Co., 1978–91; Minister of Health and Envmt, 1992–94; Minister of Education, 1995–2001. Mem. (FNM), Senate, 1992–2001 (Govt Leader, 1992–2001). *Publications:* Rose's to Mount Fitzwilliam (memoir), 2009. *Recreations:* dressmaking and design, horticulture (roses), public speaking, family. *Address:* c/o Government House, Government Hill, PO Box N8301, Nassau, Bahamas. *T:* 3221875; PO Box SS-5316, Nassau, Bahamas. *T:* 3234188.

**DUMONT, Thomas Julian Bradley;** QC 2019; *b* Hyde Park Corner, 7 May 1957; *s* of Anthony Albert Dumont and Patricia Anne Dumont (*née* Troxell); *m* 1982, Judith Anne Thompson; one *s* one *d*. *Educ:* St Paul's Sch.; Trinity Hall, Cambridge (BA 1978). Called to the Bar, Gray's Inn, 1979; in practice as a barrister, Radcliffe Chambers, 1979–. Mem., 1996–99, Vice Chm., Law Reform Cttee, 2010–17, Bar Council. Chm., Edtl Bd, STEP Jl, 2010–18. Treas., Assoc. of Contentious Trusts and Probate Specialists, 2015–. Lectr in Law, Poly. of Central London, 1979–83. FZS 1994. *Recreations:* cricket, poetry, lying in the long grass. *Address:* 11 New Square, Lincoln's Inn, WC2A 3QB. *T:* (020) 7831 0081. *E:* tdumont@radcliffechambers.com; Harting Combe House, Rake, Liss GU33 7JF.

**DUMVILLE, Prof. David Norman,** PhD; FRHistS; FRSAI, FSA, FSAScot; Professor in History, Palaeography and Celtic, University of Aberdeen, since 2005; Fellow, Girton College, Cambridge, since 1978; *b* 5 May 1949; *s* of late Norman Dumville and Eileen Florence Lillie Dumville (*née* Gibbs); *m* 1974, Sally Lois Hannay (*d* 1989); one *s*; one *d*. *Educ:* Emmanuel Coll., Cambridge (BA Hons, MA); Ludwig-Maximilians Universität, Munich; Univ. of Edinburgh (PhD 1976). FRHistS 1976; FRSAI 1989; FSAScot 1999. Fellow, Univ. of Wales, Swansea, 1975–77; Asst Prof. of English, Univ. of Pennsylvania, 1977–78; O'Donnell Lectr in Celtic Studies, Univ. of Oxford, 1977–78; Lectr in Anglo-Saxon, Norse and Celtic, Univ. of Cambridge, 1977–91; British Acad. Res. Reader in Humanities, 1985–87; Reader in Early Mediaeval History and Culture of British Isles, 1991–95, Prof. of Palaeography and Cultural History, 1995–2004, Univ. of Cambridge. Res. Associate, Sch. of Celtic Studies, Dublin Inst. for Advanced Studies, 1989– (Vis. Prof., 1996–97); Visiting Professor of Mediaeval Studies: UCLA, 1995; Univ. of Calif, Berkeley, 1997. Vice-Pres., Centre International de Recherche et de Documentation sur le Monachisme Celtique, 1986–. Hon. MA Pennsylvania, 1979. *Publications:* (with Kathryn Grabowski) Chronicles and Annals of Mediaeval Ireland & Wales, 1984; (with Michael Lapidge) The Annals of St Neots, 1985; The Historia Brittonum, 1985; (ed jtly) The Anglo-Saxon Chronicle, 1985, 1995; Histories and Pseudo-Histories of the Insular Middle Ages, 1990; Wessex and England from Alfred to Edgar, 1992; Liturgy and the Ecclesiastical History of Late Anglo-Saxon England, 1992; Britons and Anglo-Saxons in the Early Middle Ages, 1993; English Caroline Script and Monastic History, 1993; Saint Patrick, 1993; The Churches of North Britain in the First Viking-Age, 1997; Three Men in a Boat (inaugural lect.), 1997, 3rd edn 2017; Councils and Synods of the Gaelic Early and Central Middle Ages, 1997; A Palaeographer's Review, vol. 1 1999, vol. 2 2004; Saint David of Wales, 2001; Annales Cambriae, 2002–; The Annals of Iona, 2002; (with Pádraig Ó Néill) Cáin Adomnáin and Canones Adomnani, 2003; The Early Mediaeval Insular Churches and the Preservation of Roman Literature, 2004; Abbreviations used in Insular Script before AD 850, 2004, 2nd edn 2017; Brenhinoedd y Saeson, 2005–; The Mediaeval Foundations of England?, 2006; Anglo-Saxon Essays, 2007; Celtic Essays, 2 vols, 2007; Vikings in Britain and Ireland: a question of sources, 2014. *Recreations:* travelling in North America, politics and other arguments. *Address:* Department of History, University of Aberdeen, Crombie Annexe, Meston Walk, Old Aberdeen AB24 3FX. *T:* (01224) 272199.

**DUN, Peter John;** HM Diplomatic Service, retired; Foreign Policy Adviser to President and Member, President's Bureau of European Policy Advisers, European Commission, 2008–12; *b* 6 July 1947; *s* of late Herbert Ernest Dun and Joyce Hannah Dun (*née* Tozer); *m* 1984, Cheng Kiak Pang; two *s*. *Educ:* Bristol Grammar Sch.; Univ. of Birmingham (BA); Univ. of Cologne; Univ. of Freiburg; Univ. of Strasbourg. British High Commn, Kuala Lumpur, 1972–76; FCO, 1976–80; UK Repn to EU, 1980–83; UK Mission to UN, 1983–87; Dep. Hd, Disarmament Dept, FCO, 1987–89; rcds, 1989; Counsellor, British High Commission, Islamabad, 1990–93; Foreign Policy Advr and Advr on Balkans Affairs to Ext. Affairs Comr, EC, Brussels, 1993–96; Hd of Information Dept, FCO, 1996–2000; Counsellor, Berlin, 2000–02; Asst to EU Special Rep. for Afghanistan, 2002; Advr, Dir-Gen. for Ext. Relns, EC, Brussels, 2002–08. Vis. Fellow, Stiftung Wissenschaft und Politik, Berlin, 2000–. *Recreations:* music, travel, maps. *Address:* 43 Boulevard Charlemagne, 1000 Brussels, Belgium.

**DUNALLEY,** 7th Baron *cr* 1800 (Ire.), of Kilboy, Tipperary; **Henry Francis Cornelius Prittie;** Social Worker, Shetland Islands Council, 2003–13; *b* 30 May 1948; *s* of 6th Baron Dunalley and Mary Philippa, *er* d of late Hon. Philip Cary; *S* father, 1992; *m* 1978, Sally Louise, *er* *d* of Ronald Vere; one *s* three *d*. *Educ:* Gordonstoun Sch.; Trinity Coll., Dublin (BA); Bedford Coll., Univ. of London (CQSW). Probation Officer: Inner London Probation Service, 1977–80; Buckinghamshire Probation Service, 1980–83; Oxfordshire and Bucks Probation Service, 1983–2001; Thames Valley Probation Service, 2001–03. *Heir:* *s* Hon. Joel Henry Prittie, *b* 29 April 1981. *Address:* 97 Lower Seedley Road, Salford, Greater Manchester M6 5NG.

**DUNANT, Sarah;** novelist and broadcaster; *b* 8 Aug. 1950; *d* of David Dunant and Estelle (*née* Joseph); two *d* by Ian Willox. *Educ:* Godolphin and Latymer Girls' Sch.; Newnham Coll., Cambridge (BA Hons 1972). Actress, 1972–73; producer, Radio 4, 1974–76; freelance writer, TV and radio broadcaster and journalist, 1977–; The Late Show, BBC2, 1989–95. Lectr in Renaissance Studies, Univ. of Washington in St Louis, Missouri, 2009, 2011, 2014. Creative Writing Fellow, Oxford Brookes Univ., 2010–. Teacher, Faber Acad., 2011–. Hon. DLitt Oxford Brookes, 2016. *Publications:* as Peter Dunant, (with Peter

Busby): Exterminating Angels, 1983; Intensive Care, 1986; as Sarah Dunant: Snow Storms in a Hot Climate, 1988; Birth Marks, 1991; Fatlands, 1993 (Silver Dagger Award); (ed) The War of the Words, 1994; Under my Skin, 1995; (ed jtly) Age of Anxiety, 1996; Transgressions, 1997; Mapping the Edge, 1999; The Birth of Venus, 2003; In the Company of the Courtesan, 2006; Sacred Hearts, 2009; Blood and Beauty: the Borgias (novel), 2013; In the Name of the Family (novel), 2017. *Recreations:* movies, travel, nosing out renaissance frescos in churches all over Italy. *Address:* c/o Clare Alexander, Aitken Alexander Associates, 291 Gray's Inn Road, WC1X 8EB. *T:* (020) 7373 8672.

**DUNAWAY, Prof. David James,** CBE 2016; FRCS, FDSRCS; Consultant Plastic and Reconstructive Surgeon, Great Ormond Street Hospital for Children, since 2000; Professor of Craniofacial Surgery, UCL Great Ormond Street Institute of Child Health, since 2016; *b* Hampstead, London, 1956; *s* of Henry James Dunaway and Mildred Blanche Dunaway; *m* 1983, Susan Jane Goodwin; two *s* one *d*. *Educ:* Christ's Coll., Finchley; University Coll. London (BDS 1980); Univ. of Manchester (MB ChB 1989). FDSRCS 1988; FRCS 1992; FRCS(Plast) 1997. Dental Surgeon, London and Manchester, 1980–89; surgical trng, Manchester, Leeds, Adelaide, Newcastle, London, 1990–96; Consultant Plastic and Reconstructive Surgeon, Canniesburn Hosp., Glasgow, 1997–2000. *Publications:* The Clinical Management of Craniosynostosis (jtly), 2004; over 100 articles in learned jls. *Recreations:* sailing, travel, walking, ski-ing, facial surgery and teaching in Africa (Trustee, Facing Africa, 2012–). *Address:* Craniofacial Unit, Great Ormond Street Hospital for Children, Great Ormond Street, WC1N 3JH. *T:* (020) 7405 9200, *Fax:* (020) 7467 3004. *E:* david.dunaway@gosh.nhs.uk, david.dunaway@152harleystreet.com.

**DUNBABIN, Dr Jean Hymers,** FBA 2009; Fellow and Tutor, St Anne's College, Oxford, 1973–2004 (Honorary Fellow, 2011); Reader in Medieval History, University of Oxford, 1973–2004; *b* 12 May 1939; *d* of David Mackay and Peggy Mackay (*née* Stewart); *m* 1962, John Dunbabin; two *d*. *Educ:* St Leonard's Sch., St Andrews; St Hilda's Coll., Oxford (MA, DPhil 1965). Jun. Research Fellow, Somerville Coll., Oxford, 1961–63; Vice-Principal, St Anne's Coll., Oxford, 1994–97. Mem., IAS, Princeton, 1989. Ed., English Historical Rev., 2000–03. *Publications:* France in the Making 843–1180, 1985, 2nd edn 2000; A Hound of God: Pierre de la Palud and the Fourteenth Century Church, 1991; Charles I of Anjou: power, kingship and state-making in thirteenth-century Europe, 1998; Captivity and Imprisonment in Medieval Europe 1000–1300, 2002; The French in the Kingdom of Sicily, 1266–c.1305, 2011; contributions to: The Cambridge History of Later Medieval Philosophy, 1982; The Cambridge History of Medieval Political Thought, 1988; The New Cambridge Medieval History, vol. III, 1999; contrib. various jls. *Recreations:* walking, travelling. *Address:* St Anne's College, Oxford OX2 6HS. *T:* (01865) 274800.

**DUNBAR, David;** architect; Managing Director, ADF Architects Ltd, Glasgow, 1998–2019 (Director, 1991–2019); *b* Glasgow, 19 March 1959; *s* of John Dunbar and Mary Dunbar; *m* 1981, Carol Mary Shaw; three *d*. *Educ:* Hillhead High Sch.; Univ. of Strathclyde (BSc Hons Architectural Studies 1981; BArch 1983; LLM Construction Law 2004). RIBA 1984; MCIArb 2005. Partner, Dunbar and Stewart Architects, 1988–91. President: Glasgow Inst. of Architects, 2006–08; RIAS, 2009–11; Royal Glasgow Inst. of Fine Arts, 2016–18. Chair: Scottish Building Contracts Cttee, 2016–18 (Dir, 2011–); Fest. of Architecture, 2016. Dir, Dunbar Consulting Ltd, 2013–. Deacon, Incorporation of Cordiners in Glasgow, 1999–2000. Dep. Convenor, Court, Univ. of Strathclyde, 2007–11. *Recreations:* music, theatre, Partick Thistle FC.

**DUNBAR, Sir David H.;** *see* Hope-Dunbar.

**DUNBAR of Northfield, Sir Edward (Horace),** 12th Bt *cr* 1700; chartered surveyor, Peter Graham and Associates LLP, since 2012; *b* Elgin, 18 March 1977; *s* of Sir Archibald Ranulph Dunbar of Northfield, 11th Bt and of Amelia Millar Sommerville Dunbar (*née* Davidson); *S* father, 2015; *m* 2005, Caroline Mary Oliver; one *s* one *d*. *Educ:* Stonyhurst Coll.; Aberdeen Univ. (MA Geog. 1999; MA Land Econ. 2007). MRICS 2009. Chartered Surveyor, 2009–; Partner, Duffus Estate, 2009–. Director: Earthtime for All, 2014–; Outfit Moray, 2015–. Chm., Moray Coast Tourism Gp, 2016–; Mem., Moray Local Access Forum, 2014–. *Recreations:* running, cycling, golf. *Heir:* s Samuel Isaac Dunbar, Younger of Northfield, *b* 21 April 2011. *Address:* The Old Manse, Duffus, Elgin, Moray IV30 5QD. *T:* (01343) 830270.

**DUNBAR, Ian Duncan;** Sheriff of Tayside Central and Fife at Dunfermline, 2005–12; *b* 31 Oct. 1948; *s* of John Duncan Dunbar and Mary Golden; *m* 1973, Sue Young. *Educ:* Lawside Acad., Dundee; Queen's Coll., Dundee (St Andrews Univ., subseq. Dundee Univ.) (LLB 1969). Apprentice Solicitor, Soutar Reid & Mill, Dundee, 1969–71; Sneddon Campbell & Munro, Perth, later Miller Sneddon, then Miller Hendry, Perth and Dundee: Asst Solicitor, 1971–72; Partner, 1972–98; Chm., 1994–98; Floating Sheriff, 1998–2000; Sheriff of Tayside Central and Fife at Dundee, 2000–05. Pres., Law Soc. of Scotland, 1993–94 (Vice Pres., 1992–93). Trustee, Perth Coll. Develt Trust, 1995–98. *Recreations:* golf, Rugby, cooking, food, wine. *Address:* 2 New Dunbarney Gait, Bridge of Earn, Perth PH2 9FA. *Clubs:* Blairgowrie Golf (Capt., 2005–06); Royal Perth Golfing Society.

**DUNBAR, Jacqueline;** *see* Hayden, J.

**DUNBAR of Mochrum, Colonel Sir James Michael,** 14th Bt *cr* 1694 (NS), of Mochrum, Wigtownshire; *b* 17 Jan. 1950; *s* of Sir Jean Ivor Dunbar, 13th Bt and of Rose Jeanne, *d* of Henry William Hertsch; *S* father, 1993; *m* 1st, 1978, Margaret Jacobs (marr diss. 1989; she *d* 1991); two *s* one *d*; 2nd, 1989, Margaret, *d* of Roger Gordon Talbot; one *d*. Colonel, USAF, retired. *Heir:* s Michael Joseph Dunbar, *b* 5 July 1980.

**DUNBAR of Hempriggs, Sir Richard (Francis),** 9th Bt *cr* 1706 (NS); *b* 8 Jan. 1945; *s* of Lady Dunbar of Hempriggs, Btss (8th in line) and Leonard James Blake (*d* 1989); assumed the name of Dunbar, 1965; *S* to mother's Btcy, 1997; *m* 1969, Elizabeth Margaret Jane Lister; two *d*. *Educ:* Charterhouse. Businessman. *Heir:* (to father's Btcy) *d* Emma Katherine Dunbar of Hempriggs, *b* 9 Nov. 1977.

**DUNBAR of Durn, Sir Robert (Drummond Cospatrick),** 10th Bt *cr* 1698 (NS); *b* 17 June 1958; *o s* of Sir Drummond Cospatrick Ninian Dunbar, 9th Bt, MC and Sheila Barbara Mary, *d* of John B. de Fonblanque; *S* father, 2000; *m* 1994, Sarah Margaret, *yr d* of Robert Anthony Brooks; one *s* one *d*. *Educ:* Harrow; Christ Church, Oxford (MA). Associate, Soc. of Investment Professionals. Allen & Overy (Private Client Dept), 1982–86; Merrill Lynch Investment Managers, 1986–2003. *Heir:* s Alexander William Drummond Dunbar, Younger of Durn, *b* 1 March 1995.

**DUNBAR, Prof. Robin Ian MacDonald,** PhD; FBA 1998; FRAI; Professor of Evolutionary Psychology, University of Oxford, 2012–17, now Emeritus; Fellow, Magdalen College, Oxford, 2007–17, now Emeritus; *b* 28 June 1947; *s* of George MacDonald Dunbar and Betty Lilian (*née* Toon); *m* 1971, Eva Patricia Melvin; two *s* one *d*. *Educ:* Magdalen Coll. Sch., Brackley; Magdalen Coll., Oxford (BA 1969); Univ. of Bristol (PhD 1974). FRAI 1992. SERC Advanced Res. Fellow, King's Coll., Cambridge, 1977–80; Res. Fellow, Zool. Dept, Univ. of Cambridge, 1980–82; docent, Zool Inst., Univ. of Stockholm, 1983; Res. Fellow, Zool. Dept, Liverpool Univ., 1985–87; University College London: Lectr, Anthropol. Dept, 1987–92; Prof. of Biol Anthropol., 1992–94; Prof. of Evolutionary Psychol., 1994–2007, British Acad. Res. Prof., Sch. of Biol Scis, 2003–07, Univ. of Liverpool; Prof. of Evolutionary Anthropol., Univ. of Oxford, 2007–12. Vis. Prof., Dept of Computer Scis (formerly Sch. of Biomed. Engrg and Computational Sci.), Aalto Univ., Finland, 2012–. Monro Lect., Univ. of Edinburgh, 1994, 2009; Dr van Hofsten Meml Lect., Uppsala Univ., Sweden, 1997; British Assoc./BPsS Annual Lect., 2007; Stirling Lect., Univ. of Kent, 2009; RAI Huxley Lectr, 2015. Co-Dir, British Acad. Centenary Res. Project, 2003–07. Member: Animal Procedures Cttee, Home Office, 1997–2004; Internat. Adv. Cttee, Jean-Marie Delwart Foundn, Brussels, 2000–; Isle of Rum Ecol Mgt Cttee, 2000–07; Scientific Adv. Cttee, Courant Res. Centre, Univ. of Göttingen, 2007–12. Member: Assoc. for Study of Animal Behaviour, 1970–; Primate Soc., 1973– (Pres., 1990–92); British Ecol. Soc., 1979–2005; Galton Inst., 1988– (Galton Lect., 2006); Fauna and Flora Internat., 1995–; BACSA, 1998–; Chester Caledonian Assoc., 2001–. Hon. DSc Aalto, 2012. Osman Hill Medal, Primate Soc. of GB, 1994; Huxley Medal, RAI, 2015. Co-editor: Animal Behaviour, 1994–95; Jl Cultural and Evolutionary Psychol., 2003–08; Member, Editorial Board: Proc. B of Royal Soc., London; Biol. Letters; Behaviour; Internat. Jl of Primatol.; Evolutionary Psychol.; Jl of Evolutionary Psychol.; Human Nature; Primates; Jl of Ethology; Behavioral Ecol. and Sociobiol. *Publications:* Social Dynamics of Galada Baboons, 1975; Reproductive Decisions, 1984; Primate Social Systems, 1988; World of Nature, 1988; The Trouble with Science, 1995; (ed) Human Reproductive Decisions, 1995; Grooming, Gossip and the Evolution of Language, 1996; (ed) The Evolution of Culture, 1999; Primate Conservation Biology, 2000; Cousins, 2000; Human Evolutionary Psychology, 2002; The Human Story, 2004; Evolutionary Psychology: a beginner's guide, 2005; Oxford Handbook of Evolutionary Psychology, 2007; (ed) Social Brain, Distributed Mind, 2009; How Many Friends Does One Person Need?, 2010; The Science of Love and Betrayal, 2012; Thinking Big, 2014; Human Evolution, 2014; Lucy to Language, 2014; Online Social Networks: human cognitive constraints in Facebook and Twitter personal graphs, 2015. *Recreations:* poetry, Medieval and Renaissance music, hill-walking. *Address:* Department of Experimental Psychology, University of Oxford, Anna Watts Building, Radcliffe Observatory Quarter, Oxford OX2 6GG.

**DUNBAR-NASMITH, Sir James (Duncan),** Kt 1996; CBE 1976; RIBA; PPRIAS; FRSA, FRSE; Partner, Law & Dunbar-Nasmith, architects, Edinburgh, Forres, 1957–99; Professor Emeritus, Heriot-Watt University, since 1988; *b* 15 March 1927; *y s* of late Adm. Sir Martin Dunbar-Nasmith, VC, KCB, KCMG, DL and Justina Dunbar-Nasmith, CBE, DStJ. *Educ:* Lockers Park; Winchester; Trinity Coll., Cambridge (BA); Edinburgh Coll. of Art (DA; Hon. Fellow 2007). ARIBA 1954. Architekten Kammer Hessen, 1994. Lieut, Scots Guards, 1945–48. Prof. and Hd of Dept of Architecture, Heriot-Watt Univ. and Edinburgh Coll. of Art, 1978–88. President: Royal Incorporation of Architects in Scotland, 1971–73; Edinburgh Architectural Assoc., 1967–69. Member: Council, RIBA, 1967–73 (a Vice-Pres., 1972–73; Chm., Bd of Educn, 1972–73); Council, ARCUK, 1976–84 (Vice-Chm., Bd of Educn, 1977); Royal Commn on Ancient and Historical Monuments of Scotland, 1972–96; Ancient Monuments Bd for Scotland, 1966–83 (interim Chm., 1972–73); Historic Buildings Council for Scotland, 1966–93; Edinburgh New Town Conservation Cttee/Edinburgh World Heritage Trust, 1972–2004; Council, Europa Nostra, 1986–2004 (Vice-Pres., 1997–2004); Hon. Life Mem., 2005); Dep. Chm., Edinburgh Internat. Festival, 1981–85; Pres., Scottish Civic Trust, 2003– (Chm., 1995–2003); Trustee, Architectural Heritage Fund, 1976–97; Theatres Trust, 1983–95. Lifetime Achievement Award, RIAS, 2012. *Recreations:* music, theatre, ski-ing, sailing. *Address:* Sandbank, Findhorn, Moray IV36 3YY. *T:* (01309) 690445. *Clubs:* Royal Ocean Racing; New (Edinburgh).

**DUNBOYNE,** 30th Baron by Prescription, 1324, 20th Baron by Patent *cr* 1541 (Ire.); **Richard Pierce Theobald Butler;** *b* 5 July 1983; *o s* of 29th/19th Baron Dunboyne and of Diana Caroline (*née* Williams); *S* father, 2013; *m* 2012, Anneka Eileen, *d* of A. Anketell-Jones; two *d*. *Educ:* Winchester; Bristol Univ. *Heir:* cousin Michael James Butler [*b* 7 July 1944; *m* 1981, Jennifer Williams; one *d*].

**DUNCAN OF SPRINGBANK,** Baron *cr* 2017 (Life Peer), of Springbank in the County of Perth; **Ian James Duncan;** Parliamentary Under-Secretary of State: Northern Ireland Office, since 2017; Department for Business, Energy and Industrial Strategy, since 2019; *b* Alyth, Perthshire, 13 Feb. 1973; *s* of late Robert Duncan and Audrey Duncan (*née* Doig); civil partnership 2012, Benjamin Neal Brust. *Educ:* Alyth High Sch.; St Andrews Univ. (BSc 1st Cl. Hons Geol. 1994); Bristol Univ. (PhD Palaeontol. 1997). FGS. Intern: Smithsonian Instn, Washington, 1995; Mus. of Comparative Zool., Harvard Univ., 1996; Teaching Fellow, Bristol Univ., 1997–98; Policy Analyst, BP, 1998–99; Dep. Chief Exec., Scottish Fishermen's Fedn, 1999–2003; Hd, Policy and Communication, Scottish Refugee Council, 2004–05; Hd, Scottish Parlt's Office, Brussels, 2005–11; Clerk, Eur. and Ext. Relns Cttee and EU Advr, Scottish Parlt, 2011–13; Speech and Debates Officer, ESU, 2013–14. Contested (C) Aberdeen S, Scottish Parlt, 2003. Contested (C) Perth and Perthshire N, 2017. MEP (C) Scotland, 2014–17. European Parliament: Spokesman on fisheries, 2014–17, on energy and climate change, 2014–17; Chief Whip, Cons. Delegn, 2014–17; Sen. Vice-Pres., Delegn for Relns with S Asia; Vice-President: Wine and Spirits Intergp; LGBTI Intergp. Sec. Gen., New Direction - Foundn for Eur. Reform, 2014–17; Member: Bd, Eur. Forum for Renewable Energy Sources, 2015–17; Bd of Advrs, USC Schwarzenegger Inst., 2016–. Parly Under-Sec. of State, Wales Office, 2017, Scotland Office, 2017–19. Chm., ESU Scotland, 2014–. *Recreations:* geology, US politics, oil painting, carpentry. *Address:* House of Lords, SW1A 0PW. *Club:* New (Edinburgh).

**DUNCAN, Agnes Lawrie Addie, (Laura);** Sheriff of Glasgow and Strathkelvin, 1982–2006; *b* 17 June 1947; *d* of late William Smith, District Clerk, and Mary Marshall Smith McClure; *m* 1990, David Cecil Duncan, farmer, cricket coach, *y s* of late Dr and Mrs H. C. Duncan, Edinburgh; one *s*. *Educ:* Hamilton Acad.; Glasgow Univ. (LLB 1967). Admitted Solicitor, 1969; called to the Scottish Bar, 1978. Solicitor, private practice, 1969–71; Procurator Fiscal Depute, 1971–75; Standing Junior Counsel to Dept of Employment, 1982. Winner, Scottish Ladies Single handed Dinghy Championship, 1990. *Recreations:* sailing, walking.

**DUNCAN, Rt Hon. Sir Alan (James Carter),** KCMG 2014; PC 2010; MP (C) Rutland and Melton, since 1992; *b* 31 March 1957; 2nd *s* of late Wing Comdr J. G. Duncan, OBE and Anne Duncan (*née* Carter); civil partnership 2008, James Dunseath. *Educ:* Merchant Taylors' Sch.; St John's Coll., Oxford. Pres., Oxford Union, 1979. With Shell Internat. Petroleum, 1979–81; Kennedy Schol., Harvard Univ., 1981–82; oil trader, Marc Rich & Co., 1982–88; self-employed oil broker, 1988–92. PPS to Min. of State, DoH, 1993–94, to Chm. of Cons. Party, 1995–97; a Vice Chm. of Cons. Party, 1997–98; Parly Political Sec. to Leader of the Opposition, 1997; Opposition spokesman on health, 1998–99, on trade and industry, 1999–2001, on foreign affairs, 2001–03; Shadow Sec. of State for Constitutional Affairs, 2003–04, for Internat. Develt, 2004–05, for Transport, 2005, for Trade and Industry, 2005–07, for Business, Enterprise and Regulatory Reform, 2007–09; Shadow Leader, H of C, 2009; Shadow Jun. Justice Minister for Prisons, 2009–10; Minister of State, DFID, 2010–14; Special Envoy to Yemen, 2014–16; Minister of State, FCO, 2016–19. Member: Select Cttee on Social Security, 1993–95; Intelligence and Security Cttee, 2015. Contested (C) Barnsley W and Penistone, 1987. Vis. Parly Fellow, St Antony's

Coll., Oxford, 2002–03. Freeman, City of London, 1980; Liveryman, Merchant Taylors' Co., 1987. *Publications:* An End to Illusions, 1993; (with D. Hobson) Saturn's Children: how the state devours liberty, prosperity and virtue, 1995. *Address:* House of Commons, SW1A 0AA. *Club:* Beefsteak.

**DUNCAN, Alastair James;** QC (Scot.) 2012; Standing Junior Counsel to Scottish Government, since 2006; *b* Edinburgh, 3 Feb. 1969; *s* of Alan and Mary Duncan; *m* 2004, Esther Thackrey; one *d*. *Educ:* Newton Mearns Primary Sch.; Hutcheson's Grammar Sch.; Univ. of Glasgow (LLB Hons 1991; LLM 1994). Admitted Faculty of Advocates, 1999; in practice as Advocate specialising in commercial litigation. *Address:* Advocates Library, Parliament House, Edinburgh EH1 1RF. *E:* alastair.duncan@advocates.co.uk.

**DUNCAN, Dr Allan George;** environmental consultant, 2000–14; *b* 17 Oct. 1940; *s* of Donald Allan Duncan and Annabella Duncan (*née* Thom); *m* 1972, Alison Patricia Reid; two *s* one *d*. *Educ:* Robert Gordon's Coll., Aberdeen; Aberdeen Univ. (BSc Hons 1963); New Coll., Oxford, (DPhil 1966). CEnv 2006. Research Engineer: California Univ. 1966–67; US Nat. Bureau of Standards, 1967–69; UKAEA, Harwell, 1969–79; Radiochemical Inspectorate, DoE, 1979–87 (Dep. Chief Inspector, 1984–87); HM Inspectorate of Pollution, 1987–96 (Chief Inspector, 1995–96); Hd, Radioactive Substances Regulation, EA, 1996–2000. Member: EC Network of Envmtl Regulators, 1993–2000; Euratom Scientific and Tech. Cttee, 1994–2013; Envmtl Assessment Panel, UK Accreditation Service, 1994–99. MIEMA; FRSA. *Publications:* various contribs to scientific literature. *Recreations:* sailing, walking, North American history. *Address:* 14 Rawlings Grove, Abingdon, Oxon OX14 1SH. *T:* (01235) 529096.

**DUNCAN, Amanda Louise Elliot;** *see* Evans, A. L. E.

**DUNCAN, Andy;** Chief Executive, Travelopia, since 2018; *b* 31 July 1962. *Educ:* Univ. of Manchester Inst. of Sci. and Technol. (BSc). Joined Unilever, 1984; Chm., Business Unit and Mktg Controller for spreads and margarines, 1995–97, Mktg Dir, 1997–99, Van Den Bergh Foods; Eur. Gen. Man., Food and Beverages Div., 1999–2001; Dir, Marketing and Communications, subseq. Marketing, Communications and Audiences, BBC, 2001–04; Chief Executive: Channel Four, 2004–09; HR Owen plc, 2010–11; Man. Dir, 2011–14, Chief Exec., 2014–17, Camelot UK Lotteries Ltd. Founding Chm., Freeview, 2002–04. Non-executive Director: HMV plc, 2009–13; Oasis Trust, 2009–. Trustee, Media Trust, 2006– (Chm., 2006–14).

**DUNCAN, Bob;** Lord Provost and Lord-Lieutenant, Dundee, 2012–17; *b* Dundee, 1946; *m* Brenda. *Educ:* Rockwell Secondary Sch.; Duncan of Jordanstone Coll., Dundee; Stow Coll., Glasgow. Valentines of Dundee, subseq. part of Hallmark Cards: joined as apprentice; latterly Print and Graphics Manager. Mem. (SNP), Dundee CC, 2003–17. Mem. Court, Univ. of Dundee, 2012–17.

**DUNCAN, Rev. Canon Bruce,** MBE 1993; Principal, Sarum College, and Canon and Prebendary of Salisbury Cathedral, 1995–2002, now Canon Emeritus; *b* 28 Jan. 1938; *s* of late Andrew Allan Duncan and Dora Duncan (*née* Young); *m* 1966, Margaret Holmes Smith; three *d*. *Educ:* St Albans Sch.; Univ. of Leeds (BA 1960); Cuddesdon Coll., Oxford. Founder/Director: Children's Relief Internat., 1960–62; Northorpe Hall Trust, 1962–65; ordained deacon, 1967, priest, 1968; Curate, St Bartholomew, Armley, Leeds and Curate in charge, St Mary of Bethany, Leeds, 1967–69; Hon. Curate, St Mary the Less, Cambridge, 1969–70; Chaplain, Order of Holy Paraclete, Whitby, 1970–71; Chaplain to HM Ambassadors in Austria, Hungary and Czechoslovakia, based in Vienna, 1971–75; Vicar, Collegiate Church of Holy Cross and the Mother of Him Who Hung Thereon, Crediton, Devon, 1976–82; Rural Dean of Cadbury, 1976–81; Rector, Crediton and Shobrooke, 1982–86; Residentiary Canon, Manchester Cathedral and Fellow, Coll. of Christ in Manchester, 1986–95. Permission to Officiate, Dio. of Salisbury and Dio. in Europe, 2004–. Internat. Consultant, Trinity Inst. for Christianity and Culture, later Awareness Foundn, 2004–11; Development Consultant: Scargill Movt Council, 2009–14; Lee Abbey Movt, 2011–. Lazenby and St Luke's Chaplain, Exeter Univ., 2003–04; Theologian in Residence, Episcopal Ch of St Michael and All Angels, Sanibel, Fla, 2006–15. Chm. of Trustees, St Luke's Coll. Foundn, 2006–09; Trustee, Families for Children Adoption Agency, 2006–10, 2016– (Chm., 2006–10); Hon. Pres., Northorpe Hall Child and Family Trust, 1997–. FRSA 1989. Hon. Fellow, Sarum Coll., 2006. Hon. DD Graduate Theol. Foundn, Indiana, 2002. Cross of St Augustine, 2004. *Publications:* Children at Risk (ed A. H. Denney), 1968; Sich Selbst Verstehen, 1993; Pray Your Way, Your Personality and God, 1993. *Recreations:* travel, music. *Address:* 92 Harnham Road, Salisbury, Wilts SP2 8JW. *E:* canon.duncan@gmail.com. *Club:* Athenæum.

**DUNCAN, Craig;** Director of External Affairs, Royal College of Surgeons of England, 2008–10; *b* 1 May 1951; *s* of William Sneddon Duncan and of Jessie Clark Sloan Duncan (*née* Mackie); *m* 1st, 1975, Janet Elizabeth Gillespie (marr. diss. 1988); one *s* one *d*; 2nd, 1998, Jane Alison Pavitt. *Educ:* Allan Glen's Sch., Glasgow; Univ. of Strathclyde (BA 1st Cl. Hons Geog.). Administrative Assistant: Univ. of Durham, 1973–76; Univ. of Southampton, 1976–82; Royal College of Surgeons of England, 1982–2010: Admin. Asst and Asst Sec., 1982–88; Asst Sec., Inst. Basic Med. Scis, 1982–86; Secretary: Hunterian Inst., 1986–88; for Ext. Affairs, 1989–97; Senate of Surgery of GB and Ireland, 1993–97; Coll. Secretary, 1997–2001; Chief Exec., 2001–05; Advr to the Pres., 2005–08. Hon. FRCS 2010. McNeill Love Medal, RCS, 2007. *Recreations:* music, opera, reading, water-colour painting, golf. *Address:* Koos Bian, 2 Langfield Gardens, Bude, Cornwall EX23 8GU. *T:* (01288) 354785. *Club:* Bude and North Cornwall Golf.

**DUNCAN, Geoffrey Stuart,** OBE 1998; General Secretary, General Synod Board of Education and National Society for Promoting Religious Education, 1990–98; *b* 10 April 1938; *s* of Alexander Sidney Duncan and Gertude Ruth (*née* Page); *m* 1962, Shirley Bernice Matilda Vanderput; one *d* (one *s* decd). *Educ:* Hemel Hempstead Grammar Sch.; Univ. of London (BScEcon); Univ. of Exeter (MA). Served RAEC, 1960–64. School and technical coll. teaching, 1964–72; LEA Advr and Officer, 1972–82; Schs Sec. and Dep. Sec., Gen. Synod Bd of Educn and Nat. Soc. for Promoting Religious Educn, 1982–90. Part-time WEA Tutor, 1966–70; part-time Open Univ. Counsellor, 1971–72. Dir, Urban Learning Foundn, 1990–98; Company Sec., Inst. of Consumer Scis, 2000–01. Trustee: St Gabriel's Educnl Trust, 1990–98; St Christopher's Educnl Trust, 1990–98; Winchester Shoei Coll. Foundn, 1990–2015. Governor, Coll. of St Mark & St John, Plymouth, 1990–2005. MUniv Surrey, 1998. *Publications:* contributor to: Faith for the Future, 1986; Schools for Tomorrow, 1988; various educn jls. *Recreations:* campanology, travel. *Address:* Carrer Jupiter 19, Albir, Alfaz del Pi, Alicante 03581, Spain. *T:* 661139873.

**DUNCAN, George;** Chairman, Laporte plc, 1995–2001 (Director, 1987–95); *b* 9 Nov. 1933; *s* of William Duncan and Catherine Gray Murray; *m* 1st, 1965, Frauke Ulrike Schnuhr (marr. diss.); one *d*; 2nd, 2018, Shirley Mary Douglas-Mann. *Educ:* Holloway County Grammar Sch.; London Sch. of Economics (BScEcon)); Wharton Sch.; Univ. of Pennsylvania (MBA). Mem., Inst. of Chartered Accountants (FCA). Chief Executive, Truman Hanbury Buxton and Co. Ltd, 1967–71; Chief Executive, Watney Mann Ltd, 1971–72; Vice-Chm., Internat. Distillers and Vintners Ltd, 1972; Chm., Lloyds Bowmaker Finance Ltd (formerly Lloyds and Scottish plc), 1976–86; Dir, Lloyds Bank Plc, 1982–87.

Chairman: Allied Steel and Wire (Hldgs) Ltd, subseq. ASW Hldgs plc, 1986–2002; Household Mortgage Corp., 1986–94; Humberclyde Finance Gp, 1987–89; Whessoe PLC, 1987–97; Rubicon Group plc, 1992–95; Higgs and Hill plc, subseq. Swan Hill Gp, 1993–2003; Alldays plc, 1999–2001; Hurlingham School Ltd, 2000–; Director: Pauls & Whites, 1974–86; Haden plc, 1974–85 (Dep. Chm., 1984–85); Fitch Lovell plc, 1976–86; City of London Investment Trust (formerly TR City of London Trust PLC), 1977–2000; BET plc, 1981–96; Associated British Ports PLC, 1986–2003 (Dep. Chm., 1998–2003); Newspaper Publishing plc, 1986–93; Crown House PLC, 1987; Dewe Rogerson Gp Ltd, 1987–95; Calor Gp, 1990–97. Chm., CBI Companies Cttee, 1980–83; Mem., CBI President's Cttee, 1980–83. Mem., Eur. Adv. Bd, Wharton Sch., 1995–99. Freeman, City of London, 1971. *Recreations:* opera, golf. *Address:* 16 Belgrave Mews West, SW1X 8HT.

**DUNCAN, Rt Rev. Dr Gregor Duthie;** Assistant Priest, St Bride, Hyndland, Glasgow, since 2018; *b* 11 Oct. 1950; *s* of Edwin John Duncan and Janet Brown Duncan. *Educ:* Univ. of Glasgow (MA Hons 1972); Clare Coll., Cambridge (PhD 1977); Oriel Coll., Oxford (BA Hons 1983); Ripon Coll., Cuddesdon. Ordained deacon, 1983, priest, 1984; Asst Curate, Oakham with Hambleton and Egleton, and Braunston with Brooke, 1983–86; Chaplain, Edinburgh Theol Coll., 1987–89; Rector of St Columba's, Largs, 1989–99; Dean, Dio. of Glasgow and Galloway, 1996–2010; Rector, St Ninian's, Pollokshields, 1999–2010; Bishop of Glasgow and Galloway, 2010–18. *Recreations:* collecting gramophone records, cooking. *Address:* 3 Golf Road, Rutherglen, Glasgow G73 4JW. *T:* (0141) 634 1167. *E:* bishop@glasgow.anglican.org.

**DUNCAN, Hannah Gillian Isabella; Her Honour Judge Duncan;** a Circuit Judge, since 2018; *b* Southampton, 21 Feb. 1980; *d* of William Duncan and Nina Duncan; *m* 2009, Adam Richard Guthrie; one *s* one *d*. Called to the Bar, Inner Temple, 2002; barrister, 2 Harcourt Bldgs, 2002–17; a Recorder, 2016–18. *Address:* Isleworth Crown Court, Ridgeway Road, Isleworth TW7 5LP.

**DUNCAN, Jacqueline Ann,** OBE 2013; FIIDA; Founder and Principal, Inchbald School of Interior Design and Garden Design (formerly Inchbald Schools of Design and Fine Arts), since 1960, and Inchbald Online, since 2001; *b* 16 Dec. 1931; *d* of Mrs Donald Whitaker; *m* 1st, 1955, Michael John Chantrey Inchbald (marr. diss. 1964; he *d* 2013); one *s* one *d*; 2nd, 1974, Brig. Peter Trevenen Thwaites (*d* 1991); 3rd, 1994, Col Andrew Tobin Warwick Duncan, LVO, OBE. *Educ:* Convent of the Sacred Heart, Brighton; House of Citizenship, London. MBIID (FIDDA 1991); FIIDA 1994. Founded: Inchbald Sch. of Design, 1960; Inchbald Sch. of Fine Arts, 1970; Inchbald Sch. of Garden Design, 1972; Inchbald Online, 2008. Member: Monopolies Commn, 1972–75; Whitfield Cttee on Copyright and Design, 1974–76; London Electricity Cons. Council, 1973–76; Westminster City Council (Warwick Ward), 1974–78. Mem., Vis. Cttee, RCA, 1986–90; International Society of Interior Designers: Acting Pres., London Chapter, 1987–90; Chm., 1990–92. Trustee, St Peter's Research Trust, 1987–90. JP South Westminster, 1976–2001. Outstanding Contribution Award, BIDA, 2006. *Publications:* Directory of Interior Designers, 1966; Bedrooms, 1968; Design and Decoration, 1971. *Recreations:* fishing, travel. *Address:* Lime Tree House, Fifehead Magdalen, Gillingham, Dorset SP8 5RT; (office) 32 Eccleston Square, SW1V 1PB.

**DUNCAN, Sir James (Blair),** Kt 1981; Chairman: Transport Development Group, 1975–92; Boalloy Industries Ltd, 1992–2005; *b* 24 Aug. 1927; *s* of late John Duncan and Emily MacFarlane Duncan; *m* 1974, Dr Betty Psaltis (*d* 2005), San Francisco. *Educ:* Whitehill Sch., Glasgow. Qualified as Scottish Chartered Accountant. Joined Transport Development Group, 1953; Dir, 1960; Chief Exec., 1970–90; retd, 1992. Mem., LTE (part-time), 1979–82. Scottish Council: Mem. 1976–2002, and Chm. 1982–99, London Exec. Cttee; Vice Pres., 1983–99, Pres., 1999–2002. Confedn of British Industry: Mem. Council, 1980–82; Mem. 1979–90, and Chm. 1983–88, London Region Roads and Transportation Cttee; Mem., Transport Policy Cttee, 1983–92. London Chamber of Commerce: Mem. Council, 1982–; Mem., Gen. Purposes Cttee, 1983–90; Dep. Chm., 1984–86; Chm., 1986–88; Chm., Commercial Educn Trust, 1992–98. Pres., IRTE, 1984–87. FCILT (Pres., CIT, 1980–81; Spurrier Meml Lectr, 1972; Award of Merit, 1973; Herbert Crow Medal, 1978); CCMI; FRSA 1977. Liveryman, Co. of Carmen, 1983– (Award of Merit, 1992); Freeman, Co. of Watermen & Lightermen of the River Thames, 1982. *Publications:* papers on transport matters. *Recreations:* travel, reading, walking, swimming, theatre, golf. *Address:* 17 Kingston House South, Ennismore Gardens, SW7 1NF. *T:* (020) 7589 3545. *Clubs:* Hurlingham, Caledonian, Royal Automobile.

**DUNCAN, Jane Elsa,** OBE 2018; RIBA; Principal, Jane Duncan Architects Ltd, since 1992; President, Royal Institute of British Architects, 2015–17; *b* London, 7 July 1953; *d* of Leonard and Ruth Michaels; *m* 1976, Ian Martin Duncan; one *s* one *d*. *Educ:* Queen Elizabeth's Girls' Grammar Sch., Barnet; Bartlett Sch. of Architecture, University Coll. London (BSc; DipArch). Site engr, G. E. Wallis; in practice as architect, Edinburgh; with Halcrow. Director: Jane Duncan Interiors Ltd, 1992–; Jane Duncan Properties Ltd, 1992–. Vice Pres., Practice and Profession, 2007–13, Equality and Diversity Champion, 2013–15, RIBA. Pres., Architects Benevolent Soc. Hon. FAIA. *Recreations:* dancing salsa, walking, entertaining, travel, family. *Address:* The Old Warehouse, Chalfont Station Road, Little Chalfont, Bucks HP7 9PN. *T:* (01494) 766999. *E:* jane@janeduncanarchitects.co.uk.

**DUNCAN, Jo-Anne Florence;** Headmistress, Wycombe Abbey, since 2019; *b* Ont, Canada, 2 March 1974; *d* of Joseph Wright and Audrey Wright; *m* 1999, Murray Duncan; one *s* one *d*. *Educ:* Glenlola Collegiate Sch., Bangor, NI; Univ. of St Andrews (MA Hons Eng. Lit. and Theol. 1996); Univ. of Cambridge (PGCE 1997); Univ. of Leicester (Advanced Cert. Educn Mgt 2003). Teacher of Religious Studies, Latymer Sch., London, 1997–2001; Hd, Religious Studies, Benenden Sch., Kent, 2001–08; Head: Princess Helena Coll., Preston, Herts, 2008–15; Royal High Sch. Bath, 2015–19. *Recreations:* travel, literature, food and wine. *Address:* Wycombe Abbey, High Wycombe HP11 1PE. *E:* duncanj@wycombeabbey.com. *Club:* 67 Pall Mall.

**DUNCAN, John,** FRS 2008; FBA 2009; Programme Leader, MRC Cognition and Brain Sciences Unit, Cambridge; Professorial Research Fellow, Department of Experimental Psychology, University of Oxford; Fellow, St John's College, Oxford. Hon. Professor of Cognitive Neuroscience: Univ. of Cambridge; Univ. of Bangor; Professorial Res. Fellow, Univ. of Oxford. Heineken Award for Cognitive Sci., Royal Netherlands Acad. of Arts and Scis, 2012. *Publications:* (with N. Kanwisher) Attention and Performance XX, 2004; (ed jtly) Measuring the Mind, 2005; How Intelligence Happens, 2010; contribs to jls incl. Jl Exptl Psychol., Psychol. Rev., Perception and Psychophysics, Cognition, Ergonomics, Nature, Science, Cognitive Psychol. *Address:* MRC Cognition and Brain Sciences Unit, 15 Chaucer Road, Cambridge CB2 7EF.

**DUNCAN, Ven. John Finch,** MBE 1991; Archdeacon of Birmingham, 1985–2001; *b* 9 Sept. 1933; *s* of John and Helen Maud Duncan; *m* 1st, 1965, Diana Margaret Dewes (*d* 2001); one *s* two *d*; 2nd, 2011, Caroline Jane Fordham. *Educ:* Queen Elizabeth Grammar School, Wakefield; University Coll., Oxford; Cuddesdon Coll. MA (Oxon). Curate, St John, South Bank, Middlesbrough, 1959–61; Novice, Society of St Francis, 1961–62; Curate, St Peter, Birmingham, 1962–65; Chaplain, Univ. of Birmingham, 1965–76; Vicar of All Saints, Kings Heath, Birmingham, 1976–85. Chairman: Copec Housing Trust, 1970–91; Focus Housing Assoc., 1991–96. *Recreations:* golf, theatre, convivial gatherings. *Address:* 66 Glebe Rise, Kings Sutton, Banbury, Oxon OX17 3PH. *T:* (01295) 812641.

**DUNCAN, Prof. John Laing,** OBE 2015; FRCSEd; Vice President, Royal College of Surgeons of Edinburgh, 2015–18; Consultant General and Vascular Surgeon, Raigmore Hospital, Inverness, since 1992; Director of Teaching (Inverness), University of Aberdeen, since 2014; *b* Aberdeen, 13 April 1953; *s* of George and Alexina Duncan; *m* 1977, Jane Mogey; one *s* two *d*. *Educ:* Aberdeen Grammar Sch.; Univ. of Aberdeen (MB ChB 1977; ChM 1985). FRCSEd 1981; FRCSGlas 1995. Gen. clinical trng, Aberdeen Teaching Hosps, 1977–78; Lectr, Dept of Pathol., Univ. of Aberdeen, 1978–79; SHO, 1979–80, gen., orthopaedic and paediatric surgery, 1980–84, Aberdeen Teaching Hosps; Registrar, Royal Hallamshire Hosp., Sheffield, 1984–85; Sen. Registrar, Royal Hallamshire Hosp., Northern Gen. Hosp., N Derbys Royal Infirmary, Chesterfield, 1985–91. Res. Fellow, Harvard Univ., 1981–82. FACS 2005; Fellow, Faculty of Surgical Trainers, 2015. Ed. Surgeons' News, 2008–15. *Publications:* contribs to jls on surgical topics, particularly aortic aneurysm screening, patient safety and med. educn. *Recreations:* family, curling, walking, gardening. *Address:* Highland Medical Education Centre, Centre for Health Science, Raigmore Hospital, Inverness IV2 4JH. *E:* john.duncan@abdn.ac.uk.

**DUNCAN, John Lawrence,** CVO 2017; QPM 1999; Lord Lieutenant for Ayrshire and Arran, 2006–17; *b* 15 Oct. 1942; *s* of John Duncan and Emily Gordon Duncan (*née* Legge); *m* 1st, 1964, Margaret Thomson Clark (*d* 1993); one *s* one *d*; 2nd, 2005, Jess Young; one step *d*. *Educ:* Buckie High Sch. Renfrew and Bute Constabulary, 1959–75 (Cadet, 1959–61); Strathclyde Police, 1975–2001: Head, Complaints and Discipline Br., 1989–92; Divl Comdr, Ayr, 1992–95; Head: of Force Inspectorate, 1995–96; of Force Personnel, 1996; Asst Chief Constable, 1996–99; Dep. Chief Constable, 1999–2001. Chm., Ayr United FC, 2003–04. CStJ 2017 (OStJ 2011). *Recreations:* football, reading, music, art, church, Rotary. *Address:* Braeside, Stewarton, Kilmarnock KA3 5LL. *T:* (01560) 484050. *E:* johnlduncan@btinternet.com. *Club:* Glasgow Art.

**DUNCAN, Prof. John Sidney,** DM; FRCP, FMedSci; Professor of Neurology, UCL Institute of Neurology, University College London, since 1998; Clinical Director, National Hospital for Neurology and Neurosurgery, 2012–18; *b* 12 Dec. 1955; *s* of John Graham Duncan and Elizabeth Mabella Duncan; *m* 1983, Elizabeth Hills; one *s* one *d*. *Educ:* Westminster Sch.; Worcester Coll., Oxford (BM BCh 1979; MA 1980; DM 1988). FRCP 1994. Sen. Lectr in Neurology and Consultant Neurologist, Nat. Hosp. for Neurology and Neurosurgery, 1989–98. Med. Dir, Nat. Soc. for Epilepsy, 1998–2012. FMedSci 2005. *Publications:* Clinical Epilepsy, 1995; MRI Neuroanatomy, 1996; Functional Imaging of the Epilepsies, 2000; contrib. 586 papers on treatment of epilepsy and brain imaging applied to epilepsy. *Recreations:* opera, Wasps Rugby club. *Address:* Box 29, National Hospital for Neurology and Neurosurgery, Queen Square, WC1N 3BG. *T:* (020) 3448 8612. *E:* j.duncan@ucl.ac.uk.

**DUNCAN, John Stewart,** OBE 1993; HM Diplomatic Service, retired; Governor, British Virgin Islands, 2014–17; Additional Director, Southern Ocean Territories and Financial Services, Foreign and Commonwealth Office, 2017–18; *b* 17 April 1958; *s* of late Ernest Stewart Duncan and Joyce Fenner Duncan (*née* Austin); *m* 1984, Anne Marie Jacq; one *s* one *d*. *Educ:* Wycliffe Coll.; Univ. de Paris-Sorbonne (dip. langue et civilisation); Keele Univ. (BA Hons); NATO Defence Coll. Entered FCO, 1980; Scandinavia Desk, FCO, 1980–82; Chancery, Paris, 1982–84; Overseas Aid Admin, Khartoum, 1984–88; Head of Section: Defence Sales and Policy, FCO, 1988–89; Non-Proliferation, FCO, 1989–91; Asst Private Sec. to Minister for Overseas Aid and Africa, 1991–92; Chargé d'Affaires, Tirana, 1992–93; Mem., UK Delegn, NATO, 1993–96; Deputy Head: S Atlantic Dependent Territories Dept, FCO, 1996–97; Security Policy Dept, FCO, 1998; UK Pol Advr to SACEUR and Dep. SACEUR, 1998–2001; Dir, Trade and Investment, Paris, 2002–06; Ambassador for Multilateral Arms Control and Disarmament and UK Perm. Rep. to Conf. on Disarmament, Geneva, 2006–11; Special Rep. to London Conf. on Cyberspace, 2011; Dir of Engagement and Communications, FCO, 2012–13; Additional Dir, Overseas Territory Directorate, FCO, 2013–14. Chm., Falkland Is Assoc., 2018–. Trustee, Nat. Army Mus., 2017–. NATO Kosovo Medal, 2001; US Army Outstanding Civilian Service Medal, 2001. *Publications:* Rethinking NATO, 2002. *Recreations:* military history, gardening, jazz.

**DUNCAN, Laura;** *see* Duncan, A. L. A.

**DUNCAN, Lindsay Vere,** CBE 2009; actress; *b* 7 Nov. 1950; *m* Hilton McRae, actor; one *s*. *Educ:* Central Sch. of Speech and Drama. *Television:* series include: Dead Head, 1985; Traffik, 1989; GBH, 1991; A Year in Provence, 1993; Rome, 2005; Spooks, 2005–06; serials: The Rector's Wife, 1994; Oliver Twist, 1999; Shooting the Past, 1999; Perfect Strangers, 2001; Criminal Justice, 2008; Lost in Austen, 2008; Margaret, 2009; Dr Who, 2009; The Sinking of the Laconia, 2010; Christopher and His Kind, 2010; White Heat, 2012; Richard II, 2012; Black Mirror, 2012; Spy, 2012; The Honourable Woman, 2014; The Leftovers, 2017; Close to the Enemy, 2016; A Discovery of Witches, 2018; *theatre:* Les Liaisons Dangereuses, RSC, 1986 (Olivier Award); Hedda Gabler, Hampstead, 1988; Cat on a Hot Tin Roof, NT, 1988 (Evening Standard Award); A Midsummer Night's Dream, RSC; Berenice, NT, 1990; Three Hotels, Tricycle, 1993; The Cryptogram, Ambassadors, 1994; Ashes to Ashes, Royal Court Upstairs, 1996; The Homecoming, RNT, 1997; Celebration, and The Room, Almeida, 2000; Mouth to Mouth, Royal Court (Critics' Circle Award) and Albery, 2001; Private Lives, Albery, 2001, NY, 2002 (Critics' Circle, Olivier, Tony, NY Drama Desk and Variety Club Awards, 2002); That Face, Royal Court, 2007, transf. Duke of York's, 2008; John Gabriel Borkman, Abbey Th., Dublin, 2010, NY, 2011; Hay Fever, Noël Coward Th., 2012; A Delicate Balance, NY, 2014; Hansard, NT, 2019; *films:* Prick Up Your Ears, 1987; The Reflecting Skin, 1990; City Hall, 1995; A Midsummer Night's Dream, 1996; Mansfield Park, 2000; An Ideal Husband, 2000; Under the Tuscan Sun, 2003; Afterlife, 2004 (Bowmore Scottish Screen Award, Best Actress, Bratislava Film Fest.); Starter for Ten, 2006; (for TV) Longford, 2006; Alice in Wonderland, 2010; About Time, 2013; Le Weekend, 2013 (Best Actress, British Independent Film Awards, 2013); The Last Passenger, 2013; Birdman, 2014; Alice Through the Looking Glass, 2016. *Address:* c/o Dalzell & Beresford, Paddock Suite, The Courtyard, 55 Charterhouse Street, EC1M 6HA.

**DUNCAN, Martin David Anson;** freelance opera and theatre director; Joint Artistic Director, Chichester Festival Theatre, 2002–05; Artistic Adviser, Olympics Culture Festival 2012, 2009–12; *b* 12 July 1948; *s* of Ronald Francis Hamilton Anson Duncan and Margaret Elizabeth (*née* Thurlow). *Educ:* Durston House Sch., Ealing; Westminster Sch.; London Acad. of Music and Dramatic Art (Stage Mgt). Actor in rep., West End, television and film, 1968–89; composer of musical scores for over 50 theatre prodns; Associate Artist, Crucible Theatre, Sheffield, 1988; Artistic Dir, Nottingham Playhouse, 1994–99. *Theatre productions include:* Rocky Horror Show, Munich and Milan, 1985; School for Clowns, Lilian Baylis Th., 1988; Performance, Pet Shop Boys' tour (Associate Dir), 1991; The Nutcracker, Opera North (Dir and co-writer), 1992; The Comedy of Errors, Berlin, 2001; The Blacks, Johannesburg and Stockholm, 2001; *Royal Lyceum Edinburgh:* Man of La Mancha, 2007;

Private Lives, 2014; *National Theatre of Brent:* The Greatest Story Ever Told, 1987; The French Revolution, 1989; All the World's a Globe, 1990; Love upon the Throne, 1998; Massive Landmarks of the 20th Century, 1999; The Wonder of Sex, 2001; The Arts and How They Was Done, 2006; *Nottingham Playhouse:* The Nose, 1995, The Adventures of Pinocchio, 1995; Happy End, Time and the Room, 1996; Le Bourgeois Gentilhomme, 1998; Endgame, and Krapp's Last Tape, 1999; *Chichester:* The Gondoliers, 2003; Out of this World, Seven Doors, 2004; How to Succeed in Business Without Really Trying, The Government Inspector, 2005; *opera productions:* Opera North: L'heure Espagnole, Gianni Schicchi, 1990; The Thieving Magpie, 1992, 2005; Iolanta, Orpheus in the Underworld, 1992; The Adventures of Pinocchio, 2007; A Midsummer Night's Dream, 2008; Bavarian State Opera, Munich: Xerxes, 1996; La Clemenza di Tito, 1999; The Rake's Progress, 2002; Die Entführung aus dem Serail, 2003; Albert Herring, Canadian Opera Co., 1991; The Magic Flute, Scottish Opera, 1993; HMS Pinafore, Die Fledermaus, D'Oyly Carte Opera Co., 1994; Ariadne auf Naxos, Scottish Opera, 1997, Garsington Opera, 2007, Norwegian Opera, 2010; The Last Supper, Berlin State Opera, 2000; The Love of Three Oranges, Cologne Opera, 2001; The Last Supper, Glyndebourne, 2001; Pagliacci/ Cavalleria Rusticana, Royal Albert Hall, 2002; La Traviata, Flanders Opera, 2003; The Gondoliers, ENO, 2006; The Original Chinese Conjuror, Aldeburgh Fest., 2006; The Adventures of Pinocchio, Chemnitz Opera 2008, Minnesota Opera, 2009, Moscow, 2011; Artaxerxes, Royal Opera House, 2009; Armida, Garsington Opera, 2010; La Forza del Destino, Holland Park, 2010; Betrothal in a Monastery, Théâtre du Capitole Toulouse, Opéra Comique Paris, 2011; Il Turco in Italia, Garsington Opera, 2011; Moses, Theater St Gallen, 2013; Flight, Royal Acad. of Music, 2018; Fantasio, Garsington Opera, 2019; BBC Proms: Sondheim at 80, 2010; The Yeoman of the Guard, 2012; Noye's Fludde, Aldeburgh Music, 2013; Vert-Vert, Garsington Opera, 2014; Alice's Adventures in Wonderland, Opera Holland Park, 2013–16; The Corridor & The Cure, Aldeburgh Fest., 2015; Kiss Me Kate!, Oper Dortmund, 2015.

**DUNCAN, Peter;** actor, presenter, theatre director and documentary maker, since 1969; Chief Scout, 2004–09; *b* 3 May 1954; *s* of Alan Gale and Patricia Kaye; *m* 1985, Annie Francis; one *s* three *d*. *Educ:* Hawes Down Sec. Mod. Sch.; Italia Conti Stage Sch.; Open Univ. Actor: NT, Old Vic, 1970–72; *films* include: Stardust, 1974; The Lifetaker, 1975; Flash Gordon, 1980; *television* includes: Space: 1999, Survivors, Warship, 1976; King Cinder, 1977; The Flockton Flyer, 1977–78; Tumble, 2014; presenter: Blue Peter, 1980–84, 1985–86 (Gold Blue Peter Badge 2007); Duncan Dares, 1984–86; Peter Duncan's Family Travels (documentary), 2002–07; Demolition Dad, 2005–07; *theatre* includes: Pump Boy and Dinettes, Piccadilly Th.; Funny Peculiar, UK tour; The Card, Regent's Park Th., 1993; Me and My Girl, UK tour, 1995; title rôle in Barnum, UK tour, 1999; Macbeth, Fantastic Mr Fox, Regent's Park Th., 2007; Birdsong, UK tour, 2014; Hairspray, UK tour, 2015; Million Dollar Quartet, UK tour, 2017; Once Seen on Blue Peter, Assembly Rooms, Edinburgh, 2018; The Dame, Park Th., 2019. Pantomime writer and director: Oxford Playhouse, 2006–14; Lighthouse, Poole, 2016–; Cheltenham Everyman, 2017–. Patron: Action for Children's Arts, 2010–; Youth Music Th., 2011–. *Recreations:* gardening, singing, football, yoga. *Address:* 24 Wimbledon Park Road, SW18 1LT. *E:* peterduncan3@ gmail.com. *W:* www.heresoneimadeearlier.com; ARG Talent Agency, 4A Exmoor Street, W10 6BD. *E:* argall@argtalent.com.

**DUNCAN, Peter John;** politician and strategic communications consultant; media and political commentator; Managing Director, Message Matters Ltd, since 2012; *b* 10 July 1965; *s* of late Ronald Duncan and Aureen Duncan (*née* Anderson); *m* 1994, Lorna Forbes; one *s* one *d*. *Educ:* Univ. of Birmingham (BCom Hons); Manchester Business Sch. (MBA). Project Manager, Mackays Stores Ltd, 1985–88; Man. Dir, John Duncan & Son, 1988–2000; freelance business consultant, 1998–2000. MP (C) Galloway and Upper Nithsdale, 2001–05; contested (C) Dumfries and Galloway, 2005, 2010. Shadow Sec. of State for Scotland, 2003–05. Mem. (C) Dumfries and Galloway Council, 2007–12 (Chm. of Resources, 2007–12). Chm., Scottish Conservative and Unionist Party, 2004–07. Chm., Live Borders (formerly Borders Sport and Leisure Trust), 2015–18. *Recreations:* Scottish Rugby, English Test and county cricket. *Address:* East Parkside, Edinburgh EH8 8DP.

**DUNCAN, His Honour Sean Bruce;** a Circuit Judge, 1988–2009; *b* 21 Dec. 1942; *s* of late Joseph Alexander Duncan and Patricia Pauline Duncan; *m* 1974, Dr Diana Bowyer Courtney; three *s* one *d*. *Educ:* Shrewsbury Sch.; St Edmund Hall, Oxford (MA). Called to the Bar, Inner Temple, 1966; Northern Circuit (Hon. Sec., Circuit Cttee, 1985–88); a Recorder, 1984–88. Pres., Council of HM Circuit Judges, 2002 (Hon. Sec., 1996–99). Served with Cheshire Yeomanry (TA), 1963–68. Chairman: Old Swan Boys Club, Liverpool, 1974–79; Liverpool Youth Organisations Cttee, 1977–83; Vice-Chm., Liverpool Council of Voluntary Service, 1982–88. *Recreations:* theatre, sport, music. *Clubs:* Royal Liverpool Golf (Capt., 2003); Liverpool Ramblers AFC (Pres., 2000–02).

**DUNCAN, Stanley Frederick St Clair,** CMG 1983; HM Diplomatic Service, retired; *b* 13 Nov. 1927; *yr s* of late Stanley Gilbert Scott and Louisa Elizabeth Duncan; *m* 1967, Jennifer Jane Bennett; two *d*. *Educ:* Latymer Upper Sch.; Open Univ. (Dip. European Humanities 1999; BA Hons 2002). FRGS. India Office, 1946; CRO, 1947; Private Sec. to Parly Under-Sec. of State, 1954; Second Sec., Ottawa, 1954–55; Brit. Govt Information Officer, Toronto, 1955–57; Second Sec., Wellington, 1958–60; First Sec., CRO, 1960; seconded to Central African Office, 1962–64; Mem., Brit. Delegn to Victoria Falls Conf. on Dissolution of Fedn of Rhodesia and Nyasaland, 1963; First Sec., Nicosia, 1964–67; FCO, 1967–70; FCO Adviser, Brit. Gp, Inter-Parly Union, 1968–70; Head of Chancery and First Sec., Lisbon, 1970–73; Consul-General and subsequently Chargé d'Affaires in Mozambique, 1973–75; Counsellor (Political), Brasilia, 1976–77; Head of Consular Dept, FCO, 1977–80; Canadian Nat. Defence Coll., 1980–81; Ambassador to Bolivia, 1981–85; High Comr in Malta, 1985–87. Mem., UN Observer Mission to S African elections, 1994. Officer, Military Order of Christ (Portugal), 1973. *Address:* Tucksmead, Longworth, Oxon OX13 5ET.

**DUNCAN-JONES, Prof. Katherine Dorothea,** FRSL; Fellow, and Tutor in English Literature, Somerville College, Oxford, 1966–2001; Professor of English Literature, University of Oxford, 1998–2001; Senior Research Fellow, Somerville College, and Faculty of English, University of Oxford, since 2001; *b* 13 May 1941; *d* of late Prof. Austin Ernest Duncan-Jones and Elsie Elizabeth Duncan-Jones (*née* Phare); *m* 1971, Andrew N. Wilson, *qv* (marr. diss. 1990); two *d*. *Educ:* King Edward VI High Sch. for Girls, Birmingham; St Hilda's Coll., Oxford (BLitt, MA). Mary Ewart Res. Fellow, Somerville Coll., Oxford, 1963–65; Fellow, New Hall, Cambridge, 1965–66. Hon. Res. Fellow, UCL, 2000–. FRSL 1992; FEA 2000. Ben Jonson Discoveries Prize, 1996. *Publications:* (ed jtly) Miscellaneous Prose of Sir Philip Sidney, 1977; (ed) Sir Philip Sidney, 1989; Sir Philip Sidney: courtier poet (biog.), 1991; (ed) Shakespeare's Sonnets, 1997, 2nd edn 2010; Ungentle Shakespeare (biog.), 2001; Shakespeare's Life and Work, 2004; (ed jtly) Shakespeare's Poems, 2007; Shakespeare: Upstart Crow to Sweet Swan 1592–1623, 2011; Portraits of Shakespeare, 2015; contrib. numerous articles in Rev. of English Studies, TLS, and other jls. *Recreations:* swimming, theatre-going. *Address:* Somerville College, Oxford OX2 6HD. *T:* (01865) 281267.
*See also* R. P. Duncan-Jones, Viscount Runciman of Doxford.

**DUNCAN-JONES, Richard Phare,** PhD; FBA 1992; Fellow, Gonville and Caius College, Cambridge, since 1963; *b* 14 Sept. 1937; *s* of late Austin Ernest Duncan-Jones and Elsie Elizabeth Duncan-Jones; *m* 1986, Julia Elizabeth Poole. *Educ:* King Edward's Sch., Birmingham; King's Coll., Cambridge (MA, PhD). Gonville and Caius College, Cambridge: W. M. Tapp Res. Fellow, 1963–67; Domestic Bursar, 1967–84; Official Fellow, 1967–; College Lectr and Dir of Studies in Classics, 1984–2004. Mem., Inst. for Advanced Study, Princeton, 1971–72. *Publications:* The Economy of the Roman Empire, 1974, 2nd edn 1982; Structure and Scale in the Roman Economy, 1990; Money and Government in the Roman Empire, 1994; Power and Privilege in Roman Society, 2016; articles in learned jls. *Recreations:* wine tasting, continental cinema. *Address:* Gonville and Caius College, Cambridge CB2 1TA. *T:* (01223) 332394.
*See also* K. D. Duncan-Jones.

**DUNCAN SMITH, Rt Hon. (George) Iain;** PC 2001; MP (C) Chingford and Woodford Green, since 1997 (Chingford, 1992–97); *b* 9 April 1954; *s* of late Group Captain W. G. G. Duncan Smith, DSO (Bar), DFC (2 Bars) and Pamela Mary Duncan Smith (*née* Summers); *m* 1982, Hon. Elizabeth Wynne Fremantle, *er d* of 5th Baron Cottesloe; two *s* two *d. Educ:* HMS Conway (Cadet School); RMA Sandhurst; Dunchurch Coll. of Management. Scots Guards, 1975–81; ADC to Gen. Sir John Acland, 1979–81; GEC, 1981–88; Dir, Bellwinch (Property), 1988; Dir, Jane's Inf. Group, 1989–92. Vice-Chm., Fulham Cons. Assoc., 1991. Contested (C) Bradford West, 1987. Shadow Sec. of State for social security, 1997–99, for defence, 1999–2001; Leader, Cons. Party and Leader of the Opposition, 2001–03; Sec. of State for Work and Pensions, 2010–16. Member, Select Committee: on Health, 1994–95; on Nolan, 1995; on Standards and Privileges, 1996–97. Sec., Cons. Backbench Cttee on Foreign and Commonwealth Affairs, 1992–97; Vice Chm., Cons. European Affairs Cttee, 1996–97; Mem., Cons. Party Adv. Council, 2003–. Chm. and Founder, Centre for Social Justice, 2004–10, 2017– (Patron, 2010–). Trustee: Lygon Alms-house, 1985–91; Whitefield Develt Trust. Freeman, City of London. *Publications:* The Devil's Tune (novel), 2003; Breakdown Britain, 2006; Breakthrough Britain, 2007; (jtly) Early Intervention: good parents, great kids, better citizens, 2009; various pamphlets on social security, European and defence issues; occasional journalism. *Recreations:* family, painting, fishing, cricket, tennis, shooting, opera, reading. *Address:* House of Commons, SW1A 0AA. *T:* (020) 7219 2667 and 3000.

**DUNCANNON, Viscount; Frederick Arthur William Ponsonby;** *b* 9 Aug. 1974; *e s* and heir of Earl of Bessborough, *qv; m* 2005, Emily, *d* of Dr Peter D. Mott, Pittsford, NY; one *s* one *d. Educ:* Harrow; UEA. *Heir:* s Hon. William Ponsonby, *b* 6 May 2008.

**DUNCOMBE,** family name of **Baron Feversham**.

**DUNCOMBE, Sir David Philip Henry P.;** *see* Pauncefort-Duncombe.

**DUNCUMB, Dr Peter,** FRS 1977; consultant in materials analysis by X-rays and ultrasonics, 1997–2015; Director and General Manager, Tube Investments, later TI Group, Research Laboratories, 1979–87; *b* 26 Jan. 1931; *s* of late William Duncumb and of Hilda Grace (*née* Coleman); *m* 1955, Anne Leslie Taylor; two *s* one *d. Educ:* Oundle Sch.; Clare Coll., Cambridge (BA 1953, MA 1956, PhD 1957). Commnd GD Br., RAF, qualif. Pilot, 1949–50; No 22RFS Cambridge, RAFVR, 1950–54; DSIR Res. Fellow, Cambridge Univ., 1957–59; Tube Investments, subseq. TI Group, Research Laboratories: Res. Scientist and Gp Leader, 1959–67, Head, Physics Dept, 1967–72; Asst Dir, 1972–79. Hon. Prof., Warwick Univ., 1990–2000. FInstP 1969. Fellow, Microbeam Analysis Soc. of America, Legends Cl., 2018. Hon. Member: Microbeam Analysis Soc. of America, 1973; European Microbeam Analysis Soc., 1997. C. V. Boys Prize, Inst. of Physics, 1966; Henry Clifton Sorby Award, Internat. Metallographic Soc., 1996. *Publications:* numerous on electron microscopy and analysis in various jls. *Recreations:* photography, ballet, family history. *Address:* 5A Woollards Lane, Great Shelford, Cambridge CB22 5LZ. *T:* (01223) 843064.

**DUNDAS,** family name of **Marquess of Zetland,** and **Viscount Melville**.

**DUNDAS, James Frederick Trevor;** Chairman, Jupiter Fund Management plc, 2008–14; *b* 4 Nov. 1950; *s* of Sir Hugh Dundas, CBE, DSO, DFC, and of Hon. Lady Dundas; *m* 1979, Jennifer Daukes; one *s* two *d. Educ:* Eton; New Coll., Oxford (BA Hons Jurisp.). Called to the Bar, Inner Temple, 1972; Morgan Grenfell & Co. Ltd, 1972–91: Dir, 1981–91; Head, Corporate and Internat. Banking, 1987–91; Mem., Mgt Cttee, Morgan Grenfell Gp plc, 1989–91; Finance Dir, Hong Kong Airport Authy, 1992–96; Finance Dir, 1997–99, Chief Exec., 1999–2003, MEPC plc. Non-executive Director: J. Sainsbury plc, 2000–07; Standard Chartered PLC, 2004–14; Drax Gp plc, 2005–10; Francis Crick Inst., 2011–14. Dep. Pres., Macmillan Cancer Support, 2010– (Chm., 2001–10).

**DUNDAS-BEKKER, Althea Enid Philippa;** owner and administrator, Arniston House, Midlothian; *b* 4 Nov. 1939; *d* of Sir Philip Dundas, 4th Bt and Jean Marion Dundas; *m* 1972, Aedrian Ruprecht Bekker (*d* 1990); two *d. Educ:* Inverleny, Callander; Oakfield Sch., Kirkby Lonsdale. Inherited Arniston House, 1970. Mem., Royal Commn on Historical MSS, 1994–2003. DL Midlothian, 1991. *Recreations:* Scottish history and songs, walking dogs. *Address:* Arniston House, Gorebridge, Midlothian EH23 4RY. *T:* (01875) 830238.

**DUNDEE, 12th Earl of,** *cr* 1660 (Scotland); **Alexander Henry Scrymgeour;** DL; Viscount Dudhope and Lord Scrymgeour, 1641 (Scotland); Lord Inverkeithing, 1660 (Scotland); Lord Glassary (UK), 1954; Hereditary Royal Standard-Bearer for Scotland; *b* 5 June 1949; *s* of 11th Earl of Dundee, PC, and Patricia Katherine, *d* of late Col Lord Herbert Montagu Douglas Scott; *S* father, 1983; *m* 1979, Siobhan Mary (*d* 2019), *d* of David Llewellyn, Gt Somerford, Wilts; one *s* three *d. Educ:* Eton; St Andrews Univ. Contested (C) Hamilton, by-election May 1978. A Lord in Waiting (Govt Whip), 1986–89; elected Mem., H of L, 1999. DL Fife, 2003. *Heir:* s Lord Scrymgeour, *qv. Address:* Farm Office, Birkhill, Cupar, Fife KY15 4QP. *Clubs:* White's; New (Edinburgh).

**DUNDONALD, 15th Earl of,** *cr* 1669; **Iain Alexander Douglas Blair Cochrane;** Lord Cochrane of Dundonald, 1647; Lord Cochrane of Paisley and Ochiltree, 1669; Director, Anglo Scientific (formerly Anglo Digital) and associated companies, since 2001; *b* 17 Feb. 1961; *s* of 14th Earl of Dundonald and Aphra Farquhar (*d* 1972), *d* of late Comdr George Fethersonhaugh; *S* father, 1986; *m* 1987, Beatrice (marr. diss. 2011), *d* of Adolphus Russo; two *s* one *d. Educ:* Wellington College; RAC Cirencester. DipREM. Dir, Anglo Pacific Gp, 1995–98. Mem. Council, PITCOM, subseq. PICTFOR, 1994–. Hon. Consul in Scotland for Chile, 1993–. *Recreations:* rural affairs, sailing, innovation. *Heir:* s Lord Cochrane, *qv. Address:* Lochnell Castle, Benderloch, Argyll PA37 1QT.

**DUNEDIN, Bishop of,** since 2017; **Rt Rev. Dr Steven Charles Benford;** *b* Epsom; *s* of John Benford and Mary Benford; *m* 1982, Lorraine Wintrup; two *s* two *d. Educ:* Caterham Sch.; Leicester Univ. (MB ChB 1986). Anaesthetist, Oamaru, NZ, 1990–95; Associate Specialist Anaesthetist, Friarage Hosp., Northallerton, 1995–2014; ordained deacon, 2000, priest, 2001; Priest-in-charge, St Luke the Evangelist, York, 2004–14; Vicar, St Joseph the Worker, Northolt, 2014–17. *Recreations:* walking, piano, travel. *Address:* Anglican Diocese of Dunedin, PO Box 13170, Green Island, Dunedin 9052, New Zealand. *E:* frstevebenford@gmail.com.

**DUNFORD, Sir John (Ernest),** Kt 2014; OBE 1994; PhD; education consultant, retired; General Secretary, Association of School and College Leaders, 1998–2010; *b* Burnham-on-Sea, Som, 10 Nov. 1946; *s* of Leslie Donald Dunford and Mary Dunford; *m* 2001, Sue Rust D'Eye; one *s* one *d* and two step *d. Educ:* Cheltenham Coll.; Univ. of Nottingham (BSc Jt Hons Maths and Econs; PGCE); Univ. of Durham (MEd 1976; PhD 1992; Hon. Fellow, 2007). Pres. of Union, Univ. of Nottingham, 1968–69. Teacher of Maths: Mundella Sch., Nottingham, 1970–72; Hylton Red House Sch., Sunderland, 1972–73; Framwellgate Moor Comp. Sch., Durham, 1973–78 (Sen. Teacher, 1974–78); Dep. Head, Bede Sch., Sunderland, 1979–82; Hd, Durham Johnston Comprehensive Sch., 1982–98. Trustee: Step Together (formerly Worldwide) Volunteering, 1995–2018 (Chm., 2010–16); Teach First, 2003–11; Education for All, 2009–15; Chartered Inst. of Educl Assessors, 2010–14 (Chm., 2010–14); Board Member: Specialist Schs and Acads Trust, 2005–09; Future Leaders, 2006–11; Chm., Whole Educn, 2010–18. Mem. Governing Council, Nat. Coll. for Leadership of Schs and Children's Services, 2010–12. Nat. Pupil Premium Champion, 2013–15; Chair, Ind. Commn on Exam. Malpractice, 2018–19. Gov., St Andrew's C of E Primary Sch., N Kilworth, 2004–16. Conducted Review of Office of the Children's Commissioner (England), 2010. Trustee, Learn Academies Trust, 2016–. Hon. LLD Nottingham, 2013. *Publications:* Her Majesty's Inspectorate of Schools 1860–1870, 1980; Her Majesty's Inspectorate of Schools since 1944, 1998; (ed) State Schools: New Labour and the Conservative legacy, 1999; School Leadership: national and international perspectives, 2000; The Growth of Academy Chains: implications for leaders and leadership, 2012; Establishing and Leading New Types of School: challenges and opportunities for leaders and leadership, 2013; Evaluation of Teaching Schools, 2016; The School Leadership Journey, 2016. *Recreations:* cooking, birdwatching, opera, gardening, golf, walking. *Address:* Cobblestones, Church Street, North Kilworth, Leics LE17 6EZ. *E:* sirjohndunford@gmail.com.

**DUNGARVAN, Viscount; Rory Jonathan Courtenay Boyle;** naval architect (Superyachts); Burgess Technical Services Ltd, since 2007; *b* 10 Dec. 1978; *o s* and heir of Earl of Cork and Orrery, *qv; m* 2015, Lucinda Julia, *y d* of Julian C. K. Davy; one *d. Educ:* Harrow; Newcastle Univ. (BEng Hons). CEng 2008; MRINA 2008. *Recreations:* sailing, ski-ing, design, technology, country sports, reeling, limpets. *Address:* 86 Archel Road, W14 9QP. *Clubs:* Royal Yacht Squadron, Royal Northern and Clyde Yacht.

**DUNGAVELL, Ian Robert,** PhD; FSA; Chief Executive, Highgate Cemetery, since 2012; *b* 4 Sept. 1966; *s* of Robert Charles Dungavell and Barbara Marie Dungavell. *Educ:* ANU (BA Hons Art Hist. 1989); Royal Holloway, London (PhD Architectl Hist. 1999); Univ. of Reading (MSc Conservation of Historic Envmt 2010). FSA 2007. Assoc. Lectr, ANU, 1992–93; Lectr, Sotheby's Inst., 1998–2000; Dir, The Victorian Soc., 2000–12 (Dir, Summer Sch., 1998–99). Member: Exec. Cttee, Soc. of Architectl Historians of GB, 1996–99; Places of Worship Forum, English Heritage, 2006–10; Conservation Working Gp, Churches Conservation Trust, 2007–12. Hon. Sec., Jt Cttee of Nat. Amenity Socs, 2005–10. Winston Churchill Travelling Fellow, 2005. Banister Fletcher Lect., London Soc., 2008. Trustee: Cremation Soc. GB, 2015–18; Mausolea and Monuments Trust, 2016–. *Publications:* (contrib.) Birmingham (Pevsner City Guide), 2005; (ed with D. Crellin) Architecture and Englishness 1880–1914, 2006; (contrib.) Building Conservation Directory, 2007; contrib. Oxford DNB; contribs to Jl of Decorative Arts Soc., Crafts Mag., Studies in Victorian Architecture and Design. *Recreations:* architecture, cemeteries, eating. *Address:* Highgate Cemetery, Swain's Lane, Highgate, N6 6PJ. *T:* (020) 8340 1834. *E:* ian@dungavell.net.

**DUNGER, Prof. David Brian,** MD; FRCP, FRCPCH; FMedSci; Professor of Paediatrics, 2000–15, now Emeritus, and Director of Research, Department of Paediatrics, since 2015, University of Cambridge; *b* Rochford, 28 March 1948; *s* of Brian and Jean Dunger; one *d; m* 2005, Dame Jane Elisabeth Roberts, *qv;* one *s. Educ:* Charing Cross Hosp. Med. Sch., Univ. of London (MB BS 1971; MD 1983). FRCP 1993; FRCPCH 1997. Sen. Registrar in Paediatrics, Gt Ormond St Hosp., London, 1980–86; Consultant Paediatric Endocrinologist, John Radcliffe Hosp., Oxford, 1986–2000; Prof. of Paediatric Endocrinol., Univ. of Oxford, 1999–2000; Sen. Res. Investigator, NIHR, 2014–18. Banting Meml Lectr, Diabetes UK, 2016. FMedSci 2012. Andrea Prader Prize, Eur. Soc. for Paediatric Endocrinol., 2012; James Spence Medal, RCPCH, 2015. *Publications:* peer-reviewed pubns and reviews. *E:* dbd25@cam.ac.uk.

**DUNGER, Dame Jane (Elisabeth);** *see* Roberts, Dame J. E.

**DUNGLASS, Lord; Michael David Alexander Douglas-Home;** *b* 30 Nov. 1987; *s* and heir of Earl of Home, *qv.* A Page of Honour to the Queen, 1998–2000. *Address:* The Hirsel, Coldstream, Berwickshire TD12 4LP.

**DUNHILL, Rosemary Carole,** OBE 2003; FSA; County Archivist, Hampshire Record Office, 1982–2001, retired; *b* 21 June 1944; *d* of Harold John Dunhill and Freda Dunhill (*née* Best); *m* 2007, David Lloyd. *Educ:* Palmer's Girls' Sch., Grays; Cheadle Grammar Sch.; Methodist Coll., Belfast; Somerville Coll., Oxford (BA Modern Hist. 1965, MA). Archivist: Harrowby MSS Trust, 1969–71; Devon Record Office, 1972–76; Northants Record Office, 1976–82; (pt-time) Jesus Coll., Oxford, 2002–07. Member: Royal Commn on Historical MSS, 1999–2003; Lord Chancellor's Adv. Council on Public Records, 1999–2001; Adv. Council on Nat. Records and Archives, 2003–05. Chm., Assoc. of Chief Archivists in Local Govt, 1997–99. FSA 1996. Hon. DLitt King Alfred's Coll., Winchester, 2000. Ellis Prize, Soc. of Archivists, 1996. *Publications:* (with D. Burrows) Music and Theatre in Handel's World: the family papers of James Harris 1735–1780, 2002; Northamptonshire National Schools 1812–1854, 2017. *Recreations:* nephews and nieces, archives, fair trade. *Address:* 27 Sunnydown Road, Winchester, Hants SO22 4LD. *T:* (01962) 869007. *E:* rcdunhill@gmail.com.

**DUNION, Kevin Harry,** OBE 1999; Director, Centre for Freedom of Information, since 2018 (Co-Director, 2009–12; Executive Director, 2012–18); *b* 20 Dec. 1955; *s* of late Harry Dunion and Mary Leckie Bertolini; *m* 1st, 1978, Christine Elizabeth Hannam (marr. diss. 1997); two *s;* 2nd, 1997, Linda Gray. *Educ:* St Andrew's High Sch., Kirkcaldy; St Andrews Univ. (MA Hons); Edinburgh Univ. (MSc Dist.). HM Inspector of Taxes, 1978–80; Administrator, Edinburgh Univ. Students' Assoc., 1980–84; Scottish Campaign Manager, OXFAM, 1984–91; Dir, Friends of the Earth Scotland, 1991–2003; Chm., Friends of the Earth Internat., 1996–99; Scottish Information Comr, 2003–12; Lord Rector, Univ. of St Andrews, 2008–11. Vis. Prof., Univ. of Northumbria, 2011–16; Hon. Prof., Univ. of Dundee, 2012–. Member: Cabinet sub-cttee on Sustainable Scotland, Scottish Exec., 2000–03; Bd, Scottish Natural Heritage, 2000–03; Scottish Legal Complaints Commn, 2013–18; Comr, Standards Commn for Scotland, 2015– (Convener, 2017–). Member: Bd, Access to Information Appeals Bd, World Bank, 2012–; Access to Information Appeals Panel, Internat. Finance Corp., 2015–. Trustee and Mem. Bd, Scottish Fisheries Mus., 2018–. Chair, Students' Assoc. Bd, Univ. of St Andrews, 2011–14. Hon. Sen. Res. Fellow, Univ. of Strathclyde, 2000–03. Editor, Radical Scotland mag., 1981–85. FRSA 1997. Hon. LLD St Andrews, 2011. *Publications:* Living in the Real World: the international role for Scotland's Parliament, 1995; Troublemakers: the struggle for environmental justice in

Scotland, 2003; The Democracy of War, 2007; Freedom of Information in Scotland in Practice, 2011. *Recreations:* Scottish local history, curling. *Address:* Johnston Lodge, Haddfoot Wynd, Anstruther KY10 3AD.

**DUNITZ, Prof. Jack David,** FRS 1974; Professor of Chemical Crystallography at the Swiss Federal Institute of Technology (ETH), Zürich, 1957–90; *b* 29 March 1923; *s* of William Dunitz and Mildred (*née* Gossman); *m* 1953, Barbara Steuer; two *d*. *Educ:* Hillhead High Sch., Glasgow; Hutchesons' Grammar Sch., Glasgow; Glasgow Univ. (BSc, PhD). Post-doctoral Fellow, Oxford Univ., 1946–48, 1951–53; California Inst. of Technology, 1948–51, 1953–54; Vis. Scientist, US Nat. Insts of Health, 1954–55; Sen. Res. Fellow, Davy Faraday Res. Lab., Royal Instn, London, 1956–57. Overseas Fellow, Churchill Coll., Cambridge, 1968; Vis. Professor: Iowa State Univ., 1965; Tokyo Univ., 1967; Technion, Haifa, 1970; Hill Vis. Prof., Univ. of Minnesota, 1983; Fairchild Distinguished Scholar, CIT, 1985; Hooker Distinguished Vis. Prof., McMaster Univ., 1987; Alexander Todd Vis. Prof., Cambridge Univ., 1990; Oscar K. Rice Vis. Prof., Univ. of N Carolina, Chapel Hill, 1991; Robert B. Woodward Vis. Prof., Harvard Univ., 1992. Lectures: British Council, 1965; Treat B. Johnson Meml, Yale Univ., 1965; 3M Univ. of Minnesota, 1966; Reilly, Univ. Notre Dame, US, 1971; Kelly, Purdue Univ., 1971; Gerhard Schmidt Meml, Weizmann Inst. of Sci., 1973; George Fisher Baker, Cornell Univ., 1976; Centenary, Chem. Soc., 1977; Appleton, Brown Univ., 1979; H. J. Backer, Gröningen Univ., 1980; Havinga, Leiden Univ., 1980; Karl Folkers, Wisconsin Univ., 1981; A. L. Patterson Meml, Inst. for Cancer Res., Philadelphia, 1983; C. S. Marvel, Illinois Univ., 1987; Birch, Canberra, 1989; Dwyer, Sydney, 1989; Bijvoet, Utrecht Univ., 1989; Bragg, British Crystallographic Assoc., 1999. Mem., Bd of Govs, Cambridge Crystallographic Data Centre, 1987–99. Foreign Member: Royal Netherlands Acad. of Arts and Sciences, 1979; Amer. Phil Soc., 1987; Member: Leopoldina Acad., 1979; European Acad. of Scis and Arts, 1991; Foreign Associate, US Nat. Acad. of Scis, 1988; Mem., Academia Europaea, 1989; Hon. Member: Swiss Soc. of Crystallography, 1990; Swiss Chem. Soc., 2004; British Crystallographic Assoc., 2012; For. Hon. Mem., Amer. Acad. of Arts and Scis, 1997; Fellow AAAS, 1981. Hon. FRSC 2000. Hon. DSc: Technion, Haifa, 1990; Weizmann Inst. of Sci., 1992; Glasgow Univ., 1999. Tishler Award, Harvard Univ., 1985; Paracelsus Prize, Swiss Chem. Soc., 1986; Gregori Aminoff Prize, Swedish Royal Acad., 1990; Martin Buerger Award, Amer. Crystallographic Assoc., 1991; Arthur C. Cope Scholar Award, ACS, 1997. Jt Editor, Perspectives in Structural Chemistry, 1967–71; Mem. Editorial Bd: Helvetica Chimica Acta, 1971–85; Structure and Bonding, 1971–81. *Publications:* X-ray Analysis and the Structure of Organic Molecules, 1979, repr. 1995; (with E. Heilbronner) Reflections on Symmetry in Chemistry… and Elsewhere, 1993; papers on various aspects of crystal and molecular structure in Acta Crystallographica, Helvetica Chimica Acta, Jl Chem. Soc., Jl Amer. Chem. Soc., etc. *Recreations:* reading, listening to classical music. *Address:* Obere Heslibachstrasse 77, 8700 Küsnacht, Switzerland. *T:* (44) 9101723; (office) Chemistry Department, ETH-Zürich, 8093 Zürich, Switzerland. *T:* (44) 6322892.

**DUNKELD, Bishop of, (RC),** since 2013; **Rt Rev. Mgr Stephen Robson;** *b* Carlisle, 1 April 1951; *s* of Leslie and Margery Robson. *Educ:* Caldey Grange Sch., Wirral; Carlisle and Lanark Grammar Schs; Edinburgh Univ. (BSc 1974; MTh 1988); St Andrew's Coll., Drygrange; Pontifical Gregorian Univ., Rome (STL 2000; STD 2003; JCL 2006). CBiol 1985. Ordained priest, 1979; Assistant Priest: St Mary's Cathedral, Edinburgh, 1979; Our Lady of the Perpetual Succour, Kircaldy, 1979–81; teacher training in-service, 1981; Prof., St Mary's Coll., Blairs, 1981–86; Sec. to Archbishop O'Brien, 1986–88; Asst, Holy Cross, Edinburgh, 1986–88; Parish Priest, Duns, 1988–89; Novice, Ampleforth Abbey, 1989–90; Parish Priest, Dunbar, 1990–93; Asst Episcopal Vicar for Educn, 1990–93, Vicar Episcopal for Educn, 1993–98; Parish Priest: St John Vianney, Edinburgh, 1993–97; St Theresa's, East Calder, 1997–98; Spiritual Dir, Pontifical Scots Coll., Rome, 1998–2006; Prof., Pontifical Beda Coll., Rome, 1999–2001; Parish Priest, North Berwick, 2006–12; Chancellor, Archdiocese of St Andrews and Edinburgh, 2007–13; Parish Priest, SS John Cantius and Nicholas, 2012; Titular Bishop of Tunnuna, and Auxiliary Bishop, Archdiocese of St Andrews and Edinburgh, 2012–13 (Hon. Canon, Metropolitan Cathedral Chapter of St Mary, 2015–). Chaplain to His Holiness, 2008. Judge, Scottish Nat. Tribunal, 2006–; Mem., Canon Law Soc. of GB and Ireland, 2006–. Bishop Promoter for Scotland, Apostleship of the Sea, 2013–. President: Priests for Scotland, 2013; Scottish Bps Conference Commn for the Permanent Diaconate; Trustee: Scottish Catholic Internat. Aid Fund, 2013–; Charles Trotter Trust, 2013–; Scottish Catholic Heritage Collections Trust, 2014–. Gov., Anscombe Bioethics Centre, Oxford, 2014–. Conventual Chaplain (*ad honorem*), Knights of St John of Jerusalem, Rhodes and Malta, 2015–. KC★HS 2018. *Publications:* With the Spirit and Power of Elijah, 2004. *Recreations:* music, reading, cinema, theatre, gardening. *Address:* Diocese of Dunkeld, 24–28 Lawside Road, Dundee DD3 6XY.

**DUNKERLEY, Susan Margaret;** Head, Wheathampstead House (formerly Head, Juniors), St Albans High School for Girls, 1998–2009; *b* Howden, E Yorks, 18 June 1954; *d* of George Donald Whitaker and Muriel Whitaker; *m* 1977, Colin Dunkerley; two *d*. *Educ:* Goole Grammar Sch.; Homerton Coll., Cambridge (BEd Hons Newnham Coll.); Inst. of Educn, London Univ. (MA Geog. and Educn). Hd of Yr and Hd of Geog., Furzehill Middle Sch., Borehamwood, 1976–83; various posts teaching geog. with additional subjects, Beaumont Sec. Sch., St Albans, 1984–89; Haberdashers' Aske's Sch. for Girls, Elstree, 1986, 1990, 1991, 1992–98: Dir, Curriculum Studies, 1993–98; Dep. Hd, Lower Sch., 1995–98. Tutoring, 1983–91. Inspector, ISI, 2003–08. Member: Primary and Middle Sch. Cttee, Geographical Assoc., 1994–99; IAPS, 2007–. Gov., Northwood Coll., 2010–14. *Publications:* contrib. article and book reviews of geographical books for Primary Geog. mag. *Recreations:* textile art, scrapbooking, choral singing, watching Manchester United, card making, reading, travel. *E:* sue@dunkerley.com.

**DUNKLEY, Christopher;** freelance journalist and broadcaster; *b* 22 Jan. 1944; 2nd *s* of late Robert Dunkley and Joyce Mary Dunkley (*née* Turner); *m* 1967, Carolyn Elizabeth (marr. diss. 2004), *e d* of Col A. P. C. Lyons; one *s* one *d*. *Educ:* Haberdashers' Aske's (expelled). Various jobs, incl. theatre flyman, cook, hospital porter, 1961–63; general reporter, then cinema and theatre critic, Slough Observer, 1963–65; feature writer and news editor, UK Press Gazette, 1965–68; night news reporter, then mass media correspondent and TV critic, The Times, 1968–73; TV Critic, Financial Times, 1973–2002; feature writer, Daily Mail, 2002–03. Frequent radio broadcaster, 1963–; Presenter, Feedback, Radio 4, 1986–98; occasional television presenter/script writer/chairman. Critic of the Year, British Press Awards, 1976, 1986; Broadcast Journalist of the Year, TV-am Awards, 1989; Best Individual Contrib. to Radio, Voice of the Listener and Viewer Awards, 1998. *Publications:* Television Today and Tomorrow: Wall to Wall Dallas?, 1985. *Recreations:* motorcycling, collecting almost everything, especially dictionaries, tin toys, Victorian boys' books. *Address:* May Villas, 20 Byfield Road, Isleworth, Middx TW7 7AF.

**DUNLEATH,** 6th Baron *cr* 1892, of Ballywalter, co. Down; **Brian Henry Mulholland;** Bt 1945; DL; landowner and farmer; *b* 25 Sept. 1950; *o s* of 5th Baron Dunleath and Elizabeth (*d* 1989), twin *d* of Laurence B. Hyde; *S* father, 1997; *m* 1st, 1976, Mary Joan (marr. diss. 2005), *y d* of Major R. J. F. Whistler; two *s* one *d*; 2nd, 2006, Vibeke, *y d* of late Col Jens Christian Lunn, Denmark. *Educ:* Eton; Royal Agricl Coll. Director: Dunleath Estates Ltd, 1994– (Chm., 1998–); Downpatrick Race Club Ltd, 1999–. DL County Down, 2009. *Recreations:* shooting, fishing, gardening. *Heir: s* Hon. Andrew Henry Mulholland, *b* 15 Dec. 1981. *Address:* (office) The Estate Office, Ballywalter Park, Newtownards, Northern Ireland BT22 2PA. *T:* (028) 4275 8264, *Fax:* (028) 4275 8818; (home) Ballywalter Park, Newtownards, Northern Ireland BT22 2PP. *E:* bd@dunleath-estates.co.uk. *Club:* MCC.

**DUNLEAVY, Prof. Patrick John,** DPhil; FAcSS; Professor of Political Science and Public Policy (formerly of Government), London School of Economics and Political Science, since 1989; Centenary Research Professor, Institute for Governance and Policy Analysis, University of Canberra, since 2015; *b* 21 June 1952; *s* of Vincent Dunleavy and Kathleen Mary Dunleavy; *m* 1974, Sheila Dorothea Squire; two *s* one *d*. *Educ:* St Mary's Grammar Sch., Sidcup; Corpus Christi Coll., Oxford (MA 1973); Nuffield Coll., Oxford (DPhil 1978). Research Fellow, Nuffield Coll., Oxford, 1976–78; Lectr in Urban Studies, Open Univ., 1978–79; London School of Economics and Political Science: Lectr in Govt, 1979–86; Reader, 1986–89; Chair, Public Policy Gp, 1992–; Dir, MPA Prog., 2003–09. Co-Dir, Democratic Audit UK, 2013–. Mem. Exec., UK Political Studies Assoc., 1980–83, 1993–94 and 1999–2005. Councillor, Bucks CC, 1981–85. Mem., Milton Keynes CHC, 1982–90. FAcSS (AcSS 1999). Special Recognition Award, Pol Studies Assoc., 2013. Founding Editor: Politics, 1980–82; (jtly) Global Policy, 2009–; Editor: Political Studies, 1999–2005; Political Studies Review, 2003–05; mem. editl bd, various jls. *Publications:* Urban Political Analysis, 1980; The Politics of Mass Housing in Britain, 1981; (ed jtly) Developments in British Politics, vol. 1, 1983, vol. 2, 1986, vol. 3, 1990, vol. 4, 1993, vol. 5, 1997, vol. 6, 2000; (with C. T. Husbands) British Democracy at the Crossroads, 1985; Studying for a Degree, 1987; (with B. O'Leary) Theories of the State, 1987; Democracy, Bureaucracy and Public Choice, 1991; (ed with R. A. W. Rhodes) Prime Minister, Cabinet and Core Executive, 1995; (jtly) Making Votes Count, 1997; (with H. Margetts) Government on the Web, 1999; (ed jtly) British Political Science, 2000; (with H. Margetts) Government on the Web 2, 2002; Authoring a PhD, 2002; (with H. Margetts) Difficult Forms, 2003; (jtly) Citizen Redress, 2005; (jtly) Digital-Era Governance, 2006; (jtly) Government on the Internet, 2007; (with J. Dryzek) Theories of the Democratic State, 2009; (with A. White) Making and Breaking Whitehall Departments, 2010; (with L. Carrera) Growing the Productivity of Government Services, 2013; (with S. Bastow and J. Tinkler) The Impact of the Social Sciences, 2014; (with A. Park and R. Taylor) The UK's Changing Democracy, 2018; articles in learned jls. *Recreations:* family, travel, undermining the (old) constitution, advancing social media in academia, Twitter @PJDunleavy and @Write4Research. *Address:* Department of Government, London School of Economics, Houghton Street, WC2A 2AE. *T:* (020) 7955 7178. *E:* p.dunleavy@lse.ac.uk.

**DUNLOP,** family name of **Baron Dunlop**.

**DUNLOP,** Baron *cr* 2015 (Life Peer), of Helensburgh in the County of Dunbarton; **Andrew James Dunlop;** *b* Helensburgh, 21 June 1959; *s* of late Robert Jack Dunlop and Dorothy Shirley Dunlop; *m* 1991, Lucia Mary Elizabeth Campbell; three *d*. *Educ:* Trinity Coll., Glenalmond; Glasgow Acad.; Edinburgh Univ. (MA Hons Politics and Modern Hist.); King's Coll., London (Postgrad. Dip. European Competition Law). Midland Bank Internat., 1981–82; Hd of Policy and Res., Scottish Cons. Party, 1982–84; Cons. Res. Dept, 1984–86; Special Advr, Sec. of State for Defence, 1986–88; Prime Minister's Policy Unit, 1988–90; founder and Man. Dir, Politics Internat. Ltd, 1991–2008; Man. Dir, 2008–10, Exec. Chm., 2010–11, Interel Consulting UK; Mem. Mgt Bd, Interel Gp, Brussels, 2008–11; Special Advr to Prime Minister on Scotland and Devolution, 2012–15. Parly Under-Sec. of State, Scotland Office, 2015–17, NI Office, 2016–17. Mem., Constitution Cttee, H of L, 2017–. Chair: Scottish Future Growth Council, 2017–; Scottish Business Taskforce, 2017–; Member: Bd, Scottish Council for Develt and Industry, 2017–; Adv. Council, Scottish Policy Foundn, 2017–; Adv. Bd, Ionad Hiort Charitable Co. Ltd, 2017–; Civilian Expert Mem., UK Civilian Stabilisation Gp, 2017–. Member: Mgt Cttee, Sussex County, 2009–11, SE Region, 2011–12, Amateur Swimming Assoc.; Bd, Scottish Swimming, 2018–; Chair, City of Portsmouth Athletics Club, 2018–. *Recreations:* swimming, tennis, sailing, gardening, ski-ing, following football. *Address:* House of Lords, SW1A 0PW. *Clubs:* Reform; Atlantis Horsham Swimming (Chm., 2008–12).
*See also* R. A. Dunlop.

**DUNLOP, Elizabeth Sarah Ann, (Mrs C. C. H. Dunlop);** *see* Craig-McFeely, E. S. A.

**DUNLOP, Frank,** CBE 1977; theatre director; Director, Edinburgh International Festival, 1983–91; *b* 15 Feb. 1927; *s* of Charles Norman Dunlop and Mary Aaron. *Educ:* Kibworth Beauchamp Grammar Sch.; University Coll., London (Fellow, 1979). BA Hons, English. Postgrad. Sch. in Shakespeare, at Shakespeare Inst., Stratford-upon-Avon; Old Vic Sch., London. Served with RAF before going to University. Director: (own young theatre co.) Piccolo Theatre, Manchester, 1954; Arts Council Midland Theatre Co., 1955; Associate Dir, Bristol Old Vic, 1956; Dir, Théâtre de Poche, Brussels, 1959–60; Founder and Dir, Pop Theatre, 1960; Dir, Nottingham Playhouse, 1961–63; New Nottingham Playhouse, 1963–64; (dir.) The Enchanted, Bristol Old Vic Co., 1955; (wrote and dir.) Les Frères Jaques, Adelphi, 1960; Director: London Première, The Bishop's Bonfire, Mermaid, 1960; Schweyk, Mermaid, 1963; The Taming of the Shrew, Univ. Arts Centre, Oklahoma, 1965; Any Wednesday, Apollo, 1965; Too True to be Good, Edinburgh Fest., also Strand and Garrick, 1965; Saturday Night and Sunday Morning, Prince of Wales, 1966; The Winter's Tale and The Trojan Women, Edin. and Venice Festivals, also Cambridge Theatre, London, 1966; The Burglar, Vaudeville, 1967; Getting Married, Strand, 1967; A Midsummer Night's Dream and The Tricks of Scapin, Edin. Fest. and Saville Theatre, London, 1967; A Sense of Detachment, Royal Court, 1972; Sherlock Holmes, Aldwych, 1974, NY 1974; Habeas Corpus, NY 1975; The New York Idea, The Three Sisters, NY 1977; The Devil's Disciple, LA and NY, 1978; The Play's the Thing, Julius Caesar, NY, 1978; The Last of Mrs Cheyney, USA, 1978; Rookery Nook, Birmingham and Her Majesty's, 1979; Camelot, USA, 1980, London, 1996; Sherlock Holmes, Norwegian Nat. Th., Oslo, 1980; Lolita, NY, 1981; Oberon (Weber), Edinburgh, Frankfurt, 1986 (filmed); L'Elisir d'Amore, Opéra de Lyon, 1992 (filmed); My Fair Lady, European tour, 1994; Carmen, Royal Albert Hall, 1997; Ecole des Femmes, Belgium, 1998; The Invisible Man, USA, 1998–99; Scapino, Tel Aviv, 1999; Napoleon at St Helena, Waterloo, 2000, Monte Carlo, 2001; Turn of the Screw, Belgium, 2001; (adapted and dir.) Address Unknown, NY, 2004; Oscar and the Pink Lady, San Diego, 2007, NY, 2008, 2009; The Chalk Garden gala, NY, 2017; *National Theatre:* Assoc. Dir, 1967–74 and Admin. Dir, 1968–73; productions: *Nat. Theatre:* Edward II (Brecht and Marlowe); Home and Beauty; Macrune's Guevara; The White Devil; Captain of Köpenick; *Young Vic:* Founder, 1969; Mem. Bd, 1969–92; Dir, 1969–78 and 1980–83; Consultant, 1978–80; productions: (author and Dir) Scapino 1970, 1977, NY 1974, LA 1975, Australia 1975, Oslo 1975; The Taming of the Shrew, 1970, 1977; The Comedy of Errors, 1971; The Maids, Deathwatch, 1972; The Alchemist, 1972; Bible One, 1972; French Without Tears, 1973; Joseph and the Amazing Technicolor Dreamcoat (Roundhouse and Albery Theatre), 1973, NY 1976; Much Ado About Nothing, 1975; Macbeth, 1975; Antony and Cleopatra, 1976; King Lear, 1980; Childe Byron, 1981; Masquerade, 1982; *for Théâtre National de Belgique:* Pantagleize, 1970; Antony and Cleopatra, 1971; Pericles, 1972. Mem., Arts Council Young People's Panel, 1968. Governor, Central School of Arts and Crafts, 1970. Hon. Fellow of Shakespeare Inst. Hon. Dr of Theatre, Philadelphia Coll. of Performing Arts, 1978; DUniv Heriot-Watt, 1989; Dr *hc* Edinburgh, 1990. Special Olivier Award, 2017. Chevalier, Order of Arts and Literature

(France), 1987. *Recreations:* reading and looking. *Address:* c/o J. Nives, Miracle Management, 250 West 57th Street, Suite 1332, New York, NY 10107, USA. *T:* (212) 2658787.

**DUNLOP, Very Rev. John,** CBE 2004; Minister, Presbyterian Church in Ireland, 1966–2004; *b* 19 Sept. 1939; *s* of Joseph and Annie Dunlop; *m* 1965, Rosemary Willis; one *s* one *d. Educ:* QUB (BA); Univ. of Edinburgh (BD). Ordained 1966; Minister: Fitzroy Avenue Presbyterian Ch, Belfast, 1966–68; United Ch of Jamaica and Grand Cayman, 1968–78; Rosemary Presbyterian Ch, Belfast, 1978–2004; Moderator, Gen. Assembly of Presbyterian Ch in Ireland, 1992–93. Hon. DD: Presbyterian Theol Faculty of Ireland, 1992; TCD, 1993; Hon. LLD: Ulster, 2001; QUB, 2001. *Publications:* A Precarious Belonging: Presbyterians and the conflict in Ireland, 1995. *Address:* 98 Whitehouse Park, Newtownabbey BT37 9SH.

**DUNLOP, Robert Alastair;** QC (Scot.) 1990; Sheriff Principal of Tayside Central and Fife, 2000–14; Appeal Sheriff, Sheriff Appeal Court, since 2015; *b* 30 June 1951; *s* of late Robert Jack Dunlop and Dorothy Shirley Dixon or Dunlop; *m* 1st, 1975, Jane Christian Rankin (marr. diss. 1998); one *s* two *d*; 2nd, 1999, Evelyn Templeton Mackenzie. *Educ:* Trinity Coll., Glenalmond; Univ. of Dundee (LLB). Admitted solicitor, Scotland, 1976; admitted to Faculty of Advocates and called to Scottish Bar, 1978; Advocate Depute, 1985–88; Standing Jun. Counsel, Dept of Transport, 1988–90; part-time Chairman: Pensions Appeal Tribunal, 1991–2000; Employment Tribunals, 1998–2000; Mem., Scottish Court Service Bd, 2010–15. Procurator to Gen. Assembly of Ch of Scotland, 1991–2000. Comr, Northern Lighthouses, 2000–15 (Chm., 2011–13). *Recreations:* sailing, golf, music, ski-ing. *Address:* 5 Temple Village, Gorebridge, Midlothian EH23 4SQ. *T:* (01875) 830344. *Clubs:* New (Edinburgh); Royal Northern and Clyde Yacht.

**DUNLOP, Robert Daubeny, (Robin) B.;** *see* Buchanan-Dunlop.

**DUNLOP, Roderick William;** QC (Scot.) 2010; *b* Glasgow, 10 June 1970; *s* of William Dunlop, *qv*; one *s* one *d. Educ:* High Sch. of Glasgow; Univ. of Edinburgh (LLB Hons 1992; DipLP 1993). Admitted Faculty of Advocates, 1998 (Treas., 2017–). *Recreations:* Rugby, rock music. *Address:* Advocates Library, Parliament House, Edinburgh EH1 1RF. *T:* (0131) 226 5071. *E:* roddy@parliamenthouse.co.uk.

**DUNLOP, Rory James;** QC 2019; *b* Plymouth, 5 Dec. 1976; *s* of Ian Dunlop and Mary Dunlop (*née* McDougall); *m* 2009, Lia Tarkhan-Mouravi; two *d. Educ:* Eton; Magdalen Coll., Oxford (BA double 1st Lit.Hum.); City Univ. (DipLaw (distinction)). Called to the Bar, Lincoln's Inn, 2002; in practice as a barrister, specialising in immigration, professional regulation and data protection; Pegasus Scholarship to EU Ct of Human Rights, 2005; Attorney Gen.'s Panel, 2007–19. *Publications:* Detention Under the Immigration Acts: law and practice, 2015; What We Didn't Say (novel), 2016. *Recreations:* reading, writing, tennis, cricket, ski-ing, playing Scrabble with Mary and baking cakes with Connie. *Address:* 39 Essex Chambers, 81 Chancery Lane, WC2A 1DD. *T:* (020) 7832 1111. *E:* rory.dunlop@39essex.com. *Clubs:* MCC, Queen's; Hon. Company of Edinburgh Golfers, North Berwick Golf, Berkshire Golf.

**DUNLOP, Sir Thomas,** 4th Bt *cr* 1916, of Woodbourne, co. Renfrew; *b* 22 April 1951; *o s* of Sir Thomas Dunlop, 3rd Bt and of Adda Mary Alison Dunlop (*née* Smith); *S* father, 1999; *m* 1984, Eileen, *er d* of A. H. Stevenson; one *s* one *d. Educ:* Rugby; Aberdeen Univ. (BScFor). MICFor. *Heir: s* Thomas Dunlop, *b* 11 March 1990. *Address:* Bredon Croft, Bredon's Norton, Tewkesbury, Worcs GL20 7HB.

**DUNLOP, William;** QC (Scot.) 2011; Sheriff of North Strathclyde, 1995–2014; *b* 7 March 1944; *s* of William Dunlop and Catherine (*née* McKenzie); *m* 1st, 1968, Katherine Frances Howden (marr. diss. 1976); one *s* one *d*; 2nd, 1979, Janina Marthe Merecki; one *d. Educ:* High Sch. of Glasgow; Univ. of Glasgow (LLB 1965). Solicitor in family firm, 1968; called to the Scottish Bar, 1985; in practice at the Bar, 1985–95; Temp. Judge, Court of Session and High Court, 2009–19. Mem. Council, Sheriffs' Assoc., 2001–04. Six Nations Match Comr, 2000–13, Chm., Championship Appeals Panel, 2005–; Scottish Rugby Union. Governor, High Sch. of Glasgow, 1999–2011. *Recreations:* watching Rugby football, playing bad golf, enjoying good food and wine. *Address:* High Court of Justiciary, 1 Mart Street, Glasgow G1 5JT. *Clubs:* Western Baths (Glasgow); Glasgow Golf.
*See also* R. W. Dunlop.

**DUNLOP, Prof. William,** CBE 2005; PhD; FRCSE, FRCOG; Professor of Obstetrics and Gynaecology, University of Newcastle upon Tyne, 1982–2006, now Emeritus; President, Royal College of Obstetricians and Gynaecologists, 2001–04; *b* 18 Aug. 1944; *s* of Alexander Morton Dunlop and Annie Denholm Rennie (*née* Ingram); *m* 1968, Sylvia Louise Krauthamer; one *s* one *d. Educ:* Kilmarnock Acad.; Glasgow Univ. (MB ChB 1967); Univ. of Newcastle upon Tyne (PhD 1982). FRCSE 1971; MRCOG 1971, FRCOG 1984. Various junior posts in obstetrics and gynaecol., Glasgow Univ., 1969–74; seconded as Lectr, Univ. of Nairobi, 1972–73; on MRC scientific staff, 1974–75; University of Newcastle upon Tyne: Sen. Lectr, 1975–82; Hd, Dept of Obstetrics and Gynaecology, 1982–99; Hd, Sch. of Surgical and Reproductive Scis, 1999–2001. Vis. Associate Prof., Medical Univ. of S Carolina, 1980. Royal College of Obstetricians and Gynaecologists: Hon. Sec., 1992–98; Chm., Exam. Cttee, 1990–92; Chm., Specialist Trng Cttee, 1999–2001; Hon. Treasurer: European Bd and Coll. of Obstetrics and Gynaecology, 1999–2005 (Pres., 2005–08); UEMS Sect. of Obstetrics and Gynaecology, 2002–05 (Pres., 2006–10); Chm., UEMS Gp 2 (Surgical) Specialities, 2008–10. Chairman: Professional Adv. Panel, NHS Litigation Authority, 2002–04; Jt Consultants Cttee, 2003–07; Vice-Chairman: Acad. of Medical Royal Colls, 2002–04; Specialist Trng Authority, 2002–04. Chm., Assoc. of Profs of Obstetrics and Gynaecology, 1999–2002. Chm., Blair-Bell Research Soc., 1989–92. Mem. Council, GMC, 2006–08. Chm., Scientific Prog. Cttee, 20th FIGO World Congress of Gynaecology and Obstetrics, 2009–12. Hon. Member: S African Soc. of Obstetricians and Gynaecologists, 2003; Soc. of Obstetricians and Gynaecologists of Canada, 2003; Soc. of Gynaecol. and Obstetrics of Nigeria, 2003; Hon. Fellow: Acad. of Medicine, Singapore, 2002; FFPRHC 2005; Hon. Fellow *qua* Surgeon RCPSG, 2003; FRCP 2003; Hon. FACOG 2003; Hon. FRCPI 2003; Hon. FCPS (Pak) 2004; Hon. FSLCOG 2004. Dr *hc* Athens, 2006. Editor-in-Chief, Fetal and Maternal Medicine Rev., 1989–99. *Publications:* (ed jtly) High Risk Pregnancy, 1992; Recent Advances in Obstetrics and Gynaecology 22, 2003, 23, 2005, 24, 2008. *Recreations:* music, drama, literature. *Address:* 30 Eslington Terrace, Newcastle upon Tyne NE2 4RN. *T:* (0191) 281 4697.

**DUNLUCE, Viscount; Randal Alexander St John McDonnell;** DL; Partner, Sarasin & Partners (formerly Sarasin Chiswell), since 2008 (Director, 2004–08); *b* 2 July 1967; *o s* and heir of Earl of Antrim, *qv*; *m* 2004, Aurora, *d* of David Gunn; one *s* one *d. Educ:* Gresham's Sch., Holt; Worcester Coll., Oxford (MA Hons). Fund Manager: NCL Investments Ltd, 1992–97; Sarasin Investment Mgt Ltd, 1998–2004. Dir, Aberdeen Standard Asia Focus plc (formerly Aberdeen Asian Smaller Companies Investment Trust), 2013–. Director: Game Conservancy Trust, 2003–06; Irish Landmark Trust, 2004–08; Glenarm Bldgs Preservation Trust, 2005–10; Northern Salmon Co., 2006– (Chm., 2009–); Irish Grouse Conservation Trust, 2006–17. DL Co. Antrim, 2013. *Heir: s* Hon. Alexander David Somerled McDonnell, *b* 30 June 2006. *Address:* Glenarm Castle, Glenarm, Ballymena, Co. Antrim BT44 0AL. *Clubs:* Pratt's, White's.

**DUNMORE, 12th Earl of,** *cr* 1686 (Scot.); **Malcolm Kenneth Murray;** Viscount of Fincastle, Lord Murray of Blair, Moulin and Tillimet, 1686; Electrical Technical Supervisor, Air Services Australia, now retired; *b* 17 Sept. 1946; *er s* of 11th Earl of Dunmore and Margaret Joy (*d* 1976), *d* of P. D. Cousins; *S* father, 1995; *m* 1970, Joy Anne (*d* 2015), *d* of A. Partridge; one *s* one *d* (both adopted). *Educ:* Launceston Technical High School (Board A Certificate and various tech. qualifs). Patron: Tasmanian Caledonian Council; Launceston Caledonian Soc.; Armorial and Heraldry Soc. of Australasia Inc.; Scottish Australian Heritage Council; Sunnybank Br., RSL; Murray Clan Soc. of NZ; Murray Clan Edinburgh; Co. of Armigers, Australia; Lodge Amalthea No 914, A. F. & A. Masons of Victoria (Master, 2011–13); St Andrew's First Aid Australia, 2009–; Tullibardine Pipe Band NSW, 2010–; Crown Internat. Dance Assoc., 2011–; Murray Clan of N America, 2015; Patron and Member: St Andrew Soc., Tas; Murray Clan Soc. of Vic and Qld; Co-Patron: Australia Day Council (Victoria) Inc., 2009–. High Comr for Clan Murray in Australia and NZ, 2006–. Past Master: Concord Masonic Lodge, No. 10 Tasmanian Constitution, 1995–96; Devonport Masonic Lodge, No 90 Tasmanian Constitution, 2016–18; Foundn Master, Earl of Dunmore Lodge, No 1686 Victorian Constitution, 2018–19. KStJ 2008. Knight, Imperial and Royal Order of St Stanislaw (Russia), 2012. *Recreations:* flying (retired Tow Master for Soaring Club of Tasmania), astronomy, fly-fishing, music (saxophone and piano). *Heir: b* Hon. Geoffrey Charles Murray [*b* 31 July 1949; *m* 1974, Margaret Irene, *d* of H. Bulloch]. *Address:* PO Box 100E, East Devonport, Tas 7310, Australia. *E:* malc5@bigpond.com. *Clubs:* Devonport Fly Fishing, Soaring Club of Tasmania, Burns Club of Launceston (Tasmania).

**DUNMORE, Stephen Lloyd,** OBE 2011; Chief Executive, Fundraising Regulator, 2016–18; *b* 4 Dec. 1948; *s* of Leslie Alfred Dunmore and Josephine Mary Dunmore (*née* Bettles); *m* 1987, Isabel Mary Robertson; one *d. Educ:* Kettering Grammar Sch.; King's Coll. London (BA Hons Hist.). Urban Archaeol Officer, Ipswich BC, 1974–76; Department of the Environment: Inspector of Ancient Monuments, 1976–84; Principal, Housing, Construction Industry, Inner Cities, 1984–90; on secondment as Actg Chief Exec., Liverpool HAT, 1990–91; Principal, Citizen's Charter Unit, Cabinet Office, 1991; Regl Controller, Urban and Economic Affairs, Merseyside Task Force, 1991–94; Dir, Regeneration, Transport and Planning, Govt Office for Merseyside, 1994–98; Chief Executive: New Opportunities Fund, 1998–2004; Community Fund, 2003–04; Big Lottery Fund, 2004–08; Interim Chief Executive: Responsible Gambling Fund and Responsible Gambling Strategy Bd, 2009–10; Diana, Princess of Wales Meml Fund, 2009 and 2011; Lumos, 2010–11; Family and Childcare Trust, 2015; Chm., Capacitybuilders, 2009–11 (non-exec. Dir, 2008–09); Interim Dir, Transition, Consumer Focus, 2012–13; Chief Exec., Consumer Focus, 2014. Mem., Adv. Body, Office for Civil Society (formerly Office of the Third Sector), 2008–11. Chairman: Nat. Family Mediation, 2007–11; BBC Charity Appeals Adv. Cttee, 2008–13. Trustee: The Prince's Countryside Fund, 2010–17; Soc. of Antiquaries, 2017–. *Recreations:* cricket, books, walking, theatre. *Address:* 37 Pages Hill, N10 1EH. *T:* (020) 8883 3905.

**DUNN, Baroness** *cr* 1990 (Life Peer), of Hong Kong Island in Hong Kong and of Knightsbridge in the Royal Borough of Kensington and Chelsea; **Lydia Selina Dunn,** DBE 1989 (CBE 1983; OBE 1978); non-executive Director, John Swire & Sons Ltd, since 2015 (Executive Director, 1996–2015); *b* 29 Feb. 1940; *d* of Yencheun Yeh Dunn and Chen Yin Chu; *m* 1988, Michael David Thomas, *qv. Educ:* St Paul's Convent Sch., Hong Kong; Univ. of Calif, Berkeley. MLC, Hong Kong, 1976–88 (Sen. Mem., 1985–88); MEC, 1982–95 (Sen. Mem., 1988–95). Director: John Swire & Sons (HK) Ltd, 1978–2003; Swire Pacific Ltd, 1981–2015; Hongkong and Shanghai Banking Corp., 1981–96 (Dep. Chm., 1992–96); HSBC Hldgs plc, 1990–2008 (Dep. Chm., 1992–2008); Volvo AB, 1991–93 (Mem. Internat. Adv. Bd, 1985–91); Christie's Internat. plc, 1996–98; Christie's Fine Art Ltd, 1998–2000; Marconi (formerly GEC) plc, 1997–2002; Advr to Bd, Cathay Pacific Airways Ltd, 1997–2002 (Dir, 1985–97); Mem., Adv. Bd, Christie's Greater China, 2009–17. Chairman: Hong Kong/Japan Business Co-operation Cttee, 1988–95 (Mem., 1983–88); Hong Kong Trade Develt Council, 1983–91; Mem., Hong Kong/US Econ. Co-op. Cttee, 1984–93. Mem., Adv. Council, Confucius Inst. for Business, 2006–16. Chm., Lord Wilson Heritage Trust, 1993–95; Pres., Hong Kong LEP Trust, 1993–. Mem., H of L, 1990–2010. Hon. Fellow, London Business Sch., 2000. Hon. LLD: Chinese Univ. of Hong Kong, 1984; Univ. of Hong Kong, 1991; Univ. of British Columbia, 1991; Leeds Univ., 1994; Hon. DSc Univ. of Buckingham, 1995. Prime Minister of Japan's Trade Award, 1987; USA Sec. of Commerce's To Peace and Commerce Award, 1988. *Publications:* In the Kingdom of the Blind, 1983. *Recreations:* art and antiquities, music, ballet, opera. *Address:* John Swire & Sons Ltd, Swire House, 59 Buckingham Gate, SW1E 6AJ.

**DUNN, Anderson;** Assistant Commissioner, Metropolitan Police, 1994–2001; *b* 6 May 1944; adopted *s* of William Rennie and Wilma Rennie (*née* Turner); *m* 1967, Margaret Docherty; one *s* one *d. Educ:* Queen Mary Coll., London (LLB Hons; Hon. Fellow, QMW, 1998). Joined Metropolitan Police, 1963; transf. to Thames Valley Police as Chief Supt, 1987; Asst Chief Constable, Operations, 1988–93; Dep. Chief Constable, Northants, 1993–94. Former Mem. Bd, Northants Probation Service. *Recreations:* walking, reading, most sports.

**DUNN, David Hedley;** HM Diplomatic Service, retired; Chief Executive Officer, Pendragon Investments, since 2016; *b* 21 Sept. 1968; *s* of Francis Hedley Dunn and Jean Mary Dunn (*née* Osborne). *Educ:* Penrice Comp. Sch.; St Austell Coll. Joined HM Diplomatic Service, 1991; Political Attaché: Oslo, 1992–94; Suva, 1996–97; Third, later Second, Sec., NY, 1997–98; on secondment to UN, 1998–2000; First Sec., Stockholm, 2000–01; Private Sec. to the Minister for Europe, FCO, 2001–03; Dep. High Comr, Freetown, 2004–06; High Comr, Papua New Guinea, 2007–10; Counsellor (Political), FCO, 2011–12. Dir, New Business, Policy and Ext. Affairs, Arwon Capital, 2012–16; Bd Dir, Global Constructions Ltd, 2016–. *Recreations:* Cornish Rugby Union, squash, running, euchre, sea fishing. *E:* daviddunn10000@gmail.com.

**DUNN, Prof. Douglas Eaglesham,** OBE 2003; FRSL; poet and short-story writer; Professor of English, 1991–2008, now Emeritus, and Director, St Andrews Scottish Studies Institute, 1992–2008, St Andrews University; *b* 23 Oct. 1942; *s* of William Douglas Dunn and Margaret McGowan; *m* 1st, 1964, Lesley Balfour Wallace (*d* 1981); 2nd, 1985, Lesley Jane Bathgate; one *s* one *d. Educ:* Univ. of Hull (BA). Became full-time writer, 1971. St Andrews University: Fellow in Creative Writing, 1989–91; Hd, Sch. of English, 1994–99. Hon. Vis. Prof., Dundee Univ., 1987–89. Mem., Scottish Arts Council, 1992–94. FRSL 1981. Hon. Fellow, Humberside Coll., 1987. Hon. LLD Dundee, 1987; Hon. DLitt Hull, 1995. Cholmondeley Award, 1989; Queen's Gold Medal for Poetry, 2013. *Publications:* Terry Street, 1969 (Somerset Maugham Award, 1972); The Happier Life, 1972; (ed) New Poems, 1972–73, 1973; Love or Nothing, 1974 (Geoffrey Faber Meml Prize, 1976); (ed) A Choice of Byron's Verse, 1974; (ed) Two Decades of Irish Writing, 1975 (criticism); (ed) The Poetry of Scotland, 1979; Barbarians, 1979; St Kilda's Parliament, 1981 (Hawthornden Prize, 1982); Europa's Lover, 1982; (ed) A Rumoured City: new poets from Hull, 1982;

(ed) To Build a Bridge: celebration of Humberside in verse, 1982; Elegies, 1985 (Whitbread Poetry Prize, 1985; Whitbread Book of the Year Award, 1986); Secret Villages, 1985 (short stories); Selected Poems 1964–1983, 1986; Northlight, 1988 (poetry); New and Selected Poems 1966–1988, 1989; Andromache, 1990; (ed) The Essential Browning, 1990; (ed) Scotland: an anthology, 1991; (ed) Faber Book of 20th Century Scottish Poetry, 1992; Dante's Drum-Kit, 1993; Boyfriends and Girlfriends, 1995 (short stories); Oxford Book of Scottish Short Stories, 1995; The Donkey's Ears, 2000 (poetry); The Year's Afternoon, 2000 (poetry); New Selected Poems, 2003; The Noise of a Fly, 2017 (poetry); contrib. to Counterblast pamphlet series, Glasgow Herald, New Yorker, TLS, etc. *Recreations:* playing the clarinet and saxophone, listening to jazz music, philately, gardening. *Address:* School of English, St Andrews University, St Andrews, Fife KY16 9AL.

**DUNN, Hubert;** *see* Dunn, His Honour W. H.

**DUNN, Inga Margaret Amy;** *see* Grimsey, I. M. A.

**DUNN, Prof. James Douglas Grant,** PhD, DD; FBA 2006; Lightfoot Professor of Divinity, University of Durham, 1990–2003, now Professor Emeritus; *b* 21 Oct. 1939; *s* of David and Agnes Dunn; *m* 1963, Meta Russell; one *s* two *d. Educ:* Hutchesons' Boys' Grammar Sch., Glasgow; Univ. of Glasgow (MA 1961, BD 1964); Clare Coll., Cambridge (PhD 1968; BD 1976; DD 1991). Chaplain to Overseas Students, Edinburgh, 1968–70; Lectr, 1970–79, Reader, 1979–82, Univ. of Nottingham; Prof. of Divinity, 1982–90, Chm., Dept of Theol., 1984–86 and 1996–99, Univ. of Durham. Sir Derman Christopherson Foundn Fellow, 1999–2000. Numerous invited (named) and vis. lectureships. Ed., New Testament Theol. series (16 vols), 1991–2003. Pres., UK New Testament Conf., 1980–82 and 1992–96. Founder and Chm., Assoc. of Univ. Depts of Theol. and Religious Studies, 1985–92. Vice-Pres. Council, St John's Coll., Durham, 1995–2005 (Hon. Life Fellow, 2007). Pres., SNTS, 2002–03. *Publications:* Baptism in the Holy Spirit, 1970 (trans. Spanish 1977, Russian 2017), 2nd edn 2010; Jesus and the Spirit, 1975 (trans. Spanish 1981); Unity and Diversity in the New Testament, 1977, 3rd edn 2006 (trans. Russian 1997, 2009); Christology in the Making, 1980, 2nd rev. edn 1989; The Evidence for Jesus, 1985 (trans. Dutch 1987); The Living Word, 1987, 2nd edn 2009; (with J. P. Mackey) New Testament Theology in Dialogue, 1987; Word Biblical Commentary, Vol. 38, Romans, 2 vols, 1988; Jesus, Paul and the Law, 1990; The Partings of the Ways between Christianity and Judaism and their Significance for the Character of Christianity, 1991, 2nd edn 2006 (trans. Chinese 2014); Jesus' Call to Discipleship, 1992 (Japanese edn 1996, Spanish edn 2001); Christian Liberty, 1993; The Theology of Paul's Letter to the Galatians, 1993 (Japanese edn 1998); (with A. M. Suggate) The Justice of God, 1993; Epistles to the Colossians and to Philemon, 1996; The Acts of the Apostles, 1996, 2016; The Theology of Paul the Apostle, 1998 (trans. Italian 1999, Korean edn 2003); Christianity in the Making, Vol. 1: Jesus Remembered, 2003 (trans. Italian 2006, Spanish 2009, Korean 2010); (ed) The Cambridge Companion to St Paul, 2003; (Gen. Ed.) Eerdmans Commentary on the Bible, 2003; A New Perspective on Jesus, 2005 (trans. Spanish 2006, Chinese 2007, Russian 2009, Korean 2010, Italian 2011, Portuguese 2013); The New Perspective on Paul: collected essays, 2005, rev. edn 2008 (Portuguese edn 2011, Italian edn 2014); (ed with S. McKnight) The Historical Jesus in Recent Research, 2005; Christianity in the Making, Vol. 2: Beginning from Jerusalem, 2009 (trans. Spanish 2012, Italian 2012); New Testament Theology: an introduction, 2009 (Chinese edn 2012); Did the First Christians Worship Jesus?, 2010 (Spanish edn 2011, Korean edn 2016); Jesus, Paul and the Gospels, 2011 (Italian edn 2012, Spanish and Hungarian edns 2014, Hebrew edn 2015, Portuguese edn 2017); The Oral Gospel Tradition, 2013; Christianity in the Making, Vol. 3: Neither Jew Nor Greek: a contested identity, 2015 (Spanish edn 2018); (ed) Fundamentalism: threats and ideologies in the modern world, 2015; Who was Jesus?, 2016 (Swedish edn 2018); Why Believe in Jesus' Resurrection?, 2016 (Swedish edn 2018); Jesus according to the New Testament, 2019; contrib. numerous articles to jls, Festschriften, symposia and dictionaries. *Recreations:* local preaching, writing and reading, sudoku, visiting new places, checking out The Good Pub Guide, grandparental duties. *Address:* 65 Maplehurst Road, Chichester, W Sussex PO19 6RP. *T:* (01243) 527857. *E:* jdgdunn39@gmail.com.

**DUNN, Prof. John Montfort,** FBA 1989; Professor of Political Theory, University of Cambridge, 1987–2007, now Emeritus; Fellow of King's College, Cambridge, since 1966; *b* 9 Sept. 1940; *s* of Col. Henry George Montfort Dunn and Catherine Mary Dunn; *m* 1st, 1965, Susan Deborah Fyvel (marr. diss. 1971); 2nd, 1973, Judith Frances Bernal (*see* J. F. Dunn) (marr. diss. 1987); one *s* (and one *s* decd) by Prof. Heather Joan Glen; 3rd, 1997, Ruth Ginette Scurr, *qv* (marr. diss. 2013); two *d*; 4th, 2015, Anastasia Piliavsky; one *d. Educ:* Winchester Coll.; King's Coll., Cambridge (BA 1962). Harkness Fellow, Graduate Sch. of Arts and Sciences, Harvard Univ., 1964–65; Official Fellow in History, Jesus Coll., Cambridge, 1965–66; Dir of Studies in History, King's Coll., Cambridge, 1966–72; Lectr in Pol Science, 1972–77, Reader in Politics, 1977–87, Cambridge Univ. Vis. Lectr, Dept of Pol Science, Univ. of Ghana, 1968–69; Visiting Professor: Dept of Civics and Politics, Univ. of Bombay, 1979–80; Faculty of Law, Tokyo Metropolitan Univ., 1983–84; Chiba Univ., Japan, 2007–09; Distinguished Vis. Prof., Murphy Inst. of Pol Economy, Tulane Univ., New Orleans, 1986; Benjamin Evans Lippincott Dist. Prof., Minnesota Univ., 1990; Olmsted Vis. Prof., 1991, Leitner Vis. Prof. in Political Sci. and Internat. Affairs, 2008, Henry L. Stimson Lectr and Vis. Prof., 2011, Yale Univ. Foreign Hon. Mem., Amer. Acad. of Arts and Scis, 1991. Hon. Pres., Eur. Soc. for Hist. of Political Thought, 2014. Mem., Bd of Consultants, Kim Dae-Jung Peace Foundn for the Asia-Pacific Region, 1994–2002. Mem. Council, British Acad., 2004–07. FAcSS (AcSS 2009). FRSA 1993. Sir Isaiah Berlin Prize, British Political Studies Assoc., 2007. *Publications:* The Political Thought of John Locke, 1969; Modern Revolutions, 1972; Dependence and Opportunity: political change in Ahafo, 1973; (ed) West African States: failure and promise, 1978; Western Political Theory in the Face of the Future, 1979; Political Obligation in its Historical Context, 1980; Locke, 1984, rev. edn as Locke: A Very Short Introduction, 2003; The Politics of Socialism, 1984; Rethinking Modern Political Theory, 1985; (ed) The Economic Limits to Modern Politics, 1989; (ed) Contemporary West African States, 1989; Interpreting Political Responsibility, 1990; (ed) Democracy: the unfinished journey, 1992; Contemporary Crisis of the Nation State?, 1995; The History of Political Theory, 1995; (ed with Ian Harris) Great Political Thinkers, 20 vols, 1997; The Cunning of Unreason: making sense of politics, 2000; Pensare la politica, 2002; Setting the People Free: the story of democracy, 2005; (jtly) Exploring Utopian Futures of Politics, 2008; Breaking Democracy's Spell, 2014. *Address:* King's College, Cambridge CB2 1ST. *T:* (01223) 529223.

**DUNN, Prof. Judith Frances,** PhD; FBA 1996; FMedSci; Research Professor, Social, Genetic and Developmental Psychiatry Research Centre, Institute of Psychiatry, Psychology and Neuroscience (formerly Institute of Psychiatry), King's College London, 1995–2012; *d* of James Pace and Jean Stewart; *m* 1st, 1961, Martin Gardiner Bernal (marr. diss.); 2nd, 1973, John Montfort Dunn, *qv* (marr. diss. 1987); 3rd, 1987, Robert Plomin, *qv. Educ:* New Hall, Cambridge (BA 1962; MA 1968); King's Coll., Cambridge (PhD 1982). MRC Develt and Integration of Behaviour Unit, and Fellow, King's Coll., Cambridge, 1978–86; Evan Pugh Professor of Human Develt, Pennsylvania State Univ., 1986–95. FMedSci 2000. *Publications:* (jtly) First Year of Life: psychological and medical implications of early experience, 1979; (jtly) Siblings: love, envy and understanding, 1982; Sisters and Brothers, 1984; (ed with R. Plomin) Study of Temperament: changes, continuities and challenges, 1986; Beginnings of Social Understanding, 1988; (jtly) Separate Lives, 1990; (ed jtly) Children's Sibling Relationships, 1992; Young Children's Close Relationships, 1993; (ed jtly) Stepfamilies, 1994; (ed) Connections between Emotion and Understanding in Development, 1995; From One Child to Two, 1995; Children's Friendships, 2004; (ed with R. Layard) A Good Childhood, 2009.

**DUNN, Martin;** Co-owner, StreetSmartVideo.com, since 2011; *b* 26 Jan. 1955. *Educ:* Dudley Grammar Sch., Worcs. Dudley Herald, 1974–77; Birmingham Evening Mail, 1977; Birmingham Post, 1978; Daily Mail, 1978–79; freelance journalist, 1979–83; New York Correspondent, The Sun, 1983–84; The Sun, London, 1984–88; Deputy Editor: News of the World, 1988–89; The Sun, 1989–91; Editor: Today, 1991–93; The Boston Herald, 1993; Editor-in-Chief, The New York Daily News, 1993–96, 2003–10; Editor, Channel One Television, 1996–98; Managing Director: DMG New Media, 1998–2000; DMG Front of Mind Ltd, 2000–03. *Recreations:* running, golf.

**DUNN, Nicola Ann, (Nicky),** OBE 2016; Managing Director, IMD Group, since 2011; Director, London Legacy Development Corporation, since 2012; *b* Liverpool, 23 Jan. 1957; *d* of William Scott Dunn and Joan Phyllis Dunn. *Educ:* Fareham Girls' Grammar Sch.; Dorset House Coll., Oxford. Occupational therapist: Knowle Hosp., 1978–79; Torrance Meml Hosp., Calif, 1979–82; London Hosp., 1982–84; Founder and Owner, Yard Fitness Centre, 1984–88; London Arena: Event Coordinator, 1988–90; Ops Dir, 1990–91; Arena Dir, 1991–94; Commercial Dir, 1994–2000; Chief Exec., Odyssey Arena, Belfast, 2000–10. Member, Board: Ticket ABC, 2013–16; Young Vic Th., 2017–. Chair: Titanic Foundn, 2012–; E20 Stadium, 2013–; Netball World Cup 2019, 2016–; Jockey Club Live, 2017–; Mem. Bd, Princes Trust (NI), 2007–11; Trustee, Lyric Th., Belfast, 2009–16. *Recreations:* walking, yoga, gardening, friends, family, walking Trevor the dog. *Address:* 38 Flanders Road, W4 1NG. *E:* enquiries@imdgroup.co.uk. *Club:* Soho House.

**DUNN, Most Rev. Patrick James;** *see* Auckland (NZ), Bishop of, (RC).

**DUNN, Paula,** MBE 2019; Paralympic Head Coach, UK Athletics, since 2012; *b* Bradford, Yorks, 2 Dec. 1964; *d* of Kenneth and Hyacinth Louise Dunn; two *s. Educ:* Whalley Range High Sch. for Girls; Wythenshawe Coll. of Further Educn; Open Univ. (Dip. Public Admin; Dip. Social Scis). UK Athletics: Nat. Talent ID Manager, 2001–05; Talent Develt Manager, 2005–09; Paralympic Performance Transition Manager, 2009–12. Hon. Dr Manchester, 1998. *Recreations:* reading, family time. *Address:* National Performance Institute, High Performance Athletics Centre Athletics Track, Loughborough University, Loughborough LE11 3TU. *T:* 07718 526362. *E:* pdunn@uka.org.uk. *Club:* Trafford Athletics.

**DUNN, Rosamund Mary;** Chief Executive, Thames Gateway London Partnership, 2008–12; *b* 10 June 1952; *d* of Stelio Democratis and Grace Matchette; *m* 1st, 1975, Patrick Dunn (marr. diss. 2007); three *d*; 2nd, 2008, David Simon Lunts. *Educ:* Univ. of Hull (BA Hons Philosophy). HM Treasury: Head: Resource Accounting and Budgeting Team, 1995–2000; Devolved Countries and Regions Team, 2000–04; Dir, Strategy and Corporate Planning, London Develt Agency, 2004–06; Department for Communities and Local Government: Dir, Thames Gateway Strategy, 2006; Dir, Local Develt and Renewal, 2007–08; Mem., Homes and Communities Agency Set Up Team, 2008. Ind. Chair, S Kilburn Trust, 2012–. *Recreations:* theatre, cinema, socialising, holidays in France and Scotland. *Address:* Flat 20, The Old Fire Station, 46 Renfrew Road, SE11 4NA. *E:* dunnros@aol.com.

**DUNN, Shona Hunter;** Second Permanent Secretary, Home Office, since 2018; *b* Catterick, 15 Oct. 1969; *d* of William James and Patricia Nielson Dunn; *m* 2009, Simon Gerald Lamb; two *s* one *d. Educ:* Birmingham Univ. (BSc Biol.); Durham Univ. (MSc Ecol.). Policy advr, DoE, 1995–98; Asst Private Sec. to Dep. Prime Minister, DETR, 1998–2000; Head: Internat. and Central Policy, ODPM, 2002–04; of Policy, Westminster CC, 2005–06 (on secondment); Department for Communities and Local Government: Dep. Dir, Sustainable Buildings, 2007–08; Dir, Fire and Resilience, 2008–11; Dir, Planning, 2011–13; Dir Gen., Educn Standards, DFE, 2013–16; Dir Gen., Economic and Domestic Affairs Secretariat, Cabinet Office, 2016–18. Dir, Skills for Justice, 2009–11. *Recreations:* travel, reading, music (listening and playing), spending time with friends and family. *Address:* Home Office, 2 Marsham Street, SW1P 4DF.

**DUNN, Dr Stephen Phillip,** CBE 2019; Chief Executive Officer, West Suffolk Foundation Trust, since 2014; *b* Warrington, 15 Sept. 1972; *s* of Harry Dunn and Lynn Dunn; *m* 2000, Lucy; two *s* one *d. Educ:* Culcheth High Sch., Warrington; Leeds Univ. Business Sch. (BA Hons Econs 1994; MA Econs 1996; PhD Econs 2001). Mktg Asst (internship), Thurnall Engrg plc, 1991–93; University of Leeds: Lectr, Tutor and Res. Asst, 1994–97; Sen. Subwarden, Bodington Hall, 1995–99; Department of Health: Fast Stream Economist, 1997–99; Econ. Advr, 1999–2001; Econ. Advr, Wanless Rev., on secondment to HM Treasury, 2000–02; Strategy Advr, Strategy Unit, 2000–02; Dep. Dir, Foundn Trust Unit, 2002–03; Sen. Strategy Advr, Strategy Unit, 2004–05; Hd of Policy, Our Care, Our Say White Paper, 2005–06; Sen. Strategy Advr, Strategy Unit, 2006–07; Dir, Strategy and Provider Develt, NHS East of England, 2007–11; Dir, Policy and Strategy, NHS Midlands and East, 2011–13; Dir, Delivery and Develt, NHS Trust Develt Authy, 2012–14. Sen. Res. Fellow, Staffordshire Univ., 2000–02; Commonwealth Fund Harkness Vis. Fellow, Sch. of Business, Stanford Univ., 2003–04; Visiting Professor: Health Policy, LSE, 2014–16; Econs, UWE, 2014–18. Non-executive Director: Bright Stars Charity, 2017–; HelpForce CIC, 2018–. Mem. Council, St Edmundsbury Cathedral, 2017–. *Publications:* The 'Uncertain' Foundations of a Post Keynesian Economics, 2008; The Economics of John Kenneth Galbraith, 2011; John Kenneth Galbraith: the economic legacy, 4 vols, 2012; over 50 papers in jls on health policy, Keynesian econs and econs of the firm. *Recreations:* painting, tennis, running, squash, football, cricket. *Address:* West Suffolk Foundation Trust, West Suffolk Hospital, Hardwick Land, Bury St Edmunds, Suffolk IP31 3NN. *T:* (01284) 713013. *E:* stephen.dunn@wsh.nhs.uk. *W:* www.twitter.com/SteveDunnCEO.

**DUNN, William Francis N.;** *see* Newton Dunn.

**DUNN, His Honour (William) Hubert;** QC 1982; a Circuit Judge, 1993–2005, a Senior Circuit Judge, 2000–2005; Chief Immigration Adjudicator, 1998–2001; *b* 8 July 1933; *s* of William Patrick Millar Dunn and Isabel (*née* Thompson); *m* 1971, Maria Henriqueta Theresa d'Arouje Perestrello de Moser (*d* 2018); one *s* one *d. Educ:* Rockport, Co. Down, N Ireland; Winchester Coll.; New Coll., Oxford (Hons degree PPE) (Half-Blue fencing 1954–55). 2nd Lieut, Life Guards, 1956–57; Household Cavalry Reserve of Officers, 1957–64. Cholmondeley Scholar, Lincoln's Inn, 1958, called to Bar, 1958; Bencher, Lincoln's Inn, 1990. A Recorder, 1980–93. Fellow, Soc. for Advanced Legal Studies, 1998. *Recreations:* travel, literature. *Address:* 207 Ashley Gardens, Emery Hill Street, SW1P 1PA. *Club:* Boodle's.

**DUNNE, Very Rev. Dermot Patrick Martin;** Dean of Christ Church Cathedral, Dublin, since 2008; *b* Portarlington, Co. Laois, 25 March 1959; *s* of late Michael Dunne and of Brigid Dunne (*née* Whelan); *m* 1996, Celia Dorothy, *d* of late James Burl and Dorothy Burl (*née* Smith). *Educ:* Pontifical Univ., Maynooth (Dip. Phil. 1980; DipTh 1983); Church of

Ireland Theol Coll.; Chiron Centre for Integrative Psychotherapy (Cert. Psychotherapy 1995); Dublin City Univ. (BA 2004; MA 2014). Ordained deacon, 1983, priest, 1984, Church of Ireland priest, 1998; various posts in RC Church, 1983–95; Dean's Vicar, Christ Church Cathedral, Dublin, 1999–2001; Rector, Crosspatrick Gp of Parishes, Dio. of Ferns, 2001–08; Precentor, Ferns Cathedral, 2004–08; Archdeacon of Ferns, 2007–08. Warden, Cashel and Ossory Guild of Lay Readers, 2007–. *Address:* The Deanery, Werburgh Street, Dublin 8, DO8 WTCO, Ireland. *T:* (office) (1) 6778099. *E:* dean@christchurch.ie.

**DUNNE, Sir Martin,** KCVO 2013; Lord-Lieutenant of Warwickshire, 1997–2013; *b* 30 March 1938; *s* of Philip Dunne, MC and Margaret Dunne (*née* Walker); *m* 1964, Alicia Juliet Barclay; three *d*. *Educ:* Eton; Christ Church, Oxford. High Sheriff, 1982–83, JP 1984, DL 1993, Warwicks.
*See also* Sir T. R. Dunne.

**DUNNE, Nicholas Cosmo Edward;** Executive Chairman, G. Heywood Hill Ltd, since 2011; *b* Oxford, 21 June 1970; *s* of Sir Thomas (Raymond) Dunne, *qv*; *m* 2003, Lady Jasmine Cavendish, *d* of Duke of Devonshire, *qv*; three *s*. *Educ:* Eton Coll.; Univ. of Manchester (BSocSci 1992). Shipbroker, Clarkson, 1993–96; Consultant, Batey Burn, 1996–97; Asst, Enigma Productions, 2002–03; Communications Consultant, Quiller Consultants, 2003–11. Non-exec. Dir, G. Heywood Hill Ltd, 2003–11. *Recreations:* old books, new music. *Address:* G. Heywood Hill Ltd, 10 Curzon Street, W1J 5HH. *T:* (020) 7493 3742. *E:* enquiries@heywoodhill.com. *Club:* Pratt's.

**DUNNE, Rt Hon. Philip (Martin);** PC 2019; MP (C) Ludlow, since 2005; *b* 14 Aug. 1958; *s* of Sir Thomas Raymond Dunne, *qv*; *m* 1989, Domenica Margaret Anne Fraser; two *s* two *d*. *Educ:* Eton Coll.; Keble Coll., Oxford (BA 1980; MA 2006). S. G. Warburg & Co. Ltd, 1980–88; Dir, Corp. Develt, James Gulliver Associates, 1988–90; Partner, Phoenix Securities, 1991–97; a Man. Dir, Donaldson, Lufkin & Jenrette, 1997–2001; Dir, Business Develt, 2002–05, non-exec. Dir, 2006–09, Ruffer LLP. Co-founder, Dir, 1987–97, non-exec. Chm., 1997–2006, Ottakar's plc; non-exec. Chm., Baronsmead VCT 4 plc, 2001–10. Partner, Gatley Farms, 1987–. Mem. (C), S Shropshire DC, 2001–07. Asst Opposition Whip, 2008–10; Asst Govt Whip, 2010–12; Parly Under-Sec. of State (Minister for Defence Equipt, Sci. and Technol.), 2012–15, Minister of State (Minister for Defence Procurement), 2015–16, MoD; Minister of State, DoH, 2016–18. Member: Work and Pensions Select Cttee, 2005–06; Public Accounts Cttee, 2006–08; Treasury Select Cttee, 2007–08. Dep. Chm., Internat. Office, Cons. Party, 2008–10; Gov. (C) Westminster Foundn for Democracy, 2008–10. Dir, Juvenile Diabetes Res. Foundn, 1999–2005. *Address:* (office) 54 Broad Street, Ludlow, Shropshire SY8 1GP; House of Commons, SW1A 0AA.
*See also* N. C. E. Dunne.

**DUNNE, Sir Thomas (Raymond),** KG 2008; KCVO 1995; JP; retired farmer; Lord-Lieutenant for Herefordshire, 1998–2008, and for Worcestershire, 1998–2001 (Lord-Lieutenant, County of Hereford and Worcester, 1977–98); *b* 24 Oct. 1933; *s* of Philip Dunne, MC, and Margaret Walker; *m* 1957, Henrietta Crawley; two *s* two *d*. *Educ:* Eton; RMA Sandhurst. Served Army, 1951–59: Royal Horse Guards. Herefordshire CC, 1962–68. President: 3 Counties Agric. Soc., 1977; W Midlands TA Assoc., 1988–98; National Vice Pres., Royal British Legion, 1982–89. Mem., West Mercia Police Authy, 1980–99; Dir, West Regional Bd, Central TV, 1981–92. Chm., Lord-Lieutenants' Assoc., 2001–08. Chm., Hereford Cathedral Council, 2001–14. Trustee: Dyson Perrins Mus. Trust, 1980–2008; Worcester Mus. of Porcelain, 1980–2007 (Chm., 1984–2000). Hon. Colonel: 4th Worcester and Sherwood Foresters (formerly 2nd Mercian Volunteers), 1987–93; 5th Bn LI, 1993–98. High Sheriff 1970, DL 1973, Herefordshire; JP Hereford and Worcester, 1977. Hon. Fellow, Univ. of Worcester, 2008. KStJ 1978. *E:* goathollow@trippleton.com.
*See also* Sir M. Dunne, N. C. E. Dunne, Rt Hon. P. M. Dunne.

**DUNNELL, Dame Karen (Hope),** DCB 2009; National Statistician and Chief Executive, Office for National Statistics, 2005–09; *b* 16 June 1946; *d* of Richard Henry Williamson and Winifred May Beeching; *m* 1st, 1969, Keith Malvern Dunnell (marr. diss. 1976); 2nd, 1979, Prof. Michael William Adler, *qv* (marr. diss. 1994); two *d*. *Educ:* Bedford Coll., London (BSc Sociology 1967); MA Oxon, 1987. Res. Officer, Inst. of Community Studies, 1967–71; Lectr, St Thomas's Hosp. Med. Sch., 1971–74; Office of Population Censuses and Surveys, then Office for National Statistics, 1974–2009: Dep. Dir, 2000–02, Actg Dir, 2001–02, of Social Stats; Exec. Dir of Surveys and Admin. Sources, 2002–05; Registrar Gen. for England and Wales, 2005–08. Non-exec. Mem., Public Interest Body, PricewaterhouseCoopers, 2010–15. Vis. Fellow, Nuffield Coll., Oxford, 1987–95 and 2008–16; Vis. Prof., LSHTM, 1999–. Trustee, Nat. Heart Forum, 2009–14. Gov., Univ. of Westminster, 2012–. *Publications:* (with Ann Cartwright) Medicine Takers, Prescribers and Hoarders, 1972; Family Formation 1976, 1979; Nurses Working in the Community, 1982. *Recreations:* yoga, reading modern novels and biography, small house in South of France. *Address:* 53 Woodsome Road, NW5 1SA. *E:* karen.dunnell@btinternet.com.

**DUNNETT, Anthony Gordon,** CBE 2004; Co-Founder and Managing Director: Quality Medicines for All, since 2015; VAC Solar UK, since 2016; *b* 17 June 1953; *s* of Peter Sydney Dunnett and Margaret Eileen (*née* Johnson); *m* 1975, Ruth Elizabeth Barker; one *s* one *d*. *Educ:* St Dunstan's Coll.; McGill Univ. (BComm, DipCS); Exeter Univ. (MA Econs). FCIB 1981. Nat. Westminster Bank, 1975–77; Royal Bank of Canada, Montreal, 1977–80 and 1982–86, Curaçao, 1980–82; Midland Bank: Corporate Banking Dir, 1986–88; Corporate Banking Dir, Samuel Montagu, 1988–89; Corporate Dir, 1990–91; Finance Dir, Corporate and Instnl Banking, 1991–94; Dir, Industrial Develt Unit, DTI, 1994–96; Chief Executive: English Partnerships, 1996–98; SEEDA, 1999–2003. Chairman: Two-Five-Four-0 LLP, 2004–07; Esteem Resource Network, 2011–15 (Mem. Bd, 2011–15). Member: Steering Bd, Insolvency Service, 1994–96; Urban Task Force, 1998–2005; Adv. Bd, Relationships Foundn, 2000–09; Bd, Berks Learning and Skills Council, 2001–05; non-exec. Mem., Audit and Risk Assessment Cttee, DFID, 2018–. Director: Countryside Maritime, 1997–2004; Citylife Ltd, 2001–06. President: Internat. Health Partners (UK) Ltd, 2004–15; Internat. Health Partners Inc. (Dir, 2007–15); Member, Board: Health Partners Internat. of Canada, 2010–15; Mercy Ships, 2012– (Vice Chair, 2018–); non-exec. Dir, Mercy Ships Internat., 2018–. Mem., Mgt Bd, Kingsmead Homes, 1997–99. Trustee, RCPCH, 2016–. Mem., Wadhurst Parish Council, 2012–18. Mem., PCC for St Peter and St Paul's Ch, Wadhurst, 1990–. FRSA 1997; MInstD 1999. Hon. FRCOG 2012. *Recreations:* local church, gardening, theatre, opera, sports. *Address:* Shepherds Fold, Beech Hill, Wadhurst, E Sussex TN5 6JR.

**DUNNETT, Maj. Graham Thomas,** TD 1964; JP; Lord-Lieutenant of Caithness, 1995–2004; *b* 8 March 1929; *s* of late Daniel Dunnett and Elizabeth E. Macadie, Wick; *m* 1963, Catherine Elizabeth Sinclair, Westerdale (*d* 2015); three *s*. *Educ:* Wick High Sch.; Archbishop Holgate's Grammar Sch., York. 1st Seaforth Highlanders, Malaya, 1948–51; 11th Seaforth Highlanders, Caithness, 1951–71; Major and Company Comdr, 1964. DL 1975, Vice Lord-Lieutenant 1986, JP 1996, Caithness. *Recreations:* gardening, walking, country dancing. *Address:* Cathel Sheiling, Loch Calder, Thurso, Caithness KW14 7YH. *T:* (01847) 871220.

**DUNNETT, John Jacob, (Jack);** President, Football League, 1981–86 and 1988–89 (Member, Management Committee, 1977–89); *b* 24 June 1922; *m* 1951; two *s* three *d*. *Educ:* Whitgift Middle Sch., Croydon; Downing Coll., Cambridge (BA 1947; LLB 1949; MA 1950; LLM 1989). Served with Cheshire Regt, 1941–46 (Capt.). Admitted Solicitor, 1949. Middlesex CC, 1958–61; Councillor, Enfield Borough Council, 1958–61; Alderman, Enfield Borough Council, 1961–63; Councillor, Greater London Council, 1964–67. MP (Lab) Central Nottingham, 1964–74, Nottingham East, 1974–83; former PPS to: Minister of State, FCO; Minister of Transport. Mem. FA Council, 1977–89, Vice-Pres., 1981–86, 1988–89; Mem., Football Trust, 1982–89; Chm., Notts County FC, 1968–87; Vice-Chm., Portsmouth FC, 1989–90. *Recreation:* watching professional football.

**DUNNETT, Stephen Bruce,** DSc; Professor, School of Biosciences, Cardiff University, 2005–16, now Emeritus (Cardiff Professorial Research Fellow, 2000–05); *b* 28 Jan. 1950; *s* of Peter Sidney Dunnett and Margaret Eileen Dunnett (*née* Johnson); *m* 1984, Dr Sarah-Jane Richards. *Educ:* Eltham Coll.; Churchill Coll., Cambridge (BA Hons 1972; MA 1976; PhD 1981; DSc 1999); Poly. of N London (Dip in Social Work, CQSW 1976); Birkbeck Coll., Univ. of London (BSc Hons 1978). Social worker, London Borough of Southwark, 1972–78; research student, Churchill Coll., Cambridge, 1978–81; Fellow, Clare Coll., Cambridge, 1981–99; Department of Experimental Psychology, University of Cambridge: Wellcome Trust Mental Health Res. Fellow, 1982–83; Demonstrator, 1983–86; Lectr, 1986–95; Reader in Neurobiology, 1995–99; Dir, Scientific Progs, MRC Cambridge Centre for Brain Repair, 1992–99. Vis. Scientist, Univ. of Lund, Sweden, 1981–82. FMedSci 2003 (Mem. Council, 2013–16); FLSW 2011. Spearman Medal, BPsS, 1988; Alfred Meyer Medal, British Neuropathol Soc., 1998. *Publications:* (ed with S.-J. Richards) Neural Transplantation: from molecular basis to clinical application, 1990; (ed with A. Björklund): Neural Transplantation: a practical approach, 1992; Functional Neural Transplantation, 1994, Functional Neural Transplantation II, 2000, Functional Neural Transplantation III (Pts 1 and 2), 2012, Functional Neural Transplantation IV, 2017; (with R. A. Barker) Neural Repair, Transplantation and Rehabilitation, 1999; (ed jtly) Neural Transplantation Methods, 2000; (jtly) Brain Damage, Brain Repair, 2001; Dopamine, 2005; Dopamine Handbook, 2010; Animal Models of Movement Disorders (2 vols), 2011; (ed jtly) Methods in Molecular Biology: Huntington's Disease, 2018; ed jtly over 700 research papers on topics of brain function, animal models of neurodegenerative disease and neural transplantation. *Recreations:* flying, food and wine, France. *Address:* School of Biosciences, Cardiff University, Museum Avenue, Cardiff CF10 3AX. *Club:* Royal Society of Medicine.

**DUNNING, Geoffrey William;** Director, Geoff Dunning Ltd, 2014–16; *b* Pannal, 28 Nov. 1950; *s* of Oswald Dunning and May Dunning; *m* 1980, Sandra June King; two *d*. *Educ:* Harrogate Grammar Sch. Sales Rep., Ringways Garages, Leeds, 1972–75; Asst Regl Sec., Freight Transport Assoc., 1975–87; Road Haulage Association Ltd: Dist Manager, 1987–94; Regl Dir, 1994–2009; Chief Exec., 2009–14. *Recreations:* failing to stay out of trouble, manufacture of invisibility cloaks, being as good a friend, father and husband as possible, collecting mild versions of what can be serious illnesses. *T:* 07979 531470.

**DUNNING, Graham;** QC 2001; *b* 13 March 1958; *s* of late Maj. James E. Dunning and Jane P. Dunning (*née* Hunt); *m* 1986, Claire Abigael Williams; three *s* one *d*. *Educ:* King Edward VI Sch., Southampton; Emmanuel Coll., Cambridge (MA); Harvard Law Sch. (LLM). Called to the Bar, Lincoln's Inn, 1982, Bencher, 2009; joined Essex Court Chambers, 1983; in practice at commercial bar as internat. arbitrator, 1983–; Co-Head of Chambers, 2013–17. *Recreations:* travel, ski-ing, golf. *Address:* Essex Court Chambers, 24 Lincoln's Inn Fields, WC2A 3EG. *T:* (020) 7813 8000. *Clubs:* Woking Golf; Rye Golf.

**DUNNING, Sir Simon (William Patrick),** 3rd Bt *cr* 1930; *b* 14 Dec. 1939; *s* of Sir William Leonard Dunning, 2nd Bt, and Kathleen Lawrie (*d* 1992), *d* of J. P. Cuthbert, MC; S father, 1961; *m* 1975, Frances Deirdre Morton (*d* 2016), *d* of Major Patrick Lancaster; one *d*. *Educ:* Eton. *Address:* Low Auchengillan, Blanefield, by Glasgow G63 9AU. *T:* (01360) 770323. *Club:* Turf.

**DUNNINGTON-JEFFERSON, Sir John Alexander,** 3rd Bt *cr* 1958, of Thorganby Hall, East Riding of Yorks; *b* 23 March 1980; *o s* of Sir Mervyn Stewart Dunnington-Jefferson, 2nd Bt and of Caroline Anna Dunnington-Jefferson (*née* Bayley), S father, 2014; *m* 2011, Joanna Margaret Rothwell Lee; two *s* one *d*. Heir: *s* James Mervyn Rothwell Dunnington-Jefferson, *b* 13 May 2015.

**DUNROSSIL,** 3rd Viscount *cr* 1959; **Andrew William Reginald Morrison;** Director, Brundage Management Company, San Antonio, Texas, since 1990; *b* 15 Dec. 1953; *e s* of 2nd Viscount Dunrossil, CMG and of Mavis Dawn (*née* Spencer-Payne); S father, 2000; *m* 1st, 1986, Carla Marie Brundage (marr. diss. 2010); one *s* three *d*; 2nd, 2012, Mary Shell Conoly Koontz Somoza. *Educ:* Eton (KS); University Coll., Oxford (BA Lit Hum). FCO, 1978–79; Kleinwort Benson Ltd, 1979–89. Chairman: Amer. Financial Services Assoc., 2007–08; Nat. Inst. of Consumer Credit Mgt. Hon. British Consul, San Antonio, Texas, 2004–. Chm., Soc. of Scottish Armigers, 2012– (Vice Chm., 2011). Member: Standing Council of Scottish Chiefs, 2012–; Adv. Bd, Council of Scottish Clans and Assocs, 2015–. Dist. Service Award, Amer. Financial Services Assoc., 2005. Hon. Patron, American-Scottish Foundn, 2018–. *Recreations:* clan history, theology, poetry, sports. Heir: *s* Hon. Callum Alasdair Brundage Morrison, *b* 12 July 1994. *Address:* 410 Patterson Avenue, San Antonio, TX 78209, USA. *T:* (office) (210) 7359393. *Clubs:* Argyle (San Antonio); Withington Cricket (Glos).

**DUNSANY,** 21st Baron of, *cr* 1439; **Randal Plunkett;** *b* 9 March 1983; *er s* of 20th Baron of Dunsany and of Maria Alice Villela de Carvalho; S father, 2011. Heir: *b* Hon. Oliver Plunkett, *b* 26 Sept. 1985.

**DUNSMORE, Rev. Barry William;** Minister, Cathedral Church of St Machar, Aberdeen, since 2015; *b* 27 Jan. 1954; *s* of late William Dunsmore and of Mildred Dunsmore (*née* Laing); *m* 1978, Dr Hilda Burns; one *s* one *d*. *Educ:* Hillhead High Sch., Glasgow; Univ. of Glasgow (MA, BD). Post-grad. res., Univ. of Nairobi, 1980–81; ordained and inducted, Erskine Ch, Saltcoats, 1982; inducted: St Columba's Ch, Stirling, 1988; Presbytery Clerk, Presbytery of Stirling, 1994–2000; Minister: St Columba's Ch of Scotland, Pont Street, London, linked with St Andrew's, Newcastle, 2000–09; Christ Ch, Warwick, Bermuda, 2009–15; Vice-Convener, Ch of Scotland Bd of Ministry, 2003–05. *Publications:* Challenge, Comfort, Forgiveness and Welcome (book of sermons), 2007. *Recreations:* golf, music, travel. *Address:* 39 Woodstock Road, Aberdeen AB15 5EX.

**DUNSTAN, Very Rev. Gregory John Orchard;** Dean of Armagh, since 2011; Prebendary of Swords, St Patrick's Cathedral, Dublin, since 2007; *b* Abingdon, 17 Oct. 1950; *s* of Gordon Dunstan and Ruby, (Ruth), Dunstan. *Educ:* Westminster Sch.; Clare Coll., Cambridge (BA 1972); Univ. of Newcastle upon Tyne (Dip. Landscape Design 1974); Trinity Coll., Dublin (BTh 1990). Asst Landscape Architect to Mary Mitchell, 1974–77; Landscape Architect, Brady Shipman Martin, Dublin, 1977–87; ordained deacon, 1990, priest, 1991; Curate, St Patrick's, Ballymena, 1990–93; Rector, St Matthew's, Shankill, Belfast, 1993–2011; Keeper, Armagh Public Liby, 2011–18. *Recreations:* cycling, walking, music, gardening. *Address:* Library House, 43 Abbey Street, Armagh BT61 7DY. *T:* (028) 3752 3142, (home) (028) 3751 8447. *E:* gregory.dunstan@btinternet.com.

**DUNSTAN, Tessa Jane**; Director, Legal Services A, Department of Trade and Industry, 2001–04; retired; Appeal Officer for community interest companies, 2006–11; *b* 18 July 1944; *d* of Alfred Thomas Fripp and Kathleen Jennie (*née* Kimpton); *m* 1973, Richard James Rowley Dunstan; two *s* two *d. Educ*: Convent of the Sacred Heart, Woldingham, Surrey; Lady Margaret Hall, Oxford (MA). Called to the Bar, Middle Temple, 1967; Legal Asst, Solicitor's Office, BoT, 1968; Sen. Legal Asst, Solicitor's Office, DTI, 1973–84; Legal Advr, Office of Telecommunications; 1984–87; Solicitor's Office/Legal Department, Department of Trade and Industry, 1987–2000: Investigations Div., 1989–98; Grade 3, Dir Legal Services D, 1998–2001; Legal Project Dir (Co. Law Review), Legal Services, DTI, 2001. *Recreations*: opera, travel, gardening. *Address*: Shalesbrook, Forest Row, Sussex RH18 5LS. *T*: (01342) 823079.

**DUNSTONE, Sir Charles**, Kt 2012; CVO 2015; Executive Chairman, TalkTalk Telecom Group, since 2017 (Founder, 1989, Chief Executive Officer, 1989–2010, The Carphone Warehouse; non-executive Chairman, TalkTalk Telecom Group, 2010–17); Chairman, 2010–17, Senior Adviser, since 2017, Dixons Carphone (formerly The Carphone Warehouse Group); *b* 21 Nov. 1964; *s* of Denis and Anne Dunstone; *m* 2009, Celia Gordon Shute; one *s* two *d. Educ*: Uppingham Sch. Sales Manager, Communications Div., NEC, 1985–89. Non-executive Director: Halifax, 2000–01; HBOS, 2001–08; Daily Mail & Gen. Trust. Chairman: Prince's Trust, 2009–15; Trustees, Royal Museums Greenwich, 2013–. *Recreation*: sailing. *Address*: TalkTalk Telecom Group, 11 Evesham Street, W11 4AR. *Clubs*: Royal Ocean Racing, Royal Thames Yacht; Royal Yacht Squadron (Cowes).

**DUNT, Vice Adm. Sir John (Hugh)**, KCB 1998; CEng, FIET; Chief of Fleet Support and Member, Admiralty Board, 1997–2000; *b* 14 Aug. 1944; *s* of Harris Hugh Dunt and Margaret Rea Dunt (*née* Morgan); *m* 1972, Alynne Margaret Wood; two *d. Educ*: Duke of York Sch., Nairobi; RNEC Manadon (BScEng). Joined RN at BRNC Dartmouth, 1963; served in HM Ships Kent, Ajax, Dundas, Collingwood, Nubian; MoD (PE); Staff, C-in-C Fleet, 1980; Naval Operational Requirements, 1980–82; HMS Invincible, 1982–84; Staff Weapon Engr Officer to FO Sea Training, 1984; Naval Staff Duties, 1985–87; RCDS 1988; Higher Command and Staff Course, Camberley, 1989; Captain, HMS Defiance, 1989–90; Dir, Defence Systems, MoD, 1991–93; Dir, Gen. Fleet Support (Ops and Plans), 1993–95; DCDS (Systems), MoD, 1995–97. Defence Advr, Cap Gemini Ernst & Young, 2001–03. Chm. Trustees, Armed Forces Memorial Trust, 2003–16. Vice Pres., Royal Star and Garter Home, Richmond, 2016– (Chm. Govs, 2003–15). *Publications*: articles in naval and professional jls. *Recreations*: sport (golf, squash), gardening, travel. *Address*: Woodley House, Hill Brow, Liss, Hants GU33 7QG. *Clubs*: MCC; Royal Navy Cricket; Liphook Golf.
See also Vice-Adm. P. A. Dunt.

**DUNT, Vice Adm. Peter Arthur**, CB 2002; DL; Chief Executive, Royal Surrey County Hospital NHS Foundation Trust, 2015–16 (Chairman, 2010–15); *b* 23 June 1947; *s* of Harris Hugh Dunt and Margaret Rea Dunt; *m* 1974, Lesley Gilchrist; two *d. Educ*: Duke of York Sch., Nairobi; Merchant Taylors' Sch., Liverpool; BRNC, Dartmouth. Midshipman, HMS Arethusa, 1966; Sub Lieut courses, 1967–69; Captain's Sec., HMS Charybdis, 1969–71; Flag Lieut to Flag Officer, Medway, 1971–74; Dep. Supply Officer, HMS Kent, 1974; Supply Officer, HMS Aurora, 1975–77; Officer's Trng Officer, HMS Pembroke, 1977–79; Asst Sec. to Vice Chief of Naval Staff, 1979–82; Comdr, 1982; Sec. to Flag Officer, 1st Flotilla, 1982–84 (Gp Logistics Officer, HMS Hermes, Falklands Conflict); Supply Officer, BRNC, Dartmouth, 1984–86; Sec. to Dir Gen. Naval Manpower and Trng, 1986–88; Captain, 1988; Dep. Dir Naval Staff Duties, 1988; Sec. to 2nd Sea Lord, 1989–92; Captain, HMS Raleigh, 1992–94; Dir Naval Personnel Corporate Programming, 1994–97; rcds 1997; Rear Adm., 1998; COS to Second Sea Lord and C-in-C Naval Home Command, 1998–2000; Sen. Naval Directing Staff, RCDS and Chief Naval Supply Officer, 2000–02; Vice Adm., 2002; Chief Exec., Defence Estates, 2002–07. Dir, Pollen Estate, 2007–14; Non-exec. Dir, Enterprise Managed Services, 2009–11. Chm., ABTA Appeal Bd, 2010–. Mem. Council, White Ensign Assoc., 2007–17. Chairman: Govs, Queen Anne's Sch., Caversham, 2007–16; United Westminster and Grey Coat (formerly United Westminster Schs) Foundn, 2017–. FCIPD 2000. DL Surrey, 2011. *Recreations*: golf, walking, gardening, DIY. *Address*: The Lodge, Great Tangley, Guildford, Surrey GU5 0PT. *Club*: Army and Navy.
See also Vice-Adm. Sir J. H. Dunt.

**DUNTZE, Sir Daniel Evans**, 9th Bt *cr* 1774, of Tiverton, Devon; *b* 11 Aug. 1960; *o s* of Sir Daniel Evans Duntze, 8th Bt and Marietta Duntze (*née* Welsh); *S* father, 1997, but his name does not appear on the Official Roll of the Baronetage. *Educ*: Univ. of Missouri, St Louis.

**DUNWICH, Viscount; Robert Keith Rous;** *b* 17 Nov. 1961; *s* and *heir* of Earl of Stradbroke, *qv*.

**DUNWICH, Bishop Suffragan of,** since 2016; **Rt Rev. Michael Robert Harrison;** *b* Bolton, 7 March 1963; *s* of Peter Jeffrey Harrison and Kathleen Harrison; *m* 1992, Rachel Bentley; one *s* three *d. Educ*: Selwyn Coll., Cambridge (BA Maths 1984; MA 1988); Ripon Coll., Cuddesdon (BA Theol. 1989); Union Theol Seminary, NY (STM 1990); King's Coll. London (PhD Philosophy of Religion 1997); Bradford Univ. (MA Internat. Develt Studies 1999). Ordained deacon, 1990, priest, 1991; Curate, St Anne and All Saints, S Lambeth, 1990–94; Chaplain, Bradford Univ., and Bradford and Ilkley Community Coll., 1994–98; Vicar, Holy Trinity, Eltham, 1998–2006; Dir of Mission and Ministry, Dio. of Leicester, 2006–16. *Recreations*: family, fitness, travel, art. *Address*: Bishop's House, 4 Park Road, Ipswich IP1 3ST. *T*: (01473) 252829, *Fax*: (01473) 232552. *E*: Bishop.mike@cofesuffolk.org.

**DUNWOODY, Richard;** *see* Dunwoody, T. R.

**DUNWOODY, Tamsin;** Managing Director, TeeDem Ltd, since 2011; *b* 3 Sept. 1958; *d* of late Dr John Elliott Orr Dunwoody, CBE and Gwyneth Patricia Dunwoody, MP (Lab) Crewe and Nantwich; *m* 1992 (marr. diss. 2006); two *s* three *d. Educ*: Univ. of Kent (BA); Univ. of South Bank (AHSM 1982). NHS Manager, St Mary's, Whittington, Royal Northern and Royal Free Hosps, London, 1979–91; Co. Sec., St David's Care in the Community, 1992–97; small business advr/commercial tutor, 1997–2003. Mem. (Lab) Preseli Pembrokeshire, Nat. Assembly for Wales, 2003–07. Deputy Minister: for Econ. Develt and Transport, 2005–07; for Envmt Planning and the Countryside, 2005–07. Chair: Wales Adv. Gp, Coed Cymru, 2007–; Wales Adv. Gp, Woodland Trust, 2007–. Contested (Lab): Preseli Pembrokeshire, Nat. Assembly for Wales, 2007; Crewe and Nantwich, May 2008. Mem., Labour Party, 1973–. Mem., RHS, 1993–. *Recreations*: smallholder, embroidery, reading. *T*: (01348) 881510. *E*: tamsindunwoody@gmail.com.

**DUNWOODY, (Thomas) Richard,** MBE 1993; National Hunt jockey, 1982–99; *b* 18 Jan. 1964; *s* of George Rutherford and Gillian Mary Dunwoody; *m* 1988, Carol Ann Abraham (marr. diss. 2000); one *d* by Olivia Anna McDonald. *Educ*: Rendcomb Coll., Glos. Wins include: Grand National, on West Tip, 1986, on Miinnehoma, 1994; Cheltenham Gold Cup, on Charter Party, 1988; King George VI Chase, on Desert Orchid, 1989 and 1990, on One Man, 1995 and 1996; Champion Hurdle, on Kribensis, 1990; Breeders' Cup Steeplechase, on Highland Bud, 1989 and 1992; Champion National Hunt Jockey, 1992–93, 1993–94 and 1994–95. 1699 National Hunt wins, incl. ten consecutive centuries, 1999. Jt Pres., Jockeys' Assoc., 1993–99. Completed 680 mile Shackleton South Pole expedn, 2008. *Publications*: (with Marcus Armytage) Hell for Leather, 1993; (with S. Magee) Duel, 1994; (with Marcus Armytage) Hands and Heels, 1997; (with David Walsh) Obsessed: the autobiography, 2000; Horses of My Life, 2005; Method in my Madness, 2009. *Recreations*: sport, travel. *Address*: Hewins Wood House, Bradfield, Berks RG7 6DH.

**DUPAS, Gabrielle Teresa S.;** *see* Solti-Dupas.

**Du PLESSIS, Jan Petrus;** Chairman: Rio Tinto plc and Rio Tinto Ltd, 2009–18; British Telecommunications plc, since 2017; *b* 22 Jan. 1954; *m* 1978, Magdalena, (Leni), Nel; two *s* one *d. Educ*: Univ. of Stellenbosch (BCom Law 1973, LLB 1977). CA 1980 (SA). Internat. Financial Manager, Rembrandt Gp Ltd, 1981–87; Group Finance Director: Co. Financière Richemont, SA, 1988–2004; Rothmans International plc, 1990–96; Chairman: British American Tobacco plc, 2004–09; RHM, 2005–07; SABMiller, 2015–16. Non-executive Director: Lloyds Banking (formerly Lloyds TSB) Gp plc, 2005–09; Marks and Spencer Gp plc, 2008–15. *Recreations*: golf, ski-ing, scuba diving, walking. *Address*: British Telecommunications plc, BT Centre, 81 Newgate Street, EC1A 7AJ. *Club*: Beaconsfield Golf.

**DUPPLIN, Viscount; William Charles Thomas Hay;** *b* 24 June 2011; *s* and *heir* of Earl of Kinnoull, *qv*.

**Du QUESNAY, Heather Le Mercier,** CBE 1996; Chief Executive, English Schools Foundation, Hong Kong, 2005–13; *b* 10 Nov. 1947; *d* of Eric William and Agnes Elizabeth Openshaw; *m* 1969, Ian Mark Le Mercier Du Quesnay; two *d. Educ*: Univ. of Birmingham (BA, Cert Ed). Teacher, 1972–78, Dep. Head, 1978–83, Bartley Green Girls' Sch., Birmingham; Educn Officer, Cambs CC, 1983–89; Dep. Co. Educn Officer, Essex CC, 1989–90; Dir of Educn, Herts CC, 1991–96; Exec. Dir of Educn, 1996–2000, Interim Chief Exec., 2000, Lambeth BC; Chief Exec., Nat. Coll. for Sch. Leadership, 2000–05. FRSA 1994. Hon. DEd de Montfort, 1997; DUniv UCE, 2002. *Publications*: essays and articles in educ. jls and newspapers. *Recreations*: walking, food, wine, family.

**DURAND, Sir Edward (Alan Christopher David Percy),** 5th Bt *cr* 1892, of Ruckley Grange, Salop; English teacher and writer; *b* 21 Feb. 1974; *s* of Rev. Sir (Henry Mortimer) Dickon (Marion St George) Durand, 4th Bt and of Stella Evelyn Durand (*née* L'Estrange); *S* father, 1993; *m* 1st, 2004, (separated 2006; marr. diss. 2013); one *d*; 2nd, 2013, Amanda Anara Ashwood (*née* Amanda Clare Melbourne); one *s* one *d. Educ*: St Columba's Coll., Dublin; Milltown Inst., Dublin (Nat. Cert. in Philosophy); Univ. of Ulster at Coleraine (BA Phil.); Nat. Trng Authy (Dips in Herbalism and Parapsychology). *Recreations*: writing, mysticism, metaphysics, ecology, poetry, music, ancient history. *Heir*: *s* Ezra Solaris Amairgin Nehemiah Ashwood Durand, *b* 27 Sept. 2016.

**DURAND, (Julia) Alison;** *see* Noble, J. A.

**DURANT, Ian Charles;** Chairman: Greggs plc, since 2013 (non-executive Director, since 2011); DFS plc, since 2017; *b* Lusaka, 5 July 1958; *s* of John Durant and Jean Durant; *m* 1984, Sally Sharpe; one *s* two *d. Educ*: Gordonstoun; Univ. of Kent (BA). FCA 1994; FCT 1994. Trainee chartered acct, Joliffe Cork, later Thornton Baker/Joliffe Cork, 1980–84; Financial Controller, Allders, Hanson plc, 1984–89; Exec. Asst to Man. Dir, Jardine Matheson, 1989–90; Finance Dir, Dairy Farm, Asia, 1990–93; Finance Director: Hongkong Land, 1993–98; Dairy Farm Internat., 1998–2001; Thistle Hotels, 2001–03; Chief Financial Officer, SeaContainers, 2005–07; Finance Dir, Liberty Internat. plc, 2008–10. Chm., Capital & Counties Properties plc, 2010–18; non-executive Director: Westbury plc, 2003–06; Greene King, 2007–16; Home Retail Gp plc, 2011–16; Mem., Adv. Bd, Eurosite Power Inc., 2011–16. Chm., Ealing Swimming Club, 2009–12. Trustee, Richmond Parish Lands Charity, 2012–. *Recreations*: literary pursuits, golf, jazz music of Abdullah Ibrahim. *Address*: Greggs plc, Greggs House, Quorum Business Park, Newcastle upon Tyne NE12 8BU.

**DURANT, Prof. John Robert,** PhD; Director, MIT Museum, since 2005; Adjunct Professor, Science, Technology and Society Program, Massachusetts Institute of Technology, since 2005; *b* 8 July 1950; *s* of Kenneth Albert James Durant and Edna Kathleen Durant (*née* Norman); *m* 1st, 1977, Nirmala Naidoo (marr. diss. 1996); two *s* one *d*; 2nd, 2000, Prof. Anne Harrington; one *s. Educ*: Queens' College, Cambridge (MA Nat. Scis; PhD Hist. of Sci.). Staff Tutor in Biological Scis, Dept of Extramural Studies, UC Swansea, 1976–82; Staff Tutor in Biol Scis, Dept of External Studies, Univ. of Oxford, 1983–89; Hd, then Dir, Sci. Communication, Sci. Mus., 1989–2000; Chief Exec., At-Bristol, 2000–05. Imperial College London: Vis. Prof. of Hist. and Public Understanding of Sci., 1989–93; Prof., 1993–2002, Vis. Prof., 2002–05, of Public Understanding of Sci.; Vis. Prof., UWE, 2001–05. Exec. Dir, Cambridge Sci. Festival, 2007–. *Publications*: (ed) Darwinism and Divinity, 1985; (with P. Klopfer and S. Oyama) Aggression: conflict in animals and humans reconsidered, 1988; (ed) Museums and Public Understanding of Science, 1992; (ed) Public Participation in Science, 1995; (ed) Biotechnology in the Public Sphere: a European sourcebook, 1998; articles in professional jls. *Recreations*: family, the art of surviving. *Address*: MIT Museum, Building N51–201, 265 Massachusetts Avenue, Cambridge, MA 02139, USA. *T*: (617) 2535653. *E*: jdurant@mit.edu.

**DURANT, Louise;** *see* Charlton, L.

**DURANTE, Viviana Paola;** freelance ballet coach and director; Founder, Viviana Durante Company, 2010; *b* Italy, 8 May 1967; *d* of Giulio and Anna Maria Durante; *m* 2009, Nigel Cliff; one *s. Educ*: Royal Ballet School (Dip. of Dance Teaching, 2016); Trinity Coll. London (Dip. in Dance Teaching and Learning, 2016). Came to England in 1977; joined Royal Ballet Co., 1984; soloist, 1987; Principal Dancer, 1989; Guest Artist, 1996; first major rôle, Swan Lake, Covent Garden, 1988; rôles include Manon, Ondine, La Bayadère, Giselle, Kitri (in Don Quixote), Aurora, Cinderella, Juliet, Carmen, Coppelia; rôles created include: Winter Dreams; The Judas Tree. Principal Dancer, American Ballet Theatre, 1999; Principal Guest Artist: La Scala Ballet, Milan, 2002; K-Ballet, Tokyo, 2003; Associate Artist, Wilton's Music Hall; Guest Coach, Royal Ballet Co., 2016; *film*: Ogni 27 Agosto, 2005; *theatre*: Escaping Hamlet, Edinburgh Fest., 2007; Fram, NT, 2009. Dir/producer, Kenneth MacMillan: Steps Back in Time, The Pit, Barbican, 2018. Mem., Develt Bd, One Dance UK. Patron: Hammond Sch.; New English Ballet Th. Juror, Prix de Lausanne, 2011, 2016; Beijing Internat. Ballet Competition, 2017; other juror posts include: Ursula Moreton Choreographic Awards, Royal Ballet Sch., 2011; ENB Emerging Dancer, 2016; Hong Kong Ballet Gp Stars Award, 2016, 2017; Kenneth MacMillan Choreographic Award, Royal Ballet Sch., 2016. Time Out Award, 1989; Evening Standard Ballet Award, 1989; Laurence Olivier Award, 1997.

**DURÃO BARROSO, José Manuel;** non-executive Chairman, Goldman Sachs International, since 2016; President, European Commission, 2004–14; *b* 23 March 1956; *s* of Luís Barroso and Marie Elisabete Durão; *m* 1980, Maria Margarida Pinto Ribeiro de Sousa Uva Barroso; three *s. Educ*: Univ. of Lisbon (LLD Hons 1978); Univ. of Geneva (Master in Pol Sci. 1981); European Inst., Univ. of Geneva (Dip.). Lecturer: Faculty of Law, Lisbon Univ., 1978–81; Pol Sci. Dept, Geneva Univ., 1981–85; Prof. of Internat. Relns,

Universidade Lusíada (Hd of Dept, 1995–99). Vis. Scholar, 1985, Vis. Prof., 1996–98, Univ. of Georgetown, Washington. Ed., Revista de Ciência Política. MP (PSD): Lisbon, 1985–87, 1995–2004; Viseu, 1987–95; Secretary of State for: Home Affairs, 1985–87; Foreign Affairs and Co-operation, 1987–92; Minister for Foreign Affairs, Portugal, 1992–95; Prime Minister of Portugal, 2002–04. Chm., Commn for For. Affairs, Portuguese Parlt, 1995–99. Leader, PSD, 1999–2004 (Mem., Nat. Council, 1984–2004; Chm., Dept for Internat. Relns). Leader, Internat. Inst. for Democracy and Electoral Assistance mission to Bosnia Hercegovina, 1996; UN Advr, Project for Peace Process in Africa, Tanzania, 1997. Vice President: EPP, 1999–2002; Center Democrats Internat., 2001–05. Scholarship Fellow: Swiss Confedn; CEC; Volkswagenwerk Foundn; NATO; Swiss Nat. Fund for Scientific Res. *Publications*: (jtly) Governmental System and Party System, 1980; Le Système Politique Portugais face à l'Intégration Européenne, 1983; Política de Cooperação, 1990; Uma Certa Idéia de Europa, 1999; Uma Idéia para Portugal, 2000; Mudar de Modelo, 2001; Reformar: dois anos de governo, 2004; contrib. to collective works, encyclopaedias and internat. scientific jls.

**DURBIN, Prof. Richard Michael,** PhD; FRS 2004; Al-Kindi Professor, Department of Genetics, University of Cambridge, since 2017; *b* 30 Dec. 1960; *s* of Prof. James Durbin, FBA; *m* 1996, Dr Julie Ahringer; one *s* one *d*. *Educ*: Highgate Sch.; St John's Coll., Cambridge (BA Maths 1982; PhD Biology 1987). Res. Fellow, King's Coll., Cambridge, 1986–88; Vis. Fellow, Stanford Univ., 1988–90; Staff Scientist, MRC Lab. of Molecular Biology, 1990–96; Sanger Centre, later The Wellcome Trust Sanger Institute, Hinxton, Cambridge: Principal Investigator, then Sen. Gp Leader, 1992–2017; Jt Hd, 1992–94, Jt Hd, 1994–2006, Informatics Div.; Dep. Dir, 1997–2006; Jt Hd, Human Genetics Div., 2011–14; Acting Hd, Computational Genomics, 2014–16. Hon. Prof., Univ. of Cambridge, 2008–. Member: Human Genome Org., 1994–; Sci. Cttee, UK BioBank, 2003–05; EMBO, 2009–. FSS 2003; Fellow, Internat. Soc. for Computational Biology, 2011 (Mem., 2000). Mullard Medal, Royal Soc., 1994; Lord Lloyd of Kilgerran Award, 2004; Gabor Medal, Royal Soc., 2017. *Publications*: (jtly) Biological Sequence Analysis, 1998; papers in jls on genomic and computational biology. *Recreation*: walking in wild places. *Address*: Department of Genetics, University of Cambridge, Downing Street, Cambridge CB2 3EH.

**DURELL, Prof. John Leonard,** PhD; FInstP; Professor of Nuclear Physics, University of Manchester, 1998–2008, now Emeritus (Head, School of Physics and Astronomy, 2004–08); *b* 26 Oct. 1945; *s* of Leonard Joseph John Durell and Hilda Durell; *m* 1968, Susan Rolfe; two *d*. *Educ*: Beckenham Grammar Sch.; Univ. of Liverpool (BSc Hons; PhD 1970). CPhys, FInstP 1995. Royal Soc. Fellow, Max-Planck Inst., Heidelberg, 1970–71; University of Manchester: Lectr in Physics, 1971–82; Sen. Lectr, 1982–95; Reader in Physics, 1995–98; Hd, Dept of Physics and Astronomy, 2000–02; Dean, Faculty of Sci. and Engrg, 2002–04. Mem. Council, CCLRC, 2002–05. Trustee, Inst. of Physics Benevolent Fund, 2016–. *Publications*: numerous papers in acad. jls. *Recreation*: birdwatching. *Address*: 6 Elf Meadow, Poulton, Cirencester, Glos GL7 5HQ. *E*: john.durell@manchester.ac.uk.

**DURHAM, 7th Earl of,** *cr* 1833; **Edward Richard Lambton;** Baron Durham 1828; Viscount Lambton 1833; *b* 19 Oct. 1961; *o s* of Antony Claud Frederick Lambton, (Viscount Lambton), who disclaimed his peerages for life, and Belinda Bridget (*née* Blew-Jones); *S* father, 2006; *m* 1st, 1983, Christabel McEwen (marr. diss. 1995); one *s*; 2nd, 1995, Catherine (marr. diss. 2002), *e d* of late Desmond John Villiers Fitz-Gerald; 3rd, 2011, Marina Hanbury; one *s* one *d*. *Heir*: *s* Viscount Lambton, *qv*.

**DURHAM, Bishop of,** since 2014; **Rt Rev. Paul Roger Butler;** *b* 18 Sept. 1955; *s* of Denys Michael Butler and Jean Florence Butler; *m* 1982, Rosemary Jean Johnson; two *s* two *d*. *Educ*: Nottingham Univ. (BA Hons (English and History) 1977); Wycliffe Hall, Oxford (BA (Theol.) 1982; Cert. Theol. 1983). Ordained deacon, 1983, priest, 1984; Curate, Holy Trinity, Wandsworth, 1983–87; Inner London Evangelist, 1987–92, Dep. Hd of Missions, 1992–94, Scripture Union; NSM, St Paul, East Ham, 1988–94; Priest-in-charge: St Mary with St Stephen, and St Luke, Walthamstow, 1994–97; St Gabriel, Walthamstow, 1997; Team Rector, Parish of Walthamstow, 1997–2004; Area Dean, Waltham Forest, 2000–04; Bishop Suffragan of Southampton, 2004–09; Bishop of Southwell and Nottingham, 2009–14. Hon. Canon, St Paul's Cathedral, Byumba, Rwanda, 2001–. Entered H of L, 2014. Bishops' Advocate for Children, 2004–. Chairman: Church Mission Soc., 2007–10; Churches Nat. Safeguarding Cttee, 2011–16. Pres., Scripture Union, 2011–17. Hon. DD Nottingham, 2016. *Publications*: Reaching Children, 1992; Reaching Families, 1994; God's Friends, 1994; Following Jesus, 1994; Want to be in God's Family?, 1998; Growing Up in God's Family, 1998; Temptation and Testing, 2007; (contrib.) Through the Eyes of a Child, 2009; Offering the Best Children's Ministry, 2011; (jtly) Living your Confirmation, 2012; (contrib.) Being a Curate, 2014; (jtly) We Welcome You, 2016. *E*: bishop.of.durham@durham.anglican.org.

**DURHAM, Dean of;** *see* Tremlett, Very Rev. A.

**DURHAM, Archdeacon of;** *no new appointment at time of going to press.*

**DURHAM, John Clive;** HM Diplomatic Service, retired; Ambassador to Mongolia, 1997–99; *b* 12 July 1939; *s* of Fred Durham and Eva Lucy (*née* Sykes); *m* 1962, Sandra Kay, (Shan), Beaumont; one *s* one *d*. *Educ*: Castleford Grammar Sch.; Leeds Coll. of Commerce. Min. of Pensions and Nat. Insce, 1955–67; joined HM Diplomatic Service, 1967: FCO, 1967–69; 3rd Sec., Wellington, NZ, 1969–72; Vice-Consul, Mogadishu, 1972–74; seconded to DTI, 1974–77; 2nd, later 1st Sec. (Commercial), Khartoum, 1977–81; Consul (Commercial), Frankfurt, 1981–86; FCO, 1986–93; Consul-Gen., Brisbane, 1993–97. *Recreations*: fell walking, travel, genealogy, steam locomotion. *Address*: 31 Crescent Wood Road, SE26 6SA. *Club*: Royal Over-Seas League.

**DURHAM, Vivienne Mary;** Chief Executive, Girls' Schools Association, since 2017; *b* Rustington, 12 July 1961; *m* 1984, Kenneth John Durham (*d* 2016). *Educ*: St Hilda's Coll., Oxford (MA). Dep. Hd, South Hampstead High Sch., 1997–2004; Headmistress, Francis Holland Sch., Regent's Park, London, 2004–15; educational consultant, 2016–17. Mem., RSA. Best Head of a Public Sch. Award, Tatler, 2014. *Recreations*: reading, travel, theatre, music, ski-ing, riding. *Clubs*: University Women's, Lansdowne.

**DURHAM HALL, Jonathan David;** QC 1995; **His Honour Judge Durham Hall;** a Circuit Judge, since 2003; *b* 2 June 1952; *s* of Peter David Hall and Muriel Ann Hall, Sheffield; *m* 1973, Patricia Helen Bychowski (marr. diss. 1995), *d* of Stefan Bychowski, Whitehaven; one *s* one *d*; *m* 1996, J. Hilary Hart, GRSM, LRAM, *d* of late Edgar Alfred Hart, Hants. *Educ*: King Edward VII Sch., Sheffield; Nottingham Univ. (LLB Hons). Called to the Bar, Gray's Inn, 1975; joined North Eastern Circuit, 1976: Junior, 1982; Cryer, 1990–95; an Asst Recorder, 1991–95; a Recorder, 1995–2003; Resident Judge, Doncaster Crown Court, 2009–10; Resident Judge and Hon. Recorder of Bradford, 2017–. Head of Chambers, 1993–2003. Part-time Chm., Mental Health Review Tribunal, 2001–. Mem., Bar Council, 1994–95. Legal Assessor, GMC Professional Conduct Cttee, 2002–. *Recreations*: the creation and preservation of woodland, the plays of Shakespeare, all things Portuguese. *Address*: Bradford Crown Court, Bradford BD1 1JA.

**DURIE, Andrew Maule D.;** *see* Dewar-Durie.

**DURIE, Sir David Robert Campbell,** KCMG 2003 (CMG 1995); Governor and Commander-in-Chief, Gibraltar, 2000–03; *b* 21 Aug. 1944; *s* of late Frederick Robert Edwin Durie and Joan Elizabeth Campbell Durie (*née* Learoyd); *m* 1966, Susan Frances Weller; three *d*. *Educ*: Fettes Coll., Edinburgh; Christ Church, Oxford (MA Physics). Asst Principal, 1966, Pvte Sec. to Perm. Sec., 1970, Min. of Technology; Principal, DTI, 1971; First Sec., UK Delegn to OECD, 1974; Dept of Prices and Consumer Protection, 1977; Asst Sec., 1978; Dept of Trade, 1979; Cabinet Office, 1982; DTI, 1984; Under Sec., 1985–91; Dep. Sec., 1991; Minister and Dep. UK Perm. Rep. to EC/EU, Brussels, 1991–95; Dir Gen. (formerly Dep. Sec.), Enterprise and Regions, DTI, 1995–2000. Chm., Responsibility in Gambling Trust, 2004–06. Mem., Lord Chancellor's Adv. Panel on Nat. Records and Archives, 2005–14; Ind. Mem., Standards Cttee, GLA, 2008–12. CCMI (CIMgt 2000). FRSA 1996. KStJ 2000. Kt Comdr, Royal Order of Francis I, 2003. *Recreations*: outdoor exercise, (historical) story-telling on cruise ships, theatre, listening to music, admiring my grandchildren. *Address*: 62 Burlington Avenue, Kew Gardens, Richmond, Surrey TW9 4DH.

**DURKAN, (John) Mark;** *b* 26 June 1960; *s* of Brendan Durkan and Isobel Durkan (*née* Tinney); *m* 1993, Jackie Green; one *d*. *Educ*: St Columb's Coll., Derry; Queen's Univ., Belfast. Asst to John Hume, 1984–98. Mem. (SDLP) Derry CC, 1993–2000. Member: Forum for Peace and Reconciliation, Dublin, 1994–96; NI Forum (Talks Negotiator), 1996–98. Northern Ireland Assembly: Mem. (SDLP) Foyle, 1998–2010; Minister for Finance and Personnel, 1999–2001; Dep. First Minister, 2001–02; Chm., Cttee for Enterprise, Trade and Investment, 2007–09. MP (SDLP) Foyle, 2005–17; contested (SDLP) same seat, 2017. Chairperson, 1990–95, Leader, 2001–10, SDLP.

**DURKAN, Mark Henry;** Member (SDLP) Foyle, Northern Ireland Assembly, since 2011; *b* Londonderry, 3 March 1978; *s* of Patrick and Gabrielle Durkan; *m* 2013, Anne Carlin; one *d*; one *s* from previous relationship. *Educ*: St Columb's Coll.; Queen's Univ., Belfast. Formerly accountant. Health spokesman, 2011–12, social develt spokesman, 2012–13, NI Assembly; Minister for the Envmt, 2013–16. Mem. (SDLP), Derry CC, 2005–11. *Address*: Northern Ireland Assembly, Parliament Buildings, Stormont, Belfast BT4 3XX.

**DURKIN, Claire;** consultant, since 2014; Head, Global Science, Innovation and Knowledge Economy, Department for Business, Energy and Industrial Strategy (formerly Head, Global Knowledge and Innovation, Department for Business, Innovation and Skills), since 2015; *b* 18 May 1956; *d* of Richard Durkin and Mollie (*née* Frazer); *m* 1990, Stephen Morgan. *Educ*: Liverpool Univ. (BA 1st cl. Hons); Univ. of Victoria, BC (MA); Wolverhampton Poly. (PGCE). Lectr, Further and Higher Educn, Vauxhall Coll., South Bank Polytech., 1982–88; Department of Employment: Principal, 1988–89; Private Secretary: to Minister for Employment, 1989–90; to Minister for Educn, 1990–91; Asst Dir, Labour Mkt Policies, 1991–95; Asst Dir Deregulation, Central Policy Unit, DTI, 1995–97; Asst Sec., 1997–98, Sec., 1998–2000, Low Pay Commn; Dir, Consumer and Competition Policies, 2000–02, Energy Innovation and Businesses, 2003–05, Energy Markets, 2005–08, DTI, subseq. BERR; Dir, Europe and Internat. Trade Policy, then Europe, Internat. Trade and Develt Policy, later Internat. Trade, Investment and Develt, BERR, subseq. BIS, 2008–10; Vice Pres. and Regl Exec., Europe, URS Corp. Ltd, 2010–14. *Recreations*: history, politics, exploring the Welsh Marches.

**DURLACHER, Nicholas John,** CBE 1995; Chairman, Xoserve Ltd, 2011–18; *b* 20 March 1946; *s* of late John Sidney Durlacher, MC and of Alma Gabrielle (*née* Adams); *m* 1971, Mary Caroline Mclaren; one *s*. *Educ*: Stowe; Magdalene Coll., Cambridge (BA Econs). Mem., Stock Exchange, 1970–86; Partner, Wedd Durlacher, 1972–86; Director: BZW Ltd, 1986–98; BZW Futures, 1986–96; U.F.J. Internat., 2002–04; Chairman: Ennismore Smaller Cos Fund, 1999–; EMX, 2000–07; BSC Co. Ltd, 2000–10; Ffastfill, 2000–02; Elexon Ltd, 2000–10. Dir, 1984–96, Chm., 1992–95, LIFFE; Dir, 1987–95, Chm., 1995–2001, SFA; Dir, Investor's Compensation Scheme, 1992–2001; Chm., Balancing and Settlement Code Panel, 2000–10. Chm., Allied Schs, 2008–. Trustee and Dir, Brain and Spine Foundn, 1994–2011. *Recreations*: ski-ing, golf, tennis. *Address*: 10 Rutland Street, SW7 1EH. *Clubs*: White's, Hawks.

**DURMAN, David John;** Editor-in-Chief, IPC Magazines, 1994–99; *b* 10 July 1948; *s* of late John Durman and Joan Durman; *m* 1973, Hilary Pamela Aldrick. *Educ*: Leeds Univ. (BA). Dep. Editor, Woman's Own, 1986–88; Editor, Woman, 1988–94. Chm., BSME, 1996. *Recreations*: reading, theatre, life.

**DURNING, Josephine Marie;** freelance translator, French to English, since 2013; Co-Director, Europe and World Trade, Department of Trade and Industry, 2003–05; *b* 27 Aug. 1952; *d* of late Cecil and of Isobel M. Durning; *m* 1984, Paul Stephen Capella (*d* 2004); one *s* one *d*. *Educ*: Loreto Coll., St Albans; Univ. of Keele (BA Hons Eng. and Politics 1974). Entered CS as admin trainee, 1974; Private Sec. to Parly Under-Sec. of State, Dept of Employment, 1978–79; Sec. to HSE, 1982–85; Labour Attaché, Paris, 1985–89; Head of Sen. Mgt Support Unit, Dept of Employment, 1990–91; Head of Internat. and Gen. Policy, HSE, 1991–96; with Econ. and Domestic Secretariat, Cabinet Office, 1996–98; Dir, Transdeptl Gp, OST, 1998–2002, Head, Community Interest Company Team, 2002–03, DTI; ind. consultant, 2005–12. Vis. Lectr (Dip. Trans.), Univ. of Westminster, 2015–. MCIL. FRSA 2000. *Recreations*: reading, riding. *Address*: 29 Gold Street, Saffron Walden, Essex CB10 1EJ.

**DUROSE, David William;** QC 2019; *b* Stoke-on-Trent, 12 June 1973; *s* of William Durose and Joan Morvinson. *Educ*: University Coll., Oxford (BA Hons Maths); Staffordshire Univ. (CPE). Called to the Bar, Lincoln's Inn, 1996; in practice as a barrister, specialising in criminal law, 2 Paper Bldgs, 1996–2003, Furnival Chambers, 2003–. *Recreations*: reading, crosswords, misfortunes of Port Vale FC. *Address*: Furnival Chambers, 32 Furnival Street, EC4A 1JQ.

**DURR, Kent Diederich Skelton;** consultant, and trustee of family trusts, since 2005; *b* 28 March 1941; *s* of Dr John Michael Durr and Diana (*née* Skelton); *m* 1st, 1966, Suzanne Wiese (*d* 2010); one *s* two *d*; 2nd, 2011, Melanie Catherine Williamson; two *s*. *Educ*: South African Coll. Schs; Cape Town Univ. Dir, family publishing co., 1966–68; Founder and later Man. Dir, Durr Estates, 1968–84. Elected to Provincial Council of Cape, 1974; MP for Maitland, SA, 1977–91; Dep. Minister, Trade and Industry, 1984–86, Finance, 1984–88; Minister of Budget and Public Works in Ministers' Council, 1988–89; Cabinet Minister of Trade and Industry and Tourism, 1989–91; S African Ambassador to UK, 1991–94; High Comr for S Africa in London, 1994–95; Chairman: Fuel-Tech NV, 1995–97; Clean Diesel Technologies, Inc., 1995–97; Commonwealth Investment Guarantee Agency Ltd, 1997–99; Senator (African Christian Democratic Party) Western Cape Province, 1999–2004; MP (African Christian Democratic Party), 2004–05. Mem., SA Nat. Foundn for Conservation of Coastal Birds, 1985 (Award of Honour, 1987). Freeman: City of London, 1995; Vintners' Co., 1995. Spectamur Agendo award for lifetime achievement, 2016. *Publications*: numerous articles in newspapers and jls on econs, foreign affairs, constitutional affairs, urban renewal, conservation and business. *Recreations*: history, field sports, conservation, croquet, bridge. *Address*: 56 Constantia Place, Constantia, 7806 Cape Town, South Africa. *Clubs*: Royal Over-Seas League; Kelvin Grove (Cape Town, SA).

**DURRAN, Alexia Grainne; Her Honour Judge Durran;** a Circuit Judge, since 2014; Deputy Chief Coroner, since 2019; *b* London, 10 July 1971; *d* of Richard and Lesley Durran; *m* 2004, Rupert Pardoe. *Educ:* Lady Manners Sch., Bakewell, Derbys; St Catharine's Coll., Cambridge (BA Hons 1992; MA 1996); Univ. of Westminster (CPE); Inns of Court Sch. of Law. Called to the Bar, Middle Temple, 1995; in practice as criminal barrister, 1995–2014; a Recorder, 2009–14. *Recreations:* reading, cinema, family, running, theatre. *Address:* Guildford Crown Court, Bedford Road, Guildford GU1 4ST. *T:* (01483) 468500. *E:* HHJ.Alexia.Durran@ejudiciary.net.

**DURRANDS, Prof. Kenneth James,** CBE 1992; DGS (Birm), MSc, CEng, FIMechE, FIET; Vice-Chancellor and Rector, University of Huddersfield, 1992–95 (Rector, The Polytechnic, Huddersfield, 1970–92; Professor, 1985); *b* 24 June 1929; *s* of A. I. Durrands, Croxton Kerrial; *m* 1956 (marr. diss. 1971); one *s*; *m* 1983, Jennifer Jones; one *s*. *Educ:* King's Sch., Grantham; Nottingham Technical Coll.; Birmingham Univ. Min. of Supply Engrg Apprentice, ROF, Nottingham, 1947–52; Techn. Engr, UKAEA, Risley, 1954–58; Lecturer in Mechanical and Nuclear Engrg, Univ. of Birmingham, 1958–61; Head of Gen. Engrg Dept, Reactor Engrg Lab., UKAEA, Risley, 1961–67; Technical Dir, Vickers Ltd, Barrow Engrg Works, 1967–70. Vis. Lectr, Manchester Univ., 1962–68. Member: DoI Educn and Training Cttee, 1973–75 (Chm., 1975–80); DoI Garment & Allied Industries Requirements Bd, 1975–79 (Chm. Computer Cttee, 1975–79); BEC Educn Cttee, 1975–79; BEC Business Studies Bd, 1976–79; Inter-Univ. and Polytech. Council, 1978–81; Yorks Consumers' Cttee, Office of Electricity Regulation, 1990–94; British Council: Higher Educn Cttee, 1981–91; Engrg and Technology Adv. Cttee, 1981–90; Cttee, CICHE, 1985–95; Council for the Accreditation of Teacher Educn, 1991–92; Hon. Sec./Treas., Cttee of Dirs of Polytechnics, 1970–79. Educn Comr, MSC, subseq. Training Commn, 1986–89. Mem. Council, IMechE, 1963–66. Preliminary Judge, Prince of Wales Award for Industrial Innovation and Production, 1982–95. Member, Court: Leeds Univ., 1970–95; Bradford Univ., 1973–95; Mem. Council, Barnsley Coll., 1996–2000; Gov., King's Sch., Grantham, 1999– (Vice-Chm., 2004–16; Dir, Trust Mem., 2011–; Foundn Gov., 2014–). Founder Chm., Assoc. of Lincs Sch. Governing Bodies, 2005–07 (Mem. Exec. Cttee, 2005–11); Mem., Lincs Schs' Forum, 2007–. FNucI (FINucE 1959); FRSA. *Publications:* technical and policy papers. *Recreations:* gardening, reading, walking. *Address:* Church Cottage, Croxton Kerrial, Grantham, Lincolnshire NG32 1PY. *Club:* Athenæum.

**DURRANI, Prof. Tariq Salim,** OBE 2003; PhD; FRSE; FREng, FIET, FIEEE; Research Professor, Electronic and Electrical Engineering, University of Strathclyde, since 2009; *b* Amraoti, India, 27 Oct. 1943; *s* of Mohammed Salim Khan Durrani and Bilquis Jamal; *m* 1972, Clare Elizabeth Kellas; one *s* two *d*. *Educ:* E Pakistan Univ. of Engrg and Technol., Dacca (BEng Hons 1965); Univ. of Southampton (MSc 1967; PhD 1970). FIET (FIEE 1982); FIEEE 1989; FREng 1996. Res. Fellow, Univ. of Southampton, 1970–76; University of Strathclyde: Lectr, 1976–79; Sen. Lectr, 1979–82; Prof. of Signal Processing, 1982–2009; Hd, Signal Processing Div., 1982–2006; Chair, Electrical and Electronic Engrg, 1986–90; Special Advr (IT) to Principal, 1991–94; Dep. Principal, 2000–06; Special Advr to Principal, 2007–08. Vis. Professorial Fellow, 1996–98, Vis. Res. Collaborator, 2012–15, Princeton Univ.; Vis. Prof., USC, 2012–13; Hon. Prof., Univ. of Stirling, 2011–15. Director: Scottish Electronics Technol. Gp, 1986–2004; NATO Advanced Study Inst., Les Houches, 1987; UK Inst. for Systems Level Integration, 1999–2010; Scottish Inst. for Enterprise, 2001–05; Glasgow Chamber of Commerce, 2003–14; Leadership Foundn for UK Higher Educn, 2003–09; Kelvin Inst., 2004–05; SFC, 2005–09; UK Equality Challenge Unit, 2009–12; UK Nat. Commn for UNESCO, 2011–17. Mem., Parly and Scientific Cttee, Houses of Parlt, 1991–94. Member: Council, Scottish Electronics Forum, 1993–95; Coll. of Peers on IT-Communications, EPSRC, 1997–2009; Scottish Sci. Adv. Bd, 2002–04. Mem., Complaints Cttee, Law Soc. of Scotland, 1999–2004. Member: Res. Rev. Bd, Govt of Netherlands, 1999; Internat. Rev. Cttee, Min. of Educn and Industry, Carnegie Mellon-Portugal Prog., 2006–13; Internat. Cttee, RAEng, 2018–. Member: Internat. Adv. Bd, Etisalat Coll. of Technol., Sharjah, 1996–99; Bd of Councillors, US NSF Centre of Excellence in Immersive Multimedia Systems, USC, 2000–05; Adv. Bd, Centre for Multimedia Signal Processing, Hong Kong Poly. Univ., 2002–06; Great Master, III Project, Univ. of Electronic Sci. and Technol. of China, Chengdu, 2011–15. Royal Society of Edinburgh: Mem. Council, 2003–06; Vice Pres. (Natural Scis), 2007–10; Vice Pres. (Internat.), 2012–16. Institute of Electrical and Electronics Engineers: Pres., Signal Processing Soc., 1994–95; Chair: Periodicals Council, 1996–97; Periodicals Rev. Cttee, 1998–99; Vice-Chair, Tech. Activities Reg. 8, 2004–06; Pres., Engrg Mgt Soc., 2006–07; Dir, EMEA Reg., Communications Soc., 2009–11; Vice Pres., Educnl Activities Bd, 2010–11; Co-Chair, UNESCO Adv. Bd, UNESCO Engrg Report II, 2018–; Gen. Chair, China AI—Internat. Conf. on Artificial Intelligence, Urumqi, Xinqiang, China, 2019. FRSE 1994; Fellow, World Acad. of Scis, 1995. Mem., Eta Kappa Nu, 2010; Foreign Mem., US NAE, 2018. Aerospace and Electronic Systems M. Barry Carlton Honourable Mention Award, Signal Processing Soc., 1974; Meritorious Service Award, 2000, Third Millennium Medal, 2001, IEEE. *Publications:* (with C. Greated) Laser Systems in Flow Measurements, 1977; (with E. Robinson) Geophysical Signal Processing, 1986; (ed jtly) Signal Processing, 1987; (ed) Mathematics and Signal Processing, 1987; (ed) Transputer Applications 3, 1991; 360 contribs to archival jls and internat. confs. *Recreation:* occasional golf. *Address:* Department of Electronic and Electrical Engineering, University of Strathclyde, 204 George Street, Glasgow G1 1XW. *T:* (0141) 548 2540, *Fax:* (0141) 552 2487. *E:* durrani@strath.ac.uk. *Clubs:* Western (Glasgow); Ross Priory (Loch Lomond).

**DURRANT, His Honour Anthony Harrisson;** a Circuit Judge, 1991–99; *b* 3 Jan. 1931; *s* of Frank Baston Durrant and Irene Maud Durrant; *m* 1956, Jacqueline Ostroumoff (*d* 2015); one *s* two *d*. *Educ:* Sir Joseph Williamson's Mathematical Sch., Rochester. Admitted Solicitor, 1956; Partner, 1960, Sen. Partner, 1976–91, Horwood & James, Aylesbury; a Recorder, 1987–91. Dep. Chm., Agricl Land Tribunal, 1987–91. Pres., Berks, Bucks and Oxon Incorp. Law Soc., 1977–78; Chm., Berks, Bucks and Oxon Jt Consultative Cttee of Barristers and Solicitors, 1985–91.
See also A. J. Trace.

**DURRANT, Anthony Richard Charles;** Chief Executive Officer, Premier Oil, since 2015 (Finance Director, 2005–14); *b* Luton, Beds, 7 Aug. 1958; *s* of Geoffrey and Margaret Durrant; *m* 1985, Jan Rennie; one *s* one *d*. *Educ:* King's Sch., Canterbury; Corpus Christi Coll., Oxford (Schol.; BA PPE 1980). With Arthur Andersen & Co., 1980–86; Audit Senior, 1983–84; Senior, Mgt Consulting, 1985–86; Lehman Brothers, 1986–2005 (Man. Dir and Hd, Eur. Natural Resources Gp, 1997–2005). Non-executive Director: Clipper Windpower plc, 2005–; Greenenergy Fuels Hldgs Ltd, 2012–17. *Recreations:* golf, Rugby, cricket, travel. *Address:* 1 Woodborough Road, Putney, SW15 6PX. *T:* (020) 8788 6437. *E:* tdurrant@premier-oil.com.

**DURRANT, Jennifer Ann,** RA 1994; painter; began living and working in Umbria, 2000; *b* 17 June 1942; *d* of Caleb John Durrant and Winifred May (*née* Wright); *m* 1964, William Alistair Herriot Henderson (marr. diss. 1976); *m* 2000, Richard Alban Howard Oxby. *Educ:* Varndean Grammar Sch. for Girls, Brighton; Brighton Coll. of Art; Slade Sch. of Fine Art; University Coll. London (Dip. Fine Art). FRCA 1993. Postgrad. Scholar, Slade Sch. of Fine Art, 1965–66. Artist in Residence, Somerville Coll., Oxford, 1979–80. Part-time Lecturer: RCA, 1979–2000; Royal Acad. Schs, 1990–98. External Assessor: Reading Univ. MA Fine Art, 1980s; Duncan of Jordanstone Coll. of Art, Univ. of Dundee, 1993–97; Limerick and Cork Colls of Art, 1998–2001; Falmouth Coll. of Art, 1998–2002. *Solo exhibitions* include: Arnolfini Gall., Bristol, 1979; Mus. of Modern Art, Oxford, 1980; Nicola Jacobs Gall., London, 1982 and 1983; Serpentine Gall., 1987; Newlyn Orion Gall., Penzance, 1988; Concourse Gall., Barbican, 1992; Salander-O'Reilly Galls, NY, 1993 and 2000; Francis Graham-Dixon Gall., London, 1996; Friends' Room, Royal Acad., 1996 and 2005; Art First Contemporary Art, Cork St, 2005; Richmond Hill Gall., London, 2011; *group exhibitions* include: Hayward Gall., 1976, 1979, 1980 and 1990; Mus. of Fine Art, Boston, Mass and Royal Acad., 1977; Salander-O'Reilly Galls, NY, 1981; Tate Gall. and Carnegie Inst., Pittsburgh, 1982; Serpentine Gall., 1983 and 1984; Royal Acad., 1985; Mall Galls, London, 1990–92; also in provincial galls in UK, and in Europe; has exhibited at Royal Acad. Summer Exhibn, 1986, 1987 and annually, 1989–; *works in public collections* including: Arts Council, British Council; Contemporary Art Soc.; Mus. of Fine Arts, Boston, Mass; Tate Gall.; Govt Art Collection; Neue Galerie, Aachen; Trinity Coll., Cambridge; *commissions:* Newham Hosp.; R. P. Scherer 50th Anniv., Swindon, 1987; Thomas Neal, Covent Gdn, 1992; Glaxo UK, Stevenage, 1994. Arts Council Award, 1976; Arts Council Major Award, 1978; Gtr London Arts Assoc. Award, 1980; Athena Art Award, 1988; Artist of the Year, Independent on Sunday, 1996. *Recreations:* classical music, opera, archaeology, museums, painting and sculpture, the natural world. *Address:* La Vigna, Via Bondi 14, 06069 Tuoro-sul-Trasimeno (PG), Italy. *T:* and *Fax:* (075) 829010.

**DURRANT, Sir William (Alexander Estridge),** 8th Bt *cr* 1784, of Scottow, Norfolk; *b* 26 Nov. 1929; *o s* of Sir William Henry Estridge Durrant, 7th Bt and Georgina Beryl Gwendoline (*d* 1968), *d* of Alexander Purse; *S* father, 1994; *m* 1st, 1953, Dorothy (*d* 2012), *d* of Ronal Croker, Quirindi, NSW; one *s* one *d*; 2nd, 2014, Beverley Joy Bainbridge, *d* of late Reginald Walter Estridge Durrant. *Heir: s* David Alexander Durrant [*b* 1 July 1960; *m* 1st, 1989, Maria Lucia Leonard (marr. diss. 2002); three *s*; 2nd, 2006, Mary Josephine Renehan]. *Address:* Red Hill, Nundle Road, Nemingha, NSW 2340, Australia.

**DURRANT-WHYTE, Prof. Hugh Francis,** PhD; FRS 2010; FTSE, FIEEE, FREng; FAA; New South Wales Chief Scientist and Engineer, since 2018; *b* London, 6 Feb. 1961; *s* of Hugh and Dorothy Durrant-Whyte; *m* 1986, Daphne Adie; two *s* two *d*. *Educ:* Richard Hale Sch., Hertford; Queen Mary Coll., Univ. of London (BSc 1st Cl. Hons Engrg 1983); Univ. of Pennsylvania (MSE Systems Engrg 1985; PhD Systems Engrg 1986). University of Oxford: BP Res. Fellow, Dept of Engrg Sci., and Fellow, St Cross Coll., 1986–87; Univ. Lectr in Engrg Sci., and Fellow, Oriel Coll., 1987–95; Prof. of Mechatronic Engrg, Dept of Aerospace, Univ. of Sydney, 1995–2010; Dir, Aust. Res. Council Centre of Excellence for Autonomous Systems, 2003–10; CEO, NICTA, 2010–14; Prof. of Mechatronic Engrg and ARC Fedn Fellow, 2014–18, and Dir, Centre for Translational Data Sci., 2016–18, Univ. of Sydney; Chief Scientific Advr, MoD, 2017–18. Aust. Res. Council Fedn Fellow, 2002–. FTSE 2002; FIEEE 2005; FAA 2009; FREng 2018. *Publications:* five books; over 350 academic articles. *Recreations:* geology, opera, running. *Address:* Office of the NSW Chief Scientist and Engineer, GPO Box 5477, Sydney, NSW 2001, Australia.

**DURRINGTON, Prof. Paul Nelson,** MD; FRCP, FRCPath, FMedSci; Professor of Medicine, University of Manchester, since 1995; Hon. Consultant Physician, Manchester Royal Infirmary, 1982–2012; *b* 24 July 1947; *s* of Alec Edward Durrington and May Ena Durrington (*née* Nelson); *m* 1969, Patricia Joyce Gibbs; one *s* two *d*. *Educ:* Chislehurst and Sidcup Grammar Sch. for Boys; Univ. of Bristol (BSc Hons Physiol. 1969; MB ChB 1972; MD 1978). MRCP 1975, FRCP 1987; MRCPath 1982, FRCPath 1994. Hse Officer and SHO appts in medicine, paediatrics and surgery, Bristol, 1972–76; Lectr, 1976–82, Sen. Lectr, 1982–92, Reader, 1992–95, in Medicine, Univ. of Manchester. Travelling Fellow, BHF and Amer. Heart Assoc. (Vis. Prof., Div. of Metabolism, Dept of Medicine, UCSD), 1979–80. Dir, R&D, Central Manchester Healthcare NHS Trust, 1997–2001. Med. Dir, Family Heart Assoc., 1995–2002. Chm., British Hyperlipidaemia Assoc., 1992–95. Mem., Assoc. of Physicians of GB and Ireland, 1992. FMedSci 2001; Fellow, Amer. Heart Assoc. 2001; FACP 2010. *Publications:* Hyperlipidaemia, Diagnosis and Treatment, 1989, 3rd edn 2007; Pocketbook of Preventative Cardiology, 1993, 2nd edn 2001; (with A. Sniderman) Hyperlipidaemia, 2000, 5th edn 2010; contrib. articles on lipid metabolism, diabetes and coronary heart disease to learned jls. *Recreations:* angling (Mem., Prince Albert Angling Soc., Errwood Fly Fishing Club), hill-walking (Mem., Ramblers' Assoc.), good company (Mem., Old Boys' and Park Green Club). *Address:* Institute of Cardiovascular Sciences, School of Biomedicine, Core Technology Facility (3rd Floor), University of Manchester, 46 Grafton Street, Manchester M13 9NT. *T:* (0161) 275 1200, *Fax:* (0161) 275 1183. *E:* pdurrington@manchester.ac.uk.

**du SAUTOY, Prof. Marcus Peter Francis,** OBE 2010; DPhil; FRS 2016; Professor of Mathematics, since 2002, and Charles Simonyi Professor for the Public Understanding of Science, since 2008, University of Oxford; Fellow, New College, Oxford, since 2008; *b* 26 Aug. 1965; *s* of Bernard and Jennifer du Sautoy; *m* 1994, Shani Ram; one *s* twin *d* (and one *s* decd). *Educ:* Gillotts Comprehensive Sch., Henley-on-Thames; King James Sixth Form Coll., Henley-on-Thames; Wadham Coll., Oxford (BA Hons Maths 1986); DPhil Oxon 1989. SERC Postdoctoral Res. Fellow, QMW, Univ. of London, 1989–90; Postdoctoral Res. Fellow, All Souls Coll., Oxford, 1990–95; Royal Society University Research Fellow: Univ. of Cambridge, 1995–2001; Univ. of Oxford, 2001–05; Fellow, Wadham College, Oxford, 2005–08. Pres., Math. Assoc., 2012–13. Christmas Lectr, Royal Instn, 2006. BBC presenter: Mindgames, 2004–05; Music of the Primes, 2005; The Story of Maths, 2008; Horizon, 2009–12; The Code, 2011; Maestro at the Opera, 2012; Precision: The Measure of All Things, 2013; The Secret Rules of Modern Living: Algorithms, 2015; co-presenter, Dara Ó Briain's Sch. of Hard Sums, 2012–13. Berwick Prize, LMS, 2001; Michael Faraday Prize, Royal Soc., 2009; Sir George Thomson Gold Medal, Inst. of Measurement and Control, 2015. *Publications:* The Music of the Primes, 2003, 6th edn 2007; Finding Moonshine: a mathematician's journey through symmetry, 2008; The Number Mysteries, 2011; What We Cannot Know, 2016; The Creativity Code: how AI is learning to write, paint and think, 2019. *Recreations:* No 17 for Recreativo Hackney FC, playing the trumpet, theatre. *Address:* New College, Oxford OX1 3BN.

**DUTHIE, Sir Robert Grieve, (Sir Robin),** Kt 1987; CBE 1978; CA; Chairman, Scottish Development Agency, 1979–88; *b* 2 Oct. 1928; *s* of George Duthie and Mary (*née* Lyle); *m* 1955, Violetta Noel Maclean; two *s* one *d*. *Educ:* Greenock Academy. Apprentice Chartered Accountant with Thomson Jackson Gourlay & Taylor, CA, 1946–51 (CA 1952); joined Blacks of Greenock, 1952: Man. Dir, 1962; Chairman: Black & Edgington Ltd, 1972–83; Insight Internat. Tours Ltd, 1979–84; Bruntons (Musselburgh), 1984–86; Britoil, 1988–90; Tay Residential Investment Ltd, 1989–96; Neill Clerk Gp plc, 1994–98; Director: British Assets Trust, 1977–98; Royal Bank of Scotland, 1978–99; Investors Capital Trust, 1985–94; Carclo Engineering Gp, 1986–98; British Polythene Industries (formerly Scott & Robertson), 1989–99; Devol Engineering Ltd, 1994–2004. Chm., Greenock Provident Bank, 1974; Dir, Greenock Chamber of Commerce, 1967–68; Tax Liaison Officer for Scotland, CBI, 1976–79. Member: Scottish Telecommunications Bd, 1972–77; E Kilbride Develt Corp., 1976–78; Clyde Port Authority, 1971–83 (Chm., 1977–80); Council, Inst. of Chartered Accountants of Scotland, 1973–78; Scottish Econ. Council, 1980–95; Council, Strathclyde Business Sch., 1986–94; Governing Council, Scottish Business in the Community, 1987–95; Vice Chm., Adv. Bd for Scotland, BP, 1990–2002. Chm., Made Up

Textiles Assoc. of GB, 1972; Pres., Inverkip Soc., 1966; Mem. of Council, Royal Caledonian Curling Club, 1985–88. Commissioner: Queen Victoria Sch., Dunblane, 1972–89; Scottish Congregational Ministers Pension Fund, 1973–2003; Treasurer, Greenock W URC, 1970–. Fellow, Scottish Vocational Council, 1988. CCMI (CBIM 1976); FRSA 1983. Hon. FRIAS, 1989. Hon. Fellow, Paisley Coll., 1990. Hon. LLD Strathclyde, 1984; Hon. DTech Napier Coll., 1989. *Recreation:* golf. *Address:* Fairhaven, Finnart Street, Greenock PA16 8JA. *T:* (01475) 722642.

**DUTTON, Maj.-Gen. Bryan Hawkins,** CB 1997; CBE 1990 (OBE 1984; MBE 1978); Director-General, Leonard Cheshire Disability (formerly Leonard Cheshire Foundation), 1998–2008; *b* 1 March 1943; *s* of late Ralph Dutton and Honor Badcoe (formerly Dutton, *née* Morris); *m* 1972, Angela Margaret Wilson; one *s* one *d*. *Educ:* Lord Weymouth Sch.; RMA Sandhurst. Commissioned, Devonshire and Dorset Regt, 1963; served NI, British Guiana, Libya, Belize, Germany, UK; Instructor, Sch. of Infantry, 1969–71; RMCS and Staff Coll., 1974–75; C-in-C's Mission to Soviet Forces in Germany, 1976–78; Co. Comdr, 1st Devonshire and Dorset, 1978–79 (despatches 1979); Planning Staff, NI Office, 1979–81; Instructor, Staff Coll., 1981–82; MA to Adjutant-Gen., 1982–84; CO 1st Bn Devonshire and Dorset Regt, 1984–87; Ops Staff, UKLF, 1987; Comdr 39 Infantry Brigade, 1987–89; Dir, Public Relations (Army), 1990–92; Dir of Infantry, 1992–94; Comdr British Forces, Hong Kong (handover to People's Liberation Army), 1994–97. Col Comdt, POW Div., 1996–99; Col, Devonshire and Dorset Regt, 1998–2003. Chairman: Voluntary Orgns Disability Gp, 2004–08; The Keep Military Mus. of Devon and Dorset, 2008–17; Action for Stammering Children (formerly Assoc. for Res. into Stammering in Childhood), 2009–14. Gov., 1999–, Trustee, 2011–, Hayes Dashwood Foundn. FRSA; CCMI. *Recreations:* golf, fishing, wild-life, Rugby spectator, history, classical music. *Address:* Highwood, East Grimstead, Wilts SP5 3SA.

**DUTTON, Lt-Gen. Sir James Benjamin,** KCB 2010; CBE 2003; Region President for Africa, Bechtel, since 2019; *b* 21 Feb. 1954; *s* of Edgar and Aileen Dutton; *m* 1978, Elizabeth Waddell; one *s* one *d*. *Educ:* King's Sch., Chester; City Univ., London (BSc Hons (Systems and Mgt)); RCDS. Joined RM, 1972; COS, 3 Commando Bde, 1991–93; Comdr, RM Officers' Trng, 1993; Asst Dir, Jt Warfare, MoD, 1996; CO, 40 Commando, 1996–98; Dir, NATO Policy, MoD, 1998–2000; seconded to Jt Staff, Pentagon, 2001–02; Comdr, 3 Commando Bde, 2002–04; Comdr Multinat. Div. SE and GOC British Forces Iraq, 2005; Comdt Gen., Royal Marines, and Comdr, UK Amphibious Forces, 2004–06; COS (Capability) to C-in-C Fleet, 2006–07; Dep. Chief of Jt Ops (Ops), later COS (Ops), MoD, 2007–08; Dep. Comdr, ISAF, 2008–09. Infrastructure and Ops Manager, Bechtel Corp., 2010–11; Prog. Dir, Gabon Infrastructure Project, Bechtel Internat., Libreville, Gabon, 2011–13; Dir-Gen., Agence Nat. des Grands Travaux, Gabon (on secondment), 2012–13; Gov. and Comdr-in-Chief, Gibraltar, 2013–15. KStJ 2016. US Legion of Merit, 2010. *Recreation:* sailing.

**DUTTON, Prof. P(eter) Leslie,** FRS 1990; Professor of Biochemistry and Biophysics, since 1981 (Chairman, Department of Biochemistry and Biophysics, 1994–2008), and Director, Johnson Foundation for Molecular Biophysics, since 1991, University of Pennsylvania; *b* 12 March 1941; *s* of Arthur Bramwell Dutton and Mary Dutton; *m* 1965, Dr Julia R. Dwyer; two *s* one *d*. *Educ:* Univ. of Wales (BSc Hons Chem.; PhD Biochem.). PD Fellow, Dept of Biochem. and Soil Science, Univ. of Wales, 1967–68; University of Pennsylvania: PD Fellow, 1968–71, Asst Prof., 1971–76, Johnson Res. Foundn; Associate Prof., Dept of Biochem. and Biophysics, 1976–81; Hon. MA 1976. *Recreations:* painting (several one-man and group shows in Wales and USA), sailing. *Address:* Department of Biochemistry and Biophysics, University of Pennsylvania, Stellar-Chance Building, Suite 1005, 422 Curie Boulevard, Philadelphia, PA 19104–6059, USA. *T:* (215) 8980991, *Fax:* (215) 5732235; 654 West Rose Tree Road, Media, PA 19063, USA. *Clubs:* Mantoloking Yacht (NJ); Corinthian Yacht (Philadelphia).

**DUTTON, His Honour Roger Thomas;** DL; a Circuit Judge, 1996–2018; Resident Judge, Chester Crown Court, 2016–18; Hon. Recorder of Chester, 2016–18; *b* 24 March 1952; *s* of late Donald Roger Dutton and Doreen May Dutton (*née* Ankers); *m* 1977, Elaine Alison Dixon (*d* 2014); one *s* two *d*; *m* 2018, Jane Eames. *Educ:* Acton Sch., Wrexham; Grove Park Grammar Sch., Wrexham; Univ. of Kent (BA Hons Law 1973); Inns of Court Sch. of Law. Called to the Bar, Middle Temple, 1974; in practice at the Bar, 1974–96; Mem., Wales and Chester Circuit. Asst Recorder, 1988–92; Recorder, 1992–96; Liaison Judge, N Wales Magistrates, 1998–2007; Macclesfield, Crewe and Nantwich Magistrates, 2007–; Disciplinary Investigating Judge, 2007–; Interviewing Judge for Lord Chancellor's Dept, 2002–06, for Judicial Appts Commn, 2006–. Mem., Judges' Council for England and Wales, 2014. Circuit Rep., Cttee of Council of HM's Circuit Judges, 2004–05 (Hon. Treas., 2005–12; Jun. Vice-Pres., 2012; Sen. Vice-Pres., 2013; Pres., 2014); Pres., Cheshire Br., Magistrates Assoc., 2017–. Mem., Tutor Judge Panel, Judicial Coll. (formerly Judicial Studies Bd), 2007–. North Wales Institute of Higher Education, later Glyndŵr University: Mem. Bd Govs, 2002–07; Mem. Nominations Cttee, 2008–14; Hon. Fellow, 2009. Vicar Gen., Principal and Pres. of Consistory Court, and Chancellor, Dio. of St Asaph, 2010–. DL Clwyd, 2008. *Recreations:* golf, walking, travel, gardening, watching cricket, soccer, Rugby Union. *Clubs:* Lansdowne; Chester City (Pres., 2011–12), Cheshire Pitt; Wrexham Golf.

**DUTTON, Timothy Christopher;** QC 2013; *b* Essex, 1962; *s* of John Arthur and Patricia Dutton. *Educ:* Godalming Co. Grammar Sch.; Univ. of Durham (BA). Called to the Bar, Inner Temple, 1985; in practice as barrister, 1985–. Mem. Council, Incorporated Council of Law Reporting, 2014–. *Recreations:* Association Croquet, music (performing and listening), opera. *Address:* Maitland Chambers, 7 Stone Buildings, Lincoln's Inn, WC2A 3SZ. *T:* (020) 7406 1200, *Fax:* (020) 7406 1300. *Club:* Hurlingham.

**DUTTON, Timothy James,** CBE 2016; QC 1998; a Recorder, 2000–17; a Deputy High Court Judge, since 2009; *b* 25 Feb. 1957; *s* of late J. D. Dutton, MA, JP and J. R. Dutton (*née* Parsons); *m* 1987, Sappho Dias; one *d*. *Educ:* Repton Sch.; Keble Coll., Oxford (BA Jurisp. 1978). Called to the Bar, Middle Temple, 1979, Bencher, 2003; an Asst Recorder, 1998–2000. Leader, SE Circuit, 2004–06. Hd, Fountain Court Chambers, 2008–13. Chm., Bench Selection Adv. Cttee, Middle Temple, 2012–14. Advocacy teaching for Nat. Inst. for Trial Advocacy and the Bar, UK and USA, 1987–; Founder and Dir, Keble Advanced Advocacy Course, 1994–2004. Chm., Inns of Court Advocacy Trng Cttee, 2000–04; Bar Council: Vice-Chm., 2007; Chm., 2008; Vice-Chm., Direct Access Cttee, 2001–03; Chm., Wkg Party into Advocacy Trng, 2002–04; Vice-Chm., Educn and Trng Cttee, 2003–04. Founder Mem., Burma Justice Cttee, 2007–. Chair, AIM Disciplinary Tribunals, 2018–. Chm., Assoc. of Regulatory and Disciplinary Lawyers, 2009–15; Member: Admin. Law Bar Assoc.; Commercial Bar Assoc. Lectured widely on professional negligence, regulation and legal services. Dir, Burford Capital Hldgs (UK) Ltd, 2017– (Chm., Investment Cttee, 2017–). Trustee, Legal Educn Foundn (formerly Coll. of Law), 2011–. Founder and Chm., Bar Choral Soc., 2014–17. Mem., Editl Bd, Cordery on Legal Services, 2018–. Silk of the Year Professional Discipline, 2010, Lifetime Achievement Award, 2015, Chambers and Partners. *Publications:* (contrib.) Guide to the Legal Services Act 2007, 2008; contribs to Lloyds List, Financial Times, (on insce law) World Policy Review Guide. *Recreations:* music (French Horn, baritone, choral), sailing, gardening. *Address:* Fountain Court Chambers, Temple, EC4Y 9DH. *T:* (020) 7583 3335.

**DUTTON, Prof. William Harold,** PhD; Quello Chair, Department of Media and Information, and Director, Quello Center, College of Communication Arts and Sciences, Michigan State University, since 2014; *b* 23 Aug. 1947; *s* of Paul V. Dutton and Rosa Lee Dutton; *m* 1981, Diana; two *d*. *Educ:* Univ. of Missouri, Columbia (BA Hons Pol Sci. 1969); State Univ. of NY, Buffalo (MA 1971; PhD Pol Sci. 1974); MA Oxon 2002. Instructor, Dept of Pol Sci., SUNY, Buffalo, 1972–73; Asst Prof., Dept of Pol Sci., Univ. of S Florida, 1973–74; Asst Res. Pol Scientist, Public Policy Res. Orgn, Univ. of Calif, Irvine, 1974–78; Associate Prof., Sch. of Public Admin and Urban Studies, San Diego State Univ., 1978–80; Annenberg School for Communication, University of Southern California: Associate Prof., 1980–82; Associate Prof. (with tenure), 1983–89; Prof., 1990–2002; Prof. of Internet Studies, 2002–14, Founding Dir, Oxford Internet Inst., 2002–11, Univ. of Oxford; Fellow, Balliol Coll., Oxford, 2002–14. Vis. Res. Pol Scientist, Univ. of Calif, Irvine, 1979–82; Brunel University: Fulbright Schol. and Vis. Prof., Dept of Human Scis, 1986–87; Nat. Dir, Prog. on Inf. and Communication Technol., ESRC and Vis. Prof., Dept of Human Scis, 1993–95. Chm., Adv. Cttee for England, 2009–14, Mem. for SE, 2009–14, Ofcom. Fellow, Internat. Communication Assoc., 2015. *Publications:* (jtly) The Management of Information Systems, 1981; (jtly) Computers and Politics: high technology in American local governments, 1982; (with K. L. Kraemer) Modeling as Negotiating: the political dynamics of computer models in the policy process, 1985; (ed jtly) Information and Communication Technologies: visions and realities, 1996; (ed jtly) The Social Shaping of the Information Superhighway: European and American roads to the information society, 1997; Society on the Line: information politics in the digital age, 1999; (ed jtly) Digital Academe, 2002; Social Transformation in the Information Society, 2004; (ed jtly) Transforming Enterprise, 2005; (ed jtly) World Wide Research, 2010; (jtly) Freedom of Connection—Freedom of Expression, 2011; The Oxford Handbook of Internet Studies, 2013; (ed jtly) Society and the Internet, 2014; contrib. chapters in books; contrib. articles to professional jls incl. Prometheus, Information, Communication & Society. *Recreations:* walking, blogging, learning to play the piano. *Address:* Quello Center, 406 Communication Arts Building, Michigan State University, East Lansing, MI 48824–1212, USA. *T:* (517) 4328001, *Fax:* (517) 4328065. *E:* william.dutton@gmail.com, wdutton@msu.edu.

**DUVAL, Robin Arthur Philip,** CBE 2005; Director, British Board of Film Classification, 1999–2004; *b* 28 April 1941; *s* of Arthur and Jane Duval; *m* 1968, Lorna Eileen Watson; four *d* (one *s* decd). *Educ:* King Edward's Sch., Birmingham; University Coll. London (BA); Univ. of Michigan (Fulbright Schol.). Studio manager, BBC, 1964–65; TV producer, J. Walter Thompson, 1965–68; documentary and film producer, COI, 1968–78; Hd, Overseas Prodn, COI, 1978–81; Principal, Home Office, 1981–83; Hd, UK Prodn, COI, 1983–85; Chief Asst, Television, IBA, 1985–90; Dep. Dir, Programmes, ITC, 1991–98. *Publications:* novels: Bear in the Woods, 2010; Below the Thunder, 2013; Not Single Spies, 2015; articles in jls. *Recreations:* music, food, Aston Villa. *Address:* 35 Castlebar Park, Ealing, W5 1DA.

**DUVALL, Leonard,** OBE 1998; Member (Lab) Greenwich and Lewisham, since 2000, and Leader, Labour Group, since 2004, London Assembly, Greater London Authority; *b* 26 Sept. 1961; *m* (marr. diss.); two *s*. *Educ:* Hawthorn Sch., London. Mem., Greenwich LBC, 1990–2000 (Leader of Council, 1992–2000). Chairman: London Thames Gateway Partnership, 1997–2000; Local Govt Improvement and Develt Agency, 1998–2000; Dep. Chm., Assoc. of London Govt, 1996–2000; Chm., Commonwealth Local Govt Forum, 2000–05 (Vice-Chm., 1998–2000). Vice-Chm., London Develt Agency, 2000–03; Chairman: London Health Commn, 2002–04; Metropolitan Police Authy, 2004–08. Chm., Gtr London Lab. Party, 2002–. Non-exec. Dir, Tilfen Land, 2001–14. Chm., Royal Greenwich Heritage Trust, 2014–16; Trustee, Greenwich Foundn for Old Royal Naval Coll., 1997–2002; non-exec. Dir, Royal Artillery Museums Trust, 1998–2009. Chair, S London Special League, 2017–. Mem., Council of Friends, Royal Artillery Collection, 2016–. *Address:* Greater London Authority, City Hall, Queen's Walk, SE1 2AA. *T:* (020) 7983 4408/4517.

**DUXBURY, Patrick Charles;** Partner, Gowling WLG (UK) LLP (formerly Wragge & Co.), since 1999; *b* Blackburn, Lancs, 10 July 1968; *s* of Leslie John Duxbury and Ruth Duxbury; *m* 1993, Andrea Janet Allen; two *s* one *d*. *Educ:* Queen Elizabeth's Grammar Sch., Blackburn; Newcastle Univ. (BSc Hons Microbiol.); Coll. of Law, Chester (CPE Dist.; Law Soc. Finals 1st cl. Hons). Admitted solicitor, 1993; Associate, Wragge & Co., 1995–99. *Recreations:* trying to keep up with my wife and kids, the great outdoors. *Address:* High Barn House, Spring Lane, Langley, Warks CV37 0HW. *T:* 07818 003973. *E:* patrick.duxbury@gowlingwlg.com.

**DUXFIELD, Julian;** Human Resources Director, University of Oxford, since 2013; Fellow, Somerville College, Oxford, since 2013; *b* 9 Sept. 1962; *s* of John and Wendy Duxfield; partner Lucie Carrington; two *s* one *d*. *Educ:* Corpus Christi Coll., Oxford (BA PPE); London Sch. of Econs (MSc HR Mgt). HR rôles in Unilever, 1988–2000; HR Dir, Carlsberg UK, 2000–03; Dir, Human Resources, DfT, 2003–07; HR Dir, G4S Cash Solutions (formerly Cash Services UK, Gp 4 Securicor), 2007–11; UK HR Dir, G4S, 2011–12. Ext. Mem., Remuneration Cttee, Care Quality Commn, 2009–13. Member: Climbers' Club; Fell and Rock Climbing Club; Oxford Alpine Club; Oxford Mountaineering Club; VC Jericho. *Recreations:* mountaineering, cycling. *Address:* University of Oxford, Wellington Square, Oxford OX1 2JD. *E:* julian.duxfield@admin.ox.ac.uk.

**DWEK, Prof. Raymond Allen,** CBE 2013; DPhil, DSc; FRS 1998; CChem, FRSC; CBiol, FRSB; Professor of Glycobiology, and Director of Glycobiology Institute (formerly Unit), University of Oxford, 1988–2016, now Emeritus Professor and Hon. Director; Professorial Fellow, Exeter College, Oxford, 1988–2009, now Emeritus (Fellow, 1974–88); *b* 10 Nov. 1941; *s* of Victor Joe Dwek and Alice Liniado; *m* 1964, Sandra (*née* Livingstone); two *s* two *d*. *Educ:* Carmel Coll.; Manchester Univ. (BSc 1st Cl. Hons Chemistry and Mercer Scholar, 1963; MSc 1964); Lincoln Coll., Oxford (DPhil 1966; Hon. Fellow 2004); Exeter Coll., Oxford (DSc 1985). CChem, FRSC 1993; CBiol, FRSB (FIBiol 1999). Oxford University: Deptl Demonstrator, 1969–74; Lectr, 1976–88; Associate Hd, 1996–2000, Head, 2000–06, Biochem. Dept; Royal Soc. Locke Res. Fellow, 1974–76; Christ Church: Res. Lectr in Physical Chemistry, 1966–68, in Biochem., 1975–76; Lectr in Inorganic Chem., 1968–75; Lectr in Biochem., Trinity Coll., 1976–84. Vis. Royal Soc. Res. Fellow, Weizmann Inst., Rehovot, Israel, 1969; Kluge Chair of Technol. and Soc., Liby of Congress, Washington, 2007; Visiting Professor: Duke Univ., NC, seconded to Inst. of Exploratory Res., Fort Monmouth, NJ, 1968; Univ. of Trieste, Italy, 1974; Univ. of Lund, Sweden, 1977; Inst. of Enzymology, Budapest, 1980. Boyce Thompson Dist. Lectr in Glycobiology, Cornell Univ., USA, 1997; Sir Douglas Hague Lectr, Oxford Business Sch., 2010. Dir and Founding Scientist, Oxford GlycoScience (formerly Oxford GlycoSystems) Ltd, 1988–2003; Chm., Oxford University Consulting Ltd, 2000–02; Director: United Therapeutics, 2002–; Isis Innovation, 2003–08. Co-Chm., British Israel

Academic Exchange Regenerative Medicine Initiative, 2012–. Member: Oxford Enzyme Gp, 1971–88; MRC AIDS Antiviral Steering Cttee, 1987–89; Founder Mem., Oxford Oligosaccharide Gp, 1983. Mem., Bd of Scientific Governors, 2003–, and Inst. Prof., Scripps Res. Inst., La Jolla, 2008–; Special Advr on Biotechnol. to Pres., Ben Gurion Univ. of the Negev, 2001–. Pres., Inst. of Biol., 2007–09. Hon. FRCP 2007. Internat. Mem. (formerly Foreign Mem.), Amer. Philosophical Soc., 2007. Mem., editl bds. Wellcome Trust Award, for research in biochemistry related to medicine, 1994. Hon. Dr: Leuven, 1996; Univ. Coll. Dublin, 2010; Hon. PhD Ben Gurion Univ. of Negev, 2001; Hon. DSc Scripps Res. Inst., USA, 2004; Dr *hc* Causa Cluj, Romania, 2006; Dip. *hc* Romanian Acad., 2010. First Scientific Leadership Award, Hepatitis B Foundn, Philadelphia, 1997; Centennial Award, Delaware Valley Coll., Penn, 1997; Huxley Medal, Inst. Biol., 2007; K. T. Wang Prize, Taiwan, 2010. Comdr, Nat. Order for Merit (Romania), 2000. *Publications:* Nuclear Magnetic Resonance (NMR) in Biochemistry, 1973; (jtly) Physical Chemistry Principles and Problems for Biochemists, 1975, 3rd edn 1983; (jtly) NMR in Biology, 1977; (jtly) Biological Spectroscopy, 1984; articles in books and jls on physical chemistry, biochemistry and medicine; various patents. *Recreations:* family, sport, listening to music. *Address:* Exeter College, Oxford OX1 3DP. *T:* (01865) 275344; Glycobiology Institute, Department of Biochemistry, University of Oxford, South Parks Road, Oxford OX1 3QU.

**DWESAR, Sandeep,** FCA; Chief Operating and Financial Officer, Barbican Centre and Guildhall School of Music and Drama, since 2010 (Finance Director, 2007–10); *b* New Delhi, India, 7 Jan. 1960; *s* of Mahendra and Asha Dwesar; *m* 1987, Kiran Bala Makkar; one *s* one *d*. *Educ:* Bristol Poly. (BA Hons). ACA 1989, FCA 2011. Lawrence Fink & Co., 1982–86; Fraser Limebeer, 1986–87; Financial Controller, Tiphook Rail Ltd, 1988–91; Eur. Treasury Manager, J. I. Case, Tenneco Inc., 1991–92; Hd of Finance, Lewisham Directeam, 1992–95; Consultant, London Bor. of Haringey, 1995–98; Finance Dir, Barbican Centre, 1999–2007. Non-exec. Dir, Cavendish Publishing Ltd, 1999–2005. Trustee: Friends of Baale Mane, 2007–; Punchdrunk, 2010–18; Design Council, 2011–18; Help Musicians UK, 2015–. *Recreations:* history, golf, debating. *Address:* Barbican Centre, Silk Street, EC2Y 8DS. *T:* (020) 7382 7075. *E:* sandeep.dwesar@barbican.org.uk.

**DWIGHT, Reginald Kenneth;** *see* John, Sir E. H.

**DWORKIN, Prof. Gerald;** Herbert Smith Professor of European Law and Director, Centre of European Law, King's College, University of London, 1993–97, now Professor Emeritus; Director, Intellectual Property Academy, Singapore, 2003–05; *b* 8 July 1933; *s* of Louis and Rose Dworkin; *m* 1960, Celia Sharon Levin; two *s* one *d*. *Educ:* Raine's Grammar Sch., London; Univ. of Nottingham (LLB 1954). Admitted solicitor of Supreme Court, 1957; Asst Lectr, Lectr, then Reader, LSE, 1958–67; Prof. of Law, Univ. of Southampton, 1968–86; Herchel Smith Prof. of Intellectual Property Law, QMW, Univ. of London, 1986–92. Visiting Professor: Univ. of Monash, 1965–67, 1980, 1987; Univ. of NSW, 1975; Nat. Univ. of Singapore, 1985, 1991, 1997; Arizona State Univ., 1985. Mem., EC Cttee, Academic Experts on Copyright Law. Member: Council, Intellectual Property Inst. (formerly Common Law Inst. of Intellectual Property); Brit. Literary and Artistic Copyright Soc.; Law Soc. Sub-cttee on Intellectual Property. Chm., British Copyright Council. FRSA 1993. Member of Board: Mod. Law Rev.; European Intellectual Property Law Rev.; Intellectual Property Jl. *Publications:* (with R. Taylor) Guide to Copyright Law, 1989. *Address:* 30 Keverstone Court, 97 Manor Road, Bournemouth BH1 3EX. *T:* (01202) 392256.

**DWYER, Aileen Margaret;** *see* Keel, A. M.

**DWYER, Glenn N.;** *see* Neil-Dwyer.

**DWYER, Sir Joseph (Anthony),** Kt 2001; FREng; DL; Group Chairman, George Wimpey PLC, 1996–99 (Director, 1988; Group Chief Executive Officer, 1991–98); *b* 20 June 1939. CEng, FREng (FEng 1997); FICE, FCIOB. President: CIOB, 1998–99; ICE, 2000–01. Dir, ETB, 2001–02. Chairman: Liverpool Vision (Urban Regeneration Co.), 1999–2008; Construction for Merseyside Ltd, 2004–08. DL Merseyside, 2008. Hon. Fellow, Liverpool John Moores Univ., 2003. Hon. LLD Liverpool, 2002; Hon. DSc Nottingham, 2004. Citizen of Honour Award, Liverpool City, 2009.

**DWYER-JOYCE, Prof. Robert Sean,** PhD; FREng; Professor of Tribology, since 2007 and Director, Leonardo Centre for Tribology and Surface Engineering, since 2009, University of Sheffield; *b* Chelmsford, 10 March 1966; *s* of Robert Myles Dwyer-Joyce and Annette Dwyer-Joyce; *m* 1998, Yajue Wu; two *d*. *Educ:* Brentwood Sch.; Imperial Coll., London (BEng Mech. Engrg 1987; PhD Tribology 1993). FIMechE 2007. Engrg trainee, Nat. Nuclear Corp., 1983–84; Prodn Engr, Petroleum Prodn, British Gas, 1987–89; University of Sheffield: Lectr in Mech. Engrg, 1994–2000; Sen. Lectr, 2000–06; Hd, Dept of Mech. Engrg, 2008–14. FREng 2018. *Publications:* 140 papers in archival and learned soc. jls. *Address:* Department of Mechanical Engineering, University of Sheffield, Sir Frederick Mappin Building, Mappin Street, Sheffield S1 3JD. *T:* (0114) 222 7736. *E:* r.dwyerjoyce@sheffield.ac.uk.

**DYCHE, Dame Rachael (Mary),** DBE 1997 (CBE 1992); Regional Director, Midlands, Conservative Party, 1993–98; *b* 29 Nov. 1945; *d* of late George Henry Dyche and Doreen Mary Dyche (*née* Rudgard). *Educ:* Burton upon Trent Tech. High Sch. Conservative Party: Agent: Burton, 1968–72; Harwich, 1972–75; Deputy Central Office Agent: Wales, 1975–76; W Midlands, 1976–85; Wessex, 1985–88; Central Office Agent, E Midlands, 1988–93. Mem., Nat. Soc. Cons. and Unionist Agents, 1968–. Member: PCC, All Saints, Lubenham, 2003–15 (Asst Church Warden, 2004–07; Church Warden, 2007–16); Village Hall Cttee, Lubenham, 1999–2014; Heritage Gp, Lubenham, 2001–12. *Recreations:* golf, gardening, music, horse riding, walking, member of National Trust. *Address:* 2 Channing Mews, Gloucester Road, Ross-on-Wye HR9 5WH.

**DYCKHOFF, Thomas Charles;** writer, architectural historian and broadcaster; *b* St Albans, 27 Feb. 1971; *s* of Brian and Helen Dyckhoff; *m* 2009, Claire Barrett; two *s*. *Educ:* Aylesbury Grammar Sch.; Royal Grammar Sch., Worcester; Christ Church, Oxford (MA Hons Geog.); University Coll. London (MSc Hons Architectural Hist.). Asst Ed., Perspectives on Architecture, 1995–98; Dep. Ed., Space, 1998–2001, Prodn Ed., Weekend, 2001–03, The Guardian; Architecture Critic, The Times, 2003–11. TV presenter, BBC, Channel 4, 2004–. Hon. Sen. Res. Associate, UCL, 2011–16. Mem., Stirling Prize Jury, RIBA, 2008–11. Hon. FRIBA 2011. Ed., Sir Banister Fletcher's A History of Architecture, 2014–16. *Publications:* The Age of Spectacle: adventures in architecture and the 21st century city, 2017. *Recreations:* gluttony, staring out of the window, butchery and pie-making.

**DYE, Dr Christopher,** FMedSci; FRS 2012; FRSB; Director of Strategy, Policy and Information (formerly Director of Strategy), Office of Director General, World Health Organization, Geneva, 2014–18; Visiting Professor of Zoology, University of Oxford, since 2009; Visiting Fellow, All Souls College, Oxford; *b* Belfast, 15 April 1956; *s* of Albert Edward Dye and Shirley Helen Dye (*née* Wooldridge); *m* 1988, Enricke Bouma; three *s*. *Educ:* De La Salle Coll., Sheffield; Vyners Sch., Ickenham, Middx; Univ. of York (BA 1st Cl. Hons Biol. 1978); Wolfson Coll., Oxford (DPhil Zool. 1982). FRSB (FSB 2008). Postgrad. Res. Asst (desert ecol.), New Mexico State Univ., 1978–79; NERC Postdoctoral Fellow (ecol. of insect vectors of disease), Imperial Coll. London, 1982–84; London School of Hygiene and Tropical Medicine: MRC Postdoctoral Res. Fellow, 1984–85; Lectr, Sen. Lectr, then Reader in Population Biol., 1985–96; Hd, Vector Biol. and Epidemiol. Unit, 1990–96; World Health Organization, Geneva: Coordinator, Tuberculosis Monitoring and Evaluation, Tuberculosis Dept, 1996–2008; Dir, Office of Health Information, HIV/AIDS, Tuberculosis, Malaria and Neglected Tropical Diseases, 2008–14. Gresham Prof. of Physic (and other Biol Scis), Gresham Coll., London, 2006–09. Member: British Ecol Soc., 1980; British Soc. for Parasitol., 1986. FRSTM&H 1985; Scientific FZS 1994; FMedSci 2008. *Publications:* Global Tuberculosis Control, 12 vols, 1997–2008; World Malaria Report 2008, 2008; World Health Report 2013, 2013; The Population Biology of Tuberculosis, 2015; contrib. 300 articles to scientific jls and books. *Recreations:* running and cycling, all terrains.

**DYE, Air Vice-Marshal Dr Peter John,** OBE 1992; CEng; Director General, RAF Museum, 2009–14 (Deputy Director General and Director, Collections Division, 2008–09); historian and museum consultant, since 2014; *b* 17 Aug. 1953; *s* of Roy Mackenzie Dye and Margaret Mary Dye (*née* Chauffourier); *m* 1985, Anne Catherine Waine; two *d*. *Educ:* Sevenoaks Sch.; Imperial Coll., Univ. of London (BSc Eng 1975); RAF Coll., Cranwell; Univ. of Birmingham (DPhil 2014). CEng 1989; MRAeS 1989. Commnd RAF, 1972; served UK, Germany and Canada; Sen. Engrg Officer, No IX Sqdn, 1986–88; OC Engrg and Supply Wing, RAF Coltishall, 1990–91; PSO AOC-in-C, RAF Support Comd, 1991–94 and AOC-in-C, Logistics Comd, 1994; Dir, Dept of Specialist Ground Trng, 1994–96; rcds 1997; AO Wales, 1999–2001; Air Cdre Ground Trng, 2001–05; Dep. C-in-C, Personnel and Trng Comd, and COS to Air Mem. for Personnel, 2005–07; Head: RAF Process and Orgn Rev., 2006–07; Collocated HQ, 2006–08; RAF Transformation, 2007–08. Hon. Res. Fellow, Coll. of Arts and Law, Univ. of Birmingham, 2015–; Vis. Lectr, Univ. of Wolverhampton, 2019–. ACGI 1975. Pres., Cross and Cockade, First World War Aviation Histl Soc. *Publications:* The Bridge to Air Power, 2015; The Man Who Took the Rap: Sir Robert Brooke-Popham and the fall of Singapore, 2018; articles and reviews. *Recreations:* aviation history, archaeology. *Club:* Royal Air Force.

**DYER, Alexander Patrick;** Chief Executive and Deputy Chairman, BOC Group plc, 1993–96; Deputy Chairman, Bunzl plc, 1996–2005 (Chairman 1993–96); *b* 30 Aug. 1932; *m* 1954, Shirley Shine; one *s* (and one *s* decd). *Educ:* US Military Acad. (BSc Engrg); Harvard Business Sch. (MBA). US Army, 1954–57; Esso Corp., 1959–63; Air Products, 1963–89; Gp Vice Pres., Gases, 1978–87; Exec. Vice Pres., Gas and Equipment, 1987–89; Bd Dir, 1988–89; Man. Dir, Gases, BOC Gp, 1989–93. *Recreations:* golf, skeet. *Address:* 2117 Kirkland Village Circle, Bethlehem, PA 18017, USA. *Clubs:* University (New York); Saucon Valley Country; Weyhill Skeet.

**DYER, Rt Rev. Anne Catherine;** *see* Aberdeen and Orkney, Bishop of.

**DYER, Charles;** playwright and novelist; actor-director (as Raymond Dyer); *b* 7 July 1928; *s* of James Sidney Dyer and Florence (*née* Stretton); *m* 1959, Fiona Thomson, actress; three *s*. *Educ:* Queen Elizabeth's Sch., Barnet. *Plays:* Clubs Are Sometimes Trumps, 1948; Who On Earth!, 1951; Turtle in the Soup, 1953; The Jovial Parasite, 1954; Single Ticket Mars, 1955; Time, Murderer, Please, and Poison In Jest, 1956; Wanted—One Body!, 1958; Prelude to Fury, 1959 (also wrote theme music); Rattle of A Simple Man, 1962 (also in Berlin, Paris, NY, Rome and London), 1981, 2004, USA, 1985, 1990, Netherlands, 1988, Germany, 1993, Scandinavia, 1993, 1995; Staircase, 1966 (for RSC; also in NY, Paris (1968, 1982, 1986, 1992), Amsterdam, Berlin, Rome, 1988, 1992, Vienna, Brazil, 1992, trans-Germany, 1992–95); Mother Adam, Paris, Berlin, 1970, London, 1971, 1973, NY, 1974; The Loving Allelujah, 1974; Circling Dancers, 1979; Lovers Dancing, 1981, 1983; Futility Rites, 1981; as R. Kraselchik: Red Cabbage and Kings, 1960 (also wrote theme music); *screenplays:* Rattle, 1964; Insurance Italian Style, 1967; Staircase, 1968; Brother Sun and Sister Moon, 1970. Also directed plays for the stage and television. Acted in 230 plays and films; London début as Duke in Worm's Eye View, Whitehall, 1948; *films* include: Cuptie Honeymoon, 1947; Britannia Mews, 1949; Road Sense, 1950; Off The Record, 1952; Pickwick Papers, 1952; Dockland Case, 1953; Strange Case of Blondie, 1953; Naval Patrol, 1959; Loneliness of the Long Distance Runner, 1962; Mouse On The Moon, 1962; Knack, 1964; Rattle of A Simple Man, 1964; How I Won The War, 1967; *television:* Charlie in Staircase, BBC, 1986; *television series:* Hugh and I, 1964. Knight of Mark Twain (USA), 1972; Chevalier, Légion d'Honneur (France), 2015. *Publications:* (as Charles Dyer): plays: Wanted—One Body!, 1961; Time, Murderer, Please, 1962; Rattle Of A Simple Man, (Fr.) 1963; Staircase, 1966; Mother Adam, 1970; The Loneliness Trilogy, 1972; Hot Godly Wind, 1973; Red Plush and Trombones: the lonely trilogy, 2011; novels: Rattle Of A Simple Man, 1964; Charlie Always Told Harry Almost Everything, 1969 (USA and Europe, 1970); The Rising of our Herbert, 1972; Wilderness of Monkeys (autobiog.), 2005. *Recreations:* amateur music and carpentry. *Address:* Old Wob, Austenwood Common, Gerrards Cross, Bucks SL9 8SF.

**DYER, Christine Helen H.;** *see* Hewitt-Dyer.

**DYER, Prof. Christopher Charles,** CBE 2008; PhD; FBA 1995; FSA; Professor of Regional and Local History, and Director, Centre for English Local History, University of Leicester, 2001–10, now Emeritus, and Leverhulme Emeritus Fellow, 2011–12; Honorary Senior Research Fellow, Institute of Historical Research, University of London, since 2013; *b* 24 Dec. 1944; *s* of Charles James Dyer and Doris Mary Dyer; *m* 1967, Jenifer Ann Dent; one *s* one *d*. *Educ:* Univ. of Birmingham (BA, PhD). Asst Lectr in History, Univ. of Edinburgh, 1967–70; Lectr, Sen. Lectr, then Reader, 1970–90, Prof. of Medieval Social History, 1991–2001, Univ. of Birmingham. Ford Lectr in Hist., Oxford Univ., 2000–01. Leverhulme Emeritus Fellow, 2011–12; Sen. Res. Fellow, Univ. of Birmingham, 2013–14. President: Soc. for Medieval Archaeology, 1998–2001 (Vice-Pres., 2011–); Bristol and Glos Archaeol Soc., 2001–02; British Agricl Hist. Soc., 2004–07 (Vice-Pres., 2009–); Worcs Histl Soc., 2012–; Vice-President: Medieval Settlement Res. Gp, 2010– (Pres., 1997–99); English Place-Name Soc., 2014–. Chairman: Victoria County History Cttee, 1997–2004; Dugdale Soc., 2003–; Records of Social and Economic History Cttee, British Acad., 2004–10. FSA 1994; AcSS 2006–08. *Publications:* Lords and Peasants in a Changing Society, 1980; Standards of Living in the later Middle Ages, 1989; Everyday Life in Medieval England, 1994; Making a Living in the Middle Ages 850–1520, 2002; An Age of Transition, 2005; A Country Merchant 1495–1520: trading and farming at the end of the Middle Ages, 2012. *Address:* Centre for English Local History, University of Leicester, Marc Fitch House, 5 Salisbury Road, Leicester LE1 7QR. *T:* (0116) 252 2765.

**DYER, Nigel Ingram John;** QC 2006; *b* 21 Sept. 1957; *s* of late Derek Ingram Dyer and Elizabeth Dyer; *m* 1986, Victoria Duckham; one *s* one *d*. *Educ:* St Mary's Sch., Nairobi; Oratory Sch.; Durham Univ. (BA Jt Hons Law and Politics). Called to the Bar: Inner Temple, 1982; BVI, 2011; Mem., Western Circuit. Member: President's Ancillary Relief Adv. Gp, Family Div., 2000–05; Money and Property Cttee, Family Justice Council, 2005–11. *Publications:* (ed jtly) Rayden and Jackson on Divorce and Family Matters, 18th edn 2005; (ed jtly) Detection and Preservation of Assets in Financial Remedy Claims, 2014. *Recreations:* gardening, opera, theatre, running. *Address:* 1 Hare Court, Temple, EC4Y 7BE. *T:* (020) 7797 7070, *Fax:* (020) 7797 7435. *E:* dyer@1hc.com. *Clubs:* Hurlingham, MCC; Rye Tennis.

**DYER, Penelope Jane, (Penny), (Mrs N. C. J. Day);** freelance voice and dialect specialist, since 1983; *b* St Leonards-on-Sea, Sussex, 30 May 1957; *d* of Paul M. C. Dyer and June D. Dyer (*née* Guy); *m* 1996, Nicholas C. J. Day. *Educ:* Barton Sch. Kindergarten, St Leonards-on-Sea; St Mary's Sch., St Leonards-on-Sea; Central Sch. of Speech and Drama (BEd and Advanced Dip. Voice Studies). Speech, drama and English teacher, Bodiam Manor, Bedgebury, Cranbrook, St Mary's and Ancaster Hse schs, E Sussex and Kent, 1979–83; peripatetic teacher, Rose Bruford Coll. of Speech and Drama, Drama and Musical Depts of Arts Educnl Schs, Italia Conti Stage Sch. and Questors Th. Drama Course, 1984–87; Main Voice and Dialect Tutor, Actg Course and Voice Dip., Central Sch. of Speech and Drama, 1987–90; Speech and Dialect Tutor, RADA, 1991–95; Voice and Dialect Tutor, The Poor Sch., 1991–95. Work in theatre, TV and film, 1986–: *theatre* includes: Another Time, 1989; Shadowlands, Wyndhams, 1990; Cyrano de Bergerac, 1992; Mojo, Royal Court; The Blue Room, Donmar; My Fair Lady; The Crucible, RSC; Frost Nixon, Gielgud; Parade, Donmar; Fiddler on the Roof, Savoy; Boeing, Boeing, Comedy; Speed the Plow, Old Vic; Piaf, Donmar; *television* includes: A Small Dance (screenplay), 1990; Band of Gold; Longford; The Deal, 2003; Blackpool, 2004; A Short Stay in Switzerland, 2009; *films* include: Bhaji on the Beach, 1993; Elizabeth, 1998; The War Zone, 1999; The Importance of Being Earnest, 2002; Dirty Pretty Things, 2003; Ladies in Lavender, 2004; Mrs Henderson Presents, 2005; The Da Vinci Code, 2006; Infamous, 2006; The Queen, 2006; Elizabeth: the Golden Age, 2007. *Publications:* Access Accents, 2007; booklets on British and American dialects. *Recreations:* swimming, walking, reading, poetry, yoga, food, all music, maps, art, all while talking in funny voices! *E:* sarah.upson@voicecoach.tv. *Clubs:* Union, Ronnie Scott's.

**DYER, Dr Richard George,** OBE 2007; Chief Executive, Biosciences Federation, 2006–09; *b* 18 July 1943; *s* of late Comdr Charles William Dyer, RN and Dorothy Patricia Victoria Vaughan-Hogan; *m* 1st, 1967, Shirley James Foulsham (marr. diss. 1995); two *s* one *d*; 2nd, 2000, Dr Caroline Edmonds (*née* Porter); one *d*. *Educ:* Churcher's Coll., Petersfield; Univ. of London (BSc 1967); Univ. of Birmingham (MSc 1968); Univ. of Bristol (PhD 1972). Research, Dept of Anatomy, Bristol Med. Sch., 1968–74; ARC Institute of Animal Physiology, subseq. AFRC Institute of Animal Physiology and Genetics Research, then Babraham Institute: Head, Dept of Neuroendocrinology, 1985–90; Head, Cambridge Station, 1989–90; Associate Dir of Inst., 1991–93; Exec. Dir, 1993–94; Dir, 1994–2005. Teacher of Physiol., Jesus Coll., Cambridge, 1977–90; Res. Fellowships, Germany and France; Consultant for WHO, Shanghai, 1983–86. Member: AFRC Animals Res. Bd, 1992–93; AFRC Strategy Bd, 1993; various BBSRC cttees and panels, 1993–2012, incl. Animal Sci. and Psych. Cttee, 1994–96; Cttee, R&D Soc., 1998–2000; European Science Foundation: Member: Life and Envmtl Scis Standing Cttee, 1995–2000; Eur. Medical Res. Councils, 1996–2000; Exec. Bd, 1999–2007; Chm., Finance and Audit Cttee, 2004–07; Vice-Pres., 2004–07. Member, Board: Babraham Bioscience Technologies Ltd, 1998–2008 (Chm., 2000–05); Univ. of Cambridge Challenge, then Venture, Fund, 1999–2004. Medal, Soc. for Endocrinology, 1986; Medal, Polish Physiol. Soc., 1987. Former Member, Editorial Board: Exptl Brain Res.; Jl of Endocrinology. *Publications:* (ed with R. J. Bicknell) Brain Opioid Systems in Reproduction, 1989; numerous papers on neuroendocrine topics in learned jls. *Recreations:* finding bargains, escaping to mountains and sea, lively dinners.

**DYER, Prof. Richard William,** PhD; FBA 2012; Professor of Film Studies, King's College London, 2006–15, now Emeritus; Professorial Fellow in Film Studies, St Andrews University, 2011–17, now Honorary (Wardlaw Professor, 2013); *b* Leeds, 1 June 1945; *s* of Gilbert and Kathleen Dyer. *Educ:* St Andrews Univ. (MA French 1968); Centre for Contemp. Cultural Studies, Birmingham Univ. (PhD 1973). Lectr, Univ. of Keele, 1974–77; Lectr, 1979–88, Sen. Lectr, 1988–93, Prof., 1993–2006, Univ. of Warwick, 1979–2006. Dist. Adjunct Prof., UCD, 2010; Visiting Professor: Univ. of Pennsylvania, Annenberg Sch. of Communications, 1985; Univ. of Stockholm (Cinema Studies), 1996, 2006, 2010; New York Univ. (Cinema Studies), 2003; Bauhaus Univ., Weimar, 2009; Univ. of Indiana Bloomington, 2015. Lifetime Hon. Mem., Soc. for Cinema and Media Studies, 2007. Hon. DH Turku, 2009; Hon. Dr Bordeaux Montaigne, 2018. Lifetime Achievement Award, British Assoc. of Film, TV and Screen Studies, 2014; James Robert Brudner '83 Meml Prize, Yale Univ., 2014. *Publications:* Stars, 1979, new edn 1998; Heavenly Bodies, 1987, new edn 2004; Now You See It, 1990, new edn 2003; Only Entertainment, 1992, new edn 2002; The Matter of Images, 1993, new edn 2003; Brief Encounter, 1993; White, 1997; Seven, 1999; The Culture of Queers, 2002; Pastiche, 2006; Nino Rota, 2010; In the Space of a Song, 2011; Lethal Repetition: serial killing in European cinema, 2015; La Dolce Vita, 2017. *Recreations:* talking with friends, theatre, film, dance, art, novels.

**DYER, Simon Christopher;** QC 2017; *b* Warrington, 17 March 1965; *s* of Christopher and Gillian Dyer; *m* 1996, Elizabeth Selman; three *s*. *Educ:* Temple Secondary Modern Sch.; Bishopsfield Comprehensive Sch.; Price's Sixth Form Coll.; Univ. of Kent (BA Law); Inns of Court Sch. of Law. Called to the Bar, Middle Temple, 1987. *Address:* End Farm Barn, Seymour Court Lane, Marlow, Bucks SL7 3DD. *T:* 07912 653020. *E:* sd@cloisters.com.

**DYER-BENNET, Sir David,** 17th Bt *cr* 1678; *b* 21 Sept. 1954; *s* of late Prof. John Dyer-Bennet and Mary Abby Dyer-Bennet; *S* kinsman, 2018, but his name does not appear on the Official Roll of the Baronetage; *m* 1982, Pamela Collins Dean.

**DYET, Fergus John C.;** *see* Cochrane-Dyet.

**DYKE;** *see* Hart Dyke.

**DYKE, Gregory;** Chairman, Trafalgar Entertainment Group, since 2017; *b* 20 May 1947; *s* of Joseph and Denise Dyke; *m* 2009, Sue Howes; one *s* one *d*; one step *s* one step *d*. *Educ:* Hayes Grammar Sch.; York Univ. (BA Politics). Varied career, 1965–83; Editor in Chief, TV-am, 1983–84; Dir of Programmes, TVS, 1984–87; London Weekend Television: Dir of Progs, 1987–91; Dep. Man. Dir, 1989–90; Man. Dir, subseq. Gp Chief Exec., 1990–94; Chm., GMTV, 1993–94; Director: Channel Four Television, 1988–92; BSkyB, 1995; Chm. and Chief Exec., Pearson Television, 1995–99; Exec. Dir, Pearson plc, 1996–99; Chm., Channel 5 Broadcasting, 1997–99; Dir-Gen., BBC, 2000–04. Chairman: HIT Entertainment Ltd, 2005–12; Brentford FC, 2006–13; BFI, 2008–16; Ambassador Th. Gp, 2009–16; FA, 2013–16. Non-executive Director: ITN, 1990–92; Manchester United FC, 1997–99; ProSiebenSat.1 Media AG, 2004–. Chm., ITV Council, 1992–94. Chancellor, York Univ., 2004–15. Trustee: Science Museum, 1996–2005; English Nat. Stadium Trust, 1997–99. *Publications:* Inside Story (memoirs), 2004. *Recreations:* football, ski-ing, horse-riding, movies, theatre.

**DYKES,** family name of **Baron Dykes**.

**DYKES,** Baron *cr* 2004 (Life Peer), of Harrow Weald in the London Borough of Harrow; **Hugh John Maxwell Dykes;** *b* 17 May 1939; *s* of Richard Dykes and Doreen Ismay Maxwell Dykes; *m* 1965, Susan Margaret Dykes (*née* Smith) (marr. diss. 2000); two *s* (and one *s* decd). *Educ:* Weston super Mare Grammar Sch.; Pembroke Coll., Cambridge. Partner, Simon & Coates, Stockbrokers, 1968–78; Associate Mem., Quilter, Hilton, Goodison, Stockbrokers, 1978. MCSI (MSI 1993). Dir, Dixons Stores Far East Ltd, 1985. Contested (C) Tottenham, 1966. MP (C) Harrow East, 1970–97; contested (C) same seat, 1997; joined Lib Dem party, 1997; contested (Lib Dem) London Region, Eur. Parly elecns, 1999. PPS: to three Parly Under-Secs of State for Defence, 1970; to Parly Under-Sec. of State in Civil Service Dept attached to Cabinet Office, 1973; Mem., H of C EEC Select Cttee, 1983–97. Mem., European Parlt, Strasbourg, 1974–77; Chairman: Cons. Parly European Cttee, 1979–80 (Vice-Chm., 1974–79); Commons Euro-Gp, 1988–97; Vice-Pres., Cons. Gp for EEC, 1982–86 (Chm., 1978–81). Chm., European Movement, 1990–97 (Jt Hon. Sec., 1982–87); Cons., 2005–07, Pres., 2007–09, European–Atlantic Gp. Mem., Lib Dem Team on EU, Foreign Affairs and Defence Policy, 1997–2004; Lib Dem spokesman on EU, 2005–10, on Envmt, Food and Rural Affairs, 2006–10, H of L; Mem., Hybrid Instruments Cttee, H of L, 2017–. Research Sec., Bow Gp, 1965; Chm., Coningsby Club, 1969. Governor: Royal Nat. Orthopaedic Hosp., 1975–82; N London Collegiate Sch., 1982. Order of Merit (Germany), 1993; Médaille pour l'Europe (Luxembourg), 1993; Chevalier: Ordre National du Mérite (France), 1994; Légion d'Honneur (France), 2003. *Publications:* (ed) Westropp's "Invest £100", 1964, and Westropp's "Start Your Own Business", 1965; (jtly) On the Edge: Britain and Europe, 2012; many articles and pamphlets on political and financial subjects. *Recreations:* music, theatre, swimming, travel, gardening. *Address:* House of Lords, SW1A 0PW. *Clubs:* Garrick, Beefsteak.

**DYKES, David Wilmer,** MA, PhD; Director, National Museum of Wales, 1986–89; *b* 18 Dec. 1933; *s* of late Captain David Dykes, OBE and Jenny Dykes; *m* 1967, Margaret Anne George; two *d*. *Educ:* Swansea Grammar Sch.; Corpus Christi Coll., Oxford (MA); PhD (Wales). FRNS 1958 (Parkes-Weber Prize, 1954); FRSAI 1963; FRHistS 1965; FSA 1973. Commnd RN and RNR, 1955–62. Civil Servant, Bd of Inland Revenue, 1958–59; administrative appts, Univ. of Bristol and Univ. Coll. of Swansea, 1959–63; Dep. Registrar, Univ. Coll. of Swansea, 1963–69; Registrar, Univ. of Warwick, 1969–72; Sec., Nat. Museum of Wales, 1972–86, Acting Dir, 1985–86. Mem., Treasure Valuation Cttee, DCMS, 2010–14. Hon. Lectr in History, University Coll., Cardiff, later Univ. of Wales Coll. of Cardiff, 1975–95. Pres., 1999–2003, Vice-Pres., 2009–, British Numismatic Soc. (Mem. Council, 1966–70 and 1997–). Trustee, UK Numismatic Trust, 1999–. Liveryman: Worshipful Co. of Tin Plate Workers, 1985; Livery Co. of Wales (formerly Welsh Livery Guild), 1993; Freeman, City of London, 1985. KStJ 1993 (CStJ 1991; Chancellor, Priory for Wales, 1991–98; Bailiff of St Davids, 1999–2002). *Publications:* Anglo-Saxon Coins in the National Museum of Wales, 1977; (ed and contrib.) Alan Sorrell: Early Wales Re-created, 1980; Wales in Vanity Fair, 1989; The University College of Swansea: an illustrated history, 1992; Coinage and Currency in Eighteenth-Century Britain: the provincial coinage, 2011 (North Book Prize, British Numismatic Soc., 2012); articles and reviews in numismatic, historical and other jls. *Recreations:* numismatics, writing. *E:* davwd@btinternet.com. *Clubs:* Athenæum; Cardiff and County (Cardiff).

**DYKES, Richard Thornton Booth;** Chairman, Carrenza Ltd, 2001–16; *b* 7 April 1945; *s* of Alan Thornton Dykes and Myra McFie Dykes (*née* Booth); *m* 1970, Janet Rosemary Cundall (marr. diss. 1995); one *s*. *Educ:* Rossall Sch. Articled clerk, Dehn & Lauderdale, solicitors, 1965–67; EO, later HEO, Min. of Labour, 1967–73; Private Sec. to Sec. of State for Employment, 1974–76; Principal, Econ. Policy Div., Dept of Employment, 1976–77; Dir, Industrial Relns, British Shipbuilders, 1977–80; Non-exec. Dir, Austin & Pickersgill Ltd, Sunderland, 1979–80; Principal Private Sec. to Sec. of State for Employment, 1980–82; Department of Employment: Hd, Unemployment Benefit Service, 1982–85; Sec., Sen. Mgt Gp, 1985–86; Hd, Inner Cities Central Unit, 1986; Post Office Counters Ltd: Gen. Manager for Gtr London, 1986–87; Dir of Ops, 1987–92; Man. Dir, 1993–96; Gp Man. Dir, Royal Mail, and Exec. Bd Mem., The Post Office, later Consignia plc, 1996–2001. Non-exec. Dir, Employment Service, 1998–2002. Member: Forensic Sci. Service Adv. Bd, Home Office, 1991–98; EDC, BITC, 1994–2003; Design Council, 1994–2001; Chm., HSC and DTLR Work-related Road Safety Task Gp, 2000–01. *Recreations:* travel, hill-walking. *Address:* 513 Gilbert House, Barbican, EC2Y 8BD.

**DYKSTRA, Ronald Gerrit Malcolm;** Senior Partner, Addleshaw Sons & Latham, solicitors, 1987–94, retired; *b* 4 March 1934; *s* of Gerrit Abe Dykstra and Margaret Kirk Dykstra (*née* McDonald); *m* 1st, 1960, Jennifer Mary Cramer (marr. diss. 1985); three *s*; 2nd, 1986, Sonia Hoole. *Educ:* Edinburgh Academy. Admitted Solicitor, 1957; Asst Solicitor, 1957, Partner, 1961, Addleshaw Sons & Latham, Manchester. Pres., Wilmslow Green Room Soc., 2011–. *Recreations:* cycling, amateur drama, walking. *Address:* 7 Racecourse Road, Wilmslow, Cheshire SK9 5LF. *T:* (01625) 525856.

**DYLAN, Bob;** *see* Zimmerman, R. A.

**DYMOCK, Vice Adm. Sir Anthony (Knox),** KBE 2008; CB 2003; consultant on maritime security policy, European Union 2009–18; Director, Wise Pens International Maritime Security Consultancy, 2011–18; Senior Mentor, UK Defence Academy, 2010–15; consultant on international maritime security policy, 2009–18; *b* 18 July 1949; *s* of Richard Challis Dymock and Irene Mary Dymock (*née* Knox); *m* 1977, Elizabeth Mary Frewer (*d* 2015); one *s* one *d*. *Educ:* Brighton, Hove and Sussex Grammar Sch.; Univ. of E Anglia (BA Hons Russian and Philosophy); Kennedy Sch. of Govt, Harvard Univ. MNI 1992. BRNC, 1969–70; served: HMS Yarmouth, 1972–74; HMS Brighton, 1974; HMS Antrim, 1981–83 (Falklands War); i/c HMS Plymouth, 1985–88; MoD, Whitehall, 1989–91; HMS London, 1991–92 (Gulf War); i/c HMS Campbeltown, 1992–93; MoD Naval Staff, 1993–96; i/c 2nd Frigate Sqdn, HMS Cornwall, 1996–98; Dep. Comdr, UK Task Gp (HMS Invincible), Gulf and Kosovo, 1998–99; Dep. Comdr, Striking and Support Forces Southern Region, 2000–02; Defence Attaché and Hd of British Defence Staff, Washington, 2002–05; UK Mil. Rep. to NATO, 2006–08. Member: RYA; RNSA. *Publications:* (jtly) Military Capability Development in the EU, 2012. *Recreations:* sailing, ski-ing. *Clubs:* Pilgrims; Royal Cruising, Royal Yacht Squadron.

**DYMOND, Duncan Simon,** MD; FRCP; Consultant Cardiologist, Barts Health NHS Trust (formerly Barts and The London NHS Trust), since 1987; *b* North Cheam, Surrey, 25 Feb. 1950; *s* of late Sydney Dymond and Adele Dymond; partner, Christine Baldwin; one *s* one *d*. *Educ:* St Paul's Sch., London; St Bartholomew's Hosp. Med. Sch., London (MB BS 1972; MD 1980). MRCP 1974, FRCP 1991. House Physician, 1973, Registrar in Cardiol., 1975–80, St Bartholomew's Hosp.; Asst Prof. and Dir, Nuclear Cardiol., Mount Sinai Hosp. and Univ. of Wisconsin, 1980–81; Sen. Registrar in Cardiol., St Bartholomew's Hosp., 1981–86. Lead Clinician for Clinical Standards, and Chm., Clinical Governance Bd, Wellington Hosp., London, 2001–. Chm., London Consultants' Assoc., 2009–. Chm., Wkg Gp on Nuclear Cardiol., Eur. Soc. of Cardiol., 1984–88; Hon. Sec., 1990–94, Mem., Finance Cttee, 2009–, British Cardiovascular Soc. (formerly British Cardiac Soc.). Patron and Trustee, Forces Children Trust, 2009–. FACC 1983; FESC 1991. *Publications:* Atlas of Myocardial Infarction, 1994; The Jargon-Buster's Guide to Heart Disease, 1996, new edn as Plain English Guide to Heart Diseases, 2003; How to Cope Successfully with High Blood Pressure, 2003; approx. 100 articles. *Recreations:* football, tennis, cricket, ski-ing, classical piano, cinema, theatre, travel. *Address:* 34 Circus Road, NW8 9SG. *T:* (020) 7079 4260, *Fax:* (020) 7079 4269. *E:* secretary@drduncandymond.com. *Clubs:* MCC, Lord's Taverners.

**DYNEVOR**, 10th Baron cr 1780; **Hugo Griffith Uryan Rhys**; b 19 Nov. 1966; o s of 9th Baron Dynevor and of Lucy Catherine King, o d of Sir John Rothenstein, CBE; S father, 2008. Educ: Bryanston.

**DYSART**, 13th Earl of, cr 1643; **John Peter Grant of Rothiemurchus**; DL; Lord Huntingtower, 1643; b 22 Oct. 1946; o s of Colonel John Peter Grant of Rothiemurchus, MBE (d 1987) and Countess of Dysart (12th in line); S mother, 2011; m 1971, Wendy Philippa Chance; one s two d. Educ: Gordonstoun. DL Inverness-shire, 1986. Heir: s Lord Huntingtower, qv.

**DYSON, Rt Hon. Lord; John Anthony Dyson**, Kt 1993; PC 2001; Master of the Rolls and Head of Civil Justice, 2012–16; b 31 July 1943; s of late Richard Dyson and Gisella Dyson; m 1970, Jacqueline Carmel Levy; one s one d. Educ: Leeds Grammar Sch.; Wadham Coll., Oxford (Open Classics Scholar; MA; Hon. Fellow, 2001). Harmsworth Law Scholar, 1968, called to Bar, Middle Temple, 1968, Bencher, 1990 (Treas., 2017); QC 1982; a Recorder, 1986–93; a Judge of the High Court of Justice, QBD, 1993–2001; Presiding Judge, Technology and Construction Court, 1998–2001; a Lord Justice of Appeal, 2001–10; Dep. Hd of Civil Justice, 2003–06; a Justice of the Supreme Court of the UK, 2010–12. Dep. Chm., 2003–06, Chm., 2012–16, Civil Justice Council. Chm., Civil Procedure Rule Cttee, 2012–16 (Mem., 2002–06). Chairman: Adv. Council on Nat. Records and Archives, 2012–16; Magna Carta Trust, 2012–16. Member: Council of Legal Educn, 1992–96; Judicial Studies Bd, 1994–98. Visiting Professor: Queen Mary, Univ. of London, 2007–; UCL, 2016–. Hon. Freeman, 2014, Liveryman, 2017, Drapers' Co. Hon. Fellow: Soc. of Advanced Legal Studies, 1998–; Hebrew Univ. of Jerusalem, 2004. Hon. LLD: UCL, 2013; Essex, 2013; Leeds, 2014. Publications: A Judge's Journey, 2019. Recreations: piano playing, singing, walking.

**DYSON, Prof. Freeman John**, FRS 1952; Professor, School of Natural Sciences, Institute for Advanced Study, Princeton, New Jersey, 1953–94, Professor Emeritus since 1994; b 15 Dec. 1923; s of late Sir George Dyson, KCVO; m 1st, 1950, Verena Esther (née Huber) (marr. diss. 1958); one s one d; 2nd, 1958, Imme (née Jung); four d. Educ: Winchester; Cambridge; Cornell University. Operational research for RAF Bomber Command, 1943–45. Fellow of Trinity Coll., Cambridge, 1946–50, Hon. Fellow, 1989; Commonwealth Fund Fellow at Cornell and Princeton, USA, 1947–49; Mem. of Institute for Advanced Study, Princeton, USA, 1949–50; Professor of Physics, Cornell Univ., Ithaca, NY, USA, 1951–53. Mem. of National Academy of Sciences (USA), 1964; For. Associate, Acad. des Scis, Paris, 1989. Gifford Lectr, Aberdeen, 1985; Radcliffe Lectr, Oxford, 1990. Mem., Bd of Visitors, Ralston Coll. Lorentz Medal, Royal Netherlands Acad. of Sciences, 1966; Hughes Medal, Royal Soc., 1968; Max Planck Medal, German Physical Soc., 1969; Templeton Prize, 2000; Henri Poincaré Prize, Internat. Assoc. of Math. Physics, 2012. Publications: Disturbing the Universe, 1979; Values at War, 1983; Weapons and Hope, 1984; Origins of Life, 1986, 2nd edn 1999; Infinite in All Directions, 1988; From Eros to Gaia, 1991; Imagined Worlds, 1997; Technology and Social Justice, 1998; The Sun, the Genome and the Internet, 1999; The Scientist as Rebel, 2006; A Many-Colored Glass, 2007; Advanced Quantum Mechanics, 2007; Birds and Frogs: selected papers, 1990–2014, 2015; contrib. to The Physical Review, Annals of Mathematics, etc. Address: School of Natural Sciences, Institute for Advanced Study, Einstein Drive, Princeton, NJ 08540, USA.

**DYSON, Ian Christopher**, QPM 2016; Commissioner, City of London Police, since 2016; b Epsom, Surrey, 26 Oct. 1960; s of Ralph and Barbara Dyson; m 1986, Fiona Thomson; two s one d. Educ: Kingston Grammar Sch.; Univ. of Leeds (BA Hons Hist.). With Metropolitan Police, 1983–2008; Asst Chief Constable, Surrey Police, 2008–10; Comdr, 2010–12, Asst Comr, 2012–15, City of London Police. Trustee, Inst. of Business Ethics, 2015–. MInstD 2013. Liveryman, Glovers' Co. Recreations: classic car restoration, cinema, cycling. Address: City of London Police, 4th Floor, Guildhall Yard East, EC2V 5AE. E: ian.dyson@cityoflondon.police.uk.

**DYSON, Sir James**, OM 2015; Kt 2007; CBE 1998; RDI 2005; FRS 2015; FREng; FCSD; FIEE; Founder and Chairman, Dyson Ltd (formerly Prototypes Ltd, then Dyson Research), since 1992; Founder and Trustee, James Dyson Foundation, since 2002; b 2 May 1947; s of late Alec Dyson and Mary Dyson (née Bolton); m 1967, Deirdre Hindmarsh; two s one d. Educ: Gresham's Sch.; Royal Coll. of Art (MDes). FCSD 1996; FIEE 2001; FREng 2005. Dir, Rotork Marine, 1970–74 (design and manufacture of Sea Truck high speed landing craft); Man. Dir, Kirk-Dyson, 1974–79 (design and manufacture of Ballbarrow wheelbarrow); founded Dyson Res. Ltd, 1979 (developed and designed: Dyson Dual Cyclone vacuum cleaner, 1979–93; Dyson Contrarotator washing machine, 2000; Dyson Digital Motor, 2004; Dyson Airblade Hand Dryer, 2006; Dyson Ball vacuum cleaner, 2008; Dyson Digital Motor V2, 2009; Dyson Air Multiplier Fan, 2009; Dyson Hot Fan Heater, 2011; Dyson Airblade Tap, 2013; Dyson 360 Eye Robotic vacuum cleaner, 2014; Dyson Humidifier, 2014; Dyson Pure Cool Link, 2015; Dyson Supersonic hair dryer, 2016; Dyson V8 cord-free vacuum cleaner, 2016; Dyson V9 Digital motor, 2016). Mem., Design Council, 1997–; Chairman: Bath Coll. of Higher Educn, 1990–92; Design Mus., 1999–2004; Design London, 2007–. Mem., Prime Minister's Business Adv. Gp, 2010–. Provost, RCA, 2011–17 (Ext. Examr, 1993–96; Mem. Council, 1998–). Mem., Adv. Bd, MAK, Vienna. Patron: Design and Technol. Assoc., 2010–; Royal United Hosp. Bath Cancer Care Campaign, 2013–; Nat. Assoc. Inspectors and Advrs in Design and Technol. Trustee, Roundhouse Th., London, 1998. Exhibitions: Doing a Dyson, Design Mus., 1996–97; Glasgow; Arnhem. Dyson vacuum cleaners on permanent display in museums including: Sci. Mus., V&A and Design Mus., London; MOMA, NY; Boymans Mus., Rotterdam; Powerhouse Mus., Sydney; San Francisco Mus. of Modern Art; Mus. of Scotland; Design Mus., Zurich; Mus. für angewandte Kunst, Germany; Centre Georges Pompidou, Paris; Cité des Scis et de l'Industrie, Paris; MAK, Vienna; Design Mus., Lisbon; Danish Design Centre, Copenhagen; Sci. Works Mus., Melbourne; Hawke's Bay Mus., NZ; Mus. de les Arts Decoratives, Barcelona; Metropolitan Mus. of Art, NY; Magna Mus., Sheffield; Iron Bridge Gorge Mus., Shropshire. Hon. MIEEE 2017. Hon. Fellow, John Moores Univ., 1997. Hon. FRIBA 2005; Hon. FIED 2001 (Hon. MIED 1997). Hon. DLitt Staffs, 1990; Hon. DSc: Oxford Brookes, 1997; Hon. DTech Brunel, 1999; Hon. Dr: Bradford, 1998; RCA, Bath, 2000; Imperial Coll. London, 2001; Middlesex; Bristol; Liverpool John Moores; Huddersfield Univ. Business Sch.; West of England; Bath Spa. Awards incl.: Design and Innovation Award for Ballbarrow, Building Design, 1976; Internat. Design Fair Prize, Japan, 1991; Minerva Award, CSD, 1995; Gerald Frewer Trophy, Inst. Engrg Designers, 1996; Industrial Design Prize of America, 1996; Eversheds Grand Prix Trophy, Design Council, 1996; European Design Prize, EC, 1997; Prince Philip's Designers Prize, 1997; European Design Prize, 1997; French Oscar, Livre Mondial des Inventions, 1997; Award for Euro Design, Design Council, 1997; Marketer of Year, Mktg Soc., 1998; Gold Award, Industrial Design Promotion Orgn, Japan, 1999; Gal. Lafayette Prix Innovation-Design, France, 1999; Designer of Decade, Design Week, 1999; Mingay Most Innovative Product Award, Australia, 2000; Classic Design Award, Homes and Gdns, 2000; Lord Kilgerran Prize, Royal Soc., 2000; Queen's Award for Innovation, 2003; Giant of Design, USA, 2004; Queen's Award for Export, 2006; Lifetime Achievement Award, Plus X Awards, 2007; Le Janus de l'Industrie, Inst Français du Design, 2007. Publications: Doing a Dyson, 1996; Against the Odds (autobiog.), 1997; History of Great Inventions, 2001; Genius of Britain, 2010; Ingenious Britain, 2010. Recreations: running, garden design, bassoon, opera, tennis. Address: c/o Tetbury Hill, Malmesbury, Wilts SN16 0RP. T: (01666) 828282. Club: Chelsea Arts.

**DYSON, John Anthony**; see Dyson, Rt Hon. Lord.

**DYSON, Prof. Kenneth Herbert Fewster**, PhD; FRHistS; FBA 1997; FLSW; FAcSS; Distinguished Research Professor, 2003–17, Visiting Research Professor, since 2017, School of Law and Politics (formerly School of European Studies, then School of Politics and International Relations), Cardiff University; Honorary Research Professor: School of Politics and International Studies, Leeds University, since 2017; University of Luxembourg, since 2017; b 10 Nov. 1946; s of Arthur Dyson and Freda Dyson; m 1971, Patricia Ann Holmes; two s. Educ: Scarborough Grammar Sch.; London Sch. of Econs (BSc Econs, MSc Econs); Univ. of Liverpool (PhD 1980). FRHistS 1981. Lectr in Politics, 1969–79, Sen. Lectr, 1979–81, Univ. of Liverpool; Prof. of European Studies, 1982–2002, Co-Dir, European Briefing Unit, 1987–2002, Vis. Prof. of Eur. Politics, 2002–07, Univ. of Bradford. Visiting Professor: in Politics, Univ. of Konstanz, Germany, 1981–82; Inst d'Etudes Politiques de Lille, 2004. Chairman: Assoc. for Study of German Politics, 1978–81; Standing Conf. of Heads of European Studies, 1990–93; HEFCE Panel for European Studies, RAEs 1996 and 2001; British Academy: Grants Officer, Politics Section, 1999–; Mem., Overseas Policy Cttee, and Res. Grants Cttee, 2003–. FRSA 1993; FAcSS (AcSS 2000); Founding FLSW 2010 (Mem. Council, 2010–). Hon. DLitt Aston, 2003. Federal Service Cross (1st Cl.) (Germany), 1990. Publications: Party, State and Bureaucracy in Germany, 1978; The State Tradition in Western Europe, 1980; (with S. Wilks) Industrial Crisis, 1983; European Detente, 1986; The Politics of the Communications Revolution in Western Europe, 1986; Local Authorities and New Technologies, 1987; Broadcasting and New Media Policies in Western Europe, 1988; Combatting Long-Term Unemployment, 1989; Political Economy of Communications, 1990; Politics of German Regulation, 1992; Elusive Union, 1994; Culture First, 1996; (with K. Featherstone) The Road to Maastricht, 1999; The Politics of the Euro-Zone, 2000; European States and the Euro, 2002; (with K. Goetz) Germany, Europe and the Politics of Constraint, 2003; Enlarging the Euro Area: external empowerment and domestic transformation in East Central Europe, 2006; The Euro at Ten, 2008; (with M. Marcussen) Central Banking in the Age of the Euro, 2009; (with A. Sepos) Which Europe?: the politics of differentiated integration, 2010; (with L. Quaglia) European Economic Governance and Policies, Vol. I: history and institutions, Vol. II: policies, 2010; States, Debt and Power, 2014 (UACES Best Book, 2015); (with I. Maes) Architects of the Euro: intellectuals in the making of European Monetary Union, 2016. Recreations: Renaissance Florence, classical music, charity work for the disabled, walking. Address: School of Law and Politics, Cardiff University, Cardiff CF10 3YQ.

**DYSON, Nicholas Graham**; olive farmer, since 2010; sustainability and permaculture designer, practitioner and blogger, since 2011; b 29 Nov. 1945; s of Hugh Norman Dyson and Joyce Dyson; m 2010, Sharon Lynda (née Jones); one s two d by previous marriages. Educ: Brunel Univ. (BSc Maths). Work in private sector, 1967–74; Statistician, Dept of Industry, 1974–82; Consultant, European Stats Office, 1982–85; Course Dir, CS Coll., 1985–88; Nat. Statistician, Solomon Is, 1988–91; Advr to OFT, 1991–94; Dir and Chief Statistician, Information Centre, DSS, later DWP, 1994–2002; Dir of Inf. and Analysis, DWP, 2002–05; Dir of Knowledge, Analysis and Intelligence, 2005–07, Dir, Data Integration for Govt, 2007–08, HMRC. Ind. information consultant, 2008–10. Recreations: sustainable house design, off-grid living, photography.

**DYSON, Richard George**, FCA; Partner, Ernst & Young LLP (formerly Ernst & Whinney), 1983–2008; b Huddersfield, 6 April 1949; s of George Hirst Dyson and Margaret Esther Dyson; m 1st, 1986, Valerie Anne Conlen (marr. diss. 1997); two d; 2nd, 1998, Jane Veronica Kay. Educ: Clifton Coll.; Queens' Coll., Cambridge (BA 1971). ACA 1974. Articles with Whinney Murray & Co., London, 1971; Ernst & Whinney, subsequently Ernst & Young: Head: Due Diligence Services in NW, 1983–97; Forensic Accounting Services, N of England, 1997–2001; Nat. Risk Mgt Partner, 2001–06. Mem. Council, ICAEW, 2001–10 (Pres., 2006–08). Chm., Wythenshawe Hosp. Transplant Fund, 2008–; Lay Mem. for Audit, Governance and Risk, Trafford CCG, 2019–. Trustee: Charity Service Ltd, 2009– (Chm., 2009–); David Lewis Centre, 2009–18 (Chm., 2013–18); Children of Success Schs Trust, 2014– (Chm., 2015–); Dir, Gtr Manchester Centre for Voluntary Orgn, 2014–. Gov., Bell Concord Educnl Trust, 2010–. Mem. Ct, Chartered Accountants' Co., 2009–17. Recreations: golf, opera, travel. Address: Portinscale, 45 Arthog Road, Hale, Cheshire WA15 0LU. T: (0161) 980 5552. E: richard@portinscale.com. Clubs: Hawks (Cambridge); St James' (Manchester) (Hon. Treas., 2010–13); Denham Golf, Formby Golf, Hale Golf.

**DYSON, Stephen John**; journalist, media analyst, trainer and consultant; Director, Dyson Media Ltd, since 2010; b 5 March 1968; s of Rev. Colin Dyson and Frances Dyson (née Ward); m 1992, Ruth Emma Lillywhite; three s. Educ: Primrose Hill Secondary Sch.; Matthew Boulton Coll., Birmingham; Lancaster Univ. (BA 1990). Trainee journalist, Caters News Agency, 1991; reporter: Birmingham Metro News, 1992; Sunday Mercury, Birmingham, 1993; Birmingham Evening Mail: industrial corresp., 1994–96; Dep. News Ed., 1996–98; Features Ed., 1998–99; Hd of News, 1999–2001; Dep. Ed., 2001–02; Ed., Evening Gazette, Teesside, 2002–05; Ed., Birmingham Mail, 2005–09, Sunday Mercury, Birmingham, 2008–09; Ed., BQ W Midlands, 2013–18. Presenter, Hardtalk (series), 2010–11, Special Correspondent, 2010–15, BBC WM Radio; Columnist, www.holdthefrontpage.co.uk, 2010–. Chm., Birmingham Mail Charity Trust, 2005–09. Non-exec. Bd Mem., Waterloo Housing Gp, 2012–. Midland Business Journalist of Year, BT Regl Awards, 1995; Ed., Newspaper of Year, NE Press Awards, 2003; Ed., Newspaper of the Year, Midland Press Awards, 2008; Ed., Regl Newspaper of the Year, Campaign for Plain English, 2009. Publications: (jtly) We Ain't Going Away!: the battle for Longbridge, 2000. Recreations: family, travelling, walking, reading, meeting folk, drinking real ale, eating pork scratchings, learning from mistakes. Address: 29 Goldieslie Road, Sutton Coldfield, W Midlands B73 5PE. T: 07818 004575. E: steve.dysonmedia@ gmail.com. Club: Birmingham Press.

**DYSON, Prof. Timothy Peter Geoffrey**, FBA 2001; Professor of Population Studies, London School of Economics, since 1993; b 1 Aug. 1949; s of Geoffrey Dyson and Maureen (née Gardner); m 1979, Susan Ann Borman; two s. Educ: Queen's Univ., Kingston, Ont.; London Sch. of Econs (BSc Sociol. 1971, MSc Demography 1973). Res. Officer, Inst. of Develt Studies, Univ. of Sussex, 1973–75; Res. Fellow, Centre for Population Studies, LSHTM, 1975–80; Lectr in Population Studies, 1980–88, Reader, 1988–93, LSE. Publications: (ed) India's Historical Demography, 1989; (ed) Sexual Behaviour and Networking, 1992; Population and Food: global trends and future prospects, 1996; (ed jtly) Twenty-first Century India, 2005; Population and Development: the demographic transition, 2010; A Population History of India, 2018. Recreation: gardening. Address: Department of International Development, London School of Economics, Houghton Street, WC2A 2AE. T: (020) 7955 7662.

**DYTOR, Clive Idris,** MC 1982; Seminarian, St Mary's College, Oscott, since 2018; Head Master, Oratory School, 2000–15; *b* 29 Oct. 1956; *s* of (Cecil) Frederick Dytor and Maureen (Margaret) Dytor (*née* Owen); *m* 1985, Sarah Louise Payler; one *s* one *d*. *Educ*: Trinity Coll., Cambridge (MA Hons Oriental Studies); Wycliffe Hall, Oxford (MA Hons Theology). Served Royal Marines, 1980–86: officer trng, 1980–81; Troop Officer, 45 Cdo, 1981–82; Instructor, Officers' Training Wing, 1982–83; 2nd i/c Trng Team in Persian Gulf, 1983–84; Officer Recruiting Liaison Officer, 1984–86; ordained deacon 1989, priest 1990; Curate, Rushall (Dio. of Lichfield), 1989–92; Chaplain, Tonbridge Boys' Sch., 1992–94; received into RC Church, 1994; Housemaster, St Edward's Sch., Oxford, 1994–2000; Jun. Master, Bruern Abbey Sch., 2017–18. Public Sch. Headmaster of Year, Tatler, 2013. *Recreations*: sport, music, Hispanic studies, country life. *Club*: Pitt (Cambridge).

**DYVIG, Peter;** Comdr (1st cl.), Order of the Dannebrog, 1986; Chamberlain to Her Majesty Queen Margrethe II of Denmark, 1999; *b* 23 Feb. 1934; *m* 1959, Karen Dyvig (*née* Moller); one *s* one *d*. *Educ*: Copenhagen Univ. (grad. in Law). Entered Danish For. Service, 1959; bursary at Sch. of Advanced Internat. Studies, Washington, 1963–64; First Secretary: Danish Delegn to NATO, Paris, 1965–67; Brussels, 1967–69; Min. of For. Affairs, Copenhagen, 1969–74; Minister Counsellor, Washington, 1974–76; Ambassador, Asst Under-Sec. of State, Min. of For. Affairs, Copenhagen, 1976–79; Under-Sec. for Pol Affairs, 1980; State Sec., 1983–86; Ambassador: to UK, 1986–89; to USA, 1989–95; to France, 1995–99. Chairman: Exec. Bd, European Center for Minority Issues, Flensburg, Germany, 1999–2005; Exec. Bd, La Maison du Danemark, Paris, 2000–04; British Import Union, Copenhagen, 2000–06; Rohde Nielsen Holding A/S, 2006–11. Dir, various Danish cos. *Address*: Christiansgave 56, 2960 Rungsted Kyst, Denmark.

# E

**EACOTT, Rt Rev. Leonard Sidney,** AM 2007; Anglican Bishop to the Australian Defence Force, 2007–12; *b* Toowoomba, Qld, 14 June 1947; *s* of Sidney Stephen Eacott and Ivy Jane McMurray Eacott (*née* Geizer); *m* 1971, Sandra Carol Danson; one *s* one *d* (and one *s* decd). *Educ:* Queensland Agricultural Coll. (Cert. in Rural Technol. (Soil Conservation) 1971); Univ. of Queensland (BA Religion and Sociol. 1983); Univ. of South Australia (Grad. Dip. in Religious Educn 1998). Soil Conservation Advr, Queensland Dept of Primary Industries, 1969–80; Officer, Royal Australian Infantry (Reserve), 1972–84; ordained deacon and priest, 1983; Parish Priest, Dio. of Brisbane, 1983–89; Chaplain, Royal Australian Army Chaplains' Dept, 1984–2007; Regular Army Chaplain, 1990–2007; Archdeacon to Army and Principal Chaplain, Army, 2002–07. Locum Bp, Western Reg., Dio. Brisbane, 2014. Mem., Religious Adv. Cttee to Services, 2007–12. Chaplain, UN Transitional Authy in Cambodia, 1993; Sen. Chaplain, Internat. Force for E Timor, 1999–2000. Chaplain, Scouts Aust., 1996–2000. Mem. Bd, Service Personnel Anglican Help Soc., 2015–. KStJ 2012. *Recreations:* bushwalking, off-road cycling, genealogical research, reading (adventure novels in preference to theology). *Address:* 6 Springwood Avenue, Pacific Pines, Qld 4211, Australia. *Club:* United Service (Brisbane).

**EADES, His Honour Robert Mark;** a Circuit Judge, 2001–17; *b* 6 May 1951; *s* of John Robert Eades and Margaret Ursula Eades; *m* 1982, Afsaneh, (Sunny), Atri; two *d*. *Educ:* Moffats Sch., Bewdley, Worcs; Leighton Park Sch., Reading; Bristol Univ. (LLB). Called to the Bar, Middle Temple, 1974; in practice as barrister, specialising in criminal law, 1974–2001. *Recreations:* gardening, watching cricket, current affairs, English domestic architecture, local history.

**EADIE, Roland Rennie Alistair,** FRICS; Vice Lord-Lieutenant of Fermanagh, since 2014; *b* Enniskillen, Co. Fermanagh, NI, 21 Aug. 1944; *s* of Ian Chapman Eadie and Nancy Dawson Eadie; *m* 1976, Lois Cecily Sullivan. *Educ:* Gloucester House Prep. Sch., Enniskillen; Portora Royal Sch., Enniskillen. FRICS 1978. With Osborne King & Megran, Chartered Surveyors, Belfast, 1962–71; qualified as Chartered Surveyor, 1968; Sen. Partner, 1971–96, Consultant, 1996–2018, Eadie, McFarland & Co., Enniskillen. Member: Black Inquiry into Inland Fisheries in NI, 1978–80; NI Milk Quota Tribunal, 1982–84; Lord Chancellor's Adv. Cttee, Fermanagh, 1985–97. Member: Ulster Countryside Commn for NI, 1980–86; Historic Bldgs Council for NI, 1987–90. Founder Chm., Enniskillen Yacht Club Charitable Trust, 1987–2016; Hon. Sec., Fermanagh Harriers Hunt Club, 1972–92. Gov., Portora Royal Sch., Enniskillen, 1994–. DL 1978, High Sheriff, 1984, Fermanagh. *Recreations:* gardening, breeding race horses, farming, forestry, collecting early Irish glass. *Address:* Glen Lodge, 4 Carrowkeel Road, Lisbellaw, Co. Fermanagh BT94 5BP. *T:* (028) 6638 5956. *E:* rolandeadie@gmail.com. *Clubs:* Royal Over-Seas League; Kildare Street and University (Dublin).

**EADY,** family name of **Baron Swinfen**.

**EADY, Sir David,** Kt 1997; a Judge of the High Court of Justice, Queen's Bench Division, 1997–2013; *b* 24 March 1943; *s* of late Thomas William Eady and Kate Eady; *m* 1974, Catherine, *yr d* of J. T. Wiltshire; one *s* one *d*. *Educ:* Brentwood Sch.; Trinity Coll., Cambridge (Exhibnr; Pt I Moral Science Tripos, Pt II Law Tripos; MA, LLB). Called to the Bar, Middle Temple, 1966, Bencher, 1991; QC 1983; a Recorder, 1986–97. Mem., Cttee on Privacy and Related Matters (Calcutt Cttee), 1989–90. *Publications:* The Law of Contempt (with A. J. Arlidge), 1982, 4th edn (ed with A. T. H. Smith), 2011, 5th edn (with P. Londono and A. T. H. Smith), 2017.

**EADY, Hon. Dame Jennifer Jane,** DBE 2019; **Hon. Mrs Justice Eady;** a Judge of the High Court, Queen's Bench Division, since 2019; *b* 31 May 1965; *d* of Gordon James Eady and Theresa Alice Eady; *m* 2006, Paul Noordhof; one *s*. *Educ:* High Sch., Boston, Lincs; St Hugh's Coll., Oxford (BA Hons PPE 1986); Poly. of Central London (Dip. Law 1988). Called to the Bar, Inner Temple, 1989; in practice, specialising in employment law; a Recorder, 2003–13; QC 2006; a Circuit Judge, 2013–19. Chm., Employment Tribunals, later Employment Judge (pt-time), 2001–08; Mem. Council, ACAS, 2008–14. Trustee: Free Representation Unit, 2006–14; Wallace Collection, 2013–. *Recreation:* my family. *Address:* Royal Courts of Justice, Strand, WC2A 2LL.

**EAGAR, (Edward) Patrick;** freelance photographer, since 1965; *b* 9 March 1944; *s* of late Desmond Eagar and Marjorie Eagar; *m* 1968, Annabel Trench (*d* 1996); one *s* one *d*. *Educ:* Magdalene Coll., Cambridge (BA 1965). Retrospective exhibn, Lord's Cricket Ground, 2005, 2006. *Publications:* (with John Arlott) An Eye for Cricket, 1979; (with Alan Ross) A Summer to Remember, 1981; Test Decade, 1982; Summer of the All Rounder, 1982; Summer of Speed, 1983; Kiwis and Indians, 1983; Botham, 1985; An Australian Summer, 1985; Summer of Suspense, 1986; West Indian Summer, 1988; Tour of Tours, 1989; (with Richard Wilson) Caught in the Frame, 1992; The Ashes in Focus, 2005. *Recreations:* wine, golf, gardening. *Address:* Queensberry Place, Richmond, Surrey TW9 1NW. *T:* (020) 8940 9269. *Clubs:* MCC; Royal Mid-Surrey Golf.

**EAGLAND, (Ralph) Martin;** Managing Director, Eagland Planning Associates (formerly Director, Martin Eagland Economic Development Consultancy), 1995–2016; *b* 1 May 1942; *s* of Norman Albert Eagland and Jessie Eagland; *m* 1963, Patricia Anne Norton; one *s* one *d*. *Educ:* Hipperholme Grammar Sch.; Leeds Sch. of Town Planning; Univ. of Bradford (MSc); Univ. of Birmingham. Jun. planning posts, Huddersfield, Dewsbury and Halifax, 1959–67; Principal Planning Officer, City of Gloucester, 1967–72; Asst Co. Planning Officer, Northants CC, 1972–74; Chief Planner (Envmt), W Yorks CC, 1974–79, Head of Econ. Develt Unit, 1979–84; Chief Exec., Kettering Borough Council, 1984–88; Chief Exec. and Accounting Officer, Leeds Develt Corp., 1988–95. Director: Urban Regeneration Partnership, 1996–98; BURA, 2001– (Mem. Panel, 1995; Vice-Chm., 2002–04). Mem., W Yorks Cttee, CoSIRA, 1985–88; Sec., Kettering Enterprise Agency, 1986–88; Mem., Electricity Consumers' Cttee, Yorks Reg., 1997. Hon. Public Relns Officer, RTPI (Yorks Br. Exec. Cttee), 1990–92. Vice-Chm., Colne and Holme Valley Jt Cttee for the Blind, 1994–99; Mem., Rotary Club of Leeds, 1992–95. *Publications:* contribs to RTPI Jl, Instn of Highways and Transportation Jl and various property jls and publications. *Recreations:* environmental studies, music, history, gardening.

**EAGLE, Angela;** MP (Lab) Wallasey, since 1992; *b* 17 Feb. 1961; twin *d* of André and late Shirley Eagle; civil partnership 2008, Maria Exall. *Educ:* Formby High Sch.; St John's Coll., Oxford (BA PPE). Economic Directorate, CBI, 1984; Confederation of Health Service Employees: Researcher, 1984; Press Officer, 1986; Parly Officer, 1987–92. Parly Under-Sec. of State, DETR, 1997–98, DSS, 1998–2001, Home Office, 2001–02; Exchequer Sec. to HM Treasury, 2007–09; Minister of State (Minister for Pensions and Ageing Society), DWP, 2009–10; Shadow Chief Sec. to the Treasury, 2010–11; Shadow Leader, H of C, 2011–15; Shadow First Sec. of State and Shadow Sec. of State for Business, Innovation and Skills, 2015–16. Labour Party: Member: Nat. Women's Cttee, 1989–; Nat. Exec. Cttee, 2006–16 (Chair, 2013–14); Chair, Nat. Policy Forum, 2012–16. Mem., BFI. *Recreations:* chess (Jun. Internat. Hons), cricket, cinema. *Address:* House of Commons, SW1A 0AA. *T:* (020) 7219 4074.
*See also* M. Eagle.

**EAGLE, Maria;** MP (Lab) Garston and Halewood, since 2010 (Liverpool, Garston, 1997–2010); *b* 17 Feb. 1961; twin *d* of André Eagle and late Shirley Eagle. *Educ:* Formby High Sch.; Pembroke Coll., Oxford (BA Hons); Coll. of Law, Lancaster Gate. Articles, Brian Thompson & Partners, Liverpool, 1990–92; Goldsmith Williams, Liverpool, 1992–95; Sen. Solicitor, Steven Irving & Co., Liverpool, 1994–97. Contested (Lab) Crosby, 1992. Parliamentary Under-Secretary of State: DWP, 2001–05; DfES, 2005–06; NI Office, 2006–07; MoJ, 2007–09; Govt Equalities Office, 2008–09; Minister of State, MoJ and Govt Equalities Office, 2009–10; Shadow Sec. of State for Transport, 2010–13, for Envmt, Food and Rural Affairs, 2013–15, for Defence, 2015–16, for Culture, Media and Sport, 2016. *Address:* House of Commons, SW1A 0AA.
*See also* A. Eagle.

**EAGLEN, Jane;** international opera singer (soprano); *d* of late Ronald Arthur Eaglen and of Kathleen Eaglen; *m* 2000, Brian Lyson. *Educ:* Royal Northern Coll. of Music (vocal studies with Joseph Ward). Principal Soprano, ENO, 1983–91; major house débuts include: Donna Anna in Don Giovanni, Vienna State Opera, 1993; Brunnhilde in Die Walküre, La Scala, Milan, 1994; Norma, Seattle Opera, 1994; Amelia in Un Ballo in Maschera, Opéra National de Paris-Bastille, 1995; Brunnhilde in Ring Cycle, Lyric Opera, Chicago, 1996, Seattle, 2000–01, Metropolitan Opera, NY, 2000; Brunnhilde in Die Walküre, San Francisco Opera, 1995; Donna Anna, Metropolitan Opera, NY, 1996; Lady Macbeth, Macbeth, Vancouver Opera, 2006; Senta, Der Fliegende Holländer, Seattle Opera, 2007; other appearances include: La Gioconda, Chicago, 1999; Isolde, in Tristan and Isolde, Seattle and Chicago, 1999, Metropolitan Opera, NY, 2000; Julia, in La Vestale, ENO, 2002; Seattle Opera: Fidelio, 2003, Ariadne, in Ariadne auf Naxos, 2004 and 2005, Ortrud in Lohengrin, 2004, Brunnhilde in Ring Cycle, 2005, Rosalinda in Die Fledermaus, 2006; Brunnhilde in Ring Cycle, Chicago, 2005; Ariadne, Pittsburgh Opera, 2005. Recordings include Tosca, Norma, Tannhäuser (Grammy Award, 2002) and five solo discs of opera arias and song cycles. Prof. of Voice, Baldwin Wallace Coll., Ohio, 2010–13; Glasham Internat. Chair in Voice, RSAMD, later Royal Conservatoire of Scotland, 2011–; Prof. of Voice, New England Conservatory, 2013–. Hon. Dr: McGill Univ., 2005; Lincoln Bp Grosseteste, 2008. Lifetime Achievement Award, Licia Albanese-Puccini Foundn, 2008. *Recreations:* computing, sport spectator. *E:* jane.eaglen@necmusic.edu. *Club:* Rainier (Seattle).

**EAGLES, Rt Rev. Peter Andrew;** *see* Sodor and Man, Bishop of.

**EAGLESTONE, Her Honour Diana Barbara;** a Circuit Judge, 1995–2015; *b* 24 May 1949; *d* of Frank Nelson Eaglestone and Irene Eaglestone; three *d*. *Educ:* Manchester Univ. (LLB). Called to the Bar, Gray's Inn, 1971; a Recorder, 1986–95.

**EAGLETON, Prof. Terence Francis,** PhD; FBA 2003; Professor of English Literature, University of Lancaster, since 2008; *b* 22 Feb. 1943; *s* of Francis Paul Eagleton and Rosaleen (*née* Riley); *m* 1st, 1966, Elizabeth Rosemary Galpin (marr. diss. 1976); two *s*; 2nd, 1997, Willa Murphy; two *s* one *d*. *Educ:* Trinity Coll., Cambridge (MA, PhD). Fellow in English, Jesus Coll., Cambridge, 1964–69, Hon. Fellow, 2009; Oxford University: Tutorial Fellow, Wadham Coll., 1969–89; Lectr in Critical Theory, 1989–92; Fellow, Linacre Coll., 1989–92; Thomas Warton Prof. of English Lit., 1992–2001; Fellow, St Catherine's Coll., 1992–2001; Prof. of Cultural Theory and John Rylands Fellow, 2001–06, John Edward Taylor Prof. of English Lit., 2006–08, Univ. of Manchester. Adjunct Prof. of Cultural Theory, Nat. Univ. of Ireland, Galway, 2008–; Dist. Visitor, Univ. of Notre Dame, 2009–. Hon. DLitt: Salford, 1993; NUI, 1997; Santiago di Compostela, 1999; Central Lancs, 2005; Durham, 2008; Halifax, NS, 2010; E Anglia, 2010; Catholic Univ. of Peru, 2011; Sacred Heart, USA, 2012. *Publications:* Criticism and Ideology, 1976; Marxism and Literary Criticism, 1976; Literary Theory: an introduction, 1983; The Function of Criticism, 1984; The Ideology of the Aesthetic, 1990; Ideology: an introduction, 1993; Heathcliff and the Great Hunger: studies in Irish culture, 1995; Crazy John and the Bishop, and other Essays on Irish Culture, 1998; The Truth about the Irish, 1999; The Idea of Culture, 2000; The Gatekeeper: a memoir, 2002; Sweet Violence: a study of the tragic, 2002; After Theory, 2003; The English Novel: an introduction, 2004; Holy Terror, 2005; How to Read a Poem, 2006; The Meaning of Life, 2007; Trouble with Strangers, 2008; Reason, Faith and Revolution: reflections on the God debate, 2009; On Evil, 2010; Why Marx was Right, 2011; The Event of Literature, 2012; How to Read Literature, 2013; Across the Pond, 2013; Culture and the Death of God, 2014; Hope Without Optimism, 2015; Culture, 2016; Materialism, 2017; Radical Sacrifice, 2018; Humour, 2019. *Recreation:* Irish music. *Clubs:* Irish; United Arts (Dublin).

**EAGLING, Wayne John;** dancer and choreographer; Artistic Director, English National Ballet, 2005–12; *s* of Eddie and Thelma Eagling. *Educ:* P. Ramsey Studio of Dance Arts; Royal Ballet Sch. Sen. Principal, Royal Ballet, 1975–91; Artistic Dir, Dutch Nat. Ballet, 1991–2003. Has danced lead rôles in major classics including Sleeping Beauty, Swan Lake, Cinderella; first rôle created for him was Young Boy in Triad, 1972; subsequent created rôles include: Solo Boy in Gloria; Ariel in The Tempest; Woyzeck in Different Drummer. Choreographed: The Hunting of the Snark by Michael Batt; (for Royal Ballet) Frankenstein, The Modern Prometheus, 1985; Beauty and the Beast, 1986; The Wall,

Berlin, 1990; (for Dutch Nat. Ballet) Ruins of Time, 1993, Symphony in Waves, 1994, Duet, 1995, Lost Touch, 1995, Holding a Balance (for opening of Vermeer exhibn in Mauritshuis), 1996, (with Toer van Schayk) Nutcracker and Mouseking, 1996, Magic Flute, 1999, Le sacré du printemps, 2000, Frozen, 2001; (for La Scala, Milan) Alma Mahler, 1994; (for English Nat. Ballet) Resolution, 2008; Sleeping Beauty (for Nat. Ballet of Japan), 2014; (for English Nat. Ballet) The Nutcracker, 2016; (for New English Ballet Th.) Remembrance, 2018; choreographed, produced and directed various galas. *Publications:* (with Ross MacGibbon and Robert Jude) The Company We Keep, 1981. *Recreations:* golf, scuba diving, tennis, antique cars.

**EAMES,** family name of **Baron Eames.**

**EAMES,** Baron *cr* 1995 (Life Peer), of Armagh, in the County of Armagh; **Rt Rev. Robert Henry Alexander Eames,** OM 2007; PhD; Archbishop of Armagh and Primate of All Ireland, 1986–2006; *b* 27 April 1937; *s* of William Edward and Mary Eleanor Thompson Eames; *m* 1966 Ann Christine Daly (*see* Lady Eames); two *s*. *Educ:* Belfast Royal Acad.; Methodist Coll., Belfast; Queen's Univ., Belfast (LLB (hons), PhD); Trinity Coll., Dublin. Research Scholar and Tutor, Faculty of Laws, QUB, 1960–63; Curate Assistant, Bangor Parish Church, 1963–66; Rector of St Dorothea's, Belfast, 1966–74; Examining Chaplain to Bishop of Down, 1973; Rector of St Mark's, Dundela, 1974–75; Bishop of Derry and Raphoe, 1975–80; Bishop of Down and Dromore, 1980–86. Select Preacher, Oxford Univ., 1987. Irish Rep., 1984, Mem. Standing Cttee, 1985, ACC; Chairman: Commn on Communion and Women in the Episcopate, 1988–90; Commn on Inter-Anglican Relations, 1988–91; Lambeth Commn on Communion, 2004 (Windsor Report). Co-Chm., Consultative Panel on the Past, NI, 2007–08. Mem., Ind. Police Commn for England and Wales, 1985–. Governor, Church Army, 1985–90. Chairman: Armagh Observatory and Planetarium, 1986–2006; Bd, Royal Sch., Armagh, 1986–2006; Mem. Bd, St George's House, Windsor, 2008–. Hon. Bencher, Lincoln's Inn, 1998. Hon. LLD: QUB, 1989; TCD, 1992; Lancaster, 1994; Hon. DD Cambridge, 1994 and other hon. degrees from UK, Irish and US univs. *Publications:* A Form of Worship for Teenagers, 1965; The Quiet Revolution—Irish Disestablishment, 1970; Through Suffering, 1973; Thinking through Lent, 1978; Through Lent, 1984; Chains to be Broken, 1992; Unfinished Search, 2017; *relevant publication:* Nobody's Fool: the life of Archbishop Robin Eames, by Alf McCreary, 2004; contribs to New Divinity, Irish Legal Quarterly, Criminal Law Review, The Furrow. *Address:* House of Lords, SW1A 0PW.

**EAMES, Lady; Ann Christine Eames,** OBE 2006; Member, Northern Ireland Human Rights Commission, 2001–07; Lay Member, General Medical Council, since 2013; *b* 21 Jan. 1943; *d* of Captain William Adrian Reynolds Daly and Olive Margaret Daly; *m* 1966, Rt Rev. Robert Henry Alexander Eames (*see* Baron Eames); two *s*. *Educ:* Ashleigh House Sch., Belfast; Queen's Univ., Belfast (LLB Hons, MPhil). World-Wide Pres., Mothers' Union, 1995–2000. Mem. Bd, Hunterhouse Sch., Belfast, 2008–. Trustee: Leonard Cheshire Disability, 2009–13; Christian Aid (Ireland), 2009–15; Cancer Focus. Patron, Homestart; NI Cttee, Barnardo's; Vice Chm., Abbeyfield, Belfast. *Recreations:* sailing, reading. *Address:* 3 Downshire Crescent, Hillsborough, Co. Down BT26 6DD. *Clubs:* Hillsborough Tennis; Strangford Lough Yacht.

**EARDLEY-WILMOT, Sir Benjamin John,** 7th Bt *cr* 1821, of Berkswell Hall, Warwickshire; *b* 24 Jan. 1974; *er s* of Sir Michael John Assheton Eardley-Wilmot, 6th Bt and Wendy Eardley-Wilmot (*née* Wolstenholme); *S* father, 2014, but his name does not appear on the Official Roll of the Baronetage; *m* 2009, Clementine Daisy Langton; two *s*. *Heir: s* Arlo Timothy Eardley-Wilmot, *b* 28 May 2012.

**EARL, Belinda Jane,** OBE 2017; consultant; Style Director, Marks & Spencer, 2012–18; *b* 20 Dec. 1961; *d* of late Colin Lee and of Diana Lee; *m* 1985, David Mark Earl; two *s*. *Educ:* UCW, Aberystwyth (BScEcon (Econs and Business)); Hon. Fellow, 2003). Controller, Fashion Div., Harrods, 1983–85; Debenhams Retail Plc: Merchandiser (Menswear), 1985–88; Controller (Children's), 1988–92; Dir (accessories, women's), 1992–97; Trading Dir, 1997–2000; Debenhams Plc: Dir, 1999–2003; Chief Exec., 2000–03. Chm., Skillsmart, 2002–04; Chief Exec., Jaeger, 2004–12; Chm., AlexandAlexa.com, 2009–12. FCGI 2006.

**EARL, Eric Stafford;** Clerk to the Worshipful Company of Fishmongers, 1974–88, retired; *b* 8 July 1928; *s* of late Alfred Henry Earl and Mary Elizabeth Earl; *m* 1951, Clara Alice Alston (*d* 2010). *Educ:* SE Essex Technical Coll.; City of London Coll. Served with RA, 1946–48. Joined Fishmongers' Co. 1948: Accountant, 1961–68; Asst Clerk, 1969–73; Actg Clerk, 1973–74; Liveryman, 1977. Clerk to Governors of Gresham's Sch., 1974–88; formerly: Sec., City and Guilds of London Art School Ltd; Sec., Atlantic Salmon Res. Trust Ltd; Mem. Exec. and Mem. Council, Salmon and Trout Assoc.; Mem., Nat. Anglers' Council (Chm., 1983–85). Hon. Sec., Shellfish Assoc. of GB, 1974–88; Jt Hon. Sec., Central Council for Rivers Protection, 1974–88; Hon. Asst River Keeper of River Thames, 1968–88; Mem. Council, Anglers' Co-operative Assoc., 1974– (Vice Chm., 1988–). Director: Hulbert Property Co. Ltd, 1975–88; Hulbert Property Holdings Ltd, 1975–88. FZS 1988. Hon. Freeman, Watermen's Co., 1984. *Recreations:* fishing, gardening, tennis, cricket. *Address:* Dolphins, Watling Lane, Thaxted, Essex CM6 2RA. *T:* (01371) 830758.

**EARL, John,** FSA; Special Adviser, Theatres Trust, 2019 (Director, 1986–95; Consultant, 1996); *b* 11 April 1928; *s* of Philip Haywood Earl and May Florence (*née* Walsh); *m* 1952, Valerie Atkins; one *s* (one *d* decd). *Educ:* Roan Sch.; Brixton Sch. of Building. MRICS until 2019 (ARICS 1952); FSA 1978. Nat. Service, RE, 1947–49. London County Council: Architect's Dept, 1954–56; Historic Bldgs Section, 1956–61; MPBW (Special Services), 1961–65; Section Leader, GLC Historic Bldgs Div., 1965–86. Private consultancy, 1986–2016. Lectr, various bldg conservation courses, 1970–2004; External Examiner for conservation courses at: Heriot-Watt Univ., 1982–84; Architectl Assoc., 1984–86; RICS Coll. of Estate Mgt, 1990–95 (Chm., Adv. Bd, 1996–2000); Tutor for SPAB William Morris Craft Fellows, 1987–90. Pres., Frank Matcham Soc., 1999–2015, now Emeritus. Trustee: Talawa Theatre Co., 1996–2000; Raymond Mander and Joe Mitchenson Theatre Collection, 1996–2004. FRSA 1992; IHBC 1998–2019. Hon. Fellow, Coll. of Estate Mgt, 2001. *Publications:* (with J. Stanton) Canterbury Hall and Theatre of Varieties, 1982; Philosophy of Building Conservation, 1996, 3rd edn 2003; Dr Langdon-Down and the Normansfield Theatre, 1997, 2nd enlarged edn 2010 as Dr Langdon Down's Normansfield Theatre; (architectural ed.) Theatres Trust Guide to British Theatres, 2000; British Theatres and Music Halls, 2005, 2nd edn 2011; conservation plans and historical reviews for a number of listed theatres; contrib. numerous books and jls on building conservation and theatre buildings. *Recreation:* avoiding organised sport and religion.

**EARL, Prof. Michael John,** FBCS; Professor of Information Management, University of Oxford, 2002–07, now Emeritus; Dean, Templeton College, Oxford, 2002–08, now Hon. Fellow, Green Templeton College; Acting Pro-Vice-Chancellor, Development and External Affairs, University of Oxford, 2008–10; *b* 11 Jan. 1944; *s* of late Vincent and Marjorie Earl; *m* 1969, Alison Jennifer Eades; one *s* one *d*. *Educ:* Univ. of Newcastle-upon-Tyne (BA 1966); Univ. of Warwick (MSc 1971); MA Oxon 2002. FBCS 1992. Systems Analyst, United Steel Cos, 1966–68; Sen. Systems Analyst, Bowater Paper Corp., 1968–69; Gp Systems Manager, GEC Telecommunications Ltd, 1969–74; Lectr in Mgt Control, Manchester Business Sch., 1974–76; Fellow in Information Mgt, Templeton Coll., Univ. of Oxford, 1976–90; London Business School: Prof. of Information Mgt, 1991–2002; Dep. Principal, 1996–98; Actg Principal, 1998. Chm., First Residential Properties PLC, 2011–12; Founding Consultant, Formicio Ltd, 2011–. Non-executive Director: Shell Information Services BV, 1997–98; Institut V, Stockholm Sch. of Economics, 2000–. Trustee, and Chm., Finance Cttee, Oxford Philharmonic (formerly Philomusica), 2004–. Chm., Oxford Centre for the Study of Philanthropy, 2015–19. Hon. Fellow, Harris Manchester Coll., Oxford, 2008. *Publications:* (with A. M. McCosh) Accounting Control and Financial Strategy, 1978; (jtly) Developing Managerial Information Systems, 1979; (jtly) Information Society: for richer, for poorer, 1982; Perspectives on Management, 1983; Information Management: the strategic dimension, 1989; Management Strategies for Information Technology, 1989; Information Management: the organizational dimension, 1996; articles in learned and professional jls. *Recreations:* golf, music, tennis, travel. *Address:* Green Templeton College, University of Oxford, Oxford OX2 6HG. *T:* (01865) 274797, *Fax:* (01865) 284598. *E:* Michael.Earl@gtc.ox.ac.uk. *Clubs:* Oxford and Cambridge; Frewen (Oxford); Frilford Heath Golf; Burford Golf.

**EARL, Stephen,** TD 1992; His Honour Judge Earl; a Circuit Judge, since 2015; *b* 16 April 1958; *s* of Leslie Earl and Anne Earl; *m* 2002, Gillian Douglass; one *s* one *d*, and two step *s* four step *d*. *Educ:* Beverley Grammar Sch.; Manchester Polytech. (BA Hons Law); Guildford Coll. of Law. Articled clerk, Hart Scales & Hodges, 1980–82; admitted solicitor, 1982; Asst Solicitor, Gibson & Co., 1983–90; sole practitioner, Earl Galpin, 1990–2004. A Dep. Dist Judge, 2000–04; a District Judge (Magistrates' Courts), 2004–15. Mem., Criminal Procedure Rule Cttee, 2010–15. VRSM 2001. *Recreations:* family, travel, reading, staying fit. *Address:* Newcastle Crown Court, The Law Courts, The Quayside, Newcastle upon Tyne NE1 3LA.

**EARL, Col Timothy James,** OBE 2000; Private Secretary to HRH the Princess Royal, 1999–2002; *b* 2 July 1943; *s* of Rowland William Earl and Elizabeth Sylvia Earl; *m* 1968, Elizabeth Mary Ghislaine de Pelet; two *s* one *d*. *Educ:* Brentwood Sch.; RMA Sandhurst. Commnd 1st Bn King's Own Royal Border Regt, 1964; served British Guyana, Gulf States, Cyprus, Gibraltar and Germany; transf. to Life Guards, 1974; served Germany, Norway, Belize; CO, 1983–85; RCDS, 1985–87; MoD, 1987–90; HQ UKLF, 1990–93; Sec., Govt Hospitality Fund, 1993–99. Hon. Sec., Piscatorial Soc., 2008–17. *Recreations:* field sports, planting trees. *Address:* Haddon Lodge, Stourton Caundle, Dorset DT10 2LB. *T:* (01963) 362241. *Club:* Flyfishers'.

**EARLE, Sir George;** *see* Earle, Sir H. G. A.

**EARLE, Glenn Peter Jonathan;** Managing Director and Chief Operating Officer, Europe, Middle East and Africa, Goldman Sachs, 2006–11; *b* Douglas, I of M, 12 Jan. 1958; *s* of Brian Peter Earle and late Elsie Florence Earle; *m* 1983, Phyllida Charlotte Gerrard; one *s* two *d*. *Educ:* Millfield Sch.; Emmanuel Coll., Cambridge (BA Hons 1979); Harvard Business Sch. (MBA with High Dist.). With Grindlays Bank, subseq. ANZ Grindlays, 1979–85; with Goldman Sachs, incl. roles in NY, Frankfurt and London, 1987–2011 (Partner, 1996; Co-hd, EMEA M&A Adv. Gp, 1999–2003). Non-executive Director: Fiat Chrysler Automobiles, NV; Affiliated Managers Gp, Inc.; Rothesay Life Gp, 2015–18. Chm., Adv. Bd, Judge Business Sch., Cambridge Univ., 2010–15; Mem., Adv. Bd, Sutton Trust, 2013–. Trustee: RNT, 2009–17; Teach First, 2012–. *Recreations:* theatre, sport, the outdoors. *Clubs:* MCC; Queen's; Royal Ashdown Golf, Queenwood Golf; Bath and Racquets.

**EARLE, Sir (Hardman) George (Algernon),** 6th Bt *cr* 1869; *b* 4 Feb. 1932; *S* father, 1979; *m* 1967, Diana Gillian Bligh, *d* of Col F. F. B. St George, CVO; one *s* one *d*. *Heir: s* Robert George Bligh Earle [*b* 24 Jan. 1970; *m* 2007, Nico Germaine Erzsebet, *d* of Miklós Kōs; one *s* one *d*].

**EARLE, Joel Vincent, (Joe);** Senior Consultant for Japanese Works of Art, Bonhams, since 2012; *b* 1 Sept. 1952; *s* of late James Basil Foster Earle and Mary Isabel Jessie Weeks; *m* 1980, Sophia Charlotte Knox; two *s*. *Educ:* Westminster Sch.; New Coll., Oxford (BA 1st Cl. Hons Chinese). Far Eastern Department, Victoria & Albert Museum: Res. Asst, 1974–77; Asst Keeper, 1977–82; Keeper, 1982–87; Head of Public Services, V&A Mus., 1987–89; independent curator, 1990–2003; Chair, Dept of Art of Asia, Oceania and Africa, Mus. of Fine Arts, Boston, 2003–07; Vice-Pres. and Dir, Japan Soc. Gall., NY, 2007–12. Consultant, Christie's, 1998–2003. Exhibns Co-ordinator, Japan Fest. 1991, 1990–91; *other exhibitions include:* Japan Style, V&A, 1980; Japanese Lacquer, V&A, 1980; Great Japan Exhibition, RA, 1981; The Toshiba Gall. of Japanese Art, V&A, 1986; British Design, South Coast Plaza, 1990; Visions of Japan, V&A, 1991–92; London Transport Posters, 1994; Da un antico castello inglese, Milan, 1994; Shibata Zeshin, Nat. Mus. of Scotland, 1997; Splendors of Meiji, USA, 1999; Netsuke, Mus. of Fine Arts, Boston, 2001; Serizawa: Master of Japanese Textile Design, Nat. Mus of Scotland, 2001; New Bamboo: contemporary Japanese masters, Japan Soc., 2008; Buriki: Japanese tin toys from the golden age of the American automobile, Japan Soc., 2009; Fiber Futures: Japan's Textile Pioneers, Japan Soc., 2011; Silver Wind: the arts of Sakai Hoitsu (1761–1828), Japan Soc., 2012; New Forms, New Voices: Japanese ceramics from the Gitter-Yelen Collection, 2017. *Publications:* An Introduction to Netsuke, 1980, 2nd edn 1982; An Introduction to Japanese Prints, 1980; (contrib.) Japan Style, 1980; (contrib.) The Great Japan Exhibition, 1981; (trans.) The Japanese Sword, 1983; The Toshiba Gallery: Japanese art and design, 1986; Flower Bronzes of Japan, 1995; (ed) Treasures of Imperial Japan: Lacquer, 1995; (ed) The Index of Inro Artists, 1995; Shibata Zeshin, 1996; Shadows and Reflections: Japanese lacquer art, 1996; Flowers of the Chisel, 1997; R. S. Huthart Collection of Netsuke, 1998; Splendors of Meiji, 1999; Infinite Spaces: the art and wisdom of the Japanese garden, 2000; Netsuke of Iwami Province, 2000; Japanese Lacquer: The Denys Eyre Bower Collection, 2000; Netsuke: fantasy and reality in Japanese miniature sculpture, 2001; Splendors of Imperial Japan, 2002; Lethal Elegance: the art of Samurai sword fittings, 2004; Contemporary Clay: Japanese ceramics for the new century, 2005; Serizawa: master of Japanese textile design, 2009; (trans.) Melk's Golden Acres, 2011; (trans.) A White Camellia in a Vase, 2012; (contrib.) In the Moment: Japanese art from the Larry Ellison collection, 2013; Inro from a Private European Collection, 2013; (contrib. and ed) Grace Tsumugi Fine Art: Japanese works of art, 2014; (contrib. and ed) Erik Thomsen: Japanese paintings and works of art, 2014; (contrib. and ed) Erik Thomsen: Inoue Yuichi, 2014; (contrib. and ed) Bonhams 1793: the Misumi Collection of important works of lacquer art and paintings, Part I, 2014, Part II, 2015; Bonhams 1793: Transformation, Summation, Creation: masterpieces of Japanese Meiji-Era craft from a private collection, 2015; Bonhams 1793: From Edo to Tokyo: a special exhibition of masterpieces of Japanese art from a private collection, 2016; Bonhams 1793: Image and Ornament: a special exhibition of masterpieces of Japanese metalwork from a private collection, 2017; Baskets: masterpieces of Japanese bamboo art 1850–2015, 2017; Birds and Flowers: a special exhibition of masterpieces of Japanese art from a private collection, 2018; Suzuki Chōkichi: master of metal raptors, 2019; Glass Mountains, Silver Moon: a special exhibition of masterpieces of Japanese art from a

private collection, 2019; articles in learned jls. *Recreation:* translating Japanese. *Address:* 123 Middleton Road, E8 4LL. *T:* (020) 7254 5178, 07880 313351, (USA) (646) 5962939. *E:* joevearle@gmail.com.
*See also T. F. Earle.*

**EARLE, Prof. Thomas Foster,** DPhil; King John II Professor of Portuguese Studies, University of Oxford, 1996–2013; Fellow, St Peter's College, Oxford, 1996–2013, now Emeritus; *b* 5 April 1946; *s* of late James Basil Foster Earle and Mary Earle (*née* Weeks); *m* 1970, Gisèle Hilary Wilson; one *s* one *d. Educ:* Westminster Sch.; Wadham Coll., Oxford (BA 1967; DPhil 1976). University of Oxford: Lectr in Portuguese Studies, 1968–96; Fellow, Linacre Coll., 1968–96; Dir, Portuguese Studies, 1976–96; Chm., Centre for Study of Portuguese Discoveries, Linacre Coll., 1989–. Founder Mem., Associação Internacional de Lusitanistas, 1984; Corresp. Fellow, Acad. das Ciências de Lisboa, 2010. Pres., Assoc. of British and Irish Lusitanists, 2006–09. Grande oficial, Ordem do Infante D. Henrique (Portugal), 1995. *Publications:* Theme and Image in the Poetry of Sá de Miranda, 1980 (trans. Portuguese 1985); The Muse Reborn: the poetry of António Ferreira, 1988 (trans. Portuguese 1990); (ed) Castro de António Ferreira, 1990; (with J. Villiers) Albuquerque: Caesar of the East, 1990; (ed) Poemas Lusitanos de António Ferreira, 2000, 2nd edn 2008; O Livro de Eclesiastes, 2002, 2nd edn 2014; Portuguese Writers and English Readers: books by Portuguese writers published before 1640 in the libraries of Oxford and Cambridge, 2009 (trans. Portuguese, 2014); Estudos sobre literatura e cultura portuguesa do Renascimento, 2013; (ed with J. Camões) Comédias de Sá de Miranda, 2013; (ed) Almeida Garrett, Um Auto de Gil Vicente, 2017; articles in collections, learned jls, etc. *Recreations:* music, gardening, walking. *Address:* c/o St Peter's College, New Inn Hall Street, Oxford OX1 2DL.
*See also J. V. Earle.*

**EARLES, Prof. Stanley William Edward,** PhD, DScEng; FREng, FIMechE; Professor of Mechanical Engineering, King's College, University of London, 1976–94, Emeritus since 1994; *b* 18 Jan. 1929; *s* of late William Edward Earles and Winnifred Anne Cook; *m* 1955, Margaret Isabella Brown; two *d. Educ:* King's Coll., Univ. of London (BScEng, PhD, DScEng; AKC; FKC 1993). FIMechE 1976; FREng (FEng 1992). Nuffield Apprentice, Birmingham, 1944–50; King's Coll., Univ. of London, 1950–53; Scientific Officer, Royal Naval Scientific Service, 1953–55; University of London: Queen Mary College: Lectr in Mech. Engrg, 1955–69; Reader in Mech. Engrg, 1969–75; Prof. of Mech. Engrg, 1975–76; King's College: Head, Dept of Mech. Engrg, 1976–90, 1991–94; Dean of Engrg, 1986–90; Hd of Sch. of Phys. Scis and Engrg, 1990–91. James Clayton Fund prize, IMechE, 1967; Engineering Applied to Agriculture Award, IMechE, 1980. *Publications:* papers and articles in Proc. IMechE, Jl of Mech. Engrg Science, Jl of Sound and Vibration, Wear, Proc. ASME and ASLE, and Eng. *Recreations:* Real tennis, gardening, fell walking. *Address:* Woodbury, Church Lane, Wormley, Broxbourne, Herts EN10 7QF. *T:* (01992) 464616.

**EARLY, Fergus,** OBE 2009; dancer and choreographer; Founder and Artistic Director, Green Candle Dance Company, since 1987; *b* Worthing, 4 Aug. 1946; *s* of Dr Noel Early and Hilda Early (*née* West); *m* 2005, Jacky Lansley; one *d. Educ:* Royal Ballet Sch.; RAD major exams. Founder Mem., Balletmakers Ltd, 1962–69; dancer, Royal Ballet, 1964–68; Ballet Master and Resident Choreographer, Ballet for All company, Royal Ballet, 1965–70; Sen. Teacher, London Sch. of Contemp. Dance, 1971–74; Founder Member: Dance Organisation, 1975–76; X6 Dance Space, 1976–80; Chisenhale Dance Space, 1981–88. Co-Founder and Co-Ed., New Dance Mag., 1977–82. Chm., Gtr London Arts Dance Panel, 1979–84; Trustee: Scarabeus Theatre Co., 1999–2012 (Chm., 2006–11); Oxford House, Bethnal Green, 2004– (Vice Chm., 2009–). Churchill Fellow, 2010. Hon. DA De Montfort, 2011. *Publications:* Growing Bolder: a start-up guide to creating dance with older people, 1996; The Wise Body: conversations with experienced dancers, 2011; articles in dance and arts jls. *Recreations:* playing cricket, walking. *Address:* Green Candle Dance Company, Oxford House, Derbyshire Street, E2 6HG. *T:* (020) 7739 7722. *E:* fergus@greencandledance.com.

**EARNSHAW, Christopher Martin,** OBE 2015; FREng, CEng, FIET; Chairman: BRE Group, since 2014; Cranfield Group Holdings (formerly Cranfield Ventures) Ltd, since 2008; *b* Yorkshire, 4 May 1954; *s* of Frank and Bessie Earnshaw; *m* 1979, Moira Turner; two *s* one *d. Educ:* Wellington Grammar Sch.; Adams Grammar Sch., Newport; Univ. of Sheffield (BSc Hons Physics). CEng 1983; FIET 1990; FREng 1999. British Telecommunications plc: Sen. Network Project Manager, 1981–87; Gen. Manager, Network Technol., 1987–89; Dir Networks, 1989–91; Man. Dir, Worldwide Networks, 1991–93; Pres. and CEO, Concert Communications Inc., 1993–95; Man. Dir, Networks and Systems, 1995–99, Gp Engrg Dir, 1999–2002, British Telecommunications plc; Man. Dir, Oakleigh Ventures Ltd, 2002–16. Chm., Police IT Orgn, 2004–07. *Address:* c/o BRE Group, Bucknalls Lane, Watford WD25 9XX. *E:* chris@oakleighassociates.com.

**EARNSHAW, Prof. William Charles,** PhD; FMedSci; FRS 2013; FRSE; Professor of Chromosome Dynamics, Institute of Cell Biology, University of Edinburgh. *Educ:* Lenox Sch., Lenox, Mass; Colby Coll. (BA Biol. and Art 1972); Massachusetts Inst. of Technol. (PhD Microbiol. 1977). Postdoctoral Fellow: MRC Molecular Biol. Lab., Cambridge, 1977–81; Univ. of Geneva, 1981–82; Prof., Sch. of Medicine, Johns Hopkins Univ., 1982–95; Wellcome (formerly Wellcome Trust) Principal Res. Fellow, Univ. of Edinburgh, 1996–. FRSE 2002; FMedSci 2009; FAAAS; Mem. EMBO. *Publications:* Cell Biology (with Thomas Pollard), 2nd edn 2007, 3rd edn 2017. *Address:* Wellcome Centre for Cell Biology, University of Edinburgh, Michael Swann Building, Max Born Crescent, Edinburgh EH9 3BF.

**EARWICKER, Martin John,** FREng; Vice Chancellor and Chief Executive, and Personal Chair, London South Bank University, 2009–13; *b* 11 May 1948; *s* of George Allen Earwicker and Joan Mary Earwicker (*née* West); *m* 1970, Pauline Ann Josey; two *s. Educ:* Farnborough Grammar Sch.; Univ. of Surrey (BSc Hons Physics 1970). FREng 2000. Various research posts, ARE, 1970–86; Dir, Science (Sea), MoD, 1986–89; Hd, Attack Weapons Dept, 1989–90, Hd, Flight Systems Dept, 1990–92, RAE; Dir, Operational Studies, 1992–93, Dir, Air Systems Sector, 1993–96, DRA; Dep. Chief Scientist (Scrutiny and Analysis), 1996–98, Dir Gen. (Scrutiny and Analysis), 1998–99, MoD; Man. Dir, Analysis, DERA, 1998–99; Hd of Science and Engrg Base Gp, OST, DTI, 1999–2001; Chief Exec., Defence Sci. and Technol. Lab., MoD, 2001–06; Dir, NMSI, 2006–09. Vis. Prof., Faculty of Engrg, Imperial Coll., London, 2005–09. Chairman: Farnborough Coll. of Technol., 2004–10, 2015–; Tower Hamlets Coll., 2010–16. Non-exec. Dir, 2013–16, Vice Chm., 2014–16, Dorset County Hosp. NHS Foundn Trust; Chm., Berks Healthcare NHS Foundn Trust, 2016–. Trustee: Hart CAB, 2013–; Regent's Univ., London, 2014. Pres., Assoc. for Sci. Educn, 2008. Vice Pres., RAEng 2009–12. DUniv Surrey, 2010. A. B. Wood Medal and Prize, Inst. of Acoustics, 1984. *Recreations:* cycling, woodwork, music. *Address:* Fitzwilliam House, Berkshire Healthcare NHS Foundation Trust, Skimped Hill Lane, Bracknell, Berks RG12 1JX.

**EASMON, Prof. Charles Syrett Farrell,** CBE 2000; MD, PhD; Professor of Health Policy, University of West London (formerly Thames Valley University), 2003–10, now Emeritus; *b* 20 Aug. 1946; *s* of Dr McCormack Charles Farrell Easmon and Enid Winifred Easmon; *m* 1977, Susan Lynn (*née* Peach). *Educ:* Epsom Coll.; St Mary's Hospital Med. Sch. (Open Schol.; MB BS; MD); PhD London. MRCP; FRCPath. Pathology trng, St Bartholomew's Hosp., 1970–71; St Mary's Hospital Medical School: Research Asst, 1971; Lectr, 1973; Sen. Lectr, 1976; Reader and Actg Head of Dept, 1980; Personal Chair, 1983; Fleming Prof. of Med. Microbiol., 1984–92; Dean of Postgrad. Med. for NW Thames, BPMF, Univ. of London, 1992–95; Dir of Educn and Trng, N Thames, then London, Reg., NHS Exec., 1994–2002; Clin. Dir, Directorate of Health and Social Care for London, DoH, 2002–03. Dep. Chm., HPA, 2003–13. Non-exec. Dir, SW London Strategic HA, 2003–06. Chm., Darwin Centre Trust, 2015–17. Founder FMedSci 1998. *Publications:* (ed) Medical Microbiology, vol. 1 1982, vols 2 and 3 1983, vol. 4 1984; (ed) Infections in the Immunocompromised Host, 1983; (ed) Staphylococci and Staphylococcal Infections, 1983; numerous papers in learned jls. *Recreations:* music, history, fishing. *Address:* 34 St Johns Road, Clifton, Bristol BS8 2HG. *Club:* Athenæum.

**EASSIE, Rt Hon. Lord;** Ronald David Mackay; PC 2006; a Senator of the College of Justice in Scotland, 1997–2015; Chairman, Scottish Law Commission, 2002–06; *b* 1945; *s* of Robert Ostler Mackay and Dorothy Lilian Johnson or Mackay; *m* 1988, Annette Frenkel; one *s. Educ:* Berwickshire High Sch.; Univ. of St Andrews (MA Hons); Univ. of Edinburgh (LLB). Admitted to Faculty of Advocates, 1972; Official of Court of Justice of European Communities, Luxembourg, 1979–82; QC (Scot.) 1986; Advocate Depute, 1986–90. *Publications:* (ed with H. L. MacQueen) Gloag & Henderson, The Law of Scotland, 13th edn 2012 to 14th edn 2017. *Recreations:* walking, ski-ing. *Club:* New (Edinburgh).

**EASSON, Gillian;** Chairman, Stockport NHS Foundation Trust, 2012–17 (Deputy Chairman, 2007–12); *b* Stockport, 2 Dec. 1950; *d* of late Stanley and Joan Oakley; *m* 1972, Malcolm Cameron Greig Easson (*d* 2010); one *s* one *d. Educ:* Marple Hall Sch. for Girls; Girton Coll., Cambridge (BA 1972; MA 1976). Admitted as solicitor, 1975; Solicitor, Gtr Manchester Council, prosecuting for NW Prosecuting Solicitors' Dept, 1977–86; Crown Prosecutor, 1986–87; sole practitioner, 1987–2000. Mem. Bd, Ofqual, 2010–12 (Chair, Ext. Equality Adv. Gp, 2010–12; Hd, 2010 GCSE, AS and A Level Exam. Marking Inquiry, 2010–12). Chair, Manchester Univ. Press., 2010–13; non-executive Director: Christie Hosp. NHS Trust, 2000–06 (Chair: Charitable Funds Cttee, 2001–02; Audit Cttee, 2001–03; Finance Cttee, 2003–06); Project Unity Ltd, 2004; UMIP Ltd, 2005–07 (Chair, Audit Cttee, 2006–07). Member: Gtr Manchester Provider Chairs Gp, 2015–; Gtr Manchester Health and Social Care Strategic Partnership Bd, 2016–. Mem. Council and Court, UMIST, 2001–04; University of Manchester: Mem., 2004–08, Dep. Chm., 2008–12, Chm., Staffing Cttee, 2010–12, Bd of Govs; Chm., Risk Cttee, 2004–09; Pro-Chancellor, 2012–; Chair, Nominations Cttee, 2012–18; Mem., Global Leadership Bd, 2012–. Trustee and Mem. Bd, NHS Providers, 2014–17. *Recreation:* light aviation.

**EAST, John Anthony,** CBE 1996 (OBE 1982); Chairman: Continuum Group (formerly Heritage Projects Ltd), since 1997; Greenway LLP, since 2007; E-Riser Ltd, since 2014; *b* 25 May 1930; *s* of John East and Jessie Mary East; *m* 1st, 1957, Barbara Collins (marr. diss. 1980); two *s* one *d;* 2nd, 1982, Susan Finch (marr. diss. 1996); two *d. Educ:* Bromley Grammar School. Reuter's, 1954–58; Notley Advertising, 1958–60; Director: French Government Tourist Office, 1960–70; English Tourist Bd, 1970–95 (Chief Exec., 1985–95). Chairman: Watermark, 1995–97; Kent Life, 2009–16; Sustainable Villages Ltd, 2010–16; Cygnus Homes, 2016–. *Publications:* History of French Architecture, 1968; Gascony and the Pyrenees, 1969; articles on France and French architecture. *Recreations:* walking, gardening, studying things French. *Address:* Continuum Group, St Edmunds House, Margaret Street, York YO10 4UX.

**EAST, Rt Hon. Paul Clayton,** CNZM 2005; PC 1998; QC (NZ) 1995; High Commissioner for New Zealand in the United Kingdom, 1999–2002; *b* 4 Aug. 1946; *s* of Edwin Cuthbert East and Edith Pauline Addison East; *m* 1972, Marilyn Kottman; three *d. Educ:* King's Coll., Auckland; Auckland Univ. (LLB 1970); Univ. of Virginia, USA (LLM 1972). Barrister and solicitor, Auckland, 1971; Graduate Fellow, Univ. of Va Sch. of Law, 1971–72; Partner, 1974–78, Consultant, 1978–90, East Brewster, Solicitors, Rotorua. City Councillor, and Dep. Mayor of Rotorua, 1974–79 (Chm., Finance Cttee, 1977–79). MP (N) New Zealand, 1978–99 (for Rotorua, 1978–96). Opposition Spokesman, NZ Parliament: for Commerce and Customs, 1984; on Justice, Attorney-Gen. and Constitutional Affairs, 1985–90; on Health, 1986; Attorney-Gen., 1990–97; Minister: for Crown Health Enterprises, 1991–96; of State Services, 1993–97; of Defence, and for Corrections, 1996–97. Leader of House of Representatives, 1990–93. Chm., Parly Select Cttee on Official Information, 1982; Member: Nat. Exec., NZ Nat. Party, 1985–87; NZ Delegn, Council of Europe and Eur. Parlt, 1985; Dep. Chm., Commonwealth Eminent Persons Observer Gp, Kenya Elections, 2008; Chm., Commonwealth Eminent Persons Gp, Tanzania Elections, 2010. Chm., Rotorua Airport Cttee, 1977–79; Mem. Exec., Airport Authorities of NZ, 1974–79. Chm., Perpetual Capital Mgt Ltd, 2006–; Director: Taylors Gp Ltd, 2002–; Benfield Gp (formerly Grieg) (NZ) Ltd, 2002–; Agriquality Ltd; NZ Rail Corp., 2015–. Chm., Charity Gaming Assoc., 2002–. Trustee: NZ Antarctic Heritage Trust, 2002– (Chm., 2005–); Rotorua Energy Charitable Trust, 2004–. Fellow, Australia/NZ Foundn, 1983. *Publications:* numerous articles. *Recreations:* ski-ing, fishing, golf. *Address:* 30 Hamilton Road, Herne Bay, Auckland 1011, New Zealand. *Club:* Northern (Auckland).

**EAST, Ronald Joseph;** Director, Kleinwort Charter Investment Trust PLC, 1987–97; formerly Director, Kleinwort Development Fund PLC; *b* 17 Dec. 1931; *s* of Joseph William and Marion Elizabeth Emma East; *m* 1955, Iris Joyce Beckwith; two *d. Educ:* Clare Coll., Cambridge Univ. (MA). Engineering Apprenticeship, Ford Trade Sch., Ford Motor Co. Ltd, 1945–52. Troop Comdr, RA (Lieut), 1953–55. Managerial posts in economics, product planning, finance, and engineering areas of Ford Motor Co. Ltd, 1959–65; Guest, Keen & Nettlefolds Ltd: Corporate Staff Dir of Planning, 1965–70; Planning Exec., Automotive and Allied Products Sector, 1972–73; Chairman: GKN Castings Ltd, 1974–77; GKN Kent Alloys Ltd, 1974–77; GKN Shotton Ltd, 1974–77; Dir, GKN (UK) Ltd, 1974–77; Corporate Staff Dir, Group Supplies, GKN Ltd, 1976–77. Dir, Programme Analysis and Review (PAR) and Special Advisor to Chief Sec. to the Treasury, 1971–72. Chairman: Hale Hamilton Hldgs, 1981–89; Hale Hamilton (Valves), 1981–89. *Recreation:* walking. *Address:* 12 Rutland Gate, SW7 1BB.

**EAST, Trevor James;** Partner, Pitch International LLP, since 2005; *b* Derby, 22 Oct. 1950; *s* of Ralph James and Hazel Jean East; *m* 1st, 1975, Penelope Anne McLean (marr. diss. 1987); two *s* one *d;* 2nd, 1995, Katharine Judith Brown; two *s* one *d. Educ:* Bemrose Grammar Sch., Derby. Trainee journalist, then journalist, Raymonds News Agency, 1967–72; Producer and Presenter, ATV Sport, 1972–78; Presenter, Tiswas, 1973–78; Sports Ed., Central TV, 1978–84; Exec. Producer, 1984–92, Dep. Hd, 1992–94, Hd, 1994–95, ITV Sport; Dep. Man. Dir, Sky Sports, 1995–2005; Dir of Sport, Setanta, 2005–09. *Recreations:* sport, music, food, wine. *Address:* Pitch International LLP, 27 Brewhouse Lane, Putney, SW15 2JX.

**EAST ANGLIA, Bishop of, (RC),** since 2013; **Rt Rev. Alan Stephen Hopes;** *b* 17 March 1944; *s* of William Stephen and Ivy Beatrice Hopes. *Educ:* Enfield Grammar Sch.; King's Coll., London (BD, AKC 1966). Ordained deacon, 1967, priest, 1968; Assistant Curate: All Saints, E Finchley, 1967–72; St Alphage, Burnt Oak (in charge of Grahame Park Estate), 1972–78; Vicar, St Paul, Tottenham, 1978–94; Area Dean, E Haringey, 1982–88; Preb., St Paul's Cathedral, 1987–94; ordained priest in the Roman Catholic Church, 1995;

Asst Priest, Our Lady of Victories, Kensington, 1995–97; Parish Priest, Holy Redeemer, Chelsea, 1997–2001; VG, Westminster Archdiocese, 2001–03; Auxiliary Bishop of Westminster, (RC), 2003–13; Titular Bishop of Cuncacestre, 2003–13. *Recreations:* books, art, films, classical music, opera, travel. *Address:* The White House, 21 Upgate, Poringland, Norwich NR14 7SH.

**EAST RIDING, Archdeacon of;** *see* Broom, Ven. A. C.

**EASTEAL, Andrew Francis Martin; His Honour Judge Easteal;** a Circuit Judge, since 2018; *b* Ipswich, 8 Oct. 1965; *s* of Roy Easteal and Betty Easteal; *m* Elizabeth Smith; one *d*. *Educ:* Samuel Ward Upper Sch., Haverhill; Oriel Coll., Oxford (MA Juris. 1988). Called to the Bar, Inner Temple, 1990; a Recorder, 2009–18. Lectr to expert witnesses, trainee barristers and sixth form confs, 1995–2017; annual presentations to students, 2005–15, Ext. Examnr, 2008–11, Bar Professional Trng Course. *Recreations:* running exclusive taxi service for Beth and Naeve, watching horse riding, trampolining and shopping by Beth and Naeve, carrying shopping bags for Beth and Naeve, trying surreptitiously to watch football on TV without being dragged away to do something by Beth and Naeve. *Address:* Lincoln Crown Court, Lincoln LN1 3GA. *T:* (01522) 525222. *E:* hhj.andrew.easteal@ejudiciary.net.

**EASTELL, Prof. Richard,** MD; FRCP, FRCPE, FRCPath, FMedSci; Professor of Bone Metabolism, since 1995, and Director, Mellanby Centre for Bone Research, since 2008, University of Sheffield; Hon. Consultant Physician, Sheffield Teaching Hospitals NHS Trust (formerly Northern General Hospital, Royal Hallamshire Hospital and Nether Edge Hospital), since 1989; *b* 12 Feb. 1953; *s* of late Kenneth Eastell and Betty Eastell (*née* Hoare); *m* 1974, Joyce Rachel Noble; two *s* one *d*. *Educ:* Univ. of Edinburgh (BSc Hons 1974; MB ChB 1977; MD 1984). FRCP 1996; FRCPE 2000; FRCPath 2000. House Officer, Royal Infirmary and Western Gen. Hosp., Edinburgh, 1977–78; MRC Res. Fellow, 1978–80, Registrar, 1980–82, Western Gen. Hosp. Edinburgh; Registrar, Northwick Park Hosp., Harrow, 1982–84; Res. Associate and Sen. Clinical Fellow, Mayo Clinic, Rochester, Minn., 1984–89; University of Sheffield: Sen. Res. Fellow, 1989–92, Sen. Lectr, 1992–95, Dept of Human Metabolism and Clinical Biochemistry; Res. Dean, Sch. of Medicine and Biomed. Scis, 2002–05; Dir, Bone Biomedical Res. Unit, 2008–12. Director: Div. of Clinical Scis (North), 1999–2003; R&D for Sheffield Teaching Hosps Trust, 2003–05. Sen. Investigator, NIHR, 2009–. Visiting Professor in Endocrinology: Mayo Clinic, Rochester, USA, 1999; Univ. of Pittsburgh, 2002; Path West Vis. Lectr, Perth, Australia, 2005. Member: ARC Res. Cttee, 1998–2004; Res. Adv. Council, Res. into Ageing, 2001–04; MRC Physiological Systems and Clinical Scis Bd, 2003–06; MRC and NIHR Efficacy and Mechanism Evaluation Bd, 2009–. President: Bone and Tooth Soc., 2002–05; Eur. Calcified Tissue Soc., 2005–08; Chm., Nat. Osteoporosis Soc., 2007–08. FMedSci 2000. Hon. FRCPI 1998. Randall G. Sprague Award, Mayo Clinic, 1989; Corrigan Medal, RCPI, 1998; Queen's Anniversary Award for Higher Educn, 2002; Kohn Award, Nat. Osteoporosis Soc., 2004; Soc. for Endocrinol. Medal, 2004; Sen. Investigator Award, NIHR, 2009; Philippe Bordier Award for Clinical Investigation, Eur. Calcified Tissue Soc., 2012; Frederic C. Bartter Award, Amer. Soc. of Bone and Mineral Res., 2014; Linda Edwards Award, Nat. Osteoporosis Soc., 2018. *Publications:* (ed jtly) Bone Markers: biochemical and clinical perspectives, 2001; over 300 articles in med. literature. *Recreations:* golf, hill walking. *Address:* 289 Ringinglow Road, Bents Green, Sheffield, South Yorks S11 7PZ. *T:* (0114) 271 4705. *E:* r.eastell@sheffield.ac.uk.

**EASTER, Rev. Canon Ann Rosemarie;** Chaplain to the Queen, 2007–17; Associate Priest, East Ham Team, since 2011; Member (Lab), Newham London Borough Council, since 2014; *b* Upton Park, 9 Sept.; *d* of Harry Easter and Audrey Easter (*née* Boater); *m* 1987, Rev. Christopher Owens; two *s* one *d*. *Educ:* George Green's Grammar Sch.; Queen's Coll., Birmingham (Dip. in Religious Studies 1979); Univ. of East London (Dip. in Mgt Studies 1994). Ordained deaconess, 1980, deacon, 1987, priest, 1994; Parish Minister, St John, St James and Christchurch, London, 1980–89; Manager, Newham Crossroads, 1990–95; CEO, Renewal Programme, 1995–2015; Area Dean, Newham, 1996–2007. Chair: Child Bereavement UK, 2012–; Newham Healthwatch, 2016–; Sparrows Trading Co., 2016–. Chelmsford Dio. Hon. Canon, Chelmsford Cathedral, 2000–; Hon. Curate (part-time), All Saints, West Ham, 2008–10. Regular contributor: BBC religious progs, Good Morning Sunday, Pause for Thought and Daily Service; Big Brother's Bit on the Side, Channel 5, 2016–18. *Publications:* This Month We Celebrate, 1990. *Recreations:* playing the piano, entertaining and being entertained. *Address:* 67 Disraeli Road, E7 9JU. *T:* (020) 8555 6337.

**EASTERLING, Prof. Patricia Elizabeth,** FBA 1998; Regius Professor of Greek, Cambridge University, 1994–2001, and Fellow of Newnham College, Cambridge, 1994–2001 (Hon. Fellow, 1987–94 and since 2001); *b* 11 March 1934; *d* of Edward Wilson Fairfax and Annie Smith; *m* 1956, Henry John Easterling; one *s*. *Educ:* Blackburn High School for Girls; Newnham College, Cambridge (BA 1955, MA 1959). Asst Lectr, Univ. of Manchester, 1957–58; University of Cambridge: Asst Lectr, 1968; Lectr, 1969–87; Newnham College, Cambridge: Asst Lectr, 1958–60; Fellow and Lectr, 1960–87; Dir of Studies in Classics, 1979–87; Vice-Principal, 1981–86; Prof. of Greek, UCL, 1987–94. Townsend Lectr, Cornell Univ., 1990. Chm., Council of Univ. Classical Depts, 1990–93. President: Classical Assoc., 1988–89; Hellenic Soc., 1996–99. Mem., Academia Europaea, 1995. Corresp. étranger, 2004, Associé étranger, 2013, Acad. des Inscriptions et Belles-Lettres, Inst de France. Hon. Mem., Hungarian Acad. of Scis, 2013. Hon. Fellow: UCL, 1997; Inst. of Classical Studies, London, 2015. Hon. DPhil: Athens, 1996; Uppsala, 2000; Ioannina, 2002; Hon. DLitt Bristol, 1999; Hon. DLitt London, 1999. *Publications:* (with E. J. Kenney) Ovidiana Graeca, 1965; (ed) Sophocles, Trachiniae, 1982; (with B. M. W. Knox, ed and contrib.) Cambridge History of Classical Literature, vol. I, 1985; (ed with J. V. Muir) Greek Religion and Society, 1985; (ed) Cambridge Companion to Greek Tragedy, 1997; (ed with C. M. Handley) Greek Scripts, 2001; (ed with E. M. Hall) Greek and Roman Actors, 2002. *Address:* Newnham College, Cambridge CB3 9DF. *T:* (01223) 335700.

**EASTHAM, Kenneth;** *b* 11 Aug. 1927; *s* of late James Eastham; *m* 1951, Doris, *d* of Albert Howarth; one *d*. Planning engr, GEC, Trafford Park. Mem., Manchester CC, 1962–80 (Dep. Leader 1975–79; Chairman: Planning Cttee, 1971–74; Educn Cttee, 1978–79); Mem., NW Econ. Planning Council, 1975–79. MP (Lab) Manchester, Blackley, 1979–97. An Opposition Whip, 1987–92. *Address:* 12 Nan Nook Road, Manchester M23 9BZ.

**EASTMAN, Roger;** a Master, Senior (formerly Supreme) Court, Queen's Bench Division, since 2009; *b* Maidstone, 23 May 1953; *s* of late Maurice George Eastman and Marian Eastman (*née* Pettman); *m* 1994, Ruth Denton Farnsworth; one step *s* one step *d*. *Educ:* Maidstone Grammar Sch.; St John's Coll., Durham (BA 1975). Called to the Bar, Gray's Inn, 1978, Bencher 2001; in practice at the Bar, specialising in common law, Henderson Chambers, 1980–2009. Dean of Chapel, Gray's Inn, 2010–. FRSA. *Publications:* (Jt Ed.) Civil Procedure (formerly Supreme Court Practice), 2009–; (ed) Pleadings Without Tears, 8th edn 2012, 9th edn 2017; (Jt Gen. Ed.) Rev. Roger Holloway, OBE, MA: a collection of favourite sermons preached in the Chapel of Gray's Inn 1997–2010, 2012; (contrib.) Atkin's Court Forms, 2014–. *Recreations:* music (active and passive), art, cooking, gardening, enthusiastic but flawed tennis and ski-ing. *Address:* Royal Courts of Justice, Strand, WC2A 2LL. *Club:* Clapham Common All Weather Tennis.

**EASTON, Carole,** OBE 2017; PhD; Chief Executive, Young Women's Trust (formerly Platform 51), since 2013; *b* 13 July 1954; *d* of Laszlo Easton and Naomi Easton. *Educ:* Brunel Univ. (BSc; PhD); Tavistock Clinic (Child and Adolescent Psychotherapist). Child Psychotherapist, NHS, 1984–91. Counselling Manager, ChildLine, 1992–96; Hd, Clinical Services, The Place to Be, 1996–98; Chief Executive: Cruse Bereavement Care, 1998–2001; ChildLine, 2001–06; CLIC Sargent, 2006–09; Exec. Dir, Changing Faces, 2010–13. *E:* eastoncarole@gmail.com.

**EASTON, (Catharine) Jane;** Director-General, English-Speaking Union, since 2014; *b* Sunderland, 19 Oct. 1961; *d* of late Roger and Jennifer Hubbard; *m* 1985, Peter Easton (marr. diss. 2010); two *s* one *d*. *Educ:* Harrogate Grammar Sch.; Durham Univ. (BA Hons Geog.); Loughborough Univ. (Dip. Mgt). Music Officer, E Midlands Arts, 1986–88; Co-ordinator, Nat. Assoc. of Music Advrs, 1989–91; Administrator, Leicester Royal Infirmary, 1992–93; Registry Manager, Loughborough Univ., 1994–99; Faculty Manager, Univ. of Nottingham, 1999–2004; Diocesan Sec., Dio. Leicester, 2004–10; Sec.-Gen., RAFA, 2010–14. *Recreations:* music, film, theatre. *Address:* English-Speaking Union, Dartmouth House, 37 Charles Street, W1J 5ED. *E:* jane.easton@esu.org.

**EASTON, David John;** HM Diplomatic Service, retired; consultant on Arab and South Asian matters; *b* 27 March 1941; *o s* of Air Cdre Sir James Easton, KCMG, CB, CBE, and Anna, *d* of Lt-Col J. A. McKenna, Ottawa; *m* 1964, Alexandra Julie, er *d* of Kenneth W. Clark (MBE 2000), London, W8; two *s* one *d*. *Educ:* Stone House, Broadstairs; Stowe (Exhbnr); Balliol Coll., Oxford (Trevelyan Schol.; BA Hons Jurisprudence 1963, MA 1973). Apprentice, United Steel Cos, Workington, 1960. TA, 1959–65; 2nd Lieut, Oxford Univ. OTC, 1962; Lieut, Inns of Court and City Yeo., 1964. Entered Foreign Office, 1963; Third Sec., Nairobi, 1965–66; Second Sec., UK Mission to UN, Geneva, 1967–70; MECAS, Lebanon, 1970–72; First Sec., FCO, 1972–73; First Sec. (Information), Tripoli, 1973–77; Defence Dept, FCO, 1977–80; First Sec. (Chancery), later Political Counsellor, Amman, 1980–83; Counsellor, FCO, 1984–86; Counsellor (Political), New Delhi, 1986–89; FCO, 1990–94; Gen. Manager, Network Security Mgt Ltd, 1994–95; Dir (Internat. Affairs), ICAEW, 1995–97; Sec., RSAA, 1997–2001. Dir, Internat. Community Sch. (Jordan) Ltd, 1980–83 (Chm. 1981–83). Pres., Delhi Diplomatic Assoc., 1988–89; Chm., Lansdowne Residents' Assoc., 1990–96. FRSA 1996; FRGS 1998. *Recreations:* swimming, travel, antiques and antiquities.

**EASTON, Helen Alice B.;** *see* Bower-Easton, H. A.

**EASTON, James,** OBE 1986; HM Diplomatic Service, retired; Feature Writer, Accordion Times, since 1992; *b* 1 Sept. 1931; *s* of John Easton and Helen Easton (*née* Whitney); *m* 1960, Rosemary Hobbin (*d* 2006); one *s* two *d*. *Educ:* St John Cantius Catholic Sch., Broxburn. Served 3rd Hussars, 1952–55. Admiralty, 1957–60; FO, 1960; Prague, 1960–62; Paris, 1963–65; FO, 1965–68; Vice-Consul: Belgrade, 1968–71; La Paz, 1971–74; Second Sec. (Commercial), New York, 1974–78; FCO, 1978–83; First Sec., Rome, 1983–87; Counsellor (Admin) and Consul-Gen., Brussels, 1987–89. *Recreation:* music. *Address:* 6 Cedar Gardens, Sutton, Surrey SM2 5DD. *T:* (020) 8643 2432.

**EASTON, Jane;** *see* Easton, C. J.

**EASTON, Karen Elisabeth Dind;** *see* Jones, K. E. D.

**EASTON, Mark Richard Erskine;** Home Editor, BBC News, since 2004; *b* 12 March 1959; *s* of Stephen and Fiona Easton; *m* 1987, Antonia Higgs; one *s* three *d*. *Educ:* Peter Symonds Grammar Sch., Winchester. Southern Evening Echo, 1978–80; Radio Victory, 1980–81; Radio Aire, 1981–82; LBC Radio, 1982–86; Corresp., BBC, 1986–96; Political Ed., Channel 5, 1996–98; Home and Social Affairs Ed., Channel 4, 1998–2004. FRSA 2007. *Publications:* Britain etc, 2012. *Recreations:* piano blues, Arsenal FC. *E:* mark.easton@bbc.co.uk.

**EASTON, Robert Alexander,** PhD; Chief Executive, Delta plc, 1989–96; *b* 24 Oct. 1948; *s* of Malcolm Edward George Easton and Violet May Liddell Easton (*née* Taylor); *m* 1983, Lynden Anne Welch; two *d*. *Educ:* St Lawrence Coll.; Univ. of Manchester (BSc Hons); Univ. of Aston (PhD). Delta plc, 1974–96: Dir of Planning, 1980–83; Man. Dir, Industrial Services Div., 1984–87; Dep. Chief Exec., 1988–89. Director: G. E. Crane (Holdings), 1986–91; Elementis (formerly Harrisons & Crosfield) plc, 1991–2001. *Recreations:* golf, travel, medieval art and architecture.

**EASTWOOD, Basil Stephen Talbot,** CMG 1999; HM Diplomatic Service, retired; *b* 4 March 1944; *s* of late Christopher Gilbert Eastwood, CMG and Catherine Emma (*née* Peel); *m* 1970, Alison Faith Hutchings; three *d* (and one *d* decd). *Educ:* Eton (KS); Merton College, Oxford. Entered Diplomatic Service, 1966; Middle East Centre for Arab Studies, 1967–68; Jedda, 1968–69; Colombo, 1969–72; Cairo, 1972–76; Cabinet Office, 1976–78; FCO, 1978–80; Bonn, 1980–84; Khartoum, 1984–87; Athens, 1987–91; Dir of Res. and Analysis, FCO, 1991–96; Ambassador to Syria, 1996–2000; Project Dir, Middle East Inst., 2000–01; Ambassador to Switzerland, 2001–04. Chairman: Cecily's Fund, 1998–2009; Oxfordshire Historic Churches Trust, 2012–17. *Address:* Redding Wyck House, Market Street, Charlbury, Oxon OX7 3PJ.

**EASTWOOD, Clinton, (Clint);** actor, film director and producer; *b* San Francisco, 31 May 1930; *s* of Clinton and Ruth Eastwood; *m* 1st, 1953, Maggie Johnson (marr. diss. 1978); one *s* one *d*; 2nd, 1996, Dina Ruiz; one *d*; one *d* with Frances Fisher; one *d* with Roxanne Tunis; one *s* one *d* with Jacelyn Reeves. *Educ:* Oakland Tech. High Sch.; LA City Coll. Actor, TV series, Rawhide, 1959–66. *Films include: actor:* A Fistful of Dollars, 1964; For a Few Dollars More, 1965; The Good, The Bad and The Ugly, 1966; Hang 'Em High, 1968; Where Eagles Dare, Coogan's Bluff, 1968; Paint Your Wagon, 1969; Kelly's Heroes, 1970; The Beguiled, Dirty Harry, 1971; Joe Kidd, 1972; Magnum Force, 1973; Thunderbolt and Lightfoot, 1974; The Enforcer, 1976; Every Which Way But Loose, 1978; Escape from Alcatraz, 1979; Tightrope (and prod.), City Heat, 1984; The Dead Pool, 1988; Pink Cadillac, 1989; In the Line of Fire, 1993; Trouble with the Curve, 2012; *actor and director:* Play Misty for Me, 1971; High Plains Drifter, 1973; The Eiger Sanction, 1975; The Outlaw Josey Wales, 1976; Bronco Billy, 1980; The Rookie, 1990; *actor, director and producer:* Firefox, Honkytonk Man, 1982; Sudden Impact, 1983; Pale Rider, 1985; Heartbreak Ridge, 1986; White Hunter Black Heart, 1990; Unforgiven, 1992 (Academy Awards for Best Dir and Best Picture, 1993); A Perfect World, 1993; The Bridges of Madison County, 1995; Absolute Power, 1997; True Crime, 1999; Space Cowboys, 2000; Blood Work, 2002; Million Dollar Baby (Golden Globe Award for Best Dir; Academy Awards for Best Dir and Best Picture), 2005; Gran Torino, 2009; The Mule, 2019; *director and producer:* Bird, 1988 (Golden Globe Award for Best Dir, 1989); Midnight in the Garden of Good and Evil, 1997; Mystic River, 2003; Flags of Our Fathers, 2006; Letters From Iwo Jima, 2007; Changeling, 2008 (Special Prize, Cannes Film Fest., 2008); Invictus, 2010; Hereafter, 2011; J. Edgar, 2012; Jersey Boys, 2014; American Sniper, 2015; Sully, 2016; The 15:17 to Paris, 2018. Founder and owner, Malpaso Prodns, 1969–. Proprietor: Mission Ranch, Carmel, Calif; Tehama Golf Club, Carmel Valley, Calif; co-founder, Tehama, clothing co., 1997. Mayor of Carmel, Calif, 1986–88. Commandeur, Légion d'Honneur (France), 2009.

**EASTWOOD, Prof. Sir David (Stephen)**, Kt 2014; DL; DPhil; FRHistS; Vice-Chancellor and Principal, University of Birmingham, since 2009; *b* 5 Jan. 1959; *s* of Colin Eastwood and Elaine Clara Eastwood; *m* 1980, Jan Page; one *s* two *d*. *Educ*: Sandbach Sch., Cheshire; St Peter's Coll., Oxford (BA 1st Cl. Hons Modern Hist.; MA 1985; DPhil 1985; Hon. Fellow 2003). FRHistS 1991. Jun. Res. Fellow, Keble Coll., Oxford, 1983–87; Fellow and Tutor in Modern Hist., 1988–95, Sen. Tutor, 1992–95, Pembroke Coll., Oxford; Dep. Chair, Bd of Faculty of Modern Hist., Univ. of Oxford, 1994–95; University of Wales, Swansea: Prof. of Social Hist., 1995–2000; Hd, Dept of Hist., 1996–2000; Actg Hd, Dept of Philosophy, 1998–99; Dean, Faculty of Arts and Social Studies, 1997–99; Pro-Vice-Chancellor, 1999–2000; Chief Exec., AHRB, 2000–02; Vice-Chancellor, UEA, 2002–06, Emeritus Prof. of Hist., 2006; Chief Exec., HEFCE, 2006–09. British Acad. Post-Doctoral Fellow, 1986–87. Literary Dir, RHistS, 1994–2000; Chm. Editl Bd, RHistS Studies in History series, 2000–04. Chair of Examrs, A Level Hist., UODLE, O&C, OCR, 1991–2000. Chair: Adv. Gp on Benchmarking, QAA, 2003–06; Assoc. of Univs in E of England, 2003–06; City of Westminster Educn Commn, 2009; Supporting Professionalism in Admissions Prog., 2009–11; Russell Gp, 2012–15 (Mem. Bd, 2009–); Universitas 21, 2014–. Member: RAE Review Gp, HEFCE, 2002–03; Res. Support Libraries Gp, 2002–03; 14–19 Wkg Gp, DfES, 2003–04; Res. Strategic Cttee, HEFCE, 2003–06; Bd, QAA, 2004–06; Bd, UCAS, 2009–12 (Chm., 2010–12); Govt Rev. Panel on Funding and Student Finance; Ind. Rev. of Higher Educn Funding and Student Finance, 2009–11; Council, AHRC, 2011–; Director: Univs Superannuation Scheme, 2007– (Chair, 2015–); Gtr Birmingham and Solihull LEP, 2012–13 and 2019; non-executive Director: UUK, 2009–; INTO University Partnerships, 2014–. Co-founder and non-exec. Chair, Nat. Centre for Public Policy, 1998–2000. Member: Gov. Council, John Innes Centre, 2003–06 (Dep. Chm., 2004–06); Council, Sainsbury Lab., 2003–06; Adv. Bd, Higher Educn Policy Inst., 2003–18; Grants Cttee, Hong Kong Univ., 2011–. Mem., Marshall Aid Meml Commn, 2003–10 (Dep. Chair, 2006–10). FRSA. DL W Midlands, 2012. Hon. Fellow, Swansea Univ., 2010. Hon. DLitt: UWE, 2003; UEA, 2006; Reading, 2016. *Publications*: Governing Rural England: tradition and transformation in local government 1780–1840, 1994; Government and Community in the English Provinces 1700–1870, 1997; (ed with L. Brockliss) A Union of Multiple Identities: the British Isles *c* 1750–*c* 1850, 1997; (ed with N. Thompson) The Social and Political Writings of William Cobbett, 16 vols, 1998; numerous papers in scholarly jls, edited vols, etc. *Recreations*: music, collecting CDs, current affairs, walking, fine wine, watching sport. *Address*: Vice-Chancellor's Office, University of Birmingham, Birmingham B15 2TT. *T*: (0121) 414 4536, *Fax*: (0121) 414 4534. *Club*: Athenæum.

**EASTWOOD, Noel Anthony Michael**, MA; CEng, MRAeS; Chairman, InterData Group (International Publishing), 1981–93; *b* 7 Dec. 1932; *s* of Edward Norman Eastwood and Irene Dawson; *m* 1965, Elizabeth Tania Gresham Boyd, *d* of Comdr Thomas Wilson Boyd, CBE, DSO, DL and Irene Barbara Gresham; three *s*. *Educ*: The Leys School, Cambridge; Christ's College, Cambridge; AEI Gp Summer Sch., Corpus Christi Coll., Oxford, 1962. Lieut RA, 1951–54; Pilot Officer, RAFVR, 1954–57; de Havilland Aircraft Co., 1956–60; Rio Tinto, London and Southern Rhodesia, 1960–61; AEI Group, 1961–64; Director: Charterhouse Industrial Development, 1964–69; Charterhouse Japhet (Merchant Bank), 1969–79 (Pres., Charterhouse Japhet Texas, 1974–77); Charterhouse Middle East, 1975–79; Burnett & Rolfe Ltd, 1964–69 (Chm.); Wharton Crane & Hoist, 1967–70 (Chm.); Daniel Doncaster & Son (International Nickel), 1971–81; The Barden Corp., 1971–82; Hawk Publishing (UAE), 1981–87; Oryx Publishing (Qatar), 1981–87; Falcon Publishing (Bahrain), 1981–84; Caribbean Publishing, 1981–84; IDP InterData (Australia), 1984–92 and 1995–96; European Public Policy Advisers Gp, 1987–97; Spearhead Communications, 1988–99; Founder, Seafish Falklands Ltd (Port Stanley), 1990–95. Sec., RAeS, 1983. Member: London Cttee, Yorkshire & Humberside Development Assoc., 1975–94; Management Cttee, Offshore Europe Conf. and Exhibn, 1990–2000; S Atlantic Council (Westminster), 1991– (Hon. Treas., 1998–2016). Member: Much Hadham PCC, 1989–2007; Much Hadham Parish Council, 1995–97; St Albans Diocesan Synod, 1997–2006. Hon. Treas., 1992–99, Vice Chm., 2004–08, Vice Pres., 2008–, Herts Soc.; Mem. Exec. Cttee, CPRE, 1995–98 (Chm., SE Reg., 1995–2000; Vice-Chm., E of England Cttee, 1999–2005); Chm., Thames NE Area Envmt Agency Gp, 1997–2000; Mem. Exec. Cttee, E England Envmtl Forum, 1999–2006 (Founding Chm., 1999); Mem., Thames and Chilterns Regl Cttee, 2001–02, E of England (formerly E Anglia) Regl Cttee, 2002–11 (Chm., Projects and Acquisitions Gp, 2006–11), Nat. Trust. Mem., Friends Council, Firepower - Royal Artillery Mus., 2009–. Founder, Royal Artillery Heritage Campaign, 1991. *Recreations*: ski-ing, sailing, vintage sportscars, family picnics, desert travel, trekking the Grand Canyon. *Address*: 5 Mariners Terrace, Shore Road, Bosham, W Sussex PO18 8JA. *T*: (01243) 576311. *Club*: Royal Thames Yacht.

**EASTY, Prof. David Leonello**, MD; FRCS, FRCOphth; Professor of Ophthalmology and Head of Department of Ophthalmology, University of Bristol, 1982–99, now Professor Emeritus; *b* 6 Aug. 1933; *s* of Arthur Victor Easty and Florence Margaret (*née* Kennedy); *m* 1963, Božana Martinović; three *d*. *Educ*: King's Sch., Canterbury; Univ. of Manchester. MD 1963; FRCS 1969; FRCOphth (FCOphth 1988). Capt., RAMC, 1959; Med. Officer, British Antarctic Survey, 1960. Moorfields Eye Hospital: Resident, 1966–69; Lectr, 1969–72; Consultant, Bristol Eye Hosp., 1972–82. Dir, Corneal Transplant Service Eye Bank, 1986–99. Lectures: Lang, RSocMed, 1998; Doyne, Oxford Congress of Ophthalmol., 1999; Bowman, RCOphth, 2000; Castroviejo, Amer. Acad. of Ophthalmol., 2002. Nettleship Medal for Research, Ophthalmol Soc., 1999. Member: BMA; RSocMed (Pres., Sect. of Ophthalmol., 1998–2000). Member: Antarctic Club; Piscatorial Soc. *Publications*: Virus Disease of the Eye, 1985; (with G. Smolim) External Eye Disease, 1985; (ed) Current Ophthalmic Surgery, 1990; (with N. Ragge) Immediate Eye Care, 1990; Oxford Textbook of Ophthalmology, 1999. *Recreations*: fishing, running, opera, lawn tennis, Real tennis. *Address*: The Barn, Grove Place, Upton Lane, Nursling, Southampton SO16 0XY. *Clubs*: Army and Navy; Clifton (Bristol).

**EATOCK TAYLOR, Prof. (William) Rodney**, FREng; Professor of Mechanical Engineering, University of Oxford, 1989–2009, now Emeritus (Head of Department of Engineering Science, 1999–2004); Fellow of St Hugh's College, Oxford, 1989–2009, now Emeritus; *b* 10 Jan. 1944; *s* of late William Taylor, Hadley Wood, Herts and Norah O'Brien Taylor (*née* Ridgeway); *m* 1971, Jacqueline Lorraine Cannon, *d* of late Desmond Cannon Brookes; two *s*. *Educ*: Rugby Sch.; King's Coll., Cambridge (BA, MA); Stanford Univ. (MS, PhD). FRINA 1986; FIMechE 1989; FREng (FEng 1990). Engineer, Ove Arup and Partners, 1968–70; University College London: Res. Asst, 1970; Lectr, 1972; Reader, 1980; Prof. of Ocean Engineering, 1984–89; Dean, Faculty of Engineering, 1988–89. Hon. Prof., Harbin Engrg Univ., China, 2008; Vis. Prof., Nat. Univ. of Singapore, 2010–15; Adjunct Prof., Univ. of WA, 2015–. Dir, Marine Technology Directorate Ltd, 1990–95; Chm., Marine Technology Trust, 1991–. Mem., Marine Technology Foresight Panel, OST, 1995–97. Mem. Council, 2003–07, Vice Pres., 2004–07, Royal Acad. of Engrg. Gov., Queenswood Sch., 1990–2003. Associate Ed., Jl Fluids and Structures, 1990–2011; Member, Editorial Boards: Engineering Structures, 1978–2008; Applied Ocean Research, 1984–2012; Ocean Engineering, 2008–; series: Ocean Technology, 1986–2001; Engineering Science, 1990–98. Hon. Fellow, UCL, 2008. *Publications*: numerous contribs to learned jls of structural dynamics and marine hydrodynamics. *Recreations*: walking, music. *Address*: Department of Engineering Science, Parks Road, Oxford OX1 3PJ. *Club*: Athenæum.

**EATON**, family name of **Baroness Eaton**.

**EATON**, Baroness *cr* 2010 (Life Peer), of Cottingley in the County of West Yorkshire; **(Ellen) Margaret Eaton**, DBE 2010 (OBE 2003); DL; Chairman, Local Government Association, 2008–11 (Vice President, 2011–12); *b* Bradford; *d* of John and Evelyn Midgley; *m* 1969, John Eaton; one *s* one *d*. *Educ*: Hanson Grammar Sch.; Balls Park Teacher Trng Coll. (Cert Ed). Former teacher. Mem. (C), Bradford MDC, 1986– (Leader, 2000–06). Trustee: Cottingley Town Hall, 2008; Near Neighbours, 2011– (Chm., 2011–); Tracks of Peace, 2018–. Pres., Bradford Choral Soc., 2010–13. Guardian, Holy Shrine of Walsingham, 2014–. Fellow, Bradford Coll., 2012. Hon. DEd Bradford, 2012. DL W Yorks 2008. *Recreations*: music, theatre, cooking, Germany and the German language. *Address*: House of Lords, SW1A 0PW. *E*: eatonm@parliament.uk. *Clubs*: United and Cecil; Bradford (Bradford).

**EATON, Deborah Ann**; QC 2008; a Recorder, since 2004; a Deputy High Court Judge, since 2011; *b* Nottingham, 28 March 1962; *d* of Stanley Eaton and Margaret Ann Eaton. *Educ*: Univ. of Keele (BSocSci Hons 1983); City Univ., London (Dip. Law 1984). Called to the Bar, Inner Temple, 1985, Bencher; in practice as a barrister, specialising in family law; Midland Circuit, 1985–. *Publications*: (author, and ed with Stephen Wildblood) Financial Provision in Family Matters, 1998. *Address*: 1 King's Bench Walk, Temple, EC4Y 7DB. *T*: (020) 7936 1500, *Fax*: (020) 7936 1590. *E*: deatonqc@1kbw.co.uk.

**EATON, Rt Rev. Derek Lionel**, QSM 1985; Bishop of Nelson, New Zealand, 1990–2006; *b* 10 Sept. 1941; *s* of Henry Jackson Eaton and Ella Barbara (*née* McDouall); *m* 1964, Alice Janice Maslin; two *s* one *d*. *Educ*: Christchurch Boys' High Sch. (NZ); AG Graduate Sch., Missouri (MA *cum laude*); Christchurch Teachers' Coll. (Teacher Trng Cert); Switzerland (Cert. Française); Univ. of Tunis (Cert. Arabic and Islamics); Missionary Training Coll., Australia (DipTheol); Trinity Theol Coll., Bristol. School teacher, 1964. Missionary with Worldwide Evangelisation Crusade, Tunisia, 1968–78; ordained deacon and priest, 1971; Curate, St Luke's, Bristol, 1971–72; Vicar of Tunis, 1972–78; Hon. Chaplain, British Embassy, Tunis, 1972–78; Provost, Cairo Cathedral, Egypt, 1978–83 (Emeritus, 1984); Hon. Chaplain, British Embassy, Egypt, 1978–83; with Church Missionary Society, 1980–84; Associate Vicar, Papanui, Bishopdale, NZ, 1984–85; Vicar, Sumner, Redcliffs, NZ, 1985–90; Asst Anglican Bp of Egypt with N Africa and the Horn of Africa, 2007–09; Dean, All Saint's Cathedral, Cairo, 2007–09. Hon. Canon, 1985, Episcopal Canon, 1992, Cairo Cathedral. Chaplain to staff and students, Bishopdale Theol Coll., Nelson, NZ, 2009–. *Publications*: What awaits us there: between reality and illusion (Arabic), 2002; Life After Death: welcome to the future, 2004; contrib. theol and missiological jls. *Recreations*: swimming (Competitive Ocean Swimming and Masters Swimming), reading, walking and hiking. *Address*: 67 Grove Street, The Wood, Nelson 7010, New Zealand.

**EATON, Duncan**; *see* Eaton, N. D.

**EATON, Fredrik Stefan**, OC 1990; OOnt 2001; Chairman, White Raven Capital Corporation; *b* 26 June 1938; *s* of late John David Eaton and Signy Hildur Eaton (*née* Stephenson); *m* 1962, Catherine Howard (Nicky) Martin; one *s* one *d*. *Educ*: Univ. of New Brunswick (BA). T. Eaton Co. Ltd: joined 1962; positions in Victoria, London, England and Toronto, 1962–67; Dir, 1967–99; Pres. and CEO, 1979–88; Dir, Eaton's of Canada, 1969–; Chm., 1988–91; High Comr for Canada in the UK, 1991–94. Former Director: Masonite (formerly Premdor); Abitibi Consolidated; Norcen Energy; Maple Leaf Foods; Toronto-Dominion Bank; Bata Shoe Museum. Trustee: The Catherine and Fredrik Eaton Charitable Foundn; Canadian Mus. of Civilization (Chm., Bd of Trustees, 2007–11); Hon. Trustee, Univ. Health Network (Chair, Bd of Trustees, 1994–2000); Member: ICBP Rare Bird Club; Polite Soc. Patron, ESU of Canada. FRSA. Chancellor, Univ. of New Brunswick, 1993–2003. Internat. Retailer of the Year Award, Nat. Retail Merchants Assoc., NY, 1978; McGill Univ. Management Award, 1987. Hon. LLD: New Brunswick, 1983; QUB, 1995. *Recreations*: sailing, fishing. *Address*: (office) 55 St Clair Avenue West, Suite 260, Toronto, ON M4V 2Y7, Canada.

**EATON, James Thompson**, CBE 1992; TD 1963; Lord-Lieutenant, County Borough of Londonderry, 1986–2002; *b* 11 Aug. 1927; *s* of late J. C. Eaton, DL, and Mrs E. A. F. Eaton, MBE; *m* 1954, Lucy Edith Smeeton (OBE 1986); one *s* one *d*. *Educ*: Campbell Coll., Belfast; Royal Technical Coll., Glasgow. Man. Dir, Eaton & Co. Ltd, 1965–80. Mem., Londonderry Develt Commn, 1969–73 (Chm., Educn Cttee, 1969–73); Chm., Londonderry Port and Harbour Comrs, 1989–95 (Mem., 1977–95; Vice Chm., 1985). Served North Irish Horse (TA), 1950–67 (Major, 1961). Hon. Col, 1st (NI) Bn, ACF, 1992–98. High Sheriff, Co. Londonderry, 1982. *Recreations*: military history, gardening. *Address*: Cherryvale Park, Limavady, Co. Londonderry, Northern Ireland BT49 9AH.

**EATON, Keith John**, PhD; FIStructE; Chief Executive, Institution of Structural Engineers, 1999–2008; *b* 4 May 1945; *s* of John Ernest Eaton and Phyllis Marguerite (*née* Groom); *m* 1967, Janet Marion, *d* of Geoffrey and Winifred Allanson Walker; two *d*. *Educ*: Bishopshalt Grammar Sch., Hillingdon, Middx; Univ. of Birmingham (BSc Civil Engrg 1966); UCL (PhD Structural Engrg 1971). FRMetS 1971; CEng 1975; FIStructE 1986. Joined BRE, 1966; Head: Wind Loading Section, 1971–77; Overseas Develt Res. Unit, 1977–84; Structural Design Div., 1984–89; European Manager, 1989–91, Dep. Dir, 1991–99, Steel Construction Inst. Mem. Council, Hon. Sec. and Hon. Treas., IStructE, 1986–92. FCGI 2004. MASCE 1991–2009. Freeman, City of London, 2003; Liveryman, Engineers' Co., 2003–09. *Publications*: Wind Loading Handbook, 1971; Wind Effects on Buildings and Structures, 1977; Buildings and Tropical Windstorms, 1981; A Comparative Environmental Life Cycle Assessment of Modern Office Buildings, 1998; technical papers on wind loading, earthquake engrg, sustainability and envmtl issues in learned jls. *Recreations*: playing bridge, gardening, walking, being a grandfather. *Address*: 18 Sandpit Lane, St Albans AL1 4HN. *T*: (01727) 853915.

**EATON, Adm. Sir Kenneth (John)**, GBE 1994; KCB 1990; FREng, FIET; Rear Admiral of the United Kingdom, 2001–07; Chairman, Society for Nautical Research, since 2011; *b* 12 Aug. 1934; *s* of John and May Eaton; *m* 1959, Sheena Buttle; two *s* one *d*. *Educ*: Borden Grammar Sch.; Fitzwilliam Coll., Cambridge (BA). FIET (FIEE 1989); FREng (FEng 1994). HMS Victorious, 1959–61; ASWE, 1961–65; HM Ships Eagle, Collingwood and Bristol, 1965–71; Defence Communications Network, 1971–72; ASWE, 1972–76; HMS Ark Royal, 1976–78; MoD, 1978–81; ASWE, 1981–83; Dir Torpedoes, 1983–85; Dir-Gen. Underwater Weapons (Navy), 1985–87; Flag Officer, Portsmouth, and Naval Base Comdr, Portsmouth, 1987–89; Controller of the Navy, 1989–94. Chm., UKAEA, 1996–2002. Chairman: Guy's and St Thomas' NHS Trust, 1995–99; National Remote Sensing Centre (Infoterra Ltd), 1995–2001. Chm., Mary Rose Trust, 2001–07. Hon. DSc Aston, 2006. *Recreations*: art, countryside, theatre, opera, classical music. *Address*: c/o Naval Secretary, Fleet Headquarters, Whale Island, Portsmouth PO2 8BY.

**EATON, Martin Roger,** CMG 1993; HM Diplomatic Service, retired; Deputy Legal Adviser, Foreign and Commonwealth Office, 1991–2000; *b* 10 Nov. 1940; *m* 1972, Sylvia White; two *s* one *d.* Admitted Solicitor, 1968; FCO, 1970; Bonn, 1977; FCO, 1981; Legal Counsellor: FCO, 1982; UKREP Brussels, 1987; FCO, 1991. Chm., Council of Europe Steering Cttee on Human Rights, 2003–04. *Recreations:* choral singing, gardening.

**EATON, (Neil) Duncan,** FCIPS; adviser, government and commercial sector; Chairman: Kimal Holdings Ltd, since 2008; BCAS Medical Ltd, since 2016; Bladder Health UK, since 2016; *b* 28 May 1946; *s* of John and Bessie Eaton; *m* 1st, 1969, Ainsley Elizabeth Isles (marr. diss. 2006); two *d*; 2nd, 2010, Karen (*née* Fielding). *Educ:* King's Sch., Macclesfield; Manchester Coll. of Commerce (HND Business Studies); Dip. Inst. Healthcare Mgt; Dip. Chartered Inst. Purchasing and Supply. FCIPS (FInstPS 1985); MIHM 1972. Hosp. mgt and supply mgt posts, Manchester, Swindon and Wolverhampton, 1966–74; Area Supplies Officer: Tameside AHA, 1974–78; Northants AHA, 1978–83; Dir of Ops, NW Thames RHA, 1983–90; Chief Executive: Bedfordshire HA, 1990–2000; NHS Purchasing and Supply Agency, 2000–06. Non-executive Director: Policy Connect, 2008–; BCAS Biomed, 2012–. Strategic Advr, BiP Solutions, 2009–; Exec. Advr, All Party Parly Health Gp, 2008–. President: Chartered Inst. Purchasing and Supply, 1992–93; Health Care Supplies Assoc., 1996–2001. Hon. Prof., Univ. of Bath, 2013–. *Recreations:* amateur dramatics, Rugby, football. *Address:* 14 Knights Court, Linen Street, Warwick CV34 4DJ.

**EATON, Robert James;** Director, Chevron (formerly Texaco, then ChevronTexaco) Inc., 2000–12; Chairman, Daimler Chrysler (formerly Chairman and Chief Executive, Chrysler Corporation), 1993–2000; *b* 13 Feb. 1940; *s* of Gene and Mildred Eaton; *m* 1964, Cornelia Cae Drake; two *s. Educ:* Univ. of Kansas (BS Mech Eng). Joined General Motors, 1963, transf. to English staff, 1971; Chevrolet Div., 1975; Oldsmobile, 1979; Vice-Pres. in charge of Tech. Staffs, 1986; Pres., General Motors Europe, 1988–92; Mem., Bd of Dirs, Lotus Group, 1986–2000; Chm., Saab Auto, 1990–2000. Member: Industrial Adv. Board, Stanford Univ.; Business Roundtable and Business Council. Mem. Bd, Dama. Former Chm., Nat. Acad. of Engrg; FSAE.

**EATON, Hon. Dame Sara Elizabeth;** *see* Cockerill, Hon. Dame S. E.

**EATWELL,** family name of **Baron Eatwell.**

**EATWELL, Baron** *cr* 1992 (Life Peer), of Stratton St Margaret in the County of Wiltshire; **John Leonard Eatwell;** President, Queens' College, Cambridge, 1997–Sept. 2020; Professor of Financial Policy, Judge Business School (formerly Judge Institute of Management Studies), University of Cambridge, 2002–12, now Emeritus; *b* 2 Feb. 1945; *s* of Harold Jack and Mary Eatwell; *m* 1970, Hélène Seppain (marr. diss. 2002); two *s* one *d*; *m* 2006, Hon. Mrs Susan Elizabeth Digby (OBE 2007). *Educ:* Headlands Grammar Sch., Swindon; Queens' Coll., Cambridge (BA 1967; MA 1971); Harvard Univ. (PhD 1975). Teaching Fellow, Grad. Sch. of Arts and Scis, Harvard Univ., 1968–69; Res. Fellow, Queens' Coll., Cambridge, 1969–70; Fellow, Trinity Coll., Cambridge, 1970–96; University of Cambridge: Asst Lectr, 1975–77, Lectr, 1977–2002, Faculty of Econs and Politics; Dir, Cambridge Endowment for Res. in Finance, Judge Business Sch. (formerly Judge Inst. of Mgt Studies), 2002–12. Visiting Professor of Economics: New Sch. for Social Res., NY, 1982–96; USC, 2012–; Vis. Fellow, St Antony's Coll., Oxford, 2011. Econ. Advr to Rt Hon. Neil Kinnock, MP, Leader of the Labour Party, 1985–92. Opposition spokesman on Treasury affairs, and on trade and industry, H of L, 1992–93; Principal Opposition spokesman on Treasury and econ. affairs, H of L, 1993–97 and 2010–13. Mem., Jersey Financial Services Commn, 2010– (Chm., 2014–). Adviser: to E. M. Warburg Pincus & Co. Internat. Ltd, 1996–2014; to Palamon Capital Partners LLP, 2000–; Chief Econ. Advr to Chartered Mgt Inst., 2009–10. Chm., British Screen Finance Ltd, 1997–2000; Dir, SFA, 1997–2002; Mem., Regulatory Decisions Cttee, FSA, 2001–06. Trustee, Inst. for Public Policy Res., 1988– (Sec., 1988–97; Chm., 1997–2000, 2016–18); Chm., Adv. Bd, Inst. for Policy Res., Univ. of Bath, 2013–. Non-executive Director: Anglia Television Gp, 1994–2000; Cambridge Econometrics Ltd, 1996–2006; Rontech Ltd, 2003–08; NewDay Ltd (formerly SAV Credit Ltd), 2007–17; Chm., Deutsche Wealth and Asset Mgt Global Financial Inst., 2012–. Chairman: Commercial Radio Cos Assoc., 2000–04; Consumer Panel, Classic fm, 2007–11. Chm., Crusaid, 1993–98. Chm., Extempory Dance Theatre, 1990; Governor: Contemporary Dance Trust, 1991–95; Royal Ballet Sch., 2003–06; Dir, Arts Theatre Trust, Cambridge, 1991–98; Mem. Bd, Royal Opera House, 1998–2006; Chm., British Library Bd, 2001–06. Chm. Trustees, Royal Opera Hse Pension Fund, 2007–. *Publications:* (with Joan Robinson) An Introduction to Modern Economics, 1973; Whatever Happened to Britain?, 1982; (ed with Murray Milgate) Keynes's Economics and the Theory of Value and Distribution, 1983; (ed with Murray Milgate and Peter Newman): The New Palgrave: A Dictionary of Economics, 4 vols, 1987; The New Palgrave Dictionary of Money and Finance, 3 vols, 1992; Transformation and Integration: shaping the future of central and eastern Europe, 1995; (ed) Global Unemployment: loss of jobs in the '90s, 1996; Not "Just Another Accession": the political economy of EU enlargement to the East, 1997; (with L. Taylor) Global Finance at Risk: the case for international regulation, 2000; Hard Budgets, Soft States, 2000; Social Policy Choices in Central and Eastern Europe, 2002; (with L. Taylor) International Capital Markets, 2002; (jtly) Global Governance of Financial Systems: the legal and economic regulation of systemic risk, 2006; (jtly) Financial Supervision and Risk Management in the EU, 2007; (ed with P. Arestis) Issues in Finance and Industry: essays in honour of Ajit Singh, 2008; (jtly) Clearing and Settlements in the EU, 2009; (jtly) Crisis Management, Burden Sharing and Solidarity Mechanisms in the EU, 2010; (with M. Milgate) The Fall and Rise of Keynesian Economics, 2011; (ed jtly) Challenges for Europe in the World 2030, 2014; articles in sci. jls and other collected works. *Recreations:* classical and contemporary dance, Rugby Union football. *Address:* (until Sept. 2020) Queens' College, Cambridge CB3 9ET. *T:* (01223) 335532, *Fax:* (01223) 335555. *E:* president@queens.cam.ac.uk; (from Sept. 2020) Rosewood Manor, Timsbury, Bath BA2 0EU. *E:* je24@cam.ac.uk. *Clubs:* Harvard (New York), Bohemian (San Francisco).

**EAVES, Prof. Laurence,** CBE 2003; FRS 1997; Research Professor, School of Physics and Astronomy, University of Nottingham, since 2011; Professor of Physics, University of Manchester, since 2012; *b* 13 May 1948; *s* of Raymond Eaves and late Margaret Eaves (*née* Howells); *m* 1985, Dr Ffiona Helen Gilmore. *Educ:* Rhondda Co. Grammar Sch.; Corpus Christi Coll., Oxford (BA 1st Cl. Hons Physics 1969; MA 1973; DPhil 1973; Hon. Fellow, 2013). FInstP 1996. Res. Fellow, Clarendon Lab., Univ. of Oxford, 1972–74; Res. Lectr, Christ Church, Oxford, 1972–75; Miller Fellow, Univ. of Calif, Berkeley, 1974–75; University of Nottingham: Lectr, 1976–84, Reader, 1984–86, Dept of Physics; Prof. of Physics, 1986–2000; Lancashire-Spencer Prof. of Physics, 2000–11. Vis. Prof., Inst. for Solid State Physics, Univ. of Tokyo, 1991. Royal Soc. Leverhulme Sen. Res. Fellow, 1993–94; EPSRC Sen. Res. Fellow, 1994–99. Chm., Condensed Matter Div., Inst. of Physics, 1998–99; Member: Council, Royal Soc., 2002–04 (Mem., Sectional Cttee 2, 1999–2001, 2008–10, 2014–16); HEFCE RAE Physics sub-panel, 2004–08; Leverhulme Trust Res. Awards Adv. Cttee, 2008–15; HEFCE REF 2014 Physics sub-panel, 2011–14; Sci. Adv. Council for Wales, 2015–18. FLSW 2011. Mott Lectr, Inst. of Physics, 1988; European Physical Soc. Lectr, 1991. Guthrie Medal and Prize, Inst. of Physics, 2001.

*Publications:* (jtly) numerous res. articles in jls incl. Physical Rev., Physical Rev. Letters, Nature, Science, Applied Physics Letters. *Address:* School of Physics and Astronomy, University of Nottingham, Nottingham NG7 2RD. *T:* (0115) 951 5136.

**EBADI, Dr Shirin;** lawyer in private practice in Iran, specialising in human rights, since 1992; *b* 21 June 1947; *d* of late Mohammad Ali Ebadi; *m;* two *d. Educ:* Univ. of Tehran. Judge, 1969–79, Pres., 1975–79, Tehran City Court. Lectr in Law, Univ. of Tehran. Co-founder and President: Assoc. for Support of Children's Rights, 1995–2000; Human Rights Defence Centre, 2001–; Founder and Chair, Center for Supporters of Human Rights, 2013–. Nobel Peace Prize, 2003. *Publications:* Criminal Laws, 1972; The Rights of the Child, 1987 (trans. English 1993); Medical Laws, 1988; Young Workers, 1989; Copyright Laws, 1989; Architectural Laws, 1991; The Rights of Refugees, 1993; History and Documentation of Human Rights in Iran, 1993; (jtly) Tradition and Modernity, 1995; Children's Comparative Law, 1997 (trans. English 1998); The Rights of Women, 2002; Iran Awakening: a memoir of revolution and hope, 2006; Refugee Rights in Iran, 2008; The Golden Cage: three brothers, three choices, one destiny, 2011; articles in learned jls.

**EBAN, Anna Maeve;** *see* Guggenheim, A. M.

**EBBSFLEET, Bishop Suffragan of,** since 2013; **Rt Rev. Jonathan Michael Goodall,** SSC; Provincial Episcopal Visitor, Province of Canterbury, since 2013; *b* 1961; *m* Sarah; one *s* one *d. Educ:* Royal Holloway Coll., Univ. of London (BMus 1983); Wycliffe Hall, Oxford. Macmillan Publishers, 1983–86; freelance editor, 1983–; freelance singer, 1983–89; ordained deacon, 1989, priest, 1990; Asst Curate, Bicester with Bucknell, Caversfield and Launton, 1989–92; Asst Chaplain, HM Prison Bullingdon, 1990–92; Minor Canon, Chaplain and Sacrist, Westminster Abbey, 1992–98; Bishop's Chaplain, Res. Asst and Dio. Liturgical Officer, Dio. of Europe, 1998–2005; Archbishop's Chaplain and Ecumenical Officer, 2005–09; Archbishop's Personal Chaplain and Ecumenical Sec., 2009–13. Priest-Vicar, Westminster Abbey, 2004–; Hon. Canon: Gibraltar Cath., 2005–; Canterbury Cath., 2014–; Hon. Assistant Bishop, Diocese of: Oxford, 2013–; Lichfield, 2013–; Worcester, 2013–; Exeter, 2014–; Coventry, 2014–; Bristol, 2015–; Bath and Wells, 2016–; Truro, 2016–; Birmingham, 2017–. Church of England: Member: Porvoo Panel, 1999–2006; Council for Christian Unity, 2005–13; Faith and Order Adv. Gp, 2005–10 (Consultant, House of Bps Theol Gp, 2005–10); Faith and Order Commn, 2010–13; House of Bps, 2013–; Wkg Gp on Communion and Diversity, 2015–16. Member: Inter-Anglican Standing Cttee on Ecumenical Relns, 2005–08 (Consultant, Inter-Anglican Standing Commn for Unity, Faith and Order, 2010–13); Internat. Commn for Anglican-Orthodox Theol Dialogue (IV), 2009–13; ARCIC (III), 2010–13; Anglican-RC Jt Ordinariate Liaison Gp, 2011–13; Internat. Commn for Anglican-Oriental Orthodox Theol Dialogue (IV), 2013. Special Envoy to Orthodox Ch, 2015–17; Spiritual Patron, 2017–. Mem., Council of Bps, The Society, 2013–. Hon. Curate, St Matthew, Westminster, 1999–2003. Trustee: Action Around Bethlehem Children with Disability, 1995–; Nikaean Ecumenical Trust, 2005– (Guestmaster, Nikaean Club, 2005–13); Philip Usher Trust, 2008–; Mem., Internat. Adv. Bd, British Trust for Tantur, 2014–. Gov., Anglican Centre in Rome, 2008–13. Ed., C of E Lectionary, 2000–12; Chm., English Hymnal Revision Cttee, 2014–. *Recreations:* early music, fell walking, French food, reading, theatre. *Address:* Hill House, The Mount, Caversham, Reading, Berks RG4 7RE. *T:* (0118) 948 1038.

**EBDON, Sir Leslie Colin,** Kt 2018; CBE 2009; DL; PhD; CChem, FRSC; Vice-Chancellor and Chief Executive, University of Bedfordshire (formerly University of Luton), 2003–12; Director of Fair Access to Higher Education, 2012–18; *b* 26 Jan. 1947; *s* of Harold and Doris Ebdon; *m* 1970, Judith Margaret Thomas; two *s* one *d* (and one *s* decd). *Educ:* Hemel Hempstead Grammar Sch.; Imperial Coll., Univ. of London (BSc, PhD; ARCS, DIC). MCIWEM. Lectr in Chem., Makerere Univ., Uganda, 1971–73; Sen. Lectr, Sheffield City Poly., 1973–80; Plymouth Polytechnic, later Polytechnic SouthWest, then Plymouth University: Reader in Analytical Chem., 1981–89; Hd, Dept of Envmtl Scis, 1989; Prof. of Analytical Chem., 1986–2003; Dep. Dir, 1989–92; Dep. Vice-Chancellor, 1992–2003. Schs Lectr, Analytical Div., RSC, 1986. Chair, Editorial Board: Jl Analytical Atomic Spectroscopy, 1987–91; Chemistry World, 2003–08. Member: Nat. Council of Educn Excellence, 2007–10; Further Educn and Skills Ministerial Adv. Panel, 2010–. Member: Measurement Bd, BIS, then BEIS (formerly Measurement Adv. Cttee, DTI), 1999–; East of England Regl Economic Forum, 2009–10; Bd, SE Midlands LEP, 2012–. Chairman: Assoc. of Universities in East of England, 2006–11; Student Experience Policy Cttee, Universities UK, 2007–12; Million+, 2007–12. Mem. Council, RSC, 1996–2008 (Chm., Pubns Bd, 1996–2000, Strategy and Resources Bd, 2003–05); Trustee: Luton Christian Educn Trust, 2010–; RSC Pension Fund, 2010–; Bletchley Park Trust, 2011–. Pres., Luton UNA, 2009–; Vice Pres., Bedford Hosps Charity, 2010–. DL Beds, 2011. FRSA. Hon. DSc Plymouth, 2008. 13th Soc. for Analytical Chem. Silver Medal for Analytical Chem., RSC, 1986; Benedetti-Pichler Meml Award, Amer. Microchem. Soc., 1995. *Publications:* An Introduction to Analytical Atomic Spectroscopy, 1982, 2nd edn 1998; 270 contribs to refereed jls. *Recreations:* vegetable gardening, Baptist lay preacher.

**EBERS, Prof. George Cornell,** MD; FRCP, FRCPC, FMedSci; Professor of Clinical Neurology, University of Oxford, 1999–2011, now Emeritus (Head, Department of Clinical Neurology, 1999–2004); Fellow, St Edmund Hall, Oxford, since 1999; *b* Budapest, 24 July 1946; *s* of Cornell George Ebers and Leontine Amant Ebers; *m* 1997, Sharon Vitali; one *s* one *d. Educ:* De La Salle Coll.; Univ. of Toronto (MD 1970); MA Oxon. FRCPC 1977. University of Western Ontario: Asst Prof., 1977–82; Associate Prof., 1982–87; Prof., Dept of Clinical Neurol Scis, 1987–99. Numerous vis. professorships and named lectures. Member, Editorial Board: Jl Neuroimm., 1983–2011; Canadian Jl Neuro. Sci., 1985–2011; MS Res. Reports, 1987–2011; Jl Tropical Geog. Neurol., 1990–94; Neuroepidemiol., 1992–2011; Multiple Sclerosis, 1994–2011. FMedSci 2001. John Dystel Award for MS Res., Amer. Acad. of Neurol., 2013. Mem., Bayfield Histl Soc.; Mem. Bd, Bayfield River Valley Trail Assoc., 2015–. *Publications:* The Diagnosis of MS, 1984; Multiple Sclerosis, 1998; sole or jt author of over 400 peer reviewed pubns. *Recreations:* book collecting, ornithology, history of medicine, windmill restoration, woodworking. *Address:* 35957 Bayfield River Road, Bayfield, ON N0M 1G0, Canada. *Club:* Osler.

**EBRAHIM, Sir (Mahomed) Currimbhoy, (Sir Mohamed Currimbhoy),** 4th Bt *cr* 1910; BA, LLB; Advocate, Pakistan; Member, Standing Council of the Baronetage, 1961; *b* 24 June 1935; *o s* of Sir (Huseinali) Currimbhoy Ebrahim, 3rd Bt, and Alhaja Lady Amina Khanum, *d* of Alhaj Cassumali Jairajbhoy; *S* father, 1952; *m* 1958, Dur-e-Mariam, *d* of Minuchehir Ahmud Ghulamaly Nana; three *s* one *d. Recreations:* tennis (Karachi University No 1, 1957, No 2, 1958), cricket, table-tennis, squash, reading (literary), art, poetry writing, debate, quotation writing. *Heir: s* Zulfiqar Ali Currimbhoy Ebrahim [*b* 5 Aug. 1960; *m* 1984, Adila, *d* of Akhtar Halipota; one *s* one *d*].

**EBRAHIM, Prof. Shaheen Brian John,** DM; FRCP, FFPH; Professor of Public Health, London School of Hygiene & Tropical Medicine, 2005–14, now Hon. Professor; *b* 19 July 1952; *s* of Dr Donald William Ebrahim and Marjorie Sybil (*née* Evans); *m* 1st, 1984, Julia Lesley Shaw (marr. diss. 2002); 2nd, 2004, Fiona Clair Taylor. *Educ:* King Henry VIII Sch., Coventry; Nottingham Univ. Med. Sch. (BMed Sci; BM BS 1975; DM 1985). FRCP 1993; FFPH (FFPHM 1993). Wellcome Trust Clinical Epidemiology Trng Fellow, Nottingham Univ. Med. Sch., 1981–83; Lectr in Geriatric Medicine, Univ. of Nottingham,

1983–85; Wellcome Trust Lectr in Epidemiology, Dept of Social Medicine and Gen. Practice, St George's Hosp. Med. Sch., London, 1985–86; Cons. Physician and Sen. Lectr, Dept of Geriatric Medicine, Royal Free Hosp. Sch. of Medicine, 1987–89; Prof. of Geriatric Medicine, London Hosp. Med. Coll. and St Bartholomew's Hosp. Med. Coll., 1989–92; Prof. of Clinical Epidemiology, Royal Free Hosp. Sch. of Med., 1992–98; Prof. of Epidemiology of Ageing, Univ. of Bristol, 1998–2005. Vis. Prof., Christchurch Med. Sch., NZ, 1990; Nat. Heart Foundn of NZ Vis. Prof. in Stroke, 1991; Australian Veterans Vis. Prof., 1995; Visiting Professor: McMaster Univ., Canada, 1996; Sydney Univ., Australia, 2003; Univ. of Bristol, 2013–; Hon. Professor: UCL 2003–14; Public Health Foundn of India, 2009–14; Adjunct Prof., Internat. Inst. of Diarrheal Disease Res., Bangladesh, 2009–14. *Publications:* Clinical Epidemiology of Stroke, 1990, 2nd edn 1999; (ed jtly) The Health of Older Women, 1992; (with G. Bennett) Essentials of Health Care in Old Age, 1992, 2nd edn 1995; (ed jtly) Epidemiology in Old Age, 1996; (ed jtly) Handbook of Health Research Methods, 2005; scientific papers on public health, clinical epidemiology and geriatric medicine. *Recreations:* coarse fishing, music of Velvet Underground and Don Van Vliet. *Address:* Faculty of Epidemiology and Population Health, London School of Hygiene & Tropical Medicine, Keppel Street, WC1E 7HT. *Club:* Royal Society of Medicine.

**EBRINGER, Prof. Alan Martin,** MD; FRACP, FRCP, FRCPath; Professor of Immunology, King's College, London, 1995, now Emeritus; *b* 12 Feb. 1936; *s* of late Bernard Ebringer and Maria Ebringer; *m* 1960, Eva Marie Ernest; two *s* one *d. Educ:* Melbourne High Sch.; Univ. of Melbourne (BSc Maths 1961; MB BS 1962; MD 1971). FRACP 1967; MRCP 1970, FRCP 1987; FRCPath 1997. Prosector in Anatomy, Univ. of Melbourne, 1958–; Pathology Registrar, Geelong Hosp., 1964; Research Fellow: Walter and Eliza Hall Inst., Royal Melbourne Hosp., 1965–66; Austin Hosp., 1967–69; RACP Overseas Travelling Schol., Dept of Immunol., Middx Hosp., 1970; Berkeley Fellow, Middx Hosp. and Gonville and Caius Coll., Cambridge, 1971; King's College, London: Lectr, 1972–77; Sen. Lectr, 1977–82; Reader, 1982–95; Hon. Consultant Rheumatologist, UCL Hosps (formerly Middx Hosp.), i/c of Ankylosing Spondylitis Res. Clinic, 1980–2002. Appeared before Phillips Inquiry into BSE, 1998. Member: British Soc. Immunol., 1970; British Soc. Rheum., 1972; Amer. Coll. Rheumatol., 1996. Vis. Lectr, Melbourne, Edinburgh, Glasgow, Sheffield, Paris, Marseille, Brest, Madrid, Helsinki, Turku, Bratislava, Moscow, Suzdal, Innsbruck, San Antonio, Dallas, Uppsala. Life Mem., RSocMed, 2008. Hon. FRSPH (Hon. FRSH 2001). Donaldson Gold Medal, RSH, 2003. *Publications:* Rheumatoid Arthritis and Proteus, 2011; Ankylosing Spondylitis and Klebsiella, 2012; Multiple Sclerosis, Mad Cow Disease and Acinetobacter, 2014; contrib. numerous papers dealing with autoimmune diseases produced by molecular mimicry to ext. agents, esp. ankylosing spondylitis (klebsiella), rheumatoid arthritis (proteus), bovine spongiform encephalopathy (acinetobacter), multiple sclerosis (acinetobacter) and Crohn's disease (Klebsiella). *Recreations:* languages, Karl Popper, walking. *Address:* 76 Gordon Road, W5 2AR.

**ECCLES,** family name of **Viscount Eccles** and **Baroness Eccles of Moulton.**

**ECCLES,** 2nd Viscount *cr* 1964, of Chute, co. Wilts; **John Dawson Eccles,** CBE 1985; Baron 1962; Chairman, The Bowes Museum, County Durham, 2000–08; *b* 20 April 1931; *er s* of 1st Viscount Eccles, CH, KCVO, PC and Sybil (*d* 1977), *d* of 1st Viscount Dawson of Penn, GCVO, KCB, KCMG, PC; *S* father, 1999; *m* 1955, Diana Catherine Sturge (*see* Baroness Eccles of Moulton); one *s* three *d. Educ:* Winchester Coll.; Magdalen Coll., Oxford (BA). Commnd 1st 60th KRRC, 1950. Director: Glynwed International plc, 1972–96; Investors in Industry plc, 1974–88; Chairman: Head Wrightson & Co. Ltd, 1976–77 (Man. Dir, 1968); Chamberlain & Hill plc, 1982–2004; Acker Deboeck, corporate psychiatrists, 1994–2006; Courtaulds Textiles plc, 1995–2000 (Dir, 1992–2000); Director: The Nuclear Power Gp Ltd, 1968–74; Davy Internat. Ltd, 1977–81; Govett Strategic Investment Trust plc, 1996–2004. Member: Monopolies and Mergers Commn, 1976–85 (Dep. Chm., 1981–85); Industrial Develt Adv. Bd, 1989–93; Gen. Manager, subseq. Chief Exec., Commonwealth Develt Corp., 1985–94 (Mem., 1982–85). Chm., Bd of Trustees, Royal Botanic Gardens, Kew, 1983–91. Mem. Council, Eccles Centre for American Studies, BL, 2003–. Chm., Hosp. for Tropical Diseases Foundn, 2000–15. Elected Mem., H of L, March 2005. Hon. DSc Cranfield Inst. of Technology, 1989. *Recreations:* gardening, theatre. *Heir: s* Hon. William David Eccles [*b* 9 June 1960; *m* 1984, Claire Margaret Alison Seddon (*d* 2001); two *s* one *d*]. *Address:* 5 St John's House, 30 Smith Square, SW1P 3HF. *T:* (020) 7222 4040; Moulton Hall, Richmond, N Yorks DL10 6QH. *T:* (01325) 377227. *Club:* Brooks's.

**ECCLES OF MOULTON,** Baroness *cr* 1990 (Life Peer), of Moulton in the County of North Yorkshire; **Diana Catherine Eccles, (Viscountess Eccles);** DL; Chairman, Ealing, Hammersmith and Hounslow Health Authority, 1993–2000 (Chairman, Ealing District Health Authority, 1988–93); *b* 4 Oct. 1933; *d* of late Raymond Sturge and Margaret Sturge; *m* 1955, John Dawson Eccles (*see* Viscount Eccles); one *s* three *d. Educ:* St James's Sch., West Malvern; Open Univ. (BA). Voluntary work, Middlesbrough Community Council, 1955–58; Partner, Gray Design Associates, 1963–77. Director: Tyne Tees Television, 1986–94; J. Sainsbury, 1986–95; Yorkshire Electricity Gp, 1990–97; National & Provincial Building Soc., 1991–96; Opera North, 1998–2011; Ind. Nat. Dir, Times Newspapers Holdings Ltd, 1998–2015. Member: North Eastern Electricity Bd, 1974–85; British Railways Eastern Bd, 1986–92; Teesside Urban Develt Corp., 1987–98. Member: Adv. Council for Energy Conservation, 1982–84; Widdicombe Inquiry into Local Govt, 1985–86; Unrelated Live Transplant Regulatory Authority, 1990–99. Vice Chairman: Nat. Council for Voluntary Orgns, 1981–87; Durham Univ. Council, 1985–2004. Trustee: Charities Aid Foundn, 1982–89; York Minster Fund, 1989–99 and 2006–09; London Clinic, 2003–08. DL N Yorks, 1998. Hon. DCL Durham, 2015. *Address:* Moulton Hall, Richmond, N Yorks DL10 6QH. *T:* (01325) 377227; 5/30 Smith Square, SW1P 3HF. *T:* (020) 7222 4040.

**ECCLES, His Honour (Hugh William) Patrick;** QC 1990; a Circuit Judge, 2000–16; *b* 25 April 1946; *s* of late Gp Captain (retd) Hugh Haslett Eccles and Mary Eccles; *m* 1972, Rhoda Ann Eccles (*née* Moroney); three *d. Educ:* Stonyhurst Coll.; Exeter Coll., Oxford (MA). Called to the Bar, Middle Temple, 1968, Bencher, 1998; practising barrister, head of chambers, 1985–2000; a Recorder, 1987–2000; approved to sit as Dep. High Court Judge, QBD, 1997–2015, Chancery and Family Divs, 2002–15. Asst Parly Boundary Comr, 1992; Legal Mem., First-tier Tribunal (Health, Educn and Social Care Chamber) (formerly Mental Health Review Tribunal (Restricted Patients)), 2000–16. Mem., County Court Rule Cttee, 1986–91. Trustee and Sec., Friends of Church of St Birinus, 2001–14. Gov., Sch. of St Helen and St Katharine, Abingdon, 1992–2013. Shrieval Remembrancer to High Sheriffs of Oxon, 2019–. *Recreations:* playing tennis, watching Rugby and football, enjoying opera, theatre, reading, travel, mowing the lawn, walking with retired gentlemen, learning modern Greek, playing improver's bridge.

**ECCLES, Nigel;** Co-Founder and Chief Executive Officer, Flick, since 2018; *b* Co. Tyrone, NI, 1974; *m* 2003, Lesley; two *s* one *d. Educ:* Univ. of St Andrews (BSc Pure Maths); Cranfield Univ. (MPhil Mil. Operational Res.). Burlington Consultants, 1999–2000; Flutter.com, 2000–02; Betdaq, 2002–03; McKinsey & Co., 2003–06; Co-Founder and Chief Executive Officer: Hubdub, 2007–09; FanDuel, 2009–17. Non-exec. Dir, Ooni, 2019–. *Recreations:* running, reading.

**ECCLESHARE, (Christopher) William;** Chief Executive Officer, Clear Channel Outdoor Holdings Inc., since 2012 (President and Chief Executive Officer, Clear Channel International, 2009–12); *b* 26 Oct. 1955; *s* of late Colin Forster Eccleshare and Elizabeth Eccleshare; *m* 1980, Carol Ann Seigel; two *s* one *d. Educ:* Fitzjohns Primary Sch.; William Ellis Sch.; Trinity Coll., Cambridge (BA Hist. 1978). Account Exec., 1978–89, Man. Dir, 1990–92, J. Walter Thompson; Chief Exec., PPGH/JWT Amsterdam, 1993–95; Global Strategy Dir, J. Walter Thompson, 1995–96; Chief Exec., Ammirati Puris Lintas, London, 1996–99; Partner, Leader Eur. Branding Practice, McKinsey & Co., 2000–02; Chairman and Chief Executive Officer: Young & Rubicam, Europe, 2002–05; BBDO EMEA, 2005–09. Non-executive Director: Hays plc, 2004–14; Britvic plc, 2017–; Sen. Ind. Dir, Centaur plc, 2016–. Mem., Mktg Gp of GB, 2006–. Mem. Council, University Coll. Sch., 2002–12. Mem. Bd and Trustee, Donmar Warehouse Th., 2013–. FIPA 1998 (Mem. Council, 1998–2000; Judge, IPA Effectiveness Awards, 2002). *Publications:* (contrib.) The Timeless Works of Stephen King, ed J. Lannon, 2007; contribs to Campaign, Admap, Market Leader. *Recreations:* American and European politics, theatre, running, music of Bruce Springsteen. *Address:* Clear Channel Outdoor, 33 Golden Square, W1F 9JT. *T:* (020) 7478 2334. *E:* williameccleshare@clearchannel.com; Apartment S12.07, Plimsoll Building, N1C 4BP. *Club:* Thirty (Pres., 2018–19).
*See also* J. J. *Eccleshare.*

**ECCLESHARE, Julia Jessica,** MBE 2014; journalist and broadcaster; *b* 14 Dec. 1951; *d* of late Colin Forster Eccleshare and of Elizabeth Eccleshare; *m* 1977, John Lemprière Hammond, *s* of Prof. Nicholas Geoffrey Lemprière Hammond, CBE, DSO, FBA; three *s* one *d. Educ:* Camden Sch. for Girls; Girton Coll., Cambridge. Editorial assistant: TLS, 1973–78; Puffin Books, 1978–79; Fiction editor, Hamish Hamilton Children's Books, 1979–82; selector of Children's Books of Year for Book Trust, 1982–92; Children's Book corresp., Bookseller, 1993–97; Children's Books Editor, Guardian, 1997–2016; Children's Festival Dir, Hay Festivals, 2016–. Co-dir, Centre for Literacy in Primary Educn, 2004–13; Hd of Policy and Engagement (formerly of Advocacy and Policy), Public Lending Right, 2014–. Chm. Judges, Smarties Award, 1994–; Member: Adv. Body, Reading is Fundamental (UK), 1996–; Poetry Book Soc., 2012–15; Adv. Bd, Give a Book, 2017–; Trustee: Listening Books, 2000–; Volunteer Reading Help, 2003–06; Siobhan Dowd Trust, 2014–. Contributor to BBC Treasure Islands, Night Waves, Kaleidoscope, Woman's Hour and Open Book, 1985–. Hon. DLitt Worcester, 2014. Eleanor Farjeon Award, 2000. *Publications:* The Woman's Hour Guide to Children's Books, 1987; A Guide to the Harry Potter Novels, 2002; Beatrix Potter to Harry Potter, 2002; The Rough Guide to Teenage Reading, 2003; The Rough Guide to Picture Books, 2008; 1001 Children's Books You Must Read Before You Grow Up, 2009; ed numerous anthologies. *Recreations:* theatre, walking. *Address:* 37 Oak Village, NW5 4QN. *T:* (020) 7431 1295. *E:* julia.eccleshare@blueyonder.co.uk.
*See also* C. W. *Eccleshare.*

**ECCLESHARE, William;** *see* Eccleshare, C. W.

**ECCLESTON, Christopher;** actor; *b* 16 Feb. 1964; *s* of Joseph Ronald Eccleston and Elsie Lavinia Eccleston. *Educ:* Central Sch. of Speech and Drama. *Films include:* Let Him Have It, 1991; Shallow Grave, 1994; Jude, 1996; Elizabeth, A Price Above Rubies, 1998; Heart, Old New Borrowed Blue, eXistenZ, 1999; Gone in 60 Seconds, 2000; The Invisible Circus, The Others, 2001; I Am Dina, 28 Days Later, 2002; A Revenger's Tragedy, 2003; Song for Marion, Thor: The Dark World, 2013; Legend, 2015. *Television includes:* Cracker (series), 1993–94; Hearts and Minds, 1995; Our Friends in the North (series), Hillsborough, 1996; Strumpet, 2001; Flesh and Blood, Othello, Sunday, 2002; The Second Coming, 2003; Doctor Who (series), 2005; Perfect Parents, 2006; Lennon Naked, 2010; The Shadow Line, The Borrowers, 2011; Blackout, 2012; Lucan, 2013; Fortitude, Safe House, 2015; The A Word, 2016, 2017; Come Home, Dead in a Week (Or Your Money Back), 2018. *Theatre includes:* Miss Julie, Haymarket, 2000; Hamlet, 2002, Electricity, 2004, W Yorks Playhouse; Antigone, NT, 2012; Macbeth, RSC, 2018. *Publications:* I Love the Bones of You (autobiog.), 2019. *Address:* c/o Independent Talent Group Ltd, 40 Whitfield Street, W1T 2RH.

**ECCLESTONE, Bernard, (Bernie);** Chief Executive Officer, Formula One Administration Ltd and Formula One Management Ltd, until 2017, now Chairman Emeritus; *b* Suffolk, 28 Oct. 1930; *m* 1st; one *d*; 2nd, Slavica (marr. diss. 2009); two *d*; 3rd, 2012, Fabiana Flosi. *Educ:* Woolwich Polytechnic (BSc). Est. car and motorbike dealership, Midweek Car Auctions; racing car driver, F3; owner, Connaught racing team, 1957; Manager, Jochen Rindt; owner, Brabham racing team, 1970–90. Vice-Pres., Fed. Internat. de l'Automobile. Person of the Year, Motorsport Industry Assoc., Business Achievement Awards; inaugural Gold Medal, British Racing Drivers' Club. Keys to Cities of São Paulo and Rio de Janeiro. Medal (1st degree), Bahrain; Silver Medals, Monaco; Bandeirante Medal, Brazil. Grand Officer, Equestrian Order of St Agata, San Marino; Grand Decoration of Honour, Austria; Order of Merit, Hungary; Grand Officer, Order of Merit, Italy. *Address:* c/o Formula One Administration Ltd, 6 Prince's Gate, SW7 1QJ.

**ECCLESTONE, Jacob Andrew;** Assistant General Secretary, Writers' Guild, 1999–2001; *b* 10 April 1939; *s* of late Rev. Alan Ecclestone and Delia Reynolds Abraham; *m* 1966, Margaret Joan Bassett; two *s* one *d. Educ:* High Storrs Grammar Sch., Sheffield; Open Univ. (BA). Journalism: South Yorkshire Times, 1957–61; Yorkshire Evening News, 1961–62; The Times, 1962–66, 1967–81; Dep. Gen. Sec., NUJ, 1981–97 (Mem., 1977, Vice-Pres. 1978, Pres., 1979, Nat. Exec.). Member: Press Council, 1977–80; Exec., NCCL, 1982–86. *Recreations:* gardening, walking (slowly), music. *Address:* North House, 50 Mount Street, Diss, Norfolk IP22 4QG. *T:* (01379) 644949. *E:* ecclestones@btinternet.com.

**ECE;** *see* Hussein-Ece.

**ECHENIQUE, Prof. Marcial Hernan,** OBE 2009; DArch, ScD; Professor of Land Use and Transport Studies, University of Cambridge, 1993–2013, now Emeritus (Head, Department of Architecture, 2004–08); Fellow, Churchill College, Cambridge, since 1972; *b* 23 Feb. 1943; *s* of Marcial Echenique and Rosa de Echenique (*née* Talavera); *m* 1963, Maria Luisa Holzmann; two *s* one *d. Educ:* Catholic Univ. of Chile; Univ. of Barcelona (DArch); ScD Cantab 2015. MA Cantab 1972. MRTPI 1990; ARIBA 1997. Asst Lectr, Univ. of Barcelona, 1964–65; University of Cambridge: Research Officer, 1967–70; Lectr, 1970–80; Reader in Architecture and Urban Studies, 1980–93. Founder and Mem., Bd of Applied Res., Cambridge, 1969–83. Advr to Public Works and Transport Ministers, Chilean Govt, 1991–2019. Chm., Marcial Echenique & Partners Ltd, England, 1978–2001; Pres., Marcial Echenique y Compañía SA, Spain, 1988–2007; Member Board: Trasporti e Territorio SRL, Italy, 1992–2007; Autopista Vasco-Aragonesa SA, Spain, 1994–99; Tecnologica SA, Spain, 1994–96; Ferrovial-Agroman, Construcciones, Spain, 1995–2000; Dockways Ltd, Jersey, 1996–2000. Bank of Bilbao-Vizcaya of Spain: Mem. Bd, 1988–94; Trustee of Foundn, 1990–94. *Publications:* (ed jtly) La Estructura del Espacio Urbano, 1975; (ed jtly) Urban Development Models, 1975; (ed) Modelos Matemáticos de la Estructura

Espacial Urbana: aplicaciones en America Latina, 1975; (with L. Piemontese) Un Modello per lo Sviluppo del Sistema Grecia-Italia Meridionale, 1984; (jtly) Cambridge Futures, 1999; (ed jtly) Cities for the New Millennium, 2001; (jtly) Cities of Innovation: shaping places for high-tech, 2003. *Recreations:* music, reading, gardening. *Address:* Farm Hall, Godmanchester, Cambs PE29 2HQ.

**ECKERBERG, (Carl) Lennart,** Hon. KCMG 1983; Officer of Royal Northern Star 1970; Swedish Ambassador to the Court of St James's, 1991–94; *b* 2 July 1928; *s* of late Enar Lars Eckerberg and Dagmar Liljedahl; *m* 1965, Willia Fales; two *s* one *d*. *Educ:* Univ. of Stockholm (law degree 1953). Swedish Foreign Service in Stockholm, London, Warsaw and Washington, 1954–71; Disarmament Ambassador, Geneva, 1971; Minister Plenipotentiary, Washington, 1975; Ambassador, Dar es Salaam, 1977; Under Sec., Political Affairs, Stockholm, 1979; Ambassador, Bonn, 1983–91. Orders from Finland, Germany, Iceland, Spain and Mexico. *Recreations:* golf, tennis, bridge. *Address:* (summer) Martornsvägen 3, 23940 Falsterbo, Sweden. *Clubs:* Chevy Chase (Washington); Falsterbo (Sweden).

**ECKERT, Neil David;** Chairman, Aggregated Micro Power Holdings plc, since 2012 (Chief Executive Officer, Aggregated Micro Power Ltd, 2010–12); *b* 20 May 1962; *s* of Clive and Mary Eckert; *m* 1986, Nicola Lindsay; three *d*. *Educ:* Merchant Taylors' Sch., Northwood, Middx. Reinsurance broker, 1980; joined Benfield Lovick & Rees & Co. Ltd, 1986; Mem. Bd, Benfield Gp plc, 1991–2000; Brit Insurance plc: Dir, 1995–2005; CEO, 1999–2005; non-exec. Dir, 2006–08; Chief Exec., Climate Exchange plc, 2005–10. Non-executive Director: Titan (Southwest) Ltd, 2003–; Ebix Inc., 2006–; Chm., IncubEx LLC, 2017–. *Recreations:* golf, sailing, tennis, other watersports in general, going to concerts, all types of music. *Address:* Aggregated Micro Power Holdings plc, 1 Dover Street, W1S 4LD. *T:* (020) 7382 7800, *Fax:* (020) 7382 7810. *Clubs:* Royal Automobile, Hurlingham, City of London; St Enodoc Golf.

**ECONOMIDES, Alain Giorgio Maria;** Ambassador of Italy to the Court of St James's, 2010–13; *b* Rome, 6 March 1948; *s* of Alessandro Economides and Elena Economides (*née* Potsios); *m* 1975, Franca Giannini; one *s* one *d*. *Educ:* Univ. of Rome (law degree 1973). Entered Diplomatic Service, Italy, 1975; Political Directorate, Min. of For. Affairs, 1976–79; First Sec., Perm. Repn to UN, NY, 1979–83; Counsellor: (Commercial) Harare, 1983–85; Human Resources Directorate, Min. of For. Affairs, 1985; Cabinet of Sec. of State for For. Affairs, 1986–89; First Counsellor, Perm. Repn to EEC, Brussels, 1989–93; Hd, Secretariat Unit, Political Directorate, 1993, Advr to Sec. Gen., 1994–96, Min. of For. Affairs; Minister Plenipotentiary, Perm. Repn to EU, Brussels, 1996–2001; Ambassador to Dakar, and concurrently to Mauritania, Gambia, Cape Verde, Mali, Guinea and Guinea Bissau, 2001–03; Dep. Dir Gen., Internat. Develt Directorate, Min. of For. Affairs, 2003; Dep. Chef de Cabinet to Sec. of State for For. Affairs, 2004–06; Dir Gen., Internat. Develt Directorate, Min. of For. Affairs, 2006–08; Chef de Cabinet to Sec. of State for For. Affairs, 2008–10. Medaglia al Merito Croce Rossa Italiana (Italy), 2004; Gran Croce dell'Ordine al Merito Melitense; Grande Ufficiale, Ordine al Merito della Repubblica Italiana. *Publications:* articles on the law of the sea. *Recreations:* tennis, swimming, golf.

**EDBROOKE, Rowan Clare;** Headmistress, St Helen & St Katharine, Abingdon, 2008–14; *b* Belize City, 27 Oct. 1961; *d* of Dr Donald Edbrooke and Vicky Edbrooke; partner, Bill Gott. *Educ:* St Catherine's Sch., Surrey; Godalming Sixth Form Coll.; Bedford Coll. of Higher Educn (BEd Hons). Teacher, Queen Elizabeth's Girls Sch., Barnet, 1984–86; South Hampstead High School: PE Teacher, 1986–88; Hd, PE Dept, 1988–93; Hd of Middle Sch., 1989–95; Sen. Teacher, 1995–98; Hd of Sixth Form, 1998–2001, Dep. Hd, 2001–04, Haberdashers' Aske's Sch. for Girls, Elstree; Headmistress, St Margaret's Sch., Exeter, 2004–08. *Recreations:* England netball (21 caps, 1981–84); currently tennis, golf, sailing, literature, choral music. *Address:* 8 The Beacon, Exmouth, Devon EX8 2AG. *T:* (01395) 227411.

**EDDINGTON, Sir Roderick Ian, (Sir Rod),** Kt 2005; AO 2012; DPhil; non-executive Chairman, Lion, since 2012; Chairman, Asia Pacific Advisory Council, JP Morgan, since 2017 (non-executive Chairman, Australia and New Zealand, 2006–17); *b* 2 Jan. 1950; *s* of Gil and April Eddington; *m* 1994, Young Sook Park; one *s* one *d*. *Educ:* Univ. of WA (BEng Hons; MEng Sci.); Lincoln Coll., Oxford (DPhil 1979). Res. Lectr, Pembroke Coll., Oxford, 1978–79; John Swire & Sons, 1979–96 (on secondment to Cathay Pacific Airways as Man. Dir, 1992–96); Director: Swire Pacific, 1992–96; John Swire & Sons Pty Ltd, 1997–; Exec. Chm., Ansett Australia, 1997–2000; Dir, News Ltd, 1997–2000; CEO, British Airways plc, 2000–05. Non-executive Director: News Corp., 2000–13; Rio Tinto plc, 2005–11; CLP Holdings, 2006–; 20th Century Fox, 2013–19; Chairman: Victoria Major Events Co., 2006–16; Allco Finance Gp Ltd, 2006–09; Infrastructure Partnerships Australia, 2019–. Chm., Adv. Council, Infrastructure Australia, 2008–14; Member: Asia-Pacific Econ. Cooperation Business Adv. Council, 2014–; Adv. Bd, Visy Industries Australia plc, 2018–; Adv. Bd, Pratt Industries (USA) Inc., 2018–. Commnd by HM Treasury and DFT to provide long-term strategy for UK's transport infrastructure, 2005 (report, Eddington Transport Study, 2006). Grand Cordon, Order of the Rising Sun (Japan), 2015. *Recreations:* cricket, bridge. *Address:* JPMorgan, Level 31, 101 Collins Street, Melbourne, Vic 3000, Australia. *Clubs:* Vincent's (Oxford); Melbourne; Hong Kong, Shek O (Hong Kong).

**EDDLESTON, Prof. Adrian Leonard William Francis,** DM; FRCP; Professor of Liver Immunology, London University, 1982–2000, now Emeritus, and Dean, Guy's, King's College and St Thomas' School of Medicine of King's College London, 1998–2000; *b* 2 Feb. 1940; *s* of late Rev. William Eddleston and Kathleen Brenda (*née* Jarman); *m* 1966, Hilary Kay Radford; three *s* one *d*. *Educ:* St Peter's Coll., Oxford (BA 1961; MB BCh, MA 1964; DM 1972); Guy's Hosp. Med. Sch., London. MRCS 1965; LRCP 1965, MRCP 1967, FRCP 1979. House Surgeon, Casualty Officer, House Physician, Sen. House Officer and Jun. Med. Registrar, Guy's Hosp., 1965–67; Med. Registrar, KCH, 1967–68; King's College School of Medicine and Dentistry: Res. Fellow and Hon. Lectr in Med., 1968–70, Hon. Sen. Lectr, 1972–78, Liver Unit; Dean, Faculty of Clinical Med., 1992–97; Dean, 1997–98; Hon. Consultant Physician, KCH, 1982–2000. Mem., London Health Commn, 2000–04. MRC Vis. Res. Fellow, Clin. Immunol. Lab., Minnesota Univ., 1970–72. Non-exec. Dir, King's Healthcare NHS Trust, 1990–2000; Chm., Bromley Primary Care Trust, 2001–05. Vice-Chm., King's Fund Mgt Cttee, 2002–07 (Mem., 2000–07). Mem., Gen. Osteopathic Council, 2002–12 (Chm., 2008–12). Trustee: St Christopher's Hospice, 2000–01; Keswick Choral Soc., 2008– (Sec., 2010–18). Dir, Threlkeld Community Coffee Shop CIC, 2011–15. FKC 1996. Founder FMedSci 1998. *Publications:* Immune Reactions in Liver Disease, 1979; Interferons in the Treatment of Chronic Virus Infection of the Liver, 1990; contrib. learned publications on immunology of auto-immune and virus-induced liver diseases. *Recreations:* choral singing, HF electronics, computing. *Address:* 40 High Street, Corby Glen, Grantham, Lincs NG33 4LX.

**EDDY, Thomas Edward Dacombe,** CBE 2002; Secretary, Royal Commission on Environmental Pollution, 2004–09; *b* 4 Aug. 1949; *s* of Thomas Charles Eddy and Myrtle Constance Eddy (*née* Dacombe); *m* 1980, Cherry Eva; two *s*. *Educ:* Queen Elizabeth Grammar Sch., Wimborne; Pembroke Coll., Cambridge (BA Natural Scis 1970, MA 1973). Joined MAFF, 1973; Head of: Countryside Div., 1990–93, Animal Health Div., 1993–96, BSE Div., 1996–99, EU Div., 1999–2004, MAFF, subseq. DEFRA. Mem., World Ship Soc. *Recreations:* commercial shipping history, reading, croquet. *Address:* 46 Grove Way, Esher, Surrey KT10 8HL. *E:* the4eddys@hotmail.com.

**EDE, Anthony Roger;** a District Judge (Magistrates' Courts), 2006–15; a Deputy District Judge, 2016–17; *b* 20 Dec. 1945; *s* of Hugh Geoffrey Ede and Rosalie Ede; *m* 1st (marr. diss.); 2nd, Jill Frances Drower (marr. diss.); one *s* one *d*; 3rd, 2006, Akiyo Yamamoto; one *d* (one *s* decd). *Educ:* Hull Univ. (LLB Hons 1968). Admitted as solicitor, 1971; Partner, Dundon, Ede & Studdert, solicitors, Lavender Hill, 1975–88; Lectr in Law, Coll. of Law, Guildford, 1988–90; Dir, Practical Legal Trng, London, 1990–91; Law Society: Sec., Criminal Law Cttee, 1991–2000; Internat. Projects Manager, 2000–06. Dir, Ede & Edge Ltd, 2016–. Mem., Governing Council, Council for Registration of Forensic Practitioners, 1998–2005. Mem., Commonwealth Magistrates and Judges Assoc., 2011–. *Publications:* (with E. Shepherd) Active Defence, 1997, 2nd edn 2000; (with A. Edwards) Criminal Defence, 2000, 4th edn 2017; (with L. Townley) Forensic Practice in Criminal Cases, 2003. *Recreations:* world travel, food, cinema, music. *Address:* c/o Ede & Edge Ltd, 67 Westow Street, Upper Norwood, SE19 3RW.

**EDE, Ven. Dennis;** Archdeacon of Stoke-upon-Trent, 1989–97, now Emeritus; permission to officiate, Diocese of Lichfield, since 2002; *b* 8 June 1931; *m* 1956, Angela Horsman (*d* 2016); one *s* two *d*. *Educ:* Prebendal Choir Sch., Chichester; Ardingly Coll.; Portsmouth Tech. Coll.; Univ. of Nottingham (BA Theology 1955); Barnett House, Oxford (Cert. of Social Studies); Ripon Hall, Oxford; MSocSc Birmingham, 1972. Nat. Service, RAF, 1950–52; Pilot Officer, Admin. Branch. Asst Curate, St Giles, Sheldon, dio. Birmingham, 1957–60; Asst Curate-in-charge, St Philip and St James, Hodge Hill, Birmingham, 1960–64, Priest-in-charge 1964–70, Team Rector 1970–76; part-time Chaplain, East Birmingham Hosp., 1961–76; Vicar of All Saints Parish Church, West Bromwich, dio. Lichfield, 1976–89; Rural Dean, W Bromwich, 1976–89; Hon. Priest i/c, All Saints, Tilford, dio. Guildford, 1997–2002; permission to officiate: Dio. of Guildford, 2003–13; Dio. of Southwark, 2003–16. Mem., Gen. Synod of C of E, 1975–76, 1980–90. Diocese of Lichfield: Chm. House of Clergy, 1985–90; Chm. of Communications, 1983–97; Prebendary of Lichfield Cathedral, 1983–89; Hon. Canon, 1989–97. Chairman: Sandwell Volunteer, 1980–86; Faith in Sandwell, 1986–89; Shallowford House, 1990–97; Diocesan Clergy Retirement Cttee, 1990–97; Widows (Diocesan) Officers Cttee, 1990–97; Surrey and Sussex Churches Broadcasting Cttee, 1997–2002. Co-ordinator for religious bodies in Staffs in major disasters, 1990–97. Broadcaster, local radio, 1960–97; epilogian, ATV, 1961–73. *Recreation:* walking. *Address:* Tilford, 13 Park Close, Carshalton, Surrey SM5 3EU. *T:* (020) 8647 5891. *E:* dennisangelaede@aol.com.

**EDELKOORT, Lidewij de Gerarda Hillegonda;** design forecaster, strategist and educator; Founder and Chief Executive Officer, Trend Union, since 1986; *b* Wageningen, The Netherlands, 29 Aug. 1950; *d* of Jan Edelkoort and Hillegonda van der Spek; partner, Anthon Beeke. *Educ:* Acad. of Fine Arts, Arnhem (Bachelor in Fashion 1972). Stylist, De Bijenkorf, Amsterdam, 1972–75; collection developer, Exporters India Ltd and India Handicraft, Inc., 1975–79; freelancer, Comité de Coordination des Industries de la Mode, Paris, 1976–86; Founder and Forecaster, Studio Edelkoort, Paris, 1991–; Founder and Director: Edelkoort INC, 1999–; Edelkoort EAST, 2008–. In-house trend forecaster, Première Vision, 1986–93. Design Academy, Eindhoven: Hd, Man and Leisure Dept, 1991–98; Chairwoman, 1998–2008; Co-Founder and Art Dir, Sch. of Form, Poznan, 2010–; Dean, Hybrid Design Studies, Parsons Sch. of Design, The New Sch., New York and Paris, 2015–. Founder and Dir, Heartwear, 1993–; Founder and Artistic Dir, Designhuis Eindhoven, 2006; Founder and creator, Laurier, restaurant, 2007, Mem. Bd, Fondation d'entreprise, 2013–, Galeries Lafayette, Paris. Founder and creator, magazines: View on Colour, 1992–; Bloom, a Horticultural View, 1997–. Curator, exhibitions, incl. Oracles du Design, La Gaîté Lyrique, Paris, 2015. Hon. DArt Nottingham Trent, 2008. Grand Seigneur Prize, Netherlands, 2004; Prins Bernhard Cultuurfonds Prijs, Netherlands, 2012; Hon. RDI, 2014. Knight, Order of Oranje Nassau (Netherlands), 2008; Officier des Arts et des Lettres (France), 2014 (Chevalier, 2008). *Publications:* Fetishism in Fashion, 2013. *Recreations:* design, fashion, education, art, craft, trend forecasting, curating. *Address:* Trend Union, 30 Boulevard Saint Jacques, 75014 Paris, France. *T:* (1) 44086880. *E:* li@edelkoort.com.

**EDELL, Stephen Bristow;** ombudsman, 1987–2005; *b* 1 Dec. 1932; *s* of late Ivan James Edell and Hilda Pamela Edell; *m* 1958, Shirley Ross Collins; two *s* one *d*. *Educ:* St Andrew's Sch., Eastbourne; Uppingham; LLB London. Commnd RA, 1951. Articled to father, 1953; qual. Solicitor 1958; Partner, Knapp-Fishers (Westminster), 1959–75; Law Comr, 1975–83; Partner, Crossman Block and Keith (Solicitors), 1983–87; Building Societies Ombudsman, 1987–94; PIA Ombudsman, 1994–97; Waterways Ombudsman, 1997–2005. Chm., Ind. Monitoring Bd, Tinsley House Immigration Removal Centre, Gatwick, 2010–11 (Mem., 2007–11). Legal Mem., RTPI, 1971–92. Mem. Cttee, 1973–85, Vice-Pres., 1980–82, Pres., 1982–83, City of Westminster Law Soc. Oxfam: Mem., Retailing and Property Cttee, 1984–93 (Chm., 1989–93); Mem. Council, 1985–93; Mem., Exec., 1987–93. Dir, Catholic Bldg Soc., 1998–2003. Chm. Council, Hurstpierpoint Coll., 1997–2002; Donation Gov., Christ's Hosp., 2010–. Makers of Playing Cards' Company: Liveryman, 1955–2012; Mem., Ct of Assts, 1978–2000; Sen. Warden, 1980–81; Master, 1981–82; Sen. Freeman, 2012–; Tallow Chandlers' Company: Freeman, 2002–; Liveryman, 2006–. *Publications:* Inside Information on the Family and the Law, 1969; The Family's Guide to the Law, 1974; articles in Conveyancer, Jl of Planning and Environmental Law, Bulletin of Scientific Instrument Soc., Globe Studies (Vienna), and newspapers. *Recreations:* family life; music, opera, theatre; early astronomical instruments; avoiding gardening; interested in problems of developing countries. *Address:* The Old Farmhouse, Twineham, Haywards Heath, Sussex RH17 5NP. *T:* (01273) 832058.

**EDELMAN, Colin Neil;** QC 1995; barrister and arbitrator; a Recorder, 1996–2016; Deputy High Court Judge, 2008–16; *b* 2 March 1954; *s* of late Gerald Bertram Edelman and of Lynn Queenie Edelman (*née* Tropp); *m* 1978, Jacqueline Claire Seidel; one *s* one *d*. *Educ:* Haberdashers' Aske's Sch., Elstree; Clare Coll., Cambridge (MA). Called to the Bar, Middle Temple, 1977, Bencher, 2003; Asst Recorder, 1993–96; Head of Chambers, 2002–11. Dir, Bar Mutual Indemnity Fund Ltd, 2007– (Dep. Chm., 2009–13; Chm., 2013–). *Publications:* (contrib.) Insurance Disputes, 1999, 3rd edn 2011; (ed) The Law of Reinsurance, 2005, 2nd edn 2013. *Recreations:* badminton, ski-ing, walking, Luton Town FC. *Address:* Devereux Chambers, Queen Elizabeth Building, Temple, EC4Y 9BS. *T:* (020) 7353 7534, *Fax:* (020) 7583 5150.

**EDELMAN, Keith Graeme;** Chairman, Revolution Bars Group plc, since 2015; Pennpetro Energy plc, since 2017; Senior Independent Director, Headlam, since 2018; *b* 10 July 1950; *m* 1974, Susan Brown; two *s*. *Educ:* Haberdashers' Aske's Sch.; UMIST (BSc). IBM, 1971–73; Rank Xerox, 1973–78; Bank of America, 1978–83; Grand Metropolitan, 1983–84; Corporate Planning Dir and Chm., Texas Homecare, Ladbroke Group, 1984–91; Man. Dir, Carlton Communications, 1991–93; Chief Exec., Storehouse and BHS, 1993–99; Man. Dir, Arsenal Football Club, 2000–08. Chairman: Glenmorangie, 2002–05; Goals Soccer Centres plc, 2013–15; Sen. Ind. Dir, Supergroup, then Superdry plc, 2009–18; non-executive Director: Eurotunnel plc, 1995–2004; Eurotunnel SA, 1995–2004; Channel

Tunnel Gp Ltd, 1995–2004; France-Manche SA, 1995–2004; Qualceram Shires plc, 2005–09; Nirah, 2006–16; Beale plc, 2008–13; Olympic Park Legacy Co., later London Legacy Develt Corp., 2009–; Arnotts Hldgs, 2009–10; Safestore, 2009–16; Argentium, 2010–12; Thorntons plc, 2012–15; Clarion Events Ltd, 2013–15; Altitude Gp plc, 2018–. *Recreations:* tennis, ski-ing. *Address:* Laurimar, 7 Linksway, Northwood, Middx HA6 2XA. *T:* (01923) 823990.

**EDELSTEIN, Victor Arnold;** painter of portraits and interiors; *b* 10 July 1945; *s* of late Israel and Rebecca Edelstein; *m* 1973, Anna Maria Succi. Trainee Designer, Alexon, 1962–66; Asst Designer, Biba, 1966–68; formed own small dress designing co., 1968–72; Salvador, 1972–76; Designer, Christian Dior, 1976–78; founded Victor Edelstein Ltd, 1978, closed 1993. Ballet design, Rhapsody in Blue, 1989. One-man exhibitions: Sotheby's, 1996; Hopkins Thomas, Paris, 1999; Hazlitt, Gooden & Fox Gall., 2001; Didier Aaron, NY, 2004, 2015 (Gilded Interiors); (portraits) The Studio, Glebe Place, London, 2005; (pastels) Derek Johns Gall., Duke Street, London, 2011; Didier Aaron, Paris (Gilded Interiors), 2015; Views of Venice, Whichford Hse, Warwickshire, 2018; exhibn with Annamaria Succi, Souvenirs of India, Indar Pasricha, London, 2015. *Recreations:* walking, music. *Address:* Gloucestershire.

**EDEN,** family name of **Barons Auckland, Eden of Winton** and **Henley**.

**EDEN OF WINTON,** Baron *cr* 1983 (Life Peer), of Rushyford in the County of Durham; **John Benedict Eden;** PC 1972; Bt (E) 1672 and Bt (GB) 1776; Chairman, Lady Eden's Schools Ltd, 1974–2001 (Director, 1949–70); *b* 15 Sept. 1925; *s* of Sir Timothy Calvert Eden, 8th and 6th Bt and Patricia (*d* 1990), *d* of Arthur Prendergast; *S* father, 1963; *m* 1st, 1958, Belinda Jane (marr. diss. 1974), *o d* of late Sir John Pascoe; two *s* two *d*; 2nd, 1977, Margaret Ann, Viscountess Strathallan. Lieut Rifle Bde, seconded to 2nd KEO Goorkha Rifles and Gilgit Scouts, 1943–47. Contested (C) Paddington North, 1953; MP (C) Bournemouth West, Feb. 1954–1983. Mem. House of Commons Select Cttee on Estimates, 1962–64; Vice-Chm., Conservative Parly Defence Cttee, 1963–66 (formerly: Chm., Defence Air Sub-Cttee; Hon. Sec., Space Sub-Cttee); Vice-Chm., Aviation Cttee, 1963–64; Additional Opposition Front Bench Spokesman for Defence, 1964–66; Jt Vice-Chm., Cons. Parly Trade and Power Cttee, 1966–68; Opposition Front Bench Spokesman for Power, 1968–70; Minister of State, Min. of Technology, June–Oct. 1970; Minister for Industry, DTI, 1970–72; Minister of Posts and Telecommunications, 1972–74; Mem., Expenditure Cttee, 1974–76; Chairman: House of Commons Select Cttee on European Legislation, 1976–79; Home Affairs Cttee, 1981–83. Sponsored Copyright Act, 1983. Mem., H of L, 1983–2015. Vice-Chm., Assoc. of Conservative Clubs Ltd, 1964–67, Hon. Life Vice-Pres., 1970–; President: Wessex Area Council, Nat. Union of Conservative and Unionist Assocs, 1974–77; Wessex Area Young Conservatives, 1978–80. UK Deleg. to Council of Europe and to Western European Union, 1960–62; Mem., NATO Parliamentarians' Conf., 1962–66. Chm., Royal Armouries, 1986–94. Chairman: WonderWorld plc, 1982–98; Gamlestaden plc, 1987–92; Bricom Gp, 1990–93. Pres., Independent Schs Assoc., 1969–71; a Vice-Pres., Nat. Chamber of Trade, 1974–86; Vice-Pres., Internat. Tree Foundn (formerly The Men of the Trees), 1953–98. Hon. Vice-Pres., Nat. Assoc. of Master Bakers, Confectioners & Caterers, 1978–82. Chm., British Lebanese Assoc., 1990–98. Heir (to baronetcies only): *s* Hon. Robert Frederick Calvert Eden, *b* 30 April 1964. *Clubs:* Boodle's, Pratt's.

**EDEN, Prof. Colin L.,** PhD; Professor of Management Science and Strategic Management, Associate Dean and Director, International Division, Strathclyde Business School, University of Strathclyde, 2006–14; *b* 24 Dec. 1943; *s* of John and Connie Eden; *m* 1967, Christine. *Educ:* Univ. of Leicester (BSc); Univ. of Southampton (PhD). Operational Researcher, then Operational Res. Manager, then Mgt Cons., 1967–73; Lectr, then Sen. Lectr, then Reader, Sch. of Mgt, Univ. of Bath, 1974–87; Prof., Business Sch., 1988–99, Dir, Grad. Sch. of Business, 1999–2006, Univ. of Strathclyde. Advr, SHEFC; Mem., Mgt Bd, Scottish Exams Bd and Scottish Qualifications Authy. *Publications:* Management Decision and Decision Analysis, 1976; Thinking in Organizations, 1979; Messing About in Problems, 1983; Tackling Strategic Problems, 1990; Managerial and Organizational Cognition, 1998; Making Strategy, 1998; Visible Thinking, 2004; Practice of Making Strategy, 2005; over 170 papers in learned jls. *Recreations:* sailing, ski-ing, walking. *Club:* Clyde Cruising.

**EDEN, Prof. Osborn Bryan, (Tim),** FRCPE, FRCP, FRCPath, FRCPCH, FRCR; CRUK (formerly CRC) Professor of Paediatric Oncology, 1994–2005, Teenage Cancer Trust Professor of Teenage and Young Adult Cancer, 2005–08, Hon. Professor, 2008–10, now Professor Emeritus of Paediatric and Adolescent Oncology, University of Manchester; Medical Adviser: Teenage Cancer Trust UK, 2005–10; Teenage Cancer Trust in Scotland, 2010–12; *b* 2 April 1947; *s* of late Eric Victor Eden and Gwendoline Eden (*née* Hack); *m* 1970, Randi Forsgren; one *s* one *d*. *Educ:* University Coll. London (MB BS 1970). DRCOG 1972; MRCP 1974, FRCP 1992; FRCPE 1983; FRCPath 1995; FRCPCH 1997; FRCR 2007. House physician, UCH, 1970–71; house surgeon, Portsmouth, 1971; Sen. House Officer appts, IoW, UCH, Simpson Meml Pavilion and Royal Hosp. for Sick Children, Edinburgh, 1971–73; Registrar, Paediatrics and Haematology, Royal Hosp. for Sick Children, Edinburgh, 1974–76; Fellow, Stanford Univ., Calif., 1976–77; Leukaemia Res. Fellow, Edinburgh, 1977–78; Lectr, Edinburgh Univ., 1978–79; Consultant Clinical Haematologist, Bristol Children's Hosp., 1979–82; Consultant Paediatric Haematologist and Oncologist, Royal Hosp. for Sick Children, Edinburgh, 1982–91; Prof. of Paediatric Oncology, St Bartholomew's Hosp., 1991–94; Lead Clinician, Paediatric Oncology, Royal Manchester Children's Hosp., 1994–2007; Lead Clinician, Teenage Cancer Trust Young Oncology Unit, Christie Hosp. NHS Trust, 1994–2007; Hon. Consultant, Central Manchester and Manchester Children's Univ. Hosps NHS Trust, 1994–2007. Chm., UK Children's Cancer Study Gp, 1989–92 (Chm., Haematology Oncology Div., 2000–06); Member: MRC Childhood Leukaemia Working Party, 1978–2008 (Chm., 1991–2000); MRC Leukaemia Steering Cttee, 1991–2002; Cttee on Med. Effects of Radiation in the Envmt, 1991–2003; Clin. Trials Cttee, CRC, 1998–2002; Med. and Scientific Panel and Clin. Trials Cttee, Leukaemia Res. Fund, 2000–04; Clinical Trials Adv. and Awards Cttee, MRC/CRUK, 2002–04; Clinical and Translational Res. Cttee, CRUK, 2007–10; Nat. Adv. Cttee for Chronic Pain (formerly Ministerial Steering Gp on Chronic Pain), Scottish Govt, 2015–; Stakeholder and Advr on behalf of Internat. Soc. Paediatric Oncol. and World Child Cancer in Wkg Gps of WHO 5-year Global Initiative to improve childhood cancer care worldwide, 2015–. Pres., Internat. Soc. of Paediatric Oncology, 2004–07 (Chm., Scientific Cttee, 1996–99); Hon. Treas., Genetics Section, RSocMed, 2003–04 (Hon. Sec., 2001–03). Non-exec. Dir, Manchester Children's Hosps NHS Trust, 1996–2001. Med. Advr and Founding Mem., Over the Wall Gang Gp, 2001–08. Trustee, Malcolm Sargent Cancer Fund, 1985–95; Founding Medic, World Child Cancer (formerly World Child Cancer Foundn), 2007– (Med. Trustee, 2007–12; Patron and Volunteer, 2012–); Chm., World Child Cancer Global, 2013–14. Paediatric Advr, AfrOx, 2008–. Faculty Associate, Brooks Poverty Inst., Univ. of Manchester, 2008–12. Hon. Mem., Burma Med. Assoc., 1985. Fellow, Inst. of Cancer Policy, 2014. Volunteer of Year, Bond Internat. Develt, 2018; UK Point of Light Award, 2018; Vanessa Moss Prize, Oncol. Section, RSocMed, 2018. *Publications:* over 300 scientific papers, editorials and chapters on paediatric and adolescent haematology and oncology. *Recreations:* international aid projects, my family, writing, reading, theatre. *Address:* 5 South Gillsland Road, Edinburgh EH10 5DE.

**EDEN, Prof. Richard John,** OBE 1978; Professor of Energy Studies, Cavendish Laboratory, University of Cambridge, 1982–89, now Emeritus; Fellow of Clare Hall, Cambridge, 1966–89, now Emeritus (Vice-President, 1987–89; Hon. Fellow, 1993); *b* 2 July 1922; *s* of James A. Eden and Dora M. Eden; *m* 1949, Elsie Jane Greaves (*d* 2014); one *s* one *d* and one step *d*. *Educ:* Hertford Grammar Sch.; Peterhouse, Cambridge (BA 1943, MA 1948, PhD 1951). War service, 1942–46, Captain REME, Airborne Forces. Cambridge University: Bye-Fellow, Peterhouse, 1949–50; Stokes Student, Pembroke Coll., 1950–51; Clare College: Research Fellow, 1951–55; Official Fellow, 1957–66; Dir of Studies in Maths, 1951–53, 1957–62; Royal Soc. Smithson Res. Fellow, 1952–55; Sen. Lectr in Physics, Univ. of Manchester, 1955–57; Cambridge University: Lectr in Maths, 1957–64 (Stokes Lectr, 1962); Reader in Theoretical Physics, 1964–82; Head of High Energy Theoretical Physics Gp, 1964–74, Hd of Energy Res. Gp, 1974–89, Cavendish Lab. Mem., Princeton Inst. for Advanced Study, 1954, 1959, 1973, 1989; Visiting Scientist: Indiana Univ., 1954–55; Univ. of California, Berkeley, 1960, 1967; Visiting Professor: Univ. of Maryland, 1961, 1965; Columbia Univ., 1962; Scuola Normale Superiore, Pisa, 1964; Univ. of Marseilles, 1968; Univ. of California, 1969. Member: UK Adv. Council on Energy Conservation, 1974–83; Eastern Electricity Bd, 1985–93; Energy Adviser to UK NEDO, 1974–75. Syndic, CUP, 1984–95. Chm., Cambridge Energy Res. Ltd, subseq. Caminus Energy Ltd, 1985–91. Companion, Inst. of Energy, 1985. Smiths Prize, Univ. of Cambridge, 1949; Maxwell Prize and Medal, Inst. of Physics, 1970; Open Award for Distinction in Energy Economics, BIEE, 1989. *Publications:* (jtly) The Analytic S Matrix, 1966; High Energy Collisions of Elementary Particles, 1967; Energy Conservation in the United Kingdom (NEDO report), 1975; Energy Prospects (Dept of Energy report), 1976; World Energy Demand to 2020 (World Energy Conf. report), 1977; (jtly) Energy Economics, 1981; (jtly) Electricity's Contribution to UK Energy Self Sufficiency, 1984; (jtly) UK Energy, 1984; Clare College and the Founding of Clare Hall, 1998; (jtly) Clare Hall 40, 2006; Clare Hall, 2009; Sometimes in Cambridge (memoirs), 2012; papers and review articles on nuclear physics and theory of elementary particles. *Recreations:* writing, painting, reading, gardening, travel. *Address:* Clare Hall, Cambridge CB3 9AL. *T:* (01223) 332360.

**EDEN, Tim;** *see* Eden, O. B.

**EDENBOROUGH, Dr Michael Simon;** QC 2010; barrister. *Educ:* Sidney Sussex Coll., Cambridge (MA Natural Scis); Exeter Coll., Oxford (MSc Bio-organic Chem.; DPhil Biophysics). Called to the Bar, Middle Temple, 1992; in practice as a barrister, specialising in intellectual property law, 1994–. *Publications:* Organic Reaction Mechanisms: a step by step approach, 1994, 2nd edn 1999; Lecture Notes on Intellectual Property Law, 1995; Contentious Trade Mark Registry Proceedings, 2018. *Address:* Serle Court, Lincoln's Inn, WC2A 3QS.

**EDER, Prof. Andrew Howard Eric,** FDS RCSE; Dean and Professor of Dentistry, University of Buckingham Dental School, since 2018; Hon. Consultant in Restorative Dentistry, Milton Keynes University Hospital NHS Foundation Trust, since 2018; specialist in restorative dentistry and prosthodontics, since 1998; Clinical Director, Specialist Dental Care and London Tooth Wear Centre, since 1998; *b* London, 21 April 1964; *s* of Hans and Helga Eder; *m* 1988, Rosina Jayne Saideman; two *s* one *d*. *Educ:* St Paul's Sch.; King's Coll. Sch. of Medicine and Dentistry (BDS 1986); LDS RCS 1987; Eastman Dental Inst., Univ. of London (MSc 1990). MFGDP 1993; MRD RCS RCPSG 1994; FDS RCSE 2003. KCH School of Medicine and Dentistry: Hse Officer, Paediatric, Orthodontic and Restorative Dentistry, 1987–88; Clin. Asst in Restorative Dentistry, 1988–89; Eastman Dental Hospital: Registrar in Restorative Dentistry, 1990–91; Associate Specialist in Restorative Dentistry, 1998–2002; Eastman Dental Institute, subseq. UCL Eastman Dental Institute: Clin. Lectr, 1991–94, Sen. Clin. Lectr, 1995–2002, in Restorative Dentistry; Prof. of Restorative Dentistry and Dental Educn, 2002–18, now Prof. Emeritus; Dir, Continuing Professional Develt, 2002–12; Dir, Educn, 2005–12; Associate Dean for Continuing Educn, Sch. of Life and Med. Scis, 2008–12, Pro-Vice-Provost, Educn, Innovation and Enterprise, 2013–17, UCL; Hon. Consultant in Restorative Dentistry, UCLH Foundn Trust, 2002–18. Mem. Bd, Faculty of Dental Surgery, RCSE, 2017–. Member, Editorial Advisory Board: Eur. Jl Restorative Dentistry and Prosthodontics, 1995–2015; British Dental Jl, 2005–17. Postgraduate Speciality Examiner: UCL, 1999–2017; MRD RCS, 2009– (Chm., Examiners, 2016–). President: Alpha Omega, 1994–95 (Chm. Trustees, 2003–); Dental Section, RSocMed, 2001–02; British Soc. for Restorative Dentistry, 2005–06. FHEA 2002. *Publications:* (ed jtly) Tooth Surface Loss, 2000; contrib. chapters in textbooks and articles to academic jls. *Recreations:* family, bridge, snooker and pool. *Address:* University of Buckingham Dental School, Hunter Street, Buckingham MK18 1EG. *T:* (020) 7486 7180. *E:* andrew.eder@buckingham.ac.uk; Specialist Dental Care, 57A Wimpole Street, W1G 8YP. *T:* (020) 7486 7180. *E:* andreweder@restorative-dentistry.co.uk.
*See also* Hon. Sir H. B. Eder.

**EDER, Hon. Sir (Henry) Bernard,** Kt 2011; a Judge of the High Court, Queen's Bench Division, 2011–15; international arbitrator and mediator, Essex Court Chambers, since 2015; *b* 16 Oct. 1952; *s* of Hans and Helga Eder; *m* 2008, Claire Green; four *s* one *d* by a former marriage. *Educ:* Haberdashers' Aske's School, Elstree; Downing College, Cambridge (BA 1974). Called to the Bar, Inner Temple, 1975, Bencher, 2007; QC 1990; an Asst Recorder, 1996–2000; a Recorder, 2000–01. Internat. Judge, Singapore Internat. Commercial Ct, 2015–; Acting Judge, Commercial Ct, BVI, 2016. Chair, ARIAS (UK), 2015–; Legal Chair, Financial Reporting Council, 2015–19. Vis. Prof., UCL, 1999–2003. *Publications:* Jt Ed., Scrutton on Charterparties, 22nd edn, 2011, 23rd edn 2015. *Recreations:* tennis, ski-ing.
*See also* A. H. E. Eder.

**EDEY, Philip David;** QC 2009; *b* Johannesburg, SA, 23 Feb. 1971; *s* of Russell and Celia Edey; *m* 1999, Alison Baxter; three *s*. *Educ:* Eton Coll.; Lady Margaret Hall, Oxford (BA 1st Cl. Juris. 1993; MA). Called to the Bar, Gray's Inn, 1994. Chm. of Govs, Ludgrove Sch., 2013–. *Recreations:* Real Tennis, lawn tennis, golf, wine. *Address:* 20 Essex Street, WC2R 3AL. *T:* (020) 7842 1200. *Clubs:* Queen's, Garrick, Jesters; Vincent's (Oxford).

**EDGAR, (Christopher) George,** OBE 2011; HM Diplomatic Service; Ambassador of the European Union to Cambodia, since 2015; *b* 21 April 1960; *s* of Dr William Macreadie Edgar and Dr Freda Elizabeth Edgar; *m* 1994, Elena Ryurikovna Nagornichnykh; two *d*. *Educ:* Trinity Coll., Cambridge Univ. (MA Philosophy); Open Univ. (MA Envmt, Policy and Society). FCO, 1981–83; Moscow, 1984–85; Lagos, 1986–88; FCO, 1988–92; resigned 1992, reinstated 1995; FCO, 1995–97; Ambassador to Cambodia, 1997–2000; Ambassador to Macedonia, 2001–04; Consul Gen., St Petersburg, 2004–06; Envoy for Climate Security in Africa, FCO, 2006–07; Head: Consular Assistance Gp, FCO, 2007–10; Papal Visit Team, FCO, 2010; Chargé d'Affaires, Holy See, 2011; Additional Dir, Protocol Directorate, FCO, 2011–12; Ambassador to Uzbekistan, 2012–15. *Recreation:* music. *Address:* c/o Foreign and Commonwealth Office, King Charles Street, SW1A 2AH.

**EDGAR, David Burman**; author and playwright; Chair, MA in Playwriting Studies, 1989–99, Hon. Professor, since 1992, University of Birmingham; *b* 26 Feb. 1948; *s* of late Barrie Edgar and Joan (*née* Burman); *m* 1st, 1979, Eve Brook (*d* 1998); two *s*; 2nd, 2012, Stephanie Dale. *Educ*: Oundle Sch.; Univ. of Manchester (BA 1969). FRSL. Fellow in Creative Writing, Leeds Polytechnic, 1972–74; Resident Playwright, Birmingham Rep. Theatre, 1974–75; Board Mem., 1985–; UK/US Bicentennial Arts Fellow, USA, 1978–79; Literary Consultant, 1984–88, Hon. Associate Artist, 1989, RSC; Hon. Sen. Res. Fellow, 1988–92, Prof. of Playwriting Studies, 1995–99, Birmingham Univ.; Humanitas Vis. Prof. of Playwriting, Univ. of Oxford, 2014–15. Hon. Fellow, Birmingham Polytechnic, 1991; Judith E. Wilson Fellow, Clare Hall, Cambridge, 1996. Hon. MA Bradford, 1984; DUniv Surrey, 1993; Hon. DLitt: Birmingham, 2002; Warwick, 2012. *Plays*: The National Interest, 1971; Excuses Excuses, Coventry, 1972; Death Story, Birmingham Rep., 1972; Baby Love, 1973; The Dunkirk Spirit, 1974; Dick Deterred, Bush Theatre, 1974; O Fair Jerusalem, Birmingham Rep., 1975; Saigon Rose, Edinburgh, 1976; Blood Sports, incl. Ball Boys, Bush Theatre, 1976; Destiny, Other Place, 1976, Aldwych, 1977; Wreckers, 1977; Our Own People, 1977; (adaptation) The Jail Diary of Albie Sachs, Warehouse Theatre, 1978; (adaptation) Mary Barnes, Birmingham Rep., then Royal Court, 1978–79; (with Susan Todd) Teendreams, 1979; (adaptation) Nicholas Nickleby, Aldwych, 1980, Plymouth Theatre, NY, 1981; Maydays, Barbican, 1983, revival RSC, 2018; Entertaining Strangers, 1985, Nat. Theatre, 1987; That Summer, Hampstead, 1987; (with Stephen Bill and Anne Devlin) Heartlanders, Birmingham Rep., 1989; The Shape of the Table, NT, 1990; (adaptation) Dr Jekyll and Mr Hyde, Barbican, 1991; Pentecost, Other Place, 1994, Young Vic, 1995; (adaptation) Albert Speer, NT, 2000; The Prisoner's Dilemma, RSC, 2001; Continental Divide (2 play cycle, Daughters of the Revolution, and Mothers Against), Oregon Shakespeare Fest./Berkeley Rep., 2003, Barbican, 2004; (trans.) The Life of Galileo, Birmingham Rep.; Playing with Fire, NT, 2005; Testing the Echo, Out of Joint (tour), 2008; Black Tulips (part of The Great Game), Tricycle Th., 2009–10; (adaptation) Arthur & George, Birmingham Rep., 2010; (translation) The Master Builder, Chichester Th., 2010; Written on the Heart, RSC, 2011, transf. Duchess, 2012; Concerning Faith (part of Sixty-Six Books), Bush Th., 2011; If Only, Minerva, Chichester, 2013; (adaptation) A Christmas Carol, RSC, 2017; Trying It On, Warwick Arts Centre, Royal Court, 2018; *TV and radio*: The Eagle has Landed, 1973; Sanctuary, 1973; I know what I meant, 1974; Ecclesiastes, 1977; (with Neil Grant) Vote for Them, 1989; A Movie Starring Me, 1991; Buying a Landslide, 1992; Citizen Locke, 1994; Talking to Mars, 1996; (adaptation) The Secret Parts, 2000; Brave Faces, 2006; Something Wrong about the Mouth, 2007; *film*: Lady Jane, 1986. *Publications*: Destiny, 1976; Wreckers, 1977; The Jail Diary of Albie Sachs, 1978; Teendreams, 1979; Mary Barnes, 1979; Nicholas Nickleby, 1982; Maydays, 1983; Entertaining Strangers, 1985; Plays One, 1987; That Summer, 1987; The Second Time as Farce, 1988; Vote for Them, 1989; Heartlanders, 1989; Edgar Shorts, 1990; Plays Two, 1990; The Shape of the Table, 1990; Plays Three, 1991; Dr Jekyll and Mr Hyde, 1992; Pentecost, 1995; (ed) State of Play, 1999; Albert Speer, 2000; The Prisoner's Dilemma, 2001; Continental Divide, 2004; Playing with Fire, 2005; (with Stephanie Dale) A Time to Keep, 2007; Testing the Echo, 2008; How Plays Work: a practical guide to playwriting, 2009; contrib. Black Tulips, in The Great Game, 2009; Arthur & George, 2010; The Master Builder, 2010; contrib. Concerning Faith, in Sixty-Six Books, 2011; Written on the Heart, 2011; If Only, 2012; (adaptation) A Christmas Carol, 2017; Maydays and Trying It On, 2018. *Recreation*: correspondence. *Address*: c/o Alan Brodie Representation, Paddock Suite, The Courtyard, 55 Charterhouse Street, EC1M 6HA. *T*: (020) 7253 6226.

**EDGAR, George**; *see* Edgar, C. G.

**EDGAR, Pauline Claire**; Principal, Queenswood School, 2006–16; *b* Birmingham, 13 March 1956; *d* of Peter Brown and Christine Brown; *m* 1982, Hamish Edgar; two *s* one *d*. *Educ*: Dudley Girls' High Sch.; Bedford Coll., Univ. of London (BA Hons); Inst. of Educn, Univ. of London (PGCE). Hd, Sixth Form and Hd, History and Politics, Francis Holland Sch., NW1, 1988–2006. *Recreations*: travel, reading, galleries, swimming. *Clubs*: University Women's, Lansdowne.

**EDGAR, William**, CBE 2004; FREng, FIMechE; FRSE; Group Director, John Wood Group plc, 1995–2004; Chairman and Chief Executive, Wood Group Engineering Ltd, 1995–2004; Chairman, J. P. Kenny Engineering Ltd, 1995–2004; *b* 16 Jan. 1938; *s* of William Edgar and Alice Anderson McKerrell; *m* 1961, June Gilmour; two *s*. *Educ*: Royal Coll. of Science and Technology (Strathclyde Univ.), ARCST 1961; Birmingham Univ. (MSc 1962). CEng, FIMechE 1979. Develt Engr, BSC, Motherwell and Glasgow, 1954–62; Principal Aeromech. Engr, BAC, Warton, 1963–67; Chief Develt Engr, Gen. Manager Sales and Service, Gen. Works Manager, Weir Pumps, Glasgow, 1967–73; Chief Exec., Seaforth Engineering and Corporate Develt Dir, Seaforth Maritime, Aberdeen, 1973–86; Business Develt Dir, Vickers Marine Engineering, Edinburgh, 1986–88; Exec. Chm., Cochrane Shipbuilders, Yorks, 1988–90; Chief Exec., Nat. Energy Lab., 1990–95. Chairman: European Marine Energy Centre, 2005–14; Subsea UK Ltd, 2005–; Nat. Subsea Res. Inst., 2009–14; non-exec. Dir, Online Electronics Ltd, 2008–15. Vis. Prof., Strathclyde Univ., 2001–14. Chm., Offshore Contractors Assoc., 2000–03; Pres., IMechE, 2004–05 (Dep. Pres., 2002–04; Chm., Scottish Br., 1996–98). FREng 1999; FRSE 2003. Hon. FIMechE 2009. Liveryman, Engineers' Co., 2006–. Hon. DSc Aberdeen, 2009. *Recreations*: golf, walking, reading, soccer. *Club*: Sloane.

**EDGAR-JONES, Philip**; Director, Sky Arts, since 2014, and Head of Entertainment, Sky, since 2017; *b* Leeds, 13 July 1966; *s* of Edward Jones and Isabella Jones (*née* Macpherson); *m* 1990, Wendy Edgar; one *d*. *Educ*: Royal High Sch., Edinburgh; Queen Margaret Coll., Edinburgh (BA Hons Communication Studies). Journalist, Sky Mag., 1988–90; freelance sub-editor, 1990–92; presenter, Moviewatch, 1992; Series Editor: The Big Breakfast, 1993–96; Jack Docherty Show, 1996–97; The Priory, 1998–2000; Exec. Producer, Big Brother, 2000–11; Hd of Entertainment, BSkyB, 2012–14. Mem. Bd, ENO, 2016–. *Recreations*: poetry composition, opera. *Address*: BSkyB, Grant Way, Isleworth, Middx TW7 5QD. *T*: 07725 235644. *E*: philip.edgar-jones@sky.uk.

**EDGAR-WILSON, Jennifer Chase**; *see* Barnes, J. C.

**EDGCUMBE**, family name of **Earl of Mount Edgcumbe**.

**EDGE, Geoffrey**; Managing Director, Geonomics Ltd, since 2007; *b* 26 May 1943; single. *Educ*: London Sch. of Econs (BA); Birmingham Univ. Asst Lectr in Geography, Univ. of Leicester, 1967–70; Lectr in Geog., Open Univ., 1970–74. Member: Bletchley UDC, 1972–74 (Chm. Planning Sub-cttee 1973–74); Milton Keynes DC, 1973–76 (Vice-Chm. Planning Cttee, 1973–75); Bucks Water Bd, 1973–74; W Midlands CC, 1981–86 (Chm., Econ. Develt Cttee); Walsall MBC, 1983–90 (Leader, 1988–90). MP (Lab) Aldridge-Brownhills, Feb. 1974–1979; PPS to Minister of State for Educn, Feb.–Oct. 1974, 1976–77, to Minister of State, Privy Council Office, Oct. 1974–1976. Research Fellow, Dept of Planning Landscape, Birmingham Polytechnic, 1979–80; Senior Research Fellow: Preston Polytechnic, 1980–81; NE London Polytechnic, 1982–84; Hon. Res. Fellow, Birmingham Polytechnic, 1980–81; New Initiatives Co-ordinator, COPEC Housing Trust, 1984–87; Sen. Associate, P-E Inbucon, then P-E Internat., 1987–97. Chm., West Midlands Enterprise Ltd, 1982–2007; Associate Dir, W. S. Atkins plc, 1997–99; Director: Winning Pitch plc, 2007–09; BCRS Business Loans Ltd, 2017–. *Publications*: (ed jtly) Regional Analysis and Development, 1973; Open Univ. booklets on industrial location and urban development. *Recreations*: music, reading, touring. *Address*: 5 Sedgefield Close, Dudley DY1 2UU.

**EDGE, Prof. Kevin Anthony**, PhD, DSc; CEng, FREng, FIMechE; Professor of Mechanical Engineering, 1991–2015, now Emeritus, and Deputy Vice-Chancellor, 2008–15, University of Bath; *b* 1 July 1949; *s* of George and Marion Edge; *m* 2008, Delyth Ann Davies. *Educ*: Univ. of Bath (BSc 1971; PhD 1975; DSc 1995). CEng 1982; FIMechE 1990. Sen. Control Systems Engr, Rolls Royce Ltd, 1974–76; University of Bath: Res. Officer, 1976; Lectr, 1976–87; Sen. Lectr, 1987–91; Reader, 1991; Dep. Dir, Centre for Power Transmission and Motion Control, 1993–2008; Hd, Mech. Engrg, 1997–2003; Pro-Vice-Chancellor (Research), 2003–08. Trustee, Res. Inst. for Care of Older People, Bath, 2009–. FREng 2003. Hon. DEng Bath, 2016. *Publications*: papers in professional jls. *Recreations*: classical music, photography. *Address*: University of Bath, Claverton Down, Bath BA2 7AY. *E*: k.a.edge@bath.ac.uk.

**EDGE, Captain Sir (Philip) Malcolm**, KCVO 1995; FNI; Deputy Master and Chairman, Board of Trinity House, 1988–96; *b* 15 July 1931; *s* of Stanley Weston Edge and Edith Edge (*née* Liddell); *m* 1st, 1967, (Kathleen) Anne Greenwood (*d* 1994); one *s* one *d*; 2nd, 2003, Carol Mann. *Educ*: Rock Ferry High School; HMS Conway. Master Mariner. Apprenticed to Shipping subsidiary of British Petroleum, 1949, and served in all ranks; in command, world wide, 1969–78. Elder Brother and Mem. Board, Trinity House, 1978; Mem., PLA, 1980–97. Dir, Standard Steamship Owners' Protection & Indemnity Assoc. Ltd, 1988–97 (Chm., 1992–97). Mem. Council, Internat. Assoc. of Lighthouse Authies, 1988–96 (Pres., 1988–90). Freeman, City of London, 1980; Liveryman: Hon. Co. of Master Mariners, 1980–; Shipwrights' Co., 1990–2006; Master, Watermen and Lightermen's Co., 1996–97. *Recreations*: sailing, family. *Address*: c/o Trinity House, Tower Hill, EC3N 4DH. *T*: (020) 7481 6900. *Clubs*: Royal Yacht Squadron (Hon.); Royal Lymington Yacht; The Cachalots (Hon.) (Southampton).

**EDGE, Stephen Martin**; Corporate Tax Partner, Slaughter and May, since 1982; *b* Farnworth, Lancs, 29 Nov. 1950; *s* of late Harry Edge and Mary Edge; *m* 1975, Melanie Lawler (separated); two *d*. *Educ*: Canon Slade Grammar Sch., Bolton; Exeter Univ. (LLB Hons). Admitted solicitor, 1975; joined Slaughter and May, 1973 (Mem., Partnership Bd, 1986–2011). Mem., Practice Council, Internat. Tax Adv. Prog., Sch. of Law, New York Univ., 2011–. Non-exec. Dir, Bournemouth SO, 2013–. Trustee, Tommy's Charity, 2018–. Mem., Alumni Network Gp (formerly Alumni and Develt Bd), Exeter Univ., 2004– (Chm., 2014–). Pres., Amberley CC, 2000–; Vice Pres., Lancs CCC, 2011–. Hon. LLD Exeter, 2012. *Publications*: contrib. to tax pubns. *Recreations*: walking, golf, theatre, watching cricket and soccer. *Address*: Slaughter and May, 1 Bunhill Row, EC1Y 8YY. *T*: (020) 7600 1200, *Fax*: (020) 7090 5000. *E*: steve.edge@slaughterandmay.com. *Club*: MCC.

**EDGE, Titus William Clive**; Headmaster, Gordonstoun School, since 2017; *b* Hong Kong, 18 Sept. 1972; *s* of William Edge and Maria Ford; *m* 1999, Manira Ford; two *s* one *d*. *Educ*: Gordonstoun Sch.; Newcastle Univ. (BA Hons Hist. 1995); St Edmund Hall, Oxford (PGCE (Secondary) 1998). School Master: City of London Sch. for Boys, 1998–99; Dulwich Coll., 1999–2013; Dep. Hd, Gordonstoun Sch., 2013–17. Mem. Bd of Govs, Ardvreck Sch. *Recreations*: history, reading, music, walking the dog, drawing cartoons. *Address*: Headmaster's House, Gordonstoun School, Elgin, Moray IV30 5QZ. *T*: (01343) 837837. *E*: edget@gordonstoun.org.uk.

**EDGE, William**, (3rd Bt *cr* 1937); *S* father, 1984, but does not use the title and his name does not appear on the Official Roll of the Baronetage. *Heir*: *s* Edward Knowles Edge.

**EDGINGTON, Prof. Dorothy Margaret Doig**, FBA 2005; Senior Research Fellow, Department (formerly School) of Philosophy, Birkbeck, University of London, 2006–17, now Emeritus Professor; *b* 29 April 1941; *d* of late Edward Milne and Rhoda Milne (*née* Blair); *m* 1965, John Edgington; one *s* (one *d* decd). *Educ*: St Leonards Sch., St Andrews; St Hilda's Coll., Oxford (BA 1964; Hon. Fellow, 2004); Nuffield Coll., Oxford (BPhil 1967). Lectr in Philosophy, 1968–90, Sen. Lectr, 1990–96, Birkbeck Coll., London Univ.; Prof. of Philosophy, Oxford Univ., and Fellow of UC, Oxford, 1996–2001; Prof. of Philosophy, Birkbeck Coll., London Univ., 2001–03; Waynflete Prof. of Metaphysical Philosophy, Univ. of Oxford, 2003–06, now Emeritus, and Fellow of Magdalen Coll., Oxford, 2003–06. British Acad. Res. Reader in the Humanities, 1992–94; visiting posts: Univ. of British Columbia, 1974–75, 1990, 1992; Univ. Nacional Autónoma de México, 1985, 1988, 1990, 1995; Princeton Univ., 1986; Univ. of Calif, Berkeley, 1993. Pres., Mind Assoc., 2004–05. Hon. Sec., 1986–92, Pres., 2007–08, Aristotelian Soc. (Ed., Proc. of Aristotelian Soc., 1986–90). *Publications*: contrib. anthologies, and learned jls incl. Analysis, British Jl for Philos. of Sci., Crítica, Mind, Proc. of Aristotelian Soc., Revista Latinoamericana de Filosofía. *Address*: Department of Philosophy, Birkbeck, University of London, Malet Street, WC1E 7HX.

**EDINBURGH, Bishop of**, since 2012; **Rt Rev. Dr John Andrew Armes**; *b* London, 10 Sept. 1955; *m* 1983, Clare; one *s* three *d*. *Educ*: Sidney Sussex Coll., Cambridge (BA 1977; MA 1981); Manchester Univ. (PhD 1996); Salisbury and Wells Theol Coll. Ordained deacon, 1979, priest, 1980; Curate, Walney Island, Barrow in Furness, 1979–82; Chaplain: Barrow Sixth Form Coll., 1979–82; Agriculture and Rural Life, Dio. of Carlisle, 1982–86; Team Vicar, Team Ministry of Greystoke, 1982–86; Chaplain, Manchester Univ., 1986–94; Team Vicar, 1986–88, Team Rector, 1988–94, Parish of Whitworth, Manchester; Priest-in-charge, St Mary and All Saints, Goodshaw and St John's Crawshawbooth, 1994–98; Area Dean, Rossendale, 1994–98; Rector, St John the Evangelist, Edinburgh, 1998–2012; Dean of Edinburgh, 2010–12. Hon. Canon, St Mary's Cathedral, Edinburgh, 2010. *Recreations*: cinema, theatre, travel, watching sport, walking, writing unpublishable novels. *Address*: Diocesan Office, 21a Grosvenor Crescent, Edinburgh EH12 5EL. *T*: (0131) 538 7044.

**EDINBURGH, Dean of**; *see* Burberry, Very Rev. F. S.

**EDINBURGH, (St Mary's Cathedral), Provost of**; *see* Conway, Very Rev. J. A.

**EDINGTON, (George) Gordon**, CBE 2007; FRICS; an Ambassador (formerly Vice-President), Action for Children (formerly NCH, the Children's Charity), 1998–2016 (Chair of Trustees, 2001–07); *b* 7 Sept. 1945; *s* of George Adam Edington and Phyllis Mary (*née* Allan); *m* 1st, 1973, Jane Mary Adie (marr. diss. 2007); four *s*; 2nd, 2013, Paula Carrington Edmunds. *Educ*: St Mary's Sch., Kenya; St Lawrence Coll., Kent. FRICS 1970. Man. Dir, Lynton plc, 1981–94; Director: BAA plc, 1991–99; Lend Lease Corp., 1999–2013; Chm., Earls Court and Olympia Gp Ltd, 2000–01. Pres., British Property Fedn, 1998–99. Chairman: Michael Stuckey Trust, 1988–98; Public Art Develt Trust, 1992–98. Trustee: Tennis First Charitable Trust, 1999–2018 (Chm., 2007–18); Fulham Palace Trust, 2011– (Dep. Chm., 2011–18); Dir and Trustee, Sponsoring Bd, Chobham Acad., Stratford, 2013–. Jt Founder, John O'Halloran Symposium, 2016. Gov., Wilson Centre, Cambridge Internat. Land Inst., 1993–98. FRSA 1992; Mem., Henley Royal Regatta. Freeman, City of London, 1994; Liveryman, Chartered Surveyors' Co., 1994–. *Publications*: The Clowes Family of Chester Sporting Artists, 1985; Property Management: a customer focused approach, 1997; Gordon McLean Allan 1912–1942, 2014. *Recreations:* grandchildren, tennis, golf, hill walking, photography, historic Thames rivercraft. *Address:* 78 Hotham Road, SW15 1QP. *E:* gordonedington@snowshill.co.uk. *Clubs:* Royal Wimbledon Golf; Riverside Racquets; Leander (Henley).

**EDINGTON, Martin George Ritchie;** Sheriff of Lothian and Borders at Livingston, since 2009 (at Linlithgow, 2007–09); *b* 28 Oct. 1955; *s* of George and Eva Edington; *m* 1979, Susan Jane Phillips; two *s*. *Educ:* Fettes Coll.; Dundee Univ. (LLB). NP 1981; WS 1985; Partner, Turnbull, Simson & Sturrock, WS, 1983–2001; Temp. Sheriff, 1999–2000; All-Scotland Floating Sheriff, 2001–03; Floating Sheriff at Linlithgow, 2003–07. *Recreations:* fine wines and whiskies, eating, travelling, curling, Rugby, cricket, making decisions. *Address:* Sheriff Court, Howden South Road, Livingston EH54 6FF. *T:* (01506) 402400, *Fax:* (01506) 415262.

**EDIS, Hon. Sir Andrew (Jeremy Coulter),** Kt 2014; **Hon. Mr Justice Edis;** a Judge of the High Court of Justice, Queen's Bench Division, since 2014; a Presiding Judge, South Eastern Circuit, since 2017; *b* 9 June 1957; *s* of late Dr Peter Marcus Edis and Barbara Louise Edis; *m* 1984, Sandy Wilkinson; one *s* two *d*. *Educ:* Liverpool Coll.; University Coll., Oxford (MA). Called to the Bar, Middle Temple, 1980, Bencher, 2004; Junior, Northern Circuit, 1983–84; Asst Recorder, 1994–99; QC 1997; Recorder, 1999–2014; Sen. Treasury Counsel, 2009–14; Dep. High Court Judge, 2001–14. Hd of Atlantic Chambers, 2000–06. Mem., Investigatory Powers Tribunal, 2019–. *Recreations:* cricket, travel. *Address:* Royal Courts of Justice, Strand, WC2A 2LL.
See also A. W. B. Edis.

**EDIS, (Angus) William (Butler);** QC 2008; a Recorder, since 2005; *b* Liverpool, 15 June 1961; *s* of late Dr Peter Marcus Edis and Barbara Louise Edis; *m* 1996, Mary Elizabeth Pinder; two *s*. *Educ:* Liverpool Coll.; Trinity Coll., Oxford (BA Lit.Hum.; MA); City Univ. (Dip. Law). Called to the Bar, Lincoln's Inn, 1985; in practice, specialising in healthcare and disciplinary law. *Publications:* contribs to medico-legal jls. *Recreations:* family, football, explaining that I am not my brother. *Address:* (chambers) 1 Crown Office Row, Temple, EC4Y 7HH. *T:* (020) 7797 7500, *Fax:* (020) 7797 7550.
See also Hon. Sir A. J. C. Edis.

**EDKINS, Dr Antony John Jameson;** Lead Inspector, Office for Standards in Education, since 2018; *b* Hillingdon, 15 April 1969; *s* of Daisy Veronica Small, thereafter adopted and fostered; *m* 2007, Annette Mary Frances Rand; one *d* and one step *s* one step *d*. *Educ:* Univ. of Exeter (BA Hons); Ridley Hall, Cambridge (PGCE); Brunel Univ. (MEd; Postgrad. Dip.); Univ. of Leicester (MBA); Univ. of Sussex (EdD 2006); Coll. of Preceptors, London (ACP). Hd of RE, Westgate Sch., Slough, 1991–93; Hd of RE, Charters Sch., Sunningdale, 1993–96; Hd of Year and of Curriculum Develt, Longford Sch., Feltham, 1996–98; Dep. Headteacher, then Headteacher, Falmer High Sch., Brighton, 1998–2003; Hd, Secondary Sch. Improvement, E Sussex, 2003–04; Exec. Headteacher, Harrop Fold High Sch., Salford, 2004–10; Chief Exec., Landau Forte Charitable Trust, 2014–17. Hon. Asst Lectr, Univ. of Brighton and Brunel Univ., 1998–2004. Hon. Mem., Grenadier Guards Assoc., 2013 (Battle of Inkerman Award, 2016, 2017). FCollP 1997; FRSA. *Publications:* contrib. articles on educnl leadership and on factors that cause educnl failure; book reviews for British Educnl Res. Jl and Educnl Mgt and Leadership Jl. *Recreations:* opera, gym, public speaking. *Address:* 11 Stafford Road, Eccles M30 9HN. *T:* 07717 703944.

**EDMISTON,** family name of **Baron Edmiston**.

**EDMISTON,** Baron *cr* 2011 (Life Peer), of Lapworth in the County of Warwickshire; **Robert Norman Edmiston;** Chairman, IM Group Ltd, since 1988; *b* New Delhi, India, 6 Oct. 1946; *s* of Vivian Edmiston and Norma Margaret Mary Edmiston (*née* Grostate); *m* 1998, Tracie Jacqueline Spicer; one *s* two *d* by a former marriage. *Educ:* Abbs Cross Technical High Sch., Hornchurch; Barking Regl Coll. of Technol. ACMA 1974, FCMA 1991. Bank Clerk, English, Scottish and Australian Bank, 1964–66; Treasury Clerk, Chrysler International SA Treasury, 1966–67; Financial Analyst, Ford Motor Co., 1967–70; Chrysler (UK) Ltd: Sen. Analyst, 1970–71; Capital Planning Manager, 1971–72; Economic Res. Analyst, 1972; Manager, Financial Analysis and Admin, 1972–74; Financial Controller and Co. Sec., 1974–75, Dir of Finance, 1975–76, Jensen Motors Ltd; Man. Dir, Jenson Parts and Service Ltd, 1976–80; Chm., International Motors Ltd, 1980–88. Mem., H of L, 2011–15. Chm., Midlands Industrial Council, 2002–10. Founder and Trustee, Christian Vision, 1988–; Founder, Grace Foundn, 2003–; Sponsor and Gov., Grace Academies, 2003–. *Recreations:* playing guitar, golf, ski-ing, tennis, scuba.

**EDMONDS, David Albert,** CBE 2003; Chairman, NHS Shared Business Services, since 2005; *b* 6 March 1944; *s* of Albert and Gladys Edmonds; *m* 1966, Ruth Beech; two *s* two *d*. *Educ:* Helsby County Grammar School; University of Keele. BA Hons Political Institutions and History. Asst Principal, Min. of Housing and Local Govt, 1966–69; Private Sec. to Parly Sec., MHLG and DoE, 1969–71; Principal, DoE, 1971–73; Observer, CSSB, 1973–74; Vis. Fellow, Centre for Metropolitan Planning and Research, Johns Hopkins Univ., 1974–75; Private Sec. to Perm. Sec., DoE, 1975–77; Asst Sec., DoE, 1977–79; Principal Private Sec. to Sec. of State, DoE, 1979–83; Under Sec., Inner Cities Directorate, DoE, 1983–84; Chief Exec., Housing Corporation, 1984–91; Gen. Manager, then Man. Dir, Central Services, NatWest Gp, 1991–97; Dir Gen. of Telecommns, 1998–2003. Dir, Housing Finance Corp., 1988–91; Member: Bd, English Partnerships, 2000–03; Steering Bd, Radiocommunications Agency, 1998–2003; OFCOM, 2002–05; Bd, Legal Services Commn, 2004–08; Chairman: NHS Direct, 2004–08; Legal Services Bd, 2008–14; London Legacy Develt Corp. (formerly Olympic Park Legacy Co.), 2015–16 (non-exec. Dir, 2009–16). Non-executive Director: Hammerson PLC, 2003–11 (Chm., Pension Trustees, 2005–14); Wincanton plc, 2003–11 (Chm., 2008–11); William Hill plc, 2005–14; Barchester Healthcare Ltd, 2012–17; Chairman: Swanton Care and Community Ltd, 2012–14; E20 LLP, 2014–; Phone-paid Services Authy (formerly Phonepay Plus), 2015–. Pres., Internat. New Town Assoc., 1987–91; Mem. Cttee, Notting Hill Housing Trust, 1991–94. Dep. Chm., New Statesman and Society, 1988–90 (Chm., New Society, 1986–88). Mem. Bd, Social Market Foundn, 2001–09. Chair of Trustees, Crisis, 1996–2002; Chm., British Motor Racing Drivers Club Pension Trustees, 2019–. Mem. Council, Chm., Finance Cttee, and Univ. Treas., Keele Univ., 1997–2003; Chm. Governing Bd, Kingston Univ., 2012–; Mem. Bd, Trinity Laban Conservatoire, 2014–17. Hon. DLitt Keele, 2004. *Recreations:* opera, walking, golf. *Address:* 61 Cottenham Park Road, West Wimbledon, SW20 0DR. *T:* (020) 8946 3729. *Clubs:* MCC; Wimbledon Park Golf (Captain, 1997–98; Pres., 2015–18).

**EDMONDS, John Christopher Paul,** CBE 1993; Chief Executive, Railtrack, 1993–97; *b* 22 April 1936; *s* of late Frank Winston Edmonds and Phyllis Mary Edmonds; *m* 1962, Christine Elizabeth Seago; one *s* one *d*. *Educ:* Lowestoft Grammar School; Trinity College, Cambridge. Nat. Service Commission, RAF, 1955–57. Joined British Rail, 1960; Chief Freight Manager, London Midland Region, 1981; Nat. Business Manager, Coal, 1982; Dir, Provincial, 1984; Gen. Manager, Anglia Region, 1987; Bd Mem., and Man. Dir, Gp Services, 1989–93. *Recreations:* theatre, music, gardening.

**EDMONDS, John Walter;** General Secretary, GMB (formerly General, Municipal, Boilermakers and Allied Trades Union), 1986–2003; *b* 28 Jan. 1944; *s* of Walter and Rose Edmonds; *m* 1967, Linden (*née* Callaby) (*d* 2018); two *d*. *Educ:* Brunswick Park Primary; Christ's Hosp.; Oriel Coll., Oxford (BA 1965, MA 1968). General and Municipal Workers' Union: Res. Asst, 1966; Dep. Res. Officer, 1967; Reg. Officer, 1968; Nat. Industrial Officer, 1972. Mem. Council, ACAS, 1992–2000. Pres., TUC, 1997–98. Chm., TU Adv. Cttee on Sustainable Develt, 1998–2003. Director: National Building Agency, 1978–82; Unity Trust Bank, 1986–2003 (Pres., 2001–03). Mem., Royal Commn on Environmental Pollution, 1979–89; a Forestry Comr, 1995–2001; Director: EA, 2002–09; Carbon Trust, 2002–13; Chair: Inland Waterways Adv. Council, 2006–12; River Thames Alliance, 2012–16. Dir, Salix Finance, 2004–. Vice Chair, Comprehensive Future Ltd, 2015–. Vis. Fellow, Nuffield Coll., Oxford, 1986–94; Res. Fellow, KCL, 2003–; Vis. Prof., Durham Univ. Business Sch., 2014–. Mem. Council, Consumers' Assoc., 1991–96. Trustee: Inst. of Public Policy Research, 1988–2002; NSPCC, 1995–2002. Gov., LSE, 1986–95. Hon. LLD Sussex, 1994. *Publications:* with Eva Tutchell: Man-made: why so few women are in positions of power, 2015; The Stalled Revolution: is equality for women an impossible dream?, 2018. *Recreations:* cricket, carpentry. *Address:* 50 Graham Road, Mitcham, Surrey CR4 2HA. *T:* (020) 8648 9991.

**EDMONDS, Prof. Michael Edwin,** MD; FRCP; Consultant Physician, King's College Hospital, London, since 1986; *b* Wareham, Dorset, 28 Aug. 1948; *s* of Arthur Percy Edmonds and Freda Joan Edmonds; *m* 1982; one *s*. *Educ:* Swanage Grammar Sch.; King's Coll. Hosp. Med. Sch. (BSc 1969; AKC 1969; MB BS 1972; MD 1985). MRCP 1977, FRCP 1991. Jun. appts, KCH and Poole and Weymouth Hosps, 1973–77; Med. Registrar, St Stephen's Hosp., Chelsea, 1977–79; Res. Fellow and Lectr, Diabetic Dept, KCH, 1979–86; Hon. Sen. Lectr, Diabetic Dept, 1986–2007, Hon. Prof. of Diabetic Foot Medicine, 2007–, KCL. Arnold Bloom Lectr, Diabetes UK, 2015. Karel Bakker Internat. Foot Award, 2011; Edward James Olmos Award for Advocacy in Amputation Prevention, 2014. *Publications:* (with A. V. M. Foster) Managing the Diabetic Foot, 2000 (trans. Spanish, 2004), 2nd edn 2005 (trans. Japanese, 2006); (jtly) A Practical Manual of Diabetic Foot Care, 2004 (Med. Book of Year, BMA, 2004) (trans. Chinese 2006), 3rd edn 2014; (with A. V. M. Foster) A Colour Atlas of the Foot and Ankle, 2008; (with A. V. M. Foster) Diabetic Foot Care: case studies in clinical management, 2010. *Address:* Diabetic Foot Clinic, King's College Hospital, Denmark Hill, SE5 9RS. *T:* (020) 3299 3223, *Fax:* (020) 3299 4536. *E:* michael.edmonds@nhs.net.

**EDMONDS, Noel E.;** DL; television presenter; *b* 22 Dec. 1948; *s* of Dudley Edmonds and Lydia Edmonds; *m* 1st, 1971, Gillian Slater (marr. diss.); 2nd, 1986, Helen Soby (marr. diss.); four *d*; 3rd, 2009, Liz Davies. *Educ:* Brentwood Sch. Newsreader, Radio Luxembourg, 1968–69; presenter, BBC Radio, 1969–2000, incl. Breakfast Show, 1973–78; BBC TV, 1970–2000; presenter, BBC TV series: Z Shed, 1975; Multicoloured Swap Shop, 1976–81; Lucky Numbers, 1978; The Late Late Breakfast Show, 1982–86; Time of Your Life, 1983; Telly Addicts, 1985–98; Saturday Roadshow, 1987; Noel's House Party, 1991–99; presenter: Channel 4 TV series, Deal or No Deal, 2005–16, Noel's HQ, 2008–09, Cheap Cheap Cheap, 2017; Sky One series, Are You Smarter Than a 10 Year Old?, 2007–; appeared: Road to Saigon, 2018; I'm a Celebrity Get Me Out of Here, 2018. Chm., Unique Group, 1985–2007. DL Devon, 2004. *E:* john@johnmiles.org.uk.

**EDMONDS-BROWN, (Cedric Wilfred) George;** HM Diplomatic Service, retired; Executive Secretary, Canada-UK Council (formerly Colloquia), 2001–16; *b* 24 April 1939; *s* of late Maj. W. R. E. Edmonds-Brown and E. M. Edmonds-Brown; *m* 1st, 1964, Everild A. V. Hardman (*d* 1988); one *s* two *d*; 2nd, 1990, Teiko Watanabe; one *s* one *d*. *Educ:* Dame Allan's Boys' Sch., Newcastle; King's Coll., Durham Univ. Joined CRO, 1962; Lagos, 1963; Karachi, 1964–68; Third Sec., Buenos Aires, 1968–73; FCO, 1973–76; Second Sec., Bucharest, 1976–80; First Sec. and HM Consul, Caracas, 1980–85; ODA, 1985–88; Head of Chancery, Ottawa, 1988; Dep. High Comr, Barbados, 1989–91; First Sec., Rome, 1991–95, Geneva, 1995–97; Consul, Geneva, 1997–99. *Recreations:* writing, art, travel, cricket. *Address:* 4 The Willows, Wootton, Oxon OX1 5LD.

**EDMONDSON,** family name of **Baron Sandford**.

**EDMONDSON, Alex;** *see* Crawford, A. C.

**EDMONDSON, Rt Rev. Christopher Paul;** Bishop Suffragan of Bolton, 2008–16; an Honorary Assistant Bishop, Diocese of Leeds, since 2016; *b* Carlisle, 25 June 1950; *s* of Jack and Margaret Edmondson; *m* 1973, Susan Heap; two *s*. *Educ:* St John's Coll., Durham Univ. (BA 1971, MA 1981); Cranmer Hall, Durham (DipTh 1972). Ordained deacon, 1973, priest, 1974; Asst Curate, Kirkheaton, Huddersfield, 1973–79; Vicar, St George's, Halifax, 1979–86; Diocesan Officer for Evangelism, Dio. of Carlisle, 1986–92; Vicar, St Peter's, Shipley, 1992–2002; Warden, Lee Abbey, Devon, 2002–08. Hon. Chaplain, Yorks CCC, 2019–. Chair of Trustees, Scargill House, N Yorks, 2009–. Occasional Lectr, St Hild Coll., Mirfield, 2018–. Mem., British Inst. of Innkeepers, 2004. Gov., Woodhouse Grove Sch., 2017–. Chm., Aire Valley Singers, 2017–. *Publications:* Strategies for Rural Evangelism, 1989; How Shall They Hear?, 1994; Minister, Love Thyself, 2000; Fit to Lead, 2002, 3rd edn 2009; (contrib.) Vicar's Guide, 2004; (jtly) Celebrating Community, 2006; Leaders Learning to Listen, 2010. *Recreations:* cricket, football, playing piano, guitar and organ (former organ scholar), walking. *Address:* 16 Cavalier Drive, Apperley Bridge, Bradford BD10 0UF. *T:* 07817 511118. *E:* chris.edmondson@me.com.

**EDMONSTONE, Sir Archibald (Bruce Charles),** 7th Bt *cr* 1774; *b* 3 Aug. 1934; *o* surv. *s* of Sir Charles Edmonstone, 6th Bt, and Gwendolyn Mary (*d* 1989), *d* of late Marshall Field and Mrs Maldwin Drummond; *S* father, 1954; *m* 1st, 1957, Jane (marr. diss. 1967), *er d* of Maj.-Gen. E. C. Colville, CB, DSO; two *s* one *d*; 2nd, 1969, Juliet Elizabeth, *d* of Maj.-Gen. C. M. F. Deakin, CB, CBE; one *s* one *d*. *Educ:* St Peter's Court; Stowe Sch. *Heir: s* Archibald Edward Charles Edmonstone [*b* 4 Feb. 1961; *m* 1988, Ursula (marr. diss. 1994), *e d* of late Benjamin Worthington]. *Address:* Duntreath Castle, Blanefield, Stirlingshire G63 9AJ.

**EDMONTON, Area Bishop of,** since 2015; **Rt Rev. Robert James Wickham;** *b* 3 May 1972; *s* of John and Christine Wickham; *m* 2000, Helen Parker; two *s* one *d*. *Educ:* Grey Coll., Durham (BA 1994); Ridley Hall, Cambridge; King's Coll. London (MA 2012). Ordained deacon, 1998, priest, 1999; Curate: St Mary, Willesden, 1998–2001; St Mary the Virgin, Somers Town, 2001–03; Team Vicar, Old Church, St Pancras, 2003–07; Rector, St John-at-Hackney, 2007–15; Area Dean, Hackney, 2014–15. *Publications:* (contrib.) Anglican Church School Education, 2012. *Address:* 27 Thurlow Road, NW3 5PP. *E:* bishop.edmonton@london.anglican.org.

**EDMUNDS, Alan Geoffrey;** Editorial Director, Reach plc (formerly Trinity Mirror) Regionals, since 2017 (Deputy Editorial Director, 2016–17); *b* 2 Aug. 1959; *s* of Geoffrey and Carol Edmunds; *m* 1988, Susanne; three *d*. *Educ:* Bristol Univ. (LLB Hons 1984); UC Cardiff (Postgrad. Dip. Journalism 1986). Ed., Wales on Sunday, 1997–2002; Man. Dir, Media Wales Ltd, 2011–12; Ed., Western Mail, 2002–16; Man. Dir and Ed.-in-Chief,

Media Wales Ltd, 2012–16. *Recreations:* football, tennis, Rugby Union, reading, coin collecting, children's TV trivia from the 1970s. *Address:* 10 Duffryn Avenue, Lakeside, Cardiff CF23 6LF. *T:* (029) 2024 4747.

**EDMUNDS, Martin James Simpson;** QC 2006; **His Honour Judge Edmunds;** a Circuit Judge, since 2009; a Senior Circuit Judge, since 2017; Resident Judge, Isleworth Crown Court, since 2017; Hon. Recorder, Royal Borough of Kensington and Chelsea; *b* 4 Dec. 1959; *s* of Brian Edmunds and Moira Edmunds. *Educ:* Brentwood Sch., Essex; Corpus Christi Coll., Cambridge (BA 1982). Called to the Bar, Middle Temple, 1983, Bencher, 2014; barrister, Walnut House, Exeter, and 33 Chancery Lane, London; a Recorder, 1999–2009. Freeman, Stationers' Co.

**EDMUNDS, Prof. Michael Geoffrey,** PhD; Professor of Astrophysics, Cardiff University, 1997–2007, now Emeritus; *b* 18 June 1949; *s* of Geoffrey and Joyce Edmunds; *m* 1987, Margaret Morris; one *d*, and one step *d*. *Educ:* Woking Co. Grammar Sch.; Downing Coll., Cambridge (BA Natural Scis 1971; PhD 1976). FRAS 1975; FInstP, CPhys 2003. Bye-Fellow, Downing Coll., Cambridge, 1973–74; Cardiff University: Res. Fellow, 1974–76; Lectr, 1976–88; Sen. Lectr, 1988–96; Reader, 1996–97; Hd, Sch. of Physics and Astronomy, 2003–06. Chm., Antikythera Mechanism Res. Project, 2005–. Royal Astronomical Society: Darwin Lectr, 2004; Mem. Council, 2007–10; Chm., Astronomical Heritage Cttee, 2009–17; Vice-Pres., 2014–16; Chm., Curriculum Cttee, Inst. of Physics, 2013–. Member: PPARC, 2004–07 (Chm., Sci. and Soc. Adv. Panel, 2004–11); Sci. and Technol. Facilities Council, 2007–10. Vice-Pres., William Herschel Soc., 2017–. Giuseppe Sciacca Prize for Physics, Internat. Assoc. Culture and Voluntary Work, 2018. *Publications:* res. papers in Nature, Monthly Notices of RAS, Astrophysical Jl, etc. *Recreations:* walking, sailing, drama, music, old railways. *Address:* School of Physics and Astronomy, Cardiff University, Queens Buildings, The Parade, Cardiff CF24 3AA. *T:* (029) 2087 4458, *Fax:* (029) 2087 4056. *E:* mge@astro.cf.ac.uk; 3 Tyrwhitt Crescent, Roath Park, Cardiff CF23 5QP.

**EDNEY, James David;** public sector consultant and pension fund independent adviser, since 2007; *b* 22 April 1953; *s* of late James William John Edney and Alma Mary Edney; *m* 1974, Heather Anita Sayer; one *s* two *d*. *Educ:* Dr Morgan's Grammar Sch., Bridgwater; Univ. of Newcastle upon Tyne (BA Hons (Hist.)); New Coll., Durham (CPFA 1979). Asst Dir, Finance and Admin, Cambridgeshire CC, 1985–89; Deputy County Treasurer: Lincolnshire CC, 1989–91; Essex CC, 1991–2002; Chief Financial Officer, Essex CC, 2002–03; Dep. Chief Exec. and Exec. Dir of Resources, Lancashire CC, 2003–06. Non-exec. Dir, Blackpool NHS Foundn Trust, 2013–16 (Chair, Audit Cttee, 2013–16). Mem. Bd, Univ. of Central Lancashire, 2012– (Chair: Audit Cttee, 2013–16; Resources Cttee, 2016–; Vice Chair, Bd, 2018–). Treas., St Annes on the Sea URC, 2012–. *T:* 07805 322721. *E:* jde388@gmail.com.

**EDSON, Ven. Michael;** Archdeacon of Leicester, 1994–2002, now Archdeacon Emeritus; Acting Archdeacon of Barnstaple, 2014–15; *b* 2 Sept. 1942; *s* of Joseph Pratt and Elsie (*née* Edson); name changed to Edson, 1989; *m* 1968, (Ann) Frances Tuffley; three *s* one *d*. *Educ:* Univ. of Birmingham (BSc Hons 1964); Univ. of Leeds (BA Hons 1971); College of the Resurrection, Mirfield. Management Consultant, 1966–68. Ordained deacon, 1972, priest, 1973; Curate, Barnstaple, Devon, 1972–77; Team Vicar, Barnstaple, 1977–82; Chaplain, N Devon Dist Hosp., 1976–82; Vicar, Roxbourne, Harrow, 1982–89; Area Dean of Harrow, 1985–89; Warden of Lee Abbey Fellowship, Devon, 1989–94. Leicester Diocesan Evangelist, 1997–2002; Team Rector, Torridge Estuary Team Ministry, 2002–09. *Publications:* The Renewal of the Mind, 1988; Loved into Life, 1993. *Recreations:* hill-walking, people, writing, spirituality, art, upholstery. *Address:* 11 Belmont Road, Ilkley, Yorks LS29 8PE.

**EDUR, Agnes;** *see* Oaks, A.

**EDUR, Thomas,** CBE 2010; Order of White Star, 3rd Cl. (Estonia), 2001; former ballet dancer; teacher; choreographer; Artistic Director, Estonian National Ballet, since 2009; *b* 20 Jan. 1969; *s* of Enn and Ludmilla Edur; *m* 1990, Agnes Oaks, *qv* (separated); one *d*; partner, Alena Shkatula. *Educ:* Estonian State Ballet Sch. Principal Dancer: Estonian Nat. Opera, 1988–90; English Nat. Ballet, 1990–96; Birmingham Royal Ballet, 1996–97; internat. freelance dancer, and with English Nat. Ballet, 1997–2009, with Zurich Ballet, 2000–01. Guest Artist: La Scala, Milan, 1994–2001; Finnish Nat. Opera, 1999–2004; Berlin Staatsoper, 2000–02; Cape Town City Ballet, 2001–07. Choreographed: one-act ballets: Serenade de Florence, and Mozart, Estonian Th., Vanemuine, 2005; Anima, 2006; full length ballets: Modigliani, 2012; La Bayadère, 2013, The Sleeping Beauty, 2014; Swan Lake, 2016; Katarina, 2018; Romeo and Juliet, 2019; *other works:* Forever, 2000; Fete Polonaise, 2008; Silent Monologues, St Paul's Cathedral, 2009; duet, Chase, 2017; other appearances include: Concert for Diana, 2007; Royal Variety Performance, 2007. Patron: British Ballet Orgn, 2004; English Nat. Ballet Sch., 2008–. Evening Standard Award, 1994; Best Dancer Award and Unique Partnership Award (with Agnes Oaks), Critics Circle, 2003; Laurence Olivier Award for Outstanding Achievement in Dance (with Agnes Oaks), 2004. *Recreations:* cycling, nature, reading, photography. *Address:* Estonian National Ballet, National Opera and Ballet Theatre, Estonia av. 4, Tallinn 10148, Estonia. *E:* t.edur@ballet.ee.

**EDWARD, Rt Hon. Sir David (Alexander Ogilvy),** KCMG 2004 (CMG 1981); PC 2005; QC (Scotland) 1974; FRSE; Judge of the Court of Justice of the European Communities, 1992–2004 (Judge of the Court of First Instance, 1989–92); Temporary Judge, Court of Session, Scotland, 2004–09; *b* 14 Nov. 1934; *s* of J. O. C. Edward, Travel Agent, Perth; *m* 1962, Elizabeth Young McSherry; two *s* two *d*. *Educ:* Sedbergh Sch.; University Coll., Oxford (Hon. Fellow, 1995); Edinburgh Univ. Sub-Lt RNVR (Nat. Service); HMS Hornet, 1956–57. Admitted Advocate, 1962; Clerk of Faculty of Advocates, 1967–70, Treasurer, 1970–77. Pres., Consultative Cttee of Bars and Law Societies, EC, 1978–80; Salvesen Prof. of European Instns and Dir, Europa Inst., 1985–89, Hon. Prof., 1990, Prof. Emeritus, 2008, Univ. of Edinburgh. Mem. Law Adv. Cttee, British Council, 1974–88; Specialist Advr, H of L Select Cttee on EC, 1985, 1986 and 1987. Mem., Panel of Arbitrators, Internat. Centre for Settlement of Investment Disputes, 1981–89 and 2004–. Director: Continental Assets Trust plc, 1985–89 (Chm.); Adam & Co. Group plc, 1983–89; Harris Tweed Association Ltd, 1984–89. Member: Foundation Senate, Europa Universität Viadrina, Frankfurt/Oder, 1991–93; Bd of Trustees, Acad. of European Law, Trier, 1993–. Trustee: Nat. Library of Scotland, 1966–95; Industry and Parlt Trust, 1995–2013 (Vice Pres., 2013–); Carnegie Trust for Univs of Scotland, 1996–2015 (Chm., 2003–15); Council for the Defence of British Univs, 2013–. Chm., Scottish Council of Ind. Schs, 2005–10; Member: Scotland Cttee, British Council, 2008–14; Commn on Scottish Devolution, 2008–09; Commn on a Bill of Rights, 2011–12; First Minister of Scotland's Standing Council on Europe, 2016–. Vice-Pres., British Inst. Internat. and Comparative Law, 2002–. Patron, Scottish European Educn Trust, 2014–. President: Johnson Soc., Lichfield, 1995; Franco-Scottish Soc., 1996–2015; Edinburgh Sir Walter Scott Club, 2001–02. FRSE 1990 (Royal Medal, 2005). Hon. Bencher, Gray's Inn, 1992. Hon. LLD: Edinburgh, 1993; Aberdeen, 1997; Napier, 1998; Glasgow, 2003; St Andrews, 2015; DUniv Surrey, 2003; Dr (*hc*): Saarbrücken, 2001; Münster, 2001. Distinguished Cross, First Class, Order of St Raymond of Penafort (Spain), 1979; Officier de la Légion d'Honneur (France), 2012; Chevalier de l'Ordre des Arts et des Lettres (France), 2012. *Publications:* The Professional Secret, Confidentiality and Legal Professional Privilege in the EEC, 1976; (with R. C. Lane) European Community Law: an introduction, 1991, 3rd rev. edn 2013; European Union Law, 2013; articles in legal jls, etc. *Address:* 32 Heriot Row, Edinburgh EH3 6ES. *Clubs:* Athenæum; New (Edinburgh).

**EDWARDES,** family name of **Baron Kensington**.

**EDWARDS, Alan Francis;** publicist, since 1976; Chairman, Outside Organisation Ltd, since 2015 (Chief Executive Officer, 1994–2015); *b* London, 19 July 1955; *s* of Harrington and Elizabeth Edwards; four *d*. Journalist, Sounds, Record Mirror, 1973; with Keith Altham Publicity, 1974–77; formed Modern Publicity, 1977, Grant Edwards Mgt, 1980; Entertainment Dir, Rogers & Cowan, 1989; Poole Edwards PR, 1990. Contributing Ed., GQ mag., 2005–. *Recreations:* reading, watching Arsenal FC. *Address:* The Outside Organisation Ltd, Charles House, 5–11 Regent Street, St James's, SW1Y 4LR. *T:* (020) 7436 3633, *Fax:* (020) 7462 2920. *Club:* Ivy.

**EDWARDS, Rev. Canon Aled,** OBE 2006; Chief Executive, CYTÛN Churches Together in Wales, since 2006; *b* 4 Oct. 1955; *s* of David Samuel Edwards and Katie Olwen Edwards; *m* 1976, Susan Marie Ball; two *s* one *d*. *Educ:* St David's UC, Lampeter (BA Jt Hons Hist. and Theol. Wales 1977); Trinity Coll., Bristol. Ordained deacon, 1979, priest, 1980; Asst Curate, Glanogwen, 1979–82; Vicar: Llandinorwig with Penisa'rwaun, 1982–85; Botwnnog, 1985–93; Dewi Sant, Cardiff, 1993–99; CYTÛN Nat. Assembly Liaison Officer, 1999–2006. Metropolitical Canon, Llandaff Cathedral, 2014–. Wales Comr, Commn for Racial Equality, 2006–07; Mem., Wales Cttee, Equality and Human Rights Commn, 2007–. Dir, Millennium Stadium plc, 2013–. Mem., Gorsedd of Bards, 2008. Recognising Achievement Award, Welsh Assembly Govt, 2010. *Publications:* Transforming Power: a Christian reflection on Welsh devolution, 2001; From Protest to Process: stories from the National Assembly for Wales, 2003; West Wing Wales - Obama for America: a Welsh campaign experience, 2009. *Recreations:* supporting Llanelli Scarlets, watching West Wing, running ultra marathons. *Address:* CYTÛN, 58 Richmond Road, Cardiff CF24 3AT. *T:* (029) 2046 4378. *E:* aled@cytun.cymru.

**EDWARDS, (Alfred) Kenneth,** CBE 1989 (MBE 1963); Deputy Director-General, Confederation of British Industry, 1982–88; Director: Reliance Bank Ltd, 1992–2008; Salvation Army Trustee Co., 1996–2006; SATCOL Ltd, 2003–10; *b* 24 March 1926; *s* of late Ernest Edwards and Florence Edwards (*née* Branch); *m* 1st, 1949, Jeannette Lilian (*d* 2002), *d* of David Speeks, MBE; one *s* two *d*; 2nd, 2004, Jenefer, *d* of John Nicholas. *Educ:* Latymer Upper Sch.; Magdalene Coll., Cambridge; University Coll. London. Served RAF, 1944–47; RAF Coll., Cranwell, 1945, FO (Pilot). Entered HMOCS, Nigeria, 1952; Provincial Administration, Warri and Benin, 1952–54; Lagos Secretariat, 1954; Sen. Asst Sec., Nigerian Min. of Communications and Aviation, 1959; retired, 1962. Secretary, British Radio Equipment Manufrs' Assoc., 1962; Gp Marketing Manager, Thorn Elec. Industries Ltd, 1965; Internat. Dir, Brookhirst Igranic Ltd (Thorn Gp), 1967; Gp Marketing Dir, Cutler Hammer Europa, 1972; Dep. Chm., BEAMA Overseas Trade Cttee, 1973; Chief Exec., BEAMA, 1976–82. CBI: Member: Council, 1974, 1976–82; Finance and Gen. Purposes Cttee, 1977–82; Vice-Chm., Eastern Reg. Council, 1974; Chm., Working Party on Liability for Defective Products, 1978–82; Mem., President's Cttee, 1979–82. Chm., Facilities & Properties Management Plc, 1989–91; Dir, Polar Electronics PLC, 1984–96. Member: Elec. Engrg EDC, 1976; Council, Elec. Res. Assoc. Ltd, 1976–82; Exec. Cttee, ORGALIME, 1976–82; Management Bd, Eur. Cttee for Develt of Vocational Training, 1988–; BSI Bd, 1978–82, 1984–89 (Chm., British Electrotechnical Cttee and Electrotechnical Divisional Council, 1981–82; Chm., Quality Policy Cttee, 1988–); BOTB, 1982–88; BTEC, 1983–89; BBC Consultative Gp on Indust. and Business Affairs, 1983–88; Bd and Exec. Cttee, Business in the Community, 1987–88; President: CENELEC, 1977–79; Liaison Cttee for Electrical and Electronic Industries, ORGALIME, 1979–82 (Chm., 1980–82). Mem. Exec. Cttee, 1982–89, and Chm. Finance Cttee, 1983–89, UNICE. Dep. Chm., Salvation Army Adv. Bd, 1995–2000 (Mem., 1982). Mem. Court, Cranfield Inst. of Technol., 1970–75. *Publications:* contrib. technical jls; lectures and broadcasts on industrial subjects. *Recreations:* music, books, walking. *Address:* Greenfield House, Bedford Road, Rushden, Northants NN10 0ND. *Club:* Royal Air Force.

**EDWARDS, Andrew John Cumming,** CB 1994; composer and conductor; Deputy Secretary, HM Treasury, 1990–95; public sector consultant, 1995–2014; *b* 3 Nov. 1940; *s* of John Edwards and Norah Hope Edwards (*née* Bevan); *m* 1st, 1964, Charlotte Anne Chilcot (marr. diss. 1987); one *s* two *d*; 2nd, 1994, Ursula Mary Richardson; one *s*. *Educ:* Fettes Coll., Edinburgh; St John's Coll., Oxford (MA); Harvard Univ. (AM, MPA). Asst master, Malvern Coll., 1962–63; HM Treasury: Asst Principal, 1963–67; Pvte Sec. to Jt Perm. Sec., 1966–67; Principal, 1967–75; Harkness Fellow, Harvard Univ., 1971–73; Asst Sec., 1975–83; RCDS, 1979; Asst Sec., DES, 1983–85; Under Sec., HM Treasury, 1985–89. Professional advr to Greenbury Cttee, 1995; conducted reviews of BM, 1996, Financial Regulation in Crown Dependencies, 1998, Finance Ministries of Bulgaria, 1999, Slovakia, 2000, Greece, 2002, and HM Land Registry, 2000–01; Mem., Financial Issues Adv. Gp for Scottish Parliament, 1998; Chm., Acacia Prog., 2002–05; Leader, OGC Gateway Reviews, 2003–14. Chm., Bishop Gilpin Sch. Appeal, 2001–02. Gov., British Inst. of Recorded Sound, 1974–79; Sec., Bd of Dirs, Royal Opera House, 1988–2006 (Sec., Develt Bd, 1984–87); Chm. Trustees, Wimbledon Music Fest., 2009–14, 2017–18. Music Dir, Academy Choir and Orchs, Wimbledon, 1980–2016. *Publications:* Nuclear Weapons, the balance of terror, the quest for peace, 1986; (jtly) The Crisis in our Democracy, 2017; reports; *music:* Missa Brevis, 2007; The Easter Story (oratorio), 2010; The Christmas Story (oratorio), 2015. *Recreations:* reading, writing, walking. *Address:* 15 Highbury Road, SW19 7PR.

**EDWARDS, (Ann) Mererid; Her Honour Judge Mererid Edwards;** a Circuit Judge, since 2013; *b* Wrexham, 10 March 1968; *d* of William Henry Edwards and Dr Ann Eleri Edwards; *m* 1996, Adrian Philip Jackson; one *s* two *d*. *Educ:* Ysgol-Y-Berwyn, Y Bala; Yale Sixth Form Coll.; Univ. of Wales, Aberystwyth (LLB Hons). Called to the Bar, Gray's Inn, 1991; lawyer, S4C, 1990–91; in practice as barrister, Paradise Chambers, Sheffield, 1992–2013; a Recorder, 2008–13. *Recreations:* keeping up with the kids and ironing. *Address:* Cardiff Civil and Family Justice Centre, 2 Park Street, Cardiff CF10 1ET.

**EDWARDS, Prof. Anne,** PhD; FAcSS; FLSW; Professor of Education, University of Oxford, 2005–14, now Emerita (Director, Department of Education, 2010–12); Fellow, St Hilda's College, Oxford, since 2005; *b* Swansea, 31 Oct. 1946; *d* of Owen Terence Davies and Glory Marie Louise, (Jackie), Davies (*née* Jacobsen); *m* 1991, David Christopher Webb; two *d*, and one step *s* one step *d*. *Educ:* Grammar Sch. for Girls, Pontypool; Univ. of Wales, Cardiff (BA 1968; MEd 1977; PhD 1984). ESRC Postdoctoral Fellow, Dept of Psychology, University Coll. Cardiff, 1983–85; Sen. Lectr, then Principal Lectr in Postgrad. Educnl Studies, West Glamorgan Inst. of HE, 1985–87; Principal Lectr, then Prof., St Martin's Coll., Lancaster, 1987–95; Prof. of Primary Educn, Sch. of Educn, Univ. of Leeds, 1996–99; Prof. of Pedagogic Practices, Sch. of Educn, Univ. of Birmingham, 1999–2005. Visiting Professor: Faculty of Educn, Univ. of Oslo, 2006–16; Centre for Human Activity Theory, Kansai Univ., 2006–09. AFBPsS 1985; FAcSS (AcSS 2004). Hon. PhD: Helsinki, 2010; Oslo, 2012. *Publications:* (with D. Galloway) Primary School Teaching and

Educational Psychology, 1991; (with D. Galloway) Secondary School Teaching and Educational Psychology, 1992; (with R. Talbot) The Hard-Pressed Researcher: a handbook for practitioner researchers in the caring professions, 1994, 2nd edn 1999; (with P. Knight) Effective Education in the Early Years, 1994; (ed with P. Knight) The Assessment of Competences in Higher Education, 1995; (with J. Collison) Mentoring and Developing Practice in Primary Schools, 1996; (with A. Anning) Promoting Learning from Birth to Five: developing professional practice in the pre-school, 1999, 2nd edn 2006; (jtly) Rethinking Teacher Education: an interdisciplinary analysis, 2002; (ed with H. Daniels) RoutledgeFalmer Reader: the psychology of Education, 2003; (jtly) Improving Inter-professional Collaborations: multi-agency working for children's wellbeing, 2009; (ed jtly) Activity Theory in Practice: promoting learning across boundaries and agencies, 2009; (ed jtly) Learning Teaching: cultural historical perspectives on teacher education and development, 2010; Being an Expert Professional Practitioner: a relational turn, 2010; (jtly) Improving User-engagement in Educational Research, 2011; (ed jtly) Motives, Emotions and Values in the Development of Children and Young People, 2012; (ed jtly) Pedagogy in Higher Education, 2013; Working Relationally In and Across Practices, 2017; contribs in ed collections and acad. jls. *Recreations:* family, theatre, walking. *Address:* Department of Education, University of Oxford, 15 Norham Gardens, Oxford OX2 6PY. *T:* (01865) 242669, *Fax:* (01865) 274027. *E:* anne.edwards@education.ox.ac.uk.

**EDWARDS, Prof. (Anthony) David,** DSc; FRCP, FRCPCH, FMedSci, FRCR; Professor of Paediatrics and Neonatal Medicine, King's College London, since 2012; Director, Centre for the Developing Brain, King's College London (formerly at Imperial College London), since 2008; Director, Institute for Women's and Children's Health, King's Health Partners, since 2018; Consultant Neonatologist, Guy's and St Thomas' Hospitals NHS Trust, since 2012; *b* 26 Nov. 1954; *s* of Raymond Edwards and Nora Edwards; *m* 1978, Catherine James; one *s* one *d. Educ:* St Peter's Coll., Oxford (MA; Univ. Boat Race winning crew, 1976); Harvard Univ.; Guy's Hosp. Med. Sch., Univ. of London (MB BS); Imperial Coll. London (DSc 2010). FRCP 1993; FRCPCH 1997; FMedSci 2002; FRCR 2016. Sen. Lectr in Paediatrics, UCL, 1992–93; Imperial College London: Weston Prof. of Neonatal Medicine, 1993–2012; Chm., Div. of Paediatrics, Obstetrics and Gynaecol., 1998–2005; Lead for Imaging Res., 2006–08; Hd, Neonatal Medicine Gp, MRC Clin. Sci. Centre, Hammersmith Hosp., 1999–2012. Assoc. Dir, UK Medicines for Children Res. Network, 2006–12. Visiting Professor: UCL, 1994; Univ. of Hong Kong, 2000; Dept of Bioengrg, Imperial Coll. London, 2012–17. Member: Sci. Adv. Bd, Liggins Inst., Auckland, NZ, 2001; INSERM, 2004–; MRC, 2004–05; Nat. Centre for Growth and Develt, NZ, 2005–; Inst. of Child Health, UCL, 2015–. Arvo Ylppö Medal, Foundn for Paediatric Res., Finland, 2007. *Publications:* contrib. numerous papers to scientific jls. *Recreations:* Manouche jazz, the renaissance lute, sailing. *Address:* Centre for the Developing Brain, King's College London, St Thomas' Hospital, Westminster Bridge Road, Lambeth, SE1 7HY. *T:* (020) 7188 9158. *E:* ad.edwards@kcl.ac.uk. *Club:* Athenæum.

**EDWARDS, Prof. Anthony William Fairbank,** FRS 2015; Professor of Biometry, University of Cambridge, 2000–03; Fellow, Gonville and Caius College, Cambridge, since 1970; *b* London, 4 Oct. 1935; *s* of late Harold Clifford Edwards and Ida Margaret Atkinson Edwards (*née* Phillips); *m* 1958, (Elsa Helny) Catharina Edlund; one *s* two *d. Educ:* Uppingham Sch.; Trinity Hall, Cambridge (BA 1957; PhD 1961; ScD 1972; LittD 2005). Res. Fellow, Dept of Genetics, Univ. of Cambridge, 1960; Res. Assoc., Univ. of Pavia, 1961–64; Actg Asst Prof., Depts of Genetics and Maths, Stanford Univ., 1964–65; Sen. Lectr in Statistics, Univ. of Aberdeen, 1965–68; University of Cambridge: Bye Fellow, Gonville and Caius Coll., 1968–70; Asst Dir of Res., 1970–78; Reader in Biometry, 1978–2000; Sen. Proctor, 1978–79. Hon. Prof., Univ. of Pavia, 1999. *Publications:* Likelihood, 1972, 2nd edn 1992; Foundations of Mathematical Genetics, 1977, 2nd edn 2000; Pascal's Arithmetical Triangle, 1987, 2nd edn 2002; (with H. A. David) Annotated Readings in the History of Statistics, 2001; Cogwheels of the Mind, 2004; (jtly) Ending the Mendel-Fisher Controversy, 2008. *Recreations:* formerly gliding and ski-ing. *Address:* Nickersons, 104 High Street, Barton, Cambridge CB23 7BG. *T:* (01223) 262367. *E:* awfe@cam.ac.uk.

**EDWARDS, Prof. Brian,** CBE 1988; FHSM; Professor of Health Care Development, University of Sheffield, 1996–2002, now Emeritus (Foundation Dean, School of Health and Related Research, 1996–99); *b* 19 Feb. 1942; *s* of John Albert Edwards and Ethel Edwards; *m* 1964, Jean (*née* Cannon); two *s* two *d. Educ:* Wirral Grammar Sch. FHSM 1983. Jun. Administrator, Clatterbridge Hosp., 1958–62; Dep. Hosp. Sec., Cleaver Hosp., 1962–64; National Trainee, Nuffield Centre, Leeds, 1964–66; Administrator, Gen. Infirmary, Leeds 1966–67; Hosp. Sec., Keighley Victoria Hosp., 1967–68; Administrator, Mansfield HMC, 1969–70; Lectr, Univ. of Leeds, 1970–72; Dep. Gp Sec., Hull A HMC, 1972–74; Nuffield Travelling Fellow, USA, 1973; Dist Administrator, Leeds AHA(T), 1974–76; Area Administrator, Cheshire AHA, 1976–81; Regional Administrator, 1981–84, Regl Gen. Man., 1984–93, Trent RHA; Chief Exec., W Midlands RHA, 1993–96; Regl Dir, NHS Exec., 1994–96. Chm., Clinical Pathology Accreditation Ltd, 1992–2000. Vis. Lectr, Health Care Studies, 1973–93, and Associate Fellow, Nuffield Inst., 1987–93, Univ. of Leeds; Vis. Prof., Health Care Studies, Univ. of Keele, 1989; Queen Elizabeth Nuffield Fellow, Nuffield Provincial Hosps Trust, 1991; Hon. Prof., Univ. of Keele, 1993. Adviser to WHO, 1982–2005; Chairman: NHS Manpower Planning Adv. Gp, 1983–86; Regional Gen. Managers Gp, 1986–87, 1991–94; NHS Patient Empowerment Gp, 1991–94; Patient's Charter Team, 1992; Council for the Professions Supplementary to Medicine, 1997–2002; Notts Health NHS Trust, 2001–07; Member: Steering Cttee on Future of Nursing, 1988; Standing Cttee on Medical Audit, RCP, 1989–94; Ashworth Inquiry, 1997–98; Leader: Sec. of State's Task Force on Quality in NHS, 1993; UK Delegn, Hosp. Cttee for Europe, 1994–2005 (Pres., 2005–08). Chairman: ATM Consulting, 2007–09; Pain Management Solutions, 2009–10; Referrals Direct Ltd, 2010–15; Director: Shirehall Gp, 1996–99; Health on the Box Ltd, 1999–2001. Institute of Health Service Administrators: Mem., 1964–; Pres., 1982–83; Mem. Editorial Cttee, Health Care in the UK: its organisation and management, 1982–83; Pres., Assoc. of Health Service Supplies Officers, 2001–04. Patron, NHS Retirement Fellowship, 2002–07. Trustee: Marie Curie Trust, 1996–2000; Pharmacy Practice Res. Trust, 2006–. Jt Editor, Health Services Manpower Review, 1970–91; Editor, Euro Hospital Yearbook, 1998–2005. CCMI (CBIM 1988); Hon. FRCPath 1996; Professorial FRSPH 2013. DUniv UCE, 1998; Hon. MD Sheffield, 2018. *Publications:* Si Vis Pacem—preparations for change in the NHS, 1973; Profile for Change, 1973; Bridging in Health, Planning the Child Health Services, 1975; Industrial Relations in the NHS: managers and industrial relations, 1979; Manpower Planning in the NHS, 1984; Employment Policies for Health Care, 1985; Distinction Awards for Doctors, 1987; (contrib.) Doctors' Contracts, 1992; (contrib.) Public Sector Managers' Handbook, 1992; The NHS: a manager's tale, 1993, 2nd edn 1995; (contrib.) Management for Doctors, 1994; (contrib.) Managed Healthcare, 1998; (ed) NHS 50th Anniversary Lectures, 1999; The Executive Years of the NHS, 2005; An Independent NHS, 2007; A History of the NHS in the South West, 2010; A Collapse in the Culture of Care: the Stafford Inquiries, 2013; Social History of a Grave Yard, 2016; Ministers of the NHS, 2019; papers presented at numerous nat. and internat. confs; contrib. prof. jls.

*Recreation:* golf. *Address:* 3 Royal Croft Drive, Baslow, Derbyshire DE45 1SN. *T:* (01246) 583459. *Clubs:* Athenæum; Bakewell Golf (Captain, 1991; Pres., 2015), Chatsworth Golf; La Manga (Spain).

**EDWARDS, His Honour (Charles) Marcus;** a Circuit Judge, 1986–2008; *b* 10 Aug. 1937; *s* of late John Basil Edwards, CBE; *m* 1st, 1963, Anne Louise Stockdale (*d* 1970), *d* of Sir Edmund Stockdale, 1st Bt; 2nd, 1975, Sandra Wates (*née* Mouroutsos); one *d* and three step *d. Educ:* Dragon Sch., Oxford; Rugby Sch.; Brasenose Coll., Oxford (scholar; BA Jurisprudence). Trooper, RAC, 1955; 2nd Lieut, Intelligence Corps, Cyprus, 1956–57. HM Diplomatic Service, 1960–65; Third Sec., 1960, Spain, 1961, FO, 1961–62, South Africa and High Commn Territories, 1962–63, Laos, 1964; Second Sec., FO, 1965, resigned. Called to the Bar, Middle Temple, 1962; practised, London, 1966–86; Mem., Midland and Oxford Circuit; a Recorder, 1985–86. Chm., Pavilion Opera, 1987–2018. *Recreations:* gardening, walking, talking, food and drink. *Address:* Mathon Lodge, Mathon, Herefordshire WR14 4DW. *T:* (01684) 564592; Menginolle, 32730 Malabat, France. *Clubs:* Beefsteak, Vincent's.

**EDWARDS, Sir Christopher (John Churchill),** 5th Bt *cr* 1866; Adjunct Professor, University College, University of Denver, since 1999, and Affiliate Professor, Regis University, Denver, Colorado since 1999; President, Rocky Mountain Information Specialists, Westminster, Colorado, since 2007; *b* 16 Aug. 1941; *s* of Sir (Henry) Charles (Serrell Priestley) Edwards, 4th Bt and of Lady (Daphne) Edwards (*née* Birt); *S* father, 1963; *m* 1972, Gladys Irene Vogelgesang (*d* 2005); two *s. Educ:* Frensham Heights, Surrey; Loughborough Univ., Leics (DLC Hons; BSc); Regis Univ., Denver, USA (MSc). Gen. Manager, Kelsar Inc., American Home Products, San Diego, Calif, 1979–84; Vice-Pres., Valleylab Inc., Boulder, Colo, 1981–89; Dir, Ohmeda BOC Group, Louisville, 1989–92; Pres., Intermed Consultants, Westminster, Colo, 1992–99; Vice Pres., Teledyne Inc., Fort Collins, Colo, 1994–95; Exec. Vice-Pres. and Gen. Manager, RAM Electronics Corp., Fort Collins, Colo, 1995–97. Affiliate Prof. of MSc in Mgt, Regis Univ., Denver, 1999–2006; Adjunct Prof. of MSc in Inf. Technol., Organization Leadership and Envmtl Policy and Mgt, Univ. of Denver, 1999–. Ruth Murray Underhill Teaching Award, Univ. of Denver, 2006. *Heir:* s David Charles Priestley Edwards, *b* 22 Feb. 1974. *Address:* 11637 Country Club Drive, Westminster, CO 80234-2649, USA. *T:* (303) 4693156.

**EDWARDS, Sir Christopher (Richard Watkin),** Kt 2008; MD; FRCP, FRCPE, FMedSci; FRSE; Chairman: Council, British Heart Foundation, 2009–15; Hotspur (formerly Cluff) Geothermal, since 2014; Icappic Ltd, since 2015; *b* 12 Feb. 1942; *s* of Thomas Archibald Watkin Edwards and Beatrice Elizabeth Ruby Watkin Edwards; *m* 1968, Sally Amanda Kidd; two *s* one *d. Educ:* Marlborough Coll.; Christ's Coll., Cambridge (BA, MB, BChir, MA, MD). St Bartholomew's Hospital: Lectr in Medicine, 1969–75; Sen. Lectr in Medicine and MRC Sen. Res. Fellow, 1975–80; Hon. Consultant Physician, 1975–80; University of Edinburgh: Moncrieff Arnott Prof. of Clinical Medicine, 1980–95; Dean, Faculty of Medicine, 1991–95; Provost, Faculty Group of Medicine and Veterinary Medicine, 1992–95; Principal and Prof. of Medicine, ICSM, Univ. of London, 1995–2000; Vice-Chancellor, Univ. of Newcastle upon Tyne, 2001–07. Chairman: Chelsea and Westminster NHS Foundn Trust, 2007–14; NHS Medical Educn England, 2008–12. Non-executive Director: Celltech, 1997–2004; Argenta Discovery, 2000–04; One NorthEast, 2001–07. Mem., MRC, 1991–95. Gov., Wellcome Trust, 1994–2005. Trustee, Planet Earth Inst., 2012–. Founder FMedSci 1998; FIC 2003. Hon. DSc Aberdeen, 2000. *Publications:* (ed) Clinical Physiology, 5th edn, 1984; (ed) Essential Hypertension as an Endocrine Disease, 1985; Endocrinology, 1986; (ed) Recent Advances in Endocrinology Metabolism, vol. 3, 1989; (ed) Davidson's Principles and Practice of Medicine, 17th edn, 1995; 421 scientific papers and communications. *Recreations:* reading, golf, ski-ing. *Address:* 4 Thames Walk, SW11 3BG. *Club:* Athenæum.

**EDWARDS, Rev. Canon Clare;** see Edwards, Rev. Canon D. C.

**EDWARDS, David;** see Edwards, Anthony D.

**EDWARDS, David Leslie;** QC 2006; a Deputy High Court Judge, since 2017; *b* 8 Nov. 1966; *s* of late Leslie Joseph Edwards and of Angela Mary Edwards; *m* 1994, Caroline May Evans; three *s. Educ:* King's Sch., Chester; Peterhouse, Cambridge (BA 1988, MA 1991). Called to the Bar, Lincoln's Inn, 1989; in practice as barrister, 1990–, specialising in commercial law, incl. insurance, reinsurance, banking, internat. trade and professional negligence. Mem., Standards Cttee, Bar Standards Bd, 2011–15. Chm. Council, Friends of Peterhouse, 2010–16. *Recreations:* Real tennis, football, wine, classical music and opera, reading. *Address:* 7 King's Bench Walk, Temple, EC4Y 7DS. *T:* (020) 7910 8300. *Clubs:* Arts; Royal Tennis Court.

**EDWARDS, David Michael,** CMG 1990; international commercial mediator; Adjunct Professor, Singapore Management University, 2007–15; Program Director, Chief Legal Officers' Council and Emerging Markets Risk and Compliance Council (Asia Pacific), The Conference Board, since 2011; *b* 28 Feb. 1940; *s* of late Ernest William Edwards and Thelma Irene Edwards; *m* 1st, 1966, Veronica Margaret Postgate (marr. diss. 1996); one *s* one *d*; 2nd, 1996, Rain Ren; one *s* one *d. Educ:* The King's Sch., Canterbury; Univ. of Bristol (LLB Hons). Admitted to Roll of Solicitors, 1964. Solicitor of Supreme Court, 1964–67; Asst Legal Adviser, Foreign Office, 1967; Legal Adviser: British Military Govt, Berlin, 1972; British Embassy, Bonn, 1974; Legal Counsellor, 1977; Gen. Counsel and Dir, Legal Div., IAEA, Vienna, 1977–79; Legal Counsellor, FCO, 1979; Agent of the UK Govt in cases before European Commn and Court of Human Rights, 1979–82; Counsellor (Legal Adviser), UK Mission to UN, New York, and HM Embassy, Washington, 1985–88; Legal Counsellor, 1988–89, Dep. Legal Advr, 1989–90, FCO; Sen. Counsel, Bechtel Ltd, 1990; Law Officer (Internat. Law), Hong Kong Govt, 1990–95; Sen. Counsel, Bechtel Ltd, London, 1995–97; Asia Pacific Chief Counsel and Vice-Pres., Bechtel Internat. Inc., Singapore, 1997–2002; Chief Legal Counsel, Shell/CNOOC Nanhai Petrochemical Complex, Guangdong Province, China, 2002–05. *Recreations:* reading, travel, antique clocks. *Club:* Tanglin (Singapore).

**EDWARDS, Prof. David Olaf,** DPhil; FRS 1988; University Professor of Physics, Ohio State University, 1988–95, now Distinguished Professor Emeritus; *b* 27 April 1932; *s* of Robert Edwards and Margaret Edwina (*née* Larsen); *m* 1967, Wendy Lou Townsend (*d* 2009); one *s* one *d. Educ:* Holt High Sch., Liverpool; Brasenose Coll., Oxford (BA 1st cl. Hons, 1953; Sen. Hulme Schol., 1953–56; MA; DPhil 1957). FAPS. Pressed Steel Co. Res. Fellow, Clarendon Lab., Oxford Univ., 1957–58; Ohio State University: Vis. Asst Prof., 1958–60; Asst Prof., 1960–62; Associate Prof., 1962–65; Prof., 1965–88. Visiting Professor: Imperial Coll., London, 1964; Sussex Univ., 1964, 1968; Technion, Israel, 1971–72; Ecole Normale Supérieure, Paris, 1978, 1982, 1986; Vis. Scientist, Brookhaven Nat. Lab., 1975. Consultant: Brookhaven Nat. Lab., 1975–77; Los Alamos Scientific Lab., 1979–81. Sir Francis Simon Prize, British Inst. of Physics, 1983; Dist. Schol. Award, Ohio State Univ., 1984; Special Creativity Awards, US Nat. Sci. Foundn, 1981, 1986; Oliver E. Buckley Condensed Matter Physics Prize, APS, 1990. Mem. Editl Bd, Jl of Low Temperature Physics, 1990–2004. *Publications:* (ed jtly) Proceedings of the Ninth International Conference on Low Temperature Physics (LT9), 1966; numerous articles on low temp. physics in scientific jls. *Recreations:* beagling (Master, Rocky Fork Beagles, 1975–90), snorkeling (Grand Cayman), crossword puzzles, reading detective stories. *Address:* 2345 Dorset Road, Columbus, OH 43221, USA. *T:* (614) 4864553; Department of Physics, Ohio State University, 191 West Woodruff Avenue, Columbus, OH 43210–1117, USA. *Fax:* (614) 2927557.

EDWARDS, **David Stanley**, OBE 2005; Chairman: Cambridgeshire and Peterborough NHS Foundation Trust, 2012–14; Healthwatch Norfolk, since 2018; *b* 5 Oct. 1943; *s* of Stanley and May Edwards; partner, Christine Baxter; two *s*. *Educ:* Coll. of Advanced Technol., Birmingham (HND Prodn and Mech. Engrg 1966); Coll. of Commerce, Birmingham (Dip. Mgt Studies 1969). DipHSM 1981. Tech. engr, then industrial engr, British Steel, Wednesbury (Tube Prodn), 1960–67; Sen. Industrial Engr, GKN (Birwelco) Ltd, Halesowen (Engrg), 1967–68; West Midlands Regional Health Authority: Orgn and Methods Assignment Officer, 1968–70; Mgt by Objectives Advr, 1970–72; Asst Regl Orgn and Methods Work Study Manager, 1972–74; West Birmingham Health Authority: Dist Support Services Manager, 1974–77; Dist Gen. Adminr (Planning), 1977–79; Central Birmingham Health Authority: Sector Adminr, Gen., Dental and Jaffray Hosp. and Community Services, 1979–82; Dep. Dist Adminr, 1982–85; Dir, Admin and Planning, 1985–86; Dist Gen. Manager, 1986–91; Chief Executive: Queen's Med. Centre, Nottingham Univ. Hosp. NHS Trust, 1991–99; Cardiff and Vale NHS Trust, 1999–2004. Chm., NHS Great Yarmouth and Waveney, 2009–12; non-exec. Dir, James Paget Univ. Hosps NHS Foundn Trust, 2007–09. Vice Chm., Council, UEA, 2011–14 (Mem. Council, 2005–14; Chm., Audit Cttee, 2006–10); Mem. Bd, Univ. Campus Suffolk, then Univ. of Suffolk, 2010–. Fellow, Univ. of Nottingham, 1994. Companion IHM 2002; CCMI 2003. Hon. DCL UEA, 2014. *Recreations:* two sons, three granddaughters, two grandsons, antique clocks and Victorian relief moulded jugs, classic cars, scuba diving (in warm water!), squash, running and all sport, foreign travel, walking, reading for pleasure, music and playing the piano in private. *Address:* The Grove, Smee Lane, Great Plumstead, Norwich, Norfolk NR13 5AU. *T:* (01603) 717310.

EDWARDS, **Rev. Canon (Diana) Clare**; Rector, Benefice of BrookDean, Forest of Dean, since 2018; *b* 14 Feb. 1956; *d* of Bryan Reginald Edwards and Vivienne Edwards. *Educ:* London Hosp., Whitechapel (SRN 1977); Hosp. for Sick Children, Gt Ormond St (RSCN 1981); London Univ. (DipN 1983); Nottingham Univ. (BTh 1986). Staff Nurse, London Hosp., Whitechapel, 1977–79; Community Mem., Scargill House, Yorks, 1979–80; Post Registration Student, Hosp. for Sick Children, Gt Ormond St, 1980–81; Staff Nurse, Mayday Hosp., Croydon, 1981–83; ordained deaconess, 1986, deacon, 1987, priest, 1994; Deaconess, 1986–87, Deacon, 1987–90, Holy Trinity & St Peter, S Wimbledon; Curate, St Peter & St Paul with St George, Crowhurst, and Chaplain, Lingfield Hosp. Sch., 1990–95; Rector, St Mary the Virgin, Bletchingley, 1995–2004; Rural Dean, Godstone, 1997–2004; Hon. Canon, 2001–04, Dean of Women's Ministry, 2003–04, Dio. of Southwark; Canon Pastor, Canterbury Cathedral, 2004–18. *Publications:* Human Rites (contrib.), 1995; Isabella Gilmore: forerunner of today's women parish priests, 2009. *Recreations:* swimming, windsurfing, embroidery, arts and crafts. *Address:* The Rectory, High Street, Ruardean, Forest of Dean GL17 9US.

EDWARDS, **Prof. Dianne**, CBE 1999; ScD; FRS 1996; FRSE; FLSW; Distinguished Research Professor in Palaeobotany, Cardiff University (formerly University of Wales, Cardiff), since 1996; President, Linnean Society of London, 2012–15; *b* 23 Feb. 1942; *d* of William John Edwards and Enid Edwards; *m* 1965, Thomas Geoffrey Morgan (*d* 1997); one *s*. *Educ:* Girton Coll., Cambridge (BA, MA; PhD 1968; ScD 1989). Res. Fellow, Girton Coll., Cambridge, 1967–70; Fellow, Univ. of Wales, 1970–72; University College, Cardiff: Lectr in Botany, 1972–82; Sen. Lectr, 1982–86; Reader in Plant Sci., 1986–92; Prof. of Palaeobotany, 1992–96. Royal Soc. Leverhulme Trust Sen. Res. Fellow, 1994–95. Mem., Countryside Council for Wales, 2001–07. Corresp. Mem., Botanical Soc. of America, 1994. Trustee: Nat. Botanic Garden of Wales, 1997–2006; Royal Botanic Garden, Edinburgh, 1999–2006; Natural Hist. Mus., 2003–11. Founder Fellow and Vice Pres., Learned Soc. of Wales, 2010–14. FRSE 2001. Hon. Fellow, Univ. of Wales, Swansea, 1997. Hon. ScD TCD, 2005; Hon. Dr: Uppsala, 2014; Edinburgh, 2017; Wales, 2017. Ed., Botanical Jl of Linnean Soc., 1993–2006. Linnean Medal for Botany, 2010; Lapworth Medal, Palaeontological Soc., 2013. *Publications:* contrib. to jls incl. Palaeontology, Rev. of Palaeobotany and Palynology, Botanical Jl Linnean Soc., Nature. *Recreations:* gardening, Mozart, opera. *Address:* School of Earth and Ocean Sciences, Cardiff University, Cardiff CF10 3AT. *T:* (029) 2087 4264.

EDWARDS, **Douglas**; *see* Edwards, P. D.

EDWARDS, **Duncan**; *see* Edwards, John D.

EDWARDS, **Elizabeth Alice**; *see* Wilson, E. A.

EDWARDS, **Prof. Elizabeth Jane Mary**, FBA 2015; Research Professor in Photographic History and Director, Photographic History Research Centre, De Montfort University, 2011–16, now Professor Emerita; *b* Carlisle, 24 Feb. 1952; *d* of Dennis and Sheila Edwards; *m* 1977, Simon Edwards; one *d*. *Educ:* Univ. of Reading (BA); Univ. of Leicester (MA). Curator of Photographs, Pitt Rivers Mus., 1977–2005, Lectr in Visual Anthropol., 1990–2005, Univ. of Oxford; Professorial Res. Fellow, Univ. of Arts, London, 2005–11. Vis. Schol., Max Planck Inst. für Wissenschaftsgeschichte, 2008; Fellow, Inst. of Advanced Studies, Univ. of Durham, 2012; Andrew W. Mellon Vis. Prof., V&A Res. Inst., 2017–. Hon. Prof., Dept of Anthropology, UCL, 2016–. Member: Adv. Bd, Nat. Media Mus. (Science Mus.), 2015–; Scientific Adv. Bd, Kunsthistorisches Inst in Florenz (Max Planck Inst.), 2017–. Vice-Pres., RAI, 2009–12. *Publications:* Anthropology and Photography 1865–1920, 1992; Raw Histories: photographs, anthropology and museums, 2001; (ed jtly) Photographs Objects Histories, 2004; (ed jtly) Sensible Objects: colonialism, material culture and the senses, 2006; (with P. James) A Record of England, 2006; (ed jtly) Photography, Anthropology and History, 2009; Camera as Historian: amateur photographers and historical imagination 1885–1918, 2012; (ed jtly) Uncertain Images: museums and the work of photographs, 2014; (ed jtly) Photographs, Museums, Collections: between art and information, 2015; contrib. articles to Hist. and Theory, Hist. and Anthropol., Hist. of Photography. *Recreations:* chamber music, growing vegetables, architectural history. *E:* ejmedwards10@gmail.com.

EDWARDS, **Gareth Huw**; Principal, George Watson's College, Edinburgh, 2001–14; *b* Swansea, 9 April 1958; *s* of Roy and Gwyneth Edwards; *m* 1981, Jane Rees; one *d*. *Educ:* Tudor Grange Grammar Sch.; Solihull Sixth Form Coll.; Exeter Coll., Oxford (BA Hons Lit.Hum.); Univ. of Bristol (PGCE). Asst Classics Master, King Edward's Sch., Birmingham, 1981–85; Hd of Classics, Boys' Div., Bolton Sch., 1985–90; Vice-Principal, Newcastle-under-Lyme Sch., 1990–96; Rector, Morrison's Acad., Crieff, 1996–2001. *Recreations:* choral singing, Welsh Rugby fan, Hellenophile.

EDWARDS, **His Honour Gareth Owen**; QC 1985; a Circuit Judge, 1991–2006; *b* 26 Feb. 1940; *s* of Arthur Wyn Edwards and Mair Eluned Edwards; *m* 1967, Katharine Pek Har Goh; two *s* one *d*. *Educ:* Herbert Strutt Grammar Sch., Belper; Trinity Coll., Oxford (BA, BCL). Called to the Bar, Inner Temple, 1963; Army Legal Service, 1963–65; Commonwealth Office, 1965–67. Practised, Wales and Chester Circuit, 1967–91; Recorder, Crown Court, 1978–91. *Recreations:* climbing, chess. *Address:* 58 Lache Lane, Chester CH4 7LS. *T:* (01244) 677795. *Club:* Army and Navy.

EDWARDS, **Sir Gareth (Owen)**, Kt 2015; CBE 2007 (MBE 1975); retired 1978 as Welsh Rugby footballer; chairman of leisure company in S Wales; *b* 12 July 1947; *s* of Granville and Anne Edwards; *m* 1972, Maureen Edwards; two *s*. *Educ:* Pontardawe Tech. Sch.; Millfield Sch.; Cardiff College of Educn. Rugby Football: 1st cap for Wales, 1967 (*v* France); Captain of Wales on 13 occasions; youngest Captain of Wales (at 20 years), 1968; British Lions Tours: 1968, 1971, 1974; Barbarians, 1967–78. Member of Cardiff RFC, 1966–; a record 53 consecutive caps, to 1978. Director: Fairwater Enterprises Ltd, 1992–; Euro Commercials (South Wales) Ltd, 1992–; Euro Commercials Investments (Swansea) Ltd, 1995–; Cardiff Blues Ltd, 1997–; Euro Commercials Investments (Cardiff) Ltd, 1998–; Cardiff RFC Ltd, 2003–. *Publications:* Gareth: an autobiography, 1978; (jtly) Rugby Skills, 1979; Rugby Skills for Forwards, 1980; Gareth Edwards on Fishing, 1984; Rugby, 1986; Gareth Edwards' 100 Great Rugby Players, 1987; (with Peter Bills) Gareth Edwards: the autobiography, 1999; (with Peter Bills) Tackling Rugby: the changing world of professional Rugby, 2002. *Recreations:* fishing, golf. *Address:* 211 West Road, Nottage, Porthcawl, Mid-Glamorgan CF36 3RT. *T:* (01656) 785669.

EDWARDS, **Graham**, FRICS; Executive Chairman, Telereal Trillium, since 2018 (Chief Executive, 2001–18); *b* London, 4 Jan. 1964; partner, Georgina Black; one *d*, and one *s* one *d* by a previous marriage. *Educ:* Fitzwilliam Coll., Cambridge (BA Econs 1987). ACA 1990. Investment Mgt Cert. Level 3 1997. Associate Mem., ACT, 1995; Associate, UK Soc. of Investment Professionals, 1998. Auditor, 1987–90, Corporate Finance Exec., 1990–91, Stoy Hayward; Hd, Property Finance, 1991–94, Corporate Finance Manager, 1994–97, BT plc; Fund Manager, Merrill Lynch Mercury Asset Mgt, 1997–99; Chief Investment Officer, 1999–2004, Dir, 2004–12, Talisman Global Asset Mgt. Trustee: MDA, 2006–; Pennies Foundn, 2010–. FRICS 2012. *Recreations:* bridge, tennis, ski-ing, investing. *Address:* (office) Clive House, 2 Old Brewery Mews, Hampstead, NW3 1PZ. *T:* (020) 7433 0667. *E:* gedwards@telerealtrillium.com.

EDWARDS, **Helen**, CB 2012; CBE 2001; Director General, Localism, Department for Communities and Local Government, 2013–16; *b* 2 Aug. 1953; *d* of Charlton and Isobel Edwards; *m* 1987, David John Rounds; three *s*. *Educ:* Univ. of Sussex (BA Hons 1975); Univ. of Warwick (MA 1977; CQSW 1977). Social Worker, E Sussex CC, 1975–80; Dep. Project Dir, Save the Children Fund, 1980–83; National Association for Care and Resettlement of Offenders: Policy Devel Officer, 1983–85; Principal Officer, 1985–88; Asst Dir, 1988–93; Dir of Policy, Res. and Develt, 1993–96; Chief Exec., 1997–2001; Dir, Active Community Unit, 2002–04, Dir Gen., Communities Gp, 2004–05, Home Office; Chief Exec., Nat. Offender Mgt Service, Home Office, subseq. at MoJ, 2005–08; Dir Gen., Justice Policy (formerly Criminal Justice) Gp, MoJ, 2008–13. Member: New Deal Adv. Task Force, 1997–2001; Working Gp reviewing prison Bds of Visitors, 2000–01; Learning and Skills Council, 2000–02; Social Finance, 2017–. Non-exec. Dir, Central and NW London NHS Foundn Trust, 2009–19. Trustee, Lloyds Bank Foundn, 2011–18. Chair: Recovery Focus and Richmond Fellowship, 2016–; Mem. Bd, Peabody Housing Trust, 2016–. FRSA 1997. DUniv Middlesex, 2004. *Publications:* articles in jls on crime, social exclusion and criminal justice. *Recreation:* family and friends.

EDWARDS, **Huw**; Presenter: BBC News at Ten (formerly Ten O'Clock News), since 2003; BBC News at Five, since 2006; *b* 18 Aug. 1961; *s* of late Prof. Hywel Teifi Edwards and of Aerona Edwards (*née* Protheroe); *m*; five *c*. *Educ:* Llanelli Boys' Grammar Sch.; University Coll. Cardiff (BA French 1983); Univ. of Wales Trinity St David (PhD 2018). Joined BBC as trainee journalist, 1984; Parly Corresp., BBC Wales, 1986–88; Political Corresp., then Chief Political Corresp., BBC TV News and BBC News 24, 1988–99; Presenter, BBC Six O'Clock News, 1999–2002. Presenter of BBC TV and radio progs incl. Trooping the Colour, Festival of Remembrance, State Opening of Parliament, D-Day 60, The Story of Welsh, Songs of Praise, Lloyd George, Gladstone and Disraeli, The Royal Wedding, The Story of Wales, The Diamond Jubilee, Opening and Closing Ceremonies of London 2012 Olympic Games, D-Day 70, WW1 Remembered, Cymry Estron (Story of the Welsh in London), Patagonia with Huw Edwards, Aberfan: the fight for justice, and progs on classical music; newsreader cameo role, Skyfall (film), 2012. Hon. Prof. of Journalism, 2006, Pro-Chancellor, 2012–, Cardiff Univ. Hon. Fellow: Cardiff Univ., 2003; Univ. of Wales, Lampeter, 2006; Univ. of Wales, Swansea, 2007; Univ. of Wales, Newport, 2007; Swansea Inst. of Higher Educn, 2007; Bangor Univ., 2014. Ambassador, Prince's Trust. Patron: Cancer Research, Wales; Nat. Coll. of Music; George Thomas Hospice, 2007–; Bridgend Male Choir, 2008–; Trinity Hospice, London, 2010–; Ty Bryngwyn Hospice, Llanelli, 2012–; Addoldai Cymru (Welsh Religious Bldgs Trust), 2015–; President: Gwalia Male Voice Choir, 2006–17; Llanelli Community Heritage, 2006–; London Welsh Trust, 2008–; London Welsh Male Voice Choir, 2012– (Vice Pres., 2005–12); Vice-Pres., Nat. Churches Trust, 2013–. DUniv Glamorgan, 2007. Presenter of the Year, BAFTA Cymru/Wales, 2001, 2002, 2003, 2004, 2009, 2012, 2017. *Publications:* Capeli Llanelli: our rich heritage, 2009; City Mission: the story of London's Welsh chapels, 2014; contrib. Cylchgrawn Cymdeithas Hanes y Methodistiaid Calfinaidd, Welsh Hist. Rev. *Clubs:* Garrick, London Welsh (Pres., 2008–).

EDWARDS, **Huw William Edmund**; independent training consultant and political advisor, Huw Edwards Training Ltd, specialising in parliamentary processes, democratic governance and influencing the political process; trainer, Industry and Parliament Trust; *b* 12 April 1953; *s* of late Rev. Dr Ifor M. Edwards and Esme Edwards; *m* 2005, Tess Cooling; one step *s* one step *d*. *Educ:* Eastfields High Sch., Mitcham; Manchester Polytechnic; Univ. of York (BA, MA, MPhil). Lecturer in Social Policy: Coventry (Lanchester) Poly., 1980–81; Univ. of Sheffield, 1983–84; Poly. of the South Bank, 1984–85; Manchester Poly., 1985–88. Res. Associate, Low Pay Unit, 1985–97; Tutor with Open Univ., 1987–95; Sen. Lectr in Social Policy, Brighton Poly., later Univ. of Brighton, 1988–91, 1992–97; Res. Student, Constitution Unit, UCL, 2007–11; former Associate Lectr, Nat. Sch. of Govt. MP (Lab) Monmouth, May 1991–1992, 1997–2005; contested (Lab) same seat, 1992, 2005. Member: Select Cttee on Welsh Affairs, 1991–92, 1998–2001, and 2002–05; Modernisation Cttee, H of C, 1997–98. Chm., Welsh Parly Labour Gp, 2000–01; Sec., All Party Commons and Lords Rugby Club. Member: Labour campaign for Electoral Reform; Fabian Soc., 1992–. Internat. Expert, EU funded project on governance and parly reform in Libya, 2012–14. Pres., Chepstow Mencap, 1992–; Mem. Exec., Shelter Cymru, 1988–91; Mem. Monmouth Gp, Amnesty Internat., 1969–. Patron, Gwent ME Soc., 1997–. Mem., Boro' Welsh Congregational Chapel, London. Vice-Pres., Monmouth Rugby Club, 1997–. *Publications:* reports on low pay in Wales and a fair electoral system for the Welsh Assembly; articles in professional jls. *Recreations:* sport, football, Rugby, cricket, Welsh choral music (Member, Gwalia Male Voice Choir; Chairman, Monmouth Male Voice Choir). *Address:* Wyefield House, The Paddocks, Monmouth NP25 3NP. *W:* www.huwedwardstraining.com. *Club:* London Welsh Association.

EDWARDS, **Ian Anthony**; Regional Chairman of Industrial, subsequently Employment, Tribunals, Southampton, 1996–2003, a part-time Chairman, 2004–06; *b* 18 June 1940; *s* of Gordon Burrows Edwards and Florence Hilda Edwards; *m* 1976, Susan Joy Rooth; one *s* one d. *Educ:* Liverpool Inst.; Liverpool Univ. (LLB 1961); Southampton Univ. (LLM 1962). Admitted as solicitor, 1965; Partner, Paris, Smith & Randall, Southampton, 1970–87; Chm., part-time, 1985–87, full-time, 1987–96, Industrial Tribunals, Southampton. *Publications:* (ed jtly) Mead's Unfair Dismissal, 5th edn, 1994. *Recreations:* leader of Urban Saints (formerly Crusaders), walking, music, railways.

**EDWARDS, (Ifan) Prys;** Director, Prys Edwards Consultancy, since 1986; *b* 11 Feb. 1942; *m* 1966, Catherine Williams; one *s* one *d*. *Educ:* Leighton Park Sch., Reading; Welsh Sch. of Architecture, Cardiff (DipArch). RIBA 1965. Principal Partner, Prys Edwards Partnership, 1966–86. Member: Wales and the Marches Postal Bd, 1974–76; Develt Bd for Rural Wales, 1976–84; BTA, 1984–92; Chairman: Wales Tourist Bd, 1984–92; Welsh Fourth Channel Authy, 1992–98. Dir, Wales Millennium Centre, 1997–2006 (Life Vice-Pres., 2008). Hon. Pres., Urdd Gobaith Cymru (Welsh League of Youth), 1981–. *Recreations:* sailing, watching Rugby, golf. *Address:* Bryn Aberoedd, Caemelyn, Aberystwyth SY23 2HA. *T:* (01970) 623001.

**EDWARDS, Jacqueline Louise, (Jacks);** *see* Thomas, J. L.

**EDWARDS, Jennifer Fitzgerald,** CBE 2011; Chief Executive Officer, Mental Health Foundation, 2013–18; *b* Bristol, 26 Dec. 1954; *d* of William Terence Chalmers Edwards and Cora Marion Edwards; *m* 1994, Jean Pierre Ferraroli (marr. diss. 2014); one *s*. *Educ:* Torquay Girls' Grammar Sch.; Girton Coll., Cambridge (BA 1976; MA 1981). Fast Stream Civil Servant, MAFF, 1976–81; Nat. Organiser, CND, 1981–83; various posts, London Bor. of Camden, 1983–89; Nat. Coordinator, Ministry for Women Initiative, 1990–92; Sen. Policy Advr to Leader, Camden Council, 1992–93; Dir/CEO, Nat. Campaign for the Arts, 1993–98; London Dir, Ext. Relns and Develt, Arts England, 1998–2004; Chief Exec., Homeless Link, 2004–11; Interim Exec. Dir, Interights, 2012–13. Dir, Taproot Consultancy, 2011–13. Mem. (Lab), Westminster CC, 1990–93. Chair, Ashford Place, 2012–14. Fellow, Soc. of Leadership Fellows, 2016–. FRSA 1995. *Publications:* (contrib. with P. Farmer) Hidden Loneliness, 2014; (jtly) Hard Edges: mapping severe and multiple disadvantage in England, 2015. *Recreations:* gardening, opera, creative digital work.

**EDWARDS, Jeremy John Cary;** Group Managing Director, Henderson Administration Group, 1989–95; *b* 2 Jan. 1937; *s* of late William Philip Neville Edwards, CBE, and Hon. Mrs Sheila Edwards (*née* Cary); *m* 1st, 1963, Jenifer Graham (*née* Mould) (decd); one *s* one *d*; 2nd, 1974, April Philippa Harding (marr. diss. 1993); one *s*; 3rd, 1994, Mrs Amanda Barber. *Educ:* Ridley Coll., Ontario; Vinehall Sch., Sussex; Haileybury and Imperial Service Coll. Unilever, 1955–57; Hobson Bates & Co., 1957–59; Overseas Marketing and Advertising, 1959–61; Courtaulds, 1961–63; Vine Products, 1963–66; Loewe SA, 1966–68; Jessel Securities, 1968–70; Man. Dir, Vavasseur Unit Trust Management, 1970–74; Henderson Admin Gp, 1974–95; Jt Man. Dir, 1983–89. Non-executive Director: College Hill Associates, 1996–2002; Tribune Trust, 1997–2006; Liontrust First UK Investment Trust, 1999–2004. Hon. Treas., WWF (UK), 1984–2002; Children's Society (formerly C of E Children's Society): Mem. Council, 1987–2002; Vice-Chm., 1996–2002; Chm., Jewson Associates (formerly E. Jewson Services to Charities) Ltd, 2000–06; Trustee, Breast Cancer Haven (formerly Haven Trust), 1998–2008. *Address:* 59 Dorothy Road, SW11 2JJ. *T:* (020) 7228 6055. *Club:* Boodle's.

**EDWARDS, Rev. Joel,** CBE 2019; International Director, Micah Challenge, 2009–14; Strategic Adviser, Christian Solidarity Worldwide, since 2015; *b* 15 Oct. 1951; *m* 1976, Carol Munroe-Edwards; one *s* one *d*. *Educ:* London Bible Coll. (BA Theology 1975). Probation Officer, 1978–88; Gen. Sec., African and Caribbean Evangelical Alliance, 1988–92; UK Dir, Evangelical Alliance, 1992–97; Gen. Dir, Evangelical Alliance UK, 1997–2008. Pastor, 1985–95, Associate Pastor, 1996–2003, Mile End New Testament Church of God. Hon. Canon, St Paul's Cathedral, 2002. Comr, Equality and Human Rights Commn, 2007–10. Advr, Tony Blair Faith Foundn, 2008; Mem., Human Rights Adv. Gp, FCO, 2010–. Fellow, St John's Coll., Durham, 2009. Hon. DD: Caribbean Grad. Sch. of Theol., Jamaica, 2006; St Andrews, 2007. Prime Minister's Award (Jamaica), 2003. *Publications:* Lord Make Us One—But Not All the Same!, 1999; The Cradle, The Cross and The Empty Tomb, 2000; Hope, Respect and Trust: valuing these three, 2004; Falling Back on God: a Lent group study on trust, 2006; (with D. Killingray) Black Voices: the shaping of our Christian experience, 2007; Advent Hope: a spiritual focus for personal or group use, 2007; An Agenda for Change: a global call for spiritual and social transformation, 2008. *Recreations:* gym, reading.

**EDWARDS, John Coates,** CMG 1989; HM Diplomatic Service, retired; Head of UK Delegation, EC Monitoring Mission in former Yugoslavia, April–Sept. 1995, April–Aug. 1996, May–Sept. 1997, April–July 1998 and March–June 1999; *b* 25 Nov. 1934; *s* of late Herbert John and Doris May Edwards; *m* 1959, Mary Harris (*d* 2006); one *s* one *d*. *Educ:* Skinners' Co. Sch., Tunbridge Wells, Kent; Brasenose Coll., Oxford (MA). Military Service, 1953–55: Lieut, RA. Asst Principal: Min. of Supply, 1958; Colonial Office, 1960; Private Sec. to Parly Under Sec. of State for the Colonies, 1961; Principal: Nature Conservancy, 1962; Min. of Overseas Develt, 1965; First Sec. (Develt), and UK Perm. Rep. to ECAFE, Bangkok, Thailand, 1968; Asst Sec., Min. of Overseas Develt, 1971; Head of E Africa Develt Div., Nairobi, Kenya, 1972; Asst Sec., Min. of Overseas Develt, 1976; Head of British Develt Div. in the Caribbean, Barbados, 1978; UK Dir, Caribbean Develt Bank, 1978; Hd, West Indian and Atlantic Dept, FCO, 1981–84; Dep. High Comr, Kenya, 1984–88; High Commissioner: Lesotho, 1988–91; Botswana, 1991–94. Chm., Kenya Soc., 1997–2012. JP Kent, 2000. *Address:* Fairways, Back Lane, Ightham, Sevenoaks, Kent TN15 9AU. *Club:* Royal Over-Seas League.

**EDWARDS, John David; His Honour Judge John Edwards;** a Circuit Judge, since 2018; *b* Devizes, 21 March 1959; *s* of Rev. Thomas Harold David Edwards and Ann Gollan Edwards; *m* 1989, Louise Cooper; one *s* one *d*. *Educ:* Haileybury and Imperial Service Coll.; Leeds Poly. (BA Hons); Inns of Court Sch. of Law. Called to the Bar, Inner Temple, 1983; a Recorder, 2002–18. Dep. Chancellor, Birmingham Dio., 2005–. *Recreations:* Rugby Union, tennis, history. *Address:* c/o Minshull Street Crown Court, Manchester M1 3FS. *T:* (0161) 954 7500. *E:* hhj.john.edwards@ejudiciary.net. *Club:* Manchester Tennis and Racquet.

**EDWARDS, (John) Duncan;** Director, Swipecast, since 2016; Chief Executive Officer, BritishAmerican Business, since 2018 (Member, Advisory Board, since 2010); *b* 28 March 1964; *s* of Dr Vernon A. Edwards, OBE, JP and Jean Edwards; *m* 1993, Sarah Kennedy; two *s*. *Educ:* Merchant Taylors' Sch., Northwood; Univ. of Sheffield (BA Hons Geog. and Politics 1985). With Media Week Ltd, 1985–89; Publisher, Company mag., 1989–93; National Magazine Co. Ltd: Business Develt Dir, 1993–98; Dep. Man. Dir, 1998–2002; Man. Dir, later Chief Exec., 2002–09; Chm., Comag Ltd, 2002; Pres. and Chief Exec., Hearst Magazines Internat., 2009–16; Vice Chm., Hearst Magazines UK, 2009–16; Mem., Bd of Dirs, Hearst Corp., 2011–16. Dir, Foreign Policy Assoc., 2012. Dir, St George's Soc. of NY, 2014–. *Recreations:* running, triathlon, books, chopping wood, growing vegetables, leading a full life! *Clubs:* Soho House, George; Old Merchant Taylors' Rugby Football.

**EDWARDS, John Reid,** JD; attorney; Partner, Edwards Kirby, since 2013; US Senator from North Carolina, 1999–2005; *b* 10 June 1953; *s* of Wallace R. Edwards and Catherine Edwards; *m* 1977, (Mary) Elizabeth Anania (*d* 2010); one *s* two *d* (and one *s* decd). *Educ:* NC State Univ. (BS 1974); Univ. of NC at Chapel Hill (JD 1977). Called to the Bar: NC, 1977; Tenn, 1978; Associate, Dearborn and Ewing, Nashville, Tenn, 1978–81; trial lawyer, 1981; Associate, 1981–83, Partner, 1984–92, Tharrington Smith and Hargrove, Raleigh, NC; Partner, Edwards and Kirby, Raleigh, NC, 1993–99. Dir, Center on Poverty, Work and Opportunity, Univ. of N Carolina at Chapel Hill, 2005–06. Vice-Presidential cand. (Democrat), 2004, Presidential cand. (Democrat), 2008, US elections.

**EDWARDS, Jonathan;** MP (Plaid Cymru) Carmarthen East and Dinefwr, since 2010; *b* Capel Hendre, Carmarthenshire, 26 April 1976. *Educ:* Ysgol Gyfun Maes yr Yrfa; Univ. of Wales, Aberystwyth (BA Hist. and Politics; postgrad. degree in Internat. Hist.). COS to Rhodri Glyn Thomas, Mem., Nat. Assembly for Wales and Adam Price, MP; with Nat. Campaigns Directorate, Plaid Cymru, 2005–07; with Citizens Advice Cymru, 2007–10. Plaid Cymru spokesman for: Business, Innovation and Skills, 2010–; Communities and Local Government, 2010–15; Culture, Olympics, Media and Sport, 2010–15; Transport, 2010–; Treasury, 2010–; Foreign Intervention, 2015–. Mem., Welsh Affairs Select Cttee, 2010–15. *Address:* House of Commons, SW1A 0AA.

**EDWARDS, Jonathan David,** CBE 2001 (MBE 1996); athlete, retired 2003; Presenter, Eurosport, since 2017; *b* 10 May 1966; *s* of Andrew David Edwards and Jill Edwards (*née* Caulfield); *m* 1990, Alison Joy Briggs; two *s*. *Educ:* Durham Univ. (BSc Hons). Triple jump athlete: English Schs Champion, 1984; Gold Medallist: World Cup, 1992, 2002; World Championships, Gothenburg, 1995 (estabd world record, 18.29m), Edmonton, 2001; Eur. Indoor Championships, Valencia, 1998; Eur. Championships, Budapest, 1998; Olympic Games, Sydney, 2000; Commonwealth Games, Manchester, 2002. Mem. Bd, London Organising Cttee, 2012 Olympic Games, 2005–13. Mem. for England, Content Bd, Ofcom, 2003–06. Broadcaster, BBC Sport. Sports Personality of Year Award, BBC, 1995. *Publications:* A Time to Jump, 2000. *Address:* c/o MTC (UK) Ltd, 71 Gloucester Place, W1U 8JW. *T:* (020) 7935 8000.

**EDWARDS, Rev. Jonathan Page;** Special Adviser, Torch Trust, since 2017; *b* Westcliff-on-Sea, Essex, 23 Feb. 1956; *s* of Linley Gordon Edwards and Barbara Elizabeth Hindley Edwards (*née* Baker); *m* 1984, Susan Lesley Stevens; one *s* two *d*. *Educ:* Westcliff High Sch. for Boys; St John's Coll. and Regent's Park Coll., Oxford (MA). Ordained minister, 1982; Minister, Southgate Church, Bury St Edmunds, 1983–91; Sen. Minister, Orpington Baptist Church, 1991–98; Gen. Superintendent, SW Area, Baptist Union of GB, 1998–2001; Sen. Regl Minister, SW Baptist Assoc., 2001–06; Gen. Sec., Baptist Union of GB, 2006–13; Exec. Ambassador, Prospects, 2013–16. Sec., Baptist Ministers' Fellowship, 1994–99. Chm., Membership Cttee, Baptist World Alliance, 2010–15. *Recreations:* family, music, postcard collecting.

**EDWARDS, Dame Julie Andrews;** *see* Andrews, Dame J. E.

**EDWARDS, Kenneth;** *see* Edwards, A. K.

**EDWARDS, Dr Kenneth John Richard;** Vice-Chancellor, University of Leicester, 1987–99; *b* 12 Feb. 1934; *s* of John and Elizabeth May Edwards; *m* 1958, Janet Mary Gray; two *s* one *d*. *Educ:* Market Drayton Grammar Sch.; Univ. of Reading (BSc 1st class 1958); University Coll. of Wales, Aberystwyth (PhD 1961; Hon. Fellow). Nat. Service, RAF, 1952–54. Fellow, Univ. of California, 1961–62; ARC Fellow, Welsh Plant Breeding Station, Aberystwyth, 1962–63, Sen. Sci. Officer, 1963–66; Cambridge University: Lectr in Genetics, 1966–84; Head of Dept of Genetics, 1981–87; Sec. Gen. of Faculties, 1984–87; St John's College: Fellow, 1971–87; Lectr, 1971–84; Tutor, 1980–84. Vis. Lectr in Genetics, Univ. of Birmingham, 1965; Vis. Prof., INTA, Buenos Aires, 1973; Leverhulme Res. Fellow, Univ. of California, 1973. Chm., CVCP, 1993–95; Member: Marshall Aid Commemoration Commn, 1991–98; Council, ACU, 1994–99; Bd, CRE, 1994–2001 (Pres., 1998–2001). Mem. Bd, USS Ltd, 1994–97. Chm. Governing Body, Inst. of Grassland and Envmtl Res., 1994–99. Chm. Council, CRAC, 2001–08; Chm. Govs, Perse Sch., Cambridge, 2002–09. Hon. LLD: QUB, 1995; Leicester, 1999; Hon. DSc: Reading, 1995; Loughborough, 1995; Warwick, 2000; Hon. MA Nene Coll., 1997; Dr (*hc*) Babeş-Bolyai, Romania, 1998; Maribor, Slovenia, 2001; Olomouc, Czech Republic, 2002. *Publications:* Evolution in Modern Biology, 1977; articles on genetics in sci. jls. *Recreations:* music, gardening. *Address:* 10 Sedley Taylor Road, Cambridge CB2 8PW. *T:* (01223) 245680.

**EDWARDS, Lionel Antony, (Tony),** CEng, FRAeS; Head, Defence Export Services Organisation, 1998–2002; *b* 4 Nov. 1944; *s* of Lionel Victor and Marjorie Edwards. *Educ:* Abingdon Sch.; Univ. of Birmingham (BSc Hons 1966); Harvard Business Sch. (MBA 1972). CEng 1991; FRAeS 1991. Apprentice Engr, Rolls-Royce, Derby, 1962–68; Mfg Engr, General Electric, Lynn, Mass, 1968–71; Lectr, Harvard Univ., 1972–73; Manager/Dir, General Electric, Lynn and Cincinatti, Ohio, 1973–82; Gen. Manager, Storno A/S, Copenhagen, 1983–86; Corporate Vice-Pres., Motorola, Copenhagen, 1986–88; President: Challenger Exec. Jet Div., Montreal, 1988–89; Canadair Aerospace Gp, Montreal, 1989; Man. Dir, Lucas Aerospace Ltd, Solihull, 1989–92; Gp Man. Dir, Lucas Industries, 1992; Chief Exec., Dowty, and Main Bd Dir, TI Gp PLC, 1992–98; Chm. and Chief Exec., Messier-Dowty, 1994–98. Chm., Defence and Aerospace Sector Panel, OST Technology Foresight Prog., 1995–97. Member: Council, SBAC, 1989–98 (Vice-Pres. 1990–91, Pres. 1991–92, Dep. Pres. 1992–93); DTI Aviation Cttee, 1992–98; Council, Air League, 1992; Council, RAeS, 1992 (Pres., 1999–2000); NDIC, 1992–2001. Trustee: RAF Mus.; Swordfish Heritage Trust, subseq. Fly Navy Heritage Trust. *Recreations:* preservation of historic aircraft, shooting, classic cars, farming. *Address:* Wincott Hill Farm, Long Compton Road, Whichford, Warwickshire CV36 5PQ.

**EDWARDS, Hon. Sir Llewellyn (Roy),** AC 1989; Kt 1984; FRACMA; Consultant, Jones Lang La Salle (formerly Jones Lang Wootton), Brisbane, 1989–2009; *b* 2 Aug. 1935; *s* of Roy Thomas Edwards and Agnes Dulcie Gwendoline Edwards; *m* 1st, 1958, Leone Sylvia Burley (decd); two *s* one *d*; 2nd, 1989, Jane Anne Brumfield, AM. *Educ:* Raceview State Sch.; Silkstone State Sch.; Ipswich Grammar Sch.; Univ. of Queensland (MB, BS 1965). Qualified Electrician, 1955. RMO and Registrar in Surgery, Ipswich Hosp., 1965–67; gen. practice, Ipswich, 1967–74. MLA (L) Ipswich, Qld Parlt, 1972–83; Minister for Health, Qld, 1974–78; Dep. Premier and Treasurer, Qld, 1978–83; Dep. Med. Supt, Ipswich Hosp., 1983–85. Chairman: Ansvar Australia Insurance Ltd, 1984–94; World Expo 88 Authority, 1984–89; Australian Coachline Holdings Ltd, 1992–96; Micromedical Industries, 1993–96; Multi-Function Polis Develt Corp., SA, 1995–98; UQ Hldgs Pty Ltd, 1998–2009; Director: Westpac Banking Corp., 1988–2004; James Hardie Industries Pty Ltd, 1989–2001; Uniseed Pty Ltd, 2001–09. Chm., Pacific Film and Television Commn, 1991–2008; Mem., Australia Japan Foundn Bd, 1992–2006. Chancellor, Univ. of Queensland, 1993–2009 (Mem. Senate, 1984–2009). FRACMA 1984. Hon. FAIM 1988. Hon. LLD Queensland, 1988; DUniv: Griffith, 1998; Qld Univ. of Technol., 1999. *Recreations:* tennis, walking, cricket, Rugby Union. *Address:* 8 Ascot Street, Ascot, Qld 4007, Australia. *Clubs:* Brisbane, Tattersall's (Brisbane, Qld).

**EDWARDS, Malcolm John,** CBE 1985; Chairman, Coal Investments Plc, 1993–96; founded Edwards Energy Ltd, 1992; Commercial Director, British Coal (formerly National Coal Board), 1985–92; Member of the Board, British Coal, 1986–92; *b* 25 May 1934; *s* of John J. Edwards and Edith (*née* Riley), *m* 1967, Yvonne, *d* of Mr and Mrs J. A. W. Daniels, Port Lincoln, S Australia; two *s*. *Educ:* Alleyn's Sch., Dulwich; Jesus Coll., Cambridge (MA). Joined NCB as trainee, 1956; Industrial Sales Manager, 1962; Dir of Domestic and Industrial Sales, 1969; Dir Gen. of Marketing, 1973; responsible for coal utilisation R & D, 1984–92; Chm., British Fuels Gp, 1988–92; Dep. Chm., Inter Continental Fuels, 1989–92. Chm., Finance Cttee, Southwark Diocesan Bd of Educn, 1992–. *Publications:* (with J. J. Edwards) Medical Museum Technology, 1959. *Recreations:* book collecting, arts and crafts movement, music, gardening. *Address:* 80 Waller Road, SE14 5LY.

**EDWARDS, Marcus;** *see* Edwards, His Honour C. M.

**EDWARDS, Margaret Elizabeth;** Member, Civil Service Commission, since 2017; *b* 21 May 1962; *d* of Bertie Arthur John Edwards and Christine Edwards (*née* Hamilton-Bell); partner, Michael Ramsden. *Educ:* UEA (BA Hons (Econs) 1983); Univ. of Plymouth (MBA 1993); Royal Soc. of Apothecaries (DPhilMed 1996); INSEAD (top mgt prog. 1998). Planning and Inf. Manager, Norwich HA, 1983–85; various mgt posts, Plymouth HA, 1985–94; Dir of Clin. Services, 1995–98, Chief Exec., 1998–2001, Heatherwood and Wexham Park NHS Trust; Dir of Performance, 2001–02, Dir of Access, 2002–06, DoH; Chief Exec., Yorks and the Humber Strategic HA, 2006–09; Nat. Dir, NHS Productivity and Efficiency Unit, 2009; Interim Chief Exec., Wales Probation Service, 2010; Special Advr to Lord Carter, McKesson Health Solutions, 2010–11; Vice Pres., UK Commng, McKesson, 2010–15. Chairman: Nat. Oversight Gp for High Secure Mental Health Services, 2015–; Civil Service Pension Bd, 2016–; Mem., Sen. Salaries Pay Review Body, 2012–18; non-exec. Dir, Govt Internal Audit Agency, 2014–18. *Recreations:* reading, travel, philosophy and ethics.

**EDWARDS, Mererid;** *see* Edwards, A. M.

**EDWARDS, Sir Michael,** Kt 2014; OBE 2006; PhD; poet; Professor of Literary Creation in the English Language, Collège de France, since 2002; Member, Académie française, since 2013; *b* Barnes, 29 April 1938; *s* of Frank Edwards and Irene Edwards (*née* Dalliston); *m* 1964, Danielle Bourdin; one *s* one *d*. *Educ:* Kingston Grammar Sch.; Christ's Coll., Cambridge (BA 1960; MA 1964; PhD 1965; Hon. Fellow 2013). Lectr in French, Univ. of Warwick, 1965–73; Reader in Literature, Univ. of Essex, 1973–87; Prof. of English, Univ. of Warwick, 1987–2002; Eur. Chair, Collège de France, 2000–01. Hon. LittD Cantab, 2018. Commandeur des Arts et des Lettres (France), 2013; Chevalier de La Légion d'Honneur (France), 2015. *Publications:* La Tragédie racinienne, 1972; Eliot/Language, 1975; Towards a Christian Poetics, 1984; Poetry and Possibility, 1988; Of Making Many Books, 1990; Raymond Mason, 1994; Éloge de l'attente, 1996; De Poetica Christiana, 1997; Beckett ou le don des langues, 1998; Leçons de poésie, 2001; Sur un vers d'Hamlet, 2001; Ombres de lune, 2001; Un monde même et autre, 2002; Shakespeare et la comédie de l'émerveillement, 2003; Terre de poésie, 2003; Étude de la création littéraire en langue anglaise, 2004; Racine et Shakespeare, 2004; Shakespeare et l'œuvre de la tragédie, 2005; Le Génie de la poésie anglaise, 2006, 2nd edn 2014; De l'émerveillement, 2008; Shakespeare: le poète, le dramaturge, 2009; L'Étrangereté, 2010; Le Bonheur d'être ici, 2011; Le Rire de Molière, 2012; Discours de Réception à l'Académie française, 2015; Bible et poésie, 2016; Dialogues singuliers sur la langue française, 2016; Molière et Shakespeare, ou les frères amis, 2016; *poetry:* To Kindle the Starling, 1972; Where, 1975; The Ballad of Mobb Conroy, 1977; The Magic, Unquiet Body, 1985; Poèmes, 1989; Rivage mobile, 2003; Paris demeure, 2008; At the Root of Fire/À la racine du feu, 2009; Ce que dit la lumière, 2010; Paris aubaine, 2012; L'Infiniment proche, 2016; In a Wide Bewilderment of Quiet, 2018; Capitales, 2018; At the Brasserie Lipp, 2019. *Recreations:* theatre, music, art, conversation. *Address:* 22 rue de Rivoli, 75004 Paris, France. *T:* (1) 40299579. *E:* michael.edwards@college-de-france.fr. *Club:* Cambridge Union.

**EDWARDS, Dr Michael Frederick,** OBE 1993; FREng, FIChemE; Principal Engineer, Unilever, 1987–2001; *b* 27 April 1941; *s* of H. S. Edwards and J. Edwards (*née* Wallwork); *m* 1964, Margaret Roberta Thorne; one *s* one *d*. *Educ:* University Coll., Swansea (BSc, PhD). FIChemE 1980; FREng (FEng 1992). Lectr in Engrg Scis, Univ. of Warwick, 1966–69; Lectr, Sen. Lectr in Chem. Engrg, 1969–81, Prof. of Chemical Engrg, 1981–87, Bradford Univ. Mem., various research council bds and cttees. *Publications:* Mixing in the Process Industries, 1985, 2nd edn 1992; papers on process engrg in learned jls. *Recreations:* hill-walking, classical music, golf. *Address:* 44 Long Meadow, Gayton, Wirral CH60 8QQ. *T:* (0151) 342 5602.

**EDWARDS, Prof. Michael Martin;** JP; Joint Chairman, 2002–07, Chairman, 2007–08, Association of Governing Bodies of Independent Schools (Chairman, Governing Bodies Association, 1998–2002); *b* 19 July 1934; *s* of Charles Samuel and Lilian Edwards; *m* 1956, Dorothy Mildred Mayall; two *s*. *Educ:* London Sch. of Economics (BSc (Econ), PhD); London Univ. Inst. of Education (PGCE); Univ. of Maryland (Fulbright Schol.). Hd of Econs Sch., Woolwich Poly., 1959–67; Hd of Dept of Mgt and Business Studies, Hendon Coll. of Technology, 1967–71; Asst Dir, Poly. of South Bank, 1971–73; Academic Dir and Dep. Chief Exec., Middlesex Poly., 1973–91. Lectured at summer schs and confs, Univs of Bremen, Cologne, Hamburg, Heidelberg, Munich, Poznan, Trondheim and Warsaw, 1975–92; leader of educn missions to Hong Kong, Malaysia and Singapore, 1990–94. Dir, ISC, 1998– (Mem., 1998–). Non-exec. Dir, Harrow Community NHS Trust, 1991–94. Chairman: Bishop of London's Industrial Adv. Council, 1970–84; Higher and Further Educn Cttee, London Dio., 1973–80; Fulbright Awards Selection Cttee, 1984–96 (Mem., Fulbright Commn, 1986–96); John Lyon Charity, 1993–; St Mark's Hosp. Academic Inst., 1995–2001; St Mark's Res. Foundn, 1998–2011. Mem., Wkg Gp, RNT Trust, 2002–14; Hon. Mem. Council, RNT, 2014. Chairman of Governors: Harrow Coll. of Higher Educn, 1981–85; John Lyon Sch., 1982–2002; Mem. Governing Council, Oak Hill Theol Coll., 1981–91; Governor: Harrow Sch., 1982–2004; Lancing Coll., 2004–09; Mem., Council, Royal Alexandra and Albert Sch., 2008–11. Fellow, Woodard Corp., 2004–09. FRSocMed 1999. JP Harrow, 1991. *Publications:* The Growth of the British Cotton Trade 1780–1815, 1967; Aspects of Capital Investment, 1971; N. J. Smelser and the Cotton Factory Family, 1971. *Recreations:* music, Victorian literature, theatre, golf.
See also N. C. M. Edwards.

**EDWARDS, Prof. Nancy Margaret,** PhD; FBA 2016; FLSW; FSA; Professor of Medieval Archaeology, Bangor University, since 2008; *b* Portsmouth, 8 Jan. 1954; *d* of David Cyril Bonner Edwards and Ann Edwards; *m* 1983, Anthony Huw Pryce; one *s*. *Educ:* Portsmouth High Sch. for Girls; Univ. of Liverpool (BA Archaeol., Ancient and Medieval Hist. 1976); Durham Univ. (PhD 1982). FSA 1989. Lectr, 1979–92, Sen. Lectr, 1992–99, Reader, 1999–2008, UCNW, then Univ. of Wales, Bangor, later Bangor Univ. Visiting Fellow: Clare Hall, Cambridge, 1991; All Souls Coll., Oxford, 2007; Vis. O'Donnell Lectr in Celtic Studies, Univ. of Oxford, 2000. Chm., Royal Commn on Ancient and Historical Monuments of Wales, 2019–. Member: Council, Nat. Mus and Galls of Wales, 1997–2003; Ancient Monuments Adv. Bd, Cadw, 2003–10; Council, Learned Soc. for Wales, 2014–19. FLSW 2012. Chm., Gwynedd Archaeol Trust, 2004–19; Pres., Cambrian Archaeol Assoc., 2019–20. *Publications:* (ed with A. Lane) Early Medieval Settlements in Wales AD 400–1100, 1988; The Archaeology of Early Medieval Ireland, 1990; (ed with A. Lane) The Early Church in Wales and the West, 1992; (ed) Landscape and Settlement in Medieval Wales, 1997; (ed jtly) Pattern and Purpose in Insular Art, 2001; A Corpus of Early Medieval Inscribed Stones and Stone Sculpture in Wales, Vol. II, South-West Wales, 2007, Vol. III, North Wales, 2013; (ed jtly) Transforming Landscapes of Belief in the Early Insular World and Beyond, 2017; contribs in books and learned jls. *Recreations:* art, walking, swimming. *Address:* School of History, Philosophy and Social Sciences, Bangor University, Bangor, Gwynedd LL57 2DG.

**EDWARDS, Nigel Charles Michael;** Chief Executive, Nuffield Trust, since 2014; *b* Lambeth, 1961; *s* of Prof. Michael Martin Edwards, qv; *m* 1993, Virginia Burns; three *d*. *Educ:* University Coll., Oxford (BA PPE); Westminster Univ. (MBA). Ops Dir, Central Middx Hosp., 1985–90; Reform Manager, Oxford RHA, 1990–92; Dir, London Health Econs Consortium, LSHTM, 1992–99; Dir of Policy, 1999–2010, Actg Chief Exec., 2010–11, NHS Confederation; Sen. Fellow, King's Fund, 2011–14. Expert, KPMG Global Centre of Excellence on Health, 2011–14. Hon. Vis. Prof., LSHTM, 2000–. *Publications:* The Triumph of Hope over Experience: lessons from NHS reorganisation, 2010. *Address:* Nuffield Trust, 59 New Cavendish Street, W1G 7LP. *T:* (020) 7631 8450. *E:* CEO@nuffieldtrust.org.uk.

**EDWARDS, Nigel Royston;** QC 2019; *b* London, 17 March 1967; *s* of Bessie, (Betty), Edwards; *m* 2004, Hayley. *Educ:* George Dent; Mount Pleasant; Branksome; Univ. of Sheffield (LLB Hons 1993). Called to the Bar, Lincoln's Inn, 1995. *Recreations:* Rugby, kayaking, walking, travelling. *Address:* Drumlahan House, Milner Lane, Thorner, Leeds LS14 3AG. *T:* 07932 733593, (0113) 289 3554. *E:* nedbar1@me.com; St Pauls Chambers, Park Row House, 19–20 Park Row, Leeds LS1 5JF.

**EDWARDS, Norman L.;** *see* Lloyd-Edwards.

**EDWARDS, Patricia Anne, (Mrs Roger Cox),** BEM 2018; Legal Director, Office of Fair Trading, 1996–2004; *b* 29 May 1944; *d* of late Maurice James Edwards and of Marion Edwards (*née* Lewis); *m* 1970, His Honour Roger Charles Cox (*d* 2009). *Educ:* Barry and Purley County Grammar Schools; King's College London (LLB). Called to the Bar, Middle Temple, 1967, Bencher, 2003 (Lent Reader, 2017); Criminal Appeal Office, 1965–74; Law Officers' Dept, 1974–77; Home Office: Sen. Legal Asst, 1977–80; Asst Legal Adviser, 1980–88; Principal Asst Legal Advr, 1988–94; Dep. Parly Comr for Admin, 1994–96. *Recreations:* music, travel, reading, domestic pursuits.

**EDWARDS, Sir Paul;** *see* Edwards, Sir R. P.

**EDWARDS, Prof. Paul Kerr,** DPhil; FBA 1998; FAcSS; Professor of Employment Relations, Birmingham Business School, Birmingham University, 2011–19, now Emeritus (Head, Department of Management, 2011–13); *b* 18 March 1952; *s* of Ernest Edwards and Ida Vivienne Edwards (*née* Kerr); *m* 1975, Susan Jane Martin; one *s* one *d*. *Educ:* Magdalene Coll., Cambridge (BA 1973); Nuffield Coll., Oxford (BPhil 1975; DPhil 1977). Warwick University: Res. posts, 1977–88, Dep. Dir, 1988–98, Dir, 1998–2002, Indust. Relns Res. Unit; Prof. of Industrial Relns, 1992–2010; Associate Dean, Warwick Business Sch., 2007–10. Chm., Social Scis Gp, British Acad., 2006–10. Mem., Business and Mgt sub-panel, RAE 2008, 2005–08, REF 2014, 2011–14. Hon. Prof., Univ. of Warwick, 2017–; Vis. Fellow, Aston Univ., 2019–. Fellow, AIM, 2004–07. FAcSS (AcSS 2008), Ed., Work, Employment and Society, 1996–98; Associate Ed., 2006–11, Ed.-in-Chief, 2012–16, Human Relations. *Publications:* Strikes in the United States, 1981; (jtly) The Social Organization of Industrial Conflict, 1982; Conflict at Work, 1986; Managing the Factory, 1987; (jtly) Attending to Work, 1993; (ed) Industrial Relations, 1995, 2nd edn 2003; (jtly) Managers in the Making, 1997; (ed jtly) The Global Economy, National States and the Regulation of Labour, 1999; (jtly) The Politics of Working Life, 2005; (ed jtly) Social Theory at Work, 2006; (ed jtly) Studying Organizations using Critical Realism, 2014. *Recreation:* cycling.

**EDWARDS, Prof. Peter Philip,** PhD; FRS 1996; Professor of Inorganic Chemistry, University of Oxford, since 2003 (Head of Inorganic Chemistry, 2003–13); Fellow of St Catherine's College, Oxford, since 2003; *b* 30 June 1949; *s* of late Ronald Goodlass and of Ethel Mary, who later *m* Arthur Edwards; *m* 1970, Patricia Anne Clancy; two *s* one *d*. *Educ:* Univ. of Salford (BSc; PhD 1974). Fulbright Scholar and NSF Fellow, Baker Lab. of Chem., Cornell Univ., 1975–77; SERC/NATO Fellow and Ramsay Meml Fellow, Inorganic Chem. Lab., Oxford Univ., 1977–79; Cambridge University: Demonstrator in Inorganic Chem., 1979–81, Lectr, 1981–91, Univ. Chem. Labs; Dir of Studies in Chem., Jesus Coll., 1979–91; Co-Founder and Co-Dir, IRC in Superconductivity, 1988; Nuffield Sci. Res. Fellow, 1986–87; BP Venture Res. Fellow, 1988–90; Birmingham University: Prof. of Inorganic Chem., 1991–2003, of Chem. and of Materials, 1999–2003; Hd, Sch. of Chem., 1996–99; Royal Soc. Leverhulme Sen. Res. Fellow, 1996–97. Vis. Prof., Cornell Univ., 1983–86. Mem., HEFCE Res. Assessment Panel, RAE for 1996 and 2001. FRSC 1988 (Vice-Pres., Dalton Div., 1995; Corday-Morgan Medal, 1985; Tilden Medal, 1992; Liversidge Medal, 1999). Mem., German Acad. Scis, 2009. Hughes Medal, Royal Soc., 2003. *Publications:* (with C. N. R. Rao): The Metallic and Non-Metallic States of Matter, 1985; Metal-Insulator Transitions Revisited, 1995; contrib. Angewandte Chemie Internat. Edn. *Address:* St Catherine's College, Oxford OX1 3UJ.

**EDWARDS, Peter Robert;** Director, Personal Investment Authority, 1992–2001; *b* 30 Oct. 1937; *s* of Robert and Doris Edith Edwards; *m* 1st, 1967, Jennifer Ann Boys; one *s*; 2nd, 1970, Elizabeth Janet Barrett; one *d*; 3rd, 2000, Marjorie Ann Edworthy. *Educ:* Christ's Hospital. Chartered Accountant. Ernst & Young (and predecessor firms), 1955–90; Chief Exec., Secretan, 1990–92. Ind. Mem. Council, FIMBRA, 1990–94. Dir, Blackwell Green Ltd, 1992–96. *Recreations:* ornithology, gardening. *Address:* 18 Roman Fields, Chichester, West Sussex PO19 5AB.

**EDWARDS, (Philip) Douglas;** QC 2010; a Recorder, since 2019; *b* Blaina, S Wales, 10 June 1970; *s* of John Edwards and Leslie Edwards (*née* Silk). *Educ:* Nantyglo Comp. Sch.; Univ. of Birmingham (LLB Hons 1991). Called to the Bar, Lincoln's Inn, 1992, Bencher, 2016; in practice as barrister specialising in planning, envmt and public law. Asst Parly Boundary Comr, 2011–; Lead Asst Comr for E Midlands Region, 2011–. Mem., Bar Representation Cttee, 2012–16, Estates Cttee, 2015–, Hon. Soc. of Lincoln's Inn. *Recreations:* ski-ing, walking, reading, natural history, Rugby. *Address:* Francis Taylor Building, Temple, EC4Y 9DB. *T:* (020) 7353 8415. *E:* douglas.edwardsqc@ftb.eu.com.

**EDWARDS, Prys;** *see* Edwards, I. P.

**EDWARDS, Richard,** PhD; Member (Lab) Preseli Pembrokeshire, National Assembly for Wales, 1999–2003; Member, Carmarthen Town Council, 2008; *b* 1956. *Educ:* Queen Elizabeth Grammar Sch., Carmarthen; Univ. of Swansea; Univ. of Birmingham. Posts in local govt and political res. Mem., Carmarthen Town Council, 1991–99; Mayor of Carmarthen, 1997. Chair, Envmt, Planning and Transport Cttee, Nat. Assembly for Wales, 2000–03. Mem., ICSA.

**EDWARDS, Prof. Robert**, PhD; FRSC; Professor of Crop Protection, since 2014, and Head, School of Natural and Environmental Sciences, since 2017, Newcastle University; Director, Institute for AgriFood Research and Innovation, Newcastle University and Fera Science Ltd Institute, since 2015; *b* Watford, 28 Dec. 1957; *s* of Dennis and Sheila Edwards; *m* 1988, Lesley Davies; one *s* one *d*. *Educ:* Mill Hill Sch., London; Univ. of Bath (BSc Hons Biochem. 1981); St Mary's Med. Sch., Univ. of London (PhD Biochem. 1984). FRSC 2011. Postdoctoral researcher, Royal Holloway, Univ. of London, 1984–86; Team Leader, Schering Agrochemicals, 1986–88; Section Hd, Noble Foundn, Oklahoma, 1988–90; University of Durham: Lectr, 1990–98; Reader, 1998–2003; Prof., 2003–10; Hd of Sch., Biol. Dept, 2008–10; Prof. of Crop Protection, Univ. of York, 2010–14; Chief Scientist, Food and Envmt Res. Agency, 2010–14; Hd, Sch. of Agriculture, Food and Rural Develt, Newcastle Univ., 2014–17. Res. Develt Fellow, BBSRC, 2003–08. *Publications:* contrib. papers to peer-reviewed jls. *Recreations:* historic car restoration, farming, golf. *Address:* 48 Ancroft Garth, Durham DH1 2UD. *T:* (0191) 384 9541. *E:* robert.edwards@ncl.ac.uk.

**EDWARDS, Sir (Robert) Paul**, Kt 2009; Chief Executive, School Partnership Trust Academies, 2007–15; *b* Doncaster, 25 July 1957; *s* of Richard Edwards and Edna Edwards; *m* 1984, Christine; two *d*. *Educ:* Univ. of Warwick (BA Hons Eng. and Philos. 1978); Univ. of Sheffield (MA Educn Mgt 1985; PGCE Eng. (Dist.) and Drama 1985; Adv. Dip. Educn Studies 1985). Teacher of English, Stanley High Sch., Southport, 1980–83; Hd of Drama, Mexborough Sch., Doncaster, 1983–86; Dep. Hd of English, Baysgarth Sch., Barton upon Humber, 1986–88; Hd of English, Hartland Sch., Worksop, 1988–90; Dep. Hd, Garibaldi Sch., Mansfield, 1990–95; Headteacher, Knottingley High Sch., 1995–2000; Principal, Garforth Academy (formerly Community College), 2000–11; Executive Headteacher: John Smeaton, 2001–11; Agnes Stewart, 2003–11. Advr, DCSF, later DFE Academies Unit, 2004–11. *Recreations:* art, keen sportsman.

**EDWARDS, Robin Anthony**, CBE 1981; Partner with Dundas & Wilson, CS (formerly Davidson & Syme, WS), 1965–96; *b* 7 April 1939; *s* of Alfred Walton Edwards and Ena Annie Ruffell; *m* 1963, Elizabeth Alexandra Mackay (marr. diss.); one *s* one *d*; *m* 1986, Janet Cant Pow. *Educ:* Daniel Stewart's Coll., Edinburgh; Edinburgh Univ. (MA, LLB (distinction), Cl. Medallist). Former Lectr in Conveyancing, Edinburgh Univ.; Admitted Member, WS Society, 1964; Mem. Council, Law Society of Scotland, 1969–84, Vice-Pres., 1978–79, Pres., 1979–80 (youngest Pres. ever, at that time). Mem., Lands Tribunal for Scotland, 1991–2001. *Recreation:* French travel and cuisine.

**EDWARDS, Sara Elinor;** Lord-Lieutenant of Dyfed, since 2016 (Vice Lord-Lieutenant, 2011–16); *b* Cardiff, 8 Feb.; *d* of John Morris Edwards, MS, FRCS, FACNM and Gwenyth Petty, actress and broadcaster; one *d*. *Educ:* James Allen's Girls Sch.; Greenacre Girls Sch.; Epsom Coll.; Bedford Coll., Univ. of London (BA Hons Medieval and Modern Hist.). Dip. de la Petite Cuisine, Richmond. Broadcaster and writer: freelance work for BBC Wales, incl. news and current affairs, countryside documentaries, interviews; outside broadcasting for agric., the arts and hist., incl. Royal Welsh Show, Nat. Eisteddfod of Wales and Llangollen Internat. Musical Eisteddfod. Pres., Cardiff NSPCC, 2000– (Divl Vice-Pres.); Vice Pres., Nat. Parks of England and Wales. Sister, St John Cymru. Patron, Hijinx Th. Co. CStJ. *Recreations:* cooking, gardening, fishing, the countryside, reading, music, visiting museums and art galleries. *W:* www.saraedwards.co.uk.

**EDWARDS, Sian;** freelance conductor; Music Director, English National Opera, 1993–95; Head of Conducting, Royal Academy of Music, since 2013; *b* 27 Aug. 1959; *m* 1992, Ian Kemp (*d* 2011); one *s*. *Educ:* Royal Northern Coll. of Music; Leningrad Conservatoire. Since 1985 has conducted many orchestras incl. LPO, RPO, Royal Scottish Orch., City of Birmingham SO, Hallé, English Chamber Orch. and Docklands Sinfonietta; conducted Orchestre de Paris and Philharmonique de Lille in France, and Pittsburgh Symphony, Philadelphia Orch., San Francisco Symphony, Los Angeles Philharmonic, Nat. Symphony, Atlanta Symphony, Minnesota Orch. in USA, and Ensemble Modern, Südwest Funk Orchester, ND Radiofunkorchester in Germany; has also conducted orchestras in Canada, Belgium, Austria, Russia and Australia. Operatic début with Mahagonny (Weill), then Carmen, Scottish Opera, 1986; world première of Greek (Turnage), Munich Biennale and Edinburgh Fest., 1988; Glyndebourne: La Traviata, 1987; Katya Kabanova, 1988; New Year (Tippett), 1990; Royal Opera, Covent Garden: The Knot Garden (Tippett), 1988; Rigoletto, 1989; Il Trovatore, 1991; Madam Butterfly, 1992; English National Opera: The Gambler (Prokofiev), 1992; The Queen of Spades, 1993; La Bohème, Marriage of Figaro, Jenufa, The Mikado, Khovanshchina, 1995; Mahagonny, Carmen, Eugene Onegin, 1998; Peter Grimes, 2001; Coraline, 2018; La Clemenza di Tito, Bordeaux, 1996; Clara (Gefors), Opéra Comique, Paris, 1997; Don Giovanni, Danish Royal Opera, 2001; The Death of Klinghoffer (John Adams), La Damnation de Faust, Finnish Nat. Opera, 2001; A Streetcar Named Desire (Previn), 2007, Dead Man Walking (Heggie), 2008, Rape of Lucretia (Britten), 2011, La Traviata (Verdi), 2014, Theater an der Wien; A Night at the Chinese Opera (Weir), 2008, Rake's Progress, 2012, Scottish Opera; Jenufa, WNO, 2008; Hansel and Gretel, Royal Acad. of Music, 2008. Recordings incl. orchestral works by Tchaikovsky, Prokofiev, Ravel, Britten, John Adams, and opera by Judith Weir. *Address:* c/o Groves Artists, 7 St George's Court, 131 Putney Bridge Road, SW15 2PA. *T:* (020) 8874 3222.

**EDWARDS, Dr Steven**, CBE 2009; MRCVS; Consultant Editor, World Organisation for Animal Health, since 2009; Chief Executive, Veterinary Laboratories Agency, 2000–08, on secondment as interim Chief Executive, Animal Health, 2008, Department for Environment, Food and Rural Affairs (formerly Ministry of Agriculture, Fisheries and Food); *b* 9 March 1948; *s* of late William Edward Edwards and Daisy May Edwards (*née* Candelent); *m* 1976, Virginia Elizabeth Marian Lynch Evans; two *s*. *Educ:* Wolverhampton Grammar Sch.; Trinity Hall, Cambridge (MA, VetMB); Edinburgh Univ. (MSc, DVMS). MRCVS 1972. General veterinary practice, Montgomery, Powys, 1972–76; Univ. of Edinburgh, 1976–77; MAFF Veterinary Investigation Centre, Aberystwyth, 1977–78; Tech. Co-op. Officer, ODM, El Salvador, 1978–80, Bolivia, 1980; MAFF Central Veterinary Laboratory: Vet. Research Officer, 1980–92; Head of Virology Dept, 1992–98; MAFF Veterinary Laboratories Agency: Dir of Lab. Services, 1998–99; Dir of Surveillance and Lab. Services, 1999–2000. Visiting Professor: Farm Animal Studies, Univ. of Liverpool, 2001–10; Veterinary Infectious Diseases, RVC, London, 2002–09. Sec. General, 1991–2000, Vice Pres., 2000–03, Pres., 2003–09, Biological Standards Commn (formerly Standards Commn), World Orgn for Animal Health (formerly Office Internat. des Epizooties, Paris). Chm., World Orgn for Animal Health (formerly Office Internat. des Epizooties)/FAO Network on Avian Influenza, 2005–13. Founder Mem., European Soc. for Vet. Virology, 1987 (Sec., 1988–94; Hon. Mem., 1997); Pres., Vet. Res. Club, London, 1995–96. Co-founder, Sec. and Ed., Foundn for Medieval Genealogy, 2002–; Asst Sec., Harleian Soc., 2011–. Chm., St Lawrence Chobham Handbell Ringers, 2004–06. Churchwarden: St Bartholomew's, Vowchurch, 2012–18; Parish of Vowchurch and Turnastone, 2019–. Gold Medal, World Orgn for Animal Health, 2009. *Publications:* contribs and editl for veterinary jls, text books and conf. proceedings, and for genealogy jls. *Recreations:* genealogy, railway preservation, local history.

**EDWARDS, Susan;** Director, Enforcement, Insolvency and Corporate Law, Department for Business, Innovation and Skills, 2009–12; *b* Preston, 17 Feb. 1949; *d* of Maurice Wilkinson and Nora Wilkinson; *m* 1993, Peter Edwards; one *s* one *d*, and two step *s*. *Educ:* Queen Mary Sch., Lytham; Queen Mary Coll., London (LLB); London Coll. of Garden Design (Dip. Garden Design, 2016). Called to the Bar, Gray's Inn, 1972; barrister, 1972–75; Prosecutor, HM Customs and Excise, 1975–77; Lectr in Law, Suffolk Coll. of Higher and Further Educn, 1980–81; Magistrate, Stow PSD, 1981; HM Customs and Excise: Prosecutor, 1982; Criminal Law Advr, 1982–88, Tax Adv. Lawyer, 1989–92; Sen. Prosecutor, 1992–93; Hd, Criminal Adv. Team, 1993–96; Hd, Civil Litigation, 1996–99, Hd, Prosecutions, 1999–2003, DoH and DSS, later DWP; Hd, Legal, Assets Recovery Agency, 2003–07; Dir, Litigation and Ops, Solicitor's Office, HMRC, 2007. *Recreations:* reading, country walks, listening to music, truffling in charity shops, massacre of noxious weeds.

**EDWARDS, Thomas Mowbray C.;** *see* Charles-Edwards.

**EDWARDS, Timothy Peter Warren;** Chair: Storm Therapeutics Ltd, Cambridge, since 2015; Karus Therapeutics Ltd, Oxford, since 2018; *b* Brentwood, Essex, 9 Oct. 1956; *s* of Frank Edwards and Jean Edwards (*née* Short); *m* 1991, Caroline Anne Brown; three *s*. *Educ:* Dragon Sch., Oxford; St Edward's Sch., Oxford. ACA 1980. Entrepreneur, 1982–94; Dir, Corporate Finance, NatWest Mkts, London, 1994–97; Bd Dir, British Biotech plc, 1997–2004; Chm., ReOx Ltd, 2004–07; Pres. and CEO, Cellzome Inc., Boston, USA, 2004–12; Exec. Chair, Atopix Therapeutics Ltd, Oxford, 2012–16; Dir, Ervaxx Ltd, Oxford, 2017–19. Non-executive Director: UK Cell Therapy Catapult, London, 2013–15; Record plc, 2018–. Mem., Ministerial Industry Strategy Gp, DoH, 2010–13. Member: Supervisory Bd, ProtAffin AG, Graz, Austria, 2011–13; Governing Bd, Innovate UK, 2015–18. Chm. and Mem. Bd, UK BioIndustry Assoc., 2007–14. Chm. and Trustee, Mulberry Bush Sch., Standlake, Oxon, 2005–14; Trustee: Magdalen Coll. Sch., Oxford, 2012– (Chm., 2012–18), Inst. for Res. in Schs, 2018–. FRSA 1998. *Recreations:* jazz, choral music and opera, scented gardens, family lunch, Monday tennis, pilates to try to maintain the right stretch and balance. *E:* edwardstpw@gmail.com.

**EDWARDS, Tony;** *see* Edwards, L. A.

**EDWARDS, Tracy Karen**, MBE 1990; consultant on team-building, personal insolvency, leadership and management; Managing Director, Maiden Rescue 2014 Ltd, since 2014; Founder and Managing Director, Maiden Factor, since 2016; *b* 5 Sept. 1962; *d* of Antony Herbert Edwards and Patricia Edwards; one *d*; *m* twice (both marrs diss.). *Educ:* Highlands Primary Sch., Berks; Arts Educnl, Tring; Gowerton Comprehensive Sch., Swansea; Roehampton Univ. (BSc Psychol. and Criminol. 2012). Assembled first all-female crew to compete in 1989 Whitbread Round the World Race (Maiden Project), 1987; set world fastest ocean record, 1997. Man. Dir, Tracy Edwards Associates Ltd, 1990–2002; CEO, Quest Series Ltd, 2003–05; managed Oryx Quest yacht race, Qatar, 2005; Project Manager, Child Exploitation and Online Protection Centre, 2007–08. Presenter/Commentator, TV broadcasts, incl. 1993–94 Whitbread Race; Science of Sailing, 2001; On the Crest of a Wave, 2002. Dir, Safer World Trng Ltd, 2013–15. Patron: Just a Drop, 2009–; Regenerate, 2009–; Girls Network, 2016–; Trustee, Maiden Factor Foundn (formerly Maiden Rescue charity, then Maiden Educn), 2015–; Ambassador: Prince's Trust, 1990–; Duke of Edinburgh Award Scheme, 1998–; Gingerbread, 2007–. *Publications:* Maiden, 1990; Living Every Second (autobiog.), 2001. *Recreations:* riding, theatre, travel, reading, music, shooting, ski-ing. *Address:* c/o Lucas Alexander Whitley, 14 Vernon Street, W14 0RJ. *W:* www.tracyedwards.com. *Clubs:* Royal Ocean Racing, Mosimann's, Home House; Royal Yachting Association.

**EDWARDS, Dr Victoria Mary, (Mrs R. M. Taylor)**, OBE 2004; FRICS; FAAV; Chief Executive, Ernest Cook Trust, since 2016 (Trustee, 2007–16); *b* 14 Aug. 1963; *d* of George Wade Brown Edwards and Betty Kathleen Edwards (*née* Mack); *m* 1999, Richard Michael Taylor; one step *s* one step *d*. *Educ:* Birkenhead High Sch.; Univ. of Reading (BSc; PhD 1995); Univ. of Canterbury, NZ (MSc Hons). FAAV 1985; FRICS 1986. Chartered Surveyor, Dreweatt-Neate, 1984–87; Commonwealth Schol., Univ. of Canterbury, NZ, 1987–89; Consultant (pt-time), QEII Nat. Trust, Wellington, NZ, 1988–89; University of Portsmouth: Sen. Lectr, 1989–94, Principal Lectr, 1994–2006, Head, 2006–07, Faculty of Envmt; Res. Dir, Sch. of Envmtl Design and Mgt, 2007–10; Partner, Taylor-Edwards Envmtl Communications, 2010–16; Associate Prof. in Real Estate and Planning, Henley Business Sch., Univ. of Reading, 2011–16. Winston Churchill Travelling Fellow, 1991; Carthage Fellow, Pol Econ. Res. Center, Montana, 1991. Member: Countryside Commn, 1998–99; Bd, Countryside Agency, 1999–2004; Forestry Commn, 1999–2006. Mem., Burns Cttee for Inquiry into Hunting with Dogs, 1999–2000. Mem., Adv. Cttee, Sch. of Rural Econ. and Land Mgt, RAC, Cirencester, 1996–2001; Gov., Macaulay Land Res. Inst., 2001–03. Mem., Surveying Courses Bd, 1991–96, Educn and Membership Cttee, 1992–96, RICS. Trustee: Countryside Educn Trust, Beaulieu, Hants, 1998–2001; Habitat Res. Trust, 2003–09. *Publications:* Dealing in Diversity: America's market for nature conservation, 1995; Corporate Property Management: aligning real estate with business strategy, 2004; contrib. articles to envmtl jls. *Recreations:* golf, ski-ing, riding, travel, cooking for friends, walking, West Highland Terriers, the New Forest. *Address:* Ernest Cook Trust, Fairford Park, Fairford, Glos GL7 4JH. *E:* Victoria.Edwards@ernestcooktrust.org.uk.

**EDWARDS-MOSS, (Sir) David John**, (5th Bt *cr* 1868); *S* father, 1988, but does not use the title and his name does not appear on the Official Roll of the Baronetage.

**EDWARDS-STUART, Hon. Sir Antony James Cobham**, Kt 2009; international arbitrator, since 2017; a Judge of the High Court of Justice, Queen's Bench Division, 2009–16; Deputy Chair, Security Vetting Appeals Panel, since 2018; *b* 2 Nov. 1946; *s* of late Lt-Col Ivor Arthur James Edwards-Stuart and Elizabeth Aileen Le Mesurier Edwards-Stuart (*née* Deck); *m* 1973, Fiona Ann, *d* of late Paul Weaver, OBE; two *s* two *d*. *Educ:* Sherborne Sch.; RMA Sandhurst; St Catharine's Coll., Cambridge. MCIArb. Called to the Bar, Gray's Inn, 1976, Bencher, 2009; QC 1991; an Asst Recorder, 1991–97; a Recorder, 1997–2009; a Deputy High Ct Judge, 2003–09: Judge i/c, Technol. and Construction Court, 2013–16. Head of Chambers, 2005–09. Chm., Home Office Adv. Cttee on Service Candidates, 1995–98. Commnd 1st RTR, 1966; Adjutant: 1st RTR, 1973–75; Kent and Sharpshooters Sqn, Royal Yeomanry, 1976–77. *Recreations:* woodwork, restoring property in France.

**EDWARDSON, Prof. James Alexander**, PhD; Professor of Neuroendocrinology, Newcastle University, 1982–2013, now Emeritus; Director, Institute for Ageing and Health (formerly Institute for the Health of the Elderly), Newcastle University, 1994–2006; *b* 18 March 1942; *s* of James Thompson Hewson Edwardson and Isabel Ann Edwardson; *m* 1965, Caroline Hunter; one *s* two *d*. *Educ:* South Shields Grammar-Technical Sch. for Boys; Univ. of Nottingham (BSc Hons Zoology 1963); Inst. of Psychiatry, Univ. of London (PhD 1966). MRC Junior Res. Fellow, Inst. of Psychiatry, 1966–67; Lectr in Physiology, Aberdeen Univ., 1967–69; MRC Scientist and Lectr in Biochem., Imperial Coll., London, 1970–75; Sen. Lectr, then Reader, in Physiology, St George's Hosp. Med. Sch., 1975–79; Director: MRC Neurochem. Pathology Unit, 1979–2000; MRC-Newcastle Univ. Centre Develt for Clinical Brain Ageing, 2000–04. Chairman: Years Ahead - NE Regl Forum on Ageing, 2005–09; VOICE North, 2011–13. Vice-President: Alzheimer's Disease Soc., 1989–; Age Concern Newcastle, 2007–14. Mem. Council, Natural Hist. Soc. of Northumbria, 2004–18; Vice Chm., Northumbria Reg., U3A, 2012–15. *Publications:*

numerous papers on brain biochem., physiology and behaviour and on Alzheimer's Disease and related neurodegenerative disorders. *Recreations:* bird watching, poetry. *Address:* 18 Leslie Crescent, Newcastle upon Tyne NE3 4AN. *T:* (0191) 285 0159.

**EDWARDSON, Prof. (John) Michael,** PhD; Sheild Professor of Pharmacology, since 2017, and Head, Department of Pharmacology, since 2013, University of Cambridge; Fellow of Christ's College, Cambridge, since 2003; *b* Warrington, Cheshire, 30 Dec. 1954; *s* of John Edwardson and Mary Edwardson (*née* Hailey); *m* 1985, Prof. (Anne) Jennifer Morton; two *s*. *Educ:* St Augustine's Primary Sch., Latchford, Warrington; St Ambrose Coll., Hale Barns, Altrincham; Trinity Coll., Cambridge (BA 1976; PhD 1979). Lectr in Pharmacol., Sch. of Pharmacy, Univ. of London, 1981–84; University of Cambridge: Lectr in Pharmacol., 1984–2000; Reader in Molecular Pharmacol., 2000–09; Prof. of Molecular Pharmacol., 2009–17. *Publications:* articles in biol jls. *Recreation:* Cambridge United Football Club. *Address:* Department of Pharmacology, University of Cambridge, Tennis Court Road, Cambridge CB2 1PD. *T:* (01223) 334014, *Fax:* (01223) 334100. *E:* jme1000@cam.ac.uk.

**EDZARD, Christine;** film director; Managing Director, Sands Film Studios, 1975; *b* 15 Feb. 1945; *d* of Dietz Edzard and Susanne Eisendieck, painters; *m* 1968, Richard Goodwin; one *d*, and one step *s* one step *d*. *Educ:* Ecole Nationale de Science Politique, Paris (Econ degree). Asst designer to Lila de Nobili and Rostislav Doboujinsky, Paris; asst on Zeffirelli's Romeo and Juliet, 1966; designer for Hamburg Opera, WNO and Camden Town Fest.; designer, costumes and sets and wrote (with Richard Goodwin) script of film, Tales of Beatrix Potter, 1971; directed short films, The Little Match Girl, The Kitchen and Little Ida, released as Tales from a Flying Trunk; dir, The Nightingale, 1979; wrote and directed: Biddy, 1981 (first feature film); Little Dorrit, 1987 (BAFTA Award, Best Screenplay; LA Critics Award, Best Film; Orson Welles Award, Best Director); The Fool, 1991; directed and produced, As You Like It, 1992; designed and directed, Menotti's Amahl and the Night Visitors, Spoleto Fest., 1996; wrote, designed and directed: The Nutcracker, 1997; The Children's Midsummer Night's Dream, 2000; wrote and directed, The Good Soldier Schwejk, 2017. *Address:* Sands Films Costumes Ltd, 82 Saint Marychurch Street, SE16 4HZ. *T:* (020) 7231 2209, *Fax:* (020) 7231 2209.

**EEKELAAR, John Michael,** FBA 2001; Reader in Family Law, University of Oxford, 1990–2005; Academic Director, Pembroke College, Oxford, 2005–09, now Emeritus Fellow (Tutorial Fellow, 1965–2005); *b* Johannesburg, 2 July 1942; *s* of John (Jan) Eekelaar and Delphine Eekelaar (*née* Stoughton); *m* 1978, Pia Nicole Lewis; two *d*. *Educ:* King's Coll., London (LLB); University Coll., Oxford (BCL). Rhodes Schol., 1963–65; Vinerian Schol., 1965. University of Oxford: Lectr in Law, 1966–90; Res. Fellow, Centre for Socio-Legal Studies, 1976–2000; Co-Dir, Oxford Centre for Family Law and Policy, 2000–. Dist. Vis. Fellow, NZ Law Foundn, 2005. Pres., Internat. Soc. of Family Law, 1985–88. Gen. Ed., Oxford Jl Legal Studies, 1993–2005; Founding Co-ed., Internat. Jl Law Policy and the Family, 1987–. *Publications:* Family Security and Family Breakdown, 1971; Family Law and Social Policy, 1978, 2nd edn 1984 (trans. German 1983); (ed jtly) Family Violence: an international and interdisciplinary study, 1978; (ed jtly) Marriage and Cohabitation in Contemporary Societies, 1982; (jtly) The Protection of Children: state intervention and family life, 1983; (ed jtly) The Resolution of Family Conflict: comparative legal perspectives, 1984; (jtly) Maintenance after Divorce, 1986; (ed jtly) Family, State and Individual Economic Security, 1988; (ed jtly) Divorce Mediation and the Legal Process, 1988; (ed jtly) An Aging World: dilemmas and challenges for law and social policy, 1989; (jtly) The Reform of Child Care Law, 1990; Regulating Divorce, 1991; (ed jtly) Parenthood in Modern Society: social and legal issues for the Twenty-First century, 1993; (ed jtly) A Reader on Family Law, 1994; (jtly) The Parental Obligation: a study of parenthood across households, 1997; (ed jtly) The Changing Family: family law and family forms in international perspective, 1998; (jtly) Family Lawyers: the divorce work of solicitors, 2000; (ed jtly) Cross Currents: family law and policy in the US and England, 2000; Family Law and Personal Life, 2006, 2nd edn 2017; (jtly) Family Law Advocacy 2009; (ed jtly) Managing Family Justice in Diverse Societies, 2013; (jtly) Family Justice, 2013; (jtly) Lawyers and Mediators, 2016; (jtly) After the Act, 2019; contrib. articles to jls and chapters in books. *Recreation:* music. *Address:* Ridgeway Cottage, The Ridgeway, Boars Hill, Oxford OX1 5EX. *T:* (01865) 735485.

**EELES, Maj. Gen. Nicholas Henry,** CBE 2014; Executive Chairman, Royal Artillery Museums Ltd, since 2016; *b* Lyndhurst, 24 April 1961; *s* of Maj. Anthony Thomas Eeles, MC, RA and Valerie Mildred Eeles (*née* Hayes); *m* 1990, Carolyn, (Wob), Stirling Smith; one *s* two *d*. *Educ:* Homefield Coll.; Brockenhurst Coll.; Bristol Univ. (BSc Biochem. 1982); RMA Sandhurst. Commnd RA, 1983; psc 1993; Battery Comdr, C Battery, RHA, 1996–98; CO, 26 Regt RA, 2001–03; Col Manning (A), 2003–05; hcsc 2005; CRA 3 (UK) Div., 2005–07; Brig., Gen. Staff, MoD, 2007–10; Dir, RA, 2010–11; GOC 2nd Div., Scotland, and Gov., Edinburgh Castle, 2012–15. Hon. Regt Col, 26 Regt RA, 2011–15; Col Comdt, RA, 2012–17. Chairman: RA Centre for Personal Develt, 2010–16; RA Historical Trust, 2012–17. *Recreations:* tennis, modern poetry, World War I history, ornithology.

**EFFINGHAM, 7th Earl of,** *cr* 1837; **David Mowbray Algernon Howard;** DL; Baron Howard of Effingham 1554; Commander RN, retd; National President, The Royal British Legion, 2003–06; *b* 29 April 1939; *s* of Hon. John Algernon Frederick Charles Howard (*d* 1971), *yr s* of 5th Earl, and his 1st wife, Suzanne Patricia (*née* Macassey); *S* uncle, 1996; *m* 1st, 1964, Anne Mary Sayer (marr. diss. 1975); one *s*; 2nd, 1992, Mrs Elizabeth Jane Turner; two step *s*. *Educ:* Fettes Coll., Edinburgh; Royal Naval Coll., Dartmouth. Royal Navy, 1961–91. DL Essex, 2006. *Recreations:* horse racing, fishing. *Heir: s* Lord Howard of Effingham, *qv*. *Address:* (home) Readings, Blackmore End, Essex CM7 4DH. *T:* (office) (01787) 461182. *Clubs:* Royal Navy, Army and Navy; Essex.
See also C. A. F. Howard.

**EFFORD, Clive Stanley;** MP (Lab) Eltham, since 1997; *b* 10 July 1958; *s* of Stanley Charles Efford and Mary Agnes Elizabeth Christina Caldwell; *m* 1981, Gillian Vallins; three *d*. *Educ:* Walworth Comprehensive Sch. Sen. Adventure Playground Leader; Asst to Warden, Pembroke Coll. Mission; former London taxi driver. Mem. (Lab) Greenwich LBC, 1986–98 (former Gp Sec.; Chief Whip; Chm., Social Services Cttee, Health and Envmt Cttee). Contested (Lab) Eltham, 1992. Shadow Minister for the Home Office, 2010–11, for Sports, Tourism and Gambling, 2011–16; PPS to successive Ministers for Housing, DCLG, 2008–10. Member: Procedure Select Cttee, 1997–2000; Transport Select Cttee, 2002–09; DCMS Select Cttee, 2018–. Prelim. FA Coach's Badge. *Recreations:* sports, reading, cinema. *Address:* (office) 132 Westmount Road, Eltham, SE9 1UT. *T:* (020) 8850 5744. *Clubs:* Eltham Hill Working Man's, Woolwich Catholic.

**EFSTATHIOU, Prof. George Petros,** FRS 1994; Professor of Astrophysics, University of Cambridge, since 1997 (Director, Kavli Institute for Cosmology, 2008–13); Fellow, King's College, Cambridge, since 1997; *b* 2 Sept. 1955; *s* of Petros Efstathiou and Christina (*née* Parperi); *m* 1st, 1976, Helena Jane (*née* Smart) (marr. diss. 1997); one *s* one *d*; 2nd, 1998, Yvonne Nobis; two *s*. *Educ:* Somerset Comprehensive Sch., Keble Coll., Oxford (BA); Univ. of Durham (Dept of Physics) (PhD). Res. Asst, Astronomy Dept, Univ. of California, Berkeley, 1979–80; SERC Res. Asst, Inst. of Astronomy, Univ. of Cambridge, 1980–83; Jun. Res. Fellow, 1980–84, Sen. Res. Fellow, 1984–88, King's Coll., Cambridge; Institute of Astronomy, Cambridge: Sen. Asst in Res., 1984–87; Asst Dir of Res., 1987–88; Head of Astrophysics, 1988–94; Savilian Prof. of Astronomy, and Fellow, New Coll., Oxford, 1988–97; PPARC Sen. Fellow, 1994–99; Dir, 2004–08. Mem., PPARC, 2001–04. Maxwell Medal and Prize, Inst. of Physics, 1990; Bodossaki Foundn Academic and Cultural Prize for Astrophysics, 1994; Robinson Prize in Cosmology, Univ. of Newcastle, 1997; Heineman Prize for Astrophysics, Amer. Inst. of Physics, 2005; Gruber Cosmol. Prize, Peter and Patricia Gruber Foundn, 2011; Hughes Medal, Royal Soc., 2015. *Publications:* articles in astronomical jls. *Recreation:* playing the guitar. *Address:* Institute of Astronomy, Hoyle Building, Madingley Road, Cambridge CB3 0HA. *T:* (01223) 337548.

**EFUNSHILE, Althea,** CBE 2016; Founding Chair, National College for Creative and Cultural Industries, since 2016; *b* 20 Aug. 1956; *d* of Chas L. Barrett and Ena Louise Barrett; partner, David Reardon; one *s* one *d*. *Educ:* Univ. of Essex (BA Hons Sociol.); Goldsmiths' Coll., London (PGCE); Buckinghamshire Coll. (DMS). Teacher, Brent, 1980–83; Dir, Elimu Community Educn Centre, 1983–85; detached youth worker, 1987, Area Youth Worker, 1987–89, Bucks CC; Educn Officer, Harrow, 1989–93; Asst Dir of Educn, Merton, 1993–96; Exec. Dir, Educn and Culture, Lewisham, 1996–2001; Dir, Children and Young People's Unit, then Safeguarding Children Gp, subseq. Vulnerable Children Gp, DFES, 2001–06; Arts Council England: Exec. Dir, Arts Planning and Investment, 2007; Chief Operating Officer, 2009–13; Dep. Chief Exec., 2013–16; Actg Chief Exec., 2015). Non-exec. Dir, Channel 4, 2017–. *Recreations:* travel, reading, cinema.

**EGAN, Caroline Elizabeth;** see Rees, C. E.

**EGAN, Sir John (Leopold),** Kt 1986; DL; Chairman, Severn Trent plc, 2005–10; Chancellor, Coventry University, 2007–17; *b* 7 Nov. 1939; *m* 1963, Julia Emily Treble; two *d*. *Educ:* Bablake Sch., Coventry; Imperial Coll., London Univ., 1958–61 (BSc Hons; FIC 1985); London Business Sch., London Univ., 1966–68 (MScEcon). Petroleum Engineer, Shell International, 1962–66; General Manager, AC-Delco Replacement Parts Operation, General Motors Ltd, 1968–71; Managing Director, Leyland Cars Parts Div., Parts and Service Director, Leyland Cars, BLMC, 1971–76; Corporate Parts Director, Massey Ferguson, 1976–80; Chm. and Chief Exec., Jaguar Cars Ltd, 1980–85, Jaguar plc, 1985–90; Chief Exec., BAA plc, 1990–99; Chairman: MEPC plc, 1998–2000; Inchcape plc, 2000–05; Harrison Lovegrove Ltd, 2000–05; QinetiQ, 2001–02. Director: Foreign and Colonial Investment Trust, 1985–97; Legal & General Group, 1987–97 (Dep. Chm., 1993–97). Chm., 1993–97, Pres., 1998–, London Tourist Bd; Dir, BTA, 1994–97. Dep. Pres., 2001–02, Pres., 2002–04, CBI. Hon. Professor: Dept of Engrg, Warwick Univ. 1990; Aston Univ., 1990. DL Warwicks, 1988. Sen. Fellow, RCA, 1987; FCIPS 1993; FRAeS 1994; FCIT 1994. Hon. FCIM 1989. Hon. Fellow: London Business Sch., 1988; Wolverhampton Poly., 1989. Dr hc Cranfield Inst. of Technology, 1986; Hon. DTech: Loughborough, 1987; Brunel, 1997; Hon. DBA Internat. Business Sch., 1988; Hon. LLD Bath, 1988; Hon. DSc Aston, 1992. Hon. Insignia for Technology, CGLI, 1987. Internat. Distinguished Entrepreneur Award, Univ. of Manitoba, 1989. MBA Award of the Year, 1988. *Recreations:* music, ski-ing, tennis. *Clubs:* Royal Automobile, MCC; Warwick Boat.

**EGAN, Michael Flynn John;** QC 2006; Queen's Coroner and Attorney, Master of the Crown Office and Registrar of Criminal Appeals, 2011–18, and Registrar of the Court Martial Appeal Court, 2012–18; *b* Dungarvan, Co. Waterford, 14 March 1952; *s* of late Maurice Egan and Joan Egan (*née* Flynn); *m* 1976, Shelagh Patricia Terry; one *s* one *d*. *Educ:* Coll. of Law, Lancaster Gate. Articled clerk, Turberville Smith & Co., 1971–76; admitted as solicitor, 1976; Kingsley Napley & Co., 1977–81; called to the Bar, Gray's Inn, 1981 (Bencher, 2012); Asst Recorder, 1998–2000; Recorder, 2000–; Special Counsel, 2004; Special Advocate, 2009. Chair of Trustees, Dacorum Citizens' Advice, 2018–. *Recreations:* sport, horology, 2CVs.

**EGAN, Penelope Jane,** CBE 2013; Executive Director, Fulbright Commission, 2007–19; *b* 18 July 1951; *d* of late Derek A. Morris and of June E. Morris; *m* 1975, David Anthony Egan (*d* 2016); two *s*. *Educ:* St Paul's Girls' Sch.; Leicester Univ. (BA 1971). Mus. Asst, 1971–73, Press Officer, 1973–77, Victoria & Albert Mus.; Press Officer, Prime Minister's Office, 1975–77; Press and Publicity Officer, Crafts Council, 1977–82; Lecture Sec., 1986–95, Programme Develt Dir, 1995–97, Exec. Dir, 1998–2006, RSA. Mem., Design Council, 1999–2008. Trustee: Geffrye Mus., 2006–14 (Chm. Trustees, 2010–14); Demos, 2009–13; RSA Academies, 2014–. Member, Council: Warwick Univ., 2007–12 and 2013–15; Reading Univ., 2016–. Mem., Internat. Women's Forum. Hon. FRCA 2006. Hon. FRSA 2006. *Recreations:* tennis, cooking, cinema. *Address:* 11 Egliston Road, Putney, SW15 1AL. *T:* 07885 398050. *E:* penny@pennyegan.com. *Clubs:* Roehampton, Pilgrims.

**EGAN, Rt Rev. Dr Philip;** see Portsmouth, Bishop of, (R.C.).

**EGAN, Rt Rev. Mgr Canon Thomas;** Parish Priest of Our Lady of Lourdes, New Southgate, 2001–17; *b* 15 Feb. 1942; *s* of Frank and Mary Egan. *Educ:* St Joseph's Primary Sch., Macklin St, Holborn; Challoner Sec. Sch., Finchley; St Edmund's Coll., Ware; Inst. of Educn, London Univ. (BEd). Asst priest, Our Lady and St Joseph, Hanwell, 1967–72; Home Mission Team, 1972–73; asst priest, St Joan of Arc, Highbury, 1973–78; Parish Priest, St Pius X, St Charles Square, 1978–86; Pastoral Dir, Allen Hall Seminary, 1986–90; Parish Priest, Our Lady of Hal, Camden Town, 1990–93; VG, Archdio. Westminster, 1993–2001. Mem., Westminster Cath. Chapter of Canons, 2005–17, Canon Emeritus, 2017. *Recreations:* fishing, swimming, football. *Address:* Flat 2, 90 Station Road, Wood Green, N22 7SY.

**EGBUNA, Robert Obiora; His Honour Judge Egbuna;** a Circuit Judge, since 2015; *b* London, 30 Nov. 1963; *s* of Dr Robert Egbuna and Dr Phyllis Wakile; *m* 1992, Maite Gloria Ruiz-Guerrero; one *s* one *d*. *Educ:* Sibford Quaker Sch., Sibford Ferris, Banbury; Poly. of Central London (LLB Hons); Council of Legal Educn. Called to the Bar, Gray's Inn, 1988; a Recorder, 2009–15. *Recreation:* golf badly! *Address:* Derby Combined Court Centre, Morledge, Derby DE1 2XE. *T:* (01332) 622657. *Club:* Notts Golf (Hollingwell).

**EGERTON,** family name of **Duke of Sutherland**.

**EGERTON, Keith Robert,** FRICS; non-executive Director, Rowlandson Organisation, 2002–12; Chairman, Native Land Ltd, 2003–07; *b* 26 June 1942; *s* of Harold and Doris Egerton; *m* 1968, Pauline Steele; one *s* one *d*. FRICS 1988 (ARICS 1966). Development Surveyor, Laing Properties, 1970–73; Commercial Union Properties: S Area Develt Manager, 1973–75; Dir, Belgian and Dutch projects, 1975–77; Dir, 1978–82; Dir, 1977–82, Chief Exec., 1978–82, Commercial Union Property Develts Ltd; Costain plc, 1982–91: Man. Dir, 1982–85, Chief Exec., 1985–91, County & District Properties; Director: resp. for Property, 1986–90; resp. for UK Spanish and Calif Housing Ops and Property, 1990–91; joined Taylor Woodrow plc, 1991; Dir, 1992–2002; Gp Chief Exec., 1998–2002; Man. Dir, 1991–98, and Chm., 1992–99, Taylor Woodrow Property Co. Ltd; Director: Taywood Homes, 1996–98; Monarch Develt Corp., 1998–2002. *Recreations:* cycling, gardening, hill walking, country pursuits, motorbikes, vintage and other interesting cars. *Address:* The White House, Run Common, Shamley Green, Guildford, Surrey GU5 0SY. *T:* (01483) 272944.

**EGERTON, Sir William (de Malpas),** 17th Bt *cr* 1617, of Egerton and Oulton, Cheshire; *b* Bromley, 27 April 1949; *o s* of Maj.-Gen. (Sir) David Boswell Egerton, (16th Bt), CB, OBE, MC and Margaret Gillian, ARCM (*d* 2004), *d* of Canon C. C. Inge; *S* father, 2010; *m* 1971, Ruth, *d* of late Rev. George Watson; two *s*. *Educ:* St John's Coll., Cambridge (BA 1970; MA). Technical Manager, QinetiQ plc, 2005–09. *Recreation:* local history. *Heir: s* Matthew Robert Egerton, *b* 19 May 1977. *Address:* Northdown Farmhouse, 106 Sutton Road, Sutton Poyntz, Weymouth, Dorset DT3 6LW. *T:* (01305) 832872.

**EGGAR, Rt Hon. Tim(othy John Crommelin);** PC 1995; Chairman: Cape plc, 2011–17; MyCelx Technologies Corporation, since 2011; Oil and Gas Authority, since 2019; *b* 19 Dec. 1951; *s* of late John Drennan Eggar and of Pamela Rosemary Eggar; *m* 1977, Charmian Diana Minoprio; one *s* one *d*. *Educ:* Winchester Coll.; Magdalene Coll., Cambridge (MA). Called to the Bar, Inner Temple, 1976. European Banking Co., 1975–83; Director: Charterhouse Petroleum, 1984–85; LASMO plc, 1999–2000; Chairman: M W Kellogg, 1996–98; AGIP (UK) Ltd, 1997–98; Nitol Solar plc, 2007–12. Chm., Cambridge Univ. Cons. Assoc., 1972; Vice-Chm., Fedn of Cons. Students, 1973–74. MP (C) Enfield N, 1979–97. PPS to Minister for Overseas Develt, 1982–85; Parly Under-Sec. of State, FCO, 1985–89; Minister of State: Dept of Employment, 1989–90; DES, 1990–92; DTI (Minister for Energy, 1992–96, also for Industry, 1994–96). Chief Exec., Monument Oil and Gas PLC, 1998–99 (Dir, 1997–98); Vice-Chm., ABN AMRO Corporate Finance, 2000–05; Chairman: Harrison Lovegrove & Co. Ltd, 2005–08; Indago Petroleum plc, 2005–09; 3Legs Resources, 2010–15; Haulfryn Gp, 2012–18; Dir, Anglo-Asian Mining plc, 2005–08. Pres., Russo-British Chamber of Commerce, 2004–13. Chm. Govs, Shiplake Coll., 2009–. *Recreations:* ski-ing, shooting, Rugby. *Address:* Nettlebed House, Nettlebed, Oxon RG9 5DD. *T:* (01491) 642833. *Club:* Carlton.

**EGGINGTON, Dr William Robert Owen;** Chief Medical Adviser, Department of Health and Social Security, later Department of Social Security, 1986–92; part-time Medical Adviser, Nestor Disability Alliance, 1999–2002; *b* 24 Feb. 1932; *s* of Alfred Thomas Eggington and Phyllis Eggington (*née* Wynne); *m* 1961, Patricia Mary Elizabeth, *d* of Henry David and Elizabeth Grant; one *s* one *d*. *Educ:* Kingswood School, Bath; Guy's Hosp. MB, BS 1955, DTM&H 1960, DPH 1962, DIH 1963; MFCM 1970. House Surgeon, Guy's Hosp., 1955; House Physician, St John's Hosp., Lewisham, 1956. RAMC, 1957–73, retired as Lt-Col, Senior Specialist Army Health. DHSS, later DSS, 1973–92. Medical Adviser: War Pensions Agency, 1994–98; Benefits Agency, 1998. *Recreations:* Goss heraldic china, military history, football spectator. *Address:* 33 Chestnut Road, Farnborough, Hants GU14 8LD.

**EGGLESTON, Anthony Francis,** OBE 1968; Headmaster, Campion School, Athens, 1983–88, retired; *b* 26 Jan. 1928; *s* of late J. F. Eggleston and late Mrs J. M. Barnard, Harrow, Middx; *m* 1957, Jane Morison Buxton, JP (*d* 2009), *d* of late W. L. Buxton, MBE and Mrs F. M. M. Buxton, Stanmore, Middx; one *s* two *d*. *Educ:* Merchant Taylors' Sch., Northwood (Schol.); St John's Coll., Oxford (Sir Thomas White Schol.; BA 1949, MA 1953; 2nd cl. hons Chemistry). National Service, 1950–52; 2nd Lieut, RA, Suez Canal Zone. Asst Master, Cheltenham Coll., 1952–54; Sen. Science Master, English High Sch., Istanbul, 1954–56; Asst Master, Merchant Taylors' Sch., Northwood, 1956–62; Principal, English Sch., Nicosia, 1962–68; Headmaster, Felsted Sch., 1968–82. *Recreation:* looking at and talking about buildings of all periods. *Address:* 22 Cross Penny Court, Bury St Edmunds, Suffolk IP33 1XY. *T:* (01284) 705297.
See also H. M. M. Baldwin.

**EGGLESTON, Prof. James Frederick;** Professor of Education, University of Nottingham, 1972–84, now Emeritus; *b* 30 July 1927; *s* of Frederick James and Anne Margaret Eggleston; *m* 1956, Margaret Snowden; three *s* two *d*. *Educ:* Appleby Grammar Sch.; Durham Univ. (King's Coll., Newcastle upon Tyne). BSc Hons Zoology; DipEd; FRSB (FIBiol 1975). School teacher, 1953–64, Head of Biol., later Head of Sci., Hinckley Grammar Sch.; Res. Fellow, Res. Unit for Assessment and Curriculum Studies, Leicester Univ. Sch. of Educn, 1964; team leader, later consultant, Nuffield Sci. Teaching Project, 1964–68; Lectr in Educn, Leicester Univ. Sch. of Educn, 1966; apptd to Colls and Curriculum Chair of Educn, Nottingham Univ., 1973, Dean of Educn, 1975–81. *Publications:* A Critical Review of Assessment Procedures in Secondary School Science, 1965; Problems in Quantitative Biology, 1968; (with J. F. Kerr) Studies in Assessment, 1970; (jtly) A Science Teaching Observation Schedule, 1975; (jtly) Processes and Products of Science Teaching, 1976; contributions to: The Disciplines of the Curriculum, 1971; The Art of the Science Teacher, 1974; Frontiers of Classroom Research, 1975; Techniques and Problems of Assessment, 1976; (with Trevor Kerry) Topic Work in the Primary School, 1988; articles in professional jls. *Recreations:* fell walking, golf, photography. *Address:* The Old Chapel, Church Street, Fritchley, Derbys DE56 2FQ. *T:* (01773) 850255.

**EGGLETON, Anthony,** AO 1991; CVO 1970; Director, since 1996, Member of Advisory Council, since 2007, CARE Australia (National Director, 1995–96; Vice-Chairman, 2001–04; Chairman, 2004–07); Chairman, CARE International Strategy and Governance Committees, 2003–07; *b* 30 April 1932; *s* of Tom and Winifred Eggleton; *m* 1953, Mary Walker, Melbourne; two *s* one *d*. *Educ:* King Alfred's Sch., Wantage. Journalist, Westminster Press Group, 1948–50; Editorial Staff, Bendigo Advertiser, Vic, 1950–51; Australian Broadcasting Commn, 1951–60 (Dir of ABC-TV News Coverage, 1956–60); Dir of Public Relations, Royal Australian Navy, 1960–65; Press Sec. to Prime Ministers of Australia, 1965–71 (Prime Ministers Menzies, Holt, Gorton, McMahon); Commonwealth Dir of Information, London, 1971–74; Special Advr to Leader of Opposition, and Dir of Communications, Federal Liberal Party, 1974–75; Federal Dir, Liberal Party of Australia, 1975–90; Campaign Dir, Federal Elections, 1975, 1977, 1980, 1983, 1984, 1987, 1990. Sec.-Gen., 1991–95, Bd Mem., 2001–07, CARE Internat., Brussels; CEO, Centenary of Federation Council, 1997–2002. Chairman: Asia Pacific Democrat Union, 1998–2005 (Exec. Sec., 1982–84, 1985–87, Dep. Chm., 1987–90, Pacific Democrat Union); Australian Centre for Democratic Instns, 2007–10. Mem., Australian Govt Aid Adv. Council, 2002–08. Mem. Bd, Nat. Stroke Foundn, 1997–2002. Chm., C. E. W. Bean (War Correspondents) Assoc., 2002–; Chair, Commonwealth Day Cttee, Canberra, 2006–. Mem., Editl Adv. Bd, Australian Dept of Foreign Affairs, 1999–. Australian Public Relations Inst.'s 1st Award of Honour, 1968; Outstanding Service Award, Liberal Party of Australia, 1990; Centenary Medal, Australia, 2003. *Address:* 87 Buxton Street, Deakin, ACT 2600, Australia. *Clubs:* (Foundn Pres.) National Press (Canberra), Commonwealth (Canberra).

**EGGLETON, Hon. Arthur C.;** PC (Can.) 1993; Senator of Canada, 2005–18; *b* 29 Sept. 1943; *m*; one *d*. Former accountant; consultant, urban mgt and policy issues. Toronto City Council: Mem., 1969–93; Budget Chief, 1973–80; Pres., 1975–76, 1978–80; Mayor of Toronto, 1980–91; former Member: Metropolitan Police Commn; Bd, Canadian Nat. Exhibn. MP (L) York Centre, Toronto, 1993–2004; Pres., Treasury Bd, and Minister responsible for Infrastructure, 1993–96; Minister: for Internat. Trade, 1996–97; of Nat. Defence, 1997–2002; Vice-Chm., Cabinet Cttee on Economic Policy, 1997–2002. Mem. Adv. Bd Dirs, Skylink Gp of Cos Inc. Chm., Rebuilding Lives Campaign, St John's Rehabilitation Hosp. Civic Award of Merit, Toronto, 1992.

**EGILSSON, Ólafur;** attorney and diplomat; *b* 20 Aug. 1936; *s* of Egill Kristjánsson and Anna Margrjet Thuríður Ólafsdóttir Briem; *m* 1960, Ragna Sverrisdóttir Ragnars; one *s* one *d*. *Educ:* Commercial College, Iceland (grad. 1956); Univ. of Iceland, Faculty of Law (grad. 1963). Reporter on Vísir, 1956–58, Morgunblaðið, 1959–62; publishing Exec., Almenna bókafélagið, 1963–64; Head, NATO Regional Inf. Office, Iceland, 1964–66, and Gen. Sec., Icelandic Assoc. for Western Co-operation and Atlantic Assoc. of Young Political Leaders of Iceland; Icelandic Foreign Service, 1966; Foreign Ministry, 1966–69; First Sec., later Counsellor, Icelandic Embassy, Paris, and Dep. Perm. Rep. to OECD, UNESCO, 1969–71, and Council of Europe, Strasbourg, 1969–70; Dep. Perm. Rep., NATO and Dep. Head, Icelandic Delegn to EEC, Brussels, 1971–74; Counsellor, later Minister Counsellor, Political Div., Min. of Foreign Affairs, 1974–80; Chief of Protocol, with rank of Ambassador, 1980–83; Acting Principal Private Sec. to President of Iceland, Oct. 1981–June 1982; Dep. Perm. Under Sec. and Dir Gen. for Political Affairs, Min. of Foreign Affairs, 1983–87; Ambassador: to UK, 1986–89, and concurrently to the Netherlands, Ireland and Nigeria; to USSR, later Russia, 1990–94, and concurrently to Bulgaria, Japan, Romania and Ukraine; to Denmark, 1994–96, and also to Italy, Israel, Japan, Lithuania and Turkey; in charge of Arctic co-operation, 1996–98, also accredited to the Holy See and Turkey; Ambassador to China, and concurrently to Australia, Indonesia, Japan, Korea, Mongolia, New Zealand, Thailand and Vietnam, 1998–2003; Ambassador to Thailand, Singapore, Malaysia, Indonesia and Cambodia, 2003–06. Chm., Governing Bd, Icelandic Internat. Develt Agency, 1982–87; Sec., Commn revising Foreign Service Act, 1968–69. President: Nat. Youth Council of Iceland, 1963–64; Acad. Assoc. of Reykjavík, 1967–68; Executive Member: Bible Soc., 1977–87 and 1996–2013; History Soc., 1982–88. Commander, Icelandic Order of the Falcon, 1981 (Mem. Council, 2007–16); holds numerous foreign orders. *Publications:* (jtly) Iceland and Jan Mayen, 1980; (ed) Bjarni Benediktsson: Contemporaries' views, 1983; (jtly) NATO's Anxious Birth: the prophetic vision of the 1940s, 1985; (ed) Shaping Culture, 2012; contrib. articles to Iceland Rev. and Danish-Icelandic Soc. Centenary Festschrift. *Recreations:* walking, music (opera), history. *Address:* Valhusabraut 35, 170 Seltjarnarnes, Iceland. *T:* 6151121, *Fax:* 5515411. *E:* olegice@simnet.is.

**EGLIN, Philip Michael;** ceramic artist; *b* Gibraltar, 29 Nov. 1959; *s* of Jack and Mary Eglin; *m* 1987, Jennet Walters; two *s*. *Educ:* Harlow Tech. Coll.; Staffordshire Poly. (BA 1982); Royal Coll. of Art (MA Ceramics 1986). Sen. Lectr, Staffs Poly., later Staffs Univ., 1987–2011. Mem., Selected Index Cttee, Crafts Council, 1997–2000. Fellow, Arts Foundn, 1993. Solo exhibitions include: Stafford Art Gall., 1990; Oxford Gall., 1991; New Work, Scottish Gall., Edinburgh, 2004; Franklin Parrasch Gall., NY; Barrett Marsden Gall., London, 2001, 2003, 2006 and Hands Off Berbatov (ceramics), 2008; Borrowings, Nottingham Mus. and Art Gall., 2007; Dean Proj., Sculpture Objects and Functional Art Fair, NY, 2007; Spiritual Heroes (ceramics), 2008, Wakelin Award, 2017, Glynn Vivian Art Gall., Swansea; Popes, Pin-ups and Pooches, Scottish Gall., Edinburgh, 2009; Mixed Marriage(s), Blackwell Hse, Cumbria, 2011; Nice Pair of Jugs, 2013, Kick the Bucket, 2016, Marsden Woo Gall., London; Slipping the Trail, touring exhibn, Aberystwyth Arts Centre, 2015; Unfinished Business, Scottish Gall., Edinburgh, 2017; Ajar: a taste of contemporary art, Art Genève, Switzerland, 2019; *group exhibitions* include: Contemporary Applied Arts, London, 1986, 1988, 1989, 1992; Crafts Council, London, 1991, 1996, 1999; One From the Heart, Aberystwyth Arts Centre, 1995; The Nude in Clay, Chicago, 1995; Hell Fire, Stedelijk Mus. in De Nieuwe Kerk, Amsterdam, 2008; Galerie Handwerk, Munich, 2009; Inscription, Jerwood Space, London, 2010; Modern British Potters, Goldmark Gall., Uppingham, 2010; Double Take, 2010, Many a Slip, 2015, Marsden Woo Gall., London; Taiwan Ceramics Biennale, Taipei Ceramics Mus., 2010; Contemp. British Studio Ceramics, Graine Collection, Charlotte, NC, 2010; British Ceramics Biennial, Stoke-on-Trent, 2011; RA Summer Show, 2012; Gp Jug Show, 2013, Motifs, Places, Figures Libres, 2014, Helene Azziza Gall., Paris; Positions of Design, 2014, Meister der Moderne, 2014, Galerie Handwerk, Munich; Taste Contemp. Craft, Artgenève, Geneva, 2015; Ceramix, Bonnefanten Mus., Maastricht, 2015; Crafts Study Centre, Farnham, 2015; Nat. Mus. of Wales, Cardiff, 2015; V&A Mus., London, 2015; Material: Earth, Messums, Wilts, 2017; Things of Beauty Growing, Yale Centre for British Art and Fitzwilliam Mus., Cambridge, 2017; Taste Contemp. Craft, Art Genève, Switzerland, 2018; work in public collections, including: V&A Mus.; Brighton Mus.; Crafts Council, London; Portsmouth City Mus. and Art Gall.; Fitzwilliam Mus., Cambridge; York Mus.; Middlesbrough Inst. Modern Art; Stedelijk Mus., Amsterdam; Gardiner Mus., Toronto; Mint Mus., N Carolina; Sèvres Mus., Paris; La Piscine Mus., Roubaix; Nat. Mus. of Wales, Cardiff; Craft Study Centre, Farnham; Glynn Vivian Art Gall., Swansea (Wakelin Award purchase prize, 2017). Jerwood Prize for Applied Arts, Jerwood Foundn, 1996. *Publications:* Philip Eglin, 1997; (with Tony Hayward) Eglin's Etchings, 2008; *catalogues*: Borrowings, 2007; Popes, Pin-ups and Pooches, 2009; Mixed Marriage(s), 2011; Slipping the Trail, 2015; Unfinished Business, 2017; Ajar, 2019. *Recreations:* manager of football teams, Westpoint Wanderers (mini-soccer league, under 11s) and Shamblers FC (Potteries jun. youth league, under 13s).

**EGLINTON AND WINTON,** 19th Earl of, *cr* 1507; **Hugh Archibald William Montgomerie;** Lord Montgomerie, 1448; Baron Seton and Tranent, 1859; Baron Kilwinning, 1615; Baron Ardrossan (UK), 1806; Earl of Winton (UK), 1859; Hereditary Sheriff of Renfrewshire; Datacentre Storage Architect, Dell Computers, since 2004; *b* 24 July 1966; *s* of 18th Earl of Eglinton and Winton and Marion Carolina Montgomerie; *m* 1991, Sara Alexandra (marr. diss. 1998), *e d* of Niel Redpath; *m* 2001, Carol Anne Robinson, *yr d* of R. Donald Robinson Jr, Brentwood, Tenn; one *s* two *d*. *Educ:* Univ. of Edinburgh (MBA 2000). RN officer, 1988–92. Ops Manager, Gander & White Shipping Ltd, 1996–97. Intelligence Officer, 51 Highland Bde, 1997–98. Project Manager, ReServ Construction Co. Inc., 2000–04. Chm., Soc. of Scottish Armigers; Co-Chair, Historic Franklin Masonic Hall Foundn. *Heir: s* Lord Montgomerie, *qv*.

**EGLINTON, Prof. Timothy Ian,** PhD; FRS 2014; Professor of Biogeoscience, Geological Institute, ETH Zürich, since 2010; *b* UK; *s* of Prof. Geoffrey Eglinton, FRS and Pamela Joan Eglinton; *m*; three *c*. *Educ:* Plymouth Poly. (BSc Envmtl Sci. 1982); Univ. of Newcastle upon Tyne (MSc 1983; PhD Organic Chem. 1988). Postdoctoral res., Delft Tech. Univ. and Oslo Univ.; Mem., Scientific Staff, then Asst, later Associate, subseq. Sen. Scientist, Dept of Marine Chem. and Geochem., Woods Hole Oceanographic Instn, 1990–2010 (Chm. of Dept, 2007–10). Mem., Scientific Adv. Bd, Max Planck Inst. for Biogeochemistry, 2015. Mem., Bd of Dirs, Geochem. Soc., 2016–18. *Address:* Geological Institute, ETH Zürich, Sonneggstrasse 5, 8092 Zürich, Switzerland.

**EGREMONT,** 2nd Baron *cr* 1963, **AND LECONFIELD,** 7th Baron *cr* 1859; **John Max Henry Scawen Wyndham;** DL; FRSL, FSA; *b* 21 April 1948; *s* of John Edward Reginald Wyndham, MBE, 1st Baron Egremont and 6th Baron Leconfield, and Pamela, *d* of late Captain the Hon. Valentine Wyndham-Quin, RN; *S* father, 1972; *m* 1978, Caroline, *er d* of A. R. Nelson, Muckairn, Taynuilt, Argyll, and Hon. Lady Musker; one *s* three *d*. *Educ:* Eton; Christ Church, Oxford (MA Modern History). Mem., Royal Commn on Historical MSS, 1989–2001. Chm., Friends of the Nat. Libraries, 1985–2018; Trustee: Wallace Collection, 1988–2000; British Museum, 1990–2000; Nat. Manuscripts Conservation Trust, 1995–2018 (Chm., 2000–18). President: ACRE, 1993–99; Sussex Heritage Trust, 2009–. DL W Sussex, 1988. FRSL 2001; FSA 2005. *Publications:* (as Max Egremont) The

Cousins: a biographical study of Wilfrid Scawen Blunt and George Wyndham, 1977 (Yorkshire Post First Book Award); Balfour: a life of Arthur James Balfour, 1980; Under Two Flags: the life of Major-General Sir Edward Spears, 1997; Siegfried Sassoon, 2005: Forgotten Land: journeys among the ghosts of East Prussia, 2011; Some Desperate Glory: the First World War the poets knew, 2014; The Connell Guide to World War One, 2017; (with F. Carey) Käthe Kollwitz: portrait of the artist, 2017; All You Need to Know About World War 1, 2018; *novels:* The Ladies' Man, 1983; Dear Shadows, 1986; Painted Lives, 1989; Second Spring, 1993. *Heir: s* Hon. George Ronan Valentine Wyndham [*b* 31 July 1983; *m* 2019, Cruz Maria, *d* of Manuel Vallespir Machado]. *Address:* Petworth House, Petworth, West Sussex GU28 0AE. *T:* (01798) 342447. *E:* egremont@leconfield.net.

**EHLERS, Prof. Anke,** PhD; FBA 2010; FMedSci; Professor of Experimental Psychopathology, and Wellcome Principal Research Fellow, University of Oxford, since 2012; *b* Kiel, Germany, 11 Jan. 1957; *d* of Hans Werner and Hella Ehlers; *m* 1994, Prof. David Millar Clark, *qv;* two *s. Educ:* Eberhard-Karls-Univ. Tübingen (Dip. Psychol. 1983; PhD 1985); Philipps-Univ. Marburg (Dr rer. nat. habil. 1990). Res. Scholar, Stanford Univ., 1983–85; Asst Prof., Philipps-Univ. Marburg, 1985–90; Associate Prof., Free Univ. of Berlin, 1990; Prof., Georg-August-Univ. Göttingen, 1991–93; Wellcome Principal Res. Fellow, Univ. of Oxford, 1993–2000; Prof. of Experimental Psychopathology, and Wellcome Principal Res. Fellow, KCL, 2000–11. MAE 2012. Fellow, German Acad. of Scis Leopoldina, 2005. FMedSci 2014. German Psychology Prize, 2013; Oswald Külpe Prize, Univ. of Würzburg, 2013; Award for Distinguished Scientific Contribs to Clinical Psychol., Amer. Psychol Assoc., 2014; Wilhelm Wundt-William James Award, Eur. Fedn of Psychol. Assocs and Amer. Psychol Foundn, 2015. *Publications:* (ed jtly) Perspectives and Promises of Clinical Psychology, 1992; numerous articles in scientific jls. *Recreations:* theatre, art, cinema, travel. *Address:* Department of Experimental Psychology, University of Oxford, The Old Rectory, Paradise Square, Oxford OX1 1TW. *T:* (01865) 618602. *E:* anke.ehlers@psy.ox.ac.uk.

**EHRMAN, Sir William (Geoffrey),** KCMG 2007 (CMG 1998); HM Diplomatic Service, retired; Ambassador to the People's Republic of China, 2006–10; *b* 28 Aug. 1950; *s* of John Patrick William Ehrman, FBA and Susan (*née* Blake); *m* 1977, Penelope Anne, *d* of late Brig. H. W. Le Patourel, VC and of Babette Le Patourel; one *s* three *d. Educ:* Eton; Trinity Coll., Cambridge (MA); Royal Agricultural Coll. (DipAgr 2011). Joined Diplomatic Service, 1973; language student, Hong Kong, 1975–76; Third/Second Sec., Peking, 1976–78; First Secretary, UK Mission to UN, NY, 1979–83, Peking, 1983–84, FCO, 1985–89; Pol Advr, Hong Kong, 1989–93; Head, Near East and N Africa Dept, FCO, 1993–94; UK Mem., Bosnia Contact Gp, 1994–95; Prin. Pvte Sec. to Sec. of State for Foreign and Commonwealth Affairs, 1995–97; seconded to Unilever (China) Ltd, 1997–98; Ambassador to Luxembourg, 1998–2000; Dir, Internat. Security, 2000–02, Dir Gen., Defence and Intelligence, 2002–04, FCO; Chm., Jt Intelligence Cttee, and Hd, Intelligence and Security Secretariat, Cabinet Office, 2004–05. *Recreations:* sailing, walking, ski-ing. *Club:* Royal Cruising.

**EICHEL, Hans;** Member (SPD), Bundestag, 2002–09; Minister of Finance, Germany, 1999–2005; *b* Kassel, 24 Dec. 1941; *m;* two *c.* Secondary sch. teacher, Kassel, 1970–75. Mem., Kassel City Council, 1968–75; Mayor, Kassel, 1975–91; Mem. (SPD), Assembly, and Premier, Hesse Land, 1991–99. German Convention of Municipal Authorities: Mem., Presidium, 1981–91; Pres., 1985–87 and 1989–91. Joined SPD, 1964: Mem., Exec. Cttee, 1984–2005; Chm., Hesse, 1989–2005.

**EICKE, Tim;** Judge, European Court of Human Rights, since 2016; *b* Hannover, Germany, 27 July 1966; *s* of Reinhard Eicke and Gerda Adeline Eicke (*née* Loescher); *m* 1993, Andrea Elisabeth Hielscher; two *s. Educ:* Ulrichsgymnasium Norden; Passau Universität; Univ. of Dundee (LLB Hons English Law 1992; LLD 2017). Called to the Bar, Middle Temple, 1993; Jun. Counsel to the Crown, 1999–2011; QC 2011; Bencher, Lincoln's Inn, 2014. Ed., European Human Rights Reports, 1999–2016. *Publications:* (ed jtly) The Strasbourg Case Law: leading cases from the European Court of Human Rights, 2001; (jtly) Human Rights Damages: principles and practice, 2001. *Recreations:* family, cycling, cooking, bread making. *Address:* European Court of Human Rights, Council of Europe, 67075 Strasbourg, France.

**EIDENMÜLLER, Prof. Horst Gerhard Michael,** PhD; Professor of Commercial Law, University of Oxford, since 2015; Fellow, St Hugh's College, Oxford, since 2015; *b* Munich, 23 Oct. 1963; *m* Dr Kathrin; one *s* one *d. Educ:* Univ. of Vienna; Univ. of Munich (1st and 2nd Legal State Exams, 1988, 1992; PhD *summa cum laude* 1994; Habilitation 1998); Peterhouse, Cambridge (LLM 1st Cl. Hons 1989). Associate, McKinsey & Co., Düsseldorf, 1991–92; Visiting Scholar: Univ. of Calif, Berkeley, 1992; Harvard Law Sch., 1993; Prof. of Private Law, Civil Procedure, German and Internat. Business Law, Univ. of Münster, 1999–2003; University of Munich: Prof. of Private Law, German, Eur. and Internat. Commercial and Corporate Law, 2003–15; Director: Munich Centre for Dispute Resolution, 2003–15; Inst. of Internat. Law, 2003–15; Res. Prof., 2007–11. Herbert Smith Vis. Prof., Univ. of Cambridge, 2007; Visiting Professor: Univ. of Oxford, 2009–14; Harvard Law Sch., 2011; Stanford Univ., 2014; Columbia Univ., 2018; Global Vis. Prof., NY Univ. Law Sch., NY, 2013– (Mem., Global Faculty, 2013–); Vis. Fellow, Peterhouse, Univ. of Cambridge, 2002; Res. Associate, Eur. Corporate Governance Inst., 2009–. Member, Editorial Board: Eur. Corporate Governance Inst. Law Working Paper Series; Jl Corporate Law Studies; Zeitschrift für Wirtschaftsrecht; Zeitschrift für Konfliktmanagement; Recht der Internat. Wirtschaft. Member: Berlin-Brandenburg Acad. of Sci. and Humanities, 2008–; Eur. Law Inst., 2011–; Eur. Acad. Sci. and Arts, 2016–. Mem., Internat. Acad. Comparative Law, 2010–. Fellow: Inst. for Advanced Study, Berlin, 2008–09; Centre for Advanced Study, Univ. of Munich, 2008–; Inst. Law and Econs, Univ. of Chicago, 2013. *Publications:* Effizienz als Rechtsprinzip: Möglichkeiten und Grenzen der ökonomischen Analyse des Rechts, 1995, 4th edn 2015; (with A. Heldrich) Europarechtliche Regulierung der telefonischen Markt- und Sozialforschung, 1995; Unternehmenssanierung zwischen Markt und Gesetz: Mechanismen der Unternehmensreorganisation und Kooperationspflichten im Reorganisationsrecht, 1999; Vertrags- und Verfahrensrecht der Wirtschaftsmediation, 2000; (ed jtly and contrib.) Münchener Kommentar zur Insolvenzordnung, 2002, 3rd edn 2013; (jtly) Mediation in der Wirtschaft: Wege zum professionellen Konfliktmanagement, 2003, 3rd edn 2019; (ed and contrib.) Ausländische Kapitalgesellschaften im deutschen Recht, 2004; Finanzkrise, Wirtschaftskrise, und das deutsche Insolvenzrecht, 2009; (jtly) Verhandlungsmanagement, 2009, 2nd edn 2017; (jtly) Fälle zum Erbrecht, 5th edn 2010, 6th edn 2017; (jtly) Revision des Verbraucher-acquis, 2011; (ed with G. Wagner and contrib.) Mediationsrecht, 2015; (ed jtly and contrib.) Negotiating Brexit, 2017; (ed jtly and contrib.) Autonomous Systems and the Law, 2019; contrib. jls incl. to Eur. Business Orgn Law Rev., Eur. Co. and Financial Law Rev., Chicago Law Rev., American Bankruptcy Law Jl, Common Mkt Law Rev., Edinburgh Law Rev., Jl Corporate Law Studies, Eur. Rev. Contract Law. *Address:* St Hugh's College, St Margaret's Road, Oxford OX2 6LE. *T:* (01865) 284472. *E:* horst.eidenmueller@law.ox.ac.uk; Faculty of Law, University of Oxford, St Cross Building, St Cross Road, Oxford OX1 3UL.

**EILLEDGE, Elwyn Owen Morris,** CBE 2001; FCA; Chairman, Financial Reporting Advisory Board to HM Treasury, 1996–2010; Senior Partner, Ernst & Young, Chartered Accountants, 1989–95; *b* 20 July 1935; *s* of Owen and Mary Elizabeth Eilledge; *m* 1962, Audrey Ann Faulkner Ellis; one *s* one *d. Educ:* Merton College, Oxford (BA, MA). FCA 1968. Articled with Farrow, Bersey, Gain, Vincent & Co., later Binder Hamlyn, 1959–66; Whinney Murray & Co. subseq. Ernst & Whinney, now Ernst & Young, Liberia, 1966–68; Ernst & Whinney: Audit Manager, Hamburg, 1968–71; Partner, London, 1972; Managing Partner, London office, 1983–86; Dep. Sen. Partner, 1985; Sen Partner, 1986–89; Chairman: Ernst & Whinney Internat., 1988–89; Ernst & Young Internat., 1989–95. Chm., BTR, 1996–98; Dir, BG Group plc, 1997–2005. Member: Accounting Standards Bd, 1989–91; Financial Reporting Council, 1989–95. *Recreations:* gardening, swimming, tennis, listening to classical music. *Address:* Whitethorn House, Long Grove, Seer Green, Beaconsfield, Bucks HP9 2QH. *Club:* Brooks's.

**EILON, Prof. Samuel,** FREng; Professor of Management Science, Imperial College of Science, Technology and Medicine, University of London, 1963–89, Professor Emeritus, since 1989 (Senior Research Fellow, 1989–2002); industrial consultant on corporate performance and strategy; *b* 13 Oct. 1923; *s* of Abraham and Rachel Eilon; *m* 1946, Hannah Ruth (*née* Samuel); two *s* two *d. Educ:* Reali Sch., Haifa; Technion, Israel Inst. of Technology, Haifa; Imperial Coll. London. PhD London, 1955; DSc(Eng) London, 1963. FREng (Founder FEng 1976); FIMechE; FIET. Engr, Palestine Electric Co. Ltd, Haifa, 1946–48; Officer, Israel Defence Forces, 1948–52; CO of an Ordnance and workshop base depot (Major); Res. Asst, Imperial Coll., 1952–55; Lectr in Production Engrg, Imperial Coll., 1955–57; Associate Prof. in Industrial Engrg, Technion, Haifa, 1957–59; Imperial College: Head of Section, 1955–57; Reader, 1957–63; Head of Dept, 1959–87. Consultant and Lectr, European Productivity Agency, Paris, 1960–62. Professorial Research Fellow, Case Western Reserve Univ., Cleveland, Ohio, 1967–68. Vis. Fellow, University Coll., Cambridge, 1970–71. Mem., Monopolies and Mergers Commn, 1990–97. Past Mem. of several cttees of IProdE and DES; Member: Council, Operational Res. Soc., 1965–67; Council, Inst. of Management Scis, 1970–72, 1980–82; Exec. Cttee, British Acad. of Management, 1985–89. Adviser, P-E Consulting Gp, 1961–71; Principal and Dir, Spencer Stuart and Associates, 1971–74; Director: Amey Roadstone Corp., subseq. ARC, 1974–88; Campari Internat., 1978–80. Chief Editor, OMEGA, Internat. Jl of Management Science, 1972–94; Deptl Editor, Management Science, 1969–77. Hon. FCGI 1978. Two Joseph Whitworth Prizes for papers, IMechE, 1960; Silver Medal, ORS, 1982; Imperial Coll. Medal, 2019. *Publications:* Elements of Production Planning and Control, 1962; Industrial Engineering Tables, 1962; (jtly) Exercises in Industrial Management, 1966; (jtly) Industrial Scheduling Abstracts, 1967; (jtly) Inventory Control Abstracts, 1968; (jtly) Distribution Management, 1971; Management Control, 1971, 2nd edn 1979; (jtly) Applications of Management Science in Banking and Finance, 1972; (jtly) Applied Productivity Analysis for Industry, 1976; Aspects of Management, 1977, 2nd edn 1979; The Art of Reckoning: analysis of performance criteria, 1984; Management Assertions and Aversions, 1985; (jtly) The Global Challenge of Innovation, 1991; Management Practice and Mispractice, 1992, repr. 2018; Management Science: an anthology, 1995; Management Strategies: a critique of theories and practices, 1999; some 300 papers and articles in the field of management. *Recreations:* theatre, walking. *Address:* 1 Meadway Close, NW11 7BA. *T:* (020) 8458 6650.

**EIMER, Prof. Martin,** PhD; FBA 2016; Professor of Psychology, Birkbeck, University of London, since 2000; *b* Kamen, Germany, 5 Aug. 1959; *s* of Theodor Eimer and Marianne Eimer; partner, Prof. Cecilia Mary Heyes, *qv. Educ:* Univ. of Bielefeld (Dip. Psychol. 1986; PhD Philos. 1989); Univ. of Munich (Habilitation Psychol. 1995). Lecturer: Dept of Psychol., Univ. of Munich, 1990–97; Dept of Experimental Psychol., Univ. of Cambridge, 1997–2000. Mem., German Nat. Acad. of Scis (Leopoldina), 2013. *Publications:* approx. 200 articles in jls in fields of psychol., neuropsychol. and neurosci. *Recreations:* sports, travel, history. *Address:* Department of Psychological Sciences, Birkbeck, University of London, Malet Street, WC1E 7HX. *T:* (020) 7631 6358. *E:* m.eimer@bbk.ac.uk.

**EIRUG, Dr Aled;** Member, Content Board, Ofcom, since 2015; Senior Lecturer, Morgan Academy, Swansea University, since 2017; *b* London, 1 July 1955; *s* of Dewi Aled Eirug Davies and Emily Maud Davies; surname changed to Eirug by deed poll, 1974; *m* 2003, Margaret Anne Russell; one *s* and one step *s* one step *d. Educ:* Penlan Sch., Swansea; University Coll. of Wales, Aberystwyth (BA Hons Hist. 1977); London Sch. of Econs and Pol Sci. (MSc Hons Urban and Regl Planning 1982); Univ. of Cardiff (PhD 2017). Parly researcher, 1979–82; current affairs researcher and prog. ed., ITV Wales, 1982–91; BBC Wales: Hd, News, 1992–2003; Hd, Corporate Social Responsibility, 2003–06; Constitnl Advr to Presiding Officer, Nat. Assembly for Wales, 2007–11; Lang. Policy Advr to Welsh Govt, 2012–13; Strategic Policy Advr, Univ. of Swansea, 2013–17; Mem., Nominet Adv. Cttee for Wales, 2014–16. Mem., S4C Authy, 2012–15. Chair: Welsh Refugee Council, 2006–12; Wales Cttee, British Council, 2012–15. Mem. Bd, Linc Housing Assoc., 2005–09. Member: Llafur, 1974–; Inst. Welsh Affairs, 2000–; Bevan Foundn, 2009–. *Recreations:* football, Rugby, cricket, Welsh history, theatre. *Address:* 14 Denbigh Street, Cardiff CF11 9JQ. *E:* aled.eirug@mac.com. *Clubs:* Cardiff City Football; Glamorgan CC.

**EISEN, Prof. Timothy George Quentin,** PhD; FRCP; Professor of Medical Oncology, University of Cambridge, since 2006; Fellow, Homerton College, Cambridge, since 2014; Vice President, Oncology Translational Medicine Unit, AstraZeneca, since 2016 (Vice President, Clinical Discovery, 2014–16); *b* London, 13 Dec. 1963; *s* of Vuk and Phyl Eisen; *m* 2003, Julia Hardiman; one *s* one *d. Educ:* Arnold House Sch., London; Westminster Sch.; Middlesex Hosp. Med. Sch. (BSc); Gonville and Caius Coll., Cambridge (BChir 1986, MB 1987); Marie Curie Res. Inst., Surrey (PhD 1996). FRCP 2002. Clin. Res. Fellow, Marie Curie Res. Inst., 1990–94; Sen. Registrar, Royal Marsden Hosp., 1994–98; Senior Lecturer in Medical Oncology: UCL, 1998–2001; Inst. of Cancer Res., 2001–06. Chair: Lung Clin. Studies Gp, NCRI, 2004–10; Macmillan Clinical Adv. Bd (formerly Med. Adv. Cttee, Macmillan Cancer Backup), 2006–. Trustee and Med. Advr, Balkans Relief, 1996–98; Trustee: Kidney Cancer UK, 2004–; Macmillan Cancer Support, 2012–. *Publications:* (ed) Clinical Progress in Renal Cancer, 2007; (Oncology Section Ed.) Oxford Textbook of Medicine, 6th edn 2017; contribs on kidney cancer, lung cancer and melanoma. *Recreations:* hill-bagging in Cambridgeshire (and beyond), tennis, trying to find a balance between unbridled optimism and pessimism. *Address:* Department of Oncology, Box 193, Addenbrooke's Hospital, Cambridge CB2 0QQ. *T:* (01223) 769312, *Fax:* (01223) 769313. *E:* tgqe2@cam.ac.uk. *Club:* Athenæum.

**EISENBERG, Neville;** Senior Partner, Bryan Cave Leighton Paisner (formerly Berwin Leighton Paisner) LLP, Solicitors, since 2015 (Partner, 1996–99; Managing Partner, 1999–2015); *b* 12 April 1962; *s* of late Benjamin Elieser Eisenberg and of Masha Eisenberg. *Educ:* Paul Roos Primary Sch.; Paul Roos Gymnasium; Pretoria Boys High Sch.; Univ. of Witwatersrand (BCom 1982; LLB 1984); London Sch. of Econs and Pol Sci. (LLM 1988). Articled clerk, Werksmans Attorneys, 1985–87; solicitor, Berwin Leighton Paisner, 1989–95; admitted solicitor, England and Wales, 1991. Mem., London Council, CBI, 2002–08, 2011–. Chairman: Lawyers on Demand Ltd, 2012–; Managing Partner Forum, 2017–. Chm., British Israel Law Assoc., 1996–. Nat. Chm., South African Union of Jewish Students, 1982–84; Comptroller, World Union of Jewish Students, 1986–89. Assoc. Gov., Hebrew Univ. of Jerusalem, 2004–; Trustee, Tel Aviv Foundn,

2013–. *Recreations:* current affairs, theatre, music, travel. *Address:* Bryan Cave Leighton Paisner LLP, Adelaide House, London Bridge, EC4R 9HA. *T:* (020) 3400 1000, *Fax:* (020) 3400 1111. *E:* neville.eisenberg@bcplaw.com. *Club:* Home House.

**EISENSTADT, Naomi,** CB 2005; Senior Research Fellow, International Inequalities Institute, London School of Economics and Political Science, since 2018; *b* 10 Feb. 1950; *d* of Berthold and Cecilia Leidner; *m* Prof. Marc Eisenstadt (marr. diss.); one *s*; *m* Michael Moutrie. *Educ:* Univ. of Calif, San Diego (BA; Post-grad. Dip. Early Childhood Educn); Cranfield Univ. (MSc Social Policy). Centre Leader, Moorlands Children's Centre, Milton Keynes, 1978–83; Lectr, Sch. of Educn, Open Univ., 1983–86; SCF, 1986–92; NCVO, 1992–96; Chief Exec., Family Service Units, 1996–99; Dir, Sure Start and Extended Schs, DfES, 1999–2006; Chief Advr on Children's Services to Sec. of State for Children, Schs and Families (formerly for Educn and Skills), 2006–07; Dir, Social Exclusion Task Force, Cabinet Office, 2007–09. Sen. Res. Fellow, Oxford Univ., 2010–18. Ind. Advr on Poverty to Scottish Govt, 2015–18. Mem., Editl Bd, Children and Society, 2002–13. DUniv Open, 2002. Philanthropy Champions Award, Milton Keynes Community Foundn, 2011. *Recreations:* cooking, movies.

**EISNER, Prof. David Alfred,** DPhil; FMedSci; BHF Professor of Cardiac Physiology, University of Manchester, since 2000 (Professor of Cardiac Physiology, 1999–2000); *b* Manchester, 3 Jan. 1955; *s* of Herbert Eisner and Gisela Eisner (*née* Spanglet); *m* 1983, Susan Wray; two *s* one *d*. *Educ:* Manchester Grammar Sch.; King's Coll., Cambridge (BA 1976); Balliol Coll., Oxford (DPhil 1979). Lectr in Physiol., 1980–86, Wellcome Trust Sen. Lectr, 1986–90, UCL; Prof. of Veterinary Biol., Univ. of Liverpool, 1990–99. Lectures: Q. R. Murphy, Univ. of Wisconsin, 1992; Reimer, Internat. Soc. for Heart Res., 2008; Carmeliet-Coraboeuf-Weidmann, Eur. Soc. of Cardiol., 2013; G. L. Brown, Physiol Soc., 2014; Peter Harris Dist. Scientist Award, Internat. Soc. for Heart Res., 2017; Annual Rev. Prize, Physiol Soc., 2017; Naranjan Dhalla, Internat. Acad. of Cardiovascular Scis, 2017. President: Fedn of Eur. Physiol Socs, 2011–15; Eur. Section, Internat. Soc. for Heart Res., 2014–16; Physiol Soc., 2016–18. FMedSci 1999; Fellow, Internat. Soc. for Heart Res., 2000. Hon. FRCP 2010. Hon. Dr Debrecen, Hungary. Pfizer Prize for Res. in Biol., 1985; Wellcome Prize in Physiol., 1988. *Publications:* articles in physiol and cardiovascular jls. *Recreations:* photography, walking. *Address:* Institute of Cardiovascular Sciences, University of Manchester, 3.18 Core Technology Facility, 46 Grafton Street, Manchester M13 9NT. *T:* (0161) 275 2702. *E:* eisner@manchester.ac.uk.

**EISNER, Prof. Manuel Peter,** PhD; Professor of Comparative and Developmental Criminology, since 2009, Director, Violence Research Centre, since 2013, and Wolfson Professor of Criminology, since 2017, Institute of Criminology, University of Cambridge; *b* Berne, 7 May 1959; *s* of Gerhard Eisner and Marlies Eisner-Odenbreit; *m* 1991, Ruth Schmid; one *s* two *d*. *Educ:* Univ. of Zurich (MA Hist., Sociol. and Social Psychol. 1985; PhD Sociol. 1991; Habilitation (venia legendi-private docent) 1997). Res. Associate, Inst. of Sociol., Univ. of Zurich, 1985–93; Asst Prof., 1993–96, Associate Prof., 1996–2001, Dept of Sociol., Swiss Federal Inst. of Technol.; University of Cambridge: Lectr, 2000–01, Reader in Sociological Criminol., 2002–09, Inst. of Criminol.; Dir, Social Sci. Res. Methods Prog., 2009–13. *Publications:* contrib. articles to peer-reviewed jls and ed vols. *Address:* Institute of Criminology, University of Cambridge, Sidgwick Site, Cambridge CB3 9DA.

**EISNER, Michael D(ammann);** Founder and Chief Executive Officer, Tornante Company, since 2005; Chief Executive Officer, 1984–2005, Director, 1984–2006, Walt Disney Co. (Chairman, 1984–2004); *b* 7 March 1942; *s* of Lester Eisner and Margaret Eisner (*née* Dammann); *m* 1967, Jane Breckenridge; three *s*. *Educ:* Lawrenceville Sch.; Denison Univ. (BA English Lit. and Theatre 1964). ABC Entertainment Corporation: Dir of Program Develt, East Coast, 1968–71; Vice President: Daytime Programming, 1971–75; Program Planning and Develt, 1975–76; Sen. Vice Pres., Prime-Time Production and Develt, 1976; Pres. and Chief Operating Officer, Paramount Pictures Corp., 1976–84. Jt Founder, Eisner Foundn, 1996. Host, TV show, Conversations with Michael Eisner, 2006–. Member of Board: California Inst. of the Arts; American Film Inst. Chevalier, Légion d'Honneur (France). *Publications:* Work in Progress (autobiog.), 1998; Camp (autobiog.), 2005. *Address:* c/o Eisner Foundation, 9401 Wilshire Boulevard, Suite 735, Beverly Hills, CA 90212, USA.

**EISSA, Adrian Nadir;** QC 2018; a Recorder, since 2012; *b* London, 1964; *m* Kirstie. *Educ:* Christ's Coll., Finchley; Southwark Coll.; Univ. of Warwick (BA Hons 1986). Called to the Bar, Inner Temple, 1988 (Hughes Parry Prize for Trusts and Contract); in practice as a barrister, specialising in fraud and crime, Pump Court Chambers, 1989–94, Garden Court Chambers, 1994–2011, 25 Bedford Row Chambers, 2011–. *Publications:* The Confiscation Law Handbook, 2011; The Fraud Lawyers Handbook, 2014; (contrib.) The Proceeds of Crime, 5th edn 2018. *Recreations:* family life, music, football, travel, books. *Address:* 25 Bedford Row, WC1R 4HD. *T:* (020) 7067 1500. *E:* aeissa@25bedfordrow.com.

**EKANEY, Nkumbe;** QC 2011; a Deputy High Court Judge, since 2017; *b* London, 4 Aug. 1967; *s* of Thomas Kolle Ekaney and Lydia Ndolo Ekaney; *m* 1994, Lucy Monjoa; four *d*. *Educ:* Oratory Sch., Woodcote; Univ. of Bristol (LLB Hons). Called to the Bar, Gray's Inn, 1990; in practice as a barrister, specialising in family law. *Recreations:* travel, African art and music, socialising. *Address:* Garden Court Family Law, 10 Lincoln's Inn Fields, WC2A 3BP. *E:* Ekaney@1gc.com.

**EKERS, Prof. Ronald David,** AO 2019; PhD; FRS 2005; FAA; CSIRO Fellow, Australia Telescope National Facility, since 2008 (Director, 1988–2003; ARC Federation Fellow, 2003–08); *b* 18 Sept. 1941. *Educ:* Univ. of Adelaide (BSc 1963); Australian Nat. Univ. (PhD 1967). FAA 1993. Calif Inst. of Technol., 1967–70; Inst. of Theoretical Astronomy, Univ. of Cambridge, 1970–71; Kapteyn Lab., Groningen, 1971–80; Asst Dir, and Dir for Very Large Array Ops, Nat. Radio Astronomy Observatory, Socorro, USA, 1980–88. Pres., IAU, 2003–06. Mem., Amer. Philosophical Soc., 2003; Mem., NAS, 2018. Flinders Medal, Aust. Acad. of Sci., 2005; Grote Reber Medal, Grote Reber Foundn, 2014. Centenary Medal, Australia, 2003. *Publications:* 442 articles in learned jls. *Address:* Australia Telescope National Facility, CSIRO Astronomy and Space Science, PO Box 76, Epping, NSW 1710, Australia.

**EKERT, Prof. Artur Konrad,** DPhil; FRS 2016; FInstP; Professor of Quantum Physics, Oxford University, since 2007; Fellow of Merton College, Oxford, since 2007; Director, Centre for Quantum Technologies, Singapore, since 2007; *b* 19 Sept. 1961; *s* of Kazimierz and Janina Ekert; *m* 1990, Beata Wijowska. *Educ:* Jagiellonian Univ., Kraków, Poland (MSc); Wolfson Coll., Oxford (DPhil). FInstP 2004. Oxford University: Jun. Research Fellow, 1991–94, Res. Fellow, 1994–98, Merton Coll.; Prof. of Physics, 1998–2002; Fellow and Tutor, Keble Coll., 1998–2002; Leigh Trapnell Prof. of Quantum Physics, Cambridge Univ., 2002–07; Fellow, King's Coll., Cambridge, 2002–07. Howe Res. Fellow, Royal Soc., 1994–2000; Temasek Prof., Univ. of Singapore, 2002–05; Lee Kong Chian Centennial Prof., Nat. Univ. of Singapore, 2006–. Visiting Professor: Univ. of Innsbruck, 1994, 1998; Nat. Univ. of Singapore, 2001. Maxwell Medal and Prize, Inst. of Physics, 1995; (jtly) Descartes Prize, EU, 2004; Hughes Medal, Royal Soc., 2007. *Publications:* articles in scientific jls. *Recreations:* scuba diving, water sports, ski-ing, general aviation. *Address:* Mathematical Institute, University of Oxford, Andrew Wiles Building, Radcliffe Observatory Quarter, Woodstock Road, Oxford OX2 6GG. *E:* artur.ekert@qubit.org.

**EKINS, Prof. Paul Whitfield,** OBE 2015; PhD; Professor of Resources and Environmental Policy (formerly of Energy and Environment Policy), since 2009, and Director, UCL Institute for Sustainable Resources, since 2012, University College London; *b* 24 July 1950; *s* of John Robert Ekins and Lydia Mary Ekins (*née* Daukes); *m* 1979, Susan Anne Lofthouse; one *s*. *Educ:* Imperial Coll., London (BSc Eng); Univ. of Bradford (MPhil); Birkbeck Coll., London (MSc Econ 1988; PhD Econ 1996). Res. Fellow, Birkbeck Coll., London, 1990–96; Sen. Lectr, then Reader, 1996–2000, Prof. of Sustainable Develt, 2000–02, Keele Univ.; Prof. of Sustainable Develt and Hd, Envmt Gp, Policy Studies Inst., Univ. of Westminster, 2002–07; Prof. of Energy and Envmt Policy, KCL, 2008–09. Mem., Royal Commn on Envmtl Pollution, 2002–08. Mem., Internat. Resource Panel, UNEP, 2013–; Co-Chair, Global Envmtl Outlook 6, UN Envmt, Nairobi, 2016–. Mem. Bd, NCC, 1996–2002. Hon. DSc Keele, 2015. *Publications:* A New World Order, 1992; (ed jtly) Global Warming and Energy Demand, 1995; Economic Growth and Environmental Sustainability, 2000; (ed jtly) Understanding the Costs of Environmental Regulation in Europe, 2009; Trade, Globalization, and Sustainability Impact Assessment: a critical look at methods and outcomes, 2009; Carbon-Energy Taxation: lessons from Europe, 2009; (ed) Hydrogen Energy: economic and social challenges, 2010; (ed jtly) Energy 2050: the transition to a secure, low-carbon energy system for the UK, 2011; Environmental Tax Reform: a policy for green growth, 2011; (ed jtly) Global Energy: issues, potentials and policy implications, 2015; contrib. numerous jl papers and articles. *Recreations:* music, theatre. *Address:* UCL Institute for Sustainable Resources, Central House, 14 Upper Woburn Place, WC1H 0NN. *T:* (020) 3108 5990. *E:* p.ekins@ucl.ac.uk.

**EKLUND, Graham Nicholas;** QC 2002; barrister; *b* 23 Dec. 1950; *s* of Alan Nicholas Eklund and Mollie Jean (*née* Talbot); *m* 1987, Deborah Anne Bartley; one *s* one *d* (and one *s* decd). *Educ:* Auckland Univ. (BA; LLB Hons). Barrister and solicitor, Agar Keesing McLeod & Co., NZ, 1975–78; solicitor, Herbert Smith, 1981–84; called to the Bar, Inner Temple, 1984; in practice as a barrister, 1984–. *Recreations:* wine, sport, song. *Address:* 4 New Square, Lincoln's Inn, WC2A 3RJ. *T:* (020) 7822 2000, *Fax:* (020) 7822 2001. *E:* g.eklund@4newsquare.com.

**EKSERDJIAN, Prof. David Patrick Martin,** PhD; Professor of History of Art and Film, University of Leicester, since 2004; *b* 28 Oct. 1955; *s* of late Nubar Martin Ekserdjian and Mabel Brown Ekserdjian (*née* Angus); *m* 1990, Susan Moore; one *s* one *d*. *Educ:* Westminster Sch.; Trinity Coll., Cambridge (BA Modern and Medieval Langs 1977); Courtauld Inst. of Art, Univ. of London (MA 1979; PhD 1988). Christie's Jun. Res. Fellow, Balliol Coll., Oxford, 1983–86; Lectr, Courtauld Inst. of Art, 1986–87; Slade Fellow, Corpus Christi Coll., Oxford, 1987–91; with Christie, Manson & Woods, 1991–97; Editor, Apollo, 1997–2004 (Mem., Editl Adv. Panel, 2012–); Leverhulme Trust Major Res. Fellow, 2008–11. Guest Scholar, J. Paul Getty Mus., 2006; Slade Prof. of Fine Art, Univ. of Oxford, 2017–18. Member: Bd, Courtauld Inst. of Art, 1998–2002; Comitato Scientifico, Fondazione il Correggio, 2002–; Reviewing Cttee on Export of Works of Art, 2002–12; Bd, MA course in history of design, V&A/RCA, 2003–13; Adv. Bd, Bampton Opera, 2003–06. Trustee: Nat. Gall., 2005–13; Tate Gall., 2008–13; Art UK (formerly Public Catalogue Foundn), 2012–. Hon. Citizen, Correggio, 2004. *Publications:* (introd. and notes) Vasari, Lives of the Artists, 1996; Correggio, 1997; Parmigianino, 2006; Alle origini della natura morta, 2007; (notes) Benvenuto Cellini: autobiography, 2010; Correggio and Parmigianino: art in Parma during the sixteenth century, 2016; *exhibition catalogues:* (with D. Mahon) Guercino Drawings, 1986; Old Master Paintings from the Thyssen-Bornemisza Collection, 1987; Mantegna, 1992; Treasures from Budapest, 2010; Bronze, 2012; Wentworth-Fitzwilliam: an English collection, 2015; contrib. to Macmillan Dictionary of Art, Saurs Allgemeine Künstlerlexicon, etc. *Recreations:* wine, Real tennis, opera, moths. *Address:* Department of History of Art and Film, University of Leicester, University Road, Leicester LE1 7RH. *T:* (0116) 252 2905. *Club:* Beefsteak.

**ELAM, Caroline Mary, (Mrs J. H. Drury);** Senior Research Fellow, Warburg Institute, University of London, since 2012; *b* 12 March 1945; *d* of John Frederick Elam and Joan Barrington Elam (*née* Lloyd); *m* 2009, Very Rev. John Henry Drury, *qv*. *Educ:* Colchester County High Sch.; Lady Margaret Hall, Oxford (BA); Courtauld Inst. of Art, Univ. of London. MA London and Cantab. Lectr, Fine Art Dept, Univ. of Glasgow, 1970–72; Jun. Res. Fellow, King's Coll., Cambridge, 1972–76 (Hon. Fellow, 1992); Lectr, History of Art Dept, Westfield Coll., Univ. of London, 1976–87; Editor, Burlington Mag., 1987–2002; Andrew W. Mellon Prof., Center for Advanced Study in the Visual Arts, Nat. Gall. of Art, Washington, 2002–04; Ruth and Clarence Kennedy Prof. in Renaissance Studies, Smith Coll., Northampton, Mass, 2008. Villa I Tatti, Florence: Fellow, Harvard Univ. Center for Renaissance Studies, 1981–82, 2002; Vis. Prof., 2005; Accademica, Accademia Raffaello, Urbino, 2005–. Chair, SH5 Panel, Starting Grants, Eur. Res. Council, 2012. Member: Exec. Cttee, NACF, 1988–2002; Bd, Warburg Inst., 1992–97; Bd, Courtauld Inst. of Art, 1993–98; Syndic, Fitzwilliam Mus., Cambridge, 1993–2002; Trustee, Friends of Courtauld Inst., 2009–. Hon. DArts Oxford Brookes, 2005. Agnes and Elizabeth Mongan Prize, 2004. Exec. Ed., I Tatti Studies, 2004–12. *Publications:* Roger Fry and the Re-evaluation of Piero della Francesca, 2005; Roger Fry: Mantegna, 2006; Roger Fry: Giovanni Bellini, 2007; Roger Fry's Journey: from the primitive to the post-impressionists, 2008; articles in Art History, Burlington Magazine, I Tatti Studies, Mitteilungen des Kunsthistorischen Insts in Florenz, Renaissance Quarterly, Renaissance Studies, Jl of RSA, etc.
*See also* J. N. Elam.

**ELAM, (John) Nicholas,** CMG 1994; HM Diplomatic Service, retired; *b* 2 July 1939; *s* of John Frederick Elam, OBE and Joan Barrington Elam (*née* Lloyd); *m* 1967, Florence Helen, *d* of P. Lentz; two *s* one *d*. *Educ:* Colchester Royal Grammar Sch.; New Coll., Oxford (schol.). Frank Knox Fellow, Harvard Univ., 1961–62. Entered HM Diplomatic Service, 1962; served: Pretoria and Cape Town, 1964–68; Bahrain, 1971; Brussels, 1972–76; FCO, 1976–79, Dep. Head of News Dept, 1978–79; Counsellor and Dep. British Govt Rep., Salisbury, 1979; Dep. High Comr, Salisbury (later Harare), 1980–83; Consul-General, Montreal, 1984–87; Hd of Cultural Relations Dept, FCO, 1987–94; Ambassador to Luxembourg, 1994–98. Chm., Cultural Co-operation Council, Council of Europe, 1993–94. Administrator, Caine Prize for African Writing, 1999–2011; Co. Sec., Africa 95, 1999–2016; Dir, Dance Umbrella, 1999–2004; Consultant, Serious Internat. Music Producers, 1999–2002; Trustee, Triangle Arts Trust, 1998–2010; Chairman: Henri Oguike Dance Co., 2002–10; Friends of UCL Art Collections, 2003–14. Mem., British Council, 1994. Hon. Sen. Res. Fellow, Dept of History of Art, UCL, 2003–04. *Recreations:* travel, the arts. *Address:* 86 Camberwell Church Street, SE5 8QZ. *Club:* Chelsea Arts.
*See also* C. M. Elam.

**ELAND, Prof. John Hugh David,** DPhil; FRS 2006; FRCS; Professor of Physical Chemistry, University of Oxford, 1997–2006; Fellow and Tutor in Chemistry, Worcester College, Oxford, 1983–2006, now Emeritus Fellow; *b* 6 Aug. 1941; *s* of Rev. Thomas Eland and Verna Prosser Eland (*née* Reynolds); *m* 1967, Ieva Antonovics; three *s*. *Educ:* St John's Sch., Leatherhead; University Coll., Oxford (BA 1963; MA, DPhil, 1966). FRCS

2005. Physicist, Argonne Nat. Lab., USA, 1976–80; Lectr, Queen's Coll., Oxford, 1980–83. Visiting Professor: Univ. of Paris, 1981, 1995; Inst. Molecular Sci., Japan, 1989; Uppsala Univ., 1995; Tohoku Univ., Japan, 2002; Guest Prof. in Physics and Astronomy, Uppsala Univ., 2010–14; Guest Prof. in Physics, Gothenburg Univ., 2014–18. *Publications:* Photoelectron Spectroscopy, 1972, 2nd edn 1984; Double Photoionisation Spectra of Molecules, 2018; contrib. numerous articles to learned jls. *Recreations:* astronomy, linguistics, walking. *Address:* Physical and Theoretical Chemistry Laboratory, University of Oxford, South Parks Road, Oxford OX1 3QZ. *T:* (01865) 275400, *Fax:* (01865) 275410. *E:* john.eland@chem.ox.ac.uk.

**ELAND, Michael John,** CB 2006; Commissioner, 2000–12, and Director General, Enforcement and Compliance, 2005–12, HM Revenue and Customs (formerly Customs and Excise); *b* 26 Sept. 1952; *s* of George and Betty Eland; *m* 1981, Luned Rhiannon Wynn Jones; one *s* one *d. Educ:* Worksop Coll.; Trinity Coll., Oxford (BA Jurisp, MA). Called to the Bar, Middle Temple, 1975. Administration Trainee, HM Customs and Excise, 1975; Private Sec. to Chm., 1979–81; Cabinet Office, 1982–87; Private Sec. to Lord President of the Council (Viscount Whitelaw), 1987–88; Asst Sec., 1988–92, Comr, 1992–97, HM Customs and Excise; Dep. Dir-Gen., Policy, Immigration and Nationality Directorate, Home Office, 1997–2000; HM Customs and Excise, later Revenue and Customs: Dir Gen., Business Services and Taxes, 2000–03; Actg Chm., 2003–04; Dir Gen., Law Enforcement, 2004–05. *Recreations:* walking, theatre.

**ElBARADEI, Dr Mohamed Mostafa;** Director General, International Atomic Energy Agency, 1997–2009, now Emeritus; *b* Egypt, 17 June 1942; *s* of Mostafa and Aida ElBaradei; *m* 1975, Aida ElKachef; one *s* one *d. Educ:* Cairo Univ. Sch. of Law (Licence en droit 1962; Dip. Advanced Studies, Admin. Law, 1964); NY Univ. Sch. of Law (LLM 1971; JSD Internat. Law 1974). Dept of Internat. Orgns, Min. of Foreign Affairs, Egypt, 1964–67; Perm. Mission of Egypt to UN, NY, 1967–71; Sen. Fellow, Center for Internat. Studies, NY Univ., 1973–74; Special Asst to Foreign Minister, Min. of Foreign Affairs, Egypt, 1974–78; Perm. Mission of Egypt to UN, Geneva, and Alternate Rep., Cttee on Disarmament, 1978–80; Sen. Fellow and Dir, Internat. Law and Orgns Prog., UN Inst. for Trng and Res., NY, 1980–84; International Atomic Energy Agency: Rep. of Dir Gen. to UN, NY, 1984–87; Dir, Legal Div. and Legal Advr, Vienna, 1987–91; Dir, Ext. Relns, Vienna, 1991–93; Asst Dir Gen. for Ext Relns, 1993–97. Adjunct Prof. of Internat. Law, NY Univ. Sch. of Law, 1981–87. Rep. of Egypt or IAEA, to UN Gen. Assembly, UN Security Council, Cttee on Disarmament, Rev. Confs of Treaty on Non-Proliferation of Nuclear Weapons, OAU, UNDP, ILO and WHO. Has lectured widely on internat. law and orgns, arms control and non-proliferation and peaceful uses of nuclear energy. Nobel-Laureate-in-Residence, Fletcher Sch. of Law and Diplomacy, Tufts Univ., USA, 2014. Nobel Peace Prize (jtly), 2005. *Publications:* The Right of Innocent Passage through Straits, 1974; (jtly) The International Law Commission: the need for a new direction, 1981; (jtly) Crowded Agendas, Crowded Rooms, 1981; Model Rules for Disaster Relief Operations, 1982; (jtly) The International Law of Nuclear Energy, 1993; The Age of Deception, 2011; contribs to NY Univ. Jl of Internat. Law and Politics, Leiden Jl of Internat. Law, etc.

**EL BELEIDI, Cecille;** HM Diplomatic Service; Consul General, Chongqing, since 2016; *b* Singapore, 22 Nov. 1962; *d* of Frederick and Maria Greaves; *m* 1987, Magdi El Beleidi; one *d. Educ:* Weymouth Grammar Sch. Entered FCO, 1983; Desk Officer, S America Dept, FCO, 1983–85; Archivist, Kuwait, 1985–86; Desk Officer, Nationality and Treaty Dept, FCO, 1986–89; Accountant and Asst Mgt Officer, Kathmandu, 1989–92; Sen. Mgt Officer/Vice Consul/Entry Clearance Officer, Casablanca, 1992–95; ME Dept, FCO, 1995–96; Entry Clearance Officer, Cairo, 1996; Asst Private Sec. to Parly Under-Sec. of State, FCO, 1996–99; Second Sec., Political and Press and Public Affairs, Riyadh, 1999–2002; Arabic lang. trng, 2002–03; Dep. Consul Gen. and Hd, Trade and Investment, Jeddah, 2003–08; HR Transition Team, UK Border Agency, 2008–09; Regl Lead, Corporate Services Prog., FCO, 2009–10; Hd, Consular Overseas Residents Services Unit, FCO, 2010–12; Dep. Hd of Mission, Doha, 2012–15. Chm. Govs, Jeddah Prep. Sch. *Recreations:* reading, art work, puzzle solving, walking. *Address:* c/o Foreign and Commonwealth Office, King Charles Street, SW1A 2AH. *E:* Cecille.elbeleidi@fco.gov.uk; 104 Innes Gardens, Putney, SW15 3AE; 110 Weymouth Bay Avenue, Weymouth, Dorset DT3 5AA.

**ELBORN, Peter Leonard,** OBE 1990; Regional Director, East and Central Africa, and Director, Kenya, British Council, 2000–04; *b* 11 June 1945; *s* of Leonard and Joyce Elborn; *m* 1997, Sue Unsworth (*d* 2016); three *s. Educ:* UC, Swansea (BA). British Council: Mexico, 1970–74; Croatia/Slovenia, 1977–82; Iraq, 1987–91; Zimbabwe, 1991–94; Kenya, 2000–04. Mem. Bd, Acad. of Live and Recorded Arts, 2009–17. Sec., 2010–17, Events Sec., 2017–, British-Croatian Soc. Trustee, Charles Wallace Pakistan Trust, 2008–. *Recreations:* walking, swimming, reading. *Address:* 9 Belle Vue Apartments, Rowland Hill Street, NW3 2AQ. *T:* (020) 7431 3179. *E:* peterelborn@hotmail.co.uk.

**ELCHO, Lord; Francis Richard Percy Charteris;** *b* 15 Sept. 1984; *s* and *heir* of Earl of Wemyss and March, *qv. Educ:* Eton Coll.; Edinburgh Univ. (MA History). Student, Inner Temple. Volunteer, Free Representation Unit. Interest in industrial law and legal, political and military history. *Recreations:* hunting, shooting, football, boxing, hill-walking.

**ELCOAT, Dame Catherine Elizabeth,** DBE 2002; independent healthcare adviser, 2010–14; Director of Nursing and Patient Care, East Midlands Strategic Health Authority, 2006–10; *b* 26 Feb. 1954; *d* of Derrick and Johanna Goulding; *m* 1975, Richard Thomas Elcoat. *Educ:* Birmingham Univ. (MScSoc); Darlington Meml Hosp. (RGN); Univ. of Teesside (DipHV). Student Nurse, 1972–75; North Tees Hospital: Staff Nurse, 1975–77; Ward Sister, 1977–82; Clinical Nurse Specialist, 1982–87; Health Visitor, 1987–90; Quality Manager, Darlington Meml Hosp., 1990–93; Exec. Dir of Nursing and Quality, S Durham Healthcare NHS Trust, 1993–96; Nursing Officer, NHS Exec., Leeds, 1996–97; Exec. Nurse Dir, City Hosp., Birmingham, 1997–99; Dep. Hd, NHS Clinical Governance Team, 1999–2001; Exec. Chief Nurse, Univ. Hosp. Birmingham NHS Trust, 2001–06. Nat. Clinical Advr, Health Care Commn, 2005–07. Mem., NHS Reconfiguration Panel, 2004–05. Special Prof., Univ. of Nottingham, 2007–13; Adjunct Prof. of Nursing, Univ. of Tasmania, 2009–13. Hon. DSc De Montfort, 2008. *Publications:* Stoma Care Nursing, 1986, new edn 2003; contribs to various nursing, medical and professional jls. *Recreations:* embroidery, quilting, sewing, craft work. *Address:* 5 Chestnut Grove, Kinver, Stourbridge DY7 6DQ.

**ELDEN, Prof. Stuart Robert,** PhD; FBA 2013; Professor of Political Theory and Geography, University of Warwick, since 2013; *b* Ipswich, 8 Dec. 1971; *s* of Colin Richard Elden and Rosemary Jill Elden; *m* 2002, Susan Renee Rizor. *Educ:* Brunel Univ. (BSc Hons 1994; PhD 1999); Durham Univ. (DLitt 2013). Lectr in Politics, Univ. of Warwick, 1999–2002; Prof. of Political Geog., Durham Univ., 2002–13. Ed., Envmt and Planning D: Society and Space, 2006–. Globe Book Award, 2010, Meridian Book Award, 2014, Assoc. American Geographers; Murchison Award, RGS, 2011. *Publications:* Mapping the Present: Heidegger, Foucault and the project of a spatial history, 2001; Understanding Henri Lefebvre: theory and the possible, 2004; Speaking Against Number: Heidegger, language and the politics of calculation, 2006; Terror and Territory: the spatial extent of sovereignty, 2009; The Birth of Territory, 2013; Foucault's Last Decade, 2016; Foucault: the birth of power, 2017; Shakespearean Territories, 2018; Canguilhem, 2019. *Recreations:* cycling, watching cricket, music, theatre. *Address:* Department of Politics and International Studies, University of Warwick, Coventry CV4 7AL. *E:* stuart.elden@warwick.ac.uk.

**ELDER,** Baron *cr* 1999 (Life Peer), of Kirkcaldy in Fife; **Thomas Murray Elder;** Chancellor, Al-Maktoum College of Further Education (formerly Institute for Arabic and Islamic Studies), Dundee, since 2003; *b* 9 May 1950. *Educ:* Kirkcaldy High Sch.; Edinburgh Univ. (MA). Bank of England, 1972–80; Res. Asst to Shadow Trade and Industry Sec., 1980–84; Gen. Sec., Scottish Labour Party, 1988–92; Chief of Staff to Leader of Labour Party, 1992–94; Political Advr to Leader of Labour Party, 1994; Special Advr, Scottish Office, 1997–99. Contested (Lab) Ross, Cromarty & Skye, 1983. Chm. Trustees, Smith Inst. *Address:* House of Lords, SW1A 0PW.

**ELDER, Dorothy-Grace;** freelance journalist and commentator; political columnist, Scottish Daily Express, 2002–13; *m* George Welsh; one *s* two *d.* Journalist; former campaigning columnist, Scotland on Sunday. MSP, Glasgow, 1999–2003 (SNP 1999–2002, Ind. 2002–03). Hon. Prof., Robert Gordon Univ., Aberdeen, 2006–, lectrg (pt-time) on investigative journalism. Oliver Brown Award, Scots Independent, 1995; UK Reporter of the Year, UK Press Awards, 1996; London Award for campaigning for chronic pain patients, British Medical Journalists' Assoc., 2014. *E:* dg.elder@ntlworld.com.

**ELDER, Sir Mark (Philip),** CH 2017; Kt 2008; CBE 1989; conductor; Music Director, Hallé Orchestra, since 2000; Artistic Director, Opera Rara, since 2011; *b* 2 June 1947; *s* of late John and Helen Elder; *m* 1980, Amanda Jane Stein; one *d. Educ:* Bryanston Sch.; Corpus Christi Coll., Cambridge (Music Scholar, Choral Scholar; BA, MA). Music staff, Wexford Festival, 1969–70; Chorus Master and Asst Conductor, Glyndebourne, 1970–71; music staff, Covent Garden, 1970–72; Staff Conductor, Australian Opera, 1972–74; Staff Conductor, ENO, 1974, Associate Conductor, 1977, Music Dir, 1979–93; Music Dir, Rochester Philharmonic Orch., USA, 1989–94. Principal Guest Conductor: London Mozart Players, 1980–83; BBC Symphony Orchestra, 1982–85; CBSO, 1992–95. *Address:* c/o Groves Artists, 7 St George's Court, 131 Putney Bridge Road, SW15 2PA.

**ELDER, Prof. Murdoch George,** MD, DSc; FRCS, FRCOG; Professor of Obstetrics and Gynaecology, University of London, at Institute of Obstetrics and Gynaecology, Royal Postgraduate Medical School, 1978–98, now Professor Emeritus, and Hon. Fellow, since 2001, Imperial College School of Medicine; Chairman, Division of Paediatrics, Obstetrics and Gynaecology, Imperial College School of Medicine, 1996–98; *b* 4 Jan. 1938; *s* of late Archibald James and Lotta Annie Elder; *m* 1964, Margaret Adelaide McVicker; two *s. Educ:* Edinburgh Acad.; Edinburgh Univ. (MB ChB 1961, MD 1973). DSc London, 1994. FRCS 1968; FRCOG 1978. Junior posts, Edinburgh and Bristol, 1961–68; Lectr, Inst. of Obst. and Gyn. and Royal Univ. of Malta, 1968–71; Sen. Lectr and Reader, Charing Cross Hosp. Med. Sch., Univ. of London, 1971–78; Dean, Institute of Obstetrics and Gynaecology, RPMS, 1985–95. Green Armytage Scholarship, RCOG, 1976; WHO Travelling Scholarship, 1977; Dir, Clinical Res. Centre, WHO, 1980–94; Member: Steering Cttee on Contraception, WHO, 1980–86; WHO Scientific Ethics Res. Cttee, 1996–2005. Mem., Hammersmith and Queen Charlotte's Special Health Authy, 1982–90. Mem. Council, RPMS, 1979–97. Visiting Professor: UCLA, 1984, 1986 and 1997; Singapore Univ., 1987; Natal Univ., 1988. Ext Examr for DSc, PhD, Masters and MB, BS degrees of 19 univs in several countries. Silver Medal, Hellenic Obstetrical Soc., 1983; Bronze Medal, Helsinki Univ., 1996. Mem., Editl Bds, Jl of Obst. and Gyn. and Clinical Reproduction, 1985–98. *Publications:* Human Fertility Control, 1979; (ed) Preterm Labour, 1980; (ed) Reproduction, Obstetrics and Gynaecology, 1988; Preterm Labour, 1997; Obstetrics and Gynaecology, 2001; chapters in books and learned articles on biochemistry in reproduction and pre term labour, clinical obstetrics, gynaecology and contraception. *Recreations:* travel, golf, curling. *Address:* Burnholm, Broughton, Biggar ML12 6HQ. *T:* (01899) 830359. *Club:* 1942.

**ELDER, Air Vice-Marshal Ronald David,** CBE 1991; Managing Director, RED Partners LLP, 2007–18; *b* 27 May 1946; *m* Sue; one *s* one *d. Educ:* RAF Coll., Cranwell. Commissioned RAF pilot, 1968; jun. appts and RAF Staff Coll., to 1981; Central Tactics and Trials Orgn, 1981–86; Comdr No 20 Sqdn, Laarbruch, 1986–88; Stn Comdr, Tri-National Tornado Trng Estabt, RAF Cottesmore, 1988–90; RAF Comdr, Tabuk, Saudi Arabia, 1990–91; RCDS 1991; Policy Area, Central Staff, MoD, 1991–93; Dir of Airspace Policy, CAA, 1993–98; RAF retd, 1999. Civil Aviation Authority: Hd, Gen. Aviation, 1999–2000; Hd, Personnel Licensing, 2000–03; Hd, Licensing Standards Div., 2003–07. FRAeS 1997. *Recreations:* Real tennis, golf. *Club:* Royal Air Force.

**ELDERFIELD, John,** PhD; Chief Curator of Painting and Sculpture, Museum of Modern Art, New York, 2003–08, now Emeritus; Consultant, Gagosian Gallery, since 2012; Allen R. Adler, Class of 1967, Consulting Curator, Princeton University Art Museum, since 2019; *b* 25 April 1943; *s* of late Henry Elderfield and Rhoda May Elderfield (*née* Risbrough); *m* 1st, 1965, Joyce Davey (marr. diss.); two *s*; 2nd, 1989, Jill Elizabeth Moser (marr. diss.); 3rd, 2005, Jeanne Collins. *Educ:* Univ. of Manchester; Univ. of Leeds (BA 1966; MPhil 1970); Univ. of London (PhD 1975). Lectr in Hist. of Art, Winchester Sch. of Art, 1966–70; Harkness Fellow, Yale Univ., 1970–72; John Simon Guggenheim Meml Fellow, 1972–73; Lectr in Hist. of Art, Univ. of Leeds, 1973–75; Museum of Modern Art, New York: Curator of Painting and Sculpture, 1975–93; Dir, Dept of Drawings, 1980–93; Chief Curator at Large, 1993–2003; Dep. Dir for Curatorial Affairs, 1996–99. Adjunct Prof. of Fine Arts, Inst. of Fine Arts, NY Univ., 1994. Vis. Scholar, Getty Res. Inst., Calif, 2001; Vis. Fellow, Amer. Acad. at Rome, 2006. Editor, Studies in Modern Art, 1991–2008. Sen. Advr, Art.sy, 2012–16. Member, Board of Directors: Dedalus Foundn, NY, 1996–; Master Drawings Assoc., 2000–09; Members Bd, Phillips Collection, Washington, 2000–19; Member: Adv. Bd, Kate Weare Dance Co., 2010–; Art Adv. Council, Internat. Foundn for Art Res., 2012–. Member: Assoc. of Literary Scholars, Critics, and Writers, 2011–; Internat. Assoc. of Art Critics, 2012–; Soc. Paul Cézanne, 2015–. Hon. Mem., Proyecto Armando Reverón, Caracas, 2007–. Hon. DLit Leeds, 2006. Officier des Arts et Lettres (France), 2006 (Chevalier, 1989). *Publications:* Hugo Ball: the flight out of time, 1974, 2nd edn 1996; The Wild Beasts: Fauvism and its affinities, 1976; European Master Paintings from Swiss Collections: Post Impressionism to World War II, 1976; The Cut-outs of Henri Matisse, 1978; Matisse in the Collection of the Museum of Modern Art, 1978; The Modern Drawing, 1983; The Drawings of Henri Matisse, 1984; Kurt Schwitters, 1985; Morris Louis, 1986; The Drawings of Richard Diebenkorn, 1988; Helen Frankenthaler, 1988; (jtly) Matisse in Morocco, 1990; Henri Matisse: a retrospective, 1992; Pleasuring Painting: Matisse's feminine representations, 1995; (jtly) Howard Hodgkin: paintings, 1995; The Language of the Body: drawings by Pierre-Paul Prud'hon, 1996; (jtly) The Art of Richard Diebenkorn, 1997; (jtly) Bonnard, 1998; (jtly) Modern Starts, 1999; (jtly) Bridget Riley: reconnaissance, 2001; (jtly) Matisse-Picasso, 2002; Modern Painting and Sculpture: 1880 to the present, 2004; (jtly) Against the Grain, 2006; Manet's "The Execution of the Emperor Maximilian", 2006; Armando Reverón, 2007; Martin Puryear, 2007; (jtly) Matisse: radical invention, 1913–17, 2010; (jtly) Bob Dylan: the Brazil series, 2010; (jtly) Bob Dylan: the Asia series, 2011; De Kooning: a retrospective, 2011; Painted on 21st Street: Helen Frankenthaler from 1950 to 1959, 2013; (jtly) Willem de Kooning: ten paintings 1983–85,

2013; (jtly) Bob Dylan: face value, 2013; In the Studio: paintings, 2015; (jtly) Cézanne Portraits, 2017; (jtly) Cézanne Rocks, 2020. *Address:* 175 East 62 Street, #16A, New York, NY 10065, USA. *T:* (917) 2074041. *Club:* Century (New York).

**ELDON,** 6th Earl of, *cr* 1821; **John Francis, (Jock), Scott;** Baron Eldon 1799; Viscount Encombe 1821; Corporate Psychologist, Founder and Director, EC Partnership, since 2010; Warden, Incorporation of Goldsmiths, since 2017; Co-founder, Wellbeing Economy Alliance Scotland, since 2018; *b* 9 July 1962; *s* of 5th Earl of Eldon; *S* father, 2017; *m* 1993, Charlotte, *d* of Robert de Vlaming; one *s* one *d*, and one *s* one step *d*. *Educ:* Ampleforth Coll.; St Benet Hall, Oxford (MA English Lang. and Lit.); UMDS Guy's and St Thomas' Hosps (DipCAT; UKCP). Business Manager, Catalyst Publishing, 1984–87; Japanese Equity Derivative Sales, Nomura Securities, 1987–89; Hd, Japanese Equity Derivative Sales, SG Warburg, 1989–91; Series Producer, SuperChannel, 1991–93; Leadership and Orgnl Develt Consultant, Monitor & Co., 1996–99; Psychotherapist and Clinical Supervisor, UMDS Guy's and St Thomas' Hosps, 1991–2001; Founder and Dir, YSC Scotland, 1999–2010. Chm., Mercy Corps, Europe, 2007–15. *Heir: s* Viscount Encombe, *qv.*

**ELDON, David Gordon,** GBS 2004; CBE 2005; JP; Chairman: HSBC Bank Middle East Ltd, since 2011; Octopus Cards Ltd, since 2016; *b* Inverness, 14 Oct. 1945; *s* of late Leslie Gordon Eldon and Mary Forbes Eldon (*née* Smith); *m* 1975, Maria Margarita Gaus; two *s* one *d*. *Educ:* Duke of York's Royal Mil. Sch. Union Internat. Co., 1963–64; Commercial Banking Co. of Sydney, 1964–67; with British Bank of the Middle East, later HSBC Group, 1968–2005: Dist Manager, Mongkok, 1982–84; Dep. Man. Dir, Saudi British Bank, 1984–87; CEO, Malaysia, 1988–92; Exec. Dir, Internat., 1993–95; CEO, Hongkong and Shanghai Banking Corp., 1996–98. Chairman: Hang Seng Bank Ltd, 1996–2005; Hong Kong and Shanghai Banking Corp. Ltd, 1999–2005; Director: Swire Pacific Ltd, 1996–2005; HSBC Hldgs plc, 1999–2005; MTR Corp. Ltd, 1999–2008; Eagle Asset Management Ltd, 2006–11; China Central Properties Ltd, 2007–09; Shui On Construction and Materials, 2010–12; Cassis International Pte Ltd, 2010–12; Dubai Internat. Financial Centre Higher Bd, 2011–; New Lily International, 2013–; KC Maritime Ltd, 2014–15; Lead Ind. Dir, Noble Gp, 2010–15 (Chm., 2007–09; Vice Chm., 2015–18). Non-executive Chairman: Hong Kong Gen. Chamber of Commerce, 2005–07; Dubai Internat. Financial Centre Authy, 2006–11; HSBC Bank Oman SAOG, 2013–17; Octopus Hldgs Ltd, 2016–; HSBC Bank Egypt SAE, 2017–; HSBC Bank A.S. (Turkey), 2017–; HSBC Bank Middle East Hldgs BV, 2017–. Sen. Advr, PricewaterhouseCoopers, 2005–14. Founding Mem., Seoul Internat. Business Adv. Council, 2001–07 (Chm., 2002–05); Special Advr, Korea Nat. Competitiveness Council, Office of the President, 2008–12. Member: Council, Hong Kong Trade Develt Council, 1996–2007; Internat. Council, Bretton Woods Cttee, 2006–10; Adv. Bd, Unisys, 2006–10; Capital Adequacy Review Tribunal, 2007–12; Adv. Bd, Chartis Asia Pacific, 2011–13; Chairman, Advisory Board: Asiya Investments, 2010–15; HSBC Global Commercial Bank Risk Cttee, 2012–16; Alexander Proudfoot, 2014–16; Global Inst. for Tomorrow, 2015–; Advr, Southern Capital Gp, 2007–; Mem., Corporate Governance Cttee, Charoen Pokphand Gp Corp., 2016–18. Vice Patron, Community Chest, 2005–. JP Hong Kong, 2000. FCIB 1986; FCIB (Hong Kong) 1995. Hon. DBA Hong Kong City Univ., 2003; Hon. Dr Hong Kong Acad. of Performing Arts, 2011. Businessman of the Year, DHL and S China Morning Post, 2003. *Recreations:* sports, music, reading, travel. *Address:* 16th Floor, Hong Kong Club Building, 3A Chater Road, Hong Kong. *Clubs:* Hong Kong, Hong Kong Jockey (Steward, 1996–2008; Dep. Chm., 2006–08; Hon. Steward, 2008–), China.

**ELDON, Sir Stewart (Graham),** KCMG 2009 (CMG 1999); OBE 1991; HM Diplomatic Service, retired; Senior Adviser on defence and security issues, Transparency International, since 2010; *b* 18 Sept. 1953; *s* of late John Hodgson Eldon and of Rose Helen (*née* Stinton); *m* 1978, Christine Mary Mason; one *s* one *d*. *Educ:* Pocklington Sch.; Christ's Coll., Cambridge (BA Electrical Scis 1974; MSc 1976; MA 1977). MIET (MIEE 2002). Joined HM Diplomatic Service, 1976: UK Mission to UN, NY, 1976; FCO, 1977; Third, later Second Sec., Bonn, 1978–82; First Sec., FCO, 1982; Private Sec. to Minister of State, 1983–86; First Sec., UK Mission to UN, NY, 1986–90; Asst Hd, ME Dept, FCO (also Dep. Crisis Manager, Gulf War), 1990–91; Counsellor, Eur. Secretariat, Cabinet Office, 1991–93; Fellow, Center for Internat. Affairs, Harvard Univ., 1993–94; Counsellor (Political), UK Delegn to NATO, Brussels, 1994–97; Dir (Confs), FCO, 1997–98; Ambassador and Dep. Perm. Rep., UK Mission to UN, NY, 1998–2002; Ambassador to Ireland, 2003–06; UK Perm. Rep., UK Delegn to NATO, 2006–10; NATO Subject Matter Expert on Building Integrity, 2010–. Ind. Mem., Parole Bd for England and Wales, 2010–; Mem., Investigating Cttee, GDC, 2014–16. Civil Advr, HCSC, UK Defence Acad., 2011–. Vis. Fellow, Yale Univ., 2002. Ambassador Partnership accredited mediator. *Publications:* contrib. RIIA paper, to RIIA jl and to Internat. Peace Acad. pubns. *Recreations:* music, travel, science fiction, breaking computers. *W:* www.stewarteldon.com. *Club:* Athenæum.

**ELFER, His Honour David Francis;** QC 1981; a Circuit Judge, 1996–2000; *b* 15 July 1941; *s* of George and Joy Elfer; *m* 1968, Karin Ursula Strub; two *s*; *m* 1988, Alexandra Smith-Hughes; one *s*. *Educ:* St Bede's Coll., Manchester; Emmanuel Coll., Cambridge (MA). Called to the Bar, Inner Temple, 1964, Bencher, 1989; a Recorder, 1978–96. Bar Col rep. for W Circuit, 1987–89. *Recreation:* music. *Address:* c/o Circuit Office, Rose Court, 2 Southwark Bridge, SE1 9HS.

**ELGIN,** 11th Earl of, *cr* 1633, **AND KINCARDINE,** 15th Earl of, *cr* 1647; **Andrew Douglas Alexander Thomas Bruce,** KT 1981; CD 1981; JP; Lord Bruce of Kinloss, 1604, Lord Bruce of Torry, 1647; Baron Elgin (UK), 1849; 37th Chief of the Name of Bruce; Lord-Lieutenant of Fife, 1987–99; late Scots Guards; Captain; Royal Company of Archers, HM Body Guard for Scotland; Hon. Colonel, 31 Combat Engrs (The Elgins), Canada; *b* 17 Feb. 1924; *e s* of 10th Earl of Elgin, KT, CMG, TD and Hon. Katherine Elizabeth Cochrane (DBE 1938) (*d* 1989), *er d* of 1st Baron Cochrane of Cults; *S* father, 1968; *m* 1959, Victoria Mary, *o d* of Dudley Usher, MBE and Mrs Usher of Larach Bhan, Kilchrennan, Argyll; three *s* two *d*. *Educ:* Eton; Balliol College, Oxford (BA Hons, MA Hons). Served War of 1939–45 (wounded). Dir, Royal Highland and Agricultural Soc., 1973–75; Pres., Scottish Amicable Life Assurance Soc., 1975–94. Chm., Nat. Savings Cttee for Scotland, 1972–78; Mem., Scottish Post Office Bd (formerly Scottish Postal Bd), 1980–96. Chm., Scottish Money Management Assoc., 1981–95. Lord High Comr, Gen. Assembly of Church of Scotland, 1980–81. Regent, RCSE, 1997–. County Cadet Commandant, Fife, 1952–65. Hon. Col, 153(H) Regt RCT(V), TAVR, 1976–86. JP 1951, DL 1955, Fife. Grand Master Mason of Scotland, 1961–65. Brigade Pres. of the Boys' Brigade, 1963–84; Pres., Royal Caledonian Curling Club, 1968–69. Hon. LLD: Dundee, 1977; Glasgow, 1983; Hon. DLitt St Mary's, Halifax, 2014. Freeman: Bridgetown, Barbados; Regina; Port Elgin; Winnipeg; St Thomas, Ont; Moose Jaw. Order of Merit (Norway), 1994; Chevalier, Légion d'Honneur (France), 2014. *Heir: s* Lord Bruce, *qv. Address:* Broomhall, Dunfermline KY11 3DU. *T:* (01383) 872222, *Fax:* (01383) 872904. *Clubs:* Beefsteak, Caledonian, Pratt's; New (Edinburgh).
*See also* Hon. A. R. Bruce.

**ELIAS, Gerard,** CBE 2017; QC 1984; a Recorder of the Crown Court, 1984–2016; a Deputy High Court Judge, 1997–2016; *b* 19 Nov. 1944; *s* of late Leonard Elias and Patricia Elias, JP; *m* 1970, Elisabeth Kenyon; three *s*. *Educ:* Cardiff High School; Exeter University (LLB). Barrister; called to the Bar, Inner Temple, 1968, Bencher, 1993; Wales and Chester Circuit (Circuit Treasurer, 1990–92; Leader, 1993–95); Asst Comr, Boundary Commission for Wales, 1981–83, 1985–; Chancellor, Dio. of Swansea and Brecon, 1999–2016; Standards Comr for Wales, 2010–16. Mem., Bar Council, 1985–89, 1993–95; Dir, Bar Mutual Insurance Fund, 1987–97. Governor and Mem. Council, Malvern Coll., 1988–96. Chairman: Disciplinary Commn, ECB (formerly TCCB), 1996–2016; Glam CCC, 1998–2003 (Mem. Exec. Cttee, 1986–93; Dep. Chm., 1993–98); Sport Resolutions UK, 2007–13; Disciplinary Panel, MCC, 2014–. Church in Wales: Mem., Governing Body, 2000–05; Pres., Disciplinary Tribunal, 2007–15; Mem., Provincial Ct, 2015–. Chm., Finding Rhythms, 2015–. Hon. LLD S Wales, 2014. *Recreations:* music, cricket. *Address:* 13 The Cathedral Green, Llandaff, Cardiff, South Glamorgan CF5 2EB. *T:* (029) 2057 8857. *Clubs:* MCC; Cardiff and County; Royal Porthcawl Golf.
*See also* Rt Hon. Sir P. Elias.

**ELIAS, Rt Hon. Sir Patrick,** Kt 1999; PC 2009; a Lord Justice of Appeal, 2009–17; *b* 28 March 1947; *s* of late Leonard and Patricia Mary Elias; *m* 1970, Wendy Kinnersley-Haddock; three *s* one *d*. *Educ:* Cardiff High Sch.; Univ. of Exeter (LLB 1969); King's Coll., Cambridge (MA; PhD 1973). Called to the Bar, Inner Temple, 1973, Bencher, 1995; QC 1990; a Judge of the High Court, QBD, 1999–2009; Pres., Employment Appeal Tribunal, 2006–08. Fellow of Pembroke Coll., Cambridge, 1973–84, Hon. Fellow, 2010; Lectr, Univ. of Cambridge, 1975–84. Hon. LLD: Exeter, 2001; City, 2003. *Publications:* (ed) Harvey on Industrial Relations and Employment Law, 1976; (jtly) Labour Law: cases and materials, 1979; (with Keith Ewing) Trade Union Democracy, Members' Rights and the Law, 1987. *Recreations:* reading, music, painting, cricket, Rugby.
*See also* G. Elias.

**ELIAS, Rt Hon. Dame Sian,** GNZM 1999; PC 1999; Chief Justice of New Zealand, 1999–2019; *b* 12 March 1949; *m* 1970, Hugh Alasdair Fletcher, *qv*; two *s*. *Educ:* Diocesan High Sch. for Girls; Auckland Univ. (LLB Hons 1972); Stanford Univ., Calif (JSM 1972). Admitted to Bar of NZ, 1970; Tutor, Law Sch., Univ. of Auckland, 1970; solicitor, 1972–75; Barrister, 1975–95; QC 1988; Judge of the High Court of NZ, 1995. Mem., NZ Law Commn, 1985–89. Commemoration Medal (NZ), 1990. *Recreations:* chess, piano. *Address:* PO Box 11468, Ellerslie, Auckland 1542, New Zealand. *Clubs:* Northern (Auckland); Wellington (Wellington).

**ELIASSEN, Kjell,** Hon. GCMG 1981; Commander with Star, Royal Order of Saint Olav, 1982; Norwegian Ambassador to Germany, 1994–98; *b* 18 Aug. 1929; *s* of Carl August Eliassen and Bergljot (*née* Store); *m* 1953, Vesla Skretting; one *s* one *d*. *Educ:* Oslo Univ. (law degree). Entered Norwegian Foreign Service 1953; served Belgrade, Moscow, London; Counsellor, Min. of Foreign Affairs, 1963–67; Moscow, 1967–70; Dep. Dir-Gen., Min. of Foreign Affairs, 1970–72; Dir-Gen., 1972–77; Ambassador to Yugoslavia, 1977–80; Perm. Under-Sec., Min. of Foreign Affairs, 1980–84; Ambassador to USA, 1984–89; to UK, 1989–94. Numerous foreign decorations. *Address:* Generallunden 21, 0381 Oslo, Norway.

**ELIASSON, Jan;** Deputy Secretary-General, United Nations, 2012–16; Chair, Governing Body, Stockholm International Peace Research Institute, since 2017; *b* Göteborg, 1940; *m* 1967, Kerstin Englesson; one *s* two *d*. *Educ:* Swedish Naval Acad.; Sch. of Econs, Göteborg (MEcons 1965). Harare, 1980; Diplomatic Advr to Swedish Prime Minister, 1982–83; Dir Gen. for Pol Affairs, Min. for For. Affairs, 1983–87; Swedish Ambassador to the UN, NY, 1988–92; UN Under-Sec.-Gen. for Humanitarian Affairs, 1992; State Sec. for For. Affairs, 1994–2000; Swedish Ambassador to the USA, 2000–05; Pres., UN Gen. Assembly, 2005–06; Foreign Minister, Sweden, 2006. Chm., UN Trust Fund for S Africa, 1988–92; Chm., working gp on emergency relief, UN Gen. Assembly, 1991; Vice Pres., ECOSOC, 1991–92; Special Envoy of UN Sec.-Gen. for Darfur, 2007–08. Visiting Professor: Uppsala Univ., 2006–; Göteborgs Univ., 2007–. Chairman: Anna Lindh Meml Fund, 2007–11; WaterAid Sweden, 2009–12. Hon. Dr: American Univ., Washington, 1994; Göteborgs, 2001; Bethany Coll., Kansas, 2005; Uppsala, 2006. *Address:* Stockbyvägen 15, SE 18278 Stocksund, Sweden.

**ELIBANK,** 15th Lord *cr* 1643 (Scotland); **Robert Francis Alan Erskine-Murray;** Bt (Nova Scotia) 1628; *b* 10 Oct. 1964; *s* of 14th Lord Elibank and Valerie Sylvia Erskine-Murray; *S* father, 2017; *m* 1996, Antonia, *yr d* of Roger Carrington; two *d*. *Educ:* The Grove, Harrow School; Reading Univ. (BA (Hons) History and Politics, 1987). *Recreations:* golf, tennis. *Heir: b* Master of Elibank, *qv.*

**ELIBANK, Master of; Hon. Timothy Alexander Elibank Erskine-Murray;** Director, Clients Department, Baillie Gifford, since 2015; *b* 6 May 1967; *s* of 14th Lord Elibank and Valerie Sylvia Erskine-Murray; heir to 15th Lord Elibank, *qv*; *m* 2000, Clare Watkiss; two *s*. *Educ:* Eton; Exeter Univ. (BA Hons Hist. 1990); Cambridge Univ. (MBA 2001). Smith New Court, 1991–94; joined Cazenove & Co, 1994, specialising in Asian equities; Co-Manager, Asia-Pacific Pension Fund, Kames Capital, 2008–15.

**ELINGER, John;** *see* Ball, Sir C. J. E.

**ELIOT,** family name of **Earl of St Germans**.

**ELIOT, Simon Flowerdew,** MA; Headmaster, Sherborne School, 2000–10; *b* 20 July 1952; *s* of late Geoffrey Philip Eliot and Margery Hope Eliot-Sutton; *m* 1983, Olivia Margaret Cicely Roberts; one *s* one *d*. *Educ:* Radley Coll.; Queens' Coll., Cambridge (MA). Sedgwick Forbes (Marine), 1974–75; Asst Master, Radley Coll., 1975–76; Winchester College: Asst Master, 1976–2000; Housemaster, 1988–2000. *Recreations:* history, theatre, music, horse racing. *Address:* 28 Daniel Street, Bath BA2 6ND. *T:* (01225) 462156.

**ELIOTT of Stobs, Sir Rodney Gilbert Charles,** 13th Bt *cr* 1666 (NS); *b* Toowoomba, Qld, 15 July 1966; *s* of Sir Charles Joseph Alexander Eliott of Stobs, 12th Bt and Wendy Judith Eliott (*née* Bailey); *S* father, 2014; *m* 1988 (marr. diss. 1997); one *s* two *d*. *Educ:* St Mary's Christian Brothers Coll. Qualified Diesel Mechanic, 1989–. *Recreation:* motor and water sports. *Heir: s* Steven Charles Eliott, *b* 2 Aug. 1990. *Address:* Minyama, Qld, Australia. *T:* 45706686. *E:* rodo66@bigpond.net.au.

**ELIS-THOMAS,** family name of **Baron Elis-Thomas**.

**ELIS-THOMAS, Baron** *cr* 1992 (Life Peer), of Nant Conwy in the County of Gwynedd; **Dafydd Elis Elis-Thomas,** PC 2004; Member for Dwyfor Meirionnydd, National Assembly for Wales, since 2007 (Plaid Cymru, 2007–16, Ind, since 2016) (Member (Plaid Cymru) Meirionnydd Nant Conwy, 1999–2007); Deputy Minister for Culture, Sport and Tourism, since 2018; *b* 18 Oct. 1946; name changed from Thomas to Elis-Thomas by deed poll, 1992; *m* 1st, 1970, Elen M. Williams (marr. diss.); three *s*; 2nd, 1993, Mair Parry Jones. *Educ:* Ysgol Dyffryn Conwy; UC North Wales. Research worker, Bd of Celtic Studies, 1970; Tutor in Welsh Studies, Coleg Harlech, 1971; Lectr, Dept of English, UC North Wales, 1974. MP (Plaid Cymru) Merioneth, Feb. 1974–1983, Meirionnydd Nant Conwy,

1983–92. National Assembly for Wales: Presiding Officer, 1999–2011; Minister for Culture, Tourism and Sport, 2017–18; Chair, Envmt and Sustainability Cttee, 2011–14; Member: Enterprise and Business Cttee, 2012–13, 2014–16; Constitnl and Legislative Affairs Cttee, 2015, 2016–. Chm., Future Landscapes Wkg Gp, Welsh Govt, 2015–16. Pres., Plaid Cymru, 1984–91. Mem., Arts Council for Wales; Chairman: Welsh Lang. Bd, 1993–99; Screen Wales; a Gov., BFI, 1997–2000. Part-time freelance broadcaster, BBC Wales, HTV, 1970–73; has also broadcast on S4C and Radio Wales. Chancellor (formerly Pres.), Bangor Univ. (formerly Univ. of Wales, Bangor), 2001–17. Mem., Church in Wales. *Recreations:* hill walking, running, arts, Welsh literature. *Address:* 7 Bank Place, Porthmadog, Gwynedd LL49 9AA. *T:* (01766) 515028.

**ELKIN, Sonia Irene Linda,** OBE 1981 (MBE 1966); Director for Regions and Smaller Firms, Confederation of British Industry, 1985–92; *b* 15 May 1932; *d* of Godfrey Albert Elkin and Irene Jessamine Archibald. *Educ:* Beresford House Sch., Eastbourne. Overseas Dir, Assoc. of British Chambers of Commerce, 1950–66; Lloyds Bank Overseas Dept, 1966–67; Confederation of British Industry, 1967–92. Commissioner, Manpower Services Commission, 1982–85. Non-executive Director: Greggs plc, 1992–2004; Kall Kwik Printing (UK), 1993–95. Chm. Trustees, Greggs Pension Fund, 1999–2009. *Publications:* What about Europe?, 1967; What about Europe Now?, 1971. *Club:* Oxford and Cambridge (Lady Associate).

**ELKINGTON, Ven. Dr Audrey Anne;** Archdeacon of Bodmin, since 2011; *b* 1 Nov. 1957; *d* of Henry and Alexandra King; *m* 1986, David Elkington. *Educ:* St Catherine's Coll., Oxford (BA 1980); UEA (PhD 1983); St John's, Nottingham; East Anglian Ministerial Trng Course; Durham Univ. (MA 1999). Ordained deaconess, 1988, deacon, 1992, priest, 1994; Parish Deacon, St Mary the Virgin, Ponteland, 1992–93; Asst Curate, St Mary Magdalene, Prudhoe, 1993–2002; Rural Dean, Corbridge, 1999–2002; Dir of Ordinands and Bishop's Domestic Chaplain, Dio. of Newcastle, 2002–11. Bishop's Advr for Women in Ministry, Dio. of Newcastle, 2001–11; Hon. Canon, Newcastle Cathedral, 2006–11. *Address:* 4 Park Drive, Bodmin PL31 2QF.

**ELKINGTON, Benjamin Michael Gordon;** QC 2012; *b* London, 2 Aug. 1971; *s* of Prof. Andrew Robert Elkington, CBE; *m* 1998, Annabel, *d* of Robin Francis Leigh Oakley, *qv;* one *s* three *d. Educ:* Winchester Coll.; Trinity Coll., Cambridge (Univ. Schol.; Jun. and Sen. Schol.; BA 1st Cl. Hons 1993; MA); Univ. of Virginia (LLM 1994); Inns of Ct Sch. of Law (Scarman Schol. 1996). FCIArb 2017. Associate, Sullivan & Cromwell, NY, 1994–95; admitted to NY Bar, 1995; called to the Bar, Gray's Inn, 1996 (Gray's Inn Schol., 1995); in practice as barrister, specialising in commercial law, 1996–. *Publications:* (jtly) Professional Liability Precedents, 2000; (ed jtly) Jackson & Powell on Professional Liability, 5th edn 2002 to 8th edn 2017. *Recreations:* family, walking and fishing on the Isle of Mull, lighting fires in the rain. *Address:* 4 New Square, Lincoln's Inn, WC2A 3RJ. *T:* (020) 7822 2000, *Fax:* (020) 7822 2001. *E:* b.elkington@4newsquare.com.

**ELKINGTON, John Brett;** environmentalist, entrepreneur, consultant, author, speaker; Co-Founder and Director, SustainAbility Ltd, since 1987 (Chairman, 1996–2006); Chief Entrepreneur, 2006–08; Hon. Chairman, 2014–19); Founding Partner, Chairman and Chief Pollinator, Volans Ventures Ltd, since 2008; *b* Padworth, Berks, 23 June 1949; *s* of late John Francis Durham, (Tim), Elkington and of Patricia Elkington; *m* 1973, Elaine Waite; two *d. Educ:* various schs in England, NI and Cyprus; Glencot Prep. Sch., Wookey Hole; Bryanston Sch.; Univ. of Essex (BA Hons 1970); University Coll. London (MPhil 1974). Associate and Sen. Planner, Transport and Envmt Studies, 1974–78; Environmental Data Services Ltd, 1978–83, Man. Dir, 1981–83, Editor, ENDS Report, 1978–83; Editor, Biotechnology Bulletin, 1983–98; Founder Dir, John Elkington Associates, 1983–. Chairman: Envmt Foundn, later Foundn for Democracy and Sustainable Develt, 1995–2012; Adv. Council, Export Credits Guarantee Dept, 2005–07; Adv. Council, Novartis Impact Valuation, 2018–; Member: EU Consultative Forum on the Envmt and Sustainable Develt, 1994–2001; Faculty, World Econ. Forum, 2002–08; WWF-UK Council of Ambassadors, 2006–; Chm., Admissions Panel, Social Stock Exchange, 2015–18 (Mem Bd, 2015–17); Sustainability Council, Positive Luxury, 2016–. Visiting Professor: Doughty Centre for Corporate Responsibility, Sch. of Mgt, Cranfield Univ., 2007–; Imperial Coll. London, 2013–; UCL, 2013–. Chm. Bd, Envmt Faculty, Herning Inst. of Business Admin and Technol., Denmark, 1995–98. Mem. Bd, Global Reporting Initiative, Netherlands, 2009–13; Mem., Internat. Integrated Reporting Council (formerly Cttee), 2010–13; Member, Advisory Board: Instituto Ethos, Brazil, 2007–13; Zouk Ventures, 2008–; EcoVadis, France, 2008–; 2degrees Network, 2009–; Nestlé Creating Shared Value, 2009–18; Carbon War Room Gigaton awards, 2010–11; Aviva/Friends Life Stewardship Cttee of Ref. (formerly F&C Investment Cttee of Ref., later Friends Life Cttee of Ref.), 2010–18; Recyclebank, 2011–17; Vert Capital, 2017–; UBQ Materials, Israel, 2017–; Sustainian, 2018–; Chm., Impact Valuation Adv. Council, Novartis, 2018–. Member: Bd, Biomimicry 3.8 Inst., 2013–16; SunRise Adv. Bd, Covestro (formerly Bayer MaterialScience), 2013–18. Trustee, Ecological Sequestration Trust, 2014–18 (Actg Chm., Bd of Trustees, 2011–14). Hon. Fellow, The Hub, 2008. Hon. Dr Essex, 2014. FRSA. *Publications:* The Ecology of Tomorrow's World, 1980; Sun Traps: the renewable energy forecast, 1984; The Gene Factory, 1985; The Poisoned Womb, 1985; (with T. Burke) The Green Capitalists, 1987; (with J. Hailes and T. Burke) Green Pages: the business of saving the world, 1988; A Year in the Greenhouse, 1990; (with J. Hailes and P. Knight) The Green Business Guide: how to take up – and profit from – the environmental challenge, 1991; Cannibals with Forks: the triple bottom line of 21st century business, 1997; The Chrysalis Economy: how citizen CEOs and corporations can fuse values and value creation, 2001; (with P. Hartigan) The Power of Unreasonable People: how social entrepreneurs create markets that change the world, 2008; The Zeronauts: breaking the sustainability barrier, 2012; (with J. Zeitz) The Breakthrough Challenge: 10 ways to connect today's profits with tomorrow's bottom line, 2014; *with Julia Hailes:* The Green Consumer Guide: from shampoo to champagne, 1988; The Green Consumer's Supermarket Shopping Guide, 1989; The Young Green Consumer's Guide, 1990; Holidays That Don't Cost the Earth, 1992; Manual 2000: life choices for the future you want, 1998; The New Foods Guide: what's here, what's coming, what it means for us, 1999; author or jt author of over 40 reports; columnist and/or blogger for various pubns incl. China Dialogue, Director Mag., Época Negócios, GreenBiz, Eco-Business, Nikkei Ecology, CSR Wire, FastCompany.com, Monday Morning, Harvard Business Rev. and The Guardian. *Recreations:* playing with ideas, thinking around corners, conversations with unreasonable people, reading an Alpine range of books (history to science fiction) and US business and science magazines, risking life and limb as a London cyclist, catch-it-as-you-can photography, art and design, writing all hours, sleeping, pre-1944 aircraft, New World wines, 20th century popular music—and Johann Strauss II. *E:* john@volans.com, johnelkington@mac.com. *W:* www.johnelkington.com.

**ELLAM, Michael James,** CB 2014; Global Head, Public Sector Banking, Global Banking and Markets, HSBC, since 2018; *b* London, 4 Oct. 1968; *s* of Brian and Kathleen Ellam; *m* 1995, Karina Saroukhanian; one *s* one *d. Educ:* Forest Hill Sch. for Boys; Peterhouse, Cambridge (BA 1990); London Sch. of Econs (MSc Econ 1991). Economist: Credit Suisse First Boston, 1992–93; HM Treasury, 1993–94; Pvte Sec. to Chancellor of the Exchequer, 1994–96; First Sec. (Econ.), Beijing, 1996–98; HM Treasury: Economist, EMU Policy Team, 1998–2000; Head: Debt and Reserves Mgt Team, 2000; Communications, 2000–03; Perf. and Efficiency Team, Public Services Directorate, 2004; Dir of Policy and Planning, 2004–07; Dir of Communications and Prime Minister's Spokesman, Prime Minister's Office, 2007–09; Man. Dir, Internat. and Europe, then Dir Gen., Internat. Finance, HM Treasury, 2009–13; HSBC: Man. Dir, 2013–14, Vice-Chm., 2014–16, Public Sector Banking; Co-Hd, Public Sector Banking, Global Banking and Mkts, 2016–18. *Recreations:* family, cinema, golf, watching football. *Address:* HSBC Holdings plc, 8 Canada Square, E14 5HQ. *Club:* West Ham United.

**ELLAM, Prof. Robert Mark,** PhD; FRSE; Professor of Isotope Geochemistry, University of Glasgow, since 2007; *b* Shipley, W Yorks, 15 April 1962; *s* of late Derek Ellam and of Margaret Ellam (*née* Thomas); *m* 1985, Elspeth Rowena Wood; one *s* one *d. Educ:* Imperial Coll. London (BSc 1983); Open Univ. (PhD 1987). ARSM 1983. Post Doctoral Res. Asst, Univ. of Oxford, 1987–89; Lectr, 1990–2000, Reader, 2000–06, Univ. of Glasgow; Dir of Res., 2007–12, Dir, 2012–17, Scottish Universities Envmtl Res. Centre. Hon. Prof., Inst. of Surface-Earth System Sci., Tianjin Univ., 2017–. FRSE 2010. *Publications:* Isotopes: a very short introduction, 2016; more than 150 articles in learned jls. *Recreations:* grand-parenting, playing 5-string banjo and banjo ukulele, cookery. *Address:* Scottish Universities Environmental Research Centre, Rankine Avenue, East Kilbride G75 0QF. *T:* (01355) 270130, *Fax:* (01355) 229898. *E:* r.ellam@suerc.gla.ac.uk, rob.m.ellam@gmail.com.

**ELLEN, Eric Frank,** QPM 1980; LLB; Chairman and Director, First Approach Ltd, since 1999; Board Member, International Chamber of Commerce Commercial Crime Services, 1999–2001 (Executive Director, 1994–99; First Director: International Maritime Bureau, 1981–99; Counterfeiting Intelligence Bureau, 1985–99; Commercial Crime Bureau, 1992–99; Regional Piracy Centre, Kuala Lumpur, 1992–99); Consultant, ICC, 1999–2002; *b* London, 30 Aug. 1930; *s* of late Robert Frank Ellen and of Jane Lydia Ellen; *m* 1st, 1949, Gwendoline Dorothy Perkins (marr. diss. 2010); one *s* one *d;* 2nd, 2010, S. Lin Kuo-Ellen; one *d. Educ:* Wakefield Central Sch., East Ham; Holborn Coll. of Law, Univ. of London (LLB Hons, London Univ. Certificate in Criminology). CCMI (FBIM 1978). Joined PLA Police, 1951; Sgt 1956; Inspector 1961; Chief Insp. 1972; Supt and Chief Supt 1973; attended 11th Sen. Comd Course, Bramshill Police Coll., 1974; Dep. Chief Constable 1975; Chief Constable, 1975–80. Adviser on security to Ports Div. of Dept of Environment; advised Barbados Govt on formation of Barbados Port Authy Police Force, 1983; reviewed port security at Jeddah and Dammam. Sec., Internat. Assoc. of Airport and Seaport Police, 1980–88 (Pres., 1977–78 and 1978–79); Founder, Chm. and Life Mem., EEC Assoc. of Airport and Seaport Police, 1975–78; Chm., Panel on Maritime Fraud, Commonwealth Secretariat, 1982–90; Consultant, Commercial Crime Unit. Member: Internat. Assoc. of Ports and Harbours Standing Cttee on Legal Protection of Port Interests, 1977–79 (Chm., Sub-Cttee on Protection of Ports against Sabotage and Terrorism, 1977–79); Cttee of Conservative Lawyers, 1985–; Shipbrokers Cttee on Maritime Fraud; British Acad. of Forensic Sciences; Hon. Soc. of Middle Temple. Police Long Service and Good Conduct Medal, 1974. Freeman of the City of London, 1978. Police Medal Republic of China, 1979. *Publications:* (co-author) International Maritime Fraud, 1981; (ed) Violence at Sea, 2nd edn, 1987; (ed) Piracy at Sea, 1989; (ed) Ports at Risk, 1993; (ed) Shipping at Risk: the rising tide of organised crime, 1998; A Guide to the Prevention of Money Laundering, 1998; professional articles on marine fraud and counterfeiting, terrorism, piracy and port policing, money laundering and fraud in commerce (has lectured on these topics at seminars in over 50 countries). *Recreations:* golf, swimming, yoga. *Address:* 38 Tyle Green, Hornchurch, Essex RM11 2TB.

**ELLEN, Prof. Roy Frank,** PhD; FBA 2003; FLS; Professor of Anthropology and Human Ecology, 1988–2012, now Emeritus, and Director, Centre for Biocultural Diversity, 2007–12, University of Kent; *b* 30 Jan. 1947; *s* of Gerald Frank Ellen and Nancy Eileen (*née* Childs); *m* 1978, Nicola Jane Goward; two *d. Educ:* LSE (BSc; PhD); Univ. of Leiden. Lectr, LSE, 1972–73; Lectr, 1973–80, Sen. Lectr, 1980–86, Reader, 1986–88, Univ. of Kent, Canterbury. Visiting Fellow: ANU, 1981; Netherlands Inst. for Adv. Study, 1984; Vis. Prof., Univ. of Leiden, 1994. President: Anthropol. and Archaeol. Section, BAAS, 2004–05; RAI, 2007–11. Mem. Council, British Acad., 2010–13. Lectures: Curl, RAI, 1987; Munro, Univ. of Edinburgh, 1994; Stirling, Univ. of Kent, 2007; Layton, Univ. of Durham, 2013. FLS 2001. Dist. Economic Botanist Award, Soc. for Economic Botany, 2017. *Publications:* Nuaulu Settlement and Ecology, 1978; (ed with P. H. Burnham) Social and Ecological Systems, 1979; (ed with D. Reason) Classifications in Their Social Context, 1979; (ed) Environment, Subsistence and System, 1982, 2nd edn 2002; (ed) Ethnographic Research, 1984; (ed jtly) Malinowski Between Two Worlds, 1988; The Cultural Relations of Classification, 1993; Nuaulu Ethnozoology, 1993; (ed with C. W. Watson) Understanding Witchcraft and Sorcery in Southeast Asia, 1993; (ed with K Fukui) Redefining Nature, 1996, 2nd edn 2002; (ed jtly) Indigenous Environmental Knowledge and its Transformations, 2002; On the Edge of the Banda Zone, 2003; The Categorical Impulse, 2006; (ed) Ethnobiology and the Science of Humankind, 2006; (ed) Modern Crises and Traditional Strategies: local ecological knowledge in Island Southeast Asia, 2007; Nuaulu Religious Practices: the frequency and reproduction of rituals in a Moluccan society, 2012; (ed jtly) Understanding Cultural Transmission in Anthropology, 2013; Kinship, Population and Social Reproduction in the New Indonesia; a study of Nuaulu cultural resilience, 2018. *Address:* School of Anthropology and Conservation, University of Kent, Canterbury, Kent CT2 7NR. *T:* (01227) 720464, *Fax:* (01227) 827289. *E:* R.F.Ellen@kent.ac.uk.

**ELLEN, Susan Caroline;** Chairman, West Middlesex University Hospital NHS Trust, 2002–10; *b* 15 Dec. 1948; *d* of late Albert John Davies and of (Winnifred) Ivy (Caroline) (*née* Emberton); *m* 1974, Simon Tudor Ellen; two *d. Educ:* Cardiff High Sch.; Malvern Girls' Coll.; Bristol Univ. (BSc Politics and Sociol.); Dip HSM. With NHS, 1970–77; joined BUPA, 1977: Dir, 1990–95; Man. Dir, BUPA Health Services, 1990–95; Man. Dir, United Racecourses (Hldgs) Ltd, 1996–2002; Non-executive Director: Asda Gp plc, 1992–98; Birmingham Midshires Building Soc., 1996–2000; Portman Building Soc., 2001–07; Vitality (formerly Prudential Health, then PruHealth), 2006–16; Nationwide Bldg Soc., 2007–09. Member: Financial Reporting Rev. Panel, 1992–98; Financial Reporting Council, 1995–96. Trustee, St John Ambulance, 2006–17. *Recreations:* family, racing, the arts.

**ELLENA, Rt Rev. Richard;** Bishop of Nelson (NZ), 2007–18; *b* 15 Jan. 1951; *s* of Victor Albert Ellena and Helen Mae Ellena; *m* 1972, Hilary Geoghegan; one *s* one *d. Educ:* Canterbury Univ. (BMus 1976); St John's Coll., Auckland (LTh 1984). Head, Dept of Music, Rangiora High Sch., Christchurch, 1976–82; ordained priest, 1985; Vicar: St Peter's, Kensington-Otipua, 1986–91; Blenheim Anglican Parish, 1992–2006; Archdeacon, Nelson and Marlborough, 2001–06; Vicar-Gen., Dio. of Nelson, 2002–06. *Recreations:* reading, walking, sailing.

**ELLENBOGEN, Naomi Lisa, (Mrs M. S. Barklem);** QC 2010; a Recorder, since 2016; a Deputy High Court Judge, since 2017; *b* Liverpool, 20 March 1970; *d* of late Dr Wilfred Ellenbogen and of Margaret Rose Ellenbogen (*née* Ognall, later Unger, now Brin) and step *d* of late Dr Philip Carl Unger, subseq. of Dr Kenneth Brin; *m* 2008, Martyn Stephen Barklem, *qv;* two step *s. Educ:* King David Primary Sch., Liverpool; King David High Sch.,

Liverpool; New Coll., Oxford (BA Juris. 1991; MA 1996). Called to the Bar, Gray's Inn, 1992, Bencher, 2014; in practice at the Bar, specialising in employment, commercial and professional negligence law, 1993–. Jt Hd, Littleton Chambers, 2014–18. Mem., 2005–10, Vice Chm., 2011–15, Professional Conduct Cttee, Bar Standards Bd (formerly Professional Complaints and Conduct Cttee, Bar Council, then Complaints Cttee, Bar Standards Bd); Mem., 2015–, Vice Chm., 2016–, Bar Standards Bd. *Publications:* (Gen. Ed.) Butterworths Employment Law: Practice, Procedure and Precedents, 5th edn 2007. *Recreations:* sailing, travel, theatre, music, enjoying her husband's culinary delights. *Address:* Littleton Chambers, 3 King's Bench Walk North, Temple, EC4Y 7HR. *T:* (020) 7797 8600. *E:* nellenbogen@ littletonchambers.co.uk. *Clubs:* Bar Yacht; Hong Kong Cricket.

**ELLENBOROUGH,** 9th Baron *cr* 1802; **Rupert Edward Henry Law;** Senior Investment Director, Investec Wealth & Investment, since 2012; *b* London, 28 March 1955; *s* of 8th Baron Ellenborough and Rachel Mary (*née* Hedley); *S* father, 2013; *m* 1981, Hon. Grania Janet Gray, *d* of Baron Boardman, MC, TD; two *s* one *d*. *Educ:* Eton Coll. Major, Coldstream Guards, retd. *Heir: s* Hon. James Rupert Thomas Law [*b* 8 March 1983; *m* 2012, Sophie Hamilton; one *d*]. *Address:* Bridge House, Kelmarsh Road, Clipston, Market Harborough LE16 9RX. *Club:* Cavalry and Guards.

**ELLERAY, Anthony John;** QC 1993; a Recorder, since 1999; *b* 19 Aug. 1954; *s* of late Alexander John Elleray and of Sheila Mary Elleray (*née* Perkins); *m* 1982, Alison Elizabeth Potter; one *s* one *d*. *Educ:* Bishop's Stortford Coll.; Trinity Coll., Cambridge (MA). Called to the Bar, Inner Temple, 1977. *Recreations:* pictures, garden, wine. *Address:* 201 Deansgate, Manchester M3 3NW. *T:* (0161) 833 2722. *Clubs:* Oxford and Cambridge; Manchester Tennis and Racquet.

**ELLES, James Edmund Moncrieff;** Member (C) South East Region, England, European Parliament, 1999–2014 (Oxford and Buckinghamshire, 1984–94; Buckinghamshire and Oxfordshire East, 1994–99); *b* 3 Sept. 1949; *s* of late N. P. M. Elles and Baroness Elles; *m* 1977, Françoise Le Bail (marr. diss. 1997); one *s* one *d*. *Educ:* Ashdown House; Eton College; Edinburgh University. External Relations Div., EEC, 1976–80; Asst to Dep. Dir Gen. of Agriculture, EEC, 1980–83. European Parliament: EPP spokesman on the Budget, 1994–99; Vice-Pres., EPP-ED Gp, 1999–2004 (Chm., Wkg Party C); Mem., Budget Cttee; Substitute Mem., US Delegn. Founder: Transatlantic Policy Network, 1992 (Chm., 1992–99, 2009–); Founder, European Ideas Network, 2002 (Chm., 2002–08). Co-founder, European Internet Foundn, 2002. Co-founder, EU Baroque Orch. *Clubs:* Carlton; Royal and Ancient Golf (St Andrews).

**ELLETSON, Harold Daniel Hope,** PhD; Director, New Security Foundation, since 2006; *b* 8 Dec. 1960; *m* 1987, Fiona Margaret Ferguson; two *s*. *Educ:* Eton Coll.; Exeter Univ.; Voronezh Univ., USSR; Poly. of Central London; Bradford Univ. (PhD). Mem. (C) Lancashire CC, 1984–88; worked in journalism and public affairs, 1984–88; CBI and Illingworth Morris plc, 1988–90; public affairs adviser and consultant to cos trading in Eastern Europe, 1990–. Contested (C) Burnley, 1987. MP (C) Blackpool North, 1992–97; contested (C) Blackpool North and Fleetwood, 1997. Joined Liberal Democrats, 2002; Mem., Lib Dem foreign affairs team, 2003 (Chm.). Dir, NATO Forum on Business and Security, 2004. Associate, Centre for Defence and Internat. Security Studies. *Publications:* The General Against the Kremlin—Alexander Lebed: power and illusion, 1998.

**ELLICOTT, Russel;** Headteacher, Pate's Grammar School, since 2012 (Deputy Headteacher, 2008–12); *b* Newmarket, Suffolk, 26 Oct. 1970; *s* of Bryan and Jennifer Ellicott; *m* 2001, Catherine Rees; one *s* one *d*. *Educ:* Castle Manor Upper Sch., Haverhill; Royal Holloway and Bedford New Coll., Univ. of London (BA Hons); Univ. of Hull (PGCE; MEd). Teacher of History, Crypt Sch., Glos, 1994–2004; Asst Head Teacher, Marling Sch., Stroud, 2004–08. *Recreations:* enjoying all sports, travelling and time with my family, a VW Campervan enables us to enjoy time together and explore new places. *Address:* Pate's Grammar School, Princess Elizabeth Way, Cheltenham, Glos GL51 0HG. *T:* (01242) 523169. *E:* head@patesgs.org.

**ELLINGTON, Prof. Charles Porter,** PhD; FRS 1998; Professor of Animal Mechanics, University of Cambridge, 1999–2010, now Emeritus; Fellow of Downing College, Cambridge, 1979–2010, now Emeritus; *b* 31 Dec. 1952; *s* of Dr Charles Porter Ellington and Margaret Moselle Ellington; *m* 1977, Dr Stephanie Katharine Lindsay Buckley; two *s*. *Educ:* Duke Univ. (BA 1973); Downing Coll., Cambridge (MA 1979; PhD 1982). Cambridge University: Demonstrator and Lectr in Zoology, 1979–97; Reader in Animal Mechanics, 1997–99. Editor, Jl of Experimental Biology, 1990–94. Scientific Medal, Zoological Soc., 1990. *Publications:* (ed with T. J. Pedley) Biological Fluid Dynamics, 1995; (ed with J. D. Altringham) Designs for Life: the science of biomechanics, 1999; (ed with D. Floreano, J.-C. Zufferey and M. V. Srinivasan) Flying Insects and Robots, 2009; papers on mechanics and physiology of insect flight. *Recreations:* cooking, gardening, wood- and metal-working. *Address:* Department of Zoology, University of Cambridge, Downing Street, Cambridge CB2 3EJ. *T:* (01223) 336668, 336600.

**ELLINGTON, Marc Floyd,** FSA; DL; communications and heritage consultant; *b* 16 Dec. 1945; *s* of late Homer Frank Ellington, Memsie, Aberdeenshire, and of Harriette Hannah Ellington (*née* Kellas); *m* 1967, Karen Leigh, *d* of Capt. Warren Sidney Streater; two *d*. Chm., Heritage Press (Scot.); Board Member: Soundcraft Audio Guides, 1979–; Aberdeen Univ. Res. Ltd, 1980–85; Gardenstown Estates Ltd, 1983–; Grampian Enterprises Ltd, 1992–96; Partner, Heritage Sound Recordings, 1981–; Exec. Dir, Scottish Traditional Skills Trng Centre, 2013–. Composer and recording artiste; producer of documentary films and TV progs. Chm., Grampian Reg. Tourism Task Force, 1991–. Trustee, Nat. Galls of Scotland, 2002–10; non-exec. Dir, Historic Scotland, 2005–11; Member: Historic Bldg Council for Scotland, 1980–98; Cttee for Scotland, Heritage Lottery Fund, 1998–. Member: British Heritage Cttee, 1992–; HHA; PRS. DL Aberdeenshire, 1984. FSA 1987; Hon. FRIAS 2014. Dr *hc* Aberdeen, 2015. Vice-Pres., Buchan Heritage Soc., 1986; Mem., Convention of Baronetage of Scotland. Patron, Banffshire Wildlife Rehabilitation Trust. Baron of Towie Barclay; Laird of Gardenstown and Crovie. OStJ 2004. Saltire Award, 1973; Eur. Architectural Heritage Award, 1975; Civic Trust Award, 1975, 1993. *Publications:* contribs to architectural and historic jls and periodicals. *Recreations:* sailing, historic architecture, art collecting, music. *Address:* Towie Barclay Castle, Auchterless, Turriff, Aberdeenshire AB53 8EP. *T:* (01888) 511347, *Fax:* (01888) 511522. *E:* soundcraft@towiebarclay.co.uk.

**ELLIOT;** *see* Elliot-Murray-Kynynmound, family name of Earl of Minto.

**ELLIOT, Dr Alison Janet,** CBE 2018 (OBE 2003); General Secretary, Royal Society of Edinburgh, since 2018; *b* 27 Nov. 1948; *d* of Kenneth and Janet Macrae; *m* 1979, John Christian Elliot; one *s* one *d*. *Educ:* Bathgate Acad.; Edinburgh Univ. (MA 1970; PhD 1976); Sussex Univ. (MSc 1971). FRSE 2008. Lecturer in Psychology: Lancaster Univ., 1974–76; Edinburgh Univ., 1977–85; Associate Dir, Centre for Theol. and Public Issues, Edinburgh Univ., 2001–17. Elder, 1984, and Session Clerk, 2000–07, Greyfriars, Tolbooth and Highland Kirk, Edinburgh. Moderator of the Gen. Assembly, Church of Scotland, 2004–05; Convener: Church and Nation Cttee, Church of Scotland, 1996–2000; Action of Churches Together in Scotland, 2002–06; Scottish Council for Voluntary Orgns, 2007–13; Mem., Central Cttee, Conf. of European Churches, 1997–2009. Chair: Land Reform Rev. Gp, Scottish Govt, 2012–14; Scottish Fundraising Standards Panel, 2017–18; Internat. Futures Forum, 2017–. Hon. FRCPE 2007. Hon. LLD TCD, 2004; Hon. DD: St Andrews, Edinburgh, Knox Coll., Toronto, 2005; DUniv Open, 2015. *Publications:* Child Language, 1981; Scottish Churches and the Political Process Today, 1987; The Miraculous Everyday, 2005; Growing Citizens, 2009. *Recreations:* friends, family, food. *Address:* Royal Society of Edinburgh, 22–26 George Street, Edinburgh EH2 2PQ. *E:* aelliot@ therse.org.uk.

**ELLIOT, Benjamin William;** Co-Founder and Co-Chairman, Quintessentially Group, since 2000; *b* London, 11 Aug. 1975; *s* of Simon and Annabel Elliot; *m* 2011, Mary Clare Winwood; two *s*. *Educ:* Eton Coll.; Bristol Univ. (BSc Politics). Co-founder and Partner, Hawthorn Advisors, 2013–; Partner, Ding Tai Fung, 2016–. Non-exec. Dir, YouGov plc, 2009–. Govt Food Waste and Surplus Champion, 2019–. Exec. Producer, documentary, Fire in Babylon, 2011. Chm., Quintessentially Foundn, 2008–. Co-Chm., Cons. Party, 2019–. Trustee: Eranda Foundn; V&A Mus., 2017–. *Recreations:* cricket, cycling. *Address:* Quintessentially, 29 Portland Place, W1B 1QB. *T:* (020) 3073 6600. *E:* ben@ quintessentially.com. *Clubs:* White's, 5 Hertford Street, MCC (Associate Mem.).

**ELLIOT, Caroline Margaret, (Carma),** CMG 2011; OBE 2004; Regional Director, China, British Council, since 2013; *b* 24 Aug. 1964; two adopted *d*. *Educ:* Fudan Univ., Shanghai. Entered FCO, 1987; Peking, 1989–91; Brussels, 1991–94; EC Presidency Liaison Officer, Bonn, Paris and Madrid, 1994–96; Second, later First Sec., FCO, 1996–2000; Consul General: Chongqing, 2000–04; Jeddah, 2004–06; Shanghai, 2006–10; Exec. Dir, China, Half the Sky Foundn, 2011–13. *Address:* British Council, 4/f Landmark Building Tower 1, 8 North Dongsanhuan Road, Chaoyang District, Beijing 100004, China.

**ELLIOT, Iain Fleming,** OBE 2000; PhD; Director, East-West Insight, 2000–18; *b* 24 May 1943; *s* of John Darling Elliot and Isabel Elliot (*née* MacLean); *m* 1970, Dr Elisabeth Mary Robson; one *s* one *d*. *Educ:* Univ. of Glasgow (MA); Univ. of Sussex (MA); Univ. of Bradford (PhD 1974). Res. student, Univ. of Leningrad, 1967–68; res. asst and Lectr, Univ. of Bradford, 1969–70; Sen. Lectr, Univ. of Brighton, 1971–88; leader writer and specialist on Soviet affairs, The Times, 1982–86; Associate Dir, with responsibility for Russian broadcasting, Radio Liberty, subseq. also Chief Ed. and Dir, analytic research, RFE/RL Research Inst., Munich, 1987–93; Dir, Britain-Russia Centre, and British East-West Centre, 1993–2000. Ed., Soviet Analyst, 1972–88. *Publications:* The Soviet Energy Balance, 1974; (ed jtly) Demise of the USSR, 1995; contrib. books, jls and newspapers on Soviet and Russian affairs. *Address:* 42 Preston Park Avenue, Brighton, Sussex BN1 6HG. *T:* (01273) 556156.

**ELLIOT, (Robert) John,** WS; Deputy Keeper of HM Signet, 1999–2008; *b* 18 Jan. 1947; *s* of Robert Thomas Elliot and Barbara Elliot; *m* 1971, Christine Anne Glencross; one *s* one *d*. *Educ:* Craigflower Prep. Sch., Dunfermline; Loretto Sch., Musselburgh; Edinburgh Univ. (LLB). WS 1971; Admitted solicitor, 1971; with Lindsays WS, Edinburgh, 1969–2011: Partner, 1973–2011; Man. Partner, 1988–94; Chm., 1994–2010; Chm., William Simpsons, 2010–16. Pres., Law Soc. of Scotland, 1997–98 (Mem. Council, 1990–99). Chm., Age Concern Edinburgh IT, 1995. *Recreations:* golf, politics, argument, wine, literature. *Address:* 1 Lauder Loan, Edinburgh EH9 2RB. *T:* (0131) 667 9339.

**ELLIOT, Virginia Helen Antoinette,** MBE 1986; trainer of National Hunt jockeys and horses; former equestrian event rider; Eventing High Performance Coach, Horse Sport Ireland, 2008–13; *b* 1 Feb. 1955; *d* of late Col Ronald Morris Holgate, RM and of Heather Holgate; *m* 1st, 1985, Hamish Julian Peter Leng (marr. diss. 1989), *s* of Gen. Sir Peter Leng, KCB, MBE, MC; 2nd, 1993, Michael Elliot. *Educ:* Bedgebury Park, Goudhurst, Kent. Three day event equestrian team trainer, 1996 Olympic Games. Three day event wins: Junior European Champion, 1973 (Dubonnet); Mini Olympics, 1975 (Jason); Burghley, 1983 (Priceless), 1984 (Nightcap), 1985 (Priceless), 1986 (Murphy Himself), 1989 (Master Craftsman); Badminton, 1985 (Priceless), 1989 (Master Craftsman), 1993 (Houdini); European Championship, 1985 (Priceless), 1987 (Nightcap), 1989 (Master Craftsman); World Championship, 1986 (Priceless); Team Silver Olympic Medal, 1984 and 1988; Bronze Individual Olympic Medal, 1984 (Priceless), and 1988 (Master Craftsman). *Publications:* (with Genevieve Murphy) Ginny, 1986; (with Nancy Roberts) Priceless, 1987; (with Genevieve Murphy) Ginny and Her Horses, 1987; (with Genevieve Murphy) Training the Event Horse, 1990; *novels for children:* Winning, 1995; Race against Time, 1996; High Hurdle, 1997. *Recreations:* ski-ing, cooking, art, theatre. *Address:* Holliers House, Worton Road, Chipping Norton, Oxon OX7 7DU.

**ELLIOT MAJOR, Prof. Lee,** OBE 2019; Professor of Social Mobility, University of Exeter, since 2018; *b* 20 Aug. 1968; *s* of Terry William Major and Dianne Margaret Major; partner, Siobhan Scannell; one *s* one *d*. *Educ:* Isleworth and Syon Sch. for Boys; Richmond upon Thames Coll.; Univ. of Sheffield (BSc Phys; PhD Theoretical Phys 1993); Imperial Coll. London (MSc Sci. Communication). Reporter, 1995–97, Dep. Editor, 1997–99, Research Fortnight; Educn reporter, Guardian News and Media, 2000–02; Dir, Policy, Wellcome Trust, 2002–04; News Editor, THES, 2004–06; Dir of Res., 2006–12, Dir of Develt and Policy, 2012–14, Chief Exec., 2014–18, Sutton Trust. Hon. Prof., UCL Inst. of Educn; Vis. Sen. Fellow, Internat. Inequalities Inst., LSE. Member: Adv. Gp, Office for Fair Access; Social Mobility Transparency Bd. Trustee, Educn Endowment Foundn (Chm., Evaluation Adv. Bd); Mem., Res. Adv. Panel, Great Ormond Street Hosp. Children's Charity. Foundn Gov., William Ellis Sch. (Chm., Sch. Improvement Cttee). Hon. Prof., Univ. of Exeter, 2017–18. Hon. Dr Sheffield, 2017. *Publications:* (with S. Machin) Social Mobility and its Enemies, 2018; (with S. Higgins) What Works?, 2019. *Recreations:* playing EP Dad's football, playing guitar for the Spontaneous Emissions, compiling the educational backgrounds of people in Who's Who, yoga. *Address:* Graduate School of Education, University of Exeter, North Cloisters, St Luke's Campus, Heavitree Road, Exeter EX1 2LU. *T:* (01392) 724768. *E:* L.Elliot-Major@exeter.ac.uk.

**ELLIOT-MURRAY-KYNYNMOUND,** family name of **Earl of Minto**.

**ELLIOTT, Anthony Michael Manton, (Tony Elliott),** CBE 2017; non-executive Director, Time Out Group plc, since 2016; Founder and Chairman, Time Out Group, 1968–2012 (Director, 1968–2016); *b* 7 Jan. 1947; *s* of late Katherine and Alan Elliott; *m* 1st, 1976, Janet Street-Porter, *qv* (marr. diss. 1978); 2nd, 1989, Jane L. Coke; three *s* (incl. twins). *Educ:* Stowe Sch.; Keele Univ. Time Out Group publishing activities include: Time Out London and Time Out New York; internat. website timeout.com; licensed local edns of Time Out worldwide; annual guides; Time Out Markets. Time Out Trust formed 1989. Director: Roundhouse Trust, 1998–2017; Somerset House Trust, 1999–2017; Photographers' Gall., 1999–2004; Soho Th. Co., 2000–03; Film London, 2003–09; Create London, 2013–. Gov., BFI, 1997–2003 (Chm., Production Bd, 1998–2000). Dir, Human Rights Watch, 2006–15 (Chair, London Cttee, 2003–13). Goodman Award, Arts & Business Awards, 2014. *Recreations:* travel, watching television, cinema going, eating out with friends, reading newspapers and magazines, being with family. *Address:* Time Out Group plc, 77 Wicklow Street, WC1X 9JY. *T:* (020) 7813 3000, *Fax:* (020) 7813 6001.

**ELLIOTT, Prof. (Barbara) Jane**, PhD; Professor of Sociology, University of Exeter, since 2017; *b* Mancot, Flint, 25 Jan. 1966; *d* of late Keith Elliott and of Barbara Joy Elliott; *m* 2001, Jon Lawrence; one *s*. *Educ*: Sharnbrook Upper Sch.; Bedford Coll. of Higher Educn; King's Coll., Cambridge (BA 1987); Univ. of Manchester (PhD Sociol. 2001). Res. Associate, Univ. of Cambridge, 1987–92; Res. Fellow, Univ. of Manchester, 1994–99; Lectr, Univ. of Liverpool, 1999–2004; Institute of Education, University of London: Principal Investigator, 1970 and 1958 British Birth Cohort Studies, 2004–11; Prof. of Sociol., 2009–17; Dir, Centre for Longitudinal Studies, 2010–14; Chief Exec., ESRC, 2014–17. Vis. Lectr, Harvard Univ., 2002–03. *Publications*: Using Narrative in Social Research: qualitative and quantitative approaches, 2005; (with C. Marsh) Exploring Data, 2nd edn 2008; articles in major jls incl. Sociology, Eur. Sociol Rev., Soc. Sci. and Medicine, Internat. Jl of Epidemiol. *Recreations*: a cappella singing, growing vegetables, hiking, birdwatching. *Address*: Sociology, Philosophy and Anthropology, University of Exeter, Amory Building, Rennes Drive, Exeter EX4 4RJ.

**ELLIOTT, Brent**; *see* Elliott, W. B.

**ELLIOTT, Rev. Dr Charles Middleton**; Fellow, Dean and Chaplain of Trinity Hall, 1990–2001, Affiliated Lecturer in Theology, 1991–2001, in Social and Political Sciences, 1993–2001, University of Cambridge; *b* 9 Jan. 1939; *s* of Joseph William Elliott and Mary Evelyn Elliott; *m* 1962, Hilary Margaret Hambling; three *s* (one *d* decd). *Educ*: Repton; Lincoln and Nuffield Colls, Oxford (MA, DPhil). Ordained deacon, 1964; priest, 1965. Lectr in Econs, Univ. of Nottingham, 1963–65; Reader in Econs, Univ. of Zambia, 1965–69; Asst Sec., Cttee on Society, Develt and Peace, Vatican and World Council of Churches, 1969–72; Sen. Lectr in Develt Econs, Univ. of E Anglia, 1972–73; Dir, Overseas Develt Gp, UEA, 1973–77; Minor Canon, Norwich Cathedral, 1974–77; Prof. of Develt Policy and Planning, and Dir, Centre of Develt Studies, Univ. of Wales, 1977–82; Director of Christian Aid, 1982–84; Asst Gen. Sec., BCC, 1982–84; Benjamin Meaker Prof., Bristol Univ., 1985–86; Sen. Consultant, ODI, 1986–87. G. E. M. Scott Fellow, Univ. of Melbourne, 1984–85; Hon. Vis. Prof. of Christian Ethics, Univ. of Edinburgh, 1985–87; Vis. Prof. in Theology, KCL, 1986–88. Chm., Ind. Gp on British Aid, 1981–89. Prebendary of Lichfield Cathedral, 1987–95. *Publications*: The Development Debate, 1972; Inflation and the Compromised Church, 1973; Patterns of Poverty in the Third World, 1975; Praying the Kingdom: an introduction to political spirituality, 1985 (Biennial Collins Prize for Religious Lit., 1985); Comfortable Compassion, 1987; Praying through Paradox, 1987; Signs of Our Times, 1988; Sword and Spirit, 1989; Memory and Salvation, 1995; Strategic Planning for Churches: an appreciative approach, 1997; Locating the Energy for Change: an introduction to appreciative inquiry, 1999; articles in Jl of Develt Studies, Econ. Hist. Rev., Theology, World Health Forum, World Develt, Lancet, BMJ and in Proc. Royal Soc. *Recreations*: sailing, fly-fishing, walking, chatting to rural craftsmen.

**ELLIOTT, (Charles) Thomas**, CBE 1994; PhD; FRS 1988; Tom Elliott Consultancy Ltd, 1999–2006; *b* 16 Jan. 1939; *s* of Charles Thomas and Mary Jane Elliott; *m* 1962, Brenda Waistell; one *s* two *d*. *Educ*: Washington Grammar Sch.; Manchester Univ. (BSc 1960; PhD 1965). Univ. of Manchester: Research student, 1960–63; Asst Lectr/Lectr, 1963–67 (research on dielectric breakdown); joined RSRE 1967, to study electrical transport in semiconductors; SSO, 1967–73; Vis. Scientist, MIT, Lincoln Lab., USA, 1970–71; research into infrared detectors, infrared emitters, novel and ultra-high-speed semiconductor devices, 1972–2006; PSO, 1973–79, SPSO, 1979–86, DCSO, 1986–91, RSRE; CSO (Individual Merit), DRA, Electronics Sector, 1991–99; Chief Scientist, Electronics Sector, DERA, 1996–99. Part-time Prof. of Physics, 1999–2005, Hon. Prof. of Physics, 2005–, Heriot-Watt Univ. Hon. FRPS 2001. Rank Prize for optoelectronics and IEE Electronics Div. Premium Award, 1982; Churchill Medal, Soc. of Engineers, 1986; MacRobert Award for Engineering, 1991; Paterson Medal, Inst. of Physics, 1997; J. J. Thomson Medal, IEE, 1998; Progress Medal, RPS, 2001. *Publications*: numerous papers and patents. *Recreations*: reading, golf, music, motor caravanning. *Address*: Weardale, 8 Hall Green, Malvern, Worcs WR14 3QX. *T*: (01684) 562474.

**ELLIOTT, Christine Anne**; Chief Executive and Director, Institute for Turnaround (formerly Society of Turnaround Professionals), 2007–16; *b* 10 Oct. 1954; *d* of Charles Archbold Elliott and Geneviève Suzanne Marie Thérèse Elliott (*née* Colombé); marr. diss.; two *d*. *Educ*: Blyth Grammar Sch., Northumberland; Sheffield Univ. (BA Hons Law); Chambre de Commerce et d'Industrie, Paris (DS). Thomson Regl Press, 1977–78; NFWI, 1978–80; mkting and PR consultancy, 1980–93; Wiggins Gp plc and Hayklan Industries, 1994–97; Dir, Bletchley Park, 1998–2006; Chief Exec., Ramblers Assoc., 2006. Special Advr, Hadlow Gp, 2016–; Chm., Hadlow Coll. Unity Gp, 2016–. Dir, Collaborate CIC, 2018–19 (Special Advr, 2017). Sen. Ind. Dir, Coll. of Policing, 2017– (non-exec. Dir, 2015–; Chm., Coll. Consultative Gp, 2015–; Chm., 2017–18, Mem., 2018–, Audit and Risk Cttee, 2017–18; Mem., 2015–, Chm., 2019–, Nominations and Remuneration Cttee); non-exec. Advr, Lyonsdown Ltd, 2014–. Vis. Lectr, Univ. of Westminster, 1989–91; Expert Panellist, Cass Business Sch., 2005–; speaker, London Business Sch., 2010–; speaker and mentor, Inspiring the Future, 2013– (Chm., IFT Awards, 2014–). Chm., Health and Care Professionals Council, 2019–. Mem., Leadership Gp, Inst. for Turnaround Foundn, 2011–; Hon. Mem., Inst. for Turnaround, 2011. Lay Mem., Editors' Code of Practice Cttee, 2015–. Mem., Australian Digital Disruption Assoc., 2016–. Member: Poetry Soc.; Oxford-Perm Assoc. *Publications*: Bye Bye Belle (illustrated story book), 1996; Hijacking Enigma, 2003; Can You Keep a Secret?: children's codebreaking, 2004. *Recreations*: saxophone, piano, languages. *Address*: London.

**ELLIOTT, Maj.-Gen. Christopher Haslett**, CVO 2004; CBE 1994; Director, Army Sport Control Board, 2005–15; *b* 26 May 1947; *s* of late Lt-Col Blethyn Elliott and of Zara Elliott; *m* 1970, Annabel Melanie Emerson; four *d*. *Educ*: Kelly Coll., Tavistock; Mons Officer Cadet Sch.; Staff Coll., Camberley (psc). Commnd into S Wales Borderers, 1966: regtl duty appts, 1966–80 (despatches, NI, 1975); Army Staff Coll., Camberley, 1980; COS, Berlin Inf. Bde, 1981–83; Mem., Directing Staff, Army Staff Coll., Camberley, 1985–87; CO, 1st Bn, Royal Regt of Wales, 1987–90; Comdr, British Forces Belize, 1990–93; Dir, Army Recruiting, MoD, 1993–94; Comdr, Brit. Mil. Adv. and Trng Team, S Africa, 1994–97; GOC UKSC (Germany), 1997–2001; Defence Services Sec. and Dir Gen., Reserve Forces and Cadets, 2001–04. Col Comdt POW Div., 1999–2009; Col, Royal Regt of Wales, 1999–2004. Chief Exec., Army Sport Control Bd Charitable Fund, 2005–15; Chm., Army Sports Lottery Grants Cttee, 2005–15; Member: Combined Services Sports Bd, 2005–15 (Chm., 2006–09 and 2013–15); Army Grants Planning Forum, 2007–15; Army Welfare Grants Cttee, 2010–15. Mem. Council for S Africa, Royal Commonwealth Ex-Services League, 2006–. *Recreations*: fly-fishing, rough shooting, walking, watersports. *Club*: Army and Navy.
See also N. B. Elliott.

**ELLIOTT, Maj. Gen. Christopher Leslie**, CB 1999; MBE 1969; author; Director, Doctrine and Strategic Analysis, General Dynamics UK Ltd, 2002–10; Director General, Dynamics UK Research Foundation, 2002–10; *b* 18 March 1947; *s* of Peter Archibald Elliott and Evelyn Sarah (*née* Wallace); *m* 1970, Margaret Bennett; one *d* (and one *d* decd). *Educ*: Pocklington Sch., York; RMA; Royal Mil. Coll. of Sci. (BSc Hons Eng); Cranfield Inst. of Technol. (MPhil). Commnd RE, 1967 (MBE for Gallantry); emergency tours in NI, 1971, 1972 (twice), 1974, 1978; Adjt, 22 Engr Regt, 1974–76; Instructor, RMA, Sandhurst, 1976–78; DA&QMG, 22 Armd Bde, 1980–82; OC 48 Field Sqdn, RE, 1982–84 (incl. ops tour to Falkland Is, winter 1983); CO, 21 Engr Regt, 1986–88; ACOS 1 (BR) Corps, 1988–90; Comdr, 6th Armd Bde, 1990–91; Dir of Studies, Staff Coll., Camberley, 1991–92; Dir, Mil. Ops, 1993–95; UK Mil. Advr to Chm., Internat. Conf. on former Yugoslavia, 1995–96; Dir Gen. Army Trng and Recruiting, and Chief Exec., Army Trng and Recruiting Agency, 1996–99; COS, HQ QMG, 1999–2000; Dir-Gen. Develt and Doctrine, MoD, 2000–02. Comr, Royal Hosp., Chelsea, 1996–2002. Trustee, Army Central Fund, 1998–2000. Col Comdt, RE, 2000–08. Consultant, Ove Arup and Partners, 2002–12. Chm., Purple Secure Systems Ltd, 2007–09. Vis. Prof., Cranfield Univ., 2002–15; Research Fellow: Changing Character of War Centre, Faculty of History, Oxford Univ., 2013–17; Dept of Politics and Internat. Relns, Reading Univ., 2012–; Associate Fellow, RUSI, 2012–. Mem. Senate, Cranfield Univ., 1996–99; Mem. Adv. Council, RMCS, 2000–02; Pres., Instn of RE, 2002–07 (Fellow, 2007). Pres., Jt Services Paragliding and Hang-gliding Assoc., 1993–2002; Cdre, Army Sailing Assoc., 2001–02 (Vice-Cdre, 1993–94). Pres., Victim Support, Wilts, 2003–09. Mem., Easton Royal Parish Council, 2003–17 (Chm., 2014–15). *Publications*: (contrib.) Blast Damage to Buildings, 1995, repr. 2010; High Command: British military leadership in the Iraq and Afghanistan wars, 2015. *Recreations*: sailing, ski-ing, reading, good company. *E*: Molelowerfarm@gmail.com. *Clubs*: Royal Ocean Racing, Royal Cruising (Mem. Cttee, 2000–), Royal Yacht Squadron; Royal Engineer Yacht (Chatham) (Cdre, 1995–96); Royal Lymington Yacht.

**ELLIOTT, Sir David (Murray)**, KCMG 1995; CB 1987; Director General (Internal Market), General Secretariat of Council of European Union, 1991–95; *b* 8 Feb. 1930; *s* of late Alfred Elliott, ISM, and Mabel Kathleen Emily Elliott (*née* Murray); *m* 1956, Ruth Marjorie Ingram; one *d* (one *s* decd). *Educ*: Bishopshalt Grammar Sch.; London Sch. of Economics and Political Science (BScEcon); Kitchener Scholar. National Service, RAF, 1951–54; Gen. Post Office, 1954–57; seconded to Federal Ministry of Communications, Enugu, Nigeria, 1958–62; GPO, 1962–69 (Principal, 1964; Clerk in Waiting, 1964–69); Asst Secretary: Min. of Posts and Telecommunications, 1969–74 (Dep. Leader, UK Delegn to Centenary Congress, UPU, Lausanne, 1974); Dept of Industry, 1974–75; Counsellor at UK Representation to the European Communities, Brussels, 1975–78; Under Sec., European Secretariat, Cabinet Office, 1978–82; Minister and Dep. UK Perm. Rep. to the Eur. Communities, Brussels, 1982–91 (Chm., Cttee of Perm. Reps Pt 1, 1986). Advr on EU affairs under UK Know-How Fund and EU PHARE progs, 1995–98. Member Board: CARE UK, 1995–2001; CARE Internat., 1998–2001. Mem., Sen. European Experts Gp, 2000–. *Address*: 31 Ailsa Road, Twickenham, Middlesex TW1 1QJ. *Club*: Travellers.

**ELLIOTT, David Stewart Innes**; Honorary Treasurer, The Baring Foundation, since 2014 (Trustee, since 2011); *b* 6 April 1945; *s* of late John Innes Elliott, CBE and Edith Agnes Elliott; *m* 1978, Patricia Nicholson; two *s*. *Educ*: Whitgift Sch.; Oriel Coll., Oxford (MA). Commercial Evaluation Dept, 1966–68, Market and Commercial Analyst, 1969–70, Vickers Ltd; Corporate Finance Dept, Baring Brothers & Co. Ltd, 1970–80 (Asst Dir, 1978); Exec. Vice-Pres., Baring Brothers Inc., NY, 1981–84; Finance Dir, ENO, 1985–90; Dir of Finance and Admin, 1991–93, Dep. Chief Exec., 1994–97, Chief Exec., 1998–2009, Royal Albert Hall. Chm., English Touring Opera, 2009–15 (Mem. Bd, 2007–15). Chm., Benesh Inst. of Choreology, 1997–2007; Mem. Exec. Cttee, Royal Acad. Dancing, 1997–2007. Hon. Treas., Lyric Th. Hammersmith, 1999–2006. *Recreations*: opera, theatre, realising my shortcomings as a painter, sailing.

**ELLIOTT, David Stuart**; independent curator, writer, teacher and museum consultant, since 2008; Vice-Director and Senior Curator, Redtory Museum of Contemporary Art, Guangzhou, since 2017; *b* 29 April 1949; *s* of Arthur Elliott and May Elliott; *m* 1974, Julia Alison (marr. diss. 2006); two *d*. *Educ*: Loughborough Grammar Sch.; Durham Univ. (BA Hons Mod. Hist.); Univ. of London (MA Hist. of Art, Courtauld Inst.). Asst Stage Manager, Phoenix Theatre, Leicester, 1966; Asst, City Art Gallery, Leicester, 1971; Regional Art Officer, Arts Council, 1973–76; Director: Mus. of Modern Art, Oxford, 1976–96; Moderna Museet, Stockholm, 1996–2001; Mori Art Mus., Tokyo, 2001–06; Istanbul MOMA, 2007–08; Artistic Director: Sydney 17th Biennale of Art, 2008–10; Kiev First Biennale of Contemp. Art, 2011–12; 4th Internat. Biennale of work by young artists, Moscow, 2012–14; Belgrade 56th October Salon, 2014–16. Visitor, Ashmolean Mus., Oxford, 1992–2000. Rudolf Arnheim Guest Prof. of Art History, Humboldt Univ., Berlin, 2008; Vis. Prof., Dept of Mus. Studies, Chinese Univ., Hong Kong, 2008–16. Art Advr for revitalisation of Central Police Stn site in Hong Kong into centre for contemp. art and heritage, 2010–12; Advr, Redtory Arts District, Guangzhou, 2016–17; Member: Adv. Bd, Mill6 Foundn, Hong Kong, 2017–18; Arts Adv. Bd, Asia Hse, London, 2017–. Curator, 56th Belgrade Salon, 2015–16. Chairman: Bd; Triangle Arts Network, London, 2009–16; Adv. Bd, Momentum, Berlin, 2012–. Pres., Internat. Cttee for Museums and Collections of Modern Art, ICOM, 1998–2004. President of Jury: La Biennale des Arts, Dakar, 2000; Internat. Architectural Competition for Tsunami Meml, Thailand, 2005; Chm. of Judges, Sovereign Asian Art Prize, 2010–; Jury Mem., German Govt arts residency prog. at Tarabya, Istanbul, 2010–17. Contribs to radio and TV. Hon. DA Oxford Brookes, 1998. NACF Award, 1988. Orden de Mayo (Argentina), 2001. *Publications*: Alexander Rodchenko, 1979; José Clemente Orozco, 1980; New Worlds: Russian Art and Society 1900–1937, 1986; (ed jtly) Eisenstein at 90, 1988; (ed jtly) 100 Years of Russian Art 1889–1989, 1989; (ed jtly) Alexander Rodchenko: Works on Paper, 1991; (ed jtly) Engineers of the Human Soul: Soviet Socialist Realism, 1992; Photography in Russia 1840–1940, 1992; (ed) Art from Argentina 1920–1994, 1994; (ed jtly) Wounds: between democracy and redemption in contemporary art, 1998; (ed jtly) After the Wall: art and culture in post-Communist Europe, 1999; Organising Freedom: Nordic art of the '90s, 2000; (ed jtly) Happiness: a survival guide for art and life, 2003; (ed jtly) Hiroshi Sugimoto, 2005; (ed) The Beauty of Distance: songs of survival in a precarious age, 2010; Bye, Bye Kitty!!!: between heaven and hell in contemporary Japanese art, 2011; Between Heaven & Earth: contemporary art from the centre of Asia, 2011; The Best of Times, The Worst of Times: rebirth and apocalypse in contemporary art, 2012; Art from Elsewhere, 2014; contribs to art books, catalogues and magazines. *Recreations*: keeping fit, travelling. *E*: david@elliott.as.

**ELLIOTT, Edward Charles**; Head, The Perse School, Cambridge, since 2008; *b* Worcester, 27 May 1970; *s* of (Charles) Richard Elliott and Janet Elizabeth Elliott; *m* 2002, Dr Susan Broster; one *s* two *d*. *Educ*: Royal Grammar Sch., Worcester; St Anne's Coll., Oxford (BA 1991). Asst Hd, Sixth Form, Whitgift Sch., Croydon, 1995–97; Hd, Sixth Form, 1997–2004, Dep. Hd, 2004–08, The Perse Sch., Cambridge. *Publications*: University Applications (with Michael Punt), 2004; (contrib.) Leading Schools in the 21st Century: heads of department, 2008. *Recreations*: cricket, horticulture, reading political biographies. *Address*: The Perse School, Hills Road, Cambridge CB2 8QF. *T*: (01223) 403869, *Fax*: (01223) 403810. *E*: ecelliott@perse.co.uk.

**ELLIOTT, Eric Alan**; QC 2006; a Recorder, 1993–2019; *b* West Hartlepool, 12 July 1951; *s* of Alan and Sheila Elliott; *m* 1st (marr. diss.) one *s* one *d*; 2nd, 2010, Sally Bradley (*d* 2014). *Educ*: West Hartlepool Grammar Sch.; Liverpool Univ. (LLB). Called to the Bar, Gray's Inn, 1974; in practice as a barrister, until 2013, specialising in criminal law and regulatory and disciplinary law, particularly relating to equine matters; Asst Recorder, 1989–93. *Recreations:* most sports, but particularly horse racing (licensed trainer, 1995–2006) and football (especially following Hartlepool United FC), French culture, fine food and wine.

**ELLIOTT, Rt Rev. George;** *see* Elliott, Rt Rev. M. G. H.

**ELLIOTT, George,** FRICS; Senior Partner, Edmond Shipway and Partners, 1985–93; *b* 20 Aug. 1932; *s* of Harry Elliott and Nellie Elizabeth Elliott; *m* 1st, 1958, Winifred Joan (marr. diss. 1990); one *s* one *d*; 2nd, 1992, Hazel Ann Willis. *Educ:* Sir George Monoux Grammar Sch.; SW Essex Technical Coll. FRICS 1966. Founder Partner, Edmond Shipway, 1963; Chief Exec., British Urban Develt Services Unit, 1975–78. Pres., Western Australian Chapter, Naval Hist. Soc. of Australia, 2003–09. *Recreations:* travel, naval history, croquet. *Address:* 4 Langtry View, Mount Claremont, WA 6010, Australia. *T:* (8) 93842147.

**ELLIOTT, Guy Robert;** Chairman of Trustees, Sir John Soane's Museum, since 2013; *b* 1955; *s* of Robert George Ian Elliott and Susan Mary Jane Elliott (*née* De Wend Fenton); *m* 1988, Hon. Sophia Anne Sackville West, *d* of 6th Baron Sackville; one *s*. *Educ:* Harrow Sch.; Exeter Coll., Oxford; INSEAD (MBA). Chief Financial Officer, Rio Tinto plc, 2002–13. Non-executive Director: Cadbury plc, 2007–10; Royal Dutch Shell plc, 2010–17; SAB Miller plc, 2013–16. Mem., Takeover Panel, 2012–17. *Address:* Sir John Soane's Museum, 13 Lincoln's Inn Fields, WC2A 3BP. *Club:* Beefsteak.

**ELLIOTT, Sir Ivo (Antony Moritz),** 5th Bt *cr* 1917, of Limpsfield, Surrey; FRCPath; Consultant in Infectious Diseases and Microbiology, Oxford University Hospitals NHS Foundation Trust, since 2019; *b* Luzern, Switzerland, 9 May 1978; *s* of Sir Clive Christopher Hugh Elliott, 4th Bt and of Marie-Thérèse Elliott; *S* father, 2018; *m* 2008, Catriona Isobel Wootton; one *s* one *d*. *Educ:* Dragon Sch., Oxford; Eton Coll.; Univ. of St Andrews (BSc (Med. Sci.)); Univ. of Manchester (MB ChB 2003). MRCP, MRCP (Infectious Diseases); DTM&H. FRCPath 2013. Jun. Hse Officer, 2003–04, SHO, 2004–06, Ninewells Hosp., Dundee; SHO, St Thomas' Hosp., London, 2006–07; Specialist Registrar, Nottingham Univ. Hosps NHS Trust, 2007–15; Wellcome Trust Res. Trng Fellow, Laos, 2015–19. *Publications:* contribs to books and jls in clin. medicine and tropical diseases. *Recreations:* tennis, cycling, birdwatching, exotic cuisine. *Heir: s* Tristan Hugh Leighton Elliott, *b* 17 Aug. 2016. *Address:* Blue Barn House, South Leigh, Witney, Oxon OX29 6XH. *T:* (01865) 731111. *E:* ivoelliott@doctors.org.uk.

**ELLIOTT, Prof. (James) Keith,** DPhil, DD; Professor of New Testament Textual Criticism, University of Leeds, 1997–2007, now Emeritus; *b* 19 March 1943; *s* of James and Lillian Elliott; *m* 1971, Carolyn Tull; one *d*. *Educ:* Liverpool Inst. High Sch.; University Coll. of N Wales, Bangor (BA 1st Cl. Hebrew and Biblical Studies 1964); St Peter's Coll., Oxford (DPhil 1967); DD Wales 1988. Leeds University: Lectr in New Testament Lang. and Lit., 1967–89; Sen. Lectr, 1989–93, Reader, 1993–97, Dept of Theol.; Warden, Charles Morris Hall, 1971–83. Ed., 1977–87, Sec., 1987–2010, Internat. Greek New Testament Project; Asst Sec., Studiorum Novi Testamenti Societas, 1983–93; Book Rev. Ed., 1990–, Pres., Editl Bd, 2008–, Novum Testamentum (Leiden). Mem. Cttee, Vacation Term for Biblical Study, Oxford, 2003– (Vice-Chm., 2005–14 and 2016–; Chm., 2014–16). Gov., Harrogate Grammar Sch., 1989–93, 1996–2000. *Publications:* The Greek Text of the Epistles to Timothy and Titus, 1968; Questioning Christian Origins, 1982; Codex Sinaiticus and the Simonides Affair, 1982; A Survey of Manuscripts used in Editions of the Greek New Testament, 1987; A Bibliography of Greek New Testament Manuscripts, 1989, 3rd edn 2015; Essays and Studies in New Testament Textual Criticism, 1992; The Apocryphal New Testament, 1993; The Apocryphal Jesus: legends of the Early Church, 1996; (with D. R. Cartlidge) Art and the Christian Apocrypha, 2001; A Synopsis of the Apocryphal Nativity and Infancy Narratives, 2006, 2nd edn 2016; New Testament Textual Criticism: the application of thoroughgoing principles, 2010; (ed jtly) Textual Research on the Psalms and Gospels, 2012. *Recreations:* walking in the Yorkshire Dales, cycling in Austria, music (big bands, grand opera, especially Wagner). *Address:* 11 Cundall Way, Harrogate HG2 0DY. *E:* j.k.elliott@leeds.ac.uk. *Club:* Army and Navy.

**ELLIOTT, Jane;** *see* Elliott, B. J.

**ELLIOTT, Prof. John,** DLitt; FAcSS; Professor of Education, University of East Anglia, 1987–2002, Emeritus Professor, 2004 (Professorial Fellow, 2002–04); Chief Editor, Journal for Lesson and Learning Studies, 2011–16; *b* 20 June 1938; *s* of Alfred George Lewis Elliott and Mary Doris Elliott (*née* Greason); *m* 1st, 1967, Jean Marion Walford (marr. diss. 1993); three *d*; 2nd, 1998, Anne Christine O'Hanlon. *Educ:* Ashford Grammar Sch.; City of Portsmouth Trng Coll.; Bishop Otter Coll., Chichester; London Univ. Inst. of Educn (Dip. Phil. Ed. 1970; MPhil 1980); DLitt E Anglia, 2003. Horticultural researcher, E Malling Res. Stn, 1956–59; sch. teacher, 1962–67; Educnl Researcher, Schs Council, 1967–72; Lectr in Applied Educnl Res., UEA, 1972–76; Tutor in Curriculum Studies, Cambridge Inst. of Educn, 1976–84; University of East Anglia: Reader, 1984–87; Dean, Sch. of Educn and Professional Develt, 1992–95; Dir, Centre for Applied Res. In Educn, 1996–99. Adv. Prof., Hong Kong Inst. of Educn, 2000–06. R and D Advr, Curriculum Develt, Inst. of Hong Kong, 2000–07; Associate, Centre for Educnl R and D, von Hügel Inst., St Edmund's Coll., Cambridge, 2004–08. Ind. Acad. Advr, Home Office, 2003–04. Mem., Fellowship Council, RSA, 2009–14. Visiting Professor: Manchester Metropolitan Univ., 2004–; Sheffield Univ., 2004–; University Campus Suffolk, 2013–16. Member: Norfolk Learning and Skills Council, 2001–08; Norfolk 14–19 Strategy Gp, 2006–09. Pres., World Assoc. of Lesson Studies, 2009–10. Gov., Sewell Park Coll. and Kett Sixth Form Coll., Norwich, 2009–12. FRSA 1992–2018; FAcSS (AcSS 2011). Hon. DEd Hong Kong Inst. of Educn, 2002; Hon. Dr: Autonomous Univ. of Barcelona, 2003; Jönköping, 2014. *Publications:* Action Research for Educational Change, 1991; The Curriculum Experiment, 1999; (ed with H. Altrichter) Images of Educational Change, 2000; Reflecting Where the Action Is: selected works, 2007; (ed with N. Norris) Curriculum, Pedagogy and Educational Research, 2012; contrib. numerous papers to learned jls and chapters in books. *Recreations:* golf, walking with Murphy the dog and Christine in the countryside, visiting heritage sites in UK and Ireland, cinema and theatre, reading. *Address:* School of Education and Lifelong Learning, University of East Anglia, Norwich NR4 7TJ. *T:* (01603) 592859. *Club:* Royal Norwich Golf.

**ELLIOTT, John Dorman;** Chairman, Australian Product Traders Pty Ltd, 1992; Deputy Chairman, Foster's Brewing Group (formerly Elders IXL Ltd), 1990–92 (Chairman and Chief Executive, 1985–90); *b* 3 Oct. 1941; *s* of Frank Faithful Elliott and Anita Caroline Elliott; *m* 1st, 1965, Lorraine Clare (*née* Golder) (marr. diss. 1986; she *d* 2014); two *s* one *d*; 2nd, 1987, Amanda Mary Drummond Moray (*née* Bayles); one *d*. *Educ:* Carey Baptist Grammar School, Melbourne; BCom (Hons) 1962, MBA Melbourne 1965. With BHP, Melbourne, 1963–65; McKinsey & Co., 1966–72; formed consortium and raised 30 million to acquire Henry Jones (IXL), and became Man. Dir, 1972; Elder Smith Goldsbrough Mort merged with Henry Jones (IXL) to form Elders IXL, 1981; Elders IXL acquired Carlton & United Breweries, 1983, largest takeover in Aust. history. Pres., Liberal Party of Australia, 1987–90. Pres., Carlton FC, 1983–2002. *Publications:* Big Jack: my sporting life, 2003. *Recreations:* football, tennis, Royal tennis. *Address:* 44/108 Elgin Street, Carlton, Vic 3053, Australia. *T:* (3) 96060711. *Club:* Savage (Melbourne).

**ELLIOTT, Sir John (Huxtable),** Kt 1994; FBA 1972; Regius Professor of Modern History, and Fellow of Oriel College, Oxford, 1990–97 (Hon. Fellow, Oriel College, 1997); *b* 23 June 1930; *s* of late Thomas Charles Elliott and Janet Mary Payne; *m* 1958, Oonah Sophia Butler. *Educ:* Eton College; Trinity College, Cambridge (MA, PhD). Fellow of Trinity Coll., Cambridge, 1954–67, Hon. Fellow, 1991; Asst Lectr in History, Cambridge Univ., 1957–62; Lectr in History, Cambridge Univ., 1962–67; Prof. of History: KCL, 1968–73; Inst. for Advanced Study, Princeton, NJ, 1973–90. Chm., Adv. Council, Inst. for the Study of the Americas, Univ. of London, 2004–11. King Juan Carlos Vis. Prof., New York Univ., 1988; Vis. Hon. Prof., Univ. of Warwick, 2003–07. Wiles Lectr, QUB, 1969; Trevelyan Lectr, Cambridge Univ., 1982–83. Chm., Council, Omohundro Inst. of Early American Hist. and Culture, Williamsburg, 2007–10. Hon. Trustee, Prado Mus., 2015. FKC 1998. Corresp. Fellow, Real Academia de la Historia, Madrid, 1965; Fellow, Amer. Acad. Arts and Scis, 1977; Mem., Amer. Philosophical Soc., 1982; Corresponding Member: Hispanic Soc. of America, 1975 (Hon. Fellow, 1997); Real Academia Sevillana de Buenas Letras, 1976 (Hon. Mem., 2008); Royal Acad. of Letters, Barcelona, 1992; Nat. Acad. of History, Venezuela, 1992; Accademia delle Scienze di Torino, 2009; Foreign Mem., Accademia Nazionale dei Lincei, 2003; Real Academia Española, 2016. Hon. Fellow, Lady Margaret Hall, Oxford, 2013. Dr *hc*: Universidad Autónoma de Madrid, 1983; Genoa, 1992; Barcelona, 1994; Valencia, 1998; Lleida, 1999; Complutense, Madrid, 2003; Seville, 2011; Alcalá, 2012; Cantabria, 2015; Hon. DLitt: Portsmouth, 1993; Warwick, 1995; London, 2007; Carlos III, Madrid, 2008; Hon. DHL: Brown, 1996; Coll. of William and Mary, 2005; Hon. LittD Cambridge, 2013. Medal of Honour, Universidad Internacional Menéndez y Pelayo, 1987; Medalla de Oro al Mérito en las Bellas Artes, Spain, 1990; Premio Antonio de Nebrija, Univ. of Salamanca, 1993; Prince of Asturias Prize for Social Scis, 1996; Gold Medal, Spanish Inst., NY, 1997; Balzan Prize for History 1500–1800, Internat. Balzan Foundn, 1999; Premio Órdenes Españolas (Spain), 2018. Visitante Ilustre de Madrid, 1983; Comdr, 1984, Grand Cross, 1988, Order of Alfonso X El Sabio; Comdr, 1987, Grand Cross, 1996, Order of Isabel la Católica; Cross of St George (Catalonia), 1999. *Publications:* The Revolt of the Catalans, 1963; Imperial Spain, 1469–1716, 1963; Europe Divided, 1559–1598, 1968; The Old World and the New, 1492–1650, 1970; (ed with H. G. Koenigsberger) The Diversity of History, 1970; (with J. F. de la Peña) Memoriales y Cartas del Conde Duque de Olivares, 2 vols, 1978–80, 2nd edn 2013; (with Jonathan Brown) A Palace for a King, 1980, 2nd edn 2003; Richelieu and Olivares, 1984 (Leo Gershoy Award, Amer. Hist. Assoc., 1985); The Count-Duke of Olivares, 1986 (Wolfson History Prize, 1986); Spain and its World 1500–1700, 1989; (ed) The Hispanic World, 1991; (ed with Laurence Brockliss) The World of the Favourite, 1999; (ed with Jonathan Brown) The Sale of the Century, 2002; Empires of the Atlantic World (Francis Parkman Prize, Soc. of American Historians), 2006; Spain, Europe and the Wider World, 1500–1800, 2009; History in the Making, 2012; Scots and Catalans: union and disunion, 2018. *Recreation:* looking at paintings. *Address:* Oriel College, Oxford OX1 4EW; 122 Church Way, Iffley, Oxford OX4 4EG. *T:* (01865) 716703.

**ELLIOTT, John Stanley;** Chief Economist, 2007–11, and Director for Social Science, 2010–11, Home Office; *b* 26 March 1959; *s* of late Stanley Elliott and Betty Elliott (*née* Cornish); partner, Shirley Ann McClune; (one *s* decd). *Educ:* Bemrose Sch., Derby; Jesus Coll., Oxford (MA PPE 1980; MPhil Econ. 1982); Sheffield Hallam Univ. (PGCE 2014); Open Univ. (Cert. Maths 2013). Econ. Asst, MSC, 1982–83; Sen. Econ. Asst, DES, 1983–86; Econ. Advr, MoD, 1986–89; Econ. Advr, 1989–92, Sen. Econ. Advr, 1992–95, Dept of Employment; Sen. Econ. Advr, DFEE, then DFES, 1995–2004; Chief Economist, DFES, then DCSF, 2004–07. Mem. Council, Inst. for Employment Studies, 2005–12. Gov., Firth Park Acad. (formerly Firth Park Community Arts Coll.), 2006–10 and 2013–19 (Chm., 2008–09; Associate Gov., 2010–13; Co-Chm., 2015–17). *Recreations:* crosswords, rowing, part-time study for Open University maths degree, volunteer signalman on Peak Rail heritage railway. *Club:* City of Sheffield Rowing.

**ELLIOTT, Prof. Julian George,** PhD; CPsychol, FBPsS, FAcSS; Professor of Education, since 2004, and Principal, Collingwood College, since 2011, Durham University; *b* Epsom, 27 July 1955; *s* of George and Helen Elliott; *m* 1977, Ruth White; one *s* one *d*. *Educ:* Wimbledon Coll.; Durham Univ. (BEd; BA; MA; MSc; PhD 1994). CPsychol 1988; AFBPsS 1988, FBPsS 2016. Teacher (SEN), Seaham Community Home, Co. Durham, 1977–80, Ryhope Sch., Sunderland, 1980–84; educnl psychologist, 1984–90; School of Education and Lifelong Learning, Sunderland Polytechnic, later Sunderland University: Sen. Lectr, 1990–92; Principal Lectr, 1992–96; Reader, 1996–97; Prof., 1997–2004; Associate Dean (Res.), 1999–2003; Actg Dean, 2003–04. FAcSS (AcSS 2010). *Publications:* Children in Difficulty: a guide to understanding and helping, 1998, 3rd edn 2012; Frameworks for Thinking, 2005; Motivation, Engagement and Educational Performance, 2005; The Sage Handbook of Emotional and Behavioural Difficulties, 2014; The Dyslexia Debate, 2014; Dyslexia: developing the debate, 2016; (jtly) Understanding Behaviour, 2016. *Recreations:* racquetball, table tennis, walking, theatre. *Address:* Collingwood College, Durham University, South Road, Durham DH1 3LT. *E:* joe.elliott@durham.ac.uk.

**ELLIOTT, Julie;** MP (Lab) Sunderland Central, since 2010; *b* Whitburn, Sunderland, 1963; one *s* three *d*. *Educ:* Seaham Northlea Comprehensive Sch.; Newcastle Poly. (BA Govt and Public Policy). Regl Organiser, Labour Party, 1993–98; Agent, gen. election, Tynemouth, 1997; Regl Officer, Nat. Asthma Campaign, 1998–99; Regl Organiser, GMB, 1999–2010. Shadow Minister for Energy and Climate Change, 2013–15. Member: Eur. Scrutiny Select Cttee, 2010–15; Business, Innovation and Skills Select Cttee, 2011–13; Culture, Media and Sport, subseq. Digital, Culture, Media and Sport, Select Cttee, 2015–. *Address:* House of Commons, SW1A 0AA.

**ELLIOTT, Keith;** *see* Elliott, J. K.

**ELLIOTT, Lawrence Brian;** JP; Economics Editor, The Guardian, since 1995; *b* 29 Aug. 1955; *s* of Brian and Peggy Elliott; *m* 1980, Carol Ann Lelliott; two *d*. *Educ:* St Albans Sch.; Fitzwilliam Coll., Cambridge (BA Hist. 1977). Evening Post-Echo, Hemel Hempstead, 1978–83; Economics Correspondent: Press Assoc., 1983–88; The Guardian, 1988–95. Sen. Res. Fellow, Univ. of Herts. Council Mem., ODI. Mem., Scott Trust, 2001–11. JP Central Herts, 1992. *Publications:* (ed with Rowan Williams) Crisis and Recovery, 2010; with Dan Atkinson: The Age of Insecurity, 1998; Fantasy Island, 2007; The Gods that Failed, 2008; Going South, 2012; Europe Isn't Working, 2016. *Recreations:* soccer, golf, music, cooking, walking. *Address:* The Guardian, Kings Place, 90 York Way, N1 9AG. *E:* larry.elliott@guardian.co.uk.

**ELLIOTT, Margaret,** CBE 1999; solicitor in private practice, since 1976; *b* 20 March 1951; *d* of Malachy and Kathleen Trainor; *m* 1973, Acheson Elliott; two *s* (twins) one *d*. *Educ:* Our Lady's Grammar Sch., Newry; Queen's Univ., Belfast (LLB Hons). Pres., Law Soc. of NI, 1989–90; Chm., Legal Aid NI, 1990–91. Non-executive Director: Ulsterbus/Citybus, 1990–95; Northern Bank Ltd, 1992–2005; National Irish Bank, 2001–05; Oaklee Housing Assoc. Ltd, 2009–; Irish Times Ltd, 2012–. Fair Employment Comr, 1993–96; Civil Service Comr, 1995–2006. Chm., Bd of Trustees, Nat. Mus and Galls NI, 1998–2008. Gov., Irish Times Trust, 2008–. Mem., Disciplinary Tribunal, ICAI, 2008–. Hon. LLD, 2002.

*Recreations:* reading, cooking, travelling. *Address:* c/o The Elliott-Trainor Partnership, 3 Downshire Road, Newry, Co. Down BT34 1EE. *T:* (028) 3026 8116, *Fax:* (028) 3026 9208. *E:* margaret.elliott@etpsolicitors.com.

**ELLIOTT, Margaret Anne;** *see* O'Brien, M. A.

**ELLIOTT, Prof. Marianne,** OBE 2000; DPhil; FBA 2002; Andrew Geddes and John Rankin Professor of Modern History, 1993–2009, Director, Institute of Irish Studies, 1997–2014, and Blair Chair of Irish Studies, 2008–14, University of Liverpool, now Emeritus Professor; *b* 25 May 1948; *d* of Terry Burns and Sheila Burns (*née* O'Neill); *m* 1975, Trevor Elliott; one *s*. *Educ:* Queen's University, Belfast (BA Hons History); Lady Margaret Hall, Oxford (DPhil 1975). Lectr II, W London Inst. of Higher Educn, 1975–77; Univ. Res. Fellow, 1977–79, Temp. Lectr, 1981–82, UC, Swansea; Univ. Res. Fellow, 1984–87, Hon. Fellow, 1987–93, Dept of History, Univ. of Liverpool; Simon Sen. Res. Fellow, Univ. of Manchester, 1988–89; Lectr in History, Birkbeck Coll., Univ. of London, 1991–93. Visiting Professor: Iowa State Univ., 1983; Univ. of S Carolina, 1984. Part-time Tutor: Balliol Coll., Oxford, 1974–75; Westminster Tutors, 1974–75; Dept of History and WEA/Dept of Educn, Univ. of Reading, 1974–75; Course Tutor, Open Univ., 1979–85; Tutor, Univ. of Warwick, 1980–81. Ford Lectr, Oxford, 2005. Mem., 1995–98, Chm., 1998, AHRB res. panel (hist. and archaeol.); Mem., Res. Cttee, 2002–05, Council, 2006–09, British Acad. Mem., Opsahl Commn on NI, 1992–93. Hon. MRIA 2017. Hon. Fellow, Birkbeck, Univ. of London, 2018. Hon. DLitt TCD 2017. *Publications:* Partners in Revolution: the United Irishmen and France, 1982; Watchmen in Sion: the Protestant idea of Liberty, 1985; (trans.) The People's Armies, 1987; Wolfe Tone: prophet of Irish independence, 1989; (jtly) A Citizens' Inquiry: the report of the Opsahl Commission on Northern Ireland, 1993; The Catholics of Ulster: a history, 2000; (ed) The Long Road to Peace in Northern Ireland, 2002; Robert Emmet: the making of a legend, 2003; When God Took Sides: religion and identity in Ireland - unfinished history, 2009; Hearthlands: a memoir of the White City housing estate in Belfast, 2017; contribs to books and learned jls. *Recreations:* running, cycling, reading. *Address:* Institute of Irish Studies, University of Liverpool, Liverpool L69 7WY. *T:* (0151) 794 3831, *Fax:* (0151) 794 3836. *E:* melliott@liv.ac.uk.

**ELLIOTT, Marianne,** OBE 2018; Artistic Director, Elliott & Harper Productions, since 2016; *b* London, 27 Dec. 1966; *d* of Michael Elliott and Rosalind Elliott (*née* Knight); *m* 2000, Nick Sidi; one *d*. *Educ:* St Hilary's Sch., Alderley Edge; Stockport Grammar Sch.; Hull Univ. (BA). An Artistic Dir, Manchester Royal Exchange Th.; Associate Dir, Royal Court Th.; Associate Dir, NT, 2006–16. Productions include: Much Ado About Nothing, RSC, 2006; Sweet Bird of Youth, Old Vic, 2013; Heisenberg: The Uncertainty Principle, Wyndham's Th., 2017; Company, Gielgud, 2018; Death of a Salesman, Young Vic, 2019, transf. Piccadilly Th., 2019; National Theatre: Pillars of the Community, 2005 (Evening Standard Award); Therese Raquin, 2006; St Joan, 2007 (Best Revival, Olivier Awards; South Bank Show Award); Warhorse, 2007, transf. NY, 2011 (Outer Critics' Circle Award for Outstanding Dir, 2011; Tony Award for Best Dir, 2011); All's Well That Ends Well, 2009; Women Beware Women, 2010; Season's Greetings, 2010; The Curious Incident of the Dog in the Night-Time, 2012 (Olivier Award for Best Dir, 2013), transf. NY, 2014 (Tony Award for Best Dir, 2015), Piccadilly Th., 2018; Port, 2013; The Light Princess, 2013; Rules for Living, 2015; Husbands & Sons, 2015; Angels in America, 2017, transf. NY, 2018.

**ELLIOTT, Mark,** CMG 1988; HM Diplomatic Service, retired; *b* 16 May 1939; *s* of William Rowcliffe Elliott, CB, and Karin Tess Elliott (*née* Classen); *m* 1964, Julian Richardson; two *s*. *Educ:* Eton Coll. (King's Scholar); New Coll., Oxford. HM Forces (Intell. Corps), 1957–59. FO, 1963; Tokyo, 1965; FCO, 1970; Private Sec. to Perm. Under-Sec. of State, 1973–74; First Sec. and Head of Chancery, Nicosia, 1975–77; Counsellor, 1977–81, Head of Chancery, 1978–81, Tokyo; Hd of Far Eastern Dept, FCO, 1981–85; Under-Sec. on secondment to N Ireland Office, 1985–88; Ambassador to Israel, 1988–92; Dep. Under-Sec. of State, FCO, 1992–94; Ambassador to Norway, 1994–98. Grand Cross, Order of Merit (Norway), 1994. *Recreations:* fell walking, nature, music, photography.

**ELLIOTT, Prof. Martin John,** MD; FRCS; Professor of Cardiothoracic Surgery, University College London, since 2004; Consultant Paediatric Cardiothoracic Surgeon, Great Ormond Street Hospital for Children, since 1985 (Medical Director, 2010–15); Clinical Ambassador, Great Ormond Street Children's Charity, since 2015; Chief Medical Officer, Allocate Software Ltd, since 2016; *b* Sheffield, 8 March 1951; *s* of John Elliott and Muriel Elliott; *m* 1977, Lesley Rickard; one *s* (and one *s* decd). *Educ:* King Edward VII Grammar Sch., Sheffield; Univ. of Newcastle upon Tyne (MB BS 1973; MD 1983). FRCS 1978. Postgrad. surgical trng, Newcastle and Southampton, 1973–78; First Asst in Cardiothoracic Surgery, Univ. of Newcastle Upon Tyne, 1978–84; Sen. Registrar in Paediatric Cardiothoracic Surgery, 1984–85, Chm., Cardiorespiratory Services, 2006–10, Great Ormond Street Hosp. for Children. Director: Eur. Congenital Heart Defects Database, 1990–99; Nat. Service for Severe Tracheal Disease in Children, 2001–16. Gresham Prof. of Physic, Gresham Coll., London, 2014–18 (Fellow, 2018). Visiting Professor: Warsaw, 2014–; UCSF, 2014–; Vanderbilt Univ., 2014–; Medical Univ. of S Carolina, 2014–; Johns Hopkins Univ., 2015–. Over 350 invited lectures including: Alfred Blalock Lectr, Johns Hopkins Univ., 2015; Hunterian Orator, RCS, 2015; Robert E. Gross Lectr, Boston Children's Hosp., 2016. Sen. Advr, PA Consulting plc, 2019–. Non-executive Director: Royal Marsden Hosp. NHS Foundn Trust, 2017–; Children's Health Ireland, 2018–. Mem., Internat. Tribunal into Forced Organ Harvesting in China, 2019–. Mem., Industry Adv. Council, Novartis Inc., 2019–. Founder Mem., Eur. Congenital Heart Surgeons Assoc., 1991; Pres. Internat. Soc. for Nomenclature in Congenital Heart Disease, 2000–12; active in Eur. and US professional socs. *Publications:* (with R. A. Jonas) Cardiopulmonary Bypass in Neonates, Infants and Young Children, 1994; (with M. Kanani) Applied Surgical Vivas, 2004; 38 chapters in books; over 300 articles in jls relating to pathophysiol. of cardiopulmonary bypass, outcomes of surgery for congenital heart defects, teamwork and tracheal problems in children. *Recreations:* reading, cycling, cinema, music. *Address:* Cardiothoracic Unit, Great Ormond Street Hospital for Children NHS Trust, WC1N 3JH. *T:* (020) 7405 9200. *E:* martin.elliott@gosh.nhs.uk, martin.elliott@icloud.com. *W:* www.martinelliott.me.

**ELLIOTT, Rt Rev. (Matthew) George (Holden);** a Suffragan Bishop of Toronto (Area Bishop of York-Simcoe), 2001–13; *b* 17 Feb. 1949; *s* of George and Phyllis Elliott; *m* 1977, Linda Ann Martinez; one *s* one *d*. *Educ:* Univ. of Toronto (BA 1972); George Brown Coll. (Dip. Food Services Mgt 1973); Wycliffe Coll. (MDiv 1979; Hon. DD 2002). Asst Curate, St Thomas à Becket, Toronto, 1979–80; Incumbent: Parish of Minden, 1981–88; All Saints', King City, 1989–2001. Regional Dean: Victoria/Haliburton, 1985–88; Holland, 1993–2000. Director: Toronto Parish Trng Prog., 1988–91; Wycliffe Coll. Internship Prog., 1992–94. Member: Communications Inf. Resources Cttee, Nat. Church, 2007–13; Inf. and Communications Standards Develt Cttee, Ont Disability Council, 2007–09. Pres. Bd, Anglican Jl, 2008–13. Chair, Refugee Resettlement Cttee, 2015–. *Recreations:* cooking, gardening, reading. *Address:* 28 Charles Street, King City, ON L7B 1J7, Canada. *T:* (905) 8334988. *E:* bishopgeorge@sympatico.ca.

**ELLIOTT, Matthew Jim;** Editor-at-Large, BrexitCentral, since 2016; *b* Leeds, 12 Feb. 1978; *s* of Geoffrey Edward Elliott and Kathryn Georgiana Elliott (*née* Collins); *m* 1st, 2005, Florence Liselotte Sarah Heath (marr. diss. 2012); 2nd, 2014, Sarah Brunson Smith; one *d*. *Educ:* Leeds Grammar Sch.; London Sch. of Econs and Pol Sci. (BSc Govt). Press Officer, Eur. Foundn, 2000–01; Pol Sec. to Timothy Kirkhope, MEP, 2001–04; Co-Founder and Chief Exec., TaxPayers' Alliance, 2004–12; Founder and Chief Executive: Big Brother Watch, 2009–12; Business for Britain, 2013–16; Chief Exec., Vote Leave, 2015–16; Sen. Pol Advr, Shore Capital, 2017–. Sen. Fellow, Legatum Inst., 2017–. Campaign Dir, NO to AV, 2010–11. Non-exec. Dir, Wess Digital Ltd, 2013–14. Trustee, Social Affairs Unit, 2014–15. FRSA 2008. *Publications:* (jtly) The Bumper Book of Government Waste, 2006; (jtly) The Bumper Book of Government Waste 2008, 2007; (jtly) The Great European Rip-Off, 2009; (jtly) Fleeced!, 2009; contrib. Legatum Inst. papers. *Recreations:* playing pool and the organ, visiting America. *E:* mjelliott78@gmail.com. *Clubs:* Arts, 5 Hertford Street; Cheshire Pitt (Hon. Mem.).

**ELLIOTT, Michael Norman;** Mayor of Ealing, 2005–06; *b* 3 June 1932; *m* 1979, Julia Perry. *Educ:* Brunel College of Technology. Formerly res. chemist in food industry. Mem., Ealing Borough Council, 1964–86 and 2002–10 (former Leader of Council and Chm., Educn Cttee). MEP (Lab) London W, 1984–99; contested (Lab) London Region, 1999. Formerly: Member: Civil Liberties Parly Cttee (Lab party spokesperson); Parly Cttee of Inquiry into Racism and Xenophobia; Parly Jt Cttees with Poland and with Malta; Substitute Mem., Econ. and Monetary Cttee; Pres., Parly Intergroup for Animal Welfare and Conservation. Chm., Ealing Aircraft Noise Action Gp. Member: CND, 1961–; Friends of the Earth, 1985–. Hon. Fellow, Ealing Coll. of Higher Educn, 1988. Hon. Freeman, London Bor. of Ealing, 2011. *Address:* 4 Fern Dene, Ealing, W13 8AN.

**ELLIOTT, Michele Irmiter,** OBE 2008; Founder and Director, Kidscape Children's Charity, 1984–2009; *b* 7 Jan. 1946; *d* of James Irmiter and Ivy (*née* Dashwood); *m* 1968, Edward Elliott; two *s*. *Educ:* Univ. of S Florida (MA *summa cum laude* 1967); Univ. of Florida (MA *cum laude* 1969). Educational Psychologist: Booker Washington Sch., Fla, 1969–71; Amer. Sch. in London, 1971–84. Winston Churchill Fellow, 1991. Chairman: Home Office Working Gp on prevention of sexual abuse, 1988; WHO Cttee on prevention of sexual abuse, 1989. Mem., Video Consultative Council, BBFC, 1992–99. Member: Hon. Adv. Bd, NSPCC, 1994–; Nat. Toy Council, 1996–; Bd, Internet Watch Foundn, 2003–08. Mem., Soc. of Authors, 1990–. Hon. PhD Post Univ., Conn, 1993; Hon. DSc Birmingham, 2003. Children and Young People's Champion, Children & Young People Now, 2009. *Publications:* Preventing Child Sexual Assault: a practical guide to talking with children, 1985, 2nd edn 1987 (trans. Norwegian); Kidscape Primary Kit, 1986, 3rd edn 2001; Under Fives Programme, 1987, 4th edn 1999; Keeping Safe, 1988, 2nd edn 1995 (trans. German, French, Chinese, Czech, Norwegian, Polish, Slovenian, Russian); The Willow Street Kids, 1986, 2nd edn 1997; Dealing with Child Abuse, 1989; Teenscape, 1990, 3rd edn 2002; Feeling Happy Feeling Safe, 1991, 2nd edn 1999; Bullying: a practical guide to coping for schools, 1991, 3rd edn 2002 (trans. Spanish 2010); Protecting Children: a training package, 1992; Bullies Meet the Willow Street Kids, 1993, 2nd edn 1997; (ed) Female Sexual Abuse of Children: the ultimate taboo, 1993, 2nd edn 1997; (with J. Kilpatrick) How to Stop Bullying: a Kidscape training guide, 1994, 3rd edn 2002 (trans. Japanese); 501 Ways to be a Good Parent, 1996 (trans. Russian, Estonian, Chinese, Polish, German); 101 Ways to Deal with Bullying: a guide for parents, 1997 (trans. Japanese, Chinese); Bullying: wise guide, 1998; Bully Free, 1999; 601 Ways to be a Good Parent, 1999; Stop Bullying Pocketbook, 2005, 2nd edn 2010; Tackling Bullying: the essential guide, 2011; Bullies, Cyberbullies and Frenemies, 2013 (Children's Literary Gold Award, Children's Literary Classics, USA, 2013); numerous contribs to learned jls. *Recreations:* piano, cycling, walking, dancing, swimming. *Address:* Kidscape, 2 Grosvenor Gardens, SW1W 0DH. *T:* (020) 7730 3300.

**ELLIOTT, Nicholas Blethyn;** QC 1995; *b* 11 Dec. 1949; *s* of late Col Blethyn William Treharne Elliott, late South Wales Borderers, and of Zara Elliott; *m* 1976, Penelope, (Nemmy), Margaret Longbourne Browne; two *s*. *Educ:* Kelly Coll.; Bristol Univ. (LLB Hons). Called to the Bar, Gray's Inn, 1972, Bencher, 2003. Asst Boundary Comr, 2000–07, 2011–13, 2016–17. *Publications:* (ed jtly) Banking Litigation, 1999, 3rd edn 2011; (ed) Byles on Bills of Exchange and Cheques, 28th edn 2007; (contrib.) Money Laundering and Financial Services, 2003. *Recreations:* tennis, cycling, swimming, bridge, rock and roll dancing. *Address:* Old Whistley Farmhouse, Potterne, Devizes, Wilts SN10 5TD.
*See also* Maj. Gen. C. H. Elliott.

**ELLIOTT, Paul;** Finance Director, Hanover Foundations, 2007–12; *b* 27 Oct. 1949; *s* of John and Winifred Elliott; *m* 1995, Sharon Amanda Jordan; one *s* one *d*. *Educ:* Clare Coll., Cambridge (Hons Modern Langs). Joined MAFF, 1971; Private Secretary: to Perm. Sec., 1974–75; to Minister, 1975–76; Private Sec. (Agriculture), Bonn, 1984–89; Head, Milk Div., 1989–94; Rural White Paper Team, 1994–95; Prin. Finance Officer, MAFF, then DEFRA, 1996–2001; Dir, Rural Economies and Communities Directorate, DEFRA, 2001–03; Strategic Projects Officer, London Bor. of Camden, 2003–04. Clerk, Scriveners' Co., 2007–11. *Recreations:* music, photography, cricket, ICT, travel.

**ELLIOTT, Prof. Paul,** PhD; FRCP, FFPH, FMedSci; Professor of Epidemiology and Public Health Medicine, since 1995 and Head, Department of Epidemiology & Biostatistics, School of Public Health (formerly Division of Primary Care and Population Health Sciences, Faculty of Medicine), since 1998, Imperial College London; *b* 21 April 1954; *s* of Dr Arnold Elliott, OBE and Esther Elliott; *m* Nina Gay; one *s* two *d*. *Educ:* Brentwood Sch., Essex; Christ's Coll., Cambridge (BA, MA Maths and Med. Scis); UCL (MB BS 1978); LSHTM (MSc 1983; PhD 1991). FFPH (FFPHM 1995); FRCP 1998; FMedSci 2000. Med. Registrar, Edgware Gen. Hosp., Middlesex, 1981–82; Wellcome Res. Fellow, St Mary's Hosp. Med. Sch. and LSHTM, 1982–87; Lectr, 1987–88, Sen. Lectr, 1988–93, Reader, 1993–95, in Epidemiology, LSHTM. Hon. Consultant Physician, Dept of Medicine, Hammersmith Hosp., London, 1990–; Hon. Consultant: in Public Health Medicine, Kensington and Chelsea PCT (formerly Kensington, Chelsea and Westminster HA), 1995–2013; Imperial College Healthcare NHS Trust (formerly St Mary's Hosp. NHS Trust, London), 1998–. Director: UK Small Area Health Stats Unit, 1991–; MRC-PHE (formerly MRC-HPA) Centre for Envmt and Health, 2009–. *Publications:* (ed jtly) Geographical and Environmental Epidemiology: methods for small-area studies, 1992; (ed jtly) Coronary Heart Disease Epidemiology: from aetiology to public health, 1992, 2nd edn 2005; (ed jtly) Spatial Epidemiology: methods and applications, 2000; (ed jtly) Oxford Handbook of Epidemiology for Clinicians, 2012; articles in learned jls on diet and blood pressure, epidemiology, small-area health statistics and methodology. *Recreations:* family, swimming. *Address:* Department of Epidemiology & Biostatistics, School of Public Health, Imperial College London, St Mary's Campus, Norfolk Place, W2 1PG. *T:* (020) 7594 3328, *Fax:* (020) 7594 3456. *E:* p.elliott@imperial.ac.uk.

**ELLIOTT, Paul Richard;** theatrical producer, director, writer; Managing Director, Paul Elliott Ltd, 1999–2018; *b* 9 Dec. 1941; *s* of late Lewis Arthur Elliott and Sybil Elliott; *m* 1st, 1971, Jenny Logan (marr. diss. 1986); one *s*; 2nd, 1987, Linda Hayden; one *s* one *d*. *Educ:* Bournemouth Sch. Actor, 1958–63; appeared in Dixon of Dock Green, 1961–62. Man. Dir, E&B Prodns, 1964–2000; Jt Dir, Triumph Entertainment Ltd, 2000–18. London productions include: When We Are Married, Strand, 1970; The King and I, Adelphi, 1973; Grease, New London, 1973; The Pleasure of His Company, and I Do, I Do, Phoenix, 1974; Hedda Gabler, Aldwych, 1975; Hello Dolly, Theatre Royal, 1979; Run for Your Wife, Criterion, Whitehall, Aldwych, 1983–92; Buddy, Victoria Palace, Strand, 1989–2002; The Pirates of Penzance, Palladium, 1990; Jolson, Victoria Palace, 1996 (Olivier Award, Best Musical, 1996); The Goodbye Girl, Albery, 1997; Kat and the Kings, Vaudeville, 1998 (Olivier Award, Best Musical, 1999); Annie, Victoria Palace, 1998; Stones in His Pockets (Olivier and Evening Standard Awards, Best Comedy), Duke of York's, 2000, transf. NY, 2001; The Tempest, Old Vic, 2003; Thoroughly Modern Millie, Shaftesbury, 2004; The Philadelphia Story, Old Vic, 2005; As You Desire Me, Playhouse, 2006; The Last Confession, Haymarket, 2007; Macbeth, Gielgud, 2007, transf. NY, 2008; Waiting for Godot, Th. Royal, Haymarket, 2010; Private Lives, Vaudeville, 2010; Pygmalion, Garrick, 2011; Blithe Spirit, Apollo, 2011; Rosencrantz and Guildenstern are Dead, The Tempest, Haymarket, 2011; David Suchet in The Last Confession, world tour, 2014; Backbeat, 2014; Dirty Dancing, 2015; numerous pantomime prodns throughout UK; London *pantomimes* include: Aladdin, Shaftesbury, 1983; Snow White and the Seven Dwarfs, Strand, 1990; Jack and the Beanstalk, Piccadilly, 1991; Babes in the Wood, Sadler's Wells; Snow White and the Seven Dwarfs, Victoria Palace, 2004–05; *New York productions:* The Hollow Crown; Brief Lives; Run for Your Wife, 1989; Buddy, 1990; Private Lives (Tony Award), 2002 and 2011 (also Toronto); Gaslight, Toronto, 2016; touring prodns in UK and overseas incl. USA, Canada, Australia, NZ, Japan, Hong Kong, Zimbabwe, India and Europe; co-producer and writer of play, There's No Place Like a Home, 2006. Dir, SOLT, 1996–. Hon. Fellow, 2012, Hon. MA 2015, Bournemouth Univ. Award for Contribution to Provincial Theatre, Theatre Managers Assoc., 1996; Olivier Award for Services to Th. Industry, 2018. *Publications:* Keeping My Balls in the Air (autobiog.), 2018. *Recreation:* watching sport! *Address:* 16 Westbourne Park Road, W2 5PH.

**ELLIOTT, Ven. Peter;** Archdeacon of Northumberland, 1993–2005; *b* 14 June 1941; *s* of James Reginald and Hilda Elliott; *m* 1967, Evelyn Embleton; one *d. Educ:* Queen Elizabeth Grammar Sch., Horncastle; Hertford Coll., Oxford (MA Mod. History); Lincoln Theological Coll. Assistant Curate: All Saints, Gosforth, 1965–68; St Peter, Balkwell, 1968–72; Vicar: St Philip, High Elswick, 1972–80; North Gosforth, 1980–87; Embleton with Rennington and Rock, 1987–93. RD of Alnwick, 1989–93; Hon. Canon, 1990–93, Residentiary Canon, 1993–2005, Newcastle Cathedral. English Heritage: Member: Cathedrals and Churches Adv. Cttee, 1998–2001; Historic Built Envmt Cttee, 2001–03; Places of Worship Panel, 2001–05; Adv. Cttee, 2003–05. *Recreations:* genealogy, travel, railway timetables, food, wine, gardening. *Address:* 56 King Street, Seahouses, Northumberland NE68 7XS. *T:* (01665) 721133.

**ELLIOTT, Robert Anthony K.;** *see* Keable-Elliott.

**ELLIOTT, Prof. Robert Francis,** FRSE; Professor of Health Economics, Health Economics Research Unit, University of Aberdeen, 2012–16, now Emeritus (Professor of Economics, since 1990); *b* Thurlow, Suffolk, 15 June 1947; *s* of Francis Percy Elliott and Margaret Elliott (*née* Hunter); *m* 1970, Susan Gutheridge; one *s. Educ:* Haverhill Sec. Mod. Sch.; Ruskin Coll., Oxford (Special Dip. Soc. Studies 1970); Balliol Coll., Oxford (BA PPE 1972); Univ. of Leeds (MA Labour Econs 1973). University of Aberdeen: Res. Fellow, 1973–78; Lectr, 1978–82; Sen. Lectr, 1982–89; Dir, Health Econs Res. Unit, 2002–12. Dir, Scottish Doctoral Prog. in Econs, 1989–99; Chm., Rev. of Area Cost Adjustment (Elliott Rev.), 1995–96; Mem., McCrone Cttee of Inq. into Professional Conditions of Service for Teachers, 1999–2000; Ind. Mem., Low Pay Commn, 2007–15. Econ. Advr, Police Fedn of England and Wales, 1986–2016; Consultant to: HM Treasury, 1992–98; OECD, 1992–99; EC, 1994–2005. Pres., Scottish Econ. Soc., 2003–05. Visiting Professor: New York Univ., 1978–80; Stanford Univ., 1981, 1986; Cornell Univ., 1985–86; Paris II, 1995, 1997–99, 2001–02; Indiana Univ. - Purdue Univ. at Indianapolis, 1996; Univ. of Wisconsin, 2001; Università Cattolica, Milan, 2001–05; Univ. of Melbourne, 2011, 2012. FRSE 2001. *Publications:* (ed with J. L. Fallick) Incomes Policy, Inflation and Relative Pay, 1981 (trans. Spanish, 1983), re-issued 2016; (ed jtly) Incomes Policy, 1981; (jtly) Macmillan Dictionary of Modern Economics, 1981, 4th edn 1992 (trans. 14 langs); (ed with A. E. H. Speight) Unemployment and Labour Market Efficiency: a study of the Aberdeen and Grampian labour markets, 1989; (with J. L. Fallick) Pay in the Public Sector, 1991; Labor Economics: a comparative text, 1991 (trans. Turkish, 1997); (ed jtly) Public Sector Pay Determination in the European Union, 1999; (ed jtly) Advances in Health Economics, 2002; (with K. Bender) Decentralised Pay Setting: a study of collective bargaining reform in the civil service in Australia, Sweden and the UK, 2003; (jtly) Public Sector Remuneration in Scotland, 2012; articles in econs jls. *Recreations:* hillwalking, opera, jazz, all classical music, wine discovery, reading, golf. *Address:* Health Economics Research Unit, University of Aberdeen, Polwarth Building, Foresterhill, Aberdeen AB25 2ZD. *T:* (01224) 437197. *E:* pec016@abdn.ac.uk.

**ELLIOTT, Steven Ballantyne,** JD, DPhil; QC 2018; *b* Kingston, Ont, 16 Jan. 1971; *s* of Dr Murray Elliott and Mary Elliott; *m* 2000, Dr Eva Micheler; one *s* one *d. Educ:* Queen's Univ., Kingston (BA Hons 1992); Univ. of Toronto (JD Hons 1995); Merton Coll., Oxford (DPhil 2002). Called to the Bar: British Columbia, 1997; Lincoln's Inn, 2001. Clerk to British Columbia Court of Appeal, 1995–96; articles, Davis & Co., Vancouver, 1996–97; Lectr, St Catherine's Coll., Oxford, 1999–2000; Asst to Lord Chief Justice, 2000; barrister, One Essex Court, 2001–. Founder Ed., Oxford Univ. Commonwealth Law Jl, 1998–2000. *Publications:* (jtly) The Law of Rescission, 2008, 2nd edn 2014; (ed) Snell's Equity, 32nd edn 2010 to 33rd edn 2015. *Recreations:* mountaineering, ski-ing, kayaking. *Address:* One Essex Court, Temple, EC4Y 9AR. *T:* (020) 7583 2000. *E:* selliott@oeclaw.co.uk.

**ELLIOTT, Thomas;** *see* Elliott, C. T.

**ELLIOTT, Thomas;** *b* 11 Dec. 1963; *s* of late John Elliott and of Noreen Elliott; *m* 1989, Anne; one *s* one *d. Educ:* Ballinamallard Primary Sch.; Duke of Westminster High Sch., Ballinamallard; Enniskillen Coll. of Agric. Self-employed farmer, 1981–. Mem. (pt-time), UDR/Royal Irish Regt, 1982–99. Mem. (UU), Fermanagh DC, 2001–10. Mem. (UU) Fermanagh and S Tyrone, NI Assembly, 2003–June 2015. Leader, Ulster Unionist Party, 2010–12. MP (UU) Fermanagh and S Tyrone, 2015–17; contested (UU) same seat, 2017. *Recreations:* community activity, sport, church. *E:* t.elliott6@btopenworld.com.

**ELLIOTT, Prof. Timothy John,** PhD; FMedSci; FRSB; Professor of Experimental Oncology, since 2000, and Director, Southampton Centre for Cancer Immunology, since 2016, University of Southampton; *b* Sheffield, 5 July 1961; *s* of Colin and Myra Elliott; *m* 1996, Prof. Anneke Lucassen; two *d. Educ:* Balliol Coll., Oxford (BA Biochem.); Univ. of Southampton (PhD Immunol. 1986). Res. Associate, MIT, 1986–89; Lectr, Balliol Coll., Oxford, 1989–93; Sen. Res. Fellow, Inst. for Molecular Medicine, 1993–99, Prof. of Immunology, 2000, Univ. of Oxford; Res. Dean, Faculty of Medicine, 2006–15, Interim Pro Vice Chancellor (Res. and Enterprise), 2016, Univ. of Southampton. FRSB (FSB 2012); FMedSci 2014. *Publications:* contrib. articles to learned jls incl. Nature, Cell, Science, Immunity, Proc. NAS. *Recreations:* cooking, cycling, hillwalking, thinking at the interface between art and science, contemporary art. *Address:* Southampton Centre for Cancer Immunology, University Hospital Southampton, Mailpoint 824, Tremona Road, Southampton SO16 6YD. *T:* (023) 8120 6196, *Fax:* (023) 8120 6186. *E:* tje@soton.ac.uk.

**ELLIOTT, Timothy Stanley;** QC 1992; *b* 2 April 1950; *s* of John Edwin Elliott and Annie Elizabeth Stanley (*née* Lowe); *m* 1973, Katharine Barbara Lawrance (*d* 2008); one *s* one *d. Educ:* Marlborough Coll.; Trinity Coll., Oxford (Exhibnr, MA Lit. Hum. 1973). Called to the Bar, Middle Temple, 1975. *Address:* 15 Essex Street, WC2R 3AA. *T:* (020) 7544 2600.

**ELLIOTT, Tobin David, (Toby),** OBE 2007; Vice Lord-Lieutenant of Gwent, 2012–16; *b* Farnham, 22 April 1944; *s* of James Newenham Elliott, RN and Joanne Elliott; *m* 1971, Imogen Margaret Pugh; two *s* one *d. Educ:* Cranbrook Sch.; BRNC Dartmouth. Served RN, 1963–97; Commanding Officer: HMS Otter, 1974–76; HMS Resolution, 1980–82; HMS Trafalgar, 1986–88; Captain, 10th Submarine Sqdn, 1989–91; CO HMS Brilliant and Captain, 2nd Frigate Sqdn, 1991–93; Chief Exec., Ex-Services Mental Welfare Soc. (Combat Stress), 1999–2010. Dir, Highland Power Ltd, 2012–16. Trustee, Headley Court Trust, 2005–. President: Monmouth Br., RNA; Monmouth Br., RBL; Ross and Monmouth Sea Cadet Unit. Younger Brother, Trinity House, 1997. High Sheriff 2005, DL 2009, Gwent. *Recreations:* country pursuits, gardening, family and friends, sailing. *Address:* 38 Opulus Way, Monmouth, Gwent NP25 5UW. *T:* (01600) 712958. *E:* toby.elliott@btopenworld.com.

**ELLIOTT, Trudi Margaret,** CBE 2010; Chief Executive, Royal Town Planning Institute, 2011–18; *b* Croydon, 19 Sept. 1957; *d* of Patrick James Gerald Job and Sheila Mary Job; *m* 1986, Prof. Geoffrey Clifford Elliott; two *s. Educ:* Crown Woods Sch., London; University Coll. of Wales, Aberystwyth (BSc Econ (Law and Econs) 1980); Coll. of Law, Chester. MRTPI 2017. Admitted as solicitor, 1983; Solicitor and Partner, Lickfold Wiley and Powles, Solicitors, London, 1981–89; youth worker (pt-time), ILEA, 1983–85; Interview Panellist and Local Conciliator (pt-time), Solicitors Complaints Bureau, 1990–92; Planning Solicitor, Wyre Forest DC, 1992–93; Solicitor to Council, 1993–95, Chief Exec., 1995–2003, Bridgnorth DC; Dir, Local Govt Practice (W Midlands), ODPM, 2003–04; Lead Official, Walsall MBC, 2003–04; Chief Exec., W Midlands Regl Assembly and W Midlands Local Govt Authy, 2004–06; Dir, Govt Office for W Midlands, 2006–11. Internat. Observer, first elections in Czech Republic, 2002. Chair: Bridgnorth Community Safety Partnership, 1998–2000; W Midlands Regl Bd, 2006–10; Planning Inspectorate, 2018–; Member, Board: Shropshire Regeneration Partnership, 1998–2000; W Midlands Regl Skills Partnership, 2004–06; Business in the Community (W Midlands), 2007–09; Birmingham and Solihull Employment and Skills, 2007–09; Member: Birmingham Strategic Partnership, 2007–10; W Midlands Econ. Task Force, 2009–10; Taylor Rev. of Planning Practice Guidance, 2012; Nat. Infrastructure Planning Assoc. Policy Council, 2012–; Cttee, Oxford Jt Planning Law Conf., 2012–. Chair: Shropshire Active Sports Partnership, 1999–2003; W Midlands 2012 Olympics Steering Gp, 2004–06; Vice Chair, 2003–08, Actg Chair, 2004–05, W Midlands Regl Sports Bd, Sport England. Mem., editl team, Jl Planning Theory & Practice, 2012–. Mem. Council, 2008–16, Estates Cttee, 2016–, Univ. of Warwick. Gov., Shrewsbury Coll. of Arts and Technol., 1995–2000. *Recreations:* tennis, The Arsenal. *Club:* Bewdley Tennis.

**ELLIOTT, William,** OBE 2003; Director, Cormont Ltd, since 2011; *b* Boston, Lincs, 16 March 1968; *s* of Roger Elliott and Rebecca Short (*née* Fernandez); *m* 2003, Daria Chrin; one *s* three *d. Educ:* Alderman Peel High Sch., Wells, Norfolk; Wymondham Coll.; Univ. of York (BA Eng. and Related Lit.). Lectr in English, Lodz and Tbilisi, 1991–92; entered HM Diplomatic Service, 1993; Second Sec., Warsaw, 1995–98; First Secretary: FCO, 1998; Kabul, 2001–02; Dep. Hd of Mission, Tallinn, 2002–06; Consul-Gen., St Petersburg, 2006–10. *Recreations:* history and literature of Europe and S Asia, cricket, food and drink. *Club:* English (St Petersburg).

**ELLIOTT, (William) Brent,** PhD; Historian, Royal Horticultural Society, 2007–17; *b* 10 Jan. 1952; *s* of William Alfred and Annie Irene Elliott; *m* 1981, Dr Frances Margaret Clegg; one *s. Educ:* Univ. of BC (BA 1973; MA 1974); King's Coll., London (PhD 1978). Asst Librarian, 1977–82, Librarian and Archivist, 1982–2007, RHS. Ed., Garden Hist. (Jl Garden Hist. Soc.), 1984–88. English Heritage: Member: Gardens Cttee, 1985–89; Historic Landscapes Panel, 1989–93; Historic Parks and Gardens Adv. Cttee, 1994–2011. Member: Council, Garden Hist. Soc., 1979–89; Buildings Cttee, Victorian Soc., 1979– (Chm., Cemeteries Sub-cttee, 1983–89; Mem., Main Cttee, 1983–93). Ed., Occasional Papers from RHS Lindley Liby, 2009–17. FLS 1995. Veitch Meml Medal, RHS, 1994. Greensfelder Medal, Missouri Botanical Garden, 2008. *Publications:* Victorian Gardens, 1986; (with A. Clayton-Payne) Victorian Flower Gardens, 1988; (with C. Brooks) Mortal Remains, 1989; Waddesdon Manor: the gardens, 1994; Treasures of the Royal Horticultural Society, 1994; The Country House Garden, 1995; Flora: an illustrated history of the garden flower, 2001; The Royal Horticultural Society 1804–2004: a history, 2004; (with V. Buchan) Garden People, 2007; (vol. ed.) Flora: the Erbario Miniato and other drawings, in The Paper Museum of Cassiano dal Pozzo, 2007; RHS Chelsea Flower Show, 2013; Federico Cesi's Botanical Manuscripts, 2015; The Rose, 2016. *Recreations:* visiting parks, gardens and cemeteries, gardening, reading. *Address:* 56 Roxborough Park, Harrow-on-the-Hill HA1 3AY.

**ELLIS,** family name of **Baron Seaford**.

**ELLIS, Alexander Wykeham,** CMG 2013; Director General, Department for Exiting the European Union, since 2017; *b* London, 5 June 1967; *s* of Roger Wykeham Ellis, *qv*; *m* 1996, Teresa Adegas; one *s. Educ:* Dragon Sch., Oxford; Winchester Coll.; Magdalene Coll., Cambridge (BA Hons Mod. Hist. 1989). Teacher, St Edward's Sch., Oxford, 1989–90; FCO, 1990–92; Third, then Second Sec., Lisbon, 1992–96; First Sec. (Econ.), UK Repn to EU, Brussels, 1996–2001; FCO, 2001–03; Counsellor, EU, Madrid, 2003–05; Advr to Pres. of EC, 2005–07; Ambassador to Portugal, 2007–10; Dir of Strategy, FCO, 2011–13; Ambassador to Brazil, 2013–16. *Recreations:* most ball games, music, theatre, history. *Address:* Department for Exiting the European Union, 9 Downing Street, SW1A 2AS. *Clubs:* MCC; Estoril; Denham Golf.

**ELLIS, Andrew Steven,** OBE 1984; freelance consultant senior adviser on electoral, constitutional and democracy building issues, since 2014; *b* 19 May 1952; *s* of late Peter Vernon Ellis and Kathleen Dawe; *m* 1st, 1975, Patricia Ann Stevens (marr. diss. 1987); 2nd, 1990, Helen Prudence Drummond. *Educ:* Trinity Coll., Cambridge (BA Mathematics); Univ. of Newcastle upon Tyne (MSc Statistics); Newcastle upon Tyne Polytechnic (BA Law). Proprietor, Andrew Ellis (Printing and Duplicating), Newcastle upon Tyne, 1973–81; freelance Election Agent/Organizer, 1981–84; Sec.-Gen., Liberal Party, 1985–88; Chief Exec., Social and Liberal Democrats, 1988–89; freelance political consultant on elections, constitutions, democracy bldg and governance issues, 1989–93; Dir, GJW Hldgs Ltd, 1993–99; Associate Dir, GJW, subseq. GJW-BSMG Worldwide, then GJW Europe-Weber Shandwick Worldwide, 1999–2002; International Institute for Democracy and Electoral Assistance: Head of Electoral Progs, 2003–06; Dir of Ops, 2006–09; Asia and Pacific Dir, 2009–14. Consultant Nat. Agent, Welsh Liberal Party, 1984–88. Contested (L): Newcastle upon Tyne Central, Oct. 1974, Nov. 1976, 1979; Boothferry, 1983; Leader, Liberal Gp, Tyne & Wear CC, 1977–81; Vice-Chm., Liberal Party, 1980–86. Tech. Advr to Chm., Palestine Central Election Commn, 1994–96; Co-ordinator, OSCE Observation Mission for Registration of Voters, Bosnia and Hercegovina, 1997; designer of Eur. Commn electoral assistance to Cambodia, 1997–98; Sen. Advr on constitutional, electoral and decentralisation issues, Nat. Democratic Inst., Indonesia, 1998–2003. *Publications:*

Algebraic Structure (with Terence Treeby), 1971; Let Every Englishman's Home Be His Castle, 1978; (contrib.) Indonesia Matters, 2003; (contrib.) International Handbook of Electoral Systems, 2004; (jtly) Electoral System Design: the New International IDEA Handbook, 2006; (jtly) Electoral Management Design, 2006, 2nd edn 2014; (jtly) Voting Abroad, 2007; (jtly) Direct Democracy, 2008; (jtly) Electoral Justice, 2010; (jtly) The Integrity of Elections: the role of regional organizations, 2012; Citizen-led Assessment of Democracy: local and regional contexts in Pakistan, 2015; Administration of Referendums: a comparative study of independence referendums, 2018. *Recreation:* travel. *Address:* 28 Kimberley Park Road, Falmouth, Cornwall TR11 2DB.

ELLIS, Arthur John, CBE 1986; Chairman, Fyffes Group Ltd, 1984–2008 (Chief Executive Officer, 1969–95); *b* 22 Aug. 1932; *s* of Arthur Ellis and Freda Jane Ellis; *m* 1956, Rita Patricia Blake; two *s* one *d*. *Educ:* Chingford Jun. High Sch.; South West Essex Technical Coll. FCCA; FCMA; FCIS; MBCS. Joined Fyffes Gp Ltd, Finance and Admin Dept, 1954; Chief Financial Officer, 1965; Financial Dir, 1967; Dir, Fyffes plc, 1991–2001. Chm., Nat. Seed Develt Organisation Ltd, 1982–87. Chm., Intervention Bd for Agricl Produce, later Intervention Bd Exec. Agency, 1986–95. *Recreations:* golf, reading, gardening. *Club:* Farmers.

ELLIS, David Charles; Chief Executive, National Star College, since 2010; *b* 29 Dec. 1960; *s* of Oswald David Ellis and Joyce Mary Ellis; *m* 1990, Yvonne (née Pauline); two *s*. *Educ:* Exeter Univ. (BSc Hons Physics). Overseas aid worker, Southern Sudan, 1984–87; with various UK disability charities, 1987–92; Regl Dir, British Red Cross, 1992–98; Dir of Services, Guide Dogs for the Blind, 1998–2001; Chief Exec., Cancer and Leukaemia in Childhood, then CLIC Sargent, 2001–05; Dir of Business Improvement, National Trust, 2006–10. *Recreations:* photography, gardening, reading. *Address:* National Star College, Ullenwood, Cheltenham GL53 9QU. *T:* (01242) 527631.

ELLIS, His Honour David Raymond; a Circuit Judge, 1995–2014; *b* 4 Sept. 1946; *s* of Raymond Ellis and Ethel Ellis (née Gordon); *m* 1974, Cathleen Margaret Hawe; one *s* one *d*. *Educ:* St Edward's Sch., Oxford; Christ Church, Oxford (MA Jurisprudence). Called to the Bar, Inner Temple, 1970; barrister, 1970–95; a Recorder, 1991–95. Chm., Lord Chancellor's SE London Adv. Cttee, 2000–05. *Recreations:* travel, theatre, boating, the garden. *Club:* Leander (Henley).

ELLIS, Diana; QC 2001; a Recorder, since 1998; *d* of Evan Henry Ellis and Irene Sarah Jeanette Ellis (née Behrens); *m* 2001, Geoffrey Keith Watts. *Educ:* London Sch. of Econs (Dip. Social Admin); LLB Hons London. Teacher, Italia Conti Stage Sch., 1971–74; called to the Bar, Inner Temple, 1978; in practice as barrister, SE Circuit, 1978–, specialising in criminal and internat. law and human rights. *Recreations:* reading, theatre, walking and relaxing in Italy. *Address:* 25 Bedford Row, WC1R 4HD.

ELLIS, (Dorothy) June; Headmistress, The Mount School, York, 1977–86; Clerk to Central Committee, Quaker Social Responsibility and Education, 1987–90; *b* 30 May 1926; *d* of Robert Edwin and Dora Ellis. *Educ:* La Sagesse, Newcastle upon Tyne; BSc Pure Science, Durham; DipEd Newcastle upon Tyne. Assistant Mistress: Darlington High Sch., 1947–49; Rutherford High Sch., 1949–50; La Sagesse High Sch., 1950–53; Housemistress, 1953–61, Sen. Mistress, 1961–64, St Monica's Sch.; Dep. Head, Sibford Sch., 1964–77. Clerk, 1986–90, Mem., 1990–98, Swerford Parish Council; Mem., Milcombe PCC, 1999–2006, 2008–. Mem. Cttee, Bray d'Oyley Housing Assoc., 1993–96. Mem. Council, Woodbrooke Coll., 1987–93; Governor: Ellerslie Sch., Malvern, 1987–92; Friends' Sch., Saffron Walden, 1990–93; St Mary's Primary Sch., Bloxham, 2000–04. *Recreation:* home-making.

ELLIS, Eileen Mary, RDI 1984; freelance woven textile designer, retired; *b* 1 March 1933; *m* 1954, Julian Ellis; one *s* two *d*. *Educ:* Leicester, Central and Royal Colleges of Art. Des RCA 1957; FCSD (FSIAD 1976). Designer of contract and decorative woven furnishing fabrics, carpets and woven wall coverings; designed for Ascher & Co., 1957–59; Partner, Orbit Design Group, 1960–73; formed Weaveplan, to provide design and consultancy services, 1973–2005. Lecturer: Hornsey Coll. of Art/Middx Polytechnic, 1965–74; RCA, 1974–82. Director: Jamasque Ltd, 1982–96; Curragh Tintawn Carpets Ltd, 1987–95. Hon. Pres., Textile Soc., 2003–08. Textile Inst. Design Medal, 1985; Silver Medal, Weavers' Co., 2002. *Recreation:* country pursuits. *Address:* Weaveplan, The Granary Studio, Holbeam Road, Stalisfield, Faversham, Kent ME33 0HS. *T:* (01795) 890602.

ELLIS, Prof. George Francis Rayner, PhD; FRS 2007; FRSSAf; Professor of Applied Mathematics, University of Cape Town, 1973–87 and 1989–2005, now Emeritus; *b* 11 Aug. 1939; *s* of George Rayner Ellis and Gwendoline Hilda Ellis (née MacRobert); *m* 1st, 1963, Jane Mary Sue Parkes; one *s* one *d*; 2nd, 1978, Mary MacDonald Wheeldon (*d* 2008); 3rd, 2009, Carole Bloch. *Educ:* Univ. of Cape Town (BSc Hons 1960; Fellow, 1982); St John's Coll., Cambridge (PhD 1964). FRSSAf 1983 (Hon. FRSSAf, 2008). Lectr, Cambridge Univ., 1968–73; Prof., Scuola Internazionale Superiore di Studi Avanzati Trieste, 1987–89. Vis. Prof., Univs of Texas, Hamburg, Chicago, Alberta, and QMC London; Vis. Prof., Physics Dept, Oxford Univ., 2016–18. Pres., Internat. Soc. of General Relativity and Gravitation, 1987–91. Clerk, S Africa Yearly Meeting of Quakers, 1982–86; Chairman: Quaker Service, W Cape, 1978–86, 2013–16; Quaker Peace Work Cttee, W Cape, 1989–91. Pres., Royal Soc. of SA, 1992–96. Fellow, Third World Acad. of Sci., 2006. Hon. DSc: Haverford Coll., 1995; Natal Univ., 1998; London 2001; Cape Town, 2009; Hon. Dr: Witwatersrand, 2016; Pierre and Marie Curie, Paris, 2016. Herschel Medal, Royal Soc. of S Africa, 1978; Medal, SA Assoc. for Advancement of Science, 1993; Gold Medal, SA Math. Soc., 2001; Templeton Prize, 2004; De Beers Gold Medal, SA Inst. of Physics, 2010; Lemaître Prize, Univ. of Louvain, 2019. Star of S Africa Medal, 1999; Order of Mapungubwe, 2005. *Publications:* (with S. W. Hawking) The Large Scale Structure of Space-Time, 1973; (with D. Dewar) Low Income Housing Policy, 1979; Before the Beginning, 1993; (with N. Murphy) On the Moral Nature of the Universe, 1996; The Far Future Universe, 2001; (jtly) Relativistic Cosmology, 2012; How Can Physics Underlie the Mind?, 2016; (with M. Solms) Beyond Evolutionary Psychology, 2017. *Recreations:* mountain climbing, gliding. *Address:* Department of Applied Mathematics, University of Cape Town, Rondebosch 7701, Cape Town, South Africa; Flat 523 Montebello, 4 Montrose Street, Newlands 7700, South Africa. *T:* (21) 7888387. *Club:* Mountain of South Africa (Cape Town).

ELLIS, Prof. Harold, CBE 1987; MA, MCh, DM; FRCS; FRCOG; Clinical Anatomist, University of London, at Guy's campus, since 1993; *b* 13 Jan. 1926; *s* of Samuel and Ada Ellis; *m* 1958, Wendy Mae Levine; one *s* one *d*. *Educ:* Queen's Coll. (State Scholar and Open Scholar in Natural Sciences), Oxford; Radcliffe Infirmary, Oxford. BM, BCh, 1948; FRCS, MA, 1951; MCh 1956; DM 1962; FRCOG ad eundem, 1987. House Surgeon, Radcliffe Infirmary, 1948–49; Hallett Prize, RCS, 1949. RAMC, 1950–52. Res. Surgical Officer, Sheffield Royal Infirm., 1953–54; Registrar, Westminster Hosp., 1955; Sen. Registrar and Surgical Tutor, Radcliffe Infirm., Oxford, 1956–60; Sen. Lectr in Surgery, 1960–62, Hon. Consultant Surgeon, 1960–89, Westminster Hosp.; Prof. of Surgery, Univ. of London, 1962–89; Clinical Anatomist, Univ. of Cambridge and Fellow, Churchill Coll., Cambridge, 1989–93. Hon. Consultant Surgeon to the Army, 1978–89. Mem. Council, RCS, 1974–86. Member: Association of Surgeons; British Soc. of Gastroenterol.; Surgical Research Soc.; Council: RSocMed; British Assoc. of Surgical Oncology; Associé étranger, L'Academie de Chirurgie, Paris, 1983. Hon. FACS 1989; Hon. FRCP 2004. *Publications:* Clinical Anatomy, 1960; Anatomy for Anaesthetists, 1963; Lecture Notes on General Surgery, 1965; Principles of Resuscitation, 1967; History of the Bladder Stone, 1970; General Surgery for Nurses, 1976; Intestinal Obstruction, 1982; Notable Names in Medicine and Surgery, 1983; Famous Operations, 1984; Wound Healing for Surgeons, 1984; Maingot's Abdominal Operations, 1985; Research in Medicine, 1990; Cross-sectional Anatomy, 1991; Surgical Case-Histories from the Past, 1994; (ed) French's Index of Differential Diagnosis, 1996; A History of Surgery, 2000; numerous articles on surgical topics in medical journals. *Recreation:* medical history. *Address:* 16 Bancroft Avenue, N2 0AS. *T:* (020) 8348 2720.

ELLIS, Ian David; non-executive Chairman: Arcus Services Ltd, since 2011; NHS Property Services, since 2016; *b* Colchester, 4 Dec. 1955; *s* of John Douglas Vernon and Heather Ellis; *m* 1997, Clare Poyner; three *s* two *d*. FRICS 1991. District Valuer and Valuation Officer, Ipswich, 1974–83; Richard Ellis City Team, 1983–94; Shareholding Partner, Richard Ellis, 1994–98; Hd of Corporate Real Estate, Trillium, 1998–2002; Chief Exec., Land Securities Trillium, 2002–09; Dir, Land Securities Gp plc, 2002–09. Chm., 2009–14, non-exec. Dir, 2015–18, Telereal Trillium. Dir, Portman Settled Estates, 2007–. Member: Estates Bd, KCL, 2010–; Estates Cttee, Nat. Hist. Mus., 2013–. *Recreations:* family, cricket, World War II, books.

ELLIS, Prof. Ian Ogilvie, FRCPath; Professor of Cancer Pathology, University of Nottingham, since 2004; *b* Edinburgh, 24 Aug. 1955; *s* of Philip Senior Ellis and Anna Ellis (née Ure); *m* 1st, 1979, Jane Elizabeth Stevens (marr. diss. 1996); one *s* one *d*; 2nd, 2000, Eileen Jane Barrett (marr. diss. 2011); one *s*; 3rd, 2017, Carole Patricia Patrick. *Educ:* Stockport Grammar Sch.; Univ. of Nottingham (BMedSci 1976; BM BS 1978). MRCPath 1985, FRCPath 1995. Lectr in Pathol., Univ. of Nottingham, 1980–87; Consultant Pathologist, Nottingham City Hosp., 1987–97; Reader in Pathol., Univ. of Nottingham, 1997–2003. *Publications:* over 600 peer-reviewed scientific articles, chapters in medical text books and specialist text books in pathology. *Recreations:* fly fishing, wine tasting. *Address:* Yew Tree House, 2 Kenilworth Road, The Park, Nottingham NG7 1DD. *T:* (0115) 947 2186. *E:* ian.ellis@nottingham.ac.uk. *Clubs:* Oriental, Flyfishers'.

ELLIS, Dr Jeffrey Graham, FRS 2009; FAA; Senior Principal Research Scientist and Programme Leader, Program Y, Genetic Engineering for Plant Improvement, Commonwealth Scientific and Industrial Research Organisation Plant Industry, Canberra, since 2001. *Educ:* Univ. of Adelaide (BAgrSc Hons 1976; PhD 1980). CSIRO Post-doctoral Fellow, Genetics Dept, State Univ., Ghent, Belgium, 1981–82; CSIRO Plant Industry, Canberra: Queen Elizabeth II Post-doctoral Fellow, 1982–84; Res. Scientist, 1984–87; Sen. Res. Scientist and Sub-Prog. Leader, Prog. X, 1987–93; Prin. Res. Scientist, and Project Leader, Prog. Y, 1993–2001; CSIRO Fellow, 2008. Co-Ed., Plant Cell, 2001–06. FAA 2005. E. C. Stakman Award, Univ. of Minnesota, 2015. *Publications:* (contrib.) Infectious Disease: innate immunity, 2003; articles in learned jls. *Address:* CSIRO Plant Industry, Black Mountain Laboratories, Clunies Ross Street, Canberra, ACT 2601, Australia.

ELLIS, Jennifer; *see* Rowe, J.

ELLIS, John; Member, Local Government Planning Executive, 2000–03; Steel Worker, British Steel plc, Scunthorpe, 1980–89; *b* Hexthorpe, Doncaster, 22 Oct. 1930; *s* of George and Hilda Ellis; *m* 1953, Rita Butters; two *s* two *d*. *Educ:* Rastrick Gram. Sch., Brighouse. Laboratory technician, Meteorological Office, 1947–63; Vice-Chm., Staff side, Air Min. Whitley Council, 1961–63; Member Relations Officer, Co-op. Retail Services, Bristol/Bath Region, 1971–74. Member: Easthampstead RDC, 1962–66; Bristol City Council, 1971–74; Humberside County Council, 1987–96; N Lincs Council, 1995–2003 (Vice Chm., Housing Cttee, 1998–99; Chm., Planning Cttee, 1999–2003). Chairman: Humberside Social Service Council, 1992–94 (Vice-Chm., 1990–92); Social Services Children's Cttee, 1991–94; Member: Scunthorpe HA, 1988–91 (Chm., Jt Consultative Cttee, 1988–2000); NRA (formerly Lincs Land Drainage Cttee), 1988–96 (Member: Anglian Regl Flood Defence cttee; Lincs Flood Defence cttee). Contested (Lab) Wokingham, 1964; MP (Lab) Bristol North-West, 1966–70, Brigg and Scunthorpe, Feb. 1974–1979; PPS to Minister of State for Transport, 1968–70; an Asst Govt Whip, 1974–76. Formerly Mem., Select Cttee on Nationalised Industries. Chm., 1985–2002, Sec./Treas., 2002–05, Co-op. Party. JP North Riding Yorks, 1960–61. *Publications:* (jtly) Fabian pamphlet on MPs from Unions, 1974. *Recreations:* gardening, watching cricket. *Address:* 102 Glover Road, Scunthorpe DN17 1AS.

ELLIS, John; *see* Ellis, Jonathan R.

ELLIS, Ven. John Raymond, QHC 2017; Director General Chaplaincy Services, Headquarters Air Command, and Chaplain-in-Chief and Archdeacon, Royal Air Force, since 2018; *b* Malta, 3 Nov. 1963; *s* of Walter Ellis and Shirley Ellis; *m* 1985, Amanda Jane Hubbard; one *s* one *d*. *Educ:* Hamond's Grammar Sch., then Hamond's High Sch., Swaffham; St Stephen's House, Oxford (DipMin). Police Constable, Suffolk Constabulary, 1983–95. Ordained deacon, 1997, priest, 1998; Curate, Clare with Poslingford, Cavendish, etc, St Edmundsbury, 1997–2000; Priest in Charge, St John's and St George's, Bury St Edmunds, 2000–02; Team Vicar, All Saints with St John's and St George's, Bury St Edmunds, 2002–04; RAF Chaplain, 2004–; rcds, 2017–18. *Recreations:* music, history, family. *Address:* Chaplaincy Services (RAF), Headquarters Air Command, RAF High Wycombe, Bucks HP14 4UE. *T:* (01494) 493802, *Fax:* (01494) 496343. *E:* john.ellis932@mod.gov.uk. *Club:* Royal Air Force.

ELLIS, John Russell, FCILT; transport consultant, since 1997; Chairman, Cotswold Line Promotion Group, since 2009; *b* 21 May 1938; *s* of Percy Macdonald Ellis and Winifred Maud (née Bunker); *m* 1962, Jean Eileen Taylor; two *d*. *Educ:* Rendcomb Coll., Cirencester; Pembroke Coll., Oxford (BA Hons PPE). FCILT 1997. Joined BR as Grad. Management Trainee, 1962; various posts, 1963–80; Chief Freight Manager, 1980–83, Divl Manager, 1983–84, Asst Gen. Manager, 1984–85, Eastern Region; Dep. Gen. Manager, Southern Region, 1985–87; Gen. Manager, ScotRail, 1987–90; Gen. Manager, Southern Region, 1990–91; Dep. Man. Dir, InterCity, 1992–93; Dir, Production, Railtrack, 1993–95; Man. Dir, ScotRail, 1995–97. Director: GB Railfreight, 2001–10; Rail Estate Consultancy, 2002–. Trustee, Campaign for Better Transport Trust (formerly Transport 2000 Trust), 2001–13. Chairman: Nat. Railway Heritage Awards, 2001–19; Campden and District Peelers Trust, 2001–; Dir, Glos Market Towns Forum, 2004–13. *Recreations:* walking, gardening, music. *Address:* St Anne's, High Street, Chipping Campden, Glos GL55 6AL. *T:* (01386) 841253.

ELLIS, Prof. Jonathan Richard, (John), CBE 2012; PhD; FRS 1985; Senior Staff Physicist, Theoretical Studies Division, CERN, Geneva, 1994–2011 (Leader, 1988–94); Clerk Maxwell Professor of Theoretical Physics, King's College London, since 2010; *b* 1946; *s* of Richard Ellis and Beryl Lilian Ellis (née Ranger); *m* 1985, Maria Mercedes; one *s* one *d*. *Educ:* Highgate Sch.; King's Coll., Cambridge (BA, PhD; Hon. Fellow, 2006). Postdoctoral research, SLAC, Stanford, 1971–72; Richard Chase Tolman Fellow, CIT,

1972–73; Staff Mem., CERN, Geneva, 1973–2011, Advr to Dir-Gen. for relns with non-member States. Member: PPARC, 2004–07; Sci. Bd, STFC, 2007. FInstP. Maxwell Medal, Royal Soc., 1982. *Recreations:* movies, reading, travel, hiking in the mountains.

**ELLIS, June;** *see* Ellis, D. J.

**ELLIS, Prof. Katharine,** DPhil; FBA 2013; 1684 Professor of Music, University of Cambridge, since 2017. *Educ:* University Coll., Oxford (BA, DPhil); Guildhall Sch. of Music. Jun. Res. Fellow, French Studies, St Anne's Coll., Oxford; Open Univ., 1991–94; Royal Holloway, Univ. of London, 1994–2013; Dir, Inst. of Musical Res., Sch. of Advanced Study, Univ. of London, 2006–09; Stanley Hugh Badock Prof. of Music, Univ. of Bristol, 2013–17. MAE 2010. *Publications:* Music Criticism in Nineteenth-Century France, 1995; Interpreting the Musical Past, 2005; The Politics of Plainchant in fin-de-siècle France, 2013; (ed jtly) Words and Notes in the Long Nineteenth Century, 2013. *Address:* Faculty of Music, University of Cambridge, 11 West Road, Cambridge CB3 9DP.

**ELLIS, Keith;** *see* Ellis, R. K.

**ELLIS, Kevin James David;** Chairman and Senior Partner, PricewaterhouseCoopers, since 2016 (Member, Executive Board, since 2008); *b* Walthamstow, 24 July 1963; *s* of (Arthur) John Ellis and Rita Ellis; *m* 2003, Kathryn Peasley; three *s* one *d*. *Educ:* Forest Sch., Snaresbrook; Univ. of Nottingham (BA). ACA 1988. Price Waterhouse, subseq. PricewaterhouseCoopers: Audit, 1984–88; Business Restructuring Services, 1988–2008; Partner, 1996–; Hd, Advisory, 2008–12; Man. Partner, 2012–16. *Recreations:* ski-ing, running, golf, Spurs supporter. *Address:* PricewaterhouseCoopers, No 1 Embankment Place, WC2N 6RH. *T:* (020) 7804 4102. *E:* kevin.ellis@pwc.com.

**ELLIS, Luke;** *see* Ellis, S. L.

**ELLIS, Martin Arthur;** Taxing Master of the Supreme Court, 1990–2000, Costs Judge, 1999–2006; *b* 10 Jan. 1933; *s* of Walter Ellis and Phoebe Alicia Ellis; *m* 1961, Moira Herbert; one *s* (and one *s* decd). *Educ:* Beckenham Grammar School. Solicitor, admitted 1956; 2nd Lieut, 4th Regt, Royal Horse Artillery, 1957–58; Partner, Simmons & Simmons, 1973–90. *Recreations:* sport, golf, cricket. *Address:* Field House, North Road, Sandwich Bay, Kent CT13 9PJ. *T:* and *Fax:* (01304) 619375. *Clubs:* MCC; Royal St George's Golf.

**ELLIS, Michael Henry,** OBE 2007; Chairman, Skipton Building Society, 2011–17; *b* 4 Aug. 1951; *s* of late John Ellis and Joan (*née* Lawton); *m* 1973, Jeanette Booth; two *d*. *Educ:* Open Univ. (BA). Various posts in local govt sector, 1967–87; Halifax Building Society, later Halifax plc: Gp Treas., 1987–92; Gen. Manager, Treasury and Eur. Ops, 1992–95; Man. Dir, Treasury and Overseas Ops, 1995–96; Banking and Savings Dir, 1996–99; Financial Services Dir, 1999; Chief Operating Officer, 1999–2001; Gp Finance Dir, HBOS plc, 2001–04, 2008–09. Fund Comr and Chm., Fund Distribution Ltd, 2005–06. Non-exec. Dir, W H Smith plc, 2005–13. *Recreations:* travel, football, music, reading. *Club:* Royal Automobile.

**ELLIS, Rt Hon. Michael (Tyrone);** PC 2019; QC 2019; MP (C) Northampton North, since 2010; Solicitor General, since 2019; *b* Northampton, 13 Oct. 1967; *s* of Jack Ellis and Margaret Ellis (*née* Surgenor). *Educ:* Wellingborough Sch.; Univ. of Buckingham (LLB); Inns of Court Sch. of Law (BVC). Called to the Bar, Middle Temple, 1993; in practice as barrister, 1993–2010. Mem. (C) Northants CC, 1997–2001. PPS to Home Sec., 2015–16; an Asst Govt Whip, 2016–17; Parly Sec. (Dep Leader), Office of the Leader of the H of C, 2016–18; Parly Under-Sec. of State, DCMS, 2018–19; Minister of State, DfT, 2019. Member: Home Affairs Select Cttee, 2011–15; Jt Cttee on Statutory Instruments, 2010–15; Chm., All-Party Parly Gp on the Queen's Diamond Jubilee, 2010–13. Parly Advr to Co-Chm., Cons. Party, 2012–15. Pres., Commonwealth Jewish Council, 2012–14. *Recreations:* theatre, British Royal history. *Address:* House of Commons, SW1A 0AA. *T:* (020) 7219 7220. *E:* michael.ellis.mp@parliament.uk. *Club:* Carlton.

**ELLIS, Morag;** *see* Ellis, Rosalind M.

**ELLIS, Nicholas St John;** QC (Scot.) 2002; *b* 11 Nov. 1958; *s* of Anthony Brian Ellis and Pauline Ellis; *m* 1997, Victoria Craig; one *s* one *d*. *Educ:* Edinburgh Univ. (LLB). Admitted solicitor, 1981; WS 1985; called to the Scottish Bar, 1990. *Recreations:* walking, country pursuits. *Address:* Norham House, Norham, Berwick-upon-Tweed TD15 2LF. *T:* (01289) 382215. *E:* Nstje@aol.com.

**ELLIS, Dr Norman David;** Under Secretary, British Medical Association, 1980–2000 (Senior Industrial Relations Officer, 1978–82); *b* 23 Nov. 1943; *s* of late George Edward Ellis and late Annie Elsie Scarfe; *m* 1966, Valerie Ann Fenn, PhD; one *s*. *Educ:* Minchenden Sch.; Univ. of Leeds (BA); MA (Oxon), PhD. Research Officer, Dept of Employment, 1969–71; Leverhulme Fellowship in Industrial Relations, Nuffield Coll., Oxford, 1971–74; Gen. Sec., Assoc. of First Division Civil Servants, 1974–78. *Publications:* (with W. E. J. McCarthy) Management by Agreement, 1973; Employing Staff, 1984; (with J. Chisholm) Making sense of the Red Book, 1993, 3rd edn 1997; (with T. Stanton) Making sense of Partnerships, 1994; Making sense of General Practice, 1994; (with J. Lindsay) Making sense of Pensions and Retirement, 1995; General Practitioners' Handbook, 1997, 2nd edn (with D. Grantham), 2000; GP Employment Handbook, 1998; (with J. Lindsay) Staff Pensions in General Practice, 1998; various contribs to industrial relations literature. *Recreations:* maritime history, reading, travel, swimming. *Address:* 7 South Row, SE3 0RY. *T:* (020) 8852 6244.

**ELLIS, Osian Gwynn,** CBE 1971; harpist; Professor of Harp, Royal Academy of Music, London, 1959–89; *b* Ffynnongroew, Flints, 8 Feb. 1928; *s* of Rev. Tomas Griffith Ellis, Methodist Minister and Jennie Ellis; *m* 1951, Rene Ellis Jones (*d* 2012), Pwllheli; one *s* (and one *s* decd). *Educ:* Denbigh Grammar Sch.; Royal Academy of Music. Has broadcast and televised extensively. Has given recitals/concertos all over the world; shared poetry and music recitals with Dame Peggy Ashcroft, Paul Robeson, Burton, C. Day-Lewis, etc. Mem., Melos Ensemble; solo harpist with LSO, 1961–94. Former Mem., Music and Welsh Adv. Cttees, British Council. Works written for him include Harp Concertos by Hoddinott, 1957 and by Mathias, 1970, Jersild, 1972, Robin Holloway, 1985; chamber works by Gian Carlo Menotti, 1977; William Schuman, 1978; from 1960 worked with Benjamin Britten who wrote for him Harp Suite in C (Op. 83) and (for perf. with Sir Peter Pears) Canticle V, Birthday Hansel, and folk songs; from 1974 accompanied Sir Peter Pears on recital tours, Europe and USA; records concertos, recitals, folk songs, etc. Film, The Harp, won a Paris award; other awards include Grand Prix du Disque and French Radio Critics' Award. FRAM 1960. Hon. DMus Wales, 1970. *Publications:* Story of the Harp in Wales, 1991.

**ELLIS, Prof. Reginald John,** PhD; FRS 1983; Professor of Biological Sciences, University of Warwick, 1976–96, now Emeritus; *b* 12 Feb. 1935; *s* of Francis Gilbert Ellis and Evangeline Gratton Ellis; *m* 1963, Diana Margaret Warren; one *d*. *Educ:* Highbury County Sch.; King's Coll., London (BSc, PhD). ARC Fellow, Univ. of Oxford, 1961–64; Lectr in Botany and Biochemistry, Univ. of Aberdeen, 1964–70; Sen. Lectr, 1970–73, Reader, 1973–76, Dept of Biol Sciences, Univ. of Warwick; SERC Senior Res. Fellow, 1983–88. Sen. Vis. Fellow, St John's Coll., Oxford, 1992–93; Vis. Prof., Oxford Centre for Molecular Scis, 1997–2001. Mem. EMBO, 1986. LRPS 1987. Tate & Lyle Award (for contribs to plant biochem.), 1980; Internat. Gairdner Foundn Award, 2004; Internat. Medal, Cell Stress Soc., 2007; Croonian Lect. Prize, Royal Soc., 2011. Research interests include chloroplast biogenesis, protein aggregation, and molecular chaperones. *Publications:* How Science Works: evolution, 2010, 2nd edn 2016; A Devonshire Lad in the Great War, 2014; 170 papers in biochem. jls. *Recreations:* photography, hill walking.

**ELLIS, Prof. (Richard) Keith,** DPhil; FRS 2009; Professor of Physics, and Director, Institute for Particle Physics Phenomenology, Durham University, since 2015; *b* Aberdeen, 17 Nov. 1949; *s* of Richard Tunstall Ellis, OBE, and Jean Bruce Maitland Ellis, OBE; *m* 1990, Theresa Pedemonte; one *s* two *d*. *Educ:* Fettes Coll., Edinburgh; New Coll., Oxford (MA); Wadham Coll., Oxford (DPhil 1974). Royal Soc. Res. Fellow, Rome, 1974–76; Research Fellow: Imperial Coll., London, 1977; MIT, 1978–79; Calif Inst. of Technol., 1980; CERN, 1980–82; Rome, 1982–84; Scientist, 1984–2015, Hd, Theory Dept, 1992–2004, Fermi Nat. Accelerator Lab., USA. Fellow, Amer. Physical Soc., 1988. *Publications:* (jtly) QCD and Collider Physics, 1996; contribs to Physical Rev., Nuclear Physics, Jl of High Energy Physics, Physics Rev. Letters. *Address:* Institute for Particle Physics Phenomenology, Ogden Centre for Fundamental Physics, Department of Physics, University of Durham, Science Laboratories, South Road, Durham DH1 3LE. *T:* (0191) 334 3621, *Fax:* (0191) 334 3658. *E:* keith.ellis@durham.ac.uk.

**ELLIS, Richard Marriott;** Chairman, The Original Cottage Company, since 2010; *b* 23 Jan. 1955; *s* of late Martin Beazor Ellis and Janet Pamela Ellis (*née* Morgan); *m* 1987, Lesley Anne Smith; three *s* two *d*. *Educ:* Shene Grammar Sch.; Norwich City Coll. ACMA 1979. Financial Dir, Tucker Foods Ltd, 1984–92; Man. Dir, Norfolk Country Cottages, 1992–; Chief Exec., Kettle Foods Ltd, 1994–2000. Chairman: Arts and Business East, 2000–03; East of England Sustainable Develt Round Table, 2001–03; East of England Develt Agency, 2003–10; Norfolk Tourism, 2010–12. Dir, Heart Mercers Ltd, 2009–14. Chairman: Earlham Early Years Centre, 2000–04; Sheringham Little Theatre, 2010–; Visit East Anglia Ltd, 2011–18; Trustee: Norwich Th. Royal, 1999–2015; The Forum Trust, 2002–17; Norwich Heritage and Econ. Regeneration Trust, 2004–11; Rothamsted Research, 2005–08; Holt Fest., 2012–18. Gov., Norwich Univ. (formerly Norwich Univ. Coll.) of the Arts, 2011–17. FRSA. *Recreations:* travel, ski-ing badly, seeking adrenaline (bungee jumping, sky diving, etc.), finding things which aren't there, avoiding Who Was Who! *Address:* The Original Cottage Company, Bank House, Market Place, Reepham, Norfolk NR10 4JJ. *T:* (01603) 876214, *Fax:* (01603) 870304. *E:* r.ellis@tocc.co.uk.

**ELLIS, Prof. Richard Salisbury,** CBE 2008; FRS 1995; FAA; Professor of Astrophysics, University College London, since 2015 (on leave as Senior Scientist, European Southern Observatory, 2015–17); *b* 25 May 1950; *s* of late Capt. Arthur Ellis, MBE and of Marion Ellis (*née* Davies); *m* 1972, Barbara Williams; one *s* one *d*. *Educ:* Abergele GS; University Coll. London (BSc Hons 1971; Fellow, 1998); Wolfson Coll., Oxford (DPhil 1974) FRAS 1974; FInstP 1998. Durham University: Sen. Demonstrator in Physics, 1974–77; Res. Asst, 1977–81; Lectr in Astronomy, 1981–83; Principal Res. Fellow, Royal Greenwich Observatory, 1983–85; Prof. of Astronomy, Durham Univ., 1985–93; SERC Sen. Res. Fellow, 1989–94; Cambridge University: Plumian Prof. of Astronomy and Exptl Philosophy, 1993–99; Dir, Inst. of Astronomy, 1994–99; Professorial Fellow, Magdalene Coll., 1994–99; Prof. of Astronomy, 1999–2002, Steele Prof., 2002–15, Calif Inst. of Technol.; Director: Palomar Observatory, 2000–02; Caltech Optical Observatories, 2002–05; Royal Soc. Prof., Dept of Astrophysics, Univ. of Oxford, 2008–09; Fellow, Merton Coll., Oxford, 2008–09. Chm., SERC Large Telescope Panel, 1986–90; Mem., Anglo-Australian Telescope Bd, 1991–95. Associate, Canadian Inst. of Advanced Res., 1993–; Member: Space Telescope Science Inst. Council, 1995–2001; Gemini Telescopes Bd, 1996–98; Bd, W. M. Keck Observatory, 2000–05; Bd, Thirty Meter Telescope Proj., 2003–14. Visiting Professor: Space Telescope Science Inst., 1985, 2006; Anglo-Australian Observatory, 1991; CIT, 1991, 1997, 2018; Princeton, 1992; Carnegie Observatory, 1998; UCL, 2005; Toronto, 2006; Oxford, 2007; Tokyo, 2011; Tel Aviv, 2018; Carnegie Centennial Prof., Edinburgh, 2015–18; Hon. Prof., Observational Astrophysics, Univ. of Cambridge, 2000–03. Lectures: J. L. Bishop, Princeton, 1992; Halley, Oxford, 1993; Cormack, RSE, 1996; Lockyer, RAS, 1997; Sackler, Harvard, 1998; Bakerian, Royal Soc., 1998; Poynting, Birmingham, 1998; Grubb Parsons, Durham, 1999; Rosenblum, Jerusalem, 1999; Lansdowne, Victoria, 2001; Allison-Levick, Astronomical Soc., Australia, 2004; J. Bahcall, NASA, 2006; J. L. Bishop, NY, 2007; E. Spreadbury, UCL, 2008; Neils Bohr, Copenhagen, 2009; Schopp, San Diego, 2010; Oort, Leiden, 2010; Rittenhouse, Pennsylvania, 2012; J. Bahcall, Israel, 2012; Watson, Caltech, 2013; Fundación BBVA, Madrid, 2013; Darwin, Cambridge, 2015; Carnegie Centennial, St Andrews, 2016; Wilson, UCL, 2016; de Laeter, Perth, 2017; Brinson, Chicago, 2018. FAAAS 2001; FAA 2018. Hon. DSc: Durham, 2002; Edinburgh, 2019. Gruber Prize, Gruber Foundn, 2007; Gold Medal, RAS, 2011. *Publications:* Epoch of Galaxy Formation, 1988; Observational Tests of Cosmological Inflation, 1991; Large Scale Structure in the Universe, 1999; numerous articles in astronomical jls. *Recreations:* exploration, photography, music, ski-ing. *Address:* Department of Physics and Astronomy, University College London, Gower Street, WC1E 6BT. *T:* (020) 3108 7912.

**ELLIS, Rev. Dr Robert Anthony;** Principal, Regent's Park College, Oxford, since 2007; *b* Cardiff, 24 Aug. 1956; *s* of John and Joyce Ellis; *m* 1977, Susan Winters; three *s* one *d*. *Educ:* Cathays High Sch., Cardiff; Regent's Park Coll., Oxford (MA; DPhil 1984); Colgate Rochester Divinity Sch., NY. Minister: Spurgeon Baptist Ch, Bletchley, 1981–87; Tyndale Baptist Ch, Bristol, 1987–2001; Tutor, Bristol Baptist Coll., 1995–2001; Tutorial Fellow in Pastoral Studies, Regent's Park Coll., 2001–07. Mem. Council, Baptist Union of GB, 1990–; Moderator, Baptist Union Ministry Exec., 2003–09. Chm., Religious Adv. Panel, BBC Bristol, 1993–2000. Mem. Bd, Bristol Churches Housing Assoc., 1987–96. *Publications:* Answering God: towards a theology of intercession, 2005; The Games People Play: theology, religion and sport, 2014; contrib. articles to jls incl. Jl Religion, Religious Studies, Baptist Qly, Epworth Rev. *Recreations:* sports spectating, especially Rugby Union, walking the dog, reading, music, caravanning, family chilling. *Address:* Regent's Park College, Pusey Street, Oxford OX1 2LB. *T:* (01865) 288120, *Fax:* (01865) 288121. *E:* robert.ellis@regents.ox.ac.uk.

**ELLIS, Ven. Robin Gareth;** Archdeacon of Plymouth, 1982–2000; *b* 8 Dec. 1935; *s* of Walter and Morva Ellis; *m* 1964, Anne Ellis (*née* Landers); three *s*. *Educ:* Worksop Coll., Notts; Pembroke Coll., Oxford (BCL, MA). Curate of Swinton, 1960–63; Asst Chaplain, Worksop Coll., 1963–66; Vicar of Swaffham Prior and Reach, and Asst Director of Religious Education, Diocese of Ely, 1966–74; Vicar of St Augustine, Wisbech, 1974–82; Vicar of St Paul's, Yelverton, 1982–86. *Recreations:* cricket, theatre, prison reform. *Address:* Flat 1, 4 Lyndhurst Road, Exmouth, Devon EX8 3DT. *T:* (01395) 272891.

**ELLIS, Roger Wykeham,** CBE 1984; Master of Marlborough College, 1972–86; *b* 3 Oct. 1929; *s* of Cecil Ellis, solicitor, and Pamela Unwin; *m* 1964, Margaret Jean, *d* of William Hugh Stevenson; one *s* two *d*. *Educ:* St Peter's Sch., Seaford; Winchester Coll.; Trinity Coll., Cambridge (Schol., MA). Royal Navy, 1947–49. Asst Master, Harrow Sch., 1952–67, and Housemaster of the Head Master's House, 1961–67; Headmaster of Rossall Sch., 1967–72. Graduate Recruitment Manager, Barclays Bank, 1986–91. Chm., HMC, 1983.

Member: Harrow Borough Educn Cttee, 1956–60; Wilts County Educn Cttee, 1975–86. Governor: Campion Sch., Athens, 1981–2003; Cheam Sch., 1975–93 (Chm., 1987–93); Hawtreys Sch., 1975–86; Sandroyd Sch., 1982–86; Fettes Coll., 1983–94; St Edward's Sch., Oxford, 1985–2006 (Chm., 1992–99); Harrow Sch., 1987–97. Dir, Asquith Ct Schs Ltd, 1992–2000. Trustee, Hanover Foundn, 2001–05. *Publications:* Who's Who in Victorian Britain, 1997; (with Geoffrey Treasure) Britain's Prime Ministers, 2005. *Recreations:* golf, fishing, bridge. *Address:* 32 Hillcroft Crescent, Ealing, W5 2SQ. *Clubs:* East India, MCC; Denham Golf.

See also A. W. Ellis, Sir H. A. Stevenson.

**ELLIS, (Rosalind) Morag, (Mrs A. Bushell);** QC 2006; *b* 5 June 1962; *d* of Ivor and Pamela Ellis; *m* 1985, Rev. Anthony Bushell; two *s* one *d*. *Educ:* Penrhos Coll., Colwyn Bay; St Catharine's Coll., Cambridge (BA 1983); Inns of Court Sch. of Law. Called to the Bar, Gray's Inn, 1984, Bencher, 2017; in practice as a barrister, specialising in law of planning, local government and village greens. Chm., Planning and Envmt Bar Assoc., 2012–16 (Vice-Chm., 2007–12). Mem. Council, Wescott House, Cambridge, 2010–. QC Church Comr, 2019–. Commissary Gen., Dio. of Canterbury, 2011–; Dep. Chancellor, Dio. of Southwark, 2012–. Member: Archbps' Clergy Discipline Panel, 2015–; Legal Adv. Commn, C of E, 2016–. Church of England Reader. *Publications:* (contrib.) Halsbury's Laws of England, 4th edn, 1998 reissue; (contrib.) Gambling for Local Authorities, 2nd edn 2010; articles in Jl Planning and Envmt Law. *Recreations:* music: Member, Bach Choir, violin, viola. *Address:* Francis Taylor Building, Temple, EC4Y 7BY. *T:* (020) 7353 8415, *Fax:* (020) 7353 7622. *E:* morag.ellis@ftb.eu.com.

**ELLIS, (Stephen) Luke;** Chief Executive Officer, Man Group plc, since 2016; *b* London, 27 Feb. 1963; *s* of Douglas and Mary Ellis; *m* 1989, Jenny Attlee; two *s* one *d*. *Educ:* Bristol Univ. (BSc Hons Maths and Econs 1985). Managing Director: J P Morgan, 1988–98; Financial Risk Mgt, 1998–2008; Chm., GLG Multi Manager Business, 2009–10; Man Group plc: Hd and Chief Inf. Officer, Multi Manager Business, 2010–12; CEO, Man Gp PLC FRM, 2012–13; Pres., 2013–16. Trustee, Greenhouse Sports, 2015–. *Recreations:* organic farming, mountain sports, charitable fundraising expeditions. *Address:* Man Group plc, Riverbank House, 2 Swan Lane, EC4R 3AD. *T:* (020) 7144 1000. *E:* luke.ellis@man.com.

**ELLIS, Timothy David;** Deputy Director, Performance and Outcomes, Scottish Government, since 2018; *b* London, 14 April 1971; *m* 2003, Catriona Brown; three *d*. Dept of Transport, 1989–98; Scottish Office, 1998–2003; Hd, Freedom of Information Unit, Scottish Exec., 2003–06; Sen. Manager, Communities Scotland, 2006–08; Dep. Dir, Housing Investment, 2008–10, Hd, Cabinet and Corporate Secretariat, 2011–13, Scottish Govt; Chief Exec., Keeper and Registrar Gen., Nat. Records of Scotland, 2013–18.

**ELLIS, Rt Rev. Timothy William,** DPhil; Bishop Suffragan of Grantham, 2006–13; an Honorary Assistant Bishop: Diocese of Lincoln, since 2013; Diocese of Sheffield, since 2014; Diocese of Derby, since 2015; *b* 26 Aug. 1953; *s* of Albert and Betty Ellis; *m* 1976, Susan Weston; two *s* one *d*. *Educ:* King's Coll., London (AKC 1975); York Univ. (DPhil 1998). Ordained deacon, 1976, priest, 1977; Asst Curate, St John, Old Trafford, 1976–80; Vicar, St Thomas, Pendleton and Chaplain to Salford Coll. of Technol., 1980–87; Vicar, St Leonard, Norwood, 1987–2001; Priest i/c, St Hilda, Shiregreen, 1994–97; RD Ecclesfield, 1994–99; Archdeacon of Stow and Lindsey, 2001–06. Sec., 1988–94, Chm., 1999–2001, Sheffield DAC; Member, Fabric Advisory Committee: Sheffield Cathedral, 2000–; York Minster, 2000–16; Lincoln Minster, 2005–07. Hon. Canon, Sheffield Cathedral, 2000–01. Chairman: Living Stones Consortium, 2011–17; E Midlands Community Led Housing Trust (formerly Lincolnshire Community Land Trust), 2012–; Sheffield Faiths Together Exec., 2015–. *Recreations:* Sheffield Wednesday FC, wine, foreign travel, golf, gardening, DIY, hen husbandry. *Address:* 8 Mason Grove, Sheffield S13 8LL.

**ELLIS, Sir Vernon (James),** Kt 2011; Chairman, British Council, 2010–16; *b* 1 July 1947; *s* of Norman and Phyllis Ellis; *m* 1972, Hazel Marilyn Lucas; one *s* one *d*. *Educ:* Magdalen Coll. Sch., Oxford; Magdalen Coll., Oxford (MA Hons PPE 1969). FCA 1982. Andersen Consulting, later Accenture, 1969–2010: Partner, 1979; Man. Partner, UK, 1986–89; Man. Partner, Europe, ME, Africa and India, 1989–99; Internat. Chm., 1999–2008; Sen. Advr, 2008–10. Chm., Arts and Media Hons Cttee, 2013–16. Chairman: Martin Randall Travel, 2008–; Country Greenhouses Ltd, 2008–11; Passionato Ltd, 2009–11; OneMedicare LLP, 2010–14; FTI Consulting Inc., 2012–; OneMedical Gp, 2014–19. Dir, World-Links, Washington, 2002–06. Member: Bd, Prince of Wales Business Leaders Forum, 1997–2006 (Chm. Bd, 2001–05); Adv. Bd, Centre for European Reform, 1998–2010; Council, World Economic Forum, 1999–2001; Mem., 2001–04, Dep. Chm., 2002–04, Mayor of Seoul's Internat. Adv. Council. UK private sector delegate, G8 Digital Opportunities Task Force, 2000–02. Member: Develt Cttee, Magdalen Coll., Oxford, 1999–2010; Adv. Council, Saïd Business Sch., Univ. of Oxford, 1996–2006; Foundn Bd, Internat. Inst. of Mgt Develt, Lausanne, 1996–2004; Internat. Council, INSEAD, 2001–04; Bd, Arts & Business, 2003–06; Adv. Bd, Bridges Ventures, 2008–10; Council, Beacon Collaborative, 2018–. Chairman: Classical Opera, 1996–2009 (Pres., 2009–); ENO, 2006–12 (Mem., 2001–12; Pres., 2012–); Sacconi Trust, 2007–10; Nat. Opera Studio, 2012–19; Appeal Bd, Stop MS, 2015–19; Leeds Internat. Piano Comp., 2015–19; Britten-Pears Foundn, 2017–19; Live Music Now, 2018–; Co-Chm., Benjamin Britten Foundn, 2019–. Trustee: Florestan Trio, 2003–11; Royal Coll. of Music, 2004–10; Kathleen Ferrier Prize, 2004–19; Young Singers Welfare Foundn, 2008–10; Leopold Trust, 2009–13; London Music Masters, 2015–19; Royal Philharmonic Soc., 2015–. Mem., Philanthrophy Rev., 2011. Barclay Fellow, Templeton Coll., Oxford, 2002–06. Hon. Bencher, Middle Temple, 2017. Hon. Mem., Royal Soc. of Musicians, 2017. FRCM 2012. Hon. Fellow, Trinity Laban Conservatoire, 2012. Hon. DLit Goldsmiths, Univ. of London, 2011; Hon. DSc QUB, 2012; Hon. LLD Warwick, 2014. Beacon Fellow for Cultural Philanthropy, 2013. Assoc. of British Orchestra's Award, 2014. *Recreations:* music, opera, theatre, gardening, wine, cooking, photography. *E:* vernon@vernonellis.net. *Club:* Athenæum.

**ELLIS-REES, Hugh Francis,** CB 1986; Regional Director, West Midlands, Departments of the Environment and Transport, 1981–89; *b* 5 March 1929; *s* of late Sir Hugh Ellis-Rees, KCMG, CB and Lady (Eileen Frances Anne) Ellis-Rees; *m* 1956, Elisabeth de Mestre Gray; three *s* one *d*. *Educ:* Ampleforth Coll.; Balliol Coll., Oxford. Served Grenadier Guards, 1948–49. Joined War Office, 1954; DoE, 1970–89; Cabinet Office, 1972–74; Under Sec., DoE, 1974. Mem., Black Country Develt Corp., 1990–98. Chm., Burford and Dist Soc., 2005–10; Trustee, Burford Fest., 2007–13 (Chm. 2007).

**ELLISON, Jane;** Deputy Director-General for Corporate Operations, World Health Organization, since 2017; *b* Bradford, 15 Aug. 1964; *m* John Samiotis. *Educ:* St Hilda's Coll., Oxford (BA PPE). With John Lewis Partnership, London, 1986–2010: grad. trainee; Manager, Customer Direct Mktg; Sen. Manager, Edition, customer mag.; on secondment with music charity, Sing for Pleasure, 2004. Mem. (C) Barnet LBC, 1991–94, 2006–08. Contested (C): Barnsley E, Dec. 1996; Barnsley E and Mexborough, 1997; Tottenham, June 2000; Pendle, 2005. MP (C) Battersea, 2010–17; contested (C) same seat, 2017. Parly Under-Sec. of State, DoH, 2013–16; Financial Sec., HM Treasury, 2016–17. Member: Works and Pensions Select Cttee, 2012–13; Backbench Business Cttee, 2010–13. Special Advr, Chancellor of the Exchequer, 2017. *Address:* World Health Organization, Avenue Appia 20, 1202 Geneva, Switzerland.

**ELLISON, Dame Jillian Paula Anne, (Dame Jill),** DBE 2001; Director of Nursing, Heart of England Foundation Trust (formerly East Birmingham Hospital, then Birmingham Heartlands and Solihull NHS Trust), 1990–2007; *b* 31 Jan. 1955; *d* of Joseph Ellison and Mollie Yvonne Ellison (*née* North). *Educ:* St Margaret's Sch., Bushey; Birmingham Poly. (HVCert 1980); MA UCE, 2001. Trained at Middx Hosp. Sch. of Nursing, 1973–76 (SRN); Staff Nurse: Middx Hosp., London, 1976–77; Hadassah Hosp., Israel, 1978–79; (Intensive Care) Charing Cross Hosp., 1979–80; Sandwell Health Authority: Health Visitor, 1980–85; Nurse Manager, 1985–87; Dist Sen. Nurse, 1987–90. Chm., Nurse Directors Assoc., 2005–07. *Recreations:* walking, cycling. *Address:* 4 The Badgers, Barnt Green, Birmingham B45 8QR.

**ELLISON, Rt Rev. John Alexander;** Bishop of Paraguay, 1988–2007; an Hon. Assistant Bishop, Diocese of Winchester, since 2008; *b* 24 Dec. 1940; *s* of Alexander and Catherine Ellison; *m* 1964, Judith Mary Cox; one *s* two *d*. *Educ:* London College of Divinity (ALCD); Borough Road College (Teacher's Cert.). Secondary school teacher, 1961–64. Ordained deacon 1967, priest 1968; Curate, St Paul, Woking, 1967–71; missionary, church planter, evangelist; Bible school/Bible institute lecturer, 1971–79; Asst to Archdeacon, St Saviour, Belgrano, Dio. Argentina, 1979–82; Rector, Aldridge, Dio. Lichfield, 1983–88. *Recreations:* walking, gardening, family, dining out. *Address:* The Furrow, Evingar Road, Whitchurch, Hants RG28 7EU. *T:* (01256) 892126. *E:* jyjellison@btinternet.com.

**ELLISON, Lawrence J., (Larry);** Executive Chairman and Chief Technology Officer, Oracle Corporation, since 2014 (Chief Executive Officer, 1977–2014; President, 1977–96; Chairman, 1996–2004); *b* New York City, 1944; *s* of Florence Spellman; adopted by Louis and Lillian Ellison; *m* 2003, Melanie Craft. *Educ:* High Sch., Chicago; Univ. of Illinois. Formerly computer programmer, Calif; posts with Amdahl Inc., 1967–71, and Ampex Corp., 1972–77; Founder (with Bob Miner), Oracle, 1977. Dir, Apple Computer Inc., 1997–2002. Ind. Dir, Tesla, 2018–. *Address:* Oracle Corporation, 500 Oracle Parkway, Redwood Shores, CA 94065, USA.

**ELLISON, Mark Christopher;** QC 2008; a Recorder, 2000–15; a Deputy High Court Judge, 2010–15; *b* 8 Oct. 1957; *s* of late Anthony Ellison and of Arlette Maguire Ellison (*née* Blundell); *m* 1981, Kate Augusta (*née* Middleton); two *s* two *d*. *Educ:* Pocklington Sch.; Skinners' Sch.; UWIST (LLB). Called to the Bar, Gray's Inn, 1979, Bencher, 2012; in practice at the Bar, 1980–; Treasury Counsel at CCC, 1994; Sen. Treasury Counsel, 2000–08; First Sen. Treasury Counsel, 2006–08. Member: Criminal Justice Council, 2008–12; Professional Practice Cttee, Bar Council, 2009–12. *Recreations:* my children, dinghy sailing. *Address:* QEB Hollis Whiteman, 1–2 Laurence Pountney Hill, EC4R 0EU. *T:* (020) 7933 8855. *E:* barristers@qebholliswhiteman.co.uk.

**ELLISON, Robin Charles;** Consultant, Pinsent Masons, since 2016 (Partner, 2002–16); *b* 3 Feb. 1949; *s* of Cecil Ellison and Vera Ellison (*née* Glicher); *m* 1986, Micheline Harris; two *s*. *Educ:* Manchester Grammar Sch. Cecil Ellison & Co., Manchester, 1973–75; Res. Fellow, Wolfson Coll., Cambridge, 1976–81; admitted Solicitor, 1979; Sen. Partner, Ellison Westhorp, Solicitors, 1981–94; Consultant, Hammond Suddards, 1994–97; Nat. Hd of Pensions, Eversheds, 1997–2002. Visiting Professor: Pensions Law and Econs, Cass Business Sch., City Univ., 2006; Pensions Law, Birmingham City Univ., 2008–11. Chairman: Nat. Assoc. of Pension Funds, 2005–07; Instnl Investors Tort Recovery Assoc., 2012–. Chairman: Trustee Guild, 2000–; London & Colonial Assurance Gp, 2003–; Carillion Trustees, 2011–18. Chairman: Magen David Adom UK, 2003–; Lung Cancer Res., 2004–. Chm., U Party, 2010–. FPMI 1997; FRSA; FRSocMed 2007. Freeman, City of London, 2013. *Publications:* Pensions for Partners, 1978, 4th edn 1984; Private Occupational Pension Schemes, 1979; Pension Schemes for Controlling Directors, 1980, 3rd edn 1984; Pensions for Partners, 4th edn 1984; Pension Problems on Mergers and Acquisitions, 1984; Pensions Law and Practice (looseleaf), 1987–; (ed) Pensions Benefits Law Reports, 1989–; Pensions and Divorce, 1991; Pensions: Europe and equality, 1993, 2nd edn 1995; Pension Disputes, 1995; Pension Trustees Handbook, 1995, 4th edn 2006; (jtly) Family Breakdown and Pensions, 1997, 3rd edn 2006; (jtly) Pensions and Insolvency, 1997; The Pocket Pensions Guide, 1998; Pensions and Investments, 2006; Pension Fund Investment Law, 2008; (jtly) Pensions and Divorce, 2010; Pensions for You and Your Business, 2013; (ed) Halsbury's Statutes, vol. 80, 2014; Red Tape: managing excess in law, regulation and the courts, 2018. *Recreations:* walking, sailing, brutalist architecture. *Address:* 110 Frognal, NW3 6XU. *T:* (020) 7435 7330. *E:* robin@pensionslaw.net. *Clubs:* English-Speaking Union, Walbrook.

**ELLMAN, Dame Louise (Joyce),** DBE 2018; MP (Lab and Co-op) Liverpool Riverside, since 1997; *b* 14 Nov. 1945; *d* of late Harold and Annie Rosenberg; *m* 1967, Geoffrey David Ellman; one *s* one *d*. *Educ:* Manchester High Sch. for Girls; Hull Univ. (BA Hons); York Univ. (MPhil). Worked in further educn and on Open Univ., 1970–76. Member: Lancs CC, 1970–97 (Leader, Lab Gp, 1977–97; Leader, Council, 1981–97; Chm., 1981–85; Hon. Alderman, 1998–); W Lancs DC, 1974–87; Regl Exec., NW Labour Party, 1985– (Chm., 1993–98). Contested (Lab) Darwen, 1979. Member: Select Cttee on Envmt, Transport and Regl Affairs, 1997–2001; Select Cttee on Transport, 2002–17 (Chm., 2008–17); Vice Pres., All Pty Parly Cttee against Anti-semitism, 2007–; Jt Sec., All Pty Gp against Trafficking, 2007–11; Chair, All Pty Bahá'ís Gp, 2016–. Chm., PLP Regl Govt Gp, 1999. Chair: Jewish Labour Movement, 2004–16 (Pres., 2016–); Labour-Regeneration Gp, 2005–10; Vice Chair: Labour Friends of Israel, 2004–; Parly Liverpool Capital of Culture Gp, 2006–. Mem., Bd of Deputies of British Jews, 2007–. Vice-Chm., Lancashire Enterprises, 1982–97; Founder Mem., Co-operative Enterprises NW, 1979–; Founder Chm., NW Regl Assoc., 1992–93; Mem., NW Partnership, 1993–97. Youngest mem., Lancs CC, 1970; youngest mem. and first woman to be Chm., 1981. *Address:* House of Commons, SW1A 0AA.

**ELLORY, Prof. (John) Clive,** PhD; Professor of Physiology, University of Oxford, 1996, now Emeritus; Fellow of Corpus Christi College, Oxford, 1985, now Emeritus; *b* 16 April 1944; *s* of Ronald and Muriel Ellory; *m* 1969, Jane Metcalfe; one *s* one *d*. *Educ:* Latymer Upper Sch.; Univ. of Bristol (BSc Biochemistry 1964; PhD Zoology 1967); MA 1975, ScD 1995, Cantab; MA 1985, DSc 1996, Oxon. SO, 1967–71, SSO, 1971–75, PSO, 1975, Inst. of Animal Physiology, Babraham; Lectr, Dept of Physiology, Univ. of Cambridge, 1975–84; Fellow, Queens' Coll., Cambridge, 1975–84; Reader in Human Physiology, 1985–96, Hd of Physiology Dept, 1994–2006, Univ. of Oxford. Vis. Associate Prof., Yale, and Guest Fellow, Silliman Coll., 1971; Vis. Associate Prof., 1975, Vis. Prof., 1982, Univ. of Illinois; Investigator, US Antarctic Res. Program, McMurdo, Antarctica, 1980; Vis. Prof., Univ. of Nice, 1985, 1993; Royal Soc. Israel Res. Prof., Technion, Haifa, 1994. FMedSci 1999. *Publications:* jointly: Membrane Transport in Red Cells, 1977; Red Cell Membranes: a methodological approach, 1982; The Binding and Transport of Anions in Living Tissues, 1982; The Sodium Pump, 1985; Patronage and Plate at Corpus Christi College, Oxford, 1999; Red Cell Membrane Transport in Health & Disease, 2003. *Recreations:* food, antique silver, hill walking. *Address:* Corpus Christi College, Merton Street, Oxford OX1 4JF. *T:* (01865) 276760.

**ELLWOOD, Sir Peter (Brian),** Kt 2011; CBE 2001; Vice Lord-Lieutenant, Northamptonshire, 2014–18; *b* 15 May 1943; *s* of Isaac and Edith Ellwood; *m* 1968, Judy Ann Windsor; one *s* two *d. Educ:* King's Sch., Macclesfield. FCIB. Barclays Bank, 1961–89; Chief Exec., Barclaycard, 1985–89; Chief Exec., Retail Banking, TSB, 1989–92; Gp Chief Exec., TSB Gp, 1992–95; Chm., Visa International, 1994–99; Dep. Gp Chief Exec., 1995–97, Gp Chief Exec., 1997–2003, Lloyds TSB Gp plc. Dep. Chm., 2003, Chm., 2004–08, ICI PLC; Chm., Rexam PLC, 2008–12. Dir, Supervisory Bd, Akzo Nobel, 2008–14. Chairman: The Work Foundn, 2001–07; Royal Parks Adv. Bd, 2003–07; Royal Parks Foundn, 2003–08; Adv. Council, Royal Philharmonic Orchestra, 2013– (non-exec. Dir, 1996–2007). Trustee, Royal Theatre, Northampton, 1982–99. Pres., Northampton Bach Choir, 2005–. Mem., Ct of Govs, St Andrew's Healthcare, 2008–. Mem. Court, Univ. of Northampton (formerly Nene Coll., later UC Northampton), 1989–. FRSA. Hon. LLD Leicester, 1994; DUniv Central England, 1995. DL 2005, High Sheriff 2008, Northants. *Recreations:* theatre, music. *Address:* Wyndham House, Main Street, Church Stowe, Northampton NN7 4SG.

**ELLWOOD, Peter David Roger,** OBE 2002; Regional Director, Americas (formerly Latin America and Caribbean), British Council, 2009–12; consultant on international partnerships, University of Sussex, 2013–14; *b* 17 Oct. 1948; *s* of John and Eileen Ellwood; *m* 1976; one *s* two *d; m* 2010, Maria Karutina; one *s. Educ:* Trinity Hall, Cambridge (BA Hons English 1970, MA). Shell-Mex and BP, 1970–75; British Council, 1975–2012: Asst Rep., Nepal, 1975–79; Regl Officer, Middle East (based in London), 1979–81; Pvte Sec. to Dir Gen., 1981–83; Dep. Rep., Indonesia, 1983–86; Dir, Cameroon, 1986–89; Dep. Dir, France, 1989–94; Director: Sri Lanka, 1994–98; Pakistan, 1998–2002; Regional Director: Middle East, UAE, 2002–04; N and Central Europe, Sweden, 2004–07; Russia and N Europe, Prague, 2007–09. *Recreations:* travel, birdwatching, theatre, opera. *Address:* 25 Queens Park Road, Brighton BN2 0GJ.

**ELLWOOD, Rt Hon. Tobias,** PC 2017; MP (C) Bournemouth East, since 2005; *b* 12 Aug. 1966; *s* of Peter Ellwood and Dr Caroline Ellwood; *m* 2005, Hannah Ryan; two *s. Educ:* Vienna Internat. Sch.; Loughborough Univ. (BA Hons Design and Technol.); City Univ. Business Sch. (MBA); Kennedy Sch. of Govt, Harvard Univ. (Exec. Course on Nat. and Internat. Security). Served Army, RGJ, 1991–96; reservist, 77th Bde. Researcher for Rt Hon. Tom King, 1996–97; Senior Business Develt Manager: London Stock Exchange, 1998–2002; Allen & Overy, 2002–04. Shadow Minister for culture, media and sport, 2007–10; PPS to Sec. of State for Defence, 2010–11, to Minister for Europe, 2011–13, to Sec. of State for Health, 2013–14; Parly Under-Sec. of State, FCO, 2014–17, MoD, 2017–19. Mem., Parly Delegn to NATO, 2014; Parly Advr to Prime Minister for NATO Summit, 2014. Eagle Scout. *Recreations:* private pilot, wind-surfing, travel, diving, landscape gardening, military history. *Address:* House of Commons, SW1A 0AA. *T:* (020) 7219 3000. *E:* tobias.ellwood.mp@parliament.uk.

**ELLY, His Honour (Richard) Charles;** DL; a Circuit Judge, 1998–2012; Partner, Reynolds, Parry-Jones & Crawford, solicitors, 1968–98; *b* 20 March 1942; *s* of Harold Elly and Dora Ellen Elly (*née* Luing); *m* 1967, Marion Rose Blackwell; one *s* one *d. Educ:* Sir William Borlase's Sch., Marlow; Hertford Coll., Oxford (MA); Coll. of Law, London. Admitted solicitor, 1966. Secretary: Southern Assoc. of Law Socs, 1975–82; Berks, Bucks and Oxon Law Soc., 1975–82 (Pres., 1988–89); Law Society: Mem. Council, 1981–97; Dep. Vice-Pres., 1992–93; Vice-Pres., 1993–94; Pres., 1994–95. Mem., Lord Chancellor's Adv. Cttee on Legal Educn and Conduct, 1997–98. Mem., Berks CC, 1980–81. Chairman: Maidenhead Deanery Synod, 1972–79; High Wycombe and Dist CAB, 1983–88; Maidenhead Contact Centre, 2012–; Dir, Diocesan Trustees (Oxford) Ltd, 2012– (Chm., 2019–). President: Cookham Soc., 1987–97; Hertford Coll. Lawyers Assoc., 1995–98; Criminal Law Solicitors Assoc., 1995–98. Gov., Coll. of Law, 1984–2000; Gov., 1995–2011 (Chm. Govs, 1996–2001), Chm. Trustees, 2001–, Sir William Borlase's Sch. Chm., Berks Gardens Trust, 2013–. FRSA 1995. DL Berks, 2011. Hon. LLD Kingston, 1994. *Recreations:* bird-watching, theatre, walking, gardening. *Address:* Court Cottage, Dean Lane, Cookham Dean, Maidenhead, Berks SL6 9AF. *Club:* Oxford and Cambridge.

**ELMES, Caroline Myfanwy Tonge,** CMG 2001; HM Diplomatic Service, retired; *b* 20 Sept. 1948. Second Sec., FCO, 1975; First Secretary: Czechoslovakia, 1978–81; FCO, 1981–85; (Econ.), Rome, 1985–89; Dep. High Comr and Head of Chancery, Sri Lanka, 1989–92; Dep. Head of Mission, Czechoslovakia, 1992–95; Head of S Asia Dept, FCO, 1995–98; language trng, 1998; Ambassador to Angola, 1998–2002.

**ELMORE, Christopher Philip James;** MP (Lab) Ogmore, since May 2016; *b* Newport, 23 Dec. 1983; *m* 2019, Bridie Sedgebeer. *Educ:* Cardiff Metropolitan Univ. (BA Hons Modern Hist. and Culture 2005). Mem. (Lab) Vale of Glamorgan Council, 2008–17 (Cabinet Mem. for Children's Services and Schs, 2012–16). An Opposition Whip, 2016–. Member: Welsh Affairs Select Cttee, 2016–17; Justice Select Cttee, 2016; Procedure Cttee, 2017–. Mem., Cardiff and Vale Univ. Health Bd, 2013–16. *Recreations:* walking, reading. *Address:* House of Commons, SW1A 0AA.

**ELMS, Marsha Marilyn, (Marsha Carey-Elms),** OBE 2012; MA; Executive Head Teacher, Kendrick School and Reading Girls' School, 2007–12; Education Adviser, Department for Education, 2012; *b* 11 June 1946; *d* of James F. Carey and Carolyn M. Carey; *m* (marr. diss.); one *s* one *d. Educ:* Tottenham County Grammar Sch.; Bedford Coll., London Univ. (BA); Brunel Univ. (PGCE 1969); Reading Univ. (MA 1988). Featherstone High School, Southall: teacher, 1969–90; Head, Liberal Studies Faculty, 1973–75; Dep. Head, 1990; Dep. Headteacher, Magna Carta Sch., Staines, 1990–93; acting Headteacher, Ashmead Sch., Reading, Summer term 1998; Headteacher, Kendrick Girls' Sch., 1993–2007. Mem., ASCL (formerly SHA), 1994–2012 (Mem., Associates Cttee, 2012–); Pres., Assoc. of Girls' Maintained Schs, 2002–03; Chm., Berkshire Assoc. of Heads, 2009–12; Mem., Graduation Bd, Nat. Professional Qualification for Headship, 2011–. Nat. Leader of Educn, 2007–12. Exec. Hd, Kendrick Fedn, 2006–12. Governor: Reading Girls' Sch., 2007–15; Shiplake Coll., Henley, 2014– (Chm., Educn Cttee, 2015–); Altwood Sch., Maidenhead, 2014–; Trustee, Kendrick Sch., 2012–. Chm., Arts Soc., Maidenhead, 2017–. JP Middx 1982–2016 (Mem., W London Adv. Cttee, 2012–16). *Publications:* articles for ASCL and in educnl jls. *Recreations:* family, holidays, Spurs supporter, food, painting. *Address:* Roseneath, Altwood Bailey, Maidenhead, Berks SL6 4PQ. *T:* (01628) 620085. *Clubs:* Lansdowne (Mem. Council, 2017–); Phyllis Court (Henley-on-Thames).

**ELPHICK, Dr Clive Harry;** Independent Director: National Grid Gas plc, since 2014; National Grid Electricity Transmission plc, since 2014; Member, Competition Appeal Tribunal, since 2011; *b* Eastbourne, 24 Nov. 1956; *s* of late Leonard Harry Elphick and of Pamela Joan Elphick (*née* Reed); *m* 1st, 1979, Kathryn Heasman (marr. diss. 1986); 2nd, 2003, Jane Harris (*née* Adams). *Educ:* Eastbourne Grammar Sch.; Queens' Coll., Cambridge (BA 1978; MA); Univ. of Birmingham (MSc; PhD 1981). FCMA 1990. United Utilities Group plc: Gp Financial Controller, 1991–92; Econ. Regulation Dir, 1992–94; Gp Strategic Planning Dir, 1995–2005; Chief Operating Officer, Transformation, 2006–07; Man. Dir, Asset Mgt and Regulation, 2007–09. Board Member: DCMS, 2003–07; NI Authy for Utility Regulation, 2006–12; Northwest RDA, 2010–11; Envmt Agency, 2011–17. Chm., NW CBI, 2008–09. Mem., England Cttee, Wildlife Trusts, 2012–16. Trustee: Lancs Wildlife Trust, 2010–; Nat. Museums of Liverpool, 2012–16. Hon. Res. Fellow in Maths, Univ. of Birmingham, 2017–. Liveryman, Water Conservators' Co., 2009–18. FRSA. *Publications:* contrib. papers on econ. regulation, maths and graph theory. *Recreations:* hiking, mountain biking, classical music, New Zealand. *E:* clive.elphick@gmail.com.

**ELPHICKE, Charles;** MP for Dover, since 2010 (C, 2010–19; Ind, since 2019); *b* Huntingdon, 14 March 1971; *m* 1996, Natalie Cecilia Ross (*see* N. C. Elphicke); one *s* one *d. Educ:* Felsted Sch.; Nottingham Univ. (LLB Hons). Called to the Bar, Middle Temple, 1994; admitted solicitor, 1998; Partner and Hd of Tax, Reed Smith, solicitors, 2001–05; Partner and Hd of Eur. Tax, Hunton & Williams, solicitors, 2006–10. Mem. (C) Lambeth LBC, 1994–98. Contested (C) St Albans, 2001; a Lord Comr of HM Treasury (Govt Whip), 2015–16. *Publications:* papers for Centre for Policy Studies. *Recreations:* sailing, making Britain a richer, more exciting place to be. *Address:* House of Commons, SW1A 0AA. *T:* (020) 7219 3000. *E:* charlie.elphicke.mp@parliament.uk. *Club:* Royal Cinque Ports Yacht.

**ELPHICKE, Natalie Cecilia,** OBE 2015; Chief Executive, Housing and Finance Institute, since 2015; *b* Welwyn Garden City, 5 Nov. 1970; *m* 1996, Charles Elphicke, *qv*; one *s* one *d. Educ:* Queenwood Sch., Herts; Clarendon Grammar Sch., Ramsgate; Canterbury Coll.; Univ. of Kent, Canterbury (LLB Hons). Called to the Bar, Lincoln's Inn, 1994 (Hardwicke Schol.); admitted solicitor, 1999; lawyer: Inland Revenue, 1995–97; lawyer, 1997–2007, Partner, 2003–07, Wilde Sapte, then Denton Wilde Sapte; Partner: Addleshaw Goddard, 2007–09; Stephenson Harwood, 2009–12; ind. advr to Govt on housing and regeneration, 2014–16. Led (jtly) Rev. into local authority role in housing supply (Elphicke-House Report, 2015). Non-executive Director: Principality Building Soc., 2012–18 (Chair, Risk Cttee, 2014–18); Student Loans Co., 2016– (Chair, Audit and Risk Cttee, 2016–). Ind. Mem., Audit and Risk Cttee, DFE, 2016–. Freeman, City of London. *Publications:* policy publications on housing finance and housing policy. *Recreations:* social policy, volunteering at homeless shelter, kayaking. *Address:* The Edge, Bay Hill, St Margaret's Bay, Dover, Kent CT15 6DU. *E:* elphicke.gen@gmail.com.

**ELPHINSTON of Glack, Sir Alexander,** 12th Bt *cr* 1701, of Logie Elphinstone and Nova Scotia; Senior Associate Solicitor, Anthony Collins Solicitors, since 2005; *b* Gloucester, 6 June 1955; *s* of Sir John Elphinston of Glack, 11th Bt and of Margaret Doreen Elphinston (*née* Tasker); *S* father, 2015; *m* 1986, Ruth Mary Dunnett; three *s* one *d. Educ:* Repton; Durham Univ. (BA Gen. Arts 1977). Admitted solicitor, 1980; in practice, 1980–; Partner, Foot Anstey, 1991–2001. Chm., STEP, England and Wales, 2014–17 (Mem., Birmingham Cttee, 2001–18; Mem., Mental Capacity Gp, 2013–17); Member: Solicitors for the Elderly, 2001–16 (Mem., Birmingham Cttee, 2001–17); Court of Protection User Gp, 2013–. *Publications:* articles in STEP Jl. *Recreations:* walking, jazz, theatre, jigsaws. *Heir:* s Daniel John Elphinston, *b* 24 Sept. 1989. *Address:* 43 Lonsdale Road, Harborne, Birmingham B17 9QX.

**ELPHINSTONE,** family name of **Lord Elphinstone**.

**ELPHINSTONE,** 19th Lord *cr* 1509; **Alexander Mountstuart Elphinstone;** Baron (UK) 1885; *b* 15 April 1980; *e s* of 18th Lord Elphinstone and of Willa Mary Gabriel, 4th *d* of Major David Chetwode; *S* father, 1994; *m* 2007, Nicola Jane, *yr d* of Michael Hall, Beaconsfield; two *s* one *d. Educ:* Belhaven Hill Sch.; Eton Coll.; Univ. of Newcastle upon Tyne (MSc 2002); Sch. of Oriental and African Studies, London (MA Develt Studies 2005). *Heir:* s Hon. Jago Alexander Elphinstone, Master of Elphinstone, *b* 19 Aug. 2011.

**ELPHINSTONE, Sir John (Howard Main),** 6th Bt *cr* 1816, of Sowerby, Cumberland; *b* 25 Feb. 1949; *o s* of Sir Douglas Elphinstone, 5th Bt and of Helen Barbara Elphinstone (*née* Main); *S* father, 1995; *m* 1990, Diane Barbara Quilliam, *d* of Dr B. Q. Callow. *Educ:* Loretto Sch., Midlothian. *Heir:* cousin Henry Charles Elphinstone, *b* 7 July 1958. *Address:* Crooklands, Clapham, Lancaster LA2 8HY.

**ELPHINSTONE, Lucy;** Headmistress, Francis Holland School, Sloane Square, since 2012; *b* Woking, 11 May 1957; *d* of Major Myles Reynolds and Rhoda Reynolds; *m* 1981, Charles Elphinstone (marr. diss. 2004); two *s* two *d. Educ:* Didcot Girls' Grammar Sch.; Barnstaple Grammar Sch.; Newnham Coll., Cambridge (BA Hons English 1979; MA); South Bank Univ. (PGCE 1996). Promotions Exec. and Ed., Collins Publishers, 1979–81; Pastoral Counsellor, C of E, 1981–82; bookshop manager, Leics and Angus, 1982–85; hotel manager, 1990–92; Hd, Brotherton Castle Sch., Johnshaven, 1992–94; Dir of Studies and Hd of English, Lathallan Sch., Montrose, 1994–2000; Dir of Studies, Sen. Mistress and Hd of English, St Michael's Sch., Tawstock, 2000–01; Dir of Drama, Fettes Coll., Edinburgh, 2001–03; Hd of English, King's Coll., Taunton, 2003–07; Hd of Sixth Form, Downe House, 2007–12. Trustee: Katherine Low Settlement, Battersea, 2012–; Mvumi Sch., Tanzania, 2018–; Chelsea Barracks Chapel, 2018–. FRSA. *Publications:* Dana: an autobiography, 1986; (with Julie Sheldon) Dancer off her Feet, 1991; (with Julie Sheldon) One Step at a Time, 2000; educnl articles on children's mental health and wellbeing, building resilience, entrepreneurship for children. *Recreations:* tennis, ski-ing, piano, choral singing, theatre, art. *Address:* Birch Cottage, Orchard Lane, Boars Hill, Oxford OX1 5JH. *T:* (020) 7730 2971. *E:* lucy.elphinstone@fhs-sw1.org.uk. *Club:* Conduit.

**ELS, Theodore Ernest, (Ernie);** South African golfer; *b* 17 Oct. 1969; *s* of Cornelius, (Nils), and Hester Els; *m* 1998, Liezl Wehmeyer; one *s* one *d. Educ:* Delville Sch.; Jan de Klerk Tech. Coll. Professional golfer, 1989–; winner: Jun. World Championship, USA, 1984; South African Open, 1992, 1996, 1998, 2006, 2010; US Open, 1994, 1997; World Match Play Championship, 1994, 1995, 1996, 2002, 2003, 2004, 2007; European Order of Merit, 1995; South African PGA Championship, 1995; Million Dollar Challenge, Sun City, 1999; Nedbank Golf Challenge, Sun City, 2000, 2002; Open, Muirfield, 2002; Open, Royal Lytham and St Annes, 2012.

**ELSE, Jean,** MA; Headteacher, Whalley Range High School, Manchester, 1994–2006. Teacher: Counthill Sch., Oldham; various schs in Rochdale and Trafford. Co-ordinator for Manchester, DFES Excellence in the Cities, 1999. Trustee, Imperial War Mus., 2003–07.

**ELSE, Martin Thomas;** Chief Executive, Royal College of Physicians, 2005–13; *b* 21 May 1953; *s* of late Richard Else and of Lilian Margaret Else (*née* Stickells); *m* 1978, Jennifer Louise Bridges; one *s* one *d. Educ:* Farnborough Grammar Sch.; Univ. of Salford (BSc Econ); Southampton Coll. of Technol.; London Business Sch. (Sloan Fellowship with Dist.). CPFA (IPFA 1979). Finance trainee, City and Hackney HA, 1975–79; Principal Finance Planning Manager, 1979–82, Principal Asst Treas., 1982–83, NE Thames RHA; Dep. Treas., 1983–86, Dir of Finance, 1986–90, Hampstead HA; Royal Free Hampstead NHS Trust: Dir of Finance and Dep. Chief Exec., 1990–94; Chief Exec., 1994–2005. Policy Advr, DoH, 2005; Dir, RCP Regent's Park Ltd, 2005–13. Treas., Alzheimer's Disease Internat., 2005–13; Mem., Independent Age, 2010–. Royal Free Hospital: Hon. Sec. and Treas. to Special Trustees, 1986–2005; Trustee, Appeal Trust, 1988–92; Chm., Cancerkin Mgt Cttee, 1990–94; Trustee: Hampstead Wells and Campden Trust, 1996–2005; CORESS, 2006–. Health Comr, Liverpool, 2013–14. FRSocMed 2007. Hon. FRCP 2013; Hon. FMLM 2019. *Recreations:* football, cricket, golf, horseracing. *E:* martin.else@hotmail.co.uk.

**ELSEY, Robert Dermot James**; Executive Director, Technology, Bank of England, since 2016; *b* Taunton, 16 May 1980; *s* of Dermot Charles Elsey and Kathryn Elsey (*née* Tillier); *m* 2003, Zoe Victoria Mier; two *d*. *Educ*: Wellington Sch.; Birmingham City Univ. (BSc Business Systems Engrg). Call Centre Manager, Birmingham Cable, 1998–99; Credit Planning Analyst, Telewest Communications, 1999–2002; Contribution Assurance and Business Intelligence Manager, Virgin Media, 2002–04; Cable & Wireless International: Internat. Revenue Assurance Manager, 2004–06; Hd of Collections Strategy, 2006–07; Hd of Business Intelligence, 2007–08; Sen. Prog. Manager, Billing/Customer Relationship Mgt, 2008–11; Vodafone UK: Head: Business Intelligence, 2011–12; CRM, Billing and Retail Domain, 2012–13; IT, 2013–15; Chief Technol. Officer, Bank of England, 2015–16. *Recreations*: scuba diving, Rugby enthusiast, family. *Address*: Bank of England, Threadneedle Street, EC2R 8AH. *T*: (020) 3461 4444, *Fax*: (020) 3461 4771. *E*: robert.elsey@bankofengland.gsi.gov.uk.

**ELSEY, Roger William**; Resident Judge and HM Coroner, Sovereign Base Areas, Cyprus, since 2019; *b* 12 June 1954; *s* of William Gattie Elsey and Rita Alillian Elsey; *m* 1985, Susan Coull; three *d*. *Educ*: Bede Sch.; Univ. of Newcastle upon Tyne (LLB Hons); Open Univ. (MA 2008). Called to the Bar, Gray's Inn, 1977; practised in criminal law, N Eastern Circuit. Actg Stipendiary Magistrate, 1999–2004; a District Judge (Magistrates' Cts), 2004–18. Jt Ed., Signpost mag., 2000–. Mem., Durham Diocesan Synod, 2003–08. Chm., Northumbria Judicial Business Gp, 2013–. *Recreations*: cycling, theatre, walking, Anglican affairs. *Address*: Sovereign Base Areas Administration Courts, BFPO 53.

**EL-SISI, Abdel Fattah**; President of Arab Republic of Egypt, since 2014; *b* Cairo, 19 Nov. 1954; *s* of Saeed Hussein Khalil El-Sisi; *m* Entissar El-Sisi; three *s* one *d*. *Educ*: Egyptian Military Acad. (graduated 1977); Egyptian Command and Staff Coll. (Gen. Comd and Staff Course 1987); Army Command and Staff Coll., UK (Gen. Comd and Staff Course 1992); Nasser Military Acad. (War Course, Fellow, Higher War Coll., 2003); US Army War Coll. (War Course 2006). Comdr, Mechanised Inf. Bn, Egypt; Mil. Attaché, Riyadh; COS, then Comdr, Mechanised Inf. Bde; Comdr, Mechanised Inf. Div.; Comdr, Northern Mil. Zone; Dir, Mil. Intelligence and Reconnaissance Dept; Minister of Defence and Mil. Prodn, Egypt, 2012–14. Decorations and medals incl. 25 April, Dist. Service, Mil. Duty, Longevity and Exemplary, Kuwait Liberation, Mil. Courage, Republic's Mil., Training, Army. Order of Abdulaziz Al Saud (Saudi Arabia). *Recreations*: reading, cycling, working out. *Address*: Heliopolis Palace, Heliopolis, Cairo, Egypt. *T*: (2) 24177222. *E*: president.elsisi@op.gov.eg.

**ELSMORE, Ven. Guy Charles**; Archdeacon of Buckingham, since 2016; *b* Sutton Coldfield, 1966. *Educ*: Univ. of Edinburgh (BSc 1988); Ridley Hall, Cambridge. Ordained deacon, 1993, priest, 1994; Curate, St Michael's, Huyton, 1993–98; Vicar, St Basil and All Saints, Widnes, 1998–2005; Area Dean, Widnes, 2003–05; Priest-in-charge, 2005–10; Team Rector, 2010–16, St Luke in the City Team Ministry, Liverpool, 2010–16; Area Dean, Toxteth and Wavertree, 2014–16. Hon. Canon, Liverpool Cathedral, 2014–16. *Address*: Archdeacon's House, Stone, Aylesbury, Bucks HP17 8RZ.

**ELSNER, Prof. John Richard, (Jaś)**, PhD; FBA 2017; Professor of Late Antique Art, University of Oxford, since 2014; Humfry Payne Senior Research Fellow, Corpus Christi College, Oxford, since 1999; *b* London, 19 Dec. 1962; *s* of Dante Elsner and Renée Elsner; *m* 1992, Silvia Frenk; one *s* three *d*. *Educ*: University College Sch., London; King's Coll., Cambridge (BA 1985; PhD 1991); Harvard Univ.; Courtauld Inst. of Art, London. Jun. Res. Fellow, Jesus Coll., Cambridge, 1991; Lectr, 1992–98, Reader, 1998–99, Courtauld Inst. of Art, London. Visiting Professor: École des Hautes Études en Scis Sociales, Paris, 1999; Univ. of Michigan, 2000; Univ. of Chicago, 2003– (Vis. Prof. of Art and Religion, 2014–); Princeton Univ., 2007; Hebrew Univ., 2009–10; Free Univ., Brussels, 2010; UCLA, 2011; Humboldt Univ., Berlin, 2015–16. Sen. Res. Keeper, BM, 2012–18. Lead Curator, exhibitions: Imagining the Divine: Art and the Rise of the World Religions, Ashmolean Mus., 2017–18; The Archaeological Object, Beijing, 2017. Foreign Hon. Mem., Amer. Acad. of Arts and Scis, 2009. *Publications*: (ed jtly) Reflections of Nero: history, culture and representation, 1994; (ed jtly) The Cultures of Collecting, 1994 (trans. Japanese 1998); Art and the Roman Viewer, 1995; (with Simon Coleman) Pilgrimage Past and Present, 1995; (ed) Art and Text in Roman Culture, 1996; Imperial Rome and Christian Triumph: the art of the Roman Empire AD 100–450, 1998, 2nd edn 2018; (ed jtly) Voyages and Visions: reflections on the cultural history of travel, 1999; (ed jtly) Pausanias: travel and memory in Roman Greece, 2001; (ed jtly) Pilgrim Voices: narrative and authorship in Christian pilgrimage, 2003; (ed) The Verbal and the Visual: cultures of ekphrasis in antiquity, 2004; (ed jtly) Pilgrimage in Greco-Roman and Early Christian Antiquity: seeing the gods, 2005; Roman Eyes: visuality and subjectivity in art and text, 2007; (ed jtly) Visualising the Tragic, 2007; (ed jtly) Severan Culture, 2007; (ed jtly) Philostratus, 2009; (ed jtly) Images and Texts on the "Artemidorus Papyrus", 2009; (ed jtly) Life, Death and Representation: some new work on Roman sarcophagi, 2011; (ed jtly) Saints: faith at the borders, 2011; (ed jtly) Art and Rhetoric in Roman culture, 2014; (ed jtly) The Poetics of Late Latin Literature, 2017; (ed) Comparativism in Art History, 2017; (ed jtly) The Ark of Civilization: émigré scholars in Oxford in the mid twentieth century, 2017; edited articles in jls. *Recreations*: family, cooking, theatre, classical music. *Address*: Corpus Christi College, Oxford OX1 4JF. *T*: (01865) 276700, *Fax*: (01865) 276767. *E*: jas.elsner@ccc.ox.ac.uk.

**ELSON, Anthony Kenneth**; independent consultant, since 2004; *b* 15 June 1948; *s* of William and Elsie Elson; *m* 1971, Joy Waterworth. *Educ*: Birmingham Univ. (BSc 1st cl. Hons Exptl Physics 1969); Liverpool Univ. (BPhil Applied Social Studies 1972); CQSW. Social Worker, 1972–76; Principal Lectr in Social Work, Worcester Coll. of Further Educn, 1976–78; Social Services, Birmingham City Council: Team Manager, 1978–81; Area Manager, 1981–83; Asst Dir, 1983–88; Kirklees Metropolitan Borough Council: Dir of Social Services, 1988–89; Exec. Dir (Housing and Social Services), 1989–97; Exec. Dir (Social Services and Educn), 1997–98; Chief Exec., 1998–2004. Local Govt Advr, DoH, 2004. *E*: tony.elson@broomstileconsultants.co.uk.

**ELSON, Prof. Diane Rosemary**, PhD; Professor of Sociology, University of Essex, 2000–12, now Emeritus; *b* Bedworth, Warwickshire, 20 April 1946; *d* of Edwin and Vera Elson; one *s*. *Educ*: St Hilda's Coll., Oxford (BA Hons PPE 1968); Univ. of Manchester (PhD Econs 1994). Res. Asst, Inst. of Commonwealth Studies and St Antony's Coll., Oxford, 1968–71; Teaching Fellow, Dept of Economics, Univ. of York, 1971–75; Res. Officer, Inst. of Develt Studies, Univ. of Sussex, 1975–77; Temp. Lectr, Univ. of Manchester, 1978–79; part-time consultant and occasional lectr, 1979–84; University of Manchester: Hon. Res. Fellow, Internat. Develt Centre and Dept of Sociol., 1984–85; Lectr, 1985–91, Reader, 1992–95, in Develt Econs; Prof. of Develt Studies, 1995–98; Special Advr, UN Develt Fund for Women, 1998–2000; Advr, UN Women, 2012–. Member: UN Taskforce on Millennium Develt Goals, 1998–2000; Strategic Res. Bd, ESRC, 2008–10; UN Cttee on Develt Policy, 2013–. (Jtly) Leontief Prize for Advancing Frontiers of Econ. Thought, Global Develt and Envmt Inst., Tufts Univ., 2016. *Publications*: Male Bias in the Development Process, 1991, 2nd edn 1995; Progress of World's Women, 2000; Budgeting for Women's Rights, 2006; (ed jtly) Economic Policy and Human Rights Obligations, 2011; (ed jtly) Harvesting Feminist Knowledge for Public Policy, 2011; (ed jtly) Financial Governance from a Feminist Perspective, 2011; (ed jtly) Human Rights and the Capabilities Approach: an interdisciplinary dialogue, 2012; (jtly) Rethinking Economic Policy for Social Justice, 2016. *Recreations*: gardening, bird watching, campaigning for women's rights. *Address*: 159 Wick Hall, Furze Hill, Hove BN3 1NJ. *E*: drelson@essex.ac.uk.

**ELSON, Graham Peel**; Chief Executive, South West One, political and public affairs company, 1998–2015; *b* 21 Aug. 1949; *s* of George Ernest Elson and Rhoda (*née* Atkinson); *m* 1975, Jane Rosamunde Isaac. *Educ*: Palmers Endowed Sch. for Boys, Grays, Essex; NE London Polytechnic (BA Business Studies). Brand Manager, Rank Hovis McDougall Foods, 1972–74; Gen. Manager, Wilkinson Sword Gp, 1974–85. Councillor (Lib Dem) and Leader, Oxfordshire CC, 1985–89; Councillor (Lib Dem), Mid Devon DC, 1999–2003. Gen. Sec., Liberal Democrats, 1989–97. *Recreations*: boating, gardening, supporting West Ham United FC. *Address*: 12 Avenue de Beaumont, Saint Pardoux-la-Riviere 24470, France.

**ELSON, Louis Goodman**; Co-Founder and Managing Partner, Palamon Capital Partners LLP, since 1998; *b* Atlanta, Georgia, 25 Dec. 1962; *s* of Edward Elliott Elson and Suzanne Goodman Elson; one *s* two *d*; *m* 2019, Claudia Irene Huebschmann; one step *s* two step *d*. *Educ*: Phillips Acad., Andover, Mass; Eton Coll.; Harvard Univ. (AB Hons 1985); Univ. of Virginia (MBA Hons 1990). Manager, Time Inc., NY, 1985–88; E. M. Warburg, Pincus & Co.: Associate, NY, 1990–93; Vice-Pres., London, 1994; Partner, London, 1995–98. Non-executive Director: NDL Internat., 1992–95; Argent Gp, 1994–97; Cox Insce Hldgs plc, 1996–2005; Imagenet, 2001–04; Omnibus Systems, 2001–10; Newday Cards, 2002–10; Towry Gp, 2003–16; Retail Decisions, 2006–11; Integrated Dental Hldgs, 2014–; Rug Co., 2015–; Currencies Direct, 2015–; Simplify Gp, 2017–. Chair, Res. Adv. Bd, 2011–13, Dir, 2013, BVCA. Mem., Develt Bd, Prince's Trust, 2005–15; Chair, Impetus Trust, 2009–13, Vice-Chair, Impetus Private Equity Foundn, 2013–; Trustee, Voices Foundn, 2010–18; Founding Trustee, Education Endowment Foundn, 2011–; Dir, Social and Sustainable Capital, 2017–. Charter Trustee, Phillips Acad., Andover, Mass, 2004–; Trustee, Darden Sch., Univ. of Virginia, 2009–15. FRSA 2006. *Address*: Palamon Capital Partners LLP, 33 King Street, St James's, SW1Y 6RJ. *T*: (020) 7766 2000. *Clubs*: Alfred's, Buck's, Pilgrims, White's, 5 Hertford Street; Brook, Links, University (NY).

**ELSTEIN, David Keith**; Chairman, Open Democracy, since 2010; *b* 14 Nov. 1944; *s* of late Albert Elstein and Millie Cohen; *m*; one *s*. *Educ*: Haberdashers' Aske's; Gonville and Caius Coll., Cambridge (BA, MA; Hon. Fellow, 2016). BBC, 1964–68; ITV, 1968–82; founded Brook Prodns, 1982; Man. Dir, Primetime Television, 1983–86; Dir of Programmes, Thames Television, 1986–92; Hd of Programmes, BSkyB, 1993–96; Chief Exec., Channel 5 Broadcasting, 1996–2000. Visiting Professor: Univ. of Oxford, 1999; Univ. of Westminster, 2001–04; Univ. of Stirling, 2002–07. Beesley Lectr, 2009. Chairman: Nat. Film and Television Sch., 1996–2002; British Screen Adv. Council, 1997–2008; Really Useful Theatres, 2001–06; Screen Digest Ltd, 2004–10; Commercial Radio Companies Assoc., 2004–06; Sparrowhawk Investments Ltd, 2004–07; DCD Media (formerly Digital Classics), 2005–10; Luther Pendragon Hldgs, 2006–10; Vice-Chm., Kingsbridge Capital Ltd (formerly Hardt Gp (UK)), 2003–17; non-executive Director: Virgin Media (formerly NTL), 2003–08; Orion Holdings, 2006–09; Primacom AG, 2008–10. Chm., Broadcasting Policy Gp, 2003–. Writer and Producer: audio drama, July 1914: Countdown To War, 2015; audio drama, 1918: Countdown To Peace, 2018; associate producer, film, Ida, 2013. Chm., Develt Bd, Gonville and Caius Coll., Cambridge, 2008–. *Recreations*: film, theatre, bridge, reading.

**ELSTON, Christopher David**; Chief Executive, London Bullion Market Association, 1995–99; *b* 1 Aug. 1938; *s* of Herbert Cecil Elston and Ada Louisa (*née* Paige); *m* 1964, Jennifer Isabel Rampling; one *s* two *d*. *Educ*: University Coll. Sch., Hampstead; King's Coll., Cambridge (BA Classics, 1960, MA 1980); Yale Univ. (MA Econs, 1967). Bank of England, 1960–95: seconded to Bank for Internat. Settlements, Basle, Switzerland, 1969–71; Private Sec. to Governor of Bank of England, 1974–76; Asst to Chief Cashier, 1976–79; seconded to HM Diplomatic Service, as Counsellor (Financial), British Embassy, Tokyo, 1979–83; Advr, later Sen. Advr (Asia and Australasia), 1983–94. Advr, KorAm Bank London Br., 1995–2000. Ordinary Mem. Council and Chm. Business Gp, Japan Soc., 1997–2000. *Recreations*: music, garden, photography. *Address*: 23 Grasmere Avenue, Harpenden, Herts AL5 5PT. *T*: (01582) 760147.

**ELSWORTH, Prof. Yvonne Patricia**, PhD; FRS 2015; Professor of Helioseismology and Poynting Professor of Physics, University of Birmingham. *Educ*: Victoria Univ. of Manchester (BSc Hons Physics 1970; PhD 1976). Sch. of Physics and Astronomy, Univ. of Birmingham, 1984–. Mem., REF Physics Panel, 2011–. Mem. Council, US Solar Observatory, 2008–; Mem., Oversight Cttee, Kiepenheuer-Inst. für Sonnenphysik, Freiburg, 2010–. Royal Astronomical Society: Founder and Chm., Status of Women in Astronomy and Geophysics Cttee; Mem. Council, 2011–. Mem., Women in Physics Cttee, Inst. of Physics. Payne Gaposchkin Medal, Inst. of Physics, 2011. *Publications*: contribs to scientific jls incl. Astronomy and Astrophysics, Nature, Science. *Address*: School of Physics and Astronomy, University of Birmingham, Edgbaston, Birmingham B15 2TT.

**ELSY, Richard Peter, (Dick)**, CBE 2018; Chief Executive Officer, High Value Manufacturing Catapult, since 2012; *b* South Shields, 1959; *s* of Raymond Elsy and Rebecca Elsy; *m* 1984, Margaret Gale; one *d*. *Educ*: Durham Sch.; Loughborough Univ. (BTech). CEng 1991; FIMechE 2004; FIET 2016. Land Rover: Develt Engr, 1983–85; Principal Engr, 1985–86; Engrg Manager, 1986–89; Chief Engr, 1989–91; Product Dir, 1991–93; Project Dir, 1993–98; Project Dir, BMW AG, 1999; Engrg Dir, Jaguar Cars, 1999–2003; CEO, Torotrak plc, 2003–12. Dir, Rover Australia, 1997–99. Mem., STFC, 2018–. Dir and Trustee, Engrg and Technol. Bd, 2004–10; Director: AIRTO, 2015–; Henry Royce Inst., 2017–; Mem. Bd, Eur. Assoc. of Res. and Technol. Orgns, 2018–. Chm., Crescent (HiNA) Mgt Ltd. Chm., Hampton in Arden Wine Soc. Liveryman, Engineers' Co., 2017–. Silver Medal, RAEng, 1998. *Recreations*: ski-ing, shooting, gardening, fine wine, antiques, art and design. *Address*: High Value Manufacturing Catapult, The Regus Building, Blythe Valley Business Park, Shirley, Solihull B90 8AG. *T*: (01564) 711529. *E*: dick.elsy@hvm.catapult.org.uk.

**ELTOM, Mohammed Abdalla Ali**; Ambassador of the Republic of Sudan to the Court of St James's, since 2014; *b* Annuhoud, Sudan, 10 Nov. 1963; *s* of Abdalla Ali Eltom and Aysha Mukhtar Abuaagla; *m* 1994, Amani Abuaagla; four *s*. *Educ*: Univ. of Khartoum (BSc Econs, Econ. and Pol Sci.); Post Grad. Dip. Internat. Relns); Juba Univ. (MSc Peace and Develt Studies). Entered Min. of Foreign Affairs, Sudan, 1988; Second Secretary: Abu Dhabi, 1990–92; Amman, 1993–95; First Sec., Damascus, 1995–97; First Sec. and Counsellor, Min. of Foreign Affairs, Sudan, 1997–2001; Counsellor i/c Congressional Affairs, Washington, 2001–05; Amer. Affairs Dept, Min. of Foreign Affairs, Sudan, 2005–08; Minister Plenipotentiary, 2008–10; Dep. Hd of Mission, 2010–12, UK. *Recreations*: reading, walking, watching football. *Address*: Embassy of the Republic of Sudan, 3 Cleveland Row, SW1A 1DD. *T*: (020) 7839 8080. *E*: info@sudan-embassy.co.uk.

**ELTON**, family name of **Baron Elton**.

**ELTON**, 2nd Baron *cr* 1934, of Headington; **Rodney Elton**, TD 1970; a Deputy Speaker, House of Lords, 1999–2008; *b* 2 March 1930; *s* of 1st Baron Elton and of Dedi (*d* 1977), *d* of Gustav Hartmann, Oslo; *S* father, 1973; *m* 1st, 1958, Anne Frances (separated 1973; marr. diss. 1979), *e d* of late Brig. R. A. G. Tilney, CBE, DSO, TD; one *s* three *d*; 2nd, 1979, (Susan) Richenda (DCVO 2010), *y d* of late Sir Hugh Gurney, KCMG, MVO, and Lady Gurney. *Educ*: Dragon Sch., Oxford; Eton; New Coll., Oxford (MA). Farming, 1954–64. Assistant Master: Loughborough Grammar Sch., 1964–67; Fairham Comprehensive School for Boys, Nottingham, 1967–69; Lectr, Bishop Lonsdale College of Education, 1969–72. Contested (C) Leics, Loughborough, 1966, 1970. Cons. Whip, House of Lords, Feb. 1974–76, an Opposition spokesman, 1976–79; Parly Under Sec. of State, NI Office, 1979–81, DHSS, 1981–82, Home Office, 1982–84; Minister of State: Home Office, 1984–85; DoE, 1985–86. House of Lords: Mem., Delegated Powers Scrutiny Cttee, 1993–96; a Dep. Chm. of Cttees, 1997–2008; elected Mem., 1999; Member: Lord Privy Seal's Cttee on Neill Report, 2001; Offices Select Cttee, 2001–02; Select Cttee on the Constitution, 2002–07; Jt Ecclesiastical Cttee, H of L and H of C, 2002–. Mem. Exec. Cttee, Assoc. of Cons. Peers, 1986–93, 1994–97, 2001–03 (Dep. Chm., 1991–93). Chm., FIMBRA, 1987–90; Mem., Panel on Takeovers and Mergers, 1987–90. Formerly Director: Overseas Exhibition Services Ltd; Building Trades Exhibition Ltd. Dep. Chm., Andry Montgomery Ltd, 1978–79 and 1986–2001. Dep. Sec., Cttee on Internat. Affairs, Synod of C of E, 1976–78. Licensed Lay Minister, Oxford dio., C of E, 1998–. Mem. Boyd Commn to evaluate elections in Rhodesia, 1979; Chm., Cttee of Enquiry into discipline in schools, 1988. Chm., Intermediate Treatment Fund, 1990–93; Vice-Pres., Inst. of Trading Standards Administrators, 1990–; Member of Council: CGLI, 1987–91 (Chm., Quality and Standards Cttee, 1999–2005; Hon. FCGI 2005); Rainer Foundn, 1990–96; Founding Chm., DIVERT Trust, 1993–2001; Pres., Building Conservation Trust, 1990–95; Trustee: City Parochial Foundn, 1990–97; Trust for London, 1990–97. Late Captain, Queen's Own Warwickshire and Worcs Yeo.; late Major, Leics and Derbys (PAO) Yeo. Lord of the Manor of Adderbury, Oxon, 1973. *Heir: s* Hon. Edward Paget Elton [*b* 28 May 1966; *m* 2004, Claire Helen Pauline, *y d* of Sir Morgan O'Connell, 6th Bt; one *s*]. *Address*: House of Lords, SW1A 0PW. *Clubs*: Pratt's, Beefsteak, Cavalry and Guards.
*See also* Lord Gray.

**ELTON, Benjamin Charles**; author and performer; *b* 3 May 1959; *s* of late Prof. Lewis Richard Benjamin Elton and of (Kathleen) Mary Elton (*née* Foster); *m* 1994, Sophie Gare; two *s* one *d* (of whom one *s* one *d* are twins). *Educ*: Godalming Grammar Sch.; S Warwicks Coll. of Further Educn; Manchester Univ. (BA Drama). First professional appearance, Comic Strip Club, 1981; writer for television: Happy Families, 1985; Filthy Rich and Catflap, 1986; The Thin Blue Line, 1995, 1996; jointly: The Young Ones, 1982, 1984; Blackadder II, 1987; Blackadder the Third, 1988; Blackadder goes Forth, 1989; Upstart Crow, 2016–18; writer and performer: Friday Live, 1987–88; Saturday Live, 1986–87, 1988; The Man from Auntie, 1990, 1994; Stark, 1993; The Ben Elton Show, 1998; Get A Grip, 2007; writer and director: Silly Cow, Theatre Royal, Haymarket, 1991; Maybe Baby (film), 2000; We Will Rock You (musical), 2002; Tonight's the Night (musical), Victoria Palace, 2003; Blessed (TV), 2005; Three Summers (film), 2018; writer: Gasping, Theatre Royal, Haymarket, 1990; Popcorn, Apollo, 1997; The Beautiful Game (musical), 2000; (jtly) Love Never Dies (book of musical), 2010; All is True (film), 2019; actor: Much Ado About Nothing (film), 1993; numerous tours as a stand-up comic, 1986, 1987, 1989, 1993, 1996–97, 2005–06, 2019. Hon. Dr Manchester. *Publications: novels*: Stark, 1989; Gridlock, 1991; This Other Eden, 1993; Popcorn, 1996; Blast from the Past, 1998; Inconceivable, 1999; Dead Famous, 2001; High Society, 2002; Past Mortem, 2004; The First Casualty, 2005; Chart Throb, 2006; Blind Faith, 2007; Meltdown, 2009; Two Brothers, 2012; Time And Time Again, 2014; Identity Crisis, 2019; *plays*: Gasping, 1990; Silly Cow, 1991; Popcorn, 1996; Blast from the Past, 1998. *Recreations*: walking, reading, drinking, cutting firewood, Sunday lunch. *Address*: c/o Phil McIntyre, 3rd Floor, 85 Newman Street, W1T 3EU. *Club*: Groucho.

**ELTON, Sir Charles (Abraham Grierson)**, 11th Bt *cr* 1717; film and television producer; writer; *b* 23 May 1953; *s* of Sir Arthur Hallam Rice Elton, 10th Bt, and Margaret Ann (*d* 1995), *d* of Olafur Bjornson; *S* father, 1973; *m* 1990, Lucy Lauris (*see* L. L. Heller) (marr. diss. 2007), *d* of late Lukas Heller; one *s* one *d*. *Educ*: Eton Coll.; Reading Univ. Publishing, 1976–79; BBC, 1979–84; Director: Curtis Brown, 1984–91; First Choice Productions, 1991–2000; Exec. Producer, Carlton Television, subseq. ITV Productions, 2000–08. *Publications*: Mr Toppitt, 2009; The Songs, 2017. *Heir: s* Abraham William Elton, *b* 27 Sept. 1995. *Address*: Clevedon Court, Somerset BS21 6QU. *Club*: Garrick.

**ELVEDEN, Viscount; Arthur Benjamin Jeffrey Guinness**; *b* 6 Jan. 2003; *s* and *heir* of Earl of Iveagh, *qv*.

**ELVERY, Nathan Dominic**; Chief Executive, West Sussex County Council, since 2016; Clerk to the Lord Lieutenant for West Sussex, since 2017; *b* 2 June 1969; *s* of Patricia Anne Bennett and adopted *s* of Richard William Foote; *m* 2003, Silke Anette Benneckenstein; one *s* two *d*. *Educ*: Thomas Bennett Community Coll., Sussex; NE Surrey Coll. of Technol.; Lewes Tertiary Coll.; Brighton Coll.; CIPFA Educn Trng and Employment Centre. LGA Future Vision Prog. Alumni, 2015–16. MAAT 1991; CIPFA 1995, GPD 2000. Principal consultant, Crawley BC, 1995–2000; Dep. Hd of Core Finance, GLA, 2000–02; Asst Dir, Finance and Business Mgt, Westminster CC, 2002–04; London Borough of Croydon: Dir of Finance, 2004–05; Dir of Finance and Resources, 2005–07; Exec. Dir of Resources and Customer Services, 2008–11; Dep. Chief Exec. and Exec. Dir of Corporate Resources and Customer Services, 2011–13; Interim Chief Exec., 2013–14; Chief Exec., 2014–16. Chief Exec., London Councils, 2013–16; Chairman: London Authorities Mutual Ltd, 2007–09; Croydon Enterprise Loans Fund Ltd, 2008–13; Croydon Local Strategic Partnership, 2013–16; S London Partnership Chief Exec. Gp, 2014–16; Croydon Strategic Metropolitan Bd, 2014–16; Dep. Chm., Capital Ambition Efficiency Bd, 2008; Member, Board: London Finance Adv. Cttee, 2005–13; CCURV Ltd, 2008–12; Assoc. of Local Authorities Treasurers, 2011–13 (Pres., 2012–13); Mem., Local Govt Reference Panel, 2013–. Local Government Association: Mem., Chief Exec. Sounding Bd, 2013–; Mem., Rotherham Improvement Bd, 2014–16; Chief Exec. Advr, Safer and Stronger Communities Bd, 2015–; Corporate Peer Rev. Lead, 2016–. Member: Soc. of London Treasurers, 2004–13 (Pres., 2011–12); Soc. of Municipal Treasurers, 2004–13; Soc. of Local Authy Chief Execs, 2007– (Evidence-based Policy spokesman, 2019–); 30% Club, 2016–17; Assoc. of County Chief Execs, 2016– (Communities and Health spokesman, 2017–); W Sussex Chief Execs Bd, 2016– (Chair, 2017–). Dir of Finance of the Year for Public and Vol. Sector, Accountancy Age, 2005. *Publications*: articles in Public Finance, Local Govt Chronicle, Municipal Jl, Accountancy Age, PQ Mag., Public Servant, Insurance Times, Daily Mail and The Times. *Recreations*: my family, travelling, running, golf, cycling, motorcycling, charity fund raising. *Address*: West Sussex County Council, County Hall, Chichester PO19 1RQ. *E*: nathan.elvery@westsussex.gov.uk.

**ELVIDGE, Gillian**; *see* Matthews, G.

**ELVIDGE, John Cowie**; QC 2010; *b* Perth, Scotland, 27 Nov. 1964; *s* of late John Elvidge and of Flora Elvidge (*née* Cowie, now Taylor); *m* 1993, Gillian Matthews, *qv*; two *d*. *Educ*: King Edward VII Sch., Sheffield; Univ. of Newcastle upon Tyne (LLB). Called to the Bar, Gray's Inn, 1988, Bencher, 2014. Head: York Chambers, 2011; Dere Street Barristers Chambers, 2011–. Leader, NE Circuit, 2014–16. *Recreations*: sport, cinema, genealogy. *Address*: Dere Street Barristers Chambers, 14 Toft Green, York YO1 6JT. *T*: 0344 3351551; Dere Street Barristers Chambers, 33 Broad Chare, Newcastle upon Tyne NE1 3DQ.

**ELVIDGE, Sir John (William)**, KCB 2006; FRSE; Chairman, Edinburgh Airport, since 2012; *b* 9 Feb. 1951; *s* of Herbert William Elvidge and Irene Teresa Elvidge; *m* 2003, Maureen Margaret Ann McGinn. *Educ*: Sir George Monoux Sch., Walthamstow; St Catherine's Coll., Oxford (BA English Lang. and Lit.). Joined Scottish Office, 1973: Principal, 1978–84; Asst Sec., 1984–88; Dir, Scottish Homes, 1988–89 (on secondment); Asst Sec., 1989–93; Under Sec., 1993–98; Dep. Hd, Econ. and Domestic Secretariat, Cabinet Office, 1998–99 (on secondment); Hd, Educn Dept, 1999–2002, Finance and Central Services Dept, 2002–03, Scottish Exec.; Perm. Sec., Scottish Govt (formerly Scottish Exec.), 2003–10. *Recreations*: painting, film, theatre, music, modern novels, food and wine. *Address*: 6 Sciennes Gardens, Edinburgh EH9 1NR.

**ELVIN, David John**; QC 2000; a Recorder, since 2002; a Deputy High Court Judge, since 2008; *b* 30 April 1960; *s* of Walter and Margaret Elvin; *m* 1985, Helen Julia Shilling. *Educ*: A. J. Dawson Grammar Sch.; Hertford Coll., Oxford (BA 1st Cl. Hons Jurisprudence 1981, BCL 1982). Called to the Bar: Middle Temple, 1983, Bencher 2015; NI, 2009. Asst Comr, 2000–09, Mem., 2009–19, Boundary Commn. Mem. Council, RSCM, 2004–08. Accredited Mediator, 2010. *Publications*: Unlawful Interference with Land, 1995, 2nd edn 2002; (ed jtly) The Planning Encyclopaedia (loose-leaf); contrib. articles to Law Qly Rev., Judicial Rev., Jl of Planning and Envmt Law. *Recreations*: music (playing, singing, listening), opera, history. *Address*: Landmark Chambers, 180 Fleet Street, EC4A 2HG. *T*: (020) 7430 1221.

**ELVIN, Joanne**; Editor, You magazine, Mail on Sunday, since 2018; *b* Sydney, 21 Feb. 1970; *d* of Harry Elvin and Leonie Elvin; *m* 2000, Ross Jones; one *d*. *Educ*: Univ. of Western Sydney. Publicist, TV series, Neighbours, 1992; Dep. Editor, TV Hits mag., 1993–94; Editor: Sugar mag., 1994–96; B mag., 1996–98; New Woman mag., 1998–2000; Glamour mag., 2000–17. *Address*: You magazine, Mail on Sunday, Associated Newspapers Ltd, Northcliffe House, 2 Derry Street, W8 5TT. *Clubs*: Groucho, Soho House.

**ELVIN, Violetta, (Violetta Prokhorova), (Signora Fernando Savarese)**; ballerina; a prima ballerina of Sadler's Wells Ballet, Royal Opera House, London (now The Royal Ballet), 1951–56; Director, Ballet Company, San Carlo Opera, Naples, 1985–87; *b* Moscow, 3 Nov. 1923; *d* of Vassilie Prokhorov, engineer, and Irena Grimouzinskaya, former actress; *m* 1st, 1944, Harold Elvin (divorced 1952), of British Embassy, Moscow; 2nd, 1953, Siegbert J. Weinberger, New York; 3rd, 1959, Fernando Savarese, lawyer; one *s*. *Educ*: Bolshoi Theatre Sch., Moscow. Trained for ballet since age of 8 by: E. P. Gerdt, A. Vaganova, M. A. Kojuchova. Grad, 1942, as soloist; made mem. Bolshoi Theatre Ballet; evacuated to Tashkent, 1943; ballerina Tashkent State Theatre; rejoined Bolshoi Theatre at Kuibishev again as soloist, 1944; left for London, 1945. Joined Sadler's Wells Ballet at Covent Garden as guest-soloist, 1946; later became regular mem. Has danced all principal rôles, notably, Le Lac des Cygnes, Sleeping Beauty, Giselle, Cinderella, Sylvia, Ballet Imperial, etc. Danced four-act Le Lac des Cygnes, first time, 1943; guest-artist Stanislavsky Theatre, Moscow, 1944, Sadler's Wells Theatre, 1947; guest-prima ballerina, La Scala, Milan, Nov. 1952–Feb. 1953 (Macbeth, La Gioconda, Swan Lake, Petrouchka); guest artist, Cannes, July 1954; Copenhagen, Dec. 1954; Teatro Municipal, Rio de Janeiro, May 1955 (Giselle, Swan Lake, Les Sylphides, Nutcracker, Don Quixote and The Dying Swan); Festival Ballet, Festival Hall, 1955; guest-prima ballerina in Giselle, Royal Opera House, Stockholm (Anna Pavlova Memorial), 1956; concluded stage career when appeared in Sleeping Beauty, Royal Opera House, Covent Garden, June 1956. *Appeared in films*: The Queen of Spades, Twice Upon a Time, Melba. Television appearances in Russia and England. Has toured with Sadler's Wells Ballet, France, Italy, Portugal, United States and Canada. *Recreations*: reading, painting, swimming. *Address*: Hotel Le Axidie, Via Marina di Equa, 80069 Vico Equense, Napoli, Italy.

**ELWEN, His Honour Christopher**; a Circuit Judge, 1995–2011; Resident Judge, Truro Combined Courts, 2008–11; *b* 14 Sept. 1944; *s* of Kenneth Spence Elwen and Joan Marie Elwen; *m* 1967, Susan Elizabeth Allan; one *s* one *d*. *Educ*: Quarry Bank High Sch., Liverpool; Univ. of Liverpool (LLB). Called to the Bar, Gray's Inn, 1969; Wm Brandts Sons & Co. Ltd, 1970–72; Cripps Warburg Ltd, 1972–75; Holman Fenwick & Willan, 1975–89; admitted solicitor, 1976; Stephenson Harwood, 1989–95; a Recorder, 1993–95. *Recreations*: golf, mediaeval history, walking. *Address*: Dunvegan, Carlton Road, W5 2AW. *Club*: Garrick.

**ELWES, Sir Henry (William George)**, KCVO 2009; JP; Lord-Lieutenant of Gloucestershire, 1992–2010; *b* 24 Oct. 1935; *s* of John Hargreaves Elwes, MC, Major, Scots Guards (killed in action, N Africa, 1943) and late Isabel Pamela Ivy Beckwith, *g d* of 7th Duke of Richmond and Gordon, KG, GCVO, CB; *m* 1962, Carolyn Dawn Cripps; two *s* (and one *s* decd). *Educ*: Eton; RAC, Cirencester (Hon. Fellow, 2009). FRAC 2010. Served Army, Lieut, Scots Guards, 1953–56. Member: Cirencester RDC, 1959–74; Glos CC, 1970–91 (Vice-Chm., 1976–83 and 1991; Chm., 1983–85). Regl Dir, Lloyds Bank, 1985–91. Mem., Nat. Jt Council for Fire Brigades, 1979–91; Director: Colesbourne Estate Co., 1969–; Cirencester Friendly Soc. (formerly Cirencester Benefit Soc. Trustee Co.) Ltd, 1974–2000. Pres., Western Woodland Owners Ltd, 1986–2003 (Chm., 1972–86). Pro Chancellor, Univ. of Gloucestershire, 2012–. Patron, Pres. and Mem. of many Glos trusts and societies. Gloucestershire: High Sheriff, 1979–80; DL 1982; JP 1992; Hon. Alderman, 1992. Liveryman, Gardeners' Co., 2004–. Warden Emeritus, Hon. Co. of Glos, 2001. Hon. Lay Canon, Gloucester Cathedral, 2001–. Hon. DPhil Gloucestershire, 2002; Hon. LLD UWE, 2006. Confrérie des Chevaliers du Tastevin. KStJ 1992. *Address*: The Dower House, Colesbourne Park, near Cheltenham, Glos GL53 9NP.

**ELWES, Sir Jeremy (Vernon)**, Kt 1994; CBE 1984; Chairman, St Helier NHS Trust, 1990–99; *b* 29 May 1937; *s* of late Eric Vincent Elwes and Dorothea Elwes, OBE (*née* Bilton); *m* 1963, Phyllis Marion Relf, 2nd *d* of late George Herbert Harding Relf and Rose Jane Relf (*née* Luery); one *s*. *Educ*: Wirral Grammar Sch.; Bromley Grammar Sch.; City of London Coll. ACIS 1963. Technical Journalist, Heywood & Co., 1958–62; Accountant and Co. Sec., Agricultural Press, 1962–70; Sec. and Dir, East Brackland Hill Farming Development Co., 1967–70; IPC Business Press: Pensions Officer, 1966–70; Divl Personnel Manager, 1970–73; Manpower Planning Manager, 1973–78; Exec. Dir (Manpower), 1978–82; Personnel Dir, Business Press Internat., then Reed Business Publishing, 1982–93; Human Resources Dir, Reed Publishing Europe, 1993–94. Director: Periodicals Trng Council, 1986–92; Sutton Enterprise Agency Ltd, 1987–94 (Chm., 1987–90). Chairman: Cons. Political Centre Nat. Adv. Cttee, 1981–84; Cons. SE Area, 1986–90; Mem., Nat. Union Exec. Cttee, 1972–94; Co-ordinator, Specialist Gps, Cons. Pty, 2000–13; Hon. Sec., Cons. Med. Soc., 1996–2000; Pres., Sevenoaks Cons. Assoc., 2007–09. Mem. Exec. Cttee, GBGSA, 1996–99, 2000–03; Dir and Trustee, Eur. Sch. of Osteopathy, 1999–2007. Pres., Sevenoaks Div., 2000–13, Dep. County Pres., Kent, 2001–, St John Ambulance. Chm. of Governors, Walthamstow Hall, 1984–2003, now Gov. Emeritus, 2003. FRSA 1994. Liveryman: Stationers' and Newspapermakers' Co., 1991– (Master and Wardens Cttee, 1999–2002; Chm., Livery Cttee, 2000–02; Livery Rep.,

2005–07; Mem. Ct Assts, 2007–10; Chm., Hall and Heritage Cttee, 2008–10]; Chartered Secretaries' and Administrators' Co., 2003–12 (Sec., 2005–06, Chm., 2006–11, Livery Liaison Gp). Member Council: Imperial Soc. of Kts Bachelor, 2002– (Treas., 2012–17; Registrar, 2016–18; Knight Vice-Pres., 2018–); Printers' Charitable Corp., 2002–08 (Pres., 2004; Dep. Chm., 2005–06, Chm., 2006–08; Pres. Emeritus, 2009); Hospice in the Weald, 2003–11; Foundn for Liver Res., 2005–. OStJ 2009. Chevalier, Ordre des Chevaliers Bretvins (Chancelier to 1992); Kt, Habsburg-Lothringen Order of St George, 2016. *Recreations:* wine and food, reading, walking, golf. *Address:* Crispian Cottage, Weald Road, Sevenoaks, Kent TN13 1QQ. *T:* (01732) 454208. *Clubs:* City Livery; Nizels Golf and Leisure (Captain, Veterans, 1998–99).

**ELWOOD, Sir Brian (George Conway),** Kt 1990; CBE 1985; Chairman, Kiwifruit New Zealand, 2004–15; *b* 5 April 1933; *s* of Jack Philip Elwood and Enid Mary Elwood; *m* 1956, Dawn Beverley Elwood (*née* Ward); one *s* two *d*. *Educ:* Victoria Univ., Wellington (LLB); Trinity Coll., London (ATCL). Barrister and Solicitor, 1957–92. Ombudsman, 1992–94; Chief Ombudsman of NZ, 1994–2003. Chairman: Local Govt Commn, NZ, 1985–92; Survey Industry Review Commn, 1990–92; Comr, Wellington Area Health Bd, 1990–92. Mayor, Palmerston North City, 1971–85. Life Mem., Internat. Ombudsman Inst., 2002 (Regl Vice Pres., 1996–98; Internat. Pres., 1999–2002). Mem., Wellington Harbour Bd, 1968–74. Chairman: Age Concern (Wellington) Charitable Trust, 2004–15; Central Energy Trust, 2012–15 (Mem., 2006–15). Hon. Mem., NZ Inst. of Surveyors. Hon. DLitt Massey, 1994. Medal for Distinguished Public Service, Lions Club Internat., 1985; Hayward Medal for Distinguished Service to NZ Kiwifruit Industry, 2015. *Recreations:* golf, fishing, gardening. *Address:* Box 58-193, Whitby 5245, Porirua, New Zealand. *T:* (4) 2341669, (27) 2863342. *Club:* Wellington.

**ELWORTHY, Air Cdre Hon. Sir Timothy (Charles),** KCVO 2001 (CVO 1995); CBE 1986; Her Majesty's Senior Air Equerry, 1995–2001; Director of Royal Travel, 1997–2001; Extra Equerry to the Queen, since 1991; *b* 27 Jan. 1938; *e s* of Marshal of the RAF Baron Elworthy, KG, GCB, CBE, DSO, LVO, DFC, AFC and late Audrey Elworthy; *m* 1st, 1961, Victoria Ann (marr. diss.), *d* of Lt Col H. C. W. Bowring; two *d*; 2nd, 1971, Annabel, *d* of late Reginald Harding, OBE; one *s*. *Educ:* Radley; RAF Coll., Cranwell. CO 29 (Fighter) Sqn, 1975 (Wing Comdr); PSO to AO Commanding-in-Chief, Strike Comd, 1979; CO RAF Stn Leuchars, 1983 (Gp Capt.); RCDS, 1986; Dir, Operational Requirements, (Air), MoD, 1987 (Air Cdre); Captain of The Queen's Flight, 1989–95. QCVSA 1968. *Recreations:* country pursuits, wine, travel. *Address:* Coates House, Swyncombe, Henley-on-Thames, Oxon RG9 6EG. *Club:* Boodle's.

**ELY, 9th Marquess of,** *cr* 1801; **Charles John Tottenham;** Bt 1780; Baron Loftus 1785; Viscount Loftus 1789; Earl of Ely 1794; Baron Loftus (UK) 1801; Director of Admissions (formerly Head of French Department), Strathcona-Tweedsmuir School, Calgary, until 2004; *b* 2 Feb. 1943; *e s* of 8th Marquess of Ely and Katherine Elizabeth (*née* Craig); *S* father, 2006; *m* 1969, Judith Marvelle, *d* of Dr J. J. Porter, FRS, Calgary, Alberta; one *s* one *d*. *Educ:* Trinity Coll. Sch., Port Hope, Ont; Ecole Internationale de Genève; Univ. of Toronto (MA). *Heir: b* Lord Timothy Craig Tottenham [*b* 17 Jan. 1948; *m* 1973, Elizabeth Jane McAllister; two *s*]. *Address:* 153 Chaparral Circle, Calgary, AB T2X 3M2, Canada.

**ELY, Bishop of,** since 2010; **Rt Rev. Stephen David Conway;** *b* 22 Dec. 1957; *s* of late David Conway and of Dorothy Isabella (*née* Jarman, now Lambert). *Educ:* Archbishop Tenison's Grammar Sch., London; Keble Coll., Oxford (BA Mod. Hist. 1980, MA 1984; PGCE 1981); Selwyn Coll., Cambridge (BA Theol. 1985; MA 2005); Westcott House, Cambridge. Asst Master, Glenalmond Coll., 1981–83; ordained deacon, 1986, priest, 1987; Curate: Heworth, 1986–89; Bishopwearmouth, 1989–90; St Margaret, Durham, 1990–94; Diocesan Dir of Ordinands, Durham, 1989–94; Priest i/c, subseq. Vicar, Cockerton, 1994–98; Sen. Chaplain to Bishop of Durham and Diocesan Communications Officer, 1998–2002; Archdeacon of Durham, and Canon Residentiary, Durham Cathedral, 2002–06; Area Bishop of Ramsbury, 2006–10. Entered H of L, 2014. Mem., Gen. Synod of C of E, 1995–2000. Visitor: Jesus Coll., Cambridge, 2010–; Peterhouse, Cambridge, 2010–; St John's Coll., Cambridge, 2010–; Soc. of Sacred Mission, 2014–. Chairman: Develt and Appts, Gp of Hse of Bishops, 2011–14; Nat. Soc. Council of C of E, 2014–; Mem., Archbishops' Council, 2015–. Trustee, Affirming Catholicism, 2001–08 (Chm., Exec., 1997–2003; Vice Pres., 2008–). Chm., Bd of Trustees, Mental Health Matters, 2004–10. Member: Church Leaders Gp, L'Arche UK, 2009–; Internat. Church Leaders Gp, L'Arche Community, 2013–; C of E Rep., Faith and Order Commn, World Council of Churches, 2014–. Episcopal Visitor, Co. of Servers 2010–. Chm. Council, Westcott House, Cambridge, 2012–19; Mem. Council, Radley Coll., 2014–17. *Publications:* (ed) Living the Eucharist, 2001; (contrib.) This is Our Calling, 2004; (contrib.) The Vicar's Guide, 2005; (ed) Generous Ecclesiology: towards a generous ecclesiology, 2013; (contrib.) A Good Year, 2016; (contrib.) Preaching Radical and Orthodox, 2017. *Recreations:* walking, cinema, wine, travel, books. *Address:* Bishop's House, Ely, Cambs CB7 4DW. *T:* (01353) 662749. *E:* bishop@elydiocese.org. *Clubs:* Athenæum, Nobody's Friends, Nikaean; Cambridge County.

**ELY, Dean of;** *see* Bonney, Very Rev. M. P. J.

**ELY, Archdeacon of;** *see* Beer, Ven. J. S., Archdeacon of Cambridge.

**ELY, Keith;** *see* Ely, S. K.

**ELY, Philip Thomas,** OBE 2003; Chairman, Legal Services Commission, 2003–04; *b* 22 March 1936; *s* of Eric Stanley Ely and Rose Josephine Ely; *m* 1966, Diana Mary (*née* Gellibrand); two *s* three *d*. *Educ:* Douai Sch.; LLB (external) London Univ. Admitted Solicitor, 1958. National Service, RN, 1958–60 (commnd, 1959). Articled Hepherd Winstanley & Pugh, Southampton, 1953–58; joined Paris Smith & Randall, Southampton, as Asst Solicitor, 1960; Partner, 1961–98, Sen. Partner, 1981–98. Law Society: Mem. Council, 1979–93; Vice-Pres., 1990–91; Pres., 1991–92; Hampshire Incorporated Law Society: Asst Hon. Sec., 1961–66; Hon. Sec., 1966–74; Hon. Treasurer, 1974–79; Pres., 1979. Appointed by HM Treasury to conduct enquiry into powers of Inland Revenue to call for papers of tax accountants, 1994. Mem., Legal Services Commn (formerly Legal Aid Bd), 1996–2004 (Chm., Regl Legal Services Cttees, Reading, 1998–2002, London, 1998–2003); Chm., Police Disciplinary Appeals Tribunal, 1996–2003. Hon. LLD Southampton, 1992. *Recreations:* fly-fishing, gardening, music, reading. *Address:* Orchard Cottage, Crawley, Winchester, Hants SO21 2PR. *T:* (01962) 776379.

**ELY, (Sydney) Keith;** writer; *b* 17 April 1949; *s* of Charles Rodenhurst Ely and Dorothy Mary Ely (*née* Rowlands); *m* 1st, 1970, Patricia Davies (marr. diss. 1994); three *d*; 2nd, 1994, Jo Ann Beroiz. *Educ:* Maghull Grammar Sch.; Open Univ. (BA). Journalist: Liverpool Daily Post & Echo, 1968–78; Reuters, 1978–80; Daily Post, Liverpool: Business Editor, 1980–84; Acting Asst Editor, 1984; Systems Develt, 1985–86; Features Editor, 1987; Dep. Editor, 1987; Editor, 1989–95; Man. Dir, Trinity Weekly Newspapers Ltd, 1995–96; Editor and Gen. Manager, Channel One TV, Liverpool, 1996–97; Regl Ops Dir, Liverpool Daily Post & Echo Ltd, 1998–2000 (Dir, 1998–95 and 1998–2000); Man. Dir, Corporate Culture Plc, 2000–01 (Dir, 1988, 2000). Owner, Keith Ely Media Services, 2002–. *Recreations:* music, computing. *Address:* Medford, OR 97504, USA.

**ELYSTAN-MORGAN,** family name of **Baron Elystan-Morgan**.

**ELYSTAN-MORGAN,** Baron *cr* 1981 (Life Peer), of Aberteifi in the County of Dyfed; **His Honour Dafydd Elystan Elystan-Morgan;** a Circuit Judge, 1988–2003; *b* 7 Dec. 1932; *s* of late Dewi Morgan and late Mrs Olwen Morgan; *m* 1959, Alwen (*d* 2006), *d* of William E. Roberts; one *s* one *d*. *Educ:* Ardwyn Grammar Sch., Aberystwyth; UCW, Aberystwyth. LLB Hons Aberystwyth, 1953. Research at Aberystwyth and Solicitor's Articles, 1953–57; admitted a Solicitor, 1957; Partner in N Wales (Wrexham) Firm of Solicitors, 1958–68; Barrister-at-law, Gray's Inn, 1971; a Recorder, 1983–87. MP (Lab) Cardiganshire, 1966–Feb. 1974; Chm., Welsh Parly Party, 1967–68, 1971–74; Parly Under-Secretary of State, Home Office, 1968–70; front-bench spokesman on Home Affairs, 1970–72, on Welsh Affairs, 1972–74, on Legal and Home Affairs, House of Lords, 1981–85. Contested (Lab): Cardigan, Oct. 1974; Anglesey, 1979. President: Welsh Local Authorities Assoc., 1967–73; Parlt for Wales Campaign, 1979. President: Univ. Coll. of Wales, Aberystwyth, subseq. Aberystwyth Univ., 1997–2007; Welsh Sch. of Legal Studies, 1998. Hon. Fellow, Univ. of Wales, Aberystwyth, 1992. Elder, Presbyterian Church of Wales, 1971–. *Address:* Carreg Afon, Dolau, Bow Street, Dyfed SY24 5AE.

**EMANUEL, David,** FCSD; fashion designer; *b* 17 Nov. 1952; *s* of John Lawrence Morris Emanuel and late Elizabeth Emanuel; *m* 1975, Elizabeth Florence Weiner (*see* E. F. Emanuel) (separated 1990; marr. diss. 2008); one *s* one *d*. *Educ:* Cardiff Coll. of Art (Diploma); Harrow Sch. of Art (Diploma); Royal College of Art (MA). Final Degree show at RCA, 1977. Emanuel (couture business) commenced in Mayfair, W1, 1977, Jt Partner/Dir, 1977–90; The Emanuel Shop (retail), London, SW3, 1986–90; ready-to-wear business partnership in USA, 1988; formed: David Emanuel Couture, 1990; Licensed to Design Ltd, 2002; launched David Emanuel for Clogau Gold, jewellery collection, 2017. Designed: wedding gown for the Princess of Wales, 1981; ballet productions, incl. Frankenstein, the Modern Prometheus, Royal Opera House, Covent Garden, 1985 and La Scala, Milan, 1987; uniforms for Virgin Atlantic Airways, 1990; prodns for theatre, film, TV and operatic recitals. Television presenter: fashion shows, 1994–; (and Creative Dir) Say Yes to the Dress: UK, 2016–17; runner-up, I'm a Celebrity Get Me Out of Here, 2013. Ambassador for Macmillan Cancer Support, 2014–. FCSD (FSIAD 1984). Hon. FRWCMD (Hon. FWCMD 2000). *Publications:* (with Elizabeth Emanuel): Style for All Seasons, 1983; A Dress for Diana, 2006. *Recreations:* singing at private charity concerts, keeping doves, gardening. *T:* (David Emanuel Couture) 07885 380798. *E:* david@davidemanuel.com, (agent/brand manager) seamus@seamuslyte.com.

**EMANUEL, Elizabeth Florence,** FCSD; fashion designer; *b* 5 July 1953; *d* of Samuel Charles Weiner and Brahna Betty Weiner; *m* 1975, David Emanuel, *qv* (separated 1990; marr. diss. 2008); one *s* one *d*. *Educ:* City of London Sch. for Girls; Harrow Sch. of Art (Diploma with Hons); Royal Coll. of Art (MA 1977; DesRCA 1977). FCSD 1984. Emanuel (couture) commenced in Mayfair, W1, 1977; The Emanuel Shop (retail), London, SW3, 1986–90; launched internat. fashion label, Elizabeth Emanuel, 1991; set up Elizabeth Emanuel Enterprises, 1999; designer, Luxury Brand Gp, 2001–02; started new label: Art of Being, Little Venice, 2005–; launched luxury couture brand, Elizabeth, 2019. Designed: wedding gown for the Princess of Wales, 1981; advertisement campaigns for Estee Lauder with Elizabeth Hurley, 1997 and 1998; range of wedding dresses for: Berkertex, 1995; BHS, 2008; Takami Bridal, Japan, 2014–; Little Black Dress Collection, 2010; Chocolate Couture Collection, 2013; Paris 1902, 2019; ballet productions, incl. Frankenstein, the Modern Prometheus, Royal Opera House, Covent Garden, 1985 and La Scala, Milan, 1987; costumes for films: The Changeling, 1995; RosBeef, 2004; Metamorphosis, 2006; uniforms for: Virgin Atlantic Airways, 1990; Britannia Airways, 1995; prodns for theatre and operatic recitals. *Publications:* (with David Emanuel): Style for All Seasons, 1983; A Dress for Diana, 2006. *Recreations:* ballet, films, writing children's books, supporting animal charities. *Address:* Garden Studio, 51 Maida Vale, W9 1SD. *T:* (020) 7289 4545.

**EMBERTON, Prof. Mark,** MD; FRCS; Professor of Interventional Oncology, since 2010, and Dean, Faculty of Medical Sciences, since 2015, University College London; *b* Edinburgh, 16 Oct. 1960; *s* of Stephen Ewart and Esther Emberton; *m* Leah Byrne; two *d*. *Educ:* St Boniface's Coll., Plymouth; St Mary's Hosp. Med. Sch., London (BSc 1983; MB BS 1985); Univ. of London (MD 1997). FRCS 1990. Higher Surgical Trainee, N London Scheme, 1994–98; Hon. Consultant Urologist, University Coll. Hosp. NHS Foundn Trust, 1998–; Dir, Div. of Surgery and Interventional Sci., UCL, 2012–15. FMedSci 2016. *Publications:* over 300 articles in peer-reviewed jls in field of early prostate cancer. *Recreations:* reading, running, ski-ing, cooking, travel. *E:* m.emberton@ucl.ac.uk.

**EMBLEY, Lloyd William;** Editor-in-Chief, Daily Mirror and Sunday Mirror, since 2012; *b* Birmingham, 16 March 1966; *s* of David Embley and Elizabeth Jennings; *m* 1998, Soraya Khan; one *s* one *d*. *Educ:* Malvern Coll. Daily Mirror: Associate Night Ed., 1999–2001; Night Ed., 2001–04; Asst Ed., 2004–08; Ed., The People, 2008–12. *Recreations:* golf, ski-ing, wine and wine books, cooking and cook books. *Address:* Mirror, 1 Canada Square, Canary Wharf, E14 5AP. *Clubs:* Royal Cinque Ports Golf, Press Golfing Society; Ski of GB.

**EMBREY, Derek Morris,** OBE 1986; CEng, FIMechE; Technical Director, Streamwatch Ltd, 2004–10; Chairman, Turnock Ltd (formerly George Turnock Ltd), 1998–2000; Group Technical Director, AB Electronic Products Group PLC, 1973–91; *b* 11 March 1928; *s* of Frederick and Ethel Embrey; *m* 1st, 1951, Frances Margaret Stephens (marr. diss. 1995); one *s* one *d*; 2nd, 1999, Jean McKay Stevens, *d* of late Norman McKay Fairgrieve. *Educ:* Wolverhampton Polytechnic (Hon. Fellow, 1987). Chief Designer (Electronics), Electric Construction Co. Ltd, 1960–65, Asst Manager Static Plant, 1965–69; Chief Engineer, Abergas Ltd, 1969–73. Member: Engineering Council, 1982–87; Welsh Industrial Develt Adv. Bd, 1982–85; NACCB, 1985–87; Council, IERE, 1984–88 (Vice Pres., 1985–88); National Electronics Council, 1985–99; Welsh Adv. Bd, 1986–90 (Chm., 1987–90). Vis. Prof., Univ. of Technology, Loughborough, 1978–84 (External Examr, Dept of Mechanical Engrg, 1984–88); Visiting Lecturer: Loughborough Univ., 1988–97; Birmingham Univ., 1989–2000. Member: Council, UWIST, Cardiff, 1984–88; Bd, Inst. of Transducer Technol., Southampton Univ., 1986–2000; Council, IEE, 1992–95 (Chm., Management and Design Divl Bd, 1993–94); Air Cadet Council, 1988–95; Regl Civilian Chm., ATC, Wales, 1988–95; Dir and Mem. Council, BTEC, 1993–96. Freeman, City of London, 1986; Liveryman, Scientific Instrument Makers' Co., 1986–; founder Liveryman, Livery Co. of Wales (formerly Welsh Livery Guild), 1994–. Hon. Fellow UWIC, 1992. *Recreations:* fondly remembering flying and navigating powered aircraft and gliders; music, English history, archaeology, amateur radio communication (M0 GTN), family history research. *Address:* 21 Rockfield Glade, Penhow, Caldicot, Monmouthshire NP26 3JF. *T:* (01633) 400995. *Club:* Royal Air Force.

**EMBUREY, John Ernest;** Director of Cricket, Middlesex County Cricket Club, 2006–08 (Director of Coaching, 2001–06); *b* 20 Aug. 1952; *s* of John Alfred Emburey and Rose Alice Emburey (*née* Roff); *m* 1980, Susan Elizabeth Anne Booth; two *d*. *Educ:* Peckham Manor. Professional cricketer: Middx CCC, 1971–95; England Test cricketer, 1978–95; 64 Test matches (Captain, 1988); 63 one-day internationals; Manager, England A Team tour to Pakistan, 1995; Chief Coach and Manager, Northants CCC, 1996–98; coach, England A

Team tour, Zimbabwe and S Africa, 1999; player/coach, Berks CCC, 2000. *Publications:* Emburey (autobiog.), 1986; Spinning in a Fast World, 1989. *Recreations:* golf, reading. *Club:* MCC.

**EMERSON, David;** *see* Emerson, J. D.

**EMERSON, Joanna;** *see* Hardy, J.

**EMERSON, (John) David,** CBE 2015; Chief Executive, Association of Charitable Foundations, 2003–17; *b* Pembury, Kent, 7 April 1951; *s* of John Raine Emerson and Evelyn Ethel Emerson (*née* Hedge); *m* 2008, Baroness Pitkeathley, *qv*; one step *s* one step *d*. *Educ:* East Grinstead County Grammar Sch.; University Coll. London (BSc Geog. 1972); Wye Coll., Univ. of London (MSc Landscape Ecol., Design and Maintenance 1973); Webber Douglas Acad. (Postgrad. Dip. Drama 1983). Rural Officer, Cheshire Community Council, 1973–78; Dep. Hd, Rural Dept, NCVO, 1978–82; actor, West End and internat. tours, 1983–89; freelance theatre prodn and stage mgt, 1989–96; Sen. Exec., TMA, 1996–2003. Pt-time tutor, Extra Mural Studies, Univ. of Liverpool, 1975–78. Chair: nitroBEAT Theatre Co. (formerly Nitro Theatre Co.), 2009–17; ACRE, 2014–; Longleigh Foundn, 2019–; Treas., Donors and Foundns Networks in Europe, 2016–17. FRGS 1973. *Publications:* (with Jill Pitkeathley) The Only Child, 1992 (trans. 10 foreign langs); (with Jill Pitkeathley) Age Gap Relationships, 1994. *Recreations:* British orchids and managing a wild flower meadow, walking, music, theatre and tap dance, directing the village pantomime. *E:* david@demerson.co.uk.

**EMERSON, Michael Ronald,** MA; FCA; Associate Senior Research Fellow, Centre for European Policy Studies, Brussels, since 1998; *b* 12 May 1940; *s* of late James Emerson and Priscilla Emerson; *m* 1st, 1966, Barbara Brierley; one *s* two *d*; 2nd, 2000, Elena Prokhorova. *Educ:* Hurstpierpoint Coll.; Balliol Coll., Oxford (MA (PPE)). Price Waterhouse & Co., London, 1962–65; Organisation for Economic Cooperation and Development, Paris: several posts in Develt and Economics Depts, finally as Head of General Economics Div. 1966–73; EEC, Brussels: Head of Division for Budgetary Policy, Directorate-General II, 1973–76; Economic Adviser to President of the Commission, 1977; Dir for Nat. Economies and Economic Trends, 1978–81; Dir for Macroecon. Analyses and Policies, 1981–86; Dir, Economic Evaluation of Community Policies, Directorate-General II, 1987–90; Ambassador and Head of EC Delegn to USSR, subseq. Russia, 1991–96. Fellow, Centre for Internat. Affairs, Harvard Univ., 1985–86; Sen. Res. Fellow, LSE, 1996–98. Hon. DLitt Keele, 1993; Hon. DCL Kent, 1993. *Publications:* (ed) Europe's Stagflation, 1984; What Model for Europe, 1987; The Economics of 1992, 1988; One Market, One Money, 1991; Redrawing the Map of Europe, 1998; Wider Europe Matrix, 2004; (ed) Britain's Future in Europe, 2015; contribs to various economic jls and edited volumes on internat. and European economics. *Address:* CEPS, 1 Place du Congrès, 1000 Brussels, Belgium.

**EMERSON, Dr Peter Albert,** MD; FRCP; Hon. Consultant Physician, Chelsea and Westminster Hospital (formerly Westminster and Charing Cross Hospitals), since 1988; *b* 7 Feb. 1923; *s* of Albert Emerson and Gwendoline (*née* Davy); *m* 1947, Ceris Hood Price (*d* 2016); one *s* one *d*. *Educ:* The Leys Sch., Cambridge; Clare Coll., Univ. of Cambridge (MA); St George's Hosp., Univ. of London (MB, BChir 1947; MD 1954). FRCP 1964; Hon. FACP 1975. House Physician, St George's Hosp., 1947; RAF Med. Bd, 1948–52 (Sqdn Leader); Registrar, later Sen. Registrar, St George's Hosp. and Brompton Hosp., London, 1952–57; Asst Prof. of Medicine, Coll. of Medicine, State Univ. of New York, Brooklyn, USA, 1957–58; Consultant Phys., Westminster Hosp., 1959–88; Civilian Consultant Phys. in Chest Diseases to RN, 1974–88; Dean, Westminster Medical Sch., London, 1981–84. Hon. Consultant Phys., King Edward VII Hosp., Midhurst, 1969–88. Royal Coll. of Physicians: Asst Registrar, 1965–71; Procensor and Censor, 1978–80; Vice-Pres. and Sen. Censor, 1985–86; Mitchell Lectr, 1969. *Publications:* Thoracic Medicine, 1981; The Heart Hunters, 2017; articles in med. jls and chapters in books on thoracic medicine and the application of decision theory and expert systems to clinical medicine. *Address:* 3 Halkin Street, SW1X 7DJ. *T:* (020) 7235 8529. *Clubs:* Royal Air Force, Royal Society of Medicine, Caledonian.

**EMERSON, Richard Martyn;** writer; *b* 19 Dec. 1949; *s* of late Maj. Hugh Emerson and Keyna Emerson (*née* Parson); *m* 1st, 1971, Vanessa Leadam Andrews (marr. diss. 1990); two *s* one *d*; 2nd, 1991, Anne Grenfell Macdonald; one *s* one *d*. *Educ:* Wellington Coll.; Courtauld Inst. of Art, London Univ. (BA Hons). Dep. Conway Librarian, Courtauld Inst. of Art, 1971–73; Res. Asst, Nat. Monuments Record for Scotland, Royal Commn on Ancient and Historical Monuments of Scotland, 1973–78; Principal Inspector of Historic Bldgs, 1978–99; Chief Inspector of Historic Bldgs, 1999–2004, Historic Scotland. Hon. FRIAS 2006. *Publications:* Rhythm & Colour: Hélène Vanel, Loïs Hutton and Margaret Morris, 2018; contribs to architectural history jls and books. *Recreation:* practising contentment by the Mediterranean. *Address:* 4 rue de la Casette, 06570 Saint-Paul, France; 15/6 Tron Square, Edinburgh EH1 1RT. *E:* palazzo-lilo@hotmail.fr.

**EMERSON, Ronald Victor,** CBE 2017; Chairman, Amsterdam Trade Bank, since 2017; *b* Hartlepool, 22 Feb. 1947; *s* of Albert Victor Emerson and Doris Emerson; *m* 1996, Angela Jane Stephenson; four *s*. *Educ:* West Hartlepool Grammar Sch.; Manchester Univ. (BSc); Durham Univ. (MSc); Templeton Coll., Oxford (MLitt); Green Templeton Coll., Oxford (MA). Hd, Commercial Develt Formica Internat., De La Rue Gp, 1970–75; Hd of Banking UK, Northern Europe, Hd of Ops EMEA Div., Bank of America, 1975–89; Dir and Gen. Manager, Nomura Internat., 1989–90; Gp Hd, Corporate Banking, Standard Chartered Bank, 1991–96. Senior Advisor: Bank of England, 1997–2000; FSA, 1997–2000. Chairman: Fairfield Energy, 2010–16; British Business Bank plc, 2013–16; non-executive Director: Premier Oil plc, 2001–08; Ace Eur. Gp Ltd, 2004–12; Specialist Energy Gp plc, 2010–12. Associate Fellow, Said Business Sch., Univ. of Oxford, 1997–; Barclay Fellow, Green Templeton Coll., Oxford, 2014–. FInstD 2012; FRSA. *Recreations:* reading, flying (PPL). *Address:* The Reeds, Remenham Lane, Henley on Thames RG9 3DA. *E:* ronemerson@btinternet.com. *Club:* Oxford and Cambridge.

**EMERTON,** Baroness *cr* 1997 (Life Peer), of Tunbridge Wells in the co. of Kent and of Clerkenwell in the London Borough of Islington; **Audrey Caroline Emerton,** DBE 1989; RGN, RM, RNT; Chief Commander, St John Ambulance, 1998–2002; Chairman, Brighton Health Care NHS Trust, 1994–2000 (Vice Chairman, 1993–94); *b* 10 Sept. 1935; *d* of late George Emerton and Lily (*née* Squirrell). *Educ:* Tunbridge Wells GS; St George's Hosp.; Battersea Coll. of Technol.; Henley Business Sch. Sen. Tutor, Experimental 2 year and 1 year Course, St George's Hosp., SW1, 1965–68; Principal Nursing Officer, Educn, Bromley HMC, 1968–70; Chief Nursing Officer, Tunbridge Wells and Leybourne HMC, 1970–73; Regl Nursing Officer, SE Thames RHA, 1973–91. St John Ambulance, Kent: Co. Nursing Officer, 1967–85; Co. Comr, 1985–88; St John Ambulance: Chief Nursing Officer, 1988–98; Chm. of Med. Bd, 1993–96; Chief Officer, Care in the Community, 1996–97; Chief Officer, Nursing and Social Care, 1997–98. Lay Mem., GMC, 1996–2001. Mem., Prime Minister's Commn on the Future of Nursing and Midwifery, 2009–10. Pres., Assoc. of Nurse Administrators, 1979–82; Hon. Vice-Pres., RCN, 1994–99. Chairman: English Nat. Bd for Nursing, Midwifery and Health Visiting, 1983–85; UKCC, 1985–93; Vice-Pres., Attend (formerly Assoc. of Hosp. and Community Friends), 2008– (Chm., 2003–07); Pres., Florence Nightingale Foundn, 2004–16. Trustee: Kent Community Housing Trust, 1993–99; Defence Med. Welfare Service, 2001–12 (Patron, 2012–). DL Kent, 1992–2010. Hon. Fellow: Christ Church UC, Canterbury, 2003; KCL, 2009. Hon. FRCN 2009. Hon. DCL Kent, 1989; Hon. DSc Brighton, 1997; DUniv Central England, 1997; Hon. Dr of Science Kingston, 2001. GCStJ 2004. *Address:* House of Lords, SW1A 0PW.

**EMERY, Prof. Alan Eglin Heathcote,** MD, PhD, DSc; FRSE, FRCP, FRCPE; FLS; Chief Scientific Advisor, European Neuromuscular Center, Baarn, The Netherlands, since 1999 (Research Director, and Chairman, Research Committee, 1989–99); Professor of Human Genetics, University of Edinburgh and Hon. Consultant Physician, Lothian Health Board, 1968–83, now Emeritus Professor and Hon. Fellow; Hon. Fellow, Green College, later Green Templeton College, Oxford, 2006 (Hon. Visiting Fellow, 1986–2006); *b* 21 Aug. 1928; *s* of Harold Heathcote Emery and Alice Eglin; *m* 1988, Marcia Lynn (*née* Miller); three *s* three *d* from a previous marriage. *Educ:* Manchester Univ. (BSc (double 1st cl. Hons), MD, DSc; John Dalton Prize); Johns Hopkins Univ., Baltimore (PhD). FRSPH (FRIPHH 1965); FRCPE 1970; MFCM 1974; FRSE 1972; FLS 1985; FRCP 1985. Formerly Resident in Medicine and Surgery, Manchester Royal Infirmary; Fellow in Medicine, Johns Hopkins Hosp., Baltimore, 1961–64; Reader in Medical Genetics, Univ. of Manchester, 1964–68 and Hon. Consultant in Medical Genetics, United Manchester Hosps; Sen. Res. Fellow, Green Coll., Oxford, 1985–86. Hon. Vis. Prof., Peninsular Med. Sch., 2006–. Pres., British Clinical Genetics Soc., 1980–83; Council Mem., British Genetic Soc. (Mem. cttees on trng in genetics, 1976, 1979 and 1983 and NHS services, 1978, 1980, 1983 and 1989); Vice Pres., Muscular Dystrophy UK (formerly Muscular Dystrophy Campaign), 1999–; Pres., Med. Genetics Sect., RSocMed, 2002–04 (Trustee, 2007–08). Hon. Member: Assoc. of British Neurologists, 1999; Netherlands Genetic Soc., 1999. FRSA 2002. Hon. FRSSAf 1989; Hon. FACMG 1993; Hon. FRSocMed 2006. Hon. MD: Naples, 1993; Würzburg, 1995; Athens, 2008; Hon. DSc Chester, 2014. Nat. Foundn (USA) Internat. Award for Research, 1980; Gaetano Conte Award and Medal, Gaetano Conte Acad., Italy, 2000; Pro Finlandiae Gold Medal, Univ. of Helsinki, 2000; Elsevier Sci. Award, 2001; Assoc. Française Contre Les Myopathies Prize, 2001; Life-time Achievement Award, World Fedn of Neurology, 2002; Cockcroft Medal and Alumnus of the Year Award, Manchester Univ., 2006; Doubleday Medal in Medicine, Doubleday Foundn, 2007; Internat. Honoree, Internat. Congress on Neuromuscular Disorders, 2010; Internat. Award in Genetic Educn, Amer. Soc. of Human Genetics, 2012; Lifetime Achievement Award: Muscular Dystrophy Campaign, 2012; World Muscle Soc., 2015. Exec. Editor, Procs B, RSE, 1986–90. *Publications:* Elements of Medical Genetics, 1968, 15th edn as Emery's Elements of Medical Genetics (ed P. Turnpenny and S. Ellard), 2017; Methodology in Medical Genetics, 1976, 2nd edn 1986; Recombinant DNA—an introduction, 1984, 2nd edn (with S. Malcolm) 1995; Duchenne Muscular Dystrophy, 1987, 4th edn (jtly) 2015; Muscular Dystrophy: the facts, 1994, 3rd edn 2008; The History of a Genetic Disease, 1995, 2nd edn 2010; with M. Emery: Medicine and Art, 2002; Surgical and Medical Treatment in Art, 2005; Mother and Childcare in Art, 2007; editor: Modern Trends in Human Genetics, vol. 1, 1970, vol. 2, 1975; Antenatal Diagnosis of Genetic Disease, 1973; Registers for the Detection and Prevention of Genetic Disease, 1976; Principles and Practice of Medical Genetics, 1983, 6th edn as Emery & Rimoin's Principles and Practice of Medical Genetics, 2013; Psychological Aspects of Genetic Counselling, 1984; Diagnostic Criteria for Neuromuscular Disorders, 1994, 2nd edn 1997; Neuromuscular Disorders: clinical and molecular genetics, 1998; The Muscular Dystrophies, 2002; numerous scientific papers. *Recreations:* oil painting, medical and art history, writing poetry (4 published books). *Address:* c/o Green Templeton College, Oxford OX2 6HG.

**EMERY, Fred;** author and broadcaster; Presenter, Panorama, BBC TV, 1978–80 and 1982–92; *b* 19 Oct. 1933; *s* of Frederick G. L. Emery and Alice May (*née* Wright); *m* 1958, E. Marianne Nyberg; two *s*. *Educ:* Bancroft's Sch.; St John's Coll., Cantab (MA). RAF fighter pilot, 266 & 234 Squadrons, National Service, 1953. Radio Bremen, 1955–56; joined The Times, 1958, Foreign Correspondent, 1961; served in Paris, Algeria, Tokyo, Indonesia, Vietnam, Cambodia, Malaysia and Singapore until 1970; Chief Washington Corresp., 1970–77; Political Editor, 1977–81; Home Editor, 1981–82; Exec. Editor (Home and Foreign), and Actg Editor, 1982. Reporter, Watergate (TV series), 1994 (Emmy Award, 1995). Press Officer, Crystal Palace Campaign, 1999–2008. Contrib. to CBC/Radio-Canada French Service, 1977–. *Publications:* Watergate: the corruption and fall of Richard Nixon, 1994. *Recreations:* cross-country ski-ing, hill walking. *Address:* 5 Woodsyre, SE26 6SS. *T:* (020) 8761 0076. *Club:* Garrick.

**EMERY, Joyce Margaret;** *see* Zachariah, J. M.

**EMERY, Nicola Susan;** *see* Clayton, N. S.

**EMERY, Prof. Paul,** OBE 2018; MD; FRCP, FRCPE, FMedSci; Arthritis Research UK (formerly ARC) Professor of Rheumatology, University of Leeds, since 1995 (Head, Leeds Institute of Rheumatic and Musculoskeletal Medicine (formerly Division of Musculoskeletal Disease), 1995–2018); Director, Leeds Musculoskeletal Biomedical Research Centre, Leeds Teaching Hospitals Trust, since 1995; *b* 30 Nov. 1952; *s* of late Leonard Leslie Emery and Beryl Emery; *m* 1980, Shirley; two *s*. *Educ:* Cardiff High Sch.; Churchill Coll., Cambridge (BA, MA 1976). Guy's Hosp. Med. Sch.; MB BChir 1977, MD 1985 Cantab. MRCP 1979, FRCP 1992. Accredited Rheumatol. and Gen. (Internal) Medicine, JCHMT, 1985. Hse Officer and SHO rotation, Guy's Hosp., 1979; SHO, Brompton Hosp., 1980; Registrar, then Sen. Registrar in Gen. Medicine and Rheumatol., 1980–85; Hd of Rheumatol., Walter and Eliza Hall Inst., Melbourne and Hon. Consultant, Royal Melbourne Hosp., 1985–87; Sen. Lectr, Univ. of Birmingham, 1987–95. Licentiate Mem., Western Acad. Acupuncture, 1982. Pres., Eur. League Against Rheumatism, 2009–11 (Treas., 2003). FMedSci 2015. Roche Biennial Award for Clinical Rheumatol., 1991; Hosp. Dr of the Year (Rheumatol.), 1999; Outstanding contrib. to rheumatol., Eur. League against Rheumatism, 2002; Carol Nachman Award, 2012. *Publications:* Visual Diagnosis Self-tests in Rheumatology, 1996, 2nd edn 2001; Clinician's Manual on COX-2 Inhibition, 1999, 2nd edn 2002; Adalimumab and Rheumatoid Arthritis, 2003; New Treatments in Arthritis, 2003; Early Rheumatoid Arthritis: rheumatic disease clinics of North America, 2006; 73 book chapters and over 1000 peer-reviewed pubns. *Recreations:* golf, walking, music. *Address:* Leeds Institute of Rheumatic and Musculoskeletal Medicine, Chapel Allerton Hospital, Chapeltown Road, Leeds LS7 4SA. *T:* (0113) 392 4884, *Fax:* (0113) 392 4991. *E:* p.emery@leeds.ac.uk. *Clubs:* Oakdale Golf, Newport Golf, Harrogate Academy Sports.

**EMERY, Richard James,** OBE 2009; Chairman: CSC Media Group Ltd, 2008–14; Wildscreen Charitable Trust, 2008–15; *b* 21 July 1946; *s* of Frederick Harold Emery and Hilda Emery (*née* Newson); *m* 1st, 1978, Patricia Moore (marr. diss. 1993); one *s*, and one step *s*; 2nd, 1995, Hazel Susan Challis; one step *s* two step *d*. *Educ:* Reading Blue Coat Sch. Sales Controller: Anglia Television, 1976; TVS Ltd, 1982; Sales Dir, Central Independent Television Ltd, 1984; Jt Man. Dir and Founder, TSMS Ltd, 1989; Commercial Dir, ITN Ltd, 1991; Dir, Market Strategy, ITV Network Centre, 1993; Man. Dir, BBC Worldwide

TV, 1994; Chief Operating Officer, BBC Worldwide Ltd, 1997; Chief Exec., UKTV Ltd, 1998–2008. *Recreations:* Rugby, walking, reading, boating. *Address:* New Oak, Mill Road, Shiplake, Henley-on-Thames RG9 3LW. *T:* (0118) 940 6503.

**EMERY, William Hubert,** PhD; JP; Chair: Northern Ireland Authority for Utility Regulation, since 2012; Centre on Regulation in Europe, since 2012; *b* 28 June 1951; *s* of Prof. John Lewis and Marjorie Rose Emery (*née* Mytton); *m* 1975, Celia Joan Abbott, PhD; one *s* one *d*. *Educ:* Univ. of Sheffield (BEng 1972; PhD 1976); Univ. of Bradford (MBA 1981). CEng, MICE 1978. Various posts, Yorkshire Water Authy, 1975–90; Office of Water Services: Hd, Engrg Intelligence, 1990–94; Asst Dir, 1994–98; Chief Engr and Dir of Costs and Performance, 1998–2005; Chief Exec., Office of Rail Regulation, 2005–11. JP S Yorks, 1981.

**EMIN, Tracey,** CBE 2013; RA 2007; artist; *b* 1963. *Educ:* Maidstone Coll. of Art (BA 1986); Royal Coll. of Art (MA 1989). Solo exhibitions include: White Cube, London, 1993, 2001, 2005, 2009, 2014, 2019; São Paulo, 2012, Hong Kong, 2016; S London Gall., 1997; Galerie Gebauer, Berlin, 2000; Stedelijk Mus., Amsterdam, 2002; Haus der Kunst, Munich, 2002; Modern Art Oxford, 2002; Art Gall. of NSW, 2003; Platform Garanti Contemp. Art Centre, Istanbul, 2004; Venice Biennale, 2007; (retrospective) Scottish Nat. Gall. of Modern Art, 2008 (toured Malaga, 2008, Bern, 2009); (retrospective) Love is What You Want, Hayward Gall., 2011; Turner Contemporary, Margate, 2012; Xavier Hufkens Gall., Brussels, 2017. Group exhibns incl. Sensation, RA, 1997; Tracey Emin–Egon Schiele: where I want to go, Leopold Mus., Vienna, 2015. Set designer, Les Parents Terribles, Jermyn Street Th., 2004. Film, Top Spot, 2004. Founder, Tracey Emin Museum, London, 1995–98. Eranda Prof. of Drawing, Royal Acad. Schs, 2011–13. *Publications:* Strangeland, 2005; Tracey Emin: my life in a column, 2011. *Address:* c/o White Cube, 144–152 Bermondsey Street, SE1 3TQ.

**EMLEY, Miles Lovelace Brereton;** Chairman, St Ives plc, 1993–2011; *b* 23 July 1949; *s* of late Col Derek Emley, OBE and Mary Georgina Emley (*née* Lovelace); *m* 1976, Tessa Marcia Radclyffe Powell; two *s* one *d*. *Educ:* St Edward's Sch., Oxford; Balliol Coll., Oxford (MA). N. M. Rothschild & Sons Ltd, 1972–89 (Dir, 1982–89); Man. Dir, UBS Phillips & Drew, 1989–92. Non-exec. Dir, Marston's plc (formerly Wolverhampton & Dudley Breweries plc), 1998–2012. Master, Leathersellers' Co., 2011–12. *Club:* White's.

**EMLYN, Viscount; James Chester Campbell;** *b* 7 July 1998; *s* and *heir* of Earl Cawdor, *qv*.

**EMMERICH, Michael Gerard;** Founding Director, Metro Dynamics Ltd, since 2015; *b* Southport, Lancs, 4 Jan. 1967; *s* of late Heinz Gunther Alfred Emmerich and Isobel Mary Emmerich (*née* Case); *m* 1st, 1992, Andrea Howarth (marr. diss. 2017); one *s* one *d*; 2nd, 2018, Jessica Bowles. *Educ:* St John Plessington High Sch., Wythenshawe; Loreto Coll., Moss Side, Manchester; Leeds Poly. (BA Hons Econs and Public Policy 1988). Dep. Dir, Centre for Local Econ. Strategies, 1994–96; Sen. Consultant, Ernst & Young, 1996–98; Policy Advr, Productivity Team, HM Treasury, 1997–2000; Sen. Policy Advr, Prime Minister's Policy Unit, 2000–03; Dir, Inst. for Political and Econ. Governance and Associate Dean, Humanities, Univ. of Manchester, 2003–06; Chief Exec., New Economy Manchester, 2006–15. Trustee, HLF and NHMF, 2003–09; Mem., ESRC, 2018– (Mem., Res. Cttee, 2017); Mem., London Finance Commn, 2012–13. Non-executive Director: Discuss Ltd, 2013–; Residential Secure Income plc, 2018–. Trustee: Addiction Dependency Solutions, 2007–10; Tutor Trust, 2011–. Chm., Manchester Baroque, 2018–; Gov., RNCM, 2010–19 (Hon. Mem., 2019); Dir, Manchester Camerata Ltd, 2014–. Mem., Policy Cttee, Centre for Econ. Performance, LSE, 2015–. Vis. Fellow, Luiss Guido Carli Univ., Rome, 2004. Expert Projects Advr, Local Econ. and Employment Develt Prog., OECD, 2010–15; Advr, City Growth Commn. *Publications:* Britain's Cities, Britain's Future, 2017; articles in Regl Studies and Local Economy. *Recreations:* running, football (MUFC), music (early music and opera in particular), Italophile. *Address:* Metro Dynamics Ltd, Elliot House, 151 Deansgate, Manchester M3 3WD. *T:* (PA) (020) 3865 3082. *E:* mike.emmerich@metrodynamics.co.uk.

**EMMOTT, Linda Mary;** *see* Mulcahy, L.-A. M.

**EMMOTT, Stephen,** PhD; Head of Computational Science, Microsoft Research, 2004; *b* Keighley, W Yorks, 3 June 1960; *s* of James Emmott and Sandra Emmott. *Educ:* Univ. of York (BSc 1st Cl. Experimental Psychol. 1987); Univ. of Stirling (PhD Computational Neurosci. 1993). Post-doctoral Scientist, AT&T Bell Laboratories, USA, 1993–96; Dir and Chief Scientist, Advanced Res. Lab., NCR Corp., 1997–2001; Hd, Intelligent Media Initiative, UCL, 2002–03. Vis. Prof., UCL, 2003–; Vis. Prof. of Computational Sci., Univ. of Oxford, 2005–. Trustee, NESTA, 2009–12. *Publications:* Towards 2020 Science, 2005; Ten Billion, 2013. *Recreations:* cooking, reading, music, travel. *Address:* c/o Microsoft Research, 21 Station Road, Cambridge CB1 2FB.

**EMMOTT, William John, (Bill);** author and consultant; *b* 6 Aug. 1956; *s* of Richard Anthony Emmott and Audrey Mary Emmott; *m* 1st, 1982, Charlotte Crowther (marr. diss.); 2nd, 1992, Carol Barbara Mawer. *Educ:* Latymer Upper Sch., Hammersmith; Magdalen Coll., Oxford (BA Hons PPE; Hon. Fellow, 2002); Nuffield Coll., Oxford. The Economist: Brussels corresp., 1980–82; Economics corresp., 1982–83; Tokyo corresp., 1983–86; Finance Editor, 1986–88; Business Affairs Editor, 1989–93; Editor-in-chief, 1993–2006; Editorial Dir, Economist Intelligence Unit, May–Dec. 1992. Member: European Exec. Cttee, Trilateral Commn, 1999–2009; BBC World Service Governors' Consultative Gp, 2000–06; Swiss Re Chairman's Adv. Panel, 2006–; Univ. of Tokyo President's Council, 2006–; Sen. Adv. Panel, Critical Resource Ltd, 2010–; Bd, Ofcom, 2016 (Chm., Content Bd, 2016); Co-Chm., Canada-Europe Roundtable for Business, 2006–13; Econ. Advr, Stonehage Fleming Family and Partners (formerly Fleming Family & Partners), 2011–16. Non-executive Director: Development Consultants International, 2006–09; eAccess Ltd, 2009–10; Lo Stellone Ltd, 2012–16; InFacts, 2017–; Chm., Peer Index (formerly Viewsflow) plc, 2009–14. Dir, Salzburg Global Seminar, 2008–11. Vis. Prof., Shujitsu Univ., Okayama, 2014–; Visiting Fellow: Blavatnik Sch. of Govt, Univ. of Oxford, 2015–17; All Souls Coll., Oxford, 2017–18; Tokyo Coll., Univ. of Tokyo, 2019–. Chm., London Library, 2009–15; Co-Founder and Chm., Wake Up Foundn, 2013–17. Trustee, Internat. Inst. for Strategic Studies, 2009–15, 2016– (Chm., 2019–); Mem., Adv. Bd, Reuters Inst. for Study of Journalism, 2017–; Chairman: Arts and Humanities Res. Inst., Trinity Coll. Dublin, 2019–; Japan Soc., UK, 2019–. Columnist: The Times, 2010–12; La Stampa, 2019–; Nikkei Business, 2014–; Project Syndicate, 2015–; Mainichi Shimbun, 2018–. Co-writer, Girlfriend in a Coma (documentary film), 2012; Exec. Producer, The Great European Disaster Movie (documentary film), 2015. Hon. LLD Warwick, 1999; Hon. DLitt: City, 2001; Northwestern, 2008. Order of the Rising Sun (Gold Rays with Neck Ribbon) (Japan), 2016. *Publications:* The Pocket Economist (with Rupert Pennant-Rea), 1983; The Sun Also Sets, 1989; Japan's Global Reach, 1992; Kanryo no Taizai, 1996; 20:21 Vision, 2003; The Sun Also Rises, 2006; Nihon no Sentaku, 2007; Rivals: how the power struggle between China, India and Japan will shape our next decade, 2008; Sekai Choryu no Yomikata, 2008; Kawaru Sekai, Tachiokureru Nihon, 2010; Forza, Italia: come ripartire dopo Berlusconi, 2010; Good Italy, Bad Italy, 2012; The Fate of the West, 2017; Japan's Female Future, 2019. *Recreations:* cricket, dogwalking, journalism. *W:* www.billemmott.com. *Clubs:* Royal Over-Seas League, Frontline; Kildare Street and University (Dublin).

**EMMS, Peter Fawcett;** public administration consultant in former communist countries, 1995; *b* 25 April 1935; *s* of late Reginald Emms and Hetty Emms; *m* 1960, Carola Wayne; three *d*. *Educ:* Derby Sch., Derby; Magdalen Coll., Oxford, 1956–59 (Open Schol. in Mod. Langs; MA French and German). National Service, Jt Services Russian Course, 1954–56. Assistant Master: Abingdon Sch., 1959–62; Rugby Sch., 1962–74; Vis. Master, Groton Sch., Mass, 1967–68; Hd of Mod. Langs 1969–71, Housemaster of Town House 1971–74, Rugby Sch.; joined DoE as Principal, 1974, with posts in Road Safety, Construction Industries and Housing; Asst Sec., 1979; Hd of Greater London Housing, 1979–81; seconded to DES, Further and Higher Educn Br., 1981–83; Hd of Housing Management Div., and of Estate Action Unit, DoE, 1983–87; Nuffield Leverhulme Travelling Fellowship, 1987–88; Hd, Dept of Transport Internat. Transport Div., Mem., Central Rhine Commn, 1988–89; Under Sec., 1989; Regl Dir, Eastern Reg., DoE and Dept of Transport, 1989–94; Leader, Know How Fund adv. team to Ukrainian govt, 1994–95. *Publications:* Social Housing: a European dilemma?, 1990; (contrib.) Changing Housing Finance Systems, 1991. *Recreation:* travel. *Address:* 28 Sherard Court, 3 Manor Gardens, N7 6FA.

**EMPEY,** family name of **Baron Empey**.

**EMPEY,** Baron *cr* 2011 (Life Peer), of Shandon in the City and County Borough of Belfast; **Reginald Norman Morgan Empey,** Kt 1999; OBE 1994; Member (UU), Belfast City Council, 1985–2010; Chairman, Ulster Unionist Party, since 2012 (Leader, 2005–10); *b* 26 Oct. 1947; *s* of Samuel Frederick Empey and Emily Winifred (*née* Morgan); *m* 1977, Stella Ethna Donnan (MBE 2007); one *s* one *d*. *Educ:* The Royal Sch., Armagh; Queen's Univ., Belfast (BSc (Econ)). Cons. & Unionist Assoc., QUB, 1967; Publicity Officer, 1967–68, Vice-Chm., 1968–72, Ulster Young Unionist Council; Chm., Vanguard Unionist Party, 1974–75; Mem., E Belfast, NI Constitutional Convention, 1975–76. Dep. Lord Mayor, 1988–89, Lord Mayor of Belfast, 1989–90 and 1993–94. Northern Ireland Assembly: Mem. (UU) Belfast E, 1998–2011; Minister of Enterprise, Trade and Investment, 1999–2002, for Employment and Learning, 2007–10. Member: Belfast Harbour Comrs, 1985–89; Eastern Health and Social Services Bd, 1985–86; Ulster Unionist Council, 1987– (Hon. Sec., 1990–96; Vice-Pres., 1996–2004); Bd, Laganside Corp., 1992–98; Police Authy for NI, 1992–2001; European Cttee of the Regions for NI, Brussels, 1994–2002; Standing Adv. Commn on Human Rights, 1994–96. Contested: (UU) Belfast East, 2005; (UCUNF) South Antrim, 2010. *Recreations:* walking, gardening. *Address:* Knockvale House, 205 Sandown Road, Belfast BT5 6GX. *T:* (office) (020) 7219 8482.

**EMPEY, Prof. Duncan William,** FRCP; Group Medical Director, 2008–12, and Responsible Officer, 2011–16, BMI Healthcare (formerly General Healthcare Group); *b* 9 Sept. 1946; *s* of Henry Gordon Empey and Katherine Isobel (*née* Hooper); *m* 1972, Gillian Mary Charlesworth (*d* 2015); three *d*. *Educ:* Christ's Coll., Finchley; University Coll. London; Westminster Hosp. Med. Sch. (MB, BS). MRCS 1969; FRCP 1983 (LRCP 1969). NIH Fogarty Internat. Res. Fellow, Cardiovascular Res. Inst., San Francisco, 1974–75; Hon. Lectr, London Hosp. Med. Coll., 1975–79; Hon. Sen. Registrar, London Hosp., 1975–79; Consultant Physician, London Chest Hosp. and Royal London Hosp., 1979–2004; Hon. Sen. Lectr, St Bartholomew's and Royal London Sch. of Medicine and Dentistry, 1995–2004; Hon. Consultant Physician, King Edward VII Hosp. for Officers, 1995–2015; Hon. Prof., Univ. of Keele Centre for Health Planning and Mgt, 2005–; Foundn Prof. and Dean, Beds and Herts Postgrad. Med. Sch., 2005–09. Medical Director: Royal Hosps, then Barts and the London, NHS Trust, 1994–2001; NHS Executive (N Thames) Trust Unit, 1997–98; Associate Dir, Rapid Response Unit, subseq. Performance Develt Team, NHS Modernisation Agency, 2002–04. Pres., Section of Respiratory Medicine, RSocMed, 2013–14. Mem. Bd, Osteopathic Foundn, 2017–19. Trustee, British Lung Foundn, 2009–14. Ed., British Jl of Diseases of the Chest, 1984–88. Sec.-Gen., European Soc. for Clinical Respiratory Physiol., 1979–84; Mem. Council, British Thoracic Soc., 2003–06. *Publications:* (jtly) Lung Function for the Clinician, 1981; papers on medical management, asthma, chronic bronchitis, pulmonary circulation, tuberculosis and cystic fibrosis. *Recreation:* historic building conservation.

**EMPEY, Rt Rev. Walton Newcombe Francis;** Archbishop of Dublin and Primate of Ireland, 1996–2002; Bishop of Glendalough, 1996–2002; *b* 26 Oct. 1934; *m* 1960, Louise E. Hall; three *s* one *d*. *Educ:* Portora Royal School and Trinity College, Dublin. Curate Assistant, Glenageary, Dublin, 1958–60; Priest-in-charge, Grand Falls, NB, Canada, 1960–63; Parish Priest, Edmundston, NB, 1963–66; Incumbent, Stradbally, Co. Laois, Ireland, 1966–71; Dean of St Mary's Cathedral and Rector, Limerick City Parish, 1971–81; Bishop of Limerick and Killaloe, 1981–85; Bishop of Meath and Kildare, 1985–96. *Recreations:* reading, fishing, walking. *Address:* Rathmore Lodge, Rathmore, Tullow, Co. Carlow, Republic of Ireland.

**EMPTAGE, Prof. Nigel John,** PhD; Professor of Neuropharmacology, since 2010 and Head, Department of Pharmacology, since 2015, University of Oxford; Nuffield Research Fellow, Lincoln College, Oxford, since 2000; *b* Burton upon Trent, 22 Oct. 1965; *s* of George William Emptage and Joan Sylvia Emptage; *m* 2004, Dr Karin Bradley; two *d*. *Educ:* Belgrave Comp. Sch., Tamworth; Univ. of East Anglia (BSc Hons Biophys); Corpus Christi Coll., Cambridge (PhD 1992). MA Oxon. SERC-NATO Res. Fellow, Yale Univ., 1991–94; Res. Fellow, NIMR, London, 1994–2000; Lectr, Univ. of Oxford, 2000–10. *Publications:* articles in Science, Neuron and other learned jls. *Recreations:* opera, ski-ing, hiking, tennis. *Address:* Department of Pharmacology, University of Oxford, Mansfield Road, Oxford OX1 3QT. *T:* (01865) 271588. *E:* nigel.emptage@pharm.ox.ac.uk.

**EMSLEY, Dr John,** FRSC; writer and broadcaster; *s* of Charles and Mary Emsley; *m* 1963, Joan Feather; one *s* one *d*. *Educ:* Manchester Univ. (BSc, MSc; PhD 1963); DSc London 1983. FRSC 1983. Lectr, 1966–84, Reader, 1984–90, KCL; Science Writer in Residence: Imperial Coll., London, 1990–97; Dept of Chem., Univ. of Cambridge, 1997–2002. Consultant, Broadcast Advertising Clearance Centre, 1996–2007. Columnist: Molecule of the Month, Independent, 1990–96; Wired mag., 2009–13. *Publications:* (with C. D. Hall) The Chemistry of Phosphorus, 1976; The Elements, 1989, 3rd edn 1998; The Consumer's Good Chemical Guide, 1994; Molecules at an Exhibition, 1998 (Chinese edn 2012); (with P. Fell) Was it something you ate?, 1999; The Shocking History of Phosphorus, 2000; Nature's Building Blocks, 2001, 2nd edn 2011; Vanity, Vitality & Virility, 2004; Elements of Murder, 2005 (Korean edn 2012); Better Looking, Better Living, Better Loving, 2007; Molecules of Murder, 2008 (trans. Hungarian 2015); A Healthy, Wealthy, Sustainable World, 2010; Islington Green, 2012; The Newsletter, 2013; Sweet Dreams, 2013; Chemystery, 2013; Chemistry at Home, 2015; More Molecules of Murder, 2017; Chemhistory, 2017; popular sci. books trans. into foreign langs, incl. German, French, Italian, Spanish, Portuguese, Polish, Finnish, Chinese and Japanese; original res. papers on phosphorus chem. and strong hydrogen-bonded systems; contrib. numerous sci. articles and features to jls incl. New Scientist, Independent, Guardian, Chem. in Britain, ChemMatters,

Focus, Sci. Watch. *Recreation:* walking. *Address:* Alameda Lodge, 23A Alameda Road, Ampthill MK45 2LA. *T:* (01525) 404718. *E:* JohnEmsley38@aol.com, johnemsley38@btinternet.com.

**EMSLIE, Rt Hon. Lord;** Hon. George Nigel Hannington Emslie; PC 2011; a Senator of the College of Justice in Scotland, 2001–12; *b* 17 April 1947; *s* of Rt Hon. Lord Emslie, PC, MBE; *m* 1973, Heather Ann Davis; one *s* two *d*. *Educ:* Edinburgh Acad.; Trinity Coll., Glenalmond; Gonville and Caius Coll., Cambridge (BA); Edinburgh Univ. (LLB). Admitted to Faculty of Advocates, 1972; Standing Junior Counsel: to Forestry Commn in Scotland and to Dept of Agric. and Fisheries for Scotland, 1981–82; to Inland Revenue in Scotland, 1982–86; QC (Scot.) 1986. Part-time Chm., Med. Appeal Tribunals, 1988–97. Dean, Faculty of Advocates, 1997–2001. *Address:* c/o Court of Session, Parliament House, Edinburgh EH1 1RQ. *T:* (0131) 225 2595. *Clubs:* Hawks (Cambridge); New (Edinburgh).
See also Rt Hon. Lord Kingarth.

**EMSLIE, Hon. Derek Robert Alexander;** see Kingarth, Rt Hon. Lord.

**EMSLIE, Donald Gordon;** Chairman: Royal Lyceum Theatre Co., 2004–12; Thorpe Hall Leisure Ltd, since 2012; *b* 8 May 1957; *s* of Francis G. Emslie and Margaret Evelyn (*née* Campbell); *m* 1998, Sarah, *d* of Peter Gardner; two *d*. *Educ:* Jordanhill Coll., Glasgow (BEd Physical Educn). Teacher, Kingussie High Sch., 1979–82; with Bochringer Ingelheim Pharmaceuticals, 1982–85; sales, 1985–94, Commercial Dir, 1994–97, Scottish TV; Man. Dir, Broadcasting, SMG plc, 1997–99; Chief Executive: SMG Television, 1999–2006; SMG plc, 2006–07. Chairman: GMTV Ltd, 2002–04; Queuebay Ltd, 2008–11. Chairman: ITV Council, 2002–07; Scottish Industry Skills Panel, 2004–09; RZSScot, 2008–11. Chm., Castle Hotel Mgt Co., 2009–; non-executive Director: Scottish Water, 2008–16; SRU plc, 2008–11. Member, Board: Scottish Screen, 2000–07; Skillset, 2004–09; Screen Acad. Scotland, 2006–11 (Chm., Adv. Bd, 2006–11); Jt Bd, Scottish Screen and Scottish Arts Council, 2007–10. Jt Hon. Chm., BAFTA Scotland, 2004–07. FRTS; FRSA. Hon. DBA Robert Gordon, 2010. *Recreations:* golf, tennis, theatre. *Address:* 32 Drumsheugh Gardens, Edinburgh EH3 7RN. *T:* (0131) 226 3938.

**EMSLIE, Rt Hon. George Nigel Hannington;** see Emslie, Rt Hon. Lord.

**ENCOMBE, Viscount;** John James Robert Columba Scott; *b* 1996; *s* and heir of 6th Earl of Eldon, *qv*.

**ENDERBY, Charles;** see Enderby, S. C.

**ENDERBY, Sir John (Edwin),** Kt 2004; CBE 1997; FRS 1985; H. O. Wills Professor of Physics, 1981–96, now Emeritus, and Senior Research Fellow, since 1996, University of Bristol; *b* 16 Jan. 1931; *s* of late Thomas Edwin Enderby and Rheita Rebecca Hollinshead (*née* Stather); *m* Susan, *yr d* of late Harold Vincent Bowles, OBE and Colleen Bessie Bowles; one *s* two *d*, and one *d* (one *s* decd) of previous marriage. *Educ:* Chester Grammar Sch.; London Univ. (BSc, PhD). Lecturer in Physics: Coll. of Technology, Huddersfield, 1957–60; Univ. of Sheffield, 1960–67; Reader in Physics, Univ. of Sheffield, 1967–69; Prof. in Physics and Head of the Dept, Univ. of Leicester, 1969–76; Prof. of Physics, Bristol Univ., 1976–81; Head of Dept of Physics, and Dir, H. H. Wills Physics Lab., Bristol Univ., 1981–94; Directeur-Adjoint, Institut Laue-Langevin, Grenoble, 1985–88. Fellow, Argonne Nat. Lab., Ill., USA, 1989–91; Visiting Fellow, Battelle Inst., 1968–69; Visiting Professor: Univ. of Guelph, Ont., 1978; Univ. of Leiden, 1989. Humphrey Davy Lectr, Royal Soc., 1997. Member: Physics Cttee, SRC, 1974–77; Neutron Beam Res. Cttee, SRC, 1974–80 and 1988–91 (Chm., 1977–80 and 1988–91); PPARC, 1994–98. Chm., Physics Panel, 2001 RAE, HEFCE, 1999–2001. Chm., Liquids Bd, Eur. Physical Soc., 1991–96. Member: Council, Institut Laue-Langevin, Grenoble, 1973–80; Council, Royal Soc., 1990–92 (Physical Sec. and Vice-Pres., 1999–2004). Chm., Melys Diagnostics Ltd, 2004–. MAE 1989. FInstP 1970 (Chm., SW Br., 1979–83; Guthrie Medal, 1995; Pres., 2004–06). Associate Editor, Philosophical Magazine, 1975–81; Editor, Proc. Royal Soc. A, 1989–94; Editor in Chief, Jl of Physics Condensed Matter, 1997–2002; Chief Sci. Advr, Inst. of Physics Publishing, 2002–11. Hon. Fellow, Birkbeck Coll., London, 1991. Hon. FInstP 2010. Hon. DSc: Loughborough, 1996; Leicester, 2006; Bristol, 2006; Sheffield, 2006; UEA, 2007; Kent, 2008; Huddersfield, 2011; Chester, 2013. *Publications:* (jointly): Physics of Simple Liquids, 1968; Amorphous and Liquid Semiconductors, 1974; many publications on the structure and properties of liquids in: Phil. Mag. Adv. Phys, Jl Phys, Proc. Royal Soc., etc. *Recreations:* gardening, woodwork, watching Association football. *Address:* H. H. Wills Physics Laboratory, Tyndall Avenue, Bristol BS8 1TL. *T:* (0117) 928 8737; 7 Cotham Lawn Road, Bristol BS6 6DU. *T:* (0117) 973 3411.

**ENDERBY, Major (Samuel) Charles,** LVO 2010; JP; Lieutenant, Queen's Body Guard of the Yeoman of the Guard, 2006–09; *b* 18 Sept. 1939; *s* of late Col Samuel Enderby, CVO, DSO, MC and of Pamela Enderby (*née* Hornby); *m* 1973, Mary Justina Compton; two *d*. *Educ:* Wellington Coll.; RMA, Sandhurst. Commnd 12th Royal Lancers, 1959; retd 1985, in rank of Major. Queen's Body Guard of Yeoman of the Guard: Exon, 1987–2002; Ensign, 2002–04; Clerk of the Cheque, 2004–06. Chm., Hexham Steeplechase Co. Ltd, 1991–2016. JP Tynedale, 1991. *Recreations:* gardening, reading, bird ringing, shooting. *Address:* The Riding, Hexham, Northumberland NE46 4PF. *Clubs:* Army and Navy, Pratt's.

**ENDICOTT, Grattan,** OBE 1998; Chief Executive and Secretary to the Trustees, Foundation for Sport and the Arts, 1991–2004; *b* 12 Jan. 1924; *s* of late Cecil George Endicott and Annette Rose Endicott; *m* 1st, 1944, Paolina Cicoria (marr. diss. 1955); two *s*; 2nd, 1961, Jean Thurgeson (marr. diss. 1981). *Educ:* Rhyl Co. Grammar Sch. Served RN, 1941–46; Principal Linguist, Navy Sub-Commn, Allied Commn, Rome, 1944–46. Personnel Asst, ICI, 1946–57; Littlewoods Pools: Asst Permutation Manager, 1957–66; Hd, Permutation Services, 1966–89. European Bridge League: Member: Exec. Cttee, 1989–93; Appeals Cttee (Standing), 1999–2011; Laws Cttee, 1999–2011; Systems Cttee, 1999–2011; Tournament Dirs Cttee, 1999–2001 and 2003–07; World Bridge Federation: Member: Systems Cttee, 1990–95; Rules and Regulations Cttee, 1992–95 and 2000–10; Appeals Cttee (Standing), 1993–95 and 2000–10; Convention Card Cttee, 1987–89; Laws Cttee, 1987 (Vice-Chm., 1988–95; Sec., 1998–2013; Hon. Life Sec., 2013); Laws Drafting Subcttee, 2001–10. Vice Pres., English Bridge Union; Pres., Merseyside and Cheshire Contract Bridge Assoc. FRSA. Gold Medal, World Bridge Fedn, 2005; Gold Medal, English Bridge Union, 2013. *Publications:* European Bridge League Commentary on the Laws of Duplicate Contract Bridge 1987, 1992; (jtly) Draft Laws of Duplicate Bridge, 2006; (jtly) Laws of Duplicate Bridge, 2007. *Recreation:* competition (duplicate) bridge. *Address:* 14 Elmswood Court, Palmerston Road, Mossley Hill, Liverpool L18 8DJ. *T:* (0151) 724 1484. *Club:* Liverpool Bridge.

**ENDICOTT, Prof. Timothy Andrew Orville,** DPhil; Professor of Legal Philosophy, University of Oxford, since 2006 (Dean, Faculty of Law, 2007–15); Fellow, Balliol College, Oxford, since 1999; *b* Golden, BC, 9 July 1960; *s* of Orville and Julianne Endicott; one *s* one *d*. *Educ:* Harvard Univ. (AB 1983); Univ. of Oxford (MPhil 1985; DPhil 1997); Univ. of Toronto (LLB 1988). Barrister and solicitor, Oslers, Toronto, 1988–91; Lectr in Law, Jesus Coll., 1994–95, St Anne's Coll., 1995–96, St Catherine's Coll., 1996–99 (Fellow, 1998–99), Oxford. Bencher, Inner Temple, 2011. *Publications:* Vagueness in Law, 2000; Administrative Law, 2009, 4th edn 2018; articles in law and philos. jls. *Address:* Balliol College, Oxford OX1 3BJ. *T:* (01865) 271564, *Fax:* (01865) 271493.

**ENFIELD, Viscount;** Samuel Peter Byng; *b* 17 July 1998; *e* twin *s* and heir of 9th Earl of Strafford, *qv*. *Educ:* Durham Johnston Comp. Sch., Durham; Robinson Coll., Cambridge.

**ENFIELD, Harry;** comedy actor and writer; *b* 30 May 1961; *m* 1997, Lucy Lyster; one *s* one *d*. *Educ:* York Univ. (BA Hons Politics). TV programmes include: Sir Norbert Smith: a life, 1989 (Silver Rose of Montreux, Emmy Award); Smashie and Nicey: the end of an era, 1994 (Silver Rose of Montreux); Norman Ormal, 1998; Kevin's Guide to Being a Teenager, 1999; Skins, 2007, 2008; series: Harry Enfield's Television Programme, 1990, 1992; Harry Enfield's Guide to the Opera, 1993; Harry Enfield and Chums, 1994 (Writers Guild Award) and 1997 (Silver Rose of Montreux); St Albion Parish Council, 1998, 1999; Harry Enfield's Brand Spanking New Show, 2000; Celeb, 2002; Ruddy Hell! It's Harry and Paul, 2007; Harry and Paul, 2008, 2010, 2012; Skins, 2009; (narrator) Crackanory, 2013; Bad Education, 2013–14; Blandings, 2014; An Evening with Harry Enfield and Paul Whitehouse, 2015; The Windsors, 2016, 2017; Upstart Crow, 2016; Island of Dreams, 2019; also appeared regularly in: Saturday Night Live, 1986; Friday Night Live, 1988; Gone to the Dogs, 1991; Men Behaving Badly, 1992; films: Kevin and Perry Go Large, 2000; Churchill: the Hollywood Years, 2003; Tooth, 2004; Scottish Mussel, 2015; The Bad Education Movie, 2015; Swallows and Amazons, 2016. Theatre: Legends!, tour, 2015; Once in a Lifetime, Young Vic, 2016; Genesis Inc., Hampstead Th., 2018. Top BBC 1 Comedy Personality, British Comedy Awards, 1998. *Publications:* Harry Enfield and his Humorous Chums, 1997. *Address:* c/o Curtis Brown Group Ltd, Haymarket House, 28–29 Haymarket, SW1Y 4SP.

**ENGEL, Matthew Lewis;** writer; *b* 11 June 1951; *s* of late Max David and Betty Ruth Engel; *m* 1990, Hilary Davies; one *d* (one *s* decd). *Educ:* Carmel Coll.; Manchester Univ. (BA Econ). Reporter, Chronicle and Echo, Northampton, 1972–75; Reuters, 1977–79; The Guardian: journalist, 1979–2004, 2016–; cricket corresp., 1982–87; feature writer, sports columnist, occasional war, political and foreign corresp., 1987–2001; columnist, 1998–2004; Washington corresp., 2001–03; columnist, Financial Times, 2004–16. Ed., Wisden Cricketers' Almanack, 1992–2000, 2003–07. Vis. Prof. of Media, Oxford Univ., 2010–11. Co-Founder, Laurie Engel Fund, 2005. Sports Writer of the Year, What the Papers Say, 1985; Sports Journalist of the Year, British Press Awards, 1991. *Publications:* Ashes '85, 1985; (ed) Guardian Book of Cricket, 1986; (ed) Sportswriter's Eye, 1989; (ed) Sportspages Almanac, 1990, 1991, 1992; (with A. Radd) History of Northamptonshire CCC, 1993; Tickle the Public, 1996; Extracts from the Red Notebooks, 2007; Eleven Minutes Late, 2009; Engel's England, 2014; That's the Way it Crumbles, 2017. *Recreation:* wishful thinking. *Address:* Fair Oak, near Bacton, Herefordshire HR2 0AT. *Clubs:* Garrick; Northamptonshire CC (Vice-Pres.).

**ENGEL, Natascha;** Commissioner for Shale Gas, 2018–19; *b* 9 April 1967; *d* of Achaz and Christina Engel; *m* 2001, David Salisbury Jones (marr. diss. 2012); three *s*. *Educ:* King's Coll., London (BA 1st Cl. Hons Mod. Langs); Westminster Press Dip. Journalism; Westminster Univ. (MA Tech. and Specialist Translation). Journalist, Dover Express, 1990; English and German teacher, Spain, 1990–92; teletext subtitler, 1992–97; GPMU Organiser, TUC Organising Acad., 1997–98; TU Liaison, Labour Party, 1998–2001; Prog. Dir, John Smith Inst., 2001–02; Co-ordinator, TU Political Fund Ballots, 2002–03. MP (Lab) NE Derbyshire, 2005–17; contested (Lab) same seat, 2017. Second Dep. Speaker of Ways and Means, and a Dep. Speaker, 2015–17.

**ENGESET, Jetmund,** Hon. LVO 2004; FRCSE; FRCSG; Consultant Surgeon, Grampian Health Board, 1987–2004; Surgeon to the Queen in Scotland, 1985–2004; *b* 22 July 1938; *s* of Arne K. Engeset and Marta Engeset; *m* 1966, Anne Graeme (*née* Robertson); two *d*. *Educ:* Slemdal and Ris Skole, Oslo, Norway; Oslo University; Aberdeen University (MB ChB, ChM Hons). House Officer (Surgical and Medical), Aberdeen Royal Infirmary, 1964–65; Aberdeen University: Res. Assistant, Dept of Surgery, 1965–67; Surgical Registrar, 1967–70; Lectr in Surgery, 1970–74; Sen. Lectr in Surgery, 1974–87; Head of Dept of Surgery, 1982–85 (seconded to Salgrenska Hosp. Surgical Unit, Gothenburg, Sweden, 1972–74). Golden Jubilee Medal, 2002. *Publications:* papers on microcirculation, vascular surgery, organ preservation and tissue transplantation. *Recreations:* ski-ing, angling, squash, gardening. *Address:* 66 Greystoke Park, Gosforth, Newcastle-upon-Tyne NE3 2DZ. *T:* (0191) 236 3223.

**ENGLAND, Angela Catherine;** see Finnerty, A. C.

**ENGLAND, Prof. George Leslie,** DScEng; CEng, FICE, FNucI; Professor of Mechanics and Structures, Imperial College, London, 1989–2000; *b* 9 Oct. 1935; *s* of John Edward Philip England and Rose Gladys England; *m* 1968, W. Margaret Landon. *Educ:* East Barnet Grammar Sch.; King's Coll., London (Sambrooke Medal; BScEng 1st Cl. Hons; Jameson Prize (Eng); Eng. Soc. Centenary Prize, Tennant Medal (Geol); PhD 1961; DScEng 1974). King's College, London: Lectr, 1961; Reader in Engrg Mechanics, 1975; Dean, 1983–85; Vice-Dean, 1985–86; Prof. of Mechanics and Structures, 1986–89. Consultant to: HSE, NII, 1971; UN Develt Project, Central Soils and Materials Res. Station, India, 1992. MASCE. Patent holder for the design of long-span integral bridges with improved performance. *Publications:* contribs to learned jls on time-dependent service-life performance of concrete structures, behaviour of structures at high temperatures and cyclic soil-structure interaction problems. *Recreations:* landscape gardening, mountain walking. *Address:* Department of Civil and Environmental Engineering, Imperial College of Science, Technology and Medicine, SW7 2BU.

**ENGLAND, Prof. Philip Christopher,** FRS 1999; Professor of Geology, Oxford University, 2000–19; *b* 30 April 1951; *s* of Anthony Christopher England and Margaret Jean England; *m* 1978, Pamela Anne Shreeve; one *s* two *d*. *Educ:* Bristol Univ. (BSc Physics 1972); DPhil Geophysics, Oxford, 1976. NERC Research Fellow, 1977–79, IBM Res. Fellow, 1979–81, Dept Geodesy and Geophysics, Univ. of Cambridge; Asst, then Associate Prof., Harvard Univ., 1981–86; Lectr in Geophysics, Oxford Univ., 1986–99; Fellow, Exeter Coll., Oxford, 1986–2000. Fellow, Amer. Geophysical Union, 1996. Murchison Medal, Geol Soc., 2004; Love Medal, EU Geoscientists, 2010; Gold Medal, RAS, 2016; Bucher Medal, Amer. Geophysical Union, 2018. *Publications:* contribs to earth science jls. *Recreations:* family, music.

**ENGLAND, Rear-Adm. Timothy John,** FIET; maritime and transport consultant, since 1997; Chief Staff Officer (Support) to Commander-in-Chief Fleet, 1992–94; *b* Llandudno, 6 Feb. 1942; *s* of late Wilfred James England and Kathleen Helen England (*née* Stacey); *m* 1966, Margaret Ann Cullen (*d* 2017); one *s* one *d*. *Educ:* Trinity Sch. of John Whitgift, Croydon; RNEC Manadon. BScEng ext. London Univ. CEng. Joined RN at BRNC Dartmouth as Weapon Engineering specialist, 1960; served HM Ships Alert, Collingwood, London, Salisbury; Staff of DG Ships; HM Dockyard, Devonport; HMS Bristol; Staff of C-in-C Fleet; Directorate of Naval Operational Requirements, 1978–80; Weapon Engineer Officer, HMS Invincible, incl. Falklands Campaign, 1981–82; Staff Weapon Engineer

Officer to FO Sea Training, 1982–84; Defence Operational Requirements, 1984–86; RCDS 1987; Fleet Weapon Engineer Officer, 1988–89; WRNS Sea Service Implementation Team Leader, 1990; Captain, RNEC, Manadon, 1990–92. Harbour Master, River Hamble, 1995–96. MInstD. *Publications:* articles in Naval and professional jls. *Recreations:* sailing/cruising, photography, information technology. *Address:* 14 East Hill Close, Fareham, Hants PO16 8SE.

**ENGLE, Prof. Robert Fry,** PhD; Professor of Finance, 1999, and Michael Armellino Professor in the Management of Financial Services, since 2000, Leonard N. Stern School of Business, New York University; *b* Nov. 1942; *m* 1969, Marianne Eger; one *s* one *d. Educ:* Williams Coll. (BS highest Hons (Physics) 1964); Cornell Univ. (MS (Physics) 1966; PhD (Econs) 1969). Asst Prof., 1969–74, Associate Prof., 1975, MIT; University of California, San Diego: Associate Prof., 1975–77; Prof., 1977; Chair, 1990–94; Chancellors' Associates Prof. of Econs, 1993–; Prof. Emeritus and Dist. Res. Prof., 2003; New York University: Co-Founding Pres., Soc. for Financial Econometrics, 2007–11; Founder and Dir, Volatility Inst., 2009–. Fellow, Wharton Financial Instns Center, Philadelphia, 2009–10; Dist. Vis. Scholar, Kenan-Flagler Business Sch., Univ. of N Carolina Chapel Hill, 2010; Dist. Vis. Scholar, McDonough Sch. of Business, Georgetown Univ., 2012; T. C. Liu Vis. Scholar, Becker Friedman Inst., Univ. of Chicago, 2013. Principal, Robert F. Engle Econometric Services. Mem. Econ. Panel, NSF, 1979–81; Res. Associate, Nat. Bureau of Econ. Res., 1987–. Fellow: Econometric Soc., 1981 (Mem. Council, 1994); Mem., Nominating Cttee for Council, 1995); Amer. Acad. of Arts and Scis, 1995; Amer. Statistical Assoc., 2000; Amer. Finance Assoc., 2004; Inst. for Quantitative Res. in Finance, 2006. Associate Editor: Econometrica, 1975–81; Jl of Regl Sci., 1978–; Jl of Forecasting, 1985–; Jl of Applied Econometrics, 1988– (Co-Ed., 1985–89); Rev. of Econs and Stats, 1992; Adv. Ed., Empirical Finance, 1992. Hon Dr: Southern Switzerland, 2003; Savoie, 2005; HEC Paris, 2005; Williams Coll., 2007. Roger F. Murray Prize, Inst. for Quantitative Res. in Finance, 1991; (jtly) Nobel Prize for Econs, 2003. *Publications:* (ed jtly) Long Run Economic Relations: readings in cointegration, 1991; (ed jtly) Handbook of Econometrics, vol. IV, 1994; (ed jtly) ARCH: selected readings, 1995; (ed jtly) Cointegration, Causality, and Forecasting: a festschrift in honor of Clive W. J. Granger, 1999; Anticipating Correlations, 2008; contribs to Econometrica, Jl of Business and Econ. Stats, Jl of Econometrics, Jl of Finance, Review of Financial Studies, Jl of Financial Economics, etc. *Address:* Leonard N. Stern School of Business, New York University, Salomon Center, 44 West Fourth Street, Suite 9–62, New York, NY 10012, USA. *T:* (212) 9980710, *Fax:* (212) 9954220. *E:* rengle@stern.nyu.edu.

**ENGLEHART, Robert Michael;** QC 1986; a Recorder, since 1987; a Deputy High Court Judge, since 1994; *b* 1 Oct. 1943; *s* of G. A. F. and K. P. Englehart; *m* 1971, Rosalind Mary Foster; one *s* two *d. Educ:* St Edward's Sch., Oxford; Trinity Coll., Oxford (MA); Harvard Law School (LLM); Bologna Centre (Dip. in Internat. Relns). Assistente, Univ. of Florence, 1968. Called to the Bar, Middle Temple, 1969 (Astbury Scholar; Bencher, 1995); practising barrister, 1969–. Chm., London Common Law and Commercial Bar Assoc., 1990–91. Trustee, Free Representation Unit, 1991–. *Publications:* (contrib.) Il Controllo Giudiziario: a comparative study of civil procedure, 1968. *Recreations:* shooting, cricket. *Address:* Blackstone Chambers, Blackstone House, Temple, EC4Y 9BW. *T:* (020) 7583 1770. *Clubs:* Garrick, MCC.

**ENGLERT, Prof. François,** PhD; Professor, 1964–98, now Professor Emeritus, and Joint Director, Theoretical Physics Group, 1980–98, Université Libre de Bruxelles; *b* Etterbeek, Belgium, 6 Nov. 1932; *m* 1st, Esther Dujardin; two *s* one *d*; 2nd, Danielle Vindal; two *d*; 3rd, Mira Nikomarow. *Educ:* Univ. Libre de Bruxelles (Ingénieur Civil Electricien-Mécanicien 1955; Licencié en Scis Physiques 1958; PhD 1959). Asst, Univ. Libre de Bruxelles, 1956–59; Res. Associate, 1959–60, Asst Prof., 1960–61, Cornell Univ.; Chargé de Cours, Univ. Libre de Bruxelles, 1961–64. Prix Francqui, Fondn Francqui, 1982; (jtly) High Energy and Particle Physics Prize, Eur. Physical Soc., 1997; (jtly) Wolf Foundn Prize in Physics, 2004; (jtly) J. J. Sakurai Prize for Theoretical Physics, Amer. Physics Soc., 2010; (jtly) Prince of Asturias Award for Tech. and Scientific Res., Prince of Asturias Foundn, 2013; (jtly) Nobel Prize in Physics, 2013. Hon. Dr: Mons-Hainaut, 2004; Vrije, Brussels, 2005; Blaise Pascal, France, 2013. *Address:* Service de Physique Theorique, CP 225, Université Libre de Bruxelles, Boulevard du Triomphe, Campus de la Plaine, 1050 Brussels, Belgium.

**ENGLISH, Rt Hon. Bill;** *see* English, Rt Hon. S. W.

**ENGLISH, Caroline Frances; Her Honour Judge English;** a Circuit Judge, since 2015; *d* of Maureen Frances Streight; *m* 1996, Floyd Ramsey Porter. *Educ:* Nottingham Trent Univ. (LLB Hons). Called to the Bar, Inner Temple, 1989; a Recorder, 2007–15. Fee-paid Judge of First-tier Tribunal (Health, Educn and Social Care Chamber (Mental Health) (formerly Fee-paid Legal Mem., Mental Health Rev. Tribunal (England)), 2003–. *Recreations:* horse riding, foreign travel (particularly Central and South America), wildlife photography. *Address:* Snaresbrook Crown Court, 75 Hollybush Hill, Snaresbrook, E11 1QW.

**ENGLISH, Judith Frances, (Lady English);** Principal, St Hilda's College, Oxford, 2001–07; Dean of Scholars, Oxford Centre for Islamic Studies, 2010–17; *b* 1 March 1940; *d* of Dr Kenneth James Grant Milne and Dr Constance Nellie Milne; *m* 1st, 1973, Ralph Talbot (marr. diss. 2001); two *d*; 2nd, 2002, Sir Terence English, *qv. Educ:* Notre Dame High Sch., Sheffield (State Schol.); Girton Coll., Cambridge (Crewdson Prize; MA 1963; Hon. Fellow 2004); University Coll. Hosp. Med. Sch., London (MB BChir 1965). MRCP 1968; MRCPsych 1973, FRCPsych 2002. Medical house staff posts, Whittington Hosp., Brompton Hosp. and UCH, 1965–67; Lectr in Clinical Immunology, Inst. of Chest Diseases, London Univ., 1967–70; Registrar in Psychiatry, Maudsley Hosp., 1970–74; Fellow in Consultation-Liaison Psychiatry, then Staff Psychiatrist, UCLA, 1974–79; Director, Psychiatric Consultation Service: Boston Veterans' Affairs Med. Center, 1980–95; New England Med. Center, 1986–93; Chief of Staff, Boston Veterans' Affairs Med. Center, 1996–2000; Asst Prof. of Psychiatry, Tufts Univ., 1986–2000; Associate Clinical Prof. of Psychiatry, Boston Univ. Sch. of Medicine, 1998–2000. *Publications:* contribs to med. and psychiatric jls. *Recreations:* reading, poetry, dance, textile collage. *Address:* 28 Tree Lane, Iffley Village, Oxford OX4 4EY.

**ENGLISH, Prof. Richard Ludlow,** CBE 2018; PhD; FBA 2009; FRHistS; FRSE; Pro-Vice-Chancellor for Internationalisation and Engagement, Queen's University Belfast, since 2016; *b* Belfast, 16 Dec. 1963; *s* of Donald English and Bertha English (*née* Ludlow); *m* 1989, Maxine Cresswell; two *d. Educ:* Keble Coll., Oxford (BA Modern Hist.; Hon. Fellow, 2014); Keele Univ. (PhD Hist. 1990). Lectr in Politics, 1990–95, Reader in Politics, 1995–99, Prof. of Politics, 1999–2011, QUB; Wardlaw Prof. of Politics and Dir, Centre for the Study of Terrorism and Political Violence, Univ. of St Andrews, 2011–16. MRIA 2009. FRHistS 1996; FRSE 2015. *Publications:* Radicals and the Republic: socialist republicanism in the Irish Free State 1925–37, 1994; Ernie O'Malley: IRA intellectual, 1998; Armed Struggle: the history of the IRA, 2003; Irish Freedom: the history of nationalism in Ireland, 2006; Terrorism: how to respond, 2009; Modern War: a very short introduction, 2013; Does Terrorism Work?, 2016. *Recreations:* Handel, Wagner, the Arsenal. *Address:* Vice Chancellor's Office, Queen's University Belfast, University Road, Belfast BT7 1NN. *T:* (028) 9097 3131. *E:* r.english@qub.ac.uk.

**ENGLISH, Rt Hon. Sir Simon William, (Rt Hon. Sir Bill),** KNZM 2018; MP (Nat.) Clutha-Southland, New Zealand, 1996–2018; Leader of the Opposition, New Zealand, 2017–18; Leader, National Party, 2016–18; *b* 30 Dec. 1961; *s* of Mervyn English and Norah (*née* O'Brien); *m* 1987, Dr Mary Scanlon; five *s* one *d. Educ:* St Patrick's Coll., Silverstream; Otago Univ. (BCom); Victoria Univ. of Wellington (BA Hons English Lit.). Sheep farmer, Dipton, until 1987; Policy Analyst, NZ Treasury, 1987–89; MP (Nat.) Wallace, 1990–96; Parly Under-Sec. for Health and Crown Health Enterprises, 1993–96; Minister for Crown Health Enterprises, Associate Minister of Educn and Mem., Cabinet, Feb.–Dec. 1996; Minister of Health, 1996–99; Associate Minister of Revenue, 1997–99; Associate Treas., 1998–99; Minister of Finance and Minister of Revenue, 1999; Opposition spokesman for educn, 2003–06, on finance, 2006–08; Dep. Prime Minister, 2008–16; Minister for Infrastructure, 2008–11; Minister of Finance, 2008–16; Minister for Regulatory Reform, 2013–16; Prime Minister, 2016–17. Dep. Leader, 2001–02 and 2006–16, Leader, 2002–03, Nat. Party. Patron, Epilepsy NZ, 2018–. *Recreations:* Rugby, running.

**ENGLISH, Sir Terence (Alexander Hawthorne),** KBE 1991; FRCS; FRCP; Master of St Catharine's College, Cambridge, 1993–2000; Consultant Cardiothoracic Surgeon, Papworth and Addenbrooke's Hospitals, Cambridge, 1973–95; *b* 3 Oct. 1932; *s* of late Arthur Alexander English and Mavis Eleanor (*née* Lund); *m* 1st, 1963, Ann Dicey (marr. diss. 2002); two *s* two *d*; 2nd, 2002, Judith Frances Milne (see J. F. English). *Educ:* Hilton Coll., Natal; Witwatersrand Univ. (Transvaal Chamber of Mines Scholarship, 1951–54; BSc(Eng) 1954); Guy's Hosp. Med. Sch. (MB, BS 1962); MA Cantab 1977. FRCSE 1967; FRCS 1967; FRCP 1990. House appointments, Guy's Hosp., 1962–63; Demonstrator, Anatomy Dept, Guy's Hosp., 1964–65; Surgical Registrar: Bolingbroke Hosp., 1966; Brompton Hosp., 1967–68; Res. Fellow, Dept of Surgery, Univ. of Alabama, 1969; Sen. Registrar, Brompton, National Heart and London Chest Hosps, 1968–72; Dir, Papworth Heart Transplant Res. Unit, 1980–88 (performed Britain's 1st successful heart transplant, 1979); non-exec. Dir, Papworth Hosp. NHS Trust, 1997–2001. Chief Med. Advr, BUPA, 1991–99. Mem., Audit Commn, 1993–98. Chm., Asia Healthcare plc, 1995–98. Member: British Cardiac Soc., 1973–; British Transplantation Soc., 1980–; Soc. of Thoracic and Cardiovascular Surgeons, 1972– (Exec. Council, 1975–77); Thoracic Soc., 1971– (Exec. Council, 1978–81). Member: Specialists Adv. Cttee in Cardiothoracic Surgery, 1980–87; Council, BHF, 1983–87; GMC, 1983–89; Standing Med. Adv. Cttee, 1989–92; Jt Consultants Cttee, 1989–92; Supraregional Services Adv. Gp, 1990–92; Clinical Standards Adv. Gp, 1991–94; Steering Cttee, Healthcare Professionals for Assisted Dying, 2010–15. President: Internat. Soc. of Heart Transplantation, 1984–85; Soc. of Perfusionists of GB and Ireland, 1985–86; RCS, 1989–92 (Mem. Council, 1981–93; Court of Patrons, 1994; Trustee, Hunterian Mus., 1996–); Cardiothoracic Sect., RSM, 1992–93; BMA, 1995–96; Vice Pres., British Lung Foundn, 2002–15. Upjohn Lectr, Royal Soc., 1988. Capt., Guy's Hosp. RFC, 1959–60. Gov., Leys Sch., Cambridge, 1993–2001. Trustee: Northwick Park Inst. for Med. Res., 1996–2006; Comparative Clinical Science Foundn, 2003–16; IDEALS, 2003–; Med. Aid for Palestinians, 2010–15 (Patron, 2015–). Member Council: Winston Churchill Meml Trust, 1995–2009; Univ. of Cambridge, 1998. Patron: Primary Trauma Care Foundn, 2006–; Emthonjeni Trust, 2006–; Dignity in Dying, 2009–; Al-Quds Foundn for Med. Schs in Palestine, 2012–; Internat. Med. Educn Trust 2000, 2013–. Hon. Freeman, Barbers' Co., 1993. DL Cambs, 1996–2001. FACC 1986. Hon. FRCSCan 1990; Hon. FRACS 1991; Hon. FCSSA 1991; Hon. FRCS (Thailand) 1991; Hon. FCP&S (Pakistan), 1991; Hon. FRCAnaes, 1991; Hon. FDSRCS 1992; Hon. FACS 1992; Hon. FRCSI 1992; Hon. FRCSGlas 1992; Hon. FCOphth 1993; Hon. FRSocMed 2007; Hon. Fellow: St Catharine's Coll., Cambridge, 1992; Hughes Hall, Cambridge, 1993; UMDS, Guy's and St Thomas' Hosps (now KCL), 1993; Worcester Coll., Oxford, 2003. Hon. DSc: Sussex, 1992; Hull, 1996; Oxford Brookes, 2013; Hon. MD: Nantes, 1992; Mahidol, Thailand, 1993; Witwatersrand, 2008. Man of the Year, RADAR, 1980; Clement Price Thomas Award, RCS, 1986; Lifetime Achievement Award, Soc. for Cardiothoracic Surgery in GB and Ireland, 2009; Lifetime Achievement Award, Internat. Soc. of Heart and Lung Transplantation, 2014; Ray C. Fish Award for Scientific Achievement in Cardiovascular Disease, Texas Heart Inst., 2014. *Publications:* (jtly) Principles of Cardiac Diagnosis and Treatment: a surgeons' guide, 1992; Follow Your Star: from mining to heart transplants – a surgeon's story, 2011; chapter on Surgery of the Thorax and Heart in Bailey and Love's Short Practice of Thoracic Surgery, 1980; numerous articles in medical jls on matters relating to the practice of heart transplantation and cardiothoracic surgery. *Recreations:* reading, 4 x 4 rallies, travel, classic cars. *Address:* 28 Tree Lane, Iffley Village, Oxford OX4 4EY. *E:* tenglish@doctors.org.uk. *Clubs:* Athenæum; Hawks (Cambridge).

**ENGLISH, Terence Michael;** a District Judge (Magistrates' Courts) (formerly Metropolitan Stipendiary Magistrate), 1986–2009; *b* 3 Feb. 1944; *s* of John Robert English and Elsie Letitia English; *m* 1st, 1966, Ivy Joan Weatherley (*d* 1997); one *s* one *d*; 2nd, 2001, Clare Joanne Evans. *Educ:* St Ignatius Coll., London N15; London Univ. (external LLB 1967). Admitted Solicitor of the Supreme Court, 1970. Assistant, Edmonton PSD, 1962–71; Dep. Clerk to Justices, Bullingdon, Bampton E, Henley and Watlington PSDs, 1972–76; Clerk to the Justices: Newbury and Hungerford and Lambourn PSDs, 1977–85; Slough and Windsor PSDs, 1985–86. A Recorder, 1994–97. Chairman: Family Panel, 1991–92; Inner London Juvenile Ct Panel, 1989–2002. *Recreations:* philately, music, travel, arts. *Address:* c/o Chief Magistrate's Office, Westminster Magistrates' Court, 181 Marylebone Road, NW1 5BR.

**ENGLUND, Prof. Harri Mikael,** PhD; FBA 2019; Professor of Social Anthropology, University of Cambridge, since 2014; Fellow of Churchill College, Cambridge, since 2004; *b* Helsinki, 1 Nov. 1966; *s* of Börje Evald Englund and Kirsti Kyllikki Englund (*née* Seiro); *m* 2004, Gudrun Haraldsdottir (marr. diss. 2016); one *s. Educ:* Etu-Töölön Lukio; Helsinki Univ. (MA Cultural Anthropol. 1990); Univ. of Manchester (PhD Social Anthropol. 1995). Research Fellow: Univ. of Manchester, 1997–98; Nordic Africa Inst., 1998–2002; Acad. of Finland, 2003–04; Lectr, 2004–08, Reader, 2008–14, Univ. of Cambridge. *Publications:* From War to Peace on the Mozambique-Malawi Borderland, 2002; (ed) A Democracy of Chameleons: politics and culture in new Malawi, 2002; (ed jtly) Rights and the Politics of Recognition in Africa, 2004; Prisoners of Freedom, 2006; Human Rights and African Airwaves, 2011; (ed) Christianity and Public Culture in Africa, 2011; Gogo Breeze, 2018. *Recreations:* music, running. *Address:* Department of Social Anthropology, University of Cambridge, Cambridge CB2 3RF. *E:* hme2@cam.ac.uk.

**ENNALS, Sir Paul (Martin),** Kt 2009; CBE 2002; Independent Chair: Local Safeguarding Children Board: South Tyneside, since 2015; Gateshead, since 2016; Sunderland, since 2017; Independent Chair, Safeguarding Adult Board: Gateshead, since 2016; South Tyneside, since 2017; Sunderland, since 2018; *b* 7 Nov. 1956; *s* of Baron Ennals, PC, and of Eleanor Maud Ennals (*née* Caddick); *m* 1996, Christine Reid. *Educ:* King's Coll. Sch., Wimbledon; New Coll., Oxford (BA Psychology). Director: Services, SENSE, 1983–89; Educn and Employment, RNIB, 1989–98; Chief Exec., Nat. Children's Bureau, 1998–2011. Chairman: Council for Disabled Children, 1991–98; Special Educnl Consortium, 1992–97; Independent Rev. of Pre-Schools, 1999; Children's Workforce

Develt Council, 2009–12 (Shadow Chm., 2004–05); Children's Workforce Network, 2006–09; Fulfilling Lives Strategic Gp, 2014–; Voluntary Orgns Network NE, 2015–; Chm., Local Safeguarding Children Bd, Haringey, 2014–17; Vice-Chairman: Nat. Adv. Gp on Special Educnl Needs, 1997–2001; Children's Inter-agency Gp, 2008–11; Ways to Wellness Foundn, 2015–; Member: Children's Task Force, 2001–04; Children's Workforce Expert Gp, 2008–09; Child Health Adv. Gp, DoH, 2008–10; DFE (formerly DCSF) Prog. Bd for Children in Care, 2008–10. Trustee: Sightsavers, 1995–2007; Wave Trust, 2011–15. *E:* paulennals@yahoo.co.uk.

**ENNIS, Catherine Mary, (Mrs J. A. Higham);** concert organist; Organist, St Lawrence Jewry-next-Guildhall, EC2, since 1985; *b* 20 Jan. 1955; *d* of Séamus and Margaret Ennis; *m* 1988, John Arthur Higham, *qv;* two *s* one *d*, and one step *s* two step *d. Educ:* Christ's Hosp., Hertford; Kingsway Further Educn Coll.; St Hugh's Coll., Oxford (MA). Recitals, Europe and USA, 1977–; Dir of Music, St Marylebone Parish Church, 1978–90; Asst Organist, Christ Church Cathedral, Oxford, 1984–86; Professor: RAM, 1982–90; GSM, 1985–86; Mem. staff, Trinity Coll. of Music, 2001–08. Dir, John Hill Meml Recitals, 2006–. Estabd and Editor-in-Chief, London Organ Concerts Guide, 1995, now Editor Emeritus. President: IAO, 2005–07; RCO, 2013–15 (Mem. Council, 2006–08). Trustee, Nicholas Danby Trust, 1999–. Presenter, recitalist, concerto soloist and conductor on radio and TV; has made several commercial recordings. Prizewinner: GSM, 1973; Manchester Internat. Organ Comp., 1981 and 1983; RCO Medal, 2018. *Publications:* contribs to organ jls. *Recreations:* family, reading, gardening, opera. *Address:* c/o The Vestry, St Lawrence Jewry-next-Guildhall, EC2V 5AA. *E:* cmennis@aol.com.

**ENNIS, Jeffrey,** OBE 2018; *b* 13 Nov. 1952; *s* of William Ennis and Jean Ennis; *m* 1980, Margaret Angela Knight; three *s. Educ:* Redland Coll.; Univ. of Bristol (BEd Hons). Teacher: Elston Hall Jun. Sch., Fordhouses, Wolverhampton, 1976–78; Burngreave Middle Sch., Sheffield, 1978–79; Hillsborough Primary Sch., Sheffield, 1979–96. Barnsley Metropolitan Borough Council: Councillor (Lab), 1980–97 and 2012–; Dep. Leader, 1988–95; Leader, 1995–96; Mayor, 2017–18. MP (Lab) Barnsley E, Dec. 1996–1997, Barnsley E and Mexborough, 1997–2010. PPS to Minister for Public Health, DoH, 1997–99, to Minister for Employment, 1999–2001, to Chancellor of Duchy of Lancaster and Cabinet Sec., 2007–08; Dep. Minister for Yorks and Humberside, 2008–10. Mem., Educn and Skills Select Cttee, 2001–10. Mem., British-Irish Inter-Parly Body, 1998–2010; Jt Chair, All Party Racing and Bloodstock Gp, 2001–10; Treas., All Party China Gp, 2005–10; Sec., Lab back-bench Gp on Regeneration, 2005–10; Founder Mem. and Chm., All Party Brass Band Gp, 2008–10. Member: Co-op Party; TGWU; Chm., Brierley Lab. Pty Br., 1998–2010. *Recreations:* most sports, especially swimming, hill-walking, caravanning.

**ENNIS, Richard;** Managing Director, Ennis Consultancy, since 2018; *b* 9 Oct. 1965; *s* of Thomas and Wendy Ennis; *m* 1990, Theresa Dawn Jones; three *s*; partner, Alison Siggs; one *s. Educ:* W London Poly.; Harrow College (Finance and Business Studies degree 1989); Middlesex Poly. (Dip. Mgt Studies 1991); Thames Valley Univ. (ACMA 1995). Mgt Accountant, PO Ltd, 1986–90; Accountant, Slough BC, 1990–96; Finance and Systems Manager, Guildford Spectrum Leisure, 1996–98; Assistant Director, Finance: Slough Unitary Council, 1998–2000; Westminster CC, 2000–03; Exec. Dir of Finance, Lambeth LBC, 2003–05; Exec. Dir of Corporate Resources (formerly of Finance and Business Support), Ealing LBC, 2005–09; Exec. Dir of Finance and Corporate Services, Homes and Communities Agency, then Homes England, 2009–18. *Recreation:* football coach.

**ENNIS-HILL, Dame Jessica,** DBE 2017 (CBE 2013; MBE 2011); athlete, 2007–16; *b* Sheffield, 28 Jan. 1986; *d* of Vinnie Ennis and Alison Powell; *m* 2013, Andrew Hill; one *s* one *d. Educ:* King Ecgbert Secondary Sch., Sheffield; Univ. of Sheffield (BSc Psychol. 2007). Heptathlon wins include: Commonwealth Games: Bronze Medal, 2006; World Championships: Gold Medal, 2009, 2011, 2015; European Championships: Gold Medal, 2010; Olympic Games: Gold Medal, 2012; Silver Medal, 2016; pentathlon wins include: World Indoor Championships: Gold Medal, 2010; Silver Medal, 2012. Hon. LittD Sheffield, 2010. Freedom of Sheffield, 2013. *Publications:* Unbelievable (autobiog.), 2013; Evie's Magic Bracelet (series of books for children): The Silver Unicorn, 2017; The Enchanted Puppy, 2017; The Sprites' Den, 2017; The Unicorn Foal, 2017; The Clocktower Charm, 2018; The Fire Bird, 2018; The Golden Sands, 2018. *Address:* c/o JCCM Ltd, Thornton House, Thornton Road, SW19 4NG.

**ENNISKILLEN,** 7th Earl of, *cr* 1789 (Ire.); **Andrew John Galbraith Cole;** Baron Mountflorence 1760; Viscount Enniskillen 1776; Baron Grinstead (UK) 1815; company director; *b* 28 April 1942; *s* of 6th Earl of Enniskillen, MBE and Sonia (*d* 1982), *d* of Major Thomas Syers, RA; *S* father, 1989; *m* 1964, Sarah, *o d* of Maj.-Gen. J. Keith-Edwards, CBE, DSO, MC, Nairobi; three *d. Educ:* Eton. Captain, Irish Guards, 1965. Airline pilot; Man. Dir, Kenya Airways, 1979–81; CEO and Chm., AAR Health Services, 1991–2006. Gov. and Mem. Bd, Kenya Private Sector Alliance, 2002–11; Mem. Bd and Chm., Inst. of Dirs, Kenya, 2003–09. Mem., Nat. Envmt Council, Kenya, 2010–14. *Heir: cousin* Berkeley Arthur Cole [*b* 17 Dec. 1949; *m* 1978, Hon. Cecilia Anne Ridley (marr. diss. 2002), *e d* of 4th Viscount Ridley; two *s*].

**ENO, Brian Peter George St John Baptiste de la Salle,** RDI 2012; musician and artist; *b* 15 May 1948; *s* of William Arnold Eno and Maria Alphonsine Eno (*née* Buslot); *m* 1st, 1967, Sarah Grenville; one *d*; 2nd, 1988, Anthea Norman-Taylor; two *d. Educ:* Ipswich Sch. of Art; Winchester Coll. of Art. With Roxy Music, 1971–73. Vis. Prof., RCA, 1995–; Hon. Prof. of New Media, Berlin Univ. of Art, 1998–; Founder, Long Now Foundn, 1996–. Hon. DTech Plymouth, 1995. Brit Award, Best Producer, 1994. *Music:* solo recordings: Here Come the Warm Jets, 1974; Taking Tiger Mountain (By Strategy), 1974; Another Green World, 1975; Discreet Music, 1975; Before and After Science, 1977; Music for Films, 1978; Music for Airports, 1978; On Land, 1981; Thursday Afternoon, 1984; Nerve Net, 1992; The Shutov Assembly, 1992; Neroli, 1993; The Drop, 1997; Another Day on Earth, 2005; The Ship, 2016; collaborative recordings: (with David Bowie) Low, 1977, Heroes, 1977, Lodger, 1979; (with David Byrne) My Life in the Bush of Ghosts, 1980; (with Daniel Lanois and Roger Eno) Apollo: Atmospheres and Soundtracks, 1983, 2019; (with J. Peter Schwalm) Drawn from Life, 2001; (with Paul Simon) Surprise, 2006; (with David Byrne) Everything that Happens Will Happen Today, 2008; (with Tom Rogerson) Finding Shore, 2017; *productions:* Talking Heads: More Songs about Buildings and Food, Fear of Music, Remain in Light, 1978–80; U2: Unforgettable Fire, The Joshua Tree, Rattle and Hum, Achtung Baby, Zooropa, All That You Can't Leave Behind (Grammy Award, Record of the Year: for track Beautiful Day, 2000, for track Walk On, 2001), 1984–2001; David Bowie: Outside, 1995; *visual:* over 80 exhibns of video artworks and audio-visual installations in museums and galleries worldwide, incl. Stedelijk Mus., Amsterdam, 1984; Venice Biennale, 1986; Marble Palace, St Petersburg, 1997; Hayward Gall., London, 2000; San Francisco Mus. of Modern Art, 2001; Lyon Biennial, 2005; Mus. für Abgüsse Klassischer Bildwerke, Munich, 2005. *Publications:* (with Peter Schmidt) Oblique Strategies (set of cards), 1975, 5th edn 2001; A Year with Swollen Appendices, 1996. *Recreation:* perfumery.

**ENOCH, Dafydd Huw;** QC 2008; a Recorder, since 2004; *b* Chelmsford, 24 April 1961; *s* of Dr Morgan David Enoch and late Margaret Joyce Enoch; *m* 1997, Naomi Jane Hartridge; one *s* two *d. Educ:* Univ. of Buckingham (LLB 1984); Univ. d'Aix-Marseille III (Diplôme d'Etudes Juridiques). Called to the Bar, Gray's Inn, 1985; in practice as barrister specialising in criminal and disciplinary law. *Recreations:* playing the guitar and drums, travelling, sport of all types. *Address:* New Park Court Chambers, 16 Park Place, Leeds LS1 2SJ.

**ENRIGHT, Neil James,** MA; Headmaster, Queen Elizabeth's School, Barnet, since 2011; *b* London, 5 Sept. 1977. *Educ:* John Lyon Sch., Harrow; St John's Coll., Oxford (BA Geog. 1999); Nat. Coll. for Sch. Leadership (NPQH 2007); Inst. of Educn, Univ. of London (MBA 2010). Gifted and Talented Co-ordinator and Teacher of Geog., St Gregory's RC Sci. Coll., 2000–02; Hd of Geog., 2002–07, Hd of Year, 2007–08, Asst Hd, 2008–10, Dep. Headmaster, 2010–11, Queen Elizabeth's Sch., Barnet. Governor: Longfield Primary Sch., Harrow, 2009–; St Albans High Sch. for Girls, 2016–; John Lyon Sch., Harrow, 2016–; Chm., Mgt Cttee, Northgate Sch., Edgware, 2011–19. *Recreations:* family, friends, education, geography, music (clarinettist), art, cinema, theatre, travel, food and wine, watching sports, club level football (especially Luton Town FC), international cricket and Rugby. *Address:* Queen Elizabeth's School, Queen's Road, Barnet, Herts EN5 4DQ. *T:* (020) 8441 4646. *E:* hmoffice@qebarnet.co.uk.

**ENRIGHT, Seán; His Honour Judge Enright;** a Circuit Judge, since 2008; *m* Lorna. In practice as a barrister, 1982–2008. Mem., Justice Wkg Pty, Mental Health and Fair Trial, 2017–. Chairman: Discipline Panel: RFU, 2009–; Six Nations; World Rugby. Vis. Scholar, Sidney Sussex Coll., Cambridge, 2017. Consultant Ed., Halsbury's Laws, 2012–. *Publications:* Taking Liberties: criminal jury in the 1990s (with James Morton), 1990; The Trial of Civilians by Military Courts: Ireland 1921, 2012; Easter Rising 1916 - The Trials, 2013; After the Rising, 2016. *Club:* Peterborough Rugby.

**ENRIQUES, Prof. Luca,** PhD; Allen & Overy Professor of Corporate Law, University of Oxford, since 2014; Fellow, Jesus College, Oxford, since 2014; *b* Bologna, 17 Feb. 1970; *s* of Federico Enriques and Raffaella Tommasi; *m* 1997, Claudia Barbara; two *s* one *d. Educ:* Liceo Ginnasio Statale L. Galvani, Bologna (Dip.); Univ. of Bologna (degree in law *cum laude*); Harvard Law Sch. (LLM); Univ. Commerciale L. Bocconi, Milan (PhD 1999). Lawyer, Banking Supervision Dept, Legislation Div., Bank of Italy, 1996–99; Faculty of Law, University of Bologna: Asst Prof. of Business Law, 1999–2001; Associate Prof. of Business Law, 2001–04; Prof. of Business Law, 2004–12; on leave to Comr, Consob (Italian Stock Exchange), 2007–12; Prof. of Business Law, LUISS Guido Carli Univ., Rome, 2013–14. Nomura Vis. Prof. of Internat. Financial Systems, Harvard Law Sch., 2012–13. Ind. Consultant, Cleary Gottlieb, Steen & Hamilton, Rome and Milan, 2003–07. Advr on corporate, banking and financial mkts law, Min. of Econ. and Finance, Italy, 2000–06, 2014–16, 2017–18. Mem., Adv. Bd, Yale Prog. on Financial Stability, 2013–17. Mem., Bd of Dirs, Eur. Corporate Governance Inst., 2018–. *Publications:* Il conflitto d'interessi degli amministratori di società per azioni, 2000; Mercato del controllo societario e tutela degli investitori, 2002; (with Renzo Costi) Il mercato mobiliare, 2004; (contrib.) Commentario del codice civile Scialoja-Branca, 2007; (jtly) The Anatomy of Corporate Law, 2nd edn 2009, 3rd edn 2017; (jtly) Principles of Financial Regulation, 2016; contrib. to jls incl. Univ. of Pennsylvania Jl Internat. Law, Harvard Business Law Rev., Jl Corporate Law Studies, Cambridge Law Jl, Jl Econ. Perspectives, Tulane Law Rev., Cornell Law Rev., Modern Law Rev. *Address:* Jesus College, Oxford OX1 3DW.

**ENSOR, Anthony;** *see* Ensor, His Honour G. A.

**ENSOR, David,** OBE 1986; Managing Director, Croydon Advertiser Ltd, 1979–85; *b* 2 April 1924; *s* of Rev. William Walters and Constance Eva Ensor; *m* 1947, Gertrude Kathleen Brown (*d* 2015); two *s. Educ:* Kingswood Sch., Bath; London Coll. of Printing. Served Royal Signals, 1942–46, Captain; ADC to GOC Bengal Dist. Managing Director: George Reveirs, 1947–59; Charles Skipper & East, 1959–69; Knapp Drewett & Sons, 1969–79; Chairman: Methodist Newspaper Co., 1975–94; Methodist Publishing House, 1981–96. A Vice-Chm., Press Council, 1987–90 (Mem., 1982–90); Mem. Council, Newspaper Soc., 1979–94. Pres., London Printing Industries Assoc., 1976. Vice-Pres., Methodist Conf., 1981. *Address:* Sunrise, 6 Upper Kings Drive, Eastbourne, E Sussex BN20 9AN. *T:* (01323) 525097.

**ENSOR, His Honour (George) Anthony;** a Circuit Judge, 1995–2008; *b* 4 Nov. 1936; *s* of George and Phyllis Ensor; *m* 1968, Jennifer Margaret Caile, MB, ChB; two *d. Educ:* Malvern College; Liverpool University (LLB). Solicitor, 1961 (Atkinson Conveyancing Medal, 1962; Rupert Bremner Medal, 1962); Partner, 1962–92, Sen. Partner, 1992–95, Rutherfords, later Weightman Rutherfords, Solicitors, Liverpool; a Recorder, 1983–95; Dep. Sen. Judge, Sovereign Base Area, Cyprus, 2005. Deputy Coroner, City of Liverpool, 1966–95; part-time Chairman, Industrial Tribunals, 1975–95; Asst Parly Boundary Comr, 1992–95. Mem., Judicial Studies Bd, 1987–89; President, Liverpool Law Society, 1982. Trustee, Empire Theatre (Merseyside) Trust, Ltd, 1986–. Dir, Liverpool FC, 1985–93. *Recreations:* golf, theatre. *Clubs:* Artists (Liverpool); Formby Golf; Pwllheli Golf; Waterloo Rugby Union.

**ENTICKNAP, Colin,** FRICS, FCIOB; Group Chairman, Willmott Dixon Holdings Ltd, since 2005; *b* Huntingdon, 6 Sept. 1958; *s* of Colin and Pamela Enticknap; *m* 1981, Susan Hood; one *s* one *d. Educ:* Harvard Business Sch. (AMP 1998). FRICS 1985; FCIOB 2001. Mgt Trainee, Tarmac Construction, 1977–80; Chartered Quantity Surveyor, R. G. Carter, 1980–87; Dir and Gen. Manager, Willmott Dixon Chilterns, 1987–88; Man. Dir, Willmott Dixon Construction, 1988–91; Gp Chief Exec., Willmott Dixon Hldgs Ltd, 1991–2005. *Address:* Willmott Dixon Holdings Ltd, Spirella 2, Icknield Way, Letchworth Garden City SG6 4GY. *T:* (01462) 671852. *E:* colin.enticknap@willmottdixon.co.uk.

**ENTWISTLE, George;** Director General, BBC, 2012; *b* 8 July 1962; *s* of Philip and Wendy Entwistle; *m* 1992, Jane Porter; one *s* one *d. Educ:* Durham Univ. (BA Hons Philosophy and Politics 1983); St Catherine's Coll., Oxford (MSt History of Design 2015). Sub-ed. and Ed., Haymarket Magazines, 1984–89; joined BBC, 1989; broadcast journalism trainee, 1989–90; Asst Producer, Panorama, 1990–92; Producer, On The Record, 1993–94; Producer, 1994–97, Asst Ed., 1997–99, Newsnight; Dep. Ed., Tomorrow's World, 1999–2000; Dep. Ed., 2000–01, Ed., 2001–04, Newsnight; Ed., The Culture Show, 2004–05; Hd of TV Current Affairs, 2005–07; Actg Controller, BBC Four, 2007; Controller, Knowledge Commissioning, BBC TV, 2008–11; Dir, BBC Vision, 2011–12. Mem., Exec. Cttee, Edinburgh Internat. TV Fest., 2011–15 (Chair, Adv. Cttee, 2011). Trustee: Comic Relief, 2011–12; Art UK (formerly Public Catalogue Foundn), 2013–; Georgian Gp, 2016–. DPhil student (pt-time), Worcester Coll., Oxford, 2016–. *Recreations:* architectural and design history, reading, music, fell walking, armchair Rugby Union. *E:* george.entwistle@worc.ox.ac.uk.

**ENTWISTLE, John Nicholas McAlpine,** OBE 2005; Consultant Solicitor, Davies Wallis Foyster, 1992–2004; President, British Chambers of Commerce, 1998–2000; *b* 16 June 1941; *s* of Sir (John Nuttall) Maxwell Entwistle and Lady (Jean Cunliffe McAlpine) Entwistle; *m* 1968, Phillida Gail Sinclair Burgess; one *s* one *d. Educ:* Uppingham Sch.

Admitted Solicitor, 1963. Asst Attorney, Shearman & Sterling, NY, 1963–64; Partner, Maxwell Entwistle & Byrne, Solicitors, 1966–91. Regl Dir, Midshires Building Soc., 1977–87; non-exec. Dir, Rathbone Brothers plc, 1992–98. Founder Dir, Merseyside TEC, 1990–91; Dep. Dist Chm., Appeals Service, 1999–2006 (pt-time Chm., Social Security Appeals Tribunal, 1992–99); pt-time Immigration Judge, 2000–10. Member: Parole Bd, 1994–2000; Criminal Injuries Compensation Tribunal (formerly Appeals Panel), 2000–12; Disciplinary Cttee, Mortgage Code Compliance Bd, 1999–2004; Chancellor of Exchequer's Standing Cttee on Preparation for EMU, 1998–2000; Adv. Council, Migration Watch UK, 2010–15. Trustee: Nat. Museums and Galls on Merseyside, 1990–97 (Chm., Develt Trust, 1991–95); RA Trust, 2006–11, now Emeritus; Friends of the Lake District, 2014– (Chm., 2016–). Gen. Comr for Income Tax, 1978–83. Mem. (C), Liverpool CC, 1968–71. Contested (C) Huyton, 1970. DL Merseyside, 1992–2002. Hon. Fellow, Liverpool John Moores Univ., 2010. *Recreations:* collecting and painting pictures, gardening. *Address:* 40 Kentsford Road, Grange-over-Sands, Cumbria LA11 7AP. *T:* (015395) 83726. *E:* entwistlej@mail.com. *Club:* Carlton (Mem., Political Cttee, 2004–08).

**EÖTVÖS, Peter;** composer and conductor; *m* 1st, 1968, Piroska Molnar (marr. diss. 1975); one *s*; 2nd, 1976, Pi-Hsien Chen (marr. diss. 1994); one *d*; 3rd, 1995, Maria Mezei. *Educ:* Acad. of Music, Budapest; Musik Hochschule, Cologne. Composer, chamber music, electronic music, opera and orchestral music; conductor and musical director, Ensemble Intercontemporain, Paris, 1979–91; principal guest conductor, BBC Symphony Orchestra, 1985–88; first Guest Conductor, Budapest Fest. Orch., 1992–95; Chief Conductor, Radio Chamber Orch. Hilversum, 1994–2005; first Guest Conductor, Radio Symphony Orchestra Vienna, 2009–12. Professor: Musikhochschule Karlsruhe, 1992–2007; Musikhochschule Köln, 1998–2001; Founder: Internat. Eötvös Inst., for young conductors and composers, 1991; Peter Eötvös Contemporary Music Foundn, 2004. *Recreations:* walking, pipe smoking, jazz. *W:* www.eotvospeter.com.

**EPSTEIN, Sir Anthony;** *see* Epstein, Sir M. A.

**EPSTEIN, Prof. David Bernard Alper,** PhD; FRS 2004; Professor, Mathematics Institute, University of Warwick, 1969–2005, now Professor Emeritus; *b* 16 May 1937; *s* of Dr Ben Epstein and Pauline Alper Epstein; *m* 1958, Rona; one *s* two *d. Educ:* Univ. of Witwatersrand (BSc Hons 1955); Trinity Coll., Cambridge (BA 1957); PhD Cantab 1960. Instructor, Princeton Univ., 1960–61; Princeton Inst. for Advanced Study, 1961–62; Cambridge University: Fellow, Trinity Coll., 1960–62; Lectr, 1962–64; Dir, Studies in Maths, Churchill Coll., 1962–64; Reader in Maths, Univ. of Warwick, 1964–69. Scientific Dir, NSF Geometry Center, Minneapolis, 1990–91. Vis. Prof., Univ. of Paris, Orsay, 1974–75; Ordway Dist. Vis. Prof., Minnesota, 1986. *Publications:* (with N. E. Steenrod) Cohomology Operations, 1963; (jtly) Word Processing in Groups, 1992. *Recreations:* gardening, friends. *Address:* Mathematics Institute, University of Warwick, Zeeman Building, Coventry CV4 7AL. *T:* (024) 7652 2677. *E:* David.Epstein@warwick.ac.uk.

**EPSTEIN, Sir (Michael) Anthony,** Kt 1991; CBE 1985; FRS 1979; Fellow, 1986–2001, Hon. Fellow, since 2001, Wolfson College, Oxford; Professor of Pathology, 1968–85 (now Emeritus), and Head of Department, 1968–82, University of Bristol; Hon. Consultant Pathologist, Bristol Health District (Teaching), 1968–82; *b* 18 May 1921; *yr s of* Mortimer and Olga Epstein; *m* 1950, Lisbeth Knight (separated 1965; she *d* 2015); two *s* one *d. Educ:* St Paul's Sch., London; Trinity Coll., Cambridge (Perry Exhibr, 1940); Middlesex Hosp. Medical Sch. MA, MD, DSc, PhD; FRCPath. Ho. Surg., Middlesex Hosp., London, and Addenbrooke's Hosp., Cambridge, 1944; Lieut and Captain, RAMC, 1945–47; Asst Pathologist, Bland Sutton Inst., Middx Hosp. Med. Sch., 1948–65, with leave as: Berkeley Travelling Fellow, 1952–53; French Govt Exchange Scholar at Institut Pasteur, Paris, 1952–53; Vis. Investigator, Rockefeller Inst., NY, 1956; Reader in Experimental Pathology, Middx Hosp. Med. Sch., 1965–68; Hon. Consultant in Experimental Virology, Middx Hosp., 1965–68. Member: Cttee, Pathological Soc. of GB and Ire., 1969–72 (Hon. Mem., 1987); Council, and Vice-Pres., Pathology Section of RSM, 1966–72 (Hon. Mem., 1988); Study Gp on Classification of Herpes Viruses, of Internat. Commn for Nomenclature of Viruses, 1971–81; Scientific Adv. Bd, Harvard Med. Sch.'s New England Regional Primate Center, 1972–96; Cancer Research Campaign MRC Jt Cttee, 1973–77, 1982–87 (Chm. 1983–87); Cttee, British Soc. for Cell Biology, 1974–77; MRC, 1982–86 (Mem., 1979–84, Chm., 1982–84, Cell Bd; Mem., 1984–85, Chm., 1985–88, Tropical Medicine Res. Bd); Council, Royal Soc., 1983–85, 1986–91 (Foreign Sec. and a Vice-Pres., 1986–91; Assessor on MRC, 1987–91); Medical and Scientific Panel, Leukaemia Research Fund, 1982–85; Scientific Adv. Cttee, Lister Inst., 1984–87; Expert Working Party on Bovine Spongiform Encephalopathy, DoH, 1988; Exec. Bd, ICSU, 1990–93 (Chm., Cttee on Sci. in Central and Eastern Europe, 1992–95); Exec. Council, ESF, 1990–93; Program Adv. Gp, World Bank China Key Studies Project, 1992–97; Special Rep. of Dir Gen. UNESCO for Sci. in Russia, 1992. Discovered in 1964 a new human herpes virus, now known as Epstein-Barr virus, which causes infectious mononucleosis and is also causally implicated in some forms of human cancer (esp. Burkitt's lymphoma, nasopharyngeal carcinoma and post-transplant lymphomas). Fellow, 1992, Hon. Fellow, 2010, UCL. Founder FMedSci 1998. Mem., Academia Europaea, 1988. Mem. d'honneur, Belgian Soc. for Cancer Res., 1979. Hon. Professor: Sun Yat-Sen Med. Univ., Guangzhou, 1981; Chinese Acad. of Preventive Medicine, Beijing, 1988. Hon. Fellow: Queensland Inst. of Med. Research, 1983; CRUK, 2004; Bristol Univ., 2006; Hon. FRCP 1986; Hon. FRSE 1991; Hon. FRCPA 1995. Hon. MD: Edinburgh, 1986; Charles Univ., Prague, 1998; Hon. DSc Birmingham, 1996. Paul Ehrlich and Ludwig Darmstaedter Prize and Medal, Paul Ehrlich Foundn, W Germany, 1973; Markham Skerrit Prize, 1977; (jtly) Bristol-Myers Award, NY, 1982; Leeuwenhoek Prize Lectr, Royal Soc., 1983; Prix Griffuel, Assoc. pour la recherche sur le cancer, Paris, 1986; David Henderson Medal, PHLS, 1986; Samuel Weiner Distinguished Visitor Award, Univ. of Manitoba, 1988; John H. Lattimer Award, Amer. Urol Assoc., 1988; Internat. Award, Gairdner Foundn, Toronto, 1988; Jenner Medal, St George's Hosp. Med. Sch., 1989; Royal Medal, Royal Soc., 1992; Gold Medal, Charles Univ., Prague, 1998. *Publications:* over 250 scientific papers in internat. jls on tumour cell structure, viruses, tumour viruses, Burkitt's lymphoma, and the EB virus. Jt Founder Editor, The Internat. Review of Experimental Pathology (vols 1–28, 1962–86); (ed jtly) The Epstein-Barr Virus, 1979; (ed jtly) The Epstein-Barr Virus: recent advances, 1986; (ed jtly) Oncogenic γ-herpesviruses: an expanding family, 2001. *Address:* Wolfson College, University of Oxford, Linton Road, Oxford OX2 6UD. *T:* (01865) 250885.

**EPSTEIN, Paul Jeremy;** QC 2006; *b* London, 9 Aug. 1963; *s* of Maurice and late Jill Epstein; partner, Laura Binns; two *d. Educ:* Balliol Coll., Oxford (BA Hist. and Mod. Langs); City Univ., London (Dip. Law). Called to the Bar, Middle Temple, 1988, Bencher, 2013; barrister, Cloisters chambers, 1990–. *Recreation:* enthusiastic cyclist. *Address:* Cloisters, 1 Pump Court, Temple, EC4Y 7AA. *T:* (020) 7827 4000, *Fax:* (020) 7827 4100. *E:* clerks@cloisters.com.

**EPSTEIN, Sophie Lysandra;** *see* Thomas, S. L.

**ERECIŃSKA, Barbara;** *see* Tuge-Erecińska.

**EREMIN, Prof. Oleg,** MD; FRCSE, FRACS, FMedSci; Honorary Professor (formerly Special Professor) in Surgery, University of Nottingham, at Queen's Medical Centre, Nottingham, since 1998; Honorary Senior Research Fellow, United Lincolnshire Hospitals (formerly Lincoln) NHS Trust, since 2014 (Director of Research and Development, 2001–14); *b* 12 Nov. 1938; *s* of Theodor and Maria Eremin; *m* 1963, Jennifer Mary Ching; two *s* one *d. Educ:* Christian Brothers' Coll., St Kilda, Melbourne; Univ. of Melbourne. MB BS 1964; MD 1985. FRACS 1971; FRCSE 1983. Clinical posts: Royal Melbourne Hosp., 1965–72; Norfolk and Norwich Hosps, 1972–74; Research Asst-Associate, Dept of Pathology, Univ. of Cambridge, 1974–80; Sen. Lectr, Dept Clinical Surgery, Univ. of Edinburgh, 1981–85; Regius Prof. of Surgery, Univ. of Aberdeen, 1985–98. Consultant Breast Surgeon and Lead Clinician, United Lincs Hosps (formerly Lincoln) NHS Trust, 1999–2011; Clinical Dir, Trent Comp. Local Res. Network, 2007–14. Hon. Professorial Fellow, Rowett Res. Inst., 1992; Vis. Prof., Univ. of Lincoln, 2003–. Founder FMedSci 1998; Hon. FRCST 2003. Hon. DSc Lincoln. *Publications:* articles in surgical, oncological and immunological jls and textbooks. *Recreations:* music, sport, reading. *Address:* Orchard House, 51A Washdyke Lane, Nettleham, Lincoln LN2 2PX. *T:* (01522) 750669.

**ERICHT, Hon. Lord; Andrew Fleming Stewart;** a Senator of the College of Justice in Scotland, since 2016; *b* Dundee, 12 Sept. 1963; *s* of late Rev. Gordon Grant Stewart and Elspeth Margaret Stewart (*née* Farquharson); *m* 1992, Dr Lesley Katherine Dawson; two *d. Educ:* Perth High Sch.; Edinburgh Univ. (LLB Hons 1985). Admitted Faculty of Advocates, 1996; Standing Jun. Counsel to DTI, 2000–09; QC (Scot.) 2009; Advocate Depute, 2009–13; Mem., Scottish Civil Justice Council, 2014–16. Clerk of the Faculty of Advocates, 2003–09; Pres., Scottish Tax Tribunals, 2015–16. Vis. Lectr, Univ. de Lorraine (formerly Univ. de Nancy 2), 1993–2016. Chm., Scottish Churches Cttee, 2007–16. Ed., Session Cases, 2001–16. Hon. FRCPE 2017. *Publications:* articles in legal jls, etc. *Recreations:* family, Scottish dance music, golf. *Address:* Court of Session, Parliament House, Edinburgh EH1 1RQ. *Clubs:* New (Edinburgh); Blairgowrie Golf, Bruntsfield Links Golfing Society.

**ERIKSSON, Peter Eskil;** Head Coach, Athletics Canada, 2013–16; *b* Stockholm, 19 Nov. 1952; *s* of Eskil and Ellen Eriksson; *m* 1992, Rhonda Nishio; four *d. Educ:* Univ. of Stockholm (Special Educn degree 1983; MSc Physical Educn 1984). Speed skating competitor for Sweden, 1963–80; coach for speed skating, ice hockey, then athletics, 1980–87; coach, Canadian Paralympic athletes, 1987–2008; High Performance Dir, Speed Skating Canada, 1992–95; Sales Manager, Corel Corp., 1995–97; Manager, Distribn and Corporate Resellers, JefForm Corp., 1997–99; Exec. Vice-Pres., Business and Develt and Strategic Alliances, Runaware Inc., 1999–2005; Hd Coach, Athletics, US Paralympics, 2005; High Performance Advr, Own the Podium 2010 (Olympic and Paralympic Sports), 2005–08; Hd Coach and Performance Dir, Paralympic Progs, UK Athletics, 2008–12; Head Coach, UK Athletics, 2012–13. Coach of Year, Manitoba Wheelchair Sports Assoc., 1989; Coaching Association of Canada: Wittenauer Coaching Excellence Award, 1993, 1995, 1996, 1998, 2000; Petro-Canada Coaching Excellence Award, 2004, 2006, 2008; Coach of Year: Canadian Wheelchair Sports Assoc., 2004, 2008; Ontario Sports Awards, 2005; Canadian Sports Awards, 2005; Athletics Canada, 2008; UK Coaching Awards: UK Coach, 2012; High Performance Coach of Year, 2012; Order of Ikkos, US Olympic Cttee, 2008. *Publications:* Wheel into Fitness: management of spinal cord injuries, 1991; contribs to jls and conf. procs incl. Skridskonytt, Svenskidrott, Medicine and Sci. in Sports and Exercise, New England Jl Medicine, Archives of Physical Medicine and Rehabilitation, Paraplegia, Adapted Physical Activity Qly, Canadian Jl Applied Physiol. *E:* coachesforum@hotmail.com.

**ERIKSSON, Sven-Göran;** Head Coach, Philippines National Football Team, since 2018; *b* Torsby, Sweden, 5 Feb. 1948; *s* of Sven and Ulla Eriksson; *m* Ann-Kristin (marr. diss.); one *s* one *d.* Former footballer (defender); clubs include Torsby IF, Sifhalla and KB Karlskoga (all Sweden); managerial posts: Asst Manager, 1976, Manager, 1977–78, Degerfors, Sweden; Manager: IFK Gothenburg, Sweden, 1979–82; Benfica, Portugal, 1982–84; AS Roma, Italy, 1984–87; AC Fiorentina, Italy, 1987–89; Benfica, 1989–92; Sampdoria, Italy, 1992–97; SS Lazio, Italy, 1997–2000 (winners: Italian Cup, 1998; Italian Super Cup, 1998; UEFA Cup Winners Cup, 1999; UEFA Super Cup, 1999; Italian Championship, 2000); Hd Coach, England Football Team, 2001–06; Manager, Manchester City FC, 2007–08; Hd Coach, Mexico Football Team, 2008–09; Dir of Football, Notts County FC, 2009–10 (Hon. Pres., 2010); Manager: Ivory Coast Team, World Cup, 2010; Leicester City FC, 2010–11; Technical Director: Bec Tero Sasana, Thailand, 2012–13; Al-Nasr Sports Club, UAE, 2013; Chief Coach, Guangzhou R&F FC, China, 2013–14; Hd Coach, Shanghai Internat. Port Gp (formerly Shanghai East Asia) FC, 2014–16; Hd Coach, Shenzhen FC, 2016–17. *Publications:* Sven: my story (autobiog.), 2013. *Address:* c/o Athole Still Ltd, Foresters Hall, 25 Westow Street, SE19 3RY. *E:* athole@atholestill.co.uk.

**ERLEIGH, Viscount; Julian Michael Rufus Isaacs;** Corporate Financier, Cantor Fitzgerald (Europe); *b* 26 May 1986; *s* and *heir of* Marquess of Reading, *qv. Educ:* Cheltenham Coll.; Univ. of the West of England Business School, Bristol (BA 2009). *Recreations:* motorsport, tennis, Reading FC. *Address:* 7 Cecily Hill, Cirencester, Glos GL7 2EF.

**ERMISCH, Prof. John Francis,** FBA 1995; Professor of Family Demography, University of Oxford, since 2011; Senior Research Fellow, Nuffield College, Oxford, since 2011; *b* 1 July 1947; *s of* Elmer and Frances Ermisch; *m* 1977, Dianne M. Monti. *Educ:* Univ. of Wisconsin (BSc); Univ. of Kansas (MA, PhD 1973). Res. Economist, US Dept of Housing and Urban Develt, 1974–76; Res. Fellow, Centres for Environmental Studies and for the Study of Social Policy, London, 1976–78; Sen. Res. Fellow, PSI, 1978–86; Sen. Res. Officer, NIESR, 1986–91; Bonar-Macfie Prof., Univ. of Glasgow, 1991–94; Prof. of Econs, ESRC Res. Centre on Micro-Social Change, later Inst. for Social and Econ. Res., Univ. of Essex, 1994–2011. *Publications:* The Political Economy of Demographic Change, 1983; Lone Parenthood: an economic analysis, 1991; An Economic Analysis of the Family, 2003; contribs to economic and demographic jls. *Recreations:* films, music. *Address:* Department of Sociology, University of Oxford, 42–43 Park End Street, Oxford OX1 1JD.

**ERNE, 7th Earl of,** *cr* 1789; **John Henry Michael Ninian Crichton;** Baron Erne 1768; Viscount Erne (Ire.) 1781; Baron Fermanagh (UK) 1876; DL; Founder Director, John Crichton Property, since 2008; *b* 19 June 1971; *o s of* 6th Earl of Erne, KCVO and Camilla Marguerite Crichton (*née* Roberts); *S father*, 2015; *m* 2019, Harriet Elizabeth Patterson. *Educ:* Sunningdale Prep. Sch.; Shiplake Coll.; L'Institut de Touraine, Tours. Douglas & Gordon Ltd, 1992–98; Associate Dir, Lane Fox Residential Ltd, 1998–2007. Trustee, Hope for Youth, NI (formerly Women Caring Trust for NI), 2009–; DL Co. Fermanagh, 2016–. *Recreations:* theatre, amateur dramatics, shooting, ski-ing. *Heir: cousin* Charles David Blayney Crichton [*b* 31 Oct. 1953; *m* 1st, 1977, Nicola Sian Barry; 2nd, 1988, Harriet Monier-Williams; one *s* two *d*]. *Address:* Crom Castle, Newtownbutler, Co. Fermanagh, N Ireland BT92 8AP. *Clubs:* White's; Lough Erne Yacht.

**ERNEST, Rt Rev. (Gerald James) Ian,** GOSK 2006; Director, Anglican Centre in Rome, and Personal Representative of the Archbishop of Canterbury to the Pope, since 2019; *b* 30 Aug. 1954; *s of* Gerald and Jessie Ernest; *m* 1983, Kamla Ramloll; one *s. Educ:* Madras Univ., India (BCom 1979); St Paul's Theol Coll., Mauritius; Westhill Coll., Univ. of Birmingham, UK (CPS 1986); Procter Schol., Episcopal Div. Sch., Cambridge, Mass and

Boston Inst. of Theol., 2005. Ordained priest, 1985; Bishop of Mauritius, 2001–19; Archbishop of the Indian Ocean, 2006–17. Mem., 1989–93, Chm., 2001–19, Bd of Comrs, Dio. Mauritius; Member: Provincial Standing Cttee and Provincial Electoral Coll., Ch of Province of Indian Ocean, 1992–2001; Council of Religious and Spiritual Leaders of Mauritius, 1996–2019. Chm., Council of Provinces in Africa, 2007–12. Convener, Target Gp for Bps Trng, Task Force of Theol Educn for Anglican Communion, 2003–; Mem., Eight Mems Design Gp Cttee, apptd by Archbp of Canterbury to prepare for Lambeth Conf. and Anglican Gathering 2008, 2003–. Pres., Prison Fellowship Internat., Mauritius. Main translator of New Testament into Creole, 1987–91; Ed., Anglican Diocesan Mag., 1990–95. *Publications*: (jtly) Autonomy for Rodrigues Island; articles on peace, justice and family issues. *Recreations*: reading, music, swimming. *Address*: Anglican Centre in Rome, Palazzo Doria Pamphilj, Piazza del Collegio Romano 2, 00186 Rome, Italy.

**ERNST, Prof. Edzard**, MD, PhD; FMedSci, FRSB, FRCP, FRCPE; Professor of Complementary Medicine, Peninsula Medical School, Universities of Exeter and Plymouth, 2000–12 (Professor of Complementary Medicine at University of Exeter, 1993–2012, now Emeritus); *b* 30 Jan. 1948; *s* of Wolfgang Ernst and Erika (*née* Tillwichs); *m* 1983, Danielle Johnson (*née* Le Mignon). *Educ*: Maximilian Ludwig Univ., Munich (MD 1978; PhD 1985). FRCPE 1997; FRCP 2003. University of Munich: Sen. House Officer, 1977–79; Registrar, then Sen. Registrar, 1981–89; Res. Assistant, St George's Hosp., London, 1979–81; Prof. of Physical Medicine and Rehabilitation, Univ. of Hanover, 1989; Prof. of Physical Medicine and Rehabilitation, Univ. of Vienna, 1990–93. Visiting Professor: RCPS, Canada, 1999; UCLA, 2005. Member: Medicines Commn, British Medicines and Healthcare Products Regulatory Agency (formerly British Medicines Control Agency), 1993–2005; Scientific Cttee on Herbal Medicinal Products, Irish Medicines Bd. Editor-in-Chief: Perfusion, 1987–; Focus on Alternative and Complementary Therapies, 1996–. FMedSci 2009; FRSB (FSB 2010). HealthWatch Award, 2005, Amer. Botanical Council Annual Award, 2006, In Praise of Reason Award, Cttee for Skeptical Inquiry, 2012, John Maddox Prize for standing up for science, 2015, Ockham Award, 2017, and 10 other scientific awards. *Publications*: Meyler's Side Effects of Drugs, 2000; Desk Top Guide to Complementary and Alternative Medicine, 2001, 2nd edn 2006; (contrib.) Oxford Textbook of Medicine, 4th edn 2003; Oxford Handbook of Complementary Medicine, 2008; (with S. Singh) Trick or Treatment? Alternative Medicine on Trial, 2008; A Scientist in Wonderland: a memoir of searching for truth and finding trouble, 2015; Homeopathy: the undiluted facts, 2016; More Harm than Good? The Moral Maze of Complementary and Alternative Medicine, 2018; SCAM, so-called alternative medicine, 2018; numerous articles in med. jls. *Recreations*: music, writing, blogging. *Address*: 6 Aberdeen Square, Cambridge CB2 8BZ. *T*: (01223) 364035.

**ERNST, Prof. Richard Robert**; Professor of Physical Chemistry, Swiss Federal Institute of Technology (ETH-Z), 1976–98, now Emeritus; *b* 14 Aug. 1933; *s* of Prof. Robert Ernst, architect, and Irma Ernst (*née* Brunner); *m* 1963, Magdalena Kielholz; one *s* two *d*. *Educ*: Winterthur schools; ETH-Zentrum (DipChemEng 1956; PhD 1962). Mil. Service, 1956–57. Scientist, Instrument Div., Varian Associates, Calif., 1963–68; Swiss Federal Institute of Technology (ETH-Z): Lectr in Phys. Chem., 1968–70 (Group Leader in Magnetic Resonance Spectroscopy); Asst Prof., 1970; Associate Prof., 1972–76; Pres., Research Council, 1990. Mem. Bd, Spectrospin AG (Vice-Pres., 1989). Fellow, Amer. Phys. Soc.; For. Mem., Royal Soc., 1993; Member: internat. scientific bodies; editl bds of learned jls. Hon. doctorates: ETH Lausanne; Technical Univ., Munich; Zürich; Antwerp; Cluj-Napoca; Montpellier. Numerous medals and prizes, Swiss and foreign; Nobel Prize in Chemistry, 1991; Wolf Prize, 1991; Louisa Gross Horwitz Prize, 1991. *Address*: Laboratorium für Physikalische Chemie, Vladimir-Prelog-Weg 2, ETH Zürich, HCI D217, 8093 Zürich, Switzerland. *T*: (44) 6324368. *E*: richard.ernst@nmr.phys.chem.ethz.ch; Kurlistrasse 24, 8404 Winterthur, Switzerland. *T*: (52) 2427807.

**ERNST, Prof. Wolfgang**, DIur; Regius Professor of Civil Law, University of Oxford, since 2015; Fellow, All Souls College, Oxford, since 2015; *b* Bonn, Germany, 28 June 1956; *s* of Dr Hermann Ernst and Anna Elisabeth Ernst; *m* 1985, Dr Katharina von Zglinitzki; one *s* three *d*. *Educ*: Arndt Gymnasium, Bonn; Bonn Univ. (DIur 1981); Yale Law Sch. (LLM 1982). Stagiaire, Cologne Ct of Appeal, 1982–85; Res. Asst, Inst. for Roman Law, Bonn Univ., 1986–89; Prof. of Private and Roman Law, Tübingen Univ., 1990–2000; Prof. of Private Law and Dir, Inst. for Roman Law, Bonn Univ., 2000–04; Arthur Goodhart Prof. in Legal Sci., Cambridge Univ. and Fellow, Magdalene Coll., Cambridge, 2002–03; Prof. of Roman Law and Private Law, Univ. of Zurich, 2004–15. Hon. LLD: Edinburgh, 2017; Vienna, 2017. *Publications*: (with D. Fox) Money in the Western Legal Tradition, 2015; contrib. articles to law and legal history jls. *Recreations*: hiking, Abraham Lincoln studies. *Address*: All Souls College, Oxford OX1 4AL. *T*: (01865) 279379. *E*: ernst.wolfgang@gmail.com.

**ERRERA, Gérard**, Hon. CVO 2004; Officier de la Légion d'Honneur, 2009; Chairman (France), Blackstone Group, since 2012 (Special Adviser, since 2009); *b* 30 Oct. 1943; *s* of Paul and Bella Errera; *m* Virginie Bedoya; two *s* one *d*. *Educ*: Institut d'Etudes Politiques, Paris; Ecole Nationale d'Administration. Joined Min. of Foreign Affairs, 1969; First Sec., Washington, 1971–75; Special Advr to Minister of Foreign Affairs, 1975–77; Political Counsellor, Madrid, 1977–80; Special Advr to Minister of Foreign Affairs, 1980–81; Consul General, San Francisco, 1982–85; Dir for Internat. Relns, French Atomic Energy Commn, and Governor for France, IAEA, 1985–90; Ambassador, Conf. on Disarmament, Geneva, 1991–95; Ambassador to NATO, Brussels, 1995–98; Political Dir, Min. of Foreign Affairs, 1998–2002; Ambassador to the Court of St James's, 2002–07; Sec. Gen., Min. of Foreign Affairs, France, 2007–09. Director: EDF/Areva, 2007–09; Domaine Nat. de Chambord, 2017–. Special Advr, Qwant, 2016–. Dir, Musée des Arts Décoratifs, Paris, 2012–. Officier de l'Ordre National du Mérite (France), 1999; Officer: Order of the White Rose (Finland), 1976; Order of Civil Merit (Spain), 1980; Knight, Order of St Charles (Monaco), 2008. *Recreations*: opera, guitar.

**ERRINGTON, Viscount; Alexander Rowland Harmsworth Baring;** *b* 5 Jan. 1994; *s* and *heir* of Earl of Cromer, *qv*.

**ERRINGTON, Prof. Jeffery**, PhD; FRS 2003; Professor of Cell and Molecular Biosciences, since 2005, and Director, Centre for Bacterial Cell Biology, since 2012, Newcastle University (Director, Institute of Cell and Molecular Biosciences, 2005–12); *b* 3 May 1956; *s* of Sidney Errington and Elizabeth Errington (*née* Wright); *m* 1982, Veronica Mary Geoghegan; two *d*. *Educ*: Blaydon Secondary Sch.; Univ. of Newcastle upon Tyne (BSc Hons Genetics/Zoology 1977); Thames Poly. (PhD 1981); MA Oxon 1989. Oxford University: Royal Soc. Univ. Res. Fellow, 1985–89; Lectr in Chemical Pathology, 1989–2000, Prof. of Microbiology, 2000–05, Sir William Dunn Sch. of Pathology; Fellow: Magdalen Coll., 1989–2001; Wadham Coll., 2001–06; BBSRC Sen. Res. Fellow, 1997–2002. Lectures: Kluyver, Dutch Microbiology Soc., 2009; Fred Griffiths Prize Rev., Soc. for Gen. Microbiol., 2009; Inaugural Joel Madelstam Meml, Univ. of Oxford, 2009; 8th Sir William Dunn, Oxford Univ., 2011; Royal Soc. Jean Shanks Meml, 2015. Scientific Founder and Dir, Prolysis Ltd, 1998–2009; Founder and Dir, Demuris Ltd, 2007–; Dir, BIOTA Pharmaceuticals Inc. (formerly BIOTA Hldgs Ltd), 2010–13. Mem., EMBO, 2004; FMedSci 2007; Fellow: Amer. Acad. of Microbiol., 2007; Eur. Acad. of Microbiol., 2016. Trustee, EPA Cephalosporin Res. Fund, 1999–. BBSRC Anniversary Medal, 2014; Novartis Medal and Prize, Biochem. Soc., 2014; Leeuwenhoek Medal and Prize, Royal Soc., 2015; Lwoff Award, Fedn of Eur. Microbiol Socs, 2017. *Publications*: over 200 peer-reviewed scientific papers; ten patents. *Recreations*: soccer, snorkelling, ski-ing, walking, gardening. *Address*: Centre for Bacterial Cell Biology, Baddiley-Clark Building, Newcastle University, Richardson Road, Newcastle upon Tyne NE2 4AX. *T*: (0191) 208 3232, *Fax*: (0191) 208 3205.

**ERRINGTON, Sir Robin (Davenport)**, 3rd Bt *cr* 1963, of Ness in the co. Palatine of Chester; *b* Munster, 1 July 1957; *e s* of Col Sir Geoffrey Frederick Errington, 2nd Bt, OBE and of Diana Kathleen Forbes Errington (*née* Davenport); *S* father, 2015; *m* 2001, Margerita Dudek; two *s*. *Educ*: Eton Coll. Mem. Cttee, Standing Council of the Baronetage, 2017–. *Recreations*: music, flying. *Heir*: *s* Oliver Marcus Errington, *b* 14 Oct. 2001. *E*: erringtonrobin@gmail.com. *Club*: Chelsea Arts.

**ERROCH, Bruce**; QC (Scot.) 2018; *b* Elderslie, 7 May 1968; *s* of John Erroch and Elaine Erroch (*née* Stewart). *Educ*: Paisley Grammar Sch.; Univ. of Glasgow (LLB Hons; DipLP). Admitted as solicitor, 1991; Solicitor, 1991–97; Advocate, 1998–; Advocate Depute, 2009–12; Sen. Crown Counsel, 2013–17. Convener, Mental Health Tribunal for Scotland, 2016–; Legal Chm., Scottish Social Services Council, 2017–; Tribunal Chm., Parole Bd for Scotland, 2018–. Chancellor, Dio. of Glasgow and Galloway, 2018–. *Recreations*: gastronomy, oenology, political debate. *Address*: Advocates Library, Parliament House, Edinburgh EH1 1RF. *T*: (0131) 226 5071. *E*: Bruce.Erroch@advocates.org.uk.

**ERROLL**, 24th Earl of, *cr* 1452; **Merlin Sereld Victor Gilbert Hay;** Lord Hay, 1429; Baron of Slains, 1452; Bt 1685; 28th Hereditary Lord High Constable of Scotland, *cr* 1314; Celtic title, Mac Garadh Mor; 33rd Chief of the Hays (from 1171); Senior Great Officer, Royal Household in Scotland; computer consultant; *b* 20 April 1948; *er s* of 23rd Countess of Erroll and Sir Iain Moncreiffe of that Ilk, 11th Bt, CVO, QC; *S* mother, 1978 (and to baronetcy of father, 1985); *m* 1982, Isabelle Astell, *o d* of late T. S. Astell Hohler, MC; two *s* two *d*. *Educ*: Eton; Trinity College, Cambridge. Page to the Lord Lyon, 1956. Lieut, Atholl Highlanders, 1974. Chm., Cost Reduction Consultants Ltd, 1995–. Elected Mem., H of L, 1999; Member: Library and Computers Sub-Cttee, 1999–2001; Bd, POST, 2000–; Council, PITCOM, subseq. PICTFOR, 2000–; Council, European Inf. Soc. Gp, 2000–; H of L Inf. Cttee, 2001–. Prime Warden, Fishmongers' Co., 2000–01. Hon. Col, RMP TA, 1992–97. OStJ 1977. Member, Queen's Body Guard for Scotland, Royal Company of Archers, 1978. Patron, Keepers of the Quaich. *Recreation*: country pursuits. *Heir*: *s* Lord Hay, *qv*. *Address*: Woodbury Hall, Sandy, Beds SG19 2HR. *E*: errollm@parliament.uk. *Clubs*: White's, Pratt's; Puffin's (Edinburgh).

**ERSKINE;** *see* St Clair-Erskine.

**ERSKINE**, family name of **Earls of Buchan** and **Mar and Kellie**.

**ERSKINE, Gerald David**; greyhound owner, since 2013; *b* Woking, 15 Nov. 1956; *s* of late Robert Gordon Erskine, MRCVS and Nona Erskine; *m* 1987, Patricia Cumisky; one *s* one *d*. *Educ*: Ranelagh Sch., Bracknell; Oxford Poly. (BA Geog./Hist. 1978). Sales Exec., construction engrg, 1978–79; civil staff, Metropolitan Police, 1980–83; served Army (short service volunteer commn), 1984–86 (Captain); Civil Servant, MoD (posts in force structure, infrastructure and internat. arms control), 1986–2005; Hd of Enforcement and Compliance, HMRC (on attachment), 2005–08; Chief, PHIA and Strategic Horizons, Cabinet Office (on attachment), 2008–10; Civilian Mem., Overseas Basing Study Team, 2010–11, Dep. Head, Global Combat Ship Export Team, 2011, Dep. Head, Strategic Assessments, 2011–12, MoD. Served TA, 2 Wessex Regt and Intelligence Corps, 1974–84 and 1986–87. Gov., Ashburton Community Sch., Croydon, 2000–09 (Chm., 2008–09); Trustee, Ashburton Develt Trust, 2008–13. *Recreations*: dog walking, shooting, travelling, railways, horse racing. *Address*: c/o 29–31 Abercromby Place, Edinburgh EH3 6QE. *Club*: Royal Scots (Edinburgh).

**ERSKINE, Sir Peter;** *see* Erskine, Sir T. P. N.

**ERSKINE, Peter Anthony**; Chairman, Ladbrokes plc, 2009–15; *b* 10 Nov. 1951; *s* of Stanley and Winifred Erskine; *m* 1975, Jan Green; three *s* one *d*. *Educ*: Bancroft's Sch., Woodford Green; Liverpool Univ. (BA Hons Psychology 1973). Various appointments at Polycell, Colgate and Palmolive; Sen. Vice-Pres. Sales and Marketing, Unitel, 1990–93; British Telecommunications: Man. Dir, BT Mobile, 1993–95; Pres. and CEO, Concert, USA, 1995–98; CEO, BT Cellnet, 1998–2000; CEO, 2001–08 and Chm., 2006–08, BT Wireless, subseq. mmO$_2$, then O$_2$, later Telefónica O$_2$ Europe plc; Dir, 2006–08, non-exec. Dir, 2008–, Telefónica SA. Adv. Bd, Univ. of Reading Bus. Sch., 2003. Hon. LLD Reading, 2008. *Recreations*: football, family, cinema, curry.

**ERSKINE, Ralph;** *see* Erskine, T. R.

**ERSKINE, Sir (Thomas) Peter (Neil)**, 6th Bt *cr* 1821, of Cambo, Fife; DL; laird, Cambo Estate, since 1976; *b* 28 March 1950; *s* of Sir (Thomas) David Erskine, 5th Bt and Ann Erskine (*née* Fraser-Tytler); *S* father, 2007; *m* 1972, Catherine Hewlett; two *s* two *d*. *Educ*: Birmingham Univ. (BSc Psychol.); Edinburgh Univ. (DipRuralAg). LBIPP. Cambo Estate: opened farm park, 1982, photo studio, 1990; gardens opened to public and holiday accommodation in mansion, 1993; opened Kingsbarns Golf Links, 2000. Founder, Scottish Organic Producers Assoc., 1986. *Recreations*: blues guitarist and singer, garden photography, cycling, reading, theatre and arts. *Heir*: *s* Thomas Struan Erskine, *b* 6 Feb. 1977. *Address*: Cambo House, Kingsbarns, St Andrews, Fife KY16 8QD. *T*: (01333) 450054, *Fax*: (01333) 450987. *E*: peter@camboestate.com. *W*: www.camboestate.com. *Clubs*: New (Edinburgh); Royal & Ancient (St Andrews).

**ERSKINE, (Thomas) Ralph**, CB 1986; First Legislative Counsel, Northern Ireland, 1979–93; *b* 14 Oct. 1933; *m* 1966, Patricia Joan Palmer; one *s* one *d*. *Educ*: Campbell College; Queen's University, Belfast. Called to the Bar, Gray's Inn, 1962. *Publications*: (with Arthur Bauer and Klaus Herold) Funkpeilung als alliierte Waffe gegen deutsche U-Boote 1939–1945, 1997; (ed with Michael Smith) Action This Day: Bletchley Park from the breaking of the Enigma code to the birth of the modern computer, 2001; (ed with Michael Smith) The Bletchley Park Codebreakers: how ultra shortened the war and led to the birth of the computer, 2011; contrib. Oxford DNB; contribs to Cryptologia, Annals of the History of Computing, legal jls, etc. *Recreations*: researching subjects relating to signals intelligence in WW2, writing. *Address*: c/o Office of the Legislative Counsel, Parliament Buildings, Belfast BT4 3XX.

**ERSKINE-HILL, Sir (Alexander) Roger**, 3rd Bt *cr* 1945, of Quothquhan, Co. Lanark; *b* 15 Aug. 1949; *s* of Sir Robert Erskine-Hill, 2nd Bt and of Christine Alison, *o d* of late Capt. (A) Henry James Johnstone of Alva, RN; *S* father, 1989; *m* 1st 1984, Sarah Anne Sydenham (marr. diss. 1994), *er d* of late Dr R. J. Sydenham Clarke and of Mrs Charles Clarke; one *s* one *d*; 2nd, 2000, Gillian Elizabeth Borlase Mitchell, *d* of David and Sheila Surgey. *Educ*: Eton; Aberdeen Univ. (LLB). Director: Map Marketing Ltd, 1986–2002 and 2008–; The Hillbrooke Partnership Ltd, 2002–. *Heir*: *s* Robert Benjamin Erskine-Hill, *b* 6 Aug. 1986. *Address*: The Old Malthouse, Briton Street, Bampton, Devon EX16 9LN.

**ERSKINE-MURRAY,** family name of **Lord Elibank**.

**ERTL, Prof. Gerhard;** Director, Department of Physical Chemistry, Fritz-Haber-Institut der Max-Planck-Gesellschaft, Berlin, 1986–2004, now Professor Emeritus; *b* Stuttgart, 10 Oct. 1936; *s* of Ludwig and Johanna Ertl; *m* 1964, Barbara Maschek; one *s* one *d. Educ*: Technical Univ., Stuttgart (Dip. Phys. 1961); Technical Univ., Munich (Dr rer. nat. 1964). Asst and Lectr, Technical Univ., Munich, 1965–68; Professor of Physical Chemistry: Technical Univ., Hanover, 1968–73; Ludwig Maximilians Univ., Munich, 1973–86. Nobel Prize in Chemistry, 2007; many other awards and prizes. *Publications*: three books; over 600 articles in jls. *Address*: Fritz-Haber-Institute, Faradayweg 4, 14195 Berlin, Germany. *T*: (30) 84135100, *Fax*: (30) 84135106. *E*: ertl@fhi-berlin.mpg.de.

**ESAKI, Leo;** Chairman, Science and Technology Promotion Foundation of Ibaraki, Japan, since 1998; President, Yokohama University of Pharmacy (formerly Yokohama College of Pharmacy), since 2006; *b* 12 March 1925; *s* of Soichiro Esaki and Niyoko Ito; *m* 1986, Masako Kondo; one *s* two *d* by previous *m. Educ*: Univ. of Tokyo. MS 1947, PhD 1959. Sony Corp., Japan, 1956–60; IBM Research, 1960–92; IBM Fellow, 1967–92. Dir, IBM-Japan, 1976–92. President: Univ. of Tsukuba, Japan, 1992–98; Shibaura Inst. of Technol., 2000–05; Dir-Gen., Tsukuba Internat. Congress Centre, 1998. Research in tunnelling in semiconductor junctions which led to the discovery of the Esaki tunnel diode; subsequently research on man-made semiconductor superlattice in search of predicted quantum mechanical effect. Sir John Cass sen. vis. res. fellow, London Poly., 1982. Councillor-at-Large, Amer. Phys. Soc., 1971–75; Dir, Amer. Vacuum Soc., 1972–76; Member: Japan Academy, 1975; Max-Planck-Ges., 1989; For. Associate, Nat. Acad. of Sciences, USA, 1976; For. Associate, Nat. Acad. of Engineering, USA, 1977; Corresp. Mem., Academia Nacional De Ingenieria, Mexico, 1978; Hon. Academician, Academia Sinica, Taiwan, 2008. Nishina Meml Award, 1959; Asahi Press Award, 1960; Toyo Rayon Foundn Award, 1961; Morris N. Liebmann Meml Prize, 1961; Stuart Ballantine Medal, Franklin Inst., 1961; Japan Academy Award, 1965; (jtly) Nobel Prize for Physics, 1973; Science Achievement Award, US-Asia Inst., 1983; Centennial Medal, IEEE, 1984; Internat. Prize for New Materials, Amer. Physical Soc., 1985; Distinguished Foreign-born Individual Award, Internat. Center, NY, 1986; IEEE Medal of Honor, 1991; Japan Prize, 1998. Order of Culture (Japan), 1974; Grand Order of Rising Sun, First Class (Japan), 1998. *Publications*: numerous papers in learned jls. *Address*: Yokohama University of Pharmacy, Totsuka-ku, Yokohama, Kanagawa 245–0066, Japan.

**ESCHENBACH, Christoph;** conductor and pianist; Music Director, National Symphony Orchestra and John F. Kennedy Center for Performing Arts, Washington, 2010–17; *b* 20 Feb. 1940. *Educ*: Hamburg Conservatory; State Music Conservatory, Cologne. Chief Conductor, Tonhalle Orch., Zürich, and Artistic Dir, Tonhalle-Gesellschaft, Zürich, 1982–86; Music Director: Houston SO, 1988–99, now Conductor Laureate; Ravinia Fest., 1994–2003; NDR SO, 1998–2004; Orch. de Paris, 2000–10; Philadelphia Orch., 2003–08; Artistic Dir, Schleswig-Holstein Music Fest., 1999–2002; Co-Artistic Dir, Pacific Music Fest., 1992–98. *As conductor*: studied with W. Bruckner Ruggeberg, George Szell; guest appearances include: NY Philharmonic, Boston Symphony, Chicago Symphony, Cleveland Orch., Pittsburgh Symphony, Los Angeles Philharmonic, London Symphony, BBC Philharmonic, Berlin Philharmonic, Bavarian Radio Symphony Munich, Munich Philharmonic, Vienna Philharmonic, Czech Philharmonic, New Japan Philharmonic, Houston Grand Opera, Metropolitan Opera, and Vienna State Opera. *As pianist*: studied with Eliza Hansen; winner: Internat. Piano Competition, Munich, 1962; Concours Clara Haskil, 1965; Canadian début, Montreal Expo, 1967; US début, Cleveland Orch., 1969; has toured Europe, N and S America, USSR, Israel, Japan, China, Australia; and has performed as pianist with leading orchs incl. Concertgebouw Amsterdam, Orch. de Paris, London Symphony, Berlin Philharmonic, and Cleveland Orch.; festivals incl. Salzburg, Lucerne, Bonn, Aix-en-Provence, and BBC Proms. (Jtly) Best Classical Compendium, Grammy Awards, 2014. Ernst von Siemens Music Prize, 2015. Officer's Cross with Ribbon, 1990, Commander's Cross, 1993, Order of Merit (Germany).

**ESCOTT COX, Brian Robert;** *see* Cox.

**ESCUDIER, Prof. Marcel Paul,** PhD, DSc(Eng); FREng, FIMechE, FCGI; Harrison Professor of Mechanical Engineering, University of Liverpool, 1989–2008, now Emeritus Professor; *b* 17 July 1942; *s* of late Isabel Kate Escudier; *m* 1st, 1966, Sonja Kennedy Allen (marr. diss. 1973); 2nd, 1973, Agnes Margaret Simko; one *s. Educ*: Sir Walter St John's Grammar Sch., London; Imperial Coll., London Univ. (BScEng; DIC; PhD 1967); DSc(Eng) 1990. ACGI 1963; FIMechE 1995; FREng 2000; FCGI 2003. Res. Associate, MIT, 1967–69; Asst Prof., Univ. of Southern Calif, 1969–73; Mem., Plasmaphysics Res. Gp, 1973–74, Leader, Fluid Mechanics Res. Gp, 1974–86, Brown Boveri Res. Centre, Switzerland; Hd, Fluid Mechanics Res. Dept, Schlumberger Cambridge Res. Ltd, Cambridge, 1986–88; Hd, Dept of Mech. Engrg, Univ. of Liverpool, 1990–97. *Publications*: The Essence of Engineering Fluid Mechanics, 1998; (with A. G. Atkins) A Dictionary of Mechanical Engineering, 2013; Introduction to Engineering Fluid Mechanics, 2017; contrib. papers on vortex flows, non-Newtonian fluid flow, etc, to scientific jls. *Recreations*: gardening, cooking, erotic art, motor racing (non participatory), digital photography. *Address*: Silverburn, Park Road, Willaston, Neston CH64 1TJ. *T*: (0151) 327 2949.

**ESHALOMI, Florence;** Member (Lab) Lambeth and Southwark, London Assembly, Greater London Authority, since 2016; *b* Birmingham, Sept. 1980; *d* of Anthony Nosegbe and late Maria Da-Silva; *m* 2014, Matthew O. Eshalomi; one *d. Educ*: Bishop Thomas Grant Secondary Sch.; Univ. of Middlesex (BA Hons Political and Internat. Studies with Law); Utrecht Univ. Parly Caseworker Asst, H of C, 2003–04; Regl Election Organiser, Labour Party, 2004–05; Policy, Res. Support Officer, Islington Council, 2005–10; Public Affairs Manager, Runnymede Trust, 2014–15; Account Manager, Four Communications, 2015–16. Mem. (Lab), Lambeth LBC, 2006– (Cabinet Mem., Culture, Sport and 2012 Olympics, 2010–12). Gov., La Retraite RC Girls' Sch., 2012–14. *Recreation*: mentor to two local students. *Address*: Greater London Authority, City Hall, Queen's Walk, SE1 2AA. *T*: (020) 7983 4712. *E*: florence.eshalomi@london.gov.uk.

**ESHER, 5th Viscount** *cr* 1897; **Christopher Lionel Baliol Brett;** Baron 1885; *b* 23 Dec. 1936; *s* of 4th Viscount Esher and Christian (*née* Pike); *S* father, 2004; *m* 1st, 1962, Camilla Charlotte (marr. diss. 1970), *d* of Sir (Horace) Anthony Rumbold, 10th Bt, KCMG, KCVO, CB; one *s* two *d*; 2nd, 1971, Valerie Harrington; two *s* twin *d. Educ*: Eton; Magdalen Coll., Oxford. *Heir*: *s* Hon. Matthew Christopher Anthony Brett [*b* 2 Jan. 1963; *m* 1992, Hon. Emma Charlotte Denison-Pender, *e d* of 3rd Baron Pender; one *s* two *d*]. *Address*: Beauforest House, Newington, Wallingford, Oxon OX10 7AG.
*See also* M. N. C. Thomas.

**ESIPISU, (Caleb) Manoah;** High Commissioner of Kenya to the Court of St James's, since 2018; *m* Waithiegeni Kanguru. News Journalist, Kenya, 1987–90; Reuters Africa: Reporter, Kenya, 1991–93; Correspondent, East Africa, 1993–96; Emerging Markets Correspondent, East Africa, 1996–99; Correspondent, Zambia and Malawi, 1999–2002; Correspondent, Southern Africa, 2002–06; Dep. Dir and Spokesman, Communications and Public Affairs, Commonwealth Secretariat, 2006–12 (Acting Dir, 2011–12); Africa Advr, SA, Business Day Newspaper, 2012–13; Communications Asst and Public Affairs Advr to the President, African Develt Bank, 2013; Sec., Communication and State House Spokesperson, Kenya, 2013–18. Lectr, Financial Journalism, Wits Univ., 2006. Moran, Order of the Burning Spear (Kenya), 2014. *Address*: Kenya High Commission, 45 Portland Place, W1B 1AS. *T*: (020) 7636 2371. *E*: info@kenyahighcom.org.uk.

**ESIRI, Prof. Margaret Miriam,** DM; FRCPath; Professor of Neuropathology, Departments of Neuropathology and Neurology, Oxford University, 1996–2007, now Emeritus; Professorial Fellow, St Hugh's College, Oxford, 1988–2007, now Emeritus; *b* 5 Oct. 1941; *d* of William Alfred Evans and Doreen Mary (*née* Bates); *m* 1963, Frederick Obukowho Uruemuowho Esiri (*d* 2018); two *s* one *d. Educ*: Croydon High Sch. (GPDST); St Hugh's Coll., Oxford (BSc, MA, DM). FRCPath 1988. University of Oxford: preregistration med. and surgical posts and scholarship for trng in research methods, 1967–69; Jun. Res. Fellow in Neuropathology, 1970–72; trng posts in Histopathology, 1973–79; MRC Sen. Clinical Fellow in Neuropathology, 1980–85; Consultant Neuropathologist, Radcliffe Infirmary, 1986–88; Clinical Reader in Neuropathology, 1988–96. *Publications*: (with J. Booss) Viral Encephalitis, 1986; (with D. R. Oppenheimer) Diagnostic Neuropathology, 1989, 2nd edn 1996, 3rd edn (with D. Perl) 2006; (ed with J. H. Morris) The Neuropathology of Dementia, 1997, 2nd edn (ed with V. M.-Y. Lee and J. Q. Trojanowski) 2004; (with J. Booss) Human Viral Encephalitis, 2003; over 300 original pubns. *Recreation*: grandchildren. *Address*: Neuropathology Department, Level 1, West Wing, John Radcliffe Hospital, Headington, Oxford OX3 9DU. *T*: (01865) 234403. *E*: margaret.esiri@ndcn.ox.ac.uk.

**ESKENAZI, Giuseppe, (J. E. Eskenazi);** Managing Director, Eskenazi Ltd, since 1969; *b* 8 July 1939; *s* of late Isaac Eskenazi and of Lea Eskenazi; *m* 1963, Laura (*née* Bandini); one *s* one *d. Educ*: King's School, Sherborne; The Polytechnic, Regent Street; University College London. Art dealer, primarily Chinese and Japanese, 1962–; Eskenazi Ltd founded by father in 1960. Mem., steering cttee to estab. Asian Art in London, 1997–98, Chm., 2002, 2003; Member: Exec. Cttee, Asia House, 1993–2007; Council, Oriental Ceramic Soc., 1998–2002, 2004–07; Adv. Bd, Bard Grad. Center for Studies in the Decorative Arts, NY, 2000–15. Trustee, Asia House Trust (London), 2000–07. Adviser to Royal Academy for exhibitions: 100 Masterpieces of Imperial Chinese Ceramics from the Au Bak Ling Collection, 1998; Return of the Buddha, The Qingzhou Discoveries, 2002. Chevalier, Légion d'Honneur (France), 2006. *Publications*: A Dealer's Hand: the Chinese art world through the eyes of Giuseppe Eskenazi, 2012, Chinese edn 2015; over 90 exhibition catalogues. *Recreations*: sailing, opera. *Address*: Eskenazi, 10 Clifford Street, W1S 2LJ. *T*: (020) 7493 5464.

**ESLER, Gavin William James;** freelance writer, author, journalist and television presenter; *b* 27 Feb. 1953; *s* of William John Esler and Georgena Esler; *m* 1st, 1979, Patricia Margaret Warner (marr. diss.); one *s* one *d*; 2nd, 2012, Anna Phoebe McElligott; two *d. Educ*: George Heriot's Sch., Edinburgh; Kent Univ. (BA English and American Lit); Leeds Univ. (MA Anglo-Irish Lit. (Dist.)). Reporter, Belfast Telegraph, 1975–76; BBC: Reporter and Presenter, Northern Ireland, 1977–82; Reporter, Newsnight, 1982–88; Washington Corresp., 1989; Chief N America Corresp., 1989–97; presenter: Newsnight, 1997, 2003–14; BBC News 24, 1997–2002; BBC World, 1998–2017; BBC Radio Four, 2000–17. Columnist: The Scotsman, 1998–2005; The National, UAE, 2017–. Chancellor, Univ. of Kent, 2013–. Contested (Change UK) London Reg., EP, 2019. Hon. MA, 1995, Hon. DCL, 2005, Kent; Hon. Dr: Glasgow Caledonian; York. RTS Award, 1989; Sony Gold Award, 2007. FRSA 2000. *Publications*: The United States of Anger: the people and the American dream, 1997; Lessons from the Top: how leaders succeed through telling stories, 2012; novels: Loyalties, 1990; Deep Blue, 1992; The Blood Brother, 1995; A Scandalous Man, 2008; Powerplay, 2009; Lessons from the Top, 2013. *Recreations*: hiking, ski-ing, camping, especially in the American West, open water swimming, tennis.

**ESLER, Prof. Philip Francis,** DPhil, DD; FRSE; Principal and Professor of Biblical Interpretation, St Mary's University College, Twickenham, 2010–13; Portland Chair in New Testament Studies, University of Gloucestershire, since 2013; *b* 27 Aug. 1952; *s* of Patrick Joseph Esler and Evelyn Elizabeth Esler; *m* 1983, Patricia Kathryn Curran; two *s* one *d. Educ*: Sydney Univ. (BA Hons LLB, LLM); Magdalen Coll., Oxford (DPhil 1984). DD Oxford 2008. Associate to Justice W. H. Collins of NSW Supreme Court, 1977; articled clerk, then solicitor, Allen, Allen & Hemsley, Sydney, 1978–81 and 1984–86; barrister, NSW Supreme Court, 1986–92; University of St Andrews: Reader in New Testament, 1992–95; Prof. of Biblical Criticism, 1995–2010; Vice-Principal for Res., and Provost, St Leonard's Coll., 1998–2001; Chief Exec., AHRC, 2005–09. Mem. Bd, Scottish Enterprise Fife, 1999–2003. FRSE 2009. *Publications*: Community and Gospel in Luke – Acts, 1987; The First Christians in their Social Worlds, 1994; Galatians, 1998; Conflict and Identity in Romans, 2003; (with J. Boyd) Velázquez and Biblical Text, 2004; New Testament Theology, 2005; (with R. A. Piper) Lazarus, Martha and Mary, 2006; Sex, Wives and Warriors: reading biblical narrative with its ancient audience, 2011; Babatha's Orchard: the Yadin Papyri and an ancient Jewish family tale retold, 2017; God's Court and Courtiers in the Book of the Watchers: re-interpreting heaven in 1 Enoch 1–36, 2017; Ethiopian Christianity: history, theology, practice, 2019. *Recreations*: swimming, walking, tennis. *Address*: 27 Rosehill Street, Cheltenham GL52 6SQ.

**ESMONDE, Sir Thomas (Francis Grattan),** 17th Bt *cr* 1629 (Ire.), of Ballynastragh, Wexford; MD; Consultant Neurologist, Antrim Area Hospital, since 2007; *b* 14 Oct. 1960; *s* of Sir John Henry Grattan Esmonde, 16th Bt and of Pamela Mary, *d* of late Francis Stephen Bourke, FRCPI; *S* father, 1987; *m* 1986, Pauline Loretto Kearns; one *s* two *d*; *m* 2018, Rachel Elizabeth, *d* of Rev. William Paul Henry Erskine. *Educ*: Sandford Park Secondary School, Ranelagh, Dublin; Medical School, Trinity College, Dublin (MB, BCh, BAO 1984; MD 1995). MRCPI, MRCP (UK) 1987. Junior House Officer, Whiteabbey Hosp., 1984–85; SHO, Royal Victoria, Musgrave Park and Whiteabbey Hosps, 1985–87, Altnagelvin Hosp., Londonderry, 1987–88; Med. Registrar, Royal Gwent Hosp., Newport, 1988–89; Registrar in Neurology, Univ. Hosp. of Wales, 1989–90; Clinical Res. Fellow, Dept of Neurosci., Western General Hosp., Edinburgh, 1990–92; Sen. Registrar, 1992–96, Consultant Neurologist, 1996–2007, Royal Victoria Hosp., Belfast. *Recreations*: chess, fishing. *Heir*: *s* Sean Vincent Grattan Esmonde, *b* 8 Jan. 1989.

**ESOM, Steven Derek;** Chairman: BRC Global Standards, since 2011; Advantage Travel Partnership, since 2013; British Amateur Boxing Association, since 2013; Sedex, since 2016; Andrews Property Group, since 2018; *b* 13 Nov. 1960; *s* of Derek Esom and Shirley Esom (*née* Beldom); *m* 1994, Fiona (marr. diss. 2016); one *s* one *d. Educ*: St Edward's Sch., Romford; Univ. of Wales, Swansea (BSc Hons Geog.). Sen. Manager, Buying, J. Sainsbury plc, 1982–93; with US subsidiary, Shaws, Boston, 1991–99; Buying and Merchandising Dir, Texas Homecare, Ladbroke Gp, 1994–95; Vice-Pres., Global Merchandising, Hilton Internat., 1995–96; Dir of Buying, 1996–2002, Man. Dir, 2002–07, Waitrose; Dir of Food, Marks and Spencer, 2007–08; Operating Partner, Langholm Capital, 2009–13. Dir, CIES, 2004–07; Chairman: Bart Spices, 2010–13; British Retail Consortium Trading, 2011–16; Ice Orgn, 2011–. Non-executive Director: Carphone Warehouse Gp plc, 2005–09; Cranswick Foods, 2009–18; Tyrrells Potato Chips, 2009–12; Rank Gp plc, 2016–. FRSA, FIGD. *Recreations*: food & wine, ski-ing, fitness. *Address*: c/o Product Chain Ltd, 4 City Limits, Reading RG6 4UP.

**ESPEJO, Genefer D.**; Headmistress, Nonsuch High School for Girls, Cheam, 1995–2009; *b* 17 July 1949; *d* of late Rev. D. G. Larkinson and Mrs S. Larkinson; *m* 1972, Dr L. G. Espejo; one *s*. *Educ*: Queen's Univ., Belfast (BA Hons); Univ. of Sussex (PGCE). Dep. Hd, Kings' Sch., Winchester, 1985–92; Headmistress, Reading Girls' Sch., 1992–95. Mem., Ind. Monitoring Bd, HMP High Down, 2015–. Mem., Bd of Trustees, Pilgrims' Friend Soc., 2016–. *Recreations*: walking, visiting art galleries, theatre, contemporary fiction, travel.

**ESPLEN, Sir William (John Harry)**, 4th Bt *cr* 1921, of Hardres Court, Canterbury, Kent; *b* 24 Feb. 1967; *o s* of (Sir) John Graham Esplen (3rd Bt, but did not use the title) and Valerie Joan, *yr d* of Maj.-Gen. Albert Percy Lambooy, CB, OBE; *S* father, 2016, but does not use the title and his name does not appear on the Official Roll of the Baronetage; *m* 1996, Helen Chesser; one *s* two *d*. *Educ*: Cranleigh Sch. Chartered Surveyor. *Heir*: *s* Frederick William Harry Esplen, *b* 7 Feb. 2001. *Address*: The Gables, Burrows Lane, Guildford GU5 9QE. *T*: (01483) 203546.

**ESQUIVEL, Rt Hon. Sir Manuel**, KCMG 2010; PC 1986; Prime Minister of Belize, 1984–89 and 1993–98; Member, House of Representatives, Belize, 1984–98; Leader, United Democratic Party, 1982–98; *b* 2 May 1940; *s* of John and Laura Esquivel; *m* 1971, Kathleen Levy; one *s* two *d*. *Educ*: Loyola Univ., New Orleans (BSc Physics); Bristol Univ. (Cert Ed.). Instructor in Physics, St John's Coll., Belize City, 1967–82. Member: Belize City Council, 1974–80; Nat. Senate, 1979–84; Leader of the Opposition, Belize, 1989–93. Chm., Utd Democratic Party, 1976–82. Hon. DHL Loyola Univ., 1986. *Recreation*: electronics. *Address*: PO Box 1344, Belize City, Belize.

**ESSAAFI, M'hamed**; Grand Officier, Order of Tunisian Republic, 1963; Disaster Relief Co-ordinator and Under Secretary General, United Nations, 1982–92; *b* 26 May 1930; *m* 1956, Hedwige Klat; one *s* one *d*. *Educ*: Sadiki Coll., Tunis; Sorbonne, Paris. Secretariat of State for For. Affairs, 1956; 1st Sec., Tunisian Embassy, London, 1956; 1st Sec., Tunisian Embassy, Washington, 1957; Secretariat of State for For. Affairs, Tunis: Dir of Amer. Dept, 1960; America and Internat. Confs Dept, 1962; Ambassador to London, 1964–69; Ambassador to Moscow, 1970–74; Ambassador to Bonn, 1974–76; Sec.-Gen., Ministry of Foreign Affairs, Tunis, 1969–70 and 1976–78; Ambassador to Belgium and EEC, 1978–79; Permanent Rep. of Tunisia to the UN, and Special Rep. of the Sec.-Gen., 1980–81, Chief de Cabinet 1982. *Address*: rue de la Mosquée BH20, La Marsa, Tunis, Tunisia; 41 Chemin Moïse-Duboule, 1209 Geneva, Switzerland.

**ESSERY, David James**, CB 1997; Under Secretary, Scottish Office Home (formerly Home and Health) Department, 1991–97; *b* 10 May 1938; *s* of Lawrence and Edna Essery; *m* 1963, Nora Sim; two *s* one *d*. *Educ*: Royal High Sch., Edinburgh. Entered Dept of Health for Scotland, 1961; Private Sec. to Minister of State, Scottish Office, 1968; Principal, Scottish Develt Dept, 1969; Assistant Secretary: Scottish Economic Planning Dept, 1976; Scottish Develt Dept, 1981–85; Under Sec., Scottish Office Agric. and Fisheries Dept, 1985–91. Mem. Mgt Cttee, Hanover (Scotland) Housing Assoc., 2005–12. *Recreations*: reading, music, golf. *Address*: 110 Grange Loan, Edinburgh EH9 2EF.

**ESSEX, 11th Earl of**, *cr* 1661; **Frederick Paul de Vere Capell**; Baron Capell 1641; Viscount Malden 1661; *b* 29 May 1944; *s* of 10th Earl of Essex, and of Doris Margaret, *d* of George Frederick Tomlinson; *S* father, 2005. *Educ*: Skerton Boys' School; Lancaster Royal Grammar School; Didsbury College of Education, Manchester; Northern School of Music. ACP, LLCM(TD), ALCM. Assistant teacher, Marsh County Junior School, 1966–72; Deputy Head, 1972–75; Acting Head, 1975–77; Deputy Head Teacher, Marsh County Primary School, 1977–78; Head Teacher, Cockerham Parochial CE School, Cockerham, Lancaster, 1979–80; Skerton County Primary School, Lancaster: in charge of Pastoral Care, Curriculum Develt and Music, 1981–90; Dep. Head Teacher, 1990–95, Actg Head, 1992–93. Patron, Friends of Cassiobury Park, Watford, 1998–. FRSA. *Recreations*: music, gardening, gym. *Heir*: *kinsman* William Jennings Capell [*b* 9 Aug. 1952; *m* 1971, Sandra Elaine Matson; one *s* one *d*].

**ESSEX, David Albert**, OBE 1999; singer, actor and composer; *b* 23 July 1947; *s* of Albert Cook and Doris Cook (*née* Kemp); *m* 1971, Maureen Annette Neal; one *s* one *d*; *m* 2010, Susan Hallam-Wright; one *s*. *Educ*: Shipman Secondary Sch., E London. Music industry début, 1965; acting début, touring repertory co.; Jesus, in Godspell, Wyndhams, 1972 (Most Promising Newcomer Award, Variety Club of GB); Che Guevara, in Evita, Prince Edward, 1978; Byron, in Childe Byron, Young Vic, 1981; Fletcher Christian, in Mutiny, Piccadilly, 1985 (also wrote score); She Stoops to Conquer, Queen's, 1993; All the Fun of the Fair, UK tour and Garrick, 2008–10 (also wrote score); annual Christmas appearances in own musical version of Robinson Crusoe. Films include: That'll Be the Day, 1973; Stardust, 1974; Silver Dream Racer (also wrote score), 1979; Shogun Mayeda, 1991; Traveller, 2013. Many best-selling singles and albums; first concert tour of UK, 1974; tours, 1975–, incl. Europe, USA, Australia, and a world tour; TV and radio appearances, incl. BBC TV series, The River, 1988; Eastenders, 2011. Mem. Council, VSO (Ambassador, 1990–92). *Publications*: (autobiography) A Charmed Life, 2002; Over the Moon: my autobiography, 2012; Travelling Tinker Man and Other Rhymes, 2015. *Address*: c/o David Essex Management, PO Box 390, Billingshurst, W Sussex RH14 0BE.

**ESSEX, Susan Linda, (Sue)**; Member (Lab) Cardiff North, National Assembly for Wales, 1999–2007; Minister for Finance, Local Government and Public Services, 2003–07; *b* 29 Aug. 1945; *m* 1967, Richard Essex; one *s* one *d*. *Educ*: Leicester Univ. (BA). MRTPI. Lectr in Planning, Univ. of Wales, Cardiff, 1992–99. Member (Lab): Cardiff City Council, 1983–96 (former Leader); Cardiff County Council, 1995–99. Sec., then Minister, for the Envmt, Nat. Assembly for Wales, 2000–03. Member: Countryside Council for Wales, 1994–99; Commn on Devolution in Wales, 2011–12. *Address*: 29 Lon-y-Dail, Rhiwbina, Cardiff CF14 6DZ.

**ESSIG, Philippe Louis Charles Marie**; Officier de l'Ordre National du Mérite, 1984; Commandeur de la Légion d'Honneur, 1994; international consultant, since 1991; Chairman, Board of Transmanche-Link, 1988–91; *b* 19 July 1933; *s* of Jean Essig and Germaine Olivier; *m* 1960, Isabelle Lanier (*d* 2016); one *s* three *d*. *Educ*: Lycée Janson-de-Sailly; Ecole Polytechnique; Engineer, Ponts et Chaussées. Engr, Dakar-Niger railway, 1957–59; Asst Dir, Régie du chemin de fer Abidjan-Niger, 1960–61; Dir, Régie des chemins de fer du Cameroun, 1961–66; Régie autonome des transports parisiens (RATP): Chief Engr, Research Dept, 1966–71; Chief Op. Officer, Ops Dept, 1971–73; Man. Dir, Railways, Paris, 1973–81; Gen. Manager, 1982–85; Pres., SNCF, 1985–88. Sec. of State for Housing, 1988. Officier de l'Ordre de la Valeur Camerounaise, 1966. *Recreations*: walking, ski-ing, shooting. *Address*: 5 Avenue Fourcault de Pavant, 78000 Versailles, France. *E*: essigph@wanadoo.fr.

**ESSWOOD, Paul Lawrence Vincent**; singer (counter-tenor); conductor; Professor of Baroque Vocal Interpretation, Royal Academy of Music, 1985; Principal Conductor, Polish Orchestra of the XVIII Century; *b* West Bridgford, Nottingham, 6 June 1942; *s* of Alfred Walter Esswood and Freda Garratt; *m* 1st, 1966, Mary Lillian Cantrill, ARCM (marr. diss.); two *s*; 2nd, 1990, Aimée Désirée Blattmann; one *s* one *d*. *Educ*: West Bridgford Grammar Sch.; Royal Coll. of Music (ARCM). Lay-Vicar, Westminster Abbey, 1964–71. Prof., RCM, 1973–85; Specialist in baroque performance; first broadcast, BBC, 1965; co-founder: Pro Cantione Antiqua; A Cappella Male Voice Ensemble for Performance of Old Music, 1967; joined The Musicke Companye, 1998; operatic début in Cavalli's L'Erismena, Univ. of California, Berkeley, 1968; début at La Scala, Milan with Zurich Opera in L'Incoronazione di Poppea and Il Ritorno d'Ulisse, 1978; Scottish Opera début in Dido and Aeneas, 1978; world premières: Penderecki's Paradise Lost, Chicago Lyric Opera, 1979; Philip Glass's Echnaton, Stuttgart Opera, 1984; Herbert Willi's Schlafes Bruder, Zurich Opera, 1996; performed in major festivals: Edinburgh, Leeds Triennial, English Bach, Vienna, Salzburg, Zurich, Hamburg, Berlin, Naples, Israel, Lucerne, Flanders, Wexford, Holland. Has made over 150 recordings for major cos, incl. solo recitals of Purcell, Schumann, English lute songs, Benjamin Britten folk songs and Canticle II (Abraham and Isaac). Début as conductor, Chichester Fest., 2000, conducted Purcell's The Fairy Queen, King Arthur, Dido and Aeneas, Handel's Messiah and Bach's B Minor Mass; conducted modern world première, Cavalli's Pompeo Magno, Varazdin Fest., Croatia, 2002; conducted Capella Cracoviensis in Purcell's The Fairy Queen and Handel's Israel in Egypt, Cracow; conducted numerous orchs in Poland incl. Cappella Bydgostiensis, Cappella Gedanensis, Philharmonic Orch. of Krakow and Philharmonic Orch. of Katowice in works by baroque composers incl. Handel, Bach, Vivaldi; masterclasses and concerts for Acad. of Music, Krakow, Lodz, Gdansk and Bydoszcz. Hon. RAM 1990. *Recreations*: gardening (organic), apiculture. *Address*: Jasmine Cottage, 42 Ferring Lane, Ferring, West Sussex BN12 6QT. *T*: and *Fax*: (01903) 504480.

**ESTERSON, William**; MP (Lab) Sefton Central, since 2010; *b* 27 Oct. 1966; *s* of Derek and Joyce Esterson; *m* 1998, Caroline Herbert; one *s* one *d*. *Educ*: Rochester Mathematical Sch.; Leeds Univ. (BSc Maths and Phil. 1990). Accountancy trng; Dir, Leaps and Bounds (Trng) Ltd. Mem. (Lab) Medway Council, 1995–2010. Shadow Minister: BIS, then BEIS, 2015–; Internat. Trade, 2016–. Member: Envmt, Food and Rural Affairs Select Cttee, 2010–11; Educn Select Cttee, 2010–15; Communities and Local Govt Select Cttee, 2011–13; Treasury Select Cttee, 2015; Chair, All Party Parly Gp for Children in Care and Care Leavers, 2015–17, for Foetal Alcohol Spectrum Disorders, 2015–. *Address*: House of Commons, SW1A 0AA.

**ESTEVE-COLL, Dame Elizabeth Anne Loosemore**, DBE 1995; Vice-Chancellor, University of East Anglia, 1995–97; Chancellor, University of Lincoln, 2001–08; *b* 14 Oct. 1938; *o d* of P. W. and Nora Kingdon; *m* 1960, José Alexander Timothy Esteve-Coll (*d* 1980). *Educ*: Darlington Girls High Sch.; Birkbeck Coll., London Univ. (BA 1976). Head of Learning Resources, Kingston Polytechnic, 1977; University Librarian, Univ. of Surrey, 1982; Keeper, National Art Library, 1985, Dir, 1988–95, V&A Museum. *Recreations*: reading, music, foreign travel. *Address*: The Tabernacle, Millgate, Aylsham, Norfolk NR11 6HR.

**ESTLIN, Peter Kenneth**; Senior Adviser, Barclays, since 2013; Lord Mayor of London, 2018–19; *b* Portsmouth, 4 July 1961; *s* of Keith Bryan Estlin and Joan Estlin (*née* Farrage); *m* 1988, Linda, (Lindy), Susan Waters; one *s* two *d*. *Educ*: King Edward's Witley; Univ. of Bristol (BSc). FCA 1985. Partner, Coopers & Lybrand, 1993–94; Chief Financial Officer: Salomon Bros Asia, 1997–99; Citigroup Corporate and Investment Bank, 1999–2008; Gp Financial Controller and Chief Financial Officer, Barclays Retail Bank, 2008–12; Acting Gp Chief Financial Officer, Barclays, 2013. Ind. Mem., Audit Cttee, HM Treasury, 2015–. Mem., Internat. Adv. Bd, British Airways, 2007–15 (Chm., 2012–15). Comr, London Fairness Commn, 2015–16. Gov., Bridewell Royal Hosp., 1993– (Chm., 2006–16). Trustee, Morden Coll., 2015–. KStJ 2018. *Address*: 41 Warwick Park, Tunbridge Wells, Kent TN2 5EF. *T*: (01892) 548092. *E*: peter@estlin.co.uk. *Clubs*: 67 Pall Mall, Walbrook.

**ESTRIN, Prof. Saul**, DPhil; Professor of Management, London School of Economics and Political Science, since 2006; *b* 7 June 1952; *s* of Maurice Estrin and Irene Estrin (*née* Redhouse); *m* 1985, Jennifer Ann Lockwood; one *s* three *d*. *Educ*: St John's Coll., Cambridge (BA 1974; MA 1977); Univ. of Sussex (DPhil 1979). Lectr, Southampton Univ., 1977–84; Lectr, 1984–89, Sen. Lectr, 1989–90, in Econs, LSE, 1984–90; London Business School: Associate Prof. of Econs, 1990–94; Prof. of Economics, 1994–2006; Dir, CIS Middle Europe Centre, 1997–2000; Dep. Dean (Faculty and Academic Planning), 1998–2006; Res. Dir, Centre for New and Emerging Markets, 2000–06; Acting Dean, 2002; Founding Hd, Dept of Mgt, LSE, 2006–13. *Publications*: Self-Management: economic theory and Yugoslav practice, 1984; (jtly) Introduction to Microeconomics, 4th edn, 1993; (ed jtly) Competition and Competition Policy, 1993; Privatisation in Central and Eastern Europe, 1994; (ed jtly) Essential Readings in Economics, 1995; Foreign Direct Investment in Central and Eastern Europe, 1997; numerous academic papers. *Recreation*: family. *Address*: Department of Management, London School of Economics and Political Science, New Academic Building, 54 Lincoln's Inn Fields, WC2A 3LJ. *T*: (020) 7955 6629. *E*: s.estrin@lse.ac.uk.

**ETCHINGHAM, Julie Anne**; Presenter, News at Ten, ITV News, since 2008; *b* Leicester, 21 Aug. 1969; *d* of James and Sheila Etchingham; *m* 1997, Nicholas Gardner; two *s*. *Educ*: English Martyrs RC Comprehensive Sch., Leicester; Newnham Coll., Cambridge (BA Hons English 1991). Reporter, BBC, 1992–94; presenter and reporter, BBC Newsround, 1994–97; reporter, BBC News, 1997–2001; presenter, Sky News, 2002–08. Hon. DLaws Leicester, 2012. Presenter of Year, RTS, 2010, 2016. *Recreations*: reading, raising small boys. *Address*: ITV News, 200 Gray's Inn Road, WC1X 8XZ. *E*: julie.etchingham@itn.co.uk.

**ETHERIDGE, Prof. Alison Mary, (Mrs Lionel Mason)**, OBE 2017; DPhil; FRS 2015; Professor of Probability, University of Oxford, since 2003; Fellow, Magdalen College, Oxford, since 1997; *b* Wolverhampton, 27 April 1964; *d* of Arnold and Catherine Etheridge; *m* 1997, Lionel Mason; one *s* one *d*. *Educ*: Smestow Comprehensive Sch., Wolverhampton; New Coll., Oxford (MA; DPhil Maths). Sir Christopher Cox Jun. Res. Fellow, New Coll., Oxford, 1987–90; SERC Postdoctoral Fellow, Univ. of Cambridge, 1990–91; Lectr in Pure Maths, Univ. of Edinburgh, 1990–96; Neyman Asst Prof., Univ. of Calif, Berkeley, 1992; Reader in Probability and Stats, QMW, 1996–97; Lectr in Applied Maths, Oxford Univ., 1997–2002. EPSRC Advanced Fellow, 1997–2005. Mem., UKRI-EPSRC, 2018–. *Publications*: Introduction to Super Processes, 2000; A Course in Financial Calculus, 2002; (with M. Davis) Louis Bachelier's Theory of Speculation: the origins of modern finance, 2006; Some Mathematical Models from Population Genetics, 2012. *Recreations*: hill walking, theatre. *Address*: Mathematical Institute, University of Oxford, Andrew Wiles Building, Radcliffe Observatory Quarter, Woodstock Road, Oxford OX2 6GG.

**ETHERIDGE, Brian Ernest**, CBE 2010; Director of Network Services, Rail, Department for Transport, 2016–19; *b* Basingstoke, 12 May 1959; *s* of Cyril and Kathleen Etheridge; *m* 1988, Julia Brant; two *s*. *Educ*: Aston Univ. (BSc Hons Envmtl Health); Brunel Univ. (MSc Envmtl Pollution Sci.). Envmtl Health Officer, London Bor. of Brent, 1981–85; Dist Envmtl Health Officer, Basingstoke and Deane BC, 1985–87; Prin. Policy Officer, 1987–89, Asst Sec., 1989–95, Assoc. of Dist Councils; Hd, Local Envmt Mgt, DoE, 1995–97; Health and Safety Executive: Hd, Local Authy Unit, 1997–2001; Hd, Gas and Transport Safety, 2001–02; Dir of Strategy, 2002–04; Dir, London Reg., 2004–06; Dep. Dir, Prime Minister's Delivery Unit, 2006–08; Dir, Civil Service Capability, later Civil Service Capability and HR Ops, Cabinet Office, 2008–11; Man. Dir, Motoring Services,

DfT, 2011–15; Dir of Integrated Delivery, Rail Exec., DfT, 2015. Ind. Mem. Bd, Sentinel Housing Assoc., 2005–15 (Vice Chm. 2010–15). *Publications:* (contrib.) Clay's Handbook of Environmental Health, 19th edn 2004. *Recreations:* cycling, golf, gardening.

**ETHERIDGE, William;** Member for West Midlands, European Parliament, 2014–19 (UK Ind, 2014–18; Libertarian, 2018–19); *b* Wolverhampton, 18 March 1970; *s* of Alan and Valerie Etheridge; *m* 2008, Star; three step *c. Educ:* Parkfield Sch., Wolverhampton; Wolverhampton Poly. Purchasing/sales, British Steel Stainless, 1990–94; selling stainless steel for cos incl. Thyssen, 1994–2014. Campaign Exec., Dudley Conservatives, 2010; Regl Organiser, UKIP, W Midlands, 2013. Mem. (UK Ind) Dudley MBC, until 2018. Prospective Parly Candidate (UK Ind), Dudley North. *Publications:* Black Country Revolutionary, 2011; The Rise of UKIP, 2014. *Recreations:* cricket, football, Wolves season ticket. *Address:* 11 Tipton Street, Sedgeley, Dudley, W Midlands DY3 1HE. *T:* (01902) 664670. *Clubs:* Claverley Cricket; Sedgeley Working Men's.

**ETHERIDGE, Zina Ruth;** Chief Executive, Haringey Council, since 2017 (Deputy Chief Executive, 2013–17); *b* Cheltenham, 9 Nov. 1971; *d* of Colin Etheridge and Jackie Etheridge; *m* 2005, Chris Megainey; two *s* one *d. Educ:* Keble Coll., Oxford (BA Hons); Univ. of Wales, Aberystwyth (MSc Econ). Joined Dept of Transport, later DETR, 1996: various appts, then Hd, Transport and Envmt Team, 1999–2001; in-house policy consultant, 2001–04; Hd, Reform Strategy, Cabinet Office, 2004–07; Dir of Strategy and Communications, DIUS, 2007–09; Asst Chief Exec., London Bor. of Barnet, 2009–11; Exec. Dir, Civil Service Reform, Cabinet Office, 2011–12; Dir, Transformation and Strategy, Home Office, 2012–13. *T:* 07763 487900. *E:* zinaetheridge@gmail.com.

**ETHERINGTON, David Charles Lynch;** QC 1998; a Recorder, since 2000; *b* 14 March 1953; *s* of late Charles Henry Etherington and Beryl Etherington (*née* Croft). *Educ:* Keble Coll., Oxford (BA 1976, MA 2001; Special DPSA (Distinction) 1977). Called to the Bar, Middle Temple, 1979, Bencher, 2005; Asst Recorder, 1997–2000. Hd of Chambers, 2005–12. Bar Council: Chm., Professional Conduct Cttee, 2003–04; Chm., Professional Practice Cttee, 2006–08. Legal Advr, GDC, 2004–. Deputy Chancellor: Dio. of Norwich, 2005–07; Dio. of Ely, 2012–; Dep. Chancellor, 2007–09, Chancellor, 2009–, Dio. of St Edmundsbury and Ipswich. *Address:* 18 Red Lion Court, EC4A 3EB. *T:* (020) 7520 6000. *Club:* Garrick.

**ETHERINGTON, Col John,** CBE 2018 (OBE 2009); FRCP; Medical Director, Pure Sports Medicine, London, since 2019; President, Faculty of Sport and Exercise Medicine, since 2018; *b* Leeds, 26 Oct. 1961; *s* of John Ronald Etherington and Nora Etherington; *m* 1991, Nicola Jane Parker; two *s* one *d. Educ:* Leeds Grammar Sch.; Birmingham Univ. Med. Sch. (MB ChB 1986); St Bartholomew's and Royal London Sch. of Medicine and Dentistry, Queen Mary and Westfield Coll., Univ. of London (MSc 1996). MRCP 1991, FRCP 2001; Founder FFSEM (UK) 2006; FFPMRCA 2011. Commnd RAMC 2nd Lt, 1983; Regtl Med. Officer, 3 Bn Queen's Regt, 1988–89. House Physn, Gen. Hosp. and Dudley Road Hosp., Birmingham, 1986–87, gen. and higher professional trng in medicine, Queen Elizabeth Mil. Hosp., Woolwich, St Thomas' Hosp. and Royal Nat. Orthopaedic Hosp. Stanmore, 1991–97; Defence Medical Rehabilitation Centre, Headley Court: Consultant in Rheumatol. and Rehabilitation, 1997–2018; Clin. Dir, 2007–09; Dir, Defence Rehabilitation, 2009–18. Nat. Clin. Dir, Rehabilitation and Recovery in the Community, NHS England, 2013–16. Co-Chair, Rehabilitation Cttee, Regl Trauma Networks Adv. Gp; Chair, Cttee on Sport and Exercise Medicine, RCP, 2005–12. *Publications:* (contrib.) Military Medicine in Iraq and Afghanistan, 2019; articles in BMJ, Jl of Bone and Jt Surgery, Jl of RAMC, Archives of Physical Medicine and Rehabilitation, Arthritis and Rheumatism, Medicine & Sci. in Sports & Exercise. *Recreations:* reading, English history, family activities, walking, sport in general and cricket, theatre, all forms of music. *Address:* Pure Sports Medicine, 116 Cromwell Road, SW7 4XR. *T:* (020) 7788 7000. *E:* john.etherington@puresportsmed.com.

**ETHERINGTON, Sir Stuart (James),** Kt 2010; Chief Executive, National Council for Voluntary Organisations, 1994–2019; *b* 26 Feb. 1955; *s* of late Ronald Etherington and Dorothy Etherington (*née* West). *Educ:* Sondes Place Sch., Dorking; Brunel Univ. (BSc Politics 1977); Essex Univ. (MA Soc. Sci. Planning 1981); London Business Sch. (MBA 1992); SOAS (MA Internat. Relns and Diplomacy 1999). Social Worker, London Borough of Hillingdon, 1977–79; Sen. Res. Officer, Joseph Rowntree Meml Trust, Circle 33, 1980–82; Policy Advr, BASW, 1982–84; Dir, Good Practices in Mental Health, 1984–87; Dir, Public Affairs, 1987–91, Chief Exec., 1991–94, RNID. Mem. Council, ESRC, 1998–2003. Mem., Econ. and Social Cttee, EU, 2010–. Trustee: CAF, 1995–2004; BITC, 1995–2008; Civicus, 2001–07 (Treas., 2004–07); Chm., GuideStar UK, 2008–09. Member: RIIA, 1997; IISS. Mem. Council, Open Univ., 2002–07; Mem. Court, 2004–13, Pro Chancellor, 2008–13, Greenwich Univ. Visiting Professor: London South Bank Univ., 2002–16; City Univ., 2003–. Vis. Fellow, Cumberland Lodge, 2017–. Chair, London Utd, 2015–18; Chairman: Patron's Fund, 2015–17; 25th Anniversary Celebrations, Charlton FC, 2016–18. FRSA 1995. Hon. DSocSc Brunel, 2000. *Publications:* Mental Health and Housing, 1984; Emergency Duty Teams, 1985; The Sensitive Bureaucracy, 1986; Social Work and Citizenship, 1987; Voluntary Action: a way forward, 2018. *Recreations:* reading biographies, theatre, opera, watching cricket and Charlton Athletic. *Address:* 49 King George Street, Greenwich, SE10 8QB. *T:* (020) 8305 1379. *Clubs:* National Liberal, Reform, House of St Barnabas; Surrey CC; Blackheath Rugby.

**ETHERINGTON, William;** *b* 17 July 1941; *m* 1963, Irene; two *d. Educ:* Monkwearmouth Grammar Sch.; Durham Univ. Apprentice fitter, Austin & Pickersgill shipyard, 1957–63; fitter, Dawdon Colliery, 1963–83; full-time NUM official, 1983–92. Mem., NUM, 1963– (Vice-Pres., NE Area, 1988–92). MP (Lab) Sunderland N, 1992–2010. Mem., 1997–2010, Dep. Leader, 2002–10, UK delegn to Council of Europe and WEU. Secretary: Miners' Parly Gp, 1994–2010; All-Party Against Fluoridation Gp, 1998–2006.

**ETHERTON, Gillian Felicity Amanda;** QC 2011. Called to the Bar, Middle Temple, 1988; in practice as a barrister, specialising in murder, serious sex crime, child cruelty and baby shaking cases. *Recreations:* reading, swimming, playing the piano, tennis, art. *Address:* 2 Harcourt Buildings, Temple, EC4Y 9DB. *T:* (020) 7353 2112. *E:* clerks@2hb.co.uk. *Club:* Groucho.

*See also Rt Hon. Sir T. M. E. B. Etherton.*

**ETHERTON, Rt Hon. Sir Terence (Michael Elkan Barnet),** Kt 2001; PC 2008; Master of the Rolls and Head of Civil Justice, since 2016; *b* 21 June 1951; *s* of Alan Kenneth Etherton and Elaine Myrtle (*née* Maccoby); civil partnership 2006, *m* 2014, Andrew Howard Stone. *Educ:* Holmewood House Sch., Tunbridge Wells; St Paul's Sch., London (Sen. Foundn Schol.); Corpus Christi Coll., Cambridge (Open Exhibnr; MA (History and Law); LLM; Hon. Fellow, 2007). FCIArb 1993. Called to the Bar, Gray's Inn, 1974 (Uthwatt Schol., 1972; Holker Sen. Award, 1974; Arden Atkin and Mould Prize, 1975; Bencher 1998); in practice, 1975–2000; QC 1990; a Dep. High Court Judge, 2000; a Judge of the High Court, Chancery Div., 2001–08; a Lord Justice of Appeal, 2008–13; Chancellor of the High Court, 2013–16. Chm., Law Commn, 2006–09. Mem., Bar Council, 1978–81; Chm., Young Barristers' Cttee of Bar Council, 1980–81; Mem., Lord Rawlinson's Cttee on the Constitution of the Senate of the Inns of Court and the Bar, 1985–86; Vice Chm., Chancery Bar Assoc., 1999–2001; Pres., Council of the Inns of Court, 2009–12. Mem., Mental Health Review Tribunal, 1994–99; Chairman: Broadmoor Hosp. Authy, 1999–2001; West London Mental Health NHS Trust, 2000–01; Dir (non-exec.), Riverside Mental Health NHS Trust, 1992–99 (Chm., Ethics Forum, 1994–99). Claims Adjudicator, Savings and Investment Bank (IOM) Depositors' Compensation Scheme, 1993–94. Chm., DoE/MAFF Ind. Review Panel on designation of nitrate vulnerable zones under EC Nitrate Directive, 1995 (report published, 1995). Mem. Council, RHBNC, 1992–2002 (Hon. Fellow, Royal Holloway, London Univ., 2005); Chm., City Law Sch. Adv. Bd, City Univ., 2006–08. Chm., Adv. Council on Nat. Records and Archives, 2016–. Vis. Prof., Birkbeck, Univ. of London, 2010– (Fellow, 2019); Hon. Prof., Kent Univ., 2011–. Blundell Meml Lect., 1996. FRSA 2000. Hon. LLD: City, 2009; Kent, 2018. Captain, Cambridge Univ. Fencing Team, 1971–72; Mem., GB Sen. Internat. Fencing Team (Sabre), 1977–80 (World Championships, 1977, 1978, 1979); England Sabre Team Gold Medal, Commonwealth Fencing Championships, 1978; selected for Moscow Olympics, GB Fencing Team, 1980. *Publications:* articles in various legal jls. *Address:* Royal Courts of Justice, Strand, WC2A 2LL. *Club:* Hawks (Cambridge).

*See also G. F. A. Etherton.*

**ETIANG, Paul Orono,** BA London; Chairman: Rock FM Radio Ltd, 2002; Uganda Railways Corporation, 2003–06; *b* 15 Aug. 1938; *s* of late Kezironi Orono and Mirabu Achom Orono; *m* 1967, Zahra Ali Foum; two *s* two *d. Educ:* Makerere Univ. Coll. Uganda Admin Officer, 1962–64; Asst Sec., Foreign Affairs, 1964–65; 3rd Sec., 1965–66, 2nd Sec., 1966–67, Uganda Embassy, Moscow; 1st Sec., Uganda Mission to UN, New York, 1968; Counsellor, 1968–69, High Commissioner, 1969–71, Uganda High Commission, London; Chief of Protocol and Marshal of the Diplomatic Corps, Uganda, 1971; Permanent Sec., Uganda Min. of Foreign Affairs, 1971–73; Minister of State for Foreign Affairs, 1973; Minister of State in the President's office, 1974; Minister of Transport and Communications, July 1976, of Transport, Communications and Works, Mar. 1977, of Transport and Works, 1978; an Asst Sec.-Gen., OAU, Addis Ababa, 1978–87; Minister for Regl Co-operation, March–Dec. 1988; Minister: of Commerce, 1989–91; of Information, 1991–96; Third Dep. Prime Minister, 1996–98; Minister: of Labour and Social Services, 1996–98; for Disaster Preparedness and Refugees, 1998–99. *Recreations:* chess, classical music, billiards. *Address:* Kampala, Uganda.

**EUBANKS, Hyacinth, (Cynthia),** OBE 2014; Education Consultant, Cobe Consultancy Ltd, since 2016; *b* Trelawny, Jamaica, 2 Sept. 1952; *d* of Frank Alfred White and Leanora White; one *d. Educ:* Collingwood Girls Sch.; Balls Park Coll. (Cert Ed). Dep. Headteacher, Monson Primary Sch., Lewisham, 1985–95; Headteacher, Grinling Gibbons Primary Sch., 1996–2010; Exec. Headteacher, Grinling Gibbons and Lucas Vale Fedn, Lewisham, 2010–16. Nat. Leader of Educn, 2010–. *Recreations:* walking, gym, cinema, theatre, family, reading, secondary school governor. *Address:* 12 Henryson Road, Brockley, SE4 1HJ. *T:* 07887 683966.

**EUROPE, Suffragan Bishop in;** *see* Gibraltar in Europe, Suffragan Bishop of.

**EUSTACE, David Russell;** Chancellor, Edinburgh Napier University, since 2015; *b* Edinburgh, 23 Nov. 1961; adopted *s* of James and Susan Eustace, and *s* of Margarita Kellaway and step *s* of Michael Kellaway; *m* 1987, Deirdre Margaret MacDonald; one *d. Educ:* Carntyne Primary Sch., Glasgow; Smithycroft Secondary Sch., Glasgow; Edinburgh Napier Univ. (BA Photography, Film and TV (Dist.) 1991). Sales asst, 1976–77; mkt trader, 1977–78; bingo caller, 1978; served RNR, 10 Mine Countermeasures Sqdn, 1979–82; Prison Officer, HMP Barlinnie, Glasgow, 1983–89; photographic artist, 1991–; masthead contributing photographer, GQ mag., 1993–98; regular contributor to ES Mag., Telegraph Mag., Sunday Times Mag., Tatler and Vogue, 1993–98. Solo photography exhibn, Scottish Gall., Edinburgh, 2015. Hon. DArts Edinburgh Napier, 2011. *Publications:* (contrib.) The Character Project, 2008; I write to tell you of a baby born only yesterday, 2014. *Recreations:* antiques, art. *Address:* Edinburgh Napier University, Sighthill Court, Edinburgh EH11 4BN. *Clubs:* Glasgow Art; Edinburgh Oyster.

**EUSTACE, Dudley Graham,** FCA; Chairman, Smith & Nephew plc, 2000–06; *b* 3 July 1936; *s* of Albert and Mary Eustace; *m* 1964, Carol Diane Zakrajsek; two *d. Educ:* Cathedral Sch., Bristol; Univ. of Bristol (BA Econ). FCA 1972. John Barritt & Son, Hamilton, Bermuda, 1962; Internat. Resort Facilities, Ont, 1963; Aluminium Securities Ltd, Montreal, 1964–65; Aluminium Co. of Canada Ltd, Vancouver, 1966–69, Montreal, 1969–73; Alcan Aluminio America Latina, Buenos Aires, 1973–76, Rio de Janeiro, 1976–79; Empresa Nacional del Aluminio, Madrid, 1979–83; Alcan Aluminium Ltd, Montreal, 1983–84; British Alcan Aluminium PLC, Gerrards Cross, Bucks, 1984–87; BAe, 1987–92 (Finance Dir, 1988–92); Chief Financial Officer, 1992–97, Vice Pres., 1992, Exec. Vice Pres. and Dep. Chm., 1997–99, Philips Electronics NV, Eindhoven. Chm., Sendo Hldgs PLC, 2000–05; Chief Financial Officer, Royal Ahold NV, 2003; Member, Advisory Council: Bayerische Landesbank, Munich, 1995–99; Rothschilds, 2005–12; Member, Supervisory Board: Aegon NV, 1997–2010 (Chm. Bd, 2005–10); Hagemeyer NV, 1999–2006; KLM Royal Dutch Airlines, 1999–2004; Charterhouse Vermogensbeheer BV, 1999–2014; KPN NV, 2000–08; Stork NV, 2007–08; Mem., Adv. Bd, Vallstein NV, 2009–11; Member, Board: sonae.com SGPS, 1999–2003; Providence Capital NV, 2008–. Chm., Nielsen Co., 2005–09. Member: Council, ECGD, 1988–92; Bd, Assoc. for Monetary Union in Europe, 1992–99; Bd, Amsterdam Inst. of Finance, 2001–05. Mem. Council, Univ. of Surrey, 2005–14 (Vice Chm., 2007–14). Liveryman, Chartered Accountants' Co., 1991. DUniv Surrey, 2015. Officier, Order of Oranje-Nassau (Netherlands), 2013. *Recreations:* gardening, reading, fishing. *Address:* Avalon, Old Barn Lane, Churt, Surrey GU10 2NA.

**EUSTICE, (Charles) George;** MP (C) Camborne and Redruth, since 2010; Minister of State, Department for Environment, Food and Rural Affairs, since 2019; *b* Penzance, 1971; *s* of Paul Eustice and Adele Eustice. *Educ:* Truro Cathedral Sch.; Truro Sch.; Cornwall Coll.; Writtle Coll. Dir, Trevaskis Farm Ltd, 1996–99; Campaign Dir, No Campaign Against the Euro, 1999–2003; Hd of Press, Conservative Party, 2003–05; Press Sec. to Rt Hon. David Cameron, MP, 2005–07; Hd, External Relns, Conservative Party, 2008–09; Associate Dir, Portland PR, 2009–10. Parly Under-Sec. of State, 2013–15, Minister of State, 2015–19, DEFRA. *Recreation:* running. *Address:* House of Commons, SW1A 0AA. *T:* (020) 7219 7032. *E:* george.eustice.mp@parliament.uk.

**EUSTON, Earl of; Alfred James Charles FitzRoy;** *b* 26 Dec. 2012; *s* and *heir* of Duke of Grafton, *qv*.

**EVAIN, Christophe;** Senior Adviser, Intermediate Capital Group plc, since 2017 (Chief Executive Officer, 2010–17); *b* Paris 14, 14 June 1962; *m* 1988, Priscille Jeanne Genevieve; two *s* one *d. Educ:* Dauphine Univ., Paris (Master of Strategic Mgt 1987). Credit Analyst, Corporate Treasury and Ops, Credit Lyonnais, USA, 1987–88; Asst Accounts Exec., National Westminster Bank, Paris, 1988–91; Asst Dir, Strategic Finance Unit, Banque de Gestion Privée, Paris, 1991–94; Investment Dir, Paris, 1994–2001, a Man. Dir, 2001–11, Intermediate Capital Gp plc. *Recreations:* music and film, reading about history, Rugby, good quality wine.

**EVAN, Prof. Gerard Ian**, PhD; FRS 2004; FMedSci; Sir William Dunn Professor of Biochemistry, and Head, Department of Biochemistry, University of Cambridge, since 2009; *b* 17 Aug. 1955; *s* of Robert Evan (*née* Ekstein) and Gwendoline Evan; one *s* one *d*. *Educ*: St Peter's Coll., Oxford (BA, MA); King's Coll., Cambridge (PhD 1982). Asst Mem., Ludwig Inst. for Cancer Res., Cambridge, 1984–88; Principal Scientist, ICRF, London, 1988–99; Royal Soc. Napier Res. Prof., UCL, 1996–99; Gerson and Barbara Bass Bakar Distinguished Prof. of Cancer Biol., UCSF, 1999–2009. Mem., EMBO, 1996. FMedSci 1999. Joseph Steiner Prize in Cancer Res., 1996. *Publications*: contrib. numerous res. pubns to learned jls. *Recreations*: hiking, music, mountain biking. *Address*: Department of Biochemistry, University of Cambridge, Tennis Court Road, Cambridge CB2 1GA. *E*: gie20@cam.ac.uk.

**EVANS**; *see* Parry-Evans and Parry Evans.

**EVANS**, family name of **Baroness Blackstone** and **Barons Evans of Watford** and **Mountevans**.

**EVANS OF BOWES PARK**, Baroness *cr* 2014 (Life Peer), of Bowes Park in the London Borough of Haringey; **Natalie Jessica Evans**; PC 2016; Leader of the House of Lords and Lord Privy Seal, since 2016; *b* London, 29 Nov. 1975; *d* of Nicholas David Evans and Ann Elizabeth Evans; *m* 2010, James Oliver Wild. *Educ*: Henrietta Barnett Sch.; New Hall, Cambridge (BA Social and Political Sci. 1998). Hd of Policy, British Chambers of Commerce, 2006–08; Dep. Dir, Policy Exchange, 2008–11; Chief Operating Officer, 2011–12, Dir, 2012–15, New Schools Network. A Baroness in Waiting (Govt Whip), 2015–16. *Recreations*: cricket, football, theatre, travel, fine wine. *Address*: House of Lords, SW1A 0PW.

**EVANS OF TEMPLE GUITING, Lady**; *see* Michel, C. J.

**EVANS OF WATFORD**, Baron *cr* 1998 (Life Peer), of Chipperfield in the co. of Hertfordshire; **David Charles Evans**; Chairman: Senate Publishing Ltd (formerly Senate Consulting Ltd), since 2002; Kennedy Scott Ltd, since 2014; Stormount Energy, since 2015; *b* 30 Nov. 1942; *s* of Arthur and Phyllis Evans; *m* 1966, June Scaldwell (marr. diss. 2008); one *s* one *d*; one *s* by Jeanne Pieplenbosch. *Educ*: Hampden Secondary Sch.; Watford Coll. of Technology. Apprentice printer, Stone and Cox Ltd, 1957. Founded: Centurion Press Ltd, 1971; (with Susanne Lawrence) Personnel Publications Ltd, 1975; Centurion Press bv, 1975; Chairman: Centurion Press Gp, 1971–2002; Senate Media (formerly Centurion Media) Gp bv, 1974–2002; Personnel Publications Ltd, 1981–2011; Redactive Publishing (formerly Partnership Sourcing Ltd), 2002– (Fellow, 2018); TU Ink Ltd, 2005–; Newsdesk Media Ltd, 2013–14 (Dir, 2012–15); Indigo Publishing Ltd; Evans Mitchell Books; One Gold Radio; Ace Consortium Ltd; Ace Funding Ltd; Forum Print Mgt Ltd. Non-exec. Dir, Care Capital plc. Dep. Chm., Internat. Medical Educn Trust; former Dir, KISS 100 FM; former Mem. Develt Bd, UCL Hosp. Charitable Trust. Mem., H of L Select Cttee for Small and Medium Enterprises, 2012–13. Dir, RAF Mus. Trading Ltd; former Trustee, RAF Mus. Hon. Fellow, Cancer Research UK. Patron: Watford Peace Hospice; VITAL; Alma Hosp. Trust; Eliminating Domestic Violence. Freeman, Marketors' Co., 1991. FCIM 1991; FCGI 2001. *Publications*: articles on marketing, print management and purchasing. *Recreations*: theatre, art, reading, travel. *Address*: Senate Publishing Ltd, 47 Connaught Street, W2 2BB. *T*: (020) 7723 9825. *E*: lordevans@senatepublishing.co.uk.

**EVANS OF WEARDALE**, Baron *cr* 2014 (Life Peer), of Toys Hill in the County of Kent; **Jonathan Douglas Evans**, KCB 2013; DL; Director-General, Security Service, 2007–13; *b* 1958. *Educ*: Sevenoaks Sch.; Bristol Univ. (BA Classical Studies). Security Service, 1980–2013; Dep. Dir-Gen., 2005–07. Non-executive Director: HSBC, 2013–19; Ark Data Centres, 2015–. Chair, Cttee on Standards in Public Life, 2018–. Dist. Fellow (formerly Sen. Associate Fellow), RUSI, 2013– (Mem. Council, 2007–10). Hon. Prof., Univ. of St Andrews, 2013–; Vis. Prof., KCL, 2019. Mem., Adv. Bd, Darktrace, 2013–. Chm., Kent Search and Rescue, 2016–; Patron: Sevenoaks Sch., 2012–; W Kent YMCA, 2013–. Freeman, City of London, 2011; Liveryman, Skinners' Co., 2013–. DL Kent, 2015. Hon. LLD Bristol, 2008. *Recreations*: classic cars, town and country walks. *Address*: House of Lords, SW1A 0PW.

**EVANS, Adrian Anthony Joseph**, LVO 2012; Festival Director, Thames Festival Trust, since 1997; *b* London, 22 Dec. 1957; *s* of Brig. Patrick Joseph, (Paddy), Evans, CBE and Patricia Evans; *m* 1993, Bettany Hughes; two *d*. *Educ*: Oratory Sch.; Univ. of Edinburgh (MA Hons 1981). Producer, Lumiere & Son Theatre Co., 1982–87. Director: London Fest. of New Circus, 1988; Gran Gran Fiesta, 1989–95; Coin Street Fest., 1994–2009; Producer: Archaos, Cirque de Caractère, 1989–96; Art Casino, Barbican Art Gall., 1995; The African Prom, Royal Albert Hall, 1995; Director of Animations: Opening of the Channel Tunnel, 1994; Big Time, London's Official Millennium Celebrations, 1999–2000; Pageant Master, Thames Diamond Jubilee Pageant, 2009–12; Campaign Dir, Clean for the Queen, 2016. *E*: a.evans@thamesfestival.org.

**EVANS, Alan**; *see* Evans, D. A.

**EVANS, Dr Alison Margaret**; Director General, Evaluation, World Bank Group, since 2019; *b* Sutton Coldfield, 7 July 1962; *d* of Geoffrey Morris Evans and Margaret Evans; civil partnership 2007, Jan Mathew; one *s* two *d*. *Educ*: Univ. of Sussex (BA Hons 1st Cl. Econs 1983; DPhil Develt Studies 1997); Queens' Coll., Cambridge (MPhil Econs and Politics of Develt 1984). University of Sussex: Res. Officer, Inst. of Develt Studies, 1983–89; Lectr in Econs, 1990–94; Sen. Economist, 1994–97; Sen. Evaluation Officer, 1997–2000; World Bank; Dir, Progs 2006–09, Dir, 2009–13, ODI; Chief Comr, Ind. Commn for Aid Impact, 2015–18. Non-exec. Dir, Oxford Policy Mgt, 2013–15. Mem., Adv. Council, Queen Elizabeth House, Oxford, 2009–13. Trustee: BBC Media Action (formerly BBC World Service Trust), 2010–; Social Finance, 2014–. *Recreations*: film, literature, walking, theatre.

**EVANS, Alun**; *see* Evans, T. A.

**EVANS, Alun Trevor Bernard**, CBE 2018; Chief Executive and Secretary, British Academy, 2015–19; *b* 8 Dec. 1958; *s* of late Thomas Francis Evans and Marjorie Gladys Evans (*née* Macken); *m* 1986, Ingrid Elisabeth Dammers; two *d*. *Educ*: County Sch., Ashford, Middx; Essex Univ. (BA Hons); Birmingham Univ. (MPhil 1983). Civil Servant, Dept of Employment, subseq. DfEE, 1983–98: Private Sec. to Paymaster Gen. and Minister for Employment, 1986; Asst Regl Dir, Eastern Reg., 1992–93; Hd, Nuclear Safety Policy Div., HSE, 1993–94; Principal Private Sec. to Sec. of State for Employment, 1994–95, to Sec. of State for Educn and Employment, 1995–98; Hd, Strategic Communications Unit, Prime Minister's Office, 1998–2000; Dir of Communications, DETR, then DTLR, 2000–01; Sec. to Inquiry into lessons to be learned from foot and mouth disease outbreak, 2001–02; Cabinet Office, 2002–03; Dir of Civil Resilience, ODPM, subseq. of Fire and Resilience, DCLG, 2003–06; Director General: Transformation, DCLG, 2006–08; Sci. and Res., DIUS, 2008; Dir, Policy and Analysis Profession, DIUS, 2008–09; Dir, Delivery and Implementation, later Strategy, BIS, 2009–10; Sec., Detainee Inquiry, 2010–12; Dir, Scotland Office, 2012–15. Sen. Fellow (pt-time), Inst. for Government, 2011–; Gwilym

Gibbon Fellow, Nuffield Coll., Oxford, 2014–; Vis. Prof., KCL, 2015–. *Recreations*: political history, family, cricket, running, art, opera. *Clubs*: Garrick; Occasionals, Mandarins Cricket.

*See also* R. J. E. Evans.

**EVANS, Amanda Louise Elliot, (Mrs A. S. Duncan)**; freelance writer, editor and editorial consultant, since 1997; reflexologist specialising in fertility, pregnancy and babies, since 2009; *b* 19 May 1958; *d* of late Brian Royston Elliot Evans and of June Annabella (*née* Gilderdale); *m* 1989, Andrew Sinclair Duncan; one *s* two *d*. *Educ*: Tonbridge Girls' Grammar Sch. Editorial writer, Interiors magazine, 1981–83; Consultant Editor, Mitchell Beazley Publishers, 1983–84; freelance writer and stylist on A la carte, Tatler, Country Homes & Interiors, Sunday Times, 1984–86; Dep. Editor, April–Oct. 1986, Editor, 1986–96, Homes & Gardens. *Publications*: Homes and Gardens Bedrooms, 1997; Making the Most of Living Rooms, 1998. *Recreations*: mountain walking, opera, camping. *Address*: 1 Rylett Studios, 77 Rylett Crescent, W12 9RP.

**EVANS, Anne Celia**; *see* Segall, A. C.

**EVANS, Dame Anne (Elizabeth Jane)**, DBE 2000; soprano; *b* 20 Aug. 1941; *d* of late David and Eleanor, (Nellie), Evans; *m* 1st, 1962, John Heulyn Jones (marr. diss. 1981); 2nd, 1981, John Philip Lucas. *Educ*: Royal Coll. of Music; Conservatoire de Genève. Début, Annina in La Traviata, Grand Théatre, Geneva, 1967; UK début, Mimi in La Bohème, Coliseum, 1968; Principal soprano, ENO, 1968–78; subseq. major rôles at Metropolitan Opera House, NY, San Francisco Opera, Deutsche Oper, Berlin, Dresden State Opera, Vienna State Opera, Paris Opéra, Rome Opera, Théâtre de la Monnaie, Brussels, Teatro Colón, Buenos Aires, Royal Opera House, Covent Garden, WNO, Scottish Opera; rôles include: Brünnhilde in Der Ring des Nibelungen (incl. Bayreuth Fest., 1989–92), Isolde in Tristan und Isolde, Sieglinde in Die Walküre, Elsa in Lohengrin, Elisabeth in Tannhäuser, Senta in Der fliegende Holländer, Leonore in Fidelio, Cassandre in Les Troyens, Chrysothemis in Elektra, Marschallin in Der Rosenkavalier, Ariadne in Ariadne auf Naxos; recitals incl. Edinburgh Fest., Wigmore Hall; Last Night of the Proms, 1997. Trustee, Countess of Munster Musical Scholarships, 2009–. FRWCMD (FWCMD 1996). Hon. DMus Kent, 2005. *Recreations*: cooking, gardening. *Address*: c/o Groves Artists, 7 St George's Court, 131 Putney Bridge Road, SW15 2PA.

**EVANS, Anthony**; *see* Evans, D. A.

**EVANS, Anthony Clive Varteg**, FCIL; Head Master, King's College School, Wimbledon, 1997–2008; *b* 11 Oct. 1945; *s* of Edward Varteg Evans and Doris Lilian Evans; *m* 1968, Danielle Jacqueline Nicole Bégasse (*d* 1997); two *s*. *Educ*: De la Salle Grammar Sch., London; St Peter's Coll., Oxford (MA); University Coll. London (MPhil); Inst. of Educn, London Univ. (Advanced DipEd). FCIL (FIL 1975). Assistant Master: Eastbourne Coll., 1967–72; Winchester Coll., 1972–77; Hd of Mod. Langs and Hd of Humanities, Dulwich Coll., 1977–83; Headmaster, Portsmouth Grammar Sch., 1983–97. Headmasters' and Headmistresses' Conference: Chm., 1996; Mem., 1985–94, Chm., 1990–94, Acad. Policy Cttee; Mem., Common Entrance Cttee, 1988–90; Mem., Cttee, 1989–97; Mem., HMC/GSA Univ. Cttee, 1993–2002 (Co-Chm., 1993–95). Member: Admiralty Interview Bd, 1985–97; Nat. Curriculum Council, 1989–91; ISC Council, 1996–2000; HEFCE, 1999–2002; Bd, Assoc. of Governing Bodies of Ind. Schs, 2008–14; Chm., ISC Adv. Council, 1997–99; Co-Chm., ISC Unity Cttee, 1997–99; Chm., Large Ind. Day Schs Gp, 2002–06. Fellow, Winchester Coll., Hants, 1997–2006; Governor: Mall Sch., Twickenham, 1997–2007; Sevenoaks Sch., 2000–13 (Chm., 2008–13); Ecole Saint-Georges, Montreux, 2000–07; Perse Sch., Cambridge, 2003–15; Lancing Coll., 2008–17; Marlborough Coll., 2008–16; British Sch. of Paris, 2010–16. FKC 2008. *Publications*: Souvenirs de la Grande Guerre, 1985. *Recreations*: France, theatre, Southampton FC, avoiding dinner parties. *Address*: 15 Castelnau Mansions, Castelnau, Barnes, SW13 9QX; 15 Route de Saint Hubert, 33450 St Sulpice et Cameyrac, France. *Club*: East India.

**EVANS, Rt Hon. Sir Anthony (Howell Meurig)**, Kt 1985; RD 1968; PC 1992; arbitrator; a Justice of the Court of Appeal, Bermuda, 2003–15; Chief Justice, DIFC Court, Dubai, 2005–10; Chairman, Dubai World Special Tribunal, since 2009; *b* 11 June 1934; *s* of late His Honour David Meurig Evans and Joy Diedericke (*née* Sander); *m* 1963, Caroline Mary Fyffe Mackie, *d* of late Edwin Gordon Mackie; one *s* two *d*. *Educ*: Bassaleg Sec. Grammar Sch., Mon; Shrewsbury Sch.; St John's Coll., Cambridge (BA 1957; LLB 1958). Nat. Service, RNVR, 1952–54 (Lt-Comdr RNR). Called to Bar, Gray's Inn, 1958 (Arden Scholar and Birkenhead Scholar); Bencher, 1979; Treas., 2000); QC 1971; a Recorder, 1972–84; a Presiding Judge, Wales and Chester Circuit, 1986–88; a Judge of the High Court of Justice, QBD, 1984–92; Judge in charge of the Commercial Court, 1991–92; a Lord Justice of Appeal, 1992–2000. Dep. Chm., Inf. Tribunal (Pres., Nat. Security Appeals), 2000–04; Vice-Pres., Internat. Cttee on Holocaust Era Insurance Claims Appeal Tribunal, 2000–06; Chm., Commn of Inquiry, Bermuda, 2016. Mem., Melbourne, Vic, Bar, 1975–84, Hon. Mem., 1985. Dep. Chm., Boundary Commn for Wales, 1989–92. Visitor: Cardiff Univ., 1999–2013; SOAS, 2002–07. Pres., Bar Musical Soc., 1998–2008. Hon. Fellow, Internat. Acad. of Trial Lawyers, 1985; FCIArb 1986 (Patron, Wales Br., 1988–98; Hon. Pres., 1998–2001; Companion, 2007). A Vice President: British Maritime Law Assoc., 1992–; Assoc. of Average Adjusters, 1997–. Freeman, 2000, Liveryman, 2001, Shipwrights' Co. *Publications*: (Jt Editor) The Law of the Air (Lord McNair), 1964. *Recreations*: sailing, music. *Address*: Essex Court Chambers, 24 Lincoln's Inn Fields, WC2A 3EG. *Clubs*: Royal Yacht Squadron; Royal Welsh Yacht.

**EVANS, Prof. Anthony John**, PhD; Professor in Department of Information and Library Studies (formerly Library and Information Studies), 1973–95, now Emeritus Professor, and Director, Alumni Office, 1992–95, Loughborough University of Technology, now Loughborough University; *b* 1 April 1930; *s* of William John and Marian Audrey (*née* Young); *m* 1954, Anne (*née* Horwell); two *d*. *Educ*: Queen Elizabeth's Hosp., Bristol (Pres., Old Boys' Soc., 1999); Sch. of Pharmacy and University College, Univ. of London. BPharm, PhD. Lectr in Pharm. Eng. Sci., Sch. of Pharmacy, Univ. of London, 1954–58; Librarian, Sch. of Pharmacy, Univ. of London, 1958–63; University Librarian, 1964–91, and Dean, Sch. of Educnl Studies, 1973–76, Loughborough Univ. of Technology. Pres., IATUL, 1970–75 (Bd Mem. and Treasurer, 1968–70; Hon. Life Mem., 1976–); Mem. Exec. Bd, IFLA, 1983–89 (Treas., 1985–89; Consultative Cttee, 1968–76; Standing Cttee on Sci. and Tech. Libraries, 1977–87; Standing Cttee on Univ. Libraries, 1989–93; Chm., Cttee on Access to Information and Freedom of Expression, 1995–97); Pres., Commonwealth Library Assoc., 1994–96; ASLIB: Vice-Pres., 1985–88; Mem. Council, 1970–80, 1985–88; Internat. Relations Cttee, 1974–85; Annual Lecture, 1985; BSI: Mem. Bd, 1984–86; Chm., Documentation Standards Cttee, 1980–86 (Mem., 1976–86); Member: Inf. Systems Council, 1980–86. Member: Adv. Cttee, Sci. Ref. Library, 1975–83; Vice-Chancellors and Principals Cttee on Libraries, 1972–77; Jt UNESCO/ICSU Cttee for establishment of UNISIST, 1968–71; Internat. Cttee, LA, 1985–96; Adv. Council to Bd of Dirs of Engineering Information Inc., USA, 1986–91; Chm., Adv. Gp on Documentation Standards, ISO, 1983–85; consultancy work for British Council, ODA, UNESCO, UNIDO, World Bank in Africa, Asia and Latin America, especially China, Kenya and Mexico. Pres., Jaguars Wheelchair Basketball Club, 1997–2004. FCLIP (FLA 1969); Hon. FLA 1990. Medal IFLA, 1989. *Publications*: (with D. Train) Bibliography of the tabletting of medicinal substances, 1964, suppl. 1965; (with R. G. Rhodes and S. Keenan) Education and training of users of scientific and technical information, UNESCO Paris, 1977; articles in librarianship and documentation. *Recreations:* genealogy, sport, especially wheelchair basketball. *Address:* The Willows Lodge, Old Wood, Skellingthorpe, Lincoln LN6 5UA. *E:* ajevans54@btinternet.com.

**EVANS, Anthony Thomas;** a District Judge (Magistrates' Courts) (formerly Metropolitan Stipendiary Magistrate), 1990–2008; *b* 29 Sept. 1943; *s* of late Emlyn Roger Evans and Dorothy Evans; *m* 1st, 1965, Gillian Celia Mather (*d* 1988); one *s*; 2nd, 1991, Margaret Elizabeth Ryles (*née* Howorth); one step *s* one step *d. Educ:* Bishop Gore Grammar Sch., Swansea; Univ. of Manchester (LLB 1965; LLM 1968). Asst Lectr, Univ. of Manchester, 1965–68; admitted Solicitor, 1971; Partner: Haye & Reid, 1971–85; Evans & Co., 1985–89; sole practitioner, 1989–90. Chairman: Inner London Family Courts, 1991–2006; Inner London Youth Courts, 1993–2006. Chm., Stipendiary Magistrates' Legal Cttee, 1994–2000; Mem., Criminal Procedure Rules Cttee, 2004–07. Mem., British Acad. of Forensic Scis, 1994–2017. *Recreations:* reading, music, theatre.

**EVANS, Bethan;** governance trainer and consultant, since 2018; Partner, Bevan Brittan LLP, 2002–18 (Senior Partner, 2012–16); *b* Wednesbury, W Midlands, 22 Jan. 1958; *d* of Dennis Evans and Sybil Evans; partner, Steve Evans. *Educ:* Queen Mary's High Sch. for Girls, Walsall; Univ. of Bristol (LLB Hons 1980); Guildford Law Sch. (Law Soc. Finals 1981). Trainee solicitor, Veale Benson Solicitors, Bristol, 1981–83; admitted as solicitor, 1983; Solicitor: Wansdyke DC, 1983–85; Bristol CC, 1985–88; Asst County Solicitor, Avon CC, 1988–96; Dir, Corporate Services, S Gloucestershire Council, 1996–99; Dir, Syniad, Cardiff, 1999–2002. *Recreation:* living long enough to see any football team I support do anything decent (Walsall FC and England).

**EVANS, Prof. Brian Mark,** PhD; Professor of Urbanism and Landscape, and Head of Urbanism, Glasgow School of Art, since 2010; *b* St Andrews, 1953; *m* 1988, Susan Ann. *Educ:* Linlithgow Acad.; Univ. of Edinburgh (BSc Hons Earth Scis and Maths); Univ. of Strathclyde (DipURP; MSc Urban Design); Univ. of Glasgow (PhD). Partner, Gillespies LLP, 1989–2015. Tutor, Scott Sutherland Sch. of Architecture, Robert Gordon Univ., 1989–99; Prof., Sch. of Architecture, Chalmers Univ., Gothenburg, 1998–2004. Enabler, CABE, 2003–06; Dep. Chm., Architecture and Design Scotland, 2004–10; City Urbanist, Glasgow, 2019–. Founder and Dir, Acad. of Urbanism, 2005–14 (Academician). Advr, UNECE, 2015–. FRTPI; FCSD; FAcSS; FRGS. *Publications:* (jtly) Tomorrow's Architectural Heritage: the landscape setting of buildings in the countryside, 1991; (ed jtly) Space, Place, Life, 2007, 2nd edn 2011; (ed jtly) Urban Identity, 2011; (ed jtly) Growing Awareness: how green consciousness can change perceptions and places, 2016; book chapters, articles, conf. papers. *Recreations:* blethering my way into anecdotage; hunting hubris, occasionally from architects whom I otherwise adore for their relentless belief that the world can be made better by design. *Address:* Mackintosh School of Architecture, Glasgow School of Art, 167 Renfrew Street, Glasgow G3 6RQ. *T:* (0141) 353 4447. *E:* b.evans@gsa.ac.uk.

**EVANS, Carole Denise M.;** *see* Mills-Evans.

**EVANS, Catherine Angela, (Cat);** HM Diplomatic Service; Ambassador to Mali and (non-resident) Ambassador to Niger, since 2018; *b* Islington, 27 Dec. 1979; *d* of Christopher Evans and Felicity Evans. *Educ:* Fakenham Coll.; Durham Univ. (MMath 1st Cl. Hons 2002). Assoc. of Project Managers qual. 2007. Ministry of Defence: Desk Officer for Afghanistan, 2003–04; Team Leader, Prince's Trust (on secondment), 2004–05; Defence Change Prog. Manager, 2005–06; Dep. Civilian Advr to Sierra Leone MoD, 2006–07; Proj. Manager, Special Projects, 2007–08; Political/Policy Advr, Multi-Nat. Div. SE HQ, Basra, 2008–09; First Sec., Islamabad, 2009–11; Counsellor (Political), Kabul, 2011–12; Dep. Hd (Olympics), Counter-Terrorism Dept, FCO, 2012; Dep. Hd, Future of Europe Dept, FCO, 2012–14; Dep. Hd of Mission, Addis Ababa, 2015–17. *Recreations:* tennis, hiking, exploring new places, running, aspiring photographer. *Address:* British Embassy Bamako, Cité de Niger II, Bamako, Mali. *T:* 44976913. *E:* bebamako@fco.gov.uk, Cat.Evans@fco.gov.uk.

**EVANS, Charles A. W.;** *see* Wynn-Evans.

**EVANS, Christina Hambley, (Lady Evans);** *see* Brown, Tina.

**EVANS, Christopher;** radio and television presenter; Executive Producer and Writer, UMTV, since 2002; *b* 1 April 1966; *m* 1991, Carol McGiffin (marr. diss.); *m* 2001, Billie Piper (marr. diss. 2007); *m* 2007, Natasha Shishmanian; three *s* one *d* (incl. twin *s* and *d*); one *d* from a previous relationship. Started broadcasting career with Piccadilly Radio, Manchester; *radio:* producer and presenter, GLR; presenter: Radio One Breakfast Show, BBC, 1995–97; Virgin Radio Breakfast Show, 1997–2001, 2019–; The Chris Evans Show, 2005–06, Drive Time Show, 2006–09, The Chris Evans Breakfast Show, 2010–18, BBC Radio 2; *television:* presenter, Power Station, BSB Channel; Channel 4: co-presenter: The Big Breakfast, 1992–93; Top Gear, 2016; devised, wrote and presented, Don't Forget Your Toothbrush, 1993 (BAFTA Award, 1995); TFI Friday, 1997–2000, 2015. Chairman: Ginger Prodns, 1993–2000; Ginger Media Gp, 1997–2000; Virgin Radio, 1997–2001. Radio Personality of the Year, TRIC, 1997, 2012; Sony Radio Awards for Entertainment Personality and Music Radio Personality, 2007. *Publications:* It's Not What You Think (autobiog.), 2009; Memoirs of a Fruitcake, 2010; Call the Midlife, 2015. *Address:* Mr Hiten Vora, c/o News UK, The News Building, 1 London Bridge Street, SE1 9GF.

**EVANS, Christopher Charles,** MD; FRCP, FRCPI; Consultant Physician, Cardiothoracic Centre and Royal Liverpool University Hospital, 1974–2003, now Emeritus; President and Chairman, Medical Defence Union, 2006–12 (Vice President and Vice Chairman, 2001–06); *b* 2 Oct. 1941; *s* of Robert Percy Evans and Nora Carson Evans; *m* 1966, Dr Susan Fuld; one *s* two *d. Educ:* Wade Deacon Grammar Sch., Widnes; Univ. of Liverpool Med. Sch. (MB ChB 1964; MD 1973). MRCP 1968, FRCP 1979; FRCPI 1997. Hon. Sen. Lectr, Univ. of Liverpool, 1974–2003. Consulting Medical Officer: Royal Sun Alliance, 1977–2005; Swiss Life, 1990–2005. Pres., Liverpool Med. Instn, 1991–92. Academic Vice Pres., RCP, 2001–03. Chm., NW Reg., British Lung Foundn, 1993–2000. *Publications:* (ed jtly) Symptoms and Signs in Clinical Medicine, 12th edn 1997; contrib. on general med. and thoracic topics, Thorax, BMJ, Lancet. *Recreations:* tennis, ski-ing, fell-walking, watching Liverpool FC, theatre, birdwatching. *Address:* Lagom, Glendyke Road, Liverpool L18 6JR. *T:* (0151) 724 5386. *E:* christoffe58@hotmail.com. *Clubs:* Reform; XX (Pres., 1993–94), Artists (Liverpool) (Pres., 2010–11); Liverpool Cricket (Pres., 2014–15).

**EVANS, Christopher James;** MP (Lab Co-op) Islwyn, since 2010; *b* Llwynipia, Rhondda; *s* of Michael Alan Evans and Lynne Evans; *m* 2013, Julia Teresa Ockenden; one *s. Educ:* Porth Co. Comp. Sch.; Pontypridd Coll.; Trinity Coll., Carmarthen (BA Hist.). Office Manager, Jack Brown Bookmakers Ltd, 1998–2001; Personal Account Manager, Lloyds TSB Bank plc, 2001–03; Marketing Exec., Univ. of Glamorgan, 2003–04; Area Sec., Union of Finance Staff, 2004–06; Parly Researcher, Don Touhig, MP, 2006–10. Contested (Lab) Cheltenham, 2005. Hon. Fellow, Univ. of Wales Trinity St Davids, 2017. *Publications:* Fearless Freddie: the life and times of Freddie Mills, 2017. *Recreations:* running, reading, watching most sports. *Address:* (office) 6 Woodfieldside Business Park, Penmaen Road, Pontllanfraith, Blackwood NP12 2DG. *T:* (01495) 231990.

**EVANS, Dr (Christopher) Paul;** regeneration consultant, since 2008; Strategic Director of Regeneration and Neighbourhoods, London Borough of Southwark, 2001–07; *b* 25 Dec. 1948; *s* of late Colwyn and Margery Evans; *m* 1971, Margaret Beckett; two *d. Educ:* St Julian's High Sch., Newport; Trinity Coll., Cambridge (MA, DipArch, PhD). Department of the Environment, subseq. of the Environment, Transport and the Regions, then Department for Transport, Local Government and the Regions, later Office of the Deputy Prime Minister, 1975–2001: Private Sec. to Permanent Sec., 1978–80; Principal, 1980; Asst Sec., 1985; Under Sec., 1993; Dir, Urban Policy Unit, 1997–2001. Vice Chm., British Urban Regeneration Assoc., 2007–10; Dir, UK Regeneration, 2010–13; Dir, Catalyst Housing, 2010–17 (Vice Chm., 2014–17).

**EVANS, Air Marshal (Christopher) Paul (Anthony),** CB 2014; FRAeS; Surgeon General, 2012–15; *b* 1954. *Educ:* MB BCh 1978; DAvMed 1987; MSc 1999. FRAeS 2009. Joined RAF as Med. Cadet, 1975; Jun. MO, RAF Wyton and RAF Hosps at Ely, Nocton Hall and Halton, 1979–83; SMO, RAF Leeming, Coltishall and Valley, 1983–90; Comd Flight MO, RAF Support Comd, 1990–92; OC Med. Wing, RAF Hosp. Wegberg, 1992–95; Medico-Legal Advr to DGMS(RAF), 1995–96; Course Leader, RAF Staff Coll., 1996; MO responsible for clin. policy, Surgeon Gen.'s Dept, 1997–99; Dir responsible for med. policy and plans, Directorate of DGMS(RAF), 1999–2002; MO lead on Surgeon Gen.'s Change Mgt Team, 2002–03; Dir Healthcare, Surgeon Gen.'s Dept, 2003–08; COS Health and DGMS, RAF, 2008–09; Comdr, Jt Med. Comd, 2009–12. QHP 2005–16. Hon. DSc Loughborough, 2015.

**EVANS, Sir Christopher (Thomas),** Kt 2001; OBE 1995; PhD; CBiol, FRSB, CChem, FRSC; FMedSci; CSci; Founder and Chairman: Excalibur Fund Managers (formerly Merlin Biosciences Ltd), since 1996; Excalibur Group, since 2008; *b* 29 Nov. 1957; *s* of Cyril and Jean Evans; *m* 1985, Judith Anne; twin *s* two *d. Educ:* Imperial Coll., London (BSc 1979; ARCS 1979); Univ. of Hull (PhD). CBiol 1994, FRSB (FIBiol 1994); CSci 1994; CChem 1995; FRSC 1995. Postdoctoral Res., Univ. of Michigan, 1983; Alleix Inc., Toronto, 1984–86; Genzyme Biochemicals Ltd, Maidstone, 1986–87; Founder and Director: Enzymatix Ltd, 1987–; Chiroscience plc, 1992–; Celsis Internat. plc, 1992– (Chm., 1998–); Founder, Director and Chairman: Toad Innovations plc, 1993–2001; Merlin Scientific Services Ltd, 1995–; Enviros Ltd, 1995–; Cyclacel Ltd, 1996–; Founding Investor and Chairman: Biovex, 1998; Piramed, 2004; Founder and Chm., Arthurian Life Scis, 2012–; Founder and Dep. Chm., Arix Bioscience Ltd, 2016–19; Dir, Microscience Ltd, 1997. Founder: Merlin Fund, 1996; Merlin Biosciences Fund; British Growth Trust (formerly FLIT), 1997; Vectura plc, 1997; Stem Cell Foundn, 2004. Mem., Prime Minister's Council for Sci. and Technol. FRSA 1995; FMedSci 2003; Fellow: Bath Univ.; Univ. of Wales, Aberystwyth. Hon. Prof., Univs of Manchester, Liverpool, Exeter and Bath, and Imperial Coll., London; Hon. Fellow: UWCC, 1996; Univ. of Wales Swansea, 1996; Hon. FREng 2005. Hon. DSc: Hull, 1995; Nottingham, 1995; East Anglia, 1998; Cranfield, 1998; Bath, 2000. Henderson Meml Medal, Porton Down, 1997; SCI Centenary Medal, 1998; RSC Interdisciplinary Medal, 1999. *Publications:* numerous scientific papers and patents. *Recreations:* wife, Rugby, gym, fly-fishing, electric guitar, song writing. *Address:* Excalibur Group, Berkeley Square House, Berkeley Square, Mayfair, W1J 6BD.

**EVANS, Air Vice-Marshal Clive Ernest,** CBE 1982; DL; Senior Directing Staff (Air), Royal College of Defence Studies, 1988–91, retired; *b* 21 April 1937; *s* of Leslie Roberts Evans and Mary Kathleen Butcher; *m* 1963, Therese Goodrich (*d* 2013); one *s* one *d. Educ:* St Dunstan's Coll., Catford. Flying training, RAF, 1955–56; graduated as pilot, 1956, as qualified flying instr, 1960; served on Vampires, Jet Provosts, Canberras, Lightnings and F111s (exchange tour with USAF), 1960–72; RAF Staff Coll., 1972; PSO to Controller Aircraft, 1973; OC No 24 Sqn (Hercules), 1974–76; Nat. Defence Coll., 1976–77; DS RAF Staff Coll., 1977–79; Head of RAF Presentation Team, 1979–81; OC RAF Lyneham, 1981–83; RCDS, 1984; COS and Dep. Comdr, British Forces Falkland Is, 1985; Dep. Air Sec., 1985–88. Pres., Surrey Wing, ATC. DL Greater London, 1997. *Recreations:* reading, cricket, golf, gardening. *Address:* 43 Purley Bury Close, Purley, Surrey CR8 1HW. *T:* (020) 8660 8115. *Club:* Royal Air Force.

**EVANS, Colin Rodney;** Director, Weapon Systems Research Laboratory, Defence Science and Technology Organisation, Adelaide, 1989–91; *b* 5 June 1935; *s* of John Evans and Annie (*née* Lawes); *m* 1963, Jennifer MacIntosh; two *d. Educ:* Bridlington Sch.; Woolwich Polytechnic; Imperial Coll., London. BSc(Eng); HND; MIMechE. Scientific Officer, ARDE (now RARDE), 1959–60; Lectr, RNC, Greenwich, 1960–61; Scientific Officer, then Sen. Scientific Officer and PSO, ARDE, 1961–69; SO to Chief Scientist (Army), MoD, 1969–71; British Defence Staff, Washington, 1971–73; SPSO, RARDE, 1973–79; Dep. Dir, Scientific and Technical Intell., MoD, 1979–81; seconded to Sir Derek Rayner's study team on efficiency in govt, 1981; RCDS, 1982; Dep. Dir (1), RARDE, 1983–84; Asst Under Sec. of State, MoD, Dep. Dir (Vehicles) and Hd of RARDE (Chertsey), 1985–89. President: Kent Squash Rackets Assoc., 1992–2010; Maudslay Soc., 1993–99. *Recreations:* travel, tennis, bird watching, stamp collecting (Pres., Tunbridge Wells Philatelic Soc., 2014–16). *Address:* c/o HSBC, 105 Mount Pleasant, Tunbridge Wells TN1 1QP.

**EVANS, Dafna Miriam;** *see* Spiro, D. M.

**EVANS, Daniel Gwyn;** Artistic Director, Chichester Festival Theatre, since 2016; *b* Rhondda, S Wales, 31 July 1973; *s* of Gwyn and Val Evans. *Educ:* Guildhall Sch. of Music and Drama (BA Acting). Artistic Dir, Sheffield Theatres, 2009–16. *Theatre includes: as actor:* A Midsummer Night's Dream, RSC and NY tour, 1994; Cardiff East, Peter Pan, RNT, 1997; Cleansed, Royal Court, 1998; Merchant of Venice, Troilus and Cressida, Candide, 1999, RNT; Merrily We Roll Along, Donmar Warehouse, 2000 (Olivier Award for Best Actor in a Musical, 2001); Other People, 2000, 4:48 Psychosis, 2001, Where Do We Live, 2002, Royal Court; Ghosts, English Touring Th., 2002; The Tempest, Crucible, Old Vic, 2002; Measure for Measure, Cymbeline, RSC, 2003; Cloud Nine, Crucible, 2004; Grand Hotel, Donmar Warehouse, 2004; Sunday in the Park with George, Menier Chocolate Factory, transf. Wyndham's, 2006, NY 2008 (Olivier Award for Best Actor in a Musical, 2007); Total Eclipse, Menier Chocolate Factory, 2007; Sweeney Todd, Southbank Centre, 2007; The Pride, Company, Crucible, 2011; *as director:* Crucible Theatre: An Enemy of the People, 2010; Othello, Company, 2011; Macbeth, My Fair Lady (Best Regl Prodn, Whatsonstage Awards, 2014), 2012; This is My Family (Best Musical Prodn, UK Th. Awards, 2013), Oliver!, 2013 (Best Regl Prodn, Whatsonstage Awards, 2015); The Full Monty, 2013, transf. Noël Coward Th., 2014; Anything Goes, 2014; The Effect, 2015; American Buffalo, Wyndham's Th., 2015; Show Boat, 2015, transf. New London Th., 2016; Flowers for Mrs Harris, 2016; The Light in the Piazza, RFH, 2019; Chichester Festival Theatre: 40 Years On, 2017; Fiddler on the Roof, 2017; Quiz, 2017, transf. Noël Coward Th., 2018; Me and My Girl, 2018; Flowers for Mrs Harris, 2018; This is My Family, 2019. Actor: *television* includes: Great Expectations, 1999; Love in a Cold Climate, 2001; The Vice, 2001; Daniel Deronda, 2002; To the Ends of the Earth, 2005; The Passion, 2008; *films* include: A Midsummer Night's Dream, 1996; Tomorrow La Scala!, 2002; Les

Misérables, 2012. Gov. GSMD, 2012–14. DUniv Sheffield Hallam, 2012. *Recreations:* marathon running, cinema. *Address:* Chichester Festival Theatre, Oaklands Park, Chichester, W Sussex PO19 6AP. *E:* daniel.evans@cft.org.uk.

**EVANS, Dr David;** *see* Evans, Dr W. D.

**EVANS, David,** CBE 1992; Director-General, National Farmers' Union, 1985–96 (Deputy Director-General, 1984–85); Director, Federation of Agricultural Co-operatives UK, 1995–2001; *b* 7 Dec. 1935; *yr s* of late William Price Evans and Ella Mary Evans; *m* 1960, Susan Carter Connal, *yr d* of late Dr John Connal and Antoinette Connal; one *s* (one *d* decd). *Educ:* Welwyn Garden City Grammar Sch.; University Coll. London (BScEcon). Joined Min. of Agriculture, Fisheries and Food, 1959; Private Sec. to Parliamentary Sec. (Lords), 1962–64; Principal, 1964; Principal Private Sec. to Ministers, 1970–71; Asst Sec., 1971; seconded to Cabinet Office, 1972–74; Under-Sec., MAFF, 1976–80; joined NFU as Chief Economic and Policy Adviser, 1981. Mem., EU Econ. and Social Cttee, 1998–2002. Director: ACT Ltd, 1996–2004; Drew Associates Ltd, 1997–2003. *Address:* 6 Orchard Rise, Kingston upon Thames, Surrey KT2 7EY. *T:* (020) 8336 5868.

**EVANS, Rev. Canon David;** Rector of Heyford with Stowe-Nine-Churches, 1989–2001, of Flore, 1996–2001, and Brockhall, 1997–2001; *b* Llanglydwen, Carmarthenshire, 15 Feb. 1937; *o s* of late Rev. W. Noel Evans, JP, and Frances M. Evans; *m* 1962, Jenifer Margaret (*née* Cross); three *s*. *Educ:* Sherborne; Keble Coll., Oxford (MA); Wells Theological Coll. (BD London). 2nd Lieut, Royal Signals, 1956–57. Minor Canon, Brecon Cath., and Asst Curate, Brecon St Mary with Battle, 1964–68; Bishop's Chaplain to Students, UC, Swansea, and Asst Curate, Swansea St Mary with Holy Trinity, 1968–71; Bishop of Birmingham's Chaplain for Samaritan and Social Work, 1971–75; Dir, Samaritans of Swansea, 1969–71, of Birmingham, 1971–75; Jt Gen. Sec., 1975–84, Gen. Sec., 1984–89, The Samaritans; Licensed Priest, Dio. of Oxford, 1975–89; RD of Daventry, 1995–2000. Chaplain, Northamptonshire Police, 1990–2001. Non-Residentiary Canon, Peterborough Cath., 1997–2001. Mem., Church in Wales Liturgical Commn, 1969–75. *Recreations:* music, railways, bird-watching. *Address:* 3 Elm Close, Tutshill, Chepstow NP16 7DA. *T:* (01291) 630398. *E:* blind_puw@yahoo.co.uk.

**EVANS, (David) Alan;** General Counsel and Solicitor, HM Revenue and Customs, since 2019; *b* 21 Oct. 1965; *s* of David Lynn Evans and Sarah Eleanor Elvira Evans (*née* Rees). *Educ:* Olchfa, Swansea; London Sch. of Econs and Pol Sci. (BSc (Econ) Govt 1987). Macfarlanes, 1990–92; admitted as solicitor, 1992; Wilde Sapte, 1992–95; Taylor Joynson-Garrett, 1995–97; DWP, 1997–2000; Eur. Commn, 2000–02; Cabinet Office Legal Advrs, 2002–05; Director: DTI, 2005–09; HMRC, 2009–12; Dir, Legal Services, BIS, 2012–14; Legal Dir, Govt Legal Dept, 2014–18. *Address:* HM Revenue and Customs, 100 Parliament Street, SW1A 2BQ.

**EVANS, Prof. David Alan Price,** FRCP; Senior Consultant Physician (formerly Director of Medicine), Department of Medicine, Riyadh Armed Forces Hospital, Saudi Arabia, 1983–2007; Emeritus Professor of Medicine, Liverpool University, since 1994; *b* 6 March 1927; *s* of Owen Evans and Ellen (*née* Jones). *Educ:* Univ. of Liverpool (MD, PhD, DSc); Johns Hopkins Univ. RAMC, Jun. Med. Specialist, BMH Kure, Field Hosp. Korea, BMH Singapore and BMH Kinrara, Malaysia, 1953–55; Capt. RAMC, 1954–55. House Physician and House Surg. 1951–52, and Med. Registrar, 1956–58 and 1959–60, United Liverpool Hosps; Res. Fellow, Div. of Med. Genetics, Dept of Medicine, Johns Hopkins Hosp., 1958–59; Lectr 1960–62, Sen. Lectr 1962–68, Personal Chair, 1968–72, Dept of Medicine, Univ. of Liverpool; Prof. and Chm., Dept of Medicine and Dir, Nuffield Unit Medical Genetics, Univ. of Liverpool, 1972–83; Cons. Physician, Royal Liverpool Hosp. (formerly Royal Liverpool Infirmary) and Broadgreen Hosp., Liverpool, 1965–83. Visiting Professor: Karolinska Univ., Stockholm, 1968; Johns Hopkins Univ., 1972; Univ. Michigan at Ann Arbor, 1981. Lectures: Poulson Meml, Oslo Univ., 1972; first Sir Henry Dale, and Medallist, Johns Hopkins Univ., 1972; first Walter Idris Jones, Univ. of Wales, 1974; Watson Smith, RCP, 1976. Member: BMA, 1951; Assoc. of Physicians of GB and Ireland, 1964. Hon. LLD Liverpool, 2008. University of Liverpool: Roberts Prize, 1959; Samuels Prize, 1965; Thornton Prize, Eastern Psychiatric Assoc., 1964. Life Mem., Johns Hopkins Soc. of Scholars, 1972. Scientific Ed., Saudi Med. Jl, 1983–93; Member, Editorial Board: Internat. Jl of Clinical Pharmacology Res., 1980–; Jl of Saudi Heart Assoc. 1988–2005; Pharmacogenetics, 1995–2001. *Publications:* Genetic Factors in Drug Therapy, 1993; medical and scientific, principally concerned with genetic factors determining responses to drugs. *Address:* c/o 160 Rudston Road, Liverpool L16 4PJ.

**EVANS, (David) Anthony;** QC 1983; a Recorder of the Crown Court, 1980–2003; *b* 15 March 1939; *s* of Thomas John Evans, MD and May Evans; *m* 1974, Angela Bewley, *d* of John Clive Bewley, JP and Cynthia Bewley; two *d*. *Educ:* Clifton Coll., Bristol; Corpus Christi Coll., Cambridge (BA). Called to the Bar, Gray's Inn, 1965, Bencher, 2004; in practice at the Bar, Swansea, 1965–84, London, 1984–2013; Hd of Chambers, 9–12 Bell Yard, 1996–2003. DTI Inspector, 1988–92. Chm., Jt Disciplinary Scheme Tribunals, 2000–05; Mem., Accountancy Investigation and Disciplinary Bd Tribunal, 2005–13. *Recreation:* sport of all kinds. *Address:* Carey Hall, Neath, W Glamorgan SA10 7AU. *T:* (01639) 643859; Flat 3, 115 Ifield Road, SW10 9AS. *T:* (020) 7370 1025. *Clubs:* Turf, MCC; Cardiff and County (Cardiff).

**EVANS, David Christopher, (Christopher Dee);** tenor; Founder, Director and Chorus Master, Maida Vale Singers, since 1999; *b* Morriston, Wales, 13 Dec. 1960; *s* of John Leslie Evans and Avis Evans (*née* Jones). *Educ:* Royal Welsh Coll. of Music and Drama (LWCMD); Guildhall Sch. of Music and Drama. Vocal contractor: Peacock Theatre: Side by Side by Jerome Kern, 1999; Man of La Mancha, 2000; A Funny Thing Happened…, 2001; Royal Albert Hall: Spirit of Fire, 2003; Strictly Gershwin, 2008, 2011; Danny Elfman's Music from the Films of Tim Burton, 2013, 2014; Alice in Wonderland, 2015; Independence Day, 2016; Festival Hall: A Salute to New York, 2003; Candide, 2005; Sweeney Todd, 2007; BBC Proms: Oklahoma!, 2002; HMS Pinafore, 2005; 60 Years of British Film Music, 2007; 75 Years of MGM Film Musicals, 2009; A Celebration of Rodgers and Hammerstein, 2010; Hooray for Hollywood, 2011; The Broadway Sound, 2012; Bernstein Stage & Screen, 2015; The Gershwin Brothers, 2016; Sondheim Inside Out, Queen Elizabeth Hall, 2013; John Wilson Orchestra Tour, 2017; *television:* Victoria Wood Christmas Show, 2001; Never Mind the Buzzcocks, 2003; Grand Designs, 2016; *radio:* Der Kuhhandel, 2000; On Your Toes, 2002; Pal Joey, 2002; A Bernstein Celebration, 2004; Sondheim at 75, 2005; Friday Night is Music Night, 2005, 2010; Menna, 2008; A Tribute to Charles Strauss, 2008; Good Companions, 2009; Chef de choeur de Radio France, Broadway concerts, 2017. Several recordings. *Recreations:* musical theatre, opera, theatre, bridge, fine wines, fine dining, board and card games. *Address:* 7b Lanhill Road, Maida Vale, W9 2BP. *T:* (020) 7266 1358. *E:* maidavalesingers@gmail.com.

**EVANS, Air Chief Marshal Sir David (George),** GCB 1979 (KCB 1977); CBE 1967 (OBE 1962); Bath King of Arms, 1985–99; Deputy Chairman, NAAFI, 1991–2001 (Director, 1984–2001; President of Council, 1981–83); *b* Windsor, Ont, Canada, 14 July 1924; *s* of William Stanley Evans, Clive Vale, Hastings, Sussex; *m* 1949, Denise Marson Williamson-Noble (*d* 2009), *d* of late Gordon Till, Hampstead, London; two *d*, and two step *s*. *Educ:* Hodgson Sch., Toronto, Canada; North Toronto Collegiate. Served War, as Pilot, in Italy and NW Europe, 1944–45. Sqdn Pilot, Tactics Officer, Instructor, 1946–52; Sqdn Comdr, Central Flying Sch., 1953–55; RAF Staff Coll. course, 1955; OC No 11 (F) Sqdn, in Germany, 1956–57; Personal Staff Officer to C-in-C, 2nd Allied TAF, 1958–59; OC Flying, RAF, Coltishall, 1959–61; Coll. of Air Warfare course, 1961; Air Plans Staff Officer, Min. of Defence (Air), 1962–63; OC, RAF Station, Gutersloh, Germany, 1964–66; IDC, 1967; AOC, RAF Central Tactics and Trials Organisation, 1968–70; ACAS (Ops), 1970–73; AOC No 1 (Bomber) Group, RAF, 1973–76; Vice-Chief of Air Staff, 1976–77; C-in-C, RAF Strike Command, and UK NATO Air Forces, 1977–80; VCDS (Personnel and Logistics), 1981–83. Mil. Advr and Dir, BAe, 1983–92, and dir several BAe subsids; Chairman: BAe Canada Ltd, 1987–92; Arabian Gold, later Finngold Resources, plc, 1989–99; Dir, Intermin Resource Corp. Ltd, 1986 (Chm., 1989–93); Chairman: Officers Pensions Soc. Ltd; OPS Investment Co. Ltd; Trustees, OPS Widows' Fund; Dir, Airshow Canada. Queen's Commendation for Valuable Service in the Air (QCVSA), 1955. CCMI (CBIM 1978; Mem. Bd of Companions, 1983–; Dep. Chm., 1989–). *Recreations:* rep. RAF at Rugby football and winter sports (President: RAF Winter Sports Assoc.; Combined Services Winter Sports Assoc.); has rep. Gt Brit. at Bobsleigh in World Championships, Commonwealth Games and, in 1964, Olympic Games. *Address:* Royal Bank of Canada Europe Ltd, 71A Queen Victoria Street, EC4V 4DE. *Clubs:* Royal Air Force; Phyllis Court (Henley-on-Thames).

**EVANS, David Howard;** QC 1991; a Recorder of the Crown Court, 1992–2010; *b* 27 July 1944; *s* of David Hopkin Evans and Phoebe Dora Evans (*née* Reading); *m* 1973, Anne Celia Segall, *qv*; two *s*. *Educ:* London Sch. of Economics (BSc Econ 1965; MSc 1967); Wadham Coll., Oxford (BA 1970; MA 2002). Asst Economic Adviser, HM Treasury, 1967–68; called to the Bar, Middle Temple, 1972, Bencher, 2004; Asst Recorder of the Crown Court, 1987. *Recreations:* tennis, swimming, listening to music.

**EVANS, (David) Hugh;** HM Diplomatic Service; Ambassador to Lao People's Democratic Republic, 2015–19; *b* Santa Elena, Ecuador; *s* of David Evans and Mary Evans; *m* 1988, Nirmala Vinodhini; two *d*. *Educ:* St Joseph's Coll., Dumfries; Univ. of London (BA Hons 1st Mod. Hist., Econ. Hist. and Politics 1980); Univ. of Chicago (MA Pol Sci. 1982). Joined FCO, 1985; Res. Analyst, FCO, 1985–94; officer on loan to US State Dept, 1995–99; First Sec. (Pol), Nairobi, 2001–05; Dep. Hd of Mission, Khartoum, 2006–08; Mgt Counsellor, Moscow, 2008–12; Consul Gen., Erbil, 2012–14. Chm., Bd of Govs, Anglo-American Sch., Moscow, 2010–11. *Recreations:* travel, reading, theatre. *Address:* c/o Foreign and Commonwealth Office, King Charles Street, SW1A 2AH.

**EVANS, David Julian;** Director, Eastern India, British Council, 1999–2002; *b* 12 May 1942; *s* of David Thomas Evans and Brenda Muriel Evans (*née* Bennett); *m* 1967, Lorna Madeleine Jacques; three *s*. *Educ:* Fosters Sch., Sherborne; Queen Mary Coll., London Univ. (BA Hist. 1963). Teacher, Rajasthan, VSO, 1963–64; Mgt Trainee, J. Sainsbury Ltd, 1964–65; British Council: seconded to VSO, 1965–67; Sierra Leone, 1967–70; Dep. Rep., Wales, 1970–72; educn trng course, UC, Cardiff, 1972–73; Enugu, Nigeria, 1973–76; Dir, Istanbul, 1976–80; Dir Gen's Dept, 1980–81; Dep. Dir, Germany, 1981–85; Dir, Youth Exchange Centre, 1985–88; Dir, Drama and Dance, 1988–89; Dep. Dir, Arts Div., and Head, Arts Projects, 1989–94; Dir, USA, and Cultural Counsellor, British Embassy, Washington, 1994–98; Hd of Global Advice, Facilities Gp, 1999. Ind. Mem., Gen. Council, BUNAC, 2006–12. *Recreations:* the arts, history, travel, walking. *Address:* The Garret, Old Probate House, 5 Duncombe Place, York YO1 7ED.

**EVANS, David Lewis;** QC 2012; *b* Wegberg BMH, 4 Sept. 1963; *s* of Alan Evans and Janet Evans; *m* 1993, Caroline Lewis; one *s* one *d*. *Educ:* Monmouth Sch.; Christ's Coll., Cambridge (BA 1987). Called to the Bar, Middle Temple, 1988; in practice as a barrister, specialising in clinical negligence and regulatory, govt work, gp actions, public inquiries, inquests, 1988–; Mem., Attorney Gen.'s Panel of Counsel to the Crown (Common Law), 2004–12. *Recreations:* history, hill-walking, gardening, lobster-potting. *Address:* 1 Crown Office Row, Temple, EC4Y 7HH. *T:* (020) 7797 7500. *E:* david.evans@1cor.com.

**EVANS, David Lloyd C.;** *see* Carey Evans.

**EVANS, Rt Rev. David Richard John;** an Assistant Bishop, Diocese of Coventry, since 2003; *b* 5 June 1938; *s* of William Henry Reginald Evans and Beatrix Catherine Mottram; *m* 1964, Dorothy Evelyn Parsons; one *s* two *d*. *Educ:* Caius College, Cambridge (Hons degree in Mod. Langs and Theology, 1963; MA 1966). Curate, Christ Church, Cockfosters, 1965–68; Missionary Pastor and Gen. Sec., Argentine Inter-Varsity Christian Fellowship, in Buenos Aires, Argentina, 1969–77; Chaplain, Good Shepherd Church, Lima, Peru, 1977–82; Bishop of Peru, 1978–88 (with delegated jurisdiction of Bolivia from 1980); Assistant Bishop: dio. of Bradford, 1988–93; dios of Chichester, Canterbury and Rochester, 1994–97; dio. of Birmingham, 1997–2003; Associate Priest, Stourdene Gp of Parishes, 2003–10. Gen. Sec., S Amer. Mission Soc., 1993–2003. Internat. Co-ordinator, Evangelical Fellowship of the Anglican Communion, 1989–2003. Patron, Church's Ministry among Jewish People, 2018– (Vice-Pres., 2009–10; Pres., 2010–18). *Publications:* En Diálogo con Dios, 1976; Have Stick: Will Travel… Mainly South American Journeys, 2012. *Recreations:* golf, philately. *Address:* 30 Charles Street, Warwick CV34 5LQ. *T:* (01926) 258791. *E:* bishopdrjevans@talktalk.net.

**EVANS, Hon. Sir (David) Roderick,** Kt 2001; a Judge of the High Court, Queen's Bench Division, 2001–13; Pro-Chancellor, Swansea University, since 2013; *b* 22 Oct. 1946; *s* of Thomas James and Dorothy Evans; *m* 1971, Kathryn Rebecca Lewis; three *s* one *d*. *Educ:* Bishop Gore Grammar School, Swansea; University College London (LLB 1967; LLM 1968). Called to the Bar, Gray's Inn, 1970 (Bencher, 2001), Lincoln's Inn *ad eund*, 2001; a Recorder, 1987–92; QC 1989; a Circuit Judge, 1992–2001; Resident Judge: Merthyr Tydfil Crown Ct, 1994–98; Swansea Crown Ct, 1998–99; Cardiff Crown Court, 1999–2001; Recorder of Cardiff, 1999–2001; Presiding Judge: Wales and Chester Circuit, 2004–07; Wales, 2007. Comr for Standards, Nat. Assembly for Wales, 2016–. Member: Criminal Cttee, Judicial Studies Bd, 1998–2001; Parole Bd, 2011–. Sec., Assoc. of Judges of Wales, 2008–12. Trustee, Aberglasney Restoration Trust, 2013–. Hon. Mem., Gorsedd of Bards, 2002. Visitor, Aberystwyth Univ., 2014–. FLSW 2015. Fellow: Univ. of Wales, Aberystwyth, 2003; Swansea Univ., 2007; Bangor Univ., 2010. *Recreations:* Welsh ceramics, local history, walking.

**EVANS, Delyth;** Chair, Volunteer Space Ltd, since 2018; *b* 17 March 1958; *d* of David Gwynne Evans and Jean Margaret Evans; partner, Edward Charles Richards, *qv*; one *s* one *d*. *Educ:* Ysgol Gyfun Rhydfelen, Pontypridd; University Coll. of Wales, Aberystwyth (BA Hons French); Centre for Journalism Studies, Cardiff. Journalist, HTV Wales and BBC Radio 4, 1985–91; policy advr and speechwriter to John Smith, MP, Leader of Labour Party, 1992–94; Mgt Consultant, Adrian Ellis Associates, 1995–98; Special Advr to First Sec., Nat. Assembly for Wales, 1999–2000. Mem. (Lab) Mid and W Wales, Nat. Assembly for Wales, 2000–03. Contested (Lab) Carmarthen W and Pembrokeshire S, 2015. Policy and communications consultant, 2005–09; Chief Exec., Dress for Success London, subseq. Smart Works Charity, 2010–14; Interim Chief Exec., Action for Stammering Children, 2016; Chair, Welsh Govt Policy Rev. of Coleg Cymraeg Cenedlaethol, 2016–17. Mem. Bd, Film Agency for Wales, 2009–13. *Recreations:* keeping fit, reading, the arts, family activities.

**EVANS, Denise**; see Mina, D.

**EVANS, Derek**; see Evans, J. D.

**EVANS, Dylan J.**; see Jones-Evans, D.

**EVANS, (Elizabeth Gwendoline) Nerys**; Director, Deryn Consulting, since 2012; *b* 22 March 1980; *d* of Glanmor and Wendy Evans. *Educ:* Univ. of Manchester (BA Hons Govt and Pol Theory 2001); Cardiff Univ. (MSc Hons Welsh Politics 2004). Plaid Cymru: Organiser and Press Officer, Carmarthenshire CC, 2002–03; Pol Officer, Nat. Assembly for Wales, 2003–07; Dir of Policy, 2008–12; Educn Comr for Welsh Govt, 2011–12. Mem. (Plaid Cymru) Wales Mid and West, Nat. Assembly for Wales, 2007–11. Contested (Plaid Cymru) Carmarthen W and Pembrokeshire S, Nat. Assembly for Wales, 2011. Mem., Williams Commn, 2012.

**EVANS, Ena Winifred**; Headmistress, King Edward VI High School for Girls, Birmingham, 1977–96; *b* 19 June 1938; *d* of Frank and Leonora Evans. *Educ:* The Queen's Sch., Chester; Royal Holloway Coll., Univ. of London (BSc); Hughes Hall, Cambridge (CertEd). Asst Mistress, Bolton Sch. (Girls' Div.), 1961–65; Bath High School (GPDST): Head of Mathematics Dept, 1965–72; Second Mistress, 1970–72; Dep. Head, Friends' Sch., Saffron Walden, 1972–77. Pres., GSA, 1987–88. Mem., Central Birmingham DHA, 1988–90. Mem. Council: Aston Univ., 1989–98; Queen's Coll., Birmingham, 1996–2010; Birmingham Univ., 2000–05. FRSA 1986. Hon. DSc Aston, 1996. *Recreation:* music. *Address:* 26 Weoley Hill, Selly Oak, Birmingham B29 4AD.

**EVANS, His Honour Fabyan Peter Leaf**; a Circuit Judge, 1988–2005; *b* 10 May 1943; *s* of late Peter Fabyan Evans and Catherine Elise Evans; *m* 1967, Karen Myrtle (*née* Balfour), *gd* of 1st Earl Jellicoe; two *s* one *d*. *Educ:* Clifton College. Called to the Bar, Inner Temple, 1969. A Recorder, 1985–88. Resident Judge, Middx Guildhall Crown Court, 1995–2005. Chairman: Area Criminal Justice Liaison Cttee, London and Surrey, 1997–2000; London Area Criminal Justice Strategy Cttee, 2000–03. Mem., Parole Bd for England and Wales, 2005–15. *Recreations:* golf, sailing, singing (Chm., London Concert Choir, 2012–). *Clubs:* Brooks's; New Zealand Golf.

**EVANS, Hon. Gareth (John)**, AC 2012 (AO 2001); QC (Vic and ACT) 1983; Honorary Professorial Fellow, Australian National University, since 2012 (Chancellor, 2010–19); Professorial Fellow, University of Melbourne, 2011–12 (Hon. Professorial Fellow, 2009–10); *b* 5 Sept. 1944; *m* 1969, Merran Anderson; one *s* one *d*. *Educ:* Melbourne High Sch.; Melbourne Univ. (law and arts); Oxford Univ. (PPE). Lectr in Law, 1971–74, Sen. Lectr, 1974–76, Melbourne Univ.; practising Barrister, 1977–78. Senator (Lab) for Victoria, 1978–96; Shadow Attorney-General, 1980–83; Attorney-General, 1983–84; Minister for Resources and Energy, 1984–87, for Transport and Communications, 1987–88, for Foreign Affairs, 1988–96; Dep. Leader of Govt in Senate, 1987–93, Leader, 1993–96; MP (ALP) Holt, Vic, 1996–99; Dep. Leader of Opposition and Shadow Treasurer, Australia, 1996–98. Co-Chm., Internat. Commn on Intervention and State Sovereignty, 1999–2001; Pres. and Chief Exec., Internat. Crisis Gp, 2000–09, now Pres. Emeritus; Chm., World Economic Forum Peace and Security Expert Gp, 2003–06; Co-Chair, Internat. Adv. Bd, Global Centre for Responsibility to Protect, 2008–; Co-Chm., Internat. Commn on Nuclear Non-Proliferation and Disarmament, 2008–10; Convenor, Asia Pacific Leadership Network for Nuclear Non-Proliferation and Disarmament, 2011–15, now Emeritus Convenor and Patron; Member: Internat. Task Force on Global Public Goods, 2003–06; UN Sec.-Gen.'s High Level Panel on Threats, Challenges and Change, 2003–04; Commn on Weapons of Mass Destruction, 2004–06; Bd of Sponsors, Bulletin of Atomic Scientists, 2015–. Humanitas Vis. Prof. of Statecraft and Diplomacy, Univ. of Cambridge, 2013; Vis. Prof., Central European Univ., Budapest, 2014–16; Vis. Distinguished Diplomat in Residence, Indiana Univ., 2015; Simons Vis. Chair in Internat. Law and Human Security, Simon Fraser Univ., 2016–17. Hon. Fellow: Magdalen Coll., Oxford, 2004; Acad. of Social Scis in Australia, 2012; Australian Inst. of Internat. Affairs, 2012. Hon. LLD: Melbourne, 2002; Carleton, Canada, 2005; Sydney, 2008; Queen's, Canada, 2010. Franklin D. Roosevelt Four Freedoms Award for Freedom from Fear, 2010; Sir Edward 'Weary' Dunlop Asialink Medal, Univ. of Melbourne, 2016. Grand Cross, Order of Merit (Chile), 1999; Companion, Order of O. R. Tambo (Silver) (South Africa), 2015. *Publications:* (ed) Labor and the Constitution, 1972; (ed) Law, Politics and the Labor Movement, 1980; (ed) Labor Essays, 1980, 1981, 1982; (jtly) Australia's Constitution, 1983; (jtly) Australia's Foreign Relations, 1991, 2nd edn 1995; Co-operating for Peace, 1993; The Responsibility to Protect: ending mass atrocity crimes once and for all, 2008; (ed jtly) Nuclear Weapons: the state of play, 2013, 2nd edn 2015; Inside the Hawke-Keating Government: a cabinet diary, 2014; Incorrigible Optimist: a political memoir, 2017. *Recreations:* reading, writing, travel. *Address:* Melbourne, Australia. *E:* ge@gevans.org.

**EVANS, Gareth Robert William**; QC 1994; a Recorder, 1993–2019; *b* 19 Jan. 1947; *s* of late David M. J. Evans and Megan Evans; *m* 1971, Marion Green; one *s* one *d*. *Educ:* Caerphilly Grammar Tech. Sch.; Birmingham Poly.; LLB Hons London. Called to the Bar, Gray's Inn, 1973, Bencher, 2007; in practice as barrister, 1973–2018. Head of No 5 Chambers (Birmingham, London, Bristol), 2002–07; Leader, Midland Circuit, 2008–11. Acting High Ct Judge, Eastern Caribbean Supreme Court. *Recreations:* watching Rugby, reading poetry, cooking, attempting to play golf at Sapey Golf and Country Club. *Address:* The Old Rectory, Abberley, Worcs WR6 6BN. *T:* (01299) 896029. *E:* ge@no5.com.

**EVANS, Gay Jeanette H.**; see Huey Evans, G. J.

**EVANS, George James**; Sheriff of Tayside, Central and Fife at Cupar, 1997–2009; *b* 16 July 1944; *s* of Colin Evans and Caroline Catherine Kennedy MacPherson Harris; *m* 1973, Lesley Jean Keir Cowie; two *d*. *Educ:* Ardrossan Acad.; Glasgow Univ. (MA Hons); Edinburgh Univ. (LLB). Advocate, 1973; Standing Jun. Counsel, Dept of Energy, Scotland, 1982; Sheriff of Glasgow and Strathkelvin at Glasgow, 1983–97. *Publications:* contribs to legal periodicals. *Recreations:* art, literature, history, choral and individual singing, visiting English cathedrals. *Address:* Catherine Bank, Bridgend, Ceres KY15 5LS. *T:* (01334) 652121.

**EVANS, Dame Georgina (Mary)**; see Mace, Dame G. M.

**EVANS, Prof. Gillian Rosemary**, FRHistS; Professor of Medieval Theology and Intellectual History, University of Cambridge, 2002–05, now Emeritus; *b* Birmingham, 26 Oct. 1944; *d* of late Arthur Raymond Evans and Gertrude Elizabeth (*née* Goodfellow). *Educ:* King Edward VI High Sch. for Girls, Birmingham; St Anne's Coll., Oxford (BA 1966; DipEd 1967; MA 1970); Grad. Centre for Medieval Studies, Univ. of Reading (PhD 1974); DLitt Oxon 1983; LittD Cantab 1983. FRHistS 1978. Asst Mistress, Queen Anne's Sch., Caversham, 1967–72; Res. Asst, Univ. of Reading, 1974–78; Lectr in Theol., Univ. of Bristol, 1978–80; Lectr in Hist., Univ. of Cambridge, 1980–2002; British Acad. Res. Reader, 1986–88. Mem. Council, Univ. of Cambridge, 1997–2001. Called to the Bar, Gray's Inn, 2002. Vis. lectureships in USA and Canada and various European countries. Consulting Editor: Dictionary of Biblical Interpretation in English; Encyclopaedia of Medieval, Renaissance and Reformation Christian Thought; Jl Hist. of Biblical Interpretation; Jl of ADR, Mediation and Negotiation; Series Ed., I. B. Taurus History of the Christian Church, 2005–. Mem., Civil Mediation Council, 2005–. Member: Faith and Order Adv. Gp, Gen. Synod of C of E, 1986–96; Archbp's Gp on Episcopate, 1987–90; English Anglican-Roman Catholic Cttee, 1997–2002. Officer, Council for Acad. Freedom and Acad. Standards, 1994–2003; Mem., Cttee for Auctores Britannici Medii Aevi, Brit. Acad., 1980–2001. Co-Founder, Oxcheps Higher Educn Mediation Service, 2004; Project Leader, HEFCE-funded project on dispute resolution in higher educn, 2007–10; Founder Mem. and Chief Exec., Improving Dispute Resolution Adv. Service, 2010–. Freeman, Co. of Educators (formerly Guild of Educators), 2004 (Liveryman, 2014–). Hon. DLitt: Nottingham Trent, Southampton Inst. of Higher Educn, 2001. FCCT; FRSA 1996. *Publications:* include: Anselm and Talking About God, 1978; Anselm and a New Generation, 1980; Old Arts and New Theology, 1980; The Mind of St Bernard of Clairvaux, 1983; Alan of Lille, 1983; Augustine on Evil, 1983; The Anselm Concordance, 1984; The Logic and Language of the Bible, 2 vols, 1984–85; The Thought of Gregory the Great, 1986; (ed) Christian Authority, 1988; Problems of Authority in the Reformation Debates, 1992; Philosophy and Theology in the Middle Ages, 1994; The Church and the Churches, 1994; Method in Ecumenical Theology, 1996; The Reception of the Faith, 1997; Calling Academia to Account, 1998; The Medieval Epistemology of Error, 1998; Discipline and Justice in the Church of England, 1999; Bernard of Clairvaux, 2000; (ed) Managing the Church, 2000; (ed) A History of Pastoral Care, 2000; (ed) The Medieval Theologians, 2001; (jtly) Universities and Students, 2001; Law and Theology in the Middle Ages, 2002; Academics and the Real World, 2002; Faith in the Medieval World, 2002; A Brief History of Heresy, 2002; (ed) The First Christian Theologians, 2004; Inside the University of Cambridge in the Modern World, 2004; Wyclif, a Biography, 2005; Belief, 2006; The Church in the Early Middle Ages, 2007; The Good, the Bad and the Moral Dilemma, 2007; A History of Christian Europe, 2008; The Effort to Create a National System of Higher Education in Great Britain 1850–2010, 2009; The University of Cambridge: a new history, 2009; The University of Oxford: a new history, 2010; Roots of the Reformation: tradition, emergence and rupture, 2012; First Light: a history of Creation myths from Gilgamesh to the God-Particle, 2013; Edward Hicks: a pacifist bishop at war, 2014; A History of Western Monasticism, 2015; Medieval Christianity, 2017; contribs to jls, etc on medieval intellectual history, ecumenical theology, higher educn law and policy issues. *Recreation:* painting. *E:* gre1001@cam.ac.uk. *Clubs:* Nikaean, Royal Over-Seas League.

**EVANS, Dame Glynne**; see Evans, Dame M. G. D.

**EVANS, Graham**; *b* Poynton, Cheshire, 10 Nov. 1963; *s* of Gordon Evans and Violet Evans; *m* 1995, Cheryl Browne; two *s* one *d*. *Educ:* Poynton High Sch.; Manchester Metropolitan Univ. (BA Hons Business Studies 2000); Postgrad. Dip. Mktg Mgt 2001; King's Coll. London (MA Internat. Security and Strategy 2016). BAE Systems, 1982; sales mgt, Sun Chemical, 1988–99; sales mgt, Hewlett Packard, 1999–2004. Mem., Macclesfield BC, 2000–09. Contested (C) Worsley, 2005. MP (C) Weaver Vale, 2010–17; contested (C) same seat, 2017. Mem., British Transport Police Authy, 2019–. MInstD. *Recreations:* cricket, football, Rugby, running, 5-a-side, British history (military, social and economic; specialist First World War historian).

**EVANS, Sir Harold (Matthew)**, Kt 2004; author and editor; Editor at Large: The Week, 2001–12; Thomson Reuters, since 2011; *b* 28 June 1928; *s* of late Frederick and late Mary Evans; *m* 1st, 1953, Enid (marr. diss. 1978), *d* of late John Parker and of Susan Parker; one *s* two *d*; 2nd, 1981, Christina Hambley Brown (see Tina Brown); one *s* one *d*. *Educ:* St Mary's Road Central Sch., Manchester; Durham Univ. BA 1952, MA Dunelm 1966. Ashton-under-Lyne, Lancs, Reporter Newspapers, 1944–46 and 1949; RAF, 1946–49; Durham Univ., 1949–52; Manchester Evening News, 1952; Commonwealth Fund Fellow in Journalism, Chicago and Stanford Univs, USA, 1956–57; Asst Ed., Manchester Evening News, 1958–61; Ed., Northern Echo, 1961–66; Editor-in-Chief, North of England Newspaper Co., 1963–66; Sunday Times: Chief Asst to Editor, 1966; Managing Editor, 1966; Editor, 1967–81; Editor, The Times, 1981–82; Editor-in-Chief, Atlantic Monthly Press, NY, 1984–86; Founding Editor, Condé-Nast Traveler Magazine, 1986–90; Editl Dir, 1984–86, Contributing Editor, 1986–, US News and World Report, Washington; Vice-Pres. and Sen. Editor, Weidenfeld & Nicolson, NY, 1986–87; Pres. and Publisher, Random House Trade Gp, 1990–97; Editl Dir and Vice-Chm., NY Daily News Inc., US News & World Report, Atlantic Monthly, and Fast Company, 1998–99. Member, Executive Board: Times Newspapers Ltd, 1968–82 (Mem. Main Bd, 1978); International Press Inst., 1974–80; Director: The Sunday Times Ltd, 1968–82; Times Newspapers Ltd, 1978–82. Writer and presenter: Evans on Newspapers, BBC TV, 1981; A Point of View, BBC Radio 4, 2005. Hon. Vis. Prof. of Journalism, City Univ., 1978; Vis. Prof., Inst. of Public Affairs, Duke Univ., N Carolina, 1984. Fellow, Freedom Forum. Hon. FSIAD. Internat. Editor of the Year, 1975; Gold Medal Award, Inst. of Journalists, 1979; Hood Medal, RPS, 1981; Editor of the Year, 1982; President Award, D&AD, 1983; Lotos Club Medal, NY, 1993; Ortega y Gasset Prize, 2012. DUniv Stirling, 1982; Hon. DCL Durham, 1998. *Publications:* The Active Newsroom, 1961; Editing and Design (five volumes): vol. 1, Newsman's English, 1972; vol. 5, Newspaper Design, 1973; vol. 2, Newspaper Text, 1974; vol. 3, Newspaper Headlines, 1974; vol. 4, Pictures on a Page, 1977; Good Times, Bad Times, 1983, 4th edn 2011; (jointly): We Learned To Ski, 1974; The Story of Thalidomide, 1978; (ed) Eye Witness, 1981; How We Learned to Ski, 1983; Front Page History, 1984; The American Century, 1998; They Made America, 2004; My Paper Chase: true stories of vanished times (autobiog.), 2009; Do I Make Myself Clear?: why writing well matters, 2017. *Recreations:* swimming, music, chess, Sunday in the park with George and Isabel. *Clubs:* Garrick, Royal Automobile; Century, Yale (New York).

**EVANS, (Henry) Nicholas**; a District Judge (Magistrates' Courts) (formerly Metropolitan Stipendiary Magistrate), since 1995; *b* 7 Nov. 1945; 3rd *s* of Gilbert Arthur Evans and Muriel Elaine Evans (*née* Oxford); *m* 1980, Diana Claire Smith; one *s* one *d*. *Educ:* Highgate Sch. Called to the Bar, Middle Temple, 1971, Lincoln's Inn, ad eundem, 1975. *Clubs:* Garrick, Bar Yacht.

**EVANS, Prof. (Hubert) Roy**, CBE 2002; PhD; FREng; FICE, FIStructE; Vice-Chancellor, University of Wales, Bangor, 1995–2004; *b* 27 May 1942; *s* of David James Evans and Sarah Ann Evans; *m* 1966, Eira John; two *s* two *d*. *Educ:* Llandysul Grammar Sch.; University Coll. of Swansea (BSc, MSc; PhD 1967). Res. Fellow, University Coll. of Swansea, 1966–67; Asst Engr, Freeman Fox & Partners, 1967–69; University College, Cardiff, later University of Wales College of Cardiff: Lectr, 1969–75; Sen. Lectr, 1975–79; Reader, 1979–83; Prof. of Civil and Structural Engrg, 1983–95; Hd of Dept, 1984–95; Dean, 1987–88; Dep. Principal, 1990–93 and 1994–95. Vis. Prof., Univ. of W Virginia, 1983. FREng (FEng 1992); Founding FLSW 2010. Hon. Fellow: UC, Swansea, 1995; Univ. of Wales, Cardiff, 1998. Telford Premium, 1976, 1979 and 1987, George Stephenson Medal, 1980, ICE; Henry Adams Bronze Medal, IStructE, 1976; Medal, Acad. of Scis, Czech Republic, 1995. *Publications:* numerous contribs in field of structural engrg and plate structures. *Recreations:* hill-walking, gardening, cricket, soccer. *Address:* Pwllcorn, Moylegrove, Cardigan, Pembrokeshire SA43 3BS. *T:* (01239) 881274.

**EVANS, Hugh**; see Evans, D. H.

**EVANS, Huw David;** Director General, Association of British Insurers, since 2015 (Deputy Director General, and Director, Policy, 2013–15); *b* Banbury, 27 Aug. 1971; *s* of Anthony Evans and Geraldine Evans; *m* 2005, Katharine Mahoney; one *s* one *d*. *Educ:* Kingsfield Sch., Bristol; St Brendan's VIth Form Coll., Bristol; Lady Margaret Hall, Oxford (BA Hons 1993). Journalist, Newbury Weekly News, 1993–96; Press Officer, Labour Party, 1996–99; Dir, Communications, Welsh Labour Party, 1999–2001; Special Advisor: to Home Sec., 2001–04; to the Prime Minister, 2005–06; Sen. Manager, Gp Strategy, RBS, 2006–08; Dir, Ops, ABI, 2008–13. Non-executive Director: Flood Re Ltd, 2015–; TheCityUK, 2016–. *Recreations:* family, Welsh Rugby, history, reading. *Address:* Association of British Insurers, One America Square, 17 Crosswall, EC3N 2LB. *T:* (020) 7216 7401. *E:* huw.evans@abi.org.uk.

**EVANS, Iain Richard,** CBE 2013; FCA; independent strategy consultant, since 2015; Chairman, LEK Consulting (formerly L/E/K Partnership), 1991–2015, now Chairman Emeritus; *b* 17 May 1951; *s* of late Alan Caradog Crawshay Evans and Barr Hargreave Bell (*née* Dalglish); *m* 1st, 1973, Zoe Dorothy Valentine (*d* 2002); two *s*; 2nd, 1988, Jayne Doreen Almond; one *d*; 3rd, 2015, Gillian Kathryn Chruscikowska. *Educ:* John Lyon Sch.; Rotherham Sixth Form Coll.; Bristol Univ. (BSc Hons 1972); Harvard Univ. Grad. Sch. of Business Admin (MBA with High Distinction, Baker Scholar, Loeb Rhoades Fellow, 1978). ACA 1975, FCA 1977. Arthur Young McClelland Moores & Co., 1972–76; Bain & Co., 1978–83, Partner 1982; Founding Partner, L/E/K Partnership, subseq. LEK Consulting, 1983. Non-executive Director: Hyder (formerly Welsh Water Authy, then Welsh Water) plc, 1989–98 (Dep. Chm., 1992–93; Chm., 1993–98); Pennon Gp plc, 2018–. *Recreations:* gardening, travel, art. *Address:* c/o LEK Consulting, Nova South, 160 Victoria Street, SW1E 5LB.

**EVANS, Dr (Ian) Philip,** OBE 1999; FRSC; Head Master, Bedford School, 1990–2008; *b* 2 May 1948; *s* of late Joseph Emlyn Evans and Beryl Evans; *m* 1972, Sandra Veronica Waggett (*d* 2016); two *s*. *Educ:* Ruabon Boys' Grammar Sch.; Churchill College, Cambridge (BA 1970; MA 1973; 1st cl. hons Nat. Scis Tripos); Imperial College of Science and Technology (PhD, DIC). CChem, FRSC 1997. Post-Doctoral Fellow, Res. Sch. of Chemistry, ANU, 1973–75; Asst Master, St Paul's Sch., 1975–90 (Head of Chemistry Dept, 1984–90). Member: Schs Exams and Assessment Council, 1991–93; SCAA, 1993–97; Qualifications and Curriculum Authority, 1997–99. Chief Examr, A-level Chem., Univ. of London Schs Exam. Bd, 1987–90. Member Council: Nat. Trust, 1999–2001; RSC, 2007–11 (Trustee, 2007–11; Chm., Educn Policy Bd, 2007–10; Mem., Sci., Educn and Industry Bd, 2011–14). *Publications:* (with S. V. Evans) Anyone for Science?, 1994; contribs to books; papers in learned jls. *Recreations:* music, cricket, poetry, wine. *Address:* Rue du Chagnot, Monthélie, Côte d'Or, 21190, France. *Club:* East India.

**EVANS, James,** CBE 1995; Chairman, Bristol United Press, 1997–2000; *b* 27 Nov. 1932; *s* of late Rex Powis Evans and Louise Evans; *m* 1961, Jette Holmboe; two *d*. *Educ:* Aldenham School; St Catharine's College, Cambridge (MA). Called to the Bar, Gray's Inn, 1959; admitted Solicitor, 1972; recalled to the Bar, Gray's Inn, 1991, Bencher, 1993. Commissioned 26th Field Regt RA, 1951–53. Legal Dept, Kemsley Newspapers Ltd, 1956–59; practised at Bar, 1959–65; Legal Adviser: Thomson Newspapers Ltd, 1965–73; Times Newspapers Ltd, 1967–73; Sec. and Mem. Exec. Bd, 1973–78, Dir, 1978–86, Thomson Organisation Ltd; Dir, 1977–81, Chm., 1980–81, Times Newspapers Ltd; Chm., Thomson Withy Grove Ltd, 1979–84; International Thomson Organisation plc: Dir, 1978; Jt Dep. Man. Dir, 1982–84; Man. Dir and Chief Exec., 1985–86; Chm., 1986; Chm. and Chief Exec., 1982–84, Dir, 1982–96, Thomson Regional Newspapers Ltd; Dir, Liverpool Daily Post and Echo Ltd, 1996–97. Dir, 1983–90, Chm., 1987–89, Press Assoc.; Dir, Reuters Holdings, 1984–92. Mem., Monopolies and Mergers Commn, 1989–97. Dir, Press Standards Bd of Finance, 1990–2000. Trustee, Visnews, 1985–95. Member: Council, Newspaper Soc., 1984–2001 (Vice-Pres., 1998–99; Pres., 1999–2000); Press Council, 1987–90; Council of Legal Educn, 1992–94. Mem., Home Office Deptl Cttee on Official Secrets Act (Franks Cttee), 1971. *Recreations:* various. *Address:* 6 Fishpool Street, St Albans, Herts AL3 4RT. *T:* (01727) 853064. *Club:* Garrick.

**EVANS, James Humphrey R.;** *see* Roose-Evans.

**EVANS, Jane Elizabeth;** *see* Collins, Jane E.

**EVANS, Jeremy David Agard;** Director, Public Affairs, British Rail, 1990–97; *b* 20 June 1936; *s* of Arthur Burke Agard Evans and Dorothy (*née* Osborne); *m* 1964, Alison Mary (*née* White); one *s* two *d*. *Educ:* Whitgift Sch.; Christ's Coll., Cambridge (BA Hons). Ministry of Power, 1960–69; Sloan Fellow, London Business Sch., 1969–70; DTI, 1970–73; Asst Sec., DTI, 1973, Dept of Energy, 1974 (Offshore Supplies Office, 1973); seconded as Sec. to BNOC on its foundn, 1976–78; a Man. Dir, 1978; Man. Dir Corporate Develt, and Sec., 1980–82, Mem. Bd, 1981–82; Dir, Britoil plc, 1982–88. Mem., GDC, 1989–94. Gov., St Piers Sch., subseq. NCYPE, 1998–2001. *Recreations:* opera, ski-ing, walking. *Address:* Dormans House West, Dormans Park, East Grinstead, West Sussex RH19 2LY. *T:* (01342) 870518.

**EVANS, (Jeremy) Roger;** Member (C) Havering and Redbridge, 2000–16, and Deputy Mayor, 2015–16, London Assembly, Greater London Authority; *b* 23 June 1964; *s* of Ronald Evans and Doris Valentine Evans. *Educ:* Univ. of Sheffield (BSc Hons 1985); Westminster Univ. (CPE); Inns of Court School of Law. Various managerial rôles, Royal Mail, 1985–95; law student, 1995–98; called to Bar, Middle Temple, 1997; legal advr, Spring Gp, 1998–2000. Member (C): Waltham Forest LBC, 1990 (Leader, Cons. Gp, 1994–98); Havering LBC, 2006. *Recreations:* badminton, swimming, public speaking.

**EVANS, Jillian;** Member (Plaid Cymru) Wales, European Parliament, since 1999; President, Plaid Cymru, 2010–13; *b* 8 May 1959; *d* of Horace Burge and Valma Burge; *m* 1992, Syd Morgan. *Educ:* UCW, Aberystwyth (BA Hons Welsh); MPhil CNAA, 1986. Res. Asst, Poly. of Wales, Trefforest, 1980–85; self-employed administrator, 1986–89; Admin./Public Affairs Officer, 1989–93, Project Officer, 1994–97, NFWI Wales; Wales Regl Organiser, Child, Infertility Support Network, 1997–99. *Address:* 45 Gelligaled Road, Ystrad, Rhondda Cynon Taf, Wales CF41 7RQ.

**EVANS, Prof. John,** PhD; Professor of Chemistry, University of Southampton, 1990–2016, now Emeritus; *b* 2 June 1949; *s* of Leslie and Eleanor Evans; *m* 1972, Hilary Jane Fulcher; two *d*. *Educ:* Rutherford Grammar Sch., Newcastle upon Tyne; Imperial Coll. London (BSc 1970; ARCS); Sidney Sussex Coll., Cambridge (PhD 1973). Research Fellow, Princeton Univ., 1973–74; Cambridge University: ICI Res. Fellow, 1974–75; Royal Soc. Pickering Res. Fellow, 1975–76; Southampton University: Res. Fellow, 1976–78; Lectr, 1978–84; Sen. Lectr, 1984–87; Reader, 1987–90; Dean of Science, 1997–2000; Hd of School, 2007–10. Science and Engineering Research Council: Chm., Synchrotron Radiation Cttee, 1991–94; UK Deleg. to Council of European Synchrotron Radiation Facility, 1991–94 (Mem., Scientific Adv. Cttee, 1995–98); Mem., Facilities Commn, 1993–94. Sci. Prog. Advr, Diamond Light Source Ltd, 2002–07 (Vice-Chm., Diamond Scientific Adv. Cttee, 2000–02). Member: Photon Sci. Adv. Cttee, Paul Scherrer Inst., 2009–13; ALBA Panel for Sci. Review, Barcelona, 2012–14; Diamond Peer Rev. Panel, 2012–15. Royal Society of Chemistry: Sec. and Treas., Dalton Div., 1993–96; Council Mem., 1994–97. Tilden Lectr, RSC, 1994. Editor, Inorganic Chemistry Series, Oxford Chemistry Primers Text Book Series, 1991–2000. Meldola Medal, RSC, 1978. *Publications:* contrib. scientific jls, incl. Jl RSC. *Recreations:* garden work, travel. *Address:* School of Chemistry, University of Southampton, Southampton SO17 1BJ. *T:* (023) 8059 3307.

**EVANS, John;** *see* Evans, M. J.

**EVANS, John Alfred Eaton;** Headmaster, Brentwood School, 1981–93; *b* 30 July 1933; *s* of John Eaton Evans and Millicent Jane Evans (*née* Righton); *m* 1958, Vyvyan Margaret Mainstone; two *s* one *d*. *Educ:* Bristol Grammar Sch.; Worcester Coll., Oxford. MA (Lit. Hum.). Nat. Service, 1952–54, commnd RAOC. Assistant Master: Blundell's Sch., 1958–63; Rugby Sch., 1963–73; Housemaster: Phillips Acad., Andover, Mass, USA, 1968–69; Rugby Sch., 1973–81. Chm., London Div., HMC, 1993. Member selection panels: CMS, 1983–91; Admiralty, 1985–96; Army Scholarship Bd, 1990–2002; ABM, 1992–2002. Chm. Trustees, Crescent Sch., Rugby, 1968–78; Governor: Colfe's Sch., 1993–2002; Prior Park Coll., 1998–2004; Mem. Adv. Bd, St Christopher's Sch., Burnham-on-Sea, 1994–97. FRSA 1983. *Publications:* various articles on community service in education. *Recreations:* cricket, Rugby fives, piano, singing, drama, walking. *Clubs:* Vincent's (Oxford); Savage (Bristol); Jesters; Cryptics Cricket.

**EVANS, (John) Derek,** CBE 2001; Chief Conciliator, Advisory, Conciliation and Arbitration Service, 1992–2001; *b* 11 Sept. 1942; *s* of late Leslie and Mary Evans; *m* 1964, Betty Wiseman; two *d*. *Educ:* Roundhay Sch., Leeds. FCIPD. Dept of Employment, 1962–74; Advisory, Conciliation and Arbitration Service: Midlands, 1974–78; Head Office, 1978–82; Dir, Wales, 1982–88; Dir, Adv. Services, 1988–91; Dir, Conciliation and Arbitration, 1991–92. Mem., Employment Appeal Tribunal, 2003–12; Chm., Agricl Wages Bd, 2003–13. Chm., URC (Wales) Trust, 2009–12 (Dir, 2007–09). Industrial Fellow, Kingston Univ., 1994–2013. Ind. Chm., Standards Cttee, Wokingham DC, 2002–04. *Recreations:* golf, driving, music. *Address:* 23 Ty-Gwyn Road, Rhiwbina, Cardiff CF14 6NF. *T:* (029) 2115 2077. *Club:* Whitchurch Golf (Cardiff).

**EVANS, John Kerry Q.;** *see* Quarren Evans.

**EVANS, John Roger W.;** *see* Warren Evans.

**EVANS, Sir John (Stanley),** Kt 2000; QPM 1990; DL; consultant in security and counter terrorism; Special Security Advisor: to the Football Association, 2004–09; to the England and Wales Cricket Board, since 2008; *b* 6 Aug. 1943; *s* of late William Stanley and Doris Evans; *m* 1965, Beryl Smith; one *s* one *d*. *Educ:* Wade Deacon Grammar Sch., Widnes; Liverpool Univ. (LLB Hons 1972). Liverpool City, then Merseyside Police, 1960–80; Asst Chief Constable, Greater Manchester Police, 1980–84; Dep. Chief Constable, Surrey Constabulary, 1984–88; Chief Constable, Devon and Cornwall Constabulary, 1989–2002. Pres., ACPO, 1999–2000. Chm., Police Athletic Assoc., 1996–2002 (Life Vice Pres., 2002). Chm., Your Radio Ltd, 2003–06. Prince's Trust: Chm., SW England, 2001–08; Mem., Nat. Trustees Council, 2005–07; Vice Chm., English Regions Council, 2005–07. Member: Public Inquiry into alleged sectarian murder of Robert Hamill, NI; several Police Appeal Tribunals. President: Devon and Cornwall Victim Support Schemes, 2002–07; Combined Community Watch Assoc., 2002–; Life Educn Wessex, 2010–; Ind. Chm., Wakeley Stakeholders Reference Gp, NHS Northern, Eastern and Western Devon, 2015–. Patron: Dream Away, 1990–; Wooden Spoon (Devon Co.), 2002–; Ottery St Mary Help Scheme, 2019– Vice Patron, Exeter Leukaemia Fund, 2003–. Mem., Otter Valley Rotary Club, 2003– (Pres., 2012–13). DL Devon, 2000. *Recreations:* most sports (ran London Marathon, 1988, 1989), service and charitable activities. *Address:* c/o Woodbury Park Hotel, Golf & Country Club Ltd, Woodbury Castle, Woodbury, Exeter, Devon EX5 1JJ. *Club:* Woodbury Park Golf and Country (Pres., 2001–).

**EVANS, Rt Rev. (John) Wyn,** FSA, FRHistS; Bishop of St Davids, 2008–16; *b* 4 Oct. 1946; *o s* of late Ven. David Eifion Evans and Iris Elizabeth (*née* Gravelle); *m* 1997, Diane Katherine, *d* of George and Kathleen Baker. *Educ:* Ardwyn Grammar Sch., Aberystwyth; University Coll., Cardiff (BA); St Michael's Theol Coll., Llandaff (BD); Jesus Coll., Oxford. FSA 1989; FRHistS 1994. Deacon 1971, priest 1972; Curate, St Davids, 1971–75; Minor Canon, St Davids Cathedral, 1972–75; grad. student, Jesus Coll., Oxford, 1975–77, permission to officiate Oxford diocese, 1975–77; Diocesan Adviser on Archives, St Davids, 1976–83; Rector, Llanfallteg with Castell Dwyran and Clunderwen with Henllan Amgoed and Llangan, 1977–82; Exam. Chaplain to Bishop of St Davids, 1977; Diocesan Warden of Ordinands, 1978–83; Chaplain and Lectr, Trinity Coll., Carmarthen, 1982–90; Diocesan Dir of Educn, 1982–92; Hon. Canon, St Davids Cathedral, 1988–90, Canon (4th Cursal), 1990–94; Dean of Chapel, Trinity Coll., Carmarthen, 1990–94; Head, Dept of Theology and Religious Studies, 1991–94; Dean and Precentor, St Davids Cathedral, 1994–2008; Rector, Rectorial Benefice of Dewisland, 2001–08. Vis. Res. Fellow, Oxford Brookes Univ., 2016–. Visitor, Univ. of Wales Trinity St David, 2010–17. Chairman: Deans of the Church in Wales, 2001–08; Cathedral Libraries and Archives Assoc., 2001–07; Member: St Davids Diocesan Adv. Cttee, 1994–2008 (Chm., 2006–08); Cathedrals and Churches Commn, Church in Wales, 1995–; Exec., Friends of Friendless Churches, 1995–2006 (Episcopal Patron, 2009–); Rep. Body, Church in Wales, 1999–2004. Mem. Governing Body, Trinity Coll., Carmarthen, 1994–2006; Member Court: Nat. Liby of Wales, 1998–2006; Univ. of Wales Cardiff, 2002–09. Mem., Cambrian Archaeological Assoc., 1972– (Pres., 2010–11). Mem., Gorsedd of Bards (White Robe), 1997–. Hon. Fellow, Univ. of Wales, Lampeter, 2006. Hon. DD Wales, 2017. *Publications:* (with Roger Worsley) St Davids Cathedral 1181–1981, 1981; (ed jtly) St David of Wales, Cult, Church and Nation, 2007; contribs to jls, including Jl Welsh Ecclesiastical History, Carmarthen Antiquary, Diwinyddiaeth. *Recreations:* reading, music, antiquities. *Address:* 12 Ffordd Caerfai, St Davids, Haverfordwest, Carmarthen SA62 6QT. *T:* (01437) 729402. *Club:* Oxford and Cambridge.

**EVANS, Jonathan,** OBE 2005; Company Secretary of Royal Mail Group (formerly Secretary to the Post Office, then Consignia), 1999–2010; *b* 21 April 1952; *s* of Alec H. Evans and Beryl Evans; *m* 1978, Gillian Eileen Blundell; one *s* two *d*. *Educ:* King Edward VI Sch., Nuneaton; Durham Univ. (BSc Maths 1974). Joined Post Office, 1974; mgt trainee, 1974–76; Ops Exec., Midlands Postal Bd, 1976–82; Personal Asst to Chm., 1982–84; Asst Head Postmaster, Leicester, 1984–86; Asst Personnel Dir, PO Counters Ltd, 1986–92; Dir of Orgn, 1992–95; Gen. Manager, Midlands Region, 1993–95; Network Dir, 1995–99. Trustee Dir, Royal Mail Pension Plan, 2005–13; Chm., Royal Mail Sen. Exec. Pension Plan, 2007–13. Mem., Audit Cttee, Archbps' Council, 2011–17. Chm., Claverdon Community Shop Ltd, 2011–15. Trustee: Rowland Hill Fund, 2007–14 (Chm., 2010–14); Postal Heritage Trust, 2010–19 (Vice Chm., 2010–19); City of Birmingham Symphony Orch. Pension Scheme, 2016–; Gov., Foundn of Lady Katherine Leveson, 2008–. Mem. Chapter, 2013–18, Chair, Finance Cttee, 2014–18, Coventry Cathedral. *Recreations:* music, campanology, cricket. *E:* jonathan.evans3@btinternet.com.

**EVANS, Rev. Jonathan Edward;** QC 2014; Assistant Curate, Parish of the Holy Trinity, Christchurch, since 2018; *b* Maidstone, 9 Aug. 1969; *s* of late Clive Mortimer Evans and of Belinda Jane Evans; *m* 1996, Harriet Alice Tatton Brown; two *s* two *d*. *Educ:* Maidstone

Grammar Sch.; Oriel Coll., Oxford (MA); Ripon Coll., Cuddesdon. Called to the Bar, Middle Temple, 1994; barrister, Wilberforce Chambers, 1994–2016. Ordained deacon, 2018. *Recreation:* cycling the 'Cent Cols Challenge' courtesy of the incomparable P. Deeker, Esq.

**EVANS, Jonathan Peter;** solicitor; Chairman, British Insurance Brokers Association, from Jan. 2020 (non-executive Director, since 2018); *b* 2 June 1950; *s* of late David John Evans and Harriet Mary Drury; *m* 1975, Margaret Thomas; one *s* two *d*. *Educ:* Lewis Sch., Pengam; Howardian High Sch., Cardiff; Coll. of Law, Guildford and London. Admitted Solicitor of Supreme Court, 1974; Leo Abse & Cohen, Cardiff: Partner, 1974–92; Man. Partner, 1987–92; Dir of Insce, Eversheds, 1997–99, consultant, 1999–2009; Dir, NFU Mutual Insce Gp, 2000–10; Chairman: Pearl Gp Ltd, 2005–09; Phoenix Life Ltd, 2009–16; Allied World Managing Agency, 2015–. Dep. Chm., Tai Cymru (Welsh Housing Corp.), 1988–92. Contested (C): Ebbw Vale, Feb. and Oct., 1974; Wolverhampton NE, 1979; Brecon and Radnor, 1987. MP (C) Brecon and Radnor, 1992–97; contested (C) Brecon and Radnorshire, 1997; MP (C) Cardiff N, 2010–15. PPS to Minister of State, NI Office, 1992–94; Parly Under-Sec. of State, DTI, 1994–95 (Minister for Corporate Affairs, 1994–95, for Competition and Consumer Affairs, 1995); Parly Sec., Lord Chancellor's Dept, 1995–96; Parly Under-Sec. of State, Welsh Office, 1996–97; Chief Cons. Party Spokesman for Wales, 1997–98. MEP (C) Wales, 1999–2009; Leader, Conservatives, EP, 2001–05; Pres., EP Delegn for Relns with US Congress, 2004–09; Mem. Adv. Bd, Transatlantic Economic Council, 2007–09. Chm., All Party Parly Gp on Insurance and Financial Services, 2010–15; Co-Chm., All Party Parly Gp on Building Socs and Financial Mutuals, 2010–15; Chm., Associate Parly Gp on Wholesale Financial Mkts and Services, 2012–15. Mem. Bd, Cons. Party, 2002–05; Chairman: Assoc. of Cons. Clubs, 2007–15 (Pres., 2004–05); Welsh Cons. Party, 2014–17. Vice Pres., Catholic Union of GB, 2001–. Hon. Consultant on law and policy, NSPCC, 1991–94; Dep. Chm., Welsh NSPCC Council, 1991–94; Pres., Cardiff and Dist NSPCC, 1992–94. FRSA 1995. Freeman, City of London, 2015. *Recreations:* watching Rugby Union and cricket, reading. *Clubs:* Farmers, Carlton (Chm., Political Cttee, 2013–15); Cardiff and County (Cardiff).

**EVANS, Julian Ascott;** HM Diplomatic Service, retired; Director, International and Community Engagement, Commonwealth War Graves Commission, since 2018 (Director for Commonwealth Liaison, 2017–18); *b* 5 July 1957; *s* of late Frederick Evans and Glenys Evans (née Williams); *m* 1991, Gayle Evelyn Louise (née Sperring); two *d*. *Educ:* Llanelli Grammar Sch.; Price's Coll., Fareham; University Coll. London (BA Hons Geog.). Joined HM Diplomatic Service, 1978; Russian lang. trng, RAEC, Beaconsfield, 1981; Third Secretary: (Scientific), Moscow, 1982–84; (Commercial), Zurich, 1985–86; Asst Private Sec. to Minister of State, FCO, 1987–89; FCO, 1989–91; Second, later First, Sec., UKMIS to UN, NY, 1991–95; FCO, 1996–2002; Deputy High Commissioner: Islamabad, 2002–03; Ottawa, 2003–07; Consul Gen., San Francisco, 2007–11; Dep. High Comr to India, 2011–15; Dir of Protocol and Vice-Marshal of Diplomatic Corps, 2015–17. *Recreations:* travel, military history. *Address:* Commonwealth War Graves Commission, 2 Marlow Road, Maidenhead, Berks SL6 7DX.

**EVANS, Kim,** OBE 2007; arts consultant, since 2006; Chair, Clean Break Theatre Company, since 2012; *b* 3 Jan. 1951; *d* of Jon Evans and Gwendolen (née McLeod); *m* 2001, David Hucker. *Educ:* Putney High Sch.; Our Lady of Sion Convent; Warwick Univ. (BA Hons Eng. and Amer. Lit.); Leicester Univ. (MA Hons Victorian Lit. and Society). Press Asst, Design Council, 1973–74; Asst Editor, Crafts mag., 1974–76; Chief Sub-Editor, Harpers & Queen, 1976–78; South Bank Show, LWT: researcher, 1978–82; Producer/Dir, 1982–89; BBC Television: Producer, Omnibus, 1989–92; Asst Hd, Music and Arts, 1992–93; Head of Music and Arts, subseq. of Arts, BBC TV, then of BBC Arts and Classical Music, 1993–99; Exec. Dir, Arts, Arts Council of England, later Arts Council England, 1999–2006. Mem., Parole Bd, 2006–18. Trustee: Chelsea and Westminster Health Charity, 2008–12; Nat. Heritage Meml Fund, 2008–14; Nat. Portrait Gall., 2010–18 (Dep. Chair, 2017–18); Dance United, 2010–13; Arts Catalyst, 2014–. FRTS 1999. Hon. FRCA 2006. Huw Wheldon Award for Best Arts Prog., BAFTA, 1993. *Recreations:* travelling (particularly in Africa), reading, contemporary art, theatre. *Address:* c/o Clean Break Theatre Company, 2 Patshull Road, NW5 2LB.

**EVANS, Leslie Elizabeth;** Permanent Secretary, Scottish Government, since 2015; *b* 11 Dec. 1958; *d* of Philip Charles Evans and Mary Elizabeth Nora Evans (née Else); *m* 1990, Derek George McVay; one *s*. *Educ:* Liverpool Univ. (BA Hons Music). Asst to Dir, Greenwich Fest., 1981; Entertainments Officer, London Bor. of Greenwich, 1981–83; Arts Co-ordinator, Sheffield CC, 1983–85; Sen. Arts Officer, Edinburgh DC, 1985–87; Principal Officer, Stirling CC, 1987–89; Asst Dir of Recreation, 1989–99, Strategic Projects Manager, 1999–2000, City of Edinburgh Council; Scottish Executive, later Scottish Government: Head: Local Govt, Constitution and Governance, 2000–03; Public Service Reform, 2003–05; Tourism, Culture and Sport, Scottish Exec. Educn Dept, 2006–07; Dir, Culture, Ext. Affairs and Tourism (formerly Europe, Ext. Affairs and Culture), 2007–09; Dir Gen., Educn, 2009–11; Dir Gen., Learning and Justice, 2011–15. Mem., Scotch Malt Whisky Soc. *Recreations:* Ashtanga yoga, Scotland's wilderness, the arts, baking, sleeping. *Address:* Scottish Government, St Andrews House, Edinburgh EH1 3DG. *E:* leslie.evans@gov.scot.

**EVANS, Lewis Jones;** Chairman, Post Office Board, Wales and the Marches, 1997–2000; *b* 14 Feb. 1938; *s* of Evan Jones Evans and Jane Jones Evans (née Morgans); *m* 1961, Siân, *e d* of Rev. Harri Hughes and Blodwen Hughes, Penclawdd; two *s* one *d*. *Educ:* Tregaron County Sch.; Trinity Coll., Carmarthen (DipEd; Hon. Fellow, 2006); Harvard Sch. of Mgt (AMP 1983). FCIB 1986. Schoolmaster, 1960–62; Lloyds Bank plc, 1962–90: branch and head office appts incl. Manager, Llanelli Br., 1970–73; Sen. Manager, Newcastle upon Tyne, 1982–84; Regl Dir and gen. mgt, 1984–90; Dir, Lloyds Develt Capital Ltd, Alex Lawrie Factors Ltd, and Internat. Factors Ltd, 1989–90; Dep. Man. Dir, 1990–91, Man. Dir, 1991–96, Girobank; Dir, Alliance and Leicester Building Soc., 1991–96. Mem., Post Euro Giro Council, 1991–96; Mem. Council, British Bankers' Assoc., 1992–96. Member: Wales Tourist Bd, 1996–2004; Wales Adv. Bd, BITC, 1996–2000 (Chairman: Professional Firms Gp, Cardiff, 1996–99; Community Loan Fund for Wales, 1997–2000; Mem. Council, UK Local Investment Fund, 1997–2000); Wales Adv. Bd, Barclays Wealth (formerly Gerrard Ltd), 2000–08; Panel of Ind. Assessors for Public Appts, 2000–04; Chairman: Cwlwm Busnes, Caerdydd, 1998–2006; GSL Farm and Pet Place Ltd, 2000–02. Member: Council, Royal Nat. Eisteddfod of Wales, 1999–2006 (Chm., Resources and Finance Cttee, 1999–2006); Council, CBI for Wales, 1997–2000; Dir, Cardiff Bay Opera Trust Ltd, 1994–97. Jt Chm., Action Res. Project on the Underachievement of Boys, 1996–98; Dep. Chm., NPFA, 2004–07 (Chm., NPFA Cymru, 2000–07). Hon. Vice-Pres., London Welsh Trust and Assoc., 1994–2000. Hon. Treas. and Mem. Council, Univ. of Wales, Lampeter, 1993–99; University of Wales: Member: Court, 1996–2002; Audit Cttee, 1997–2000; Council, 2004–07; Bd, Univ. of Wales Press, 2004–07. Governor: Univ. of Glamorgan, 1999–2002; Trinity Univ. Coll. (formerly Trinity Coll.), Carmarthen, 2006–10; Univ. of Wales Trinity St David, 2010–14; Swansea Metropolitan Univ., 2011–14. CCMI (CIMgt 1994); FRSA 1994. Hon. Druid, Gorsedd of Bards, Isle of Britain, 1994. Hon. DSc Econs Wales, 2014. *Recreations:* family, music, sport. *Clubs:* Cardiff and County (Cardiff); Crawshays Rugby Football; Royal Porthcawl Golf.

**EVANS, Lindsay;** *see* Evans, W. L.

**EVANS, Lyndon Rees,** CBE 2001; PhD; FRS 2010; Project Leader, Large Hadron Collider, Organisation Européenne pour la Recherche Nucléaire (CERN), 1994–2010; *b* Aberdare, 24 July 1945; *m* 1967, Lynda Mear; one *s* one *d*. *Educ:* Aberdare Boys' Grammar Sch.; Univ. of Wales, Swansea (BSc 1st Cl. Hons Physics 1966; PhD Physics 1970; Hon. Fellow 2002). CERN: Fellow, Linac Gp, 1969; Res. Fellow, Proton Synchrotron Div., 1970–71; joined 300 GeV project, 1971; Dep. Leader, Super Proton Synchrotron Div., 1988–89; Leader, Super Proton Synchrotron—Large Electron Positron Div., 1990–93; Associate Dir, Future Accelerators, 1994. Fellow, APS, 1991. Robert R. Wilson Prize, APS, 2008; Glazebrook Medal, Inst. of Physics, 2013. *Address:* c/o CERN, 1211 Geneva 23, Switzerland.

**EVANS, Dame (Madelaine) Glynne (Dervel),** DBE 2000; CMG 1992; PhD; HM Diplomatic Service, retired; Senior Adviser: Olive Group Ltd, since 2006; Restrata Ltd, since 2013; *b* 23 Aug. 1944. *Educ:* Univ. of St Andrews (MA Hons 1st cl. Mediaeval and Modern Hist. 1966); University Coll. London (PhD 1971). Res. Fellow, Centre for Latin American Studies, Univ. of Liverpool, 1969–70; Vis. Lectr, Coll. of William and Mary, Williamsburg, 1970–71; Second Sec., FCO, 1971; Buenos Aires, 1972; First Sec., FCO, 1975; Pte Sec. to Parly Under-Sec. of State, 1977; on loan to UN Secretariat, NY, 1978; First Sec., UKMIS NY, 1979; First Sec., subseq. Counsellor, FCO, 1982; Counsellor and Dep. Hd of Mission, Brussels, 1987; Head of UN Dept, FCO, 1990–96; Res. Associate, IISS, 1996–97; Ambassador to Chile, 1997–2000; Dist. Vis. Scholar, NATO Defense Coll., Rome, 2000–01; Ambassador to Portugal, 2001–04. Advr to Dir, Defence Acad. of the UK, 2006–07. Associate Fellow, RUSI, 2004–09. Advr, CAB, 2005–06. *Publications:* Responding to Crises in the African Great Lakes, 1997; articles on internat. peacekeeping and conflict management. *Address:* c/o Olive Group Ltd, 23 Buckingham Gate, SW1E 6LB. *E:* gevans@olivegroup.com.

**EVANS, Sir Malcolm (David),** KCMG 2016; OBE 2004; DPhil; Professor of Public International Law, University of Bristol, since 1999; *b* Cardiff, 31 Dec. 1959; *s* of Albert Osborn Evans and Eunice Myra Evans; *m* 1986, Rev. Dr Alison Ruth Measures; three *d*. *Educ:* Llanrumney High Sch., Cardiff; Regent's Park Coll., Oxford (BA 1982; MA 1986; DPhil 1987). University of Bristol: Lectr in Law, 1988–95; Sen. Lectr in Law, 1995–98; Reader in Internat. Law, 1998–99; Hd, Sch. of Law, 2003–05; Dean, Faculty of Social Scis and Law, 2005–09. Co-Gen. Ed., Internat. and Comparative Law Qly, 2013–. Member: Adv. Council on Freedom of Religion or Belief, OSCE, 2004–13; Subcttee for Prevention of Torture, UN, 2009– (Chm., 2011–); Ind. Inquiry into Child Sexual Abuse in England and Wales, 2015–; Adv. Bd, UN Global Study of Children in Detention, 2016–; Commn on Religious Educn, 2016–18. Chm., Meeting of UN Chairs of Human Rights Treaty Bodies, 2014–15. Chm. Coll. Council and Governing Body, Regent's Park Coll., Oxford, 2011–. Trustee, Cumberland Lodge, 2009–. Gov., Marling Sch., Stroud, 2009–16; Mem., Cotswold Beacon Acad. Trust, 2016–. Hon. Fellow, Univ. of Bangor, 2012. *Publications:* Relevant Circumstances and Maritime Delimitation, 1989; Religious Liberty and International Law in Europe, 1997; (with R. Morgan) Preventing Torture: a study of the European Convention for the Prevention of Torture, 1998; (with R. Morgan) Combating Torture in Europe, 2001; (ed) International Law, 2003, 5th edn 2018; Manual on the Wearing of Religious Symbols in Public Areas, 2009; (jtly) The Optional Protocol to the UN Convention Against Torture, 2011; (ed jtly) The Changing Nature of Religious Rights Under International Law, 2015; (with C. Bicknell and R. Morgan) Preventing Torture in Europe, 2018. *Recreations:* reading, theatre, opera, cinema. *Address:* School of Law, University of Bristol, Wills Memorial Building, Queens Road, Bristol BS8 1RJ. *T:* (0117) 954 5335. *E:* m.d.evans@bristol.ac.uk.

**EVANS, His Honour (Maldwyn) John;** a Circuit Judge, 2005–15; *b* 11 July 1950; *s* of late Comdr David Anthony Evans and of Margaret Evans; *m* 1998, Miriam Dorothy Swaddle (née Beaumont); one step *s* two step *d*, and two *s* one *d* from former marriage. *Educ:* Royal Hospital Sch., Holbrook; Newcastle upon Tyne Polytechnic (BA Hons 1972). Called to the Bar, Gray's Inn, 1973; a Recorder of the Crown Court, 1998; Hd, New Court Chambers, Newcastle, 1999–2005. Gov., King's Sch., Tynemouth, 2000–; Fellow, Woodard Corp., 2002. *Recreations:* sport, ski-ing, sailing, cricket, Rugby in particular, holidays, walking, contemporary cinema.

**EVANS, Prof. Margaret;** *see* McCaskill, M.

**EVANS, Mark;** QC 1995; a Recorder, 1996–2009; a Deputy High Court Judge; *b* 21 March 1946; *s* of Rev. Clifford Evans and Mary (née Jones); *m* 1971, Dr Barbara Skew (marr. diss. 1995); one *s* one *d*; *m* 2001, Carolyn Poots, barrister. *Educ:* Christ Coll., Brecon; King's Coll., London (LLB Hons). Called to the Bar, Gray's Inn, 1971; practice in Bristol, 1973; founded St John's Chambers, 1978. *Recreations:* music, vintage cars. *Club:* Savages (Bristol).

**EVANS, Mark Armstrong,** CVO 1994; Director, British Council, Austria, 1996–2000; *b* 5 Aug. 1940; *s* of late Charles Tunstall Evans, CMG, Birmingham, and Kathleen Armstrong, Newcastle; *m* 1965, Katharine, *d* of Alfred Bastable, Brecon; one *s* one *d*. *Educ:* Marlborough Coll.; Clare Coll., Cambridge (BA 1962; MA 1966); Moscow State Univ.; Bristol Univ. (PGCE 1964). Head, Russian and German, Chichester High Sch. for Boys, 1964–69; apptd to British Council, 1969; Bahrain, 1969–71; Frankfurt, 1971–73; MECAS, Lebanon, 1973–74; Dir, UAE in Dubai, 1974–77; temp. posting, Kabul, 1977; Asst Dir, Educnl Contracts, 1977–79; Dep. Rep. and Cultural Attaché, France, 1979–85; Head, Office Services, 1985–88; Dir, Canada, and Cultural Counsellor, Ottawa, 1988–92; Dir, and Cultural Counsellor, Russia, 1992–96. Chm., Chailey Parish Council, 2005–09, 2014–17. Mem., E Sussex Valuation Tribunal, 2002–12. Member: RSAA, 1972; Adv. Bd, Österreich Institut, 1999–2008. Gov., RNLI, 1995. Gov., Chailey Sch., 2004–. Mem., Bluebell Railway Preservation Soc., 1997–. *Recreation:* garden history. *Address:* High Field, North Chailey, Sussex BN8 4JD. *Club:* Union (Cambridge).

**EVANS, Sir Martin (John),** Kt 2004; PhD; ScD; FMedSci; FRS 1993; Chancellor, Cardiff University, 2012–17 (President, 2009–12); Director, Cardiff School of Biosciences, and Professor of Mammalian Genetics, 1999–2009; Founder, Chairman and Chief Scientific Officer, Celixir Ltd (formerly Cell Therapy Ltd), since 2009; *b* 1 Jan. 1941; *s* of Leonard Wilfred Evans and Hilary Joyce (née Redman); *m* 1966, Judith Clare Williams, MBE; two *s* one *d*. *Educ:* St Dunstan's Coll., Catford; Christ's Coll., Cambridge (BA Pt II in Biochem., MA; Hon. Fellow 2004); PhD London 1969; ScD Cambridge 1996. University College London: Res. Assistant, Dept of Anatomy and Embryology, 1963–66; Asst Lectr, 1966–69; Lectr, 1969–78; Cambridge University: Lectr, Dept of Genetics, 1978–91; Reader, 1991–94; Prof. of Mammalian Genetics, 1994–99; Fellow, St Edmund's Coll., Cambridge, 1998–99; Vice Provost, Sch. of Medicine, Biol., Health and Life Scis, Cardiff Univ., 2004–06. Discovered embryonic stem cells, 1981. Member: CMO's expert gp on Therapeutic Cloning, 1999–2000; Steering Cttee, UK Stem Cell Bank and for Use of Stem Cell Lines, 2002–07; UK Nat. Stem Cell Network Steering Cttee, 2006–09. Trustee, Breakthrough Breast Cancer, 2004–15; Pres., Techniquest, 2009. Mem., EMBO, 1990; Founder FMedSci 1998 (Hon. FMedSci 2008). Hon. Mem. Biochem. Soc., 2008. Liveryman, Livery Co. of Wales (formerly Welsh Livery Guild), 2005; Hon. Freeman, Soc. of Apothecaries of London, 2008. Hon. Fellow, St Edmund's Coll., Cambridge, 2002.

Hon. DSc: Mount Sinai Sch. of Medicine, 2002; Bath, 2005; Buckingham, 2009; Hon. DSc (Med) UCL, 2008; Hon. Dr: Athens, 2008; Univ. of Wales, 2008. March of Dimes Prize in Develtl Biol., 1999; Albert Lasker Award for Basic Medical Research, 2001; Special Achievement Award, Miami Nature Biotechnol. Winter Symposium, 2003; (jtly) Nobel Prize for Medicine, 2007; Morgan Stanley Great Britons Award for Sci. and Innovation, 2007; Gold Medal, RSocMed, 2008; Copley Medal, Royal Soc., 2009. *Publications*: numerous contribs to scientific works. *Recreations*: family, walking, golf.

**EVANS, Martyn Robert Rowlinson;** Executive Chair, Alex Ferry Foundation, since 2019; *b* Hamilton, Bermuda, 11 July 1952; *s of* Lt Col John Evans and Connie Evans; *m* 2004, Angela Morton; two *s*. *Educ*: City of Birmingham Poly. (BA Hons); Univ. of Manchester (MA Econs). Housing Aid Officer, Thamesside Housing Aid Centre, 1977–79; Housing Aid Worker, Glasgow Shelter Housing Aid Centre, 1980–84; Dep. Dir, 1984–87, Dir, 1987–92, Shelter (Scotland); CEO, Citizens Advice Scotland, 1992–97; Dir, Scottish Consumer Council, 1998–2008; Sen. Dir, Consumer Focus, 2008–09; Chief Exec., Carnegie UK Trust, 2009–19. Vis. Prof. of Law, Univ. of Strathclyde, 1996–2003. Chair, Quality Improvement Scotland, 2009–10 (Vice Chair, 2004–09). Member, Board: IPPR Scotland, 2018–; Scottish Police Authy, 2019–. FRSA 2011. *Address*: Alex Ferry Foundation, 88 Kingsway, WC2B 6AA.
*See also* R. E. R. Evans.

**EVANS, Michael;** *see* Evans, His Honour T. M.

**EVANS, Michael Ritho;** QC 2014; **His Honour Judge Michael Evans;** a Circuit Judge, since 2018; *b* London, 4 July 1963; *s of* Dai Evans and Verena Evans; *m* 1994, Maria Arnolda Henrica Dionysia Walravens; one *s* two *d*. *Educ*: BA Hons. Called to the Bar, Middle Temple, 1988; a Recorder, 2009–18. *Recreations*: sports, playing golf (if that counts), tennis and cycling, most of time spent trying to keep up with my children, watching Wales play Rugby (but only if winning). *Club*: Harlequins Rugby.

**EVANS, Michael Stephen James;** freelance defence writer, The Times, since 2013; *b* 5 Jan. 1945; *s of* Reginald and Beatrix Evans; *m* 1971, Robyn Nicola Coles; three *s*. *Educ*: Christ's Hosp.; QMC, London Univ. (BA Hons English). Reporter, 1968–69, News Editor, Loughton office, 1969–70, Express and Independent; Daily Express: Reporter, Action Line consumer column, 1970–72; Reporter, 1972–77; Home Affairs Correspondent, 1977–82; Defence and Diplomatic Correspondent, 1982–86; The Times: Whitehall Correspondent, 1986–87; Defence Correspondent, 1987–98; Defence Editor, 1998–2010; Pentagon Correspondent in Washington, 2010–13. *Publications: fiction:* A Crack in the Dam, 1978; False Arrest, 1979; Double Lives, 2011; *non-fiction*: Great Disasters, 1981; South Africa, 1987; The Gulf Crisis, 1988; First with the News, 2016. *Recreations*: cricket, golf, tennis, playing piano. *Address*: c/o The Times, 1 London Bridge Street, SE1 9GF. *T*: 07768 081797.

**EVANS, Nerys;** *see* Evans, E. G. N.

**EVANS, Nicholas;** *see* Evans, H. N.

**EVANS, Nicholas Henry Robert;** Command Secretary, Land Forces, Ministry of Defence, 2006–10; *b* 21 July 1950; *s of* Ivor Robert Evans and Esther Jane Evans; *m* Sally Vera Carter; two *s*. *Educ*: Reading Sch.; St John's Coll., Oxford (MA Hons Modern History). Joined MoD, 1971; posts in RN, Army and Air Force policy, planning and finance, incl. Private Sec. to Under-Sec. of State for the Army, 1974–75, and Civil Advr to GOC NI, 1975–77; Asst Private Sec. to Sec. of State, 1981–84; Head: Naval Manpower and Trng, 1985–87; Mgt Services Div., 1987–90; Next Steps Implementation Team, 1990–92; Resources and Progs (Air), 1992–95; Asst Under-Sec. of State (Quartermaster), 1995–99; Exec. Dir (Finance), Defence Procurement Agency, 1999–2000; Dir Gen., Defence Logistics (Finance and Business Planning), then Resources, Defence Logistics Orgn, 2000–02; Dir Gen., Mgt and Orgn, 2003–06. *Recreations*: walking, gardening, house maintenance, reading history.

**EVANS, Nigel Martin;** MP (C) Ribble Valley, since 1992; *b* 10 Nov. 1957; *s of* late Albert Evans and Betty Evans. *Educ*: Swansea Univ. (BA Hons). Retail Newsagent, family business, 1979–90. West Glamorgan County Council: Councillor (C), 1985–91; Dep. Leader, 1989. Chm., Welsh Cons. Candidates Policy Gp, 1990; Pres., Cons. NW Parly Gp, 1991. Contested (C): Swansea West, 1987; Pontypridd, Feb. 1989; Ribble Valley, March 1991. PPS to Sec. of State for Employment, 1993–94; to Chancellor of Duchy of Lancaster, 1994–95; Opposition front bench spokesman on Welsh and constitutional affairs, 1997–2001; Shadow Welsh Sec., 2001–03; First Dep. Chm. of Ways and Means and a Dep. Speaker, H of C, 2010–13. Mem., Select Cttee on Transport, 1993, on Envmt, 1996–97, on Public Service, 1996–97, on Trade and Industry, 2003–05, on Culture, Media and Sport, 2005–09, on Internat. Develt, 2009–10, 2015–; Sec., 1992–97, Chm., 2010–12, NW Gp of Cons. MPs; Secretary: Manufacturing Cttee; All-Party Tourism Cttee; Chairman: All-Party Music Gp, 1996–97 (Vice-Chm., 2002–10); All-Party Identity Fraud Gp, 2006–10; All-Party Egypt Gp, 2007–10; Co-Chair: All-Party Drugs Gp, 1997–2010; Taiwan All-Party Parly Gp, 2015–; Vice Chair, Internat. Trade Cttee, 2016–; President: All-Party Beer Gp, 2010–; Parly Space Cttee, 2010–. Vice-Chm., Cons. Party (Wales), 1999–2001. Director: Made in the UK Ltd; Small Business Bureau. *Recreations*: tennis, swimming, theatre, tourism, new technology, defence, broadcasting. *Address*: Brooklyn Cottage, Main Street, Pendleton, Clitheroe, Lancs BB7 1PT. *T*: (01200) 443875; House of Commons, SW1A 0AA. *Clubs*: Carlton, Royal Automobile, Lansdowne, Groucho.

**EVANS, Dame Oremi,** DBE 2015; Headteacher, Brookfield School, Hereford, 2001–16; Executive Headteacher, Hereford Integrated Behaviour Outreach Service, 2017–18 (Executive Headteacher, Behaviour, Herefordshire Council, 2011–16); *b* Lagos, Nigeria, 7 Oct. 1956; *d of* Sir Mobolaji Bank-Anthony, KBE and Mrs Suzy Iseli (*née* Gray); *m* 1975, Clifford Evans; two *d*. *Educ*: Queen's Coll., Lagos; Avery Hill Higher Educn Coll. (BEd Hons); Univ. of Worcester (MSc). Teacher of Sci., 1979–89, Special Educnl Needs Coordinator, 1989–94, Whitecross High Sch., Hereford; Dep. Hd, 1994–99, Headteacher, 1999–2001, John Venn Unit, Hereford. *Recreations*: music, theatre, ballet, opera, travelling. *Address*: 58 Three Elms Road, Hereford HR4 0RH. *T*: (01432) 354142. *E*: dameoremi@gmail.com.

**EVANS, Ven. Patrick Alexander Sidney;** Archdeacon of Canterbury, and a Canon Residentiary, Canterbury Cathedral, 2002–07, now Archdeacon Emeritus; *b* 28 Jan. 1943; *m* 1969, Jane Kemp; two *s* one *d*. *Educ*: Clifton College, Bristol; Lincoln Theological Coll. Curate: Holy Trinity, Lyonsdown, Barnet, 1973–76; Royston, 1976–78; Vicar: Gt Gaddesden, 1978–82; Tenterden, 1982–89; RD of West Charing, 1988–89; Archdeacon of Maidstone, 1989–2002; Diocesan Dir of Ordinands, Canterbury, 1989–94. Selector, ABM, 1992–95. Mem., Gen. Synod, 1996–2005; Chairman: Bd of Mission, 1994–95, and Pastoral Cttee, 1994–2002, dio. of Canterbury; Canterbury & Rochester Church in Society (formerly Council for Social Responsibility), 1997–2007. Trustee, Dorset Historic Churches Trust, 2008–12. *Address*: Wills Tenement, Trehan, Trematon, Cornwall PL12 4QN. *E*: patrickevans120@hotmail.co.uk.

**EVANS, Paul;** *see* Evans, Christopher P.

**EVANS, Air Marshal Paul;** *see* Evans, Air Marshal C. P. A.

**EVANS, Paul Anthony,** CBE 2019; Clerk of Committees, House of Commons, 2016–19; *b* 15 Oct. 1955; *s of* late John Evans and Cecilia Evans (*née* Monks); *m* 1991, Katharine; one *s* one *d*. *Educ*: St Peter's RC Primary Sch., Winchester; Peter Symonds, Winchester; Sevenoaks Sch.; King's Coll., Cambridge (BA 1977). Vis. Schol., Univ. of Siena, 1976; Vis. Fellow, Univ. of Heidelberg, 1980; Jun. Res. Fellow, St Edmund's House, Cambridge, 1980–81; Clerk, House of Commons, 1981–2019: Health Cttee, 1991–93; Defence Cttee, 1997–2001; Human Rights Cttee, 2001–04; Principal Clerk: Delegated Legislation, 2005–06; Select Cttees, 2006–11; Table Office, 2011–14; Clerk of the Jls, 2014–16. Presidential Advr, Parly Assembly of Council of Europe, 2003–06. Chair, Study of Parlt Gp, 2005–07; Trustee, Industry and Parlt Trust, 2010–15. Associate, Inst. for Govt, 2011–; Hon. Res. Associate, UCL, 2014; Hon. Res. Fellow, Centre for British Politics and Public Life, Birkbeck, Univ. of London, 2019. FAcSS 2012; FRSA 2012. *Publications*: (contrib.) Parliamentary Accountability, 1995; Dod's Handbook of House of Commons Procedure, 1997, 8th edn 2011; (contrib.) The Future of Parliament, 2005; (with Paul Silk) Parliamentary Assembly of the Council of Europe: practice and procedure, 10th edn 2008, 11th edn 2013; (ed) A History of Parliamentary Procedure: essays in honour of Thomas Erskine, 2017; (contrib.) Parliament and the Law, 2nd edn 2018; articles in jls on parly matters. *Recreations*: British Constitution, Victorian and 20th century architecture, walking, silence and empty places, Wales.

**EVANS, Paul Gareth;** Lecturer, Leadership and Management Development, Alliance Manchester Business School (formerly Manchester Business School), since 2012; *b* 9 Sept. 1963; *s of* Thomas Neville Evans and Rosamund Sheila Evans; *m* 1998, Barbara Shih Wen Chan; one *s* two *d*. *Educ*: Chilwell Comprehensive Sch.; Univ. of Surrey (BSc Hons); Univ. of Manchester (MBA; PhD). Project Manager, Kirin Beer, Tokyo, 1993; Area Manager, Whitbread Inns, 1994–98; Regl Ops Dir, Rank Holidays Div., Rank Orgn plc, 1998–2000; Chief Operating Officer, 2000–03; Master and Chief Exec., 2003–08, Royal Armouries. *Recreation*: fly fishing.

**EVANS, Paul William;** independent educational consultant, since 2015; *b* Plymouth, 10 April 1960; *s of* William and Eileen Evans; *m* 1983, Serena Pratt; one *d*. *Educ*: Coll. of St Mark and St John, Plymouth (BEd Hons 1983); Bulmershe Coll. of Higher Educn, Reading (MEd 1988). NPQH 2001. Sci. Teacher, Park House Sch., Newbury, 1983–86; Hd of Biol., 1986–89, Hd of Maths and Sci., 1989–97, Theale Green Sch., Reading; Dep. Headteacher, 1997–2008, Headteacher, 2008–15, Colyton Grammar Sch.; OFSTED Inspector, 2016–18. FCollT 2007; FRSA 2012. *Recreations*: walking, photography, listening to classical music, theatre. *Address*: 14 Banfield Way, Honiton, Devon EX14 2GB. *E*: pwevans@me.com. *Club*: Lansdowne.

**EVANS, Peter,** CBE 1986; National Secretary, General Workers' Trade Group, Transport & General Workers' Union, 1974–90; *b* 8 Nov. 1929; *m* 1st, 1957, Christine Pamela (marr. diss.); one *d*; 2nd, 1975, Gillian Rosemary (decd); 3rd, 1980, Joy Elizabeth (decd). *Educ*: Culvert Road Secondary School, Tottenham. London bus driver, 1955–62; District Officer, TGWU, 1962–66; Regional Trade Group Sec., Public Services, 1966–74. *Recreations*: talking, reading (history books, biographies), films. *Clubs*: Victoria, Players' Theatre.

**EVANS, Dr Peter Glyn Howard;** Director, Sea Watch Foundation, since 1990; *b* London, 12 Aug. 1949; *s of* David Evans and Sybil Victoria Evans. *Educ*: Whitgift Sch.; Bromley Coll. of Technol. (HNC 1972); Univ. of Aberdeen (BSc 1976); St Peter's Coll., Oxford (DPhil 1980). NERC Postdoctoral Res. Fellow, Univ. of Oxford, 1980–82; Principal Investigator, Dominica Multiple Land Use Proj., 1981–90. Consultant Editor, Encyclopaedia of Mammals, 1983. Vis. Lectr on Marine Vertebrate Ecol., Univ. of Reykjavik, 1984; Hon. Sen. Lectr, Sch. of Ocean Scis, Bangor Univ., 2007–. Member: BOU; British Trust for Ornithol.; Seabird Gp; Mammal Soc.; British Ecol Soc.; Eur. Cetacean Soc.; Soc. of Marine Mammalogy. Educn and Outreach Award, UNEP/ASCOBANS, 2009; Conservation Award, Eur. Cetacean Soc., 2010. *Publications*: (ed jtly) Status and Conservation of the World's Seabirds, 1984; The Natural History of Whales and Dolphins, 1987; Birds of the Eastern Caribbean, 1990; Whales, 1990; Dolphins, 1994; Guide to the Identification of Whales, Dolphins and Porpoises in European Seas, 1995; (jtly) Dominica, Nature Island of the Caribbean, 8 vols, 1997; (ed jtly) Marine Mammals: biology and conservation, 2001; (jtly) Atlas of Cetacean Distribution in North-West European Waters, 2001; European Whales, Dolphins and Porpoises, 2019; approx. 200 articles in learned jls. *Recreations*: photography, writing, hiking, bird watching. *Address*: Ewyn y Don, Bull Bay, Amlwch, Isle of Anglesey LL68 9SD. *T*: (01407) 832892. *E*: peter.evans@bangor.ac.uk.

**EVANS, Philip;** *see* Evans, I. P.

**EVANS, Dr Philip Richard,** FRS 2005; Member of Scientific Staff, Medical Research Council Laboratory of Molecular Biology, Cambridge, 1976–2016; *b* 25 May 1946; *s of* Maurice Lionel Evans and Janette Marjorie (*née* Burridge); two *s* one *d*. *Educ*: Christ's Hosp.; Wadham Coll., Oxford (MA, DPhil 1974). IBM Res. Fellow, Oxford Univ., 1974. *Publications*: contrib. res. papers to scientific jls. *Recreations*: playing bassoon, walking. *Address*: MRC Laboratory of Molecular Biology, Francis Crick Avenue, Cambridge CB2 0QH. *T*: (01223) 267000. *E*: pre@mrc-lmb.cam.ac.uk.

**EVANS, Rebecca Mary;** Member (Lab) Gower, National Assembly for Wales, since 2016 (Wales Mid and West, 2011–16); Minister for Finance and Trefnydd, since 2018; *b* Bridgend, 2 Aug. 1976; *d of* Ven. Alun Wyn Evans and Everly Evans; *m* 2010, Paul Michael Evans. *Educ*: Univ. of Leeds (BA Hons Hist. 1997); Sidney Sussex Coll., Cambridge (MPhil Histl Studies 1998); Sheffield Hallam Univ. (Postgrad. Cert. Asperger Syndrome, 2011). Mid and W Wales Organiser, Welsh Labour, 2004–06; Sen. Researcher and Communications Officer for Carl Sargeant, Mem., Nat. Assembly for Wales, 2006–09; Policy and Public Affairs Officer, Nat. Autistic Soc., Cymru, 2009–11. Dep. Minister for Farming and Food, 2014–16, Minister for Social Services and Public Health, 2016–17, Minister for Housing and Regeneration, 2017–18, Welsh Govt. *Address*: National Assembly for Wales, Cardiff Bay CF99 1NA. *T*: 0300 200 7160. *E*: rebecca.evans@assembly.wales.

**EVANS, Sir Richard (Harry),** Kt 1996; CBE 1986; Independent Director, SWF Samruk-Kazyna JSC, Kazakhstan; *b* 1942; *m*; three *d*. *Educ*: Royal Masonic Sch. Joined Civil Aviation section, Min. of Transport, 1960; Min. of Technology, 1961; Govt Contracts Officer, Ferranti, 1967; British Aerospace (formerly British Aircraft Corporation): Contracts Officer, 1969, Commercial Dir, 1978, Asst Man. Dir, 1981, Dep. Man. Dir, 1983, Marketing Dir, 1985, Mktg Dir, 1987; Chairman: British Aerospace (Dynamics), 1988; BAe (Military Aircraft), 1988; Chief Exec., 1990–98, Chm., 1998–2004, BAe plc, then BAE SYSTEMS. Former Chm., Royal Ordnance; Dir, Panavia, 1981; Chm., United Utilities, 2001–08 (non-exec. Dir, 1997–2008). Chancellor, Univ. of Central Lancs, 2001–15.

**EVANS, Richard Jeremy;** *b* 28 June 1953; *s of* late George Evans and Helen Maud Evans; *m* 1976, Alison Mary Thom. *Educ*: Ipswich Sch., Suffolk. Journalist: East Anglian Daily Times, 1974–78; Cambridge Evening News, 1978–79; with The Times, 1979–99 (Racing Correspondent, 1991–99); Racing Correspondent, Daily Telegraph, 1999–2005. Racing

Journalist of the Year, Horserace Writers' Assoc., 1995. *Recreations:* golf, bridge. *Address:* Old Village Hall, Stansfield, Suffolk CO10 8LP. *T:* (01284) 789478. *E:* richardevans53@me.com.

**EVANS, Sir Richard (John),** Kt 2012; FBA 1993; FRHistS, FRSL, FLSW; Regius Professor of History (formerly Regius Professor of Modern History), University of Cambridge, 2008–14, now Emeritus; President, Wolfson College, Cambridge, 2010–17, now Hon. Fellow; Provost, Gresham College, London, since 2014; *b* 29 Sept. 1947; *s* of late Ieuan Trefor Evans and Evelyn Evans (*née* Jones); *m* 1st, 1976, Elín Hjaltadóttir (marr. diss. 1993); 2nd, 2004, Dr Christine L. Corton; two *s*. *Educ:* Forest Sch., London; Jesus Coll., Oxford (Open Schol.; 1st Cl. Hons Mod. Hist. 1969; Stanhope Hist. Essay Prize 1969; Hon. Fellow, 1998); St Antony's Coll., Oxford (MA, DPhil 1973); Hamburg Univ. (Hanseatic Schol.); LittD East Anglia, 1990. Lectr in History, Univ. of Stirling, 1972–76; University of East Anglia: Lectr, 1976; Prof. of European History, 1983–89; Birkbeck College, London: Prof. of History, 1989–98; Vice-Master, 1993–97; Acting Master, 1997; Hon. Fellow, 1999; Prof. of Modern History, Univ. of Cambridge, 1998–2008; Fellow, Gonville and Caius Coll., Cambridge, 1998–2010 (Hon. Fellow, 2011). Vis. Associate Prof. of European History, Columbia Univ., 1980; Vis. Fellow, Humanities Res. Centre, ANU, Canberra, 1986; Alexander von Humboldt Fellow, Free Univ. of Berlin, 1981, 1985, 1989; Douglas Southall Freeman Prof. of History, Univ. of Richmond, Va, 2018; Dist. Fellow, Munk Centre for Global Affairs, Univ. of Toronto, 2018–. FRHistS 1978; FRSL 2000; Founding FLSW 2010. Hon. DLit: London, 2012; Oxon, 2015. Wolfson Literary Award for History, 1988; William H. Welch Medal, Amer. Assoc. for Hist. of Medicine, 1989; Medaille für Kunst und Wissenschaft der Hansestadt Hamburg, 1993; Fraenkel Prize in Contemporary History, Inst. of Contemp. Hist., 1994; Norton Medlicott Medal, Histl Association, 2014; Leverhulme Medal and Prize, British Acad., 2015. *Publications:* The Feminist Movement in Germany 1894–1933, 1976; The Feminists, 1977; (ed) Society and Politics in Wilhelmine Germany, 1978; Sozialdemokratie und Frauenemanzipation im deutschen Kaiserreich, 1979; (ed jtly) The German Family, 1981; (ed) The German Working Class, 1982; (ed jtly) The German Peasantry, 1986; (ed jtly) The German Unemployed, 1987; Comrades and Sisters, 1987; Rethinking German History, 1987; Death in Hamburg, 1987; (ed) The German Underworld, 1988; (ed) Kneipengespräche im Kaiserreich, 1989; In Hitler's Shadow, 1989; Proletarians and Politics, 1990; (ed jtly) The German Bourgeoisie, 1992; Rituals of Retribution, 1996; Rereading German History, 1997; In Defence of History, 1997; Tales from the German Underworld, 1998; Telling Lies About Hitler, 2002; The Coming of the Third Reich, 2003; The Third Reich in Power, 2005; The Third Reich at War, 2008; Cosmopolitan Islanders, 2009; Altered Pasts, 2014; (essays) Third Reich in History and Memory, 2015; The Pursuit of Power: Europe 1815–1914, 2016; Eric Hobsbawm: a life in history, 2019. *Recreations:* playing the piano, opera, reading, cooking for friends, walking, gardening. *Address:* Rushing Wells, Burrs Lane, Barkway, Royston, Herts SG8 8EL.

**EVANS, Richard Llewellyn;** JP; Director of Social Services, Birmingham City Council, 1994–99; *b* 1 June 1949; *s* of Robert Ellis Evans and Sarah Christine (*née* Cassidy); *m*; one *s* one *d*. *Educ:* Chiswick Poly.; Dundee Univ. (Dip. Social Work; CQSW; Dip. TMHA). Aircraft engr, BAC, 1964–69; Surrey County Council: Instructor, 1969–72; Dep. Manager, 1972–73; Trng Officer, Lothian Regl Council, 1973–77; Manager, Emergency Duty Team, Wilts CC, 1977–79; Principal Officer, Lothian Regl Council, 1979–81; Develt Officer, London Boroughs' Regl Children's Planning Cttee, 1981–83; Avon County Council: Asst Dir of Social Services, 1983–90; Dir, Social Services, 1990–94. Chm., BBC Children in Need Appeal for South and West, 2004–06. JP Bristol and North Avon, 2006. *Recreations:* music, cinema, entertaining.

**EVANS, Sir Robert,** Kt 1994; CBE 1987; FREng; FIMechE, FInstE; Chairman, British Gas plc, 1989–93 (Chief Executive, 1983–92 and Member of the Board, 1983–89); *b* 28 May 1927; *s* of Gwilym Evans and Florence May Evans; *m* 1950, Lilian May (*née* Ward) (*d* 2009); one *s* one *d*. *Educ:* Old Swan Coll., Liverpool; Blackburn Coll.; City of Liverpool Coll. (Tech.). FREng (FEng 1991). D. Napier & Son Ltd, 1943–49; North Western Gas Bd, 1950–56; Burmah Oil Co., 1956–62; Dir of Engrg, Southern Gas Bd, 1962–70; Dep. Dir (Ops), Gas Council, 1972; Dir of Operations, British Gas, 1972–75; Dep. Chm., North Thames Gas, 1975–77; Chm., E Midlands Gas Region, 1977–82; Man. Dir, Supplies, British Gas Corp., 1982–83. President: Instn of Gas Engrs, 1981–82; Inst. of Energy, 1991–92; Pipeline Industries Guild, 1990–94. Founder Chm., Indo British Partnership, 1991–97. Founder Chm., Nat. Council for Hospice and Specialist Palliative Care Services. FInstE (MInstE 1988); Hon. FIGasE 1961; CCMI (CBIM 1983); Hon. FCGI. Freeman, City of London, 1974; Mem., Engineers' Co., 1984. *Recreations:* reading, golf.

**EVANS, Prof. Robert,** PhD; FRS 2005; FInstP; H. O. Wills Professor of Physics, University of Bristol, 2005–11, now Emeritus; *b* 7 April 1946; *s* of John David Evans and Mary Evans; *m* 1967, Margaret Hume; one *s*. *Educ:* A. J. Dawson Grammar Sch., Wingate; Univ. of Birmingham (BSc); Univ. of Bristol (PhD 1970). FInstP 1981. University of Bristol: Lectr, 1978–84; Reader, 1984–92; Prof. of Physics, 1992–2005; Hd, Dept of Physics, 2005–11. Res. Prof., Univ. of Wuppertal, 1997–98; A. von Humboldt Res. Prof., Max Planck Institut, Stuttgart, 2002–05; Kramers Prof. of Theoretical Physics, Univ. of Utrecht, 2011. *Publications:* contrib. numerous articles to learned jls. *Address:* H. H. Wills Physics Laboratory, University of Bristol, Tyndall Avenue, Bristol BS8 1TL.

**EVANS, Robert John Emlyn;** independent consultant, trainer and freelance journalist, specialising in Europe and South Asia; Lecturer and Visiting Tutor, Royal Holloway, University of London, since 2014; *b* 23 Oct. 1956; *s* of late T. F. Evans and Marjorie Evans. *Educ:* County Sch., Ashford, Middlesex; Shoreditch Coll. of Educn; Inst. of Educn, London Univ. (BEd 1978; MA 1993). Teacher: Thames Ditton Middle Sch., 1978–83; Woodville Middle Sch., Leatherhead, 1983–85; Dep. Headteacher, Town Farm Middle Sch., 1985–89; Headteacher, Crane Jun. Sch., Hanworth, Hounslow, 1990–94. MEP (Lab): London NW, 1994–99, London Region, 1999–2009; European Parliament: Member: Youth, Culture, Educn and Media Cttee, 1994–2001; Rules of Procedure Cttee, 1994–99 (Vice Pres., 1997–99); Cttee on Citizens' Freedoms and Rights, Justice and Home Affairs, 1999–2004 (Vice Pres., 1999–2004); Cttee on Transport and Tourism, 2004–09; Mem. Delegn for Relns with Countries of S Asia, 1994–09 (Chm., 2007–09), with Romania, 1997–2006, with Georgia, Armenia and Azerbaijan, 2004–09, with Moldova, 2005–09, with Afghanistan, 2007–09; Chief EU Observer, Cambodian Elections, 2003; Rapporteur: mobility for students, volunteers, teachers and trainers, 2001; prevention of trafficking in human organs, 2003; certification of seafarers, 2004; access to aircraft for disabled people and passengers of reduced mobility, 2005. Contested (Lab): Berkshire East, 1987; Uxbridge, 1992; Brent E, Sept. 2003; London South and Surrey, European Parly election, 1989. Mem. (Lab), Surrey CC, 2013–. Member: NUT (Pres., Leatherhead Br., 1984–85); GMB; Nat. Exec., Socialist Educnl Assoc., 1989–98; League Against Cruel Sports, 1976– (Hon. EP Consultant, 1997–2009; Vice-Pres.). Trustee: Interact Worldwide, 2003–07; BRAC (UK), 2009–; NGO Shipbreaking Platform, 2013–. Mem. Corp., Coll. of NW London, 2004–15. DUniv Brunel, 1998. *Recreations:* cricket, hockey, swimming, cycling, ski-ing, cinema, psephology, mowing the lawn, theatre, travel, history of education. *E:* rjeevans@globalnet.co.uk, robert.evans@surreycc.gov.uk. *Clubs:* MCC; Ruskin House Labour (Croydon); Ashford Hockey, Ashford Cricket (Middlesex); Middlesex County Cricket, Incogniti Cricket.

*See also A. T. B. Evans.*

**EVANS, Prof. Robert John Weston,** PhD; FBA 1984; Regius Professor of History (formerly Modern History), University of Oxford, 1997–2011; Fellow, Oriel College, Oxford, 1997–2011, now Hon. Fellow; *b* 7 Oct. 1943; *s* of Thomas Frederic and Margery Evans (*née* Weston), Cheltenham; *m* 1969, Kati Róbert; one *s* (one *d* decd). *Educ:* Dean Close School; Jesus College, Cambridge (BA 1st Cl. with distinction 1965, PhD 1968). Oxford University: Fellow, Brasenose Coll., 1968–97, Emeritus Fellow, 2010; Lectr, 1969–90; Reader in Modern History of E Central Europe, 1990–92; Prof. of European History, 1992–97. Mem., Inst. for Advanced Study, Princeton, 1981–82. Fellow: Hungarian Acad. of Scis, 1995; Austrian Acad. of Scis, 1997; Learned Soc. of Czech Republic, 2004; Founding FLSW 2010. Hon. DPhil: Charles Univ., Prague, 2005; Eötvös Loránd Univ., Budapest, 2014; Hon. LittD Cambridge, 2018. František Palacký Medal, Czechoslovakia, 1991; Ehrenkreuz für Wissenschaft und Kunst, Austria, 2009. Jt Editor, English Historical Review, 1985–95. *Publications:* Rudolf II and his World, 1973; The Wechel Presses, 1975; The Making of the Habsburg Monarchy, 1979 (Wolfson Literary Award for History, 1980; Anton Gindely Preis, Austria, 1986); (ed with H. Pogge von Strandmann) The Coming of the First World War, 1988; (ed with T. V. Thomas) Crown, Church and Estates: Central European politics, 1991; (ed with H. Pogge von Strandmann) The Revolutions in Europe, 1848–9, 2000; Austria, Hungary and the Habsburgs: essays on Central Europe c 1683–1867, 2006; (ed with M. Cornwall) Czechoslovakia in a Nationalist and Fascist Europe 1918–48, 2007; (ed with T. Charles-Edwards) Wales and the Wider World, 2010; (ed with G. Marchal) The Uses of the Middle Ages in Modern European States: history, nationhood, and the search for origins, 2011; (ed jtly) The Holy Roman Empire 1495–1806, 2011; (ed jtly) The Holy Roman Empire 1495–1806: a European perspective, 2012; Tales from God's Acre, 2016. *Recreations:* music, walking, natural (and unnatural) history. *Address:* Oriel College, Oxford OX1 4EW; Rowan Cottage, 45 Sunningwell, Abingdon, Oxon OX13 6RD.

**EVANS, Maj.-Gen. Robert Noel,** CB 1981; Postgraduate Dean and Commandant, Royal Army Medical College, 1979–81; *b* 22 Dec. 1922; *s* of William Evans and Norah Moynihan; *m* 1950, Mary Elizabeth O'Brien (*d* 2007); four *s* one *d*. *Educ:* Christian Brothers Sch., Tralee, Co. Kerry; National University of Ireland (MB, BCh, BAO 1947). DTM&H 1961; FFARCS 1963. Commnd RAMC 1951; Consultant Anaesthetist, 1963; CO BMH Rinteln, 1969–71; ADMS 4th Div., 1971–73; DDMS HQ BAOR, 1973–75; Comdt, RAMC Trng Centre, 1975–77; DMS, HQ BAOR, 1977–79; QHP 1976–81. Col Comdt, RAMC, 1981–86. MFCM 1978. OStJ 1978. *Recreations:* gardening, walking, music.

**EVANS, Robin Edward Rowlinson,** FRICS; Chief Executive, Canal and River Trust (formerly British Waterways), 2002–13; *b* 24 March 1954; *s* of Lt Col John and Connie Evans; *m* 1978, Hilary; two *s* one *d*. *Educ:* Reading Univ. (BSc Estate Mgt). FRICS 1990. Land Agent, NT, 1979–87; Dir, Landmark Trust, 1987–95; Palaces Dir, Historic Royal Palaces, 1995–99; Commercial Dir, British Waterways, 1999–2002. Mem. Bd, Valuation Tribunal Service, 2014–18 (Chair, 2018–). Trustee, Volunteer England, 2012–13. Mem. Council, Univ. of Reading, 2009– (Chm., Investments Cttee, 2011–18; Chair, Remuneration Cttee, 2017–; Vice Pres., 2017–). CCMI 2007. *Recreations:* family, walking, tennis. *T:* (01494) 863482.

*See also M. R. R. Evans.*

**EVANS, Hon. Sir Roderick;** *see* Evans, Hon. Sir D. R.

**EVANS, Roger;** *see* Evans, Jeremy R.

**EVANS, Roger Kenneth;** barrister; a Recorder, since 2000; *b* 18 March 1947; *s* of late G. R. Evans and Dr A. M. Evans; *m* 1973, June Rodgers, MA, barrister; two *s*. *Educ:* The Grammar Sch., Bristol; Trinity Hall, Cambridge (MA). President: Cambridge Union, 1970; Cambridge Georgian Gp, 1969; Chm., Cambridge Univ. Conservative Assoc., 1969. Called to the Bar: Middle Temple, 1970 (Astbury Schol.); Inner Temple, *ad eundem*, 1979; in practice, 1970–94, 1997–; an Asst Recorder, 1998–2000. Contested (C): Warley West, Oct. 1974, 1979; Ynys Môn, 1983; Monmouth, May 1991. MP (C) Monmouth, 1992–97; contested (C) same seat, 1997, 2001. Parly Under-Sec. of State, DSS, 1994–97. Member: Welsh Affairs Select Cttee, 1992–94; Ecclesiastical Cttee of Parlt, 1992–97. Chairman: Friends of Friendless Churches, 1998–; Prayer Book Soc., 2001–06 (Vice-Pres., 1995–2001); Mem., Ecclesiastical Law Soc., 1988–. Freeman, City of London, 1976. *Recreations:* architectural and gardening history, building, gardening. *Address:* 2 Harcourt Buildings, Temple, EC4Y 9DB. *E:* revans@harcourtchambers.co.uk. *Clubs:* Carlton, Coningsby (Chm., 1976–77; Treas., 1983–87).

**EVANS, Roger W.;** *see* Warren Evans.

**EVANS, Roy;** *see* Evans, H. R.

**EVANS, Russell Wilmot,** MC 1945; Chairman, Rank Organisation, 1982–83; *b* 4 Nov. 1922; *s* of William Henry Evans and Ethel Williams Wilmot; *m* 1956, Pamela Muriel Hayward (*d* 1989); two *s* one *d*. *Educ:* King Edward's Sch., Birmingham; Birmingham Univ. LLB Hons. Served HM Forces, 1942–47; commnd Durham LI, 1942, Major, 1945. Admitted Solicitor, Birmingham, 1949; Solicitor with Shakespeare & Vernon, Birmingham, 1949–50; Asst Sec., Harry Ferguson, 1951; Sec., Massey-Ferguson (Hldgs) and UK subsids, 1955–62; Dir, gp of private cos in construction industry, 1962–67; joined Rank Organisation, 1967: Dep. Sec., 1967–68; Sec., 1968–72; Dir, 1972–83; Man. Dir, 1975–82; Dep. Chm., 1981; Dir, principal subsid. and associated cos incl. Rank Xerox, 1975–83; Fuji Xerox, 1976–83; Chm., Rank City Wall, 1976–83. Director: Eagle Star Holdings, 1982–87; Oxford Economic Forecasting Ltd, 1986–96; Medical Cyclotron Ltd, 1988–2011. *Recreations:* formerly tennis, golf and photography. *Address:* Walnut Tree, Roehampton Gate, SW15 5JR. *T:* (020) 8876 2433. *Clubs:* English-Speaking Union, Roehampton (Dir 1971–87, Chm., 1984–87, Pres., 1991–).

**EVANS, Ruth Elizabeth;** Chair: Payments Strategy Forum, since 2015; Independent Parliamentary Standards Authority, since 2016; non-executive Director, Serious Fraud Office, since 2015; *b* 12 Oct. 1957; *d* of Peter Evans and Dr Anne Evans; one *d*. *Educ:* Girton Coll., Cambridge (MA Hist.). Dir, Maternity Alliance, 1981–86; Dep. Dir, then Actg Dir, Nat. Assoc. for Mental Health (MIND), 1986–90; Gen. Sec., War On Want, 1990; Mgt Consultant, 1990–91; Dir, Nat. Consumer Council, 1992–98; Chairman: Inquiry into Paediatric Cardiac Services, Royal Brompton and Harefield NHS Trust, 1999–2001; Ind. Inquiry into Drug Testing at Work, 2002–04. Non-executive Director: Financial Ombudsman Service, 1999–2002; Liverpool Victoria Gp, 1999–2002; Nationwide Bldg Soc., 2002–05; PhonePay Plus, 2008; Nat. Audit Office, 2010–12 (Chair, Remuneration Bd, 2010–12); Alacrity Entrepreneurship Foundn, 2011 (Founding Trustee, 2010); Mem. Adv. Bd, ING Direct, UK, 2007–10; Sen. Ind. Dir, CPP Gp plc, 2013–16 (Chair, Remuneration Cttee, 2013–16). Mem., Central R&D Cttee, NHS, 1995–99; Chm., Standing Adv. Gp on Consumer Involvement, NHS R&D Prog., 1995–99; Dep. Chm., Ofcom Consumer Panel, 2002–; Chair, Assoc. of Television on Demand, 2010–15;

Member: Ind. Rev. Panel for advertising of medicines for human use, 1999–2003; Human Genetics Commn, 1999–2002; Medicines Commn, 2002–03; Law Soc. Governance Review Gp, 2003–04. Lay Mem., 1999–2007, and Chm., Standards and Ethics Cttee, 2004–06, GMC. Chm., Bar Standards Bd, 2006–08. Member: UK Round Table on Sustainable Develt, 1995–99; Expert Panel on Sustainable Develt, DETR, 1998–99; Commn on Taxation and Citizenship, Fabian Soc., 1999–2000; BBC Licence Fee Review Panel, DCMS, 1999; Bd, Financial Services Ombudsman Scheme, subseq. Financial Ombudsman Service, 1999–2002; Panel of Ind. Assessors, Office of Comr for Public Appts, 1999–2005; Council, Britain in Europe, 1999–2004; Ind. Complaints Panel, Audit Commn, 2004–06; Queen's Counsel Selection Panel, 2005–08; Customer Impact Panel, ABI, 2006–09; Ind. Police Complaints Commn, 2009– (Chair, Remuneration Bd, 2009–). Trustee, Money Advice Trust, 1994–2000 (Chm., Adv. Gp of UK money advice agencies, 1994–2000). *Recreations:* daughter, writing, music, swimming. *Address:* 24 Falkland Road, NW5 2PX. *T:* (020) 7482 0420, 07973 370677. *E:* ruth@ruthevans.org.

**EVANS, Sally Anne;** Deputy Legal Adviser, Home Office, 1995–2000; *b* 20 March 1948; *d* of late Arthur Francis Gardiner Austin and Joy Austin (*née* Ravenor); *m* 1977, Richard Maurice Evans. *Educ:* High Sch. for Girls, Darlington; Univ. of Manchester (LLB Hons 1970). Called to the Bar, Gray's Inn, 1971; Barclays Bank DCO, then Barclays Bank Internat. Ltd, 1970–72; Western American Bank Ltd, 1972–73; Legal Adviser's Br., Home Office, 1974–2000. Vice Chm., Friends of The Royal Marsden, 2006–08. *Recreations:* theatre, cooking, summer gardening.

**EVANS, Sarah Hauldys,** OBE 2014; educational consultant, since 2013; Principal (formerly Headmistress), King Edward VI High School for Girls, 1996–2013; Acting Principal, Elmhurst School for Dance, 2015–17; *b* 4 March 1953; *d* of Nancy and Wyndham Evans; *m* 1989, Andrew Romanis Fowler; one *s. Educ:* King James' Grammar Sch., Knaresborough; Univ. of Sussex (BA Hons English); Univ. of Leicester (MA Victorian Studies); Univ. of Leeds (PGCE). English Teacher, Leeds Girls' High Sch., 1976–84; Dep. Head, Fulneck Girls' Sch., 1984–89; Head, Friends' Sch., Saffron Walden, 1989–96. *Recreation:* the arts.

**EVANS, Stephen James;** Chief Executive, Learning and Work Institute, since 2016 (Deputy Chief Executive, 2014–16); *b* Leicester, 19 May 1979; *s* of Paul and Christine Evans; *m* 2008, Nicola McCulloch. *Educ:* Queen's Coll., Cambridge (BA Econs); Birkbeck Coll., Univ. of London (MSc Econs). Sen. Policy Advr, HM Treasury, 2001–06; Chief Economist, Social Mkt Foundn, 2006–07; Dir, Employment and Skills, London Develt Agency, 2007–11; Dir, Policy and Strategy, Working Links, 2011–14. *Recreations:* sport, travel, theatre. *Address:* Learning and Work Institute, 21 De Montfort Street, Leicester LE1 7GE. *T:* (0116) 204 2819. *E:* stephen.evans@learningandwork.org.uk.

**EVANS, Stephen Nicholas,** CMG 2002; OBE 1994; HM Diplomatic Service; Senior Directing Staff, Royal College of Defence Studies (on secondment), since 2016; *b* 29 June 1950; *s* of late Vincent Morris Evans and Doris Mary Evans (*née* Braham); *m* 1975, Sharon Ann Holdcroft; one *s* two *d. Educ:* King's Coll., Taunton; Bristol Univ. (BA); Corpus Christi Coll., Cambridge (MPhil). Royal Tank Regt (Lieut), 1971–74; FCO, 1974; language student (Vietnamese), SOAS, 1975; FCO, 1976; First Sec., Hanoi, 1978–80; FCO, 1980–82; language training (Thai), Bangkok, 1982–83; First Sec., Bangkok, 1983–86; FCO, 1986–90; First Sec. (Political), Ankara, 1990; Counsellor (Econ., Commercial, Aid), Islamabad, 1993–96; seconded to UN Special Mission to Afghanistan, 1996–97; Counsellor and Head: OSCE and Council of Europe Dept, FCO, 1997–98; S Asian Dept, FCO, 1998–2002; Chargé d'Affaires, Kabul, 2002; High Comr, Sri Lanka, 2002–06; Ambassador to Afghanistan, 2006–07; Dir, Afghanistan Inf. Strategy, FCO, 2007–08; High Comr, Bangladesh, 2008–11; Asst Sec. Gen. for Ops, NATO, 2011–15 (on secondment). *Recreations:* military and naval history, golf, cycling. *Address:* c/o Foreign and Commonwealth Office, King Charles Street, SW1A 2AH. *Club:* Athenæum.

**EVANS, Steven David; His Honour Judge Steven Evans;** a Circuit Judge, since 2019; *b* Bicester, 23 Nov. 1959; *s* of David Evans and Beryl Evans; *m* 1986, Deborah Jayne Horsley; three *d. Educ:* Sheffield City Poly. (CQSW, DipSW 1985); De Montfort Univ., Leicester (LLB Hons 1996); Inns of Court Sch. of Law (BVC 1997). Probation Officer, 1985–87; Project Manager, Nat. Children's Home, 1987–90; Unit Manager, Northants Diversion Unit, 1990–95; called to the Bar, Middle Temple, 1997; barrister, 1997–2019; a Recorder, 2009–19; a Fee-paid Judge, 2018–19, a Judge, 2019–, First-tier Tribunal, Health, Educn and Social Care Chamber (Restricted Patients Panel). Chair, Police Disciplinary Panels, 2015–19. *Recreations:* adventures to meet a decent midlife crisis (swim run/triathlon), grandchildren. *Address:* c/o Luton Crown Court, 7 George Street, Luton LU1 2AA. *T:* (01582) 522000.

**EVANS, Susan Louise Carr;** QC 2010; **Her Honour Judge Susan Evans;** a Circuit Judge, since 2011; *b* Arbroath, 16 June 1966; *d* of Anthony Evans and Jeanette Carr; *m* 2000, John Pemberton. Called to the Bar, Gray's Inn, 1989; Recorder, 2005–11. *Address:* Winchester Combined Court, High Street, Winchester SO23 9EL. *E:* HHJ.Susan.Evans.QC@ejudiciary.net.

**EVANS, (Thomas) Alun,** CMG 1994; HM Diplomatic Service, retired; *b* 8 June 1937; *s* of late Thomas Evans and Mabel Elizabeth (*née* Griffiths); *m* 1964, Bridget Elisabeth, *d* of late Peter Lloyd, CBE and of Nora Kathleen Williams (*née* Patten); three *s. Educ:* Shrewsbury Sch.; University Coll., Oxford (MA). Army, 1956–58, commd KOYLI. Entered HM Foreign Service, 1961; Third Sec., Rangoon, 1962–64; Second Sec., Singapore, 1964–66; FO, 1966–70; First Sec., Geneva, 1970–74; FCO, 1974–79; Counsellor: Pretoria, 1979–82; FCO, 1983–95. Internat. Risk and Internat. Affairs Advr, British Airways, 1995–2002; Internat. Affairs Advr, Cathay Pacific Airways, 2002–08; Director: Fleming, subseq. J. P. Morgan, Asian Investment Trust, 2001–12; Sigma Internat. Ltd, 2002–04; Advr, Nimbus Trng, 2003–06; Chairman: Lexicon Data Ltd, 2007–; Oceanfoil Ltd, 2012–. Dir, British Iranian and Central Asian Assoc., 2000–01; Vice-Chairman: British Iranian Chamber of Commerce, 2001–16; Thames Concerts, 2008–11. Trustee, Pimpernel Trust, 1997–2005. *Recreations:* France, music, travel. *Clubs:* Travellers, Sloane.

**EVANS, His Honour (Thomas) Michael;** QC 1973; a Circuit Judge, 1979–98; *b* 7 Sept. 1930; *s* of late David Morgan Evans, Barrister, and of Mary Gwynydd Lloyd; *m* 1957, Margaret Valerie Booker; one *s* four *d. Educ:* Brightlands Prep. Sch., Newnham, Glos; Marlborough Coll., Wilts; Jesus Coll., Oxford (MA (Juris.)). Called to the Bar, Gray's Inn, 1954; Wales and Chester Circuit, 1955; a Recorder of the Crown Court, 1972–79. Legal Chm., Mental Health Review Tribunal for Wales, 1970. Chancellor, Diocese of St Davids, 1986–2005; Pres., Provincial Court, Church in Wales, 1997–2007. Gov., Christ Coll., Brecon, 1992–2009 (Chm. of Govs, 1999–2003). *Recreations:* walking, fishing, genealogy. *Address:* 31 Saxon Road, Manor Park, Tavistock, Devon PL19 8JS.

**EVANS, Timothy Hugh David,** LVO 2016; Apothecary to the Queen and to the Royal Households of London, since 2003; Private General Practitioner, since 1990; *b* 3 May 1955; *s* of late David Lawrence Evans and Betty Joan Evans; *m* 2000, Annabel Clare Blake (*d* 2008); one *s* one *d. Educ:* Marlborough Coll.; Westminster Hosp. Med. Sch. (MB BS); MRCS 1979, LRCP 1979; DRCOG 1984; MRCGP 1985; DA 1987. House Officer, Westminster Hosp., 1979–80; SHO, Andrew Fleming Hosp., Harare, 1980–81; Dist MO, Kariba Hosp., Zimbabwe, 1981–83; SHO, Obstetrics, Cheltenham Gen. Hosp., 1984; GP Registrar, Tewkesbury, 1985; SHO, Anaesthetics, Cheltenham Gen. Hosp., 1986; RMO, London Clinic, Portland Hosp. for Women and Children, 1987–89. Med. Dir, Blossom House Sch., 1997; Founder and Med. Dir, Grace Belgravia, 2012–19. Trustee, Mothers2Mothers (UK) Ltd, 2016–. Mem., Chelsea Clinical Soc., 1993–. *Recreations:* golf, tennis, sailing, music, theatre. *Address:* Bazeley House, Bazeley Copse Lane, Micheldever, Hants SO21 3AA. *Club:* Royal Wimbledon Golf.

**EVANS, Lt Gen. Timothy Paul,** CB 2016; CBE 2012 (MBE 2000); DSO 2008; senior adviser, and defence and security consultant, since 2017; *b* Iserlöhn, Germany, 21 Sept. 1962; *s* of Col Peter Benwell Evans and Ray Evans; *m* 1987, Helen Mary O'Reilly; two *d. Educ:* Monkton Combe Jun. Sch.; Monkton Combe Sen. Sch.; Royal Military Acad., Sandhurst. Commnd 1982; Platoon Comdr, 1st Bn LI, then Trng Platoon Comdr, Light Div. Depot, 1984–86; ADC to GOC Wales, 1986–87; Ops Officer, 3rd Bn LI, 1988–89; Troop Comdr, Special Forces, 1990–93; Staff Coll., 1994; Ops Officer, HQ DSF, 1995–96; Co. Comdr, 1st Bn LI, 1997; Sqdn Comdr, Special Forces, 1998–2000; Jt Doctrine and Concept Centre, 2000–01; CO, 1st Bn LI, 2001–02; COS, 3(UK) Div., 2002–05; Bde Comdr, 19 Light Bde, 2006–08; Comdr, Jt Force Ops, PJHQ, 2008–09; COS ISAF Jt Comd HQ, Afghanistan, 2010–11; COS HQ ARRC, 2009–12; Comdt, RMA, 2012–13; Comdr Allied Rapid Reaction Corps, 2013–16. *Recreations:* running, hill walking, water ski-ing, ski-ing, bridge.

**EVANS, Dr Trevor John;** consultant in governance and change management; *b* 14 Feb. 1947; *o s* of late Evan Alban Evans and Margaret Alice Evans (*née* Hilton); *m* 1973, Margaret Elizabeth (*née* Whitham); three *s* one *d. Educ:* King's Sch., Rochester; University Coll., London (BSc (Eng) 1968, PhD 1972; Fellow, 1997; Hon. Fellow, 2010); Univ. of Liverpool (MA Dist. 2013). CEng, FIChemE (Hon. FIChemE 2006). Res. Officer, CSIR, Pretoria, 1968–69; Ford Motor Co., Aveley, Essex, 1972–73; Institution of Chemical Engineers: Asst Sec., Technical, 1973–75; Dep. Sec., 1975–76; Gen. Sec., 1976–94; Chief Exec., 1994–2006; Chief Exec., Ergonomics Soc., 2007; Chief Exec., AATSE, 2007–08. Member: Bd, Council of Science and Technology Institutes, 1976–87; Exec. Cttee, Commonwealth Engineers Council, 1976–2004; Steering Cttee, DTI Action for Engrg Prog., 1995–96, Bd, Science Council, 2001–06; Bd, Engrg Council (UK), 2002–06 (Dep. Chm., 2005–06); Engrg and Technology Bd, 2005–07; Chm. Exec. Cttee, World Chem. Engrg Council, 2006. Vis. Prof., UCL, 2011–14. Jt Hon. Sec., 1976–2006, Hon. Mem., 2008, European Fedn of Chem. Engrg. Mem. Ct, Imperial Coll., London, 1998–2006. FRSA. Hon. Mem., Czech Soc. of Chemical Engrg, 2006. Kurnakov Meml Medal, USSR Acad. of Scis, 1991; Titanium Achema Plaque, 1997. *Publications:* scientific and historical papers and general articles in Chemical Engrg Science, The Chem. Engr, etc. *Recreations:* study of slavery, 18th, 19th century and WW1 history. *Address:* Welsh Row House, 50 Welsh Row, Nantwich, Cheshire CW5 5EJ.

**EVANS, Very Rev. Trevor Owen;** Dean of Bangor, 1998–2003; *b* 10 July 1937; *s* of John James Pierce Evans and Elizabeth Jane Evans; *m* 1962, Ann Christine Stephens; one *s* one *d. Educ:* Dolgellau Boys' Grammar Sch.; UCW, Aberystwyth (BSc); Coll. of the Resurrection, Mirfield. Ordained deacon, 1961, priest, 1962; Diocese of Bangor: Curate, Barmouth, 1961–64; Curate, 1964–70, Vicar, 1970–75, Llandudno; Vicar, Llanidloes, 1975–89; RD, Arwystli, 1976–89; Preb. and Canon of Bangor Cathedral, 1982–98; Rector of Trefdraeth, 1989–99; Dir of Ministry, 1989–98; Rector of Llanfair PG with Penmynydd, 1990–98, also with Llanddaniel-Fab and with Llanedwen, 1997–98; Surrogate, 1978–98. *Recreations:* hill-walking, wood-turning, ornithology, geology, geomorphology. *Address:* Hafan, 3 Coed y Castell, Bangor LL57 1PH.

**EVANS, Maj.-Gen. William Andrew,** CB 1993; DL; Secretary, Council of TAVRAs, 1993–2001; *b* 5 Aug. 1939; *s* of late Maj.-Gen. Roger Evans, CB, MC and Eileen Evans; *m* 1964, Virginia Susan (*d* 2014), *e d* of late William Robert Tomkinson and Helen Mary Tomkinson, MBE; two *d. Educ:* Sherborne; RMA Sandhurst; Christ Church, Oxford (MA). Commnd 5th Royal Inniskilling Dragoon Guards, 1959; served in BAOR, Middle East, Cyprus, Libya, N Ireland; Staff Coll., Bracknell, 1971; Army Instructor, RAF Cranwell, 1974–75; Instructor, Army Staff Coll., 1978–80; CO 5th Royal Inniskilling Dragoon Guards, 1980–82 (despatches, 1981); Col, Asst Dir (Policy), Defence Policy Staff, 1982–83; Comdr 4 Armd Bde, 1983–85; RCDS 1986; DCS, HQ BAOR, 1987–89; GOC Eastern Dist, 1989–92, retired. Pres., Essex, Army Benevolent Fund, 1997–2008; Vice Chm., Royal Dragoon Guards Regtl Assoc., 1992–2002; Member Council: ACFA, 1993–2001; Union Jack Club, 1995–2009. Pres., Army Cricket Assoc., 1989–91; Chm., Combined Services Cricket Assoc., 1990. Trustee, Daws Hall Trust, 2000–08. Mem., Court, Essex Univ., 1994–2009. Liveryman, Broderers' Co., 1992–2014. DL Essex, 1998. *Recreations:* fishing, birdwatching, golf, grandchildren. *Club:* Essex.

**EVANS, Dr (William) David;** Director, Innovation and International, Department for Business, Innovation and Skills (formerly Department for Innovation, Universities and Skills), 2008–09; *b* 20 April 1949; *s* of late Harold Evans and Gladys Evans (*née* Webber); *m* 1980, Elizabeth Crowe; three *s* one *d. Educ:* Haberdashers' Aske's School, Elstree; St Catherine's College, Oxford (BA 1971; DPhil 1974; Senior Scholar). FRAS 1975. Dept of Energy, 1974–80; First Sec., Science and Technology, British Embassy, Bonn, 1980–83; Asst Sec., 1984–89, Chief Scientist, 1989–92, Dept of Energy; Department of Trade and Industry: Hd of Envmt Div., 1992–94; Hd of Technology and Innovation Div., 1994–96; Director: Technol. and Standards, later Technol. and Standards Directorate, 1996–98; Competitiveness, 1998–2001; Dep. Chief Exec., Small Business Service, 2001–03; Dir, Finance and Resource Mgt, 2003–05; Acting Dir Gen., Services Gp, 2005–06; Dir, Technol. and Innovation, DTI, later Dir, Innovation, DIUS, 2006–08. Member: NERC, 1989–92; EPSRC, 1994–98; PPARC, 1994–98; Assessor, SERC, ACORD, 1989–92. Interim Chief Exec., 2007, Sen. Govt Advr, 2009–13, Technol. Strategy Bd. Institution of Engineering and Technology: Chm., Standards Cttee, 2013–; Chm., Knowledge Services Bd, 2014–; Vice Pres. and Trustee, 2014–. Senator, Engrg Council, 1996–98; Hon. Treas., Science Council, 2009–13. Adjunct Prof., Imperial Coll. Business Sch., 2010. *Publications:* scientific papers in professional jls. *Recreations:* music, reading, history of technology.

**EVANS, (William) Lindsay;** DL; freelance lecturer, television actor and presenter; Trustee, National Heritage Memorial Fund, 1992–99; Chairman, Committee for Wales, Heritage Lottery Fund, 1998–99; *b* 22 March 1933; *o s* of John Evans and Nellie (*née* Davies). *Educ:* Swansea GS; Univ. of Wales (BA, MA, DipEd); Jesus Coll., Oxford (MLitt 1961). School teacher, Middlesex CC, 1958–60; freelance newsreader, BBC, 1960–61; Asst Master, Llandovery Coll., 1961–65; Lectr in Drama, Bangor Normal Coll., 1965–67; Prin. Lectr and Hd of Drama Dept, Cartrefle Coll., Wrexham, 1967–91. Lectr, summer schools, Extra-Mural Dept, UCNW, Bangor, 1967–70; Standish Barry Lectr, Irish Georgian Soc., 2005. Member: Exec. Cttee, N Wales Arts Assoc., 1973–76; Welsh Arts Council, 1982–88; Historic Bldgs Council for Wales, 1977–99; Welsh Cttee, NT, 1984–90. Trustee, Patti Theatre Preservation Trust, 2004–. Hon. Fellow, Glyndŵr Univ., 2012. DL Clwyd, 1999. Author of numerous radio and television plays and documentaries in English and Welsh. Exhibn, Open Eyes: the Lindsay Evans Collection, MOMA Machynlleth, 2018.

*Publications:* Y Gelltydd (novel), 1980; The Castles of Wales, 1998; *contributed to:* Everyman's Guide to England & Wales, 2000; Treasures of Britain, 2002; The Twentieth Century Great House, 2002; Art and Industry, 2012; articles on aspects of built envmt. *Recreations:* friends, music, discovering places and buildings. *Address:* 100 Erddig Road, Wrexham LL13 7DR.

**EVANS, Rt Rev. Wyn;** *see* Evans, Rt Rev. J. W.

**EVANS-ANFOM, Emmanuel,** FRCSE 1955; Commissioner for Education and Culture, Ghana, 1978–88; Member, Council of State, 1979; Chairman, National Education Commission, since 1984; *b* 7 Oct. 1919; *m* 1952, Leonora Francetta Evans (*d* 1980); three *s* one *d*; *m* 1984, Elise Henkel. *Educ:* Achimota School; Edinburgh University (MB ChB 1947; DTM&H; Alumnus of the Year Award, 1996). House Surgeon, Dewsbury Infirmary, 1948–49; Medical Officer, Gold Coast Medical Service, 1950–56, Specialist Surgeon, 1956–67; Senior Lecturer, Ghana Medical School, 1966–67; Vice-Chancellor, Univ. of Science and Technology, Kumasi, 1967–74. Mem., WHO Expert Panel on Med. and Paramed. Educn, 1977–; Chairman: Nat. Council for Higher Educn, 1974–78; W African Exams Council, 1991–94; Chairman: Med. and Dental Council; Akrofi-Christaller Centre for Mission Res. and Applied Theology, 1986–; Inter-church and Ecumenical Relations Cttee, Presbyterian Church of Ghana, 1990–. Titular Mem., Internat. Assoc. Surgeons; Past President: Ghana Medical Assoc.; Assoc. of Surgeons of W Africa; FICS. Fellow: Ghana Acad. Arts and Sciences, 1971 (Pres., 1987–91); African Acad. of Scis, 1986. Chm., Ghana Hockey Assoc. Pres., Ghana Boys' Brigade Council, 1987–. Hon. DSc: Salford, 1974; Kwame Nkrumah Univ. of Sci. and Technol., 2003; Hon. DLitt Akrofi-Christaller Inst., 2012. Millennium Excellence Award of Ghana, 2000; Life Achievement Award, Ghana Med. and Dental Council, 2004. Mem., Order of the Star of Ghana, 2006. *Publications:* Aetiology and Management of Intestinal Perforations, Ghana Med. Jl, 1963; Traditional Medicine in Ghana: practice problems and prospects, 1986; To the Thirsty Land: autobiography of a patriot, 2003. *Recreations:* hockey, music, art. *Address:* PO Box M135, Accra, Ghana.

**EVANS-BEVAN, Sir Martyn Evan,** 2nd Bt *cr* 1958; *b* 1 April 1932; *s* of Sir David Martyn Evans-Bevan, 1st Bt, and Eira Winifred, *d* of late Sidney Archibald Lloyd Glanley; *S* father, 1973; *m* 1957, Jennifer Jane Marion, *d* of Robert Hugh Stevens; four *s*. *Educ:* Uppingham. Entered family business of Evan Evans Bevan and Evans Bevan Ltd, 1953. High Sheriff of Breconshire, 1967; Liveryman, Worshipful Co. of Farmers; Freeman, City of London. *Recreations:* shooting, fishing. *Heir: s* David Gawain Evans-Bevan [*b* 16 Sept. 1961; *m* 1987, Philippa, *y d* of Patrick Sweeney; two *s* one *d*]. *Address:* Spring Box, Rue de Creux, Baillot St Ouen, Jersey, CI JE3 2DR. *Club:* Carlton.

**EVANS-FREKE,** family name of **Baron Carbery**.

**EVANS-GORDON, Jane-Anne Mary; Her Honour Judge Evans-Gordon;** a Circuit Judge, since 2014; *b* Northampton; *d* of Dr J. G. O'Hagan and P. J. O'Hagan; *m* 1982, Alastair Kenmure Evans-Gordon; one *s*. *Educ:* Univ. of Reading (LLB 1st Cl. Hons 1991). Called to the Bar, Inner Temple, 1992, Bencher, 2017; in practice as a barrister, New Square Chambers, 1993–2014; Recorder, 2009–14. Guardian, Staffs Hoard, Birmingham Mus. *Publications:* (contrib.) Cohabitation: law and precedents, 1999–; (contrib.) Williams, Mortimer and Sunnucks, Executors, Administrators and Probate, 20th edn, 2013; (contrib.) Theobald on Wills, 18th edn, 2015.

**EVANS-LOMBE, Hon. Sir Edward (Christopher),** Kt 1993; a Judge of the High Court of Justice, Chancery Division, 1993–2008; *b* 10 April 1937; *s* of Vice-Adm. Sir Edward Evans-Lombe, KCB, and Lady Evans-Lombe; *m* 1964, Frances Marilyn MacKenzie, DL; one *s* three *d*. *Educ:* Eton; Trinity Coll., Cambridge (MA). National Service, 1955–57: 2nd Lieut Royal Norfolk Regt. Called to the Bar, Inner Temple, 1963, Bencher, 1985. Standing Counsel to Dept of Trade in Bankruptcy matters, 1971; QC 1978; a Recorder, 1982–93. Chm., Agricultural Land Tribunal, S Eastern Region, 1983–93. *Recreations:* fishing, ornithology, amateur archaeology. *Address:* c/o Royal Courts of Justice, Strand, WC2A 2LL. *Club:* Norfolk (Norwich).

**EVANS-TIPPING, (Sir) David Gwynne,** (5th Bt *cr* 1913, of Oaklands Park, Awre, Co. Gloucester); *b* 25 Nov. 1943; *e s* of Sir Francis Loring Gwynne-Evans, 4th Bt (who assumed name of Evans-Tipping, 1943–58), and his 1st wife, Elisabeth Fforde, *d* of J. Fforde-Tipping; *S* father, 1993, but does not use the title, and his name does not appear on the Official Roll of the Baronetage; *m* 2003, Françoise Lucie Saldes. *Educ:* Trinity Coll., Dublin (BAgrSc). *Heir: b* Christopher Evan Evans-Tipping [*b* 27 Feb. 1946; *m* 1974, Fenella Catherine Morrison; one *s* one *d*].

**EVATT, Hon. Elizabeth Andreas,** AC 1995 (AO 1982); Member: World Bank Administrative Tribunal, 1998–2006; International Commission of Jurists, 2003–18; *b* 11 Nov. 1933; *d* of Clive Raleigh Evatt, QC and Marjorie Hannah (*née* Andreas); *m* 1960, His Honour Robert Joseph Southan (*d* 2015); one *d* (one *s* decd). *Educ:* Sydney Univ. (LLB); Harvard Univ. (LLM). Called to the Bar: NSW, 1955; Inner Temple, 1958. Chief Judge, Family Court of Australia, 1976–88. Dep. Pres., Australian Conciliation and Arbitration Commn, 1973–89; Chairperson, Royal Commn on Human Relationships, 1974–77; Dep. Pres., Australian Ind. Relns Commn, 1989–94; Pres., Australian Law Reform Commission, 1988–93 (Mem., 1993–94). Member: UN Cttee on Elimination of Discrimination against Women, 1984–92 (Chairperson, 1989–91); UN Human Rights Cttee, 1993–2000; Human Rights and Equal Opportunity Commn, Australia, 1995–98; Corrective Services NSW Women's Adv. Council, 2016–. Chancellor, Univ. of Newcastle, 1988–94. Fellow, Aust. Inst. of Internat. Affairs, 2010. Hon. LLD: Sydney, 1985; Macquarie, 1989; Queensland, 1992; Flinders, 1994; Univ. of NSW, 1996; Hon. Dr Newcastle, 1988; Hon. LittD Western Sydney, 2016. *Publications:* Guide to Family Law, 1986, 2nd edn 1991. *Recreation:* music. *Address:* Unit 2003, 184 Forbes Street, Darlinghurst, NSW 2010, Australia.

**EVE,** family name of **Baron Silsoe**.

**EVE, Judith Mary,** CBE 2005 (OBE 1998); DL; Legal Chairman (part-time) for the Appeals Service, since 1984; *b* 13 April 1949; *d* of Edward Steele and Adele Steele (*née* Barnes); *m* 1st, 1971, Richard Eve (marr. diss. 1987); one *s*; 2nd, 1992, John McQuoid (*d* 2013). *Educ:* Queen's Univ. of Belfast (LLB 1971). Called to the Bar, NI, 1973; Queen's University of Belfast: Lectr in Law, 1971–82; Sen. Lectr, 1982–92; Dean, Faculty of Law, 1986–89; Internat. Liaison Officer, 1989–2002. Member: Rent Assessment Panel for NI, 1985–91 and 1994–97; Mental Health Commn for NI, 1986–90; EOC for NI, 1992–98; Bd, Public Appts Service (Ireland), 2011– (Chm., 2014–); Mem., 1993–2006, Chair, 1998–2006, CS Comrs for NI. Non-exec. Dir, N and W Belfast HSS Trust, 1993–2000. Mem., NI Council for Postgrad. Med. and Dental Educn, 2002–04; Mem. and Dep. Chm., NI Med. and Dental Trng Agency, 2004–13. Ind. Assessor, OCPA (NI), 2004–13. Mem., Bd of Visitors, Maghaberry Prison, 1990–92. Dir, Helm Housing (formerly BIH Housing Assoc.), 1984–2012 (Chm., 1985–87). Member, Board: Odyssey Trust Co., 2008–16; Northern Regl Coll. (NI), 2013–; Trustee: Victoria Housing Estates, 2016–; HarmonI (formerly NI Inst. for the Disabled), 2017–; South Ulster Housing Assoc., 2018. DL Belfast, 2016. *Recreation:* travel.

**EVE, Trevor John;** actor, since 1974; producer, since 1997; *b* 1 July 1951; *s* of Stewart Frederick Eve and Elsie (*née* Hamer); *m* 1980, Sharon Maughan; two *s* one *d*. *Educ:* Bromsgrove Sch.; Kingston Sch. of Architecture; Royal Acad. of Dramatic Art (Bancroft Gold Medal). *Theatre* includes: John, Paul, George, Ringo and Bert, 1975, Filumena, 1977, Lyric; A Bit of Rough, Soho Poly, 1977; Children of a Lesser God, Albery (Best Actor, Olivier Awards and Variety Club of GB), 1981; The Genius, Royal Court, 1983; High Society, Victoria Palace, 1986; Man Beast and Virtue, RNT, 1989; A Winter's Tale, Young Vic, 1991; Inadmissible Evidence, RNT, 1993; Uncle Vanya, Albery (Best Actor in Supporting Role, Olivier Awards and British Regl Th. Awards), 1997; *films* include: Dracula, 1979; Scandal, 1989; Aspen Extreme, 1993; The Tribe, Appetite, 1998; Possession, 2002; Troy, 2004; She's Out of My League, 2008; Death of a Farmer, 2014; Bees Make Honey, 2017; *television* includes: Shoestring, 1979–81 (Best TV Actor, Variety Club of GB, 1980); Jamaica Inn, 1983; A Wreath of Roses, 1986; Shadow of the Sun, 1987; A Sense of Guilt, 1988; Parnell and the Englishwoman, 1990; A Doll's House, 1992; Murder in Mind, Black Easter, The Politician's Wife, 1994; Heat of the Sun, 1997; An Evil Streak, 1998; David Copperfield, 1999; Waking the Dead, 2000–10; Lawless, 2004; The Family Man, 2006; Hughie Green, Most Sincerely, 2008; Framed, 2009; Bouquet of Barbed Wire, 2010; Death Comes to Pemberley, 2013; The Interceptor, 2015; Unforgotten, 2015; Strike Back, 2017; A Discovery of Witches, 2018–19; The American Guest, 2019. CEO and Exec. Prod. for Projector Pictures: Alice Through the Looking Glass, 1998; Cinderella, 2000; Twelfth Night, 2003; Kidnap and Ransom (and actor), 2011, 2012. Patron: Childhope Internat., 1998–. Hon. DLitt Newman Univ., Birmingham, 2014. *Publications:* Lomita for Ever (novel), 2019. *Recreations:* tennis, golf, painting, architecture. *E:* film@projector.co.uk. *Clubs:* Chelsea Arts, Hurlingham, Queen's; Wentworth.

**EVENNETT, Rt Hon. Sir David (Anthony),** Kt 2018; PC 2015; MP (C) Bexleyheath and Crayford, since 2005; *b* 3 June 1949; *s* of late Norman Thomas Evennett and Irene Evennett; *m* 1975, Marilyn Anne Smith; two *s*. *Educ:* Buckhurst Hill County High School for Boys; London School of Economics and Political Science (BSc (Econ) Upper Second Hons, MSc (Econ)). School Master, Ilford County High School for Boys, 1972–74; Marine Insurance Broker, Lloyd's, 1974–81; Mem., Lloyd's, 1976–92; Dir, Lloyd's Underwriting Agency, 1982–91; Commercial Liaison Manager, Bexley Coll., 1997–2001; mgt lectr and consultant, 2001–05. Consultant, J & H Marsh and McLennan (UK), then Marsh (UK), Ltd, 1998–2000. Redbridge Borough Councillor, 1974–78. Contested (C) Hackney South and Shoreditch, 1979; MP (C) Erith and Crayford, 1983–97; contested (C) Bexleyheath and Crayford, 1997, 2001. PPS to Minister of State, Dept of Educn, 1992–93, to Sec. of State for Wales, 1993–95, to Minister of State, Home Office, 1995–96, to Sec. of State for Educn and Employment, 1996–97, to Sec. of State for Educn, 2010–12; an Opposition Whip, 2005–09; Shadow Minister for Univs and Skills (formerly Innovation, Univs and Skills), 2009–10; acting Parly Under-Sec. of State, DCMS, 2016; a Lord Comr of HM Treasury (Govt Whip), 2012–18. Member, Select Committee: on Educn, Science and the Arts, 1986–92; for Educn and Skills, 2005; on Selection, 2015–18; on Procedure, 2018–; on European Statutory Instruments, 2018–. *Recreations:* my family, reading, history, music, cinema. *Address:* House of Commons, SW1A 0AA. *Club:* Bexleyheath Conservative.

**EVENS, Rt Rev. Robert John Scott;** Bishop Suffragan of Crediton, 2004–12; an Honorary Assistant Bishop: Diocese of Gloucester, since 2013; Diocese of Bristol, 2013–18; Bishop's Visitor to Cheltenham Network Church, since 2016; *b* 29 May 1947; *s* of Reginald Evens and Sheila (*née* Scott); *m* 1972, Sue Hayes; one *s* one *d*. *Educ:* Maidstone Grammar Sch.; Trinity Coll., Bristol (DipTh); ACIB. Nat. Westminster Bank, 1964–74; ordained deacon, 1977, priest, 1978; Assistant Curate: St Simon's, Southsea, 1977–79; St Mary's, Portchester, 1979–83; Vicar, St John's, Locks Heath, 1983–96; RD of Fareham, 1993–96; Archdeacon of Bath, 1996–2004. *Recreations:* gardening, walking with Sue. *Address:* 30 Highland Road, Charlton Kings, Cheltenham GL53 9LT.

**EVERALL, Prof. Ian Paul,** PhD, DSc; FRCPsych, FRCPath, FRANZCP; Executive Dean, Institute of Psychiatry, Psychology and Neuroscience, King's College London, since 2017; *b* Stafford, 5 Aug. 1961; *s* of Alan Vincent Everall and Shirley Ann Everall; *m* 2008, Philippe Michel Savoy; one *s*. *Educ:* Blessed William Howard High Sch., Stafford; Sch. of Medicine, Univ. of Leicester (BSc Hons Med. Scis 1982, MB ChB Hons 1985); King's Coll. London (PhD 1993); Univ. of Melbourne (DSc 2014). MRCPsych 1989, FRCPsych 2004; FRCPath 2004; FRANZCP 2010. Bethlem Royal and Maudsley Hospitals: SHO and Registrar in Psychiatry, 1986–89; Sen. Registrar in Psychiatry, 1989–93; Institute of Psychiatry, King's College London: MRC Clin. Trng Fellow, 1989–92; MRC Clinician Scientist Fellow, 1992–96; Sen. Lectr in Psychiatry, 1993–99; Prof. of Experimental Neuropathol. and Psychiatry, 1999–2004; Prof. of Psychiatry, UCSD, 2004–09; Cato Prof., and Hd, Dept of Psychiatry, Univ. of Melbourne, 2009–17. Hon. Sen. Lectr, King's Coll. Sch. of Medicine, 1992–99; Hon. Professorial Fellow, Florey Inst. of Neurosci. and Mental Health, Univ. of Melbourne, 2012–17; Hon. Prof., Mental Health Centre, Shantou Univ., 2014–; Adjunct Professorial Fellow, Dept of Electrical and Electronic Engrg, Melbourne Sch. of Engrg, Univ. of Melbourne, 2015–17. Honorary Consultant Psychiatrist: King's Healthcare NHS Trust, 1992–2004; S London and Maudsley NHS Trust, 1992–2004; S London and Maudsley NHS Foundn Trust, 2017– (non-exec. Dir, 2017–). Director: UCSD Outpatient Services, 2004–09; Mental Health Res., NW Mental Health, Royal Melbourne Hosp., Melbourne 2009–17. Non-executive Director: Nat. Ageing Res. Inst., Vic, 2009–17; Phoenix Australia, Nat. Centre for Posttraumatic Mental Health, Vic, 2010–17; Neurosci. Trials Australia, Vic, 2014–17. *Publications:* HIV Associated Dementia: brain pathology, clinical features and treatment, 1999; (jtly) The Postmortem Brain in Psychiatric Research, 2002; (ed jtly) The Neurology of AIDS, 2nd edn 2005 to 3rd edn 2012; 15 chapters in books; over 200 papers in learned jls incl. Lancet, Nature Medicine, Procs of NAS, Molecular Psychiatry, Biol Psychiatry, Archives of Gen. Psychiatry, Psychol Medicine. *Recreations:* concerts, art, reading, gardening. *Address:* Institute of Psychiatry, Psychology and and Neuroscience, King's College London, 16 De Crespigny Park, SE5 8AF. *T:* (020) 7848 0593, *Fax:* (020) 7848 0560. *E:* ian.everall@kcl.ac.uk. *Club:* Reform.

**EVERALL, Mark Andrew;** QC 1994; **His Honour Judge Everall;** a Circuit Judge, since 2006; *b* 30 June 1950; *s* of late John Everall, FRCP and Pamela Everall; *m* 1978, Anne Perkins; two *d*. *Educ:* Ampleforth Coll., York; Lincoln Coll., Oxford (MA). Called to the Bar, Inner Temple, 1975, Bencher, 1998; Asst Recorder, 1993–96; a Recorder, 1996–2006. *Publications:* (ed jtly) Rayden and Jackson on Divorce and Family Matters, 17th edn 1997 to 18th edn 2005; (jtly) International Movement of Children, 2004. *Recreations:* walking, music, architecture. *Address:* 1 Hare Court, Temple, EC4Y 7BE.

**EVERARD, Sir Henry Peter Charles, (Sir Harry),** 5th Bt *cr* 1911, of Randlestown, co. Meath; *b* 6 Aug. 1970; *s* of Sir Robin Charles Everard, 4th Bt and of Ariel Ingrid (*née* Cleasby-Thompson); *S* father, 2010; *m* 2003, Nicola Anne de Poher, *y d* of late Geoffrey de la Poer Wilkinson; two *s* one *d*. *Educ:* Gresham's Sch., Holt; RMA Sandhurst. Late Queen's Royal Lancers. Hd of Ops, Massive Ltd; Proj. Manager, Castlecomer Discovery Park; Estate Manager, Mount Congreve; Rural Recreation Officer. *Heir: s* Benjamin Richard Nugent Everard, *b* 1 Jan. 2005.

**EVERARD, Gen. Sir James (Rupert)**, KCB 2016; CBE 2005 (OBE 2000); Deputy Supreme Allied Commander Europe, 2017–April 2020; *b* Tilton-on-the-Hill, Leics, 23 Sept. 1962; *s* of late Simon Everard and Jo Everard (*née* Holt); *m* 1992, Caroline Mary Simpson; two *s* one *d*. *Educ*: Uppingham Sch.; RMAS. Commnd 17th/21st Lancers, 1982; acsc 1994; COS 4th Armoured Bde, 1994–95; CO Queen's Royal Lancers, 2000–02; DACOS J5(B) PJHQ, 2002–04; HCSC 2005; CDS Liaison Officer to Chm. Jt Chiefs of Staff, 2005; Comdr 20th Armoured Bde, 2006–07; Dir Commitments HQ Land Forces, 2008–09; GOC 3rd (UK) Div., 2009–11; Asst Chief of Gen. Staff, 2011–13; DCDS Mil. Strategy and Ops, 2013–14; Comdr Land Forces, later Field Army, 2014–16. Colonel Commandant: RAC, 2012–17; RAVC, 2012–17; Scottish, Welsh, Irish (formerly POW) Div., 2013–; Hon. Col, FANY, 2014–18. CCMI 2015. Army Champion, LGBT Forum, 2011–16. Chm., Army Cresta, 2013–19; Pres., UK Armed Forces Polo Assoc., 2017–. QCVS 1996 and 2007. Gold Cross of Honour, Bundeswehr (Germany), 2017; Common Security and Defence Policy Medal for Extraordinary Meritorious Service, 2019. *Recreations*: walking, travel, shooting. *Address*: Home Headquarters, Queen's Royal Lancers, Lancer House, Prince William of Gloucester Barracks, Grantham, Lincs NG31 7TJ. *T*: (0115) 957 3195. *E*: james.everard882@hotmail.co.uk. *Clubs*: Cavalry and Guards, Army and Navy.

**EVERARD, John Vivian;** HM Diplomatic Service, retired; Ambassador to the Democratic People's Republic of Korea, 2006–08; independent media commentator, since 2013; *b* 24 Nov. 1956; *s* of William Ralph Everard and Margaret Nora Jennifer Everard (*née* Massey); *m* 1990, Heather Ann Starkey. *Educ*: King's Sch., Chester; King Edward VI Sch., Lichfield; Emmanuel Coll., Cambridge (BA 1978; MA 1986); Peking Univ.: Manchester Business Sch. (MBA 1986); London Film Acad. (Cert. 2013). Joined HM Diplomatic Service, 1979: FCO, 1979–81; Third (later Second) Sec., Peking, 1981–83; Second Sec., Vienna, 1983–84; Manchester Business Sch., 1984–86; Metapraxis Ltd, 1986–87; FCO, 1987–90; First Sec., Santiago, 1990–93; Chargé d'Affaires, Minsk, 1993; Ambassador, Belarus, 1993–95; OSCE Mission to Bosnia and Hercegovina, 1995–96; Dep. Hd, Africa (Equatorial) Dept, FCO, 1996–98; Counsellor (Political, Econ. and Develt), Peking, 1998–2000; Ambassador, Uruguay, 2001–05. Co-Ordinator, UN Panel of Experts on Sanctions on the Democratic People's Republic of Korea, 2011–12. Vis. Fellow, Stanford Univ., 2010–11. Trustee: YHA, 2009–10; London Cycling Campaign, 2009–10. Patron, UK Defence Forum, 2014–. *Publications*: Only Beautiful Please: a British diplomat in North Korea, 2012. *Recreations*: reading, travel, cats, cycling.

**EVERARD, Richard Anthony Spencer**, OBE 2011; DL; Chairman, Everards Brewery Ltd, since 1988 (Director, since 1983); Vice Lord-Lieutenant of Leicestershire, 2003–13; *b* 31 March 1954; *s* of late Maj. Richard Peter Michael Spencer and Bettyne Ione (*née* Everard; formerly Lady Newtown-Butler); name changed to Everard by deed poll, 1971; *m* 1981, Caroline Anne Hill; one *s* one *d*. *Educ*: Eton; RMA Sandhurst. Commnd 1973, Lieut 1975, Royal Horse Guards 1st Dragoons, 1973–77. Pres., Age Concern Leics, 1992–; Trustee, County Air Ambulance, 1999–. Hon. Col, Leics, Northants and Rutland ACF, 2007–. Master, Co. of Brewers, 2004. DL 1997, High Sheriff, 2002–03, Leics. Hon. DLaws Leicester, 2009. *Recreations*: shooting, ski-ing, motorcycling, tennis, golf. *Address*: Everards Brewery Ltd, Castle Acres, Narborough, Leics LE19 1BY. *T*: (0116) 201 4307, *Fax*: (0116) 281 4198. *Clubs*: MCC; Eton Ramblers; Luffenham Heath Golf.

**EVERARD, Timothy John**, CMG 1978; HM Diplomatic Service, retired; Secretary General, Order of St John, 1988–93; *b* 22 Nov. 1929; *s* of late Charles M. Everard and Monica M. Everard (*née* Barford); *m* 1955, Josiane Romano; two *s* two *d*. *Educ*: Uppingham Sch.; Magdalen Coll., Oxford. BA (Mod. Langs). Banking: Barclays Bank DCO, 1952–62, in Egypt, Sudan, Kenya, Zaire. Entered Foreign (later Diplomatic) Service: First Sec., FO, 1962–63; First Sec., Commercial, Bangkok, 1964–66; resigned to take up directorship in Ellis & Everard Ltd, 1966–67. Rejoined Foreign and Commonwealth Office, Oct. 1967: First Sec., FO, 1967–68; Bahrain, 1969–72 (First Sec. and Head of Chancery, HM Political Residency); seconded to Northern Ireland Office, FCO, April–Aug. 1972; Consul-Gen., then Chargé d'Affaires, Hanoi, 1972–73; Economic and Commercial Counsellor, Athens, 1974–78; Commercial Counsellor, Paris, 1978–81; Minister, Lagos, 1981–84; Ambassador to GDR, 1984–88. Trustee, Dresden Trust, 1994–2005. Freeman, City of London, 1991. KStJ 1988. *Address*: 10 The Dene, Sevenoaks, Kent TN13 1PB. *Club*: Reform.

**EVERED, David Charles;** Special Adviser, International Agency for Research on Cancer, World Health Organisation, 2001–03; *b* 21 Jan. 1940; *s* of late Thomas Charles Evered and Enid Christian Evered; *m* 1st, 1964, Anne Elizabeth Massey Lings, (Kit) (*d* 1998), *d* of John Massey Lings, Manchester; one *s* two *d*; 2nd, 2000, Sheila May Pusinelli, *d* of Charles Cecil Lennox Pusinelli and Margaret Chaloner Pusinelli, Thornton-le-Dale, Yorks. *Educ*: Cranleigh Sch., Surrey; Middlesex Hosp. Med. Sch. (BSc 1961, MB 1964, MD 1971). MRCP 1967, FRCP 1978; FRSB (FIBiol 1979). Junior hospital appointments, London and Leeds, 1964–70; First Asst in Medicine, Wellcome Sen. Res. Fellow and Consultant Physician, Univ. of Newcastle upon Tyne and Royal Victoria Infirmary, 1970–78; Dir, Ciba Foundn, 1978–88; Second Sec., MRC, 1988–96. Member: British Library Medical Information Review Panel, 1978–80; Council, St George's Hosp. Med. Sch. 1983–91; Cttee, Assoc. of Med. Res. Charities, 1981–84, 1987–88 (Vice-Chm., 1987–88); COPUS, Royal Soc., 1986–88; Media Resource Service Adv. Cttee, NY, 1986–88; NW Thames RHA, 1988–90; Hammersmith & Queen Charlotte's SHA, 1989–94; Bd, Hammersmith Hosps NHS Trust, 1995–96; Council, Internat. Agency for Res. into Cancer (Lyon), 1988–96; Council, RPMS, 1994–96; Vice-Pres., Science Cttee, Louis Jeantet Fondation de Médecine, 1984–91; Chairman: Anglia & Oxford Res. Ethics Cttee, 1997–99; Nuffield Orthopaedic Centre NHS Trust, 1998–2001. FRSocMed; Scientific Fellow, Zool Soc. of London (Mem. Council, 1985–89). Member: Soc. for Endocrinology; Eur. Thyroid Assoc. (Mem. Exec. Cttee, 1977–81, Sec.-Treas., 1983–89). *Publications*: Diseases of the Thyroid, 1976; (with R. Hall and R. Greene) Atlas of Clinical Endocrinology, 1979, 2nd edn 1990; (with M. O'Connor) Collaboration in Medical Research in Europe, 1981; Beyond the Arch (novel), 2018; numerous papers on medicine, education and science policy. *Recreations*: reading, history, tennis, Real tennis, gardening. *Address*: Dudley House, The Street, Mortimer Common, Berkshire RG7 3RD.

**EVEREST, Anne Christine;** Head, St George's School for Girls, Edinburgh, 2010–16; *b* E Riding of Yorks, 23 Sept. 1956; *d* of Charles Vincent and Bessie Flanagan; *m* 1977, Paul Andrew Everest; two *s* one *d*. *Educ*: Univ. of Hull (BA 1st Cl. Hons; PGCE Classics); Univ. of Aberdeen (PGCE Guidance and Pupil Support). Lectr in Classics (pt-time), Univ. of Hull, 1980–81 and 1988–90; Robert Gordon's College, Aberdeen: teacher of Classics, 1992–2007; Principal Teacher of Guidance (Careers), 2001–02; Deputy Hd, 2002–07; Hd, St Margaret's Sch. for Girls, Aberdeen, 2007–10 (Mem., Gov. Council, 2014–). *Recreations*: reading, walking, writing.

**EVEREST, Prof. Kelvin Douglas**, PhD; FEA; Andrew Cecil Bradley Professor of Modern Literature, 1991–2016, now Emeritus, Director, Academic Affairs for China, 2008–16, and Pro-Vice-Chancellor, 2010–16, University of Liverpool; *b* 9 Sept. 1950; *s* of Les and Catherine Everest; *m* 1971, Faith Mary Rissen; three *d*. *Educ*: Reading Univ. (BA 1972; PhD 1977). Lectr, St David's UC Lampeter, 1975–79; Lectr, then Reader, Leicester Univ., 1979–91; Sen. Pro-Vice-Chancellor, Univ. of Liverpool, 2001–07. Mem., NW Regl Bd, NT, 2006–11. Mem. Bd of Govs, RNCM, 2006–11. An Associate Ed., Oxford DNB, 1997–. Foundn FEA 1999. *Publications*: Coleridge's Secret Ministry, 1979; (ed) Shelley Revalued, 1983; (ed) The Poems of Shelley, vol. 1 1989, vol. 2 2000, vol. 3 2011, vol. 4 2013; English Romantic Poetry, 1990; (ed) Revolution in Writing, 1991; (ed) Bicentenary Essays on Shelley, 1992; (ed with A. Yarrington) Reflections of Revolution, 1993; Keats, 2002; contrib. numerous articles and chapters. *Recreations*: cricket, Liverpool FC, jazz guitar, wildlife, cooking, drinking. *Address*: 37 Christchurch Road, Prenton, Merseyside CH43 5SF. *T*: 07387 074625. *E*: k.d.everest@liverpool.ac.uk.

**EVERETT, Bernard Jonathan**, CVO 1999; HM Diplomatic Service, retired; Chairman, Goddard Consultants CIC, since 2009; *b* 17 Sept. 1943; *s* of late Arnold Edwin Everett and Helene May Everett (*née* Heine); *m* 1970, Maria Olinda, *d* of late Raul Correia de Albuquerque and Maria de Lourdes Gonçalves de Albuquerque; two *s* one *d* (and one *d* decd). *Educ*: King's Coll. Sch., Wimbledon; Lincoln Coll., Oxford (BA 1965). Researcher, Reader's Digest, 1965; entered HM Diplomatic Service, 1966; Third, later Second Sec., Lisbon, 1967; FCO, 1971; Consul, Luanda, 1975; FCO, 1976; Head of Chancery, Lusaka, 1978; Consul (Commercial), Rio de Janeiro, 1980; Asst Head, Information Dept, FCO, 1983; on secondment as Head, Sub-Saharan Africa Br., DTI, 1984; Ambassador to Guatemala, 1987–91; Consul-Gen., Houston, 1991–95; High Comr, Mozambique, 1996–2000; Consul-Gen., São Paulo and Dir of Trade and Investment for Brazil, 2000–03. Member: Public Liaison Cttee, British Thoracic Soc., 2013–16; Governor Policy Bd, NHS Providers, 2014–15. Public Governor, Chesterfield Royal Hospital Foundn Trust, 2007–15. Vice-Chair, Foundn Trust Governors' Assoc., 2011–14. *Recreations*: sport, performing arts, walking, gardening, family history, local issues.

**EVERETT, Charles William Vogt;** *b* 15 Oct. 1949; *s* of Dr Thomas Everett and Ingeborg Everett (*née* Vogt); *m* 1978, Elizabeth Vanessa Ellis; three *s*. *Educ*: Bryanston Sch.; Reading Univ. Admin. trainee, Lord Chancellor's Dept, 1971; Asst Private Sec. to Lord Chancellor, 1974–76; Dept of Transport, 1982–84; Lord Chancellor's Department: Asst Sec., 1984; Under Sec., 1991; Head of Policy and Legal Services Gp, 1991–94; Dir, Resource and Support Services, The Court Service, 1994–99; Home Office, 1999–2006: Director: Fire and Emergency Planning, 1999–2002; Corporate Develt and Services, 2002–06. Chair, Hastings and Rother PCT, 2007–11; Vice-Chair: NHS Sussex, 2011–13; Hastings and Rother CCG, 2013–15. Member: Sussex Probation Bd, 2007–10; Surrey and Sussex Probation Trust Bd, 2010–14. Trustee, St Michael's Hospice, Hastings, 2012–.

**EVERETT, Christopher Harris Doyle**, CBE 1988; MA; Director General and Secretary, Daiwa Anglo-Japanese Foundation, 1990–2000; *b* 20 June 1933; *s* of late Alan Doyle Everett, MBE, MS, FRCS, and Annabel Dorothy Joan Everett (*née* Harris); *m* 1955, Hilary (Billy) Anne (*née* Robertson); two *s* two *d*. *Educ*: Winchester College; New College, Oxford (MA 1st cl. Class. Mods and 1st cl. Lit. Hum.). Nat. Service, 2nd Lieut, Grenadier Guards, 1951–53. HM Diplomatic Service, 1957–70: posts included MECAS, Lebanon, Embassies in Beirut and Washington, and Foreign Office (Personnel Dept and Planning Staff); Headmaster: Worksop Coll., 1970–75; Tonbridge Sch., 1975–89. Chm., 1986, Vice-Chm., 1987, HMC. Pt-time Chm., CSSB, 1972–92; Mem., Extended Interview Bd for Police Service, 1975–2013, for Prison Service, 1998–2011; pt-time assessor, Home Office Promotion and Selection Bds, 2002–13. Trustee: Guild of Aid (formerly for Gentlefolk), 1995– (Chm., Cttee of Mgt, 1995–2007); Professional Classes Aid Council, 1995– (Pres., 2007–; Chm., Exec. Cttee, 2007–); Daiwa Anglo-Japanese Foundation, 2005–13. Non-exec. Dir, The Learning Trust, Hackney, 2007–12. Hon. Liveryman, Skinners' Co., 1993– (Mem., Ct of Assts, 1997–; Master, 2002–03); Chm., Skinners' Co. Sch. for Girls, 2001–10; Chm., Friends of Skinners' Kent Acad., 2011–). JP Worksop, 1971–75, Tonbridge and W Malling, 1976–89. FRSA 1988. Hon. FCP 1988. *Recreations*: family, reading, walking, current affairs. *Address*: Lavender House, 12 Madeira Park, Tunbridge Wells, Kent TN2 5SX. *T*: (01892) 525624. *E*: christopher@twells.freeuk.com.

**EVERETT, Eileen, (Mrs Raymond Everett);** see Diss, E.

**EVERETT, Prof. Martin George**, DPhil; Professor of Social Network Analysis, University of Manchester, since 2009; *b* 25 May 1955; *s* of late Reginald Douglas Walter Everett and Joan Gladys Everett; *m* 1981, Vanessa Ann Kendrick; two *s*. *Educ*: Loughborough Univ. (BSc Maths 1976); Trinity Coll., Oxford (MSc Maths 1977; DPhil 1980). Thames Polytechnic, then University of Greenwich: Lectr, 1980–83; Sen. Lectr, 1983–86; Prin. Lectr, 1986–88; Reader, 1988–89; Prof., 1990–2003; Hd of Computing and Maths, 1991–2003; Campus Provost and Pro Vice-Chancellor, Univ. of Westminster, 2003–07; Vice-Chancellor, UEL, 2007–09. Vis. Hon. Fellow, Dept of Sociol., Univ. of Surrey, 1989–92. Treas., UK Heads of Depts of Mathematical Scis, 1999–2003. Mem., London Higher Bd, 2007–09. Mem. Bd, Internat. Network of Social Network Analysts, 1994–2010 (Pres., 2000–03). FAcSS (AcSS 2004). *Publications*: (jtly) Ucinet for Windows: software for social network analysis, 2002; (jtly) Analyzing Social Networks, 2013; Social Network Analysis for Ego-Nets, 2015; papers on methods for social network analysis. *Recreations*: wine, theatre, Charlton Athletic FC. *Address*: School of Social Sciences, University of Manchester, Oxford Road, Manchester M13 9PL.

**EVERETT, Oliver William**, CVO 1991 (LVO 1980); Librarian, Windsor Castle and Assistant Keeper of The Queen's Archives, 1985–2002, Librarian Emeritus, since 2002; lecturer, since 2005; *b* 28 Feb. 1943; *s* of Charles Everett, DSO, MC and Judy Rothwell; *m* 1965, Theffania Vesey Stoney (separated 2003); two *s* two *d*; partner, 2003, Diana Jervis-Read. *Educ*: Felsted Sch.; Western Reserve Acad., Ohio, USA; Christ's Coll., Cambridge; Fletcher Sch. of Law and Diplomacy, Mass, USA; London Sch. of Econs and Pol Sci. HM Diplomatic Service, 1967–81: First Secretary: New Delhi, 1969–73; Madrid, 1980–81; Asst Private Sec. to HRH The Prince of Wales, 1978–80; Private Sec. to HRH The Princess of Wales, 1981–83. *Recreations*: lecturing, film, baseball. *Address*: Cawdles Barn, Keeres Green, Great Dunmow, Essex CM6 1PQ. *T*: (01245) 231364. *E*: o.everett05@tiscali.co.uk. *Clubs*: Chelsea Arts, Jesters.

**EVERETT, Rupert;** actor; *s* of late Major Anthony Everett and of Sara Everett. *Educ*: Ampleforth Coll.; Central Sch. of Speech and Drama. Trained with Glasgow Citizens' Theatre, 1979–82; *stage* includes: Glasgow Citizens' Theatre: Waste of Time; Don Juan; Heartbreak House; The Vortex, 1988, transf. Garrick, 1989; The Picture of Dorian Gray, 1993; The Milk Train Doesn't Stop Here Anymore, 1994, transf. Lyric, Hammersmith, 1997; Another Country, Greenwich, transf. Queen's, 1982; Mass Appeal, Lyric, Hammersmith; L'importance d'être Constant, Théâtre de Chaillot, Paris, 1996; Some Sunny Day, Hampstead, 1996; Blithe Spirit, Broadway, NY, 2009; Pygmalion, Chichester Festival Th., 2010; Six Actors in Search of a Director, Charing Cross Th., 2012; The Judas Kiss, Hampstead Th., transf. Duke of York's, 2012, revival, BAM Harvey Th. NY, 2016; Amadeus, Chichester Fest. Th., 2014; (also dir.) Uncle Vanya, Th. Royal, Bath, 2019; *films* include: A Shocking Accident, 1982; Another Country, 1984; Dance with a Stranger, 1985; Duet for One, 1986; The Comfort of Strangers, 1990; Inside Monkey Zetterland, 1992; Prêt-à-Porter, 1994; The Madness of King George, 1995; My Best Friend's Wedding, 1997; B Monkey, 1998; An Ideal Husband, Shakespeare in Love, A Midsummer Night's Dream, 1999; The Next Best Thing, 2000; Unconditional Love, The Importance of Being Earnest, 2002; To Kill a King, 2003; Stage Beauty, 2004; Separate Lies, 2005; St Trinian's, 2007; St Trinian's 2: the Legend of Fritton's Gold, 2009; Wild Target, 2010; Hysteria, 2011; A

Royal Night Out, 2015; Miss Peregrine's Home for Peculiar Children, 2016; The Happy Prince (also writer and dir), 2018; *television* includes: The Far Pavilions, 1982; The Musketeers, 2016; 50 Shades of Gay, 2017; Quacks, 2017. *Publications:* Hello Darling, Are You Working?, 1992; The Hairdressers of St Tropez, 1995; Red Carpets and Other Banana Skins (autobiog.), 2006; Vanished Years (autobiog.), 2012. *Address:* c/o Independent Talent Group Ltd, 40 Whitfield Street, W1T 2RH.

**EVERETT, Steven George; His Honour Judge Everett;** a Circuit Judge, since 2007; Resident Judge, Chester Crown Court, since 2019; Honorary Recorder of Chester, since 2019; *b* 21 July 1956; *s* of George and Jean Everett; *m* 1985, Melinda Birch; two *s. Educ:* Newport High Sch.; Lanchester Poly., Coventry (BA Business Law 1978); Coll. of Law, Chester. Admitted as solicitor, 1981; called to the Bar, Gray's Inn, 1989; criminal defence solicitor, 1981–83; prosecuting solicitor, 1983–86; Crown Prosecutor, 1986–89; barrister, Wales and Chester Circuit, 1989–2007; Asst Recorder, 1999–2000, Recorder, 2000–07. Bar Council: Member: Panel, Complaints Adv. Service, 1995–2007; Professional Conduct Cttee, 2005–07. A Panel Chm., Parole Bd, 2010–12. Judicial College: Tutor Judge, 2012–; Course Dir, Serious Sexual Offences Seminar, 2017–. Council of Circuit Judges: Mem. Cttee, 2015–18; Hon. Treas., 2018–. Mem., Adv. Editl Bd, Blackstone's Criminal Practice, 2018–. *Recreations:* circuit training (i.e. keeping fit - not training advocates), campanology, visiting places of interest (especially NT properties), watching most sport (especially following Everton FC, Newport County and Welsh Rugby), eating out with my family, watching decent TV, trying to keep up with the latest films at the cinema (could do better), reading. *Address:* Chester Crown Court, The Castle, Chester, Cheshire CH1 2AU.

**EVERETT, Thomas Henry Kemp;** Deputy Special Commissioner of Income Tax, 2000–03 (Special Commissioner of Income Tax, 1983–2000); *b* 28 Jan. 1932; *s* of late Thomas Kemp Everett and Katharine Ida Everett (*née* Woodward); *m* 1st, 1954, June (*née* Partridge) (*d* 2012); three *s*; 2nd, 2015, Jocelyn Heather Payne (*née* Trease). *Educ:* Queen Elizabeth Hospital, Bristol; Univ. of Bristol (LLB Hons 1957). Solicitor (Hons), admitted 1960; Partner, Meade-King & Co., 1963–83. Clerk to General Commissioners, Bedminster Div., 1965–83. Chairman: Service 9, 1972–75; Bristol Council of Voluntary Service, 1975–80; St Christopher's Young Persons' Residential Trust, 1976–83; Mem., Governing Council, St Christopher's School, Bristol, 1983–89; Gov., Queen Elizabeth Hosp., 1974–92 (Vice-Chm. Govs, 1980–91); Pres., Queen Elizabeth Hosp. Old Boys' Soc., 1990–91. *Recreations:* music, motoring, gardening. *Address:* Aries, 26a Sidcot Lane, Winscombe, Som BS25 1LP. *T:* (01934) 842380.

**EVERHART, Prof. Thomas Eugene,** PhD; President, and Professor of Electrical Engineering and Applied Physics, California Institute of Technology, 1987–97, now President Emeritus and Professor Emeritus; *b* 15 Feb. 1932; *s* of William E. Everhart and Elizabeth A. Everhart (*née* West); *m* 1953, Doris A. Wentz; two *s* two *d. Educ:* Harvard Coll. (AB 1953); Univ. of California (MSc 1955); Clare Coll., Cambridge (PhD 1958). Department of Electrical Engineering and Computer Science, University of California, Berkeley: Asst Prof., 1958–62; Associate Prof., 1962–67; Prof., 1967–78; Dept Chm., 1972–77; Dean, Coll. of Engrg, Cornell Univ., 1979–84; Chancellor, Univ. of Illinois, Urbana-Champaign, 1984–87; Pro-Vice-Chancellor, Cambridge Univ., 1998. Director: General Motors Corp., 1989–2002; Hewlett-Packard Co., 1991–99; Reveo Inc., 1994–2003; Saint Gobain, 1996–2008; Raytheon Co., 1998–2006; Hughes Electronics Corp., 1999–2002; Agilent Technologies, 1999–2002. Trustee: CIT, 1998–; Harvard Bd of Overseers, 1999–2005 (Pres., 2004–05). Mem., NAE (USA), 1978; Foreign Mem., Royal Acad. of Engrg, 1996. Hon. LLD: Ill Wesleyan, 1990; Pepperdine, 1990; Hon. DEng Colo Sch. of Mines, 1990. Centennial Medal, 1984, Founders Medal, 2002, IEEE; Benjamin Garver Lamme Award, 1989, Centennial Medal, 1993, ASEE; Clark Kerr Award, Univ. of Calif., Berkeley, 1992; Okawa Prize, Okawa Foundn, 2002. *Publications:* Microwave Communications, 1968; over 90 articles in jls, book chapters, etc, 1955–96. *Recreations:* hiking, fishing, ski-ing. *Address:* President Emeritus, Mail Code 202–31, California Institute of Technology, Pasadena, CA 91125, USA. *T:* (805) 8797697. *Club:* Athenæum (CIT).

**EVERINGTON, Sir Anthony Herbert, (Sir Sam),** Kt 2015; OBE 1999; general practitioner, Bromley-By-Bow Partnership, since 1989; Chair, NHS Tower Hamlets Clinical Commissioning Group, since 2013; *b* UK, 1957; *s* of Geoffrey Devas Everington and Laila Nissen Everington; one *s* one *d* by Dr Pui-Ling Li; *m* 2014, Linda Aldous; two step *s* one step *d. Educ:* Inns of Court Sch. of Law; Royal Free Sch. of Medicine, Univ. of London (MB BS 1984). MRCGP 1989. Called to the Bar, Gray's Inn, 1978. Mem. Council, BMA, 1989–. Fellow, 2015–, Hon. Prof., 2016–, QMUL. Chair, London Clinical Commissioning Council, 2018–. Trustee, Stanton Guild Hse, 2005–. Gov., Gatehouse Primary Sch., 2012–. *Publications:* contrib. papers to BMJ on discrimination. *Recreations:* Norway (speaks Norwegian), wood carving, sailing. *Address:* Bromley-By-Bow Centre, St Leonards Street, E3 3BT. *T:* (020) 8709 9700. *E:* sam.everington@me.com.

**EVERITT, Anthony Michael;** writer; Secretary-General, Arts Council of Great Britain, 1990–94 (Deputy Secretary-General, 1985–90); *b* 31 Jan. 1940; *s* of late Michael Anthony Hamill Everitt and Simone Dolores Cathérine (*née* Vergriette; she *m* 2nd, John Brunel Cohen). *Educ:* Cheltenham Coll.; Corpus Christi Coll., Cambridge (BA Hons English, 1962). Lectured variously at National Univ. of Iran, Teheran, SE London Coll. of Further Educn, Birmingham Coll. of Art, and Trent Polytechnic, 1963–72; The Birmingham Post: Art Critic, 1970–75; Drama Critic, 1974–79; Features Editor, 1976–79; Director: Midland Gp Arts Centre, Nottingham, 1979–80; E Midlands Arts Assoc., 1980–85. Vis. Prof., Performing and Visual Arts, Nottingham Trent Univ., 1996–2010. Lead Reviewer, HK Arts Develt Council, 1998; Reviewer of Arts Councils: of NI, 2000; of Wales, 2001; of Ireland, 2001; of I of M, 2005. Chairman: Ikon Gall., Birmingham, 1976–79; Birmingham Arts Lab., 1977–79; Vice-Chm., Council of Regional Arts Assocs, 1984–85; Member: Drama Panel, 1974–78, and Regional Cttee, 1979–80, Arts Council of GB; Cttee for Arts and Humanities, 1986–87, Performing Arts Cttee, 1987–92, CNAA; General Adv. Council, IBA, 1987–90. Gov., Liverpool Inst. of Performing Arts, 2006–11 (Companion, 2003). Hon. Fellow, Dartington Coll. of Arts, 1995. *Publications:* Abstract Expressionism, 1974; In from the Margins, 1996; Joining In, 1997; The Governance of Culture, 1997; The Creative Imperative, 2000; Cicero: a turbulent life, 2001; New Voices, 2003; New Voices: an update, 2004; The First Emperor, Caesar Augustus and the Triumph of Rome, 2006; Hadrian, 2009; Rise of Rome, 2012; SPQR: a Roman miscellany, 2014; The Rise of Athens, 2016; Alexander the Great, 2019; contribs to The Independent, The Guardian, Financial Times, Studio Internat., Country Life, etc. *Address:* Westerlies, Anchor Hill, Wivenhoe, Essex CO7 9BL.

**EVERITT, Prof. Barry John,** PhD, ScD; FRS 2007; FMedSci; Master, Downing College, Cambridge, 2003–13 (Fellow, 1976–2003; Hon. Fellow, 2013); Professor of Behavioural Neuroscience, Department of Psychology, University of Cambridge, 1997–2013, now Emeritus Professor and Director of Research; Provost, Gates Cambridge Trust, since 2013; *b* 19 Feb. 1946; *s* of Frederick John Everitt and Winifred Doris Everitt; *m* 1st, 1966, Valerie Sowter (marr. diss. 1978); one *s*; 2nd, 1979, Dr Jane Carolyn Sterling; one *d. Educ:* Univ. of Hull (BSc Zool. 1967); Univ. of Birmingham (PhD 1970); MA, ScD 2004, Cantab. MRC Res. Fellow, Univ. of Birmingham Med. Sch., 1970–73; MRC Travelling Res. Fellow, Karolinska Inst., Sweden, 1973–74; Department of Anatomy, University of Cambridge: Demonstrator, 1974–79; Lectr, 1979–91; Reader in Neurosci., 1991–97; Dir of Studies in Medicine, Downing Coll., Cambridge, 1978–98. Ciba-Geigy Sen. Res. Fellow, Karolinska Inst., 1982–83; Vis. Prof., Univ. of Calif, San Francisco, 2000; Sterling Vis. Prof., Univ. of Albany, NY, 2005; Internat. Dist. Scientist, Riken Inst., Tokyo, 2006; Lectures: EBBS Review, Madrid, 1993; Maudsley Bequest, 1997; Grass, Texas, 1997; Swammerdam, Amsterdam, 1999; Swedish Neurosci. Review, 1999; Hillarp, Miami, 1999; Soc. for Neurosci., Orlando, 2002; NIH Dir's, Washington, 2004; Internat. Narcotics, Kyoto, 2004; Spanish Psychobiol. Soc., 2004; Marazzo, Univ. of Portland, Oregon, 2005; Dalbir Bindra, McGill, Canada, 2006; Grass Internat., UCLA, 2006; Johns Hopkins Univ., 2007; BMI Lausanne, 2007; Wallenberg, Stockholm, 2007; Elsevier, EBBS, Trieste, 2008; Internat. Basal Ganglia Soc., Amsterdam, 2008; President's, Fedn of Eur. Neurosci. Socs, 2008; Stephan von Apáthy, Hungarian Acad. of Sci., 2009; Nat. Inst. on Drug Abuse, Baltimore, 2009; Karolinska Res., Stockholm, 2009; John P. Flynn Meml, Yale Univ., 2010; Bryan Kolb, Univ. of Calgary, 2011; French Neurosci. Soc., 2013; Fondation Fyssen, Waterloo, 2017; MIT Picower Inst., 2017; Plenary, British Neurosci. Assoc. Fest. of Neurosci., 2019. Editor-in-Chief: Physiol. and Behavior, 1994–99; European Jl Neurosci., 1997–2008; Reviewing Ed., Science, 2003–; Mem. Editl Bd, Philos. Trans of Royal Soc. B, 2014–. Scientific Counsellor, Nat. Inst. on Drug Abuse, USA, 2002–06. Chairman: MRC Res. Studentships and Trng Awards Panel, 1995–97; Human Sci. Frontier Prog. Fellowships Cttee, 1994–96; Scientific Adv. Bd, Astra Arcus, Sweden, 1998–2001, Astra-Zeneca, 2001–04; Neurogenetics and Behavior Center, Johns Hopkins Univ., 2002–10; Ecole des Neurosciences de Paris, 2008–13; Prog. Cttee, Soc. for Neurosci., 2011–13 (Mem., 2005–08); Member: Helsinki Neurosci. Centre, 2000–10; MRC Neurosci. and Mental Health Bd, 2001–05; Cttee on Cttees, Soc. for Neurosci., 2010–12; DrugScience (formerly Ind. Sci. Cttee on Drugs), 2010–; Video Standards Council Appeals Cttee, 2012–. Member, Scientific Advisory Board: Brain-Mind Inst., Lausanne, 2008–20; Centre for Research on Sex Differences, Univ. of Michigan, 2011–14; Portland Alcohol Research Center, Univ. of Portland, Oregon, 2012–15; Wellcome Trust Centre for Neuroimaging, UCL, 2012–16; Inst. of Experimental Medicine, Hungarian Acad. of Scis, 2013–20; Chair, Scientific Adv. Bd, Sainsbury-Wellcome Centre on Neural Circuits, UCL, 2018–20. President: Brit. Assoc. Psychopharmacology, 1992–94; Eur. Brain and Behaviour Soc., 1998–2000; Eur. Behavioural Pharmacology Soc., 2003–05; Fedn of Eur. Neurosci. Socs, 2016–18; Soc. for Neurosci., 2019–Oct. 2020. Mem., EMBO, 2014–. Fellow, Amer. Coll. of Neuropsychopharmacology, 1999 (Mem. Council, 2013–16); FMedSci 2008. Highly Cited Neurosci. Researcher, Inst. Scientific Information, 2002–. Hon. DSc: Hull, 2009; Birmingham, 2010; Hon. MD Karolinska Inst., Stockholm, 2015. Dist. Sci. Contribn Award, Amer. Psychol Assoc., 2011; Dist. Achievement Award, Eur. Behavioural Pharmacol. Soc., 2011; Fed. of Eur. Neurosci. Socs-Eur. Jl of Neurosci. Award, 2012; Lifetime Achievement Award, British Assoc. of Psychopharmacol., 2012; Fondation Ipsen Neuronal Plasticity Prize, 2014. *Publications:* Essential Reproduction, 1980, 5th edn 1999; over 450 papers in scientific jls. *Recreations:* opera, wine (Mem., 1995–, Sec., 2018–, Saintsbury Club), cricket. *Address:* Downing College, Cambridge CB2 1DQ.

**EVERITT, Father (Charles) Gabriel,** OSB; Master of Studies, since 2015, Prior Administrator and Acting Superior, since 2018, Ampleforth Abbey; *b* 7 Jan. 1956; *s* of Prof. William Norrie Everitt and Katharine Elisabeth Everitt (*née* Gibson). *Educ:* Dundee High Sch.; Edinburgh Univ. (MA History 1978); Balliol Coll., Oxford (MA Theol. 1985; DPhil History 1986); St Stephen's House, Oxford. Asst Curate, St Aidan and St Columba, Hartlepool, 1986–89; recd into RC Church, 1989; entered Ampleforth Abbey, 1990, professed, 1991; ordained priest, 1994; Ampleforth College: Asst Master, 1992–97, Head, 1997–2003, Dept of Christian Theol.; Housemaster: St Aidan's, 1997–98; St Oswald's, 1998–2003; Third Master, 2000–03; Headmaster, 2004–14. Dir, Centre for Benedictine Educn, 2014–18. Librarian, St Benet's Hall, Oxford, 2015–18. *Recreations:* reading, cinema. *Address:* Ampleforth Abbey, York YO62 4EN.

**EVERITT, Rev. Canon Michael John;** Canon Pastor, Durham Cathedral, since 2019; *b* Banbury, 26 Aug. 1968; *s* of Raymond Edward Everitt and Edna Dorothy Everitt (*née* Scotford); *m* 1992, Ruth Anne, *d* of Rev. Canon Rex Anthony Chapman, *qv*; one *s* one *d. Educ:* Warriner Sch., Bloxham; Banbury Sch.; King's Coll., London (BD Hons 1990; AKC 1990); Queen's Coll., Birmingham (DipTh 1992); Venerable English Coll., Rome. Office clerk, Zoffany Ltd, 1988–90; lay worker, St Paul's, Covent Garden, 1988–90; ordained deacon, 1992, priest, 1993; Asst Curate, St Andrew's, Cleveleys, 1992–95; Succentor, 1995, Precentor, 1996–98, Bloemfontein Cathedral; Anglican Chaplain, Nat. Hosp., Bloemfontein, 1995–98; Anglican Chaplain and Asst Lectr, Univ. of Orange Free State, 1996–98; Sen. Coll. Chaplain, St Martin's Coll., Lancaster, 1998–2002; Asst Dir Ordinands, Blackburn dio., 2000–02; Rector, Standish, 2002–11; Priest in Charge, Appley Bridge, 2006–10; Area Dean, Chorley, 2004–11; Hon. Canon, Blackburn, 2010–11; Archdeacon of Lancaster, 2011–19; Interim Vicar, St John's Minster, Preston and St George the Martyr, 2018–19. Member: Blackburn Diocesan Synod, 1994–95, 2002–19; Bloemfontein Diocesan Synod, 1995–98; Bishop's Panel, 1999–2010; Gen. Synod, 2013–19; Church Bldg Council, 2014–. Chm., Lancaster City Council of Churches, 1999–2001; Bishops' Advr, Ministry Div., C of E, 2013–. Mem., Panel, Blackburn Diocesan Adoption Agency, 2003–07; Dir, Blackburn Diocesan Bd of Finance, 2011–19, of Educn, 2013–19 (Chm., 2014–19). Tutor, Carlisle and Blackburn Diocesan Trng Inst., 2002–10. Mem., Cidari Multi Acad. Trust, 2013–19 (Dir and Chm., 2016–19). Governor: St Wilfrid's C of E Prim. Sch., Standish, 2002–11 (Vice Chm., 2006–07, 2011–; Chm., 2006–07); Standish Community High Sch., 2002–11; All Saints Appley Bridge Prim. Sch., 2006–10; St Aidan's C of E Technol. Coll., Preesall, 2011–13; St Hilda's C of E Primary Sch., Carleton, 2012–14 (Chm., 2012–14). President: Standish Arts Fest., 2002–11; St Wilfrid's Bowling Club, 2002–11. *Publications:* (contrib.) The Bible Uncovered, 1993. *Recreations:* drawing, watercolour painting, photography, travel. *Address:* 15 The College, Durham DH1 3EQ. *T:* 07715 490144. *E:* everitts@hotmail.co.uk. *Club:* Nikaean.

**EVERITT, Richard Leslie,** CBE 2014; Chief Executive, Port of London Authority, 2004–14; *b* 22 Dec. 1948. Admitted solicitor; five yrs in private practice; joined legal dept, BAA, 1978, Head of Legal, 1984–90; Dir, Planning and Regulatory Affairs, 1990; Chief Exec., NATS Ltd, 2001–04. Non-exec. Dir, Air Partner plc, 2004–17 (Chm., 2012–17).

**EVERITT, William Howard,** FREng; FIMechE, FIET; Group Managing Director, Technology, T & N plc, 1995–96; *b* 27 Feb. 1940; *s* of H. G. H. Everitt and J. S. Everitt; *m* Antha Cecilia; two *s. Educ:* Leeds Univ. (BSc). Director of Operations, IBM Europe, 1974; Managing Director: Wellworthy, AE, 1975–76; Bearings, AE, 1977–79; AE plc, 1983–86 (Dir, 1978); Dir, T & N plc, 1987–96; Man. Dir, Automotive, T & N, 1990–93. Non-exec. Dir, Domino Printing Services plc, 1997–2008. FREng (FEng 1988). *Recreation:* golf. *Address:* Horley House, Hornton Lane, Horley, near Banbury, Oxon OX15 6BL. *T:* (01295) 730603.

**EVERITT-MATTHIAS, David Richard;** Co-proprietor and chef, Le Champignon Sauvage, Cheltenham, since 1987; *b* 29 Oct. 1960; *m* 1985, Helen. *Educ:* Sir Walter St John's Grammar Sch., London; Ealing Coll. of Higher Educn (C&G). Chef, Inn on the Park, London, 1978–83; Head Chef: Grand Café, 1983–85; Steamer's Fish Restaurant, 1985–86; Fingal's Restaurant, Putney, 1986–87. Member: Acad. Culinaire de France; Sir Walter St John's Old Boys' Assoc. Hon. PhD Glos, 2009. Awards include: Acorn Award,

Midland Chef of Year, 1995, 1996; Egon Ronay Dessert Chef of Year, 1996; Nat. Chef of Year, Craft Guild of Chefs, 1996, 1997; Chef of Year: Cotswold Life, 2005; Catey Awards, 2007; Good Food Guide, 2014; Observer Outstanding Contribn Award, 2013. Restaurant awards: Michelin Star, 1995–99, 2 Michelin Stars, 2000–; 4 Rosettes, AA Guide, 1997–; 2 Egon Ronay Stars, 2005; Restaurant of Year, Good Food Guide, 2005. *Publications*: Essence: recipes from Le Champignon Sauvage, 2006; Dessert: dessert recipes from Le Champignon Sauvage, 2009; Beyond Essence, 2013. *Recreations*: cricket, squash, art, jazz, reading. *Address*: Le Champignon Sauvage, Suffolk Road, Cheltenham, Glos GL50 2AQ.

**EVERSHED, Prof. Richard Peter,** PhD; FRS 2010; Professor of Biogeochemistry and Director, Biogeochemistry Research Centre, University of Bristol, since 2000; *b* 25 July 1956. *Educ*: Trent Poly., Nottingham (BSc Applied Chem. 1978); Univ. of Keele (PhD 1982). FRSC 2011. Postdoctoral res., Sch. of Chem., Univ. of Bristol, 1981–84; Dept of Biochem., Univ. of Liverpool, 1984–93; Lectr, 1993–96, Reader, 1996–2000, Sch. of Chem., Univ. of Bristol. Dir, Bristol node, NERC Life Scis Mass Spectrometry Facility; Mem., NERC Peer Review Coll. Theophilus Redwood Lect., Analytical Div., RSC, 2002; Elliott Lect., Rothamsted Res., 2007. Interdisciplinary Award, RSC, 2003; Royal Soc. Wolfson Res. Merit Award, 2009–14; Aston Medal, British Mass Spectrometry Soc., 2010; Robert Boyle Prize, RSC, 2016. *Publications*: (with N. Temple) Sorting the Beef from the Bull: the science of food fraud forensics, 2016; *c* 400 pubns incl. *c* 300 in peer-reviewed jls, with *c* 20 papers in Nature, Science and PNAS. *Address*: Organic Geochemistry Unit, School of Chemistry, University of Bristol, Cantock's Close, Bristol BS8 1TS. *T*: (0117) 928 7671, *Fax*: (0117) 925 1295. *E*: r.p.evershed@bristol.ac.uk.

**EVERSON, John Andrew;** *b* 26 Oct. 1933; *s* of Harold Leslie Everson and Florence Jane Stone; *m* 1961, Gilda Ramsden; two *s. Educ*: Tiffin Boys' Sch., Kingston-upon-Thames; Christ's Coll., Cambridge (MA); King's Coll., London (PGCE). Teacher: Haberdashers' Aske's Sch., Elstree, 1958–65; City of London Sch., 1965–68; Schools Inspectorate, DES, later Dept for Educn, 1968–92; Chief Inspector for Secondary Educn, 1981–89; seconded to Peat Marwick McLintock, 1989; Chief Inspector for Teacher Training, 1990–92. *Publications*: (with B. P. FitzGerald) Settlement Patterns, 1968; (with B. P. FitzGerald) Inside the City, 1972. *Recreations*: opera, walking, theatre, chess. *Address*: 74 Longdown Lane North, Epsom, Surrey KT17 3JF. *T*: (01372) 721556. *Club*: Athenæum.

**EVERSON, Simon John;** Headmaster, Merchant Taylors' School, Northwood, since 2013; *b* 31 Oct. 1965; *s* of John and Gilda Everson; *m* 2001, Virginia Murphy. *Educ*: St Alphege Jun. Sch.; Solihull Sch.; Fitzwilliam Coll., Cambridge (BA 1987; PGCE 1990; MA 2004); Nottingham Univ. (MA 1999). NPQH 2006. English teacher: Bretton Woods Community Coll., 1990–92 and 1993–94; Myokokogen Jun. High Sch., Japan, 1992–93; Nottingham High Sch. for Boys, 1994–99; Hd of English, Arnold Sch., 1999–2003; Dep. Headmaster, Westcliff High Sch. for Boys, 2003–06; Headmaster, The Skinners' Sch., Tunbridge Wells, 2006–13. Chm., Grammar Sch. Heads Assoc., 2010. *Recreations*: reading, music, philosophy, wine, prehistory. *Address*: Merchant Taylors' School, Sandy Lodge, Moor Park, Middx HA6 2HT.

**EVERT, Christine Marie;** American tennis player, retired 1989; founder, Chris Evert Charities Inc., 1989; *b* 21 Dec. 1954; *d* of late James and of Colette Evert; *m* 1st, 1979, John Lloyd (marr. diss. 1987); 2nd, 1988, Andy Mill (marr. diss.); three *s*; 3rd, 2008, Gregory John Norman, *qv* (marr. diss. 2009). *Educ*: St Thomas Aquinas High Sch., Fort Lauderdale. Amateur tennis player, 1970–72, professional player, 1972–89. Semi-finalist in US Open at age of 16; won numerous titles, including: Wimbledon: 1974, 1976, 1981 (doubles, 1976); French Open: 1974–75, 1979–80, 1983, 1985–86; US Open: 1975–78, 1980, 1982; Australian Open: 1982, 1984. Represented USA in Wightman Cup, 1971–73, 1975–82, and in Federation Cup, 1977–82. Pres., Women's Tennis Assoc., 1982–91. *Address*: 7200 West Camino Real, Suite 310, Boca Raton, FL 33433, USA.

**EVERY, Sir Henry (John Michael),** 13th Bt *cr* 1641, of Egginton, Derbyshire; FCA; DL; Chairman of Governors, Repton School, since 2012 (Governor, since 2003); Chairman, Tala PR, 2010–13; *b* 6 April 1947; *s* of Sir John Simon Every, 12th Bt and Janet Marion, *d* of John Page; *S* father, 1988; *m* 1974, Susan Mary, *er d* of Kenneth Beaton, JP, Eastshotte, Hartford, Cambs; three *s. Educ*: Malvern College. Qualified as Chartered Accountant, 1970; worked in South Africa, 1970–74; Partner, Josolyne Layton-Bennett, Birmingham, 1979–81; merged with BDO Binder Hamlyn, 1982, then with Touche Ross, 1994, to form Deloitte & Touche; retired as Partner, 2001. Chairman: Burton Hosps NHS Trust, 2003–04; Derby Cathedral Council, 2003–12. Pres., Birmingham and West Midlands Dist Soc. of Chartered Accountants, 1995–96 (Chm., Dist Trng Bd, 1991–93). Mem., Egginton Parish Council, 1987–2006 and 2012–. Mem. Cttee, Lunar Soc., 1993–2003. Trustee: Egginton Meml Hall, 1986– (Chm., 2015–); Repton Foundn, 2002–04, 2006–; Consultant to Nat. Meml Arboretum, 2003–13 (Trustee, 1996–2003); Chm., Derbys Crimebeat, 2009–13; Patron: Derbys Children's Holiday Centre, 2012–; Children and Families of the Far East Prisoners of War, 2015–. Mem., Adv. Panel, McCarthy & Stone, 2012–15. FRSA 1996. DL, 2006, High Sheriff, 2009–10, Derbys. *Recreations*: travel, National Trust, gardening; supporter of Nottingham Forest FC. *Heir*: *s* Edward James Henry Every [*b* 3 July 1975; *m* 2007, Sosennah Mary, *e d* of David Siviter; one *s* one *d*]. *Address*: Cothay, Egginton, Derby DE65 6HJ.

**EVES, David Charles Thomas,** CB 1993; Deputy Director General, 1989–2002 and HM Chief Inspector of Factories, 1985–88 and 1992–2002, Health and Safety Executive; *b* 10 Jan. 1942; *s* of Harold Thomas Eves and Violet Eves (*née* Edwards); *m* 1964, Valerie Ann Carter; one *d. Educ*: King's Sch., Rochester; University Coll., Durham (BA Hons). Teacher, Kent CC, 1963–64; HM Inspector of Factories, Min. of Labour, 1964–74; Health and Safety Executive, 1974–2002: Under Sec., 1985–89, Dep. Sec., and Dep. Dir Gen., 1989–2002; Dir, Resources and Planning Div., 1988–89. Associate Dir, Sancroft Internat. Ltd, 2002–09. International Association of Labour Inspection: Vice Pres., 1993–99; Sec. Gen., 1996–99; Technical Advr, 1999–2005; Ambassador, Nat. Exam. Bd for Occupational Safety and Health, 2006–. Ext. Examiner, Sch. of Law, Univ. of Warwick, 2007–12. Hon. Vice Pres., Safety Gps UK (formerly Nat. Health and Safety Gps Council), 2004–12. FIOSH (Hon. Vice Pres., 1992–). Hon. Fellow, IIRSM, 2009. *Publications*: (jtly) Questioning Performance: the Director's essential guide to health, safety and the environment, 2005; Disasters: learning the lessons for a safer world, 2010; Two Steps Forward, One Step Back: a brief history of health and safety law in the United Kingdom, 2014. *Recreations*: music, reading, painting, gardening, wood turner.

**EVES, Ernest (Larry);** Founder and Chairman, Justin Eves Foundation, since 2005; *b* Windsor, Ont, 17 June 1946; *s* of Harry Eves and Julie Eves (*née* Hawrylechko); *m* one *d* (one *s* decd). *Educ*: Vincent Massey High Sch.; Univ. of Toronto; Osgoode Law Sch. (LLB 1970). Called to the Bar, Ont, 1972; QC (Ont) 1983. MPP (PC) Parry Sound, 1981–99, Parry Sound-Muskoka, 1999–2001, Dufferin-Peel-Wellington-Grey, Ontario, 2002–05. Government of Ontario: Parly Asst to Minister of Educn and Minister of Colls and Univs, 1983; Minister: of Skills Develt, 1985; of Resource Develt and Provincial Sec. for Resources, 1985; of Community and Social Services, 1985; PC Party Chief Whip, 1985–90, House Leader, 1990; Govt House Leader, 1995–96; Dep. Premier and Minister of Finance, 1995–2001; Vice-Chm., Policy and Priorities Bd, and Mgt Bd, Cabinet, 1995–2000; Premier of Ontario, Pres. of the Council, and Minister of Intergovtl Affairs, 2002–03; Leader of Opposition, 2003–04. Leader, PC Party, Ont, 2002–04. Partner, Green and Eves, 1972–81; Vice Chm. and Sen. Advr, Credit Suisse First Boston (Toronto), 2000–02; Lawyer, Borden, Ladner, Gervaise LLP, 2001–02. Chairman: Jacob Securities Inc., 2007; Gilla Inc., 2012–; Gravitas Financial Inc., 2013–; PACE Securities Corp., 2014–; Timeless Herbal Care, 2015–; Director: Medifocus, 2011–; Canada Lithium Corp., 2013–; Nighthawk Gold Corp., 2013–; RB Energy, 2013–14. Chm., Ont Olympic Sports and Waterfront Develt Agency, 2000–01; Chm. and Special Advr, Ontario Trade and Investment Adv. Council, 2006–; Dir, CB Richard Ellis Ltd (Canada), 2009–.

**EVISON, Raymond John,** OBE 2000; VMH 1995; FLS, FCIHort; nurseryman and breeder, horticultural exhibitor and judge, lecturer, author and photographer; Founder and Chairman: Guernsey Clematis Nursery Ltd, since 1984; Raymond J. Evison Ltd, since 1997; *b* Shrewsbury, 9 March 1944; *s* of Eric John William Evison and Edith Annie Evison (*née* Trow); three *d. Educ*: Diddlebury and Burford Primary Schs; Ludlow Secondary Mod. Sch. Man. Dir and Jun. Partner, Treasures of Tenbury Ltd, 1969–87. Chm., Mont Rose of Guernsey Ltd, 2008–16. Exhibitor at RHS Shows, incl. Chelsea Flower Show (numerous Gold medals, 6 Williams Meml Medals, 2 Lawrence Medals). Judge: garden exhibits, Chelsea Flower Show, 1985–2013; leading flower shows in USA, 1994–. Garden Designer, Internat. Expo, Beijing, 2019. Lectured in UK, Europe, USA, Canada, China, Japan and NZ. Designer of stamps: Guernsey postage stamps, 2004; Wild Flora Guernsey stamps, issue 1, 2008, issue 2, 2009. Royal Horticultural Society: Mem. Council, 1985–96; Chm., Shows Cttee, 1988–95; Vice Pres., 2005–; Trustee and Mem. Council, 2007–12; Chm., Woody Plant Cttee, 2009–14; Chm., Plants Adv. Cttee, 2010–12; Mem., Awards Cttee, 2010–. Member: Nat. Council for Conservation of Plants and Gardens, 1980–88 (Chm., Guernsey Gp, 1999–2011); Horticultural Bd, 2012–14. Founder, Internat. Clematis Soc., 1984 (Pres., 1989–91); International Plant Propagators' Society: Vice-Pres., 1976, Pres., 1977, GB and NI Reg.; Internat. Vice-Pres., 1981, Internat. Pres. 1982. Pres., Guernsey Botanical Trust, 2007–. FCIHort (FIHort 1993); FLS 2016. Trustee, Caritas, Guernsey, 2007–19. Hon. Fellow, Kew Guild, 2016. Rose Bowl Award, Plant Propagators' Soc., 1979; Reginald Cory Meml Cup, RHS, 2004; Achievement in Horticulture Award, Inst. of Horticulture, 2012; Contributor Award, Perennial Plant Assoc., USA, 2014. *Publications*: Making the Most of Clematis, 1979, 2nd edn 1991 (Dutch edn 1987); The Gardener's Guide to Growing Clematis, 1997 (Dutch edn 1998); Clematis for Everyone, 2000; Clematis du 3$^e$ millénaire, 2002; Clematis for Small Spaces, 2007. *Recreations*: hockey, swimming, tennis, gardening, conservation work with native and cultivated plants, wildlife. *Address*: Guernsey Clematis Nursery Ltd, Braye Vinery, Route Militaire, Vale, Guernsey GY3 5RP. *T*: (01481) 245942, *Fax*: (01481) 248987. *E*: raymondjevison@guernsey-clematis.com. *Club*: Sloane.

**EWAN, Pamela Wilson,** CBE 2007; FRCP, FRCPath; Consultant Allergist, Addenbrooke's Hospital, Cambridge, since 1997; *b* Forfar, 23 Sept. 1945; *d* of Norman Ewan and Frances Ewan; *m* 1979, Sir (David) Keith Peters, *qv*; two *s* one *d. Educ*: Forfar Acad., Angus; Royal Free Hosp. Med. Sch., London (MA, MB BS 1969). FRCP 1986; FRCPath 1997. Jun. hosp. posts, Royal Free, Guy's and Hammersmith Hosps, London, 1969–80; Sen. Lectr and Hon. Consultant, St Mary Hosp. Med. Sch., London 1980–88; MRC Clinical Scientist and Hon. Consultant Allergist, Addenbrooke's Hosp., Cambridge, 1988–97. Pres., British Soc. for Allergy and Clin. Immunol., 1999–2002; Chm., Nat. Allergy Strategy Gp, 2005–. Leader of translational res. to develop peanut oral immunotherapy and allergy services nationally. William Frankland Award, 2000, Jack Pepys Award, 2014, British Soc. for Allergy and Clin. Immunol.; Silver Medal, Chelsea Flower Show, 2003, 2004; Lifetime Achievement Award, Allergy UK, 2011. *Publications*: scientific papers and chapters on allergy, esp. nut allergy and anaphylaxis. *Recreations*: cats, art. *Address*: 7 Chaucer Road, Cambridge CB2 7EB. *T*: (01223) 217777, *Fax*: (01223) 216953. *E*: pamela.ewan@addenbrookes.nhs.uk.

**EWART, David Scott;** QC 2006; barrister; *b* 29 April 1964; *s* of David and Christina Ewart; *m* 2011, Sarah Dunn; two *s* three *d*, and one *s* one *d* from a previous marriage. *Educ*: Hamilton Grammar Sch.; Trinity Coll., Oxford (BA 1986). Called to the Bar, Gray's Inn, 1988. *Recreation*: bridge. *Address*: Pump Court Tax Chambers, 16 Bedford Row, WC1R 4EF. *T*: (020) 7414 8080. *Club*: Young Chelsea Bridge.

**EWART, Dr Michael;** Director, Scottish International Education Trust, since 2009; *b* 9 Sept. 1952; *s* of late James Ewart and Joyce Goulden; *m* 2010, Dr Sally Anderson; one *s* one *d. Educ*: Jesus Coll., Cambridge (BA Hons 1974); York Univ. (DPhil 1977). Scottish Office, 1977–81; Asst Private Sec. to Sec. of State for Scotland, 1981–82; CS Fellow in Politics, Univ. of Glasgow, 1982–83; Health Service Mgt Reform, 1983–86; Hd, Schs Div., Scottish Educn Dept, 1986–91; Dep. Dir, Scottish Courts Admin, 1991–93; Chief Exec., Scottish Court Service, 1993–99; Hd, Schs Gp, 1999–2002, Hd of Dept, 2002–06, Scottish Exec. Educn Dept; Chief Exec., Scottish Prison Service, 2007–09. Member: Bd, Scottish Ballet, 2007–13; Bd, Quality Scotland, 2007–09; Bd, Phoenix Futures, 2012–19; Mgt Adv. Bd, Education Scotland, 2012–19; Chm., Phoenix Futures Scotland, 2013–19. Lay Mem., Judicial Appts Bd for Scotland, 2010–18. *Recreations*: music, books, military history, running, climbing (ice and rock), ski-ing, geocaching. *Address*: Scottish International Education Trust, Turcan Connell, Princes Exchange, 1 Earl Grey Street, Edinburgh EH3 9EE.

**EWART, Sir Michael;** *see* Ewart, Sir W. M.

**EWART, Penelope Jane Clucas;** *see* Marshall, P. J. C.

**EWART, Sir (William) Michael,** 7th Bt *cr* 1887, of Glenmachen, Co. Down and of Glenbank, Co. Antrim; *b* 10 June 1953; *o s* of Sir (William) Ivan (Cecil) Ewart, 6th Bt and Pauline Preston (*d* 1964); *S* father, 1995. *Educ*: Radley. *Recreations*: racing, ski-ing, travel. *Heir*: none. *Address*: Hill House, Hillsborough, Co. Down BT26 6AE. *Club*: Naval.

**EWEN, Air Vice-Marshal Peter Ronald,** CB 2015; CEng; FRAeS; Engineering Director, MTR Corporation, since 2016; *b* London, 1959; *s* of Ronald and Marion Ewen; one *d* (and one *d* decd); *m* 2016, Sqn Ldr Hazel Reed; one *s. Educ*: Campion Sch.; BSc 1st Cl. Hons Engrg; Postgrad. Dip Mgt Studies; Postgrad. Dip. Mgt Consultancy; DPhil 2008. FRAes 2004; CEng 2005. Head: Nimrod, 2009–11; Air, Intelligence, Surveillance, Target Acquisition and Reconnaissance, 2011–12; COS, Support and Exec. Officer, RAF, 2012–13; Dir Air Support, Defence Equipment and Support, MoD, 2013–15. Procurement Advr, Rail Franchising, DfT, 2015; Hd of Air, Airbus Defence and Space, 2015–16. *Recreations*: classic cars, Rugby, travel.

**EWENS, Prof. Warren John,** PhD; FRS 2000; Professor of Biology, University of Pennsylvania, 1972–2005, now Emeritus; *b* 23 Jan. 1937; *s* of John and Gwendoline Ewens; *m* 1st, 1961, Helen Wiley (marr. diss.); one *s* one *d*; 2nd, 1981, Kathryn Gogolin. *Educ*: Trinity Coll., Melbourne Univ. (MA); Australian Nat. Univ. (PhD 1964). Professor, Department of Mathematics: La Trobe Univ., 1967–72; Monash Univ., 1977–96. *Publications*: Population Genetics, 1969; Mathematical Population Genetics, 1979; Probability and Statistics in Bioinformatics, 2000. *Recreations*: tennis, bridge, reading. *Address*: 324 Leidy Laboratories, University of Pennsylvania, PA 19104, USA. *T*: (215) 8987109.

**EWER, Graham Anderson**, CB 1999; CBE 1991; President, 2004–06, Vice President, 2006–08, Hon. Member, since 2009, European Logistics Association; *b* 22 Sept. 1944; *s* of late Robert and Maud Ewer; *m* 1969, Mary Caroline Grant; two *d*. *Educ*: Truro Cathedral Sch.; RMA, Sandhurst. FCILT (FILT 1999; FCIT 1999). Commnd RCT, 1965; served Germany, UK and ME, 1966–75; Army Staff Coll., 1976; Lt Col, Directing Staff, Army Staff Coll., 1984; CO, 8 Regt RCT, Munster, 1985–87; Col, DCS, G1/4 HQ 1st Armd Div., Verden, Germany and Gulf War, 1988–91; Comdt, Army Sch. of Transportation, 1991; Col, Logistic Support Policy Secretariat, 1992; Brig. 1993; Comd, Combat Service Support Gp, Germany and Guetersloh Garrison, 1993–94; Dir, Logistic Planning (Army), 1995; Maj. Gen. 1996; ACDS (Logistics), 1996–99; Chief Exec., Chartered Inst. of Logistics and Transport (UK), 1999–2004; ind. logistics consultant, 2004–14. Col Comdt, RLC, 1999–2009. *Publications*: (contrib.) Blackadder's War, ed M. S. White, 1995; (contrib.) Sustainable Supply Chain Management: the bestLog textbook, 2010; contrib. to various jls. *Recreations*: sailing, military history, motorcycling, cycling, model railways. *Address*: c/o HSBC, 17 Boscawen Street, Truro, Cornwall TR1 2QZ.

**EWING**; see Orr-Ewing and Orr Ewing.

**EWING, Rt Rev. Allan**; Bishop of Bunbury, 2010–17; *b* Hemel Hempstead, 3 Nov. 1951; *s* of William and Patricia Ewing; *m* 1972, Tricia Fowler; two *s*. *Educ*: Hemel Hempstead Grammar Sch.; Australian Coll. of Theology (BTh). ACA 1975, FCA 1980; ordained priest, Australia, 1988; Asst Priest, Canberra, 1988–89; Rector: Holbrook, NSW, 1989–93; Batemans Bay, NSW, 1993–96; St John's, Canberra, 1996–2004; Archdeacon of N Canberra, 1996–2004; Asst Bishop, Canberra and Goulburn, 2004–09.

**EWING, Annabelle Janet**; solicitor; Member (SNP) Cowdenbeath, Scottish Parliament, since 2016 (Scotland Mid and Fife, 2011–16); *b* 20 Aug. 1960; *d* of late Stewart Martin Ewing and of Winifred Margaret Ewing, *qv*. *Educ*: Craigholme Sch., Glasgow; Univ. of Glasgow (LLB Hons); Bologna Center, Johns Hopkins Univ.; Europa Inst., Amsterdam Univ. Apprentice lawyer, Ruth Anderson and Co., 1984–86; admitted solicitor, 1986; Legal Service, DG XIV, CEC, 1987; Associate, Lebrun de Smedt and Dassesse, Brussels, 1987–89; Associate, 1989–92, Partner, 1993–96, Akin Gump, Brussels; Special Counsel, McKenna and Cuneo, Brussels, 1996; EC lawyer, 1997; Associate, 1998–99, Partner, 1999–2001, Ewing & Co., solicitors, Glasgow; Consultant, Leslie Wolfson & Co., solicitors, Glasgow, 2001–03. MP (SNP) Perth, 2001–05; contested (SNP) Ochil and South Perthshire, 2005, 2010. Minister for Youth and Women's Employment, 2014–16, for Community Safety and Legal Affairs, 2016–18, Scottish Parlt. *Address*: Scottish Parliament, Edinburgh EH99 1SP.

**EWING, Bernadette Mary**; see Kelly, B. M.

**EWING, Maria Louise**; soprano; *b* Detroit, 27 March 1950; *y d* of Norman Ewing and Hermina Ewing (*née* Veraar); *m* 1982, Sir Peter Reginald Frederick Hall, CBE (marr. diss. 1990; he *d* 2017); one *d*. *Educ*: High School; Cleveland Inst. of Music. Studied with Marjorie Gordon, Eleanor Steber, Jennie Tourel, Otto Guth. First public performance, Meadowbrook, 1968 (Rigoletto), débuts Metropolitan Opera and La Scala, 1976; sings at Covent Garden, Glyndebourne, Salzburg, Paris, Metropolitan Opera, LA Opera, La Scala and other major venues; rôles include Begbick, Blanche, Carmen, Geschwitz, Jezibaba, Klythaemnestra, Lucretia, Lady Macbeth, Mélisande, La Périchole, Poppea; concerts and recitals.

**EWING, Mrs Winifred Margaret**; Member (SNP) Highlands and Islands, Scottish Parliament, 1999–2003; *b* 10 July 1929; *d* of George Woodburn and Christina Bell Anderson; *m* 1956, Stewart Martin Ewing, CA (*d* 2003); two *s* one *d*. *Educ*: Queen's Park Sen. Sec. Sch.; University of Glasgow (MA, LLB). Qual. as Solicitor, 1952. Lectr in Law, 1954–56; Solicitor, practising on own account, 1956–. Sec., Glasgow Bar Assoc., 1961–67, Pres., 1970–71. MP (SNP): Hamilton, Nov. 1967–1970; Moray and Nairn, Feb. 1974–1979; contested (SNP) Orkney and Shetland, 1983. MEP (SNP), 1975–99, elected Mem. for Highlands and Is, 1979–99; Vice-Pres., Animal Welfare Intergp, EP, 1989–99. President: Scottish National Party, 1987–2005; European Free Alliance, 1991–; Mem., Lomé Assembly, 1981–. Pres., Glasgow Central Soroptimist Club, 1966–67. FRSA 1990. DUniv: Open, 1993; Stirling, 2012; Hon. LLD Glasgow, 1995; Hon. LLD Aberdeen, 2004. Freeman, City of Avignon, 1985; Comptroller of Scottish Privileges, Veere, Netherlands, 1997–2011. Médaille d'Or, Fondation du Mérite Européen, 2014.
See also A. J. Ewing.

**EWINS, (David) James**; QC 2016; *b* England, 7 Jan. 1973; *s* of Peter David Ewins, *qv*; *m* 1998, Rev. Tiffany-Alice Perschke; two *s* two *d*. *Educ*: Woolmer Hill Secondary Sch., Haslemere; New Coll., Oxford (BA Juris.); Inns of Court Sch. of Law. Called to the Bar, Middle Temple, 1996; in practice as barrister, specialising in divorce, internat. and big money financial relief claims, pre-nuptial contracts, 1996–; Field Officer Dir, Bangalore, 2008–09, Internat. Advocate, 2011–, Internat. Justice Mission. Dep. Chm., Modern Slavery Wkg Gp, Centre for Social Justice, 2011–13; Special Advr to Jt Select Cttee on Modern Slavery Bill, 2014–15. Ind. Reviewer of Overseas Domestic Worker Visa, 2015–16. Governor: St Cecilia's C of E Sch., Wandsworth, 2017–; Lady Margaret Sch., Fulham, 2019–. Trustee, Just Love, 2019–. *Recreations*: family, faith-life, sailing, running, ski-ing. *Address*: Queen Elizabeth Building, Temple, EC4Y 9BS. *T*: (020) 7797 7837. *E*: j.ewins@qeb.co.uk.

**EWINS, Prof. David John**, FRS 2006; FREng, FIMechE; Professor of Vibration Engineering, 1983–2013, Distinguished Research Fellow, since 2014, Imperial College London (formerly Imperial College of Science, Technology and Medicine); Professor of Vibration Engineering, University of Bristol, 2007–15; *b* 25 March 1942; *s* of W. J. and P. Ewins; *m* 1st, 1964, Brenda Rene (*née* Chalk) (marr. diss. 1997); three *d*; 2nd, 2007, Rosemary Gillian (*née* Siddall). *Educ*: Kingswood Grammar Sch., Bristol; Imperial Coll., London (BScEng, ACGI, DScEng); Trinity Coll., Cambridge (PhD). FIMechE 1990; FREng (FEng 1995). Res. Asst for Rolls-Royce Ltd, Cambridge Univ., 1966–67; Imperial College, London University: Lectr, then Reader, in Mech. Engrg, 1967–83; formed Modal Testing Unit, 1981; Dir, Rolls-Royce sponsored Centre of Vibration Engrg, 1990–2002; Pro-Rector, Internat. Relations, 2001–05; Dir, Bristol Lab. for Advanced Dynamic Engrg, Univ. of Bristol, 2007–15. Temasek Prof., and Dir, Centre for Mechanics of Microsystems, Nanyang Technol Univ., Singapore, 1999–2002. Sen. Lectr, Chulalongkorn Univ., Bangkok, 1968–69; Maître de Conférences, INSA, Lyon, 1974–75; Visiting Professor: Virginia Poly. and State Univ., USA, 1981; ETH, Zürich, 1986; Inst. Nat. Polytechnique de Grenoble, 1990; Nanyang Technol Univ., Singapore, 1994, 1997; Hon. Professor: Nanjing Aero Inst., 1988; Shandong Polytechnic Inst., 1991. Partner, ICATS, 1989–2012. Consultant to: Rolls-Royce, 1969–; MoD, 1977–; NASA, 2017–, and other organisations in Europe, S America and USA. Chm., then Pres., Dynamic Testing Agency, 1990–99; Chm., EU CleanSky Sci. and Technol. Adv. Bd, 2010–14. FCGI 2002. Foreign Fellow, Indian Nat. Acad. of Engrg, 2012; Fellow, Soc. of Experimental Mechanics (USA), 2014; Fellow (Mem. Titulaire), Acad. de l'Air et l'Espace (France), 2015. *Publications*: Modal Testing: theory and practice, 1984, 9th edn 1996; Modal Testing: theory, practice and application, 2000; (ed with D. J. Inman) Structural Dynamics, 2000; (ed jtly) Encyclopedia of Vibration, 2002; papers on vibration engrg in technical jls in UK, USA, France. *Recreations*: music (piano, choral singing), moorland walking, travel, good food, French, Italian, bridge. *Address*: Imperial College, Exhibition Road, SW7 2AZ. *T*: (020) 7594 7068.

**EWINS, James**; see Ewins, E. J.

**EWINS, Peter David**, CB 2001; FREng; FRAeS; Chief Executive, Meteorological Office, 1997–2004; *b* 20 March 1943; *s* of John Samuel Ewins and Kathleen Ewins; *m* 1968, Barbara Irene Howland; two *s* one *d*. *Educ*: Imperial College London (BSc Eng); Cranfield Inst. of Technology (MSc). FREng (FEng 1996); FRAeS 1996. Joined RAE Farnborough, 1966, research on structl applications of composite materials; section head, 1974; staff of Chief Scientist, RAF, MoD, 1978; Head of Helicopters Res. Div., RAE, 1981; seconded to Cabinet Office (Civil Service personnel policy), 1984; Dir, Nuclear Projects, MoD, 1987; Dir, ARE, MoD (PE), 1988; Man. Dir (Maritime and Electronics), 1991, Man. Dir, Command and Maritime Systems Gp, 1992, Man. Dir (Ops), 1993–94, DRA; Chief Scientist, MoD, 1994–97. Mem. Council, Royal Acad. of Engrg, 1999. Hon. DSc Exeter, 2006. *Publications*: technical papers on structural composite materials in learned jls. *Recreations*: horticulture, bee-keeping, walking.
See also D. J. Ewins.

**EXETER, 8th Marquess of**, *cr* 1801; **William Michael Anthony Cecil**; Baron Burghley 1571; Earl of Exeter 1605; *b* 1 Sept. 1935; *s* of 7th Marquess of Exeter and Edith Lilian Csanady de Telegd (*d* 1954); S father, 1988; *m* 1st, 1967, Nancy Rose (marr. diss. 1992), *d* of Lloyd Arthur Meeker; one *s* one *d*; 2nd, 1999, Barbara Anne, *d* of Eugene Magat. *Educ*: Eton. Rancher and businessman in 100 Mile House, BC, Canada, 1954–96. *Publications*: (jtly) Spirit of Sunrise, 1979; The Long View, 1985; The Rising Tide of Change, 1986; Living at the Heart of Creation, 1990. *Heir*: *s* Lord Burghley, *qv*. *Address*: 307–1521 Church Street, Victoria, BC V8P 5T7, Canada. *T*: (778) 4331521. *E*: wmacecil@icloud.com.

**EXETER, Bishop of**, since 2014; **Rt Rev. Robert Ronald Atwell**; *b* Ilford, Essex, 5 Aug. 1954; s of Ronald Victor Atwell and Marcia Blanche Atwell (*née* Newton). *Educ*: Wanstead High Sch.; St John's Coll., Durham Univ. (BA 1975; MLitt 1979); Westcott House, Cambridge; Venerable English Coll., Rome. Ordained deacon, 1978, priest, 1979; Asst Curate, John Keble, Mill Hill, 1978–81; Chaplain, Trinity Coll., Cambridge, 1981–87; Benedictine Monk, Burford Priory, 1987–98; Vicar, St Mary-the-Virgin, Primrose Hill, 1998–2008; Bishop Suffragan of Stockport, 2008–14. *Publications*: Spiritual Classics from the Early Church, 1995; Celebrating the Saints, 1998, enlarged edn, 2004; Celebrating the Seasons, 1998; Gift: 100 readings - celebration of birth and parenthood, 2005; Love: 100 readings - celebration of marriage and love, 2005; Remember: 100 readings for those in grief and bereavement, 2005; The Contented Life: spirituality and the gift of years, 2011; The Good Worship Guide, 2013; Peace at the Last: leading funerals well, 2014. *Recreations*: theatre, gardening, hill-walking. *Address*: The Palace, Exeter EX1 1HY. *T*: (01392) 272362. *E*: bishop.of.exeter@exeter.anglican.org.

**EXETER, Dean of**; see Greener, Very Rev. J. D. F.

**EXETER, Archdeacon of**; see Beane, Ven. A. M.

**EXLEY, Margaret**, CBE 2001; Chief Executive, SCT Consultants Ltd, since 2011; *d* of Ernest and Elsie Exley; *m* 1984, Malcolm Grant (*d* 2007); one *s* one *d*. *Educ*: Univ. of Manchester (BA Hons Econ); Univ. of Warwick (MBA). Res. Fellow, Manchester Business Sch., 1971–73; Principal, Cabinet Office, 1973–80; Dir, Hay Mgt Consultants, 1980–84; Chief Exec., Kinsley Lord Ltd, 1984–95; European Managing Partner, Towers Perrin, 1995–2001; Chm., Mercer Delta UK Ltd, 2001–07; Founder and Chm. Stonecourt Consulting Ltd, 2007–11. Non-executive Director: St Mary's NHS Trust, 1997–2000; Field Gp, 1997–99; HM Treasury, 1999–2005; Barts Health NHS Trust, 2018–. Mem., Employment Appeal Tribunal, 1992–95. Mem., Charter Renewal Steering Gp, BBC, 2006–07. Chm., Corporate Adv. Bd, NPG, 2000–12; Trustee, NPG Portrait Fund, 2012–19. FRSA 1996. *Publications*: various, on strategy and leadership, in learned and popular jls. *Recreations*: social history, politics, music, comedy, cinema. *Address*: 11 Launceston Place, Kensington, W8 5RL. *T*: (020) 7376 1973. *E*: margaret.exley@sctconsultants.com. *Club*: Reform.

**EXMOUTH, 10th Viscount** *cr* 1816; **Paul Edward Pellew**; Bt 1796 (Pellew of Treverry); Baron 1814; Marqués de Olias (Spain *cr* 1652); *b* 8 Oct. 1940; *s* of 9th Viscount Exmouth and Maria Luisa (*d* 1994), *d* of late Luis de Urquijo, Marqués de Amurrio, Madrid; *S* father, 1970; *m* 1st, 1964, Krystina Garay-Marques (marr. diss. 1974); one *d*; 2nd, 1975, Rosemary Countess of Burford (marr. diss. 2000); twin *s*. *Educ*: Downside. Formerly cross bencher, House of Lords. *Heir*: er twin *s* Hon. Edward Francis Pellew, *b* 30 Oct. 1978. *E*: PaulExmouth@aol.com.

**EXNER, Most Rev. Adam**; Archbishop of Vancouver, (RC), 1991–2004, now Archbishop Emeritus; *b* 24 Dec. 1928. *Educ*: St Joseph's Coll., Yorkton, Sask; Gregorian Univ., Rome (LPH 1954; STB 1956 STL 1958). Ottawa Univ. (STD 1960). Entered novitiate, Oblates of Mary Immaculate, St Norbert, Manitoba, 1950; ordained Roviano, Rome, 1957; St Charles Scholasticate, Battleford, Saskatchewan: Prof., 1960–64 and 1971–72; Rector and Superior, 1965–71; Prof. of Moral Theology, Newman Theol Coll., Edmonton, Alberta, 1972–74; Bishop of Kamloops, BC, 1974–82; Archbishop of Winnipeg, 1982–91. Secretary: BC and Yukon Conf. of Bishops, 1974–79 (Chm., 1991); Conf. of Catholic Bishops, 1974–80. Canadian Conference of Catholic Bishops: Mem., Admin. Bd, 1976–83; Rep. of Western Conf. of Bishops, 1981–83; Mem., Episcopal Commn for Christian Educn, 1983–88; Mem., Social Communications Commn, 1989–91; Rep. of W Reg. of Bishops on Permanent Council, 1989–93; Mem., Cttee on Sexual Abuse, 1990–92; Mem., Theol. Commn, 1991–93, 1995– (Pres., 1993–95); Mem., Working Gp Residential Schs, 1992–95; Mem., Progs and Priorities Cttee, 1993–95; Chm., Catholic Orgn for Life and Family, 1995. Chm., Conf. of Bishops of Manitoba, 1983–91; Member: Sacred Congregation for Bishops, 1984–90; Nat. Catholic-Lutheran Dialogue, 1987–89. Chaplain, Knight of Columbus, 1974–82; Liaison Bp and Chaplain, Catholic Sch. Trustees Assoc. of BC, 1974–82; Mem., St Paul's Coll. Bd, Univ. of Manitoba, 1982. *Publications*: contrib. to Catholic Press, 1960–82. *Recreations*: playing piano and accordion, golf, working out, cross country ski-ing, jogging.

**EXON, Richard Douglas**; Co-founder, Joint, since 2012; *b* Birmingham, 12 Aug. 1971; *s* of Dr and Mrs Peter Exon; *m* 2001, Melanie Copeland; two *d*. *Educ*: Yarlet Hall; Shrewsbury Sch.; Univ. of Durham (BA Hons 1993). Account Exec., Ogilvy & Mather, 1993; Account Manager to Global Business Develt Dir, Bartle Bogle Hegarty, 1994–2007; Man. Dir, 2007, CEO, 2007–12, Rainey Kelly Campbell Roalfe/Y&R. IPA Effectiveness Award, 1998. *Recreations*: winter sports, field sports, ball sports, cooking. *Address*: Joint, 30 Market Place, W1W 8AP. *T*: (020) 7637 0079. *Clubs*: Ivy, Every House.

**EXTON-SMITH, Jasmine**; see Whitbread, J.

**EYERS, Patrick Howard Caines**, CMG 1985; LVO 1966; HM Diplomatic Service, retired; *b* 4 Sept. 1933; *s* of late Arthur Leopold Caines Eyers and Nora Lilian Eyers; *m* 1960, Heidi, *d* of Werner Rüsch, Dipl. Ing, and Helene (*née* Feil); two *s* one *d*. *Educ*: Clifton Coll.; Gonville and Caius Coll., Cambridge (BA Hons 1957); Institut Universitaire de Hautes

Etudes Internationales, Geneva. RA, 1952–54. Asst Editor, Grolier Soc. Inc., New York, 1957; HM Foreign (now Diplomatic) Service, 1959; ME Centre for Arabic Studies, 1960; Dubai, 1961; Brussels, 1964; FO, 1966; Aden, 1969; Abidjan, 1970; British Mil. Govt, Berlin, 1971; FCO, 1974; Counsellor, Bonn, 1977; Head, Republic of Ireland Dept, FCO, 1981; RCDS, 1984; Ambassador: to Zaire, the Congo, Rwanda and Burundi, 1985–87; to Algeria, 1987–89; to GDR, 1990; to Jordan, 1991–93. Officer, Order of Leopold, Belgium, 1966. *Recreations:* music, sailing. *Address:* c/o Barclays Bank, 86 Queens Road, Bristol BS8 1RB. *Clubs:* Hurlingham; Bosham Sailing.

**EYKYN, George William;** Director of Corporate Affairs, Smart Data Communications Company, Capita plc, since 2018; *b* Oxford, 4 May 1966; *s of* Jamie and Angela Eykyn; *m* 1993, Anne Lennon; one *s* one *d*. *Educ:* Radley Coll., Oxon; Magdalen Coll., Oxford (MA Hons Modern Langs). Joined BBC, 1987: trainee, News, 1987–89; regl journalist, then TV reporter, NI, 1989–92; reporter, Breakfast News, 1992–94; news corresp., BBC News, 1994–2004; presenter, BBC World, 1997–2004; Sen. Consultant, PricewaterhouseCoopers LLP, 2004–08; Dir of Communication, DCLG, 2008–14; Dir of Communications, British Gas, 2014–18. *Recreations:* cricket, ski-ing, motorcycling, fishing. *E:* geykyn@btopenworld.com. *Club:* MCC (playing Mem.).

**EYLES, Timothy George;** Managing Partner, and Chairman, International Board, Taylor Wessing, 2009–18; Chairman, Royal Society of Arts, since 2018; *b* Dewsbury, W Yorks, 20 Nov. 1956; *s of* Reginald Eyles and Judith Eyles; *m* 2000, Heide; one *s*, and one step *s* one step *d*. *Educ:* Queen Elizabeth Grammar Sch., Wakefield; Univ. of Birmingham (LLB Law). Chm., Risk Advisory Gp, 2019–. Chairman: Jerwood Charitable Foundn, 2005–; Theatres Trust, 2015–. *Recreations:* yoga, tennis, theatre. *Address:* c/o Royal Society of Arts, 8 John Adam Street, WC2N 6EZ. *E:* tgeyles@gmail.com. *Clubs:* Soho House, Groucho.

**EYRE, Prof. Deborah Mary;** Chief Executive Officer, DEL International Consultancy, since 2008; Founder and Executive Chair, High Performance Learning, since 2015; *b* 22 Jan. 1954; *d of* Philip and Mary Davis; *m* 1976, John Eyre; one *s* one *d*. *Educ:* Hunmanby Hall Sch., Filey; Westminster Coll., Oxford (Cert Ed); Univ. of Reading (MEd). Teacher, primary schs, 1976–83; educn consultant on gifted and talented, 1983–89; advr on gifted and talented, Oxon LEA, 1989–97; Oxford Brookes University: Dir, Res. Centre for Able Pupils, and Dep. Dean of Educn, 1997–2002; Prof. of Educn, 2002; University of Warwick: Dir, Nat. Acad. for Gifted and Talented Youth, 2002–07; Prof. of Educn, 2007–08, now Hon. Prof. Chief Executive, Deborah Eyre Ltd, 2008–10; Educn Dir, Nord Anglia Educn Ltd, 2010–14. Member, Executive Board: Center for Talented Youth, Johns Hopkins Univ., 2005–; Trng and Develt Agency for Schs, 2006–09; Governing Council Observer, Nat. Coll. for Sch. Leadership, 2006–09; Vice-Pres., World Council for Gifted and Talented Children, 2006–09; Educn Dir, Mawhiba Schs Partnership Initiative, King Abdulaziz and his Companions Foundn for the Gifted, Saudi Arabia, 2009–. Non-executive Director: Inspiring Futures Foundn, 2007–17; Kingshurst CTC Acad., Birmingham, 2009–16; Dir, Centre for Economics in Educn, 2016–; Centre for Talented Youth, Ireland, 2015–. Mem. Bd, 21st Century Learning Alliance, 2007–; Dir, Council of Overseas British Internat. Schs, 2015–. Vis. Senior Res. Fellow, St Hugh's Coll., Univ. of Oxford, 2007–; Adv. Prof., Hong Kong Inst. of Educn, 2008–09. Adviser: Educn Select Cttee, H of C, 1998–99; Ministerial Task Force for Gifted and Talented, DfES, 1998–2001. Dir, River Learning Trust, 2016–; Trustee, Academies Enterprise Trust, 2018–. FRSA. Liveryman, Educators' Co., 2015–. *Publications:* School Governors and More Able Children, 1995; Able Children in Ordinary Schools, 1997; (ed jtly) Curriculum Provision for the Gifted and Talented in the Primary School, 2001; (ed jtly) Curriculum Provision for the Gifted and Talented in the Secondary School, 2002; Gifted and Talented International: international handbook for gifted education, 2007; (ed) Major Themes in Gifted Education (4 vols), 2009; Room at the Top: inclusive education for high performance, 2010; High Performance Learning: how to become a world class school, 2016; (jtly) Great Minds and how to Grow Them, 2018. *Recreations:* modern fiction, food and wine, family and friends. *Address:* 59 Linkside Avenue, Oxford OX2 8JE. *T:* (01865) 510045. *E:* Deborah.Eyre@highperformancelearning.co.uk.

**EYRE, James Henry Robert,** OBE 2003; Director, Wilkinson Eyre Architects Ltd, since 1989; *b* 24 Jan. 1959; *s of* late Michael Robert Giles Eyre and of Susan Bennett; *m* 1983, Karen Fiona Turner; one *s* one *d*. *Educ:* Oundle Sch.; Liverpool Univ. (BA Hons 1980); Architectural Assoc. (AA Dip. 1983). RIBA 1985. Architect, Michael Hopkins & Partners, 1980–85; joined Chris Wilkinson Architects, subseq. Wilkinson Eyre Architects, 1985, Partner, 1986–; *projects include:* Stratford Market Depot for Jubilee Line Extension, 1996; South Dock Footbridge for LDDC, 1997; Hulme Arch, Manchester, 1997; Stratford Station for Jubilee Line Extension, 2000; Gateshead Millennium Bridge, 2001; Making the Modern World gall., Science Mus.; Bridge of Aspiration, Floral Street, for Royal Ballet Sch., 2003; Mus. of London entrance and gall., 2003; Ceramics Gall. Bridge, V&A Mus., 2010; 435m Guangzhou Internat. Finance Centre Tower, 2011; Gardens by the Bay Conservatories, Singapore, 2011; Power Station at Battersea, 2013; Weston (new Bodleian) Library for special collections, Oxford, 2015. Comr, Royal Commn for the Exhibition 1851, 2014–. Trustee: Design Council CABE, 2011–; AA Foundation, 2013–. Pres., AA, 2007–09. Hon. DLaws Liverpool, 2009. President's Medal, RAEng, 2004; Bodley Medal, Bodleian Libraries, 2015. *Publications:* (contrib.) The Architecture of Bridge Design, 1997; (jtly) Bridging Art and Science, 2001; Exploring Boundaries, 2007; Wilkinson Eyre Architects: works, 2015; contribs World Architecture, Architects Jl, The Architecture of Bridge Design. *Recreations:* designing, making, reading, game fishing. *Address:* (office) 33 Bowling Green Lane, EC1R 0BJ. *T:* (020) 7608 7900.

**EYRE, Major John Vickers;** JP; DL; Vice Lord-Lieutenant of Gloucestershire, 2007–11; *b* 30 April 1936; *s of* Nevill Cathcart Eyre and Maud Evelyn Eyre (*née* Truscott); *m* 1974, Sarah Margaret Aline Heywood; one *s* one *d*. *Educ:* Winchester; Staff Coll., Camberley. Commnd, 1955, RHA, 1957, 14th/20th Kings Hussars, 1962; retd, 1973. Asst to Chm., Savoy Hotel, 1973–75; Administrator, Brian Colquhoun and Partners, consulting engrs, 1975–79; Proprietor, Haresfield Garden Centre, 1981–86; Man. Dir, George Truscott Ltd, 1986–2003. Royal Glos Hussars, TA, 1980–83 (Patron, 1997–). Dist Comr, Berkeley Hunt Pony Club, 1986–95; Chm., Berkeley Hunt, 2005–11. Gloucestershire: JP 1987; DL 2000; High Sheriff, 2000–01. Pres., Glos, RBL, 2008–11. *Recreation:* country pursuits. *Address:* Barn Cottage, Tytherington, Wotton-under-Edge, Glos GL12 8UG. *T:* (01454) 412220. *E:* jve@boyts.co.uk. *Club:* Army and Navy.

**EYRE, Patrick Giles Andrew;** Master of the Senior (formerly Supreme) Court, Queen's Bench Division, 1992–2012; *b* 11 March 1940; *s of* late Edward Joseph Eyre and Hon. Dorothy Elizabeth Anne Pelline Lyon-Dalberg-Acton; *m* 1977, Victoria Mary Bathurst Barthorp; one *s*, and one step *d*. *Educ:* Downside; Trinity Coll., Oxford (MA). Farmer, 1965–72. Called to the Bar, Inner Temple, 1974. *Publications:* articles on law, computers, horses and country pursuits. *Recreations:* books, bridge, horses, hunting, languages, music.

**EYRE, Richard Anthony,** CBE 2014; Chairman: Internet Advertising Bureau Ltd, since 2003; Next 15 plc, since 2011; *b* 3 May 1954; *s of* Edgar Gabriel Eyre and Marjorie (*née* Corp); *m* 1977, Sheelagh Colquhoun; one *s* one *d*. *Educ:* King's Coll. Sch., Wimbledon; Lincoln Coll., Oxford (MA); Harvard Business Sch. (AMP). Media buyer, Benton & Bowles, 1975–79; TV airtime salesman, Scottish TV, 1979–80; media planner, Benton & Bowles, 1980–84; Media Director: Aspect, 1984–86; Bartle Bogle Hegarty, 1986–91; Chief Executive: Capital Radio plc, 1991–97; ITV, 1997–2000; Pearson Television, 2000–01; Dir, Strategy and Content, RTL Gp, 2000–01. Chairman: RDF Media plc, 2001–09; GCap Media plc, 2007–08; Rapid Mobile, 2008–11; Eden Project Ltd, 2009–13 (non-exec. Dir, 2003–09); Founder, RadioCrimson.com, 2014–; non-executive Director: Guardian Media Gp, 2004–07; MGt, 2007–15; Results Internat. Gp, 2007–15; Grant Thornton LLP, 2010–15. FRSA 1997. Chm., Media Trust, 2014–; Trustee, Walking with the Wounded, 2013–16. Mackintosh Medal, Advertising Assoc., 2013. *Publications:* The Club (novel), 2005. *Recreations:* music, travel. *Address:* Internet Advertising Bureau, 67–68 Long Acre, WC2E 9JD. *Club:* Thirty.

**EYRE, Sir Richard (Charles Hastings),** CH 2017; Kt 1997; CBE 1992; theatre, film and TV director; Artistic Director, Royal National Theatre, 1988–97 (Associate Director, 1981–88); *b* 28 March 1943; *m* 1973, Susan Elizabeth Birtwistle, *qv*; one *d*. *Educ:* Sherborne Sch.; Peterhouse, Cambridge (BA; Hon. Fellow, 2001). Asst Dir, Phoenix Theatre, Leicester, 1966; Lyceum Theatre, Edinburgh: Associate Dir, 1967–70; Dir of Productions, 1970–72; freelance director: Liverpool, 7:84 Co., West End; tours for British Council: W Africa, 1971; SE Asia, 1972; Artistic Dir, Nottingham Playhouse, 1973–78; Prod./Dir, Play for Today, BBC TV, 1978–80. A Gov., BBC, 1995–2003. Director: The Churchill Play, Nottingham, 1974; Comedians, Old Vic and Wyndham's, 1976; Touched, Nottingham, 1977; Hamlet, Royal Court, 1980; Edmond, Royal Court, 1985; Kafka's Dick, Royal Court, 1986; National Theatre: Guys and Dolls, 1982, revived 1996 (SWET Director of the Year, 1982, Standard Best Director, 1982, Critics' Circle Best Dir Award, 1997); The Beggar's Opera, and Schweyk in the Second World War, 1982; The Government Inspector, 1985; Futurists, 1986 (Best Production Award, Time Out, 1986); The Changeling, Bartholomew Fair, 1988; Hamlet, The Voysey Inheritance, 1989; Racing Demon, Richard III, 1990; White Chameleon, Napoli Milionaria, Murmuring Judges, 1991; Night of the Iguana, 1992; Macbeth, The Absence of War, 1993; Johnny on a Spot, Sweet Bird of Youth, 1994; La Grande Magia, 1995; Skylight, 1995, transf. Wyndham's, then NY, 1996, UK tour, then Vaudeville, 1997; The Prince's Play, John Gabriel Borkman (Critics' Circle Best Dir Award, 1997), 1996; Amy's View, 1997, NY, 1999; King Lear (Olivier Award, 1998), The Invention of Love (Evening Standard Award, 1997), 1997; Vincent in Brixton, transf. Wyndham's, 2002, NY, 2003 (Drama League Award); The Reporter, 2007; The Observer, 2009; Welcome to Thebes, 2010; Liolà, 2013; The Judas Kiss, Playhouse, transf. NY, 1998; (also trans.) The Novice, Almeida, 2000; The Crucible, NY, 2002; Mary Poppins, Prince Edward, 2004, Bristol Hippodrome, 2015; (also trans.) Hedda Gabler, Almeida, transf. Duke of York's, 2005 (Olivier Award, 2006); The Last Cigarette, Minerva, Chichester, 2009; Private Lives, Vaudeville, 2010; A Flea in Her Ear, Old Vic, 2010; Betty Blue Eyes, Novello, 2011; The Last of the Duchess, Hampstead Th., 2011; The Dark Earth and the Light Sky, Almeida, 2012; Quartermaine's Terms, Wyndham's, 2013; The Pajama Game, Minerva, Chichester, 2013, transf. Shaftesbury Th., 2014; Ghosts, Almeida, 2013, transf. Trafalgar Studios, 2014 (Evening Standard Award for Best Dir, 2013; Olivier Award for Best Revival, 2014); Stephen Ward, Aldwych, 2013; Mr Foote's Other Leg, Hampstead Th., transf. Th. Royal, Haymarket, 2015; Little Eyolf, Almeida, 2015; Long Day's Journey into Night, Bristol Old Vic, 2016, transf. Wyndham's Th., 2018; The Stepmother, Minerva, Chichester, 2017; My Name is Lucy Barton, Bridge Th., 2018, 2019; The Bay at Nice, Menier Chocolate Factory, 2019; Blithe Spirit, Th. Royal Bath, 2019; 8 Hotels, Minerva, Chichester, 2019. *Opera:* La Traviata, Covent Gdn, 1994, 2019; Le Nozze di Figaro, Aix-en-Provence, 2001; Carmen, 2009, Werther, Le Nozze di Figaro, 2014, Metropolitan Opera, NY; Manon Lescaut, Baden-Baden Festspielhaus, 2014, Metropolitan Opera, NY, 2016. *Films:* The Ploughman's Lunch (Evening Standard Award for Best Film, 1983), Loose Connections, 1983; Laughterhouse, 1984, released as Singleton's Pluck, USA, 1985 (TV Prize, Venice Film Fest.); Iris, 2002 (Humanitas Prize; Efebo d'Oro Award); Stage Beauty, 2004; Notes on a Scandal, 2007; The Other Man, 2009; The Children Act, 2018; *for television:* The Imitation Game, Pasmore, 1980; Country, 1981; The Insurance Man, 1986 (Special Prize, Tokyo TV Fest., 1986); Past Caring, 1986; Tumbledown, 1988 (BAFTA Award for best single drama, Italia RAI Prize, RTS Award, Press Guild Award, Tokyo Prize); v., 1988 (RTS Award); Suddenly Last Summer, 1992; The Absence of War, 1995; King Lear, 1998 (Peabody Award, 1999), 2018; writer and presenter, Changing Stages (series), 2000; Henry IV, 2012; The Dresser, 2015. Cameron Mackintosh Vis. Prof. of Contemporary Theatre, Oxford Univ., 1997. Hon. Fellow: Goldsmiths' Coll., 1993; KCL, 1994. Hon. DLitt: Nottingham Trent, 1992; South Bank, 1994; Liverpool, 2003; Nottingham, 2008; DUniv Surrey, 1998; Hon. DDra RSAMD, 2000; Hon. Dr Oxford Brookes, 2003. STV Awards for Best Production, 1969, 1970 and 1971; De Sica Award, Sorrento Film Fest., 1986; Laurence Olivier and South Bank Show Awards for Outstanding Achievement, 1997; Lifetime Achievement Awards, Critics' Circle, and Directors' Guild, 1997. Officier de l'ordre des Arts et des Lettres (France), 1998. *Publications:* Utopia and Other Places, 1993; The Eyre Review (report of inquiry into running of Royal Opera House), 1998; (with Nicholas Wright) Changing Stages: a view of British theatre in the twentieth century, 2000; Iris (screenplay), 2002; National Service, 2003 (Theatre Bk Award, 2004); Hedda Gabler (adaptation), 2005; Talking Theatre: interviews with theatre people, 2009; Ghosts (adaptation), 2013; What Do I Know? (essays), 2014; Little Eyolf (adaptation), 2015; Place to Place, 2019. *Address:* c/o Judy Daish Associates, 2 St Charles Place, W10 6EG. *T:* (020) 8964 8811.

**EYRE, Stephen John Arthur;** QC 2015; **His Honour Judge Eyre;** a Circuit Judge, since 2015; a Specialist Civil Circuit Judge, since 2017; *b* Stourbridge, 17 Oct. 1957; *s of* Leslie Eyre and Joyce Eyre (*née* Whitehouse); *m* 1989, Margaret Goodman. *Educ:* Solihull Sch.; New Coll., Oxford (BA 1979; BCL 1980; MA); Cardiff Univ. (LLM 2010). Called to the Bar, Inner Temple, 1981; barrister, 1 Fountain Court, 1982–2002, St Philips Chambers, 2002–15; a Recorder, 2005–15; a Judge, First-tier Tribunal (Mental Health) (formerly Legal Mem., Mental Health Review Tribunal), 2007–15. Dep. Chancellor, dio. of Southwell, 2007–12; Chancellor: dio. of Coventry, 2009–; dio. of Lichfield, 2012–. Mem. (C), Solihull MBC, 1983–91, 1992–96. Contested (C) Birmingham Hodge Hill, 1987, July 2004, Strangford, 1992, Stourbridge, 2001. *Recreations:* reading, opera, theatre, walking, gardening. *Address:* Manchester Civil Justice Centre, 1 Bridge Street West, Manchester M60 9DJ.

**EYRE, Susan Elizabeth, (Lady Eyre);** see Birtwistle, S. E.

**EYSENCK, Prof. Michael William;** Professor of Psychology, Royal Holloway (formerly Royal Holloway and Bedford New College), University of London, 1987–2009, now Emeritus (Head of Department of Psychology, 1987–2005), Honorary Fellow, 2013; Professorial Fellow, Roehampton University, since 2010; *b* 8 Feb. 1944; *s of* late Prof. Hans Jürgen Eysenck and Margaret Malcolm Eysenck (*née* Davies); *m* 1975, Mary Christine Kabyn; one *s* two *d*. *Educ:* Dulwich Coll.; University College London (BA Psych. 1st cl. Hons; Rosa Morrison Medal for outstanding arts graduate, 1965); Birkbeck Coll., London (PhD Psych). Asst Lectr, Lectr and Reader in Psychology, Birkbeck Coll., Univ. of London, 1965–87. Vis. Prof., Univ. of S Florida, Tampa, 1980. Chm., Cognitive Psych. Section, BPsS, 1982–87; Pres., Internat. Soc. for Stress and Anxiety, 2006–08 (Pres.-elect, 2004–06; Past Pres., 2008–10). Fellow, Assoc. for Psychol Sci., 2019. Editor, European Jl of Cognitive Psych., 1989–91. *Publications:* Human Memory, 1977; (with H. J. Eysenck)

Mindwatching, 1981; Attention and Arousal: cognition and performance, 1982; A Handbook of Cognitive Psychology, 1984; (with H. J. Eysenck) Personality and Individual Differences, 1985; (with J. T. Richardson and D. W. Piper) Student Learning: research in education and cognitive psychology, 1987; (with H. J. Eysenck) Mindwatching: why we behave the way we do, 1989; Happiness: facts and myths, 1990; (ed) The Blackwell Dictionary of Cognitive Psychology, 1990; International Review of Cognitive Psychology, 1990; (with M. T. Keane) Cognitive Psychology: a student's handbook, 1990; Anxiety: the cognitive perspective, 1992; (with M. Weller) The Scientific Basis of Psychiatry, 1992; (with A. Gale) Handbook of Individual Differences: biological perspectives, 1992; Principles of Cognitive Psychology, 1993; Perspectives on Psychology, 1994; Individual Differences: normal and abnormal, 1994; Simply Psychology, 1996; Anxiety and Cognition: a unified theory, 1997; Psychology: an integrated approach, 1998; Psychology: a student's handbook, 2000; (with C. Flanagan) Psychology for A2 Level, 2001; Key Topics in A2 Psychology, 2003; Psychology for AS Level, 2003; Perspectives in Psychology, 2004; Fundamentals of Cognition, 2006, 3rd edn (with M. Brysbaert), 2016; (with P. Buchwald and T. Ringeisen) Stress and Anxiety owns the life span: recent developments and challenges, 2008; Fundamentals of Psychology, 2009; (with A. Baddeley and M. C. Anderson) Memory, 2009; (with T. Marusz and M. Fajkowska) Warsaw Lectures on Personality and Social Psychology, vol 1: personality from biological, cognitive and social perspectives, 2009; (jtly) Handbook of Managerial Behaviour and Occupational Health, 2009; (with M. Fajkowska and T. Marusgewski) Warsaw Lectures on Personality and Social Psychology, vol. 2: personality, cognition and emotion, 2012, vol. 4: anxiety, depression and attentional control, 2014; (with D. Groome) Cognitive Psychology: revisiting the classic studies, 2015; (with D. Groome) An Introduction to Applied Cognitive Psychology, 2nd edn, 2016; (jtly) Psychology of the Paranormal, 2019; numerous book chapters and contribs to Qly Jl of Exptl Psychology, Jl of Exptl Psychology, Jl of Abnormal Psychology, British Jl of Clin. Psychology, Jl of Personality and Social Psychology, Psychol Bull., Emotion, and others. *Recreations:* travel, tennis, golf, walking, bridge, croquet. *Address:* Department of Psychology, Roehampton University, Whitelands College, Holybourne Avenue, SW15 4JD. *T:* (020) 8392 3510. *Clubs:* Campden Hill Lawn Tennis; Surbiton Croquet.

**EYTON, Anthony John Plowden,** RA 1986 (ARA 1976); RWS 1988 (ARWS 1985); RWA 1984; RCA 1993; *b* 17 May 1923; *s* of late Captain John Seymour Eyton, ICS, author, and Phyllis Annie Tyser, artist; *m* 1960, Frances Mary Capell, MA (marr. diss.); three *d. Educ:* Twyford Sch.; Canford Sch.; Dept of Fine Art, Reading Univ.; Camberwell Sch. of Art (NDD). Served War, 1939–45, Cameronians (Scottish Rifles), Hampshire Regt, and Army Educn Corps. Abbey Major Scholarship in Painting, 1950–51. Elected Mem., London Gp, 1958. One Man Exhibitions: St George's Gall., 1955; Galerie de Seine, 1957; New Art Centre, 1959, 1961, 1968; New Grafton Gall., 1973; William Darby Gall., 1975; Newcastle Polytechnic Art Gall., 1978; Browse & Darby, 1978, 1981, 1985, 1987, 1990, 1993, 1996, 2000, 2005, 2009, 2013, 2016; Austin Desmond Gall., 1990; A. T. Kearney Ltd, 1997; King's Road Gall., 2002; Woodlands Art Gall., 2003; Eleven Spitalfields Gall., 2011, 2015; Avalanche, Academicians in Focus series, RA, 2017; Retrospective Exhibn, S London Art Gall., Towner Art Gall., Eastbourne, and Plymouth Art Gall., 1981; Hong Kong and the New Territories exhibn, Imperial War Museum, 1983 (subsequent to commission); Evolution of a Cornish China Clay Pit exhibn, Eden Project, 2009–10 (resident artist, 1999–2009); work included in British Painting 1945–77, RA; Drawing Inspiration, Abbot Hall Art Gall., Lakeland Arts Trust, 2006; resident artist, Stowe Sch., 2015–. Work in public collections: Tate Gall.; Arts Council; Plymouth Art Gall.; Towner Art Gall., Eastbourne; Carlisle Art Gall.; DoE; RA; Government Picture Coll.; BR; Contemp. Art Soc.; Guildhall Art Gall. Fellowship awarded by Grocers' Co. (for work and travel in Italy), 1974. Hon. Fellow, Univ. of Arts, London, 2011. Hon. Mem., Pastel Soc., 1986; Hon. ROI 1988. Prize, John Moore's Exhibn, Liverpool, 1972; First Prize, Second British Internat. Drawing Biennale, Middlesbrough, 1975; Charles Wollaston Award, RA, 1981. *Relevant publication:* Eyton's Eye, by Jenny Pery, 2005. *Recreation:* gardening. *Address:* c/o Browse & Darby Ltd, 19 Cork Street, W1S 3LP.

# F

**FABER, David James Christian**; writer; Headmaster, Summer Fields School, Oxford, since 2010; *b* 7 July 1961; *s* of late Julian Tufnell Faber and Lady (Ann) Caroline Faber, *e d* of 1st Earl of Stockton, OM, PC, FRS; *m* 1st, 1988, Sally Elizabeth Gilbert (marr. diss. 1996); one *s*; 2nd, 1998, Sophie Amanda Hedley; two *d*. *Educ:* Summer Fields Sch., Oxford; Eton Coll.; Balliol Coll., Oxford (MA Mod. Langs). Conservative Central Office, 1985–87; Director: Sterling Marketing Ltd, 1987–2002; Freestream Aircraft Ltd, 1998–; Quintus Public Affairs Ltd, 2006–09. Contested (C) Stockton North, 1987; MP (C) Westbury, 1992–2001. PPS to Min. of State, Foreign Office, 1994–96, to Sec. of State for Health, 1996–97; Opposition frontbench spokesman on foreign and commonwealth affairs, 1997–98. Member: Social Security Select Cttee, 1992–97; Culture, Media and Sport Select Cttee, 1998–2001; Public Accounts Cttee, 2000–01; Sec., Cons. back bench Educn Cttee, 1992–94. Trustee: Rehabilitation for Addicted Prisoners Trust, 1993–2001; Clouds House, 1992–2007 (Chm., 2003–07). Member, Board of Governors: Summer Fields Sch., Oxford, 2001–09; Aysgarth Sch., 2012–; Harrow Sch., 2016–. *Publications:* Speaking for England, 2005; Munich, 2008. *Recreations:* Chelsea FC, cricket, golf. *Address:* Summer Fields, Mayfield Road, Oxford OX2 7EN. *Clubs:* Garrick, MCC (Mem. Cttee, 1997–2000, 2001–04, 2005–08, 2011–; Chm., Arts and Library Cttee, 2013–), Lord's Taverners; Vincent's (Oxford); Sunningdale Golf; Royal and Ancient Golf (St Andrews).

**FABER, Her Honour Diana**; a Circuit Judge, 2000–17; *b* 23 Oct. 1955; *d* of T. G. Faber and Mrs D. Swan, and step *d* of A. C. Swan. *Educ:* Putney High Sch.; University Coll. London (LLB Hons). Called to the Bar, Gray's Inn, 1977; barrister, 1977–82; admitted solicitor, 1983; joined Richards Butler, 1982, Partner, 1987–93; a Law Comr, 1994–2000; a Recorder, 1998–2000. Bencher, Lincoln's Inn, 2009. *Publications:* (General Ed.) Multimodal Transport: avoiding legal problems, 1997; numerous articles in legal and commercial jls and newspapers.

**FABER, His Honour Trevor Martyn**; a Circuit Judge, 2001–12; *b* 9 Oct. 1946; *s* of Harry Faber and Millicent Faber (*née* Waxman); *m* 1985, Katrina Sally Clay. *Educ:* Clifton Coll.; Merton Coll., Oxford (MA; 3 boxing blues and Capt.). Called to the Bar, Gray's Inn, 1970; in practice, Midland and Oxford Circuit, 1970–2001; a Recorder, 1989–2001. *Recreations:* music, sport, theatre, literature, cooking. *Club:* Vincent's (Oxford).

**FABIAN, Prof. Andrew Christopher**, OBE 2006; FRS 1996; Acting Director, Institute of Astronomy, University of Cambridge, 2015–17, now Emeritus Professor (Director, 2013–15); Fellow of Darwin College, Cambridge, 1983–2015, now Emeritus (Vice-Master, 1997–2012); *b* 20 Feb. 1948; *s* of John Archibald and Daphne Monica Fabian; *m* 1st, 1971 (marr. diss. 1991); one *s* one *d*; 2nd, 1991, Prof. Carolin Susan Crawford, *qv*; two *s*. *Educ:* Daventry Grammar Sch.; King's Coll., London (BSc Physics); University Coll. London (PhD). SRC post doctoral research asst, University Coll. London, 1972–73; Institute of Astronomy, Cambridge: SRC post doctoral Fellow, 1973–75; SRC PDRA, 1975–77; Radcliffe Fellow in Astronomy, 1977–81; Royal Soc. Res. Prof., 1982–2013, Prof., 2002–13. Pres., RAS, 2008–10. Foreign Associate, US Nat. Acad. of Scis, 2016; MAE 2016. Hon. Dr l'Observatoire de Paris, 2018. Asteroid 25157 Fabian, 2016. (Jtly) Rossi Prize, AAS, 2001; Dannie Heineman Prize for Astrophysics, Amer. Inst. Physics and AAS, 2008; Gold Medal, RAS, 2012; Mohler Prize, Univ. of Michigan, 2012; Catherine Wolfe Bruce Gold Medal, Astronomical Soc. of the Pacific, 2016. *Publications:* contribs to Monthly Notices RAS, Astrophys. Jl, Nature, etc. *Address:* Institute of Astronomy, Madingley Road, Cambridge CB3 0HA.

**FABIAN, Carolin Susan**; *see* Crawford, C. S.

**FABIANI, Linda**; Member (SNP) East Kilbride, Scottish Parliament, since 2011 (Central Scotland, 1999–2011); Deputy Presiding Officer, Scottish Parliament, since 2016; *b* 14 Dec. 1956; *d* of late Giovanni Aldo Fabiani and Claire Fabiani (*née* Smith). *Educ:* Napier Coll., Edinburgh (SHND); Glasgow Univ. (Dip Housing 1988). Admin. Sec., Yoker Housing Assoc., Glasgow, 1982–85; Housing Officer, Clydebank Housing Assoc., 1985–88; Develt Manager, Bute Housing Assoc., Rothesay, 1988–94; Dir, E Kilbride Housing Assoc., 1994–99. Scottish Parliament: Dep. shadow spokesperson on social justice, housing and urban regeneration, 1999–2003; SNP Dep. Business Manager and Whip, 2003–05; Convenor, European and External Relations Cttee, 2005–07; Minister for Europe, Ext. Affairs and Culture, 2007–09; Mem., Scottish Parlt Corporate Body, 2011–16; Convenor, Scotland Bill Cttee, 2011–13; Member: Referendum Bill Cttee, 2012–14; Welfare Reform Cttee, 2012–13. Hon. FRIAS 2009. Cavaliere, Order of Star of Italian Solidarity (Italy), 2007. *Recreations:* reading, theatre, music, holidays. *Address:* Scottish Parliament, Edinburgh EH99 1SP. *T:* (0131) 348 5698.

**FABIUS, Laurent**, Hon. KCMG 2014; Grand Croix, Ordre National du Mérite; Grand Officier, Légion d'Honneur; President, Constitutional Council, France, since 2016; *b* 20 Aug. 1946; *s* of André Fabius and Louise Fabius (*née* Mortimer). *Educ:* Lycée Janson-de-Sailly; Lycée Louis-le-Grand; Ecole Normale Supérieure, Paris; Institut d'Etudes Politiques, Paris (Agrégé des lettres); Ecole Nationale d'Administration. Conseil d'Etat, 1973–81; Deputy for Seine Maritime, French Nat. Assembly, 1978–81, re-elected 1981, 1986, 1993, 1997, 2002, 2007 (Pres., 1988–92, 1997–2000); Nat. Sec., Parti Socialiste (responsible for the press), 1979–81; Junior Minister, Ministry of Economy and Finance (responsible for the budget), 1981–83; Minister of Industry and Research, 1983–84; Prime Minister of France, 1984–86; MEP, 1989–92; Finance Minister and Dep. Prime Minister, 2000–02; Minister of Foreign and European Affairs, then Foreign and Internat. Develt, 2012–16; Pres., Paris Agreement (COP21), 2015. First Sec., Socialist Party, 1992–93; Pres., Socialist Gp, Nat. Assembly, 1995–97. Mem., Conseil d'Etat, 1981–93. First Dep. Mayor, 1977–95 and 2000–, Mayor, 1995–2000, Grand Quevilly. *Publications:* La France inégale, 1975; Le Coeur du Futur, 1985; C'est en allant vers la mer, 1990; Les Blessures de la Vérité, 1995; Cela commence par une balade, 2003; Une certaine idée de l'Europe, 2005; Le Cabinet des Douze: regards sur des tableaux qui font la France, 2010; 37 Quai d'Orsay, 2016. *Address:* Conseil Constitutionnel, 2 rue de Montpensier, 75001 Paris, France.

**FABRE, Prof. Cécile**, DPhil; FBA 2011; Professor of Political Philosophy, University of Oxford, 2010–14; Senior Research Fellow, All Souls College, Oxford, since 2014; *b* Paris, France, 2 Feb. 1971; *d* of Francois Fabre and Geneviève Fabre (*née* Thélot); one *s*. *Educ:* Univ. of La Sorbonne, Paris (BA Hist. 1992); Univ. of York (MA Pol Theory 1993); Univ. of Oxford (DPhil Pols 1997). Postdoctoral Fellow, Nuffield Coll., Oxford, 1998–2000; Lectr, then Sen. Lectr, LSE, 2000–07; Prof. of Pol Theory, Univ. of Edinburgh, 2007–10; Fellow, and Tutor in Philosophy, Lincoln Coll., Oxford, 2010–14. *Publications:* Social Rights under the Constitution, 2000; Whose Body is it Anyway?, 2006; Justice in a Changing World, 2007; Cosmopolitan War, 2012; Cosmopolitan Peace, 2016; articles in Ethics, Jl of Pol Philos., British Jl of Pol Sci., Utilitas. *Recreations:* reading and watching thrillers, doing nothing. *Address:* All Souls College, Oxford OX1 4AL. *T:* (01865) 279282. *E:* cecile.fabre@all-souls.ox.ac.uk.

**FÁBREGA, Daniel Eduardo**; Ambassador of Panama to the Court of St James's, 2014–19; *b* Panama, 15 March 1975; *s* of Julio J. Fábrega III and Mary Faith Fábrega Venier; *m* 2001, Amparo Arrocha; one *s* one *d*. *Educ:* Valley Forge Mil. Acad., Wayne (Bachelor of Sci. and Letters 1993); ITESO, Univ. Jesuita de Guadalajara; Clarkson Univ., Potsdam; Loyola Univ. (Bachelor of Business Admin 1997); Univ. Latinoamericana de Ciencia y Tecnología (MBA 2004). Brand Manager, Ron Bacardi, 1998–2000; Commercial Vice Pres. of Exports, Varela Hermanos, SA, 2000–14. *Recreations:* ski-ing, boxing, swimming, general fitness. *Clubs:* Naval and Military; Union (Panama).

**FABREGAT, Fernando L.**; *see* Lopez-Fabregat.

**FABRICANT, Michael Louis David**; MP (C) Lichfield, since 1997 (Mid-Staffordshire, 1992–97); *b* 12 June 1950; *s* of late Isaac Nathan Fabricant and of Helena (*née* Freed). *Educ:* Loughborough Univ. (BA Law and Econs); Univ. of Sussex (MSc Systems). CEng, FIET. Postgrad. doctoral res., mathematical econs, London Univ., Oxford Univ. and Univ. of S California, LA. Formerly: Broadcaster, current affairs, BBC Radio; Man. Dir, Commercial Radio Gp; Founder Dir, Internat. Broadcast Electronics and Investment Gp, 1979–91. PPS to Financial Sec., HM Treasury, 1996–97; Opposition front-bench spokesman on economic affairs, 2003–05; an Opposition Whip, 2005–10; a Lord Comr of HM Treasury (Govt Whip), 2010–12. Member, Select Committee: Nat. Heritage, 1993–96, 1997–2005; Culture, Media and Sport, 1997–99, 2001–05; Home Affairs, 1999–2001; Information, 2001–03 (Chm., 2001–03); Member: European Legislation Scrutiny Cttee B, 1993–97; Finance and Services Cttee, 2001–03; Liaison Cttee, 2001–03; Admin Cttee, 2015–; Dep. Chm., All Party Cable and Satellite Gp, 1997–99 (Treas., 1995–97); Vice Chairman: All Party Gp on Smoking and Health, 1997–2010; All Party Anglo-German Gp, 1997–2010; All Party Gp on Film Industry, 1997–2010; Jt Chm., All Party Internet Gp, 1998–2003; Chairman: Royal Marines All Party Parly Gp, 2005–10 (Jt Chm., 1999–2005); Cons. Friends of America, 2008–; Dep. Chm., Cons. Parly Media Cttee, 1992–96. Vice Chm., Cons. Party, 2012–14. FCMI; FRSA. *Publications:* various newspaper articles and pamphlets. *Recreations:* fell-walking, reading, music (Mozart to rock), ski-ing, listening to the Archers. *Address:* House of Commons, SW1A 0AA. *Club:* Blacks.

**FACENNA, Gerald Carlo**; QC 2016; *b* Glasgow, 1975; *s* of Geraldo Facenna and Edith Facenna (*née* Gillies); *m* 2016, Dameeli Coates; three *s*. *Educ:* High Sch. of Glasgow; Clare Coll., Cambridge (BA 1996); Univ. of Edinburgh (LLB 1998). Called to the Bar, Lincoln's Inn, 2001; in practice as barrister, specialising in admin., competition and EU law, 2001–; Advocate, Faculty of Advocates, Scotland, 2006–. *Publications:* EU Competition Law: procedures and remedies, 2006; (contrib.) Halsbury's Laws of England: Rights and Freedoms, 2013; (contrib.) Information Rights: law and practice, 2014. *Recreations:* children, swimming, wine, music. *Address:* Monckton Chambers, 1 & 2 Raymond Buildings, Gray's Inn, WC1R 5NR. *T:* (020) 7405 7211. *E:* gfacenna@monckton.com.

**FACER, Roger Lawrence Lowe**, CB 1992; Deputy Under-Secretary of State, Ministry of Defence, 1988–93; *b* 28 June 1933; *s* of late John Ernest Facer and Phyllis Facer; *m* 1960, Ruth Margaret, *o d* of late Herbert Mostyn Lewis, PhD, Gresford, Clwyd; three *d*. *Educ:* Rugby; St John's Coll., Oxford (MA); Royal Holloway, Univ. of London (MA 2000). HM Forces, 2nd Lieut, East Surrey Regt, 1951–53. War Office, 1957; Asst Private Sec. to Secretary of State, 1958; Private Sec. to Permanent Under-Sec., 1958; Principal, 1961; Cabinet Office, 1966; Ministry of Defence, 1968–93: Private Sec. to Minister of State (Equipment), 1970; Asst Sec., 1970; Internat. Inst. for Strategic Studies, 1972–73; Counsellor, UK Delegn, MBFR Vienna, 1973–75; Private Sec. to Sec. of State for Defence, 1976–79; Asst Under-Sec. of State, 1979–81; Under Sec., Cabinet Office, 1981–83; Rand Corporation, Santa Monica, USA, 1984; Asst Under-Sec. of State, MoD, 1984–87. *Publications:* Weapons Procurement in Europe—Capabilities and Choices, 1975; Conventional Forces and the NATO Strategy of Flexible Response, 1985; articles in Alpine Garden Soc. Bulletin. *Recreations:* Alpine gardening, opera. *Address:* Kennett Lodge, Hambledon, Hants PO7 4SA.

**FACEY, Dr Karen Maria, (Mrs Philip Gaskell)**; evidence based health policy consultant, since 2003; *b* Braunton, Devon, 13 Dec. 1963; *d* of late Frederick Facey and Ivy Facey; *m* 2006, Dr Philip Gaskell. *Educ:* Braunton Sch. and Community Coll.; North Devon Coll.; City Univ., London (BSc 1st Cl. Stats); Univ. of Reading (PhD Stats 1991). CStat 1998. Statistician, Pfizer, 1986–87; Res. Fellow, Univ. of Reading, 1990–92; Statistics Manager, Roche UK, 1992–95; Sen. Statistical Assessor, MHRA, 1995–99; Chief Exec., Health Technol. Bd for Scotland, 2000–03; Mem., Scottish Health Technologies Gp, 2011–. Dir, Health Technol. Assessment Internat., 2017–. Sen. Res. Fellow, Usher Inst. of Population Health Scis and Informatics, Univ. of Edinburgh, 2018–. Hon. Officer, Royal Statistical Soc., 2016–. FRSocMed 2006. Hon. MFPH 2002. *Publications:* (ed jtly) Patient Involvement in Health Technology Assessment, 2017; articles in Internat. Jl of Technol. Assessment in Health Care, Patient, New England Jl of Medicine, Health Policy, Orphanet. *Recreations:* Scottish Episcopal Church, classical concerts, enjoying Scottish countryside. *Address:* Woodlands Lodge, Buchanan Castle Estate, Drymen G63 0HX. *T:* and *Fax:* (01360) 660316. *E:* k.facey@btinternet.com.

**FAGAN, Anne Marie**, CBE 2000; Head Teacher, John Ogilvie High School, Hamilton, 1991–2007; *b* 17 Dec. 1947; *d* of Edward Irons and Helen (*née* Muir); *m* 1969, Bernard Fagan; two *c*. *Educ:* St Patrick's High Sch., Coatbridge; Strathclyde Univ. (BA); Jordanhill Coll. (PGCE Dist.). Teacher of Business Educn, Columba High Sch., Coatbridge, 1969–79; Principal Teacher of Business Educn, Cardinal Newman High Sch., 1979–84;

Asst Hd Teacher, Curriculum/Middle Sch., John Ogilvie High Sch., 1984–91. Pres., Catholic Headteachers Assoc. of Scotland, 2000–02 (Vice-Pres., 1998–2000); Mem. Exec., Head Teachers Assoc. of Scotland. Chair, Conforti Inst. (formerly Global Educn Centre) (Bd Mem., 2005–10); Mem., Nat. Adv. Gp, Schs of Ambition Prog., 2005–07. Former GTC Rep. on Bd of Govs, St Andrew's Coll. of Educn, Bearsden, Glasgow. Mem. Bd, Lanarkshire Orchestral Soc., 1996–98. FRSA. Lady Capt., Hamilton Golf Club, 2017. *Recreations:* singing (leading lady in light operatic society, 1986–96), playing piano, keep fit, running, painting, golf.

**FAGAN, Sir David (Alexander),** KNZM 2016 (ONZM 2007; MNZM 1999); farmer; Chairman, Shearing Sports New Zealand, since 2015; *b* Te Kuiti, NZ, 13 Oct. 1961; *s* of Christopher and June Fagan; *m* 1990, Wendy Hawkins; one *s* one *d*. *Educ:* Piopio Primary Sch.; Piopio Coll. Shearing contractor, 1990–2007. Champion sheep shearer: winner: 642 open championships incl. 16 NZ Open titles and 17 times Golden Shears champion; 7 world team championships; represented NZ 120 times in team events; retired 2015, ranked No 1 in NZ. Ambassador, Lister Shearing Equipt in UK, 2005–. *Address:* PO Box 91, Te Kuiti 3941, New Zealand. *E:* fagan.david@xtra.co.nz.

**FAGAN, Lady (Florence) Mary,** LG 2018; DCVO 2009; JP; Lord-Lieutenant of Hampshire, 1994–2014; *b* 11 Sept. 1939; *o d* of Col George Vere-Laurie, JP, DL, Carlton Hall, Newark, Notts and Judith Caroline Vere-Laurie (*née* Franklin); *m* 1960, Capt. Christopher Fagan, Grenadier Guards; one *s* (and one *s* decd). *Educ:* Southover Manor, Sussex. Chm., Countess of Brecknock Hospice Trust, Andover, 1989–. Chm., Hants Magistrates Adv. Cttee, 1994–2014. President: Hants and IoW Youth Options, 1994–2014; Hants Br., Army Benevolent Fund, 1994–2014; Gift of Sight, 2011–; Vice-President: Southern Regl Assoc. for the Blind, 1994–2014; Mary Rose Trust, 1994–; Fortune Centre of Riding Therapy, 1994–2014; SSAFA; Patron: Rowans Hospice, Portsmouth, 1994–; Hants Music Trust, 1994–; Hants Br., BRCS, 1994–; Oakhaven Hospice, 1995–; Home-Start Eastleigh, 2002–14; New Forest Show, 2012. Chairman: Winchester Cathedral Develt Trust, 2000–; Portsmouth Cathedral Develt Trust, 2004–14. Hon. Prof. and Chancellor, Univ. of Winchester, 2006–15, now Chancellor Emeritus. Hon. Colonel: ACF, 1995–2009; 457 Battery, RA, 1998–2010; REME (Vol.) 4th Div., 2010–; Hon. Rear Admiral, RN, 2013–14 (Hon. Captain, 2001–07; Hon. Cdre, 2007–13). Liveryman, Saddlers' Co., 1996–. JP Hants, 1994; High Steward of Winchester, 2012. Freedom: City of Southampton, 2013; New Forest, 2013. Hon. DLitt Southampton, 1997; Hon. Dr jur Portsmouth, 2000. DStJ 1994. *Recreation:* country activities. *Address:* Deane Hill House, Deane, near Basingstoke, Hants RG25 3AX.

**FAGAN, Maj.-Gen. Patrick Feltrim,** CB 1990; MBE (mil.) 1966; FRICS 1971; FRGS 1966; *b* 8 Dec. 1935; *s* of late Air Cdre Thomas Patrick Feltrim Fagan and Hon. Isabel Mairi, *yr d* of 15th Baron Arundell of Wardour; *m* 1967, Veronica Thompson (*née* Lorant) (*d* 2003), *widow* of Captain C. J. C. Thompson, RE; two *s*. *Educ:* Stonyhurst Coll.; RMA, Sandhurst; University Coll. London (MSc (Hons) 1969). Commnd RE, 1955; served in Gibraltar, Germany, Aden and Oman. Internat. Scientific Expedn to Karakoram, 1961–62; UAE-Oman Border Survey, 1964; Jt Services Expedn to S Georgia, 1964–65; Ordnance Survey, 1969–73; Geographic Advr, AFCENT, 1979–83; Chief Geographic Officer, SHAPE, 1983–85; Dir, Survey Operations and Prodn, 1985–87; Dir Gen. of Military Survey, 1987–90. Member: Council, RGS, 1987–92 and 1993–95 (Vice-Pres., 1990–92); Council, BSES, 1987–90; Cttee of Management, Mt Everest Foundn, 1989–95 (Chm., 1992–94); Nat. Cttee for Photogrammetry and Remote Sensing, 1987–91; Adv. Bd, Inst. of Engrg, Surveying and Space Geodesy, Nottingham Univ., 1987–91; Council, RICS Land Surveyors, 1988–91; RICS Pres.'s Disciplinary and Appeals Tribunal, 1989–95; Pres., Defence Surveyors' Assoc., 2004–12. Dep. Pres., Army RU, 1989–91. Col Comdt, RE, 1991–96, Rep. Col Comdt, 1992. Chm., James Caird Soc., 2000–06. FCMI (FBIM 1971). *Publications:* articles on surveying and mapping in Geographical Jl, Photogrammetric Record, Survey Rev., Chartered Surveyor, and on ski mountaineering in subject jls. *Recreations:* mountain sports, cricket, reading, photography, opera, travel. *Clubs:* Royal Over-Seas League, Alpine (Vice Pres., 1999–2001), Alpine Ski (Pres., 1995–98), Eagle Ski (Pres., 1988–90), MCC, Geographical.

**FAGGE, Sir John Christopher,** 12th Bt *cr* 1660, of Wiston, Sussex; *b* 30 April 1942; *o s* of Sir John William Frederick Fagge, 11th Bt and Ivy Gertrude (*née* Frier); *S* father, 2000, but his name does not appear on the Official Roll of the Baronetage; *m* 1974, Evelyn Joy Golding.

**FAHEY, Hon. John Joseph,** AC 2002; Chairman, World Anti-Doping Agency, 2007–13; *b* 10 Jan. 1945; *s* of Stephen Fahey and Annie (*née* Fahey); *m* 1968, Colleen Maree McGurren; one *s* two *d*. *Educ:* St Anthony's Convent, Picton, NSW; Chevalier Coll., Bowral, NSW; Univ. of Sydney Law Extension Cttee (Dip. Law). Practised law, Camden, NSW, 1971–86. New South Wales: MLA (L) Camden, 1984–88, Southern Highlands, 1988–96; Minister for Ind. Relns and Minister assisting the Premier, 1988–90; Minister for Ind. Relns, Further Educn, Trng and Employment, 1990–92; Premier, 1992–95; Treasurer, 1992–93; Minister for Econ. Develt, 1993–95. Australia: MHR (L) Macarthur, NSW, 1996–2001; Minister for Finance, 1996–2001, for Admin, 1997–2001. Chairman: Australian Rugby League Develt, 2002–12; Lane Cove Tunnel, 2005–11; Commonwealth Reconstruction Authy, 2011–15; Assetinsure Hldgs Pty Ltd, 2003–16; Sydney Olympic Park Authy, 2016–; Australian Bldg Codes Bd, 2017–. Sen. Advr, Business Adv. Council, J. P. Morgan Australia, 2002–. Director: Avant Insurance Gp, 2004–; Endeavour Energy Ltd, 2002–12. Chancellor, Australian Catholic Univ., 2014–. Hon. DLitt Western Sydney, 2013. Centenary Medal (Australia), 2001. *Recreations:* tennis, Rugby, cricket, gardening, reading.

**FAHY, Sir Peter (Martin),** Kt 2012; QPM 2004; Director of Structural Reform, Hope for Justice, since 2018 (Chief Executive Officer, Retrak, 2015–18); *b* London, 18 Jan. 1959; *m* 1981, Jenny; four *c*. *Educ:* Univ. of Hull (BA Hons 1981); Univ. of E Anglia (MA 1998). Joined Police Force, 1981; Asst Chief Constable, Surrey, 1997–2002; Chief Constable: Cheshire Constabulary, 2002–08; Greater Manchester Police, 2008–15. Hon. Prof. of Criminal Justice, Univ. of Manchester, 2015–. *Recreations:* running, charity work, theatre, singing. *Address:* Hope for Justice, PO Box 5527, Manchester M61 0QU.

**FAINT, John Anthony Leonard, (Tony),** CBE 2002; consultant on international development, since 2003; Director (International), Department for International Development, 1997–2002; *b* 24 Nov. 1942; *s* of Thomas Leonard Faint and Josephine Rosey Faint (*née* Dunkerley); *m* 1st, 1978, Elizabeth Theresa Winter (*d* 2002); 2nd, 2004, Dorothy Isobelle Rankin (*d* 2015). *Educ:* Chigwell Sch.; Magdalen Coll., Oxford (BA Lit.Hum. 1965); MA Development Economics, Fletcher Sch., Mass, 1969. Ministry of Overseas Development (later Overseas Development Administration), London, 1965–71 (study leave in Cambridge, Mass, 1968–69); First Secretary (Aid), Blantyre, Malawi, 1971–73; ODM/ODA, London, 1974–80; Head of SE Asia Develt Div., Bangkok, 1980–83; Head of Finance Dept, ODA, FCO, 1983–86; Alternate Exec. Dir, World Bank, Washington, 1986–89; Head, E Asia Dept, 1989–90, Under Sec., Internat. Div., 1990–91, ODA; on secondment as UK Dir, EBRD, 1991–92; Under Sec. (Eastern Europe), ODA, 1991–93; Under Sec. (Eastern Europe and Western Hemisphere), ODA, later DFID, 1993–97. Chm., Trustees, Most Mira, 2017–. *Recreations:* music, bridge, walking, ski-ing. *Address:* 7 The Leyes, Deddington, Oxon OX15 0TX.

**FAIRBAIRN, Alasdair Chisholm;** Chief Executive, Sea Fish Industry Authority, 1997–2002; *b* 23 Jan. 1940; *s* of late Douglas Chisholm Fairbairn, CIE, CBE and Agnes Fairbairn (*née* Arnott); *m* 1964, Charlotte Henriette Tichelman; two *s* one *d*. *Educ:* Trinity Coll., Glenalmond, Perthshire; Corpus Christi Coll., Cambridge (MA Hons). Man. Dir, Conimex BV, Netherlands, 1975–78; Reckitt & Colman plc: Chief Manager, Planning and Evaluation, 1978–80; Regl Dir, 1980–84; Dir, LR Overseas Ltd, 1984–91; Chief Exec., Potato Mktg Bd, 1991–97. *Recreations:* walking, computers, concerts.

**FAIRBAIRN, Andrew Finlay,** FRCPsych; Consultant in Old Age Psychiatry, Newcastle General Hospital, 1989–2008; Medical Director, Northumberland, Tyne and Wear NHS Trust, 2006–08 (Acting Chief Executive, 2007–08); *b* 16 April 1950; *s* of Thomas Andrew Fairbairn and Pauline Mary Fairbairn; *m* 1971, Andrea Mary Hudson; one *s* two *d*. *Educ:* George Watson's Coll., Edinburgh; Newcastle upon Tyne Univ. (MB BS 1974). FRCPsych 1989. Consultant Psychiatrist, St Nicholas' Hosp., Newcastle upon Tyne, 1981–88. Medical Director: Newcastle Mental Health Trust, 1992–94; Newcastle City Health, 2000–01; Newcastle, N Tyneside and Northumberland Mental Health Trust, 2002–06 (Jt Med. Dir, 2001–02). Sen. Policy Advr (pt-time), 1994–98, Mem., Nat. Taskforce for Older People, 2000–04, DoH; Chm., Jt NICE/SCIE Guidelines Develt Gp on Dementia, 2004–06. Non-exec. Dir, Gateshead Hosps NHS Foundn Trust, 2009–15. Hon. Chm., Faculty for Psychiatry of Old Age, 1998–2002, Hon. Registrar, 2002–05, RCPsych. *Recreations:* house in France, 19th century history and biography. *Address:* 3 Killiebrigs, Heddon on the Wall, Northumberland NE15 0DD. *T:* (01661) 852686.

**FAIRBAIRN, Dame Carolyn (Julie),** DBE 2019; Director-General, Confederation of British Industry, since 2015; *b* 13 Dec. 1960; *d* of late David Ritchie Fairbairn, OBE; *m* 1991, Peter Harrison Chittick; one *s* two *d*. *Educ:* Wycombe High Sch. for Girls; Bryanston (Schol.); Gonville and Caius Coll., Cambridge (Hon. Sen. Scholar, MA); Univ. of Pennsylvania (Thouron Schol., MA); INSEAD, Fontainebleau (MBA). Economist, World Bank, Washington, 1984–85; financial writer, The Economist, 1985–87; Mgt Consultant, McKinsey & Co., London and Paris, 1988–94; Mem., Prime Minister's Policy Unit, 1995–97; Dir of Strategy, BBC Worldwide, 1997–99; Dir of Strategy, then of Strategy and Distribution, BBC, 2000–04; Principal, McKinsey & Co., London, 2006–07; Dir of Gp Develt and Strategy, ITV, 2007–11. Non-executive Director: FSA, 2008–11; UK Statistics Authy, 2013–15; Competition and Mkts Authy, 2013–15. Non-executive Director: Vitec Gp plc, 2012–15; Lloyds Banking Gp, 2012–15; Capita plc, 2014–15. Mem., Cttee on Standards in Public Life, 2014–15. Chair, RTS, 2010–11 (Vice-Chair, 2008–10). Trustee, Marie Curie Cancer Care, 2012–16. *Recreations:* tennis, travel. *Address:* Winchester, Hants.

**FAIRBAIRN, Erik;** Founder and Chief Executive Officer, POD Point Ltd, since 2009; *b* Redhill, 27 Feb. 1977. *Educ:* Univ. of Sheffield (BEng Hons 1999). Engr, MSX Internat., 2000–03; Innovation Manager, Britvic Soft Drinks, 2004–05; Founder and CEO, ecurie25 Ltd, 2005–09. Mem., Young Presidents' Orgn. *Recreation:* cycling. *Address:* POD Point Ltd, Discovery House, 28–42 Banner Street, EC1Y 8QE. *E:* erik.fairbairn@pod-point.com.

**FAIRBAIRN, James Bennett,** OBE 2007; FREng; FRSE; Chief Executive Officer, Megger Group Ltd, since 2017; *b* Edinburgh, 18 Oct. 1968; *s* of James and Mary Fairbairn; *m* 2002, Teresa Turner; one *d*. *Educ:* Denny High Sch.; Univ. of Strathclyde (BEng Mech. Engrg 1992); Loughborough Univ. (MBA 2002). FREng 2013. Lead Engr, Wood Gp, 1995–96; Engrg Dir, 1996–2000, Man. Dir, 2000–07, Clyde Bergemann; Divl CEO, Clyde Process Solutions, 2008–09; Man. Dir, Howden Compressors, 2009–11; Exec. Dir, Howden Gp, 2011–17. FRSE 2017. *Publications:* Nothing Changes Until You Do, 2004; The Game of Business, 2016. *Recreations:* golf, football, ski-ing, running. *Address:* Megger Group Ltd, Archcliffe Road, Dover CT17 9EN. *T:* (01304) 502100. *E:* jim.fairbairn@megger.com. *Club:* Turnberry Golf.

**FAIRBAIRN, John Sydney;** Trustee, 1966–2008, and Chairman, 1988–2003, Esmée Fairbairn Foundation (formerly Esmée Fairbairn Charitable Trust); *b* 15 Jan. 1934; *s* of Sydney George Fairbairn, MC and Angela Maude Fairbairn (*née* Fane); *m* 1968, Mrs Camilla Fry (*d* 2000), *d* of late G. N. Grinling; one *s* two *d*, and two step *s* two step *d*; *m* 2001, Felicity, *widow* of 3rd Baron Milford; two step *s* three step *d*. *Educ:* Eton; Trinity College, Cambridge (MA). 2nd Lt, 17/21 Lancers, 1952–54. ACA 1960. With M & G Group, 1961–99: Dep. Chm., 1979–89; non-exec. Dir, 1989–99. Dep. Chm., Lautro, 1986–89. Chairman: Unit Trust Assoc., 1989–91; Central European Growth Fund plc, 1994–2000. Council Mem. and Treasurer, King's College London, 1972–84 (Fellow 1978); Council Member: Univ. of Buckingham, 1986–95; Policy Studies Inst., 1991–97. Trustee: Monteverdi Trust, 1991–96; Royal Pavilion, Art Gall. and Mus of Brighton, 1993–2001; Dulwich Picture Gall., 1994–97 DL West Sussex, 1996–2001. DUniv Buckingham, 1992. *Address:* The Old Vicarage, Powerstock, Dorset DT6 3TE. *Clubs:* Beefsteak, Brooks's.

**FAIRBAIRN, Sir Robert (William),** 7th Bt *cr* 1869, of Ardwick; Senior Managing Director, BlackRock Inc., since 2016; *b* Cambridge, 10 April 1965; *s* of Sir (James) Brooke Fairbairn, 6th Bt and Mary Fairbairn (*née* Russell Scott); *S* father, 2017; *m* 1990, Sarah Frances Colleypriest, *e d* of Roger Griffin; two *s* two *d*. *Educ:* King's Sch., Ely; Durham Univ. (BA 1987). Investment manager, GT Mgt; Lazard Investors, 1990–93; Mercury Asset Mgt, 1993–99; Hd, EMEA Sales Div., 1999–2001, Chief Operating Officer, EMEA Pacific Reg., 2001, Sen. Vice Pres. and Mem. Exec. Cttee, Merrill Lynch Investment Managers; BlackRock Inc.: Hd, Global Client Gp and Chm., Internat. Businesses, 2012; Global Hd, Retail and iShares, 2012–16; Mem., Global Exec. Cttee; Mem., Global Operating Cttee; Co. Chair, Human Capital Cttee; Mem. Bd, Equity Bond Mutual Fund. Trustee, Pitzer Coll., Calif. *Recreations:* fly fishing, boating. *Heir:* *s* Jack Edmund Brooke Fairbairn, *b* 22 March 1995. *E:* robandgriff@btinternet.com. *Club:* Mill Reef (Antigua).

**FAIRBANK, Judith;** *see* Pallot, J.

**FAIRBURN, Prof. Christopher James Alfred Granville;** Wellcome Principal Research Fellow, 1996–2017, and Professor of Psychiatry, 1996, University of Oxford, now Emeritus Professor; *b* 20 Sept. 1950; *s* of Ernest Alfred Fairburn and Margaret Isabel Fairburn; *m* 1st, 1979, Susan Margaret Russam (marr. diss. 2007); one *s* one *d*; 2nd, 2009, Kristin Sonja Bohn; one *s*. *Educ:* Malvern Coll.; Worcester Coll., Oxford (BM BCh); DM. FRCPsych. University of Oxford: Res. Psychiatrist, 1981–84; Wellcome Trust Sen. Lectr, 1984–96; Hon. Clinical Reader, 1991–96. Hon. Consultant Psychiatrist, Oxford Health NHS Foundn Trust (formerly Oxfordshire Mental Healthcare NHS Trust), 1984–. Governor: Wellcome Trust, 2008–11; MQ: Research for Mental Health, 2011–17. FMedSci 2001. *Publications:* Binge Eating: nature, assessment and treatment, 1993; Eating Disorders and Obesity: a comprehensive handbook, 1995, 2nd edn 2002; Science and Practice of Cognitive Behaviour Therapy, 1997; Cognitive Behavior Therapy and Eating Disorders, 2008; contrib. numerous articles to learned jls. *Recreations:* design, wine, travelling off the beaten track.

**FAIRCLOUGH, Oliver Noel Francis**, FSA; Honorary Research Fellow, Amgueddfa Cymru—National Museum Wales (formerly National Museums and Galleries of Wales), Cardiff, since 2015 (Keeper of Art, 1998–2015); *b* 27 March 1950; *s* of late Arthur Basil Rowland Fairclough and Jean McKenzie Fairclough (*née* Fraser); *m* 1977, Caroline Mary Latta; one *s* two *d. Educ:* Bryanston Sch.; Trinity Coll., Oxford (BA); Univ. of Keele (MA). AMA 1978; FSA 2009. Asst, Liverpool Mus., 1971–74; Asst Keeper, Art, 1975–79, Dep. Keeper, Applied Art, 1979–86, Birmingham Museums and Art Gall.; Asst Keeper, Applied Art, Nat. Mus. of Wales, 1986–98. Lectr and author. Mem., various adv. bodies and learned socs. Chm., French Porcelain Soc., 2015–. Trustee, Peak Cymru (formerly Arts Alive Wales), 2015–. *Publications:* (with E. Leary) Textiles by William Morris, 1981; The Grand Old Mansion, 1984; (with M. Evans) Companion Guide to the National Art Gallery, 1993, 2nd edn 1997; The Llanthony Valley: a borderland, 2018; contribs to exhibn catalogues; contrib. to Burlington Mag. and other art Jls. *Recreations:* walking, travel, architectural history, naval and military history. *Address:* Tyn y Llwyn, Partrishow, Crickhowell, Breconshire NP7 7LT. *T:* (01873) 890540.

**FAIREY, Michael Edward;** Chairman, Hastings Group Holdings Ltd, 2015–18; *b* 17 June 1948; *s* of late Douglas and Marjorie Fairey; 1973, Patricia Ann Dolby; two *s. Educ:* King Edward VI Grammar Sch., Louth. ACIB 1974. Barclays Bank, 1967–92: Asst Dir, Watford Gp, 1986; Ops Dir, Barclaycard, 1986–88; Exec. Dir, Barclays Card Services, 1988–92; Dir, Retail Credit, and Gp Credit Dir, 1992, Gp Dir, Credit and Ops, 1993–96, TSB Gp; Lloyds TSB Group plc: IT and Ops Dir, 1996–97; Gp Dir, Central Services, 1997–98; Dep. Gp Chief Exec., 1998–2008. Chairman: APR Energy plc (formerly Horizon), 2010–14; Vertex Data Sci. Ltd, 2012 (Dir, 2007); One Savings Bank, 2014–17; non-executive Director: Energy Saving Trust; VTX Bidco; Bibby Financial Services, 2017–. Chm., Race for Opportunity; Bd Mem., Business in the Community. Former Pres., British Quality Foundn. *Recreations:* tennis, opera, football.

**FAIREY, Michael John**, CB 1989; Chief Executive, The Royal London Hospital and Associated Community NHS Trust, 1991–94; *b* 20 Sept. 1933; *s* of late Ernest John Saunder Fairey and Lily Emily (*née* Pateman); *m* 1st, 1958 (marr. diss. 1989); two *s* one *d*; 2nd, 1990, Victoria Frances Hardman. *Educ:* Queen Elizabeth's Sch., Barnet; Jesus Coll., Cambridge (MA). Served RA, 1952–53. Jun. Administrator, St Thomas' Hosp., 1957–60; Gp Develt Sec., Westminster Hosp., 1960–62; Deputy House Governor, The London Hosp., 1962, House Governor 1972; Regional Administrator, NE Thames RHA, 1973; Dir, Planning and Inf., NHS Management Bd, DHSS, later Dept of Health, 1984–89; Dir of Information Systems, NHS Management Exec., Dept of Health, 1989–91. Sec., London Hospital Med. Coll., 1994–96. Gov., St Catherine's Sch., Ware, 1995–2018 (Chm., 1997–2000). *Publications:* various articles in med. and computing jls. *Recreations:* church music, history of medieval exploration, Rugby football. *Club:* Athenæum.

**FAIRFAX,** family name of **Lord Fairfax of Cameron**.

**FAIRFAX OF CAMERON**, 14th Lord *cr* 1627; **Nicholas John Albert Fairfax;** Director, Sovcomflot (UK) Ltd, since 2005; Chairman, SCF Overseas Holdings Ltd, since 2012; *b* 4 Jan. 1956; *e s* of 13th Lord Fairfax of Cameron and Sonia, *yr d* of late Capt. Cecil Gunston, MC; *S* father, 1964; *m* 1982, Annabel, *er d* of late Nicholas and of Sarah Gilham Morriss; three *s. Educ:* Eton; Downing Coll., Cambridge (LLB in international law subjects, 1981). Called to the Bar, Gray's Inn, 1977. Director: Thomas Miller P and I, and Thomas Miller Defence, 1987–90; Sedgwick Marine & Cargo Ltd, 1995–96; North of England P&I Assoc. Ltd, 2012–. Chm., Adv. Bd, Hawki Worldwide Ltd, 2016–. Elected Mem., H of L, 2015–. Patron: AMUR Tiger and Leopard Charity, 2006–; Tyoply Dom (Warm House), 2016–; Downside Up, 2016–. *Recreations:* sailing, adventure motorcycling, photography. *Heir: s* Hon. Edward Nicholas Thomas Fairfax, *b* 20 Sept. 1984. *Address:* 10 Orlando Road, SW4 0LF. *Club:* Royal Yacht Squadron (Cowes).

**FAIRFAX-LUCY, Sir Edmund (John William Hugh Cameron-Ramsay-)**, 6th Bt *cr* 1836; painter, chiefly of still-life and interiors; *b* 4 May 1945; *s* of Sir Brian Fulke Cameron-Ramsay-Fairfax-Lucy, 5th Bt and Hon. Alice Caroline Helen Buchan (*d* 1993), *o d* of 1st Baron Tweedsmuir, PC, GCMG, GCVO, CH; *S* father, 1974; *m* 1994, Erica, *d* of Warren Loane, Crocknaerieve, Enniskillen; two *s. Educ:* City and Guilds of London Art Sch.; Royal Academy Schs of Art. Regular exhibitor, RA Summer Exhibn, 1967–; one-man shows, numerous mixed exhibitions. *Heir: s* Patrick Samuel Thomas Fulke Fairfax-Lucy, *b* 3 April 1995.

**FAIRHAVEN**, 3rd Baron *cr* 1929 and 1961 (new creation); **Ailwyn Henry George Broughton;** JP; Vice Lord-Lieutenant, Cambridgeshire, 1977–85; *b* 16 Nov. 1936; *s* of 2nd Baron Fairhaven and Hon. Diana Rosamond (*d* 1983), *o d* of late Captain Hon. Coulson Fellowes; *S* father, 1973; *m* 1960, Kathleen Patricia, *d* of late Col James Henry Magill, OBE; three *s* two *d* (and one *s* decd). *Educ:* Eton; RMA, Sandhurst. Royal Horse Guards, 1957–71. Mem., Jockey Club, 1977– (Steward, 1981–82, Sen. Steward, 1985–89). DL Cambridgeshire and Isle of Ely, 1973; JP South Cambridgeshire, 1975. KStJ 1992. *Recreations:* gardening, cooking. *Heir: s* Major Hon. James Henry Ailwyn Broughton [*b* 25 May 1963; *m* 1990, Sarah Olivia, *d* of late Harold Digby Fitzgerald Creighton; one *s* two *d*]. *Address:* Kirtling Tower, Cambs CB8 9PA. *Club:* White's.

**FAIRHEAD**, Baroness *cr* 2018 (Life Peer), of Yarm in the County of North Yorkshire; **Rona Alison Fairhead,** CBE 2012; *b* 28 Aug. 1961; *m*; three *c. Educ:* Yarm Grammar Sch.; St Catharine's Coll., Cambridge (BA; Hon. Fellow 2012); Harvard Business Sch. (MBA). Associate Consultant, Bain & Co., 1983–87; analyst, Morgan Stanley Internat., 1988; Manager, Bain & Co., 1989–90; ind. consultant, British Aerospace plc, 1991; Short Bros plc, later Bombardier Inc.: joined 1991; Vice-President: Corp. Strategy and Public Affairs, 1994–95; UK Aerospace Services, 1995–96; ICI plc: Dir of Planning and Acquisitions, 1996–97; Executive Vice President: for Planning and Communications, 1997–98; Strategy and Control, 1998–2001; Dep. Finance Dir, 2001–02, Chief Financial Officer, 2002–06, Pearson plc; Chm. and Chief Exec., Financial Times Gp, 2006–13; Chm., BBC Trust, 2014–17. Non-executive Director: Lagansile Corp., Belfast, 1994–2000; HSBC Hldgs plc, 2004–16; PepsiCo, 2014–17; Mem. Bd of Dirs, Oracle, 2019–. Minister of State for Trade and Export Promotion, DIT, 2017–19. *Address:* House of Lords, SW1A 0PW.

**FAIRHEAD, Melissa Anne;** *see* Leach, M. A.

**FAIRHURST, Robert John D.;** *see* Douglas-Fairhurst.

**FAIRLEY, Douglas;** QC (Scot.) 2012; *b* Glasgow, 20 Feb. 1968; *s* of late John A. Fairley and of Marjorie Fairley; *m* 2000, Una Doherty; one *s* one *d. Educ:* Hutcheson's Grammar Sch., Glasgow; Glasgow Univ. (LLB Hons). Admitted as solicitor, 1992; Solicitor, Maclay Murray & Spens, 1992–98; called to Faculty of Advocates, 1999; Employment Judge, Scotland and England, 2009–13; Advocate Depute, 2011–15. Dir, Tennis Scotland, 2014–16. *Publications:* Contempt of Court in Scotland, 2000. *Recreations:* tennis, ski-ing, music. *Address:* Advocates Library, Parliament House, Edinburgh EH1 1RF. *T:* (0131) 226 5071. *E:* douglas.fairley@advocates.org.uk. *Clubs:* Victory Services; New (Edinburgh).

**FAIRLEY, John Alexander;** Chairman: Highflyer Productions, since 1996; Trainers House Enterprises, since 2004; *s* of Alexander Miller Fairley and Madge Irene Fairley; *m*; three *d. Educ:* Merchant Taylors' Sch., Crosby; Queen's Coll., Oxford (MA). Midshipman, RNVR. Journalist: Bristol Evening Post, 1963; London Evening Standard, 1964; Producer: BBC Radio, 1965–68; Yorkshire TV, 1968–78; freelance writer and broadcaster, 1979–84; Dir of Programmes, Yorkshire TV, 1984–92; Managing Director: Yorkshire TV Programmes, 1992–93; Yorkshire TV, 1993–95; Chief Exec., UK TV, 1995–96; Chairman: ITV Broadcast Bd, 1995; K Max Radio, 1995–97; Channel 4 Racing, 1997–2012; Highfield Racing, 2006. TV presenter, Mysterious World (series), 2016. Mem., British Horseracing Bd Stud and Stable Staff Commn, 2004. Trustee, Injured Jockeys Fund, 1999–2016. FRTS 1994; FRSA. *Publications:* (jtly) The Monocled Mutineer, 1978; (jtly) Arthur C. Clarke's Mysterious World, 1980, and subseq. vols, 1984, 1987; Great Racehorses In Art, 1984; Racing In Art, 1990; (jtly) The Cabinet of Curiosities, 1991; The Art of the Horse, 1995; Horses of the Great War: the story in art, 2015; (jtly) Heartbeat and Beyond, 2017; The Armistice and the Aftermath: the story in art, 2018. *Recreations:* writing, racing, hunting. *Address:* Trainers House, Eddlethorpe, Malton, Yorks YO17 9QS.

**FAIRLEY, Josephine;** *b* London, 10 July 1956; *d* of Peter Alan Fairley and Vivienne Fairley; *m* 1991, Craig Lynn Sams, *qv. Educ:* Bromley High Sch. for Girls. Editor: Look Now mag., 1979–82; Honey mag., 1982–85; columnist, Ecosphere, The Times, 1988–91; Co-Founder: Green & Black's Chocolate, 1991; The Perfume Society, 2014. Hon. DBA Kingston, 2006. *Publications:* The Ultimate Natural Beauty Book, 2004; (with Craig Sams) Sweet Dreams: the story of Green & Black's, 2008; (with Sarah Stacey) The Green Beauty Bible, 2008; (with Sarah Stacey) The Anti-Ageing Beauty Bible, 2011; Yoga for Life, 2012; (with Sarah Stacey) The Ultimate Natural Beauty Bible, 2014; (with Lorna McKay) The Perfume Bible, 2014. *Recreations:* sea bathing, yoga, kindle reading, travel. *Address:* 106 High Street, Hastings, E Sussex TN34 3ES. *T:* (01424) 203751. *E:* jo@josephinefairley.com. *Clubs:* Groucho, House of St Barnabas.

**FAIRLEY, Una Frances;** *see* Doherty, U. F.

**FAIRLIE-CUNINGHAME, Sir Robert (Henry)**, 17th Bt *cr* 1630, of Robertland, Ayrshire; *b* 19 July 1974; *o s* of Sir William Henry Fairlie-Cuninghame, 16th Bt and of Janet Menzies, *d* of R. M. Saddington; *S* father, 1999; *m* 2005, Mary Louise, *d* of Captain Geoffrey Hugh Belasyse-Smith, Broadstairs; one *d. Heir: cousin* David Hastings Fairlie-Cuninghame [*b* June 1937; *m* 1963, Susan Gai White; one *s* one *d*]. *Address:* 29a Orinoco Street, Pymble, NSW 2073, Australia.

**FAIRS, Marcus;** Founder and Editor-in-Chief, Dezeen, since 2006; *b* Rinteln, West Germany, 27 Nov. 1967; *s* of David Fairs and Georgina Fairs (now Ledward); *m* 1998, Rupinder Bhogal; one *s* one *d. Educ:* Harrow Way Sch., Andover; Cricklade Coll., Andover; Winchester Sch. of Art (Foundn Course Art and Design); Wolverhampton Poly. (BA Hons 3D Design). News Ed., Building Design mag., 1997–2000; Dep. Editor, Building mag., 2000–03; Editor, icon mag., 2003–06. Mem., Ind. Expert Adv. Panel for UK City of Culture 2021, 2017–. Hon. FRIBA 2017. *Publications:* Twenty-first Century Design, 2006, 3rd edn 2011; Green Design, 2008; Dezeen Book of Ideas, 2011; Dezeen Book of Interviews, 2014. *Recreations:* travel, gardening. *Address:* Dezeen Ltd, Third Floor, 8 Orsman Road, N1 5QJ. *T:* 07961 315705. *E:* marcus@dezeen.com. *Club:* Soho House.

**FAIRWEATHER, Prof. Denys Vivian Ivor**, MD; FRCOG; Secretary-General of International Federation of Gynaecology and Obstetrics, 1985–94; Professor and Head of Department of Obstetrics and Gynaecology, 1966–90, and Vice-Provost, 1984–90, University College London; Pro-Vice-Chancellor for Medicine and Dentistry, University of London, 1989–92; *b* 25 Oct. 1927; *s* of late Albert James Ivor Fairweather and Gertrude Mary Forbes; *m* 1956, (Gwendolen) Yvonne Hubbard (*d* 2014); one *s* two *d. Educ:* Forfar Acad.; Websters Seminary, Kirriemuir; St Andrews Univ. (MB, ChB 1949; MD 1966). FRCOG 1967 (MRCOG 1958). Served RAF Med. Br., 1950–55, Sqn Leader. Sen. Lectr, Univ. of Newcastle upon Tyne, 1959–66; Fulbright Scholar, Western Reserve Univ., USA, 1963–64; Dean, Faculty of Clinical Science, UCL, 1982–84; Vice Provost (Medicine) and Head, University Coll. London Sch. of Medicine, later University Coll. and Middx Sch. of Medicine of UCL, 1984–89; Hon. Fellow, UCL, 1985. Member: GMC, 1988–92; Internat. Med. Adv. Panel, IPPF, 1988–94; Vice Pres., FPA, 1985–98 (Patron, 1998). Hon. FAARM 1969; Hon. FACOG 1993. Freeman, City of Krakow, 1989. Dist. Service Award, FIGO, 1997. *Publications:* Amniotic Fluid Research and Clinical Applications, 1973, 2nd edn 1978; Labour Ward Manual, 1985; over 160 pubns in scientific jls, on perinatal mortality, rhesus disease, genetics, antenatal diagnosis, very low birthweight, medical education. *Recreations:* gardening, fishing, do-it-yourself. *Address:* 4 Kingston Farm Road, Woodbridge, Suffolk IP12 4BD.

**FAIRWEATHER, Eric John**, FCIB; financial consultant, retired; *b* 9 Nov. 1942; *s* of late John Walter William Fairweather and Lilian Emma Fairweather; *m* 1st, 1966, Frances Mary Ewer (marr. diss.); two *d*; 2nd, 1991, Deborah Chubb; two *s. Educ:* Carlisle Grammar Sch. CeMAP 2005; CeRGI 2006. Entered Midland Bank at Carlisle, 1961; Manager, Corporate Finance Div., 1978–81; Sen. Asst Man., Poultry and Princes Street, 1981–84; on secondment as Dir, Industrial Develt Unit, DTI (Under Sec.), 1984–86; Manager, UK Business Sector, Midland Bank, 1986; Manager, Central Management and Planning, 1986–87; Corporate Banking Area Manager, Manchester, 1987–93; Area Manager: Manchester, 1993–94; Sheffield, 1994–95; Regl Gen. Manager, NW, Co-operative Bank, 1995–98; Hd of Asset Finance, Co-operative Bank PLC, 1999–2002. Non-executive Director: Cartel Mktg Ltd, 2004–07; Cartel Gp Hldgs plc, 2004–07; SD Healthcare Ltd, 2008–09. Director: Sheffield TEC, 1994–95; Wigan Borough Partnership, 1996–2002. Sen. Consultant, Ultraforce Gp, 2011–13. Gov., Bolton Sch., 2006–. *Recreations:* classical music, Association football (Bolton Wanderers), golf. *Address:* 1 Talbenny Close, Heaton, Bolton BL1 5FG.

**FAIRWEATHER, Sir Patrick (Stanislaus)**, KCMG 1992 (CMG 1986); HM Diplomatic Service, retired; Senior Adviser, Citigroup (formerly Schroders, then Schroder Salomon Smith Barney), 1996–2007; Director, Butrint Foundation, 1997–2004; *b* 17 June 1936; *s* of John George Fairweather and Dorothy Jane (*née* Boanas); *m* 1962, Maria (*née* Merica) (*d* 2010); two *d. Educ:* Ottershaw Sch., Surrey; Trinity Coll., Cambridge (Hons History). National Service in Royal Marines and Parachute Regt, 1955–57. Entered FCO, 1965; 2nd Secretary, Rome, 1966–69; FCO, 1969–70; 1st Secretary (Economic), Paris, 1970–73; FCO, 1973–75; 1st Sec. and Head of Chancery, Vientiane, 1975–76; 1st Sec., UK Representation to EEC, Brussels, 1976–78; Counsellor (Economic and Commercial), Athens, 1978–83; Head of European Community Dept (Internal), FCO, 1983–85; Ambassador to Angola, 1985–87; Asst Under-Sec. of State, FCO, 1987–90; Dep. Under-Sec. of State (ME/Africa), FCO, 1990–92; Ambassador to Italy and (non-resident) to Albania, 1992–96. *Recreations:* travel, gardening, photography. *Club:* Garrick.

**FAIRWOOD, Ian Stuart;** a District Judge, 1996–2014; a Recorder, since 2001; *b* 16 May 1951; *s* of George Centenus Fairwood and Kathleen Florence Fairwood; *m* 1976, Hilary Joan Middleton; two *s. Educ:* Carlton Cavendish Secondary Modern; UCL (LLB). Bar Sch., 1974–75; called to the Bar, Middle Temple, 1974; Dep. Dist Judge, 1993–96; NE Circuit. *Recreations:* golf, tennis, gardening. *Clubs:* Notts County Football; Easingwold Golf.

**FAIZAL, Dr Farahanaz,** PhD; Ambassador of the Republic of Maldives to the Court of St James's, since 2019; *m* Dr Mohamed Ahmed Didi; one *d. Educ:* Univ. of Keele (BA Internat. Relns 1989); Queens' Coll., Cambridge (MPhil Internat. Relns 1991); Univ. of Hull (PhD Politics 1996). Res. Officer, 1989–91, Sen. Res. Officer, 1991–92, For. Relns Section, President's Office, Malé; Nat. Programme Officer, UN Population Fund, 1996–98; independent analyst and consultant with res. speciality of security problems of small island states, gender and internat. relns, 1998–2008; Advr to Min. of For. Affairs, 2008–09; High Comr for the Maldives in UK, 2009–12. Mem., Maldivian Democratic Party, 2006–. *Address:* Embassy of the Republic of Maldives, 22 Nottingham Place, W1U 5NJ.

**FALCON, David;** international public management consultant, 1992–2014; *b* 3 Jan. 1946; *s* of Arnold and Barbara Falcon; *m* 1st, 1967 (marr. diss. 1991); two *s*; 2nd, 1998, Simoné Mondesir. *Educ:* Helston County Grammar Sch.; University College London (BSc); Lancaster Univ. (MA); Univ. of Pennsylvania. Research Associate, Univ. of Lancaster, 1969–72; Lectr, Leeds Polytechnic, 1972–74; Sen. Lectr, Sheffield Polytechnic, 1974–76; Asst Dir, Sen. Asst Dir, Dep. Dir of Education, Humberside CC, 1976–85; Dir of Education, ILEA, 1985–88; Dir-Gen., RIPA, 1988–92. Mem., Manchester United Supporters' Trust, 2006–. Assoc., Fest. Pablo Casals, 2018–. *Publications:* articles in educn and management jls. *Recreations:* music, opera, photography, travel, bricolage. *Address:* 45 rue du Pérou, 66500 Prades, France. *T:* (4) 68057458.

**FALCONER,** family name of **Baron Falconer of Thoroton.**

**FALCONER OF THOROTON,** Baron *cr* 1997 (Life Peer), of Thoroton in the co. of Nottinghamshire; **Charles Leslie Falconer;** PC 2003; QC 1991; a Senior Counsel, Gibson, Dunn and Crutcher (formerly Gibson Dunn) LLP, since 2008; *b* 19 Nov. 1951; *s* of John Leslie Falconer and late Anne Mansel Falconer; *m* 1985, Marianna Catherine Thoroton Hildyard, *qv*; three *s* one *d. Educ:* Trinity Coll., Glenalmond; Queens' Coll., Cambridge (Hon. Fellow, 2003). Called to the Bar, Inner Temple, 1974, Bencher, 1997. Solicitor-General, 1997–98; Minister of State: Cabinet Office, 1998–2001; for Housing, Planning and Regeneration, DTLR, 2001–02; for Criminal Justice, Sentencing and Law Reform, Home Office, 2002–03; Sec. of State for Justice (formerly for Constitutional Affairs) and Lord Chancellor, 2003–07; Shadow Lord Chancellor and Shadow Sec. of State for Justice, 2015–16. Chairman: Amicus Horizon Gp Financing Ltd, 2008–12; 1NG Ltd, 2009–15. Chm., John Smith Meml Trust, 2007. Visitor, Queens' Coll., Cambridge, 2007–. Hon. DCL Northumbria, 2015. *Address:* House of Lords, SW1A 0PW. *E:* falconerc@parliament.uk.

**FALCONER OF THOROTON, Lady;** *see* Hildyard, M. C. T.

**FALCONER, Anthony Dale,** OBE 2014; DM; FRCOG; Consultant Obstetrician and Gynaecologist, Derriford Hospital, Plymouth, 1986–2013; President, Royal College of Obstetricians and Gynaecologists, 2010–13; *b* Edinburgh, 11 March 1949; *s* of Dale Falconer and Hermione Falconer; *m* 1979, Elizabeth Mallaband, three *s* one *d. Educ:* Wellington Coll., Berks; Napier Coll., Edinburgh; Univ. of Bristol (MB ChB 1972); Univ. of Nottingham (DM 1984). FRCOG 1991. Trainee Obstetrician and Gynaecologist, Edinburgh, Nottingham and Cape Town, 1974–86; Lectr in Physiology and Pharmacology, Univ. of Nottingham, 1979–81. Sen. Vice Pres., RCOG, 2007–10. Trustee, Acad. of Med. Royal Colls, 2011. Mem. Court, Queen Margaret Univ., Edinburgh, 2013–. FRCPE 2012. Hon. FICOG 2012; Hon. FCOG(SA) 2012; Hon. FACOG 2012. Hon. DSc: Plymouth, 2011; Bristol, 2013. *Publications:* articles on sympatho-adrenal activity in fetuses, cancer and global health issues affecting maternity. *Recreations:* hockey, golf, walking, music. *Club:* Murrayfield Golf.

**FALCONER, Prof. Kenneth John,** PhD; FRSE; Professor of Pure Mathematics, since 1993, and Regius Professor of Mathematics, since 2017, University of St Andrews; *b* Hampton Court, Middx, 25 Jan. 1952; *s* of Angus Duncan Falconer and Ivy Magdalene Muriel Falconer; *m* 1978, Isobel Jessie Nye; one *s* one *d. Educ:* Kingston Grammar Sch.; Corpus Christi Coll., Cambridge (BA 1974; PhD 1979; MMath 2014). Res. Fellow, Corpus Christi Coll., Cambridge, 1977–80; Lectr, 1980–88, Reader, 1988–93, Univ. of Bristol. Visiting Professor: Oregon State Univ., 1985–86; Isaac Newton Inst., Cambridge, 1999, 2011, 2015; Institut des Hautes Études Scientifique, Paris, 2005; ANU, Canberra, 2009; East China Normal Univ., Shanghai, 2010; Mittag-Leffler Inst., 2017. Mem. Council, LMS, 2000–09 (Pubns Sec., 2006–09). FRSE 1998. *Publications:* The Geometry of Fractal Sets, 1985; Fractal Geometry: mathematical foundations and applications, 1990, 3rd edn 2014; (jtly) Unsolved Problems in Geometry, 1991; Techniques in Fractal Geometry, 1997; Fractals: a very short introduction, 2013; 115 papers in res. jls, mainly on fractal geometry. *Recreations:* hillwalking (climbed Munros twice and Corbetts once), long distance walking (Chair, Long Distance Walkers Assoc., 2000–03, Editor, Strider jl, 1987–92 and 2007–12; Mem., Centurions 1911), reading P G Wodehouse. *Address:* Mathematical Institute, North Haugh, St Andrews, Fife KY16 9SS. *T:* (01334) 463733. *E:* kjf@st-andrews.ac.uk; (home) Lumbo Farmhouse, St Andrews, Fife KY16 8NS.

**FALCONER, Prof. Roger Alexander,** FREng; FLSW; Professor of Water Management, School of Engineering, Cardiff University, 1997–2018 (part-time, 2016–18), now Emeritus Professor of Water Engineering; Director, Roger Falconer Water Consultancy Ltd, since 2016; *b* 12 Dec. 1951; *s* of late Cyril Thomas Falconer and Winifred Mary Matilda Falconer (*née* Rudge); *m* 1977, Nicola Jane Wonson; two *s* one *d. Educ:* King's Coll., London (BSc(Eng)); Univ. of Washington, USA (MScE); Imperial Coll., London (PhD 1976; DIC 1976); Univ. of Birmingham (DEng 1992); Univ. of London (DSc(Eng) 1994). CEng 1982; FCIWEM 1990; FICE 1992; FREng (FEng 1997). Engr, Sir M. MacDonald and Partners, Cambridge, 1976–77; Lectr in Hydraulic Engrg, Dept of Civil Engrg, Univ. of Birmingham, 1977–86; University of Bradford: Prof. of Water Engrg, 1987–97; Hd, Dept of Civil and Envmtl Engrg, 1993–97. Hon. Prof., China Inst. of Water Resources and Hydropower Research, 2013–. Co-Chm., Gp of Experts, Internat. Tribunal for Law of the Sea Malaysia *v* Singapore Land Reclamation Case, 2003–05. Member: Govt Expert Panel on Severn Tidal Power Studies, 2008–10; Expert Panel, Hafren Power, 2012–14. Pres., Internat. Assoc. for Hydro-Envmt Engrg and Res. (formerly Internat. Assoc. for Hydraulic Res.), 2011–15 (Mem. Council, 1999–2007); Member, Council: CIWEM, 1997–2002 (Mem., Trustee Bd, 2016–); ICE, 2000–03. FASCE 1993; FCGI 1997; FLSW 2011. Ippen Award, Internat. Assoc. Hydraulic Res., 1991; Telford Premium, 1994, Robert Carr Prize, 2003, 2007, ICE; Silver Medal, Royal Acad. of Engrg, 1999; Hai He Award, China, 2004. *Publications:* edited: (jtly) Hydraulic and Environmental Modelling of Coastal, Estuarine and River Waters, 1989, 1992; (jtly) Wetland Management, 1994; over 400 jl and conf. papers, and over 80 tech. reports on hydro-envmtl modelling of coastal, estuarine and river waters. *Recreations:* music, walking, travel, Formula 1. *Address:* School of Engineering, Cardiff University, The Parade, Cardiff CF24 3AA. *T:* 07775 640468. *E:* FalconerRA@cardiff.ac.uk; 24 Moorfield Road, Ilkley, W Yorks LS29 8BL. *T:* (01943) 605847. *E:* rogerfalconer@btinternet.com.

**FALDO, Sir Nicholas Alexander, (Sir Nick),** Kt 2009; MBE 1988; professional golfer; Chairman, Faldo Design, since 1991; lead golf analyst for CBS Sports and The Golf Channel, since 2007; *b* 18 July 1957; *s* of George and Joyce Faldo; *m* (marr. diss.); one *s* three *d. Educ:* Welwyn Garden City. Won English Amateur Golf Championship, 1975; Professional golfer, 1976; Mem., Ryder Cup team, 1977–97, Captain, 2008; many championship titles include: Open, Muirfield, 1987, 1992, St Andrews, 1990; US Masters, 1989, 1990, 1996; French Open, 1983, 1988, 1989; GA Eur. Open, 1992; World Match Play Championship, 1992; Irish Open, 1991, 1992, 1993. *Publications:* Golf: the winning formula, 1989; In Search of Perfection, 1994; A Swing for Life, 1995; Life Swings, 2004. *Recreations:* helicopter flying, fly fishing, motor sports, cycling, photography. *E:* info@nickfaldo.com.

**FALK, Hon. Dame Sarah (Valerie),** DBE 2019; **Hon. Mrs Justice Falk;** a Judge of the High Court of Justice, Chancery Division, since 2018; *b* London, 1 June 1962; *d* of John Falk and late Annette Falk; *m* 1985, Marcus Flint; one *s* one *d. Educ:* St Albans High Sch.; Sidney Sussex Coll., Cambridge (BA 1983). Admitted solicitor, 1986; Freshfields, 1984–2018, Partner, 1994–2013, Consultant, 2013–18; Fee-paid Dep. Judge, Upper Tribunal (Tax and Chancery Chamber), 2015–18. Chm., Pro Corda Trust, 2008–18. *Recreations:* family, classical music (active and passive participation), walking (preferably with dog), horse riding. *Address:* Royal Courts of Justice, Rolls Building, Fetter Lane, EC4A 1NL. *T:* (020) 7947 7501. *E:* MrsJustice.Falk@ejudiciary.net.

**FALKINER, Sir Benjamin (Simon) Patrick,** 10th Bt *cr* 1778, of Annemount, Cork; *b* 16 Jan. 1962; *s* of Sir Edmond Charles Falkiner, 9th Bt and of his 1st wife, Janet Iris, *d* of Arthur Edward Bruce Derby; *S* father, 1997, but his name does not appear on the Official Roll of the Baronetage; *m* 1998, Linda Louise Mason (*d* 2006); one *s* one *d. Educ:* Queen Elizabeth's Grammar Sch. for Boys, Barnet. *Heir: b* Matthew Terence Falkiner, *b* 9 Jan. 1964. *Address:* 29 Glebeland, Hatfield, Herts AL10 8AA.

**FALKLAND,** 15th Viscount *cr* 1620 (Scot.), of Falkland, Co. Fife; **Lucius Edward William Plantagenet Cary;** Lord Cary 1620; Premier Viscount of Scotland on the Roll; *b* 8 May 1935; *s* of 14th Viscount Falkland, and Constance Mary (*d* 1995), *d* of late Captain Edward Berry; *S* father, 1984; *m* 1st, 1962, Caroline Anne (marr. diss. 1990), *o d* of late Lt-Comdr Gerald Butler, DSC, RN, and late Mrs Patrick Parish; one *s* two *d* (and one *d* decd); 2nd, 1990, Nicole, *o d* of late Milburn Mackey; one *s. Educ:* Wellington Coll.; Alliance Française, Paris. Late 2nd Lieut 8th King's Royal Irish Hussars. Export marketing consultant, formerly Chief Executive, C. T. Bowring Trading (Holdings) Ltd. House of Lords: Mem., Select Cttee on Overseas Trade, 1984–85; Dep. Whip, Lib Dem, 1989–2002; spokesman on culture, media and sport (formerly nat. heritage), 1995–2005; elected Mem., 1999; Mem., Pre-legislative Jt Cttee on Gambling, 2006–07; Chm., Works of Art Cttee, 2008–10; crossbencher, 2012–. *Recreations:* reading, motorcycling, racing, cinema. *Heir: s* Master of Falkland, *qv. Address:* c/o House of Lords, SW1A 0PW. *Clubs:* Brooks's; Cercle de Deauville.

**FALKLAND, Master of; Hon. Lucius Alexander Plantagenet Cary;** Co-Executive Producer, Homeland, US TV, 2011–14; *b* 1 Feb. 1963; *s* and *heir* of 15th Viscount Falkland, *qv*; *m* 1993, Linda (marr. diss. 1999), *d* of Raymond Purl, Colorado City, USA; one *s*; one *s* by another relationship; *m* 2013, Jennifer Marsala. *Educ:* Loretto School; RMA Sandhurst. Late Captain, 2nd Battalion, Scots Guards. Executive Producer, TV series: Lie to Me (USA), 2010–11; Legends, 2014; Taken, (USA) 2017. *Recreations:* ski-ing, golf. *Club:* Cavalry and Guards.

**FALKNER,** family name of **Baroness Falkner of Margravine.**

**FALKNER OF MARGRAVINE,** Baroness *cr* 2004 (Life Peer), of Barons Court in the London Borough of Hammersmith and Fulham; **Kishwer Falkner;** *b* 9 March 1955; *m* 1996, Robert Falkner; one *d. Educ:* St Joseph's Convent Sch., Karachi; LSE (BSc(Econ) 1992); Univ. of Kent (MA). Dir, Internat. Affairs, Lib Dems, 1993–99; Chief Prog. Officer, Political Affairs Div., Commonwealth Secretariat, 1999–2003; Chief Exec., Students Partnership Worldwide, 2003–04. Member: H of L/H of C Jt Cttee on Human Rights, 2005; H of L Cttee on the Constitution, 2011–15; Jt Cttee on Nat. Security Strategy, 2014–17; EU Cttee, H of L, 2015–; Chm., EU Sub-cttee on Financial Affairs, H of L, 2015–. Contested (Lib Dem): Kensington and Chelsea, 2001; London, European Parlt, 2004. Chancellor, Univ. of Northampton, 2008–16. Mem., Lib Dem Federal Exec., 2010–12. *Address:* House of Lords, SW1A 0PW.

**FALL,** Baroness *cr* 2015 (Life Peer), of Ladbroke Grove in the Royal Borough of Kensington and Chelsea; **Catherine Fall;** Senior Adviser, Brunswick Group, since 2016; *d* of Sir Brian (James Proetel) Fall, *qv*; *m* 1996, Ralph Ward-Jackson (marr. diss.); one *s* one *d. Educ:* King's Sch., Canterbury (music schol.); St Hilda's Coll., Oxford (BA PPE 1986). Res. asst to Patricia Rawlings, MEP; Special Advr to Dep. Dir Gen., CBI; Conservative Research Department: desk officer for Europe and agric., 1995–97; work for Shadow Foreign Sec., then Hd, Home Affairs Section, 1997; Dep. COS to Leader of the Opposition, 2005–10; Dep. COS to the Prime Minister, 2010–16. Trustee, Atlantic Partnership, 2016– (Dir, 2001–05); Mem., Adv. Bd, Onward, 2018–.

**FALL, Sir Brian (James Proetel),** GCVO 1994; KCMG 1992 (CMG 1984); HM Diplomatic Service, retired; British Government Special Representative for the South Caucasus, 2002–12; *b* 13 Dec. 1937; *s* of John William Fall, Hull, Yorkshire, and Edith Juliette (*née* Proetel); *m* 1962, Delmar Alexandra Roos; three *d. Educ:* St Paul's Sch.; Magdalen Coll., Oxford; Univ. of Michigan Law Sch. Served HM Forces, 1955–57. Joined HM Foreign (now Diplomatic) Service, 1962; served in Foreign Office UN Dept, 1963; Moscow, 1965; Geneva, 1968; Civil Service Coll., 1970; FO Eastern European and Soviet Dept and Western Organisations Dept, 1971; New York, 1975; Harvard Univ. Center for Internat. Affairs, 1976; Counsellor, Moscow, 1977–79; Head of Energy, Science and Space Dept, FCO, 1979–80; Head of Eastern European and Soviet Dept, FCO, 1980–81; Prin. Private Sec. to Sec. of State for Foreign and Commonwealth Affairs, 1981–84; Dir, Cabinet, Sec. Gen. of NATO, 1984–86; Asst Under-Sec. of State (Defence), FCO, 1986–88; Minister, Washington, 1988–89; High Comr to Canada, 1989–92; Ambassador to Russian Fedn, and to Republics of Armenia, Georgia, Moldova and Turkmenistan, 1992–95, also to Azerbaijan, Belarus, Kazakhstan, Kyrgyzstan and Uzbekistan, 1992–93; Principal, LMH, Oxford, 1995–2002 (Hon. Fellow, 2002). Advr, Rio Tinto, 1996–2010; Chm., MC Russian Market Fund, 1996–2002; Mem., Internat. Adv. Bd, La Poste, 2006–14; Dir, Rio Tinto Alcan Fund, 2008–10. Chm., ICC (UK) Cttee on Anti-Corruption, 2005–11. Gov., ESU, 2002–08. Dir, UK Foundn, Univ. of BC, 2005–08. Gov., St Mary's Sch., Calne, 1996–2005. Hon. LLD York Univ., Toronto, 2002. *Recreation:* France. *Address:* 2 St Helena Terrace, Richmond, Surrey TW9 1NR. *Club:* Garrick.
*See also* Baroness Fall.

**FALL, David William,** CMG 2007; HM Diplomatic Service, retired; Ambassador to Thailand and Laos, 2003–07; *b* 10 March 1948; *s* of George William Fall and Susan Fall; *m* 1973, Margaret Gwendolyn Richards; three *s. Educ:* St Bartholomew's Grammar Sch., Newbury; New Coll., Oxford (MA Mod. Hist.). VSO, Papua-New Guinea, 1970–71; joined FCO, 1971; language student, later 2nd then 1st Sec., Bangkok, 1973–77; seconded to Cabinet Office, 1977–78; FCO, 1978–80; 1st Sec., Cape Town and Pretoria, 1981–85; FCO, 1985–90; Counsellor, 1989; Head of Narcotics Control and AIDS Dept, FCO, 1989–90; Dep. Hd of Mission, Bangkok, 1990–93; Dep. High Comr, Canberra, 1993–97; Ambassador to Socialist Republic of Vietnam, 1997–2000; Estate Sales Prog., subseq. Estate

Modernisation, Manager, FCO, 2000–03. Board Member: POWER International, 2008–09; Anglo-Thai Society, 2008–18 (Chm., 2009–12). Internat. Trustee, British Red Cross, 2008–13 (Vice Chm., 2011–13). Mem. Council, Royal Over-Seas League, 2012–18 (Vice Chm., 2016–18). *Recreations:* long distance walking, 19th century military and naval history, War of 1812, Monty Python.

**FALLAS, Diana Elizabeth Jane;** *see* Burrell, D. E. J.

**FALLICK, Prof. Anthony Edward,** PhD; FRSE; Professor of Isotope Geosciences, University of Glasgow, 1996–2012, now Emeritus; *b* 21 April 1950; *s* of Edward Henry Fallick and Helen Fallick (*née* Murray); partner, Dr Charlotte Bryant; one *d. Educ:* Univ. of Glasgow (BSc Hons Natural Philosophy 1971; PhD Nuclear Geochem. 1975). Research Fellow, McMaster Univ., 1975–78; Vis. Schol., Cambridge Univ., 1978–80; Res. Fellow, 1980–85, Lectr, 1985–90, Reader, 1990–96, Univ. of Glasgow; Dir, Scottish Univs Envmtl Res. Centre, 1999–2007. Hon. Professor: Univ. of Edinburgh, 2000–; Univ. of St Andrews, 2000–; Univ. of Glasgow, 2014–. Chm. Adv. Cttee, British Geol Survey, 2010–12. Mem., AC Milanda AFC, 1969– (player, 1969–75). FRSE 1993; FRSA 1997; FMinSoc 1998 (Schlumberger Medal, 1997; Dist. Lectr, 2009–10); Founding Fellow, Inst. of Contemp. Scotland, 2000. Richard A. Glenn Award, ACS, 2001; Coke Medal, Geol Soc., 2004; Clough Medal, Edinburgh Geol Soc., 2014. *Publications:* contrib. numerous articles and papers to peer-reviewed jls and symposia vols. *Recreations:* wine, song. *Address:* 0/2 28 Partickhill Road, Glasgow G11 5BP. *E:* anthony.fallick@glasgow.ac.uk. *Club:* Four Forty Five (Hamilton, Ont.).

**FALLON, Her Honour Hazel Rosemary;** a Circuit Judge, 1978–96; *b* 7 Jan. 1931; *d* of late Arthur Henry Counsell and Elsie Winifred Counsell; *m* 1980, His Honour Peter Fallon, QC (*d* 2016). *Educ:* Clifton High Sch.; Switzerland; Univ. of Bristol (LLB). Called to the Bar, Gray's Inn, 1956; Western Circuit, 1956–96; a Recorder of the Crown Court, 1976–77. Legal Dept, Min. of Labour, 1959–62. Mem. of Council, Univ. of Bristol, 1992–97. Hon. LLD UWE, 1996. *Recreations:* reading, swimming, travel. *Address:* c/o The Law Courts, Small Street, Bristol BS1 1DA.

**FALLON, Ivan Gregory;** Deputy Chairman, N. Brown Group plc, 2009 (Director, 1994–2017); *b* 26 June 1944; *s* of Padraic and Dorothea Fallon; *m* 1st, 1967, Susan Mary Lurring (marr. diss. 1997); one *s* two *d;* 2nd, 1997, Elizabeth Rees-Jones. *Educ:* St Peter's Coll., Wexford; Trinity Coll., Dublin (BBS). Irish Times, 1964–66; Thomson Provincial Newspapers, 1966–67; Daily Mirror, 1967–68; Sunday Telegraph, 1968–70; Deputy City Editor, Sunday Express, 1970–71; Sunday Telegraph, 1971–84: City Editor, 1979–84; Dep. Editor, Sunday Times, 1984–94; Chief Executive Officer: Ind. Newspapers of S Africa, then Ind. News & Media of SA, 1994–2002; Independent News & Media UK, 2002–10. Chm., iTouch plc, 1998–2005; Dir, Independent Newspapers plc, Ireland, 1995–2010. Mem., Council of Governors, United Med. and Dental Schs of Guy's and St Thomas' Hosps, 1985–94; Trustee, Project Trust, 1984–. *Publications:* (with James L. Srodes) DeLorean: the rise and fall of a dream-maker, 1983; (with James L. Srodes) Takeovers, 1987; The Brothers: the rise and rise of Saatchi and Saatchi, 1988; Billionaire: the life and times of Sir James Goldsmith, 1991; Paper Chase, 1993; The Player: the life of Tony O'Reilly, 1994; (with James B. Sherwood) Orient Express: a personal journey, 2012; Black Horse Ride: the inside story of Lloyds and the banking crisis, 2015; (with Philip Harris) Magic Carpet Ride, 2017. *Recreations:* walking, tennis. *Address:* 17 Kensington Mansions, Trebovir Road, SW5 9TF; Prospect House, Klein Constantia Road, Constantia, Cape Town 7806, South Africa. *Clubs:* Garrick, Beefsteak, Political Economy.

**FALLON, John Joseph;** Chief Executive Officer, Pearson plc, since 2013; *b* Blackpool, 25 Aug. 1962; *s* of Jack and Maureen Fallon; *m* 1988, Della Broome; two *d. Educ:* Cardinal Langley Sch., Middleton, Gtr Manchester; Hull Univ. (BA Hons Econs, Politics and Sociol.). Communications and public policy rôles with local govt and Parliament; Communications Director: Powergen plc, 1995–97; Pearson plc, 1997–2003; Chief Executive Officer: Pearson Educn, EMEA, 2003–08; Pearson Internat., 2008–13. *Recreations:* running, football, golf. *Address:* Pearson plc, 80 Strand, WC2R 0RL.

**FALLON, Kieren;** flat race jockey, retired 2016; *b* Crusheen, Co. Clare, 22 Feb. 1965; *s* of Frank and Maureen Fallon; *m* 1993, Julie Bowker; one *s* two *d.* With Lynda Ramsden stable, 1993–97; stable jockey for Henry Cecil, 1997–2000, for Michael Stoute, 2000–05, for Aidan O'Brien, 2005–07; rode first British winner, 1988; rode 200 winners in season, 1997. Winner: Lincoln Handicap, on High Premium, 1993; 1,000 Guineas, on Sleepytime, 1997, on Wince, 1999, on Russian Rhythm, 2003, on Virginia Waters, 2005; Oaks, on Reams of Verse, 1997, on Ramruna, 1999, on Ouija Board, 2004; Grosser Preis von Baden, Germany, on Borgia, 1997; Prix de la Forêt, France, on Tomba, 1998; Derby, on Oath, 1999, on Kris Kin, 2003, on North Light, 2004; Irish Oaks, on Ramruna, 1999, on Ouija Board, 2004, on Alexandrova, 2006; Tattersalls Gold Cup, Ireland, on Shiva, 1999; 2,000 Guineas, on King's Best, 2000, on Golan, 2001, on Footstepsinthesand, 2005, on George Washington, 2006, on Night of Thunder, 2014; King George VI and Queen Elizabeth Diamond Stakes, on Golan, 2002; Filly and Mare Turf, Breeders' Cup, on Islington, 2003, on Ouija Board, 2004; Irish Derby, on Hurricane Run, 2005, on Dylan Thomas, 2006; Prix de l'Arc de Triomphe, on Hurricane Run, 2005, on Dylan Thomas, 2007; French 2,000 Guineas, on Aussie Rules, 2006. Champion Jockey, 1997, 1998, 1999, 2001, 2002, 2003. *Publications:* Form (autobiog.), 2017.

**FALLON, Martin;** *see* Patterson, H.

**FALLON, Rt Hon. Sir Michael,** KCB 2016; PC 2012; MP (C) Sevenoaks, since 1997; *b* 14 May 1952; *s* of late Martin Fallon, OBE, FRCSI and of Hazel Fallon; *m* 1986, Wendy Elisabeth, *e d* of late Peter Payne, Holme-on-Spalding Moor, Yorks; two *s. Educ:* St Andrews Univ. (MA Hons 1974). European Educnl Res. Trust, 1974–75; Opposition Whips Office, House of Lords, 1975–77; EEC Officer, Cons. Res. Dept, 1977–79; Jt Man. Dir, European Consultants Ltd, 1979–81; Dir, Quality Care Homes plc, 1992–97; Chief Exec., Quality Care Develts Ltd, 1996–97; Man. Dir, Just Learning Ltd, 1996–2009; Director: Bannatyne Fitness Ltd, 1999–2000; Collins Stewart Tullett plc, 2004–06; Tullett Prebon plc, 2006–12; Attendo AB, 2008–12; Chm., Avanton Ltd, 2018–; non-exec. Dir, Infinite Percent Ltd, 2019–. Mem., Internat. Adv. Bd, Investcorp Internat. Ltd, 2018–. Sec., Lord Home's Cttee on future of House of Lords, 1977–78; Assistant to Baroness Elles, 1979–83. MP (C) Darlington, 1983–92; contested (C) Darlington, 1992. PPS to Sec. of State for Energy, 1987–88; an Asst Govt Whip, 1988–90; a Lord Comr of HM Treasury, 1990; Parly Under-Sec. of State, DES, 1990–92; Opposition spokesman on trade and industry, 1997, on Treasury matters, 1997–98; Minister of State: BIS, 2012–14; DECC, 2013–14; Minister for Portsmouth, 2014; Sec. of State for Defence, 2014–17. Mem., Treasury Select Cttee, 1999–2012; Chm., All Party Classics Gp, 2005–09. Mem., Exec., 1922 Cttee, 2005–07. Dep. Chm., Cons. and Unionist Party, 2010–12. Member: HEFCE, 1993–97; Adv. Council, Social Market Foundn, 1994–2001; Govt's Deregulation Task Force, 1994–97; Council, 2009, Adv. Bd, 2018–, Centre for Policy Studies. Dir, Internat. Care and Relief, 1997–2003; Pres., Royal Soc. for Blind Children (formerly Royal London Soc. for the Blind), 2010–. Gov., Whitefield Schs, 1994–99. *Publications:* The Quango Explosion (jtly), 1978; Sovereign Members?, 1982; The Trojan Horse of the Euroquango, 1982; Brighter Schools, 1993; Social Mobility, 2007; contribs to journals. *Recreations:* books, skiing, visiting classical sites. *Address:* House of Commons, SW1A 0AA. *Club:* Academy.

**FALLON, Paul Michael,** OBE 2014; independent health and social care consultant, 2007–17; Head of Children's Services and Director of Social Services, London Borough of Barnet, 2001–07; *b* 11 July 1952; *s* of Michael and Doreen Fallon; *m* 2003, Joanne (*née* Katz); one *s. Educ:* Barking Abbey Grammar Sch.; Redbridge Tech. Coll.; Southampton Univ. (BSc, CQSW, DASS). Youth and Community Worker, 1975–78, Sen. Social Worker and Team Leader, 1978–82, Solihull MBC; Principal Officer (Child Care), 1982–89, Operational Services Manager, 1989–94, Coventry CC; Asst Dir (Child Care), Islington LBC, 1994–99; Quality Protects Develt Officer, DoH, 1999–2000. Co-Chm., ADSS Children and Families Policy Cttee, 2005–07; Ind. Chm., Croydon Safeguarding Children Bd, 2011–15; Dir, Assoc. of Independent LSCB Chairs, 2013–15. Non-exec. Dir, Pathway Care, 2008–11. Trustee and Board Member: Change, Grow, Live (formerly Crime Reduction Initiatives), 2009–18; Ambitious about Autism, 2011–14. JP Sussex Central, 2009–15. *Recreations:* travel, songwriting, playing the guitar. *E:* paulfallonuk@yahoo.co.uk.

**FALLOWELL, Duncan Richard,** FRSL; author; *b* London, 26 Sept. 1948; *s* of Thomas Edgar Fallowell and Celia Fallowell (*née* Waller). *Educ:* Palmer's Sch.; St Paul's Sch.; Magdalen Coll., Oxford (BA Hist. 1970; MA 2010). FRSL 2015. *Publications:* Drug Tales, 1979; April Ashley's Odyssey, 1982; Satyrday, 1986; The Underbelly, 1987; To Noto, 1989; One Hot Summer in Saint Petersburg, 1994; Twentieth Century Characters, 1994; A History of Facelifting, 2003; Going As Far As I Can, 2008; How To Disappear, 2011 (PEN Ackerley Prize, 2012); *e-publications:* Three Romes, 2014; The Rise and Fall of the Celebrity Interview, 2014; opera libretto: Gormenghast, composer, Irmin Schmidt, 1998; song lyrics for Can and for Irmin Schmidt, 1974–. *Recreations:* swimming, rural motoring. *Address:* c/o Aitken Alexander Associates, 291 Gray's Inn Road, WC1X 8EB. *E:* reception@aitkenalexander.co.uk. *Club:* Groucho.

**FALLOWFIELD, Dame Lesley (Jean),** DBE 2016; DPhil; Professor of Psycho-Oncology, and Director, Sussex Health Outcomes Research and Education in Cancer, University of Sussex, since 2001; *b* Southampton, 31 Oct. 1949; *d* of William and Jean Mason; one *s* one *d. Educ:* Parkstone Girls Grammar Sch., Poole; Guy's Hosp., London (SRN 1971); Univ. of Sussex (BSc 1980; DPhil 1984). Staff Nurse, Guy's Hosp., 1971, Royal Sussex County Hosp., Brighton, 1971–73; Res. psychologist, CRC Trials Unit, KCH, 1984–87; Lectr, 1987–89, Sen. Lectr, 1989–94, in Health Psychol., London Hosp. Med. Coll.; Reader in Psycho-Oncol., 1994–97, Prof. of Psycho-Oncol., and Dir, CRC Psychological Oncol. Gp, 1997–2001, UCL. *Publications:* The Quality of Life: the missing measurement in health care, 1990; The Experience of Breast Cancer, 1991; (ed with H. Davis) Counselling and Communication in Health Care, 1991; contrib. res. papers to peer reviewed jls. *Recreations:* playing golf badly, cooking for friends and family, getting irritated by politicians, theatre and cinema, walking along windy beaches, driving my children mad. *Address:* Sussex Health Outcomes Research and Education in Cancer, Brighton & Sussex Medical School, University of Sussex, Science Park Road, Falmer, Brighton BN1 9RX. *T:* (01273) 873015. *E:* l.j.fallowfield@sussex.ac.uk.

**FALLOWS, Albert Bennett,** CB 1987; Hon. RICS; Chief Valuer, Inland Revenue Valuation Office and Commissioner of Inland Revenue, 1984–88; *b* 7 Dec. 1928; *s* of Bennett and May Fallows; *m* 1955, Maureen James; two *d. Educ:* Leek High School. Private practice, surveying, 1945–56; local govt service, Staffs, 1956–63; joined CS, 1963; Dist Valuer, Basingstoke, 1973–75; Superintending Valuer, Liaison Officer, DoE/Dept of Transport, 1975–77; Board of Inland Revenue: Superintending Valuer, North West, Preston, 1977–80; Asst Chief Valuer, 1980–83; Dep. Chief Valuer, 1983. *Address:* 1 Meadow Drive, Bude, Cornwall EX23 8HZ. *T:* (01288) 354434.

**FALLOWS, Prof. David Nicholas,** PhD; FBA 1997; Professor of Musicology, University of Manchester, 1997–2010, now Emeritus; *b* 20 Dec. 1945; *yr s* of late William John Fallows and Winifred Joan Fallows (*née* Sanderson); *m* 1st, 1976, Paulène Oliver (marr. diss. 2008); one *s* one *d;* 2nd, 2013, Dagmar Hoffmann-Axthelm. *Educ:* Shrewsbury Sch.; Jesus Coll., Cambridge (BA 1967); King's Coll., London (MMus 1968); Univ. of Calif at Berkeley (PhD 1978). Assistant, Studio der Frühen Musik, Munich, 1968–70; Lectr, Univ. of Wisconsin-Madison, 1973–74; Lectr, 1976–82, Sen. Lectr, 1982–92, Reader in Music, 1992–97, Univ. of Manchester. Vis. Associate Prof., Univ. of N Carolina, Chapel Hill, 1982–83; Prof. invité de musicologie, Ecole Normale Supérieure, Paris, 1993; visiting posts: Univ. of Basel, 1996, 2004, 2009; Univ. of Vienna, 1999; Harvard Univ., 2002. Pres., Internat. Musicological Soc., 2002–07 (Hon. Mem. 2017); Vice-Pres., Royal Musical Assoc., 2000–10. Corresp. Mem., Amer. Musicol Soc., 1999. Reviews Editor, Early Music, 1976–95, 1999–2000; Gen. Editor and Founder, Royal Musical Assoc. Monographs, 1982–98; Member, Editorial Board: Musica Britannica, 1985–; Jl of Royal Musical Assoc., 1986–88; Basler Jahrbuch für historische Musikpraxis, 1988–2019; Early Music History, 1991–; Muziek en Wetenschap, 1992–2001; Early English Church Music, 1994–. Dr hc Tours, 2010. Chevalier, Ordre des Arts et des Lettres (France), 1994. *Publications:* Dufay, 1982, 2nd edn 1987; (jtly) Chansonnier de Jean de Montcheneu, 1991; (ed jtly) Companion to Medieval and Renaissance Music, 1992, 2nd edn 1997; The Songs of Guillaume Dufay, 1995; (ed and introd) Oxford Bodleian Library MS Canon Misc. 213 (Late Medieval and Early Renaissance music in facsimile, vol. 1), 1995; Songs and Musicians in the Fifteenth Century, 1996; The Songbook of Fridolin Sicher, 1996; A Catalogue of Polyphonic Songs 1415–1480, 1999; (ed) Josquin des Prez, Secular Works for Four Voices (New Josquin Edn vol. 28), 2005; Chansonnier de Jean de Montcheneu (ca. 1475): commentary to the facsimile, 2008; Josquin, 2009; Composers and their Songs, 1400–1521, 2010; The Henry VIII Book: facsimile with introduction, 2014; (ed) Secular Polyphony 1380–1480, Musica Britannica, vol. 97, 2014; Henry VIII and the Earliest English Carols, 2018. *Address:* Martin Harris Centre for Music and Drama, University of Manchester, Bridgeford Street, Manchester M13 9PL. *T:* 07714 184655. *E:* david.fallows@manchester.ac.uk.

**FALMOUTH,** 9th Viscount *cr* 1720; **George Hugh Boscawen;** 26th Baron Le Despencer, 1264; Baron Boscawen-Ros, 1720; Lord-Lieutenant of Cornwall, 1977–94; *b* 31 Oct. 1919; 2nd but *e* surv. *s* of 8th Viscount Falmouth; *S* father, 1962; *m* 1953, Elizabeth Price Browne (*d* 2007), OBE 2002, DL; four *s. Educ:* Eton Coll.; Trinity Coll., Cambridge. Served War, 1939–46, Italy. Capt., Coldstream Guards. DL Cornwall, 1968. *Heir: s* Hon. Evelyn Arthur Hugh Boscawen [*b* 13 May 1955; *m* 1st, 1977, Lucia Vivian-Neal (marr. diss. 1995), *e d* of R. W. Vivian-Neal; one *s* one *d;* 2nd, 1995, Katharine Maley; two *s* one *d*].

**FALVEY, Dr David Alan,** FGS; Managing Director, Research Connect Pty Ltd, since 2008; *b* Sydney, 19 Dec. 1945; *s* of late Keith Falvey and Ella Falvey (*née* Hendley); *m* 1969, Margaret Kaye (*d* 1984); one *s* one *d; m* 1986, Gillian Tidey. *Educ:* Univ. of Sydney (BSc Hons 1967); Univ. of New South Wales (PhD 1972). FGS 1998. Explorationist, Shell Develt, Australia, 1972–74; Lectr, then Sen. Lectr, Univ. of Sydney, 1974–82; Chief, Marine Div., Bureau of Mineral Resources, 1982–89; Associate Dir, Petroleum and Marine Geoscis, Australian Geol Survey Orgn, 1989–94; Dir, Ocean Drilling Program, Jt Oceanographic Instns, Washington, 1994–98; Executive Director: British Geological Survey, NERC, 1998–2006; Physics, Chem. and Geosci., Australian Res. Council,

2006–08. Managing Director: Tamboran, 2009–11; Palatine Energy, 2011–19. CCMI 2003. Hon. DSc Nottingham Trent, 2001. *Publications:* numerous scientific contribs to learned jls. *Recreation:* golf.

**FAMA, Prof. Eugene F.**, PhD; Robert R. McCormick Distinguished Service Professor of Finance, University of Chicago, since 1993; *b* Boston, Mass, 14 Feb. 1939; *m* 1958, Sallyann Dimeco; two *s* two *d*. *Educ:* St James Catholic Grammar Sch., Medford; Boys' Catholic High Sch., Malden; Tufts Univ. (BA 1960); Grad. Sch. of Business, Univ. of Chicago (MBA 1963; PhD 1964). Graduate School of Business, University of Chicago: Asst Prof. of Finance, 1963–65; Associate Prof., 1966–68; Prof. of Finance, 1968–73; Theodore O. Yntema Prof. of Finance, 1973–84; Theodore O. Yntema Dist. Service Prof. of Finance, 1984–93. Visiting Professor: Catholic Univ. of Leuven and Eur. Inst. for Advanced Studies in Mgt, Belgium, 1975–76; Anderson Grad. Sch. of Mgt, UCLA, 1982–95. Associate Editor: Jl Finance, 1971–73, 1977–80; Amer. Econ. Rev., 1975–77; Jl Monetary Econs, 1984–96; Adv. Ed., Jl Financial Econs, 1974–. Mem., Bd of Dirs, Dimensional Fund Advrs, 1982–. Fellow: Amer. Finance Assoc., 2001; Econometric Soc. Deutsche Bank Prize in Financial Econs, 2005; Award for Excellence in Finance, Morgan Stanley American Finance Assoc., 2007; Onassis Prize in Finance, 2009; (jtly) Nobel Prize in Econ. Scis, 2013. *Publications:* (with M. Miller) The Theory of Finance, 1972; (contrib.) Studies in the Theory of Capital Markets, 1972; Foundations of Finance, 1976; contribs to jls. *Address:* Booth School of Business, University of Chicago, 5807 South Woodlawn Avenue, Chicago, IL 60637, USA.

**FAME, Georgie;** musician, vocalist, songwriter; *b* 26 June 1943; *s* of James and Mary Anne Powell; *né* Clive Powell, name changed by impresario Larry Parnes, 1960; *m* 1971, Nicolette (*d* 1993); two *s*. *Educ:* Leigh Central Co. Secondary Sch., Lancs. Professional musician, 1959–; toured with Eddie Cochran, Gene Vincent and Billy Fury, 1960; leader of own band, The Blue Flames, 1962–; toured with Count Basie Orch., 1967 and 1968; rep. UK, Fest. Internat. da Canção Popular, Brazil, 1967; in partnership with Alan Price, 1970–73; collaborated with Van Morrison, 1988–98; Founder Mem., Bill Wyman's Rhythm Kings, 1998; hosted own series, BBC Radio 2, 2000; featured guest soloist with all of Europe's major jazz orchs; has composed and performed music for various feature films, television and radio commercials. Over 30 albums released under own name inc. Poet in New York, 2000 (Prix Billie Holiday, Acad. du Jazz de France); 13 hit singles, incl. 3 Number Ones: Yeh Yeh, 1965; Getaway, 1966; Ballad of Bonnie and Clyde, 1968. Hon. Mem. Swedish Exec. Jazz Soc., 2002. *Recreations:* aviation, crosswords.

**FANCOURT, Hon. Sir Timothy Miles**, Kt 2018; **Hon. Mr Justice Fancourt;** a Judge of the High Court, Chancery Division, since 2018; President, Upper Tribunal (Lands Chamber), since 2019; *b* 30 Aug. 1964; *s* of Dr Philip Fancourt and Georgina Mary Fancourt (*née* Brown); *m* 2000, Emily Windsor; one *d*. *Educ:* Whitgift Sch.; Gonville and Caius Coll., Cambridge (MA). Called to the Bar, Lincoln's Inn, 1987; QC 2003; a Recorder, 2009–17; a Dep. High Court Judge, 2013–17. Chm., Chancery Bar Assoc., 2012–14 (Vice-Chm., 2010–12). *Publications:* Enforceability of Landlord and Tenant Covenants, 1997, 3rd edn 2014; Megarry's Assured Tenancies, 2nd edn 1999. *Recreations:* cricket, classical music. *Address:* Royal Courts of Justice, Rolls Building, Fetter Lane, EC4A 1NL.

**FANE,** family name of **Earl of Westmorland.**

**FANE, Andrew William Mildmay,** OBE 2017; FCA; President, Emmanuel Society, since 2009; *b* 9 Aug. 1949; *s* of late Robert Fane and Valerie Fane (*née* Borthwick); *m* 1989, Clare Lucy Marx (*see* Dame C. L. Marx). *Educ:* Radley Coll.; Emmanuel Coll., Cambridge (MA Law; Hon. Fellow 2012). FCA 1974. Chief Exec., Whitburgh Investments Ltd, 1982–92; Dep. Chm., Borthwicks plc, 1988–92. Non-exec. Dir, Great Ormond St Hosp. for Children NHS Trust, 2001–11 (Chm., Audit Cttee, 2006–08; Chm., Clinical Governance Cttee, 2008–11). Chairman: Friends of the Children of Gt Ormond St Hosp., 1992–2012; Special Trustees, Gt Ormond St Hosp. Children's Charity, 1999–2006 (Special Trustee, 1996–2007); Govs, The Children's Hosp. Sch. at Gt Ormond St Hosp. and UCH, 2000–12. Councillor, RBK&C, 1987–94 (Chm., Planning Cttee). Mem., Royal Commn on Histl Monuments of England, 1999–2003; English Heritage: Comr, 1995–2004; Dep. Chm., 2001–04; Chm., Audit Cttee, 2002–11. Chairman: Historic Bldgs and Areas Adv. Cttee, 1995–2001; London Adv. Cttee, 1999–2004 (Mem., 1994–2004). Mem., E Anglia Regl Cttee, NT, 1994–2002. Chm. Bd of Govs, Framlingham Coll., Suffolk, 2001–17 (Gov., 1995–2017); Mem. Council, Radley Coll., Oxon, 2003–11 (Trustee, Radley Foundn, 2002–14). Chm. Trustees, Inst. of Child Health, 2006– (Hon. Fellow, 2001); Trustee: Foundling Mus., 2007–12 (Chm., 2009–12); Britten-Pears Foundn, 2009–17 (Chm., Bldg Cttee, 2009–13); Chairman: Stowe House Preservation Trust, 2007–; Chiswick House and Gardens Trust, 2011–; Suffolk Preservation Soc., 2013–. *Recreations:* farming, conservation. *Address:* Hoo House, Woodbridge, Suffolk; 64 Ladbroke Road, W11 3NR. *T:* (020) 7221 2748.

**FANE, Dame Clare Lucy;** *see* Marx, Dame C. L.

**FANE, Mark William;** Co-Founder and Chief Executive, Crocus.co.uk Ltd, since 2003; *b* London, 21 June 1958; *s* of Michael Francis Fane and Carole Daisy Fane; *m* 1986, Emma Mary Bonnor-Maurice (marr. diss. 2014); one *s* one *d*; *m* 2017, Alexandra Mary Wellesley-Wesley. *Educ:* Eton Coll.; Univ. of Exeter (BA Politics and Econs); INSEAD Business Sch. (MBA 1986). Dir, Foreign & Colonial Ventures, 1987–91; Chm., Waterers Landscape plc, 1991–2003. Non-exec. Chm., Graphite Enterprise plc, 2010–. Non-exec. Chm., Garden Mus., 2011–; Mem., Council, RHS, 2009–; Dir, Chatsworth House Trust, 2015–. Freeman, Grocers' Co. *Address:* Fryern Court, Upper Burgate, Fordingbridge, Hants SP6 1NF. *E:* mark.fane@crocus.co.uk. *Clubs:* White's, Royal Thames Yacht; Sunningdale Golf.

**FANE TREFUSIS,** family name of **Baron Clinton.**

**FANELLI, Sara;** artist and illustrator; *b* 20 July 1969; *d* of Giovanni Fanelli and Rosalia (*née* Bonito); one *d* by Dario Marianelli. *Educ:* Liceo Classico Michelangelo, Florence (Maturità Classica); Camberwell Coll. of Art (BA Hons Graphic Design); Royal Coll. of Art (MA Illustration). Projects include: stamp design for Royal Millennium Collection, 1999 (D&AD Silver Award); timeline 40 metres long and design of 4 gallery entrances at Tate Modern, 2005–; (with Thomas Heatherwick) mural design for Nanyang Technology Univ., Singapore, 2014; book jackets for Penguin, Orion, Bloomsbury, Random House, Pan MacMillan and Faber and Faber; magazine illustrations for: New Yorker, NY Times, New Scientist, Guardian, TES, Radio Times, Daily Telegraph, Independent on Sunday; work for: BBC English; BBC Worldwide; British Council; Amnesty; Virgin Classics; Orange; Edinburgh Fest.; Royal Exchange Th., Manchester; Lyric Th., London; Nat. Westminster Bank; Nickelodeon (US); Alessi; Issey Miyake; Ron Arad. Mem., AGI, 2000–. Hon. RDI 2006. Numerous awards including: Parallel Prize, 1995; Nat. Art Liby Illustration Award, V&A, 1995, Commended Winner, 1997, 1998, 2000; D&AD Silver Award, for poster illustration, 2003; V&A Illustration Award, 2004; TITAN Internat. Illustration in Design Prize, 2009. *Publications: written and illustrated:* Button, 1994 (MacMillan Prize for a Children's Picture Book, 1992); My Map Book, 1995, 2nd edn 2006; Cinderella: Picture Box, 1996; Pinocchio: Picture Box, 1996; Wolf!, 1997; A Dog's Life, 1998; It's Dreamtime, 1999; Dear Diary, 2000; First Flight, 2002; Mythological Monsters, 2002; The Onion's Great Escape, 2012; *illustrated:* Dibby Dubby Dhu, 1997; The Folio Book of Short Novels, 1998; The New Faber Book of Children's Verse, 2001; Pinocchio, 2003; Sometimes I Think, Sometimes I Am, 2007 (D&AD Silver Award, for book design/illustration, 2008). *Recreations:* film, music, reading, travelling, flea markets, playing games, the moon. *Address:* c/o Walker Books, 87 Vauxhall Walk, SE11 5HJ. *W:* www.sarafanelli.com.

**FANNING, Michael Leonard;** a District Judge (Magistrates' Courts), since 2012; a Recorder, since 2019; *b* Edinburgh, 18 Sept. 1967; *s* of Brian and Patricia Fanning; *m* 1993 (marr. diss.); two *d*. *Educ:* Keswick Sch., Cumbria; Leeds Poly. (LLB Hons). Admitted as solicitor, 1993; Solicitor, 1993–2012; a Dep. Dist Judge (pt-time) (Magistrates' Courts), 2008–12. Solicitor Mem. (pt-time), Solicitors' Disciplinary Tribunal, 2009–12. *Recreations:* fell-running (former Member, Borrowdale Fell Runners; Member, Holmfirth Harriers AC), Member, Keswick Mountain Rescue Team, 1989–2006. *Address:* Kirklees Magistrates' Court, The Court House, Civic Centre, Huddersfield, W Yorks HD1 2NH.

**FANTONI, Prof. Barry Ernest;** writer, performer, jazz musician; Member of editorial staff of Private Eye, 1963–2010; Professor of Communications and Media Studies, University of Salerno, since 1997; Director, All This Time Theatre Co., since 1998; *b* 28 Feb. 1940; *s* of late Peter Nello Secondo Fantoni and Sarah Catherine Fantoni; became Italian citizen, 1997; *m* 1972, Teresa Frances, (Tessa), Reidy (separated 1998). *Educ:* Archbishop Temple Sch.; Camberwell Sch. of Arts and Crafts (Wedgwood Scholar). Cartoonist of The Listener, 1968–88; contrib. art criticism to The Times, 1973–77; record reviewer, Punch, 1976–77; Diary cartoonist, The Times, 1983–90; Dir, Barry Fantoni Merchandising Co., 1985–93; designer of film and theatre posters and illustrator of book jackets; mural for Queen Elizabeth II Conf. Centre, London, 1985; film and television actor; From the Dragon's Mouth (one-man show for stage), 1991–; plays: Jeanne, performed Battersea Arts Centre, 1997; Modigliani, My Love, Paris, 1999; Rooms of the House, 2001; The Piano Tuner, 2005, Extra Time, 2006, (with Barry Booth) Café de Paris, 2006, (adapted and dir) Lady Windermere's Fan, 2006, (dir) Death of an Elephant, 2007, Loving Art, 2008, Put On a Happy Face - The Life and Songs of Charles Strouse, 2009, Landor Th.; Picasso is Coming, Pentameters and St James Th., 2013; (writer and dir) Seven Paintings of Joan de Llum, Heatherley School of Fine Art, 2010; creator, Ronnie's Horns (perf. with O. T. Fagbenly), RADA, 2002; travelling act (with Dominic Alldis) An Evening with E. J. Thribb; presenter and writer, Barry Fantoni's Chinese Horoscopes, BBC Radio 4 series, 1986; writer, My Turn for Lunch, Radio 4, 2015. One-man shows: Woodstock Gall., London, 1963; Comara Gall., LA, 1964; Brunel Univ., 1974; Times cartoon exhibition, Charlotte Lampard Gall., 1990; retrospective: Cadogan Contemporary Gall., 1991; Caricatures by Barry Fantoni, NPG, 2007; Thomas Williams Fine Art Gall., 2009; two-man shows (with Peter Fantoni): Langton Gall., London, 1977; Annexe Gall., London, 1978; Katherine House Gall., 1983; Fulford Cartoon Gall., 1983; New Grafton Gall., 1985; Green & Stone, Cirencester, 1986; work exhibited: AIA Gall., London, 1958, 1961 and 1964; D and AD Annual Exhibn, London, 1964; Royal Acad. Summer Exhibn, 1963 (as Stuart Harris, with William Rushton), 1964, 1975 and 1978 (with Richard Napper); Tate Gall., 1973; Bradford Print Biennale, 1974; National Theatre, 1977; Browse and Darby, 1977; Gillian Jason Gall., 1983; Three Decades of Art Schools, RA, 1983; Piers Feetham Gall., 2002; The British Art of Illustration, Chris Beetles Gall., 2014, 2015. Founder, Dépêchism art movement, 2012, exhibn (with Andrew Aarons), Thomas Williams Fine Art, 2014. Collections of work at London Museum, 1980; V&A, 1984; Cartoon Museum, 1993; Univ. of Kent, 2005; BL, 2006; NPG, 2007. Musical compositions include: popular songs (also popular songs with Marianne Faithfull and with Stanley Myers); The Cantors Crucifixion (musical improvisation for 13 instruments), 1977; (with John Wells) Lionel (musical), 1977; (with Barry Booth) We Are Your Future (official Unicef anthem), 1996; Mass of the Holy Spirit, 1999. Formed: (with John Butler) Barry Fantoni Duo, 1990–; Barry Fantoni's Jazz Circus, 1992 (a performance jazz trio); created (with Andy Cleyndert and Mark Sanders) Fish Factory, 2017 (free jazz trio). Patron: Landor Th., 2005–; British Musical Archive, 2011–. Editor, St Martin's Review, 1969–74; weekly columnist on Chinese Horoscopes: Today, 1986–87; Woman, 1987–88; Plus magazine, 1989; The Guardian, 1990. Male TV Personality of the Year, 1966. *Publications:* (with Karl Dallas) Swinging London, 1966; (with Richard Ingrams) Private Pop Eye, 1968; (as Old Jowett, with Richard Ingrams) The Bible for Motorists, 1970; Tomorrow's Nicodemus, 1974; (as Sylvie Krin, with Richard Ingrams) Love in the Saddle, 1974; Private Eye Cartoon Library 5, 1975; (as E. J. Thribb, with Richard Ingrams) So Farewell Then…and Other Poems, 1978; Mike Dime, 1980; (as Sylvie Krin, with Richard Ingrams) Born to be Queen, 1981; Stickman, 1982; (ed) Colemanballs, 1982; (ed) Colemanballs 2, 1984; The Times Diary Cartoons, 1984; Barry Fantoni's Chinese Horoscope, annually 1985–, retitled Barry Fantoni's Complete Chinese Horoscope, 1991; (ed) Colemanballs 3, 1986; Barry Fantoni Cartoons: a personal selection from The Times and The Listener, 1987; The Royal Family's Chinese Horoscopes, 1988; (ed) Colemanballs 4, 1988; Chinese Horoscope Guide to Love, Marriage and Friendship, 1989; (ed) Colemanballs 5, 1990; (ed) Colemanballs 6, 1992; (ed) Colemanballs 7, 1994; (ed) A Hundred Years of Neasden Football Club, 1995; (ed) Colemanballs 8, 1996; (ed) Colemanballs 9, 1998; (ed) Colemanballs 10, 2000; (ed) Colemanballs 11, 2002; (ed) Colemanballs 12, 2004; (ed) Colemanballs 13, 2006; (ed) Colemanballs 14, 2008; Scenes You Seldom See, 2005; (ed) Colemanballs 15, 2010; Harry Lipkin P.I., 2010; Harry Lipkin, 2012; A Whole Scene Going On, 2019; *illustrations for:* How To Be a Jewish Mother, 1966; The BP Festivals and Events in Britain, 1966; (with George Melly) The Media Mob, 1980; The Best of Barry Fantoni Cartoons, 1990. *Recreation:* animal welfare. *Address:* c/o Elaine Steel, 49 Greek Street, W1D 4EG. *T:* 01273 739022. *E:* info@elainesteel.com. *Clubs:* Arts, Chelsea Arts (Chm., 1978–80).

**FARAGE, Nigel Paul;** Member for South East Region, England, European Parliament, since 1999 (UK Ind, 1999–2018; Ind, 2018–19; Brexit, since 2019); Leader, Brexit Party, since 2019; *b* 3 April 1964; *s* of Guy Farage and Barbara Stevens; *m* 1st, 1988 (marr. diss. 1997); two *s*; 2nd, 1999, Kirsten Mehr; two *d*. *Educ:* Dulwich Coll. Commodity Broker: Drexel Burnham Lambert, 1982–86; Credit Lyonnais Rouse Ltd, 1986–93; Refco Overseas Ltd, 1994–2002; Natexis Metals, 2003–04. UK Independence Party: Founder Mem., 1993; Chm., 1998–2000; Spokesman, 2000–18; Leader, 2006–09 and 2010–16. Co-Pres., UK Ind): Eastleigh, June 1994; Salisbury, 1997; Bexhill & Battle, 2001; Buckingham, 2010; S Thanet, 2015; Itchen, Test & Avon, EP elecns, 1994. Pres., Gadfly Club, 2006–. Radio presenter, LBC, 2017–; contrib. to Fox News, 2017–. *Publications:* The Purple Revolution: the year that changed everything, 2015. *Recreations:* military history 1914–18, sea angling, proper English pubs. *Address:* 1 Darwin Villas, Single Street, Berrys Green, Westerham, Kent TN16 3AA. *T:* (office) (01903) 885573. *Club:* East India.

**FARAH, Sir Mohamed, (Sir Mo),** Kt 2017; CBE 2013; athlete; *b* Mogadishu, Somalia, 23 March 1983; *m* 2010, Tania Nell; twin *d* and one step *d*. Gold Medal: for 5000m, Eur. Jun. Championships, 2001; Eur. Jun. Cross Country Championships, 2001; Silver Medal for 5000m, Eur. Under 23 Championships, 2003; debut for GB, 2005; Silver Medal for 5000m, Eur. T&F Championships, 2006; Gold Medal, 2006, Silver Medal, 2008, 2009, Eur. Cross Country Championships; Gold Medal for 3000m, Eur. Indoor Championships,

2009, 2011; Gold Medal for 5000m and for 10,000m, 2010, Gold Medal for 5000m, 2012, Gold Medal for 10,000m, 2014, Gold Medal for 5000m, 2014, Eur. Athletics Championships; Gold Medal for 5000m, Silver Medal for 10,000m, World Athletics Championships, 2011; Gold Medal for 5000m and for 10,000m, Olympic Games, London, 2012; Gold Medal for 5000m and for 10,000m, World Athletics Championships, 2013, 2015; winner: New York Half Marathon, 2011; New Orleans Half Marathon, 2013; Great North Run, 2014, 2015, 2016, 2017, 2018, 2019; Lisbon Half Marathon, 2015; IAAF Diamond League 5000m, 2017; Vitality Big Half, 2018, 2019; Chicago Marathon, 2018; Gold Medal for 5000m and for 10,000m, Olympic Games, Rio de Janeiro, 2016; Gold Medal for 10,000m, Silver Medal for 5000m, World Athletics Championships, 2017. Founder, Mo Farah Foundn, 2011. Male Athlete of Year, British Athletics Writers' Assoc., 2006, 2010, 2011, 2013; Sen. Athlete of Year, UK Athletics, 2010; Eur. Athlete of Year, Eur. Athletics Assoc., 2011, 2012; BBC Sports Personality of the Year, 2017. *Publications:* Twin Ambitions (autobiog.), 2013; (jtly) Ready, Steady, Mo!, 2016. *Address:* c/o PACE Sports Management, 6 The Causeway, Teddington, Middx TW11 0HE.

**FARBEY, Hon. Dame Judith (Sarah),** DBE 2018; **Hon. Mrs Justice Farbey;** a Judge of the High Court, Queen's Bench Division, since 2018; President, Upper Tribunal Administrative Appeals Chamber, since 2019; *b* London, 21 Oct. 1965; *d* of Alan David Farbey and Barbara Astrid Farbey; *m* 2011, Prabhat Vaze. *Educ:* Magdalen Coll., Oxford (BA Hons 1989); City Univ., London (DipLaw 1991). Called to the Bar, Middle Temple, 1992, Bencher, 2013; QC 2011; a Recorder, 2016–18. A Dep. Judge (part-time), Upper Tribunal (Administrative Appeals Chamber), 2014–. Member: Bar Law Reform Cttee, 2003–15; Middle Temple Educn and Trng Cttee, 2014–; Bar Standards Bd, 2016–. Asst Boundary Comr (Lead, London Reg.), 2011–12. Bar Pro Bono Award (first winner), 1997. *Publications:* (jtly) The Law of Habeas Corpus, 3rd edn 2011. *Recreations:* watching plays at Hampstead Theatre, using English Heritage membership, hanging out with Prabhat in Camden Town. *Address:* Royal Courts of Justice, Rolls Building, Fetter Lane, EC4A 1NL.

**FARDON, Prof. Richard Osborne,** PhD; FBA 2004; Professor of West African Anthropology, School of Oriental and African Studies, University of London, 1996–2018, now Emeritus Professor of Anthropology (Head, Doctoral School, 2012–16); *b* 16 Jan. 1952; *s* of Arthur Dennis Fardon and Hilda Fardon (*née* Davidson); partner, Prof. Catherine Davies; one *s*, and two step *d*. *Educ:* Sir Roger Manwood's Grammar Sch., Sandwich; UCL (BSc (Econs) 1973; PhD 1980). Lectr in Social Anthropol., Univ. of St Andrews, 1980–88; Lectr in W African and Caribbean Anthropol., 1988–91, Reader, 1991–96, SOAS; Chm., Centre of African Studies, Univ. of London, 1993–97 and 2001–05. Chair, Assoc. of Social Anthropologists of UK and Commonwealth, 2001–05. Chair: Trustees, Internat. African Inst., 2016–; S3 (Anthropol. and Geog.), British Acad., 2018–. Hon. Ed., Africa: Jl of Internat. African Inst., 2001–07. *Publications:* (ed) Power and Knowledge, 1985; Raiders and Refugees: trends in Chamba political development 1750–1950, 1988; (ed) Localizing Strategies, 1990; Between God, the Dead and the Wild, 1991; (ed with P. T. Baxter) Voice, Genre, Text, 1991; (ed with Graham Furniss) African Languages, Development and the State, 1994; (ed) Counterworks: managing the diversity of knowledge, 1995; Mary Douglas: an intellectual biography, 1999; (ed and introd with Jeremy Adler) Franz Baermann Steiner: selected writings, vol. 1, Taboo, Truth and Religion, vol. 2, Orientpolitik, Value and Civilisation, 1999; (ed jtly) Modernity on a Shoestring, 1999; (ed with Graham Furniss) African Broadcast Culture, 2000; (ed jtly) From Prague Poet to Oxford Anthropologist Franz Baermann Steiner Celebrated: essays and translations, 2003; (with Christine Stelzig) Column to Volume, 2005; Lela in Bali: history through ceremony in Cameroon, 2006; Fusions: masquerades and thought style east of the Niger-Benue confluence, West Africa, 2007; (with Marla Berns and Sidney Kasfir) Central Nigeria Unmasked: arts of the Benue River valley, 2011; (ed jtly) Sage Handbook of Social Anthropology, 2012; (ed with Maria Berns) Nigéria: arts de la vallée de la Bénoué, 2012; (ed) Mary Douglas—A Very Personal Method: anthropological writings drawn from life, 2013; (ed) Mary Douglas—Cultures and Crises: understanding risk and resolution, 2013; Tiger in an African Palace, and other thoughts about identification and transformation, 2014; (with Sènga la Rouge) Learning from the Curse: Ousmane Sembene's Xala, 2017. *Recreations:* following opera and the fortunes of Tottenham Hotspur FC. *Address:* Department of Anthropology and Sociology, School of Oriental and African Studies, University of London, Thornhaugh Street, Russell Square, WC1H 0XG. *T:* (020) 7898 4406. *E:* rf@soas.ac.uk.

**FARHI, Nicole, (Lady Hare),** Hon. CBE 2007; sculptor, since 2012; *b* 25 July 1946; *d* of Ephraim Farhi and Marcelle (*née* Babani); one *d* by Stephen Marks; *m* 1992, Sir David Hare, *qv*. *Educ:* Lycée Calmette, Nice; Cours Berçot Art Sch., Paris. Fashion designer; first designed for Pierre d'Albi, 1968; founded French Connection with Stephen Marks, 1973; founder and designer, Nicole Farhi Co., 1983–2012; launched Nicole Farhi For Men, 1989; opened Nicole's Restaurant, 1994; opened Nicole Farhi US flagship store, NY, 1999. Solo exhibitions: From the Neck Up, 2014, The Human Hand, 2016, Bowman Sculpture, Duke Street; Folds, Beaux Arts, London, 2019; Heads and Hands, Gainsborough House, 2019; Canwood Gall., 2019; Literary Heads, Fine Arts Soc., Edinburgh, 2019. Mem. RSS (Mem. RBS 2017). British Classics award, 1989, Best Contemporary Designer, 1995, 1996 and 1997, British Fashion Awards; Menswear Designer of the Year, FHM Awards, 2000; British Designer of the Year, Maxim Awards, 2001; Lifetime Achievement Award, CBI, 2008; French Woman of the Year, Grandes Ecoles City Circle, 2008. Chevalier, Legion d'Honneur (France), 2010.

**FARINGDON, 3rd Baron** *cr* 1916; **Charles Michael Henderson,** KCVO 2008; Bt 1902; Partner, Cazenove & Co., 1968–96; Chairman, Witan Investment Trust (formerly Witan Investment Company) plc, 1980–2003; a Lord in Waiting to the Queen, 1998–2008; *b* 3 July 1937; *s* of Lt-Col Hon. Michael Thomas Henderson (*d* 1953) (2nd *s* of Col Hon. Harold Greenwood Henderson, CVO, and *g s* of 1st Baron) and Oonagh Evelyn Henderson, *er d* of late Lt-Col Harold Ernest Brassey; *S* uncle, 1977; *m* 1959, Sarah Caroline, *d* of late J. M. E. Askew, CBE; three *s* one *d*. *Educ:* Eton College; Trinity College, Cambridge (BA). Treasurer, Nat. Art Collections Fund, 1984–91; Chm., RCHME, 1994–99; Comr, English Heritage, 1998–2001. Chm. Bd of Governors, Royal Marsden Hosp., 1980–85 (Mem., 1975–85); Chm., Bd of Management, 2001–05 (Mem., 1980–2000), Fellow, 2000, Inst. of Cancer Res. Pro-Chancellor, Univ. of West London, 2014–. *Heir:* s Hon. James Harold Henderson [*b* 14 July 1961; *m* 1986, Lucinda, *y d* of late Desmond Hanson, Knipton, Lincs; two *s* one *d*]. *Address:* Plantation House, Buscot Park, Faringdon, Oxon SN7 8BU. *E:* farbuscot@aol.com.

**FARISH, William Stamps,** III; Ambassador of the United States of America to the Court of St James's, 2001–04; *b* Houston, Tex, 1938; *m* Sarah Sharp; one *s* three *d*. *Educ:* Univ. of Virginia. Formerly: Stockbroker, Underwood, Neuhaus & Co., Houston; Pres., Navarro Exploration Co.; Founding Director: Eurus Inc., NY; Capital Nat. Bank, Houston; Pres., W. S. Farish & Co., Houston. Owner, Lane's End Farm, Versailles, Ky, 1980–; formerly Chairman: Churchill Downs Inc., Ky; Exec. Cttee, Breeders Cup Ltd; Vice-Chm., US Jockey Club; Dir, Thoroughbred Breeders and Owners Assoc.

**FARLEY, Mary-Rose Christine, (Mrs R. D. Farley);** *see* Bateman, M.-R. C.

**FARMELO, Dr Graham Paul;** author and consultant in science communication, since 2003; Affiliate Professor of Physics, Northeastern University, Boston, since 1990; Fellow, Churchill College, Cambridge, since 2017; *b* London, 18 May 1953; *s* of Cyril Albert John Farmelo and Joyce Alice Farmelo (*née* Puttock). *Educ:* Tubbenden Lane Primary Sch., Orpington; Cray Valley Tech. Sch., Sidcup; Univ. of Liverpool (BSc Mathematical Physics 1974; PhD Theoretical Physics 1977). Lectr in Physics, Open Univ., 1977–90; Hd, contemp. sci. exhibns and progs, Science Mus., London, 1990–2002. Has led internat. initiatives in sci. engagement in Europe and US; co-dir, internat. confs, incl. Sci. and Society: Closing the Gap (in collaboration with AAAS), 2007; has participated in strategic cttees, incl. Sci. and Technol. Facility Council Large Hadron Collider public engagement policy cttee, 2007–08; Chair, Internat. Rev. Panel on Communications and Engagement in Sci. Foundn Ireland, for Irish Govt, 2012. Senator James E. O'Neill Meml Lectr, Saginaw Valley State Univ., Michigan, 2014. Director's Visitor: Inst. for Advanced Study, Princeton, 2014–17, 2018–19; Perimeter Inst., Waterloo, Canada, 2016; Simons Center, Stony Brook Univ., 2018. Writer-in-residence, Kavli Inst., UCSB, 2015. Burns Lect., Defence Acad. of the UK, 2016. Hon. Fellow, British Sci. Assoc., 2011. Kelvin Prize and Medal, Inst. of Physics, 2012. *Publications:* (ed with S. Bicknell) Visitor Studies in the 90s, 1993; (ed with J. Carding) Here and Now, 1996; (ed) It Must be Beautiful, 2003; (ed) Creating Connections: museums and the public understanding of research, 2004; The Strangest Man, 2007 (Costa Prize for Biography, Book of Year, Physics World, 2009); Churchill's Bomb, 2013; The Universe Speaks in Numbers, 2019; contrib. papers to specialist physics jls; articles and book reviews in mags and newspapers, incl. Nature and Scientific American. *Recreations:* books, theatre, movies, music, exhibitions, walking, eating well, searching for the perfect espresso, not writing. *E:* graham@ grahamfarmelo.com. *W:* www.grahamfarmelo.com, www.twitter.com/grahamfarmelo.

**FARMER,** family name of **Baron Farmer**.

**FARMER, Baron** *cr* 2014 (Life Peer), of Bishopsgate in the City of London; **Michael Stahel Farmer;** Founding Partner, RK Capital Management LLP, since 2004; *b* Dec. 1944; *m* Jennifer Dorothy Rochfort; one *s* two *d*. *Educ:* King Alfred's Grammar Sch., Wantage. Global Hd, Base Metals, Phibro Salomon, 1986–88; Man. Dir, The Metal and Commodity Co. Ltd, 1989–2002. Co-Treas., Cons. Party, 2012–. Trustee: Kingham Hill Trust, 2002–; The Cross Trust, 2008–. *Recreations:* military and political history, Biblical studies, running, cycling. *Club:* Royal Automobile.

**FARMER, Bruce;** *see* Farmer, E. B.

**FARMER, Prof. David Malcolm,** PhD; FRS 2006; FRSC; Dean and Professor of Oceanography, Graduate School of Oceanography, University of Rhode Island, 2001–11, now Dean and Professor Emeritus. *Educ:* McGill Univ. (MS 1969); Univ. of British Columbia (PhD 1972). FRSC 1993. Physical Oceanographer, Inst. of Ocean Scis, Sidney, BC, now Scientist Emeritus. Adjunct Prof., Sch. of Earth and Ocean Scis, Univ. of Victoria, BC. *Publications:* 113 articles in learned jls.

**FARMER, Dr (Edwin) Bruce,** CBE 1997; FREng; FIMMM; Chairman: Scottish & Southern Energy plc, 2000–05 (Deputy Chairman, 1999–2000); Southern Electric, 1998; *b* 18 Sept. 1936; *s* of Edwin Bruce Farmer and Doris Farmer; *m* 1962, Beryl Ann Griffiths; one *s* one *d*. *Educ:* King Edward's, Birmingham; Univ. of Birmingham (BSc, PhD). CEng 1994; FIMMM (FIM 1994); FREng (FEng 1997). Dir and Gen. Manager, Brico Metals, 1967–69; Man. Dir, Brico Engineering, 1970–76; Man. Dir, Wellworthy, 1976–81; The Morgan Crucible Co. plc: Dir, 1981–83; Chm., Thermal Ceramics Div., 1981–83; Man. Dir and Chief Exec., 1983–97; Chm., 1998–2003. Chairman: Allied Colloids Gp plc, 1996–98; Devro plc, 1998–2001; Bodycote Internat. plc, 1999–2002; Director: Scapa Gp plc, 1993–99; Foreign & Colonial Smaller Cos plc, 1999–2007 (Sen. Ind. Dir, 2005–07). Member: Council, CBI, 1990–2002; Adv. Bd, Imperial Coll. Management Sch., 1991–2003; Finance Cttee, Cancer Res. UK (formerly ICRF), 1997–2008; Court, Surrey Univ., 1998–2005. Pres., Inst. of Materials, 1999–2002 (Sen. Vice-Pres., 1997–99); Chm., Mgt Bd, 2002–04 (Platinum Medal, 2004), Chm., Communications Bd, 2006–14, IMMM. CCMI (CIMgt 1984); FRSA 1995. Freeman, City of London, 1994; Liveryman, Scientific Instrument Makers' Co., 1995–. *Recreations:* music, cricket, hill walking. *Address:* Weston House, Bracken Close, Wonersh, Surrey GU5 0QS. *Club:* Athenæum.

**FARMER, George Wallace;** President, Immigration Appeal Tribunal, 1991–97 (Vice President, 1982–91); *b* 4 June 1929; *s* of George Lawrence Farmer and Blanche Amy (*née* Niccolls); *m* 1961, Patricia Mary Joyce (*d* 2012); three *d*. *Educ:* The Lodge, Barbados; Harrison Coll., Barbados. Called to the Bar, Middle Temple, 1950. Private practice, Barbados, 1950–52; Magistrate, Barbados, 1952–56; Resident Magistrate, Uganda, 1956–63, Sen. Resident Magistrate, 1963–64; Dir of Public Prosecutions, Uganda, 1964–65; attached to Cottle Catford & Co., Solicitors, Barbados, 1965–67; Legal Manager, Road Transport Industry Trng Bd, 1967–70; Adjudicator, Immigration Appeals, 1970–82. *Recreation:* enjoying the company of grandchildren. *Address:* 7 Coney Acre, West Dulwich, SE21 8LL.

**FARMER, Ian Peter;** Chief Executive Officer, Lonmin plc, 2008–12; *b* Petersfield, Hants, 25 March 1962; *s* of Brian John Farmer and Alice Kathleen Farmer; *m* 1994, Diane Chilangwa; three *s* one *d*. *Educ:* Springs Boys' High Sch.; Univ. of S Africa (BCompt Hons). CA S Africa. Audit Senior: Campbell, Bode, Brown & Stewart, 1980–84; Coopers & Lybrand, 1985–86; Gp Accountant and Treas., Lonmin plc, 1986–89; Financial Controller, Lonmin Zambia, 1990–95; Finance Dir, Lonmin Platinum, 1995–2000; Chief Strategic Officer, Lonmin plc, 2001–08. Non-executive Director: VTTI Energy Partners LP, 2014–17; The Royal Marsden NHS Foundn Trust, 2014–. *Recreations:* family time, reading, travelling, Rugby spectator.

**FARMER, Prof. Lindsay,** PhD; FBA 2019; Professor of Law, University of Glasgow, since 1999; *b* Birmingham, 31 Oct. 1963; *s* of Micheal Farmer and Anne Farmer; *m* Sarah Armstrong; two *s*. *Educ:* Univ. of Edinburgh (LLB 1985); Wolfson Coll., Cambridge (MPhil 1986); European University Inst., Florence (PhD 1993). Lectr, Strathclyde Univ., 1987–90; Lectr, then Sen. Lectr, Birkbeck Coll., Univ. of London, 1993–99. *Publications:* Criminal Law, Tradition and Legal Order, 1997; (jtly) The Trial on Trial, Vol. III, Towards a Normative Theory of the Criminal Trial, 2007; Making the Modern Criminal Law, 2016. *Address:* School of Law, University of Glasgow, Glasgow G12 8QQ. *T:* (0141) 330 4181. *E:* lindsay.farmer@glasgow.ac.uk.

**FARMER, Paul David Charles,** CBE 2016; Chief Executive, Mind, since 2006; *b* 8 Oct. 1966; *s* of David and Ann Farmer; *m* 1994, Claire Dwyer (*d* 2019); two *s*. *Educ:* Oratory Sch., Reading; St Peter's Coll., Oxford (BA Modern Hist.; Hon. Fellow). Communications Manager, Samaritans, 1994–97; Dir, Public Affairs, Rethink, 1997–2006. Chm., Mental Health Alliance, 2000–06. Mem., BBC Appeals Adv. Cttee, 2007–12. Chm., Disability Charities Consortium, 2009–14. Member: Catholic Bishops Mental Health Reference Gp, 2008–14; Harrington Review on Disability Benefits, 2010–12; Ind. Commn on Mental Health and Policing, 2012–13; Bd, ACEVO, 2014–18 (Chm., 2015–18); Chm., NHS Mental Health Taskforce, 2015–16; Co-Chair, PM's Rev. on Employers and Mental Health, 2017. Comr, Historic England, 2018–. Trustee: Samaritans, 1998–2001; Directory of Social Change, 2000–10 (Chm., 2003–05); Mental Health Providers Forum, 2006–14; Lloyds Bank Foundn, 2014–. FRSA. Hon. DSc East London, 2012. Co-author, Realising Ambitions, DWP, 2009. *Publications:* contribs to jls on anti-discrimination and stigma. *Recreations:* cricket, Rugby, tennis, film, cookery, listening. *Address:* c/o Mind, 15–19 Broadway, Stratford, E15 4BQ. *T:* (020) 8215 2295. *E:* p.farmer@mind.org.uk.

**FARMER, Peter John;** Planning Director, Office of the Legal Services Complaints Commissioner, 2004–05; *b* 5 Nov. 1952; *s* of Alec and Norah Farmer; *m* 1986, Christine Ann Tetley. *Educ:* King Edward VI Sch., Southampton; Gonville and Caius College, Cambridge (Maths; MA); London Univ. (Cert. Psych.); Open Univ. (DipEcon 2007; BSc 2009). Joined HM Customs and Excise, 1975; HM Treasury, 1979; Lord Chancellor's Dept, 1981; Circuit Principal, Leeds, 1983; Asst Sec., 1987; Asst Public Trustee, 1988; Public Trustee and Accountant Gen. of Supreme Court, 1991; Circuit Administrator, NE Circuit, 1994–2002; Tribunal Appts Project Dir, LCD, 2002–03; Judicial Inf. and Planning Dir, Dept for Constitutional Affairs, 2003–04. Mem., Lord Chancellor's Adv. Cttee on Justices of the Peace for Leeds, 2005–11, for W Yorks, 2011–14 (Mem., sub-cttee for Leeds, 2011–14). Chm., Judicial Appts Panels, DCA, 2005–06; Panel Chm., Judicial Appts Commn, 2006–08. Consultant, Office of the Legal Services Complaints Comr, 2006–09. *Recreations:* English folk dancing, hill walking, classical music, photography (LRPS 2011; Pres., Ilkley Camera Club, 2016–18), bridge.

**FARMER, Sir Thomas,** Kt 1997; CVO 2009; CBE 1990; FRSE; DL; Founder, Kwik-Fit, 1971; *b* 10 July 1940; *s* of John Farmer and Margaret (*née* Mackie); *m* 1966, Anne Drury Scott; one *s* one *d*. *Educ:* St Mary's Primary Sch., Edinburgh; Holy Cross Acad., Edinburgh. Chm. and Chief Exec., Kwik-Fit, 1984–2002. Chairman: Scottish BITC, 1990–2000; Investors in People Scotland, 1991–97; Mem. Bd, Scottish Enterprise, 1990–96. Chm., Bd of Trustees, Duke of Edinburgh Award, 2001–10. Chancellor, Queen Margaret Univ., Edinburgh, 2007–16. FRSE 2009. DL Edinburgh, 1996. KCSG 1997. *Recreations:* tennis, swimming, ski-ing. *T:* (0131) 315 2830.

**FARNELL, Graeme,** FMA; Managing Director, MuseumsEtc Ltd, since 2009; *b* 11 July 1947; *s* of Wilson Elliot Farnell and Mary Montgomerie Wishart Farnell (*née* Crichton); *m* 1969, Jennifer Gerda (*née* Huddlestone); one *s*. *Educ:* Loughborough Grammar Sch.; Edinburgh Univ. (MA); London Film Sch. (DipFilm Studies). FMA 1989; FSAScot 1976; MBIM. Asst Keeper, Mus. of East Anglian Life, 1973–76; Curator, Inverness Mus. and Art Gall., 1976–79; Dir, Scottish Museums Council, 1979–86; Dir Gen., Museums Assoc., 1986–89; Man. Dir, The Development (formerly Museum Development) Co. Ltd, 1989–94; Publishing Ed., IMS Publications, 1994–96; Man. Dir, Heritage Development Ltd, 1996–2008; Director: Heritage Business International, 2005–08; Heritage Development International, 2006–08. Publisher: New Heritage (formerly Heritage Development) magazine, 1996–2003; Heritage Business.net (formerly Heritage Insider, then Heritage Business) newsletter, 1998–2008; Heritage Retail mag., 1999–2003; Heritage Restoration mag., 2000–03; Heritage 365 mag., 2003–08. Director of films: Documentary, 1970; Jagger, 1971; Capital, 1972. *Publications:* (ed) The American Museum Experience, 1986; The Handbook of Grants, 1990, 2nd edn, 1993; (ed) The European Heritage Directory, 1998; (ed) New Museums in China, 2005; (ed) Museums of Ideas: commitment and conflict, 2011; (ed) The Photographer and the Collection, 2013; High Ground, 2013; (ed) Interpreting the Art Museum, 2015; (ed) The Museum Blog Book, 2017; *photobooks:* A Lot of Mud to Work In, 2019; This Miraculous Saint Grants Everything, 2019; Bayble: capital of poetry, 2019; contribs to Museums Jl, Internat. Jl of Mus. Management and Curatorship, Museum (Unesco), Industrial Soc. *Recreations:* baroque opera, contemporary music, photography.

**FARNELL, John Bernard Patrick;** writer and researcher on China's external economic relations; Director, Coordination and International Affairs, Enterprise and Industry Directorate-General, European Commission, 2008–12 (Director, Competitiveness, 2006–07); *b* 24 Aug. 1948; *s* of James Farnell and Laura (*née* O'Connell); *m* 1976, Susan Mary Janus; two *s*. *Educ:* Downside Sch.; Christ's Coll., Cambridge (MA Hist.); London Sch. of Econs (MSc Econ). Economist, BEA, 1970–72; CBI, 1973–74; with European Commission, 1975–2012: Ext. Relns, 1975–77; Fisheries, 1977–82; Industry, 1982–93 (Internat. Questions Unit, 1982–87; Head: Standardisation and Certification Unit, 1987–93; Tech. Legislation Unit, 1993); Hd, Operation of Internal Mkt and Econ. Analysis Unit, Directorate-Gen. of Internal Mkt and Financial Services, 1993–97; Dir, Horizontal Measures and Markets, 1997–2001, Conservation Policy, 2001–06, Fisheries Directorate-General. Mem., Impact Assessment Bd, EC, 2008–12; Sen. Advr, EU-Asia Centre, Brussels, 2013–. EU Fellow, 2011–12, Academic Visitor, 2014–, St Antony's Coll., Oxford; Academic Visitor, 2017–18, Associate Mem., 2018–, Univ. of Oxford China Centre. *Publications:* Public and Private Britain, 1975; (with James Elles) In Search of a Common Fisheries Policy, 1984; (with Paul Irwin Crookes) The Politics of EU-China Economic Relations: an uneasy partnership, 2016. *Recreations:* opera, sailing. *Address:* 61 Chalfont Road, Oxford OX2 6TJ.

**FARNES, Richard Haworth;** Music Director, Opera North, Leeds, 2004–16; *b* Cuckfield, Sussex, 15 Jan. 1964; *s* of Alexander and Christine Farnes; *m* 2001, Juliet Welchman; two *s*. *Educ:* King's Coll. Sch., Cambridge; Eton Coll.; King's Coll., Cambridge (BA Music 1986). Freelance conductor, Glyndebourne, Scottish Opera, Royal Opera and ENO, 1988–. *Recreations:* earth sciences, astronomy, photography, walking, travel. *Address:* c/o Maestro Arts, One Eastfields Avenue, SW18 1FQ. *T:* (020) 3637 2789. *E:* info@maestroarts.com.

**FARNHAM,** 13th Baron *cr* 1756; **Simon Kenlis Maxwell;** Bt (NS) 1627; *b* 12 Dec. 1933; *s* of Hon. Somerset Arthur Maxwell, MP and Angela Susan (*née* Roberts); *S* brother, 2001; *m* 1964, Karol Anne (*d* 2014), *d* of Maj.-Gen. George Erroll Prior-Palmer, CB, DSO; two *s* one *d* (of whom one *s* one *d* are twins). *Educ:* Eton. Late Lt, 10th Royal Hussars. *Heir: s* Hon. Robin Somerset Maxwell [*b* 15 Sept. 1965; *m* 1993, Tessa Shepherd; two *s* one *d*]. *Address:* The Dower House, Church Westcote, near Chipping Norton, Oxon OX7 6SF.
*See also* Viscountess Knollys.

**FARNHAM, Diana, Lady; Diana Marion Maxwell,** DCVO 2010 (CVO 1998); Lady of the Bedchamber to the Queen, since 1987; *b* London, 24 May 1931; *d* of Nigel Eric Murray Gunnis and Elizabeth Gunnis (*née* Morrison); *m* 1959, 12th Baron Farnham; two adopted *d*. *Educ:* Hatherop Castle Sch.; House of Citizenship. Vice-Pres., Dance Teachers' Benevolent Fund, 2012 (Trustee, 1989–2012); Trustee, British Kidney Patient Assoc., 2003–11; Patron, Friends of the Elderly, 1990–. *Address:* 3 Astell House, Astell Street, SW3 3RX.

**FARNISH, Christine,** (Mrs J. Hayes), CBE 2013; a Civil Service Commissioner, 2012–14; *b* 21 April 1950; *d* of Harry Farnish and Agnes Monica Farnish; *m* John Hayes; three *s* one *d*. *Educ:* Ipswich High Sch.; Manchester Univ. (BSc Botany and Geog. 1971); University Coll. London (MSc Conservation 1972). Asst Chief Exec., Cambridge CC, 1988–94; Consumer Dir, 1992–97, Actg Dep. Dir Gen., 1998, OFTEL; Consumer Dir, FSA, 1998–2002; Chief Exec., Nat. Assoc. of Pension Funds, 2002–06; Man. Dir, Public Policy, Barclays PLC, 2006–11. Mem. Council, ASA, 2002–08; non-exec. Dir, OFT, 2003–06; Director: Consumer Focus (formerly NCC), 2008–14 (Chm., 2010–14); ABTA, 2010–16; Aggregate Industries, 2012–14; Brighton and Sussex Univ. Hosps NHS Trust, 2013–16; Ofwat, 2014–; Gas and Electricity Mkts Authy, 2016–; non-exec. Dir, Zopa Gp Ltd, 2018–; Chair, Zopa P2P Ltd, 2018–. Chm., Peer-to-Peer Finance Assoc., 2012–18. Chm., Family and Parenting Inst., 2010–13. *Recreations:* singing, trekking, family. *Address:* Flat 3, 3 Palmeira Square, Hove, East Sussex BN3 2JA. *T:* 07712 530119.

**FARNSWORTH, Ian Ross;** Director, Coutts & Co., 1992–97 (Deputy Chairman and Chief Executive, 1992–95); *b* 15 Feb. 1938; *s* of Frederick Sutcliffe and Winifred Ruby Bryan; *m* 1964, Rosalind Amanda Baker; one *s* one *d*. *Educ:* Nottingham High Sch. ACIB. Westminster Bank, later National Westminster Bank: joined 1954; seconded Nat. Bank of N America, 1979–80; Exec. Vice-Pres., NatWest N America, 1981–84; Asst Gen. Manager, NatWest, 1987–88; Dir, European Businesses, 1988–90; Gen. Manager, NatWest, 1990–91; Dep. Chm., Coutts & Co. AG, Zürich, 1991–94; Mem., Supervisory Bd, F. van Lanschot Bankiers, Holland, 1991–95. Chm., Willowbrite Ltd, 1997–2010; Dir, Finsbury Foods plc, 1997–2014. Director: PEC Concerts Ltd, 1995–2000; New Sadler's Wells Ltd, 1996–2002; Gov., Sadler's Wells Foundn, 1995–2004. Mem., Develt Cttee, 1996–2008, Mem. Court, 2008–14, Univ. of Herts. Liveryman, Information Technologists' Co., 1994–2005. *Recreations:* music, golf. *Address:* 15 Dellcroft Way, Harpenden, Herts AL5 2NQ. *T:* (01582) 712518.

**FARNSWORTH, His Honour John David;** a Circuit Judge, 1991–2008; *b* 20 June 1935; *s* of George Arthur Farnsworth and Mary Lilian Farnworth; *m* 1964, Carol Gay Mallett; one *s* two *d*. *Educ:* Bedford Sch.; St Edmund Hall, Oxford (BA). Bigelow Teaching Fellow, Univ. of Chicago Law Sch., 1958–59. Admitted Solicitor, 1962; a Recorder, 1986–91. *Recreations:* golf, cricket, snooker, art galleries. *Clubs:* MCC; Bedfordshire Golf.

**FARNWORTH, Judith Margaret;** HM Diplomatic Service; Ambassador to Armenia, 2015–19; *b* Sutton Coldfield, 25 April 1966; *d* of Roy Farnworth and Kathleen Mary Hulme. *Educ:* Univ. of Durham (BA Hons Russian 1988); Univ. of East Anglia (MA Internat. Relns 1990). Joined FCO, 1991; Sen. Res. Analyst, Res. and Analysis Dept, FCO, 1991–95; Second Sec., Political/Press Public Affairs, Kyiv, 1996–2000; Hd, Political Section, Prague, 2000–04; Deputy Head of Mission and Consul: Riga, 2005–08; Kyiv, 2008–12; Ambassador to the Kyrgyz Republic, 2012–15. *Address:* c/o Foreign and Commonwealth Office, King Charles Street, SW1A 2AH. *E:* judith.farnworth@fco.gov.uk.

**FAROOKHI, Imtiaz;** entrepreneur; Chairman, Land Data CIC, since 2006; *b* 17 Jan. 1951; *s* of Mumtaz and Anwar Farookhi; two *s* one *d*. *Educ:* King Alfred Sch.; Acton Tech. Coll.; Univ. of Kent at Canterbury; Birkbeck Coll., London Univ. FRICS 2011. Asst Chief Exec., Hackney LBC, 1983–88; Head of Co-ordination, Wakefield MDC, 1988–89; Dir of Policy and Admin, Southwark LBC, 1988–91; Chief Executive: Leicester CC, 1991–96; Nat. House-Building Council, 1997–2012. CEO, The Lowdown, 2016–18. Member: Bd, Envmt Agency, 1995–97; BURA, 1998–2004; British Bd of Agrément, 1999–; LSC, 2001–04; CITB Construction Skills Council, 2004–; SEEDA, 2004–12; London Thames Gateway UDC, 2004–13; Chm., Vistage, 2013–14. Chm., Forum for Construction Skills, 2003–06. Ind. Mem., Audit Cttee, Milton Keynes Council, 2015–. FRSA 1994. *Publications:* articles in jls. *Recreations:* cycling, family life. *Club:* QPR Supporters'.

**FARQUHAR, Maj. Gen. Andrew Peter,** CBE 2003 (MBE 1981); DL; Managing Director, UK, GardaWorld Consulting (UK) Ltd, since 2011; *b* Leeds, 1953; *s* of John and Elizabeth Farquhar; *m* 1981, Alison Jane Grey; three *s* one *d*. *Educ:* Pocklington Sch., Yorks; Sheffield Univ. (BEng Hons Mech. Engrg 1975); Army Staff Coll. (psc† 1985). Commnd Green Howards, 1975; MA to ACDS (I), 1986–88; Chief Instructor, RMA Sandhurst, 1990–92; CO, 1 Green Howards, 1994–96; MA to Adjt Gen., 1996–98; COS, HQ Infantry, 1998–2000; Commander: 15 (NE) Bde (York), 2000–02; Multinat. Div. (SW) Bosnia Herzegovina, 2002–03; COS to Comdr Regl Forces, 2003–04; Dep. Comdg Gen., Multi-Nat. Corps Iraq, 2004–05; GOC 5th Div., 2005–08. Man. Partner, Millbrook Partnership, 2008–10. Dep. Col, then Col, Green Howards, 2001–06; Dep. Col, Yorks Regt, 2006–11; Col, Royal Mercian and Lancastrian Yeomanry, 2008–17. Trustee, Nat. Meml Arboretum, 2011–. Vice Pres., Pocklington RFC, 2001–. FCMI 2008. Shrewsbury Drapers' Co., 2010–. DL Staffs, 2009. QCVS 1995. Officer, Legion of Merit (USA), 2005. *Recreations:* offshore sailing (Yachtmaster Offshore), slowly running marathons, shooting, carpentry, horology, classical music, watching cricket and Rugby. *Address:* GardaWorld Consulting (UK) Ltd, 2 London Bridge, SE1 9RA. *Club:* MCC.

**FARQUHAR, Prof. Graham Douglas,** AO 2013; PhD; FRS 1995; FAA; Distinguished Professor, Australian National University, Canberra, since 2003; *b* 8 Dec. 1947. *Educ:* Australian Nat. Univ. (BSc 1968; PhD 1973); Queensland Univ. (BSc Hons Biophysics 1969). FAA 1988. Dept of Energy Plant Res. Lab., Michigan State Univ., 1973–76; Australian National University: Res. Fellow, 1976–80; Sen. Res. Fellow, 1980–; Fellow, 1980–83; Sen. Fellow, 1983–88; Prof. of Biology, 1988–2003; Research School of Biological Sciences, later Research School of Biology: Leader, Plant Envtml Biology Gp, 1988–89; Envtml Biology Gp, 1994–2009; Associate Dir, 2005–09; Lab. Leader, Plant Sci. Div., 2010–. Prime Minister's Prize for Science, 2015. *Publications:* (ed jtly) Stomatal Function, 1987; (ed jtly) Perspectives of Plant Carbon and Water Relations for Stable Isotopes, 1993; numerous research texts. *Address:* RN Robertson Building 46, Plant Science Division, Research School of Biology, Australian National University, Canberra, ACT 0200, Australia. *T:* (2) 61253743, *Fax:* (2) 61244919.

**FARQUHAR, Margaret (Elizabeth),** CBE 1999; JP; Lord Provost and Lord-Lieutenant of Aberdeen, 1996–99; *b* Aberdeen, 1930; *née* Burnett; *m* 1951, William Farquhar (*d* 1993); one *s* one *d*. *Educ:* Ruthrieston Secondary Sch., Aberdeen; Webster's Coll., Aberdeen. Clerical work: N of Scotland Coll. of Agric., 1947–48; Charles Michie, haulage contractor, 1948–51; Cordiners Sawmills, 1963–65; William Walker, haulage contractor, 1969–77. Member (Lab): Aberdeen DC, 1971–96 (Vice-Chm., 1994–96); Aberdeen CC, 1995–99. Mem., Planning Cttee, 1985–86, 1988–92, Aberdeen Council rep., 1992–99, COSLA. Dir, Grampian Enterprise, 1991–92. Member: Mgt Cttee, Aberdeen CAB, 1986–; Mgt Cttee, Northfield Community Centre, 1993–. Labour Party: Sec., Bridge of Don Br., 1980–81; Sec. and Chm., Cummings Pk Br., 1971–79; Chm., Aberdeen Women's Council, 1971–72. Hon. Pres., Grampian Girls' Bde, 1988–. Chm., Aberdeen Br., RNLI, 2003–. Chm., Friends of Gordon Highlanders Mus., 2001–. JP Aberdeen, 1972. Hon. LLD: Aberdeen, 1996; Robert Gordon, 1998. Paul Harris Fellowship, Rotary Internat., 1998. *Recreations:* working with the elderly and the young, bowling, driving, watching television.

**FARQUHAR, Sir Michael (Fitzroy Henry),** 7th Bt *cr* 1796; of Cadogan House, Middlesex; farmer; *b* 29 June 1938; *s* of Sir Peter Walter Farquhar, 6th Bt, DSO, OBE, and Elizabeth Evelyn (*d* 1983), *d* of Francis Cecil Albert Hurt; *S* father, 1986; *m* 1963, Veronica Geraldine Hornidge; two *s*. *Educ:* Eton; Royal Agricultural College. *Recreations:* fishing, shooting. *Heir: s* Charles Walter Fitzroy Farquhar [*b* 21 Feb. 1964; *m* 2004, Sarah Josephine Wynne-Williams; one *s* one *d*]. *Address:* Manor Farm, West Kington, Chippenham, Wilts SN14 7JG. *T:* (01249) 782671. *Club:* White's.

**FARQUHAR, Stuart Alastair; His Honour Judge Farquhar;** a Circuit Judge, since 2013; Judge of the Court of Protection, since 2013; *b* Weybridge, 4 June 1962; *s* of late Laurence Farquhar and Grace Fairweather Farquhar; *m* 1991, Rebecca Jane Saunders; one *s* one *d*. *Educ:* Esher Grammar Sch.; Univ. of Manchester (LLB 1983); Inns of Court Sch. of Law. Called to the Bar, Inner Temple, 1985; in practice as barrister, 1985–2005; Dep. Dist Judge, 1999–2005; Dist Judge, 2005–13; Recorder, 2009–13. *Recreations:* supporting AFC Wimbledon, walking my dog in the rain, preferably past a real ale pub. *Address:* Brighton County and Family Court, William Street, Brighton BN2 0RF. *T:* (01273) 811333.

**FARQUHARSON, Alex;** Director, Tate Britain, since 2015. *Educ:* Univ. of Exeter (BA); City Univ. (MA). Curator, 1994–96, Exhibns Dir, 1996–98, Spacex, Exeter; Exhibns Dir, Centre for Visual Arts, Cardiff, 1999–2000; independent curator and writer, 2000–07; Dir, Nottingham Contemporary, 2007–15. Vis. Lectr and Reader, RCA, 2000–07. Hon. DLitt Nottingham, 2016. *Address:* Tate Britain, Millbank, SW1P 4RG. *T:* (020) 7887 8048.

**FARQUHARSON of Invercauld, Captain Alwyne Arthur Compton,** MC 1944; JP; Head of Clan Farquharson; *b* 1 May 1919; *er s* of late Major Edward Robert Francis Compton, JP, DL, Newby Hall, Ripon, and Torloisk, Isle of Mull, and Sylvia, *y d* of A. H. Farquharson; recognised by Lord Lyon King of Arms as Laird of Invercauld (16th Baron of Invercauld *S* aunt 1941), also as Chief of name of Farquharson and Head of Clan, since 1949; assumed (surname) Compton as a third forename and assumed surname of Farquharson of Invercauld, by warrant granted in Lyon Court, Edinburgh, 1949; *m* 1st, 1949, Frances Strickland Lovell (*d* 1991), *d* of Robert Pollard Oldham, Seattle, Washington, USA; 2nd, 1993, Patricia Gabrielle Estelle Parry de Winton, *d* of Henry Norman Simms-Adams, Brancaster Hall, Norfolk. *Educ:* Eton; Magdalen Coll., Oxford. Joined Royal Scots Greys, 1940. Served War, 1940–45, Palestine, N Africa, Italy, France (wounded); Captain 1943. County Councillor, Aberdeenshire, 1949–75, JP 1951. *Address:* Valley Farm, Brancaster Staithe, King's Lynn, Norfolk PE31 8DB.

**FARQUHARSON, Very Rev. Hunter Buchanan;** Provost, St Ninian's Cathedral, Perth, since 1999; *b* 19 July 1958; *s* of Cameron Bruce Farquharson and Thelma Alice Buchanan Farquharson. *Educ:* Birmingham Sch. of Speech (ALAM, LLAM); Edinburgh Theol Coll. (General Ministerial Exams; Luscombe Scholar, 1989). Deacon 1988, priest 1989; Curate, West Fife Team, 1988–91; Rector, St Luke's, Glenrothes, 1991–97; Leader of Central Fife Team, 1995–97; Rector, Holy Trinity, Dunfermline and Leader of West Fife Team, 1997–99. Chm., Perth and Kinross Assoc. of Voluntary Services, 2000–08 (Advr to Bd, 2008–). Chm., Scottish Flat-coated Retriever Club, 2005–11 (Vice-Chm., 2002–05). Dir, 2005–10, Vice-Chm., 2007–10, Chm., 2010–11, Ochil Tower Sch. (Camphill), Auchterarder. *Recreations:* showing and breeding flat-coated retrievers and Toulouse Geese, fishing, hill-walking. *Address:* Upper Greenside, by Abernethy, Perthshire KY14 6EL. *T:* (01738) 850987. *E:* huntfar@gmail.com. *Clubs:* Scottish Arts (Edinburgh); Flat-coated Retriever Society; Scottish Kennel (Edinburgh).

**FARQUHARSON, Paul Hiram,** QPM; High Commissioner of the Bahamas to the United Kingdom, and Ambassador to the European Union, Belgium, France, Germany and Italy, 2008–12; *b* 10 Jan. 1949; *s* of late Ural Farquharson and Martha Deveaux; *m* 1969, Sharon Major; one *s* two *d*. *Educ:* Univ. of Louisiana (BAppSci); Univ. of Cambridge (Dip. Applied Criminol. and Police Studies); Atlanta Univ., Georgia (Cert. Criminal Justice, Admin and Principles of Mgt); Police Staff Coll., Bramshill (Strategic Comd Course; Overseas Comd Course). Enlisted Royal Bahamas Police Force, 1966: Corporal, 1971; Sergeant, 1974; Inspector, 1981; Chief Inspector, 1985; Asst Superintendent, 1988; Chief Superintendent, 1994; Asst Comr, 1998; Actg Comr of Police, 2000; Comr of Police, 2001–08. Aide-de-Camp: to Gov. Gen. of the Bahamas, 1984–88; to Rt Hon. Dr Robert Runcie, 1984–88; to Robert Mugabe, 1989; to HRH Duke of Edinburgh, 1993. Pres., Assoc. of Caribbean Comrs of Police, 2005; International Association of Chiefs of Police: Exec. Mem.; Mem., Firearms Cttee; Regl Chm. for Caribbean and Central America; Mem., Internat. Assoc. of Police Community Relns Officers. Mem., Bahamas Film and TV Commn. Salvation Army: Mem., Exec. Bd; Mem., Adv. Bd, Bahamas Div.

**FARQUHARSON-ROBERTS, Surgeon Rear Adm. Michael Atholl,** CBE 2001; FRCS; Medical Director General (Navy), 2003–07; *b* 23 Sept. 1947; *s* of Rev. Donald Arthur Farquharson-Roberts (Captain, RM) and Violet Farquharson-Roberts (*née* Crooks); *m* 1974, Jean Neilsen (*née* Harding); three *s* three *d*. *Educ:* Dorking County Grammar Sch.; Westminster Hosp. Sch. of Medicine (MB BS); RCDS/KCL (MA 2002); Exeter Univ. (PhD Maritime Hist. 2013). FRCS 1976. Orthopaedic trng, Nuffield Orthopaedic Centre, Oxford, Addenbrooke's Hosp., Cambridge and Royal Nat. Orthopaedic Hosp.; Consultant Orthopaedic Surgeon, Royal Hosp. Haslar, 1983–84 and 1986–2000; Principal Med. Officer, HMS Illustrious, 1985–86; rcds, 2001; Change Manager, Defence Med. Trng Orgn, 2001–02; Dir Med. Ops (Navy), 2002–03. Defence Consultant Advr in Orthopaedics, 1996–2000; Mem., Intercollegiate Specialist Adv. Cttee in Orthopaedics, 1996–2000. QHS 1997–2007. Gov., Royal Star and Garter Homes, 2003–18; Trustee, Help for Heroes, 2007–08. Freeman: Apothecaries' Soc.; City of London, 2011. OStJ 2002. Gulf War Medal, 1991. *Publications:* A History of the Royal Navy: World War I, 2014; From War to War: the executive branch of the Royal Navy 1918–1939, 2015; articles in learned jls incl. Jl of Bone and Joint Surgery, BMJ and Jl of RUSI. *Recreations:* golf (badly), sailing, ship modelling. *Address:* 45 Bury Road, Gosport, Hants PO12 3UE. *E:* mfr@globalnet.co.uk. *Clubs:* Army and Navy; Hornet Sailing.

**FARR, Clarissa Mary;** High Mistress, St Paul's Girls' School, 2006–17; *b* 30 June 1958; *d* of late Alan Farr and Wendy Farr; *m* 1993, John Goodbody; one *s* one *d*. *Educ:* Bruton Sch. for Girls; Exeter Univ. (BA Hons Eng. Lit., MA); Bristol Univ. (PGCE). Teacher: Farnborough Sixth Form Coll., 1981–83; Filton High Sch., 1983–86; Head of Sixth Form, Shatin Coll., Hong Kong, 1986–89; Sen. Mistress, Leicester GS, 1990–92; Dep. Head, 1992–96, Principal, 1996–2006, Queenswood Sch., Hatfield. Chm., Boarding Schs' Assoc., 2001–02; Pres., GSA, 2005. Trustee: African Gifted Foundn, 2014–; British Mus., 2016–. Gov., Royal Ballet Sch., 2010–. Fellow, Winchester Coll., 2013. *Recreations:* running, literature, theatre.

**FARR, David Charles;** playwright; Associate Director, Royal Shakespeare Company, since 2009; *b* 29 Oct. 1969; *s* of Martin and Maureen Farr; *m* 2000, Anne Siddons; two *d*. *Educ:* Trinity Hall, Cambridge (MA double 1st cl. Hons (English) 1991). Associate Dir, Gate Th., London, and freelance Dir, Almeida Opera, 1991–95; Artistic Director: Gate Th., 1995–98; (Jt) Bristol Old Vic, 2003–05; Lyric Th., Hammersmith, 2005–08. Director: Coriolanus, 2002, Julius Caesar, 2004, The Winter's Tale, 2009 and 2010, King Lear, 2010, The Homecoming, 2011, Twelfth Night, The Tempest, 2012, Hamlet, 2013, RSC; A Midsummer Night's Dream, 2018 (TMA Award for Best Dir), (also adapted) The Odyssey, 2005, Bristol Old Vic; writer/director: The Nativity, Young Vic, 1999; Crime and Punishment in Dalston, Arcola Th. and radio, 2002; Night of the Soul, RSC, 2002; The UN Inspector, NT, 2005; dir/adapter, Tamburlaine, Barbican/Young Vic, 2005; writer, The Heart of Robin Hood, RSC, 2011; adapter, The Hunt, Almeida Th., 2019; TV screenplay: The Night Manager, John le Carré, 2016; Troy: Fall of a City, 2018; writer and dir, The Ones Below (film), 2016. *Publications: plays:* Elton John's Glasses, 1998 (Writers' Guild Best Play); The Nativity, 1999; The Danny Crowe Show, 2001; Night of the Soul, 2001; Plays 1, 2005. *Recreations:* guitar, cinema, football, walking, Shamanism. *Address:* c/o Curtis Brown, 5th Floor, Haymarket House, 28-29 Haymarket, SW1Y 4SP. *Club:* Anorak.

**FARR, Jennifer Margaret,** MBE 2003; Vice Lord-Lieutenant of Nottinghamshire, 1999–2008; *b* 20 July 1933; *d* of late Charles Percival Holliday and Vera Margaret Emily (*née* Burchell); *m* 1956, Sydney Hordern Farr (*d* 1981); two *s* one *d*. *Educ:* Nottingham Girls' High Sch.; Middlesex Hosp.; Royal Victoria Hosp., Newcastle upon Tyne. Physiotherapist, Nottingham City Hosp., 1954–56. National Society for Prevention of Cruelty to Children: Mem., Nottingham & Dist Cttee, 1959–; Nat. Council Mem., 1973–94; a Nat. Vice-Pres., 1994–; Member: Notts Centenary Appeal, 1983–85; Midlands Regions Bd, 2003–07; Chairman: Nottingham Br., 1983–98 (Pres., 1998–); Notts Full Stop Appeal, 1999–2004; Notts 125 Years Anniversary, 2015–; 60 years with NSPCC celebrated by Jenny Farr Diamond Appeal, 2018–20; Pres., Child's Voice Appeal, E Midlands, 2009–11. Pres., League of Friends, Queen's Med. Centre, 1999–2012. Member: Nottingham Convent Council, 1992–98; Southwell 2000 Appeal, 1992–96; Develt Bd, Nottingham Trent Univ., 2008–16; Cttee, Motor Neurone Disease Appeal for Specialised Wheelchairs, 2010–12. Trustee, Mary Potter Convent Hosp. Trust, 1998–2014. Master Patron, Notts, Public Catalogue Foundn, 2007–09. Pres., Newark and Notts Agricl Soc., 2003 (Hon. Mem. Council, 2004). Gov., Nottingham High Sch. for Girls, 2001–10. Pres., Thurgarton Cricket Club, 1981–99. JP Notts, 1979–89; DL 1993, High Sheriff 1998–99, Notts. Hon. DLitt, Nottingham Trent, 2011. *Recreations:* bridge, gardening, music, sports, theatre, family life. *Club:* Sloane.

**FARR, Susan Jane;** Special Adviser, Chime Communications plc, since 2015 (Executive Director, 2003–15); *b* Yorks, 29 Feb. 1956; *d* of Derek Fairburn and Margaret, (Peggy), Fairburn; *m* 1st, 1979, Richard Peter Farr (marr. diss. 2002); 2nd, 2009, Anthony Christopher Mair. *Educ:* Sheffield High Sch. for Girls; Univ. of Reading (BA Hons Politics). Grad. trainee, Northern Foods plc, 1977–79; Mktg Consultant, KAE and Mintel, 1979–84; Account Director: Dorlands, 1984–86; CDP, 1986–87; WCRS, 1987–89; Dir, Corporate Communications, Thames TV plc, 1989–91; Mktg Dir, UK Gold, 1991–92; Director of Marketing: BBC Radio, 1993–95; BBC, 1995–2000; Chm., Golin Harris, 2000–02; Dir, Corporate Affairs, Vauxhall, 2002–03. Non-executive Director: New Look plc, 1994–96; Motivcom plc, 2008–14; Dairy Crest plc, 2011–; Millennium and Copthorne Hotels plc, 2013–18; Accsys, 2014–; British American Tobacco, 2015–; Dolphin Capital Investors Ltd, 2016–18. Trustee, Historic Royal Palaces, 2007–13. Chm., Mktg Soc., 1990–92; Mem., Mktg Gp of GB, 1993– (Chm., 1999–2001). Hon. DBA Bedfordshire, 2010. *Recreations:* horse riding, travelling, reading, enjoying life. *Address:* E1, Montevetro, 100 Battersea Church Road, SW11 3YL; Chime Communications plc, 62 Buckingham Gate, SW1E 6AJ. *E:* sfarr@chimegroup.com.

**FARRAN, Rt Rev. Brian George;** Bishop of Newcastle, NSW, 2005–12; *b* 15 Dec. 1944; *s* of George Farran and Dorothy Barnes; *m* 1971, Robin Jeanne Marsden; one *s* two *d*. *Educ:* ANU (BA); St John's Theol Coll., Morpeth (ThL); Deakin Univ. (BLitt Hons); Melbourne Coll. of Divinity (DMin Studies 2005). Ordained deacon, 1967, priest, 1968; Curate: St Phillips, O'Connor, 1968; St Alban's, Griffith, 1969–71; Rector: Ch of the Epiphany, Lake Cargelligo, 1972–75; St Barnabas, N Rockhampton, 1975–79; St Saviour's, Gladstone, 1979–82; Dean of St Paul's Cathedral, Rockhampton, Queensland, 1983–89; Regl Dir, Australian Bd of Missions, Province of Victoria, 1989–92; an Asst Bp of Perth, WA, 1992–2005 (Bp of Goldfields Region, 1992–98, of Northern Region, 1998–2005). Vice-Chm., Gen. Bd of Religious Educn, Anglican Church of Australia, Vic, 1984–2000. Chm., Commn on Ministry, 2001–; Mem., Standing Cttee, Gen. Synod, 1998–. Chm. Council, Peter Moyes Anglican Community Sch., Mindarie, Perth, WA, 2000–; President: Bishop Tyrrell Anglican Coll., 2005–12; Lakes Grammar, 2005–12; Manning Valley Anglican Coll., 2005–12; Scone Grammar Sch., 2005–12. Fellow, Guildford Grammar Sch., Guildford, Perth, WA, 2001. *Recreations:* gardening, music, films, reading. *Address:* 4 Leicester Close, Raworth, NSW 2321, Australia.

**FARRANCE, Roger Arthur,** CBE 1988; Chief Executive, Electricity Association, 1990–93; Chairman: Electricity Association Services Ltd, 1991–93; Electricity Association Technology Ltd, 1991–93; *b* 10 Nov. 1933; *s* of Ernest Thomas Farrance and Alexandra Hilda May (*née* Finch); *m* 1956, Kathleen Sheila (*née* Owen); one *d*. *Educ:* Trinity School of John Whitgift, Croydon; London School of Economics (BScEcon). CCIPD; FIET (FIEE 2002). HM Inspector of Factories, Manchester, Doncaster and Walsall, 1956–64; Asst Sec., West of England Engineering Employers' Assoc., Bristol, 1964–67; Industrial Relations and Personnel Manager, Foster Wheeler John Brown Boilers Ltd, 1967–68; Dep. Director, Coventry and District Engineering Employers' Assoc., also Coventry Management Trng Centre, 1968–75; Electricity Council: Dep. Industrial Relations Adviser (Negotiating), 1975–76; Industrial Relations Adviser, 1976–79; Mem., 1979–88; Dep. Chm., 1989–90. Chm., Power Aid Logistics, 1993–94. Dir, Caswell Bay Court Mgt Co. Ltd, 2000–05 (Chm., 2002–05). Member Council: ACAS, 1983–89; CBI, 1983–93 (Chm., Health and Safety Policy Cttee, 1990–93); Mem., Directing Cttee, Union Internationale des Producteurs et Distributeurs d'Energie Electrique, 1991–94 (Chm., Human Factors Cttee, 1991–94). President: IPM, 1991–93; Electricity Supply Industry Ambulance Centre, St John's Amb. Assoc., 1979–93; St John's 210 (London Electricity) Combined Div., 1989–94. Chairman: Devonshire House Management Trustees, 1989–94; Management Bd, Electrical and Electronics Industry Benevolent Assoc., 1987–93. Councillor (C), London Borough of Merton, 1994–98. Chm. Govs, Pentyrch Primary Sch., 2002–06. Freeman, City of London, 1985; Liveryman, Basketmakers' Co., 1986–98. FRSA 1985. OStJ 1983. *Recreations:* painting, woodwork, music, walking. *Address:* 47 Clos Goch, Pentyrch, Cardiff CF15 9RA.

**FARRAND, Julian Thomas;** legal editor and writer; *b* 13 Aug. 1935; *s* of J. and E. A. Farrand; *m* 1st, 1957, Winifred Joan Charles (marr. diss. 1992); one *s* two *d*; 2nd, 1992, Brenda Marjorie Hoggett (*see* Baroness Hale of Richmond). *Educ:* Haberdashers' Aske's Sch.; University Coll. London (LLB 1957, LLD 1966). Admitted Solicitor, 1960. Asst Lectr, then Lectr, KCL, 1960–63; Lectr, Sheffield Univ., 1963–65; Reader in Law, QMC, 1965–68; Prof. of Law, 1968–88, Dean of Faculty of Law, 1970–72, 1976–78, Manchester Univ. Visiting Professor: UCL, 1990–2001; London Guildhall, subseq. London Metropolitan Univ., 2001–06. A Law Comr, 1984–88; Insce Ombudsman, 1989–94; Pensions Ombudsman, 1994–2001. Chairman: Gtr Manchester and Lancs Area, Rent Assessment Panel, 1973–84 (Vice-Pres., 1977–84); Supplementary Benefit Appeals Tribunal, 1977–80; Nat. Insce Local Tribunal, 1980–83; Social Security Appeal Tribunal, 1983–88; Leasehold Valuation Tribunals and RACs for London Area, Rent Assessment Panel, 1984–2010; Govt Conveyancing Cttee, 1984–85; Disciplinary Sub-Cttee, Banking Code Standards Bd, 2001–05; Adjudicator, Ind. Cttee for Supervision of Standards of Telephone Inf. Services, subseq. PhonepayPlus, 2001–08. Chm., Pensions Compensation Bd, 1996–2001; Mem. Adv. Cttee, English Longitudinal Study of Ageing, 2001–05. Non-exec. Dir, First Title plc, 1996–2005 (Consultant, 2010–11). Mem., ADR Chambers (UK) Ltd, 2000–14. Mem., Consumer Policy Adv. Council, Brunel Univ., 2001–05. Mem., UK Assoc. of Women Judges, 2015–. Hon. Prof. of Law, Essex Univ., 2000–12. FCIArb 1994–2005. Hon. QC 1994. Hon. LLD Sheffield, 1990. Editor: Emmet & Farrand on Title, 1967–; Conveyancer and Property Lawyer, 1974–84. *Publications:* Contract and

Conveyance, 1963–64, 4th edn 1983; (ed) Wolstenholme and Cherry, Conveyancing Statutes, 13th edn (vols 1–6) 1972, Consultant Ed., revd edn of vol. 6 as Wolstenholme and Cherry's Land Registration Act 2002, 2004; The Rent Acts and Regulations, 1978, 2nd edn (with A. Arden) 1981; (novel) Love at all Risks, 2001. *Recreations:* chess, bridge, wine, fiction. *Address:* Sandford House, Easby, Richmond, N Yorks DL10 7EW.

**FARRANT, Graham Barry;** Chief Executive, Bournemouth, Christchurch and Poole Council, since 2019; *b* London, 7 June 1960; *s of* John Farrant and Barbara Farrant; *m* 1997, Linda Lillis; four *d. Educ:* Thames Poly. (BSc Hons); Brunel Univ., London (MSc). Student Envmtl Health Officer, 1978–82, Envmtl Health Officer, 1982–85, Westminster CC; Asst Principal Envmtl Health Officer, RBK&C, 1985–86; Asst Divl Dir of Housing, Westminster CC, 1986–90; Birmingham City Council: Asst Dir, 1990–94; Chief Exec., City Challenge, 1994–97; Dir of Housing, 1997–2000; Chief Executive: London Bor. of Barking and Dagenham, 2000–04; Leisure Connection Ltd, 2004–09; pmpgenesis, 2009–10; Thurrock Council, 2010–15; London Bor. of Barking and Dagenham, 2012–14; Chief Exec. and Chief Land Registrar, Land Registry, 2015–18. *Recreations:* hockey, tennis, angling.

**FARRAR, Catherine;** *see* Finnegan, R. H.

**FARRAR, Sir Jeremy (James),** Kt 2019; OBE 2005; DPhil; FMedSci; FRS 2015; Director, Wellcome Trust, since 2013; *b* Singapore, 1 Sept. 1961; *s of* Eric Farrar and Anne Farrar (*née* Melton); *m* 1998, Christiane Dolecek; two *s* one *d. Educ:* University Coll. London (BSc; MB BS); New Coll., Oxford (DPhil). Dir, Oxford Univ. Clin. Res. Unit, Hosp. for Tropical Diseases, Ho Chi Minh City, Viet Nam, 1996–2013; Prof. of Tropical Medicine and Global Health, Univ. of Oxford, 2000–13. Adv. roles on several WHO cttees; Member: Internat. Adv. Bd on Global Health, Federal Ministry of Health, Germany, 2017–; Internat. Panel, Temasek, Singapore, 2019–. Co-Founder and Chm., Farrar Foundn, 2011–. Mem., Nat. Acad. of Medicine, USA, 2018. FMedSci 2007. Ho Chi Minh City Medal, 2004; Frederick Murgatroyd Prize for Tropical Medicine, RCP, 2006; Bailey Ashford Award, Amer. Soc. for Tropical Medicine and Hygiene, 2006; Jimmy and Rosalynn Carter Humanitarian Award, Nat. Foundn for Infectious Diseases, 2019. Meml Medal (Viet Nam), 2013. *Publications:* 600 scientific papers on infectious diseases, global health and emerging infections. *Recreations:* all sports, walking in the Alps. *Address:* Wellcome Trust, 215 Euston Road, NW1 2BE. *T:* (020) 7611 8888.

**FARRAR, Mark Jonathan,** FCA; Chief Executive, Association of Accounting Technicians, since 2014; *b* 14 Aug. 1961; *s of* Ronald and late Doreen Farrar; *m* 2005, Francesca Ann Beckerleg; one *s* one *d,* and two step *s. Educ:* Univ. of Wales, Swansea (BSc Hons). FCA 1988. Finance Dir, Corporate and Instns Gp, Barclays Bank, 1992–94; Asst Dir of Finance, Allied Dunbar, 1994–95; Hd, Planning and Analysis, Norwich Union, 1995–2000; Finance and Resources Dir, 2000–04, Chief Exec., 2004–07, CEFAS; Corporate Services Dir, 2007–08, Chief Exec., 2008–13, ConstructionSkills. Mem., Adv. Bd, Skills Funding Agency, 2011–17. Trustee, BRE, 2009–13. Chm., Barking and Dagenham Coll., 2017–. Mem., ACT. *Recreation:* sailing (RYA Yachtmaster: Ocean). *Address:* Association of Accounting Technicians, 140 Aldersgate Street, EC1A 4HY. *E:* mark.farrar@aat.org.uk.

**FARRAR, Michael,** CBE 2005; Chief Executive, NHS Confederation, 2011–13; *b* Rochdale, 31 July 1960; *s of* Jack and Betty Farrar; partner, Rosamond Roughton; one *s* three *d. Educ:* Bury Grammar Sch.; Nottingham Univ. (BA Hons Geog. 1981); Leeds Univ. (Postgrad. Dip. Health Educn 1985). Middle and sen. mgt appts, NHS, 1982–98; Hd of Primary Care, DoH, 1998–2000; Chief Executive Officer: Tees HA, 2000–02; S Yorks Strategic HA, 2002–05; W Yorks Strategic HA, 2005–06; NW Strategic HA, 2006–11. Director: York Health Econs Consortium, 2000–; Unique Health Solutions, 2012–13. Chm., Strategic HAs CEO Gp (NHS), 2002–09. Nat. Dir for Sport and Health, 2009. Mem. Bd, Sport England, 2005–13 (Interim Chm., 2008–09); Chm., Gp Bd, Amateur Swimming Assoc., 2015–. Chm., Rugby League Players Welfare Bd. Chm., Huddersfield Town/Huddersfield Giants Community Sporting Trust; Trustee, Football League Trust. Hon. FRCGP 2009. Hon. Fellow, Univ. of Central Lancs, 2011. *Recreations:* all sports, films, family life.

**FARRAR-HOCKLEY, Maj.-Gen. (Charles) Dair,** MC 1982; Senior Fellow, Institute for Statecraft, since 2013; Director General (formerly Secretary General), Chartered Institute of Arbitrators, 1999–2006; *b* 2 Dec. 1946; *s of* Gen. Sir Anthony Farrar-Hockley, GBE, KCB, DSO, MC and Margaret Bernadette (*née* Wells); *m* 1969, Vicki King; two *s* one *d. Educ:* Exeter Sch. Commissioned Parachute Regt, 1967; Staff Coll., 1978–79; BM, Berlin, 1979–81; Co. Comdr, 2nd Para Bn, 1982, incl. Falkland Islands campaign; MA to Sec. to Chiefs of Staff Cttee, SHAPE, 1983; Directing Staff, Staff Coll., 1984; CO 3rd Para Bn, 1984–86; Special Briefer to COS, SHAPE, 1987; Higher Command and Staff Course, and Service Fellowship, KCL, 1988; Comdr 19 Inf. Bde, 1989–91; RCDS, 1992; Comdr Inf. Training, 1993–95; British Liaison Officer to Czech Chief of Defence, 1995–96; GOC 2nd Div., 1996–99. Consultant in commercial dispute resolution, 2006–15. Trustee: Airborne Forces Museum, 1993–98 (Chm., 1998–2008); Airborne Forces Security Fund, 1998–2014; Chm., Appeal Bd, Airborne Assault, 2004–09; Patron, Second World War Experience Centre, 1999–. Special Comr, Duke of York's Royal Mil. Sch., 2005–10. Trustee, Holy Trinity Monastery, 2012–. FCMI (FIMgt 1999); MCIArb 1999. Freeman, City of London, 1991. *Publications:* articles on causes and effects of human migration incl. contrib. European Security, vol. 3, Issue 1, 1994. *Recreations:* cricket, wine, photography, supporting Arsenal Football Club. *Address:* c/o Personal Banking Office, National Westminster Bank, Farnborough, Hants GU14 7YU. *Clubs:* Moulsford Cricket (Pres., 2007–16); Travellers' Hockey; Vagrants' Hockey.

**FARRELL, David Anthony;** QC 2000; **His Honour Judge Farrell;** a Circuit Judge, since 2011; Resident Judge, Cambridgeshire Crown Courts; *b* 27 May 1956; *s of* Joseph Anthony Farrell and Valerie Mabel Farrell; *m* 1981, Sandra Nicole Hibble; four *s* one *d. Educ:* Ashby-de-la-Zouch Grammar Sch.; Manchester Univ. (LLB Hons 1977). Called to the Bar, Inner Temple, 1978, Bencher, 2017; Asst Recorder, 1996–2000; Recorder, 2000–11. Hon. Recorder of Cambridge and Peterborough. *Recreations:* tennis, sailing, walking, music. *Address:* Cambridge Crown Court, 83 East Street, Cambridge CB1 1BT.

**FARRELL, James Aloysius;** QC (Scot.) 2013; Sheriff of Lothian and Borders at Edinburgh, 1986–2009; *b* 14 May 1943; *s of* James Stoddart Farrell and Harriet Louise McDonnell; *m* 1st, 1967, Jacqueline Allen (marr. diss.); two *d*; 2nd, 1996, Patricia McLaren. *Educ:* St Aloysius College; Glasgow University (MA); Dundee University (LLB). Admitted to Faculty of Advocates, 1974; Advocate-Depute, 1979–83; Sheriff: Glasgow and Strathkelvin, 1984; S Strathclyde, Dumfries and Galloway, 1985; Temporary Sheriff Principal: Glasgow and Strathkelvin, 2010; Tayside, Central and Fife, 2010, 2011; S Strathclyde, Dumfries and Galloway, 2012, 2013; Temp. High Court Judge, 2012, 2013. *Recreations:* sailing, hillwalking, cycling. *Address:* 8B Merchiston Park, Edinburgh EH10 4PN. *Club:* New (Edinburgh).

**FARRELL, Michael Arthur;** *b* 27 April 1933; *s of* Herbert and Marjorie Farrell; *m* 1st, 1957, Myra Shilton (*d* 1973); two *d*; 2nd, 1976, Beryl Browne (*d* 2011). *Educ:* Beverley Grammar Sch., Yorks; Holly Lodge Grammar Sch., Birmingham. Design Draughtsman, 1949–51; Nat. Service, RASC, 1951–53; Planning Engineer, 1953–61; Representative, 1961–74; Sales Manager, Lillywhites Cantabrian, 1974–80; Sales Executive, En-Tout-Cas, 1980–82; Gen. Sec., AAA, subseq. British Athletic Fedn, 1982–91; Export Sales Dir, Cantabrian Athletics Ltd, 1992–93; consultant, 1994–96; restaurateur, 1996–99. Mem., South Cams DC, 1994–96. Fifth position, 800m final (track and field), 1956 Olympics. *Recreations:* painting, walking, cycling.

**FARRELL, Prof. Paul James,** PhD; FMedSci; Professor of Tumour Virology, Imperial College, London, since 1994; *b* 10 July 1953; *s of* James Patrick Farrell and Audrey Winifred Farrell; *m* 1977, Diana Elizabeth Hamilton Kirby; one *s* one *d. Educ:* Churchill Coll., Cambridge (BA 1974); Clare Hall, Cambridge (PhD 1978). FRCPath 1995. Res. Fellow, Yale Univ., 1977–80; Res. Scientist, MRC Lab. of Molecular Biology and Ludwig Inst., Cambridge, 1980–86; Dir, St Mary's Br., Ludwig Inst. for Cancer Research, 1986–2005. Chm., Res. Cttee, Leukaemia and Lymphoma Res. (Bloodwise), 2009–16. FMedSci 2003. *Publications:* res. pubns on molecular biology of viruses and cancer, particularly Epstein-Barr virus. *Recreations:* sailing (Sec., 2009–13, Chm., 2013–15, 2019–, Gerrards Cross Sailing Assoc.), gardening. *Address:* Section of Virology, Faculty of Medicine, Imperial College, St Mary's Campus, Norfolk Place, W2 1PG. *T:* (020) 7594 2005, *Fax:* (020) 7594 3973. *E:* p.farrell@imperial.ac.uk.

**FARRELL, Simon Henry;** QC 2003; a Recorder, since 2006; *b* 17 Jan. 1960; *s of* Thomas and Joyce Farrell; *m* 1988, Kathryn Wood; three *s* one *d. Educ:* King's Sch., Canterbury; Gonville and Caius Coll., Cambridge (MA 1981); City Univ. (Dip. Law). Called to the Bar, Lincoln's Inn, 1983; barrister specialising in law of commercial fraud, money laundering, tax evasion, civil and criminal confiscation of assets. *Publications:* (jtly) The Proceeds of Crime Act 2002, 2002; (jtly) Asset Recovery, Criminal Confiscation and Civil Recovery, 2003; (jtly) The Fraud Act 2006, 2007. *Recreations:* squash, running, watching Tottenham Hotspur FC, wine, family. *Address:* 3 Raymond Buildings, Gray's Inn, WC1R 5BH.

**FARRELL, Sir Terence, (Sir Terry),** Kt 2001; CBE 1996 (OBE 1978); Principal, Farrells (formerly Terry Farrell & Partners), since 1980; *b* 12 May 1938; *s of* Thomas and Molly Farrell (*née* Maguire); *m* 1st, 1960, Angela Rosemarie Mallam; two *d*; 2nd, 1973, Susan Hilary Aplin; two *s* one *d*; 3rd, 2007, Mei Xin Wang; one step *s. Educ:* St Cuthbert's Grammar Sch., Newcastle; Newcastle Univ. (BArch, 1st class hons); Univ. of Pennsylvania (MArch, MCP). ARIBA 1963; MRTPI 1970; FCSD (FSIAD 1981). Harkness Fellow, Commonwealth Fund, USA, 1962–64. Partner in Farrell Grimshaw Partnership, 1965–80. Major projects include: redevelt of Charing Cross Station; Edinburgh Internat. Conf. Centre; British Consulate-Gen., Hong Kong; Vauxhall Cross (MI6), London; Kowloon Station, Hong Kong; Internat. Centre for Life, Newcastle; Deep Aquarium, Hull; Greenwich Peninsular masterplan; Home Office HQ, London; regeneration of Marylebone-Euston Road, London; Transportation Centre, Inchon Internat. airport, Seoul; Univ. of Newcastle masterplan; Manchester Southern Gateway masterplan; Manchester Univ. masterplan; Regent's Place, London; Great North Museum, Newcastle upon Tyne; The Royal Institution, London; Beijing South Station. *Exhibitions:* RIBA Heinz Gall., London, 1987; RIBA, London, 1995; V&A Mus., 2011. Design Champion: City of Edinburgh, 2004–09; Thames Gateway, 2007–; Ashford's Future, 2009–; Vision Champion, Kent CC, 2009–. Comr, English Heritage, 1990–96; Member: Royal Parks Adv. Bd, 2003–; Mayor of London's Design Adv. Panel, 2009–. Chm., Walking Co-ordination Gp, Central London Partnership, 2003–. Vis. Prof., Univ. of Westminster, 1998–2001. Hon. FRIAS 1996; Hon. FAIA 1998. Hon. DCL Newcastle, 2000; Hon. DA Lincoln, 2003. *Publications:* Architectural Monograph, 1985; Urban Design Monograph, 1993; Place: a story of modelmaking, menageries and paper rounds (life and work: early years to 1981), 2004; Shaping London: the patterns and forms that make the metropolis, 2009; Terry Farrell Interiors and the Legacy of Postmodernism, 2011; articles in numerous British and foreign jls; *relevant publications:* Terry Farrell: selected and current works, 1994; Ten Years: Ten Cities: the work of Terry Farrell & Partners 1991–2001, 2002; Continuum, 2012; Collage & Context, 2013. *Recreations:* walking, swimming. *Address:* (office) 7 Hatton Street, NW8 8PL.

**FARRELL, Timothy Robert Warwick;** Organist, Liberal Jewish Synagogue, St John's Wood, since 1975; *b* 5 Oct. 1943; *m* 1st, 1975, Penelope Walmsley-Clark (marr. diss. 1995); one *s*; 2nd, 1996, Jane Emmanuel. *Educ:* Diocesan Coll., Cape Town; Royal Coll. of Music, London; Paris; etc. FRCO, ARCM (piano and organ). Asst Organist, St Paul's, Knightsbridge, 1962–66; Asst Organist, St Paul's Cath., 1966–67; Sub-organist, Westminster Abbey, 1967–74; Organ Tutor at Addington Palace, RSCM, 1966–73; Organist, Choirmaster and Composer, HM Chapels Royal, 1974–79. Broadcaster, recordings, electronic and orchestral music, etc. *Recreations:* golf, walking, sailing, flying. *Address:* Liberal Jewish Synagogue, 28 St John's Wood Road, NW8 7HA. *T:* (020) 7286 5181.

**FARRELLY, (Christopher) Paul;** MP (Lab) Newcastle-under-Lyme, since 2001; *b* Newcastle-under-Lyme, 2 March 1962; *s of* late Thomas Farrelly and Anne Farrelly (*née* King); *m* 1998, Victoria Perry; one *s* two *d. Educ:* St Edmund Hall, Oxford (BA Hons PPE). Manager, Corporate Finance Div., Barclays de Zoete Wedd, 1984–90; Corresp., Reuters Ltd, 1990–95; Dep. City and Business Ed., Independent on Sunday, 1995–97; City Ed., The Observer, 1997–2001. Mem., Culture, Media and Sport, subseq. Digital, Culture, Media and Sport, Select Cttee, 2005–. *Recreations:* Rugby, football, writing. *Address:* House of Commons, SW1A 0AA. *T:* (020) 7219 8262. *Clubs:* Holy Trinity Catholic, Halmer End Working Men's (Newcastle-under-Lyme); Trentham Rugby Union Football, Finchley Rugby Football, Commons and Lords Rugby Union Football.

**FARREN, Dr Sean;** Member (SDLP) Antrim North, Northern Ireland Assembly, 1998–2007; *m* 1967, Patricia Clarke; one *s* three *d. Educ:* National Univ. of Ireland (BA 1960; HDE 1961); Essex Univ. (MA 1970); Univ. of Ulster (DPhil 1989). Teacher, Sierra Leone, Switzerland, Ireland, 1961–68; University Lectr in Educn, Univ. of Ulster, 1970–98. Fellow, Saltzburg Internat. Seminar, 1989. Minister of Higher and Further Educn, Trng and Employment, 1999–2001, of Finance and Personnel, 2001–02, NI. Contested (SDLP) Antrim N, 2001. *Publications:* The Politics of Irish Education 1920–1965, 1995; (with Robert Mulvihill) Paths to a Settlement in Northern Ireland, 1999; The SDLP: the struggle for agreement in Northern Ireland 1970–2000, 2010; (ed jtly) John Hume - Peacemaker, 2015; contributed to: Motivating the Majority—Modern Languages, Northern Ireland, 1991; Whose English, 1994; Irish Educational Documents, Vol. III, 1995; Language, Education and Society in a Changing World, 1996; A New History of Ireland, Vol. VII, 1998; Fiction, Multi-media and Intertextuality in Mother Tongue Education, 1998; contribs to Aspects of Educn, History of Educn, Etudes Irlandaises, Lang. Culture and Curriculum, Oxford Internat. Rev., Southeastern Pol Rev.; res. reports. *Recreations:* reading, swimming, cycling, theatre. *Address:* 3 Mill Square, Lissadell Avenue, Portstewart, Co. Derry BT55 7TB. *T:* (028) 7083 3042.

**FARRER, Sir (Charles) Matthew,** GCVO 1994 (KCVO 1983; CVO 1973); Private Solicitor to the Queen, 1965–94; Partner in Messrs Farrer & Co., Solicitors, 1959–94; *b* 3 Dec. 1929; *s* of late Sir (Walter) Leslie Farrer, KCVO, and Hon. Lady Farrer; *m* 1962, Johanna Creszentia Maria Dorothea Bennhold; one *s* one *d*. *Educ*: Bryanston Sch.; Balliol Coll., Oxford (MA). Admitted solicitor, 1956. A Trustee, British Museum, 1989–99; Comr, Royal Commn on Historical Manuscripts, 1991–2002; Mem., British Library Bd, 1994–2000. Trustee, Lambeth Palace Library, 1991–2002. Pres., Selden Soc., 2001–03. Mem., Ct of Assts, Fishmongers' Co., 1995– (Prime Warden, 2007–08). *Address*: 6 Priory Avenue, Bedford Park, W4 1TX. *T*: (020) 8994 6052; Charlwood Place Farm, Horley Road, Charlwood, Surrey RH6 0BJ. *T*: (01293) 862413.

**FARRER, Rt Rev. David;** *see* Farrer, Rt Rev. R. D.

**FARRER, David John;** QC 1986; a Recorder, 1983; *b* 15 March 1943; *s* of John Hall Farrer and Mary Farrer; *m* 1969, Hilary Jean Bryson; two *s* one *d*. *Educ*: Queen Elizabeth's Grammar Sch., Barnet; Downing Coll., Cambridge (MA, LLB). Called to the Bar, Middle Temple, 1967, Bencher, 1998. Dep. Chm., Information Tribunal, 2005. Mem., Bar Council, 1986–94; Chm., Bar Services Cttee, 1989–94. Contested (L): Melton, 1979; Rutland and Melton, 1983. *Recreations*: tennis, cricket, Liberal Party politics. *Club*: National Liberal.

**FARRER, Sir Matthew;** *see* Farrer, Sir C. M.

**FARRER, Paul Ainsworth;** QC 2006; **His Honour Judge Farrer;** a Circuit Judge, since 2011; *b* 15 March 1965; *s* of His Honour Brian Ainsworth Farrer, QC and of Gwendoline Valerie Farrer; *m* 2004, Emma Louise Kelly; two *d*. *Educ*: Nottingham Univ. (LLB Hons 1986); Inns of Court Sch. of Law. Called to the Bar, Gray's Inn, 1988; in practice as barrister, 1988–2011, specialising in criminal law; Recorder, 2004–11. *Recreations*: golf, skiing, tennis, travel. *Address*: Birmingham Crown Court, 1 Newton Street, Birmingham B4 7NA. *Clubs*: Little Aston Golf, Aberdovey Golf.

**FARRER, Rt Rev. (Ralph) David;** Locum Vicar, All Saints' Church, East St Kilda, Vic, Australia, 2015; Locum Priest, St James the Great Church, East St Kilda, Vic, Australia; *b* 7 May 1944; *s* of Alexander John Farrer and Jacquelyn Mary Westacott Farrer (*née* Pattison); *m* 1969, Helen Belfield Walker; two *s*. *Educ*: Mentone Grammar Sch.; Ringwood High Sch.; St Barnabas Theol Coll. (ThL Hons; ThSchol Hons). Asst Curate, Good Shepherd, Plympton, SA, 1968–71; ordained priest, 1969; Priest i/c, St John the Baptist, Hillcrest, SA, 1971–73; Asst Priest, St Peter, Eastern Hill, Melbourne, 1973–75; Vicar: Christ Church, Brunswick, Vic, 1975–90; St Mary, Nottingham, 1988–89 (exchange); St Peter, Eastern Hill, 1990–98. Canon, St Paul's Cathedral, Melbourne, 1985–98; Archdeacon: La Trobe, Vic, 1994–96; Melbourne, 1996–98; Bishop of Wangaratta, Vic, 1998–2008; Vicar, St Nicholas, Arundel, with Tortington and South Stoke, 2008–15; an Hon. Asst Bishop, Dio. of Chichester, 2008–15. Dir, Inst. for Spiritual Studies, Melbourne, 1990–98. Chaplain to Parlt, Vic, 1992–98. CHLJ 1991; CMLJ 1996. *Publications*: Orthodoxy Down Under: tracts for our times, 1983; Wilderness Transformed, 1992. *Recreations*: reading, travel, golf. *E*: dfarrerarundel@gmail.com. *Club*: Melbourne (Melbourne).

**FARRINGTON, Rev. Canon Christine Marion;** Vicar of St Mark's, Cambridge, 1996–2002; Chaplain to the Queen, 1998–2012; *b* 11 June 1942; *d* of late Wilfred Bourne Farrington and Doris Violet Farrington. *Educ*: Cheshunt Grammar Sch.; Birkbeck Coll., London (BA Hons); Univ. of Nottingham (Dip. in Applied Social Studies); Univ. of Middlesex (MA in Deviancy and Social Policy); St Albans MTS. Ordained deaconess 1982, deacon, 1987, priest, 1994. Asst librarian, 1960–62; primary school teacher, 1962–65; probation officer, Hemel Hempstead, 1967–71; social work lectr, Middlesex Poly., 1971–79; sen. probation officer, Harrow, 1979–86; asst prison chaplain, 1986–87; Asst Dir of Pastoral Studies, Lincoln Theol Coll., 1986–87; Deacon, Salisbury Cathedral, 1987–93; Dir, Sarum Christian Centre, 1987–93; Co-Diocesan Dir of Ordinands and Dir of Women's Ministry, Dio. of Ely, 1993–2002; Hon. Canon, Ely Cathedral, 1993–2002, now Canon Emeritus; Chaplain, N Thames Ministerial Trng Course, 2003–07; RD, Wheathampstead, 2004–07; Associate Minister, Kirkwall Cathedral, Orkney, 2007–08. Hon. Chaplain: Wolfson Coll., Cambridge, 1993–2002; St John Ambulance Bde, Cambs, 2000–02. *Recreations*: gardening, walking, entertaining, reading, theatre and concerts. *Address*: 4 Pondesmeade, Redbourn, St Albans, Herts AL3 7LD.

**FARRINGTON, Prof. David Philip,** OBE 2004; PhD; FBA 1997; FMedSci; Professor of Psychological Criminology, University of Cambridge, 1992–2012, now Emeritus; Leverhulme Trust Emeritus Fellow, 2012–15; *b* 7 March 1944; *s* of William Farrington and Gladys Holden (*née* Spurr). *m* 1966, Sally Chamberlain; three *d*. *Educ*: Clare Coll., Cambridge (BA, MA; PhD Psychology 1970). Joined staff of Cambridge Univ. Inst. of Criminology, 1969; Reader in Psychol Criminology, 1988–92; Fellow, Darwin Coll., Cambridge, 1980–83. Mem., Parole Bd for England and Wales, 1984–87. Chm., Div. of Criminological and Legal Psychology, British Psychological Soc., 1983–85; President: British Soc. of Criminology, 1990–93; Eur. Assoc. of Psychology and Law, 1997–99; Amer. Soc. of Criminology, 1998–99 (Chm., Div. of Develt and Life-Course Criminology, 2012–16); Acad. of Experimental Criminology, 2001–03. Vice-Chm., US Nat. Acad. of Scis Panel on Violence, 1989–92; Co-Chairman: US Office of Juvenile Justice and Delinquency Prevention Study Gp on Serious and Violent Juvenile Offenders, 1995–97, on Very Young Offenders, 1998–2000; High Security Psychiatric Services Commng Bd, Network on Primary Prevention of Adult Antisocial Behaviour, DoH, 1997; US Center for Disease Control Expert Panel on Promotive and Protective Factors for Youth Violence, 2007–12; US Nat. Inst. of Justice Study Gp on Transitions from Juvenile Delinquency to Adult Crime, 2008–12; Chm., UK DoH Adv. Cttee, Nat. Prog. on Forensic Mental Health, 2000–03. FMedSci 2000. Hon. FBPsS, 2012. Hon. ScD Trinity Coll., Dublin, 2008. Sellin-Glueck Award, 1984, Sutherland Award, 2002, Vollmer Award, 2014, Bloch Award, 2018, Amer. Soc. of Criminology; Joan McCord Award, Acad. of Experimental Criminology, 1988; Award for Dist. Contribns, US Office of Juvenile Justice and Delinquency Prevention, 1998; Joan McCord Award, Acad. of Experimental Criminology, 2005; Beccaria Gold Medal of Criminology, Soc. of German-Speaking Countries, 2005; Sen. Prize, Div. of Forensic Psychology, BPsS, 2007; Award for Outstanding Career-long Contribs to the Scientific Study of Law and Human Behaviour, Eur. Assoc. of Psychol. and Law, 2009; Jerry Lee Award, Div. of Experimental Criminology, American Soc. of Criminology, 2010; Robert Boruch Award, Campbell Collaboration, 2012; Stockholm Prize in Criminology, Sweden, 2013; Freda Adler Dist. Scholar Award, Amer. Soc. of Criminology, 2013; Internat. Award, Juvenile Justice Without Borders, 2014; John Paul Scott Award, Internat. Soc. for Res. on Aggression, 2018. *Publications*: Who Becomes Delinquent?, 1973; The Delinquent Way of Life, 1977; Behaviour Modification with Offenders, 1979; Psychology, Law and Legal Processes, 1979; Abnormal Offenders, Delinquency and the Criminal Justice System, 1982; Aggression and Dangerousness, 1985; Reactions to Crime, 1985; Prediction in Criminology, 1985; Understanding and Controlling Crime, 1986; Human Development and Criminal Behaviour, 1991; Offenders and Victims, 1992; Integrating Individual and Ecological Aspects of Crime, 1993; Psychological Explanations of Crime, 1994; Building a Safer Society, 1995; Understanding and Preventing Youth Crime, 1996; Biosocial Bases of Violence, 1997; Serious and Violent Juvenile Offenders, 1998; Antisocial Behaviour and Mental Health Problems, 1998; Evaluating Criminology and Criminal Justice, 1998; Sex and Violence, 2001; Offender Rehabilitation in Practice, 2001; Child Delinquents, 2001; Costs and Benefits of Preventing Crime, 2001; Evidence-Based Crime Prevention, 2002; Early Prevention of Adult Antisocial Behaviour, 2003; Crime and Punishment in Western Countries, 2005; Integrated Developmental and Life-course Theories of Offending, 2005; Reducing Crime, 2006; Preventing Crime, 2006; Key Issues in Criminal Career Research, 2007; Saving Children from a Life of Crime, 2007; Violence and Serious Theft, 2008; (ed) Dictionary of Forensic Psychology, 2008; Making Public Places Safer, 2009; Young Homicide Offenders and Victims, 2011; Oxford Handbook of Crime Prevention, 2012; From Juvenile Delinquency to Adult Crime, 2012; Young Adult Offenders, 2012; Scholarly Influence in Criminology and Criminal Justice, 2012; Explaining Criminal Careers, 2012; Offending from Childhood to Middle Age, 2013; Labelling Theory: empirical tests, 2014; Most-Cited Scholars in Criminology and Criminal Justice, 2014; Effects of Parental Incarceration on Children, 2014; Criminal Recidivism: explanation, prediction and prevention, 2016; Offending from Childhood to Young Adulthood, 2016; What Works in Crime Prevention and Rehabilitation, 2016; The Psychology of Crime, Policing and Courts, 2016; Female Delinquency from Childhood to Young Adulthood, 2017; Protecting Children Against Bullying and its Consequences, 2017; International Perspectives on Cyberbullying, 2018; (ed jtly) The Oxford Handbook on Developmental and Life-Course Criminology, 2019; (jtly) Communities That Care, 2019; (jtly) Crime in Japan, 2019. *Address*: Institute of Criminology, Sidgwick Avenue, Cambridge CB3 9DA. *T*: (01223) 335360.

**FARRINGTON, Sir Henry (William),** 8th Bt *cr* 1818, of Blackheath, Kent; *b* 27 March 1951; *s* of Sir Henry Francis Colden Farrington, 7th Bt and Anne, *e d* of Major W. A. Gillam, DSO; *S* father, 2004; *m* 1979, Diana Donne, *yr d* of late Geoffrey Broughton; two *s*. *Educ*: Haileybury; RAC Cirencester. MRICS. *Heir*: *s* Henry John Albert Farrington, *b* 4 Jan. 1985. *Address*: Castle, Wiveliscombe, Taunton, Somerset TA4 2TJ.

**FARRINGTON, Paul;** freelance vocal coach and consultant, and specialist remedial voice therapist; *b* 25 Feb. 1959; *s* of Brian and Mary Farrington. *Educ*: Birmingham Sch. of Music (GBSM, ABSM). Dir of Music, Birmingham Sch. of Speech and Drama, 1986–96; Opera Dir, Guildford Sch. of Acting, 1990–95; Vocal Tutor: Welsh Coll. of Music and Drama, 1990–97; RAM, 1994–99; Clinical Vocal Consultant, University Hosp., Birmingham, 1990–; Vocal Consultant: Samling Foundn, 1996–; Birmingham Sch. of Acting, 2001–; Internat. Vocal Tutor, NZ Opera Sch. for Emerging Artists, 2006–; Technical Vocal Coach, Young Artists Prog., Royal Opera, Covent Gdn, 2007–. Visiting Vocal Coach: Göteborgs Operan, 2004–; Tokyo New Nat. Th., 2009–; Frankfurt Neue Opera, 2010–; Lindemann Young Artists Prog., Met. Opera, NY, 2010–. Vis. Prof., Operahogskolan, Stockholm, 2010–; Prof. of Opera and Vocal Pedagogy, Kunsthogskolan, Oslo, 2014–. Vocal Coach and Musical Dir, film, Quartet, 2012; Music Consultant, Vocal Coach and Orchestral Cond., film, The Theory of Everything, 2015. *Recreations*: dining, gym, travel, theatre, fine wine, cooking, gardening, Pilates (keeping fit). *T*: 07970 268933. *E*: paulfarrington@me.com. *W*: www.paulfarrington.org.

**FARRON, Timothy James;** MP (Lib Dem) Westmorland and Lonsdale, since 2005; *b* 27 May 1970; *s* of Christopher Farron and Susan Farron (*née* Trenchard); *m* 2000, Rosemary Alison Cantley; two *s* two *d*. *Educ*: Univ. of Newcastle upon Tyne (BA Hons Politics 1991). Lancaster University: Adult Educn Officer, 1992–96; Special Needs Student Advr, 1996–8; Asst to Acad. Registrar, 1998–2002; Hd, Faculty Admin, St Martin's Coll., 2002–05. Member (Lib Dem): Lancs CC, 1993–2000; S Ribble BC, 1995–99; S Lakeland DC, 2004–08. Pres., 2011–14, Leader, 2015–17, Liberal Democrats. Mem., Amnesty Internat., 1993–. Mem., Cumbria Wildlife Trust, 2003–. Mem. PCC, Milnthorpe St Thomas, 2004–. Chm., Milnthorpe Youth Gp, 2004–. *Publications*: A Better Ambition: confessions of a faithful liberal, 2019. *Recreations*: walking, football (both playing and watching, respectively as an average goalkeeper and a Blackburn Rovers fan), music. *Address*: House of Commons, SW1A 0AA; Acland House, Yard 2, Strickland Gate, Kendal LA9 4ND. *T*: (01539) 723403, *Fax*: (01539) 740800. *E*: tim@timfarron.co.uk. *Club*: Kendal and South Westmorland Liberal (Pres.).

**FARROW, Christopher John;** Chairman, Aga Foodservice Group, 2001–04; *b* 29 July 1937; *s* of late Thomas and Evangeline Dorothea Farrow; *m* 1961, Alison Brown; one *s* one *d*. *Educ*: Cranleigh Sch.; King's Coll., Cambridge (BA). Board of Trade, 1961; Harkness Fellowship and visiting scholar, Stanford Univ., USA, 1968–69; Private Sec. to Pres. of BoT and Minister for Trade, 1970–72; Dept of Trade and Industry, 1972–74; Cabinet Office, 1975–77; Dept of Industry, 1977–83; Asst Dir, Bank of England, 1983–87; Dir, Kleinwort, Benson Ltd, 1987–92; Dir-Gen., British Merchant Banking and Securities Houses, then London Investment Banking, Assoc., 1993–99. Director: London Metal Exchange Ltd, 1987–99 (Vice Chm., 1997–99); Glynwed International, 1993–2001 (Chm., 2000–01). Member: Engrg Council, 1984–86; Financial Reporting Review Panel, 1992–2002. *Recreation*: gardening.

**FARROW, Christopher John;** Chairman, Ellesmere Port Development Board, since 2016 (Member, since 2010); *b* 19 Nov. 1947; *s* of Sydney A. Farrow; *m* 1980, Susan Thomas; three *d*. *Educ*: Claysmore Sch., Dorset; Univ. of London (BA Hons); Polytechnic of Central London (DipTP Dist.). Planner, London Borough of Newham, 1974–81; Dir, LDDC, 1981–91; Chief Exec., Merseyside Develt Corp., 1991–98; Man. Dir, North, then Exec. Dir, N Wales, WDA, 1998–2006; Chief Exec., Central Salford Urban Regeneration Co., 2006–11. Non-executive Director: Greenland Dock Develt Co., 1985–90; Mersey Partnership, 1992–98. Mem. Bd, Cheshire Sci. Corridor Enterprise Zone. Trustee, Surrey Docks City Farm. *Publications*: planning papers on urban develt and economy.

**FARROW, Gary,** OBE 2011; Founder, Chairman and Chief Executive Officer, The Corporation, since 2005; *b* Orpington, 25 Aug. 1955; *s* of late Lesley Farrow and Evelyn Joyce Farrow; *m* 2002, Jane Moore; two *d*, and one step *d*. *Educ*: Midfield Sch. for Boys, later Walsingham Boys' Sch., Orpington; St Martin's Sch. of Art. Worked in shop, One Stop Records, London, 1973; runner, Rocket Records, 1974; joined EMI records, 1976; Man. Dir, Chinnichap, songwriting partnership, 1978; Founder, Gary Farrow Enterprises Media Mgt Co., 1980; Vice Pres., Communications, Sony Music Entertainment, 1995–2004. Deputy Chairman: Music Industry Trust, 1994–2010; Radio Acad., 1996–2004; PR Cttee, BPI, 2001–; Member: Cttee, HMV Charities, 1994; Cttee, BRITs, 1994–; Patron: Elton John Aids Foundn; Nordoff Robins; Fashion Rocks. Fellow, Radio Acad. Outstanding Achievement Award, Nordoff Robins, 2006; Scott Piering Award, Music Industry Trust, 2006. *Recreations*: photography, music, films, Chelsea Football Club, cooking. *Clubs*: Groucho, Soho House, Mark's.

**FARROW, Mia (Villiers);** actress; *b* 9 Feb. 1945; *d* of late John Villiers Farrow and Maureen O'Sullivan; *m* 1st, 1966, Frank Sinatra (marr. diss. 1968; he *d* 1998); 2nd, 1970, André George Previn, Hon. KBE (marr. diss. 1979; he *d* 2019); three *s*, two adopted *d* (and one adopted *d* decd); one *s* by Woody Allen, *qv*; two adopted *s* three adopted *d* (and one adopted *s* and one adopted *d* decd). TV series: Peyton Place, 1965; A Girl Thing, 2001; *films*: Secret Ceremony, 1968; Rosemary's Baby, 1969; John and Mary, 1970; The Public Eye, 1972; The Great Gatsby, 1974; Full Circle, Death on the Nile, A Wedding, 1978; Hurricane, 1980; A Midsummer Night's Sex Comedy, 1982; Zelig, 1983; Broadway Danny Rose, 1984; The Purple Rose of Cairo, 1985; Hannah and her Sisters, 1986; Radio Days,

1987; September, 1988; Another Woman, 1989; Crimes and Misdemeanours, 1990; Alice, 1990; Husbands and Wives, 1992; Shadows and Fog, 1992; Widows' Peak, 1994; Miami Rhapsody, 1995; Reckless, 1995; Angela Mooney, 1996; Coming Soon, 1999; Purpose, 2002; The Omen, 2006; Be Kind Rewind, 2008; Dark Horse, 2012; *stage*: The Importance of Being Earnest, NY, 1963; Mary Rose, Shaw, 1973; The Three Sisters, Greenwich, 1974; The House of Bernarda Alba, Greenwich, 1974; Peter Pan, 1975; The Marrying of Ann Leete, RSC, 1975; The Zykovs, Ivanov, RSC, 1976; A Midsummer Night's Dream, Leicester, 1976; Romantic Comedy, NY, 1979. David Donatello Award, Italy, 1969; Best Actress awards: French Academy, 1969; San Sebastian, 1969; Rio de Janeiro, 1970. *Publications*: What Falls Away (memoirs), 1997. *Address*: Bridgewater, CT, USA.

**FARRY, Stephen Anthony,** PhD; Member (Alliance) North Down, Northern Ireland Assembly, since 2007; *b* 22 April 1971; *s* of Vincent Farry and Margaret Farry (*née* Greer); *m* 2005, Wendy Watt, PhD. *Educ*: Queen's Univ., Belfast (BSocSc 1st Cl. Pols 1992; PhD Internat. Relns 2000). Mem. (Alliance), N Down BC, 1993– (Dep. Mayor, 2002–03; Mayor, 2007–08). Gen. Sec., 2000–07, Dep. Leader, 2016–, Alliance Party of NI. Contested (Alliance) N Down, 2010. Minister for Employment and Learning, NI, 2011–16. Mem., Finance and Personnel Cttee, 2007–11, Economy Cttee, 2016–17, NI Assembly; Dep. Chm., Cttee for the Office of First Minister and Dep. First Minister, 2010–11. Member: Community Relns Council, 2007–11; NI Policing Bd, 2016–17. Sen. Fellow, US Inst. of Peace, 2005–06. *Publications*: various jl and newspaper articles. *Recreations*: travel, international affairs. *Address*: Parliament Buildings, Stormont, Belfast BT4 3XX. *E*: stephen.farry@allianceparty.org.

**FARTHING, Alan John,** MD; FRCOG; Consultant Gynaecological Surgeon, Imperial College Healthcare NHS Trust (formerly St Mary's NHS Trust), since 1997; Surgeon Gynaecologist to the Queen, since 2013 (to the Royal Household, 2008–13); *b* Winchester, 8 June 1963; *s* of John Farthing and Barbara Farthing; *m* 2008, Janet Stowell; two *s. Educ*: Queen Elizabeth Sch., Wimborne; St George's Hosp. Med. Sch., London (MB BS 1986; MD 1996). MRCOG 1991, FRCOG 2003. Postgrad. trng posts, St Mary's NHS Trust, Guy's Hosp. and Perth, WA; Res. into human papillomavirus in cervical cancer, Ludwig Inst. of Cancer Res., 1992–94. Hon. Sen. Lectr, Imperial Coll. London, 1997–. *Publications*: articles on laparoscopic surgery in gynaecology and fertility sparing surgery in gynaecological cancer. *Recreations*: golf, cricket, Western Australian wine. *Address*: 148 Harley Street, W1G 7LG. *E*: alanfarthing@aol.com.

**FARTHING, Prof. Michael John Godfrey,** MD, DSc (Med); FRCP, FRCPE, FRCPGlas, FMedSci; Vice-Chancellor, University of Sussex, 2007–16; *b* 2 March 1948; *s* of Dennis Jack Farthing and Joan Margaret Farthing (*née* Godfrey); *m* 1979, Alison Mary McLean; two *s. Educ*: Henry Thornton Sch., London; University Coll., London (BSc); UCH Med. Sch. (MB BS); MD London 1981; DSc (Med) London 2001. FRCP 1988; FRCPE 2001; FRCPGlas 2001. Res. Fellow, St Mark's Hosp., 1974; Med. Registrar, Addenbrooke's Hosp., 1975–77; Res. Fellow and Hon. Lectr, 1977–80, Wellcome Tropical Lectr, 1980–83, St Bart's Hosp.; Vis. Asst Prof., Tufts Univ. Sch. of Medicine, 1981–83; St Bartholomew's Hospital Medical College, subseq. St Bartholomew's and Royal London Hospital School of Medicine and Dentistry, QMW: Wellcome Sen. Lectr, 1983–91; Prof. and Head of Dept of Gastroenterology, 1990–2000; Dir, Digestive Diseases Res. Centre, 1990–2000; Dean, Faculty of Clin. Medicine, 1995–97; Prof. of Medicine and Exec. Dean, Faculty of Medicine, Univ. of Glasgow, 2000–03; Prof. of Medicine and Principal, St George's Hosp. Med. Sch., subseq. St George's, Univ. of London, 2003–07; Pro-Vice-Chancellor for Medicine, Univ. of London, 2005–07. Hon. Cons. Gastroenterologist, St George's Healthcare NHS Trust, 2003–07; Hon. Consultant: St Mark's Hosp., 1987–; St Luke's Hosp. for Clergy, 1990–; to the Army, 1991–; UCL Hospitals, 2016– (Hon. Prof., UCL, 2016–). Non-executive Director: E London and City HA, 1998–2000; Greater Glasgow NHS Bd, 2001–03; SW London Strategic HA, 2004–06; Brighton and Sussex Univ. Hosp. Trust, 2010–15. Editor, Gut, 1996–2002. Mem., GMC, 2001–08, 2013–17 (Mem., Educn Cttee, 2001–08; Chm., Audit and Risk Cttee, 2017). Chairman: Cttee on Publication Ethics, 1997–2003; Scientific Cttee, United European Gastroenterology Fedn, 2004–09; Health and Soc. Care Policy Cttee, Universities UK, 2009–16; 1994 Gp of Universities, 2011–13; Clinical Academic Staff Adv. Gp, UCEA, 2015–16; Royal Medical Benevolent Fund, 2017–; Vice Chm., UK Res. Integrity Office, 2006–; Hon. Sec., 1990–94, Pres., 2007–08, British Soc. of Gastroenterology; Pres., Eur. Assoc. of Gastroenterology and Endoscopy, 1998–2001; Pres., United Eur. Gastroenterology Fedn, 2014–15; Vice-Pres., World Orgn of Gastroenterology, 2005–09. Trustee, Digestive Disorders Foundn, 2003–08; Chair: Charleston Trust, 2016–; West Pier Trust, Brighton, 2017–. Founder FMedSci 1998. Mem. Ct of Assistants, Apothecaries' Soc., 2003– (Master, 2019–Aug. 2020). *Publications*: Enteric Infection: mechanisms, manifestations and management, vol. 1 1989, vol. 2 1995; Clinical Challenges in Gastroenterology, 1996; Drug Therapy for Gastrointestinal and Liver Diseases, 2001; Fraud and Misconduct in Biomedical Research, 2008; (with Stephen Farthing) Leonardo da Vinci: under the skin, 2019; India Calling, 2019; many papers on intestinal disorders. *Recreations*: theatre, modern literature, jazz, running, watersports. *Address*: UCL Medical School, University College London, Gower Street, WC1E 6BT. *E*: m.farthing@ucl.ac.uk. *Club*: Glasgow Art.
*See also* S. F. G. *Farthing.*

**FARTHING, Stephen Frederick Godfrey,** RA 1998; artist; Rootstein Hopkins Chair of Drawing, University of the Arts London, 2004–17; *b* 16 Sept. 1950; *s* of Dennis Jack Farthing and Joan Margaret (*née* Godfrey); *m* 1st, 1975, Joni Elizabeth Jackson (marr. diss. 2004); one *d*; 2nd, 2010, Ami Jihan Abou-bakr. *Educ*: St Martin's Sch. of Art; Royal Coll. of Art; British Sch. at Rome. Lectr in Painting, Canterbury Coll. of Art, 1977–79; Tutor in Painting, RCA, 1980–85; Head of Painting, W Surrey Coll. of Art and Design, Farnham, 1985–90; Ruskin Master of Drawing, Oxford Univ., and Professorial Fellow, St Edmund Hall, Oxford, 1990–2000, now Emeritus Fellow; Exec. Dir, NY Acad. of Art, 2000–04. Artist in Residence, Hayward Gall., London, 1989. *One-man shows* include: Nat. Mus. of Modern Art, Kyoto; Museo Carrillo Gil, Mexico City; Arnolfini, Bristol; Edward Totah Gall., London; Royal Acad. of Arts; Royal W of England Acad., Bristol; Salisbury Cathedral; Candida Stevens Gall. British School at Rome: Chm., Arts Faculty, 1996–2000; Mem., Council, 1998–2009. Mem., Bd of Dirs, MBNA Europe Bank Ltd, 2003–06. Chm., Exhibns Cttee, Royal Acad. of Arts, 2012–19. *Publications*: The Intelligent Persons Guide to Modern Art, 2000; (ed) 1001 Paintings You Must See Before You Die, 2006; (ed) 501 Artists, 2008; Art: the whole story, 2010; Derek Jarman: the sketchbooks, 2013; (with David Kastan) On Color, 2018; (with Michael Farthing) Leonardo da Vinci: under the skin, 2019. *Recreations*: watercolours, tennis, swimming. *Address*: 1412 Clearwater Way, Twin Falls, ID 83301, USA.
*See also* M. J. G. *Farthing.*

**FARWELL, Prof. Ruth Sarah,** CBE 2015; PhD; DL; Professor and Vice Chancellor, Buckinghamshire New University (formerly Buckinghamshire Chilterns University College), 2006–15; *b* Leigh-on-Sea, Essex, 22 Feb. 1954; *d* of Frederick Farwell and Vera Farwell; *m* 2001, Dr Martin Daniels. *Educ*: Westcliff High Sch.; Univ. of Kent (BSc Hons Maths; PhD Applied Maths 1980). Sen. Lectr, Maths, 1982–86, Hd, Maths Dept, 1986–89, St Mary's University Coll.; Dir of Studies, 1990–93, Univ. Modular Co-ordinator, 1993–95, Hd, Strategic Planning, 1995–98, Univ. of Brighton; Pro Vice Chancellor, London South Bank Univ., 1998–2006. Mem. Bd, HEFCE, 2009–15. Member, Board: Buckinghamshire Business First, 2011–14; Buckinghamshire Thames Valley LEP, 2012–15; Aylesbury Coll., 2012–15; ifs University Coll. (formerly ifs Sch. of Finance), 2012–15; Southampton Solent Univ., 2015–; Pearson Coll. London, 2017–. Trustee: GuildHE, 2007–14 (Chair, 2009–13); Univs and Colls Employers Assoc., 2008–11; SE Reg., Open Coll. Network, 2008–12; Buckinghamshire Univ. Tech. Coll., 2012–17 (Chair, 2014–17); Buckinghamshire Educn Skills and Trng, 2013–15. Hon. Pres., AUA, 2014–17. DL 2015, High Sheriff 2018, Bucks. *Publications*: over 20 papers in jls of physics and maths, 14 papers in conf. procs; chapters in books. *Recreations*: gardening, jazz music, bee keeping, cinema.

**FASSENFELT, John Arthur,** OBE 2014; Chairman, Magistrates' Association, 2011–13 (Deputy Chairman, 2009–11); *b* Stepney, 17 May 1947; *s* of Arthur Edward and Joyce Fassenfelt; partner, Julie Evans; one *s* one *d. Educ*: Abbs Cross Tech. High Sch.; Medway and Maidstone Coll. (Dip. Mgt Studies 1985). CStat 1977. Section Engr, Kent CC, 1985–88; Sen. Manager, 1989, Asst Chief Personnel Officer, 1989–99, London Borough of Bexley. Mem., Kent Magistrates' Cttee, 1998–2001; Dep. Chm., Sittingbourne Bench, 2002–04; Magistrates' Association: Chm., Youth Courts Cttee, 2005–07; Trustee, 2008–13; Vice Pres., 2010–16, Pres., 2017–, Kent Br. Chairman: Govs, Sittingbourne Community Coll., 2013–17; Swale Acads Trust, 2014–17 (Dir, 2010–17; Chm., 2015–17); Gov., Fulston Manor Sch., 2017–. JP Maidstone, 1992–2017. *Recreations*: golf, walking, going on holiday. *E*: johnfassenfelt@googlemail.com. *Club*: Durban (S Africa).

**FASSETT, Kaffe,** Hon. MBE 2018; textile designer; *b* 7 Dec. 1937; *s* of William Elliot Fassett and Madeleine Fassett. Self-educated. Retrospective exhibitions: Tokyo, 1986; V&A Museum, 1989; Copenhagen, Stockholm, Oslo, Melbourne, Toronto and Helsinki, 1990; Vancouver, Holland, 1993; Osaka, Iceland, 1996; Minneapolis, 1997; Fashion and Textile Mus., London, 2013; Mottisfont, Hants, 2017; Victoria Gall., Bath, 2018; American Mus., Bath, 2019. DUniv Huddersfield, 2016. *Publications*: Glorious Knitting, 1985; Glorious Needlepoint, 1987; Kaffe Fassett at the V & A, 1988, 4th edn, as Glorious Colour, 1991; Family Album, 1989; Glorious Inspiration, 1991; Kaffe's Classics, 1993; Glorious Interiors, 1995; Mosaics, 1997; Glorious Patchwork, 1997; Glorious Knitting, 1999; Welcome Home, 1999; Passionate Patchwork, 2001; Kaffe's Pattern Library, 2003; A Colourful Journey, 2003; Caravan of Quilts, 2004; Kaffe Fassett's V & A Patchwork Quilts, 2005; Kaffe Fasssett's Quilt Road, 2005; At Home with Pattern, 2006; The New Country Style, 2006; Kaffe Fassett's Kaleidoscope of Quilts, 2006; Kaffe Knits Again, 2007; Kaffe Fassett's Quilts in the Sun, 2007; Kaffe Fassett's Country Garden Quilts, 2008; Kaffe Fassett's Quilt Romance, 2009; Kaffe Fassett's Simple Shapes Spectacular Quilts, 2010; Kaffe Fassett's Quilts en Provence, 2010; Kaffe Fassett's Quilts in Sweden, 2011; (with Brandon Mably) Knitting with The Color Guys, 2012; Dreaming in Colour (autobiog.), 2012; Kaffe Quilts Again, 2012; Kaffe Fassett Quilts Shots and Stripes, 2013; Kaffe Fassett's Quilt Grandeur, 2013; Kaffe Fassett's Quilts in Morocco, 2014; Kaffe Fassett's Heritage Quilts, 2015; Kaffe Fassett's Bold Blooms, 2016; Kaffe Fassett's Brilliant Little Patchwork Cushions and Pillows, 2016; Kaffe Fassett's Quilts in Italy, 2016; Kaffe Fassett's Adventures in Colour, 2017; Kaffe Fassett's Sew Artisan, 2017; Kaffe Fassett's Quilts in Ireland, 2017; Kaffe Fassett's Quilts in America, 2018. *Address*: Kaffe Fassett Studio, London. *W*: www.kaffefassett.com.

**FATTORINI, Maj. Gen. Charles Sebastian;** Director, Strix Orbis Ltd, since 2018; Senior British Loan Service Officer, Oman, 2014–17; *b* Harrogate, N Yorks, 4 July 1962; *s* of late David William Fattorini and of Jennifer Susan Melville Fattorini (*née* Wills; she *m* 2nd, 17th Viscount Mountgarret); *m* 1993, Cecilia Anstice Birkmyre; one *s* one *d* (and one *s* decd). *Educ*: Ampleforth Coll.; RMA, Sandhurst; Royal Mil. Coll. of Sci. (MA Mil. Studies 1993). Commnd Army, 1982; psc 1994; Comdr, Queen's Royal Lancers, 2002–04; Sen. British Liaison Officer, Pakistan, 2006; Dep. Asst COS - Trng, HQ Land Forces, 2006–09; Col Officer, Liabilities, Army Personnel Centre, 2009–10; Defence Advisor, British High Commission: Islamabad, 2010–12; Nairobi and Dar-es-Salaam, 2012–14. *Recreations*: photography, wild life conservation, travel, fishing, kayaking. *Address*: c/o Army Personnel Centre, Kentigern House, 65 Brown Street, Glasgow G2 8EX. *Club*: Cavalry and Guards.

**FAUCONBERG,** Barony cr 1295, **AND CONYERS,** Barony cr 1509; in abeyance. *Co-heiresses*: Hon. Anthea Theresa Lycett [*b* 21 June 1954; *née* Marcia Anne Miller; renamed on adoption by Major Michael Lycett, CBE but retains her right to the succession]; Hon. Beatrix Diana Armstrong [*b* 23 Aug. 1955; *m* 1991, Simon William Jones Armstrong (*d* 2012); two *s*].

**FAULKNER,** family name of **Baron Faulkner of Worcester**.

**FAULKNER OF WORCESTER,** Baron cr 1999 (Life Peer), of Wimbledon in the London Borough of Merton; **Richard Oliver Faulkner;** *b* 22 March 1946; *s* of late Harold Ewart and Mabel Faulkner; *m* 1968, Susan Heyes; two *d. Educ*: Merchant Taylors' Sch., Northwood; Worcester Coll., Oxford (MA PPE; Hon. Fellow, 2002). Research asst and journalist, Labour Party, 1967–69; PRO, Construction Ind. Trng Bd, 1969–70; Editor, Steel News, 1971; Account dir, F. J. Lyons (PR) Ltd, 1971–73; Dir, PPR International, 1973–76; communications advisor: to Leader of the Opposition and Labour Party (unpaid), gen. elections, 1987, 1992, 1997; to the Bishop at Lambeth, 1990; Govt relations adviser: rly trade unions, 1975–76; C. A. Parsons & Co., 1976–77; Pool Promoters Assoc., 1977–99; British Rlys Bd, 1977–97; Prudential Assurance Co., 1978–88; IPU, 1988–90; Southampton City Council, 1989–91; CAMRA, 1989; Barclays de Zoete Wedd, 1990–92; Standard Life Assurance, 1990–99; S Glam CC, 1991–96; Cardiff CC, 1996–99; Cardiff Bay Develt Corp., 1993–98; Littlewoods Orgn, 1994–99; FSA, 1998–99; Actg Hd of Communications, SIB, 1997; Jt Man. Dir, Westminster Communications Gp, 1989–97; Deputy Chairman: Citigate, Westminster, 1997–99; Cardiff Millennium Stadium, 2004–08 (Dir, 1997–2004); Strategy Adviser: Sportech Gp plc (formerly Littlewoods Pools), 1999–2009; Dept of Transport, NSW Govt, 2012; Chairman: Adv. Bd, Great Western Railway (formerly First Great Western), 2014– (Mem., 2009, 2010–); Alderney Gambling Control Commn, 2014– (Strategy Advr, 2005–08; Mem., 2013–). A Dep. Chm., 2007–09 and Dep. Speaker, 2008–09, 2010–, H of L; a Lord in Waiting (Govt Whip), 2009–10; Dept Liaison Peer, DETR, 2000–01, Cabinet Office, 2001–05; House of Lords: Member: Sub-cttee B, 2000–03, Sub-cttee F, 2009 and 2013–15, EC Select Cttee; Delegated Powers and Regulatory Reform Cttee, 2007–09; Rookery South (Resource Recovery Facility) Order 2011 Cttee, 2012–13; Cttee of Selection, 2013–18; EU Home Affairs Sub-cttee, 2015–16; Information Cttee, 2015–16; Equality Act 2010 and Disability Select Cttee, 2015–16; Secondary Legislation Scrutiny Cttee, 2017–; Nat. Envmt and Rural Communities 2006 Act Cttee, 2017–18; Jt Scrutiny Cttee, Draft Gambling Bill, 2003–04; London Local Authy Private Bill Cttee, 2006; Chm., London Local Authorities and Transport for London Private Bill Cttee, 2009; Mem., Olympic Legacy Select Cttee, 2013; Mem., Ecclesiastical Cttee, 2018–; Mem., Works of Art Panel, 2018–; Mem., Jt Cttee on the Draft Registration of Overseas Entities Bill, 2019; EU Cttee, 2019–; EU Ext. Sub Cttee, 2019–; Chm., Inquiry into Betting on Sport, 2005. Treas., All Party Railways Gp, 2000–09, 2010–15; Graduate Mem., Armed Forces Parly Scheme, attached to RN, 2002–07; Sec., British-Namibian Parly Gp, 2004–09; Vice-Chairman: Football Gp, 2004–09, 2010–; British-Cyprus Gp, 2005–09; Betting and Gaming Gp, 2005–09; Abolition of Death Penalty Gp, 2007–09,

2010–; British Caribbean Gp, 2000–09; British-S African Gp, 2002–09; British-Danish Parly Gp, 2005–09; British-Channel Islands Gp, 2007–09, 2015–; Heritage Rail Gp, 2011–; East-West Rail Gp, 2015–; British-Norwegian Parly Gp, (Sec., 2000–09, 2010–15); British-Argentine Parly Gp, 2015 (Sec., 2001–09, 2010–15); Jt Treas., British-Swedish Parly Gp, 2001–09; Chairman: All Party War Graves and Battlefields Heritage Gp, 2002–09; All Party Sustainable Aviation Gp, 2003–09; Co-Chm., British-Taiwanese Parly Gp, 2005–09, 2010–16 (Sec., 2000–05); War Heritage Gp, 2015– (Chm., 2010–15). Mem., Govt Adv. Bd on WW1 Centenary Commemoration, 2013–19; Govt's Trade Envoy for Taiwan, 2016–. Football Trust: Foundn Trustee, 1979–82; Sec., 1983–86; First Dep. Chm., 1986–98; Chm., Sports Grounds Initiative, 1995–2000; Vice Chm., Govt's Football Task Force, 1997–99; Member: Sports Council, 1986–88; Football League enquiry into membership schemes, 1984, anti-hooliganism cttee, 1987–90; FIFA Wkg Gp on betting, 2006–09; Chm., Women's Football Assoc., 1988–91; non-exec. Dir, Football Assoc. of Wales, 2007–09. Vice-Chm., 1986–99, Vice-Pres., 2000–09, 2010–, Campaign for Better Transport (formerly Transport 2000 Ltd); Chm., Worcester Live, 2014–18 (Dir, 2011–18); Mem., Railway Heritage Cttee, 2002–09 (Chm., 2004–09); President: Heritage Railway Assoc., 2011–; Cotswold Line Promotion Gp, 2007–09, 2010–; Scottish Railway Preservation Soc., 2019–; Quainton Railway Soc., 2019–. Pres., 2001–04, Vice Pres., 2004–, RoSPA; Vice-President: Football Conf., 2007–09, 2010–15; Level Playing Field (formerly Nat. Assoc. for Disabled Supporters), 2007–09, 2010–; Nat. League, 2015–. Trustee: Foundn for Sport and the Arts, 2000–12; Gamcare, 2005–09; Nat. Mus. for Sci. and Industry, 2007–09; Sci. Mus. Gp, 2011–19 (Dep. Chm., 2015–19; Chairman: MOSI Adv. Bd, 2013; Railway Heritage Designation Adv. Bd, 2013–19 (Co-Chm., 2019–)); Nat. Football Mus., 2007–09, 2011–17; ASH, 2007–09; Patron: Roy Castle Lung Cancer Foundn, 1999– (Trustee, 2003–07); Myriad Centre Worcester, 2012–; Guild of Battlefield Guides, 2013–; Worcs Industrial Archaeology and Local Hist. Soc., 2016–. Chairman: Worcester Coll. Appeal, 1996–2003; Adv. Cttee, Worcester Coll. Soc., 2003–13, Pres., 2013–; Mem. Ct, Bedfordshire Univ. (formerly Luton Univ.), 1999–2009; Pres., Old Merchant Taylors' Soc., 2011–12 (Vice-Pres., 2006–11). Mem., Merton Borough Council, 1971–78; contested (Lab) Devizes 1970, Feb. 1974, Monmouth, Oct. 1974, Huddersfield W, 1979. Co-founder, parly jl The House mag. (Mem., Editl Bd, 2003–). Fellow, Univ. of Worcester, 2008– (Mem., Develt Cttee, 2009–14; Pres., Coll. of Fellows, 2014–18). Hon. LLD Beds (formerly Luton), 2003. Friendship Medal of Diplomacy (Taiwan), 2004; Order of the Brilliant Star with Grand Cordon (Taiwan), 2008. *Publications:* (with Chris Austin) Holding the Line: how Britain's railways were saved, 2012 (Railway and Canal Historical Soc. Award, 2014); Disconnected!: broken links in Britain's Rail Policy, 2015. *Recreations:* collecting Lloyd George memorabilia, tinplate trains, watching Association Football, travelling by railway. *Address:* House of Lords, SW1A 0PW. *E:* faulknerro@parliament.uk.
*See also* D. E. R. *Faulkner.*

**FAULKNER, David Ewart Riley,** CB 1985; Senior Research Associate, University of Oxford Centre for Criminology (formerly for Criminological Research), since 1992; *b* 23 Oct. 1934; *s* of Harold Ewart and Mabel Faulkner; *m* 1961, Sheila Jean Stevenson; one *s* one *d*. *Educ:* Manchester Grammar Sch.; Merchant Taylors' Sch., Northwood; St John's Coll., Oxford (MA Lit Hum). Home Office: Asst Principal, 1959; Private Sec. to Parly Under-Sec. of State, 1961–63; Principal, 1963; Jt Sec. to Inter-Party Conf. on House of Lords Reform, 1968; Private Sec. to Home Sec., 1969–70; Asst Sec., Prison Dept, 1970, Establishment Dept, 1974, Police Dept, 1976; Asst Under-Sec. of State, 1976; Under Sec., Cabinet Office, 1978–80; Home Office; Asst Under-Sec. of State, Dir of Operational Policy, Prison Dept, 1980–82; Dep. Under-Sec. of State, 1982; Head of Criminal and Res. and Statistical Depts, 1982–90; Principal Estab. Officer, 1990–92. Fellow, St John's Coll., Oxford, 1992–99. Chm., Howard League for Penal Reform, 1999–2002. Member: UN Cttee on Crime Prevention and Control, 1984–91; Adv. Bd, Helsinki Inst. for Crime Prevention and Control, 1988–93; Council, Magistrates' Assoc., 1992–98; Council, Justice, 1993–97; Commn on the Future of Multi-Ethnic Britain, 1998–2000. Trustee, Gilbert Murray Trust, 1992–, Thames Valley Partnership, 1992–, and other charities. *Publications:* Darkness and Light, 1996; Crime, State and Citizen, 2001, 2nd edn 2006; Civil Renewal, Diversity and Social Capital in a Multi-Ethnic Britain, 2004; Better Government: more justice, 2009; (with R. Burnett) Where Next for Criminal Justice?, 2011; Servant of the Crown: a civil servant's story of criminal justice and public service reform, 2014; contribs to jls. *Recreations:* railways, birds. *Address:* c/o Centre for Criminology, Manor Road, Oxford OX1 3UR.
*See also* Baron *Faulkner of Worcester.*

**FAULKNER, Graham John;** Chief Executive, National Society for Epilepsy, 2000–13; *b* 26 Sept. 1948; *s* of William and Edna Faulkner; *m* 1st, 1975, Jennifer Barkway (marr. diss. 1998); one *s* one *d*; 2nd, 1999, Dorothy, (Dee), Napier (marr. diss. 2002). *Educ:* UC of Swansea (BSc Hons Psychol. 1970); Univ. of Leicester (postgrad. res.); Univ. of Birmingham (CQSW 1984; MSocSc). Local Govt O R Unit, RIPA, 1973–75; Planning Dept, 1975–77, Social Services Dept, 1977–85, Warwickshire CC; Dir, Retirement Security Ltd, 1985–92; Dir and Gen. Sec., Leonard Cheshire Foundn, 1992–98; Chief Exec., Rehab UK, 1999–2000. Chm., Queen Square Enterprises, 2011–; Dir, Healthwatch Bucks, 2015–. Gov., UCLH NHS Foundn Trust, 2004–11; Mem. Adv. Bd, Greenwich Hosp., 2015–. Trustee, Roald Dahl Marvellous Children's Charity; Chm. Trustees, St Loye's Foundn, 2013–18. *Publications:* contributor to: White Media and Black Britain, 1975; Solving Local Government Problems, 1981; This Caring Business, 1988; contrib. jls and res. reports. *Recreations:* theatre, music, Rugby, golf, watching Coventry City and Wasps.

**FAULKNER, Gregory;** *see* Faulkner, L. G.

**FAULKNER, John Richard Hayward;** theatre and management consultant; international impresario; *b* 29 May 1941; *s* of Capt. Richard Hayward Ollerton and Lilian Elizabeth (*née* Carrigan), and step *s* of late Herbert Andrew Faulkner; *m* 1st, 1970, Janet Gill (*née* Cummings) (*d* 1994); two *d*, and two step *d*; 2nd, 2001, Christie Dickason; two step *s*. *Educ:* Archbishop Holgate's Sch., York; Keble Coll., Oxford (BA). Worked with a number of theatre companies, Prospect Productions, Meadow Players, Century Theatre, Sixty-Nine Theatre Co., Cambridge Theatre Co., toured extensively, UK, Europe, Indian Sub-Continent, Australia, 1960–72; Drama Director: Scottish Arts Council, 1972–77; Arts Council of GB, 1977–83; Head, Artistic Planning, Nat. Theatre, 1983–88. Touring Consultant, The Entertainment Corp., 1988–92; Consultant, later Gen. Manager, Pleasance Theatre Fest., 1992–94; Associate: Prince Res. Consultants, 2001–09; Theatre Futures Ltd, 2003–. Mem., Assessors' Panel, Nat. Lottery Dept, Arts Council, 1995–2001. Director: Minotaur Films, 1988–92; Visionhaven Ltd, 1991–2003; New Zoo Develts Ltd, 1992. Proprietor, Ollerton Press, 2006–. Member: Pubns & Communication Commn, Orgn Internat. des Scénographes, Techniciens et Architectes de Théâtre, 1994– (Chm., 1999–2001); Internat. Soc. for the Performing Arts, 1997–; Council, Assoc. of British Theatre Technicians, 1998–2001 (sometime Chm.; Fellow, 2014); Sec., Pleasance Theatre Trust, 1997–. Trustee: The Arts Educational Schools, 1986–92; The Arts for Nature, 1990–99; Performing Arts Labs, 1991–2001; Pension Scheme for Admin. and Tech. Staff in the Arts, 1996–2012; Orange Tree Th. Trust, 1998–2008 (Jt Chm., 1999–2004, Chm., 2004–08 and 2010–11). *Recreations:* intricacies and wildernesses. *Address:* 28 Ellesmere Road, Chiswick, W4 4QH. *T:* (020) 8995 3041.

**FAULKNER, (Leo) Gregory;** HM Diplomatic Service, retired; Ambassador to Chile, 2000–03; *b* 21 Sept. 1943; *s* of late James and Teresa Faulkner; *m* 1970, Fiona Hardie (*née* Birkett); three *d*. *Educ:* Manchester Univ. (BA Hons Spanish). FCO, 1968–72; Lima, 1972–76; Lagos, 1976–79; EC Internal Dept, FCO, 1979–82; Head of Chancery, Madrid, 1982–84; Head, Internat. Telecoms Br., DTI, 1984–86, on secondment; Commercial Counsellor, The Hague, 1986–90; Dep. Head of Mission, Buenos Aires, 1990–93; Head, Latin America Dept, FCO, 1993–96; High Commissioner, Trinidad and Tobago, 1996–99. Consultant (pt-time), UK Trade and Investment, 2009–15. *Recreations:* golf, theatre, political history. *Club:* Canning.

**FAULKNER, Sarah Donaldson;** *see* Wootton, S. D.

**FAULKS,** family name of **Baron Faulks.**

**FAULKS,** Baron *cr* 2010 (Life Peer), of Donnington in the Royal County of Berkshire; **Edward Peter Lawless Faulks;** QC 1996; Chairman, Independent Press Standards Organisation, from Jan. 2020; *b* 19 Aug. 1950; *s* of His Honour Peter Ronald Faulks, MC and Pamela Faulks (*née* Lawless); *m* 1990, Catherine Frances Turner, *d* of Lindsay Turner and Anthea Cadbury; two *s*. *Educ:* Wellington Coll.; Jesus Coll., Oxford (MA; Hon. Fellow 2014). FCIArb. Called to the Bar, Middle Temple, 1973, Bencher, 2002. Literary Agent, Curtis Brown, 1980–81; Asst Recorder, 1996–2000; Recorder, 2000–10. Chairman: Professional Negligence Bar Assoc., 2002–04; Res. Soc. of Conservative Lawyers, 2010–12. Special Advr to DCA on compensation culture, 2005–06. Mem., Commn on a Bill of Rights, 2012. Minister of State, MoJ, 2014–16. Justice, Astana Internat. Financial Centre Court, 2018–. *Publications:* (contributing ed.) Local Authority Liabilities, 1998, 5th edn 2012. *Recreations:* sports, the arts. *Address:* 33 Ladbroke Grove, W11 3AY; 1 Chancery Lane, WC2A 1LF. *T:* 0845 634 6666; House of Lords, SW1A 0PW. *Clubs:* Garrick, Beefsteak.
*See also* S. C. *Faulks.*

**FAULKS, His Honour Esmond James;** a Circuit Judge, 1993–2011; *b* 11 June 1946; *s* of Hon. Sir Neville Faulks, MBE, TD and Bridget Marigold (*née* Bodley); *m* 1972, Pamela Margaret Ives; one *s* one *d*. *Educ:* Uppingham Sch.; Sidney Sussex Coll., Cambridge (Exhibitioner; MA). Called to the Bar, Inner Temple, 1968; a Recorder, 1987–93. Member: Parole Bd, 2002–08; Mental Health Rev. Tribunal, 2011–16. Hon. Vis. Prof. of Law, Samford Univ., Ala, 2005. *Recreation:* country pursuits.

**FAULKS, Sebastian Charles,** CBE 2002; author; *b* 20 April 1953; *s* of His Honour Peter Ronald Faulks, MC and Pamela Faulks (*née* Lawless); *m* 1989, Veronica Youlten; two *s* one *d*. *Educ:* Wellington Coll. (Scholar); Emmanuel Coll., Cambridge (Exhibnr; BA 1974; Hon. Fellow 2007). Editor, New Fiction Society, 1978–81; Daily Telegraph, 1978–82; feature writer, Sunday Telegraph, 1983–86; Literary Editor, Independent, 1986–89; Dep. Editor, 1989–90, Associate Editor, 1990–91, Independent on Sunday; columnist: The Guardian, 1992–98; London Evening Standard, 1997–99; Mail on Sunday, 1999–2000. Writer and presenter: Churchill's Secret Army (television), 2000; Faulks on Fiction (television), 2011; panellist, The Write Stuff, Radio 4, 1998–2015. FRSL 1995. Hon. DLitt: Tavistock Clinic/UEL, 2007; Hertfordshire, 2012. Hon. Bencher, Middle Temple, 2015. *Publications:* A Trick of the Light, 1984; The Girl at the Lion d'Or, 1989; A Fool's Alphabet, 1992; Birdsong, 1993; The Fatal Englishman, 1996; Charlotte Gray, 1998 (filmed 2002); (ed with Jörg Hensgen) The Vintage Book of War Stories, 1999; On Green Dolphin Street, 2001; Human Traces, 2005; Pistache, 2006; Engleby, 2007; Devil May Care, 2008; A Week in December, 2009; Faulks on Fiction, 2011; A Possible Life, 2012; Jeeves and the Wedding Bells, 2013; (ed with Hope Wolf) A Broken World: letters, diaries and memories of the Great War, 2014; Where My Heart Used to Beat, 2015; Pistache Returns, 2016; Paris Echo, 2018; contribs to newspapers and magazines. *Address:* c/o Aitken Alexander Associates, 291 Gray's Inn Road, WC1X 8EB.
*See also* Baron *Faulks.*

**FAULL, Sir Jonathan (Michael Howard),** KCMG 2017; Chair, European Public Affairs, Brunswick Group, since 2017; *b* 20 Aug. 1954; *s* of Gerald Faull and June Faull (*née* Shepherd); *m* 1979, Sabine Garrel; two *s*. *Educ:* Univ. of Sussex (BA); Coll. of Europe, Bruges (MA). European Commission, 1978–2016: Administrator, then Principal Administrator, various depts, 1978–87; Asst to Dir Gen., Directorate Gen. for Competition, 1987–89; Mem., Cabinet of Sir Leon Brittan, Vice-Pres., EC, 1989–92; Directorate General for Competition: Hd, Transport and Tourism Unit, 1992–93; Hd, Co-ordination and Gen. Policy Unit, 1993–95; Dir, Competition Policy, Co-ordination, Internat. Affairs and Relns with other Instns, 1995–99; Dep. Dir Gen. of Competition, 1999; Hd of Press and Communication Service, later Dir Gen., Press and Communication, 1999–2003; Dir Gen., Justice and Home Affairs, later Justice, Freedom and Security, 2003–10; Dir Gen., Internal Market and Services, later Financial Stability, Financial Services and Capital Markets Union, 2010–15; Dir Gen., UK Referendum Task Force, 2015–16. Advr to British Chamber of Commerce, Belgium, 2003–. Prof. of Law, Inst. of European Studies, Free Univ. of Brussels, 1989–2012, now Emeritus (Mem. Bd, 2005–); Vis. Prof., Coll. of Europe, Bruges, 2009–; Hon. Prof., KCL, 2017– (Vis. Fellow, Policy Inst., 2013–); Hon. Prof. and Fellow, UK Trade Policy Observatory, Univ. of Sussex Business Sch., 2018–; Montague Burton Prof. of Internat. Relns, Univ. of Edinburgh, 2018–19; Vis. Lectr, Inst. d'Etudes Politiques, Paris, 1992–95, 2019–; Vis. Fellow, Centre for Eur. Legal Studies, Cambridge Univ., 1997–2001 (Mem., Adv. Bd, 2018–). Member: Conseil d'Administration, Institut Jacques Delors - Notre Europe, 1996–; Adv. Bd, Security and Defence Agenda, Brussels, 2006–; Comitato di direzione, Mercato Concorrenza Regole, 2008–; Res. Council, European University Inst., 2011–16; Adv. Bd, Centre for Eur. Reform, 2017–. Mem., editl or adv. boards of various law jls, incl. Common Market Law Reports, Eur. Business Law Rev., UK Competition Law Reports, and World Competition Review; EC corresp., Eur. Law Review, 1980–89. Hon. LLD Sussex, 2018. *Publications:* The EC Law of Competition, 1999, 3rd edn as The EU Law of Competition, 2014; contrib. articles on various topics of EC law and policy. *Address:* Place Albert Leemans 13/24, 1050 Brussels, Belgium.

**FAULL, Dr Margaret Lindsay,** OBE 2009; Museum Director and Company Secretary, National Coal Mining Museum for England, 1986–2015; *b* Sydney, Australia, 4 April 1946; *d* of Norman Augustus Faull and Myra Beryl Faull (*née* Smith). *Educ:* Fort St Girls' High Sch., Sydney; Sydney Univ. (BA Archaeol. 1966; DipEd 1967); Macquarie Univ. (MA Hons English Lang. 1970); Leeds Univ. (PhD Archaeol. 1979); Sheffield Univ. (MA Leisure Mgt 1990). Teacher of English and History, NSW, 1970–71; Sub-Warden, Oxley Hall, Univ. of Leeds, 1972–75; field archaeologist, 1975–83, Dep. Co. Archaeologist, 1983–85, W Yorks MCC; Project Manager, Thwaite Mills Industrial Mus., 1985–86. Non-executive Director: Wakefield HA, 2000–02; Local Care Direct, 2005–13; Mid Yorks Hosps NHS Trust, 2008–12. Ind. Mem., Wakefield Dist Housing, 2003–13. Chair: Wakefield Dist Med. Res. Ethics Cttee, 2000–07; Leeds Central Med. Res. Ethics Cttee, 2007–13. Mem., Deptl Adv. Bd, Univ. of Bradford Archaeol Scis, 1998–2010; Trustee, 2000–04, Vice Pres., 2004–08, Council for British Archaeol.; Vice-Pres., Archaeol. Section, Assoc. for

Advancement of Sci., 1997. Chair: Soc. for Church Archaeol., 2005–10; Network of European Coal Mining Museums, 2016–18, now Hon. Pres. Vice-Chair and Trustee, Soc. for Landscape Studies, 1986–; Sec., Chair and Agent, Thwaite Mills Soc., 1986–2011. *Publications:* (ed with M. Stinson) Domesday Book, 30: Yorkshire, 2 vols, 1986. *Recreations:* watching cricket, attending opera and ballet, collecting African carvings. *Address:* 39 Leeds Road, Wakefield WF1 3JW. *T:* (01924) 379690. *E:* margaret.faull@googlemail.com.

FAULL, Sir Richard (Lewis Maxwell), KNZM 2017 (ONZM 2005); PhD, DSc; FRSNZ 1998; Director, Centre for Brain Research, since 2009 and University Distinguished Professor of Anatomy, since 2012, University of Auckland (Professor of Anatomy, since 1993); *b* Marton, NZ, 21 Oct. 1945; *s* of Wilfred Faull and Phyllis Faull; *m* 1970, Diana Stewart; two *s* three *d*. *Educ:* Tikorangi Primary Sch.; Waitara High Sch.; New Plymouth Boys' Sch.; Otago Univ. (BMedSci 1967; MB ChB 1970); Univ. of Auckland (PhD 1975; DSc 1994). MRC Doctoral Trng Fellow, Univ. of Auckland, 1972–75; Postdoctoral Res. Fellow in Neurosci., Harkness Fellow and MRC Overseas Res. Fellow, NASA-Ames Res. Centre, Calif, MIT and Harvard Univ., 1975–78; University of Auckland: Sen. Lectr in Anatomy, 1978–87; Associate Prof. in Anatomy, 1987–93; Preclinical Sub Dean, 1987–88; Hd, Dept of Anatomy, 1988–2000; John Hood Fellow, 2015. Wellcome-MRC Res. Travel Fellow, Babraham Inst., Univ. of Cambridge, 1989. Distinguished Speaker, RSNZ, 2010; Sir Paul Reeves Meml Lect., Leadership NZ, 2013. Liley Medal, Health Res. Council, 2005; New Zealander of the Yr Award, NZ Herald, 2007; Rutherford Medal, RSNZ, 2007; World Class NZ Award, Kea, 2010; 25th Anniv. Sen. Res. Excellence Award, Health Res. Council, 2016. *Publications:* approx. 310 refereed res. papers; 50 reviews and book chapters. *Recreations:* reading, classical music, opera, medical history, walking, family, travelling. *Address:* Department of Anatomy and Medical Imaging, Centre for Brain Research, Faculty of Medical and Health Sciences, University of Auckland, Private Bag 92019, Auckland 1142, New Zealand. *T:* (9) 9236708. *E:* rlm.faull@auckland.ac.nz. *Club:* Northern (Auckland).

FAULL, Rt Rev. Vivienne Frances; *see* Bristol, Bishop of.

FAULTLESS, Prof. Margaret; violinist; Director of Performance, Faculty of Music, University of Cambridge, since 2010; Head, Historical Performance, since 2012 and Professor, since 2018, Royal Academy of Music, London; *b* Solihull, 9 Dec. 1960; *d* of Geoffrey Faultless and Dinah Faultless; *m* 1st, 1997, Simon Whistler (*d* 2005); 2nd, 2011, Richard Heacock. *Educ:* King Edward VI High Sch. for Girls, Edgbaston, Birmingham; Clare Coll., Cambridge (BA Music 1983). FTCL 1979; ARCM 1979. Freelance soloist, dir and concert-master, 1985–. Co-Leader, Orch. of the Age of Enlightenment, 1989–; Concert-Master, Amsterdam Baroque Orch., 1994–2004; Founder and Artistic Dir, Music for Awhile, 1996–; Dir of Studies, EU Baroque Orch., 2000–. Dir of Music, Girton Coll., Cambridge, 2018. Hon. FRBC (Hon. FBC 2012); Hon. RAM 2016. *Recreations:* yoga, swimming, walking. *E:* mf413@cam.ac.uk.

FAURE, Danny Antoine Rollen; President of the Republic of Seychelles, since 2016; *b* Kilembe, Uganda, 8 May 1962; *s* of Jean Faure and Violet Faure; *m* (marr. diss.); one *s* four *d*. *Educ:* Univ. of Havana (BA Political Sci. 1985). Asst Curriculum Officer, Min. of Educn, 1985–89; Lectr, Nat. Youth Service and Seychelles Polytechnic, 1985–89; Dir, Nat. Youth Service, 1989–91. Leader, Govt Business, Nat. Assembly, 1993–98; Minister: of Educn, 1998–2006; of Finance, 2006–10; Designated Minister, 2004–10; Vice Pres., 2010–16. Champion of Blue Economy in Africa, 2018; Nat. Geographic Planetary Leadership Award, 2019. *Recreation:* reading. *Address:* State House, PO Box 55, Victoria, Mahé, Republic of Seychelles. *T:* 4295656. *W:* www.dannyfaure.com.

FAVELL, Anthony Rowland, MBE 2013; solicitor; *b* 29 May 1939; *s* of Arnold Rowland Favell and Hildegard Favell; *m* 1966, Susan Rosemary Taylor; one *s* one *d*. *Educ:* St Bees School, Cumbria; Sheffield University (LLB). Founder and Sen. Partner, Favell, Smith & Lawson solicitors, Sheffield, 1966–87. MP (C) Stockport, 1983–92; PPS to Rt Hon. John Major, MP, 1986–90. Contested (C) Stockport, 1992. Chm., Tameside and Glossop Acute Services NHS Trust, 1993–97. Part-time Chairman: Mental Health Review Tribunals, 1995–2008; FHSA Appeal Tribunals, 1996–2002; Mem., Criminal Injuries Appeal Panel, 2000–08; Tribunal Judge, 2008–09. Member: High Peak BC, 2007–15; Peak Dist Nat. Park Authy, 2007– (Chm., 2011–14); E Midlands Regl Assembly, 2009–10; Chm., National Parks UK, 2013–14. *Recreations:* music, gardening, hill walking, dry stone walling. *Address:* Skinners Hall, Edale, Hope Valley S33 7ZE. *T:* (01433) 670281. *Club:* Lansdowne.

FAWCETT, Dame Amelia (Chilcott), DBE 2010 (CBE 2002); CVO 2018; Chairman, Kinnevik AB, Sweden, since 2018; Chairman, Standards Board for Alternative Investments (formerly Hedge Fund Standards Board), since 2011; *b* 16 Sept. 1956; *d* of Frederick John Fawcett, II and Betsey Sargent Chilcott. *Educ:* Pingree Sch., Mass; Wellesley Coll. (BA 1978); Univ. of Virginia Sch. of Law (JD 1983). Admitted to New York Bar, 1984. Sullivan & Cromwell: NY, 1983–85; Paris, 1986–87; Morgan Stanley International, 1987–2007: Vice Pres., 1990; Exec. Dir, 1992; Man. Dir and Chief Admin. Officer, 1996–2002; Mem., Eur. Exec. Cttee, 1996–2007; Vice Chm. and Chief Operating Officer, 2002–06; Sen. Adviser, 2006–07. Chairman: Pensions First LLP, 2007–10; Guardian Media Gp plc, 2009–13 (non-exec. Dir, 2007–13); non-executive Director: State St Corp., Boston, 2006– (Chm., Risk Cttee, 2008–18); Millicom Internat. Cellular SA, Luxembourg, 2014–16. Mem. Court, Bank of England, 2004–09 (Chm., Audit Cttee, 2005–09); non-exec. Dir, HM Treasury, 2012–18. Member: Practitioner Forum, FSA, 1998–2001; Competitiveness Council, DTI, 1999–2000; New Deal Task Force, 1999–2001; Dep. Chm., Nat. Employment Panel, 2001–04. Member: Adv. Bd, Community Links, 1992–2001; BITC, 2005–09. Chm. Trustees, Royal Botanic Gdns, Kew, 2019–; Trustee: Nat. Portrait Gall., 2003–11 (Chm., Devclt Bd, 2002–11; Dep. Chm., 2005–11); Nat. Maritime Mus., Cornwall, 2004–06; Project Hope (UK), 2010–; Prince of Wales's Charitable Foundn, 2011–18 (Chm., 2012–18). Chm., London Internat. Fest. of Theatre, 2002–10. Mem. Council, Univ. of London, 2002–08 (Chm., Audit Cttee, 2003–08); Gov., London Business Sch., 2010–18 (Dep. Chm., 2014–18); Comr, UK-US Fulbright Commn, 2010–17. Lady Usher of the Purple Rod, Order of the British Empire, 2013–. Hon. DIB American Univ., Richmond, 2006. Prince of Wales' Ambassador Award, 2004. *Recreations:* fly fishing, hill walking, lavender farming, sailing, photography. *Address:* Kinnevik AB, Skeppsbron 18, PO Box 2094, 103 13 Stockholm, Sweden. *E:* amelia.fawcett@kinnevik.com. *Clubs:* Reform, Oswald's; Cradoc Golf; St Mawes Sailing; Manchester Yacht (USA).

FAWCETT, Prof. James William, PhD; FRCP; Chairman, Cambridge University Centre for Brain Repair, since 2001, and Merck Company Professor of Experimental Neurology, 2002–17, now Emeritus Professor, University of Cambridge; Fellow, since 1986, and Director of Studies in Medicine, since 1999, King's College, Cambridge; *b* 13 March 1950; *s* of late Edward Fawcett, OBE and Jane Fawcett, MBE; *m* 1980, Kay-Tee Khaw, *qv*; one *s* one *d*. *Educ:* Westminster Sch.; Balliol Coll., Oxford, (BA 1972); St Thomas's Hospital Med. Sch. (MB BS 1975); PhD London Univ. 1982. MRCP 1979, FRCP 2000. House Surgeon, St Thomas' Hosp., 1976; House Physician, Addenbrooke's Hosp., 1977; SHO Intensive Care, St Thomas' Hosp., 1977–78; SHO Immunology, Northwick Park Hosp., 1978–79; Scientist, NIMR, London, 1979–82; Asst Prof., Salk Inst., La Jolla, 1982–86; Lectr in Physiol., Cambridge Univ., 1986–2001. Res. Dir, Centre for Reconstructive Neurosci., Inst. of Experimental Medicine, Acad. of Scis, Czech Republic. FMedSci 2003. *Publications:* (jtly) Formation and Regeneration of Nerve Connections, 1992; (jtly) Brain Damage, Brain Repair, 2002. *Recreations:* bagpiping, sailing, old machinery. *Address:* Cambridge University Centre for Brain Repair, Robinson Way, Cambridge CB2 2PY. *T:* (01223) 331160. *E:* JF108@cam.ac.uk. *Clubs:* Pinstripe Highlanders; Brancaster Staithe Sailing, Royal Highland Yacht.

FAWCETT, Prof. Jeremy James, FBA 2010; Professor of International Commercial Law, University of Nottingham, 1995–2013, now Emeritus; *b* Isleworth, 18 May 1949; *s* of Sydney and Kathleen Fawcett; *m* 1971, Jane Rowe; two *d*. *Educ:* Altrincham Grammar Sch.; Univ. of Nottingham (LLB 1970); Univ. of Bristol (PhD 1980). Admitted as solicitor, 1973; Lectr in Law, 1973–87, Reader in Law, 1988, Univ. of Bristol; Prof. of Law, 1988–95, Dean, Faculty of Law, 1993–95, Univ. of Leicester. Vis. Sen. Fellow, NUS, 1987–88. *Publications:* (with P. M. North) Cheshire and North's Private International Law, 11th edn 1987 to 14th edn (with J. M. Carruthers) as Cheshire, North and Fawcett: Private International Law, 2008, (consultant ed) 15th edn 2017; Declining Jurisdiction in Private International Law, 1995; (with P. Torremans) Intellectual Property and Private International Law, 1998, 2nd edn 2011; (jtly) International Sale of Goods in the Conflict of Laws, 2005; (jtly) Human Rights and Private International Law, 2016. *Recreations:* gardening, art, walking coastal paths, theatre. *Address:* School of Law, University of Nottingham, University Park, Nottingham NG7 2RD. *T:* (0115) 951 5737. *E:* james.fawcett@nottingham.ac.uk.

FAWCETT, John Harold, CMG 1986; HM Diplomatic Service, retired; *b* 4 May 1929; yr *s* of late Comdr Harold William Fawcett, OBE, RN, and of late Una Isobel Dalrymple Fawcett (*née* Gairdner); *m* 1st, 1961, Elizabeth Shaw (*d* 2002); one *s*; 2nd, 2004, Linda Garnett. *Educ:* Radley (Scholar); University Coll., Oxford (Scholar). 1st cl. Hon. Mods 1951, 2nd cl. Lit. Hum. 1953. Nat. Service, RN (Radio Electrician's Mate), 1947–49. British Oxygen Co., 1954–63 (S Africa, 1955–57). Entered Foreign Service, 1963; FO, 1963–66; 1st Sec. (Commercial), Bombay, 1966–69; 1st Sec. and Head of Chancery, Port-of-Spain, 1969–70; Asst, Caribbean Dept, FCO, 1971–72; Head of Icelandic Fisheries Unit, Western European Dept, FCO, 1973; Amb. to Democratic Republic of Vietnam, 1974; Counsellor and Head of Chancery, Warsaw, 1975–78; Dep. High Comr, Wellington, 1978–86; Counsellor (Commercial and Economic, 1978–83, Political and Economic, 1983–86), and Head of Chancery, 1983–86, Wellington; Amb. to Bulgaria, 1986–89. Mem., 1998–2002, Chm., 2000–02, Dent Parish Council. Mem., 1989–94, Lay Chm., 1994–99, 2008–11, Ewecross Deanery Synod, dio. of Bradford; Member: Bradford Diocesan Synod, 2009–11; Kendal Deanery Synod, Dio. of Carlisle, 2012–15. Trustee: Bradford Dio. Church Buildings Fund, 1996–99; Sedbergh and Dist Community Trust, 1998–2005. Chm., Morecambe Bay Gp, CS Pensioners' Alliance, 1994–2000. Clerk, 1989–94, Chm. of Govs, 1994–2001, Dent Grammar Sch. Educnl Foundn; Governor, Dent C of E Primary Sch., 1994–99. Pres., Dent CC, 2001–05. One of the Twenty-four Sidesmen of Dent. *Publications:* contrib. SYMmetryplus mag. *Recreations:* gardening, collecting books, mathematical models, fractal development of the octagon, design of experimental multi-hull sailing craft. *Address:* Strait End, Dent, Cumbria LA10 5QW. *Clubs:* Savile, MCC; Wellington Racing (Wellington); Royal Bombay Yacht.

FAWCETT, Kay-Tee; *see* Khaw, Kay-Tee.

FAWCUS, Maj.-Gen. Graham Ben, CB 1991; Chief of Staff and Head of UK Delegation, Live Oak, SHAPE, 1989–91, retired; *b* 17 Dec. 1937; *s* of late Col Geoffrey Arthur Ross Fawcus, RE and Helen Sybil Graham (*née* Stronach); *m* 1966, Diana Valerie, *d* of Dr P. J. Spencer-Phillips of Bildeston, Suffolk; two *s* one *d*. *Educ:* Wycliffe College; RMA Sandhurst (Sword of Honour); King's College, Cambridge (BA 1963, MA 1968). Commissioned RE, 1958; served UK, Cyprus, BAOR, MoD; OC 39 Field Squadron RE, BAOR, 1973–74; MoD, 1975–76; GSO1 (DS), Staff College, 1977–78; CO 25 Engineer Regt, BAOR, 1978–81; Cabinet Office, 1981; Comdt, RSME, 1982–83; ACOS, HQ 1 (Br) Corps, 1984–85; Chief, Jt Services Liaison Orgn, Bonn, 1986–89. Col Comdt RE, 1991–2000. Chm., RE Widows Soc., 1992–2000. Chm., Ipswich & Suffolk Small Business Assoc., 1996–99. Gov., 1995–2006, Chm. of Govs, 2006–09, Wycliffe Coll. *Recreations:* ski-ing, tennis, Scottish country dancing, furniture restoration, bridge. *Address:* Church Cottage, The Green, Flowton, Ipswich, Suffolk IP8 4LG.

FAWKES, Wally; cartoonist, 1945–2005; *b* 21 June 1924; *m* 1st, 1949, Sandra Boyce-Carmichele (marr. diss. 1964; she *d* 2005); one *s* two *d* (and one *d* decd); 2nd, 1965, Susan Clifford; one *s* one *d*. *Educ:* Sidcup Central Sch.; Sidcup Sch. of Art; Camberwell Sch. of Art. Came from Vancouver, BC, to England, 1931. Joined Daily Mail, 1945; started Flook strip, 1949, transferred to The Mirror, 1984. Political cartoons for: Spectator, 1959; Private Eye, and New Statesman, 1965; Observer, 1965–95; Punch, 1971–92; Today, 1986–87; London Daily News, 1987; Times mag., 1995–96; Sunday Telegraph, 1996–2005; cartoons for Daily Express, 1994; caricatures for Oldie mag., 1996–2005; covers for The Week, 1997. Co-Founder, Humphrey Lyttelton Band, 1948. Hon. DLitt Kent, 2001. Cartoonist of the Year, British Press Awards, 2004. *Publications:* World of Trog, 1977; Trog Shots, 1984; Trog: 40 Graphic Years, 1987; collections of Flook strips. *Recreations:* playing jazz (clarinet and soprano saxophone), cooking, cricket. *Address:* 8 Glenhurst Avenue, NW5 1PS. *T:* (020) 7267 2979.

FAY, Dr Christopher Ernest, CBE 1999; FREng; Chairman: Brightside plc, 2008–14; Iofina plc, 2009–14 (non-executive Director, 2008–14); *b* 4 April 1945; *s* of Harry Thomas Fay and Edith Margaret Fay (*née* Messenger); *m* 1971, Jennifer Olive Knight (*d* 2019); one *s* two *d*. *Educ:* Leeds Univ. (BSc Civil Eng. 1967; PhD 1970). CEng 1974; FICE 1994 (MICE 1973; Hon. FICE 1998); FEI (FInstPet 1994); FREng (FEng 1996). Joined Shell Internat. Petroleum Co., 1970, as offshore design engr; Shell-BP Develt Co., Nigeria, 1971–74; Head, Engrg Planning and Design and Offshore Construction, Sarawak Shell Berhad, Malaysia, 1974–78; Develt Manager, Dansk Undergrunds Consortium, Copenhagen, on secondment from Dansk Shell, 1978–81; Technical Manager, Norske Shell Exploration and Production, Stavanger, 1981–84; Dir, Exploration and Production, Norway, 1984–86; Gen. Manager and Chief Exec., Shell Cos, Turkey, 1986–89; Man. Dir, Shell UK Exploration and Production and a Man. Dir, Shell UK, 1989–93; Chm. and Chief Exec., Shell UK, 1993–98. Chairman: Expro Internat. Gp plc, 1999–2008; Tuscan Energy Gp Ltd, 2002–05; non-executive Director: BAA, 1998–2006; Stena Internat., 1999– (Chm.); Stena Drilling Ltd, 1999–; Anglo American plc, 1999–2010; Weir Gp plc, 2001–03; Conister Financial Gp plc, 2006–08. Chm., Adv. Cttee on Business and the Envmt, 1999–2003. Member: CBI President's Cttee, 1993–98; INSEAD UK Cttee, 1993–95; British Cttee, Det Norske Veritas, 1994–95 and 1996–2001; Bd, Oil, Gas and Petrochemicals Supplies (formerly Oil and Gas Projects and Supplies) Office, 1994–98; Exec. Cttee, British Energy Assoc., 1994–98; Chm., Oil Industries Emergency Cttee, 1993–98. Gov., Motability, 1999–2001 (Mem. Council, 1993–98). CCMI (CIMgt 1994); FRSE 1996; FRSA 1994. *Recreations:* gardening, ski-ing, golf, tennis. *Address:* Merrifield, Links Road, Bramley, Guildford GU5 0AL. *Clubs:* Sunningdale Golf, Bramley Golf.

FAY, Sir (Humphrey) Michael (Gerard), Kt 1990; Principal, Fay, Richwhite & Co. Ltd, Merchant Bankers, since 1974 (Joint Chief Executive, 1990–96); *b* 10 April 1949; *s* of James and Margaret Fay; *m* 1983, Sarah Williams; one *s* two *d*. *Educ:* St Patrick's Coll.,

Silverstream, Wellington; Victoria Univ., Wellington (LLB 1971). Jt Chief Exec., Capital Markets, 1986–90; Dir, Bank of New Zealand, 1989–92. Chairman: Australia/NZ Bicentennial Commn, 1988; Expo 1988 Commn, 1987–88; Expo 1992 Commn, 1989–92; NZ Ireland Fund, 1995–98. Hon. Consul General for Thailand, 1996–98. Chm., NZ Americas Cup Challenges, 1987, 1988, 1992. Chm., Manu Samoa Rugby Club, 1997–2004. *Recreations:* horse breeding and racing, fishing, swimming, running, golf. *Clubs:* Royal New Zealand Yacht Squadron, Auckland Racing, Mercury Bay Boating.

**FAY, Margaret,** CBE 2010 (OBE 2004); DL; Chairman, One NorthEast, 2003–10; *b* 21 May 1949; *d* of Oswald and Joan Allen; *m* 1st, 1968, Matthew Stoker (marr. diss. 1978); one *s*; 2nd, 1982, Peter Fay (marr. diss. 1993). *Educ:* South Shields Grammar Sch. for Girls. Joined Tyne Tees TV, 1981; Dir of Ops, 1995–97; Man. Dir, 1997–2003. Dir, Newcastle Gateshead Initiative, 1999–2003; Member Board: English Partnerships, 2004–08; Homes and Communities Agency, 2008–10; Chm., South Tyneside MBC Econ. Regeneration Bd, 2010–. Non-executive Director: Darlington Building Soc., 2000–08; Northumbrian Water, 2010–; Fabrick Gp, 2011–14; Thirteen Group, 2014–17. Vice Chm., The Sage Gateshead, 2010–18; Chm., Customs House, South Shields, 2018–. Governor: Teesside Univ., 1998–2007; Sunderland Univ., 2011–. DL Tyne and Wear, 2011. *Recreations:* travel, theatre, wine, grandchildren, food.

**FAY, Sir Michael;** *see* Fay, Sir H. M. G.

**FAY, Stephen Francis John;** journalist and author; *b* 14 Aug. 1938; *s* of Gerard Fay and Alice (*née* Bentley); *m* 1964, Prudence Butcher; one *s* one *d*. *Educ:* Highgate Sch.; Univ. of New Brunswick, Canada (BA, MA). On edtl staff: Glasgow Herald, 1961–64; Sunday Times, 1964–84; freelance writer, 1984–86, 1991–96; Ed., Business Mag., 1986–89; Dep. Ed., Independent on Sunday, 1989–91 and 1996–99; Ed., Wisden Cricket Monthly, 2000–03. British Press Special Award, 1978, 1979. *Publications:* Measure for Measure: reform in the Trade Unions, 1970; (with L. Chester and M. Linklater) Hoax, 1972 (Edgar Award for Best Crime Fact Book, 1973); (with P. Knightley) The Death of Venice, 1976; The Great Silver Bubble, 1980; The Ring: anatomy of an opera, 1984; Portrait of an Old Lady: turmoil at the Bank of England, 1987; Power Play: the life and times of Peter Hall, 1995; The Collapse of Barings, 1996; (contrib.) The Secrets of the Press, 1999; Tom Graveney at Lord's, 2005; (with David Kynaston) Arlott, Swanton and the Soul of English Cricket (Book of the Year, Cricket Writers' Club), 2018. *Recreations:* theatre, watching sport, reading broadsheets. *Address:* 5A Furlong Road, N7 8LS. *T:* (020) 7607 8950. *E:* stephen@sandpfay.co.uk. *Clubs:* Garrick, MCC.

**FAYERS, Norman Owen;** City Treasurer and Director of Financial Services, Bristol City Council, 1990–96; Managing Director, Norman Fayers Consultancy Ltd, 2002–09; *b* 8 Jan. 1945; *s* of Claude Lance Fayers and Winifred Joyce (*née* Reynolds); *m* 1966, Patricia Ann Rudd; two *s*. *Educ:* Northgate Grammar Sch. for Boys, Ipswich; BA Open Univ. CPFA 1967; IRRV 1990; FMAAT 1999. Ipswich CBC, 1961–66; Eastbourne CBC, 1966–70; Group Accountant (Educn), Royal Borough of Kingston upon Thames, 1970–73; Chief Accountant, RBK & C, 1973–77; Chief Officer, Finance, London Borough of Ealing, 1977–90. Chartered Institute of Public Finance and Accountancy: Mem. Council, 1991–92; Pres., S Wales and W England Reg., 1993–95 (Vice Pres., 1991–93); Association of Accounting Technicians: Mem. Council, 1992–2001, 2004–07; Chm., Bristol Br., 2000–03. Treas., Life Educn Centres Bristol Ltd, 2009–. Gov., Orchard Sch., Bristol, 2011–. *Recreations:* golf, music, bridge. *Clubs:* Rotary (Bristol; Pres., 2008–09; Treas., 2009–); Kendleshire Golf.

**FAZAKERLEY, Prof. John Kneale,** PhD; FRCPath; FRSB; Professor of Virology and Dean, Faculty of Veterinary and Agricultural Sciences, University of Melbourne, since 2016; *b* Liverpool, 23 July 1957; *s* of John Ernest Fazakerley and Edna Fazakerley (*née* Kneale); *m* 1986, Ann Walker. *Educ:* Wilmslow Grammar Sch.; Univ. of Durham (BSc Hons); St Thomas' Hosp. Med. Sch. (PhD 1985); Univ. of Edinburgh (MBA). FRCPath 2005; FRSB (FSB 2011). Postdoctoral Fellow, Dept of Microbiol., Univ. of Pennsylvania, 1986–88; Sen. Res. Associate, Neuropharmacol., Scripps Res. Inst., La Jolla, Calif, 1988–91; Sen. Res. Fellow, Pathol., Univ. of Cambridge, 1991–94; University of Edinburgh: Veterinary Pathol., and Centre for Infectious Diseases, 1994–2011; Prof. of Virol., Coll. of Medicine and Veterinary Medicine, 2004–11, now Hon. Prof.; Dir, Pirbright Inst. (formerly Inst. for Animal Health), 2011–16. Vis. Fellow, Nuffield Dept of Medicine, Univ. of Oxford, 2013–. *Address:* Faculty of Veterinary and Agricultural Sciences, Building 142, University of Melbourne, Vic 3010, Australia. *E:* John.Fazakerley@unimelb.edu.au.

**FAZIO, Antonio;** Governor, Bank of Italy, 1993–2005; *b* 11 Oct. 1936; *m* Maria Cristina Rosati; one *s* four *d*. *Educ:* Univ. of Rome (BSc *summa cum laude* Econs and Business 1960); MIT. Asst Prof. of Demography, Univ. of Rome, 1961–66; Consultant to Res. Dept, Bank of Italy, 1961–66; Bank of Italy: Dep. Head, subseq. Head, Unit of Econometric Res., 1966–72; Dep. Dir, Monetary Sector, 1972, Head, 1973–79, Res. Dept; Central Manager for Economic Res., 1980–82; Dep. Dir Gen., 1982–93. Chm., Italian Foreign Exchange Office, 1993–2005; Member: Bd of Dirs, BIS, 1993–2005; Governing Council, Eur. Central Bank (formerly Eur. Monetary Inst.), 1993–2005. Hon. Mem., Circolo San Tommaso d'Aquino, 2009. Hon. Dr Econs and Business Bari, 1994; Hon. DHL Johns Hopkins, 1995; Hon. Dr Pol Sci. Macerata, 1996; Hon. LLB Cassino, 1999; Hon. Dr Stats and Econs Milan, 1999; Hon. Dr Computer Engrg Lecce, 2000; Hon. Dr Banking Econs Verona, 2002; Hon. LLD St John's, 2002; Hon. DPhil Catania, 2002; Hon. Dr Moral Theol. Pontificia Salesiana, 2003. Ezio Tarantelli Prize for most original theory in Economic Policy, Club dell'Economia, 1995; Saint Vincent Prize for Economics, Centro Culturale Saint-Vincent, 1997; Pico della Mirandola Prize for Econs, Finance and Business, Fondazione Cassa di Risparmio di Mirandola, 1997–98; Internat. Award in the Humanities, Accad. di Studi Mediterranei, 1999; Keynes-Sraffa Prize, London, 2003; Fiaccola d'oro, Circolo San Tommaso d'Aquino, 2012. Kt Grand Cross, Order of Merit (Italy), 1993. *Publications:* Razionalità economica e solidarietà, 1996; Globalizzazione: politica economica e dottrina sociale, 2008; L'enciclica Caritas in Veritate: Prospettiva storica e attualità, 2011; Sviluppo e declino demografico in Europa e nel Mondo, 2012; (contrib.) Studi in onore di Giuseppe Di Taranto, 2018; scientific articles, mainly on monetary theory and monetary policy issues. *Address:* c/o Bank of Italy, Via Nazionale 91, 00184 Rome, Italy; Via della Camilluccia, u. 741, 00135 Rome, Italy.

**FEACHEM, Sir Richard (George Andrew),** KBE 2007 (CBE 1995); PhD, DSc (Med); FREng; Professor of Global Health (formerly International Health), since 1999, and Director, Global Health Group, since 2007, University of California, San Francisco and Berkeley; *b* 10 April 1947; *s* of late Charles George Paulin Feachem and Margaret Flora Denise Greenhow; *m* 1st, 1970, Zuzana Sedlarova (marr. diss. 1999); one *s* one *d*; 2nd, 1999, Neelam Sekhri. *Educ:* Wellington Coll.; Univ. of Birmingham (BSc 1969); Univ. of NSW (PhD 1974); DSc (Med) London, 1991. MICE 1980; FIWEM 1987; FICE 1990; FREng (FEng 1994). Volunteer, Solomon Is, 1965–66; Research Fellow: Univ. of NSW, 1970–74; Univ. of Birmingham, 1974–76; London School of Hygiene and Tropical Medicine: Lectr and Sen. Lectr, 1976–82; Reader, 1983–87; Prof. of Tropical Envmtl Health, 1987–95; Dean, 1989–95; Dir, Health, Nutrition and Population, World Bank, 1995–99; Prof. of Internat. Health, Univ. of Calif, San Francisco and Berkeley, and founding Dir, Inst. for Global Health, 1999–2002; founding Exec. Dir, Global Fund to Fight AIDS, Tuberculosis and Malaria, and Under Sec.-Gen., UN, 2002–07 (on leave of absence). Vis. Prof., LSHTM, 1995–; Adjunct Professor: Johns Hopkins Univ., 1996–2001; George Washington Univ., 1997–2001; Hon. Prof., Univ. of Qld, 2005–. Consultant, WHO, 1982–83; Principal Public Health Specialist, World Bank, 1988–89; Chairman: Adv. Cttee, World Develt Report, 1992–93; Adv. Cttee, TB Programme, WHO, 1992–95; Bd, Initiative on Public Private Partnerships for Health, 2000–02; Bd, Global Forum for Health Res., 2001–04; Malaria Elimination Gp, 2008–17; Commn on Malaria Eradication, 2017–; Co-Chair, Asia Pacific Malaria Elimination Network, 2008–15; Member: Adv. Cttee, Caribbean Epidemiology Centre, 1990–95; Mgt Cttee, Inst. of Child Health, 1989–91; Bd on Internat. Health, US NAS, 1992–97, 2001–03; Bd, Internat. AIDS Vaccine Initiative, 1996–2003; Adv. Cttee, Aust. Nat. Centre for Epidemiology and Public Health, 1996–2001; Commn on Macroeconomics and Health, 2000–02; Commn on HIV/AIDS and Governance in Africa, 2003–06; Commn on Investing in Health, 2012–; Strategic Adv. Gp on Malaria Eradication, WHO, 2016–; Bd, Asia Pacific Leaders Malaria Alliance, 2018–. Member Council: RSTM&H, 1978–81; VSO, 1991–2007; Water Aid, 1994–95; Patron, Assoc. for Promotion of Healthcare in former Soviet Union, 1992–96. Trustee, Internat. Centre for Diarrhoeal Diseases Research, Bangladesh, 1985–89. Chm., Health Policy Adv. Bd, Gilead Sciences Inc., 2010– (Mem., 2007–); Member: Adv. Bd, Sure Chill Ltd, 2011–16; Bd, Vital Connect Inc., 2011–. Mem., Nat. Acad. of Medicine (formerly Inst. of Medicine), 2002. Hon. FFPH (Hon. FFPHM 1990); Hon. Fellow, LSHTM, 2000. Hon. DEng Birmingham, 2007; Hon. MD Queensland, 2015. Dean's Medal, Johns Hopkins Sch. of Public Health, 2003; Sir Frank Whittle Medal, RAEng, 2010; Richard T. Hewitt Award, RSocMed, 2016. Member, Editorial Board: Transactions of the RSTM&H, 1979–88; Jl of Tropical Medicine and Hygiene, 1979–96; Current Issues in Public Health, 1993–2002; Health and Human Rights, 1993–2002; Tropical Medicine and Internat. Health, 1996–2001; Global Public Health, 2005–10; Editor-in-Chief, WHO Bulletin, 1999–2002. *Publications:* Water, Wastes and Health in Hot Climates, 1977; Subsistence and Survival: rural ecology in the Pacific, 1977; Water, Health and Development, 1978; Evaluation for Village Water Supply Planning, 1980; Sanitation and Disease, 1983; Environmental Health Engineering in the Tropics, 1983; Evaluating Health Impact, 1986; Disease and Mortality in Sub-Saharan Africa, 1991; The Health of Adults in the Developing World, 1992; Shrinking the Malaria Map, 2009; over 220 papers in scientific jls. *Recreations:* mountaineering, ski-ing. *Club:* Travellers.

**FEALY, Michael;** QC 2014; *b* Drogheda, Ireland, 6 May 1970; *s* of Peter and Rose Fealy; *m* 2003, Della Burnside (marr. diss. 2016). *Educ:* National Univ. of Ireland (BCL); Sidney Sussex Coll., Cambridge (LLM 1992). Called to the Bar: King's Inns, Dublin, 1995; Middle Temple, 1997. Lectr, QMW, subseq. QMUL, 1992–97; in practice as barrister, 1998–. Mem., Chatham House (RIIA), 2014–. *Publications:* (with I. Grainger) An Introduction to the Civil Procedure Rules, 1999. *Recreations:* reading, running, travel. *Address:* 1 Essex Court, Temple, EC4Y 9AR. *T:* (020) 7583 2000. *E:* mfealy@oeclaw.co.uk. *Clubs:* Reform, Ivy.

**FEAN, Sir (Thomas) Vincent,** KCVO 2005; HM Diplomatic Service, retired; Consul-General, Jerusalem, 2010–14; *b* 20 Nov. 1952; *s* of Joseph Peter Fean and Brigid Fean (*née* Walsh); *m* 1978, Anne Stewart; one *s* two *d*. *Educ:* St Theodore's RC Secondary Sch., Burnley; Sheffield Univ. (BA French and German 1975). Joined FCO, 1975; Second Sec., Baghdad, 1978; First Sec., Damascus, 1979–82; EU and Berlin issues, FCO, 1982–85; UK Repn to EU, Brussels, 1985–89; Personnel Mgt Dept, FCO, 1989–92; Counsellor, Press and Public Affairs, Paris, 1992–96; Head, Counter-Terrorism Policy Dept, FCO, 1996–99; Dir, Asia Pacific, Internat. Gp, Trade Partners UK, 1999–2002; High Comr, Malta, 2002–06; Ambassador to Libya, 2006–10. Chm., Libyan British Business Council, 2016–. Trustee, Medical Aid for Palestinians, 2015–; Chair, Trustees, Balfour Project, 2018–; Patron, Britain Palestine Friendship and Twinning Network, 2016–. *Recreations:* supporting Burnley FC and Lancashire CCC, travel, walking, cycling, folk music. *Club:* Burnley Football.

**FEAR, Kevin David;** Headmaster, Nottingham High School, since 2007; *b* Watford, 12 June 1963; *s* of late Derek Fear and Gwen Fear; one *s* one *d*. *Educ:* Douai Sch.; Southampton Univ. (BA Hons Hist.); Nottingham Univ. (PGCE). Hd of Hist., King's Sch., Chester, 1986–2000; Sen. Teacher, 2000–04, Dep. Hd, 2004–07, Nottingham High Sch. *Recreations:* children, following fortunes of Arsenal FC, running. *Address:* Nottingham High School, Waverley Mount, Nottingham NG7 4ED. *T:* (0115) 978 6056, *Fax:* (0115) 924 9716. *E:* fear.kd@nottinghamhigh.co.uk. *Clubs:* East India, Lansdowne.

**FEARN,** family name of **Baron Fearn**.

**FEARN,** Baron *cr* 2001 (Life Peer), of Southport in the County of Merseyside; **Ronald Cyril Fearn, (Ronnie),** OBE 1985; *b* 6 Feb. 1931; *s* of James Fearn and Martha Ellen Fearn; *m* 1955, Joyce Edna Dugan; one *s* one *d*. *Educ:* King George V Grammar School. FCIB. Banker with Williams Deacons Bank, later Williams & Glyn's Bank, later Royal Bank of Scotland. MP (L 1987–88, Lib Dem 1988–92 and 1997–2001) Southport; contested (Lib Dem) Southport, 1992. Lib Dem spokesman on health and tourism, 1988–89, on local govt, 1989–90, on transport, housing and tourism, 1990–92. Mem., Select Cttee on Culture, Media and Sport, 1997–2001. Councillor, Sefton MBC, 1974–2016. Mem., H of L, 2001–18. *Recreations:* badminton, amateur dramatics, athletics. *Address:* Norcliffe, 56 Norwood Avenue, Southport, Merseyside PR9 7EQ. *T:* (01704) 228577.

**FEARNLEY-WHITTINGSTALL, Hugh Christopher Edmund;** writer, broadcaster, cook and food campaigner, since 1989; Founder and Director: River Cottage Cookery School and River Cottage Kitchens; Keo Films Ltd; *b* 14 Jan. 1965; *s* of Robert and Jane Fearnley-Whittingstall; *m* 2001, Marie Derôme; two *s* two *d*. *Educ:* Eton Coll.; St Peter's Coll., Oxford (BA Hons Philos. and Psychol.). Sous chef, River Cafe, 1989; journalist: Punch, 1989–92; Sunday Times, 1990–92; Daily Telegraph, 1993–98; Independent on Sunday, 2000–02; Observer, 2002. Food columnist: Observer (monthly), 2003–06; Guardian Weekend Mag., 2006–13. Television includes series: A Cook on the Wild Side, 1995, 1997; Escape to River Cottage, 1998–99; Return to River Cottage, 2000; River Cottage Forever, 2002; Beyond River Cottage, 2004; River Cottage Road Trip, 2005; The View from River Cottage, 2005; The River Cottage Treatment, 2006; River Cottage: Gone Fishing, 2007; Hugh's Chicken Run, 2008; River Cottage Spring, 2008; River Cottage Autumn, 2008; River Cottage: Summer's Here, 2009, Winter's on the Way, 2009; River Cottage Every Day, 2010; Hugh's Fish Fight, 2011; River Cottage Veg, 2011; River Cottage Mash Up, Three Go Mad, 2012; Three Good Things, 2012; Hugh's Fish Fight: Save Our Seas, 2013; River Cottage to the Core, 2013; Scandimania, 2014; Hugh's Fish Fight: Hugh's Last Stand, 2014; Big Blue UK, 2015; Hugh's War on Waste, 2015, 2016; Ingenious Animals, 2016; Saving Africa's Elephants: Hugh and the Ivory War, 2016; Hugh's Wild West, 2018; Britain's Fat Fight, 2018, 2019; War on Plastic with Hugh and Anita, 2019. Member: Devon Cattle Breeders' Assoc., 2004–; Greenpeace, 2010–. Patron: FARMA; Switchback; Countryside Restoration Trust. Vice-Pres., Fauna and Flora Internat. *Publications:* A Cook on the Wild Side, 1995; The River Cottage Cookbook, 2001; The River Cottage Year, 2003; The River Cottage Meat Book, 2004; The River

Cottage Family Cookbook, 2005; (with Nick Fisher) The River Cottage Fish Book, 2007; Hugh Fearlessly Eats It All, 2007; River Cottage Every Day, 2009; River Cottage Veg Every Day!, 2011; Hugh's Three Good Things on a Plate, 2012; River Cottage Fruit Every Day!, 2013; River Cottage Light & Easy, 2014; Love Your Leftovers, 2015; River Cottage A to Z, 2016; River Cottage Much More Veg, 2017. *Recreations:* fishing, diving, growing vegetables, charcuterie. *Address:* c/o Antony Topping, Greene & Heaton, 37 Goldhawk Road, W12 8QQ. *Clubs:* Century, Soho House, Frontline, Conduit.

**FEARON, Prof. Douglas Thomas**, MD; FRS 1999; FRCP, FMedSci; Professor, Cold Spring Harbor Laboratory, USA, since 2014; Walter B. Wriston Professor of Pancreatic Cancer Research, Weill Cornell Medicine, Cornell University, since 2014; Senior Group Leader, CRUK Cambridge Research Institute, University of Cambridge, since 2011; Fellow, Trinity College, Cambridge, since 2001; *b* 16 Oct. 1942; *s* of late Dr Henry Dana Fearon and of Frances Hudson (*née* Eubanks); *m* 1st, 1972, Margaret Andrews (marr. diss. 1975); 2nd, 1977, Clare MacIntyre (*née* Wheless); one *s* one *d*. *Educ:* Williams Coll. (BA 1964); Johns Hopkins Med. Sch. (MD 1968). FRCP 1994. Major, US Army Med. Corps, 1970–72 (Bronze Star and Army Commendation Medal, 1972). Med. Res., Johns Hopkins Hosp., 1968–70; Helen Hay Whitney Foundn Post-Doctoral Res. Fellow, 1974–77; Harvard Medical School: Res. Fellow in Medicine, 1972–75; Instr in Medicine, 1975–76; Asst Prof., 1976–79, Associate Prof., 1979–84, Prof., 1984–87, of Medicine; Prof. of Medicine, and Director, Div. of Rheumatology and of Grad. Prog. in Immunology, Johns Hopkins Univ. Sch. of Medicine, 1987–93; University of Cambridge: Wellcome Trust Prof. of Medicine, 1993–2003; Sheila Joan Smith Prof. of Immunology, 2003–10, now Prof. Emeritus; Dir, Wellcome Trust PhD Prog. in Infection and Immunity, 2005–10. Principal Res. Fellow, Wellcome Trust, 1993–2001; Hon. Consultant in Medicine, Addenbrooke's Hosp., 1993–. Member: Scientific Adv. Bd, Babraham Inst., 1998; Scientific Bd, Ludwig Inst. for Cancer Res., 1998–; Scientific Adv. Bd, Max Planck Institut für Immunobiologie, 2001; Scientific Adv. Cttee, Rita Allen Foundn, 2002–. Member: EMBO, 2001; NAS, USA, 2001; Hon. For. Mem., Amer. Acad. of Arts and Scis, 1999. Founder FMedSci 1998. Hon. MA Harvard, 1984. Merit Award, NIH, 1991. *Publications:* articles on immunology in learned jls. *Recreation:* golf. *Address:* 4 Lloyd Point Drive, Lloyd Harbor, NY 11743, USA. *Clubs:* Gog Magog Golf; The Country (Brookline, USA).

**FEAST, Prof. William James, (Jim)**, CBE 2007; FRS 1996; CChem, FRSC; Courtaulds Professor of Polymer Chemistry, Durham University, 1989–2003, now Emeritus Professor; *b* 25 June 1938; *s* of William Edward Feast and Lucy Mary Feast (*née* Willis); *m* 1967, Jenneke Elizabeth Catherina van der Kuijl, Middelburg, Netherlands; two *d*. *Educ:* Sheffield Univ. (BSc 1960); Birmingham Univ. (PhD 1963). CChem, FRSC 1981; FIM 1994. Durham University: Lectr, 1965–76; Sen. Lectr, 1976–86; Prof., 1986–2003; Dir, IRC in Polymer Sci. and Technol., 1994–2002. Gillette Internat. Res. Fellow, Leuven, Belgium, 1968–69; Vis. Prof., Max Planck Institut für Polymerforschungs, 1984–88. Pres., RSC, 2006–08. *Publications:* numerous res. papers, reviews in learned jls. *Recreations:* walking, gardening, theatre, fine arts. *Address:* Chemistry Department, Durham University, South Road, Durham DH1 3LE. *T:* (0191) 386 8646. *E:* w.j.feast@durham.ac.uk.

**FEATES, Prof. Francis Stanley**, CB 1991; PhD; CEng, FIChemE; FRSC; CChem; Professor of Environmental Engineering, University of Manchester Institute of Science and Technology, 1991–95; *b* 21 Feb. 1932; *s* of Stanley James Feates and Dorothy Marguerite Jenny Feates (*née* Orford); *m* 1953, Gwenda Grace Goodchild; one *s* three *d*. *Educ:* John Ruskin Sch., Croydon; Birkbeck Coll. London (BSc Special Chem.; PhD). FRSC 1972; FIChemE 1991; CEng 1991. Wellcome Res. Foundn, 1949–52; Chester-Beatty Cancer Res. Inst., Univ. of London, 1952–54. Chemistry Lectr, Goldsmiths' Coll., London, 1954–56; AERE, Harwell, UKAEA, 1956–78; Argonne Nat. Lab., Univ. of Chicago, Illinois, 1965–67; Department of the Environment: Dir, Nuclear Waste Management, 1978–83; Chief Radiochemical Inspector, 1983–86; Chief Inspector, Radioactive Substances, HM Inspectorate of Pollution, 1986–88; Dir and Chief Inspector, HM Inspectorate of Pollution, 1989–91. Consultant to EC (formerly EEC) on nuclear matters, 1991–. Director: Sir Alexander Gibb & Partners, 1991–94; Siemens Plessey Controls Ltd, 1991–92; Grundon Waste Management, 1991–92. Expert Mem., Scientific and Technical Cttee, EEC, Brussels, 1989–92; Member: Steering Cttee, Nuclear Energy Agency, OECD, Paris, 1988–91; Steering Bd, Lab. of Govt Chemist, 1991–94; Observer Mem., NRPB, 1988–91. Founder Editor, Jl of Hazardous Materials, 1975–85. *Publications:* Hazardous Materials Spills Handbook, 1982; Integrated Pollution Management, 1995; numerous scientific papers on pollution issues, nuclear power, electrochemistry, thermodynamics, waste management, electron microscopy. *Recreations:* walking, cycling, travel.

**FEATHER, Prof. John Pliny**; Professor of Book History, School of Arts, English and Drama, Loughborough University, 2013–14, now Emeritus Professor (Professor of Information and Library Studies, 1988–2013); *b* 20 Dec. 1947; *m* 1971, Sarah, *d* of late Rev. A. W. Rees and Mrs S. M. Rees. *Educ:* Heath Sch., Halifax; Queen's Coll., Oxford (BLitt, MA); MA Cambridge, PhD Loughborough. FCLIP (FLA 1986). Asst Librarian, Bodleian Liby, Oxford, 1972–79; Munby Fellow in Bibliography, Cambridge Univ., 1977–78; Loughborough University: Lectr, then Sen. Lectr, 1979–88; Hd, Dept of Information and Liby Studies, then Information Sci., 1990–94 and 2003–06; Dean of Educn and Humanities, 1994–96; Pro-Vice-Chancellor, 1996–2000; Dean, Graduate Sch., 2010–13. Vis. Prof., UCLA, 1982. Pres., Oxford Bibliographical Soc., 1988–92. Mem., many nat. and internat. professional cttees; consultancy and teaching in many countries and for UNESCO, EEC and British Council, 1977–. Gov., Loughborough Endowed Schs, 2001–. FRSA 1994. *Publications:* The Provincial Book Trade in Eighteenth-Century England, 1985; A Dictionary of Book History, 1987; A History of British Publishing, 1988, 2nd edn 2005; Preservation and the Management of Library Collections, 1991, 2nd edn 1996; Index to Selected Bibliographical Journals 1971–1985, 1991; Publishing, Piracy and Politics: a history of copyright in the British book trade, 1994; The Information Society, 1994, 6th edn 2013; (with James Dearnley) The Wired World, 2001; Managing Preservation in Libraries and Archives, 2002; Publishing: communicating knowledge in the 21st century, 2003; (ed) Book Publishing: critical concepts in media and cultural studies, 4 vols, 2011; articles and reviews in academic and professional jls, conf. procs, etc. *Recreations:* photography, music, travel, cooking. *Address:* 36 Farnham Street, Quorn, Leicestershire LE12 8DR. *Club:* Athenæum.

**FEATHER, Robert;** Chief Executive Officer, Fenwick Ltd, since 2018; *b* Bradford, 21 Oct. 1967; *s* of Duncan Feather and Ruth Feather; *m* 1996, Annabel Landon O'Dwyer; three *d*. *Educ:* Ratcliffe Coll., Leics; Magdalene Coll., Cambridge (BA Law 1989). Called to the Bar, Inner Temple, 1991; Pupillage, Keating Chambers, 1992; Mgt Consultant, COBA Gp, 1993–96; Category Manager, Asda, 1996–99; Co-founder, Feather and Black, 1999–2009; Buying Dir, John Lewis Partnership, 2009–11; Gen. Merchandise Dir, 2011–13, Online Dir, 2013–16, J. Sainsbury; Commercial Dir, Argos, 2016–17. Non-executive Director: Retail, BHF, 2013–17; New West End Co., 2018–. *Recreations:* family, gardening, sailing, exercise. *Address:* Hoggs Lodge, Upper Lanham, Alresford, Hants SO24 9RL. *E:* robbiefeather1@gmail.com.

**FEATHERBY, William Alan;** QC 2008; a Recorder, since 2002; *b* Clifton, Bristol, 16 May 1956; *s* of Joseph Alan Featherby and Patricia Annie Featherby (*née* Davies); *m* 1980, Clare Frances, JP, *d* of Ian Richard Posgate; five *s* five *d*. *Educ:* Ripley Court Sch., Ripley; Haileybury; Trinity Coll., Oxford (MA, Scholar). Called to the Bar, Middle Temple, 1978 (Astbury Law Scholar); practises in common law, esp. personal injury and clinical negligence. Arbitrator. Member: Professional Conduct Cttee, Bar Council, 1995–2000; Civil Procedure Rules Cttee, 2008–14. Mem., Southwark Dio. Synod, 2006–10. A Church Comr, 2016–18. *Publications:* A Yorkshire Furrow, 1992. *Recreations:* opera, Richard Strauss, reading, walking. *Address:* 12 King's Bench Walk, Temple, EC4Y 7EL. *Club:* Carlton.

**FEATHERSTONE,** family name of **Baroness Featherstone**.

**FEATHERSTONE,** Baroness *cr* 2015 (Life Peer), of Highgate in the London Borough of Haringey; **Lynne Choona Featherstone;** PC 2014; *b* 20 Dec. 1951; *d* of Joseph and Gladys Ryness; *m* 1982, Stephen Featherstone (marr. diss. 2003); two *c*. *Educ:* South Hampstead High Sch.; Oxford Poly. (Dip. in Communications and Design). Various design posts, 1975–80; Man. Dir, own design co., Inhouse Outhouse Design, 1980–87; strategic design consultant, 1987–97. Dir, Ryness Electrical Supplies Ltd, 1991–2002. Member (Lib Dem): Haringey LBC, 1998–2006 (Leader of the Opposition, 1998–2002); London Assembly, GLA, 2000–05. MP (Lib Dem) Hornsey and Wood Green, 2005–15; contested (Lib Dem) same seat, 2015. Lib Dem Shadow Sec. of State for Internat. Develt, 2006–10; Lib Dem Spokesperson for Youth and Equalities, 2007–10; Parliamentary Under-Secretary of State: (Minister for Equalities and Criminal Information), Home Office, 2010–12; DFID, 2012–14; Minister of State (Minister for Crime Protection), Home Office, 2014–15. Lib Dem spokesperson for energy and climate change, 2015–. Contested (Lib Dem) Hornsey and Wood Green, 2001. *Publications:* (as Lynne Choona Ryness) Marketing and Communication Techniques for Architects, 1992; Equal Ever After: the fight for same-sex marriage and how I made it happen, 2016. *Recreations:* writing, food, television. *Address:* House of Lords, SW1A 0PW.

**FEATHERSTONE, Jane Elizabeth;** Chief Executive, Sister Pictures, since 2016; *b* 24 March 1969; *d* of John Robert Featherstone and Elizabeth Ann Featherstone. *Educ:* Old Palace Sch., Croydon; Leeds Univ. (BA Jt Hons Hist. and German). PA, Paul Gascoigne Promotions, 1991–92; Producer: Hat Trick Prodns, 1992–95; United TV, 1995–97; Wall to Wall, 1998–99; Kudos Film and Television Ltd: Hd of Drama, 2000–02; Exec. Producer, 2002; Jt Man. Dir, 2002; Creative Dir, 2008; CEO, 2011–15; Jt Chm., UK Shine Gp, 2012–15; Producer or Executive Producer: Touching Evil, 1997; Sex 'n' Death, 1999; Glasgow Kiss, 2000; Spooks (series 1–6), 2002–11; Hustle (series 1–4), 2004–06; Life on Mars (series 1–2), 2006, 2008; Tsunami, the Aftermath, 2006; Secret Life; The Hour, 2001–12; Pleasureland; Wide Sargasso Sea, 2006; Ashes to Ashes, 2008–10; Law & Order: UK, 2009–14; Outcasts, 2011; Hunted, Eternal Law, 2012; Broadchurch, 2013–17; Gracepoint, 2014; River, Humans, 2015; The Split, 2018. *Recreations:* family, friends, shops full of old things, ski-ing averagely, saying "quite frankly", good food and wine, the beach, wonderful writing.

**FEATHERSTONE-WITTY, Mark,** OBE 2014; Founding Principal and Chief Executive Officer, Liverpool Institute for Performing Arts Learning Group (formerly Liverpool Institute for Performing Arts), since 1994; *b* 2 June 1946; *s* of late Philip and Evy Featherstone-Witty; *m* 1972, Alison Thomas; one *s*. *Educ:* Univ. of Durham (BA, PGCE); Rollins Coll., Florida (MEd). Asst Ed., Macmillan Educnl Publishing, 1974–76; English teaching jobs in both private and maintained sector, 1976–80; Founder and Principal, Capital Coll., 1980–89; Chief Exec., London Sch. of Publishing, 1982–89; Co-founder and Principal, London Sch. of Insce, 1983–89; Co-founder, Rainbow Educn Prodns, 1983–86; Consultative Educn Ed., Quartet Books, 1984–86; Founder, and Sen. Educnl Advr, Brit Sch., 1989–91; Dir, Sell a Door, Theatre Co., 2014–. Chair, Assoc. of Tutors, 1985–88. Founder Trustee, Schs for Performing Arts Trust, 1985–2009; Trustee: Liverpool Royal Court Th. Foundn, 2000–; Nat. Acad. of Writing, 2003–11; The British Music Experience, 2017–; Member, Board: The Music Lives Foundn, 2006–08; Drama UK, 2012–; Dir, Conference of Drama Schs, 2010–12. Judge, Liverpool Music Awards, 2012–. Chm., Sefton Park Palm House Preservation Trust, 2004–12. Member and Director: LIPA Primary Sch., 2012–; LIPA Sixth Form Coll., 2013–; LIPA 4–19 Acad. Hon. Fellow: Inst. of the Arts, Barcelona, 2017; Liverpool John Moores Univ., 2017. Kt (1st cl.), Royal Norwegian Order of Merit, 2015. *Publications:* Optimistic, Even Then, 2000; LIPA in Pictures: the first ten years, 2006. *Recreations:* reading comic crime books, entertainment, walking, projects. *Address:* Liverpool Institute for Performing Arts, Mount Street, Liverpool L1 9HF. *T:* (0151) 330 3000. *E:* m.featherstone-witty@lipa.ac.uk. *Clubs:* Lansdowne, Savile.

**FEAVER, William Andrew;** writer, art critic and painter; *b* 1 Dec. 1942; *s* of Rt Rev. Douglas Russell Feaver; *m* 1st, 1964, Victoria Turton (marr. diss.); one *s* three *d*; 2nd, 1985, Andrea Rose; two *d*. *Educ:* St Albans School; Nottingham High School; Keble College, Oxford. Teacher: South Stanley Boys' Modern Sch., Co. Durham, 1964–65; Newcastle Royal Grammar Sch., 1965–71; Sir James Knott Res. Fellow, Newcastle Univ., 1971–73; art critic: The Listener, 1971–75; Financial Times, 1974–75; art adviser, Sunday Times Magazine, 1974–75; art critic, The Observer, 1975–98. Vis. Prof., Nottingham Trent Univ., 1994–. Exhibitions curated include: George Cruikshank, V&A, 1974; Thirties, Hayward Gall., 1979; The Ashington Gp, Beijing, 1980; Lucian Freud, Kendal, 1996, Tate Gall., and La Caixa, Barcelona, 2002, Mus. of Contemp. Art, LA, 2002–03; Museo Correr, Venice, 2005; Michael Andrews: lights, Thyssen-Bornemisza Mus., Madrid, 2000; Michael Andrews, Tate Gall., 2001; John Constable, Grand Palais, Paris, 2002. Trustee, Ashington Gp, 1989–. Critic of the Year, 1983, Commended, 1986, UK Press Awards. *Publications:* The Art of John Martin, 1975; When We Were Young, 1976; Masters of Caricature, 1981; Pitmen Painters, 1988; James Boswell: unofficial war artist, 2006; Lucian Freud, 2007; Frank Auerbach, 2009; The Lives of Lucian Freud: volume I: 1922–1968, 2019. *Address:* 1 Rhodesia Road, SW9 9EJ. *T:* (020) 7737 3386.
*See also* W. Horbury.

**FEDERER, Roger;** professional tennis player, since 1998; *b* Basle, 8 Aug. 1981; *s* of Robert Federer and Lynette Federer (*née* Durand); *m* 2009, Mirka Vavrinec; twin *s* twin *d*. Ranked World No. 1 as Jun., 1998; winner: Wimbledon Jun. title, 1998; singles titles include: Milan, 2001; Hamburg TMS, 2002, 2005; Sydney, 2002; Vienna, 2002, 2003; Marseilles, 2003; Tennis Masters Cup, Houston, 2003, 2004; Wimbledon, 2003, 2004, 2005, 2006, 2007, 2009, 2012, 2017; Halle, Germany, 2003, 2004, 2005, 2006, 2008, 2013, 2014, 2015, 2017, 2019; Munich, 2003; Dubai, 2003, 2004, 2005, 2007, 2012, 2014, 2015, 2019; Australian Open, 2004, 2006, 2007, 2010, 2017, 2018; Bangkok, 2004, 2005; Canada AMS, 2004; Gstaad, 2004; Hamburg AMS, 2004, 2007; Toronto, 2004, 2006; US Open, 2004, 2005, 2006, 2007, 2008; Cincinnati, 2005, 2007, 2010, 2012, 2014, 2015; Doha, 2005, 2006, 2011; Miami, 2005, 2006, 2017, 2019; Rotterdam, 2005, 2018; Basle, 2006, 2007, 2008, 2010, 2014, 2015; Madrid, 2006, 2012; Masters Cup, Shanghai, 2006, 2007, 2014, 2017; Tokyo, 2006; Estoril, 2008; French Open, 2009; Stockholm Open, 2010; Istanbul Open, 2014, 2015; Stuttgart, 2018; Barclays ATP World Tour Finals, London, 2010, 2011; Silver Medal, London Olympics, 2012; doubles titles: Rotterdam, 2001, 2002; Gstaad,

2001; Moscow, 2002; Vienna, 2003; Miami TMS, 2003; Halle, 2005; Beijing Olympics, 2008; 27 Davis Cup ties, 1999– (40 singles wins, 12 doubles wins; winning Swiss team, 2014). Founder, Roger Federer Foundn, 2003. Pres., ATP Player Council, 2008–. Swiss Personality of Year, 2003; ATP Eur. Player of Year, 2004; BBC Overseas Sports Personality of Year, 2004, 2006, 2007, 2017; Laureus World Sportsman of Year, 2005, 2006, 2007, 2008. *Recreations:* golf, soccer, ski-ing, friends, PlayStation, music, playing cards. *Address:* c/o Lynette Federer, POB 209, 4103 Bottmingen, Switzerland.

**FEDOTOV, Yury Viktorovich;** Executive Director, United Nations Office on Drugs and Crime, and Director-General, United Nations Office, Vienna, since 2010; *b* 14 Dec. 1947; *m* 1973, Elena Fedotova; one *s* one *d*. *Educ:* Moscow State Inst. of Internat. Relns. Joined USSR Diplomatic Service, 1971; served: Algeria, 1974–80; Ministry of For. Affairs, Moscow, 1980–83; India, 1983–88; Ministry of For. Affairs, Moscow, 1988–94; Dep. Perm. Rep., then Actg First Dep. Perm. Rep. of Russian Fedn to UN, NY, 1994–99; Ministry of For. Affairs, Moscow, 1999–2002; Dep. Minister of Foreign Affairs, 2002–05; Ambassador of the Russian Federation to the Court of St James's, 2005–10. Order of Friendship (Russia); Distinguished Mem. of Diplomatic Service (Russia). *Address:* United Nations Office on Drugs and Crime, Vienna International Centre, PO Box 500, 1400 Vienna, Austria. *Club:* Athenæum.

**FEEHAN, Francis Thomas, (Frank);** QC 2010; a Recorder, since 2005; *b* Liverpool, 26 Oct. 1964; *s* of Francis John Feehan and Angela Feehan (*née* Wilson); civil partnership 2006, Simon Owers. *Educ:* All Saints RC Comp. Sch., Sheffield; Emmanuel Coll., Cambridge (BA Hons 1987). Called to the Bar, Lincoln's Inn, 1988; in practice as a barrister, 1988–. *Recreations:* travel, friends. *Address:* 1 King's Bench Walk, Temple, EC4Y 7DB. *Club:* Travellers'.

**FEENEY, Jason,** CBE 2011; Chief Executive, Food Standards Agency, since 2017; *b* Leeds, 13 Jan. 1963; *s* of Douglas Feeney and Patricia Feeney; *m* 1988, Wendy Baxter; one *s* one *d*. Pension Service: Hd, Future Pensions, 2002–04; Hd, Central Design Authy, 2004–06; Business Design Dir, 2006–008; Department for Work and Pensions: Strategy Dir, 2008–09, Chief Operating Officer, 2009–10, Pension Service; Pensions Dir, 2010–12, Benefits Dir, 2012–14; Chief Operating Officer, Food Standards Agency, 2015–17. *Recreations:* fell running, cycling, gardening. *Address:* Food Standards Agency, Floor 6 & 7, Clive House, 70 Petty France, SW1H 9EX. *E:* jason.feeney@food.gov.uk.

**FEENY, Patrick, (Paddy);** communications consultant, since 2016; Head of Communications, Christie's, 2014–16; *b* 27 June 1965; *s* of Victor Francis Foy Feeny and Joan Aïda (*née* Dunbar-Stuart); partner, Alan Davey, *qv*. *Educ:* St Brendan's Coll., Bristol; King's Coll., London (BD 1987). Asst Press Sec., Prime Minister's Office, 1993–96; Press. Sec., DFID, 1996–98; Policy and Commns Manager, Social Exclusion Unit, Cabinet Office, 1998–2000; Commns Advr, Teenage Pregnancy Unit, DoH, 2000–01; Hd of News, 2001–05, Communications Dir, later External Relations Dir, 2005–08, DCMS; Communications Dir, DECC, 2008–11; Head of Communications, BBC News, 2012–14. *Recreations:* music, theatre, books and walking. *E:* paddy.feeny@btinternet.com. *Club:* 2 Brydges.

**FEESEY, Air Vice-Marshal John David Leonard,** AFC 1977; retired, 1999; *b* 11 Oct. 1942; *s* of Leonard Ewart Feesey and Maisie Veronica Lillian Feesey; *m* 1968, Glenda Doris Barker; two *s*. *Educ:* Oldershaw Grammar Sch., Wallasey, Cheshire. RAF Officer Cadet, 1961; commnd General Duties Br., 1962; RAF pilot (Hunter, Harrier), 1962–83; OC No 1 (Fighter) Sqdn (Harrier), 1983–86; Stn Comdr, RAF Wittering, 1986–88; Comd Exec. Officer, HQ AAFCE, 1989–91; Dir Airspace Policy, 1991–93, Dir Gen., Policy and Plans, 1993–96, HQ NATS; Dep. Comdr, Combined Air Ops Centre 4, 1996–98. Vice-Pres., CCF Assoc., 1999–2009; President: No. 1 (Fighter) Sqdn Assoc., 2006–12; Pelynt and Lanreath Br., RBL, 2006–. Chm., Lanreath Community Assoc., 2014–. Hon. Treas., 2000–, Local Worship Leader, 2012–, Lansallos Church. *Recreations:* hill walking, gardening. *Club:* Royal Air Force.

**FEEST, Adam Sebastian;** QC 2016; a Recorder, since 2009; *b* Newcastle upon Tyne, 23 Jan. 1970; *s* of Terry George Feest, *qv*, and Gillian Jane Foote (*née* Endersby); *m* 1995, Charlotte Mary Garnett; one *s* three *d*. *Educ:* Exeter Sch., Exeter; Keble Coll., Oxford (BA Hons Juris. 1992); Inns of Court Sch. of Law. Called to the Bar, Inner Temple, 1994; in practice as barrister: London, 1994–2011; Winchester, 2011– (Hd, Crime Gp, 2016–). Mem., Attorney Gen.'s list of Special Advocates, 2005–; Legal Assessor: GMC, 2010–18; NMC, 2011–16. *Recreations:* my family, running through the woods with my dog. *Address:* 3 Paper Buildings, 4 St Peter Street, Winchester, Hants SO23 8BW. *E:* adam.feest@3pb.co.uk.

**FEEST, Terry George,** MD; FRCP; Consultant Nephrologist, Richard Bright Renal Unit, 1991–2009, and Clinical Director, Renal and Transplant Services, 1991–2006, Southmead Hospital, North Bristol NHS Trust; *b* 16 Feb. 1944; *s* of Sydney George Feest and Doris May Feest; *m* 1991, Kathleen Alexis Blosick; one step *s*; one *s* one *d* by a previous marriage. *Educ:* Sidney Sussex Coll., Cambridge (BA 1965; MB BChir 1968; MD 1980); King's Coll. Hosp., London. FRCP 1986. Consultant Physician and Nephrologist, Royal Devon and Exeter Hosp., 1978–91. Hon. Prof. of Clinical Nephrology, Univ. of Bristol, 1995–. Renal Physician, Auckland City Hosp., 2009–10. Asst Dir, UK Renal Registry, Renal Assoc., 2011–13 (Chm., 1990–2006; Dir, 2010–11); Mem. Appraisal Cttees, NICE, 2000–06. *Publications:* UK Renal Registry Annual Report, 1998–2013; papers in internat. renal and gen. med. jls. *Recreations:* travel, walking, cooking, theatre, music, gardening, chess, fly-fishing, swimming. *E:* terry@feest.co.uk.
See also A. S. Feest.

**FEILDEN, Sir Henry (Rudyard),** 7th Bt *cr* 1846 of Feniscowles, Lancashire; Principal of Small Animal Practice, Poole Road Veterinary Surgery, since 1998; *b* Burwash, E Sussex, 26 Sept. 1951; *o s* of Sir Henry Wemyss Feilden, 6th Bt and Ethel May (*née* Atkinson); *S* father, 2010; *m* 1st, 1982, Anne, *d* of William Frank Bonner Shepperd (marr. diss. 1997); one *s*; 2nd, 1998, Geraldine, *d* of late Major Gerald Rayland Kendall; one *s* one *d*. *Educ:* Kent Coll., Canterbury; Bristol Univ. (BVSc 1975). MRCVS. Veterinary Surgeon: Tuckett Gray and Partners, Aylesbury, Bucks, 1976–78; Fraser and Smith, Binfield, Berks, 1978–83; L. A. Gould, Rossendale, Lancs, 1983–84; Riverside Veterinary Surgery, Bishopstoke, Eastleigh, Hants, 1996–98. Veterinary Advr, Solvay-Duphar Veterinary, Southampton, 1984–96. *Recreations:* DIY, natural history, military history, travel, fine wine, antiques, digital photography, genealogy, good company, visiting Bath. *Heir: s* William Henry Feilden, *b* 5 April 1983. *Address:* 340 Poole Road, Branksome, Poole, Dorset BH12 1AW. *T:* (01202) 765431. *Club:* Old Canterburians.

**FEILDING,** family name of Earl of Denbigh.

**FEILDING, Viscount; Peregrine Rudolph Henry Feilding;** *b* 19 Feb. 2005; *s* and heir of Earl of Denbigh, *qv*.

**FEINSTEIN, Elaine Barbara,** FRSL; writer, since 1966; *b* 24 Oct. 1930; *d* of Isidore Cooklin and Fay Cooklin (*née* Compton); *m* 1956, Arnold Feinstein; three *s*. *Educ:* Wyggeston Grammar Sch. for Girls, Leicester; Newnham Coll., Cambridge (Exhibnr, English Tripos; MA). Mem., editl staff, CUP, 1959–62; Asst Lectr, Comparative Lit. Dept, Univ. of Essex, 1968–71. Rockefeller Foundn Fellow, Bellagio, 1998. Writer of reviews for The Times, Daily Telegraph, TLS, The Guardian and other newspapers, 1975–2002; Writer in Residence: for British Council, Singapore, 1993; Tromsø, 1995. Mem. Council, RSL, 2004–11. Writer: *for television:* Breath, 1975; Lunch, 1981; The Edwardian Country Gentlewoman's Diary (12 part series), 1984; A Brave Face, 1985; *for radio:* Echoes, 1980; A Late Spring, 1981; A Day Off, 1983; Marina Tsvetaeva: a life, 1985; If I Ever Get On My Feet Again, 1987; The Man in Her Life, 1990; Foreign Girls (trilogy), 1993; A Winter Meeting, 1994; Lawrence's Women in Love (4 part adaptation), 1996; Cloudberries, 1999. Chm. Judges, T. S. Eliot Award, 1995. FRSL 1981. Hon. DLitt Leicester, 1990. Cholmondeley Award for Poetry, 1990; Soc. of Authors Travel Award, 1991. *Publications: novels:* The Circle, 1970; The Amberstone Exit, 1972; The Glass Alembic, 1973 (US edn as The Crystal Garden, 1974); Children of the Rose, 1975; The Ecstasy of Dr Miriam Garner, 1976; The Shadow Master, 1978; The Survivors, 1982; The Border, 1984; Mother's Girl, 1988; All You Need, 1989; Loving Brecht, 1992; Dreamers, 1994; Lady Chatterley's Confession, 1996; Dark Inheritance, 2001; The Russian Jerusalem, 2008; *poems:* In a Green Eye, 1966; The Magic Apple Tree, 1971; At the Edge, 1972; The Celebrants and Other Poems, 1973; Some Unease and Angels, 1977; Selected Poems, 1977; The Feast of Euridice, 1980; Badlands, 1987; City Music, 1990; Selected Poems, 1994; Daylight, 1997; (ed) After Pushkin, 1999; Gold, 2000; Collected Poems, 2002; Talking to the Dead, 2007; Cities, 2010; Portraits, 2015; The Clinic, Memory: new and selected poems, 2017; *poems in translation:* The Selected Poems of Marina Tsvetaeva, 1971, 5th revd edn 1999 (Arts Council Translation Awards, 1970, 1972); Three Russian Poets: Margarite Aliger, Yunna Moritz, Bella Akhmadulina, 1976; Bride of Ice: new selected poems by Marina Tsvetaeva, 2009; *biography:* Bessie Smith, 1986; A Captive Lion: the life of Marina Tsvetaeva, 1987; Lawrence's Women, 1993 (US edn as Lawrence and The Women, 1993); Pushkin, 1998; Ted Hughes: the life of a poet, 2001; Anna of All the Russias: a life of Anna Akhmatova, 2005; *short stories:* Matters of Chance, 1972; The Silent Areas, 1980; *autobiography:* It Goes with the Territory: memoirs of a poet, 2013; *editor:* Selected Poems of John Clare, 1968; (with Fay Weldon) New Stories, 1979; New Poetry, 1988. *Recreations:* books, music, travel, the conversation of friends. *Address:* c/o Rogers Coleridge & White, 20 Powis Mews, W11 1JN. *T:* (020) 7722 3688. *E:* ebfeinstein@btinternet.com. *Clubs:* Athenæum; PEN.

**FELDMAN,** family name of **Barons Feldman** and **Feldman of Elstree**.

**FELDMAN,** Baron *cr* 1995 (Life Peer), of Frognal in the London Borough of Camden; **Basil Feldman,** Kt 1987; a Party Treasurer, Conservative and Unionist Party, 1996; *b* 23 Sept. 1926; *s* of late Philip and Tilly Feldman; *m* 1952, Gita Julius; two *s* one *d*. *Educ:* Grocers' School. National Union of Conservative and Unionist Associations: Mem., 1975–98, Chm., 1991–96, Exec. Cttee; Vice-Chm., 1982–85, Chm., 1985–86; Vice-Pres., 1986–98; Jt Nat. Chm., Cons. Party's Impact 80s Campaign, 1982–87; Chairman: Team 1000, 1989–93; Renaissance Forum, 1996–2010; Member: Policy Gp for London, 1975–81, 1984–87; Nat. Campaign Cttee, 1976 and 1978; Adv. Cttee on Policy, 1981–86; Cttee for London, 1984–87; Greater London area: Dep. Chm., 1975–78; Chm., 1978–81; Pres., 1981–85; Vice Pres., 1985; Vice-Pres., Greater London Young Conservatives, 1975–77; President: Richmond and Barnes Cons. Assoc., 1976–84; Hornsey Cons. Assoc., 1978–82; Patron, Hampstead Cons. Assoc., 1981–86. Contested GLC Elections, Richmond, 1973; Member: GLC Housing Management Cttee, 1973–77; GLC Arts Cttee, 1976–81. Mem., H of L, 1995–2017. Mem., Free Enterprise Loan Soc., 1977–84. Chairman: Martlet Services Gp Ltd, 1973–81; Solport Ltd, 1980–85; The Quality Mark, 1987–92. Chairman: Better Made in Britain Campaign, 1983–98 (organising 22 exhbns in 14 different business sectors); Market Opportunities Adv. Gp, DTI, 1991–93; Shopping Hours Reform Council, 1988–93 (Pres., 1993–95); Better Business Opportunities, 1990–96; Watchpost Ltd, 1983–; Dir, Young Entrepreneurs Fund, 1985–95. Underwriting Mem. of Lloyd's, 1979–96. Membre Consultatif, Institut Internat. de Promotion et de Prestige, Geneva (affiliated to Unesco), 1978–96. Member: Post Office Users National Council, 1978–81 (Mem., Tariffs Sub-Cttee, 1980–81); English Tourist Board, 1986–96; Chairman: Clothing EDC (NEDO), 1978–85; Maker/User Working Party (NEDO), 1988–89. Gov., Sports Aid Foundn, 1990–2002. Chairman: London Arts Season 1993–97; Festival of Arts and Culture, 1995; Salzburg Festival Trust, London, 2000–03 (Vice Chm., 1997–2000); Mem., Internat. Council, Los Angeles Philharmonic, 1995–. Chm., Fresh Hope Trust, 2003–. Freeman, City of London, 1984. FRSA 1987. Silver Decoration of Honour, Salzburg, 2003. *Publications:* Some Thoughts on Job Creation (for NEDO), 1984; Constituency Campaigning: a guide for Conservative Party workers; several other Party booklets and pamphlets. *Recreations:* golf, tennis, theatre, opera, travel, watching football. *Club:* Carlton.

**FELDMAN OF ELSTREE,** Baron *cr* 2010 (Life Peer), of Elstree in the County of Hertfordshire; **Andrew Simon Feldman;** PC 2015; Principal, Andrew Feldman Associates, since 2016; Partner, Macro Advisory Partners, since 2017; *b* London, 25 Feb. 1966; *s* of late Malcolm Roger Feldman and of Marcia Feldman (*née* Summers); *m* 1999, Gabrielle Josephine Gourgey; two *s* one *d*. *Educ:* Haberdashers' Aske's Sch., Elstree; Brasenose Coll., Oxford (BA 1st Cl. Juris.); Inns of Court Sch. of Law. Mgt Consultant, Bain & Co., 1988–90; commercial barrister, 1 Essex Court, 1991–95. Dir, Jayroma (London) Ltd, 1995–2018. Conservative Party: Dep. Treas., 2005–08; Chief Exec., 2008–10; Chm., 2010–16; Chm. Bd, 2010–16; Mem. Bd, Cons. Party Foundn, 2010–16. Senior Advisor: Towerbrook; Tulchan Communications Gp; Policy Exchange. Trustee, BHF, 2017–. *Recreations:* tennis, golf, ski-ing, reading. *Address:* House of Lords, SW1A 0PW. *Clubs:* 5 Hertford Street, Carlton, George.

**FELDMAN, Prof. David John,** FBA 2006; Rouse Ball Professor of English Law, University of Cambridge, 2004–18, now Emeritus; Fellow of Downing College, Cambridge, 2003–18, now Emeritus; *b* 12 July 1953; *s* of late Alec Feldman and Valerie Feldman (*née* Michaelson); *m* 1983, Naomi Jill Newman; one *s* one *d*. *Educ:* Brighton, Hove and Sussex Grammar Sch.; Exeter Coll., Oxford (MA, DCL). Lectr in Law, 1976–89, Reader, 1989–92, Bristol Univ.; University of Birmingham: Barber Prof. of Jurisprudence, 1992–2000; Dean of Law, 1997–2000; Prof. of Law, 2000–04; Chm., Faculty Bd of Law, 2006–09, Faculty of Human, Social and Political Sci., 2013–16, Univ. of Cambridge. Vis. Fellow, ANU, 1989; Miegunyah Dist. Vis. Fellow, 2006, Hon. Sen. Fellow, 2019, Univ. of Melbourne; Sir J. C. Smith Sen. Vis. Scholar, Univ. of Nottingham, 2010. Legal Advr to Jt Select Cttee on Human Rights, Houses of Parlt, 2000–04. A Judge of Constitutional Court of Bosnia and Herzegovina, 2002–10 (a Vice-Pres., 2006–09). Pres., Soc. of Legal Scholars, 2010–11. FRSA. Hon. Bencher, Lincoln's Inn, 2003. Hon. QC 2008. Hon. LLD Bristol, 2013. *Publications:* Law Relating to Entry, Search and Seizure, 1986; Criminal Confiscation Orders: the new law, 1988; (ed) Criminal Investigation: reform and control, 1991; Civil Liberties and Human Rights in England and Wales, 1993, 2nd edn 2002; (ed jtly) Corporate and Commercial Law: modern developments, 1996; (ed) English Public Law, 2004, 2nd edn 2009; (ed) Law in Politics, Politics in Law, 2013; (ed jtly) Cambridge Companion to Public Law, 2015; contrib. articles on public law, human rights and criminal procedure. *Recreations:* music, dog-walking, cooking, history, theatre, cinema, law. *Address:* Downing College, Cambridge CB2 1DQ. *T:* 07816 894706.

**FELDMAN, Sally Joy**; media trainer, journalist, humanist celebrant; Honorary Fellow, Creative Industries, University of Westminster, 2016 (Senior Fellow, 2012–16); *b* 10 March 1948; *d* of Reuben Feldman and Karola Landau; *m* 1st, 1981, Tony Russell (marr. diss. 2010); one *s* one *d*; 2nd, 2010, Prof. Laurence John, (Laurie), Taylor, *qv*. *Educ*: Univ. of Reading (BA Hons English 1970); Univ. of Manitoba (MA English 1972). Freelance and editorial posts, 1970s; Press Officer, CRC and CRE, 1976–78; Editor, range of magazines: Love Affair, New Love, Loving, Woman's World, 1978–83; Woman's Hour, BBC Radio 4: Producer, 1983–86; Dep. Editor, 1986–89; Presenter, Weekend Edition, 1986; Editor, 1990–97, and Editor, range of other progs; Launch Editor, Treasure Islands; Dean: Sch. of Media, London Coll. of Printing, 1998–2002; Sch. of Media, Arts and Design, Univ. of Westminster, 2002–12. Freelance broadcaster, and journalist and reviewer. Mem., Bd of Trustees, Rationalist Assoc., 2007–. Associate Ed., New Humanist Mag. *Publications*: The Complete Desk Book, 1978; (with Laurie Taylor) In Confidence: talking frankly about fame, 2013; *novels for teenagers* (as Amber Vane): Hopelessly Devoted, 1995; Blazing Kisses, 1996; Freezing Heart, 1996; Follow the Sun, 1996; I Taught Him a Lesson He'll Never Forget, 1998. *Recreations*: voracious reading, talking, film, clothes, travel, friends and family. *T*: 07930 314259. *E*: sallyjoyfeldman@gmail.com.

**FELDMANN, Sir Marc**, Kt 2010; AC 2014; PhD; FRCP, FRCPath; FMedSci; FRS 2006; FAA; Professor, Kennedy Institute of Rheumatology, University of Oxford, 2011–14, now Emeritus; Head, Kennedy Institute of Rheumatology, University of Oxford (formerly at Faculty of Medicine, Imperial College London), 2002–14 (Head, Cytokine Biology and Immunology, 1992–2014); *b* 2 Dec. 1944; *s* of Elie and Cyla Feldmann; *m* 1966, Tania Gudinski; one *s* one *d*. *Educ*: Univ. of Melbourne (MB BS 1967, BSc Med Hons 1970; PhD 1972). FRCPath 1984; FRCP 1998. Sen. Scientist, 1974–77, Principal Scientist, 1977–85, ICRF; Prof. of Cellular Immunology, Univ. of London, 1985–2011; Dep. Dir, Charing Cross Sunley Res. Centre, 1985–92. Pres., Internat. Cytokine Soc., 2002–03. Mem., EMBO, 2006–. FMedSci 2001; FAA 2005. Crafoord Prize (with Sir R. Maini), Royal Swedish Acad. of Sci., 2000; Albert Lasker Award for Clin. Med. Res. (with Sir R. Maini), NY, 2003; Cameron Prize for Therapeutics (with Sir R. Maini), Edinburgh Univ., 2004; Internat. Rheumatoid Arthritis Award (with Sir R. Maini), Japan Rheumatism Foundn, 2007; Curtin Medal, ANU, 2007; Lifetime Achievement, Eur. Inventor Award, Europ. Patent Office, 2007; Dr Paul Janssen Award for Biomed. Res. (with Sir R. Maini), Johnson & Johnson, New York, 2008; Ernst Schering Prize (with Sir R. Maini), Ernst Schering Foundn, 2010; Canada Gairdner Award, Gairdner Foundn, 2014. *Publications*: (ed with J. J. Oppenheim) Cytokine Reference, 2001; (with R. N. Maini) Pocket Reference to TNFα Antagonist and Rheumatoid Arthritis, 2001; over 730 articles in scientific jls; 90 patents. *Recreations*: tennis, hiking, keeping fit, art, theatre. *Address*: Kennedy Institute of Rheumatology, Nuffield Department of Orthopaedics, Rheumatology and Musculoskeletal Sciences, University of Oxford, Botnar Research Centre, Windmill Road, Headington, Oxford OX3 7LD. *E*: marc.feldmann@kennedy.ox.ac.uk. *Club*: Queen's.

**FELL, Sir David**, KCB 1995 (CB 1990); novelist; Pro-Chancellor, Queen's University Belfast, 2005–14; *b* 20 Jan. 1943; *s* of Ernest Fell and Jessie (*née* McCreedy); *m* 1967, Sandra Jesse (*née* Moore); one *s* one *d*. *Educ*: Royal Belfast Academical Instn; The Queen's University of Belfast (BSc: Pure and Applied Mathematics, also (1st Cl. Hons) Physics). Sales Manager, Rank Hovis McDougall Ltd, 1965–66; Teacher, 1966–67; Research Associate, 1967–69; Civil Servant, 1969–97: Dept of Agriculture (NI), 1969–72; Dept of Commerce (NI), 1972–82 (Under Secretary, 1981); Under Secretary, Dept of Economic Development (NI), 1982; Dep. Chief Exec., Industrial Develt Bd for NI, 1982–84; Permanent Sec., Dept of Economic Develt (NI), 1984–91; Hd of NICS, and Second Perm. Under Sec. of State, NI Office, 1991–97. Chairman: Northern Bank, 1998–2005; Boxmore Internat. plc, 1998–2000; Nat. Irish Bank, 1999–2005; Harland & Wolff Gp plc, 2001–02; Titanic Quarter Ltd, 2001–03; Titanic Properties Ltd, 2001–03; Canal Corp. (USA), 2009–11; Novenso (formerly Litelighting) Ltd, 2010–12; non-exec. Chm., Goldblatt McGuigan, 2005–12; non-executive Director: Dunloe Ewart plc, 1998–2002; Nat. Australia Gp (Europe) Ltd, 1998–2012; Fred Olsen Energy ASA, 1999–2003; Chesapeake Corp. (USA), 2000–09 (Chm., 2005–09); Clydesdale Bank plc, 2004–12. Chairman: Opera NI, 1998–99; Prince's Trust Volunteers (NI), 1998–99; Prince's Trust (NI), 1999–2005; Pres., Extern Orgn, 1998–. Mem. Council, Industrial Soc., 1998–2001. CCMI; FRSA; FCIB. DUniv Ulster, 2003; Hon. LLD QUB, 2014. *Recreations*: music (opera), reading, Rugby Union, writing. *Clubs*: Old Instonians, Ulster Reform (Belfast).

**FELL, Richard Taylor**, CVO 1996; HM Diplomatic Service, retired; *b* 11 Nov. 1948; *s* of late Eric Whineray Fell and Margaret Farrer Fell (*née* Taylor); *m* 1981, Claire Gates; three *s*. *Educ*: Bootham Sch., York; Bristol Univ. (BSc); Univ. of London (MA). Joined HM Diplomatic Service, 1971; Ottawa, 1972–74; Saigon, 1974–75; Vientiane, 1975; First Sec. and Chargé d'Affaires ai, Hanoi, 1979; First Sec., UK Delegn to NATO, 1979–83; First Sec. and Head of Chancery, Kuala Lumpur, 1983–86; FCO, 1986–88; on secondment to Thorn EMI, 1988–89; Counsellor, Ottawa, 1989–93; Dep. Hd of Mission, Bangkok, 1993–96; Counsellor, FCO, 1997–2000; Acting Consul-Gen., Toronto, 2000; RCDS, 2001; High Comr, New Zealand, Governor (non-res.) of Pitcairn, Henderson, Ducie and Oeno Is, and High Comr (non-res.), Samoa, 2001–06. Chm., NZ–UK Link Foundn, 2008–11. Book Reviews Editor, RSAA, 2010–. *Publications*: Early Maps of South-East Asia, 1988. *Recreations*: antiques, reading, sport.

**FELL, William Varley**, CMG 2002; International Affairs Adviser, Cathay Pacific Airways, 2009–18; *b* 4 March 1948; *s* of late John Richmond Fell and Cicely Juliet Fell (*née* Varley); *m* 1970, Jill Pauline Warren; two *s* one *d*. *Educ*: Charterhouse; Bristol Univ. (BA Hons). With Hambros Bank, 1969–71; entered HM Diplomatic Service, 1971; 3rd Sec., Vienna, 1973–75; 2nd Sec., Havana, 1976–78; 1st Secretary: Warsaw, 1979–82; FCO, 1982–88; Counsellor, Athens, 1988–92; FCO, 1992–2002. Internat. Risk Advr, British Airways, 2002–08; Advr, Aegis Defence Services Ltd, 2009–16. Gov., Skinners' Sch., Tunbridge Wells, 2006–12 (Chm., Finance and Gen. Purposes Cttee, 2008–12). Liveryman, Skinners' Co., 2003– (Extra Mem. Ct, 2006–08; Master, 2012–13; Second Warden, 2015–16; Chairman: Lawrence Atwell's Charity, 2011–16; Charity Cttee, 2015–). Hon. Col 39 (The Skinners) Signal Regt Army Reserve, 2015–19. Trustee, Dartmoor Preservation Assoc., 2017–. *Recreations*: walking, especially on Dartmoor and in Greece, history, travel.

**FELLGETT, (Terence) Robin**, CB 2007; PhD; Deputy Head, Economic and Domestic Affairs Secretariat, Cabinet Office, 2003–11; *b* 1 Oct. 1950; *s* of Prof. Peter Berners Fellgett, FRS, and Mary Briggs; *m* 1976, Patti Douglas (marr. diss.); one *s* one *d*; *m* 2009, Rebecca Collings; one step *s*. *Educ*: Univ. of Warwick (PhD Maths 1976); Birkbeck Coll., London Univ. (MSc Econs 1984); INSEAD (AMP 1995). BP Chemicals, 1969; Asst Prof., Univ. of Maryland, 1976–78; MSC, 1979; CSD 1979–83; joined HM Treasury, 1983: held posts in expenditure, privatisation and internat. finance; Dep. Dir, then Dir, Financial Sector, 1998–2003. *Recreations*: music, travel, relaxation. *Clubs*: Jazz Café, Vortex.

**FELLNER, Eric**, CBE 2005; film producer; Co-Chairman, Working Title Films, since 1992; *b* 10 Oct. 1959; *m* (marr. diss.); three *s*; partner, Laura Bailey; one *s* one *d*. *Educ*: Cranleigh Sch.; Guildhall Sch. of Music and Drama. *Films include*: Sid and Nancy, 1986; Pascali's Island, 1988; The Rachel Papers, 1989; Hidden Agenda, 1990; A Kiss Before Dying, Liebestraum, 1991; Wild West, 1992; Posse, Romeo is Bleeding, 1993; Four Weddings and a Funeral, The Hudsucker Proxy, 1994; Loch Ness, French Kiss, Dead Man Walking, Moonlight and Valentino, Panther, 1995; Fargo, 1996; Bean, The Borrowers, The Matchmaker, 1997; Elizabeth, The Big Lebowski, What Rats Won't Do, 1998; Notting Hill, Plunkett & Macleane, 1999; O Brother, Where Art Thou?, Billy Elliot, The Man Who Cried, 2000; Bridget Jones's Diary, Captain Corelli's Mandolin, The Man Who Wasn't There, Long Time Dead, 2001; 40 Days and 40 Nights, About A Boy, Ali G Indahouse, The Guru, My Little Eye, 2002; Love Actually, Calcium Kid, Ned Kelly, Shape of Things, Johnny English, Thirteen, 2003; Thunderbirds, Bridget Jones: The Edge of Reason, Shaun of the Dead, Wimbledon, Inside I'm Dancing, 2004; Mickybo and Me, Pride and Prejudice, Nanny McPhee, The Interpreter, 2005; Sixty Six, United 93, Hot Stuff, 2006; The Golden Age, Atonement, Mr Bean's Holiday, Hot Fuzz, Gone, Smokin' Aces, 2007; Definitely Maybe, Wild Child, Burn After Reading, 2008; Frost/Nixon, State of Play, The Soloist, The Boat That Rocked, Hippie Hippie Shake, A Serious Man, 2009; Green Zone, Nanny McPhee and the Big Bang, 2010; Paul, Senna, Johnny English Reborn, Tinker, Tailor, Soldier, Spy, 2011; Anna Karenina, Les Misérables, Big Miracle, Contraband, 2012; I Give It a Year, Closed Circuit, About Time, Rush, The World's End, 2013; Two Faces of January, 2014; The Theory of Everything, Trash, Everest, Legend, We Are Your Friends, 2015; The Danish Girl, Hail Caesar, Grimsby, Bridget Jones's Baby, 2016; Baby Driver, Victoria & Abdul, The Snowman, 2017; Darkest Hour, 7 Days in Entebbe, King of Thieves, Johnny English Strikes Again, 2018; Mary Queen of Scots, The Kid Who Would Be King, 2019. Four Academy Awards; 36 BAFTA awards. *Address*: Working Title Films, 26 Aybrook Street, W1U 4AN. *T*: (020) 7307 3000; Working Title Films, 4th Floor, 9720 Wilshire Boulevard, Beverly Hills, CA 90212, USA. *T*: (310) 777 3100.

**FELLNER, Dr Peter John**; Chairman, Vernalis (formerly British Biotech) plc, since 2002 (Director, 1988–90); *b* 31 Dec. 1943; *s* of late Hans Julius Fellner and Jessica (*née* Thompson); *m* 1st, 1969, Sandra Head (*née* Smith); one *d* and one step *s*; 2nd, 1982, Jennifer Mary Zabel (*née* Butler); two step *s*. *Educ*: Sheffield Univ. (BSc Biochem. 1965); Trinity Coll., Cambridge (PhD 1968). Post-doctoral Res. Fellow, 1968–70, Associate Prof., 1970–73, Strasbourg Univ.; Searle UK Research Laboratories: Sen. Res. Investigator, 1973–77; Dir of Chem., 1977–80; Dir of Res., 1980–84; Dir of Res., Roche UK Res. Centre, 1984–86; Man. Dir, Roche UK, 1986–90; Chief Exec., 1990–2003, Chm., 2003–04, Celltech, then Celltech Chirosci., subseq. Celltech Gp plc. Chairman: Astex Pharmaceuticals (formerly Astex Technol., then Astex Therapeutics) Ltd, 2002–11 (Vice-Chm., 2011–13); Ionix Pharmaceuticals Ltd, 2002–05; Acambis plc, 2006–08; Premier Research Gp plc, 2007–08; Optos plc, 2010–15; Biotie Therapies Corp., 2010–14; Ablynx NV, 2013–18; Mereo BioPharma plc, 2015–; non-executive Director: Colborn Dawes Ltd, 1986–90; Synaptica Ltd, 1999–2002; QinetiQ Gp plc, 2004–09; UCB SA, 2005–14; Evotec AG, 2005–11; Consort Medical (formerly Bespak) plc, 2005– (Chm., 2009–). Mem., MRC, 2000–07. *Address*: Vernalis plc, 100 Berkshire Place, Wharfedale Road, Winnersh, Berkshire RG41 5RD. *T*: (0118) 938 0019.

**FELLOWES**; see Kitchener-Fellowes, family name of Baron Fellowes of West Stafford.

**FELLOWES**, family name of **Barons De Ramsey** and **Fellowes**.

**FELLOWES**, Baron *cr* 1999 (Life Peer), of Shotesham in the county of Norfolk; **Robert Fellowes**, GCB 1998 (KCB 1991; CB 1987); GCVO 1996 (KCVO 1989; LVO 1983); QSO 1999; PC 1990; Chairman, Barclays Private Bank (formerly Barclays Private Banking), 2000–09 (Vice-Chairman, 1999–2000); Secretary and Registrar of the Order of Merit, since 2003; *b* 11 Dec. 1941; *s* of Sir William Fellowes, KCVO; *m* 1978, Lady Jane Spencer, *d* of 8th Earl Spencer, LVO; one *s* two *d*. *Educ*: Eton. Scots Guards (short service commission), 1960–63. Director, Allen Harvey & Ross Ltd, Discount Brokers and Bankers, 1968–77; Asst Private Sec. to the Queen, 1977–86, Dep. Private Sec., 1986–90; Private Sec. to the Queen and Keeper of the Queen's Archives, 1990–99. Non-exec. Dir, SABMiller (formerly South African Breweries), 1999–2010. Mem., UK Governing Body, Internat. Chamber of Commerce, 2004–15. Vice-Chm., Commonwealth Educn Trust (formerly Commonwealth Inst.), 2000–16; Chm., Prison Reform Trust, 2001–08; Mem., British Liby Bd, 2007–16. Trustee: Rhodes Trust, 2000–10; Winston Churchill Meml Trust, 2001–16 (Chm., 2009–16); Mandela-Rhodes Trust, 2003–10; Chm., Voices Foundn, 2004–12. Pres., Adv. Council, Goodenough Coll., 2008–13. Gov., King Edward VII Hosp., Sister Agnes, 2010–13. *Recreations*: reading, watching cricket, golf. *Address*: No 1 Millbank, House of Lords, SW1P 3JU. *Clubs*: White's, Pratt's, MCC.

**FELLOWES OF WEST STAFFORD**, Baron *cr* 2011 (Life Peer), of West Stafford in the County of Dorset; **Julian Alexander Kitchener-Fellowes**; DL; screenwriter, actor, producer, director and lecturer (as **Julian Fellowes**); *b* 17 Aug. 1949; *s* of late Peregrine Edward Launcelot Fellowes and Olwen Mary (*née* Stuart-Jones); *m* 1990, Emma Kitchener, LVO (Lady-in-Waiting to HRH Princess Michael of Kent), *d* of Hon. Charles Kitchener; one *s*. *Educ*: Ampleforth Coll., Yorkshire; Magdalene Coll., Cambridge (BA, MA); Webber Douglas Acad. As actor: *theatre includes*: Joking Apart, Queen's, 1978; Present Laughter, Vaudeville, 1981; Futurists, RNT; *television includes*: For the Greater Good, 1991; Our Friends in the North, 1996; Aristocrats, 1999; Monarch of the Glen, 1999–2005; *films include*: Shadowlands, 1993; Damage, 1993; Tomorrow Never Dies, 1997; Place Vendôme, 1998; (co-prod.) A Married Man, 1982. As writer: *television*: Little Lord Fauntleroy, 1994 (Internat. Emmy, 1995); The Prince and the Pauper (also co-prod.), 1997; Downton Abbey (also exec. prod.), 2010, 2011, 2012 (Emmy Award for writing, 2011), 2013, 2014, 2015; Titanic, 2012; Doctor Thorne, 2016; Agatha Christie's Crooked House, 2017; *films*: Gosford Park, 2001 (NY Film Critics' Circle Award, Best Screenplay, 2001; Nat. Soc. of Film Critics of America Award, Best Screenplay, 2001; Screenwriter of Year, ShoWest, 2002; Writer's Guild Award, Best Orig. Screenplay, 2002; Academy Award, Best Orig. Screenplay, 2002); Separate Lies (also dir), 2005 (Best Directorial Debut, Nat. Bd of Review, 2006); Vanity Fair, 2005; The Young Victoria, 2009; From Time to Time, 2010 (Best Picture, Chicago Children's Film Fest., Seattle Internat. Film Fest. Youth Jury Award, Fiuggi Family Fest., Rome, Cinemagic Belfast Young Jury Award, 2010); The Tourist, 2010; Romeo & Juliet, 2013; Downton Abbey, 2019; *theatre*: Mary Poppins, Prince Edward Th., 2004, New Amsterdam, NY, 2006, Bristol Hippodrome, 2015; School of Rock, NY, 2015; Half a Sixpence, Chichester Festival Th., 2016; The Wind in the Willows, UK tour, 2016. Vice-President: Weldmar Hospicecare Trust, 2006–; RNIB, 2017– (Chm., Talking Books Appeal, 2005–); President: Thomas Hardy Soc., 2007–; Trollope Soc., 2019–; Patron, Help the Aged, Dorset, 2007–. Paul Harris Fellowship, Rotary Club, 2007. DL Dorset, 2008. Hon. DLitt Bournemouth, 2007; Hon. DArts Southampton Solent, 2010. Internat. Emmy Founders Award, 2015. *Publications*: Snobs (novel), 2004; The Curious Adventures of the Abandoned Toys (children's stories), 2007; Past Imperfect (novel), 2008; Downton Abbey: the complete scripts, Season One, 2012, Season Two, 2013, Season Three, 2014; Belgravia (novel), 2016. *Recreations*: too little sport and too much eating. *Address*: c/o 42, Palladium House, 1–4 Argyll Street, W1F 7TA. *Clubs*: Boodle's, Pratt's, 5 Hertford Street.

**FELLOWES, Julian**; see Baron Fellowes of West Stafford.

**FELLOWS, Derek Edward**, FIA; Executive Director, Securities and Investments Board, 1989–91; *b* 23 Oct. 1927; *s* of late Edward Frederick Fellows and of Gladys Fellows; *m* 1948, Mary Watkins (*d* 2013); two *d*. *Educ:* Mercers' Sch. FIA 1956. Entered Prudential Assurance Co. Ltd, 1943; Gp Pensions Manager, 1973–81; Chief Actuary, 1981–88; Man. Dir, Gp Pension Div., 1984–88; Dir, Prudential Corp. plc, 1985–88; non-exec. Dir, Countrywide Assured (formerly Hambro Guardian Assurance, then Hambro Assured), 1992–99. Mem., Occupational Pensions Bd, 1974–78; Chm., Bd of Trustees, South Bank Centre Retirement Plan, 1993–2001; Trustee, C of E Pensions Bd, 1998–2002. Church Comr, 1996–2002 (Mem., Audit Cttee, 1994–2001). FPMI 1976; Vice Pres., Inst. of Actuaries, 1980–83. *Publications:* contrib. Jl of Inst. of Actuaries. *Recreations:* music, theatre, bridge. *Club:* Actuaries'.

**FELLOWS, Jeffrey Keith**; Technical Consultant, BAE Systems, since 1999; *b* 17 Sept. 1940; *s* of Albert and Hilda May Fellows; *m* 1965, Mary Ewins; one *s*. *Educ:* Handsworth Grammar Sch.; Birmingham Univ. (BSc (Phys) Hons 1962). Royal Aircraft Establishment: joined Weapons Dept, 1962, Sect. Leader, 1973; Div. Leader, Systems Assessment Dept, 1976; Head of: Combat Mission Systems Div., 1981; Flight Systems Dept, 1983; seconded to BNSC as Dir (Projects and Technol.), 1986; Dep. Dir (Mission Systems), RAE, Farnborough, 1988–89; Asst Under Sec. of State, MoD, 1989–95; Technical Planning Dir, BAe plc, 1995–99; retired. *Publications:* various, for AGARD, IBA, US Nat. Space Foundn, etc. *Recreations:* tennis, aeromodelling.

**FELLOWS, John Walter**, CEng, FICE, FCIHT; independent transportation consultant, since 1996; *b* 27 July 1938; *s* of William Leslie Fellows and Lavinia Keziah (*née* Chilton); *m* 1964, Maureen Joyce Lewis; two *s*. *Educ:* Dudley Technical High Sch.; Wolverhampton Polytechnic; Birmingham Univ. (MSc). FICE 1990; FCIHT (FIHT 1989). Civil Engineer (pupil), Contractors Wilson Lovatt & Sons Ltd, 1954–59; Civil Engineer: CBs of Wolverhampton, Coventry and Dudley, 1959–69; joined Department of Transport, 1969: Asst Sec., Highway Maintenance Div., 1984–88; Dir, SE, 1988–90; Regl Dir (SE), DoE/DoT, 1990–94; Bd Dir, Highway Agency, 1994–96. *Publications:* papers to ICE and IHT. *Recreations:* boating, sailing, golf, music, theatre. *Address:* 17 Chinthurst Park, Shalford, Guildford, Surrey GU4 8JH. *E:* jwfellows@btopenworld.com.

**FELLOWS, Marion**; MP (SNP) Motherwell and Wishaw, since 2015; *b* 5 May 1949; *d* of John Fullarton and Marion Fullarton (*née* Wyllie); *m* 1971, George Fellows; three *c*. *Educ:* Heriot-Watt Univ. (BA Accountancy and Finance). Lectr in Business Studies, W Lothian Coll., 1992–2011. Mem. (SNP), N Lanarkshire Council, 2012–15. *Address:* House of Commons, SW1A 0AA.

**FELLS, Prof. Ian**, CBE 2000; FREng; FRSE; Professor of Energy Conversion, University of Newcastle upon Tyne, 1975–90, now Emeritus; *b* 5 Sept. 1932; *s* of late Dr Henry Alexander Fells, MBE and Clarice Fells, Sheffield; *m* 1st, 1957, Hazel Denton Scott (*d* 2017); four *s*; 2nd, 2018, Candida Jane Whitmill. *Educ:* King Edward VII School, Sheffield; Trinity College, Cambridge. MA, PhD. FInstE, FIChemE; FREng (FEng 1979); FRSE 1996. Chief Wireless Officer, British Troops in Austria, 1951–52; Lectr and Dir of Studies, Dept of Fuel Technology and Chem. Engineering, Univ. of Sheffield, 1958–62; Reader in Fuel Science, King's Coll., Univ. of Durham, 1962; Public Orator, Univ. of Newcastle upon Tyne, 1970–73. Lectures: Brough, Paisley Coll., 1977; Allerdale Wylde, Cumbria Science Socs, 1986; Fawley, Southampton Univ., 1987; Robert Spence, RSC, 1988 and 1990; Charles Parsons' Meml, Royal Soc., 1988; Clancey, City Univ., 1992; Erasmus Darwin, Lichfield Sci. and Engrg Soc., 1994; Hunter Meml, IEE, 1999; Higginson, Durham Univ., 2000; Idris Jones Meml, Cardiff, 2000; Hawksley Meml, IMechE, 2001. Pres., Inst. of Energy, 1978–79; Scientific Advr, World Energy Council, 1990–98; Special Advisor: to H of L Select Cttee for the European Communities, 1991–92; to H of C Select Cttee on Envmt, 1993–94, and on Trade and Industry, 1995–96; on Energy, Commonwealth Business Council, 2011–14. Member: Electricity Supply Res. Council, 1979–90; Sci. Consultative Gp, BBC, 1976–81; CNAA, 1987–93. Chm., New and Renewable Energy Centre, Blyth, Northumberland, 2002–05. Technical Dir, Penultimate Power UK Ltd, 2013–. Hon. Life Vice Pres., Internat. Centre for Life, 2010– (Trustee, 1995–2010). Hatfield Meml Prize, 1974; Beilby Meml Medal and Prize, 1976; Faraday Medal and Prize, 1993, Collier Medal and Lect., 1999, Royal Soc.; Melchett Medal and Lect., Royal Instn, 1999; Kelvin Medal, Royal Philosophical Soc. of Glasgow, 2002. Participator in TV series: Young Scientist of the Year, 1970; The Great Egg Race, 1970–85; Earth Year 2050, 1983; Men of Science, 1984; Take Nobody's Word For It, 1987, 1989; QED, 1987, 1991; The Human Element, 1992; What If... the Lights Go Out?, 2004. *Publications:* Energy for the Future, 1973, 2nd edn 1986; UK Energy Policy Post-Privatisation, 1991; Energy for the Future, 1995; World Energy 1923–98 and Beyond, 1998; A Pragmatic Energy Policy for the UK, 2008; contribs to professional jls. *Recreations:* sailing, painting. *Address:* 29 Rectory Terrace, Newcastle upon Tyne NE3 1YB. *T:* (0191) 285 5343. *Club:* Naval and Military.

**FELTON, Ian**; HM Diplomatic Service; Languages Team Leader, Diplomatic Academy, since 2017; *b* 16 May 1966; *m* Judith Fairbairn. Entered FCO, 1986; Southern Eur. Dept, FCO, 1986–87; Chancery, Brussels, 1987–89; worldwide floater, 1990–95, UN Dept, FCO, 1993–95; UK Mission to UN, NY, 1995–99; Dep. Hd of Mission, Cambodia, 2000–03; Prog. Manager, Engaging with the Islamic World, FCO, 2003–06; Team Leader, SE Asia and Pacific Gp, FCO, 2006–08; Ambassador to Guinea, 2008–11; Dep. High Comr, Bangalore, India, 2011–15; Global Learning and Develt Team, Human Resources Dept, FCO, 2015–17. *Address:* c/o Foreign and Commonwealth Office, King Charles Street, SW1A 2AH.

**FELTON, Lt Gen. Richard Friedrich Patrick**, CBE 2011 (OBE 2006; MBE 1997); Director General, Defence Safety Authority, 2017–19; *b* Irvine, Scotland, 13 June 1964; *s* of Richard and Marga Felton; *m* 2007, Mia Shackleton; one *s*. *Educ:* West Buckland Sch.; Hull Univ. (BSc Hons); Cranfield Univ. (MA). Joined Army, 1985; Glos Regt, NI, Germany and Canada, 1986–92 (mentioned in despatches, 1990); Recce Flt Comdr, Hildesheim, 1992–95; COS 7 Armd Bde, 1996–99; Chief of Ops, HQ Multi-Nat. Div. (SE), Bosnia, 1997; OC 669 Sqdn AAC, 1999–2001; SO Directorate of Operational Capability, MoD, 2001–03; CO 9 Regt, AAC, 2004–06; Comdr, Jt Helicopter Force, Afghanistan, 2006; Chief of Staff: 1st (UK) Armd Div., 2007–09; Multi-Nat. Div. (SW), Iraq, 2007–08; Commander: 4th Mechanized Bde, 2009–11; Task Force Helmand, Afghanistan, 2010; Chief, Jt Force Ops, 2011–13; Comdr, Jt Helicopter Comd, 2014–17; Col Comdt, AAC, 2017–. QCVS 2013. *Recreations:* fine art (Aidan Meller Galleries), scuba diving, running, poker and backgammon. *T:* 07880 730736. *E:* rfpf2@aol.com.

**FELWICK, Wing Comdr David Leonard**, CBE 2004; RAF retired; Deputy Chairman, John Lewis Partnership, 2002–04 (Director of Trading (Food), 1991–2002); *b* 9 Nov. 1944; *s* of Leonard Felwick and Mary J. Felwick (*née* Rolling); *m* 1970, Lynne Margaret Yeardley; two *s*. *Educ:* Devonport High Sch., Plymouth; RAF Coll., Cranwell. Served RAF, 1962–82. Joined John Lewis Partnership, 1982; Man. Dir, John Lewis, Welwyn, 1985–87; Dir of Selling, 1987–91, Man. Dir, 1991–2002, Waitrose Ltd. MInstD 1985. *Recreations:* ski-ing, shooting, tennis, golf. *Address:* Grange Barn, Moulsford, Wallingford OX10 9JD. *Club:* Royal Air Force.

**FENBY, Jonathan Theodore Starmer**, CBE 2000; author, analyst and journalist; *b* 11 Nov. 1942; *s* of late Charles Fenby and June (*née* Head); *m* 1967, Renée Wartski; one *s* one *d*. *Educ:* West House Sch., Birmingham; King Edward VI Sch., Birmingham; Westminster Sch.; New Coll., Oxford (BA). Reuters, 1963–77, Ed., Reuters World Service, 1973–77; correspondent in France and Germany, Economist, 1982–86; Asst Ed. and Home Ed., The Independent, 1986–88; Dep. Ed., The Guardian, 1988–93; Editor: The Observer, 1993–95; South China Morning Post and Sunday Morning Post, Hong Kong, 1995–99; Business Europe.com, 2000–01; Associate Ed., Sunday Business, 2000–01; Man. Partner, China, Trusted Sources, 2006–16; China Chm. and Dir, Eur. Political Res., TS Lombard, 2016–; contrib. to press and broadcasting in UK, Europe, US, Canada and Far East. Res. Associate, SOAS, 2002–; Associate Fellow, LSE Ideas, 2015–. Mem. Exec. Bd, China Dialogue, 2012–. Chevalier: Ordre Nat. du Mérite (France), 1992; Légion d'Honneur (France), 2013. *Publications:* Fall of the House of Beaverbrook, 1979; Piracy and the Public, 1983; International News Services, 1986; On the Brink: the trouble with France, 1998, 2nd edn 2002, updated edn as France on the Brink, 2014; Comment peut-on être français, 1999; Dealing with the Dragon: a year in the new Hong Kong, 2000; Generalissimo: Chiang Kai-shek and the China he lost, 2003; The Sinking of the Lancastria, 2005; Alliance, 2007; 70 Wonders of China, 2007; The Dragon Throne, 2008; China's Journey, 2008; The Penguin History of Modern China, 2008, 3rd edn 2019; The General: Charles de Gaulle and the France he saved, 2010; Tiger Head, Snake Tails: today's China, how it got there and where it is heading, 2012; Will China Dominate the 21st Century?, 2014, 2nd edn 2017; The Siege of Tsingtao, 2014; A History of Modern France, 2015, 2nd edn 2016; Crucible: thirteen months that forged our world, 2018; (contrib. text) Magnum China, 2018. *Recreations:* walking, belote, jazz. *Address:* 101 Ridgmount Gardens, Torrington Place, WC1E 7AZ.

**FENDER, Benjamin James**, OBE 2014; HM Diplomatic Service; Ambassador to Somalia, since 2019; *b* Oxford, 30 May 1973; *s* of Alan Fender and Hilary Fender. *Educ:* Winchester Coll.; Balliol Coll., Oxford (BA 1st Cl. PPE 1995); Harvard Univ. Entered FCO, 1996; Middle East Directorate, FCO, 1996–97; Second Sec., 1999–2001, First Sec., 2001–03, Beijing; Hd, Iran Team, FCO, 2003–07; First Sec. (Pol-Mil.), Paris, 2007–11; Political Counsellor, Kabul, 2012–14; Dep. Hd, UK Ebola Response, Sierra Leone, 2014–15; Chargé d'Affaires, 2015–16, Dep. Hd of Mission, 2016, Tehran; Hd, Security Dept, FCO, 2016–19. *Address:* c/o Foreign and Commonwealth Office, King Charles Street, SW1A 0AH.

**FENDER, Sir Brian (Edward Frederick)**, Kt 1999; CMG 1985; Chairman, BTG plc, 2003–08 (Board Member, British Technology Group, then BTG, 1992–2003); Chief Executive, Higher Education Funding Council for England, 1995–2001; *b* 15 Sept. 1934; *s* of late George Clements and of Emily Fender; *m* 1st, 1956; one *s* three *d*; 2nd, 1986, Ann Linscott (*d* 2011). *Educ:* Carlisle Grammar Sch.; Sale County Grammar Sch.; Imperial College London (ARCS, BSc 1956; DIC, PhD 1959; FIC 1997); MA Oxon 1963. FRSC; FInstP. Research Instructor, Univ. of Washington, Seattle, 1959–61; Senior Research Fellow, Nat. Chem. Lab. (now NPL), 1961–63; University of Oxford: Dept Demonstrator in Inorganic Chemistry, 1963–65; Lectr, 1965–84; Senior Proctor, 1975–76; Mem., Hebdomadal Council, 1977–80; St Catherine's College: Fellow, 1963–84 (Hon. Fellow 1986); Sen. Tutor, 1965–69; Chm., Management Cttee, Oxford Colls Admissions Office, 1973–80; Vice-Chancellor, Univ. of Keele, 1985–95. Institut Laue-Langevin, Grenoble: Asst Dir, 1980–82; Dir, 1982–85; Mem., Steering Cttee, 1974–77; Mem., Scientific Council, 1977–80. Member: SERC, 1985–90; CERN Review Cttee, 1986–87; Chairman: Science Board, SERC, 1985–90 (Mem., 1974–77); Neutron Beam Res. Cttee, 1974–77 (Mem., 1969–71); Science Planning Group for Rutherford Lab. Neutron Scattering Source, 1977–80; Member: Defence Meteorol Bd, subseq. UK Meteorol Bd, 1991–2004; Adv. Cttee, Tate Gall., Liverpool, 1988–93; West Midlands Arts Bd, 1995–2002; Bd of Conservatoire for Dance and Drama, 2002–04; Dir, Higher Aims Ltd, 2002–; Chairman: Univs and Colls Employers Assoc., 1994–95; New Victoria Th. Trust, Staffs, 2003–15; Nat. Council for Drama Trng, 2004–11; Waterways Partnership (London), 2012–18; Mitchell Arts Centre, 2012–. Pres., NFER, 1999–2007; Pres., Inst. of Knowledge Transfer, 2006–14 (Chm., 2006–11). Chm. Trustees, Willoughbridge Garden Trust, Staffs, 2008–. Member: HK UGC, 2003–07; Canals and Rivers Trust Council, 2012–18. CCMI (CBIM 1989). FInstKT 2011. Hon. Fellow, Univ. of Wales, Cardiff, 1996; Hon. FRVC 2001; Hon. FTCL 2001; Hon. FRCA 2003. DUniv: Keele, 1996; Staffordshire, 2001; Hon. DSc Ulster, 2001; Hon. DCL Northumbria, 2001; Hon. Dr jur Lincoln, 2002; Hon. DEd UWE, 2002. *Publications:* scientific articles on neutron scattering and solid state chemistry. *Recreations:* theatre, gardening, watching Manchester United. *Address:* Bishops Offley Manor, Bishops Offley, Stafford ST21 6ET. *Clubs:* Athenæum; Potters' (Stoke-on-Trent).

**FENECH-ADAMI, Hon. Dr Edward**, KUOM 1990; LLD; President of Malta, 2004–09; *b* Birkirkara, Malta, 7 Feb. 1934; *s* of late Luigi Fenech-Adami and Josephine (*née* Pace); *m* 1965, Mary (*née* Sciberras) (*d* 2011); four *s* one *d*. *Educ:* St Aloysius Coll., Malta; Royal Univ. of Malta (BA 1955, LLD 1958). Entered legal practice in Malta, 1959. Nationalist Party: Mem. Nat. Exec., 1961; Asst Gen. Sec., 1962–75; Pres., Gen. and Admin. Council, 1975–77; Leader, 1977–2004. MP Malta, 1969–2004; Shadow Minister for Labour and Social Services, 1971–77; Leader of the Opposition, 1977–82, 1983–87, 1996–98; Prime Minister, 1987–96, 1998–2004; Foreign Minister, 1989–90. Vice-Pres., European Union of Christian Democrat Parties, 1979–99. Editor, Il-Poplu (Party Newspaper), 1962–69. *Publications:* (with Steve Mallia) Eddie: my journey (autobiog.), 2014.

**FENHALLS, Richard Dorian**; Chairman, After Strand Ltd, since 2012; *b* 14 July 1943; *s* of Roydon Myers and Maureen Rosa Fenhalls; *m* 1967, Angela Sarah Allen; one *s* one *d*. *Educ:* Hilton Coll., Univ. of Natal (BA); Christ's Coll., Cambridge (MA, LLM). Attorney, S Africa, 1969. Goodricke & Son, Attorney, S Africa, 1969–70; Citibank, 1970–72; Senior Vice President: Marine Midland Bank, 1972–77; American Express Bank, 1977–81; Dep. Chm. and Chief Exec., Guinness Mahon & Co. Ltd, 1981–85; Chief Exec., Henry Ansbacher Hldgs, 1985–93; Chm., Henry Ansbacher & Co. Ltd, 1985–93; Chief Exec., 1993–2007, Dep. Chm., 2006–07, Exec. Chm., 2007–09, Chief Exec. and Dep. Chm., 2009–13, Strand Partners, later Strand Hanson Ltd. *Recreations:* sailing, veteran cars, historic car rallying. *Address:* 8b St James's Gardens, W11 4RB. *Clubs:* Royal Ocean Racing, Royal Thames Yacht; Royal Southern Yacht (Hamble); Veteran Car of GB.

**FENLON, Prof. Iain Alexander**, FSA, FRHistS; Professor of Historical Musicology, University of Cambridge, since 2005; Fellow, King's College, Cambridge, since 1976; *b* 26 Oct. 1949; *s* of Albert Fenlon and Joan (*née* Rainey); *m* 1st, 1993, Nicoletta Guidobaldi (marr. diss. 2008); 2nd, 2014, Maria José de la Torre Molina. *Educ:* Reading Univ. (BA); Birmingham Univ. (MA); St Catharine's Coll., Cambridge; King's Coll., Cambridge (MA, PhD 1977). FSA 1989; FRHistS 2016. Hayward Research Fellow, Birmingham Univ., 1974–75; Fellow, Villa I Tatti (Harvard Univ. Center for Italian Renaissance Studies), Florence, 1975–76; King's College, Cambridge: Jun. Res. Fellow, 1976–79; Sen. Res. Fellow, 1979–83; Vice-Provost, 1986–91; Sen. Tutor, 2005–08; University of Cambridge: Asst Lectr, 1979–84; Lectr, 1984–96; Reader in Historical Musicology, 1995–2005. Vis. Scholar, Harvard Univ., 1984–85; Visiting Fellow: All Souls Coll., Oxford, 1991–92; New Coll., Oxford, 1992; British Acad. Res. Reader, 1996–98; Visiting Professor: Ecole Normale Supérieure, Paris, 1998–99; Univ. of Bologna, 1999–2000; Heidelberg Univ.,

2017; Regensburg Univ., 2018. Leverhulme Res. Award, 2000–03. Founding Ed., Early Music History, 1981–. Dent Medal, Internat. Musicological Soc./Royal Musical Assoc., 1984. *Publications:* Music and Patronage in Sixteenth-Century Mantua, 2 vols, 1980, 1982; (ed) Music in Medieval and Early Modern Europe, 1981; (with J. Haar) The Early Sixteenth-Century Italian Madrigal, 1988; (with P. Miller) The Song of the Soul: understanding Poppea, 1992; Music, Print and Culture in Early Sixteenth-Century Italy, 1995; Giaches de Wert: letters and documents, 1999; Music and Culture in Late Renaissance Italy, 2002; The Ceremonial City: history, memory and myth in Renaissance Venice, 2007; Piazza San Marco, 2009; (ed with I. Groote) Heinrich Glarean's Books: the intellectual world of a sixteenth-century musical humanist, 2013; articles in various musicol jls, TLS, London Review of Books, etc. *Recreations:* travel, wine. *Address:* King's College, Cambridge CB2 1ST. *T:* (01223) 331100. *Club:* Oxford and Cambridge.

**FENLON, Yvonne Gabrielle;** *see* Doyle, Y. G.

**FENN, Robert Dominic Russell;** HM Diplomatic Service; Deputy Ambassador to Indonesia, since 2017; *b* 28 Jan. 1962; *s* of Sir Nicholas Maxted Fenn, GCMG; *m* 2002, Julia Lloyd Williams; two *s*. *Educ:* Kingswood Sch., Bath; Peterhouse, Cambridge (BA 1st Cl. Hons Classics 1983). Entered FCO, 1983; Third Sec., The Hague, 1985–88; Second Sec., Lagos, 1988–89; First Secretary: S Africa Desk, FCO, 1989–92; Human Rights, UKMIS, NY, 1992–97; (EU/Econ.), Rome, 1997–2001; Dep. Hd, Southern Eur. Dept, later Team Leader, E Mediterranean (Cyprus/Greece/Turkey), FCO, 2001–04; Dep. High Comr, Nicosia, 2004–08; High Comr, Brunei, 2009–13; Hd, Human Rights and Democracy Dept, FCO, 2013–17. *Recreations:* reading, poetry, armchair architecture. *Address:* c/o Foreign and Commonwealth Office, King Charles Street, SW1A 2AH. *E:* rob.fenn@fco.gov.uk.

**FENNELL, Alister Theodore, (Theo);** jewellery designer; Creative Director, Theo Fennell Ltd, since 1997; Founder, Original Design Partnership, 2008; *b* Egypt; *s* of Maj. Alister Fennell and Verity Fennell (*née* Frith); *m* 1977, Louise MacGregor; two *d*. *Educ:* Eton Coll.; Byam Shaw Sch. of Art. Office boy, Edward Barnard & Sons, 1973–75; formed Theo Fennell, 1975; Man. Dir, Theo Fennell Ltd, 1982–97; designer and Man. Dir, Theo Fennell plc, 1997. *Recreations:* most sports and games, music, art, drawing, reading, strumming guitar with tuneless vocals, musical theatre. *Address:* Theo Fennell Ltd, 2B Pond Place, SW3 6TF. *E:* theo.fennell@theofennell.com. *Clubs:* Chelsea Arts, Saints and Sinners, Tramp; MCC, I Zingari.

**FENTEM, Prof. Peter Harold,** MBE 2011; FRCP; Emeritus Professor, University of Nottingham, 1997 (Stroke Association Professor of Stroke Medicine, 1992–97); Hon. Consultant, Nottingham City Hospital NHS Trust (formerly Nottingham Health Authority), 1976–97; *b* 12 Sept. 1933; *s* of Harold and Agnes Fentem; *m* 1958, Rosemary Hodson; two *s* two *d*. *Educ:* Bury Grammar Sch.; Univ. of Manchester (BSc 1st cl. hons 1955; MSc 1956; MB ChB Hons 1959). FRCP 1989. Hosp. appts, Manchester Royal Inf., 1959–60; Demonstrator in Path., Univ. of Manchester, 1960–61; Manchester and Cardiff Royal Infs, 1961–64; Lectr in Physiol., St Mary's Hosp. Med. Sch., 1964–68; University of Nottingham: Sen. Lectr in Physiol., 1968; Reader, 1975; Prof. of Physiol., 1975–92; Dean of Medicine, 1987–93. Chm., BSI Tech. Sub-Cttee on Compression Hosiery, 1978–89; Sci. Sec., Fitness and Health Adv. Gp, Sports Council, 1981; Civil Consultant to RAF, 1983–2000; Hon. Consultant to Army, 1989–97; Member: Army Personnel Res. Cttee, 1983–93 (Chm., Applied Physiol. Panel, 1986–93); GMC, 1988–93; Trent RHA, 1988–90; DoH Physical Activity Task Force, 1993–96; Nat. Alliance for Physical Activity, 1997–99; Nat. Heart Forum, 1997–. Trustee: Age Concern Essex, 1999–2008; Stroke Assoc., 2000–08. *Publications:* (jt author): Exercise: the facts, 1981; Work Physiology, in Principles and Practice of Human Physiology, 1981; The New Case for Exercise, 1988; Benefits of Exercise: the evidence, 1990; (Adv. Editor) Physiology Integrated Clinical Science, 1983. *Recreations:* gardening, walking.

**FENTIMAN, Prof. Richard Griffith;** Professor of Private International Law, University of Cambridge, since 2011; Fellow, Queens' College, Cambridge, since 1981; *b* Sevenoaks, Kent, 3 April 1956; *s* of late Denis and Olwen Fentiman; *m* 1986, Alicia Jewett. *Educ:* St John's Sch., Leatherhead; Brasenose Coll., Oxford (Collins Schol.; BA 1977; BCL 1978; MA 1980). Admitted as solicitor, 1981; Articled Clerk and Solicitor, Clifford Chance, 1979–81; University of Cambridge: Asst Lectr in Law, 1985–89; Lectr in Law, 1989–2000; Reader in Private Internat. Law, 2000–12; Chm. Bd, Faculty of Law, 2015–18. Vis. Fellow in Private Internat. Law, British Inst. of Internat. and Comparative Law, 1989–97; Visiting Professor: Inst. of Comparative Law in Japan, Tokyo, 1989; Cornell Law Sch., 1992; Walter Ganshof van der Meersch Prof., Univ. Libre de Bruxelles, 2001; delivered Special Course, Hague Acad. of Internat. Law, 2002. Member: Internat. Acad. of Comparative Law, 2004–; Amer. Law Inst., 2007–. Member, Editorial Board: Jl Private Internat. Law, 2005–; Law and Financial Mkts Rev., 2010–. Hon. QC 2019. Hon. Dr Athens, 2018. Pilkington Prize, Univ. of Cambridge, 2014. *Publications:* (ed) Conflict of Laws, 1996; Foreign Law in English Courts, 1998; (ed jtly) L'espace judicaire européen en matières civile et commercial, 1999; International Commercial Litigation, 2010, 2nd edn 2015; contrib. articles on private internat. law and internat. civil procedure. *Recreations:* wine, conversation, travel. *Address:* Queens' College, Cambridge CB3 9ET. *T:* (01223) 335511. *E:* rgf1000@cam.ac.uk.

**FENTON, Ernest John;** Director General, Association of Investment Trust Companies, 1993–97; *b* 14 Oct. 1938; *s* of Forbes Duncan Campbell Fenton and Janet Burnfield Fenton (*née* Easson); *m* 1965, Ann Ishbel Ramsay; one *s* two *d*. *Educ:* Harris Acad., Scotland. CA 1961; CFA (AIIMR 1972). Partner, W. Greenwell & Co., 1968–87; Chm. and Chief Exec., Greenwell Montagu Stockbrokers, 1987–92. Non-executive Director: Fleming Income & Capital Investment Trust PLC, 1991–2002; Cotesworth & Co. Ltd (Lloyd's Managing Agents), 1994–2001; Renaissance US Growth and Income Trust PLC, 1996–2014 (Chm., 2004–14); US Special Opportunities (formerly BFS US Special Opportunities) Trust plc, 2001–08. Farmer, Kent and Sussex, 1973–. Proprietor, Fenton's Rink, Kent, 2004–. Mem. Investment Cttee, CRC, 1995–98. MCSI (MSI 1986); MInstD 1994. FRSA 1993. *Recreation:* curling. *Address:* Dundale Farm, Dundale Road, Tunbridge Wells, Kent TN3 9AQ.

**FENTON, Frances Ellen;** *see* McCarthy, F. E.

**FENTON, James Martin,** FRSL; FSA; writer; Professor of Poetry, University of Oxford, 1994–99; *b* 25 April 1949; *s* of late Rev. Canon John Charles Fenton and Mary Hamilton (*née* Ingoldby). *Educ:* Durham Choristers Sch.; Repton Sch.; Magdalen Coll., Oxford (MA). Hon. Fellow, 1999). FRSL 1983; FSA 2006. Asst Literary Editor, 1971, Editorial Asst, 1972, New Statesman; freelance correspondent in Indo-China, 1973–75; Political Columnist, New Statesman, 1976–78; German Correspondent, The Guardian, 1978–79; Theatre Critic, Sunday Times, 1979–84; Chief Book Reviewer, The Times, 1984–86; Far East Corresp., 1986–88, columnist, 1993–95, The Independent. Trustee, Nat. Gall., 2002–09; Visitor, Ashmolean Mus., 2002. FRSA 2003. Queen's Gold Medal for Poetry, 2007; PEN Pinter Prize, 2015. *Publications:* Our Western Furniture, 1968; Terminal Moraine, 1972; A Vacant Possession, 1978; A German Requiem, 1980; Dead Soldiers, 1981; The Memory of War, 1982; (trans.) Rigoletto, 1982; You Were Marvellous, 1983; (ed) The Original Michael Frayn, 1983; Children in Exile, 1984; Poems 1968–83, 1985; (trans.) Simon Boccanegra, 1985; The Fall of Saigon, in Granta 15, 1985; The Snap Revolution, in Granta 18, 1986; (ed) Cambodian Witness: the autobiography of Someth May, 1986; (with John Fuller) Partingtime Hall (poems), 1987; All the Wrong Places: adrift in the politics of Asia, 1988; Manila Envelope, 1989; (ed) Underground in Japan, by Rey Ventura, 1992; Out of Danger (poems), 1993; Leonardo's Nephew, 1998; The Strength of Poetry, 2001; A Garden from a Hundred Packets of Seed, 2001; An Introduction to English Poetry, 2002; The Love Bomb (3 dramatic works for music), 2003; Selected Poems, 2006; Samuel Taylor Coleridge: poems selected by James Fenton, 2006; School of Genius: a history of the Royal Academy, 2006; (ed) The New Faber Book of Love Poems, 2006; (ed) D. H. Lawrence: selected poems, 2008; Yellow Tulips: poems 1968–2011, 2012; (adapted) The Orphan of Zhao, 2012. *Address:* United Agents Ltd, 12–26 Lexington Street, W1F 0LE. *E:* wasserman@kwlit.com.

**FENTON, Mark Alexander,** PhD; Chief Executive, Grammar School Heads Association, since 2019; *b* 20 Oct. 1965; *s* of Prof. George and Dr Sylvia Fenton. *Educ:* Peterhouse, Cambridge (BA 1987; MA); Anglia Poly. Univ. (MSc 1993; PhD 1997); Univ. of Buckingham (DipEd Law 1998). Teacher of Hist., Boswells Sch., Chelmsford, 1988–91; Head of Hist. and Politics, 1991–97, Sen. Teacher, 1994–97, King Edward VI Grammar Sch., Chelmsford; Dep. Headteacher, Sir Joseph Williamson's Mathematical Sch., Rochester, 1997–2001; Headmaster, Dr Challoner's Grammar Sch., Amersham, 2001–16; Exec. Headteacher, Ealing Fields Acad. Trust, 2014–16; Chief Master, King Edward's Sch., Birmingham, 2016–18; Headmaster, Schs of King Edward VI in Birmingham, 2016–18. Chm., Grammar Sch. Hds Assoc., 2012–13 (Nat. Vice Chm., 2011–12 and 2013–14). Bd Mem., Bucks Acad. of Sch. Leadership, 2004–10 (Chm., 2005–08); a Nat. Leader of Educn, 2009–18. Gov., Berkhamsted Schs Gp, 2014–. Trustee: The Cricket Foundn, 2005–08; Internat. Boys' Schs Coalition, 2014–18. Dir, Ramsey Singers, 1987–; Manager, Bucks County U13 Cricket, 2001–05, U15 Cricket, 2005–; Schools' Rep., 2002–10, Youth Cricket Dir, 2012–16, Bucks Cricket Bd; Chm., Bucks Schs Cricket Assoc., 2004–16 (on secondment to British Council SLANT Project (Trinidad and Tobago), 2006–11). *Publications:* articles in educn mgt jls. *Recreations:* singing in and conducting choirs; watching, coaching, umpiring and talking about cricket; golf. *Clubs:* Lansdowne, MCC.

**FENTON, Shaun Alan,** MA, MEd; Headmaster, Reigate Grammar School, since 2012; *b* Liverpool, 1969; *s* of late Shane Fenton (*né* Bernard William Jewry), (Alvin Stardust) and Iris Fenton; two *s*. *Educ:* Haberdashers' Aske's Sch., Elstree; Keble Coll., Oxford (BA, MA PPE; MEd Educnl Leadership; PGCE); Nat. Coll. for Sch. Leadership (NPQH). Teacher: Bishopshalt Sch., 1994–96; The Ridings Sch., Yorks, 1996–98; Dep. Headteacher, Sandringham Sch., 1998–2000; Mem., Sch. Mgt and Improvement Service, Herts Educn Authy, 2000–01; Headteacher, Sir John Lawes Sch., Harpenden, 2001–06; Headmaster, Pate's Grammar Sch., Cheltenham, 2006–12; Principal, Pate's Acad., 2010–12. Partner, Cheltenham All Saints Acad. (Gov., 2011). Mem., Partnership Adv. Gp, Univ. of Herts, 2004–06. Chairman: Nat. GS Heads' Assoc., 2008–10; HMC, 2018–19 (Addnl Mem., 2007, Full Mem., 2012–); Member: Nat. GS Assoc., 2006–; Nat. Headteacher Steering Gp for Sci. Colls, 2010–; Cttee, Freedom and Autonomy for Schs – Nat. Assoc. (formerly Foundn, Aided Schs and Academies Nat. Assoc.); Partnership Gp, UCAS. Trustee, AQA, 2012–18. Local Leader of Educn, 2010–11, Nat. Leader, 2011–. FRSA. *Address:* Reigate Grammar School, Reigate Road, Reigate, Surrey RH2 0QS. *Clubs:* Lansdowne, East India, National Liberal.

**FENWICK, John James,** CBE 2013; Vice Lord-Lieutenant, Tyne and Wear, 2002–07; Deputy Chairman, Fenwick Ltd, 1972–79 and 1997–2013 (Managing Director, 1972–82; Chairman, 1979–97); Director, Northern Rock plc (formerly Northern Rock Building Society), 1984–99; *b* 9 Aug. 1932; *e s* of James Frederick Trevor Fenwick; *m* 1957, Muriel Gillian Hodnett; three *s*. *Educ:* Rugby Sch.; Pembroke Coll., Cambridge (MA). Chairman: Northumberland Assoc. of Youth Clubs, 1966–71; Retail Distributors Assoc., 1977–79; Vice Chm., National Assoc. of Citizens Advice Bureaux, 1971–79; Regional Dir, Northern Bd, Lloyds Bank, 1982–85. Member: Newcastle Diocesan Bd of Finance, 1964–69; Retail Consortium Council, 1976–79; Post Office Users' Nat. Council, 1980–82; Civic Trust for NE, 1979–96. Governor: Royal Grammar Sch., Newcastle upon Tyne, 1975–2000 (Chm. Govs, 1987–2000); St Paul's Girls' Sch., 1988–2001 (Chm. Govs, 1995–2001); Moorfields Eye Hosp., 1981–86; Royal Shakespeare Theatre, 1985–2002. Master, Mercers' Co., 1991–92. DL Tyne and Wear, 1986. Hon. DCL Northumbria, 1993. *Recreations:* travel, reading, walking. *Address:* London, SW6. *Clubs:* Garrick, MCC.

**FENWICK, Justin Francis Quintus;** QC 1993; a Recorder, since 1999; a Deputy High Court Judge, since 2003; *b* 11 Sept. 1949; *s* of David and Maita Fenwick; *m* 1975, Marcia Mary Dunn; one *s* three *d*. *Educ:* Ampleforth Coll., York; Clare Coll., Cambridge (MA Mod. Langs and Architectural Hist.). Commnd Grenadier Guards, 1968; Adjt, 2nd Battalion, 1977–79; Temp. Equerry to HRH the Duke of Edinburgh, 1979–81. Called to the Bar, Inner Temple, 1980, Bencher, 1997. Hd of Chambers, 4 New Square, 2000–05. Dir, Bar Mutual Indemnity Fund Ltd, 1997–2013 (Chm., 1999–2013); Dir, 1982–, Man. Dir, 2006–, By Pass Nurseries Ltd; Dir, 1984–, Man. Dir, 2006–, Chelsea Gardener Ltd. Comr, Royal Hospital Chelsea, 2011–17 (Dep. Chm., 2015–17). *Recreations:* wine, shooting, reading. *Address:* 4 New Square, Lincoln's Inn, WC2A 3RJ. *T:* (020) 7822 2000. *Club:* Garrick.

**FENWICK, Sir Leonard (Raymond),** Kt 2008; CBE 2000; Chief Executive, Newcastle upon Tyne Hospitals NHS Foundation Trust (formerly NHS Trust), 1998–2017; *b* Newcastle upon Tyne, 10 Aug. 1947; *s* of late Leo Stanislaws Fenwick and Hilda May Fenwick (*née* Downey); *m* 1969, Jacqueline Simpson; one *d*. Joined NHS as mgt trainee; mgt roles at Newcastle Gen. Hosp., then at Freeman Hosp.; Chief Exec., Freeman Gp of Hosps NHS Trust, 1990–98. Hon. DSc Newcastle upon Tyne, 2006.

**FENWICK, Lex;** Chairman and Chief Executive Officer, Heckyl Technologies, New York, since 2017; Founder, Selector Consultancy LLC, 2014; *b* 21 March 1959; *s* of Benedict and Deirdre Fenwick; *m* 1990, Sophie Crichton-Stuart; two *d*. Bloomberg LP, 1996–2012: Man. Dir, Bloomberg Europe, ME and Africa, 1996–2000; Chief Operating Officer, 2001–02; CEO, 2002–08; Founder and CEO, Bloomberg Ventures, 2008–12; CEO, Dow Jones & Co., 2012–14. Non-executive Director: Phorm Corpn, 2015–; DueDil, 2015–17. *Recreations:* art, music.

**FENWICK, Mark Anthony;** Director, 1977–2017, and Chairman, 1997–2017, Fenwick Ltd; Manager of Roger Waters, since 1991; *b* Newcastle upon Tyne, 11 May 1948; *s* of John and Sheila Fenwick; *m* 1972, Margaret Kathleen Hue-Williams; one *s* one *d*. *Educ:* Millfield. Joined EG Management; on tour with T-Rex; Manager: Emerson Lake and Palmer; Roxy Music and Bryan Ferry, 1972–85; worked in the property business, 1985–91. *Address:* MFM Ltd, 7 Melbray Mews, 158 Hurlingham Road, SW6 3NS. *E:* markfenwick@mfm.london. *Club:* George.

**FENWICK, Mary;** *see* Nightingale, M.

**FENWICK, Peter Brooke Cadogan,** FRCPsych; Consultant Neuropsychiatrist, Maudsley Hospital, 1977–96, now Emeritus; President, Scientific and Medical Network, since 2003 (Chairman, 1987–2000); *b* 25 May 1935; *s* of Anthony Fenwick and Betty (*née*

Darling); *m* 1963, Elizabeth Roberts; one *s* two *d*. *Educ*: Stowe Sch.; Trinity Coll., Cambridge (BA 1957; MB BChir 1960); DPM London 1966. FRCPsych 1986. House Officer, St Thomas' Hosp., 1960–62; SHO in Psychiatry, Middlesex Hosp., 1962–64; MRC Fellow, Nat. Hosp., 1964–66; Registrar, then Sen. Registrar, Maudsley Hosp., 1967–74; Consultant Neurophysiologist: Westminster Hosp., 1974–77; St Thomas' Hosp., 1974–96, now Hon. Consulting Neurophysiologist; Cons. Neuropsychiatrist, Radcliffe Infirmary, Oxford, 1989–2002, now Emeritus; Hon. Cons. Neurophysiologist, Broadmoor Special Hosp., 1972–; Hon. Sen. Lectr, Inst. of Psychiatry, London Univ., 1974–; Sen. Vis. Scientist, 2000, Res. Fellow, 2001–09, RIKEN IBrain Sci. Inst., Japan, 2000–09. Forensic expert on automatism and sleep disorders; has given expert neuropsychiatric evidence in many civil and criminal legal cases; res. into experiences of dying in hospices and nursing homes in UK and Holland; internat. lectr. Consultant, Music and the Brain documentary series, 1986. Ver Hayden de Lancey Prize, Cambridge Univ., 1987. *Publications*: with Elizabeth Fenwick: The Truth in the Light, 1995; The Hidden Door, 1997; Past Lives, 1999; The Art of Dying, 2008; over 200 contribs to learned jls. *Recreations*: flying, hill walking, wind and water turbines, the study of consciousness. *Address*: 42 Herne Hill, SE24 9QP. *T*: (020) 7274 3154.

**FENWICK, Rt Rev. Dr Richard David**; Bishop of St Helena, 2011–18; *b* 3 Dec. 1943; *s* of Ethel May and William Samuel Fenwick; *m* 1975, Dr Jane Elizabeth Hughes; one *s* one *d*. *Educ*: Glantâf Secondary Modern Sch.; Monkton House; Canton High Sch., Cardiff; Univ. of Wales, Lampeter (BA, MA, PhD); Trinity Coll., Dublin (MusB, MA); Fitzwilliam Coll., Cambridge; Ridley Hall, Cambridge. FLCM; FTCL. Ordained deacon, 1968, priest, 1969; Assistant Curate: Skewen, 1968–72; Penarth with Lavernock, 1972–74; Priest-Vicar, Succentor and Sacrist of Rochester Cathedral, 1974–78; Minor Canon, 1978–83, Succentor, 1979–83, Warden of the Coll. of Minor Canons, 1981–83, St Paul's Cathedral; Vicar, St Martin's, Ruislip, 1983–90; Priest-Vicar of Westminster Abbey, 1983–90; Canon Residentiary and Precentor, 1990–97, Sub-Dean, 1996–97, Guildford Cathedral; Dean of Monmouth, 1997–2011. Chm., Liturgical Commn of the Church in Wales, 1998–2011. Chm., Cttee for Archbp of Wales' Award in Church Music, 1997–2011. Warden, Guild of Church Musicians, 1998–2011. Liveryman, Musicians' Co.; Hon. Liveryman, Co. of Gold and Silver Wyre Drawers. Hon. FVCM, 1990; Hon. FGCM, 2004. OStJ 2001. Hon. DLitt Central Sch. of Religion, 2011. Hon. Archbishop of Wales's Award in Church Music, 2012. *Publications*: contribs to various musical and theol jls. *Recreations*: travel, reading, music. *Address*: St Anne's, 1 Insole Close, Llandaff, Cardiff CF5 2HQ. *T*: (029) 2021 9291.

**FENWICK, Sir Robert (George Mappin)**, KNZM 2016 (CNZM 2007); environmentalist, professional director and entrepreneur; *b* Auckland, NZ, 5 May 1951; *s* of Dr George Fenwick and Ethel Fenwick (*née* Mappin); *m* 1988, Jennie Beatty; three *d*. *Educ*: King's Coll., Auckland. Reporter: Auckland Star, 1969–71; Radio Hauraki, 1972–73; consultant: Fenwick PR Ltd, 1974–76; Allan Fenwick McCully, 1977–86; Co-founder: NZ Natural Ltd, bottled water, 1986; Living Earth Ltd, organic waste processing, 1994; Te Matuku Bay Oysters Ltd, 1999 (Dir, 1999–). Co-founder: NZ Business Council for Sustainable Develt, 1998 (Emeritus Chm., 1998–); BlueGreens Envmtl Policy Unit, 1998. Chairman: Govt Waste Adv. Bd, 2009–14; Sustainable Adv. Bd, Air NZ, 2014–. Chm., Adv. Bd, Westpac Bank, 2015–. Chairman: Antarctic Heritage Trust, 1996–2007; Landcare Res., 1997–2007; Antarctica NZ, 2007–14; NZ Antarctic Res. Inst., 2011–. Chairman: Fred Hollows Foundn NZ, 2009–15; Kiwi Trust, 2009–; Predator Free NZ, 2010–; Sustainable Seas Nat. Sci. Challenge, 2015–. Co-founder, Progressive Green Party, 1996. Director: Ngati Whatua o Orakei, 2014–; Te Papa Tongarewa Nat. Mus., 2016–. Patron: NZ Plant Conservation Network; Outlook for Someday; Trees for Survival. Chancellor, Order of St John, NZ, 2005–09. KStJ 2005. Hon. Dr Nat. Resources, Lincoln, NZ, 2006. Sir Peter Blake Medal, Sir Peter Blake Trust, 2015. *Recreations*: family, farming, gardening, sailing, reading. *Address*: Te Matuku, RD1 Orapiu Road, Waiheke Island, New Zealand. *E*: rob@fenwick.kiwi.

**FERDINAND, Nikita**; *see* Kanani, N.

**FERGUS, Prof. Sir Howard (Archibald)**, KBE 2001 (CBE 1995; OBE 1979); PhD; Deputy Governor, Montserrat, 1976–2009; Professor, University of West Indies, 2001–04; *b* 22 July 1937; *s* of Simon and Priscilla Fergus; *m* 1970, Eudora Edgecombe; one *s* two *d*. *Educ*: Univ. of W Indies (BA, PhD 1984); Univ. of Bristol (CertEd); Univ. of Manchester (MEd). Primary sch. teacher, 1955–64; secondary sch. teacher, 1964–70; Chief Educn Officer, Montserrat, 1970–74; Lectr, 1974–81, Sen. Lectr, 1981–2001, Sch. of Continuing Studies, Univ. of WI. Mem. and Speaker, Legislative Council, Montserrat, 1975–2001; Speaker, Legislative Assembly, 2014–15. Supervisor of Elections, 1978–2009. Hon. DD WI Sch. of Theology, Trinidad and Tobago, 2010. *Publications*: Calabash of Gold (poetry), 1993; Montserrat: history of a Caribbean colony, 1994, 2nd edn 2004; Gallery Montserrat: prominent people in our history, 1996; Montserrat Versus Volcano, 1996; Hope (poetry), 1998; Lara Rains and Colonial Rites (poetry), 1998; (jtly) Montserrat: report of the election commissioners, 1999; Volcano Song: poems of an island in agony, 2000; Montserrat in the Twentieth Century: trials and triumphs, 2001; Volcano Verses, 2003; A History of Education in the British Leeward Islands, 1838–1945, 2003; (jtly) Montserrat and Montserratians, 2005; Love, Labor, Liberation in Lasana Sekou, 2007; (jtly) Breaking down the Walls, 2007; I Believe (poetry), 2008; Death in the Family: E. A. Markham 1939–2008, 2008; The Arrow Poems and Saturday Soup, 2010; Poems From Behind God Back, 2011; Obama and Other Poems, 2012; Festival at Fifty, 1962–2012, 2012; Road from Long Ground: my personal path (autobiog.), 2005; A Cloud of Witnesses: some Pentecostal Pastors of Montserrat, 2014; September Remember (poems), 2014; contrib. several book chapters and articles to learned jls. *Recreations*: reading, writing, poetry. *Address*: (home) Olveston, Montserrat, W Indies. *T*: 4912414, 4962888.

**FERGUSON, Sir Alexander Chapman**, Kt 1999; CBE 1995 (OBE 1984); Director, Manchester United Football Club Ltd, since 2013; Manager, Manchester United Football Club, 1986–2013; *b* Govan, Glasgow, 31 Dec. 1941; *s* of Alexander and Elizabeth Ferguson; *m* 1966, Catherine Holding; three *s*. *Educ*: Govan High Sch., Glasgow. Footballer; played for: Queen's Park, 1957–60; St Johnstone, 1960–64; Dunfermline Athletic, 1964–67; Glasgow Rangers, 1967–69; Falkirk, 1969–73; Ayr United, 1973–74; Manager: East Stirlingshire, 1974; St Mirren, 1974–78 (Scottish First Div. 1977); Aberdeen, 1978–86 (Scottish Premier League, 1980, 1984, 1985; Scottish Cup, 1982, 1983, 1984, 1986; Scottish League Cup, 1986; European Cup Winners Cup, 1983; UEFA Super Cup, 1983); wins with Manchester United: FA Cup, 1990, 1994, 1996, 1999, 2004; Charity Shield, later Community Shield, 1990, 1993, 1994, 1996, 1997, 2003, 2007, 2008, 2010, 2011; Premier Div., 1992–93, 1993–94, 1995–96, 1996–97, 1998–99, 1999–2000, 2000–01, 2002–03, 2006–07, 2007–08, 2008–09, 2010–11, 2012–13; League Cup, 1992, 2006, 2009, 2010; European Cup Winners Cup, 1991; UEFA Super Cup, 1991; UEFA Champions League, 1999, 2008; European-S American Cup, 1999; FIFA Club World Cup, 2008. Lectr, Business of Entertainment, Media and Sports, Harvard Business Sch., 2014–. *Publications*: A Light in the North, 1985; Six Years at United, 1992; Just Champion, 1993; A Year in the Life: the Manager's diary, 1995; (with David Meek) A Will to Win: the Manager's diary, 1997; (with Hugh McIlvanney) Managing My Life: my autobiography, 1999; The Unique Treble: achieving our goals, 2000; Alex Ferguson: my autobiography, 2013; (with Sir Michael Moritz) Leading, 2015. *Recreations*: golf, snooker.

**FERGUSON, Dr Archibald Thomas Graham**, CPhys, FInstP; Nuclear Weapons Safety Advisor, Ministry of Defence, 1994–97; *b* 27 Dec. 1928; *s* of Francis Ferguson and Annie Orr Ferguson (*née* Graham); *m* 1956, Margaret Watson; two *d*. *Educ*: Irvine Royal Acad.; Glasgow Univ. (MA 1950; PhD 1954). CPhys 1974; FInstP 1974. United Kingdom Atomic Energy Authority, Harwell Laboratory, 1953–93: Nuclear Physics Div., 1953–65; Gp Leader, High Voltage Lab., 1961–81; on secondment to Neils Bohr Inst., Copenhagen, 1965–66; Head: Scientific Admin, 1982–85; Nuclear Physics Div., 1985–90; Safety, Culham and Harwell, 1990–93. *Publications*: contrib. numerous articles in learned jls; conf. proceedings. *Recreations*: sailing, gardening.

**FERGUSON, Duncan George Robin**, FIA; Senior Independent Director, Royal London Mutual Insurance Society, 2010–17; *b* 12 May 1942; *s* of Dr R. L. Ferguson and K. I. Ferguson; *m* 1966, Alison Margaret Simpson; one *s* one *d* (and one *s* decd). *Educ*: Fettes Coll., Edinburgh; Trinity Coll., Cambridge (MA Maths and Econs 1964; DipAgSci (Agricl Econs) 1965). FIA 1970. Actuarial student, Bacon & Woodrow, 1965–69; Actuary and Asst Gen. Manager, Metropolitan Life, Cape Town, 1969–72; Actuary and Dir, Nation Life, 1972–75; Dir, Internat. Div., Eagle Star, 1975–88; Partner, 1988, Sen. Partner, 1994–2001, Bacon & Woodrow; Sen. Partner, B & W Deloitte, and Partner, Deloitte & Touche, 2001–03. Non-executive Director: HBOS Financial Services (formerly Halifax), 1994–2007; Illium Insce, 2003–05; Windsor Life, 2004–11; Henderson, 2004–13; non-exec. Chm., Phoenix Life Assurance Ltd (formerly Resolution Gp Life Assurance Co.), 2003–09. Pres., Inst. of Actuaries, 1996–98. *Publications*: Unit Linked Life Assurance in South Africa, 1972; Life Assurance Solvency and Insolvency, 1976; Business Projections: a critical appraisal, 1980; Review of Law Relating to Insolvent Life Assurance Companies and Proposals for Reform, 1984; Reasonable Expectations of Policy Holders, 1984. *E*: dferguson@europe.com.

**FERGUSON, Edward Alexander de Poulton**; Minister Counsellor Defence, Washington, since 2018; *b* Oslo, 15 March 1978; *s* of Brig. John Gordon Goddard de Poulton Ferguson, OBE, DL and Celia Mary Ferguson, MBE; *m* 2007, Caroline Evelyn Vera Harris; one *s* two *d*. *Educ*: Trinity Coll., Oxford (BA 1st Cl. Hons Lit.Hum. 2001); London Sch. of Econs and Pol Sci. (MSc Dist. Diplomacy and Internat. Strategy 2012). Ministry of Defence: fast-stream grad. posts, 2001–04; Proj. Manager, Defence Estates, 2004–06; Political Advr, Maysaan Battlegroup, Iraq, 2006; Asst Hd, N America and Western Europe, 2006–07; Private Sec. to Sec. of State for Defence, 2007–09; Head: Afghanistan and Pakistan Policy, 2009–11; Defence Strategy and Priorities, 2011–14; Ambassador to Bosnia and Herzegovina, 2014–18. Hon. Fellow, Strategy and Security Inst., Univ. of Exeter, 2019–. Assembly Mem., Centre for Investigative Journalism, Bosnia and Herzegovina, 2019–. *Recreations*: family, singing, theatre, long walks and a good book. *Address*: HBDS, British Embassy Washington DC, BFPO 2. *E*: edward.ferguson956@mod.gov.uk.

**FERGUSON, George Robin Paget**, CBE 2010; Founder and Owner, Tobacco Factory Arts Centre, South Bristol, since 1995; Director, Tobacco Factory Enterprises Ltd, since 2003; Chairman, Ferguson Mann (formerly Acanthus Ferguson Mann) Architects, 2002–12 (Director, 1988–2012); *b* 22 March 1947; *s* of late Robert Spencer Ferguson and Eve Mary Ferguson; *m* 1969, Lavinia (*née* Clerk) (marr. diss. 2000); one *s* two *d*. *Educ*: Wellington Coll.; Univ. of Bristol (BA, BArch). RIBA. Mem. (L), Bristol CC, 1973–79. Contested (Lib/Alliance) Bristol West, 1983, 1987. First Elected Mayor of Bristol (Ind.), 2012–16. Commenced own architectural practice as sole practitioner, 1971; Founder and Dir, Acanthus Associated Architectural Practices Ltd, 1986–2005; Dir, Concept Planning Gp, 1991–2003. Pres., RIBA, 2003–05. Dir, Acad. of Urbanism, 2006–11. Chm., Bristol Beer Factory (Bristol Brewing Co. Ltd), 2006–; Director: Pierian Centre Community Interest Co., 2008–11; Brewery Lofts Ltd, 2017–. Presenter: The Architecture Show, TV, 1998; Demolition, C4, 2005–06; Building Britain, BBC, 2007; Columnist, Bristol Evening Post, 2008–10. Chm., Bristol Exploratory, 1993–2001; Pres., Avon Youth Assoc., 1999–2015; Dir, Canteen West Ltd, 2010–; Trustee: Greater Bristol Foundn, 1995–2001; Bristol Cathedral Trust, 1999–2002; Demos, 2008–10; Arnolfini Art Gall., 2009–12; Bristol Univ. Student Union, 2011–15. Gov., UWE, 1995–99. Architect to RWA, 1997–2007. High Sheriff, Bristol, 1996–97. Hon. Mem., AIA, 2004. Hon. FRIAS 2011. Hon. MA Bristol, 1999; Hon. DDes UWE, 2003. RIBA Awards; Civic Trust Awards; RICS Awards. *Publications*: Races Against Time, 1983. *Recreations*: the arts, travel, people, ideas, challenging the establishment, making things happen. *Address*: Tobacco Factory, Raleigh Road, Bristol BS3 1TF. *W*: peopleandcities.com, www.twitter.com/georgefergusonx.

**FERGUSON, Iain William Findlay**; QC (Scot.) 2000; *b* 31 July 1961; *s* of James Thomas Ferguson and Catherine Doris (*née* Findlay); *m* 1992, Valérie Laplanche; two *s*. *Educ*: Univ. of Dundee (LLB Hons; DipLP). Admitted Faculty of Advocates, 1987; Standing Junior Counsel: MoD (Army), 1991–98; Scottish Exec., Planning, 1998–2000. *Recreations*: cycling, cooking. *Address*: 16 McLaren Road, Edinburgh EH9 2BN. *T*: (0131) 667 1751.

**FERGUSON, Ian Stewart**, CBE 2005; Director and Chairman of Trustees, Employee Benefit Trust, Metaswitch Networks (formerly Data Connection Ltd), since 1988 (Chief Executive, 1981–2008; Chairman, 1981–2010); *b* 22 Feb. 1943; *s* of John Smith Ferguson and Victoria Alexandra Ferguson (*née* Luscombe); *m* 1st, 1967, Wilma Murray (marr. diss. 1991); one *s* one *d*. *Educ*: High Sch. of Glasgow; Univ. of Glasgow (BSc Hons Maths 1965). Unilever, 1965–70; IBM, 1970–81. Dir, Business Link London, 1995–97. Member: Modern Apprenticeship Adv. Cttee, DfES, 2001; LSC, 2001–10 (Chm., Young Peoples' Learning Cttee, 2004–07); 14–19 Govt Wkg Gp, 2003–04; Skills Commn, 2011–; Deputy Chairman: Apprenticeship Task Force, 2003–05; Apprenticeship Ambassadors Network, 2006–14; Member, Board: QCA, 2003–08 (Chm., Qualifications and Skills Adv. Gp, 2003–08); UK Skills, 2004–15; Trng and Develt Agency for Schs, 2006–09; Mem., Young People's Learning Agency, 2010–12; non-exec. Dir and Chair, Risk and Audit Cttee, DFE, 2016–; Chm. Bd, Educn and Skills Funding Agency, 2017–19. Confederation of British Industry: Mem., Nat. Council, 1998–99; Member: Educn and Skills (formerly Educn and Trng Affairs) Cttee, 2003–12; Educn Funding Agency Adv. Gp, 2012–17. Mem., Educn Adv. Gp, RSC, 2012–. FRSA 2006. *Recreations*: theatre, opera, music, skiing, food, wine, family, philosophy, human condition. *Address*: Metaswitch Networks, 100 Church Street, Enfield EN2 6BQ. *T*: (020) 8366 1177, *Fax*: (020) 8363 5062. *E*: ian.ferguson@metaswitch.com.

**FERGUSON, Sir Mark Edward J.**; *see* Johnson-Ferguson.

**FERGUSON, Prof. Mark William James**, CBE 1999; PhD; FMedSci; FDSRCSE, FFDRCSI; Professor, Faculty of Life Sciences (formerly School of Biological Sciences), University of Manchester, 1984–2012, now Honorary Professor of Life Sciences; Director General, Science Foundation Ireland, and Chief Scientific Adviser to the Government of Ireland, since 2012; *b* 11 Oct. 1955; *s* of late James Ferguson and of Elenor Gwendoline Ferguson; *m* (marr. diss.); two *d*; *m* Dr Sharon O'Kane; one *d*. *Educ*: Queen's Univ., Belfast (BSc 1st Cl. Hons Anatomy 1976; BDS 1st Cl. Hons Dentistry 1978; PhD Anatomy and Embryology 1982). FFDRCSI 1990; FDSRCSE 1997. Winston Churchill Travelling Fellow, 1978; Lectr in Anatomy, QUB, 1979–84; Head, Dept of Cell and Structural Biology, 1986–92, Dean, Sch. of Biol Scis, 1994–96, Univ. of Manchester. Founder and Chm. of Bd, Manchester Biotechnology Ltd, 1997–99; Founder, 1998, CEO, 2000–11, non-exec. Chm., 2011–12, Renovo Ltd, later Renovo Gp plc. Chm., Health and Life Scis Panel, Tech. Foresight Prog., OST, 1994–99; Member: Lord Sainsbury's Biotech. Cluster Cttee, DTI, 1999; Biol Sub Cttee, Cttee of Safety of Medicines, 1999–2005; Genome Valley Steering Gp, DTI, 2000–01; Preclinical Medicine, Anatomy, Physiol. and Pharmacol. Panel, RAE 2001, HEFCE; Life Sci. Mktg Bd, UK Trade & Investment, 2008–11; Bd, Sci. Foundn Ireland, 2012–; Bd, Forfás, 2012–14. Chm., EU country review of Hungarian Res. and Innovation Systems, 2016; Member: High Level Gp for H2020, EU Commn, 2017; Governing Bd, EC Jt Res. Centre, 2017–; Governing Bd, Global Res. Council, 2018–; Chm., Internat. Rev. Panel, Innovation Fund Denmark, 2018–19. President: Med. Scis Section, BAAS, 1997; Bd, BioIndustry Assoc., 2001–03; European Tissue Repair Soc., 2002–03 (Sec., 1996–2007); Manchester Med. Soc., 2009–10. Gov., Res. into Ageing, 1995–2000. Steeger Vis. Prof. and Lectr, NY Univ. Med. Center, 1992; Lectures: Teale, RCP, 1994; Kelvin, IEE, 1995; Broadhurst, Harvard Med. Sch., 1996; Distinguished, Amer. Soc. of Human Genetics, 1998; Northcroft, British Orthodontic Soc., 2001; Langdon-Brown, RCP, 2002; Cairns, British Soc. Neurol Surgery, 2008; Sir Bernard Crossland, QUB, 2015. British Council lecture tours: India, 1999, China, 2002. Founder FMedSci 1998. Mem., World Econ. Forum, Davos, 2007– (Tech. Pioneer, 2007–09). Hon. FIAE 2014. Hon. DMedSci QUB, 2002. John Tomes Prize and Medal, 1990, Charles Tomes Prize and Medal, 1998, RCS; Carter Medal, Clin. Genetics Soc., 1997; Internat. Assoc. for Dental Res. Award, 2000; Körber European Science Award, 2002; N. Rowe Lecture and Prize, BAOMS, 2003; Eur. Biotechnia Award, Eur. Biotechnol. Orgn, 2007; Fergal Nally Lect. and Medal, RCSI, 2013. *Publications:* The Structure, Development and Evolution of Reptiles, 1984; Egg Incubation: its effects on embryonic development in birds and reptiles, 1991; (ed) Gray's Anatomy, 38th edn, 1995; more than 350 scientific papers, patents and contribs to books on wound healing, prevention of scarring, cleft palate and sex determination. *Recreations:* travel, wildlife, reading, antiques, scientific research. *Address:* Science Foundation Ireland, Wilton Park House, Wilton Place, Dublin D02 NT99, Ireland. *T:* (1) 6073175.

**FERGUSON, Martin John**, AM 1996; Strategic Director Natural Resource, SGH Energy Pty Ltd (formerly Group Executive Director, Natural Resources, SGH Energy, Seven Group Holdings), since 2013; *b* 12 Dec. 1953; *s* of Laurie John Ferguson and Mary Ellen Clare Ferguson (*née* Bett); *m* 1981, Patricia Jane Waller; one *s* one *d*. *Educ:* St Patrick's Convent, Guildford; St Patrick's Coll., Strathfield; Sydney Univ. (BEc Hons). Federated Miscellaneous Workers Union of Australia: Federal Research Officer, 1975–81; Asst Gen. Sec., 1981–84; Gen. Sec., 1984–90; Pres., ACTU, 1990–96. MP (ALP) Batman, Australia, 1996–2013; Asst to Ldr of Opposition on multicultural affairs, 1997–98; Opposition Shadow Minister, Australian Parliament: for employment and trng, 1996–98; for population, 1997–2001; for immigration, 1997–98; for regl develt and infrastructure, 1999–2002; for regl services, 1999–2001; for transport, 1999–2002; for urban develt, 2001–03; for regl develt, transport infrastructure and tourism, 2002–03; for urban and regl develt, transport and infrastructure, 2003–04; for resources, forestry and tourism, 2004–06, and for primary industries, 2005–06; for transport, roads and tourism, 2006–07; Minister for Resources and Energy, and Minister for Tourism, 2007–13. Non-exec. Dir, BG Group, 2014–16. Chairman: Adv. Bd, APPEA, 2013–; CO2 Co-operative Res. Centre, 2013–; Adelaide Bd, UCL, 2014–18; Tourism Accommodation Australia, 2015–. Mem., Governing Body, ILO, 1990–96. Member: Trade Develt Council, 1990–96; Econ. Planning Adv. Council, 1990–96; Australian Govt's Agric. Food Council, 1992–96; Exec. Bd, Construction Ind. Develt Agency, 1992–96; Leadership Council, CEDA, 2014–; Member: Bd, Nat. Liby of Australia, 1999–2007; Bd of Trustees, Energy and Minerals Inst., Univ. of Western Australia, 2013–19.

**FERGUSON, Sir Michael (Anthony John)**, Kt 2019; CBE 2008; PhD; FRS 2000; FRSE; Regius Professor of Life Sciences, since 2013, and Professor of Molecular Parasitology, since 1994, University of Dundee (Dean of Research, 2007–14); *b* 6 Feb. 1957; *s* of Dr Anthony John Alexander Ferguson and Pamela Mary (*née* Gray); *m* 1st, 1982, Sheila Duxbury (marr. diss. 1988); 2nd, 1992, Dr Maria Lucia Sampaio Güther; one *s*. *Educ:* St Peter's Sch., York; UMIST (BSc Hons Biochem. 1979); Charing Cross Hosp. Med. Sch., Univ. of London (PhD Biochem. 1982). Post-doctoral Research Fellow: Rockefeller Univ., NY, 1982–85; Oxford Univ., 1985–88; Res. Fellow, Pembroke Coll., Oxford, 1986–88; University of Dundee: Lectr, 1988–91; Reader, 1991–94. Member: Bd of Govs, Wellcome Trust, 2012– (Dep. Chm., 2018–); Bd of Dirs, Medicines for Malaria Venture, 2012–. FRSE 1994; FMedSci 2007. Mem. EMBO 1999. Colworth Medal, Biochemical Soc., 1991; C. A. Wright Medal, Brit. Soc. of Parasitol., 2006; Royal Medal, Royal Soc. of Edinburgh, 2013; Alice and C. C. Wang Award, Amer. Soc. of Biochem. and Molecular Biol., 2016. *Recreation:* travel. *Address:* Wellcome Centre for Anti-Infectives Research, School of Life Sciences, University of Dundee, Dundee DD1 5EH. *T:* (01382) 386672.

**FERGUSON, Prof. Niall Campbell**, DPhil; Senior Fellow, Hoover Institution, Stanford University, since 2016 (Adjunct Senior Fellow, 2003–16); *b* 18 April 1964; *s* of late Dr James Campbell Ferguson and of Molly Archibald Ferguson (*née* Hamilton); *m* 1st, 1994, Susan Margaret Douglas, *qv* (marr. diss. 2011); two *s* one *d*; 2nd, 2011, Ayaan Hirsi Ali; two *s*. *Educ:* Glasgow Acad.; Magdalen Coll., Oxford (BA 1st Cl. Hons; DPhil 1989). Hanseatic Schol., Hamburg, 1986–88; Research Fellow, Christ's Coll., Cambridge, 1989–90; Official Fellow and Lectr, Peterhouse, Cambridge, 1990–92; University of Oxford: Lectr in Mod. Hist., 1992–2000; Prof. of Pol and Financial Hist., 2000–02; Vis. Prof. in Modern Eur. Hist., 2003–; Sen. Res. Fellow, Jesus Coll., Oxford, 2003–14; John E. Herzog Prof. of Financial History, Leonard N. Stern Sch. of Business, NY Univ., 2002–04; Laurence A. Tisch Prof. of History, Harvard Univ., 2004–16; William Ziegler Prof. of Business Admin, Harvard Business Sch., 2006–11; Philippe Roman Prof. of History and Internat. Affairs, LSE, 2010–11. Houblon-Norman Fellow, Bank of England, 1998–99. Reith Lectr, BBC, 2012. Dir, Chimerica Media Ltd, 2007–; Man. Dir, Greenmantle LLC, 2011–. Presenter, TV series: Empire, 2003; American Colossus, 2004; War of the World, 2006; The Ascent of Money, 2008; Civilization: Is the West History?, 2011; China: Triumph and Turmoil, 2012; The Pity of War, 2014. Ed., Jl of Contemp. History, 2004–08; contributing ed., FT, 2008–11. *Publications:* Paper and Iron: Hamburg business and German politics in the era of inflation 1897–1927, 1995; (ed) Virtual History: alternatives and counterfactuals, 1997; The World's Banker: the history of the house of Rothschild, 1998; The Pity of War, 1998; The Cash Nexus, 2001; Empire: how Britain made the modern world, 2003; Colossus: the rise and fall of the American Empire, 2004; The War of the World: history's age of hatred, 2006; The Ascent of Money: a financial history of the world, 2008; High Financier: the lives and time of Siegmund Warburg, 2010; Civilization: the West and the rest, 2011; The Great Degeneration: how institutions decay and economies die, 2013; Kissinger, vol. 1, 2015; The Square and the Tower: networks, hierarchies and the struggle for global power, 2017; contrib. English Historical Rev., Past & Present, Econ. Hist. Rev., Jl of Econ. Hist. *Recreations:* double bass, surfing, ski-ing. *Address:* Hoover Institution, 434 Galvez Mall, Stanford University, Stanford, CA 94305–6003, USA. *Clubs:* Beefsteak, Savile, Royal Automobile; Gridiron (Oxford); Brook (New York).

**FERGUSON, Nicholas Eustace Haddon**, CBE 2013; Chairman, Savills plc, since 2016; *b* 24 Oct. 1948; *s* of Captain Derrick Ferguson, RN and Betsy Ferguson; *m* 1976, Margaret Jane Dura Collin; two *s* one *d*. *Educ:* Univ. of Edinburgh (BSc Econs 1970); Harvard Business Sch. (MBA 1975, Baker Scholar). CEO, Singapore Internat. Merchant Bankers, 1980–83; Chm., Schroder Ventures, 1983–2001; CEO, 2001–06, Chm., 2006–12, SVG Capital plc (formerly Schroder Ventures Internat. Investment Trust); Chm., Sky (formerly BSkyB) plc, 2012–16 (Dir, 2004–16). Non-executive Director: Schroders plc, 1998–2001; Tamar Energy Ltd, 2010–; Maris Ltd, 2014–; Chm., Alta Hldgs Ltd, 2008–. Chairman: Courtauld Inst. of Art, 2002–12; Inst. for Philanthropy, 2003–11. Chm., Kilfinan Trust, 2004–; Trustee, EDF, 2014–. *Recreations:* collecting and studying Medieval art, country pursuits, ski-ing, gardening. *Club:* Brooks's.

**FERGUSON, Patricia Josephine**; Member (Lab) Glasgow Maryhill and Springburn, Scottish Parliament, 2011–16 (Glasgow Maryhill, 1999–2011); *b* 24 Sept. 1958; *d* of John Ferguson and Andrewina Ferguson (*née* Power); *m* 1988, William Gerard Butler, *qv*. *Educ:* Garnethill Convent Secondary Sch., Glasgow; Glasgow Coll. of Technology (part-time) (SHNC Public Admin). Greater Glasgow Health Board: Admin. Trainee, 1976–78; Administrator, 1978–83; Sec., Greater Glasgow SE Local Health Council, 1983–85; Administrator: Capital Services, Lanarkshire Health Bd, 1985–90; Scottish TUC, 1990–94; Organiser, South West of Scotland Lab. Party, 1994–96; Scottish Officer, Scottish Lab. Party, 1996–99. Scottish Parliament: Dep. Presiding Officer, 1999–2001; Minister: for Parly Business, and Govt Chief Whip, 2001–04; for Tourism, Culture and Sport, 2004–07; Shadow Minister for Europe, External Affairs and Culture, 2007; Shadow Cabinet Sec. for Culture and External Affairs, 2011–14. Contested (Lab) Glasgow Maryhill and Springburn, Scottish Parlt, 2016. *Recreations:* reading, driving, travel, theatre, music.

**FERGUSON, Rt Rev. Paul John;** *see* Whitby, Bishop Suffragan of.

**FERGUSON, Peter William;** QC (Scot.) 2005; Advocate, since 1987; *b* 22 March 1961; *er s* of late John Lambie Ferguson and of Joyce Robertson Ferguson (*née* Carrol). *Educ:* Portobello High Sch., Edinburgh; Univ. of Edinburgh (LLB Hons 1983; MSc Dist. 1998); Univ. of Strathclyde (DipLP 1984). Admitted Advocate, 1987. Mem., Scottish Criminal Cases Review Commn, 2011–19. *Publications:* Crimes Against the Person, 1989, 2nd edn 1998; contrib. legal pubns. *Address:* Advocates' Library, Parliament Square, Edinburgh EH1 1RF. *Club:* Scottish Arts (Edinburgh).

**FERGUSON, Susan Margaret;** *see* Douglas, S. M.

**FERGUSON, Veronica Mary Geneste**, LVO 2014; FRCS, FRCOphth; Consultant Ophthalmic Surgeon, Imperial College Healthcare NHS Trust (formerly Hammersmith Hospitals NHS Trust and St Mary's Hospital NHS Trust), since 1996; Surgeon Oculist to the Queen, since 2018; *b* 18 May 1960; *d* of late Geoffrey Crosby Ambrose and of Dympna Mary Ambrose (*née* Bourke); *m* 1988, James Malcolm Ferguson, TD. *Educ:* Convent of the Sacred Heart, Woldingham; Guy's Hosp. Med. Sch., London Univ. (MB BS 1983). FRCS 1987; FRCOphth 1989. Sen. House Officer, Guy's Hosp., Royal Free Hosp., Southampton Eye Hosp., and St Thomas' Hosp., 1984–89; Registrar, Southern Gen. Hosp., Glasgow, 1989–91; Sen. Registrar, St George's Hosp. and Moorfields Eye Hosp., 1991–96; Consultant Ophthalmic Surgeon: King Edward VII's Hosp. (Sr Agnes), 1997–; St Luke's Hosp. for the Clergy, 2002–; Ophthalmologist, Blind Veterans UK (formerly St Dunstan's Charity for Blind Ex-servicemen), 2004–; Surgeon Oculist to HM Household, 2002–18. Hon. Sen. Lectr, Imperial Coll., London, 1996–. Mem. Council, Royal Coll. Ophthalmologists, 1999–2005. *Publications:* contribs on cataract surgery, ocular inflammation and strabismus to ophthalmic jls. *Recreations:* horses, gardening, bee-keeping, ski-ing. *Address:* King Edward VII's Hospital, Beaumont Street, W1G 6AA. *T:* (020) 7487 2838. *E:* v.ferguson@doctors.org.uk.

**FERGUSON, William James**, OBE 1996; FRAgS; farmer; Vice Lord-Lieutenant of Aberdeenshire, 1998–2008; Chairman, Aberdeen Milk Company, since 1994; *b* 3 April 1933; *s* of William Adam Ferguson and Violet (*née* Wiseman); *m* 1961, Carroll Isabella Milne; one *s* three *d*. *Educ:* Turriff Acad.; North of Scotland Coll. of Agriculture (Cert. of Agric.). Nat. Service, 1st Bn Gordon Highlanders, serving in Malaya, 1952–54. Chm., North of Scotland Coll. of Agric., 1986–91; Vice Chm., Scottish Agricl Colls, 1991–97 (Hon. Fellow, 1999). Former Chm., Grampian Farm Wildlife Adv. Gp; Member: Rowett Res. Inst., 1980–82; Technical Cttee, Crichton Royal Dairy Farm, Dumfries, 1980–83; Macaulay Inst. of Soil Res., 1983–85; Scottish Farm Bldgs Investigation Unit, 1984–86; Scottish Country Life Mus., 1986–96; Trustee, Aberdeen Endowments Trust, 2003– (Convenor, Land and Finance Cttee, 2003–). FRAgS 1995. DL Aberdeenshire, 1988. *Recreations:* golf, ski-ing, field sports. *Address:* Nether Darley, Auchterless, Turriff, Aberdeenshire AB53 8LH. *Club:* Farmers.

**FERGUSON DAVIE, Sir Michael**, 8th Bt *cr* 1847, of Creedy, Devonshire; retired stockbroker; *b* 10 Jan. 1944; *er s* of Sir John Ferguson Davie, 7th Bt and (Joan) Zoë (Charlotte), *d* of Raymond Hoole, Vancouver, BC; *S* father, 2000; *m* 1st, 1968, (Margaret) Jean (marr. diss. 1992), *d* of Douglas Macbeth; one *s* decd; 2nd, 2001, Sarah, *d* of John Seyfried and Lady Cathleen Hudson (*née* Eliot), and former wife of Peter M. Smith; two step *s*. *Educ:* St Edward's Sch., Oxford. Grenfell & Co. (later Grenfell & Colegrave), 1961–79; Fielding Newson-Smith & Co., 1979–86; Dir, NatWest Markets, 1986–95; Consultant, Madoff Securities Ltd, 1995–98; Partner, Footloose, 1997–2003. Trustee: SCF Endowment, 2006–10; Somerset Community Foundn, 2007–13 (Treas., 2007–10); Somerset Sight, 2010–15. Mem., Treasury Cttee, Lord's Taverners, 2014–. *Recreations:* writing, bridge, travel, Real tennis, cricket, Rugby football. *Heir: b* Julian Anthony Ferguson Davie [*b* 6 July 1950; *m* 1976, Louise, *d* of John Marsden; three *s*]. *Address:* 26 Lower Oldfield Park, Bath BA2 3HP. *T:* (01225) 334692. *Clubs:* Pratt's, City of London, MCC.

**FERGUSON-SMITH, Prof. Anne Carla**, PhD; FRS 2017; FMedSci; Arthur Balfour Professor of Genetics, since 2015, and Head, Department of Genetics, since 2013, University of Cambridge (Professor of Genetics, 2012–15); Fellow, Darwin College, Cambridge, since 1997; *b* Baltimore, USA, 23 July 1961; *d* of Prof. Malcolm Andrew Ferguson-Smith, *qv*; *m* 1988, Mark Gregory McHarg; one *s* one *d*. *Educ:* Univ. of Glasgow (BSc Hons); Yale Univ. (PhD 1989). FMedSci 2012. *Address:* Department of Genetics, University of Cambridge, Downing Street, Cambridge CB2 3EH.

**FERGUSON-SMITH, Prof. Malcolm Andrew**, FRS 1983; FRSE 1978; Professor of Pathology, University of Cambridge, 1987–98, now Emeritus; Professorial Fellow, Peterhouse, Cambridge, 1987–98, now Emeritus; Director, Cambridge University Centre for Medical Genetics, 1989–98; *b* 5 Sept. 1931; *s* of John Ferguson-Smith, MA, MD, FRCP and Ethel May (*née* Thorne); *m* 1960, Marie Eva Gzowska; one *s* three *d*. *Educ:* Stowe Sch.; Univ. of Glasgow (MB ChB 1955). MRCPath 1966, FRCPath 1978; MRCPGlas 1972, FRCPGlas 1974; FRCOG 1993. Registrar in Lab. Medicine, Dept of Pathology, Western Infirmary, Glasgow, 1958–59; Fellow in Medicine and Instructor, Johns Hopkins Univ. Sch. of Medicine, 1959–61; Lectr, Sen. Lectr and Reader in Med. Genetics, Univ. of Glasgow, 1961–73, Burton Prof. of Med. Genetics, 1973–87; Hon. Consultant: in Med. Paediatrics, Royal Hosp. for Sick Children, Glasgow, 1966–73; in Clin. Genetics, Yorkhill and Associated Hosps, 1973–87; in Med. Genetics, Addenbrooke's NHS Trust, 1987–98; Director: W of Scotland Med. Genetics Service, 1973–87; E Anglian Regl Clin. Genetics Service, 1987–95. President: Clinical Genetics Soc., 1979–81; Eur. Soc. of Human

Genetics, 1997–98; Internat. Soc. for Prenatal Diagnosis, 1998–2002; Assoc. of Clinical Cytogeneticists, 2002–05. Mem., Johns Hopkins Univ. Soc. of Scholars, 1983; For. Mem., Polish Acad. of Scis, 1988; For. Corresp. Mem., Nat. Acad. of Medicine of Buenos Aires, 2002. Founder FMedSci 1998; Hon. ARCVS 2002. Hon. DSc: Strathclyde, 1992; Glasgow, 2002. Bronze Medal, Univ. of Helsinki, 1968; Makdougall-Brisbane Prize, RSE, 1988; San Remo Internat. Prize for Genetic Res., 1990; Baschirotto Award, Eur. Soc. of Human Genetics, 1996. Founding Editor, Prenatal Diagnosis, 1980–2006. *Publications*: (ed) Early Prenatal Diagnosis, 1983; (jtly) Essential Medical Genetics, 1984, 6th edn 2011; (ed) Prenatal Diagnosis and Screening, 1992; papers on cytogenetics, gene mapping, human genetics and evolutionary biology in med. and biol. jls. *Recreations*: swimming, sailing, fishing. *Address*: Department of Veterinary Medicine, Cambridge University, Madingley Road, Cambridge CB3 0ES.
*See also* A. C. Ferguson-Smith.

**FERGUSSON, Adam (Dugdale)**, FRSL; writer; *b* 10 July 1932; *yr s* of Sir James Fergusson of Kilkerran, 8th Bt, LLD, FRSE, and Frances Dugdale; *m* 1965, Penelope (*d* 2009), *e d* of Peter Hughes, Furneaux Pelham Hall; two *s* two *d*. *Educ*: Eton; Trinity Coll., Cambridge (BA History, 1955). Glasgow Herald, 1956–61: Leader-writer, 1957–58; Diplomatic Corresp., 1959–61; Statist, 1961–67: Foreign Editor, 1964–67; Feature-writer for The Times on political, economic and environmental matters, 1967–77. Special Advr on European Affairs, FCO, 1985–89; consultant on European affairs, 1989–. European Parliament: Member (C) West Strathclyde, 1979–84; Spokesman on Political Affairs for European Democratic Gp, 1979–82; Vice-Chm., Political Affairs Cttee, 1982–84; Mem., Jt Cttee of ACP/EEC Consultative Assembly, 1979–84; contested (C) London Central, European elecn, 1984. Vice-Pres., Pan-European Union, 1981–2004; Mem., Scotland Says No Referendum Campaign Cttee, 1978–79. Dir, Murray International Trust PLC, 1995–2001. Gov., Howick Trust, 1976–2002; Vice-Pres., Bath Preservation Trust, 1997–. FRSL 2009. *Publications*: Roman Go Home, 1969; The Lost Embassy, 1972; The Sack of Bath, 1973; When Money Dies, 1975; Scone: a likely tale, 2004; *musical comedies*: book and lyrics for: State of Emergency, 1962; Gibbon Slept Here, 1964; Just One of those Thanes, 2009; various pamphlets; articles in national and internat. jls and magazines. *Address*: 15 Warwick Gardens, W14 8PH. *T*: (020) 7603 7900.

**FERGUSSON of Kilkerran, Sir Charles**, 9th Bt *cr* 1703; *b* 10 May 1931; *s* of Sir James Fergusson of Kilkerran, 8th Bt, and Frances (*d* 1988), *d* of Edgar Dugdale; *S* father, 1973; *m* 1961, Hon. Amanda Mary Noel-Paton, *o d* of Lord Ferrier, ED; two *s*. *Educ*: Eton; Edinburgh and East of Scotland Coll. of Agriculture. *Heir*: *s* Maj. Adam Fergusson [*b* 29 Dec. 1962; *m* 1989, Jenifer, *yr d* of Adam Thomson; one *s* two *d*].

**FERGUSSON, Rev. Prof. David Alexander Syme**, OBE 2016; DPhil; FBA 2013; FRSE; Professor of Divinity, University of Edinburgh, since 2000 (Principal, New College, 2008–18; Vice-Principal, 2009–11); a Chaplain to the Queen in Scotland, since 2015; *b* Glasgow, 3 Aug. 1956; *s* of Thomas Fergusson and Charis Fergusson; *m* 1985, Margot Evelyn McIndoe; two *s*. *Educ*: Univ. of Glasgow (MA 1977); Univ. of Edinburgh (BD 1980); Univ. of Oxford (DPhil 1984). Licensed, 1980, ordained, 1984, C of S; Asst Minister, St Nicholas, Lanark, 1983–84; Associate Minister, St Mungo's, Cumbernauld, 1984–86; Lectr in Systematic Theol., Univ. of Edinburgh, 1986–90; Prof. of Systematic Theol., Univ. of Aberdeen, 1990–2000. Lectures: Cunningham, Univ. of Edinburgh, 1996; Bampton, Univ. of Oxford, 2001; Gifford, Univ. of Glasgow, 2008; Warfield, Princeton Theol Seminary, 2009; Birks, McGill Univ., 2013; Mackay, Taiwan Theol Coll., 2017. FRSE 2004. Hon. DD Aberdeen, 2014. *Publications*: Bultmann, 1992; Christ, Church and Society, 1993; John and Donald Baillie, 1997; The Cosmos and the Creator, 1998; Community, Liberation and Christian Ethics, 1998; John Macmurray: critical perspectives, 2002; Church, State and Civil Society, 2004; Scottish Philosophical Theology, 2007; Faith and Its Critics, 2009; (ed) Blackwell Companion to 19th Century Theology, 2010; (ed) Cambridge Dictionary of Christian Theology, 2011; Creation, 2014; Christian Theology: 21st century challenges, 2015; (ed) Cambridge Companion to Reformed Theology, 2016; The Providence of God, 2018. *Recreations*: golf, football. *Address*: 23 Riselaw Crescent, Edinburgh EH10 6HN. *T*: (0131) 447 4022. *E*: David.Fergusson@ed.ac.uk. *Clubs*: New, Mortonhall Golf (Edinburgh).

**FERGUSSON, George Duncan Raukawa**; HM Diplomatic Service, retired; Governor and Commander-in-Chief of Bermuda, 2012–16; Senior Adviser, UK Governance Group, Cabinet Office, 2016–17; *b* 30 Sept. 1955; *s* of Brig. Bernard Fergusson, later Baron Ballantrae, KT, GCMG, GCVO, DSO, OBE; *m* 1981, Margaret Sheila Wookey; three *d* (one *s* decd). *Educ*: Ballantrae Jun. Secondary Sch.; Hereworth Sch., NZ; Eton Coll.; Magdalen Coll., Oxford. Murray and Tait, Solicitors, 1977–78; joined Northern Ireland Office, 1978; seconded to NI Dept of Commerce, 1979–80; Private Sec. to Min. of State for NI, 1982–83; First Sec., Dublin, 1988–91; joined Diplomatic Service, 1990; FCO, 1991–93; First Sec., Seoul, 1994–96; FCO, 1996–99; Head: Republic of Ireland Dept, 1997–99; Devolved Admins Dept, 1999; Consul Gen., Boston, 1999–2003; Counsellor, Cabinet Office, 2003–06; High Comr, New Zealand, Governor (non-res.) of Pitcairn, Henderson, Ducie and Oeno Is, and High Comr (non-res.), Samoa, 2006–10; FCO, 2010–12.

**FERGUSSON, Kenneth James**, CEng, FIMechE; Chief Executive, Coal Authority, 1997–2001; Trustee, UCG Association, 2010–12 (Senior Adviser, Underground Coal Gasification Partnership, 2008–10); *b* 1938; *s* of Robert Brown Millar Fergusson and Agnes Tattersall Fergusson; *m* 1961, Beryl Foster; two *s* one *d*. *Educ*: Robert Gordon's Coll., Aberdeen; Harrow County Grammar Sch.; Imperial Coll., London (BSc 1st cl. Hons Engrg); Harvard Business Sch. (AMP). CEng 1966; FIMechE 1976; FIMMM until 2015 (FIMM 1999). ICI Agricl Div., 1959–68; RTZ Gp, 1968–86: Geschäftsführer, Duisburger Kupferhütte, 1981–85; Man. Dir, Rio Tinto Zimbabwe, 1985–86; Project Dir, European Transonic Windtunnel, Cologne, 1986–88; Man. Dir, Docklands Light Railway, 1988–90; Chief Exec., Hub Power Co., Karachi, 1992–93; Regl Dir, BESO, 1995–97. Trustee, Industrial Trust, 1998–2010. Pres., Combustion Engrg Assoc., 2002–06. FIMgt 1984–2002; MInstD 1987–2010; FRSA 1998–2002. Freeman, City of London, 1990; Liveryman, Co. of Engineers, 1995–2014. *Recreations*: advanced motoring and motorcycling, swimming, archaeology, music, current affairs, travel. *Address*: 24F Thorney Crescent, Morgans Walk, SW11 3TT. *T*: (020) 7585 1294.

**FERLEGER BRADES, Susan Deborah**; Director, Hayward Gallery, London, 1996–2004; *b* 7 July 1954; *d* of Alvin Ferleger and Beatrice Ferleger (*née* Supnick); *m* 1st, 1979, Peter Eric Brades (*d* 2001); one *s*; 2nd, 2006, Rhett Davies. *Educ*: Courtauld Inst. of Art (MA); Univ. of Mass, Amherst (BA 1976; magna cum laude; Phi Beta Kappa); Barnard Coll., Columbia Univ., NY. Curatorial Co-ordinator, Solomon R. Guggenheim Mus., NY, 1975–79; Nat. Endowment for Arts Fellowship, 1975–76; Researcher, British Sculpture in the Twentieth Century, Whitechapel Art Gall., London, 1979–80; Hayward Gallery: Exhibn Organiser, Arts Council of GB, S Bank Centre, 1980–88; Sen. Exhibn Organiser, Exhibns Dept, S Bank Centre, 1988–93 (Public Art Programme Co-ordinator, 1990); Dep. Dir, Hayward Gall., S Bank Centre, 1993–96. Purchaser, Arts Council Collection, 1983–2004; Visual Arts Advr, John Lyons Charity, 2004–; Consultant, Bldg Project and Artist Engagement, London Liby, 2005–10. Trustee, IVAM Centro Julio Gonzalez, Valencia, 2000–04; Review Panel Mem., Course Validation Panel, Academic Standards, RCA, 2009–11. *E*: susanbrades@gmail.com.

**FERLIE, Prof. Ewan Balfour**, PhD; FBA 2016; Professor of Public Services Management, King's College London, since 2008; *b* Leamington Spa, 3 May 1956; *s* of Thomas Ferlie and Joyce Ferlie; *m* 2014, Luis Canizares. *Educ*: Kenilworth Grammar Sch.; Balliol Coll., Oxford (BA Hist. 1977; MSc Social Res. and Social Policy 1979); Univ. of Kent at Canterbury (PhD Social Policy 1986). Res. posts, Personal Soc. Services Res. Unit, Univ. of Kent, 1979–86; University of Warwick: res. posts, Centre for Corporate Strategy and Change, Warwick Business Sch., 1986–96; personal chair, 1996–97; Prof. of Public Services Mgt, Imperial Coll. London, 1997–2003; Prof. of Public Services Mgt and Hd, Sch. of Mgt, Royal Holloway, Univ. of London, 2003–08; Hd, Dept of Mgt, KCL, 2008–11. Hon. Chm., Soc. for the Study of Organizing in Health Care, 2012–. FAcSS (AcSS 2008) FRSA 2012. *Publications*: (jtly) Efficiency Improving Innovations in the Community Care of the Elderly, 1989; (jtly) Shaping Strategic Change, 1992; (jtly) Managing Crisis and Change in Health Care, 1994; (jtly) The New Public Management in Action, 1996; (ed jtly) New Public Management, 2001; (with T. McNulty) Reengineering Health Care: the complexities of organizational transformation, 2002; (ed jtly) The Oxford Handbook of Public Management, 2005; (jtly) Organizing and Reorganizing: power and change in health care organizations, 2008; (jtly) University Governance: Western comparative perspectives, 2009; (jtly) Leadership in the Public Services: promises and pitfalls, 2012; (jtly) Making Wicked Problems Governable?, 2013; (with E. Ongaro) Strategic Management and Public Services Organizations: concepts, schools and contemporary issues, 2015; (ed jtly) Managing Change: from health policy to practice, 2015; Analysing Health Care Organizations: a personal anthology, 2016; (ed jtly) The Oxford Handbook of Health Care Management, 2016. *Recreations*: tennis, reading, art, travel. *Address*: King's College London, Franklin Wilkins Building, 150 Stamford Street, SE1 9NH. *T*: (020) 7848 4466. *E*: ewan.ferlie@kcl.ac.uk.

**FERMOR-HESKETH**, family name of **Baron Hesketh**.

**FERMOY**, 6th Baron *cr* 1856; **Maurice Burke Roche**; *b* 11 Oct. 1967; *s* of 5th Baron Fermoy and of Lavinia Frances Elizabeth, *o d* of late Captain John Pitman; name changed from Patrick Maurice Burke Roche by deed poll, 2010; *S* father, 1984; *m* 1998, Tessa Fiona Ledger, *e d* of Major David Pelham Kayll; two *d*. *Educ*: Eton. A Page of Honour to the Queen Mother, 1982–85. Commnd, Blues and Royals, 1987–95; Capt. With Bass Taverns, 1996–99; Dir, Horse Fair Properties Ltd (formerly Arrow Pubs Ltd), 1999–. Mem., Cherwell DC, 2000–04. Jt Hon. Sec., Warwickshire Hunt, 2014–. *Recreation*: country sports. *Heir*: *b* Hon. (Edmund) Hugh Burke Roche [*b* 5 Feb. 1972; *m* 2004, Phillipa Long; one *s* two *d*]. *Address*: Handywater Farm, Sibford Gower, Banbury, Oxon OX15 5AE.
*See also* Hon. P. H. C. Stanley.

**FERN, Georgina Jane**; *see* Harrisson, G. J.

**FERN, John Christopher**; Headmaster, Royal Grammar School, Newcastle upon Tyne, since 2017; *b* Leicester, 20 Sept. 1974; *s* of Ernest Fern and Iris Fern. *Educ*: Loughborough Grammar Sch.; Exeter Coll., Oxford (BA Hons Mod. Hist. 1996; PGCE 1997). Teacher of Hist., 1997–2002, Hd of Hist., 2002–05, Oakham Sch.; IB Co-ordinator, Fettes Coll., 2005–09; Dep. Hd (Acad.), King Edward's Sch., Birmingham, 2009–17. *Recreations*: theatre, classical music, singing, ballet, opera, walking, travel. *Address*: Royal Grammar School, Eskdale Terrace, Newcastle upon Tyne NE2 4DX. *T*: (0191) 281 5711. *E*: hm@rgs.newcastle.sch.uk.

**FERNANDES, Anthony Francis**, Hon. CBE 2011; Group Chief Executive Officer, AirAsia Berhad, 2001–12 and since 2013 (non-executive Director, 2012–13; Executive Director, since 2013). *Educ*: ACCA 1991, FCCA 1996; ACA 2008. Financial Controller, Virgin Communications London, 1987–89; Sen. Financial Analyst, 1989–92, Man. Dir, 1992–96, Warner Music Internat. London; Dir, Warner Music, Malaysia, 1992–96; Regl Man. Dir, ASEAN, 1996–99; Vice Pres., Warner Music SE Asia, 1999–2001. Co-Founder, Tune Gp of Cos, 2001. Principal, Caterham F1 Team, 2010–12; Chm., Caterham Gp; Chm., Queens Park Rangers FC, 2011–18. Commandeur, Légion d'Honneur (France), 2013 (Officier, 2010). *Recreations*: sports, football, hockey. *Address*: AirAsia Berhad, LCC Terminal, Jalan Klia S3, Southern Support Zone, Klia, 64000 Sepang, Selangor Darul Ehsan, Malaysia. *T*: 386604333, *Fax*: 386601100. *E*: tonyfernandes@airasia.com.

**FERNANDES, Prof. Kiran Jude**, PhD; CEng, FIET; FAcSS; Professor of Operations Management, since 2013 and Associate Dean for Internationalisation, since 2018, Durham University Business School (Head, Department of Management, 2013–17); *b* Mysore, India, 15 Nov. 1973. *Educ*: Walchand Inst. of Technol. (BEng 1995); Mississippi State Univ. (MS 1997); Massachusetts Inst. of Technol. (Professional Prog. 1998); Univ. of Warwick (PhD 2004). CEng 2003; FIET 2006. Boeing Sub-Systems Engr, NASA John C. Stennis Space Center, 1997–99; EPSRC/Internat. Manufg Res. Centre Sen. Res. Fellow, Warwick Manufg Gp, Univ. of Warwick, 1999–2004; York Management School, University of York: 40th Anniv. Lectr in Ops Mgt, 2004–07; Sen. Lectr in Ops Mgt, 2007–11; Prof. of Ops Mgt, 2011–13; Hd, Ops Mgt, 2010–13; Pro-Dean for Res., 2011–13. Non-exec. Dir, UK Nat. Commn for UNESCO, 2013–. FHEA 2007; FRSA 2012; FCILT 2015; FAcSS 2016. *Publications*: (with V. Raja) Reverse Engineering: an industrial perspective, 2008; articles in learned jls. *Address*: Durham University Business School, Mill Hill Lane, Durham DH1 3LB. *T*: (0191) 334 5512. *E*: k.j.fernandes@durham.ac.uk.

**FERNANDES, Sue-Ellen Cassiana, (Suella)**; *see* Braverman, S. E. C.

**FERNÁNDEZ, Mariano**; Ambassador of Chile to the Holy See, 2016–18; consultant on international affairs; *b* Santiago, 21 April 1945; *s* of Mariano Fernández and María Angélica Amunategui; *m* 1969, María Angélica Morales; two *s* one *d*. *Educ*: Universidad Católica de Santiago (law degree 1970); Bonn Univ. (major in pol sociol.). Mem., Foreign Service, Chile, 1967–74; Third Sec., Embassy of Chile, Germany, 1971–74; in exile, Bonn, 1974–82: Ed., Develt and Co-opn Mag.; Chief Editor: IPS-Dritte welt Nachrichtenagentur (news agency); Handbuch der Entwicklungshilfe; returned to Chile, 1982; Researcher and Mem. Exec. Cttee, Centre of Studies for Develt, 1982–90; Ambassador: to EC, 1990–92; to Italy and (non-resident) to Malta, 1992–94; Vice Minister for Foreign Affairs, 1994–2000; Ambassador: to Spain and (non-resident) to Andorra, 2000–02; to UK, 2002–06, and (non-resident) to Libya, 2005–06; to USA, 2006–09; Minister of Foreign Affairs, Chile, 2009–10; Under-Sec.-Gen. and Special Rep. to Haiti, and Hd of Peacekeeping Mission in Haiti, UN, 2011–13; Ambassador to Germany, 2014–16. Board Member: Fintesa Financial Agency, 1982–84; Radio Cooperativa, 1982–90; Editorial Board Member: Mensaje, 1984–86; Fortin Mapocho, 1986–88; Apsi, 1986–89. President: European-Latin American Relations Inst., Madrid, 1992–93 (Vice-Pres., 1992); Internat. Council, Latin-American Centre for Relations with Europe, 1996–98; Vice-Pres., Italo-Latin American Inst., Rome, 1994; Mem. Exec. Cttee, Jacques Maritain Inst., Rome, 1994–96. Hd, Chilean Commn, Internat. Whaling Commn, 2003–07; Chilean Rep., IMO, 2006. Member: Pol Sci. Assoc. of Chile; Cofradía del Mérito Vitivinícola de Chile; Jurade de St Emilion; Commanderie de Médoc et Graves; Europaische Weinritterschaft;

Slow Food. Mem. Bd, Universidad Mayor, Santiago, until 2011. Hon. President: Chilean Assoc. of Sommeliers; Acad. Internat. du Vin. Grand Cross of: Argentina; Brazil; Colombia; Ecuador; Finland; Germany; the Holy See; Italy; Mexico; Netherlands; Panama; Peru; Portugal; Spain; Grand Officer of: Croatia; Germany; Sweden. *Publications*: articles in mags and jls, mainly on internat. policy and on wine tasting.

**FERNANDO, Most Rev. Nicholas Marcus;** Archbishop of Colombo, (RC), 1977–2002, now Emeritus; *b* 6 Dec. 1932. *Educ*: St Aloysius' Seminary, Colombo; Universitas Propaganda Fide, Rome. BA (London); PhL (Rome); STD (Rome). Ordained priest, 1959. Pres., Catholic Bishops' Conf. of Sri Lanka, 1989–95. Former Mem., Sacred Congregation for Evangelization of Peoples. *Address*: Emmaus, No 202, National Basilica Mawatha, Tewatta, Ragama, Sri Lanka.

**FERNEYHOUGH, Prof. Brian John Peter,** FRAM; composer; William H. Bonsall Professor in Music, Stanford University, since 2000; *b* 16 Jan. 1943; *s* of Frederick George Ferneyhough and Emily May (*née* Hopwood); *m* 1990, Stephany Jan Hurtik. *Educ*: Birmingham Sch. of Music; RAM (FRAM 1998); Sweelinck Conservatory, Amsterdam; Musikakademie, Basel. Mendelssohn Schol., 1968; Stipend: City of Basle, 1969; Heinrich-Strobel-Stiftung des Südwestfunks, 1972; Composition teacher, Musikhochschule, Freiburg, 1973–86 (Prof., 1978–86); Principal Composition Teacher, Royal Conservatory, The Hague, 1986–87; Prof. of Music, UCSD, 1987–99. Guest Artist, Artists' Exchange Scheme, Deutsche Akad. Austauschdienst, Berlin, 1976–77; Lectr, Darmstadt Summer Sch., 1976–96 and 2004 (Comp. course co-ordinator, 1984–94); Guest Prof., Royal Conservatory, Stockholm, 1981–83, 1985; Vis. Prof., Univ. of Chicago, 1986. Master Class, Civica Scuola di Musica di Milano, 1985–87. Mem., ISCM Internat. Jury, 1977, 1988. Hon. FRBC (Hon. FBC 1996); Hon. DMus Goldsmiths, Univ. of London, 2012. Prizes, Gaudeamus Internat. Comp., 1968, 1969; First Prize, ISCM Internat. Comp., Rome, 1974; Koussevitsky Prize, 1978; Royal Philharmonic Soc. Award, 1996, 2011; Ernst von Siemens Music Prize, 2007. Chevalier, l'Ordre des Arts et des Lettres, 1984. *Compositions include*: Sonatas for String Quartet, 1967; Epicycle, for 20 solo strings, 1968; Firecycle Beta, for large orch. with 5 conductors, 1971; Time and Motion Studies I–III, 1974–76; Unity Capsule, for solo flute, 1975; Funérailles, for 7 strings and harp, 1978; La Terre est un Homme, for orch., 1979; 2nd String Quartet, 1980; Lemma-Icon-Epigram, for solo piano, 1981; Carceri d'Invenzione, for various ensembles, 1981–86; 3rd String Quartet, 1987; Kurze Schatten II, for guitar, 1988; La Chute d'Icare, for clarinet ensemble, 1988; Trittico per G. S., 1989; 4th String Quartet, 1990; Bone Alphabet, for percussionist, 1991; Terrain, for violin and eight instruments, 1992; On Stellar Magnitudes, for voice and ensemble, 1994; String Trio, 1995; Incipits, for viola, percussion and small ensemble, 1996; Kranichtänze II, for piano, 1996; Maisons Noires, for ensemble, 1997; Unsichtbare Farben, for solo violin, 1999; Doctrine of Similarity, for choir and instruments, 2000; Opus Contra Naturam, for speaking pianist, 2000; Stele for Failed Time, for choir and electronics, 2001; Shadowtime, 1999–2004; Dum transisset I–IV, for string quartet, 2005–06; 5th String Quartet, 2006; Plötzlichkeit, for orch., 2006; Chronos-Aion, for large ensemble, 2008; Exordium, 2008; 6th String Quartet, 2010, Renvoi/Shards, 2009; Sisyphus Redux, for alto flute, 2009; Liber Scintillarum, for six instruments, 2012; Finis Terrae, for six voices and ensemble, 2012; Quiril, for solo piano, 2013; Schatten aus Wasser und Stein, for quarter-tone oboe and string quartet, 2013. *Publications*: Collected Writings, 1996; articles in Contrechamps, Musiktexte, and Contemp. Music Rev. *Recreations*: reading, wine, cats. *Address*: Department of Music, Braun Music Center, Stanford University, Stanford, CA 94305–3076, USA.

**FERNIE, Prof. Eric Campbell,** CBE 1995; FBA 2002; FSA; FSA (Scot.); FRSE; Director, Courtauld Institute of Art, University of London, 1995–2003, now Honorary Fellow; *b* Edinburgh, 9 June 1939; *s* of Sydney Robert and Catherine Reid Fernie; *m* 1964, Margaret Lorraine French; one *s* two *d*. *Educ*: Univ. of the Witwatersrand (BA Hons Fine Arts); Univ. of London (Academic Diploma). FSA 1973; FSA (Scot.) 1984; FRSE 1993. Lectr, Univ. of the Witwatersrand, 1963–67; University of East Anglia: Lectr and Sen. Lectr, 1967–84; Dean, Sch. of Fine Art and Music, 1977–81; Public Orator, 1982–84; Watson Gordon Prof. of Fine Art, Univ. of Edinburgh, 1984–95 (Dean, Faculty of Arts, 1989–92). Chm., Ancient Monuments Bd for Scotland, 1989–95; Trustee: Nat. Galleries of Scotland, 1991–97; Scotland Inheritance Fund, 1992–2005; Samuel Courtauld Trust, 1995–2003; Heather Trust for the Arts, 1997–2001; Comr, English Heritage, 1995–2001; Mem., RCHME, 1997–99. Pres., Soc. of Antiquaries of London, 2004–07 (Vice-Pres., 1992–95). Hon. DLitt UEA, 2011. *Publications*: An Introduction to the Communar and Pitcaner Rolls of Norwich Cathedral Priory (with A. B. Whittingham), 1973; The Architecture of the Anglo-Saxons, 1983; An Architectural History of Norwich Cathedral, 1993; Art History and its Methods, 1995; The Architecture of Norman England, 2000; Romanesque Architecture: the first style of the European Age, 2014; (ed jtly) Tomb and Temple: re-imagining the sacred buildings of Jerusalem, 2018; contribs to British and overseas architectural jls. *Address*: 82 Bradmore Way, Old Coulsdon, Surrey CR5 1PB. *T*: (01737) 559553.

**FERRAN, Brian;** Chief Executive, Arts Council of Northern Ireland, 1991–2000; *b* 19 Oct. 1940; *s* of late Bernard and Susan Ferran; *m* 1963, Denise Devine; one *s* one *d*. *Educ*: St Columb's Coll., Derry; St Mary's Coll., Belfast (ATD); Courtauld Inst., London Univ. (BA 1973); Queen's Univ., Belfast (DBA 1975). Art Teacher, Derry, 1963–66; Visual Arts Dir, Arts Council of NI, 1966–91. Commissioner: Paris Biennale, 1980; São Paolo Biennial, 1985; Orgnr, exhibn of NI artists, Houston Internat. Fest. and US tour, 1990. HRUA 1980; HRHA 1998. Leverhulme European Award, 1969; Douglas Hyde Gold Medal for historical painting, 1965, 1976; Conor Prize, 1979, Gold Medal, 2014, Royal Ulster Acad. *Publications*: Basil Blackshaw: painter, 1995. *Recreation*: visiting museums. *Address*: Goorey Rocks, Malin, Inishowen, Co. Donegal, Ireland. *T*: 749370934.

**FERRAN, Prof. Eilís Veronica, (Mrs Roderick Cantrill),** PhD; FBA 2013; Professor of Company and Securities Law, since 2005, and Pro-Vice-Chancellor for Institutional and International Relations, since 2015, University of Cambridge; Fellow, St Catharine's College, Cambridge, since 1987; *b* Belfast, 14 March 1962; *d* of Edward Gerald and Kathleen Ferran; *m* 1992, Roderick Cantrill; one *s* one *d*. *Educ*: St Dominic's RC High Sch., Belfast; St Catharine's Coll., Cambridge (BA 1983; MA 1986; PhD 1992). Articled clerk, Coward Chance, 1984–86; admitted as solicitor, 1986; Lectr, St Catharine's Coll., Cambridge, 1986–88; Asst Lectr, 1988–91, Lectr, 1991–2000, Reader in Corporate Law and Financial Regulation, 2000–05, Chm., Faculty of Law, 2012–15, Univ. of Cambridge. Non-exec. Dir, Euroclear SA/NV, 2018–. Hon. Bencher, Middle Temple, 2014. *Publications*: Mortgage Securitisation, 1992; Building an EU Securities Market, 2004; Principles of Corporate Finance Law, 2008, 2nd edn 2014; (jtly) The Regulatory Aftermath of the Global Financial Crisis, 2012; (ed jtly) The Oxford Handbook of Financial Regulation, 2015; (jtly) Brexit and Financial Services, 2018. *Recreation*: family activities. *Address*: St Catharine's College, Cambridge CB2 1RL. *T*: (01223) 338335, 330041, *Fax*: (01223) 338400. *E*: evf1000@cam.ac.uk.

**FERRAROLI, Jennifer Fitzgerald;** *see* Edwards, J. F.

**FERRERO-WALDNER, Benita Maria;** Member, European Commission, 2004–10; Partner, Cremades and Calvo-Sotelo Abogados, Madrid, since 2014; *b* 5 Sept. 1948; *d* of Bruno and Emilie Waldner; *m* 1993, Prof. Francisco Ferrero Campos. *Educ*: Univ. of Salzburg (DIur). Export Dept, Paul Kiefel, Freilassing, Germany, 1971–72; Dir for Export Promotion, Gerns and Gahler, Freilassing, 1972–78; Sales Dir for Europe, P. Kaufmann Inc., NY, 1978–81; Chief Mgt Asst, Gerns and Gahler, 1981–83; Special Consultancy, Austrian Embassy, Madrid, 1984; Federal Ministry for Foreign Affairs, Austria: Depts of Econ. Affairs, Political Affairs and Consular Affairs, 1984–86; First Sec., Dakar, 1986; Dept for Develt Co-operation, 1986–87; Counsellor for Econ. Affairs, 1987–90, Minister-Counsellor, Dep. Chief of Mission and Chargé d'Affaires, 1990–93, Paris; Dep. Chief of Protocol, 1993; Chief of Protocol, Exec. Office of Sec. Gen., UN Secretariat, NY, 1994–95; State Sec. for Foreign Affairs, 1995–2000; Minister for Foreign Affairs, Austria, 2000–04. Pres., EU-LAC Foundn, 2011–15. Member, Advisory Board: Bertelsmann Foundn, 2011–; Munich Re, 2010–. Mem., Fundación Principe de Girona, 2011–. Grand Decoration of Honour in Gold with Sash (Austria), 1999; holds numerous foreign decorations, including: Grand Cross: Order of Isabel la Católica (Spain), 1995; Royal Order of Merit (Norway), 1996; 2nd Cl., Order of Merit (FRG), 1997; SMO (Malta), 1999. *Publications*: Globale Ethik, 1998; Zukunft der Entwicklungszusammenarbeit, 1999; Die Entwicklungzusammenarbeit - Herausforderungen und Visionen (Development Cooperation: challenges and visions), 1999; Kurs setzen in einer veränderten-Welt (Charting Course in a Changing World), 2002; Biregional Relations: European Union, Latin America and the Caribbean: speeches, 2012; contrib. articles and essays to internat. and European books and jls. *Recreations*: reading, travelling, theatre, concerts, swimming, yoga.

**FERRERS,** 14th Earl *cr* 1711; **Robert William Saswalo Shirley,** FCA; Viscount Tamworth 1711; Bt 1611; Managing Director: Ruffer Management (formerly Ruffer Investment Management) Ltd, 1999–2011 (Director, since 1994); Ruffer LLP, 2004–11, now Director; *b* 29 Dec. 1952; *s* of 13th Earl Ferrers, PC and Annabel Mary (*née* Carr); *S* father, 2012; *m* 1980, Susannah, *y d* of late C. E. W. Sheepshanks, Arthington Hall, Yorks; two *s* one *d*. *Educ*: Ampleforth. Teaching in Kenya, under CMS's Youth Service Abroad Scheme, 1971–72. Admitted to ICAEW, 1976. Articled to Whinney Murray & Co., CA, 1972–76; employed at Ernst & Whinney, 1976–82, Asst Manager, 1981–82; Gp Auditor, 1982–85, Sen. Treasury Analyst, 1986, BICC plc; Director: Viking Property Gp Ltd, 1987–88 (Financial Controller and Company Sec., 1986–87); Ashby Securities, subseq. Norseman Hldgs, 1987–92; Derbyshire Student Residences Ltd, 1996–2003. Dir, Assoc. of Private Client Investment Managers and Stockbrokers, 2007–13. Trustee: Auckland Castle Trust, 2012–15; Orders of St John Care Trust, 2013–. Kt SMO Malta, 2005. *Recreations*: the British countryside and related activities, the garden. *Heir*: *s* Viscount Tamworth, *qv*. *Address*: Ditchingham Hall, Ditchingham, Norfolk NR35 2JX. *Clubs*: Boodle's, Pratt's.

**FERRIE, Dr John,** CBE 2004; CEng, FREng; FRAeS; FIMechE; Executive Director and Group Managing Director, Aerospace, Smiths Group plc, 2000–07; *b* 17 Jan. 1947; *s* of Hugh Ferrie and Barbara Ferrie (*née* Miller); *m* 1968, Helen Allan; two *s*. *Educ*: Univ. of Strathclyde (BSc 1st Cl. Hons Mech. Eng. 1970); Univ. of Warwick (DEng 1998). CEng, FREng 2000; FRAeS 1995; FIMechE 1996. With Rolls Royce, 1964–2000: Director: Manufacturing, 1992–96; Mil. Engines, 1996–98; Exec. Vice-Pres., Business Ops, 1998–2000; Company Officer, GE Aviation, 2007–08. Non-exec. Dir, Westbury plc, 2004–06. Mem. Council, Univ. of Warwick, 2014–. *Recreations*: golf, music, world travel. *E*: john.ferrie17@btinternet.com.

**FERRIER, Margaret;** *b* Glasgow; one *d*. Commercial Sales Supervisor, Terex Equipt Ltd, Motherwell, until 2015. MP (SNP) Rutherglen and Hamilton W, 2015–17; contested (SNP) same seat, 2017.

**FERRIS, Jonathan Moreton; His Honour Judge Ferris;** a Circuit Judge, since 2017; *b* Reynoldston, Gower, July 1955; *s* of late Paul Frederick Ferris and Gloria Ferris; three *s*; partner, Helen Wragg; three step *s*. *Educ*: Latymer Upper Grammar Sch.; Durham Univ. (BA); Central London Poly. (DipLaw). Called to the Bar, Middle Temple, 1979; barrister in private practice, 1979–2011; a Recorder, 2000–17; Employment Judge, 2011–17. *Clubs*: Garrick; Monmouth Rowing, Leander, Furnivall Sculling, Quintin.

**FERRIS, Rt Rev. Ronald Curry;** Assisting Bishop for Missionary Planning, Anglican Network in Canada, since 2018 (Assisting Bishop, 2009–18); sessional lecturer, Anglican Studies Program, Faculty of Regent College, Vancouver, since 2018; *b* 2 July 1945; *s* of Herald Bland Ferris and Marjorie May Ferris; *m* 1965, Janet Agnes (*née* Waller); two *s* four *d*. *Educ*: Toronto Teachers' Coll. (diploma); Univ. of W Ontario (BA); Huron Coll., London, Ont. (MDiv); Pacific Sch. of Religion (DMin 1995). Teacher, Pape Avenue Elem. School, Toronto, 1965; Principal Teacher, Carcross Elem. School, Yukon, 1966–68. Incumbent, St Luke's Church, Old Crow, Yukon, 1970–72; Rector, St Stephen's Memorial Church, London, Ont., 1973–81; Bishop of Yukon, 1981–95; Bishop of Algoma, 1996–2008; Rector, Anglican Church of the Ascension, Langley, BC, 2009–17. Hon. DD Huron Coll., London, Ont, 1982; Hon. STD Thorneloe Univ., Ont, 1995. *Address*: 7137 194B Street, Surrey, BC V4N 5Z3, Canada.

**FERRIS, William Stephen,** OBE 2011; DL; Chief Executive, Chatham Historic Dockyard Trust, since 2000; *b* 3 June 1958; *s* of Harold Sydney Ferris and Grace Eileen Ferris; *m* 1982, Honor Margaret Gregory; two *s*. *Educ*: Tavistock Comprehensive Sch.; Aston Univ. (BSc 1st Cl. Hons Managerial and Admin. Studies). Self-employed baker, 1982–88; Commercial Manager, Yorkshire Mining Mus., 1988–90; various posts, Heritage Projects (Mgt) Ltd, 1990–2000 (Ops Dir, 1996–2000). Chm., Assoc. of Ind. Mus, 2002–12. Bd Mem., Visit Kent Ltd, 2008–; Mem., SE Cttee, HLF, then NLHF, 2012–. DL Kent, 2016. *Recreations*: trout fishing, mountaineering, ski-ing, Rugby football, gardening, family. *Address*: Chatham Historic Dockyard Trust, Historic Dockyard, Chatham ME4 4TZ. *T*: (01634) 823806, *Fax*: (01634) 823801. *E*: bferris@chdt.org.uk.

**FERRY, Bryan,** CBE 2011; musician; *b* 26 Sept. 1945; *s* of late Frederick Charles Ferry and Mary Ann Ferry (*née* Armstrong); *m* 1st, 1982, Lucy Helmore (marr. diss. 2003; she *d* 2018); four *s*; 2nd, 2012, Amanda Sheppard (marr. diss. 2014). *Educ*: Newcastle upon Tyne Univ. (BA Fine Art). Vocalist and founder mem., Roxy Music, 1971–83, subseq. solo recording artist; *albums include*: (with Roxy Music): Roxy Music, 1972; For Your Pleasure, 1973 (Grand Prix du Disque, Montreux, 1973); Stranded, 1973; Country Life, 1974; Siren, 1975; Viva Roxy Music, 1976; Manifesto, 1979; Flesh & Blood, 1980; Avalon, 1982; The High Road, 1983; Streetlife, 1986; (solo): These Foolish Things, 1973; Another Time Another Place, 1974; Let's Stick Together, 1976; In Your Mind, 1977; The Bride Stripped Bare, 1978; Boys and Girls, 1985; Bête Noire, 1987; Taxi, 1993; Mamouna, 1994; As Time Goes By, 2000; Frantic, 2002; Dylanesque, 2007; Olympia, 2010; The Jazz Age, 2012; Yellow Cocktail Music, 2013; Avonmore, 2014; Bitter-Sweet, 2018; numerous singles. Hon. DMus Newcastle, 2014. Officier, Ordre des Arts et des Lettres (France), 2012. *Recreations*: tennis, reading, shooting.

**FERRY, Joe David;** creative director and inventor; Art and Design Director, Belmond UK Ltd, since 2017; *b* Southampton, 20 April 1969; *s* of late Alan James Ferry and of Gillian Clare Ferry; *m* 2019, Rebecca Brooks-Daw. *Educ*: Bitterne Park Comp. Sch., Southampton; Richard Taunton Coll., Southampton; Brunel Univ. (BSc Hons Industrial Design 1993; Hon. Fellow 2010); Royal Coll. of Art (MA Industrial Design Engrg 1996); Imperial Coll., London (DIC 1996). Virgin Atlantic Airways: Design Manager, 1996–2001;

Head of Design, 2001–10; Intercontinental Hotels Group: Sen. Vice Pres., Guest Experience and Design, 2010–12; Hd of Brand Experience, Vertu, 2012–13; Global Hd of Design, Mars, 2013–15; Hd of Guest Experience-Interior Design, Etihad Airways, 2016–17. Member: Design Council, 2009–11; Cabinet Office Innovators Council, 2009–10. Mem., Exec. Bd, D&AD, 2009–12. Vis. Tutor, RCA, 2013–. FRSA 2011. *Publications:* 9 patents on aircraft seating and vehicle accommodation. *Recreations:* travelling, ski-ing, cycling, triathlons. *Address:* Patty's Farm House, Brook Lane, Cropthorne, Worcs WR10 3JX. *T:* 07973 657476. *E:* joeferry@me.com.

**FERSHT, Sir Alan (Roy),** Kt 2003; MA, PhD; FRS 1983; Emeritus Member, MRC Laboratory of Molecular Biology, Cambridge, since 2018 (Emeritus Group Leader, 2010–17); Herchel Smith Professor of Organic Chemistry, University of Cambridge, 1988–2010, now Emeritus Professor; Life Fellow, Gonville and Caius College, Cambridge, since 2018 (Fellow, 1988–2018, Master, 2012–18); *b* 21 April 1943; *s* of Philip and Betty Fersht; *m* 1966, Marilyn Persell; one *s* one *d*. *Educ:* Sir George Monoux Grammar Sch.; Gonville and Caius Coll., Cambridge (MA, PhD). Res. Fellow, Brandeis Univ., 1968; Scientific Staff, MRC Lab. of Molecular Biology, Cambridge, 1969–77; Fellow, Jesus Coll., Cambridge, 1969–72 (Hon. Fellow, 2017); Eleanor Roosevelt Fellow, Stanford Univ., 1978; Wolfson Res. Prof. of Royal Society, Dept of Chemistry, Imperial Coll. of Science and Technology, 1978–89 (FIC 2004); Hon. Dir, MRC Unit for Protein Function and Design, later Cambridge Centre for Protein Engrg, 1989–2010; Hon. Fellow, Darwin Coll., Cambridge, 2014. Wellcome Vis. Prof. in Basic Med. Scis, Univ. of Calif, San Francisco, 1997–98; Manchot Prof., Munich, 2009–. Lectures: Smith Kline & French, Berkeley, 1984; Edsall, Harvard, 1984; B. R. Baker, Univ. of California at Santa Barbara, 1986; Frank Mathers, Univ. of Indiana, 1986; Cornell Biotechnol Program, 1987; Ferdinand Springer, FEBS, 1988–89; Calvin, Berkeley, 1990; Walker, Edinburgh, 1990; Max Tishler Prize, Harvard Univ., 1991–92; Jubilee, Biochemical Soc., E. Gordon Young Meml, Canada, and Brändström, Gothenberg, 1993; Sternbach, Yale, 1994; Sunner Meml, Lund, 1994; Heatley, Oxford, Chan, Berkeley, Rudin, Columbia, and Hofmann, German Chemical Soc., 1995; Herriott, Johns Hopkins, Fritz Lipmann, German Biol Chem. Soc., and Merck-Frosst, Montreal, 1996; Hong Kong Advanced Chems Ltd Dist., Dewey-Kelley Internat. Award, Univ. of Nebraska, Kolthoff, Univ. of Minn, Max Gruber, Groningen, 1998; Upper Rhine, NIH Dir's, 1999; Stauffer, Stanford, 2000; W. H. Stein, Rockefeller, 2003; Walker Ames, Seattle Univ., Albert Neuberger Meml, Jerusalem, 2005; Robert Robinson Meml, Oxford, Drummond, Queen Mary Coll., Kendrew, Weizmann Inst., 2006; Henry Kamin, Duke Univ., 2007; Marion Koshland, and G. N. Lewis, Berkeley, 2008; Summer, Cornell, 2009. Hon. Treas., Fedn of European Biochemical Socs, 2012–. Mem., EMBO, 1980; MAE 1989; FMedSci 2007. Hon. For. Mem., Amer. Acad. of Arts and Sci., 1988; For. Associate, Nat. Acad. of Scis, USA, 1993; Foreign Member: Amer. Philosophical Soc., 2008; Accademia Nazionale dei Lincei, 2013. Essex County Jun. Chess Champion, 1961; Pres., Cambridge Univ. Chess Club, 1964 (Half Blue, 1965). Hon. DPhil: Uppsala, 1999; Weizmann Inst., 2004; Dr *hc* Free Univ. of Brussels, 1999; Hebrew Univ., 2006; Aarhus Univ., 2008. FEBS Anniversary Prize, 1980; Novo Biotechnology Prize, 1986; Charmian Medal, 1986, Natural Products Award, 1999, RSC; Gabor Medal, 1991, Davy Medal, 1998, Royal Medal, 2008, Royal Soc.; Harden Medal, Biochemical Soc., 1993; Feldberg Foundn Prize, 1996; Distinguished Service Award, Miami, 1997; Anfinsen Award, 1999, Stein and Moore Award, 2001, Protein Soc.; Bader Award, Amer. Chem. Soc., 2005; Linderstrøm-Lang Prize and Medal, 2005; Bijvoet Medal, Utrecht Univ., 2008; G. N. Lewis Medal, Berkeley, 2008; Wilhelm Exner Medal (Austria), Österreichischer Gewerbeverein, 2009. *Publications:* Enzyme Structure and Mechanism, 1977, 2nd edn 1984; Structure and Mechanism in Protein Science, 1999; Jaques Staunton Chess Sets 1849–1939, 2007; Jaques and British Chess Company Chess Sets, 2010; papers in scientific jls. *Recreations:* chess, horology, bird photography. *Address:* Gonville and Caius College, Cambridge CB2 1TA. *T:* (01223) 763092.

**FERT, Prof. Albert,** Grand Croix, Ordre National du Mérite, 2015 (Grand Officier 2008); Commandeur de la Légion d'Honneur, 2012; DèsSc; Professor of Physics, University of Paris Sud 11, 1976, now Emeritus; Scientific Director, Unité Mixte de Physique CNRS/Thales, since 1995; *b* Carcassonne, France, 7 March 1938; *s* of Charles and Irmine Fert; *m* 1967, Marie-Josée; one *s* one *d*. *Educ:* Ecole Normale Supérieure, Paris (DèsSc). Lectr, Univ. of Grenoble, 1962–70; Asst Prof., Univ. of Paris Sud, 1970–76. (Jtly) Nobel Prize in Physics, 2007. *Publications:* 400 contribs to books and learned jls. *Recreations:* music (jazz), windsurfing, mountaineering, cinema, cycling. *Address:* Unité Mixte de Physique, CNRS/Thales, 1 Avenue Fresnel, 91767 Palaiseau, France. *T:* (1) 69415864. *E:* albert.fert@thalesgroup.com.

**FESTING, Andrew Thomas,** MBE 2008; RP 1992; painter, since 1981; President, Royal Society of Portrait Painters, 2002–08; *b* 30 Nov. 1941; *s* of Field Marshal Sir Francis Wogan Festing, GCB, KBE, DSO and Mary Festing (*née* Riddell); *m* 1968, Virginia Fyffe; one *d*. *Educ:* Ampleforth; RMA Sandhurst. Commnd Rifle Bde, 1961. Joined Sotheby & Co., 1969, Dir, English Picture Dept, 1977–81. Paintings in permanent collections incl. Nat. Gall. of Ireland, Palace of Westminster, Royal Collection, NPG. Notable commissions include HM the Queen, Queen Elizabeth the Queen Mother, group portrait of whole Royal family; group picture of MPs in Library at Palace of Westminster, H of L in Session, Speakers Boothroyd and Martin; set of five pictures of famous cricketers for Lord's. Hon. DLitt Northumbria, 2010. *Recreations:* country sports, gardening. *Address:* 3 Hillsleigh Road, W8 7LE. *T:* (020) 7727 9287.

**FETHERSTON-DILKE, Mary Stella,** CBE 1968; RRC 1966; Organiser, Citizens' Advice Bureau, 1971–83, retired; *b* 21 Sept. 1918; *d* of late B. A. Fetherston-Dilke, MBE. *Educ:* Kingsley Sch., Leamington Spa; St George's Hospital, London (SRN). Joined QARNNS, 1942; Matron-in-Chief, QARNNS, 1966–70, retired. OStJ 1966. *Recreation:* antiques.

**FETHERSTON-DILKE, Michael Charles,** FCA; Vice Lord-Lieutenant of Warwickshire, since 2017; *b* Southsea, 30 Dec. 1948; *s* of Capt. Charles Beaumont Fetherston-Dilke, RN and Pauline (*née* Stanley-Williams); *m* 1983, Rosemary Ann Keith; two *s* one *d*. *Educ:* Rugby Sch.; Univ. of Bristol (BSc SocSci). FCA 1973. Peat, Marwick, Mitchell, 1970–78; Nat. Enterprise Bd (on secondment), 1978–79; Sen. rôles, BET plc, 1980–92, incl. Develt Dir, United Transport Internat., 1988–92; Finance Dir, Nightspeed Gp Ltd, 1994–99; Chm. and non-exec. dir, private equity-backed service businesses, 2000–13. Non-exec. Dir, CLA, 2014–. Regl Chm., Heart of England, Historic Houses, 2013–18. DL Warwickshire, 2009. *Recreations:* archery (Mem., Woodmen of Arden), golf, country pursuits. *Address:* Maxstoke Castle, Coleshill, Warwickshire B46 2RD. *T:* (01675) 466532. *Clubs:* Boodles; Royal West Norfolk Golf.

**FETHERSTONHAUGH, Guy Cuthbert Charles,** QC 2003; *b* 29 Jan. 1955; *s* of late Theobald Henry Robert Fetherstonhaugh and Genevieve Fetherstonhaugh (*née* Moreau); *m* 1991, Alexia Jane Musson Lees; two *s* one *d*. *Educ:* Stonyhurst Coll.; Bristol Univ. (BSc). FCIArb 2014. Served 2nd Bn, RGJ, 1978–81. Called to the Bar, Inner Temple, 1983, Bencher, 2014. Hon. RICS 2011; Hon. Arbrix 2012. *Publications:* (jtly) Handbook of Rent Review, 1991 and Supplements; (contrib.) The Litigation Practice, 1999–2003; Commonhold, 2004; The Electronic Communications Code and Property Law: practice and procedure, 2018. *Recreations:* my family, woodwork, gardening, cycling. *Address:* Falcon Chambers, Falcon Court, EC4Y 1AA. *T:* (020) 7353 2484. *Clubs:* Rifles Officers', Royal Automobile.

**FETHERSTONHAUGH, Henry George,** OBE 2001; FRAgS; farmer, forester and property manager; Lord-Lieutenant of Clwyd, since 2013; *b* 16 Oct. 1954; *s* of David Henry Fetherstonhaugh and Hon. Maria Victoria, *d* of 8th Viscount Galway, PC, GCMG, DSO, OBE; *m* 1st, 1978, Nicola Payne-Gallwey (marr. diss. 1994); two *s*; 2nd, 1996, Davina MacLeod; two *s*. *Educ:* Eton Coll.; Royal Agricl Coll., Cirencester. Game business, 1974–78; farming and forestry enterprises, 1978–; Finance Dir, Timber Growers UK, 1989–94. Forestry Comr for Wales, 1995–2001. Mem., Home Grown Timber Adv. Cttee, 1990–95. Royal Welsh Agricultural Society, 1978–: Hon. Show Dir, 1994–; Vice-Chm., Bd of Dirs, 1994–; Chair, Show Admin, 1994–; Chair, Livestock, 1998–2000; Chm., Finance; Chm., Bd of Dirs, 2002–04. Chm. Govs, Ysgol-Y-Plas Voluntary Aided Sch., 1979–2014. Pres., Denbigh and Flints Agricultural Assoc., 2014. *Recreations:* shooting, ornithology, tennis. *Address:* Coed Coch, Dolwen, Abergele, N Wales LL22 8AY. *T:* and *Fax:* (01492) 680357. *Club:* Boodle's.

**FETTIPLACE, Prof. Robert,** FRS 1990; Steenbock Professor of Neural and Behavioral Sciences, University of Wisconsin, since 1991; *b* 24 Feb. 1946; *s* of George Robert Fettiplace and Maisie Fettiplace (*née* Rolson); *m* 1977, Merriel Cleone Kruse. *Educ:* Nottingham High Sch.; Sidney Sussex Coll., Cambridge (BA 1968; MA 1972; PhD 1974). Research Fellow: Sidney Sussex Coll., Cambridge, 1971–74; Stanford Univ., 1974–76; Elmore Res. Fellow, Cambridge, 1976–79; Howe Sen. Res. Fellow, Royal Soc., 1979–90. Fellow, Amer. Acad. of Arts and Scis, 2012. Kavli Prize in Neurosci., 2018; Passano Award for Med. Sci., 2019. *Publications:* contribs to Jl Physiology, Jl Neuroscience and other learned jls. *Recreations:* bird watching, listening to music. *Address:* Department of Neuroscience, University of Wisconsin, 1300 University Avenue, Madison, WI 53706-1510, USA.

**FEUCHTWANG, Anna;** Chief Executive, National Children's Bureau, since 2014; *b* London, 27 March 1964; *d* of Stephan Feuchtwang and Miranda Feuchtwang; two *s*. *Educ:* Holland Park Comp. Sch.; London Coll. of Printing (HND Journalism). Croydon Advertiser: indentured; Chief Reporter, 1986–89; Press Officer/Hd of Communications, Oxfam, 1989–99; Dir, On the Line, 1999–2001; Dir, Communications and Public Affairs, Assoc. of London Govt, 2001–04; Chief Exec., EveryChild, 2004–14. Trustee and Chair of Board: Action Aid, 2001–04; Bond, 2005–11; Asylum Aid, 2012–14; Trustee, Juconi, Mexico, 2017–. Mem., Charity Appeals Adv. Cttee, BBC, 2014–17. *Address:* National Children's Bureau, WeWork, 115 Mare Street, E8 4RU. *T:* 07508 741176. *E:* afeuchtwang@ncb.org.uk. *W:* www.twitter.com/AnnaFeuchtwang.

**FEVERSHAM, 7th Baron** *cr* 1826; **Jasper Orlando Slingsby Duncombe;** *b* 14 March 1968; *e s* of 6th Baron Feversham and Shannon (*d* 1976), *d* of Sir Thomas Foy, CSI, CIE; *S* father, 2009; *m* 2009, Candida, *d* of Clive Boddington; one *s*. *Heir: s* Hon. Orlando Balthazar Duncombe, *b* 16 July 2009.

**FEWSTER, Dr Kevin John,** AM 2001; Director, Royal Museums Greenwich (formerly National Maritime Museum), since 2007; *b* Perth, WA, 1 Dec. 1953; *s* of Geoffrey and Audrey Fewster; *m* 1996, Carol Scott; one *d*. *Educ:* Glyn Grammar Sch., Ewell; Haileybury Coll., Melbourne; Australian National Univ. (BA Hons); Univ. of New South Wales (PhD 1980). Teaching Fellow, Royal Mil. Coll. Duntroon, Univ. of NSW, 1976–80; Tutor, 1981–82, Sen. Tutor, 1983–84, History Dept, Monash Univ.; Director: S Australian Maritime Mus., Port Adelaide, 1984–89; Australian Nat. Maritime Mus., Sydney, 1989–2000; Powerhouse Mus., Sydney, 2000–07. Dir, Visit Greenwich Destination Mgt Co., 2013–. Member: Collections Council of Australia, 2004–07; Nat. Museums Directors' Council, 2007–; Exec., Maritime Greenwich World Heritage Site, 2007– (Chm., 2010–14). Chm., Council of Australian Mus. Dirs, 2004–07. Vice Pres., 1993–96, Pres., 1996–99 and 2014–15, Internat. Congress of Maritime Mus. Pres., Darling Harbour Business Assoc., 2000–02. FRSA. Hon. DLitt Greenwich, 2016. *Publications:* Gallipoli Correspondent: the frontline diary of C. E. W. Bean, 1983, 3rd edn 2007; (jtly) A Turkish View of Gallipoli: Canakkale, 1985, 2nd edn 2005. *Recreations:* tennis, football. *Address:* Royal Museums Greenwich, Greenwich, SE10 9NF. *Club:* Sydney Cricket Ground.

**FFOLKES, Sir Robert (Francis Alexander),** 7th Bt *cr* 1774; OBE 1990; Save the Children UK, 1974–2003; *b* 2 Dec. 1943; *o s* of Captain Sir (Edward John) Patrick (Boschetti) ffolkes, 6th Bt, and Geraldine (*d* 1978), *d* of late William Roffey, Writtle, Essex; *S* father, 1960. *Educ:* Stowe Sch.; Christ Church, Oxford. *Recreations:* mountain ecology development and conservation, esp. in the Himalayas and Central Asia. *Address:* Coast Guard House, Morston, Holt, Norfolk NR25 7BH. *E:* robertffolkes@gmail.com.

**FFOWCS WILLIAMS, Prof. John Eirwyn,** FREng; Rank Professor of Engineering, University of Cambridge, 1972–2002, now Emeritus; Master, Emmanuel College, Cambridge, 1996–2002 (Professorial Fellow, 1972–96; Life Fellow, 2002); *b* 25 May 1935; *m* 1959, Anne Beatrice Mason; two *s* one *d*. *Educ:* Friends Sch., Great Ayton; Derby Techn. Coll.; Univ. of Southampton (BSc, PhD 1960); MA, ScD Cantab 1986. CEng, FREng (FEng 1988); FRAeS, FInstP, FIMA, FIOA, Fellow Acoustical Soc. of America, FAIAA. Engrg Apprentice, Rolls-Royce Ltd, 1951–55; Spitfire Mitchell Meml Schol. to Southampton Univ., 1955–60 (Pres., Students' Union, 1957–58); Aerodynamics Div., NPL, 1960–62; Bolt, Beranek & Newman Inc., 1962–64; Reader in Applied Maths, Imperial Coll. of Science and Technology, 1964–69; Rolls Royce Prof. of Theoretical Acoustics, Imperial Coll., 1969–72. Chairman: Concorde Noise Panel, 1965–75; Topexpress Ltd, 1979–89; Dir, VSEL Consortium plc, 1987–95. Chm., Noise Research Cttee, ARC, 1969–76. FRSA; FLSW 2012. Honour Prof., Beijing Inst. of Aeronautics and Astronautics, 1992–; Emeritus Hon. Prof., Wales Inst. of Math. and Computational Scis, 2011. Foreign Hon. Mem., Amer. Acad. Arts and Scis, 1989; Foreign Associate, NAE, USA, 1995. Gov., Felsted Sch., 1980–94. Hon. ScD Southampton 2003. AIAA Aero-Acoustics Medal, 1977; Rayleigh Medal, Inst. of Acoustics, 1984; Silver Medal, Société Française d'Acoustique, 1989; Gold Medal, RAeS, 1990; Per Bruel Gold Medal, ASME, 1997; Sir Frank Whittle Medal, Royal Acad. Engrg, 2002; Aeroacoustics Award, Confedn of European Aerospace Socs, 2004. *Publications:* (with A. P. Dowling) Sound and Sources of Sound, 1983; articles in Philosophical Trans Royal Soc., Jl of Fluid Mechanics, Jl IMA, Jl of Sound Vibration, Annual Reviews of Fluid Mechanics, Random Vibration, Financial Times; (jtly) film on Aerodynamic Sound. *Recreations:* friends, vintage cars, thinking. *Address:* Emmanuel College, Cambridge CB2 3AP.

**FFRENCH,** family name of **Baron ffrench.**

**FFRENCH, 8th Baron** *cr* 1798; **Robuck John Peter Charles Mario ffrench;** Bt 1779; *b* 14 March 1956; *s* of 7th Baron ffrench and of Sonia Katherine, *d* of late Major Digby Cayley; *S* father, 1986; *m* 1987, Dörthe Marie-Louise, *d* of Captain Wilhelm Schauer; one *d*. *Educ:* Blackrock, Co. Dublin; Ampleforth College, Yorks. *Heir:* none.

**ffRENCH BLAKE, Col Robert John William;** Extra Equerry to the Prince of Wales, since 1995; international sporting consultant, since 1991; *b* Salisbury, Wilts, 21 June 1940; *s* of late Lt Col Desmond O'Brien Evelyn ffrench Blake and Elizabeth Iris (*née* Cardale, later

Mrs Anthony Hogg); *m* 1976, Ilynne Sabina Mary Eyston; three *d*. *Educ:* Eton; RMA Sandhurst; Army Staff Coll. Commnd 13th/18th Royal Hussars, 1960; psc 1972; CO, 1981–83. Asst Mil. Attaché, Washington, 1985–88. Chief Exec., Guards Polo Club, 1989–91. Hon. Colonel: 13th/18th Royal Hussars, 1990–93; Light Dragoons, 1993–95. Mem., HM Body Guard, Hon. Corps of Gentlemen-at-Arms, 1990–2010 (Harbinger, 2007–10). *Recreations:* shooting, ski-ing, polo, Alpaca farmer. *Address:* Gillans, Minterne Parva, Dorchester, Dorset DT2 7AP. *T:* 07970 444447. *E:* rfb@gillans.net. *Clubs:* Cavalry and Guards, Pratt's.

**FFRENCH-CONSTANT, Prof. Charles Kenvyn**, PhD; FRCP, FMedSci; FRSE; Professor of Medical Neurology, 2008–16, now Professorial Fellow, Co-Director, Centre for Multiple Sclerosis Research, since 2008, Co-Director, Anne Rowling Regenerative Neurology Clinic, since 2013, and Dean of Research, College of Medicine and Veterinary Medicine, since 2017, University of Edinburgh; *b* 5 Nov. 1954; *m* Jennifer Wimperis, DM, FRCP, FRCPath; one *s* one *d*. *Educ:* Pembroke Coll., Cambridge (BA 1976; BChir 1979; MA 1980; MB 1980); University College London (PhD 1986). MRCP 1982, FRCP 1999. Lucille Markey Postdoctoral Fellow, MIT, 1986–88; Wellcome Trust Sen. Res. Fellow, Wellcome/CRC Inst. of Develt Biol., 1991–96, Prof. of Neurological Genetics, 1999–2008, Univ. of Cambridge; Fellow, Pembroke Coll., Cambridge, 1999–2008; Hon. Consultant in Med. Genetics, Addenbrooke's Hosp., Cambridge, 1996–2008; Dep. Dir, 2008–11, Dir, 2011–16, MRC Centre for Regenerative Medicine, Univ. of Edinburgh. FMedSci 2017; FRSE 2018. *Publications:* papers on develtl and regenerative biol. *Recreation:* fishing. *Address:* Scottish Centre for Regenerative Medicine, Edinburgh bioQuarter, 5a Little France Drive, Edinburgh EH16 4UU; 420 Unthank Road, Norwich NR4 7QH.

**FFYTCHE, Timothy John**, LVO 1997; FRCS; Surgeon-Oculist to the Queen, 1999–2001; Consultant Ophthalmologist: Moorfields Eye Hospital, 1975–2001; Hospital for Tropical Diseases, 1988–2006; Consultant Ophthalmic Surgeon to King Edward VIIth Hospital for Officers, 1980–2006; *b* 11 Sept. 1936; *s* of late Louis ffytche and Margaret (*née* Law); *m* 1961, Bärbl, *d* of late Günther Fischer; two *s*. *Educ:* Lancing Coll.; St George's Hosp., London. MB, BS; DO 1961; FRCS 1968. Registrar, Moorfields Eye Hosp., 1966–69; Wellcome Lectr, Hammersmith Hosp., 1969–70; Sen. Registrar, Middlesex Hosp., 1970–73; Ophthalmic Surgeon, St Thomas' Hosp., 1973–99; Surgeon-Oculist to HM Household, 1980–99. Sec., OSUK, 1980–82. Mem., Medical Adv. Bd, LEPRA, 1982–2008; Vice-Pres., Ophthalmol Sect., RSocMed, 1985–88; UK rep. to Internat. Fedn of Ophthalmic Socs, 1985–89; Mem., Adv. Cttee to Internat. Council of Ophthalmology, 1985–2002. Founder, Ophthalmic Aid to Eastern Europe, 1990–; Chm., European Sect., Internat. Agency for Prevention of Blindness, 1999–2008 (Co-Chm., 1994–99); President: Med. Soc. of London, 2001–02; Moorfields Assoc. (formerly Moorfields Alumni Assoc.), 2010–18. Clayton Meml Lectr, LEPRA, 1984. Hon. FRCOphth 2011. Editorial Committee: Ophthalmic Literature, 1968–82; Transactions of OSUK, 1984–89, Eye, 1989–96; European Jl of Ophthalmology, 1990–2006. *Publications:* articles on retinal diagnosis and therapy, retinal photography and the ocular complications of leprosy, in The Lancet, British Jl of Ophthalmol., Trans OSUK, Proc. Royal Soc. Med., Leprosy Review and other specialist jls. *Recreation:* occasional fishing. *Address:* (home) 1 Wellington Square, SW3 4NJ.

**FIDDES, Rev. Prof. Paul Stuart**, DPhil, DD; Professor of Systematic Theology, University of Oxford, since 2002; Professorial Research Fellow and Director of Research, Regent's Park College, Oxford, since 2007; Ecumenical Canon, Christ Church, Oxford, 2012–18, now Emeritus Canon; Ecumenical Prebendary, Collegiate Church of St Endelienta, North Cornwall, since 2012; *b* 30 April 1947; *s* of James Stuart Fiddes and Lois Sleeman Fiddes; *m* 1973, Marion Downing Anness; one *s* (and one *s* decd). *Educ:* Drayton Manor Grammar Sch.; St Peter's Coll., Oxford (BA Eng. Lang. and Lit. 1968; Theol 1970, MA 1972; Hon. Fellow 2004); Regent's Park Coll., Oxford (DPhil 1975; DD 2004). Ordained to Baptist Ministry, 1972; Regent's Park College, Oxford: Res. Fellow in OT, 1972–75; Tutorial Fellow in Christian Doctrine, 1975–89; Principal, 1989–2007, now Principal Emeritus; Lectr in Theol., St Peter's Coll., Oxford, 1979–85; Chm. Bd, Faculty of Theology, Oxford Univ., 1996–98. Joint Editor: Ecclesiology; Ecclesial Practices. Hon. Dr Bucharest, 2004. *Publications:* The Creative Suffering of God, 1988; Past Event and Present Salvation: the Christian idea of atonement, 1989; Freedom and Limit: a dialogue between literature and Christian doctrine, 1991; (ed) Reflections on the Water: understanding God and the world through the baptism of believers, 1996; (ed jtly) Pilgrim Pathways, 1999; The Promised End, 2000; Participating in God: a pastoral doctrine of the Trinity, 2000; (ed) The Novel, Spirituality and Modern Culture, 2000; (ed) Faith in the Centre: Christianity and culture, 2001; Tracks and Traces: baptist identity in church and theology, 2003; (ed jtly) Flickering Images: theology and film in dialogue, 2005; (ed) Under the Rule of Christ, 2008; (ed) The Spirit and the Letter, 2013; (ed jtly) The Rhetoric of Evil, 2013; Seeing the World and Knowing God: Hebrew wisdom and Christian doctrine in a late-modern context, 2013; (jtly) Baptists and the Communion of Saints: a theology of covenanted disciples, 2014; (jtly) Two Views on the Doctrine of the Trinity, 2014; (jtly) Sharing the Faith at the Boundaries of Unity, 2015; Shakespeare and Religion, 2015; (ed) A World Order of Love: Baptists and the peace movements of 1914, 2017; (jtly) Dissenting Spirit: a history of Regent's Park College 1752–2017, 2017; (ed jtly) David Jones: a Christian Modernist? Approaches to his art, poetry and cultural theory, 2018; A Unicorn Dies: a novel of mystery and ideas, 2018. *Recreations:* music, literature, travel, inland waterways. *Address:* Regent's Park College, Oxford OX1 2LB. *E:* paul.fiddes@regents.ox.ac.uk.

**FIDDICK, Peter Ronald**; journalist and broadcaster; *b* 21 Oct. 1938; *s* of late Wing-Comdr Ronald Fiddick and Phyllis Fiddick (*née* Wherry); *m* 1966, Jane Mary Hodlin; one *s* one *d*. *Educ:* Reading Sch.; Magdalen Coll., Oxford (BA English Lang. and Lit.). Journalist, Liverpool Daily Post, 1962–65; Leader writer, Westminster Press, 1965–66; Asst Editor, Nova, 1968; The Guardian: reporter, 1966–67 and 1969; Asst Features Editor, 1970–75; Television Columnist, 1971–84; Media Editor, 1984–88; Editor: The Listener, 1989–91; Television (RTS), 1991–2001; Research (Market Res. Soc.), 1992–99; RADA, The Magazine, 1993–2006; Media Columnist, Admap, 1997–2002. Newspaper Reviewer, BBC Breakfast News, 1989–99; Media Critic, BBC Radio Arts Programme, 1990–2001. Mem., Bd, George Foster Peabody Awards, USA, 2000–06 (Chm., 2005–06). FRTS 1992; Associate, RADA. Wrote and presented television series: Looking at Television, 1975–76; The Television Programme, 1979–80; Soviet Television - Fact and Fiction, 1985. *Publications:* (with B. Smithies) Enoch Powell on Immigration, 1969. *Recreations:* music, food, theatre, Saturdays.

**FIDLER, John Allan**, RIBA; FSA; Principal, John Fidler Preservation Technology Inc., Los Angeles, since 2012; *b* 1 Sept. 1952; *s* of late Eddie Fidler and Joan Margaret Fidler (*née* Edwards); *m* 1992, Jeanne Marie Teutonico. *Educ:* Sheffield Univ. (BA Hons; DipArch, MA Arch); Manchester Univ. (MA Conservation); Architectural Assoc., London (Grad. Dip. Conservation). RIBA 1979; IHBC 1998. Casework officer, Historic Bldgs Div., GLC, 1978–83; Historic Bldgs architect, City of London Corp., 1983–84; English Heritage: Conservation Officer for bldgs at risk, 1984–86; Superintending Architect, 1986–90; Head: Architectural and Survey Services, 1990–91; Bldg Conservation and Res., 1991–2002; Conservation Dir, 2002–06; Staff Consultant, 2006–12, Practice Leader, 2007–12, Preservation Technol., Simpson Gumpertz & Heger Inc., LA. Chm., Cttee B/209-7 drafting codes of practice, BSI, 2001–06. Member: Council, ICCROM, 2001–07 (Vice Pres., 2005–07); Conservation Cttee, Getty Foundn (formerly J. P. Getty Trust Grants Prog.), 2001–07. FAPT 2000; FSA 2002; FIIC 2006; FRICS 2007. FRSA 1980. *Publications:* (ed) English Heritage Directory of Building Sands and Aggregates, 2000; (ed) Stone, Vol. 2, English Heritage Research Trans, 2002; contrib. technical papers to ASCHB Trans, Bull. Assoc. for Preservation Technol. *Recreations:* hiking, visiting historic sites. *Address:* (office) 4640 Admiralty Way, Suite 500, Marina Del Rey, CA 90292, USA. *T:* (310) 4965730. *E:* johnfidler@jf-pt.com.

**FIDLER, Prof. (John) Kelvin**, PhD; FREng, Hon. FIET; consultant on engineering and higher education, since 2008; Vice-Chancellor and Chief Executive, University of Northumbria at Newcastle, 2001–08; *b* 11 May 1944; *s* of Samuel Fidler and Barbara Fidler; *m* 1st, 1966, Jadwiga Sorokowska (marr. diss. 1995); one *s* one *d*; 2nd, 2002, Nadine Cleaver. *Educ:* Harrow Co. Sch. for Boys; King's Coll., Univ. of Durham (BSc); Univ. of Newcastle upon Tyne (PhD 1968). CEng 1972, FREng 2005; FIET (FIEE 1982), Hon. FIET 2010. Sen. Res. Associate, Univ. of Newcastle upon Tyne, 1968–69; Lectr, 1969–74, Sen. Lectr, 1974–80, Reader, 1980–83, Univ. of Essex; Professor of Electronics: Open Univ., 1984–88; Univ. of York, 1989–2001. Chm., Engineering Council, 2005–11; Member: EngineeringUK (formerly Engrg and Technol. Bd), 2005–11; Standing Cttee on Educn and Trng, 2011–15, Visiting Professors Mgt Gp, 2017– (Dep. Chair, 2019–), Royal Acad. of Engrg; UCL Centre for Engrg Educn Adv. Gp, 2015–; Hon. Consultant, New Models in Technol. and Engrg (formerly Teaching Engrg) Curriculum Adv. Gp, 2015–18. Mem., Prime Minister's Adv. Cttee, Queen's Award for Enterprise, 2005–11. Non-exec. Dir, Arden Univ. (formerly Resource Develt Internat.) Ltd, 2010–16. Chm., Ind. Commn on Northumberland, 2008–09. Chm., Subject Benchmark Rev. Gp for Engrg, QAA, 2013–15. Chm., Associates of Discovery Mus., 2008–11. Hon. Consultant, Graduate Excellence Curriculum Gp, Food and Drink Fedn, 2012–15. Chm., Industrial Adv. Cttee, Univ. of Huddersfield, 2012–14. Institution of Engineering and Technology: Member: Fellows Standing Panel, 2013–16; Scholarships and Awards Cttee, 2014–15; Educn and Skills Policy Panel, 2015–18; Acad. Adv. Gp, 2016–. Hon. DSc Huddersfield, 2007; DUniv York, 2009; Hon. DCL Northumbria, 2010. *Publications:* Computer Aided Circuit Design, 1978; Introductory Circuit Theory, 1980, 2nd edn 1989; Continuous Time Active Filter Design, 1998; Skills for the Nation: engineering undergraduates in the UK, 2013; numerous contribs on electronics to learned jls. *Recreations:* varied.

**FIDLER, Prof. Peter Michael**, CBE 2012 (MBE 1993); DL; President, University of Sunderland, 2014–15 (Vice-Chancellor and Chief Executive, 1999–2014). *Educ:* Univ. of Salford (MSc). Town planner. Formerly: Dean, Dept of Built Envmt, UWE; Dep. Chancellor (Academic Affairs), Oxford Brookes Univ.; Past Pres., Royal Town Planning Inst. Ind. Gov., London S Bank Univ. Non-exec. Dir, Together for Children Sunderland Ltd, 2017–. Hon. DEd Sunderland, 2015. DL Tyne and Wear, 2005.

**FIDLER-SIMPSON, John Cody**; *see* Simpson.

**FIELD, Barry John Anthony**, TD 1984; *b* 4 July 1946; *s* of Ernest Field and late Marguerite Eugenie Field; *m* 1969, Jaqueline Anne Miller; one *s* one *d*. *Educ:* Collingwood Boys' Sch.; Mitcham Grammar Sch.; Bembridge Sch.; Victoria Street Coll. Chm., J. D. Field & Sons Ltd, 1993–94 (Dir, 1981–94); Dir, Great Southern Cemetery & Crematorium Co. Ltd, 1969–94. Councillor, Horsham Dist Council, 1983–86 (Vice-Chm., Housing, 1984–85, Chm., Housing, 1985–86); Mem., IoW CC, 1986–89. MP (C) Isle of Wight, 1987–97. Chm., H of C Deregulation Cttee, 1995–97. Major RCT TA; Liveryman, Turners' Co.; Mem., Watermen and Lightermen's Co. *Recreations:* sailing, theatre, ski-ing. *Address:* Medina Lodge, 25 Birmingham Road, Cowes, Isle of Wight PO31 7BH. *T:* (01983) 292871. *Club:* Island Sailing (Cowes).

**FIELD, Dr Clive Douglas**, OBE 2007; FRHistS; FEA; Director of Scholarship and Collections, British Library, 2001–06; *b* 27 June 1950; *o s* of Joseph Stanley Field and Lily Field (*née* Battams); *m* 1972, Verena Duss; one *s*. *Educ:* Dunstable Grammar Sch.; Wadham Coll., Oxford (BA Modern History 1971; MA 1975; DPhil Modern History 1975); Westminster Coll., Oxford (PGCE 1975). FRHistS 2001; FEA 2008. SSRC Post-Doctoral Fellow, Wadham Coll., Oxford, 1975–77; Asst Librarian, 1977–87, Sub-Librarian, 1987–90, John Rylands Univ. Liby of Manchester; University of Birmingham: Dep. Librarian, 1990–95; Librarian and Dir of Inf. Services, 1995–2001; Associate Mem., 1992–2001, Hon. Res. Fellow, 2006–, Dept of Modern History. Hon. Res. Fellow, Inst. for Social Change, Univ. of Manchester, 2010–. Project Director: Ensemble: towards a distributed nat. liby resource for music, 1999–2002; Revelation: unlocking research resources for 19th and 20th century church history and Christian theology, 2000–02. Co-Dir, British Religion in Numbers, 2008–. Chairman: Internat. English Short Title Catalogue Cttee, 2001–06; Full Disclosure Implementation Gp, 2001–05; Jt Cttee on Voluntary Deposit, 2001–03; Jt Cttee on Legal Deposit, 2004–06; Member: Bd of Dirs, Consortium of Univ. Res. Libraries, 1996–2001, 2003–06 (Chm., 2000–01); Cttee on Electronic Inf., 1999–2001, Cttee for Content Services, 2002–05, and Cttee for Support of Res., 2003–04, Jt Inf. Systems Cttee; Midlands Metropolitan Area Network Mgt Cttee, 1999–2001; HEFCE Strategic Adv. Cttee for Res., 2003–06; Legal Deposit Adv. Panel, 2005–06; Adv. Council on Nat. Records and Archives, 2007–14; Forum on Historical Manuscripts and Academic Res., 2010–14; Academic Adv. Cttee, Ushaw Coll. Liby, 2011–17; Bd of Dirs, Birmingham Res. Park Ltd, 1999–2001. Dir and Trustee, Pastoral Res. Centre Trust, 2008–18. Pres., Religious Archives Gp, 2007–16. Bibliography Ed., Wesley Historical Soc., 1976–; Ed., The People Called Methodists microfiche project, 1988–98; Chm., Editl Bd, Bulletin of John Rylands Univ. Liby, Univ. of Manchester, 2008–12. Hon. DLitt Birmingham, 2006. *Publications:* Non-Recurrent Christian Data: reviews of UK Statistical Sources, 1987; Anti-Methodist Publications of the Eighteenth Century, 1991; Church and Chapel in Early Victorian Shropshire, 2004; Lutonian Odyssey, 2008; Britain's Last Religious Revival?, 2015; Secularization in the Long 1960s, 2017; British Religion and the World Wars, 2019; Periodizing Secularization, 2019; professional papers; articles, bibliographies and reviews on the social history of religion in Great Britain since 1689, with special reference to religious statistics, religious practice, and the history of Methodism. *Recreations:* historical research and writing, visiting (incl. virtually) secondhand bookshops. *Address:* 35 Elvetham Road, Edgbaston, Birmingham B15 2LZ. *E:* c.d.field@bham.ac.uk.

**FIELD, David Anthony**; Chief Executive, Zoological Society of East Anglia, since 2018; *b* 9 Jan. 1967; *s* of Derek and Jean Field; *m* 1997, Dr Lesley Dickie. *Educ:* Foxyards Primary Sch.; Dudley Sch.; University Coll., Cardiff (BSc Hons Zool.); Open Univ. (MBA). SO, UFAW, 1988–90; Senior Zookeeper: Penscynor Wildlife Park, 1990–93; Edinburgh Zoo, 1993–98; Asst Dir, Dublin Zoo, 1998–2002; Curator, Whipsnade Zoo, 2002–03; Curator of Mammals, 2003–04, Hd of Animal Care, 2004–06, Zool Dir, 2006–18, Zool Soc. of London. Hon. Prof., RVC, 2015–. Member: Council, British and Irish Assoc. of Zoos and Aquaria, 2005–16 (Chm., 2011–16); Bd, Internat. Species Information Systems, 2008–15 (Chm., 2010–15); DEFRA Zoos Forum, 2008–; World Assoc. of Zoos and Aquaria, 2015–.

Trustee: Wild Vets Internat., 2006–07; Gorilla Orgn, 2010–12. FLS 2010. *Recreations:* zoo history, golf. *Address:* Zoological Society of East Anglia, The Grove, Kenninghall Road, Banham, Norfolk NR16 2HE.

FIELD, Prof. **David John**, DM; FRCPE, FRCPCH; Professor of Neonatal Medicine, University of Leicester, 1996–2018, now Emeritus; Hon. Consultant Neonatologist, University Hospitals of Leicester, 1989–2015; *b* Barnet, Herts, 12 March 1953; *s* of George and Joan Field; *m* 1974, Caroline Stainer; one *s* one *d*. *Educ:* Sandown Grammar Sch., IoW; King's Coll. Hosp., London (MB BS 1976). DCH 1978; FRCPE 1988; FRCPCH 1996. MRC Res. Fellow, Nottingham Univ., 1983–85; Lectr, 1985–89, Sen. Lectr, 1989–96, Univ. of Leicester. Neonatal Lead for MBBRACE-UK Collaboration, 2013–. Hon. Sec., 2001–04, Pres., 2008–11, British Assoc. of Perinatal Medicine. *Publications:* (with J. Stroobnant) Case Studies in Paediatrics, 1987; (jtly) Tutorials in Differential Diagnosis, 1989; (jtly) Paediatric Grey Courses, 1994; (ed jtly) Paediatrics: an illustrated colour text, 1997 (internat. edn 2002); (ed with J. Stroobnant) Handbook of Paediatric Investigations, 2001; (ed jtly) Paediatric Differential Diagnosis, 2nd edn 2005; (ed jtly) Multiple Pregnancy, 2006; contrib. chapters in books; contribs to Seminars in Neonatol., Paediatric Pulmonol., Archives of Diseases in Childhood, BMJ, Early Human Develt, Jl Perinatal Medicine, Lancet, Acta Paediatrica, etc. *Recreations:* gardening, travel, walking, opera and ballet. *Address:* Department of Health Sciences, University of Leicester, Centre for Medicine, University Road, Leicester LE1 7RH. *T:* (0116) 252 5468. *E:* df63@le.ac.uk.

FIELD, **His Honour Douglas John**; a Circuit Judge, 2006–15; a Deputy Circuit Judge, since 2015; *b* 17 April 1947; twin *s* of Robert Henry Field and Ivy May Field (*née* Dicketts); *m* 1969, Karen Heather Strubbe; one *s* one *d*. *Educ:* Ottershaw Sch.; Coll. of Law, Guildford. Admitted solicitor, 1972; called to Bermuda Bar, 1974; in practice as barrister and attorney, Bermuda, 1972–76; a District Judge, 1995–2006; Resident Judge, Swindon Combined Court, 2007–14. *Recreations:* watching cricket and Rugby, playing golf, cinema.
*See also* Hon. Sir R. A. Field.

FIELD, **(Edward) John**, CMG 1991; HM Diplomatic Service, retired; High Commissioner, Sri Lanka, 1991–96; *b* 11 June 1936; *s* of late Arthur Field, OBE, MC, TD, and Dorothy Agnes Field; *m* 1960, Irene Sophie du Pont Darden; one *s* one *d*. *Educ:* Highgate Sch.; Corpus Christi Coll., Oxford; Univ. of Virginia. Courtaulds Ltd, 1960–62; FCO, 1963–96: 2nd, later 1st Sec., Tokyo, 1963–68; Amer. Dept, FCO, 1968–70; Cultural Attaché, Moscow, 1970–72; 1st Sec. (Commercial), Tokyo, 1973–76; Asst Head, S Asian Dept, FCO, 1976–77; Dept of Trade, 1977–79 (Head, Exports to Japan Unit); Counsellor: (Commercial), Seoul, 1980–83; at Harvard Univ., 1983–84; UK Mission to UN, 1984–87; Minister, Tokyo, 1988–91. Mem. Bd. WHRO, Virginia, 2011–17. Pres., Virginia Opera Assoc., 2003–05. Trustee, Chrysler Mus. of Art, Norfolk, Virginia, 2002–10. *Recreations:* riding, listening to music. *Address:* 21 Dawson Place, W2 4TH; Jericho Farm, 19637 Governor Darden Road, Courtland, VA 23837, USA. *Club:* Travellers.

FIELD, Rt Hon. **Frank**; PC 1997; DL; MP for Birkenhead, since 1979 (Lab, 1979–2018; Ind, since 2018); *b* 16 July 1942; *s* of late Walter and of Annie Field. *Educ:* St Clement Danes Grammar Sch.; Univ. of Hull (BSc (Econ)). Director: Child Poverty Action Gp, 1969–79; Low Pay Unit, 1974–80. Minister of State (Minister for Welfare Reform), DSS, 1997–98. Chairman: Select Cttee on Social Services, 1987–90; Select Cttee on Social Security, 1991–97; Jt Select Cttee on Draft Modern Slavery Bill, 2014; Select Cttee on Work and Pensions, 2015–; Co-Chm., All Party Parly Inquiry into hunger in UK, 2014. Chm., Pensions Reform Gp, 1999– (reports: Universal Protected Pension: modernising pensions for the millennium, 2001; Universal Protected Pension: the following report, 2002). Chairman: Ind. Review on Poverty and Life Chances, 2010 (report, Preventing Poor Children becoming Poor Adults, 2010); Modern Slavery Bill Evidence Rev., 2013 (report, Establishing Britain as a World Leader in the Fight against Modern Slavery, 2013). Vice Chm., Human Trafficking Foundn, 2011–. Co-Founder, Cool Earth, 2007. Chm., King James Bible Trust, 2007–. DL Merseyside, 2011. *Publications:* (ed jtly) Twentieth Century State Education, 1971; (ed jtly) Black Britons, 1971; (ed) Low Pay, 1973; Unequal Britain, 1974; (ed) Are Low Wages Inevitable?, 1976; (ed) Education and the Urban Crisis, 1976; (ed) The Conscript Army: a study of Britain's unemployed, 1976; (jtly) To Him Who Hath: a study of poverty and taxation, 1976; (with Ruth Lister) Wasted Labour, 1978 (Social Concern Book Award); (ed) The Wealth Report, 1979; Inequality in Britain: freedom, welfare and the state, 1981; Poverty and Politics, 1982; The Wealth Report—2, 1983; (ed) Policies against Low Pay, 1984; The Minimum Wage: its potential and dangers, 1984; Freedom and Wealth in a Socialist Future, 1987; The Politics of Paradise, 1987; Losing Out: the emergence of Britain's underclass, 1989; An Agenda for Britain, 1993; (jtly) Europe Isn't Working, 1994; (jtly) Beyond Punishment: pathways from workfare, 1994; Making Welfare Work, 1995; How to Pay for the Future: building a stakeholders welfare, 1996; Stakeholder Welfare, 1997; Reforming Welfare, 1997; Reflections on Welfare Reform, 1998; The State of Dependency: welfare under Labour, 2000; Making Welfare Work: reconstructing welfare for the millennium, 2001; Neighbours from Hell: the politics of behaviour, 2003; The Ethic of Respect: a left wing cause, 2006; Attlee's Great Contemporaries, 2009; Saints and Heroes, 2010. *Address:* House of Commons, SW1A 0AA. *T:* (020) 7219 5193.

FIELD, **Brig. Jill Margaret**, CBE 1992; RRC 1988; Matron-in-Chief (Army) and Director of Defence Nursing Services, 1989–92; *b* 20 June 1934; *d* of late Major Charles Euston Field, Royal Signals, and Mrs Eva Gladys Field (*née* Watson). *Educ:* High School for Girls, Southend-on-Sea; St Bartholomew's Hosp., London (SRN). Joined QARANC, 1957; appointments include: service in Mil. Hosps in UK, BAOR, N Africa, Cyprus, Singapore; Instructor, QARANC Trng Centre, 1971–74; Liaison Officer QARANC, MoD, 1980–83; Matron, BMH Hannover, 1984–85; Dep. Medical (Nursing), BAOR, 1985–87; Matron, Cambridge Mil. Hosp., Aldershot and Chief Medical (Nursing) SE and SW Dist, 1987–89. QHNS 1989–92. *Recreations:* gardening, reading, music.

FIELD, **John**; *see* Field, E. J.

FIELD, Prof. **John Edwin**, OBE 1987; PhD; FRS 1994; Professor of Applied Physics, Department of Physics, University of Cambridge, 1994–2003, now Emeritus; Head of Physics and Chemistry of Solids Section, Cavendish Laboratory, Cambridge, 1987–2003; Fellow of Magdalene College, Cambridge, 1964–2003, now Emeritus; *b* 20 Sept. 1936; *s* of William Edwin Field and Madge (*née* Normansell); *m* 1963, Ineke Tjan; two *s* one *d*. *Educ:* Univ. of London (BSc); Univ. of Cambridge (PhD 1962). Graduate Tutor, Magdalene Coll., Cambridge, 1974–87; Asst Lectr, 1966–71, Lectr, 1971–90, Reader, 1990–94, Dept of Physics, Univ. of Cambridge. Hon. FRSSAf 2002. Hon. DSc: Univ. of Luleå, Sweden, 1989; Cranfield, 2002. Duddell Medal, Inst. of Physics, 1990; John S. Rinehart Award, DYMAT Assoc., 2009. *Publications:* (ed) The Properties of Diamond, 1979, 2nd edn 1991; (ed) The Properties of Natural and Synthetic Diamond, 1992; (ed) 3 conf. proc.; over 440 scientific papers. *Recreations:* mountain walking, running, ski-ing. *Address:* 11A Church Street, Stapleford, Cambs CB22 5DS. *T:* (01223) 846515.

FIELD, **Sir Malcolm (David)**, Kt 1991; Senior non-executive Director, Hochschild Mining plc, 2006–16; non-executive Director: Odgers Berndston (formerly Odgers), 2002–16; Petropavlovsk, since 2009; *b* 25 Aug. 1937; *s* of Stanley Herbert Raynor Field and Constance Frances (*née* Watson); *m* (marr. diss.); one *d*; *m* 2001, Anne Charlton. *Educ:* Highgate Sch.; London Business Sch. National Service, commnd Welsh Guards (2nd Lieut), 1955–57 (served in Cyprus and Germany). PA to Dir, ICI (Paints Div.), 1957; joined family business, 1960 (taken over by W. H. Smith, 1963); Wholesale Dir, 1970–82, Man. Dir, Retail Gp, 1978–82, Gp Man. Dir, 1982–93, Chief Exec., 1994–96, W. H. Smith. Chairman: Bd of Management, NAAFI, 1986–93 (Mem., Bd of Management, 1973–86; Dep. Chm., 1985–86); CAA, 1996–2001; Sofa Workshop, 1998–2002; Tube Lines Ltd, 2003–06; Aricom plc, 2004–06 (Sen. non-exec. Dir, 2006–09); non-executive Director: MEPC, 1989–99; Scottish & Newcastle Breweries, 1993–98; Phoenix Group Ltd, 1995–97; Stationery Office, 1996–2001; Walker Greenbank, 1997–2002; Evolution Beeson Gregory (formerly Beeson Gregory), 2000–04; Garden Centre Gp, 2011–12. Ext. Policy Advr, DfT, 2001–06. Mem. Council, RCA, 1991–2001; Mem. Bd, English Nat. Ballet Sch., 1997–2007; Gov., Highgate Sch., 1994–2004 (Dep. Chm., 1999–2004). CCMI (CBIM 1988); CRAeS 1997; FRSA 1989. *Recreations:* watching cricket, tennis, golf, building a garden in Dorset, reading biographies, collecting modern art, grandchildren, playing golf and tennis. *Address:* 21 Embankment Gardens, SW3 4LH. *Clubs:* Garrick, MCC.

FIELD, Rt Hon. **Mark (Christopher)**; PC 2015; MP (C) Cities of London and Westminster, since 2001; *b* 6 Oct. 1964; *s* of late Maj. Peter Field and Ulrike Field (*née* Peipe); *m* 1st, 1994, Michele Louise Acton (marr. diss. 2006); 2nd, 2007, Victoria Margaret Philadelphia Elphicke; one *s* one *d*. *Educ:* Reading Sch.; St Edmund Hall, Oxford (MA Hons Juris.); Coll. of Law, Chester. Trainee solicitor, Richards Butler, 1988–90; Solicitor, Freshfields, 1990–92; employment consultant, 1992–94; Man. Dir, Kellyfield Consulting (publishing/recruiting firm), 1994–2001. Adviser: Bd, Ellwood Atfield, 2011–15; Cains, 2011–17. Councillor (C), RBK&C, 1994–2002. An Opposition Whip, 2003–04; Shadow Minister for London, 2003–05; Shadow Financial Sec. to the Treasury, 2005; Shadow Minister for Culture, 2005–06; Minister of State, FCO, 2017–19. Member: Select Cttee on LCD, 2003, on Procedure, 2008–10; Intelligence and Security Cttee, 2010–15. Chm., All Party Parly Gp on Venture Capital and Private Equity, 2010–17 (Vice Chm., 2004–10); Vice-Chm., All Party Parly Gp on Bangladesh, 2009–17, on Football, 2010–17. Member Standing Committee for: Proceeds of Crime Act, 2002; Enterprise Act, 2002; Finance Act, 2002; Licensing Act, 2003; Housing Act, 2004; Railways Act, 2005; Finance Act (No. 2), 2005; Regn of Financial Services (Land Transactions) Act, 2006; Nat. Insurance Contributions Act, 2006; National Lottery Act, 2006; Crossrail Act, 2008; Finance Act, 2008; Nat. Insce Contribns Act, 2008; Dormant Bank and Building Socs Accounts Act, 2008; Business Rates Supplements Act, 2009; Finance Act, 2009. Vice Chm. (Internat. Affairs), Cons. Party, 2015–17. Mem., Adv. Cttee, London Sch. of Commerce, 2005–17. Regular broadcaster on radio and TV and newspaper columnist on H of C, economic and financial affairs, and London issues. *Publications:* Reforming the City (contrib.), 2009; Between the Crashes, 2013; The Best of Times, 2016. *Recreations:* cricket, football, researching local history, reading political biographies and diaries, walking in London, listening to popular/rock music. *Address:* House of Commons, SW1A 0AA. *T:* (020) 7219 8155.

FIELD, **Marshall Hayward**, CBE 1985; Director, Phoenix Assurance, 1980–85 (Actuary, 1964–85, General Manager, 1972–85); *b* 19 April 1930; *s* of Harold Hayward Field and Hilda Maud Field; *m* 1960, Barbara Evelyn Harris (*d* 1998); two *d*. *Educ:* Dulwich College. FIA 1957. With Pearl Assce, 1948–58; joined Phoenix Assurance, 1958. Director: TSB Trust Co. Ltd, 1985–89; TSB Gp, 1990–95; Ark Life Assurance Co., Dublin, 1991–2003; Consultant, Bacon & Woodrow, 1986–2000. Institute of Actuaries: Hon. Sec., 1975–77; Vice-Pres., 1979–82; Pres., 1986–88; Vice Pres., International Actuarial Assoc., 1984–90; Chm., Life Offices' Assoc., 1983–85. Mem., Fowler Inquiry into Provision for Retirement, 1984; Consultant, Marketing of Investments Bd Organising Cttee, 1985–86. Mem., Dulwich Picture Gall. Cttee, 1985–94; Trustee, Dulwich Picture Gall., 1994–2002; Chm., Dulwich DFAS, 2002–05. Governor: Dulwich Coll. Estates, 1973–95 (Chm., 1988–90); Dulwich Coll., 1987–97; James Allen's Girls' School, 1981–95. Mem., Ct of Assistants, Actuaries' Co., 1989– (Master, 1996–97). *Recreations:* theatre, architecture. *Address:* 12 Gainsborough Court, College Road, SE21 7LT.

FIELD, Hon. **Michael Walter**, AC 2003; Chancellor, University of Tasmania, since 2013; *b* 28 May 1948; *s* of William Field and Blanche (*née* Burrows); *m* 1975, Janette Elizabeth Mary Fone; one *s* two *d*. *Educ:* Railton Primary Sch., Tasmania; Devonport High Sch., Tasmania; Univ. of Tasmania (BA Pol Sci./History). Teacher, 1971–75; Community Develt Officer, 1975–76. Government of Tasmania: MHA (Lab) Braddon, 1976–97; Minister for Transport, Main Roads, Construction and Local Govt, 1979–82; Shadow Minister for: Transport, 1982–83; Education and Ind. Relns, 1982–86; State Development, 1992–97; Dep. Leader of Opposition and Shadow Minister for Forestry, Ind. Relns and Energy, 1986–88; Leader of the Opposition, 1988–89 and 1992–97; Premier, Treas. and Minister for State Develt and Finance, 1989–92; Shadow Minister for Educn, Trng, and Youth Affairs, 1996–97. Board Member: John Curtin House Ltd, 1997–2012; Tasmanian Electricity Code Change Panel, 1999–2005. Chairman: Tasmanian Innovations Adv. Bd, 1999–2009; Bd, Australian Innovation Res. Centre, 2006–12. Dir, Port Arthur Historic Site Mgt Authy, 2005–. Life Mem. ALP, 2001. Hon. LLD Tasmania, 2000. *Recreations:* fishing, reading, music, kayaking.

FIELD, **Patrick John**; QC 2000; **His Honour Judge Patrick Field;** a Circuit Judge, since 2012; *b* 19 March 1959; *s* of late Michael Edward and Patricia Field; *m* Helen McCubbin; one *s* two *d*. *Educ:* Wilmslow Co. Grammar Sch.; King's Coll. London (LLB Hons). Called to the Bar, Gray's Inn, 1981, Bencher, 2007; Northern Circuit, 1982– (Junior, 1985); a Recorder, 2001–12. *Recreations:* fishing, travel. *Address:* Courts of Justice, Crown Square, Manchester M3 3FL.

FIELD, Hon. **Sir Richard (Alan)**, Kt 2002; a Judge of the High Court, Queen's Bench Division, 2002–14; Judge in charge of Commercial List, 2014; a Justice of Court of Dubai International Financial Centre, and of Court of Appeal, Cayman Islands, since 2014; *b* 17 April 1947; twin *s* of Robert Henry Field and Ivy May Field; *m* 1st, 1968, Lynne Hauskind (*d* 2007); two *s* two *d*; 2nd, 2009, Marion Nitch-Smith. *Educ:* Ottershaw Sch.; Bristol Univ. (LLB); London School of Economics (LLM with Dist.). Asst Prof., Univ. of British Columbia, 1969–71; Lectr in Law, Hong Kong Univ., 1971–73; Associate Prof., McGill Univ., Montreal, 1973–77; called to the Bar, Inner Temple, 1977, Bencher, 1998. QC 1987; a Dep. High Court Judge, 1998–2001; a Recorder, 1999–2001; a Presiding Judge, Western Circuit, 2009–13; in practice as internat. commercial arbitrator, One Essex Court, 2015–. Cheng Yu Tung Vis. Prof., Faculty of Law, Hong Kong Univ., 2014–15. *Recreations:* cricket, opera, theatre, learning Italian. *Clubs:* Garrick, Roehampton.
*See also* D. J. Field.

FIELD, **Stephen Brian**; UK Executive Director, International Monetary Fund, 2013–18; *b* London, 30 May 1972; *s* of Brian Albert Field and Jean Alice Field (*née* Ixer); *m* 2013, Helen Mary Lewis; one *s* one *d*. *Educ:* Dame Alice Owen's Sch.; British Sch. of Brussels; Queens' Coll., Cambridge (BA Hons Econs 1994). HM Customs and Excise, 1994–95; HM Treasury: Economic Asst, 1995–97; Private Sec. to Paymaster Gen., 1997–99; Economic Advr, 1999–2005, various posts incl. Dep. Press Sec., 2001–04; Dep. Dir,

Europe, 2005–07; Press Sec. to Chancellor of the Exchequer, 2007–09; Dir, Strategy and Communication, 2009–10; Prime Minister's Spokesman, 2010–12. *Recreations:* cooking, piano, playing with my children, Arsenal FC.

**FIELD, Stephen John**, CBE 2010; FRCP, FRCGP, FFPH; Chairman, Royal Wolverhampton NHS Trust, since 2019; *b* Stourbridge, Worcs, 22 June 1959; *s* of Derek and Yvonne Field; *m* 1992, Lynn Kennedy (*d* 2016); twin *d*; *m* 2019, Elizabeth Chidgey. *Educ:* Univ. of Birmingham Med. Sch. (MB ChB with Dist. in Social Medicine 1982); Univ. of Dundee (Dip. Med. Educn 1994; MMEd 2001). Family Planning Cert. 1986; DRCOG 1987; JCPTGP Cert. 1987; MRCGP 1987, FRCGP 1997; FRCP 2009; FFPH 2011. Hse surgeon, Worcester Royal Infirmary, 1982–83; Hse physician, Kidderminster Gen. Hosp., 1983; Worcester Royal Infirmary: Senior House Officer: Anaesthetics, 1983–84; Paediatrics, 1984–85; Obstetrics and Gynaecol., 1985–86; Worcester Vocational Trng Scheme for Gen. Practice, 1986–87; GP, Qld, 1986; SHO, A&E, Worcester Royal Infirmary, 1987; Principal in General Practice: (Sen. Partner), Corbett Med. Practice, Droitwich Spa, Worcs, 1987–97; (part-time) Bellevue Med. Centre (Modality Partnership), Birmingham, 1997–2017. Regl Advr and Dir, Postgrad. Gen. Practice Educn, W Midlands, 1995–2001. Regl Postgrad. Med. and Dental Dean, 2001–10; Hd of Workforce Develt, 2006–07, NHS W Midlands; Dep. Nat. Med. Dir, NHS England, 2012–13; Chm., NHS Future Forum, 2011–13. Chm. Council, RCGP, 2007–10; Chm., Nat. Inclusion Health Bd, 2010–16; Chief Inspector of Gen. Practice and Integrated Care, Care Quality Commn, 2013–19. Hon. Professor: of Med. Educn, Univ. of Warwick, 2002–; Sch. of Medicine, Univ. of Birmingham, 2003–. Mem. Faculty, Harvard Macy Inst. Prog. for Leaders in Health Care Innovation and Educn, Harvard Univ., 2003–. Broadcaster; contrib. radio and TV progs on ethical and health issues, UK and overseas, 2007–. FHEA 2007; Mem., Acad. Med. Educators, 2008; Fellow, Faculty of Homelessness and Inclusion Health, 2019. DUniv: Staffordshire, 2006; Birmingham City, 2012; Hon. MSc Worcester, 2010; Hon. DSc: Keele, 2011; Exeter, 2015. Gold Award, Adv. Cttee on Clin. Excellence Awards, DoH, 2005. *Publications:* (jtly) Watching You, Watching Me…: an introduction to communication skills in general practice, 1996, 2nd edn 1998; (jtly) Those Things You Say…: consultation skills and the MRCGP examination (interactive video and workbook), 1998; (jtly) Sexual Health History Taking, 1998; (jtly) Medical Careers: opportunities and options, 2000; (jtly) Quality in General Practice, 2000; (jtly) Continuing Professional Development in Primary Care: making it happen, 2000; (with P. Middleton) The GP Trainer's Handbook, 2000; (ed jtly) The General Practice Jigsaw, 2001; (jtly) Prescription for Learning: getting the message across, 2002; (jtly) Appraisal for the Apprehensive - or, being appraised and making it work for you, 2002; (jtly) Guiding Doctors in Managing Careers: a toolkit for tutors, trainers, mentors and appraisers, 2006; (jtly) The Future Direction of General Practice: a roadmap, 2007; (jtly) The Condensed Curriculum Guide for GP Training and the New MRCGP, 2007; (jtly) Primary Care Federations: putting patients first, 2008; contrib. educn and res. papers to learned jls on med. educn, continuing professional develt, revalidation, leadership, primary care and health policy. *Recreations:* tennis, hillwalking, supporting W Bromwich Albion, watching England win Test matches!

**FIELD, Stuart**, MBE 2013; FRCR; Consultant Radiologist, Kent and Canterbury Hospital, 1974–2004; Director, Kent Breast Screening Programme, 1988–2004; *b* 22 June 1944; *s* of Walter Frederick William Field and Maisie Field (*née* Marlow); *m* 1968, Margaret Shirley Dawes; two *d*. *Educ:* Watford Grammar Sch. (Head Boy); Gonville and Caius Coll., Cambridge (BA 1st Cl. Hons Natural Sci. Tripos, MA, MB BChir). DMRD 1972; FRCR 1974. Houseman to Professorial Med. and Surgical Units, 1969–70, Registrar in Radiol., 1970–74, KCH. Royal College of Radiologists: Dean, Faculty of Clinical Radiology, 1991–93, Vice-Pres., 1993; Pres. Kent Postgrad. Med. Centre, 1994–2000; Hon. Prof., Kent Inst. of Medicine and Health Scis, Univ. of Kent at Canterbury, 1998–2007. Mem., DoH Adv. Cttee for Breast Cancer Screening, 1994–2003. Chairman: Breast Gp, 1997–99; League of Friends, Kent and Canterbury Hosp., 2007–15. Gov., E Kent Hosps Univ. NHS Foundn Trust, 2009–12. Hon. Mem., Romanian Radiol. Soc., 1993. Chm., Arts Soc. Canterbury (formerly Canterbury Decorative and Fine Arts Soc.), 2016–19. President's Medal, RCR, 2002. *Publications:* numerous chapters in textbooks of radiol. on the plain abdominal radiograph in the acute abdomen; contrib. articles on breast cancer screening and other radiol topics to specialist radiol. jls. *Recreations:* gardening, walking, DIY, classical music, the family, Porchlight (homelessness charity based in Canterbury). *Address:* Bournes Corner, Bekesbourne Road, Bridge, Canterbury, Kent CT4 5AE.

**FIELD, Ven. Susan Elizabeth**; Archdeacon of Coventry, since 2018; a Chaplain to the Queen, since 2017; *b* Birmingham, 10 May 1959; *d* of Donald Field and Cynthia Field. *Educ:* King Edward VI High Sch. for Girls, Birmingham; Univ. of York (BA Hons Mathematics 1980); Univ. of Birmingham (PGCE 1981); Queen's Coll., Birmingham; Westminster Coll., Oxford (MTh 1998); DipABRSM 2003. Ordained deacon, 1987, priest, 1994; Asst Curate, Coleshill and Maxstoke, Birmingham, 1987–90; Chaplain, Loughborough Univ. and Colleges, 1991–98; Team Vicar, Emmanuel, Loughborough and St Mary in Charnwood, 1998–2014; Vicar, St Mary in Charnwood, Nanpantan, 2015–18. Dir of Post Ordination Trng, 1995–2004, Advr for Women's Ministry, 1997–2004, Dir of Ordinands, 2004–18, Dio. of Leicester. Hon. Canon, Leicester Cathedral, 2004–18, now Canon Emeritus. *Recreations:* music, reading, walking. *Address:* Diocesan Office, 1 Hill Top, Coventry CV1 5AB. *T:* 07885 714829. *E:* sue.field@covcofe.org.

**FIELD-SMITH, Robin**, MBE 1983; Lay Member, Professional Conduct Committee, Bar Standards Board, since 2016; Independent Member, Chief Police Officer Appointments, since 2012; HM Inspector of Constabulary, 2000–09; Senior Police Assessor, since 2009; *b* Brighton, 24 Jan. 1948; *s* of John and Meriel Field-Smith; *m* 1970, Mary Paffett; two *s* one *d*. *Educ:* Manor House Sch.; Hurstpierpoint Coll.; Univ. of Liverpool (BA 1970); Churchill Coll., Cambridge (PGCE 1971); Open Univ. (MA 1993). FCIPD 1999. Commissioned: TA, 1970; RAEC, 1971; regtl duties, 1972–79; Staff Coll., 1980; SO2 HQ BAOR, 1981–82; BAOR and MoD, 1983–86; JSDC 1986; SO1 HQ AFCENT, 1987–89; Comd ETS, Berlin, 1990–92; SO1 HQ AGC, 1992–93; Comd ETS, BAOR, 1993–94; CO ASTS, 1995–97; Dep. Dir, ETS(A), 1997–99; Defence Trng Review, 1999–2000. Lay Chm., Army Synod, 1990–2000; Lay Member: GDC, 2009–13; Equality and Diversity Cttee, Bar Standards Bd, 2009–15; Employment Tribunals (England and Wales), 2010–14. Vice-Pres., Nat. Assoc. of Chaplains to the Police, 2008–18. Vis. Prof., Univ. of Portsmouth, 2010–17. Member: Quality and Standards Cttee, C&G, 2010–17; Recognition of Prior Learning Steering Gp, Open Univ., 2015–17. Dir, Wilts TEC, 1996–2000; Gov., Chippenham Coll., 1997–2001; Chair of Trustees, Royal Sch. Hampstead Trust, 2009–16 (Trustee, 2003–09); Trustee: Learning from Experience Trust, 2003–17 (Chair, 2008–10); Eric Frank Trust, 2010–16. Churchwarden, St Mary's, Teddington, 2018–. CCMI 2007; CMgr 2013. Freeman, City of London, 2008. Hon. MCGI 2004. *Publications:* over 60 inspection and independent member reports. *Recreations:* choral singing, family, steam railways, walking, DIY, golf. *E:* robin@field-smith.com.

**FIELDEN, Jonathan Mark**, FRCA, FRCP, FFICM; Director, JF Health Solutions, since 2017; Director, Specialised Commissioning, and Deputy National Medical Director, NHS England, 2016–17; *b* Greenfield, Yorks, 9 Sept. 1963; *s* of Barry and Margaret Fielden; *m* 1st, 1990, Kate Emerson (marr. diss. 2008); one *s*; 2nd, 2010, Christine Yeates (marr. diss. 2019). *Educ:* Bedford Sch.; Bristol Univ. (BSc Hons Pharmacol. 1985; MB ChB 1988). FRCA 1994; FRCP 2009; FFICM 2011. Hse Officer, 1988–89, SHO, 1989–91, Bristol Royal Infirmary; SHO, Royal United Hosps, Bath, 1992–93; Registrar, Bristol Royal Infirmary, 1993–94; Prov. Fellow, St Vincent's Hosp., Sydney, 1994–95; Specialist Registrar: Bristol Royal Infirmary and Royal United Hosps, Bath, 1995–96; Southampton Univ. Hosp. and Portsmouth Hosp., 1996–98; Royal Berkshire Hospital: Consultant in Anaesthesia and Intensive Care Medicine, 1998–2012; Dir, Med. Educn and Develt, 2008–10; CMO/Med. Dir, 2009–12; Consultant in Intensive Care Medicine and Med. Dir (Medicine), UCLH, 2012–16. Bd Dir, Health Services Labs, 2014–16. Dep. Chm., 2004–06, Chm., 2006–09, Central Consultants and Specialists Cttee, BMA. Mem., Governing Body, Aylesbury Vale CCG, 2012–15. Member: Council, RCAnaes, 1997–2001; Faculty of Med. Leadership and Mgt, 2010–. Trustee, Nuffield Trust, 2015–16. *Publications:* contrib. learned papers on med. leadership, Accelerated Evidence Based Co-Design and intensive care. *Recreations:* travel, swimming, hill walking, most things French, fine wine, mindfulness, ski-ing a little slower than my son Alex, but running half marathons (for charity CALM) that bit quicker.

**FIELDEN, Lara Anne**; regulator and author, since 2011; *b* London, 29 April 1967; *d* of Brian Fielden and Judy Fielden (*née* Yarrow); *m* 1997, Jeremy Watson; two *c*. *Educ:* South Hampstead High Sch., London; St Catherine's Coll., Oxford (BA Hons PPE). Graduate trainee, LWT, 1989–90; BBC TV, 1990–2000: researcher, Assignment, 1990–92; asst producer, Panorama, 1993–94; producer/director: First Sight, 1995–96; Newsnight, 1996; Panorama, 1996–97; current affairs documentaries incl.: The Price of Peace, 1998; The Forgotten Children, 2000. Broadcasting Standards Exec., 2005–06, Fairness and Privacy Standards Manager, 2007–08, Project Manager, Broadcasting Code Rev., 2009–10, Ofcom. Vis. Fellow, 2011–12, Res. Associate, 2013–, Reuters Inst. for the Study of Journalism, Univ. of Oxford. Mem., tribunal panel, 2013–17, Strategic Adv. Bd, 2018–, Bar Tribunals and Adjudication Service, 2013–17; Lay Mem., Bar Standards Bd, 2018–. Ind. Mem., Complaints Cttee, IPSO, 2014–; Mem., Code of Practice for Stats steering gp, UK Stats Authy, 2016. Author, Regulating the Press report, 2012, used extensively in Leveson Inquiry. Mem. Bd, London Probation Trust, 2011–14 (Vice Chair, 2013–14); Lead nonexec. Dir, London Community Rehabilitation Co.. 2014–15. Gov., Children's Hosp. Sch., Great Ormond Street Hosp. and UCH, 2006–17 (Chair of Govs, 2012–17). Lay Examnr, RCOG, 2016–17; Panel Chair, British Assoc. for Counselling and Psychotherapy, 2016–17. Mem. Adv. Bd, Dept of Journalism Studies, Univ. of Sheffield, 2019–. JP City of Westminster, 2003–11. *Publications:* Regulating for Trust in Journalism, 2011; reports on the press and press regulation; submissions to Parly inquiries; articles in Jl Media Law and Internat. Jl Res. into New Media Technols. *Recreations:* walking the dogs, Torcross, Ai Chi.

**FIELDER, Prof. Alistair Richard**, FRCS, FRCP, FRCOphth; Professor of Ophthalmology, City University, 2005–07, now Emeritus; Hon. Consultant Ophthalmologist: St Mary's Hospital NHS Trust, 1995–2007; Hillingdon Hospital NHS Trust, 1996–2007; *b* 3 Sept. 1942; *s* of late Alfred Emmanuel Hugh Fielder and Elizabeth Rachel Fielder (*née* Hutchinson); *m* 1965, Gillian Muriel Slough; one *s* three *d*. *Educ:* St George's Hosp. Med. Sch., London Univ. (MB BS 1966). FRCS 1974; FRCOphth (FCOphth 1988), Hon. FRCOphth 2012; MRCP 1991, FRCP 1994; FRCPCH 1999. RSO, Moorfields Eye Hosp., 1973–76; Consultant Ophthalmologist, Derby Hosps, 1977–82; Reader in Ophthalmology, Leicester Univ., 1982–88; Professor of Ophthalmology: Birmingham Univ., 1988–95; ICSTM, later ICL, 1995–2004. Vice Pres., 1995–99, Sen. Vice Pres., 1997–99, Royal Coll. of Ophthalmologists (Hon. Fellow, 2012); British Rep., Societas Ophthalmologica Europæa, 1998–2009. Trustee: RNIB, 1990–2002 (Mem., Nat. Assembly, 2002–09); Fight for Sight, 2003–16; Nat. Fedn of Families with Visually Impaired Children (LOOK), 2003–09 (Chm. Trustees, 2003–07); Action for Blind People, 2006–16; Vice Chm. Trustees, Vision 2020 UK, 2002–07. *Publications:* scientific articles and contribs to books on the developing visual system and paediatric ophthalmology. *Recreation:* escaping on narrow boats and Dutch barges. *Address:* 18 Melrose Gardens, W6 7RW. *T:* (020) 7602 4790, 07850 742900. *Club:* Royal Society of Medicine.

**FIELDHOUSE, Brian**; DL; Chief Executive, West Sussex County Council, 1990–95; *b* 1 May 1933; *s* of late Harry and Florence Fieldhouse; *m* 1959, Sonia J. Browne; one *s* one *d*. *Educ:* Barnsley Holgate Grammar Sch.; Keble Coll., Oxford (MA PPE). CPFA (IPFA 1960). Formerly, Treasurer's Departments: Herts CC; Hants CC; Flints CC; County Treasurer: Lincs parts of Lindsey CC, 1970–73; W Sussex CC, 1973–90. Comr, Public Works Loans Bd, 1988–92. Principal Financial Advr, ACC, 1980–85. Pres., Soc. of Co. Treasurers, 1983. Trustee, Chichester Fest. Theatre, 1995–97. Sec., Rees Jeffreys Road Fund, 1995–2005. DL West Sussex, 1996. FRSA 1984. *Recreations:* hill farming, theatre going. *Address:* 13 The Avenue, Chichester PO19 5PX.

**FIELDING, Emma Georgina Annalies**; actress; *b* 7 Oct.; *d* of late Johnny Fielding, CBE and Sheila Fielding (*née* Brown); *m* 2004, Michael Ashcroft; one *s*. *Educ:* Royal Scottish Acad. of Music and Drama (Dip. Dramatic Art). BBC Radio Drama Co., 1991; Sheffield Crucible, 1992; Almeida Th., 1993, 1995, 1997, 2005; NT, 1993, 1999, 2005; RSC, 1994, 1998, 2003; plays include: Private Lives, Albery Th., 2001, NY, 2002 (Theater World Award, outstanding Broadway debut, 2002); Rock 'n' Roll, Duke of York's, 2007; Decade, Headlong Th., 2011; The King's Speech, Yvonne Arnaud, Guildford and tour, 2012; Heartbreak House, Chichester, 2012; In the Republic of Happiness, Royal Court, 2012; Rapture, Blister, Burn, Hampstead Th., 2014; The Massive Tragedy of Madame Bovary!, Liverpool Everyman, 2016; Terror, Lyric Hammersmith, 2017; *films* include: Pandaemonium, 2000; The Discovery of Heaven, 2001; Shooters, 2002; The Great Ghost Rescue, 2011; Twenty8K, Fast Girls, 2012; *television* includes: Tell Tale Hearts, 1992; The Maitlands, 1993; A Dance to the Music of Time, 1997; A Respectable Trade, 1998; Big Bad World, 1999; Other People's Children, 2000; My Uncle Silas, 2003; The Government Inspector, The Ghost Squad, 2005; Cranford, 2007; Return to Cranford, 2009; The Suspicions of Mr Whicher, 2011; Kidnap and Ransom, 2011; many radio performances. Associate Artist, RSC. London Critics' Circle Award, most promising newcomer, 1993. *Publications:* Twelfth Night: actors on Shakespeare, 2002. *Recreation:* walking. *Address:* c/o Rebecca Blond Associates, 69a Kings Road, SW3 4NX. *T:* (020) 7351 4100.

**FIELDING, Helen Elizabeth**; novelist and screenwriter; *b* Yorkshire, 19 Feb. 1958; *d* of late Michael Fielding and of Nellie Fielding; partner, Kevin Curran; one *s* one *d*. *Educ:* Wakefield Girls' High Sch.; St Anne's Coll., Oxford (MA English 1979). BBC TV researcher and producer, 1979–90; journalist, Independent, Sunday Times, Guardian, Telegraph, 1990–. Ambassador, Save the Children, 2013–. Writer of screenplays: Bridget Jones's Diary, 2001 (Evening Standard Award for Best Screenpaly, 2002); Bridget Jones: The Edge of Reason, 2004; Bridget Jones's Baby, 2016. *Publications: novels:* Cause Celeb, 1994; Bridget Jones's Diary, 1996 (British Book of Year, Nat. Book Awards, 1997); Bridget Jones: The Edge of Reason, 1999; Olivia Joules and the Overactive Imagination, 2003; Bridget Jones: Mad About the Boy, 2013; Bridget Jones's Baby: the diaries, 2016; *short stories:* Ox-Tales, 2009. *Recreations:* hiking, salsa, scuba, ski-ing, Googling imaginary holidays. *Address:* c/o Aitken Alexander Associates Ltd, 291 Gray's Inn Road, WC1X 8EB. *Club:* Soho House.

**FIELDING, Sir Leslie**, KCMG 1988; Vice-Chancellor, University of Sussex, 1987–92; *b* 29 July 1932; *o s* of late Percy Archer Fielding and of Margaret (*née* Calder Horry); *m* 1978, Dr Sally P. J. Harvey, FSA, FRHistS, sometime Fellow of St Hilda's Coll., Oxford; one *s* one *d. Educ*: Queen Elizabeth's Sch., Barnet; Emmanuel Coll., Cambridge (First in History; MA; Hon. Fellow 1990); School of Oriental and African Studies, London; St Antony's Coll., Oxford (MA; Vis. Fellow, 1977–78). Served with Royal Regt of Artillery, 1951–53; TA, 1953–56. Entered HM Diplomatic Service, 1956; served in: Tehran, 1957–60; Foreign Office, 1960–64; Singapore, 1964; Phnom Penh (Chargé d'Affaires), 1964–66; Paris, 1967–70; Dep. Head of Planning Staff, FCO, 1970–73; seconded for service with European Commn in Brussels, 1973; Dir (External Relns Directorate Gen.), 1973–77; permanent transfer 1979; Head of Delegn of Commn in Tokyo, 1978–82; Dir-Gen. for External Relns, Brussels, 1982–87. UK Mem., High Council of European Univ. Inst. in Florence, 1988–92. Chm., Nat. Curriculum Geography Wkg Gp, 1989–90. Adviser: IBM Europe, 1989–95; Panasonic Europe, 1990–96. Hon. Pres., Univ. Assoc. for Contemporary European Studies, 1990–2000; Founder Mem., Japan-EC Assoc., then Europe-Japan Business Forum, 1988–98; Mem., UK-Japan 2000 Gp, 1993–2001. Mem. Ct, Univ. of Sussex, 2000–. Mem., Gen. Synod, C of E, 1990–92. Admitted to office of Reader by Bishop of Exeter, 1981; served dios of Exeter, Tokyo, Gibraltar, Chichester and Hereford; Reader Emeritus, 2007. Patron, Soc. of King Charles the Martyr, 1992– (Companion, 2019). Mem., Soc. of Authors, 2006–. FRSA 1989; FRGS 1991 (Mem. Council, 1992–95). Hon. Fellow, Sussex European Inst., 1993. Hon. LLD Sussex, 1992. Grand Officer, Order of St Agatha (San Marino), 1987; Knight Commander Order of the White Rose (Finland), 1988; Grand Silver Medal of Honour with Star (Austria), 1989. *Publications*: Europe as a global partner: the external relations of the European Community, 1991; (contrib.) Travellers' Tales, 1999; (contrib.) More Travellers' Tales, 2005; Before the Killing Fields: witness to Cambodia and the Vietnam War, 2008; Kindly Call Me God: the misadventures of Fielding of the FO, Eurocrat Extraordinaire and Vice-Chancellor Semipotentiary, 2009; Twilight Over The Temples: the close of Cambodia's Belle Epoque, 2011; The Mistress of the Bees, 2011; Mentioned in Dispatches - Phnom Penh, Paris, Tokyo, Brussels: Is Diplomacy Dead?, 2012; (contrib.) Changing Horizons: memories of Britain's European pioneers 1973, 2013; Is Diplomacy Dead?, 2014; Germansweek and its Parish Church, 2014; articles on internat. relations, higher educn and ecclesiastical matters. *Recreations*: life in the country, theology. *Address*: Wild Cherry Farm, Elton, Ludlow, Shropshire SY8 2HQ. *Club*: Travellers.

**FIELDING, Dame Pauline**, DBE 1999; PhD; Professional Adviser to the Healthcare Commission, 2002–09; Director of Nursing: Preston Acute Hospitals NHS Trust, 1993–2002; Chorley and South Ribble NHS Trust, 1998–2002; *m* Rev. Michael Fielding; one *s* one *d. Educ*: Univ. of Southampton (BSc Hons; PhD 1981). Ward Sister, 1982, Sen. Nurse, then Dir of Clinical Nursing Res., Middx Hosp.; formerly Nursing Dir, Forest Healthcare Trust. Hon. Professor of Nursing: Univ. of Central Lancashire, 2000; Southampton Univ., 2003. Chm., Lancaster and Morecambe Univ. of the Third Age, 2008–11. Churchwarden, Lancaster Priory, 2018. DUniv Southampton, 2003. *E*: paulinefielding@aol.com.

**FIELDING, Richard Walter**; Chairman, Richard Fielding Ltd, 1992–2000; *b* 9 July 1933; *s* of late Walter Harrison Fielding, MBE, and Marjorie Octavia Adair (*née* Roberts); *m* 1st, 1961, Felicity Ann Jones (*d* 1981); one *s* three *d*; 2nd, 1983, Jacqueline Winifred Digby (*née* Hussey). *Educ*: Clifton Coll., Bristol. National Service, Royal Engineers (Lieut), 1951–53. Broker to Dir, Bland Welch & Co. Ltd, 1954–68; Dir to Man. Dir, C. E. Heath & Co. Ltd, 1968–75; Founder and Chm., Fielding and Partners, 1975–86; Chairman: C. E. Heath PLC, 1987–92; Sharelink PLC, 1993–95. Chm., Syndicate Capital Trust, 1996–98 (Dir, 1993–96); Dir, Hambros Insurance Services, 1993–98. High Sheriff, Dorset, 1997. *Recreations*: hunting, country sports. *Address*: Ryeclose Farm House, Bishops Down, Sherborne, Dorset DT9 5PN.

**FIELDS, Sir Allan (Clifford)**, KCMG 2005; Chairman, Banks Holdings Ltd, 1999–2012 (Managing Director, 1988–99); *b* 19 Sept. 1942; *s* of James Percival Fields and Gwendolyn Fields; *m* 1944, Irene Elizabeth Smith; one *s* one *d. Educ*: Harrison Coll., Barbados; Stow Coll. of Engrg, Glasgow. Engr, Barbados Light & Power, 1966–78; Managing Director: Neal & Massy, 1978–88; Barbados Shipping & Trading, 1999–2005 (Chm., 2005–07). Chm., Cable & Wireless (Barbados), 2002–. Chm., Private Sector Assoc., 1999–2004. Senator (Ind) Barbados Parlt, 2003–08. *Recreations*: reading, gardening, cooking. *Address*: Morning Mist, Stepney, St George, Barbados. *T*: 4265195, *Fax*: 4294664. *E*: afields@caribsurf.com.

**FIENNES**, family name of **Baron Saye and Sele**.

**FIENNES, Joseph Alberic**; actor; *b* 27 May 1970; *s* of late Mark Fiennes and Jennifer Fiennes (*née* Lash); *m* 2009, María Dolores Diéguez; two *d. Educ*: Guildhall Sch. of Music and Drama. *Theatre includes*: The Woman in Black, Fortune, 1993; A Month in the Country, Albery, 1994; A View from the Bridge, Strand, 1995; Real Classy Affair, Royal Court, 1998; Edward II, Crucible, Sheffield, 2001; Love's Labour's Lost, NT, 2003; Epitaph for George Dillon, Comedy, 2005; Unicorns, Almost (one-man play), Old Vic, 2006; 2,000 Feet Away, Bush Th., 2008; Cyrano de Bergerac, Chichester, 2009; Ross, Chichester, 2016; Royal Shakespeare Company: Son of Man, Les Enfants du Paradis, Troilus and Cressida, The Herbal Bed, 1996; As You Like It, 1997. *Television includes*: The Vacillations of Poppy Carew, 1995; FlashForward (series), 2009; Camelot (series), 2011; The Handmaid's Tale (series), 2017–. *Films include*: Stealing Beauty, 1996; Elizabeth, Martha - Meet Frank, Daniel and Laurence, 1998; Shakespeare in Love, Forever Mine, 1999; Rancid Aluminium, 2000; Enemy at the Gates, Dust, 2001; Killing Me Softly, Leo, 2002; Luther, 2003; The Merchant of Venice, 2004; Man to Man, The Great Raid, 2005; The Darwin Awards, 2006; Running with Scissors, Goodbye Bafana, 2007; The Escapist, Spring 41, 2008; Red Baron, 2008; Against the Current, 2009; Hercules 3D, 2014; Risen, 2016; dir, The Spirit, 2008 (Best Short Film, Cinema for Peace). *Address*: c/o The Artists Partnership, 21–22 Warwick Street, W1B 5NE.

*See also* R. N. *Fiennes*.

**FIENNES, Ralph Nathanial**; actor; *b* 22 Dec. 1962; *s* of late Mark Fiennes and Jennifer Fiennes (*née* Lash). *Educ*: Bishop Wordsworth's Sch., Salisbury; RADA. *Theatre includes*: Open Air Theatre, Regent's Park: Twelfth Night, Ring Round the Moon, 1985; A Midsummer Night's Dream, 1985, 1986; Romeo and Juliet, 1986; Royal National Theatre: Six Characters in Search of an Author, Fathers and Sons, Ting Tang Mine, 1987; The Talking Cure, 2002; Oedipus, 2008; Man and Superman, 2015; Antony and Cleopatra, 2018; Royal Shakespeare Company: The Plantagenets, Much Ado About Nothing, 1988; Playing With Trains, 1989; Troilus and Cressida, King Lear, 1990; The Man Who Came to Dinner, 1991; Brand, transf. Th. Royal Haymarket, 2003; Almeida Theatre: Hamlet, 1995 (also Hackney Empire and Broadway, NY); Ivanov, 1997; Richard II, Coriolanus (transf. NY), 2000; Julius Caesar, Barbican, 2005; Faith Healer, Gate Th., Dublin, transf. NY, 2006; God of Carnage, Gielgud, 2008; The Tempest, Th. Royal, Haymarket, 2011; The Master Builder, Old Vic, 2016; Richard III, Almeida, 2016; *films*: Wuthering Heights, 1992; Baby of Macon, Schindler's List, 1993; Quiz Show, 1994; Strange Days, 1995; The English Patient, 1997; Oscar and Lucinda, The Avengers, 1998; Onegin, 1999 (also exec. producer); Sunshine, The End of the Affair, 2000; Red Dragon, Maid in Manhattan, 2002; Spider, 2003; Chromophobia, The Constant Gardener, Wallace and Gromit in the Curse of the Were-Rabbit, Harry Potter and the Goblet of Fire, 2005; The White Countess, Land of the Blind, 2006; Harry Potter and the Order of the Phoenix, Bernard and Doris, The Chumscrubber, 2007; In Bruges, The Duchess, 2008; The Reader, The Hurt Locker, 2009; Cemetery Junction, Nanny McPhee and the Big Bang, Clash of the Titans, 2010; Harry Potter and the Deathly Hallows, Pt 1, 2010, Pt 2, 2011; Coriolanus (also dir), Wrath of the Titans, Skyfall, Great Expectations, 2012; The Invisible Woman (also dir), The Grand Budapest Hotel, 2014; Spectre, 2015; A Bigger Splash, 2016; Hail, Caesar!, 2016; Holmes and Watson, 2018; The White Crow (also dir), 2019; *television* includes: A Dangerous Man, 1991; The Cormoran, 1992; Page Eight, 2011; Turks & Caicos, Salting the Battlefield, 2014. *Recreation*: books. *Address*: c/o Dalzell & Beresford Ltd, Paddock Suite, The Courtyard, 55 Charterhouse Street, EC1M 6HA. *T*: (020) 336 0531.

*See also* J. A. *Fiennes*.

**FIENNES, Sir Ranulph Twisleton-Wykeham-**, 3rd Bt *cr* 1916; OBE 1993; *b* 7 March 1944; *s* of Lieut-Col Sir Ranulph Twisleton-Wykeham-Fiennes, DSO, 2nd Bt (died of wounds, 1943) and Audrey Joan (*d* 2004), *yr d* of Sir Percy Newson, 1st Bt; *S* father, 1944; *m* 1st, 1970, Virginia Pepper (*d* 2004) (first female member of Antarctic Club, 1985; first woman to be awarded Polar Medal, 1987); 2nd, 2005, Louise Millington; one *d. Educ*: Eton. Liveryman, Vintners' Company, 1960. French Parachutist Wings, 1965. Lieut, Royal Scots Greys, 1966, Captain 1968 (retd 1970). Attached 22 SAS Regt, 1966, Sultan of Muscat's Armed Forces, 1968 (Dhofar Campaign Medal, 1969; Sultan's Bravery Medal, 1970). T&AVR 1971, Captain RAC. Leader of British expeditions: White Nile, 1969; Jostedalsbre Glacier, 1970; Headless Valley, BC, 1971; (Towards) North Pole, 1977; (with Charles Burton) Transglobe (first surface journey around the world's polar axis), 1979–82, reached South Pole, 15 Dec. 1980, reached North Pole, 11 April 1982 (first man in history to reach both Poles by surface travel); North Polar Unsupported Expeditions: reached 84°48´N on 16 April 1986; reached 88°58´N on 14 April 1990 (Furthest North Unsupported record); (with Dr Mike Stroud) South Polar Unsupported Expedition: first crossing of Antarctic Continent and longest unsupported polar journey in history (1,345 miles), 1992–93; (with Dr Mike Stroud) Land Rover 7x7x7 Challenge (7 marathons in 7 days on 7 continents), 2003; climbed North Face of Eiger, 2007; climbed Everest, 2009 (first OAP to scale highest summit, and first human to scale Everest and cross both icecaps). Life Mem., Highland Soc. of London, 2010. FRGS 1970; Fellow, British Exploring Soc., 2018. Hon. MRIN 1997. Hon. Fellow, Univ. of Glamorgan, 2012. Hon. DSc: Loughborough, 1986; Portsmouth, 2000; Sheffield, 2005; Abertay Dundee, 2007; Plymouth, 2011; DUniv Birmingham, 1995; Hon. DLitt Glasgow Caledonian, 2002. Inst. of Navigation Award, 1977; Guinness Book of Records World Hall of Fame, World's Greatest Living Explorer award, 1984. Livingstone Gold Medal, RSGS, 1983; Explorers' Club of New York Medal (and Hon. Life Membership), 1983; Founder's Medal, RGS, 1984; Polar Medal, 1987, clasp 1995; ITN Award, for the Event of the Decade, 1990; Millennium Award for Polar Exploration, British Chapter, Explorers' Club; Oldies of the Year Award, 2004; Great British Sportsman of Year Award, ITV, 2007. *Films*: (cameraman) To the Ends of the Earth, 1983; (writer) Killer Elite, 2011. Just Giving Award, 2011. *Publications*: A Talent for Trouble, 1970; Ice Fall in Norway, 1972; The Headless Valley, 1973; Where Soldiers Fear To Tread, 1975; Hell on Ice, 1979; To the Ends of the Earth, 1983; (with Virginia Fiennes) Bothie, the Polar Dog, 1984; Living Dangerously (autobiog.), 1987, rev. and expanded 1994; The Feather Men, 1991; Atlantis of the Sands, 1992; Mind Over Matter, 1993; The Sett, 1996; Fit for Life, 1998; Beyond the Limits, 2000; The Secret Hunters, 2001; Captain Scott, 2003; Mad, Bad and Dangerous to Know: the autobiography, 2007; Mad Dogs and Englishmen, 2009; My Heroes, 2011; Cold, 2013; Agincourt: my family, the battle and the fight for France, 2014; Heat, 2015; Fear, 2016. *Recreations*: langlauf, photography. *Heir*: none. *Club*: Travellers (Hon. Mem.).

**FIENNES-CLINTON**, family name of **Earl of Lincoln**.

**FIETH, Robin Paul**, FCA; Chief Executive, Building Societies Association, since 2013; *b* Sheffield, Yorks, 8 Dec. 1963; *s* of Eric and Eileen Fieth; *m* 1991, Fiona MacGregor; one *s* two *d. Educ*: Downside Sch.; Durham Univ. (BA Hons Geog.). FCA 1990. Price Waterhouse, 1986–96; Finance Dir, GiroVend Cashless Systems plc, 1996–2000; Gp Finance Dir, Transacsys plc, 2000–01; Finance Dir, 2002–07, Exec. Dir, 2007–13, ICAEW. Dir, Co-operatives UK, 2018–. Trustee, Chartered Accountants Benevolent Assoc., 2010–19. *Recreations*: cycle touring, philately. *Address*: Building Societies Association, York House, 23 Kingsway, WC2B 6UJ. *T*: (020) 7520 5900. *E*: robin.fieth@bsa.org.uk.

**FIFE, 4th Duke of**, *cr* 1899; **David Charles Carnegie**; Lord Carnegie of Kinnaird (Scot.), 1616; Earl of Southesk and Lord Carnegie of Kinnaird and Leuchars (Scot.), 1633; Bt (NS), 1663; Baron Balinhard, 1869; Earl of Macduff, 1899; Chairman, Elsick Development Co., since 2008; *b* 3 March 1961; *s* of 3rd Duke of Fife and of Hon. Caroline Cicely Dewar (now Hon. Lady Worsley), *er d* of 3rd Baron Forteviot, MBE; *S* father, 2015; *m* 1987, Caroline, *d* of Martin Bunting, *qv*; three *s. Educ*: Eton; Pembroke Coll., Cambridge (BA Law 1982; MA 1986); Royal Agricultural College, Cirencester; Edinburgh Univ. (MBA 1990). Cazenove & Co., 1982–85; Bell Lawrie & Co., 1988–89; chartered accountant, Reeves & Neylan, to 1997. Partner, Southesk Farms. Mem. Council, HHA for Scotland. Vice-Patron, Braemar Royal Highland Soc. Hon. President: Montrose and Dist Angling Club; Angus Show; Hon. Patron, Edinburgh Angus Club. *Heir*: *s* Earl of Southesk, *qv*.

**FIFE, Robert Donald Mathieson**; Sheriff of Lothian and Borders at Edinburgh, since 2017; Specialist Sheriff, all-Scotland Personal Injury Court, since 2018; *b* Edinburgh, 2 Sept. 1955; *s* of Robert and Kathleen Fife; *m* 1975, Jean McVitie; two *s. Educ*: Edinburgh Acad.; Univ. of Edinburgh (LLB). Admitted solicitor, 1978; Partner, Strathern & Blair WS, subseq. Anderson Strathern LLP, 1982–2014. Temp. Sheriff, 1998–2000, pt-time Sheriff, 2000–14; Sheriff of N Strathclyde at Paisley, 2014–17. Chair, Appeals Cttee, Inst. of Chartered Accountants of Scotland, 1999–2013. *Recreations*: travel, walking, sports, cultural events. *Address*: Edinburgh Sheriff Court, Sheriff Court House, 27 Chambers Street, Edinburgh EH1 1LB. *T*: (0131) 225 2525, *Fax*: (0131) 225 8899. *E*: sheriffrdmfife@scotcourts.gov.uk.

**FIGEL, Ján**; Leader, Christian Democratic Movement, Slovakia, 2009–16; Special Envoy for promotion of freedom of religion or belief outside the European Union, European Commission, since 2016; *b* 20 Jan. 1960; *s* of Stefan Figel and Mária Figelova; *m* 1983, Maria; three *s* one *d. Educ*: Tech. Univ., Kosice (MSc Electronic Engrg); Georgetown Univ., Washington (Internat. Affairs); UFSIA, Antwerp (European Econ. Integration). MP, Slovak Republic, 1992–98; State Sec., Min. of Foreign Affairs, 1998–2002; Chm., Internat. Cttee, 2002–04. Mem., Parly Assembly to Council of Europe, Strasbourg, 1993–98 (Vice Chm., Agric. and Rural Develt; Chm., Internat. Econ. Relns). Chief Negotiator of Slovak Republic for accession to EU, 1998–2002. Mem., Eur. Commn, 2004–09. Dep. Prime Minister, and Minister of Transport, Posts and Telecommunications, 2010–12. *Publications*: European Foreign Affairs Review: Slovakia's difficult but promising task, 1999; (jtly) Slovakia on the Road to the EU, 2002; (ed and contrib.) Slovakia on the Road to the European Union, 2003.

**FIGES, Prof. Orlando Guy,** PhD; FRSL; Professor of History, Birkbeck College, London University, since 1999; *b* 20 Nov. 1959; *s* of late John Figes and Eva Figes (*née* Unger); *m* 1990, Stephanie Palmer; two *d. Educ:* Gonville and Caius Coll., Cambridge (BA History 1982); Trinity Coll., Cambridge (PhD 1987). Fellow, 1984–99, Dir of Studies in History, 1988–98, Trinity Coll., Cambridge; University Lectr in History, Cambridge, 1987–99. FRSL 2003. *Publications:* Peasant Russia Civil War: the Volga countryside in revolution 1917–21, 1989, 3rd edn 2000; A People's Tragedy: the Russian Revolution 1891–1924, 1996 (Wolfson History Prize, W. H. Smith Lit. Award, NCR Book Award, Los Angeles Times Book Prize, 1997); (with B. Kolonitskii) Interpreting the Russian Revolution: the language and symbols of 1917, 1999; Natasha's Dance: a cultural history of Russia, 2002; The Whisperers: private life in Stalin's Russia, 2007; Crimea: the last crusade, 2010; Just Send Me Word: a true story of love and survival in the Gulag, 2012; Revolutionary Russia, 1891–1991, 2014; The Europeans: three lives and the making of a cosmopolitan culture, 2019. *Recreations:* soccer, music, gardening, wine, anything Italian. *Address:* Birkbeck College, Malet Street, WC1E 7HX.

**FIGGIS, Sir Anthony (St John Howard),** KCVO 1996; CMG 1993; HM Diplomatic Service, retired; HM Marshal of the Diplomatic Corps, 2001–08; *b* 12 Oct. 1940; *s* of Roberts Richmond Figgis and Philippa Maria Young; *m* 1964, Miriam Ellen, (Mayella), Hardt (*d* 2017); two *s* one *d. Educ:* Rugby Sch.; King's Coll., Cambridge (Mod Langs). Joined HM Foreign (later Diplomatic) Service, 1962; Third Sec., Belgrade, 1963–65; Commonwealth Office, 1965–68; Second Sec., Pol Residency, Bahrain, 1968–70; FCO, 1970–71; First Sec. (Commercial), Madrid, 1971–74; CSCE delegn, Geneva, 1974–75; FCO, 1975–79; Madrid: Head of Chancery, 1979–80; Commercial Counsellor, 1980–82; Counsellor, Belgrade, 1982–85; Head of E European Dept, FCO, 1986–88; Counsellor and Head of Chancery, Bonn, 1988–89; Dir of Res., subseq. of Res. and Analysis, FCO, 1989–91; Asst Under-Sec. of State, FCO, and HM Vice-Marshal of the Diplomatic Corps, 1991–96; Ambassador to Austria, 1996–2000. Pres., Internat. Social Service (UK), 2001–08 (Patron, 2008–17). Trustee: Guildhall Sch. Trust, 2001–09; Swinfen Charitable Trust, 2008–17; Curriculum for Cohesion, 2017–; Gov., Goodenough Coll. for Overseas Graduates, 2004–15; Royal Over-Seas League: Mem., Central Council, 2004–15, Exec. Cttee, 2006–15; Vice-Chm., 2007–09; Chm., 2009–15. Gentleman Usher of the Blue Rod, Order of St Michael and St George, 2002–15. Freeman, City of London, 1996. *Recreations:* family, fly-fishing, tennis, music (piano). *Address:* 5 Bellevue Road, SW13 0BJ. *Club:* Royal Over-Seas League.
See also B. A. H. Figgis.

**FIGGIS, Benedict Allen Howard;** Headmaster, Ardingly College, since 2014; *b* London, 2 July 1968; *s* of Sir Anthony St John Howard Figgis, *qv*; *m* 1996, Joanna; one *s* two *d. Educ:* Girton Coll., Cambridge (BA Hist. 1990); Univ. of Buckingham (MEd; PGCE Hist.). Account Exec., Ogilvy & Mather, 1990–92; Asst Producer, Pro7, Munich, 1992–94; Asst News Producer, Sky News, 1994–96; Housemaster, Abingdon Sch., 1996–2004; Dep. Hd, Oakham Sch., 2005–14. *Recreations:* tennis, theatre, cooking without recipes. *Address:* Headmaster's House, Ardingly College, College Road, Haywards Heath RH17 6SQ. *T:* (01444) 893000. *E:* head@ardingly.com. *Club:* Lansdowne.

**FIGGURES, Lt-Gen. Andrew Collingwood,** CB 2009; CBE 1998; FREng; Chief Executive, British Transport Police Authority, 2010–16; *b* 13 Nov. 1950; *s* of Colin Norman Figgures and Ethel Barbara Figgures (*née* Wilks); *m* 1978, Poppy Felicity Ann Ogley; one *d. Educ:* Loughborough Grammar Sch.; Welbeck Coll.; RMA Sandhurst; St Catharine's Coll., Cambridge (MA); Open Univ. (MBA). CEng 1991; MIEE 1991, FIET (FIEE 2005); FIMechE 1992; FREng 2011. Commnd, REME, 1970; served UK, Cyprus, BAOR, Former Republic of Yugoslavia, Iraq; attended Army Staff Coll., HCSC and RCDS; Comdr, Equipment Support, Land Comd, 1995; DOR (Land), Defence Systems, MoD, 1999–2000; Capability Manager (Manoeuvre), MoD, 2000–03; Dep. Commanding Gen., Jt Task Force 7, Iraq, 2003–04; Master Gen. of the Ordnance, and Tech. Dir, Defence Procurement Agency and Defence Logistics Orgn, MoD, 2004–06; Dep. Chief of Defence Staff (Equipment Capability), 2006–09. Col Comdt, 2002–11, Master Gen., 2012–17, REME. Trustee, Imperial War Mus., 2018–. MAPM 2005; FRAeS 2006; FCGI 2014. QCVS 2004. Hon. DSc Cranfield, 2008. *Clubs:* Royal Over-Seas League; Leander.

**FIGUERES, Christiana;** Executive Secretary, UN Framework Convention on Climate Change, 2010–16; Vice Chair, Global Covenant of Mayors for Climate & Energy, since 2016; *b* San Jose, Costa Rica, 7 Aug. 1956; *d* of Jose Figueres Ferrer and Karen Olsen; two *d. Educ:* London Sch. of Econs and Pol Sci. (MA Anthropol.). Minister Counsellor, Embassy of Costa Rica in Bonn, 1982–85; Dir, Internat. Cooperation, Min. of Planning, Costa Rica, 1987–88; COS to Minister of Agric., 1988–90; Dir, Tech. Secretariat, Renewable Energy in the Americas, 1993–94; Founder and Exec. Dir, Center for Sustainable Develt of the Americas, 1995–2003; Mem., Costa Rican climate change negotiating team, 1995–2009; Mem. Exec. Bd, Clean Develt Mechanism, and Vice Pres., Bureau of Conf. of the Parties, 2008–09. Hero for the Planet, 2001; Energy Efficiency Visionary, Energy Efficiency Global Forum, 2011; Climate Leadership Award, American Carbon Registry, 2013; Leadership Award, Climate Gp, 2014; Global Citizen Award, Unilever, 2015. *Publications:* chapters in: The UN Framework Convention on Climate Change Activities Implemented Jointly Pilot, 1999; Global Environmental Governance: options and opportunities, 2002; Global Environmental Governance: perspectives on the current debate, 2007; contribs to jls incl. Climate Policy, Envmtl Finance, Our Planet, Jl Envmt and Develt, Jl Sustainable Develt, Law and Policy. *Recreations:* long distance running, biking, hiking. *E:* christianafigueres@gmail.com.

**FILBEY, Air Vice-Marshal Keith David,** CBE 1993; Chairman, 2008–17, and Managing Director, 2015–17, AirTanker Services Ltd (Chief Executive, 2004–08); *b* 16 Dec. 1947; *s* of late Sqn Ldr Cecil Hayward Filbey and of Barbara Filbey; *m* 1982, Anne Feaver; one *s* one *d. Educ:* Brentwood Sch.; Royal Air Force Coll., Cranwell. Royal Air Force: Pilot, 214 Sqn, 1969–76; Flt Comdr 51 Sqn, 1976–78; Personnel Officer, 1978–79; RAF Staff Coll., 1980; Staff Officer, HQ 1 Gp, 1981–83; OC, 216 Sqn, 1983–86; staff appts, MoD and HQ 1 Gp, 1986–90; OC, RAF Brize Norton, 1990–92; RCDS, 1993; Dep. Chief of Assessments Staff, Cabinet Office, 1993–96; Dir, Air Ops, 1997; Sen. DS (Air), RCDS, 1998–99; AOC No 38 Gp, 2000; AOC No 2 Gp, 2000–02. Business Develt Advr, Cobham PLC, 2003–04. Mem., Air League, 1999–. Pres., RAF Cricket Assoc., 2000–02. Gov., Sherborne Sch. for Girls, 2005–09. Upper Freeman, Hon. Co. of Air Pilots (formerly GAPAN), 2000–. *Recreations:* walking, golf, choral music, ski-ing, wine collecting, cooking. *Clubs:* Royal Air Force, Innominate; Adastrian Cricket; Aero Golfing Soc. (Capt., 2013–14), Lilley Brook Golf.

**FILBY, Ian Francis;** Chairman, Joules Group plc, since 2018; *b* London, 27 Jan. 1959; *s* of Peter Michael Raymond Filby and Francisca Carmen Maria Filby; *m* Susan; one *s* two *d. Educ:* Queen Elizabeth's Hospital Sch., Bristol; St Catharine's Coll., Cambridge (BA Hons Chem. 1981). Boots Co. plc, later Alliance Boots: Sales and Marketing Dir, Fads/Homestyle, 1997; Commercial Gen. Manager, Fragrance and Cosmetics, 1998–2003; Commercial Dir, Lifestyle, 2003–05; Exec. Dir, Beauty and Lifestyle, 2005–07; Exec. Trading Dir, 2007–09; CEO, DFS, 2010–18. Chm., Shoe Zone plc, 2014–16. Mem. Bd, 2014–, Chm., Policy Bd, 2014–, British Retail Consortium. Trustee, Pennies Charity, 2015–. *Recreations:* tennis, ski-ing, good food and wine. *Address:* Joules Group plc, Joules Building, The Point, Rockingham Road, Market Harborough, Leics LE16 7QU.

**FILDES, (David) Christopher,** OBE 1994; financial journalist; *b* 10 Nov. 1934; *s* of late David Garland Fildes and Shelagh Fildes (*née* Jones), Manley, Cheshire; *m* 1st, 1969, Susan Patricia Mottram (*d* 1978); one *d* decd; 2nd, 1986, Frederica Bement Lord (*d* 1992); one step *d. Educ:* Clifton; Balliol Coll., Oxford. Financial journalist, 1963–; columnist, editor and broadcaster (The Times, Spectator, Daily Mail, Euromoney, Evening News, Investors Chronicle, Business Prog.); financial columnist: Euromoney, 1969–98; Daily Telegraph, 1984–2005; Spectator, 1984–2006; Evening Standard, 2005–09. Director: The Spectator (1828) Ltd, 1990–2004; London Mozart Players, 2000–09. Member: Council, GDST, 1999–2008; Rly Heritage Cttee, 1999–2010. Hon. Freeman, Drapers' Co., 2010. Hon. LittD Sheffield, 1999. Wincott Award for financial journalism, 1978 and 1986. *Publications:* A City Spectator, 2004. *Recreations:* racing, railways. *Address:* 4 Scarsdale Villas, W8 6PR. *Club:* Garrick.

**FILER, Denis Edwin,** CBE 1992; TD 1965 and 1977; FREng, FIMechE, FIChemE; Director of Engineering, ICI, 1981–88; *b* 19 May 1932; *s* of Francis and Sarah Filer; *m* 1957, Pamela Armitage; one *s* two *d. Educ:* Manchester Central Grammar Sch.; Manchester Univ. (Hons BSc Mech. Eng.); BA Open 1987. Commissioned REME (Nat. Service); served in Germany; REME TA, 1955–: Col, 1975–77; Hon. Col, 1978–87. ICI: Works Maintenance Engineer, 1960–67; Project Manager, Manchester, 1967–71; Project Manager, Holland (ICI Europa), 1971–73; Div. Maintenance Advisor, Organics Div., 1973; Plastics Div., Wilton Works: Works Engineer, 1973–76; Engineering Manager, Welwyn Garden City, 1976–78; Engineering & Production Dir, 1978–81; Dir-Gen., Engrg Council, 1988–95 (Mem., 1986–88; Chm., Continuing Educn and Trng Cttee; Mem., Standing Cttee for Industry). Chairman: Rolinx, 1978–81; Adwest Gp, then Adwest Automotive plc, 1994–97 (Dir, 1991–97); Electra Innvotec Corporate Ventures Ltd, then Innvotec Corporate Ventures Ltd, 2000–01 (Dir, 1989–2001); Director: Bexford, 1978–80; Engineering Services Wilton, 1978–81; Eur. Adv. Dir, Callidus Technologies Inc., 1991–99. Member: Council, IMechE, 1983–89 (Vice-Pres., 1987–89, 1996–98; Dep. Pres. 1998–2000; Pres., 2000–01; Chm., Process Industries Div. Bd, 1985–87); Board, Lloyd's Register of Quality Assurance, 1986–88, Gen. Cttee, Lloyd's Register, 1988–95. Chm., F and GP Cttee, 2002–04. Gov., Univ. of Hertfordshire, 1996– (Vice-Chm., 2002–04; Chm., 2004–07). FREng (FEng 1985). Liveryman, Engineers' Co., 1990– (Mem. Court, 1995–). Hon. DSc Herts, 1993. *Recreations:* tennis, sport, reading. *Address:* Brambles, Perrywood Lane, Watton Green, Watton-at-Stone, Hertford SG14 3RB. *T:* (01920) 830207. *Club:* Army and Navy.

**FILER, (Douglas) Roger,** FCA; Chairman, D & S Travel Supplies Ltd, since 2012 (Managing Director, 1997–2012); *b* 25 Feb. 1942; *s* of Horace Filer and Raie (*née* Behrman); *m* 1979, Vivienne Sara Green; one *s* one *d. Educ:* Clifton Coll.; St John's Coll., Oxford (MA); FCA 1970. Called to the Bar, Gray's Inn, 1979. Joined Association Television Group, 1967; Chief Accountant, Ambassador Bowling, 1967–69; Financial Controller, Bentray Investments, 1969–70; Financial Dir, M. Berman then Bermans & Nathans, 1971–73; Financial Controller, Stoll Theatres Corp./Moss Empires, 1974; Dir, 1982–92, Man. Dir, 1990–92, Stoll Moss Theatres; Man. Dir, Maybox Gp, subseq. Mayfair Theatres and Cinemas Ltd, 1993–96. *Recreations:* golf, history, walking. *Address:* Four Brim Hill, Hampstead Garden Suburb, N2 0HF. *T:* (020) 8455 7392.

**FILKIN,** family name of **Baron Filkin**.

**FILKIN, Baron** *cr* 1999 (Life Peer), of Pimlico in the City of Westminster; **David Geoffrey Nigel Filkin,** CBE 1997; Chairman, Centre for Ageing Better, 2013–19; *b* 1 July 1944; *s* of Donald Geoffrey and Winifred Filkin; *m* Camilla Hubback (marr. diss. 1973); *m* 1974, Elizabeth Tompkins (*see* Elizabeth Filkin) (marr. diss. 1994); two *d*; *m* 2005, Brigitte Paupy. *Educ:* King Edward VI Sch., Five Ways, Birmingham; Clare Coll., Cambridge (MA Hist.); Manchester Univ. (DipTP); Birmingham Univ. (postgrad. study). Formerly MRTPI. Teacher on VSO, Ghana, 1966–67; Planner, Redditch Develt Corp., 1969–72; Manager, Brent Housing Aid Centre, London Borough of Brent, 1972–75; Dep. Chief Exec., Merseyside Improved Houses, 1975–79; Borough Housing Officer, Ellesmere Port and Neston Council, 1979–82; Dir of Housing, London Borough of Greenwich, 1982–88; Chief Exec., Reading BC, 1988–91; Sec., ADC, 1991–97. Dir, New Local Govt Network, 1995–2001. A Lord in Waiting (Govt Whip), 2001–02; Parliamentary Under-Secretary of State: Home Office, 2002–03; DCA, 2003–04; DFES, 2004–05. Chairman: All Party Parly Business Services Gp, 2000; H of L Merits Cttee, 2005–09; H of L Select Cttee on Public Services and Demographic Change, 2012–13; Founder and Chairman: The Parlt Choir, All Party Parly Gp, 2000–; Public Sector Res. Gp, 2005–07; 2020 Public Services Trust, 2007–11. Non-exec. Dir, Accord, 2005–07. Chairman: Beacon Council Adv. Panel, 1999–2001; St Albans Cathedral Music Trust, 2006–10. Adviser: on local govt, Joseph Rowntree Foundn, 1997–2001; H of C Envmt Cttee, 1998; Capgemini, 2005–12; NSL (Services) (formerly NCP), 2006–12; Serco (Civil Govt), 2006–13. Trustee, Southbank Sinfonia, 2008–18. *Publications:* (jtly) Better Outcomes, 2009; pamphlets, papers and articles on housing and local govt policy. *Recreations:* music, walking, swimming. *Address:* c/o House of Lords, SW1A 0PW. *T:* (020) 7219 0640.

**FILKIN, Elizabeth Jill,** CBE 2014; Chairman, Annington (formerly Annington Homes) Ltd, 2008–19; Chair, Employers' Initiative on Domestic Abuse, since 2017; *b* 24 Nov. 1940; *d* of Frances Trollope and John Tompkins; *m* 1st, 1963, Michael David Radford (marr. diss. 1974); one *d*; 2nd, 1974, David Geoffrey Nigel Filkin (marr. diss. 1994); two *d*; 3rd, 1996, Michael John Honey, *qv. Educ:* Birmingham Univ. (BSocSci). Organiser, Sparkbrook Assoc., 1961–64; Whyndham Deedes Fellowship, Israel, 1964; Res. Asst, Associate Lectr, Birmingham Univ., 1964–68; Lectr and Community Worker, Nat. Inst. for Social Work, 1968–71; Community Work Services Officer, London Borough of Brent, 1971–75; Lectr in Social Studies, Liverpool Univ., 1975–83; Chief Exec., Nat. Assoc. of CABx, 1983–88; Dir of Community Services, 1988–90, Asst Chief Exec., 1990–92, LDDC; Revenue Adjudicator, 1993–95; The Adjudicator, Inland Revenue, Customs and Excise, and Contribs Agency, 1995–99; Parly Comr for Standards, 1999–2002; Comr, Audit Commn, 1999–2004; Mem., 2002–08, Dep. Chm., 2005–08, Regulatory Decisions Cttee, FSA. Ind. Advr, Metropolitan Police Service, 2011–12. Non-executive Director: Britannia Bldg Soc., 1992–98; Hay Management Consultants, 1992–98; Logica, 1995–98; Weatherall, Green & Smith, 1997–99; Jarvis plc, 2003–10; Sen. Ind. non-exec. Dir, Stanelco plc, 2003–10 (Chm., 2002–03); Chm., HBS, 2005–08; Chair, Ind. Adv. Gp, Marston Hldgs, 2014–. Chm., Lord Chancellor's Adv. Cttee on Legal Aid, 1991–94. Chairman: Rainer Foundn, 2004–08; Television (formerly Video) on Demand Assoc., 2004–10; Appts Gp, RPSGB, 2005–10; Advertising Adv. Cttee, 2005–11; Appts Cttee, Gen. Pharmaceutical Council, 2010–17. Trustee: Tiri, 2008–12; Vodafone Foundn, 2009–. Dep. Chm. Council, Univ. of E London, 1999–2004. City Fellow, Hughes Hall, Cambridge Univ., 2003–06. *Publications:* The New Villagers, 1968; What a Community Worker Needs to Know, 1974; Community Work and Caring for Children, 1979; Caring for Children, 1979; (ed) Women and Children First, 1984. *Recreations:* walking, swimming.

**FILLINGHAM, David James,** CBE 2005; Chief Executive, Advancing Quality Alliance, since 2010; *b* 28 March 1960; *s* of Thomas Fillingham and Irene Fillingham (*née* Webster); *m* 1982, Janet Green; two *d. Educ:* Cowley High Sch.; Peterhouse, Cambridge (MA History 1982); Henley Coll. (MBA 1993). Personnel Officer, Pilkington plc, 1982–84; Personnel Manager, 1984–88, Product Develt Manager, 1988–89, Pilkington Glass; Regl Personnel Manager, Mersey RHA, 1989–91; Gen. Manager, Wirral FHSA, 1991–93; Chief Executive: St Helens and Knowsley HA, 1993–97; N Staffordshire Hosp. NHS Trust, 1997–2001; Dir, NHS Modernisation Agency, 2001–04; Chief Exec., Royal Bolton Hosp. NHS Foundn Trust (formerly Bolton Hosps NHS Trust), 2004–10. Sen. Vis. Fellow, King's Fund, 2012–17. Non-exec. Dir, Aintree Hosp. NHS Foundn Trust, 2013– (Dep. Chm., 2013–). Chair: Healthier Wigan Partnership, 2016–; Trafford Local Care Alliance, 2018–. MIPM 1986. *Publications:* Lean Healthcare, 2008; various articles in mgt jls and health service pubns. *Recreations:* hill-walking, watching Rugby League, keen but inexpert skier. *Address:* Advancing Quality Alliance, St James's House, Pendleton Way, Salford M6 5FW; Springfield, Millbrow, St Helens, Merseyside WA10 4QQ. *T:* (01744) 29600.

**FILLON, François Charles Amand;** Partner, Tikehau Capital, since 2017; Prime Minister of France, 2007–12; *b* Le Mans, 4 March 1954; *m* 1980, Penelope Clarke; four *s* one *d. Educ:* Univ. du Maine, Le Mans (Master's degree Public Law 1976); Univ. René Descartes, Paris (Dip. d'études appliquées Public Law 1977). Intern, Agence France-Presse, Paris, 1976; Parly Asst to Joël Le Theule, MP, 1976–77; Dep. Hd, private office of Joël Le Theule, 1978–80; Hd, legislation dept, private office of André Giraud, 1981. Mayor, Sablé-sur-Sarthe, 1983–2001; Chm., Sarthe Gen. Council, 1992–98; Pays de la Loire Regional Council: Chm., 1998–2002; First Vice-Chm., 2002–04; Mem., 2004–07; Chm., Community of Communes of Sablé sur Sarthe, 2001. MP (RPR) Sarthe, 1981–93, 1997–2002, 2007; Mem. of Senate for Sarthe, 2004–07. Minister: of Higher Educn and Res., 1993–95; for Information Technol. and the Post Office, 1995; Minister Delegate with responsibility for the Post Office, Telecommns and Space, 1995–97; Minister: of Social Affairs, Labour and Solidarity, 2002–04; for Nat. Educn, Higher Educn and Res., 2004–05. Pol Advr to Nicolas Sarkozy, UMP, 2004–07. Mem. (UMP) Paris, Nat. Assembly, 2012–17. Chm., France.9 think-tank, 2002; Founder Mem., Union en Mouvement, 2002. Nat. Sec., 1997, Spokesman, 1998, RPR. *Publications:* La France peut supporter la vérité, 2006. *Recreations:* mountain climbing, ski-ing, hiking, motor racing, running, mountain biking, cinema, reading.

**FILMER-SANKEY, Dr William Patrick,** FSA; Partner, Alan Baxter & Associates, since 2008 (Senior Engineer, 2000; Associate, 2002; Senior Associate, 2005–08); *b* 13 Oct. 1957; *s* of late Patrick Hugh Filmer-Sankey and Josephine Filmer-Sankey; *m* 1981, Caroline Frances Sparrow; one *s* one *d. Educ:* Downside Sch.; New Coll., Oxford (BA Hons Mod. Hist. 1979); Inst. of Archaeology, Oxford (Dip. European Archaeol. 1981; DPhil 1989). Associate Archaeol Consultant, Oxford Archaeological Associates Ltd, 1990–93; Dir, Victorian Soc., 1993–2000. Dir, Snape Historical Trust, 1987–95; Hon. Sec., 1994–2000, Vice Pres., 2000–, British Archaeol Assoc.; Mem. Council, Soc. of Antiquaries, 2002–05. Vis. Fellow, Dept of Archaeol., Univ. of York, 2005–08. FSA 1997; FRSA 1998. Editor, Anglo-Saxon Studies in Archaeology and History, 1991–94. *Publications:* From the Dust of the Earth Returning: excavations of the Anglo-Saxon cemetery at Snape, Suffolk, 1990; (contrib.) Maritime Celts, Frisians and Saxons, 1991; (contrib.) The Age of Sutton Hoo, 1992; Snape Anglo-Saxon Cemetery: excavations and surveys 1824–1992, 2001; articles and papers. *Recreations:* archaeology, ornithology, sailing, deer stalking, Germany. *Address:* 57 Lavington Road, Ealing, W13 9LS. *T:* (020) 8579 0425.

**FILOCHOWSKI, Jan;** writer and speaker on National Health Service and management; consultant on healthcare management nationally and internationally, 2014–18; Chief Executive Officer, Great Ormond Street Hospital for Children NHS Foundation Trust, 2012–13; *b* England, 27 April 1950; *s* of Tadeusz Filochowski and Jean Filochowski (*née* Royce); *m* 2006, Prof. Naomi Fulop; one *s* one *d* from a former marriage. *Educ:* Churchill Coll., Cambridge (BA 1972); Newcastle Univ. (MA 1973); Linacre Coll., Oxford. Civil Servant, DoH, 1975–85; Unit General Manager: Southend HA, 1986–87; Barts and St Mark's Hosps, 1987–88; Chief Executive Officer: Poole Hosps NHS Trust, 1989–97; Southmead Hosp. NHS Trust, 1998–99; Medway Hosps NHS Trust, 1999–2002; Royal United Hosps, Bath NHS Trust, 2002–03; Sen. Mgt Advr, NHS Authorities, SE, 2003–07; Advr to Prime Minister's Delivery Unit (pt-time), 2004–06; CEO, W Herts Hosps NHS Trust, 2007–12. Inspection Chair, CQC, 2014–16. Vis. Prof., Brunel Univ., 2004–16; Vis. Fellow, Harvard Univ., 1997–98; NHS Univ. Fellow and Associate, Judge Business Sch., Univ. of Cambridge, 2004–05; Sen. Mem., Wolfson Coll., Cambridge, 2004–. Advr, Namibian Min. of Health, 2015–16. *Publications:* Too Good to Fail?, 2013 (trans. Korean, 2014, Chinese, 2017); articles on state and future of NHS in Guardian, BMJ, Health Services Jl. *Recreations:* swimming, ski-ing, walking.
*See also Julian Filochowski.*

**FILOCHOWSKI, Julian,** CMG 2004; OBE 1998; international development consultant, 2005–14; Strategic Development and Advocacy Adviser, Jesuit Missions (GB), 2010–14; *b* 9 Dec. 1947; *s* of Tadeusz Filochowski and Jean Filochowski (*née* Royce); civil partnership 2006, Martin Pendergast. *Educ:* St Michael's Coll., Leeds; Churchill Coll., Cambridge (MA Econs). Economic Planning Advr, Min. of Finance, Belize, 1969–70; Central America Regl Co-ordinator, British Volunteer Prog., 1970–73; Co-ordinator, Educn Dept, Catholic Inst. for Internat. Relations, 1973–82; Dir, CAFOD, 1982–2003. Dir, Tablet Publishing Co., 2003–17. Vis. Fellow, Clare Coll., Cambridge, 2005. Chm., Archbp Romero Trust, 2005–; Trustee: Thomson Foundn, 2008–12; Denis Hurley Assoc., 2011–16; The Friars Aylesford, 2011–18. Patron, Nat. Justice and Peace Network, 2012–. Dr *hc.* Univ. Centroamericana, San Salvador, 2004; Roehampton, 2006. *Publications:* Reflections on Puebla, 1980; Archbishop Romero, Ten Years On, 1991; (ed jtly) Opening Up: speaking out in the Church, 2005. *Recreation:* swimming. *Address:* 57 Lyme Grove, E9 6PX.
*See also Jan Filochowski.*

**FINALDI, Dr Gabriele Maria;** Director, National Gallery, since 2015; *b* Barnet, 28 Nov. 1965; *s* of Remo and Iwonka Finaldi; *m* 1987, María Inés Luisa Irene Guerrero Parra; one *s* five *d. Educ:* St Joseph's Acad., Blackheath; Istituto Cristoforo Colombo, Piacenza, Italy; Dulwich Coll.; Courtauld Inst. of Art, London Univ. (BA 1987; MA 1989; PhD Hist. of Art 1995). Curator, Later Italian and Spanish Painting, National Gall., 1992–2002; Dep. Dir for Collections and Res., Museo del Prado, Madrid, 2002–15. Cavaliere dell'Ordine al Merito (Italy), 2006; Medalla de Oro al Merito de las Bellas Artes (Spain), 2015; Grande Ufficiale dell'Ordine della Stella d'Italia, 2017. *Publications:* Discovering the Italian Baroque: the Denis Mahon collection, 1997; Orazio Gentileschi at the Court of Charles I, 1999; The Image of Christ, 2000; El trazo oculto: dibujos subyacentes en pinturas de los siglos XV y XVI, 2006; The Art of Friendship, Murillo and Justino de Neve, 2012; Jusepe de Ribera: the drawings, 2016; contrib. articles to Burlington Mag., Apollo, Boletín del Museo del Prado. *Recreation:* playing the piano. *Address:* National Gallery, Trafalgar Square, WC2N 5DN.

**FINCH, Alan Arthur,** CBE 2015; Co-Managing Director, Cameron Mackintosh Ltd, since 2016; *b* Mansfield, Notts, 9 April 1965; *s* of Geoffrey Finch and Margaret Finch; *m* 1989, Alison Margaret Roberts; one *s* one *d. Educ:* Brunts Sch., Mansfield. Electrician, 1984–89, Prodn Manager, 1989–94, Nottingham Playhouse; Gen. Manager, Th. Royal, Plymouth, 1994–2004; Exec. Dir, Chichester Festival Th., 2005–16. Chm. Trustees, Children on the Edge, 2008–. *Recreations:* cinema, family, theatre, school governor. *Address:* Cameron Mackintosh Ltd, 1 Bedford Square, WC1B 3RB. *T:* (020) 7637 8866. *E:* alan@camack.co.uk.

**FINCH, Henrietta Lucy Anne, (Henny);** Executive Producer, Donmar Warehouse, since 2019; *b* London, 1975; *d* of Graham Finch and Mary Finch; *m* 2004, Rory Fisher; one *s* one *d. Educ:* Bath High Sch.; St John's Coll., Oxford (BA Lit.Hum. 1997). Develt Officer, Almeida Th., 1997–99; Agent's Asst, London Management, 1999–2000; Asst Producer, Act Prodns, 2000–04; Executive Director: Headlong, 2005–16; Hofesh Shechter Co., 2016–19. Clore Fellow, 2013–14. *Recreations:* theatre, visual art, contemporary fiction. *Address:* Donmar Warehouse, 41 Earlham Street, WC2H 9LX.

**FINCH, Hilary Ann;** freelance writer and broadcaster, since 1980; *b* 2 May 1951; *d* of Francis Richard Finch and Hilda Grace (*née* Davey). *Educ:* Univ. of Exeter (MA); Hughes Hall, Cambridge (PGCE). Asst to Arts Editor, TES, 1976–80; feature writer and Music Critic, The Times, 1980–2015. *Recreations:* walking in Iceland, playing the violin. *Address:* 51 Victoria Road, Mortlake, SW14 8EX. *T:* (020) 8878 0957.

**FINCH, Dame Janet (Valerie),** DBE 2008 (CBE 1999); DL; PhD; FAcSS; Vice-Chancellor, Keele University, 1995–2010; *b* 13 Feb. 1946; *d* of Robert Bleakley Finch and Evelyn Muriel (*née* Smith); *m* 1st, 1967, Geoffrey O. Spedding (marr. diss. 1982); 2nd, 1994, David H. J. Morgan. *Educ:* Merchant Taylors' Sch. for Girls, Crosby; Bedford Coll., London (BA Hons Sociol.; Hon. Fellow, RHC, 1999); Univ. of Bradford (PhD Sociol. 1975). Lectr, Endsleigh Coll., Hull, 1974–76; Lancaster University: Lectr, then Sen. Lectr, 1976–88; Prof. of Social Relations, 1988–95; Pro-Vice-Chancellor, 1992–95. Non-executive Director: NW Regl HA, 1992–96; ONS, 1999–2008; HM Passport Service (formerly Identity and Passport Service), 2008–13; Office of the Health Professions Adjudicator, 2010–12; Chm., Ombudsman Services Ltd, 2010–16; Member: Bd, QAA, 1997–2004; Council for Science and Technology, 2004–11 (Ind. Co-Chm., 2007–11); Ind. Panel, BBC Charter Review, 2004–05; Sci. and Technol. Honours Cttee, 2009–15; Chairman: Health Cttee, Universities UK, 2003–06; Social Scis, REF, 2010–14; Rev. on Expanding Access to Res. Pubns, 2012–13; Chm., Nursing and Midwifery Council, 2015–18. Chm., Preston CRC, 1980–85; Mem. Bd, Staffs Environmental Fund Ltd, 2000–04; Chm., Staffs Connexions Ltd, 2002–04. Member, Council: ESRC, 1993–97 (Chm., Res. Grants Bd, 1994–97); MRC, 2014–18; Research England, 2018–. Chm. Exec., Brit. Sociol. Assoc., 1983–84. Governor: City of Stoke-on-Trent Sixth Form Coll., 1999–2002; Manchester Metropolitan Univ., 2002–10; Chm., Governing Bd, Life Study, 2011–15; Mem. Council, Leicester Univ., 2017–. Trustee, Nat. Centre for Soc. Res., 2002–12 (Chm., 2007–12). DL Staffs, 1999. FAcSS (AcSS 1999). Hon. Fellow, Liverpool John Moores Univ., 2001. Hon. DLitt UWE, 1997; Hon. DSc: Edinburgh, 2000; Southampton, 2001; Manchester, 2017; Hon. DEd: Lincoln, 2002; Queen Margaret UC, Edinburgh, 2003. *Publications:* Married to the Job, 1983, reprint 2012; Education as Social Policy, 1984; Research and Policy, 1986; Family Obligations and Social Change, 1989; Negotiating Family Responsibilities, 1993; Wills, Inheritance and Families, 1996; Passing On, 2000. *Recreation:* theatre-going. *Address:* The Cottage, 39 Millfields, Nantwich, Cheshire CW5 5HR. *Club:* Athenæum.

**FINCH, John;** Chief Information Officer, Refinitiv, since 2018; *b* UK, 8 Sept. 1965; *m* 1994, Hilary; one *d. Educ:* Aireborough Grammar Sch., Leeds; Univ. of Hull (BSc (Econ) Hons Business Econs 1987). Mercury Communications, Cable & Wireless, 1988–95; Sen. Business Analyst, Heinz, 1995–97; Hd of Intranet Develt, Unipart, 1997–98; Hd of Internet/Intranet Develt, Nat. Bank of Kuwait, 1998–2001; Hd of Develt, SHL plc, 2002–05; Global Hd of Product Develt, 2005–11, Chief Information Officer, 2011–13, Experian; Exec. Dir, Inf. Services and Technol., and Chief Inf. Officer, Bank of England, 2013–16; Chief Technol. Officer, Thomson Reuters Financial and Risk, 2016–18. Tech. Advr, RSocMed, 2015–. Non-exec. Dir, OPP Ltd, 2011–15. Mem. Council, Nottingham Univ., 2014–18 (Mem., Audit Cttee, 2012–18). *Recreations:* Leeds United FC supporter, England cricket watcher. *Address:* Refinitiv, 5 Canada Square, Canary Wharf, E14 5AQ. *E:* john.finch@refinitiv.com.

**FINCH, (John) Russell,** OBE 2017; FCIArb; Judge, Royal Court of Guernsey, since 2005; *b* 15 Feb. 1950; *s* of Reginald John Peter Fergusson Finch and Winifred Joan Finch (*née* Woods); *m* 1990, Anne Elizabeth Sergeant (*née* Lowe), *widow* of Peter Sergeant; one step *s. Educ:* Southern Grammar Sch. for Boys, Portsmouth; Queen Mary Coll., London (LLB); Univ. de Caen; Open Univ. (BA Hons, DipHErUm); Sheffield Hallam Univ. (MA 2004). FCIArb 1999. Articled to Clerk to Fareham and Gosport Justices, 1972–74; admitted solicitor, 1974; Court Clerk, 1974–75; Principal Asst, Aylesbury Gp of Magistrates' Courts, 1975–79; joined Dept of DPP, 1979; served on S, Metropolitan and Police Complaints Divs, 1979–86; Asst Br. Crown Prosecutor, Inner London CPS (Sen. Principal), 1986–88; joined Chambers of HM's Procureur (Attorney-Gen.) for Guernsey, 1988; Advocate, Royal Court of Guernsey, 1993; Crown Advocate, 1994; Stipendiary Magistrate and Coroner, 1997–2005, Sen. Magistrate, 2004–05, Guernsey; Lt-Bailiff and Judge, Matrimonial Causes Div., 1999–2011. Examr in Family Law and Criminal Law, Guernsey Bar, 2000–. Chm., Guernsey Inf. Exchange, 1999–2005. Member: US Naval Inst., Annapolis; HMS Hood Assoc. *Publications:* Practical Police Prosecuting, 1977; contrib. articles to various jls on magisterial law and practice. *Recreations:* chess (mainly correspondence) (former Vice-Pres., English Chess Fedn), history, listening to opera recordings. *Address:* Royal Court House, St Peter Port, Guernsey GY1 2NZ. *T:* (01481) 726161. *E:* russell.finch@gov.gg. *Club:* Civil Service.

**FINCH, Hon. Lance (Sidney George),** OBC 2017; Associate Counsel, Guild Yule LLP, since 2014; *b* 16 June 1938; *s* of Herbert George and Rita Muriel Finch; *m* 1963, Judith A. C. Jack; one *s* two *d. Educ:* Univ. of British Columbia (LLB 1962). Barrister and solicitor, 1963–83; Justice: Supreme Court of BC, 1983–93; BC and Yukon Courts of Appeal, 1993–2001; Chief Justice of BC and Yukon Courts of Appeal, Chief Justice of BC, and Adminr of Govt, Province of BC, 2001–13. Hon. QC 2014. *Club:* Vancouver.

**FINCH, Lucie;** see Skeaping, L.

**FINCH, Paul,** OBE 2002; Director, World Architecture Festival, since 2008; Editorial Director, Architectural Review and Architects' Journal, since 2009; *b* 2 March 1949; *s* of William and Nancy Finch; *m* 1973, Susanna Phillips; one *s. Educ:* Woolverstone Hall, Suffolk; Selwyn Coll., Cambridge (MA). Dep. Ed., Estates Times, 1976–83; Ed., Building Design, 1983–94; Jt Ed., Planning in London, qly jl, 1991–; Ed., Architects' Jl, 1994–99; Editl Dir, Emap Construct, 1999–2008; Ed., The Architectural Rev., 2005–08. Dep. Chm., 1999–2005, Chm., 2009–14, CABE, then Design Council Cabe. Hon. Mem., Architectural Assoc., 2014. Hon. FRIBA 1994; Hon. Fellow, UCL, 2006. Hon. DSc Westminster, 2007. *Recreations:* cinema, novels, weekend cooking. *Address:* (office) Telephone House, 69–77 Paul Street, EC2A 4NA. *E:* paul.finch@emap.com. *Clubs:* Reform, Chelsea Arts.

**FINCH, Raymond Terence;** Member (UK Ind) South East England, European Parliament, 2014–19; *b* Liverpool, 2 June 1963; *s* of Raymond Walter and Lily Finch; *m* 1989, Debra Anne; one *s*. *Educ:* Cantril Farm Primary Sch.; Liverpool Inst. High Sch. for Boys. Mem. (UK Ind) Hants CC, 2013–17. Fisheries spokesman, 2014–16, Dep. Whip, 2014–16, Housing spokesman, 2016–19, UKIP Gp, EP; Hd, UKIP Delegn to EP, 2016–19. Mem., Nat. Exec. Cttee, UKIP, 2015–17. Contested (UK Ind): SE England, EP, 2009; Eastleigh, 2010; Lewes, 2015. Hon. Sec., Gadfly Club. *Recreations:* watching Everton FC, sea angling, electric guitar.

**FINCH, Russell;** *see* Finch, J. R.

**FINCH, Stephen Clark,** OBE 1989; independent consultant, since 1989; *b* 7 March 1929; *s* of Frank Finch and Doris Finch (*née* Lloyd), Haywards Heath; *m* 1975, Sarah Rosemary Ann, *d* of Adm. Sir Anthony T. F. G. Griffin, GCB; two *d*. *Educ:* Ardingly; Sch. of Signals; RMCS. FInstAM; FCMA. Commnd Royal Signals 1948; served Korea, UK and BAOR; retired 1968. Joined British Petroleum Co. Ltd, 1968: Gp Telecommunications Manager, 1968–81; Sen. Adviser, Regulatory Affairs, 1981–84; Asst Co-ordinator, Inf. Systems Admin, 1984–89. Member: Adv. Panel on Licensing Value Added Network Services, 1982–87; Competition (formerly Monopolies and Mergers) Commn, 1985–2000. Member: Inst. of Administrative Management, 1968– (Mem. Council, 1981–84; Medallist, 1985); Communications Mgt Assoc. (formerly Telecommunications Managers Assoc.), 1968– (Exec. Cttee, 1971–91; Chm., 1981–84; Regulatory Affairs Exec., 1984–87; Dir, External Affairs, 1988–91); Council, Internat. Telecommunications Users Gp, 1981–94 (Chm., 1987–89). Member: City of London Deanery Synod, 1981– (Lay Chm., 1994–2008); London Diocesan Synod, 1994– (Bishop's Council, 1994–); City Churches Grants Cttee, 1994–2008; London DAC for Care of Churches, 1995–2006; City Churches Develt Gp, 1997–2002; Two Cities Area Council, 1997–2008 (Vice-Chm., 2001–07); Archdeacon of London's Finance Adv. Gp, 1999–2008; City Deanery Bishop's Adv. Gp, 2003–08. Trustee: Oxford Churches Trust, 1996 (Sec., 1997); Dick Lucas Trust, 1999 (Chm., 1999). Churchwarden, St Martin Outwich, 1987–2010. Freeman, City of London, 1975. FCMI. *Publications:* occasional contribs to learned jls. *Recreations:* sailing, ski-ing, swimming, music. *Club:* National.

**FINCH, Stephen John;** Consultant, Excello Law, since 2015; *b* Carshalton, 28 Nov. 1950; *s* of Harry John and Evelyn Louise Finch; three *s* one *d*. *Educ:* London Univ. (LLB). Admitted solicitor, 1975; Solicitor: practising in Sydney and London, 1975–78; Lloyds Bowmaker, 1978–82; Citibank Internat., 1982–85; Partner: Hill Bailey, 1985–89; Salans, 1989–2012 (Chm., 2005–10); Partner, 2012–13, Consultant, 2014–15, Locke Lord LLP. *Publications:* (contrib.) Practical Commercial Precedents. *Recreations:* anything involving mainstream sports, spending time with family and friends, restaurant owner. *Address:* c/o Excello Law, 5 Chancery Lane, WC2A 1LG. *T:* 07887 644297. *E:* sfinch@excellolaw.co.uk.

**FINCH HATTON,** family name of **Earl of Winchilsea and Nottingham.**

**FINCH-KNIGHTLEY,** family name of **Earl of Aylesford.**

**FINCHAM, Peter Arthur;** Co-Chief Executive Officer, Expectation Entertainment, since 2016; *b* 26 July 1956; *s* of late Arthur and Joan Fincham; *m* 1995, Clare Lewthwaite; two *s* two *d*. *Educ:* Tonbridge Sch.; Churchill Coll., Cambridge (BA English 1977). Man. Dir, TalkBack Prodns, 1986–2002; Chief Exec., talkbackThames, 2003–05; Controller, BBC1, 2005–07; Dir of Television, ITV, 2008–16. *Address:* Expectation Entertainment, 8B Ledbury Mews North, W11 2AF.

**FINDLATER, (John) Donald;** child protection worker and commentator; Director, Research and Development, Lucy Faithfull Foundation, 2008–18 (Manager, Wolvercote Clinic, 1995–2002; Deputy Director, 1997–2007); Director, Stop it Now! UK and Ireland, 2008 (Manager, UK and Ireland helpline, 2002–07); *b* 23 March 1955; *s* of Robert and Mary Findlater; *m* 1977, Jacqueline Durrant; four *s* one *d*. *Educ:* King George V Grammar Sch., Southport; Univ. of Kent, Canterbury (BA Hons Law 1976); Univ. of East Anglia (MA Soc. Work 1981; CQSW 1981). Probation Officer, Hereford and Worcester Probation Service, 1981–85; Probation Officer, then Sen. Probation Officer, Surrey Probation Service, 1985–97. Consultant: to Home Office, DfES, later DCSF, and DoH on sexual abuse prevention; to RC, Anglican and Methodist Churches on sexual abuse prevention and sex offender rehabilitation; Member: Sir Roger Singleton's panel of child protection experts, 2006–08; Ind. Safeguarding Authy, 2008–12; Disclosure and Barring Service, 2012–13. Trustee: Langley House Trust, 2003–08; Sanctuary, 2006–08. FRSA. *Publications:* (contrib.) Eradicating Child Maltreatment, 2015; contrib. to professional jls and ref. texts. *Recreations:* spending time with my family, DIY, gardening, walking, visiting historic buildings, finding and sharing hope. *T:* 07778 532851.

**FINDLAY, Alastair Donald Fraser,** FCIWEM; Chief Executive, North of Scotland Water Authority, 1995–2000; *b* 3 Feb. 1944; *s* of late Rev. Donald Fraser Findlay and Isobel Ellis Findlay (*née* Louden); *m* 1969, Morag Cumming Peden; one *s* three *d*. *Educ:* Pitlochry High Sch.; Kelso High Sch.; Univ. of Edinburgh (MA (Hons) Mental Philosophy). FCIWEM 1996. Asst Principal, Dept of Agriculture and Fisheries for Scotland, 1966–70; Private Sec. to Jt Parly Under Sec. of State, Scottish Office, 1970–71; Principal, Scottish Office, 1971–74; on loan to FCO as First Sec. (Agric. and Food), The Hague, 1975–78; Asst Sec., Higher Educn Div., Scottish Educn Dept, 1979–82; Fisheries Div., 1982–85, Livestock Products Div., 1985–88, Dept of Agric. and Fisheries for Scotland; Under Sec., IDS, then Scottish Office Industry Dept, 1988–93; Fisheries Sec., Scottish Office Agric. and Fisheries Dept, 1993–95. Advr to Scottish Fishermen's Orgn, 2005–15. Mem., Barnardo's Scottish Cttee, 2002–05. Trustee: Lloyds TSB Foundn for Scotland, 1998–2004 (Dep. Chm., 2003–04); Univ. of Highlands and Islands Develt Trust (formerly Univ. of Highlands and Islands Millennium Inst. Develt Trust), 2003–08; The Queen Mother's Memorial Fund for Scotland, 2003–09. Treas., Boroughmuir RFC, 2001–08 (Dir, 2004–09). *Recreations:* walking, motor cars, Rugby spectating, gardening.

**FINDLAY, Donald Russell;** QC (Scot.) 1988; after dinner and motivational speaker; *b* 17 March 1951; *s* of James Findlay and Mabel Findlay (*née* Muirhead); *m* 1982, Jennifer Edith (*née* Borrowman). *Educ:* Harris Academy, Dundee; Univ. of Dundee (LLB 1st cl. Hons); Univ. of Glasgow (MPhil). Mem., Faculty of Advocates, 1975– (Chm., Faculty Services Ltd, 2003–05; Chm., Criminal Bar Assoc., 2010–12); Lectr in Law, Heriot-Watt Univ., 1976–77. Mem., Lothian Health Bd, 1987–91. Vice Chm., Glasgow Rangers FC, 1992–99 (Dir, 1991–99); Chm., Cowdenbeath FC, 2010–. Vice Chairman: N Cunninghame Cons. and Unionist Assoc., 1989–92; Leith Cons. and Unionist Assoc., 1985–88. Rector, St Andrews Univ., 1993–99. Vice Pres., Assoc. for Internat. Cancer Res., 1996–. Columnist, Scottish Daily Express, 1995–97; radio and television broadcaster. FRSA 1997. *Publications:* Three Verdicts (novel), 1998; contribs to Scots Law Times and various medico-legal publications. *Recreations:* avoiding the ageing process, suffering along with every other supporter of Cowdenbeath FC, remaining constantly cheery. *Address:* Optimum Advocates, Glasgow High Court, 1 Mart Street, Saltmarket, Glasgow G1 5JT; Faculty of Advocates, Parliament House, Edinburgh EH1 1RF. *T:* (0131) 226 2881.

**FINDLAY, Irene, (Irene Paterson Hesford),** OBE 2004; executive coach, since 2011; Managing Director, Hurria, 2011–15; *b* Greenock, Scotland; 24 Oct.; *d* of John Kerrigan Findlay and Olive Findlay (*née* Maddock). *Educ:* Greenock Acad.; Univ. of E Anglia (CQSW); John Moores Univ., Liverpool (MBA); ILM Dip. Exec. Coaching. Asst Dir of Social Services, Wirral MBC, 1991–2000; Dep. Dir, Social Services Inspectorate, 2001–03; Advr on Social Care Reconstruction, Iraq, 2003–04; Dir of Adult Social Services, 2004–10, Dir of Health Integration, 2010–11, London Bor. of Barnet. FRSA 2005–12. *Recreations:* sailing (competent crew), ski-ing, internet/technology, wine (WSET Level 3 Merit). *T:* 07867 537535. *E:* irenepatersonhesford@gmail.com.

**FINDLAY, James de Cardonnel;** QC 2008; QC (Scot.) 2017; *b* Girvan, 27 June 1961; *s* of late John Findlay and Rosemary Findlay; *m* 1994, Caroline Pedersen; two *s* one *d*. *Educ:* Trinity Coll., Glenalmond; Magdalene Coll., Cambridge (BA 1983). Called to the Bar, Middle Temple, 1984; admitted Advocate, 2008; in practice as barrister specialising in administrative, planning and licensing law in England and Scotland. *Recreations:* walking, supporting Scottish Rugby. *Address:* Cornerstone Barristers, 2–3 Gray's Inn Square, WC1R 5JH. *T:* (020) 7242 4986. *E:* jamesf@cornerstonebarristers.com. *Club:* Lansdowne.

**FINDLAY, Neil;** Member (Lab) Lothian, Scottish Parliament, since 2011; *b* Broxburn, 6 March 1969; *s* of Ian Findlay and Margaret Findlay (*née* McAuley); *m* 1998, Fiona Miller; one *d*. *Educ:* St Kentigern's Acad., Blackburn; Univ. of Strathclyde (BA 1996); Univ. of Glasgow (PGCE 2003). Apprentice and tradesman bricklayer, 1986–93; Housing Official, various housing orgns, 1996–2002; teacher, several schs, Falkirk Council, 2003–11. Mem. (Lab), West Lothian Council, 2003–12. Member: UNITE; EIS; Campaign for Socialism; Cuba Solidarity Campaign. *Recreations:* golf, cooking, going for a pint, gardening. *Address:* Scottish Parliament, Edinburgh EH99 1SP. *T:* (0131) 348 6896. *E:* neil.findlay.msp@parliament.scot.

**FINDLAY, Ralph Graham;** Chief Executive, Marston's plc (formerly The Wolverhampton & Dudley Breweries plc), since 2001; *b* 9 Jan. 1961; *s* of James Findlay and Margaret Findlay (*née* Teesdale); *m* 1990, Louise Mackenzie; one *s* one *d*. *Educ:* James Gillespie's High Sch., Edinburgh; Univ. of Edinburgh (BSc Hons 1983). FCA 1988; MCT (Dip). Price Waterhouse, 1984–90; Treasury Manager, Bass plc, 1990–92; Chief Accountant, Geest plc, 1992–94; joined Wolverhampton & Dudley Breweries plc, 1994, Gp Finance Dir, 1996–2001. Non-exec. Dir, Bovis Homes Gp plc, 2015–. Chm., British Beer and Pub Assoc., 2009–11. Pro-Chancellor and Chm., Governing Council, Keele Univ., 2014–18. *Recreations:* family, reading, music, running, sport. *Address:* Marston's plc, Marston's House, Brewery Road, Wolverhampton WV1 4JT. *T:* (01902) 329530, *Fax:* (01902) 778007. *E:* ralph.findlay@marstons.co.uk. *Club:* Wolverhampton and Newbridge Lawn Tennis and Squash.

**FINDLAY, Richard Martin;** entertainment lawyer and business affairs consultant, 2012–15; Entertainment Law Partner, 1990–2012, Head of Hospitality and Leisure and Charity Law Team, 2009–12, Tods Murray, LLP; *b* 18 Dec. 1951; *s* of late Ian Macdonald Semple Findlay and Kathleen Lightfoot or Findlay. *Educ:* Gordon Schs, Huntly; Univ. of Aberdeen (LLB). Trainee Solicitor, Wilsone & Duffus, Advocates, Aberdeen, 1973–75; Asst Solicitor, Maclay Murray & Spens, Glasgow, 1975–79; Partner, Ranken & Reid, SSC, Edinburgh, 1979–90. Mem., Business in the Arts Placement Scheme, 1994–2012; Associate Mem., 1996–2000, Mem., 2000–13, Theatrical Management Assoc. Chm., Red FM Ltd, 2004–05; Director: Krazy Kat Theatre Co., 1984–86; Edinburgh Music Theatre Co. Ltd, 1985–88; Gallus Theatre Co. Ltd, 1996–98; Dance Base Ltd, 1997–98; Royal Lyceum Theatre Co. Ltd, 1999–2013 (Vice-Chm., 2002–13); Audio Description Film Fund Ltd, 2000–09; Hill Adamson (formerly Scottish Nat. Photography Centre) Ltd, 2002–12; Scottish Screen, 2003–07; Scottish Screen Enterprises, 2003–07; Luxury Edinburgh Ltd, 2006–12; David Hughes Dance Productions Ltd, 2010–15 (Chm., 2012–15); Angel Scene Ltd, 2011–12; Scottish Documentary Inst., 2014–16; Stills Gallery, 2015– (Vice Chm., 2016–). Company Secretary: Edinburgh Arts and Entertainment Ltd, 1987–2000; Duddingston Coachworks Ltd, 1988–91; Edinburgh Internat. Jazz and Blues Fest. Ltd, 1988–2012; Edinburgh Capital Gp Ltd, 1989–2001; French Film Fest. Ltd, 1992–2000; Centre for Moving Image, 1993–95; Filmhouse Trading Ltd, 1993–95; Italian Film Fest. Ltd, 1994–2002; Great Distribution Ltd, 1995–2000; Scottish Screen Locations 1996–2000; Moonstone Ltd, 1997–2008; Assoc. of Integrated Media, Highlands and Islands Ltd, 2002–09. Dir, Lothian Gay and Lesbian Switchboard Ltd, 1998–2002; Company Secretary: Gay Men's Health Ltd, 1995–2012; Positive Voice, 1999–2006. Member: Internat. Assoc. of Entertainment Lawyers, 1990–2012; Internat. Entertainment & Multimedia Law & Business Network, 1995–2012; Scottish Media Lawyers Soc., 1995–2012; IBA, 1993–99; BAFTA, 1990– (Mem. Mgt Cttee, BAFTA (Scotland), 1998–2004); Writers' Guild, 1993–2002; New Producers Alliance, 1993–98; Inst. of Art and Law, 1996–98; RTS, 2003–05. Mem., Fedn of Scottish Theatre, 1997–2012; Founder Mem., Screen Academy Scotland Adv. Bd, 2006–12. Hon. Patron, Pitlochry Fest. Th., 2013–. Trustee: Peter Darrell Trust, 1996–2004; Frank Mullen Trust, 2004–08. Part-time Lectr on Law of Film, Napier Univ., then Screen Acad., Scotland, 1997–2016. Man. Editor, i-2-i–the business journal for the international film industry (formerly Internat. Film Business, Finance and Law Rev.), 1995–97; Scotland Ed., Methuen Amateur Theatre Handbook; Mem., Edibl Bd, The Firm Mag., 2009–12. *Recreations:* photography, theatre, travel, film, music, Highland Games, genealogy, reading. *Address:* 1 Darnaway Street, Edinburgh EH3 6DW. *T:* (0131) 226 3253, 07850 327725. *E:* richardmfindlay@icloud.com.

**FINE, Anne,** OBE 2003; FRSL; writer; Children's Laureate, 2001–03; *b* 7 Dec. 1947; *d* of Brian Laker and Mary Baker; *m* 1968, Kit Fine (marr. diss. 1991); two *d*. *Educ:* Northampton High School for Girls; Univ. of Warwick (BA Hons History and Politics). Hon. DLitt: Central England, 2003; Warwick, 2005; Teesside, 2007; Leicester, 2017. Guardian Children's Fiction Award, 1990; Carnegie Medal, 1990, 1993; Children's Author of the Year, Publishing News, 1990, 1993. FRSL 2003. *Publications: for older children:* The Summer House Loon, 1978; The Other Darker Ned, 1978; The Stone Menagerie, 1980; Round Behind the Icehouse, 1981; The Granny Project, 1983; Madame Doubtfire, 1987; Goggle-Eyes, 1989; The Book of the Banshee, 1991; Flour Babies, 1992 (Whitbread Award, 1993); Step by Wicked Step, 1995; The Tulip Touch, 1996 (Whitbread Award, 1997); Very Different, 2001; Up on Cloud Nine, 2002; The Road of Bones, 2006; The Devil Walks, 2011; Blood Family, 2013; Blue Moon Day, 2014; *for younger children:* Scaredy-Cat, 1985; Anneli the Art Hater, 1986; Crummy Mummy and Me, 1988; A Pack of Liars, 1988; Stranger Danger, 1989; Bill's New Frock, 1989 (Smarties Award, 1990); The Country Pancake, 1989; A Sudden Puff of Glittering Smoke, 1989; A Sudden Swirl of Icy Wind, 1990; Only a Show, 1990; Design-a-Pram, 1991; A Sudden Glow of Gold, 1991; The Worst Child I Ever Had, 1991; The Angel of Nitshill Road, 1991; Same Old Story Every Year, 1992; The Chicken Gave it to Me, 1992; The Haunting of Pip Parker, 1992; How To Write Really Badly, 1996; Press Play, 1996; Jennifer's Diary, 1997; Loudmouth Louis, 1998; Roll Over, Roly, 1999; Charm School, 1999; Bad Dreams, 2000; The Jamie and Angus Stories, 2002 (Boston Globe Horn Book Award, 2003); The More the Merrier, 2003; Return of The Killer Cat, 2003; Frozen Billy, 2004; Nag Club, 2004; The Killer Cat Strikes Back, 2006; Ivan the Terrible, 2007; The Killer Cat's Birthday Bash, 2008; The Killer Cat's Christmas, 2009; Eating Things on Sticks, 2009; Under a Silver Moon, 2010; Trouble in Toadpool, 2012; The Killer Cat Runs Away, 2013; The Only Child Club,

2013; Party Club, 2015; Under the Bed, 2015; Sixteen Sisters, 2017; Magic Ball, 2017; *picture books:* Poor Monty, 1991; Ruggles, 2002; Let It Snow!, 2017; *novels:* The Killjoy, 1986; Taking the Devil's Advice, 1990; In Cold Domain, 1994; Telling Liddy, 1997; All Bones and Lies, 2001; Raking the Ashes, 2005; Fly in the Ointment, 2008; Our Precious Lulu, 2009; Battle of Wills, 2016. *Recreations:* reading, walking. *Address:* c/o David Higham Associates, 6th Floor, Waverley House, 7–12 Noel Street, W1F 8GQ.

**FINE, Prof. Leon Gerald,** FRCP, FRCPGlas, FACP, FMedSci; Director, Program in the History of Medicine, Cedars-Sinai Medical Center and University of California, Los Angeles, since 2017 (Chairman, Department of Biomedical Sciences, 2007–17; Vice-Dean for Research and Graduate Research Education, 2013–17); *b* 16 June 1943; *s* of Matthew Fine and Jeanette (*née* Lipshitz); *m* 1966, Brenda Sakinovsky; two *d*. *Educ:* Univ. of Cape Town, SA (MB, ChB). FACP 1978; FRCP 1986; FRCPGlas 1993. Internship and Residency in Internal Medicine, Tel Aviv Univ. Med. Sch., Israel, 1967–70; Asst Prof. of Medicine, Albert Einstein Coll. of Medicine, NY, 1975–76; University of Miami School of Medicine: Asst Prof., 1976–78; Associate Prof., 1978–82; Prof. of Medicine and Chief, Div. of Nephrology, UCLA, 1982–91; University College London: Prof. and Hd, Dept of Medicine, 1991–2002; Dean, Faculty of Clinical Sci., Royal Free and UC Med. Sch., 2002–06. Founder FMedSci 1998. Editor-in-Chief, Nephron, 2003–14. *Publications:* contribs in professional jls on pathophysiology of chronic renal disease, renal growth control, renal growth responses to acute and chronic injury, genetic manipulation of the kidney, and history of medicine. *Recreations:* collecting rare books on the history of medicine, fine printing and photography, book-binding. *Address:* Cedars-Sinai Medical Center, Thalians E 113A, 8730 Alden Drive, Los Angeles, CA 90048, USA. *E:* leon.fine@cshs.org. *Clubs:* Athenæum; Grolier (New York).

**FINE, Nigel,** CEng, FICE, FIET; Chief Executive, Institution of Engineering and Technology, since 2009; *b* Cardiff, 21 June 1957; *s* of Mossey and Esther Fine; *m* 1982, Ruth; two *s* one *d*. *Educ:* Cardiff High Sch.; Univ. of Manchester Inst. of Sci. and Technol. (BSc Civil Engrg); London Business Sch. (MBA 1984). MICE 1982, FICE 2011; CEng 1983; FIET 2009. Grad. and Project Engr, John Laing plc, 1978–82; EMEA Strategy and Business Develt Dir, Internat. Paint Ltd, 1984–94; Associate Partner, Andersen Consulting (Accenture), 1994–99; Man. Dir, EMEA and Asia Pacific, Experian plc, 1999–2009. *Recreations:* family, theatre, travel, sport. *Address:* Institution of Engineering and Technology, Savoy Place, WC2R 0BL. *T:* (020) 7344 5400. *E:* nfine@theiet.org.

**FINER, Dr Elliot Geoffrey,** FRSC; Director General, Chemical Industries Association, 1996–2002; *b* 30 March 1944; *s* of Reuben and Pauline Finer; *m* 1970, Viviane Kibrit; two *s*. *Educ:* Royal Grammar Sch., High Wycombe; Cheadle Hulme Sch.; East Barnet Grammar Sch.; St Catharine's Coll., Cambridge (BA 1965); Univ. of East Anglia (MSc 1966; PhD 1968). CChem, FRSC 1993. Unilever Research, Welwyn, 1968–75; Dept of Energy, 1975–90; Dir for Industry and Commerce, 1983–86, Dir Gen., 1988–90, Energy Efficiency Office; Under Secretary, 1988; Head of Management Develt Gp, Cabinet Office, 1990–92; Head of Chemicals and Biotechnology Div., DTI, 1992–95. Director: Spillers Foods Ltd, 1989–92; Vestry Court Ltd, 1997–. Dir, Enfield PCT, 2003–08. Mem., BBSRC, 1994–95. Pres., Assembly of European Chemical Industry Fedns, 1998–2000. Mem. Council, RSC, 2002–09 (Hon. Treas., 2005–09). Chm., Ramsay Meml Fellowship Trust, 2007–15. Hon. FEI (CIE 1985). *Publications:* scientific papers and articles in learned jls. *Recreations:* home and family, reading, writing, DIY. *Club:* Athenæum.

**FINESTEIN, Jonathon Eli;** a District Judge (Magistrates' Courts), Manchester and Salford, 2012–15; *b* 9 April 1950; *s* of Gustav Finestein and Esther Finestein; *m* 1985, Elaine March; one *d*. *Educ:* Hull Grammar Sch.; Leeds Univ. (LLB). Called to the Bar, Gray's Inn, 1973; practice in Hull; Asst Stipendiary Magistrate, 1989–92; Stipendiary Magistrate for Lancs and Merseyside, 1992–2001; Stipendiary Magistrate, later a District Judge (Magistrates' Courts), Salford, 2001–12; Asst Recorder, 1992–96; Recorder, 1996–2008. *Recreations:* watching all sports, walking. *E:* jfinestein@gmail.com.

**FINGLETON, John,** DPhil; Chief Executive Officer, Fingleton Associates, since 2013; *b* 21 Sept. 1965. *Educ:* Trinity Coll., Dublin (BA Mod 1987); Nuffield Coll., Oxford (MPhil Econs 1989, DPhil 1991). Researcher, LSE, 1991; Lectr in Econs, Trinity Coll., Dublin, 1991–2000; Chm., Competition Authy of Ireland, 2000–05; CEO, OFT, 2005–12; Senior Adviser: Cabinet Office, 2012–13; HM Treasury, 2012–13. Visiting Scholar: Université Libre de Bruxelles, 1995; Univ. of Chicago, 1998–2000. *Publications:* (jtly) Competition Policy and the Transformation of Central Europe, 1996; (jtly) The Dublin Taxi Market: re-regulate or stay queuing?, 1998; contrib. Global Agenda.

**FINGRET, His Honour Peter;** a Circuit Judge, 1992–2005; *b* 13 Sept. 1934; *s* of late Iser and Irene Fingret; *m* 1st, 1960, June Moss (marr. diss. 1980); one *s* one *d*; 2nd, 1980, Dr Ann Lilian Mary Hollingworth (*née* Field) (*d* 2011). *Educ:* Leeds Modern Sch.; Leeds Univ. (LLB Hons); Open Univ. (BA). President, Leeds Univ. Union, 1957–58. Admitted Solicitor, 1960. Partner: Willey Hargrave & Co., Leeds, 1964–75; Fingret, Paterson & Co., Leeds, 1975–82. Stipendiary Magistrate for Co. of Humberside sitting at Kingston-upon-Hull, 1982–85; Metropolitan Stipendiary Magistrate, 1985–92; a Recorder, 1987–92; a Pres., Mental Health Rev. Tribunal, 1993–2005. Mem., Parole Bd, 2003–16. Chm., Lord Chancellor's Adv. Cttee on JPs for Cities of London and Westminster, 2005–07. Councillor, Leeds City Council, 1967–72; Member: Court, Univ. of Leeds, 1975–85; Cttee, Leeds Internat. Piano Competition, 1981–85. Freeman: Musicians' Co., 2002– (Liveryman, 2010–); City of London, 2004–. *Recreations:* golf, music, theatre. *E:* peterfingret@hotmail.com. *Clubs:* Garrick, MCC.

**FINK,** family name of **Baron Fink**.

**FINK, Baron** *cr* 2011 (Life Peer), of Northwood in the County of Middlesex; **Stanley Fink**; Chairman, International Standard Asset Management, 2015–18 (Chief Executive, 2008–15); *b* 15 Sept. 1957; *s* of Louis and Janet Fink; *m* 1981, Barbara Paskin; two *s* one *d*. *Educ:* Manchester Grammar Sch.; Trinity Hall, Cambridge (MA Law). ACA. Qualified chartered accountant, Arthur Andersen, 1979–82; Financial Planning, Mars Confectionery, 1982–83; Vice Pres., Citibank NA, 1983–86; Man Group plc: Dir, 1987–2008; Gp Finance Dir, 1992–96; Man. Dir, Asset Mgt, 1996–2000; Chief Exec., 2000–07; Dep. Chm., 2007–08; Chm., Man Investments, 2002–07. Principal Treas., Cons. Party, 2010–13 (Co-Treas., 2010–11). *Recreations:* golf, ski-ing. *Address:* House of Lords, SW1A 0PW. *E:* finkstanley@gmail.com.

**FINK, Prof. George,** FRCPE; FRSE; FRSB; Professorial Research Fellow, University of Melbourne and Mental Health Research Institute of Victoria, Australia, 2007–13 (Scientific Director and Chief Executive Officer, 2004–06; Director of Laboratory Research, 2003–04); Honorary Professor and Professorial Research Fellow, Florey Institute of Neuroscience and Mental Health, University of Melbourne, since 2014; *b* 13 Nov. 1936; *s* of John H. Fink and Therese (*née* Weiss); *m* 1959, Ann Elizabeth Langsam; one *s* one *d*. *Educ:* Melbourne High Sch. (Dist. Old Boy); Univ. of Melbourne (MB BS Hons 1960; MD 1978); Hertford Coll., Univ. of Oxford (DPhil 1967). FRSE 1989; FRCPE 1998. Jun. and sen. house officer, Royal Melbourne and Alfred Hosps, Victoria, Australia, 1961–62; Demonstrator in Anatomy, Monash Univ., Victoria, 1963–64; Nuffield Dominions Demonstrator, Oxford Univ., 1965–67; Sen. Lectr in Anatomy, Monash Univ., 1968–71; Univ. Lectr 1971–80, Official Fellow in Physiology and Med., Brasenose Coll., 1974–80, Oxford Univ.; Dir, MRC Brain Metabolism Unit, 1980–99, Hon. Prof., 1984–2000, Univ. of Edinburgh; Vice-Pres. of Res., 1999–2003, consultant, 2003–04, Pharmos Corp. Royal Soc.-Israel Acad. Exchange Fellow, 1979, Vis. Scientist, Neurobiol., 2009–, Weizmann Inst. of Sci., Israel; Walter Cottman Fellow and Vis. Prof., Monash Univ., 1985, 1989; Arthur Bishop Prof., Mt Sinai Med. Sch., NY, 1988; Visiting Professor: Neurobiol., Mayo Clinic, Minnesota, 1993; Neurobiol. and Behavior, Rockefeller Univ., NY, 1996–2000; Honorary Professor: Melbourne Univ., 2004–06; Monash Univ., 2004–06. Prosector in Anatomy, Melbourne Univ., 1956; Wolfson Lectr, Univ. of Oxford, 1982; first G. W. Harris Lectr, Physiol Soc., Cambridge, 1987. Pres., European Neuroendocrine Assoc., 1991–95; Member: Council, European Neuroscience Assoc., 1980–82, 1994–98; Mental Health Panel, Wellcome Trust, 1984–89; Steering Cttee, British Neuroendocrine Group, 1984–88 (Trustee, BNG, 1990–); Co-ordinating Cttee, ESF Network on Neuroimmunomodulation, 1990–93. Chm., 5 Year Assessment Biomed. Prog., 1991–96; Monitor, EU Biomed. 2 Prog., 1995. Senior Member: Physiological Soc., 1967; Soc. for Endocrinology, 1967; British Pharmacological Soc., 1990; Mem., Internat. Coll. of Neuropsychopharmacology, 2010. FRSB (FSB 2015); FPhysiol 2018. Hon. Mem., British Neuroendocrine Soc., 2005. Emeritus Member: Soc. for Neurosci., 2008; Endocrine Soc., 2008; Genetics Soc. of America, 2009. Lifetime Achievement Award, Internat. Soc. of Psychoneuroendocrinology, 2000. Trustee, Jl of Neuroendocrinology, 1990–2003. *Publications:* (ed with L. J. Whalley) Neuropeptides: Basic and Clinical Aspects, 1982; (ed with A. J. Harmar and K. W. McKerns) Neuroendocrine Molecular Biology, 1986; (ed) Transmitter Molecules in the Brain, 1987; (ed with A. J. Harmar) Neuropeptides: A Methodology, 1989; (Ed. in Chief) Encyclopedia of Stress, 2000, 2nd edn 2007 (BMA commendation for contrib to mental health, 2001); (ed) Stress Science: neuroendocrinology, 2010; (ed) Stress Consequences: mental, neuropsychological and socioeconomic, 2010; (ed) Stress of War, Conflict and Disaster, 2010; (ed with D. W. Pfaff and J. Levine) Handbook of Neuroendocrinology, 2011; (ed and contrib.) Handbook of Stress, Vol. 1, Stress: concepts, cognition, emotion and behavior, 2016 (Highly Commended, BMA Med. Book Awards, 2017), Vol. 2, Stress: neuroendocrinology and neurobiology, 2017, Vol. 3, Stress: Physiology, Biochemistry and Pathology, 2019; more than 360 scientific publications on neuroendocrinol., molecular neuroendocrinol., neuropharmacol. and psychopharmacol. *Recreations:* ski-ing, scuba diving. *Address:* Florey Institute of Neuroscience and Mental Health, Kenneth Myer Building, University of Melbourne, 30 Royal Parade (corner of Genetics Lane), Melbourne, Vic 3010, Australia. *T:* (3) 90356634, 408961002, *Fax:* (3) 90358768. *E:* george.fink@florey.edu.au. *W:* www.georgefink.com.

**FINK, Laurence Douglas, (Larry);** Co-Founder, Chairman and Chief Executive, BlackRock, since 1988; *m* Lori; three *c*. *Educ:* Univ. of Calif, Los Angeles (BA Pol Sci. 1974; MBA 1976). First Boston Corporation, 1976–88: Mem., Mgt Cttee; a Man. Dir; Co-Head, Taxable Fixed Income Div.; started Financial Futures and Options Dept. Co-Chm., Partnership for New York City. Mem., Bd of Trustees, New York Univ.; Co-Chm., Bd of Trustees, New York Univ. Langone Med. Center. Member, Board: MOMA; Council on Foreign Relns; Robin Hood. *Address:* BlackRock, 55 East 52nd Street, New York, NY 10055, USA. *T:* (212) 8105300.

**FINKELSTEIN,** family name of **Baron Finkelstein**.

**FINKELSTEIN, Baron** *cr* 2013 (Life Peer), of Pinner in the County of Middlesex; **Daniel William Finkelstein,** OBE 1997; Associate Editor, 2001–10 and since 2013, and Columnist, since 2013, The Times (Executive Editor, 2010–13; Chief Leader Writer, 2008–13; Comment Editor, 2004–08); *b* 30 Aug. 1962; *s* of late Prof. Ludwik Finkelstein, OBE and Mirjam Emma Finkelstein (*née* Wiener); *m* 1993, Dr Nicola Ruth, *d* of Henry and Frances Connor; three *s*. *Educ:* Hendon Prep. Sch.; University College Sch.; London School of Economics (BSc Econs 1984); City Univ. (MSc 1986). Journalist, Network magazine, 1987–89; Editor, Connexion, 1989–92; Columnist, Jewish Chronicle, 2004–; Editor, Comment Central (weblog), Times Online, 2006–. Director: Social Market Foundn, 1992–95; Conservative Res. Dept, 1995–98; Policy Unit, Conservative Central Office, 1999–2001; Associate Editor, New Moon magazine, 1990–97. Res. Asst, RCA, 1984–87; Political Advr to Dr David Owen, MP, 1986–91. Contested: (SDP) Brent E, 1987; (C) Harrow W, 2001. Mem., Nat. Cttee, SDP, 1986–90. Founder and Bd Mem., Enterprise Europe, 1990– (Chm., 1990–95). *Publications:* (with Craig Arnall) The Open Network and its Enemies, 1990; Conservatives in Opposition: Republicans in the US, 1994. *Recreations:* US political memorabilia, Chinese food. *Address:* c/o The Times, 1 London Bridge Street, SE1 9GF. *T:* (020) 7782 7188. *Club:* Reform.
*See also* A. C. W. Finkelstein, T. M. Finkelstein.

**FINKELSTEIN, Prof. Anthony Charles Wiener,** CBE 2016; PhD; CEng, FIET, FREng; CITP; FBCS; FCGI; Professor of Software Systems Engineering: University College London, since 1997 (Head of Computer Science, 2002–10; Dean, Faculty of Engineering Sciences, 2010–15); Alan Turing Institute, since 2015; Chief Scientific Adviser for National Security to HM Government, since 2016; *b* London, 28 July 1959; *s* of late Prof. Ludwik Finkelstein, OBE and of Mirjam Emma Finkelstein (*née* Wiener); *m* 1985, Judith Fishman; two *s*. *Educ:* Univ. of Bradford (BEng); London Sch. of Econs and Pol Sci. (MSc); Royal Coll. of Art (PhD 1985). FREng 2012. Post-doctoral Res. Fellow, 1985–88, Lectr, 1988–94, Imperial Coll., London; Prof. of Computer Sci., 1994–97, Hd, Computer Sci., 1995–97, City Univ. Dist. Vis. Prof., Nat. Inst. of Informatics, Tokyo, 2007–; Vis. Prof., Imperial Coll., London, 2008–. Mem., EPSRC, 2013–18. MAE 2013. FCGI 2013. Hon. DSc City, 2018. *Publications:* contrib. IEEE Transactions on Software Engrg, ACM Transactions on Software Engrg Methods, Internat. Conf. on Software Engrg and other learned jls. *Recreations:* capoeira, reading, art, antiques, family life. *Address:* Alan Turing Institute, British Library, 96 Euston Road, NW1 2DB. *E:* afinkelstein@turing.ac.uk. *Club:* Athenæum.
*See also* Baron Finkelstein, T. M. Finkelstein.

**FINKELSTEIN, Tamara Margaret, (Mrs M. Isaacs);** Permanent Secretary, Department for Environment, Food and Rural Affairs, since 2019; *b* 24 May 1967; *d* of late Prof. Ludwik Finkelstein, OBE and Mirjam Emma Finkelstein (*née* Wiener); *m* 1997, Michael Isaacs; one *s* two *d*. *Educ:* Haberdashers' Aske's Sch. for Girls; Balliol Coll., Oxford (BA Engrg Sci. 1989; London Sch. of Econs (MSc Econs 1992). HM Treasury: Economic Advr, 1992–97; Private Sec. and Speechwriter to Chancellor of the Exchequer, 1997–99; Sen. Advr, Gen. Expenditure Policy, 2000–01; Dep. Dir, Sure Start, 2001–04; HM Treasury: Hd, Permt Sec.'s Strategy Team, 2004; Dir of Ops, 2005; Dir, Govt Treasury Mgt, 2006–08; Dir, UK Border Agency Integration Prog., 2008–10; Dir, Ind. Public Service Pension Commn, HM Treasury, 2010–11; Dir, Public Services, HM Treasury, 2011–14; Chief Operating Officer and Dir Gen., Gp Ops, 2014–16, Dir Gen., Community Care, 2016–18, DoH, then DHSC; Dir Gen., Bldg Safety, MHCLG, 2017–18; Dir Gen., EU Exit Delivery, DEFRA, 2018–19. *Recreations:* family, book club, women's group. *Address:* Department for Environment, Food and Rural Affairs, Seacole Building, 2 Marsham Street, SW1P 4DF.
*See also* Baron Finkelstein, A. C. W. Finkelstein.

**FINLAY OF LLANDAFF,** Baroness *cr* 2001 (Life Peer), of Llandaff in the County of South Glamorgan; **Ilora Gillian Finlay,** FRCP, FRCGP; Hon. Professor in Palliative Medicine, since 1996, and Vice-Dean, School of Medicine, 2000–05, Cardiff University (formerly University of Wales College of Medicine); President: Royal Society of Medicine, 2006–08; British Medical Association, 2014–15; *b* 23 Feb. 1949; *d* of Charles Beaumont Benoy Downman and Thaïs Helène Downman (*née* Barakan); *m* 1972, Andrew Yule Finlay; one *s* one *d*. *Educ:* Wimbledon High Sch.; St Mary's Hosp. Med. Sch., Univ. of London (MB, BS 1972). DObstRCOG 1974; DCH 1975. FRCGP 1992; FRCP 1999. GP, 1981–86; first Med. Dir, Holme Tower Marie Curie Centre, Cardiff, 1987–2000. Consultant in Palliative Medicine, Velindre NHS Trust, Cardiff, 1994–. Course Dir, Dip. and MSc in Palliative Medicine, Cardiff Univ. (formerly UWCM), 1989–2014. Non-exec. Dir, Gwent HA, 1995–2001. Founder Mem., Cancer Res. UK, 2002–04 (Mem., Sci. and Educn Cttee). Mem., Internat. Scientific Expert Panel, Cicely Saunders Foundn, 2012–. House of Lords: Mem., Select Cttee on Sci. and Technol., 2002–06, and on Assisted Dying for Terminally Ill Bill, 2005–07; Chm., Allergy Inquiry, 2006–07; Dep. Speaker and Dep. Chair of Cttees, 2018–. Chairman: Allergy Services: still not meeting the unmet need, RCP, 2008–10; Commn on Generalism, RCGP, 2010–11; Vice Chair, NICE guideline rev. on ME/CFS, 2018–20. Chairman: Nat. Council for Palliative Care, 2015–; Nat. Mental Capacity Forum, 2015–; Co-Chm., Living and Dying Well, 2010–. Mem., Bevan Commn, 2017–. President: Assoc. for Palliative Medicine, 1995–98; Medical Women's Fedn, 2001–02; Hon. Pres., CSP, 2003–; Vice Pres., Marie Curie Cancer Care, 2009–. Gov., Howell's Sch., Llandaff, GDST, 2000–05; Ind. Gov., Cardiff Metropolitan Univ., 2012–14 (Chair, 2018–). Patron: Shalom Hospice, St David's, Pembrokeshire, 2001–; Coping and Living in Pain, 2002–10; MND Assoc., 2008–. Member, Editorial Board: Lancet Oncology, 2002–; Quality in Healthcare, 2002–; Medical Humanities, 2002–. FMedSci 2014; Hon. Fellow, Cardiff Univ., 2002. Hon. Prof., Groningen Univ., 2006–07 (Vis. Prof., 2000–02). Hon. DSc: Glamorgan, 2002; UWIC, 2005. *Publications:* (ed jtly) Care of the Dying: a clinical handbook, 1984; (ed jtly) Medical Humanities, 2001; (ed jtly) Oral Care in Advanced Disease, 2005; (ed jtly) Handbook of Communication in Oncology and Palliative Care, 2010; papers in peer-reviewed med. jls and other pubns. *Address:* House of Lords, SW1A 0PW; Velindre NHS Trust, Cardiff CF14 2TL.

**FINLAY, Amanda Jane,** CBE 2001; Director, Legal Aid Strategy, Ministry of Justice (formerly Department for Constitutional Affairs), 2005–09; *b* 3 Sept. 1949; *d* of John Alexander Robertson Finlay, QC (His Honour Judge Finlay) and Jane Little Hepburn, CBE; *m* 1975, Richard Bevan Butt, *qv*; two *s*. *Educ:* Newnham Coll., Cambridge (BA English 1971). Lord Chancellor's Department, then Department for Constitutional Affairs, subseq. Ministry of Justice: fast stream entrant, 1971; Principal, 1976; Sec. to Legal Aid Adv. Cttee, 1981; Asst Sec., 1993; Sec. to Lord Woolf's inquiry, Access to Justice, 1994–96; implementation of Human Rights Act, 1997–99; Grade 3, 1999; Director: Public and Private Rights, 1999–2004; Legal Services and Civil and Administrative Justice, 2004–05. Member: Council, Justice, 2009–18 (Mem., Exec. Bd, 2010–); Mem., Wkg Gp, Justice in an Age of Austerity, 2014; Mem., Wkg Gp on What is a Court?, 2015; Chair, Preventing Digital Exclusion from Online Justice, 2018); Civil Justice Council, 2009–13 (Mem., Working Gp on Self Represented Litigants, 2011–); Public Legal Educn Strategy Gp, MoJ, 2009–10; Vice Chair, Low Commn on the Future of Advice and Legal Support, 2012–; Chm., Adv. Gp on Role of Advice Services in Health Outcomes, 2014–. Public Gov., Oxleas NHS Foundn Trust, 2008–17. Chm., Friends of Greenwich Univ. Legal Advice Centre, 2016–. Trustee: Law Works, 2009–16; Law for Life, 2011– (Chm., 2016–). *Recreations:* travel, music, gardening. *E:* amandajfinlay@gmail.com.

**FINLAY, Prof. Bland James,** PhD; FRS 2004; Professor of Microbial Ecology, Queen Mary University of London, 2007–13, now Honorary Professor; *b* 16 March 1952; *s* of Bland and Mabel Finlay; *m* 1996, Genoveva Esteban; one *s* one *d*. *Educ:* Univ. of Stirling (BA; PhD). Lectr in Biol., Univ. of Jos, Nigeria, 1977; PSO, Freshwater Biol Assoc., UK, 1984–92; NERC, 1992–2007 (Dep. CSO, 2005–07). Guest Prof., Univ. of Aarhus, 1982. Field work and expeditions in field of protozoology: Nigeria, 1977–78; Kenya (soda lakes), 1985; Spain (solution lakes), 1987 and 1990; Australia (volcanic crater lakes), 1997. Chm., Grant Cttee, Royal Soc., 2005–07. Fellow, Royal Danish Acad. of Scis and Letters. Scientific Medal, Zool Soc. of London, 1991. *Publications:* Ecology and Evolution in Anoxic Worlds (with T. Fenchel), 1995; over 200 scientific articles. *Recreations:* being on holiday with my wife, listening to J. S. Bach, continuously searching for my spectacles. *Address:* c/o The River Laboratory, Wareham, Dorset BH20 6BB. *T:* (01929) 401885. *E:* b.j.finlay@qmul.ac.uk.

**FINLAY, Sir David (Ronald James Bell),** 2nd Bt *cr* 1964, of Epping, Co. Essex; *b* 16 Nov. 1963; *s* of Sir Graeme Bell Finlay, 1st Bt, ERD and of June Evangeline, *y d* of Col Francis Collingwood Drake, OBE, MC, DL; *S* father, 1987; *m* 1998, Camilla, *d* of Peter Newton Acheson; one *s* one *d*. *Educ:* Marlborough College; Bristol Univ. (BSc Hons Economics/Philosophy). Peat Marwick McLintock, 1986–91; Hill Samuel Financial Services, 1992–94; Gerrard Vivian Gray, 1994–97; Greig Middleton, 1997; Cater Allen Asset Management, 1998–2001; Royal Bank of Canada, 2002–11; Coutts & Co. Channel Islands, 2011–17; Intertrust Gp, 2017–. Freeman, City of London, 1991. *Recreations:* skiing, shooting. *Heir: s* Tristan James Bell Finlay, *b* 5 April 2001.

**FINLAY, Larry;** Managing Director, Transworld Publishers, since 2001; *b* London, 20 Jan. 1960; *s* of Harry Finlay and Tess Matz; *m* 2002, Claire Calman; one *s*. *Educ:* University College Sch., London; Univ. of Manchester (BA Econ. and Soc. Studies). Transworld Publishers: copywriter, 1983–86; Advertising and Promotions Dir, 1986–90; Mktg Dir, 1990–96; Paperback Publisher, 1997–99; Dep. Publisher, 1999–2001. *Recreations:* reading, gardening, reading to my son, arguing about God, eating my wife's wonderful food, shouting at the TV, teaching my son to swim, unleashing nematodes on unsuspecting slugs. *Address:* Transworld Publishers, 61–63 Uxbridge Road, W5 5SA. *T:* (020) 8579 2652.

**FINLAYSON, Sir Garet (Orlando),** KCMG 2007; OBE 1999; Chairman and Chief Executive, Associated Bahamian Distillers & Brewers Ltd, 1981; *b* Andros, Bahamas, 4 Aug. 1937; *s* of Hastings and Maud Finlayson; *m* 1963, Rowena Frances Rolle; two *s* two *d*. *Educ:* Evelyn Wood Inst.; La Salle Univ., Chicago (home study course in business): Bahamas Teachers' Coll., Nassau. Primary sch. teacher, 1949–52; tailor, 1950–61; waiter, 1961–68; car salesman, 1968–71; owner: car dealerships, 1972–92; Bahamas Catering Ltd, 1972–; Davinci Restaurant, 1973–94; Atlantis Hotel and Night Club, 1974–93; Bethell Robertson & Co. Ltd, 1981–; City Markets Food Stores, 2010–. Owner and Chairman: Burns House Ltd, 1980–; Bahamas Distillers Ltd, 1981–; Butler & Sands Ltd, 2004–; Solomon's Mines Ltd, 2004–; Chairman: Gen. Bahamian Cos Ltd, 1981–; Wholesale Wines & Spirits Ltd, 2004–; Todhunter-Mitchell Co. Ltd, 2004–; Deputy Chairman: Bahamas In-Flight Ltd, 1972–; Commonwealth Brewery Ltd, 1988–. Mem., World Presidents Orgn. Silver Jubilee Award in Business, Bahamas, 1998. *Recreations:* reading, yachting, fishing. *Address:* PO Box N1019, Nassau, Bahamas. *T:* 3282833, *Fax:* 3233211.

**FINLAYSON, George;** HM Diplomatic Service, retired; *b* 22 April 1943; *s* of late George Finlayson and Alison Boath (*née* Barclay); *m* 1966, Patricia Grace Ballantine; two *s*. *Educ:* Tynecastle High Sch., Edinburgh. Joined HM Diplomatic Service, 1965; Reykjavik, 1967–69; Prague, 1969–71; Lagos, 1971–75; FCO, 1975–78; 2nd Sec., New Delhi, 1978–81; 1st Sec., FCO, 1981–83; 1st Sec. and Head of Chancery, Montevideo, 1983–87; Consul (Commercial) and Dep. Dir for Trade Promotion, New York, 1987–90; Dep. High Comr, Dhaka, 1990–93; Consul-Gen., Melbourne, 1994–98; High Comr to Malawi, 1998–2001. Mem., Internat. Develt Adv. Gp, Scottish Govt, 2008–12. Dir, Challenges Africa, 2012–. Dep. Chm., Scots Australian Council, 2002–14. Trustee: Malawi Tomorrow, 2005–; Scotland Malawi Business Gp, 2007–. Mem., Scottish Charity Appeals Panel, 2006–10. *Recreations:* drawing, painting. *Address:* 95 Craigleith Crescent, Edinburgh EH4 3LA.

**FINLAYSON, George Ferguson,** CMG 1979; CVO 1983; HM Diplomatic Service, retired; *b* 28 Nov. 1924; *s* of late G. B. Finlayson; *m* 1st, 1951, Rosslyn Evelyn (*d* 1972), *d* of late E. N. James; one *d*; 2nd, 1982, Anthea Judith (*d* 2014), *d* of late F. D. Perry. *Educ:* North Berwick High Sch. Royal Air Force, 1943–47. Apptd HM Foreign (later Diplomatic) Service, 1949; 2nd Sec. (Inf.), HM Embassy, Rangoon, 1952–54; FO, 1955–59; First Sec., 1959; HM Consul, Algiers, 1959–61; First Sec., HM Embassy, Bamako, 1961–63; HM Consul (Commercial), New York, 1964–68; Counsellor, 1968; Counsellor (Commercial), British High Commn, Singapore, 1969–72; Head of Trade Relations and Exports Dept, FCO, 1972–73; Counsellor (Commercial) Paris, 1973–78; Consul-General: Toronto, 1978–81; Los Angeles, 1981–84. Admin. Advr, British Neurological Res. Trust, 1987–2001. *Recreations:* travel, walking, swimming. *Address:* 2 Craigleith View, Station Road, North Berwick EH39 4BF. *T:* (01620) 890987. *Club:* Oriental.

**FINLAYSON, Niall Diarmid Campbell,** OBE 1998; PhD; FRCSE, FRCP, FRCPE; Chief Medical Officer, Royal London Insurance, since 2004; Chairman, LifeCare, Edinburgh, 2006–15; *b* 21 April 1939; *s* of Duncan Iain Campbell Finlayson and Helen Rita Blackney; *m* 1972, Dale Kristin Anderson; one *s* one *d*. *Educ:* Loretto Sch., Musselburgh; Edinburgh Univ. (BSc (Hons) 1962; MB, ChB 1964; PhD 1972). FRCPE 1977; FRCP 1982; FRCSE 1999. Asst Prof. of Medicine, New York Hospital-Cornell Medical Center, NY, 1970–73; Consultant Physician, Centre for Liver and Digestive Disorders, Royal Infirmary Edinburgh, 1973–2003. Hon. Sen. Lectr, Edinburgh Univ. Medical Sch., 1973–2003; Hon. Fellow (Clinical Teaching), Coll. of Medicine and Veterinary Medicine, Edinburgh Univ., 2004–. Pres., RCPE, 2001–04. *Publications:* (ed jtly) Diseases of the Gastrointestinal Tract and Liver, 1982, 3rd edn 1997; about 100 publications in learned jls and as contributions to books. *Recreations:* music, history. *Address:* 10 Queens Crescent, Edinburgh EH9 2AZ. *T:* (0131) 667 9369. *E:* niall.finlayson@icloud.com.

**FINLEY, Gerald Hunter,** CBE 2017; OC 2014; FRCM; baritone; *b* Montreal, 1960; *s* of Eric Gault Finley and Catherine Rae Finley; *m* 1st, 1990, Louise Winter, opera singer (marr. diss. 2009); two *s*; 2nd, 2010, Heulwen Keyte, artist agent; one *d*. *Educ:* Glebe Collegiate Inst., Ottawa; Univ. of Ottawa; Royal Coll. of Music (ARCM 1980; Dip. 1986); King's Coll., Cambridge (BA 1983; MA 1986); Nat. Opera Studio. FRCM 2007. St Matthew's Church Choir, Ottawa, 1970–79; Ottawa Choral Soc., 1976–79; Ontario Youth Choir, 1977–78; King's Coll. Choir, 1981–83; Glyndebourne Chorus, 1986–88; *débuts:* Figaro in Le Nozze di Figaro, Downland Opera, 1984; Antonio in Le Nozze di Figaro, Nat. Arts Centre Opera, 1987; Graf Dominik in Arabella, Glyndebourne, 1989; Graf in Capriccio, Chicago Lyric Opera, 1994; Figaro in Le Nozze di Figaro, LA Music Centre, 1994, Royal Opera House, Covent Garden, 1995; Valentin in Faust, Opéra de Paris, 1997; Papageno in Die Zauberflöte, NY Met. 1998; Mr Fox in Fantastic Mr Fox, LA Opera (world première), 1998; Harry Heegan in The Silver Tassie, ENO (world première), 2000; Robert Oppenheimer in Doctor Atomic, San Francisco Opera (world première), 2005, Barbican, 2017; Iago in Otello, Barbican, 2009; Don Giovanni, Munich State Opera, 2010; Graf Almaviva, Vienna State Opera, 2012; Scarpia in Tosca, Deutsche Oper, 2018; *other rôles include:* Forester in Cunning Little Vixen, title rôle in Don Giovanni, Royal Opera, 2003; Guglielmo in Così fan tutte, Salzburg, Olivier in Capriccio, Paris Opera, and Jaufre Rudel in L'amour de Loin (Sariaaho), Helsinki, 2004; Giorgio Germont in La Traviata, Royal Opera, and title rôle in Eugene Onegin, ENO, 2005; Count in Le Nozze di Figaro, Royal Opera, 2006 and 2014; Guillaume Tell, Accademia di Santa Cecilia, Rome, 2010, Royal Opera, 2015, NY Metropolitan Opera, 2016, Munich State Opera, 2017; Howard K. Stern in Anna Nicole, Royal Opera (world première), 2011; Hans Sachs in Die Meistersinger, Glyndebourne, 2011, Opéra de Paris, Glyndebourne, 2016; Don Giovanni, Salzburg Fest., 2011, Royal Opera, Metropolitan Opera, 2012; Il Prigioniero, NY Philharmonic, 2013; Don Alfonso in Così fan tutte, Salzburg Fest., 2013; Amfortas in Parsifal, Royal Opera, 2013, Vienna State Opera, 2017, Berlin Philharmoniker, Baden Baden, 2018; Falstaff, Canadian Opera, 2014 (Dora Award for best male perf.); Wolfram in Tannhäuser, Lyric Opera, Chicago, 2015; Nick Shadow in Rake's Progress, NY Met, 2015; Golaud in Pelléas et Mélisande, Berlin Phil., 2015, LSO, 2016; Priest and Angel of Agony, The Dream of Gerontius, Barbican, 2016; Michonnet in Adriana Lecouvreur, Royal Opera, 2017; Lear in Lear, Salzburg Fest., 2017; Athanael in Thaïs, NY Metropolitan Opera, 2017; Iago in Otello, Munich State Opera, 2018, Canadian Opera, 2019; Bluebeard at NY Metropolitan Opera, 2019; Last Night of the Proms, Royal Albert Hall, 2018; *world première performances:* Mark Anthony Turnage, The Torn Field, Berlin Philharmonie Kammermusik Saal, and Three Songs, Wigmore Hall, 2001; When I Woke, LPO, 2004; Peter Lieberson Songs of Love and Sorrow, Boston SO, 2010; Huw Watkins, Look down, fair moon, Wigmore Hall, 2011; Kaija Saariaho, True Fire, LA Philharmonic Orch., 2015; Einojuhani Rautavaara, Rubáiyát, Wigmore Hall, 2015, Helsinki Philharmonic Orch., 2016; In the Stream of Life, Helsinki Philharmonic Orch., 2016. Vis. Prof., Royal Coll. of Music, 2000. Numerous opera and recital recordings, and recitals and masterclasses at festivals and music institutions worldwide. John Christie Award, Glyndebourne, 1989; Juno Award, Canadian Acad. of Recording Arts, 1998, 2011, 2015; Singer's Award, Royal Philharmonic Soc., 2000; Editor's Choice Award, Gramophone mag./Classic FM, 2006; Vocal Award, Gramophone mag., 2008, 2009, 2011; Oscar della Lirica—baritono 2012, Internat. Opera Award, Confederazione Italiana Associazioni e Fondazioni per al Musica Lirica e Sinfonica; Paul de Hueck and Norman Walford Award, Ont. Arts Council, 2018. Hon. DLitt Saskatchewan, 2015. Grammy Award for best opera DVD, 2012. *Recreations:* wine, cooking, astronomy, successfully climbed Mt Kilimanjaro Aug. 2014. *Address:* c/o Stefania Almans, IMG Artists Europe, Capital Tower, 91 Waterloo Road, SE1 8RT. *T:* (020) 7957 5800. *E:* salmansi@imgartists.com; c/o Alison Pybus, Alison Pybus Personal Management, 3117 Caves Road, Owings Mill, MD 21117, USA. *T:* (410) 4802095. *E:* alisonpybus73@gmail.com. *Club:* Two Brydges.

**FINLEY, Michael John;** Governor, International Press Foundation, 1988–97; *b* 22 Sept. 1932; *s* of late Walter Finley and Grace Marie Butler; *m* 1st, 1955, Sheila Elizabeth Cole (*d* 1992); four *s*; 2nd, 2001, Maureen Elizabeth Crocker. *Educ:* King Edward VII Sch., Sheffield. Editor, 1964–69, Sheffield Morning Telegraph (formerly Sheffield Telegraph); Editorial Dir, 1969–79, and Dir and Gen. Man., 1979–82, Kent Messenger Gp; Exec. Dir, Periodical Publishers Assoc., 1983–88; Dir, Internat. Fedn of Periodical Publishers, 1989–92. Hon. Mem. and Past Chm., Parly and Legal Cttee, Guild of British Newspaper Editors. Chm., Inst. of Dirs (Kent branch), 1980–83. Member: BBC Regional Adv. Council, 1967–69; BBC Gen. Adv. Council, 1971–77; Exec. Cttee, Internat. Fedn of Periodical Publishers, 1983–89; Bd, Fedn of Periodical Publishers in EEC, 1984–92; Bd,

Internat. Press Centre, London, 1984–88; Gov., Cranbrook Sch., 1978–98. *Publications*: contrib. Advertising and the Community, 1968. *Recreations*: golf, Rugby (spectator), snooker, walking. *Address*: 22 Rochester Close, Eastbourne BN20 7TW.

**FINN**, family name of **Baroness Finn**.

**FINN**, Baroness *cr* 2015 (Life Peer), of Swansea in the County of West Glamorgan; **Simone Jari Finn**; Partner, FMA Partners, since 2017; Director, FMAP Ltd, since 2018; *b* 10 June 1968; *d* of Prof. Jan Kubes and Morwenna Talfan Davies (*née* Lewis); *m* 1996, Alexander William Galletly Finn; one *s* one *d*. *Educ*: Lady Margaret Hall, Oxford (BA Hist.). ACA 1995. Coopers & Lybrand, later PricewaterhouseCoopers, 1991–98; Sen. Acct, Financial Services Authy, 1998–2001; Advr on industrial relations to Cabinet Office, 2010–11; Special Advr to Minister for the Cabinet Office, 2012–15, to Sec. of State for Business, Innovation and Skills and Minister for Trade and Investment, 2015–16. Member: Adv. Bd, Centre for Politics, Philosophy and Law, KCL, 2016–; Bd, Open Europe, 2019–. Dir, Conservative Party Foundn Ltd, 2018–. Mem., Audit Cttee, Arbuthnot Latham & Co. Ltd, 2018–. Vis. Parly Fellow, St Antony's Coll., Oxford, 2018. Trustee, Demos, 2019–. *Address*: House of Lords, SW1A 0PW.

**FINN, Benjamin James**, OBE 2007; Co-founder and Director, Sibelius Software Ltd, 1993–2006; *b* 29 Nov. 1968; *s* of Timothy Finn and Anthea, (Widget), Finn (*née* Fox-Male). *Educ*: King's Coll. Choir Sch., Cambridge; King's Sch., Canterbury; Royal Coll. of Music; King's Coll., Cambridge (BA 1991; MPhil). *Recreations*: thinking, dabbling.
*See also J. H. Finn*.

**FINN, Jonathan Humbert**, OBE 2007; Co-founder and Director, Sibelius Software Ltd, 1993–2006; *b* 29 Nov. 1968; *s* of Timothy Finn and Anthea, (Widget), Finn (*née* Fox-Male). *Educ*: King's Coll. Choir Sch., Cambridge; King's Sch., Canterbury; Christ Church, Oxford (BA Music 1990). Vis. Prof. of Notation Technol., Royal Acad. Music, 1995. *Publications*: The Scorpion Control Computer, 1987. *Recreations*: follies, etymologies, in-between colours.
*See also B. J. Finn*.

**FINN, Leo Peter**; Chief Executive, Northern Rock PLC, 1997–2001; *b* 13 July 1938; *s* of Thomas Leo Finn and Jenny Finn (*née* Davison); *m* 1963, Alice Patricia Harold; two *s* two *d*. *Educ*: Carlisle Grammar Sch.; Newcastle upon Tyne Polytechnic (BA Hons). FCIB. Sec., 1982–89, Exec. Dir, 1989–91, Dep. Man. Dir, 1991–97, Northern Rock Building Soc.; Dir, Bellway plc, 1995–2009. Chairman: Newcastle/Gateshead Housing Market Restructure Pathfinder, 2002–05; Northern Recruitment Group PLC, 2005–09; Dir, Eden Housing Assoc., 2005–12 (Vice Chm., 2008–11; Chm., 2011–12). Lay Mem., Public Protection Panel Cumbria, 2002–10. Chm., Joseph Rowntree Enquiry into home ownership 2010 and beyond, 2004–05. Chm., Newcastle Coll., 2001–06. Chm., Northern Rock Foundn, 2004–06 (Trustee, 1997–2006). Hon. DCL Northumbria, 2005. *Recreations*: walking, opera, cooking.

**FINNEGAN, Joseph**; a Judge of the Supreme Court of Ireland, 2006–12; *b* 1 Oct. 1942; *s* of Isaac Finnegan and Charlotte Finnegan (*née* Sheridan); *m* 1968, Kathleen Gilligan; one *s* three *d*. *Educ*: Marist Coll., Dundalk; University Coll., Dublin (BCL, LLB). Admitted solicitor, Ireland; called to the Bar, King's Inns, Dublin (Bencher, 1999); in practice as solicitor, 1966–68 and 1973–78; Asst Sec., Incorporated Law Soc. of Ireland, 1968–73; Jun. Counsel, 1978–90; Sen. Counsel, 1990–99; Judge of the High Court of Ireland, 1992–2001; Pres. of the High Court, 2001–06. Bencher, Middle Temple, 2006. *Recreations*: National Hunt racing, golf. *Clubs*: Blackrock College Rugby Football; Bray Golf, El Saler Golf (Valencia, Spain).

**FINNEGAN, Kevin James**; QC (NI) 1985; **His Honour Judge Finnegan**; a County Court Judge, Northern Ireland, since 2001; *b* 3 June 1947; *s* of James Finnegan and Sheila Finnegan; *m* 1976, Anne Frances Aubrey; six *s*. *Educ*: St Malachy's Coll., Belfast; Queen's Univ., Belfast (LLB Hons 1970). Called to the Bar, NI, 1973. *Recreations*: golf, reading, listening to the radio, sleeping, going to Van Morrison, John Prine and Ray Davies concerts. *Address*: Royal Courts of Justice, Belfast BT1 3JF. *Club*: Malone Golf.

**FINNEGAN, Prof. Ruth Hilary**, OBE 2000; DPhil; FBA 1996; Visiting Research Professor, Open University, since 1999 (Professor in Comparative Social Institutions, 1988–99, Emeritus Professor, 2002); *b* 31 Dec. 1933; *d* of Tom Finnegan and Agnes (*née* Campbell); *m* 1963, David John Murray; three *d*. *Educ*: Mount Sch., York; Magee Univ. Coll.; Somerville Coll., Oxford (BA 1956; Dip in Anthropology 1959; BLitt 1960; Hon. Fellow, 1997); Nuffield Coll., Oxford (DPhil 1963). Teacher, Malvern Girls' Coll., 1956–58; Lectr in Social Anthropol., UC of Rhodesia and Nyasaland, 1963–64; Lectr in Sociol., 1965–67, Sen. Lectr, 1967–69, Ibadan Univ.; Open University: Lectr in Sociol., 1969–72; Sen. Lectr in Comparative Social Instns, 1972–75 and 1978–82; Reader, 1982–88; Reader in Sociol. and Head of Sociol. Discipline, Univ. of S Pacific, Suva, 1975–78. Vis. Prof., Univ. of Texas at Austin, 1989. Mem., Internat. Res. Council on Humanities and Social Scis Studies on Africa, 2013–. Mem., Governing Body, SOAS, 1999–2007 (Vice-Chm., 2003–06). Trustee, Mass-Observation Archive, 1998–2011. Pres., Mount Old Scholars' Assoc., 2003–05. Associate Mem., Finnish Lit. Soc., 1989; Folklore Fellow, Finnish Acad. of Sci. and Letters, 1991; Hon. Mem., Assoc. of Social Anthropologists of UK and Commonwealth, 2002; Internat. Fellow, Amer. Folklore Soc., 2017. Rivers Memorial Medal, RAI, 2016; internat. awards for fiction, non-fiction and scriptwriting. *Publications*: Survey of the Limba people of Northern Sierra Leone, 1965; Limba Stories and Story-telling, 1967; Oral Literature in Africa, 1970, 1976, 2nd (illustrated) edn 2012; Oral Poetry, 1977, 2nd edn 1992; Literacy and Orality, 1988; The Hidden Musicians, 1989, 2nd edn 2007; Oral Traditions and the Verbal Arts, 1992; Tales of the City, 1998; Communicating: the multiple modes of human interconnection, 2002, 2nd edn 2014; The Oral and Beyond: doing things with words in Africa, 2007; Why Do We Quote?: the culture and history of the quotation, 2011; The Search for African Orality, 2012; Music and Creation, 2012; Thoughts and Reflections on Language, Literature and Performance, 2013; Love Enpictured, 2013; Studying Oral Texts, 2013; Where is Language?, 2015 (Bronze Medal, Readers Favourite Book Award, 2016); Entrancement, 2016; Where Does Fiji's Music Come From?, 2017; Time for the World To Learn From Africa, 2019; *edited*: The Penguin Book of Oral Poetry, 1978, reissued as A World Treasury of Oral Poetry, 1982; Participating in the Knowledge Society: researchers beyond the university walls, 2005; Cato's Distichs: the oldest Latin primer, 2012; Peace Writing, 2013; Short Story Writing, 2013; He Came All So Stille: the home anthology of beautiful verse, 2014; *edited jointly*: Modes of Thought, 1973, 2nd edn 2013; Essays on Pacific Literature, 1978; Conceptions of Inquiry, 1981; New Approaches to Economic Life, 1985; Information Technology: social issues, 1987; From Family Tree to Family History, 1994; Sources and Methods for Family and Community Historians, 1994; South Pacific Oral Traditions, 1995; (series) Hearing Others' Voices, 2018–; *fiction*: Black Inked Pearl: a girl's quest, 2015 (Silver Award, Literary Titan, 2017) (screenplay (Genre Winner, Capital Fund Screenplay Contest), 2017); The Heavenly Rocker, 2016; Soa the Wicked, 2016; Pearl of the Seas, 2017 (Hungry Monster Silver Award, 2017); (poetry) Kate's Black Ink Poems, 2016; as Catherine Farrar: The Little Angel and the Three Wisdoms, 2012; Three Ways of Loving, 2012; L'il Ole Lil the Heavenly Rocker, 2012; The Dragon's Tale, 2012; The Wild Thorn Rose, 2012; contrib. to encyclopaedias and learned jls. *Recreations*: writing, singing, listening to music, learning with and from grandchildren, visiting New Zealand, dreaming, running indie Callender Press (founder, director and senior editor). *Address*: 125 Church Green Road, Bletchley, Milton Keynes MK3 6DE.

**FINNERTY, Angela Catherine; Her Honour Judge Finnerty**; a Circuit Judge, since 2000; Designated Family Judge for North Yorkshire, since 2011; *b* 22 March 1954; *d* of late Michael Peter Finnerty and of Mary Elizabeth Finnerty; *m* 1st (marr. diss.); one *s* one *d*; 2nd, 2012, Clive William Heaton, *qv*. *Educ*: Bury Convent Grammar Sch.; Leeds Univ. (LLB 1st Cl. Hons); Coll. of Law, London. Called to the Bar, Middle Temple, 1976 (Harmsworth Scholar), Bencher, 2015; in practice as barrister, 1976–2000. *Address*: York County Court, Piccadilly House, 55 Piccadilly, York YO1 9WL.

**FINNEY, Denise Kathryn**; see Plumpton, D. K.

**FINNEY, Rt Rev. John Thornley**; Bishop Suffragan of Pontefract, 1993–98; Hon. Assistant Bishop, diocese of Southwell and Nottingham (formerly diocese of Southwell), since 1998; *b* 1 May 1932; *s* of Arthur Frederick and Elaine Mary Finney; *m* 1959, Sheila Elizabeth Russell (*d* 2018); three *d*. *Educ*: Charterhouse; Hertford College, Oxford (BA Jurisp.; Dip. Theol.). Ordained 1958; Curate, All Saints, Headington, 1958–61; Curate in Charge, Aylesbury, 1961–65; Rector, Tollerton, Notts, 1965–71; Vicar, St Margaret's, Aspley, Nottingham, 1971–80; Adviser in Evangelism to Bishop of Southwell, 1980–89; Officer for Decade of Evangelism, 1990–93. Manager, Research Project in Evangelism, BCC, 1989–92. Chm. Council, Lee Abbey, 1999–2003. *Publications*: Saints Alive!, 1983; Understanding Leadership, 1989; The Well Church Book, 1991; Church on the Move, 1992; Finding Faith Today, 1992; Stories of Faith, 1995; Recovering the Past: Celtic and Roman mission, 1996; Fading Splendour?, 2000; Emerging Evangelism, 2004; To Germany with Love: die evangelische Kirche in Deutschland aus der Sicht eines Anglikaners, 2011. *Recreations*: golf, growing old gracefully. *Address*: Greenacre, Crow Lane, South Muskham, Newark, Notts NG23 6DZ. *T*: and *Fax*: (01636) 679791. *E*: john.finney2@talktalk.net.

**FINNIE, (James) Ross**, CA; Chairman, Food Standards Scotland, since 2015; *b* 11 Feb. 1947; *s* of late James Ross Finnie and Elizabeth Main Finnie; *m* 1971, Phyllis Sinclair; one *s* one *d*. *Educ*: Greenock Acad. Director: James Finlay Bank Ltd, 1975–86; Singer & Friedlander Ltd, 1986–91; Partner, Ross Finnie & Co., Chartered Accountants, 1991–99. Mem., Exec. Cttee, Scottish Council (Develt and Industry), 1976–87. Member (L then Lib Dem): Inverclyde DC, 1977–96; Inverclyde Council, 1995–99. Mem. (Lib Dem) W of Scotland, Scottish Parlt, 1999–2011; contested (Lib Dem) Greenock and Inverclyde, 2011. Minister for Rural Affairs, then for Envmt and Rural Develt, Scottish Exec., 1999–2007; Lib Dem Shadow Cabinet Sec. for Health and Wellbeing, 2007–11. Vice Convenor, Health and Sport Cttee, 2007–11, Convenor, End of Life Assistance Bill Cttee, 2010, Scottish Parlt. Chm., Scottish Lib Party, 1982–86. Contested: (L) Renfrewshire W, 1979; (L/All) Stirling, 1983. Dir, Scotland's Futures Forum Ltd, 2009–11. Non-executive Member: Water Industry Commn for Scotland, 2012–; NHS Greater Glasgow and Clyde Health Bd, 2012– (Vice Chm., 2016–). Pres., Scottish Envmt LINK, 2011–15. *Address*: 91 Octavia Terrace, Greenock PA16 7PY. *T*: (01475) 631495. *E*: finnie80@btinternet.com.

**FINNIE, John Bradford**; Member (Green) Highlands and Islands, Scottish Parliament, since 2016 (SNP, 2011–12, Ind, 2012–16); *b* Clunes, Inverness-shire, 31 Dec. 1956; *m* Bernadette; one *s* one *d*. *Educ*: Achnacarry Primary Sch.; Lochaber High Sch.; Oban High Sch. Constable: Lothian and Borders Police, 1976–79; Northern Constabulary, 1979–2006. Sec., Northern Br., Scottish Police Fedn, 1992–2006. Mem. (SNP), Highland Council, 2007–12. *Recreations*: family, football, music. *Address*: Scottish Parliament, Edinburgh EH99 1SP. *T*: (0131) 348 6898. *E*: john.finnie.msp@parliament.scot.

**FINNIE, Ross**; see Finnie, J. R.

**FINNIGAN, Judith, (Judy)**; television presenter; *b* 16 May 1948; *d* of late John Finnigan and of Anne Finnigan; *m* 1986, Richard Holt Madeley, *qv*; one *s* one *d*, and two *s* from previous marriage. Researcher, Granada TV, 1971–73; reporter, Anglia TV, 1974–77; presenter: Granada TV, 1980–2001; Channel 4, 2001–08; programmes include: This Morning, 1988–2001; Richard and Judy, 2001–08; British Book Awards, 2004–; Richard and Judy's New Position, Watch, 2008–09. *Publications*: (with R. Madeley) Richard & Judy: the autobiography, 2001; (novel) Eloise, 2012; (novel) I Do Not Sleep, 2015. *Address*: c/o James Grant Management, 4th Floor, 180 Great Portland Street, W1W 5QZ. *T*: (020) 8742 4950.

**FINNIGAN, Peter Anthony**; QC 2009; *b* Leigh, Lancs, 14 Sept. 1955; *s* of Geoffrey Finnigan and Anne Finnigan; *m* 1982, Sarah Jane Farmbrough; one *s* two *d*. *Educ*: Sevenoaks Sch.; Univ. of Newcastle upon Tyne (LLB Hons). Called to the Bar, Lincoln's Inn, 1979; Standing Counsel to HMRC, 1996–2006. Mem., Glyndebourne Fest. Soc. *Recreations*: opera, travel, ski-ing, sailing, watching and supporting lacrosse and Rugby. *Address*: QEB Hollis Whiteman Chambers, 1–2 Laurence Pountney Hill, EC4R 0EU. *T*: (020) 7933 8855. *E*: peter.finnigan@qebholliswhiteman.co.uk. *Club*: Harlequin Football.

**FINNIGAN, Stephen James**, CBE 2010; QPM 2006; DL; Chief Constable, Lancashire Constabulary, 2005–17; *b* Liverpool, 29 June 1957; *s* of James Francis Finnigan and late Veronica Finnigan (*née* Ramsey); *m* 1990, Jaqueline Marie Brammer; one *s* one *d*. *Educ*: Maricourt Comprehensive Sch.; St John's Coll., Cambridge (BA 1992); Univ. of Cambridge (Dip. Applied Criminol. and Police Studies 2000). Merseyside Police, 1976–2001: Sergeant, 1980–87; Inspector, 1987–93; Chief Inspector, 1993–96; Superintendent, 1996–2001; Lancashire Constabulary: Asst Chief Constable, 2001–02, Dep. Chief Constable, 2002–05. DL Lancs 2017. *Recreations*: running, watching football (Everton FC), spending time with young family.

**FINNIS, Jane**; Chief Executive, Culture24 (formerly 24 Hour Museum), since 2001 (on secondment to Culture is Digital Culture Project, Department for Digital, Culture, Media and Sport, 2017); *b* Walton-on-Thames, Oct. 1965; *d* of Richard Finnis and Hazel Finnis (*née* Hoare); *m* 2006, Nick Brown; one *s* one *d*. *Educ*: Brighton Poly. (BA Hons 1st Cl. Expressive Arts 1987). Freelance video and TV prod. and dir, 1987–90; Dir, Lighthouse Arts & Training Ltd, 1989–2001. Mem., Adv. Bd, Place To Be, Brighton and Hove Council, 2000–03. Chm. and Founder Mem., Internat. Steering Cttee, Culturemondo, 2003–13. Mem. Bd and Trustee, South East Dance Agency, 1998–2001; Member: South East Film Task Force, 2000–01; Prog. Cttee, Museums and the Web, 2010–. Trustee, Photoworks, 2007–15. *Publications*: (contrib.) Learning to Live: museums, young people and education, 2009; (contrib.) Digital Culture: the changing dynamics, 2009; (contrib.) Let's Get Real: how to evaluate online success, 2011; (contrib.) Let's Get Real 2: a journey towards understanding and measuring online engagement, 2013; (contrib.) The Digital Media Handbook, 2013; (contrib.) Let's Get Real 3: is your content fit for purpose?, 2014; (contrib.) ReProgram: technology innovation and culture in a new era of museums, 2015; Let's Get Real 4: what's the story?, 2016. *Recreations*: drawing, singing, writing, travel. *Address*: c/o Culture24, 28 Kensington Street, Brighton BN1 4AJ. *E*: jane@culture24.org.uk. *W*: https://medium.com/@janefinnis.

**FINNIS, Prof. John Mitchell,** AC 2019; DPhil; FBA 1990; Professor of Law and Legal Philosophy, Oxford University, 1989–2010, now Emeritus; Fellow and Praelector in Jurisprudence, 1966–2010, Stowell Civil Law Fellow, 1973–2010, Vice Master, 2001–10, University College, Oxford (Honorary Fellow, since 2011); Biolchini Family Professor of Law, University of Notre Dame du Lac, USA, since 1995; *b* 28 July 1940; *s* of Maurice and Margaret Finnis; *m* 1964, Marie Carmel McNally; three *s* three *d* (and one *d* decd). *Educ:* St Peter's Coll., Adelaide, SA; St Mark's Coll., Univ. of Adelaide (LLB 1961); University Coll., Oxford (Rhodes Scholar for SA, 1962; DPhil 1965). Called to the Bar, Gray's Inn, 1970. Associate in Law, Univ. of Calif at Berkeley, 1965–66; Rhodes Reader in Laws of British Commonwealth and United States, Oxford Univ., 1972–89; Prof. and Head of Dept of Law, Univ. of Malawi, 1976–78. Huber Distinguished Vis. Prof., Boston Coll. Law Sch., 1993–94. Special Adviser to Foreign Affairs Cttee, House of Commons, on role of UK Parlt in Canadian Constitution, 1980–82; Consultor, Pontifical Commn, Iustitia et Pax, 1977–89; Member: Pontifical Council de Iustitia et Pace, 1990–95; Catholic Bishops' Jt Cttee on Bio-Ethical Issues, 1981–88; Internat Theol Commn, The Vatican, 1986–91; Pontifical Acad. for Life, 2001–16. Governor, Anscombe Centre, Oxford (formerly Linacre Centre, London), 1981–96, 1998–2007, 2010–16 (Vice-Chm., 1987–96, 2002–07). Hon. QC 2017. Hon. LLD: Notre Dame, Australia, 2011; Adelaide, 2017. *Publications:* Commonwealth and Dependencies, in Halsbury's Laws of England, 4th edn, Vol. 6, 1974, revised 1991, 2003, 5th edn, Vol. 13, 2009; Natural Law and Natural Rights, 1980, 2nd edn 2011; Fundamentals of Ethics, 1983; (with Joseph Boyle and Germain Grisez) Nuclear Deterrence, Morality and Realism, 1987; Moral Absolutes, 1991; Aquinas: moral, political, and legal theory, 1998; Collected Essays, Vols I–V, 2011. *Address:* University College, Oxford OX1 4BH.

**FINNISSY, Prof. Michael Peter;** composer; Professor of Composition, University of Southampton, 1999–2018; *b* 17 March 1946; *s* of George Norman Finnissy and Rita Isolene Finnissy (*née* Parsonson). *Educ:* Hawes Down Jun. Sch.; Bromley Tech. High Sch.; Beckenham and Penge Grammar Sch.; Royal Coll. of Music. Lectr, Music Dept, London Sch. of Contemporary Dance, 1969–74; Artist-in-Residence, Victorian Coll. of the Arts, Melbourne, Australia, 1982–83; Lectr, Dartington Summer Sch., 1981, 1990, 1992–; Consultant Tutor in Composition, Winchester Coll., 1988–; Res. Fellow in Music, Univ. of Sussex, 1989–99; Mem., Composition Faculty, Royal Acad. of Music, 1990–2001; KBC Prof. of New Music, Katholieke Univ., Leuven, 1999–2001; Mem., St John's Coll., Cambridge, 2017–. Pres., ISCM, 1990–96 (Hon. Mem., 1998–). Hon. FRCM 2008. *Compositions include:* Beat Generation Ballads (piano), 1961–2014; Four Organ Symphonies, 1962–2008; Eighteen Songs, 1963–76; World (vocal/orchestral), 1968–74; Tsuru-Kame (stage work), 1971–73; Mysteries (stage work), 1972–79; Verdi Transcriptions (piano), 1972–88; Cipriano (choral), 1974; Seven Piano Concertos, 1975–81; Pathways of Sun & Stars (orchestral), 1976; English Country-Tunes (piano), 1977; Alongside (orchestral), 1979; Sea and Sky (orchestral), 1979–80; Kelir (choral), 1981; Undivine Comedy (stage work), 1985–2017; Thérèse Raquin (stage work), 1992; Folklore (piano), 1993–94; Liturgy of S Paul (vocal), 1993–95; Shameful Vice (stage work), 1994; Speak its Name! (orchestral), 1996; The History of Photography in Sound (piano), 1993–2000; This Church (choral), 2000–03; Six Sexy Minuets Three Trios (string quartet), 2003; Molly-House (open ensemble), 2004; Second String Quartet, 2006–07; Grieg Quintettsatz, 2007; Mankind (stage work), 2007–08; Third String Quartet, 2007–09; The Transgressive Gospel, 2008–09; Three Piano Quartets, 2009–10; Completion of Grieg's Piano Quintet in B Flat, 2007–12; Awaz-e Niyaz (for lupophone doubling quarter-tone oboe and piano), 2012–13; Sesto Libro di Gesualdo (vocal), 2012–13; Remembrance Day, 2013–14; Janne (orchestra), 2014–15; Beethoven's Robin Adair (piano), 2012–16; Andersen-Liederkreis, 2015–16; Vervollständigung von Schuberts D840 (piano), 2016–17; Mu-Fa (two ensembles), 2016; Maat Strikt (soloist and ensemble), 2016–17; Pious Anthems and Voluntaries, 2016–19; Easy Things to Do (choral), 2018; Beddoes (soprano and piano), 2018–19. *Address:* c/o Verlag Neue Musik, Grabbeallee 15, 13156 Berlin, Germany; 26 Hadley Road, Sheringham, Norfolk NR26 8PZ.

**FINUCANE, Brendan Godfrey Eamonn;** QC 2003; **His Honour Judge Finucane;** a Circuit Judge, since 2017; *b* 16 March 1952; *s* of Raymond and Feardar Finucane; *m* 1998, Fiona Rosalie Horlick; two *s* two *d* from former marriage. *Educ:* Bedford Coll., Univ. of London (BSc Hons Sociol. and Social Admin). Called to the Bar, Middle Temple, 1976, Bencher, 2006; in practice, specialising in criminal law and regulatory and professional discipline work; Asst Recorder, 2000–01; Recorder, 2001–17. Member Council: Tate Members, 2001–11; Friends of BM, 2002–12. Chm., Equipment for Independent Living (Charity), 1996–2011. Member: Bd of Dirs, City & Guilds of London Art Sch., 2006– (Chm., Develt Cttee, 2004–); Bd of Advrs, Delfina Foundn, 2007–; Finance and Gen. Purposes Cttee, Art Fund, 2011– (Chm. of Patrons, 2015–); non-exec. Dir, Design and Artists Copyright Soc., 2010–16. Mem. Council, RA, 2013– (Chm., Ethics Adv. Gp, 2016–18; Vice Chair, 2018–); Dir, Barts Heritage Trust, 2017–. Trustee: Paintings in Hosps, 2007–14; Pallant House Gall., 2009–18; East Malling Trust, 2014–15; Art 360 Foundn, 2017–. *Recreations:* collecting art, architecture, theatre, cinema, visiting art galleries, music. *Address:* Woolwich Crown Court, 2 Belmarsh Road, SE28 0EY. *Clubs:* Athenæum, Chelsea Arts.

**FINUCANE, Joanne;** *see* Lomas, J.

**FINZI, Claudio V.;** *see* Vita-Finzi.

**FIORINA, Carleton S., (Carly);** Chairman and Chief Executive Officer, Carly Fiorina Enterprises; *b* Austin, Texas, 6 Sept. 1954. *Educ:* Stanford Univ. (BA 1976); Univ. of Maryland (MBA 1980); Sloan Sch. of Mgt, MIT (MSc 1989); UCLA. Joined AT&T, 1980: posts included account exec., Sen. Vice-Pres. of Global Mktg, and Pres., Atlantic and Canadian Region; Lucent Technologies (formerly subsid. of AT&T), 1996–99: Vice-Pres. of Corp. Ops; Pres., Global Service Provider Business; Chm. and CEO, Hewlett-Packard Co., 1999–2005. Formerly Director: Kellogg Co.; Merck & Co. Inc.; Cybertrust, 2005–07; Revolution Health Gp, 2005–08; non-exec. Dir, Cisco Systems Inc., 2001. Chm., Good360, 2012; Founder and Chm., Unlocking Potential. Mem., US China Bd of Trade. *Publications:* Tough Choices: a memoir, 2006; (jtly) Our Shared Opportunity: a vision for global prosperity, 2013; Rising to the Challenge: my leadership journey, 2015.

**FIRE, Prof. Andrew Zachary,** PhD; George D. Smith Professor in Molecular and Genetic Medicine, and Professor of Pathology and of Genetics, since 2003, Stanford University School of Medicine; *b* Santa Clara Co., Calif, 27 April 1959. *Educ:* Fremont High Sch.; Univ. of Calif, Berkeley (AB 1978); Massachusetts Inst. of Technol. (PhD 1983). Helen Hay Whitney Foundn Fellow, MRC Lab. of Molecular Biol., Cambridge, 1983–86; Staff Associate, 1986–89, Staff Mem., 1989–2003, Dept of Embryology, Carnegie Instn of Washington, Baltimore. Adjunct Prof., Dept of Biol., Johns Hopkins Univ., 1989–2009. (Jtly) Nobel Prize in Physiol. or Medicine, 2006. *Publications:* articles in learned jls. *Address:* Departments of Pathology and Genetics, Stanford University School of Medicine, 300 Pasteur Drive - L235, Stanford, CA 94305–5324, USA.

**FIRMIN, Carlene Emma,** MBE 2011; Senior Research Fellow and Head of MsUnderstood Programme, University of Bedfordshire, since 2013; *b* London, Oct. 1983; *d* of John Firmin and Anita Pearson. *Educ:* St Michael's Catholic Grammar Sch.; Univ. of Cambridge (BA Hons Philosophy 2005); London Sch. of Econs and Pol Sci. (MSc Social Policy and Planning 2008). Race on the Agenda: Building Bridges Coordinator and Office Adminr, 2005–08; Senior Policy Officer, 2008–09; Female Voice in Violence Coordinator, 2009–11; Asst Dir, Policy and Res., Youth Justice and Child Sexual Exploitation, Barnardo's, 2011; Principal Policy Advr and Hd of Secretariat, Office of the Children's Comr's Inquiry into Child Sexual Exploitation in Gangs and Gps, Office of the Children's Comr, 2011–13. Columnist, Society Guardian, 2010–. Founder Bd of Dirs, GAG Project. Trustee: Prison Reform Trust; Hibiscus. *Recreations:* funky dance classes, looking after my Godchildren, baking, cooking for friends and family. *Address:* University of Bedfordshire, University Square, Luton, Beds LU1 3JU. *E:* carlenefirmin@hotmail.com.

**FIRRELL, Hon. Dame Lucy Morgan;** *see* Theis, Hon. Dame L. M.

**FIRTH, Colin,** CBE 2011; actor; *b* 10 Sept. 1960; *s* of David and Shirley Firth; one *s* by Meg Tilly; *m* 1997, Livia Giuggioli; two *s*. *Educ:* Montgomery of Alamein Sch., Winchester; London Drama Centre. *Stage includes:* Another Country, Queen's, 1983; The Lonely Road, Old Vic, 1985; The Elms, Greenwich, 1987; The Caretaker, Almeida, 1991; Chatsky, Almeida, 1993; Three Days of Rain, Donmar Warehouse, 1999; *films include:* Another Country, 1983; A Month in the Country, 1986; Valmont, 1988; Wings of Fame, 1989; The Hour of the Pig, 1992; Circle of Friends, 1995; The English Patient, 1996; Fever Pitch, 1997; Shakespeare in Love, The Secret Laughter of Women, 1999; My Life So Far, Relative Values, 2000; Bridget Jones's Diary, 2001; The Importance of Being Earnest, 2002; Hope Springs, What A Girl Wants, Love Actually, 2003; Girl with a Pearl Earring, Trauma, Bridget Jones: The Edge of Reason, 2004; Nanny McPhee, Where the Truth Lies, 2005; And When Did You Last See Your Father?, The Last Legion, St Trinian's, 2007; The Accidental Husband, Mamma Mia!, Easy Virtue, 2008; Genova, Dorian Gray, St Trinian's 2: the Legend of Fritton's Gold, 2009; A Single Man (BAFTA Award for Best Actor), 2010; The King's Speech (Academy, Golden Globe and BAFTA Awards for Best Actor), Tinker, Tailor, Soldier, Spy, 2011; Gambit, 2012; The Railway Man, 2013; Devil's Knot, Arthur & Mike, Before I Go to Sleep, Magic in the Moonlight, 2014; Kingsman, 2015; Genius, Bridget Jones's Baby, 2016; Kingsman: The Golden Circle, 2017; The Mercy, The Happy Prince (and co-producer), Mamma Mia! Here We Go Again, Mary Poppins Returns, 2018; Kursk: the last mission, 2019; producer, Eye in the Sky, 2016; *television includes:* Dutch Girls, 1984; Tumbledown, 1987; Out of the Blue, 1990; The Deep Blue Sea, 1994; Pride and Prejudice, 1995; Nostromo, 1996; The Turn of the Screw, 1999; Donovan Quick, 2000. *Address:* c/o Independent Talent Group Ltd, 40 Whitfield Street, W1T 2RH. *T:* (020) 7636 6565.

**FIRTH, Prof. David,** PhD; FBA 2008; Professor of Statistics, University of Warwick, since 2003; *b* Wakefield, Yorks, 22 Dec. 1957; *s* of Allan Firth and Betty Firth (*née* Bailey); *m* 1987, Julie McCormack; one *s* two *d*. *Educ:* Trinity Hall, Cambridge (BA Maths 1980); Imperial Coll. London (MSc 1982; PhD Stats 1987). Asst Prof., Univ. of Texas at Austin, 1987–89; Lectr, Univ. of Southampton, 1989–93; Prof. of Social Stats, University of Oxford, 1993–2003. Professorial Fellow, ESRC, 2003–06. Guy Medal in Bronze, 1998, Guy Medal in Silver, 2012, Royal Statistical Soc. *Publications:* contrib. articles to learned jls incl. Biometrika, Jl Royal Statistical Soc., BMJ. *Recreations:* cycling, walking. *Address:* Department of Statistics, University of Warwick, Coventry CV4 7AL. *T:* (024) 7657 4855. *E:* d.firth@warwick.ac.uk.

**FIRTH, Ian Peter Thomas,** FREng, FICE, FIStructE; independent engineering consultant, since 2018; Chief Operating Officer, COWI UK (formerly Flint & Neill) Ltd, 2008–18; *b* Rustington, Sussex, 17 Feb. 1956; *s* of Thomas Mark Bernard Firth and Anne Firth; *m* 1981, Rachel Maureen Clamp; one *s* two *d*. *Educ:* Marlborough Coll.; Univ. of Bristol (BSc Civil Engrg 1979); Imperial Coll. of Sci. and Technol., London (MSc Structural Steel Design 1982; DIC 1982). FICE 1998; FIStructE 2000; FREng 2007. Joined Flint & Neill Partnership, 1979, Partner, 1990–2008. Chm., British Gp, Internat. Assoc. for Bridge and Structural Engrg, 2013–. Chm., Trustees, Bridges to Prosperity UK Charitable Trust, 2014–. Pres., IStructE, 2017. Member: RSPB; Nat. Trust. Hon. FRIBA 2017. *Publications:* over 20 tech. papers in engrg and other professional jls. *Recreations:* church, choir, music, theatre. *Address:* London and Wiltshire.

**FIRTH, Mrs Joan Margaret,** CB 1995; PhD; Chair, Bradford Health Authority, 1998–2000 (Vice Chair, 1996–98); Deputy Director of NHS Finance, Department of Health, 1990–95; *b* 25 March 1935; *d* of Ernest Wilson and Ann (*née* Crowther); *m* 1955, Kenneth Firth. *Educ:* Lawnswood High Sch., Leeds; Univ. of Leeds (1st Cl. BSc Colour Chemistry; PhD Dyeing of Wool). Research Asst, Leeds Univ., 1958–60; Head of Science, Selby High Sch., 1960–62; Sen. Lecturer in General Science, Elizabeth Gaskell Coll., Manchester, 1962–66; Lectr in Organic Chemistry, Salford Univ., 1966–67; joined Civil Service as Direct Entry Principal, 1967; Asst Sec., 1974; Under-Sec., DHSS, 1981; Under-Sec., Social Security Div. C, DHSS, later DSS, 1987–90. Member: ESRC, 1988–92; Training Bd, 1990–92. Mem., Audit Cttee, Inst. Cancer Res., 1994–98. *Publications:* contrib. Jl Textile Inst., 1958. *Recreations:* wine, bridge.

**FIRTH, Kathryn;** Director of Urban Design, NBBJ Design, Boston, since 2017; *b* Toronto; *d* of Anthony Firth and Marianne Firth; *m* 1996, Derek Pajaczkowski; one *s*. *Educ:* Univ. of Toronto (BArch); Graduate Sch. of Design, Harvard (MArch). Sen. Urban Designer, David Dixon/Goody Clancy (USA), 1994–95; Associate Dir, Chan Krieger & Associates (USA), 1995–97; Projects Dir, Architecture Foundn, 1998–99; Sen. Urban Designer, Jeremy Dixon.Edward Jones Architects, 2000–02; Director: MSc City Design and Soc. Sci., Cities Prog., LSE, 2002–05; Urban Design, PLP|KPF Architects, 2004–11; Chief of Design, London Legacy Develt Corp., 2011–15; Dir of Develt, Urban Design and Master Planning, Publica Associates, 2015–16; Partner, FPDesign, 2016–17. Vice-Chm., Old Oak Park Royal Rev. Gp, 2015–; Mem., Camden Design Rev. Panel, 2016–. Mem., Exec. Cttee, London Soc., 2014–; Dir, Sadler's Wells Foundn, 2015–; Trustee, Architecture Sans Frontières, UK, 2016–17. Mem., Bd of Dirs, Acad. of Urbanism, 2016–18. *Publications:* articles in Jl of London Soc., Architectural Design. *E:* kfirth@public-realm.net.

**FIRTH, Paul James;** writer (part-time); a District Judge (Magistrates' Courts), Lancashire, 2001–05; *b* 2 June 1951; *s* of Albert and Violet Firth; *m* 1979, Ann Barbara Whitehead; one *s*. *Educ:* Bradford Grammar Sch.; Queen's Coll., Oxford (Hastings Exhibnr; MA 1973). Admitted solicitor, 1980; Trainee Court Clerk, Keighley Magistrates' Court, 1973–74; Trainee Court Clerk, Court Clerk, then Sen. Court Clerk, Leeds Magistrates' Court, 1975–81; Dep. Clerk to Justices (Legal), Manchester City Magistrates' Court, 1981–86; Clerk to Justices, Rotherham Magistrates' Court, 1986–95; Actg Stipendiary Magistrate, 1991–95; Stipendiary Magistrate, subseq. Dist Judge (Magistrates' Cts), Merseyside, 1995–2001. Pt-time Lectr, 2006–16, Hon. Fellow in Criminal Justice Studies, Directorate of Social Scis, 2011–16, Univ. of Salford. *Publications:* Four Minutes to Hell: the story of the Bradford City fire, 2005; Bobby Campbell: they don't make them like him any more, 2012; contrib. The City Gent, Boy from Brazil, Yorkshire Post. *Recreations:* running any distance up to 10 km, various sports (mainly watching, especially Bradford City), reading anything except law books. *E:* paulfirth@blueyonder.co.uk. *Club:* Yorkshire CC.

**FIRTH, Rt Rev. Peter James**; Bishop Suffragan of Malmesbury, 1983–94; an Hon. Assistant Bishop, diocese of Gloucester, since 2003; *b* 12 July 1929; *s* of Atkinson Vernon Firth and Edith Pepper; *m* 1955, Felicity Mary Wilding; two *s* two *d* (and one long-term foster *d*). *Educ*: Stockport Grammar School; Emmanuel Coll., Cambridge (Open Exhibnr, MA, DipEd; Pres., Cambridge Footlights, 1953); St Stephen's House Theol Coll., Oxford. Ordained, 1955; Assistant Curate, St Stephen's, Barbourne in Worcester, 1955–58; Priest-in-charge, Church of the Ascension, Parish of St Matthias, Malvern Link, Worcs, 1958–62; Rector of St George's, Abbey Hey, Gorton in Manchester, 1962–66; Religious Broadcasting Assistant, North Region, BBC, 1966–67; Religious Broadcasting Organiser and Senior Producer, Religious Programmes, BBC South and West, Bristol, 1967–83. Religious Advr to HTV West, 1983–2003; Mem., W of England TV Council, 2003–. Pres., Religious Drama Soc. of GB, 1994–2009. Trustee, Bristol Cancer Help Centre, 1995–2007. Governor: Millfield Sch., 1994–2002. Clifton Coll., 1995–2007; Internat. Radio Festival winner, Seville, 1975. *Publications*: Lord of the Seasons, 1978; The Love that moves the Sun, 1996; As Far As I Can See (poetry), 2013; This is my House (poetry) 2016; I Wish I Knew More (poetry), 2018. *Recreations*: theatre, photography, music, travel, Manchester United. *Address*: Mill House, Silk Mill Lane, Winchcombe GL54 5HZ. *T*: (01242) 603669. *E*: peter.united4@btinternet.com.

**FIRTH, Tazeena Mary**; designer; *b* 1 Nov. 1935; *d* of Denis Gordon Firth and Irene (née Morris). *Educ*: St Mary's, Wantage; Châtelard Sch. Theatre Royal, Windsor, 1954–57; English Stage Co., Royal Court, 1957–60; partnership in stage design with Timothy O'Brien estabd 1961; output incl.: The Bartered Bride, The Girl of the Golden West, 1962; West End prodns of new plays, 1963–64; London scene of Shakespeare Exhibn, 1964; Tango, Days in the Trees, Staircase, RSC, and Trafalgar at Madame Tussaud's, 1966; All's Well that Ends Well, As You Like It, Romeo and Juliet, RSC, 1967; The Merry Wives of Windsor, Troilus and Cressida (also Nat. Theatre, 1976), The Latent Heterosexual, RSC, 1968; Pericles (also Comédie Française, 1974), Women Beware Women, Bartholomew Fair, RSC, 1969; Measure for Measure, RSC, Madame Tussaud's in Amsterdam, and The Knot Garden, Royal Opera, 1970; Enemies, Man of Mode, RSC, 1971; La Cenerentola, Oslo, Lower Depths, and The Island of the Mighty, RSC, As You Like It, OCSC, 1972; Richard II, Love's Labour's Lost, RSC, 1973; Next of Kin, NT, Summerfolk, RSC, and The Bassarids, ENO, 1974; John Gabriel Borkman, NT, Peter Grimes, Royal Opera (later in Paris), The Marrying of Ann Leete, RSC, 1975; Wozzeck, Adelaide Fest., The Zykovs, RSC, and The Force of Habit, NT, 1976; Tales from the Vienna Woods, Bedroom Farce, NT, and Falstaff, Berlin Opera, 1977; The Cunning Little Vixen, Göteborg, Evita, London (later in USA, Australia, Vienna), A Midsummer Night's Dream, Sydney Opera House, 1978; Peter Grimes, Göteborg, The Rake's Progress, Royal Opera, 1979; Turandot, Vienna State Opera, 1983. Designed independently: The Two Gentlemen of Verona, RSC, 1969; Occupations, RSC, 1971; The Rape of Lucretia, Karlstad, 1982; Katherina Ismailova, Göteborg, 1984; La Traviata, Umeå, The Trojan Woman, Göteborg, and Bluebeard's Castle, Copenhagen, 1985; Il Seraglio, Göteborg, 1986; The Magic Flute, Rigoletto, Umeå, 1987; Romeo and Juliet, Malmö, 1988; The Rake's Progress, Göteborg, and, Dido and Aeneas, Copenhagen, 1989; From the House of the Dead, Göteborg, and, Barbarians, RSC, 1990; Macbeth, Göteborg, 1990; Lady Macbeth of Mtsensk, Copenhagen, La Bohème, Malmö, and Il Seraglio, Stockholm, 1991; Don Giovanni, Prague, 1991; Rigoletto, Oslo, and Carmen, Copenhagen, 1992; Carmen, Stockholm, Drot og Mask, Copenhagen, Magic Flute, Prague and Peter Grimes, Copenhagen, 1993; Vox Humana, Göteborg, 1994; Don Giovanni, Japan, Dido and Aeneas, and Oh Come Ye Sons of Art, Dröttningholm, Bluebeard's Castle, and Jenůfa, Göteborg, 1995; Peter Grimes, Göteborg and Finnish Nat. Opera, and Jenůfa, Copenhagen, 1998; Peter Grimes, New Israeli Opera, Tel Aviv, 2002. (Jtly) Gold Medal for Set Design, Prague Quadriennale, 1975. *Recreations*: sailing, walking. *Address*: Faraway, Keyhaven Marshes, Lymington SO41 0TR.

**FIRTH, Timothy David**; playwright, composer and lyricist; *b* Chester, 13 Oct. 1964; *s* of Gordon Firth and Kathleen Firth; *m* 1993, Katy Sayer; two *s* one *d*. *Educ*: King's Coll., Cambridge (BA Hons Eng. 1987). Writer: *theatre* includes: Neville's Island, 1992; The Safari Party, 2002; Our House, 2002; The Flint Street Nativity, 2006; Sign of the Times, 2009; Calendar Girls, 2008; This is My Family, 2013; (jtly) The Girls, 2015; The Band, 2017; *television* includes: Money for Nothing, 1994; All Quiet on the Preston Front, 1994–97; The Rottentrolls, 1995–99; The Flint Street Nativity, 1999; Cruise of the Gods, 2000; *films* include: Blackball, 2003; Calendar Girls, 2003; Kinky Boots, 2005. Solo album, Harmless Flirting, 2004. Hon. DLitt Chester, 2010. *Publications*: A Man of Letters, 1992; Neville's Island, 1994; The End of the Food Chain, 1995; The Safari Party, 2003; The Flint Street Nativity, 2009; Calendar Girls, 2010; Sign of the Times, 2011. *Recreations*: running, playing rhythm piano. *Address*: c/o Alan Brodie Representation Ltd, Paddock Suite, The Courtyard, 55 Charterhouse Street, EC1M 6HA. *T*: (020) 7253 6226. *E*: mia@alanbrodie.com.

**FISCHEL, David Andrew**; Chief Executive, Intu Properties (formerly TransAtlantic Holdings, then Liberty International, then Capital Shopping Centres Group) plc, 2001–19; *b* 1 April 1958. ACA 1983. Touche Ross & Co., 1980–85; with TransAtlantic Holdings, later Liberty International, then Capital Shopping Centres Group plc, subseq. Intu Properties plc, 1985–2018: Man. Dir, 1992–2001.

**FISCHEL, Robert Gustav**; QC 1998; Chambers of Robert Fischel, QC, Estepona, Spain, since 2001; Consultant, Verralls Barristers and Solicitors, since 2018; *b* 12 Jan. 1953; *s* of Bruno Rolf Fischel and Sophie Fischel (née Kruml); *m* 1st, 1989, Louise Kim Halsall (marr. diss. 1997); 2nd, 1999, Anna Louise (*d* 2012), *d* of Patrick Landucci; two *d*; 3rd, 2014, Susan Maria Kelly. *Educ*: City of London Sch.; Univ. of London (LLB). Called to the Bar, Middle Temple, 1975; in practice at the Bar, 1975–; Chambers of Brian Higgs, QC, 1977–2001; called to the Gibraltar Bar, 2012; Consultant: Governor's Street Chambers, Gibraltar, 2011–13; Chambers of Stephen Bullock, Gibraltar, 2012–13; HM Govt of Gibraltar, 2013–18. Former proprietor, El Molino de la Cala hotel, Estepona. Freeman, City of London, 1974. *Recreations*: cooking, horse riding, ski-ing, travel.

**FISCHELIS, Suzy**; *see* Klein, S.

**FISCHER, Dr Edmond Henri**; Professor Emeritus, University of Washington, since 1990; *b* Shanghai, China, 6 April 1920; *s* of Oscar Fischer and Renee Tapernoux; *m* 1st, Nelly Gagnaux (*d* 1961); two *s*; 2nd, 1963, Beverley Bullock (*d* 2006). *Educ*: Univ. of Geneva (Licencié ès Sciences 1943; Diplôme d'Ingénieur 1944; DSc 1947). Asst, Labs of Organic Chem., Univ. of Geneva, 1946–47; Fellow, Swiss Nat. Foundn, 1948–50; Res. Fellow, Rockefeller Foundn, 1950–53; Res. Associate, Div. of Biol., CIT, 1953; University of Washington: Asst Prof. of Biochem., 1953–56; Associate Prof., 1956–61; Prof., 1961–90. Associate, Neurosciences Res. Prog., Neuroscience Res. Inst., La Jolla, Calif, 1995–. Member: Biochem. Section, NIH, 1959–64; Editl Adv. Bd, Biochemistry, Jl of ACS, 1961–66 (Associate Editor, 1966–92); Adv. Bd, ACS, 1962; Sci. Adv. Bd, Friedrich Miescher Inst. CIBA-GEIGY, 1976–84 (Chm., 1981–84); Council, Amer. Soc. Biol Chemists, 1980–83; Scientific Council on Basic Sci., Amer. Heart Assoc., 1977–80; Bd of Scientific Govs, Scripps Res. Inst., 1987–; Scientific Adv. Cttee, Muscular Dystrophy Assoc., 1980–89; Scientific Adv. Bd, Basel Inst. for Immunology, 1996–; Bd Govs, Weizmann Inst. of Sci., Israel, 1997–; Chm., Task Force, Muscular Dystrophy Assoc. Res. Centres, 1985–89. Member: Amer. Soc. Biol Chemists; ACS; Amer. Acad. of Arts and Scis, 1972; AAAS 1972; NAS 1973; Amer. Assoc. of Univ. Profs. Foreign Mem., Royal Society, 2010. Pres., Pole Universitaire de Montpellier, 1993–96. Hon. PhD: Montpellier 1985; Basel 1988; Med. Coll. of Ohio, 1993; Indiana, 1993; Ruhr-Univ., 1994. Numerous awards, medals and prizes; Nobel Prize in Physiology or Medicine, 1992. *Publications*: numerous. *Recreations*: playing classical piano, private pilot. *Address*: Department of Biochemistry, Box 357350, University of Washington, Seattle, WA 98195–7350, USA. *T*: (206) 5431741.

**FISCHER, Hartwig**; Director, British Museum, since 2016; *b* Hamburg, 14 Dec. 1962; *m* 1990, Ilaria Piqueras. *Educ*: Univ. of Bonn (Doctorate Philos.). Curator, 19th-century and Modern Art, Kunstmuseum, Basel, 2001–06; Dir, Museum Folkwang, Essen, 2006–12; Dir-Gen., Dresden State Art Collections, 2012–16. *Address*: British Museum, Great Russell Street, WC1B 3DG. *E*: directorate@britishmuseum.org.

**FISCHER, Iván**; conductor; Founder and Music Director, Budapest Festival Orchestra, since 1983; Music Director, Konzerthaus Berlin, and Principal Conductor, Konzerthaus Orchester, Berlin, 2012–18, now Honorary Conductor; *b* Budapest, 20 Jan. 1951; *s* of Sándor Fischer and Éva Boschán; two *s* two *d*. *Educ*: Béla Bartók Music Conservatory, Budapest; Wiener Hochschule für Musik; Mozarteum, Salzburg. Début in London with RPO, 1976; Music Director: Northern Sinfonia, Newcastle, 1979–82; Kent Opera, 1984–89; Lyon Opera House, 1999–2003; Principal Guest Conductor, Cincinnati SO, 1989–96; Principal Guest Conductor, 2006–08, Principal Conductor, 2008–10, Nat. SO, Washington. Concert tours with LSO, to Spain, 1981, USA, 1982, world tour, 1983; concerts with orchestras, including: Berlin Philharmonic, Concertgebouw; Munich Philharmonic; Israel Philharmonic; Orch. de Paris; Orch. of Age of Enlightenment; LA and NY Philharmonics; Cleveland; Philadelphia; San Francisco Symphony; Chicago Symphony; opera prodns in London, Paris, Vienna. Has made over 70 recordings. Patron, British Kódaly Acad.; Founder, Hungarian Mahler Soc. Premio Firenze, 1974; Rupert Foundn Award, BBC, 1976; Gramophone Award for Best Orchestral Recording of Year, 1998; Crystal Award, World Econ. Forum, 1998. Golden Medal Award (Hungary), 1998; Kossuth Prize (Hungary), 2006; Royal Philharmonic Award, 2011; Dutch Ovatie Prize, 2011. Chevalier des Arts et des Lettres (France). *Address*: Budapest Festival Orchestra, Polgár u. 8–10, 1033 Budapest, Hungary.

**FISCHER, Joseph Martin, (Joschka)**; Minister of Foreign Affairs and Deputy Chancellor, Germany, 1998–2005; Managing Partner, Joschka Fischer and Company, since 2009; *b* 12 April 1948; *m* 1st, 1967, Edeltraud (marr. diss. 1984); 2nd, 1984, Inge (marr. diss. 1987); one *s* one *d*; 3rd, 1987, Claudia Bohm (marr. diss. 1999); 4th, 1999, Nicola Leske (marr. diss. 2003); 5th, 2005, Minu Barati. Mem., Green Party, Germany, 1982– (former Leader). State of Hesse: Minister for the Envmt and Energy, 1985–87; Mem., Landtag, 1987–91 (Chm., Green Party); Minister for the Envmt, Energy and Fed. Affairs, and Dep. to Minister-Pres., 1991–94; Mem., Bundestag, 1983–85, 1994–2006; Dep. Mem., Bundesrat, 1985–87; Parly spokesman, Alliance '90/Green Party, Bundestag, 1994–98. Vis. Lectr, Woodrow Wilson Sch. of Public and Internat. Affairs, Princeton Univ., 2006–07. *Publications*: The Red-Green Years (autobiog.), 2007.

**FISCHER BOEL, (Else) Mariann**; Member, European Commission, 2004–10; *b* 15 April 1943; *d* of Hans Boel and Valborg Boel; *m* 1967, Hans Fischer Boel. Mgt Sec., 1965–67, Finance Manager, 1967–71, export co., Copenhagen. Mem., Munkebo Municipal Council, 1982–91, 1994–97. MP (L) Denmark, 1990–2004; Minister for Food, Agriculture and Fisheries, 2001–04.

**FISCHLER, Dr Franz**; Member, European Commission, 1995–2004; Consultant, Franz Fischler Consult GmbH, since 2004; President, European Forum Alpbach, since 2012; *b* 23 Sept. 1946; *s* of Josef Fischler and Theodora Fischler; *m* 1973, Adelheid Hausmann; two *s* two *d*. *Educ*: Univ. for Soil Sci., Vienna (Dr in Natural Scis 1978). Univ. Asst, Dept of Regl Agricl Planning, Inst. for Farm Mgt, Vienna, 1973–79; Tyrol Chamber of Agriculture: Mem., 1979–84; Dir, 1985–89; elected Mem., Nationalrat, 1990, 1994; Fed. Minister of Agric. and Forestry, 1989–94. Grosse Goldene Ehrenzeichen am Bande (Austria), 1993. *Address*: Dörferstrasse 30B, 6067 Absam, Austria.

**FISH, David John**, PhD; non-executive Chairman, United Biscuits, 2004–06 and 2011–14 (Executive Chairman, 2006–11); Director, Fishdance Ltd, since 2013; *b* 31 May 1948; *s* of George Henry and Edith Doreen Fish; *m* 1976, Linda Pamela Robinson; one *s* two *d*. *Educ*: Gateway Grammar Sch., Leicester; Univ. of Sheffield (BSc 1st cl. 1969, Mappin Medal; PhD Metal Physics 1972). Unilever, 1972–74; joined Mars, 1974; Operating Bd, Mars Inc., 1994–2001; Pres., European Snackfoods, 1998–2000; Jt Pres., Masterfoods Europe, 2000–01. Chm., Christian Salveson, 2003–07. Non-exec. Dir, Royal Mail, 2003–08. *Recreations*: cricket, football, ski-ing, golf, breeding and racing horses (flat). *Clubs*: Royal Automobile; Berkshire Golf.

**FISH, Sir David Royden**, Kt 2014; MD; FRCP; Managing Director, UCL Partners, 2009–16; *b* 5 June 1956; *s* of George Henry Fish and Sadie Fish; *m* 1986, Glenda Joyce Parker; one *s* one *d* (twins). *Educ*: Selwyn Coll., Cambridge (BA 1978); King's Coll., London (MB BS 1981; MD 1989). FRCP 1994. Asst Prof., Neurology, McGill Univ., Montreal, 1988–89; Consultant Physician, Nat. Hosp. for Neurology and Neurosurgery, 1989–2010; Prof. of Clinical Neurophysiology and Epilepsy, UCL, 2000–10. Prof. Med. Dir (Specialist Hosps), UCL Hosps NHS Foundn Trust, 2001–09. *Publications*: contribs to learned jls and books on medical subjects incl. epilepsy, brain imaging, safety of video games and health care. *Recreations*: trekking, English music hall.

**FISH, David Stanley**, CBE 2007; Head, Zimbabwe, Department for International Development, 2009–12; *b* 4 Oct. 1948; *s* of John and Phyllis Fish; *m* 1st, 1971, Sandra Templeton (marr. diss. 1990); two *d*; 2nd, 1992, Marion Fleming Semple; two *d*. *Educ*: Baines Grammar Sch., Poulton-le-Fylde. Department for International Development: Head: Develt Educn Unit, 1979–81; Manpower Policy Unit, 1981–84; Dependent Territories Section, British Develt Div. in the Caribbean, Barbados, 1985–86; Accounts Dept, 1986–88; Overseas Pensions Dept, 1988–92; Procurement, Appts and NGO Dept, 1993–97; Eastern Africa, Nairobi, 1997–99; Dir of Human Resources, 2000–04; Dir, Africa, then E and Central Africa, 2004–09. *Recreations*: sport, politics, dog walking, supporting Blackpool and Crystal Palace. *Address*: 34 Shawton Road, Chapelton, Strathaven, Lanarkshire ML10 6RY. *Club*: Chapelton Inn Racing.

**FISH, David Thomas**; QC 1997; a Recorder, 1994–2006; *b* 23 July 1949; *s* of Tom Fish and Gladys (née Durkin); *m* 1989, Angelina Brunhilde Dennett; one *s* one *d*. *Educ*: Ashton-under-Lyne Grammar Sch.; Univ. of Econs (LLB). Called to the Bar, Inner Temple, 1973. Non-exec. Chm., 32 Red plc, 2005. *Recreations*: horse-racing, golf. *Address*: Deans Court Chambers, 24 St John Street, Manchester M3 4DF. *T*: (0161) 214 6000.

**FISH, Dame Jocelyn (Barbara)**, DNZM 2009 (DCNZM 2001); CBE 1991; voluntary community worker, since 1959; farming partner, 1959–90; *b* 29 Sept. 1930; *d* of John Arthur Green and Edna Marion Green (née Garton); *m* 1959, Robert John Malthus Fish; one *s* two *d*. *Educ*: Hamilton High Sch., New Zealand; Auckland Univ. (BA); Auckland Teachers' College (cert.). Secondary school teacher, NZ and UK, 1953–59. Nat. Pres., Nat.

Council of Women of NZ, 1986–90; (various offices) NZ Fedn of Univ. Women, and Anglican Women; Chm. Policy Cttee, survey, NZ Women—family, employment and education, Centre for Population Studies, Univ. of Waikato, 1995–98. NZ Deleg., UN Conf. on Women, Nairobi, 1985. Member: Film Censorship Bd of Review, 1981–84; Nat. Commn for Australian Bicentenary, 1987–88; Nat. Commn for UNESCO, 1989–94; Broadcasting Standards Authority, 1989–91; Transport Accident Investigation Commn, 1990–95; Hamilton Dist Legal Services Cttee, 1992–97; NZ Dental Council Complaints Assessment Cttee, 1995–2001. Member, Board: Waikato Br., Fedn of Univ. Women, 1991–99 (Chm.); Hamilton Community Law Centre Trust, 1994–2000 (Chm.); Hamilton Combined Christian Foodbank Trust, 1997–99; Waikato Anglican Social Services Trust, 2000–04 (Chm.). Councillor, Piako County Council, 1980–89. JP 1984–2010. Hon. Fellow, Waikato Inst. of Technol., 2003. NZ Sesquicentenary Commemoration Medal, 1990; NZ Suffrage Commemoration Medal, 1993; Univ. of Waikato Medal, 2012. *Recreations:* music, literature, family, travel, watching politics. *Address:* 63 Gilbass Avenue, Hamilton, New Zealand. *T:* (7) 839 1512.

**FISH, His Honour Peter Stuart;** a Circuit Judge, 1994–2005; *b* 18 Dec. 1938; *s* of Geoffrey Chadwick Fish and Emma (*née* Wood); *m* 1963, Nola Ann Worrall; two *s* one *d* (and one *d* decd). *Educ:* Rydal Sch.; Trinity Hall, Cambridge (MA). Admitted solicitor, 1963; practised in Southport, 1964–87; Dist Registrar, subseq. Dist Judge, Manchester, 1987–94; a Recorder, 1991–94. *Recreations:* music, gardening, golf, bridge, woodcarving.

**FISH, Wendy;** Director, British Architectural Library, Royal Institute of British Architects, since 2013; *b* Dulwich, London; *d* of John Alfred Fish and Elsie Joy Fish; *m* 2002, Andrew Geoffrey Greenhalgh. *Educ:* Kingsdale Comp. Sch., Dulwich; Leicester Poly. (BA Hons 1981); Poly. of North London (DipLib). Curator, 1984–89, Inf. Services Manager, 1989–96, Nat. Art Liby, V&A Mus.; Hd, User Services, Wellcome Liby, Wellcome Trust, 1996–2009; Dep. Dir, British Architl Liby, RIBA, 2010–13. *Recreations:* art, architecture, current affairs, walking, sport, Arsenal FC. *Address:* Royal Institute of British Architects, 66 Portland Place, W1B 1AD. *T:* (020) 7307 3695. *E:* wendy.fish@riba.org.

**FISHBURN, (John) Dudley;** Chairman: Bluecube Technology Ltd, since 2009; Mulvaney Capital Management, since 2011; Baring Vostok Investments Ltd, since 2013; GFI Markets Ltd, since 2015; *b* 8 June 1946; *s* of John Eskdale Fishburn and Bunting Fishburn; *m* 1981, Victoria, *y d* of Sir John Dennis, (Sir Jack), Boles, MBE; two *s* two *d*. *Educ:* Eton Coll.; Harvard Univ. (BA). Exec. Editor, The Economist, 1979–88. MP (C) Kensington, July 1988–1997. Parliamentary Private Secretary: FCO, 1989–90; DTI, 1990–93. Chairman: HFC Bank, 1998–2009; Henderson Smaller Cos Investment Trust plc, 2003–11. Non-executive Director: Saatchi & Saatchi, 1998–2003; Philip Morris Inc. (formerly Atria Inc.), 1998–2014; Beazley Gp plc, 2002–10; HSBC Bank plc, 2003–09; GFI Ltd, 2010–; Kyte Gp Ltd, 2010–15; Adviser: J. P. Morgan, 1988–96; T. T. Internat., 1997–2011; Baring Private Equity, 1997–2008. Chm., Standing Cttee on Social Scis, 1993–96, Library Cttee, 1996–2006, Harvard Univ.; Mem., Bd of Overseers, Harvard Univ., 1989–95; Pres., Harvard Club of London, 1970–90. Governor, English National Ballet, 1989–95; Chairman: Trustees, Open Univ., 1995–2001; Library Vis. Cttee, Cambridge Univ., 2005–14; Member of Council: Nat. Trust, 1993–2005 (Hon. Treas., 1996–2002); Prison Reform Trust, 1993–2000; Foundn for Liver Res. (formerly Liver Res. Trust), 1995–; Dulwich Picture Gall. Council, 1997–2001; Royal Oak Foundn (USA), 1997–2004; Reading Univ. Council, 2002–12. Chm., Theale Green Acad., 2013–. Gov., Peabody Trust, 2000–11; Trustee, Heritage of London Trust, 2010– (Chm., 2011–). Pres., W Berks Conservative Assoc., 2000–. Chm., Friends of Silchester Archaeological Site, 2003–. Fellow, Centre for the Advanced Study of India, Univ. of Penn, 2005–13. Editor, The Economist's World in 1993, and annually until 2003; Associate Editor, The Economist, 1989–2003. DUniv: Open, 2002; Reading, 2013. Parly Radical of the Year, 1992. *Recreations:* sailing, cooking. *Address:* The Old Rectory, Englefield, Berks RG7 5EP. *Club:* Brooks's.

See also N. E. C. Boles.

**FISHER,** family name of **Baron Fisher**.

**FISHER,** 4th Baron *cr* 1909, of Kilverstone, co. Norfolk; **Patrick Vavasseur Fisher;** *b* Cambridge, England, 14 June 1953; *er s* of 3rd Baron Fisher, DSC and of Elizabeth Ann Penelope Holt; *S* father, 2012; *m* 1977, Lady Karen Jean Carnegie, *er d* of 13th Earl of Northesk; two *s* four *d* (of whom one *s* one *d* are twins) (and one *s* decd). *Educ:* Cheam Sch., Newbury; Stowe. *Recreations:* shooting, woodland management. *Heir: er* surv. *s* Hon. Benjamin Carnegie Vavasseur Fisher, *b* 2 June 1986. *Address:* Kilverstone Hall, Thetford, Norfolk IP24 2RL. *T:* (01842) 751122. *E:* patrick.fisher@kilverstonehall.com. *Club:* Royal Thames Yacht.

**FISHER, Adrian;** maze designer, inventor and author; Founder and Chairman, Adrian Fisher Design (formerly Adrian Fisher Mazes) Ltd, since 1983; *b* 5 Aug. 1951; *s* of Dr James Frederick Fisher and Rosemary (*née* Sterling-Hill); *m* 1st, 1975, Dorothy Jane Pollard (marr. diss. 1996; she *d* 2009); two *d*; 2nd, 1997, Marie Ann Butterworth; one *s*. *Educ:* Oundle Sch.; Portsmouth Poly. Over 700 mazes created in 40 countries, 1979–; designer: world's first cornfield maize maze, Pennsylvania, 1993, and subseq. over 400 maize mazes; over 40 hedge mazes, including: Leeds Castle; Blenheim Palace; Scone Palace; Speke Hall; pioneer: of over 60 mirror mazes, including mazes at: Wookey Hole Caves; Hamburg Dungeon; Navy Pier, Chicago; Birmingham Sea Life Centre; Absolut Amaze, at Oxo Gall., London, 2002; Warwick Castle; Tokyo Dome; Hollywood Wax Mus., TN; PortAventura theme park, Spain; Tokyo Tower, Singapore Sci. Centre, 2017; Jewel, Changi Airport, Singapore; of brick-path-in-grass mazes, and foaming fountain water mazes; walk-through parting waterfalls, foaming fountain gates and wrought-iron maze gates in mazes; inventor: 7-sided Fisher Paver system for decorative brick paving; (jtly) Mitre Tile system for paving, tiling and decorative patterns, including 24ft high Mitre mosaic in SciTec Bldg, Oundle Sch.; designer of puzzles for 2000 and 2006 World Puzzle Championships; one-man show: An Amazing Art: Contemporary Labyrinths, Norton Mus. of Art, W Palm Beach, Florida, 1997. Set 6 Guinness world records for progressively larger cornfield mazes in USA and England, 1993–2003; Guinness world record: (200 metres) for world's tallest maze on facades of Maze Tower, Dubai, 2015; for world's largest hedge maze, Ningbo, China, 2017. Dir, 1991—The Year of the Maze, British tourism campaign. Mem., Eur. Bd, Themed Entertainment Assoc., 2005–08. Liveryman: Soc. of Apothecaries, 1979–; Gardeners' Co., 1991–. Gold Medal for Beatles' Maze, Liverpool Internat. Garden Fest., 1984; Resorgimento Award, Univ. of Tennessee at Knoxville, 2003. *Publications:* The Art of the Maze, 1990; Secrets of the Maze, 1997; Mazes and Follies, 2004; Mazes and Labyrinths, 2004; The Amazing Book of Mazes, 2006. *Recreations:* gardening, photography, water-colour painting, recreational mathematics, keeping sheep, flying quadcopter. *Address:* Adrian Fisher Design Ltd, Portman Lodge Studios, Durweston, Dorset DT11 0QA. *T:* (01258) 458845. *E:* adrian@adrianfisherdesign.com. *W:* www.adrianfisherdesign.com.

**FISHER, Andrew;** see Fisher, J. A.

**FISHER, Andrew Charles;** Chief Executive, Towry Group (formerly JS & P Holdings, then Towry Law Group), 2006–14; *b* 22 June 1961; *s* of Harold Fisher and Jessie Fisher (now Stanley); *m*; two *s*; *m* 2009, Caroline Gina (*née* Moss); one *d*. *Educ:* Birmingham Univ. (BSc Hons Econs). Mktg Manager, Unilever PLC, 1982–87; Partner, Coopers & Lybrand Mgt Consultancy, 1987–91; Sales and Mktg Dir, Standard Chartered Bank, Equitor Div., 1991–94; Man. Dir, Rangeley Co. Ltd, 1994–97; Strategic Advr, NatWest Wealth Mgt, 1997–98; Gp Commercial Dir, Coutts NatWest Gp, 1998–2000; Chief Exec., Coutts Gp, 2000–02; Partner, Carlyle Gp, 2002–03; Chief Exec., CPP Gp, 2003–04; Gp CEO, Cox Insurance, 2004; Exec. Chm., JS & P Hldgs, 2005–06. Non-executive Director: Benfield Gp Ltd, 2003–08; C. Hoare & Co., 2015–; Smith & Williamson, 2018–; Adviser: Ondra Partners, 2014–; Davy Gp, 2015–. *Recreations:* ski-ing, golf, squash, scuba diving. *Clubs:* Mosimann's; Wentworth Golf.

**FISHER, Most Rev. Anthony Colin Joseph;** see Sydney, Archbishop of, (RC).

**FISHER, Carol Ann;** Chief Executive, COI Communications (formerly Central Office of Information), 1999–2002; *b* 13 April 1954; *d* of Joseph and Gladys Fisher. *Educ:* Univ. of Birmingham (BA Hons Medieval and Modern Hist.). Brand Manager, Bisto, RHM Foods, 1979–81; Sen. Mktg Manager and various other posts, Grand Metropolitan Brewing, 1982–88; Mktg Dir, Holsten Distributors, 1989–94; Gen. Manager, Mktg and Commercial, Courage Internat., 1994–95; Man. Dir, CLT-UFA UK Radio Sales, 1996–98. Chief Advr to Govt on Mktg Commns, 2002. Member: Women in Advertising and Communications (Pres., 2000–01); Mktg Soc.; Mktg Gp GB. *Recreations:* walking, long haul travel.

**FISHER, Christopher Charles;** Chair, Marshall Aid Commemoration Commission, since 2016; *b* Weston-super-Mare, 5 Oct. 1953; *s* of Edward Charles and Jean Fisher; *m* 1981, Carole Ann Wilson; two *d*. *Educ:* Woodroffe Sch., Lyme Regis; Univ. of Reading (BA Hist. 1976); Kennedy Sch. of Govt, Harvard Univ. (MPP 1978). Pres., Students' Union, Reading Univ., 1974–75; Kennedy Schol., 1976–78; economist, Econ. Directorate, CBI, 1978–80; Lazard Bros, 1980–2003: Lazard NY (on secondment), 1984–85; Dir, 1987–2003; Man. Dir, 2000–03; Vice-Chm., Corporate Finance, KPMG, 2004–06; Sen. Partner, Penfida, 2006–14 (Sen. Advr, 2014–). Non-executive Director: Kelda Gp plc, 2003–08; Segro plc, 2012–; Nat. Savings & Investments, 2017–; Chairman: Southern Cross Healthcare, 2011; Bank of Ireland UK, 2012–16 (non-exec. Dir, 2010–12). Trustee, Imperial War Mus., 2002–10. Pres. Council, Univ. of Reading, 2009–16. Hon. DLitt Reading, 2016. Liveryman, Cutlers' Co., 1998– (Master, 2011–12). *Address:* Penfida Ltd, One Carey Lane, EC2V 8AE.

**FISHER, (Christopher) Mark,** CBE 2010; Director General, Cabinet Office, and Secretary, Grenfell Tower Inquiry, since 2017; *b* 8 Oct. 1960; *s* of late Christopher Forsyth Fisher and of (Nadia) Ruth Reeve Fisher (*née* Angel); *m* 1997, Helen, *d* of late Patrick Daniel Fitzgibbon and of Marie Fitzgibbon, Lymm, Cheshire. *Educ:* King Edward's Sch., Bath; Lady Margaret Hall, Oxford (BA Hons PPE). Jun. posts, DHSS, 1983–87; Principal: Social Security Policy Gp, DSS, 1988–90; Econ. Secretariat, Cabinet Office, 1990–92; speech writer for Sec. of State for Social Security, 1992; mgt posts, 1993–97, Personnel and Communications Dir, 1997–2000, Benefits Agency; Human Resources Dir, DSS, subseq. DWP, 2000–01; Dir, Performance and Product Mgt, then Business Strategy, Jobcentre Plus, DWP, 2001–05; Chief Exec., Sector Skills Develt Agency, 2005–08; Dir, Benefit Strategy and Skills, then Jobseekers and Skills, DWP, 2008–11; Social Justice Dir, DWP, 2011–14; Dir, Office for Civil Society and Innovation, Cabinet Office, then Office for Civil Society, DCMS, 2014–17. *Recreations:* good company, railways, canals. *Club:* Reform.

**FISHER, David Paul;** QC 1996; a Recorder, since 1991; *b* 30 April 1949; *s* of late Percy Laurence Fisher and Doris Mary Fisher; *m* 1st, 1971, Cary Maria Cicely Lamberton (*d* 1977); one *d*; 2nd, 1979, Diana Elizabeth Dolby. *Educ:* Felsted Sch. Called to the Bar, Gray's Inn, 1973, Bencher, 2003; Asst Recorder, 1987. Hd of Chambers, 2010–16. Member: Gen. Council of the Bar, 1997–2000; Advocacy Studies Bd, 1997–2001; Criminal Procedure Rule Cttee, 2004–08. *Recreations:* travel, sport, gardening, cinema.

**FISHER, Duncan Mark,** OBE 2009; Research Policy and Innovation (formerly International Programmes Director), Family Initiative, since 2016; *b* 3 Nov. 1961; *s* of Humphrey and Helga Fisher; *m* Clare; two *d*. *Educ:* Corpus Christi Coll., Cambridge (BA Natural Scis 1984; MPhil Theol 1986); School of Slavonic and East European Studies, London (MA Area Studies 1989). Founder and CEO, East West Environment, 1989–95; Founder and CEO, 1994–2003, Trustee, 2003–08, Action for Conservation through Tourism, subseq. Travel Foundn; Co-Founder and Chief Exec., Fathers Direct, subseq. Fatherhood Inst., 1999–2009; Co-Founder and Dir, Family Info Ltd, 2007–11; Project Director: Kids in the Middle, 2012–16; Child&Family Blog, 2014–16; Family Included, 2015–16. Mem., Equal Opportunities Commn, 2005–07. Hon. Fellow, Faculty of Health and Social Care, Univ. of Chester, 2009–14. *Recreations:* making lists, eating very good chocolate, early music, travelling with my family, log fires. *Address:* 37 Upper House Farm, Crickhowell, Powys NP8 1BZ. *T:* 07950 028704.

**FISHER, Her Honour Elisabeth Neill;** a Circuit Judge, 1989–2015; *b* 24 Nov. 1944; *d* of late Kenneth Neill Fisher and Lorna Charlotte Honor Fisher. *Educ:* Oxford High Sch. for Girls (GPDST); Cambridge Univ. (MA); Cardiff Univ. (LLM Canon Law, 2011). Called to the Bar, Inner Temple, 1968, Bencher, 2003. A Recorder, 1982–89. Mem. Senate, Inns of Court, 1983–86; Pres., Council of HM Circuit Judges, 2004. Member: Criminal Cttee, Judicial Studies Bd, 1995–98; Criminal Justice Consultative Council, 1992–99. Chm., Home Sec.'s Adv. Bd on Restricted Patients, 1998–2003. Dep. Chancellor, Bangor Diocese, 2014–16; Licensed Reader, Anglican Ch, 2018. DUniv UCE, 1997. *Address:* c/o Queen Elizabeth II Law Courts, Newton Street, Birmingham B4 7NA.

**FISHER, Henrietta Lucy Anne, (Henny);** see Finch, H. L. A.

**FISHER, Dame Jacqueline, (Dame Jackie),** DBE 2010 (CBE 2005); Chief Executive, NCG, until 2013; *b* 10 March 1956; *d* of Stanley and Anne Walton; *m* 1st, 1974, Thomas Fisher (marr. diss. 1978); two *s*; 2nd, 1996, David Collier. *Educ:* Leeds Univ. (BA Hons 1979; MA 1980; MSc 1989). Asst Principal, St Helen's Coll., 1989–94; Vice Principal, 1994–97, Chief Exec. and Principal, 1997–2000, Tameside Coll.; Chief Exec. and Principal, Newcastle Coll., 2000; interim Chief Exec., Barnfield Fedn, 2014. Member: Bd, One North East, RDA, 2000–07; Council, HEFCE, 2001–08. FCGI. *Recreations:* cinema, food, walking, travel in Central and Eastern Europe.

**FISHER, (Jervis) Andrew;** QC 2009; *b* 23 Oct. 1955; *s* of John George Fisher and Joyce Fisher (*née* Horton); *m* 1982, Catherine Maura Swatman; one *s* one *d*. *Educ:* Malvern; Queen Mary Coll., Univ. of London (LLB). Called to the Bar, Gray's Inn, 1980; in practice as a barrister, Midland Circuit, 1980–. Hd, Citadel Chambers, 2004–. *Address:* Citadel Chambers, 190 Corporation Street, Birmingham B4 6QD. *T:* (0121) 233 8500, *Fax:* (0121) 233 8501. *E:* andrew.fisher@citadelchambers.com.

**FISHER, Joan;** Headteacher, King Edward VI Camp Hill School for Girls, Birmingham, 1992–2003; *b* 24 Sept. 1939; *d* of late A. R. Bowler and R. Bowler (*née* Byatt); *m* 1969, Ronald William Fisher; four *d* (incl. triplets). *Educ:* Univ. of Leeds (BA Modern Langs); Univ. of York (Schoolteacher Fellowship); Inst. of Educn, London (MA). Teacher in comprehensive schs, Yorkshire and Surrey, 1962–89: Holme Valley GS, 1962–66; Middlesbrough Girls' High, 1966–69; Acklam High, 1970–72; Framwellgate Moor, 1972–73; Glebelands, 1974–82; Tomlinscote, 1982–89; Dep. Headteacher, Westcliff High

Sch. for Girls, 1989–92. Chm. Govs, Northway Infant Sch., Tewkesbury, 2007–. FRSA 1997. *Publications:* teaching materials for German, including: Achtung! Achtung!, 1985; Begegnungen, 1985; Lesekiste, A, 1987, B, 1988; Pack's An!, 1991.

**FISHER, Prof. John,** CBE 2011; PhD, DEng; CEng, FREng, FIMechE, FIPEM; FMedSci; Professor of Mechanical Engineering, University of Leeds, since 1993 (Deputy Vice-Chancellor, 2006–16); *b* 10 Aug. 1955; *s* of James Fisher and Joan Fisher; *m* 1995, Eileen Ingham; two *d*. *Educ:* Univ. of Birmingham (BSc 1st Cl. Physics 1976); Univ. of Glasgow (PhD Bioengrg 1986); Univ. of Leeds (DEng 1996). CEng 1983; FIMechE 1995; FIPEM 1998; CSci 2005; FREng 2009. Bioengr, Dept of Clinical Phys and Bioengrg, Greater Glasgow Health Bd, 1978–87; University of Leeds: Lectr, 1987–93; Dir, Inst. of Med. and Biol Engrg, 2001–16; Pro-Vice-Chancellor, 2001–06. Chm., Tissue Regenix Ltd, 2007–12; Dir, Bitecic Ltd, 2006–11. Mem., EPSRC, 2011–15. FMedSci 2012. *Publications:* 350 articles in jls. *Recreations:* walking, swimming, running. *Address:* School of Mechanical Engineering, University of Leeds, Leeds LS2 9JT. *T:* (0113) 343 2128. *E:* j.fisher@leeds.ac.uk.

**FISHER, Jonathan Simon;** QC 2003; *b* 24 Feb. 1958; *s* of Aubrey and Pauline Fisher; *m* 1980, Paula Goldberg; two *s* two *d*. *Educ:* Poly. of N London (BA 1st Cl. Hons); St Catharine's Coll., Cambridge (LLB; LLM). Called to the Bar, Gray's Inn, 1980; Lectr, Chelmer Inst., 1981–82; Mem. *ad eund*, Inner Temple, 1984; in practice as barrister, specialising in business crime and contentious tax cases, 1982–; Standing Counsel to IR, CCC and London Crown Courts, 1991–2003; Associate Mem., Red Lion Chambers, London, 2016–. Comr, Bill of Rights Commn, MoJ, 2011–12. Member: Steering Gp, Assets Recovery Agency, 2003–06; Legal Panel, Accountancy Investigation and Disciplinary, then Accountancy Actuarial and Discipline, Bd, 2005–09; Red Tape Initiative, 2017–; Trustee Dir, Fraud Adv. Panel, 2006–10. Hon. Mem., Steering Gp, London Fraud Forum, 2007–. Specialist Advr, Treasury Cttee, H of C, 2014–. Exec. Mem., 2005–06 and 2011–13, Chm. of Res., 2006–10, Hon. Sec., 2015–17, Soc. of Conservative Lawyers. Sen. Vis. Fellow, City Univ., 1986–2004; Visiting Professor: Cass Business Sch., City Univ., 2004–07; LSE, 2006– (Vis. Fellow, 2004–06); Hebrew Univ., Jerusalem, 2013–14, 2015–18; Hon. Vis. Prof., City Law Sch., City Univ., 2011–13. Fellow, Chartered Inst. of Taxation, 2009–; Accredited Trusts and Estates Practitioner, 2010–; Reg. Practitioner, Dubai Internat. Financial Court, 2015–. Gen. Ed., Lloyds Law Reports: Financial Crime, 2008–; Mem., Editl Bd, Simon's Taxes, Butterworths Looseleaf, 2011–. Hon. LLD UWE, 2015. *Publications:* (jtly) Pharmacy Law and Practice, 1995, 4th edn 2006; (jtly) Law of Investor Protection, 1997, 2nd edn 2003; (contrib.) Fighting Financial Crime in the Global Economic Crisis, 2014; (contrib.) The British Bill of Rights: protecting freedom under the law, 2015; (jtly) Criminal Finances Act 2017, 2018; contrib. articles to Conservative Liberty Forum, Policy Exchange, British Tax Review, Law and Financial Markets Review, Criminal Law Review. *Recreations:* theatre, football, arts, history, travelling. *Address:* Bright Line Law, Central Court, 25 Southampton Buildings, WC2A 1AL. *T:* (020) 3709 9471. *E:* jf@brightlinelaw.co.uk. *Clubs:* Carlton, Walbrook.

**FISHER, Laura Mary;** see Clarke, L. M.

**FISHER, Mark,** FSA; *b* 29 Oct. 1944; *s* of Sir Nigel Fisher, MC and of Lady Gloria Flower; *m* 1971, Ingrid Geach (marr. diss. 1999); two *s* two *d*; *m* 2010, Gillian FitzHugh; two step *d*. *Educ:* Eton College; Trinity College, Cambridge (MA). Documentary film producer and script writer, 1966–75; Principal, Tattenhall Centre of Education, 1975–83. Mem., Staffs CC, 1981–85 (Chm., Libraries Cttee, 1981–83). Contested (Lab) Leek, 1979. MP (Lab) Stoke-on-Trent Central, 1983–2010. An Opposition Whip, 1985–87; Opposition spokesman on the arts, 1987–92, 1993–97, on Citizen's Charter, 1992–93; Parly Under-Sec. of State, Dept for Culture, Media and Sport, 1997–98. Mem., Treasury and CS Select Cttee, 1983–85. Chm., Parliament First, 2003–10. Dep. Pro-Chancellor, Keele Univ., 1989–97. Vis. Fellow, St Antony's Coll., Oxford, 2000–01. Member: BBC Gen. Adv. Council, 1988–95; Council, PSI, 1989–95; Acceptance in Lieu Panel, 1998–2012; Museums and Galls Commn, 1998–2002; Develt Cttee, RA, 2010–. Trustee: Britten-Pears Foundn, 1998–2007; Estorick Collection of Modern Italian Art, 2000–14; Hunterian Museum, 2005–14; Friends of the Nat. Libraries, 2005–09; British Sporting Art Trust, 2011–17; Member: Bd, Qatar Mus Authy, 2007–10 (Mem., Internat. and Policy Cttees, 2010–); Fitzwilliam Mus. Develt Trust, 2011–. FSA 2006. Hon. FRIBA 1992; Hon. FRCA 1993. Author of stage plays: Brave New Town, 1974; The Cutting Room, 1990. Patron, Ledbury Poetry Fest., 2011–. *Publications:* City Centres, City Cultures, 1988; (ed jtly) Whose Cities?, 1991; (with Richard Rogers) A New London, 1992; Britain's Best Museums and Galleries, 2004; Hwaet! (poetry), 2016. *Address:* 111 Sixth Avenue, W10 4HH. *T:* (020) 8969 4067. *Club:* Grillions.

**FISHER, Mark;** see Fisher, C. M.

**FISHER, Prof. Michael Ellis,** FRS 1971; Distinguished University Professor and Regents' Professor, Institute for Physical Science and Technology, University of Maryland, 1993–2012, now Emeritus (Wilson H. Elkins Distinguished Professor, 1987–93); Horace White Professor of Chemistry, Physics and Mathematics, Cornell University, 1973–89, Emeritus Professor, 2012; *b* 3 Sept. 1931; *s* of Harold Wolf Fisher and Jeanne Marie Fisher (née Halter); *m* 1954, Sorrel Castillejo; three *s* one *d*. *Educ:* King's Coll., London. BSc 1951, PhD 1957, FKC 1981. Flying Officer (Educn), RAF, 1952–53; London Univ. Postgraduate Studentship, 1953–56; DSIR Sen. Research Fellow, 1956–58. King's College, London: Lectr in Theoretical Physics, 1958–62; Reader in Physics, 1962–64; Prof. of Physics, 1965–66; Cornell University: Prof. of Chemistry and Maths, 1966–73; Chm., Dept of Chemistry, 1975–78. Guest Investigator, Rockefeller Inst., New York, 1963–64; Vis. Prof. in Applied Physics, Stanford Univ., 1970–71; Walker Ames Prof., Univ. of Washington, 1977; Vis. Prof. of Physics, MIT, 1979; Sherman Fairchild Disting. Scholar, CIT, 1984; Vis. Prof. in Theoretical Physics, Oxford, 1985; Lorentz Prof., Leiden, 1993; Vis. Prof., Nat. Inst. of Sci. and Technol., USA, 1994. Lectures: Buhl, Carnegie-Mellon, 1971; 32nd Richtmyer Meml, 1973; 17th Fritz London Meml, 1975; Morris Loeb, Harvard, 1979; H. L. Welsh, Toronto, 1979; Bakerian, Royal Soc., 1979; Welch Foundn, Texas, 1979; Alpheas Smith, Ohio State Univ., 1982; Laird Meml, Univ. of Western Ontario, 1983; Fries, Rensselaer Polytechnic Inst., NY, 1984; Amos de-Shalit Meml, Weizmann Inst., Rehovoth, 1985; Cherwell-Simon, Oxford, 1985; Marker, Penn. State Univ., 1988; Nat. Sci. Council, Taiwan, 1989; Hamilton Meml, Princeton Univ., 1990; 65th J. W. Gibbs, Amer. Math. Soc., Condon, Univ. of Colorado, and M. S. Green Meml, Temple Univ., 1992; R. and B. Sackler, Tel Aviv, 1992; Lennard-Jones, RSC, 1995; G. N. Lewis, UC Berkeley, 1996; Hirschfelder, Wisconsin Univ., 1995; Baker, in Chemistry, Cornell Univ., 1997; F. G. Brickwedde, in Physics, Johns Hopkins Univ., 1998; Michelson, Case Western Reserve Univ., 1999; T. A. Edison Meml, Naval Res. Lab., Washington, 2000; J. R. Oppenheimer, Univ. of Calif, Berkeley, 2006; C. V. Raman Meml, Indian Inst. Sci., Bangalore, 2007; Homi Bhabha Meml, Tata Inst. Fundamental Res., Mumbai, 2007; E. L. Hudspeth Centennial, Univ. of Texas, Austin, 2007; Mark Kac Meml, Los Alamos Nat. Lab., 2008; Seymour Sherman Meml, Indiana Univ., 2009; Loeb-Lee Harvard Univ., 2017; Philip Taylor Celebration, Case Western Reserve Univ., 2018. Mem. Council and Vice-Pres., Royal Soc., 1993–95. Mem., Amer. Philos. Soc., 1993. John Simon Guggenheim Memorial Fellow, 1970–71, 1978–79; Fellow, Amer. Acad. of Arts and Scis, 1979; FAAAS 1986; For. Associate, National Acad. of Sciences, USA, 1983; Foreign Member: Brazilian Acad. of Scis, 1996; Royal Norwegian Soc. of Scis and Letters, 2003–. Hon. FRSE 1986; Hon. Fellow, Indian Acad. of Scis, Bangalore, 2000. Hon. DSc Yale, 1987; Hon. DPhil Tel Aviv, 1992; Hon. PhD Weizman Inst. of Sci., 2009; Dr *hc* École Normale Supérieure de Lyon, 2012. Irving Langmuir Prize in Chemical Physics, Amer. Phys. Soc., 1970; Award in Phys. and Math. Scis, NY Acad. of Scis, 1978; Guthrie Medal, Inst. of Physics, 1980; Wolf Prize in Physics, State of Israel, 1980; Michelson-Morley Award, Case-Western Reserve Univ., 1982; James Murray Luck Award, National Acad. of Sciences, USA, 1983; Boltzmann Medal, Internat. Union of Pure and Applied Physics, 1983; Lars Onsager Medal, Norwegian Inst. of Technol., 1993; Onsager Meml Prize, Amer. Phys. Soc., 1995; Hildebrand Award, Amer. Chem. Soc., 1995; Royal Medal, Royal Soc., 2005; Frontiers of Knowledge Award in Basic Scis, BBVA Foundn, Madrid, 2010; Rudranath Capildeo Award for Applied Sci. and Technol., Gold Medal, State of Trinidad and Tobago, 2015. *Publications:* Analogue Computing at Ultra-High Speed (with D. M. MacKay), 1962; The Nature of Critical Points (Univ. of Colorado) 1964, (Moscow) 1968; contribs to Proc. Roy. Soc., Phys. Rev., Phys. Rev. Lett., Jl Sci. Insts, Jl Math. Phys., Arch. Rational Mech. Anal., Jl Chem. Phys., Commun. Math. Phys., Rept Prog. Phys., Rev. Mod. Phys., Physica, Proc. Nat. Acad. Sci., USA, Biophys. Jl, etc. *Recreations:* Flamenco guitar, travel. *Address:* Institute for Physical Science and Technology, University of Maryland, College Park, MD 20742–8510, USA. *T:* (301) 4054819.

**FISHER, Dr Paul Gregory;** Chairman, London Bullion Market Association, since 2016; *b* Rochford, 7 Sept. 1958; *s* of late Jack Nichol Archibald Fisher and Maisie Joan Fisher; *m* 1983, Susan Mary Gill; one *s* one *d*. *Educ:* Univ. of Bristol (BSSocSci Econs with Stats 1980); Univ. of Warwick (MA Econs 1983; PhD Econs 1990). Res. Associate, ESRC Macroeconomic Modelling Bureau, Univ. of Warwick, 1983–90; Bank of England: Analyst, then Manager, 1990–94; Hd, Conjunctural Assessment and Projections Div., 1995–98; Private Sec. to Governor, 1999–2001; Hd, Foreign Exchange Div., 2002–08; Mem., Monetary Policy Cttee Secretariat, 1998 and 2006–08; Chm., Foreign Exchange Jt Standing Cttee, 2002–08; Exec. Dir, Mkts and Mem., Monetary Policy Cttee, 2009–14; Mem., Interim Financial Policy Cttee, 2011–13; Exec. Dir, Supervisory Risk Specialists and Regulatory Ops, and Dep. Hd, Prudential Regulation Authy, 2014–16; Member: High-Level Experts Gp on Sustainable Finance, EC, 2016–18; UK Green Finance Task Force, 2017–18. Associate, Systemic Policy Partnership LLP, 2016–. Chm., 2011–, Vis. Prof., 2019–, London Inst. of Banking & Finance (formerly ifs Sch. of Finance, later ifs UC); non-exec. Dir, UK Debt Mgt Office, 2016–. Fellow, Inst. for Sustainable Leadership, Univ. of Cambridge, 2018– (Sen. Associate, 2016–18); Sen. Res. Fellow, DAFM Res. Centre, KCL Business Sch., 2018–. Mem. Adv. Bd, Centre for Competition Policy, UEA, 2012–. Vis. Prof., Richmond, Amer. Internat. Univ. in London, 2012–. *Publications:* (contrib.) Models of the UK Economy: a review by the ESRC Macroeconomic Modelling Bureau, 1984, a second review, 1985, a third review, 1986, a fourth review, 1987; Rational Expectations in Macroeconomic Models, 1992; articles in Econ. Jl, Jl of Econ. Dynamics and Control, Econ. Modelling, Oxford Bulletin of Econ. Statistics, etc. *Address:* London Bullion Market Association, 1–2 Royal Exchange Buildings, Royal Exchange, EC3V 3LF. *E:* pgfpolicy@btinternet.com.

**FISHER, Paul Richard;** Chief Executive (formerly Group Managing Director), Jockey Club Racecourses Ltd, since 2008; *b* Gillingham, Kent, 24 Jan. 1965; *s* of Victor and Sheila Fisher; *m* 1998, Jacqueline Schooling; one *s* one *d*. *Educ:* Poly. of Central London (BA Hons). CPFA 1991. Sen. Accountant, 1990–92, Asst Chief Exec., 1992–95, Rochester CC; Dep. Finance Dir, Medway Council, 1995–97; Finance Director: Gillingham FC, 1997–2000; United Racecourses, 2000–05; Man. Dir, Kempton Park Racecourse, 2005–08. *Recreations:* cricket, football, horseracing, all sports, family, wine! *Address:* Jockey Club, 75 High Holborn, WC1V 6LS. *E:* paul.fisher@thejockeyclub.co.uk. *Clubs:* Ivy; Bobbing Court Cricket; Reigatians Rugby Football, Reigate Priory Cricket, Reigate Heath Golf.

**FISHER, Rev. Canon Peter Timothy;** Vicar, Maney, 2002–10; *b* 7 July 1944; *s* of late Rev. James Atherton Fisher; *m* 1968, Elizabeth Lacey; two *s*. *Educ:* City of London Sch.; Durham Univ. (BA, MA); Cuddesdon Coll., Oxford. Ordained deacon, 1970, priest 1971; Curate, St Andrew's, Bedford, 1970–74; Chaplain, Surrey Univ., 1974–78; Sub-Warden, Lincoln Theol Coll., 1978–83; Rector, Houghton-le-Spring, 1983–94; Principal, The Queen's Coll., subseq. The Queen's Foundn for Ecumenical Theol Educn, Birmingham, 1994–2002. Mem., Faith and Order Commn, WCC, 2008–16. Hon. Canon, Birmingham Cathedral, 2000–. *Publications:* Outside Eden, 2009. *Recreations:* piano and water-colours, both strictly incognito. *Address:* Eden, Unicorn View, Bowes, Barnard Castle, County Durham DL12 9HW. *T:* (01833) 628001.

**FISHER, Richard, (Rick);** lighting designer (freelance), since 1980; Chairman, Association of Lighting Designers, 1995–2011 (Fellow, 2011); *b* Pennsylvania, 19 Oct. 1954; *s* of Samuel M. Fisher and Helene K. Fisher. *Educ:* Dickinson Coll., Carlisle, PA (BA 1976). Lighting designs for theatre and dance productions include: An Inspector Calls, NT, 1992, transf. NY (Tony Award, Drama Desk Award, 1994); Matthew Bourne's Swan Lake, London, 1995, transf. Los Angeles and NY; Via Dolorosa, Royal Court, transf. NY, 1998; Disney's The Hunchback of Notre Dame, Berlin, 1999; Blue/Orange, NT, 2000, Duchess, 2001; A Number, Royal Court, 2002; Far Away, NY, 2002; Jerry Springer the Opera, NT, transf. Cambridge Th., 2003; Old Times, 2004, The Philanthropist, 2005, Donmar; Billy Elliot, Victoria Palace, 2005, transf. Australia, 2007, New York, 2008 (Tony Award, Drama Desk Award, 2009); Landscape with Weapon, NT, 2007; The Family Reunion, Donmar Warehouse, 2008; Tribes, Royal Court, 2010; The Sound of Music, Buenos Aires, 2011; Hero, Royal Court, 2012; The Judas Kiss, Hampstead Th., transf. Duke of York's, 2012, Toronto and Brooklyn Acad. of Music, 2016; Chariots of Fire, Hampstead Th., transf. Gielgud, 2012; The Audience, Gielgud, 2013, transf. Apollo Th. and NY, 2015; Inside Wagner's Head, Linbury Studio Th., 2013; Sunny Afternoon, Hampstead Th., transf. Pinter, 2014; Waste, NT, 2016; Rent, St James, 2017; Consent, W End; for Royal Shakespeare Company: Merchant of Venice, 2011, transf. Almeida, 2014; Richard III, 2012; Galileo, 2013; opera productions include: Opera North: La Bohème, 1996, Gloriana, 1999; Bolshoi: Turandot, 2002; The Fiery Angel, 2004; Royal Opera: Wozzeck, 2002; Tsarina's Slippers, 2009; A Midsummer Night's Dream, La Fenice, Venice, 2004; Santa Fe: Peter Grimes, 2005; Billy Budd, Radamisto, 2008; Madame Butterfly, Albert Herring, 2010; Wozzeck, La Bohème, The Last Savage, 2011; Daughter of the Regiment, Rigoletto, Salome, 2015; The Little Prince, Houston, 2003, NY, 2005; Betrothal in a Monastery, Glyndebourne, 2006; Sweeney Todd, Paris, 2011, Houston, San Francisco, 2015; King and I, 2014; La Traviata, ROH, Muscat; Man of La Mancha, ENO. Olivier Award for Best Lighting Design, 1994 and 1998; Bronze Medal for Lighting Design, World Stage Design Expo, Toronto, 2005; Helpmann Award, Australia, 2008; Stage Lighting Designer of Year, Live Design Internat., 2008; Enrico Caironi Award for Lifetime Achievement, Knights of Illumination Awards, 2017. *Recreations:* theatre going, travel, eating!, camping. *Address:* c/o Dennis Lyne Agency, 503 Holloway Road, N19 4DD.

**FISHER, Richard Alan;** QC 2015; *b* Coventry, 14 Oct. 1971; *s* of Alan and Mai Fisher; *m* 2007; one *s* one *d*. *Educ:* King Henry VIII Sch., Coventry; Bristol Univ. (LLB 1993); Inns of Court Sch. of Law. Called to the Bar, Lincoln's Inn, 1994; in practice as barrister, specialising in fraud and in advice and litigation relating to proceeds of crime. *Publications:* (jtly) Blackstone's Guide to the Proceeds of Crime Act 2002, 2003, 5th edn 2015. *Recreation:* sports (former English schools sprint hurdles champion, representative Rugby, Warwickshire schools and Bristol University). *Address:* Doughty Street Chambers, 53–54 Doughty Street, WC1N 2LS. *T:* (020) 7404 1313, *Fax:* (020) 7404 2283. *E:* r.fisher@doughtystreet.co.uk.

FISHER, Robert Reginald James, AM 2003; JP; Agent General for Western Australia, 2001–05; *b* 13 Oct. 1942; *s* of Albert Reginald Fisher and Irene Fisher; *m* 1967, Lynette Fulford; one *s* one *d*. *Educ:* Univ. of Western Australia (BA, BEd). Member, Australian Trade Commissioner Service, 1970–80: Lima, 1971–73; Russian lang. trng, 1973–74; Moscow, 1974–76; New Delhi, 1976–77; San Francisco, 1977–80; Government of Western Australia, 1980–2005: Chief Executive: Dept of Industrial Develt, 1980–87; Countertrade Office, 1987–88; Dept of Trade Develt, 1988–91; Regl Develt, 1991–92; Family and Children's Services, 1993–2001. Chairman: Aquatic Adv. Cttee, WA, 2012–15; Forest Products Commn, WA, 2013–15; Mem. Bd, Defence Housing Authy, 2016– . Comr, Nat. Commn of Audit, 2013–14. JP Western Australia, 2001. *Recreations:* swimming, golf. *Address:* 12 Sutcliffe Street, Dalkeith, WA 6009, Australia.

FISHER, Roger Anthony, FRCO(CHM); Organist and Master of Choristers, Chester Cathedral, 1967–96; *b* 18 Sept. 1936; *s* of Leslie Elgar Fisher and Vera Althea (*née* Salter); *m* 1st, 1967, Susan Mary Green (marr. diss. 1983); one *d*; 2nd, 1985, Gillian Rushforth (*née* Heywood). *Educ:* Bancroft's Sch., Woodford Green, Essex; Royal Coll. Music; Christ Church, Oxford (Organ schol.); MA 1964). FRCO(CHM); ARCM; ATCL. Organist, St Mark's, Regent's Park, 1957–62; Asst Organist, Hereford Cathedral, 1962–67; Asst Lectr in Music, Hereford Coll. of Educn, 1963–67. Music Critic, Liverpool Echo, 1976–79; Associate Editor, Organists' Rev., 1996–2004. Recital tours incl. N America, Europe, Scandinavia, S Africa and Australia. Recordings in GB, Europe, USA and S Africa; BBC broadcasts as organist and with Chester Cathedral Choir. Conductor, choral socs and orchestras; Organ Consultant to churches and cathedrals. Geoffrey Tankard Prize for Solo Organ, RCM, 1959. *Publications:* Master Class with Roger Fisher, 2006; Towards Keyboard Fluency, 2010; articles about the organ and related subjects in several periodicals. *Recreations:* railway interests, walking, motoring. *Address:* The Old Chapel, Trelogan, Holywell, Flintshire CH8 9BD. *W:* www.rfisher.me.

FISHER, Steven Mark; HM Diplomatic Service; Ambassador to the Republic of Moldova, since 2019; *b* Stratford upon Avon, 7 Feb. 1965; *s* of Dennis John Fisher and Janet Mary Fisher; *m* 1990, Linda Westwood (marr. diss. 2010); three *s*; partner, Kriszta Fogarasi; one *d*. *Educ:* Cubbington C of E Jun. Sch.; Warwick Sch.; Wadham Coll., Oxford (BA French and Hist. 1987). IT Consultant, Andersen Consulting, 1987–92; bookseller, The Book Shop, Amersham, 1992–93; joined FCO, 1993; Second Sec. (Econ./Commercial), Singapore, 1995–98; Hd, Ukraine, Belarus, Moldova Sect., Eastern Dept, FCO, 1998–2001; Hd, Press Sect., EU Dept, FCO, 2001; Dep. Hd of Mission, Caracas, 2002–06; First Sec. EU, then Dep. Hd of Mission, Budapest, 2006–09; Ambassador to Dominican Republic and (non-resident) to Haiti, 2009–15; Human Rights and Democracy Dept, FCO, 2015–19. *Recreations:* keeping up with my children, restoring a farmhouse in Spain, maintaining old friendships, reading and writing history, music. *Address:* 3 Castle Rise, Castle Street, High Wycombe HP13 6FQ. *E:* steven.fisher@fco.gov.uk, stevenfisher2009@gmail.com.

FISHER CROUCH, Corinne Louise Teague; see Searle, C. L. T.

FISHLOCK, Trevor; journalist, foreign correspondent, author; *b* 21 Feb. 1941; *s* of Edward and Ada Fishlock; *m* 1st, 1965; two *s* one *d*; 2nd, 1978, Penelope Symon. *Educ:* Churcher's Coll., Petersfield; Southern Grammar Sch., Portsmouth. Portsmouth Evening News, 1957–62; freelance and news agency reporter, 1962–68; The Times: Wales and W England staff correspondent, 1968–77; London and foreign staff, 1978–80; S Asia correspondent, Delhi, 1980–83; New York correspondent, 1983–86; Daily Telegraph: roving foreign correspondent, 1986–89, 1993–96; Moscow correspondent, 1989–91; foreign correspondent, The Sunday Telegraph, 1991–93. Writer-presenter, Wild Tracks, 1995–2008 (BAFTA Award, 2000), Fishlock's Wales, 2003–13, ITV Wales. Fellow, World Press Inst., St Paul, Minnesota, 1977–78. Mem., Council for the Welsh Language, 1973–77. Hon. Fellow, Univ. of Wales, Lampeter, 2008. Hon. MA Wales, 2008. David Holden Award for foreign reporting (British Press Awards), 1983; Internat. Reporter of the Year (British Press Awards), 1986. *Publications:* Wales and the Welsh, 1972; Talking of Wales, 1975; Discovering Britain: Wales, 1979; Americans and Nothing Else, 1980; India File, 1983; The State of America, 1986; Indira Gandhi (for children), 1986; Out of Red Darkness: reports from the collapsing Soviet Empire, 1992; My Foreign Country: Trevor Fishlock's Britain, 1997; Cobra Road: an Indian journey, 1999; Conquerors of Time, 2004; In This Place, centenary vol. for Nat. Liby of Wales, 2007; Senedd: the National Assembly for Wales building, 2010; Pembrokeshire: journeys and stories, 2011; A Gift of Sunlight: the fortune and quest of the Davies sisters, 2014; Reporter, 2017. *Recreation:* sailing. *Address:* 7 Teilo Street, Cardiff CF11 9JN. *Club:* Naval.

FISHWICK, Dr Nicholas Bernard Frank, CMG 2009; HM Diplomatic Service, retired; *b* Ashbourne, 23 Feb. 1958; *s* of Roland Frank Fishwick and Dorothy May Fishwick (*née* Ford); *m* 1987, Rouane Theresa Mendel; two *s* one *d*. *Educ:* Staveley Netherthorpe Grammar Sch.; Hertford Coll., Oxford (BA 1st Cl. Hons Mod. Hist. 1979; DPhil 1985). Entered FCO, 1983; First Sec. (Press and Inf.), Lagos, 1988–91; Consul (Pol), Istanbul, 1994–97; on secondment to HM Customs and Excise, 2001–04; Counsellor: (Pol), Kabul, 2006–07; FCO, 2007–12. Advr, Financial System Vulnerabilities Cttee, HSBC, 2013– ; non-exec. Dir, HSBC Latin America, Argentina, Mexico, 2016– . *Publications:* English Football and Society 1910–1950, 1989; (contrib.) New DNB. *Recreations:* family, walks, running, football, churches, music (Beethoven, Wagner, David Bowie, Morrissey). *E:* nick.fishwick@hotmail.co.uk.

FISK, Prof. David John, CB 1999; ScD, PhD; FREng; Laing O'Rourke Professor, Systems Engineering and Innovation, Imperial College London, 2011–17, now Emeritus; *b* 9 Jan. 1947; *s* of late John Howard Fisk and of Rebecca Elizabeth Fisk (*née* Haynes); *m* 1972, A. Anne Thoday; one *s* one *d*. *Educ:* Stationers' Company's Sch., Hornsey; St John's Coll., Cambridge (BA, MA, ScD); Univ. of Manchester (PhD). FCIBSE 1983 (Hon. FCIBSE 1998); FREng (FEng 1998); FInstP 1999. Joined Building Res. Estabt (traffic noise res.), 1972; Higher Sci. Officer, 1972–73; Sen. Sci. Officer (energy conservation res.), 1973–75; PSO, 1975–78; SPSO, Hd Mechanical and Elec. Engrg Div., 1978–84; Department of the Environment: Asst Sec., Central Directorate of Environmental Protection, 1984–87; Under Sec., 1987; Dep. Chief Scientist, 1987–88; Chief Scientific Advr, OPDM (formerly Dept of the Envmt, then DETR, later DTLR), 1998–2006. Director: Air, Climate and Toxic Substances Directorate, 1990–95; Envmt & Internat. Directorate, 1995–98; Central Strategy Directorate, DETR, then DTLR, 1999–2002. RAEng Prof. of Engrg for Sustainable Develt, Imperial Coll. London, 2002–11. Member: Gas and Electricity Mkts Authy, 2009–17; Nat. Infrastructure Commn, 2017– . Pres, CIBSE, 2011–12 (Vice Pres., 2010–11). Dir, Watford Palace Th., 2000–08. Hon. FRIBA 2009. *Publications:* Thermal Control of Buildings, 1981; Energizing Sustainable Cities, 2013; numerous papers on technical innovation, bldg sci., systems theory and economics. *Recreations:* modern theatre, music. *Address:* Imperial College London, South Kensington Campus, SW7 2AZ. *Club:* Athenæum.

FISON, Sir Charles (William), 5th Bt *cr* 1905, of Greenholme, Burley-in-Wharfedale, West Riding of Yorkshire; *b* 6 Feb. 1954; *o s* of Sir (Richard) Guy Fison, 4th Bt, DSC, and Elyn Hartmann (*d* 1987); *S* father, 2008, but his name does not appear on the Official Roll of the Baronetage. *Educ:* Eton. *Heir:* none.

FISON, David Gareth, CEng, FICE; Chairman, Pontoonworks Ltd, since 2015; Director and Chairman, Humphrey Farms Ltd, since 2017; *b* Rochester, Kent, 14 March 1952; *s* of Joseph Edward Fison and Monica Irene Fison; *m* 1979, Honor Mary Borwick; one *s* one *d*. *Educ:* Marlborough Coll.; Trinity Hall, Cambridge (BA 1973; MA). CEng 1978; FICE 1992. Managing Director: Balfour Beatty Civil Engrg, 1994–96; Balfour Beatty Rail, 1996–98; Chief Executive: Skanska UK plc, 2002–08; Geoffrey Osborne Ltd, 2009–15. Non-executive Director: Olympic Delivery Authy, 2009–14; Harwich Haven Authy, 2014–15; London City Airport, 2017– . Gov., UAL, 2017– . *Recreations:* house in Suffolk, sailing, cooking. *E:* davidgfison@gmail.com.

FITCHETT, Robert Duncan; HM Diplomatic Service, retired; *b* 10 June 1961; *s* of late John Charles Fitchett and of Sheila Mary Fitchett; *m* 1985, Adèle Thérèse Hajjar; one *s* two *d*. *Educ:* Northampton Sch. for Boys; Univ. of Bradford (BA Hons Mod. Langs (French and German) 1983). Joined FCO, 1983; Dakar, 1984–87; Bonn, 1987–90; FCO, 1990–93; Cabinet Office, 1993–94; First Sec., Paris, 1994–98; FCO, 1998–2003; Dep. Hd of Mission, Manila, 2003–06; FCO, 2007–08; Dep. Hd of Mission and Consul Gen., Mexico City, 2008–11; FCO, 2011–13. *Recreations:* horse racing, opera, classical music, reading, walking, Vice Chairman of Southern Golden Retriever Society.

FITKIN, Graham; Composer in Residence, London Chamber Orchestra, since 2009; *b* Cornwall, 19 April 1963; *s* of Norman Wayland Fitkin and Joan Fitkin; partner, Ruth Wall. *Educ:* Humphry Davy Sch., Penzance; Univ. of Nottingham (BA Hons Music 1984); Koninklijk Conservatorium, The Hague (MMus Music Composition 1986). Founder, Nanquidno Gp, 1985; Composer in Association, Royal Liverpool Philharmonic Orch., 1994–96; compositions for Tokyo SO, BBC Philharmonic Orch., Royal Scottish Nat. Orch., NY City Ballet, Umeå Capital of Culture 2014, Decca Records; *compositions* include: Still Warm, 2007; Reel (for Royal Ballet), 2009; Cello Concerto (for Yo-Yo Ma and BBC Proms), 2011; Home (for Royal Opera Hse), 2012; Intimate Curve (for Royal Liverpool Philharmonic Orch.), 2015. Hon. Fellow, University Coll. Falmouth, 2010. UK Composer Award, 1990; British Composer Award, BASCA, 2009 and 2011; RPS Composer Award, 2015. *Publications:* ballet, opera and orchestral works. *Recreations:* running, swimming, cycling. *Address:* c/o Jane Ward, 60 Shrewsbury Road, Oxton, Merseyside CH43 2HY. *T:* (0151) 513 2716. *E:* info@fitkin.com.

FITT, Prof. Alistair David, DPhil; Vice-Chancellor, Oxford Brookes University, since 2015; *b* London, 23 Nov. 1957; *s* of Kenneth Walter Fitt and late Enid Phyllis Fitt; *m* 2012, Prof. Anne Trefethen; one step *s* one step *d*. *Educ:* Dr Challoner's Grammar Sch., Amersham; Lincoln Coll., Oxford (MA, MSc; DPhil 1984). Sen. Res. Fellow, RMCS, Shrivenham, 1984–89; University of Southampton: Lectr, 1989–94; Sen. Lectr, 1994–96; Reader, 1996–99; Prof. of Maths, 1999–2011; Dean, Faculty of Maths, 2002–08; Pro Vice Chancellor (Internat.), 2008–11; Pro Vice-Chancellor (Res. and Knowledge Exchange), Oxford Brookes Univ., 2011–15. Mem. Bd, Oxon LEP, 2014– . Mem. Council, IMA, 2000– (Pres., 2018–); Exec. Sec., Internat. Council for Industrial and Applied Maths, 2007–15. Trustee, Oxford Trust, 2014– . *Publications:* contrib. scientific papers to peer-reviewed jls. *Recreations:* golf, cricket. *Address:* Office of the Vice-Chancellor, Oxford Brookes University, Headington Campus, Oxford OX3 0BP.

FITTALL, Sir William (Robert), Kt 2016; Secretary-General, Archbishop's Council and General Synod of the Church of England, 2002–15; *b* 26 July 1953; *s* of Arthur Fittall and Elsie Fittall; *m* 1978, Barbara Staples; two *s*. *Educ:* Dover Grammar Sch.; Christ Church, Oxford (MA). Entered Home Office, 1975; Private Sec. to Minister of State, 1979–80; Ecole Nationale d'Administration, Paris, 1980–81; Broadcasting Dept, 1981–85; Private Sec. to Home Sec., 1985–87; Sec., Review of Parole System, 1987–88; Prison Service HQ, 1988–91; Principal Private Sec. to Sec. of State for NI, 1992–93; Police Dept, Home Office, 1993–95; Chief of Assessments Staff, Cabinet Office, 1995–97; Dir, Crime Reduction and Community Progs, Home Office, 1997–2000; Associate Political Dir, NI Office, 2000–02. Chairman: Folkestone Rainbow Centre, 2016– ; Robert Thompson Charities, 2018– . Ind. Reviewer, Women Bishops Legislation, 2015– . Anglican Lay Reader, 1977– . *Recreations:* playing church organs, choral singing, reading.

FITTER, Prof. Alastair Hugh, CBE 2010; PhD; FRS 2005; Professor of Ecology, University of York, 1992–2013, now Emeritus; *b* 20 June 1948; *s* of late Richard Sidney Richmond Fitter and Alice Mary, (Maisie), Fitter; *m* 1969, Rosalind Morris (*d* 2014); two *s* one *d*. *Educ:* New Coll., Oxford (BA 1969); Univ. of Liverpool (PhD 1973). University of York: Lectr and Sen. Lectr in Ecology, 1972–92; Hd of Dept of Biol., 1997–2004; Pro-Vice-Chancellor for Res., 2004–10. Dir, UK Population Biology Network, 2004–07. Mem., NERC, 2005–11. Joint Editor: Advances in Ecological Research, vols 18–30, 1987–99; Jl of Ecology, 1992–96; Ed., New Phytologist, 1988–2013. Pres., British Ecol Soc., 2003–05; Vice-Pres., Internat. Assoc. for Ecology, 2009–13. Hon. Member: British Naturalists' Assoc., 2006; Botanical Soc. of British Isles, 2007; British Mycol Soc., 2007. Chair of Trustees, Castle Howard Arboretum Trust, 2011– . *Publications:* (with M. Blamey and R. Fitter) Wild Flowers of Britain and Northern Europe, 1974, 5th edn 1996; An Atlas of the Wild Flowers of Britain and Northern Europe, 1976; (with C. Smith) A Wood in Ascam: a study in wetland conservation, Askham Bog 1879–1979, 1979; Trees, 1980; (with R. K. M. Hay) Environmental Physiology of Plants, 1981, 3rd edn 2002; (with N. Arlott and R. Fitter) The Complete Guide to British Wildlife, 1981; (with R. Fitter and J. Wilkinson) Collins Guide to the Countryside, 1984; (with R. Fitter and A. Farrer) Grasses, Sedges, Rushes and Ferns of Britain and Northern Europe, 1984; (ed) Ecological Interactions in the Soil: plants, microbes and animals, 1985; (with R. Fitter) Collins Guide to the Countryside in Winter, 1988; (ed jtly) Mycorrhizas in Ecosystems, 1992; (with M. Blamey and R. Fitter) Wild Flowers of Britain and Ireland, 2003, 2nd edn 2013. *Address:* Department of Biology, University of York, York YO10 5DD.

FITTON, David John, CMG 2004; HM Diplomatic Service, retired; Executive Director, UK-Japan 21st Century Group, since 2017; *b* 10 Jan. 1955; *s* of Jack and Joan Fitton; *m* 1989, Hisae Iijima; one *s* one *d*. *Educ:* Durham Univ. (BA Hons; MA). Entered FCO, 1980; appts in New Delhi, Tokyo and London, 1980–96; Political Counsellor, Tokyo, 1996–2000; Dep. Hd of Mission, Ankara, 2001–04; Actg Consul-Gen., Istanbul, 2003–04; Hd, Crisis Gp, Consular Directorate, FCO, 2004–07; Minister, Tokyo, 2008–12; High Comr to Jamaica and Bahamas, 2013–17. *Recreations:* tennis, medieval French manuscripts, football, golf. *Address:* c/o Japan Society, 13/14 Cornwall Terrace, NW1 4QP. *E:* david@fitton.org.uk.

**FITTON, Michael David Guy**; QC 2006; **His Honour Judge Fitton**; a Circuit Judge, since 2015; b Nairobi, 28 April 1957; s of O. V. A. Fitton and E. N. Fitton; m 1981, Susan Booker; one s one d. Educ: King George V Grammar Sch., Southport, Lancs; Lincoln Coll., Oxford (MA Juris.). Admitted Solicitor, 1981; Partner, Bobbetts Mackan, Bristol, 1985–91; called to the Bar, Gray's Inn, 1991; a Recorder, 2000–15; Hd, Albion Chambers, Bristol, 2009–15. Legal Mem., Mental Health Rev. Tribunal, Wales, 2012–. Recreations: family, walking, photography, early classical music, African jazz, supporting Wales at Rugby and Cardiff FC at football. Address: Cardiff Crown Court, The Law Courts, Cathays Park, Cardiff CF10 3PG.

**FITTON-BROWN, Edmund Walter**; HM Diplomatic Service; UN Monitoring Team Coordinator, since 2018 (Expert, supporting Security Council Committees responsible for sanctions against Al Qaeda, ISIL/Daesh and Taliban, 2017); b 5 Oct. 1962; s of Anthony David and Daphne Mary Fitton-Brown; m 1995, Julie Ann Herring; two s one d. Educ: Wyggeston Boys' Sch., Leicester; Corpus Christi Coll., Cambridge (BA Hons Hist. 1984). Joined FCO, 1984; Third Sec., 1987–88, Second Sec., 1988–89, Helsinki; FCO, 1989–91; First Secretary: FCO, 1991–93; Cairo, 1993–96; FCO, 1996–98; Kuwait, 1998–2001; FCO, 2001–03; Counsellor: Cairo, 2003–05; Riyadh, 2005–06; FCO, 2006–09; Rome, 2009–11; Dubai, 2011–15; Ambassador to Yemen, 2015–17. Recreations: squash, football, tennis, golf, bridge. Address: c/o United Nations, DC2, East 44th Street, New York, NY 10017, USA. E: edmund.fitton-brown@un.org.

**FITZALAN-HOWARD**, family name of **Duke of Norfolk**.

**FITZGERALD**, family name of **Duke of Leinster**.

**FitzGERALD, Sir Adrian (James Andrew Denis)**, 6th Bt cr 1880, of Valencia, Co. Kerry; 24th Knight of Kerry; b 24 June 1940; o s of Major Sir George FitzGerald, 5th Bt, MC and Angela Dora (née Mitchell); S father, 2001. Educ: Harrow. Editor, Monday World, political qly, 1967–74; hotelier, 1983–90. Mem. (C) Council, Royal Borough of Kensington and Chelsea, 1974–2002 (Mayor, 1984–85; Chief Whip, 1986–95; Chm., Educn and Libraries Cttee, 1995–98; Chm., Highways and Traffic Cttee, 1999–2001). Dep. Leader, London Fire and Civil Defence Authy, 1989–90. Pres., Anglo-Polish Soc., 2001– (Chm., 1989–92); Vice-Chm., London Chapter, Irish Georgian Soc., 1990–2009; Pres., Benevolent Soc. of St Patrick, 1997–2013; Patron, Latin Mass Soc., 2012–. Gov., Cardinal Vaughan Meml Sch., 1999–2009, 2010–13 (Vice-Chm., 2002–03; Chm., 2003–09). Kt Grand Cross, SMO, Malta, 2015 (Pres., Irish Assoc., 2009–15). Publications: (contrib.) Education, Church and State, ed M. R. O'Connell, 1992; (contrib.) The Knights of Glin: seven centuries of change, ed Tom Donovan, 2009. Heir: cousin Anthony Desmond FitzGerald [b 24 Dec. 1953; m 1986, Janine Miller (marr. diss. 2003); one s]. Clubs: Beefsteak, Pratt's; Kildare Street and University (Dublin).

**FitzGERALD, Sir (Andrew) Peter**, 5th Bt cr 1903, of Geraldine Place, St Finn Barr, co. Cork; b 31 July 1950; s of John Finbarr FitzGerald and Margaret FitzGerald (née Hogg); S cousin, 2016, but his name does not appear on the Official Roll of the Baronetage; m 1974, Bridette, d of William Enright; one s one d. Heir: s William John FitzGerald [b 9 June 1976; m 2003, Elaine Kelly; one s two d].

**FitzGERALD, Christopher Francis**; Chairman, Regulatory Decisions Committee, Financial Services Authority, 2001–04; b 17 Nov. 1945; s of late Lt Comdr Michael Francis FitzGerald, RN and Anne Lise FitzGerald (née Winther); m 1st, 1968, Jennifer (née Willis) (marr. diss. 1984); one s two d; 2nd, 1986, Jill (née Freshwater); two step d. Educ: Downside Sch.; Lincoln Coll., Oxford (Classics Schol.; BA Juris. 1967; MA). Admitted solicitor, 1971; Partner, Slaughter and May, 1976–95; Gen. Counsel, and Mem., Exec. Dirs' Cttee, NatWest Gp, 1995–2000. Non-executive Director: Intercare Gp plc, 2001–03; City Merchants High Yield Trust plc, 2007–12; Mimecast Ltd, 2007–; Chm., Macfarlane Trust, 2007–12. Member: Finance Cttee, Lincoln Coll., Oxford, 2003–; Financial Reporting Review Panel, 2006–12. Recreations: travelling, opera, theatre and concert going, appreciating fine wines. Address: 26 Lower Addison Gardens, W14 8BQ.

**FITZGERALD, Edward Hamilton**, CBE 2008; QC 1995; a Recorder, since 2002; b 13 Aug. 1953; s of Carrol James Fitzgerald and Cornelia (née Claiborne); m 1988, Rebecca Fraser; three d. Educ: Downside; Corpus Christi Coll., Oxford (BA 1st cl. Hons Lit. Hum. 1975); MPhil Cantab 1979. Called to the Bar, Inner Temple, 1978, Bencher, 2002. Times Justice Award, 1998. Recreations: reading history and novels, visiting the seaside, travel. Address: (chambers) 54 Doughty Street, WC1N 2LS. T: (020) 7404 1313.

**FITZGERALD, Frances**; Member of the Dáil (TD) (FG) Dublin Mid-West, Ireland, since 2011; b 1 Aug. 1950; m; three s. Educ: University Coll. Dublin (BSocSc); London Sch. of Econs and Pol Sci. (MSc Social Admin). Chm., Council for Status of Women, 1989–92. Mem. of the Dáil (TD) (FG) Dublin SE, 1992–2002; Senator, and Leader of Opposition, Ireland, 2007–11; Minister for Children and Youth Affairs, 2011–14, for Justice and Equality, 2014–17, for Business, Enterprise and Innovation, 2017; Tánaiste (Dep. Prime Minister), 2016–17. Address: (office) 9 Main Street, Clondalkin, Dublin 22, D22 V4X2, Ireland.

**FITZGERALD, Frank**, CBE 1989; PhD; FREng; consultant, since 1992; Director, Sheffield Forgemasters Ltd, 1993–98; b 11 Nov. 1929; s of George Arthur Fitzgerald and Sarah Ann (née Brook); m 1956, Dorothy Eileen Unwin (d 2010); two s one d. Educ: Barnsley Holgate Grammar Sch.; Univ. of Sheffield (BScTech; PhD). FEI (FInstE 1965); FREng (FEng 1977); FIMMM (FIM 2000). Dedicatee, Frank Fitzgerald Medal and Travel Award, IMMM. Ministry of Supply, RAE, Westcott, Bucks, 1955; United Steel Cos, Swinden Laboratories, Rotherham, 1960–68; British Steel plc (formerly British Steel Corporation), 1968–92: Process Res. Manager, Special Steels Div., 1970; Head Corporate Advanced Process Laboratory, 1972; Director, R&D, 1977; Man. Dir, Technical, 1981–92; Dir, 1986–92; Chairman: British Steel Corp. (Overseas Services), subseq. British Steel Consultants, 1981–89; British Steel Stainless, 1989–91. Hon. Fellow, Queen Mary, Univ. of London, 2004. Hon. DEng Sheffield, 1993. Hadfield Medal, Iron and Steel Inst., for work on application of combustion and heat transfer science to industrial furnaces, 1972; Melchett Medal, Inst. of Energy, 1988; Bessemer Gold Medal, Inst. of Metals, 1991; Esso Energy Award, Royal Soc., 1991. Publications: papers in learned jls on heat and mass transfer and metallurgical processes. Recreations: rock climbing and mountain literature, classical music. Clubs: Alpine; Climbers'.

**FITZGERALD, Prof. Garret Adare**, MD; FRS 2012; FRCPI, FACP; Professor of Medicine and Pharmacology, since 1994, McNeil Professor of Translational Medicine and Therapeutics, since 2007, Chair, Department of Pharmacology, since 1996, Director, Institute for Translational Medicine and Therapeutics, since 2004, and Associate Dean for Translational Research, since 2004, University of Pennsylvania; b Dublin. Educ: Belvedere Coll., Dublin; University Coll. Dublin (MB BCh 1974; MD (Pharmacol.) 1980); Sch. of Hygiene, Univ. of London (MSc Stats 1979). MRCPI 1976, FRCPI 1982; MRCP 1977; FACP 1984. Intern, 1974–75, SHO, 1975–76, St Vincent's Hosp., Dublin; SHO, 1976–77, Res. Registrar, 1977, Mater Hosp., Dublin; Res. Fellow, RPMS, 1977–79; Neurol. Res. Fellow, Univ. of Cologne, 1979–80; Vanderbilt University School of Medicine, Nashville: Res. Fellow, 1980; Asst Prof., 1981–84, Associate Prof., 1984–87, Medicine and Pharmacol.; Prof. of Medicine and Pharmacol., 1987–91; William Stokes Prof. of Experimental Therapeutics, 1989–91; Dir, Centre for Cardiovascular Sci., 1991–94, and Prof. and Chm., Dept of Experimental Therapeutics, 1991–94, UCD; Consultant Physician, Mater Hosp., Dublin, 1991–94; University of Pennsylvania: Dir, Center for Experimental Therapeutics, and Dir, Clin. Res. Centre, 1994–2004; Robinette Foundn Prof. of Cardiovascular Medicine, 1994–2004; Elmer Bobst Prof. of Pharmacol., 1999–2007. Adjunct Prof., RCSI, 1995–2004; Visiting Scientist: Wellcome Trust Centre for Human Genetics and Dept of Anatomy and Human Genetics, Oxford Univ., 2002–03; Scripps Res. Inst. and Genomics Inst. of Novartis Foundn, La Jolla, Calif, 2003. FAAAS 1998. Boyle Medal, Royal Dublin Soc., 2005. Publications: articles in learned jls. Address: 10th Floor, Room 122, 3400 Civic Center Boulevard Building 421, Institute for Translational Medicine and Therapeutics, University of Pennsylvania, Philadelphia, PA 19104–5158, USA.

**FITZGERALD, Hon. Gerald Edward, (Hon. Tony)**, AC 1991; arbitrator, mediator, private dispute adjudicator; b Brisbane, 26 Nov. 1941; m 1968, Catherine Glynn-Connolly; one s two d. Educ: Univ. of Queensland (LLB). Admitted Queensland Bar, 1964; QC Queensland 1975 and subseq. QC NSW and Victoria; Judge of Federal Court of Australia, 1981–84; Judge of Supreme Court of ACT, 1981–84; Pres., Court of Appeal, Supreme Court of Qld, 1991–98; Judge of Ct of Appeal, Supreme Ct of NSW, 1998–2001. Presidential Mem., Administrative Appeals Tribunal, 1981–84; Mem., Australian Law Reform Commn, 1981–84; Chairman, Commission of Inquiry: into official corruption, Qld, 1987–89; into the Conservation, Management and Use of Fraser Is. and the Gt Sandy Reg., Qld, 1990–91; Chairman: Litigation Reform Commn, Qld, 1991–92; Cape York Justice Study, 2001; Nat. Pro Bono Resource Centre, 2004–06; former Chm., Law and Justice Foundn. Dir, Australian Res. Alliance for Children and Youth. Chm., Australian Heritage Commn, 1990–91. Chairman: Nat. Inst. for Law, Ethics and Public Affairs, 1992–95; Key Inst. for Ethics, Law, Justice and Governance, Griffith Univ., 1999– (Hon. Prof., 2003–); Vis. Scholar, New York Univ. Sch. of Law, 1997; Professorial Fellow, Univ. of Melbourne Law Sch., 1999–. Chancellor, Sunshine Coast UC, 1994–98. Dep. Chm., Gov. Bd, Mater Health Services, 1995–98. Mem., Adv. Bd, Legal Information Access Centre, State Liby of NSW, 2002–05. Jury Mem., Internat. Justice in the World Prize, Justice in the World Foundn, Internat. Assoc. of Judges, 2002–03. Fellow, Australian Centre for Internat. Commercial Arbitration Ltd. Mem., List of Neutrals, Arbitration and Mediation Center, WIPO. DUniv: Qld Univ. of Technol., 1995; Sunshine Coast, 1999; Griffith, 2003. Recreations: tennis, reading, music. Address: Level 34, New Chambers, 126 Phillip Street, Sydney, NSW 2000, Australia. T: (4) 07870084. E: tonyfitzqc@icloud.com.

**FITZGERALD, Gerard, (Ged)**; Chief Executive, Liverpool City Council, 2011–18; b Liverpool, 26 Aug. 1961; s of Timothy and Patricia Fitzgerald; m 1999, Karen Morris (marr. diss. 2014); one d. Educ: Goldsmiths' Coll., Univ. of London (BA Hons); Univ. of Salford (MBA). ACIS 1986; DMS 1992. Sefton MBC, 1983–87; Eur. Officer, Knowsley MBC, 1987–88; Policy Officer, Sefton MBC, 1988–91; Econ. Devel. Manager, Knowsley MBC, 1991–94; Exec. Dir, Bootle City Challenge, 1994–96; Hd, Econ. Devel and Eur. Affairs, Liverpool CC, 1996–98; Dep. Chief Exec., Calderdale MBC, 1998–2001; Chief Executive: Rotherham MBC, 2001–04; Sunderland CC, 2004–08; Lancs CC, 2008–10. Recreations: family, football - Liverpool FC fan, travel.

**FITZGERALD, Kevin Jeffrey**, CMG 2013; FRGS; Directeur, Cabinet du Directeur Général, United Nations World Intellectual Property Organisation, since 2015; b Oxford, 16 Jan. 1960; s of late Thomas John Fitzgerald and Pamela Rosemary Fitzgerald, OStJ. Educ: Greyfriars Hall, Oxford (MA). With Thomas Cook plc, 1997–2002, incl. Man. Dir, Thomas Cook Publishing, and Hd of Content, ThomasCook.com; Man. Dir, Rough Guides, Pearson plc, 2002–06; CEO, Copyright Licensing Agency, 2007–14. Chm., Eur. Gp, 2008–14, Dir, 2012–14, Internat. Fedn of Reprodn Rights Orgns; Chm., Regulation Gp, British Copyright Council, 2010–14. Non-exec. Dir, B of England Tourist Bd, 2006–11. Independent Member: Public Diplomacy Partners Gp, FCO, 2007–12; British Waterways Ombudsman, 2014– (Chm., 2018–). Trustee, Prisoners Abroad, 2009–14 (Chm., 2009–14), Patron, 2018–). FRGS 2004; FInstD 2014. Club: Travellers.

**FITZGERALD, Prof. Maria**, PhD; FRS 2016; FRCA, FMedSci; Professor of Developmental Neurobiology, University College London, since 1995; b Hampstead, London, 10 April 1953; d of Desmond John Lyon Fitzgerald and Penelope Mary Fitzgerald (née Knox); m 1978, John Burton Lake; two s one d. Educ: Godolphin and Latymer Sch.; Lady Margaret Hall, Oxford (BA Hons Physiol Sci. 1975); University Coll. London (PhD Physiol. 1978). University College London: MRC Trng Fellow, 1978–82, MRC Res. Associate, 1982–85, Cerebral Functions Gp; Lectr, 1985–90, Reader, 1990–95, Dept of Anatomy and Develtl Biol. FMedSci 2000; FRCA 2013. Jeffrey Lawson Award, Amer. Pain Soc., 2010. Publications: over 220 articles in learned jls. Recreations: gardening, tennis, travelling, art. Address: Department of Neuroscience, Physiology and Pharmacology, University College London, Gower Street, WC1E 6BT. T: (020) 7679 1303. E: m.fitzgerald@ucl.ac.uk.

**FitzGERALD, Michael Frederick Clive**, OBE 2002; QC 1980; b 9 June 1936; s of Sir William James FitzGerald, MC, QC, and Mrs E. J. Critchley; m 1st, 1966, Virginia Grace Cave (marr. diss. 1992); one s three d; 2nd, 1999, Nicola Mary Rountree (née Norman-Butler). Educ: Downside; Christ's Coll., Cambridge, 1956–59 (MA). 2nd Lieut 9th Queen's Royal Lancers, 1954–56. Called to the Bar, Middle Temple, 1961, Bencher, 1987. Leader, Parly Bar, 1997–2002. Chm., Adv. Panel on Standards for Planning Inspectorate Exec. Agency, 1992–2000. Recreations: opera, field sports. Address: 9 Bearwater, Charnham Street, Hungerford, Berks RG17 0NN. Club: Boodle's.

**FitzGERALD, Niall William Arthur**, Hon. KBE 2002; Deputy Chairman, Thomson Reuters, 2008–11 (Chairman, Reuters PLC, 2004–08; non-executive Director, Thomson Reuters (formerly Reuters PLC), 2003–11); b 13 Sept. 1945; s of William FitzGerald and Doreen Chambers; m 1st, 1970, Monica Cusack (marr. diss. 2003); two s one d; 2nd, 2003, Ingrid Van Velzen; one d. Educ: St Munchin's Coll., Limerick; University College Dublin (MComm). FCT 1986. Unilever, 1968–2004: North America, 1978–80; Chief Exec. Officer, Foods, S Africa, 1981–85; Group Treasurer, 1985–86; Financial Dir, 1987–89; Exec. Dir, 1987–96; Vice-Chm., 1994–96; Chm., 1996–2004; Director: Unilever Foods, 1990–91; Unilever Detergents, 1992–96. Non-executive Director: Bank of Ireland, 1990–99; Prudential Corp., 1992–99; Ericsson, 2000–02; Merck, 2000–03; Chairman: Hakluyt & Co. Ltd, 2008–13; Adv. Bd, Hakluyt Internat., 2013–. A Sen. Advr, Allen & Co. LLP. Chairman: CBI Europe Cttee, 1995–2001; Conference Bd, 2003–05; Co-Chairman: Transatlantic Business Dialogue, 2004–05; Investment Climate Facility for Africa, 2005–10. Chm., Internat. Business Council, 2006–08; Member: EU-China Business Council, 1997; US Business Council, 1998–2006; Trilateral Commn, 1999; Council: Co-operation Ireland; World Econ. Forum, 1999–2011; Member: President of South Africa's Internat. Investment Adv. Council, 2000–07; Mitsubishi Internat. Adv. Cttee, 2014–; Chm., Munster Rugby Commercial Bd, 2015–. Chairman: NiJaCo, 2006–; Brand Learning, 2013–; Smurfit Business Sch., UCD, 2014–18. Pres., Advertising Assoc., 2000–05. CCMI. Chm., Bd of Trustees, BM, 2006–14. Chm., Nelson Mandela Legacy Trust (UK), 2005–08; Trustee, Leverhulme Trust, 1996– (Chm., 2013–). Chm., Bd of

Govs, Cumnor House Sch., 2014–19. FRSA. Patron, British Irish Chamber of Commerce, 2015–. Presidential Dist. Service Award (Ireland), 2015. *Recreations:* observing humanity, music (opera and jazz), Irish Rugby, running, golf, creating an exotic garden in Sussex. *Club:* Royal Automobile.

**FITZGERALD, Prof. Patrick John;** Adjunct Professor of Law, Carleton University, Ottawa, since 1996 (Professor of Law, 1971–96); *b* 30 Sept. 1928; *s* of Dr Thomas Walter and Norah Josephine Fitzgerald; *m* 1959, Brigid Aileen Judge (*d* 2011); two *s* one *d*. *Educ:* Queen Mary's Grammar Sch., Walsall; University Coll., Oxford. Called to the Bar, Lincoln's Inn, 1951; Ontario Bar, 1984. Fellow, Trinity Coll., Oxford, 1956–60. Professor of Law: Leeds Univ., 1960–66; Univ. of Kent at Canterbury, 1966–71. Visiting Prof., University of Louisville, 1962–63. Consultant, Law Reform Commn of Canada, 1973–92. *Publications:* Criminal Law and Punishment, 1962; Salmond on Jurisprudence (12th edn), 1966; This Law of Ours, 1977; Looking at Law, 1979, 6th edn 2010; (ed) Crime, Justice and Codification, 1986. *Recreations:* music, bridge, creative writing. *Address:* 246–3310 Southgate Road, Ottawa, ON K1V 8X4, Canada.

**FitzGERALD, Sir Peter;** *see* FitzGerald, Sir A. P.

**FitzGERALD, Presiley Lamorna, (Mrs R. K. FitzGerald);** *see* Baxendale, P. L.

**FITZGERALD, Prof. Rebecca Clare,** MD; FRCP; FMedSci; Professor of Cancer Prevention, since 2014, and Programme Leader, MRC Cancer Unit, Hutchison/MRC Research Centre, since 2002, University of Cambridge; Director of Studies in Medicine, and College Lecturer in Medical Sciences, Trinity College, Cambridge, since 2002; Lead for Early Detection of Cancer Programme, Cambridge Cancer Centre, University of Cambridge, since 2015; *b* Sheffield, 30 Sept. 1968; *d* of Robert Parker and Linda Parker (*née* Clarke, now McKinley); *m* 1992, Shaun David Fitzgerald, *qv*; four *s*. *Educ:* St Brandon's Sch., Clevedon, Avon; Girton Coll., Cambridge (BA Hons Med. Scis 1989; MB BChir 1991; MA 1993; MD 1997). MRCP 1995, FRCP 2006. Hse surgeon, Hinchinbrooke Hosp., Huntingdon, 1992; hse physician, 1992–93, SHO, 1993–95, Addenbrooke's Hosp., Cambridge; Res. Fellow, Dept of Gastroenterol., Stanford Univ. Center for Molecular Biol. in Medicine, 1995–97; Specialist Registrar Rotation, Gastroenterol. and Gen. Medicine, NE Thames, 1997–2001; Postdoctoral Res. Trng, Digestive Diseases Res. Centre, St Bart's and the Royal London NHS Trust, 1997–2001 (MRC Clinician Scientist, 1999); Sen. Clinician Scientist, Cancer Cell Unit, Hutchison/MRC Res. Centre, Cambridge, 2001–02; Speciality Registrar, 2001–03, Hon. Consultant in Gastroenterol., Addenbrooke's Hosp. and Dept. of Oncol., Univ. of Cambridge, 2003–. Vis. Postdoctoral Res. Fellow, Dept of Cellular and Molecular Medicine, Stanford Univ., 1999. FMedSci 2013. *Publications:* book chapters; contribs to jls, incl. Nat. Medicine, Nat. Genetics and Gastroenterology. *Recreations:* classical music (piano, clarinet, singing), organizing church and community musical fundraising events. *Address:* MRC Cancer Unit, Hutchison/MRC Research Centre, University of Cambridge, Box 197, Cambridge Biomedical Campus, Cambridge CB2 0XZ. *T:* (01223) 763287, *Fax:* (01223) 763241. *E:* rcf29@mrc-cu.cam.ac.uk.

**FITZGERALD, Dr Shaun David,** FREng; Director, Royal Institution of Great Britain, since 2018; *b* Crawley, W Sussex, 12 Nov. 1966; *s* of Alan and Susan Fitzgerald; *m* 1992, Rebecca Clare Parker (*see* R. C. Fitzgerald); four *s*. *Educ:* Girton Coll., Cambridge (BA 1989; MA); Darwin Coll., Cambridge (PhD 1994). FREng 2014. Actg Asst Prof., Stanford Univ., 1995–97; Consultant, Bain & Co., 1997–2001; Researcher, Univ. of Cambridge, 2001–05; CEO, Breathing Buildings, 2006–18. Fellow, Girton Coll., Cambridge, 2004–. *Recreation:* trumpet with Prime Brass. *Address:* The Wix, 147 High Street, Harston, Cambs CB22 7QD. *T:* (01223) 870420; Girton College, Huntingdon Road, Cambridge CB3 0JG. *T:* (01223) 338999.

**FitzGERALD, Susanna Patricia;** QC 1999; *d* of late Frederick Patrick FitzGerald, FRCSI, PPICS and Zina Eveline FitzGerald (*née* Moncrieff), FRCP; *m* 1983, Wendell, (Nick), Clough; two *s*. *Educ:* Benenden Sch.; Bristol Univ. (LLB Hons). Called to the Bar, Inner Temple, 1973, Bencher, 2007; in practice at the Bar, 1973–; specialises in gambling and licensing law. Dir, Business in Sport and Leisure, 1994–2013; Chm., Business in Licensing. Dir, Inst. of Licensing, 2008–. Mem., Internat. Masters of Gaming Law, 2011–. Trustee, Gamcare. *Publications:* (contributing ed.) Law of Betting, Gaming and Lotteries, 2nd and 3rd edns; (contrib.) Gambling and Public Policy, 1991; contributing ed., Halsbury's Laws of England, vol. 4(1), Betting, Gaming and Lotteries, 4th edn reissue, 2002. *Recreation:* renovating old houses. *Address:* 1 Essex Court, Temple, EC4Y 9AR. *T:* (020) 7583 2000.

**FitzGERALD, Sylvia Mary Denise,** FLS; Head of Library and Archives (formerly Chief Librarian and Archivist), Royal Botanic Gardens, Kew, 1979–99; *b* 7 May 1939; *d* of Audoen Aengus FitzGerald and Doris Winifred (*née* Dickinson). *Educ:* Our Lady of Sion Sch., Worthing; Open Univ. (BA Hons 1977); Univ. of Surrey (MA Pastoral Theology 2005). MCLIP (ALA 1962). Assistant: Science Mus. Liby, 1956–57; Brit. Mus. (Natural Hist.) Zool. Liby, 1957–63; Assistant Librarian: Patent Office Liby, 1963–65; MAFF, 1965–67; Librarian-in-charge: MAFF Food & Nutrition Liby, 1967–72; MAFF Tolworth Liby for State Vet. Service and Vertebrate Pest Control, 1972–78. Member, Library Committee: Linnean Soc. of London, 1985–2003; RHS, 1993–. FLS 1992. *Publications:* contrib. State Librarian, Aslib Prog., Archives, etc. *Recreations:* friends, music. *Address:* 139 London Road, Ewell, Epsom, Surrey KT17 2BT.

**FITZGERALD, Hon. Tony;** *see* Fitzgerald, Hon. G. E.

**FITZGIBBON, Dr Andrew William,** FREng; Partner Scientist, Microsoft (formerly Principal Researcher, Microsoft Research), Cambridge, since 2005; *b* Dublin, 1968; *s* of Frank and Barbara Fitzgibbon; *m* 2003, Elizabeth Barry; *d* of. *Educ:* University Coll., Cork (BSc 1986); Heriot Watt Univ. (MSc 1989); Univ. of Edinburgh (PhD 1997). FBCS 2012; FREng 2014. Res. Asst, Univ. of Edinburgh, 1990–96; Res. Associate, 1996–99, Royal Soc. Univ. Res. Fellow, 1999–2005, Univ. of Oxford. Chm., British Machine Vision Assoc., 2010–13. Roger Needham Award, BCS, 2006; (jtly) MacRobert Award, 2011, Silver Medal, 2013, RAEng. *Recreation:* ski-ing. *Address:* Microsoft, 21 Station Road, Cambridge CB1 2FB. *E:* awf@microsoft.com.

**FitzGIBBON, Francis George Herbert Dillon;** QC 2010; *b* Dorchester, 18 July 1961; *s* of late Constantine FitzGibbon and Marion FitzGibbon (*née* Gutmann); *m* 1986, Camilla Beresford; one *s* one *d*. *Educ:* Westminster Sch.; Magdalen Coll., Oxford (BA Lit.Hum.; MA). Called to the Bar, Middle Temple, 1986, Bencher, 2017; Immigration Judge, 2002–. Chm., Criminal Bar Assoc., 2016–17. Trustee: Turner Contemp., Margate, 2008–16; Chaos Theory, 2016–. FRSA. *Recreations:* family, music, running. *Address:* 23 Essex Street, WC2R 3AA. *E:* francisfitzgibbon@23es.com.

**FitzHARRIS, Viscount; James Hugh Carleton Harris;** *b* 29 April 1970; *s* and *heir* of Earl of Malmesbury, *qv*; *m* 1997, Jemima, *d* of Captain M. Fulford-Dobson, *qv*; two *s* one *d*. *Educ:* Eton; Christ Church, Oxford (MEng); RAC Cirencester (DipAgr). ACA 1997. *Heir:* s Hon. James Michael Oswald Harris, *b* 26 April 1999. *Address:* Sydling Court, Sydling St Nicholas, Dorchester, Dorset DT2 9PA.

**FITZHARRIS, Ven. Robert Aidan;** Archdeacon of Doncaster, 2001–11, Archdeacon Emeritus, since 2012; *b* 19 Aug. 1946; *s* of late John Joseph and Margaret Louisa Fitzharris; *m* 1971, Lesley Margaret Mary Rhind; three *d*. *Educ:* St Anselm's Coll., Birkenhead; Sheffield Univ. (BDS 1971); Lincoln Theol Coll. (Gen. Ministerial Exam. 1989). General dental practice, 1971–87; part-time Clinical Asst to Prof. of Child Dental Health, Charles Clifford Dental Hosp., Sheffield, 1978–85. Ordained deacon, 1989, priest, 1990; Asst Curate, Dinnington, 1989–92; Vicar of Bentley, 1992–2001; Substitute Chaplain, HMP Moorland, 1992–2001; Area Dean, Adwick-le-Street, 1995–2001. Hon. Associate Chaplain, Doncaster Royal Infirmary and Mexbrough Montague Hosp. Trust, 1995–2001; Hon. Canon, Sheffield Cathedral, 1998; Hon. Associate Priest, Doncaster Minster, 2014–; Hon. Chaplain to Civic Mayor of Doncaster, 2014–15; Hon. Chaplain to High Sheriff of S Yorks 2015–16. Chairman: Sheffield Diocesan Strategy Gp, 1999–2001; Sheffield Diocesan Bd of Educn, 2001–11; Sheffield Diocesan Parsonages Cttee, 2001–11; Doncaster Minster Develt Cttee, 2005–07; Together for Regeneration Project, 2004–10; Refurnish Ltd (formerly Doncaster Refurnish Ltd), 2007–; Member: Doncaster Adv. Gp, Common Purpose S Yorks, 2004–; Res. Ethics Cttee, Sheffield Univ., 2007–. Founding Chm., Bentley Assoc. for Supportive Help, 1995–2001; Chairman: Doncaster Cancer Detection Trust, 2003–; Doncaster Freeman Gp, 2015– (Vice Chm., 2014–15). Chm., Wildwood Project (Bentley) Ltd, 1998–2004. Chm., Friends of Doncaster Mansion House, 2015–; Vice-Patron, Doncaster and Dist Family Hist. Soc., 2006–; Patron, Doncaster and Dist Heritage Assoc., 2016–. Life Mem., Royal and Ancient Polar Bear Soc. of Hammerfest, Norway, 2012. Hon. Freeman, Bor. of Doncaster, 2008. Occasional broadcaster, BBC Radio 2 Pause for Thought; regular contributor, BBC Radio Sheffield. *Recreations:* travelling the world to cuddle local and and antipodean grandchildren, cooking for them, and attempting to read at the same time. *Address:* Amberley, Old Bawtry Road, Finningley, Doncaster DN9 3BY. *T:* (01302) 773220. *E:* lesleyfitzharris@waitrose.com.

**FITZHERBERT,** family name of **Baron Stafford**.

**FitzHERBERT, Giles Eden,** CMG 1985; HM Diplomatic Service, retired; *b* Dublin, 8 March 1935; *e s* of late Captain H. C. FitzHerbert, Irish Guards, and Sheelah, *d* of J. X. Murphy; *m* 1st, 1962, Margaret Waugh (*d* 1986); one *s* three *d* (and one *s* decd); 2nd, 1988, Alexandra Eyre; three *s* one *d*. *Educ:* Ampleforth Coll.; Christ Church Oxford; Harvard Business Sch. 2nd Lieut, 8th King's Royal Irish Hussars, 1957–58. Vickers da Costa & Co., 1962–66. First Secretary: Foreign Office, 1966; Rome, 1968–71; FCO, 1972–75; Counsellor: Kuwait, 1975–77; Nicosia, 1977–78; Head of Eur. Community Dept (Ext.), FCO, 1978–82; on sabbatical leave, LSE, 1982; Inspector, FCO, 1983; Minister, Rome, 1983–87; Ambassador to Venezuela and concurrently (non-resident) to the Dominican Republic, 1988–93. Contested (L) Fermanagh and South Tyrone, Gen. Elect., 1964. *Address:* Woodbrook House, Killanne, Enniscorthy, Co. Wexford, Ireland. *Club:* Beefsteak.

**FitzHERBERT, Sir Richard (Ranulph),** 9th Bt *cr* 1784, of Tissington, Derbyshire; *b* 2 Nov. 1963; *s* of Rev. David Henry FitzHerbert, MC (*d* 1976) and Charmian Hyacinthe (*d* 2006), *yr d* of late Samuel Ranulph Allsopp, CBE; *S* uncle, 1989; *m* 1st, 1993, Caroline Louise (marr. diss. 2007), *d* of late Major and Mrs Patrick Shuter; one *s* one *d*; 2nd, 2011, Fiona Alison, *d* of late Dr and Mrs John Fitzgerald. *Educ:* Eton College. Mem. (C) Derbys Dales DC, 2011–. President: Derbys Community Foundn, 1995–; Derbys Rural Community Council, 1996–; Derbys Scouts, 2005–; Member, Board: E Midlands Tourism, 2004–07; Visit Peak District and Derbyshire Destination Mgt Partnership, 2005–12; Historic Houses (formerly HHA), 2009– (Mem., 1995, Chm., 1999–2006, E Midlands HHA). Patron, Soc. of Derbys Golf Captains. *Recreations:* cricket, shooting, restoring family estate. *Heir:* s Frederick David FitzHerbert, *b* 23 March 1995. *Address:* Tissington Hall, Ashbourne, Derbys DE6 1RA. *E:* tisshall@dircon.co.uk. *Clubs:* White's, MCC; I Zingari, Stansted Hall Cricket, S Anselms Strollers Cricket, Strawberry Cricket.

**FitzHUGH, (Edmund Francis) Lloyd,** OBE 1995; JP; barrister; Vice Lord-Lieutenant for the County of Clwyd, since 2008; *b* 2 Feb. 1951; *s* of late Godfrey Edmund FitzHugh and Burness Grace FitzHugh (*née* Clemson); *m* 1975, Pauline Davison; two *s*. *Educ:* Eton; Shuttleworth Agricl Coll. Chairman: Bd of Mgt, Royal Welsh Agricl Soc., 1991–98; NE Wales NHS Trust, 1999–2005. Dep. Chm., Local Govt Boundary Commn for Wales, 1995–2002. Chm., Dangerpoint charity, 2013–; Trustee, Community Foundn in Wales, 2013–. JP Wrexham 1990; DL 1996, High Sheriff, 2011–12, Clwyd. *Recreations:* church music, wining and dining. *Address:* Garden House, Plas Power, Bersham, Wrexham LL14 4LN. *T:* (01978) 263522.

**FITZMAURICE;** *see* Petty-Fitzmaurice, family name of Marquess of Lansdowne.

**FITZPATRICK, Brian;** advocate; *b* 9 June 1961; *s* of late Patrick Fitzpatrick and Kathleen (*née* Strong); *m* 1986, Marie Macdonald; one *s* two *d*. *Educ:* Univ. of Glasgow (LLB Juris 1984). Called to Scottish Bar, 1993; Solicitor, Glasgow, Edinburgh and London, 1984–92; Mem., Faculty of Advocates, 1993–. Hd of Policy, First Minister's Policy Unit, Scottish Parlt, 1999–2000. MSP (Lab) Strathkelvin and Bearsden, June 2001–2003. Contested (Lab) Strathkelvin and Bearsden, Scottish Parlt, 2003. *Recreations:* swimming, cinema, reading, poetry, travel, wine, politics. *Address:* c/o Advocates' Library, Parliament House, Edinburgh EH1 1RF.

**FITZPATRICK, Francis Paul;** QC 2015; a Deputy High Court Judge, since 2018; *b* Birmingham, 16 April 1967; *s* of Thomas Fitzpatrick and Catherine Fitzpatrick (*née* Coote); *m* 1997, Jessica; one *s* one *d*. *Educ:* Handsworth Grammar Sch.; Worcester Coll., Oxford (BA 1st Cl. Hons Law; BCL). Called to the Bar, Inner Temple, 1990. *Recreations:* ski-ing, tennis, croquet, theatre. *Address:* 1st Floor, 11 New Square, Lincoln's Inn, WC2A 3QB.

**FITZPATRICK, James, (Jim);** MP (Lab) Poplar and Limehouse, since 2010 (Poplar and Canning Town, 1997–2010); *b* 4 April 1952; *s* of James Fitzpatrick and Jean Fitzpatrick (*née* Stones). *Educ:* Holyrood Sch., Glasgow. Trainee, Tytrak Ltd, Glasgow, 1970–73; driver, Mintex Ltd, 1973–74; Firefighter, London Fire Brigade, 1974–97. PPS to Sec. of State for Health, 1999–2001; an Asst Govt Whip, 2001–02; a Lord Comr of HM Treasury (Govt Whip), 2002–03; Vice-Chamberlain of HM Household, 2003–05; Parliamentary Under-Secretary of State: ODPM, 2005–06; DTI, 2006–07; DfT, 2007–09; Minister of State, DEFRA, 2009–10; Shadow Minister for Envmt, Food and Rural Affairs, 2010, for Transport, 2010–13. Mem., NEC, Fire Bdes Union, 1988–97. Mem. Exec., Gtr London Lab. Party, 1988–2000 (Chm., 1991–2000). Fire Bde Long Service and Good Conduct Medal, 1994. *Recreations:* cycling, reading, football (West Ham Utd), television and films. *Address:* House of Commons, SW1A 0AA. *T:* (020) 7219 5085.

**FITZPATRICK, Air Marshal Sir John (Bernard),** KBE 1984; CB 1982; Royal Air Force, retired; *b* 15 Dec. 1929; *s* of Joseph Fitzpatrick and Bridget Fitzpatrick; *m* 1954, Gwendoline Mary Abbott; two *s* one *d*. *Educ:* RAF Apprentice Sch., Halton; RAF Coll. Cranwell. Officer Commanding: No 81 Sqdn, 1966–68; No 35 Sqdn, 1971–72; Gp Captain Plans to AOC No 18 Gp, 1973; OC, RAF Scampton, 1974–75; RCDS, 1976; Dir of Ops (Strike), RAF, 1977–79; SASO, HQ Strike Command, 1980–82; Dir Gen. of Organisation, RAF, 1982–83; AOC No 18 Gp, RAF, and Comdr Maritime Air Eastern Atlantic and Channel, 1983–86. Ind. Panel Inspector, Depts of the Envmt and Transport, 1986–99. *Recreations:* good food with good company, DIY.

**FitzPATRICK, Joseph Martin;** Member (SNP) Dundee City West, Scottish Parliament, since 2011 (Dundee West, 2007–11); Minister for Public Health, Sport and Wellbeing, since 2018; *b* 1 April 1967; *s* of Joseph K. FitzPatrick and Margaret M. FitzPatrick (*née* Crabb). *Educ:* Univ. of Abertay Dundee (BSc Hons). Mem., Dundee CC, 1999–2007. Minister for Parly Business, Scottish Parlt, 2012–18. Contested (SNP) Dundee W, 2005. *Recreations:* hill-walking, trekking, scuba diving. *Address:* (office) 37 Dock Street, Dundee DD1 3DR. *T:* (01382) 623200, *Fax:* (01382) 903205. *E:* dundee@joefitzpatrick.net.

**FITZPATRICK, Prof. Raymond Michael,** PhD; Professor of Public Health and Primary Care, University of Oxford, since 1996; Fellow, Nuffield College, Oxford, since 1986; *b* 8 Oct. 1950; *s* of James Fitzpatrick and Maureen Fitzpatrick; *m* 1979, Mary Boulton. *Educ:* UC, Oxford (BA); Bedford Coll., London Univ. (MSc; PhD 1986). Lecturer: Bedford Coll., London Univ., 1978–86; Oxford Univ., 1986–. Mem., MRC, 1998–2003 (Chm., Health Services and Public Health Res. Bd, 1998–2003). *Publications:* (jtly) The Experience of Illness, 1984; (ed with G. Albrecht) Quality of Life in Health Care, 1994; (jtly) Understanding Rheumatoid Arthritis, 1995; (ed jtly) Health Services Research Methods, 1998. *Recreations:* music, theatre. *Address:* Nuffield College, Oxford OX1 1NF. *T:* (01865) 278500.

**FitzROY,** family name of **Duke of Grafton** and of **Baron Southampton**.

**FitzROY NEWDEGATE,** family name of **Viscount Daventry**.

**FITZSIMONS, Anthony;** see Fitzsimons, P. A.

**FITZSIMONS, Prof. James Thomas,** FRS 1988; Professor of Medical Physiology, University of Cambridge, 1990–95, now Emeritus Professor; Fellow of Gonville and Caius College, Cambridge, since 1961 (President, 1997–2005); *b* 8 July 1928; *s* of Robert Allen Fitzsimons, FRCS and Dr Mary Patricia (*née* McKelvey); *m* 1961, Aude Irène Jeanne, *d* of Gén. Jean Etienne Valluy, DSO and Marie (*née* Bourdillon); two *s* one *d*. *Educ:* St Edmund's Coll., Ware; Gonville and Caius Coll., Cambridge (1st cl. Pts I and II, Nat. Sci. Tripos; BA 1949; BChir 1953; MB 1954; MA 1954; PhD 1960; MD 1967, Sir Lionel Whitby Medal; ScD 1979); Charing Cross Hosp. House appts, Leicester Gen. and Charing Cross Hosps, 1954–55; RAF, Inst. of Aviation Medicine, 1955–57 (Flight Lieut); Cambridge University: MRC Scholar, Physiol. Lab., 1957–59; Univ. Demonstrator in Physiol., 1959–64, Lectr, 1964–76, Reader, 1976–90; Gonville and Caius College: Tutor, 1964–72; Coll. Lectr in Physiol., 1964–93; Dir of Studies in Medicine, 1978–93. Visiting Scientist: CNRS Lab. des Régulations Alimentaires, Coll. de France, 1967; Inst. of Neurol Scis, Univ. of Pennsylvania, 1968, 1972; CNRS Lab. de Neurobiol., Coll. de France, 1975; Lectures: Stevenson Meml, Univ. of Western Ontario, 1979; Halliburton, KCL, 1982. Royal Soc. rep., British Nat. Cttee for Physiol. Scis, 1976–82; Mem., Physiol. Soc. Cttee, 1972–76 (Chm., 1975–76); Mem., IUPS Commn on Physiol. of Food and Fluid Intake, 1973–80 (Chm., 1979–80). Member, Editorial Boards: Jl of Physiol., 1977–84; Neuroendocrinology, 1979–84; Editor, Biological Reviews, 1984–95. Hon. MD Lausanne, 1978. Dist. Career Award, Soc. for Study of Ingestive Behavior, 1998. *Publications:* The Physiology of Thirst and Sodium Appetite, 1979; scientific papers in professional jls. *Recreations:* Irish language and literature, cats, music, photography, grandchildren, gardening. *Address:* Gonville and Caius College, Trinity Street, Cambridge CB2 1TA. *T:* (01223) 332429; 91 Thornton Road, Girton, Cambridge CB3 0NR. *T:* (01223) 276874.

**FITZSIMONS, Lorna, (Mrs S. B. Cooney);** Director, Lorna Fitzsimons Consulting Ltd, since 2013; Co-Founder and Chief Executive Officer, MK-LF Partnership (The Pipeline), since 2013; Director, Alliance Project and N Brown Textile Growth Programme, since 2012; *b* 6 Aug. 1967; *d* of late Derek Fitzsimons and of Barbara Jean Taylor; *m* 2000, Stephen Benedict Cooney; one *s*, and one step *s* one step *d*. *Educ:* Wardle High Sch.; Rochdale Coll. of Art and Design; Loughborough Coll. of Art and Design (BA Hons Textile Design 1988; a Vice Pres., Students' Union, 1988–89). National Union of Students: part-time Nat. Exec. Officer, 1989–90; Vice Pres., Educn, 1990–92; Pres., 1992–94; Rowland Public Affairs: Account Manager, 1994–95; Account Dir, 1995–96; Associate Dir, 1996–97. Mem. Bd, Endsleigh Insce, 1992–94. Chair, Student Forum, EU, 1990–94; Mem., Quality Cttee, FEFC, 1993–94. Member National Executive: Fabian Soc., 1996–97; Lab. Co-ordinating Cttee, 1995–97, Campaign of Electoral Reform, 1997, Labour Party. MP (Lab) Rochdale, 1997–2005; contested (Lab) same seat, 2005. PPS to Minister of State, FCO, 2000–01, to Leader of H of C, 2001–03. Treas., 1997–2003, Chm., 2003–05, All Party Parly Gp on Kashmir. Chair, 1997–2001, Vice Pres., 2001–05, Women's Cttee, PLP. Supporter, Labour Friends of Israel, 1997–2005. Lorna Fitzsimons Consulting, 2005–06; CEO, Britain Israel Communications & Res. Centre, 2006–12. Sen. Associate Fellow, UK Defence Acad. Advanced Res. and Assessment Gp, 2005. Dir, Regl Growth Fund, 2013–. Governor: Wardle High Sch., 1982–83, 2003; Loughborough Coll. of Art and Design, 1988–89; Sheffield Hallam Univ., 1995–96. *Recreations:* watching films, cooking, walking, travelling, dancing or listening to music. *E:* mail@lornafitzsimons.net.

**FITZSIMONS, P. Anthony;** Chairman: Ruton Management Ltd, since 1994; Prisoner Escort and Custody Services Lay Observers' National Council, since 2015; *b* 16 March 1946; two *s*. *Educ:* LSE (BSc Econ.). Rank Xerox: Australia, 1972–75; Southern Europe, 1975–76; Australasia, Middle East, 1976–79; Regional Control Dir, London, 1979–81; Grand Metropolitan: Finance Systems and Strategy Dir, Brewing and Retail Div., 1981–83; Man. Dir, Host Group, 1983–85; Man. Dir, Personal Banking, Citibank, 1985–89; Chief Exec. and Man. Dir, Bristol & West Bldg Soc., 1989–93. Chm., Avon TEC. Chairman: Great Western Ambulance Service NHS Trust, 2006–12; Gloucestershire Probation Trust, 2007–14. *Recreations:* squash, riding, music, sailing. *Address:* Hill House, Hannington, Wilts SN6 7RS.

**FitzWALTER,** 22nd Baron *cr* 1295; **Julian Brook Plumptre;** *b* 18 Oct. 1952; *s* of 21st Baron FitzWalter and Margaret Melesina (*née* Deedes); *S* father, 2004; *m* 1988, Sally, *o d* of late I. M. T. Quiney; three *s*. *Educ:* Radley; Wye Coll., London Univ. *Heir: s* Hon. Edward Brook Plumptre, *b* 26 April 1989.

**FIVET, Edmond Charles Paul,** CBE 2008; FRCM; Principal, Royal Welsh College of Music and Drama, 1989–2007; *b* 12 Feb. 1947; *s* of Paul Fivet and Lorna (*née* Edwards); *m* 1st, 1969, Christine Partington (marr. diss. 1976); one *s* one *d*; 2nd, 1978, Elizabeth Page. *Educ:* Royal Coll. of Music; Coll. of St Mark and St John; City Univ. (MA); Open Univ. (BA). FRCM 1988. Registrar, 1973–83, Dir, 1983–89, Jun. Dept, Royal Coll. of Music; Music Dir, Audi Jun. Musician, 1986–98. Member: Music Cttee, Welsh Arts Council, 1991–94; Steering Cttee, NYO of Wales, 1991–2002; Music Cttee, Cardiff Internat. Fest., 1992–95; Council, Arts Council of Wales, 2000–03; Vice-Pres., Richmond upon Thames Arts Council, 1986–98. Member: Assoc. of European Conservatoires, 1989–2007; Heads of Higher Educn, Wales, 1996–2007. Music Director: Aldeburgh Music Club, 2008–; Phoenix Singers, 2008–12; Conductor, Prometheus Orch., 2008–. Chairman: Bury St Edmunds Concert Club, 2008–17; Making Music Concert Promoters Gp (formerly Cttee), 2010–15; Adjudicators, Bromsgrove Internat. Young Musicians' Competition, 2012–17. Gov., Dartington Coll. of Arts, 1997–2004. Trustee: Millennium Stadium Charitable Trust, 2001–06; Nat. Children's Orchestras, 2014–16. Hon. FRBC (Hon. FBC 2006); Fellow, RWCMD, 2007. DUniv Glamorgan, 2007. *Recreations:* golf, music, theatre, reading, current affairs. *Address:* Fair Winds, 11 North Warren, Aldeburgh, Suffolk IP15 5QF. *Club:* Aldeburgh Golf.

**FLACH, Timothy Irvine;** photographer, specialising in conceptual images of animals, since 1983; *b* London, 16 April 1958; *s* of late Robert Thomas Francis Flach and Mary Irvine Flach, TD (*née* Friend; she *m* 2nd 5th Baron Crofton); *m* 2008, Yu Sun; one *s*. *Educ:* Launceston Coll., Cornwall; North East London Poly. (BA Hons Communication Design 1980); St Martin's Sch. of Art (Postgrad. Photography and Painted Structures 1983). Works in public collections incl. Nat. Media Mus., UK. FBIPP 2013. Hon. FRPS 2013. Hon. Dr Norwich Univ. of Arts, 2013. Fine Art Photographer of Year, USA, Internat. Photography Awards, 2006; Best in Book, Creative Rev. Photography Annual UK, 2010, 2012, 2013. *Publications:* Equus, 2008 (German and French edns 2008, Chinese edn 2011); Dogs Gods, 2010 (German, French, Australian edns 2010, Chinese edn 2011); More Than Human, 2012 (German and Australian edns 2012); Stern Portfolio NI.74 Evolution, 2013; Endangered, 2017; contribs to Nat. Geographic mag., NY Times, Sunday Times. *Recreations:* dancing, running, table tennis. *Address:* 58 Eastern Street, EC2A 3QR. *E:* tim@timflach.com.

**FLACK, John;** JP; Member (C) East of England, European Parliament, 2017–19; *b* Romford, 3 Jan. 1957; *s* of William James Flack and Edith Alice Flack (*née* Clarke); *m* 1st, 1980, Susan Ritchie (marr. diss. 2004); four *s*; 2nd, 2017, Louise Bradley. *Educ:* Abbs Cross High Sch.; Univ. of Reading. Chm., EALP Ltd, 1983–. European Parliament: Cons. Spokesman, Regl Develt Cttee; Member: PECH (Fisheries) Cttee; Animal Welfare Intergp. Contested (C) East of England, EP, 2019. Founding Chm., Greenfields Community Housing, 2006–08. JP Essex, 1988.

**FLACK, Rt Rev. John Robert;** an Honorary Assistant Bishop: Diocese in Europe, since 2004; Diocese of Leeds, since 2017; *b* 30 May 1942; *s* of Edwin John Flack and Joan Annie Flack; *m* 1968, Julia Clare Slaughter; one *s* one *d*. *Educ:* Hertford Grammar Sch.; Univ. of Leeds (BA 1964); Coll. of the Resurrection, Mirfield. Ordained, deacon, 1966, priest, 1967; Assistant Curate: St Bartholomew, Armley, Leeds, 1966–69; St Mary the Virgin, Northampton, 1969–72; Vicar: Chapelthorpe (Wakefield dio.), 1972–81; Rippondon with Rishworth and Barkisland with West Scammonden, 1981–85; Brighouse, 1985–92 (Team Rector, 1988–92); Rural Dean of Brighouse and Elland, 1986–92; Archdeacon of Pontefract, 1992–97; Bishop Suffragan of Huntingdon, 1997–2003; Dir, Anglican Centre in Rome, and Archbp of Canterbury's Rep. to the Holy See, 2003–08; an Hon. Asst Bp, Dio. of Peterborough, 2013–17, Dio. of Ely, 2013–17; Priest-in-charge, Nassington with Yarwell and Woodnewton, and of Apethorpe, 2008–12. Hon. Canon of Peterborough Cathedral, 2004–12, now Canon Emeritus. *Recreations:* cricket, Mozart. *Address:* 6 Oakhall Park, Crigglestone, Wakefield WF4 3HG. *E:* johnflack67@yahoo.com.

**FLAHERTY, Patrick John;** Chief Executive, Somerset County Council, since 2014; *b* Stoke-on-Trent, 23 Sept. 1968; *s* of Vincent and Rosemary Flaherty; *m* 1993, Alison Ball; one *s* one *d*. *Educ:* St Thomas More High Sch. and Sixth Form Coll., Stoke-on-Trent; Bolton Inst. of Higher Educn (BEng Hons Civil Engrg 1997); Univ. of Salford (MSc Transport Engrg 2000). Hd of Regeneration, Stafford BC, 2002–06; Somerset County Council: Hd of Regeneration, 2006–11; Dir, Envmt Services, 2011–12; Gp Dir Ops, 2012–14. Gov., Richard Huish Sixth Form Coll., Taunton, 2013–. *Recreations:* cycling, literature, family. *Address:* Somerset County Council, County Hall, The Crescent, Taunton, Som TA1 4DY.

**FLAHIVE, Daniel Michael; His Honour Judge Flahive;** a Circuit Judge, since 2009; *b* London, 1 Oct. 1958; *s* of Jeremiah and Eileen Flahive; *m* 1989, Cheryl Ulmer; two *s*. *Educ:* London Sch. of Econs (LLB Hons); Inns of Court Sch. of Law. Called to the Bar, Gray's Inn, 1982; in practice specialising in criminal law, London, 1982–2009; Recorder, 2003–09. Judicial Mem., Parole Bd, 2010–13. *Recreation:* travel. *Address:* Croydon Combined Court Centre, The Law Courts, Altyre Road, Croydon CR9 5AB. *T:* (020) 8410 4700.

**FLANAGAN, Andrew Henry;** a Civil Service Commissioner, 2014–19; Chairman, Scottish Police Authority, 2015–17; *b* 15 March 1956; *s* of Francis Desmond Flanagan and Martha Donaldson Flanagan; *m* 1992, Virginia Walker; two *s* one *d*. *Educ:* Glasgow Univ. (BAcc). CA. Touche Ross, 1976–79; Price Waterhouse, 1979–81; Financial Control Manager, ITT, 1981–86; Finance Dir, PA Consulting Gp, 1986–91; Gp Finance Dir and Chief Financial Officer, BIS Ltd, 1991–94; Finance Dir, Scottish Television plc, 1994–96; Man. Dir, Scottish Television plc, 1996–97; Chief Exec., SMG (formerly Scottish Media Gp) plc, 1997–2006; Chm., Fleming Media, 2007–08; Chief Exec., NSPCC, 2009–13. Chm., Heritage House Gp, 2008–12 (Dir, 2008–12); Dir, Phonepayplus, 2008–09. Non-executive Director: NHS North and East London Commissioning Support Unit, 2013–; Criminal Injuries Compensation Authy, 2014–; NHS Business Services Authy, 2014– (Chair, Audit and Risk Cttee, 2015–); CIPFA Business Services Ltd, 2014–17. Non-exec. Dir, Scottish RU, 2005–. Trustee, NESTA, 2006–09. *Recreations:* golf, ski-ing, television.

**FLANAGAN, Caroline Jane;** Partner, Ross & Connel, Solicitors, Dunfermline, since 1990; President, Law Society of Scotland, 2005–06; *b* 12 Jan. 1961; *d* of Leslie and Sheila Ebbutt; *m* 1986, Roy Flanagan; one *s* one *d*. *Educ:* Dollar Acad.; Edinburgh Univ. (LLB, DipLP). Trainee, then asst solicitor, 1982–90. Dean, Dunfermline and Dist Soc. of Solicitors, 2000–02; Vice-Pres., Law Soc. of Scotland, 2004–05. *Recreations:* ski-ing, walking, reading, music. *Address:* Ross & Connel, 18 Viewfield Terrace, Dunfermline KY12 7JH. *T:* (01383) 721156. *E:* cflanagan@ross.connel.co.uk.

**FLANAGAN, Charles;** Member (FG) of the Dáil (TD) for Laois-Offaly, 1987–2002 and since 2007; Minister for Justice and Equality, Ireland, since 2017; *b* Dublin, 1 Nov. 1956; *s* of Oliver J. Flanagan and Mai Flanagan (*née* McWey); *m* 1984, Mary McCormack; two *d*. *Educ:* University Coll., Dublin (BA Hist. and Politics 1977). Admitted as solicitor, Ireland, 1982; legal practice in Portlaoise specialising in family and criminal law, 1982–87. FG spokesperson on NI, 1997–2000; Chief Whip (FG), 2000–02; Opposition spokesperson: on Justice, Equality and Defence, 2007–10; on Children and Youth Affairs, 2010–11; Minister for Children and Youth Affairs, 2014, for Foreign Affairs and Trade, 2014–17. Chairperson, FG Parly Party, 2011–14. Vice-Chm., British-Irish Parly Gp, 1997–2000. Member (FG): Mountmellik Town Council, 1987–91; Laois CC, 1987–2004. Mem., FG Party Exec. Council, 1995–2002 and 2010–14. *Recreations:* hill walking, following football and Gaelic games. *Address:* Department of Justice and Equality, 51 St Stephen's Green, Dublin 2, Ireland. *E:* charlie.flanagan@oir.ie. *Club:* Rotary (Portlaoise).

**FLANAGAN, Michael Joseph;** Director, Finance and Planning, Cheshire Constabulary, 1995–2000; Company Secretary, FFBA Ltd, since 2004; *b* 21 Nov. 1946; *s* of Daniel and Margaret Constance Flanagan; *m* 1968, Patricia Holland; two *s* one *d*. *Educ:* St Joseph's Coll., Blackpool; Southampton Coll. of Higher Educn. IPFA 1972; DMS 1983. Trainee Accountant, Lancs CC, 1965–69; Preston County Borough, 1969–70; Southampton City

Council, 1970–72; Accountant, 1972, Asst Dir of Finance, 1981–87, Telford Develt Corp.; Dir of Finance and Tech. Services, 1987–90, Chief Exec., 1990–95, Develt Bd for Rural Wales. *Recreations:* sport, esp. football, golf, tennis; family activities. *Club:* Lancs CC.

FLANAGAN, Sir Ronald, GBE 2002 (OBE 1996); Kt 1999; QPM 2007; HM Chief Inspector of Constabulary, 2005–08; Strategic Adviser to the Minister of Interior, United Arab Emirates, since 2009; Chairman, Anti-Corruption and Security Unit, International Cricket Council, since 2010; *b* 25 March 1949; *s* of John Patrick Flanagan and Henrietta Flanagan; *m* 1968, Lorraine Nixon; three *s*. *Educ:* Belfast High Sch.; Univ. of Ulster (BA, MA); Graduate: FBI Nat. Acad., 1987; FBI Nat. Exec. Inst., 1996. Joined Royal Ulster Constabulary, as Constable, 1970: Sergeant, Belfast, 1973; Inspector, Londonderry, 1976, Belfast, 1977–81; Detective Inspector, 1981; Detective Chief Inspector, 1983; Detective Superintendent, Armagh, 1987; Chief Superintendent, Police Staff Coll., Bramshill, 1990; Asst Chief Constable, Belfast, 1992; Actg Dep. Chief Constable, 1995, affirmed Feb. 1996; Chief Constable, RUC, 1996–2002; HM Inspector of Constabulary, 2002–05. Advr on illegal tobacco trade, British American Tobacco, 2013–. *Recreations:* walking, Rugby, reading (particularly Yeats' poetry), music (particularly Van Morrison), but very varied taste. *Club:* Royal Ulster Yacht (Bangor, Co. Down).

FLANDERS, Stephanie Hope; Head, Bloomberg Economics, and Senior Executive Editor for Economics, Bloomberg News, since 2017; *b* 5 Aug. 1968; *d* of late Michael Flanders, OBE and Claudia Flanders, OBE; partner, John Arlidge; one *s* one *d*. *Educ:* St Paul's Girls' Sch., Hammersmith; Balliol Coll., Oxford (Schol.; BA 1st Cl. Hons PPE); John F. Kennedy Sch. of Govt, Harvard Univ. (Kennedy Schol.; MPA). Research Officer: London Business Sch., 1990–91; Inst. for Fiscal Studies, 1991–92; Teaching Fellow, Dept of Govt, Harvard Univ., and Kennedy Sch. of Govt, 1993–94; econs leader-writer and columnist, Financial Times, 1994–97; Sen. Advr and speechwriter to Lawrence H. Summers, US Treasury Dept, 1997–2001; reporter, NY Times, 2001; Econs Ed., Newsnight, BBC TV, 2002–08; Econs Ed., BBC, 2008–13; Stephanomics (series), BBC Radio 4, 2011–13; Chief Market Strategist, Europe, JP Morgan Asset Mgt, 2013–17. Mem., Council on Foreign Relns, 2001–. Mem., Gen. Council, REconS, 2007–. FRSA 2006. *Publications:* Principal Editor: World Bank World Development Reports, 1996, 1997; UN Human Development Report, 2002. *Recreations:* cycling, collecting jokes. *E:* Flanders@bloomberg.net. *Club:* Soho House.

FLANNERY, Liz; *see* Pichon, L.

FLANNERY, Louis Kruschev; QC 2018; Partner, since 2008, and Head, International Arbitration Group, since 2009, Stephenson Harwood LLP, solicitors; *b* London, 22 July 1963; *s* of Nollaig Flannery and Evelyne Shine (*née* Dunton); partner, Ania Farren; three *s* two *d*. *Educ:* Langley Park Sch. for Boys; Univ. of Southampton (LLB Hons 1985); Coll. of Law, Guildford. FCIArb 2002. Articled clerk and solicitor, Church Adams Tatham & Co., 1988–92; solicitor: Wedlake Bell, 1994–97; S J Berwin & Co., 1997–2003; solicitor and Partner, Howes Percival LLP, 2003–08. FRGS 2001. *Publications:* (with Robert Merkin) Arbitration Act 1996, 4th edn 2008, 5th edn 2014; Consultant Ed., Merkin's Arbitration Law, 2003–. *Recreations:* children (creating and raising), pink fizz, trying to avoid being ejected from London hotels for indulging in too much of the latter, telling tall tales to anyone who will listen, supporting Irish Rugby team, enjoying other sports, eating snow. *Address:* Stephenson Harwood LLP, One Finsbury Circus, EC2M 7SH. *T:* (020) 7809 2319. *Club:* Gravetye Manor.

FLAPAN, Andrew Daniel, MD; FRCP; Consultant Cardiologist, New Royal Infirmary of Edinburgh, since 1994; Physician to the Queen in Scotland, since 2009; *b* London, 20 Sept. 1956; *m* 1994, Christiane Thöennes; two *s*. *Educ:* Epsom Coll.; London Hosp. Med. Coll. (MB BS 1981); Univ. of London (MD 1993). FRCP 2008. *Recreations:* Fly Fishing, Association football (Chelsea FC). *Address:* New Royal Infirmary of Edinburgh, Little France, Edinburgh EH16 4SA. *T:* (0131) 242 1847. *E:* andrew.flapan@luht.scot.nhs.uk.

FLATHER, family name of Baroness Flather.

FLATHER, Baroness *cr* 1990 (Life Peer), of Windsor and Maidenhead in the Royal County of Berkshire; Shreela Flather; JP; DL; Councillor, Royal Borough of Windsor and Maidenhead, 1976–91 (first ethnic minority woman Councillor in UK), Mayor, 1986–87 (first Asian woman to hold this office); *b* Lahore, India; *née* Shreela Rai; *m* Gary Denis Flather OBE, QC (*d* 2017); two *s*. *Educ:* University Coll. London (LLB; Fellow 1992). Called to the Bar, Inner Temple, 1962. Infant Teacher, ILEA, 1965–67; Teacher of English as a second lang., Altwood Comp. Sch., Maidenhead, 1968–74; Broadmoor Hosp., 1974–78. Chairman: Consortium for Street Children Charities, 1992–94; Disasters Emergency Cttee, 1993–96; Vice Chm., Refugee Council, 1991–94; Member: W Metropolitan Conciliation Cttee, Race Relations Bd, 1973–78; Cttee of Inquiry (Rampton, later Swann Cttee) into Educn of Children from Ethnic Minority Gps, 1979–85; Comr, CRE, 1980–86 (Chm., Educn, Housing and Services Cttee, and Welsh Consultative Cttee, 1980–86); UK Rep., EC Commn into Racism and Xenophobia, 1994–95. Member: Police Complaints Board, 1982–85; HRH Duke of Edinburgh's Inquiry into British Housing, 1984–85; Lord Chancellor's Legal Aid Adv. Cttee, 1985–88; Social Security Adv. Cttee, 1987–90; Econ. and Social Cttee, EC, 1987–90; Carnegie Inquiry into the Third Age, 1990–93; H of L Select Cttee on Med. Ethics, 1993–94; Equal Opportunities Cttee, Bar Council, 2002–03; Chm., Alcohol Educn and Res. Council, 1996–2002; Dir, Marie Stopes Internat., 1996–2017. President: Cambs, Chilterns and Thames Rent Assessment Panel, 1983–97; Community Council for Berks, 1991–98; Member: Thames and Chilterns Tourist Bd, 1987–88; Berks FPC, 1987–88; Jt Pres., FPA, 1995–98; Vice-Pres., BSA, 1988–91. Member: Cons. Women's Nat. Cttee (formerly Cons. Women's Nat. Adv. Cttee), 1978–89; Exec. Cttee, Anglo-Asian Cons. Soc., 1979–83; NEC, Cons. Party, 1989–90; Sec., Windsor and Maidenhead Cons. Gp, 1979–83. Chm., Star FM, 1992–97; Director: Daytime Television, 1978–79; Thames Valley Enterprise, 1990–93; Meridian Broadcasting, 1991–2001; Cable Corp., 1997–2000; Kiss FM, 2000–02; Pres., Global Money Transfer, 1997–2001. Member: BBC S and E Regl Adv. Cttee, 1987–89; Cttee of Management, Servite Houses Ltd, 1987–94; LWT Prog. Adv. Bd, 1990–94. Member: Bd of Visitors, Holloway Prison, 1981–83; Broadmoor Hosp. Bd, 1987–88 (Chm., Ethics Cttee, 1993–97; Equal Opportunities Cttee, 1994–97; Pres., League of Friends, 1991–98); Dir, Hillingdon Hosp. Trust, 1990–98. Vice President: Townswomen's Guilds; Servite Houses Housing Assoc.; Carers Nat. Assoc.; British Assoc. for Counselling and Psychotherapy, 1999–2009. Chm., Memorial Gates Trust, later Memorial Gates Council, 1998–2016 (Life Pres., Meml Gates on Constitution Hill, 2016); Member Council: Winston Churchill Meml Trust, 1993–2008; St George's Hse, Windsor Castle, 1996–2002; Mem., UK Adv. Council, Asia House, 1996–; Chm., ClubAsia, 2002–07; Trustee: Berks Community Trust, 1978–90; Borlase Sch., Marlow, 1991–97; Rajiv Gandhi UK Foundn, 1993–2001; BookPower (formerly Educational Low Priced Sponsored Texts), 2001–07; Pan African Health Foundn, 2004–11; Patron: Population Matters, 2011–; JAN Trust, Asian Women's Resource Centre, 2012–; Founder Chm., Women Matter, 2015–. Governor: Commonwealth Inst., 1993–98; Altwood Comp. Sch., Maidenhead, 1978–86; Slough Coll. of Higher Educn, 1984–89; Mem. Council, Atlantic Coll., 1994–98. Pres., Alumni Assoc., 1998–2000, Lay Mem., Council, 2000–06, UCL. Sec./Organiser Maidenhead Ladies' Asian Club, 1968–78; Founder, LINK (club for Asian conservatives in

H of L), 1994–98; Chm., New Star Boys' Club, 1969–79; Vice Chairman: Maidenhead CAB, 1982–88; Maidenhead CRC, 1969–72; formerly Vice Chairman: Maidenhead Police Consultative Cttee; Maidenhead Volunteer Centre. FRSA 1999. JP Maidenhead, 1971; DL Berks, 1994. DUniv Open, 1994; Hon. LLD Leeds, 2008; Hon. Dr Northampton, 2010. Asian of the Year, 1996; Asian Jewel Award, Lloyds TSB, 2003; Lifetime Achievement Award, Global NRI Inst., 2011. Pravasi Diwas Samman (India), 2009. *Publications:* Stepping Stones (Adult English Training Scheme), 1973; Woman—Acceptable Exploitation for Profit, 2010. *Recreations:* travel, cinema, swimming. *Address:* House of Lords, SW1A 0PW. *T:* (020) 7219 5353.

FLATT, Julie; *see* James, J.

FLAUX, Rt Hon. Sir Julian Martin, Kt 2007; PC 2016; Rt Hon. Lord Justice Flaux; a Lord Justice of Appeal, since 2016; *b* 11 May 1955; *s* of late Louis Michael Flaux and Maureen Elizabeth Brenda Flaux; *m* 1983, Matilda Christian (*née* Gabb); three *s*. *Educ:* King's Sch., Worcester; Worcester Coll., Oxford (BCL, MA; Hon. Fellow). Called to the Bar, Inner Temple, 1978, Bencher, 2002; in practice, 1979–2007; QC 1994; a Recorder, 2000–07; a Dep. High Ct Judge, 2002–07; a Judge of the High Ct, QBD, 2007–16; a Presiding Judge, Midland Circuit, 2010–13; Judge in Charge of Commercial Court, 2014–15. Pres., Special Immigration Appeals Commn, 2016. *Recreations:* opera, reading, walking. *Address:* Royal Courts of Justice, Strand, WC2A 2LL.

FLAVELL, Prof. Richard Anthony, PhD; FRS 1984; Sterling Professor of Immunobiology, Yale University School of Medicine, since 2002 (Professor of Immunobiology, since 1988; Chair of Immunobiology, 1988–2016); Investigator of the Howard Hughes Medical Institute, since 1988; *b* 23 Aug. 1945; *s* of John T. and Iris Flavell; *m* Madlyn (*née* Nathanson); one *d*; two *s* of former *m*. *Educ:* Dept of Biochemistry, Univ. of Hull (BSc Hons Biochem. 1967; PhD 1970). Royal Soc. Eur. Fellow, Univ. of Amsterdam, 1970–72; EMBO Post-doctoral Fellow, Univ. of Zürich, 1972–73; Wetenschappelijk Medewerker, Univ. of Amsterdam, 1973–79; Head, Lab. of Gene Structure and Expression, NIMR, Mill Hill, 1979–82; Pres., Biogen Res. Corp., 1982–88; Principal Res. Officer and CSO, Biogen Gp, 1984–88. Darwin Trust Vis. Prof., Univ. of Edinburgh, 1995; Adjunct Prof., Scripps Res. Inst., Fla, 2009; Co-Dir, Shanghai Jiao Tong Univ. Sch. of Medicine-Yale Univ. Inst. for Immune Metabolism, 2019. Mem., EMBO, 1978–. MRI 1984–; Mem., Amer. Assoc. of Immunologists, 1990– (Excellence in Mentoring Award, 2016); FAAAS 2000; MNAM; MNAS 2006; Member: Inst. of Medicine, NAS, 2006; Henry Kunkel Soc., 2007; Eur. Res. Inst. for Integrated Cellular Pathology, 2009; Yale Comprehensive Cancer Center, Yale Univ., 2010; Eur. Acad. for Tumour Immunology, 2011; Bd of Hon. Advisors, IUBMB, 2012; Lifetime Honorary Member: Scandinavian Soc. for Immunology, 2013; British Soc. for Immunology, 2014; Pres., Internat. Cytokine and Interferon Soc., 2014–15. Hon. Professor: Wuhan, China, 2007; Nan Kai Univ., China, 2007; Suzhou Univ., China, 2010; Div. of Infection and Immunity, UCL, 2011; Hon. Dir, Internat. Immunology Center, Biomedical Translational Res. Inst., Jinan Univ., Guangzhou, 2013–. Hon. DSc: Hull; Zurich, 2018. Anniversary Prize, FEBS, 1980; Colworth Medal, Biochem. Soc., 1980; Rabbi Shai Shacknai Meml Prize in Immunology and Cancer Res., Lautenberg Center, Hebrew Univ. Med. Sch., 2008; AAI-Invitrogen Meritorious Career Award, 2008; Andrew Lazarovitz Award, Canadian Soc. of Transplantation, Quebec, 2011; Gold Medal and Cert. of Honor, Cell Signaling Networks, Merida, Yacatan, 2011; William B. Coley Award for Dist. Res. in Basic and Tumour Immunology, 2012; Vilcek Prize in Biomedical Sci., 2013; Star of Hope Award, JDRF Connecticut Chapter, 2014; AAI Excellence in Mentoring Award, 2016; Hans Bloemendal Medal, Radboud Inst. for Molecular Life Sci., Netherlands, 2017; Seymour & Vivian Milstein Award for Excellence in Interferon and Cytokine Res., Internat. Cytokine and Interferon Soc., 2017. *Publications:* chapters in: Handbook of Biochemistry and Molecular Biology, ed Fasman, 3rd edn 1976; McGraw-Hill Yearbook of Science and Technology, 1980; Eukaryotic Genes: their structure, activity and regulation, ed jtly with Maclean and Gregory, 1983; Globin Gene Expression: hematopoietic differentiation, ed Stamatoyannopoulos and Nienhuis, 1983; Regulation of the Immune System, 1984; Lyme Disease: molecular and immunologic approaches, ed Schutzer, 1992; Tumor Necrosis Factor: molecular and cellular biology and clinical relevance, ed Fiers and Buurman, 1993; Analysis of the Immune System Utilizing Transgenesis and Targeted Mutagenesis, ed Blüthmann and Ohashi, 1994; Current Directions in Autoimmunity, ed von Herrath, 2001; Apoptosis and Autoimmunity: from mechanisms to treatments, ed Kalden and Herrmann, 2003; Therapeutic Targets of Airway Inflammation, ed Eissa and Huston, 2003; Cancer Immunotherapy: immune suppression and tumor growth, ed Prendergast and Jaffee, 2007; New Generation Vaccines, ed Levine, 4th edn, 2007; more than 1000 articles in numerous scientific jls, incl. Nature, Cell, Proc. Nat. Acad. Sci., EMBO Jl, Jl Exp. Med. Sci., Science, and Immunity; contrib. Proceedings of symposia. *Recreations:* music, ornithology, horticulture. *Address:* Department of Immunobiology, Yale University School of Medicine, 300 Cedar Street, TAC S-569, New Haven, CT 06520-8011, USA. *E:* richard.flavell@yale.edu.

FLAVELL, Dr Richard Bailey, CBE 1999; FRS 1998; Chair, International Wheat Yield Partnership, since 2014; Chief Scientific Officer, Ceres Inc., 1998–2013; Chief Scientist, Inariag, Boston, Mass, 2016–18; *b* 11 Oct. 1943; *s* of Sidney Flavell and Emily Gertrude Flavell (*née* Bailey); *m* 1966, Hazel New; two *d*. *Educ:* Univ. of Birmingham (BSc 1964); Univ. of East Anglia (PhD 1967). Research Associate, Univ. of Stanford, California, 1967; Plant Breeding Institute, 1969–88 (Head, Molecular Genetics Dept, 1985–88); Dir, John Innes Inst., subseq. Centre, and John Innes Prof. of Biology, UEA, 1988–98; Chm. Mgt Cttee, AFRC Inst. of Plant Sci. Res., 1990–94. Chief Scientist, Indigoag, Boston, 2015–16. Hon. Prof., King's College London, 1986–90. Fellow, EMBO, 1990; Pres., Internat. Soc. for Plant Molecular Biology, 1993–95. *Publications:* scientific papers and books. *Recreations:* music, gardening. *Address:* International Wheat Yield Partnership, Texas A & M University College Station, TX 77843, USA.

FLAVELL, Prof. Wendy Ruth, DPhil; CChem, CPhys, FInstP; Professor of Surface Physics, since 1998, Vice Dean for Research, Faculty of Science and Engineering (formerly of Engineering and Physical Sciences), since 2018 (Assistant Vice Dean, 2016–18), and Deputy Head of School, School of Physics and Astronomy, since 2017, University of Manchester (formerly University of Manchester Institute of Science and Technology); *b* Bilston, W Midlands, 1 Sept. 1961; *d* of Maurice and June Flavell; partner, Stephen Allen. *Educ:* Wolverhampton Girls' High Sch.; St John's Coll., Oxford (BA Natural Scis (Chem.) 1983; MA 1983; DPhil 1986). CChem 1995; CPhys 1998; FInstP 1999. MRSC. SERC Postdoctoral Fellow, 1986–88, Royal Soc. Univ. Res. Fellow, 1988–90, Dept of Chem., Imperial Coll. London; University of Manchester Institute of Science and Technology: Lectr, 1990–94, Reader, 1994–96, Dept of Chem.; Reader, Dept of Physics, 1996–98. Chair, UK Synchrotron Radiation Source Sci. Adv. Council, 2002–04; Dep. Chair, Physics sub-panel REF, 2014; Interdisciplinary Advr, Physics sub-panel, REF 2021; Mem., beamtime allocation panels for internat. synchrotron sources, including: SOLEIL, France, 2006–17; SLS, Switzerland, 2009–11; MAX-lab, Sweden, 2012–14, 2016–; Member: Physical Sci. Strategic Adv. Team, EPSRC, 2007–09; Physics sub-panel, RAE, 2008; Council, Inst. of Physics, 2017–. *Publications:* contribs to scientific jls on electronic structure of functional materials, incl. semiconductor nanocrystals, oxide catalysts and photocatalysts.

*Recreations:* singing (St George's Singers, Poynton), generally futile gardening, beachcombing, testing deck chairs. *Address:* Photon Science Institute, University of Manchester, Alan Turing Building, Oxford Road, Manchester M13 9PL. *T:* (0161) 306 4466, *Fax:* (0161) 275 1001. *E:* wendy.flavell@manchester.ac.uk.

**FLAXEN, David William;** Director of Statistics, Department of Transport, 1989–96; statistics consultant to overseas governments, especially in Central and Eastern Europe and Africa, 1996–2009; *b* 20 April 1941; *s* of late William Henry Flaxen and Beatrice Flaxen (*née* Laidlow); *m* 1969, Eleanor Marie Easton; two *d*. *Educ:* Manchester Grammar Sch.; Brasenose Coll., Oxford (MA Physics); University Coll. London (DipStat). Teacher, Leyton County High School for Boys, 1963; UK Government Statistical Service, 1963–96: Central Statistical Office and Min. of Labour, 1964–71; UNDP Advr, Swaziland, 1971–72; Statistician, Dept of Employment, 1973–75; Chief Statistician: Dept of Employment, 1975–76; Central Statistical Office, 1976–77 and 1981–83; Inland Revenue, 1977–81; Asst Dir (Under-Sec.), Central Statistical Office, 1983–89. Creator of Tax and Price Index, 1979. *Publications:* contribs to articles in Physics Letters, Economic Trends, Dept of Employment Gazette, etc. *Recreations:* bridge, wine, cooking, music. *Address:* 65 Corringham Road, NW11 7BS. *T:* (020) 8458 5451. *E:* dflaxen@easynet.co.uk.

**FLECK, Andrew Arthur Peter,** MA; Principal (formerly Headmaster), Sedbergh School, since 2010; *b* Chichester, 18 Aug. 1962; *s* of Peter Hugo Fleck and Fiona Charis Elizabeth Fleck (*née* Miller); *m* 1987, Anne Judith Jennison; twin *d*. *Educ:* Marlborough Coll.; Nottingham Univ. (BSc Hons Geol. 1983); University Coll., N Wales (PGCE 1985); Sussex Univ. (MA Educn 1993). Kayak expedns around Newfoundland, Japan and Norway, 1986–88; Hd of Geog., Hurstpierpoint Coll., 1988–96; Dep. Headmaster, St Bedes Sch., 1996–2003; Headmaster, Ashville Coll., 2003–10. Dir, Eggbase Ltd, 2012–. Governor: Westville Hse Sch., 2008–16; Terra Nova Sch., 2012–; St Mary's, Melrose, 2014–. *Recreations:* sailing, writing. *Address:* Sedbergh School, Sedbergh, Cumbria LA10 5HG. *T:* (01539) 620535. *E:* principal@sedberghschool.org.

*See also* R. J. H. Fleck.

**FLECK, Prof. Norman Andrew,** PhD; FRS 2004; FREng, CEng, FIMMM; Professor of Mechanics of Materials, Cambridge University, since 1997; Fellow of Pembroke College, Cambridge, since 1982; *b* 11 May 1958; *s* of William and Roberta Fleck; *m* 1st, 1983, Vivien Christine Taylor (*d* 2007); one *s* one *d*; 2nd, 2016, Maureen Clare Birch. *Educ:* Jesus Coll., Cambridge (BA 1979; MA 1981); PhD Cantab 1982. FIMMM (FIM 1997); FREng 2008. Maudslay Res. Fellow, Pembroke Coll., Cambridge, 1983–84; Lindemann Fellow, Harvard Univ., 1984–85; Cambridge University: Lectr in Engineering, 1985–94; Reader in Mechanics of Materials, 1994–97; Dir, Cambridge Centre for Micromechanics, 1996–. For. Mem., US NAE, 2014. Hon. Dr Eindhoven, 2014. *Publications:* (jtly) Metal Foams: a design guide, 2000; numerous papers in mechanics and materials jls. *Recreations:* running, ski-ing, wine, church. *Address:* Cambridge University Engineering Department, Trumpington Street, Cambridge CB2 1PZ. *T:* (01223) 748240.

**FLECK, Richard John Hugo,** CBE 2009; Consultant, Herbert Smith Freehills (formerly Herbert Smith), since 2009 (Partner, 1980–2009); *b* Leamington, 30 March 1949; *s* of Peter Hugo Fleck and Fiona Charis Elizabeth Fleck (*née* Miller); *m* 1983, Mary Gardiner; one *s* one *d*. *Educ:* Marlborough Coll.; Southampton Univ. (LLB Hons). Solicitor, Herbert Smith, 1971–2009. Mem., Auditing Practices Bd, 1986–2012 (Chm., 2003–12); Dir, Financial Reporting Council Ltd, 2004–13 (Chm., Financial Reporting Review Panel, 2012–15; Chm., Conduct Div., 2013–14); Dep. Chm., Internat. Ethics Standards Bd for Accountants, 2016– (Chm., Consulting and Adv. Gp, 2006–13). Non-executive Director: Nat. Audit Office, 2009–12; Natural Capital Consortium, 2012–. Chm., Incorporated Council of Law Reporting of England and Wales, 2012–. Chm., Holbourne Mus., 2012–16. Mem., Council, Marlborough Coll., 1997–2010. Liveryman, Tallow Chandlers' Co., 1980 (Master, 2016–17). *Recreations:* sailing, Real tennis, golf, shooting, rackets. *Address:* Hill Farm, Ebbesbourne Wake, Salisbury, Wilts SP5 5LW. *T:* (01722) 780644. *E:* richardfleck@btinternet.com. *Clubs:* Athenæum, MCC, Royal Yacht Squadron, Royal Ocean Racing, Jesters; City Law; Itchenor Sailing; Petworth Real Tennis.

*See also* A. A. P. Fleck.

**FLECKER, James William,** MA; Founder/Director, European Language Year, 2003–10; Headmaster, Ardingly College, 1980–98; *b* 15 Aug. 1939; *s* of Henry Lael Oswald Flecker, CBE, and Mary Patricia Flecker; *m* 1967, Mary Rose Firth; three *d*. *Educ:* Marlborough Coll.; Brasenose Coll., Oxford (BA, now MA Lit. Hum., 1962). Asst Master: Sydney Grammar Sch., 1962–63; Latymer Upper Sch., 1964–67; (and later Housemaster), Marlborough Coll., 1967–80. Recruitment Manager, Students Partnership Worldwide, 1998–2001 (Trustee, 2001–08); Recruiter, BESO, 2001–05; Short Term Placement Advr, VSO, 2005–06. Trustee: Alive and Kicking, 2003– (Chm., 2005–09); Good Earth Trust, 2006–13 (Chm., 2006–11). Governor: Reed's Sch., Cobham, 1998–2010; Royal Masonic Sch. for Girls, Rickmansworth, 2007–19. Chm., Friends of Gt Bedwyn Ch, 2012–. *Recreations:* hockey, cricket, flute playing, writing children's operas, golf, vegetable gardening. *Address:* Easter Cottage, 42 Church Street, Great Bedwyn, Wilts SN8 3PQ. *T:* (01672) 870079. *E:* james@flecker.com.

**FLEET, Dr Andrew James,** FGS; Assistant Director of Science, Natural History Museum, 2013–15 (Keeper of Mineralogy, 1996–2012; Head, Department of Earth Sciences, 2012–13); *b* 14 June 1950; *s* of late Rupert Stanley Fleet and Margaret Rose Fleet (*née* Aitken); *m* 1976, Susan Mary Adamson; one *s* one *d*. *Educ:* Bryanston Sch.; Chelsea Coll., Univ. of London (BSc; PhD 1977). FGS 1976. UNESCO Fellow in Oceanography, Open Univ., 1975–79; Lectr in Geochem., Goldsmiths' Coll., Univ. of London, 1979–80; Research and Exploration, BP, 1980–95, Head, Petroleum Geochem. Res., 1987–95. Vis. Prof. in Geol., ICSTM, 1997–2000. Geological Society: Special Pubns Ed., 1993–2002; Mem. Council, 1997–2000, 2002–05 and 2006–11; Sec. (Publications), 2002–05; Treas., 2006–11; Member: Finance and Planning Cttee, 2011–16; Publications and Inf. Cttee, 2016–18. Mem., Finance Cttee, Internat. Union of Geol Scis, 2018–. Custodian Trustee, Mineralogical Soc. of GB and Ireland, 2012–16; Trustee, Dorset Natural History and Archaeological Soc., 2015– (Chm., 2017–). Ed.-in-Chief, Geoscientist, 2018–. *Publications:* edited jointly: Marine petroleum source rocks, 1987; Lacustrine petroleum source rocks, 1988; Petroleum migration, 1991; Coal and coal-bearing strata as oil-prone source rocks?, 1994; Muds and mudstones: physical and fluid flow properties, 1999; Petroleum Geology of Northwest Europe: proceedings of the 5th conference, 1999; contrib. papers in scientific jls on petroleum and sedimentary geochemistry and marine geology. *Recreations:* archaeology, cricket, cooking, wine. *Address:* Stour Brook House, Cookswell, Shillingstone, Blandford Forum, Dorset DT11 0QZ.

**FLEETWOOD, Gordon;** Sheriff of Grampian, Highland and Islands at Inverness, since 2014; *b* Elgin, Moray, 3 Oct. 1951; *s* of John Fleetwood and Isabel Fleetwood; *m* 1975, Jean Arthur; two *d*. *Educ:* Elgin Acad.; Univ. of Edinburgh (LLB Hons 1973). Admitted Solicitor, 1975, Solicitor Advocate, 1994; Solicitor: More and Co., 1977–82; Sutherland and Co., 1982–86; Fleetwood and Robb, 1986–2004; principal in own practice, 2004–08; part-time Sheriff, 2003–14; Legal Mem., Parole Bd for Scotland, 2010–14. *Recreations:* salmon fishing, curling. *Address:* Sheriff Court House, The Castle, Inverness IV2 3EG. *T:* (01463) 230782.

**FLEGG, Dr James John Maitland,** OBE 1997; FCIHort; consultant on horticulture and environment; *b* Hong Kong, 23 April 1937; *s* of Jack Sydney Flegg and Lily Elizabeth (*née* Sponner); *m* 1976, Caroline Louise Coles; two *s*. *Educ:* Melbourne, Australia; Gillingham Grammar Sch.; Imperial Coll. of Science and Technol. (BSc, PhD). ARCS 1962; FCIHort (FIHort 1993). Nematologist, E Malling Res. Stn, 1956–66; MAFF, 1966–68; Dir, Brit. Trust for Ornithology, Tring, 1968–75; Hd, Zool. Dept, E Malling Res. Stn, 1976–87; Dir of Inf. Services, 1987–95, Hd of Stn, 1990–95, Dir, Ext. Affairs, 1995–97, Horticulture Res. Internat., East Malling; Chm., Meiosis Ltd, 2000–15. Presenter, Country Ways, Meridian TV. Sec., European Soc. of Nematologists, 1965–68; Mem. Council, RSPB, 1978–83; Pres., Kent Ornithol. Soc., 1986–2004. MBOU 1966. Chm., Romney Marsh Res. Trust, 1990–2000; Mem., Conservation Panel, Nat. Trust, 2003–11. Trustee, Dungeness Bird Observatory, 1958–. Editor, Collins New Naturalist Series, 2006–. Freeman, City of London; Liveryman, Co. of Fruiterers. *Publications:* books include: In Search of Birds, 1983; Oakwatch, 1985; Birdlife, 1986; Field Guide to the Birds of Britain and Europe, 1990; Poles Apart, 1991; Deserts, 1993; Classic Birds (60 Years of Bird Photography): a biography of Eric Hosking, 1993; Photographic Field Guide to the Birds of Australia, 1996; Time to Fly: exploring bird migration, 2004; numerous papers and articles on nematological, ornithological and envmtl topics. *Recreations:* grandchildren (Jack, Toby and Jessica), wildlife, rural history, environmental affairs, gardening, music. *Address:* Divers Farm, E Sutton, Maidstone, Kent ME17 3DT.

**FLELLO, Robert Charles Douglas;** *b* 14 Jan. 1966; *s* of Douglas Flello and Valerie Swain; *m* 1990, Teresa (*née* Gifoli) (marr. diss.); one *d*, and one step *s*. *Educ:* University Coll. of N Wales, Bangor (BSc Hons). Consultant, Price Waterhouse, 1989–94; Manager, Arthur Andersen, 1994–99; Dir, Platts Flello Ltd, 1999–2003; CEO, Malachi Community Trust, 2003–04. MP (Lab) Stoke-on-Trent S, 2005–17; contested (Lab) same seat, 2017. Associate: Royal Inst. Taxation, 1990–; Soc. Financial Advrs, 1998–. *Recreations:* reading, running, ancient history, cooking, riding my motorbike.

**FLEMING, Anne Elizabeth;** film archive consultant, since 2005; *b* 12 Aug. 1944; *d* of Harry Gibb Fleming and Agnes Wilkie Fleming (*née* Clark); *m* 2003, Taylor Downing. *Educ:* Univ. of Edinburgh (MA Hons English Lit. and Lang.). Films Administrator, Edinburgh Film Fest., 1966, 1967, 1968, 1969; teacher of English as a foreign lang., Acad. of Langs, Catania, Sicily, 1967–68; Imperial War Museum; Res. Asst, Dept of Film Programming, 1970–72; Res. Asst, Dept of Film, 1972–73; Dep. Keeper, 1973–83, Keeper, 1983–90, Dept of Film; Dep. Curator, 1990–97, Curator, 1997–2000, BFI Nat. Film and TV Archive; Hd of Content, MAAS Media Online, British Univs Film and Video Council, 2001–05. Mem., Wellcome Trust Liby Adv. Cttee, 2006–09. Co-ordinating Juror, FOCAL Internat. Film Restoration and Preservation Award, 2003–19. *Publications:* contribs to catalogues and data-bases. *Recreations:* cinema, reading, walking, cooking, growing herbs. *E:* anneefleming@btinternet.com.

**FLEMING, Ven. David;** Chaplain-General to HM Prisons and Archdeacon of Prisons, 1993–2001; Chaplain to the Queen, 1995–2007; *b* 8 June 1937; *s* of John Frederick Fleming and Emma (*née* Casey); *m* 1966, Elizabeth Anne Marguerite Hughes; three *s* one *d*. *Educ:* Hunstanton County Primary School; King Edward VII Grammar School, King's Lynn; Kelham Theological Coll. National Service with Royal Norfolk Regt, 1956–58. Deacon 1963; Asst Curate, St Margaret, Walton on the Hill, Liverpool, 1963–67; priest 1964; attached to Sandringham group of churches, 1967–68; Vicar of Great Staughton, 1968–76; Chaplain of HM Borstal, Gaynes Hall, 1968–76; RD of St Neots, 1972–76; RD of March, 1977–82; Vicar of Whittlesey, 1976–85; Priest-in-Charge of Pondersbridge, 1983–85; Archdeacon of Wisbech, 1984–93; Vicar of Wisbech St Mary, 1985–88. Hon. Canon of Ely Cathedral, 1982–2001. Chm. of House of Clergy, Ely Diocesan Synod, 1982–85. *Recreations:* tennis, chess, extolling Hunstanton. *Address:* Fair Haven, 123 Wisbech Road, Littleport, Ely, Cambs CB6 1JJ. *Club:* Whittlesey Rotary.

**FLEMING, Dr David,** OBE 1997; Professor of Public History, Liverpool Hope University, since 2018; *b* 25 Dec. 1952; *s* of Jack and Doreen Fleming; *m* 2007, Alison Jane Hastings, *qv*; one *d*, and two *s* one *d* from a previous marriage. *Educ:* London Sch. of Econs; Leeds Univ. (BA Hons); Leicester Univ. (MA; PhD 1981). Curator: Yorkshire Mus. of Farming, 1981–83; Collection Services, Leeds Mus, 1983–85; Principal Keeper of Mus, Hull Mus, 1985–90; Asst Dir, 1990–91, Dir, 1991–2001, Tyne & Wear Museums; Dir, Nat. Mus and Galls on Merseyside, later Nat. Mus Liverpool, 2001–18. Vis. Prof., Liverpool Hope Univ., 2013–18. Mem., Exec. Bd, ICOM (UK), 1997–2000; Chm., Finance and Resources Cttee, 2011–15, Mem., Ethics Cttee and Mus. Definition Cttee, 2017–, ICOM. Chairman: Social History Curators Gp, 1986–87; Museum Professionals Gp, 1986–90; Liverpool Culture Partnership, 2003–05; Liverpool Heritage and Regeneration Adv. Gp, 2005–06; Liverpool Find Your Talent Mgt Cttee, 2008–11; Liverpool Mayor's Task Gp on Cultural Heritage, 2012–14; Member: Liverpool Mayor's Creative Commn, 2014–16; Liverpool Mayor's Beatles Legacy Gp, 2016–; Tourism Scrutiny Panel, Liverpool CC, 2017–18. Convenor: Gp for Large Local Authority Museums, 1998–2001; Social Justice Alliance of Mus, 2013–; Vice Chairman: Liverpool First Culture Task Gp, 2009–10; European Mus. Forum, 2009–15 (Treas., 2012–13); Member: NW Cultural Consortium, 2003–04; Culture Cttee, UK Nat. Commn for UNESCO, 2005–09; Creative Apprenticeship Task Force, 2005–07. Mem. Adv. Cttee on the Export of Works of Art, 1991–93; Special Advisor: Min. of Educn, Culture and Sci., Netherlands, 2005–06; Internat. Mus. for Democracy, Rosario, Argentina, 2013– (Trustee, 2018–); Mem., Expert Panel, Stuttgart City Mus., 2007; Expert Advr, Grand Egyptian Mus. Project, 2008. Lecturer: Baltic Museology Sch., 2009; Lithuanian Cultural Administrators Trng Centre, 2011. External Examiner: Dept of Mus. Studies, Leicester Univ., 2003–10; Dept of Heritage and Mus. Studies, Bournemouth Univ., 2010–12. Trustee: Yorks and Humberside Museums Council, 1986–90; Nat. Mus. of Labour History, 1990–92; North of England Mus. Service, 1990–2001; Nat. Football Mus., 1996–2003; NE Cultural Consortium, 1999–2001; Cultural Heritage Nat. Trng Orgn, 2000–01; NE Museums, Libraries and Archives Council, 2001; NW Museums Service, 2001–02; Liverpool Capital of Culture Co., 2001–03; St George's Hall, 2001–08; Bluecoat Arts Centre, 2004–09; SS Daniel Adamson, 2015–; Best in Heritage, 2017–; Muzeum Slaskie, Katowice, Poland, 2017–. President: Museums Assoc., 2000–02 and 2015–18 (Trustee, 2011–; Chm., Ethics Cttee, 2014–15); Internat. Cttee on Mus. Mgt, 2004–10; Fedn of Internat. Human Rights Museums, 2010–; Luciano Becchio Appreciation Soc., 2010–13. Patron, St James in the City, 2013–17. *Recreations:* my family, history, travel, film, literature, Leeds United, collecting CDs. *Address:* Faculty of Arts and Humanities, Liverpool Hope University, Hope Park, Liverpool L16 9JD.

**FLEMING, Prof. David,** OBE 2016; DBA; Vice-Chancellor, 2010–15, and Professor of Land Economics, 2010–15, now Emeritus, York St John University; *b* Southport, 24 Sept. 1959; *s* of Norman Fleming and Shirley Fleming; *m* Lesley; one *s* one *d*. *Educ:* King William's Coll., IOM; Sheffield City Poly. (BSc Hons, PGDip, MBA, DBA 2001). FRICS 1986. Man. Dir, Pannon Pacific, 1988–91; Sen. Lectr, 1991–99, Principal Lectr, 1999–2002, Nottingham Trent Univ.; Dean, Sch. of Built Envmt, Northumbria Univ., 2002–07; Dep. Vice-Chancellor, Univ. of Sunderland, 2007–10. *Publications:* articles in jls on behavioural analysis of building occupants. *Recreations:* golf, sailing.

**FLEMING, Fergus Hermon Robert**; writer, since 1991; *b* 13 Oct. 1959; *s* of Richard and Charm Fleming; partner, Elizabeth Hodgson; one *s* one *d*. *Educ*: Magdalen Coll., Oxford (MA); City Univ., London. Trainee accountant, Ernst & Whinney, 1981–82; acad. trng as barrister, 1982–83; furniture maker, Christopher Clark Workshops, 1984–85; writer and ed., Time-Life Books, 1985–91. Director: Ian Fleming Pubns Ltd, 2003–; The Book Collector, 2016–; Publisher, Queen Anne Press, 2007–. *Publications*: Amaryllis Fleming, 1993; The Medieval Messenger, 1996; The Greek Gazette, 1997; The Viking Invader, 1997; Stone Age Sentinel, 1998; Barrow's Boys, 1998; Killing Dragons, 2000; Ninety Degrees North, 2001; The Sword and the Cross, 2003; Tales of Endurance, 2004; (ed) The Explorer's Eye, 2005; (ed) The Travellers Daybook, 2011; (ed) The Man with the Golden Typewriter: Ian Fleming's James Bond letters, 2015. *Address*: c/o Aitken Alexander Associates, 291 Gray's Inn Road, WC1X 8EB. *T*: (020) 7373 8672. *Club*: Leander (Henley-on-Thames).

**FLEMING, Prof. George**, PhD; FREng, FICE; FCIWM; FRSE; Professor of Civil Engineering, University of Strathclyde, 1985–2003, now Emeritus; Chairman, EnviroCentre, since 2007 (Managing Director, 1993–2011); *b* Glasgow, 16 Aug. 1944; *s* of Felix and Catherine Fleming; *m* 1966, Irene MacDonald Cowan; two *s* one *d*. *Educ*: Univ. of Strathclyde (BSc 1st cl. Hons; PhD 1969). FICE 1982; FREng (FEng 1987); FRSE 1992; FASCE 2000; FCIWM 2002 (MIWM 1987). Res. Fellow, Stanford Univ., 1967; University of Strathclyde: Res. Asst, 1966–69; Lectr, 1971–76; Sen. Lectr, 1976–82; Reader, 1982–85; Dir and Vice Pres., Hydrocomp Internat., 1969–77. Consultant, Watson Hawkesley, 1980–92; non-exec. Dir, WRAP, 2001–07. Member: Overseas Projects Bd, DTI, 1991–95; British Waterways Bd, 2001–07; Port of Tyne Bd, 2005–10. Pres., ICE, 1999–2000; Mem., Smeatonian Soc. of Civil Engrs, 1998. Hon. Mem., British Hydrol Soc. *Publications*: Computer Simulation in Hydrology, 1971; The Sediment Problem, 1977; (ed) Recycling Derelict Land, 1991; (contrib.) Geochemical Approaches to Environmental Engineering of Metals, 1996; (contrib.) Energy and the Environment: geochemistry of fossil, nuclear and renewable resources, 1998. *Recreations*: DIY, travelling. *Address*: EnviroCentre, Unit 2B, Craighall Business Park, 8 Eagle Street, Glasgow G4 9XA.

**FLEMING, Prof. Graham Richard**, PhD; FRS 1994; Professor of Chemistry, University of California, Berkeley, since 1997; Berkeley Director, Institute for Quantitative Biomedical Research (QB3), University of California, 2001–09; *b* 3 Dec. 1949; *s* of Maurice Norman Henry Fleming and Lovima Ena Winter; *m* 1977, Jean McKenzie; one *s*. *Educ*: Bristol Univ. (BSc Hons); Royal Instn (PhD London). Res. Fellow, CIT, 1974–75; Univ. Res. Fellow, Univ. of Melbourne, 1975–76; Leverhulme Fellow, Royal Instn, 1977–79; University of Chicago: Asst Prof., 1979–83; Associate Prof., 1983–85; Prof., 1985–87; Arthur Holly Compton Dist. Service Prof., Dept of Chem., 1987–97; Dep. Dir, Lawrence Berkeley Nat. Lab., 2005–07, Vice-Chancellor for Res., 2009–15, Univ. of Calif, Berkeley. Member: NAS, 2007–; Amer. Philosophical Soc., 2011. Fellow, Amer. Acad. of Arts and Scis, 1991. Hon. DSc: Bristol, 2012; Vilnius, 2013. *Publications*: Chemical Applications of Ultrafast Spectroscopy, 1986; numerous articles in learned jls. *Recreation*: hiking. *Address*: Department of Chemistry, B84 Hildebrand #1460, University of California, Berkeley, CA 94720–1460, USA. *T*: (510) 6432735, *Fax*: (510) 6426340. *E*: fleming@berkeley.edu, grfleming@lbl.gov.

**FLEMING, Grahame Ritchie**; QC (Scot.) 1990; Sheriff of Lothian and Borders, 1993–2014; *b* 13 Feb. 1949; *s* of Ian Erskine Fleming and Helen Ritchie Wallace or Fleming; *m* 1st, 1984, Mopsa Dorcas Robbins (*d* 2008); one *d*; 2nd, 2013, Evelyn Mary Donaldson. *Educ*: Forfar Acad.; Univ. of Edinburgh (MA, LLB). Admitted Faculty of Advocates, 1976. Standing Jun. Counsel to Home Office in Scotland, 1986–89. *Recreations*: food, travel, supporting the Scottish Rugby team, playing pétanque. *Address*: Advocates Library, Parliament House, Edinburgh EH1 1RF.

**FLEMING, Iain Macdonald**; Sheriff of North Strathclyde at Greenock, since 2014; *b* London, 24 Aug. 1962; *s* of Archibald Macdonald Fleming and Joan Fleming (*née* Moore); *m* 1990, Louise Alexandra Cumming; one *d*. *Educ*: High Sch. of Glasgow; Kelvinside Acad., Glasgow; Univ. of Strathclyde (LLB Hons 1983; DipLP 1984). Admitted Solicitor, 1986, Solicitor Advocate, 2001; part-time Sheriff, 2005–14; Convenor, Mental Health Tribunals, 2011–. Mem., Judicial Panel, Scottish FA, 2011–. President: Glasgow Bar Assoc., 1998–99; Part-Time Sheriffs' Assoc., 2011–13. *Recreations*: Association football, martial arts, golf, works of Robert Burns. *Address*: Greenock Sheriff Court, Nelson Street, Greenock PA15 1TR. *E*: sheriffifleming@scotcourts.gov.uk. *Club*: Glasgow Golf.

**FLEMING, Prof. Ian**, FRS 1993; Professor of Organic Chemistry, University of Cambridge, 1998–2002, now Emeritus (Reader in Organic Chemistry, 1986–98); Fellow of Pembroke College, Cambridge, 1964–2002; *b* 4 Aug. 1935; *s* of David Alexander Fleming and Olwen Lloyd Fleming (*née* Jones); *m* 1st, 1959, Joan Morrison Irving (marr. diss. 1962); 2nd, 1965, Mary Lord Bernard. *Educ*: Pembroke Coll., Cambridge (MA, PhD 1963; ScD 1982). Cambridge University: Res. Fellow, Pembroke Coll., 1962; Univ. Demonstrator, 1964–65; Asst Dir of Research, 1965–80; Univ. Lectr, 1980–86. *Publications*: (with D. H. Williams) Spectroscopic Methods in Organic Chemistry, 1966, 6th edn 2007; (with D. H. Williams) Spectroscopic Problems in Organic Chemistry, 1967; Selected Organic Syntheses, 1973; Frontier Orbitals and Organic Chemical Reactions, 1976; Pericyclic Reactions, 1998, 2nd edn 2015; Molecular Orbitals and Organic Chemical Reactions: student edition, 2009, reference edition, 2010; 273 papers in chem. jls. *Recreations*: watching movies, reading, music. *Address*: Pembroke College, Cambridge CB2 1RF. *T*: (01223) 362862.

**FLEMING, James Randolf G.**; see Gibson Fleming.

**FLEMING, Prof. Karen**; Professor of Textiles, since 2008 and Head, Belfast School of Art, since 2016, Ulster University (formerly University of Ulster); *b* Belfast, 21 June 1965; *d* of Thomas Fleming and Anna Fleming (*née* Calvert); *m* 1987, (Donald) Peter Young (*d* 2006); one *d*. *Educ*: Belmont Primary Sch.; Strandtown Primary Sch.; Strathearn Grammar Sch. for Girls; Loughborough Coll. of Art (Dip. Foundn Studies Art and Design 1984); Univ. of Ulster (1st Cl. BA Hons degree Fashion and Textiles 1987; Postgrad. Dip. Art and Design (distinction) 1988; MEd (distinction) 1992). University of Ulster: pt-time and Vis. Lectr, 1989–91; Lectr in Art and Design, 1991–2004; Reader, 2004–08; Leader, Interface Centre for Res. in Art, Technols and Design, 2004–08. Dir, Northern Bridge Consortium, 2018–. Non-exec. Dir, Craft NI, 2000–08. Trustee: Nat. Mus and Galls NI, 2012–; Council for Higher Educn in Art and Design, 2012–; Peer Rev. Coll. Mem. and Panel Mem., AHRC, 2012–; Mem., Art and Design Panel, REF 2021, 2018–. Reg. Lead Verifier for Scotland, Ireland, NE England and Cumbria, C&G, 1991–2006. Curated exhibitions include: Reinventing Linen, Smithsonian Inst., Washington and Millennium Court Gall., Portadown, 2005–07; Linen Diaspora, Biennale Internationale du Lin de Portneuf, Quebec, 2011. Works include: Polisher, Perm. Collection, Ulster Mus., 2007; (developed jtly) Incisions Gown I, 2008. *Recreations*: art, craft, cinema, travel, food. *E*: k.fleming@ulster.ac.uk.

**FLEMING, Kenneth Anthony**, DPhil; FRCPath; FRCP; Clinical Reader in Pathology, University of Oxford, 1981–2000 and 2008–10, now Emeritus; Fellow of Green Templeton College (formerly Green College), Oxford, 1981–2010, now Emeritus (Virginia Swanson Fellow in Pathology, 2004–10); Senior Consultant for Pathology, Center for Global Health, National Cancer Institute, Washington, DC, 2015–18; *b* 7 Jan. 1945; *s* of Thomas and Margaret Fleming; *m* 1969, Jennifer; two *s* one *d*. *Educ*: Univ. of Glasgow (MB ChB); Merton Coll., Oxford (DPhil; MA). FRCPath 1988; FRCP 2007. University of Glasgow: Sen. House Officer, 1969–70; Registrar in Pathology, 1970–72; Lectr in Pathology, 1972–76; Wellcome Res. Fellow in Pathology, Univ. of Oxford, 1976–80; MRC Travelling Fellow, Roche Inst. for Molecular Biology, USA, 1980–81; University of Oxford: Dir of Planning and Develt, 1995–97; Dean, Faculty of Clinical Medicine, 1997–2000; Hd, Med. Scis Div., 2000–08. Hon. Consultant in Pathology, Oxford Radcliffe Hosps Trust, 1981–2008. Associate Hd, Academic Affairs, Oxford Deanery, 2009–12. Chair, Ind. Appt Panel, Bar Standards Bd, 2010–16. Member: Council, RVC, 2009–12; Adv. Bd, Li Ka Shing Res. Inst., Chinese Univ. of Hong Kong, 2010–15; UK Lead, Project to develop MMEd in Pathology, Univ. of Zambia, Tropical Health Educn Trust, 2010–15; Dir of Internat. Activities, RCPath, 2011–14. Sen. Res. Fellow, Inst. for Preventative Res., Lyon, 2010–; Co-founder, Global Health Policy and Mgt in Medicine Progs, 2012–; Health Advr, Emerging Markets Symposium, Green Templeton Coll., Oxford, 2010–18. *Publications*: around 200 articles in learned jls on aspects of molecular biology and pathology. *Recreations*: walking, reading. *Address*: 2 The Winnyards, Cumnor, Oxford OX2 9RJ. *T*: (01865) 864793. *E*: kenneth.fleming@icloud.com.

**FLEMING, Prof. Peter John**, CBE 2001; PhD; FRCP, FRCPC, FRCPCH; Professor of Infant Health and Developmental Physiology, University of Bristol, since 1995 (Head, Division of Child Health, 1996–2002); Consultant Paediatrician, Royal Hospital for Children, Bristol, since 1982; *b* 19 Aug. 1949; *s* of Nora Eileen Page and step *s* of Peter John Page; *m* 1973, Dr Josephine Olwen Allen; four *s*. *Educ*: Gillingham Grammar Sch., Kent; Univ. of Bristol (MB ChB 1972; PhD 1993). MRCP 1975, FRCP 1988; FRCPC 1981; FRCPCH 1997. Senior House Officer: Southmead Hosp., Bristol, 1974–75; Gt Ormond St Hosp., 1975–76; Sen. Resident, 1976–77, Fellow in Neonatal Medicine, 1977–78, Hosp. for Sick Children, Toronto; Sen. Registrar, Paediatrics, Royal Hosp. for Children, Bristol, 1978–81. Chm. of Overview Panel, and co-author of report, Confidential Inquiry into Premature Deaths of People with Learning Disabilities, 2013. Pres., Assoc. of Clinical Profs of Paediatrics, 2002–05; Member: Neonatal Soc., 1979–; British Assoc. Perinatal Medicine, 1980–; Paediatric Intensive Care Soc., 1987–. FRSA 1996. *Publications*: A Neonatal Vade Mecum, 1986, 3rd edn 1998; The Care of Critically Ill Children, 1993; Sudden Unexpected Death in Infancy, 2000; Unexpected Death in Childhood, 2007; contrib. numerous original and rev. articles on neonatal medicine, developmental physiology, learning disability, the epidemiology and prevention of cot death and paediatric intensive care to learned jls. *Recreations*: being with my family, working on and caring for our land, running, listening to and playing music, reading. *Address*: Centre for Academic Child Health, Level D, St Michael's Hospital, Southwell Street, Bristol BS2 8EG. *T*: (0117) 342 5144, *Fax*: (0117) 342 5154. *E*: peter.fleming@bris.ac.uk.

**FLEMING, Raylton Arthur**; freelance journalist specialising in international affairs, music and Mallorca; editorial adviser, Majorca Daily Bulletin; *b* 1 Sept. 1925; *s* of Arthur and Evelyn Fleming; *m* 1967, Leila el Doweini; one *s*. *Educ*: Worksop Coll. Associate Producer, World Wide Pictures Ltd, 1952; Head of Overseas Television Production, Central Office of Information, 1957; Dep. Dir, Films/Television Div., COI, 1961; Asst Controller (Overseas) COI, 1968; Actg Controller (Overseas), 1969; Dir, Exhibns Div. COI, 1971; Controller (Home), COI, 1972–76; Controller (Overseas), COI, 1976–78; Dir of Inf., UN Univ., Japan, 1978–83; Dir, UN Univ. Liaison Office, NY, 1983–84; Liaison Officer, UN Univ., World Inst. for Develt Econs Res., Helsinki, 1984–86. *Recreations*: music, opera. *Address*: Camino del Castillo, 07340 Alaro, Mallorca, Spain.

**FLEMING, Renée L.**; soprano; *b* 14 Feb. 1959; *d* of Edwin Davis Fleming and Patricia (Seymour) Alexander; *m* 1989, Richard Lee Ross (marr. diss. 2000); two *d*; *m* 2011, Timothy Jessell. *Educ*: Potsdam State Univ. (BM Music Educn 1981); Eastman Sch. of Music (MM 1983). Studied at Juilliard American Opera Center, 1983–84, 1985–87; Fulbright Schol., Frankfurt, 1984–85. Débuts include: Houston Grand Opera, 1988; NYC Opera, 1989; Covent Garden, 1989; San Francisco Opera, 1991; Met. Opera, Paris Opera, Bastille, 1991; Teatro Colon, Buenos Aires, 1991; La Scala, Milan, 1993; Lyric Opera, Chicago, 1993; performed at Nobel Peace Prize ceremony, 2006, US Presidential inauguration, 2009, Diamond Jubilee Concert for HM Queen Elizabeth II, Buckingham Palace, 2012, and (US nat. anthem) Super Bowl, 2014; Creative Consultant, Lyric Opera, Chicago, 2010; Artistic Advr-at-Large, John F. Kennedy Center for Performing Arts, 2016. Winner, Met. Opera Nat. Auditions, 1988; George London Prize, 1988; Richard Tucker Award, 1990; Solti Prize, 1998; Grammy Award, 1999, 2003, 2010, 2013; Classical Brit Award, 2004, 2018; Polar Music Prize, 2008; Fulbright Lifetime Achievement Medal, 2011; US Nat. Medal of Arts, 2012; Edison Award, 2018. Hon. Mem., RAM, 2003; Hon. DMus: Juilliard, 2003; Eastman Sch. of Music, 2011; Hon. Dr: Carnegie Mellon, 2012; Harvard, 2015; Duke, 2015; Pennsylvania, 2016; Northwestern, 2018. Commandeur des Arts et des Lettres (France), 2002; Chevalier de la Légion d'Honneur (France), 2005; Victoire d'Honneur, Victoires de la Musique, 2012; Cross of Order of Merit (Germany), 2015. *Publications*: The Inner Voice, 2004.

**FLEMING, Robert, (Robin)**, CBE 2013; DL; Chairman, Robert Fleming Holdings, 1990–97; *b* 18 Sept. 1932; *s* of late Major Philip Fleming and Joan Cecil Fleming (*née* Hunloke); *m* 1962, Victoria Margaret Aykroyd; two *s* one *d*. *Educ*: Eton College; Royal Military Academy, Sandhurst. Served The Royal Scots Greys, 1952–58. Joined Robert Fleming, 1958; Director: Robert Fleming Trustee Co., 1961–2016 (Chm., 1985–91); Robert Fleming Holdings, 1974–97 (Dep. Chm., 1986–90). High Sheriff, 1980, DL 1990, Oxfordshire. *Recreation*: most country pursuits. *Address*: Church Farm, Steeple Barton, Bicester, Oxon OX25 4QR. *T*: (01869) 347177.

**FLEMING, Roderick John**; Director: Fleming Family & Partners, 2000–08; Highland Star Group, since 2000; Chairman, Robert Fleming Holdings Ltd, 2000 (Director, 1994–2000; Deputy Chairman, 1999–2000); *b* 12 Nov. 1953; *s* of Richard Evelyn Fleming and Hon. Dorothy Charmian Fleming; *m* 1979, Diana Julia Wake; twin *d*. *Educ*: Eton Coll.; Magdalen Coll., Oxford (MA History). Trainee: Cazenove, 1974–75; Morgan Guaranty, NY, 1975–76; Corporate Finance Dept, Robert Fleming, 1976–80; joined Jardine Fleming, Singapore, 1980, Man. Dir, 1982–84; Dir, Jardine Fleming Internat. Ltd, with responsibility for internat. corporate finance, Jardine Fleming, Tokyo, 1984–86; International Portfolios Gp, Robert Fleming: joined, 1986; est. Product Develt Gp, 1989; Product Develt Gp Dir, 1990–2000; Director: Capital Mkts, 1991–2000, Corporate Finance UK, 1993–2000, Robert Fleming; Robert Fleming Trustee Co. Ltd, 1991–; Dover Corp., 1995–2002; Ian Fleming (Glidrose) Pubns Ltd, 1996– (Chm., 2000–). *Recreation*: country pursuits. *Address*: Fleming Family & Partners (Liechtenstein) AG, AM Schrägen Weg 2, Postfach 740, 9490 Vaduz, Liechtenstein. *Clubs*: White's, Mark's.

**FLENLEY, William David Wingate**; QC 2010; *b* 28 April 1964; *s* of late Prof. David Caton Flenley and of Hilary Elizabeth Flenley (*née* Wingate); *m* 2001, Hannah Keturah Coombe; one *s* one *d*. *Educ*: Exeter Coll., Oxford (Open Exhibnr; MA; BCL; Editor, Isis mag.); Cornell Law Sch., NY (St Andrew's Soc. of State of NY Schol.; LLM). Called to the Bar, Middle Temple, 1988, Bencher, 2014; in practice, Hailsham Chambers, specialising in professional liability and insce law, 1990–. Lectr in Law (pt-time), LSE, 1988–89. Member: Mgt Cttee, Bondway Housing Assoc., 1990–2001; Bd of Mgt, Thames Reach Housing Assoc., 2001–. Vice Chm., 2011–13, Chm., 2013–15, Professional Negligence Bar Assoc. Asst Gen. Ed., Lloyd's Reports: Professional Negligence, 2000–03. *Publications:* (jtly) The Mareva Injunction and Anton Piller Order, 2nd edn 1993; (ed and contrib.) Cordery on Legal Services (formerly Cordery on Solicitors), 9th edn, 1995–2011; (with T. Leech) Solicitors' Negligence and Liability, 1999, 3rd edn 2012; (contrib.) Professional Negligence and Liability, 2001. *Address:* Hailsham Chambers, 4 Paper Buildings, Temple, EC4Y 7EX.

**FLESCH, Michael Charles;** QC 1983; *b* 11 March 1940; *s* of late Carl and Ruth Flesch; *m* 1972, Gail Schrire; one *s* one *d*. *Educ:* Gordonstoun Sch.; University College London (LLB 1st Cl. Hons; Hon. Fellow, 2011). Called to the Bar, Gray's Inn, 1963 (Lord Justice Holker Sen. Schol.), Bencher, 1993. Bigelow Teaching Fellow, Univ. of Chicago, 1963–64; Lectr (part-time) in Revenue Law, University Coll. London, 1965–82. Practice at Revenue Bar, 1966–. Chairman: Taxation and Retirement Benefits Cttee, Bar Council, 1985–93; Revenue Bar Assoc., 1993–95. Governor of Gordonstoun Sch., 1976–96. *Publications:* various articles, notes and reviews concerning taxation, in legal periodicals. *Recreations:* all forms of sport, backgammon. *Address:* (home) 38 Farm Avenue, NW2 2BH. *T:* (020) 8452 4547; (chambers) Gray's Inn Chambers, 36 Queen Street, EC4R 1BN. *T:* (020) 7242 2642, *Fax:* (020) 7831 9017. *E:* mf@taxbar.com. *Clubs:* MCC, Royal Automobile, Arsenal Football.

*See also* S. B. Lucas.

**FLESHER, Timothy James,** CB 2002; adviser and consultant, since 2010; *b* 25 July 1949; *s* of James Amos Flesher and Evelyn May Flesher (*née* Hale); *m* 1986, Margaret McCormack; two *d*. *Educ:* Hertford Coll., Oxford (BA). Lectr, Cambridge Coll. of Arts and Technol., 1972–74; Admin. Trainee/HEO, Home Office, 1974–79; Sec. to Prisons Bd, 1979–82; Private Sec. to Prime Minister, 1982–86; Home Office: Head of: After Entry and Refugee Div., 1986–89; Personnel Div., 1989–91; Probation Service Div., 1991–92; Dir of Admin, OFSTED, 1992–94; Dep. DG (Ops), Immigration and Nationality Directorate (formerly Dept), Home Office, and Chief Inspector, Immigration Service, 1994–98; a Comr, 1998–2003, a Dep. Chm., 1999–2003, Inland Revenue; Dep. Chief of Defence Logistics, MoD, 2003–07; Chief of Corporate Services, Defence Equipment and Support Orgn, MoD, 2007–10. Chm., Crown Hosting Data Centres, 2015–. Mem., Armed Forces Pay Rev. Body, 2014–; Chair, Prison Service Pay Rev. Body, 2019–. Chm., Home Office Retired and Reunited Civil Servants, 2015–. Chair of Govs, Farnborough Hill Sch., 2018–.

**FLETCHER;** *see* Aubrey-Fletcher.

**FLETCHER, Andrew Fitzroy Stephen;** QC 2006; *b* 20 Dec. 1957; *s* of Fitzroy Fletcher and Brygid Fletcher (*née* Mahon); *m* 1st, 1984, Felicia Taylor (marr. diss. 1999); 2nd, 2010, Eri Aso, three *s* one *d*. *Educ:* Eton Coll.; Magdalene Coll., Cambridge (BA 1980; MA 1983). 2nd Lieut, Welsh Guards, 1976. Called to the Bar, Inner Temple, 1980; in practice specialising in commercial litigation. Liveryman, Grocers' Co., 1994–. *Recreations:* Real Tennis, travel, cricket, wine, reading. *Address:* 3 Verulam Buildings, Gray's Inn, WC1R 5NT. *T:* (020) 7831 8441. *E:* afletcher@3vb.com. *Clubs:* Boodle's, Pratt's, MCC.

**FLETCHER, Dame Ann Elizabeth Mary;** *see* Leslie, Dame A. E. M.

**FLETCHER, Prof. Anthony John;** Professor of English Social History, University of London, at the Institute of Historical Research, 2001–03, now Emeritus; *b* 24 April 1941; *s* of John Molyneux Fletcher and Delle Clare Chenevix-Trench; *m* 1st, 1967, Tresna Dawn Russell (marr. diss. 1999); two *s*; 2nd, 2006, Brenda Joan Lockhart-Smith (*née* Knibbs). *Educ:* Wellington Coll.; Merton Coll., Oxford (BA 1962). History Master, King's Coll. Sch., Wimbledon, 1964–67; Lectr, Sen. Lectr, then Reader in History, Sheffield Univ., 1967–87; Prof. of Modern History, Durham Univ., 1987–95; Prof. of History, Essex Univ., 1995–2000; Dir and Gen. Ed., Victoria County History, Inst. of Histl Res., Univ. of London, 2001–03. Auditor, QAA (formerly HEQC), 1994–2001. Pres., Ecclesiast. Hist. Soc., 1996–97; Vice-Pres., RHistS, 1997–2001 (Mem. Council, 1992–96). Convenor, History at the Univs Defence Gp, 1997–2000; Chair, QAA History Subject Benchmarking Gp, 1998–99. *Publications:* Tudor Rebellions, 1967; A County Community in Peace and War, 1975; The Outbreak of the English Civil War, 1981; (ed jtly) Order and Disorder in Early Modern England, 1985; Reform in the Provinces, 1986; (ed jtly) Religion, Culture and Society in Early Modern Britain, 1994; Gender, Sex and Subordination in England 1500–1800, 1995; (ed jtly) Childhood in Question: children, parents and the state, 1999; Growing Up in England: the experience of childhood 1600–1914, 2008; Life, Death and Growing Up on the Western Front, 2013; Love, Sex and Marriage in the English Country House, 2020; articles and reviews in learned jls. *Recreations:* theatre, opera, travel. *Address:* 40 Coachmans Court, Station Road, Moreton-in-Marsh, Glos GL56 0DE. *E:* afletcher1@btinternet.com.

**FLETCHER, Augustus James Voisey,** OBE 1977; GM 1957; HM Diplomatic Service, retired; Foreign and Commonwealth Office, 1982–89; *b* 23 Dec. 1928; *s* of James Fletcher and Naomi Fletcher (*née* Dudden); *m* 1956, Enyd Gwynne Harries; one *s* one *d*. *Educ:* Weston-super-Mare Grammar Sch.; Oriental Language Institute, Malaya. Colonial Service, Palestine, 1946–48, Malaya, 1948–58; Min. of Defence, 1958–64; FCO, 1964–89: Hong Kong (seconded HQ Land Forces), 1966–70; FCO, 1970–73; Hong Kong, 1973–76; FCO, 1976–79; Counsellor, New Delhi, 1979–82. *Recreations:* trout fishing, walking, food/wine, theatre. *Club:* Travellers.

**FLETCHER, Rt Rev. Colin William;** *see* Dorchester, Area Bishop of.

**FLETCHER, Colleen Margaret;** MP (Lab) Coventry North East, since 2015; *b* Coventry, 23 Nov. 1954; *d* of William Charles Dalton and Dot Dalton; *m* Ian Richard Fletcher (*d* 2018); two *s*. *Educ:* Lyng Hall Comprehensive Sch.; Henley Coll. GEC, Coventry; Customer Services Officer, Orbit Housing Gp. Mem. (Lab), Coventry CC, 1992–2000, 2002–04 and 2011–15. An Opposition Whip, 2017–. *Address:* House of Commons, SW1A 0AA.

**FLETCHER, David Edwin,** MBE 1986; Owner and Director, Hebden Bridge Mill, since 1972; President, Pennine Heritage Environmental Trust, since 2015 (Founder Chairman, 1979–2015); restoration and regeneration specialist; *b* 15 July 1933; *s* of Edwin and Winifred Fletcher; marr. diss. 1990; two *d*; *m* 2005, Hilary Darby. *Educ:* Hebden Bridge Grammar Sch.; Calder High Sch.; Sheffield Univ. (BSc Jt Hons); Leeds Univ. (PGCE); Bradford Univ. (MSc). Schoolmaster and Head of Biology, Bingley GS, 1957–60, Calder High Sch., 1960–69; Manchester Polytechnic: Sen. Lectr, 1970–74; Principal Lectr, 1974–80; Head, Envmt and Geographical Dept, 1980–88; Exec. Dir, Transpennine Campaign, 1988–2005. Mem., Hebden Royd UDC, 1967–74 (Chm., Planning Cttee, 1969–74); Founder Chm., Calder Civic Trust, 1965–75; Dir, Adv. Services, Civic Trust NW, 1970–76. Commissioner: Countryside Commn, 1988–96; Rural Develt Commn, 1993–2000. Chairman: Action for Market Towns, 1998–2005; Hebden Bridge (formerly Hebden Royd Town) Partnership, 2002–11; Upper Calder Valley Renaissance, 2003–07; Chm. of Trustees, X-PERT Health Charity, 2010–. Member: NW Council for Sport and Recreation, 1972–78; Yorks and Humber Cttee, Heritage Lottery Fund, 2001–06. *Publications:* ASK - Amenity, Society Knowhow, 1976; Industry Tourism, 1988; England's North West: a strategic vision for a European region, 1992; research and consultancy reports; contribs to acad. jls; environmental pamphlets. *Recreations:* walking, ski-ing, travel, meeting interesting people in interesting situations, restoring and finding new uses for wonderful old mills in the Pennines; engaged in returning 700 year old Bridge Mill, Hebden Bridge, to its sustainable energy origins, independent of the grid, through solar and hydropower solutions plus twin water-source heat pumps. *Address:* Hebden Bridge Mill, Hebden Bridge, W Yorks HX7 8ET. *T:* 07785 280479.

**FLETCHER, Dr David John,** CBE 2002; CEng, FREng, FIET; Chief Executive, British Waterways, 1996–2002; *b* 12 Dec. 1942; *s* of late John Fletcher and Edna Fletcher; *m* 1967, Irene Mary Luther; one *s* one *d*. *Educ:* The Crypt Grammar Sch., Gloucester; Univ. of Leeds (BSc (Elect. Eng, High Frequency Electronics), DEng). FCIWEM; FREng 2004. General Electric Company, 1965–95: GEC Applied Electronics Labs, Stanmore, 1965–80; Gen. Manager, Stanmore Unit, Marconi Space and Defence Systems, 1980–84; Man. Dir, Marconi Defence Systems, 1984–87; GEC Marconi, 1987–95 (Dep. Chm., 1993–95). Dir, Easynet Group PLC, 2001–06; Chm., Infrared Systems Ltd, 2004–06. Mem., Partnerships UK Adv. Council, 1999–2002. Chm., Assoc. of Inland Navigation Authorities, 1997–2003; Director: Co. of Proprietors Stroudwater Navigation, 2003–; Stroud Valley Canal Co., 2012–. President: Sleaford Navigation, 2003–; Wendover Arm Trust, 2003–; Vice-President: Inland Waterways Assoc., 2002–; Cotswold Canal Trust, 2003–; Bedford/Milton Keynes Canal Trust, 2003–06; Wilts and Berks Canal Trust, 2015–; Trustee, Waterways Trust, 1999–2012. Director Trustee, Nat. Coal Mining Mus., 1997–2015. Chm., Nat. Horse Brass Soc., 2016–18. Member: Rare Breed Survival Trust; Nat. Trust. *Recreations:* boating, classic cars. *Address:* Beverley House, Nettleden Road, Little Gaddesden, Herts HP4 1PP.

**FLETCHER, David Robert,** CBE 2010; **His Honour Judge David Fletcher;** a Circuit Judge, since 2004; *b* 6 May 1957; *s* of late Donald Fletcher and of Alice Fletcher (*née* Worrall); *m* 1982, Janet Powney; one *s* one *d*. *Educ:* Biddulph Grammar Sch.; Biddulph High Sch.; Univ. of Liverpool (LLB Hons 1978). Admitted solicitor, 1981; Higher Courts Advocate, 1999; Charltons, Solicitors: articled clerk, 1979–81; Asst Solicitor, 1981–84; Partner, 1984–96; Partner: Beswicks, Stoke-on-Trent, 1996–2001; Stevens, Stoke-on-Trent, Stafford and Wolverhampton, 2001–03. Actg Stipendiary Magistrate, 1998–2000; Dep. Dist Judge (Magistrates' Courts), 2000–03; a Dist Judge (Magistrates' Courts), Sheffield, 2003–04; Presiding Judge, N Liverpool Community Justice Centre, 2004–12. Chm., Judicial Business Gp, Staffs and W Mercia, 2013–18. Mem. Bd, Internat. Assoc. of Drug Treatment Courts, 2008–. Mem. Council, Tate Liverpool, 2008–12. Chm. Govs, Biddulph High Sch., 1996–2004. *Recreations:* swimming, hill walking, travel, cooking, music, speaking and learning Spanish, watching Port Vale FC. *Address:* Trent Combined Court Centre, Bethesda Street, Hanley, Stoke on Trent ST1 3BP.

**FLETCHER, Hugh Alasdair;** Chairman, Fletcher Brothers Ltd, since 1997; Deputy Chairman, Reserve Bank of New Zealand, 2009–12 (Director, 2002–12); *b* 28 Nov. 1947; *s* of Sir James Muir Cameron Fletcher, ONZ and of Margery Vaughan Fletcher; *m* 1970, Sian Seerpoohi Elias (*see* Rt Hon. Dame Sian Elias); two *s*. *Educ:* Auckland Univ. (MCom Hons, BSc); Stanford Univ., USA (MBA 1972). Fletcher Holdings: Asst to Ops Res., 1969–70; PA to Man. Dir, 1972–76; Dep. Man. Dir, 1976–79; CEO, 1979–81; Fletcher Challenge Ltd: non-exec. Dir, 1981–2001; Man. Dir, 1981–87; CEO, 1987–97; Chairman: CGNU Australia Holdings Ltd (formerly CGU Insurance Australia), 1998–2003; New Zealand Insurance, 1998–2003. Non-exec. Chm., Air New Zealand Ltd, 1985–89; Director: Australasian Adv. Bd, Merrill Lynch, 1998–2000; Rubicon, 2001–; Fletcher Bldg, 2001–12; Ports of Auckland, 2002–06; IAG NZ, 2004–; IAG, 2007–; Vector, 2007–17. Chairman: NZ Thoroughbred Marketing, 1998–2000; Ministerial Inquiry into Telecommunications, 2000; Member: Prime Minister's Enterprise Council, 1995–97; Asia Pacific Adv. Cttee, New York Stock Exchange, 1995–2005; World Business Council for Sustainable Develt, Geneva, 1993–96; Adv. Cttee, UN Office for Project Services, 2000–07. Chancellor, Univ. of Auckland, 2005–08 (Mem. Council, 2000–11). Hon. LLD Auckland, 2012. *Recreations:* horse riding, horse breeding and racing, chess, Go. *Address:* PO Box 11468, Ellerslie, Auckland 1542, New Zealand.

**FLETCHER, Ian Raymond;** Managing Partner, InPhySec Security Ltd, Wellington, since 2016; *b* New Zealand, 25 Aug. 1959; *s* of Raymond William Fletcher and Elizabeth Ruth (*née* Millin); *m* 1st, 1990, Lorna Windmill (marr. diss. 2007); 2nd, 2008 Elizabeth Claire McNabb (separated 2016); partner, Maxine Anderson; one *d*. *Educ:* Burnside High Sch., Christchurch, NZ; Canterbury Univ. (MA Hons 1982). NZ Diplomatic Service, 1982–89; Monopolies and Mergers Commn, UK, 1989–91; Department of Trade and Industry: general trade policy, 1992–94; telecommunications policy, 1994–95; EC, on secondment, 1996–98; DTI and British Trade Internat., 1998–99; Dir-Gen., UN Customs Service and Hd, Dept of Trade and Industry, UN Admin, Kosovo, 2000; Dir, Gas and Electricity, DTI, 2000–02; Principal Private Sec. to Sec. of the Cabinet, 2002–04; Dir, Internat. Trade Develt, UK Trade and Investment, 2004–07; Chief Exec., Intellectual Property Office (Patent Office), 2007–09; Dir-Gen., Dept of Employment, Econ. Develt and Innovation, Qld, 2009–12; Dir, Govt Communications Security Bureau, NZ, 2012–15; Chief Exec., Australian Wagering Council, 2015–16. *Address:* PO Box 12068, Wellington 6144, New Zealand.

**FLETCHER, His Honour John Edwin;** a Circuit Judge, 1986–2006; *b* 23 Feb. 1941; *s* of late Sydney Gerald Fletcher and Cecilia Lane Fletcher; *m* 1st, 1971, Felicity Jane Innes Dick (marr. diss.); 2nd, 1996, Mrs Susan Kennedy-Hawkes. *Educ:* Munro Coll., Jamaica; St Bees Sch., Cumbria; Clare Coll., Cambridge (MA). Called to the Bar, Inner Temple, 1964; Midland and Oxford Circuit, 1965–86; a Recorder, 1983–86. Mem. Panel of Chairmen, Medical Appeal Tribunals, 1981–86. *Recreations:* walking, photography, classical guitar.

**FLETCHER, Kim Thomas;** Partner, Brunswick, since 2011; *b* 17 Sept. 1956; *s* of Jack Fletcher and Agnes Fletcher (*née* Coulthwaite); *m* 1991, Sarah Sands; one *s* one *d*, and one step *s*. *Educ:* Heversham Grammar Sch., Westmorland; Hertford Coll., Oxford (BA Law); UC Cardiff (Dip. Journalism Studies). Journalist: The Star, Sheffield, 1978–81; Sunday Times, 1981–86; Daily Telegraph, 1986–87; Sunday Telegraph, 1988–98; Editor, Independent on Sunday, 1998–99; Editl Dir, Hollinger Telegraph New Media, 2000–03; Editl Dir, Telegraph Gp Ltd, 2003–05; Man. Dir, Trinity Mgt Communications, 2007–11. Chm., NCTJ, 2004–. Ed., British Journalism Rev., 2012–. *Publications:* The Journalist's Handbook, 2005. *Recreation:* family life. *Address:* (home) Apartment 409, 3 Television Centre, W12 7FS. *E:* kim.fletcher@me.com. *Clubs:* Groucho, Soho House.

**FLETCHER, Malcolm Stanley,** MBE 1982; FREng; FICE; Consultant, Halcrow Group (formerly Sir William Halcrow & Partners) Ltd, Consulting Civil Engineers, 1996–2012; *b* 25 Feb. 1936; *s* of Harold and Clarice Fletcher; *m* 1965, Rhona Christina Wood; one *s* two *d*. *Educ:* Manchester Grammar Sch.: Manchester Univ. (MSc); Imperial Coll., London (DIC). FICE 1976; FREng (FEng 1993). Pupil, Binnie & Partners, 1957–60; Sir William Halcrow & Partners, 1968–96: Partner, 1985–96; Chm., 1990–96. Resident Engineer: Jhelum Bridge, Pakistan, 1965–67; Giuliana Bridge, Libya, 1968–74; Design Team Leader, Orwell Bridge, Ipswich, 1976–82; Dir of Design, Second Severn Crossing, 1988–96; Adviser: Dartford River Crossing, 1985–90; Lantau Fixed Crossing, Hong Kong, 1990–96. *Recreation:* cycling. *Address:* 8 The Green, Aldbourne, Marlborough, Wilts SN8 2BW.

**FLETCHER, Margaret Ann**; see Cable, M. A.

**FLETCHER, Martin Guy**; Chief Executive Officer, Australian Health Practitioner Regulation Agency, since 2010; b Sydney, Australia, 3 April 1961; s of Brian and Beverley Fletcher; m 1988, Therese Hanna; two s one d. Educ: Univ. of Sydney (BSocStud); Macquarie Univ. (BA Hons); Univ. of Technol., Sydney (MMan). Manager, Care Plus (ACT) Pty Ltd, 1996–98; Dir, Australian Dept of Health and Ageing, 1998–2000; Dir, Australian Council for Safety and Quality in Health Care, 2000–03; Asst Dir, Nat. Patient Safety Agency, 2003–04; Hd, Patient Safety, WHO World Alliance for Patient Safety, 2004–07; Chief Exec., Nat. Patient Safety Agency, 2007–10. *Publications*: contrib. articles on patient safety to jls incl. Med. Jl of Australia, Quality and Safety in Healthcare and Internat. Jl for Quality in Health Care. *Recreations*: swimming, reading, travel, running. *Address*: Australian Health Practitioner Regulation Agency, 111 Bourke Street, Melbourne, Vic 3001, Australia. *E*: Martin.Fletcher@ahpra.gov.au. *Club*: Royal Society of Medicine.

**FLETCHER, Michael John**; Sheriff of Tayside Central and Fife, 2000–14; b 5 Dec. 1945; s of Walter Fletcher and Elizabeth Fletcher (née Pringle); m 1968, Kathryn Mary Bain; two s. Educ: High Sch. of Dundee; Univ. of St Andrews (LLB). Admitted solicitor, 1968; apprenticeship, Kirk Mackie & Elliot, SSC, Edinburgh, 1966–68; Asst, then Partner, Ross Strachan & Co., Dundee, 1968–88; Partner, Hendry & Fenton, later Miller Hendry, Dundee, 1988–94; Sheriff of South Strathclyde, Dumfries and Galloway, 1994–99; Sheriff of Lothian and Borders, 1999–2000. Mem., Sheriff Court Rules Council, 2002–11; Pres., Sheriffs' Assoc., 2009–11; Vice Pres., Atlantic and Mediterranean Reg., Commonwealth Magistrates and Judges Assoc., 2012–18. Lectr (part-time) in Civil and Criminal Procedure, Univ. of Dundee, 1974–94. Editor, Scottish Civil Law Reports, 1999–. *Publications*: (jtly) Delictual Damages, 2000. *Recreations*: golf, badminton, gardening, learning Japanese.

**FLETCHER, Neil**; Hon. Research Associate, Institute for Education, and Fellow, Post-14 Centre for Education and Work, University College London, 2015; education consultant, since 2003; Head of Education, Local Government Association, 1998–2003; b 5 May 1944; s of Alan and Ruth Fletcher; m 1967, Margaret Monaghan; two s. Educ: Wyggeston Sch., Leicester; City of Leeds Coll. of Educn (Teachers' Cert.); London Univ. (BA Hons); London Business Sch. (MBA 1994). Charter FCP 1990. Schoolteacher, 1966–68; Lectr, 1969–76; Admin. Officer, 1976–91, Hd of Educn, 1991–94, NALGO; Hd of Strategic Projects, UNISON, 1994–95; mgt consultant, 1995–98. Member: Camden Bor. Council, 1978–86 (Dep. Leader, 1982–84); ILEA, 1979–90 (Chair, Further and Higher Educn Sub-Cttee, 1981–87; Leader, 1987–90); Chair: Council of Local Educn Authorities, 1987–88, 1989–90; Educn Cttee, AMA, 1987–90 (Vice-Chair, 1986–87). Advr, London Skills and Employment Bd, 2006–08. Governor: Penn Sch., 1985–2006; London Inst., 1986–99; LSE, 1990–2001; City Literary Inst., 1996–2006 (Chair of Govs, 2003–06). FRSA 1989. *Recreations*: cricket, soccer, theatre, cookery, walking. *Address*: 111 Cholmley Gardens, West Hampstead, NW6 1UP. *T*: (020) 7435 5306. *E*: neil@neilfletcher.org.uk.

**FLETCHER, Nicholas Hugo Martin**; QC 2014; barrister and arbitrator, 4 New Square, since 2014; b London, 8 Nov. 1958; s of Barbara Fletcher; m 1985, Geraldine Caruana; two s. Educ: Reed's Sch., Cobham; Balliol Coll., Oxford (BA Hons Juris 1980); London Sch. of Econs and Pol Sci. (LLM 1981). Called to the Bar, Lincoln's Inn, England and Wales, 1982; admitted to Bar of New York, 1985; admitted as solicitor, 1991 (in practice, 1991–2015); Associate, Haight Gardner Poor & Havens, NY, 1983–86; Associate, 1986–98, Partner, 1998–2009, Coward Chance, subseq. Clifford Chance LLP; Partner, and Hd of Internat. Arbitration, Berwin Leighton Paisner LLP, 2009–14. Member: London Court of Internat. Arbitration, 2000–; Exec. Cttee, Foundn for Internat. Arbitration Advocacy, 2008–; ICC Task Force on New York Convention, 2008–; IBA, 2009–; ICCA, 2012–; ICC Commn on Arbitration and Alternative Dispute Resolution, 2018–. *Recreations*: sailing, golf, opera, theatre, reading, travelling, supporting Chelsea Football Club. *Address*: 4 New Square, Lincoln's Inn, WC2A 3RJ. *T*: (020) 7822 2125. *E*: n.fletcher@4newsquare.com. *Clubs*: Royal Southampton Yacht; Dulwich and Sydenham Hill Golf.

**FLETCHER, Philip John**, CBE 2006; Chairman, Water Services Regulation Authority (Ofwat), 2006–12 (Director General, Water Services, 2000–06); b 2 May 1946; s of late Alan Philip Fletcher, QC and Annette Grace Fletcher (née Wright); m 1977, Margaret Anne Boys; one d (and one d decd). Educ: Marlborough Coll.; Trinity Coll., Oxford (MA). Asst Principal, MPBW, 1968; Department of the Environment: Private Sec. to Permanent Sec., 1978; Asst Sec., Private Sector Housebuilding, 1980, local govt expenditure, 1982–85; Under Secretary: Housing, Water and Central Finance, 1986–90; Planning and Develt Control, 1990–93; Chief Exec., PSA Services, 1993–94, and Dep. Sec., Property Holdings, 1994; Dep. Sec., Cities and Countryside Gp, 1994–95; Receiver for the Metropolitan Police District, 1996–2000. Mem. Bd, Ofqual, 2010–16 (Mem. Cttee, 2008–10). Reader, Church of England; Mem., Archbishops' Council, 2007–16 (Chair, Mission and Public Affairs Council, 2012–16); Chair, Southwark Diocesan Adv. Cttee, 2018–. Trustee, Church Urban Fund, 2016–. Gov., Canterbury Christ Church Univ., 2017–. *Recreation*: walking.

See also Area Bishop of Dorchester.

**FLETCHER, Richard George Hopper**, CMG 1996; HM Diplomatic Service, retired; Managing Director, West Mercian Property Ltd, since 2014; b 8 Nov. 1944; s of late George Hopper Fletcher, CBE, FCA and Kathleen Mary Parsons; m 1967, Celia Rosemary Soord; two d. Educ: Leys Sch., Cambridge; Balliol Coll., Oxford. Joined Foreign Office, 1966–67; Athens, 1968; Nicosia, 1969–72; First Sec., Bucharest, 1973–76; FCO, 1977–83; Counsellor: Athens, 1984–88; FCO, 1989–98; Vice-Pres., Govt Relns and External Affairs, Europe, Nortel Networks, 1998–2001; Public Policy Advr, Cogent Defence and Security Networks Ltd, 2001–02; re-employed, FCO, 2003–05. Sen. Policy Advr, EADS Defence and Security Systems, 2005–09; Senior Adviser: Ernst & Young, 2010–11; Hakluyt, 2010–11. Sen. Advr, Anthem Corporate Finance, 2010–16. *Recreations*: forestry, gardening, bridge, golf. *Clubs*: Wimbledon Park Golf (Dir, 2002–07; Capt., 2007); Sapey Golf.

**FLETCHER, Prof. Ronald Stanley**, FRAeS; Professor of Thermal Power, 1972–2003, now Emeritus, and Deputy Vice-Chancellor, 1994–2003, Cranfield University (formerly Cranfield Institute of Technology); b 12 Dec. 1937; s of Reginald and Dorothy Fletcher; m 1965, Pamela Alys, d of Gwilym and Alys Treharne; one s twin d. Educ: Imperial College, London Univ. (PhD, DIC); UMIST (BSc Tech). FRAeS 1994. Senior Engineer, Northern Research & Engineering Corp., Cambridge, USA, 1965–70; Consultant, Northern Research & Engineering Corp., Herts, 1970–72; Cranfield Institute of Technology: Head of Mechanical Engineering, 1977–87; Dean of Engineering, 1982–85; Pro-Vice-Chancellor, 1985–93; Head of Cranfield Campus, 1989–94; Chairman: Cranfield Mgt Develt Ltd, 1993–2004; Cranfield Aerospace Ltd, 1996–98. Visiting Professor: Cairo, 1975; Brazil, 1977; China (Beijing Inst. of Aero. and Astro.), 1979. Member: ARC, 1974–77; Governing Body, AFRC Inst. of Engrg Res. (formerly Nat. Inst. of Agricl Engrg), 1978–93 (Chm., Finance Cttee, 1982–86); Council, British Hydro. Res. Assoc., 1979–89; AGARD (NATO) Propulsion and Energetics Panel, 1980–99 (Chm., 1997–98); Scientific Bd, Univ. de Technologie de Compiègne, 1989–94; Conseil Scientifique, Inst. Méditerranéen de Technologie, 1989–94. Governor, Bedford Modern Sch., 1986–89. Médaille Gustave Trasenster, Liège, 1990; Prix Formation Etranger, Acad. Nat. de l'Air et de l'Espace, France, 1991. Chevalier, 1990, Officier, 1994, Ordre des Palmes Académiques (France). *Publications*: papers on combustion. *Recreations*: sailing, music. *Address*: 34 Brecon Way, Bedford MK41 8DD. *T*: (01234) 358483. *Club*: Parkstone Yacht.

**FLETCHER, Sarah Kate**; High Mistress, St Paul's Girls' School, since 2017; b Wantage, 6 Feb. 1963; d of Dr Cedric Turberfield and Sheila Turberfield; m 1988, Andrew Fletcher; two s. Educ: King Alfred's Sch., Wantage; New Coll., Oxford (MA 1st Cl.); Univ. of Exeter (PGCE). NPQH 2006. Teacher of Hist., Wycombe Abbey, 1985–90; Hd, Hist. and Careers, St George's Sch., Montreux, 1990–92; Head of History: Haberdashers' Aske's Sch. for Girls, Elstree, 1992–94; Lawrence Sheriff Sch., Rugby, 1994–96; House Mistress, 1996–99, Dir of Studies and Dep. Head, 1999–2009, Rugby School; Head, Kingston Grammar Sch., 2009–14; Head Teacher, City of London Sch., 2014–17. *Publications*: (contrib.) Liberating Learning: widening participation, 2009; contrib. articles in SecEd mag. and New DNB. *Recreations*: clarinet (semi professional orchestral and chamber musician), music, theatre, opera, art, walking. *Address*: St Paul's Girls' School, Brook Green, W6 7BS.

**FLETCHER, Stuart Barron**, OBE 2003; Chairman, Welsh Ambulance Services NHS Trust, 2006–13; b 28 July 1945; s of Arthur Barron Fletcher and Bertha Fletcher; m 1970, Dilys Roberts; two s one d. Educ: King George V Grammar Sch., Southport; Oriel Coll., Oxford (MA). MHSM, DipHSM. Entered Health Service as Nat. Trainee Administrator, 1968; NHS posts include: Hosp. Sec., Broadgreen Hosp., Liverpool, 1972–74; Area Gen. Administrator, St Helens and Knowsley HA, 1974–78; Dist Administrator, E Birmingham HA, 1978–82; Chief Exec., N Staffs HA, 1982–91; Regl Man. Dir, subseq. Chief Exec., W Midlands RHA, 1992–93; Chief Exec., Pembs, subseq. Pembs and Derwen, NHS Trust, 1994–2003; Chief Exec., Health Commn Wales, NHS Dept, Welsh Assembly Govt, 2003–05. Member: NHS Trng Authy, 1985–91; NHS Trng Adv. Bd, 1991–93. Pres., IHSM, 1991–92 (Mem., Nat. Council, 1981–95). Mem. Council and Trustee, Stroke Assoc., 2011–. Sec. to Trustees, Welsh Livery Guild Charitable Trust, 2012–. Liveryman, Livery Co. of Wales (formerly Welsh Livery Guild), 2002 (Master, 2011–12; Dep. Master, 2012–13). Chm., St John Pembrokeshire Council, 2013–. OStJ 2012. *Recreations*: Rugby, fell walking, photography, theatre. *Address*: 5 Douglas James Close, Haverfordwest, Pembrokeshire SA61 2UF. *T*: (01437) 760103. *Club*: Cardiff and County.

**FLETCHER, Thomas Stuart Francis**, CMG 2011; Visiting Professor of International Relations, New York University, since 2015; b Kent, 27 March 1975; s of Mark and Deborah Fletcher; m 2006, Louise Fitzgerald; two s. Educ: Harvey Grammar Sch., Folkestone; Hertford Coll., Oxford (BA 1st Cl. Hons Hist.; MA Hist.; Hon. Fellow, 2015). Entered FCO, 1997; Second Sec., Nairobi, 1998–2001; Private Sec. to Parly Under Sec. of State, FCO, 2002–04; Hd, Internat. Policy, Paris, 2004–07; Private Sec., 2007, Private Sec. for Foreign Affairs and NI, 2007–10, Foreign Policy Advr, 2010–11, to the Prime Minister (on secondment); Ambassador to the Lebanon, 2011–15. Sen. Associate, St Antony's Coll., Oxford, 2011–. Chm., Internat. Adv. Council, UK Creative Industries Fedn, 2016–. Adviser: Global Business Coalition for Educn, 2015–; Emirates Diplomatic Academy, Abu Dhabi, 2016–; Founder, Foundn for Opportunity, 2018–. *Publications*: Naked Diplomacy: power and statecraft in the digital age, 2016. *Recreations*: mountains, cricket, history. *Address*: New York University Abu Dhabi, PO Box 129188, Saadiyat Island, Abu Dhabi, United Arab Emirates. *Clubs*: 2020 (Co-Pres., 2002–); Strollers Cricket (Cowden).

**FLETCHER-VANE**, family name of **Baron Inglewood**.

**FLETCHER-VANE, Hon. Christopher John**; Chester Herald of Arms, since 2017; b Carlisle, 27 March 1953; s of 1st Baron Inglewood, TD and Mary (d 1982), e d of Major Sir Richard Proby, 1st Bt, MC; m 1990, Margaret Eisenklam; two s one d. Educ: Eton; Trinity Coll., Cambridge (MA 1978). Called to the Bar, Inner Temple, 1976; Chancery Bar, Newcastle upon Tyne, 1977–2013. Portcullis Pursuivant, 2012–17. *Address*: Morton House, Calthwaite, Penrith, Cumbria CA11 9PZ. *E*: chester@college-of-arms.gov.uk. *Club*: Travellers.

See also Baron Inglewood.

**FLEWITT, Neil**; QC 2003; **His Honour Judge Flewitt**; a Circuit Judge, since 2015; b 3 July 1959; s of Robert Arthur Flewitt and Caroline Mary Flewitt; m 1987, Melanie Ann Carter; two s one d. Educ: St Edward's Coll., Liverpool; Liverpool Univ. (LLB 1980). Called to the Bar, Middle Temple, 1981; joined chambers, Liverpool, 1981; in practice as a barrister in criminal law (prosecution and defence); a Recorder, 1998–2015. Mem., Criminal Bar Assoc. *Recreations*: films, food, football. *Address*: Liverpool Crown Court, Queen Elizabeth II Law Courts, Derby Square, Liverpool L2 1XA.

**FLIGHT**, family name of **Baron Flight**.

**FLIGHT**, Baron cr 2011 (Life Peer), of Worcester in the County of Worcestershire; **Howard Emerson Flight**; Chairman: Flight and Partners, since 2007; Aurora Investment Trust plc, since 2011; Director, Investec Asset Management Ltd (formerly Guinness Flight), 1987–2019 (Joint Chairman, 1999–2003); b 16 June 1948; s of late Bernard Thomas Flight and Doris Mildred Emerson Flight; m 1973, Christabel Diana Beatrice Norbury; one s three d. Educ: Brentwood Sch.; Magdalene Coll., Cambridge (MA Hist. Pt 1, Econs Pt 2); Univ. of Michigan (MBA 1971). Investment Adviser: N. M. Rothschild & Sons, 1970–73; Cayzer Ltd, 1973–77; Wardley Ltd (Hong Kong Bank), Hong Kong and India, 1977–79; Investment Dir, Guinness Mahon Co. Ltd, 1979–86; Jt Man. Dir, Guinness Flight Global Asset Mgt, 1986–99; Dep. Chm., Guinness Flight Hambro, 1997–98. Contested (C) Bermondsey, Feb. and Oct. 1974. MP (C) Arundel and South Downs, 1997–2005. Shadow Econ. Sec. to Treasury, 1999–2001; Shadow Paymaster Gen., 2001–02; Shadow Chief Sec. to HM Treasury, 2002–04; Dep. Chm., Cons. Party, 2004–05. Mem., Envmt Select Cttee, 1997–98, Social Security Select Cttee, 1998–99. Jt Chm., All Party H of C Hong Kong Cttee, 1998–2005. Mem., EU Cttee, Econs and Financial Affairs, 2011–16, Delegated Powers and Regulatory Reform Cttee, 2016–, H of L. Chairman: CIM Investment Mgt, 2006–16; Loudwater Trust Ltd, 2007–12; CorporActive Fund (HK), 2008–13; Downing Four VCT (formerly Protected Opportunities VCT 1, then Structured Opportunities VCT 1) plc, 2009–16 (Dir, 2009–); non-exec. Dir, Metro Bank plc, 2010–19; Director: Marechale Capital Ltd (formerly St Helen's Capital), 2005–; R5 FX Trading, 2015–; Mercantile Ports and Logistics Ltd, 2016–; Consultant: Tax Incentives Savings Assoc. (formerly PEP and ISA Mgt Assoc.), 1998–; Duff and Phelps (formerly Kinetic Partners), 2005–; Arden Partners, 2014–. Member: Adv. Council, Financial Services Forum, 2005–; Adv. Bd, Guinness Renewable Energy EIS Fund, 2011–. Mem., Guernsey Financial Services Commn, 2005–; Chm., Enterprise Investment Scheme Assoc., 2005–. Vice Pres., Elgar Foundn, 2005– (Trustee, 1979–); Trustee, Africa Res. Inst., 2006–. Governor, Brentwood Sch., 1989–. Liveryman, Carpenters' Co., 1999– (Master, 2019). FRSA. *Publications*: All You Need to Know About Exchange Rates, 1988; monthly articles in Conservative Home. *Recreations*: classical music, antiques, gardening, ski-ing. *Address*: 6 Barton Street, Westminster, SW1P 3NG. *E*: hflight@btinternet.com. *Clubs*: Pratt's, Boodle's.

**FLIKSCHUH, Prof. Katrin**, PhD; FBA 2014; Professor of Political Theory, London School of Economics and Political Science. Educ: Univ. of Essex (BA Govt; PhD Philosophy); Sch. of Oriental and African Studies, Univ. of London (MSc African Politics).

Lecturer: in Politics, Univ. of Manchester; in Philosophy, Univ. of Bristol; in Philosophy, Univ. of Essex, until 2003; Reader in Political Theory, LSE, 2003. Sen. Res. Fellow, Justitia Amplificata Project, Goethe Univ., Frankfurt, 2012–13. *Publications:* Kant and Modern Political Philosophy, 2000; Freedom: contemporary liberal perspectives, 2007; (ed with Lea Ypi) Kant and Colonialism, 2014; contribs to jls. *Address:* Department of Government, London School of Economics and Political Science, Houghton Street, WC2A 2AE.

**FLINDALL, Jacqueline;** Regional Nursing Officer, Wessex Regional Health Authority, 1983–85; *b* 12 Oct. 1932; *d* of Harry and Lilian Flindall. *Educ:* St David's Sch., Ashford, Middx; University Coll. Hosp., London (DipN). SRN, SCM, UCH, 1950–54; Midwifery, St Luke's Mat. Hosp., Guildford and Watford, 1955; exchange student, Mount Sinai Hosp., NY, 1956; Ward Sister and Clinical Teacher, UCH, 1957–63; Asst Matron, Wexham Park Hosp., 1964–66; Dep. Supt of Nursing, Prince of Wales and St Anne's, 1967–69; Chief Nursing Officer: Northwick Park Hosp., 1969–73; Oxfordshire HA, 1973–83. Associate Consultant, PA Management Consultants, 1986–94. Non-exec. Dir, Royal Nat. Orth. Hosp. NHS Trust, Stanmore, 1991–95. Vice Chm., Hosp. Chaplaincies Council, 1997–2003. Professional Organization Mem., RCN; Hon. FRCN 1983. JP Oxford, 1982, Salisbury, 1987–2002; Mem., Wilts Magistrates' Courts Cttee, 1995–2002. *Recreations:* painting, voluntary work.

**FLINDERS, Prof. Matthew Vincent,** PhD; Professor of Parliamentary Government and Governance, since 2009, and Founding Director, Sir Bernard Crick Centre for Public Understanding of Politics, since 2013, University of Sheffield; *b* London, 19 Aug. 1972; *s* of Terence George Flinders and Margaret Anne Flinders (*née* Sadler); *m* 2001, Tamsin Jane Burton Ryder; one *s* three *d*. *Educ:* St Catherine's Sch., Swindon; St Joseph's Sch., Swindon; Swindon Coll.; Loughborough Univ. (BA Hons); Univ. of Sheffield (PhD 1999). Department of Politics, University of Sheffield: Lectr, 2000–03; Sen. Lectr, 2003–05; Reader, 2005–08; Dep. Dean, Faculty of Social Scis, 2004–05. Leverhulme Res. Fellow, 2005; Whitehall Fellow, Cabinet Office, 2006. Adjunct Dist. Prof. of Governance and Public Policy, Sir Walter Murdoch Sch. of Public Policy and Internat. Affairs, Murdoch Univ., Perth, 2013–15; Global Associate, Sydney Democracy Network, Univ. of Sydney, 2016–; H of C Professorial Res. Fellow, 2016–19; ESRC Professorial Leadership Fellow, 2018–20. Special Advr to H of L Select Cttee on Citizenship and Civic Participation, 2017–18. Mem., ESRC-UKRI, 2018– (Mem., Capability Cttee, 2016–18; ESRC Overall Nat. Impact Champion, 2018–19). Gov., Sheffield Health and Social Care NHS Trust, 2008–11. Member: Exec. Cttee, Political Studies Assoc., 2011– (Chm., 2014–17; Pres., 2017–); Bd, Acad. of Social Scis, 2016–. Writer and presenter, BBC Radio 4 documentaries: In Defence of Politics, 2010; When Politics and Comedy Collide, 2013; University Unchallenged, 2018. FAcSS (AcSS 2011). FRSA 2012. Harrison Prize, 2002, Richard Rose Prize, 2004, W. J. M. Mackenzie Prize, 2009, Pol Studies Assoc.; Communicator of Year Award, Pol Studies Assoc., 2012; Sam Aaronovitch Meml Prize, Local Econ. Jl, 2012; Impact Champion Prize, ESRC, 2013; Democratic Innovation of Year Award, Pol Studies Assoc., 2016. *Publications:* Quangos, Accountability and Reform, 1999; The Politics of Accountability in the Modern State, 2001; Multi-Level Governance, 2004; New Politics, New Parliament?, 2005; Democratic Drift, 2008; Oxford Handbook of British Politics, 2009; Walking Without Order, 2009; Defending Politics, 2012; (jtly) Multi-Level Governance and Climate Change, 2015; (ed with I. Bache) Multi-Level Governance, 2 vols, 2015; (ed with M. Wood) Tracing the Political: depoliticisation, democracy and the state, 2015; (ed with M. Wood) Anti-Politics, Depoliticization and Governance, 2017; What Kind of Democracy is This?, 2017; The Political Imagination, 2017; contrib. res. articles and book chapters. *Recreations:* fell running, Rugby, dog walking and training (Short-haired German Pointers). *Address:* Department of Politics, University of Sheffield, Elmfield, Northumberland Road, Sheffield S10 2TU. *T:* (0114) 222 1680, *Fax:* (0114) 222 1717. *E:* m.flinders@sheffield.ac.uk. *Club:* Penn.

**FLINT, Prof. Anthony Patrick Fielding,** PhD, DSc; FRSB; Professor of Animal Physiology, School of Biosciences (formerly Department of Physiology and Environmental Science), University of Nottingham, 1993; *b* 31 Aug. 1943; *s* of Maurice Fielding Flint and Patricia Joan (*née* Ince); *m* 1967, Chan Mun Kwun; two *s*. *Educ:* Hill Crest Sch., Swanage; King's Sch., Bruton; Univ. of St Andrews (Queen's Coll., Dundee) (BSc 1966); Univ. of Bristol (PhD 1969; DSc 1984). FRSB (FIBiol 1982). Res. Fellow, Univ. of Western Ontario, 1969–72; Sen. Res. Biochemist in Obs and Gyn., Welsh Nat. Sch. of Medicine, Cardiff, 1972–73; Lectr, Nuffield Dept of Obs and Gyn., Oxford Univ., 1973–77; Staff Mem., AFRC Inst. of Animal Physiology and Genetics Res., Cambridge, 1977–87; Dir of Science and Dir of Inst. of Zool., Zool Soc. of London, 1987–93. Special Lectr, 1985–87, Special Prof. in Molecular Biol., 1987–93, Univ. of Nottingham Sch. of Agric.; Visiting Professor: Dept of Biology, UCL, 1989–; Biosphere Scis Div., KCL, 1989–. Member: Cttee, Soc. for Study of Fertility, 1981–89 (Sec., 1985–89); Steering Cttee, WHO Task Force on Plants for Fertility Regulation, 1982–87 (Chm., 1985). Member: Council of Management, Journals of Reproduction and Fertility Ltd, 1981–87 (Mem. Exec. Cttee, 1983–87); Bd of Scientific Editors, Jl of Endocrinology, 1983–87. Medal, Soc. for Endocrinology, 1985. *Publications:* (ed jtly) Embryonic Diapause in Mammals, 1981; Reproduction in Domestic Ruminants, 1991; papers in physiol, endocrinol and biochemical jls. *Recreations:* playing Bach on the organ or cello, coasting in small ships. *Address:* c/o School of Biosciences, University of Nottingham, Sutton Bonington, Loughborough, Leics LE12 5RD.

**FLINT, Rt Hon. Caroline Louise;** PC 2008; MP (Lab) Don Valley, since 1997; *b* 20 Sept. 1961; *d* of late Wendy Flint (*née* Beasley); *m* 1st, 1987 (marr. diss. 1990); one *s* one *d*; 2nd, 2001, Phil Cole; one step *s*. *Educ:* Univ. of East Anglia (BA Hons American History and Lit.). Mgt Trainee, 1983–84; Policy Officer, 1984–86, GLC/ILEA; Head of Women's Unit, NUS, 1988–89; Principal Officer, Lambeth, 1989–93; Sen. Researcher and Political Officer, GMB, 1994–97. Parliamentary Private Secretary: to Minister of State, FCO, 1999–2000 and 2001–02, Minister for Energy, DTI, 2001; to Minister without Portfolio and Labour Party Chair, 2003; Parly Under-Sec. of State, Home Office, 2003–05, DoH, 2005–06; Minister of State, DoH, 2006–07, DWP, 2007–08; Minister for Yorks and the Humber, 2007–08; Minister for Housing, DCLG, 2008; Minister of State (Minister for Europe), FCO, 2008–09; Shadow Sec. of State for Communities and Local Govt, 2010–11, for Energy and Climate Change, 2011–15. *Recreations:* cinema, family and friends. *Address:* House of Commons, SW1A 0AA. *T:* (020) 7219 4407.

**FLINT, Charles John Raffles;** QC 1995. *Educ:* Trinity College, Cambridge (BA 1973; MA 1980). Called to the Bar, Middle Temple, 1975, Bencher, 2001; Junior Counsel to the Crown (Common Law), 1991–95. Jt Hd, Blackstone Chambers, 1998–2005. Mem., Investigatory Powers Tribunal, 2012–; Chm., ITF Tribunal, 2017–. Pres., Nat. Anti-Doping Panel, 2015–. Dir, Dubai Financial Services Authy, 2013–. *Address:* Blackstone Chambers, Blackstone House, Temple, EC4Y 9BW.

**FLINT, (David) Jonathan,** CBE 2012; FREng, FInstP; Chief Executive Officer, Oxford Instruments plc, 2005–16; President, Institute of Physics, since 2019; *b* London, 8 Feb. 1961; *s* of Alan Flint and Gillian Flint; *m* 2012, Claire Goulding; one *s* two *d*. *Educ:* Imperial Coll. London (BSc Phys 1982); Univ. of Southampton (MBA 1998). FInstP 2007; FREng 2011. Marconi: Systems Engr, 1982–87; Business Develt Manager, 1987–91; Matra Marconi Space Systems: Divl Manager, 1991–94; Dir, Business Unit, 1994–96; Divisional Managing Director: GEC Marconi, 1996–98; BAE Systems, 1998–2002; Man. Dir, Vislink plc, 2002–04. Non-executive Director: Cobham plc, 2013–17; Stadium plc, 2017–; Oxford Univ. Innovation, 2018–; Marshalls of Cambridge, 2019–. Mem. Council, Inst. of Physics, 2009–12. *Recreations:* hill walking, being lost without an inside pocket. *Club:* Savile.

**FLINT, Prof. Jonathan,** FRCPsych; FRS 2019; Professor of Psychiatry and Biobehavioral Sciences, University of California, Los Angeles, since 2015 (Director, Depression Grand Challenge, 2015); *b* Sutton, 22 Jan. 1958; *s* of Michael Frederick Flint, *qv*; *m* 1980, Alison Shaw; one *s* two *d*. *Educ:* Westminster Sch.; Merton Coll., Oxford (BM BCh 1988). FRCPsych 2006. Registrar in Psychiatry, 1989–92, Sen. Registrar, 1992, Maudsley Hosp., London; University of Oxford: Wellcome Trust Career Develt Fellow, 1992–97; Wellcome Trust Sen. Fellow, 1997–2007; Wellcome Trust Principal Fellow, 2007–15; Prof. of Molecular Psychiatry, 2005–07; Michael Davys Prof. of Neurosci., 2007–15; Fellow, Merton Coll., Oxford, 2007–15; Hon. Consultant Psychiatrist, Warneford Hosp., Oxford, 1996–2015. Genetics Soc. Medal, 2014. *Publications:* 200 articles in jls and contrib. to text books on the genetics of behaviour. *Recreation:* work. *Address:* Brain Research Institute, University of California, Los Angeles, 695 Charles E Young Drive S, Los Angeles, CA 90095, USA.

**FLINT, Jonathan;** see Flint, D. J.

**FLINT, Michael Frederick,** FSA; artist printmaker; President, Orford Museum, since 2014 (Chairman, 1997–2014); *b* 7 May 1932; *s* of Frederick Nelson La Fargue Flint and Nell Dixon Smith; *m* 1st, 1954, Susan Kate Rhodes (marr. diss.) two *s* one *d*; 2nd, 1984, Phyllida Margaret Medwyn Hughes. *Educ:* St Peter's Sch., York; Kingswood Sch., Bath. Admitted Solicitor 1956; Denton Hall & Burgin, subseq. Denton Hall Burgin & Warrens, then Denton Wilde Sapte: Articled Clerk, 1951–56; Asst Solicitor, 1956–60; Partner, 1960–66 and 1972–93; Man. Partner, 1979–82; Chm., 1990–93; Consultant, 1993–2000. Paramount Pictures Corporation: Asst Vice-Pres., 1967; Vice-Pres., 1968–70; Consultant, Henry Ansbacher & Co., 1970; Chairman: London Screen Enterprises, 1970–72 (Exec. Producer, feature film, Glastonbury Fayre, 1972); Sudbourne Park Printmakers, 2003–13. Dir, Portman Entertainment Group Ltd, 1995–2001; Chm., Renaissance Films Ltd, 2002–04. Dir, and Chm. Council, 1995–99, Intellectual Property Inst. (formerly Council of Common Law Inst. of Intellectual Property; founder Mem.); Chm., Intellectual Property, Entertainment and Telecommunications Cttee, Internat. Bar Assoc., 1985–90. Vice-Pres., Brit. Archaeol Assoc., 1988–. Member: BAFTA, 1984–; British Screen Adv. Council, 1991– (Dep. Chm., 1995–); Council, Aldeburgh Music (formerly Aldeburgh Prodns), 1998–2009. Chm., Esmond House Day Care Centre, 2000–10. One-man exhibitions of etchings: Aldeburgh Cinema Gall.; Snape Maltings Concert Hall Gall.; other exhibitions: Peter Pears Gall.; Strand Gall.; Thackeray Gall.; Caroline Wiseman Prints; P-Dram Gall., Paris; Re+Art, Woodbridge; North House Gall., Manningtree; Seaview Gall., Walberswick; Aldeburgh Garage Gall.; Printroom Studio, Sweffling; Cork Brick Gall.; Christchurch Mansion, Ipswich. FSA 1965 (Life Mem.). *Publications:* A User's Guide to Copyright, 1979, (jtly) 7th edn 2017; (jtly) Television by Satellite: legal aspects, 1987; (jtly) Intellectual Property: the new law, 1989. *Recreations:* painting, etching, golf, opera. *Address:* Green Lane House, Castle Green, Orford, Suffolk IP12 2NF. *Clubs:* Garrick; Aldeburgh Golf; Orford Sailing.
*See also* J. Flint.

**FLINT, Simon Coleridge R.;** see Russell Flint.

**FLÖCKINGER, Gerda,** CBE 1991; designer maker/lecturer/photographer; *b* Innsbruck, 8 Dec. 1927; *d* of Karl Flöckinger and Anna (*née* Frankl); naturalised British citizen, 1946; *m* 1954, R. S. Houghton (marr. diss. 1962). *Educ:* Primary Sch., Innsbruck; Maidstone Girls' GS; Dorchester Co. High Sch. for Girls; S Hampstead High Sch.; St Martin's Sch. of Art; Central Sch. of Arts and Crafts. Came to England, 1938. Lectr, Hornsey Coll. of Art, 1962–68 (created New Modern Jewellery course). *Solo shows:* British Crafts Centre, London, 1968; V&A Mus., 1971 and 1986; Bristol City Art Gall. and Mus., 1971; Dartington Cider Press Gall., 1977; Crafts Council Shop at V&A, 1991; V&A, 2006; Electrum Gall., London, 2007; Boston Mus. of Fine Arts, MA, 2007–08; *numerous group shows* in UK, USA and internationally, including: ICA, 1954–64; V&A Mus.; Arnolfini Gall., Bristol; Goldsmiths' Hall; Design Centre; Electrum Gall., London; Crafts Council, London; Goldsmiths' Centre, 2015; work in *collections:* Bristol City Mus. and Art Gall.; Crafts Council; Nottingham Castle Mus.; Royal Scottish Mus., Edinburgh; Pompidou Centre, Paris; Schmuckmuseum, Pforzheim, Germany; V&A Mus.; Goldsmiths' Co., London. Hon. Fellow, Univ. of the Arts London, 2006. Freeman, Goldsmiths' Co., 1998. *Recreations:* growing camellias, breeding Iris Germanica, pistol-shooting.

**FLOOD, David Andrew;** Organist and Master of the Choristers, Canterbury Cathedral, since 1988; *b* 10 Nov. 1955; *s* of Frederick Flood and June Flood (*née* Alexander); *m* 1976, Alayne Nicholas; two *s* two *d*. *Educ:* Royal Grammar School, Guildford; St John's Coll., Oxford (MA); Clare Coll., Cambridge (PGCE). FRCO(CHM). Assistant Organist, Canterbury Cathedral, 1978–86; Organist and Master of Choristers, Lincoln Cathedral, 1986–88. Vis. Prof., Canterbury Christ Ch Univ., 2012–; Vis. Fellow, St John's Coll., Durham, 2009–. Mem., Royal Soc. of Musicians, 1996–; Hon. Sen. Mem., Darwin Coll., Univ. of Kent, 1989–; Hon. Fellow, Canterbury Christ Church Univ., 2008. Hon. FGCM 2000. Hon. DMus Kent, 2002. *Recreations:* motoring, cooking, travel. *Address:* 6 The Precincts, Canterbury, Kent CT1 2EE. *T:* (01227) 865242. *E:* davidf@canterbury-cathedral.org.

**FLOOD, Prof. John Lewis,** PhD; FRHistS; Senior Research Fellow, University of London Institute of Modern Languages Research (formerly of Germanic Studies), since 2002 (Deputy Director, 1979–2002; Leverhulme Emeritus Research Fellow, 2002–04); Professor of German, University of London, 1993–2002, now Emeritus; *b* 22 Sept. 1938; *s* of late William Henry Flood and Ethel Mary Flood (*née* Daffern); *m* 1973, Ann Matthews, BA, MCLIP, *d* of late Edward Matthews; three *s*. *Educ:* Alderman Newton's Grammar Sch., Leicester; Univ. of Nottingham (BA 1961; MA 1963); Univ. of Munich; Univ. of Kiel; PhD London 1980. Lektor for English, Univ. of Erlangen-Nuremberg, 1963–64; Asst Lectr in German, Univ. of Nottingham, 1964–65; King's College London: Asst Lectr in German, 1965–67; Lectr, 1967–72; Sen. Lectr, 1972–79; Reader in German, Univ. of London, 1980–93. Chm., Panel for German, Dutch and Scandinavian Langs, RAEs 1996 and 2001, HEFCE; Mem., Coll. of Peer Review Assessors, AHRC (formerly AHRB), 2004–09; Peer Reviewer, European Res. Council, 2008–13. Hon. Sec., Conf. of Univ. Teachers of German in GB and Ireland, 1971–92. Hon. Treas., 1984–2001, Vice-Pres., 2001–, Henry Sweet Soc. for Hist. of Linguistic Ideas; Vice-Pres., 1993–2004, Sen. Vice-Pres., 2002–04, Pres., 2004–06, Bibliographical Soc.; Member, Council: Philological Soc., 1998–2003; Viking Soc. for Northern Res., 2002–04. Adv. Ed., Oxford DNB, 2008–. Fellow, Centre for the Book, British Library, 1993–94. Corresp. Mem., Historical Commn, Börsenverein des Deutschen Buchhandels, Frankfurt am Main, 1995–. FRHistS 2002. Jacob und Wilhelm Grimm Prize, GDR, 1988. Officer's Cross, Order of Merit (FRG), 2002. *Publications:* (ed) Modern Swiss Literature, 1985; (ed) Ein Moment des erfahrenen Lebens, 1987; (ed) Mit regulu bithuungan, 1989; (ed) Kurz bevor der Vorhang fiel, 1990; (ed) Common Currency?, 1991; Die Historie von Herzog Ernst, 1992; (ed) The German Book

1450–1750, 1995; Johannes Sinapius 1505–1560, 1997; (with M. Davies) Proper Words in Proper Places: studies in lexicology and lexicography, 2001; Incunabula: German vernacular literature, 2003; Poets Laureate in the Holy Roman Empire: a bio-bibliographical handbook, 4 vols, 2006, vol. 5: supplement, 2019; (with A. Simon) Glanz and Abglanz: two centuries of German studies in the University of London, 2017; contrib. numerous essays in British, American, French, German, Italian, Hungarian and Estonian books and jls. *Recreation*: writing. *Address*: University of London School of Advanced Study, Institute of Modern Languages Research, Senate House, Malet Street, WC1E 7HU. *T*: (020) 7862 8966.

**FLOOD, John Martin**; Director, Weapons Systems Sector, 1991–93, Technical Director, 1993–94, Defence Research Agency; *b* 3 Oct. 1939; *s* of late Harry Flood and Rita Flood (*née* Martin); *m* 1962, Irene Edwards; one *s*. *Educ*: Merchant Taylors' School, Crosby; Leeds Univ. (BSc Physics, 1st cl.). CEng 1991; FRAeS 1991. Graduate Apprentice, English Electric, Stevenage, 1962; joined RAE, 1963; Asst Dir, Dir Air Guided Weapons and on Army Chief Scientist staff, 1978–83; joined RAE, 1983; Head, Attack Weapons and Defensive Systems Depts, RAE, 1985–89; Dep. Dir (Mission Systems), RAE, 1989–91; Technical Dir, RAE, 1991–92. Non-exec. Dir, Hunting Engrg Ltd, 1994–99. *Recreations*: bird watching, walking, theatre, reading (political biography). *Address*: 38 Kings Road, Ilkley LS29 9AN.

**FLOOD, Michael Donovan, (Mik)**; arts consultant, since 1997; *b* 7 May 1949; *s* of late Gp Capt. Donovan John Flood, DFC, AFC and of Vivien Ruth (*née* Alison); *m* 1st, 1975, Julie Ward (marr. diss. 1989); one *d*; 2nd, 2000, Ionela Nicolae (separated 2013). *Educ*: St George's Coll., Weybridge; Llangefni County Sch., Anglesey. Founder and Artistic Dir, Chapter Arts Centre, Cardiff, 1970–81; Develt Dir, Baltimore Theater Project, USA, 1981–82; Administrator, Pip Simmons Theatre Gp, 1982–83; Arts consultancy, 1983–85; Dir, Watermans Arts Centre, Brentford, 1985–90; Dir, ICA, 1990–97. Producer of large-scale events: Woyzeck, Cardiff, 1976; Deadwood, Kew Gdns, 1986; Offshore Rig, River Thames, 1987. Member: Film Cttee, Welsh Arts Council, 1976–80; Exec. Cttee, SE Wales Arts Assoc., 1980–81; Co-Founder, Nat. Assoc. of Arts Centres, 1976. Exec. Bd, European Forum for Arts and Heritage, 2004–08; Board of Directors: Pip Simmons Theatre Gp, 1977–83; Thames Fest., 2004–08. Pres., Informal European Theatre Meeting, 1998–2002. Mem., Ct of Govs, RCA, 1990–97. Silver Jubilee Medal, 1977. *Publications*: book reviews in nat. newspapers; contribs on arts and cultural politics to British and European periodicals. *Recreations*: sailing, ichthyology, travel. *Address*: 1 Marshall House, Dorncliffe Road, SW6 5LF. *T*: (020) 7736 8668. *E*: mik@mikflood.com.

**FLOOD, Philip James**, AO 1992; High Commissioner for Australia in the United Kingdom, 1998–2000; *b* 2 July 1935; *s* of Thomas and Maxine Flood; *m* 1990, Carole, *d* of Cuthbert and Nicole Henderson; two *s* one *d*. *Educ*: North Sydney Boys' High Sch.; Univ. of Sydney (BEc Hons). Australian Embassy and Mission to EC, Brussels, 1959–62; Australian Embassy and Mission to OECD, Paris, 1966–69; Asst Sec., Dept of Foreign Affairs, 1971–73; High Comr, Bangladesh, 1974–76; Minister, Washington, 1976–77; Special Trade Rep., 1977–80; First Asst Sec., Dept of Trade, 1981–84; Dep. Sec., Dept of Foreign Affairs and Trade, 1985–88; Ambassador to Indonesia, 1989–93; Director General: Australian Internat. Devel Assistance Bureau, 1993–95; Office of Nat. Assessments, 1995–96; Sec., Dept of Foreign Affairs and Trade, 1996–98. Mem., Minister's Foreign Affairs Council, 2004–07. Head: Inquiry into Immigration Detention, 2000–01; Inquiry into Australian Intelligence Agencies, 2004; Chm., Plasma Fractionation Review, 2006; Consulting Mem., Human Rights Inquiry, 2009. Vis. Fellow, ANU, 2001–06. Mem., Commonwealth War Graves Commn, 1998–2000; Trustee, Imperial War Mus., 1998–2000. Chm., Australia/Indonesia Lang. Foundn, 1989–90; Mem., 1996–2004, Chm., 2001–04, Australia Indonesia Inst.; Dir, 2004–09, Dep. Chm., 2006–09, Asialink. Mem. Bd, Austrade, 1996–98; Dir and Dep. Chm., CARE Australia, 2003–11. Member: Admin. Rev. Council, 1986–89; Council, Australasia Centre Asia Soc., 1997–2005. President: Australian Inst. of Public Admin, 1982–83; Order of Australia Assoc., 2016–19. FIPAA; FAIIA. Order of Merit (Indonesia), 1993; Order of Friendship (Laos), 1995; Centenary Medal (Australia), 2003. *Publications*: Odyssey by the Sea, 2005; Dancing with Warriors: a diplomatic memoir, 2011. *Recreations*: reading, theatre, walking, tennis, swimming. *Address*: 96 Jervois Street, Deakin, ACT 2600, Australia. *Club*: Commonwealth (Canberra).

**FLOOD, Thomas Nicholas Oliver**, CBE 2004; Chief Executive, Conservation Volunteers (formerly British Trust for Conservation Volunteers), 2001–12 (Marketing Director, 1986–2001); *b* 21 May 1947; *s* of Thomas Joseph Flood and Elizabeth Gerard Flood (*née* Byrne); adopted British citizenship, 1999; civil partnership 2006, Paul Cornes. *Educ*: University Coll., Dublin (BA Eng, Metaphysics and Politics). Mkt res., W. S. Atkins Ltd, 1970–72; sales and mktg, 3M UK plc, 1972–86. Chm., Red Admiral Aids Charity, 1994–99. Member: Treasury Adv. Gp on Third Sector, 2008; Ministerial Taskforce on Climate Change, Envmt and Sustainable Develt, 2009–10; Partnership Bd, DCLG, 2011–12; Department for Environment, Food and Rural Affairs: Mem., Third Sector Adv. Bd, 2009–; Co-Chair, Civil Soc. Adv. Bd, 2009–14; Chairman: Water Sector Innovation Leadership Gp, 2013–15; DEFRA Civil Society Partnership Network, 2014–; Dir, UK Water Partnership, 2015–. Mem. Bd, Acevo, 2008–11 and 2011–12 (Chm., Special Interest Gp on Sustainable Develt, 2009–11); Chm., Acevo Solutions Ltd, 2011–14; Independent non-executive Director: EST Hldgs Ltd, 2015–; Energy Saving Trust, 2016–. Chm., Strategic Adv. Bd, Twenty65, 2016–. Mem. Cttee, Queen's Awards for Voluntary Service, 2013–14. Patron, Charity Leaders' Exchange—Knowledge Peers, 2011–15. Trustee, Energy Saving Trust, 2012– (Mem., Audit Cttee, 2013–); Trustee and Chm., Energy Saving Trust Foundn, 2015–; Mem. Council, NT, 2012–16; Ambassador, FoodCycle, 2012–13. Vice Pres., CPRE, 2012–. FRSA 1995; CCMI 2010 (FCMI 1995). Freeman, City of London, 2015; Mem., Guild of Freemen, 2016–; Liveryman, Water Conservators' Co., 2015–. *Recreations*: walking, cooking, opera, cinema, reading my Kindle, growing fruit and vegetables, exploring the wonderful Dorset countryside. *Address*: 24 Keith Road, Bournemouth BH3 7DU. *T*: 07711 262198. *E*: tomnflood@hotmail.co.uk.

**FLOOK, Adrian John**; Director (formerly Consultant), CTF Partners, since 2013; *b* 9 July 1963; *s* of late John Harold Julian Flook and late Rosemary Ann Flook (*née* Richardson); *m* 2003, Frangelica O'Shea; one *d*. *Educ*: King Edward's Sch., Bath; Mansfield Coll., Oxford (MA Hons Mod. Hist.). Stockbroker, Warburg Securities, and others, 1985–98; Financial Dynamics (business communications consultancy), 1998–2003. MP (C) Taunton, 2001–05; contested (C) same seat, 2005. Consultant, M:Communications, 2005–13. *Address*: 37 Simpson Street, SW11 3HW.

**FLORENCE, Prof. Alexander Taylor**, CBE 1994; PhD, DSc; FRSE; FRPharmS, FRSC; Dean, School of Pharmacy, University of London, 1989–2006; *b* 9 Sept. 1940; *s* of late Alexander Charles Gerrard Florence and Margaret Florence; *m* 1st, 1964, Elizabeth Catherine McRae (marr. diss. 1995); two *s* one *d*; 2nd, 2000, Dr Florence Madsen, *d* of Bernard Madsen, Paris. *Educ*: Royal Coll. of Science and Technology, Glasgow and Univ. of Glasgow (BSc Hons 1962; PhD 1965); DSc Strathclyde, 1984. FRSC 1977; FRPharmS 1987. University of Strathclyde: MRC Jun. Res. Fellow, 1965–66; Lectr in Pharmaceutical Chemistry, 1966–72; Sen. Lectr in Pharm. Chem., 1972–76; J. P. Todd Prof. of Pharmacy, 1976–88. Member: Cttee on Safety of Medicines, 1983–98 (Mem., Sub-cttee on Chemistry, Pharmacy and Standards of Cttee on Safety of Medicines, 1972–98); Nuffield Inquiry into Pharmacy, 1984–86. Pres., Eur. Assoc. of Faculties of Pharmacy, 1997–2001; Vice Pres., Internat. Pharmaceutical Fedn, 1998–2000 (Host-Madsen Medal, 1996); Pres., Controlled Release Soc., 2002–03 (Vice Pres., 2001–02). Co-Editor in Chief, Jl of Drug Targeting, 1993–97; Ed.-in-Chief, Internat. Jl of Pharmaceutics, 2008–15 (Ed.-in-Chief (Europe), 1997–2008). FRSE 1987; FRSA 1989. DUniv: Hoshi, Tokyo, 2003; Strathclyde, 2004; Danish Univ. of Pharmaceutical Scis, 2006; Hon. ScD UEA, 2007; Hon. DSc London, 2009. British Pharmaceutical Conf. Science Award, 1972; Harrison Meml Medal, Royal Pharmaceutical Soc., 1986; Scheele Prize, Swedish Acad. of Pharmaceutical Scis, 1993; GlaxoSmithKline Internat. Achievement Award, 2001; Maurice-Marie Janot Award, Assoc. de Pharmacie Galénique Industrielle, France, 2006; Higuchi Prize, Acad. of Pharmaceutical Sci. and Technol., Japan, 2006; Founder's Award, Controlled Release Soc., 2009; Dist. Service Award, Controlled Release Soc., 2019. *Publications*: Solubilization by Surface Active Agents, 1968; Physicochemical Principles of Pharmacy, 1981, 6th edn 2015; Surfactant Systems, 1983; (ed) Materials Used in Pharmaceutical Formulation, 1985; (ed) Formulation Factors in Adverse Reactions, 1990; (ed jtly) Liposomes in Drug Delivery, 1992; Physical Pharmacy, 2008, 2nd edn 2012; (ed jtly) Modern Pharmaceutics, 2009; Introduction to Clinical Pharmaceutics, 2010; pubns on drug delivery and targeting, surfactants, dendrimers and nanotechnology. *Recreations*: music, writing, painting. *Address*: 18 Marine Parade, City Quay, Dundee DD1 3BN. *T*: (01382) 200135; La Providence, 7G rue Sincaire, 06300 Nice, France. *T*: 493130397.

**FLORENCE, Peter Kenrick**, CBE 2018 (MBE 2005); Founder and Director, Hay Festival, since 1988; *b* 4 Oct. 1964; *s* of late Norman Samuel Florence and of Rhoda Lewis; *m* 1996, Becky Shaw; four *s*. *Educ*: Ipswich Sch.; Jesus Coll., Cambridge (BA Hons Mod. and Medieval Langs 1987, MA); Université Paris-Sorbonne (Paris IV). Designer: Festivaletteratura, Mantova, 1996; The Word, London, 1999; Festa Literária Internacional de Paraty (FLIP), Brazil, 2002; Beirut 39, Lebanon, 2010; Hay Festivals: Cartagena, Colombia, 2005; Segovia, Spain, 2006; Alhambra, Spain, 2008; Storymoja, Kenya, 2009; Belfast, 2009; Zacatecas, Mexico, 2010; Kerala, India, 2010; Xalapa, Mexico, 2011; Merthyr Rock, Wales, 2011; Beirut, Lebanon, 2011; Dhaka, Bangladesh, 2011; Budapest, Hungary, 2012; Kells, Ireland, 2013; Abu Dhabi, UAE, 2020. Chair, Jury, Booker Prize, 2019. Fellow: Hereford Art Coll., 2008; RWCMD, 2010; Hon. Fellow: Cardiff Univ., 2013; Bangor Univ., 2013. Hon. FRSL 2018. Hon. DLitt: Glamorgan, 2004; Open, 2010; Worcester, 2017; QMUL 2018. Colombiano de Corazón, 2010. *Publications*: OxTales, 2009; (ed jtly) OxTravels, 2011; OxCrimes, 2014. *Recreations*: walking, food, family. *Address*: Hay Festival, 25 Lion Street, Hay HR3 5AD. *E*: peter@hayfestival.org. *Clubs*: Groucho; Hawks (Cambridge).

**FLOREY, Prof. Charles du Vé**; Professor of Public Health Medicine (formerly Community Medicine), University of Dundee, 1983–99; *b* 11 Sept. 1934; *s* of Howard Walter Florey and Mary Ethel Florey; *m* 1966, Susan Jill Hopkins; one *s* one *d*. *Educ*: Univ. of Cambridge (MD); Yale Univ. (MPH). FFCM 1977; FRCPE 1986. Instructor, 1965, Asst Prof., 1966–69, Yale Univ. School of Medicine; Mem. Scientific Staff, MRC, Jamaica, 1969–71; St Thomas's Hospital Medical School, London: Sen. Lectr, 1971–78; Reader, 1978–81; Prof., 1981–83. Pres., Internat. Epidemiol Assoc., 1999–2002. *Publications*: (with S. R. Leeder) Methods for Cohort Studies of Chronic Airflow Limitation, 1982; (jtly) Introduction to Community Medicine, 1983; A European Concerted Action: maternal alcohol consumption and its relation to the outcome of pregnancy and child development at eighteen months, 1992; (ed) Epilex: a multilingual lexicon of epidemiological terms, 1993; (jtly) The Audit Handbook: improving health through clinical audit, 1993; (jtly) The Pocket Guide to Grant Applications, 1998; (jtly) Studying Populations: a computer assisted learning package, 2017. *Recreations*: photography, sailing, walking, computing. *Address*: 76 Alton Road, Poole, Dorset BH14 8SS.

**FLÓREZ, Juan Diego**; tenor; *b* Lima, Peru, 13 Jan. 1973; *s* of Ruben Flórez and Maria Teresa Flórez (*née* Salom, later French); *m* 2007, Julia Trappe; one *s* one *d*. *Educ*: Conservatory of Lima; Curtis Inst., Philadelphia. Début in Matilde di Shabran, Rossini Opera Fest., 1996; has performed at: La Scala, Milan; Comunale of Florence; Rossini Opera Fest., Pesaro; Opera of Rome; Metropolitan Opera, NY; Staatsoper, Vienna; San Francisco Opera; Royal Opera Hse, Covent Gdn; Bayerische Staatsoper, Munich; Gran Teatre del Liceu, Barcelona; Paris Opera; Lyric Opera, Chicago; Deutsche Oper, Berlin. Founder and Pres., Sinfonía Por el Perú, 2011–. UNESCO Goodwill Ambassador, 2012. Kammersänger, Austria, 2012. Abbiati Prize, Rossini d'Oro, Pesaro. Gran Cruz, Orden del Sol (Peru). Readers' Award, Internat. Opera Awards, 2017. *E*: barbara@juandiegoflorez.com.

**FLORMAN, (Carl Alan) Mark**; Chairman and Chief Executive, Time Partners Ltd, since 2013; *b* London, 2 Nov. 1958; *s* of late Charles Florman and Madeleine Florman; *m* 1987, Alexia Anninos; three *d*. *Educ*: Harrow Sch.; London Sch. of Econs and Pol Sci. (BSc Econs of Industry and Trade 1981). Vice Pres., Northern Trust Co., 1981–85; Dir, Capital Mkts, County NatWest, 1985–87; Partner, Enskilda Securities, 1988–91; Founder and CEO, Maizels Westerberg, 1991–2000; Man. Dir, Doughty Hanson & Co., 2001–08. Chairman: LM Glasfiber, 2003–06; Spayne Lindsay, 2009–. Founder, 8 Miles LLP, 2009. CEO, BVCA, 2011–13. Chm., Swedish Chamber of Commerce, 2006–. Sen. Advr, MCF Corporate Finance, 2013–. Vis. Prof., Policy Inst., KCL, 2016–; Vis. Sen. Fellow, Inst. of Global Affairs, LSE, 2016–; Vis. Lectr, INSEAD, 2015–. Hon. Pres., B Lab UK, 2015–. Chm., Centre for Social Justice, 2010–16; Trustee: for England, BBC Trust, 2015–17; Foundn for Future London, 2015–16; Commonwealth Educn Trust, 2015–; Mem. Adv. Cttee, Palaeontological Scientific Trust, 2014–; Ambassador, Royal Albert Hall, 2004–. *Publications*: The Florman Guide to Europe's Best Restaurants, 2001. *Recreations*: inspecting my schools in Africa, politics, fast ski-ing, lunch in Courchevel, painting. *Address*: Time Partners Ltd, 33 St James's Square, SW1Y 4JS. *T*: 07767 420491. *E*: mark@florman.co.uk.

**FLOUD, Sir Roderick (Castle)**, Kt 2005; FBA 2002; Provost, Gresham College, London, 2008–14 (Member of Council, 1998–2014); Vice-Chancellor, 2002–04, President, 2004–06, now President Emeritus, London Metropolitan University; *b* 1 April 1942; *s* of late Bernard Francis Castle Floud, MP and Ailsa (*née* Craig); *m* 1964, Cynthia Anne (*née* Smith); two *d*. *Educ*: Brentwood Sch.; Wadham Coll., Oxford (MA; Hon. Fellow, 1999); Nuffield Coll., Oxford (DPhil 1970). Asst Lectr in Economic History, UCL, 1966–69; Lectr in Economic History, Univ. of Cambridge and Fellow of Emmanuel Coll., Cambridge, 1969–75 (Hon. Fellow, 2003); Prof. of Modern History, Birkbeck Coll., Univ. of London, 1975–88; Provost, City of London Poly., subseq. London Guildhall Univ., 1998–2002; Acting Dean, Sch. of Advanced Study, Univ. of London, 2007–09. Vis. Prof. of European History and of Economics, Stanford Univ., Calif, 1980–81. Associate Mem., Nuffield Coll., Oxford, 2007–17. Research Associate, Nat. Bureau of Economic Research, USA, 1978–2018; Research Programme Dir, Centre for Economic Policy Research, 1983–88. Member: Council: ESRC, 1993–97; UUK (formerly CVCP), 1999–2005 (Pres., 2001–03); Convenor, London Higher Educn Consortium, 1999–2001; Mem. Bd, European Univ. Assoc., 2001–07 (Vice-Pres., 2005–07). Chair, Sci. Rev. Gp (formerly Standing Cttee) for Social Scis, Eur. Sci. Foundn, 2007–15. Mem., Lord Chancellor's Adv. Council on Public Records, 1978–84. Mem. Bd, London Develt Partnership, 1998–2001; Observer, London Devel Agency, 2001–06. Mem., Tower Hamlets Coll. Corp., 1997–2001. Trustee, Samaritans, 2006–08. Treas., Oxford Union Soc., 1966. Freeman:

City of London, 1995; Information Technologists' Co., 1996 (Liveryman, 2005); Co. (formerly Guild) of Educators, 2000 (Master, 2005–06). MAE 2012. FCGI 2001. FAcSS (AcSS 2001). Hon. Fellow, Birkbeck Coll., 1994; Centenary Fellow, Historical Assoc., 2006. Hon. DLitt: City, 1999; Westminster, 2006. *Publications:* An Introduction to Quantitative Methods for Historians, 1973, 2nd edn 1980; (ed) Essays in Quantitative Economic History, 1974; The British Machine Tool Industry 1850–1914, 1976; (ed) The Economic History of Britain since 1700, 1981, 2nd edn 1994; (ed) The Power of the Past, 1984; (jtly) Height, Health and History, 1990; The People and the British Economy 1830–1914, 1997; (ed) Health and Welfare during Industrialisation, 1997; (ed) London Higher, 1998; (ed) The Cambridge Economic History of Modern Britain, 2004, 2nd edn 2014; (jtly) The Changing Body, 2011; (ed) Humanism Challenges Materialism in Economics and Economic History, 2017; An Economic History of English Gardens, 2019; articles in Economic History Review, Social Science History, etc. *Recreations:* family, walking, music. *Address:* 15 Flint Street, Haddenham, Bucks HP17 8AL. *T:* (01844) 291086. *Club:* Athenæum.

**FLOWER,** family name of **Viscount Ashbrook.**

**FLOWER, Antony John Frank, (Tony),** MA, PhD; Founding Chairman, 2005–07, Senior Fellow, since 2007, The Young Foundation; *b* 2 Feb. 1951; *s* of late Frank Robert Edward Flower and Dorothy Elizabeth (*née* Williams). *Educ:* Chipping Sodbury Grammar Sch.; Univ. of Exeter (BA Hons Philosophy and Sociology; MA Sociology); Univ. of Leicester (PhD Mass Communications). Graphic Designer, 1973–76; Co-founder with Lord Young of Dartington, and first Gen. Sec., Tawney Soc., 1982–88; Dir, Res. Inst. for Econ. and Social Affairs, 1982–92. Co-ordinator, Argo Venture (Nat. Space Mus.), 1984–2002, Dir, Argo Trust, 1986–95; Director: Healthline Health Inf. Service, 1986–88; Health Information Trust, 1987–88 (Trustee, 1988–90); Environmental Concern Centre in Europe, 1990–92; Institute of Community Studies: Trustee, 1993–2005; Dep. Dir, 1994–96; Sen. Fellow, 1996–2001; Acting Dir, 2001; Chm., 2001–05; Dep. Dir, 1994–96, Chm., 2001–04, Mutual Aid Centre (Trustee, 1990–2004). Chm., ContinYou, 2003–05. Mem. Adv. Bd, The Earth Centre, 1990–2000; Sec., Ecological Studies Inst., 1990–92. Associate: Redesign Ltd, 1989–92; Nicholas Lacey & Partners (Architects), 1989–2005; Consultant: CIRIA, 1992–96; Rocklabs Geochemical Analysis CC, 1993–2005; Cambridge Female Educn Trust, 1999–2005. Co-ordinator, Campaign for Educnl Choice, 1988–89. Trustee: Gaia, 1988–2001; Educn Extra, 1995–2004 (Chm. of Trustees, 2001–03); Consultant, Joseph Rowntree Reform Trust Ltd, 1993–2003; Co-founder and Patron, Tower Hamlets Summer Univ. Trust, 1995–2005; Patron, Nat. Space Centre, 1996–. Mem., Council for Social Democracy, 1982–84; Dir of Develt, Green Alliance, 1991–92. Associate: Open Coll. of the Arts, 1988–2002; Inst. for Public Policy Res., 1989–95; Family Covenant Assoc., 1994–2000. Editor, Tawney Journal, 1982–88; Co-founder and Man. Editor, Samizdat Magazine, 1988–90. FRSA 1991. *Publications:* (with Graham Mort) Starting to Write: a course in creative writing, 1990; (ed with Ben Pimlott and Anthony Wright) The Alternative, 1990; (ed jtly) Young at Eighty: the prolific public life of Michael Young, 1995; Trusting in Change: a history of the Joseph Rowntree Reform Trust, 2004. *Recreations:* collecting junk, sailing, making and restoring musical instruments, attempting to write poetry. *Address:* c/o 18 Victoria Park Square, E2 9PF.

**FLOWER, Gwynneth Gabrielle,** CEng, FIET; Chairman, Werneth Enterprises, since 2001; *b* Chester, 29 June 1938; *d* of William Denis Flower and Gertrude Molly Flower (*née* Jacob). *Educ:* Royal Masonic Sch.; King's Coll. London (BSc Eng. Hons); Cranfield Univ. (MBA). CEng 1967; FIET (FIEE 1968). Served Army, 1965–80. Mktg Manager, Scicon Consultancy (BP), 1980–82; Commercial Dir, Plessey Electronics, 1982–85; Dir, Sales and Mktg, GEC Marconi, 1986–90; Chief Exec., Central London Training and Enterprise Council, 1990–97; Man. Dir, Action 2000, 1998–2000; Chairman: CMB Technologies, 2000–03; UK Transplant SHA, 2003–05. Dir, 2 Change, 2003–10; Nat. Meteorological Prog., Met Office, 2004–07. Non-executive Director: Ordnance Survey, 1997–2002; European Tech. Mktg Services, 2000–03; Army Base Repair Orgn, 2001–03; Dir, Fitzgeorge & Fitzjames Freehold Ltd, 2016–. Hon. Treas., Royal Instn of GB, 2006–09 (Mem., 1998–). Mem., Forum UK, Internat. Women's Forum, 1995–. Liveryman: Engrs' Co., 2000–; Clockmakers' Co., 2010–. Chm., Govs, Our Lady of Victories Primary Sch., Kensington, 1996–2017; Vice Chm., Kensington and Chelsea FE Coll., 1997–2003. DUniv Open, 1995; Hon. DTech De Montfort, 1997. *Recreations:* arts, antique clocks, Victorian London, gardening, sailing, ski-ing. *Address:* Royal Institution of Great Britain, 21 Albemarle Street, W1S 4BS. *T:* (020) 7409 2992. *E:* gwynneth.flower@btinternet.com. *Club:* Defence Technology.

**FLOWER, Robert Philip;** HM Diplomatic Service, retired; Counsellor, Foreign and Commonwealth Office, 1994–96; *b* 12 May 1939; *s* of Philip Edward Flower and Dorothy Agnes Elizabeth (*née* Beukers); *m* 1964, Anne Daveen Tweddle (marr. diss. 2011); two *s*. *Educ:* Christ's Hosp.; Magdalene Coll., Cambridge (BA). Called to the Bar, Middle Temple, 1964. FCO, 1967–96; served in Malawi, Malaysia, UK Delegn to NATO, Bonn and London; Dep. Head of Mission, The Hague, 1990–93. Trustee, Skipton Choral Soc., 2014–. *Recreations:* fell-walking, reading, music. *Address:* The Old Cottage, Appletreewick, Skipton BD23 6DD.

**FLOWER, Prof. Roderick John,** PhD, DSc; FMedSci; FRS 2003; FBPhS; Professor of Biochemical Pharmacology, William Harvey Research Institute, Barts and the London, Queen Mary's School of Medicine and Dentistry (formerly St Bartholomew's and the Royal London School of Medicine and Dentistry, Queen Mary and Westfield College), London, 1994–2016, now Emeritus; *b* 29 Nov. 1945; *s* of Lesley Ralph Flower and Audrey Ellen Eckett; *m* 1994, Lindsay Joyce Riddell. *Educ:* Univ. of Sheffield (BSc 1st class Hons Physiol. 1971); PhD 1974, DSc 1985, London. Wellcome Res. Labs, Beckenham, 1973–84, Sen. Scientist, 1975–84; University of Bath: Prof. of Pharmacol., 1984–89; Hd, Sch. of Pharmacy and Pharmacol., 1987–89; Medical College of St Bartholomew's Hospital, London, then St Bartholomew's and Royal London Sch. of Medicine and Dentistry, QMW: Lilly Prof. of Biochem. Pharmacol., 1989–94; pt-time Actg Hd of Clinical Pharmacol., 1993–96; William Harvey Research Institute: Mem., 1989; Head of Inst., 1998–2002; Wellcome Trust Principal Res. Fellow, 1994–2007; a Dir and founding Mem., William Harvey Res. Ltd, 1989–2012. Pres., British Pharmacological Soc., 2000–03 (Fellow, 2005). Hon. Fellow, Sch. of Pharmacy, 2008. Hon. LLD Bath, 2011; Hon. DSc Sheffield, 2016. *Publications:* (ed with N. J. Goulding) Glucocorticoids, 2001; (ed jtly) Rang & Dale's Pharmacology, 6th edn 2008 to 9th edn 2018; 320 peer reviewed articles and over 200 other publications incl. reviews, book chapters, abstracts, conf. procs, editorials and pubd correspondence. *Recreations:* the camera, history of science, travel. *Address:* Department of Biochemical Pharmacology, William Harvey Research Institute, Barts and the London School of Medicine, Charterhouse Square, EC1M 6BQ. *T:* (01225) 863751. *E:* r.j.flower@qmul.ac.uk.

**FLOWERDEW, Robert John;** horticultural consultant, since 1986; *b* Yaxley, Suffolk, 30 April 1953; *s* of Richard Flowerdew and late Pamela Flowerdew; *m* 2002, Vonnetta Angeleta Crossman; one *s* one *d* (twins). *Educ:* Hatfield Poly. (BA Hons Business Studies). Panellist, Gardeners' Question Time, BBC Radio 4, 1993–; presenter, Gardeners' World, BBC TV, 1995–97. Mem., 1983–, Ambassador, 2006–, Henry Doubleday Res. Assoc. (Garden Organic); Life Mem., Soil Assoc., 1989–; Pres., Norfolk Organic Gp (formerly Norfolk Organic Gardeners), 1996– (Mem., 1982–); Patron: NWA1 Rethink Rubbish campaign, 2002–; Send a Cow to Africa, 2007–; Dig It, 2007–; Cuddalore Health and Agriculture Trust India, 2008–; Paxton Horticl Soc., 2009–; Champion for: Millennium Greens, 1998–; Woodland Trust, 1999–. *Publications:* (jtly) The Complete Manual of Organic Gardening, 1992; The Organic Gardener, 1993; Bob Flowerdew's Organic Garden, 1993; The Complete Book of Companion Gardening, 1993; Complete Fruit Book, 1995; Organic Bible, 1998; (jtly) Gardeners' Question Time All Your Gardening Problems Solved, 2000; Go Organic, 2002; The No-Work Garden, 2002; (jtly) The Complete Book of Vegetables, Herbs and Fruit, 2002; (jtly) Gardeners' Question Time Plant Chooser, 2003; (jtly) Gardeners' Question Time Tips and Techniques, 2005; The Gourmet Gardener, 2005; Organic Garden Basics, 2007; Going Organic, 2007; Grow Your Own, Eat Your Own, 2008; Simple Green Pest and Disease Control, 2010; Composting, 2010, Pruning, Training and Tidying, 2010; Companion Planting, 2010; Weeding Without Chemicals, 2010; Re-cycle and Re-use Stuff in Your Garden, 2014; Pulpit in the Potting Shed, 2015; Really Help Your Plants, 2015; Really Help Butterflies, 2016; Really Help Your Ecology, 2016; Really Help Your Crops, 2016; contrib. Amateur Gardening, BBC Gardeners' World mag. *Recreations:* gardening!, scented plants, good food, cats, beautiful women, conversation, reading, etymology, inventing, outrageous ideas, public speaking, scuba diving, whingeing on about the state of things. *E:* bob@bobflowerdew.com. *W:* bobflowerdew.com, www.twitter.com/flowerdewbob.

**FLOWERS, Angela Mary;** Chairman, Angela Flowers Gallery Ltd, since 1989; *b* 19 Dec. 1932; *d* of Charles Geoffrey Holland and Olive Alexandra Holland (*née* Stiby); *m* 1st, 1952, Adrian Flowers (marr. diss. 1973; he *d* 2016); three *s* one *d*; 2nd, 2003, Robert Heller (partner, 1973–2003; *d* 2012); one *d*. *Educ:* Westonbirt Sch., Glos; Wychwood Sch., Oxford; Webber Douglas Sch. of Singing and Dramatic Art. Posts in stage, film and advertising, until 1967; founded Angela Flowers Gallery, 1970: Lisle St, 1970–71; Portland Mews, 1971–78; Tottenham Mews, 1978–88; Richmond Rd, 1988–2001; Kingsland Rd, 2001–. Mem. Bd, Nat. Youth Jazz Orch., 1988–93. Trustee, John Kobal Foundn, 1992–97. Sen. Fellow, RCA, 1994. Hon. DArt, E London, 1999. *Recreations:* piano, singing, trombone, cooking, jazz, collecting contemporary art. *Address:* Flowers East, 82 Kingsland Road, E2 8DP. *T:* (020) 7920 7777, *Fax:* (020) 7920 7770. *E:* angelaflowers1932@gmail.com.

**FLOWERS, Michael James;** Chief Executive Officer, Chemring Group plc, 2014–18; *b* Melbourne, 2 Aug. 1961; *s* of Allan James Flowers and Margaret Mary Flowers; *m* 1990, Linda McCauley; two *d*. *Educ:* Christian Brothers' Coll., St Kilda, Melbourne; Univ. of New South Wales (Bachelor Mech. Engrg); Australian Army Comd and Staff Coll.; Royal Mil. Coll. of Sci.; Univ. of Queensland (MBA). Australian Army, 1979–2001; Prog. Manager, BAE Systems Australia, 2001–06; Man. Dir, Chemring Australia, 2006–13; Gp Dir Munitions, Chemring Gp plc, 2013–14. *Recreations:* travel, cricket, Australia football, art and its history, wine.

**FLOYD, Rt Hon. Sir Christopher (David),** Kt 2007; PC 2013; **Rt Hon. Lord Justice Floyd;** a Lord Justice of Appeal, since 2013; *b* 20 Dec. 1951; *s* of David and Hana Floyd; *m* 1974, Rosalind Jane Arscott; one *s* two *d*. *Educ:* Westminster Sch.; Trinity Coll., Cambridge (MA Nat. Scis and Law). Called to the Bar, Inner Temple, 1975, Bencher, 2001; called to the Bar of Republic of Ireland, 1988. QC 1992; Asst Recorder, 1994–2000; a Dep. High Court Judge (Patents Court), 1998–2007; Recorder, 2000–07; a Judge of the High Ct of Justice, Chancery Div., 2007–13; Judge i/c, Patents Court, 2011–13. Dep. Chm., Copyright Tribunal, 1995–2007; Chm., Competition Appeal Tribunal, 2007–; Supervising Lord Justice, Intellectual Property Appeals, 2018–. Chm., QC's Complaints Cttee, 2013–; Member: Bar Council Chm.'s Arbitration/Conciliation Panel, 1996–2007; Bar Council Professional Conduct and Complaints Cttee, 1998–2002; Bar Council, 2000–04; Bar Council European Cttee, 2003–04; Litigation Accreditation Bd Appeal Panel, Chartered Inst. Patent Attorneys, 2005–07; Enlarged Bd of Appeal, European Patent Office, 2011–15; Chm., Intellectual Property Bar Assoc., 1999–2004. Chm., Perm. Exhibn of Legal Costume, 2009–. Trustee, Rolls Bldg Art and Educnl Trust, 2011–. *Recreations:* cricket, ski-ing, walking. *Address:* Royal Courts of Justice, Strand, WC2A 2LL. *Club:* Garrick.

**FLOYD, Sir Giles (Henry Charles),** 7th Bt *cr* 1816; Director, Burghley Estate Farms, since 1958; *b* 27 Feb. 1932; *s* of Sir John Duckett Floyd, 6th Bt, TD, and Jocelin Evadne (*d* 1976), *d* of late Sir Edmund Wyldbore Smith; *S* father, 1975; *m* 1st, 1954, Lady Gillian Moyra Katherine Cecil (marr. diss. 1978), 2nd *d* of 6th Marquess of Exeter, KCMG; one *s* (and one *s* decd); 2nd, 1985, Judy Sophia Lane, *er d* of late W. L. Tregoning, CBE, and D. M. E. Tregoning. *Educ:* Eton College. High Sheriff of Rutland, 1968. *Heir: s* David Henry Cecil Floyd [*b* 2 April 1956; *m* 1981, Caroline, *d* of John Beckly, Manor Farm, Bowerchalke, Salisbury, Wilts; two *d*]. *Address:* Tinwell Manor, Stamford, Lincs PE9 3UF. *T:* (01780) 762676. *Club:* Turf.

**FLUCK, Nicholas Peter;** Partner, Stapleton & Son, Solicitors, Stamford, since 1984; President, Law Society of England and Wales, 2013–14; *b* 11 Dec. 1956; *s* of late Canon Peter Ernest Fluck and Jane Maureen Fluck (*née* Snaddon); *m* 1993, Dr Susan Ruth Wheatley; one *d* (and one *d* decd). *Educ:* Huddersfield Poly. (BA Hons Humanities 1979); Leeds Poly. (CPE 1981; Law Soc. Finals 1982). Admitted as solicitor, 1984. Dep. Vice-Pres., 2011–12, Vice-Pres., 2012–13, Law Soc. of England and Wales. Mem. Council, NHBC, 2017–. DUniv Huddersfield, 2014. *Publications:* articles in legal press and online on gen. legal issues and land law matters. *Recreations:* reading, playing piano and church organ, listening to music, spending time with my family. *Address:* 16 Mayfair Gardens, Boston PE21 9NZ. *T:* 07836 792187. *E:* nick@fluck.org.

**FLUCK, Peter Nigel;** freelance artist; sculptor of abstract kinetics, since 1994; founded (with Roger Law) Spitting Image, 1982; *b* 7 April 1941; *s* of Herbert William Fluck and Ada Margaret (*née* Hughes); *m* 1963, Anne-Cécile de Bruyne; one *d* one *s*. *Educ:* Cambs High Sch. for Boys; Cambridge Sch. of Art. Artist-reporter, illustrator, 1961–70; cartoonist and caricaturist, 1970–82; Luck & Flaw (with Roger Law), 1974–82; Spitting Image (18 TV series), 1982–94. Exhibitions: Chaotic Constructions (with Tony Myatt) Tate Gall., St Ives and Edin. Fest., 1997, Hong Kong Univ. of Sci. and Technol. 1998, RIBA, 2000, Festi Ventu, Corsica, 2002, Study Gall., Poole, 2004; Yew Tree Gall., Cornwall, (ceramics and prints) 2004, (Sans Words; mobiles and calligraphy), 2018; (mobiles) Kestle Barton Gall., Cornwall, 2011; All That Remains (with Tony Myatt), Tremenheere Gall., Cornwall, 2018. *Recreations:* fly fishing, cooking, reading to reinforce prejudice. *Address:* White Feather, Cadgwith, Cornwall TR12 7LB. *T:* (01326) 290546.

**FLUGGE, Klaus;** Founder, Publisher and Chairman (formerly Managing Director), Andersen Press Ltd, since 1976; *b* 29 Nov. 1934; *s* of Werner and Emmi Flügge; *m* 1964, Joëlle Dansac; one *s*. *Educ:* German Book Trade Sch., Leipzig (Dip.). Asst to Pres., Abelard-Schuman, NY, 1959–61; Man. Dir, Abelard-Schuman Ltd, 1963–76. Eleanor Farjeon Award for distinguished services to children's books, 1999. *Recreations:* book collecting, jazz, swimming. *Address:* c/o Andersen Press Ltd, 20 Vauxhall Bridge Road, SW1V 2SA. *T:* (020) 7840 8701. *Club:* Groucho.

**FLYNN, Douglas Ronald;** Chairman, Konekt Ltd, since 2012; *b* 8 June 1949; *s* of Ronald Norman Flynn and Rhona Ellen Flynn; *m* 1975, Lynne Cecily Harcombe; two *s. Educ:* Newcastle Boys' High Sch., Australia; Univ. of Newcastle, Australia (BEng Hons 1972); MBA Melbourne Univ. 1979. Australian Sales Manager, ICI Australia, Melbourne, 1975–80; Gen. Manager, ICI Explosives, Hong Kong, 1980–82; Regl Manager, Perth, 1982–85, Manager Strategic Planning, Melbourne, 1985–86, ICI Australia Ltd; Deloitte Haskins & Sells, 1986–87; Chief Exec., Hobart, Davies Bros Ltd, 1987–90; Man. Dir, News Ltd Suburban Newspapers, Sydney, 1990–94; Dep. Man. Dir, News Internat. Newspapers, London, 1994–95; Man. Dir, News Internat. plc, 1995–99; Chief Executive Officer: Aegis Gp, 1999–2005; Rentokil Initial plc, 2005–08. Non-exec. Dir, Seven West Media (formerly West Australian Newspapers) Ltd, 2008. *Recreation:* sailing. *Address:* Konekt Ltd, Level 3, 338 Pitt Street, Sydney, NSW 2000, Australia. *Clubs:* Tasmanian (Hobart); Royal Corinthian Yacht, Royal Hong Kong Yacht, Royal Sydney Yacht Squadron.

**FLYNN, Sister Ellen Teresa,** DSL; Daughter of Charity of St Vincent de Paul; *b* Nairobi, 15 Feb. 1953; *d* of Daniel Flynn and Dorothy Flynn. *Educ:* St Mary's Sch., Hereford; Christ's Coll., Liverpool (BEd 1989; Dip Mgt Studies 2001). DSL 1989. Teaching, 1981–88; liturgy and music consultant, 1989–99; CEO, 2000–09, Chm., 2009–16, The Passage. Provincial Councillor, 2009–15, Provincial Leader, 2015–, British Province, Sisters of Charity of St Vincent de Paul; Chm., Daughters of Charity Services, 2012–. Hon. Fellow, St Margaret's Univ. Coll., Twickenham, 2009. *Recreation:* music (grade 6 piano, grade 8 singing, Associated Bd RSM).

**FLYNN, James Edward;** QC 2003; barrister; *b* 21 June 1956; *s* of late Ronald Joseph Flynn and of Margaret Rose Flynn (*née* Crossland, now Harris); *m* 1st, 1983, Catherine Clare Gibson (marr. diss. 2008); one *s* one *d;* 2nd, 2013, Anna Margaret Morfey; one *d. Educ:* Loughborough Grammar Sch.; Brasenose Coll., Oxford (BA Jurisprudence 1977; MA 2012). Called to the Bar, Middle Temple, 1978, Bencher, 2016; admitted solicitor, 1984; with Linklaters & Paines, London and Brussels, 1982–86 and 1989–96; Legal Sec., European Court of Justice, 1986–89; Partner, Linklaters & Paines, Brussels, 1993–96; in practice as a barrister, London and Brussels, 1996–. Chm., Competition Law Assoc., 2009–; UK Mem., CCBE Perm. Delegn to European Cts. *Publications:* (jtly) Competition: understanding the 1998 Act, 1999; (jtly) The Law of State Aid in the EU, 2003; Arriving at the Capital (poems), 2016; articles in jls and poems in literary reviews. *Recreations:* poetry, singing, music. *Address:* Brick Court Chambers, 7–8 Essex Street, WC2R 3LD. *T:* (020) 7379 3550. *E:* james.flynn@brickcourt.co.uk.

**FLYNN, John Gerrard,** CMG 1992; HM Diplomatic Service, retired; Ambassador to Venezuela, and concurrently (non-resident) to the Dominican Republic, 1993–97; *b* 23 April 1937; *s* of late Thomas Flynn and Mary Chisholm; *m* 1973, Drina Anne Coates (*d* 2015); one *s* one *d. Educ:* Glasgow Univ. (MA). Prof. of English, Federal Univ. of Paraiba, Brazil, 1961; Asst Lectr, Dept of Spanish, Univ. of Bristol, 1963; Foreign Office, 1965; Second Sec., Lusaka, 1966; First Sec., FCO, 1968; seconded to Canning House as Asst Dir-Gen., 1970; First Sec. (Commercial) and Consul, Montevideo, 1971; Rhodesia Dept, FCO, 1976; Chargé d'Affaires, Luanda, 1978; Political Counsellor and Consul-Gen., Brasilia, 1979; Econ. Counsellor and Dir of Trade, Madrid, 1982; High Comr, Swaziland, 1987; Ambassador to Angola and (non-resident) to São Tomé and Príncipe, 1990–93. British Special Rep. for Sierra Leone, 1998. Pol Advr, Chevron, 1997–; Consultant, De La Rue, 2002–08. Chairman: Anglo Latin American Foundn, 1998–2003; Anglo-Venezuelan Soc., 1999–2005; British Venezuelan Chamber of Commerce, 1999–2003. Order of the Liberator Simon Bolivar (Venezuela), 1997. *Recreations:* hill-walking, golf. *Clubs:* Travellers, Caledonian.

**FLYNN, Mary Eileen Patricia, (Mo);** Chief Executive, Rehab Group, since 2015; *b* Mullingar, Ireland, 26 Aug. 1960; *d* of Michael Paul Flynn and Patricia Flynn; *m* 1998, Stephen Wescott; two step *s. Educ:* Loreto Coll., Mullingar; Univ. of Ulster (BSc Social Admin and Social Work; CQSW 1982); King's Coll. London (MSc Gerontol. 1991). Social worker, Ireland, 1982–85; Res. Social Worker, Melbourne, 1986; Sen. Social Worker, City of Westminster, 1987–90; Team Manager, Social Services, Tower Hamlets LBC, 1990–93; Continuing Care Coordinator, Bromley Health, 1993–98; Service Develt Advr, Older People, Health Advisory Service, UK, 1998–2001; Sen. Comr, Eastern Regl Health Authy, Ireland, 2001–05; Nat. Care Gp Manager, Health Services Exec., Ireland, 2005–06; Chief Exec., Our Lady's Hospice and Care Services, 2006–14. Member: Bd, Health Inf. and Quality Authy, 2013–14; Health and Social Care Professionals Council, 2014–. Chair and Mem. Bd, Carers Assoc., 2012–14. Pres., Irish Gerontol Soc., 2014–17. *Recreations:* gardening, cookery, family, travel to ancient sites. *Address:* Rehab Group, Roslyn Park, Sandymount, Dublin DO4 FH28, Ireland. *T:* (1) 2057355. *E:* mo.flynn@rehab.ie.

**FLYNN, Padraig;** Member, European Commission (formerly Commission of the European Communities), 1993–99; *b* 9 May 1939; *m* 1963, Dorothy Tynan; one *s* three *d. Educ:* St Gerald's Secondary Sch., Castlebar, Co. Mayo; St Patrick's Trng Coll., Dublin (DipEd). Mayo County Council: Mem., 1967–87; Vice-Chm., 1975–77. TD (FF), 1977–93; Minister of State, Dept of Transport and Power, 1980–81; Minister for: Gaeltacht, March–Oct. 1982; Trade, Commerce and Tourism, Oct.–Dec. 1982; spokesman on trade, commerce and tourism, 1982–87; Minister for: the Envmt, 1987–91; Justice, Feb.–Dec. 1992; Industry and Commerce, Nov.–Dec. 1992. Mem., Irish Nat. Teachers' Orgn, 1957. Mem., Gaelic Athletic Assoc., 1959–. *Recreations:* golf, reading, world affairs. *Address:* Carrowbrinogue Lodge, Castlebar, Co. Mayo, Ireland.

**FLYNN, Roger;** Chief Executive Officer, Springboard Group Ltd, since 2004; Chairman: Want2bethere Ltd, 2011–18; Olive Communications Solutions, since 2013; Clearvac Group, since 2014; Decisive Media Group, since 2016; *b* 4 Nov. 1962; *s* of late Peter Flynn and Shirley Flynn; *m* 1986, Lisa Eyre; two *d. Educ:* Imperial Coll., London (BSc 1st Cl. Hons Physics). ACA 1987. With Arthur Andersen, 1984–88; Corporate Finance Exec., Virgin Gp plc, 1988–91; Commercial Dir, Virgin Communications Ltd, 1991–95; Gen. Manager, World Sales and Distribution, BA plc, 1995–98; Man. Dir, Prudential Retail, 1998–2000; CEO, BBC Ventures Gp Ltd, 2001–04. Chm., Luxtrupper, 2018–. Pres., Internat., SDI Media Gp Inc., 2006–09. MInstP 1985; MRI 1985. Trustee, Youth Culture Television, 1994–2007. Mem., Magic Circle. *Recreations:* Rugby, tennis ski-ing, film. *Address:* 28 Alexandra Terrace, Exmouth, Devon EX8 1BD. *E:* roger@springboard.uk.com.

**FLYNN, Vernon James Hennessy;** QC 2008; *b* London, 1 Sept. 1966; *s* of James and Alice Flynn; *m* 1996, Angela Porta; one *s* two *d. Educ:* Trinity Coll., Cambridge (BA 1989). Called to the Bar, Lincoln's Inn, 1991. Vis. Fellow, LSE, 2003–09. *Address:* Essex Court Chambers, 24 Lincoln's Inn Fields, WC2A 3EG.

**FLYVBJERG, Prof. Bent;** Knight, Order of the Dannebrog, 2002; PhD; BT Professor and Chair of Major Programme Management, Saïd Business School, University of Oxford, since 2009; *s* of Thorkild and Regina Flyvbjerg. *Educ:* Univ. of Aarhus (BSc Geog. and Econs 1975; MSc Geog. and Econs 1979); Univ. of Aarhus (PhD Econ. Geog. 1985); Aalborg Univ. (Dr Techn. 1991; Dr Scient. 2007). Department of Development and Planning, Aalborg University: Asst Prof., 1979–82; Associate Prof., 1983–92; Prof. of Planning, 1993–2009; non-exec. Dir, 1980–84; Prof. and Chair in Infrastructure Policy and Planning, Faculty of Technol., Policy and Mgt, Delft Univ. of Technol., 2006–09. Vis. Fulbright Scholar, UCLA, 1981–82 and 1985–86; Dist. Res. Scholar, Nat. Sci. Council, Copenhagen, 1985–88; Vis. Fellow, Eur. University Inst., Florence, 1994. Mem., Danish Govt Commn on Infrastructure, Copenhagen, 2006–08. Non-executive Director: Nordic Section, Regl Sci. Assoc., Aalborg, 1983–85; Nordic Inst. of Planning, Stockholm, 1990–98; Danish Court Admin, Copenhagen, 1999–2005. *Publications:* Rationality and Power: democracy in practice, 1998, 5th edn 2005; Making Social Science Matter: why social inquiry fails and how it can succeed again, 2001, 10th edn 2007; (with Nils Bruzelius and Werner Rothengatter) Megaprojects and Risk: an anatomy of ambition, 2003, 7th edn 2006; (ed with Hugo Priemus and Bert van Wee) Decision-Making on Mega-Projects: cost-benefit analysis, planning, and innovation, 2008; (with Todd Landman and Sanford Schram) Real Social Science, 2012; Megaproject Planning and Management, 2014; The Oxford Handbook of Megaproject Management, 2017; numerous book chapters and articles in learned jls. *Recreations:* jogging, bike-racing, ski-ing, music.

**FOALE, (Colin) Michael,** CBE 2005; PhD; Astronaut, US National Aeronautics and Space Administration, 1987–2013; Chief Executive Officer, Foale Aerospace Inc., since 2013; *b* 6 Jan. 1957; dual UK/US nationality; *s* of late Air Cdre Colin Henry Foale and Mary Katherine Foale (*née* Harding); *m* 1987, Rhonda Butler; one *s* one *d. Educ:* King's Sch., Canterbury; Queens' Coll., Cambridge (BA 1st Cl. Hons Nat. Sci. Tripos 1978; PhD Lab. Astrophysics 1982; Hon. Fellow, 1998). National Aeronautics and Space Administration (US): Payload Officer, 1983–87; Space Shuttle Missions: Atlas 1, 1992; Atlas 2, 1993; Space Suit Test, 1995; Russian Space Station Mir, May–Oct. 1997; Hubble Telescope Repair, 1999; Asst Dir (Technical), 1998; Chief of Expedn Corps, Astronaut Office, Johnson Space Center, 1999; Comdr, Internat. Space Stn Expedn 8, 2003–04; Dep. Assoc. Adminr, Exploration Ops, NASA HQ, 2005–06; Chief, Soyuz Branch, Astronaut Office, 2010–13. Hon. FRAeS 1997. DUniv: Kent, 2000; Lincs and Humberside, 2000. Founder's Medal, Air League, 1993; Barnes Wallis Award, GAPAN, 1994. *Recreations:* flying, wind surfing, diving, ski-ing, theoretical physics, electric flight.

**FOALE, Rodney Alan,** FRCP, FACC, FESC, FCSANZ; Consultant Cardiologist, since 1985, and Clinical Director of Surgery, Cardiovascular Science and Critical Care, 1999–2010, St Mary's Hospital, London; *b* 11 Sept. 1946; *s* of Maurice Foale; *m* 1st, 1981, Emma Gordon (marr. diss. 2007); two *s;* 2nd, 2010, Dr Samina Showghi (marr. diss. 2015); one *d. Educ:* Univ. of Melbourne (MB BS 1971). FACC 1985; FESC 1990; FRCP 1994; FCSANZ 2003. Sen. Clin. Fellow, Harvard Univ. and Massachusetts Gen. Hosp., 1980–82; Sen. Registrar (Cardiol.), Hammersmith Hosp., 1982–85. Mem., British Shell Collectors. *Recreations:* sea, sand, rivers, field. *Address:* 66 Harley Street, W1G 7HD. *T:* (020) 7323 4687, *Fax:* (020) 7631 5341. *E:* raf@smht-foale.co.uk. *Clubs:* Flyfishers', Chelsea Arts, Oriental.

**FOBERT, Jamie;** Director, Jamie Fobert Architects, since 1996; *b* Kingston, Ont, 5 Nov. 1962; *s* of Glenn Fobert and Norma Fobert; *m* 2015, Dominique Gagnon. *Educ:* Univ. of Toronto (BArch 1987). Architect of private houses, exhibns and retail concepts for luxury brands; projects as architect include: Kettle's Yard, Cambridge, 2004–18; New Tate St Ives, 2005–17; NPG, 2018–. Visiting Professor: AA, 2000–02; École polytechnique fédérale de Lausanne, 2007; RCA, 2013–15. Trustee: Camden Arts Centre, 2017–; Architecture Foundn, 2019. *Publications:* Working in Architecture: Jamie Fobert Architects, 2015. *Recreations:* art exhibitions, theatre, opera, cycling, cooking. *Address:* Jamie Fobert Architects, Rochelle, 22 Club Row, E2 7EY. *T:* (020) 7553 6560. *E:* mail@jamiefobertarchitects.com.

**FOCKE, His Honour Paul Everard Justus;** QC 1982; a Circuit Judge, 1997–2007; a Senior Circuit Judge, 2000–07; *b* 14 May 1937; *s* of late Frederick Justus Focke and Muriel Focke; *m* 1973, Lady Tana Marie Alexander, *er d* of 6th Earl of Caledon; two *d. Educ:* Downside; Exeter Coll., Oxford; Trinity Coll., Dublin. National Service, 1955–57; Territorial Army, 1957–66, Cheshire Yeomanry (Captain). Called to the Bar, Gray's Inn, 1964 (Bencher, 1992), to the Bar of NSW and to the NZ Bar, 1982; QC NSW 1984; a Recorder, 1986–97. Dir, Bar Mutual Indemnity Fund, 1988–97. Judicial Mem., Parole Bd, 2007–. *Recreations:* travelling, aeroplanes. *Clubs:* Pratt's, Turf, Beefsteak, Cavalry and Guards.

**FODEN, (Arthur) John;** Chairman, PA Consulting Group, 1986–95; *b* 4 Oct. 1939; *s* of Air Vice-Marshal Arthur Foden, CB, CBE and Constance Muriel Foden (*née* Corkill); *m* 1963, Virginia Caroline Field; two *d. Educ:* Abingdon Sch., Oxon. Joined Whitbread and Co. Ltd, 1959, Industrial Relns Manager, 1967; PA Consulting Group, 1967–95: Gp Human Resources Dir, 1975–79; Chief Exec. of PA Germany, 1979–80, of PA Personnel Services, 1980–85; Chief Exec., 1985–92; Chm., 1986–95. Chm., Scottish Provident Instn, 1998–2001 (non-exec. Dir, 1995–2001); non-executive Director: Media Audits Ltd, 1992–2001; Scottish Mutual Assce plc, 2001–03. *Publications:* Paid to Decide, 1991. *Recreations:* travel, cooking.

**FODOR, Prof. Ervin,** DPhil; Professor of Virology, University of Oxford, since 2011; Fellow, Exeter College, Oxford, since 2011; *b* Želiezovce, Czechoslovakia, 12 April 1965; *s* of Ferenc and Rozália Fodor. *Educ:* Slovak Univ. of Technol., Bratislava (MSc 1987); Worcester Coll., Oxford (DPhil 1996). Res. Asst, Inst. of Virol., Slovak Acad. of Scis, Bratislava, 1987–92; Postdoctoral Res. Associate, Mt Sinai Sch. of Medicine, NY, 1997–98; University of Oxford: Postdoctoral Res. Asst, 1998–2002; MRC Sen. Res. Fellow, 2002–07; Res. Councils UK Acad. Fellow, 2008–10; Lectr, 2010–11. *Publications:* contrib. articles to jls incl. Nature, Cell, Nature Microbiol., Nature Communications, Proc. NAS, USA, Public Liby of Sci. Pathogens, Jl Virol., Virol., Jl Gen. Virol., Viruses, Vaccine, RNA Biol., Rev. Med. Virol. *Recreations:* theatre, cinema, walking, art, gardening. *Address:* Sir William Dunn School of Pathology, University of Oxford, South Parks Road, Oxford OX1 3RE. *T:* (01865) 275580, *Fax:* (01865) 275515. *E:* ervin.fodor@path.ox.ac.uk.

**FOËX, Prof. Pierre,** DPhil; FRCA, FANZCA, FMedSci; Nuffield Professor of Anaesthetics, 1991–2002, and Fellow, 1991–2002, Supernumerary Fellow, since 2002, Pembroke College, University of Oxford; *b* 4 July 1935; *s* of Georges and Berthe Foëx; *m* 1958, Anne-Lise Schürch; two *s. Educ:* Univ. of Geneva (DM); professional qualifying Swiss State Exam. in Medicine and Surgery, 1960; DPhil Oxon 1973. FRCA (FFARCS 1985); FANZCA 1993. University Hospital, Geneva: Asst, 1961–62 and Chef de Clinique, 1962–63, Dept of Neurology; Asst, 1963–65, Chef de Clinique-adjoint, 1966–68 and Chef de Clinique, 1969–70, Dept of Medicine; Nuffield Department of Anaesthetics, University of Oxford: Res. Fellow, 1970–71; Lectr, 1971–73; Univ. Lectr, 1973–76; Clinical Reader and Hon. Consultant (Clinical Physiology), 1976–91; Emer. Fellow, Worcester Coll., Oxford, 1993 (Fellow, 1976–91). Mem., Exec. Cttee, Anaesthetic Res. Soc., 1982–86; Senator, European Acad. of Anaesthesiology, 1988–99 (Vice-Pres., 1991–93); Mem. Council, RCAnaes, 1996–2002. Non-exec. Dir, Oxford Radcliffe Hosps NHS Trust, 1992–99. Vis. Prof., univs in Australia, Canada, Europe, NZ, USA. Founder FMedSci 1998. Hon. FCA(SA) 2008. *Publications:* Anaesthesia for the Compromised Heart, 1989; Principles and Practice of Critical Care, 1997; Cardiovascular Drugs in the Perioperative Period, 1999; chapters and papers on cardiac physiology, cardiovascular physiology applied to anaesthesia, myocardial ischaemia, cardiovascular pharmacology, anaesthesia, hypertension, implications of coronary revascularisation and perioperative beta-blockade. *Recreations:* walking, foreign travel. *Address:* 26 Jack Straw's Lane, Oxford OX3 0DW. *T:* (01865) 761771.

**FOGARTY, Monica Irmela;** Chief Executive, Warwickshire County Council, since 2019 (Joint Managing Director, 2017–19); *b* London, 21 May 1966; *d* of Joseph Fogarty and Margaret Fogarty; *m* 1994, Dr John Graves; one *s* one *d.* *Educ:* Trinity Coll. Dublin (BBS Hons 1988; MA 1990). Coventry CC, 1990–99; Warwickshire County Council: sen. posts, 1999–2011; Strategic Dir for Communities, 2011–17. *Recreations:* running, motorbike riding. *Address:* Warwickshire County Council, Shire Hall, Market Square, Warwick CV34 4RR. *E:* monicafogarty@warwickshire.gov.uk.

**FOGLE, Bruce,** MBE 2004; DVM; veterinary surgeon, writer, broadcaster; *b* 17 Feb. 1944; *s* of Morris Fogle and Aileen (*née* Breslin); *m* 1973, Julia Foster; one *s* two *d.* *Educ:* Ontario Vet. Coll., Univ. of Guelph (DVM 1970). MRCVS 1970. Clinical Veterinary Surgeon, London Vet. Clinic (formerly Portman Vet. Clinic), London, 1973–; Founder and Partner, Emergency Vet. Clinic, London, 1980–; Partner, Elizabeth Street Vet. Clinic, London, 1980–. Co-Founder and Vice Chm., Hearing Dogs for Deaf People, 1982–. Chm., Humane Soc. Internat., 2012–. Television: Presenter: Petwatch, 1986; Good Companions, 1987; London Walkies, 1988; People and Pets, 1989–90; radio: Resident Vet, The Jimmy Young Prog., 1992–2003, The Jeremy Vine Show, 2003–, Radio 2; columnist: Today, 1986–89; Prima mag., 1986–92; Dogs Today mag., 1990–; Daily Telegraph, 1992–97; feature writer, The Times. Consultant to internat. pet food ind. cos, Pet Plan, Encyclopedia Britannica, Microsoft Encarta. Member: BVA, 1970; British Small Animal Vet. Assoc., 1970 (Hon. Life Mem., 2013). Consumer Writer of Year, PPA, 1991; Dist. Alumnus Award, Ontario Vet. Coll., 2018. *Publications:* Interrelations Between People and Pets (ed and contrib.), 1981; Pets and their People, 1983; Games Pets Play, 1986; Paws Across London, 1989; The Dog's Mind, 1990; The Cat's Mind, 1991; People and Pets, 1991; Know Your Cat, 1991; Know Your Dog, 1992; The Complete Dog Care Manual, 1993; 101 Questions Your Cat Would Ask its Vet if Your Cat Could Talk, 1993; 101 Questions Your Dog Would Ask its Vet if Your Dog Could Talk, 1993; The Complete Dog Training Manual, 1994; 101 Essential Tips: caring for your dog, 1995; First Aid for Cat Owners, 1995; First Aid for Dog Owners, 1995; The Encyclopedia of the Dog, 1995; The Cocker Spaniel Handbook, 1996; The Golden Retriever Handbook, 1996; The Labrador Retriever Handbook, 1996; The German Shepherd Handbook, 1996; The Dachshund Handbook, 1997; The Poodle Handbook, 1997; The Secret Life of Cat Owners, 1997; The Secret Life of Dog Owners, 1997; 101 Essential Tips: training your dog, 1997; 101 Essential Tips: caring for your puppy, 1997; The Encyclopedia of the Cat, 1997; Cat's Christmas, 1998; Natural Dog Care, 1999; Natural Cat Care, 1999; The New Encyclopedia of the Dog, 2000; The New Encyclopedia of the Cat, 2001; The New Complete Dog Training Manual, 2001; What's up with my Dog?, 2001; What's up with my Cat?, 2001; The Dog Owner's Manual, 2002; The Cat Owner's Manual, 2002; Caring for your Dog, 2003; Dialogues with Dogs, 2004; Travels with Macy, 2005; If Only They Could Talk, 2006; A Dog Abroad, 2007; Eyewitness Companions: Dogs, 2006; Cats, 2006; Dog Talk, 2009; Complete Cat Care, 2011; Barefoot at the Lake: a memoir of summer people and water creatures, 2015; Complete Puppy and Dog Care, 2018; *contributions to:* New Perspectives on our Lives with Companion Animals, 1983; The Veterinary Annual, 1986; Eye to Eye: the psychology of relationships, 1988; Animals and People Sharing the World, 1988; contribs to learned jls in Eur. and N America, and to many newspapers and magazines. *Recreations:* stalking painted Gustavian furniture in rural Sweden, acting as putty in my dog's paws. *Address:* 86 York Street, W1H 1QS. *T:* (020) 7723 2068, *Fax:* (020) 7723 9009. *E:* bruce@brucefogle.com. *Club:* Garrick.

**FOISTER, Dr Susan Rosemary,** FSA; Curator of Early Netherlandish, German and British Paintings, since 1990, Deputy Director, since 2010, and Director of Public Programmes and Partnerships, since 2018, National Gallery; *b* 12 May 1954; *d* of late Philip and Pamela Foister; *m* 1985, Richard Bulkeley Ritchie; two *s* one *d.* *Educ:* Hastings High Sch.; St Anne's Coll., Oxford (BA English 1975); Courtauld Inst. of Art (MA 1977; PhD 1982). FSA 2010. Jun. Res. Fellow, Warburg Inst., 1979–81; Curator, Victorian Portraits, NPG, 1983–89; National Gallery: Hd, Curatorial Dept, 2000–04; Dir of Collections, 2004–13, of Public Engagement, 2013–18. Dir, Nat. Gall. Co. Ltd, 2005–. Member: Adv. Bd, Renaissance Studies, 1997–2013; Adv. Panel, Public Catalogue Foundn, 2003–; Adv. Bd, Making Art in Tudor Britain Project, NPG, 2007–12; Peer Rev. Coll., AHRC, 2011–14. Chm., Soc. of Renaissance Studies, 1992–95. *Publications:* Drawings by Holbein from the Royal Library, Windsor Castle, 1983; Cardinal Newman, 1990; (jtly) Giotto to Dürer, 1991; (ed jtly) Robert Campin: new directions in scholarship, 1996; (jtly) Making and Meaning: Holbein's Ambassadors, 1997; (jtly) Dürer to Veronese, 1999; (ed jtly) Investigating Jan van Eyck, 2000; (jtly) Art in the Making: Renaissance underdrawing, 2002; Dürer and the Virgin in the Garden, 2004; Holbein and England, 2004; Holbein in England, 2006; Art of Light: German Renaissance stained glass, 2007; (jtly) Renaissance Faces: Van Eyck to Titian, 2008; (jtly) Reflections: Van Eyck and the Pre-Raphaelites, 2017; contrib. articles to Burlington Mag., Apollo. *Address:* National Gallery, Trafalgar Square, WC2N 5DN. *T:* (020) 7839 3321, *Fax:* (020) 7742 2472.

**FOKAS, Prof. Athanasios Spyridon,** MD; PhD; Professor of Nonlinear Mathematical Science, University of Cambridge, since 2002; Fellow, Clare Hall, Cambridge, since 2005; *b* 30 June 1952; *s* of Spyridon and Anastasia Fokas; *m* 1996, Regina Karousou; one *s* two *d.* *Educ:* Imperial Coll., London (BS 1975); CIT (PhD 1979); Sch. of Medicine, Univ. of Miami (MD 1986). Saul Kaplun Res. Fellow in Applied Maths, CIT, 1979–80; Asst Prof., 1980–82, Prof. and Chm., 1986–93, Dept of Maths and Computer Sci., Clarkson Univ.; Prof., Dept of Maths, Univ. of Loughborough, 1993–95; Prof. of Applied Maths, Dept of Maths, Imperial Coll., London, 1996–2001. Vis. Prof., Dept of Maths, Stanford Univ., 1987–88; Vis. Prof. of Engrg, Univ. of Southern California, 2015–. Ambassador of Hellenism, Greece, 2010. Co-Founder, Jl Nonlinear Science, 1991; Member, Editorial Board: Selecta Mathematica, 1998–; Proc. Royal Soc., 2002–08; Jl Math. Physics, 2002–08. Mem., Acad. of Athens, 2004. Guggenheim Fellow, 2009; Fellow, Eur. Acad. of Scis, 2010. Hon. DSc: Tech. Univ. of Crete, 2004; Athens, 2006; Western Macedonia, 2008; Hon. Dr: Applied Maths and Phys. Scis, Tech. Univ. of Athens, 2004; Maths Patras, 2005; Materials Sci. and Engrg Univ. Ioannina, 2013. Naylor Prize, LMS, 2000; Aristeion Prize: Acad. of Athens, 2004; Bodossaki Foundn (Greece), 2006. Comdr, Order of the Phoenix (Greece), 2005. *Publications:* (with M. J. Ablowitz) Introduction and Applications of Complex Variables, 1997; (jtly) Painlevé Transcendents, the Riemann-Hilbert Approach, 2006; A Unified Approach to Boundary Value Problems, 2008; edited jointly: Important Developments in Soliton Theory, 1993; Nonlinear Processes in Physics, 1993; Algebraic Aspects of Integrable Equations, 1996; Unified Transform for Boundary Value Problems, 2015; conference procs; about 300 papers. *Address:* Department of Applied Mathematics and Theoretical Physics, University of Cambridge, Wilberforce Road, Cambridge CB3 0WA. *T:* (01223) 339733, *Fax:* (01223) 765900. *E:* t.fokas@damtp.cam.ac.uk.

**FOKINE, Yuri Evgenievich;** Adviser to Rector, Diplomatic Academy, Ministry of Foreign Affairs, Russian Federation, since 2006 (Rector, 2000–06); *b* 2 Sept. 1936; *s* of Evgeni G. Fokine and Ekaterina I. Fokine; *m* 1958, Maya E. Klimova; one *s* (one *d* decd). *Educ:* Moscow State Inst. for Internat. Relations (grad 1960). Entered Diplomatic Service, 1960; posts in USSR Perm. Mission to UN, Dept of Internat. Orgns, USSR Foreign Min., and Secretariat, USSR Foreign Min.; Dep. Perm. Rep. to UN, 1976–79; Ministry of Foreign Affairs: Dep. Sec.-Gen., 1979–80; Sec.-Gen. and Mem. of Collegium, 1980–86; Ambassador to Cyprus, 1986–90; Dir, 2nd Eur. Dept, Min. of Foreign Affairs, 1990–95; Ambassador to Norway, 1995–97, to UK, 1997–2000. Head, Assoc. for Contacts with UK. Member, Editorial Council: Internat. Affairs Mag., Moscow, 2000–; Diplomatic Service Mag., Moscow, 2009–; Ed., Diplomatic Yearbook, 2000–14. Grand Gold Cross, Order of Merit (Austria), 1995; Royal Order of Merit (Norway), 1997; also national decorations. *Publications:* A. Akaev: president, 2004; articles in jls. *Recreations:* art, ballet, reading, tennis. *Address:* Diplomatic Academy, 53/2 Ostozhenka, Moscow 119021, Russia.

**FOLDES, Prof. Lucien Paul;** Professor of Economics, University of London, at London School of Economics and Political Science, 1979–96, then Emeritus; *b* 19 Nov. 1930; *s* of Egon and Marta Foldes; *m* Carol Rosalind Hewlett. *Educ:* Bunce Court Sch.; Monkton Wyld Sch.; London School of Economics (BCom, MScEcon, DBA). National Service, 1952–54. London School of Economics and Political Science: Asst Lecturer in Economics, 1954–55; Lectr, 1955–61; Reader, 1961–79. Rockefeller Travelling Fellow, 1961–62. *Publications:* articles in Rev. of Economic Studies, Economica, Jl of Mathematical Economics, Stochastics, Mathematical Finance, Jl of Economic Dynamics and Control, and others. *Recreation:* mathematical analysis. *Address:* London School of Economics, Houghton Street, WC2A 2AE. *T:* (020) 7405 7686.

**FOLEY,** family name of **Baron Foley**.

**FOLEY,** 9th Baron *cr* 1776, of Kidderminster; **Thomas Henry Foley;** *b* 1 April 1961; *s* of 8th Baron Foley and of Patricia De Meek, *d* of Joseph Zoellner III; *S* father, 2012. *Heir:* cousin Rupert Thomas Foley [*b* 16 March 1970; *m* 2013, Rachel Staines; one *s*].

**FOLEY, Hugh Smith;** Principal Clerk of Session and Justiciary, Scotland, 1989–97. *Educ:* Dalkeith High Sch. (Joint Dux). Student Actuary, Standard Life Assce Co., 1956–59; nat. service, RAF, 1959–61; entered Scottish Court Service, Court of Session Br., 1962; Asst Clerk of Session, 1962–71; Depute Clerk of Session, 1972–80; seconded to Sheriff Court, Edinburgh, 1980–81; Prin. Sheriff Clerk Depute, Glasgow, 1981–82; Sheriff Clerk, Linlithgow, 1982; Dep. Prin. Clerk of Session, 1982–86; Sen. Dep. Principal Clerk, 1986–89. Member: Lord President's Cttee on Procedure in Personal Injuries Litigation in Court of Session, 1978–79; Lothian Valuation Appeal Panel, 1997–2007. *Recreations:* walking, painting.

**FOLEY, Johanna Mary, (Jo);** journalist, editor and media consultant specialising in spa, health and wellness retreats, luxury travel and lifestyle; *b* 8 Dec. 1945; *d* of John and Monica Foley. *Educ:* St Joseph's Convent, Kenilworth; Manchester Univ. (BA Jt Hons English and Drama, 1968). Sen. Asst Editor, Woman's Own, 1978; Woman's Editor, The Sun, 1980; Editor, Woman, 1982; Exec. Editor (Features), The Times, 1984–85; Man. Editor, The Mirror, 1985–86; Editor: Observer Magazine, 1986–87; Options, 1988–91. Editor of the Year, British Soc. of Magazine Editors, 1983. *Recreations:* eating, reading, walking, cinema, opera, travel.

**FOLEY, His Honour John Dominic;** a Circuit Judge, 1994–2009; *b* 17 Jan. 1944; *s* of Cyril Patrick Foley and Winifred Hannah (*née* McAweeny); *m* 1978, Helena Frances McGowan (marr. diss. 1986); two *d.* *Educ:* St Brendan's Coll., Bristol; Exeter Univ. (LLB Hons). Called to the Bar, Inner Temple, 1968; Western Circuit, 1969–2009; Attorney-Gen. Special Prosecutor, NI, 1971–73; Asst Recorder, 1986–89; Recorder, 1990–93; an Investigating Judge (Judicial Discipline), 2006–09. Vice-Pres., Immigration Appeal Tribunal, 1998–2005; Mem., Special Immigration Appeal Commn, 2002–05. Ind. Arbitrator (Discipline), RFU and Internat. Rugby Bd, 2005–09. Pres., Bracton Law Soc., Exeter Univ., 1966–67. *Recreations:* Rugby (formerly 1st XV, Exeter Univ.), cricket, travel, rock. *Clubs:* Clifton Rugby Football, Bristol Rugby Football; Somerset County Cricket; Carlton Cricket (Barbados), Barbados Cricket Assoc.

**FOLEY, Lt-Gen. Sir John (Paul),** KCB 1994 (CB 1991); OBE 1979; MC 1976; Vice Lord-Lieutenant, Herefordshire, 2010–14; *b* 22 April 1939; *s* of Henry Thomas Hamilton Foley, MBE and Helen Constance Margaret Foley (*née* Pearson); *m* 1972, Ann Humphries; two *d.* *Educ:* Bradfield College; Mons OCS; Army Staff College (psc). Lieut, Royal Green Jackets, 1959; RMCS and Army Staff Coll., 1970–71; Regimental Duty, 1972–74; Chief of Staff, 51 Inf. Bde, Hong Kong, 1974–76; Instructor, Army Staff Coll., 1976–78; CO 3rd Bn RGJ, 1978–80; Comdt Jun. Div., Staff Coll., 1981–82. Dir, SAS, 1983–85; RCDS 1986; Chief, British Mission to Soviet Forces in Germany, 1987–89; Dir Gen. Intelligence (Rest of World), 1989–92; Comdr, British Forces Hong Kong, and Maj.-Gen. Brigade of Gurkhas, 1992–94; Chief of Defence Intelligence, MoD, 1994–97. Col Comdt, 1st Bn, Royal Green Jackets, 1991–94, The Light Div., 1994–97. Lieut Gov. and Comdr-in-Chief, Guernsey, Channel Is, 2000–05. Non-exec. Dir, AD Systems (UK) Ltd, 2010–11. Chm., British Greyhound Racing Bd, 1999–2000. Mem., Royal Patriotic Fund Corp., 2000–01. Pres., BRIXMIS Assoc., 2002–. Liveryman, Skinners' Co., 1972– (Mem. Court, 1995–2000). DL Herefords, 2006; High Sheriff, Herefords and Worcs, 2006–07. KStJ 2000. Officer, Legion of Merit (USA), 1997. *Recreations:* tennis, walking, shooting, reading. *Club:* Boodle's.

**FOLEY, Prof. Robert Andrew,** PhD, ScD; FBA 2007; Leverhulme Professor of Human Evolution, since 2003, and Co-Founder and Co-Director, Leverhulme Centre for Human Evolutionary Studies, since 2001, University of Cambridge; Fellow, King's College, Cambridge, since 1987; *b* 18 March 1953; *s* of late Nelson Foley and Jean Foley; *m* 2003, Marta Mirazon Lahr; two *s*, and two step *s.* *Educ:* Peterhouse, Cambridge (BA 1974; PhD 1980); King's Coll., Cambridge (ScD 1996). Lectr in Anthropology, Univ. of Durham, 1977–85; Lectr in Biol Anthropology, 1986–98, Reader in Evolutionary Anthropology, 1998–2003, Univ. of Cambridge. Vis. Prof., Centre for GeoGenetics, Univ. of Copenhagen, 2013–. Pres., Soc. of Libyan Studies, 2016–. *Publications:* Off-Site Archaeology, 1981; Hominid Evolution and Community Ecology, 1984; Another Unique Species, 1987; Comparative Socioecology of Humans and Other Mammals, 1989; The Origins of Human Behaviour, 1991; Humans Before Humanity, 1995; (with P. Donnelly) Genes, Fossils and Behaviour, 2001; (with R. Lewin) Principles of Human Evolution, 2003; many scientific papers. *Recreations:* travel, cricket, gadgets. *Address:* King's College, Cambridge CB2 1ST. *T:* (01223) 331459, *Fax:* (01223) 335460.

**FOLJAMBE,** family name of **Earl of Liverpool**.

**FOLKESTONE, Viscount; Jacob Pleydell-Bouverie;** *b* 7 April 1999; *s* and *heir* of Earl of Radnor, *qv*.

**FOLKSON, Richard,** CEng, FIMechE; President, Institution of Mechanical Engineers, 2015–16; *b* Westminster, London, 31 Jan. 1955; *s* of Dr Aleck Folkson and Sheila Sybil Folkson; *m* 1993, Patricia Carole Thomas; two *d.* *Educ:* Haywards Heath Grammar Sch.; Imperial Coll. London (BSc Engrg 1977). ACGI 1977; CEng 1986; FIMechE 1995. Ford Motor Co. Ltd: Supervisor, Product Strategy, 1990–92; Project Manager, Transit, 1992–98; Chief Program Engr, 1997–98; Manager, Product Verification and Testing, 1998–2004; Chief Engr, 2004–06. Engrg consultant, low carbon vehicle technol., 2006–. Non-exec.

Dir, Evalu8 Transport Innovations, 2008–16. Vis. Prof., 2004–, RAEng Vis. Prof., 2007–, Univ. of Hertfordshire. Chm., Essex West, Remap UK, 2013–. Trustee: Smallpiece Trust, 2017–; IMechE Pension Scheme, 2017–. Member: Chelmsford Model Engrg Soc.; Romford Model Engrg Club; Aston Martin Owners Club. *Publications:* Alternative Fuels and Advanced Vehicle Technologies for Improved Environmental Performance, 2014. *Recreations:* model engineering, classic sports cars, motorcycling, Thundersley Brass Band (cornet), Big Band (trumpet). *Address:* The Black Mill, Wheelers Lane, Navestock Side, Brentwood, Essex CM14 5RN. *T:* (01277) 374389. *E:* rfolkson@aol.com.

**FOLLETT, Barbara;** *see* Follett, D. B.

**FOLLETT, Sir Brian (Keith),** Kt 1992; DL; FRS 1984; Research Fellow, University of Oxford, since 2001; *b* 22 Feb. 1939; *m* 1961, Deb (*née* Booth); one *s* one *d*. *Educ:* Bournemouth Sch.; Univ. of Bristol (BSc 1960, PhD 1964); Univ. of Wales (DSc 1975). Res. Fellow, Washington State Univ., 1964–65; Lectr in Zool., Univ. of Leeds, 1965–69; Lectr, subseq. Reader and Prof. of Zool., University Coll. of N Wales, Bangor, 1969–78; Bristol University: Prof. of Zool., 1978–93, AFRC Res. Prof., 1989–93; Hd of Dept of Zool., 1978–89; Chm., Sch. of Biol Scis, 1989–93; Vice-Chancellor, Warwick Univ., 1993–2001; Chairman: AHRB, then AHRC, 2001–07; TTA, then TDA, 2003–09. Chm., Infectious Diseases Inquiry, Royal Soc., 2001–02. Chairman: ESRC-British Acad. Working Party on the Future of Funding Res. in the Humanities, 1992; Adv. Bd, British Library, 2000–07; Res. Support Librarians Review Gp, 2001–03; Adv. Forum, STEM Strategy Gp, DfES, later DIUS, then BIS, 2007–11; Member: Biol Sci. Cttee, SERC, 1981–84; AFRC, 1984–88 (Mem., Animals Cttee, 1984–88); Biol Sci. Cttee, UGC, 1985–88; UFC, 1989–93; HEFCE, 1992–96 (Chairman: Libraries Review Gp, 1992–97; Strategic Subjects Adv. Gp, 2007–); Council, BBSRC, 1994–2001 (Chm., Sci. and Engrg Bd, 1994–97); Royal Commn on Envmtl Pollution, 2000–05. Trustee, BM (Natural Hist.), 1989–98. Biol Sec. and Vice-Pres., Royal Soc., 1987–93; Member of Council: Soc. for Study of Fertility, 1972–87 (Prog. Sec., 1976–78; Treas., 1982–87); Soc. for Endocrinology, 1974–77; Bristol Zoo, 1978–93; Wildfowl Trust, Slimbridge, 1983–86; Zool Soc. of London, 1983–86. Pres. ASE, 1997. Lectures: Amoroso, Soc. for Study of Fertility, 1985; Annual Zool., Liverpool Univ., 1991; Barrington Meml, Nottingham Univ., 1992. Gov., RSC, 2007–17; Pres., Stratford-upon-Avon Soc., 2003–. Chm., Liby and Archive Gp, The Globe, 2013–14. Mem., Academia Europaea, 1988. DL West Midlands, 2000. Hon. FCLIP (Hon. FLA 1997); Hon. FZS 2004. Hon. Fellow: UCNW, Bangor, 1990; Worcester, 2008. Hon. LLD: Wales, 1992; Calgary, 2001; St Andrews, 2002; Bristol, 2005; Lancaster, 2012; Hon. DSc: Univ. Teknologi, Malaysia, 1999; Leicester, 2001; Warwick, 2002; East Anglia, 2003; London, 2004; Bedfordshire, 2008; Bournemouth, 2008; Hon DLitt Oxford, 2012. Scientific Medal, 1976, Frink Medal, 1993, Zool Soc. of London; Dale Medal, Soc. of Endocrinology, 1988. Editorial Bds: Jl of Endocrinology, 1971–78; Gen. & Comparative Endocrinology, 1974–82; Jl of Biol Rhythms, 1986–2000; Proc. of Royal Soc., 1987–90. *Publications:* over 260 scientific papers on biol clocks and reproductive physiology. *Address:* Department of Zoology, University of Oxford, Oxford OX1 3PS. *E:* brian.follett@zoo.ox.ac.uk; 120 Tiddington Road, Stratford-upon-Avon, Warwicks CV37 7BB. *E:* follett@stratford.u-net.com.

**FOLLETT, (Daphne) Barbara;** *b* 25 Dec. 1942; *d* of late William Vernon Hubbard and Charlotte Hubbard (*née* Goulding); *m* 1st, 1963, Richard Turner (marr. diss. 1971); two *d*; 2nd, 1971, Gerald Stonestreet (marr. diss. 1974); 3rd, 1974, Leslie Broer (marr. diss. 1985); one *s*; 4th, 1985, Ken Follett, *qv*; one step *d* (one step *s* decd). *Educ:* London Sch. of Economics (BSc Econ); Open Univ. Teacher, Berlitz Sch. of Language, Paris, 1963–64; Jt Manager, fruit farm, Stellenbosch, S Africa, 1966–77; acting Regl Sec., S African Inst. of Race Relations, Cape Town, 1970; Regl Manager (Cape and Namibia), 1971–74, Nat. Health Educn Dir, 1975–78, Kupugani; Asst Course Orgnr and Lectr, Centre for Internat. Briefing, Farnham, 1980–84; freelance lectr and consultant, 1984–92. Vis. Fellow, Inst. of Public Policy Research, 1993–95. Contested (Lab): Woking, 1983; Epsom and Ewell, 1987. MP (Lab) Stevenage, 1997–2010. Parliamentary Under-Secretary of State: DWP, 2007; Govt Equalities Office, 2008; DCMS, 2008–09; DCLG, 2009–10; Minister for E of England, 2007–10. CEO, The Follett Office, 2010–. Founder Member: EMILY's List UK, 1992– (also Dir); Women's Movt for Peace, S Africa, 1976; Labour Women's Network (Mem., Steering Cttee, 1988–); Member: Fawcett Soc., 1993; Nat. Alliance of Women's Orgns, 1993; Nat. Women's Network, 1993. Hon. LLD Hertfordshire, 2010. *Recreations:* photography, Scrabble, Star Trek.

**FOLLETT, Ken,** CBE 2018; FRSL; author, since 1977; *b* 5 June 1949; *s* of late Martin Dunsford Follett and Lavinia Cynthia (Veenie) Follett (*née* Evans); *m* 1st, 1968, Mary Elson (marr. diss. 1985); one *d* (one *s* decd); 2nd, 1985, Barbara Broer (see D. B. Follett). *Educ:* Harrow Weald Grammar Sch.; Poole Tech. Coll.; University Coll. London (BA; Fellow 1994). Trainee journalist, S Wales Echo, 1970–73; Reporter, London Evening News, 1973–74; Everest Books: Editl Dir, 1974–76; Dep. Man. Dir, 1976–77. Dir, Stevenage Leisure Ltd, 1997–2005. Mem. Council, Nat. Literary Trust, 1996–2010 (Trustee, 2005–10); Chm., Nat. Year of Reading, 1998–99; Bd Dir, Nat. Acad. of Writing, 2003–10. Pres., Dyslexia Inst., 1998–2008. Vice-Pres., Stevenage Bor. FC, 2000–02; Trustee, Stevenage Community Trust, 2002– (Chm., 2005–13; Pres., 2013–); Patron, Home Start Hertfordshire (formerly Stevenage Home-Start), 2000–. Chm. Govs, Roebuck Primary Sch. and Nursery, 2001–05. Mem., Yr Academi Gymreig, 2000 (Fellow, 2011); FRSL 2018. Hon. DLitt: Glamorgan, 2007; Saginaw Valley State, 2007; Exeter, 2008; Herts, 2018; Warwick, 2019. Olaguibel Prize, Colegio Oficial de Arquitectos Vasco-Navarro, 2008; Thriller Master Award, Internat. Thriller Writers, 2010; Grand Master, Mystery Writers of America, 2013. Officier de l'ordre des arts et des lettres (France), 2019. *Publications:* Eye of the Needle (Edgar Award, Mystery Writers of Amer.), 1978; Triple, 1979; The Key to Rebecca, 1980; The Man from St Petersburg, 1982; On Wings of Eagles, 1983; Lie down with Lions, 1986; The Pillars of the Earth, 1989; Night over Water, 1991; Mrs Shiblak's Nightmare (pamphlet), 1992; A Dangerous Fortune, 1993; A Place Called Freedom, 1995; The Third Twin, 1997; The Hammer of Eden, 1998; Code to Zero, 2000; Jackdaws, 2001 (Corine Buchpreis, 2003); Hornet Flight, 2002; Whiteout, 2004; World Without End, 2007; Fall of Giants, 2010 (Libri Golden Book Award, Hungary, 2010; Que Leer Prize, 2011); Winter of the World, 2012; Edge of Eternity, 2014; A Column of Fire, 2017; various articles, screenplays and short stories. *Recreations:* bass guitarist in a blues band; Labour Party supporter and campaigner. *Address:* The Follett Office, Follett House, Primett Road, Stevenage, Herts SG1 3EE. *Clubs:* Athenæum, Groucho, Reform.

**FONAGY, Prof. Peter,** OBE 2013; PhD; FMedSci; FBA 1997; FAcSS; Professor of Contemporary Psychoanalysis and Developmental Science, since 2016, and Head, Division of Psychology and Language Sciences, since 2017, University College London; Chief Executive, Anna Freud National Centre for Children and Families, since 2003 (Director of Research, 1989–2003); National Clinical Advisor, Children and Young People's Mental Health, Department of Health, then NHS England, since 2011; *b* 14 Aug. 1952; *s* of Ivan Fonagy and Judith (*née* Barath); *m* 1990, Dr Anna Higgitt; one *s* one *d*. *Educ:* UCL (BSc Hons 1974; PhD 1980). Dip. Clin. Psych. 1980. Lectr, 1977–88, Sen. Lectr, 1988–92, in Psychology, Univ. of London; Freud Meml Prof. of Psychoanalysis, Univ. of London, at Univ. Coll., 1992–2016; Dir, Sub-Dept of Clin. Health Psychol., 1995–2007, Hd, Res. Dept of Clinical, Educnl and Health Psychol., 2008–17, UCL. Menninger Clinic: Co-ordinating Dir, Child and Family Center, 1995–2003, Clin. Protocols and Outcome Center, 1996; Voorhees Distinguished Prof., 1995; Consultant, Child and Family Prog., Menninger Dept of Psychiatry, Baylor Coll. of Medicine, Houston, 2003–. Prog. Dir, Mental Health and Wellbeing Theme (formerly Integrated Mental Health Prog.), UCLPartners, 2011– (Interim Prog. Dir, 2010–11). Interim Clinical Lead, IAPT for Children and Young People, DoH, 2011; NIHR Sen. Investigator, 2011–15, 2015–19, now Emeritus. Visiting Professor: Hebrew Univ. of Jerusalem, 1993; Univ. of Haifa, 1993, 1995; Cornell Med. Coll., NY, 1994; Adjunct Prof. of Clin. Psychol., Kansas Univ., 1995–2002; Marie and Scott S. Smith Chair in Child Develt, Karl Menninger Sch. of Psychiatry and Mental Health Scis, Kansas, 1999–2003; Adjunct Prof. of Psychiatry, Baylor Coll. of Medicine, 2003–; Clin. Prof. of Psychiatry, Sch. of Medicine, Yale Univ., 2005–; Vis. Clin. Prof., Harvard Univ., 2011–15. Hon. Principal Investigator, Tavistock and Portman NHS Foundn Trust, 2011–. Mem., 1988–, and Trng and Supervising Analyst, 1995–, British Psycho-Analytical Soc. FMedSci 2014; FAcSS 2016. *Publications:* (with A. Higgitt) Personality Theory and Clinical Practice, 1985; (with A. D. Roth) What Works for Whom?: a critical review of psychotherapy research, 1996 (trans. Italian, 1996), 2nd edn 2005; (jtly) Psychodynamic Developmental Therapy for Children: a manual, 2000; Attachment Theory and Psychoanalysis, 2001 (trans. German 2003, French 2004, Danish 2006; Korean); (jtly) What Works for Whom?: a critical review of treatments for children and adolescents, 2002, 2nd edn 2014 (trans. Italian 2003); (jtly) Affect Regulation, Mentalization and the Development of the Self, 2002 (trans. German 2004, Italian 2005, Danish 2007); (jtly) Drawing on the Evidence: advice for mental health professionals working with children and adolescents, 2002; (with M. Target) Psychoanalytic Theories: perspectives from developmental psychopathology, 2003 (trans. Italian 2005, Hungarian 2005, Czech 2005); (with A. Bateman) Psychotherapy for Borderline Personality Disorder: mentalization based treatment, 2004 (trans. Spanish 2005, Italian 2006, German 2008); (with A. Bateman) Mentalization-Based Treatment for Borderline Personality Disorder: a practical guide, 2006 (trans. Dutch 2007, Norwegian 2007, Danish, Italian 2010, Korean 2010, Finnish 2014, Turkish 2015); (with J. G. Allen) Handbook of Mentalization-Based Treatment, 2006; (jtly) Development Science and Psychoanalysis: integration and innovation, 2007; (jtly) Mentalizing in Clinical Practice, 2008 (trans. Dutch 2009, Danish 2010, Italian 2010, Hungarian 2011, Japanese 2014, Polish 2014); (jtly) Social Cognition and Developmental Psychopathology, 2008; (with J. F. Clarkin and G. O. Gabbard) Psychodynamic Psychotherapy for Personality Disorders: a clinical handbook, 2010; (jtly) Brief Dynamic Interpersonal Therapy: a clinician's guide, 2011; (jtly) Handbook of Mentalizing in Mental Health Practice, 2012, 2nd edn 2019; (with D. Cottrell, J. Phillips, D. Bevington, D. Glaser and E. Allison) What Works for Whom?: a critical review of treatments for children and adolescents, 2014, 2nd edn 2016; (with A. Bateman) Mentalization-Based Treatment for Personality Disorders: a practical guide, 2016 (trans. Spanish 2016); (jtly) Adaptive Mentalization-Based Integrative Treatment: a guide for teams to develop systems of care, 2017; 500 papers, 246 contribs books. *Recreations:* ski-ing, theatre, gardening. *Address:* Division of Psychology and Language Sciences, University College London, 26 Bedford Way, WC1H 0AP. *T:* (020) 7679 1943. *E:* p.fonagy@ucl.ac.uk.

**FONTAINE, Barbara Janet;** Senior Master of the Senior Courts, Queen's Bench Division, and Queen's Remembrancer, since 2014; *b* 29 Dec. 1953; *d* of late John Fontaine and Brenda Fontaine (*née* Taylor); *m* 1990, Trevor John Watkins; twin *s*. *Educ:* Stockport High Sch. for Girls; KCL (LLB). Admitted solicitor, 1978; articled Bird & Bird, 1976–78; Solicitor: Hill, Dickinson, London, 1978–83; Coward Chance, later Clifford Chance, 1983–87; Baker & McKenzie, Hong Kong, 1987–93 (Partner, 1989); Dep. Queen's Bench Master, 1997–2003; Master of the Senior (formerly Supreme) Court, QBD, 2003–14. *Recreations:* theatre, art, history, travel. *Address:* Royal Courts of Justice, Strand, WC2A 2LL.

**FOOKES, Baroness** *cr* 1997 (Life Peer), of Plymouth in the co. of Devon; **Janet Evelyn Fookes,** DBE 1989; DL; *b* 21 Feb. 1936; *d* of late Lewis Aylmer Fookes and Evelyn Margery Fookes (*née* Holmes). *Educ:* Hastings and St Leonards Ladies' Coll.; High Sch. for Girls, Hastings; Royal Holloway Coll., Univ. of London (BA Hons; Hon. Fellow, 1998). Teacher, 1958–70. Councillor for County Borough of Hastings, 1960–61 and 1963–70 (Chm. Educn Cttee, 1967–70). MP (C): Merton and Morden, 1970–74; Plymouth, Drake, 1974–97. Mem., Speaker's Panel of Chairmen, 1976–97; Second Dep. Chm. of Ways and Means and Dep. Speaker, H of C, 1992–97. Sec., Cons. Parly Educn Cttee, 1971–75; Chairman: Educn, Arts and Home Affairs Sub-Cttee of the Expenditure Cttee, 1975–79; Parly Gp for Animal Welfare, 1985–92 (Sec., 1974–82); Member: Unopposed Bills Cttee, 1973–75; Services Cttee, 1974–76; Select Cttee on Home Affairs, 1984–92; Armed Forces Parly Scheme, 2001–. A Dep. Speaker, H of L, 2002–; a Dep. Chm. of Cttees, H of L, 2002–; Chm., Refreshment Cttee, H of L, 2003–07; Member: Jt Select Cttee on Draft Mental Capacity Bill (formerly Mental Incapacity Bill), 2003; Select Cttee on Crossrail Bill, 2008; Select Cttee on Communications, 2010–15; Delegated Powers and Regulatory Reform Select Cttee, 2013– (Chm., 2015–17); Select Cttee on Bribery Act, 2018–19; Chm., All Party Parly Gardening and Horticulture Gp, 2010–. Chm., Cons. West Country Mems Cttee, 1976–77, Vice-Chm., 1977. Fellow, Industry and Parlt Trust, 1978. Pres., Hastings and Rye Cons. Assoc., 1998–. Member: Council, RSPCA, 1975–92 (Chm., 1979–81; Vice-Pres., 1992–); Council, SSAFA, 1980–98 (Vice-Pres., 1998–); Council, Stonham Housing Assoc., 1980–92; Commonwealth War Graves Commn, 1987–97; Council, Coll. of St Mark and St John, 1989–2004. President: Hastings, St Leonards on Sea, Bexhill and Dist Br., NSPCC, 2000–; War Widows Assoc., 2005–. Chm., Plymouth Ambassadors' Gp of Tomorrow's People (formerly Patron, Plymouth Workroute, later Regl Patron, Tomorrow's People), 1998–2016. Gov., Kelly Coll., 2002–14. Hon. Freeman, Plymouth, 2000. Member: RHS; Nat. Trust; Art Fund. DL E Sussex, 2001. Hon. DLitt Plymouth, 1993. *Recreations:* theatre, gardening, swimming, yoga. *Address:* House of Lords, SW1A 0PW.

**FOOT, David Lovell,** CB 1998; FICFor; Head of Forestry Authority, 1995–99; *b* 20 May 1939; *s* of late John Bartram Lovell Foot, MBE and of Bertha Lilian Foot; *m* 1964, Verena Janine Walton; one *s* one *d*. *Educ:* John Lyon Sch., Harrow; Edinburgh Univ. (BSc Hons 1961). FICFor 1980. Dist Officer, Forestry Commn, 1961–64; Silviculturist, Dept of Forestry and Game, Govt of Malawi, 1964–70; Forestry Commission: various appts in S Scotland, N Wales and E Scotland, 1970–86; Comr, 1986–99. Trustee, Woodland Trust, 1999–2008. *Recreations:* walking, writing, photography, natural history.

**FOOT, Michael David Kenneth Willoughby,** CBE 2003; Special Advisor, Promontory Financial Group, 2015–18 (Global Vice-Chairman, 2012–15); *b* 16 Dec. 1946; *s* of Kenneth Willoughby Foot and Ruth Joan (*née* Cornah); *m* 1972, Michele Annette Cynthia Macdonald; one *s* two *d*. *Educ:* Pembroke Coll., Cambridge (MA); Yale Univ., USA (MA). Joined Bank of England, 1969; manager, 1978; sen. man., 1985; seconded to IMF, Washington, as UK Alternate Exec. Dir, 1985–87; Head: Foreign Exchange Div., 1988–90; European Div., 1990–93; Banking Supervision Div., 1993–94; Dep. Dir, Supervision and Surveillance, 1994–96; Exec. Dir, Bank of England, 1996–98; Man. Dir, Deposit Takers and Mkts, FSA, 1998–2004; Inspector of Banks, Central Bank of the Bahamas, 2004–07. Chm., Promontory Financial Gp (UK) Ltd, 2007–12. *Publications:* contrib. essays on monetary econs to books and jls. *Recreations:* choral singing, tennis, voluntary youth work.

**FOOT, Prof. Mirjam Michaela,** DLitt; FSA; Professor of Library and Archive Studies, University College London, 2000–06, now Emeritus; *b* 11 Oct. 1941; *d* of Carl Paul Maria Romme and Anthonia Maria Wiegman; *m* 1972, Michael Richard Daniell Foot, CBE, TD (*d* 2012); *m* 2017, Adrian Heywood Seville. *Educ:* Amsterdam Univ. (BA, MA, DLitt 1979). FSA 1986. Asst Lectr, Bedford Coll., Univ. of London, 1965–66; British Library: Asst Keeper, Rare Book Collection, 1966–84; Curator, Preservation Service, 1984–87; Dep. Dir, Hd of W European Collections and Hd of Acquisitions, 1987–90; Dir of Collections and Preservation, 1990–99. Associate, Clare Hall, Cambridge, 1970–72; Sandars Reader in Bibliography, Univ. of Cambridge, 2002–03; Hon. Sen. Res. Fellow, Sch. of Advanced Study, Univ. of London, 2006–. Ed., British Liby Jl, 1977–85. Bibliographical Society: Hon. Sec., 1975–94; Vice-Pres., 1990–2000; Pres., 2000–02; Gold Medal, 2014. Vice-Pres., Soc. of Antiquaries, 2001–05. Hon. Fellow, Designer Bookbinders, 1986. *Publications:* The Henry Davis Gift: Vol I: Studies in the History of Bookbinding, 1978; Vol II: North European Bindings, 1983; Vol III: South European Bindings, 2010; Pictorial Bookbindings, 1986; (with H. M. Nixon) The History of Decorated Bookbinding in England, 1992; Studies in the History of Bookbinding, 1993; The History of Bookbinding as a Mirror of Society, 1998; The Decorated Bindings in Marsh's Library, Dublin, 2004; (ed) Eloquent Witnesses: bookbindings and their history, 2004; Bookbinders at Work: their roles and methods, 2005; contrib. articles in Book Collector, The Liby, British Liby Jl, Revue française d'histoire du livre, Proc. and Bulletins of Assoc. Internat. de Bibliophilie, Paper Conservator. *Recreations:* music, reading, walking. *Address:* Elms Barn, 146 High Street, Barkway, Royston, Herts SG8 8EG.

**FOOT, Prof. Rosemary June,** PhD; FBA 1996; John Swire Senior Research Fellow in International Relations, St Antony's College, Oxford, 1990–2014, now Emeritus; Professor of International Relations, 1997–2014, now Emeritus, and Senior Research Fellow, Department of Politics and International Relations and Research Associate, China Centre, since 2014, University of Oxford; *b* 4 June 1948; *d* of Leslie William Foot, MBE and Margaret Lily Frances Foot; *m* 1996, Timothy C. S. Kennedy. *Educ:* Univ. of Essex (BA Hons Govt 1972); SOAS, London Univ. (MA Area Studies (Far East) 1973); LSE (PhD Internat. Relns 1977). Lectr in Internat. Relns, Univ. of Sussex, 1978–90. Fulbright Scholar and American Council of Learned Socs Fellow, E Asian Inst., Columbia Univ., NY, 1981–82; Vis. Scholar, Renmin Univ., Beijing, 1986; Sen. Fellow, Belfer Center, Kennedy Sch. of Govt, Harvard Univ., 2006; S. Rajaratnam Prof. of Strategic Studies, Nat. Tech. Univ., Singapore, 2006; Visiting Fellow: Dr Seaker Chan Center, Fudan Univ., 2013; Nobel Inst., 2014; Sir Howard Kippenberger Vis. Prof., Victoria Univ. of Wellington, 2014; Prof. Desmond Ball Vis. Prof., ANU, 2017; Fudan Fellow, Fudan Univ., 2018. *Publications:* The Wrong War: American policy and the dimensions of the Korean conflict 1950–1953, 1985; A Substitute for Victory: the politics of peacemaking at the Korean Armistice talks, 1990; (ed jtly) Migration: the Asian experience, 1994; The Practice of Power: US relations with China since 1949, 1995; (ed jtly) Hong Kong's Transitions 1842–1997, 1997; Rights Beyond Borders: the global community and the struggle over human rights in China, 2000; (ed jtly) Order and Justice in International Relations, 2003; (ed jtly) US Hegemony and International Organisations, 2003; Human Rights and Counter-terrorism in America's Asia Policy, 2004; (ed jtly) Does China Matter?: a reassessment, 2004; Framing Security Agendas: US counter-terrorist policies and Southeast Asian responses, 2008; (jtly) China, the United States, and Global Order, 2011; (ed) China Across the Divide: the domestic and global in politics and society, 2013; (ed jtly) The Oxford Handbook of the International Relations of Asia, 2014. *Recreations:* walking, music, swimming. *Address:* St Antony's College, Oxford OX2 6JF.

**FOOT, Rev. Canon Prof. Sarah Rosamund Irvine,** PhD; FRHistS, FSA; Regius Professor of Ecclesiastical History, University of Oxford, since 2007; *b* 23 Feb. 1961; *d* of late Michael Richard Daniell Foot, CBE, TD, and Elizabeth Mary Irvine Foot (*née* King); *m* 1st, 1986, Geoffrey Martin Kenneth Schrecker (marr. diss. 1999); one *s*; 2nd, 2002, Prof. Michael John Bentley. *Educ:* Withington Girls' Sch., Manchester; Newnham Coll., Cambridge (BA 1984, MA 1986; PhD 1990); Ripon Coll. Cuddesdon (Oxford Ministry Course 2017). FSA 2001; FRHistS 2001. Res. Fellow, Gonville and Caius Coll., Cambridge, 1989–93; University of Sheffield: Lectr, 1993–2001; Sen. Lectr, 2001–04; Prof. of Early Medieval Hist., 2004–07. Lay Canon, Christ Ch, Oxford, 2007–17; ordained deacon and priest, 2017; Residentiary Canon, Christ Ch, Oxford, 2017–. *Publications:* Veiled Women: the disappearance of nuns from Anglo-Saxon England, 2 vols, 2000; Monastic Life in Anglo-Saxon England *c* 600–900, 2006; Athelstan: the first King of England, 2011. *Recreations:* music, fiction, travel. *Address:* Christ Church, Oxford OX1 1DP. *T:* (01865) 286078. *E:* sarah.foot@chch.ox.ac.uk.

**FOOTMAN, John Richard Evelegh,** CBE 2019; an Executive Director, since 2003, and Secretary, since 2009, Bank of England; *b* 6 Sept. 1952; *s* of Jack and Joyce Footman; *m* 1983, Elaine Watkiss; two *s* three *d*. *Educ:* Clifton Coll., Bristol. Joined Bank of England, 1969; Private Sec. to Gov., 1986–89; Head of Information, 1989–94; Sec., 1994–97; Dep. Dir, 1997–99; Dir of Personnel, 1999–2003. *Address:* Bank of England, EC2R 8AH. *T:* (020) 3461 5765.

**FOOTTIT, Rt Rev. Anthony Charles;** Bishop Suffragan of Lynn, 1999–2003; an Honorary Assistant Bishop, Diocese of Norwich, since 2004; *b* 28 June 1935; *s* of Percival Frederick and Mildred Foottit; *m* 1977, Rosamond Mary Alyson Buxton; one *s* two *d*. *Educ:* Lancing Coll.; King's Coll., Cambridge (MA). Asst Curate, Wymondham, 1961–64; Vicar, Blakeney Group, 1964–71; Rector, Camelot Group, 1971–81; RD of Cary, 1979–81; St Hugh's Missioner for Lincolnshire, 1981–87; Hon. Canon of Lincoln Cathedral, 1986–87; Archdeacon of Lynn, 1987–98. *Publications:* Mission and Ministry in Rural France, 1967; A Gospel of Wild Flowers, 2006; A Calendar of Wild Flowers, 2018. *Recreations:* gardening, botany, rambling. *Address:* 1 The Dial, Reepham, Norfolk NR10 4LX. *T:* (01603) 870340.

**FOPP, Dr Michael Anton;** Director General (formerly Director), Royal Air Force Museum, 1988–2010; *b* 28 Oct. 1947; *s* of late Sqdn Ldr Desmond Fopp, AFC, AE and of Edna Meryl Fopp; *m* 1968, Rosemary Ann Hodgetts; one *s*. *Educ:* Reading Blue Coat Sch.; City Univ., London (MA 1984; PhD 1989). FMA; FRAeS. Dep. Keeper 1979–82, Keeper 1982–85, Battle of Britain Mus.; Co. Sec., Hendon Mus. Trading Co. Ltd, 1983–85; Dir, London Transport Mus., 1985–88. Hon. Sec. 1976–86, Chm. 1986–88, Soc. of Friends of RAF Mus. President: London Underground Rly Soc., 1987–88; Internat. Assoc. of Transport Museums, 1992–98. Chairman: Museums' Documentation Assoc., 1995–98; London Transport Flying Club Ltd, 1986–97. Dir, RAF Mus. Amer. Foundn, 2000–10. Trustee: Air Safety Trust, 2011–17 (Chm., 2012–17); Air Pilots (formerly Guild of Air Pilots) Trust, 2011–17 (Chm., 2012–17). Freeman, City of London, 1984; Liveryman, 2002–, Master, 2010–11, Hon. Co. of Air Pilots (formerly GAPAN). Hon. DSc City, 2011. Cruise ship lecturer, 2011–. *Publications:* The Boeing Washington, 1980; The Battle of Britain Museum Guide, 1980; The Bomber Command Museum Guide, 1982; The RAF Museum Guide, 1985; (ed) A Junior Guide to the RAF Museum, 1985; (ed) Battle of Britain Project Book, 1989; Royal Air Force Museum, 1992, 2nd edn 2003; (ed) High Flyers, 1993; Managing Museums and Galleries, 1997; The Implications of Emerging Technologies for Museums and Galleries, 1997; The Tradition is Safe, 2003; The Spirit of the Royal Air Force, 2018; various articles on aviation, museums and management, in magazines and jls. *Recreations:* computers, flying, gliding, Chinese cookery, Radio Yacht Racing, bell ringing, model railways. *Address:* Honourable Company of Air Pilots, Air Pilots House, 52a Borough High Street, SE1 1XN. *T:* (020) 7404 4032. *Clubs:* Royal Air Force; Royal Air Squadron.

**FORAN, (Mary) Shirley;** Sheriff of North Strathclyde at Kilmarnock, since 2014; *b* Glasgow, 6 July 1957; *d* of Alexander and Mary Stewart; *m* 1979, John Foran; one *s* two *d*. *Educ:* St Michael's Acad., Kilwinning; Glasgow Univ. (LLB). Admitted Solicitor, 1980; Asst, 1980–90, Litigation Partner, 1990–2014, Black Hay, Solicitors, Ayr and Prestwick; Sheriff (pt-time), 2006–14. *Recreations:* reading, gardening, watching and pretending to play tennis. *Address:* Kilmarnock Sheriff Court, St Marnock Street, Kilmarnock KA1 1ED. *T:* (01563) 550024.

**FORBES,** family name of **Lord Forbes** and of **Earl of Granard**.

**FORBES, 23rd Lord** *cr* 1445 or before; **Malcolm Nigel Forbes;** DL; Premier Lord of Scotland; landowner; *b* 6 May 1946; *s* of 22nd Lord Forbes and Hon. Rosemary Katharine Hamilton-Russell, *o d* of 9th Viscount Boyne; *S* father, 2013; *m* 1st, 1969, Carole Jennifer Andrée (marr. diss. 1982), *d* of N. S. Whitehead, Aberdeen; one *d* (one *s* decd); 2nd, 1988, Jennifer Mary Gribbon, *d* of I. P. Whittington, Tunbridge Wells. *Educ:* Eton; Aberdeen Univ. Director, Instock Disposables Ltd, 1974–2009; Chm., Castle Forbes Collection Ltd, 1996–. DL Aberdeenshire, 1996. *Heir: g s* Master of Forbes, *qv*. *Address:* Castle Forbes, Alford, Aberdeenshire AB33 8BL. *T:* (01975) 562574; 3 Steeple Close, SW6 3LE. *T:* (020) 7736 0730.

**FORBES, Viscount; Jonathan Peter Hastings Forbes;** *b* 24 Dec. 1981; *e s* and heir of Earl of Granard, *qv*.

**FORBES, Master of; Geordie Malcolm Andrew Ross Forbes,** *b* 28 Nov. 2010; *s* of late Hon. Neil Malcolm Ross Forbes, Master of Forbes and of Maria Elfgyva Forbes (*née* Martell); heir of Lord Forbes, *qv*.

**FORBES, Major Sir Andrew (Iain Ochoncar),** 13th Bt *cr* 1630 (NS), of Craigievar, Aberdeenshire and of Corse; *b* 28 Nov. 1945; *s* of Lt-Col Patrick Walter Forbes of Corse, OBE, DL and Margaret Hawthorne Forbes (*née* Lydall); *S* kinsman, 2000, but his name does not appear on the Official Roll of the Baronetage; *m* 1984, Jane Elizabeth Dunbar-Nasmith (*d* 2005); two *s* two *d*. *Educ:* Trinity Coll., Glenalmond; RMA Sandhurst; St Catherine's Coll., Oxford (BA 1969); Cranfield Sch. of Mgt (MBA 1979). Major, Gordon Highlanders, retired. *Heir: s* James Patrick Ochoncar Forbes, *b* 1 Nov. 1986.

**FORBES, Andrew Malcolm;** Founder, Contentious Music Ltd; *b* London, 15 April 1963; *s* of Gordon and Adriana Forbes; *m* 1997, Charlotte Matthews; one *s* two *d*. *Educ:* Belle Vue Boys' Sch., Bradford; Univ. of E Anglia (LLB 1986); Coll. of Law, Chancery Lane. Lead guitarist, punk band, The Wall, 1980–81. Admitted solicitor, 1989; Solicitor: Richards Butler, 1989–92; Simkins Partnership, 1992–96 (Partner, 1996–98); Partner, Statham Gill Davies, 1998–2001; Founding Partner, Forbes Anderson, later Forbes Anderson Free, 2001–16; Hd, Dispute Resolution, Lee & Thompson LLP, 2016–18. *Recreations:* musician and songwriter, mountaineer and hill walker, polar adventurer, potholer, creator of The Spider. *T:* 07973 296565. *E:* andrewforbes@contentiousmusic.co.uk.

**FORBES, Colin,** RDI 1974; Consulting Partner, Pentagram Design AG, since 1993; *b* 6 March 1928; *s* of Kathleen and John Forbes; *m* 1961, Wendy Schneider; one *s* one *d*, and one *d* by a previous marriage. *Educ:* Sir Antony Browne's, Brentwood; LCC Central Sch. of Arts and Crafts. Design Asst, Herbert Spencer, 1952; freelance practice and Lectr, LCC Central Sch. of Arts and Crafts, 1953–57; Art Dir, Stuart Advertising, London, 1957–58; Head of Graphic Design Dept, LCC Central Sch. of Arts and Crafts, 1958–61; freelance practice, London, 1961–62; Partner: Fletcher/Forbes/Gill, 1962–65; Crosby/Fletcher/Forbes, 1965–72; Pentagram Design Ltd, 1972–78; Pentagram Design Inc., NY, 1978–93. Mem., Alliance Graphique Internationale, 1965– (Internat. Pres. 1976–79); Pres., Amer. Inst. Graphic Arts, 1984–86. *Publications:* Graphic Design: visual comparisons, 1963; A Sign Systems Manual, 1970; Creativity and Communication, 1971; New Alphabets A to Z, 1973; Living by Design, 1978; Pentagram: the compendium, 1993. *Address:* Forbes Farm, 2879 Horseshoe Road, Westfield, NC 27053, USA. *T:* (336) 3513941.

**FORBES, Very Rev. Graham John Thomson,** CBE 2004; Provost, St Mary's Cathedral, Edinburgh, 1990–2017; *b* 10 June 1951; *s* of J. T. and D. D. Forbes; *m* 1973, Jane T. Miller; three *s*. *Educ:* George Heriot's School, Edinburgh; Univ. of Aberdeen (MA); Univ. of Edinburgh (BD). Curate, Old St Paul's Church, Edinburgh, 1976–82; Provost, St Ninian's Cathedral, Perth, 1982–90. Dir, Theol Inst. of Scottish Episcopal Ch, 2002–04. HM (Lay) Inspector of Constabulary, 1995–98. Member: Armed Forces Pay Rev. Body, 2009–14; Security Vetting Appeals Panel, 2009–15. Member: Parole Bd for Scotland, 1990–95; Scottish Consumer Council, 1995–98; GMC, 1996–2008; Scottish Criminal Cases Rev. Commn, 1998–2008 (Chm., 2001–08); Clinical Standards Bd for Scotland, 1999–2002; NHS Quality Improvement Scotland, 2002–05; Chairman: MMR Expert Gp, Scottish Exec., 2001–02; UK Cttee on Ethical Aspects of Pandemic Influenza, 2006–; Mental Welfare Commn for Scotland, 2011–; Office of Scottish Charity Regulator, 2011–. Mem., Historic Bldgs Council (Scotland), 2000–02. Chm., Court, Edinburgh Napier Univ., 2012–; Chair, Cttee of Scottish Univ. Chairs, 2016–. DUniv Napier, 2006; Hon. LLD Aberdeen, 2015. *Recreations:* running, fly-fishing. *Address:* The Priory, Pittenweem, Fife KY10 2LJ. *T:* 07711 199297.

**FORBES, Adm. Sir Ian (Andrew),** KCB 2003; CBE 1994; Supreme Allied Commander Atlantic, 2002–03; Deputy Supreme Allied Commander Transformation, 2003–04; *b* 24 Oct. 1946; *s* of late James and Winifred Forbes; *m* 1975, Sally, *d* of late Ronald Statham and Cynthia Statham; two *d*. *Educ:* Eastbourne Coll.; BRNC. Sea-going appointments, 1969–83: HM Ships Hermes, Upton, HM Yacht Britannia, USS W. H. Stanley; RAF Staff Coll., 1982–83; HM Ships Whitby, Kingfisher (CO), Apollo, Juno, Glamorgan, Diomede (CO), 1984–86; Chatham (CO), 1989–91; MoD, 1991–94; RCDS 1994; HMS Invincible (CO), 1995–96; MA to UN High Rep., Sarajevo, 1996–97; Comdr, UK Task Gp and Comdr, Anti-Submarine Warfare Striking Force, 1997–2000; Flag Officer Surface Flotilla, 2000–01; Dep. SACLANT, 2002. Chm., Naval Review, 2007–13. Sen. Advr, Strategy& (formerly Booz Allen Hamilton, later Booz & Co.), 2006–13. Chm. Council, Eastbourne Coll., later Eastbourne Coll. and St Andrews Sch., 2005–13; Gov., Portsmouth High Sch., 2001–09; Mem. Adv. Bd, Occidental Coll., Calif., 2001–. President: Portsmouth Sea Cadets, 2006–13; Forces Pension Soc., 2013–; Chm., Royal Navy Club of 1765 and 1785, 2010–13. Sen. Associate FRUSI, 2010–. Hon. Citizen, City of Norfolk, Va, 2004. QCVS 1996; Legion of Merit (US); NATO Meritorious Service Medal, 2003. *Recreations:* tennis, history, gardening. *Clubs:* Army and Navy, Pilgrims.

**FORBES, James Alexander,** CBE 2003; CEng; non-executive Director, Atlantis Resources Corporation and Chairman, Atlantis Operations (UK) Ltd, 2010–12; *b* 6 Aug. 1946; *s* of James A. Forbes and Verna Kelman; *m* 1969, Jean Clark; four *s*. *Educ:* Paisley Coll. of Technol. (BSc (1st cl. hons) Elect. Engrg); Loughborough Univ. of Technol. (MSc Electro-heat). MIEE. Scottish Power: Student Apprentice, 1964; Commercial Engr, 1973–84; Area Commercial Officer, 1984–86; Mktg Manager, 1986–89; Northern Electric: Commercial Dir, 1989–90; Distribn Dir, 1990–91; Southern Electric: Ops Dir, 1991–94;

Man. Dir, Electricity, 1994–96; Chief Operating Officer, 1996; Chief Exec., 1996–98; Chief Exec., Scottish and Southern Energy plc, 1998–2002. Non-exec. Chm., Thames Water, 2006; non-exec. Dir, FirstGroup plc, 2000–09. *Recreation:* golf.

**FORBES, Sir James Thomas Stewart**, 8th Bt *cr* 1823, of Newe, Aberdeenshire; *b* 28 May 1957; *o s* of Major Sir Hamish Stewart Forbes, 7th Bt, MBE, MC and Jacynthe Elizabeth Mary (*née* Underwood); *S* father, 2007; *m* 1986, Kerry Lynne, *o d* of Rev. Lee Toms, Sacramento; two *d*. *Educ*: Eton; Bristol Univ. (BA). Patron, Lonach Highland and Friendly Soc., 2007–. Owner, Bear's Head Prodns, Napa Valley, 1997–; creator: This is Your Fridge, TV show, 1991–92 (Sweden, Germany, Norway), 2012 (Sweden); Dramophone, app for smartphone.

**FORBES, Vice-Adm. Sir John Morrison**, KCB 1978; *b* 16 Aug. 1925; *s* of late Lt-Col R. H. Forbes, OBE and Gladys M. Forbes (*née* Pollock); *m* 1950, Joyce Newenham Hadden (*d* 2004); two *s* two *d*. *Educ*: RNC, Dartmouth. Served War: HMS Mauritius, Verulam and Nelson, 1943–46. HMS Aisne, 1946–49; Gunnery course and staff of HMS Excellent, 1950–51; served in RAN, 1952–54; Staff of HMS Excellent, 1954–56; HMS Ceylon, 1956–58; Staff of Dir of Naval Ordnance, 1958–60; Comdr (G) HMS Excellent, 1960–61; Staff of Dir of Seaman Officers' Appts, 1962–64; Exec. Officer, Britannia RN Coll. 1964–66; Operational Comdr and 2nd in Comd, Royal Malaysian Navy, 1966–68; Asst Dir, Naval Plans, 1969–70; comd HMS Triumph, 1971–72; comd Britannia RN Coll., Dartmouth, 1972–74; Naval Secretary, 1974–76; Flag Officer, Plymouth, Port Adm. Devonport, Comdr, Central Sub Area, Eastern Atlantic, and Comdr, Plymouth Sub Area, Channel, 1977–79. Naval ADC to the Queen, 1974. Kesatria Manku Negara (Malaysia), 1968. *Recreation:* country pursuits. *Address:* Rosapenna, Tanfield Park, Wickham, Fareham, Hants PO17 5NP. *Club:* RN Sailing Association.

**FORBES, John Stuart**; Sheriff of Tayside, Central and Fife at Dunfermline, 1980–2002; part-time Sheriff, whole of Scotland, 2003–05; *b* 31 Jan. 1936; *s* of late John Forbes and Dr A. R. S. Forbes; *m* 1963, Marion Alcock; two *d* (and one *s* decd). *Educ:* Glasgow High Sch.; Glasgow Univ. (MA, LLB). RA, TA, 1958–63 (Lieut). Solicitor, 1959–61; Advocate, Scottish Bar, 1962–76; Standing Jun. Counsel, Forestry Commn, 1972–76; Sheriff of Lothian and Borders, 1976–80. Pres., Glasgow Juridical Soc., 1963–64. Life Trustee, Carnegie, Dunfermline and Hero Fund Trusts, 1985–2002; Trustee, Carnegie UK Trust, 1990–2002. *Recreations:* tennis, golf, fishing. *Address:* 8 Croftwynd, Milnathort, Kinross KY13 9GH. *Clubs:* Royal Scots (Edinburgh), Edinburgh Sports.

**FORBES, Lisa**; MP (Lab) Peterborough, since June 2019. *Address:* House of Commons, SW1A 0AA.

**FORBES, Matthew Keith**, OBE 2007; HM Diplomatic Service; Head, Governor's Office, Grand Cayman, since 2016; *b* Yateley, 19 April 1966; *s* of Keith Forbes and Angela Norris (*née* Parsons); *m* 1988, Lydia Mary Bagg; three *s* one *d*. *Educ:* Clark's Coll., Guildford; Univ. of Leicester (MSc (Dist.) 2019). Practitioner, Inst. Internal Auditors. Joined FCO, 1987; Attaché, Peking, 1989–90; Vice Consul, Colombo, 1990–94; Dep. High Comr, Maseru, 1999–2002; First Sec., Wellington, NZ, and Dep. Gov., Pitcairn, 2002–06; Hd, Mexico, Central America, Cuba and Hispaniola Section, FCO, 2007–09; High Comr to the Seychelles, 2009–12; Dep. Consul Gen., Shanghai, 2012–16. *Recreations:* scuba diving, flying (PPL S Africa 2002), football. *Address:* c/o Foreign and Commonwealth Office, King Charles Street, SW1A 2AH. *E:* matthew.forbes@fco.gov.uk.

**FORBES, Nanette**; *see* Newman, N.

**FORBES, Hon. Sir Thayne (John)**, Kt 1993; a Judge of the High Court of Justice, Queen's Bench Division, 1993–2009; *b* 28 June 1938; *s* of late John Thomson Forbes and Jessie Kay Robertson Stewart Lorimer; *m* 1960, Celia Joan; two *s* one *d*. *Educ:* Winchester College (Quirister); Wolverton Grammar Sch.; University College London (LLB, LLM). Served Royal Navy (Instructor Lieutenant), 1963–66. Called to Bar, Inner Temple, 1966, Governing Bencher, 1991; QC 1984; a Recorder, 1986–90; a Sen. Circuit Judge (Official Referee), 1990–93; Presiding Judge, Northern Circuit, 1995–99; Judge i/c Technology and Construction Ct, 2001–04. Chm., Al Sweady Public Inquiry, 2009–15. *Recreations:* music, reading, sailing, bird watching, astronomy, beekeeping, watercolour painting. *Club:* Garrick.

**FORBES, Sir William (Daniel) Stuart-**, 13th Bt *cr* 1626 (NS), of Pitsligo and of Monymusk, Aberdeenshire; *b* 21 Aug. 1935; *s* of William Kenneth Stuart-Forbes (*d* 1946), 3rd *s* of 10th Bt, and Marjory Gilchrist; *S* uncle, 1985; *m* 1st, 1956, Jannette (*d* 1997), *d* of late Hori Toki George MacDonald; three *s* two *d*; 2nd, 2001, Betty Dawn Ward, *d* of William Henry Gibson and Ellen Dorothy Neilson. *Heir:* s Kenneth Charles Stuart-Forbes [*b* 26 Dec. 1956; *m* 1981, Susan, *d* of Len Murray; one *s* two *d*]. *Address:* 169 Budge Street, Blenheim, Marlborough 7201, New Zealand.

**FORBES, Captain William Frederick Eustace**; Vice Lord-Lieutenant of Stirling and Falkirk, 1984–96; Forestry Commissioner, 1982–88; *b* 6 July 1932; *er s* of late Lt-Col W. H. D. C. Forbes of Callendar, CBE and Elisabeth Forbes; *m* 1st, 1956, Pamela Susan (*d* 1993), *er d* of Lord McCorquodale of Newton, KCVO, PC; two *d*; 2nd, 1995, Venetia, Hon. Lady Troubridge, *widow* of Sir Peter Troubridge, 6th Bt. *Educ:* Eton. Regular soldier, Coldstream Guards, 1950–59; farmer and company director, 1959–. Chairman: Scottish Woodland Owners' Assoc., 1974–77; Nat. Hunting Fields Assoc., Scottish Branch, 1980–90. *Recreations:* country pastimes, golf, cricket, travel. *Address:* Earlstoun Lodge, Dalry, Castle Douglas, Kirkcudbrightshire DG7 3TY. *T:* (01644) 430213. *Clubs:* MCC; New (Edinburgh).

**FORBES ADAM, Sir Nigel (Colin)**, 5th Bt *cr* 1917, of Hankelow Court, co. Chester; *b* London, 7 Dec. 1930; *s* of late Colin Gurdon Forbes Adam, CSI, 3rd *s* of 1st Bt and Hon. Irene Constance Lawley, *d* of 3rd Baron Wenlock; *S* brother, 2019; *m* 1st, 1954, Teresa Hermione Idena Robertson (*d* 2005); four *s*; 2nd, 1987, Mildred Malise Hare Ropner (*née* Armitage); three *s* and one step *d*. *Educ:* Eton; King's Coll., Cambridge (BA). Estate owner and manager, 1960–2010. *Recreations:* reading, writing, gardening, thinking, walking. *Heir:* s Charles David Forbes Adam [*b* 8 Oct. 1957; *m* 1982, Rosalind Cecilia Colvile; two *s* one *d*]. *Address:* Brook House, Byland Abbey, York YO61 4BD. *T:* (01347) 868101.

**FORBES-LEITH of Fyvie, Sir George Ian David**, 4th Bt *cr* 1923, of Jessfield, co. Midlothian; *b* 26 May 1967; *e s* of Sir Andrew George Forbes-Leith, 3rd Bt and Jane Kate (*née* McCall-McCowan); *S* father, 2000; *m* 1995, Camilla Frances Ely; two *s* one *d*. *Educ:* RAC, Cirencester. *Recreations:* shooting, ski-ing, fishing. *Heir:* s Alexander Philip George Forbes-Leith, *b* 4 Feb. 1999. *Address:* Tifty, Fyvie, Turriff AB53 8JT.

**FORBES-MEYLER, John William**, OBE 1990; HM Diplomatic Service, retired; Ambassador to Ecuador, 1997–2000; *b* 3 July 1942; *s* of late J. J. C. Forbes and Moira Patricia (*née* Garvey, who later *m* James Robert Meyler); changed name by Deed Poll, 1963 to Forbes-Meyler; *m* 1st, 1964, Margaret Goddard (marr. diss. 1979); (one *d* decd); 2nd, 1980, Mary Read (*née* Vlachou); one step *s*. *Educ:* grammar sch., etc. Joined HM Diplomatic Service, 1962: CRO, 1962–64; Lagos, 1964–68; Chicago, 1968–69; Boston, 1969–70; FCO, 1970–71; NY, 1971–72; FCO, 1972–75; Athens, 1975–80; FCO, 1980–83; 1st Sec. (Econ.), Bonn, 1983–86; on loan to MoD, 1986–88; Deputy Head of Mission: Bogota, 1988–92; Vienna, 1992–96. *Recreations:* walking, music, reading. *E:* johnforbesmeyler@gmail.com. *Club:* Special Forces.

**FORBES SMITH, Michael**; *see* Smith, M. F.

**FORBES WATSON, Anthony David**; Managing Director, Pan Macmillan Publishers Ltd, since 2008; *b* 25 Sept. 1954; *s* of late Ian and Evelyn Forbes Watson; *m* 1983, Jennifer Ann Curnow; one *s* one *d*. *Educ:* Charterhouse Sch.; York Univ. (BA English and Related Lit.). Internat. Sales, OUP, 1977–80; Harper Collins: Internat. Sales Mgt, 1980–86; Sales and Mktg Dir, 1986–90; Managing Director: Pitman Publishing, 1990–91; Ladybird Books Ltd, 1991–96; Chief Exec., Penguin Gp (UK), 1996–2005. Pres., Publishers' Assoc. of UK, 2002–03. Governor, Loughborough Coll. of Art and Design, 1993–95. *Recreations:* drawing, ski-ing, golf. *Address:* The Granary, 27–31 High Street, Watlington, Oxon OX49 5PZ. *Clubs:* Garrick; Huntercombe Golf.

**FORD,** family name of **Baroness Ford**.

**FORD, Baroness** *cr* 2006 (Life Peer), of Cunninghame in North Ayrshire; **Margaret Anne Ford**, OBE 2019; Chairman, STV Group plc, since 2013; *b* 16 Dec. 1957; *d* of Edward and Susan Garland; *m* 1990, David Arthur Bolger; one *s* one *d* by a previous marriage. *Educ:* Glasgow Univ. (MA Hons, MPhil). Scottish Organiser, BIFU, 1982–87; Managing Consultant, Price Waterhouse & Co., 1987–90; Dir, Scottish Homes, 1990–93; Man. Dir, 1993–2000, Chm., 2000–02, Eglinton Mgt Centre; Chief Exec., Good Practice Ltd, 2000–04 (Dep. Chm., 2004–05); Chm., English Partnerships, 2002–07; Man. Dir, Royal Bank of Canada Capital Mkts, 2007–09. Chairman: Lothian Health Bd, 1997–2000; Irvine Bay URC, 2006–11; Olympic Park Legacy Co., 2009–12. Non-executive Director: Scottish Prison Service, 1994–98; Ofgem, 2000–03; Thus plc, 2002–05; Serco plc, 2003–10; Grainger plc, 2008–16; Segro plc, 2013–18; Taylor Wimpey plc, 2013–16; Sen. Ind. non-exec. Dir, New River REIT, 2017– (Chair, 2018–); Chairman: May Gurney plc, 2011–13; Barchester Healthcare Ltd, 2012–15. Nat. Pres., British Epilepsy Assoc., 2008–. Mem. Bd, BOA, 2017–; Chm., Tennis Foundn, 2016–19; Councillor, LTA, 2019–. Hon. Prof., Urban Studies Dept, Univ. of Glasgow, 2008–. Hon. DBA Napier, 2008; DUniv Stirling, 2008. Hon. MRICS 2008. FRSE 2015. *Recreations:* family, sport, fine art, travel. *Address:* House of Lords, SW1A 0PW.

**FORD, Rev. Adam**; Chaplain, St Paul's Girls' School, London, 1976–2001 (Head of Lower School, 1986–92); *b* 15 Sept. 1940; *s* of John Ford and Jean Beattie Ford (*née* Winstanley); *m* 1st, 1969, Veronica Rosemary Lucia Verey (marr. diss. 1993); two *s* two *d*; 2nd, 2011, Rosemary Roscoe. *Educ:* Minehead Grammar Sch.; King's Coll., Univ. of London (BD Hons, AKC 1964); Lancaster Univ. (MA Indian Religion 1972). Asst, Ecumenical Inst. of World Council of Churches, Geneva, 1964; ordained deacon and priest, 1965; Curate, Cirencester Parish Church, Glos, 1965–69; Vicar of Hebden Bridge, W Yorkshire, 1969–76; Priest-in-Ordinary to the Queen, 1984–90. Regular contributor to Prayer for the Day, Radio 4, 1978–; writer and narrator, Whose World?, series of TV progs on sci. and religion, 1987. Hon. FRAS 1960. *Publications:* Spaceship Earth, 1981; Weather Watch, 1982; Star Gazers Guide to the Night Sky (audio guide to astronomy), 1982; Universe: God, Man and Science, 1986; The Cuckoo Plant, 1991; Mr Hi-Tech, 1993; Faith and Science, 1999; The Art of Mindful Walking, 2010; Seeking Silence in a Noisy World, 2011; Mindfulness and the Art of Urban Living, 2011; Galileo and the Art of Ageing Mindfully, 2015; Stars: a family guide to the night sky, 2015; Mindful Thoughts for Walkers, 2017; Mindful Thoughts for Birdwatchers, 2018; articles in The Times and science jls on relationship between science and religion, also on dialogue between religions; regular contrib. Church Times. *Recreations:* painting birds, feathers and flints, travelling, writing. *Address:* Bramble Cottage, Weaver's Lane, Alfriston, E Sussex BN26 5TH.

*See also* Anna Ford.

**FORD, Lt Col Sir Andrew (Charles)**, GCVO 2018 (KCVO 2012); Comptroller, Lord Chamberlain's Office, 2006–18; *b* 5 Feb. 1957; *s* of Charles and Irmgard Ford; *m* 1985, Rosalind Birkett; two *s*. *Educ:* King's Coll., Taunton; RMA Sandhurst; JSDC Greenwich. Commnd Grenadier Guards, 1977; Comd, 1st Bn Welsh Guards, 1999–2002; Extra Equerry to the Queen, 2005. *Address:* c/o Hedley Foundation, 1–3 College Hill, EC4R 2RA. *Clubs:* Pratt's, Cavalry and Guards.

**FORD, Sir Andrew (Russell)**, 3rd Bt *cr* 1929, of Westerdunes, Co. of East Lothian; Head of Sport and Leisure, 1974–96, Senior Lecturer in English, 1996–2003, Wiltshire College (formerly Chippenham College); *b* 29 June 1943; *s* of Sir Henry Russell Ford, 2nd Bt, TD and Mary Elizabeth (*d* 1997), *d* of late Godfrey F. Wright; *S* father, 1989; *m* 1968, Penelope Anne, *d* of Harry Relph; two *s* one *d*. *Educ:* Winchester; New Coll., Oxford (half-blue, athletics, 1962); Loughborough Coll. (DLC); London Univ. (BA external); Birmingham Univ. (MA external). Schoolmaster: Blairmore Sch., Aberdeens, 1967–71; St Peter's Sch., Cambridge, NZ, 1971–74. Hon. BSc Loughborough, 2009. *Heir:* s Toby Russell Ford, *b* 11 Jan. 1973. *Address:* 20 Coniston Road, Chippenham, Wilts SN14 0PX. *T:* (01249) 655442.

**FORD, Anna**; broadcaster, BBC, 1989–2006; *b* 2 Oct. 1943; *m* 1981, (Charles) Mark (Edward) Boxer (*d* 1988); two *d*. *Educ:* Manchester Univ. (BA Hons Econ 1966; DipAE 1970). Work with Internat. Students, Manchester Univ., 1966–69; Lecturer: Rupert Stanley Coll. of Further Educn, Belfast, 1970–72; NI Reg., Open Univ., 1972–74; presenter and reporter in news and current affairs for Granada TV, ITN and BBC, 1974–2006. Non-executive Director: Sainsbury's, 2006–12; N. Brown Gp plc, 2009–. Chair, Index on Censorship, 2005–08. Trustee: Royal Botanic Gardens, Kew, 1995–2002; Forum for the Future, 2006–09. Chancellor, 2001–04, Co-Chancellor, 2004–08, Univ. of Manchester. FRGS 1990; Hon. Fellow, Lucy Cavendish Coll., Cambridge, 2006. Hon. Bencher, Middle Temple, 2002. Hon. LLD Manchester, 1998; DUniv Open, 1998; Hon. DLitt St Andrews, 2006. *Publications:* Men: a documentary, 1985. *Recreations:* gardening, walking, drawing.

*See also* Rev. Adam Ford.

**FORD, Anthony**; *see* Ford, J. A.

**FORD, Antony**, CMG 1997; HM Diplomatic Service, retired; Ambassador to Austria, 2000–03; *b* Bexley, 1 Oct. 1944; *s* of late William Ford and Grace Ford (*née* Smith); *m* 1970, Linda Gordon Joy; one *s* one *d*. *Educ:* St Dunstan's Coll.; UCW, Aberystwyth (BA). Joined HM Diplomatic Service, 1967; Third, later Second, Sec., Bonn, 1968–71; Second Sec., Kuala Lumpur, 1971–73; First Secretary: FCO, 1973–77; Washington, 1977–81; FCO, 1981–84; Counsellor: East Berlin, 1984–87; FCO, 1987–90; Consul-Gen., San Francisco, 1990–94; Chm., CSSB, on secondment to RAS Agency, 1994–96; Minister, Berlin, 1996–99; on secondment to Andersen Consulting, 1999–2000. *Publications:* Learning to Suffer, 2010. *Recreations:* reading, wine, cricket. *Club:* Morgan Sports Car.

**FORD, Benjamin Thomas**; DL; *b* 1 April 1925; *s* of Benjamin Charles Ford and May Ethel (*née* Moorton); *m* 1950, Vera Ada (*née* Fawcett-Fancet); two *s* one *d*. *Educ:* Rowan Road Central Sch., Surrey. Apprenticed as compositor, 1941. Mem., Home Guard (Corporal), 1941–43; War Service, 1943–47, Fleet Air Arm (Petty Officer). Electronic Fitter/Wireman,

1951–64; Convener of Shop Stewards, 1955–64. Pres., Harwich Constituency Labour Party, 1955–63; Mem., Clacton UDC, 1959–62; Alderman Essex CC, 1959–65; JP Essex, 1962–67. MP (Lab) Bradford N, 1964–83; contested (Lab Ind.) Bradford N, 1983. Mem., H of C Select Cttee (Services), 1970–83 (Chm., Accommodation and Admin Sub-Cttee, 1979–83); Chm., Jt Select Cttee on Sound Broadcasting, 1976–77; Chairman: British-Portuguese Parly Gp, 1965–83; British-Argentinian Parly Gp, 1974–81; British-Brazilian Parly Gp, 1974–79; British-Malaysian Parly Gp, 1975–83; British-Venezuelan Parly Gp, 1977–83; All-Party Wool Textile Parly Gp, 1974–83; Vice-Chairman: British-Latin American Parly Gp, 1974–79; PLP Defence Cttee, 1979–82; Mem. Exec. Cttee, IPU British Gp, 1971–83 (Chm., 1977–79); Sec., British-Namibian Parly Gp, 1980–83. Chm., Leeds NW Lib Dems, 1988–91; Pres., Leeds Fedn of Lib Dems, 1991–97. Bd Mem., Bradford & Northern Housing Assoc., 1975–95 (Chm., Yorks and Humberside Regl Cttee). President: English Shooting Council, 1996–2001 (Chm., 1982–96); English Target Shooting Fedn, 2001–04; Yorks Rifle Assoc., 2004–12 (Chm., 1999–2004); Vice-Pres., British Assoc. for Shooting and Conservation, 1983–; Mem. Council, Nat. Rifle Assoc., 1968–94 (Vice-Pres., 1984–). President: Yorks and Humberside Region, Mencap, 1986–91; Bradford Civic Soc., 1988–96; RBL, Bramhope, 2009–. Freeman, City of London, 1979; Liveryman, Gunmakers' Co., 1978–99. DL W Yorks, 1982. Hon. FAIA 1983. Grand Officer, Order of the Southern Cross (Brazil), 1976. *Publications*: Piecework, 1960. *Recreations*: music, shooting, family, reading. *Address*: 9 Wynmore Crescent, Bramhope, Leeds LS16 9DH. *Club*: East Ward Labour (Bradford).

**FORD, Colin John**, CBE 1993; lecturer, writer and broadcaster on films, theatre and photography; exhibition organiser; Chairman, PEEL Entertainment Group (formerly Partnership Events & Entertainment), 1999–2011; *b* 13 May 1934; *s* of John William and Hélène Martha Ford; *m* 1st, 1961, Margaret Elizabeth Cordwell (marr. diss.); one *s* one *d*; 2nd, 1984, Susan Joan Frances Grayson; one *s*. *Educ*: Enfield Grammar Sch.; University Coll., Oxford (MA). Manager and Producer, Kidderminster Playhouse, 1958–60; Gen. Man., Western Theatre Ballet, 1960–62; Vis. Lectr in English and Drama, California State Univ. at Long Beach and UCLA (Univ. Extension), 1962–64; Dep. Curator, Nat. Film Archive, 1965–72. Organiser, 30th Anniv. Congress of Internat. Fedn of Film Archives, London, 1968; Dir, Cinema City Exhibn, 1970; Programme Dir, London Shakespeare Film Festival, 1972; Keeper of Film and Photography, Nat. Portrait Gall., 1972–81; founding Hd, Nat. Mus. of Photography, Film and Television, 1982–93; Dir, Nat. Mus. of Wales, then Nat. Museums & Galls of Wales, 1993–98. Chm., Kraszna-Krausz Foundn, 2003–10; Vice-Pres., Julia Margaret Cameron Trust, 2005–. Hon. FRPS 1999. Hon. MA Bradford, 1989. *Film*: Masks and Faces, 1966 (BBC TV version, Omnibus, 1968). *Publications*: (with Roy Strong) An Early Victorian Album, 1974, 2nd edn 1977; The Cameron Collection, 1975; (principal contrib.) Oxford Companion to Film, 1975; (ed) Happy and Glorious: Six Reigns of Royal Photography, 1977; Rediscovering Mrs Cameron, 1979; People in Camera, 1979; (with Brian Harrison) A Hundred Years Ago (Britain in the 1880s), 1983; Portraits (Gallery of World Photography), 1983; (ed) The Story of Popular Photography, 1988; Lewis Carroll, 1998; André Kertész and the Avant Garde, 1999; (ed) Performance!, 2000; (with Julian Cox) Julia Margaret Cameron: the complete photographs, 2003; Julia Margaret Cameron: 19th century photographer of genius, 2003; (with Péter Baki and George Szirtes) Eyewitness: Hungarian photography in the twentieth century, 2011; (with Karl Steinorth): You Press the Button, We Do the Rest: the birth of snapshot photography, 1988; Lewis Carroll: photographs, 1991; Ferenc Berko: 60 Years of Photography, 1991; articles in many jls. *Recreations*: travel, music. *Address*: 7 Gentleman's Row, Enfield EN2 6PT.

**FORD, Prof. David Frank**, Hon. OBE 2013; PhD; Regius Professor of Divinity, Cambridge University, 1991–2015, now Emeritus; Fellow of Selwyn College, Cambridge, 1991–2015; *b* 23 Jan. 1948; *s* of George Ford and Phyllis (née Woodman); *m* 1982, Deborah Perrin Hardy, *d* of late Rev. Prof. Daniel Wayne Hardy; one *s* two *d* (and one *d* decd). *Educ*: Trinity Coll. Dublin (BA (Mod) 1970); St John's Coll., Cambridge (MA 1976; PhD 1977); Yale Univ. (STM 1973); Tübingen Univ. Lectr in Theology, Birmingham Univ., 1976–91; Cambridge University: Chairman: Faculty Bd of Divinity, 1993–95; Mgt Cttee, Centre for Advanced Religious and Theol Studies, 1995–2013; Dir, Cambridge Inter-faith Prog., 2002–15; Member: Arts and Humanities Personal Promotions Cttee, 2003–08; Gen. Bd Adv. Cttee on Sen. Appts, 2005–08. Mem., CUP Syndicate, 1993–2004. Mem. Bd, Kalam Res. and Media, 2009–. Pres., Soc. for Study of Theology, 1997–98. Member: World Econ. Forum Council of 100 Leaders, 2003–08; AHRC Peer Review Coll., 2005–12; Bd of Reference, Westminster Abbey Inst., 2014–18. Trustee: Center of Theological Inquiry, Princeton, 2007–; Cambridge Muslim Coll., 2012–; Rose Castle Foundn, 2014–. Member: Bd of Advrs, John Templeton Foundn, 2008–11; Inst. for Comparative Scripture and Inter-religious Dialogue, Minzu Univ., Beijing, 2012–; Elijah Interfaith Inst., Jerusalem, 2017–. Hon. DD: Birmingham, 2000; Bolton, 2016; Aberdeen, 2016; Hon. DLitt Dev Sanskriti Vishwavidyalaya, Haridwar, India, 2017. Gold Medallion for Inter-Faith Relns, Sternberg Foundn, 2008; Coventry Internat. Prize for Peace and Reconciliation, 2012. *Publications*: Barth and God's Story: biblical narrative and the theological method of Karl Barth in the Church Dogmatics, 1981; (with Daniel W. Hardy) Jubilate: Theology in praise, 1984; (with Frances M. Young) Meaning and Truth in 2 Corinthians, 1987; (ed) The Modern Theologians, vols I and II, 1989, 3rd edn 2005; (ed jtly) Essentials of Christian Community, 1996; The Shape of Living, 1997; Self and Salvation: being transformed, 1999; Theology: a very short introduction, 1999, 2nd edn 2013; (ed jtly) Jesus, 2002; (ed jtly and contrib.) Reading Texts, Seeking Wisdom: scripture and theology, 2003; (ed jtly) Fields of Faith: theology and religious studies for the twenty-first century, 2005; (ed jtly) The Promise of Scriptural Reasoning, 2006; Christian Wisdom: desiring God and learning in love, 2007; (ed jtly) Musics of Belonging: the poetry of Micheal O'Siadhail, 2007; Shaping Theology: engagements in a religious and secular world, 2007; (jtly) Wording a Radiance: parting conversations on God and the Church, 2010; The Future of Christian Theology, 2011; (ed jtly) The Modern Theologians Reader, 2012; (ed jtly) Interreligious Reading After Vatican II: scriptural reasoning, comparative theology and receptive ecumenism, 2013; The Drama of Living: becoming wise in the spirit, 2014; (ed jtly) Say But the Word: poetry as vision and voice, 2015. *Recreations*: gardening, poetry, drama, walking. *Address*: Selwyn College, Grange Road, Cambridge CB3 9DQ. *T*: 07482 719922.

**FORD, David R. J.**; Member (Alliance) Antrim South, Northern Ireland Assembly, since 1998; Leader, Alliance Party, 2001–16; *b* 24 Feb. 1951; *s* of late Eric Ford and Jean Ford; *m* 1975, Anne Murdock; one *s* three *d*. *Educ*: Dulwich Coll.; Queen's Univ., Belfast (BSc Econ 1972); Northern Ireland Poly. (Cert. Social Work 1976). Social worker, then sen. social worker, Northern Health and Social Services Bd, Antrim, Newtownabbey and Carrickfergus, 1972–90; Gen. Sec., Alliance Party, 1990–98. Mem. (Alliance), Antrim BC, 1993–2010. Contested S Antrim, NI Forum, 1996. Contested (Alliance) S Antrim, 1997, Sept. 2000, 2001, 2005. Alliance Chief Whip, 1998–2001. Minister of Justice, NI, 2010–16. *Address*: Northern Ireland Assembly, Parliament Buildings, Stormont, Belfast BT4 3XX.

**FORD, Prof. Gary Ashley**, CBE 2013; FMedSci; Chief Executive Officer, Oxford Academic Health Science Network, since 2013; Consultant Physician, Oxford University Hospitals NHS Foundation Trust, since 2013; Professor of Stroke Medicine, University of Oxford, since 2019; Fellow, Green Templeton Coll., Oxford, since 2016; *b* Coventry, 18 Nov. 1958; *s* of Ashley Greg Ford and Eileen Mary Ford (née Painter); *m* 1987, Angela Mary Lewis; two *s* one *d*. *Educ*: King Henry VIII Sch., Coventry; Clare Coll., Cambridge (BA 1979); King's Coll. Hosp. Med. Sch., London (BA Hons; MB BChir 1983). MRCP 1985; FRCP 1996. Sen. House Officer, Addenbrooke's Hosp., Cambridge, 1983–85; Registrar, Glos Royal Hosp., 1985–87; Post-doctoral Res. Fellow in Clin. Pharmacol., Stanford Univ., Calif, 1987–89; Sen. Registrar in Geriatric and Gen. Medicine (Clin. Pharmacol.), Freeman Hosp., Newcastle upon Tyne, 1989–92; University of Newcastle upon Tyne and Newcastle upon Tyne Hospitals NHS Trust: Sen. Lectr and Cons. Physician in Clin. Pharmacol. and Geriatric Medicine, 1992–2000; Prof. of Pharmacology of Old Age, 2000–06; Hon. Consultant Physician in Stroke Medicine, 2000–; Director: Newcastle Clin. Res. Centre, 2005–08; NIHR (formerly UK) Stroke Res. Network, 2005–14; Jacobson Prof. of Clin. Pharmacol., 2006–13; Clin. Dir, R&D, Newcastle upon Tyne Hosps NHS Foundn Trust, 2006–13. FBPhS (FBPharmacolS 2014); FMedSci 2014. NIHR Res. Legend, 2018. *Recreations*: music, cooking, travel. *Address*: Oxford Academic Health Science Network, Magdalen Centre North, Oxford Science Park, Oxford OX4 4GA. *T*: (01865) 338439.

**FORD, Dr Gillian Rachel, (Mrs N. I. MacKenzie)**, CB 1981; FRCP; Medical Director, Marie Curie Cancer Care (formerly Marie Curie Memorial Foundation), 1991–97; *b* 18 March 1934; *d* of Cecil Ford and Grace Ford; *m* 1988, Prof. Norman I. MacKenzie (*d* 2013). *Educ*: Clarendon Sch., Abergele; St Hugh's Coll., Oxford; St Thomas' Hosp., London. MA, BM, BCh; FRCP 1985. Junior hospital posts, St Thomas', Oxford, Reading, 1959–64; Medical Officer, Min. of Health, 1965, Sen. Med. Officer, 1968; SPMO, 1974–77, Dep. Chief MO (Dep. Sec.), 1977–89, DHSS, later Dept of Health; on secondment as Dir of Studies, St Christopher's Hospice, Sydenham, 1985–88; Med. Sec., Standing Cttee on Postgrad. Med. Educn, 1989–90. Vice Pres., St Christopher's Hospice, 1999–; Vice Chm., Hospice in the Weald, 1999–2003. *Publications*: papers on health services research, terminal care, audit, palliative medicine and care in sundry med. publications. *Recreations*: music, ski-ing, children's literature, gardening. *Address*: 20 Winterbourne Mews, Lewes, E Sussex BN7 1HG. *T*: (01273) 479206.

**FORD, Glyn**; see Ford, J. G.

**FORD, Harrison**; actor; *b* Chicago, 13 July 1942; *m* 1st, Mary Ford (marr. diss. 1978); two *s*; 2nd, 1983, Melissa Mathison (marr. diss. 2004; she *d* 2015), screenwriter; one *s* one *d*; 3rd, 2010, Calista Flockhart. *Educ*: Ripon Coll., Wis. *Films* include: Dead Heat on a Merry-Go-Round, 1966; Journey to Shiloh, 1968; Getting Straight, 1970; The Conversation, 1974; American Graffiti, 1974; Star Wars, 1977; Force 10 from Navarone, 1978; Apocalypse Now, 1979; The Frisco Kid, 1979; The Empire Strikes Back, 1980; Raiders of the Lost Ark, 1981; Blade Runner, 1982; Return of the Jedi, 1983; Indiana Jones and the Temple of Doom, 1984; Witness, 1985; Mosquito Coast, 1986; Frantic, 1988; Indiana Jones and the Last Crusade, 1989; Presumed Innocent, 1990; Regarding Henry, 1991; The Fugitive, 1992; Patriot Games, 1992; Clear and Present Danger, 1994; Sabrina, 1995; Devil's Own, 1996; Air Force One, 1997; Six Days, Seven Nights, 1998; Random Hearts, 1999; What Lies Beneath, 2000; K-19: The Widowmaker, 2002; Hollywood Homicide, 2003; Firewall, 2006; Indiana Jones and the Kingdom of the Crystal Skull, Crossing Over, 2008; Extraordinary Measures (also prod.), 2010; Morning Glory, Cowboys and Aliens, 2011; Ender's Game, 2013; Star Wars: Episode VII - the Force Awakens, The Age of Adeline, 2015; Blade Runner 2049, 2017; numerous TV appearances, including The Virginian, Gunsmoke, Ironside. *Address*: United Talent Agency, 9336 Civic Center Drive, Beverly Hills, CA 90210, USA.

**FORD, (James) Glyn**; *b* 28 Jan. 1950; *s* of late Ernest Benjamin Ford and Matilda Alberta Ford (née James); *m* 1st, 1973, Hazel Nancy Mahy (marr. diss. 1992); one *d*; 2nd, 1992, Daniela Zannelli (marr. diss. 2005); one *s*. *Educ*: Marling; Reading Univ. (BSc Geol. with Soil Sci.); UCL (MSc Marine Earth Sci.); Manchester Univ. Undergraduate Apprentice, BAC, 1967–68; Course Tutor in Oceanography, Open Univ., 1976–78; Teaching Asst, UMIST, 1977–78; Res. Fellow, Sussex Univ., 1978–79; Manchester University: Res. Asst, 1976–77; Res. Fellow, 1979; Lectr, 1979–80; Sen. Res. Fellow, Prog. of Policy Res. in Engrg Sci. and Technol., 1980–84; Hon. Vis. Res. Fellow, 1984–. Vis. Prof., Tokyo Univ., 1983. Mem., Lab Party NEC, 1989–93 (Member: Sci. and Technol. Policy Sub-Cttee, 1981–83; Review Gp on Trade Union/Labour Party Links, 1992–93). MEP (Lab): Gtr Manchester E, 1984–99; SW Region, England, 1999–2009. European Parliament: Chm., Cttee of Inquiry into Growth of Racism and Fascism in Europe, 1984–86; Vice-Chm., Sub-Cttee on Security and Disarmament, 1987–89; first Vice-Pres., Group of Party of European Socialists, 1989–93; Vice Chm., Delegn, Japanese Diet, 1992–94, 1996–99; Leader, 1989–93, Dep. Leader, 1999–2004, Eur. PLP. Mem., Consultative Cttee on Racism and Xenophobia, Council of Ministers of EU, 1994–98. EU Chief Observer: Indonesian elections, 2004; Aceh, 2006–07. Mem., Exec. Cttee, Labour Movement for Europe, 2010– (Chm., SW, 2003–18); SW Regn., Labour Party Nat. Policy Forum, 2010–18; Mem., Labour Party Internat. Cttee, 2014–18. Treas., Anti Nazi League. Mem., Steering Cttee, UNITE Against Fascism. Contested (Lab): Hazel Grove, 1987; SW England and Gibraltar, EP, 2014. Founder: Polint, 2009; Track2Asia, 2015. *Publications*: (with C. Niblett and L. Walker) The Future for Ocean Technology, 1987; Fascist Europe, 1992; The Evolution of a European, 1994; Changing States, 1996; Making European Progress, 2002; Left in Europe, 2008; (with S. Kwon) North Korea on the Brink, 2008; (ed with J. Priestley) Our Europe, Not Theirs, 2013, 2nd edn 2016; Talking to North Korea, 2018. *Recreation*: Asia. *Clubs*: Groucho, Soho House.

**FORD, John**; see Ford, S. J.

**FORD, (John) Anthony**, OBE 1998; Director, Crafts Council, 1988–99 (Deputy Director, 1985–88); *b* 28 April 1938; *s* of Frank Everatt Ford and Dorothy Mary Ford; *m* 1st, 1963, Caroline Rosemary Wharrad (marr. diss.); one *d*; 2nd, 1984, Sandra Edith Williams. *Educ*: Epsom Coll.; St Edmund Hall, Oxford (MA). Admitted Solicitor, 1963. Dir, Art Services Grants, 1974–79; Crafts Council, 1979–99. Mem., Visual Arts Adv. Cttee, British Council, 1988–99. Vice-Pres. for Europe, World Crafts Council, 1987–93 (Advr, 1993–). Mem., Fabric Adv. Cttee, Rochester Cathedral, 1990–2004. Member: Court, RCA, 1989–99; Court of Govs, London Inst., 1993–2000; Board of Governors: Kent Inst. of Art and Design, 2001–05 (Dep. Chm., 2002–05); Univ. (formerly UC) for the Creative Arts at Canterbury, Epsom, Farnham, Maidstone and Rochester, 2005–10. Trustee: Craft Pottery Charitable Trust, 1991–2010 (Chm., 2004–10); Idlewild Trust, 2000– (Chm., 2009–). *Recreations*: theatre, cinema, the arts. *Address*: 64 Wood Vale, SE23 3ED. *T*: (020) 8693 4837.

**FORD, Rt Rev. John Frank**; Bishop of The Murray, 2013–19; *b* 14 Jan. 1952; *s* of Royston and Ivy Ford; *m* 1981, Bridget Barnard; three *s*. *Educ*: Charles Chute Sch., Basingstoke; Southampton Coll. of Technol.; Chichester Theol Coll.; University Coll., Chichester (MA 2004). Ordained deacon, 1979, priest, 1980; Curate, Christ Ch, Forest Hill, 1979–82; Vicar: St Augustine, Lee, 1982–91; Lower Beeding, and Domestic Chaplain to Bp of Horsham, 1991–94; Diocesan Missioner, Chichester, 1994–2000; Chichester Cathedral: Canon and Preb., 1997–2000; Precentor and Canon Residentiary, 2000–05; Bishop Suffragan of Plymouth, 2005–13; Asst Bishop, Dio. of Truro, 2011–13. *Recreations*: cricket, theatre, food and wine, travel, Middle Eastern politics and culture.

**FORD, Leigh-Ann Maria;** see Mulcahy, L.-A. M.

**FORD, Prof. Mark Nicholas,** DPhil; Professor of English and American Literature, University College London, since 2005; *b* Nairobi, Kenya, 24 June 1962; *s* of Don and Mary Ford; *m* 2003, Kate Bomford; two *d. Educ:* St Paul's Sch., London; Lincoln Coll., Oxford (BA English Lit.; DPhil 1991). Lectr, UCL, 1988–90; Lectr, Kyoto Univ., 1991–93; Lectr, 1995–2002, Sen. Lectr, 2002–05, UCL. *Publications:* Landlocked, 1992; Raymond Roussel and the Republic of Dreams, 2000; Soft Sift, 2001; A Driftwood Altar, 2005; Mr and Mrs Stevens, 2011; Six Children, 2011; Selected Poems, 2014; This Dialogue of One, 2014; Thomas Hardy: half a Londoner, 2016; Enter, Fleeing, 2018. *Recreations:* tennis, football, music. *Address:* English Department, University College London, Gower Street, WC1E 6BT. *T:* (020) 7679 3129. *E:* m.ford@ucl.ac.uk.

**FORD, Prof. Michael David;** QC 2013; Professor of Law, University of Bristol, since 2015; *b* Cyprus, 1961; *s* of Michael and Maureen Ford; partner, Sarah Leverton; two *s. Educ:* Gravesend Grammar Sch.; Univ. of Bristol (LLB 1st Cl. Hons 1986; BSc 1st Cl. Hons 2010); Univ. of Sheffield (MA Socio-Legal Studies 1989). Mem., GB cycling squad, 1983–84. Solicitor, Slaughter and May, 1987–89; admitted as solicitor, 1989; Lectr, Univ. of Manchester, 1990–92; called to the Bar, Middle Temple, 1992; in practice as barrister, specialising in labour law, 1992–; Lectr, Univ. of London, 1996–98; an Employment Judge (pt-time), 2003–. Vis. Fellow, LSE, 1996–2006. Trustee, Bat Conservation Trust, 2003–13. *Publications:* (jtly) Redgrave's Health and Safety, 2nd edn 1996 to 7th edn 2010; Munkman on Employer's Liability, 12th edn 1995 to 13th edn 2001; Privacy and Surveillance at Work, 1998; contrib. articles to jls incl. Industrial Law Jl, Modern Law Rev. *Recreations:* cycling, wildlife, film, French, Spanish, my boys. *Address:* Old Square Chambers, 10–11 Bedford Row, WC1R 4BU. *T:* (020) 7269 0300; Old Square Chambers, 9 Queen Square, Bristol BS1 4JE. *T:* (0117) 930 5100.

**FORD, Peter George Tipping;** Secretary, Medical Protection Society, 1983–90; *b* 18 Sept. 1931; *s* of late Raymond Eustace Ford, CBE; *m* 1958, Nancy Elizabeth Procter; four *d. Educ:* Epsom Coll.; St Bartholomew's Hosp. Med. Coll., Univ. of London (MB, BS); MRCGP, DObstRCOG. Nat. Service, RAMC, 1957–59. Gen. practice, Hythe, 1960–68; Asst Sec., Med. Protection Soc., 1968–72, Dep. Sec., 1972–83. Sec., Jt Co-ordinating Cttee, UK Defence Organizations, 1985–89. Mem., Soc. of Apothecaries. FRSocMed. Medal of Honour, Med. Defence Soc. of Queensland, 1984. *Publications:* contribs to medico-legal periodicals. *Recreations:* baroque choral music, gardening, bridge. *Address:* 14 Admirals Walk, South Road, Hythe, Kent CT21 6AL. *T:* (01303) 267896.

**FORD, Peter John,** CBE 1998; Chairman, London Transport, 1994–98; *b* 21 Nov. 1938; *s* of John Frederick Arthur Ford and Hazel Mary Ford; *m* 1966, Olivia Mary Temple; two *s* two *d. Educ:* King's Sch., Canterbury; Christ Church, Oxford (MA Chem.); Harvard Business Sch. (MBA). With Shell Chemical Co., 1961–65; McKinsey & Co., NY, 1967–70; Exec. Dir, Sterling Guarantee Trust, 1970–85; Exec. Dir, P&OSNCo., 1985–93. Director: Countrywide Assured Gp, 1994–2002; Palliser Furniture, Winnipeg, Canada, 2001–; Cambridge Biostability Ltd, 2004–09. Pres., Sheffield Chamber of Commerce, 1985–86; Dep. Pres., London Chamber of Commerce and Industry, 1998–2000. Chm., NW Surrey Short Stay Schools, 2009–; Governor: Kingston Univ., 1993–98; Collingwood Coll., 2001–10. *Recreations:* walking, music. *Address:* 2B The Downs, SW20 8HN. *T:* (020) 8944 7207. *Club:* Royal Automobile.

**FORD, Peter William;** HM Diplomatic Service, retired; Senior Regional Representative, United Nations Relief and Works Agency for Palestinian Refugees, 2006–14; *b* 27 June 1947; *s* of Alec and Gertrude Ford; *m* 1st, 1974, Aurora Garcia Mingo (marr. diss. 1992); 2nd, 1992, Alganesh Haile Beyene. *Educ:* Helsby Grammar Sch.; Queen's Coll., Oxford (BA Hons). FCO, 1971–72; Beirut, 1972–73; Second, then First, Sec., Cairo, 1974–78; Eur. Integration Dept, FCO, 1978–80; First Sec., Paris, 1980–85; Asst Hd, EC Dept, FCO, 1985–87; Counsellor (Commercial), Riyadh, 1987–90; Vis. Fellow, Harvard Univ., 1990–91; Dep. High Comr and Counsellor (Econ. and Commercial), Singapore, 1991–94; Hd, Near East and N Africa Dept, FCO, 1994–99; Ambassador to Bahrain, 1999–2003; Ambassador to Syria, 2003–06. Internat. Fellow, Brandeis Univ., 2001–03. *Recreations:* sport, reading, travel.

**FORD, Robert Stanley;** HM Diplomatic Service, retired; *b* 30 Nov. 1929; *s* of late Robert Hempstead Ford and Janet Mabel Elliot; *m* 1957, Cynthia Valerie Arscott, *d* of late Ronald Prowse Arscott, Bexhill-on-Sea, Sussex; one *s* two *d. Educ:* Daniel Stewart's Coll., Edinburgh; Univ. of Edinburgh (MA). Joined HM Diplomatic Service, 1949; HM Forces, 1949; FCO, 1951; Third Sec., Moscow, 1955; Consul, Dakar, 1958; FCO, 1959; Information Officer, NY, 1963; First Sec., Managua, 1965; Consul, Naples, 1968; FCO, 1972; Consul-Gen., Madrid, 1978; FCO, 1982; Counsellor (Admin), Paris, 1984–86. *Recreations:* music, photography, travel. *Address:* 31 Seabright, West Parade, Worthing, W Sussex BN11 3QS. *T:* (01903) 537033.

**FORD, Sarah Louise;** QC 2017; *b* Redhill, 22 Aug. 1978; *d* of David Frederick Stevens, CBE, QPM and Patricia Anne Stevens; *m* 2006, Stuart Charles Howard Ford; three *d. Educ:* Univ. of Warwick (LLB Law with Eur. Law 2000); Harvard Law Sch. (LLM 2001); BVC 2002. Called to the Bar, Lincoln's Inn, 2002; in practice as a barrister specialising in competition and EU law, 2002–. *Recreations:* family, ski-ing, scuba diving. *Address:* Brick Court Chambers, 7–8 Essex Street, WC2R 3LD. *T:* (020) 7379 3550, *Fax:* (020) 7379 3558.

**FORD, Steven Charles;** QC 2010; barrister; *b* London, 11 June 1965; *s* of Charles Ford and Pamela Ford; *m* 2000, Jane Elizabeth Ettridge; two *d. Educ:* Tiffin Boys' Sch.; Royal Acad. of Music (LRAM 1986); Kingston Univ. (LLB 1991). Called to the Bar, Middle Temple, 1992. *Recreations:* cooking, wine. *Address:* 7 Bedford Row, WC1R 4BS. *T:* (020) 7242 3555. *E:* clerks@7br.co.uk.

**FORD, (Sydney) John,** CBE 1999; PhD; Chief Executive, Driver and Vehicle Licensing Agency 1995–2000; *b* 23 Aug. 1936; *s* of Sydney James Ford and Barbara Ford (*née* Essenhigh); *m* 1st, 1960, Beryl Owen (marr. diss. 1990); two *s*; 2nd, 1990, Morag Munro. *Educ:* Bromsgrove High Sch.; Swansea Grammar Sch.; UC Swansea, Univ. of Wales (BSc Maths; PhD Maths; Hon. Fellow, 1999). British Aluminium Co. plc, 1966–82 (Dir, 1977–82; Man. Dir, 1982); Dep. Man. Dir, British Alcan Aluminium plc, 1982–85; UK Ops Dir, Williams Hldgs plc, 1985–88; Dir, European Distribn, Christian Salvesen plc, 1988–93; Chief Exec., Driving Standards Agency, 1993–94. Chm., Ofwat CSC Wales, subseq. WaterVoice Wales, 2001–05; Mem., Consumer Council for Water, Midlands, 2005–07. *Recreations:* artist and art tutor, qualified Rugby referee and coach. *Address:* Shenval, 1 Evertons Close, Droitwich Spa WR9 8AE.

**FORD, Prof. Tamsin Jane, (Mrs J. A. Cromwell),** CBE 2019; PhD; FRCPsych; Professor of Child and Adolescent Psychiatry, University of Cambridge, since 2019; *b* London, 17 Sept. 1966; adopted 1968 by Betty Ford and Barbara Tobias; *m* 2000, James Andrew Cromwell; two *d. Educ:* Ipstock Place Froebel Sch., Roehampton; Godolphin and Latymer Sch. for Girls; United Med. Schs of Guy's and St Thomas' (MB BS 1990); London Sch. of Hygiene and Tropical Medicine (MSc Epidemiol. (Dist.) 2000); Inst. of Psychiatry, King's Coll. London (PhD 2004). FRCPsych 2014. Core Psychiatry Trng, Royal London Hosp. Trng Scheme, 1992–95; Specialist Child and Adolescent Psychiatry Trng, Bethlem and Maudsley Trng Scheme, 1995–98; Wellcome Clin. Trng Fellow, KCL, 1999–2005; MRC Clinician Scientist Fellow, KCL, 2005–07; Univ. of Exeter Med. Sch., 2007–10; Prof. of Child and Adolescent Psychiatry, Univ. of Exeter Med. Sch., 2013–19 (Vis. Prof., 2019–). Member: BMA, 1990–; Bd, Assoc. of Child and Adolescent Mental Health, 2010–; Child Psychiatry Res. Soc. (Mem., Exec. Cttee). *Recreations:* running, swimming, yoga, reading, live music, comedy and theatre. *Address:* Department of Developmental Psychiatry, University of Cambridge, Douglas House, 18b Trumpington Road, Cambridge CB2 8AH. *E:* t.j.ford@exeter.ac.uk.

**FORD, Victoria Grace;** MP (C) Chelmsford, since 2017; *b* Omagh, NI, 21 Sept. 1967; *d* of Dr Anthony Pollock and Deborah Marion (*née* Bliss, now Lady Cassidi); *m* 1996, Dr Hugo Ford; two *s* one *d. Educ:* Omagh Acad. Prep. Dept; St Paul's Girls' Sch.; Marlborough Coll.; Trinity Coll., Cambridge (BA 1989). JP Morgan, 1989–2001; Bear Stearns, 2001–03. Mem. (C) S Cambs DC, 2006–09. MEP (C) Eastern, 2009–17. Chair, Internal Market and Consumer Protection Cttee, EP, 2014–17. *Recreations:* fly fishing, music, gardening. *Address:* House of Commons, SW1A 0AA.

**FORD, William Clay, Jr;** Executive Chairman, Ford Motor Company, since 2006 (Director, since 1988; Chairman, 1999; Chief Executive, 2001–06); Founding Partner, Fontinalis Partners LLC, since 2009; *b* Detroit, 3 May 1957; *m. Educ:* Princeton Univ. (BA 1979); MIT (Alfred P. Sloan Fellow, 1983–84, MBA 1984). Ford Motor Company: Product Planning Analyst, Advanced Vehicle Develt, Design Center, then Manufg Engr, Automobile Assembly Div., subseq. NY Zone Manager, Ford Div., 1979–82; Mktg Strategy Analyst, N Amer. Automobile Ops, and Advertising Specialist, Ford Div., 1982–83; Internat. Finance Specialist, 1984–85; Planning Manager, Car Product Develt, 1985–86; Dir, Commercial Vehicle Mktg, Ford of Europe, 1986–87; Chm. and Man. Dir, Ford of Switzerland, 1987–89; Manager, Heavy Truck Engrg and Manufg, Ford Truck Ops, 1989–90; Dir, 1990–91, Exec. Dir, 1991–92, Business Strategy, Ford Auto Gp; Gen. Manager, Climate Control Div., 1992–94; Vice Pres., Commercial Truck Vehicle Center, Ford Automotive Ops, 1994–95; Chm., Finance Cttee, 1995–99. Mem., Bd of Trustees, The Henry Ford (formerly Henry Ford Mus. and Greenfield Village); Trustee, Henry Ford Health System; Chm., Detroit Economic Club, 2005–17; Mem., Business Leaders for Michigan. Vice Chm., Detroit Lions (prof. football team). *Address:* Ford Motor Company, One American Road, Dearborn, MI 48126–2798, USA. *T:* (313) 3223000.

**FORD, Sir William Sam St C.;** see St Clair-Ford.

**FORDE, Helen,** PhD; FSA; archivist; lecturer; *b* Oxford, 26 May 1941; *d* of Antony Andrewes and Alison Andrewes (*née* Hope); *m* 1962, Thomas Middleton Forde; one *s* one *d. Educ:* Oxford High Sch. for Girls; University Coll. London (BA Hist. 1962); Univ. of Liverpool (DAA 1968); Univ. of Leicester (PhD 1977). FSA 2001. Archivist, Nottingham City, 1970–73; Urban Res. Asst, Council for British Archaeol., 1973–75; Archivist, Liby of the Soc. of Friends, 1978–79; Public Record Office: Asst Keeper, 1979–2001; Head: Liby and Mus., 1979–82; Conservation Dept, 1982–92; Preservation Services, 1992–2001. Extra mural tutor: Nottingham Univ., 1970–73; London Univ., 1975–89; Lectr, Sch. of Liby, Archive and Inf. Studies, 1989–2007, Hon. Res. Fellow, UCL, 2008–. Society of Archivists: Chm., 1993–95; Pres., 2002–05; Vice Pres., 2005–. Chm., Preservation Cttee, 1992–2000, Mem., Cttee of Prog. Mgt, 2000–04, Internat. Council on Archives; Museums, Libraries and Archives Council: Chm., Designation Panel, 2004–12; Chm., E Midlands, 2005–09; Mem. Bd, 2007–11; Member: Northants Archives Panel, 1994–2014; (and Vice Chm.) Lincoln Cath. Liby Council, 2001–06; (and Chm.) Expert Panel for Mus, Libraries and Archives, Heritage Lottery Fund, 2001–05; British Postal Mus. and Archive, 2001–15 (Chm., 2011–15); Documentary Heritage Review of C of E, 2004–05; Member, Council: Soc. of Antiquaries of London, 2012–16 (Vice-Pres., 2014–16); Friends of Nat. Archives, 2012–13; Mem., Adv. Council, Nat. Records and Archives, 2016–. Trustee: Marc Fitch Fund, 2001–; Friends of the Bodleian Lib., 2015–; VCH Northants, 2015–. Chm., Banbury Histl Soc., 2008–11, 2018–; Mem., Banbury Mus. Trust, 2012– (Mem., Shadow Bd, 2012–13). *Publications:* Domesday Preserved, 1986; Preserving Archives, 2007, 2nd edn (with J. Rhys Lewis) 2013; contrib. archive, liby and historical jls; ed professional works and online information sources. *Recreations:* music, gardening, travelling. *Address:* Lovells, The Square, Kings Sutton, Banbury OX17 3RE. *T:* (01295) 811247. *E:* helenforde1@gmail.com.

**FORDE, Martin Andrew;** QC 2006; *b* 1961; *s* of Ralph and Cynthia Forde; *m* 2004, Nadège Vidal; one *s* three *d. Educ:* Langley Grammar Sch.; Brasenose Coll., Oxford (BA Hons Juris). Called to the Bar, Middle Temple, 1984 (Harmsworth Exhibnr, 1983), Bencher, 2010; in practice, specialising in professional negligence, employment, professional regulatory and public law. Mem., Judicial Appointments Commn, 2012–18. *Recreations:* sport, music, travel. *Address:* 1 Crown Office Row, Temple, EC4Y 7HH. *E:* martin.forde@1cor.com.

**FORDE, Hon. (Mary Marguerite) Leneen,** AC 1993; Chancellor, Griffith University, Queensland, 2000–15; Governor of Queensland, 1992–97; *b* 12 May 1935; *d* of John Alfred Kavanagh and Evelyn Philomena Kavanagh (*née* Bujold); *m* 1st, 1955, Francis Gerard Forde (*d* 1966), *s* of Rt Hon. Francis Michael Forde, PC; three *s* two *d*; 2nd, 1983, (Albert) Angus McDonald (*d* 1999). *Educ:* Lisgar Collegiate, Ottawa (Dip.); Univ. of Queensland (LLB). Student Med. Lab. Technician, Ottawa Gen. Hosp., 1952–53; Med. Lab. Technician, Drs Rousell and Gagne, Ottawa, 1953–54; Haematol. Dept, Royal Brisbane Hosp., 1954–56; medical lab. work, 1956–58; articled Law Clerk, Alexander McGillivray, 1969–70; Solicitor, Cannan & Peterson, 1971–74; Partner, Sly, Weigall, Cannan & Peterson, subseq. Deakins, 1974–92. Comr, Royal Commn of Inquiry into Abuse of Children in Queensland Instns, 1998–99; Nat. Chm., Australian Defence Reserves Support Council, 2002–05. Board Member: St Leo's Coll., 1998–2000; Brisbane Coll. of Theol., 1999–2000; Brisbane City Council Arts and Envmt Trust, 1999–2000; Qld Ballet, 2000–11; Qld Govt Forde Foundn, 2000–07; Qld Community Foundn, 2008–; All Hallow's Sch., 2008–09; Searchlight Educn, 2008–11; Chair, Qld Educn Commn, 2016–. Founder, Qld Women Lawyers' Assoc., 1976; Member: Qld Law Soc., 1971–; Women Chiefs of Enterprises Internat., 1989–; Zonta Club of Brisbane Inc., 1971–; President: Zonta Internat., 1990–92; Scout Assoc. of Aust., 1997–2003 (Vice-Pres., 2003–10). Patron, Nat. Pioneer Women's Hall of Fame, 1999–. Paul Harris Fellow, Rotary Club of Brisbane, 1990; Woman of Substance Award, Qld Girl Guides' Assoc., 1990; Queenslander of the Year, 1991; Queensland Great, 2009. DUniv: Griffith, 1992; Qld Univ. of Technology, 1993; Australian Catholic, 2000; Southern Qld, 2000; Hon. DLitt Queensland, 1996. DStJ 1992. *Publications:* Queensland Annual Law Review, 1991, 1992. *Recreations:* theatre, art, music, ballet, surfing.

**FORDE, Very Rev. Stephen Bernard;** Dean of Belfast, since 2018; *b* 1961. *Educ:* Campbell Coll., Belfast; Edinburgh Univ. (BSc); Trinity Coll. Dublin. Ordained deacon, 1986, priest, 1987; Curate, St Mary's Parish, Belfast, 1986–89; Minor Canon, Belfast Cathedral, 1989–91; Bishop's Domestic Chaplain, Dio. of Connor, 1990–95; Rector: St Philip and St James, Booterstown, Dublin, 1995–99; Larne and Inver with Glynn and Raloo, 1999–2018; Archdeacon of Dalriada, 2006–18. Dean of Residence: QUB, 1989–95; UCD, 1995–99. *Address:* The Deanery, 5 Deramore Drive, Belfast BT9 5JQ.

**FORDHAM, His Honour (John) Jeremy**; a Circuit Judge, 1986–99; *b* 18 April 1933; *s* of John Hampden Fordham, CBE and Rowena Fordham (*née* Day, later Langran); *m* 1962, Rose Anita (*née* Brandon), *d* of Philip Brandon, Wellington, New Zealand; one *s* one *d*. *Educ*: Gresham's Sch.; Univ. of New Zealand. LLB (NZ). Merchant Navy, 1950–55 (2nd Mate (Foreign Going) Cert.); labourer, fireman etc, 1955–60; Barrister and Solicitor, New Zealand, 1960–64; called to Bar, Inner Temple, 1965; practised 1965–71, 1976–78; Sen. Magistrate, Gilbert and Ellice Islands, 1971–75; a Metropolitan Stipendiary Magistrate, 1978–86; a Recorder, 1986; a Dep. Circuit Judge, 1999–2001. Legal Chm., Immigration Appeal Tribunal, 1999–; Asst Surveillance Comr, 2001–07. *Recreations*: boats, games. *Clubs*: Garrick; Barnes Bowling.

**FORDHAM, Max**; *see* Fordham, S. M.

**FORDHAM, Michael John**; QC 2006; a Recorder, since 2010; a Deputy High Court Judge, since 2013; *b* 21 Dec. 1964; *s* of John and Margaret Fordham; *m* 1993, Alison Oxley (marr. diss. 2017); one *s* two *d*. *Educ*: Spalding Grammar Sch.; Hertford Coll., Oxford (BA Hons, BCL); Univ. of Virginia (LLM). Called to the Bar, Gray's Inn, 1990 (Prince of Wales Schol., Karmel Schol., Mould Schol., 1989), Bencher, 2009; Lectr, Hertford Coll., Oxford, 1989–; in practice as barrister, 1990–. Mem., Adv. Bd, British Inst. Internat. and Comparative Law, 2003–. Vis. Fellow, Bingham Centre for the Rule of Law, 2011–12. Human Rights Lawyer of the Year, 2005; Bar Pro Bono Award, 2006; Human Rights and Public Law Silk of the Year, 2008. Co-Ed., Judicial Rev., 1996–. *Publications*: Judicial Review Handbook, 1994, 6th edn 2012. *Recreation*: St Albans Hockey Club (Pres., 2014–). *Address*: Blackstone Chambers, Temple, EC4Y 9BW. *T*: (020) 7583 1770. *E*: michaelfordham@blackstonechambers.com.

**FORDHAM, (Sigurd) Max**, OBE 1994; RDI 2008; FREng; Member, Max Fordham LLP, since 2001; Director, Max Fordham Consulting Ltd, 2004–17; *b* Highgate, 17 June 1933; *s* of Dr Michael Scott Montague Fordham and Molly Fordham (*née* Swabey); *m* 1960, Thalia Aubrey Dyson; three *s*. *Educ*: DeCarteret Sch., Mandeville, Jamaica; Dartington Hall Sch., Totnes; Trinity Coll., Cambridge (BA 1957; MA 1960). CEng, FREng 1992. National Service, 1952–54: served RN, FAA (Temp. actg Sub-Lt (A) RNVR). Develt engr, Weatherfoil Ltd, 1958–61; engr, Arup Bldg Gp, later Arup Associates, 1961–66; Max Fordham Consulting Engr Building Services, 1966–73; Max Fordham & Partners, 1973–2001; Max Fordham Associates, 1985–2001. *Building projects* include: Alexandra Rd housing scheme, London, 1969; Royal Exchange Th., Manchester, 1977; Southern Water, Sparrow Grove, Hants, 1985; RMC Internat. HQ, Egham, 1992; Grove Rd Primary Sch., London, 1993 (HVCA/Independent on Sunday Green Bldg of Year); Queens Bldg, De Montfort Univ., 1995 (HVCA/Independent on Sunday Green Bldg of Year); Tate Gall., St Ives, 1995 (Civic Trust Award); MCC Cricket Sch., Lord's Ground, London, 1995 (Balthasar-Neumann Prize, Assoc. of German Master Builders, Architects and Engrs); Judge Inst. of Mgt Studies, Cambridge Univ., 1997; Bedales Sch. Th., Hants, 1998 (Royal Fine Arts Commn Bldg of Year); Royal Exchange, Manchester, 1999 (Lighting Project of Year, Bldg Services Awards); Nat. Botanic Gdn of Wales, 2000 (RICS Bldg Efficiency Award); Beaufort Court Zero Emissions Bldg, Kings Langley, 2005 (RICS Regl Sustainability Award). Vis. Prof., Building Design, Sch. of Civil Engrg and Architecture, Univ. of Bath, 1990–. Dir, Nestar Ltd, 1987–99. External Examiner: Univ. of Edinburgh, 1992–94; AA, 1995–97, 2007–12; Cambridge Univ., 1996–98. Mem., Judging Panel, RIBA Stirling Prize, 2005. Pres., CIBSE, 2001–02. MCIBS (MIHVE); FCIBSE. Hon. FRIBA 1996. Gold Medal, CIBSE, 1997; Prince Philip Designers Prize, 2008. *Publications*: (contrib.) European Directory of Sustainable and Energy Efficient Buildings, 1998; papers to conferences and contrib. papers and articles to jls incl. RSA Jl, Architectural Rev., Dubai. *Recreations*: mucking about in boats mostly on the East coast of England, walking in the Lake District, gardening, reading and writing about my work of improving the design of buildings. *Address*: 3 Camden Square, NW1 9UY. *T*: (020) 7485 5113. *E*: max@maxf.co.uk.

**FOREMAN, Dr Amanda Lucy, (Mrs J. L. E. Barton)**; historian; *b* London, 30 June 1968; *d* of Carl Foreman, Hon. CBE and of Evelyn Foreman; *m* 2000, Jonathan Luke Elliott Barton; one *s* four *d*. *Educ*: Lady Margaret Hall, Oxford (MPhil; DPhil 1998). Writer, consultant and presenter, BBC TV documentaries, 1998–, including: The Ascent of Woman, 2015; journalist and contributor to US and UK newspapers and periodicals, 1998–; Adjunct Prof., Faculty of Writing, Gallatin Sch., New York Univ., 2002; Vis. Sen. Res. Fellow in Hist., Faculty of Arts, QMUL, 2004–. Member: Bd, Sarah Lawrence Coll., 2000–04; Adv. Council, Lady Margaret Hall, Oxford, 2005–; Adv. Council, NY Public Liby, 2009–. Founder, House of Speakeasy Foundn, 2013–; Trustee, Whiting Foundn. Judge: PEN/Hessell-Tiltman Prize for Hist., 2012; Man Booker Prize for Fiction, 2012 (Chair, 2016). Member: Virginia Histl Soc.; Columbia Histl Soc. FRSA 2001. *Publications*: Georgiana, Duchess of Devonshire, 1998 (Whitbread Prize for Biog.); (contrib.) New Dictionary of National Biography, 2002; (Series Ed.) Making History, 2004; (contrib.) What Might Have Been, 2004; A World on Fire: an epic history of two nations divided, 2010 (Fletcher Pratt Award for Civil War Hist., Civil War Round Table of NY, 2011). *Recreations*: gardening, cooking, film, television, screenwriting, journalism. *Address*: The Wylie Agency, 17 Bedford Square, WC1B 3JA. *T*: (020) 7908 5901. *E*: mail@wylieagency.co.uk. *Clubs*: Colony, Century Association (NY).

**FOREMAN, Michael**, RDI 1985; AGI; writer and illustrator; *b* 21 March 1938; *s* of Walter and Gladys Mary Foreman; *m* 1st, 1959, Janet Charters (marr. diss. 1966); one *s*; 2nd, 1980, Louise Phillips; two *s*. *Educ*: Notley Road Secondary Modern Sch., Lowestoft; Royal College of Art, London (ARCA 1st Cl. Hons and Silver Medal). Freelance, 1963–; six animated films produced, 1967–68. Hon. FRCA 1989. Hon. DArts Plymouth, 1998. Awarded Aigle d'Argent, Festival International du Livre, Nice, 1972; (jtly) Kurt Maschler Award, 1982; Graphics Prize, Bologna, 1982; Kate Greenaway Medal, Library Assoc., 1983 and 1989. *Publications*: author and illustrator: The Perfect Present, 1967; The Two Giants, 1967; The Great Sleigh Robbery, 1968; Horatio, 1970; Moose, 1971; Dinosaurs and all that Rubbish, 1972 (Francis Williams Prize, 1972); War and Peas, 1974; All The King's Horses, 1976; Panda's Puzzle and his Voyage of Discovery, 1977 (Francis Williams Prize, 1977); Panda and the Odd Lion, 1980; Trick a Tracker, 1982; Land of Dreams, 1982; Panda and the Bunyips, 1984; Cat and Canary, 1984; Panda and the Bushfire, 1985; Ben's Box, 1986; Ben's Baby, 1987; The Angel and the Wild Animal, 1988; War Boy (autobiog.), 1989; One World, 1990; Michael Foreman's World of Fairytales, 1990; Michael Foreman's Mother Goose, 1991, reissued as Michael Foreman's Nursery Rhymes, 1998; The Boy Who Sailed with Columbus, 1991; Jack's Fantastic Voyage, 1992; War Game, 1993; Grandfather's Pencil and the Room of Stories, 1993; Dad! I Can't Sleep, 1994; Surprise! Surprise!, 1995; After the War Was Over, 1995; Panda (Panda's Puzzle, Panda and the Odd Lion), 1996; Seal Surfer, 1996; The Little Reindeer, 1996; Look! Look!, 1997; Angel and the Box of Time, 1997; Jack's Big Race, 1998; Chicken Licken, 1998; Little Red Hen, 1999; Michael Foreman's Christmas Treasury, 1999; Rock-a-Doodle Do!, 2000; Cat in the Manger, 2000; Memories of Childhood (War Boy, After the War was Over), 2000; Saving Sinbad!, 2001; Wonder Goal, 2002; Dinosaur Time, 2002; Michael Foreman's Playtime Rhymes, 2002; Evie and the Man who Helped God, 2003; Cat on the Hill, 2003; Hello World, 2003; Can't Catch Me, 2005; Classic Fairy Tales, 2005; Norman's Ark, 2006; Fox Tale, 2006; Mia's Story, 2006; The Littlest Dinosaur, 2008; A Child's Garden, 2009; The Littlest Dinosaur's Big Adventure, 2009; Why the Animals Came to Town, 2010; Fortunately, Unfortunately, 2010; Superfrog!, 2011; Oh! If Only…, 2011; Friends, 2012; Newspaper Boy and the Origami Girl!, 2012; Superfrog and the Big Stink!, 2013; I Love You Too!, 2013; The Amazing Tale of Ali Pasha, 2013; Cat and Dog, 2014; The Seeds of Friendship, 2015; The Little Bookshop and the Origami Army, 2015; A Life in Pictures, 2015; Tufty, The Little Lost Duck Who Found Love, 2016; Jamal's Journey, 2017; Hello, Mr World, 2017; Travels with My Sketchbook, 2017; Stubby: a true story of friendship, 2018; illustrator of many books by other authors. *Recreations*: football, travelling. *Address*: 11 Howards Lane, SW15 6NX. *Club*: Chelsea Arts.

**FORESTER**; *see* Weld Forester, family name of Baron Forester.

**FORESTER, 9th Baron** *cr* 1821; **Charles Richard George Weld Forester**; land agent, since 2004; *b* 8 July 1975; *o s* of 8th Baron Forester and of Catherine Elizabeth Weld Forester; *S* father, 2004; *m* 2009, Lydia, *d* of George Baugh; one *s* one *d*. *Educ*: Harrow; RAC Cirencester. *Recreations*: sport (cricket, tennis, ski-ing), bridge, reading, countryside pursuits. *Heir*: *s* Hon. Brook George Percival Weld Forester, *b* 29 March 2014.

**FORESTIER-WALKER, Sir Michael (Leolin)**, 6th Bt *cr* 1835; General Manager, Leatherhead Theatre, 2003–10 (Development Manager, 2002–03); *b* 24 April 1949; *s* of Lt-Col Alan Ivor Forestier-Walker, MBE (*d* 1954) (*g s* of 2nd Bt), and Margaret Joan Forestier-Walker (*née* Marcoolyn) (*d* 1988); *S* cousin, 1983; *m* 1988, Elizabeth Hedley, *d* of Joseph Hedley, Bellingham, Northumberland; one *s* one *d*. *Educ*: Wellington College, Crowthorne; Royal Holloway College, London Univ. (BA Hons). Teacher, Feltonfleet Sch., 1975–2002. *Heir*: *s* Joseph Alan Forestier-Walker, *b* 2 May 1992. *Address*: Bibury, 116 Hogshill Lane, Cobham, Surrey KT11 2AW.

**FORGAN, Dame Elizabeth (Anne Lucy)**, DBE 2006 (OBE 1999); writer and broadcaster; Chair, National Youth Orchestra of Great Britain, 2013–19; *b* 31 Aug. 1944; *d* of late Thomas Moinet Forgan and Jean Margaret Muriel. *Educ*: Benenden Sch.; St Hugh's Coll., Oxford (BA; Hon. Fellow 2014). Journalist: Teheran Journal, 1967–68; Hampstead and Highgate Express, 1969–74; Evening Standard, 1974–78; The Guardian, 1978–81; Channel Four TV: Sen. Commissioning Editor, 1981–86; Dir of Progs, 1988–93; Man. Dir, Network Radio BBC, 1993–96. Dir, Guardian Media Gp, 1998–2004. Non-exec. Dir, DCMS, 2008–09. Member: HFEA, 1990–98; Churches Conservation Trust, 1998–2001 (Chm., 1999–2001); Chair: NHMF and HLF, 2001–08; Arts Council England, 2009–13; Scott Trust, 2004–16; Bristol Old Vic Th., 2014–. Trustee: Conservatoire for Dance and Drama, 2002–09; British Mus., 2008–16 (Dep. Chm., 2012–16); The Art Fund, 2012–; Landmark Trust, 2016–. Patron: St Giles Trust, 2007–18; Schola Cantorum of Oxford, 2011–; Pier Arts Centre, Stromness, 2013–. FRTS 1988; FRSA 1989; Hon. Fellow, Girton Coll., Cambridge, 2009; Hon. FBA 2014. Hon. DLitt: Keele, 1994; Kent, 2009; Hon. MA Salford, 1995; Hon. Dr Univ. of the Arts, 2013. Chevalier de l'ordre des arts et des lettres (France), 1990. *Recreations*: church music, cheap novels, Scottish islands. *Address*: Most Media Ltd, 112 Regent's Park Road, NW1 8UG. *Club*: Reform.

**FORLIN, Gerard**; QC 2010; *b* Ayrshire; *s* of late Prof. Joseph Forlin and Moira Forlin (*née* Conway). *Educ*: London Sch. of Econs and Pol Sci. (LLB Hons, LLM); Trinity Hall, Cambridge (MPhil); Inst. of World Affairs (Dip. Air and Space Law). Called to the Bar, Lincoln's Inn; in practice as barrister, specialising in corporate manslaughter, health and safety, envmtl, disaster litigation, aviation, public inquiries and inquests. Pt-time lectr and speaker, incl. internat. confs, in over 60 countries, lectures for FCO, UN and ASEAN corporate social responsibility on UK Bribery Act. *Publications*: (Gen. Ed.) Corporate Liability: work related deaths and criminal prosecutions, 2004, 4th edn 2019; contrib. books and articles. *Recreations*: swimming, travel, amateur dramatics, script writing, music, after dinner speaking. *Address*: c/o Cornerstone Chambers, 2–3 Gray's Inn Square, Gray's Inn, WC1R 5JH; c/o Denman Chambers, Level 7/185 Elizabeth Street, Sydney, NSW 2000, Australia; c/o Maxwell Chambers, 3 Temasek Avenue, #16–01, Singapore 039190.

**FORMAN, Air Vice-Marshal Graham Neil**, CB 1989; Director of Legal Services, Royal Air Force, 1982–89; *b* 29 Nov. 1930; *s* of Stanley M. Forman and Eva Forman (*née* Barrett); *m* 1957, Valerie Fay (*née* Shaw) (*d* 2011); one *s* two *d*. *Educ*: Boston Grammar School; Nottingham Univ. Law School; Law Society's School of Law; admitted solicitor 1953. Commissioned RAF Legal Branch, 1957; served HQ Far East Air Force, Singapore, 1960–63 and 1965–68; Dep. Dir, RAF Legal Services, HQ Near East Air Force, Cyprus, 1971–72 and 1973–76; Dep. Dir, RAF Legal Services, HQ RAF Germany, 1978; Dep. Dir, Legal Services (RAF), 1978–82. *Clubs*: Royal Air Force (Life Mem.), Middlesex CC (Life Mem.).

**FORMANTINE, Viscount; Ivo Alexander Ninian Gordon**; *b* 18 July 2012; *s* and heir of Earl of Haddo, *qv*.

**FORNA, Aminatta**, OBE 2017; FRSL; writer, since 1999; *b* Glasgow, 7 May 1964; *d* of late Mohamed Sorie Forna and of Maureen Margaret Forna (*née* Christison); *m* 1994, Simon John Westcott; one *s*. *Educ*: Malvern Girl's Coll.; University Coll. London (LLB Hons Laws); Univ. of California at Berkeley (Harkness Fellow 1996). FRSL 2012. Reporter, Arts, News and Current Affairs, BBC Television, 1989–99. Prof. of Creative Writing (part-time), Bath Spa Univ., 2013–; Lannan Prof. of Poetics, Georgetown Univ., 2015– (Interim Dir, Lannan Center, 2018–19). Member: Council, Caine Prize for African Writing, 2005–; Bd, Index on Censorship, 2007–09; Adv. Cttee, Royal Literary Fund, 2008–15; Bd, National Th., 2012–15; Council, RSL, 2014–15. *Publications*: The Devil that Danced on the Water (memoir), 2002; Ancestor Stones, 2006; The Memory of Love, 2010 (Commonwealth Writer's Prize for Best Book, 2011); The Hired Man, 2013; Happiness, 2018. *Recreation*: running. *Address*: c/o David Godwin Associates Ltd, 55 Monmouth Street, WC2H 9DG. *T*: (020) 7240 9992. *E*: assistant@davidgodwinassociates.co.uk. *Clubs*: Groucho, Quo Vadis.

**FORRES, 4th Baron** *cr* 1922; **Alastair Stephen Grant Williamson**, MARAC; Bt 1909; Chairman, Agriscot Pty Ltd; Director, Jaga Trading Pty Ltd; *b* 16 May 1946; *s* of 3rd Baron Forres and of Gillian Ann Maclean, *d* of Major John Maclean Grant, RA; *S* father, 1978; *m* 1969, Margaret, *d* of late G. J. Mallam, Mullumbimby, NSW; two *s*. *Educ*: Eton. Alderman, Orange City Council, 1987. Pres., Big Brother Movt, 1986–. Patron, Sydney Scottish Week, 1981–. *Heir*: *s* Hon. George Archibald Mallam Williamson [*b* 16 Aug. 1972; *m* 1st, 2002, Charlotte, *e d* of Timothy and Sara Barrett; 2nd, 2009, Frances Louise, *d* of John Lindsay Merity; one *s* one *d*]. *Clubs*: Union, Australian Jockey, Sydney Turf (Sydney).

**FORREST, Prof. (Alexander) Robert (Walker)**, FRCP, FRCPE, FRCPath; CSci, CChem, FRSC; Assistant Coroner (formerly Assistant Deputy Coroner): South Yorkshire (West), since 1989; East Riding of Yorkshire and Kingston-upon-Hull, since 2008; *b* 5 July 1947; *s* of Alexander Muir Forrest and Rose Ellen Forrest (*née* Ringham); *m* 1999, Dr Wendy Susan Phillips; two *s*. *Educ*: Stamford Sch.; Univ. of Edinburgh (BSc Hons 1970; MB ChB 1973); Cardiff Law Sch. (LLM). DObstRCOG 1975; MCB 1981; CChem, FRSC 1983; FRCPE 1989; FRCP 1992; FRCPath 1992; Eurotox Registered Toxicologist 1997; CSci 2004. Sen. Registrar, Royal Infirmary, Glasgow, 1979–81; Consultant in Clin. Chem. and Toxicol., Sheffield Univ. Hosps NHS Trust at Royal Hallamshire Hosp., Sheffield, 1981–98 (Hon. Consultant, 1998–2007); Sheffield University: Prof. of Forensic Toxicol., 1998–2005; Hon. Prof. of Forensic Chem., 2005–16; Hon. Prof., Sch. of Law,

2016–. HM Sen. Coroner (formerly HM Coroner), S Lincs, 2012–16. Pres., Forensic Sci. Soc., 2005–07; Vice-Pres. (Medical Coroners), Faculty of Forensic and Legal Medicine, RCP, 2016–19. *Publications:* numerous contribs to med. and scientific literature on forensic toxicology and related subjects. *Recreations:* family, computers, books. *Address:* 37 Marlborough Road, Sheffield S10 1DA. *T:* (0114) 2669769. *Club:* Athenæum.

**FORREST, Prof. Sir (Andrew) Patrick (McEwen)**, Kt 1986; Regius Professor of Clinical Surgery, University of Edinburgh, 1970–88, now Professor Emeritus; *b* 25 March 1923; *s* of Rev. Andrew James Forrest, BD, and Isabella Pearson; *m* 1955, Margaret Beryl Hall (*d* 1961); one *s* one *d*; *m* 1964, Margaret Anne Steward; one *d*. *Educ:* Dundee High Sch.; Univ. of St Andrews. BSc 1942; MB, ChB 1945; ChM hons, University Gold Medal, 1954; MD hons, Rutherford Gold Medal, 1958; FRCSE 1950; FRCS 1952; FRCSGlas 1962; FRSE 1976; FRSB (FIBiol 1986); FRCPE 1999. Surg.-Lt RNVR, 1946–48. Mayo Foundation Fellow, 1952–53; Lectr and Sen. Lectr, Univ. of Glasgow, 1955–62; Prof. of Surgery, Welsh Nat. Sch. of Medicine, 1962–70. Hon. Consultant Surgeon: Royal Inf. of Edinburgh, until 1988; Royal Prince Alfred Hosp., Sydney; Civilian Consultant to RN, 1977–88. Chief Scientist (pt-time), SHHD, 1981–87. McIlrath Vis. Prof., Royal Prince Alfred Hosp., Sydney, 1969; Nimmo Vis. Prof., Royal Adelaide Hosp., 1973; McLauchlin-Gallie Prof., RCP of Canada, 1974; numerous other visiting professorships; Vis. Scientist, Nat. Cancer Inst., 1989–90; Associate Dean, Internat. Med. Coll., Kuala Lumpur, 1993–96. Eponymous lectures include: Lister Meml, Canadian Med. Assoc., 1970; Inaugural Bruce Wellesley Hosp., Toronto, 1970; Inaugural Peter Lowe, RCP Glas., 1980. Member: Medical sub-cttee, UGC, 1967–76; MRC, 1974–79; Scientific Adv. Cttee, Cancer Res. Campaign, 1974–83; ABRC, 1982–85. Asst Editor and Editor, Scottish Med. Jl, 1957–61; Hon. Secretary: Scottish Soc. for Experimental Medicine, 1959–62; Surgical Research Soc., 1963–66, Pres., 1974–76; Chairman: British Breast Gp, 1974–77; Working Gp on Breast Cancer Screening (reported, 1986); Scottish Cancer Foundn, 1998–2003. Member Council: Assoc. of Surgeons of GB and Ireland, 1971–74 (Pres., 1988–89); RCSE, 1976–84, 1986–89; Member: Internat. Surgical Gp, 1963–; James IV Assoc. of Surgeons Inc., 1981–; Scottish Hosp. Endowments Res. Trust, 1990–94. Mem., Kirk Session, St Giles' Cathedral, 1979–. Hon. Fellow, Amer. Surgical Assoc., 1981; Hon. FACS 1978; Hon. FRACS 1987; Hon. FRCR 1988; Hon. FRCSCan 1989; Hon. FFPH (Hon. FFPHM 2001). Hon. DSc: Wales, 1981; Chinese Univ. of Hong Kong, 1986; Hon. LLD Dundee, 1986; Hon. MD Internat. Medical Univ., 2007. Lister Medal, RCS, 1987; Gold Medal, Netherlands Surgical Assoc., 1988; Gimbernat Prize, Catalan Soc. of Surg., 1996; Breast Cancer Award, European Inst. of Oncology, 2000. *Publications:* (ed jtly) Prognostic Factors in Breast Cancer, 1968; (jtly) Principles and Practice of Surgery, 1985; Breast Cancer: the decision to screen, 1991; various papers in surgical jls, mainly on gastro-intestinal disease and breast cancer. *Address:* 19 St Thomas Road, Edinburgh EH9 2LR. *T:* (0131) 667 3203.

**FORREST, Robert;** *see* Forrest, A. R. W.

**FORREST, Rev. Canon Robin Whyte;** Dean of Moray, Ross and Caithness, 1992–98; Canon of St Andrew's Cathedral, Inverness, 1986–98, now Hon. Canon; Rector of St John's, Forres, 1979–98; *b* 1933. *Educ:* Edinburgh Theol Coll., 1958. Ordained deacon, 1961, priest, 1962; Asst Curate, St Mary, Glasgow, 1961–66; Rector: Renfrew, 1966–70; Motherwell, 1970–79, with Wishaw, 1975–79; St Columba's, Nairn, 1979–92. Synod Clerk, Moray, 1991–92. *Address:* Landeck, Cummingston, Elgin, Moray IV30 5XY. *T:* (01343) 835539.

**FORRESTER, David Michael;** education consultant; Director, Further Education and Youth Training, Department for Education and Employment, 1995–2001; *b* 22 June 1944; *s* of late Reginald Grant Forrester and Minnie Forrester (*née* Chaytow); *m* 1st, 1978, Diana Douglas (marr. diss. 1983); 2nd, 1993, Helen Mary Williams, *qv*; one *s* one *d*. *Educ:* St Paul's Sch.; King's Coll., Cambridge (BA Hons 1st Cl. 1966, MA); Kennedy Sch. of Govt, Harvard Univ. (an inaugural Kennedy Scholar, 1966–67). DES, 1967; Private Sec. to Parly Under Sec., 1971–72; Principal, DES, 1972–76; HM Treasury, 1976–78; Asst Sec., DES, 1979–85; DTI, 1985–87; Under Sec., DES, subseq. DFE, then DFEE, 1988; Hd of Further Educn Br., 1994–95. FRSA 1999. *Recreations:* cricket, squash, music, esp. opera, mountain walking. *Address:* 340 Liverpool Road, N7 8PZ. *T:* (020) 7607 1492. *E:* davidforrester@btinternet.com. *Club:* Pretenders'.

**FORRESTER, His Honour Giles Charles Fielding;** a Circuit Judge, 1986–2011; a Senior Circuit Judge and Permanent Judge at the Central Criminal Court, 1995–2011; *b* 18 Dec. 1939; *s* of late Basil Thomas Charles Forrester and Diana Florence Forrester (*née* Sandeman); *m* 1966, Georgina Elizabeth Garnett; one *s* one *d*. *Educ:* Rugby School; Grenoble Univ.; Trinity College, Oxford (MA Jurisp.). Account Exec., Pritchard Wood and Partners, 1962–66. Called to the Bar, Inner Temple, 1966, Bencher, 2008; practised, SE Circuit, 1966–86; Asst Recorder, 1981–86; Recorder of the Crown Court, 1986. Judicial Mem., Parole Bd, 2002–07. Mem., HAC Infantry Bn, 1963–67, Veteran Mem., 1994–; Pres., HAC RFC, 1994–98. Mem. Council, Magistrates' Assoc., 1998–2008 (Pres., SW London Br., 1991–2007). FRGS 2004. Freeman, City of London, 1997; Freedom, Weavers' Co., 1998 (Mem., Ct of Assts, 2008–18; Upper Bailiff, 2011–12). *Recreations:* a wide variety, mainly sporting. *Address:* 21 Tideswell Road, Putney, SW15 6LJ. *T:* (020) 8789 7386. *E:* gcf.forrester@gmail.com. *Clubs:* Boodle's, Roehampton; Royal Western Yacht; St Enodoc Golf; New Zealand Golf (Weybridge).

**FORRESTER, Helen Mary;** *see* Williams, Helen M.

**FORRESTER, Ian Stewart;** QC (Scot.) 1988; Judge, General Court of European Union, since 2015; *b* 13 Jan. 1945; *s* of late Alexander Roxburgh Forrester and Elizabeth Richardson Forrester (*née* Stewart); *m* 1981, Sandra Anne Therese Keegan, Louisiana lawyer; two *s*. *Educ:* Kelvinside Acad., Glasgow; Univ. of Glasgow (MA 1965; LLB 1967); Tulane Univ. of Louisiana (MCL 1969). Mem., British Univs debating team, 1966; Commonwealth expedn to India, 1967. Admitted Faculty of Advocates, Scots Bar, 1972; admitted Bar of State of NY, following order of NY Court of Appeals, 1977; admitted English Bar, Middle Temple, 1996, Bencher, 2012. With Maclay, Murray & Spens, 1968–69; Davis Polk & Wardwell, 1969–72; Cleary Gottlieb Steen & Hamilton, 1972–81; estab. ind. chambers, Brussels, 1981; co-founder, Forrester & Norall, 1981 (Forrester Norall & Sutton, 1989; White & Case, 1998–2015), practising before European Commn and Courts. Chm., British Conservative Assoc., Belgium, 1982–86. Vis. Prof., European Law, Univ. of Glasgow, 1991–2010, now Hon. Prof. Mem., Eur. Adv. Bd, 1992–2006, Dean's Adv. Bd, Law Sch., 2006–, Tulane Univ. Pres., Franco-British Lawyers Soc., 2018–. Trustee: EU Baroque Orch., 2005–; Les Orgues de l'Ourthe, La Roche, Belgium, 2013–. Elder, St Andrew's Church of Scotland, Brussels, 1997–. Hon. LLD Glasgow, 2009. *Publications:* numerous articles on EEC customs, dumping and trade law, competition law, German civil and commercial codes. *Recreations:* politics, wine, cooking, tree planting, preaching, sailing. *Address:* General Court of European Union, L–2925 Luxembourg; Advocates' Library, Parliament House, Edinburgh EH1 1RF. *Clubs:* Athenæum; International Château Ste-Anne (Brussels); Royal Yacht Club of Belgium.

**FORRESTER, James William;** Executive Director, Manchester International Festival, 2012–16; *b* 25 Feb. 1952; *s* of Dr Sam Forrester and Dr Marion Forrester; *m* 1988, Caroline Slinger (*d* 2008); one *s* one *d*. *Educ:* Univ. of Durham (BA Hons English Lit. and Lang. 1973); Univ. of Leicester (Mus Dip.). Apprentice boatbuilder, 1974–76; journeyman boatbuilder, 1976–84; Ship and Boat Conservator, 1984–88, Public Progs Officer, 1988–96, Merseyside Maritime Mus.; Gen. Manager, NMGM Trading Co., 1996–2001; Dir, Imperial War Mus. North, 2002–12. Chairman: N Wales and Borders Partnership Bd, Canal and River Trust, 2012–14; Bd of Trustees, Greater Manchester Arts Centre, 2012–15; Bd, Super Slow Way, 2015–18. *Recreations:* travel, boats, life's unfolding tapestry. *E:* jim.forrester@btinternet.com.

**FORRESTER, Prof. John Vincent,** MD; FRCSE, FRCOphth, FRCSGlas, FRCPE, FMedSci, FRSE, FRSB; Cockburn Professor of Ophthalmology, University of Aberdeen, 1984–2011, now Emeritus; Professor of Ocular Immunology, University of Western Australia, since 2012; *b* 11 Sept. 1946; *m* Anne Gray; two *s* two *d*. *Educ:* St Aloysius Coll., Glasgow; Glasgow Univ. (MD Hons 1980). FRCSE 1975; FRCSGlas 1985; FRCOphth 1990; FRCPE 1996. FRSB (FIBiol 2009). Various hosp. appts, Glasgow, 1971–78; MRC Travelling Fellow, Columbia Univ., NY, 1976–77; Consultant Ophthalmologist, Southern Gen. Hosp., Glasgow, 1979–83. Spinoza Prof., Univ. of Amsterdam, 1997; Adjunct Prof., Univ. of Western Australia, 2010; Visiting Professor: Univ. of Pittsburgh, 2010; Univ. of Kentucky, 2012. Master, Oxford Ophthalmol Congress, 2000–02. Pres., European Assoc. of Eye and Vision Res., 2001–02. Ian Constable Lect., 2013. Ed., British Jl Ophthalmol., 1992–2000. FMedSci 1998; FRSE 2003; Fellow, Assoc. for Res. in Vision and Ophthalmol., 2009. McKenzie Medal, 2006; Doyne Medal, 2007; Mooney Medal, 2010; Bowman Medal, 2012; Donders Medal, 2012; Mildred Wiesenfeld Award, 2012. *Publications:* (jtly) The Eye, 4th edn, 2015. *Recreation:* family. *Address:* Division of Applied Medicine, Institute of Medical Sciences, Foresterhill, Aberdeen AB25 2ZD. *T:* (01224) 437505.

**FORRESTER, Lisa;** *see* Appignanesi, L.

**FORRESTER-PATON, His Honour Douglas Shaw;** QC 1965; a Circuit Judge (formerly a Judge of County Courts), 1970–86; *b* 22 June 1921; 3rd *s* of late Alexander Forrester-Paton, JP; *m* 1948, Agnete (*d* 2015), *d* of Holger Tuxen; one *s* two *d*. *Educ:* Gresham's Sch., Holt; Queen's Coll., Oxford (BA). Called to Bar, Middle Temple, 1947; North East Circuit. Served RAF, 1941–45. Recorder: Middlesbrough, 1963–68; Teesside, 1968–70. *Address:* 5 King's Bench Walk, Temple, EC4Y 7DB.

**FORSDICK, Prof. Charles Richard Allerton,** PhD; James Barrow Professor of French, University of Liverpool, since 2001; *b* West Runton, 26 June 1969; *s* of late Michael Edward Forsdick and of Brenda Forsdick (*née* Whitehead, now Townsend); *m* 1994, Rev. Dr Christine Margaret Dutton; two *s* one *d*. *Educ:* Norwich Sch.; New Coll., Oxford (BA 1992); Lancaster Univ. (PhD 1995). Lectr in French, Univ. of Glasgow, 1995–2001. Dir, Liverpool Univ. Press., 2017–. British Acad. Sen. Res. Fellow, 2004–05; AHRC Theme Leadership Fellow, 2012–. Chm., Modern Langs and Linguistics Sub-panel, REF2021, 2018–. Foundn Mem. Council, Univ. of Chester, 2017–. Pres., Soc. for French Studies, 2012–14. MAE 2011. Philip Leverhulme Prize, Leverhulme Trust, 2005. *Publications:* Victor Segalen and the Aesthetics of Diversity, 2000; Travel in 20th-Century French and Francophone Cultures, 2005; Oasis Interdites, 2008; Toussaint Louverture: a Black Jacobin in the age of revolutions, 2017. *Recreations:* travel, languages, ceramics, history of Norfolk. *Address:* Department of Modern Languages and Cultures: French, University of Liverpool, Liverpool L69 7ZR. *T:* (0151) 794 2740. *E:* craf@liv.ac.uk.

**FORSDICK, David John;** QC 2014; *b* Woking, Surrey, 11 Jan. 1969; *s* of Brian and Joan Forsdick; *m* 1999, Natalie O'Shea; one *s* one *d*. *Educ:* Heathside Co. Sch.; Strodes VIth Form Coll.; Warwick Univ. (BA Hons Modern Eur. Hist.). Called to the Bar: Gray's Inn, 1993; NI, 2012; in practice as barrister, specialising in envmtl, planning and public law, 1994–; Mem., A Panel of Jun. Counsel to the Crown, 2005–. Chm. Govs, St Luke's and Moreland Fedn (formerly Primary Sch.), Islington, 2001–. *Recreations:* ski-ing, walking, running. *Address:* Landmark Chambers, 180 Fleet Street, EC4A 2HG. *T:* (020) 7430 1221.

**FORSHAW, Christian;** saxophonist and composer; Professor of Saxophone, Guildhall School of Music and Drama, since 2002; *b* Harrogate, 22 May 1972; *s* of Brian Forshaw and Margaret Forshaw; *m* 2006, Sarah Allen; two *s*. *Educ:* Guildhall Sch. of Music and Drama (BMus Hons 1995). Founder, Sanctuary Ensemble (saxophone, voice, organ, percussion), 1996. Recordings incl. Sanctuary, 2004, Songs of Solace, 2012. *Recreations:* cooking, walking, cycling, family. *E:* mail@christianforshaw.com.

**FORSHAW, Sarah Anne;** QC 2008; *b* Gloucester, 2 July 1964; *d* of late Brig. Peter Forshaw, CBE and Helen Forshaw (*née* Cliff); *m* 1991 (marr. diss. 2002); two *s*. *Educ:* King's Coll., Taunton; King's Coll. London (LLB). Called to the Bar, Middle Temple, 1987, Bencher, 2013; in practice as barrister specialising in crime; Co-Hd, 5 King's Bench Walk Chambers, 2009–; Leader, S Eastern Circuit, 2012–14. *Address:* 5 King's Bench Walk, Temple, EC4Y 7DN. *T:* (020) 7353 5638.

**FORSTER, Prof. Anthony William,** DPhil; Vice-Chancellor, University of Essex, since 2012; *b* Chiseldon, Wilts, 19 May 1964; *s* of William A. Forster and Patricia Forster; *m* 1994, Victoria. *Educ:* Denstone Coll., Uttoxeter; Univ. of Hull (BA 1st Cl. Hons Politics 1985); St Antony's Coll., Oxford (MPhil Eur. Politics and Society 1993); St Hugh's Coll., Oxford (DPhil 1996); Univ. of Nottingham (Postgrad. Cert. Acad. Practice 1999). Army Officer, RCT, 1985–91. Stipendiary Lectr, St Hilda's Coll., Oxford, 1995–96; Lectr, Sch. of Politics, Univ. of Nottingham, 1996–2000; Dir of Res. and Sen. Lectr, 2000–02, Reader, 2002, in Eur. Foreign and Security Policy, Defence Studies Dept, KCL; University of Bristol: Dir, Governance Res. Centre, 2002–06; Prof. of Politics, 2002–04; Hd, Dept of Politics, 2004–06; Durham University: Exec. Dean (Social Scis and Health), 2006–08; Prof. of Politics, 2006–08; Pro-Vice-Chancellor (Educn), 2008–11; Hon. Prof. of Politics, 2008–12; Dep. Vice-Chancellor, 2011–12. FHEA 2007; FAcSS (AcSS 2009); Fellow, Leadership Foundn for HE, 2014. *Publications:* Britain and the Maastricht Negotiations, 1999; (with A. Blair) The Making of Britain's European Foreign Policy, 2001; Euroscepticism in Contemporary British politics: opposition to Europe in the British Conservative and Labour Parties since 1945, 2002; (with A. Cottey) Reshaping Defence Diplomacy: new roles for military cooperation and assistance, 2004; Armed Forces and Society in Europe, 2006; (with T. Edmunds) Out of Step: the case for change in British armed forces, 2007; edited with T. Edmunds and A. Cottey: Democratic Control of the Military in Postcommunist Europe, 2001; The Challenge of Military Reform in Postcommunist Europe: building professional armed forces, 2002; Soldiers and Societies in Postcommunist Europe, Legitimacy and Change, 2003; Civil-Military Relations in Postcommunist Europe, 2006. *Recreations:* Italian Greyhounds, twentieth century architecture. *Address:* University of Essex, Wivenhoe Park, Colchester, Essex CO4 3SQ. *T:* (01206) 872000, *Fax:* (01206) 869493. *E:* vc@essex.ac.uk. *Club:* Athenæum.

**FORSTER, Dr Eliot Richard;** Chief Executive Officer, F-Star Ltd, since 2018; Chairman, MedCity Ltd, since 2014; *b* Sunderland, 27 Feb. 1966; *s* of Robert Eliot Forster and Pauline Forster; *m* 1992, Gillian Margaret Strauss; two *s* one *d*. *Educ:* St Aidan's RC Sch.,

Sunderland; Univ. of Liverpool (BSc Hons; PhD 1991); Henley Management Coll. (MBA). Clin. Proj. Manager, Glaxo, then Glaxo Wellcome, 1992–96; Pfizer: Clin. Proj. Manager, 1996–98; Develt Team Leader, 1998–2002; Hd, EU Drug Develt, 2002–07; Chief Executive Officer: Solace Pharmaceuticals, Inc., 2007–10; Creabilis SA, 2010–15; Immunocore Ltd, 2015–18. Chm., Bd of Dirs, Avacta plc, 2018–; non-executive Director: Oxford BioTherapeutics, 2006–14; Spinifex Pty Ltd, 2010–14; Persica Pharmaceuticals Ltd, 2011–14. Member: Bd, Office for Strategic Co-ordination Health Res., 2017–; Nat. Genomic Bd, 2018–. Visiting Professor: Univ. of Liverpool, 2017–; Univ. of Pavia, Italy, 2018–. Mem. Council, Univ. of Kent, 2007–13. Trustee, Poet in the City, 2010–15. FRSocMed 2004; FRSB 2013; FRSA 2011. *Publications:* 18 scientific papers. *Recreations:* cricket (village), jogging, walking, field sports, poetry. *Address:* Immunocore Ltd, 101 Park Drive, Milton Park, Abingdon, Oxon OX14 4RY. *T:* (01235) 438600. *E:* eliot.r.forster@gmail.com.

**FORSTER, Jilly, (Mrs R. A. Lamond);** Founder and Chair, Forster Communications (formerly The Forster Co.), 1996–2017; *b* 8 Dec. 1955; *d* of Dr Matthew Forster and Dr Margaret Forster; *m* 1979, Robert Andrew Lamond; two *s*. *Educ:* N London Collegiate Sch.; The Priory, Lewes. Founding Dir, Munro & Forster, 1984–89; Dir, Body Shop Internat. plc, 1989–96; Dir, Big Issue, 1991–93. Trustee: Children on the Edge, 2004–09; Forgiveness Project, 2004–09; Royal Parks Foundn, 2004–08; Jamie Oliver Foundn, 2010–16. *Recreations:* semiology, social enterprise, land art. *Address:* Forster Communications, The Loom, 14 Gower's Walk, E1 8PY. *T:* (020) 7403 2230. *E:* jilly@forster.co.uk.

**FORSTER, Rt Rev. Peter Robert;** Bishop of Chester, 1996–2019; *b* 16 March 1950; *s* of Thomas and Edna Forster; *m* 1978, Elisabeth Anne Stevenson; two *s* two *d*. *Educ:* Merton Coll., Oxford (MA 1973); Edinburgh Univ. (BD 1977; PhD 1985); Edinburgh Theol Coll. Ordained deacon, 1980, priest, 1981; Asst Curate, St Matthew and St James, Mossley Hill, Liverpool, 1980–82; Senior Tutor, St John's Coll., Durham, 1983–91; Vicar, Beverley Minster and Asst Curate, Routh, 1991–96. Introduced to H of L, 2001. *Recreations:* woodcrafts, family.

**FORSTER, Prof. Piers Maxwell de Ferranti,** PhD; Professor of Physical Climate Change, University of Leeds, since 2008; *b* Oxford, 1968; *s* of Roger and Trödissita Forster; *m* 2000, Stella; one *d*. *Educ:* Monkton Combe Sch., Bath; Imperial Coll. London (BSc Hons 1990; ARCS); Univ. of Reading (PhD Meteorol. 1994). NERC Advanced Res. Fellow, 2000–05; Res. Fellow, Univ. of Colorado, 2002; Reader, Univ. of Leeds, 2005–08. Royal Soc. Wolfson Merit Award Holder, 2011–. Mem., Expert Panel, Airport Commn, 2013–. Climate Scientist, Cttee on Climate Change, 2018–. Trustee and Dir, United Bank of Carbon Charity, 2009–. *Publications:* contrib. Intergovtl Panel for Climate Change Assessment Reports and peer-reviewed papers on aspects of climate change. *Recreations:* ski touring, hill walking, tennis, singing in the sun, marmalade, sheep farming. *Address:* School of Earth and Environment, University of Leeds, Leeds LS2 9JT. *T:* (0113) 343 6476. *E:* p.m.forster@leeds.ac.uk.

**FORSYTH,** family name of **Baron Forsyth of Drumlean**.

**FORSYTH OF DRUMLEAN,** Baron *cr* 1999 (Life Peer), of Drumlean in Stirling; **Michael Bruce Forsyth,** Kt 1997; PC 1995; *b* 16 Oct. 1954; *s* of John T. Forsyth and Mary Watson; *m* 1977, Susan Jane Clough; one *s* two *d*. *Educ:* Arbroath High School; St Andrews University (MA). Pres., St Andrews Univ. Cons. Assoc., 1972–75; Nat. Chm., Fedn of Cons. Students, 1976–77. Dir, Flemings, 1997–99; Vice-Chm., Investment Banking Europe, JP Morgan, 1999–2001; Dep. Chm., JP Morgan UK, 2002–05; Sen. Advr, 2006–07; Sen. Man. Dir, 2007–, Evercore Partners Ltd; non-executive Director: J & J Denholm Ltd, 2005–; Denholm Logistics Ltd, 2011–; Hyperion Insce Gp, 2012–15 (Chm., 2014–15); Secure Trust Bank, 2014– (Chm., 2015–). MP (C) Stirling, 1983–97; contested (C) same seat, 1997. PPS to Sec. of State for Foreign and Commonwealth Affairs, 1986–87; Parly Under-Sec. of State, 1987–90, Minister of State, 1990–92, Scottish Office; Minister of State: Dept of Employment, 1992–94; Home Office, 1994–95; Sec. of State for Scotland and Lord Keeper of the Great Seal of Scotland, 1995–97. Chm., Econ. Affairs Cttee, H of L, 2017–; Member: Select Cttee on Economic Affairs, H of L, 2009–13, 2015–; Select Cttee on Soft Power, H of L, 2013–14; Jt Cttee on Nat. Security Strategy, 2014–15. Chm., Scottish Cons. Party, 1989–90. Mem., Westminster City Council, 1978–83. Mem. Develt Bd, Nat. Portrait Gall., 1999–2003. Dir, Centre for Policy Studies, 2006–13. President: Royal Highland and Agricl Soc. of Scotland, 2015–16; Steamboat Assoc., 2017–. Patron: Children in Need Inst. UK, 2008–13. *Recreations:* photography, gardening, fly-fishing, mountaineering, ski-ing, amateur astronomy. *Address:* House of Lords, SW1A 0PW.

**FORSYTH OF THAT ILK, Alistair Charles William;** JP; FSCA, FSAScot; FInstPet; Baron of Ethie; Chief of the Name and Clan of Forsyth; *b* 7 Dec. 1929; *s* of Charles Forsyth of Strathendry, FCA, and Ella Millicent Hopkins; *m* 1958, Ann, OStJ, *d* of Col P. A. Hughes, IA; four *s*. *Educ:* St Paul's Sch.; Queen Mary Coll., London. FInstPet 1973; FSCA 1976; FSAScot 1979. National Service, 2nd Lieut The Queen's Bays, 1948–50; Lieut The Parachute Regt, TA, 1950–54. Chm., Hargreaves Reiss & Quinn Ltd, 1981–99. Mem., Angus DC, 1988–92. Mem., Standing Council of Scottish Chiefs, 1978–. Merchant and Burgess, City of Edinburgh, 1974; Freeman, City of London, 1993; Liveryman, Scriveners' Co., 1993–. CStJ 1982 (OStJ 1974). JP NSW, 1965; JP Angus, 1987. KHS 1992. *Heir: s* Alistair James Menteith Forsyth, yr of that Ilk, barrister and advocate, *b* 21 Dec. 1960. *Address:* Monteleone, Condom-en-Armagnac 32100, France.

**FORSYTH, Allegra Elizabeth Jane;** *see* Stratton, A. E. J.

**FORSYTH, Bill;** film director and script writer; *b* Glasgow, 1947; one *s* one *d*. *Educ:* National Film Sch. *Films directed:* That Sinking Feeling, 1980; Gregory's Girl, 1981; Local Hero, 1983 (adapted for stage, 2019); Comfort and Joy, 1984; Housekeeping, 1988; Breaking In, 1990; Being Human, 1993; Gregory's Two Girls, 1999. TV film, Andrina, 1981. BAFTA Award: best screenplay, 1982; best dir, 1983. Hon. DLitt Glasgow, 1984; DUniv Stirling, 1989. *Address:* c/o United Agents, 12–26 Lexington Street, W1F 0LE.

**FORSYTH, Frederick,** CBE 1997; author; *b* 25 Aug. 1938; *m* 1st, 1973, Carole Cunningham; two *s*; 2nd, 1994, Sandy Molloy. *Educ:* Tonbridge Sch. RAF, 1956–58. Reporter, Eastern Daily Press, Norfolk, 1958–61; joined Reuters, 1961: Reporter, Paris, 1962–63; Chief of Bureau, E Berlin, 1963–64; joined BBC, 1965; radio and TV reporter, 1965–66; Asst Diplomatic Correspondent, BBC TV, 1967–68; freelance journalist, Nigeria and Biafra, 1968–69. *Publications: non fiction:* The Biafra Story, 1969, 2nd edn 1977; The Outsider: my life in intrigue (autobiog.), 2015; *fiction:* The Day of the Jackal, 1971 (filmed, 1973); The Odessa File, 1972 (filmed, 1975); The Dogs of War, 1974 (filmed, 1981); The Shepherd, 1975; The Devil's Alternative, 1979; No Comebacks (short stories), 1982; Emeka, 1982; The Fourth Protocol, 1984 (filmed, 1987); The Negotiator, 1988; The Deceiver, 1991; (ed) Great Flying Stories, 1991; The Fist of God, 1993; Icon, 1996; The Phantom of Manhattan, 1999; The Veteran and Other Stories, 2001; Avenger, 2003; The Afghan, 2006; The Cobra, 2010; The Kill List, 2013; The Outsider, 2015; The Fox, 2018. *Address:* c/o Transworld, 62/63 Uxbridge Road, W5 5SA.

**FORSYTH, Justin;** *see* Forsyth, R. J. A.

**FORSYTH, Prof. Murray Greensmith,** FRHistS; Professor of Politics, University of Leicester, 1990–94, now Emeritus; *b* 30 Oct. 1936; *s* of Maj. Henry Russell Forsyth and Marie Elaine Forsyth; *m* 1964, Marie Denise Edelin de la Praudière; one *s* two *d*. *Educ:* Wellington Coll.; Balliol Coll., Oxford (BA Mod. Hist. 1959; MA 1964); College of Europe, Bruges. FRHistS 1991. Research Officer, Political and Econ. Planning, London, 1960–64; University of Leicester: Lectr in Politics, 1964–70; Reader in Internat. Politics, 1971–90; Dir, Centre for Federal Studies, 1988–94; Prof. of Govt and Pol Sci., Hong Kong Baptist Univ., 1995–97. British Acad. Wolfson Fellow, Paris, 1977; Bradlow Fellow, S African Inst. of Internat. Affairs, 1983; Vis. Prof., Coll. of Europe, Bruges, 1993–94; Robert Schuman Vis. Prof., Fudan Univ., Shanghai, 1998. Pres., European Consortium for Regl and Federal Studies, 1993–94. *Publications:* The Parliament of the European Communities, 1964; (jtly) Economic Planning and Policies in Britain, France and Germany, 1968; (ed jtly) The Theory of International Relations, 1970; Unions of States: the theory and practice of confederation, 1981; Reason and Revolution: the political theory of the Abbé Sieyes, 1987; (ed jtly) The Political Classics: Plato to Rousseau, 1988; (ed) Federalism and Nationalism, 1989; (trans.) The Spirit of the Revolution of 1789, 1989; (ed jtly) The Political Classics: Hamilton to Mill, 1993, Green to Dworkin, 1996. *Recreations:* collecting prints and watercolours, browsing in second-hand bookshops. *Address:* Blackmore House, Blackmore Park Road, Malvern, Worcs WR14 3LF. *T:* (01684) 560901.

**FORSYTH, Rt Rev. Robert Charles;** Bishop of South Sydney and an Assistant Bishop, Diocese of Sydney, 2000–15; *b* 8 June 1949; *m* 1970, Margaret Diane Shelley; two *s* two *d*. *Educ:* Meadowbank Boys' High Sch.; Sydney Univ.; Moore Coll. Assistant Minister: Glenbrook, 1976–77; Holy Trinity, Adelaide, 1978–83; Rector, St Barnabas', Broadway and Chaplain, Sydney Univ., 1983–2000. Sydney Gen. Synod Rep., 1990– (Mem., Strategic Issues Adv. Panel, 1999–2001; Mem., Standing Cttee, 2000–); Member: Sydney Standing Cttee, 1990–2015; Archbishop's Liturgical Panel, 1993–2015; St Andrew's Cathedral Chapter, 1993–2010; Sydney Doctrine Commn, 1994–; Archbishop's Selection Panel, 1996–2015 (Examining Chaplain, 1991–94); Episcopal Standards Commn, Anglican Church of Australia, 2017–. Sydney Anglican Cursillo Spiritual Dir, 1995–97. Chairman: EU Graduates Fund, 1995–; Langham Partnership Australia, 2000–07. Sen. Fellow, Centre for Ind. Studies, 2017–. Columnist, Southern Cross newspaper, 1989–2000; co-author and developer, LifeWorks evangelism prog. Deck Hand, James Craig, Sydney Heritage Fleet, 2016–. *Club:* Australian (Sydney).

**FORSYTH, (Robert) Justin (Alexander);** Director, North End Strategy, since 2018; *b* Paisley, 17 June 1965; *s* of Robert Forsyth and Maureen Forsyth (*née* Irvine); *m* 2012, Lisa Stevens; one *s*. *Educ:* Oxford Poly. (BA Hons Hist. and Pols 1988). Oxfam: Advr on Africa, 1989–95; Internat. Advocacy Dir, Washington, DC, 1995–99; Policy Dir, 1999–2002; Dep. Dir (Campaigns and Policy), 2003–05; Special Advr to the Prime Minister, 2005–08; Dir of Campaigns and Strategic Communications for the Prime Minister, 2008–10; Chief Exec., Save the Children UK, 2010–16; Dep. Exec. Dir, UNICEF UK, and Asst Sec. Gen., UN, 2016–18. *Recreations:* tennis, reading, African history and politics.

**FORSYTHE, John Leslie Robert,** FRCS, FRCSEd, FRCPEd; Consultant Transplant Surgeon, Royal Infirmary of Edinburgh, since 1995; Honorary Professor in Surgery, School of Clinical Sciences and Community Health, University of Edinburgh, since 2011 (Reader in Surgery, 2006–11); Medical Director, Organ Donation and Transplantation, NHS Blood and Transplant, since 2016; *b* 27 Feb. 1958; *s* of Rev. Canon John Leslie Forsythe and Margaret Forsythe; *m* 1st, 1982, Jo-ann E. G. Harvey (marr. diss. 2007); one *s* two *d*; 2nd, 2008, Lorna P. Marson. *Educ:* Univ. of Newcastle upon Tyne (MB BS 1981; MD 1991). FRCSEd 1986; FRCS 2001; FRCPEd 2014. Surgical trng, Newcastle upon Tyne; Consultant Transplant Surgeon and Hon. Sen. Lectr, Royal Victoria Infirmary, Newcastle upon Tyne, 1991–95. Specialist Advr to CMO, Scotland, 2000–07; Lead Clinician for Organ Donation and Transplantation Scotland, 2008–16. Chairman: Scottish Transplant Gp, 2001–; Kidney Pancreas Adv. Gp, UK Transplant SHA, 2002–06 (Mem., 1996–2001); Adv. Cttee on Safety of Blood, Tissues and Organs, DoH, 2007–15. Member: Bd, NHS Quality Improvements Scotland, 2003–08; Bd, NHS Blood and Transplant, 2006–14. Pres., British Transplantation Soc., 2005–07 (Vice-Pres., 2003–05); Gen. Sec., 2009–13, Pres., 2013–15, Eur. Soc. of Transplantation. FEBS 2009. *Publications:* A Companion to Specialist Surgical Practice, Vol. VII, 1997, 5th edn 2013; Principles and Practice in Surgery, 2002, 6th edn 2012; Abdominal Organ Retrieval and Transplantation Bench Surgery, 2013; numerous reviewed contribs to learned jls. *Address:* Transplant Unit, Royal Infirmary of Edinburgh, 51 Little France Crescent, Old Dalkeith Road, Edinburgh EH16 4SA. *T:* (0131) 242 1715, *Fax:* (0131) 242 1739. *E:* john.forsythe@nhslothian.scot.nhs.uk.

**FORSYTHE, Dr (John) Malcolm;** Chairman, South West Kent Primary Care Trust (formerly Tunbridge Wells Primary Care Group), 1998–2004; *b* 11 July 1936; *s* of late Dr John Walter Joseph Forsythe and Dr Charlotte Constance Forsythe (*née* Beatty); *m* 1961, Delia Kathleen Moore (marr. diss. 1984); one *s* three *d*; *m* 1985, Patricia Mary Barnes. *Educ:* Repton Sch., Derby; Guy's Hosp. Med. Sch., London Univ. BSc(Hons), MB, BS, MSc; DObstRCOG, FRCP; FFPH. Area Medical Officer, Kent AHA, 1974–78; SE Thames Regional Health Authority: Dir of Planning, 1985–89; Regl MO, 1978–92; Regl Dir of Public Health and Service Develt, 1989–92; Professorial Fellow in Public Health, Kent Univ., 1992–2001; Sen. Lectr, King's Coll. Sch. of Medicine and Dentistry, 1992–2001. Hon. Consultant, Univ. of Kent Health Services Res. Unit, 1977–92. Vis. Prof., Univ. of N Carolina, Chapel Hill, 1973, 1976, 1993; Adjunct Prof., Univ. of St Georges, Grenada, 1995–; Jack Masur Fellow, Amer. Hosp. Assoc., 1976. Head, UK Deleg., Hospital Cttee, EEC, 1980–85, 1989–90; Consultant, Urwick Orr Ltd; Chm., GMC Wkg Pty on Performance Assessment in Public Health Medicine, 1995–97; Member: Resource Allocation Wkg Pty and Adv. Gp on Resource Allocation, 1975–78; Technical Sub Gp, Review of Resource Allocation Working Party Formula, 1986–87; DHSS Med. Manpower Planning Review, 1986–88; NHS Computer Policy Cttee, 1981–85; Standing Med. Adv. Cttee to Sec. of State, 1982–86; PHLS Bd, 1986–95; Central Council for Postgrad. Med. Educn, 1986–88; Health Services Res. Cttee, MRC, 1988–91; Bd of Governors, UMDS of Guy's and St Thomas', 1982–92; Delegacy, King's Coll. Hosp. Med. and Dental Schs, 1978–95. External Examiner to Univ. of London, 1987–89. Member: Bd of Mgt, Horder Health Care (formerly Horder Centre for Arthritis), Crowborough, 1992–2016 (Chm., 1996–2000; Chm., Remuneration Cttee, 2011–15) (Trustee, 1992–); Tech. Bd, BUPA Ltd, 1992–2007; John Fry Cttee, KCL, 2011– (Treas., 2012–). Trustee, Sick Doctors Trust, 1996–2012. Vice-Pres., Epidemiology Sect., RSM, 2001–04 (Pres., 1998–2000); Mem. Editl Bd, RCP, 1999–2003. Member: Hyde Housing Assoc., 1999–2008; Bd, Chichester Diocesan Housing Assoc., 2001–07; Bd, In Touch, 2006–10. Chm., Ind. Remuneration Panel, Tonbridge & Malling BC, Sevenoaks DC and Tunbridge Wells BC, 2001–07. Mem., Veteran's Assoc., Guy's and St Thomas' NHS Foundn Trust, 2018–. Council of Europe Fellowship, 1975; Silver Core Award, IFIP, 1977; KCL Alumni Award, 2012. *Publications:* (ed jtly) Information Processing of Medical Records, 1969; Proceedings of First World Conference on Medical Informatics, 1975. *Recreations:* ornithology, bridge, wine. *Address:* Buckingham House, 1 Royal Chase, Tunbridge Wells, Kent TN4 8AX. *T:* (01892) 522359. *Club:* Royal Society of Medicine (Hon. Sec., 2006–10, Vice-Chm., 2010–11, Retired Fellows Section).

**FORSYTHE, William;** choreographer; Professor of Dance and Artistic Advisor, Choreographic Institute, Glorya Kaufman School of Dance, University of Southern California, since 2015; *b* NYC, 1949; *m*; two *s* one *d*. *Educ*: Jacksonville Univ., Florida; Joffrey Ballet Sch., NY. Joined Stuttgart Ballet as dancer, 1973, subseq. house choreographer and freelance choreographer; Dir, Frankfurt Ballet, 1984–2004; Artistic Dir, The Forsythe Co., 2005–15. A.D. White Prof.-at-Large, Cornell Univ. 2009–15. *Works choreographed* include: Urlicht, 1976; Gänge, 1983; France/Dance, 1983; Artifact, 1984; Steptext, 1985; Die Befragung des Robert Scott, 1986; In the Middle, Somewhat Elevated, 1988; Impressing the Czar, 1988; Limb's Theorem, 1991; The Loss of Small Detail, 1991; Herman Schmerman, 1992; Eidos: Telos, 1995; The Vertiginous Thrill of Exactitude, 1996; Approximate Sonata, 1996; workwithinwork, 1998; Endless House, 1999; One Flat Thing, reproduced 2000; Kammer/Kammer, 2000; Decreation, 2003; Three Atmospheric Studies, 2005; You made me a monster, 2005; Human Writes, 2005; Heterotopia, 2006; The Defenders, 2007; Yes we can't, 2008; I don't believe in outer space, 2008; The Returns, Theatrical Arsenal II, 2009; Rearray, Sider, 2011; Stellenstellen, Study # 1, Neue Suite, Study # 3, 2012; Blake Works I, 2016; Playlist (Track 1, 2), A Quiet Evening of Dance, 2018; works performed by NYC Ballet, Kirov Ballet, San Francisco Ballet, Nat. Ballet of Canada, Royal Ballet, Royal Ballet of Flanders, Royal Swedish Ballet, etc. Installation art works exhibited at the Louvre, Tate Modern Gall., Whitney Biennale, Venice Biennale, Munich Pinakothek der Moderne, NY MOMA, Hayward Gall., Hamburg Deichtorhallen, Zurich Migros Museum für Gegenwartskunst, Centre Pompidou, Museo d'Arte Contemporanea Roma, 20th Sydney Biennale, etc. *Address*: Forsythe Productions GmbH, Basaltstrasse 58, 60487 Frankfurt am Main, Germany.

**FORTE, Hon. Sir Rocco (John Vincent),** Kt 1995; FCA; Chairman, Rocco Forte Hotels (formerly RF Hotels Ltd), since 1996; *b* 18 Jan. 1945; *s* of Baron Forte; *m* 1986, Aliai, *d* of Prof. Giovanni Ricci, Rome; one *s* two *d*. *Educ*: Downside Coll.; Pembroke Coll., Oxford (MA). Trusthouse Forte, subseq. Forte: Dir of Personnel, 1973–78; Dep. Chief Exec., 1978–82; Jt Chief Exec., 1982–83; Chief Exec., 1983–92; Chm., 1992–96. Pres., BHA. Dir, BTA, 1986–97. *Recreations*: triathlon, golf, country pursuits. *Address*: (office) 70 Jermyn Street, SW1Y 6NY.
*See also Hon. O. Polizzi.*

**FORTESCUE,** family name of **Earl Fortescue.**

**FORTESCUE,** 8th Earl *cr* 1789; **Charles Hugh Richard Fortescue;** Baron Fortescue, 1746; Viscount Ebrington, 1789; *b* 10 May 1951; *s* of 7th Earl and his 1st wife, Penelope Jane (*d* 1959), *d* of Robert Evelyn Henderson; S father, 1993; *m* 1974, Julia, *er d* of Air Commodore J. A. Sowrey; three *d*. *Heir*: cousin John Andrew Francis Fortescue [*b* 27 March 1955; *m* 1990, Phoebe Anne Cecilia, *d* of late Rev. John Eustace Burridge; two *s* one *d*].

**FORTESCUE, Hon. Seymour Henry;** consultant, World Bank, since 2014; *b* 28 May 1942; *s* of 6th Earl Fortescue, MC, TD and late Sybil, *d* of 3rd Viscount Hardinge, CB; *m* 1st, 1966, Julia Mary Blair Pilcher (marr. diss. 1990); one *s* one *d*; 2nd, 1990, Jennifer Ann Simon; one *d*. *Educ*: Eton Coll.; Trinity Coll., Cambridge (MA); London Business Sch. (MSc). With Barclays Bank plc, 1964–91: Local Dir, Luton, 1972–77; Hd, Mktg, 1977–80; Chief Exec., Barclaycard, 1980–85; Dir, UK Personal Sector, 1986–91; Dir, Voluntary Income, ICRF, 1991–96; Chief Executive: HEA, 1996–99; Banking Code Standards Bd, 1999–2006. Chairman: UK Remittances Task Force, 2006–09; Portman Gp, 2009–13; Short-term Lending Compliance Bd, 2013–14. Hon. Treas., LEPRA, 1985–96; Chm., BookPower (formerly Educnl Low-Priced Sponsored Texts), 2001–07. Mem. Council, London Univ., 2006–08; Governor, Oundle Sch., 1999–2004. Mem., Court of Assistants, Grocers' Co., 1987– (Master, 1997–98). *Recreations*: gardening, travel, opera, country activities. *Address*: Canon Bridge House, Madley, Hereford HR2 9JF. *T*: 07785 992453.

**FORTEVIOT,** 4th Baron *cr* 1917, of Dupplin, Perthshire; **John James Evelyn Dewar;** Bt 1907; farmer, landowner; *b* 5 April 1938; *s* of 3rd Baron Forteviot, MBE, and Cynthia Monica Starkie (*d* 1986); S father, 1993; *m* 1963, Lady Elisabeth Waldegrave (*d* 2003), 3rd *d* of 12th Earl Waldegrave, KG, GCVO; one *s* three *d*. *Educ*: Eton. Nat. Service, Black Watch (RHR), 1956–58. John Dewar & Sons Ltd, 1959–62; ADC to Governor General of NZ, 1962–63; John Dewar & Sons, 1963–98. *Recreations*: fishing, shooting, birdwatching, travel. *Heir*: *s* Hon. Alexander John Edward Dewar [*b* 4 March 1971; *m* 1997, Donryn (*née* Clement); two *s* one *d*]. *Club*: Royal Perth Golfing and Country and City.

**FORTEY, Dr Richard Alan,** FRS 1997; FRSL; Research Associate, Natural History Museum, since 2006 (Merit Researcher, 1986–2006); *b* 15 Feb. 1946; *s* of Frank Allen Fortey and Margaret Fortey (*née* Wilshin); *m* 1st, 1968, Bridget Elizabeth Thomas (marr. diss.); one *s*; 2nd, 1977, Jacqueline Francis; one *s* two *d*. *Educ*: Ealing Grammar Sch.; King's Coll., Cambridge (BA, MA; PhD 1971; ScD 1986). Res. Fellow, 1970–73, SSO, 1973–77, BM (Natural Hist.); PSO, Natural Hist. Mus., 1978–86. Howley Vis. Prof., Meml Univ. of Newfoundland, 1977–78; Vis. Prof. of Palaeobiology, Univ. of Oxford, 2000–09; Collier Prof. of Public Understanding of Sci. and Technol., Univ. of Bristol, 2002–03. Presenter, BBC TV series: Survivors, 2012; Fossil Wonderlands, 2014; Nature's Wonderlands: islands of evolution, 2016. Pres., Geol Soc. of London, 2006–08 (Mem., 1972–); Mem., Brit. Mycological Soc., 1980– (Vice-Pres., 2014–). FRSL 2010. Hon. Fellow, BAAS, 2008. Hon. DSc: St Andrews, 2006; Birmingham, 2010; Leicester, 2014; DUniv Open, 2006. Lyell Medal, Geol Soc., 1996; Frink Medal, Zool Soc. of London, 2001; Lewis Thomas Prize, Rockefeller Univ., 2003; Linnean Medal for Zoology, 2006; Michael Faraday Prize, Royal Soc., 2006; Linnean Legacy Award, State Univ. Arizona, 2009; Lapworth Medal, Palaeontol Assoc., 2014; Silver Medal, Zool Soc. London, 2017. *Publications*: Fossils: the key to the past, 1982, 4th edn 2009; The Hidden Landscape, 1993, 2nd edn 2010; Life: an unauthorized biography, 1997; Trilobite!, 2000; The Earth: an intimate history, 2004; Dry Store Room No 1: the secret life of the Natural History Museum, 2008; Survivors: the animals and plants that time has left behind, 2011; The Wood for the Trees: the long view of nature from a small wood, 2016; (as Roderick Masters) The Roderick Masters Book of Money Making Schemes, 1981. *Recreations*: mushrooms and toadstools, East Anglia, conviviality. *Address*: Natural History Museum, South Kensington, Cromwell Road, SW7 5BD. *T*: (020) 7942 5493.

**FORTUNE, Robert Andrew;** QC 2003; *b* 4 July 1953; *s* of Hamish Campbell Fortune and Hazel Phoebe Fortune. *Educ*: Millfield Sch.; London Sch. of Econs (LLB Hons). Called to the Bar, Middle Temple, 1976; barrister, specialising in criminal law. *Publications*: Alaric's Gold, 2014. *Recreations*: travel, reading, archaeology. *T*: 07973 117860. *E*: robert.fortune@btinternet.com.

**FORTY, Prof. Arthur John,** CBE 1991; PhD, DSc; FRSE; FRSA; Principal and Vice-Chancellor, Stirling University, 1986–94; *b* 4 Nov. 1928; *s* of Alfred Louis Forty and Elisabeth Forty; *m* 1950, Alicia Blanche Hart Gough; one *s*. *Educ*: Headlands Grammar Sch.; Bristol Univ. (BSc; PhD 1953; DSc 1967). FRSE 1988, FRSA 1989. Served RAF, 1953–56. Sen. Res. Scientist, Tube Investments Ltd, 1956–58; Lectr, Univ. of Bristol, 1958–64; University of Warwick: Foundn Prof. of Physics, 1964–86; Pro-Vice-Chancellor, 1970–86. Visiting scientist: Gen. Electric Co., USA; Boeing Co.; Nat. Bureau of Standards, Washington, USA. Member: SRC Physics Cttee, 1969–73; SRC Materials Cttee, 1970–73; Computer Bd, 1982–85; University Grants Committee: Mem., 1982–86, Vice-Chm., 1985–86; Chairman: Physical Sciences Sub-cttee, 1985–86; Equipment Sub-cttee, 1985–86; Chairman: Jt ABRC, Computer Bd and UGC Working Party on Future Facilities for Advanced Res. Computing (author, Forty Report), 1985; Management Cttee for Res. Councils' Supercomputer Facility, 1986–88; UFC Cttee for Information Systems (formerly Computer Bd for Univs and Res. Councils), 1988–91; Jt Policy Cttee for Advanced Res. Computing, 1988–94; Cttee of Scottish Univ. Principals, 1990–92; Edinburgh Parallel Computing Centre, 1994–97; Adv. Cttee, Scottish Science Liby, 1995–2001; Member: British Library Bd, 1987–94; Bd of Trustees, Nat. Liby of Scotland, 1995–2001; Academic Adv. Bd, Univ. of the Highlands and Islands, 1999–. Chm., ICIAM 99 Ltd, 1995–96. Hon. Fellow, Edinburgh Univ., 1994. Hon. LLD St Andrew's, 1989; DUniv Stirling, 1995; Hon. DSc Warwick, 2005. *Publications*: papers in Proc. Royal Soc., Phil Magazine and other learned jls. *Recreations*: sailing, gardening, the ancient metallurgy of gold. *Address*: Port Mor, St Fillans, by Crieff, Perthshire PH6 2NF.

**FORWELL, Prof. George Dick,** OBE 1993; PhD; FRCP; Chief Administrative Medical Officer, 1973–93, and Director of Public Health, 1989–93, Greater Glasgow Health Board; *b* 6 July 1928; *s* of Harold C. Forwell and Isabella L. Christie; *m* 1957, Catherine F. C. Cousland; two *d*. *Educ*: George Watson's Coll., Edinburgh; Edinburgh Univ. (MB, ChB 1950; PhD 1955). MRCPE 1957, DIH 1957, DPH 1959, FRCPE 1967, FFCM 1972, FRCPGlas 1974, FRCP 1985. House Officer and Univ. Clin. Asst, Edinburgh Royal Infirm., 1950–52; RAF Inst. of Aviation Med., 1952–54; MRC and RCPE grants, 1954–56; pneumoconiosis field res., 1956–57; Grad. Res. Fellow and Lectr, Edinburgh Univ. Dept of Public Health and Social Med., 1957–60; Asst Dean, Faculty of Med., Edinburgh Univ., 1960–63; Dep. Sen. and Sen. Admin. MO, Eastern Reg. Hosp. Bd, Dundee, 1963–67; PMO, Scottish Home and Health Dept, 1967–73. Vis. Prof., Dept of Public Health, Glasgow Univ., 1990–93; Hon. Prof., Sch. of Biol and Med. Scis, St Andrews Univ., 1993–98. QHP, 1980–83. Mem., GMC, 1984–89. *Publications*: papers on clin. res. and on health planning and services, in med. and other jls. *Recreation*: running. *Address*: 20 Irvine Crescent, St Andrews, Fife KY16 8LG. *Club*: Royal Air Force.

**FORWOOD,** family name of **Baroness Arlington.**

**FORWOOD, Sir Nicholas (James),** Kt 2016; QC 1987; barrister; Judge, General Court of the European Union (formerly Court of First Instance, European Community), 1999–2015; *b* 22 June 1948; *s* of late Lt-Col Harry Forwood and Wendy Forwood. *Educ*: Stowe Sch.; St John's Coll., Cambridge (Open Schol., MA, Pt I Mechanical Scis, Pt II Law). Called to the Bar: Middle Temple, 1970, Bencher, 1998; Ireland, 1981. *Recreations*: ski-ing, golf, walking across Europe, opera. *Club*: Oxford and Cambridge.

**FOSKETT, Hon. Sir David (Robert),** Kt 2007; a Judge of the High Court of Justice, Queen's Bench Division, 2007–19; *b* 19 March 1949; *s* of late Robert Frederick Foskett and Ruth (*née* Waddington); *m* 1975, Angela Bridget Jacobs; two *d*. *Educ*: Warwick Sch.; King's Coll., London (LLB Hons; Pres., Faculty of Laws, 1969–70; Pres., Union Soc., 1970–71; Mem., Delegacy, 1970–72; FKC 2009). FCIArb 1992. Called to the Bar, Gray's Inn, 1972, Bencher, 1999 (Treas. 2018); Mem., Midland Circuit; QC 1991; Asst Recorder, 1992–95; Recorder, 1995–2007; a Dep. High Ct Judge, 1998–2007. Judge in charge, QBD Civil List, 2015–18. Member: Civil Procedure Rule Cttee, 1997–2001; Civil Justice Council, 2012–14; Chm., Law Reform Cttee, Bar Council, 2005–07. President: KCL Assoc., 1997–2000; Old Warwickian Assoc., 2000, 2014; Mem. Council, KCL, 2010–19. *Publications*: The Law and Practice of Compromise, 1980, 8th edn as Foskett on Compromise, 2015; Settlement Under the Civil Procedure Rules, 1999; various articles. *Recreations*: theatre, music, poetry, cricket, golf. *Clubs*: Athenæum; MCC; Woking Golf.

**FOSKETT, Prof. Nicholas Hedley,** PhD; Vice-Chancellor, Keele University, 2010–15; *b* Burslem, Stoke-on-Trent, 12 March 1955; *s* of Eric and Beryl Foskett; *m* 1979, Rosalind Arnold; one *s* one *d*. *Educ*: Wolstanton Co. Grammar Sch., Newcastle-under-Lyme; Keble Coll., Oxford (BA Hons 1977; PGCE 1978; MA 1981); Univ. of Southampton (PhD 1995). Geog. teacher, 1978–86, Hd of Geog., 1984–86, Haywards Heath Coll., W Sussex; Co-ordinator, Schools Prog., Aston Univ., 1987–89; University of Southampton: Lectr in Educn, 1989–95; Sen. Lectr, 1995–2000; Hd of Sch., 2000–05; Dean, Faculty of Law, Arts and Social Scis, 2005–10. Hon. DLitt Keele, 2016. *Publications*: (ed) Managing External Relations in Schools, 1992; (ed with A. R. Cook) Fieldwork, Development and Practice, 1996; (ed with B. Marsden) A Bibliography of Geographical Education 1970–1997, 1998 and Supplement 1998–1999, 2002; (ed with J. Lumby) Managing External Relations in Schools and Colleges, 1999; (with J. Hemsley-Brown) Choosing Futures: young people's decision-making in careers, education and training markets, 2001; (with J. Lumby) Leading and Managing Education: the international dimension, 2003; (with J. Lumby) 14–19 Education: policy, leadership and learning, 2005; (ed with F. Maringe) Globalisation and Internationalisation in Higher Education: theoretical, strategic and management perspectives, 2010; *with Rosalind Foskett*: Land, Man and Weather, 1981; The Wealden Landscape, 1983; Wealden Perspectives, 1984; People and the Rural Landscape, 1987; Conservation, 1999; (*et al*.) Geography AS/A2 Study Guide, 2001, 2nd edn 2005, rev. edn 2009; (and C. Burnett) Geography AS Fast Track, 2001; Postgraduate Study in the UK: the international student's guide, 2006; contrib. chapters in books; contrib. papers to acad. jls and res. reports. *Recreations*: sport, walking, family, theatre, music, travel.

**FOSTER,** family name of **Barons Foster of Bath, Foster of Bishop Auckland** and **Foster of Thames Bank.**

**FOSTER OF BATH,** Baron *cr* 2015 (Life Peer), of Bath in the County of Somerset; **Donald Michael Ellison Foster;** PC 2010; *b* 31 March 1947; *s* of late Rev. J. A. Foster and Iris Edith (*née* Ellison); *m* 1968, Victoria (*d* 2017), 2nd *d* of late Major Kenneth Pettegree, OBE, TD and Jean Pettegree; one *s* one *d*. *Educ*: Lancaster Royal Grammar Sch.; Univ. of Keele (BA Hons; Cert Ed 1969); Univ. of Bath (MEd 1982). Science teacher, Sevenoaks Sch., Kent, 1969–75; Science Curriculum Proj. Dir, Avon LEA, 1975–81; Science Educn Lectr, Bristol Univ., 1981–89; Head, Science Educn Centre; teacher trainer; organiser of link with Univ. of Zambia; Managing Consultant, Pannell Kerr Forster, 1989–92. Mem., Avon CC, 1981–89 (Leader, Liberal Gp; Chm., Educn Cttee, 1987–89). Mem. Exec. Cttee, ACC, 1985–89. Contested (L/All) Bristol East, 1987. MP (Lib Dem) Bath, 1992–2015. Lib Dem spokesman: on educn, 1992–99; on envmt, transport and the regions, 1999–2001; on transport, local govt and the regions, 2001–02; on transport, 2002–03; Parly Under-Sec. of State, DCLG, 2012–13; Comptroller of HM Household (Dep. Chief Whip), 2013–15. Co-Chair, Lib Dem Party Policy Cttee for culture, Olympics, media and sport, 2010–12; Member: Select Cttee on Educn and Employment, 1996–99; Bd, Westminster Foundn for Democracy, 2010–15. Mem. Bd, Olympic and Paralympic Games 2012, 2010–12. Treas., All-Party Yugoslav Gp, 1994–97. Vice-Chm., British Assoc. for Central and Eastern Europe, 1994–97. Pres., Nat. Campaign for Nursery Educn, 1999–2001 (Vice-Chm., 1993–99); Hon. Pres., British Youth Council, 1992–99; Trustee: Open Sch., 1992–99; Educn Extra, 1992–99. Hon. Fellow, Bath Coll. of Further Educn, 1994; Hon. DLaws Bath, 2016. *Publications*: Resource-based Learning in Science, 1979; Science with Gas, 1981; (jtly) Aspects of Science, 1984; (jtly) Reading about Science, 1984; (jtly) Nuffield Science, 1986; (ed) Teaching Science 11–13, 1987; From the Three

Rs to the Three Cs, 2003; science curriculum resources and educn papers. *Recreations:* watching all forms of sport (former rower and Rugby player), reading, films, music. *Address:* Willow Tree Barn, Lymballs Lane, Westleton, Suffolk IP17 3EQ.

**FOSTER OF THAMES BANK,** Baron *cr* 1999 (Life Peer), of Reddish in the county of Greater Manchester; **Norman Robert Foster,** OM 1997; Kt 1990; RA 1991 (ARA 1983); RWA 1994; RDI 1988; RIBA, FCSD, FAIA; architect; Founder and Executive Chairman, Foster + Partners, London; *b* Reddish, 1 June 1935; *s* of late Robert Foster and Lilian Smith; *m* 3rd, 1996, Dr Elena Ochoa; one *s* one *d*. *Educ:* Univ. of Manchester Sch. of Architecture (DipArch 1961, CertTP); Yale Univ. Sch. of Architecture (Henry Fellow, Jonathan Edwards Coll., March 1962). Founded: Foster Associates, 1967; Foster and Partners, 1992; in collab. with Dr Buckminster Fuller, 1968–83; Cons. Architect, UEA, 1978–87. Mem. Council: AA, 1969–70, 1970–71 (Vice Pres., 1974); RCA, 1981. Taught at: Univ. of Pennsylvania; AA, London; Bath Acad. of Arts; London Polytechnic; Visiting Professor: Bartlett Sch. of Architecture, 1998; Harvard Univ. Grad. Scholar of Design, 2000; Sch. of Geog. and Envmt, Univ. of Oxford, 2010–; Hon. Prof., Buenos Aires, 1997; IBM Fellow, Aspen Conf., 1980. External Examr, 1971–73 and Mem. Visiting Bd of Educn, RIBA. Founder Trustee, Architecture Foundn, London, 1991–; Pres., Norman Foster Foundn. Mem., H of L, 1999–2010. Major projects include: Head Office for Willis Faber & Dumas, Ipswich, 1975 (First Trustees', Medal, RIBA, 1990); Sainsbury Centre for Visual Arts, UEA, Norwich, 1977; UK headquarters for Renault, 1983; Nomos Furniture System, 1985; new HQ, Hongkong and Shanghai Banking Corp., Hong Kong, 1986; RA Sackler Galls, 1991; Stansted Airport, 1991; ITN HQ, 1991; Century Tower, Tokyo, 1991; inner harbour, Duisburg, 1991–2003; Barcelona Telecom Tower, 1992; Arts Centre, Nîmes, 1993; school, Fréjus, 1993; German Parlt bldg (Reichstag), Berlin, 1999; Bilbao Metro System, 1995; Univ. of Cambridge Faculty of Law, 1996; American Air Mus., Duxford, 1997 (RIBA Stirling Prize, 1998); HQ for Commerzbank, Frankfurt, 1997; Hong Kong Internat. Airport, 1998; Congress Centre, Valencia, 1998; Great Court, BM redevelt, 2000; City Hall, London, 2002; Swiss Re Tower, London (RIBA Stirling Prize), 2004; McLaren Technol. Centre, Woking, 2004; Sage Centre, Gateshead, 2004; Millau Viaduct, France, 2004; Hearst Tower, NY, 2006; Wembley Stadium, 2007; Beijing Capital Internat. Airport, 2008; Elephant Hse, Copenhagen Zoo, 2008; Masdar masterplan, Abu Dhabi, 2008; Torre Cepsa Madrid, 2009; YachtPlus Boat Fleet, 2009; Winspear Opera Hse, Dallas, 2009; Circle Hosp. Bath, 2009; Bodegas Portia, Faustino Winery, Spain, 2010; Masdar Inst., Abu Dhabi, 2010; Boston Museum of Fine Art, 2010; Sperone Westwater, NY, 2010; Queen Alia Internat. Airport, 2012; Bloomberg HQ, London, 2017 (Stirling Prize, RIBA, 2018); Apple Park, Calif, 2018; Norton Mus. of Art, Florida, 2019; Samson Pavilion, Case Western Reserve Univ. and Cleveland Clinic, 2019; Comcast Innovation and Technol. Center, Philadelphia, 2019. Work exhibited: Antwerp, Barcelona, Berlin, Bordeaux, Hanover, London, Lyon, Manchester, Madrid, Milan, Munich, NY, Nîmes, Paris, Seville, Tokyo, Valencia, Zurich, Dallas, Taipei, Dubai, Copenhagen, Hong Kong, Beijing, Shanghai, Mexico City, Frankfurt, Venice; permanent collections: MOMA, NY; Centre Georges Pompidou, Paris. Freeman, City of London, 2017. Hon. FAIA 1980; Hon. FREng; Hon. FIStructE; Hon. FRIAS 2000; Hon. Fellow, Inst. of Art and Design, Kent; Hon. Mem., Bund Deutscher Architekten, 1983; Member: Internat. Acad. of Architecture, Sofia; French Order of Architects; Eur. Acad. of Scis and Arts; Foreign Member: Royal Acad. of Fine Arts, Sweden; Amer. Acad. of Arts and Scis; Associate, Académie Royale de Belgique, 1990. Hon. Dr: E Anglia, Bath, Valencia, Humberside, Manchester, RCA, Eindhoven, Oxford, London, Negev, London Inst., Durham, Aberdeen, Dundee, Hong Kong, Yale, Madrid. Practice awards: over 800 for design excellence, including: R. S. Reynolds Internat. Awards, USA, 1976, 1979, 1986; 70 RIBA Awards and Commendations; Financial Times Awards for outstanding Industrial Architecture; Structural Steel Awards; Internat. Design Award; RSA Award, 1976; Ambrose Congreve Award, 1980; Civic Trust Awards; IStructE Special Awards; Premio Compasso d'Oro Award, 1987; Interiors Awards (USA); British Construction Industry Awards; Aluminium Imagination Awards; Best Building of the Year Award, Royal Fine Art Commn/Sunday Times, 1992, 1993, Royal Fine Art Commn/BSkyB, (jtly) 1998; BCO Awards; Queen's Award for Export, 1995; Regl Arch. Award, AIA, 1995. Personal awards include: RIBA Gold Medal, 1983; Kunstpreis, Berlin, 1989; Japan Design Foundn Award, 1987; Mies van der Rohe Award, Barcelona, 1991; Gold Medal, French Acad. of Arch., 1991; Brunner Meml Award, AAIL, 1992; Gold Medal, AIA, 1994; Gold Medal, Univ. Internacional Menéndez Pelayo, Santander, 1995; Best Internat. Promotion of Barcelona Award, 1997; Silver Medal, CSD, 1997; Berliner Zeitung Kultur-preis, 1998; special prize for positive contribution to British-German relations, German-British Forum, 1998; Pritzker Architecture Prize, 1999; special prize, 4th Internat. Biennial of Architecture, São Paulo, 1999; Walpole Medal of Excellence, 1999; Visual Arts Award, South Bank Show, 2001; Auguste Perret Prize, IUA, 2002; City of Rome Lifetime Achievement Award and Medaglia di Roma, 2003; Transatlantic Bridge Award, Friends of Free Univ. of Berlin, 2004; Prince Philip Designers Prize, Design Council, 2004; China Friendship Award, State Admin of Foreign Experts Affairs, 2008; Laureate, Prince of Asturias Award for the Arts, 2009; Humanitarian Award, UN Assoc. of New York, 2009; Save the Children Award, 2011; British Inspiration Award, 2012; Nat. German Sustainability Award, 2012; Gold Medal, Queen Sofia Spanish Inst., NY, 2012; Bilbao Architecture Award, 2014; Menschen in Europa Award, 2014; Louis Kahn Meml Award, 2015; Guillon d'Or Award, 2015; Scopus Award, Hebrew Univ., Jerusalem, 2016; Lifetime Achievement Award, Design Futures Council, 2016; Gold Medal, Amer. Acad. Achievement, 2017; American Prize for Design, 2018. Officer, Order of Arts and Letters (France), 1994; Order of North Rhine Westphalia; Kt Comdr's Cross, OM (Germany), 2009 (Comdr's Cross 1999). *Relevant publications:* The Work of Foster Associates, 1979; Norman Foster, 1988; Stansted: Norman Foster and the architecture of flight, 1992; Norman Foster Sketches, 1992; Foster Associates, 1992; Foster and Partners, 1996; Sir Norman Foster, 1997; The Master Architect Series II: Norman Foster, 1997; Norman Foster 30 Colours, 1998; The Norman Foster Studio, 2000; On Foster…Foster On, 2000; Norman Foster Works: vol. 1, 2003, vol. 2, 2005, vol. 3, 2006, vol. 4, 2004, vol. 5, 2009, vol. 6, 2012; Foster Catalogue, 2001, 2005, 2008, 2012; Norman Foster: the architect's studio, 2001; Architecture is About People: Norman Foster, 2001; Norman Foster and the British Museum, 2001; Reichstag Berlin, 2002; Blade of Light: the story of the Millennium Bridge, 2002; Reichstag Graffiti, 2003; Reflections, 2005; 30 St Mary Axe: a tower for London, 2006; Foster 40, 2007; Wembley Stadium: venue of legends, 2008; Norman Foster: a life in architecture, 2010; Norman Foster: drawings 1958–2008, 2010; Moving: Norman Foster on Art, 2013; Building with History, 2014; Portfolio, 2019. *Recreations:* cycling, flying, ski-ing. *Address:* (office) Riverside, 22 Hester Road, SW11 4AN. *T:* (020) 7738 0455, *Fax:* (020) 7738 1107. *E:* info@fosterandpartners.com.

**FOSTER, Alicia Christian, (Jodie);** American film actress and director; *b* 19 Nov. 1962; *d* of Lucius Foster and Evelyn Foster (*née* Almond); two *s*; *m* 2014, Alexandra Hedison. *Educ:* Yale Univ. (BA Eng. Lit. 1985). *Films* include: Napoleon and Samantha, 1972; Kansas City Bomber, 1972; Tom Sawyer, 1973; Alice Doesn't Live Here Anymore, 1975; Taxi Driver, 1976; Bugsy Malone, 1976; The Little Girl Who Lives Down the Lane, 1977; Candleshoe, 1977; Foxes, 1980; Carny, 1980; Hotel New Hampshire, 1984; Siesta, 1987; Five Corners, 1988; The Accused, 1988 (Academy Award for Best Actress, 1989); Little Man Tate, 1991 (also dir); The Silence of the Lambs, 1991 (Academy Award for Best Actress, 1992); Shadows and Fog, 1991; Sommersby, 1993; Maverick, 1994; Nell, 1994 (also prod.); dir and prod., Home for the Holidays, 1995; Contact, 1997; Anna and the King, 1999; Panic Room, 2002; Flight Plan, 2005; Inside Man, 2006; The Brave One, 2007; Nim's Island, 2008; The Beaver, 2011 (also dir); Carnage, 2012; Elysium, 2013; dir, Money Monster, 2016; Hotel Artemis, 2018; *television* includes: Mayberry, 1969; Bonanza; Paper Moon, 1974–75. Cecil B. De Mille Award, Golden Globe Awards, 2013.

**FOSTER, Hon. Dame Alison (Lee Caroline), (Lady Havelock-Allan),** DBE 2019; **Hon. Mrs Justice Foster;** a Judge of the High Court, Queen's Bench Division, since 2019; *b* 22 Jan. 1957; *o d* of Leslie Francis Foster and Marie Anne Foster (*née* MacIntosh-Hudson); *m* 1986, (Anthony) Mark (David) Havelock-Allan (*see* Sir A. M. D. Havelock-Allan, Bt); one *s* two *d*. *Educ:* Bexhill Grammar Sch. for Girls; Jesus Coll., Oxford (BA Hons English 1979; MA); Courtauld Inst. of Art, London Univ. (MPhil 1981); City Univ. (Dip. Law 1983). Called to the Bar, Inner Temple, 1984, Bencher, 2002; QC 2002; in practice, specialising in administrative law regulation and tax; Jt Hd, 39 Essex Chambers, 2015–19; a Deputy High Court Judge, Chancery Div., 2008–19, Admin. Court, 2018–19. *Recreations:* painting, rose-growing. *Address:* Royal Courts of Justice, Strand, WC2A 2LL. *Clubs:* Groucho, Royal Automobile.

**FOSTER, Andrew Kevin,** CBE 2005; Chief Executive, Wrightington, Wigan and Leigh NHS Foundation Trust, since 2007; *b* 3 March 1955; *s* of late Kevin William Foster and Doreen Foster; *m* 1981, Sara Gillian Daniels; one *s* two *d*. *Educ:* Millfield Sch.; Keble Coll., Oxford (BA Hons PPE, MA). Mktg Manager, Rowntree Mackintosh plc, 1976–81; Dir, Worldcrest Ltd, 1981–. Chairman: W Lancs NHS Trust, 1993–96; Wigan & Leigh NHS Trust, 1996–2001; Policy Dir, NHS Confedn, 1998–2001; Dir of Human Resources, then of Workforce, DoH, 2001–06; Dir of HR and Organisational Develt, Blackpool, Fylde and Wyre Hosps NHS Trust, 2006–07; Interim Chief Exec., Heart of England Foundn Trust, 2015. *Recreation:* golf.

**FOSTER, Sir Andrew (William),** Kt 2001; Chairman, Vitality Health, since 2017; *b* 29 Dec. 1944; *s* of George William and Gladys Maria Foster; *m* 1st, 1967, Christine Marquiss (marr. diss. 2000); one *s* one *d*; 2nd, 2001, Jadranka Porter. *Educ:* Abingdon School; Newcastle Polytechnic (BSc Sociol.); LSE (Postgrad. Dip. Applied Social Studies). Social Worker, London, 1966–71; Area Social Services Officer, 1971–75; Asst Dir of Social Services, Haringey, 1975–79; Dir of Social Services, Greenwich, 1979–82, N Yorks, 1982–87; Regional Gen. Manager, Yorks RHA, 1987–91; Dep. Chief Exec., NHS Management Exec., 1991–92; Controller, Audit Commn, 1992–2003; Dep. Chm., Royal Bank of Canada, 2003–12. Non-executive Director: Nestor Healthcare, 2004–11; Nat. Express Gp, 2004–15; Prudential Health Ltd, 2004–17. Chair: Foster Review Group Athletics, 2004; Further Education Review Gp, 2005; Commonwealth Games England, 2007–; 2020 Public Services Commn, 2008–10; Review of Capital Prog. in Further Educn, 2009; Review of Intercity Express Prog., DfT, 2010. Non-exec. Dir, Sport England, 2003–09. Hon. DCL Northumbria at Newcastle, 1996. *Recreations:* golf, walking, travel, theatre, food, wine.

**FOSTER, Angiolina,** CBE 2011; Chief Executive Officer, NHS 24, since 2016; *b* 1 Feb. 1956; *d* of Andrew Seath and Vera Seath; *m* 1983, Michael Foster; one *s* one *d*. *Educ:* Univ. of Glasgow (MA Hons); Glasgow Caledonian Univ. (Dip. Mgt Studies). Glasgow DC, 1979–85; Chief Housing Benefits Officer, Edinburgh DC, 1985–87; Depute Dir, Housing, City of Edinburgh Council, 1987–2001; Dir, Regulation and Inspection, Communities Scotland, 2001–02; Actg Chief Exec., Glasgow Housing Assoc., 2002–03; Chief Exec., Communities Scotland, 2004–07; Scottish Government: Dir, Strategy and Ministerial Support, 2007–12; Dir, Health and Social Care Integration, 2012–14; Chief Exec., Healthcare Improvement Scotland, 2014–16. *Recreations:* long distance walks, charity runs, food and wine with good friends, cinema, theatre. *Address:* NHS 24, Caledonia House, Fifty Pitches Road, Cardonald Park, Glasgow G51 4EB.

**FOSTER, Rt Hon. Arlene (Isobel);** PC 2016; Member (DemU) Fermanagh and South Tyrone, Northern Ireland Assembly, since 2003; First Minister of Northern Ireland, 2016–17; Leader, Democratic Unionist Party, since 2015; *b* 17 July 1970; *d* of John William Kelly and Julia Georgina Kelly (*née* Sills); *m* 1995, William Brian Johnston Foster; two *s* one *d*. *Educ:* Collegiate Grammar Sch. for Girls, Enniskillen; Queen's Univ., Belfast (LLB Hons 1993; CPLS 1996). Solicitor, private practice, 1996–2005, pt-time, 2005–07. Mem. (DemU), Fermanagh DC, 2005–07. Minister of the Envmt, 2007–08, Minister of Enterprise, Trade and Investment, 2008–15, Minister of Finance and Personnel, 2015–16, Acting First Minister, 2015, NI. Mem., NI Policing Bd, 2006–07. *Recreations:* reading (especially political and historical biographies), listening (and singing along to) music of all types. *Address:* (constituency office) 27 East Bridge Street, Enniskillen BT74 7BW. *T:* (028) 6632 0722. *E:* arlene@arlenefoster.org.uk.

**FOSTER, Brendan,** CBE 2008 (MBE 1976); television athletics commentator, since 1981; Chairman, The Great Run Company (formerly Nova International Ltd), since 2000; *b* 12 Jan. 1948; *s* of Francis and Margaret Foster; *m* 1972; one *s* one *d*. *Educ:* St Joseph's Grammar Sch., Hebburn, Co. Durham; Sussex Univ. (BSc); Carnegie Coll., Leeds (DipEd). School Teacher, St Joseph's Grammar Sch., Hebburn, 1970–74; Sports and Recreation Manager, Gateshead Metropolitan Bor. Council, 1974–81; UK Man. Dir, Nike Internat., 1981–87; Chm., Nike (UK), 1981–86; Man. Dir, Nike Europe, 1985–87; Vice Pres. Marketing, Nike Inc. Oregon, USA, 1986–87. Commonwealth Games: Bronze medal: 1500m, 1970; 5000m, 1978; Silver medal, 5000m, 1974; Gold medal, 10,000m, 1978; European Games: Bronze medal, 1500m, 1971; Gold medal, 5000m, 1974; Olympic Games: Bronze medal, 10,000m, 1976; World Records: 2 miles, 1973; 3000m, 1974. BBC Sports Personality of the Year, 1974. Chm. and Founder, Great North Run, 1981–. Chancellor, Leeds Metropolitan Univ., 2005–09. Freeman, Gateshead, 2009; Hon. Freedom, City of Newcastle upon Tyne, 2016. Hon. Fellow, Sunderland Polytechnic, 1977; Hon. MEd Newcastle, 1978; Hon. DLitt Sussex, 1982; Hon. DArts Leeds Metropolitan, 2004; Hon. DCL Northumbria, 2003. Golden Order of Merit, IAAF, 2017. *Publications:* Brendan Foster, 1978; Olympic Heroes 1896–1984, 1984. *Recreations:* running (now only a recreation), sport (as spectator).

**FOSTER, Prof. Brian,** OBE 2003; DPhil; FRS 2008; CPhys, FInstP; Professor of Experimental Physics, since 2003, and Donald H. Perkins Professor of Experimental Physics, since 2016, University of Oxford; Fellow of Balliol College, Oxford, since 2003; Alexander von Humboldt Professor, University of Hamburg and Deutsches Elektronen-Synchrotron, since 2010; *b* 4 Jan. 1954; *s* of John and Annie Foster; *m* 1983, Sabine Margot Koch; two *s*. *Educ:* Wolsingham Secondary Sch.; Queen Elizabeth Coll., Univ. of London (BSc 1975); St John's Coll., Oxford (DPhil 1978); MA Oxon 2003. CPhys, FInstP 1992. Research Associate: Rutherford Appleton Lab., 1978–82; Imperial Coll. of Science and Technology, 1982–84; Bristol University: Lectr, 1984–92; SERC, subseq. PPARC, Advanced Fellow, 1991–97; Reader, 1992–96; Prof. of Experimental Physics, 1996–2003, Emeritus, 2004. Institute of Physics: Hon. Sec., High Energy Particle Physics Gp, 1985–89; Chm., Nuclear and Particle Physics Div., 1989–93; Mem. Council, 2009–13; Mem., Resources (formerly Investment) Cttee, 2009–13; Recorder, Physics Section, BAAS, 1994–97; Mem., PPARC, 2001–06 (Mem., 1995, and Chm., 1996–99, Particle Physics

Cttee; Jt Chm., 1996–99, Mem., 2001–07, Science Cttee); Mem., Physics Sub-Panel, 2008 RAE; Chm., Physics Sub-Panel, 2014 REF. Chm., Mgt Cttee, Oxford e-Science Res. Centre, 2010–17. Member: various adv. cttees, CERN, 1993–2000; Extended Scientific Council, Deutsches Elektronen-Synchrotron, 1998–2009; Evaluation Commn, Sci. Council of Germany, 2001–07; Scientific Policy Cttee, CERN Council, 2002–05; Chm., European Cttee for Future Accelerators, 2002–05. Spokesman, ZEUS Collaboration, 1999–2003; European Director: Global Design Effort for the Internat. Linear Collider, 2005–13; Linear Collider Collaboration, 2013–16. Mem. Council, 2015–18, Mem., Public Engagement Cttee, 2015–, Vice-Pres., 2018, Royal Soc. Ed.-in-Chief, Oxford Res. Encyclopaedia of Physics, 2017–. Chm. Trustees and Admin Dir, Oxford May Music Fest., 2008–. Hon. Vice-Pres., Ernest Bloch Soc., 2008–. Alexander von Humboldt-Stiftung Res. Prize, 1999–2000; Max Born Medal, Inst. of Physics and German Physical Soc., 2003. *Publications:* (ed) Topics in High Energy Particle Physics, 1988; (ed jtly) Forty Years of Particle Physics, 1988; (ed and contrib.) Electron-Positron Annihilation Physics, 1990; numerous papers in learned jls, articles on science in popular press. *Recreations:* collecting first editions, violin playing, history and politics, hill walking. *Address:* Denys Wilkinson Building, Keble Road, Oxford OX1 3RH; 48 Great Clarendon Street, Oxford OX2 6AX. *T:* (01865) 273323.

**FOSTER, Sir Christopher (David),** Kt 1986; MA; Member, Board of Governors, Better Government Initiative, since 2013 (Chairman, 2006–13); Vice-President: RAC, since 2003 (Vice-Chairman, 1998–99; non-executive Director, 1994–98); RAC Foundation, since 2003 (Chairman, 1999–2003); *b* 30 Oct. 1930; *s* of George Cecil Foster and Phyllis Joan Foster (*née* Mappin); *m* 1958, Kay Sheridan Bullock; two *s* three *d*. *Educ:* Merchant Taylors' Sch.; King's Coll., Cambridge (Scholar) (History Tripos Pt I, Economics Tripos Pt II, 1954; MA 1959). Commnd into 1st Bn Seaforth Highlanders, Malaya, 1949. Hallsworth Research Fellow, Manchester Univ., 1957–59; Senior Research Fellow, 1959–64, Official Fellow and Tutor, 1964–66, Hon. Fellow, 1992, Jesus Coll., Oxford; Dir-Gen. of Economic Planning, MoT, 1966–70; Head of Unit for Res. in Urban Economics, LSE, 1970–76; Prof. of Urban Studies and Economics, LSE, 1976–78; a Dir and Head of Econ. and Public Policy Div., Coopers & Lybrand Associates, 1978–84; a Dir, Public Sector Practice Leader and Economic Advr, Coopers & Lybrand, 1984–86; Commercial Adviser to British Telecom, 1986–88; Mem. Bd, Coopers & Lybrand, 1988–90; Sen. Public Sector and Econs Partner, Coopers & Lybrand Deloitte, later Coopers & Lybrand, 1990–98; Advr to Chm., Coopers & Lybrand, 1994–99. Governor, 1967–70, Dir, 1976–78, Centre for Environmental Studies; Visiting Professor: of Economics, MIT, 1970; LSE, 1978–86. Special Economic Adviser (part time), DoE, 1974–77; Special Advr on BR Privatisation to Sec. of State for Transport, 1992–94; Mem. Bd, Railtrack, 1994–2000. Member: (part time), PO Bd, 1975–77; Audit Commn, 1983–88; ESRC, 1985–89; Chm., NEDO Construction Industry Sector Gp, 1988–92. Chm., Cttee of Inquiry into Road Haulage Licensing, 1977–78; Mem., Cttee of Inquiry into Civil Service Pay, 1981–82; Economic Assessor, Sizewell B Inquiry, 1982–86. Member: Econ. and Financial Cttee, CBI, 1987–94; LDDC, 1988–96. Chairman: Circle 33 Housing Assoc., 1986–90; Construction Round Table, 1993–97. Governor: RSC, 1991–; Inst. for Govt, 2009–12. *Publications:* The Transport Problem, 1963; Politics, Finance and the Role of Economics: an essay on the control of public enterprise, 1972; (with R. Jackman and M. Perlman) Local Government Finance, 1980; Privatisation, Public Ownership and the Regulation of Natural Monopoly, 1993; (with F. J. Plowden) The State Under Stress, 1996; British Government in Crisis, 2005; papers in various economic, political and other journals. *Address:* 6 Holland Park Avenue, W11 3QU. *T:* (020) 7229 6581. *Clubs:* Reform, Royal Automobile.

**FOSTER, Christopher Norman;** consultant on horseracing matters, 2006; Keeper of the Match Book, The Jockey Club, 1983–2016; *b* 30 Dec. 1946; *s* of Maj.-Gen. Norman Leslie Foster, CB, DSO; *m* 1981, Anthea Jane Sammons, MVO (separated 2011); two *s*. *Educ:* Westminster Sch. ACA 1969, FCA 1979. Cooper Brothers & Co., Chartered Accountants, 1965–73; Weatherbys, 1973–90; The Jockey Club: Sec., 1983–90; Exec. Dir, 1993–2006. Vice Chm., Internat. Fedn of Horseracing Authorities, 2000–06. Director: Wincanton Racecourse, 2006–13; The National Stud, 2008–16. Trustee: Retraining of Racehorses, 2006–13; Home of Horseracing Trust, 2009–; Racing Welfare, 2013–16. Governor, Westminster Sch., 1990–. *Recreations:* racing, shooting, fishing, gardening. *Address:* Summerhurst Farm, Union Lane, Headley, Berks RG19 8LR. *Clubs:* Jockey, MCC.

**FOSTER, Rt Rev. Christopher Richard James;** see Portsmouth, Bishop of.

**FOSTER, Prof. Christopher Stuart,** MD; PhD; DSc; FRCPath; George Holt Professor of Pathology, and Director of Cellular Pathology and Molecular Genetics, University of Liverpool, 1994–2012, now Emeritus Professor; Consultant Histopathologist, Royal Liverpool and Broadgreen University Hospitals NHS Trust, 1993–2012; Medical Director, HCA Healthcare UK, since 2012; *b* Pilling, Lancs, 22 Oct. 1947; *s* of Geoffrey Stuart Foster and Dilys Joan Foster (*née* Hughes); *m* 1992, Joan Elizabeth Hardie; one *s* one *d*. *Educ:* Midsomer Norton Grammar Sch.; Dover Boys' Grammar Sch.; University Coll. London (BSc Physiol. and Biochem. 1966); Westminster Med. Sch. (MB BS 1974); Ludwig Inst. for Cancer Res., London (PhD 1983); Children's Hosp. of Philadelphia (MD 1987); Inst. of Cancer Res. (DSc 2002). LRCP, MRCS 1973; MRCPath 1984, FRCPath 1995. Exptl Officer, RN Physiol Lab., Alverstoke, 1966–68; SHO, Royal Marsden Hosp., Sutton, 1975–76; Registrar: in Gen. Medicine, Redhill Gen. Hosp., 1976–77; in Histopathol., Greenbank Hosp., 1977–79; Clin. Scientist, Ludwig Inst. for Cancer Res., London, 1979–83; Res. Fellow, ICRF and Sen. Registrar in Pathol., St Bartholomew's Hosp., London, 1983–85; Sen. Res. Fellow, Children's Hosp. of Philadelphia, 1985–87; Sen. Lectr in Pathol., RPMS and Hammersmith Hosp., London, 1987–94; Hd, Sch. of Clin. Lab. Scis, Univ. of Liverpool, 2004–06. Visiting Professor: Medunsa Univ., S Africa, 1990; Al Quds Med. Univ., Palestine, 1998; Univ. of Beijing, 2003–04. European Editor: Human Pathol., 1995–2005; Amer. Jl Clin. Pathol., 1999–2005. Chm., NHS-NW Reg. Pathol. Modernisation Cttee, 2000–01; Mem., Nat. Steering Cttee, Pathol. Modernisation, DoH, 2001–06. Reference Pathologist, WHO Prostate Cancer, 1999–; Co-Chm., Pathol. Section, WHO Internat. Consultation on Prostate Cancer, 1999; Chm., Pathol. Section, WHO Cttee on Benign Prostatic Hyperplasia, 2000; Sen. Pathologist, Transatlantic Prostate Gp, 2004–. Dir, Workforce Planning, RCPath, 2004–07. Mem. Council, ACP, 1995–98. Dir, Safer Medicines, 2016–. *Publications:* Diagnostic Liver Pathology, 1993; Pathology of the Prostate, 1997; Pathology of the Urinary Bladder, 2004; Molecular Oncology of Prostate Cancer, 2007; contrib. papers on tumour pathology, particularly develt of novel biomarkers applied to diagnosis and prognosis of cancer. *Recreations:* ski-ing, sailing, fly-fishing, cooking. *Club:* Athenæum.

**FOSTER, Ian Hampden;** a Master of the Senior (formerly Supreme) Court, Queen's Bench Division, 1991–2011; a Recorder, 1998–2011; *b* 27 Feb. 1946; *s* of Eric Hampden Foster and Irene Foster (*née* Warman); *m* 1975, Fiona Jane (*d* 2011), *d* of Rev. J. N. and Mrs Robertson-Glasgow; one *s* one *d*. *Educ:* Battersea Grammar Sch.; Univ. of Exeter (LLB Hons 1968). Called to the Bar, Inner Temple, 1969; practice at common law bar, 1969–91. Adv. Editor, Atkin's Court Forms, 1991–2003; Jt Editor, Supreme Court Practice, 1993–98. *Recreation:* watching cricket. *Address:* c/o Royal Courts of Justice, Strand, WC2A 2LL. *Club:* Travellers.

**FOSTER, Dame Jacqueline,** DBE 2019; Member (C) North West Region, European Parliament, 1999–2004 and 2009–19; *d* of late Samuel and Isabella Renshaw; *m* 1975, Peter Laurance Foster (marr. diss. 1981). *Educ:* Prescot Girls' Grammar Sch., Lancashire. Cabin Services, BEA, then British Airways, 1969–81; Area Manager, Austria, Horizon, 1981–85; Cabin Services, British Airways, 1985–99; Founder Mem. and Exec. Officer, Cabin Crew '89 (Airline Trade Union), 1989–99; aerospace consultant, Brussels, 2004–09. European Parliament: Chm., Cons. backbench cttee, 1999–2004; Mem. Industry and Transport (Aviation) Cttees, 1999–2004; Cons. spokesman on transport and tourism, 2001–04, 2009–19; Vice-President, Parliamentary Intergroup: Sky and Space, 2009–19; Animal Welfare, 2009–19. Mem., Eur. Aviation Club, Brussels. *Recreations:* ski-ing, travel, golf. *Club:* Carlton.

**FOSTER, Joanna Katharine,** CBE 2002; leadership coach; Chair, Crafts Council, 2006–13; *b* 5 May 1939; *d* of late Michael and of Lesley Mead; *m* 1st, 1961, Jerome Foster (marr. diss. 2002); one *s* one *d*; 2nd, 2016, Nicholas Tresilian. *Educ:* Benenden School; Univ. of Grenoble. Sec. and Editl Asst, Vogue Magazine, London and NY, 1958–59; journalist, San Francisco Chronicle, 1959; Management Adviser, Industrial Soc., 1966–72; Dir, Centre Actif Bilingue, Fontainebleau, 1972–79; Press Attachée and Editor, INSEAD, Fontainebleau, 1972–79; Educn and Trng Dir, Corporate Services, Western Psychiatric Inst. and Clinic, Univ. of Pittsburgh, 1980–82; Industrial Society: Management Adviser, 1982–85; Head of Pepperell Unit for Women's Leadership Develt, 1985–88; Mem. Council, 1990–2000; Chair: Equal Opportunities Commn, 1988–93; UK Council, UN Internat. Year of the Family 1994, 1993–95; Dir, 1995–97, Chm., 1997–2001, BT Communication Forum; Chm., Nat. Work-Life Forum, 1998–2002. Pres., European Commn Adv. Cttee on Equal Opportunities, 1991–92 (Vice Pres., 1990, 1991, 1993); Member: Nat. Adv. Council for Careers and Educnl Guidance, 1993–94; Sec. of State for Employment's Women's Issues Adv. Gp, 1991–93; Target Team for Business in the Community's Opportunity 2000 Initiative, 1992–99; Govt Adv. Gp on Work-Life Balance, 2000–02. Chair, Adv. Cttee, European Public Policy Inst., Warwick Univ., 1993–95. Chm., Lloyds TSB (formerly TSB) Foundn, 1997–2003 (Dep. Chm., 1991–97). Dir, WNO, 1990–94; Mem., Central TV Adv. Bd, 1991–95; Member, Advisory Board: Econ. Regl Analysis, 1997–; Common Purpose Oxfordshire, 2004–; What Next? prog., 2007–; Dir, Pennell Initiative for Women's Health, 1997– (Chm., 2003–); Chair, Nuffield Orthopaedic Centre NHS Trust, 2001–10. President: Relate, 1993–96; Oxfordshire Craft Guild, 2004–. Trustee: Employment Policy Inst., 1995–98; Open Univ. Foundn, 2004–; Arts at the Old Fire Stn. Mem., Adv. Council, Oxford Philomusica, 2006–. Associate Fellow, 2010–14, Dir, NHS Chairs' Forum, 2010–14, Saïd Business Sch., Oxford; Chm., US.PEX - Health Experiences Res. Gp, Oxford Univ., 2015–. Governor: Oxford Brookes Univ., 1993– (Dep. Chm., 1998–2003); Birkbeck Coll., Univ. of London, 1996–98. Hon. Fellow, St Hilda's Coll., Oxford, 1988. Hon. DLitt Kingston, 1993; DU Essex, 1993; Hon. LLD: Oxford Brookes, 1993; West of England, 1993; Strathclyde, 1994; Salford, 1994; Bristol, 1996. *Recreations:* family, friends, food. *Club:* Reform.

**FOSTER, Jodie;** see Foster, A. C.

**FOSTER, John Edward,** CBE 2008; Chief Executive, London Borough of Islington, 2008–11; *b* 30 Dec. 1948; *s* of John and Ethel Foster; *m* 2003, Pauline de Silva; one *s* three *d* from a former marriage. *Educ:* Univ. of London (BSc Hons ext. 1970); Univ. of Durham. Community worker, Northumberland CC, 1971; Community Develt Officer, Durham CC, 1972; Community Develt Project, Home Office, 1973–92; various rôles with N Tyneside MBC and NALGO, 1979–92; Exec. Dir, North Tyneside MBC, 1992–97; Chief Executive: Middlesbrough Council, 1998–2002; City of Wakefield MDC, 2003–08. Dir, New Local Govt Network, 2002. Trustee, Yorkshire Sculpture Park, 2011– (Chair, Finance Bd, 2015–). FRSA 2007. *Recreations:* weekends away from it all, Friends of the Royal Academy and the Tate. *Address:* Stray House, 14a Church Square, Harrogate HG1 4SP.

**FOSTER, John Graham;** District Judge (Magistrates' Court), South Yorkshire, 2001–17; *b* 28 April 1947; *s* of James Beaumont Foster and Margaret Foster; *m* 1971, Susan Boothroyd; three *s*. *Educ:* Woodhouse Grove Sch.; Sheffield Univ. (LLB Hons). Admitted Solicitor, 1973; in private practice with Morrish & Co., Solicitors, Leeds, 1970–2001 (Partner 1975–2001); Dep. Dist Judge, 1997–2001. *Recreations:* after dinner speaking, theatre, films, music, sport, especially badminton and cricket.

**FOSTER, His Honour Jonathan Rowe;** QC 1989; a Circuit Judge, 2004–15; *b* 20 July 1947; *s* of Donald Foster and Hilda Eaton; *m* 1978, Sarah Anne Mary da Cunha; four *s*. *Educ:* Oundle Sch.; Keble Coll., Oxford (Exhibr). Called to the Bar, Gray's Inn, 1970, Bencher, 1998; a Recorder, 1988–2004; a Dep. High Ct Judge, 1994–2015; Hd of Chambers, 1997–2004. Treas., Northern Circuit, 1992–97. Mem., Criminal Injuries Compensation Bd and Appeal Panel, 1995–2004. Gov., Ryleys Sch., 1990–2006. Trustee, Acorn Recovery Projects, 2012–18. *Recreations:* bridge, gardening, golf. *Clubs:* St James's (Manchester); Hale Golf.

**FOSTER, Kevin John;** MP (C) Torbay, since 2015; Parliamentary Under Secretary of State, Wales Office, since 2019; an Assistant Government Whip, since 2019; *b* Plymouth, 31 Dec. 1978; *s* of Michael Foster and late Linda Foster; *m* 2017, Hazel Noonan. *Educ:* Hele's Sch., Plympton; Univ. of Warwick (LLB Law 2000; LLM Internat. Econ. Law 2001); Inns of Court Sch. of Law (BVC 2002). Barman, Coventry Cons. Club, 2000–03; Asst to Philip Bradbourne, MEP, 2002–03; Paralegal, Howell and Co. Solicitors, 2003–04. PPS to MHCLG (formerly DCLG), 2017–18, to Chancellor of Duchy of Lancaster, Cabinet Office, 2018–19. Mem. (C), Coventry CC, 2002–14. Contested (C) Coventry S, 2010. *Recreations:* military history, cinema, music, church. *Address:* House of Commons, SW1A 0AA. *T:* (01803) 214989. *E:* kevin.foster.mp@parliament.uk. *Clubs:* Royal Air Force; Preston Conservative (Paignton).

**FOSTER, Lawrence;** conductor; Music Director, Opéra de Marseille and Orchestre Philharmonique de Marseille, since 2013; Artistic Director and Chief Conductor, Polish National Radio Symphony Orchestra, since 2019; *b* Los Angeles, 23 Oct. 1941; *s* of Thomas Foster and Martha Wurmbrandt; *m* 1972, Angela Foster; one *d*. *Educ:* Univ. of California, LA; studied under Fritz Zweig, Bruno Walter and Karl Böhm. Asst Conductor, Los Angeles Philharmonic, 1965–68; British début, Royal Festival Hall, 1968; Covent Garden début, Troilus and Cressida, 1976; Chief Guest Conductor, Royal Philharmonic Orchestra, 1969–74; Music Dir and Chief Conductor, Houston Symphony Orchestra, 1971–78; Chief Conductor, Orchestre National (later Orchestre Philharmonique) of Monte Carlo, 1978–95; Gen. Music Dir, Duisburg concert series, 1982–86; Prin. Guest Conductor, Düsseldorf Opera, 1982–86; Music Director: Lausanne Chamber Orch., 1985–90; Aspen Fest., 1991–96; Barcelona SO and Nat. Orch. of Catalonia, 1996–2002; Orch. and Nat. Opera of Montpellier, 2009–12; Artistic Dir and Chief Conductor, Gulbenkian Orch., Lisbon, 2002–13, now Conductor Laureate; Artistic Dir, Georg Enescu Fest., 1998–2001; Guest Conductor: Deutsche Oper Berlin; LA Music Centre Opera; LA Philharmonic Orch.; Hallé Orch.; Pittsburgh, Chicago, Montreal, and Jerusalem Symphony Orchs; Orchestre de Paris. *Recreations:* reading European history, films. *Address:* c/o HarrisonParrott, The Ark, 201 Talgarth Road, W6 8BJ.

**FOSTER, Michael George;** active in range of non-executive roles, early stage companies and family art businesses; Director, Angles of Art Ltd, since 2016; Adviser, Alexander Foster Fine Art Ltd, since 2016; *b* 17 Feb. 1953; *s* of Brian and Betty Foster; *m* 1977, Marion Frances Chambers; one *s* one *d*. *Educ:* Nottingham High Sch.; Peterhouse, Cambridge (BA 1975, MA 1979); Council of Legal Educn. Called to the Bar, Inner Temple, 1977; barrister in private practice, 1977–85; admitted solicitor, 1989; GKN plc: Sen. Commercial Lawyer, 1985–88; Asst Gp Treas., 1988–93; Dep. Hd, Corporate Finance, 1993–94; Gp Treas., Trafalgar House plc, 1994–95; Chief Executive: Kvaerner Metals (Davy), 1995–98; Kvaerner Engrg & Construction Div., 1998–2000; Exec. Dir, RMC plc, 2000–04; Commercial Dir, 2005–06, Chief Exec., 2006–11, Charter International (formerly Charter) plc. Chairman: Impression Technologies Ltd, 2013–16; Microtech Ceramics Ltd, 2014–16; non-executive Director: Charter plc, 2001–04; Chas A. Blatchford and Sons Ltd, 2011–13. Trustee, St Mungo's Broadway, 2013–17. Fellow, ACT, 2007. *Recreations:* family, theatre and film, opera, blues, rock and roll, literature, travel, clay pigeon shooting.

**FOSTER, Michael Jabez;** DL; solicitor specialising in employment law; Principal, Michael Foster Law, since 2010; *b* Hastings, 26 Feb. 1946; *s* of Dorothy Foster; *m* 1969, Rosemary, *d* of Eric and Hilda Kemp; two *s*. *Educ:* Hastings Secondary Sch.; Hastings Grammar Sch.; Leicester Univ. (LLM). Admitted Solicitor, 1980; ACIArb 1997. Partner, 1980–99, Consultant, 1999–2009, Fynmores, solicitors, Bexhill-on-Sea. Member: Hastings CBC, 1971–74 (Ldr, Lab. Gp, 1973); Hastings BC, 1973–79, 1983–87 (Ldr, Lab. Gp and Dep. Ldr of Council, 1973–79); E Sussex CC, 1973–77, 1981–97 (Dep. Leader, Lab Gp, 1984–93); Mem., Sussex Police Authy, 1991–96; Mem., E Sussex AHA, later Hastings HA, 1974–91. Contested (Lab) Hastings, Feb. and Oct. 1974, 1979. MP (Lab) Hastings and Rye, 1997–2010; contested (Lab) same seat, 2010. PPS to Attorney General, 1999–2003; Parly Under-Sec. of State, Govt Equalities Office, 2009–10. Pres., Hastings Law Soc., 2014–15. DL 1993, High Sheriff 2016–17, E Sussex. Freeman, Bor. of Hastings, 2010. *Address:* 3 Cambridge Gardens, Hastings TN34 1EH. *T:* (01424) 203040. *E:* mail@michaelfosterlaw.co.uk.

**FOSTER, Michael John;** Chief Executive, Energy and Utilities Alliance, since 2011; *b* 14 March 1963; *s* of Brian and Edna Foster; *m* 1985, Shauna Ogle; one *s* two *d*. *Educ:* Great Wyrley High Sch., Staffs; Wolverhampton Poly. (BA Hons Econs 1984); Univ. of Wolverhampton (PGCE 1995). ACMA. Management Accountant, Jaguar Cars, 1984–91; Lectr, Worcester Coll. of Technology, 1991–97. MP (Lab) Worcester, 1997–2010; contested (Lab) same seat, 2010. Department of Education and Skills: PPS to Minister of State for Lifelong Learning and Higher Educn, 2001–03; for Children, 2003–04; Departmental PPS, 2004–05; PPS to Sec. of State for NI, 2005–06; an Asst Govt Whip, 2006–08; Parly Under-Sec. of State, DFID, 2008–10. Mem., Educn Select Cttee, 1999–2001. Hd of Communications, WaterAid, 2010–11. Chm., Affordable Warmth Solutions. *Recreations:* most sports, gardening. *Club:* Worcestershire County Cricket.

**FOSTER, Nikolai Sergei;** Artistic Director, Curve Theatre, Leicester, since 2015; *b* Copenhagen, 27 Jan. 1980; *s* of Ritva Foster. *Educ:* Drama Centre, London (BA Hons Acting). Trng, Crucible, Sheffield, under Regl Th. Young Dir Scheme, and NT Studio. Freelance internat. theatre dir, 2001–; productions include: Evita, Zouk Amphitheatre, Beirut, 2003; My Fair Lady, Larnaka Internat. Fest. 2006, Esplanade Th. Singapore, 2007, Kuala Lumpur Convention Centre, 2008; Macbeth, Singapore Rep. Th., 2011; As You Like It, Grosvenor Park Open Air Th., Chester, 2011; The Diary of Anne Frank, York Th. Royal, and tour, 2011; Merrily We Roll Along, Clwyd Theatr Cymru, 2012; Sherlock Holmes - The Best Kept Secret, West Yorkshire Playhouse, Leeds, 2013; The Good Person of Sichuan, Mercury, Colchester, 2013; The Memory of Water, New Vic, Stoke and Stephen Joseph, Scarborough, 2014; The Hired Man, St James, 2014; Calamity Jane, Watermill, Newbury, and tour, 2015–16; Annie, Piccadilly, London, 2017; Associate Dir, West Yorkshire Playhouse, Leeds, 2008–12, productions: Bollywood Jane, 2007, Salonika, Animal Farm, 2008, A Christmas Carol, White Christmas, 2010; Curve, Leicester, 2015–, productions: Beautiful Thing (with Nottingham Playhouse and tour), performance to celebrate reveal of tomb of King Richard III at Leicester Cath., Our Country's Good, Richard III, A Streetcar Named Desire, 2015; The Witches, 2015–16 (with Rose Th., Kingston, Lyric Th., Hong Kong, West Yorkshire Playhouse, Leeds and tour); Breakfast at Tiffany's (and Haymarket, London and nat. tour), Legally Blonde (and Daegu Internat. Fest., South Korea), Spring Awakening (with Nat. Youth Music Th.), The Importance of Being Earnest (with Birmingham Rep, UK tour), 2016; Grease, 2016–17 and 2019–20 (and Dubai and UK nat. tour); What the Butler Saw (with Th. Royal Bath), Sunset Boulevard, 2017 (UK tour); Scrooge the Musical, 2017; An Officer and a Gentleman, UK tour, 2018; White Christmas, 2018; Memoirs of an Asian Football Casual, 2018. *Recreations:* walking the dog, horse riding, theatre, aviation, dance, art, travel. *E:* n.foster@curvetheatre.co.uk.

**FOSTER, Richard John Samuel; His Honour Judge Foster;** a Circuit Judge, since 2004; a Deputy High Court Judge, since 2003; *b* 28 May 1954; *s* of late Samuel Geoffrey Foster and Beryl Foster; *m* 1st, 1980, Ann Scott (*d* 2002); one *d*; 2nd, 2004, Susan Claire Sansome (*née* Brodie); one step *s* one step *d*. *Educ:* Bromsgrove Sch.; Coll. of Law, Guildford. Qualified solicitor, 1979; Partner, 1987–97, Jt Sen. Partner, 1997–98, Vizards, London; Sen. Partner, Vizard Oldham, London, 1998–2002; Partner and Hd, Health Care Law, Weightman Vizards, subseq. Weightmans Solicitors, 2002–04. Asst Recorder, 1997–2000; Recorder, 2000–04; Resident Judge, Luton Crown Court, 2012–. Hon. Recorder of Luton, 2013–. Mem., Beds Probation Bd, 2006–10. Election Comr, Election Petition Office, 2019. Chm. Trustees, Royal British Legion Pension Fund, 2004; Trustee, Bromsgrove Sch. Foundn, 2011–. Mem., Appeals Court, United Grand Lodge of England, 2011–. Lay Mem., Consistory Ct, Dio. of St Albans, 2000–10. *Publications:* (ed) Morrell and Foster on Local Authority Liability, 1998, 6th edn 2015. *Recreations:* golf, gardening, running smallholding, bridge. *Address:* c/o Luton Crown Court, 7 George Street, Luton LU1 2AA. *Club:* Reform.

**FOSTER, Richard Scot,** CBE 2007; Chairman, Criminal Cases Review Commission, 2008–18; *b* 26 March 1950; *s* of Frank Walter Foster and Betty Lilian Foster; *m* 1997, Susan Warner Johnson; one *s* one *d*. *Educ:* Devonport High Sch.; Pembroke Coll., Cambridge (MA Hons Moral Scis). Joined Dept of Employment, 1973; Sec., MSC, 1975–77; Private Sec. to Minister, 1977–78; on secondment to FCO, Stockholm, 1981–84; Industrial Relations legislation, 1984–86; Head of Deptl Strategy Unit, 1986–88; Director: Finance and Planning, Employment Service, 1988–90; Trng Commn, 1990–92; Employment Service, 1992–98; Dir, Welfare to Work, DFEE, subseq. at DWP, 1998–2001; Chief Exec., CPS, 2002–07. Chm., SE Coast Ambulance NHS Foundn Trust, 2017–18. Trustee, Refugee Council of GB, 2007–17 (Chm., 2013–16). Chm., St George's Hill Lawn Tennis Club, 2018–. *Recreations:* ski-ing, opera, theatre, tennis.

**FOSTER, Robert;** Commissioner, Gambling Commission, 2013–15 (Commissioner, National Lottery Commission, 2005–13); *b* 12 May 1943; *s* of David and Amelia Foster; *m* 1967, Judy Welsh; one *s* one *d*. *Educ:* Oundle Sch.; Corpus Christi Coll., Cambridge (BA 1964; MA 1967). CEng, FIET (FIEE 1993); FRAeS 1996. Parkinson Cowan, 1964–66; Automation Ltd, 1966–71; Exec. Engineer, Post Office Telecommunications, 1971–76; DTI, 1977–92; Under Sec., OST, Cabinet Office, 1992–93, DTI, 1993–2000; Chief Exec. and Sec., Competition Commn, 2001–04. Non-exec. Dir, Jersey Competition Regulatory Authy, 2004–12; Vice Chair, 2004–12, Lay Chair, Consultant Appointments, KCH NHS Foundn Trust, 2012–; Chm., Equinox Care, 2012–14. *Recreations:* theatre, golf, music. *Address:* 9 Holmdene Avenue, Herne Hill, SE24 9LB.

**FOSTER, Prof. Robert Fitzroy, (Roy),** PhD; FRSL; FRHistS; FBA 1989; Carroll Professor of Irish History, University of Oxford, 1991–2016, now Emeritus Professor; Professor of Irish History and Literature, Queen Mary University of London, since 2017; *b* 16 Jan. 1949; *s* of Frederick Ernest Foster and Elizabeth (*née* Fitzroy); *m* 1972, Aisling O'Conor Donelan; one *s* one *d*. *Educ:* Newtown Sch., Waterford; St Andrew's Sch., Middletown, Delaware, USA; Trinity Coll., Dublin (MA; PhD 1975; Hon. Fellow, 2017). FRHistS 1979; FRSL 1992. Lectr, 1974, Reader, 1983, Professor of Modern British Hist., 1988–91, Hon. Fellow, 2005, Birkbeck Coll., London Univ. Alistair Horne Fellow, St Antony's Coll., Oxford, 1979–80; British Acad. Res. Reader in the Humanities, 1987–89; Fellow, IAS, Princeton, and Vis. Fellow, Dept of English, 1988–89, Whitney J. Oates Fellow, 2002, Princeton Univ. Wiles Lectr, QUB, 2004; Clark Lectr, Trinity Coll., Cambridge, 2009; Wolfson Foundn Res. Prof., 2009–12; Vis. Prof., UCD, 2010; James Ford Lectr, Univ. of Oxford, 2012. Parnell Fellow, Magdalen Coll., Cambridge, 2015–16; Hon. Fellow, Hertford Coll., Oxford, 2016. Hon. FRCPI 2017. Hon. MRIA 2010. Hon. DLitt: Aberdeen, 1997; QUB, 1998; TCD, 2003; NUI, 2004; Hon. DLaws: Queen's Univ., Ontario, 2007; Univ. Coll., Dublin, 2016; Hon. LittD Edinburgh, 2013. Irish Post Community Award, 1982; Sunday Independent/Irish Life Arts Award, 1988; M. L. Rosenthal Award, Yeats Soc. of NY, 2003; James Joyce Award, Lit. and Histl Soc., UCD, 2012. *Publications:* Charles Stewart Parnell: the man and his family, 1976, 2nd edn 1979; Lord Randolph Churchill: a political life, 1981, 3rd edn 1987; Political Novels and Nineteenth Century History, 1983; Modern Ireland 1600–1972, 1988; (ed) The Oxford Illustrated History of Ireland, 1989; (ed) The Sub-Prefect Should Have Held His Tongue and other essays, by Hubert Butler, 1990; Paddy and Mr Punch: connections in English and Irish history, 1993; The Story of Ireland, 1995; W. B. Yeats: a life, Vol. 1 The Apprentice Mage 1865–1914, 1997 (James Tait Black Prize for biog., 1998), Vol. 2 The Arch-Poet 1915–1939, 2003; The Irish Story: telling tales and making it up in Ireland, 2001 (Christian Gauss Award for literary criticism, 2004); (with Fintan Cullen) Conquering England: Ireland in Victorian London, 2005; Luck and the Irish, 2007; Words Alone: Yeats and his inheritances, 2011; Vivid Faces: the revolutionary generation in Ireland, 2014 (British Acad. Medal, 2015; Morris D. Forkosch Prize, Amer. Histl Assoc., 2016); numerous essays and reviews. *Recreation:* recreation. *Address:* Hertford College, Oxford OX1 3BW.

**FOSTER, Prof. Russell Grant,** CBE 2015; PhD, DSc; FRS 2008; FMedSci, FRSB; Professor of Circadian Neuroscience, since 2006, Chair, Nuffield Laboratory of Ophthalmology, since 2007, and Founder and Director, Sleep and Circadian Neuroscience Institute, since 2012, University of Oxford; Fellow, Brasenose College, Oxford, since 2006; *b* Aldershot, 19 Aug. 1959; *s* of Donald and Doreen Foster; *m* 1984, Elizabeth Ann Downes; one *s* two *d*. *Educ:* Heron Wood Sch., Aldershot; Farnborough 6th Form Coll.; Univ. of Bristol (BSc 1980; PhD 1984; DSc 2015). Asst Prof., Dept of Biol., Univ. of Va, 1988–95; Imperial College London: Governor's Lectr, Dept of Biol., 1995–97; Reader in Zool., 1997–99; Prof., Dept of Integrative and Molecular Neurosci., 2000–03; Dep. Chair, Dept of Visual Neurosci., 2003–06. Biotechnology and Biological Sciences Research Council: Chm., Animal Scis Cttee, 2002–06; Mem., Strategy Bd, 2007–11; Mem., Council, 2011–15. Mem., UK Panel for Res. Integrity in Health and Biomed. Scis, 2006–15. Mem. Faculty, Lundbeck Internat. Neurosci. Foundn, Denmark, 2007–. Trustee, Sci. Mus. Gp, 2015–. Chair: Adv. Bd, Mus. of Sci. and Industry, Manchester; Cheltenham Sci. Festival, 2011–15. Mem. Bd, Cheltenham Festivals, 2011–15. Royal Society: Chair, Public Engagement Cttee, 2013–; Chair, Sectional Cttee 8, 2014–15; Mem. Council, 2017–. Pres., British Neurosci. Assoc., 2013–15. FRSB 2009; FMedSci 2013. *Publications:* (with L. Kreitzman) Rhythms of Life: the biological clocks that control the daily lives of every living thing, 2005 (multiple trans); (with L. Kreitzman) Seasons of Life: the biological rhythms that living things need to thrive and survive, 2009 (multiple trans); (with S. Lockley) Sleep: a very short introduction, 2012 (multiple trans); (with L. Kreitzman) Circadian Rhythms: a very short introduction, 2017 (multiple trans); 250 peer-reviewed articles in scientific jls. *Recreations:* listening to opera, Wagner when possible, doing anything that involves laughter, hunting for fossils, swimming, being in or near the sea, food, cocktails and wine with family and friends. *Address:* Sleep and Circadian Neuroscience Institute, Nuffield Department of Clinical Neurosciences, Sir William Dunn School of Pathology, Oxford Molecular Pathology Institute, University of Oxford, South Parks Road, Oxford OX1 3RE. *T:* (01865) 618661. *E:* russell.foster@eye.ox.ac.uk. *Club:* Athenæum.

**FOSTER, Sir Saxby Gregory,** 4th Bt *cr* 1930, of Bloomsbury, co. London; *b* 3 Sept. 1957; *s* of Sir John Gregory Foster, 3rd Bt, and of Jean Millicent, *d* of late Elwin Watts; *S* father, 2006; *m* 1989, Rowan Audrey, *d* of late Reginald Archibald Ford; two *s*. *Heir: s* Thomas James Gregory Foster, *b* 1 May 1991. *Address:* PO Box 37, Golden Beach, Qld 4551, Australia. *T:* (7) 54922942, *Fax:* (7) 54957655; 125 Landsborough Parade, Golden Beach, Qld 4551, Australia. *E:* fosters4mail@gmail.com, rfoster@smccab.qld.edu.au.

**FOSTER, Simon Ridgeby;** retired farmer; *b* 1 Sept. 1939; *s* of Sir Ridgeby Foster and of Lady Nancy Foster (*née* Godden); *m* 1st, 1966, Mairi Angela Chisholm (marr. diss.); one *s* two *d*; 2nd, 1990, Philippa Lucy Back (*see* P. L. Foster Back). *Educ:* Shrewsbury Sch.; Jesus Coll., Cambridge (MA Hist.); London Business Sch. (Sloane Fellow); Wye Coll., London Univ. (MSc Sustainable Agric. 1995). Pres. and Dir Gen., Dunlop France, 1983–88; Dir, SMMT, 1988–91; Man. Dir, Toyota GB, 1991–93. Médaille d'Allier, 1987. *Publications:* Politique Industrielle, 1990. *Recreations:* farming, Dutch sailing barges.

**FOSTER BACK, Philippa Lucy,** CBE 2014 (OBE 2006); Director, Institute of Business Ethics, since 2001; *b* Swardeston, Norwich, 13 Nov. 1954; *d* of Philip John Quarles Back and June Debenham Back; *m* 1990, Simon Ridgeby Foster, *qv*. *Educ:* Berkhamsted Sch. for Girls; University Coll. London (BA Hons Geog. 1976). CDipAF 1986; CDir 2006. Asst Manager, Citibank NA, 1977–79; Gp Treas., Bowater Industries plc, 1979–88; Finance Dir, DC Gardner Gp plc, 1988–90; self-employed consultant, 1990–93; Gp Treas., Thorn EMI plc, subseq. EMI Gp plc, 1993–2000. Member: Woolf Cttee, ethical business conduct in BAE Systems plc, 2007–08; Clause 7 MoJ UK Bribery Act Steering Cttee, 2009–10; ICSA review of Higgs Guidance Steering Gp, 2009–11; Whitehall Corporate Governance Steering Gp, 2009–11; Wates Cttee on Corporate Governance Principles for Large Private Cos, BEIS/Financial Reporting Council, 2018–. Tax Comr, 1992–98; non-executive Director: MoD, 1994–2007 (Mem., Defence Bd, 2002–07; Chm., Defence Audit Cttee, 2002–07); Investors Compensation Scheme, 1995–2001; Highways Agency, 2001–05; Ind. Mem., Health Devolt Council, 1995–2001; Comr, UK Debt Mgt Office, 2004–09; Chm., UK Antarctic Place-names Cttee, 2009–. Non-exec. Dir, Barrier Biotech Ltd, 1996–; Mem., Adv. Bd, RAND Europe, 2008–20. Non-exec. Dir, Norfolk and Norwich Univ. Foundn NHS Trust, 2007–11 (Chm., Audit Cttee, 2007–11). Member: Assoc. of Corporate Treasurers, 1982– (Pres., 1999–2000; Hon. Fellow, 2015); IoD, 1999–2013 (Vice Chm. and Sen. Ind. Dir, 2010–13; Hon. Fellow, 2013); Trustee and non-exec. Dir, Assoc. for Project Mgt, 2007–09 (Hon. Fellow, 2018). Trustee: UK Antarctic Heritage Trust, 2001–13 (Chm., 2006–13); South Georgia Heritage Trust, 2015–19 (Chm., 2016–19). Mem. Adv. Bd, Centre for Corporate Reputation, Saïd Business Sch., Univ. of Oxford, 2008–. FRGS. Hon. LLD Warwick, 2018. *Publications:* Corporate Cash

Management: strategy and practice, 1987; Setting the Tone: ethical business leadership, 2005. *Recreations:* polar issues (former Chm., Friends of Scott Polar Research Inst., Cambridge), travelling (three trips to Antarctica and two to Barren Lands, N Canada), current affairs, corporate governance, Dutch Barge sailing. *Address:* c/o Institute of Business Ethics, 24 Greencoat Place, SW1P 1BE. *T:* (020) 7798 6040. *E:* pfb@ibe.org.uk. *Clubs:* Royal Over-Seas League; Norfolk (Norwich).

FOTHERBY, Gordon; *b* 15 Nov. 1950; *m* 1974, Victoria Eloise (marr. diss. 2014); one *s*. *Educ:* Hull GS; Sheffield Univ. (LLB Hons 1972). Called to the Bar, Inner Temple, 1973; Capt., Army Legal Corps, 1973–77; Solicitor's Office, HM Customs and Excise, later HM Revenue and Customs, 1977–2005: Asst Sec., Legal, 1986–93; on secondment to EC, 1989–91; Dep. Solicitor and Hd of Advisory and European, 1993–99, Hd of Prosecutions, 1999–2005; Sen. Legal Counsellor, Internat. Policy, 2005; with The Khan Partnership, LLP, 2006–08; Sen. Manager for Tax, KPMG, 2008–09; legal consultant, 2009–12.

FOTHERGILL, Alastair David William, OBE 2019; Director, Silverback Films, since 2012; *b* 10 April 1960; *s* of David and Jaqueline Fothergill; *m* 1994, Melinda Jane Barker; two *s*. *Educ:* Harrow Sch.; St Andrews Univ.; Durham Univ. (BSc). Joined BBC Natural History Unit, 1983, Head, 1992–98; series producer: Life in the Freezer, 1993; The Blue Planet, 2001; Planet Earth, 2006; exec. prod., Frozen Planet, 2011; series producer, Our Planet, Netflix, 2019. Director of films: Deep Blue, 2004; Earth, 2007; DisneyNature African Cats, 2011; DisneyNature Chimpanzee, 2012; DisneyNature Bears, 2014. *Publications:* Life in the Freezer, 1993; The Blue Planet, 2001; Planet Earth, 2006; Frozen Planet, 2011. *Recreations:* painting, walking. *Address:* Lodge Farm, St Catherine, Bath BA1 8HA. *E:* Alastair.fothergill@silverbackfilms.tv.

FOU TS'ONG; concert pianist; *b* 10 March 1934; *m* 1st, 1960, Zamira Menuhin (marr. diss. 1970); one *s*; 2nd, 1973, Hijong Hyun (marr. diss. 1976); 3rd, 1987, Patsy Toh; one *s*. *Educ:* Shanghai and Warsaw. Debut, Shanghai, 1953. Concerts all over Eastern Europe including USSR up to 1958. Arrived in Great Britain, Dec. 1958; London debut, Feb. 1959, followed by concerts in England, Scotland and Ireland; subsequently has toured all five Continents. Recordings include: Chopin, Mozart, Schumann, Debussy, Scarlatti, Handel, Haydn and Bach. Hon. DLitt Hong Kong, 1983. *Recreations:* bridge, Scrabble, watching sport, Chinese painting. *Address:* 62 Aberdeen Park, N5 2BL. *T:* and *Fax:* (020) 7226 9589.

FOULDS, Adam Samuel James, FRSL; novelist and poet; *b* London, 8 Oct. 1974; *s* of Rabbi Michael Foulds, OBE and Ruth Foulds; *m* 2012, Charla Jones. *Educ:* Bancroft's Sch., Woodford Green, Essex; St Catherine's Coll., Oxford (BA English Lang. and Lit.); Univ. of E Anglia (MA Creative Writing). FRSL 2009. Hon. Fellow, Univ. of Roehampton, 2015. Best of Young British Novelists list, Granta mag., 2013; Next Generation Poet, Poetry Book Soc., 2014. *Publications:* The Truth About These Strange Times, 2007; The Broken Word, 2008; The Quickening Maze, 2009; In the Wolf's Mouth, 2014; Dream Sequence, 2019. *Recreations:* internal martial arts, playing the violin, music, visual art, film. *Address:* c/o The Wylie Agency, 17 Bedford Square, WC1B 3JA. *T:* (020) 7908 5900. *E:* mail@wylieagency.co.uk.

FOULDS, (Hugh) Jon; Chairman: L Huntsworth plc, 2000–08; Fauchier Partners Ltd, 1995–2009; Halifax plc (formerly Halifax Building Society), 1990–99 (Director, 1986–99); *b* 2 May 1932; *s* of late Dr E. J. Foulds and Helen Shirley (*née* Smith); *m*; two *s*. *Educ:* Bootham Sch., York. Dir and Chief Exec., 1976–88, Dep. Chm., 1988–92, Investors in Industry, subseq. 3i Gp plc; Director: Brammer plc, 1980–91 (Chm., 1988–91); London Smaller Companies (formerly London Atlantic) Investment Trust, 1983–95; Pan-Holdings SA, 1986–2008; Eurotunnel plc, 1988–96; Mercury Asset Management Gp plc, 1989–98. Mem. Bd of Banking Supervision, Bank of England, 1993–96. Hon. MA Salford, 1987. *Recreations:* tennis, ski-ing, shooting, pictures. *Address:* 28 Grosvenor Crescent Mews, SW1X 7EX. *Clubs:* Chelsea Arts, Garrick, Hurlingham.

FOULGER, Keith, BSc(Eng); CEng, MIMechE; FRINA, RCNC; Chief Naval Architect, Ministry of Defence, 1983–85, retired; *b* 14 May 1925; *s* of Percy and Kate Foulger; *m* 1951, Joyce Mary Hart; one *s* one *d*. *Educ:* Univ. of London (Mech. Eng.); Royal Naval Coll. Greenwich. Asst Constructor, 1950; Constructor, 1955; Constructor Comdr, Dreadnought Project, USA, 1959; Staff Constructor Officer to C-in-C Western Fleet, 1965–66; Chief Constructor, 1967; Asst Director, Submarines, 1973; Deputy Director: Naval Construction, 1979; Naval Ship Production, 1979–81; Submarines, Ship Dept, 1981–83; Asst Under-Sec. of State, 1983. *Recreations:* travel, gardening, photography. *Address:* Lindley, North Road, Bathwick, Bath BA2 6HW.

FOULIS, Lindsay David Robertson; Sheriff of Tayside, Central and Fife at Perth, since 2001; *b* 20 April 1956; *s* of Henry Edwards Foulis and Mary Robertson Foulis; *m* 1981, Ellenore Brown; two *s* one *d*. *Educ:* High Sch. of Dundee; Univ. of Edinburgh (LLB Hons 1978). Legal apprentice, 1978–80, legal asst, 1980–81, Balfour and Manson, Edinburgh; asst, 1981–84, Partner, 1984–2000, Reid Johnston Bell and Henderson, subseq. Blackadder Reid Johnston, Dundee; Temp. Sheriff, 1998–99; All Scotland Floating Sheriff, Perth, 2000–01. Dundee University: Lectr (pt-time), 1994–2000; Hon. Prof. in Scots Law, 2001–. Mem. Council, Sheriff Court Rules, 1996–2000. *Publications:* (jtly) Civil Court Practice materials for Diploma in Legal Practice, 2001; contrib. articles on civil procedure to Jl Law Soc. of Scotland. *Recreations:* sport, now mainly golf (played badly), music. *Address:* Sheriff's Chambers, Sheriff Court House, Tay Street, Perth PH2 8NL.

FOULIS, Michael Bruce; Director, Children and Families, Scottish Government, 2011–15; *b* 23 Aug. 1956; *s* of Kenneth Munro Foulis and Edith Lillian Sommerville (*née* Clark); *m* 1981, Gillian Margaret Tyson; one *s* one *d*. *Educ:* Kilmarnock Acad.; Edinburgh Univ. (BSc Geog.). Joined Scottish Office, 1978: Private Sec. to Parly Under Sec. of State, 1987–89; on secondment to Scottish Financial Enterprise as Asst Dir, 1989–91; Scottish Educn Dept, 1991–93; Principal Private Sec. to Sec. of State for Scotland, 1993–95; Hd of Div., Agric, Envmt and Fisheries Dept, 1995–97; on secondment to Cabinet Office as Dep. Hd, Devolution Team, Constitution Secretariat, 1997–98; Hd of Gp, Educn and Industry Dept, 1998–99; Scottish Executive, later Scottish Government: Hd of Gp, Enterprise and Lifelong Learning Dept, 1999–2001; Hd, Envmt Gp, Envmt and Rural Affairs Dept, 2001–05; on secondment to Mining (Scotland) Ltd, subseq. Scottish Resources Gp, to work on corp. strategy, 2006–07; Dir, Housing and Regeneration, 2007–10; Dir, Strategy and Performance, 2011. Board Member: Children 1st, 2002–08; Wasps Artists' Studios, 2008–11; Morvern Community Develt Co., 2015–18; Drimnin Community Broadband CIC, 2017–. Vis. Prof., Strathclyde Univ., 2015–. *Recreations:* appreciating lithographs, chopping wood, walking.

FOULKES, family name of **Baron Foulkes of Cumnock**.

FOULKES OF CUMNOCK, Baron *cr* 2005 (Life Peer), of Cumnock in East Ayrshire; **George Foulkes**; PC 2002; JP; *b* 21 Jan. 1942; *s* of late George and Jessie M. A. W. Foulkes; *m* 1970, Elizabeth Anna Hope; two *s* one *d*. *Educ:* Keith Grammar Sch., Keith, Banffshire; Haberdashers' Aske's Sch.; Edinburgh Univ. (BSc 1964). President: Edinburgh Univ. SRC, 1963–64; Scottish Union of Students, 1965–67; Manager, Fund for Internat. Student Cooperation, 1967–68. Scottish Organiser, European Movement, 1968–69; Director: European League for Econ. Co-operation, 1969–70; Enterprise Youth, 1970–73; Age Concern, Scotland, 1973–79. Councillor: Edinburgh Corp., 1970–75; Lothian Regional Council, 1974–79; Chairman: Lothian Region Educn Cttee, 1974–79; Educn Cttee, Convention of Scottish Local Authorities, 1975–78. MP (Lab and Co-op) S Ayrshire, 1979–83, Carrick, Cumnock and Doon Valley, 1983–2005. Opposition spokesman on European and Community Affairs, 1984–85, on Foreign Affairs, 1985–92, on Defence, 1992–93, on Overseas Develt, 1994–97; Parly Under-Sec. of State, DFID, 1997–2001; Minister of State, Scotland Office, 2001–02. Mem., Select Cttee on Foreign Affairs, 1981–83. Jt Chm., All Party Pensioners Cttee, 1983–97 (Sec./Treasurer 1979–83); Mem., Jt Select Cttee on Nat. Security Strategy, 2010–. UK Delegate to Parly Assembly of Council of Europe, 1979–81, 2002–05, 2015–; Mem., Parly Assembly, WEU, 2002–05. MSP (Lab) Lothians, 2007–11. Member: Sub Cttee F, European Scrutiny Cttee, H of L, 2006–08; Intelligence & Security Cttee, H of L, 2007–10; EU Select Cttee, H of L, 2011–16; EU Sub Cttee on Social Policy and Consumer Protection, 2011–12; Sub Cttee C, Foreign Affairs, Defence and Internat. Develt, 2012–16; Liaison Cttee, H of L, 2016–. Treas., Parliamentarians for Global Action, 1993–97 (Mem. Council, 1987–97); Member: UK Exec., CPA, 1987–97, 2002–05, 2011–; IPU, 1989–97 (Mem., British Cttee, 2002–08). Member: Scottish Exec. Cttee, Labour Party, 1981–89; Exec., Socialist Internat., 2003–08; Chm., Labour Movt for Europe in Scotland, 2002–17. President: Caribbean-Britain Business Council, 2002–11; Caribbean Council, 2011–16; Vice-Chm., Cuba Initiative, 2005–16. Rector's Assessor, Edinburgh Univ. Court, 1968–70, Local Authority Assessor, 1971–79. Chairman: Scottish Adult Literacy Agency, 1976–79; John Wheatley Centre, 1990–97. Mem. Exec., British/China Centre, 1987–93. Director: St Cuthbert's Co-op. Assoc., 1975–79; Co-op. Press Ltd, 1990–97. Trustee, Age Scotland, 2014– (Vice Chair, 2015–16; Chair, 2016–); Trustee and Treas., Climate Parliament, 2014–16. JP Edinburgh, 1975. Wilberforce Medal, City of Hull, 1998. Order of Merit (Dominican Republic), 2006. *Publications:* Eighty Years On: history of Edinburgh University SRC, 1964; (contrib.) A Claim of Right, ed Owen Dudley Edwards, 1989. *Recreations:* boating, watching Heart of Midlothian FC (Chm., 2004–05). *Address:* House of Lords, SW1A 0PW. *T:* (020) 7219 3474.

FOULKES, Sir Arthur (Alexander), GCMG 2010 (KCMG 2001); ON 2018; Governor-General of the Bahamas, 2010–14 (Deputy Governor-General, 2008–10); *b* 11 May 1928; *s* of late Dr William Alexander Foulkes and Julie Blanche Foulkes (*née* Maisonneuve); *m* 1st, Naomi Louise Higgs; 2nd, Joan Eleanor Bullard. *Educ:* Public Sch., Inagua, Bahamas; Western Central Sch., Nassau, Bahamas; privately tutored in journalism. News Editor, The Tribune, 1950–62; Editor, Bahamian Times, 1962; Founder/Chm., Diversified Services (PR), 1967. MP Bahamas, 1967; Chm., Bahamas Telecommunications Corp., 1967; Cabinet Minister, 1968; Co-Founder, Free Nat. Movement, 1970; Mem., Senate, 1972. Delegate: Bahamas Petition to UN Cttee on Decolonization, 1965; Bahamas Constitutional Conf., London, 1972. High Comr to UK and Ambassador to France, Italy, Germany, Belgium and the EC, 1992–99; Ambassador (non-resident) to China and to Cuba, 1999–2002. Chairman: Bahamas Broadcasting Corp., 2001–02; Bahamas Parly Salaries Commn, 2001; Bahamas Order of Merit Cttee, 2001; Dir, Bahamas Information Services, 2007–10. Hon. LLD Saint John's Univ., Minnesota, 2010. *Recreations:* theatre, music, art, literature. *Address:* Gambier, West Bay Street, PO Box CB–12366, Nassau, Bahamas.

FOULKES, Rebeccah Louise Elizabeth Ann; *see* Slater, R. L. E. A.

FOULKES, Brig. Thomas Howard Exton, OBE 2012; CEng; FICE; Chairman, Bradbury Robinson Ltd, since 2018; Director General, Institution of Civil Engineers, 2002–11; *b* 31 Aug. 1950; *s* of late Maj.-Gen. Thomas Herbert Fischer Foulkes, CB, OBE and of Delphine Foulkes (*née* Exton Smith); *m* 1976, Sally Winter; two *d*. *Educ:* Clifton Coll.; RMA Sandhurst; RMCS Shrivenham (BSc); Open Univ. (MBA 2001). FIMechE 1997; FICE 1998; MInstRE 2005; FIET 2008. Commnd RE, 1971; Troop Comdr, Ind. Field Troop, AMFL, 1976–79; OC, 1st Field Sqn RE, 1985–87; CO, 28 Amphibious Engr Regt, 1989–92; Project Manager, Gen. Engr Equipment, MoD PE, 1992–95; Col ES42, HQ QMG, 1995–98; rcds, 1998; Dir, Army Estates Orgn, 1999–2002. Dep. Chm., Thomas Telford Ltd, 2002–11; Chairman: Cyntra Ltd, 2009–12; Victoria Business Improvement Dist, 2011–15. Sec.-Gen., 2002–09, Pres., 2009–11, Commonwealth Engrs Council. Vis. Prof. of Civil Engrg, Univ. of Surrey, 2010–. Mem., Smeatonian Soc., 2004–; Trustee, RE Museum Foundn, 2010–. Gov., Clifton Coll., 2010–. FAPM 2009. Liveryman, Engineers' Co., 2005. *Publications:* contribs to RE Jl, chiefly on military bridging and walks in Whitehall. *Recreations:* monuments in Whitehall, history of ideas, obituaries, football, photography, gardening, cycling. *Clubs:* Athenæum; Royal Engineers Assoc. Football (Pres., 1992–2002).

FOULSER, Jeff; Chairman and Chief Executive Officer, Sunset + Vine Productions, since 2005; *b* London, 21 Aug. 1952; *s* of George and Rose Foulser; *m* 1981, Clementine Robinson; one *s* one *d*. *Educ:* Claremont High Sch., Harrow. Asst Prod., LWT, 1970–73; Prod., The Big Match, 1973–76; Exec. Producer, ITV Sport, 1976–89; Exec. Producer, 1989–95, Man. Dir, 1995–2000, Sunset + Vine Prodns; Chief Exec., Television Corp. plc, 2000–05. *Recreations:* golf, walking, ski-ing, theatre, cinema. *Address:* 13 Spencer Road, Twickenham, Middx TW2 5TH. *T:* (020) 7478 7310. *E:* jeff.foulser@sunsetvine.com. *Clubs:* MCC, Annabel's; Royal Wimbledon Golf.

FOULSHAM, Richard Andrew, CMG 2006; HM Diplomatic Service, retired; *b* 24 Sept. 1950; *s* of William Foulsham and Lilian Elizabeth Foulsham (*née* Monro); *m* 1982, Deirdre Elizabeth Strathairn; one *s* one *d*. *Educ:* Univ. of St Andrews (MA Hons 1973). Argyll and Sutherland Highlanders, 1973–79; joined FCO, 1982; Second Sec., FCO, 1982–84; First Secretary: Brunei, 1984–86; Lagos, 1986–90; FCO, 1990–95; Counsellor (Political), Rome, 1995–99; Counsellor: FCO, 1999–2001; Ottawa, 2001–03; FCO, 2003–05. Chief Exec., Hope and Homes for Children, 2005–11. Trustee, Child Health Internat, 2005–15. *Recreation:* walking in mountains. *Address:* Hope and Homes for Children, East Clyffe, Salisbury, Wilts SP3 4LZ.

FOUNTAIN, Charles Anthony, (Tony); Chairman, Nayara Energy (formerly Essar Oil Co.) Ltd, since 2017; *b* Newquay, Cornwall, 23 Sept. 1960; *s* of Air Cdre C. Fountain and Winifred Fountain; one *d*. *Educ:* Loughborough Grammar Sch.; Warwick Univ. (BSc Econs and Internat. Studies); St Antony's Coll., Oxford (MPhil Econs). Economist, latterly Gp Vice Pres., Refining and Mktg, BP, 1984–2009; CEO, Nuclear Decommissioning Authy, 2009–11; CEO, Refining and Marketing, Reliance Industries Ltd, 2011–16. Chm., Sellafield Ltd, 2016–17. *Recreations:* horse riding, running, golf. *Address:* Nayara Energy Ltd, 5th Floor, Jet Airways Gadrej BKC, Bandra Kurla Complex, Bandra East, Mumbai 400051, India. *Club:* Ashdown Forest Golf.

FOUNTAIN, Hon. Sir Cyril (Stanley Smith), Kt 1996; Chief Justice, Supreme Court of Bahamas, 1996, retired; *b* 26 Oct. 1929; *s* of Harold Jackson Fountain and Winifred Olive Helen Fountain (*née* Smith); *m* 1954, Dorothy Alicia Hanna; two *s* one *d*. *Educ:* St Benedict's Coll., Atchison, Kansas (BA *cum laude* Econs); King's Coll. London (LLB Hons 1962). Head Teacher, Bd of Educn, Bahamas, 1955–58; articled law student to Sir Leonard J. Knowles, 1958–59; called to the Bar: Gray's Inn, 1963; Bahamas, 1963; Partner, Cash, Fountain & Co., 1963–93; Supreme Court of Bahamas: Actg Judge, April 1985 and April–Aug. 1990; Justice, 1993–94; Sen. Justice, 1994–96. MP (FNM) Long Island, Rum

Cay and San Salvador, 1972–77. *Recreations:* swimming, historical reading. *Address:* c/o Cash Fountain Law Firm, Armstrong Street, PO Box N 476, Nassau, Bahamas. *T:* (home) 3936493, (office) 3222956/7.

**FOUNTAIN, Ian Matthew;** concert pianist; Professor of Piano, Royal Academy of Music, since 2001; *b* Welwyn Garden City, 15 Oct. 1969; *s* of Nigel and Joan Fountain; partner, Erika Geldsetzer. *Educ:* New Coll. Sch., Oxford; Winchester Coll.; Royal Northern Coll. of Music (GRNCM 1991). ARCO 1985. Winner: Viotti-Valsesia Internat. piano competition, 1986; Arthur Rubinstein Internat. Piano Masters Competition, 1989. Has performed worldwide: London début, Queen Elizabeth Hall, 1991; NY, Berlin, Paris, Israel, Far East; China début, 2018. Has made recordings. Hon. ARAM 2007; Hon. RAM 2014. Echo-Preis, Germany, 2014. *Recreations:* horse racing, literature. *Address:* Royal Academy of Music, Marylebone Road, NW1 5HT. *T:* (020) 7873 7405. *E:* fountain_ian@yahoo.co.uk.

**FOURACRE, Joanna Dorothy;** *see* Haigh, J. D.

**FOURCADE, Jean-Pierre;** Commandeur de l'ordre national du Mérite, 2011; Senator, French Republic, for Hauts-de-Seine, 1977–2011, now Honorary Senator; *b* 18 Oct. 1929; *s* of Raymond Fourcade (Médecin) and Mme Fourcade (*née* Germaine Raynal); *m* 1958, Odile Mion; one *s* two *d*. *Educ:* Collège de Sorèze; Bordeaux Univ. Faculté de Droit, Institut des Etudes politiques (Dip.); Ecole Nationale d'Administration; higher studies in Law (Dip.). Inspecteur des Finances, 1954–73. Cabinet of M. Valéry Giscard d'Estaing: Chargé de Mission, 1959–61; Conseiller technique, 1962, then Dir Adjoint to chef de service, Inspection gén. des Finances, 1962; Chef de service du commerce, 1966–68; Dir-gén. du Commerce intérieur et des Prix, 1968–70; Dir-gén. adjoint du Crédit industriel et commercial, 1970, Dir-gén., 1972, and Administrateur Dir-gén., 1973; Ministre de l'Economie et des Finances, 1974–76; Ministre de l'Equipement et de l'Aménagement du Territoire, 1976–77. Senate: Pres., Commn des Affaires Sociales, 1983–98; Mem., Commn des Affaires Etrangères, de la Défense et des Forces Armées, 2004–. Mayor of Saint-Cloud, 1971–92; Conseiller général du canton de Saint-Cloud, 1973–89; Conseiller régional d'Ile de France, 1976– (Vice-Président, 1982–95); Mayor of Boulogne-Billancourt, 1995–2007. Président: Clubs Perspectives et Réalités, 1975–82; Comité des Finances Locales, 1980–2004; Commn Consultative d'Evaluation des Changes, 2005–11. Vice-Pres., Union pour la Démocratie Française, 1978–86 (Mem. Bureau, 1986); Mem., UMP, 2002–. *Publications:* Et si nous parlions de demain, 1979; La tentation social-démocrate, 1985; Remèdes pour l'Assurance-Maladie, 1989; Mon expérience peut-elle éclairer l'avenir?, 2015. *Address:* 8 Parc de Béarn, 92210 Saint-Cloud, France.

**FOURMAN, Prof. Michael Paul,** DPhil; Professor of Computer Systems, University of Edinburgh, since 1988; *b* Oxford, 12 Sept. 1950; *s* of Lucien Paul Rollings Fourman and Julia Mary Fourman (*née* Hunton); *m* 1982, Jennifer Robin Head (marr. diss. 2001); two *s* one *d*. *Educ:* Univ. of Bristol (BSc Maths 1971); Univ. of Oxford (MSc Mathematical Logic 1972; DPhil 1974). Joseph Fels Ritt Asst Prof., Dept of Maths, Columbia Univ., NY, 1977–82; Reader, 1982–86, Prof. of Formal Systems, Dept of Electronic and Electrical Engrg, 1986–88, Brunel Univ. SRC Fellow, Univ. of Cambridge, 1979; Visiting Scientist: Sydney Univ., 1982; McGill Univ., Montreal, 1983. Founder and Technical Dir, Abstract Hardware Ltd, 1986–96; consultancies for Siemens, Soft Image Systems, Higher Order Logic, Showbusiness, etc. FBCS; CITP; FRSE. *Publications:* articles in jls incl. Pure and Applied Algebra and Automated Reasoning. *Recreations:* cooking, sailing. *Address:* School of Informatics, University of Edinburgh, Informatics Forum, 10 Crichton Street, Edinburgh EH8 9AB. *T:* (0131) 651 3266, *Fax:* (0131) 651 1426. *E:* Michael.Fourman@ed.ac.uk.

**FOURNIER, Bernard;** non-executive Chairman, Xerox Ltd, 1998–2001 (Chief Executive Officer, 1995–98); *b* 2 Dec. 1938; *s* of Jean Fournier and Solange Hervieu; *m* 1st; two *s*; 2nd, 1980, Françoise Chavailler; one *s*. *Educ:* Philo Lycée (Baccalauréat); Louis Le Grand, Paris; Ecole des Hautes Etudes Commerciales, Lille. Joined: Publiart SA, 1964; Sanglier SA, 1965; Rank Xerox, 1966: Regional Manager Africa, Eastern Europe, 1980; Gen. Manager, RX France, 1981; Pres., Amer. Ops, Xerox, 1988; Man. Dir, Rank Xerox Ltd, 1989–95. Non-exec. Dir, AEGIS, 2001–09. Chm. Govs and Mem., Internat. Adv. Bd, Ecole des Hautes Etudes Commercial du Nord, 2008–12. *Recreations:* cooking, oenology, stamps, antiques, golf.

**FOVARGUE, Yvonne Helen;** MP (Lab) Makerfield, since 2010; *b* Sale, 29 Nov. 1956; *d* of Kenneth Gibbon and Irene, (Renee), Gibbon (*née* Reed); one *d*; *m* 2009, Paul Kenny. *Educ:* Sale Girls Grammar Sch.; Leeds Univ. (BA Hons Eng.). Housing Officer, Manchester CC, 1979–86; Chief Exec., St Helens CAB, 1986–2010. Mem. (Lab) Warrington BC, 2004–10. Opposition Whip, 2011–13; Shadow Parly Under Sec. of State for Transport, 2013; Shadow Minister: for Defence, 2013–14, 2015; for Young People, 2014–15; for Business, Innovation and Skills, 2015–16; for Communities and Local Govt, 2017–19. Chm., All Party Parly Gp on Debt and Personal Finance, 2010–, on Legal Aid, 2010, on Consumer Protection. Mem., MENSA. *Recreations:* crime fiction, music of David Bowie. *Address:* (office) Wigan Investment Centre, Waterside Drive, Wigan WN3 5BA. *T:* (01942) 824029. *E:* yvonne.fovargue.mp@parliament.uk. *W:* www.twitter.com/Y_FovargueMP, www.facebook.com/YvonneFovargue4Makerfield.

**FOWDEN, Prof. Garth Lowther,** DPhil; FBA 2015; Sultan Qaboos Professor of Abrahamic Faiths, University of Cambridge, since 2013; *b* Norwich, 14 Jan. 1953; *s* of late David Fowden and of Joy Fowden; *m* 1st, 1977, Polymnia Athanassiadi (marr. diss. 1990); one *s*; 2nd, 1990, Elizabeth Key; one *s*. *Educ:* Merton Coll., Oxford (BA 1974; MA 1978; DPhil 1979). Research Fellow: Peterhouse, Cambridge, 1978–82; Darwin Coll., Cambridge, 1982–83; Lectr in Byzantine and Modern Greek Hist., Groningen Univ., 1983–86; researcher, Nat. Res. Foundn, Athens, 1985–2013. *Publications:* The Egyptian Hermes: an historical approach to the late pagan mind, 1986, 2nd edn 1993; Empire to Commonwealth: consequences of monotheism in late antiquity, 1993; Qusayr Amra: art and the Umayyad elite in late antique Syria, 2004; Before and After Muhammad: the first millennium refocused, 2014. *Recreation:* mountain walking. *Address:* Faculty of Divinity, University of Cambridge, West Road, Cambridge CB3 9BS. *E:* garth.fowden@divinity.cam.ac.uk; Limni, Euboia 34005, Greece.

**FOWKE, Sir David (Frederick Gustavus),** 5th Bt *cr* 1814, of Lowesby, Leics; *b* 28 Aug. 1950; *s* of Lt-Col Gerrard George Fowke (*d* 1969) (2nd *s* of 3rd Bt) and Daphne (*née* Monasteriotis) (*d* 2010); *S* uncle, 1987. *Educ:* Cranbrook School, Sydney; Univ. of Sydney (BA 1971). *Heir:* none.

**FOWLER,** family name of **Baron Fowler**.

**FOWLER,** Baron *cr* 2001 (Life Peer), of Sutton Coldfield in the County of West Midlands; **Peter Norman Fowler,** Kt 1990; PC 1979; Chairman, Aggregate Industries, 2000–06; Lord Speaker, House of Lords, since 2016; *b* 2 Feb. 1938; *s* of late N. F. Fowler and Katherine Fowler; *m* 1979, Fiona Poole, *d* of John Donald; two *d*. *Educ:* King Edward VI Sch., Chelmsford; Trinity Hall, Cambridge (MA). Nat. Service commn, Essex Regt, 1956–58; Cambridge, 1958–61; Chm., Cambridge Univ. Conservative Assoc., 1960. Joined staff of The Times, 1961; Special Corresp., 1962–66; Home Affairs Corresp., 1966–70; reported Middle East War, 1967. Mem. Council, Bow Group, 1967–69; Editorial Board, Crossbow, 1962–69; Vice-Chm., North Kensington Cons. Assoc., 1967–68; Chm., E Midlands Area, Cons. Political Centre, 1970–73. MP (C): Nottingham S, 1970–74; Sutton Coldfield, Feb. 1974–2001. Chief Opposition spokesman: Social Services, 1975–76; Transport, 1976–79; Opposition spokesman, Home Affairs, 1974–75; PPS, NI Office, 1972–74; Sec. of State for Transport, 1981 (Minister of Transport, 1979–81), for Social Services, 1981–87, for Employment, 1987–90; Chief Opposition front bench spokesman on the envmt, transport and the regions, 1997–98; Shadow Home Sec., 1998–99. Mem., Parly Select Cttee on Race Relations and Immigration, 1970–74; Jt Sec., Cons. Parly Home Affairs Cttee, 1971–72, 1974 (Vice-Chm., 1974); Chairman: Cons. Parly Cttee on European Affairs, 1991–92; H of L Select Cttee on BBC, 2005, on Communication, 2007–10, on HIV and AIDS, 2011–12. Joint President: Commonwealth Parly Assoc., 2016–; Inter-Parly Union, British Gp, 2016–. Special Advr to Prime Minister, 1992 Gen. Elecn; Chm., Cons. Party, 1992–94; Mem. Exec., Assoc. of Cons. Peers, 2001–04 (Vice Chm., 2004–10). Chairman: Midland Independent Newspapers, 1991–98; Regl Independent Media (Yorks Post gp of newspapers), 1998–2002; Numark Ltd, 1998–2005; Thomson Foundn, 2007–13; Director: NFC plc, 1990–97; Holcim Ltd, 2006–09; non-exec. Dir, ABTA, 2010–16. Chm., NHBC, 1992–98. *Publications:* After the Riots: the police in Europe, 1979; Ministers Decide: a memoir of the Thatcher years, 1991; A Political Suicide, 2008; AIDS: don't die of prejudice, 2014; political pamphlets including: The Cost of Crime, 1973; The Right Track, 1977. *Address:* House of Lords, SW1A 0PW.

**FOWLER, Dr Aidan Lewis,** FRCS; National Director of Patient Safety, and Deputy Chief Medical Officer, NHS Improvement, since 2018; *b* Herne Bay, Kent, 12 May 1966; *m* 1993, Clare Amanda; two *d*. *Educ:* Kent Coll., Canterbury; University Coll. London (MB BS 1990). Consultant Surgeon, Glos, 2003–15; Nat. Dir of Quality Improvement and Patient Safety, Wales, 2015–18. Mem., BMA. *Publications:* book chapters; articles in jls. *Recreations:* walking, cycling. *Address:* NHS England/Medical Directorate, Skipton House, 80 London Road, SE1 6LH.

**FOWLER, Prof. Alastair David Shaw,** CBE 2014; FBA 1974; Professor of English, University of Virginia, 1990–98; Regius Professor of Rhetoric and English Literature, University of Edinburgh, 1972–84, now Emeritus (University Fellow, 1985–87 and since 2007); *b* 17 Aug. 1930; *s* of David Fowler and Maggie Shaw; *m* 1950, Jenny Catherine Simpson (*d* 2019); one *s* one *d*. *Educ:* Queen's Park Sch., Glasgow; Univ. of Glasgow; Univ. of Edinburgh; Pembroke Coll., Oxford. MA Edin. 1952 and Oxon 1955; DPhil Oxon 1957; DLitt Oxon 1972. Junior Res. Fellow, Queen's Coll., Oxford, 1955–59; Instructor, Indiana Univ., 1957–58; Lectr, UC Swansea, 1959–61; Fellow and Tutor in English Lit., Brasenose Coll., Oxford, 1962–71. Visiting Professor: Columbia Univ., 1964; Univ. of Virginia, 1969, 1979, 1985–90; Mem. Inst. for Advanced Study, Princeton, 1966, 1980; Visiting Fellow: Council of the Humanities, Princeton Univ., 1974; Humanities Research Centre, Canberra, 1980; All Souls Coll., Oxford, 1984. Lectures: Witter Bynner, Harvard, 1974; Churchill, Bristol Univ., 1979; Warton, British Acad., 1980; Ballard Matthews, Univ. of Wales, 1981; Coffin, UCL, 1984; Read-Tuckwell, Bristol Univ., 1991; Shakespeare, British Acad., 1995; Croston, Oxford, 2003; Bateson, Oxford, 2008; MacDiarmid, 2012. Mem., Agder Akademi, 2003. Mem., Scottish Arts Council, 1976–77. Milton Soc. of America Honoured Scholar, 2013. Adv. Editor, New Literary History, 1972–2003; Gen. Editor, Longman Annotated Anthologies of English Verse, 1977–80; Member, Editorial Board: English Literary Renaissance, 1978–2003; Word and Image, 1984–91, 1992–97; The Seventeenth Century, 1986–2003; Connotations, 1990–98; Translation and Literature, 1990–2014; English Review, 1990–98. *Publications:* (trans. and ed) Richard Wills, De re poetica, 1958; Spenser and the Numbers of Time, 1964; (ed) C. S. Lewis, Spenser's Images of Life, 1967; (ed with John Carey) The Poems of John Milton, 1968; Triumphal Forms, 1970; (ed) Silent Poetry, 1970; (ed with Christopher Butler) Topics in Criticism, 1971; Seventeen, 1971; Conceitful Thought, 1975; Catacomb Suburb, 1976; Edmund Spenser, 1977; From the Domain of Arnheim, 1982; Kinds of Literature, 1982; A History of English Literature, 1987; The New Oxford Book of Seventeenth Century Verse, 1991; The Country House Poem, 1994; Time's Purpled Masquers, 1996; (ed) Paradise Lost, 1998; Renaissance Realism, 2003; How to Write, 2006; Literary Names, 2012; The Mind of the Book, 2017; contribs to jls and books. *Address:* 11 East Claremont Street, Edinburgh EH7 4HT.

**FOWLER, Anne Elizabeth;** *see* Heal, A. E.

**FOWLER, Prof. (Christine) Mary Rutherford,** PhD; Master, Darwin College, Cambridge, 2012–Sept. 2020; *b* 1950; *d* of Peter and Rosemary Fowler; *m* 1975; one *s* two *d*. *Educ:* Girton Coll., Cambridge (BA 1st Cl. Maths 1972); Darwin Coll., Cambridge (PhD 1976). Royal Soc. Eur. Fellow, ETH Zürich, 1977–78; University of Saskatchewan: Professional Res. Associate, 1981–82, 1983–91; Asst Prof., 1982–83; Adjunct Prof., 1991–2001; Royal Holloway, University of London: Lectr, then Sen. Lectr (pt-time), 1992–2003; Prof. of Geophysics, 2003–12; Hd, Dept of Earth Scis, 2002–08; Deputy Dean Res. (Sci.), 2009–11; Dean of Science, 2011–12. Chm., Cttee Heads of Univ. Geosci Depts, 2010–11. Associate Editor: Reviews of Geophysics, 1991–94; Jl Geophysical Res., 1998–2004. Dir, Sask Energy, 1992. Mem. Mgt Bd, Seed Enterprise Investment Scheme UK, 2000–03. Mem., res. grant, assessment and interview panels, NERC, 1993–2000, 2013; Mem., Industry Fellowship Panel, 2006–08, Res. Appts Panel, 2011–13, Royal Soc.; Dep. Chair, Earth Systems and Envmtl Sci., HEFCE, RAE, 2008; REF, 2013; Mem., Leverhulme Trust Panel, 2010–18; Mem., Adv. Bd, Faraday Inst., 2012–18; Mem., Res. Councils Individual Merit Promotion Panel, 2014–18. Mem. Council, 1998–2002, Vice-Pres., 2000–02, RAS; Mem. Council, Geol. Soc., 2007–10; Mem., Adv. Cttee, British Geol Survey, 2012–15. Member: Bureau, Internat. Lithosphere Prog., 1997–2002; Governing Bd, Sch. of Cosmic Physics, Dublin Inst. for Advanced Studies, 2006–15. Mem., RAE 2001. Fellow, Royal Canadian Geographic Soc., 2016. Hon. Fellow, RHUL, 2015. Hon. DSc: Edinburgh, 2018; Leeds, 2018. Prestwich Medal, Geol. Soc., 1996. *Publications:* (ed with E. G. Nisbet) Heat Metamorphism and Tectonics, 1988; The Solid Earth: an introduction to global geophysics, 1990, 2nd edn 2005; (ed jtly) The Early Earth: physical, chemical and biological development, 2002; contrib. learned jls. *Address:* Darwin College, Silver Street, Cambridge CB3 9EU. *T:* (01223) 335660.

**FOWLER, Christopher B.;** *see* Brocklebank-Fowler.

**FOWLER, Prof. David,** CBE 2005; PhD; FRS 2002; FRSE; Senior Scientist, Biogeochemistry, Centre for Ecology and Hydrology, Natural Environment Research Council, Edinburgh, 2008–17 (Science Director, 2003–08); *b* 1 June 1950; *s* of late Roy Fowler and of Phyllis Joan Fowler (*née* Lee); *m* 1976, Annette Francesca Odile Rossetti; one *s* two *d*. *Educ:* City Sch., Lincoln; Univ. of Nottingham (BSc 1972; PhD 1976). Institute of Terrestrial Ecology, subseq. Centre for Ecology and Hydrology, Edinburgh: HSO, 1975–78; SSO, 1978–85; PSO, 1985; Section Hd, Air Pollution, 1986; Grade 6, 1991; Grade 5, 1998; Hd, Atmospheric Scis Div., 2002–03. Hon. Lectr, Univ. of Edinburgh, 1988; Special Prof. of Envmtl Sci., Univ. of Nottingham, 1991. Chairman: UK Photochemical Oxidants Rev. Gp, 1990–98; UK Nat. Expert Gp on Transboundary Air Pollution, 1999. FRSE 1999. Member Editorial Board: Tellus, 1995; Environmental Pollution, 2000. *Publications:* (with M. H. Unsworth) Acid Deposition at High Elevation, 1988; Ozone in the United Kingdom, 1997; Acidification, Eutrophication and Ozone in the UK, 2001; (with C. E. R. Pitcairn and J. W. Erisman) Air-Surface Exchange of Gases and Particles; many scientific papers in Qly Jl RMetS, Atmospheric Envmt, Envmtl Pollution, Tellus, New Phytologist and Nature. *Recreations:* hill walking, gardening, music, photography, natural history, cycling. *Address:* Centre for Ecology and Hydrology, Bush Estate, Penicuik, Midlothian EH26 0QB. *T:* (0131) 445 4343, *Fax:* (0131) 445 3943. *E:* dfo@ceh.ac.uk.

FOWLER, Sir (Edward) Michael (Coulson), Kt 1981; Mayor of Wellington, New Zealand, 1974–83; architectural consultant, since 1989; former company chairman and director; *b* 19 Dec. 1929; *s* of William Coulson Fowler and Faith Agnes Netherclift; *m* 1953, Barbara Hamilton Hall (*d* 2009); two *s* one *d. Educ:* Christ's Coll., Christchurch, NZ; Auckland Univ. (MArch). Architect, London office, Ove Arup & Partners, 1954–55; own practice, Wellington, 1957–59; Partner, Calder Fowler Styles and Turner, 1959–89. Wellington buildings designed and supervised: Overseas Passenger Terminal, 1963; The Reserve Bank, 1970; Dalmuir House, 1971; Church of the Immaculate Conception, Taumarunui, 1975; St Andrew's Presbyterian Church, Blenheim, 1976; Greenock House, 1978; alterations and additions, Old St Mary's Convent, Blenheim, 1986; Highfield Winery, Marlborough, 1995–2000; many country and urban houses. Director: New Zealand Sugar Co., 1983–95; Cigna Insurance New Zealand Ltd, 1985–89. Chm., Queen Elizabeth II Arts Council, 1983–87. Wellington City Councillor, 1968–74. Nat. Pres., YHA of NZ, 1984–87. Medal of Honour, NZIA, 1983; Alfred O. Glasse Award, NZ Inst. of Planning, 1984. *Publications:* Wellington Sketches: Folio I, 1971, Folio II, 1974; Country Houses of New Zealand, 1972, 2nd edn 1977; The Architecture and Planning of Moscow, 1980; Eating Houses in Wellington, 1980; Wellington Wellington, 1981; Eating Houses of Canterbury, 1982; Wellington—A Celebration, 1983; The New Zealand House, 1983; Buildings of New Zealanders, 1984; Michael Fowler's University of Auckland, 1993. *Recreations:* sketching, reading, writing, history, politics. *E:* michael.fowler@xtra.co.nz. *Club:* Wellington (Wellington, NZ).

FOWLER, Mary Rutherford; *see* Fowler, C. M. R.

FOWLER, Sir Michael; *see* Fowler, Sir E. M. C.

FOWLER, Michael Glyn; His Honour Judge Fowler; a Circuit Judge, since 2009; *b* Wantage, Oxon, 20 Nov. 1951; *s* of Gordon Fowler and Elizabeth Aled Fowler; *m* 1977, Ruth Mary Adgey-Edgar; two *d. Educ:* King's Coll. London (LLB 1973); Chancery Lane Sch. of Law. Called to the Bar, Middle Temple, 1974; Asst Recorder, 1996–2000; Recorder, 2000–09. Member: Civil Service Sports Council; Civil Service Sailing Assoc. *Recreations:* sailing, family and friends. *Address:* Northampton Crown Court, 85–87 Lady's Lane, Northampton NN1 3HQ. *T:* (01604) 470400, *Fax:* (01604) 470445. *Club:* Bar Yacht.

FOWLER, Neil Douglas; Associate Member, Nuffield College, Oxford, 2009–10 and since 2011 (Guardian Research Fellow, 2010–11; Interim Bursar, 2014–15); senior executive media and communications adviser and consultant, since 2008; *b* 18 April 1956; *s* of late Arthur Vincent Fowler and Helen Pauline Fowler; *m* 1989, Carol Susan (*née* Cherry); one *d*, and one step *s. Educ:* Southend High Sch. for Boys; Univ. of Leicester (BA Social Scis). Reporter, Leicester Mercury, 1978–81; Dep. News Editor, then Asst Chief Sub-editor, Derby Evening Telegraph, 1981–84; Asst to Editor, Asst Editor, then Editor, Lincolnshire Echo, 1984–87; Editor: Derby Evening Telegraph, 1987–91; The Journal, Newcastle upon Tyne, 1991–94; The Western Mail, 1994–2002; Proprietor, Neil Fowler Communications, 2002–03; CEO and Publisher, Toronto Sun, 2003–05; Editor, Which? mag., 2006–08; media consultant, 2008–12; Dir, Creative and Content, then Publishing Dir, 2012–14, Man. Dir, 2014, Headlines Corporate News Ltd. Dir, Publishing NTO, 2000–03. Columnist, Publishing mag., 2011–. Mem., Nunnykirk Parish Council, 2018–. FRSA 1999. Pres., Society (formerly Guild) of Editors, 1999–2000 (Vice-Pres., 1998–99). Trustee and Dir, Trinity Retirement Benefit Scheme, 2019–. Trustee, Northampton Theatres Trust, 2009–16. Mem., Audit Cttee, Nuffield Coll., Oxford, 2010–15. Regional Editor of Year, Newspaper Focus magazines, 1994; BT Welsh Journalist, 1999. *Publications:* (contrib.) Face the Future: tools for the modern media age, 2011; (contrib.) Charitable and Trust Ownership of News Organisations, 2011; (contrib.) Investigative Journalism, 2011; (ed jtly) What We Mean by Local?, 2012; (ed jtly) Last Words: how can journalism survive the death of print?, 2016; (ed jtly) Brexit, Trump and the Media, 2017; (ed jtly) Anti-Social Media?: the impact on journalism and society, 2018; (ed jtly) Do They Mean Us?, 2018; (ed jtly) The Case for Brexit, 2018; (ed jtly) Keeping the Wheels on the Road: UK auto post-Brexit, 2019; (ed jtly) Will the Tory Party Ever be the Same?, 2019. *Recreations:* Essex cricket, cinema, bridge, music of Frank Zappa, Northumberland, golf. *E:* neildfowler1@aol.com, neil.fowler@nuffield.ox.ac.uk.

FOWLER, Prof. Patrick William, PhD; FRS 2012; Professor of Theoretical Chemistry, University of Sheffield, since 2005. *Educ:* Univ. of Sheffield (BSc Chem. 1977; PhD 1980). SERC Postdoctoral Fellow, Univ. of Cambridge, 1980–83; Sen. Demonstrator, Durham Univ., 1984–85; Postdoctoral Res. Fellow, Univ. of Cambridge, 1985; University of Exeter: Lectr in Physical Chem., 1985–90; Reader, 1990–95; Prof., 1995–2005. Visiting Professor: Ecole Nationale Supérieure, Paris, 1996–2005; Univ. Paul Sabatier, Toulouse, 2007. Corday-Morgan Medal, 1992, Tilden Medal, 2004, RSC. *Address:* Department of Chemistry, University of Sheffield, Sheffield S3 7HF.

FOWLER, Peter James, CMG 1990; HM Diplomatic Service, retired; International Adviser, Cairn Energy PLC, since 2001 (non-executive Director, 1996–2001); *b* 26 Aug. 1936; *s* of James and Gladys Fowler; *m* 1962, Audrey June Smith (*d* 2015); one *s* three *d*; *m* 2017, Selina Mohsin. *Educ:* Nunthorpe Grammar Sch., York; Trinity Coll., Oxford (BA). Army Service, 1954–56. FCO, 1962–64; Budapest, 1964–65; Lisbon, 1965–67; Calcutta, 1968–71; FCO, 1971–75; East Berlin, 1975–77; Counsellor, Cabinet Office, 1977–80; Comprehensive Test Ban Delegn, Geneva, 1980; Counsellor, Bonn, 1981–85; Head of N America Dept, FCO, 1985–88; Minister and Dep. High Comr, New Delhi, 1988–93; High Comr to Bangladesh, 1993–96. Vice-Chm., Diplomatic Service Appeal Bd, 1997–2003. Chm., Britain-Nepal Chamber of Commerce and Industry, 2010–14. Chm., Charles Wallace Trust (Bangladesh), 1996–; Hon. Pres., Bangladesh-British Chamber of Commerce, 1998–2007. *Recreations:* reading, South Asia, opera, grandchildren. *Address:* 33 Northdown Street, N1 9BL.

FOWLER, Peter Jon, PhD; FSA; Professor of Archaeology, University of Newcastle upon Tyne, 1985–96, now Emeritus; painter, since 2003; *b* 14 June 1936; *s* of W. J. Fowler and P. A. Fowler; *m* 1959, Elizabeth (*née* Burley) (marr. diss. 1993); three *d. Educ:* King Edward VI Grammar Sch., Morpeth, Northumberland; Lincoln Coll., Oxford (MA 1961). Univ. of Bristol (PhD 1977). FSA 1963. Investigator on staff of RCHM (England), Salisbury office, 1959–65; Staff Tutor in Archaeology, Dept of Extra-Mural Studies, 1965–79, and Reader in Arch., 1972–79, Univ. of Bristol; Sec., Royal Commn on Historical Monuments (England), 1979–85; Leverhulme Fellow, Univ. of Newcastle upon Tyne, 1996–99; world heritage consultant, 2000–11. Member: Historic Bldgs and Ancient Monuments Adv. Cttees, Historic Buildings and Monuments Commn, 1983–86 (Ancient Monuments Bd, 1979–83); Council, National Trust, 1983–2000; World Heritage Panel, DCMS, 2010–11; Pres., Council for British Archaeol., 1981–83 (Vice-Pres., 1979–81). Archaeological consultant, Forestry Commn, 1988–2000; Mem., Landscape Adv. Cttee, DoT, 1990–95. Chm., Jarrow 700AD Ltd, 1991–2000. *Publications:* Regional Archaeologies: Wessex, 1967; (ed) Archaeology and the Landscape, 1972; (ed) Recent Work in Rural Archaeology, 1975; (ed with K. Branigan) The Roman West Country, 1976; Approaches to Archaeology, 1977; (ed with H. C. Bowen) Early Land Allotment in the British Isles, 1978; (with S. Piggott and M. L. Ryder) Agrarian History of England and Wales, I, pt 1, 1981; The Farming of Prehistoric Britain, 1983, re-issued 2009; Farms in England, 1983; (with P. Boniface) Northumberland and Newcastle upon Tyne, 1989; (jtly) Who Owns Stonehenge?, 1990; (with M. Sharp) Images of Prehistory, 1990; The Past in Contemporary Society: then, now, 1992; (jtly) Cadbury Congresbury 1968–73: a late/post-Roman hilltop settlement in Somerset, 1992; (with P. Boniface) Heritage and Tourism in 'the global village', 1993; (jtly) The Experimental Earthwork Project 1960–1992, 1996; (with I. Blackwell) The Land of Lettice Sweetapple, 1998; Landscape Plotted and Pieced: landscape history and local archaeology in Fyfield and Overton, Wiltshire, 2000; (with I. Blackwell) An English Countryside Explored, 2000, re-issued 2009; Farming in the First Millennium AD, 2002; World Heritage Cultural Landscapes, 1992–2002, 2003; Landscapes for the World, 2004; (jtly) Inventory of Cultural and National Heritage Sites of Potential Outstanding Universal Value in Palestine, 2005, re-issued 2006 (Arabic), 2009 (English, Arabic); contribs to learned jls and numerous pubns. *Recreations:* writing, music, gardening, sport. *T:* (020) 7638 6762.

FOWLER, Prof. Robert Louis Herbert, DPhil; FBA 2015; Henry Overton Wills Professor of Greek, University of Bristol, 1996–2017, now Emeritus; *b* 19 May 1954; *s* of Rev. Dr Louis Heath Fowler and Helen Minto Fowler (*née* Wilson); *m* 1976, Judith Lee Evers; two *s. Educ:* Univ. of Toronto Schs; Univ. of Toronto (BA 1976, MA 1977); Wadham Coll., Oxford (DPhil 1980). Fellow, Calgary Inst. for the Humanities, 1980; Department of Classical Studies, University of Waterloo, Canada: Asst Prof., 1981–86; Associate Prof., 1986–94; Chm. of Dept, 1988–96; Prof., 1994–96; Dean of Arts, Univ. of Bristol, 2004–09. Chm. Council, Classical Assoc., 2002–07. President: Soc. for Promotion of Hellenic Studies, 2014–17; Classical Assoc., 2016–17. Ed., Jl Hellenic Studies, 2001–05. *Publications:* The Nature of Early Greek Lyric, 1987; Early Greek Mythography, vol. I, 2000, vol. II, 2013; (ed) The Cambridge Companion to Homer, 2004; contrib. articles to learned jls. *Recreations:* piano, golf. *Address:* 22 Arbutus Drive, Coombe Dingle, Bristol BS9 2PJ. *T:* (0117) 968 5361.

FOWLER, Prof. Robert Stewart, OBE 2001; Principal and Chief Executive, Central School of Speech and Drama, 1986–2001; *b* 1 Feb. 1932; *s* of William Fowler and Breta Bell Fowler (*née* Stewart); *m* 1965, Penelope Jessie Hobbs; two *s* one *d. Educ:* Queen's Coll., Oxford (MA); Queen's Univ., Belfast (DipEd); Guildhall Sch. of Music and Drama (LGSM). Served RAEC, 1950–52. Asst in English, Drama and Latin, Royal Belfast Acad. Instn, 1955–58; Hd of Dept, Forest Gate Sch., 1958–60; Warden, Bretton Hall Coll., Wakefield, 1960–66; Dep. Principal and Principal Elect, Sittingbourne Coll. of Educn, 1966–76; HMI with resp. for theatre, the arts in teacher trng and staff inspector, teacher trng, 1976–86. Chief Ext. Examr (Theatre Design), Nottingham Trent Univ., 1996–98; Ext. Examr (Theatre Studies), TCD, 1997–99. Vis. Prof., Birmingham City Univ. (formerly Univ. of Central England), 1995–. Vice-Pres., European League Inst. of Arts, 1998–2002; Member: Bd, Univs and Colls Employers' Assoc., 1996–2000; Nat. Council for Drama Trng, 1996–2000. Panel Chm., Hong Kong Council for Academic Accreditation, 1996–. Chm. Govs, Keswick Sch., 2007–10 (Foundn Gov., 2004–; Trustee repr. Queen's Coll., Oxford, 2007–); Dir and Mem., Keswick Sch. Multi Acad. Trust, 2017–. Sec., Oxford Univ. Soc. Cumbria, 2005–14. Student Mentor, Queen's Coll., Oxford, 2015–. FRSA 1990. NW Vision Film Writing Award, 2003. *Publications:* Themes in Life and Literature, 1967; (jtly) English 11/16, 5 books, 1971–73; The Hobbit Introduced for Schools, 1973; (jtly) English: a literary foundation course, 1975; Fairy Story in New Fiction, 1992; Silver Wedding in New Fiction, 1993; Art Rush in Seattle in Blunter Edge, 2008; Private Verses, 2009; (jtly) Dreams of Longing: a song cycle, 2010; Tricky Trumtrot The Last Dragon Slayer, 2012; Sing with Joy, 2016. *Recreations:* living, loving, life-saving, laughing, Lake District, Provence, family, friends, writing. *Address:* Gutherscale, Newlands, Keswick, Cumbria CA12 5UE.

FOWLER, Sarah Hauldys; *see* Evans, S. H.

FOWLIE, John Kay, MBE 2017; JP; Vice Lord-Lieutenant of Banffshire, 2003–11; *b* 28 Jan. 1936; *s* of late Spencer Stephen Fowlie, MC and Agnes Howatson (*née* Kay); *m* 1960, Catherine Ann Coull Flett; one *s* one *d* (and one *s* decd). *Educ:* Buckie High Sch.; Jordanhill Coll. of Educn, Glasgow (Teaching Dip. in PE 1960). Nat. Service, 3rd Bn Parachute Regt, Cyprus and Suez, 1955–57; served TA 3rd Bn Gordon Highlanders, 1964–68. Teacher, then Principal Teacher of PE, Keith Grammar Sch., 1960–77; Principal Teacher (Guidance), Buckie High Sch., 1977–96. Mem., then Chm., Moray Children's Panel Adv. Cttee, 1985–96. RNLI: fundraising, 1970–; Station Hon. Sec., Launch Authy, Buckie Lifeboat, 1985–2003; Member: Steering Gp Cttee for RNLI Family Assoc., 2002–03; Scottish Lifeboat Council, 1999–2003; Cttee Mem., Buckie & District Fishing Heritage Mus., 2002–; Bd Mem., Buckie and District Fishing Heritage Gp, 2002–. Elder, Buckie S & W Church, 1975–; Hon. Sec., Buckie & District Seamen's Meml Chapel, 2004–. JP Moray, 1995; DL Banffshire, 1998. *Publications:* The Times, the People, and the Buckie Fishermen's Choir, 2005. *Recreations:* walking, gardening, local history, reading. *Address:* Dunedin, 16 Titness Street, Buckie, Banffshire AB56 1HR. *T:* (01542) 832429.

FOX, family name of **Baron Fox**.

FOX, Baron *cr* 2014 (Life Peer), of Leominster in the County of Herefordshire; **Christopher Francis Fox;** Executive Chair, Vulpes Advisory Ltd, since 2017; *b* Haslemere, 27 Sept. 1957; *s* of Andrew Fox and Elizabeth Fox; *m* Sarah, (Essie), Bengry; one *d. Educ:* Imperial Coll. London (BSc). ARCS 1980. Front of house, King's Head Th., 1980; Field Engr, 1981–85, Communications Manager, 1990–98, Schlumberger Oilfield Services; Editor, Offshore Engineer, 1985–90; Dir, Corporate Relns, Tate & Lyle, 1998–2005; Dir, Communications, Smiths Gp, 2005–09; Chief Exec., Lib Dems, 2009–11; Dir, Gp Communications, GKN plc, 2012–17. *Recreations:* mountains, tai chi, cigars. *Address:* 9 Claremont Road, Windsor SL4 3AX. *E:* foxc@parliament.uk. *Clubs:* MCC, Arsenal Football.

FOX, Dr Alan Martin; Clerk to Governors, Jews Free School, 2000–02 and since 2009; *b* 5 July 1938; *s* of Sidney Nathan Fox and Clarice Solov; *m* 1965, Sheila Naomi Pollard; one *s* two *d. Educ:* Bancroft's Sch., Essex; Queen Mary Coll., London (BSc Hons II1, Physics 1959; PhD Math. Phys. 1963). ACIArb 1997, MCIArb 1999. Home Civil Service by Open Competition, 1963; Ministry of Aviation: Private Sec. to Parly Sec., 1965–67; 1st Sec. (Aviation and Defence) on loan to FCO, Paris, 1973–75; MoD, 1975–78; RCDS, 1979; MoD, 1980–98; Asst Under Sec. of State (Ordnance), 1988–92; Vis. Fellow, Center for Internat. Affairs, Harvard, 1992–93; Asst Under-Sec. of State (Quartermaster), 1994–95, (Export Policy and Finance), 1995–98. Lectr (part-time), UCL, 1998–2000. Clerk to Trustees, St Marylebone Almshouses, 1999–2019; Member: London Rent Assessment Panel, 1999–2008; Compliance and Supervision Cttee, 2000–01, Adjudication Panel, 2002–08, SRA (formerly Office for the Supervision of Solicitors); Review Cttee on Non-

Competitive Contracts, 2000–07. Clerk to Governors: Henrietta Barnett Sch., 1998–2003; King Solomon High Sch., 2008–13. *Recreations:* grandchildren, computer games, watching Rugby, cricket, TV, travel. *Address:* 4 Woodside Avenue, N6 4SS.

**FOX, Dr (Anthony) John,** FFPH; Visiting Professor, University College London, since 2006; *b* 25 April 1946; *s* of Fred Frank Fox, OBE, and Gertrude Price; *m* 1971, Annemarie Revesz; one *s* two *d*. *Educ:* Dauntsey's School; University College London (BSc); Imperial College London (PhD, DIC). FFPH (FFPHM 2000). Statistician: Employment Medical Adv. Service, 1970–75; OPCS, 1975–79; Prof. of Social Statistics, City Univ., 1980–88; Chief Medical Statistician, OPCS, 1988–96; Dir, Census, Population and Health Gp, ONS, 1996–99; Dir of Statistics, DoH, 1999–2005; Strategic Advr, Research, Information Centre for Health and Social Care (formerly Dir, Customer and Stakeholder Engagement, NHS Health and Social Care Information Centre), 2005–06. Vis. Prof., LSHTM, 1990–. Trustee, N London Hospice, 2007. Hon. DSc City, 1997. *Publications:* Occupational Mortality 1970–72, 1978; Socio-Demographic Mortality Differentials, 1982; Health Inequalities in European Countries, 1989; (jtly) Health and Class: The early years, 1991. *Recreations:* family, tennis, bridge, theatre. *Address:* Department of Epidemiology and Public Health, University College London, 1–19 Torrington Place, WC1E 6BT.

**FOX, Sir Ashley (Peter),** Kt 2019; Member (C) South West England and Gibraltar, European Parliament, 2009–19; *b* Sutton Coldfield, 15 Nov. 1969; *s* of Clive and Diana Fox; *m* 1997, Julia Glynis David; one *s* one *d*. *Educ:* The King's School, Worcester; Bristol Poly. (LLB (Hons)); Coll. of Law, Chester. Admitted solicitor, 1994; former Solicitor, Morgan Cole. Mem. (C) Bristol CC, 2002–10. Contested (C) SW Reg., EP, 2019. *Recreations:* bridge, poker, swimming.

**FOX, Brian Michael,** CB 1998; Head of Civil Service Corporate Management (Grade 2), Cabinet Office, 1998–2000; *b* 21 Sept. 1944; *s* of Walter Frederick and Audrey May Fox; *m* 1966, Maureen Ann Shrimpton; one *d*. *Educ:* East Ham Grammar School for Boys. Joined CS, HM Treasury, 1963–98: Private Sec. to Financial Sec., 1967–69; secondment to 3i Gp, 1981–82; Dep. Estabt Officer, 1983–87; Head of Defence Policy and Materiel Div., 1987–89; Principal Estabt and Finance Officer, 1989–93; Dir (Grade 3), Sen. and Public Appts Gp, later Sen. CS Gp, Cabinet Office (on loan), 1994–98. Trustee, Help The Aged, 1998–2009; Property Trustee, Civil Service Benevolent Fund, 2001–12. Chm., Anim-Mates, 2006–11. *Recreations:* bowls, soccer. *Club:* Elm Park Bowls.

**FOX, Sir Christopher,** Kt 2006; QPM 1996; Managing Director, Chris Fox Consulting Ltd, 2006–13; *b* 21 July 1949; *s* of late Douglas Charles Fox and Olive Eileen Fox (*née* Vigar); *m* 1972, Carol Ann Wortley; one *s* two *d*. *Educ:* Broomhill Primary Sch.; Robert Gordon's Coll., Aberdeen; W Bridgford GS, Nottingham; Loughborough Univ. (BSc Physics and Electronic Engrg; DIS); Cabinet Office (Top Mgt Prog. 1995). Joined Notts Constabulary, 1972; detective and uniform duties, 1972–83; Superintendent, Mansfield, 1984–87; Chief Supt, Nottingham N Div., 1987–90; Actg Asst Chief Constable, Nottingham, 1990–91; Asst Chief Constable, 1991–94, Dep. Chief Constable, 1994–96, Warwickshire; Chief Constable, Northants, 1996–2003; Pres., ACPO, 2003–06. Chm., Civil Nuclear Police Authy, 2009–11. Pres., Endeavour, 2017– (Vice Pres., 2009–16). Trustee, Police Foundn, 2005–. Dir, Stratford Oaks Golf Club Ltd, 2016– (Chm.). *Recreations:* played Rugby at first class level (Nottingham), keen Rugby supporter of Wasps at Coventry, golf, laid back cruiser sailing. *T:* 07714 689219.

**FOX, Claire;** Founder and Director, Academy (formerly Institute of Ideas, since 2000; Member (Brexit) North West Region, European Parliament, since 2019; *b* 5 June 1960; *d* of late John Fox and of Maura Fox. *Educ:* Warwick Univ. (BA Hons English and American Lit.); Thames Poly. (PGCE 1992). Mental health social worker for variety of orgns in voluntary sector, incl. Cyrenians and MIND, 1981–87; Lectr and Tutor in English Lang. and Lit., Thurrock Tech. Coll., 1987–90 and W Herts Coll., 1992–99; Publisher, Living Marxism, subseq. LM mag., 1997–2000. Panellist, Moral Maze, BBC Radio 4, 2000–; columnist, MJ mag., 2000–. Convenor, Battle of Ideas Fest., 2005–. *Publications:* contributed chapters to: Debating Education: issues for the new millennium, 1996; Dumbing Down, 2000; (also ed) Maybe I Do: marriage and commitment in the singleton society, 2002; The McDonaldisation of Higher Education, 2002; The Routledge Falmer Guide to Key Debates in Education, 2004; A Lecturer's Guide to Further Education, 2006; The Lottery Debate, 2006; Panic Attack, 2006; No Strings Attached!: why arts funding should say no to instrumentalism, 2008; I Still Find That Offensive, 2018. *Recreation:* putting my head above the parapet, saying the unsayable and stirring up intellectual debate. *Address:* Academy of Ideas, Unit 208, Cocoa Studios, The Biscuit Factory, Drummond Road, SE16 4DG. *T:* (020) 7269 9223. *E:* clairefox@academyofideas.org.uk.

**FOX, Colin;** Member (Scot Socialist) Lothians, Scottish Parliament, 2003–07; National Convenor, Scottish Socialist Party, since 2005; *b* 17 June 1959; *s* of John Fox and Agnes Fox (*née* Mackin); partner, Zillah Jones; one *s* one *d*. *Educ:* Our Lady's High Sch., Motherwell; Bell Coll., Hamilton (SHND Accounting); Open Univ. (BSc Hons Soc. Sci. 2012). Political organiser (militant), 1983–95; Scottish Socialist Alliance organiser, 1995–98; Scottish Socialist Party: Founder Mem., 1998; Organiser, 1998–2003. Contested (Scot Socialist): Edinburgh SW, 2010; Edinburgh S, 2015. Mem., 'Yes Scotland' Adv. Bd for Independence, 2012–. Co-organiser, Edinburgh Mayday Fest., 1998–; Founder/Organiser, 2002–, Dir, 2010–, Edinburgh People's Fest. Contested (Rise) Lothian, Scottish Parlt, 2016. *Publications:* Motherwell is Won for Moscow, 1991; (jtly) Whose Justice, 2006; End Fuel Poverty and Power Company Profiteering, 2012. *Recreations:* golf, reading, travel, running.

**FOX, Edward,** OBE 2003; actor; *b* 13 April 1937; *s* of late Robin and Angela Muriel Darita Fox; *m* 1st, 1958, Tracy (*née* Pelissier) (marr. diss. 1961); one *d*; 2nd, 2004, Joanna David; one *s* one *d*. *Educ:* Ashfold Sch.; Harrow Sch. RADA training, following National Service, 1956–58; entry into provincial repertory theatre, 1958, since when, films, TV films and plays, and plays in the theatre, have made up the sum of his working life. *Theatre includes:* Knuckle, Comedy, 1973; The Family Reunion, Vaudeville, 1979; Anyone for Denis, Whitehall, 1981; Quartermaine's Terms, Queen's, 1981; Hamlet, Young Vic, 1982; Interpreters, Queen's, 1985; Let Us Go Then, You and I, Lyric, 1987; The Admirable Crichton, Haymarket, 1988; (also dir) Another Love Story, Leicester Haymarket, 1990; The Philanthropist, Wyndham's, 1991; The Father, tour, 1995; A Letter of Resignation, Comedy, 1997; The Chiltern Hundreds, Vaudeville, 1999; The Browning Version, and The Twelve-Pound Look, Th. Royal, Bath, 2002; The Winslow Boy, tour, 2002; The Old Masters, Comedy, 2004; You Never Can Tell, Th. Royal, Bath, 2005, Garrick, 2005–06; Legal Fictions, tour, 2007; Lloyd George Knew My Father, tour, 2009–10; Trollope in Barsetshire, tour, 2010, Riverside Studios, 2011; The Audience, Gielgud, 2013; An Ideal Husband, Chichester Fest. Th., 2014; Sand in the Sandwiches, UK tour, 2016. T. S. Eliot's Four Quartets, tours in provinces, 2000–, Riverside Studios, 2011; An Ideal Husband, Vaudeville, 2018. *Films include:* The Go-Between, 1971 (Soc. of Film and Television Arts Award for Best Supporting Actor, 1971); The Day of the Jackal, A Doll's House, 1973; Galileo, 1976; The Squeeze, A Bridge Too Far (BAFTA Award for Best Supporting Actor, 1977), The Duellists, The Cat and the Canary, 1977; Force Ten from Navarone, 1978; The Mirror Crack'd, 1980; Gandhi, 1982; Never Say Never Again, The Dresser, 1983; The Bounty, 1984; The Shooting Party, 1985; A Month by the Lake, 1996; Stage Beauty, 2004.

*Television series include:* Hard Times, 1977; Edward and Mrs Simpson, 1978 (BAFTA Award for Best Actor, 1978; TV Times Top Ten Award for Best Actor, 1978–79; British Broadcasting Press Guild TV Award for Best Actor, 1978; Royal TV Soc. Performance Award, 1978–79); They Never Slept, 1991; A Dance to the Music of Time, 1997; Daniel Deronda, 2002; Oliver Twist, 2007. *Recreations:* music, reading, walking. *Club:* Savile.
*See also* J. Fox, R. M. J. Fox, Viscount Gormanston.

**FOX, Fiona Bernadette, (Mrs Kevin Rooney),** OBE 2013; Founding Director and Chief Executive, Science Media Centre, since 2001; *b* Mancot, Wales, 12 Nov. 1964; *d* of late John Fox and of Maura Fox; *m* 1996, Kevin Rooney; one *s*. *Educ:* St Richard Gwyn High Sch., Flint; Poly. of Central London (BA Hons Journalism). Press Manager, NCOPF, 1984–86; Press Officer, EOC, 1986–92; Asst Press Officer, Thames Poly., 1992–93; Sen. Press Manager, Brook Adv. Centres, 1993–95; Hd of Media, CAFOD, 1995–2001. Chair, Science and the Media: securing the future, BIS report, 2010. Hon. FBPhS 2018. *Publications:* (contrib.) Communicating Biological Sciences, 2009. *Recreations:* news junkie, Celtic FC supporter. *Address:* Science Media Centre, 215 Euston Road, NW1 2BE. *T:* (020) 7611 8300. *E:* fiona@sciencemediacentre.org.
*See also* Claire Fox.

**FOX, Hazel Mary, (Lady Fox),** CMG 2006; Director, British Institute of International and Comparative Law, 1982–89; General Editor, International and Comparative Law Quarterly, 1987–98; *b* 22 Oct. 1928; *d* of J. M. B. Stuart, CIE; *m* 1954, Rt Hon. Sir Michael Fox, PC (*d* 2007); three *s* one *d*. *Educ:* Roedean Sch.; Somerville Coll., Oxford (1st Cl. Jurisprudence, 1949; MA). Called to the Bar, Lincoln's Inn, 1950 (Buchanan Prize); Bencher, 1989); practised at the Bar, 1950–54 and 1994–2011; Fellow of Somerville Coll., Oxford, 1976–81, Hon. Fellow 1988. Chairman: London Rent Assessment Panel, 1977–98; London Leasehold Valuation Tribunal, 1981–98; Mem., Home Office Deptl Cttee on Jury Service, 1963–65. Mem., Institut de droit international, 2001. Hon. QC 1993. JP London, 1959–77; Chm., Tower Hamlets Juvenile Court, 1968–76. *Publications:* (with J. L. Simpson) International Arbitration, 1959; (ed) International Economic Law and Developing States, vol. I 1988, vol. II 1992; (ed) Joint Development of Offshore Oil and Gas, vol. I 1989, vol. II 1990; (ed jtly) Armed Conflict and the New Law, vol. II: Effecting Compliance, 1993; The Law of State Immunity, 2002, rev. 3rd edn (with P. Webb) 2015. *Address:* 4/5 Gray's Inn Square, WC1R 5AH. *T:* (020) 7404 5252, *Fax:* (020) 7242 7803.

**FOX, James;** actor; *b* 19 May 1939; *s* of late Robin and Angela Fox; changed forename from William to James, 1962; *m* 1973, Mary Elizabeth Piper; four *s* one *d*. *Educ:* Harrow Sch.; Central Sch. of Speech and Drama. National Service, 1959–61. Entered acting as child, 1950; left acting to pursue Christian vocation, 1970–79; returned to acting, 1980. Main *films* include: The Servant, 1963; King Rat, 1964; Thoroughly Modern Millie, 1965; The Chase, 1966; Isadora, 1968; Performance, 1969; A Passage to India, 1984; Runners, 1984; Farewell to the King, 1987; Finding Mawbee (video film as The Mighty Quinn), 1988; She's Been Away, 1989; The Russia House, 1990; Afraid of the Dark, 1991; The Remains of the Day, 1993; Anna Karenina, 1997; Mickey Blue Eyes, 1999; Up the Villa, 1999; Sexy Beast, 1999; The Golden Bowl, 1999; The Prince and Me, 2004; Charlie and the Chocolate Factory, 2005; Mr Lonely, 2006; Sherlock Holmes, 2009; A Long Way From Home, 2012; The Double, 2012; Effie, 2013; Surviving Christmas with the Relatives, 2018; *screenplay:* Under Western Eyes, 2009; *theatre* includes: Uncle Vanya, NY, 1995; Resurrection Blues, Old Vic, 2006; Dear Lupin, Apollo Th., 2015; *television* includes: The Choir (serial), 1995; Gulliver's Travels, 1996; The Lost World, 2001; The Falklands (play), 2002; Suez, 2006; Margaret, 2008. Writer and Dir, Lara and Zhivago, 2010; Utopia, 2012; London Spy, 2014; writer, Zhivago, 2017. *Publications:* Comeback: an actor's direction, 1983. *Recreations:* Russian language and culture, wind surfing. *Address:* c/o Dalzell & Beresford Ltd, Paddock Suite, The Courtyard, 55 Charterhouse Street, EC1M 6HA.
*See also* E. Fox, R. M. J. Fox.

**FOX, (James) Robert (Rutherford),** MBE 1982; Defence Editor, Evening Standard, since 2013 (Defence Correspondent, since 1999); *b* Ratley, Warks, 21 Sept. 1945; *s* of George and Patricia Fox; *m* 1971, Fyne Marianne Ockinga; one *s* one *d*. *Educ:* Blundell's Sch.; Magdalen Coll., Oxford (BA Hons Modern Hist. 1967; MA 1970). News Producer, 1968–71, Producer, Talks and Documentaries, 1971–73, BBC Radio; Nat. Reporter, then Internat. Corresp., BBC, 1973–87; Defence Chief Foreign Corresp., Daily Telegraph, 1987–97; Special Corresp., Evening Standard, 1998–99. Churchill Fellow, 1982; Associate Fellow, Centre for Defence Studies, KCL, 2000–; Hon. Fellow, Strategic Studies Inst., Exeter Univ., 2013. Comr, Commonwealth War Graves Commn, 2012–18. *Publications:* Eye Witness Falklands, 1982; Inner Sea: Mediterranean and its people, 1990; Camera in Conflict, 1995; Eyewitness to History, 2008. *Recreations:* small boats, Italy, standing and staring, music. *T:* (office) (020) 7607 6148. *E:* robfox45@gmail.com. *Clubs:* Garrick, Academy, Beefsteak, Frontline.

**FOX, John;** *see* Fox, A. J.

**FOX, Prof. Keith Alexander Arthur,** FRCPE, FMedSci; Duke of Edinburgh Professor of Cardiology, 1989–2014, British Heart Foundation Professor of Cardiology, 1989–2014, and Head, Cardiology Section, Centre for Cardiovascular Sciences, until 2014, University of Edinburgh, now Emeritus Professor of Cardiology; *b* 27 Aug. 1949; *m* Aileen Fox; one *s* one *d*. *Educ:* Falcon Coll.; Univ. of Edinburgh (BSc Hons 1972; MB ChB 1974). FRCPE 1987; FACC 2009. Asst Prof. of Medicine, Univ. of Washington, 1980–85; Sen. Lectr in Cardiol. and Hon. Cons. Cardiologist, UWCM, 1985–89. President: British Cardiovascular Soc., 2009–12; Action on Smoking and Health (Scotland), 2009– (Chm. Bd, 1999–2008). FESC 1988 (Chm., Clinical Cttee, 2012–14); FMedSci 2001. *Publications:* 658 contribs to scientific and med. jls on coronary arterial disease, mechanisms and treatments. *Address:* Centre for Cardiovascular Science, Chancellor's Building, 49 Little France Crescent, Edinburgh EH16 4SB; An Sionnach, Nethy Bridge PH25 3EF.

**FOX, Kenneth Lambert,** FCIPS; public sector consultant, since 1986; *b* 8 Nov. 1927; *s* of J. H. Fox, Grimsby, Lincolnshire; *m* 1959, P. E. Byrne; one *d*. *Educ:* City of London Coll.; Univ. of London. BSc (Hons), MIIM. Plant Manager, Rowntree Gp, 1950–63; Supply Manager, Ford Motor Co. (UK), 1963–67; Sen. Management Conslt, Cooper & Lybrand Ltd, 1967–70; Manager of Conslts (Europe), US Science Management Corp., 1971–72; Supply Management, British Gas Corp., 1972–75; Dir of Supplies, GLC, 1975–86. *Recreations:* tennis, painting, bird watching, DIY. *Address:* 9 Dolphin Lane, Melbourn, Royston, Herts SG8 6AF. *T:* (01763) 206573.

**FOX, Prof. Kevin Dyson,** PhD; FMedSci; Professor of Neuroscience, Cardiff University, since 1996; *b* London, 1957; *s* of Kenneth Fox and Peggy Fox; *m* 1st, 1990, Helena Williams (marr. diss. 2003); two *s*; 2nd, 2009, Anwen John; two *s*. *Educ:* Buckhurst Hill Co. High Sch.; Univ. of Bath (BSc Hons Electrical and Electronic Engrg); London Hosp. Medical Coll., Univ. of London (PhD Neurophysiol. 1986). McDonnell Fellow, Sch. of Medicine, Washington Univ., St Louis, 1987–90; Res. Asst Prof., Brown Univ., Providence, 1990–93; Asst Prof., Sch. of Medicine, Univ. of Minnesota, 1993–96. Dep. Chm., Neurosci. and Mental Health Bd, MRC, 2008–12. Mem., REF 2014 Assessment Panel, 2014. MAE 2010; FMedSci 2013. *Publications:* Barrel Cortex, 2008; articles in Nature, Sci.,

Nature Neurosci., Neuron, Procs NAS. *Recreations:* music, film, poetry, hiking, ski-ing, running. *Address:* Cardiff School of Biosciences, Sir Martin Evans Building, Museum Avenue, Cardiff CF10 3AX. *E:* foxkd@cardiff.ac.uk.

**FOX, Dr the Rt Hon. Liam;** PC 2010; MP (C) North Somerset, since 2010 (Woodspring, 1992–2010); *b* 22 Sept. 1961; *s* of William Fox and Catherine Young; *m* 2005, Dr Jesmé Baird. *Educ:* St Bride's High Sch., E Kilbride; Univ. of Glasgow (MB ChB 1983). MRCGP 1989. General Practitioner, Beaconsfield, 1987–91; Army MO (civilian), RAEC, 1981–91; Divl Surgeon, St John's Ambulance, 1987–91. Contested (C) Roxburgh and Berwickshire, 1987. PPS to Home Sec., 1993–94; an Asst Govt Whip, 1994–95; a Lord Comr of HM Treasury (Govt Whip), 1995–96; Parly Under-Sec. of State, FCO, 1996–97; Opposition spokesman on constitutional affairs, 1997–99, on health, 1999–2001; Shadow Health Sec., 2001–03; Co-Chm., Cons. Party, 2003–05; Shadow Foreign Sec., 2005; Shadow Defence Sec., 2005–10; Sec. of State for Defence, 2010–11; Sec. of State for Internat. Trade and Pres. of the Board of Trade, 2016–19. Mem., Select Cttee on Scottish Affairs, 1992; Secretary: Cons. back bench Health Cttee, 1992–93; Cons. West Country Members Group, 1992–93. *Publications:* Making Unionism Positive, 1988; (contrib.) Bearing the Standard, 1991; Rising Tides: facing the challenges of a new era, 2013; contrib. to House of Commons Magazine. *Recreations:* tennis, swimming, cinema, theatre. *Address:* House of Commons, SW1A 0AA. *T:* (020) 7219 4086.

**FOX, Lindsay Garrett,** MBE 2013; Vice Lord-Lieutenant for Hampshire, 2014–17; *b* Washington, DC, 4 Dec. 1942; *d* of Sir Donald Forsyth Anderson and Margaret Elaine Anderson (*née* Llewellyn); *m* 1962, Robert Trench Fox, *qv*; two *s* two *d. Educ:* Cheltenham Ladies' Coll. Voluntary advr, Winchester CAB, 1977–87; Dir, Rank Foundn, 1991–2012 (Chm., 2010–12). Member: Adv. Cttee to children's home, 1976–88 (Chm., 1983–88); Council, Winchester Cath., 2000–09. Founder, Blue Lamp Trust (formerly Hants Bobby Trust), 1998–2017 (Patron, 2018–). JP Hants, 1979–2012 (Chm., S Hants Bench, 1992–95); High Sheriff, 1997–98, DL 1998, Hants. *Recreations:* family, travel, theatre.

**FOX, Ven. Michael John;** Archdeacon of West Ham, 1996–2007; *b* 28 April 1942; *s* of John and Dorothy Fox; *m* 1966, Susan Cooper; one *s* one *d. Educ:* Barking Abbey GS; Hull Univ. (BSc); Coll. of the Resurrection, Mirfield. Ordained deacon, 1966, priest, 1967; Curate: St Elizabeth, Becontree, 1966–70; Holy Trinity, S Woodford, 1970–72; Vicar: Ch. of the Ascension, Victoria Docks, and Missioner, Felsted Sch., 1972–76; All Saints, Chelmsford, 1976–88; Asst RD and RD, Chelmsford, 1982–88; Rector, St James, Colchester, 1988–93; Archdeacon of Harlow, 1993–96. Hon. Canon, Chelmsford Cathedral, 1991–. *Recreations:* walking, photography, West Ham. *Address:* 17A Northgate Street, Colchester, Essex CO1 1EZ. *T:* (01206) 710701.

**FOX, Sir Paul (Leonard),** Kt 1991; CBE 1985; Managing Director, BBC Television Network, 1988–91; *b* 27 Oct. 1925; *m* 1948, Betty Ruth (*née* Nathan) (*d* 2009); two *s. Educ:* Bournemouth Grammar Sch. Served War, Parachute Regt, 6th Airborne Division, 1943–46. Reporter, Kentish Times, 1946; Scriptwriter, Pathé News, 1947; joined BBC Television, 1950: Scriptwriter, Television Newsreel; first Editor, Sportsview, 1953, Panorama, 1961; Head, Public Affairs, 1963, Current Affairs, 1965; Controller, BBC1, 1967–73; Dir of Progs, 1973–84, Man. Dir, 1977–88, Yorkshire Television. Chairman: ITN, 1986–88 (Dir, 1980–86); BBC Enterprises Ltd, 1988–91; Stepgrades Consultants, 1991–2002; Director: Trident Television, 1973–80; Channel Four, 1985–88; World Television News, 1986–88; Thames Television, 1991–95. Sports columnist, The Daily Telegraph, 1991–2003. Chm., Racecourse Assoc. Ltd, 1993–97; Director: British Horseracing Bd, 1993–97; Horseracing Betting Levy Bd, 1993–97. Chm., Disasters Emergency Cttee, 1996–99; Member: Royal Commn on Criminal Procedure, 1978–80; Inquiry into Police Responsibilities and Rewards, 1992–93. Pres., RTS, 1985–92; Mem. Cttee, Nat. Mus. of Film, Photography and TV, 1985–95; Trustee, Cinema and Television Benevolent Fund, 1987–90 and 1995–2002 (Pres., 1992–95). BAFTA Fellow, 1990. CCMI (CBIM 1987). Hon. LLD Leeds, 1984; Hon. DLitt Bradford, 1991. Cyril Bennett Award, for outstanding television programming, 1984; Founders Award, Internat. Council, US Nat. Acad. of TV Arts and Scis, 1989; RTS Gold Medal, for outstanding services to television, 1992. *Recreations:* travel, theatre, films. *Address:* 20 The Rose Walk, Radlett, Herts WD7 7JS. *E:* fox.sirpaul@gmail.com. *Club:* Garrick.

**FOX, Peter Kendrew;** University Librarian, University of Cambridge, 1994–2009, now Emeritus Librarian; Fellow of Selwyn College, Cambridge, since 1994; *b* 23 March 1949; *s* of Thomas Kendrew Fox and Dorothy Fox; *m* 1983, Isobel McConnell; two *d. Educ:* Baines GS, Poulton-le-Fylde; King's Coll., London (BA, AKC 1971); Sheffield Univ. (MA 1973); MA Cantab 1976; MA Dublin, 1984. ALA 1974; ALAI 1989. Cambridge University Library: grad. trainee, 1971–72; Asst Liby Officer, 1973–77; Asst Under-Librarian, 1977–78; Under-Librarian, 1978–79; Trinity College Dublin: Dep. Librarian, 1979–84; Librarian and Coll. Archivist, 1984–94; Vis. Fellow, 2011. Curator, Oxford Univ. Library Services, 2007–09. Chairman: SCONUL Adv. Cttee on Inf. Services, 1987–90; Bd of Dirs, Consortium of Univ. Res. Libraries, 1997–2000; Brotherton Collection Adv. Cttee, 1999–2002 (Mem., 1995–2002, 2009–11); Wellcome Trust Liby Adv. Cttee, 2000–05 (Mem., 1996–2005); Bd, Nat. Preservation Office, 2002–05 (Member: Mgt Cttee, 1996–2002; Bd, 2002–09); Gen. Sec., 2003–06, Vice-Pres., 2007–08, LIBER; Member: An Chomhairle Leabharlanna, Dublin, 1982–94; Cttee on Liby Co-operation in Ireland, 1983–94; Nat. Preservation Adv. Cttee, 1984–95; Adv. Cttee for Document Supply, 1991–95, Arts, Humanities and Social Scis Adv. Cttee, 2000–02, British Liby; Lord Chancellor's Adv. Council on Nat. Records and Archives (formerly Public Records), 2001–06; Legal Deposit Adv. Panel, DCMS, 2005–08; Long Room Hub Ext. Adv. Bd, TCD, 2008–12. Hon. Fellow, TCD, 2019. *Publications:* Reader Instruction Methods in British Academic Libraries, 1974; Trinity College Library, Dublin, 1982; Trinity College Library Dublin: a history, 2014; *edited:* Treasures of the Library: Trinity College Dublin, 1986; Book of Kells: commentary vol. to facsimile edn, 1990; Cambridge University Library: the great collections, 1998; Proc. Internat. Confs on Library User Education, 1980, 1982, 1984; contrib. learned jls. *Address:* Selwyn College, Cambridge CB3 9DQ.

**FOX, Prof. Renée Claire,** PhD; FAAAS; Annenberg Professor of the Social Sciences, University of Pennsylvania, 1969–98, now Emerita (also Professor of: Sociology in Psychiatry, 1969–98; Sociology in Medicine, 1972–98; Sociology, School of Nursing, 1978–98); Senior Fellow, Center for Bioethics, University of Pennsylvania, 1999–2005, now Emerita; *b* 15 Feb. 1928; *d* of Paul Fred Fox and Henrietta Gold Fox. *Educ:* Smith Coll., Northampton, Mass (BA *summa cum laude* 1949); Harvard Univ. (PhD Sociol. 1954). Teaching Fellow, Harvard Univ., 1950–51; Columbia University: Res. Asst, Bureau of Applied Social Res., 1953–55; Res. Associate, 1955–58; Barnard College, New York: Lectr in Sociol., 1955–58; Asst Prof., 1958–64; Associate Prof., 1964–66; Harvard University: Lectr in Sociol., 1967–69; Res. Fellow, Center for Internat. Affairs, 1967–68; Res. Associate, Program on Technol and Soc., 1968–71; Consultant, Social Sci. Curriculum, Lincoln Center Coll., Fordham Univ., NY, 1968–70; University of Pennsylvania: Faculty Asst to Pres., 1971–72; Chm., Dept of Sociol., 1972–78. Res. Associate, Queen Elizabeth House, Internat. Develt Centre, Univ. of Oxford, 1999–2006. Numerous distinguished visiting appointments and lectureships; George Eastman Vis. Prof., Oxford Univ., 1996–97. Fellow, Amer. Acad. of Arts and Scis, 1971; FAAAS 1978; Member: Inst. of Med., US NAS, 1975; Amer. Philosophical Soc., 2012. Fellow, Explorers Club, 2014. Hon. Mem., Alpha Omega Alpha Honor Med. Soc., 2004. Hon. Dr: Medical Coll. of Pennsylvania, 1974; Smith Coll., Northampton, Mass, 1975; Katholieke Univ., Leuven, 1978; St Joseph's Univ., Philadelphia, 1978; La Salle, 1988; Hahnemann, 1991; Nottingham, 2002; Harvard, 2010; KCL, 2010; Hon. DSc Pennsylvania, 2011. Chevalier, Order of Leopold II (Belgium), 1995. *Publications:* (with W. de Craemer) The Emerging Physician: a sociological approach to the development of a Congolese medical profession, 1968; Experiment Perilous: physicians and patients facing the unknown, 1974, repr. with new epilogue, 1997; (with J. P. Swazey) The Courage to Fail: a social view of organ transplants and dialysis, 1974, rev. edn 1978; Essays in Medical Sociology: journeys into the field, 1979, 2nd edn 1988; (ed) The Social Meaning of Death, 1980; L'Incertitude Médicale, 1988; (jtly) Spare Parts: organ replacement in American society, 1992 (trans. Japanese 1999); The Sociology of Medicine: a participant observer's view, 1989 (trans. Korean 1993); In the Belgian Château: the spirit and culture of European society in the age of change, 1994 (French edn, with new epilogue, 1997); (ed jtly) Meanings and Realities of Organ Transplantation, 1996; (ed jtly) After Parsons: a theory of social action for the twenty-first century, 2005; (with J. P. Swazey) Observing Bioethics, 2008; In the Field: a sociologist's journey, 2010; Doctors Without Borders: humanitarian quests, impossible dreams of Médecins Sans Frontières, 2014; contrib. numerous articles on medical sociology, incl. articles on organ donation and transplantation, bioethics, med. res. and educn, and med. humanitarian action, to scientific and learned jls worldwide. *Address:* Sociology Department, University of Pennsylvania, 3718 Locust Walk, Philadelphia, PA 19104–6299, USA; The Wellington # 1104, 135 South 19th Street, Philadelphia, PA 19103, USA. *T:* (215) 5634912.

**FOX, Prof. Robert,** FSA; Professor of the History of Science, University of Oxford, and Fellow of Linacre College, 1988–2006; *b* 7 Oct. 1938; *s* of Donald Fox and Audrey Hilda Fox (*née* Ramsell); *m* 1964, Catherine Mary Lilian Roper Power; three *d. Educ:* Doncaster Grammar Sch.; Oriel Coll., Oxford (BA 1961; MA 1965; DPhil 1967; Hon. Fellow 2006). Asst Master, Tonbridge Sch., 1961–63; Clifford Norton Junior Res. Fellow, Queen's Coll., Oxford, 1965–66; University of Lancaster: Lectr, 1966; Sen. Lectr, 1972; Reader, 1975; Prof. of History of Science, 1987. Mem., Inst. for Advanced Study, Princeton, 1974–75 and 1985; Vis. Prof. and Mem., Davis Center for Historical Studies, Princeton Univ., 1978–79; Visiting Professor: Ecole des Hautes Etudes en Scis Sociales, Paris, 1984 and 2000; Johns Hopkins Univ., Baltimore, 2007; East Carolina Univ., Greenville, 2009; Dir, Centre de Recherche en Histoire des Sciences et des Techniques, Cité des Sciences et de l'Industrie, Paris, and Dir de recherche associé, Centre Nat. de la Recherche Scientifique, 1986–88; Asst Dir, Science Museum, 1988. President: IUHPS, 1995–97 (Pres., Div. of History of Science, 1993–97); European Soc. for History of Science, 2004–06. Mem., Eur. Acad. of Scis, 2015. George Sarton Medal, Hist. of Sci. Soc., 2015; Alexandre Koyré Medal, Internat. Acad. of History of Sci., 2016; Gustav Neuenschwander Prize, Eur. Soc. for Hist. of Sci., 2018. Chevalier de l'Ordre des Palmes Académiques (France), 1998; Chevalier de l'Ordre des Arts et des Lettres (France), 2005. *Publications:* The Caloric Theory of Gases from Lavoisier to Regnault, 1971; Sadi Carnot: Réflexions sur la puissance motrice du feu, 1978 (trans. English 1986, German 1987, Italian 1992); (ed jtly) The Organization of Science and Technology in France 1808–1914, 1980; The Culture of Science in France 1700–1900, 1992; (ed jtly) Education, Technology and Industrial Performance in Europe 1850–1939, 1993; Science, Technology, and the Social Order in Post-revolutionary France, 1995; (ed) Technological Change: methods and themes in the history of technology, 1996; (ed jtly) Luxury Trades and Consumerism in Ancien Régime Paris, 1998; (ed jtly) Natural Dyestuffs and Industrial Culture in Europe 1750–1880, 1999; (jtly) Laboratories, Workshops and Sites, 1999; (ed) Thomas Harriot: an Elizabethan man of science, 2000; (ed jtly) Physics in Oxford 1839–1939, 2005; (ed) Thomas Harriot: mathematics, exploration and natural philosophy in Early Modern England, 2012; The Savant and the State, 2012; (ed jtly) Oxford Handbook of the History of Physics, 2013; Science without Frontiers: cosmopolitanism and national interests in the world of learning, 2016. *Address:* Museum of the History of Science, Broad Street, Oxford OX1 3AZ. *T:* 07967 594708. *Club:* Athenæum.

**FOX, Robert;** *see* Fox, J. R. R.

**FOX, Dr Robert McDougall,** FRCP, FRCPE; Editor: The Lancet, 1990–95; Journal of the Royal Society of Medicine, 1996–2005; *b* 28 Dec. 1939; *s* of Sir Theodore Fortescue Fox and Margaret Evelyn McDougall; *m* 1969, Susan Clark; two *s* one *d. Educ:* Univ. of Edinburgh (MB ChB); Open Univ. (Dip. Music 2009). MRCP 1993, FRCP 1996; FRCPE 1990. House physician, Western Gen. Hosp., Edinburgh; house surgeon, Royal Infirmary, Edinburgh; joined staff of The Lancet, 1968, Dep. Editor, 1976–90. Associate Editor, Circulation, 1995–2005. *Recreations:* bassoon and hoe. *Address:* 2 Green Square, Wadhurst, E Sussex TN5 6BU. *T:* (01892) 782 925.

**FOX, Robert Michael John;** theatre, film and television producer; Managing Director, Robert Fox Ltd, since 1980; *b* 25 March 1952; *s* of late Robin Fox and Angela Fox; *m* 1st, 1975, Celestia Sporborg (marr. diss. 1990); one *s* two *d*; 2nd, 1990, Natasha Jane Richardson (marr. diss. 1994; she *d* 2009); 3rd, 1996, Fiona Golfar; one *s* one *d. Educ:* Harrow. Actor; runner for John Heyman at World Film Services; Asst Dir, Royal Court Th., 1971–73; PA, Michael White Ltd, 1973–80. *Productions* include: *theatre:* Goose Pimples, Garrick, 1981; Anyone For Denis?, Whitehall, 1981; Another Country, Queen's, 1982; The Seagull, Queen's, 1985; Chess, Prince Edward, 1986; Lettice and Lovage, Globe, 1987, NY, 1990; A Madhouse In Goa, Apollo, 1989; Anything Goes, Prince Edward, 1989; Burn This, Lyric, 1990; The Big Love, NY, 1991; When She Danced, Globe, 1991; The Ride Down Mount Morgan, Wyndham's, 1991; The Importance of Being Earnest, Aldwych, 1993; Vita & Virginia, Ambassadors, 1992, NY, 1994; Three Tall Women, Wyndham's, 1994; Burning Blue, Haymarket, 1995; Skylight, Wyndham's, 1995, 2014, NY, 1996, 2015, Vaudeville, 1997; Who's Afraid of Virginia Woolf?, Almeida, transf. Aldwych, 1996; Master Class, Queen's, 1997; A Delicate Balance, Haymarket, 1997; Amy's View, RNT, transf. Aldwych, 1997, NY 1999; Closer, RNT, transf. Lyric, 1998, NY 1999; The Judas Kiss (co-producer), Almeida, transf. Playhouse, NY, 1998, Duke of York's, 2013; The Boy from Oz (co-producer), Australia, 1998; The Lady in the Van, Queen's, 1999; The Blue Room, NY, 1999; The Caretaker, Comedy, 2000; The Breath of Life, Haymarket, 2002; Salome: the reading, NY, 2003, LA, 2006; Gypsy, NY, 2003; The Boy From Oz, NY, 2003, arena tour, 2006; The Pillowman, NY, 2005; Hedda Gabler, Almeida, transf. Duke of York's, 2005; Frost/Nixon, Gielgud, 2006, NY, 2007; The Vertical Hour, NY, 2006; The Lady from Dubuque, Haymarket, 2007; The Harder They Come, Playhouse, 2008; God of Carnage, NY, 2009, LA, 2011; Exit The King, NY, 2009; A Behanding in Spokane, NY, 2010; Hugh Jackman Back on Broadway, 2011; South Downs and The Browning Version, Harold Pinter Th., 2012; The Audience, Gielgud, 2013, Apollo, 2015, NY, 2015; Stephen Ward, Aldwych, 2014; Fatal Attraction, Haymarket, 2014; Skylight, Wyndham's, 2014, NY 2015; Hangmen, Wyndham's, 2015; Lazarus, King's Cross, 2017; *films:* A Month by the Lake, 1996; Iris, 2001; The Hours, 2002; Closer, 2004; Notes on a Scandal, 2006; Atonement, 2007; Wilde Salome, 2011; *television:* Oscar's Orchestra, 1996; Working with Pinter, 2007; The Crown, 2016–. *Address:* (office) 29 Wingate Road, W6 0UR.

*See also* E. Fox, J. Fox.

**FOX, Robert Trench, (Robin),** CBE 1993; Chairman, InvestUK, 2012–17; *b* 1 Jan. 1937; *s* of Waldo Trench Fox and Janet Mary Kennedy Fox (*née* Bassett); *m* 1962, Lindsay Garrett Anderson (*see* L. G. Fox); two *s* two *d*. *Educ*: Winchester Coll.; University Coll., Oxford (MA). FCIB. Kleinwort Benson Group, 1961–99; Vice-Chm., Kleinwort Benson Gp, 1989–97; Pres., Kleinwort Benson Asia Ltd, 1997–99. Chairman: Whiteaway Laidlaw Bank, 1997–2008 (Dir, 1992–2008); Boyer Allan Pacific Fund, 1998–2012; Lombard Risk Consultants, 2000–15; Stone Drum Pacific Opportunities Fund, 2012–15; Gaman Greater Europe Opportunities Fund, 2012–15. Chm., Export Guarantees Adv. Council, 1992–98; Mem., Overseas Projects Bd, 1988–98. Chm. Council, City Univ. Business Sch., 1991–99. *Recreations:* sailing, theatre, reading. *Address:* The Garden House, Cheriton, Alresford, Hants SO24 0QQ. *T:* (01962) 771230. *Club:* Brooks's.

**FOX, Robin James L.;** *see* Lane Fox.

**FOX, Ronald David;** Solicitor of the Senior Courts; Partner, Fox & Partners, since 2017; *b* London, 1946; *s* of Walter and Eva Fox; *m* 1973, Sonya Birshan; one *s* one *d*. *Educ*: Mercers' Sch.; City of London Sch.; Lincoln Coll., Oxford (MA Hons Juris 1968). Admitted as solicitor, 1972; Partner, Herbert Oppenheimer, Nathan & Vandyk, 1974–88; Denton Hall, Burgin & Warrens, 1989; Founder and Sen. Partner, Fox Williams, 1989–2005; Founder and Principal, Fox Lawyers, 2006–17. Law Society of England and Wales: Member: Completion Cheque Scheme Wkg Party, 1981–82; Company Law Cttee, 1985–89; Council Membership Cttee, 1990–97; Steering Gp, Law Mgt Section, 1998–99; Employment Law Cttee, 2001–04; Remuneration Cttee, 2005–10. Founder and Chm., Assoc. of Partnership Practitioners, 1998–2001 (Pres., 2003–08; Hon. Mem., 2009–). International Bar Association: Mem., 1984–; Chairman: Practice Mgt Sub-cttee, 1995–98; Sen. Lawyers' Cttee, 2008–10. City of London Solicitors' Co.: Liveryman, 1984–; Member: Problems of Practice Sub-cttee, 1985–93; Wkg Party on Future of Legal Profession, 1986; Chair, Wkg Party on Work and Orgn of Legal Profession, 1989; Mem. Court, 1991–; Master, 1998–99. Motoring corresp., City Solicitor, 2008–16. Mem., Appeal Bd, Tank Mus., 2008–10. Dist. Service Award, City of London Solicitors' Co., 1989; Legal Business Star of Year, 2000. *Recreations:* opera, theatre, cinema, ski-ing, swimming, scuba diving, motoring and management studies; passionate about chocolate; never miss an episode of The Archers. *Address:* Fox & Partners, 4–6 Throgmorton Avenue, EC2N 2DL. *T:* (020) 7618 2400, *Fax:* (020) 7618 2409. *E:* rdfox@foxlawyers.com. *Clubs:* Royal Automobile (Member: Pall Mall House Cttee, 2006–12; Main Bd, 2012–18), City of London.

**FOX, Dr Simon James;** QC 2016; *b* Cardiff, 17 June 1967. *Educ*: Cheltenham Coll.; Charing Cross and Westminster Med. Sch. (MB BS); City Univ. (Postgrad. DipLaw). Called to the Bar, Inner Temple, 1994; in practice as barrister, 1994–; Assistant Coroner: Avon, 2010–; Glos, 2016–. *Recreation:* hill running. *Address:* No 5 Chambers, 38 Queen Square, Bristol BS1 4QS.

**FOX-PITT, William,** MBE 2018; international three day event rider, since 1993; *b* 2 Jan. 1969; *s* of late Oliver Fox-Pitt and of Marietta Fox-Pitt; *m* 2003, Alice Plunkett; two *s* two *d*. *Educ*: Eton Coll.; Goldsmiths' Coll., London Univ. (BA Hons French 1993). Three day event rider, first competed at jun. level, 1984, also trainer, 1993–; winner: Burghley Horse Trials, 1994, 2002, 2005, 2007, 2008, 2011; British Open Championships, 1995, 2000, 2005; Badminton Horse Trials, 2004, 2015; Open European Championships: team Gold Medal, 1995; team Gold and individual Bronze Medal, 1997; team Gold Medal, 2001, 2003; team Gold and individual Silver Medal, 2005; team Gold, 2009; World Championships: team Bronze Medal, 2002; team Silver Medal, 2006; team Gold and individual Silver Medal, 2010; team Silver and individual Bronze Medal, 2014; team Silver Medal, Olympic Games, Athens, 2004; team Bronze Medal, Olympic Games, Beijing, 2008; team Silver Medal, Olympic Games, London, 2012; represented GB in team at Atlanta Olympics, 1996; ranked British No 1, 2001, 2002, 2003, 2004, 2005, 2006, 2008, 2010 and 2011, World No 1, 2002, 2009, 2010 and 2014, World No 2, 2003, 2004, 2005, 2006 and 2011. Board Director: Professional Event Riders' Assoc., 1998–; British Eventing (formerly British Horse Trials Assoc.), 2000–. *Publications:* Schooling for Success, 2004; What Will Be: the autobiography, 2007. *Recreations:* ski-ing, jogging, travel.

**FOX-STRANGWAYS,** family name of **Earl of Ilchester**.

**FOXALL, Colin,** CBE 1995; rail industry adviser, since 2015; reinsurance consultant, since 1997; Chairman, Passenger Focus, 2005–15; *b* 6 Feb. 1947; *s* of Alfred George Foxall and Ethel Margaret Foxall; *m* 2013, Helen Patricia Kaye. *Educ*: Gillingham Grammar Sch., Kent. MIEx; FICM. Joined ECGD, 1966; Dept of Trade, 1974; ECGD, 1975–91: Underwriter, Eastern Bloc, 1975; Dep. Hd, For. Currency Branch, 1977; Hd, Financial Planning, 1979; Asst Sec., ME Project Gp, 1982; Under Sec., and Dir of Comprehensive Guarantee, subseq. Insce Services, Gp, 1986–91; Man. Dir and Chief Exec., NCM Credit Insurance Ltd, 1991–97; Vice-Chm., NCM (Hldg) NV, 1996–97. Dir, Radian Asset Assurance Ltd, 2003–08; Bd Advr, Classic Construction, 2003–04; Advr, Aon Benfield, 2007–10. Member: Rail Passengers Council, 2004–05; British Transport Police Authy, 2005–13. *Recreations:* cycling, walking.

**FOXCROFT, Victoria Jane;** MP (Lab) Lewisham, Deptford, since 2015. *Educ*: De Montfort Univ. (BA 2000). Research Officer, AEEU, 2002–05; Political Officer, Amicus the Union, 2005–09; Finance Sector Officer, Unite the Union, 2009–15. Mem. (Lab) Lewisham LBC, 2010–14. An Opposition Whip, 2015–. *Address:* House of Commons, SW1A 0AA.

**FOXON, Prof. (Charles) Thomas (Bayley),** PhD; FRS 2006; Professor of Physics, University of Nottingham, 1991, now Emeritus Research Professor. *Educ*: BSc, PhD. Sen. Principal Scientist, Philips Res. Labs, until 1991. *Publications:* articles in learned jls. *Address:* School of Physics and Astronomy, University of Nottingham, University Park, Nottingham NG7 2RD.

**FOXTON, David Andrew;** QC 2006; PhD; a Recorder, since 2009; a Deputy High Court Judge, Queen's Bench Division and Chancery Division, since 2016; *b* 14 Oct. 1965; *s* of Adrian and Catherine Foxton; *m* 1992, Heather Crook; two *s* two *d*. *Educ*: Glasgow Acad.; Magdalen Coll., Oxford (MA, BCL); King's Coll. London (PhD). Called to the Bar, Gray's Inn, 1989, Bencher, 2009; in practice, specialising in commercial law; Hd of Chambers, Essex Court Chambers, 2017–. Vis. Prof. of Law, Univ. of Nottingham, 2007–. Mem. Cttee, Church Urban Fund, 2006–16. Trustee: St Albans Cathedral Music Trust, 2009–16; Magdalen Coll. Develt Trust, 2009–. Freeman, City of London, 2009. *Publications:* (with Sir Bernard Eder) Scrutton on Charterparties and Bills of Lading, 20th edn 2008 to 23rd edn 2015; Revolutionary Lawyers: Sinn Fein and Crown Courts in Britain and Ireland 1916–1923, 2008; The Life of T. E. Scrutton, 2013; (ed) Singapore International Arbitration: law and practice, 2014, 2nd edn 2018; articles in legal jls. *Recreations:* Irish history, travel, good food. *Address:* Essex Court Chambers, 24 Lincoln's Inn Fields, WC2A 3EG. *T:* (020) 7813 8000, *Fax:* (020) 7813 8080. *Club:* Athenæum.

**FOY, John Leonard;** QC 1998; a Recorder, 2000–16; *b* 1 June 1946; *s* of late Leonard James Foy and Edith Mary Foy; *m* 1972, Colleen Patricia Austin (*d* 2006); one *s*. *Educ*: Dartford GS; Birmingham Univ. (LLB Hons 1967). Called to the Bar, Gray's Inn, 1969, Bencher, 2004; in practice at the Bar, 1969–. Judge (formerly Mem.), Mental Health Review Tribunal, 2003–16. *Publications:* contribs to various legal books and jls. *Recreations:* watching West Bromwich Albion, football, Rugby, reading modern literature. *Address:* 9 Gough Square, EC4A 3DG. *T:* (020) 7832 0500.

**FOYLE, (William Richard) Christopher;** DL; Chairman, W & G Foyle Ltd, 1999–2018; *b* London, 20 Jan. 1943; *s* of William Richard Foyle and Alice Foyle (*née* Kun); *m* 1983, Catherine Mary Jelleyman; one *s* three *d*. *Educ*: Radley Coll.; Univ. of Oxford (Wainwright Schol.; Leavers' Near East Archaeol Prize 1961). Trainee bookseller, W & G Foyle Ltd, London, 1962; trng in bookselling and publishing, Tübingen, Berlin, Helsinki and Paris, 1962–65; Manager, W & G Foyle Ltd, London, 1965–72; Partner, Emson & Dudley, and Dir, Emson & Dudley Securities Ltd, 1972–78; Proprietor, Christopher Foyle Aviation Leasing Co., 1977–97; Founder and Chairman: Air Foyle Ltd, 1978–2012; Air Foyle Exec. Ltd, 1988–2009; Air Foyle Charter Airlines Ltd, subseq. Air Foyle Passenger Airlines Ltd, 1994–2003; Chm., City Jet Ltd, Dublin, 1999–2000; Chm. and Jt CEO, Air Foyle Heavy Lift Ltd, 2001–12; Dir and Alternating Chm., Noved Investment Co./Gp, 1999–; non-exec. Dir, Air Charter Service Gp plc, 2007–12. International Air Cargo Association: Trustee and Mem. Bd, 1992–; Chm., Develt Cttee, 1992–95; Vice-Pres. and Vice-Chm. of Bd, 1995–97; Pres. and Chm. of Bd, and CEO, 1997–99; Mem., Chairmen's Council, 1999–. Member: Transport Cttee, Gen. Aviation Manufrs' and Traders' Assoc., 1986–94; Small Business Trng Cttee, Air Transport Industry Trng Assoc., 1987–93. Chm., British Cargo Airline Alliance, 1999–2008. Mem. Bd, 2001–, Chm., 2006–08, Dep. Pres. (Overseas), 2008–, Air League; Pres., Air League of Monaco, 2013–. Pres., Foyle Res. Inst. of Monaco, 2016–. Freeman, City of London; Liveryman, Co. of Air Pilots and Air Navigators, 1996–. DL Essex, 2007. Trustee, Foyle Foundn, 2006–08. Patron, BTBS, Book Trade Charity, 2002–; Hon. Patron, Anthony Burgess Foundn, 2017–. Member: Soc. of Authors; Private Liby Assoc.; Soc. of Bookmen. Fellow, Aspen Inst., 2012–. FRAeS 1997; FCILT (FILT 1998); FRGS 2000; FRHS 2012. Special Achievement Award, IFW, 1997; Nat. Award, and E of England Building Conservation Award, RICS, 2008. Chevalier, Confrérie Tastevin Bourgogne, 2008. *Publications:* John Foyle of Shaftesbury and Kimpton 1564 and 1648 and His Family and Descendants, 1997; The Family of George Foyle of Portsmouth 1809–1900, 1997; (contrib.) Foyles - a Celebration, 2003; (ed and contrib.) History of Air Cargo and Air Mail, 2004; Foyles Philavery: a treasury of unusual words, 2007, 3rd edn 2009; Foyles Further Philavery: a cornucopia of lexical delights, 2008; (jtly) Pioneers to Partners: a photographic history of British aircraft from 1945, 2009; Beeleigh Abbey: a history and guide, 2012. *Recreations:* travel, flying, reading 5 daily newspapers and non-fiction books (history, ancient history, archaeology, scientific investigation of anomalous phenomena), not watching or reading about any sport except for men's tennis, mud wrestling, occasional ranting. *Address:* Beeleigh Abbey, Maldon, Essex CM9 6LL. *Clubs:* Royal Air Squadron, White's, Garrick; Essex; Yacht of Monaco, Monte Carlo, Automobile of Monaco, Etrangers de Monaco, Churchill (Monaco); Explorers' (New York); Caribou (Aspen).

**FRACKOWIAK, Prof. Richard Stanislaus Joseph,** MD, DSc; FRCP, FMedSci; Professor of Neurology, Chairman of Department of Clinical Neurosciences, and Head of Neurology Service, Centre Hospitalier Universitaire Vaudois, University of Lausanne, 2009–15, now Professeur ordinaire ad hominem and médecin associé; Titular Professor, Faculty of Life Sciences, Ecole Polytechnique Fédérale de Lausanne, since 2013; *b* 26 March 1950; *s* of Joseph Frackowiak and Wanda (*née* Majewska); *m* 1st, 1972, Christine Jeanne Françoise Thepot (marr. diss. 2004); one *s* two *d*; 2nd, 2004, Laura Frances Spinney. *Educ*: Latymer Upper Sch.; Peterhouse, Cambridge (Wilhelm Brauer Open Schol.; MA); Middlesex Hosp. Med. Sch. (MB BChir; MD 1983); DSc London 1996. FRCP 1987. Sen. Lectr, 1984–91, Prof. of Neurology, 1990–94, RPMS and Hammersmith Hosp.; Consultant Neurologist: Hammersmith Hosp., 1984–95; Nat. Hosp. for Neurology and Neurosurgery, 1984–; MRC Trng Fellow, 1980–81; MRC Clinical Scientist, 1984–94; Wellcome Principal Res. Fellow, 1994–2003; Institute of Neurology, London University: Prof. and Chm., Wellcome Dept of Cognitive Neurol., 1994–2002; Dir, Leopold Muller Functional Imaging Lab., 1994–2002; Dean, 1998–2002; Vice-Provost, UCL, 2002–09; Emeritus Prof., UCL; Hd, Dépt d'Etudes Cognitives, Ecole Normale Supérieure, Paris, 2004–09. Adjunct Prof. of Neurology, Cornell Univ. Med. Sch., NY, 1990; Visiting Professor: Wellcome Lab. of Neurobiol., UCL, 1991–95; Cath. Univ., Louvain, Belgium, 1996–97; Harvard Med. Sch., 1999; Yale Med. Sch., 2001; Hon. Prof. and Advr to Provost-Pres., UCL, 2009–10. Scientific Advr to Dir-Gen. and Pres., Inserm, Paris, 2007–13; Consultant, Lab. di neuroimagine, IRCCS Santa Lucia, Rome, 2003–13; Dir (Medicine), Human Brain Project, EU, 2013–16. Non-exec. Dir, UCLH NHS Foundn Trust Bd, 2003–08. Chair, Med. Scis Cttee, Science Europe, 2012–16; Mem., Steering Cttee, Scientific Panel for Health, Eur. Commn, 2015–. Member: Assoc. of British Neurologists, 1984; American Neurological Assoc., 1988 (Hon. Mem., 2000); Soc. Française de Neurologie, 1993; Academia Europaea, 1995; L'Academie Royale de Médecine de Belgique, 1995. Foreign Associate, Acad. Nat. de Médecine de France, 2000; Foreign Mem., Inst. of Medicine, Amer. Nat. Acads, 2009; Corresp. Mem., Polish Acad. of Scis, 2013. Founder FMedSci 1998 (Mem. Council, 2000–03). Hon. Dr Liège 1999. Wilhelm Feldberg Foundn Prize, 1996; (jtly) Ipsen Prize for Neuronal Plasticity, Ipsen Foundn, Paris, 1997; Klaus Joachim Zulch Prize, Gertrud Reemtsma Foundn and Max Planck Soc., 2004; Ottorino Rossi Prize, Univ. of Pavia, 2016. *Publications:* (jtly) Human Brain Function, 1997, 2nd edn 2004; Brain Mapping: the disorders, 2000; Le Grand Atlas du cerveau, 2018; numerous on functional anatomy and organisation of the human brain using non-invasive monitoring techniques. *Recreations:* motorcycling, reading, retirement. *Address:* c/o Laboratory of Cognitive Neuroscience, Département d'etudes cognitives, Ecole Normale Supérieure, 29 rue d'Ulm, Paris 75005, France. *Club:* Athenæum.

**FRADD, Dame Elizabeth (Harriet),** DBE 2009; DL; *b* Worcester Park, Surrey; *d* of Rev. Dr Norman Alan Birtwhistle and Edith Harriet Birtwhistle (*née* Abey); *m* 1976, Simon Oakley Fradd (marr. diss. 1998). *Educ*: Westminster Hosp. (SRN 1970; RSCN 1971); King's College Hosp. (SCM 1973); Croydon Coll. (HVCert 1981); Nottingham Univ. (MSc 1994). Sen. Nurse Manager, Children's Services, Nottingham Hosps, 1983–94; Nursing Officer, Children, DoH, 1994–95; Dir of Nursing and Educn, NHS West Mid. Reg., 1995–99; Asst Chief Nurse, DoH, 1999–2000; Dir of Nursing and Dir for Review and Inspection, Commn for Health Improvement, 2000–04. Hon. Sen. Lectr, Univ. of Birmingham, 1995–2003; Vis. Prof. of Nursing, UCE, 1996; Special Prof. of Nursing, 2000, Mem. Council, 2009–18, Vice Pres., 2012–18, Univ. of Nottingham. Chm., Health Visitor Taskforce, 2011–15; Mem., Children and Young People's Health Outcomes Forum, 2012–15. Trustee, Sue Ryder Care, 2004–10 (Vice-Chm., 2008–10); Vice-Pres., Rainbows Children's Hospice, 2005–17; Patron: Together for Short Lives (formerly Ambassador, Children's Hospice UK), 2010–; Datum Foundn, 2018. Chm., Magdala Trust, 2000–15. Fellow: Queen's Nursing Inst., 2000; Inst. of Health Visiting, 2017. FRCN 2004. Hon. FRCPCH 2000. Hon. MFPH 2000. Mem., RSA, 2003–08. Mem. Court, Needlemakers' Co., 2008 (Master, 2016–17). DL Notts, 2016. Hon. DSc Wolverhampton, 2001; DUniv UCE, 2002; Hon. LLD Nottingham, 2003. *Publications:* over 30 articles in professional jls incl. Nursing Times, Nursing Standard, Paediatric Nursing, Jl of Clin.

**FRAME, Frank Riddell;** Deputy Chairman, Hongkong and Shanghai Banking Corporation, 1986–90; b 15 Feb. 1930; s of late William Graham Frame; m 1958, Maureen Willis Milligan (d 2018); one s one d. Educ: Hamilton Academy; Univ. of Glasgow (MA, LLB); admitted solicitor, 1955. North of Scotland Hydro-Electric Board, 1955–60; UK Atomic Energy Authority, 1960–68; Weir Group plc, 1968–76 (Dir, 1971–76); joined Hongkong and Shanghai Banking Corp., as Gp Legal Advr, 1977, Exec. Dir, 1985–90; Advr to Bd, HSBC Hldgs plc, 1990–98. Chairman: South China Morning Post Ltd, 1981–87; Far Eastern Economic Review Ltd, 1981–87; Wallem Group Ltd, 1992–2004; Director: Marine Midland Banks Inc., 1986–90; The British Bank of the Middle East, 1986–91; Swire Pacific Ltd, 1986–90; Consolidated Press Internat. Ltd, 1988–91; Securities and Futures Commn, Hong Kong, 1989–90; Baxter Internat. Inc., 1992–2001; Edinburgh Dragon Trust plc, 1994–2011; Northern Gas Networks Ltd, 2004–11; Northumbrian Water Ltd, 2012–19. DUniv Glasgow, 2001. Publications: (with Prof. Harry Street) The Law relating to Nuclear Energy, 1966. Recreations: travel, Scottish art. Address: The Old Rectory, Bepton, Midhurst, W Sussex GU29 0HX. Club: Brook's.

**FRAME, Ronald William Sutherland;** author; b 23 May 1953; s of late Alexander D. Frame and Isobel D. Frame (née Sutherland). Educ: High Sch. of Glasgow; Univ. of Glasgow (MA Hons; Foulis Scholarship; Bradley Medal); Jesus Coll., Oxford (MLitt). Full-time author, 1981–; first Betty Trask Prize (jtly), 1984; Samuel Beckett Prize 1986; Television Industries' Panel's Most Promising Writer New to TV Award, 1986. Television films: Paris, 1985; Out of Time, 1987; Ghost City, 1994; A Modern Man, 1996; M. R. James (Ghost Stories for Christmas), 2000; Darien: Disaster in Paradise, 2003; Cromwell, 2003; (contrib.) The Two Loves of Anthony Trollope, 2004; radio drama includes: Winter Journey, 1984; Cara, 1989; The Lantern Bearers, 1997; The Hydro (serial), 1997, 2nd series 1998, 3rd series 1999; Havisham, 1998; Maestro, 1999; Pharos, 2000; Sunday at Sant' Agata, 2001, 2013; Greyfriars, 2002; The Shell House, 2008; Blue Wonder, 2008; Pinkerton, 2010; The Dreamer, 2012; (adaptations): Don't Look Now, 2001; The Servant, 2005; The Razor's Edge, 2005; A Tiger for Malgudi, 2006; The Other Simenon: The Blue Room, 2007, Monsieur Monde Vanishes, 2009, Sunday, Striptease, 2010, In Case of Emergency, The Cat, The Little Man from Archangel, 2011; The Other Simenon 2: Teddy Bear, The Neighbours, The Venice Train, 2012; Before the Fact, 2013; The Other Simenon 3: Three Beds in Manhattan, The Confessional, A New Lease of Life, 2014. Publications: Winter Journey, 1984; Watching Mrs Gordon, 1985; A Long Weekend with Marcel Proust, 1986; Sandmouth People, 1987; A Woman of Judah, 1987; Paris, 1987; Penelope's Hat, 1989; Bluette, 1990; Underwood and After, 1991; Walking My Mistress in Deauville, 1992; The Sun on the Wall, 1994; The Lantern Bearers, 1999 (Scottish Book of the Year, Saltire Soc., 2000; Stonewall-Barbara Gittings Honor Award in Fiction, Amer. Liby Assoc., 2003); Permanent Violet, 2002; Time in Carnbeg, 2004; Unwritten Secrets, 2010; Havisham, 2012; contrib. weekly Carnbeg story, The Herald, 2008, The Scotsman, 2008–09; regular contrib. to Sunday Herald's Scottish Review of Bks. Recreations: swimming, walking in the wind, jazz. Address: c/o Faber & Faber Ltd (Authors), Bloomsbury House, 74–79 Great Russell Street, WC1B 3DA. T: (020) 7927 3800, Fax: (020) 7927 3801. W: www.carnbeg.com.

**FRAME, Rt Rev. Prof. Thomas Robert,** AM 2019; PhD; Director, Public Leadership Research Group and Howard Library, School of Humanities and Social Sciences, UNSW Canberra, since 2017; b 7 Oct. 1962; s of Robert and Doreen Catherine Frame; m 1983, Helen Mary (née Bardsley); two d. Educ: Royal Australian Naval Coll. HMAS Creswell; Univ. of NSW (BA Hons 1985, PhD 1992); Univ. of Melbourne (DipEd 1986) MTh Sydney Coll. of Divinity 1993; Univ. of Kent at Canterbury (Lucas Tooth Schol., 1996–97; MA Hons 1997). Officer, RAN, 1979–92; ordained deacon, 1993, priest, 1994; Asst Priest, Wagga Wagga, 1993–95; Rector: Binda, 1995–99; Bungendore, 1999–2001; Anglican Bishop to Australian Defence Force, 2001–07; Dir, St Mark's Nat. Theol Centre, 2007–14; Prof., Sch. of Humanities and Social Scis, 2014–17, Dir, Australian Centre for Study of Armed Conflict and Society, 2014–17, Univ. of NSW, then UNSW Canberra. Res. Fellow, Mt Stromlo Observatory, ANU, 1999–2003; Lectr in Public Theol., St Mark's Nat. Theol Centre, 2000–02; Charles Sturt University: Vis. Fellow, Sch. of Humanities, 2000–06; Prof., 2007–14; Hd, Sch. of Theol., 2007–08. Vis. Prof., Sch. of Humanities and Social Scis, Univ. of NSW, 2013–14. W. J. Liu Prize for Excellence in Chinese Studies, Univ. of NSW, 1985. Publications: First In Last Out!: the Navy at Gallipoli, 1990; (with G. Swinden) The Garden Island, 1990; (ed jtly) Reflections on the RAN, 1991; Where Fate Calls: the HMAS Voyager tragedy, 1992; Pacific Partners: a history of Australian-American naval relations, 1992; HMAS Sydney: loss and controversy, 1993; Where the Rivers Run: a history of the Anglican parish of Wagga Wagga, 1995; (with G. Webster) Labouring in Vain: a history of Bishopthorpe, 1996; (with G. Webster) The Seven Churches of Binda, 1998; Binding Ties: an experience of adoption and reunion in Australia (autobiog.), 1999; The Shores of Gallipoli: naval aspects of the Anzac campaign, 2000; A Church for a Nation, 2000; (with K. Baker) Mutiny!: naval insurrections in Australia and New Zealand, 2001; (with D. Faulkner) Stromlo: an Australian observatory, 2003; Living by the Sword?: the ethics of armed intervention, 2004; 'No Pleasure Cruise': the story of the Royal Australian Navy, 2004; The Cruel Legacy: the tragedy of HMAS Voyager, 2005; The Life and Death of Harold Holt, 2005; (ed) Agendas for Australian Anglicanism, 2006; Church and State: Australia's imaginary wall, 2006; Anglicans in Australia, 2007; Children on Demand: the ethics of defying nature, 2008; Evolution in the Antipodes: Charles Darwin and Australia, 2009; Losing My Religion: unbelief in Australia, 2009; A House Divided: the Anglican quest for unity, 2010; (ed) Moral Injury: unseen wounds in an age of barbarism, 2015; (ed) Anzac Day: then and now, 2016; (ed) On Ops: lessons and challenges for the Australian Army since East Timor, 2016; (ed) The Long Road: Australia's train, advise and assist missions, 2017; Widening Minds: the University of New South Wales and the education of Australia's defence leaders, 2017; (ed) The Ascent to Power, 1996: The Howard Government vol. I, 2017; Back from the Brink, 1997–2001: The Howard Government vol. II, 2018; Trials and Tribulations, 2001–2004: The Howard Government vol. III, 2019; The Desire for Change, 2004–2007: The Howard Government vol. IV, 2020. Recreations: Rugby, reading biographies. Address: Howard Library, UNSW Canberra, South East Wing, Old Parliament House, 18 King George Terrace, Parkes, ACT 2600, Australia. E: t.frame@adfa.edu.au.

**FRAMLINGHAM,** Baron cr 2011 (Life Peer), of Eye in the County of Suffolk; **Michael Nicholson Lord,** Kt 2001; b 17 Oct. 1938; s of John Lord and Jessie Lord (née Nicholson); m 1965, Jennifer Margaret (née Childs); one s one d. Educ: Christ's College, Cambridge. MA. FArborA. Arboricultural consultant. MP (C) Suffolk Central, 1983–97, Central Suffolk and N Ipswich, 1997–2010. PPS: to Minister of State, MAFF, 1984–85; to Chief Secretary to the Treasury, 1985–87; Second Dep. Chm. of Ways and Means and a Dep. Speaker, 1997–2010. Member: Select Cttee on Parly Comr for Admin, 1990–97; Council of Europe, 1987–91; WEU, 1987–91. Recreations: golf, sailing, gardening, trees.
See also Hon. T. M. Lord.

**FRANCE, Annette Stephanie;** Headteacher, Beaconsfield High School, 2012–15; b Hitchin, Herts, 20 April 1952; d of Colin and Iris France; m (marr. diss.); two d. Educ: Thetford Grammar Sch. for Girls; Helsby Co. Grammar Sch. for Girls; Keele Univ. (BA Hons English and Psychol.); Nottingham Univ. (MEd; MSc). NPQH. Teaching posts in 14–19 Community Colls, Leics, 1975–2000; on secondment to Nat. Grid, 1995; Headteacher: Heart of England Sch., 2001–07; Chipping Campden Sch., 2007–12. Churchill Fellow, 1982. Nat. Leader of Educn, 2010–. Publications: Remembering and Forgetting, 1991; Perception, 1991. Recreations: travel, reading, writing, grandchildren. Address: Candle Cottage, Anchor Lane, Harvington, Worcs WR11 8NR. E: penlan52@gmail.com.

**FRANCE, Elizabeth Irene,** CBE 2002; Chairman: Security Industry Authority, since 2014; Police Advisory Board for England and Wales, since 2014; b 1 Feb. 1950; d of Ralph Salem and Elizabeth Joan Salem (née Bryan); m 1971, Dr Michael William France; two s one d. Educ: Beauchamp Sch., Leics; UCW, Aberystwyth (BScEcon Pol Sci.). Home Office: Admin. Trainee, 1971; Principal, 1977; Asst Sec., 1986; Police Dept, Criminal Justice and Constitutional Dept, IT and Pay Services, 1986–94; Data Protection Registrar, subseq. Comr, then Inf. Comr, 1994–2002; Telecommunications Ombudsman, 2002–09; Energy Supply Ombudsman, 2006–09; Surveyors Ombudsman, 2007–09; Chm., Office for Legal Complaints, 2009–14; Deputy Chair: Regulatory Decisions Cttee, FCA, 2015–; Enforcement Decisions Cttee, Payment Systems Regulator, 2015–. Non-exec. Dir, Serious and Organised Crime Agency, 2005–10. Member: Commn for control of Interpol's files, 2001–05; Compliance Cttee, Aarhus Convention, 2003–05; British Transport Police Authy, 2010–18; Ofgem Enforcement Decision Panel, 2014–; Chm., UK Public Affairs Council, 2010–13. Mem., Gen. Assembly (formerly Court), Univ. of Manchester, 2002–15; Pro-Chancellor (formerly Vice-Pres.), Aberystwyth Univ., 2008–18. Fellow, Univ. of Wales, Aberystwyth, 2003. FRSA 1995. Hon. FCICM (FICM 1999); Hon. Fellow, Inst. for Mgt of Inf. Systems, 2003. Hon. DSc De Montfort, 1996; Hon. DLitt Loughborough, 2000; Hon. LLD Bradford, 2002. Address: Security Industry Authority, PO Box 74957, London, E14 1UG.

**FRANCE, Prof. Peter,** DPhil; FBA 1989; FRSE; Professor of French, University of Edinburgh, 1980–90, now Emeritus (University Endowment Fellow, 1990–2000); b Londonderry, 19 Oct. 1935; s of Edgar France and Doris Woosnam Morgan; m 1961, Siân Reynolds; three d. Educ: Bridlington Sch.; Bradford Grammar Sch.; Magdalen Coll., Oxford (MA; DPhil). FRSE 2003. Lectr, then Reader, in French, Univ. of Sussex, 1963–80. French Editor, MLR, 1979–85. Jt Gen. Editor, Oxford History of Literary Translation in English (5 vol. series), 2005–. Mem., Chuvash Nat. Acad., 1991. Dr hc Chuvash State Univ., 1996. Officer de l'Ordre des Palmes Académiques (France), 1990; Chevalier, Légion d'Honneur (France), 2001. Publications: Racine's Rhetoric, 1965; Rhetoric and Truth in France, 1972; Poets of Modern Russia, 1982; Racine: Andromaque, 1977; Diderot, 1983; Rousseau: Confessions, 1987; trans., An Anthology of Chuvash Poetry, 1991; Politeness and its Discontents, 1992; (ed) New Oxford Companion to Literature in French, 1995; trans., Gennady Aygi, Selected Poems, 1997; (ed) Oxford Guide to Literature in English Translation, 2000; (ed) Mapping Lives: the uses of biography, 2002; (ed jtly) Oxford History of Literary Translation in English, vol. 4: 1790–1900, 2006; trans., Gennady Aygi, Field-Russia, 2007; (ed jtly) After Lermontov: translations for the bicentenary, 2014; trans., Yevgeny Baratynsky, Half-Light, 2015; Writings form the Golden Age of Russian Poetry: Konstantin Batyushkov, 2017. Address: 10 Dryden Place, Edinburgh EH9 1RP. T: (0131) 667 1177.

**FRANCE, Valerie Edith, (Lady France),** OBE 1994; MA; Headmistress, City of London School for Girls, 1986–95; b 29 Oct. 1935; d of Neville Larman, DFC and Edith Larman; m 1961, Sir Christopher Walter France, GCB (d 2014); one s one d. Educ: St Hugh's Coll., Oxford (MA); CertEd Cantab. Deputy Headmistress, Bromley High Sch., GPDST, 1984–86; Acting Hd, Atherley Sch., Oct.–Dec. 1996. Mem., Eco-Schs Adv. Panel, 1996–2000. Member Council: Cheltenham Ladies' Coll., 1995–98; Francis Holland Schs Trust, 1997–2005 (Chm. Council, 1999–2005); Mem. Court, Whitgift Foundn, 1994–97; Gov., Trinity Sch., 1997–2003. FRGS 1959; FRSA 1991. Freeman, City of London, 1988; Liveryman, Needlemakers' Co., 1992–. Recreations: family, friends, places.

**FRANCES DOMINICA, Sister;** see Ritchie, Sister F. D. L.

**FRANCIES, Michael Shaul;** Managing Partner, London Office, Weil, Gotshal & Manges, since 1998; b Tiberius, Israel, 14 Oct. 1956; s of Anthony and Iris Francies; m 1979, Claire Heather Frome; three s. Educ: Kingsbury High Sch.; Manchester Univ. (LLB Hons); Coll. of Law, Lancaster Gate. Clifford Turner, subseq. Clifford Chance: articled clerk, 1979–81; Asst Solicitor, 1981–83 and 1984–86; Partner, 1986–98; Asst Dir and Co. Sec., Carlton Communications, 1983–84. Recreations: family, football, Rugby, reading, music. Address: Weil, Gotshal & Manges, 110 Fetter Lane, EC4A 1AT. T: (020) 7903 1000, Fax: (020) 7903 0990. E: michael.francies@weil.com.

**FRANCIS, Arthur;** see Francis, F. A. S.

**FRANCIS, Barney;** Managing Director, Sky Sports, since 2009; b Leicester, 23 June 1971; s of Tony and Jane Francis; m 2000, Amy; two s. Educ: Univ. of Liverpool (BA Hons Econ. Hist.). Granada TV, 1993–96; Sky TV, 1996–98; BBC, 1998–99; Sky TV, 1999–. Address: Sky Sports, British Sky Broadcasting Ltd, Grant Way, Isleworth, Middx TW7 5QD. E: barney.francis@bskyb.com.

**FRANCIS, Prof. Becky,** PhD; FAcSS; Director, UCL Institute of Education, University College London, since 2016; b Keynsham, 7 Nov. 1969; d of Nicolas and Diana Francis; m 1997, Daniel Hew; two s. Educ: Ralph Allen Comprehensive Sch.; Univ. of Wales, Swansea (BA Hons English 1992); Univ. of N London (PhD Women's Studies and Educn (Schol.) 1996). FAcSS 2015. Sen. Res. Fellow, Sch. of Post-Compulsory Educn and Trng, Univ. of Greenwich, 1998–2000; Reader in Educn, and Dep. Dir, Inst. for Policy Studies in Educn, London Metropolitan Univ., 2000–06; Prof. of Educn, and Dir, Centre for Educnl Res. in Equalities, Policy and Practice, Roehampton Univ., 2006–10; Dir of Educn, RSA, 2010–12; Prof. of Educn and Social Justice, KCL, 2012–16; Dir, Pearson Think Tank (on secondment), 2012–13. Hon. Prof., Univ. of Warwick, 2016–. Dist. Internat. Schol., Univ. of Qld, 2008; Chen Yidan Global Vis. Fellow, Harvard, 2018–. Trustee, Impetus-PEF, 2015–. Publications: Power Plays: primary school children's construction of gender, power and adult work, 1998; Boys, Girls and Achievement: addressing the classroom issues, 2000; (ed with C. Skelton) Investigating Gender: contemporary perspectives in education, 2001 (trans. Greek 2007); (ed with C. Skelton) Boys and Girls in the Primary Classroom, 2003; (with C. Skelton) Reassessing Gender and Achievement, 2005; (with C. Skelton) A Feminist Critique of Education, 2005; (ed with C. Leathwood) Gender and Lifelong Learning, 2006; (ed jtly) Handbook of Gender and Education, 2006 (trans. Chinese 2008); (with L. Archer) Understanding Minority Ethnic Achievement: race, gender, class and 'success', 2007; (with C. Skelton) Feminism and the Schooling Scandal, 2009; (jtly) The Identities and Practices of High Achieving Pupils: negotiating achievement and peer cultures, 2011 (First Prize, Soc. for Educnl Studies Book Prizes, 2012); (jtly) Reassessing

Ability Grouping, 2019. *Recreations:* politics, film and literature, gardening, school governor (secondary). *Address:* UCL Institute of Education, 20 Bedford Way, WC1H 0AL. *T:* (020) 7612 6004. *E:* B.Francis@ucl.ac.uk.

**FRANCIS, Clare Mary,** MBE 1978; writer; *b* 17 April 1946; *d* of late Owen Francis, CB and Joan St Leger (*née* Norman); *m* 1977, Jacques Robert Redon (marr. diss. 1985); one *s*. *Educ:* Royal Ballet Sch.; University Coll. London (BScEcon; Fellow, 1978). Crossed Atlantic singlehanded, Falmouth to Newport, in 37 days, 1973; Observer Transatlantic Singlehanded Race: women's record (29 days), 1976; Whitbread Round the World Race (fully-crewed), first woman skipper, 1977–78. Chm., Soc. of Authors, 1997–99. Chm., Govt Adv. Cttee on PLR, 2000–03. Pres., Action for ME, 1990–. Hon. Fellow, UMIST, 1981. *Publications: non-fiction:* Come Hell or High Water, 1977; Come Wind or Weather, 1978; The Commanding Sea, 1981; *novels:* Night Sky, 1983; Red Crystal, 1985; Wolf Winter, 1987; Requiem, 1991; Deceit, 1993 (televised, 2000); Betrayal, 1995; A Dark Devotion, 1997; Keep Me Close, 1999; A Death Divided, 2001; Homeland, 2004; Unforgotten, 2008. *Recreations:* opera, walking. *Address:* c/o Johnson & Alcock Ltd, Bloomsbury House, 74–77 Great Russell Street, WC1B 3DA.

**FRANCIS, (David) Hywel,** PhD; FRHistS; *b* 6 June 1946; *s* of late David Francis and of Catherine Francis (*née* Powell); *m* 1968, Mair Georgina Price; one *s* one *d* (and one *s* decd). *Educ:* UC, Swansea (BA 1968; PhD 1978). Admin. Asst, TUC, 1971–72; University College, Swansea, subseq. University of Wales Swansea: Sen. Res. Officer, 1972–74; Tutor/Lectr, Contg Educn, 1974–87; Dir, Contg Educn, 1987–99; Prof., Contg Educn, 1992–99; Prof. Emeritus, 2006. Chm., Wales Congress in Support of Mining Communities, 1984–86; Nat. Convenor, Yes for Wales Campaign, 1997; Special Policy Advr, Sec. of State for Wales, 1999–2000. MP (Lab) Aberavon, 2001–15. Chair: Select Cttee on Welsh Affairs, 2005–10 (Mem., 2001–10); Jt Cttee on Human Rights, 2010–15; Member, All-Party Parliamentary Group: on Steel, 2001–15 (Sec., 2002–05; Chm., 2005–10); on Carers, 2005–15 (Chm., 2005–10); on Archives and History, 2010–15 (Chm., 2010–15); on Down's Syndrome, 2010–15 (Vice Chm., 2010–15). Introd Private Mem.'s Bill, Carers (Equal Opportunities), which received Royal Assent in 2004. Trustee: Paul Robeson Wales Trust, 2001– (Chm., 2001–08); Bevan Foundn, 2001–. Chm., Richard Burton Adv. Bd, 2005–. Hon. Prof., 2013–, Swansea Univ. Pres., S Wales Miners' Mus., 2001–. Chm., Onllwyn and Dist Welfare Assoc. Mem., Gorsedd of Bards, 1986. FRSA 1987; FRHistS 2011. Hon. DLitt Swansea, 2012. *Publications:* (with David Smith) The Fed: a history of the South Wales miners in the twentieth century, 1980, 2nd edn 1998; Miners against Fascism: Wales and the Spanish Civil War, 1984, 3rd edn 2012; Wales: a learning country, 1999; History on Our Side: Wales and the 1984–85 miners' strike, 2009, 2nd edn 2015; (with Sian Williams) Do Miners Read Dickens?: origins and progress of the South Wales Miners' Library 1973–2013, 2013; Stories of Solidarity, 2018. *Recreations:* photography, walking, reading. *Address:* Swansea University, Singleton Park, Swansea SA2 8PP. *Clubs:* Port Talbot Cricket (Pres.); Aberavon Rugby Football (Vice-Pres.); Seven Sisters Rugby Football (Pres.).

**FRANCIS, Elizabeth Ann, (Lisa);** Member (C) Wales Mid and West, National Assembly for Wales, 2003–07; *b* 29 Nov. 1960; *d* of late Thomas Foelwyn and Dilys Olwen Francis. *Educ:* Ardwyn Grammar Sch.; W London Inst. of Higher Educn. PA to Gp Chief Exec., Lead Industries Gp Ltd; Managerial Sec., African Dept, Glaxo Gp; Manager, Queensbridge Hotel, Aberystwyth, 1985–2002; Dir, Mid Wales Tourism Co., 2002–. *Recreations:* reading, travel, theatre, opera, swimming in the sea, cooking for friends.

**FRANCIS, Canon Prof. (Frederick) Arthur (Stratton);** Professor of Management and Dean, Bradford University School of Management, 1998–2010, now Emeritus Professor; *b* 16 Dec. 1944; *s* of late Arthur James Stratton Francis and Jessie Margery Francis; *m* 1969, Janice Mary Taylor (*d* 2017); one *s* two *d*. *Educ:* Warwick Sch.; Imperial Coll., London (BSc Eng). Res. student and Res. Officer, Imperial Coll., London, 1967–73; Res. Officer, Nuffield Coll., Oxford, 1973–76; Lectr, then Sen. Lectr, Imperial Coll. Sch. of Mgt, 1976–92; University of Glasgow: Prof. of Corporate Strategy, Business Sch., 1992–98; Associate Dean (Res.), Faculty of Soc. Scis, 1992–98. Sen. Res. Fellow, ESRC, 1986–91; Member: ESRC Cttee on Mgt Res., 1991–93; ESRC Res. Progs Bd, 1991–94. Vis. Prof., Kobe Univ., 1989. Nat. Rep., European Gp for Organizational Studies, 1973–90; Chm., EC COST A3 Action on Mgt and New Technol., 1993–96. Vice Chm., then Chm., Assoc. of Business Schs, 2002–06 (Companion, 2008); Dean, Coll. of Fellows, British Acad. of Mgt, 2014. Chair, Abbeyfield The Dales Ltd, 2014–19; Dir, Clarke-Foley Trust, 2014–. Chm. Council, Bradford Cathedral, 2000–14; Member: Bradford Diocesan Synod, 2014–; Leeds Diocesan Synod, 2014–; Diocesan Bd of Educn, 2013–14. Hon. Lay Canon, Bradford Cathedral, 2008–. Gov., Bradford Grammar Sch., 2008–. Fellow British Acad. of Mgt, 1997; CCMI 2000; FAcSS (AcSS 2009). *Publications:* (ed jtly) Power, Efficiency and Institutions, 1982; (jtly) Office Automation, Organisation and the Nature of Work, 1984; (jtly) Innovation and Management Control: labour relations at BL Cars, 1985; New Technology at Work, 1986; (ed jtly) New Technologies and Work: capitalist and socialist perspectives, 1989; (ed jtly) The Competitiveness of European Industry, 1989; (jtly) The Structure of Organizations, 1992; (ed jtly) Design, Networks and Strategies, 1995; articles in Sociology, Cambridge Jl of Econs, Organization Studies, Strategic Mgt Jl and Internat. Jl of Ops and Prodn Mgt. *Address:* High House, Main Street, Addingham, Ilkley, W Yorks LS29 0LY. *T:* (01943) 830264. *E:* a.francis@bradford.ac.uk.

**FRANCIS, His Holiness Pope, (Jorge Mario Bergoglio),** SJ; *b* Buenos Aires, 17 Dec. 1936; *s* of Mario Jose Bergoglio and Regina Maria Sivori. *Educ:* Escuela Nacional de Educacion Técnica; Immaculada Concepción Seminary, Villa Devoto, Buenos Aires; Colegio de San José, San Miguel (LPh 1960); Sankt Georgen Graduate Sch. of Philosophy and Theology, Frankfurt. Chemical Technician, Hickethier-Bachmann Laboratory; entered Soc. of Jesus, 1958; Teacher of Literature and Philosophy: Immaculate Conception Coll., Santa Fé, 1964–65; Colegio del Salvatore, Buenos Aires, 1966; ordained priest, 1969; Master of Novices and Prof. of Theology, Facultades de Filosofía y Teología de San Miguel; final profession, Soc. of Jesus, 1973; Provincial Superior, Soc. of Jesus, Argentina, 1973–79; Rector, Colegio de San José, San Miguel, 1980–86; Spiritual Dir and Confessor, Jesuit Church in Córdoba; Titular Bishop of Auca and Aux. Bishop of Buenos Aires, 1992–97; Episcopal Vicar, Flores District; Vicar-Gen., Archdiocese, 1993; Coadjutor Bishop of Buenos Aires, 1997; Archbishop and Primate of Argentina, 1998–2013; apptd Cardinal, 2001; elected Pope 13 March 2013. *Publications:* Meditaciones para religiosos, 1982; Reflexiones sobre la vida apostólica, 1992; Reflexiones de esperanza, 1992; The Name of God is Mercy, 2016. *Address:* Apostolic Palace, 00120 Vatican City State.

**FRANCIS, Sir (Horace) William (Alexander),** Kt 1989; CBE 1976; FREng; FICE; Director, British Railways Board, 1994–97; *b* 31 Aug. 1926; *s* of Horace Fairie Francis and Jane McMinn Murray; *m* 1949, Gwendoline Maud Dorricott; two *s* two *d*. *Educ:* Royal Technical Coll., Glasgow. Dir, Tarmac Civil Engineering Ltd, 1960; Man. Dir, Tarmac Construction Ltd, 1963; Dir, Tarmac Ltd, 1964, Vice-Chm., 1974–77; Director: Trafalgar House Ltd, 1978–85; Trafalgar House Construction Hldgs, 1979–85; Trafalgar House Oil and Gas, 1986–88; Mining (Scotland) Ltd, 1995–98; Barr Holdings Ltd, 1994–2000; Chairman: Fitzpatrick Internat. Ltd, 1993–99; Enhanced Recovery Systems, 1999–2009. Member: Export Credit Guarantees Adv. Council, 1974–80; British Overseas Trade Bd, 1977–80; Chairman: Overseas Projects Bd, 1977–80; Black Country UDC, 1987–94; Midlands Enterprise Fund, 1996–99. Mem., Engrg Council, 1995–96. Pres., ICE, 1987–88 (Vice-Pres., 1984–87). Lt-Col, Engr and Transport Staff Corps, TA, 1982. FREng (FEng 1977). FRSA 1989. Hon. LLD Strathclyde, 1988; Hon. DSc Aston, 1990. *Recreations:* fishing, construction. *Address:* The Firs, Cruckton, near Shrewsbury, Shropshire SY5 8PW. *T:* (01743) 860796, *Fax:* (01743) 860969. *E:* sirwilliam@francis.uk.net. *Clubs:* Livery, Directors'.

**FRANCIS, Hywel;** *see* Francis, D. H.

**FRANCIS, Jennifer Faure;** Gallery Director, Flowers Gallery, London, since 2018; *b* 13 July 1959; *d* of Luke Redmond Faure and Clytie Jeanne Francis; two *s*. *Educ:* St Augustine's C of E Sch., London; City Univ. (DipCAM; MA Cultural Leadership Policy and Mgt 2011). MCIPR (MIPR 1989). Br. Manager, Brook Street Bureau, 1980–83; PR, Cannons Sports Club, 1983–85; freelance PR, 1985–86; Man. Dir, Networking Public Relations, then Head of African, Caribbean, Asian and Pacific Gp, Pielle Public Relations, 1986–92; PR, LAPADA, 1999; Mktg Dir and Fest. Organiser, Carriacou Maroon Music. Fest., 2000–07; Diversity Project Manager, London Tourist Bd, 2003; Dir of Communications, The Drum, 2003–04; Hd of Press and Marketing, RA, 2004–12; Exec. Dir of Mktg, Philadelphia Mus. of Art, 2012; Dir of Mktg, Communications and Visitor Services, Louvre Abu Dhabi. Actg Hd of Media Relations, V&A Mus., 1998; Actg Dir of Public Relations—The Show, RCA, 1999. Member: Media Adv. Gp, CRE, 1990–91; Nat. Consumer Council, 1991–94; ITC Advertising Adv. Cttee, 1992–99; Prince's Youth Business Trust Ethnic Minority Adv. Gp, 1993–99; Radio Authority, 1994–99; London Regl Bd, Arts Council England, 2009–12; Chm., Women's Enterprise Develt Agency, 1990–93. Board Member: ICOM-US; Arts and Business Council of Greater Philadelphia; ArtTable; Fleisher Art Meml. Black Business Woman of the Year, 1989. *Publications:* contrib. to periodicals. *Recreations:* watercolours, travel, current affairs, music, art fairs.

**FRANCIS, Dr John Michael,** FRSE; Consultant and Adviser, UNESCO, since 2000 (Chair: UK National Commission, 1999–2003; Sustainable Development, Peace and Human Rights, UK UNESCO, 1999–2003; Deputy Chair, Scotland Committee, 2007–15); *b* 1 May 1939; *s* of late William Winston Francis and Beryl Margaret Francis (*née* Savage); *m* 1963, Eileen Sykes, Cyncoed, Cardiff; two *d*. *Educ:* Gowerton County Grammar Sch.; Royal Coll. of Sci., Imperial Coll. of Sci. and Technol., Univ. of London (BSc, ARCS, PhD, DIC). FRIC 1969; FRSGS 1990; FRSE 1991; FRZSScot 1992. Res. Officer, CEGB, R&D Dept, Berkeley Nuclear Labs, 1963–70; First Dir, Society, Religion and Tech. Project, Church of Scotland, 1970–74; Sen. Res. Fellow in Energy Studies, Heriot-Watt Univ., 1974–76; Scottish Office, Edinburgh, 1976–84; Dir Scotland, Nature Conservancy Council, 1984–91 (Mem., Adv. Cttee for Scotland, 1974–76); Chief Exec., NCC for Scotland, 1991–92; Asst Sec., Envmt Dept, 1992–95, Sen. Policy Advr, Home Dept, 1995–99, Scottish Office. Member: Oil Devel Council for Scotland, 1973–76; Ind. Commn on Transport, 1974; Adv. Cttee on Marine Fishfarming Crown Estate Commn, 1989–92. Chm., Francis Group (Consultants), 1992–99. Consultant on Sci., Tech. and Social Ethics, WCC, Geneva, 1971–83; Church of Scotland: Chm., Cttee on Society, Religion and Technol., 1980–94; Trustee, Society, Religion and Technol. Project Trust, 1998–2007; Member: Church and Nation Cttee, 2000–05; Church and Society Council, 2005–12. Chm., Edinburgh Forum, 1984–93. Mem. Council, Nat. Trust for Scotland, 1985–92. Mem., St Giles' Cathedral, Edinburgh. Associate, Scottish Inst. of Human Relations, 1974–94; Member: Scottish Univs Policy, Res. and Advice Network, 1999–2012; Internat. Develt Gp, Scottish Parlt, 2001–; Steering Gp, Scottish Sustainable Develt Forum, 2004–11; Exec. Bd, Centre for Theology and Public Issues, Univ. of Edinburgh, 2005–10; Governing Bd, UNESCO Centre for Water Law, Policy and Sci., Univ. of Dundee, 2008–; Internat. Cttee, RSE, 2009–12. Trustee, RSE Scotland Foundn, 2004–07. Fellow, Inst. for Advanced Studies in the Humanities, Edinburgh Univ., 1988; Hon. Fellow, Edinburgh Univ., 2000–10; Vis. Fellow, Centre for Values and Social Policy, Univ. of Colorado at Boulder, 1991; UK Rep., Millennium Proj., UN Univ., 1992–2004. Professional Mem., World Futures Soc., Washington DC, 1991–; Mem., UNA, 2004– (Convener, UNA Edinburgh, 2006–07). Mem., John Muir Trust, 1994–2010. *Publications:* Scotland in Turmoil, 1973; (jtly) Changing Directions, 1974; (jtly) The Future as an Academic Discipline, 1975; Facing up to Nuclear Power, 1976; (jtly) The Future of Scotland, 1977; (jtly) North Sea Oil and the Environment, 1992; (jtly) Democratic Contracts for Sustainable and Caring Societies, 2000; (jtly) Conserving Nature, 2005; contribs to scientific and professional jls and periodicals, and to RSE programmes on public understanding of science. *Recreations:* writing on environmental values, accessing spiritual paths, discovering Aquitaine.

**FRANCIS, Rev. Canon Prof. Leslie John,** PhD, ScD, DD, DLitt; FBPsS, FCCT, FAcSS; Professor of Religions and Education, Centre for Education Studies (formerly Institute of Education), University of Warwick, since 2007; *b* 10 Sept. 1947; *s* of Ronald Arthur Francis and Joan Irene Francis. *Educ:* Colchester Royal Grammar Sch.; Pembroke Coll., Oxford (BA (Theol.) 1970, MA 1974); Westcott House, Cambridge; Queens' Coll., Cambridge (PhD (Educn) 1976); Univ. of Nottingham (MTh 1976); Inst. of Educn, Univ. of London (MSc (Psychol.) 1977); Oxford Univ. (BD (Theol.) 1990; DD 2001); Univ. of Cambridge (ScD 1997); Univ. of Wales, Bangor (DLitt 2007). FBPsS 1988; CPsychol 1989. Ordained deacon, 1973, priest, 1974; Curate, St Mary's, Haverhill, 1973–77; Leverhulme Res. Fellow, London Central YMCA/Westminster Med. Sch., 1977–82; non-stipendiary Priest-in-charge, St Mary's, Gt Bradley and Holy Trinity, Little Wratting, Suffolk, 1978–82; Res. Officer, 1982–86, Sen. Res. Officer, 1986–88, Culham Coll. Inst.; non-stipendiary Priest-in-charge, All Saints, N Cerney and St Margaret's, Bagendon, Glos, 1982–85; non-stipendiary Priest, Dio. of Oxford, 1985–88; Trinity College, Carmarthen: Mansel Jones Fellow, 1989–99; Principal Lectr in Religious Studies, 1989–91; Dir, Centre for Theol. and Educn and Dir of Res., 1992–99; Asst Chaplain, 1989–94; Dean of Chapel, 1994–99; D. J. James Prof. of Pastoral Theol., Univ. of Wales, Lampeter, 1992–99; Prof. of Practical Theol. and Dir, Welsh Nat. Centre for Religious Educn, Univ. of Wales, Bangor, 1999–2007; non-stipendiary Priest, Dio. of Bangor, 1999–2006; Hon. Asst Curate, Llanfairpwll and Llanddaniel-fab with Penmynydd, 2006–12; non-stipendiary Assoc. Priest, Seintiau Braint a Chefni, 2012–17; Canon Theologian: Cath. of St John the Baptist, Newfoundland, 2017–; Liverpool Cath., 2019–; Permission to Officiate, United Dio. Dublin and Glendalough, Ireland, 2018–. Hon. Canon, St Davids Cath., 1998–99; Hon. Canon, 2006–11, Cursal Canon (Secundus), 2011–12, Canon Theologian 2006–16, Canon Treas., 2012–16, Bangor Cath.; Hon. Dist. Canon, Manchester Cath., 2017–. Chairman: Census 2001 Wkg Party, CCBI, 1995–2001; Religious Affiliation Subgp, Census Content Wkg Gp, ONS, 1996–98; Religious Affiliation Gp, 2001 Census, 1998–. Church in Wales: Chairman: Continuing Ministerial Educn Cttee, 1992–2001; Children's Sector, 1995–2001; Mem., Governing Body, 1997–2001. National Council of YMCAs: Mem., Wkg Party on use and abuse of alcohol, 1983–84; Chm., Educn and Prog. Develt, 1985–90; Mem., Exec. Cttee and Nat. Bd, 1985–90. Consultant, Archbps' Commn on Rural Areas, 1989–90. British Psychological Society: Mem., Standing Cttee on teaching psychol. to other professional gps, 1990–2000; Trustee, Welfare Fund, 1992–2002. Trustee: Alister Hardy Trust, 1999– (Chm., 2002–; Chm., Res. Cttee, 1999–2002); St Deiniol's Liby, Hawarden, 2002–10; Network for the Study of Implicit Religion, 2002–; Internat. Seminar for Religious Educn and Values, 2003–; Intereuropean Commn on Church and School, 2005–. FCP 1994. *Publications:* Youth in Transit, 1982; Experience of Adulthood, 1982; Young and Unemployed, 1984; Teenagers and the Church, 1984; Rural Anglicanism: a future for young Christians?, 1985; Partnership in Rural Education: church schools and teacher attitudes, 1986; Religion in the Primary School, 1987; (with K. Williams) Churches in Fellowship: local councils of churches in England, 1991; (with W. K. Kay) Teenage Religion and Values, 1995; (with W. K. Kay) Drift from the Churches: attitudes towards Christianity during childhood and adolescence, 1996; Church Watch: Christianity in the countryside, 1996; (with J. Martineau) Rural Praise, 1996; Personality Type and Scripture: exploring Mark's Gospel, 1997; (with P. Richter) Gone but not Forgotten: church leaving and returning, 1998; (with M. Robbins) The Long Diaconate 1987–1994: women deacons and the delayed journey to priesthood, 1999; (jtly) Rural Ministry, 2000; (with P. Atkins) Exploring Luke's Gospel: a guide to the gospel readings in the Revised Common Lectionary, 2000; The Values Debate: a voice from the pupils, 2001; (with J. Martineau) Rural Visitors, 2001; (with J. Martineau) Rural Youth, 2001; (with P. Atkins) Exploring Matthew's Gospel: a guide to the gospel readings in the Revised Common Lectionary, 2001; (with J. Martineau) Rural Mission, 2002; (with J. Astley) Children, Churches and Christian Learning, 2002; (with P. Atkins) Exploring Mark's Gospel: an aid for readers and preachers using year B of the Revised Common Lectionary, 2002; (with S. H. Louden) The Naked Parish Priest: what priests really think they're doing, 2003; Faith and Psychology: personality, religion and the individual, 2005; (with M. Robbins and J. Astley) Fragmented Faith: exposing the fault-lines in the Church of England, 2005; (with M. Robbins) Urban Hope and Spiritual Health: the adolescent voice, 2005; (with J. M. Haley) British Methodism: what circuit ministers really think, 2006; (with P. Richter) Gone for Good?: church-leaving and returning in the 21st century, 2007; (with A. Village) Preaching with all our Souls: a study in hermeneutics and psychological type, 2008; The Gospel in the Willows, 2009; (with A. Village) The Mind of the Anglican Clergy: assessing attitudes and beliefs in the Church of England, 2009; (jtly) Ordained Local Ministry in the Church of England, 2012; *edited books:* (with A. Thatcher) Christian Perspectives for Education: a reader in the theology of education, 1990; (with J. Astley) Christian Perspectives on Faith Development: a reader, 1992; (with D. W. Lankshear) Christian Perspectives on Church Schools: a reader, 1993; (with J. Astley) Critical Perspectives on Christian Education, 1994; (jtly) Fast-moving Currents in Youth Culture, 1995; (with J. Astley) Christian Theology and Religious Education, 1996; (with S. H. Jones) Psychological Perspectives on Christian Ministry: a reader, 1996; (jtly) Research in Religious Education, 1996; (jtly) Theological Perspectives on Christian Formation: a reader on theology and Christian education, 1996; (with W. K. Kay) Religion in Education: vol. 1, 1997, vol. 2, 1998, vol. 3, 2000, vol. 4 (also with K. Watson), 2003; (with J. Francis) Tentmaking: perspectives on self-supporting ministry, 1998; Sociology, Theology and the Curriculum, 1999; (with Y. J. Katz) Joining and Leaving Religion: research perspectives, 2000; (jtly) The Fourth R for the Third Millennium: education in religion and values for the global future, 2001; (with J. Astley) Psychological Perspectives on Prayer: a reader, 2001; (jtly) Changing Rural Life: a Christian response to key rural issues, 2004; (jtly) Making Connections: a reader on preaching, 2005; (jtly) The Idea of a Christian University: essays on theology and higher education, 2005; (jtly) Religion, Education and Adolescence: international empirical perspectives, 2005; (jtly) Peace or Violence: the ends of religion and education, 2007; (jtly) Empirical Theology in Texts and Tables: qualitative, quantitative and comparative perspectives, 2009; (jtly) International Handbook of Education for Spirituality, Care and Wellbeing, 2009; (jtly) The Public Significance of Religion, 2011; (jtly) Teaching Religion, Teaching Truth: theoretical and empirical perspectives, 2012; (jtly) Rural Life and Rural Church: theological and empirical perspectives, 2012; (jtly) Religious Education and Freedom of Religion and Belief, 2012; (with J. Astley) Exploring Ordinary Theology: everyday Christian believing and the Church, 2013; (jtly) History, Remembrance and Religious Education, 2015; (jtly) Anglican Cathedrals in Modern Life: the science of cathedral studies, 2015; (with J. Astley) Diversity and Intersectionality: studies in religion, education and values, 2016; (with M. Robbins) The Empirical Science of Religious Education, 2016; (jtly) Lessons in Spiritual Development, 2017; (jtly) Values, Human Rights and Religious Education, 2018; has also written 14 bks for teachers and clergy, and over 30 bks for children, incl. (with N. M. Slee) Teddy Horsley Bible Books series. *Recreations:* music, the countryside and architecture. *Address:* Warwick Religions and Education Research Unit, Centre for Education Studies, University of Warwick, Coventry CV4 7AL. *T:* (024) 7652 2539, *Fax:* (024) 7657 2638. *E:* leslie.francis@warwick.ac.uk.

**FRANCIS, Lisa;** *see* Francis, E. A.

**FRANCIS, Mary Elizabeth,** CBE 2005; LVO 1999; non-executive Director: Ensco plc, since 2013; Barclays plc, since 2016; *b* 24 July 1948; *d* of Frederick Henry George and Barbara Henrietta George (*née* Jeffs); *m* 1st, Dr Roger John Brown, *qv* (marr. diss.); 2nd, 1991, Prof. Peter William Francis (*d* 1999); 3rd, 2001, Ian Campbell Ferguson Rodger. *Educ:* James Allen's Girls' Sch., Dulwich; Newnham Coll., Cambridge (MA Hist.). Res. Asst to Prof. Max Beloff, All Souls Coll., Oxford, 1970–72; CS Dept and HM Treasury, 1972–90 incl. secondment to Hill Samuel & Co. Ltd, 1984–86, then Asst Sec., 1986–90; Economic Counsellor, British Embassy, Washington, 1990–92; Private Sec. to Prime Minister, 1992–95; Asst Private Sec. to the Queen, 1996–99, Dep. Private Sec., Feb.–June 1999; Dir-Gen., ABI, 1999–2005. Non-executive Director: Bank of England, 2001–07; Centrica plc, 2004–14 (Sen. Ind. Dir, 2006–14); St Modwen Properties Plc, 2005–09; Aviva plc, 2005–12; Alliance & Leicester plc, 2007–08; Cable and Wireless Communications plc, 2009–12; Swiss Re Gp, 2012–18. Member: Press Complaints Commn, 2001–05; Takeover Appeal Bd, 2016–. Member: Adv. Bd, NCC, 2002–08; Adv. Bd, Cambridge Univ. Centre for Business Res., 2006–10; Adv. Panel, Inst. of Business Ethics, 2015–; Sen. Advr, Chatham House (RIIA), 2008–. Gov., Pensions Policy Inst., 2002–09. Trustee, Almeida Th., 2002–10 (Treas., 2008–10). Associate Fellow, Newnham Coll., Cambridge, 1995–98. Chm. of Govs, James Allen's Girls' Sch., Dulwich, 2009–13 (Gov., 1992–2001). *Recreations:* reading, swimming, ballet, walking.

**FRANCIS, Hon. Sir Nicholas;** *see* Francis, Hon. Sir P. N.

**FRANCIS, Paul Richard,** FRICS, PPISVA; Surveyor Member, Upper Tribunal (Lands Chamber) (formerly Lands Tribunal), 1998–2018; *b* 14 Feb. 1948; *o s* of Richard Francis and Pamela Francis (*née* Rouse); *m* 2006, Mollie Labercombe. *Educ:* King's Sch., Harrow. FSVA 1974; FRICS 2000. Midland Marts (Banbury), 1967–70; E. J. Brooks & Son, Chartered Surveyors, 1970–75; Partner, A. C. Frost & Co., 1975–86; Nat. Survey and Valuation Dir, Prudential Property Services Ltd, 1986–98. Pres., ISVA, 1994–95. Chm. Adv. Bd, Cert. in Residential Estate Agency, Coll. of Estate Mgt, 1997–2000; Vice-Chm., RICS Dispute Resolution Faculty Bd, 2001–07. *Recreations:* motor sailing, golf, shooting, gardening. *Club:* Royal Southampton Yacht.

**FRANCIS, Rev. Peter Brereton;** Warden and Chief Librarian, Gladstone's (formerly St Deiniol's) Library, Hawarden, since 1997; *b* 18 June 1953; *s* of Richard and Pauline Francis; *m* 1st, 1976, Denise Steele (marr. diss. 1997); 2nd, Helen Grocott; one step *d*. *Educ:* Malvern Coll.; St Andrews Univ. (MTh 1977); Queen's Coll., Birmingham. Ordained deacon, 1978, priest, 1979; Curate, Hagley, Worcs, 1978–81; Chaplain, QMC, 1981–87; Rector, Holy Trinity, Ayr, 1987–92; Provost and Rector, St Mary's Cathedral, Glasgow, 1992–96. Vis. Prof., Glyndwr Univ., Wrexham, 2009–. Dir, Gladstone Project, 1997–. Trustee, Nat. Liberal Club, 2011– (Chm., 2017–). Hon. DD Chester, 2012. *Publications:* The Grand Old Man, 2000; The Gladstone Umbrella, 2001; (ed jtly) Changing Rural Life, 2004; (ed Jtly) Cinema Divinité, 2005; (ed) Rebuilding Communion, 2007; (contrib.) Pieces of Ease and Grace, 2013; Bible and Cinema, 2013; (contrib.) Oxford Dictionary of Christian Art and Architecture, 2013; (contrib.) Matthew and Mark Across Perspectives, 2015. *Recreations:* cinema, theatre, contemporary literature. *Address:* The Warden's Lodge, Gladstone's Library, St Deiniol's, Church Lane, Hawarden, Flintshire CH5 3DF. *T:* (01244) 532350, 531659, *Fax:* (01244) 520643.

**FRANCIS, Hon. Sir (Peter) Nicholas,** Kt 2016; **Hon. Mr Justice Francis;** a Judge of the High Court of Justice, Family Division, since 2016; *b* 22 April 1958; *s* of Peter and Jean Francis; *m* 2000, Penny Seguss; two *s*, and one *d* from previous marriage. *Educ:* Radley Coll.; Downing Coll., Cambridge (MA). Called to the Bar, Middle Temple, 1981; Asst Recorder, 1998–99; a Recorder, 1999–2016; QC 2002; Head of Chambers, 29 Bedford Row, 2002–16; a Dep. High Ct Judge, 2011–16. *Recreations:* sailing, theatre, wine. *Address:* Royal Courts of Justice, Strand, WC2A 2LL.

**FRANCIS, Richard Mark;** barn restorer and art historian; *b* 20 Nov. 1947; *s* of Ralph Lawrence and Eileen Francis; *m* 1976, Tamar Janine Helen Burchill; one *d*. *Educ:* Oakham Sch.; Cambridge Univ.; Courtauld Inst. Walker Art Gall., Liverpool, 1971–72; Arts Council of GB, 1973–80; Asst Keeper, Tate Gall., London, 1980–86; Curator, Tate Gall., Liverpool, 1986–90; Chief Curator, Mus. of Contemp. Art, Chicago, 1993–97; Christie's, NY, 1997–2002. *Publications:* Jasper Johns, 1984.

**FRANCIS, Sir Robert (Anthony),** Kt 2014; QC 1992; a Recorder, since 2000; a Deputy High Court Judge, since 2014; *b* 4 April 1950; *s* of late John Grimwade Francis and of Jean Isobel Francis; *m* 1st, 1976, Catherine Georgievsky (marr. diss. 2005); one *s* two *d*; 2nd, 2007, Alison Meek. *Educ:* Uppingham Sch.; Exeter Univ. (LLB Hons). Pres., Exeter Univ. Guild of Students, 1971–72. Called to the Bar, Inner Temple, 1973, Bencher, 2002. Asst Recorder, 1996–2000. Legal Assessor, Chartered Soc. of Physiotherapists, 1991. Mem. Exec. Cttee, Professional Negligence Bar Assoc., 2000–06 (Vice Chm., 2002; Chm., 2004); Chm., Educn and Trng Cttee, Inner Temple, 2010–13. Chairman: Mid Staffs NHS Foundn Trust Public Inquiry, 2010–13 (report, 2013); Healthwatch England, 2019–. Chm., Freedom to Speak Up Rev., 2014–15 (report, 2015). Non-exec. Dir, Care Quality Commn, 2014–. Pres., Patients' Assoc., 2013–. Pres., Medico-Legal Soc., 2019–. Trustee: Peper Harow Orgn, 1992–2002; Prostate Cancer Res. Centre, 2014–; Point of Care Foundn, 2014–. Churchwarden, St John's Parish Church, Milford, Surrey, 1984–92. Hon. FRCAnaes 2014; Hon. FRCSE 2016; Hon. FRCPath 2016. Hon. LLD Exeter, 2016. Consultant Ed., Medical Law Reports (formerly Lloyd's Law Reports: Medical, later LS Law Medical), 1999–. *Publications:* (jtly) Medical Treatment Decisions and the Law, 2001, 2nd edn 2010; (contrib.) Medical Treatment Decisions and the Law, 3rd edn 2016. *Recreation:* cricket. *Address:* Serjeants' Inn Chambers, 85 Fleet Street, EC4Y 1AE. *T:* (020) 7427 5000.

**FRANCIS, Sheena Vanessa;** *see* Wagstaff, S. V.

**FRANCIS, Stewart Alexander Clement,** MA; Headmaster, Colchester Royal Grammar School, 1985–2000; *b* 25 Feb. 1938; *s* of Clement Francis and Patricia Francis (*née* Stewart); *m* 1965, Valerie Stead; one *s* one *d*. *Educ:* St Andrew's Sch., Eastbourne; St Edward's Sch., Oxford; St John's Coll., Cambridge (MA Classics, Cert Ed). Assistant Master: Mill Hill Sch., London, 1963; Maidenhead GS, 1963–66; temp. teaching posts in S Africa and England, 1966–67; Hd, Lower Sch., Maidenhead GS, 1967–69; Hd of English and Hd of Sixth Form, William Penn Sch., Rickmansworth, 1969–74; Dep. Head, Southgate Sch., London, 1974–79; Headmaster, Chenderit Sch., Middleton Cheney, Northants, 1979–84. OFSTED sch. inspector, 2005–08; sch. improvement partner, 2006–10. Pres., NE Essex Headteachers' Assoc., 1987–88. Trustee, Colchester Blue Coat Sch. Foundn, 1985–. Mem. Court, Univ. of Essex, 1996–2000. Gov., Philip Morant Sch. and Coll., Colchester, 2011–17. FRSA 1995. Mem., Cricket Soc., 2005–; Men's squash champion, Bucks, 1970. Life Mem., Cambridge Union, 1958–; Member: Johnian Soc., 1958–; London Schools and Colleges Dining Club, 1985–2011; Brightwine, 2000–; Colchester Breakfast Club, 2001–15; Tate, 2010–12, 2015–; Friend: Bankside Gall., 2006–; Rotary Club of Colchester, 2008– (Mem., 2001–08); Royal Acad., 2010–12, 2016–; Chm., Colchester Twinning Soc., 2012–13. Hon. Life Vice Pres., Old Colcestrian Soc., 2018. Paintings in group exhibitions: Bankside Gp, London, 2010–12; Mersea Is. Art Gp, Mersea Is. Mus., Essex, 2011–12. Chevalier du Sacavin d'Anjou, 2008. *Publications:* contrib. Cricket Qly; letters in nat. newspapers; poems in Cricket Soc. News Bulletin, The Eagle, Poetry Wivenhoe pubns, Wivenhoe News, Mersea Island Courier, AMTV (Andy Merz films); contrib. Essex Co. Standard. *Recreations:* cricket and other sports, reading, writing, theatre, drawing and painting, visiting art galleries. *Address:* 32 The Lane, West Mersea, Essex CO5 8NT. *T:* (01206) 386084. *E:* stewartfrancis7@gmail.com. *Clubs:* Eagles, Victory Services, MCC, Jesters Cricket.

**FRANCIS, Vanessa; Her Honour Judge Francis;** a Circuit Judge, since 2019; *b* Neath, W Glamorgan, 28 Dec. 1968; *d* of Dennis Brian Francis and Roberta Anne Francis; partner, Julian Price; one *d*. *Educ:* Bryn Celynnog Comprehensive Sch., Beddau, Pontypridd; Cardiff Univ. (LLB). Admitted as a solicitor, 1993; Founding Partner, St James Solicitors, Exeter, 2002–17; a Recorder, 2012–19; called to the Bar, Lincoln's Inn, 2018. Legal Chair (pt-time), Restricted Patients Panel, 2018–. *Recreations:* mostly cake and patisserie, related with a nod to gentle exercise occasionally.

**FRANCIS, Sir William;** *see* Francis, Sir H. W. A.

**FRANCIS-DEHQANI, Rt Rev. Gulnar Eleanor;** *see* Loughborough, Bishop of.

**FRANCIS-WARD, Jayne;** Corporate Director for Resources and Monitoring Officer, Nottinghamshire County Council, 2012–18; *b* England, 20 March 1963; *d* of George and Joan Williams; *m* 2009, Geoffrey Ward; two *s* and one step *s*. *Educ:* Bramcote Hills Comprehensive Sch.; Univ. of Leicester (LLB Hons 1984); Nottingham Trent Univ.; Univ. of Buckingham (Postgrad. Dip. Educn Law 1999). Asst Solicitor, Derbys CC, 1987–88; Nottinghamshire County Council, 1988–2018: Service Dir, Legal and Democratic Services, 2007–09; Asst Chief Exec., 2009–12. Clerk: to Queen Elizabeth Endowed Sch. Trust, 2015–; to Allotments for Labouring Poor Trust, 2015–. Chm., Mgt Bd, EM LawShare, 2004–. Gov., Nethergate Acad., 2012–. *Publications:* contrib. articles to public sector pubns. *Recreations:* shoe shopping, theatre, family, equalities issues. *E:* jaynetrustwales@gmail.com.

**FRANCKE, Ann P.;** Chief Executive, Chartered Management Institute, since 2012; *m* Barry King; one *d*. *Educ:* Stanford Univ. (BA Distinction Russian and Politics 1980); Berlin Univ. (Deutscher Akademischer Austauschdienst Schol.); Columbia Univ., NY (MBA, MS). Procter & Gamble, Inc., 1986–99; Eur. Vice Pres. (Petcare Portfolio), Mars, Inc., 1999–2002; Dir, Strategic Mktg, Boots Gp plc, 2003; Chief Mktg Officer, Yell Gp plc, 2004–06; Co-Founder and Pres., Beutorium LLC, 2007–09; Global Man. Dir, BSI Gp, 2009–12. *Publications:* FT Guide to Management: how to make a difference and get results, 2014. *Address:* 52 Antrobus Road, W4 5HZ. *E:* annpfrancke@gmail.com.

**FRANCOIS, Rt Hon. Mark (Gino);** PC 2010; MP (C) Rayleigh and Wickford, since 2010 (Rayleigh, 2001–10); *b* London, 14 Aug. 1965; *m* 2000, Karen Thomas (marr. diss. 2006). *Educ:* Nicholas Comprehensive Sch., Basildon; Univ. of Bristol (BA 1986); King's Coll. London (MA 1987). Mgt trainee, Lloyds Bank, 1987; Consultant and Dir, Market Access Internat. Public Affairs Consultancy, 1988–95; Public Affairs Consultant, Francois Associates, 1996–2001. Mem. (C) Basildon DC, 1991–95. Opposition Jun. Whip, 2002; Shadow Econ. Sec., HM Treasury, 2004; Shadow Paymaster Gen., 2005–07; Opposition spokesman on Europe, 2007–09; Shadow Minister for Europe, 2009–10; Vice-Chamberlain of HM Household (Govt Whip), 2010–12; Minister of State, MoD, 2012–15, DCLG, 2015–16. Mem., Envmtl Audit Cttee, 2001–05, Defence Cttee, 2017–, H of C. Contested (C) Brent East, 1997. Served TA, 1983–89 (Lieut). Mem., RUSI. Fellow, Huguenot Soc. of GB and Ire., 2001–. Freeman, City of London, 2004; Liveryman, Co. of Wheelwrights, 2005–. Pres., Palace of Westminster Lions Club, 2006–12. *Recreations:* reading, travel, walking, history (including military history). *Address:* (office) 25 Bellingham Lane, Rayleigh, Essex SS6 7ED; c/o House of Commons, SW1A 0AA. *T:* (020) 7219 3000. *Clubs:* Carlton, Royal Air Force; Rayleigh Conservative (Pres., 2010–).

**FRANCOME, John,** MBE 1986; writer; racing presenter, Channel 4 Television, until 2012; first jockey to F. T. Winter, 1975–85; *b* 13 Dec. 1952; *s* of Norman and Lillian Francome; *m* 1976, Miriam Strigner (marr. diss.). *Educ:* Park Senior High School, Swindon. First ride, Dec. 1970; Champion Jockey (National Hunt), 1975–76, 1978–79, 1980–81, 1981–82, 1982–83, 1983–84, 1984–85; record number of jumping winners (1,036), May 1984; retired March 1985 (1,138 winners). *Publications:* Born Lucky (autobiog.), 1985; How to Make Money Betting—or at least how not to lose too much, 1986; Twice Lucky: the lighter side of steeplechasing, 1988; *novels:* Blood Stock, 1989; Stud Poker, 1990; Stone Cold, 1991; Rough Ride, 1992; Outsider, 1993; Break Neck, 1994; Dead Ringer, 1995; False Start, 1996; High Flyer, 1997; Safe Bet, 1998; Tip Off, 1999; Lifeline, 2000; Dead Weight, 2001; Inside Track, 2002; Stalking Horse, 2003; Back Hander, 2004; Cover Up, 2005; Free Fall, 2006; Winner Takes All, 2006; Dark Horse, 2007; Final Break, 2008; Deadly Finish, 2009; Storm Rider, 2010; (with James MacGregor): Eavesdropper, 1986; Riding High, 1987; Declared Dead, 1988. *Recreations:* tennis, music. *Address:* Beechdown Farm, Sheepdrove, Lambourn, Berks RG17 7UN.

**FRANK, Sir Andrew;** *see* Frank, Sir R. A.

**FRANK, David;** Chief Executive, Dial Square 86, since 2013; Chairman, TRX (formerly The RightsXchange), since 2014; *b* 24 Sept. 1958; *s* of late Peter James Frank and Joyce Miriam Frank (*née* Sollis); *m* 1983, Isabelle Turquet de Beauregard; two *s* one *d*. *Educ:* Trinity Coll., Oxford (BA Juris.). Manager: Hill Samuel & Co. Ltd, 1982–85; Swiss Bank Corp. Internat., 1985–87; freelance journalist, 1987–89; reporter, BBC TV, 1989–92; Chief Exec., RDF Media, later Zodiak Media Gp, 1993–2013. *Recreations:* football, scuba-diving, golf, fly-fishing. *Address:* Dial Square 86, Somerset House, Strand, WC2R 1LA. *E:* david.frank@dialsquare86.com. *Clubs:* Roehampton, Soho House, Winchester House.

**FRANK, Prof. Joachim,** PhD; Professor, Department of Biochemistry and Molecular Biophysics, and Professor, Department of Biological Sciences, Columbia University, since 2008; Investigator, Howard Hughes Medical Institute, 1998–2017; *b* Weidenau, Sieg, Germany, 9 Sept. 1940; *s* of Dr Wilhelm Frank and Charlotte Frank (*née* Manskopf); *m* 1983, Carol Saginaw; one *s* one *d*. *Educ:* Univ. of Freiburg (BS Physics 1993); Univ. of Munich (MS 1967); Tech. Univ. of Munich (PhD 1970). Res. Asst, Max-Planck Inst. für Eiweiss-und Lederforschung, 1967–70; postdoctoral res. in USA at CIT, Univ. of Calif, Berkeley and Cornell Univ., 1970–72; Vis. Scientist, Max-Planck Inst. for Biochem., 1972–73; Sen. Res. Asst, Electron Microscopy Gp, Cavendish Lab., Univ. of Cambridge, 1973–75; Sen. Res. Scientist, Wadsworth Center, NY State Dept of Health, 1975–98; Lab. Chief, Lab. for Computational Biol. and Molecular Imaging, 1994–; Res. Prof., Dept of Cell Biol., New York Univ., 1997–; Sen. Lectr, Dept of Biochem. and Molecular Biophysics, Columbia Univ., 2003–08; Dist. Prof., SUNY, 2007. Mem., NAS, 2006. FAAAS 1997; Fellow: Biophysical Soc., 2001; Amer. Acad. Arts and Scis, 2006; Amer. Acad. Microbiol., 2006; Microscopy Soc. of America, 2009. (Jtly) Elizabeth Roberts Cole Award, Biophys. Soc., 1993; Humboldt Res. Award, Alexander von Humboldt Foundn, 1994; Franklin Medal for Life Sci., Franklin Inst., Philadelphia, 2014; Wiley Prize in Biomed. Sci., 2017; (jtly) Nobel Prize for Chem., 2017. *Publications:* (ed) Electron Tomography, 1992, 2nd edn 2006; Three-dimensional Electron Microscopy of Macromolecules, 1996; (jtly) Electron Crystallography of Biological Macromolecules, 2006; (ed) Molecular Machines in Biology: workshop of the cell, 2011; (ed) Found in Translation: collection of original articles on single-particle reconstruction and the structural basis of protein synthesis, 2013; (ed with G. Herman) Computational Methods for Three-Dimensional Microscopy Reconstruction, 2014; contrib. papers to scientific learned jls. *Recreations:* fiction, photography. *Address:* 650 West 168th Street, Black Building, 2–221, New York, NY 10032, USA. *E:* jf2192@cumc.columbia.edu.

**FRANK, Prof. John William,** MD; FRSE; Professor of Public Health Research and Policy, University of Edinburgh, since 2008; *b* Guelph, Ont, 23 June 1949; *s* of William Frank and Marion Frank; *m* 1976, Eden Anderson; three *s*. *Educ:* Univ. of Toronto (BSc 1971; MD 1974); Coll. of Family Physicians of Canada (Cert. Coll. of Family Practice 1976); London Sch. of Hygiene and Tropical Medicine (MSc 1981). FRCPC 1982. Med. Officer and MA Instructor, Mbeya, Tanzania, 1976–79; Staff Physician, York Community Services, Toronto, 1979–80; Prof., Faculty of Medicine, Univ. of Toronto, 1983–2008, now Emeritus; Dir, Res., Inst. for Work and Health, Toronto, 1991–97; Adjunct Prof., Sch. of Public Health, Univ. of Calif, Berkeley, 1997–2000; Inaugural Scientific Dir, CIHR Inst. of Popn and Public Health, 2000–08; Dir, Scottish Collaboration for Public Health Res. and Policy, 2008–18. FCAHS 2006; FFPH 2009; FRSE 2013. Hon. LLD Waterloo, 2017. *Publications:* over 25 book chapters and monographs; 290 articles in jls. *Recreations:* natural history, singing, Scottish country dancing, travel. *Address:* Teviot Hall, Teviot Place, Edinburgh EH8 9AG. *E:* john.frank@ed.ac.uk.

**FRANK, Sir (Robert) Andrew,** 4th Bt *cr* 1920, of Withyham, Co. Sussex; freelance event management and training consultant, since 2000; owner, Baronet Communications, since 2009; *b* 16 May 1964; *s* of Sir Robert John Frank, 3rd Bt, FRICS, and Margaret Joyce (*d* 1995), *d* of Herbert Victor Truesdale; *S* father, 1987; *m* 1st, 1990, Zoë, *m d* of S. Å. Haas (marr. diss. 2010); 2nd, 2014, Dr Rehanwant Singh Gomez. *Educ:* Ludgrove Prep. School; Eton College. *Recreations:* travel, theatre, cinema. *Heir:* none.

**FRANKEL, Dr Hans Ludwig,** OBE 1993; FRCP; Consultant in Spinal Injuries, National Spinal Injuries Centre, Stoke Mandeville Hospital, 1966–2002, now Honorary Consultant; *b* 7 April 1932; *s* of late Dr Paul Frankel, CBE and Helen Frankel; *m* 1956, Mavis Anne Richardson; two *s*. *Educ:* Dauntsey's Sch.; University Coll. London; University Coll. Hosp. Med. Sch. (MB BS 1956). MRCS 1956; LRCP 1956, MRCP 1964, FRCP 1977. Casualty officer, Hampstead Gen. Hosp., 1957; Stoke Mandeville Hospital, 1957–: Hse Physician, 1957–58; National Spinal Injuries Centre: Registrar, 1958–62; Sen. Registrar, 1962–66; Dep. Dir, 1969–77; Mem., Exec. Bd, 1991–98; Clin. Dir, 1993–98. Hon. Consultant, Star & Garter Home, Richmond, 1979–. Vis. Prof., ICSTM, 2000–. Member: Editorial Board: Paraplegia; Annales de Readaptation et de Médecine Physique; Clinical Autonomic Res.; Editl Adv. Bd, Annals of Sports Medicine. Buckinghamshire Area Health Authority: Vice-Chm., 1976–77, Chm., 1978–80, Med. Adv. Cttee. International Medical Society of Paraplegia: Hon. Treas., 1966–78; Hon. Sec., 1976–87; Vice Pres., 1987–91; Pres., 1996–2000; Chm., Scientific Cttee, 1992–96. President: Brit. Cervical Spine Soc., 1990–92; Chiltern Gp, Spinal Injuries Assoc., 1989–98. Mem., Exec. Cttee, Brit. Paraplegic Sports Soc., 1977–91. Chm. Trustees, Internat. Spinal Res. Trust, 1983–97; Mem., Mgt Council, Brit. Neurol Res. Trust, 1989–. Numerous lectures in UK, Europe, USA and throughout the world, incl. Arnott Demonstrator, RCS 1987, Sandoz Lectr, Inst. of Neurol., London, 1988 and 1992. *Publications:* (ed) volume on Spinal Cord Injuries in Handbook of Clinical Neurology, 1992; contrib. chapters on spinal cord injuries to text books. *Recreations:* ski-ing, opera. *Address:* Seytons Manor, Terrick, Aylesbury, Bucks HP17 0UA.

**FRANKEL, Prof. Stephen John,** DM, PhD; FRCP, FFPH; Professor of Epidemiology and Public Health, University of Bristol, 1993–2007, now Emeritus; *b* 4 Nov. 1946; *s* of Eric and Constance Frankel; *m* 1st, 1972, Hermione Jane Dennis (marr. diss. 2003); one *s* one *d*; 2nd, 2004, Elizabeth-Jane Grose. *Educ:* Corpus Christi Coll., Oxford (BM BCh 1970; MA 1970; DM 1983); Corpus Christi Coll., Cambridge (PhD 1981). MFPHM 1985, FFPH (FFPHM 1991); FRCP 2000. District Medical Officer, Papua New Guinea, 1972–74; Res. Officer, Dept of Social Anthropology, Cambridge Univ., 1977–81; Res. Fellow, Clare Hall, Cambridge, 1981–84; Senior Lecturer in Epidemiology: Univ. of Wales Coll. of Medicine, 1985–89; Univ. of Bristol, 1989–92. Consultant, WHO, 1985–2001; Director: Health Care Evaluation Unit, Univ. of Bristol, 1989–93; R&D, South Western Reg., NHS, 1992–96; NHS Cancer Res. Prog., 1993–96; MRC Health Services Res. Collaboration, 1996–97. Chair, Bd of Dirs, Wadebridge Renewable Energy Network, 2011–16. Vis. Prof., Energy Policy Gp, Univ. of Exeter, 2011–16. Mem. Bd, Cornwall and Isles of Scilly Local Nature Partnership, 2013–15. Hon. DSc Bristol, 2017. SW Sustainable Energy Champion, SW Green Energy Awards, 2013. *Publications:* The Huli Response to Illness, 1986; (ed jtly) A Continuing Trial of Treatment, 1988; (ed) The Community Health Worker, 1992; (ed jtly) Rationing and Rationality in the National Health Service: the persistence of waiting lists, 1993; (ed jtly) Priority Setting: the health care debate, 1996; numerous articles in med. and sci. jls concerning the aetiology of disease, disease prevention and health service research. *Recreations:* the usual things, plus windsurfing, sailing a Southerly, gigging with Spot the Dog and the O'Frankel Family Band. *Address:* Carhart Mill, Wadebridge, Cornwall PL27 7HZ. *T:* (01208) 816818.

**FRANKL, Peter;** pianist; *b* Hungary, 2 Oct. 1935; *s* of Laura and Tibor Frankl; adopted British nationality, 1967; *m* 1958, Annie Feiner; one *s* one *d*. *Educ:* Liszt Ferenc Acad. of Music, Budapest. First Prize, several internat. competitions; London début, 1962; New York début, with Cleveland Orch. under George Szell, 1967; performances with Berlin Philharmonic, Amsterdam Concertgebouw, Israel Phil., Leipzig Gewandhaus, Orchestre de Paris, and with all London and major Amer. orchs (Chicago, Philadelphia, Boston, Washington, Los Angeles, San Francisco, Pittsburg, etc); many tours in Japan, Australia, NZ and SA, playing with orchs, in recitals and chamber music concerts; over 20 appearances, BBC Promenade Concerts, London; regular participant at Edinburgh, Cheltenham, Aldeburgh, Verbier and Kuhmo Fests; regular guest artist at summer fests in Aspen, Chautauqua, Hollywood Bowl, Marlboro, Norfolk, Ravinia, Santa Fé and Prades. Vis. Prof. of Piano, Yale Univ. Sch. of Music, 1987–2017. Hon. Prof., Liszt Acad., Budapest, 2006. Recordings include: complete solo works for piano by Schumann and Debussy; complete works for piano and orch. by Schumann; (with ECO) Mozart concerti; (with Tamás Vásáry) complete 4-hand works by Mozart; (with Lindsay Quartet) Brahms, Schumann, Dvorak and Martinu quintets; (with Kyung Wha Chung) Brahms Violin Sonatas; Brahms Piano Concerti; (with G. Pauk and R. Kirshbaum) Brahms Piano Trios; (with Fine Arts Quartet) Dohnanyi Quintets. Officer's Cross, Order of Merit (Hungary), 1995; Middle Cross Award (Hungary), 2005. Gustave Stoeckel Award for Excellence in Teaching, Yale University, 2015. *Recreations:* football, opera, theatre. *Address:* 5 Gresham Gardens, NW11 8NX. *T:* (020) 8455 5228. *E:* pafrankl@aol.com.

**FRANKLAND,** family name of **Baron Zouche**.

**FRANKLAND, (Anthony) Noble,** CB 1983; CBE 1976; DFC 1944; MA, DPhil; historian and biographer; *b* 4 July 1922; *s* of late Edward Frankland, Ravenstonedale, Westmorland; *m* 1st, 1944, Diana Madeline Fovargue (*d* 1981), *d* of late G. V. Tavernor, of Madras and Southern Mahratta Rly, India; one *s* one *d*; 2nd, 1982, Sarah Katharine (*d* 2015), *d* of His Honour the late Sir David Davies, QC and late Lady Davies (Margaret Kennedy). *Educ:* Sedbergh; Trinity Coll., Oxford. Served Royal Air Force, 1941–45 (Bomber Command, 1943–45). Air Historical Branch Air Ministry, 1948–51; Official Military Historian, Cabinet Office, 1951–58. Rockefeller Fellow, 1953. Deputy Dir of Studies, Royal Institute of International Affairs, 1956–60; Dir, Imperial War Museum (at Southwark, 1960–82, Duxford Airfield, 1976–82, and HMS Belfast, 1978–82). Lees Knowles Lecturer, Trinity Coll., Cambridge, 1963. Historical advisor, Thames Television series, The World At War, 1971–74. Vice-Chm., British Nat. Cttee, Internat. Cttee for Study of Second World War, 1976–82. Mem., Council, Morley Coll., 1962–66; Trustee: Military Archives Centre, KCL, 1963–82; HMS Belfast Trust, 1971–78 (Vice-Chm., 1972–78); HMS Belfast Bd, 1978–82. Chevalier de la Légion d'honneur (France), 2016. *Publications:* Documents on International Affairs: for 1955, 1958; for 1956, 1959; for 1957, 1960; Crown of Tragedy, Nicholas II, 1960; The Strategic Air Offensive Against Germany, 1939–1945 (4 vols) jointly with Sir Charles Webster, 1961; The Bombing Offensive against Germany, Outlines and Perspectives, 1965; Bomber Offensive: the Devastation of Europe, 1970; (ed jtly) The Politics and Strategy of the Second World War (8 vols), 1974–78; (ed jtly) Decisive Battles of the Twentieth Century: Land, Sea, Air, 1976; Prince Henry, Duke of Gloucester, 1980; general editor and contributor, Encyclopaedia of 20th Century Warfare, 1989; Witness of a Century: the life and times of Prince Arthur Duke of Connaught, 1993; History at War: the campaigns of an historian, 1998; The Unseen War (novel), 2007; Belling's War (novel), 2008; historical chapter in Manual of Air Force Law, 1956; contrib. to Encyclopaedia Britannica; other articles and reviews; broadcasts on radio and TV. *Address:* 26/27 River View Terrace, Abingdon, Oxfordshire OX14 5AE. *T:* (01235) 521624.

*See also* M. D. P. O'Hanlon.

**FRANKLIN, Andrew Cecil;** Founder and Managing Director, Profile Books Ltd, since 1996; *b* 6 March 1957; *s* of Norman Albert Jessel Franklin and Jill (*née* Leslie); *m* 1981, Caroline Elton; two *s* one *d*. *Educ:* Leighton Park Sch.; Balliol Coll., Oxford (MA PPE). HM Factory Inspector, 1979–81; bookseller, Hatchards Bookshop, 1981–82; editl asst, Faber and Faber, 1982–83; editor: Methuen, 1983–84; Penguin Books, 1984–89; Publishing Dir, Hamish Hamilton, and Dir, Penguin Books, 1989–95. Vis. Prof., City Univ. London, 2011–18. Chm., Jewish Community Centre for London, 2004–10. Dir, Rare Recruitment Ltd, 2007–. Fellow, Jerusalem Book Fair, 1985; Aspen Fellow, 1987. Trustee and Director: Jewish Literary Trust, 1987–2010 (Chm., 1994–96); Edinburgh Internat. Book Fest., 2006–14. Hon. FRSL 2018. Stanley Unwin Fellowship Award, Publishers Assoc., 1986; Friend of Jerusalem Award, City of Jerusalem, 2005. *Publications:* contrib. various newspapers. *Recreations:* my family and making trouble (separately and together). *Address:* Profile Books, 3 Holford Yard, Bevin Way, WC1X 9HD. *T:* (020) 7841 6300. *E:* andrew.franklin@profilebooks.com.

**FRANKLIN, Caryn Dawn,** MBE 2013; fashion commentator and campaigner for body diversity and emotionally considerate fashion practice; *b* Isleworth, 11 Jan. 1959; *d* of Brian Henry Charles Franklin and Pamela Ann Franklin (*née* Pollard); one *d* by Mandu Saldaan; *m* 2000, Ian Phillip Denyer; one *d*. *Educ:* Feltham Comprehensive Sch.; Richmond upon Thames Coll.; Kingston Poly. (BA Hons Graphic Design 1981); St Martin's School of Art; London Coll. of Fashion (MSc Applied Psychol. in Fashion 2016). Fashion Ed. and Co-Ed., 1982–88, Contributing Ed., 1988–, i-D Mag.; presenter and researcher, SWANK, Channel 4, 1984; Fashion Ed., C4 Network 7, 1986; Presenter and Dir, World-wide-audience, The Clothes Show, BBC TV, 1986–98; Presenter and Educnl Ambassador, Clothes Show Live, 1989–; freelance producer and presenter, fashion documentary features, BBC, Channel 4, ITV, Discovery, Granada and UKTV Style, 1998–2006; Co-founder, Moet & Chandon Fashion Tributes, ITV, 1999–2003; contrib., nat. newspapers and magazines, 1984–. Lectr, ext. assessor and course validator, 1984–; Prof. of Diversity in Fashion, Kingston Univ., 2016–. Co-Chair, Fashion Targets Breast Cancer, 1996–. Ambassador, Centre for Sustainable Fashion, London Coll. of Fashion, 2008–; Co-Founder, All Walks Beyond the Catwalk, 2009–; established: Diversity Network, Edinburgh Coll. of Art, 2011; Body Confidence Awards, All-Party Parly Gp on body image, 2012. Vis. Fellow, London Coll. of Fashion, 2011; Hon. Fellow, Arts Univ. Bournemouth, 2011. Hon. Dr Kingston, 2013. Ultimate Women Award, Cosmopolitan Mag., 2009; Red Hot Women Award, Red Mag., 2012. *Publications:* (with G. Goodman) Breast Health Handbook, 1996; Franklin on Fashion, 1997; Woman in the Mirror, 1998; Fashion UK, 2003. *Recreation:* feminist. *Address:* c/o Jo Wander, 110 Gloucester Avenue, Primrose Hill, NW1 8HX. *E:* caryn@carynfranklin.co.uk.

**FRANKLIN, Daniel,** PhD; Executive Editor, since 2006, Diplomatic Editor, since 2018, and Editor, The World In series, since 2003, The Economist; *b* London, 27 Nov. 1955; *s* of Colin and Charlotte Franklin; *m* 1987, Gaby; one *s* one *d*. *Educ:* University College Sch., London; St John's Coll., Oxford (MA French and Russian); Aston Univ., Birmingham (PhD). Joined The Economist, 1983; Europe Ed., 1986–92; Britain Ed., 1992–93; Washington Bureau Chief, 1993–97; Editl Dir, Economist Intelligence Unit, 1997–2006; Ed. in Chief, economist.com, 2006–09; Business Affairs Ed., 2010–14. *Publications:* (ed jtly) Megachange: the World in 2050, 2012; (ed) Megatech: technology in 2050, 2017. *Recreations:* travel, learning languages. *Address:* The Economist, 25 St James's Street, SW1A 1HG. *T:* (020) 7576 1185, *Fax:* (020) 7925 0651. *E:* danielfranklin@economist.com. *Club:* Lansdowne.

**FRANKLIN, John;** *see* Franklin, W. J.

**FRANKLIN, John Richard;** Head Master, Christ's Hospital, 2007–17; *b* 17 May 1953; *s* of late Richard Franklin and of Jean Franklin; *m* 1980, Kim Gillespie. *Educ:* Lockyer High Sch.; Ipswich Grammar Sch.; Univ. of Southern Qld (Dip. Teaching; BA); Univ. of New England, Australia (MEd Admin). Teacher: of English and Drama, Qld Educn Dept, 1976–79; and Housemaster and Hd of Sen. Sch., Toowoomba GS, 1980–88; Sedbergh Sch., 1989; Marlborough Coll., 1989–92; Dep. Headmaster, St Peter's Coll., Adelaide, 1993–98; Headmaster, Ardingly Coll., 1998–2007. Liveryman, Salters' Co., 2014. *Recreations:* theatre, travel, golf. *Address:* Hardwicke Lodge, Vera's Walk, Storrington RH20 3JF. *Clubs:* East India, Lansdowne.

**FRANKLIN, Kim;** QC 2016; *b* Guildford, 28 Feb. 1960; *d* of late Paul Franklin and of Margaret Franklin (now Yates); *m* Gordon Catford (marr. diss. 2008); one *s* one *d*. *Educ:* Eggar's Grammar Sch., Alton; Univ. of Warwick (LLB 1983). Called to the Bar, Middle Temple, 1984; in practice as a barrister, Lamb Chambers, 1989–2000, Crown Office Chambers, 2000–. FCIArb 1994; Chartered Arbitrator 2000. Mem., Soc. of Construction Arbitrators, 2005–. Liveryman, Arbitrators' Co., 2004. Jt Ed., Construction Law Jl, 1989–. *Recreations:* writing fiction, creating and collecting art, children and property. *Address:* Crown Office Chambers, 2 Crown Office Row, Temple, EC4Y 7HJ. *T:* (020) 7797 8100. *E:* franklin@crownofficechambers.com.

**FRANKLIN, Lucy;** *see* Hughes-Hallett, L.

**FRANKLIN, Prof. Raoul Norman,** CBE 1995; FREng; FInstP, FIMA; Visiting Professor, Open University, 1998; Vice Chancellor, 1978–98, and Professor of Plasma Physics and Technology, 1986–98, The City University, London; *b* 3 June 1935; *s* of Norman George Franklin and Thelma Brinley Franklin (*née* Davis); *m* 1st, 1961, Faith (*d* 2004), *d* of Lt-Col H. T. C. Ivens and Eva (*née* Gray); two *s*; 2nd, 2005, Christine Penfold, *d* of Henry Harold and Irene Josephine (*née* Matthews). *Educ:* Howick District High Sch.; Auckland Grammar Sch., NZ (Augusta Award 2014); Univ. of Auckland (ME, DSc; Dist. Alumnus Award 2004); Christ Church, Oxford (MA, DPhil, DSc). FInstP 1968; FIMA 1970; FIET (FIEE 1986); FREng (FEng 1990). Officer, NZ Defence Scientific Corps, 1957–75. Sen. Res. Fellow, RMCS, Shrivenham, 1961–63; University of Oxford: Tutorial Fellow, 1963–78, Dean, 1966–71, Hon. Fellow, 1980, Keble Coll.; Univ. Lectr in Engrg Science, 1966–78; Mem., Gen. Bd, 1967–74 (Vice Chm., 1971–7); Mem., Hebdomadal Council, 1971–74, 1976–78. Chairman: Associated Examining Bd, 1994–98; Assessment and Qualifications Alliance, 1998–2003. Consultant, UKAEA Culham, 1968–2001. Dep. Editor, Jl of Physics D, 1986–90. Member: UGC Equipment Sub Cttee, 1975–78; Physics Commn, IUPAP, 1971–79; Science Bd, SERC, 1982–85; Exec. Council, Business in the Community, 1982–90; Management Cttee, Spallation Neutron Source, 1983–86; Technology Educn Project, 1986–88; UK-NZ 1990 Cttee, 1988–90; Internat. Scientific Cttee, Eur. Sectional Conf. on Atomic and Molecular Processes in Ionized Gases, 1993–97. Chairman: Internat. Science Cttee, Phenomena in Ionized Gases, 1976–77; City Technology Ltd, 1978–93 (Queen's Award for Technol., 1982, 1985, for Export, 1988, 1991). Mem., London Pensions Fund Authority, 1989–95. Trustee: Ruskin School of Drawing, 1975–78; Lloyds Tercentenary Foundn, 1990–2007. Member Council: Gresham Coll., 1981–98; C&G, 1994–2000. Governor: Ashridge Management Coll., 1986–99; Univ. of Buckingham, 2000–06. Freeman, City of London, 1981. Liveryman, Curriers' Co., 1984 (Master, 2002–03); Foundn Master, Educators' Co. (formerly Guild of Preceptors, then Guild of Educators), 1999–2002. Hon. Mem. RICS, 1992; Hon. GSMD 1993. CCMI (CBIM 1986); FRSA. Hon. DCL City, 1999. *Publications:* Plasma Phenomena in Gas Discharges, 1976; papers on plasmas, gas discharges and granular materials. *Recreations:* walking, gardening, sudoku.

**FRANKLIN, Prof. Robin James Milroy,** PhD; FRCPath, FMedSci, FRCVS; Professor of Stem Cell Medicine, Wellcome (formerly Wellcome Trust)-MRC Cambridge Stem Cell Institute, University of Cambridge, since 2014; Fellow, Pembroke College, Cambridge; *b* Barnet, Herts, 15 Aug. 1962; *s* of Sir Michael David Milroy Franklin, KCB, CMG and of Dorothy Joan Franklin; two *s*; *m* 2018, Prof. Giovanna Rachele Mallucci, *qv*. *Educ:* Haberdashers' Aske's Sch., Elstree; University Coll. London (BSc 1985); Royal Veterinary Coll. (BVetMed 1988); Univ. of Cambridge (PhD 1991). MRCVS 1988; FRCPath 2006. University of Cambridge: Wellcome Trust Res. Fellow, 1991–94; Wellcome Trust Res. Career Develt Fellow, 1994–99; Wellcome Trust Lectr, 1999–2000; Sen. Lectr in Exptl Neurol., 2000–02; Reader in Exptl Neurol., 2002–05; Prof. of Neurosci., 2005–13. FMedSci 2016. *Publications:* contrib. articles to neurosci. and stem cell jls. *Recreations:* bird watching, music, reading. *Address:* Wellcome-MRC Cambridge Stem Cell Institute, Clifford Allbutt Building, Cambridge Biomedical Campus, University of Cambridge, Cambridge CB2 0AH. *T:* (01223) 762034. *E:* rjf1000@cam.ac.uk.

**FRANKLIN, Prof. Sarah Brooks,** PhD; FRSB; FAcSS; Professor of Sociology, since 2011, and Head of Sociology, since 2017, University of Cambridge; Fellow, Christ's College, Cambridge, since 2012; *b* Cambridge, Mass, 9 Nov. 1960; *d* of late John Thomas Franklin and of Susan Brooks Franklin; partner, 2001, Sara Ahmed. *Educ:* Smith Coll., Mass (BA 1982); Univ. of Kent (MA 1984); New York Univ. (MA 1986); Univ. of Birmingham (PhD 1992). FRSB (FSB 2011). Res. Associate, Dept of Anthropol., Univ. of Manchester, 1990–93; Lancaster University: Lectr, 1993–97 (pt-time, 1990–93); Sen. Lectr, 1997–99; Reader in Cultural Anthropol., 1999–2001; Prof. of Anthropol. of Sci., 2001–04; Prof. of Social Study of Biomedicine, LSE, 2004–11. Mem., Presidential Adv. Bd, Smith Coll., 2007–13. Mem., Royal Danish Acad. Scis and Letters, 2019. FAcSS 2017. Trustee: Anne McLaren Fund, 2011– (Chair, 2015–); Edwards and Steptoe Fund, 2014–. Smith Coll. Medal, 2011; Mentoring Prize, Soc. for Social Studies of Sci., 2018. *Publications:* (jtly) Off-Centre: feminism and cultural studies, 1991; (jtly) Technologies of Procreation: kinship in the age of assisted conception, 1993, 2nd edn 1999; The Sociology of Gender, 1996; Embodied Progress: a cultural account of assisted conception, 1997; (with H. Ragone) Reproducing Reproduction: kinship, power and technological innovation, 1998; (jtly) Global Nature, Global Culture, 2000; (with S. McKinnon) Relative Values: reconfiguring kinship study, 2001; (with M. Lock) Remaking Life and Death: toward an anthropology of the biosciences, 2003; (with C. Roberts) Born and Made: an ethnography of preimplantation genetic diagnosis, 2006; Dolly Mixtures: the remaking of genealogy, 2007; Biological Relatives: IVF, stem cells and the future of kinship, 2013; (with M. Strathern) Before and After Gender: sexual mythologies in everyday life, 2016. *Address:* Department of Sociology, Free School Lane, University of Cambridge, Cambridge CB2 3RQ.

**FRANKLIN, Prof. Simon Colin,** DPhil; FBA 2012; Professor of Slavonic Studies, since 2004, and Head, School of Arts and Humanities, 2009–14, University of Cambridge; Fellow, Clare College, Cambridge, since 1980; *b* 11 Aug. 1953; *s* of Colin and Charlotte Franklin; *m* 1975, Natasha Gokova; one *s* one *d*. *Educ:* University Coll. Sch.; King's Coll., Cambridge (BA 1976); St Antony's Coll., Oxford (DPhil 1981). Jun. Fellow, Dumbarton Oaks Center for Byzantine Studies, Washington, 1979–80; University of Cambridge: Res. Fellow, Clare Coll., 1980–83; Univ. Lectr in Russian, 1983–99; Reader, 1999–2003; Prof. of Russian Studies, 2003–04. Chm., Pushkin House Trust, 2004–09. Lomonosov Gold Medal, Russian Acad. of Scis, 2008. *Publications:* (trans with A. Boyars) The Face Behind the Face: new poems by Yevgeny Yevtushenko, 1979; (with A. Kazhdan) Studies in Byzantine Literature of the Eleventh and Twelfth Centuries, 1984; Sermons and Rhetoric of Kievan Rus, 1991; (with J. Shepard) The Emergence of Rus 750–1200, 1996; Writing, Society and Culture in Early Rus c.950–1300, 2002; (ed with E. Widdis) National Identity in Russian Culture: an introduction, 2004; (ed with K. Bowers) Information and Empire: mechanisms of communication in Russia, 1600–1850, 2017; The Russian Graphosphere, 1450–1850, 2019. *Recreations:* old books, watching football. *Address:* Clare College, Cambridge CB2 1TL. *T:* (01223) 333263. *E:* scf1000@cam.ac.uk.
*See also* D. Franklin.

**FRANKLIN, Thomas Gerald;** Chief Executive, Young Citizens (formerly Citizenship Foundation), since 2016; *b* 24 June 1969; *s* of Gerald Joseph Franklin and Jillian Ruth Franklin. *Educ:* King Edward VI Upper Sch., Bury St Edmunds; Univ. of Hull (BA Politics). Account Dir, Rowland Public Affairs, 1996–2000; Chief Executive: Living Streets (The Pedestrians Assoc.), 2002–07; Rambler's Assoc., 2007–12; Think Global, 2012–16. Mem. (Lab) Lambeth BC, 1994–06 (Leader, 2000–02). Trustee, Canal and River Trust, 2011–16. *Recreations:* marathon running, cycling, walking, cinema, travelling, long distance triathlons. *Address:* Young Citizens, 37 Heneage Street, E1 5LJ.

**FRANKLIN, (William) John;** DL; Deputy Chairman, Chartered Trust plc, 1986–97 (Director, 1982–97); Chairman: Howells Motors Ltd, 1986–89; Powell Duffryn Wagon, 1986–89; *b* 8 March 1927; *s* of late William Thomas Franklin and Edith Hannah Franklin; *m* 1951, Sally (*née* Davies) (*d* 2003); one *d*. *Educ:* Monkton House Sch., Cardiff. W. R. Gresty, Chartered Accountants, 1947–50; Peat Marwick Mitchell, Chartered Accountants, 1950–55; Powell Duffryn, 1956–86: Director, Cory Brothers, 1964; Man. Dir, Powell Duffryn Timber, 1967–70; Dir, 1970–86; Man. Dir and Chief Exec., 1976–85; Dep. Chm., Jan.–July 1986. Treas., UC of Swansea, 1989–92. DL Mid Glamorgan, 1989. *Recreation:* golf.

**FRANKLYN, Prof. Jayne Agneta, (Mrs Michael Gammage),** MD, PhD; FRCP; FMedSci; William Withering Professor of Medicine, 2011–14, now Emeritus (Professor of Medicine, 1995–2014), and Head, School of Clinical and Experimental Medicine, College of Medical and Dental Sciences, 2008–14, University of Birmingham; Consultant Physician, Queen Elizabeth Hospital, Birmingham, 1988–2014; *b* Birmingham, 7 July 1956; *d* of late Ivor George Franklyn and Joyce Helen Franklyn; *m* 1980, Prof. Michael Gammage; one *s* one *d*. *Educ:* Univ. of Birmingham (MB ChB Hons 1979; MD 1985; PhD 1988). MRCP 1982; FRCP 1991. University of Birmingham: MRC Trng Fellow, 1994–95; Wellcome Trust Sen. Res. Fellow in Clin. Sci., 1988–89; Sen. Lectr, then Reader in Medicine, 1989–95; Associate Dean, Grad. Sch., 2002–08. Chairman: Specialist Adv. Cttee in Endocrinol. and Diabetes, JRCPTB, 2006–09; Clinical Cttee, Soc. for Endocrinol., 2011; Mem. Council, Acad. of Med. Scis, 2012–14. Pres., British Thyroid Assoc., 2008–11. FMedSci 2000. *Publications:* contrib. papers on thyroid disease pathogenesis, treatment and long term effects. *Recreations:* gardening, enjoying the Devon coast and sea. *Address:* The Old Rectory, Plymtree, Devon EX15 2JP. *E:* j.a.franklyn@bham.ac.uk.

**FRANKLYN, Rear-Adm. Peter Michael,** CB 1999; MVO 1978; Chief Executive, Royal Hospital for Neuro-disability, 2000–09; Chairman, Royal National Hospital for Rheumatic Diseases NHS Foundation Trust, Bath, 2010–13; *b* 10 Sept. 1946; *s* of late Roy Vernon Bolton Franklyn and Yvonne Beryl Franklyn (*née* Hooper); *m* 1977, Caroline Barbara Anne Jenks; one *s* one *d*. *Educ:* King's Coll., Taunton. Joined RN, 1963; Comdr, 1980; CO, HMS Active, 1980–82; Trng Comdr, BRNC, Dartmouth, 1982–84; SO Ops FO 3rd Flotilla, 1984–86; Captain, 1986; Naval Asst to 1st Sea Lord, 1986–88; CO, HMS Bristol, 1988–90; RCDS, 1991; Capt., Sch. of Maritime Ops, 1991–93; Dir Naval Officers' Appts (Seaman), 1993–94; Rear-Adm., 1994; Comdr, UK Task Gp, 1994–96; Flag Officer, Sea Training, 1996–97; Flag Officer, Surface Flotilla, 1997–2000. Mem., RNSA, 1993–. Trustee, St John's Foundn (formerly Hospital Charitable Trust), Bath, 2010–. Younger Brother, Trinity House, 1996. *Recreation:* outdoor activities.

**FRANKOPAN, Prof. Peter Doimi de,** DPhil; FRHistS, FRGS; Professor of Global History, since 2017, and Director, Oxford Centre for Byzantine Research, since 2011, University of Oxford; Senior Research Fellow, Worcester College, Oxford, since 2000; *b* London, 22 March 1971; *s* of late Prince and of Princess Louis Doimi de Frankopan Šubić; *m* 1997, Jessica, *d* of Rt Hon. Sir Timothy Alan Davan Sainsbury, *qv*; two *s* two *d*. *Educ:* Eton Coll.; Jesus Coll., Cambridge (BA Hist.); Corpus Christi Coll., Oxford (MPhil); Worcester Coll., Oxford (DPhil 1998). FRHistS 2012; FRGS 2017. Jun. Res. Fellow, Worcester Coll., Oxford, 1997–2000. Stanley J. Seeger Vis. Fellow in Hellenic Studies, Princeton Univ., 2002–03; President's Internat. Council Scholar, Getty Centre, 2017–18;

Vis. Scaliger Prof., Leiden Univ., 2017. Sen. Advr, Transport Corridors in S Asia project, World Bank and DFID, 2017–18. Chair: A Curious Gp of Hotels, 1999–; Frankopan Nekretnine, 2001–; Peckwater PR, 2014–. Mem., Horizon Scanning Panel, Office for Students, 2019–. Mem., Guild of Benefactors, Cambridge Univ., 2012–. Gov., Wellington Coll., 2006–. Trustee: Staples Trust, 1996–; Jerusalem Trust, 2008–; World Monument Fund, 2010–15; Oxford Philomusica, 2013–17. FRSA 2001; FRAS 2014; FRAI 2014; FIH 2017; Fellow, Sutton Trust, 2015. All-England Single Wicket Cricket Champion, 2016. *Publications:* (trans.) Anna Komnene, The Alexiad, 2009; The First Crusade: the call from the East, 2012; The Silk Roads: a new history of the world, 2015; The New Silk Roads: the present and future of the world, 2018. *Recreations:* astrochronology, dendrochronology, ice-age science. *Address:* Worcester College, Oxford OX1 2HB. *T:* (01865) 278300. *E:* peter.frankopan@history.ox.ac.uk. *Clubs:* Hurlingham, Authors' Cricket, Century.

**FRANKS, Alan Lewis Duder;** author and journalist; *b* London, 3 March 1948; *s* of Arthur Henry Franks and Vera Wilson Franks (*née* Duder); *m* 1st, 1976, Susan Law (marr. diss. 1987); two *s* one *d*; 2nd, 2006, Ruth Gledhill, *qv*; one *s*. *Educ:* Kings House, Richmond; Westminster Sch.; University Coll., Oxford (BA English). Reporter, sports and arts corresp., London local newspapers, 1971–75; Ed., Richmond Herald, 1976–78; sub-ed. and writer, THES, 1979; The Times: feature writer and columnist, 1980–2010; Alan Franks's Diary, 1983–84; Ed., PHS, Times Diary, 1986–87; contrib., Guardian, Observer, Radio Times, 2010–. Mem., Bd of Dirs, Shared Experience Th. Co., 2002–08. Writer of plays: The Changing, Irish Th. Co., 1984; Our Boys, Falcon Th. Co., Camden, 1984; A Wing and a Prayer, 1991, Augusta, 2008, New End, Hampstead; The Mother Tongue, Greenwich Th., 1992; The Edge of the Land, Eastern Angles, 2004; Previous Convictions, Orange Tree, Richmond, 2005; A World Elsewhere, Theatre503, Battersea, 2014; Looking At Lucian, Th. Royal, Bath, 2017; composer and performer of songs; albums with Patty Vetta: Will, 1995; Ladders of Daylight, 1997; The Arms of the Enemy, 2002; Bird in Flames, 2006; Only Natural, 2011; album with various artists, Wherever You Go, 2016. First Prize, Wigtown Internat. Poetry Competition, 2007; First Prize, Wilfred Owen Assoc. Poetry Competition, 2014. *Publications:* Real Life with Small Children Underfoot: collected episodes of Alan Franks's Diary, 1984; *novels:* Boychester's Bugle, 1982; Going Back, 2009; The Sins of the Sons, 2010; The Notes of Dr Newgate, 2013; The Adventures of Wendy Howard-Watt, 2015; The Thickness of the Door, 2018; *plays:* The Mother Tongue, 1992; A World Elsewhere, 2014; *poetry:* Unmade Roads, 2010. *Recreations:* singing, books, country walking. *Address:* c/o Curtis Brown, Haymarket House, 28–29 Haymarket, SW1Y 4SP. *T:* (020) 7393 4400. *E:* alan@alanfranks.com.

**FRANKS, Mark William;** Director, Welfare, Nuffield Foundation, since 2018; *b* Birmingham, 16 Jan. 1973; *s* of William Franks and Dawn Franks; *m* 2006, Alison Willott; two *d*. *Educ:* Bishop Vesey Grammar Sch.; Univ. of Essex (BA Hons Econs); Merton Coll., Oxford (MPhil Econs). Economist: DFEE, 1997; Business Strategies Ltd, 1997–99; DFEE, subseq. DFES, 1999–2005; Sen. Policy Advr, HM Treasury, 2005–06; Sen. Economist, Home Office, 2006–07; Hd, Secretariat, Migration Adv. Cttee, 2007–12; Hd, Res. and Innovation Analysis, BIS, 2012–15; Chief Economist, Office of Manpower Econs, 2015–18. *Recreations:* running, cycling. *Address:* Nuffield Foundation, 28 Bedford Square, WC1B 3JS. *T:* (020) 7681 9604. *E:* mfranks@nuffieldfoundation.org. *Club:* Petts Wood Runners.

**FRANKS, Prof. Nicholas Peter,** PhD; FRS 2011; FRSB, FRCA, FMedSci; Professor of Biophysics and Anaesthetics, Imperial College London, since 1993; *b* London, 14 Oct. 1949; *s* of Leonard Maurice Franks and Mary Franks; *m* 1975, Marie Ange de Vena; two *s*. *Educ:* Mill Hill Sch.; King's Coll., London (PhD 1975). FRCA 2007; FRSB (FSB 2011). Lectr in Biophysics, 1977–89, Reader in Biophysics, 1989–93, Imperial Coll. London. Hon. Dr Montreal, 2011. FMedSci 2004. Gold Medal, RCAnaes, 2003; Excellence in Res. Award, Amer. Soc. Anesthesiologists, 2006. *Publications:* contribs to sci. and med. jls. *Recreations:* food and wine, watching almost any sport, collecting modern art. *Address:* Department of Life Sciences, Sir Ernst Chain Building, Wolfson Laboratories, Imperial College London, SW7 2AZ. *T:* (020) 7594 7629. *E:* n.franks@imperial.ac.uk.

**FRANKS, Simon;** Founder and Chairman, Redbus (media group), since 1998; Chairman, Lionsgate UK, since 2005; *b* 23 Aug. 1971; *s* of David and Brenda Franks. *Educ:* UMIST (BSc Hons). Executive: J. P. Morgan, 1992–95; BNP Paribas, 1995–97; Co-Founder and Chief Exec., Redbus Film Distribution, 1998–2005. *Recreations:* politics, film. *Address:* Redbus Group, 5th Floor, Orwell House, 16–18 Berners Street, W1T 3LN. *E:* sef@thefff.org.

**FRANSMAN, Laurens François, (Laurie);** QC 2000; *b* 4 July 1956; *s* of Henri Albert, (Harry), Fransman and Hannah Lena, (Helen), Fransman (*née* Bernstein); *m* 1st, 1977, Claire Frances Goodman (marr. diss. 1985); one *s*; 2nd, 1994, Helena Mary Cook; two *s*. *Educ:* King David High Sch., Johannesburg; Hebrew Univ. of Jerusalem; Leeds Univ. (LLB 1978). Called to the Bar, Middle Temple, 1979; in practice at the Bar, 1979–. Co-Founder, 1983 and Mem. Exec. Cttee, Immigration Law Practitioners' Assoc.; Member: Bar European Gp; Justice; Liberty. Participated in UNHCR and Open Soc. policy develt initiatives on nationality and statelessness, 2009–. Member, Editorial Board: Immigration and Nationality Law and Practice, 1987–; Immigration and Internat. Employment Law, 1999–2001. *Publications:* British Nationality Law and the 1981 Act, 1982; (jtly) Tribunals Practice and Procedure, 1985; (UK contrib. Ed.) Immigration Law and Practice Reporter, 1985; (jtly) Immigration Emergency Procedures, 1986; Fransman's British Nationality Law, 1989, 3rd edn 2011; Halsbury's Laws of England, 4th edn, cons., Nationality sect., 1991, Ed., and principal contrib., British Nationality, Immigration and Asylum, 2002, 5th edn (consultant ed) vol. 57, British Nationality, 2011; (jtly) Blackstone's Guide to The Borders, Citizenship and Immigration Act 2009, 2010; (contrib.) The Constitution of the United Kingdom, 1991; (contrib.) Strangers and Citizens, 1994; (contrib.) Citizenship and Nationality Status in the New Europe, 1998; (ed jtly and contrib.) Immigration, Nationality and Asylum under the Human Rights Act 1998, 1999; (contrib.) Immigration Law and Practice, 2001; (contrib.) Immigration Law and Practice in the United Kingdom, 7th edn 2008; (contrib.) Max Planck Encyclopedia of Public International Law, 2009; (jtly) Blackstone's Guide to the Borders, Citizenship and Immigration Act 2009, 2010; numerous articles on law practice, procedure and policy. *Recreations:* family, guitar, ski-ing, theatre, travel. *Address:* Garden Court Chambers, 57–60 Lincoln's Inn Fields, WC2A 3LJ. *T:* (020) 7993 7600.

**FRANZ, Kevin Gerhard;** Head, Department of Pastoral and Spiritual Care, Mental Health Partnerships, Greater Glasgow and Clyde Health Board, 2009–17; *b* 16 June 1953; *m* 1976, Veda Fairley; one *s* one *d*. *Educ:* Univ. of Edinburgh (MA 1974; BD 1979; PhD 1992); Edinburgh Theol Coll. Ordained deacon, 1979, priest 1980; Curate, St Martin, Edinburgh, 1979–83; Rector, St John's, Selkirk, 1983–90; Provost, St Ninian's Cathedral, Perth, 1990–99, Canon, 2000–05; General Secretary: Action of Churches Together in Scotland, 1999–2007; Quaker Peace and Social Witness, 2007–09. Chm., Scottish Religious Adv. Cttee, BBC, 2002–05. Chm., Perth and Kinross Assoc. of Voluntary Services, 1995–2001. Trustee: Mindfulness Scotland, 2012–15; Claremont Trust, 2015–. *Publications:* (contrib.) Mental Health Ethics: the human context, 2010. *Address:* 14 Comely Bank, Perth PH2 7HU. *T:* (01738) 443175. *E:* kgfranz53@gmail.com.

**FRASER,** family name of **Barons Fraser of Corriegarth, Lovat** and **Strathalmond,** and of **Lady Saltoun.**

**FRASER OF CORRIEGARTH,** Baron *cr* 2016 (Life Peer), of Corriegarth in the County of Inverness; **Alexander Andrew Macdonell Fraser;** landowner; Treasurer, Conservative Party, 2015–16; *b* 2 Dec. 1946; *o s* of Baron Fraser of Tullybelton, PC; *m* 1st, 1982, Sarah Joanna Jones (marr. diss. 1985); one *s*; 2nd, 2010, Rebecca Shaw-Mackenzie. *Educ:* Eton; St John's Coll., Oxford (MA PPE). With Vickers De Costa, Sun Hung Kai Securities and Henderson Crosthwaite from 1970; joined Baring Securities, 1984, CEO, 1993; Chairman: Equity Partners Ltd; Bridge Securities; Dir, Asia Frontier Capital Ltd. Treas., Better Together campaign, Scottish Referendum, 2014. Mem., sub-cttee on effect of Brexit on Financial Services Sector, H of L. *Address:* House of Lords, SW1A 0PW.

**FRASER, Alex;** *see* Fraser, J. A.

**FRASER, (Alexander) Malcolm;** Co-founder and Director, Fraser/Livingstone Architects Ltd, since 2018; *b* 21 July 1959; *s* of William Fraser and Margaret (*née* Watters); *m* 1998, Helen Lucas; one *s* two *d*. *Educ:* George Watson's Coll., Edinburgh; Edinburgh Univ. (MA Hons; DipArch 1985). ARB. Founder, 1993, Dir, 2006–15, Malcolm Fraser Architects; Dir, Halliday Fraser Munro, 2015–18. Vis. Prof., UWE, 2003–09; Geddes Hon. Professorial Fellow, Univ. of Edinburgh, 2009–. Dep. Chm., Architecture+Design Scotland, 2005–07. Chm., Scottish Govt's Town Centre Rev., 2013–. Principal buildings completed: Scottish Poetry Liby, Edinburgh, 1999; Dance Base, Edinburgh, 2001; Dance City, Newcastle, 2005; Scottish Storytelling Centre, Edinburgh, 2006; HBOS HQ, Edinburgh, 2006; Scottish Ballet, Glasgow, 2009; Dovecot Studios, Edinburgh, 2009; Royal Conservatoire of Scotland Speirs Locks Studio, 2010; Burgh Halls, Linlithgow, 2011; Edinburgh Centre for Carbon Innovation, Edinburgh Univ., 2013; Arcadia Nursery, Edinburgh Univ., 2014; West Pilton Crescent (council housing), Edinburgh, 2015; Stromness Warehouse, Library and Council Hub, Orkney, 2015; Lewis Castle and Museum nan Eilean, Stornoway, 2016. *Address:* 6 Hartington Place, Edinburgh EH10 4LE. *E:* malcolm@malcolmfraser.scot.

**FRASER, Andrew John,** CMG 2001; Senior Adviser, Mitsubishi Corporation, since 2000; Director, Mitsubishi Corporation International (Europe) plc, since 2013; *b* 23 Oct. 1950; *s* of John and Mary Fraser; *m* 1st, 1976, Julia Savell (marr. diss. 1987); two *d*; 2nd, 1996, Jane Howard. *Educ:* Univ. of Sussex (BA); ESU Schol., Harvard Sch.; exchange schol., UCLA. Account Dir, Young and Rubicam, London, 1972–76; Man. Dir, McCann Erickson, Thailand, 1976–80; Exec. Vice Pres., Dir of Business Develt, Saatchi and Saatchi Worldwide, 1981–92; Man. Dir, cdp Europe (Dentsu Worldwide), 1992–94; Chief Exec., Invest in Britain Bureau, later INVEST.UK, 1994–2000. Dir, UK-Japan 21st Century Gp, 1998–2004; non-exec. Dir, English Partnerships, 1999–2000; Mem., Internat. Adv. Bd, FTI Consulting (Strategic Communications) (formerly Financial Dynamics), 2003–17. Dir, Think London (formerly London First Centre), 2002–12. Advr, Arup Gp, 2001–05. Pres., Worldaware, 2002–05; Member: Develt Council, 2001–06, Trust Bd, 2006–14, Council, 2014–, Shakespeare's Globe; Council, Chatham House (RIIA), 2006–12; Council, Japan Soc., 2006–11 (Chm., Business Gp, 2006–). *Recreations:* sports, theatre, food and drink, conversation. *Clubs:* Royal Automobile, MCC, ESU, Pilgrims; V&A Cricket; Woking Golf; Royal Wimbledon Golf.

**FRASER, Dr Andrew Kerr,** OBE 2018; FRCPE, FRCPGlas, FFPH; Director of Public Health Science, NHS Health Scotland, since 2012; *b* 10 Dec. 1958; *s* of Sir William Kerr Fraser, GCB and Lady Marion Anne Fraser, LT; *m* 1st, 1985 (marr. diss. 2010); three *s* one *d*; 2nd, 2012, Barbara Pettigrew Allison. *Educ:* George Watson's Coll.; Univ. of Aberdeen (MB ChB 1981); Univ. of Glasgow (MPH 1990). FRCPE 1998; FFPH (FFPHM 1999); FRCPGlas 2001. Med. Dir, Nat. Services Div., CSA, 1993–94; Dir of Public Health, Highland Health Bd, 1994–97; Dep. CMO, Scottish Office, subseq. Scottish Exec., 1997–2003; Head of Health, 2003–06, Dir of Health and Care, 2006–12, Scottish Prison Service. *Recreations:* music, mountain walking. *Address:* NHS Health Scotland, Meridian Court, Cadogan Street, Glasgow G2 6QE. *T:* (0131) 314 5450.

**FRASER, Angus Robert Charles,** MBE 1999; Managing Director, Cricket, Middlesex County Cricket Club, since 2009; Selector, England Cricket Team, since 2014; *b* 8 Aug. 1965; *s* of Donald and Irene Fraser; *m* 1996, Denise Simmonds; one *s* one *d*. *Educ:* Gayton High Sch.; Orange Hill Sen. High Sch. Played for Middlesex CCC, 1984–2002 (Captain, 2000–02); England Test Cricketer, 1989–99: 46 Test matches (took 177 Test wickets); 42 One-day Internationals. Sponsorship consultant, Whittingdale, 1991–93 (whilst injured). Cricket Corresp., Independent, 2002–08. *Publications:* Fraser's Tour Diaries, 1998. *Recreations:* golf, wine, Liverpool FC, watching children play sport. *Address:* Middlesex County Cricket Club, Lord's Cricket Ground, NW8 8QN. *Clubs:* MCC, Stanmore Cricket, Middlesex County Cricket.

**FRASER, Angus Simon James;** Chairman of Trustees, Caldecott Foundation, 2009–14 (Trustee, 2004–14; Vice Chairman, 2006–09); *b* 28 Feb. 1945; *s* of Baron Fraser of Kilmorack, CBE and Elizabeth Chloë Fraser (*née* Drummond); *m* 1970, Jennifer Ann, *d* of Colin McKean Craig, FRCS and Irene Joan Craig (*née* Yeldham); two *s* one *d*. *Educ:* Fettes Coll., Edinburgh; Selwyn Coll., Cambridge (MA); European Inst. of Business Admin (INSEAD), France (MBA). Dunlop Co. Ltd, 1968–70; Mercantile Credit Co. Ltd, 1971–76; Chloride Group PLC, 1976–2006: Chm., Chloride Europe, 1983–85; Exec. Dir, Industrial Operations, 1985–87, Corporate Operations, 1987–88; non-exec. Dir, 1988–2006; Man. Dir, Imperial Coll. of Sci., Technol. and Medicine, 1989–94 (Gov., 1990–94); Chief Exec., Scruttons plc, 1995–97; Chm., Benitec Ltd, 1998–2002. Non-executive Director: Davies, Laing and Dick Ltd, 1998–2002 (Chm., 2000–02); Technology Enterprise Kent, 1998–2005; Singapore Para Rubber Estates plc, 1999–2001; Bertam Hldgs plc, 2001–05 (Dep. Chm., 2001–05); Shepherd Bldg Gp Ltd, 2002–07; IdaTech plc, 2007–11; Chm., Alpha Plus (formerly DLD) Hldgs Ltd, 2002–07. *Recreations:* opera, golf, fly-fishing, painting, gardening, walking, family and friends.

**FRASER, Air Cdre Anthony Walkinshaw;** company director; *b* 15 March 1934; *s* of late Robert Walkinshaw Fraser and Evelyn Elisabeth Fraser; *m* 1st, 1955, Angela Mary Graham Shaw (marr. diss. 1990); one *s* three *d*; 2nd, 1990, Grania Ruth Eleanor Stewart-Smith. *Educ:* Stowe Sch. MIL. RAF Pilot and Flying Instructor, 1952–66; sc Camberley, 1967; MA/VCDS, MoD, 1968–70; Chief Instructor Buccaneer OCU, 1971–72; Air Warfare Course, 1973; Directing Staff, National Defence Coll., 1973; Dep. Dir, Operational Requirements, MoD, 1974–76; Comdt, Central Flying Sch., 1977–79. ADC to the Queen, 1977–79. Dir, SMMT, 1980–88. Chairman: Personal Guard, 1992–94; Chlorella Products Ltd (formerly Nature's Balance Marketing), 1994–2007; Enhanced Office Environments Ltd, 2001–07; Dir, Nissan UK Ltd, 1989–91. President: Comité de Liaison de la Construction Automobile, 1980–83; Organisation (formerly Bureau Perm.) Internat. des Constructeurs d'Automobiles, 1983–87 (Vice-Pres., 1981–83). FCMI. *Recreations:* fishing, languages. *Address:* 31 Grove End Road, NW8 9LY. *T:* (020) 7286 1616. *Club:* Royal Air Force.

**FRASER, Lady Antonia, (Lady Antonia Pinter)**, CH 2018; DBE 2011 (CBE 1999); writer; b 27 Aug. 1932; d of 7th Earl of Longford, KG, PC, and late Elizabeth, Countess of Longford, CBE; m 1st, 1956, Rt Hon. Sir Hugh Fraser, MBE, MP (marr. diss. 1977, he d 1984); three s three d; 2nd, 1980, Harold Pinter, CH, CBE (d 2008). Educ: Dragon School, Oxford; St Mary's Convent, Ascot; Lady Margaret Hall, Oxford (MA; Hon. Fellow, 2007). General Editor, Kings and Queens of England series. Chairman: Soc. of Authors, 1974–75; Crimewriters' Assoc., 1985–86; Vice Pres., English PEN, 1990– (Mem. Cttee, 1979–88; Pres., 1988–89; Chm., Writers in Prison Cttee, 1985–88, 1990); Pres., Literary Soc., 2019–; Goodman Lecture, 1997. Pres., Gaieties CC, 2011–. FRSL 2003; Centenary Fellow, Histl Assoc., 2006. Norton Medlicott Medal, Histl Assoc., 2000. Hon. DLitt: Hull, 1986; Sussex, 1990; Nottingham, 1993; St Andrews, 1994. Officier, Ordre des Palmes Académiques, 2012. Publications: (as Antonia Pakenham): King Arthur and the Knights of the Round Table, 1954 (reissued, 1970); Robin Hood, 1955 (reissued, 1971); (as Antonia Fraser): Dolls, 1963; A History of Toys, 1966; Mary Queen of Scots (James Tait Black Memorial Prize, 1969), 1969 (reissued illus. edn, 1978; reissued 50th Anniv. edn, 2019); Cromwell Our Chief of Men, (in USA, Cromwell the Lord Protector), 1973; King James: VI of Scotland, I of England, 1974; (ed) Kings and Queens of England, 1975 (reissued, 1988); (ed) Scottish Love Poems, a personal anthology, 1975 (reissued, 1988), new edn 2002; (ed) Love Letters: an anthology, 1976, rev. edn 2002; Quiet as a Nun (mystery), 1977, adapted for TV series, 1978; The Wild Island (mystery), 1978 (reissued as Tartan Tragedy, 2005); King Charles II, (in USA, Royal Charles), 1979; (ed) Heroes and Heroines, 1980; A Splash of Red (mystery), 1981 (basis for TV series Jemima Shore Investigates, 1983); (ed) Mary Queen of Scots: poetry anthology, 1981; (ed) Oxford and Oxfordshire in Verse: anthology, 1982; Cool Repentance (mystery), 1982; The Weaker Vessel: woman's lot in seventeenth century England, 1984 (Wolfson History Award, 1984; Prix Caumont-La Force, 1985); Oxford Blood (mystery), 1985; Jemima Shore's First Case (mystery short stories), 1986; Your Royal Hostage (mystery), 1987; Boadicea's Chariot: the Warrior Queens, 1988 (paperback, The Warrior Queens, 1989, in USA, The Warrior Queens, 1989); The Cavalier Case (mystery), 1990; Jemima Shore at the Sunny Grave (mystery short stories), 1991; The Six Wives of Henry VIII, 1992, reissued illus. edn, 1996 (Schloss Bauverein Preis, 1997; in USA, The Wives of Henry VIII); (ed) The Pleasure of Reading, 1992 (reissued 2015); Political Death (mystery), 1994; The Gunpowder Plot: terror and faith in 1605, 1996 (CWA Non Fiction Gold Dagger, 1996) (in USA, Treason and Faith: the story of the gunpowder plot; St Louis Literary Award, 1996); Marie Antoinette: the Journey, 2001 (Enid McLeod Lit. Award, Franco-British Soc., 2002); First Jemima Shore Anthology (Quiet as a Nun, Tartan Tragedy, A Splash of Red), 2005; Second Jemima Shore Anthology (Oxford Blood, Cool Repentance, Your Royal Hostage), 2006; Love and Louis XIV: the women in the life of the Sun King, 2006; Must You Go? My life with Harold Pinter, 2010 (Prix du meilleur livre étranger essai, 2010); Perilous Question: the drama of the Great Reform Bill 1832, 2013 (in USA, Perilous Question: reform or revolution? Britain on the brink); My History: a memoir of growing up, 2015; Our Israeli Diary 1978, 2017; My Ethiopian Diary 1964, 2017; The King and the Catholics: the fight for rights 1829, 2018; various mystery stories in anthols, incl. Have a Nice Death, 1983 (adapted for TV, 1984); TV plays: Charades, 1977; Mister Clay, Mister Clay (Time for Murder series), 1985. Recreations: swimming, grandchildren. Address: 52 Campden Hill Square, W8 7JR. Clubs: Athenæum, PEN; Literary Society.
See also F. Fraser, O. G. Fraser.

**FRASER, Sir Benjamin (James)**, 4th Bt cr 1943, of Tain, co. Ross; Senior Fire Fighter, Fire and Emergency, New Zealand, since 2014; b Colombo, Sri Lanka, 6 April 1986; s of Sir Iain Michael Duncan Fraser, 3rd Bt and of Sheryle Ann Fraser (née Gillespie, later Barrak); S father, 2019; m 2011, Megan Jayne Stone; one s. Educ: Rangitoto Coll.; NZ Fire Service Coll. Served NZ Army, Royal NZ Engrs, 2005–09. NZ Army Gen. Service Medal, 2011. Recreations: hunting, off road driving, family. Heir: s Duncan James Fraser, b 17 July 2016. Address: 248C Watershed Road, RD 10, Palmerston North 4470, New Zealand. T: 0276466686. E: bjfraser00@gmail.com.

**FRASER, Sir Charles (Annand)**, KCVO 1989 (CVO 1985; LVO 1968); WS; non-executive Vice Chairman, United Biscuits (Holdings), 1986–95 (Director, 1978–95); Partner, W & J Burness, WS, Edinburgh, 1956–92; b 16 Oct. 1928; o s of late Very Rev. John Annand Fraser, MBE, TD; m 1957, Ann Scott-Kerr; four s. Educ: Hamilton Academy; Edinburgh Univ. (MA, LLB). Purse Bearer to Lord High Commissioner to General Assembly of Church of Scotland, 1969–88. Chairman: Morgan Grenfell (Scotland), 1985–86; Adam & Co., 1989–98; Lothian & Edinburgh Enterprise Ltd, 1991–94; NSM, 1992–94; Director: Scottish Widows' Fund, 1978–94; British Assets Trust, 1969–; Scottish Media Group plc (formerly Scottish Television Ltd), 1979–98, and other companies. Chm., Sec. of State for Scotland's Adv. Cttee on Sustainable Develt, 1995–98. Trustee, WWF (UK), 1998–2000. Mem. Council, Law Society of Scotland, 1966–72; Governor of Fettes, 1976–86; Mem. Court, Heriot-Watt Univ., 1972–78. Hon. Res. Fellow, Royal Botanic Gardens, Edinburgh, 2008. WS 1959; DL East Lothian, 1984–2003. Dr hc Edinburgh, 1991; Hon. LLD Napier, 1992. Recreations: gardening, ski-ing, piping. Address: Shepherd House, Inveresk, East Lothian EH21 7TH. T: (0131) 665 2570. Clubs: New, Hon. Co. of Edinburgh Golfers (Edinburgh); Royal and Ancient (St Andrews).

**FRASER, Christopher James**, OBE 2013; Chairman, International Communications Group. Mem., Three Rivers DC, 1992–96. MP (C) Mid Dorset and N Poole, 1997–2001, SW Norfolk, 2005–10. PPS to Leader of the Opposition, H of L, 1999–2001. Member: Culture, Media and Sports Select Cttee, 1997–2001; NI Select Cttee, 2005–10; NI Grand Cttee; Speaker's Panel of Chairmen; Vice Chm., All-Party Forestry Gp, 1997–2001; Mem., Parly Inf. and Technol. Cttee, 1997–2001; Chm., Parly Mgt Consultancy Gp, 2000–01; Vice Chm., Cons. Trade and Industry Cttee, 2000–01; Chm., All Party Parly Gp on NI. Member: IPU, 1997–2010; CPA, 1997–2010; Council of Europe, 2005–07; WEU, 2005–07. Director: Small Business Bureau, 1997–2005; Genesis Foundn. Patron, Firmlink, 1995–2001. Appeals Chm., Pramacare, 1996–2007; Mem., County Cttee, Holton Lee Charity Appeal, 1997–2001. Mem., Soc. of Dorset Men, 1997–2001. Freeman, City of London, 1992.

**FRASER, Prof. Derek**, FRHistS; Vice-Chancellor, University of Teesside, 1992–2003; Independent Football Ombudsman, since 2008 (Chairman, Independent Football Commission, 2001–08); b 24 July 1940; s of Jacob and Dorothy Fraser; m 1962, Ruth Spector; two s one d. Educ: Univ. of Leeds (BA, MA, PhD). Schoolteacher, 1962–65; Lectr, Sen. Lectr, Reader and Prof. of Modern History, Univ. of Bradford, 1965–82; Prof. of English History, UCLA, 1982–84; HMI (History and Higher Educn), 1984–88; Staff Inspector (Higher Educn), DES, 1988–90; Asst/Dep. Principal, Sheffield City Polytechnic, 1990–92. Chairman: Graduate Apprenticeship Nat. Steering Cttee, 1998–2000; Univ. Vocational Awards Council, 1999–2001; Standards Verification UK, 2005–11; Member: NACETT, 1999–2001; One NorthEast RDA, 1999–2001; Educn Cttee, RICS, 2006–19; Lifelong Learning UK, 2011–12. Resident Historian, Viking Cruises, 2018. Levinson Scholar in Residence, St Andrew's Sch., Delaware, 2014. Hon. LLD Teesside, 2003. Publications: The Evolution of the British Welfare State, 1973, 5th edn 2017; Urban Politics in Victorian England, 1976; Power and Authority in the Victorian City, 1979; (ed) A History of Modern Leeds, 1980; (ed jtly) The Pursuit of Urban History, 1980; (ed) Municipal Reform and the Industrial City, 1982; (ed) Cities, Class and Communication: essays in honour of Asa Briggs, 1990; The Welfare State, 2000; (ed) Leeds and its Jewish Community: a history, 2019. Recreations: cruising, bridge, music, football and other spectator sports. Address: Office of the Independent Football Ombudsman, Suite 49, 33 Great George Street, Leeds LS1 3AJ.

**FRASER, Edward**; see Fraser, J. E.

**FRASER, Flora, (Mrs Flora Soros)**; writer; b 30 Oct. 1958; d of Rt Hon. Sir Hugh Charles Patrick Joseph Fraser, MBE, MP, and of Lady Antonia Fraser, qv; m 1st, 1980, Robert James Powell-Jones (marr. diss. 1989); one d; 2nd, 1997, Peter Ross Soros (marr. diss. 2010); two s. Educ: St Paul's Girls' Sch.; British Inst., Florence; Wadham Coll., Oxford (BA Lit. Hum.). Member: Exec. Cttee, Friends of Nat. Libraries, 1999–2003; Develt Council Exec., Wadham Coll., Oxford, 2011–; Georgian Papers Academic Steering Cttee, 2019–. Trustee, NPG, 1999–2008. Co-Founder, Elizabeth Longford Grants for Historical Biographers, 2003–15; Co-Founder and Judge, Elizabeth Longford Prize for Historical Biog., 2003–. Judge Guggenheim Lehrman Prize in Military History, 2015–16; Gilder Lehrman Prize for Military History, New York Histl Soc., 2017–19. Patron, freeopenairtheatre.org, 2013–18. Hon. DLit KCL, 2019. Publications: Double Portrait, 1983; Maud: the diaries of Maud Berkeley, 1985; Beloved Emma: the life of Emma, Lady Hamilton, 1986; The English Gentlewoman, 1987; Tamgar, 1990; The Unruly Queen: the life of Queen Caroline, 1996; Princesses: the six daughters of George III, 2004; Venus of Empire: the life of Pauline Bonaparte, 2009; George & Martha Washington: a revolutionary marriage, (US edn as The Washingtons: George and Martha), 2015 (George Washington Book Prize, Washington Coll., Gilder Lehrman Inst. of Amer. Hist. and Mount Vernon Ladies' Assoc., 2016). Recreation: swimming in Greece. Address: c/o Georgina Capel Associates Ltd, 29 Wardour Street, W1D 6PS. W: www.florafraser.com. Club: Athenæum.
See also O. G. Fraser.

**FRASER, Rev. Canon Dr Giles Anthony**; Rector, St Mary's, Newington, since 2019 (Priest-in-charge, 2012–19); columnist, Church Times, 2003–13; b 27 Nov. 1964; s of Wing Comdr Anthony Fraser and Gillian Fraser; m 1993, Sally Aagaard; one s two d. Educ: Uppingham Sch.; Univ. of Newcastle-upon-Tyne (BA Hons Philosophy 1984); Ripon Coll., Cuddesdon (BA Hons Theol. (Oxon) 1992; MA (Oxon) 1997); Univ. of Lancaster (PhD 1999). Ordained deacon, 1993, priest, 1994; Curate, All Saints, Streetly, 1993–97; Chaplain, Univ. Church of St Mary the Virgin, Oxford, 1997–2000; Wadham College, Oxford: Chaplain, 1997–2000; Lectr in Philosophy, 2000–07; Team Rector, Parish of Putney, 2000–09; Canon Chancellor, St Paul's Cathedral, 2009–11. Mem., Gen. Synod, C of E, 2003–09. Founder, 2003–, Pres., 2005–, Inclusive Church. Regular contrib. to Radio 4's Thought for the Day, Guardian. Publications: Christianity and Violence, 2001; Redeeming Nietzsche, 2002; Christianity with Attitude, 2007. Recreations: golf, food, politics.

**FRASER, Dame Helen (Jean Sutherland)**, DBE 2017 (CBE 2010); Chief Executive, Girls' Day School Trust, 2010–16; b 8 June 1949; d of George Sutherland Fraser and Paddy Fraser; m 1982, Grant James McIntyre; two d, and two step d. Educ: St Anne's Coll., Oxford (BA Eng. Lang. and Lit. 1970, MA). Editor: Methuen Academic, 1972–74; Open Books, 1974–77; Editor, then Editl Dir, William Collins, 1977–87; Publisher, then Man. Dir, Reed Trade Books, 1987–97; Man. Dir, Penguin General, 1997–2001; Man. Dir, Penguin UK, 2001–09. Chm. of Judges, Bailey's Women's Prize for Fiction, 2014. Trustee, Spitalfields Music, 2008–14. Churchwarden, St Bride's Fleet St, 2013–18. Hon. DLitt Bristol, 2010. Recreations: opera, ballet, theatre, concerts.
See also B. P. K. McIntyre.

**FRASER, (James) Edward**, CB 1990; Secretary of Commissions for Scotland, 1992–94; an Assistant Local Government Boundary Commissioner for Scotland, 1997–2011; b 16 Dec. 1931; s of late Dr James F. Fraser, TD, Aberdeen, and late Dr Kathleen Blomfield; m 1959, Patricia Louise Stewart; two s. Educ: Aberdeen Grammar Sch.; Univ. of Aberdeen (MA); Christ's Coll., Cambridge (BA). FSAScot. Royal Artillery, 1953; Staff Captain 'Q', Tel-el-Kebir, 1954–55. Asst Principal, Scottish Home Dept, 1957–60; Private Sec. to Permanent Under Sec. of State, 1960–62, and to Parly Under-Sec. of State, 1962; Principal: SHHD, 1962–64; Cabinet Office, 1964–66; HM Treasury, 1966–68; SHHD, 1968–69; Asst Sec., SHHD, 1970–76; Asst Sec., 1976, Under Sec., 1976–81, Local Govt Finance Gp, Scottish Office; Under Sec., SHHD, 1981–91. Pres., Scottish Hellenic Soc. of Edinburgh and Eastern Scotland, 1987–93. Pres., Former Pupils' Club, Aberdeen GS, 1997–98 (Hon. Vice-Pres., 1998–). Recreations: reading, music, walking, Greece ancient and modern, DIY. Address: 59 Murrayfield Gardens, Edinburgh EH12 6DH. T: (0131) 337 2274.

**FRASER, James Mackenzie**, CBE 2014; Principal, 2009–13, and Vice-Chancellor, 2011–13, University of the Highlands and Islands (formerly University of the Highlands and Islands Millennium Institute); b Poolewe, Ross-shire, 29 July 1948; s of Duncan Fraser and Anne Fraser; m 1st, 1975, Janet Sinclair (d 1986); one d; 2nd, 1987, Sheila Macfarlane; one s one d. Educ: Plockton High Sch., Ross-shire; Univ. of Edinburgh (MA Hons Mental Philos.); Univ. of Stirling (MEd). Lectr, Inverness Technical Coll., 1971–77; Tutor, Open Univ. in Scotland, 1971–77; Sen. Asst Registrar, Univ. of Stirling, 1977–87; Coll. Sec., Queen Margaret Coll., Edinburgh, 1987–89; Sec., Paisley Coll., subseq. Univ. of Paisley, 1989–2002; Sec., 2002–07, Depute Principal-Sec., 2007–09, UHI Millennium Inst. Dir, Free Church Nominees Co., 1989–; Chairman: Bd of Trustees, Free Church of Scotland, 2007; Solas Centre for Public Christianity, 2017–. Chm., Highland Community Care Forum, 2015–. Recreations: music, genealogy, cinema, travel. Address: The Old Manse, Camault Muir, Kiltarlity, Beauly IV4 7JH. E: james@jamesmfraser.com. Club: New (Edinburgh).

**FRASER, Hon. John Allen**; PC (Can.) 1979; OC 1995; OBC 1995; CD 1962; QC (Can.) 1983; Chairman, BC Pacific Salmon Forum, Canada, 2005–09; b Japan, 15 Dec. 1931; m 1960, Catherine Findlay; three d. Educ: Univ. of British Columbia (LLB 1954). Law practice, Victoria, Powell River, Vancouver, 1955–72. MP (PC) Vancouver S, 1972–94; Opposition Critic, Environment, 1972–74, Labour, 1974–79; Minister of Environment and Postmaster General, 1979–80; Opposition Critic, Environment, Fisheries, Post Office, and Solicitor-General, 1980–84; Minister of Fisheries and Oceans, 1984–85; Speaker of H of C, Canada, 1986–94; Ambassador for the Envmt, Dept of Foreign Affairs and Internat. Trade, Canada, 1994–98. Chm., Pacific Fisheries Resource Conservation Council, 1998–2005. Chairman: Nat. Defence Minister's Monitoring Cttee on Change, 1998–2005; Parly Precinct Oversight Adv. Cttee, 2000–. Hon. LLD: St Lawrence Univ., 1999; Simon Fraser Univ., 1999; British Columbia, 2004. Hon. Lt-Col, Seaforth Highlanders of Canada, 1994– (Hon. Col).

**FRASER, John Stewart**; Chairman and Chief Executive, Ciba-Geigy plc, 1990–96; b 18 July 1931; s of Donald Stewart Fraser and Ruth (née Dobinson); m 1st, 1955, Diane Louise Witt (marr. diss. 1996); two s one d; 2nd, 1996, Lynette Ann Murray. Educ: Royal Melbourne Inst. of Technology. ARACI. Technical Rep., Australian Sales Manager and Australian Marketing Manager, Monsanto Australia Ltd, 1953–68; Marketing Manager, Ilford (Australia) Pty Ltd, 1968–73; Ilford Ltd, UK: Marketing Dir, 1973–78; Man. Dir and Chief Exec., 1978–84; Corporate Man. Dir, Ciba-Geigy Plastics and Additives Co., UK,

1982–84; Ciba-Geigy plc, UK: Gp Man. Dir, 1984–87; Gp Man. Dir and Chief Exec., 1987–90. Non-exec. Dir, Westminster Health Care, 1993–99. Chm., Assoc. for Schools' Sci., Engrg and Technol. (formerly Standing Conf. on Schools' Sci. and Technol.), 1996–2000. Pres., Chemical Industries Assoc., 1994–95. *Recreations:* swimming, walking. *Address:* 3091/3029 The Boulevard, Carrara, Qld 4211, Australia.

**FRASER, Julian Alexander, (Alex);** Chief Executive, London Institute of Banking & Finance (formerly ifs University College), since 2015; *b* 23 July 1959; *s* of Peter Marshall Fraser, MC, FBA and Ruth Fraser. *Educ:* Abingdon Sch., Oxon; Manchester Univ. (BA Hons Classics 1987). Teacher, Latin and Computer Studies, Lawrence House Sch., St Annes on Sea, Lancs, 1978–84; Database Researcher, CEDIM srl, Ancona, 1987–89; Information Consultant, Atefos SpA, Turin, 1989–90; Manager, Inf. Resource Centre, Merrill Lynch Europe Ltd, 1990–93; Asst Dir and Head of Inf. Systems, West Merchant Bank Ltd, 1993–95; J. Henry Schroder & Co. Ltd: Manager, Inf. Centre, 1995–96; Head of Ops, European Corporate Finance Div., 1996–97; Dir and Global Head, Corporate Finance Support Services, 1997–2000; Director: Logistics, HM Customs and Excise, 2000–03; Get Well UK Ltd, 2003–05; CEO, Land Data Ltd, 2005–09; Chief Operating Officer, Cass Business Sch., City Univ. London, 2009–15. *Recreation:* equine. *Address:* London Institute of Banking & Finance, Peninsular House, 36 Monument Street, EC3R 8LJ.

**FRASER, Kenneth John Alexander;** international marketing consultant; *b* 22 Sept. 1929; *s* of Jack Sears Fraser and Marjorie Winifred (*née* Savery); *m* 1953, Kathleen Grace Booth (*d* 2013); two *s* one *d*. *Educ:* Thames Valley Grammar Sch., Twickenham; London School of Economics (BScEcon Hons). Joined Erwin Wasey & Co. Ltd, 1953, then Lintas Ltd, 1958; Managing Director, Research Bureau Ltd, 1962; Unilever: Head of Marketing Analysis and Evaluation Group, 1965; Head of Marketing Division, 1976–79, 1981–89; Hd of Internat. Affairs, 1985–89; Hd of External Affairs, 1989–90; seconded to NEDO as Industrial Dir, 1979–81. Advr, European Assoc. of Branded Goods Manufacturers, 1991–93. Member: Consumer Protection Adv. Cttee, Dept of Prices and Consumer Protection, 1975; Management Bd, ADAS, MAFF, 1986–92; Chairman: CBI Marketing and Consumer Affairs Cttee, 1977; Internat. Chamber of Commerce Marketing Commn, 1978; Vice Chm., Advertising Assoc., 1981–90; Dir, Direct Mail Services Standards Bd, 1991–94. Mem., Advocacy Cttee, Nat. Children's Home, 1987–95. FRSA 1980. *Recreations:* walking, music, reading.

**FRASER, (Mae) Rosalie;** *see* Craig, M. R.

**FRASER, Malcolm;** *see* Fraser, A. M.

**FRASER, Mark Thomas,** CVO 2019 (LVO 2014); AO 2019 (OAM 2003); Head of Commonwealth Protocol and First Assistant Secretary, Department of Prime Minister and Cabinet, Australia, since 2018; *b* Hobart, 6 March 1975; *s* of John and Sharyn Fraser; partner, 1998, Cüneyt Mermercan. *Educ:* Bond Univ. (BA Internal Relns, PR and Journalism 1994); Monash Univ. (MA Foreign Affairs and Trade 2001); Univ. of Sydney (Exec. MBA 2013); Harvard Kennedy Sch. (Sen. Managers in Govt Course 2017). Grad. prog., Australian Taxation Office, 1995; entered Dept of Foreign Affairs and Trade, 1996; Cultural Relns Branch, then Internat. Media Centre, 1996–98; Consul, Ankara, 1998–2001; Southern Europe Sect., Ministerial and Exec. Liaison Sect., then Audit and Evaluation Sect., 2001–04; Consul-Gen., The Hague, 2004–07; Dir, Remuneration, Entitlements and Conditions Sect., 2007–09; Dep. Official Sec., 2009–14, Official Sec., 2014–18, to Gov.-Gen. of Australia; Secretary: Council for Order of Australia, 2014–18; Australian Bravery Decorations Council, 2014–18; Nat. Emergency Medal Cttee, 2014–18. Co-Founder and CEO, Make A Mark Australia, 2009–. *Recreations:* charity works, travel. *Address:* Department of Prime Minister and Cabinet, 1 National Circuit, PO Box 6500, Barton, ACT 2600, Australia. *E:* mark.fraser@pmc.gov.au.

**FRASER, Murdo Mackenzie;** Member (C) Scotland Mid and Fife, Scottish Parliament, since Aug. 2001; *b* 5 Sept. 1965; *s* of Sandy Fraser and Barbara Fraser (*née* MacPherson); *m* 1994, Emma Jarvis; one *s* one *d*. *Educ:* Inverness Royal Acad.; Univ. of Aberdeen (LLB 1986; Dip. Legal Studies). Admitted solicitor, 1988; practised in Aberdeen and Edinburgh; Associate Partner, Ketchen and Stevens WS, Edinburgh, 1994–2001. Chairman: Scottish Young Conservatives, 1989–92; Nat. Young Conservatives, 1991–92; former Dep. Chm., Edinburgh Central Cons. Assoc. Dep. Leader, Scottish Cons. and Unionist Party, 2005–11. Contested (C): East Lothian, 1997; N Tayside, 2001; N Tayside, 1999, 2003, 2007, Perthshire N, 2011, 2016, Scottish Parlt. *Publications:* The Rivals: Montrose and Argyll and the struggle for Scotland, 2015. *Recreations:* hillwalking, football, Scottish history, classic cars. *Address:* Scottish Parliament, Edinburgh EH99 1SP. *T:* (0131) 348 5293; (office) Control Tower, Perth Airport, Scone, Perth PH2 6PL. *T:* (01738) 553990. *E:* murdo.fraser.msp@parliament.scot.

**FRASER, Prof. Murray,** PhD; RIBA; Professor of Architecture and Global Culture, Bartlett School of Architecture, University College London, since 2011; *b* Glasgow, 7 July 1958; *s* of James Leslie Fraser and Amelia Ann Fraser; *m* (marr. diss.); two *s*; *m* 2017; two step *c*. *Educ:* Hemel Hempstead Grammar Sch.; University Coll. London (BSc Architecture 1979; DipArch 1981; MSc Architectl Hist. 1983; Professional Practice 1983; PhD 1993). ARB 1984; RIBA 1984. Architectl Asst, Ansell Bailey Architects, 1981–84; Architect, London Borough of Haringey, 1985–86; Vis. Lectr, Bartlett Sch. of Architecture, UCL, 1987–85; Architect, Architype Ltd, 1989–90; Sen. Lectr, then Prof. of Architecture, Oxford Brookes Univ., 1990–2003; Prof. of Architecture, Univ. of Westminster, 2003–11. Chm., Res. and Innovation Gp, RIBA, 2011–15. Mem., Council, Eur. Assoc. of Architectl Educn, 2012–13; Founding Mem., Architectural Res. in Europe Network Assoc., 2013–; Co-Ed., Jl of Architecture, 2007–12; Ed.-in-Chief, Arena Jl of Architectl Res., 2016–. Annie Spink Award, RIBA, 2018. *Publications:* John Bull's Other Homes, 1996; Critical Architecture, 2007; Architecture and the Special Relationship, 2007; Design Research in Architecture, 2013; Architecture and Globalisation in the Persian Gulf, 2013; (Gen. Ed.) Sir Banister Fletcher's Global History of Architecture, 21st edn, 2019; contrib. essays to internat. jls on architecture, architectl hist. and theory, and urbanism. *Recreations:* sport, watching football with my sons, cinema, dining out, socialising. *Address:* Bartlett School of Architecture, University College London, 22 Gordon Street, WC1H 0QH. *T:* 07988 914802. *E:* murray.fraser@ucl.ac.uk.

**FRASER, Nancy Margaret;** *see* Reid, N. M.

**FRASER, Dr Nicholas Campbell;** Keeper of Natural Sciences, National Museums Scotland, since 2007; *b* Nottingham, 14 Jan. 1956; *s* of Hugh Mckenzie Fraser and Patricia Margaret Fraser; *m* 1982, Christine Mary; two *d*. *Educ:* Univ. of Aberdeen (BSc Zool. 1978; PhD Geol. 1984). Res. Fellow, Girton Coll., Cambridge, 1985–90; Curator of Vertebrate Paleontol., 1990–2007, Dir of Res. and Collections, 2004–07, Virginia Mus. of Natural Hist. Adjunct Professor of Geology: Virginia Tech, 1993–; N Carolina State Univ., 2007–. Ed., Memoirs Series, Soc. Vertebrate Paleontol. Hon. MA Cantab 1985. *Publications:* (ed with Hans-Dieter Sues) In the Shadow of the Dinosaurs, 1994; Dawn of the Dinosaurs, 2006; (with Hans-Dieter Sues) Triassic Life on Land: the great transition, 2010; (ed with Hans-Dieter Sues) Terrestrial Conservation Lagerstaetten: windows into the evolution of life on land, 2017; contrib. peer-reviewed jls. *Recreations:* soccer, hill-walking, travel. *Address:* National Museums Scotland, Chambers Street, Edinburgh EH1 1JF. *T:* (0131) 247 4007, *Fax:* (0131) 220 4819. *E:* nick.fraser@nms.ac.uk.

**FRASER, Orlando Gregory;** QC 2014; *b* London, 9 May 1967; *s* of Rt Hon. Sir Hugh Charles Patrick Joseph Fraser, MBE, MP and of Lady Antonia Fraser, *qv*; *m* 2006, Clementine Hambro; one *s* three *d*. *Educ:* St Paul's Ind. Sch., Barnes; British Inst., Florence; Fitzwilliam Coll., Cambridge (BA Hons Hist. 1989). Asst to Patricia Rawlings, MEP, 1989; stagiaire, DG1, EC, 1990; GEC Plessey Telecommunications, Paris, Coventry, 1990–92; called to the Bar, Inner Temple, 1994; in practice as barrister, 1995–. Member: Adv. Council, NCVO, 2009–14; Bd, Charity Commn of England and Wales, 2013–17; Civil Justice Council, 2016–. Mem., Mgt Cttee, Westside Housing, 2001–03. Centre of Social Justice: Mem., Social Justice Commn, 2006–07; Founding Fellow, 2008. Contested (C) N Devon, 2005. Mem., Bd of Govs, Ilfracombe Community Coll., 2003–05. Chm., Bosnian Winter Appeal, 1992. *Recreations:* fishing, golf, Scrabble. *Address:* 4 Stone Buildings, Lincoln's Inn, WC2A 3XT. *T:* (020) 7242 5524. *E:* clerks@4stonebuildings.com. *Club:* MCC.

**FRASER, Hon. Sir Peter (Donald),** Kt 2015; **Hon. Mr Justice Fraser;** a Judge of the High Court, Queen's Bench Division, since 2015; Judge in Charge, Technology and Construction Court, since 2018; *b* Co. Down, NI, 6 Sept. 1963; *s* of Donald and Jean Fraser; *m* 2002, Samantha Hurrell; three *d*. *Educ:* Harrogate Grammar Sch.; St John's Coll., Cambridge (Open Exhibnr; BA 1986; LLM 1988). Called to the Bar, Middle Temple, 1989 (Harmsworth Exhibnr; Astbury Schol.); in practice as barrister, specialising in construction, engineering and international arbitration, 1990–2015; a Recorder, 2002–15; QC 2009. Member: Judicial Panel (Disciplinary and Anti-Drug), RFU, 2012–; Appeals Panel, World Rugby, 2016–. *Publications:* How to Pass Law Exams, 1991; (Ed.) Building Law Reports, 1990–. *Recreations:* Rugby Union, triathlon, endurance sport, wine, shooting. *Address:* Royal Courts of Justice, Strand, WC2A 2LL. *Clubs:* Reform; Hawks (Cambridge); Leander (Henley-on-Thames).

**FRASER, Peter John;** photographer, since 1982; *b* Cardiff, 1 April 1953; *s* of Jack Fraser and Doreen Fraser (*née* Evans); *m* 1st, Claire McNamee (marr. diss. 1983); 2nd, 1992, Christy Johnson (marr. diss. 1994); 3rd, 2008, Urve Opik. *Educ:* Cardiff High Sch. for Boys; Manchester Poly. (Dip. Photography 1976). Solo exhibitions include: The Flower Bridge Impressions Gall., York, 1982; Photographers' Gall., London, 1986, 2002; St Louis Mus. of Art, 1995; Ffotogallery, Cardiff, 2010; Brancolini Grimaldi Gall., London, 2012; 30 year retrospective, Tate St Ives, 2013; Mathematics, Royal Botanical Gdns, Madrid, 2017, Camden Arts Centre, London, 2018. Hon. FRPS 2013. *Publications:* Two Blue Buckets, 1988, enlarged edn as Two Blue Buckets, Director's Cut, 2017; Ice and Water, 1993; Deep Blue, 1997; Material, 2002; Lost for Words, 2010; A City in the Mind, 2012; Mathematics, 2017; photographs included in internat. pubns. *Recreation:* still searching for a hobby which my wife thinks would be good for me. *Address:* Dulwich, London. *Club:* 2 Brydges.

**FRASER, Robert William,** MVO 1994; DL; **His Honour Judge Fraser;** a Circuit Judge, since 2007; Resident Judge, Guildford Crown Court, since 2016; *b* Birkenhead, 23 Sept. 1955; *s* of Gordon Smith Fraser and Kathleen Mary Fraser; *m* 1990, Isobel Patricia Mary Clapham; two *d*. *Educ:* Birkenhead Sch.; Univ. of Liverpool (LLB Hons). Called to the Bar, Gray's Inn, 1984; Recorder, 2000–07. Royal Navy, 1974–2007: HMS Yarmouth, 1985–86; HMS Battleaxe, 1986–87; Equerry to the Prince of Wales, 1991–94; Briefing Officer to First Sea Lord, 1997–98; Dir of Staff, NATO HQ, Naples, 2000–02; rcds, 2002; Sec. to Chiefs of Staff Cttee, 2004–05; Cdre, 2005; Dir Naval Legal Services, 2005–07. DL Surrey, 2019. *Publications:* (contrib.) Seaford House Papers, 2002. *Recreations:* sailing, skiing, motor cars. *Address:* Guildford Crown Court, Bedford Road, Guildford GU1 4ST.

**FRASER, Sir Simon James,** GCMG 2016 (KCMG 2013; CMG 2009); Managing Partner, Flint Global Ltd, since 2015; *b* 3 June 1958; *s* of late James Stuart Fraser and of Joan Fraser; *m* Shireen; two *d*. *Educ:* St Paul's Sch.; Corpus Christi Coll., Cambridge (MA). Joined FCO, 1979; Second Secretary: Baghdad, 1982–84; Damascus, 1984–86; First Sec., FCO, 1986–88; Private Sec. to Minister of State, FCO, 1989–90; Policy Planning Staff, FCO, 1991–92; Asst Head, Non-Proliferation and Defence Dept, FCO, 1992–93; First Sec., Financial and Eur. Affairs, Paris, 1994–96; Dep. Chef de Cabinet of Vice-Pres. of EC, 1996–99; Pol Counsellor, Paris, 1999–2002; Dir for Strategy and Innovation, FCO, 2002–04; Chief of Staff to Peter Mandelson, EC, 2004–08; Dir Gen. for Europe and Globalisation, FCO, 2008–09; Permanent Sec., BERR, later BIS, 2009–10; Permanent Under-Sec. of State, FCO, and Head of Diplomatic Service, 2010–15. Mem. Council, RIIA, 2015– (Dep. Chm., 2016–). Mem. Internat. Adv. Bd, Amundi, 2016–. Gov., St Paul's Sch., London, 2017–. Trustee, Patchwork Foundn, 2018–. *Recreations:* cricket, football, opera, art.

**FRASER, Simon William Hetherington;** Sheriff of North Strathclyde at Dumbarton, 1989–2014; *b* 2 July 1951; *s* of late George MacDonald Fraser, OBE, author and Kathleen Margarette (*née* Hetherington); *m* 1st, 1979, Sheena Janet Fraser (marr. diss. 2009); one *d*; 2nd, 2010, Fiona Petrie. *Educ:* Glasgow Acad.; Glasgow Univ. (LLB). Solicitor, 1973–89 (Partner, Flowers & Co., Glasgow, 1976–89). Temp. Sheriff, 1987–89. Pres., Glasgow Bar Assoc., 1981–82; Mem. Council, Sheriffs' Assoc., 2007–10. *Recreations:* watching Partick Thistle, cricket. *Club:* Avizandum (Glasgow).

**FRASER, Stuart John,** CBE 2012; Deputy Chairman, Policy and Resources Committee, City of London Corporation, 2012–13 (Chairman, 2008–12); *b* Bexley, Kent, 13 April 1946; *s* of Kenneth and Anne Fraser; *m* 1967, Laura Mary Byford. *Educ:* University Sch., Bexley; Cannock House Sch. Trainee stockbroker, 1963; James Capel, 1963–66; Charterhouse Gp, 1966–68; Sheppards & Co., 1968–73; Capel-Cure Myers, 1973–78; Williams de Broë, 1978–99; Divl Dir, Brewin Dolphin Securities Ltd, 1999– (Chm., Asset Allocation Cttee). Corporation of London, later City of London Corporation: Mem., Court of Common Council, 1993–; Chm., Planning and Transportation Cttee, 1997–2000. Mem., London Stock Exchange, 1982–86. Mem. Bd and Regl Chm., London & Quadrant Housing Assoc., 1997–2007. CFA (Associate, Soc. of Investment Analysts 1976); FCSI (FSI 1978). Chm., Greenwich Br., MS Soc., 1973–92; Director: Blackheath Concert Halls, 1987–90; Blackheath Rugby Club, 1988–91. Gov., Legacy Trust, 2007–10; Chm., Bd of Govs, City of London Freemans Sch., 2013–16. Liveryman, Fletchers' Co., 1999 (Master, 2016–17). *Recreations:* walking, theatre, reading. *Address:* 19 Lock Chase, SE3 9HB. *T:* (020) 8852 6248. *E:* stuartfraser2@me.com. *Club:* Reform.

**FRASER, Prof. Thomas Grant,** MBE 2006; PhD; FRHistS; Professor of History, 1991–2006, now Professor Emeritus and Hon. Professor of Conflict Research, University of Ulster (Provost of Magee Campus, 2002–06); *b* 1 July 1944; *s* of Thomas Fraser and Annie Grant Alexander; *m* 1970, Grace Frances Armstrong; one *s* one *d*. *Educ:* Univ. of Glasgow (MA Medieval and Modern Hist. 1966; Ewing Prize); London Sch. of Economics (PhD 1974). New University of Ulster, subseq. University of Ulster: Lectr, 1969–85; Sen. Lectr, 1985–91; Hd, Dept of Hist., 1988–94; Hd, Sch. of Hist., Philosophy and Politics, 1994–98. Fulbright Scholar-in-Residence, Indiana Univ. South Bend, 1983–84. Adviser: Cordia Educn Complex, Sanghol, India, 2012–; Gingko Liby, London, 2016–18. Chm., NI Museums Council, 1998–2006; Trustee, Nat. Museums and Galls of NI, 1998–2002.

Dir, Playhouse Community Arts Centre, Derry, 2003–18. FRHistS 1992; FRSA 2000; FRAS 2013. *Publications:* (ed) The Middle East 1914–1979, 1980; Partition in Ireland, India and Palestine, 1984; The USA and the Middle East since World War 2, 1989; (ed with P. Lowe) Conflict and Amity in East Asia: essays in honour of Ian Nish, 1992; (ed with K. Jeffery) Men, Women and War: historical studies XVIII, 1993; The Arab-Israeli Conflict, 1995, 4th edn 2015 (Spanish edn 2008; Italian edn 2015); (ed with S. Dunn) Europe and Ethnicity: the First World War and contemporary ethnic conflict, 1996; (ed) The Irish Parading Tradition: following the drum, 2000; Ireland in Conflict 1922–1998, 2000; (with D. Murray) America and the World since 1945, 2002; Chaim Weizmann: the Zionist dream, 2009; (with A. Mango and R. McNamara) The Makers of the Modern Middle East, 2011, 2nd edn 2015 (Turkish edn 2011); (ed) India's Rural Transformation and Development: issues, processes and direction, 2012; (ed with J. Hume and L. Murray) Peacemaking in the 21st Century, 2013; (ed) The First World War and its Aftermath: the shaping of the modern Middle East, 2015; (ed with M. Aggarwal) Ethics, Governance and Corporate Social Responsibility in India: issues and perspectives, 2016; articles in academic jls and chapters in edited collections. *Recreations:* travel, cooking. *Address:* 45 Blackthorn Manor, Londonderry BT47 5ST. *T:* (028) 7131 2290.

**FRASER, Veronica Mary;** Diocesan Director of Education, Diocese of Worcester, 1985–93; *b* 19 April 1933; *o d* of late Archibald Fraser. *Educ:* Richmond County Sch. for Girls; St Hugh's Coll., Oxford. Head of English Department: The Alice Ottley Sch., Worcester, 1962–65; Guildford County Sch. for Girls, 1965–67 (also Librarian); Headmistress, Godolphin Sch., Salisbury, 1968–80; Adviser on Schools to Bishop of Winchester, 1981–85. Pres., Assoc. of Sen. Members, St Hugh's Coll., Oxford, 1994–98. Gov., SPCK, 1994–98.

**FRASER, Vincent;** QC 2001; a Recorder, since 2002; a Deputy High Court Judge, since 2010; *b* 18 Oct. 1958; *s* of Martin and Monica Fraser; *m* 1994, Mary Elizabeth Sweeney; one *s* three *d*. *Educ:* St Mary's Coll., Crosby; University Coll., Oxford (Open Schol.; MA Juris.; Sweet & Maxwell Prize). Called to the Bar, Gray's Inn, 1981. *Publications:* Planning Decisions Digest, 1987, 2nd edn 1992. *Recreations:* literature, music, football. *Address:* Kings Chambers, 36 Young Street, Manchester M3 3FT. *T:* (0161) 832 9082, *Fax:* (0161) 835 2139. *E:* vfraser@kingschambers.com.

**FRASER, Prof. William Irvine,** CBE 1998; MD; FRCPE, FRCPsych, FMedSci; Professor of Developmental Disability, University of Wales College of Medicine, 1989–2002, now Emeritus; *b* 3 Feb. 1940; *s* of late Duncan Fraser and Muriel (*née* Macrae); *m* 1964, Joyce Carrol; two *s*. *Educ:* Greenock Acad.; Glasgow Univ. (MBChB 1963; DPM 1967; MD (with commendation) 1969). FRCPsych 1979; FRCPE 2000. Physician Superintendent, Mental Handicap Service, Fife, 1974–78; Hon. Sen. Lectr in Psychology, Univ. of St Andrews, 1973–89; pt-time Sen. Lectr, Psychiatry, Univ. of Edinburgh, 1973–89; Consultant Psychiatrist, Royal Edinburgh Hosp., 1978–89. Ed., Jl of Intellectual Disability Research, 1982–2003. Trustee, Bailey Thomas Charitable Fund, 1999–; Autism Cymru, 2001– (Chair, 2008–); Pres., Welsh Psychiatry Soc., 2006–. Res. Medallist, Burden Inst., 1989; Fellow, Internat. Assoc. for Scientific Study of Intellectual Disability, 1997 (Dist. Achievement Award, 1996); FMedSci 2001. *Publications:* (with R. McGillivray) Care of People with Intellectual Disabilities, 1974, 9th edn, 1998; (with R. Grieve) Communicating with Normal and Retarded Children, 1981; (with M. Kerr) Seminars in Learning Disabilities, 2003. *Recreation:* sailing. *Address:* 146 Wenallt Road, Cardiff CF14 6TQ. *T:* (029) 2052 1343.

**FRASER-HOPEWELL, Peter David,** CMG 2009; MBE 1986; consultant; Head, Group Security, Enrichment Technology, 2008; *b* Sheldon, Warks, 26 Nov. 1953; *s* of David Hopewell and Isobel Hopewell (*née* Smart); *m* 1990, Clare Mary Steven; one *d*. *Educ:* Marshill Boys Grammar Sch., Birmingham; London Coll. of Printing (HND Business Studies 1975). Jun. mgt in printing industry, 1976–80. Commnd TA, 1974; Commnd Royal Scots, 1981, as regular officer; Co. Comdr, 1989–91 and 1993–96 (despatches 1983, 1991); CO, 1996–99; Chief Special Forces, HQ Allied Rapid Reaction Corps, 1999–2001; Deputy Commander: 3 Inf. Bde, 2001–03; 16 Air Assault Bde, 2003–05; COS UN Force in Cyprus and Comdr British Contingent, 2005–08. QCVS 1996. *Recreations:* ski-ing, running, triathlon, cycling, history. *E:* fraserhopewells@talktalk.net. *Clubs:* Royal Scots, Special Forces.

**FRATTINI, Franco;** President, Società Italiana per l'Organizzazione Internazionale, since 2012; *b* 14 March 1957. *Educ:* La Sapienza Univ., Rome (LLB). State Attorney, 1981; Attorney, State Attorney-Gen.'s Office, 1984; Magistrate, Regl Admin. Tribunal, Piedmont, 1984–86; Council of State Judge, 1986; Legal Adviser: to Minister of Treasury, 1986–90; to Dep. Prime Minister, 1990–91; to Prime Minister, 1992; Dep. Sec.-Gen., 1993, Sec.-Gen., 1994–95, Prime Minister's Office; Minister for the Civil Service and Regl Affairs, 1995–96; MP (Forza Italia), 1996–2004; Minister for Civil Service and for Co-ordination of Intelligence and Security Services, 2001–02; Minister for Foreign Affairs, 2002–04; MP (Popolo della Libertà) Italy, 2008–13; Minister for Foreign Affairs, 2008–11. Mem., EC, 2004–08. Mem., Rome CC, 1997–2000. *Address:* Società Italiana per l'Organizzazione Internazionale, Palazzetto Venezia, Piazza di San Marco 51, 00186 Rome, Italy.

**FRAWLEY, Dame Carolyn;** *see* McCall, Dame C.

**FRAWLEY, Thomas Jude,** CBE 2008; Assembly Ombudsman for Northern Ireland and Northern Ireland Commissioner for Complaints, 2000–16; *b* Limerick, 4 Feb. 1949; *s* of Joseph and Bride Frawley; *m* 1983, Marie Mallon; two *s* one *d*. *Educ:* St Mary's Grammar Sch., Belfast; Trinity Coll., Dublin (BA). Grad. Trainee, NHS, 1971–73; Unit Administrator, Ulster Hosp., Dundonald, 1973–77; Asst Dist Administrator, Lisburn, 1977–80; Dist Administrator for Londonderry, Limavady and Strabane Dist, 1980; Chief Admin. Officer, 1980–85, Gen. Manager, 1985–2000, Western Health and Social Services Bd. Dir-Gen., Co-operation and Working Together Initiative, 1990–2000; led project to support health system in Zimbabwe, 1994. King's Fund Travel Bursary, 1983; King's Fund Internat. Fellowships, 1988 and 1992; Eisenhower Fellowship, 1989. Mem., Ministerial Adv. Bd on Health Estates, NI, 1998–2000; Chairman: Expert Panel on Review of Public Admin, 2002; Gp on Review of Ambulance Service, NI, 1998–2000. Ind. Mem., NI Policing Bd, 2018–. Trustee, NHS Confedn, 1998–2000. Vice Pres., World Bd, Internat. Ombudsman Inst., 2006. Mem., BITC, 1998–2000. Gov., Lumen Christi Coll., 1998–2000. Rep. of Ire., Alumni Adv. Council, Eisenhower Fellowship, 2004. DUniv Ulster, 2003. *Recreations:* current affairs, sport (played Rugby and Gaelic football).

**FRAY, Prof. Derek John,** FRS 2008; FREng; Professor of Materials Chemistry, Cambridge University, 1996–2007, now Emeritus (Head, Department of Materials Science and Metallurgy, 2001–05); Professorial Fellow, Fitzwilliam College, Cambridge, 1996–2007, now Life Fellow; *b* 26 Dec. 1939; *s* of Arthur Joseph Fray and Doris Lilian Fray; *m* 1965, Mirella Christine Kathleen Honey (marr. diss. 2004); one *s* one *d*. *Educ:* Emanuel Sch.; Imperial Coll., Univ. of London (BSc Eng, ARSM 1961; PhD, DIC 1965). FIMMM (FIM 1988); FREng (FEng 1989); FRSC 2001. Asst Prof. of Metallurgy, MIT, 1965–68; Gp Leader, Imperial Smelting Corp., Bristol, 1968–71; Cambridge University: Lectr, Dept of Materials Sci. and Metallurgy, 1971–91; Fitzwilliam College: Fellow, 1972–90; Tutorial and Estates Bursar, 1974–86; Bursar, 1986–88; Investment and Estates Bursar, 1988–90; Prof. of Mineral Engrg, Univ. of Leeds, 1991–96 (Head of Dept). Hon. Professor: Beijing Univ. of Sci. and Technol., 1995–; Hubei Poly. Univ., 2006–; Liaoning Univ. of Sci. and Technol., 2009–; Vis. Prof., Univ. of Leeds, 1996–; Nuffield-NSERC Vis. Fellow, 1981. Dist. Extractive Metallurgy Lectr, Minerals, Metals and Materials Soc., USA, 2000; Fray Internat. Symposium, Cancun, Mexico, 2011; Mine to Metal Conf., IMMM, 2015. Director: Cambridge Advanced Materials, 1989–2006; Ion Science Ltd, 1989–2010; British Titanium plc, 1998–2007; EMC Ltd, 2000–; Metalysis Ltd, 2002–04; Inotec AMD Ltd, 2005–; Camfridge Ltd, 2005–; Chinuka Ltd, 2007–; La Serena Technologies Ltd, 2012–; Welding Alloys Gp Ltd, 2012–. Numerous medals and awards, UK and overseas, incl. Matthey Prize, 1967; American Instn of Metallurgical Engrs Extractive Metallurgy Technol. Award, 1980; John Phillips Medal, MIRO, 1991; Light Metals Reactive Metals Technol. Award, Minerals, Metals and Materials Soc., USA, 2000, 2004; Armourers and Brasiers' Prize, Royal Soc., 2002; Innovation Award and Prize, Federation of European Materials Socs, 2009; Max Bredig Award, US Electrochemical Soc., 2012; Sir George Beilby Medal and Prize, 1981, Kroll Medal and Prize, 1987, Inst. of Metals; Billiton Medal, 2000, Gold Medal, 2000, IMMM; Futers Gold Medal, 2015. *Publications:* (jtly) Worked Examples in Mass Heat Transfer in Materials Technology, 1983; numerous papers and granted patents on material chemistry and allied topics. *Recreations:* reading, cinema, walking. *Address:* 7 Woodlands Road, Great Shelford, Cambridge CB22 5LW. *T:* (01223) 842296.

**FRAY, Sarah Amy,** CEng; Senior Teaching Fellow in Civil Engineering Design, Department of Civil, Environmental and Geomatic Engineering, University College London; *b* Chorley, 11 Sept. 1957; *d* of Alan Fray and Joan Mary Fray (*née* Moorhouse); one *s*. *Educ:* Plymouth Poly. (BSc Hons Civil Engrg 1982). CEng 1987; MICE 1987; MIStructE 1990. Technician Engr, Coventry City Engrs, 1974–79; Grad. Engr, Michael Dew Associates, 1982–83; Grad. Civil Engr, Lemon & Blizzard Consulting Engrs, 1983–86; Structural Engr, Peter Brett Associates, 1986–87; Sen. Structural Engr, James Cunniffe Partnership, 1987–88; Project Engr, Anthony Ward Partnership, 1988–91; Prin. Structural Engr, Southampton CC, 1991–94; Associate Dir, Upton McGougan plc, 1994–96, Oscar Faber, 1995–97; Sen. Structural Engr, Arqiva, 1997–2009; Dir, Engrg and Tech. Services, IStructE, 2009–15; Exec. Sec., Geol Soc., 2015–16. *Recreations:* ski-ing, contemporary art, choral music, travel.

**FRAYLING, Sir Christopher (John),** Kt 2001; MA, PhD; Professor of Cultural History, 1979–2009, now Emeritus, Rector and Vice-Provost, 1996–2009, Royal College of Art, London; Chairman, Arts Council England, 2004–09; *b* 25 Dec. 1946; *s* of late Arthur Frederick Frayling and Barbara Kathleen (*née* Imhof); *m* 1981, Helen Snowdon. *Educ:* Repton Sch.; Churchill Coll., Cambridge (BA, MA, PhD). FCSD 1994. Churchill Research Studentship, 1968–71; Lectr in Modern History, Univ. of Exeter, 1971–72; Tutor, Dept of General Studies, Royal College of Art, 1972–73, Vis. Lectr, 1973–79; Research Asst, Dept of Information Retrieval, Imperial War Mus., 1973–74; Lectr in the History of Ideas and European Social History, Univ. of Bath, 1974–79; Royal College of Art: founder, 1979, and Head of Dept, 1979–96, Dept of Cultural History (ex General Studies); founded courses: History of Design, 1982; Conservation, 1987; Visual Arts Admin, subseq. Curating Contemporary Art, 1991; Pro-Rector, 1993–96. Visiting Professor: Shanghai Univ. of Technol., 1991; Univ. of Lancaster, 2010–; Fellow, Churchill Coll., Cambridge, 2009–. Chancellor, Arts Univ., Bournemouth, 2014–. Historian, lectr, critic; regular contributor, as writer and presenter, to radio (incl. Kaleidoscope, Stop the Week, Meridian, Critics' Forum, Third Opinion, Third Ear, Nightwaves, Front Row, Back Row, Archive Hour, The Film Programme, Saturday Rev.; series: The American Cowboy; America: the movie (Silver Medal, NY Internat. Radio Fest., 1989); Britannia: the film; Print the Legend; Cinema Cities) and TV (incl. series Scene, Art of Persuasion (Gold Medal, NY Internat. Film and TV Fest., 1985), Busting the Block—or the Art of Pleasing People, Design Classics, Design Awards, Timewatch, Movie Profiles, The Face of Tutankhamun, Strange Landscape, and Nightmare: the birth of horror). Curator of exhibitions: (co-curator) Designs of the Times, RCA, 1996; Once Upon a Time in Italy, Autry Nat. Center, LA, 2005 (Humanities Prize for scholarship); (co-curator) Gothic Nightmares—Fuseli, Blake and the Romantic Imagination, Tate Britain, 2006; (co-curator) Hollywood Costume, V&A, 2012; Sergio Leone—c'era una volta in Italia, Nat. Mus. of Cinema, Turin, 2014. Chm., Design Council, 2000–04; Mem., Crafts Council, 1982–85. Arts Council of England (formerly of GB): Mem., 1987–2000; Mem., Art Panel, 1983–94 (Dep. Chm., 1984–87; Chm., 1987–94); Chm., Film, Video and Broadcasting Panel, 1994–97; Chm., Educn and Trng Panel, 1996–98; Chm., Combined Arts Cttee, 1989–95; Chm., New Collaborations Cttee, 1990–94. Chairman: Curriculum Develt Bd, Arts Technol. Centre, 1989–94; Design Sub-Gp, Liturgical Publishing Commn, 1999–2000; Royal Mint Design Adv. Cttee, 2000–11. Chm. of Trustees, Crafts Study Centre, Bath, 1982–2004; Foundn Trustee, Holburne of Menstrie Mus., Bath, 1985–2000; Chm., Free Form Arts Trust, 1984–88; Trustee: V&A Museum, 1984–2009 (Hon. Res. Fellow, 2011–); Member: Adv. Council, 1981–83; Sen. Staff Appts Cttee, 1987–91; S Kensington Jt Planning Cttee, 1989–95; Educn and Res. Cttees, 1990–97; Chm., Bethnal Green Mus. Cttee, 1995–99; Chm., Contemporary Projects Cttee, 1999–2002; Chm., S Kensington Cultural Gp, 1999–2004); Koestler Trustees for Art in Prisons, 1992–99; Royal Mint Mus., 2011–. Member: Litmus Gp for Millennium Dome, 1998–2000; Bd, Design Mus., 1999–2004 and 2009–19; AHRB, 1999–2004; Council, Catalyst, 2004–09; Blue Plaques Cttee, English Heritage, 2009–16; Royal Commn for 1851 Exhibn, 2009–; Royal Fine Art Commn Trust, 2014–19; UK Supreme Court Arts Trust, 2014–18; Chm., Design Adv. Bd, RSA, 2017–18. Governor, BFI, 1982–87 and 2009–12 (Mem., 1982–86, Chm. 1984–86, Educn Cttee); Member: Art and Design Sect., Leverhulme Team on Arts in Higher Educn, 1982; Working Party on art and design advising NAB, 1985–87. Chm., Soc. of Designer-Craftsmen, 1997–2004. Patron: Guild of Handicraft Trust, 1989–; Parnham Trust for Makers in Wood, 1989–2003. FRSA 1984 (Bicentennial Medal, 2001); Hon. Life Fellowship, 2006); Sen. Fellow, Hereford Coll. of Arts, 2010; Hon. Fellow, Cardiff Univ., 2013. Hon. FRIBA 2005; Hon. RCM 2007; Hon. FGSM 2010; Hon. FBKSTS 2015. Hon. DLitt: NSW, 1999; Lancaster, 2008; Brighton, 2009; DUniv: Staffordshire, 2002; Sheffield Hallam, 2011; Hon. DArts: UWE, 2003; Bath, 2003; UAL, 2009; Hon. DHL Richmond, 2005; Hon. Dr Birmingham City, 2014; Hon. DArt Nottingham Trent, 2014. Sir Misha Black Medal, CSD, 2003; Maitland Medal, IStructE, 2006; Leonardo da Vinci Medal, Arts Club, 2009. Radio play, The Rime of the Bounty (Sony Radio Award, 1990). *Publications:* Napoleon Wrote Fiction, 1972; (ed) The Vampyre—Lord Ruthven to Count Dracula, 1978; Spaghetti Westerns: Cowboys and Europeans, from Karl May to Sergio Leone, 1981; The Schoolmaster and the Wheelwrights, 1983; The Royal College of Art: one hundred and fifty years of art and design, 1987; Vampyres, 1991; (ed) Beyond the Dovetail: essays on craft, skill and imagination, 1991; Clint Eastwood, 1992; The Face of Tutankhamun, 1992; (with Helen Frayling) The Art Pack, 1992; Research in Art and Design, 1994; Strange Landscape: a journey through the Middle Ages, 1995; Things to Come: a classic film, 1995; (ed jtly) Design of the Times: one hundred years of the Royal College of Art, 1996; Nightmare: the birth of horror, 1996 (Hamilton Deane AMD 1997); Tim Mara: the complete prints, 1998; Art and Design: 100 years at the Royal College of Art, 1999; Sergio Leone: something to do with death, 2000; (ed) The Hound of the Baskervilles, 2001; Ken Adam: the art of production design, 2005; Once Upon a Time in

Italy, 2005; Mad, Bad and Dangerous?: images of the scientist in film, 2005; (with Sir Kenneth Adam) Ken Adam Designs the Movies, 2008; Horace Walpole's Cat, 2009; Bill Gold: posterworks, 2010; Henry Cole and the Chamber of Horrors, 2010; On Craftsmanship, 2011; The Innocents: a classic film, 2013; The Yellow Peril: Dr Fu Manchu and the rise of Chinaphobia, 2014; The 2001 File, 2015; Inside the Bloody Chamber, 2015; Vampyres: genesis and resurrection, 2016; Frankenstein: the first two hundred years, 2017; Once Upon a Time in the West: shooting a masterpiece, 2019; contribs to: Reappraisals of Rousseau—studies in honour of R. A. Leigh, 1980; Cinema, Politics and Society in America, 1981; Rousseau et Voltaire en 1978, 1981; Rousseau After Two Hundred Years: Proc. of Cambridge Bicentennial Colloquium, 1982; Eduardo Paolozzi: perspectives and themes, 1984; Rape: an interdisciplinary study, 1987; The Cambridge Guide to the Arts in Britain, Vol. IX (post 1945), 1988; BFI Companion to the Western, 1988; Craft Classics since the 1940s, 1988; Eduardo Paolozzi: Noah's Ark, 1990; Ariel at Bay: reflections on broadcasting and the arts, 1990; Objects and Images: essay on design and advertising, 1992; BFI Companion to Horror, 1996; Fear: essays on the meaning and experience of fear, 2007; Age of Experience, 2009; It Came From the 1950s: popular culture, popular anxieties, 2012; Tanner Lectures: modern art and religion in the twentieth century, 2012; Hollywood Costume, 2012; Bram Stoker Centenary Essays, 2013; La revolución Mexicana en el Cine, 2013; Critical Perspectives on the Western, 2016; The Art of Horror Movies, 2017; La Révolution Sergio Leone, 2018; articles on film, popular culture and the visual arts/crafts in Cambridge Rev., Cinema, Film, Sight & Sound, London Magazine, New Statesman & Society, Crafts, Burlington Magazine, Art and Design, Designer, Design Week, Design, THES, TLS, Time Out, Punch, Designer, Craft History, Creative Review, Blueprint, Independent Magazine, Independent on Sunday, Culture Magazine, Listener, Times, Sunday Times, Guardian, Daily Telegraph, Christie's Magazine, RA Magazine, and various learned jls and catalogues. *Recreation:* finding time. *Address:* Garden House, Mill Lane, Bathampton, Bath, Avon BA2 6TS.
*See also Very Rev. N. A. Frayling.*

**FRAYLING, Very Rev. Nicholas Arthur;** Dean of Chichester, 2002–14, now Dean Emeritus; Dean, Priory of England and the Islands of the Most Venerable Order of the Hospital of St John of Jerusalem, since 2014; *b* 29 Feb. 1944; *s* of late Arthur Frederick Frayling, OBE and Barbara Kathleen (*née* Imhof). *Educ:* Repton Sch.; Exeter Univ. (BA Theology 1969); Cuddesdon Theol Coll., Oxford. Management training, retail trade, 1962–64; Temp. Probation Officer (prison welfare), Inner London Probation and After-Care Service, 1965–66, pt-time, 1966–71. Deacon, 1971; priest, 1972; Asst Curate, St John, Peckham, 1971–74; Vicar, All Saints, Tooting Graveney, 1974–83; Canon Residentiary and Precentor, Liverpool Cathedral, 1983–87, Hon. Canon, 1989–2002; Rector of Liverpool, 1987–2002. Chaplain: St Paul's Eye Hosp., Liverpool, 1987–90; Huyton Coll., 1987–91; to High Sheriff of Merseyside, 1992–93, 1997–98 and 1999–2000; Hon. Chaplain, British Nuclear Tests Veterans' Assoc., 1988–. Chairman: Southwark Diocesan Adv. Cttee for Care of Churches, 1980–83; Religious Adv. Panel, BBC Radio Merseyside, 1988–2002; Welfare Orgns Cttee, Liverpool CVS, 1992–2002; Mersey Mission to Seafarers, 2000–02; Church in Society Adv. Gp, Dio. of Chichester, 2003–09; Diocesan European Ecumenical Cttee, 2009–14. Trustee, Inst. of Food, Brain and Behaviour (formerly Natural Justice), 1995– (Chm., 2005–07). Chm. of Govs, Prebendal Sch., Chichester, 2002–14. Liveryman, Skinners' Co., 1980– (Chaplain, 2011–). Hon. Fellow, Liverpool John Moores Univ., 2003. Hon. LLD Liverpool, 2001. Hon. Freeman, City of Chichester, 2014. Canon of Honour, Chartres Cathedral, 2015. *Publications:* Pardon and Peace: a reflection on the making of peace in Ireland, 1996. *Recreations:* music, friends. *Address:* Flat 5, 27 South Parade, Southsea, Hants PO5 2JF. *T:* (023) 9281 7041. *E:* nicholasfrayling@gmail.com. *Clubs:* Oriental; Liverpool Artists (Life Mem.).
*See also Sir C. J. Frayling.*

**FRAYN, Claire, (Mrs Michael Frayn);** *see* Tomalin, C.

**FRAYN, Michael,** CLit 2007; writer; *b* 8 Sept. 1933; *s* of late Thomas Allen Frayn and Violet Alice Lawson; *m* 1st, 1960, Gillian Palmer (marr. diss. 1989); three *d;* 2nd, 1993, Claire Tomalin, *qv. Educ:* Kingston Gram. Sch.; Emmanuel Coll., Cambridge (Hon. Fellow, 1985). Reporter, Guardian, 1957–59; Columnist, Guardian, 1959–62; Columnist, Observer, 1962–68. Cameron Mackintosh Prof. of Contemporary Drama, Univ. of Oxford, 2009–10; Fellow, St Catherine's Coll., Oxford, 2009–10, now Emeritus. Foreign Hon. Mem., Amer. Acad. of Arts and Scis, 2000. Hon. DLitt Cambridge, 2001. *Television:* plays: Jamie, 1968 (filmed as Remember Me?, 1997); Birthday, 1969; First and Last, 1989 (Internat. Emmy Award, 1990); A Landing on the Sun, 1994; *documentaries:* Imagine a City Called Berlin, 1975; Vienna—the Mask of Gold, 1977; Three Streets in the Country, 1979; The Long Straight, 1980; Jerusalem, 1984; Prague—the Magic Lantern, 1993; Budapest: Written in Water, 1996; *stage plays:* The Two of Us, 1970; The Sandboy, 1971; Alphabetical Order, 1975 (Evening Standard Drama Award for Best Comedy); Donkeys' Years, 1976 (SWET Best Comedy Award); Clouds, 1976; Liberty Hall, 1980; Make and Break, 1980 (New Standard Best Comedy Award); Noises Off, 1982 (Standard Best Comedy Award; SWET Best Comedy Award); Benefactors, 1984 (Standard Best Play Award; Laurence Olivier (formerly SWET) Award for Play of the Year; Plays and Players London Theatre Critics' Best New Play); Look Look, 1990; Here, 1993; Now You Know, 1995; Copenhagen, 1998 (Evening Standard Best Play, South Bank Show Award for Theatre, Critics' Circle Best New Play, 1998; Prix Molière, 1999; Tony Award, Best Play, 2000); Alarms and Excursions, 1998; Democracy, 2003 (Best Play, Evening Standard, 2003; South Bank Show Award, 2003; Best New Play, Critics' Circle Awards, 2004); The Crimson Hotel, 2007; Afterlife, 2008; Matchbox Theatre, Hampstead Th., 2015; Wild Honey, Hampstead Th., 2016; *opera:* La Belle Vivette, 1995; *filmscripts:* Clockwise, 1986; Remember Me?, 1997. Hon. FBA 2019. Nat. Press Award, 1970; Heywood Hill Literary Prize, 2002; Golden PEN Award, 2003; Saint Louis Literary Award, 2006; McGovern Award, Cosmos Club Foundn, 2006; Writers' Guild Lifetime Achievement Award, 2011; Olivier Special Award, 2013. Bundesverdienstkreuz (Germany), 2004. *Publications:* collections of columns: The Day of the Dog, 1962; The Book of Fub, 1963; On the Outskirts, 1964; At Bay in Gear Street, 1967; The Original Michael Frayn, 1983; Speak After the Beep, 1995; The Additional Michael Frayn, 2000; Michael Frayn: collected columns, 2007; Stage Directions, 2008; Travels with a Typewriter, 2009; *non-fiction:* Constructions, 1974; (with David Burke) Celia's Secret, 2000; The Human Touch, 2006; My Father's Fortune: a life (memoir), 2010 (PEN/Ackerley Award); *novels:* The Tin Men, 1965 (Somerset Maugham Award); The Russian Interpreter, 1966 (Hawthornden Prize); Towards the End of the Morning, 1967; A Very Private Life, 1968; Sweet Dreams, 1973; The Trick of It, 1989; A Landing On the Sun, 1991 (Sunday Express Book of the Year Award, 1991); Now You Know, 1992; Headlong, 1999; Spies, 2002 (Bollinger Everyman Wodehouse Prize, 2002; Whitbread Novel of the Year, 2003); Skios, 2012; Matchbox Theatre, 2014; Pocket Playhouse (collection of sketches), 2017; *translations:* Tolstoy, The Fruits of Enlightenment, 1979 (prod. 1979); Anouilh, Number One, 1984; Chekhov: The Cherry Orchard, 1978 (prod. 1978, 1989); Three Sisters, 1983 (prod. 1985); Wild Honey, 1984 (prod. 1984); The Seagull, 1986 (prod. 1986); Uncle Vanya, 1988 (prod. 1988); The Sneeze (adapted from one-act plays and short stories), 1989 (prod. 1988); Trifonov, Exchange, 1986 (prod. 1986, 1990). *Address:* c/o Greene & Heaton Ltd, 37a Goldhawk Road, W12 8QQ.

**FRAYNE, Very Rev. David;** Dean (formerly Provost) of Blackburn, 1992–2001, now Emeritus; *b* 19 Oct. 1934; *s* of late Philip John Frayne and Daisy Morris Frayne (*née* Eade); *m* 1961, Elizabeth Ann Frayne (*née* Grant); one *s* two *d. Educ:* Reigate Grammar Sch.; St Edmund Hall, Oxford (BA 1958 (2nd cl. Hons PPE); MA 1962); The Queen's Coll., Birmingham (DTh 1960). Pilot Officer, RAF, 1954–55. Ordained deacon, 1960, priest, 1961; Asst Curate, St Michael, East Wickham, 1960–63; Priest-in-charge, St Barnabas, Downham, Lewisham, 1963–67; Vicar of N Sheen, Richmond, 1967–73; Rector of Caterham, 1973–83; Vicar of St Mary Redcliffe with Temple, Bristol and St John the Baptist, Bedminster, 1983–92. Rural Dean of Caterham, 1980–83; Hon. Canon, Southwark Cathedral, 1982, Emeritus, 1983; Rural Dean of Bedminster, 1986–92; Proctor in Convocation, 1987–90; Hon. Canon of Bristol Cathedral, 1991. A Church Comr, 1994–98; Mem., Redundant Churches Cttee, 1995–2001. *Recreations:* walking, music. *Address:* 30 Coleridge Vale Road South, Clevedon BS21 6PB. *T:* (01275) 873799. *E:* davidfrayne666@btinternet.com. *Club:* Oxford Society.

**FRAZER, Prof. Ian Hector,** AC 2012; MD; FRCPE, FRCPA; FRS 2011; FRSE; FAA; Chairman, TRI Foundation, Translational Research Institute Pty Ltd, Brisbane, since 2015 (Chief Executive Officer and Director of Research, 2011–15); *b* Glasgow, 6 Jan. 1953; *s* of Sam Frazer and Marion Frazer; *m* 1976, Caroline Nicoll; three *s. Educ:* George Watson's Coll., Edinburgh; Robert Gordon's Coll., Aberdeen; Univ. of Edinburgh (BSc Hons Pathol. 1974; MB ChB 1977); Univ. of Melbourne (MD 1988). FRCPE 1988; FRCPA 1988. Sen. Res. Officer and Asst Physician, Clin. Res. Unit, Walter and Eliza Hall Inst. of Medical Res., 1981–85; Sen. Lectr, Dept of Medicine, Univ. of Queensland, 1985–91; Dir, 1991–2011, Prof., 1993–2011, Univ. of Queensland Diamantina Inst. (formerly Centre for Immunol. and Cancer Res.). Pres., Cancer Council Australia, 2006–10; Chm., Scientific Adv. Council, Internat. Agency for Res. on Cancer, 2011. FAICD 2002; FTSE 2004; FAA 2005; FRACGP 2009; FASM 2011; FRSE 2018. *Publications:* over 200 res. articles. *Recreations:* snow ski-ing, classical music, bush walking, cycling. *Address:* Translational Research Institute Pty Ltd, 37 Kent Street, Woolloongabba, Brisbane, Qld 4102, Australia. *T:* (7) 34436962, *Fax:* (7) 34437779. *E:* ianhfrazer@gmail.com. *Clubs:* Queensland, Brisbane (Brisbane).

**FRAZER, Lucy Claire;** QC 2013; MP (C) South East Cambridgeshire, since 2015; Minister of State, Ministry of Justice, since 2019; *d* of Colin and Jocelyn Frazer; *m* 2002, David Leigh; one *s* one *d. Educ:* Leeds Girls' High Sch.; Newnham Coll., Cambridge (BA 1994). Called to the Bar, Middle Temple, 1996; in practice as barrister, 1998–2015. Parly Under-Sec. of State, MoJ, 2018–19; Solicitor Gen., 2019. *Publications:* (contrib.) Rowlatt on Principal and Surety. *Address:* House of Commons, SW1A 0AA.

**FREAN, Jennifer Margaret, (Jenny),** RDI 1998; Founder, and Head, First Eleven Studio, since 1986; *b* 17 April 1947; *d* of Theodore Farbridge and Isobel Farbridge (*née* Reid-Douglas); *m* 1970 (Christopher) Patrick Frean; one *d. Educ:* City of London Sch. for Girls; Hornsey Coll. of Art (BA Hons); Royal Coll. of Art (MA 1972). Design Consultant, Centro Design Montefibre, Milan, 1974; set up Jenny Frean Associates, textile design studio, 1975; portraitist, 1984–86; founded First Eleven Studio; working with textile manufacturers worldwide on every aspect of colour and surface decoration, 1986. *Recreations:* music (especially opera), all art forms, gardening. *Address:* Christmas Cottage, Ingrams Green, Midhurst, W Sussex GU29 0LJ. *T:* (01730) 812337.

**FREARS, Stephen Arthur;** film director; *b* 20 June 1941; *s* of late Dr Russell E. Frears and Ruth M. Frears; *m* 1st, 1968, Mary-Kay Wilmers, *qv* (marr. diss. 1974); two *s;* 2nd, 2002, Anne Rothenstein; one *s* one *d. Educ:* Gresham's Sch., Holt; Trinity Coll., Cambridge (BA Law). Director of films: Gumshoe, 1971; Bloody Kids, 1980; Going Gently, 1981; Walter, 1982; Saigon, 1983; The Hit, 1984; My Beautiful Laundrette, 1985; Prick Up Your Ears, 1986; Sammy and Rosie Get Laid, 1987; Dangerous Liaisons, 1989; The Grifters, 1990; Accidental Hero, 1992; The Snapper, 1993; Mary Reilly, 1996; The Van, 1996; The Hi-Lo Country, 1999; High Fidelity, 2000; Liam, 2001; Dirty Pretty Things, 2002; Mrs Henderson Presents, 2005; The Queen, 2006; Chéri, 2009; Tamara Drewe, 2010; Lay the Favorite, 2011; Mohammed Ali's Greatest Fight, 2012; Philomena, 2013; The Program, 2015; Florence Foster Jenkins, 2016; Victoria and Abdul, 2017; television: Fail Safe, 2000; The Deal, 2003; A Very English Scandal, 2018; State of the Union, 2019. *Recreation:* reading. *Address:* c/o Casarotto Co. Ltd, 7–12 Noel Street, W1F 8GQ. *T:* (020) 7287 4450.

**FRÉCHETTE, Louise,** OC 1999; Deputy Secretary-General, United Nations, 1998–2006; *b* 16 July 1946. *Educ:* Collège Basile Moreau (BA 1966); Univ. of Montreal (LèsL Hist. 1970); Coll. of Europe, Bruges (Post-grad. Dip. Econ. Studies 1978). Joined Dept of External Affairs, Govt of Canada, 1971; Ambassador to Argentina and Uruguay, 1985–88; Assistant Deputy Minister: for Latin America and Caribbean, Min. of Foreign Affairs, 1988–91; for Internat. Econ. and Trade Policy, 1991–92; Ambassador to UN, 1992–94; Associate Dep. Minister, Dept of Finance, 1994–95; Dep. Minister of Defence, Canada, 1995–98. Member, Board: CARE Canada, 2007–15 (Chair, 2011–15); Essilor Internat., France, 2012–; Chm., CARE Internat. Supervisory Bd, 2016–. Distinguished Fellow, Centre for Internat. Governance Innovation, Canada, 2006–12. Hon. LLD St Mary's Univ., Halifax, 1993; hon. drs from Univs of Ottawa, Laval, Montreal, Carleton, Waterloo, Toronto, McGill, St Francis-Xavier, Guelph, Quebec, Kyung Hee, Turin. *Recreations:* golf, reading.

**FREDERICK, Sir Christopher (St John),** 11th Bt *cr* 1723, of Burwood House, Surrey; *b* 28 June 1950; *s* of Sir Charles Frederick, 10th Bt and of Rosemary, *er d* of Lt-Col R. J. H. Baddeley, MC; *S* father, 2001; *m* 1990, Camilla Elizabeth, *o d* of Sir Derek Gilbey, 3rd Bt; one *s* one *d. Heir: s* Benjamin St John Frederick, *b* 29 Dec. 1991.

**FREDMAN, Prof. Sandra Debbe,** FBA 2005; Rhodes Professor of the Laws of the British Commonwealth and the USA, University of Oxford, since 2011 (Professor of Law, 1999–2011); Fellow, Pembroke College, Oxford, since 2011; barrister; *b* 28 July 1957; *d* of Michael Geoffrey Fredman and Naomi Pauline Fredman (*née* Greenstein); *m* 1985, Alan Leslie Stein; two *s* one *d. Educ:* Univ. of Witwatersrand (BA 1st Cl. Maths and Philosophy 1977); Wadham Coll., Oxford (Rhodes Schol., 1979–82; BA 1st Cl. Hons Jurisp. 1981; BCL 1st Cl. Hons 1982). Political and econs journalist, Financial Mail, S Africa, 1978–79; articled clerk, Lawford & Co., Gray's Inn, 1983–84; Lectr in Law, KCL, 1984–88; Fellow and Lectr in Law, Exeter Coll., Oxford, 1988–2011. Leverhulme Major Res. Fellow, 2004–07. Scientific Dir, European Network of Legal Experts in the Non-Discrimination Field, 2005–07; Dir, Oxford Human Rights Hub, 2012–. Fellow, Gray's Inn, 2007–. Hon. QC 2012. *Publications:* (with M. Nell and P. Randall) The Narrow Margin: how black and white South Africans view change in South Africa, 1983; (with B. Hepple) Labour Law and Industrial Relations in Great Britain, 1986, 2nd edn 1992; (with G. Morris) The State as Employer: labour law in the public services, 1989; Women and the Law, 1997; (ed) Discrimination and Human Rights, 2001; Discrimination Law, 2002, 2nd edn 2011; (ed with S. Spencer) Age as an Equality Issue, 2003; Human Rights Transformed: positive rights and positive duties, 2008; articles in legal jls. *Recreations:* outdoor activities, literature, theatre, travel. *Address:* Pembroke College, Oxford OX1 1DW. *T:* (01865) 276444; Old Square Chambers, 10–11 Bedford Row, WC1R 4BU. *T:* (020) 7269 0300.

**FREE, Maj. Gen. Julian Richard,** CBE 2009 (OBE 2006; MBE 2001); Deputy Vice Chancellor (People Services and Operations), University of Lincoln, since 2017; *b* Plymouth, 30 Jan. 1963; *s* of Paul and Christine Free; *m* 1990, Barbara, (Babs), Woodward; one *s* one *d*. *Educ*: Queen's Coll., Taunton; St Luke's Coll., Exeter Univ. (BEd Hons 1986); RMA Sandhurst; Army Comd and Staff Coll., Camberley (psc, MA 1995). RA Young Officers' Course, Larkhill, 1987; Comd Post Officer, 1987–88, Gun Position Officer, 1989, Forward Observation Officer (Saudi Arabia, Kuwait), 1990–91, 1 RHA; Forward Observation Officer, 1991–92, Adjt, 1992–94, 7 Para. RHA; SO 2 (Weapons) c, Equipment Support 22a, 1995–98; Batt. Comdr, G Parachute Batt. (Mercer's Troop) RHA (Kosovo, Sierra Leone), 1998–2000; Batt. Comdr, Aviation Batt. 7 Para. RHA, 2000; MA to COS, HQ Kosovo Force 4, 2000–01; MA to QMG, 2001–03; CO, 26 Regt RA (Iraq, Cyprus), 2003–05; DACOS Future Structures, HQ Land, 2005–07; hcsc 2007; Comdr, 4 Mechanised Bde (Iraq), 2007–09; rcds 2009; Director: Collective Trng Gp, 2009–10; Campaign and Transition Assessment Gp, HQ ISAF Jt Comd, Afghanistan, 2011; COS, HQ ARRC, 2012–14; Comdt, JSCSC, 2014–17. Fellow, Soc. for Educn and Trng, 2015. CCMI. *Recreations*: keen sportsman now relegated to watching his favourite ball sports (Rugby, hockey, cricket and football) but still running, cycling and keeping fit, shooting, fishing, reading (sports science, travelogue and crime novels), cinema. *Address*: University of Lincoln, Brayford Pool, Lincoln LN6 7TS.

**FREEDBERG, Prof. David Adrian;** Professor of Art History, since 1984, Pierre Matisse Professor of History of Art, since 2007, and Director, Italian Academy for Advanced Studies in America, since 2000, Columbia University; Director, Warburg Institute, 2015–17; *b* 1 June 1948; *s* of William Freedberg and Eleonore Kupfer; one *s* one *d*. *Educ*: S African Coll. High Sch., Cape Town; Yale Univ. (BA); Balliol Coll., Oxford (DPhil). Rhodes Scholar, Oxford, 1969–72; Lectr in History of Art: Westfield Coll., Univ. of London, 1973–76; Courtauld Inst. of Art, Univ. of London, 1976–84; Slade Prof. of Fine Art, Univ. of Oxford, 1983–84. Baldwin Prof., Oberlin Coll., Ohio, 1979; Andrew W. Mellon Prof. of Fine Art, Nat. Gall. of Art, Washington, 1996–98; Nat Robertson Prof. of Sci. and Society, Emory Univ., 2006; Vis. Mem., Inst. for Advanced Study, Princeton, NJ, 1980–81; Gerson Lectr, Univ. of Groningen, 1983; VUB-Leerstoel, Brussels Univ., 1988–89; Wittkower Prof., Bibliotheca Hertziana, Rome, 2008–09; Visiting Fellow: Wissenschaftskolleg, Berlin, 2009; Stellenbosch Inst. for Advanced Study, 2012; Sen. Res. Scholar, Getty Res. Inst., 2015; Slade Prof. of Fine Art, Univ. of Cambridge, 2016–17. Fellow: Amer. Acad. of Arts and Scis, 1997; Amer. Philosophical Soc., 1997; Accademia Nazionale di Agricoltura, 2003; Istituto Veneto di Scienze, Lettere e Arti, 2011. Hon. PhD Ghent, 2017; Sigillum Magnum, Univ. of Bologna, 2019. *Publications*: Dutch Landscape Prints of the Seventeenth Century, 1980; The Life of Christ after the Passion (Corpus Rubenianum Ludwig Burchard, VII), 1983; Iconoclasts and their Motives, 1985; Iconoclasm and Painting in the Revolt of the Netherlands 1566–1609, 1988; The Power of Images, 1989 (many translations); (ed) The Prints of Pieter Bruegel the Elder, 1989; (ed with Jan De Vries) Art in History/History in Art: studies in seventeenth century Dutch culture, 1991; Joseph Kosuth: The Play of the Unmentionable, 1992; Peter Paul Rubens: paintings and oil sketches, 1995; (with Enrico Baldini) Citrus Fruit: the Paper Museum of Cassiano dal Pozzo B I, 1997; (with Andrew Scott) Fossil Woods and other Geological Specimens: the Paper Museum of Cassiano dal Pozzo B III, 2000; The Eye of the Lynx: Galileo, his friends, and the beginnings of modern natural history, 2003; (with David Pegler) Fungi vols I-III: the Paper Museum of Cassiano dal Pozzo B II, 2005; Las Mascaras de Aby Warburg, 2013; Iconoclasia, 2018; articles in Burlington Magazine, Revue de l'Art, Gentse Bijdragen, Art Bulletin, Münchner Jahrbuch der Bildenden Kunst, Jl of Warburg and Courtauld Insts, Print Quarterly, Quaderni Puteani, Trends in Cognitive Science, Frontiers in Human Neurosci. *Address*: Italian Academy for Advanced Studies in America, Columbia University, 1161 Amsterdam Avenue, New York, NY 10027, USA.

**FREEDLAND, Jonathan Saul;** Executive Editor, Opinion, since 2014, and Columnist, since 1997, The Guardian; *b* 25 Feb. 1967; *s* of late Michael Freedland and Sara Freedland; *m* 2000, Sarah Peters; two *s*. *Educ*: University Coll. Sch., London; Wadham Coll., Oxford (BA Hons PPE). Reporter, Sunday Correspondent, 1989–90; news trainee, BBC, 1990; reporter, BBC News and Current Affairs, 1991–93; Laurence Stern Fellow, as staff writer, Washington Post, 1992; Washington Corresp., 1993–97, Policy Editor, 1997–2014, The Guardian. Monthly Columnist: Jewish Chronicle, 1998–; Daily Mirror, 2002–04; Presenter, The Long View, Radio 4, 1999–. Dir and Trustee, Index on Censorship, 2002–09. Columnist of the Year, What the Papers Say Awards, 2002; David Watt Prize for Journalism, Rio Tinto, 2008. *Publications*: Bring Home the Revolution, 1998 (Somerset Maugham Award for Non-fiction); Jacob's Gift: a journey into the heart of belonging, 2005; The 3rd Woman, 2015; *as Sam Bourne*: The Righteous Men, 2006 (Gold Book Award, Nielsen, 2007); The Last Testament, 2007; The Final Reckoning, 2008; The Chosen One, 2010; Pantheon, 2012; To Kill the Truth, 2019; contribs to NY Times. *Recreations*: family, music, movies. *Address*: The Guardian, Kings Place, 90 York Way, N1 9AG. *T*: (020) 3353 2000. *E*: Jonathan.freedland@guardian.co.uk.

**FREEDLAND, Prof. Mark Robert,** DPhil; FBA 2002; Professor of Employment Law, 1996–2012, now Emeritus and Research Fellow, Institute of European and Comparative Law, since 2014, University of Oxford (Senior Research Fellow, Law Faculty, 2012–14); Fellow and Tutor in Law, St John's College, Oxford, 1970–2012, now Emeritus Research Fellow; *b* 19 April 1945; *s* of Nathaniel Freedland and Esther (*née* Bendas); *m* 1st, 1973, Lalage Lewis (*d* 1976); one *s* one *d*; 2nd, 1997, Geraldine Field. *Educ*: Hendon Co. Grammar Sch.; University Coll. London (LLB); Brasenose Coll., Oxford (MA; DPhil 1970). Called to the Bar, Gray's Inn, 1971, Bencher, 1998; University of Oxford: Lectr, 1971–94; Reader, 1994–96; Dir, Inst. of European and Comparative Law, 2001–04; Leverhulme Major Res. Fellow, 2005–08. Visiting Professor: European Univ. Inst., Florence, 1995; Univ. of Paris I, 1996–98; Univ. of Paris II, 1999–2002; Hon. Prof., Faculty of Laws, UCL, 2012–. Hon. QC 2013. Dr *hc* Paris II, 2000. *Publications*: The Contract of Employment, 1976; (with P. L. Davies) Labour Law Text and Materials, 1979, 2nd edn 1983; (ed with P. L. Davies) Kahn-Freud's Labour and the Law, 1983; (with P. L. Davies) Labour Legislation and Public Policy, 1993; (jtly) Public Services and Citizenship in European Law, 1998; The Personal Employment Contract, 2003; (with P. L. Davies) Towards a Flexible Labour Market, 2005; (with N. Kountouris) The Legal Construction of Personal Work Relations, 2012; (with N. Kountouris) Resocialising Europe, 2013; (with C. Costello) Migrants at Work, 2014; (with J. Prassl) Viking, Laval and Beyond, 2015; (ed) The Contract of Employment, 2016; contrib. articles to Public Law, Industrial Law Jl. *Recreation*: living village life in France. *Address*: St John's College, Oxford OX1 3JP. *T*: (01865) 277387. *E*: mark.freedland@sjc.ox.ac.uk.

**FREEDMAN, Amelia, (Mrs Michael Miller),** CBE 2006 (MBE 1989); FRAM; Artistic Director and Founder, Nash Ensemble, since 1964; Head of Classical Music, South Bank Centre, 1995–2006; *b* 21 Nov. 1940; *d* of Miriam Freedman (*née* Claret) and Henry Freedman; *m* 1970, Michael Miller; two *s* one *d*. *Educ*: St George's Sch., Harpenden; Henrietta Barnett, London; RAM (LRAM (piano), ARCM (clarinet); ARAM 1977, FRAM 1986). Music teacher, 1961–72: King's Sch., Cambridge; Perse Sch. for Girls, Cambridge; Chorleywood College for the Blind; Sir Philip Magnus Sch., London. Presented annual themed series, Wigmore Hall, 1979–; Artistic Director: Bath Internat. Fest., 1984–93; Bath Mozartfest, 1995–; Bath Bachfest, 2012–; Musical Adviser, Israel Fest., 1989–90; Programme Adviser, Philharmonia Orch., 1993–95; chamber music consultant for various projects at South Bank Centre and Barbican, and for LSO; has commnd 171 new works for Nash Ensemble and presented 270 world premières; sang in film, A Hard Day's Night, 1964. Trustee, Nash Concert Soc., 1968–. Freeman, City of London, 2003. FRSA 2004. Hon. DMus Bath, 1993. Walter Wilson Cobbett Gold Medal, Musicians' Co., 1996; Leslie Boosey Award, PRS/Royal Philharmonic Soc., 2000; Internat. Artist Managers' Assoc. Award, 2011. Chevalier, l'Ordre des Arts et des Lettres (France), 1983; Czech Govt Medal for services to Czech music in UK, 1984; Chevalier, l'Ordre National du Mérite (France), 1996; Officier, l'Ordre des Arts et des Lettres (France), 2009. *Recreations*: theatre, cinema, ballet, opera; spectator sport—cricket, rugger, football (supporting Arsenal); children. *Address*: 14 Cedars Close, Hendon, NW4 1TR. *T*: (020) 8203 3025, *Fax*: (020) 8203 9540. *E*: info@nashensemble.org.uk.

**FREEDMAN, Hon. Sir (Benjamin) Clive,** Kt 2018; **Hon. Mr Justice Freedman;** a Judge of the High Court, Queen's Bench Division, since 2018; *b* 16 Nov. 1955; *s* of Lionel and Freda Freedman; *m* 1980, Hadassa Helen Woolfson; one *s* three *d*. *Educ*: Manchester Grammar Sch.; Pembroke Coll., Cambridge (MA). Called to the Bar, Middle Temple, 1978, Bencher, 2005; Jt Hd, Littleton Chambers, 2006–13; Mem., Northern Circuit, 1980–2018; QC 1997; an Asst Recorder, 1997–2000; a Recorder, 2000–18; a Dep. High Court Judge, 2003–18. *Recreations*: Manchester City FC, Test Match Special. *Address*: Royal Courts of Justice, Strand, WC2A 2LL.

**FREEDMAN, Her Honour Dawn Angela, (Mrs N. J. Shestopal);** a Circuit Judge, 1991–2007; *b* 9 Dec. 1942; *d* of Julius and Celia Freedman; *m* 1970, Neil John Shestopal (*d* 2016). *Educ*: Westcliff High Sch. for Girls; University Coll., London (LLB Hons). Called to the Bar, Gray's Inn, 1966; Metropolitan Stipendiary Magistrate, 1980–91; a Recorder, 1989–91. Mem. Parole Bd, 1992–96. Chm., Jewish Marriage Council, 1998–2002. Mem. Council, London Sch. of Jewish Studies, 1998–2002. Trustee, Jewish Women's Aid, 2008–. *Recreations*: theatre, television, cooking. *Address*: c/o Harrow Crown Court, Hailsham Drive, Harrow HA1 4TU.

**FREEDMAN, Jeremy Stuart; His Honour Judge Jeremy Freedman;** a Circuit Judge, since 2013; *b* Newcastle upon Tyne, 20 April 1959; *s* of Roland and Valerie Freedman; *m* 1989, Julia Anne Chapman; one *s* one *d*. *Educ*: Oundle Sch.; Manchester Univ. (BA Hons); City Univ. (DipLaw); Gray's Inn (Bar Vocational Course). Called to the Bar, Middle Temple, 1982; in practice as a barrister, specialising in personal injury and clinical negligence; Asst Recorder, 1998–2000; Recorder, 2000–13; Dep. Asst Coroner, Durham, 2010–13. *Recreations*: Real tennis, golf, ski-ing, reading, food and wine. *Address*: Newcastle upon Tyne. *E*: jeremy.freedman@btinternet.com. *Clubs*: Northern Counties (Newcastle upon Tyne); Northumberland Golf.

**FREEDMAN, Prof. Judith Anne, (Lady Freedman),** CBE 2013; FBA 2016; Professor of Taxation Law and Policy, since 2019, and Director of Legal Research, Oxford University Centre for Taxation, since 2008, University of Oxford (Pinsent Masons Professor of Taxation Law (formerly Professor of Tax Law), 2001–19); Fellow of Worcester College, Oxford, since 2001; *b* 10 Aug. 1953; *d* of Harry Hill and Estella Hill; *m* 1974, Lawrence David Freedman (*see* Rt Hon. Prof. Sir Lawrence Freedman); one *s* one *d*. *Educ*: North London Collegiate Sch.; Lady Margaret Hall, Oxford (BA 1st Class Hons Jurisprudence, MA). Articled Clerk, Stanleys & Simpson North, 1976–78; Solicitor of Supreme Court, 1978; Solicitor, Corporate Tax Dept, Freshfields, 1978–80; Lectr in Law, Univ. of Surrey, 1980–82; London School of Economics: Lectr, Law Dept, 1982–91; Sen. Lectr, 1991–96; Reader in Law, 1996–2000; Prof. of Law, 2000–01; Sen. Res. Fellow in Company and Commercial Law, Inst. of Advanced Legal Studies, 1989–92; Develt Coordinator, then Assoc. Dean for Develt and Communications, Faculty of Law, Univ. of Oxford, 2013–16. Anton Philips Vis. Prof., Tilburg Univ., 2007–08; Adjunct Prof., Australian Sch. of Business, Univ. of NSW, 2011–. Member: Tax Law Review Cttee, 1994–; DTI Company Law Review Working Party on Small Businesses, 1998–2000; Office of Tax Simplification Consultative Cttee on Small Business Taxation, 2010–12; on Small Companies, 2015–; Tax Avoidance Study Gp to advise Exchequer on Gen. Anti-avoidance Rule, 2010–12. Mem Council, Inst. for Fiscal Studies, 2003–. Gov., Wimbledon High Sch. (GDST), 2009–. Hon. Fellow, Chartered Inst. of Taxation, 2015. European Editor, Palmer's Company Law, 1991–2003; Jt Editor, British Tax Review, 1997– (Asst Ed., 1988–97); Member, Editorial Board: Fiscal Studies, 2000–11; The Tax Jl, 2002–; eJournal of Tax Res., Univ. of NSW, 2003–; Modern Law Rev., 2004– (Mem., Editl Cttee, 1987–2004); Canadian Tax Jl, 2005–; Australian Tax Rev., 2011–. *Publications*: (jtly) Property and Marriage: an integrated approach, 1988; (ed jtly) Law and Accounting: competition and co-operation in the 1990s, 1992; Employed or Self-employed? tax classification of workers and the changing labour market, 2001; (ed jtly) Taxation: an interdisciplinary approach to research, 2005; (ed) Beyond Boundaries: developing approaches to tax avoidance and tax risk management, 2008; (ed jtly) The Delicate Balance: tax, discretion and the Rule of Law, 2011; (contrib.) The Jurisprudence of Lord Hoffman, 2015; (contrib.) Tax Simplification, 2015; contrib. articles to jls. *Recreations*: family, friends, doodling. *Address*: Worcester College, Oxford OX1 2HB. *W*: www.law.ox.ac.uk/profile/freedmanj.

**FREEDMAN, Rt Hon. Prof. Sir Lawrence (David),** KCMG 2003; CBE 1996; PC 2009; DPhil; FBA 1995; Professor of War Studies, King's College, London, 1982–2014, now Emeritus; *b* 7 Dec. 1948; *s* of late Lt-Comdr Julius Freedman and Myra Freedman; *m* 1974, Judith Anne Hill (*see* J. A. Freedman); one *s* one *d*. *Educ*: Whitley Bay Grammar Sch.; BAEcon Manchester; BPhil York; DPhil Oxford. Teaching Asst, York Univ., 1971–72; Research Fellow, Nuffield Coll., Oxford, 1974–75; Research Associate, IISS, 1975–76 (Mem. Council, 1984–92 and 1993–2002); Research Fellow, 1976–78, Head of Policy Studies, 1978–82, RIIA; King's College London: Hd, Dept of War Studies, 1982–97; Hd, Sch. of Social Sci. and Public Policy, 2000–03; Vice-Principal, 2003–13. Vis. Prof., Blavatnik Sch. of Govt, Univ. of Oxford, 2015–. Mem., Iraq Inquiry, 2009–16. Hon. Dir, Centre for Defence Studies, 1990–2000. Chm., Cttee on Internat. Peace and Security, Social Science Res. Council (US), 1993–98. Trustee, Imperial War Mus., 2001–09. FKC 1992. FRSA 1991; FRHistS 2000. FAcSS (AcSS 2001). Chesney Gold Medal, RUSI, 2006; Dist. Scholar Award, Internat. Studies Assoc., 2007; George Webb Prize for Strategic Studies Leadership, Canadian Internat. Council, 2008. *Publications*: US Intelligence and the Soviet Strategic Threat, 1977, 2nd edn 1986; Britain and Nuclear Weapons, 1980; The Evolution of Nuclear Strategy, 1981, 4th edn (jtly) 2019; (jtly) Nuclear War & Nuclear Peace, 1983; (ed) The Troubled Alliance, 1983; The Atlas of Global Strategy, 1985; The Price of Peace, 1986; Britain and the Falklands War, 1988; (jtly) Signals of War, 1990; (ed) Population Change and European Security, 1991; (ed) Britain in the World, 1991; (jtly) The Gulf Conflict 1990–1991, 1993; War: a Reader, 1994; (ed) Military Intervention in Europe, 1994; (ed) Strategic Coercion, 1998; The Politics of British Defence, 1999; Kennedy's Wars, 2000; The Cold War, 2001; (ed) Superterrorism, 2002; Deterrence, 2004; The Official History of the Falklands Campaign, vols I and II, 2005; A Choice of Enemies, 2008 (Lionel Gelber Prize, 2009; Duke of Westminster Prize for Military Lit., RUSI, 2009); (ed) Scripting Middle East Leaders, 2013; Strategy: a history, 2013 (W. J. M. Mackenzie Book Prize, Pol Studies Assoc., 2014); The Future of War: a history, 2017; The Ladybird

Book of Nuclear Deterrence, 2018; Ukraine and the Art of Strategy, 2019. *Recreations:* political caricature, grandchildren. *Address:* c/o Department of War Studies, King's College London, Strand, WC2R 2LS. *T:* 07920 221312.

**FREEDMAN, Susan Rachel;** *see* Prevezer, S. R.

**FREELAND, Anne Elizabeth;** *see* Studd, A. E.

**FREELAND, Henry John,** FSA; RIBA; Partner, Freeland Rees Roberts Architects, 1981–2005; Director, Freeland Rees Roberts Trustees (formerly Freeland Rees Roberts Architects) Ltd, since 2005; *b* 16 Jan. 1948; *s* of Lt-Gen. Sir Ian Henry Freeland, GBE, KCB, DSO and Mary Freeland; *m* 1971, Elizabeth Margaret Sarel Ling; one *s* three *d*. *Educ:* Eton Coll.; Bristol Univ. (BA 1st Cl. Hons Architecture 1970; BArch 1st Cl. Hons 1973). ARCUK, RIBA 1975; AABC. Twist and Whitley, Architects, Cambridge, 1972–74; Cecil Bourne, Architects, Cambs, 1974–77; Whitworth & Hall, Architects, Bury St Edmunds, 1977–81. Surveyor to the Fabric, King's Coll. Chapel, Cambridge, 1987–2017; Architect and Surveyor: Ickworth House, 1988–2014; Guildford Cath., 1995–2010; Norwich Cath., 1996–; Burghley House, 2003–; St John's Coll. Chapel, Cambridge, 2014–; Clare Coll. Chapel, Cambridge, 2015–; Millennium Project Architect, St Edmundsbury Cath., 2007–12. Member: Ely DAC, 2001–; Fabric Adv. Cttee, Cath. and Abbey Ch of St Alban, 2006–; Fabric Adv. Cttee, St George's Chapel, Windsor, 2010– (Chm., 2018–). Member: Ecclesiastical Architects' and Surveyors' Assoc., 1978–; Cathedral Architects' Assoc., 1995–; Life Mem., SPAB, 1970. FSA 2006. Freeman, City of London, 1985; Liveryman, Co. of Chartered Architects, 1986–. Trustee, D'Oyly Carte Trust, 2001–. *Recreations:* cooking, family, painting, archaeology, fossils, gardening, building and working with timber. *Address:* Freeland Rees Roberts Architects, 25 City Road, Cambridge CB1 1DP. *T:* (01223) 366555, *Fax:* (01223) 312882. *E:* hf@frrarchitects.co.uk. *Club:* Surveyors' (Trustee, 2009–).

**FREELAND, Simon Dennis Marsden;** QC 2002; **His Honour Judge Freeland;** a Circuit Judge, since 2007; *b* 11 Feb. 1956; 2nd *s* of late Dennis Marsden Freeland and of Rosemary Turnbull Tarn; *m* 2000, Anne Elizabeth Studd, *qv*; one *s* one *d*. *Educ:* Malvern Coll.; Manchester Univ. (LLB Hons). Called to the Bar, Gray's Inn, 1978, Bencher, 2007; in practice at the Bar, 1978–2007, specialising in police law and civil liberties; Head of Chambers, 5 Essex Court, 2002–07; Recorder, 2000–07. *Recreations:* horse-racing, walking, good food and fine wine, family. *Address:* Central London County Court, Thomas More Building, Royal Courts of Justice, Strand, WC2A 2LL.

**FREELING, Dr Anthony Nigel Stanley;** President, Hughes Hall, Cambridge, since 2014 (Fellow, 2008–14); *b* London, 6 Aug. 1956; *s* of Dr Paul Freeling and Shirley Valerie Freeling; *m* 1989, Laurel Claire Powers (*see* L. C. Powers-Freeling); two *d*. *Educ:* Haberdashers' Aske's Sch., Elstree; St John's Coll., Cambridge (BA (1st Cl.) Maths 1978; MPhil Control Engrg and Operational Res. 1980; PhD Mgt Studies 1985). Decision Analyst, Decision Science Consortium, 1978–83; Sen. Mgt Scientist, Mars Inc., 1984–86; McKinsey & Company, 1986–2004: Principal, 1992–99; Dir, 1999–2004. Dir, Strategic Mgt Centre, Ashridge Business Sch., 2005–15; Mem. Council, Open Univ., 2006–14. Res. Dir, Retailing Res. Councils, Asia and Europe, Coca-Cola Co. Inc., 2010–15. Trustee: UnLtd, 2004–14; PHG Foundn, 2012–; Dir, Capacitybuilders, 2008–11. Mem. Council, Univ. of Cambridge, 2017–. *Publications:* Agile Marketing, 2011. *Recreations:* food and wine, tennis, motor racing, music. *Address:* Hughes Hall, Cambridge CB1 2EW. *T:* (01223) 761087. *E:* president@hughes.cam.ac.uk. *Club:* Oxford and Cambridge.

**FREELING, Laurel Claire P.;** *see* Powers-Freeling.

**FREEMAN,** family name of **Baron Freeman**.

**FREEMAN,** Baron *cr* 1997 (Life Peer); **Roger Norman Freeman;** PC 1993; MA; FCA; *b* 27 May 1942; *s* of Norman and Marjorie Freeman; *m* 1969, Jennifer Margaret Watson (*see* Lady Freeman); one *s* one *d*. *Educ:* Whitgift Sch., Croydon; Balliol Coll., Oxford (MA PPE). Chartered Accountant, 1969; FCA 1979. Articled with Binder Hamlyn & Co., 1964–69 (Hons Prize, 1968); General Partner, Lehman Brothers, 1969–86. MP (C) Kettering, 1983–97; contested (C) same seat, 1997. Parliamentary Under-Secretary of State: for the Armed Forces, 1986–88; DoH, 1988–90; Minister of State: Dept of Transport, 1990–94; MoD, 1994–95; Chancellor of the Duchy of Lancaster, 1995–97. Partner, 1997–99, Chm., Corp. Finance Adv. Bd, then UK Adv. Bd, 1999–2017, PricewaterhouseCoopers. Dir, Thales SA, 1997–2013; Chm., Thales UK Pension Fund, 2000–18. A Vice-Chm., Cons. Party, 1997–2001. Chairman: Skill Force Develt Ltd, 2004–16; Cambridge Enterprise Ltd (formerly Cambridge Univ. Venture Bd), 2005–10. President: British Internat. Freight Assoc., 1999–2002; RFCA (formerly TAVRA) Council, 1999–2010. *Publications:* Professional Practice, 1968; Fair Deal for Water, 1985; (ed) UK Rail Privatisation 1992–1997, 2000; (ed) University Spin-out Technology Companies, 2004. *Address:* House of Lords, SW1A 0PW. *Club:* Carlton.

**FREEMAN, Lady; Jennifer Margaret Freeman,** OBE 2012; FSA; architectural historian, writer, specialist in building conservation and developer of listed buildings; Director, Historic Chapels Trust, 1993–2012; Chairman, Freeman Historic Properties Ltd, since 1992; *b* 28 Oct. 1944; *d* of Malcolm Woodward Watson and Margaret Hannah Watson; *m* 1969, Roger Norman Freeman (later Baron Freeman); one *s* one *d*. *Educ:* Withington Girls' Sch., Manchester; Univ. of Manchester (BA Hons); Architectural Assoc. (Dip. Building Conservation); Inst. of Historic Bldg Conservation. Project Co-ordinator, Save the City: a conservation study of the City of London, report published 1976, 2nd edn 1979. Member: Cttee, Save Britain's Heritage, 1977–; London Adv. Cttee, English Heritage, 1986–2003; Council for the Care of Churches, 1991–2003. Dir and Trustee, Waltham Abbey Royal Gunpowder Mills Operating Co., 2013– (Chm., 2017–). Pres. and Trustee, Friends of Kensal Green Cemetery, 2004– (Chm., 2015–); Vice-President: Friends of the City Churches, 1996–; Nat. Churches Trust (formerly Historic Churches Preservation Trust), 2003–; Mem. Council, Nat. Chapels Soc., 2013–. Sec., Victorian Soc., 1982–85. Trustee: Heritage Link, 2002–08; Constable Trust, 2003–10. Pres., Kettering Civic Soc., 2004–. Hon. Life Mem., Rothwell Preservation Trust, 1997. Assessor, City Heritage Award, 1978–. FRSA 2003; FSA 2005. Freeman, City of London, 1998. Brother, Art Workers Guild, 2014. Hon. DArts De Montfort, 1997. *Publications:* (jtly) Kensal Green Cemetery, 2001; W. D. Caröe (1857–1938): his architectural achievement, 1990; contrib. various articles to learned jls. *Recreations:* embroidery, art gallery and museum-going, country walking, theatre, reading, travel. *E:* jmfhproperties@gmail.com.

**FREEMAN, Catherine;** Director, Dove Productions, since 1989; *b* 10 Aug. 1931; *d* of Harold Dove and Eileen Carroll; *m* 1st, 1958, Sir Charles Wheeler, CMG; 2nd, 1962, Rt Hon. John Freeman, MBE, PC (marr. diss. 1976; he *d* 2014); two *s* one *d*. *Educ:* Convent of the Assumption; St Anne's Coll., Oxford (MA Hons). Joined BBC as trainee producer, 1954; Producer/director: Panorama, Brains Trust, Monitor, Press Conference, 1954–58; joined Thames Television as Sen. Producer in Features Dept, 1976; Editor, Daytime progs, 1976–82; originator and series producer of Citizen 2000 for Channel 4; Controller, Documentaries, Features and Religion, 1982–86; Controller, Features and Religion, 1986–89. Member: Devlin Cttee on Identification Procedures, 1974–76; Literature Panel, Arts Council, 1981–84; Broadcasting, Film and Video panel, Arts Council, 1986–88;

Council, ICA, 1983–93. Dir, One World Broadcasting Trust, 1990–95. *Address:* Davies Cottage, Torriano Cottages, NW5 2TA.
*See also* M. J. A. Freeman.

**FREEMAN, David Charles;** Founder/Director of Opera Factory; freelance opera and theatre director; *b* 1 May 1952; *s* of Howard Wilfred Freeman and Ruth Adair Nott; *m* 1985, Marie Angel (marr. diss. 2012); one *s* one *d*. *Educ:* Sydney Univ., NSW (BA Hons). Opera Factory Sydney, 1973–76; Opera Factory Zürich, 1976–95: directed 20 prodns, appearing in 5, writing the text of 4; Opera Factory London, 1981–98: directed 21 prodns (8 televised by Channel Four), writing text of two; founded Opera Factory Films, 1991; Associate Artist, ENO, 1981–95: prodns include world première of The Mask of Orpheus, 1986; directed: Goethe's Faust, Pts I and II, Lyric, Hammersmith, 1988; (also adapted) Malory's Morte d'Arthur, Lyric, Hammersmith, 1990; The Winter's Tale, Shakespeare's Globe (opening prodn), 1997; Madam Butterfly, 1998 (and six revivals), Tosca, 1999, Carmen, Royal Albert Hall, 2002 (and four revivals); Carmen, O2 Centre, 2010 (first opera prodn); Magic Flute, Sydney Opera House, 2006; Gadaffi (world première), ENO, 2006; Sweeney Todd, RFH, 2007; Wozzeck, Brussels, 2008; Messiah, Royal Danish Opera, 2012, Frankfurt Opera, 2016; The Wonderful Adventures of Nils (musical), China, 2013 (Golden Lion award, 2014); The 8th Wonder, Sydney, 2016; Whiteley (world première), Opera Australia, 2019; opera prodns in New York, Houston, Paris, Germany and St Petersburg; has also worked in Senegal and India (Zangoora). Founder, Factory Edge, 2011. Chevalier de l'Ordre des Arts et des Lettres, France, 1985.

**FREEMAN, Prof. Ernest Michael,** PhD; FREng; Professor of Applied Electromagnetics, Imperial College of Science, Technology and Medicine, London University, 1980–2003, now Emeritus Professor of Electromagnetics; *b* 10 Nov. 1937; *s* of Ernest Robert Freeman and Agnes Maud Freeman; *m* 1987, Helen Anne Rigby. *Educ:* Colfe's Grammar Sch., Lewisham; King's Coll., London (BScEng; PhD 1964). Lectr, King's Coll., London, 1960–63 and 1966–70; Engrg Designer, AEI, Rugby (on secondment), 1959–65; Reader: Brighton Polytechnic, 1970–73; Imperial Coll. of Science and Technology, 1973–80. Chm., Infolytica Ltd, 1978–2008; Vice Pres., Infolytica Corp., 1978–2017. FREng (FEng 1987). *Publications:* papers in learned society jls on magnetics. *Recreations:* Anglo-Saxon period, pre-conquest churches, architecture, military and electrical engineering history, industrial archaeology. *Address:* Electrical and Electronic Engineering Department, Imperial College London, South Kensington Campus, SW7 2AZ. *E:* e.freeman@imperial.ac.uk.

**FREEMAN, George William;** MP (C) Mid Norfolk, since 2010; Minister of State, Department for Transport, since 2019; *b* Cambridge, 12 July 1967; *s* of late Arthur Freeman and of Joanna Stockbridge (*née* Philipson); *m* 1996, Eleanor Holmes (marr. diss. 2016); one *s* one *d*. *Educ:* Radley Coll., Oxon; Girton Coll., Cambridge (BA Geog. 1989; MA). Parly Officer, NFU, 1990–92; Founder, Local Identity Agency, 1992–96; Dir, Early Stage Ventures, Merlin Biosciences, 1997–2001; CEO, Amedis Pharmaceuticals, 2001–03; Man. Dir, 4D Biomedical, 2003–10. PPS to Minister of State, DECC, 2010–11; Parly Under-Sec. of State (Minister for Life Scis), BIS and DoH, 2014–16. Chm., All Party Parly Gp on Agricl Sci. and Technol., 2010–14; Govt Advr on Life Scis, 2011–14; Prime Ministerial Trade Envoy to Philippines, 2013–14. Chm., Prime Minister's Policy Bd, 2016–17. Chm., Conservative Policy Forum, 2016–. Mem. Bd, Gtr Cambridge Partnership, 2005–09. Trustee, Cambridge Union Soc., 2005–08. Chm., The Norfolk Way, 2007–11. Contested (C) Stevenage, 2005. *Recreations:* sailing, wildfowling. *Address:* House of Commons, SW1A 0AA. *T:* (020) 7219 1940. *E:* george.freeman.mp@parliament.uk. *Club:* Norfolk (Norwich).

**FREEMAN, Sir James (Robin),** 3rd Bt *cr* 1945; *b* 21 July 1955; *s* of Sir (John) Keith (Noel) Freeman, 2nd Bt and Patricia Denison (*née* Thomas); *S* father, 1981, but his name does not appear on the Official Roll of the Baronetage. *Heir:* none.

**FREEMAN, Jeane Tennent,** OBE 1996; Member (SNP) Carrick, Cumnock and Doon Valley, Scottish Parliament, since 2016; Cabinet Secretary for Health and Sport, since 2018; *b* Ayr, 28 Sept. 1953. *Educ:* Ayr Acad.; Glasgow Coll. of Technol. (MA Hons Politics and Sociol.). Pres., NUS Scotland; Gen. Sec., British Youth Council. Estabd Apex Scotland, 1987; Special Advr to First Minister of Scotland; estabd public affairs consultancy, 2005. Minister for Social Security, Scottish Parlt, 2016–18. Member: Judicial Appts Bd for Scotland; Parole Bd for Scotland; Bd, Scottish Police Authy. Chm. Bd, Golden Jubilee Foundn. *Address:* (office) 46–48 Glaisnock Street, Cumnock KA18 1BY. *T:* (01290) 425876. *E:* jeane.freeman.msp@parliament.scot.

**FREEMAN, Jennifer Margaret;** *see* Freeman, Lady.

**FREEMAN, Joan;** *see* Freeman, S. J.

**FREEMAN, John;** a Judge of the Upper Tribunal (Immigration and Asylum Chamber) (formerly a Vice-President, Immigration Appeal Tribunal, later a Senior Immigration Judge, Asylum and Immigration Tribunal), 2000–19; a Recorder, since 2003; *b* 13 July 1951; *s* of late E. A. Freeman, FRCS and Joan (*née* Horrell); *m* 1st, 1983, Alison Gwenllian Wornsnop (marr. diss. 1988); 2nd, 2015, Amanda Elaine Paul. *Educ:* Winchester Coll.; Corpus Christi Coll., Cambridge (MA); Univ. of Warwick (LLM). Practised at Bar, Midland and Oxford Circuit, 1976–83, 1986–89; Resident Magistrate, Registrar and Commissioner of High Court and Court of Appeal, actg Dir of Public Prosecutions, Solomon Islands, 1983–86; consultant, ODA and UNHCR, 1987–92; Immigration Appeal Adjudicator, 1989–90, 1991–2000. Part-time Legal Mem., Special Immigration Appeals Commn, 2001–19. *Recreation:* breeding Staffordshire bull terriers. *Address:* c/o Field House, 15–25 Bream's Buildings, EC4A 1DZ. *Club:* Royal Geographical Society.

**FREEMAN, Prof. Kenneth Charles,** AC 2017; PhD; FRS 1998; FAA; Duffield Professor, Research School of Astronomy and Astrophysics, since 2000 (Professor, Mount Stromlo and Siding Spring Observatories, 1987–2000), Institute of Advanced Studies, Australian National University; *b* 27 Aug. 1940; *s* of Herbert and Herta Freeman; *m* 1963, Margaret Leigh Cook; one *s* three *d*. *Educ:* Scotch Coll.; Univ. of Western Australia (BSc Hons Mathematics 1962); Trinity Coll., Cambridge (PhD 1965). FAA 1981. Res. Fellow, Trinity Coll., Cambridge, 1965–69; McDonald Postdoctoral Fellow in Astronomy, Univ. of Texas, 1966; Mount Stromlo and Siding Spring Observatories, Australian National University: Queen Elizabeth Fellow, 1967–70; Fellow, 1970–74; Sen. Fellow, 1974–81; Professorial Fellow, 1981–87. Sen. Scientist, Kapteyn Lab., Univ. of Groningen, 1976; Vis. Mem., IAS, Princeton, 1984, 1988; Distinguished Vis. Scientist, Space Telescope Science Inst., Baltimore, 1989; Oort Prof., Univ. of Leiden, 1994; Vis. Fellow, Merton Coll., Oxford, 1997; Tinsley Prof., Univ. of Texas, 2001; Blaauw Prof., Univ. of Groningen, 2003; de Vaucouleurs Lectr, Univ. of Texas, 2003; Henry Norris Russell Lectr, AAS, 2013; Foreign Associate, US Nat. Acad. of Scis, 2017. Chm., Nat. Cttee on Astronomy, Australian Acad. of Science, 1984–86 (Pawsey Medal, 1972). ARAS 2002. Hon. DSc WA, 1999. Heineman Prize, Amer. Inst. of Physics and Amer. Astronomical Soc., 1999; Citation Laureate Award, Thomson ISI, 2001; Johann Wempe Award, Astrophysical Inst. Potsdam, 2008; Prime Minister's Sci. Prize, Australia, 2012; Matthew Flinders Medal, Australian Acad. of Sci., 2013; Gruber Cosmology Prize, 2014; Dirac Medal, Univ. of NSW, 2016. *Publications:* (with G. McNamara) In Search of Dark Matter, 2006; (with D. Block) Shrouds of the

Night, 2008; more than 750 articles in learned astronomical jls. *Recreations:* bushwalking, birdwatching, classical music. *Address:* Mount Stromlo Observatory, Cotter Road, Weston Creek, ACT 2611, Australia. *T:* (2) 61250264. *E:* kcf@mso.anu.edu.au.

**FREEMAN, Dr Marie Joyce,** FFCM; Health Service Management Consultant, 1988–95; *b* 14 April 1934; *d* of Wilfrid George Croxson and Ada Mildred (*née* Chiles); *m* 1958, Samuel Anthony Freeman (decd); one *s*. *Educ:* Royal Free Hospital Sch. of Medicine (MB BS, DPH). Specialist in Community Medicine, Avon AHA, 1974; District MO, Southmead HA, 1982; Actg Regl MD, SW RHA, 1986–88. *Address:* Wingfield House, Darlington Place, Bath BA2 6BY. *T:* (01225) 466670; Hameau de la Lauze, 84570 Blauvac, Vaucluse, France.

**FREEMAN, Dr Matthew John Aylmer,** FRS 2006; FMedSci; Professor of Pathology and Head of Department, Sir William Dunn School of Pathology, University of Oxford, since 2013; *b* 16 June 1961; *s* of Rt Hon. John Freeman, MBE, PC and of Catherine Freeman, *qv*; *m* 1990, Rose Taylor; one *s* one *d*. *Educ:* King Alfred's Sch.; Pembroke Coll., Oxford (BA Hons); Imperial Coll., London (PhD 1987). Postdoctoral Fellow, Univ. of Calif, Berkeley, 1987–92; MRC Laboratory of Molecular Biology, Cambridge: Mem., Perm. Scientific Staff, 1992–2012; Jt Hd, 2007–08, Hd, 2008–12, Div. of Cell Biol. Chairman: British Scientists Abroad, 1990–92; British Soc. for Develtl Biology, 2004–09; Member: Exec., Campaign for Sci. and Engrg (formerly Save British Sci.), 1992–2012; Agric. and Envmt Biotechnol. Commn, 2000–05; Council, Royal Soc., 2009–11; Dir, Co. of Biologists, 2003– (Chm., 2015–). Ed., Develtl Biol., 2003–12. Mem., EMBO, 1999– (Gold Medal, 2001). FMedSci 2015. Hooke Medal, British Soc. for Cell Biology, 2003; Novartis Medal and Prize, Biochemical Soc., 2015. *Publications:* contrib. primary res. articles and reviews in specialist and gen. sci. jls. *Recreation:* sailing. *Address:* Sir William Dunn School of Pathology, University of Oxford, South Parks Road, Oxford OX1 3RE. *T:* (01865) 275500.

**FREEMAN, Prof. Michael David Alan,** FBA 2009; Professor of English Law, University College London, 1984–2011, now Emeritus; *b* London, 25 Nov. 1943; *s* of Raphael and Florence Freeman; *m* 1967, Vivien Ruth Brook; one *s* one *d*. *Educ:* Hasmonean Grammar Sch., Hendon; University Coll. London (LLB, LLM; Fellow 2000). Called to the Bar, Gray's Inn, 1968. Lectr, E London Coll. of Commerce, 1965–66; Asst Lectr, 1966–67, Lectr, 1967–69, Univ. of Leeds; Lectr, 1969–79, Reader, 1979–84, UCL. Vis. Hon. Prof. of Children's Rights, Univ. of Liverpool, 2016–; Hon. Res. Prof., QUB, 2016–. Editor: Current Legal Problems, 1992–2004; Internat. Jl Children's Rights, 1993–; Current Legal Issues, 1997–2012; Internat. Jl of Law in Context, 2005–13. *Publications:* The Legal Structure, 1974; The Rights and Wrongs of Children, 1983; The Moral Status of Children, 1997; Understanding Family Law, 2007; Introduction to Jurisprudence, 3rd edn 1972 to 9th edn 2014; Law and Childhood Studies, 2012; Law and Language, 2013; Law and Global Health, 2014; The Human Rights of Children, 2015; A Magna Carta for Children?, 2015; The Definition of a Child, 2017. *Recreations:* listening to the symphonies of Bruckner and the operas of Mozart, reading the plays of Ibsen and Brecht, watching first division county cricket, Jewish history. *Address:* Faculty of Laws, University College London, Bentham House, Endsleigh Gardens, WC1H 0EG. *T:* (020) 7679 1443. *E:* mdaf@bamps.com. *Club:* Middlesex CC.

**FREEMAN, Morgan Porterfield;** actor; *b* Memphis, 1 June 1937; *m* 1st, 1967, Jeanette Adair Bradshaw (marr. diss. 1979); two *c*; 2nd, 1984, Myrna Colley-Lee (marr. diss. 2010); two *c*. *Educ:* LA City Coll. USAF, 1955–59. *Stage* productions include: The Nigger Lovers (debut), 1967; Hello Dolly, NY, 1969; Coriolanus, Julius Caesar, NY Shakespeare Fest., 1979; Mother Courage and Her Children, 1980; Othello, All's Well That Ends Well, Dallas Shakespeare Fest., 1982; The Country Girl, NY, 2008; *films* include: Who Says I Can't Ride a Rainbow, 1971; Brubaker, 1980; Eyewitness, 1981; Harry & Son, 1984; Street Smart, 1987; Clean and Sober, 1988; Lean on Me, Johnny Handsome, Driving Miss Daisy (Golden Globe Award), Glory, 1989; Bonfire of the Vanities, Robin Hood: Prince of Thieves, 1991; Unforgiven, 1992; The Shawshank Redemption, Outbreak, Se7en, 1995; Chain Reaction, 1996, Moll Flanders, Amistad, 1997; Deep Impact, 1998; Nurse Betty, 2000; Under Suspicion, Along Came a Spider, 2001; High Crimes, The Sum of All Fears, 2002; Dreamcatcher, Bruce Almighty, 2003; Levity, The Big Bounce, 2004, Million Dollar Baby (Screen Actors' Guild Award, Academy Award for Best Supporting Actor), Batman Begins, War of the Worlds (narrator), Edison, March of the Penguins (narrator), 2005; An Unfinished Life, Lucky Number Slevin, 2006; Gone Baby Gone, The Bucket List, Wanted, The Dark Knight, 2008; Thick as Thieves, 2009; Invictus, Red, 2010; The Dark Knight Rises, 2012; Oblivion, Olympus Has Fallen, Now You See Me, 2013; Transcendence, Lucy, 2014; Ted 2, Ruth & Alex, 2015; Ben-Hur, 2016; Going in Style, 2017; The Nutcracker and the Four Realms, 2018; Angel Has Fallen, 2019; *television* includes: The Electric Company, 1971–77; Death of a Prophet, 1981; Ryan's Hope, 1981; Another World, 1982–84; The Atlanta Child Murders, 1985; The Civil War, 1990; Freedom: a history of Us, 2003; Slavery and the Making of America (narrator), 2005. *Address:* Creative Artists Agency, 2000 Avenue of the Stars, Los Angeles, CA 90067, USA.

**FREEMAN, Paul Illife,** CB 1992; PhD; Controller and Chief Executive of HM Stationery Office, and the Queen's Printer of Acts of Parliament, 1989–95; *b* 11 July 1935; *s* of late John Percy Freeman and Hilda Freeman; *m* 1959, Enid Ivy May Freeman; one *s* one *d*. *Educ:* Victoria University of Manchester (BSc (Hons) Chemistry, PhD). Post Doctoral Fellow, Nat. Research Council of Canada, 1959–61; Research Scientist, Dupont De Nemours Co. Ltd, Wilmington, Del, USA, 1961–64; Nat. Physical Laboratory: Sen. Scientific Officer, 1964–70; Principal Scientific Officer, 1970–74; Exec. Officer, Research Requirements Bds, DoI, 1973–77; Director: Computer Aided Design Centre, 1977–83; National Engrg Lab., 1980–83; Central Computer and Telecommunications Agency, HM Treasury, 1983–88. Member: CS Coll. Adv. Council, 1983–88; Bd, NCC, 1983–88; Bd, DVLA, 1990–92; Council, UEA, 1994–2003. Vis. Prof. Univ. of Strathclyde, 1981–86. CCMI (CIMgt 1995). *Publications:* scientific papers. *Recreations:* fishing, reading, walking, gardening.

**FREEMAN, Peter David Mark,** CBE 2001; Principal Finance Officer, Department for International Development, 2000–01; *b* 8 Dec. 1947; *s* of Dr Victor Freeman and Ethel (*née* Halpern); *m* 1980, Anne Tyndale; two *d*. *Educ:* Merton Coll., Oxford (BA Hons); Univ. of Toronto (MA). Asst Private Sec. to Minister for Overseas Develt, 1973–75; Office of UK Exec. Dir, World Bank, 1975–78; British High Commn, Zimbabwe, 1980–83; Overseas Development Administration, then Department for International Development: Head: EC Dept, 1984–88; Central and Southern Africa Dept, 1988–90; Aid Policy Dept, 1990–91; Internat. Div., 1991–93; Personnel, Orgn and Services Div., 1993–96; Dir, Africa Div., 1996–99. Non-executive Director: Shared Interest Soc. Ltd, 2003–13; Brighton Housing Trust, 2012–. Mem., Audit Cttee, Sightsavers Internat., 2001–09. Trustee: Internat. HIV/AIDS Alliance, 2002–11; Shared Interest Foundn, 2005–13; IDS, 2006–13; Brighton Peace and Envmt Centre, 2010–12. Governor: Stanford Jun. Sch., Brighton, 1988–2014 (Chm., 1992–96); Dorothy Stringer High Sch., Brighton, 1996–99; Brighton, Hove and Sussex Sixth Form Coll., 2001–18 (Chm., 2005–18); Coombe Road Primary Sch., Brighton, 2014– (Chm., 2018–); Chm., Brighton and Hove Schs Forum, 2003–. *Address:* 7 Windlesham Road, Brighton BN1 3AG.

**FREEMAN, Peter John,** CBE 2010; Chairman, Competition Appeal Tribunal, since 2013 (Member, 2011–13); *b* 2 Oct. 1948; *s* of Comdr John Kenneth Herbert Freeman, LVO, RN retd and Jean Forbes Freeman (*née* Irving); *m* 1972, Elizabeth Mary Rogers; two *s* two *d*. *Educ:* King Edward's Sch., Bath; Kingswood Sch., Bath; Goethe Inst., Berlin; Trinity Coll., Cambridge (Exhibnr; MA); Univ. Libre de Bruxelles (Licence Spéciale en Droit Européen). Called to the Bar, Middle Temple, 1972; admitted solicitor, 1977; Simmons & Simmons: asst, 1973; Partner, 1978–2003; Hd, EC and Competition Gp, 1987–2003; Managing Partner, Commercial and Trade Law Dept, 1994–99. Sen. Consultant, Cleary Gottlieb Steen & Hamilton LLP, 2011–13. Mem., 2003–11, Dep. Chm., 2003–05, Chm., 2006–11, Competition Commn; Member: Competition Service Bd, 2017–; Bd, Single Source Regulations Office, 2017–. Chm., Regulatory Policy Inst., Oxford, 1998–2007. Jt Gen. Ed., Butterworth's Competition Law, 1991–2005. Gov., Kingswood Sch., 2014–. Mem. Sci. Bd, Concorrência e Regulação, Lisbon, 2010–. Hon. QC 2010. *Publications:* (with R. Whish) A Guide to the Competition Act 1998, 1999; articles on competition law. *Recreations:* studying naval history, painting in oils, playing the piano. *Address:* Competition Appeal Tribunal, Victoria House, Bloomsbury Place, WC1A 2EB. *E:* Peter.Freeman@catribunal.org.uk. *Clubs:* Oxford and Cambridge, Reform.

**FREEMAN, Prof. Raymond,** MA, DPhil, DSc (Oxon); FRS 1979; John Humphrey Plummer Professor of Magnetic Resonance, University of Cambridge, 1987–99, now Emeritus; Fellow of Jesus College, Cambridge, since 1987; *b* 6 Jan. 1932; *s* of late Albert and Hilda Frances Freeman; *m* 1958, Anne-Marie Périnet-Marquet; two *s* three *d*. *Educ:* Nottingham High Sch. (scholar); Lincoln Coll., Oxford (open scholar). Ingénieur, Centre d'Etudes Nucléaires de Saclay, Commissariat à l'Energie Atomique, France, 1957–59; Sen. Scientific Officer, Nat. Phys. Lab., Teddington, Middx, 1959–63; Man., Nuclear Magnetic Resonance Research, Varian Associates, Palo Alto, Calif, 1963–73; Lectr in Physical Chemistry, 1973–82, Aldrichian Praelector in Chemistry, 1982–87, and Fellow, Magdalen Coll., 1973–87, Oxford Univ. Fellow, Internat. Soc. of Magnetic Resonance, 2008. Hon. DSc Durham, 1988. Chem. Soc. Award in Theoretical Chem. and Spectroscopy, 1978; Leverhulme Medal, Royal Soc., 1990; Longstaff Medal, RSC, 1999; Queen's Medal, Royal Soc., 2002; Günther Laukien Prize, Experimental NMR Conf., 2006; Russell Varian Prize, Varian Inc., 2012. *Publications:* A Handbook of Nuclear Magnetic Resonance, 1987; Spin Choreography: basic steps in high resolution NMR, 1997; Magnetic Resonance in Chemistry and Medicine, 2003; articles on nuclear magnetic resonance spectroscopy in various scientific journals. *Recreations:* swimming, traditional jazz. *Address:* Jesus College, Cambridge CB5 8BL.

**FREEMAN, Rt Rev. Robert John;** Bishop Suffragan of Penrith, 2011–18; Honorary Assistant Bishop, Diocese of Leicester, since 2018; *b* 26 Oct. 1952; *s* of Ralph and Constance Freeman; *m* 1974, Christine Weight; three *d*. *Educ:* Durham Univ. (BSc Psychol. 1974); Fitzwilliam Coll., Cambridge (MA Theol. 1976). Ordained deacon, 1977, priest, 1978; Asst Curate, Blackpool Parish Ch., 1977–81; Team Vicar, Chigwell (St Winifred), 1981–85; Vicar, Ch of the Martyrs, Leicester, 1985–99; Nat. Evangelism Advr, Archbishops' Council, 1999–2003; Archdeacon of Halifax, 2003–11. RD, Christianity South (Leicester), 1994–98; Hon. Canon, Leicester Cathedral, 1994–2003. Dir and Chm., rejesus.co.uk, 2001–16; Chm. and Trustee, Christian Enquiry Agency, 2006–11; Trustee, Simeon's and Hyndman's Trustees, 2007–10; Dir, Active Faith Communities, 2005–10. Mem., Churches Regional Commn Yorks and Humberside, 2004–10. *Publications:* (jtly) 20 from 10: insights from the Decade of Evangelism, 2000; (ed) Mission-shaped Church, 2004. *Recreations:* Motown, electric blues and rock, puddings, computer games, walking, adventure and detective novels. *Address:* 40 Eastfield Road, Leicester LE3 6FE. *E:* frmnfrmn@gmail.com.

**FREEMAN, Dr (Sally) Joan,** PhD; CPsychol, FBPsS; private psychology practice, London, since 1989; Visiting Professor, School of Lifelong Learning and Education, Middlesex University, since 1992; author; *b* 17 June 1935; *d* of late Phillip Casket and Rebecca (*née* Goldman); *m* 1957, Hugh Lionel Freeman (d 2011); three *s* one *d*. *Educ:* Broughton High Sch.; Univ. of Manchester (BSc, PhD 1980, MEd, DipEdGuidance). FBPsS 1985; CPsychol 1988; FCP 1990. Sen. Lectr in Applied Psychol., Preston Poly., 1975–81; Hon. Tutor, Dept of Educn, Univ. of Manchester, 1975–89; Hon. Lectr, Inst. of Educn, Univ. of London, 1988–94. Ed., High Ability Studies, 1995–98. Dir, Gulbenkian Res. Project on Gifted Children, 1973–88. Founder Pres., European Council for High Ability, 1987–92. Mem., various cttees and projects on the educn of children of high ability, incl. Adv. Bd on Exceptionally Able Pupils, SCAA, 1994–, and Govt Adv. Gp, Gifted and Talented Children, 1998–. Chair and Founder, Tower Educn Gp (UK), experts on gifts and talents, 2007–; consultant and contributor, Channel 4 TV series, Child Genius, 2006. Vis appts, scholarships and consultancies, Italy, Bulgaria, Canada, SA, Hong Kong and Australia; Executive: Eur. Talent Support Centres, Budapest, 2013–; Hungarian Templeton Prog., 2015–17. College of Preceptors, now College of Teachers: Member: Bd of Examnrs, 1987–; Council, 1995–; Exec. Cttee, 1999–; Sen. Vice-Pres., 2002–; Chm., Publications Bd, 1998–; British Psychological Society: Mem., Nat. Council, 1975–86; Chm., Northern Br., 1978–86; Mem., Standing Press Cttee, 1980–85; Lifetime Achievement Award, 2007. Mem., Strategic Thinking Forum, Centre for British Teachers. Mem., Fawcett Soc., 1984–. Patron, Nat. Assoc. for Able Children in Educn, 2006–. Hon. FCollT 2006. European Talent Networking Award, Eur. Council for High Ability, 2014; Lifetime Achievement Award, Internat. Mensa, 2015. *Publications:* Human Biology and Hygiene, 1968, 2nd edn 1981; In and Out of School: an introduction to applied psychology in education, 1975 (trans. Portuguese, Hebrew and Spanish); Gifted Children: their identification and development in a social context, 1979; Clever Children: a parents' guide, 1983 (trans. German, Finnish and Thai); (ed) The Psychology of Gifted Children: perspectives on development and education, 1985 (trans. Spanish); Gifted Children Growing Up, 1991; Bright as a Button: how to encourage your children's talents 0–5 years, 1991 (trans. Indonesian); Quality Basic Education: the development of competence, 1992 (trans. French); (with S. Ojanen) The Attitudes and Experiences of Headteachers, Classteachers and Highly Able Pupils Towards the Education of the Highly Able in Finland and Britain, 1994; (ed jtly) Actualising Talent: a lifelong challenge, 1995; Highly Able Girls and Boys, 1996; How to Raise a Bright Child, 1996 (trans. Russian and Chinese); Educating the Very Able: current international research, 1998 (trans. Thai); International Out-of-school Education for the Gifted and Talented, 1998; (with Z. C. Guenther) Educando os Mais Capazes: idéias e ações comprovadas, 2000; Gifted Children Grown Up, 2001; (with J. Fořtiková) Volnočasové aktivity: pro nadané a talentované u nás a ve světě, 2009; Gifted Lives: what happens when gifted children grow up, 2010; numerous academic papers and chapters in books; contrib. numerous articles and book reviews on child develt, psychol. and educn for both professional and lay jls. *Recreations:* photography, theatre, travel. *Address:* 21 Montagu Square, W1H 2LF. *T:* (020) 7486 2604. *E:* joan@joanfreeman.com. *W:* www.joanfreeman.com.

**FREEMAN, Sarah Anne;** *see* Barker, S. A.

**FREEMAN-ATTWOOD, Prof. Jonathan,** CBE 2018; Principal, Royal Academy of Music, since 2008 (Vice-Principal, 1995–2008); Professor, University of London, since 2001; *b* Woking, 4 Nov. 1961; *s* of late Harold Warren Freeman-Attwood and of Marigold Diana Sneyd Freeman-Attwood (*née* Philips); *m* 1990, Henrietta Paula Christian Parham; one *s* one *d*. *Educ:* Univ. of Toronto (BMus Hons); Christ Church, Oxford (MPhil). Royal

Academy of Music: GRSM Tutor, 1990–91; Associate Dean, 1991–92, Dean, 1992–95, of Undergraduate Studies; Dir of Studies, 1995–96. Vis. Prof., KCL, 2007–; Dist. Vis. Prof., Tokyo Univ. of the Arts, 2018–. Pres., RAM Club, 2006–07. Critic, Gramophone, 1992–; freelance writer mainly on 18th century music, esp. Bach, performance traditions and recordings; regular contrib. to Record Review (formerly CD Review), BBC Radio 3, 1992–. Trumpet player for many ensembles; solo recordings: Albinoni for Trumpet, 1993; Bach Connections, 1999; The Trumpets that Time Forgot, 2003; La Trompette Retrouvée, 2007; Trumpet Masque, 2008; Romantic Trumpet Sonatas, 2011; A Bach Notebook for Trumpet, 2013; (world premiere) Lydia's Vocalises, by Fauré, 2014; The Neoclassical Trumpet, 2015; An English Sett for Trumpet, 2018. Producer of over 250 commercial recordings (7 Gramophone Awards incl. Record of the Year, 2010 and several Diapason d'Ors). Member: Cheltenham Fest. Adv. Cttee, 2011–; Adv. Council, Acad. of Ancient Music, 2016–. Trustee: Young Classical Artists (formerly Young Concert Artists) Trust, 2008–18; Countess of Munster Trust, 2008–; Winifred Christie Trust, 2008–; Associated Bd of Royal Schs of Music, 2008–; Harriet Cohen Trust, 2008–; Lucille Graham Trust, 2008–; Mendelssohn and Boise Foundn, 2008–; British Library Saga Trust, 2008–; Christ Church Oxford Music Trust, 2011–; Univ. of London, 2011–15; Garsington Opera, 2012– (Chair, Artistic Adv. Cttee, 2012–); Artistic Advr, Nat. Orch. For All, 2014–; Vice Pres., Nat. Youth Wind Orch. of GB, 2013–. Patron: London Youth Choirs, 2012; Cavatina Chamber Music Trust, 2013; Hon. Patron, Lionel Tertis Fest. and Competition, 2008. FRNCM 2013; FRCM 2017. Hon. RAM 1997 (Hon. ARAM 1993); Hon. FKC 2009. *Publications:* (contrib.) The New Grove Dictionary of Music and Musicians, 2nd edn 2000; (contrib.) The Cambridge Companion to Recorded Music, 2009. *Recreations:* lots of Bach, watching cricket, French wine châteaux from a distance, Liverpool FC, reading, walking. *Address:* c/o Royal Academy of Music, Marylebone Road, NW1 5HT. *T:* (020) 7873 7377. *E:* j.freeman-attwood@ram.ac.uk.

**FREEMAN-GRENVILLE,** family name of **Lady Kinloss**.

**FREEMANTLE, Andrew,** CBE (civ.) 2007 (MBE (mil.) 1982); Chief Executive, Royal National Lifeboat Institution, 1999–2009; *b* 26 Sept. 1944; *s* of Lt-Col Arthur Freemantle and Peggy Frances Freemantle (*née* Wood); *m* 1972, Patricia Mary Thompson; four *d*. *Educ:* Framlingham Coll.; RMCS; RCDS; Sheffield Univ. Commnd Royal Hampshire Regt, 1965; Australian Army, 1969–72; Royal Hampshire Regt, 1972–76; sc, Camberley, 1978; Directing Staff, Staff Coll. Camberley, 1983–84; CO 1st Bn Royal Hampshire Regt, 1985–87 (despatches 1987); Brigadier 1987; Comd 19 Infantry Bde, 1987–89; Mem., RCDS, 1990. Chief Exec., Scottish Ambulance Service NHS Trust, 1991–99; Gov., SW Ambulance Service NHS Trust, 2018–. Trustee: ABF The Soldiers' Charity, 2008–16; Royal Commonwealth Ex-Services League, 2016–; Trustee and Council Mem. for Australia, Royal Commonwealth Ex-Services League, 2016–. Freeman, City of London, 2001. CCMI 2003. Hon. DBA Bournemouth, 2007. Officier, Ordre du Mérite Maritime (France), 2010. *Recreations:* cycling, cooking.

**FREEMONT, Prof. Anthony John,** MD; FRCP, FRCPath; Professor of Osteoarticular Pathology, since 1993, Procter Professor of Pathology, since 2010, and Director, Manchester Molecular Pathology Innovation Centre, since 2015, University of Manchester; Consultant, Manchester University NHS Foundation Trust (formerly Central Manchester University Hospitals NHS Foundation Trust), since 1988; *b* Plymouth, 27 March 1953; *s* of Walter Freemont and Sarah Freemont; *m* 1st, 1976, Susan Murray (marr. diss. 2006); one *d*; 2nd, 2008, Cordelia Warr. *Educ:* Latymer Upper Sch., Hammersmith; St Thomas' Hosp. Med. Sch., London (BSc 1973; MB BS 1976; MD 1984). FRCP 1995; FRCPath 1996. ARC Lectr, 1983–88, Sen. Lectr, 1988–93, in Osteoarticular Pathology, Univ. of Manchester. *Publications:* Atlas of Synovial Fluid Cytopathology (with J. Denton), 1991 (Glaxo Med. Atlas Book Award, 1992); 46 book chapters; over 300 articles in jls on aspects of bone, joint and soft tissue pathology. *Recreations:* church bell ringing, collecting brass threepenny pieces. *Address:* Firwood, Turners Lane, Llynclys, Shropshire SY10 8LL. *T:* (01691) 831233. *E:* tonyfreemont@hotmail.com.

**FREER, Maj. Gen. Adrian Robert,** OBE 1994; Director, Civil Nuclear Security, Office for Nuclear Regulation (formerly Health and Safety Executive), 2011–17 (Assistant Director, 2008–11); *b* 17 April 1952; *s* of Air Chief Marshal Sir Robert William George Freer, GBE, KCB and of Margaret Freer; *m* 1983, Caroline Mary Henderson; two *d*. *Educ:* Trent Coll., Long Eaton, Notts. Commnd Parachute Regt, 1972; served 1 Para, 1972–80; Instructor, NCO Tactical Wing, Brecon, 1980–81; served 3 Para, 1982–83; Army Staff Coll., 1984; COS, 48 Gurkha Bde, 1985–86; Co. Comd 3 Para, 1987–88; Chief Instructor, RMA Sandhurst, 1989–90; Directing Staff, Army Staff Coll., 1990–91; CO 2 Para, 1992–94; Comdt, Inf. Trng Centre, 1994–97; Comd 5 Airborne Bde, 1997–99; rcds 2000; ACOS, J7 PJHQ, 2001–02; Comd Internat. Military Adv. Team, Sierra Leone, 2003–04; Co-ordinator, Kosovo Protection Corps, 2004–05. Chm., Airborne Assault Mus., 2008–. *Recreations:* all sports, particularly golf! *E:* adrianfreer@btinternet.com. *Clubs:* MCC, Army and Navy; Blairgowrie Golf, Royal Perth Golfing Society and County and City.

**FREER, Maj. Gen. Ian Lennox,** CB 1994; CBE 1988 (OBE 1985); Principal, Lennox Freer and Associates Pty Ltd, since 1997; Chairman, Ocean Software Pty Ltd, since 2009 (Director, 2004–16; Managing Director, 2004–09); *b* 18 May 1941; *s* of late Lt-Col George Freer, OBE and Elizabeth (*née* Tallo), Edinburgh; *m* 1970, Karla Thwaites; one *s* two *d*. *Educ:* George Watson's Coll., Edinburgh; RMA Sandhurst; Royal College of Defence Studies. Commnd Staffordshire Regt (Prince of Wales's), 1961; served UK, Kenya, Germany, Gulf States, Belize, Gibraltar; Staff Capt. to QMG, 1972–73; MA to COS, BAOR, 1975–77; SO1, Instr Staff Coll., 1980–81; CO 1st Bn, Staffords Regt, 1982–84; Div. Col, Staff Coll., 1985; Comdr, 39 Inf. Bde (NI), 1986–87; Chief, BRIXMIS (Berlin), 1989–91; Comdr, Land Forces, NI, 1991–94; GOC Wales and Western Dist, later 5th Div., 1994–96. Col, Staffordshire Regt, 1990–94; Col Comdt, POW Div., 1993–96. Dir, Woodleigh Sch., Vic, 1999–2012; Mem. Council, RUSI, Vic, 1999–. Mem., Pacific Inst. of Aust. *Recreations:* sailing, gardening. *Club:* Melbourne.

**FREER, Michael Whitney;** MP (C) Finchley and Golders Green, since 2010; a Lord Commissioner of HM Treasury (Government Whip), since 2018; *b* Manchester, 29 May 1960; *s* of Herbert and Marian Freer; civil partnership 2007, *m* 2015, Angelo Crolla. *Educ:* Chadderton Grammar Sch., Manchester; St Aidan's Sch., Carlisle. Mem. (C) Barnet LBC, 1990–94 and 2001–10 (Leader, 2006–09). Exec. Mem., London Councils, 2008–09. Non-exec. Dir, London Develt Agency, 2008–10. Contested (C) Harrow West, 2005. an Asst Govt Whip, 2017–18. *Recreations:* cycling, keep fit, learning French. *Address:* House of Commons, SW1A 0AA. *T:* (020) 7219 7071. *E:* mike.freer.mp@parliament.uk.

**FREER, Dame Yve Helen Elaine;** *see* Buckland, Dame Y. H. E.

**FREETH, Peter Stewart,** RA 1991 (ARA 1990); RE 1991 (ARE 1987); Tutor, Etching, Royal Academy Schools, since 1966; *b* 15 April 1938; *s* of Alfred William Freeth and Olive Walker; *m* 1967, Mariolina Meliadó; two *s*. *Educ:* King Edward's Grammar School, Aston, Birmingham; Slade School, London (Dip Fine Art). Rome Scholar, Engraving, British Sch., Rome, 1960–62; teacher of Printmaking, Camden Inst., 1979–2007. One man shows: Christopher Mendez Gall., London, 1987–89; Friends' Room, RA, 1991; S Maria a Gradillo, Ravello, Italy, 1997; Word Play, RA, 2001; Christ Church Coll. Gall., Oxford, 2006; North House Gall., Manningtree, 2006; My Affair with Resin, Tennant Room, RA, 2008–09; Previous Conviction, Highgate Literary and Scientific Soc., 2013; represented in collections: British Museum; V&A; Fitzwilliam Mus., Cambridge; Arts Council; Metropolitan Mus., NY; Nat. Gall., Washington; Hunterian Mus., Glasgow; Ruth Borchard, Portrait Collection; Ashmolean Mus., Oxford; Pallant House, Chichester. Mem., Royal Soc. of Painter Printmakers. *Recreations:* music, books, yet more work. *Address:* 83 Muswell Hill Road, N10 3HT.

**FREI, Matt;** Europe Editor and Presenter, Channel 4 News (Chief Washington Correspondent, 2011–13); *b* 26 Nov. 1963; *s* of Peter and Anita Frei; *m* 1996, Penny Quested; one *s* three *d*. *Educ:* Westminster Sch.; St Peter's Coll., Oxford (MA Hist. and Spanish). Joined BBC, 1988; BBC Television: Southern Europe Corresp., 1991–96; Asia Corresp., 1996–2002; Chief Washington Corresp., 2002–11. Writer and presenter, television: Berlin (series), 2009; The Mad World of Donald Trump, 2016; Meet the Trumps, 2017; Trump and Russia: Sex, Spies and Scandal, 2017; Obama: The President Who Inspired the World, 2018; radio presenter, Saturday Morning Show, LBC, 2016–. RTS Award, 2000; Peabody Award, 2010; DuPont Award, 2011; RTS Journalist of the Year, 2015, 2017. *Publications:* Italy: the unfinished revolution, 1996, 2nd edn 1998; Only in America, 2008. *Recreation:* painting.

**FREIER, Most Rev. Philip Leslie;** *see* Melbourne, Archbishop of.

**FREMANTLE,** family name of **Baron Cottesloe**.

**FRENCH,** family name of **Baron De Freyne**.

**FRENCH, David;** Partner, Hilliard French Associates, executive coaching, since 2014; *b* 20 June 1947; *s* of late Captain Godfrey Alexander French, CBE, RN, and Margaret Annis French; *m* 1974, Sarah Anne, *d* of late Rt Rev. (Henry) David Halsey; four *s*. *Educ:* Sherborne Sch.; Durham Univ. (BA). Henley Gen. Mgt Course, 1984; Cabinet Office Top Mgt Prog., 1995. MCIPD. Nat. Council of Social Service, 1971–74; Hd of Social Services Dept, RNID, 1974–78; Dir of Services, C of E Children's Soc., 1978–87; Dir, Nat. Marriage Guidance Council, then Relate, 1987–95; consultant on family policy, 1995–97; Dir Gen., subseq. Chief Exec., Commonwealth Inst., 1997–2002; Chief Exec., Westminster Foundn for Democracy, 2003–09; Sen. Advr, European Partnership for Democracy, 2010–11; Associate Dir, Transform, 2011–13. Exec. Dir, 2011–14, Advr, 2011–17, Alexandria Trust. Chairman: London Corrymeela Venture, 1973–76; St Albans Internat. Organ Fest., 1985–87; Twenty First Century Foundn, 1996–2001; Y Care International, 2016–. Trustee: Charity Appts, 1984–91; British Empire and Commonwealth Mus., 1999–2003; The Round Table: Commonwealth Jl of Internat. Affairs, 2001–08; Nekton Foundn, 2015–17. Mem. Governing Council, Family Policy Studies Centre, 1989–2001. Mem., St Albans Cathedral Council, 1996–99. Liveryman, Glaziers' Co., 1990–2017. MRSocMed 1988, FRSocMed 2008 (Life Fellow, 2009). FRSA 1993. *Recreation:* challenging projects. *Address:* Molly Bawn, Stoke Abbott, Beaminster, Dorset DT8 3JT. *T:* (01308) 868241. *E:* david@conveners.eu.

**FRENCH, Air Vice-Marshal David Rowthorne,** CB 1993; MBE 1976; engineering consultant, 1994–2008; *b* 11 Dec. 1937; *s* of Norman Arthur French and late Edna Mary French (*née* Rowthorne); *m* 1st, 1963, Veronica Margaret Mead (marr. diss. 1982); two *s* one *d*; 2nd, 1984, Philippa Anne Pym, *d* of Sir Alexander Ross; one *s* one *d*. *Educ:* Gosport County Grammar Sch.; RAF Technical Coll., Henlow. CEng, MRAeS 1969. Commnd Engr Br., RAF, 1960; various engrg appts, 1960–69; Sen. Engrg Officer, No 14 Sqn, RAF Bruggen, 1970–71; OC Airframe Systems Sqn, CSDE, RAF Swanton Morley, 1971–72; RAF Staff Coll., Bracknell, 1973; Sen. Engrg Officer, No 54 Sqn, RAF Coltishall, 1974–76; OC Engrg Wg, RAF Lossiemouth, 1976–79; Air Warfare Coll., RAF Cranwell, 1979; SO for Offensive Support Aircraft, HQ Strike Comd, 1980; Dep. Dir of Engrg Policy, MoD, 1981–82; Comd Mech. Engr, HQ RAF Germany, 1983–86; Dir of Policy, Directorate Gen., Defence Quality Assurance, MoD (PE), 1986–87; AO Wales and Stn Comdr, RAF St Athan, 1988–90; Comd Mech. Engr, HQ Strike Comd, 1990–91; AO Maintenance and Chief Exec. Maintenance Gp Defence Support Agency, RAF Support Comd, 1991–94, retd. Mem. (C), Broadland DC, 2007–11. Chairman: RAF Germany Golf, 1983–86; RAF Support Comd Golf, 1988–90; Capt., RAF Germany Golf Club, 1985–86. *Recreations:* golf, ski-ing, gardening, wine. *Address:* Milestone Piece, 109 Yarmouth Road, Blofield, Norwich, Norfolk NR13 4LQ. *Clubs:* Royal Air Force; Royal Norwich Golf.

**FRENCH, Douglas Charles;** Chairman, Westminster and City Programmes, since 1997; *b* London, 20 March 1944; *s* of late Frederick Emil French and Charlotte Vera French; *m* 1978, Sue, *y d* of late Philip Arthur Phillips; two *s* one *d*. *Educ:* Glyn Grammar Sch., Epsom; St Catharine's Coll., Cambridge (MA). Called to the Bar, Inner Temple. Exec., then Dir, P. W. Merkle Ltd, 1966–87. Asst to Rt Hon. Sir Geoffrey Howe, Shadow Chancellor, 1976–79; Special Advr to Chancellor of the Exchequer, 1981–83. Contested (C) Sheffield, Attercliffe, 1979; MP (C) Gloucester, 1987–97; contested (C) same seat, 1997. PPS to Minister of State, FCO, 1988–89, ODA, 1989–90, MAFF, 1992–93, DoE, 1993–94, to Sec. of State for the Envmt, 1994–97. Chm., All Party Cttee on Building Socs, 1996–97. Initiated Building Socs (Jt Account Holders) Act 1995, and Building Socs (Distributions) Act 1997. Chm., Bow Gp, 1978–79. Pres., Gloucester Conservative Club, 1989–97. Pres., Glyn Old Boys' Assoc., 2005–11. Gov., Glyn Sch., Epsom, 2000–15 (Vice-Chm., 2003–05); Chm., 2006–09). *Publications:* articles and reviews. *Recreations:* gardening, renovating period houses, ski-ing, squash, dragon boat racing. *Address:* 231 Kennington Lane, SE11 5QU. *Club:* Royal Automobile.

**FRENCH, Air Chief Marshal Sir Joseph Charles, (Sir Joe),** KCB 2003; CBE 1991 (OBE); FRAeS; defence and security consultant, since 2007; Commander-in-Chief Strike Command, 2006–07; Air Aide-de-Camp to the Queen, 2006–07; *b* 15 July 1949. Joined RAF, 1967; rcds; psa; postings in ME, Germany, Hong Kong and UK; ADC to CDS; Central Trials and Tactics Orgn; OC, 7 Sqdn, RAF Odiham, 1984–86; PSO to AOC-in-C Strike Comd, 1986–88; Hd, RAF Presentation Team, RAF Staff Coll., Bracknell, 1988; Station Comdr, RAF Odiham, 1989–91; Dir, Air Force Staff Duties, MoD, 1992–95; ACDS (Policy), 1995–97; Dir Gen. Intelligence and Geographic Resources, MoD, 1997–2001; Chief of Defence Intelligence, 2001–03; Air Mem. for Personnel and C-in-C PTC, 2003–06. Comr, CWGC, 2008–16 (Vice-Chm., 2013–16). Trustee, Nuffield Trust for the Forces of the Crown, 2009–16; Vice-Patron, Blind Veterans UK (formerly St Dunstan's), 2009–19.

**FRENCH, Ven. Judith Karen;** Archdeacon of Dorchester, since 2014; *b* Portsmouth, 18 Nov. 1960. *Educ:* St David's Coll., Lampeter (BA 1989); St Stephen's House, Oxford; Sarum Coll., Salisbury (MA Univ. of Wales, Lampeter 2008). Ordained deacon, 1991, priest, 1994; Parish Deacon, All Saints, Botley, 1991–94; Asst Curate, St Mark, Bilton, 1994–97; Vicar, St Mary the Virgin, Charlbury, 1997–2014; Area Dean, Chipping Norton, 2007–12; Hon. Canon, Christ Church, 2012–14. *Address:* 11 Broad Field Road, Yarnton, Kidlington OX5 1UL.

**FRENCH, Lady Lucy Kathleen Olivia,** OBE 2019; Founder and Chief Executive Officer, Never Such Innocence, since 2013; *b* London, 11 April 1975; *d* of 3rd Earl of Ypres and Deborah (*née* Roberts); *m* 2011, Simon Barry; two *d*. *Educ:* Queen's Coll., Harley St, London. Man. Dir, Ladybird PR, 1999–2004; Develt Manager, Hampstead Th., 2004–09; Dir, Develt, Open Air Th., Regent's Park, 2009–11; Dir, St James Th., London, 2012–16. Mem. Bd, Victoriabid, 2012–16; Trustee: Churches Conservation Trust, 2013–19; Commonwealth War Graves Foundn, 2018–. *Publications:* (ed) Never Such Innocence: the centenary of the First World War: children's responses through poetry, art and song, 2018. *Recreation:* exploring historic/ancient churches and buildings. *E:* lf@neversuchinnocence.com. *Club:* Western (Glasgow).

**FRENCH, Hon. Robert Shenton,** AC 2010; Chief Justice of Australia, 2008–17; non-permanent Justice, Hong Kong Court of Final Appeal, since 2017; International Judge, Singapore International Commercial Court, since 2018; *b* Perth, WA, 19 March 1947; *s* of Robert William Shenton French and Kathleen Carina French; *m* 1976, Valerie Jean Lumsden; three *s*. *Educ:* St Louis Sch.; Univ. of Western Australia (BSc, LLB). Admitted barrister and solicitor, WA, 1972; Chm., Aboriginal Legal Service of WA, 1973–75; commenced practice at Ind. Bar, 1983; Judge, Federal Court, 1986–2008; pt-time non-resident Mem., Supreme Court of Fiji, 2003–08; Addnl Judge, Supreme Court, ACT, 2004–08. Associate Mem., Trade Practices Commn, 1983–86; Dep. Chm., 1983–86, Chm., 1986, Town Planning Appeals Tribunal, WA; Member: Law Reform Commn, WA, 1986; (pt-time), Australian Law Reform Commn, 2006–08; Pres., Nat. Native Tribunal, 1994–98; Dep. Pres., Australian Competition Tribunal, 2005–08. Hon. Prof., ANU, 2016–; Adjunct Prof., 2016–, Chancellor, 2017–, Univ. of WA. Chm., 1988–90, Chancellor, 1991–97, WA Coll. of Advanced Educn, later Edith Cowan Univ.; Mem. Council, Australian Inst. of Judicial Admin, 1992–98. Foundn Fellow, Australian Acad. of Law (Foundn Mem., 2007); Pres., Australian Assoc. for Constitnl Law, 2001–05. Hon. FASSA, 2010. Hon. Bencher: Gray's Inn, 2008; Lincoln's Inn, 2008. Hon. DLaws: Edith Cowan Univ., WA, 1998; Univ. of WA, 2011. Centenary Medal, 2003. *Publications:* (jtly) Reflections on the Australian Constitution, 2003. *Recreation:* tennis. *Address:* Suite 2, Level 13, Allendale Square, 77 St George's Terrace, Perth, WA 6000, Australia.

**FRENCH, Roger;** HM Diplomatic Service, retired; Counsellor (Management) and Consul-General, Tokyo, 2003–07; *b* 3 June 1947; *s* of Alfred Stephen George French and Margaret (*née* Brown); *m* 1969, Angela Cooper (*d* 2011); one *s* one *d*. *Educ:* County Grammar Sch., Dagenham. Joined Foreign and Commonwealth Office, 1965; Havana, 1970; Vice-Consul: Madrid, 1971–73; Puerto Rico, 1973–76; UN Dept, FCO, 1977–80; Second, later First, Sec., (Chancery), Washington, 1980–84; First Sec. (Commercial), Muscat, 1985–88; Dep. Hd of N America Dept, FCO, 1988–92; Dep. Consul-Gen., Milan, 1992–96; Counsellor (Mgt) and Consul-Gen., Washington, 1997–2001; Actg Dep. High Comr, Nigeria, 2001; Hd of Inf. Mgt Gp, FCO, 2001–03. Chm., SPUC, Milton Keynes, 2011–. Commnd Kentucky Col, 1998. *Recreation:* music. *E:* angrog1969@hotmail.co.uk.

**FRENK, Prof. Carlos Silvestre,** CBE 2017; PhD; FRS 2004; Ogden Professor of Fundamental Physics and Director, Institute for Computational Cosmology, University of Durham, since 2002; *b* 27 Oct. 1951; *s* of Silvestre Frenk and Alicia Mora de Frenk; *m* 1978, Susan Frances Clarke; two *s*. *Educ:* Nat. Autonomous Univ. of Mexico (BSc Theoretical Physics 1976); King's Coll., Cambridge (Math. Tripos Part III 1977); Inst. of Astronomy, Univ. of Cambridge (PhD 1981). Postdoctoral Research Fellow: Dept of Astronomy, Univ. of Calif at Berkeley, 1981–83; Astronomy Centre, Univ. of Sussex, 1983–85; Asst Res. Physicist, Inst. for Theoretical Physics, Univ. of Calif at Santa Barbara, 1984; University of Durham: Lectr in Astronomy, Dept of Physics, 1985–91; Reader in Physics, 1991–93; Prof. of Astrophysics, 1993–2002. Withrow Lect., 2006, George Darwin Lect., 2010, RAS. Alexander von Humboldt Fellow, 2012; Oort Prof., Leiden Observatory, 2015. Occasional broadcasts, radio and television, 1988–. Mem. Council, 2012–15, Chm., Public Engagement Cttee, 2019, Royal Soc. Member: IAU, 1985; AAS, 1993. FRAS 1981. Wolfson Res. Merit Award, Royal Soc., 2006; Daniel Chalonge Medal, Internat. Sch. of Astrophysics, 2007; Hoyle Medal, Inst. of Physics, 2010; Advanced Investigator Award Grant, ERC, 2011; Gruber Cosmology Prize, Gruber Foundn, 2011; Humboldt Res. Award, Alexander von Humboldt Foundn, 2013; Gold Medal, RAS, 2014; Max Born Prize, German Phys. Soc., 2017. *Publications:* (ed) The Epoch of Galaxy Formation, 1989; (ed) Observational Tests of Cosmological Inflation, 1991; more than 650 scientific papers in prof. jls, incl. Nature, Astrophys. Jl, Monthly Notices RAS, Phys. Rev. Letters. *Recreations:* literature, opera, ski training. *Address:* Department of Physics, Ogden Centre for Fundamental Physics, University of Durham, Science Laboratories, South Road, Durham DH1 3LE. *T:* (0191) 334 3641.

**FRENKEL, Prof. Daniel,** PhD; FRSC; Professor of Theoretical Chemistry, 2007–15, and Head, Department of Chemistry, 2011–15, University of Cambridge; Fellow, Trinity College, Cambridge, 2008–15 (Hon. Fellow, 2016); *b* Amsterdam, 27 July 1948; *s* of Maurits Frenkel and Herta G. Tietz; *m* 1st, 1986, Alida H. Bolliger (*d* 1995); two *d*; 2nd, 2004, Dr Erika Eiser. *Educ:* Barlaeus Gymnasium, Amsterdam; Univ. of Amsterdam (Masters degree in Phys. Chem. 1972; PhD 1977). FRSC 2010. Post-doctoral Res. Fellow, UCLA, 1977–80; Res. Scientist, Shell Res., Amsterdam, 1980–81; University of Utrecht: Lectr, then Reader, Dept of Physics, 1981–86; Prof. of Computational Chem. (pt-time), 1987–; Prof. of Macromolecular Simulations (pt-time), Univ. of Amsterdam, 1998–2007; Gp Leader, 1987–2007, Scientific Advr, 2007–, Inst. for Atomic and Molecular Physics, Foundn for Fundamental Res. on Matter, Amsterdam. Hon. Prof., Beijing Univ. of Chem. Technol., 2005–; Concurrent Prof. (Hon.), Nanjing Univ., 2011–. Chm., Amsterdam Centre for Multiscale Modelling, 2007–. Member: Royal Dutch Acad. of Scis, 1998; Hollandsche Maatschappij der Wetenschappen, Netherlands, 2002. Foreign Mem., Royal Soc. (London), 2006; Foreign Hon. Mem., Amer. Acad. Arts and Scis, 2008; Associate Fellow, World Acad. of Scis (formerly Acad. of Scis for Developing World), 2012; Foreign Associate, US NAS, 2016. MAE 2013. Hon. DSc Edinburgh, 2007. Boltzmann Medal, IUPAP, 2016. *Publications:* (jtly) Simulation of Liquids and Solids, Molecular Dynamics and Monte Carlo Methods in Statistical Mechanics, 1987; (jtly) Understanding Molecular Simulation: from algorithms to applications, 1996, 2nd edn 2002; contrib. internat. jls. *Address:* Department of Chemistry, University of Cambridge, Lensfield Road, Cambridge CB2 1EW. *T:* (01223) 336376. *E:* df246@cam.ac.uk.

**FRENNEAUX, Prof. Michael Paul,** MD; FRCP, FRCPE, FMedSci; Dean, Norwich Medical School, University of East Anglia, since 2015; *b* Hull, 11 Feb. 1957; *s* of Jack Frenneaux and Margaret Frenneaux; *m* 1978, Cheryl Christina Lord; one *s* one *d*. *Educ:* Beverley Grammar Sch.; Westminster Hosp. Med. Sch., London (MB BS Hons, Gold Medal, 1980; MD 1991). FRCP 1998; FRCPE 2009. Hse Officer, Westminster Hosp., 1980–81; SHO, Hammersmith and Brompton Hosps, and Nat. Hosp. for Nervous Diseases, Queen Square, 1981–83; Registrar, Aberdeen, 1983–84; Registrar (Cardiology): Edinburgh, 1984–85; Hammersmith Hosp., 1985–88; Consultant Cardiologist, Canterbury Hosp. Bd, NZ, 1988–91; Prof. of Medicine and Dir of Cardiol., Univ. of Queensland and Royal Brisbane Hosp., 1991–96; BHF Sir Thomas Lewis Prof. of Cardiol., Univ. of Wales Coll. of Medicine, 1996–2004; BHF Prof. of Cardiovascular Medicine, Univ. of Birmingham, 2004–09; Regius Prof. of Medicine, Univ. of Aberdeen, 2009–15. FRACP 1988; FACC 1995; FESC; FMedSci 2008. *Publications:* papers on cardiovascular physiol. and pathophysiol., particularly in heart failure and the cardiomyopathies. *Address:* Norwich Medical School, University of East Anglia, Norwich Research Park, Norwich NR4 7TJ. *T:* (01603) 593959. *E:* s.florescu@uea.ac.uk.

**FRERE, Vice-Adm. Sir Richard Tobias, (Sir Toby),** KCB 1994; Chairman, Prison Service Pay Review Body, 2001–05; Member, Armed Forces Pay Review Body, 1997–2002; *b* 4 June 1938; *s* of late Alexander Stewart Frere and Patricia Frere; *m* 1968, Jane Barraclough; two *d*. *Educ:* Eton College; Britannia Royal Naval College. Joined RNVR as National Serviceman; transf. RN 1956; commissioned 1958; submarines 1960; served Canada, 1961–62, Australia, 1966–67, 1973; commanded HM Submarines Andrew, Odin and Revenge and Frigate HMS Brazen. JSSC Canberra, 1973; RCDS London, 1982; Dir Gen. Fleet Support, Policy and Services, 1988–91; Flag Officer Submarines, and Comdr Submarines Eastern Atlantic, 1991–93; Chief of Fleet Support and Mem., Admiralty Bd, 1994–97. Chm. Govs, Oundle Sch., 2007–10. Master, Grocers' Co., 2004–05. *Recreation:* sailing. *Address:* c/o Naval Secretary, Fleet Headquarters, Whale Island, Portsmouth PO2 8BY. *Clubs:* Garrick, Naval, MCC.

**FRESHWATER, Prof. Dawn,** PhD; FRCN; Vice Chancellor, University of Western Australia, since 2017; *b* Nottingham. *Educ:* Univ. of Manchester (BA Hons Educn 1993); Univ. of Nottingham (PhD 1998). RN 1983; RNT 1993; Dip. Advanced Psychotherapy; FRCN 2001. University of Leeds: Prof. of Mental Health, then Adjunct Prof., 2007–; Hd of Sch., 2007–11; Pro-Vice Chancellor, 2011–14; Sen. Dep. Vice Chancellor and Registrar, Univ. of Western Australia, 2014–17. Chair, Instl Res. Rev. Panel for Res. Assessment and Impact Case Measurement, Ire., 2016–18; Exec. Mem., Yorkshire Univs Mgt Gp, 2011–14; Member: Exec. Cttee, Council of Deans, 2010–13; HEFCE REF Main Panel A (Sub-panel C), 2011–14; Exec. Bd, WA Health Translation Network, 2014–; Women in Health Sci. Cttee, NH&MRC, 2015–17; Exec. Cttee, Aust. Higher Educn Industrial Assoc., 2016–18 (Vice-Chair, 2017). Gov., Leeds Partnership Foundn Trusts (Mental Health), 2009–14. GAICD 2018. *Publications:* (with C. Johns) Transforming Nursing through Reflective Practice, 1998, 2nd edn 2005; (jtly) Critical Reflection for Nursing and the Helping Professions: a users guide, 2001, 2nd edn 2011; (ed) Therapeutic Nursing: improving patient care through self-awareness and reflection, 2002; (with C. Robertson) Needs and Emotions: core concepts in psychotherapy, 2002 (trans. Hebrew); Counselling Skills for Nurses, Midwives and Health Visitors, 2003 (trans. Italian, Chinese, Greek); (with S. Maslin-Prothero) Blackwell's Dictionary of Nursing, 2004 (trans. Hungarian); (with V. Bishop) Nursing Research in Context: appreciation, application and professional development, 2004; (with G. Rolfe) Everything and Nothing: deconstructing evidence based practice, 2004; Mental Health and Illness: questions and answers for counsellors and therapists, 2005; (with I. Holloway) Narrative Research in Nursing, 2007; (ed jtly) International Textbook of Reflective Practice, 2008; (ed jtly) Practitioner Based Research: power, discourse and transformation, 2008; over 50 book chapters; approx. 70 articles in learned jls. *Recreations:* running, swimming, reading. *Address:* Vice-Chancellery, University of Western Australia, 35 Stirling Highway, Crawley, WA 6009, Australia. *T:* (8) 64883500. *E:* dawn.freshwater@uwa.edu.au.

**FRESKO, Adrienne Sheila,** CBE 2003; Partner, GE Healthcare Finnamore, 2014–17; *b* 22 Feb. 1957; *d* of Mendal and Esther Marcus; *m* 1979, Marc Marcos Fresko; two *d*. *Educ:* Manchester High Sch. for Girls; St Anne's Coll., Oxford (MA Exptl Psychol.); Birkbeck Coll., London (MSc Occupational Psychol.). Mem., BPsS, 1998. Vice-Pres., Human Resources, Citibank, 1985–86; Principal, Adrienne Fresko Consulting, 1989–97; Audit Commission: Mem., 1996–2000; Dep. Chair, 2000–03; Actg Chair, 2001–02; Hd, Centre for Public Governance, Office of Public Mgt, 2000–04; Co-founder and Dir, Foresight Partnership, 2004–14. Chairman: Croydon Dist HA, 1992–96; Croydon HA, 1996–2000; Lead Chm., Croydon Health Commng Agency, 1994–96. Dir, Accountancy Foundn, 1999–2003; Mem., 2004–13, Vice Chm., 2009–13, Health Foundn. Ind. Mem. Council, Univ. of Sussex, 2013– (Vice Chm., 2018–). MCIPD (MIPD 1991); FRSA 2000. *Publications:* Making a Difference: women in public appointments, 2001; The Good Governance Standard for Public Services, 2005; The Healthy NHS Board: principles for good governance, 2010, 2nd edn 2013; Governing GP Commissioning, 2011. *Recreations:* family, travel, community, choral singing.

**FREUD,** family name of **Baron Freud.**

**FREUD, Baron** *cr* 2009 (Life Peer), of Eastry, in the County of Kent; **David Anthony Freud;** PC 2015; *b* London, 24 June 1950; *s* of Anton Walter Freud and Annette Vibeke Freud (*née* Krarup); *m* 1978, Priscilla Jane Dickinson; one *s* two *d*. *Educ:* Whitgift Sch.; Merton Coll., Oxford (BA PPE 1972; MA 1989). Journalist, Western Mail, 1972–75; Econs/Tax Reporter, and Lex Corresp., Financial Times, 1976–83; S. G. Warburg, later UBS Investment Bank, 1984–2003 (Vice Chm., Investment Banking, 2000–03); CEO, The Portland Trust, 2006–08. Author, ind. report for DWP, Reducing Dependency, Increasing Opportunity: options for the future of welfare to work, 2007; Advr, DWP, 2008. Shadow Minister for Welfare Reform, 2009–10; Parly Under-Sec. of State (Minister for Welfare Reform), 2010–15, Minister of State (Minister for Welfare Reform), 2015–16, DWP. *Publications:* Freud in the City, 2006. *Recreations:* swimming, cycling, ski-ing. *Address:* House of Lords, SW1A 0PW. *T:* (020) 7219 4907. *E:* freudd@parliament.uk. *Club:* Athenæum.

**FREUD, Anthony Peter,** OBE 2006; General Director, since 2011 and President and Chief Executive Officer, since 2016, Lyric Opera of Chicago; *b* 30 Oct. 1957; *s* of Joseph Freud and Katalin Lowi. *Educ:* King's Coll. London (LLB 1978); Inns of Court Sch. of Law. Called to the Bar, Gray's Inn, 1979; Th. Manager, Sadler's Wells Th., 1980–84; Company Sec. and Dir, Opera Planning, WNO, 1984–92; Exec. Producer, Philips Classics, 1992–94; Gen. Dir, WNO, 1994–2005; Gen. Dir and CEO, Houston Grand Opera, 2006–11. Chairman: Opera Europa, 2003–05; Opera America, 2008–12. Honorary Fellow: Cardiff University, 2005; RWCMD, 2006. *Address:* Lyric Opera of Chicago, 20 N Wacker Drive, Chicago, IL 60606, USA. *T:* (312) 3322244, *Fax:* (312) 4190820. *E:* afreud@lyricopera.org.

**FREUD, Emma Vallency,** OBE 2011; associate film producer; script editor, broadcaster; Director, Red Nose Day, since 2000; *b* 25 Jan. 1962; *d* of Sir Clement (Raphael) Freud and June Beatrice, (Jill), Freud; partner, Richard Whalley Anthony Curtis, *qv*; three *s* one *d*. *Educ:* St Mary's Convent; Queen's College London; Bristol Univ.; Royal Holloway Coll., Univ. of London (BA Hons Drama and Film Studies). Played Vincent Price's daughter in Ardele, West End, 1975; backing singer for Mike Oldfield on Tubular Bells tour, 1978; Mem. of The Girls (cabaret band), 1984–2004; Co-Dir and Musical Dir, Open Air Th., Regents Park, 1985–86; presenter: *television:* 6 O'Clock Show, 1986–88, Pillowtalk, 1987–89, Theatreland, 1996–98, ITV; The Media Show, 1989–91, Turner Prize, 1991, Channel 4; Everyman, 1992–94, Edinburgh Nights, 1994–96, BAFTA Awards, 1994, BBC2; *radio:* Loose Ends, BBC Radio 4, 1987–; morning show, BBC GLR, 1988–90; lunchtime show, BBC Radio 1, 1995–96; *theatre:* National Theatre Live, NT, 2009–. Script editor to Richard Curtis on: *films:* Four Weddings and a Funeral, 1994; Bean, 1997; Notting Hill, 1999; Bridget Jones's Diary, 2001; Love Actually, 2004; About Time, 2013; *television:* The Vicar of Dibley, 1995–2007; Doctor Who, 2010; Associate Producer, film: The Boat That Rocked, 2009; Yesterday, 2019. Chm., Christmas Quiz, NT, 2000–. Key Mem., Make Poverty History campaign and co-prod., Live 8 concerts, 2005. Trustee, Comic

Relief, 1998–; Patron, White Ribbon Alliance, 2008–. Columnist: Tatler, 2011–; Telegraph, 2015–16; BBC Good Food Mag., 2015–. *Publications:* contribs to The Times Mag., Guardian, Telegraph, Sunday Times, Radio Times, BBC Good Food Mag. *Recreations:* cooking with alcohol, patting small furry animals. *T:* (office) (020) 3784 6961.
*See also* M. R. Freud.

**FREUD, Matthew Rupert;** Chairman, Freuds (formerly Freud Associates, then Freud Communications), since 1985; *b* 2 Nov. 1963; *s* of Sir Clement Raphael Freud; *m* Caroline Victoria Hutton (marr. diss.); two *s*; *m* Elisabeth Murdoch, *qv* (marr. diss. 2015); one *s* one *d. Educ:* St Anthony's, Westminster. Hon. Trustee, Comic Relief, 2000–. *Address:* (office) 1 Stephen Street, W1T 1AL. *T:* (020) 3003 6300.
*See also* E. V. Freud.

**FREW, Henry Forrest;** Vice Lord-Lieutenant of Berwickshire, since 2019; Managing Director, Cheviot Trees Ltd, since 1987; *b* Stirling, 1954; *s* of Bill Frew and Anne Frew; *m* 1979, Patricia Cowe; one *s* one *d. Educ:* Malvern Coll.; Shuttleworth Agricl Coll. (HND Agric.). Farmer, 1978–. *Recreations:* family, Rugby, cricket, sports, outdoor activities, walking. *Address:* Kirkbanny Farm, Foulden, Berwick on Tweed, Scottish Borders TD15 1UH. *T:* (01289) 386755. *E:* harry@cheviot-trees.co.uk. *Clubs:* Berwick Rugby; Manderston Cricket.

**FREYBERG**, family name of **Baron Freyberg**.

**FREYBERG**, 3rd Baron *cr* 1951, of Wellington, New Zealand and of Munstead, Co. Surrey; **Valerian Bernard Freyberg;** *b* 15 Dec. 1970; *o s* of 2nd Baron Freyberg, OBE, MC, and of Ivry Perronelle Katharine, *d* of Cyril Harrower Guild, Aspall Hall, Debenham, Suffolk; *S* father, 1993; *m* 2002, Dr Harriet Atkinson, *d* of late John Atkinson and of Jane (who *m* 2nd, John Watherston, *qv*); one *s* two *d. Educ:* Eton Coll.; Camberwell Coll. of Art; Slade Sch. of Fine Art (MA Fine Art 2006). Elected Mem., H of L, 1999. Mem., Design Council, 2001–04. *Heir:* s Hon. Joseph John Freyberg, *b* 21 March 2007. *Address:* House of Lords, SW1A 0PW.

**FRICKER, His Honour (Anthony) Nigel;** QC 1977; a Deputy Circuit Judge, 2001–05 (a Circuit Judge, 1984–2001); *b* 7 July 1937; *s* of late Dr William Shapland Fricker and Margaret Fricker; *m* 1960, Marilyn Ann, *d* of late A. L. Martin, Pa, USA; one *s* two *d. Educ:* King's School, Chester; Liverpool Univ. (LLB 1958). President of Guild of Undergraduates, Liverpool Univ., 1958–59. Called to Bar, Gray's Inn, 1960. Conf. Leader, Ford Motor Co. of Australia, Melbourne, 1960–61. Recorder, Crown Court, 1975–84; Prosecuting Counsel to DHSS, Wales and Chester Circuit, 1975–77; an asst comr, Boundary Commn for Wales, 1981–84; Mem. Bd, Children and Family Court Adv. and Support Service, 2001. Member: Bar Council, 1966–70; Senate and Bar Council, 1975–78; County Court Rule Cttee, 1988–92; Family Proceedings Rule Cttee, 1997–2001; Mental Health Review Tribunal, 2001–08. Pres., Council of HM Circuit Judges, 1997. Fellow, Internat. Acad. of Trial Lawyers, 1979–. Mem. Court: Liverpool Univ., 1977–2011; York Univ., 1984–2012. Confrérie des Chevaliers du Tastevin. *Publications:* (jtly) Family Courts: Emergency Remedies and Procedures, 1990, 3rd edn (loose-leaf) as Emergency Remedies in the Family Courts (Gen. Ed., 1990–99, Consulting Ed., 1999–2002); (with David Bean) Enforcement of Injunctions and Undertakings, 1991; (consulting ed.) The Family Court Practice, (annually) 1993–2002; contrib. legal periodicals in UK and USA (Family and Conciliation Courts Rev.). *Address:* 6 Park Square, Leeds LS1 2LW; Farrar's Building, Temple, EC4Y 7BD.
*See also* C. R. Burn.

**FRIED, Bradley;** Managing Partner, Grovepoint (formerly Grovepoint Capital LLP), since 2010; *b* Cape Town, SA, 12 Aug. 1965; *s* of Louis and Joan Fried; *m* 1996, Lauren Roth; two *s. Educ:* Univ. of Cape Town (BCom with Dist. 1986); Wharton Sch., Univ. of Pennsylvania (Palmer Scholar; MBA with Dist. 1993). Trainee Accountant, Arthur Andersen, 1988–91; CA, S Africa, 1991; Partner, McKinsey & Co., NY, 1993–99; Chief Operating Officer, 1999–2003, CEO, 2003–10, Investec Bank plc; CEO-in-Residence, Judge Business Sch., Univ. of Cambridge, 2010–15. Non-executive Director: London and Johannesburg Listed Investec Gp, 2010–16; Court, Bank of England, 2012– (Dep. Chm., 2014–18; Chm., 2018–; Chm., Audit and Risk Cttee, 2014–18); Financial Conduct Authy, 2016–18; Payment Systems Regulator, 2016–18. Fellow, Magdalen Coll., Cambridge, 2010–. Gov., London Business Sch., 2016–. *Recreations:* family, visual arts. *Address:* 8–12 York Gate, NW1 4QG. *T:* (020) 7486 5954. *E:* bradley@grovepoint.co.uk.

**FRIEDBERGER, Maj.-Gen. John Peter William,** CB 1991; CBE 1986 (MBE 1975); Administrator, Sovereign Base Areas and Commander, British Forces, Cyprus, 1988–90; *b* 27 May 1937; *s* of late Brig. John Cameron Friedberger, DSO, DL and Phyllis Grace Friedberger, JP; *m* 1966, Joanna Mary, *d* of Andrew Thorne, ERD; one *s* two *d. Educ:* Red House School, York; Wellington College; RMA Sandhurst. Commissioned, 10th Royal Hussars (PWO), 1956; seconded to Northern Frontier Regt, Sultan's Armed Forces, Oman, 1961–63; Australian Army Staff Coll., 1969; CO The Royal Hussars (PWO), 1975–78; RCDS, 1978–79; Comdr, Royal Brunei Armed Forces, 1982–86; ACOS, HQ Northern Army Group, 1986–88. Chief Exec., British Helicopter Adv. Bd, 1992–2002. Hon. Colonel: The Royal Hussars (PWO), 1991–92; The King's Royal Hussars, 1992–97. Chm., Railfuture (Wessex), 2006–12. FRGS 1990. Dato, DPKT (Negara Brunei Darussalam) 1984. *Recreation:* travel. *Address:* c/o Home HQ, The King's Royal Hussars, Peninsula Barracks, Winchester, Hants SO23 8TS. *Club:* Cavalry and Guards.

**FRIEDLAND, Prof. Jonathan Samuel,** PhD; FRCP, FRCPE, FRCPI, FMedSci; Deputy Principal (Research and Enterprise), St George's, University of London, since 2018; *b* London, 6 Sept. 1960; *s* of Albert and Rosalind Friedland; *m* 1995, Joanna Catherine Porter; one *s* one *d. Educ:* St Paul's Sch., London; Corpus Christi Coll., Cambridge (BA 1981; MA 1985); King's Coll. Hosp. Med. Sch., Univ. of London (MB BS 1984); London Univ. (PhD 1993). FRCP 1999; FRCPE 1999; FRCPI 2010. Registrar, Nuffield Dept of Medicine, John Radcliffe Hosp., Oxford, 1987–89; MRC Trng Fellow, 1989–92; Univ. Lectr and Hon. Sen. Registrar in Communicable Diseases, St George's Hosp. and Med. Sch., 1992–94; Sen. Lectr in Infectious Diseases, 1994–2000, Reader in Infectious and Tropical Diseases, 2000–03, RPMS/Imperial Coll. London; Prof. of Infectious Diseases and Hd, Infectious Diseases and Immunity, 2004–18, Dir (formerly Dean), Hammersmith Campus, 2010–18, Imperial Coll. London; Hon. Consultant in Infectious Diseases and Medicine, 1994–2018, Lead Clinician, Clinical Infection, 2004–13, Imperial Coll. Healthcare (formerly Hammersmith Hosps) NHS Trust. Vis. Prof., Imperial Coll. London, 2018–. Member: Tropical Medicine Interest Gp, Wellcome Trust, 2002–04; UK Jt Cttee on Vaccination and Immunisation, 2005–13; Nat. Expert Panel of New and Emerging Infections, 2007–12; Clin. Trng and Career Develt Panel, MRC, 2009–13; Commn on Human Medicines, MHRA, 2014–; Chm., Expert Adv. Gp on Infection, MHRA, 2015–. Pres., British Infection Soc., 2007–09 (Chm., Grants Cttee, 1998–2001). FMedSci 2008; Fellow, Eur. Soc. of Clinical Microbiology and Infectious Disease, 2017. Weber-Parkes Prize Medal, RCP, 2005. *Publications:* papers on infectious diseases, innate immunity and migrant health with a special interest in tuberculosis. *Recreations:* family, chess, theatre. *Address:* St George's, University of London, Jenner Wing, Cranmer Terrace, SW17 0RE. *T:* (020) 8725 2437. *E:* jonfriedland@sgul.ac.uk.

**FRIEDMAN, David Peter;** QC 1990; *b* 1 June 1944; *s* of Wilfred Emanuel Friedman and Rosa Lees; *m* 1972, Sara Geraldine Linton. *Educ:* Tiffin Boys' School; Lincoln College, Oxford (BCL, MA). Called to the Bar, Inner Temple, 1968, Bencher, 1999; a Recorder, 1998–2005. *Recreations:* good food (cooked by others), reading. *Address:* 4 Pump Court, Temple, EC4Y 7AN. *T:* (020) 7842 5555.

**FRIEDMAN, Prof. Jerome Isaac,** PhD; Professor of Physics, 1967, William A. Coolidge Professor, 1988–90, Institute Professor, 1990, now Emeritus, Massachusetts Institute of Technology; *b* 28 March 1930; *m* Tania Baranovsky Friedman; two *s* two *d. Educ:* Univ. of Chicago (AB 1950; MS 1953; PhD Physics 1956). Research associate: Univ. of Chicago, 1956–57; Stanford Univ., 1957–60; MIT: Asst Prof. and Associate Prof., 1960–67; Dir, Nuclear Science Lab., 1980–83; Head of Dept of Physics, 1983–88. Fellow: Amer. Phys. Soc.; Nat. Acad. of Scis; Amer. Acad. of Arts and Scis. (Jtly) W. H. K. Panofsky Prize for Physics, 1989; (jtly) Nobel Prize for Physics, 1990. *Publications:* numerous papers in learned jls on particle physics, esp. the division of protons and neutrons into smaller particles, leading to different types of quarks. *Address:* Department of Physics, Massachusetts Institute of Technology, 77 Massachusetts Avenue, Cambridge, MA 02139–4307, USA.

**FRIEDMAN, Sonia Anne Primrose,** OBE 2016; Producer, Sonia Friedman Productions, since 2002; *b* 19 April 1965; *d* of Leonard and Clair Friedman. *Educ:* St Christopher Sch., Letchworth; Central Sch. of Speech and Drama (HND Stage Mgt; Hon. Fellow, 2014). Hd of Mobile Prodns, RNT, 1990–93; Producer and Co-Founder, Out of Joint Theatre Co., 1993–98; Producer, Ambassador Theatre Gp, 1998–2002. Producer of the Year, Stage Awards, 2015, 2016, 2017, 2019. *Address:* 5th Floor, 65 Chandos Place, WC2N 4HG. *T:* (020) 7845 8750, *Fax:* (020) 7845 8759. *E:* office@soniafriedman.com.

**FRIEDMANN, Prof. Peter Simon,** MD; FRCP, FMedSci; Professor of Dermatology, University of Southampton, 1998–2008, now Emeritus; *b* 18 Nov. 1943; *s* of Charles Aubrey Friedmann and Atersia Friedmann (née Le Roux); *m* 1967, Bridget Ann Harding; one *s* one *d. Educ:* Trinity Coll., Cambridge (BA 1966); University Coll. Hosp., London (MB BChir 1969; MD 1977). FRCP 1984. Wellcome Trng Fellow, RCS, 1973–77; University of Newcastle upon Tyne: Lectr in Dermatology, 1977–81; Sen. Lectr, 1981–90; University of Liverpool: Prof. of Dermatology, 1990–97; Actg Hd, Dept of Medicine, 1996–97. Hon. Res. Fellow, Tufts Univ., Boston, 1985–86. Med. Advr to All-Party Parly Gp on Skin, 1996–2008. Chm., Scientific Cttee, Nat. Eczema Soc., 1995–2001. Founder FMedSci 1998. *Publications:* contrib. book chapters; numerous scientific papers. *Recreations:* music (playing flute), bird-watching, tennis. *Address:* Dermatology Unit, Southampton General Hospital, Tremona Road, Southampton SO16 6YD.

**FRIEL, Anna;** actress; *b* Rochdale, Lancs; one *d* by David Thewlis. *Stage* appearances: Look Europe, Almeida, 1997; Closer, NY, 1998 (Drama Desk Award for Outstanding Featured Actress in a Play, 1999); Lulu, Almeida, 2001, transf. NY (Helen Hayes Award for Outstanding Lead Actress, 2002); Breakfast at Tiffany's, Th. Royal, Haymarket, 2009; Uncle Vanya, Vaudeville Th., 2012; *films* include: The Tribe, The Stringer, Land Girls, 1998; All For Love, Rogue Trader, A Midsummer Night's Dream, Mad Cows, 1999; Sunset Strip, 2000; Everlasting Piece, Me Without You, 2001; War Bride, 2002; Timeline, 2003; Goal!, 2005; Niagara Motel, Irish Jam, 2006; Goal! II, 2007; Land of the Lost, 2009; London Boulevard, You Will Meet a Tall Dark Stranger, 2011; The Look of Love, 2013; *television* includes: GBH, 1991; Brookside, 1993–95 (Nat. Television Award for Most Popular Actress, 1995); Our Mutual Friend, 1998; The Jury, 2004; Pushing Daisies, 2007–09; The Street, 2009; Without You, 2011; Odyssey, 2015; Marcella, 2016, 2018 (Best Actress, Internat. Emmy Awards, 2017); Broken, 2017; Butterfly, 2018; Deep Water, 2019. *Address:* c/o The Artists Partnership, 21–22 Warwick Street, W1B 5NE.

**FRIEND, Andrew Erskine;** Chairman, Basalt (formerly Balfour Beatty) Infrastructure Partners, since 2010; *b* 25 June 1952; *s* of Philip Friend and Eileen (née Erskine); *m* 1985, Jennifer Elizabeth Keating; one *s* two *d. Educ:* Christ's Hosp.; Peterhouse, Cambridge (BA 1973). MAICD 1994; CCMI 2006. Policy Advr, GLC, 1982–84; City of Melbourne: Dir, Econ. Develt, 1985–89; Corporate Manager, 1990–95; Chief Exec., 1995–97; Associate Dir, Macquarie Bank, 1997–99; Man. Dir, Laing Investments, 1999–2003; Chief Exec., John Laing plc, 2003–06; Commercial Advr, DfT, 2006–08. Non-executive Director: ING European Infrastructure Fund, 2006–09; Partnerships UK, 2007–10; Financial Security Assurance (UK) Ltd, 2007–09; DfT, 2009–10; HS2 Ltd, 2009–12; Strategic Advr, India Infrastructure plc, 2008–10. Chm., Investment Cttee, InfraMed Infrastructure SAS, 2010–. Trustee, Oxfam, 2007–12. Mem. Council, City Univ., 2013–. Curator, Ravilious & Co., UK touring exhibn, 2017–18. *Publications:* Slump City: the politics of mass unemployment, 1981; Ravilious & Co: the pattern of friendship, 2017; res. pubns on housing, econ. and urban develt. *Recreations:* golf, walking, reading history, lino-cuts, growing vegetables.

**FRIEND, John Richard,** DM; FRCOG; Consultant Obstetrician and Gynaecologist, Plymouth General Hospital, 1973–2000 (Medical Director, 1999–2000); Senior Vice President, Royal College of Obstetricians and Gynaecologists, 1995–98; *b* 31 Jan. 1937; *s* of George Chamings Friend and Gwendoline Mary Lewis Friend; *m* 1971, Diana Margaret Fryer; one *s* two *d* (incl. twin *s* and *d*). *Educ:* St Edward's Sch. (schol.); St Edmund Hall, Oxford (MA; BM, BCh, DM); St Thomas' Hosp. MRCOG 1968, FRCOG 1987; MRCP 1999. Queen Charlotte's Hosp. and Chelsea Hosp., 1965–66; MRC Fellow, 1969–70; Hammersmith Hosp., 1966–67; KCH, 1967–73. Hon. Consultant Gynaecologist, RN, 1987–. *Publications:* articles in jls. *Recreations:* golf, tennis. *Address:* Holme House, Stoke Hill Lane, Crapstone, Yelverton, Devon PL20 7PP. *T:* (01822) 852527. *Clubs:* Royal Western Yacht; Yelverton Golf.

**FRIEND, Lionel;** conductor; Music Director, British Youth Opera, since 2015; *b* 13 March 1945; *s* of Moya and Norman A. C. Friend; *m* 1969, Jane Hyland; one *s* two *d. Educ:* Royal Grammar School, High Wycombe; Royal College of Music; London Opera Centre. ARCM 1964; LRAM 1965, Hon. ARAM 2014. Glyndebourne Opera, 1969–72; Welsh National Opera, 1969–72; Kapellmeister, Staatstheater, Kassel, Germany, 1972–75; Staff Conductor, ENO, 1978–89; Musical Dir, New Sussex Opera, 1989–96; Conductor-in-residence, Birmingham Conservatoire, 2003–10. Guest Conductor: BBC orchestras; Philharmonia; Royal Philharmonic; City of Birmingham SO; Royal Liverpool Philharmonic; Royal Ballet; Oper Frankfurt; Opera Australia; Opéra National, Brussels; State Symphony, Hungary; Nash Ensemble, Royal Danish Opera, Polish Nat. Opera, etc. Hon. FRBC (Hon. FBC 2012). *Recreations:* reading, theatre. *Address:* 136 Rosendale Road, SE21 8LG. *T:* (020) 8761 7845.

**FRIEND, Prof. Peter John,** MD; FRCS; Professor of Transplantation, University of Oxford, since 1999; Fellow, Green Templeton College (formerly Green College), Oxford, since 1999; Hon. Consultant Surgeon, Oxford University Hospitals NHS Trust (formerly Oxford Radcliffe NHS Trust), since 1999; Co-Founder, and Chief Medical Officer, since 2008, OrganOx Ltd; *b* 5 Jan. 1954; *s* of late John Friend and (Dorothy) Jean Friend (née Brown); *m* 2001, Prof. Laurie Elizabeth Maguire. *Educ:* Rugby Sch.; Magdalene Coll., Cambridge (MA, MB, BChir, MD); St Thomas's Hosp. Med. Sch. FRCS 1983. St Thomas' Hosp., London, W Norwich Hosp., Bedford Gen. Hosp., Addenbrooke's Hosp., Cambridge, 1978–88; Vis. Asst Prof., Indiana Univ., USA, 1988–89; Lectr in Surgery, Univ. of Cambridge and Hon. Consultant Surgeon, Addenbrooke's Hosp., 1989–99;

Fellow, Magdalene Coll., Cambridge, 1993–99. Pres., British Transplantation Soc., 2007–09. *Publications:* papers on transplantation and surgery in scientific jls. *Address:* Nuffield Department of Surgical Sciences, Oxford Transplant Centre, Churchill Hospital, Oxford OX3 7LE.

**FRIEND, Sir Richard (Henry),** Kt 2003; FRS 1993; FREng, FIET; Cavendish Professor of Physics, University of Cambridge, since 1995; Fellow, St John's College, Cambridge, since 1977; *b* 18 Jan. 1953; *s* of John Henry Friend and Dorothy Jean (*née* Brown); *m* 1979, Carol Anne Maxwell (*née* Beales); two *d*. *Educ:* Rugby Sch.; Trinity Coll., Cambridge (MA, PhD; Hon. Fellow, 2004). FInstP 1999 (Hon. FInstP 2008); FREng 2002; FIET (FIEE 2002). Res. Fellow, St John's Coll., Cambridge, 1977–80; University of Cambridge: Demonstrator in Physics, 1980–85; Lectr, 1985–93; Reader in Experimental Physics, 1993–95. R&D Dir, 1996–98, Chief Scientist, 1998–2007, Cambridge Display Technology; Chief Scientist, Plastic Logic Ltd, 2000–06. Vis. Prof., Univ. of Calif, Santa Barbara, 1986–87; Nuffield Science Res. Fellowship, 1992–93; Mary Shepard B. Upson Vis. Prof., Cornell Univ., 2003; Miller Vis. Prof., 2014, Heising-Simons Fellow, 2015, Univ. of Calif at Berkeley. Mem., EPSRC, 2012–18. Lectures: Mott, Inst. of Physics, 1994; Kelvin, IEE, 2004; Holst Meml, Tech. Univ. of Eindhoven and Philips Res., 2004; (inaugural) Nakamura, Univ. of Calif, Santa Barbara, 2005; Clifford Paterson, Royal Soc., 2006; Menelaus, S Wales Inst. of Engineers, Cardiff, 2008; Kolthoff, Univ. of Minnesota, 2008; Leibniz, Kolleg Potsdam, 2008; Konarka-Tripathy, Univ. of Mass, Lowell, 2010; Georg Kanig, Berlin-Brandenburgischer Verband, Berlin, 2010; International, Internat. Centre for Materials Science, JNCASR, Bangalore, 2010; Golden Jubilee, Indian Inst. of Technol., Delhi, 2010. Hon. FRSC 2004; Hon. Fellow: Univ. of Wales, Bangor, 2006; Indian Acad. of Scis, 2011; Foreign Associate, NAE, 2013. Hon. DSc: Linköping, 2000; Mons, 2002; Heriot-Watt, 2006; Nijmegen, 2008; Montreal, 2009; Hasselt, 2013. C. V. Boys Prize, Inst. of Physics, 1988; Interdisciplinary Award, RSC, 1991; Hewlett-Packard Prize, European Physical Soc., 1996; Rumford Medal and Prize, Royal Soc., 1998; Italgas Prize for res. and technol innovation, 2001; Silver Medal, 2002, MacRobert Prize, 2002, Royal Acad. of Engrg; Faraday Medal, IEE, 2003; Gold Medal, Eur. Materials Res. Soc., 2003; Descartes Prize, Eur. Commn, 2003; Jan Rachmann Prize, Soc. for Information Displays, 2005; (jtly) Daniel E. Noble Award, IEEE, 2007; Inaugural Award, Rhodia de Gennes Prize for Sci. and Technol., Paris, 2008; (jtly) King Faisal Internat. Prize for Sci., 2009; (jtly) Business and Innovation Gold Medal, Inst. of Physics, 2009; Millennium Prize Laureate, Finnish Acad. of Technol., 2010; Harvey Prize, Israel Inst. of Technol., 2011; Internat. Medal for Materials Sci. and Technol., Materials Res. Soc. of India, 2013; Von Hippel Award, Materials Res. Soc., 2015. *Publications:* papers on chem. physics and solid-state physics in scientific jls. *Address:* Cavendish Laboratory, J. J. Thomson Avenue, Cambridge CB3 0HE. *T:* (01223) 337218. *E:* rhf10@cam.ac.uk.

**FRIEND, Victoria;** *see* Richardson, V.

**FRIER, Prof. Brian Murray,** MD; FRCPE, FRCPGlas; Consultant Physician, Royal Infirmary of Edinburgh, 1987–2012; Hon. Professor of Diabetes, University of Edinburgh, since 2001; *b* Edinburgh; *s* of Murray and Christina Frier; *m* 1985, Isobel Wilson; one *d*. *Educ:* George Heriot's Sch., Edinburgh; Univ. of Edinburgh (BSc 1st Cl. Hons Physiol. 1969; MB ChB 1972; MD 1981). MRCP(UK) 1974; FRCPE 1984; FRCPGlas 1986. Jun. med. posts, Edinburgh, 1972–74; Med. Registrar, Ninewells Hosp., Dundee, 1974–76; Clin. Res. Fellow, Cornell Univ. Med. Center, New York Hosp., NY, 1976–77; Sen. Med. Registrar, Royal Infirmary, Edinburgh, 1978–82; Consultant Physician, Western Infirmary and Gartnavel Gen. Hosp., Glasgow, 1982–87. Chair: Hon. Adv. Panel on Driving and Diabetes to Sec. of State for Transport, 2001–12 (Mem., 1993–2012); Diabetes Res. Gp, Chief Scientist Office, 2003–06. Mem. Council, 2002–08, Vice-Pres., 2008–12, RCPE. Member: Diabetes Panel, CAA, 2010–; Internat. Hypoglycaemia Study Gp, 2013–. R. D. Lawrence Lectr, British Diabetic Assoc., 1986; Banting Meml Lectr, Diabetes UK, 2009; Camillo Golgi Prize Lect., Eur. Assoc. for Study of Diabetes, 2017. Somogyi Award, Hungarian Diabetes Assoc., 2004. Co-Ed., Diabetes/Metabolism Res. and Reviews, 1998–2008; Ed., Diabetic Hypoglycemia, 2008–14; Mem., Internat. Editl Bd, Clinical Diabetes and Endocrinology, 2014–; Mem., Editl Bd, Diabetes, Sci. and Technol., 2018–. *Publications:* (ed with B. M. Fisher) Hypoglycaemia and Diabetes: clinical and physiological aspects, 1993; (ed with B. M. Fisher) Hypoglycaemia and Clinical Diabetes, 1999, 3rd edn (ed with S. R. Heller and R. J. McCrimmon) 2014; (with M. W. J. Strachan) Insulin Pocketbook, 2013; 500 scientific papers, review articles and book chapters on hypoglycaemia, diabetes and diabetic complications. *Recreations:* appreciation of the arts, ancient and modern history, sport. *Address:* University of Edinburgh/BHF Centre for Cardiovascular Science, Queen's Medical Research Institute, 47 Little France Crescent, Edinburgh EH16 4TJ; 100 Morningside Drive, Edinburgh EH10 5NT. *Clubs:* Heriot's Former Pupils, Heriot's Rugby; Merchants of Edinburgh Golf.

**FRIES, Richard James;** Chief Charity Commissioner, 1992–99; Visiting Fellow, Centre for Civil Society, London School of Economics, 2000–06; *b* 7 July 1940; *s* of late Felix Theodore Fries and Joan Mary Fries (subseq. Mrs John Harris); *m* 1970, Carole Anne Buick; one *s* two *d*. *Educ:* King's Coll., Cambridge. Home Office, 1965–92. Chm. Bd, Internat. Center for Not-for-Profit Law, Washington, 1999–2005. *Recreations:* chess, music.

**FRISBY, Audrey Mary;** Metropolitan Stipendiary Magistrate, 1972–99; *b* 22 June 1928; *d* of Hugh and Olive Jennings, Ashbrook Range, Sunderland; *m* 1961, Roger Harry Kilbourne Frisby, QC (marr. diss. 1980; he *d* 2001); two *s* one *d*. *Educ:* Durham High Sch.; Durham Univ. (BA); Oxford Univ. (DPA). Children's Officer, City and County of Cambridge, 1952–56. Called to Bar, Middle Temple, 1956 (Harmsworth Schol.); practised at Criminal Bar, London, 1956–61 and 1967–72. Occasional opera critic, Musical Opinion. *Publications:* Bar Maid, 2016. *Recreations:* theatre, music, gardening, writing short stories.

**FRISBY, Terence;** playwright, actor, producer, director, author; *b* 28 Nov. 1932; *s* of William and Kathleen Frisby; *m* 1963, Christine Vecchione (marr. diss.); one *s*. *Educ:* Dobwalls Village Sch.; Dartford Grammar Sch.; Central Sch. of Speech Training and Dramatic Art. Substantial repertory acting and directing experience, also TV, films and musicals, 1957–63; appeared in A Sense of Detachment, Royal Court, 1972–73 and X, Royal Court, 1974; Clive Popkiss, in Rookery Nook, Her Majesty's, 1979, and many since. Productions: Once a Catholic (tour), 1980–81; There's a Girl in My Soup (tour), 1982; Woza Albert!, Criterion, 1983; The Real Inspector Hound/Seaside Postcard (tour), 1983–84; Comic Cuts, 1984. Has written: many TV scripts, incl. series Lucky Feller, 1976; That's Love, 1988–92 (Gold Award, Houston Film Festival); film, There's A Girl in My Soup, 1970 (Writers Guild Award, Best British Comedy Screenplay); stage musical, Just Remember Two Things…, 2004, retitled as Kisses on a Postcard, Queen's Th., Barnstable, 2011. *Publications:* Outrageous Fortune (an autobiog. story), 1998; Kisses on a Postcard (childhood memoir), 2009; *plays:* The Subtopians, 1964; There's a Girl in My Soup, 1966; The Bandwagon, 1970; It's All Right if I Do It, 1977; Seaside Postcard, 1978; Just Remember Two Things: It's Not Fair And Don't Be Late, 1989 (radio play; Giles Cooper Award, 1988); Rough Justice, 1995; Funny About Love, 2002. *Address:* c/o The Agency, 24 Pottery Lane, Holland Park, W11 4LZ. *T:* (020) 7727 1346. *Club:* Richmond Golf.

**FRISCHMANN, Wilem William,** CBE 1990; PhD; FREng; FICE; FIStructE; FCGI; Chairman: Pell Frischmann Group: Pell Frischmann Consulting Engineers Ltd, since 1985; Pell Frischmann Consultants Ltd, since 1986; Conseco International, since 1985; *s* of Lajos Frischmann and Nelly Frischmann; *m* 1957, Sylvia Elvey; one *s* one *d*. *Educ:* Hungary; Hammersmith College of Art and Building; Imperial Coll. of Science and Technology (DIC); City University (PhD). MASCE. FIStructE 1964; FREng (FEng 1985); FCGI 1988; FConsE 1993; FICE 2004. Engineering training with F. J. Samuely and Partners and W. S. Atkins and Partners; joined C. J. Pell and Partners, 1958, Partner, 1961. Dep. Chm., Building & Property Management Services Ltd, 1993–96. Structural Engineer for Nat. Westminster Tower (ICE Telford Premium Award), Centre Point, Drapers Gardens tower (IStructE Oscar Faber Prize) and similar high buildings, leisure buildings, hotels and hospitals; Engineer for works at Bank of England, Mansion House and Alexandra Palace; particular interest and involvement in tall economic buildings, shear walls and diaphragm floors, large bored piles in London clay, deep basements, lightweight materials for large span bridges, monitoring and quality assurance procedures for offshore structures; advisory appts include: Hong Kong and Shanghai Bank HQ, Malayan Banking Berhad, Kuala Lumpur. Hon. DSc. Lifetime Achievement Award, Eur. CEO Awards, 2013; Outstanding Personal Contrib. Award, British Expertise Internat. Awards, 2013; Golden Global Excellence Award, Inst. of Economic Studies, India, 2013; Rashtriya Udyog Ratan Award, 2013. *Publications:* The use and behaviour of large diameter piles in London clay (IStructE paper), 1962; papers to learned socs and instns, originator of concepts: English Channel free-trade port; industrial complex based on Varne and Colbart sandbanks; two-mile high vertical city. *Recreations:* ski-ing, jogging, chess, architecture, design. *Address:* (office) 5 Manchester Square, W1A 1AU. *T:* (020) 7486 3661, *Fax:* (020) 7487 4153; Haversham Grange, Haversham Close, Twickenham, Middx TW1 2JP. *Club:* Arts.

**FRISK, Monica Gunnel Constance C.;** *see* Carss-Frisk.

**FRISTON, Prof. Karl John,** FRS 2006; Professor of Neuroscience, since 1998, and Wellcome Principal Research Fellow, Wellcome Centre for Human Neuroimaging (formerly Wellcome Department of Imaging Neuroscience, then Wellcome Trust Centre for Neuroimaging), since 1999, Institute of Neurology, University College London; *b* 12 July 1959; *s* of Anthony Harpham Friston and Audrey Agnes Friston (*née* Brocklesby); *m* 1987, Ann Elisabeth Leonard; three *s*. *Educ:* Gonville and Caius Coll., Cambridge (Exhibnr; BA Med. Scis Tripos 1980); King's Coll. Med. Sch., Univ. of London (MB BS 1983); MA Cantab 1985. MRCPsych 1988. Pre-registration, Surgery, Bromley Hosp. and Medicine, Farnborough Hosps, 1984–85; Post-registration, Rotational Trng Scheme in Psychiatry, Dept of Psychiatry, Univ. of Oxford, 1985–88; Hon. Senior Registrar: Dept of Psychiatry, Charing Cross and Westminster Med. Sch., 1988–91; RPMS, 1991–94 (Hon. Lectr, 1991–92); Sen. Lectr, 1994–97, Reader, 1997–98, Inst. Neurol., UCL. Research: Wellcome Trust Fellow, MRC Clin. Neuropharmacol. Unit, Oxford Univ., 1987–88; Wellcome Trust Res. Fellow, 1988–91, MRC Clin. Scientist (Sen. Grade), 1991–92, MRC Cyclotron Unit, Hammersmith Hosp.; W. M. Keck Foundn Fellow in Theoretical Neurobiol., Neurosci Inst., La Jolla, Calif, 1992–94; Wellcome Sen. Res. Fellow in Clin. Sci., Inst. of Neurol., 1994–99. Hon. Consultant, Nat. Hosp. for Neurol. and Neurosurgery, Queen Sq., 1999–. FMedSci 1999. *Publications:* (ed jtly) Human Brain Function, 1997, 2nd edn 2004; (ed jtly) Statistical Parametric Mapping and Causal Models for Brain Imaging, 2006; contrib. numerous peer-reviewed articles to acad. lit. *Recreation:* painting. *Address:* Wellcome Centre for Human Neuroimaging, 12 Queen Square, WC1N 3BG. *T:* (020) 3448 4347. *E:* k.friston@ucl.ac.uk.

**FRITCHIE,** family name of **Baroness Fritchie**.

**FRITCHIE,** Baroness *cr* 2005 (Life Peer), of Gloucester in the county of Gloucestershire; **Irene Tordoff Fritchie,** DBE 1996; Chair, Lloyds Bank Foundation for England and Wales, since 2015; Consultant on Leadership and Change, Mainstream Development, since 1991; *b* 29 April 1942; *d* of Charles Fredrick Fennell and Eva (*née* Tordoff); *m* 1960, Don Jamie Fritchie; one *s* (and one *s* decd). *Educ:* Ribston Hall Grammar Sch. for Girls. Admin. Officer, Endsleigh Insce Brokers, 1970–73; Sales Trng Officer, Trident Insce Ltd, 1973–76; Head of Trng Confs and Specialist Trng Advr on Women's Develt, Food and Drink ITB, 1976–80; Consultant, Social Ecology Associates, 1980–81; Dir, Transform Ltd, 1981–85; Rennie Fritchie Consultancy, 1985–89; Man. Dir, Working Choices Ltd, 1989–91; Vice Chair, Stroud and Swindon Bldg Soc., 2002–08 (Bd Mem., 1995–2008). Chair: Gloucester HA, 1988–92; South-Western RHA, 1992–94; S and W Region, NHS Executive (formerly S and W RHA), 1994–97; 2gether Gloucestershire NHS Foundn Trust, 2008–12. Member: NHS Policy Bd, 1994–97; GMC, 1996–99; Board, British Quality Foundn, 1994–99; Selection Panel, Glos Police Authy, 1994–99; Comr for Public Appts, 1999–2005; Civil Service Comr, 1999–2005; Chair: Ind. Appts Selection Bd, RICS, 2006–12; Adv. Bd, Web Sci. Res. Initiative, Southampton/MIT, 2006–09; Nominet, 2010–17; Vice-Chm., Audit Cttee, Scottish Public Service Ombudsman, 2007–10; non-exec. Dir, UK Shared Business Service, 2013–15. Mem., Forum UK, IHSM, 1993. Pres., Pennell Initiative for Women's Health in Later Life, 1999–2006 (Chair, 1997–99); Chm., Chronic Pain Policy Coalition, 2006–; Vice-Chm., British Lung Foundn, 2006–. Patron: Healing Arts, 1995–2002; SHARE young persons counselling service, 1997–2002; Meningitis Trust, 1998–2002; Westbank League of Friends, 1998–2002; Bart's Cancer Centre, 1998–2000; Effective Intelligence, 2000–02; SPACE, 2000–02; Swindon Arts Foundn, 2000–02; Lord Mayor's Appeal, 2000–01; Pied Piper Appeal, 2002–; Winston's Wish (grief support charity for children), 2002–06 (Pres., 1996–2000; Ambassador, 2006–); Women in Banking and Finance, 2008–11; Pres., Hosp. Caterers Assoc., 2009–10. Vis. Associate Prof., York Univ., 1996–; Pro-Chancellor, University Sussex, 1998–2008 (Chm. Council, 1998–2000). Mem., British and Irish Ombudsman Assoc., 2002–. Mem., Editl Adv. Bd, Revans Inst., 2002–. CCMI (CIMgt 2000). Fellow: Glos Univ. (formerly Cheltenham & Gloucester Coll. of Higher Educn), 1996– (Chancellor, 2012–); Sunningdale Inst., Nat. Sch. of Govt, 2006–; FCGI, 2002. Hon. PhD Southampton, 1996; DUniv: York, 1998; Oxford Brookes, 2001; Open, 2003; QUB, 2005; Hon. LLD St Andrews, 2002; Hon. DLitt Hull, 2006. *Publications:* Working Choices, 1988; The Business of Assertiveness, 1991; Resolving Conflicts in Organisations, 1998. *Recreations:* family, reading, gardening, swimming, theatre, cooking, the 'Archers'. *Address:* Mainstream Development, 51 St Paul's Road, Gloucester GL1 5AP. *T:* (01452) 414542.

**FRITH, Prof. Christopher Donald,** PhD; FRS 2000; FBA 2008; Professor in Neuropsychology, University College London, 1994–2008, now Emeritus; Visiting Professor, University of Aarhus, Denmark, since 2007; Quondam Fellow, All Souls College, Oxford, since 2013 (Fellow, 2011–13); Research Fellow, Institute of Philosophy, University of London, since 2015; *b* 16 March 1942; *s* of Donald Alfred Frith, OBE; *m* 1966, Uta Aurnhammer (*see* U. Frith); two *s*. *Educ:* Leys Sch., Cambridge; Christ's Coll., Cambridge (MA 1963); Inst. of Psychiatry, London Univ. (Dip. Psych. 1965; PhD 1969). Res. Asst, Inst. of Psychiatry, 1965–75; MRC Scientific Staff: Clin. Res. Centre, Div. of Psychiatry, Northwick Park Hosp., 1975–92; MRC Cyclotron Unit, Hammersmith Hosp., 1992–94; Wellcome Principal Res. Fellow, Wellcome Trust Centre for Neuroimaging (formerly Wellcome Dept of Cognitive Neurology), Inst. of Neurology, UCL, 1994–2008. FRSA 1996; FMedSci 1999; FAAAS 2000. Kenneth Craik Award, St John's Coll., Cambridge, 1999; (jtly) European Latsis Prize, Eur. Sci. Foundn, 2009; Internat. Fyssen

Prize, Fyssen Foundn, 2009; (jtly) Jean Nicod Prize, 2014. *Publications:* Cognitive Neuropsychology of Schizophrenia, 1992; Schizophrenia: a very short introduction, 2003; Making up the Mind, 2007; papers on cognitive neuropsychology in various scientific jls. *Recreations:* music, study of consciousness, interacting minds. *Address:* Wellcome Centre for Human Neuroimaging, 12 Queen Square, WC1N 3BG. *T:* (020) 7833 7457.

**FRITH, David Edward John;** cricket author and journalist; Founder, 1979, Editor and Editorial Director, 1979–96, Wisden Cricket Monthly; *b* 16 March 1937; *s* of Edward Frith and Patricia Lillian Ethel Frith (*née* Thomas); *m* 1957, Debbie Oriel Christina Pennell; two *s* one *d*. *Educ:* Canterbury High Sch., Sydney. First grade cricket, Sydney, 1960–64. Editor, The Cricketer, 1972–78. Vice-Pres., Cricket Memorabilia Soc., 1987–. Hon. Life Mem., Assoc. of Cricket Statisticians and Historians, 2013. Cricket Soc. Literary Award, 1970, 1987 and 2003; Cricket Writer of the Year, Wombwell Cricket Lovers Soc., 1984; Magazine Sports Writer of the Year, Sports Council, 1988; Ian Jackson Award for Dist. Service to Cricket, Cricket Soc., 2011. *Publications:* Runs in the Family (with John Edrich), 1969; (ed) Cricket Gallery, 1976; My Dear Victorious Stod, 1977; (with Greg Chappell) The Ashes '77, 1977; The Golden Age of Cricket 1890–1914, 1978; The Ashes '79, 1979; Thommo, 1980; The Fast Men, 1981; The Slow Men, 1984; (with Gerry Wright) Cricket's Golden Summer, 1985; (ed) England *v* Australia Test Match Records 1877–1985, 1986; Archie Jackson, 1987; Pageant of Cricket, 1987; Guildford Jubilee 1938–1988, 1988; England *v* Australia: A Pictorial History of the Test Matches since 1877, 1990; By His Own Hand, 1991; Stoddy's Mission, 1995; (ed) Test Match Year, 1997; Caught England, Bowled Australia (autobiog.), 1997; The Trailblazers, 1999; Silence of the Heart, 2001; Bodyline Autopsy, 2002; The Ross Gregory Story, 2003; The Battle for the Ashes, 2005; The Battle Renewed 2006–07, 2007; Inside Story: unlocking Australian cricket's archives, 2007 (Aust. Cricket Soc. Book Award, 2008); The David Frith Archive, 2009; Frith on Cricket, 2010; Cricket's Collectors, 2012; Guildford's Cricket Story, 2013; Frith's Encounters, 2014; 'Stoddy': England's finest sportsman, 2015; Alec Hurwood's 1930 Tour Diary, 2019. *Recreations:* collecting cricketana, watching documentaries. *Address:* 6 Beech Lane, Guildford, Surrey GU2 4ES. *T:* (01483) 532573. *Club:* MCC.

**FRITH, James Richard;** MP (Lab) Bury North, since 2017; *b* London, 23 April 1977; *s* of Rt Rev. Richard Michael Cokayne Frith, *qv*; *m* 2008, Nikki Cohen; two *s* two *d*. *Educ:* Monkton Combe Sch., Bath; Taunton Sch.; Manchester Metropolitan Univ. (BA Politics and Econs 2000). Sen. Finance Recruitment Consultant, Badenoch & Clark, 2000–04; Campaign and Communications Manager, Labour Party, 2004–05; Business, Educn and Skills Policy Manager, Gt Manchester Chamber, 2005–07; Hd of Strategic Develt, 2007–10, Man. Dir, 2010–12, U-Explore; Dir, Indicate Online, 2013–16; Founder and CEO, Pull Together Ltd, 2013–. Mem. (Lab), Bury MBC, 2011–15. PPS to Shadow Housing Minister, 2018–. Mem., Educn Select Cttee, H of C, 2017–; Chm., All Party Parly Gp on Hospice and Palliative Care. Contested (Lab) Bury N, 2015. *Recreations:* music (singer in a band, 1997–2009), sport. *Address:* House of Commons, SW1A 0AA. *W:* jamesfrith.org. *Club:* MCC.

**FRITH, Mark;** Editorial Director, Radio Times, since 2017; *b* 22 May 1970; *s* of John and Monica Frith; *m* Gaby; one *s* one *d*. *Educ:* Norton Free Primary Sch., Sheffield; Gleadless Valley Secondary Sch., Sheffield; Univ. of E London. Editor: Overdraft mag. (UEL mag.), 1989–90; Smash Hits mag., 1994–95; Sky mag., 1995–97; Editor-in-Chief, heat mag., 1999–2008; Editor, Time Out, 2009–11; Lifestyle Editl Dir, Bauer Media, 2011–12; presenter, Liquid News, BBC TV, 2002–03; Contributing Editor, LOVE mag., 2008–09; Editor-in-Chief, Now mag., 2015–17. *Publications:* (ed) The Best of Smash Hits: the eighties, 2006; The Celeb Diaries, 2008. *Recreations:* music, cinema, Sheffield UFC, talking too fast, clumsiness, finding things to read in other people's recycling bins.

**FRITH, Rt Rev. Richard Michael Cokayne;** Bishop of Hereford, 2014–19; *b* 8 April 1949; *s* of Roger Cokayne Frith and Joan Agnes Frith; *m* 1st, 1975, Jill Richardson (marr. diss. 2000); two *s* two *d*; 2nd, 2006, Kay Gledhill. *Educ:* Marlborough Coll.; Wiltshire; Fitzwilliam Coll., Cambridge (BA 1972; MA 1976); St John's Coll., Nottingham. Ordained deacon, 1974, priest 1975; Asst Curate, Mortlake with East Sheen, Southwark, 1974–78; Team Vicar, Thamesmead, Southwark, 1978–83; Team Rector, Keynsham, Bath and Wells, 1983–92; Archdeacon of Taunton, 1992–98; Bishop Suffragan of Hull, 1998–2014. *Recreations:* cricket, squash, theatre. *Address:* 64 Oakland Avenue, York YO31 1DF. *T:* 07817 856422. *E:* richardfrith@hotmail.com. *Club:* MCC.
See also J. R. Frith.

**FRITH, Prof. Simon Webster,** OBE 2017; PhD; FBA 2011; Tovey Professor of Music, Reid School of Music, Edinburgh College of Art, University of Edinburgh, 2006, now Emeritus; *b* 25 June 1946; *s* of Donald Frith and Mary Frith (*née* Tyler); *m* 1999, Jenny McKay; one *d*. *Educ:* Balliol Coll., Oxford (BA PPE); Univ. of Calif, Berkeley (MA; PhD Sociol. 1976). Lectr, then Sen. Lectr in Sociol., Warwick Univ., 1972–87; Professor: of English Studies, Univ. of Strathclyde, 1987–99; of Film and Media, Univ. of Stirling, 1999–2005. Dir, Media Econs and Media Culture Res. Prog., ESRC, 1995–2000. Chair of Judges, Mercury Music Prize, 1992–. *Publications:* Sound Effects, 1983; Music for Pleasure, 1988; Performing Rites, 1996; Music and Copyright, 2004; Taking Popular Music Seriously, 2007; The Art of Record Production, 2012; History of Live Music in Britain 1950–1967, 2013. *Recreation:* music. *E:* simon.frith@ed.ac.uk.

**FRITH, Prof. Uta,** Hon. DBE 2012; PhD; FMedSci; FRS 2005; FBA 2001; Professor of Cognitive Development, Institute of Cognitive Neuroscience, University College London, 1996–2006, now Emeritus (Deputy Director, 1998–2006); Visiting Professor, Interacting Minds Centre (formerly Guest Professor, Niels Bohr Project on Interacting Minds), Aarhus University, 2007–15; *b* 25 May 1941; *d* of Wilhelm Aurnhammer and Anne (*née* Goedel); *m* 1966, Prof. Christopher Donald Frith, *qv*; two *s*. *Educ:* Univ. des Saarlandes (Vordiplom. Psychol. 1964); Inst. of Psychiatry, Univ. of London (Dip. Abnormal Psychol. 1966; PhD Psychol. 1968). CPsychol. MRC Scientific Staff: Scientist, 1968–80; Sen. Scientist, 1980–98; Special Appt, 1998–. Pres., British Sci. Assoc., 2017–18. FMedSci 2001. Hon. FBPsS 2006. Hon. Fellow: UCL, 2007; Newnham Coll., Cambridge, 2008. Hon. DPhil: Göteborg, 1998; St Andrews, 2000; Palermo, 2005; York, 2005; Nottingham, 2007; Cambridge, 2012; Aston, 2015; Bath, 2016. *Publications:* Autism: explaining the enigma, 1989, 2nd edn 2003; (ed) Autism and Asperger's Syndrome, 1991; (with Rab Houston) Autism in History, 2000; (ed jtly) Autism: mind and brain, 2004; (with Sarah-Jayne Blakemore) The Learning Brain: Lessons for Education, 2005; Autism: a very short introduction, 2008. *Recreations:* collecting art and antiques, tidying and polishing, enjoying my husband's cooking. *Address:* Institute of Cognitive Neuroscience, University College London, Alexandra House, 17 Queen Square, WC1N 3AZ. *T:* (020) 7679 1177.

**FRITSCH, Elizabeth,** CBE 1995; potter; *b* Shropshire, 1940; *d* of Welsh parents; one *s* one *d*. *Educ:* Royal Acad. of Music; Royal Coll. of Art (Silver Medallist, 1970). Established own workshop, E London, 1985. *One-woman exhibitions* include: Bing and Grondahl, Copenhagen, 1972; Waterloo Place Gall., London, 1974; British Craft Centre, 1976; Leeds Galls, Temple Newsham, 1978, touring to Glasgow, Bristol, Bolton and V & A; Cross Rhythms and Counterpoint, Edinburgh, 1990; Hetjens Mus., Düsseldorf, 1991; Retrospective, Pischeur Fine Art, London, 1992–93; Vessels from Another World, Northern Centre for Contemp. Art, Sunderland, touring to Aberdeen, Birmingham, Cardiff, London and Norwich, 1993–95, Osiris Gall., Brussels, 1994; Order and Chaos, Bellas Artes, Santa Fe, 1994–95; Metaphysical Pots, Bellrive Mus., 1995; Retrospective, touring to Munich, Karlsruhe, Halle and Bellerive, Zurich, 1995–96; Sea Pieces, Contemp. Applied Arts, London, 1998; Memory of Architecture, Pt II, Besson Gall., London, 2000; Metaphysical Vessels, Mobilia Gall., Cambridge, Mass, 2000; Anthony Hepworth Gall., Bath, 2007; Retrospective, Bonhams, London, 2007; Fine Art Soc., London, 2008; Dynamic Structures: Painted Vessels, Nat. Mus. of Wales, Cardiff, 2010; *group exhibitions* include: Oxford Gall., 1974; ICA, 1985; Künstlerhaus, Vienna, 1986; Fischer Fine Art, London, 1987; Kyoto and Tokyo Nat. Museums of Modern Art, 1988; Crafts Council, touring to Amsterdam, 1988; Sotheby's, 1988; 35 Connaught Square, London (Lord Queensbery), 1991; Stuttgart, 1991; Oriel Gall., Cardiff, 1991; Marianne Heller Gall., Heidelberg, 1999; Mus. of Modern Ceramic Art, Gifu, 2003; Hayward Gall., London, 2003–04; *works in public collections:* V & A; Crafts Council; Lotherton Hall, Leeds City Art Galls; Royal Mus. of Scotland; Glasgow, Bolton, Bristol and Birmingham City Art Galls. Judge, Fletcher Challenge Internat. Ceramics Competition, NZ, 1990. Major influences on work: music, fresco painting, topology. Sen. Fellow, RCA, 1995. Herbert Read Meml Prize, 1970; Winner, Royal Copenhagen Jubilee Competition, 1972; Gold Medal, Internat. Ceramics Competition, Sopot, Poland, 1976; Gold Medal, Internat. Handwerksmesse, Munich, 1993. *Recreations:* literature, music, mountains, art.

**FRIZZELL, Edward William,** CB 2000; Head, Scottish Executive Enterprise, Transport and Lifelong Learning (formerly Enterprise and Lifelong Learning) Department, 1999–2006; *b* 4 May 1946; *s* of late Edward Frizzell, CBE, QPM and Mary McA. Russell; *m* 1969, Moira Calderwood; two *s* one *d*. *Educ:* Paisley Grammar School, Glasgow Univ. (MA Hons). Scottish Milk Marketing Board, 1968–73; Scottish Council (Develt and Industry), 1973–76; Scottish Office, 1976–78; First Sec., Fisheries, FCO UK Rep. Brussels, 1978–82; Scottish Office, then Scottish Executive, 1982–2006: SED, 1982–86; Finance Div., 1986–89; Industry Dept/SDA (Dir, Locate in Scotland), 1989–91; Under Sec., 1991; Chief Exec., Scottish Prison Service, 1991–99. Non-exec. Dir, Scottish Ambulance Service, 2011–. Vis. Prof. in Public Service Mgt, Queen Margaret Univ., Edinburgh, 2006–16. Chm. Court, Abertay Univ. (formerly Univ. of Abertay, Dundee), 2013–18 (Mem. Court, 2006–12). Chairman: Trefoil House, 2012–18; Edinburgh Sculpture Workshop, 2018–. Mem., Scotch Malt Whisky Soc. *Recreations:* running, cycling, painting. *Club:* Mortonhall Golf.

**FROGGATT, Anthony Grant;** Chief Executive Officer, Scottish & Newcastle PLC, 2003–07; *b* 9 June 1948; *s* of Sir Leslie Trevor Froggatt and of Jessie Elizabeth Froggatt (*née* Grant); *m* 1999, Chris Bulmer; three *s*. *Educ:* Queen Mary Coll., Univ. of London (LLB Hons); Columbia Business Sch., NY (MBA). Man. Dir, Swift & Moore, Sydney, Australia, 1983–88; CEO, Cinzano Internat., Geneva, 1988–92; President: Asia Pacific, 1992–95, Europe, 1995–98, Internat. Distillers & Vintners; Europe and Africa, Seagram, 1999–2002. Consultant Dir, Rothschild Australia, 2003. Non-executive Director: Brambles Ltd, 2006–; Billabong Ltd, 2008–13; AXA Asia Pacific Hldgs Ltd, 2008–11; Coca-Cola Amatil Pty Ltd, 2010–17. Chm., Foodbank Australia, 2015–. *Recreations:* tennis, travel, historical letters/signature collection. *Address:* 277 Whale Beach Road, Whale Beach, NSW 2107, Australia; 1601/2 Elizabeth Bay Road, Elizabeth Bay, Sydney, NSW 2011, Australia.

**FROGGATT, Sir Peter,** Kt 1985; MD; FRCP, FRCPI; Trustee, National Museums and Galleries of Northern Ireland, 1998–2003; Pro-Chancellor, University of Dublin, 1985–2003 (Senior Pro-Chancellor, since 1999); President and Vice-Chancellor, Queen's University of Belfast, 1976–86; *b* 12 June 1928; *s* of Albert Victor and Edith (*née* Curran); *m* 1958, Norma Cochrane; four *s* (and one *s* decd). *Educ:* Royal Belfast Academical Institution; Royal Sch., Armagh (Schol.); Trinity Coll., Dublin (BA; MB; BCh; BAO 1952; MA 1956; MD 1957; Welland Prize; Cunningham Medal; Begley Schol.); Queen's Univ., Belfast (DPH 1956; PhD 1967; Carnwath Prize). MRCPI 1972; FRCPI 1973; FFPH (FFCM 1973); MRCP 1974; FFOMI 1975; FFCMI 1976; MRIA 1978; FRCP 1980. House Surgeon and Physician, Sir Patrick Dun's Hosp., Dublin, 1952–53; Nuffield Res. Student, 1956–57; Med. Officer, Short Bros and Harland Ltd, 1957–59; Queen's University, Belfast: Lectr, 1959–65; Reader, 1965–68; Prof. of Epidemiology, 1968–76; Dean, Faculty of Medicine, 1971–76; Consultant, Eastern Health and Social Services Board, 1960–76. Hon. Prof., St Bartholomew's Hosp. Med. Sch., 1986–94. Chairman: Independent Scientific Cttee on Smoking and Health, 1980–91 (Mem., 1977–80); Tobacco Products Res. Trust, 1981–97; ASME, 1987–92; Central Ethical Compliance Gp, Unilever, 1991–97. Director: AIB Gp plc, 1984–95; TSB Bank (Northern Ireland), later First Trust Bank, 1991–98. President: Biol Scis Section, British Assoc., 1987–88; BMA, 1999–2000; Member: Bd, 1983–85, Adv. Cttee, NI, 1988–94, British Council; Gen. Adv. Cttee, BBC, 1986–88; Supervisory Bd, NHS NI, 1986–92; British Occupational Health Res. Foundn, 1991–2000. Hon. Member: Soc. for Social Medicine; Soc. of Occupational Medicine. Lectures: Robert Adams, 1977, Kirkpatrick, 1984, Abrahamson, 1986, RCSI; Apothecaries, SOM, 1978; Freyer, NUI, 1984; Bayliss, RCP, 1989; Smiley, FOMI, 1989; Bartholomew Mosse, Rotunda Hosp., 1992; John Snow, Assoc. of Anaesthetists, 2001; Doctors Award Redistribution Enterprise, FPHM, 2001. Trustee, Mater Infirmorum Hosp., Belfast, 1994–2002; Chm., Scotch-Irish Trust of Ulster, 1990–. Freeman, City of London, 1990. FSS 1963; Hon. FRCSI 1988; Hon. Fellow, Royal Acad. of Medicine in Ireland; CCMI (CBIM 1986). Hon. LLD: Dublin, 1981; QUB, 1991; Hon. DSc NUI, 1982. Dominic Corrigan Gold Medal, RCPI, 1981. *Publications:* (jtly) Causation of Bus-driver Accidents: Epidemiological Study, 1963; (ed jtly) Nicotine, Smoking and the Low Tar Programme, 1988; articles in jls on human genetics, occupational medicine, med. history, med. educn, epidemiology and smoking policies. *Recreations:* golf, music, travel. *Address:* Rathganley, 3 Strangford Avenue, Belfast BT9 6PG.

**FROLOVA-WALKER, Prof. Marina,** PhD; FBA 2014; Professor of Music History, University of Cambridge, since 2015; Fellow and Director of Studies in Music, Clare College, Cambridge; *b* Moscow. *Educ:* Moscow Conservatoire Coll.; Moscow Conservatoire (PhD 1994). Posts at Univ. of Ulster, Goldsmiths Coll., Univ. of London and Univ. of Southampton, 1994–2000; Reader in Music Hist., until 2015. *Publications:* Russian Music and Nationalism from Glinka to Stalin, 2007; (with J. Walker) Music and Soviet Power, 1917–32, 2012; (contrib.) Cambridge Companion to Grand Opera; (contrib.) Cambridge Companion to Twentieth-Century Opera; contrib. articles on Russian operatic repertoire to jls incl. Cambridge Opera Jl, Twentieth Century Music, Opera Qly. *Address:* Faculty of Music, University of Cambridge, 11 West Road, Cambridge CB3 9DP.

**FROOME, Christopher Clive,** OBE 2016; professional cyclist; *b* Nairobi, Kenya, 20 May 1985; *s* of Clive and Jane Froome; *m* 2014, Michelle; one *s* one *d*. Professional cyclist: Team Konica Minolta, 2007; Team Barloworld, 2008–09; Team Ineos (formerly Team Sky), 2010–. 2nd, British Nat. Time Trial Championships, 2010; winner, 2011, winner, 2017, Vuelta a España; 2nd overall, 2012, winner, 2013, 2015, 2016, 2017, Tour de France; Bronze Medal, Olympic Games, London, 2012, Rio de Janeiro, 2016; winner, Criterium du Dauphiné, 2013, 2015, 2016; winner, Tour de Ramandie, 2013, 2014; winner, Giro d'Italia, 2018. *Publications:* The Climb, 2014.

**FROST, Alan John**; DL; FIA; Chairman, Dorset Opera, 2005–19; b 6 Oct. 1944; s of Edward George Frost and Ellen Lucy Jamieson; m 1973, Valerie Jean Bennett; two s. Educ: Stratford County Grammar Sch., London; Manchester Univ. (BSc Hons). FIA 1970. Pearl Assurance Co., 1966–67; Australian Mutual Provident Soc., 1967–72; Laurie, Milbank & Co., 1972–74; London & Manchester Assurance Gp, 1974–84; Sun Life Assurance Soc., 1984–86; Man. Dir, Abbey Life Assurance Co., 1986–98; Gp Chief Exec., United Assce Gp plc, 1998–2000; Dep. Chief Exec., Royal London Gp, 2000–01; Chm., Queen Mab Consultancy Ltd, 2001–04. Chairman: Teachers' Bldg Soc., 2004–10 (non-exec. Dir, 2001–10); Tapper and Sons (Poole) Ltd Funeral Plans Trust, 2017–; non-executive Director: INVESCO Pensions Ltd, 2001–18; Bournemouth Univ., 2001–10 (Chm., 2004–10); NFU Mutual Insce Co., 2002–09; Car Crash Line Gp, 2002–06; Hamworthy plc, 2004–12. Vice-Chm., St Peter's Develt Project, Bournemouth, 2015–19. Chm., Bournemouth Chamber Music Soc., 2012–19. Liveryman, Co. of Actuaries, 1986– (Master, 2004–05). DL 2010, High Sheriff, 2011–12, Dorset. Hon. DBA Bournemouth, 2011. *Publications:* (with D. P. Hager) A General Introduction to Institutional Investment, 1986; (with D. P. Hager) Debt Securities, 1990; A Light Frost, 2005; actuarial papers. *Recreation:* opera. *E:* mail@alanfrost.co.uk. *Club:* Reform.

**FROST, (Angela) Jane**, CBE 2011; Chief Executive, Market Research Society, since 2011; b 14 July 1957; d of Dr William Derek Walsh and Julia Margaret Walsh; m 1981, Martin John Frost; one s one d. Educ: New Hall, Cambridge (BA 1978). Trainee manager to Product Gp Manager, Lever Brothers Ltd, 1978–85; Hd of Mktg, Shell Middle East Ltd (Dubai), 1985–88; Shell International Trading Company plc: Brand Coordinator Lubricants, 1988–91; Internat. Brand Coordinator, 1991–94; Planning and Mktg Dir (Far East and Australasia), 1995; Controller, Brand Mktg, BBC, 1995–2000; Dir, Mktg and Strategy, BBC Technol. Ltd, 2000–01; Dir, Greystones Consulting, 2001–02; Dir, Consumer Strategy, subseq. Strategy, DCA, 2003–06; Dir, Individual Customers, HMRC, 2006–11. Mem. Supervisory Bd, Wolters Kluwer NV, 2000–09. Chair, Legal Services Reform Consumer Panel, 2006–09; Dir, Audit Cttee, DirectGov, 2007–11; Mem., Governance Cttee, JobCentre Plus, 2008–11; Chm., Audit Cttee (Personal Tax Gp), HMRC, 2010–11. Member: Adv. Bd, Women on Bds Ltd, 2013–17; Internat. Bd, Women in Research, 2016–19. Dir, BBC Children in Need Ltd, 1997–2015. Trustee: Market Res. Benevolent Assoc., 2015–; Archive of Market and Social Res., 2018–. Non-exec. Dir, 2003–, Trustee, 2005–, Lowry Arts Centre; Mem. Council of Trustees, Heads, Teachers and Industry, 2003–11 (Vice Chair, 2008–11; Patron, 2011–14); Chm., Heads, Teachers and Industry Trust, 2005–08; Vice Chm., Fairtrade Foundn, 2013–. Co-Chm., Red Cross Tiffany Circle, 2019–. FCIM; FRSA. *Recreations:* my children, my dogs, Georgian glass. *Address:* Market Research Society, 15 Northburgh Street, EC1V 0JR. *T:* (020) 7490 4911. *E:* jane.frost@mrs.org.uk. *Club:* Women in Advertising and Communications London.

**FROST, Dame Barbara (Mary)**, DBE 2017; Chief Executive, WaterAid, 2005–17; b London, 18 Oct. 1952; d of William Frost and Jeannette Frost (née Norris); m 2017, Keith Bradbridge Smith. Educ: Bruton Sch. for Girls; Keele Univ. Lab. technician, Perth Hosp. for Women, WA Govt, 1973–74; Administrator, Housing Cost Enquiry, NSW Govt, 1975–76; Passport Officer, Australian Commonwealth Public Service, 1976–80; PA to Minister for Consumer Affairs, NSW Govt, 1980–83; Neighbourhood Centre Coordinator, Bellingen, NSW, 1983–86; State Manager of Service Develt, Home Care Service, NSW Govt, 1986–89; Country Dir, Community Aid Abroad, Mozambique, 1989–91; Asst Hd, Southern Africa Office, SCF, 1991–93; Dep. Dir, 1993–95, Dir, 1995–96, ActionAid, Malawi; Chief Exec., Action on Disability and Develt, 1996–2005. Vice Chair, ACEVO, 1998–2004. Trustee, Joffe Trust, 2017–. Hon. DSc Cranfield, 2011; Hon. LLD Exeter, 2011. *Recreations:* gardening, walking, birdwatching. *E:* bfrost@gn.apc.org.

**FROST, Christopher Ian**; Co-Director, East West Offender Management Consultancy Services (supporting development of justice services and promoting human rights in developing countries), since 2008; b 17 April 1949; s of late Joffre and Emily Frost; m Sandra Lomax; one s two d. Educ: Lewes County Grammar Sch. for Boys; Nottingham Univ. (MEd). Teacher, subseq. Hd of Dept, Sir William Nottidge Sch., 1970–77; Hd, Community Educn, Wigan, 1977–81; Dep. Educn Officer, Notts LEA, 1981–84; Educn Officer, Leics LEA, 1984–91; NVQ Development Officer, Home Office, 1991–93; Dir, City Coll., Manchester, 1994–2001; Chief Exec., Rathbone (educn and trng for disadvantaged young people), 2001–04. Sen. expert on justice matters in European projects supporting develts in Russia, Georgia and Serbia, 2004–; expert in criminal justice for Council of Europe in Ukraine, Moldova and Kazakhstan, 2011–13, in Armenia and Bosnia, 2011–16; Consultant, Council of Europe, 2017–. Conseiller municipale, Charlas, France, 2014–. *Publications:* Using Group Work in Anger Management Work (in Russian), 2008; reports and newspaper articles on supporting develt of democracy for offenders and of new trng initiatives for prison governors in Russia. *Recreations:* musical theatre, travel, ski-ing, performing folk music.

**FROST, David George Hamilton**, CMG 2006; Prime Minister's Europe Adviser, Cabinet Office, since 2019; b 21 Feb. 1965; s of George Leonard Frost and Margaret Elsie Frost; m 1993, Jacqueline Elizabeth Dias (marr. diss. 2018); one s one d; m 2018, Harriet Lucy Mathews, qv. Educ: St John's Coll., Oxford (BA Hons; MA). Entered FCO, 1987: London, 1987–89; Third Sec. (Political), Nicosia, 1989–90; KPMG Peat Marwick (on secondment), 1990–92; FCO, 1992–93: First Secretary (Economic): UK Repn to EU, 1993–96; UKMIS to UN, NY, 1996–98; Private Sec. to Perm. Under Sec., FCO, 1998–99; Dep. Hd, EU Dept, FCO, 1999–2001; Counsellor (Econ. and EU), Paris, 2001–03; Dir, EU (Internal) (formerly Dep. Dir, Europe), FCO, 2003–06; Ambassador to Denmark, 2006–08; Dir of Policy Planning Staff (formerly for Strategy, Policy Planning and Analysis), FCO, 2008–10; Dir, Europe, Trade and Internat. Affairs, BIS, 2010–13 (on secondment); Chief Exec., Scotch Whisky Assoc., 2014–16; Special Advr to Sec. of State for Foreign and Commonwealth Affairs, 2016–18; Chief Exec., LCCI, 2019. Mem., Adv. Council of Open Europe, 2014–16. *Recreations:* history, art and architecture, modern languages and historical linguistics, detective fiction, free-market economic theory, EU policy and politics. *Address:* Cabinet Office, 70 Whitehall, SW1A 2HQ.

**FROST, David Stuart**, CBE 2011; DL; Chairman, Stoke on Trent and Staffordshire Local Enterprise Partnership, since 2014; b 22 Feb. 1953; s of George William Stuart Frost and Winifred Leslie Frost; m 1981, Mari Doyle; two d. Educ: Thames Poly. (BA Hons Pol Economy); Poly. of the South Bank (Dip Internat. Financial Studies). Economist, London Chamber of Commerce, 1976–79; Dir of Services, Walsall Chamber of Commerce, 1979–86; Chief Executive: Walsall Chamber of Commerce and Industry, 1986–96; East Mercia Chamber of Commerce, 1996–2000; Coventry and Warwickshire Chamber of Commerce, 2000–02; Dir-Gen., British Chambers of Commerce, 2002–11. Chairman: Studio Schs Trust, 2010–12, now Ambassador; LEP Network, 2011–14; vInspired, 2012–. Chm., Coventry Univ. Coll., 2015–. Liveryman, Co. of Loriners, 1986 (Master, 2013). DL W Midlands, 2012. DUniv Birmingham City, 2008. *Recreations:* cycling, motorcycling, sailing. *Address:* 5 Norfolk Gardens, Sutton Coldfield, West Midlands B75 6SS. *T:* (0121) 355 7788. *E:* dsfrost@yahoo.com.

**FROST, Ven. George**; Archdeacon of Lichfield and Canon Treasurer of Lichfield Cathedral, 1998–2000; b 4 April 1935; s of William John Emson Frost and Emily Daisy Frost; m 1959, Joyce Pratt; four s. Educ: Hatfield Coll., Durham Univ. (BA 1956, MA 1961); Lincoln Theological Coll. Schoolmaster, Westcliff High School, 1956–57; labourer, Richard Thomas and Baldwin Steelworks, Scunthorpe, 1958–59; Asst Curate, St Margaret, Barking Parish Church, 1960–64; Minister, Ecclesiastical District of St Mark, Marks Gate, 1964–70; Vicar: St Matthew, Tipton, 1970–77; St Bartholomew, Penn, Wolverhampton, 1977–87; RD of Trysull, 1984–87; Archdeacon of Salop, 1987–98; Vicar of Tong, 1987–98. Prebendary of Lichfield Cathedral, 1985–87, Hon. Canon, 1987–98. *Recreations:* walking, wild flowers, photography. *Address:* 23 Darnford Lane, Lichfield, Staffs WS14 9RW. *T:* (01543) 415109.

**FROST, Gerald Philip Anthony**; author and journalist; b 8 Nov. 1943; s of Sidney and Flora Frost; m 1970, Margaret Miriam Freedman; two s. Educ: Univ. of Sussex (BA Hons; mature student). Junior reporter, Ilford and East London newspapers, 1960–64; reporter: Recorder Newspapers, Ilford, 1964–65; Yorkshire Post, 1965–67; Chief reporter, Morning Telegraph, 1967–68; Sub-editor: Daily Express, Manchester, 1968–69; Press Assoc., 1969–71; research staff, Centre for Policy Studies, 1974–80 (Sec. and Mem. Bd, 1977–80); Chief Leader Writer, Evening Standard, 1979–80; Director: Inst. for European Defence and Strategic Studies, 1980–92; Centre for Policy Studies, 1992–95; Trade and Policy Unit, IEA, 1997–2001; Dep. Dir, 2013–14, Dir, 2014–17, Danube Inst. Ed., eurofacts, 2001–09. Consultant Dir, New Atlantic Initiative, 1996–98. *Publications:* Protest and Perish: a critique of unilateralism (with P. Towle and I. Eliott), 1983; Antony Fisher: champion of liberty, 2002; (with John Blundell) Friend or Foe?: what Americans should know about the European Union, 2004; (with Anthony Scholefield) Too 'Nice' to be Tories: how the modernisers have damaged the Conservative Party, 2011; Making Things Happen: the life and original thinking of Nigel Vinson, 2015; *editor and contributor:* Europe in Turmoil, 1991; In search of Stability, 1992; Hubris: the tempting of modern conservatives, 1992; Loyalty Misplaced, 1997; Unfit to Fight: the cultural subversion of the armed forces in Britain and America, 1999; contribs to British and US newspapers and jls. *Recreations:* family pursuits, reading, wine. *Address:* Pear Tree Cottage, Downs Road, Epsom, Surrey KT18 5HN. *Club:* Reform.

**FROST, Jane;** see Frost, A. J.

**FROST, Jeffrey Michael Torbet**; Executive Director, London & Continental Bankers, 1983–89 (Associate Director, 1982–83); b 11 June 1938; s of late Basil Frost and Dorothy Frost. Educ: Diocesan Coll., Cape, South Africa; Radley Coll.; Oriel Coll., Oxford; Harvard Univ. Admin. Asst, Brazilian Traction, Light and Power Co., Toronto and Brazil, 1965–70; Economics Dept, Bank of London and S America, 1971–73; Asst Dir, 1974–75, Exec. Dir, 1976–81, Cttee on Invisible Exports. Hon. Sec., Anglo-Brazilian Soc., 1977–84. Liveryman, Worshipful Co. of Clockmakers. Freeman, City of London, 1980. FRSA. *Recreations:* bridge, ballet, walking. *Address:* 34 Paradise Walk, SW3 4JL. *T:* (020) 7352 8642; The Reading Room, Kintbury, near Hungerford, Berks RG17 9UP. *Clubs:* White's; Leander (Henley-on-Thames).

**FROST, Rt Rev. Jonathan Hugh**; Dean of York, since 2019; an Honorary Assistant Bishop, Diocese of York, since 2019; b 26 Sept. 1964; s of late Peter Clifford Frost and of Jean Lucelle Frost; m 1988, Christine Cuckow; three c. Educ: Univ. of Aberdeen (BD 1988); Nottingham Univ. (MTh 1999); Ridley Hall, Cambridge. Ordained deacon, 1993, priest, 1994; Asst Curate, St Giles, Bridgford, 1993–97; Rector, St Peter's, Ash, 1997–2002; Chaplain, Univ. of Surrey, 2002–10; Canon Res., Guildford Cathedral, 2002–10; Bishop Suffragan of Southampton, 2010–19; an Hon. Asst Bishop, Diocese of Portsmouth, 2016–19. Tutor, Local Ministry Prog., Dio. of Guildford, 1999–2010; Bishop of Guildford's Advr for Inter-Faith Relns, 2007–10. DUniv Surrey, 2012. *Recreation:* lifelong supporter of Fulham Football Club. *E:* dean@yorkminster.org.

**FROST, Michael Edward**, LVO 1983; HM Diplomatic Service, retired; Consul-General, San Francisco, 1998–2001; b 5 July 1941; s of Edward Lee Frost and Ivy Beatrice (née Langmead); m 1964, Carole Ann Beigel; three s. Educ: Torquay Grammar Sch. FCO, 1959–62; Algiers, 1962–67; Commercial Officer, Kuala Lumpur, 1967–71; 3rd Sec., later 2nd Sec. Commercial, Bucharest, 1972–75; FCO, 1975–78; Consul (Commercial), Seattle, 1978–83; FCO, 1983–84; on secondment to ICI, 1984–87; Dep. Head of Mission, Sofia, 1987–90; Dep. Consul Gen. and Dir (Investment), British Trade and Investment Office, NY, 1991–95; Head of Migration and Visa Dept, FCO, 1995–97. *Recreations:* watercolours, golf, travel. *Address:* 25 Waldens Park Road, Woking, Surrey GU21 4RN.

**FROST, Prof. Robert Ian**, PhD; FBA 2016; FRHistS; Burnett Fletcher Chair in History, University of Aberdeen, since 2013; b Edinburgh, 20 June 1958; s of Robert Craddock Frost and Anne Doris Frost (née Hempson); m 1994, Prof. Karin Friedrich; one s one d. Educ: Edinburgh Acad.; George Watson's Coll.; Univ. of St Andrews (MA Hons 1st Cl. 1980); Jagiellonian Univ., Kraków (Dip. Polish Lang. and Culture 1981); Sch. of Slavonic and East European. Studies, Univ. of London (PhD 1990). Asst Master, Charterhouse, 1984–87; Lectr, 1987–2000, Reader, 2000–04, KCL; Prof. of Early Mod. Hist., Univ. of Aberdeen, 2004–13. FRHistS 1991 (Mem. Council, 2004–09). *Publications:* After the Deluge: Poland-Lithuania and the Second Northern War, 1655–1660, 1993; The Northern Wars: war, state and society in Northeastern Europe, 1558–1721, 2000 (trans. Estonian 2005); (ed with Anne Goldgar) Institutional Culture in Early Modern Society, 2004; The Oxford History of Poland-Lithuania, vol. 1, The Making of the Polish-Lithuanian Union, 1385–1569, 2015 (trans. Polish 2018; Pro Historia Polonorum Prize, 2017). *Recreations:* guitar, opera, ski-ing, golf. *Address:* 50 Forest Road, Aberdeen AB15 4BP. *T:* (01224) 322824. *E:* robert.frost@abdn.ac.uk.

**FROST, Thomas Pearson**, FCIB; Group Chief Executive, National Westminster Bank, 1987–92; b 1 July 1933; s of James Watterson Frost and Enid Ella Crawte (née Pearson); m 1958, Elizabeth (née Morton); one s two d. Educ: Ormskirk Grammar Sch. FCIB (FIB 1976). Joined Westminster Bank, 1950; Chief Exec. Officer and Vice Chm., NBNA (later National Westminster Bank USA), 1980; National Westminster Bank: Gen. Man., Business Develt Div., 1982; Dir, 1984–93; Dep. Gp Chief Exec., 1985–87; Dep. Chm., 1992–93; Chm., London Clearing House Ltd, 1993–96. Chairman: Five Oaks Investments PLC, 1995–98 (non-exec. Dir, 1993–95); WSPA (UK), 2003–07 (Mem. Adv. Council, 2007–08); non-executive Director: Freedom Food Ltd, 1994–2003; Fenchurch PLC, 1993–97. Member: BOTB, 1986–93; UK Adv. Bd, British-American Chamber of Commerce, 1987–93; Business in the Cities, 1988–91; Policy Adv. Cttee, Tidy Britain Gp, 1988–92; Adv. Bd, World Economic Forum, 1990–93; Chairman: CBI Business & Urban Regeneration Task Force, 1987–88; Exec. Cttee, British Bankers' Assoc., 1991–92. Trustee, British Sports Trust, 1988–92; Gov., Royal Ballet Sch., 1988–98. Fellow, World Scout Foundn, 1984. Freeman, City of London, 1978. FCIM 1987; CompOR 1987; CCMI (CIMgt 1987); Companion, BITC, 1993; FRSA 1993. OStJ 1991. *Recreations:* orchids, theatre. *Clubs:* Carlton, MCC.

**FROST, Vince**; Graphic Designer, Creative Director and Chief Executive Officer, Frost*collective (formerly Frost Design), since 1994; b 23 Nov. 1964; s of Alan Frost and Irene Frost; m 1997, Sonia Della Grazia-Frost; two s one d. Educ: W Sussex Coll. of Art and

Design. Joined Pentagram, 1989, Associate Dir, 1992; founded own practice, Frost Design, 1994. Exhibns incl. Frost*bite: Graphic Ideas by Vince Frost, Sydney Opera House Exhibn Hall, 2006. Member: D&AD; Chartered Soc. of Designers; Internat. Soc. of Typographic Designers; Aust. Graphic Design Assoc.; AGI. Over 300 design awards. *Publications:* Frost*(sorry trees), 2006; Design Your Life®, 2014. *Recreations:* surfing, walking, playing with my kids. *Address:* Frost*collective, 16 Eveleigh Street, Redfern, NSW 2016, Australia.

**FROSTICK, Prof. Lynne Elizabeth,** PhD; Research Professor in Physical Geography, University of Hull, 2010–14, now Professor Emerita; *b* Gillingham, Kent, 2 Feb. 1949; *d* of Victor Alec John Frostick and Kathleen Frances Frostick; *m* Prof. Ian Reid; three *s*. *Educ:* Dartford Grammar Sch. for Girls; Univ. of Leicester (BSc (Hons) Geol. 1970); Univ. of East Anglia (PhD Envmtl Scis 1973). FGS 1976; CGeol 1989; FRGS 1996; CGeog 2002. Lectr in Geol., Birkbeck Coll., Univ. of London, 1973–85; Lectr, 1985–88, Sen. Lectr, 1989, in Geol., RHBNC; Sen. Lectr in Sedimentology, Univ. of Reading, 1989–96; Prof. of Physical Geog., 1996–2010, Pro Vice Chancellor, 2000–03, Univ. of Hull. Chm., Govt's Expert Gp for Women in Sci., Engrg and Technol., 2004–10; Member: Sub-panel 17, REF 2010–14; Equality and Diversity Adv. Panel, REF, 2011–14; Equalities Adv. Gp, BIS, then BEIS, 2011–15; Bd, Envmt Agency, 2015–. Pres., Geol Soc., 2008–10; Chm., British Soc. for Geomomorph., 2008–09. Hon. DSc: RHUL, 2014; Hull, 2016. Cuthbert Peek Award for Res., RGS, 2005. *Publications:* Sedimentation in the African Rifts, 1986; Desert Sediments: ancient and modern, 1987; Tectonic Controls and Signatures in Sedimentary Successions, 1993; (ed jtly) Sediment Flux to Basins: causes, control and consequences, 2002; (ed jtly) A Users Guide to Physical Modelling and Experimentation, 2011; (ed) A Users Guide to Ecohydraulic Modelling and Experimentation, 2014; over 100 papers in jls incl. Sedimentology, Sedimentary Res., Jl of Geol Soc., Jl of Hydraulic Res. *Recreations:* cycling, reading, walking, travelling on Caledonian MacBrayne ferries amongst islands off Oban in Scotland. *Address:* Highwood Cottage, Kilnwick, E Yorks YO25 9JF. *T:* 07854 651166. *E:* l.e.frostick@hull.ac.uk.

**FROSTRUP, Mariella;** journalist and broadcaster; Presenter: Open Book, since 1998, Bringing up Britain, since 2006, BBC Radio 4; The Big Painting Challenge, BBC1, since 2017; columnist: The Observer, since 1999; Telegraph Travel, since 2017; *b* Oslo, 12 Nov. 1962; *d* of late Peter Trulls Frostrup and of Joan Drysdale McMurray Blair; *m* 2003, Jason Daniel McCue, *qv*; one *s* one *d*. *Educ:* schs in Ireland. Presenter: The Book Show, Sky Arts, until 2013; Books to Live By, BBC Sounds, 2019; Harrods True Tales of Luxury, iTunes, 2019. Founder and Trustee, The Great Initiative. Mem. Council, RA. Mem., BAFTA. Hon. DLit Nottingham Trent, 2008. *Publications:* Dear Mariella, 2005; (ed jtly) Desire: 100 of literature's sexiest stories, 2016; Wild Women, 2019. *Recreations:* travelling, walking, reading, film, scuba diving. *T:* (020) 7221 5363. *E:* mariella.frostrup@observer.co.uk. *Clubs:* Groucho, Ivy, Soho House.

**FROUDE, Ven. Christine Ann;** Archdeacon of Malmesbury, 2011–18; Chaplain, Trinity College Bristol; *b* 6 June 1947; *d* of Winifred Woolcock and Frederick Woolcock; *m* 1972, David Froude; one *s* one *d*. *Educ:* Southern Diocesan Ministerial Trng Scheme. Various roles with Midland Bank incl. Hd of Trng Res., City of London Internat. Div.; ordained deacon, 1995, priest, 1996; non-stipendiary Minister, St Mary Magdalene, Stoke Bishop, 1995–99; Chaplain, Univ. Hosps Bristol NHS Foundn Trust, 1999–2001; Dean, Women's Ministry, Dio. of Bristol, 2000–11; Priest-in-charge, St Mary, Shirehampton, 2001–11; Acting Archdeacon of Bristol, 2013–18. Hon. Canon, Bristol Cathedral, 2001–11. Trustee, St Monica Trust. *Address:* 24 Waterloo Street, Clifton, Bristol BS8 4BT.

**FROW, Prof. John Anthony,** PhD; Professor of English, University of Sydney, since 2013; *b* 13 Nov. 1948; *s* of Anthony Gaunt Frow and Nola Marjorie Frow; *m* 1970, Mayerlene Engineer (marr. diss. 1985); one *s*; partner, 1978, Christine Alavi; one *d*; partner, 2001, Sandra Hawker. *Educ:* Australian National Univ. (BA); Cornell Univ. (MA 1974; PhD 1977). Lectr in American Lit., Universidad del Salvador, Buenos Aires, 1970; Lectr in English Lit., then Sen. Lectr, Murdoch Univ., WA, 1975–88; Visiting Professor: Univ. of Minnesota, 1988–89; Univ. of Qld, 1989–2000; Regius Prof. of Rhetoric and English Lit., Univ. of Edinburgh, 2000–04; Prof. of English, Univ. of Melbourne, 2004–12. FAHA 1998. *Publications:* Marxism and Literary History, 1986; Cultural Studies and Cultural Value, 1995; Time and Commodity Culture, 1997; (jtly) Accounting for Tastes, 1999; Genre, 2006; The Practice of Value, 2013; Character and Person, 2014; On Interpretive Conflict, 2019. *Address:* Department of English, University of Sydney, NSW 2006, Australia.

**FRY, Anthony Michael;** Chairman: Dairy Crest plc, 2010–14 (Deputy Chairman, 2009); CALA Group Ltd, 2010–15; *b* Worthing; *s* of Denis Fry and Doris, (Trixie), Fry (*née* Barter); *m* 1985, Anne Elizabeth Birrell; two *s* one *d*. *Educ:* Stonyhurst Coll.; Magdalen Coll., Oxford (BA 1st Cl. Hons Mod. Hist. 1977); Harvard Business Sch. (AMP 2007). Mem., Exec. Bd, N M Rothschild & Sons, 1977–96; Man. Dir, Credit Suisse, 1996–2004; Hd, UK Investment Banking, Lehman Brothers, 2004–07; Sen. Advr, Evercore Partners, 2008–11. Non-executive Director: Southern Water, 1990–96; Mowlem, 2000–06; Control Risks, 2007–. Chairman: LCC Ventures, 2010–12; Banco Espirito Santo UK, 2011–12 (Sen. Advr to Bd, 2012–14); Premier League, 2013–14. Non-exec. Dir, BSI, 2000–04; Trustee, BBC, 2008–13. Vice Chm., British Lung Foundn, 1996–2002; Member Board: Natural Hist. Mus., 1992–2004; LAMDA, 1998–2004; Nat. Film and TV Sch., 2001–04; SOAS, 2004– (Chm., Develt Bd, 2009–); The Sixteen, 2006–; ENO, 2009–; Paintings in Hosps, 2009–; Twig World, 2010–16; Member, Advisory Board: Project Associates, 2012–; Board Intelligence, 2012–. *Recreations:* discovering London monuments, cricket, opera, American Civil War, 18th century prints, political toby jugs. *T:* 07767 374567. *E:* amf@fryassociates.co.uk. *Clubs:* Soho House, Carlton, Century, Bonnetmakers; Armadillos Cricket, Incogniti Cricket, Sussex CC, Primrose Hill Cricket.

**FRY, Sir Graham (Holbrook),** KCMG 2006; HM Diplomatic Service, retired; Ambassador to Japan, 2004–08; *b* 20 Dec. 1949; *s* of Wing Comdr Richard Holbrook Fry and Marjorie Fry; *m* 1st, 1977, Mayko Iida (marr. diss. 1991); two *s*; 2nd, 1994, Toyoko Ando. *Educ:* Brasenose Coll., Oxford (BA 1972). Entered HM Diplomatic Service, 1972; Third, later Second, Sec., Tokyo, 1974–78; seconded to Invest in Britain Bureau, DoI, 1979–80; FCO, 1981–83; First Sec., Paris, 1983–87; FCO, 1987–88; Political Counsellor, Tokyo, 1989–93; Head, Far Eastern Dept, later Far Eastern and Pacific Dept, FCO, 1993–95; Dir, Northern Asia and Pacific, FCO, 1995–98; High Comr, Malaysia, 1998–2001; Dep. Under-Sec. of State, FCO, 2001–03; Dir Gen., Econ., FCO, 2003–04. Mem. Bd, Eisai Co. Ltd, 2012–17. Mem., Governing Body, SOAS, Univ. of London, 2008–15. Chm., Wildlife Trust for Beds, Cambs and Northants, 2016–; Trustee, Wildfowl and Wetlands Trust, 2009–15.

**FRY, Gregory John;** Executive Director, 1986–2016 and Chairman, 2011–16, St George plc; Divisional Executive Director, The Berkeley Group plc, 2011–16 (Director, 1996–2010); *b* 29 April 1957; *s* of Wilfred John Fry, Freeman of the City of London. *Educ:* Lord Wandsworth Coll., Hants. ACA 1983; FCA. Joined Berkeley Homes, 1982. Gov., Richmond upon Thames Coll., 2000–04. FInstD 1990. *Recreation:* Rugby. *Club:* Harlequins Rugby.

**FRY, Jonathan Michael;** Chairman, Control Risks Holdings Ltd, 2000–07; *b* 9 Aug. 1937; *s* of late Stephen Fry and Gladys Yvonne (*née* Blunt); *m* 1st, 1970, Caroline Mary Dunkerly (marr. diss. 1997); four *d*; 2nd, 1999, Marilyn Diana Russell. *Educ:* Repton Sch.; Trinity Coll., Oxford (Lit. Hum., MA). Engagement Manager and Consultant, McKinsey & Co., 1966–73; Unigate Foods Division: Man. Dir, 1973–76; Chm., 1976–78; Gp Planning Dir, Burmah Oil Trading Ltd, 1978–81; Chief Executive: Burmah Speciality Chemicals Ltd, 1981–87; Castrol Internat., 1987–93; Burmah Castrol: Man. Dir, 1990–93; Chief Exec., 1993–98; Chm., 1998–2000. Chm., Christian Salvesen plc, 1997–2003; non-executive Director: Northern Foods plc, 1991–2002 (Dep. Chm., 1996–2002); Elementis (formerly Harrisons & Crosfield), 1997–2004 (Chm., 1997–2004). Mem. Council, RIIA, 1998–2002. Chm. Govs, Repton Sch., 2003–12. *Recreations:* cricket, ski-ing, archaeology, wine, gardening. *Address:* Beechingstoke Manor, Pewsey, Wilts SN9 6HQ. *Clubs:* Beefsteak, MCC; Vincent's (Oxford).

**FRY, Lt-Gen. Sir Robert (Alan),** KCB 2005; CBE 2001 (MBE 1981); Vice President, Hewlett Packard, since 2009; *b* 6 April 1951; *s* of Raymond and Elizabeth Fry; *m* 1977, Elizabeth Woolmore; two *d*. *Educ:* Bath Univ. (BScEcon); King's Coll., London (MA). Worked in commerce, NY, 1972–73; joined Royal Marines, 1973: COS, 3 Commando Bde, 1989–91; CO 45 Commando, 1995–97; Dir Naval Staff, MoD, 1997–99; Comdr 3 Commando Bde, 1999–2001; Comdt-Gen., Royal Marines, 2001–02; COS, Perm. Jt HQ, 2002–03; DCDS (Commitments), MoD, 2003–06; Dep. Comdg Gen., Multinational Force, Iraq, 2006. CEO, EDS Defence and Security, 2007–09. Director: Injazat Data Services, Abu Dhabi, 2008–; Meeza Corp., Doha, 2008–; McKinney Rogers Internat., 2008–13 (Exec. Chm., 2010–13); non-exec. Chm., Albany Associates, 2012–. Mem., RBS Middle East Adv. Gp, 2011–. Visiting Professor: Dept of Politics and Internat. Relns, Univ. of Reading, 2009–; Dept of War Studies, KCL, 2014; Fellow, Changing Character of War, Oxford Univ., 2009–. Trustee: Help for Heroes, 2009–; RUSI, 2010–. Freeman, City of London, 2003. Hon. LLD Bath, 2014. Officer, Legion of Merit (USA), 2006. Occasional columnist, Wall St Jl; Feature writer, Prospect Mag., 2012–. *Publications:* (contrib.) War in a Time of Peace, 2014; contrib. to RUSI Jl, US Naval Inst. Proc., Bull. d'Etudes de la Marine, Huffington Post, City AM, Forbes Mag., Wall Street Jl, Prospect Mag. *Recreations:* Welsh Rugby, cinema, photography, history, cooking. *Address:* Albany Associates, 18–24 Turnham Green Terrace, W4 1QP. *Club:* Special Forces.

**FRY, Sir Roger (Gordon),** Kt 2012; CBE 2002 (OBE 1993); Chairman: King's Group, since 1981; King's Group Academies, since 2014; *b* Portsmouth, 10 Jan. 1943; *s* of Gordon Fry and Doris Fry (*née* Chopping); *m* 1st, 1966; one *s* one *d* (and one *s* decd); 2nd, 1983, Begoña Jauregui Campuzano; one *s* two *d*. *Educ:* primary and grammar schs, Portsmouth; King's Coll. London (BD; AKC); Inst. of Educn, Univ. of London (PGCE); Inst. of Dirs, London (Dip. Co. Direction). Lectr, Univ. of Comillas, Madrid, 1968–71; Founder, 1969, Headteacher, 1969–81, King's Coll., Madrid. Mem., Gen. Synod of C of E, 1990–95, 2005–10. Chm., Council of British Internat. Schs (formerly Council of British Ind. Schs in EC), 1996–2011 (Pres., 2011–); Dir, Ind. Schs Council, 2008–11. Nat. Pres., Brussels Chamber of Commerce in Spain, 2006–08. Founder, 1981, Chm., 1981–93, British Hispanic Foundn. Member: Multi Academy Trust, Worcester Dio., 2015–; Educn Adv. Bd, 2015–18, Internat. Educn Adv. Bd, 2019–, British Council; Council, Imperial Soc. of Knights Bachelor, 2017–. Gov., Royal Grammar Sch., Worcester, 1993–. Sir Thomas Pope Hon. Fellow, Trinity Coll., Oxford, 2009. Reader, C of E, 1969–2013. Freeman, City of London, 2002: Liveryman: Co. of Carmen, 2002–; Educators' Co., 2014–. Hon. DLitt Portsmouth, 2006. Internat. Medal, Complutense Univ., Madrid, 2019. Commander: Order of Civil Merit (Spain), 1994; Order of King Alfonso X The Wise (Spain), 2016. *Recreations:* study of world religions and cultures, current affairs, travel, family, classic cars, walking, gastronomy. *Address:* King's Group, Oldwood Road, St Michael's, Tenbury Wells, Worcs WR15 8PH. *E:* roger.fry@kingsgroup.org. *Clubs:* East India; Royal Naval, Royal Albert Yacht (Portsmouth); Rolls Royce Enthusiasts'; Financiero Genova, Gran Peña, Nuevo, de Campo, Rotary (Madrid).

**FRY, Sarah McC.;** *see* McCarthy-Fry.

**FRY, Stephen John;** writer, actor, comedian; *b* 24 Aug. 1957; *s* of Alan John Fry and Marianne Eve (*née* Newman); *m* 2015, Elliott Spencer. *Educ:* Uppingham Sch.; Queens' Coll., Cambridge (MA; Hon. Fellow, 2005). *TV series:* Blackadder, 1987–89; A Bit of Fry and Laurie, 1989–95; Jeeves in Jeeves and Wooster, 1990–92; Gormenghast, 2000; Absolute Power, 2003, 2005; Kingdom, 2007–09; Bones, 2007–09, 2017; 24: Live Another Day, 2014; The Great Indoors, 2016–17; presenter: QI, 2003–15; Stephen Fry: Gadget Man, 2012; Stephen Fry's Key to the City, 2013; writer and presenter: Stephen Fry in America, 2008; Last Chance To See, 2009; Fry's Planet Word, 2011; *TV documentary:* Stephen Fry: the secret life of a manic depressive, 2006 (Emmy Award, 2007); Stephen Fry: Out There, 2013; Fry's Central America, 2015; The Not So Secret Life of the Manic Depressive: 10 years on, 2016; *theatre:* Forty Years On, Queen's, 1984; The Common Pursuit, Phoenix, 1988; Twelfth Night, Shakespeare's Globe, transf. Apollo Th., 2012; *films:* Peter's Friends, 1992; I.Q., 1995; Wilde, 1997; Cold Comfort Farm, 1997; The Tichborne Claimant, 1998; Whatever Happened to Harold Smith?, 2000; Relative Values, 2000; Gosford Park, 2002; (dir) Bright Young Things, 2003; Tooth, 2004; The Life and Death of Peter Sellers, 2004; (for TV) Tom Brown's Schooldays, 2005; V for Vendetta, 2006; St Trinian's, 2007; Sherlock Holmes: A Game of Shadows, 2011; (for TV) The Borrowers, 2011; (for TV) Doors Open, 2012; The Look of Love, The Hobbit: The Desolation of Smaug, 2013; The Hobbit: The Battle of the Five Armies, 2014; The Man Who Knew Infinity, Love & Friendship, 2016; Missing Link, 2019; *radio series:* Fry's English Delight, 2008–. Numerous audiobook recordings incl. Harry Potter series. Columnist: The Listener, 1988–89; Daily Telegraph, 1990–91; The Guardian, 2007–. *Publications:* Me and My Girl, 1984 (musical performed in West End and on Broadway); A Bit of Fry and Laurie: collected scripts, 1990; Moab is My Washpot (autobiog.), 1997; The Ode Less Travelled, 2005; Stephen Fry in America, 2008; The Fry Chronicles: an autobiography, 2010; The Library Book, 2012; More Fool Me: a memoir, 2014; Mythos: the Greek myths retold, 2017 (adapted for stage, 2019); Heroes, 2018 (adapted for stage as Mythos: Heroes, 2019); *novels:* The Liar, 1991; The Hippopotamus, 1994; Making History, 1996; The Stars' Tennis Balls, 2000. *Recreations:* smoking, drinking, swearing, pressing wild flowers. *Address:* c/o Hamilton Hodell Ltd, 20 Golden Square, W1F 9JL. *Clubs:* Savile, Oxford and Cambridge, Groucho, Chelsea Arts, Garrick.

**FRYAR, Rt Rev. Godfrey Charles;** Bishop of Rockhampton, 2003–13; *b* 5 Feb. 1950; *s* of Neville Gordon Fryar and Norma Emma Fryar (*née* Kloske); *m* 1977, Bronwyn Anne Horrocks; two *s* one *d*. *Educ:* All Souls' Sch., Charters Towers, Qld; St Francis Coll. (ThL 1972). Ordained deacon, 1973, priest, 1974; Bush Brother, Longreach, Cunnamulla and Quilpie, 1973–76; Parish Priest, Dawson Valley, N Rockhampton, N Mackay, Stafford, 1977–93; Dean, St Saviour's Cathedral, Goulburn, 1993–98; Asst Bishop, Wagga Wagga, and Vicar Gen., Dio. of Canberra and Goulburn, 1998–2003. Protector Little Brother of St Francis, 2008–; Visitor, Soc. Sacred Advent Sisters, 2007–; Liaison Bp, Mission to Seafarers, 2004–09. Chm., Liturgy Commn, Anglican Ch Australia, 2008–13. Chair: Refugee Settlement Cttee, Dio. of Brisbane, 1989–92 (active involvement in refugee settlement,

1989– ); Anglicare Dio. of Canterbury and Goulburn, 2001–03; Anglicare Central Qld, 2004–05. Founding Mem. Bd, Riverina Anglican Coll., 1999–2003. *Recreation:* bush walking (walked Kokoda Track, 2006).

**FRYER, Dr Geoffrey,** FRS 1972; Deputy Chief Scientific Officer, Windermere Laboratory, Freshwater Biological Association, 1981–88; *b* 6 Aug. 1927; *s* of W. and M. Fryer; *m* 1953, Vivien Griffiths Hodgson; one *s* one *d. Educ:* Huddersfield College. DSc, PhD London. Royal Navy, 1946–48. Colonial Research Student, 1952–53; HM Overseas Research Service, 1953–60: Malawi, 1953–55; Zambia, 1955–57; Uganda, 1957–60; Sen., then Principal, then Sen. Principal Scientific Officer, Freshwater Biological Assoc., 1960–81. H. R. Macmillan Lectr, Univ. of British Columbia, 1963; Distinguished Vis. Schol., Univ. of Adelaide, 1985; Distinguished Lectr, Biol Scis Br., Dept Fisheries and Oceans, Canada, 1987; Hon. Prof., Inst. of Environmental and Natural (formerly Biol) Scis, Lancaster Univ., 1988–2008. Mem. Council, Royal Soc., 1978–80. Mem., Adv. Cttee on Science, Nature Conservancy Council, 1986–91. Pres., Yorks Naturalists' Union, 1993. Frink Medal, Zool Soc. of London, 1983; Linnean Medal for Zoology, Linnean Soc., 1987; Elsdon-Dew Medal, Parasitological Soc. of Southern Africa, 1998. *Publications:* (with T. D. Iles) The Cichlid Fishes of the Great Lakes of Africa: their biology and evolution, 1972; A natural history of the lakes, tarns and streams of the English Lake District, 1991; The Freshwater Crustacea of Yorkshire: a faunistic and ecological survey, 1993; (ed with V. R. Alexeev) Diapause in the Crustacea, 1996; numerous articles in scientific jls. *Recreations:* natural history, history of science, walking, church architecture, photography. *Address:* Greystones, Church Lane, Stonehouse, Glos GL10 2BG.

**FRYER-SPEDDING, John Henry Fryer,** CBE 2003 (OBE 1982); Vice Lord-Lieutenant of Cumbria, 2006–12; *b* 23 Jan. 1937; *s* of Lieut Col James Eustace Spedding, OBE and Mary Catherine Spedding (*née* Fryer); *m* 1968, Clare Caroline Ewbank, JP, *d* of Ven. Walter Frederick Ewbank; two *s. Educ:* Trinity Coll., Cambridge (BA 1958, MA 1961). Royal Green Jackets, 1958–68: served Germany, Cyprus and Borneo; retd Maj. 1968. Called to the Bar, Gray's Inn, 1970; a Recorder, 1990–97. Mem., Lake Dist Nat. Park Authy, 1997–2001. Pres., Royal Forestry Soc., 2003–05. Vice-Pres., Cumbria Community Foundn, 2007– (Trustee, 1997–2007; Chm., 1997–2002); Pres., Calvert Trusts (for disabled people), 2008–13 (Trustee, 1976–2006; Chm. Council, 2002–06; Vice-Pres., 2005–08). Fellow, Wordsworth Trust, 2000– (Trustee, 1978–2000); Vice-Pres., Tennyson Soc., 1984–. Hon. Fellow, Univ. of Cumbria, 2016. DL 1985, High Sheriff, 1997–98, Cumbria. DLI (TA), 1969–78: CO 7th Bn, 1976–78; retd Lt Col, 1978. *Recreations:* forestry, beekeeping. *Club:* Lansdowne.

**FUAD, Kerim Selchuk;** QC 2010; *b* Kampala, Uganda, 19 Jan. 1968; *s* of late Kutlu Tekin Fuad, CBE; *m* 1998, Tania Danielle Stevenson. *Educ:* Charterhouse Sch.; London Univ. (LLB Hons 1990). Called to the Bar, Inner Temple, 1992; in practice as barrister, specialising in criminal defence, 1992– ; Jt Hd of Chambers, 1 Inner Temple Lane, 2010–13; Hd of Chambers, Church Court Chambers, 2014– . Member, Executive: Criminal Bar Assoc., 2012–17; S Eastern Circuit, 2013– (Leader, 2017–18). Co-founder and Co-Chm., Cypriot Lawyers Soc., 2013– . Chm., Herts and Beds Bar Mess, 2013–17. Mem., nat. and local cttee, Better Case Mgt, 2015–16. *Recreations:* fire lighting, the works of Hergé, Liverpool FC, talk of exercise, friends, red wine, gardening, getting lost, making lists, enjoying my wife's great cooking, gnome collecting. *Address:* Church Court Chambers, Second Floor, Goldsmith Building, Temple, EC4Y 7BL. *T:* (020) 7936 3637. *E:* k.fuadqc@churchcourtchambers.co.uk.

**FUCHS, Prof. Anne,** Dr phil; FBA 2014; Director, Humanities Institute, University College Dublin, since 2016. *Educ:* Univ. of Konstanz (MA German and Eng. 1988; Dr phil 1991). UCL: Lectr, Sen. Lectr, then Prof. of Modern German Lit. and Culture, UCD, 1992–2010; Prof. of German, Univ. of St Andrews, 2011; Prof. of German Studies, Univ. of Warwick, 2012–16. MRIA 2009. *Publications:* Die Schmerzensspuren der Geschichte: zur Poetik der Erinnerung in W. G. Sebalds Prosa, 2004; Phantoms of War in Contemporary German Literature, Films and Discourse, 2008; (ed jtly) Debating German Cultural Identity since 1989, 2011; After the Dresden Bombing: pathways of memory, 1945 to the present, 2012; (ed with Jonathan Long) Time in German Literature and Culture, 1900–2015, 2015. *Address:* Humanities Institute, University College Dublin, Stillorgan Road, Belfield, Dublin 4, Ireland.

**FUGARD, Athol;** playwright, director, actor; *b* 11 June 1932; *s* of Harold David Fugard and Elizabeth Magdalene Potgieter; *m* 1956, Sheila Meiring; one *d. Educ:* Univ. of Cape Town. Directed earliest plays, Nongogo, No Good Friday, Johannesburg, 1960; acted in The Blood Knot, touring S Africa, 1961; Hello and Goodbye, 1965; directed and acted in The Blood Knot, London, 1966; Boesman and Lena, S Africa, 1969; directed Boesman and Lena, London, 1971; directed Serpent Players in various prodns, Port Elizabeth, from 1963, directed co-authors John Kani and Winston Ntshona in Sizwe Bansi is Dead, SA, 1972, The Island, 1973, and London, 1973–74; acted in film, Boesman and Lena, 1972; directed and acted in Statements after an Arrest under the Immorality Act, in SA, 1972, directed in London, 1973; wrote Dimetos for Edinburgh Fest., 1975; directed and acted in, A Lesson from Aloes, SA, 1978, London, 1980 (directed, NY 1981, winning NY Critics Circle Award for Best Play); directed: Master Harold and the Boys, NY, 1982 (Drama Desk Award), Johannesburg, 1983, Nat. Theatre, 1983 (Standard award for Best Play); The Road to Mecca, Yale Repertory Theatre, 1984; (also wrote) My Children! My Africa!, NY, 1990; (also wrote) Playland, SA, 1992, NY and London, 1993; (also wrote and acted in) Valley Song, Royal Court, 1996; (also wrote and acted in) The Captain's Tiger, NY, 1999, London, 2000; (also wrote) Sorrows and Rejoicings, London, 2002; Exits and Entrances, LA, 2004; Victory, SA, 2006; Coming Home, 2009; The Train Driver, SA, 2010; (also wrote) The Painted Rocks at Revolver Creek, 2015. Hon. DLitt: Natal, 1981; Rhodes, 1983; Cape Town, 1984; Emory, 1992; Port Elizabeth, 1993; Hon. DFA Yale, 1983; Hon. DHL Georgetown, 1984. *Films:* Boesman and Lena, 1973; The Guest, 1977; (acted in) Meetings with Remarkable Men (dir, Peter Brook), 1979; (wrote and acted in) Marigolds in August (Silver Bear Award, Berlin), 1980; (acted in) Gandhi, 1982; (co-dir and acted in) Road to Mecca, 1991. Adjunct Prof. of Playwriting, Acting and Directing, Univ. of Calif, San Diego. Playwright-in-residence, Signature Th., New York, 2012. Tony Award for lifetime achievement, 2011. *Publications:* The Blood Knot, 1962; People Are Living There, Hello and Goodbye, 1973; Boesman and Lena, 1973; (jtly) Three Port Elizabeth Plays: Sizwe Bansi is Dead, The Island, Statements after an Arrest under the Immorality Act, 1974; Tsotsi (novel), 1980 (also USA) (filmed 2005); A Lesson from Aloes, 1981 (also USA); Master Harold and the Boys, US 1982, UK 1983; Notebooks 1960–1977, 1983 (also USA); Road to Mecca, 1985; A Place with the Pigs, 1988; Cousins: a memoir, 1994. *Recreations:* angling, skin-diving, bird-watching. *Address:* c/o ICM Partners, 730 5th Avenue, New York, NY 10019, USA.

**FUGGER, Prof. Lars,** MD, PhD, DMSc; Professor of Neuroimmunology, University of Oxford, since 2007; Fellow of Oriel College, Oxford, since 2007; Honorary Consultant, Department of Clinical Immunology, John Radcliffe Hospital, Oxford, since 2003; *b* Copenhagen, 15 Aug. 1960; *s* of Henrik Fugger and Inger Fugger; *m* 1991, Astrid Kristine Nagel Iversen, MD, PhD; two *s* two *d. Educ:* Rungsted Gymnasium (BA Maths 1979); Univ. of Copenhagen (MD 1987; PhD 1990, DMSc 1993). Internships and residencies, various hosps, Denmark, 1987–90; Postdoctoral Fellow, Dept of Microbiol. and Immunol., Stanford Univ., 1990–94; Clin. Fellow, Dept of Clin. Immunol., Rigshospitalet, Copenhagen Univ. Hosp., 1994–96; Prof. of Clin. Immunology, Aarhus Univ. Hosp., 1996– ; Sen. Clin. Fellow, MRC Human Immunol. Unit, Weatherall Inst. of Molecular Medicine, John Radcliffe Hosp., Oxford, 2002–07; Prof. of Clin. Immunol., Univ. of Oxford, 2004– . Chm., Danish MRC, 2007– . Mem. Bd of Dirs, Novo Nordisk Foundn, Denmark, 2013– . FMedSci 2010. Gold Medal, Univ. of Aarhus, 1985; Anders Jahre Nordic Med. Res. Prize for young scientists, 1998; Descartes Prize, EC, 2002; August Krogh Prize, Danish Med. Soc., 2003; Award for Excellence in Clin. Sci., Eur. Soc. of Clin. Investigation, 2005; Sobek Internat. Res. Prize, Sobek Foundn, Germany, 2009; MS Res. of Year Award, MS Soc. (UK), 2012. Knight, Order of Dannebrog (Denmark), 2011. *Address:* Department of Clinical Neurology and MRC Human Immunology Unit, Weatherall Institute of Molecular Medicine, John Radcliffe Hospital, University of Oxford, Oxford OX3 9DS. *T:* (01865) 222351, *Fax:* (01865) 222502. *E:* lars.fugger@imm.ox.ac.uk.

**FUHR, Michael John,** CBE 2012 (OBE 1999); independent corporate consultant, since 2010; Chairman, ITSO Ltd, 2011–19; *b* 5 June 1949; *s* of late Max Fuhr and of Betty Fuhr (*née* Neuman); *m* 1975, Susan Harrington; two *d. Educ:* Bradford Grammar Sch.; Univ. of Surrey (BSc Hons 1973). Admin. trainee, 1974, Principal, 1978, DoE; Department of Transport, then DETR, subseq. DTLR, 1979–2001; Asst Sec., 1989; Project Dir, Channel Tunnel Rail Link, 1996–99; Dir, London Underground Task Gp, 1999–2001; Dir of Corporate Strategy, Treasury Solicitor's Dept, 2001–03; Dir, Cross London Rail Links Ltd, 2004–09; Dir, later Commercial Advr, DfT, 2009–16. Mem. Council, Univ. of Sussex, 2009–18 (Chm., Audit Cttee, 2016–18). *Recreations:* most sports, photography, technology, following the variable fortunes of Bradford City AFC. *E:* mike.office@ntlworld.com.

**FUJII, Hiroaki;** Chairman, Mori Arts Center, Tokyo, since 2004; Senior Executive Adviser, Mori Building, since 2004; Adviser, Japan Foundation, Tokyo, since 2003 (President, 1997–2003); *b* 21 Aug. 1933; *m* 1963, Kiyoko Shimoda; three *d. Educ:* Tokyo Univ.; Amherst Coll., USA (BA 1958). Entered Min. of Foreign Affairs, Japan, 1956; Dir, Econ. Affairs Div., UN Bureau, 1971–72; Private Sec. to Minister for Foreign Affairs, 1972–74; Dir, 2nd Econ. Co-operation Div., Econ. Co-operation Bureau, 1974–75; Dir, 1st N American Div., American Affairs Bureau, 1975–76; Fellow, Center for Internat. Affairs, Harvard Univ., 1976; Counsellor, Embassy of Japan, Washington, 1977–79; Ministry of Foreign Affairs: Dir, Personnel Div., Minister's Secretariat, 1979–81; Dep. Dir Gen., Asian Affairs Bureau, 1981–83; Consul-Gen., Hong Kong, 1983–85; Ministry of Foreign Affairs: Dir Gen., N American Bureau, 1985–88; Dep. Vice-Minister, 1988–89; Ambassador to: OECD, Paris, 1989–92; Thailand, 1992–94; Court of St James's, 1994–97. Hon. DCL: Durham, 1997; UEA, 1999; Hon. LLD Birmingham, 1997. Kt Grand Cross (1st Cl.), Most Exalted Order of White Elephant (Thailand), 1994. *Address:* Mori Arts Center, Roppongi Hills Mori Tower, 6–10–1 Roppongi, Minato-ku, Tokyo 106–6150, Japan. *T:* (3) 64066133, *Fax:* (3) 64066518.

**FULBROOK, Prof. Mary Jean Alexandra,** PhD; FRHistS; FBA 2007; Professor of German History, University College London, since 1995; *b* 28 Nov. 1951; *d* of Prof. Arthur J. C. Wilson and Dr Harriett C. Wilson (*née* Friedeberg); *m* 1973, Dr Julian Fulbrook; two *s* one *d. Educ:* Sidcot Sch., Somerset; King Edward VI High Sch., Birmingham; Newnham Coll., Cambridge (BA 1973 Double 1st Cl. Hons; Schol., Sen. Schol., Helen Gladstone Meml Schol.; MA 1977); Harvard Univ. (AM 1975; PhD 1979). FRHistS 1987. Harvard Center for European Studies Krupp Fellow, LSE, 1976–77; Temporary Lecturer: LSE, 1977–78; Brunel Univ. 1978–79; Lady Margaret Res. Fellow, New Hall, Cambridge, 1979–82; Res. Associate, KCL, 1982–83; University College London: Lectr, 1983–91, Reader, 1991–95, in German Hist.; Dir, Centre for European Studies, 1991–2010; Hd, German Dept, 1995–2006; Mem., Council, 2003–07; Vice-Dean (Inter-Disciplinarity), Faculty of Arts and Humanities, 2010–13; Dir, European Inst., 2013–16; Dean, Faculty of Social and Histl Scis, 2013–17. Vis. Fellow, Forschungsschwerpunkt Zeithistorische Studien, Potsdam, 1994; Vis. Bye-Fellow, Newnham Coll., Cambridge, 1998; Vis. Prof., Univ. of Jena, 2013. Jt Founding Ed., German History, 1984–94. Member: Jt Cttee on W Europe of ACLS/SSRC, 1990–94; Adv. Bd, German Historical Inst., London, 2002–10; AHRC (formerly AHRB) Res. Panel for Hist., 2004–07; Adv. Bd, Stiftung Gedenkstätten Buchenwald und Mittelbau-Dora, 2007– ; Adv. Bd, Bundeskanzler-Willy-Brandt-Stiftung, 2008–18; Adv. Bd, Foundn for Flight, Expulsion and Reconciliation, 2017– . Chm., German Hist. Soc., 1996–99. Vice-Chairman of Governors: Great Ormond Street Hosp. Sch. for Sick Children, 1980–85; Haverstock Sch., 1999–2001; Chm. Govs, S Camden Community Sch., 1992–94. Mayoress, London Bor. of Camden, 1985–86. *Publications:* Piety and Politics: religion and the rise of absolutism in England, Württemberg and Prussia, 1983; A Concise History of Germany, 1990, 3rd edn 2018 (trans. incl. Hungarian, Spanish, Swedish, Korean, Romanian, Chinese, Japanese); The Divided Nation: Germany 1918–1990, 1991 (trans. Italian), 4th edn as A History of Germany 1918–2008: the divided nation, 2014; The Two Germanies 1945–1990: problems of interpretation, 1992, 2nd edn as Interpretations of the Two Germanies 1945–1990, 2000; (ed) National Histories and European History, 1993; Anatomy of a Dictatorship: inside the GDR 1949–89, 1995; (ed with D. Cesarani) Citizenship, Nationality and Migration in Europe, 1996; (ed with J. Breuilly) German History since 1800, 1997; German National Identity after the Holocaust, 1999 (trans. Hungarian); (ed) The Short Oxford History of Europe 1945–2000, 2000 (trans. Spanish and Polish); (ed with M. Swales) Representing the German Nation, 2000; (ed) Twentieth-century Germany: politics, culture and society 1918–1990, 2001; Historical Theory, 2002; Hitler, Book 1, 2004, Book 2, 2005; The People's State: East German society from Hitler to Honecker, 2005 (trans. German 2008); (ed) Uncivilising Processes? Excess and Transgression in German Society and Culture, 2006; (ed) Power and Society in the GDR, 1961–1979, 2009; Dissonant Lives: generations and violence through the German dictatorships, 2011; A Small Town near Auschwitz: ordinary Nazis and the Holocaust, 2012 (Fraenkel Prize, Wiener Liby for Study of Holocaust and Genocide) (trans. Dutch, German); (ed with A. Port) Becoming East German: socialist structures and sensibilities after Hitler, 2013; Erfahrung, Erinnerung, Geschichtsschreibung: neue Perspektiven auf die deutschen Diktaturen, 2016; (ed jtly) Reverberations of Nazi Violence in Germany and Beyond, 2016; Reckonings: legacies of Nazi persecution and the quest for justice, 2018; numerous articles in jls and chapters in books. *Recreations:* swimming, jogging (London marathon 2002), reading novels, spending time with my family. *Address:* Department of German, University College London, Gower Street, WC1E 6BT. *T:* (020) 7679 7120. *E:* m.fulbrook@ucl.ac.uk.

**FÜLE, Štefan;** Special Envoy for the OSCE and the Western Balkans, Ministry of Foreign Affairs, Czech Republic; Member, European Commission, 2010–14; *b* Sokolov, 24 May 1962; *m* Hana; one *s* two *d. Educ:* Charles Univ., Prague; Moscow State Inst. of Internat. Relns. Desk Officer, UN Dept, Czechoslovakian Min. of Foreign Affairs, 1987–90; First Sec., Czechoslovakian, subseq. Czech Perm. Delegn to the UN, 1990–95; Mem., Czech Delegn, and Alternate Rep. to UN Security Council, 1994–95; Czech Ministry of Foreign Affairs: Dir, UN Dept, 1995–96; Dir, Security Policy Dept, 1996–98; Ambassador to Lithuania, 2000–01; First Dep. Defence Minister, 2001–02; Ambassador to the UK, 2003–05; Perm. Rep. to NATO, 2005–09; Eur. Affairs Minister, 2009.

**FULFORD, Rt Hon. Sir Adrian Bruce,** Kt 2002; PC 2013; **Rt Hon. Lord Justice Fulford;** a Lord Justice of Appeal, since 2013; Senior Presiding Judge of England and Wales, 2016–17 (Deputy Senior Presiding Judge, 2015); Vice-President, Court of Appeal (Criminal Division), since 2019; *b* 8 Jan. 1953; *s* of Gerald John Fulford and Marie Bettine (*née* Stevens). *Educ:* Elizabeth Coll., Guernsey; Southampton Univ. (BA Hons). Housing Advr, Shelter's Housing Aid Centre, 1974–75; called to the Bar, Middle Temple, 1978, Bencher, 2002; QC 1994; a Recorder, 2001–02; a Judge of the High Ct, QBD, 2002–13; a Judge of the Internat. Criminal Ct, The Hague, 2003–12 (Pres., Trial Div., 2008–12; Presiding Judge, Trial Chamber I, 2007–12; Mem., Adv. Cttee on Nominations, 2016–); a Presiding Judge, S Eastern Circuit, 2010–13; Judge in charge of Technol., 2014–17. Investigatory Powers Comr, 2017–19. Ed., UK Human Rights Reports, 2000–14. Hon. DLaws Southampton, 2011. *Publications:* (contrib.) Atkin's Court Forms, 1987; (ed) Archbold Criminal Pleading and Practice, 1992; (jtly) A Criminal Practitioner's Guide to Judicial Review and Case Stated, 1999; (jtly) Judicial Review: a practical guide, 2004; (ed jtly) Archbold International Criminal Courts, 2005, 4th edn 2014. *Recreations:* riding, golf. *Address:* Royal Courts of Justice, Strand, WC2A 2LL. *Club:* Garrick.

**FULFORD, Prof. Michael Gordon,** CBE 2011; PhD; FSA; FBA 1994; Professor of Archaeology, University of Reading, since 1993; *b* 20 Oct. 1948; *s* of Comdr E. G. J. D. Fulford, RN (retd) and E. Z. Fulford (*née* Simpson); *m* 1972, Charlotte Jane Hobbs; one *s* one *d. Educ:* St Edward's Sch., Oxford; Univ. of Southampton (BA Hons 1970; PhD 1975). DES Res. Student, 1970; Research Assistant: Univ. of Southampton, 1971–72; Univ. of Oxford, 1972–74; University of Reading: Lectr in Archaeol., 1974–85; Reader, 1985–88; Leverhulme Res. Fellow, 1987; Personal Prof., 1988–93; Dean, Faculty of Letters and Social Scis, 1994–97; Pro-Vice-Chancellor, 1998–2004; Leverhulme Major Res. Fellow, 2004–07. Chm., Archaeol. Panel, RAE 2001, Main Panel H, RAE 2008, HEFCE. Dalrymple Lectr, Glasgow Univ., 1996. Pres., Soc. for Promotion of Roman Studies, 2005–08 (Vice-Pres., 2008–18; Hon. Vice-Pres., 2018; Editor, Britannia, 1994–99); Chm., Roman Res. Trust, 2008–17. Historic England (formerly English Heritage): Chm., Hadrian's Wall Adv. Panel, 1989–97 (Mem., 1985–97); Mem., Ancient Monuments Adv. Cttee, 1991–97; Comr, 2014–19; Mem., Adv. Cttee, 2019– (Chm., 2014–19); Comr, RCHM, 1993–99; Member: Archaeology Adv. Cttee, Nat. Mus. of Wales, 1991–99; SE Mus., Library and Archive Council, 2002–06. Vice-Pres., Royal Archaeol Inst., 1996–2001; Mem., Council, British Acad., 2003–15 (Mem., Humanities Res. Bd, 1995–98; Chm., Acad.-Sponsored Insts and Socs Cttee, 2005–10; Treas., 2010–15); Member: Council, British Sch. at Rome, 2003–05; Sen. Academic Promotions Cttee, Univ. of Cambridge, 2008–14. Trustee, Roman Res. Trust, 2017–. Chm., Aimhigher, Berks, 2004. FSA 1977. *Publications:* New Forest Roman Pottery, 1975; (with B. Cunliffe) CSIR Great Britain I: Bath and the Rest of Wessex, 1982; Silchester Defences, 1984; (with D. Peacock) Excavations at Carthage: The British Mission, The Pottery and other Ceramics, Vol. 1, 1984, Vol. 2, 1994; The Silchester Amphitheatre, 1989; Excavations at Sabratha 1948–1951, Vol. 2, pt i (ed with M. Hall), 1989, pt ii (ed with R. Tomber), 1994; (ed jtly) Developing Landscape of Lowland Britain: the archaeology of the British gravels, 1992; (ed jtly) England's Coastal Heritage, 1997; (with J. R. Timby) Late Iron Age and Roman Silchester: excavations on the site of the Forum-Basilica 1977 and 1980–86, 2000; (jtly) Life and Labour in Late Roman Silchester: excavations in Insula IX since 1997, 2006; (jtly) Iron Age and Romano-British Settlements and Landscapes of Salisbury Plain, 2006; (jtly) Silchester: city in transition, 2011; (jtly) Pevensey Castle, Sussex, 2011; (ed) Silchester and the Study of Romano-British Urbanism, 2012; (jtly) A Late Roman Town House and its Environs, 2014; (ed jtly) New Visions of the Countryside of Roman Britain, vol. 1, 2016, vol. 2, 2017, vol. 3, 2018; (jtly) Late Iron Age Calleva: the pre-conquest occupation at Silchester Insula IX, 2018. *Recreations:* music, walking, sailing. *Address:* Department of Archaeology, University of Reading, PO Box 227, Reading, Berks RG6 6AB. *T:* (0118) 378 8048.

**FULFORD-DOBSON, Captain Michael,** CVO 1999; OBE 2008; JP; RN; Lord-Lieutenant of Dorset, 1999–2006; *b* 6 April 1931; *e s* of late Lt-Col Cyril Fulford-Dobson, OBE and Betty Bertha Fulford-Dobson (*née* Bendelack-Hudson-Barmby); *m* 1966, Elizabeth Barbara Mary Rose Tate; three *d. Educ:* Pangbourne Coll.; RN Coll., Dartmouth; RN Coll., Greenwich. Royal Navy, 1949–84 (served Korean War, Suez Operation, first Cod War; 3 Sea Comds); Gentleman Usher to the Queen, 1985–99, Extra Gentleman Usher, 1999–. Chm., W Dorset Hosps NHS Trust, 1991–98. Chm., Dorset Trust, 1991–2000; President: Dorset Br., CPRE, 1995–2008; Dorset Natural History and Archaeol Soc., 2010–14; Dorset Health Trust, 2011–; Poole Maritime Trust, 2013–; Trustee, Cancer Care Dorset, 1998–2007; Patron: Bournemouth Natural Sci. Soc., 1999–2006; Community Foundn for Dorset (formerly for Bournemouth, Dorset and Poole), 2000–; Bournemouth Soc. for Visually Impaired, 2001–; President: Dorset Army Cadet League, 1999–2006; Dorset Scout Council, 2002–; Jt Patron, Dorset and Somerset Sea Cadet Assoc., 2001–06. Dir, In and Out Ltd, 1993–96. Member of Court: Exeter Univ., 1999–2007; Southampton Univ., 1999–2007; Governor, Sherborne Sch., 1999–2007. Patron, European Coll. of Chiropractice, 2000–06. Patron, Dorset Yeomanry, 2002– (Trustee, Comrades Assoc., 1999–). Church Warden, St Mary's Cerne Abbas, 1992–2012 (Chm. of Friends, 2018–). High Sheriff of Dorset, 1994–95; DL 1995, JP 1999, Dorset. KStJ 1999 (Pres., St John Council for Dorset, 1999–2006). Hon. Dr Arts Bournemouth, 2007. *Recreations:* restoration of historic buildings, Freemasonry. *Address:* Cerne Abbey, Dorset DT2 7JQ. *T:* (home) (01300) 341284, (office) (01300) 341948. *E:* cerneabbey@hotmail.com. *Clubs:* White's, Royal Over-Seas League.
*See also* Viscount FitzHarris.

**FULHAM, Bishop Suffragan of,** since 2013; **Rt Rev. Jonathan Mark Richard Baker;** Guild Vicar, St Andrew Holborn, since 2015; *b* 6 Oct. 1966; *s* of Sir John William Baker, *qv*; *m* 1st, 1992, Jacqueline Norton (marr. diss. 2013); two *s* one *d*; 2nd, 2015, Susie Page. *Educ:* Merchant Taylors' Sch., Northwood; St John's Coll., Oxford (BA 1988, MPhil 1990, MA (Eng. Lit.)); St Stephen's House, Oxford (BA Theol. 1992). Ordained deacon, 1993, priest, 1994; Asst Curate, All Saints, Ascot Heath, 1993–96; Priest i/c, 1996–99, Vicar, 1999–2003, Holy Trinity, Reading and St Mark, Reading; Principal, Pusey House, Oxford, 2003–13; Asst Curate, St Thomas with St Frideswide, Oxford, 2008–11; Asst Bishop, Dioceses of Bath and Wells, Lichfield, Worcester, Oxford, and Salisbury, 2011–13; Bishop Suffragan of Ebbsfleet, 2011–13; Guild Vicar, St Dunstan-in-the-West, Fleet Street, 2013–15. Hon. DD Nashotah House, Wisconsin, 2009. *Publications:* (ed) Consecrated Women?, 2004; (ed jtly) Who Is This Man?, 2006. *Recreations:* music, theatre, poetry, crime fiction, continental holidays. *Address:* The Vicarage, 5 St Andrew Street, EC4A 3AF.

**FULLBROOK, Lorraine;** *b* Glasgow, 28 July 1959; *d* of late Ian and Margo; *m* 1987, Mark Fullbrook. *Educ:* Glasgow Caledonian Univ. Mem. (C) Hart DC, 2000–04 (Leader, 2001–04). Contested (C) S Ribble, 2005. MP (C) S Ribble, 2010–15. Mem., Home Affairs Select Cttee, 2010–15. FRSA.

**FULLER, Anne Rosemary,** OBE 2000; JP; Vice President, Magistrates' Association, since 1999 (Deputy Chairman of Council, 1993–96, Chairman, 1996–99); *b* 27 Sept. 1936; *d* of Ronald Clifford Dent and Clara Vera Dent (*née* Murray); *m* 1960, John Acland Fuller (*d* 2006); two *s* one *d. Educ:* St Anne's Sch., Windermere; Royal Holloway Coll., Univ. of London (BA Hons 1957); KCL and LSE (Dip. in Law 1992). Market Research Executive: McCann Erickson, then Marplan, 1958–60; Bureau of Commercial Research, 1960–65; freelance market res. consultant, 1965–. Member: Nat. Forum, SCAA, 1996–97; Home Secretary's Task Force on Youth Justice, 1997–98; Compliance and Supervision Cttee, Office for Supervision of Solicitors, 1998–2001; Sentencing Adv. Panel, 2000–10; Adjudication Panel: Law Soc., 2001–07; SRA, 2007–08; Tribunal Mem., Disciplinary Cttee, 2000–09, Review Panel, 2009–, ICAEW. Dir and Trustee, Soc. of Voluntary Associates, 2000–04. Asst Hosp. Manager, Priory Hosp., Roehampton, 2010–14. JP Kingston-upon-Thames, 1975 (Dep. Chm., 1991–95); Chm., Betting Licensing Cttee, 1986–89; Mem., Magistrates' Courts Cttee, 1987–96; Chm., Youth Panel, 1990–93; Vice Pres., Magistrates' Assoc., 1999– (Mem. Council, 1984–; Vice Chm., Sentencing Cttee, 1991–93); Mem., Magistrates' Courts Consultative Council, 1993–99 (Mem., Trial Issues Gp, 1996–99); Nat. Co-ordinator, Magistrates in Community Project, 1993–97. Mem., Chatham House, RIIA, 2009–. FRSA 1997. *Publications:* (ed jtly) International Directory of Market Research Organisations, 1974, 11th edn 1994; numerous articles on magisterial matters. *Recreations:* music, theatre, cookery, international affairs, travel, gardening. *Address:* 41 Savery Drive, Long Ditton, Surrey KT6 5RJ. *T:* (020) 8224 5308.

**FULLER, Brian Leslie,** CBE 1989; QFSM 1981; Commandant Chief Executive, Fire Service College, 1990–94; *b* 18 April 1936; *s* of Walter Leslie Victor Fuller and Eliza May Fuller; *m* 1957, Linda Peters; three *s. Educ:* St Albans County Grammar Sch. for Boys. FIFireE 1975. Station Officer: Herts Fire Brigade, 1960–66; Warwicks Fire Brigade, 1966–68; Asst Divl Officer, Notts Fire Brigade, 1968–69; Divl Commander, Essex Fire Brigade, 1969–72; Dep. Chief Fire Officer, Glamorgan Fire Brigade, 1972–74; Chief Fire Officer: Mid Glamorgan Fire Brigade, 1974–80; Notts Fire Brigade, 1980–81; W Midlands Fire Service, 1981–90. Gen. Manager and Principal, Fire Safety Engrg Coll., Oman, 1997–2001; Chm., BFA Develts Internat., 2001–04. Mem. (C), Bromsgrove DC, 2003–07. Hon. DSc South Bank, 1993. *Recreations:* cricket, music, reading. *Address:* Honey Cottage, Honey Lane, Angmering, Littlehampton, W Sussex BN16 4AB.

**FULLER, Prof. Christopher John,** PhD; FBA 2007; Professor of Anthropology, London School of Economics and Political Science, 1994–2009, now Emeritus. *Educ:* Peterhouse, Cambridge (BA 1970; PhD 1974). Lectr, Dept of Social Anthropology, Univ. of Manchester, 1974–79; Lectr in Anthropology, 1979–87, Reader in Anthropology, 1987–94, LSE. Specialist on anthropology of India; fieldwork: Nayars and Syrian Christians, Kerala, 1971–72; Temple of Madurai, Tamilnadu, 1976–2001; ESRC research projects: on regionalism, nationalism and globalisation in India, 2003–05; on Tamil Brahman community, 2005–08. *Publications:* Servants of the Goddess: the priests of a South Indian temple, 1991; (with V. Bénéï) The Everyday State and Society in Modern India, 2001; The Renewal of the Priesthood: modernity and traditionalism in a South Indian temple, 2003; The Camphor Flame: popular Hinduism and Indian society, 2004; (ed with J. Assayag) Globalizing India: perspectives from below, 2005; (with Haripriya Narasimhan) Tamil Brahmans: the making of a middle-class caste, 2014; contribs to jls incl. Contribs to Indian Sociol., Anthropol. Today, Social Anthropol., Modern Asian Studies, Econ. and Political Weekly, Comparative Studies in Society and Hist. *Address:* c/o Department of Anthropology, London School of Economics and Political Science, Houghton Street, WC2A 2AE.

**FULLER, Eleanor Mary,** OBE 2013; JP; HM Diplomatic Service, retired; Director of Advocacy and Commonwealth Engagement, Queen Elizabeth Diamond Jubilee Trust, since 2013; *b* Aldershot, 31 Dec. 1953; *d* of Peter and Ruth Breedon; *m* 1984, Simon William John Fuller, *qv*; three *s. Educ:* Somerville Coll., Oxford (MA Modern Langs). Joined FCO, 1975; FCO, 1975–77; Paris, 1978–81; FCO, 1981–83; on loan to ODA, 1983–86; Second, later First Sec., FCO, 1990–93; UNRWA for Palestine refugees in Near East, Vienna, 1993–96; First Sec., UK Delegn to OSCE, Vienna, 1998–99; First Sec., UK Mission to UN and WTO, Geneva, 2000–04; on loan to DFID, 2004–06; FCO, 2006–07; Perm. Rep. of UK to Council of Europe, Strasbourg, 2007–12; FCO, 2012. JP SE London 2014. *Recreations:* gardens, music. *Address:* Queen Elizabeth Diamond Jubilee Trust, 128 Buckingham Palace Road, SW1W 9SA. *E:* eleanor.fuller@qejubileetrust.org.
*See also* T. J. Breedon.

**FULLER, Sir James (Henry Fleetwood),** 4th Bt *cr* 1910, of Neston Park, Corsham, Wiltshire; manager, Neston Park; *b* 1 Nov. 1970; *e s* of Major Sir John William Fleetwood Fuller, 3rd Bt and of Lorna Marian (*née* Kemp-Potter); *S* father, 1998; *m* 2000, Venetia, *d* of Col Robin Mactaggart; two *s. Educ:* Milton Abbey Sch. Commnd The Life Guards, 1991; Belize, 1993; Bosnia, 1994; Knightsbridge, 1995–98; with Fuller Smith & Turner plc, 1998–2003 (non-exec. Dir, 2010–). *Heir: s* Archie Mungo Fleetwood Fuller, *b* 7 Aug. 2001. *Address:* Neston Park, Corsham, Wiltshire SN13 9TG. *T:* (01225) 810211.

**FULLER, John Leopold,** FRSL 1980; writer; Fellow of Magdalen College, Oxford, and Tutor in English, 1966–2002, now Fellow Emeritus; *b* 1 Jan. 1937; *s* of late Roy Broadbent Fuller, CBE, FRSL; *m* 1960, Cicely Prudence Martin; three *d. Educ:* St Paul's School; New Coll., Oxford (BLitt, MA). Vis. Lectr, State Univ. of NY at Buffalo, 1962–63; Asst Lectr, Univ. of Manchester, 1963–66. *Publications:* Fairground Music, 1961; The Tree that Walked, 1967; A Reader's Guide to W. H. Auden, 1970; The Sonnet, 1972; Cannibals and Missionaries, 1972, and Epistles to Several Persons, 1973 (Geoffrey Faber Meml Prize, 1974); Squeaking Crust, 1973; The Last Bid, 1975; The Mountain in the Sea, 1975; Lies and Secrets, 1979; The Illusionists (Southern Arts Lit. Prize), 1980; The Extraordinary Wool Mill and other stories, 1980; Waiting for the Music, 1982; Flying to Nowhere (Whitbread Prize for a First Novel), 1983; The Beautiful Inventions, 1983; (ed) The Dramatic Works of John Gay, 1983; Come Aboard and Sail Away, 1983; The Adventures of Speedfall, 1985; Selected Poems 1954–1982, 1985; (with James Fenton) Partingtime Hall, 1986; Tell It Me Again, 1988; The Grey Among the Green, 1988; The Burning Boys, 1989; (ed) The Chatto Book of Love Poetry, 1990; The Mechanical Body, 1991; Look Twice, 1991; The Worm and the Star, 1993; Stones and Fires, 1996 (Forward Prize, Forward Poetry Trust, 1997); Collected Poems, 1996; A Skin Diary, 1997; W. H. Auden: a commentary, 1998; (ed) The Oxford Book of Sonnets, 2000; The Memoirs of Laetitia Horsepole, 2001; Now and for a Time, 2002; Ghosts, 2004; Flawed Angel, 2005; The Space of Joy, 2006; Song & Dance, 2008; Pebble & I, 2010; (with David Hurn) Writing the Picture, 2010; Who is Ozymandias? and other Puzzles in Poetry, 2011; Dream Hunter (chamber opera libretto), 2011; New Selected Poems 1983–2008, 2012; Sketches from the Sierra de Tejeda, 2013; The Dice Cup, 2014; You're Having Me On, 2014; Gravel in my Shoe, 2015; (with Andrew Wynn Owen) AWOL, 2015; A Week in Bern, 2016; The Stone Flowers, 2016; Double Dactyls, 2017; The Clock in the Forest, 2019. *Recreations:* correspondence chess, music. *Address:* Magdalen College, Oxford OX1 4AU.

**FULLER, Jonathan Paul;** QC 2002; **His Honour Judge Fuller;** a Circuit Judge, since 2014; *b* 27 Feb. 1954; *s* of Edward and Joan Fuller; *m* 1988, Karon J. Quinn (*d* 2019); two *s* one *d. Educ:* Ampleforth; Liverpool Poly. (LLB Lond. (ext.)); Inns of Court Sch. of Law. Called to the Bar, Lincoln's Inn, 1977; a Recorder, 1999–2014. *Address:* Courts of Justice, Deansleigh Road, Bournemouth, Dorset BH7 7DS.

**FULLER, Rev. Canon Dr Michael Jeremy;** Senior Teaching Fellow, New College, Edinburgh, since 2018 (Teaching Fellow, 2014–18); *b* 7 Jan. 1963; *s* of Peter Roy Fuller and Mary Eileen Fuller; *m* 1993, Susan Rigby, *qv*; two *s. Educ:* King Edward VI Grammar

Sch., Chelmsford; Worcester Coll., Oxford (BA 1985, MA 1989; DPhil 1989); Westcott House and Queens' Coll., Cambridge (BA 1991). Ordained deacon 1992, priest 1993; Curate, All Saints', High Wycombe, 1992–95; Associate Rector, St John's, Princes Street, Edinburgh, 1995–99; Theological Institute of Scottish Episcopal Church: Pantonian Prof., 2000–14; Principal, 2000–02; Initial Ministerial Educn Officer, 2002–04; Provincial Ministerial Develt Officer, 2004–14. Canon, 2000–14, Hon. Canon, 2015–, St Mary's Cathedral, Edinburgh. Chair, Science and Religion Forum, 2013–18. Hon. Vis. Fellow, New Coll., Edinburgh, 1998–2014; Hon. Vis. Fellow, Univ. of Glasgow, 2008–18. Vice Pres. for Publications, Eur. Soc. for Study of Sci. and Theol., 2014–. *Publications*: Atoms and Icons, 1995; Matter and Meaning, 2010; Is Religion Natural?, 2012; Inspiration in Science and Religion, 2012; The Concept of the Soul, 2014; What is Life?, 2015; Do Emotions Shape the World?, 2016; Are We Special?, 2017; articles and reviews in Zygon, Science and Christian Belief, Theology, Modern Believing, New Blackfriars, Musical Times, Wagner Jl, etc. *Recreations*: opera, reading, walking. *Address*: New College, Mound Place, Edinburgh EH1 2LX. *Club*: New (Edinburgh).

**FULLER, Michael John;** Director and Chief Executive Officer, Bank of Kuwait and Middle East, 2003–06; *b* 1932; *m* 1st, 1955, Maureen Rita Slade (marr. diss. 1989); two s two d; 2nd, 1990, Elizabeth Frost. *Educ*: Wallington County Grammar Sch. FCIB 1980. National Service, commnd RAF, 1950–52. Midland Bank, 1948–90: various branch, regl and head office posts; Gp Public Affairs Advr, 1977–79; Regl Dir, Southampton, 1979–81; Gen. Manager, Midland and Wales, 1981–82; Gen. Manager, Business Develt Div., 1982–85; UK Operations Dir, 1985–87; Dep. Chief Exec., 1987–89, Chief Exec., 1989–90, UK Banking Sector; Gen. Man., Nat. Bank of Abu Dhabi, 1991–92; Dir and CEO, Al Ahli Commercial Bank BSC, subseq. Ahli United Bank (Bahrain) BSC(c), 1992–2002. Chm., ais>BrandLab, 2007–08. *Recreations*: reading, travelling. *Club*: Royal Air Force.

**FULLER, Richard;** *b* Bedford. *Educ*: University Coll., Oxford (BA); Harvard Business Sch. (MBA). Former Partner: technol. venture capital firm; mgt consultancy. Contested (C) Bedford, 2005. MP (C) Bedford, 2010–17; contested (C) same seat, 2017. Nat. Chm., Young Conservatives, 1985–87.

**FULLER, Simon;** Founder, XIX Entertainment Ltd, 2010; Co-founder, XIX Globosport, 2013; Founder and Chief Executive Officer, 19 Entertainment Ltd, 1985–2010; *b* 17 May 1960; *m* 2008, Natalie Swanston. Chrysalis Music, 1981–85; founder of 19 Entertainment, comprising management, merchandising, music recording and TV production operations; manager of artists incl. Annie Lennox, Cathy Dennis, Spice Girls, Emma Bunton, S Club 7, Will Young, Gareth Gates, David and Victoria Beckham, Carrie Underwood, Adam Lambert, Andy Murray, Daughtry, Lisa Marie Presley, Roland Mouret, Lewis Hamilton. Dir, CKX, 2005–09. Creator and producer, TV series, Pop Idol, 2001, American Idol, 2002–10, So You Think You Can Dance, 2005–10, If I Can Dream, 2010; exec. producer, Bel Ami (film), 2011; Serengeti, 2019.

**FULLER, Simon William John,** CMG 1994; HM Diplomatic Service, retired; UK Permanent Representative to the Office of the United Nations and other international organisations, Geneva, 2000–03; *b* 27 Nov. 1943; *s* of late Rowland William Bevis Fuller and Madeline Fuller (*née* Bailey); *m* 1984, Eleanor Mary Breedon (*see* E. M. Fuller); three s. *Educ*: Wellington College; Emmanuel College, Cambridge (MA Hist.). Served Singapore and Kinshasa, 1969–73; First Sec., Cabinet Office, 1973–75; FCO, 1975–77; UK Mission to UN, New York, 1977–80; FCO, 1980–86 (Counsellor, 1984); Dep. Hd of Mission, Tel Aviv, 1986–90; Hd of NE and N African Dept, FCO, 1990–93; Hd of UK Delegn to CSCE, then OSCE, Vienna, 1993–99. *Recreation*: cooking. *Address*: 27 Carlisle Mansions, Carlisle Place, SW1P 1EZ. *T*: (020) 7828 5484. *Clubs*: Brooks's, MCC.

**FULLER, Susan;** *see* Rigby, S.

**FULLERTON, Hance,** OBE 1995; Chairman: Grampian University Hospitals NHS Trust, 1996–2002; Angle plc (formerly AngleTechnology Ltd), 1996–2007; *b* 6 Dec. 1934; *s* of late Robert Fullerton and Jessie Fullerton (*née* Smith); *m* 1958, Jeannie Reid Cowie; three d. *Educ*: Anderson Educnl Inst., Lerwick; Aberdeen Univ. (BSc). Technical, prodn and operational mgt in paper industry, 1958–78; Gen. Manager, Aberdeen, 1978–81, Divl Dir, 1981–86, Wiggins Teape Ltd; Gen. Manager, Grampian Health Bd, 1986–91; Chief Exec., Grampian Enterprise Ltd, 1991–96. Chairman: Aberdeen Univ. Res. and Industrial Services Ltd, 1996–2000; Cordah Ltd, 1996–99. Hon. LLD Aberdeen, 1996. *Recreations*: golf, walking, reading, theatre.

**FULLERTON, William Hugh,** CMG 1989; HM Diplomatic Service, retired; Ambassador to Morocco and Mauritania, 1996–99; *b* 11 Feb. 1939; *s* of late Major Arthur Hugh Theodore Francis Fullerton, RAMC, and of Mary (*née* Parker); *m* 1968, Arlene Jacobowitz; one d. *Educ*: Cheltenham Coll.; Queens' Coll., Cambridge (MA Oriental Langs). Shell Internat. Petroleum Co., Uganda, 1963–65; FO, 1965; MECAS, Shemlan, Lebanon, 1965–66; Information Officer, Jedda, 1966–67; UK Mission to UN, New York, 1967; FCO, 1968–70; Head of Chancery, Kingston, Jamaica (also accredited to Haiti), 1970–73, Ankara, 1973–77; FCO, 1977–80; Counsellor (Economic and Commercial), 1980–83 and Consul-Gen., 1981–83, Islamabad; Ambassador to Somalia, 1983–87; on loan to MoD, 1987–88; Gov., Falkland Is, and Comr for S Georgia and S Sandwich Is, 1988–92; High Comr, British Antarctic Territory, 1988–89; Ambassador to Kuwait, 1992–96. Mem. Adv. Bd, Intrinsic Value Investors LLP, 2011–. Trustee, Arab-British Centre, London, 2002–12 (Dir, 2000–02; Chm., 2002–07). Member: Falkland Is Assoc., 1992–; Friends of Kuwait, 2000–; Life Member: Nat. Trust, 1968; CPRE. Trustee: Soc. for Protection of Animals Abroad, 2000–15; Lord Caradon Lectures Trust, 2004–18. Kuwait Medallion, First Class, 1995; Comdr, Ouissam Alaouite (Morocco), 1999. *Recreations*: travelling in remote areas, sailing, reading, walking. *Club*: Travellers.

**FULLJAMES, Abigail;** *see* Pogson, A.

**FULTON, Andrew;** *see* Fulton, R. A.

**FULTON, Prof. Helen Elizabeth,** PhD; FSA, FLSW; Professor of Medieval Literature, University of Bristol, since 2015; *b* Frankston, Vic, 3 June 1952; *d* of Sir Brian John Maynard Fulton, KCMG and of Elizabeth Mary Christopher; *m* 1st, 1971, Glenn Richard Fulton (marr. diss. 1985); two s; 2nd, 1988, Geraint Gwilym Evans. *Educ*: St Paul's Girls' Sch., Hammersmith, London; Narrabeen Girls' High Sch., Sydney; Univ. of Sydney (BA Hons 1st; PhD 1983); Linacre Coll., Oxford (Dip. Celtic). Postdoctoral Fellow, Univ. of Wales, Aberystwyth, 1985–87; Leverhulme Postdoctoral Fellow, 1987–88; Lectr, 1988–91, Associate Prof., 1991–2005, Univ. of Sydney; Prof. of English, Swansea Univ., 2005–10; Prof. of Medieval Literature, Univ. of York, 2010–15. Vis. Res. Fellow, Corpus Christi Coll., Cambridge, 2003–04; Sen. Vis. Res. Fellow, St John's Coll., Oxford, 2013–14. Member: Peer Rev. Coll., AHRC, 2007–15; Council, Learned Soc. of Wales, 2017–. Chm., Editl Panel, Univ. of Wales Press, 2017–. Trustee: Swansea Univ. Pension Scheme, 2006–10; Historic Towns Trust, 2017–. FSA 2014; FRSA 2014–19; FLSW 2015. Ed., Trans of Honourable Soc. of Cymmrodorion, 2007–; Series Ed., New Century Chaucer, 2012–. *Publications*: (ed) Medieval Celtic Literature and Society, 2005; Narrative and Media, 2005; (ed jtly) Medieval Cultural Studies, 2006; Welsh Prophecy and English Politics, 2008; (ed) Companion to Arthurian Literature, 2009, 2nd edn 2012; (ed) Urban Culture in Medieval Wales, 2012; (ed jtly) Anglo-Italian Cultural Relations in the Later Middle Ages, 2018; (ed jtly) The Cambridge History of Welsh Literature, 2019. *Recreations*: family, film, theatre, opera, reading, writing, afternoon tea. *Address*: Department of English, University of Bristol, 11 Woodland Road, Bristol BS8 1TB. *T*: (0117) 331 7932. *E*: helenefulton@me.com.

**FULTON, Norman Cecil;** Deputy Secretary, and Head, Food and Farming Group, Department of Agriculture, Environment and Rural Affairs, Northern Ireland, since 2016; *b* Strabane, 30 Aug. 1963; *s* of (James) Cecil Fulton and Annie Fulton; *m* 1988, Jennifer Rea; three c. *Educ*: Omagh Acad.; Queen's Univ. Belfast (Bachelor Agric. 1985); Univ. of Ulster (Post Grad. Dip. Mgt Studies 1989). Chief Agricl Economist, Dept of Agric. and Rural Develt, NI, 2005–16. *Recreation*: fixer of broken things. *Address*: Department of Agriculture, Environment and Rural Affairs, Dundonald House, Upper Newtownards Road, Belfast BT4 3SB. *T*: (028) 9052 4655. *E*: norman.fulton@daera-ni.gov.uk.

**FULTON, (Paul) Robert (Anthony);** *b* 20 March 1951; *s* of George Alan Fulton and Margaret Fulton (*née* Foxton); *m* 1981, Lee Hong Tay. *Educ*: Nunthorpe Grammar Sch., York; Churchill Coll., Cambridge (BA Hons French and Russian). Home Office, 1973–2003: Private Sec. to Perm. Sec., 1977–78; Radio Regulatory Dept, 1978–83; Police Dept, 1984–88; Prison and Criminal Policy Depts, 1988–91; Dir of Prison Service Industries and Farms, 1991–96; Principal Finance Officer, 1996–2000; Dir, Strategy and Performance, 2000–02; Implementation Dir, Assets Recovery Agency, 2002–03. Chairman: CHAS (Central London) 2006–10 (Treas., 2004–06); Ducane Housing Assoc., 2004–11; Vice-Chm., SOVA (formerly Soc. of Voluntary Associates), 2004–12. Mem., Finance and Audit Cttee, Skills for Justice, 2008–10; Treasurer: Clinks, 2009–16; Concern and Help for E Elmbridge Retired, 2009–. Trustee: Voluntary Action Elmbridge, 2010–12; Salvaire, 2012–. *Recreations*: learning new things, re-learning old things. *Address*: 1 Meadow Close, Hinchley Wood, Esher, Surrey KT10 0AY.

**FULTON, (Robert) Andrew;** HM Diplomatic Service, retired; Chairman: Validate ID Ltd, since 2017; GloblMed Ltd, since 2018; CSTechnologies Ltd, since 2018; *b* 6 Feb. 1944; *s* of late Rev. Robert M. Fulton and Janet W. Fulton (*née* Mackenzie); *m* 1970, Patricia Mary Crowley; two s one d. *Educ*: Rothesay Academy; Glasgow University (MA, LLB). Foreign and Commonwealth Office, 1968; Third later Second Secretary, Saigon, 1969; FCO, 1972; First Sec., Rome, 1973; FCO, 1977; First Sec., E Berlin, 1978; FCO, 1981; Counsellor, Oslo, 1984; FCO, 1987; UK Mission to UN, NY, 1989; FCO, 1992; Counsellor: Washington, 1995–99; FCO, 1999. Dir, Scotland, Control Risks Gp, 2002–06; Internat. Business Advr, Memex Technology, 2003–12; Global Business Adviser: Dynamic Knowledge Corp., 2005–08; Armor Gp, 2006–08; Advr, G4S, 2008–10. Chairman: Scottish N American Business Council, 2000–10 (Pres., 2010–); Adv. Bd, Proudfoot Consulting, 2003–09; Edo Midas, 2004–09; nation 1, 2005–08; Huntswood, 2006–09; GPW Ltd, 2006–17; Scottish Conservative and Unionist Party, 2008–11. Senior Adviser: Source8, 2009–11; Indigo Vision, 2010–11 (non-exec. Dir, 2011–17). Mem., Nat. Adv. Gp, Internat. Street Papers, 2013–. Vis. Prof., Univ. of Glasgow Sch. of Law, 1999–2003. *Recreations*: golf, racing, reading, cinema. *Address*: 7 Crown Road South, Glasgow G12 9DJ.

**FULTON, Lt-Gen. Sir Robert (Henry Gervase),** KBE 2005; Chief Executive, Global Leadership Foundation, since 2010; *b* 21 Dec. 1948; *s* of late James Fulton and Cynthia Fulton (*née* Shaw); *m* 1975, Midge Free; two s. *Educ*: Eton Coll.; Univ. of East Anglia (BA Hons). Entered RM, 1972: 42 Commando, 1973–75; 40 Commando, 1976–78; Instructor, Sch. of Signals, Blandford, 1978–80; student, Army Staff Coll., Camberley, 1980–81; Instructor, Jun. Div. Staff Coll., 1981–83; 42 Commando, 1983–85; SO2 Ops, HQ Training, Reserve and Special Forces, 1985–87; SO2 Commitments, Dept of Comdt Gen., 1987–90; SO1 DS, Army Staff Coll., Camberley, 1990–92; CO, 42 Commando, 1992–94; Asst Dir, CIS Operational Requirements, MoD, 1994–95; RCDS, 1996; Comdr, 3 Commando Bde, 1997–98, Comdt Gen., 1998–2001, RM; Capability Manager (Inf. Superiority), 2001–03; DCDS (Equipment Capability), 2003–06; Governor and C-in-C, Gibraltar, 2006–09. Chm. Govs, Haberdashers' Aske's Schs Elstree, 2012–17. Mem. Council, White Ensign Assoc., 2006–; Vice Pres., RN and RM Charity, 2009–18. Trustee, Nat. Mus. of RN, 2012–15. King of Arms, Order of the British Empire, 2015–. Liveryman, Haberdashers' Co. (Mem., Ct of Assts, 2012–17). KStJ 2009. *Recreations*: playing and watching sport, military history. *Clubs*: Army and Navy, MCC.

**FUNNELL, Christina Mary;** Director, Christina Funnell (formerly Funnell Associates) Consultancy, 1997–2011; *b* 24 Aug. 1947; *d* of Joanna Christina Beaumont (*née* Lenes) and Norman Beaumont; *m* 1970 (marr. diss. 1994); one s one d. *Educ*: Hull Univ. (BA Spec. Hons Soc. Admin. 1968). W Riding CC Social Services, 1964; Methodist Assoc. of Youth Clubs, 1965–68; London Council of Social Service, 1971; Herts CC Youth Service, 1973; Nat. Eczema Soc., 1982–96 (Dir, 1987–96; Chief Exec., Skin Care Campaign, 1995–96). Mem., Standing Adv. Gp on consumer involvement in NHS R&D prog., 1996–98; Chm., Consumer Health Inf. Centre, 1997–99; Organising Sec., Health Coalition Initiative, 1997–2008; Sec. and Co-ordinator, Patient Information Forum, 2001–03; Patient and Public Involvement Consultant, Perf. Develt Team, NHS Modernisation Agency, 2003–05; Patient Consultant, N and E Yorks and N Lincs Strategic Health Authy, 2005–07; Patient Engagement Officer, Patient Opinion, 2007–10. Lay Member: Nat. Clin. Assessment Authy, 2001–05; NMC, 2002–08; Health Technol. Devices Prog., DoH, 2002–12; non-exec. Mem., BeIndependent, 2014–. Mem. Council, Gen. Pharmaceutical Council, 2010–16; Mem., N Yorks Fire and Rescue Authy, 2009–11. Panel Mem., Richard Neale Inquiry, 2005. Feasibility Consultant to North Bank Estate, Muswell Hill, London, 1998–99. Vice-Chm., Socialist Health Assoc., 2005–13; Trustee: Pharmacy Practice Res. Trust, 2005–12; York Council of Voluntary Service, 2009–13; St Nicholas Envmt Centre, 2009–14; York Allotments Community Assoc., 2019–; Mem. Exec., York Older People's Assembly, 2008–10. Mem. (Labour), City of York Council, 2007–19 (Chm., Health Overview and Scrutiny Cttee, 2007–08, 2011–13); Dir, City of York Trading Co., 2017–19. Member: Wesley's Chapel, 1996–97; Christian Socialist Movt, 2009– (Mem. Exec., 1998–2003); Council, Socialist Health Assoc., 2015–17. Mem., Cathedral Council, 2017–; Community Cttee, 2017–; York Minster. Associate Mem., Iona Community, 1997–2000. Gov., Burnholme Community Coll., 2008–14. Chm., Tang Hall Community Centre, 2012–17. *Publications*: (contrib.) Clinical and Experimental Dermatology, 1993; (contrib.) Developing New Clinical Roles: a guide for health professionals, 2000. *Recreations*: walking with the York Minster Walkers, gardening, travel, social and political history, current affairs. *Address*: 6 Upper Price Street, off Scarcroft Road, York YO23 1BJ. *T*: and *Fax*: (01904) 613041. *E*: tinafunnell@btinternet.com.

**FUNNELL, Philippa Rachel,** MBE 2005; event rider; *b* 7 Oct. 1968; *d* of George and Jennifer Nolan; *m* 1993, William Funnell. *Educ*: Wadhurst Coll. Young Rider Gold Medallist, 1987; British Open Champion, 1992 and 2002; European Championships: Team and Individual Champion, 1991 and 2001; Team Champion and Individual Bronze Medallist, 2003; Olympic Games: Team Silver Medallist, Sydney, 2000; Team Silver and Individual Bronze Medallist, Athens, 2004; winner: Badminton Horse Trials, 2002, 2003, 2005; Rolex Grand Slam (Badminton, Burghley and Kentucky), 2003; Bramham Internat.

Horse Trials, 2010. *Publications:* Training the Young Horse, 2002; My Story (autobiog.), 2004; Tilly's Ponytails (series for children), 2009–. *Recreations:* tennis, cooking. *Address:* c/o British Eventing, Stoneleigh Park, Kenilworth, Warwicks CV8 2RN.

**FURBER, James;** *see* Furber, W. J.

**FURBER, (Robert) John;** QC 1995; *b* 13 Oct. 1949; *s* of late (Frank) Robert Furber and Anne Wilson Furber; *m* 1st, 1977, Amanda Cherry Burgoyne Varney (marr. diss. 2010); one *s* two *d*; 2nd, 2011, Dr Virginia Taylor. *Educ:* Westminster Sch.; Gonville and Caius Coll., Cambridge (MA). Called to the Bar, Inner Temple, 1973. Chm., Field Lane Foundn, 2004–06, 2009–12. Chm., Property Bar Assoc., 2011–14. *Publications:* (ed jtly) Halsbury's Laws of England: Landlord and Tenant, 4th edn 1981, Compulsory Acquisition of Land, 4th edn reissue 1996; (ed jtly) Hill and Redman's Landlord and Tenant, 17th edn 1982, 18th edn (looseleaf) 1988–2019; (jtly) Guide to the Commonhold and Leasehold Reform Act, 2002. *Address:* Wilberforce Chambers, 8 New Square, Lincoln's Inn, WC2A 3QP. *T:* (020) 7306 0102; 1 Hallgate, Blackheath Park, SE3 9SG. *T:* (020) 8852 7633. *Clubs:* Buck's, Beefsteak, Pratt's.

*See also* S. A. Coakley, W. J. Furber.

**FURBER, Prof. Stephen Byram,** CBE 2008; FRS 2002; FREng; ICL Professor of Computer Engineering, University of Manchester, since 1990 (Head, Department of Computer Science, 2001–04); *b* 21 March 1953; *s* of Benjamin Neil Furber and Margaret Furber (*née* Schofield); *m* 1977, Valerie Margaret Elliott; two *d*. *Educ:* St John's Coll., Cambridge (BA Maths 1st Cl. 1974; PhD Aerodynamics 1980). FREng 1999. Rolls Royce Res. Fellow, Emmanuel Coll., Cambridge, 1978–81; Hardware Design Engr, then Design Manager, Acorn Computers Ltd, Cambridge, 1981–90. Non-executive Director: Manchester Informatics Ltd, 1994–2010; Cogency Technology Inc., 1997–99; Cogniscience Ltd, 2000–; Transitive Technologies Ltd, 2001–04; Silistix Ltd, 2004–06; Mindtrace Ltd, 2018–. *Publications:* VLSI RISC Architecture and Organization, 1989; (ed jtly) Asynchronous Design Methodologies, 1993; ARM System Architecture, 1996; ARM System-on-Chip Architecture, 2000; (ed jtly) Principles of Asynchronous Circuit Design: a systems perspective, 2001; over 200 conf. and jl papers. *Recreations:* 6-string and bass guitar (Church music group), badminton. *Address:* School of Computer Science, University of Manchester, Oxford Road, Manchester M13 9PL. *T:* (0161) 275 6129, *Fax:* (0161) 275 6236. *E:* steve.furber@manchester.ac.uk.

**FURBER, (William) James;** Partner, Farrer & Co., since 1985 (Senior Partner, 2008–11); *b* 1 Sept. 1954; *s* of late (Frank) Robert Furber; *m* 1982, Rosemary Elizabeth Johnston (marr. diss. 2010); two *s* one *d*. *Educ:* Westminster Sch.; Gonville and Caius Coll., Cambridge (BA 1975, MA 1979). Admitted solicitor, 1979; joined Farrer & Co. (Solicitors), 1976, Associate Partner, 1981. Solicitor to Duchy of Cornwall, 1994–. Trustee: Leonard Cheshire Foundn, 2000–06; Arvon Foundn, 2000–07; Trinity Coll. of Music, 2003–06; Trinity Coll. of Music Trust, 2006–; Cambridge Univ. Musical Soc., 2014–; Secretary: St Bartholomew's Med. Coll. Charitable Trust, 1996–2012; Art Workers Guild Trust, 2007–10. Reader, C of E, 1991–2010. Treas., Lowtonian Soc., 2003–. High Sheriff, Gtr London, 2017–18. *Publications:* (contrib.) Encyclopedia of Forms and Precedents, vol. 36, 1990. *Recreations:* golf, literature, wine, cooking, avoiding boring people. *Address:* c/o Farrer & Co., 66 Lincoln's Inn Fields, WC2A 3LH. *T:* (020) 3375 7000, *Fax:* (020) 3375 7001. *E:* james.furber@farrer.co.uk. *Clubs:* Garrick; Norfolk; Hawks (Cambridge); Royal & Ancient Golf (St Andrews), Royal St George's Golf (Sandwich), Royal West Norfolk Golf (Brancaster), Royal Blackheath Golf; Honourable Company of Edinburgh Golfers.

*See also* S. A. Coakley, R. J. Furber.

**FUREDI, Ann Marie;** Chief Executive Officer, British Pregnancy Advisory Service, since 2003; *b* Wolverhampton, 31 Oct. 1960; *d* of Joseph and Joan Bradley; *m* 1982, Ferenc, (Frank), Furedi; one *s*. *Educ:* Univ. of Kent (BA Hons 1982). Med. journalist and political activist, 1982–91 (Mem., Political Cttee, Revolutionary Communist Party); Press Officer, FPA, 1991–92; Dep. Dir, 1992–95, Dir, 1995–98, Birth Control Trust; Dir of Communications, British Pregnancy Adv. Service, 1998–2002; Dir, Policy and Communications, HFEA, 2002–03. Mem., Bd of Trustees, IBIS Reproductive Health, 2011–. Chair, 2017–, Bd of Govs, Mid Kent Coll. (Vice Chair, 2012–17). *Publications:* Unplanned Pregnancy: your choices, 1995; The Moral Case for Abortion, 2016; contribs to BMJ, British Jl Med. Ethics, British Jl Family Planning. *Recreations:* wandering, wondering, cuddling cats, and avoiding alliteration. *Address:* 9 Newton Road, Faversham, Kent ME13 8DZ. *E:* ann.furedi@bpas.org.

**FURLONG, Prof. John,** OBE 2017; PhD; FAcSS; Professor of Educational Studies, University of Oxford, 2003–12, now Emeritus (Director, Department of Educational Studies, later of Education, 2003–10); Fellow of Green Templeton College (formerly Green College), Oxford, 2003–12, now Emeritus; *b* 7 May 1947; *s* of late William James Furlong and Ann Furlong, *né* Vivian Anthony Furlong; changed name to John by deed poll 2005; *m* 1972, Ruth Roberts; two *s*. *Educ:* Hertford Grammar Sch.; Middx Poly. (BA 1968); City Univ. (PhD 1978); Corpus Christi Coll., Cambridge (MA 1984). Teacher, Paddington Sch., London, 1971–74; post-doctoral Res. Fellow, Univs of Manchester and Brunel, 1975–81; Lectr in Educn, Univ. of Cambridge, 1981–92; Professor and Head: Dept of Educn, Univ. of Swansea, 1992–95; Grad. Sch. of Educn, Univ. of Bristol, 1995–2000; Prof., Sch. of Social Scis, Cardiff Univ., 2000–03. Pres., British Educnl Res. Assoc., 2003–05; Vice Pres., British and Foreign Schs Soc., 2015–. Member: Social Scis Panel, Internat. Evaluation of Sci. and Innovation Policy in Latvia, 2013; International Expert Panel for review of teacher educn in Rep. of Ireland, 2013, of teacher training infrastructure in NI, 2014; UK REF Educn Panel, 2014; Chair: BERA-RSA Inquiry into res. and teacher educn, 2014; Teacher Educn Accreditation Bd for Wales, 2017–; Convenor, Hong Kong RAE Educn Panel, 2014; Expert Advr to Welsh Govt on Initial Teacher Training, 2014–. FRSA 1995; FAcSS (AcSS 2003). Jt Ed., Oxford Rev. of Educn, 2012–17. *Publications:* The Language of Teaching (with A. D. Edwards), 1978; The Deviant Pupil: sociological perspectives, 1985; (jtly) Initial Teacher Training and the Role of the School, 1988; (with T. Maynard) Mentoring Student Teachers: the growth of professional knowledge, 1995; (ed jtly) The Role of Higher Education in Initial Teacher Education, 1996; (jtly) Teacher Education in Transition: re-forming professionalism?, 2000; (ed jtly) Education, Reform and the State: policy, politics and practice, 2001; (jtly) Screenplay: children and computing in the home, 2003; (jtly) Adult Learning in the Digital Age, 2005; (ed jtly) Understanding Quality in Applied and Practice-Based Research, 2007; (ed jtly) Politics and Policy in Teacher Education: international perspectives, 2008; (ed jtly) Disciplines of Education: their role in the future of education research, 2010; Education: an anatomy of the discipline, Rescuing the University project?, 2013 (First Prize, Soc. for Educnl Studies, 2015); (ed jtly) Knowledge and the Study of Education: an international exploration, 2017; (ed jtly) Education in a Federal UK, 2018; over 100 articles in educnl jls and books. *Recreations:* gardening, keeping chickens, cooking, travel, entertaining. *Address:* Department of Education, University of Oxford, 15 Norham Gardens, Oxford OX2 6PY. *T:* (01865) 274024, *Fax:* (01865) 274027. *E:* john.furlong@education.ox.ac.uk.

**FURMSTON, Prof. Michael Philip,** TD 1966; Professor of Law: University of Bristol, 1978–98, now Emeritus; Singapore Management University, 2007–15, now Emeritus (Dean, School of Law, 2007–12); Sunway University, Malaysia, since 2015; *b* 1 May 1933; *s* of late Joseph Philip Furmston and Phyllis (*née* Clowes); *m* 1964, Ashley Sandra Maria Cope; three *s* seven *d*. *Educ:* Wellington Sch., Somerset; Exeter Coll., Oxford (BA 1st Cl. Hons Jurisprudence, 1956; BCL 1st Cl. Hons 1957; MA 1960). LLM Birmingham, 1962. Called to the Bar, Gray's Inn, 1960 (1st Cl. Hons), Bencher, 1989. National Service, RA, 1951–53 (2nd Lieut); Major, TA, 1966–78, TAVR. Lecturer: Univ. of Birmingham, 1957–62; QUB, 1962–63; Fellow, Lincoln Coll., Oxford, 1964–78 (Sen. Dean, 1967–68; Sen. Tutor and Tutor for Admissions, 1969–74); Univ. Lectr in Law, 1964–78, Curator, University Chest, 1976–78, Oxford; Lectr in Common Law, Council of Legal Educn, 1965–78; Dean, Faculty of Law, 1980–84 and 1995–98, Pro-Vice-Chancellor, 1986–89, Univ. of Bristol. Chm., COMEC, 1996–2000. Visiting Professor: City Univ., 1978–82; Katholieke Universiteit, Leuven, 1980, 1986, 1992 and 1999; Nat. Univ. of Singapore, 1987, 1999; Singapore Mgt Univ., 2006; McWilliam Vis. Prof. of Commercial Law, Univ. of Sydney, 2005. Sen. Fellow, Univ. of Melbourne, 2003–05. Liveryman, Arbitrators' Co. Jt Editor, 1985–97, Editor, 1997–2015, Construction Law Reports. DUniv Open, 2010. *Publications:* (ed) Cheshire, Fifoot and Furmston's Law of Contract, 8th edn 1972 to 17th edn 2017; Contractors Guide to ICE Conditions of Contract, 1980; Misrepresentation and Fraud, in Halsbury's Law of England, 1980, 1998; Croner's Buying and Selling Law, 1982; (ed jtly) The Effect on English Domestic Law of Membership of the European Communities and Ratification of the European Convention on Human Rights, 1983; (jtly) A Building Contract Casebook, 1984, 5th edn 2012; (jtly) Cases and Materials on Contract, 1985, 5th edn 2007; (ed) The Law of Tort: policies and trends in liability for damage to property, 1986; (ed) You and the Law, 1987; Croner's Model Business Contracts, 1988; (jtly) 'A' Level Law, 1988, 4th edn 2002; Sale of Goods, 1990; Sale and Supply of Goods, 1994, 3rd edn 2000; (jtly) Commercial Law, 1995, 2nd edn 2001; Contract Formation and Letters of Intent, 1998; (ed) The Law of Contract, 1999, 6th edn 2017; (jtly) Contract Formation, Law and Practice, 2010, 2nd edn 2016; (jtly) Commercial and Consumer Law, 2010, 2nd edn 2013; (jtly) Privity of Contract, 2015; (jtly) Malaysian Insurance Law, 2018. *Recreations:* chess (Member, English team, Postal Olympiads), watching cricket, dogs. *Address:* 51 Grenville Court, Bridgwater, Somerset TA6 3TY. *T:* (01278) 421676; Faculty of Law, University of Bristol, Wills Memorial Building, Queen's Road, Bristol BS8 1RJ; Room AE 726, Level 7, Sunway University, 5A Jalan Universiti Bandar Sunway, 47500 Selangor Darul Ehsan, Malaysia. *Clubs:* Reform, Naval and Military, MCC.

**FURNESS, Alan Edwin,** CMG 1991; HM Diplomatic Service, retired; Secretary-General, British Association of the Order of Malta, 2013–17; *b* 6 June 1937; *s* of late Edwin Furness and Marion Furness (*née* Senton); *m* 1971, Aline Elizabeth Janine Barrett; two *s*. *Educ:* Eltham Coll.; Jesus Coll., Cambridge (BA, MA). Researcher, University Coll. of W Indies, Jamaica, 1959–60; Commonwealth Relations Office, 1961; Private Sec. to Parliamentary Under-Secretary of State, 1961–62; Third, later Second Secretary, British High Commn, New Delhi, 1962–66; First Secretary, DSAO (later FCO), 1966–69; First Sec., UK Delegn to European Communities, Brussels, 1969–72; First Sec. and Head of Chancery, Dakar, 1972–75; First Sec., FCO, 1975–78; Counsellor and Head of Chancery, Jakarta, 1978–81; Counsellor and Head of Chancery, Warsaw, 1982–85; Head of S Pacific Dept, FCO, 1985–88; Dep. High Comr, Bombay, 1989–93; Ambassador to Senegal and, concurrently, to Cape Verde, Guinea, Guinea Bissau and Mali, 1993–97. Resident Rep. in Senegal, 1998–2008, Advr, 2008–, Business Council for Africa (formerly W Africa Cttee). Ambassador of Order of Malta to Senegal, 2000–11. Knight Grand Cross of Magistral Grace, 2018 (Knight of Magistral Grace, 1999), Grand Cross pro Merito Melitensi, 2011, Order of Malta. *Publications:* (trans.) Le Cavalier et son ombre by Boubacar Boris Diop, as The Knight and his Shadow, 2015; The Tharp Estates in Jamaica, 2018. *Recreations:* music, literature. *Address:* 40 Brunswick Court, 89 Regency Street, SW1P 4AE. *Club:* Oxford and Cambridge.

**FURNESS, (Hugh) Jonathan;** QC 2003; **His Honour Judge Furness;** a Circuit Judge, since 2015; a Deputy High Court Judge, since 2008; *b* 8 Nov. 1956; *s* of late Thomas Hogg Batey Furness and Hilda Anita Furness; *m* 1984, Anne Margaret Jones; three *s* one *d*. *Educ:* St John's Coll., Cambridge (MA). Called to the Bar, Gray's Inn, 1979; in practice, specialising in divorce and child care work; a Recorder, 1998–2015. Chm., Shadwell Opera, 2015–. *Recreations:* golf, cricket, music. *Address:* Cardiff Crown Court, The Law Courts, Cathays Park, Cardiff CF10 3PG. *Clubs:* Cardiff and County; Mitres Cricket (Llandaff); Royal Porthcawl Golf.

**FURNESS, His Honour Mark Richard;** a Circuit Judge, 1998–2016; *b* 28 Nov. 1948; *m* 1974, Margaretta Trevor Evans; one *s* one *d*. *Educ:* Hereford Cathedral Sch.; St John's Coll., Cambridge (BA 1970; MA 1972). Called to the Bar, Lincoln's Inn, 1970; an Asst Recorder, 1992–96; a Recorder, 1996–98. Chairman: Social Security Appeal Tribunal, 1987–94; Disability Appeal Tribunal, 1991–98. Chm., Baygroup Investments Shareclub, 2016–. Chairman: Marie Curie Cttee for Wales, 2001–07; Trustees and Managing Cttee, Swansea Children Contact Centre, 2002–09; Mem., Marie Curie Welsh Develt Bd, 2007–15. *Recreations:* gardening, motoring, literature, music, DIY, travel. *Clubs:* Cardiff and County (Chm., 2018–19); Saba Rock Yacht.

**FURNESS, Michael James;** QC 2000; a Deputy High Court Judge, since 2004; *b* 2 Sept. 1958; *s* of late Harry Furness and of Rosemary Nancy Furness; *m* 2008, Frances Marguerite Shore. *Educ:* Emmanuel Coll., Cambridge (MA); St Edmund Hall, Oxford (BCL). Called to the Bar, Lincoln's Inn, 1982, Bencher, 2009; First Standing Jun. Counsel to Inland Revenue, 1998–2000. *Recreations:* acting, walking. *Address:* Wilberforce Chambers, 8 New Square, Lincoln's Inn, WC2A 3QP. *T:* (020) 7306 0102.

**FURNESS, Prof. Peter Norman,** PhD; FRCPath; Consultant Histopathologist, since 1990, and Lead Medical Examiner, since 2016, University Hospitals of Leicester; Hon. Professor of Renal Pathology, University of Leicester, since 2001; *b* Barnsley, S Yorks, 2 Sept. 1955; *s* of Harold and Kathleen Furness; *m* 1979, Sarah Haddon (*see* S. H. Furness); one *d*. *Educ:* Fitzwilliam Coll., Cambridge (BA 1st Cl. Natural Scis 1977); Wolfson Coll., Oxford (BM BCh Clin. Medicine 1981); Univ. of Nottingham (PhD 1989). FRCPath 1989. Lectr in Pathol., Univ. of Nottingham, 1984–89; Sen. Lectr in Pathol., Univ. of Leicester, 1990–2001; Asst Medical Dir, 2011–16, Responsible Officer, 2015–16, University Hosps of Leicester. Nat. Medical Examiner, 2013–15. Mem., Nuffield Council for Bioethics, 2013–15. Pres., 2008–11, Dir of Prof. Standards, 2015–18, RCPath; Vice Chair, Acad. of Medical Royal Colls, 2009–11. *Recreations:* woodwork, house and car renovation, dogwalking, horology, metal and foundry work, bellringing, beekeeping, making broken things work again. *Address:* Department of Histopathology, Sandringham Building, Leicester Royal Infirmary, Leicester LE1 5WW.

**FURNESS, Robin;** *see* Furness, Sir S. R.

**FURNESS, Dr Sarah Haddon;** Lord-Lieutenant of Rutland, since 2018; *b* Dorchester, 3 June 1956; *d* of Roger Spurgeon and Eileen Webb; *m* 1979, Peter Norman Furness, *qv*; one *d*. *Educ:* Notre Dame Sch., Plymouth; Lewes Girls Grammar Sch.; Lewes Priory Sch.; Univ. of Essex (BA 1st Cl. Art History, Theory and Philosophy; PhD Philos. 1986); Univ. of Oxford. Taught philos. and ethics at Univs of Essex and Leicester. Voluntary work for charities (NADFAS, Macmillan, Red Cross; opened garden for 16 years for Nat. Garden Scheme). Chair, Visits Prog., Garden Mus., 2010–. High Sheriff Rutland, 2016–17. *Publications:* (contrib.) Principles of Healthcare Ethics, 1996, 2nd edn 2001. *Recreations:*

garden design and history, gardening, bee keeping, hen keeping, interior design, walking, art history. *Address*: The Old Vicarage, Whissendine, Rutland LE15 7HG. *T*: (01664) 474549.

**FURNESS, Col Simon John**, MBE 2012; Vice Lord-Lieutenant of Berwickshire, 1990–2009; *b* 18 Aug. 1936; 2nd *s* of Sir Christopher Furness, 2nd Bt and Violet Flower Chipchase Furness, OBE (*d* 1988), *d* of Lieut-Col G. C. Roberts, Hollingside, Durham. *Educ*: Charterhouse; RMA Sandhurst; Royal Naval Staff College. Commissioned 2nd Lieut Durham Light Infantry, 1956; served Far East, UK, Germany; active service, Borneo and NI (despatches 1973); Comd 5th Bn LI, 1976–78, retired 1978. Dep. Col (Durham), LI, 1989–93. Trustee, Gunsgreen Hse Trust, 2002–15 (Chm., 2012–15). DL Berwickshire, 1984. OStJ 2009. *Recreations*: gardening, country sports, fine arts. *Address*: The Garden House, Netherbyres, Eyemouth, Berwickshire TD14 5SE. *T*: (01890) 750337. *Club*: Army and Navy.

**FURNESS, Sir Stephen (Roberts)**, 3rd Bt *cr* 1913, of Tunstall Grange, West Hartlepool; farmer and sporting/landscape artist (as Robin Furness); *b* 10 Oct. 1933; *e s* of Sir Christopher Furness, 2nd Bt, and Flower, Lady Furness, OBE (*d* 1988), *d* of late Col G. C. Roberts; *S* father, 1974; *m* 1961, Mary, *e d* of J. F. Cann, Cullompton, Devon; one *s* one *d*. *Educ*: Charterhouse. Entered RN, 1952; Observer, Fleet Air Arm, 1957; retired list, 1962. NCA, Newton Rigg Farm Inst., 1964. Member: Armed Forces Art Soc.; Darlington Art Soc.; Associate Mem., Soc. of Equestrian Artists. *Recreations*: looking at paintings, racing. *Heir*: *s* Michael Fitzroy Roberts Furness [*b* 12 Oct. 1962; *m* 1998, Katrine Oxtoby]. *See also S. J. Furness.*

**FURNHAM, Prof. Adrian Frank**, DSc, DPhil, DLitt; Professor of Psychology, University College London, 1992–2018; *b* 3 Feb. 1953; *s* of late Leslie Frank Furnham and Lorna Audrey (*née* Cartwright); *m* 1990, Dr Alison Clare Green; one *s*. *Educ*: Natal Univ. (BA Hons, MA; DLitt 1997); LSE (MSc Econ 1976; DSc 1991); Strathclyde Univ. (MSc 1977); Wolfson Coll. and Pembroke Coll., Oxford (DPhil 1982). Oxford University: Res. Officer, Dept Exptl Psychol., 1979–81; Lectr in Psychol., Pembroke Coll., 1980–82; University College London: Lectr, 1981–87; Reader, 1988–92. Visiting Lecturer: Univ. of NSW, 1984; Univ. of WI, 1986; Univ. of Hong Kong, 1994–96; Vis. Prof., Henley Mgt Coll., 1999–2001; Adjunct Prof., Norwegian Sch. of Mgt, Oslo, 2009–; Honorary Professor: Univ. of KwaZulu-Natal, S Africa, 2015–; Univ. of Exeter; Adjunct Prof., Perdana Univ. Kuala Lumpur. Founder Dir, ABRA, business consultancy, 1986–2002; Dir, Applied Behavioural Res. Associates; Principal Psychologist, Stamford Associates. Ext. Examr at various univs. Mem., Internat. Adv. Council, Social Affairs Unit, 1995–. Dir, Internat. Soc. for Study of Individual Differences, 1996–2001 (Pres., 2003–05). Mem., editl bd of 11 internat. scientific jls. *Publications*: books include: Culture Shock, 1986; Lay Theories, 1988; The Protestant Work Ethic, 1990; Personality at Work, 1992; Corporate Assessment, 1994; All in the Mind, 1996, 3rd edn 2016; The Myths of Management, 1996; The Psychology of Behaviour at Work, 1997; Complementary Medicine, 1997; The Psychology of Money, 1998; The Psychology of Managerial Incompetence, 1998; Children as Consumers, 1998; Personality and Social Behaviour, 1999; Body Language at Work, 1999; The Hopeless, Hapless and Helpless Manager, 2000; Designing and Analysing Questionnaires and Surveys, 2000; Children and Advertising, 2000; The Psychology of Culture Shock, 2001; Assessing Potential, 2001; The 3D Manager: dangerous, derailed and deranged, 2001; Mad, Sad and Bad Management, 2003; The Incompetent Manager, 2003; Management and Myths, 2004; The Dark Side of Behaviour at Work, 2004; Personality and Intellectual Competence, 2005; The People Business, 2005; Learning at Work, 2005; Just for the Money, 2005; Management Mumbo-Jumbo, 2006; The Body Beautiful, 2007; Dim Sum Management, 2008; The Psychology of Physical Attractiveness, 2008; Head and Heart Management, 2008; Personality and Intelligence at Work, 2008; Management Intelligence, 2008; The Economic Socialisation of Young People, 2008; 50 Psychology Ideas You Really Need to Know, 2009; The Psychology of Personnel Selection, 2010; The Elephant in the Board Room, 2010; Body Language in Business, 2010; Bad Apples, 2011; Managing People in a Downturn, 2011; Leadership: all you want to know, 2012; The Talented Manager, 2012; The Resilient Manager, 2013; The New Psychology of Money, 2014; Mental Illness at Work, 2014; High Potential, 2014; Backstabbers and Bullies, 2015; Leadership: all you need to know, 2016; Motivation and Performance, 2017; Myths of Work, 2018; 1300 scientific papers; contrib. articles and columns to newspapers, incl. Daily Telegraph, Sunday Times. *Recreations*: travel, theatre, arguing at dinner parties and utopian speculation. *Address*: 45 Thornhill Square, Islington, N1 1BE. *T*: (020) 7607 6265. *E*: adrian@adrianfurnham.com.

**FURNISS, Gill**; MP (Lab) Sheffield, Brightside and Hillsborough, since May 2016; *b* Sheffield; *m* 1st; one *s* two *d*; 2nd, 2013, (Robert) Harry Harpham, MP (*d* 2016); one step *s* one step *d*. *Educ*: Chaucer Comprehensive Sch., Sheffield; Leeds Metropolitan Univ. (MA Library and Information Studies 1998). Liby asst, Firth Park Liby, then libraries in Parson Cross and Burngreave, 1973–79; Shirecliffe Coll., 1979–85; Sheffield Coll. 1986–2000; records office, Northern Gen. Hosp. Shadow Minister for Steel, Postal Services and Consumer Protection, 2016–. Mem., Women and Equalities Select Cttee, 2016. Mem. (Lab) Sheffield CC, 1999–2016. *Address*: House of Commons, SW1A 0AA.

**FURNISS, Prof. Graham Lytton**, OBE 2013; PhD; FBA 2009; Professor of African-Language Literature, School of Oriental and African Studies, University of London, 1999–2014, now Emeritus; *b* 21 June 1949; *s* of Alfred Lytton and Margaret Elizabeth Furniss; *m* 1977, Wendy Jane de Beer; one *s* two *d*. *Educ*: Sch. of Oriental and African Studies, Univ. of London (BA; PhD 1977). Lectr, Dept of Langs and Linguistics, Univ. of Maiduguri, Nigeria, 1977–79; School of Oriental and African Studies, University of London: Lectr, then Sen. Lectr in Hausa, 1979–96; Reader in Hausa Cultural Studies, 1996–99; Hd, Lang. Centre, 1995–98; Dean: of Langs, 1995–97; Faculty of Langs and Cultures, 2002–04; Pro-Dir (Res. and Enterprise), 2008–13. Chm., Africa sub-panel, 2001 RAE Panel 46: African and ME Studies. Comr, Commonwealth Scholarship Commn, 2010–16. Vice-Pres., Royal African Soc., 2000–08; President: Internat. Soc. for Oral Lit. in Africa, 1998–2002; African Studies Assoc. of UK, 2004–06. Gov., John Lyon's Foundn, 2007–19 (Trustee, 2007–19); Trustee, Britain-Nigeria Educnl Trust, 2008–. *Publications*: (ed with R. Fardon) African Languages, Development and the State, 1994; (ed with E. Gunner) Power, Marginality and African Oral Literature, 1995; Ideology in Practice: Hausa poetry as exposition of values and viewpoints, 1995; Poetry, Prose and Popular Culture in Hausa, 1996; (ed with R. Fardon) African Broadcast Cultures: radio in transition, 2000; Orality: the power of the spoken word, 2004. *Recreations*: hill-walking, beach-combing, pottery, painting, tropical plants, gardening, cooking. *Address*: Faculty of Languages and Cultures, School of Oriental and African Studies, University of London, Thornhaugh Street, Russell Square, WC1H 0XG. *E*: gf1@soas.ac.uk.

**FURNISS, (Mary) Jane**, CBE 2012; Chief Executive, Independent Police Complaints Commission, 2006–13; *b* 28 March 1954; *d* of Eric Richard Sanders and late Catherine Lilly Sanders; *m* 1977, David Kenneth Furniss. *Educ*: Burton-on-Trent Girls' High Sch.; Bradford Univ. (BSc Hons 1975); York Univ. (MSW 1978). West Yorkshire: Probation Officer, 1975–76, 1978–85; Sen. Probation Officer, 1985–90; Asst Chief Probation Officer, 1990–95; Home Office: HM Inspector of Probation, 1995–97; HM Dep. Chief Inspector, 1997–2001; Hd, Justice and Victims Unit, 2001–02; Dir, Criminal Policy, then Criminal Justice, Gp, 2002–05; Dir, Criminal Justice, Office for Criminal Justice Reform, 2005–06. Mem., Audit and Risk Cttee, Children's Comr, 2010–11; Associate and Bd Mentor, Criticaleye, 2013– (Mem., Adv. Bd, 2010–12); Sen. Ind. Dir, Solicitors Regulation Authy, 2014–17; non-exec. Dir, Nat. Crime Agency, 2013–19; Comr, Judicial Appts Commn, 2017–. Judge, Contrarian Prize Panel, 2013–18. Trustee: Crisis, 2006–16 (Dep. Chm., 2013–16); Cumberland Lodge, 2016–. *Recreations*: music (listening), art (viewing), the world (exploring), learnt to swim in 2013!

**FURNIVALL, Barony** *cr* 1295; in abeyance. *Co-heiresses*: Hon. Rosamond Mary Dent (Sister Ancilla, OSB); *b* 3 June 1933; Hon. Patricia Mary Dent [*b* 4 April 1935; *m* 1st, 1956, Captain Thomas Hornsby (marr. diss., 1963; he *d* 1967); one *s* one *d*; 2nd, 1970, Roger Thomas John Bence; one *s* one *d*].

**FURSDON, (Edward) David**; Chairman, Beeswax (Dyson) Farming Ltd (formerly Beeswax Farming Ltd), since 2014; Lord-Lieutenant of Devon, since 2015; *b* Sevenoaks, 20 Dec. 1952; *s* of Maj. Gen. (Francis William) Edward Fursdon, CB, MBE and Joan Fursdon; *m* 1978, Catriona Margaret McCreath; three *s*. *Educ*: Sherborne Sch.; St John's Coll., Oxford (Scholar; BA 1975; Cricket Blue); RAC, Cirencester. FRICS 1998. Owner/manager, Fursdon Estate, 1981–; Officer, 6th QEO Gurkha Rifles, 1971–72; civil servant, MoD and UN, Geneva, 1975–79; Teacher, Blundell's Sch., 1979–84; RAC, Cirencester, 1984–86; Land agent, 1986–94; Partner, Stags, 1994–2007. Chm., 2003–05, Pres., 2005–07, CLA. A Crown Estate Comr, 2008–16; Commissioner: English Heritage, 2010–14; Food, Farming and Countryside Commn, 2017–. Dir, HHA, 2005–15; Mem., Duchy of Cornwall Rural Cttee, 2008–; Mem. Bd of Trustees, Nat. Trust, 2016–. Chm., Future of Farming Rev., 2013–14. Chairman: SW Bd for 2012 Games, 2010–12; SW Rural and Farming Network, 2011–; SW Rural Productivity Commn, 2017; Mem. Bd, SW RDA, 2009–12. Trustee, Prince's Countryside Fund, 2019. Gov., Blundell's Sch., 1984–2011 (Chm., 2000–11). FAAV 1988; FRAgS 2011 (ARAgS 2007). Hon. Fellow, RAU, 2016. Hon. DSc Harper Adams, 2019. DL, 2004, High Sheriff, 2009–10, Devon. CStJ 2018. *Recreations*: planting trees, appreciating landscape, buildings and gardens, moving from playing to watching sport. *Address*: c/o Savills, York House, Blackbrook Business Park, Taunton TA1 2PX. *E*: david.fursdon@fursdon.co.uk. *Clubs*: Farmers, MCC; Vincent's (Oxford).

**FURSE, Dame Clara (Hedwig Frances)**, DBE 2008; Chief Executive, London Stock Exchange plc, 2001–09; Chairman, HSBC UK, since 2017; *b* 16 Sept. 1957; 2nd *d* of Herman Werner Siemens and Cornélie Siemens-Gravin Schimmelpenninck; *m* 1981, Richard Furse; two *s* one *d*. *Educ*: St James's Sch., W Malvern; London Sch. of Econs (BScEcon). Joined UBS, 1983, Man. Dir, 1995–98; Gp Chief Exec., Credit Lyonnais Rouse, 1998–2000. Dep. Chm., LIFFE, 1997–99. Non-executive Director: Legal & General, 2009–13; Nomura International, 2009–13; Nomura Europe Hldgs, 2009–13; Nomura Hldgs, 2010–17; Amadeus IT Hldgs SA, 2010–; DWP, 2011–17; Vodafone, 2014–. Mem., Financial Policy Cttee, Bank of England, 2013–16.

**FURSSEDONN-WOOD, Scott**; HM Diplomatic Service; Deputy Private Secretary to the Prince of Wales and the Duchess of Cornwall, since 2017; *b* Harrow, 13 Feb. 1978; *s* of Leonard and Joan Furssedonn; *m* 2005, Elizabeth Wood; one *s* two *d*. *Educ*: Hatch End High Sch.; Northwood Sch.; Merton Coll., Oxford (BA Hons PPE); Open Univ. (MBA). Entered FCO, 2000; FCO, 2000–01; Second Sec., 2001–04; First Sec., 2004–06, UK Perm. Representation to EU; Private Sec. to Minister of State for Middle East and S Asia, 2006–08; First Sec., Washington, 2008–13; Dep. High Comr, Kolkata, 2013–16. *Recreations*: travel, being a dad, long walks with the dog. *Address*: c/o Foreign and Commonwealth Office, King Charles Street, SW1A 2AH. *E*: scott.furssedonn@fco.gov.uk. *Club*: Tollygunge (Kolkata).

**FURST, David Anthony**; Director: Robert Hitchins Group Ltd, since 2012; Gordon Dadds, since 2017; *b* London, 4 Sept. 1950; *s* of Arthur Gerald Furst and Aline Verity Furst; *m* 1987, Anne Elizabeth Fleming; two *s* two *d*. *Educ*: Leighton Park Sch., Reading. FCA 1973. Horwath Clark Whitehill, later Crowe Clark Whitehill: Partner, 1984–2012; Chief Exec., 1998–2004; Chm., 2004–12; Finance Dir, Powell Gilbert LLP, 2012–16. Founder Mem. Cttee, Assoc. of Partnership Practitioners, 1998–2004. Mem. Bd, Crowe Horwath (formerly Horwath) Internat., 2002–08. Pres., ICAEW, 2008–09; Chm., CCAB, 2008–09. Mem., Takeover Panel, 2008–09. *Publications*: Essential Guide to Self Assessment, 1994; regular contrib. to legal and accountancy jls. *Recreations*: bridge, ski-ing, watching motor racing, Rugby, cricket and football. *Address*: Dial House, Shepperton Road, Laleham, Middx TW18 1SE. *Clubs*: MCC; Goodwood Road Racing, Silverstone Racing.

**FURST, Stephen Andrew**; QC 1991; a Recorder, 1999–2017; a Deputy High Court Judge, 2010–17; *b* 8 Feb. 1951; *s* of Herbert and Viviane Furst; *m* 1979, Bridget Collins (marr. diss. 2013); one *s* one *d*. *Educ*: Edinburgh Academy; St Edmund Hall, Oxford (BA Hons); Leeds Univ. (LLB Hons). Called to the Bar, Middle Temple, 1975, Bencher, 2000. An Asst Recorder, 1993–99. *Publications*: (ed jtly) Keating on Construction Contracts, 9th edn 2012, 10th edn 2016. *Recreations*: bee-keeping, watercolour painting. *Address*: Keating Chambers, 15 Essex Street, WC2R 3AA. *T*: (020) 7544 2600.

**FURTADO, Peter Randall**, FRHistS; Director, Shilbrook Associates, since 2012; *b* 20 May 1952; *s* of Robert Audley Furtado and Marcelle Elizabeth Furtado (*née* Whitteridge); *m* 1st, 1977, Roberta Jane Day (marr. diss.); 2nd, 1983, (Margaret Elizabeth) Ann Swoffer; three *d*. *Educ*: Whitgift Sch., Croydon; Oriel Coll., Oxford (BA 1st Cl. Hons 1973; Dip. Hist. Art 1974). Sen. ed., Hamlyn Books, 1977–83; freelance ed., 1983–87; sen. ed., Equinox Books, 1987–91; Exec. Ed., Andromeda Books, 1991–97; Ed., History Today, 1997–2008. Managing Editor: The Ordnance Survey Atlas of Great Britain, 1981; The Illustrated History of the 20th Century, 10 vols, 1989–92; The Cassell Atlas of World History, 1996. Chm., Bd of Dirs, Shintaido Foundn, 1994–97, 2002–09; Dir, Internat. Shintaido Foundn, 2003–12; Lead Consultant, SiftGroups Ltd, 2010–12. FRHistS 2002. Hon. DLitt Oxford Brookes, 2009. *Publications*: 1001 Days That Shaped the World, 2008; Living Histories: Restoration England, 2010; History's Daybook, 2011; The Histories of Nations, 2012; History Day by Day, 2019; Great Cities Through Travellers' Eyes, 2019. *Recreations*: life, liberty, pursuit of happiness. *Address*: The Paddock, Windsoredge, Nailsworth, Glos GL6 0NR. *T*: (01453) 751272. *E*: pfurtado1543@gmail.com.

**FURY, Alexander Louis**; Fashion Features Director, AnOther Magazine, since 2017; Men's Critic, Financial Times, since 2018; *b* Bolton, 15 Dec. 1982; *s* of Paul and Janet Fury. *Educ*: Central St Martins Coll. of Art and Design (BA Hons Fashion Hist. and Theory). Fashion Dir, SHOWstudio.com, 2008–12; Ed., Love Mag., 2012–13; Fashion Ed., The Independent and i, 2013–16; Men's Critic, American Vogue, 2016; Chief Fashion Correspondent, T: New York Times Style Mag., 2016–18. *Publications*: Pattern, 2013; (jtly) Isabella Blow: Fashion Galore!, 2014; (with Chris Moore) Catwalking: photographs by Chris Moore, 2017; Dior Catwalk, 2017; (with Laziz Hamani) Dior by Gianfranco Ferre, 2018. *Recreations*: fashion, 18th century French history, rabbits.

**FUTCHER, Ven. Christopher David**; Archdeacon in Cyprus, and Chaplain of St Helena's, Larnaca, since 2019; *b* Luton, 6 Jan. 1958; *s* of David and Brenda Futcher; *m* 1986, Rev. Anne Myers; one *s* one *d*. *Educ*: Strode's Grammar Sch., Egham; Univ. of Edinburgh

(BD 1980); Heythrop Coll., Univ. of London (MTh 2004); King's Coll. London (MA 2011). Ordained deacon, 1982, priest, 1983; Asst Curate, Borehamwood Team Ministry, 1982–85; Asst Curate, 1985–88, Vicar, 1988–96, All Saints, Pin Green, Stevenage; Vicar, St Stephen's, St Albans, 1996–2000; Rector, Harpenden, 2000–12; Archdeacon of Exeter, 2012–19. *Recreations:* reading, walking, sailing, music, theatre.

**FYFE, Maria;** Chair, Remember Mary Barbour Association, since 2014; *b* 25 Nov. 1938; *d* of James O'Neill and Margaret Lacey; *m* 1964, James Joseph Fyfe (decd); two *s*. *Educ:* Strathclyde Univ. (BA Hons Economic History 1975). Senior Lecturer, Trade Union Studies Unit, Glasgow Central College of Commerce, 1978–87. Mem., Labour Party, 1960–, Scottish Exec., 1981–88; Mem., Glasgow District Council, 1980–87 (Vice-Convener, Finance Cttee, 1980–84; Convener, Personnel Cttee, 1984–87). MP (Lab) Glasgow, Maryhill, 1987–2001. Dep. Shadow Minister for Women, 1988–91; Convener, Scottish Gp of Labour MPs, 1991–92; Scottish front bench spokesperson, 1992–95. Chair: Labour Deptl Cttee on Internat. Develt, 1997–2001; Labour Gp, UK Delegn to Council of Europe, 1997–2001; Mem., Scottish Policy Forum, 2008–15, Better Politics Commn, 2010–15, Nat. Policy Forum, 2010–, Labour Party. Vice-Chair, Glasgow Housing Assoc., 2001–06. DUniv Glasgow, 2002. Columnist on Scottish affairs, Tribune mag., 2014–. *Publications:* A Problem Like Maria: a woman's eye view of life as an MP, 2014; Women Saying No: making a positive case against independence, 2014. *Address:* 10 Ascot Avenue, Glasgow G12 0AX. *T:* (0141) 334 6737.

**FYFIELD, Frances;** novelist; solicitor; *b* 8 Nov. 1948; *d* of Dr Andrew George Hegarty and Winifred Doris Hegarty (*née* Fyfield). *Educ:* convent and grammar schools, Newcastle upon Tyne; Newcastle upon Tyne Univ. (BA English Lit. 1970); Coll. of Law. Admitted solicitor, 1973; a solicitor: for Metropolitan Police, 1973–80; for DPP, 1980–86; CPS, 1986–97, pt-time, 1997–2005; lawyer and novelist, 1987–2000. Registrar, Royal Literary Fund. Presenter, Tales from the Stave, Radio 4, 2007–09, 2011–15. *Publications:* A Question of Guilt, 1988 (televised 1994); Shadows on the Mirror, 1989; Trial by Fire, 1990 (televised 1999); Deep Sleep (Silver Dagger Award, CWA), 1990; Shadow Play, 1991; Perfectly Pure and Good, 1992; A Clear Conscience, 1994 (Grand Prix de Literature Policière, 1998); Without Consent, 1996; Blind Date, 1998 (televised 2000); Staring at the Light, 1999; Undercurrents, 2000; Helen West Omnibus, 2002 (televised, as Helen West, 2002); The Nature of the Beast, 2001; Seeking Sanctuary, 2003; Looking Down, 2004; Safer Than Houses, 2005; The Art of Drowning, 2006; Blood from Stone (Gold Dagger Award, CWA), 2008; Cold to the Touch, 2009; Gold Digger, 2013; Casting the First Stone, 2014; *as Frances Hegarty:* The Playroom, 1990; Half Light, 1992; Let's Dance, 1995. *Recreations:* tobacco and fine wine, paintings, company, watching the sea. *Address:* c/o Rogers Coleridge and White, 20 Powis Mews, W11 1JN.

**FYSH, Marcus John Hudson;** MP (C) Yeovil, since 2015; *b* Australia, 8 Nov. 1970; *m* 2011, Jenny; two *d*. Sen. Vice Pres. and Fund Manager, Mercury Asset Mgt, 1993–2001; set up own business, 2003. Member (C): S Somerset DC, 2011–15; Somerset CC, 2013–17. Mem., Select Cttee on Internat. Trade, 2016–, on Public Admin and Constitutional Affairs, 2016–. *Address:* House of Commons, SW1A 0AA.

**FYSH, His Honour (Robert) Michael;** QC 1989; QC (NI) 1990; a Circuit Judge, Patents County Court, 2001–10; *b* 2 Aug. 1940; *s* of Dr Leslie Fysh and Margaret Fysh, Ashford, Kent; *m* 1971, Mary Bevan; three *s*. *Educ:* Downside Sch.; Exeter Coll., Oxford (MA). Called to the Bar, Inner Temple, 1965, Bencher, 1999; NI, 1974; NSW, 1975; Ireland, 1975; India, 1982; Pakistan, 1987; SC Trinidad and Tobago Bar, 1990; SC Dublin, 1994. A Dep. High Court Judge, Chancery Div., 1997–2010; an Additional Judge, Technol. and Construction Court, 2002–10. Chm., Copyright Tribunal, 2006–10. Mem., Rules Cttee, Unified Patents Court, 2015–16. CEDR Mediator, 2011. Vis. Prof., Intellectual Property Inst., New Delhi, 2002. Hon. LLD Wolverhampton, 2005. *Publications:* Russell-Clarke on Registered Designs, 4th edn 1974; The Industrial Property Citator, 1982, 2nd edn 1996; (ed) The Spycatcher Cases, 1989; (consulting ed.) The Modern Law of Patents, 2005, 2nd edn 2010. *Recreations:* forestry, swimming, travel. *Address:* c/o 8 New Square, Lincoln's Inn, WC2A 3QP. *Club:* Kildare Street and University (Dublin).

**FYSON, Anne Elizabeth;** *see* Howells, A. E.

# G

**GABBANA, Stefano**; President, Dolce & Gabbana; *b* 14 Nov. 1962. Asst in design studio, Milan; with Domenico Dolce opened fashion consulting studio, 1982; Co-founder, Dolce & Gabbana, 1985; first major women's collection, 1986; knitwear, 1987; beachwear, lingerie, 1989; men's collection, 1990; women's fragrance, 1992; D&G line, men's fragrance, 1994; eyewear, 1995; opened boutiques in major cities in Europe, America and Asia. *Publications*: (with Domenico Dolce): 10 Years Dolce & Gabbana, 1996; Wildness, 1997; Mémoires de la Mode, 1998; Animal, 1998; Calcio, 2004; Music, 2005; 20 Years Dolce & Gabbana, 2005; (with Eve Claxton and Domenico Dolce) Hollywood, 2003. *Address*: Dolce & Gabbana, Via Goldoni 10, 20129 Milan, Italy.

**GABBITAS, Peter**; Executive Director, Caring Services and Partnerships, Marie Curie, since 2016; *b* 15 Aug. 1961; *s* of Robert and Mary Gabbitas; *m* 1986, Karen Brown; one *d*. *Educ*: St Thomas Aquinas RC Grammar Sch.; Durham Univ. (BA Gen. Arts 1984); Warwick Univ. (MBA Dist. 1994). DipHSM 1987. NHS gen. mgt trainee, 1984–86; Director: of Service Devlt, Solihull Acute Trust, 1989–91; of Ops, Dudley Gp of Hosps, 1991–97; Chief Executive: E and Midlothian NHS Trust, 1997–99; W Lothian Healthcare NHS Trust, 1999–2005; Dir of Health and Social Care, Edinburgh CC, 2005–15. *Recreations*: golf, gardening, swimming, stained and fused glass, Latin and ballroom dancing (Member, North Berwick Dance Club). *Address*: Marie Curie, 89 Albert Embankment, SE1 7TP. *E*: peter.gabbitas@mariecurie.org.uk. *Club*: Glen Golf.

**GABER, Prof. Ivor Harold**; Professor of Political Journalism (formerly of Journalism), University of Sussex, since 2015; freelance journalist, consultant and trainer; *b* High Wycombe; *m* 1974, Jane; three *d*. *Educ*: Woodberry Down Comp. Sch., London; Univ. of Warwick (BA Hist. and Pols 1970); Univ. of Sussex (MA Industrial Relns 1972); City Univ. London (PhD Journalism Studies 2013). Asst Ed., Drugs and Society mag., 1971–73; TV journalist, Reuters TV, London, Sydney and Rome, 1973–76; Industrial Corresp., Evening Post-Echo, Hemel Hempstead, 1976–78; scriptwriter and investigative reporter, ITN, 1978–82; producer and reporter, BBC TV Current Affairs, 1982–86; Prof. and Hd, Dept of Media and Communications, Goldsmiths' Coll., Univ. of London, 1986–2000, now Emeritus Prof. of Broadcast Journalism; Res. Prof. in Media and Politics, Univ. of Bedfordshire, 2006–14; Prof. of Political Journalism and Dir, Political Journalism MA Course, City Univ. London, 2008–14; freelance TV and radio presenter and editor, BBC, ITN, Channel 4 and Sky News, 1986–. Ind. Editl Advr, BBC Trust, 2010–. Member: UK Delegn to UNESCO Gen. Conf., Paris, 2001, 2003, 2007; Freedom of Expression Panel, FCO, 2004–; Internat. Adv. Bd, Centre for Study of Global Media and Democracy, 2006–; Munro Inquiry into Child Protection, 2011; Vice Chm., Communications Sector, UK UNESCO Nat. Commn, 2006–; UK Rep., Inter-Govtl Council, Internat. Prog. for Develt Communication, UNESCO, 2010–. Mem., Adv. Council, Hansard Soc., 2006–. Member: Jury, RTS Television News Awards, 2008, 2009; Judging Panel, One World Media Awards, 2011. FAcSS (AcSS 2009); FHEA 2013. *Publications*: (with J. Aldridge) In the Best Interests of the Child: culture, identity and transracial adoption, 1994; (jtly) Environmentalism and the Mass Media: the north-south divide, 1997; (with S. Barnett) The Westminster Tales: the 21st century crisis in political journalism, 2001; (jtly) Culture Wars: the media and the British Left, 2006; Live from Africa: a handbook for African radio journalists, 2007; articles on media, politics and public affairs in learned jls, nat. newspapers and magazines incl. Guardian, Sunday Times, New Statesman, Tribune and THES. *Recreations*: playing tennis, supporting Queens Park Rangers, ski-ing, visiting the cinema, theatre, opera, travel. *E*: ivorgaber@gmail.com.

**GABITASS, Jonathan Roger**, MA; Head Master, Merchant Taylors' School, 1991–2004; *b* 25 July 1944; *s* of William Gabitass and Nell Gabitass (*née* Chaffe); *m* 1967, Fiona Patricia Hoy; two *d*. *Educ*: Plymouth Coll.; St John's Coll., Oxford (MA English Lang. and Lit., PGCE). Asst English teacher, Clifton Coll., Bristol, 1967–73; Head of English, 1973–78, Second Master, 1978–91, Abingdon Sch., Oxon. Governor: Godolphin and Latymer Sch., 2004–; Abingdon Sch., 2005–; Abingdon Prep. Sch., 2005–; St Helen and St Katharine's Sch., 2007–. Liveryman, Merchant Taylors' Co., 2005–. *Recreations*: Rugby football, Cornish coastal path walking, 18th and 19th Century caricature, art galleries and theatre. *Clubs*: East India; Vincent's (Oxford).

**GABRA, Prof. Hani**, PhD; FRCP, FRCPE; Professor of Medical Oncology, Imperial College London, since 2003; Hon. Consultant Medical Oncologist, Imperial College Healthcare NHS Trust, since 2003; Chief Physician Scientist, Vice President and Head, Clinical Discovery Unit, Early Clinical Development, iMED Biotech Unit, AstraZeneca, since 2017; *b* Cairo, 15 Jan. 1963; *s* of Gamal and Samira Gabra; *m* 1st, 1992, Laura Lee (marr. diss. 2015); two *s* one *d*; 2nd, 2016, Diana Manih. *Educ*: Carluke High Sch., Carluke, Lanarkshire; Univ. of Glasgow (BSc Hons 1984; MB ChB 1987); Univ. of Edinburgh (MSc 1993; PhD 1996). MRCP 1990, FRCP 2005; FRCPE 2003. ICRF Clin. Scientist and Hon. Consultant Med. Oncologist, CRUK Med. Oncol. Unit, Western Gen. Hosp., Edinburgh, 1998–2003; Dir, Ovarian Cancer Action Res. Centre, 2006–17, Lead for Cancer Clin. Trials, 2012–17, Imperial Coll. London; Dep. Hd, Div. of Cancer, 2013–17; Hd of Medical Oncology, Imperial Coll. Healthcare NHS Trust, 2013–17; Lead for Div. 1 and Associate Dir, NIHR Clinical Res. Network for NW London, 2014–17. Pres., Eur. Translational Ovarian Cancer Network, 2010–17. *Recreations*: cycling, stargazing. *Address*: Department of Surgery and Cancer, 4th Floor, Institute of Reproductive and Developmental Biology, Imperial College London, Hammersmith Campus, Du Cane Road, W12 0NN. *T*: (020) 7594 2792, *Fax*: (020) 7594 2154. *E*: h.gabra@imperial.ac.uk. *Club*: Caledonian.

**GABRIEL, Peter**; singer, musician and songwriter; *b* 13 Feb. 1950; *m* 1st, 1971, Jill Moore (marr. diss.); two *d*; 2nd, 2002, Meabh Flynn; two *s*. *Educ*: Charterhouse. Mem., Genesis, 1966–75; solo artist, 1975–. Founder: World of Music, Arts and Dance (annual festivals), 1982; Real World Gp, 1985; Real World Studios, 1986; Real World Records, 1989; Real World Multimedia, 1994; Jt Founder, Witness (human rights programme), 1992; Co-founder, theElders.org, 2000. *Albums* include: *with Genesis*: From Genesis to Revelation, 1969; Nursery Crime, 1971; Foxtrot, 1972; Selling England by the Pound, 1973; The Lamb Lies Down on Broadway, 1974; *solo*: Peter Gabriel I, 1977, II, 1978, III, 1980, IV, 1982; So, 1986; Us, 1992; Ovo, 2000; Up, 2002; Scratch My Back, 2010; *film soundtracks*: Birdy, 1984; Last Temptation of Christ, 1988; Rabbit-Proof Fence, 2002; WALL·E, 2008. *Address*: Real World Studios, Mill Lane, Corsham, Wilts SN13 8PL.

**GABRYS, Prof. Jennifer Chloe**, PhD; Professor of Media, Culture and Environment, University of Cambridge, since 2018; *b* USA, 1973. *Educ*: Univ. of Minnesota (BA 1996; MLA 1999); McGill Univ. (PhD 2007). Res. Associate, Univ. of Minnesota, 1995–98; Designer and Project Manager: Coen + Partners, 1998–2000; Dry Design, 2000–01; Rios Clementi Hale Studios, 2001–02; Research Fellow: McGill Univ., 2002–04; Concordia Univ., 2003–06; Goldsmiths, University of London: Lectr, 2006–09, Sen. Lectr, 2009–12, in Design; Sen. Lectr in Sociol., 2013–14; Reader in Sociol., 2014–17; Prof. of Sociol., 2017–18. FRSA. Mem., Editl Team, Big Data & Society, 2017–. *Publications*: Airdrop, 2004; Digital Rubbish: a natural history of electronics, 2011; (ed jtly) Accumulation: the material politics of plastic, 2013; Program Earth: environmental sensing and the making of a computational planet, 2016; How to Do Things with Sensors, 2019; contrib. technol. and envmt-related articles to academic, professional and popular jls. *Address*: Department of Sociology, University of Cambridge, Free School Lane, Cambridge CB2 3RQ. *E*: jg899@cam.ac.uk. *W*: www.jennifergabrys.net.

**GADD, Ruth Maria**; see Kelly, Rt Hon. R. M.

**GADDES, (John) Gordon**; Chairman and Trustee, Langa Township Pre-Schools Trust UK, since 2011; *b* 22 May 1936; *s* of late James Graham Moscrop Gaddes and of Irene Gaddes (*née* Murray; who later married E. O. Kine); *m* 1st, 1958, Pamela Jean (*née* Marchbank) (*d* 2015); one *s* one *d*; 2nd, 2017, Rosina Louisa Pocock. *Educ*: Carre's Grammar Sch., Sleaford; Selwyn Coll., Cambridge (MA Hons Geography); London Univ. (BScEcon Hons 1966; MA Philosophy and Religion 2005). Asst Lectr in Business Studies, Peterborough Technical Coll., 1960–64; Lectr in Business Studies, later Head of Business Studies, then Vice-Principal, Dacorum Coll. of Further Educn, Hemel Hempstead, 1964–69; Head of Export Services: British Standards Instn, 1969–72; Quality Assurance Dept, 1972–73; Dir, BSI Hemel Hempstead Centre, 1973–77; Commercial Dir, BSI, 1977–81; Dir, Information, Marketing and Resources, BSI, 1981–82; Dir Gen., BEAMA, 1982–97; UK Deleg., 1997, Sec. Gen., 1998–2001, Pres., 2001–03, European Orgn for Testing and Certification, subseq. for Conformity Assessment; Dir, DENS Ltd (formerly Dacorum Emergency Night Shelter), 2003–10 (Chm., 2003–07). Dir, Gaddes Associates Ltd, 1998–2007. Secretary, BSI Quality Assurance Council, 1976–80; Member: Council, 1982–97, President's Cttee, 1984–86, Production Cttee, 1984–88, CBI; NACCB, 1984–90 (Chm., Assessment Panel, 1985–90); Project Leader for ISO/UNESCO inf. network study, 1974–75; variously, consultant to UNIDO, EC and HMG; UK Rep., ORGALIME, 1982–97 (Chairman: Electrical and Electronic Inds Liaison Cttee, 1982–86; Finance and Admin Cttee, 1986–88; Exec. Cttee, 1988–90); Pres., CENELEC, 1989–91 (Dep. Pres., 1987–89, 1994–95); Chairman: Eur. Electrotechnical Sectoral Cttee for Testing and Certification, 1992–95; ASTA Certification Services, 1994–98; UK Ex Forum, 1995–97; Kennedy Mgt Develt, 1998–99. Member: (Lab) Hemel Hempstead BC, 1968–71, 1972–74 (Leader of Council and Chair, Policy and Finance, 1972–74); (Soc Dem) Dacorum BC, 1987–91 (Leader of the Opposition, 1987–89). Gov., Adeyfield Sch., 2001–12 (Vice-Chm., 2005–12). Mem., Fabian Soc., 2011–. Dir, Dacorum Heritage Trust, 2016–. Vice-Chm., 2005–08, Treas., 2015–17, Warden, 2019–, Parish of St Mary and St Paul, Hemel Hempstead. *Publications*: Cape Town Stories: apartheid - its effects and its ending, 2016. *Recreations*: golf, swimming, family, church and community affairs. *Clubs*: Athenæum; Whipsnade Park Golf.

**GADHIA, Baron** *cr* 2016 (Life Peer), of Northwood in the County of Middlesex; **Jitesh Kishorekumar Gadhia**; Senior Managing Director, Blackstone Advisory Partners LP, 2010–15; *b* Kampala, Uganda, 27 May 1970; *s* of Kishore and Hansa Gadhia; *m* 2001, Angeli Saujani; one *s* one *d*. *Educ*: Fitzwilliam Coll., Cambridge (BA Hons Econs 1991); London Business Sch. (Sloan Fellow; MSc Mgt). Baring Bros, 1991–98; Manek Investment Mgt, 1998–99; ABN AMRO, 2001–08; Man. Dir, Global Head of Advisory, Barclays Capital, 2008–10. Mem. Bd, UK Govt Investments (formerly UK Financial Investments), 2014–. Trustee: Guy's and St Thomas' Charity, 1999–2009; NESTA, 2007–14. *Recreations*: charitable activities, reading, walking, cinema, travel. *Address*: House of Lords, SW1A 0PW.

**GADHIA, Dame Jayne-Anne**, DBE 2019 (CBE 2014); Chief Executive: Snoop, since 2019; Salesforce (UK and Ireland), since 2019; *b* Stourbridge, 19 Oct. 1961; *d* of Geoffrey and Gwendoline Finch; *m* 1984, Ashok Gadhia; one *d*. *Educ*: Univ. of London (BA Hons Hist.). CA 1989. Trainee chartered accountant, Ernst & Young, 1982–87; Hd, Unit Trust Mktg/Business and Finance Manager, Norwich Union, 1987–94; Ops and Compliance Dir, Virgin Direct, 1994–98; Man. Dir, Virgin One Account, 1998–2001; Hd, Gp Mortgages, RBS, 2001–07; CEO, Virgin Money, 2007–18. Non-exec. Dir, Stagecoach Gp, 2019. Trustee, Tate, 2016–. FCIB; FRSE 2018. *Publications*: The Virgin Banker, 2017. *Recreations*: horses, music, film, France.

**GADNEY, Jane Caroline Rebecca**; see Parker-Smith, J. C. R.

**GADSBY, Prof. David Christopher**, PhD; FRS 2005; Patrick A. Gerschel Family Professor, Laboratory of Cardiac/Membrane Physiology, Rockefeller University, since 2007. *Educ*: Trinity Coll., Cambridge (BA 1969, MA 1973); University Coll. London (PhD 1978). Rockefeller University: Asst Prof., 1978–84, Associate Prof., 1984–91, Lab. of Cardiac Physiol.; Prof. and Hd, Lab. of Cardiac/Membrane Physiol., 1991–2007. *Publications*: contrib. learned jls. *Address*: Laboratory of Cardiac/Membrane Physiology, Rockefeller University, 1230 York Avenue, New York, NY 10065, USA.

**GAFFNEY, Hugh Lawrence**; MP (Lab) Coatbridge, Chryston and Bellshill, since 2017. Royal Mail Gp. Mem. (Lab), North Lanarkshire Council, 2017–. Mem., Scottish Affairs Cttee, H of C, 2017–. *Address*: House of Commons, SW1A 0AA.

**GAFFNEY, John Campion B.**; see Burke-Gaffney.

**GAGE**, family name of **Viscount Gage**.

**GAGE, 8th Viscount** cr 1720 (Ire.); **Henry Nicholas Gage**; DL; Bt 1622; Baron Gage (Ire.) 1720; Baron Gage (GB) 1790; b 9 April 1934; yr s of 6th Viscount Gage, KCVO and his 1st wife, Hon. Alexandra Imogen Clare Grenfell (d 1969), yr d of 1st Baron Desborough, KG, GCVO; S brother, 1993; m 1st, 1974, Lady Diana Adrienne Beatty (marr. diss. 2002); two s; 2nd, 2009, Alexandra Murray Templeton; one s. Educ: Eton; Christ Church, Oxford. 2nd Lt Coldstream Guards, 1953. DL East Sussex, 1998. Recreation: country and other pursuits. Heir: s Hon. Henry William Gage, b 25 June 1975. Address: Firle Place, Lewes, East Sussex BN8 6LP. T: (01273) 858535.

**GAGE, Rt Hon. Sir William (Marcus)**, Kt 1993; PC 2004; a Lord Justice of Appeal, 2004–08; a Surveillance Commissioner, 2009–15; b 22 April 1938; s of late His Honour Conolly Gage; m 1962, Penelope Mary Groves; three s. Educ: Repton; Sidney Sussex Coll., Cambridge. MA. National Service, Irish Guards, 1956–58. Called to the Bar, Inner Temple, 1963, Bencher, 1991; QC 1982; a Recorder, 1985–93; a Judge of the High Court of Justice, QBD, 1993–2004. Presiding Judge, S Eastern Circuit, 1997–2000. Chancellor, diocese of Coventry, 1980–2009, of Ely, 1989–2012. Chm., Baha Mousa Public Inquiry, 2008–11 (report published 2011); Member: Criminal Injuries Compensation Bd, 1987–93; Parole Bd, 2001–04. Recreations: fishing, travel. Address: Office of Surveillance Commissioners, PO Box 29105, SW1V 1ZU.

**GAGEBY DENHAM, Susan**; see Denham.

**GAGEN, Heather Jacqueline**; see Yasamee, H. J.

**GAHAGAN, Michael Barclay**, CB 2000; Director, Housing (formerly Housing, Private Policy and Analysis) Directorate, Office of the Deputy Prime Minister (formerly Department for the Environment, Transport and the Regions, then Department for Transport, Local Government and the Regions), 1997–2003; b 24 March 1943; s of Geoffrey and Doris Gahagan; m 1967, Anne Brown; two s. Educ: St Mary's Coll., Southampton; Univ. of Manchester (MA Econs, BA). MRICS. W. H. Robinson & Co., Chartered Surveyors, Manchester, 1964–66; DEA (NW), 1966–69; Min. of Housing and Local Govt (NW), 1969–71; DoE, Central Res. and Inner Cities Directorates, NW, SE and London Regl Offices, 1971–88; seconded to DTI Inner Cities Unit, 1988–91; Dir, Inner Cities, subseq. Cities and Countryside Policy, then Regeneration, Directorate, DoE, 1991–96. Pres., Internat. Urban Develt Assoc., 1995–99. Chairman: S Yorks Housing Market Renewal Pathfinder, 2003–11; Doncaster Housing Improvement Bd, 2011–12; Member, Board: Paradigm Housing Gp, 2003–13 (Chm., Homes (formerly Ops) Bd, 2008–13); Centre of Refurbishment Excellence, 2011–16 (Chm., 2012–16); Red Kite Community Housing, 2016– (Chm., 2017–); Chm., Paradigm Foundn, 2013–16. Recreations: soccer, bridge.

**GAIMSTER, Dr David Richard Michael**, FSA; FRSE; Director, Auckland War Memorial Museum, New Zealand, since 2017; b 3 Jan. 1962; s of late Rev. Leslie Rayner Gaimster and of Mareike Gaimster (née Döhler); m 1st 1990, Märit Thurborg (marr. diss. 2004); one s one d; 2nd, 2005, Amy Clarke; one s two d. Educ: Longsands Sch., St Neots, Cambs; Durham Univ. (BA Hons Archaeol. 1984); University Coll. London (PhD Medieval Archaeol. 1991). Asst Keeper, Dept of Medieval and Later Antiquities, BM, 1986–2001; Sen. Policy Advr, Cultural Property Unit, DCMS, 2002–04; Gen. Sec. and Chief Exec., Soc. of Antiquaries, 2004–10; Dir, The Hunterian (formerly Hunterian Mus. and Art Gall.), Univ. of Glasgow, 2010–17. Associate Prof. in Historical Archaeol., Dept of Cultural Scis, Univ. of Turku, Finland, 2000– ; Vis. Prof., Sch. of Archaeol. and Ancient History, Leicester Univ., 2009– ; Hon. Res. Fellow, Inst. of Archaeol., UCL, 2000–17. Mem., Culture Cttee, 2005–11, Dir, 2009–11, UK Nat. Commn for UNESCO. Member, Board: Museums Galleries Scotland, 2012–17; Historic Envmt Scotland, 2015–17; Council of Australasian Museum Dirs, 2018– . FSA 1996; FMA 2001); FRSE 2016; MCIfA (MIFA 1987). OM, Soc. of Historical Archaeol of N America, 2005. Publications: German Stoneware 1200–1900: archaeology and cultural history, 1997; (ed jtly) The Age of Transition: the archaeology of English culture 1400–1600, 1997; (ed jtly) Pottery in the Making: world ceramic traditions, 1997; Maiolica in the North: the archaeology of tin-glazed earthenware in NW Europe c 1500–1600, 1999; (ed jtly) Novgorod: the archaeology of a Russian medieval city and its hinterland, 2001; (ed jtly) The Archaeology of Reformation 1480–1580, 2003; The Historical Archaeology of Pottery Supply and Demand in the Lower Rhineland, AD 1400–1800, 2006; (ed jtly) Making History: antiquaries in Britain 1707–2007, 2007; (ed jtly) International Handbook of Historical Archaeology, 2009; Director's Choice: the Hunterian, University of Glasgow, 2012; (ed jtly) The Routledge Handbook of Material Culture in Early Modern Europe, 2016; Director's Choice: Auckland Museum, 2018; contribs to archaeol and historical monographs and learned jls. Recreations: antiques, historic buildings and interiors, international travel. Address: Auckland War Memorial Museum, The Domain, Private Bag 92018, 1142 Auckland, New Zealand. E: dgaimster@aucklandmuseum.com.

**GAINFORD**, Barony of cr 1917; title not used by 4th Baron (see Pease, G.);

**GAINS, Sir John (Christopher)**, Kt 2003; CEng, FICE; Chairman, CCS Group plc, since 2008; Chief Executive, Mowlem (formerly John Mowlem & Co.) PLC, 1995–2004 (Director, 1992–2005); b 22 April 1945; s of Albert Edward Gains and Grace (née Breckenridge); m 1st, 1969, Ann Murray (d 1999); one s one d; 2nd, 2012, Shirley Anne Pearce (see Dame S. A. Pearce). Educ: King Henry VIII Sch., Coventry; Loughborough Univ. (BSc). CEng 1970; FICE 1992. Joined John Mowlem & Co. PLC, 1966; Dir, Mowlem Civil Engineering, 1983–95. Chm., Aktrion Hldgs Ltd, 2005–09; non-executive Director: SGB plc, 1997–2000; Heiton Gp plc, 2002–05; Thames Water Utilities Ltd, 2005–06. Mem. Council, Loughborough Univ., 2006–16. Hon. DTech Loughborough, 2004. Recreations: golf, sailing, walking. Address: Norfolk. Club: Reform.

**GAINSBOROUGH**, 6th Earl of, (2nd) cr 1841; **Anthony Baptist Noel**; Bt 1781; Baron Barham, 1805; Viscount Campden, Baron Noel, 1841; b 16 Jan. 1950; e s of 5th Earl of Gainsborough and Mary (née Stourton); S father, 2009; m 1972, Sarah Rose (LVO 1996, DL), er d of Col T. F. C. Winnington; one s. Educ: Ampleforth; Royal Agricultural Coll., Cirencester. Heir: s Viscount Campden, qv. Address: Hall Farmhouse, Cottesmore Road, Exton, Oakham, Rutland LE15 8AN. T: (01572) 812458.

**GAINSFORD, Sir Ian (Derek)**, Kt 1995; FDSRCS, FDSRCSE; Dean of King's College School of Medicine and Dentistry, King's College London, 1988–97; Vice-Principal, King's College London, 1994–97; Vice-Principal Emeritus, 2008; b 24 June 1930; s of late Rabbi Morris Ginsberg, MA, PhD, AKC, and Anne Freda; m 1957, Carmel Liebster; one s two d. Educ: Thames Valley Grammar Sch., Twickenham; King's Coll. and King's College Hosp. Med. Sch., London (BDS; FKC 1984); Toronto Univ., Canada (DDS Hons). FDSRCS 1967; FDSRCSE 1998. Junior Staff, King's College Hosp., 1955–57; Member staff, Dept of Conservative Dentistry, London Hosp. Med. Sch., 1957–70; Sen. Lectr/Consultant, Dept of Conservative Dentistry, King's College Hosp., 1970–97; Dep. Dean of Dental Studies, 1973–77; Dir of Clinical Dental Services, KCH, 1977–87 (Dean of Dental Studies, KCHMS, 1977–83); Dean, Faculty of Clinical Dentistry, KCL, 1983–87. President, British Soc. for Restorative Dentistry, 1973–74; Member: BDA, 1956– (Pres., Metropolitan Br., 1981–82); Internat. Dental Fedn, 1966– ; American Dental Soc. of London, 1960– (Pres., 1982); Amer. Dental Soc. of Europe, 1965– (Hon. Treas. 1971–77; Pres., 1982); GDC, 1986–94 (Chm., Educn Cttee, 1990–94; Chm., Specialist Trng Adv. Cttee, 1996–2000). Examiner for Membership in General Dental Surgery, RCS, 1979–84 (Chm., 1982–84); External Examiner: Leeds Univ. Dental Sch., 1985–87; Hong Kong Dental Sch., 1988–90; Fellow, and Mem., 1967– , Hon. Mem., 1996, Pres., 1993–94, Odontological Sect., RSM; a Regent, RCSE, 2002–10, now Regent Emeritus. Non-exec. Dir, SE Thames RHA, 1988–93. President: Western Marble Arch Synagogue, 1998–2000; The Maccabaeans, 2000–07; St Marylebone Soc., 2001–04. Hon. Pres., British Friends of Magen David Adom, 1995–2009. Hon. Mem., Amer. Dental Assoc., 1983. Hon. Scientific Advr, British Dental Jl, 1982. FICD 1975; MGDS RCS 1979; FACD 1988; FRSA 1996. Hon. FRCSE 2006. Publications: Silver Amalgam in Clinical Practice, 1965, 3rd edn 1992. Recreations: theatre, canal cruising. Address: Flat 1, 19 Tzvi Graetz, Jerusalem 9311714, Israel. T: (2) 563 3050. Clubs: Athenæum, Royal Society of Medicine.

**GAISFORD, Rt Rev. John Scott**; Bishop Suffragan of Beverley, 1994–2000; Episcopal Visitor for the Province of York, 1994–2000; Hon. Assistant Bishop of Ripon, 1996–2000; b 7 Oct. 1934; s of Joseph and Margaret Thompson Gaisford; m 1962, Gillian Maclean; one s one d. Educ: Univ. of Durham (Exhibnr, St Chad's Coll., Durham; BA Hons Theol. 1959, DipTh with Distinction 1960, MA 1976). Deacon 1960, priest 1961, Manchester; Assistant Curate: S Hilda, Audenshaw, 1960–62; S Michael, Bramhall, 1962–65; Vicar, S Andrew, Crewe, 1965–86; RD of Nantwich, 1974–85; Hon. Canon of Chester Cathedral, 1980–86; Archdeacon of Macclesfield, 1986–94. Proctor in Convocation, Mem. Gen. Synod, 1975–95; Church Commissioner, 1986–94; Member: Church of England Pensions Bd, 1982–97; Churches Conservation Trust (formerly Redundant Churches Fund), 1989–98. Address: 5 Trevone Close, Knutsford, Cheshire WA16 9EJ. T: (01565) 633531, 07429 340155. E: jsandg.gaisford@gmail.com. Club: Athenæum.

**GAISMAN, Jonathan Nicholas Crispin**; QC 1995; b 10 Aug. 1956; o s of Peter and Bea Gaisman; m 1982, Tessa Jardine Paterson (MBE 1990); one s two d. Educ: Summer Fields; Eton College (King's Scholar); Worcester Coll., Oxford (BCL; MA 1st cl Hons Jurisp.). Called to the Bar, Inner Temple, 1979, Bencher, 2004; Asst Recorder, 1998–2000; Recorder, 2000–08. Mem., Legal Panel, Red Tape Initiative, 2017– . Director: English Chamber Orchestra and Music Soc. Ltd, 1992–96; Internat. Musicians' Seminar, Prussia Cove, 1994– ; Streetwise Opera, 2002– . FRSA 1997. Recreations: the arts, travel, country pursuits. Address: 7 King's Bench Walk, Temple, EC4Y 7DS. T: (020) 7910 8300. Clubs: Beefsteak; I Zingari.

**GAITSKELL, Robert**; QC 1994; PhD; CEng, FIET, FIMechE; FCIArb; a Recorder, 2000–10; Vice President, Institution of Electrical Engineers, 1998–2001; b 19 April 1948; s of late Stanley Gaitskell and late Thelma Phyllis Gaitskell (née Holmes); m 1974, Dr Deborah Lyndall Bates; one d. Educ: Hamilton High Sch., Bulawayo, Zimbabwe; Univ. of Cape Town (BSc Eng); KCL (PhD 1998; AKC 1998). CEng 1993; FIET (FIEE 1993); FCIArb 1995; FIMechE 1998. CEDR Accredited and Registered Mediator, 1999. Grad. trainee, Reyrolle Parsons, 1971–73; Engr, Electricity Dept, Bulawayo CC, Zimbabwe, 1973–75; Electrical Engr, GEC (South Africa), 1975–76; called to the Bar, Gray's Inn, 1978, Bencher, 2003; in practice at Bar in construction cases; arbitrator; Asst Recorder, 1997–2000. Lectr, Centre of Construction Law and Mgt, KCL, 1993–2003, for LLM, on Internat. Infrastructure Arbitration, 2006–08, and other professional bodies. Institution of Electrical Engineers: Mem. Council, 1994–2001; Chairman: Bd of Mgt and Design Div., 1995; Professional Gp on Engrg and the Law, 1994; Internat. Bd, 1998–99; Public Affairs Bd, 1999–2000; Professional Bd, 2000; Dispute Bd, ITER (F4E) nuclear fusion project, France, 2014– . Mem. Council, Inns of Ct Tribunal Appts Body, 2012–14. Mem., Heilbron Cttee on Civil Procedure, 1993; Chm., IET/IMechE Jt Cttee on Model Forms, 2001– . Senator, Engrg Council, 1998–2002 (Chairman: Election Cttee, 1999–2001; Code of Conduct Cttee, 1999–2001). Member: Arbitration Panel, Dubai Internat. Arbitration Centre, 2006– ; Official Referees Bar Assoc., 1987–93; Gray's Inn Barristers, 2002–03. Legal columnist, Engrg Mgt Jl, 1994–2003; Mem. Editl Bd, Construction and Engrg Law Jl, 1998–2005. Methodist local preacher. Liveryman: Engineers' Co., 1997– ; Arbitrators' Co., 2002– (Mem., Ct Assts, 2010–17). Publications: (ed) Engineers' Dispute Resolution Handbook, 2006; (ed) Construction Dispute Resolution Handbook, 2nd edn 2011, 3rd edn as Keating Construction Dispute Resolution Handbook, 2016; papers and articles on law and engrg. Recreations: walking, theatre, travel. Address: Keating Chambers, 15 Essex Street, WC2R 3AA. Club: Athenaeum.

**GALASKO, Prof. Charles Samuel Bernard**; Professor of Orthopaedic Surgery, University of Manchester, 1976–2004, now Professor Emeritus; Consultant Orthopaedic Surgeon, Hope Hospital, 1976–2004 (Medical Director, 1993–96); Director of Education and Training, Salford Royal Hospitals NHS Trust, 2003–05; b 29 June 1939; s of David Isaac Galasko and Rose Galasko; m 1967, Carol Freyda Lapinsky; one s one d. Educ: King Edward VII Sch., Johannesburg; Univ. of Witwatersrand (MB BCh 1st Cl. Hons 1962; ChM 1969). MSc Manchester 1980. FRCS 1966; FRCSEd 1966. Med. surg. and orth. trng, Johannesburg Gen. Hosp. and Univ. of Witwatersrand, 1963–66; House Surgeon and Surg. Registrar, Hammersmith Hosp. and RPMS, 1966–69; Lord Nuffield Schol. in Orthopaedic Surgery, Univ. of Oxford, 1969; Orth. and Trauma Registrar and Sen. Registrar, Radcliffe Infirmary and Nuffield Orth. Centre, Oxford, 1970–73; Cons. Orth. Surgeon, Dir of Orth. Surgery, and Asst Dir, Div. of Surgery, RPMS and Hammersmith Hosp., 1973–76; Cons. Orth. Surgeon, Royal Manchester Children's Hosp., 1976–2002. Member, Management Board: Royal Manchester Children's Hosp., 1989–92; Salford Royal Hosps NHS Trust, 1989–96; Gov., Stockport NHS Foundn Trust, 2013– . Hunterian Prof., RCS, 1971; Sir Arthur Sims Commonwealth Prof., 1998. Lectures: Hunterian, 1972; Annandale, 1979; Batson, 1979; Stanford Cade, 1993; Malkin, 1996; David Fuller, 1996; Chatterjee, 1997; Francois P. Fouche, 1999; Robert Jones, 1999; Hunterian Orator, 2003; Lord Henry Cohen, 2010; Naughton Dunn, 2010. Chm., Jt Cttee on Higher Surgical Trng, UK and Ire., 1997–2000. Member: Med. Cttee, British Olympic Assoc., 1988–2002; Internat. Cttee, 1990–93, Internat. Adv. Bd, 1994–96, SICOT (A. O. Internat. Award, 1981); President: SIROT, 1990–93; British Orthopaedic Assoc., 2000–01 (Vice Pres., 1999–2000; Mem. Council, 1988–91, 1998–2003); Faculty of Sport and Exercise Medicine, 2006–09 (Chm., Intercollegiate Academic Bd of Sport and Exercise Medicine, 2002–05); Vice President: Sect. of Oncology, RSM, 1987 (Mem. Council, 1980–87); RCS, 1999–2001 (Mem. Council, 1991–2003; Chm., Hosp. Recognition Cttee, 1992–95; Chm., Trauma Cttee, 1992–95; Chm., Trng Bd, 1995–99). Vice Pres., British Amateur Wrestling Assoc., 1996–2002 (Chm., 1992–96; Med. Advr, 1987–2002); Vice-Chm., English Olympic Wrestling Assoc., 1998–2000 (Med. Advr, 1987–2000). SICOT Fellow, 1972; ABC Fellow, 1978; Aust. Commonwealth Fellow, 1982. Hon. Fellow: British Orth. Assoc.; S African Orth. Assoc.; Amer. Fracture Assoc.; British Orthopaedics Res. Soc.; Emeritus Mem., Amer. Orth. Assoc.; Corresp. Mem., Columbian Soc. of Orth. Surgery and Traumatology. FMedSci 2002; FFSEM (Ireland) 2003; FFSEM (UK) 2006, Hon. FFSEM 2014. Hon. FCMSA 2002. Moynihan Prize, Assoc. of Surgeons, 1969. Publications: (ed jtly) Radionuclide Scintigraphy in Orthopaedics, 1984; (ed) Principles of Fracture Management, 1984; Skeletal Metastases, 1986; (ed) Neuromuscular Problems in

Orthopaedics, 1987; (ed jtly) Recent Developments in Orthopaedic Surgery, 1987; (ed jtly) Current Trends in Orthopaedic Surgery, 1988; (ed jtly) Imaging Techniques in Orthopaedics, 1989; (jtly) Competing for the Disabled, 1989; articles and contribs to books on aspects of orthopaedics and trauma, surgical educn, skeletal metastasis, neuromuscular conditions, sport and exercise medicine. *Recreations:* sport, opera, music. *Address:* Flat 1, Barfield House, 3 Spath Road, Didsbury, Manchester M20 2BX.

**GALBRAITH**, family name of **Baron Strathclyde**.

**GALBRAITH, Anne,** CBE 2010 (OBE 2005); Chairman, Valuation Tribunal Service, 2004–16; *b* 7 July 1940; *d* of Edward and Hannah Wilks; *m* 1965, John Gordon Galbraith; one *s* one *d*. *Educ:* Blyth Grammar Sch.; Durham Univ. (LLB). Sen. Lectr in Law, Newcastle Coll. of Commerce, then Newcastle Poly., subseq. Univ. of Northumbria, 1965–97 (latterly pt-time); Chair, Newcastle CAB, 1983–88; Mem., Northern RHA, 1988–91; Chair, Royal Victoria Infirmary Hosp. Trust, Newcastle, 1991–97. Member: Prime Minister's Adv. Panel for Citizen's Charter, 1994–2001; Lord Chancellor's Council on Tribunals, 1997–2003; Chm., NHS Prescription Pricing Authy, 2000–06. Non-exec. Dir, NHS Business Authy, 2006–14. Chair, Council, Univ. of Durham, 2006–12. *Recreations:* gardening, reading. *Address:* The Vicarage, Beltingham, Northumberland NE47 7BZ.

**GALBRAITH, Colin Archibald,** PhD; Director, Colin Galbraith Environment Ltd, since 2010; *b* 4 Feb. 1959; *s* of Lorne Galbraith; *m* 1987, Maria; one *s* one *d*. *Educ:* Minard Primary Sch.; Lochgilphead Sec. Sch.; Oban High Sch.; Paisley Univ. (BSc Hons Biol. 1981); Univ. of Aberdeen (PhD Zool. 1987). Ecologist, Nature Conservancy Council, 1987–91; Joint Nature Conservation Committee: Hd, Vertebrate Ecology, 1991–96; Hd, Biodiversity Service, 1996–97; Scottish Natural Heritage: Hd, Adv. Services, 1997–2001; Dir, Scientific and Adv. Services, 2001–07; Dir of Policy and Advice, 2007–10. Hon. Prof., Univ. of Stirling, 2002–. Chm., 1999–2005, Vice Chm., 2005–, Scientific Council, Convention on Migratory Species; Chairman: intergovtl negotiations on develt of global agreement on Conservation of Birds of Prey, 2007–08; Bd of Dirs, Langholm Grouse Moor Recovery Project, 2007–10; Cttee for Scotland, RSPB, 2013–. Member: Bd, Millennium Ecosystem Assessment, 2002–05; Exec. Bd, RZSScot, 2008–15. *Publications:* (ed jtly) Mountains of Northern Europe, 2005; (ed jtly) Farming, Forestry and the Natural Heritage, 2006; (ed jtly) Waterbirds around the World, 2006; (ed jtly) Energy and the Natural Heritage, 2008; (ed jtly) Species Management: challenges and solutions for the 21st century, 2010. *Recreations:* bird watching, hill walking, photography, travel, antiques. *Address:* 45 Mounthooly Loan, Edinburgh EH10 7JD.

**GALBRAITH, Prof. Graham Harold,** PhD; CEng; Vice-Chancellor, University of Portsmouth, since 2013; *b* Scotland, 16 Oct. 1960; *s* of late William Galbraith and Jean Galbraith; *m* 1987, Caroline Wilson; two *s* one *d*. *Educ:* High Sch. of Glasgow; Shawlands Acad., Glasgow; Strathclyde Univ. (BSc 1st Cl. Hons Envmt Engrg 1981; MSc Mech. Engrg 1986; PhD Mech. Engrg 1992). CEng 1983; MCIBSE 1983. Scientific Officer, BRE, Scotland, 1981–83; Lectr, Strathclyde Univ., 1983–93; Tech. Dir, 3E Consultants and Dir, 3E Consultants Ltd: a Strathclyde Univ. co., 1991–93; Glasgow Caledonian University: Sen. Lectr, 1993–96, Reader, 1996–98, Prof. of Building Physics, 1998–2000, Dept of Building and Surveying; Actg Hd, Dept of Energy and Envmtl Technol., 2000–01; Exec. Dean, 2001–05, Asst Principal, 2004–05, Sch. of Engrg, Sci. and Design; Pro Vice-Chancellor, Univ. Exec., 2005–08; Dep. Vice-Chancellor, Univ. of Herts, 2008–13. Vis. Prof., Tech. Univ. of Denmark, 2001–02; Vis. Schol., Faculty of Architecture, Inst. for Building Physics, Tech. Univ. of Dresden, 2002–05. Non-exec. Dir, Watford Enterprise Agency, 2010–14. Mem. Council, CBI E of England, 2011–13, SE of England, 2013–. FHEA 2001. MInstD 2012. *Publications:* res. reports; contribs to scientific jls. *Recreations:* walking, reading, theatre going. *Address:* University of Portsmouth, University House, Winston Churchill Avenue, Portsmouth PO1 2UP. *T:* (023) 9284 3191, *Fax:* (023) 9284 3400. *E:* graham.galbraith@port.ac.uk.

**GALBRAITH-MARTEN, Jason Nicholas;** QC 2014; Director, Assurety Training, since 2011; *b* London, 7 Jan. 1967; *s* of Gavin and Lesley Galbraith-Marten; *m* 2010, Joanne White; one *s* two *d*. *Educ:* Campion Sch., Hornchurch; Magdalene Coll., Cambridge (BA 1989). Called to the Bar, Middle Temple, 1991; in practice as barrister, 1991–. Pegasus Schol., NZ, 1994. Chair, Industrial Law Soc., 2010–13. FRSA 2015. *Recreations:* fine wine and dining, motor racing, Manchester United. *Address:* Cloisters, 1 Pump Court, Temple, EC4Y 7AA. *T:* (020) 7827 4000. *E:* jgm@cloisters.com, jason@assuretytraining.com.

**GALE,** Baroness *cr* 1999 (Life Peer), of Blaenrhondda in the county of Mid Glamorgan; **Anita Gale;** General Secretary, Wales Labour Party, 1984–99; *b* 28 Nov. 1940; *d* of late Arthur and Lillian Gale; *m* 1959 (marr. diss. 1983); two *d*. *Educ:* Pontypridd Tech. Coll.; University Coll., Cardiff (BSc Econ). Machinist, clothing factory, 1955–56 and 1965–70; grocery shop asst, 1956–59; returned to full-time educn, 1970–76; Women's Officer and Asst Organiser, Wales Labour Party, 1976–84. Shadow Spokesperson on Women and Equalities, H of L, 2017–. Member: Inf. Select Cttee, H of L, 2001–04; Jt Cttee on Statutory Instruments, 2004–07; Sub Cttee G, EU Select Cttee, 2006–09; Parly Delegn, Council of Europe, 2008–10; Works of Art Cttee, H of L, 2010–16; Lord Speaker's Works of Art Adv. Panel, 2017–. All Party Parliamentary Groups: Member: British/Taiwan, 2002–; Vice-Chm., Children in Wales, 2017– (Jt Sec., 2008–12); Co-Chm., Parkinson's, 2016– (Chm., 2007–16); Mem., Associate Parly Gp on animal welfare, 2000– (Vice-Chm., 2000–01; Jt Sec., 2001–05). Vice-Chm., Labour Animal Welfare Soc., 1990–; Vice-Chm., PLP Women's Cttee, 2013–; Mem., CPA, 2004–. Mem., IPU, 1999–. Comr for Wales, Women's Nat. Commn, 2004–09. President: Treherbert and Dist Br., RBL, 2000–; Nat. Assoc. of Old Age Pensioners Wales, 2010–; Cardiff and Dist Rhondda Soc., 2014–; Patron: Kidney Wales Foundn, 2008–; Bees for Develt, 2013–; Cardiff and Dist Rhondda Soc., 2014–. *Recreations:* walking, swimming, reading. *Address:* House of Lords, SW1A 0PW. *T:* (020) 7219 3000. *E:* galea@parliament.uk.

**GALE, Audrey Olga Helen;** *see* Sander, Her Honour A. O. H.

**GALE, Benjamin Anthony;** Co-founder and Managing Director, Little Gem, since 2014; *b* London, 23 March 1967; *m* 2001, Leeanne Vinson; one *s* two *d*. *Educ:* Pimlico Sch., London; Manchester Univ. (BA Politics and Modern Hist.). BBC Television: prodn trainee, 1990–92; series producer, documentaries, 1992–98; Exec. Producer, Lion Television, 1998–2003; Series Ed., Who Do You Think You Are?, Wall to Wall Television, 2003–04; Commng Exec., 2004–06, Commng Ed., 2007–08, BBC TV; Dir of Progs, Channel Five, 2008; Head, Bristol Factual, BBC Vision Productions, 2009–12; Dir of Progs, Maverick Television, 2012–14. *Recreations:* cooking, running, ski-ing, reading, cycling. *Address:* Little Gem, G18–21, Shepherds Building Central, Charecroft Way, W14 0EE.

**GALE, Prof. Edwin Albert Merwood,** FRCP; Professor of Diabetic Medicine, Bristol University, 1997, now Emeritus; *b* 21 March 1945; *s* of George Edwin Gale and Carole Fisher Gale; *m* 1982, Lone Brogaard; one *s* two *d*. *Educ:* Sevenoaks Sch.; Sidney Sussex Coll., Cambridge (MA, MB BChir). Sen. Lectr, 1984–92, Prof. of Diabetes, 1992–97, St Bartholomew's Hosp. *Publications:* (with R. B. Tattersall) Diabetes: clinical management, 1990; papers on causes, prediction and possible prevention of type 1 diabetes. *Recreations:* ancient coins, fossils.

**GALE, Air Vice-Marshal Ian David,** MBE 2004; Assistant Chief of Air Staff, Ministry of Defence, since 2019; *s* of Peter John Gale; *m* 2006, Sally Carmichael. *Educ:* Sir Thomas Picton Sch.; King's Coll. London (MA Defence Studies, Internat. Relns 2006); Open Univ. (MBA 2012); Major Projects Leadership Acad., Saïd Business Sch., Oxford. Joined RAF, 1989; fast jet pilot and weapons instructor, 1989–2005; Prog. Manager, MoD, 2007; OC, 31 Sqdn, 2008–10; Hd, Complex Weapons, 2010–11; CO, RAF Lossiemouth, 2011–13; Hd, Air Progs, Jt Forces Comd, 2013–15; Sen. Responsible Owner, Comd, Control, Intelligence and Surveillance Prog., RAF, 2015–19. Mem., Honourable Co. of Air Pilots, 2004. *Recreations:* photography, hill walking, competition aerobatics. *Address:* 5-I-31, Ministry of Defence, Main Building, Whitehall, SW1A 2HB. *T:* (020) 7218 6565. *Club:* Royal Air Force.

**GALE, John,** OBE 1987; theatre producer; *b* 2 Aug. 1929; *s* of Frank Haith Gale and Martha Edith Gale (*née* Evans); *m* 1950, Liselotte Ann (*née* Wratten); two *s*. *Educ:* Christ's Hospital; Webber Douglas Academy of Dramatic Art. Formerly an actor; presented his first production, Inherit the Wind, London, 1960; has since produced or co-produced, in London, British provinces, USA, Australia, New Zealand and S Africa, over 150 plays, including: Candida, 1960; On the Brighter Side, 1961; Boeing-Boeing, 1962; Devil May Care, 1963; Windfall, 1963; Where Angels Fear to Tread, 1963; The Wings of the Dove, 1963; Amber for Anna, 1964; Present Laughter, 1964, 1981; Maigret and the Lady, 1965; The Platinum Cat, 1965; The Sacred Flame, 1966; An Evening with G. B. S., 1966; A Woman of No Importance, 1967; The Secretary Bird, 1968; Dear Charles, 1968; Highly Confidential, 1969; The Young Churchill, 1969; The Lionel Touch, 1969; Abelard and Héloïse, 1970; No Sex, Please—We're British, 1971; Lloyd George Knew My Father, 1972; The Mating Game, 1972; Parents' Day, 1972; At the End of the Day, 1973; Birds of Paradise, 1974; A Touch of Spring, 1975; Separate Tables, 1977; The Kingfisher, 1977; Sextet, 1977; Cause Célèbre, 1977; Shut Your Eyes and Think of England, 1977; Can You Hear Me at the Back?, 1979; Middle Age Spread, 1979; Private Lives, 1980; A Personal Affair, 1982. The Secretary Bird and No Sex, Please—We're British set records for the longest run at the Savoy and Strand Theatres respectively; No Sex, Please—We're British is the longest running comedy in the history of World Theatre and passed 6,000 performances at the Garrick Theatre in Nov. 1985. Chichester Festival Theatre: Exec. Producer, 1983–84; Director, 1984–89. Director: John Gale Productions Ltd, 1960–90; Gale Enterprises Ltd, 1960–90; West End Managers Ltd, 1972–89; Lisden Productions Ltd, 1975–90. President, Soc. of West End Theatre Managers, 1972–75; Chm., Theatres National Cttee, 1979–85. Governor, 1976–, and Almoner, 1978–95, Christ's Hospital; Chm. of Govs, Guildford Sch. of Acting, 1989–2000. Member, Amicable Soc. of Blues, 1981–. *Recreations:* travel, rugby. *Address:* East Dean Cottage, East Dean, near Chichester, W Sussex PO18 0JA. *T:* (01243) 811407. *Club:* London Welsh Rugby Football (Richmond) (Chairman, 1979–81).

**GALE, Michael;** QC 1979; a Recorder of the Crown Court, 1977–97; *b* 12 Aug. 1932; *s* of Joseph Gale and Blossom Gale; *m* 1963, Joanna Stephanie Bloom; one *s* two *d*. *Educ:* Cheltenham Grammar Sch.; Grocers' Sch.; King's Coll., Cambridge (Exhibnr; BA History and Law, 1954, MA 1958). National Service, Royal Fusiliers and Jt Services Sch. for Linguists, 1956–58. Called to the Bar, Middle Temple, 1957, Bencher, 1988; Harmsworth Law Scholar, 1958. Mem., Gen. Council of the Bar, 1987–94; Legal Assessor: GMC, 1995–2002; GDC, 1995–2002; Gen. Osteopathic Council, 1998–2002; CIPFA, 2000–02; Chm., Review and Complaints Cttee, Nat. Heritage Meml Fund and Heritage Lottery Fund, 1996–2001. *Publications:* jointly: A Guide to the Crime (Sentences) Act, 1997; Fraud and the PLC, the Criminal Justice and Police Act 2001: a guide for practitioners, 1999. *Recreations:* the arts, country living. *Clubs:* Garrick, MCC.

**GALE, Rt Hon. Sir Roger (James),** Kt 2012; PC 2019; MP (C) North Thanet, since 1983; *b* Poole, Dorset, 20 Aug. 1943; *s* of Richard Byrne Gale and Phyllis Mary (*née* Rowell); *m* 1st, 1964, Wendy Dawn Bowman (marr. diss. 1967); 2nd, 1971, Susan Sampson (marr. diss.); one *d*; 3rd, 1980, Susan Gabrielle Marks; two *s*. *Educ:* Southbourne Prep. Sch.; Hardye's Sch., Dorchester; Guildhall Sch. of Music and Drama (LGSM). Freelance broadcaster, 1963–72; freelance reporter, BBC Radio, London, 1972–73; Producer, Current Affairs Gp, BBC Radio (progs included Newsbeat and Today), 1973–76; Producer/Dir, BBC Children's Television, 1976–79; Producer/Dir, Thames TV, and Editor, teenage unit, 1979–83. Joined Conservative Party, 1964; Mem., Cttee, Greater London Young Conservatives, 1964–65. PPS to Minister of State for Armed Forces, 1992–94. Member: Select Cttee on Televising of Proceedings of the House, 1988–91; Home Affairs Select Cttee, 1990–92; Broadcasting Select Cttee, 1997–2005; Procedure Select Cttee, 2010–15; All Party Parly Gp, Fund for Replacement of Animals in Med. Experiments, 1983–86; Chm., All Party Animal Welfare Gp, 1992–98; Mem., Chairman's Panel, 1997–. Vice Chm., Cons. Party, 2001–03. Founding Mem., Police and Parlt Scheme, 1996. Delegate, 1987–89 and 2011–15, Leader, UK Delegn, 2016–, Council of Europe. Contested Birmingham, Northfield, Oct. 1982 (Lab. majority, 289). Mem., Gen. Council, BBC, 1992–94. Founder, East Kent Development Assoc., 1984–86. Fellow: Industry and Parlt Trust, 1985; Parlt and Armed Forces Fellowship, 1992; Postgrad. Fellowship, Parlt Armed Forces Scheme, 2001–02. Pres., Cons. Animal Welfare Gp, 2003–. Special Constable, British Transport Police, 2003–06. *Recreations:* swimming, sailing. *Address:* House of Commons, Westminster, SW1A 0AA. *E:* galerj@parliament.uk. *Clubs:* Farmers, Lord's Taverners.

**GALE, William Stuart;** QC (Scot) 1993; *b* 10 June 1955; *s* of William Grimshaw Gale and Patricia Sheila (*née* Nicol); *m* 1981, Michele Marie Keklak (marr. diss.); one *d*. *Educ:* Univ. of Dundee (LLB Hons 1977); Tulane Univ., New Orleans (LLM 1978). Advocate of Scottish Bar, 1980–93; Standing Jun. Counsel to FCO in Scotland, 1987–93. Chm., Police Appeals Tribunal Scotland, 2001–. *Recreation:* modern jazz. *Address:* Terra Firma Chambers, Parliament House, Edinburgh EH1 1RF.

**GALETTI, Monica;** Chef Proprietor, Mere Restaurant, since 2017; television presenter; *b* Apia, Western Samoa, 26 Aug. 1975; *d* of Eric Faafiti and Mere Papalii; *m* 2004, David Galetti; one *d*. *Educ:* Naenae Coll., NZ (Dip. Hospitality Mgt 1997). Chef, Le Gavroche, 1999–2015 (Head Chef, Le Gavroche des Tropiques, Mauritius, 2004–05). Presenter, television series: MasterChef: The Professionals, 2008–; Amazing Hotels: life beyond the lobby, 2017–. Patron, Royal London Blind Soc., 2014–. *Publications:* Monica's Kitchen, 2012; The Skills, 2016. *Recreations:* family and friends, walking, spa days. *Address:* Mere Restaurant, 74 Charlotte Street, W1T 4QH. *T:* (020) 7268 6565. *Club:* 1 Greek Street.

**GALIONE, Prof. Antony Giuseppe,** PhD; FRS 2016; FMedSci; Professor of Pharmacology, University of Oxford, since 2006; Fellow, Lady Margaret Hall, Oxford and Extraordinary Lecturer in Biochemical Pharmacology, New College, Oxford, since 2006; *b* Chelmsford, 13 Sept. 1963; *s* of Angelo and Margaret Galione; *m* 1992, Angela Clayton. *Educ:* Felsted (Lord Butler of Saffron Walden Schol.); Trinity Coll., Cambridge (Sen. Schol.; BA 1985; PhD 1989). Harkness Fellow, 1989–91, Dmitri d'Arbeloff Fellow in Biol., 1990–91, John Hopkins Univ.; University of Oxford: Beit Meml Fellow for Med. Res.,

Dept of Pharmacol., 1991–94; Hayward Jun. Res. Fellow, Oriel Coll., 1992–95; Lectr in Med. Scis, St Hilda's Coll., 1993–95; Wellcome Trust Career Develt Fellow, Dept of Pharmacol., 1994–97; Staines Med. Res. Fellow, Exeter Coll., 1995–98; Lectr in Molecular and Cellular Biochem., St Catherine's Coll., 1997–98; Wellcome Trust Sen. Fellow in Basic Biomed. Sci., Dept of Pharmacol., 1997–2005; Fellow and Tutor in Biochem. Pharmacol., New Coll., 1998–2005; Titular Prof. of Pharmacol., 2002–05; Hd, Dept of Pharmacol., 2006–15. Herbert Rand Vis. Fellow, Marine Biol Lab., Woods Hole, Mass, 1993; Vis. Sen. Fellow, Inst. of Advanced Studies, Hong Kong Univ. of Sci. and Technol., 2011–; Vis. Prof. of Pharmacol., Univ. of Kuwait, 2011–14. Mem., Physiol. and Pharmacol. Panel, 2002–05, Basic Sci. Interest Cttee, 2006–09, Sen. Investigator, 2014–, Wellcome Trust. Co-Chair, Cttee of Heads of Pharmacol. and Therapeutics Depts UK, 2014–16. Member: Amer. Biophysical Soc., 1995–; British Marine Biol Assoc., 1995–; British Pharmacol Soc., 1997– (Trustee and Council Mem., 2014–16); British Neurosci. Assoc., 1997–. FMedSci 2010. Ed., Biochem. Jl, 1997–2006; Mem., Editl Bd, Zygote, 1998–2015. Dr hc Univ. of Medicine and Pharmacy, Craiova, 2011. Novartis Prize, British Pharmacol. Soc., 2001. *Publications:* contrib. scientific papers on cell signalling to jls incl. Nature, Science and Cell. *Recreations:* Egyptology, cats, Jack Russell terriers, gardening, Cotswold village life. *Address:* Department of Pharmacology, Oxford University, Mansfield Road, Oxford OX1 3QT. *T:* (01865) 271862, *Fax:* (01865) 271853. *E:* antony.galione@pharm.ox.ac.uk.

**GALL, Anthony Robert S.;** *see* Scott-Gall.

**GALL, Henderson Alexander, (Sandy),** CMG 2011; CBE 1988; freelance writer and broadcaster; Foreign Correspondent, Independent Television News, 1963–92 (Newscaster, 1968–90); *b* 1 Oct. 1927; *s* of Henderson Gall and Jean Begg; *m* 1958, Eleanor Mary Patricia Ann Smyth (*d* 2018); one *s* three *d*. *Educ:* Glenalmond; Aberdeen Univ. (MA). Foreign Correspondent, Reuters, 1953–63, Germany, E Africa, Suez Invasion (1956), Hungary, S Africa, Congo; joined ITN, 1963, working in Middle East, Africa, USA, Vietnam, Far East, China, Afghanistan; Newscaster on News at Ten, 1970–90; Producer/Presenter/Writer, documentaries on: King Hussein, 1972; Afghanistan, 1982, 1984, 1986; Cresta Run, 1984; George Adamson: lord of the lions, 1989; Richard Leakey, the man who saved the animals, 1995; Empty Quarter, 1996; Veil of Fear (Taliban rule in Afghanistan), 1996; Imran's Final Test, 1997; Sandy's War: face of the Taliban, 2001; Afghanistan: war without end, 2004. Chm., Sandy Gall's Afghanistan Appeal, 1983–. Rector, Aberdeen Univ., 1978–81 (Hon. LLD, 1981). Sitara-i-Pakistan, 1986; Lawrence of Arabia Medal, RSAA, 1987. *Publications:* Gold Scoop, 1977; Chasing the Dragon, 1981; Don't Worry About the Money Now, 1983; Behind Russian Lines, 1983; Afghanistan: Agony of a Nation, 1988; Salang, 1989; Lord of the Lions, 1991; News from the Front, 1994; The Bushmen of Southern Africa: slaughter of the innocent, 2001; War Against the Taliban: why it all went wrong in Afghanistan, 2012. *Recreations:* gardening, swimming. *Address:* Doubleton Oast House, Penshurst, Tonbridge, Kent TN11 8JA. *Clubs:* Turf; St Moritz Tobogganing (Hon. Mem.).

**GALLACHER, Bernard,** OBE 1996; professional golfer; golf professional, Wentworth Golf Club, 1975–96; *b* 9 Feb. 1949; *s* of Bernard and Matilda Gallacher; *m* 1974, Lesley Elizabeth Wearmouth; one *s* two *d*. *Educ:* St Mary's Academy, Bathgate. Golf tournaments won: Scottish Open Amateur Championship, 1967; PGA Schweppes, W. D. & H. O. Wills Open, 1969; Martini Internat., 1971, 1982; Carrolls Internat., 1974; Dunlop Masters, 1974, 1975; Spanish Open, 1977; French Open, 1979; Tournament Players Championship, 1980; Gtr Manchester Open, 1981; Jersey Open, 1982, 1984. Harry Vardon Trophy, 1969. Scottish Professional Champion, 1971, 1973, 1974, 1977, 1984. Ryder Cup Team, 1969, 1971, 1973, 1975, 1977, 1979, 1981, 1983, European Captain, 1991, 1993, 1995. Pres., Golf Foundn, 1996–2001. *Publications:* (with Mark Wilson) Teach Yourself Golf, 1988; (with Renton Laidlaw) Captain at Kiawah, 1991. *Recreations:* walking dogs, reading. *Address:* c/o Wentworth Club, Virginia Water, Surrey GU25 4LS.

**GALLAGHER, Ann;** Director (formerly Head) of Collections (British Art), Tate, since 2006; *b* Nottingham, 14 May 1957; *d* of Eugene Gallagher and Diana Gallagher (née Greaves); *m* 2001, David Batchelor. *Educ:* Mackie Acad., Stonehaven; Bedford Coll., Univ. of London (BA Hons). Nigel Greenwood Gall., London, 1984–89; Dir, Anthony Reynolds Gall., London, 1989–94; Sen. Curator, Visual Arts Dept, British Council, London, 1994–2005; Hd, British Art Post 1900, Tate Collection, London, 2005–06. Mem. of Faculty, British Sch. at Rome, 2005–10. Trustee, Whitechapel Art Gall., London, 2008–. *Publications:* (ed) Rachel Whiteread, 1997; Landscape, 2000; (ed) Mark Wallinger, 2001; Still Life, 2002; Sodio y Asfalto, 2004; Chris Ofili: the Upper Room, 2006; Rachel Whiteread Drawings, 2010; (ed) Susan Hiller, 2011; Damien Hirst, 2012; Rachel Whiteread, 2017; (ed) Zarina Bhimji: Lead White, 2018. *Recreations:* architecture and design, film, literature. *Address:* c/o Tate, Millbank, SW1P 4RG.

**GALLAGHER, Edward Patrick,** CBE 2001; FREng, FIET, FCIWEM; Chair, Centre for Low Carbon Futures, 2009–14; *b* 4 Aug. 1944; *m* 1969, Helen Wilkinson; two *s*. *Educ:* Univ. of Sheffield (BEng Hons; Diploma in Business Studies; Mappin Medal, 1966; John Brown Award, 1966). MRI 1992. Systems Analyst, Vauxhall Motors, 1963–68; Corporate Planning Manager, Sandoz Products, 1968–70; Computer Services Manager, Robinson Willey, 1970–71; with Black and Decker, 1971–86: Director: Marketing Services, 1978–79; Service and Distribn, 1979–81; Business Analysis, 1981–83; Market and Product Develt, 1983–86; Amersham International: Dir of Corporate Develt, 1986–88; Divl Chief Exec., 1988–90; Mfg Dir, 1990–92; Chief Executive and Board Member: NRA, 1992–95; EA, 1995–2001. Dir, ECUS Ltd, 2001–11; Chm., Enviro-fresh Ltd, 2003–06. Chair: Energywatch, 2004–08; Renewable Fuels Agency, 2008–11; Mem., NCC, 2008; Mem. Bd, Consumer Focus, 2008–11. Vice-Pres., Council for Envmtl Educn, 1997–2006; Mem. Bd and Chm. Audit Cttee, English Nature, 2001–06. Chm., Pesticides Forum, DEFRA, 2003–06. A CS Comr, 2001–06. Middlesex University: Vis. Prof., Business Sch. and Faculty of Technol., 1994–97, Sch. of Health, Biol and Envmtl Sci., 1997–; Mem., Faculty of Technol. Adv. Gp, 1994–97; Gov., 1994–2004 (Chm., Bd of Govs, 2001–04); Chairman: Audit Cttee, 1995–2000; Planning and Resources Cttee, 2000–01; Governance Cttee, 2000–01; Bristol University: Mem. Council, 1994–98; Mem. Finance Adv. Gp, 1994–2001; Chm. Adv. Bd, Centre for Social and Econ. Res. on Global Envmt, UEA, 2004–08 (Mem., 2001–04). Mem. Council, 1998–2001, Mem., Envmt and Energy Policy Cttee, 1999–2002 (Chm., 2002–04), IEE; Royal Academy of Engineering: Mem., Sustainable Develt Educn Panel, 1999–2003; Mem., Awards Cttee, 2001–04; Chm., Health, Safety and Envmt Cttee, EEF, 2001–04. Advr, Maidenhead Waterways Restoration Gp, 2008–. Patron, Envmtl Industries Commn, 2001–13. Trustee: Living Again Trust, Royal Hosp. for Neurodisability (formerly Royal Hosp. and Home, Putney), 1993–2003; Envmtl Vision, 2001–11 (Chm., 2004–11). FRSA 1995–2007; CCMI (CIMgt 1996). Freeman, City of London; Liveryman, Co. of Water Conservators (Mem., Ct of Assistants, 1999–2001). Hon. DEng Sheffield, 1996; Hon. DSc: Tomsk, 1998; Plymouth, 1998; Brunel, 1999; DUniv Middx, 2005. *Recreations:* tennis, walking, guitar, clocks. *Address:* 154 Whyteladyes Lane, Cookham, Maidenhead, Berks SL6 9LA.

**GALLAGHER, Eileen Rose,** OBE 2010; Chief Executive, Shed Productions, 2008 (Co-owner and co-founder, 1998); Managing Director, then Chief Executive, Shed Media, 1998–2008); *b* 26 Nov. 1959; *d* of Mathew Gallagher and Christine McAvoy. *Educ:* Glasgow Univ. (MA Hons Politics); UC Cardiff (Dip. Journalism). Freelance journalist, 1980–84; Scottish Television: Press Officer, 1984–87; Head of Programme Planning, 1987–91; Head of Broadcasting Div., 1991–92; Dir of Broadcasting, 1992–94; Man. Dir, Granada/LWT Broadcasting, then Man. Dir, LWT and Dep. Man. Dir, Granada UK Broadcasting, 1994–98; Man. Dir, Ginger TV, 1999. Director: Granada, 1995–98; LWT, 1995–98. Mem. Bd, Glasgow 2014, 2010–14.

**GALLAGHER, Francis Xavier,** OBE 1986; HM Diplomatic Service, retired; Head of Panel 2000 Unit, Foreign and Commonwealth Office, 1998; *b* 28 March 1946; *s* of F. P. H. Gallagher and Carmen Imelda Gallagher (née Wilson); *m* 1981, Marie-France Martine Guiller; one *d*. *Educ:* Oxford Univ. (Chancellor's Essay and Matthew Arnold Meml Prizes; BA, BPhil). Tutor, Villiers Park Educnl Trust, Oxon, 1970; joined FCO, 1971: MECAS, Lebanon, 1972–74; served FCO, NY, then Dep. Hd of Mission, Beirut, Khartoum, Kuwait, Copenhagen, 1974–98. Officier, Ordre National du Lion (Senegal), 1988. *Recreations:* music, walking. *Address:* 102 rue de la Tour, 75016 Paris, France.

**GALLAGHER, James Daniel,** CB 2005; FRSE; Associate Member, Nuffield College, Oxford, since 2014 (Gwilym Gibbon Fellow, 2010–14); Visiting Professor of Government, University of Glasgow, since 2005; *s* of William Gallagher and Bridget Gallagher (née Hart); *m* 1978, Una Mary Green; one *s* two *d*. *Educ:* Glasgow Univ. (BSc Hons Chemistry and Nat. Phil. 1976); Edinburgh Univ. (MSc Public Policy 1986). Joined Scottish Office, 1976: Private Sec. to Minister for Home Affairs, 1979; Head of Criminal Policy and Procedure Brs, 1981–85; Sec., Mgt Gp, 1985–88; Head of Urban Policy Div., 1988–89; Private Sec. to successive Secs of State for Scotland, 1989–91; Dir (Human Resources), Scottish Prison Service, 1991–96; Hd, Local Govt Finance Gp, later Local Govt and Europe Gp, Scottish Office, 1996–99; Dep. Head of Economic and Domestic Secretariat, Cabinet Office, 1999; Policy Advr, Prime Minister's Policy Unit, 1999–2000; Hd, Scottish Exec. Justice Dept, 2000–04; Prof. of Govt, Univ. of Glasgow, 2005–07 (on secondment); Dir Gen., Devolution, MoJ and Prime Minister's Office, 2007–10. Vis. Prof., 2005–08, Hon. Prof., 2007, Centre for Ethics in Public Policy and Corporate Life, Glasgow Caledonian Univ.; Hon. Prof., Sch. of History, Univ. of St Andrews, 2017–. Director: Scottish Mutual Assurance, 1999–2003; Abbey National Life, 1999–2003; Scottish Provident Life Assurance, 2001–03; Admin Re UK Services Ltd (formerly Admin Re UK Ltd), 2010–; ReAssureUK (formerly Windsor Life) Ltd, 2010–; Barclays Life Ltd, 2010–13. Chairman: Supervisory Cttee, Scottish Provident, 2003–09; With Profits Cttee, Police Mutual Assce Soc., 2015–; With Profits Cttee, Legal and General Assce, 2017–; Member: Abbey Nat. Policy Holder Review Cttee, 2003–06; Fairness Cttee, Royal London Insce Gp, 2012–. Non-exec. Dir, Lothian and Borders Police, 2006–13. Mem. Council, Law Soc. of Scotland, 2011–17. Dir, Scottish Catholic Internat. Aid Fund, 2013–. FRSE 2007. *Publications:* England and the Union, 2012; Scotland's Choices, 2013; Where Next for the UK and Scotland, 2014; All Aboard the Constitution Express, 2015; Algebra and the Constitution, 2016; The Brexit Shambles, 2017. *Address:* Nuffield College, University of Oxford OX1 1NF.

**GALLAGHER, John David Edmund;** barrister, since 1974; Chancellor and Vicar General, Diocese of Rochester, since 2005; *b* Wimbledon, 13 Sept. 1950; *s* of William Norman Gallagher, MA, ICS and Zoe Kathleen Gallagher (née Covell); *m* 1974, Gillian Amanda Battersby; three *s* two *d* (and one *d* decd). *Educ:* Belmont Prep Sch.; Mill Hill Sch.; King's Coll. London (Masom Scholar in Classics 1970; BA Classics, AKC Theol. 1972); Coll. of Law. Called to the Bar, Gray's Inn, 1974, Bencher, 2014; Asst Recorder, 1995; Recorder, 2000. Chm., Drugs Tribunal, ICC Champions Trophy, 2004; Professional Mem., Sports Dispute Resolution Panel, 1999–2007. Pres., ICS Assoc., 2006–. Life Mem., Pakistan Soc., 1998–. Trustee, Samaritans Purse, 2005–. Ct Asst, Co. of Pewterers, 2012– (Master, 2019–Sept. 2020). Member, Parochial Church Council: Priory Church of St Bartholomew the Gt, Smithfield, 1980–87; All Souls, Langham Place, 1992–2001; Dep. Chancellor, Dio. of Chelmsford, 2003–. Chm., Islington and Finsbury Cons. Assoc., 1977–84. *Recreations:* cricket, Rugby, theatre, horse-riding. *Address:* Hardwicke Building, New Square, Lincoln's Inn, WC2A 3SB. *T:* (020) 7242 2523. *E:* allgallaghers@hotmail.com. *Clubs:* MCC, HAC Mess, HAC Cricket (Pres., 2008–13), Old Millhillians (Vice Pres., 2019–20; Chm., RFC, 2014–19), Highgate Irregulars Cricket.

**GALLAGHER, Sister Maire Teresa,** CBE 1992 (OBE 1987); SND; Sister Superior, Convent of Notre Dame, Dumbarton, 1987–94, retired; *b* 27 May 1933; *d* of Owen Gallagher and Annie McVeigh. *Educ:* Notre Dame High Sch., Glasgow; Glasgow Univ. (MA Hons 1965); Notre Dame Coll. of Educn (Dip. 1953). Principal Teacher of History, Notre Dame High Sch., Glasgow, 1965–72; Lectr in Secondary Educn, Notre Dame Coll., 1972–74; Head Teacher, Notre Dame High Sch., Dumbarton, 1974–87. Chair, Scottish Consultative Council (formerly Scottish Consultative Cttee) on the Curriculum, 1987–91 (Mem., 1976–91; Chair, Secondary Cttee, 1983–87); Mem., Sec. of State's Cttee of Enquiry into Teachers' Pay and Conditions of Service, (Main Cttee), 1986; Pres., Scottish Br., Secondary Heads Assoc., 1980–82. Member: Central Council, Action of Churches Together in Scotland, 1990–2003 (Convener, 1999–2003); Assembly, CCBI, 1990–2002; Steering Cttee, CTBI, 2004–06. Fellow: SCOTVEC, 1989; Scottish Qualifications Authority, 1997. Hon. MEd CNAA, 1992. *Publications:* papers and articles in jls on teaching and management of schools. *Recreations:* homemaking skills, reading. *Address:* Sisters of Notre Dame, 2/2 90 Beith Street, Glasgow G11 6DQ. *T:* (0141) 357 4576.

**GALLAGHER, Mark;** Founder, Pagefield Communications Ltd, since 2010; Co-Founder, Pagefield Global, since 2017; *b* Poole, Dorset, 2 July 1970; *s* of John Brian and Margaret Anne Gallagher; *m* (marr. diss.); one *s* one *d*. *Educ:* Ferndown Upper Sch.; St Anne's Coll., Oxford (BA PPE 1991). Exec., Industry and Parliament Trust, 1991–96; Hd, Public Affairs, Ind. Television Assoc., 1996–99; Director: of Public Affairs, ITN, 1999–2003; of Corporate Affairs, and Bd Dir, Camelot, 2003–07; of Corporate Affairs, ITV plc, 2007–10. Comr, Royal Hosp., Chelsea, 2014–. Member: Adv. Bd, Radius, 2013–; Archbishop of Canterbury's Adv. Bd, 2015–. Mem. Bd, Queen's Diamond Jubilee Pageant, 2011–12. Trustee, Mus Assoc., 2011–14. *Recreations:* politics, family, travel. *Address:* Pagefield Communications Ltd, The Courtyard Studio, 18 Marshall Street, W1F 7BE. *T:* (020) 3327 4051. *E:* mark.gallagher@pagefield.co.uk. *Club:* Harry's.

**GALLAGHER, Paul,** CBE 1996; General Secretary, Amalgamated Engineering and Electrical Union, 1995–96; *b* 16 Oct. 1944; *s* of Joe and Annie Gallagher; *m* 1974, Madeleine. *Educ:* St Anne's, Droylesden, Manchester. Electrical, Electronic, Telecommunication and Plumbing Union: full-time officer, 1966–78; Exec. Councillor for Manchester and N Wales, 1978–91; Pres., 1986–91; Gen. Sec., 1992–95. Mem., HSC, 1990–96. *Recreations:* gardening, music, reading.

**GALLAGHER, Thomas Joseph;** Member (SDLP) Fermanagh and South Tyrone, Northern Ireland Assembly, 1998–2011; *b* 17 Aug. 1942; *s* of Thomas and Nellie Gallagher; *m* 1968, Eileen Carty; two *s* one *d*. *Educ:* St Joseph's Coll.; Queen's Univ., Belfast. Mem., NI Forum, 1996. Mem. (SDLP), Fermanagh DC, 1989–2001. Contested (SDLP) Fermanagh and S Tyrone, 2001, 2005; contested (SDLP) Fermanagh and S Tyrone, NI Assembly, 2011. Mem., Western Educn and Library Bd, 1989–2001. *Recreations:* Gaelic games, horse racing. *Address:* 164 Boa Island Road, Keenaghan, Belleek, Co. Fermanagh BT93 3ES. *T:* (028) 6865 8355. *Club:* Erne Gaels Gaelic Football.

**GALLAGHER, Tony;** Editor-in-Chief, The Sun, since 2015; b London, 2 Nov. 1963; s of Tony Gallagher and Winifred Gallagher; m 1991, Catherine Elliott; one s two d. Educ: Finchley Catholic High Sch., London; Univ. of Bristol (BA Hons); City Univ., London (Postgrad. Dip. Newspaper Journalism). Reporter: Southern Evening Echo, Southampton, 1985–86; South West News Service, Bristol, 1987–88; Today, 1988–89; Daily Mail: Reporter, 1990–96; NY Corresp., 1996–97; Dep. News Ed., 1997–99; News Ed., 1999–2006; Dep. Ed., 2007–09, Ed., 2009–14, Daily Telegraph; Dep. Ed., Daily Mail, 2014–15. Recreations: family, West Ham United.

**GALLAGHER PATRICKSON, David;** Ambassador of Chile to the Court of St James's, since 2018; b Valparaíso, Chile, 8 Aug. 1944; s of Joseph Gallagher and Inez Patrickson; m 1993, Margarita Sara Crespo Ureta; two d, and one step s one step d. Educ: Grange Sch., Santiago, Chile; Downside Sch.; Queen's Coll., Oxford (BA 1st Cl. Mod. Langs (Russian main)). Lectr in Lit. of Latin America, Univ. of Oxford and Fellow, St Antony's Coll., Oxford, 1968–74; Dir, Morgan Grenfell Internat., 1977–84; Founder, Partner and Chm., Asset-Chile SA, 1984–2017. Mem., Bd of Dirs, Cencosud SA, 2010–18. Mem. Bd, Centro de Estudios Políticos, 1983–. Member: Bd, Teatro del Lago, 2014–; Bd, Chile Mujeres, 2016–; Adv. Bd, Peggy Guggenheim Collection, Venice, 1998–. Publications: Modern Latin American Literature, 1973; Improvisaciones, 1992; Otras Improvisaciones, 2004. Recreations: literature, opera, art. Address: (residence) 92 Eaton Place, SW1X 8LW; Embassy of Chile, 37–41 Old Queen Street, SW1H 9JA. T: (020) 7222 2361, ext. 218. E: ambassadorspa@embachile.co.uk. Clubs: Boodle's, Hurlingham; Golf Los Leones.

**GALLAN, Patricia Ferguson,** QPM 2006; Assistant Commissioner, Specialist Crime and Operations, Metropolitan Police Service, 2015–18; b Paisley, Scotland, 26 Oct. 1965; d of Rev. Alexander Gallan and Sarah Gallan. Educ: Wishaw High Sch.; Univ. of Strathclyde (BA Hons Politics and Modern Hist.); Univ. of Iowa (jun. honour year); Birkbeck Coll., Univ. of London (MSc Politics and Admin); London Guildhall Univ. (CPE Law); Inns of Court Sch. of Law; Univ. of Cambridge (Dip. Applied Criminol. and Police Mgt). Called to the Bar, Middle Temple, 1999; Metropolitan Police Service: Constable (Grad. Entrant) to Detective Chief Superintendent, 1987–2005; Hostage Negotiator, 1997; Asst Chief Constable, Nat. Crime Squad, 2005–06; Asst Chief Constable, 2006–09, Temp. Dep. Chief Constable, 2009–10, Merseyside Police; Temp. Dep. Chief Constable, Home Office, 2011; Metropolitan Police Service: Deputy Assistant Commissioner: Directorate of Professionalism, 2012–13; Security and Protection, 2013–15. Alumna, British-American Project, 1992. Recreations: physical training, ski-ing, horse riding, American history and politics.

**GALLARD, Jill,** CMG 2018; HM Diplomatic Service; Deputy Political Director, Foreign and Commonwealth Office, since 2018; b Omagh, 11 June 1968; d of Leslie Parkinson and Margaret Parkinson (née Thompson); m 2007, Dominic John Gallard; two s. Educ: Univ. of Edinburgh (MA Hons French and Spanish). Joined HM Diplomatic Service, 1991; FCO, 1991–94; on secondment to EC, 1994; Third Sec. (Pol), 1994–97, Second Sec. (EU/Econ.), 1997–99, Madrid; Hd, Turkey Section, FCO, 1999–2001; Dep. Hd, Common For. and Security Policy Team, FCO, 2001–03; Hd, Pol/EU/Econ. Sections, Prague, 2004–07; Private Sec. to Perm. Under-Sec. of State, FCO, 2007–08; Asst Dir, HR Ops, FCO, 2008–10; Ambassador to Portugal, 2011–14; Human Resources Dir, FCO, 2014–18. Address: c/o Foreign and Commonwealth Office, King Charles Street, SW1A 2AH. E: jill.gallard@fco.gov.uk.

**GALLEY, Roy;** Director, Planning, Post Office Property Holdings, 1998–2006; b 8 Dec. 1947; s of late Kenneth Haslam Galley and Letitia Mary Chapman; m 1976, Helen Margaret Butcher; one s one d. Educ: King Edward VII Grammar Sch., Sheffield; Worcester Coll., Oxford (MA). North-East Postal Bd, 1969–83: started as management trainee; Asst Controller, Projects (regional manager), 1980–83; Head of Project Control, London Building and Estates Centre, Royal Mail Letters, 1987–91; Royal Mail, London: Dir, Facilities, 1992–95; Dir, Restructuring, 1995–96; Dir, Operations, 1996–98. Chm., Kingston and Richmond (formerly Kingston and Esher) DHA, 1989–98. Member: Calderdale MBC, 1980–83; Maresfield Parish Council, 2006–10; Wealden DC, 2007– (Portfolio Holder, Planning, 2008–13, Economic Regeneration, 2013–15, Economic Develt and Waste Mgt, 2015–); E Sussex CC, 2013–; E Sussex Fire Authy, 2013–; Chm., E Sussex Standing Adv. Cttee on Religious Educn, 2014–. Mem., Bd of Conservators, Ashdown Forest, 2008– (Chm., 2013–16). Chm., Yorks Young Conservatives, 1974–76; contested (C): Dewsbury, 1979; Halifax, 1987. MP (C) Halifax, 1983–87. Sec., Cons. Backbench Health Cttee, 1983–87; Mem., Social Services Select Cttee, 1984–87. Chm., Kingston and St George's Coll. of Nursing, 1993–96. Recreations: history, European literature, theatre, music, gardening, riding. Address: Fairplace Farm, Nutley, Uckfield, East Sussex TN22 3HE.

**GALLI, Paolo;** Italian Ambassador to the Court of St James's, 1995–99; b 10 Aug. 1934; s of Carlo Galli and Bianca Metral-Lambert; m 1959, Maria Giuliana Calioni; two d. Educ: Univ. of Padua (law degree). Entered Italian Diplomatic Service, 1958; Minister of State's Private Office, 1958–61; Vice Consul, Cardiff, 1961–63; Second Sec., Washington, 1963–65; First Sec., Co-ordination Dept, Sec.-Gen's Office, Min. for Foreign Affairs, 1965–68; First Sec., later Counsellor and First Counsellor, London, 1968–72; First Counsellor, Warsaw, 1972–75; Min. for Foreign Affairs, Econ. Affairs Dept, 1975–79; Foreign Minister's Private Office, 1979–80; Minister-Counsellor, Dep. Perm. Rep. to EEC, Brussels, 1980–85; promoted to rank of Minister, 1985; Ambassador to Warsaw, 1986–88; Dir-Gen., Aid and Co-operation Dept, Min. for Foreign Affairs, 1988–91; promoted to rank of Ambassador, 1989; Ambassador to Tokyo, 1992–95. Cavaliere di Gran Croce, Ordine al Merito della Repubblica Italiana, 1997. Recreations: classical music, the arts, fencing. Address: Zattere 1404, 30123 Venice, Italy.

**GALLIANO, John Charles,** CBE 2001; RDI 2002; Company Director and Couturier for Maison John Galliano, since 1984; Artistic Director: L'Etoile, since 2014; Maison Martin Margiela, since 2014; b 28 Nov. 1960. Educ: Wilson's Grammar Sch. for Boys; St Martin's Sch. of Art and Design (BA; Hon. Fellow, London Inst., 1997). Regular seasonal collections, 1985–. Designer of Haute Couture and Prêt-à-Porter: for Givenchy, 1995–96; for Dior, 1996–2011. British Designer of the Year, British Fashion Council, 1987, 1994, 1995, 1997 (jtly); Telva Award for Best Internat. Designer, Mejor Creador International, 1995; VH1 Best Women's Wear Designer Award, 1998; Internat. Designer Award, Council of Fashion Designers of America, 1998.

**GALLIE, Prof. Duncan Ian Dunbar,** CBE 2009; DPhil; FBA 1995; Professor of Sociology, University of Oxford, since 1996; Official Fellow, Nuffield College, Oxford, 1985–2014, now Emeritus Fellow; b 16 Feb. 1946; s of Ian Gallie and Elsie (née Peers); m 1971, Martine Josephine Jurdant. Educ: St Paul's Sch., London (Scholar); Magdalen Coll., Oxford (Demyship; BA 1st Cl. Hons History); LSE (MSc); St Antony's Coll., Oxford (DPhil). Research Fellow, Nuffield Coll., Oxford, 1971–73; Lectr in Sociology, Univ. of Essex, 1973–79; Reader in Sociology, Univ. of Warwick, 1979–85; Dir, ESRC Social Change and Economic Life Initiative, 1985–90. Advr, Comité Nat. d'Evaluation de la Recherche, 1991; Member, Scientific Committee: IRESCO, 1989–93; IFRESI, 1993–98; Member: EU Adv. Gp on Social Scis and Humanities in European Res. Area, 2002–06; Scientific Council, Paris Sch. of Econs, 2009–18. Vice-Pres., 2004–11, Foreign Sec., 2006–11, British Acad. Dist. Contrib. to Scholarship Award, Amer. Sociol. Assoc., 1985. Publications: In Search of the New Working Class, 1978; Social Inequality and Class Radicalism in France and Britain, 1983; (ed jtly) New Approaches to Economic Life, 1985; (ed) Employment in Britain, 1988; (ed jtly) Social Change and the Experience of Unemployment, 1994; (ed jtly) Trade Unionism in Recession, 1996; (jtly) Restructuring the Employment Relationship, 1998; (ed jtly) Welfare Regimes and the Experience of Unemployment in Europe, 2000; (ed) Resisting Marginalization, 2004; (ed) Employment Regimes and the Quality of Work, 2007; (ed) Economic Crisis, Quality of Work and Social Integration: the European experience, 2013; (ed jtly) Unequal Britain at Work, 2015; articles in learned jls. Recreations: travelling, music, museum gazing. Address: Nuffield College, Oxford OX1 1NF. T: (01865) 278500; 149 Leam Terrace, Leamington Spa, Warwickshire CV31 1DF. T: (01926) 314941.

**GALLIE, Gail Elizabeth;** Co-founder and Creative Lead, Project Everyone, since 2015; b Newcastle, 12 March 1971; d of Gerard and Irene Nuttney; m 2003, James Duncan Gallie; one s one d. Educ: Dame Allan's Sch.; Balliol Coll., Oxford (BA Hons Modern Langs (Italian/French)). Advertising Exec., DMB&B, 1992–94; Advertising Dir, BMP DDB Needham, 1994–97; Hd of Mktg, BBC, 1997–2007; Founder, Gallie Godfrey, 2008–10; CEO, Fallon London, 2010–14. Founder, Outdoor Swimming Soc. Recreations: nature, travel, music, family. E: gailgallie@me.com.

**GALLIERS, Margaret Mary,** CBE 2009; Chair, Company Board, Learning and Work Institute, since 2016; b Coventry, 17 April 1952; d of Alexander Michael Donald and Ella Mary Donald; m 1st, 1973, Simon Godfrey (marr. diss. 1987); two s one d; 2nd, 1987, David John Galliers (d 2017); one s. Educ: Barr's Hill Sch., Coventry; Univ. of Exeter (BA Social Policy and Social Admin); Univ. of Warwick (PGCE). Teacher/lectr, 1974–90; Dep. Associate Principal, 1990–92, Dep. Principal, 1992–97, Tile Hill Coll.; Principal, Henley Coll., Coventry, 1997–2002; Principal and Chief Exec., Leicester Coll., 2002–13. Pres., Assoc. of Colleges, 2012–13. Member: Quality Assessment Cttee, FEFC, 1998–2001; Young People's LSC, 2001–07; Apprenticeship Task Force, 2003–05; Bd, Quality Improvement Agency, 2006–09; Teaching Quality and Student Experience Cttee, HEFCE, 2007–13; Nat. Learning and Skills Council, 2008–10; Bd, QCA, 2008–10; Bd, Office of Qualifications and Exams Regulation, 2010–17 (Chm., Audit and Risk Cttee, 2015–17); Company Bd, Nat. Inst. of Adult Continuing Educn, 2007–15 (Chair, 2012–15); Council, Open Univ., 2018–. Nat. Leader in Governance, 2014–16. Trustee, Learning Without Limits Academy Trust, 2016–19 (Vice Chair, 2017–19). Chair, City Coll., Coventry, 2013–17. Hon. DEd Beds, 2013. Recreations: walking, gardening, kayaking. Address: Learning and Work Institute, 4th Floor, Arnhem House, 31 Waterloo Way, Leicester LE1 6LP. E: cally.sadler@learningandwork.org.uk.

**GALLIFORD, Rt Rev. David George;** Bishop Suffragan of Bolton, 1984–91; b 20 June 1925; s of Alfred Edward Bruce and Amy Doris Galliford; m 1st, 1954, Enid May Drax (d 1983); one d; 2nd, 1987, Claire Margaret Phoenix. Educ: Bede Coll., Sunderland; Clare Coll., Cambridge (Organ Scholar, 1942, BA 1949, MA 1951); Westcott House, Cambridge. Served 5th Royal Inniskilling Dragoon Guards, 1943–47. Curate of St John Newland, Hull, 1951–54; Minor Canon of Windsor, 1954–56; Vicar of St Oswald, Middlesbrough, 1956–61; Rector of Bolton Percy and Diocesan Training Officer, 1961–70; Canon of York Minster, 1969; Canon Residentiary and Treasurer of York Minster, 1970–75; Bishop Suffragan of Hulme, 1975–84. Asst Bishop, dio. York, 1991–2011. SBStJ 1992. Publications: God and Christian Caring, 1973; Pastor's Post, 1975; (ed) Diocese in Mission, 1968. Recreations: music, composition, water colours. Address: Connaught Court, Royal Masonic Benevolent Institution, St Oswalds Road, Fulford, York YO10 4FA. T: (01904) 626208.

**GALLIGAN, Prof. Denis James,** DCL; Professor of Socio-Legal Studies, 1993–2017, now Emeritus, and Director, Centre for Socio-Legal Studies, 1993–2008, University of Oxford; Fellow, Wolfson College, Oxford, 1993–2017, now Emeritus; b 4 June 1947; s of John Felix Galligan and Muriel Maud Galligan; m 1972, Martha Louise Martinuzzi; one s one d. Educ: Univ. of Queensland (LLB 1970); Univ. of Oxford (BCL 1974; MA 1976; DCL 2000). Barrister, Supreme Court of Qld, 1970; called to the Bar, Gray's Inn, 1996. Rhodes Scholar, Magdalen Coll., Oxford, 1971–74; Lectr, Faculty of Law, UCL, 1974–76; Fellow, Jesus Coll., and CUF Lectr, Oxford Univ., 1976–81; Sen. Lectr, Univ. of Melbourne, 1982–84; Prof. of Law, Univ. of Southampton, 1985–92 (Dean, Law Faculty, 1987–90); Prof. of Law, Univ. of Sydney, 1990–92. Visiting Professor: Central European Univ., 1993–2004; Princeton Univ., 2002–; Jean Monnet Prof., Univ. of Siena, 2003–. AcSS 2000. Publications: Essays in Legal Theory, 1984; Law, Rights and the Welfare State, 1986; Discretionary Powers, 1986; Australian Administrative Law, 1993; Socio-Legal Readings in Administrative Law, 1995; Socio-Legal Studies in Context, 1995; Due Process and Fair Procedures, 1996; Administrative Justice in the New Democracies, 1998; Western Concepts of Administrative Law, 2002; Law and Informal Practices, 2003; Law in Modern Society, 2006; (ed jtly) The Social and Political Foundations of Constitutions, 2013; (ed) Constitutions and the Classics, 2014; (ed) Constitution in Crisis, 2017. Recreations: reading, gardening. Address: Wolfson College, Linton Road, Oxford OX2 6UD; The Rosary, Beckley, Oxford OX3 9UU. T: (01865) 284220 and 351281.

**GALLIVER, Philippa Ann;** see Helme, P. A.

**GALLOP, Prof. Angela Mary Cecilia,** DPhil; CBE 2015; Co-Founder and Chief Executive, Axiom International Ltd, since 2010; Professor of Practice, and Strategic Director, Centre for Forensic Science, University of Strathclyde, since 2016; b Oxford, 2 Jan. 1950; d of Kenneth Knowles and Eunice Knowles; partner, David Russell; one s by a previous marriage. Educ: Headington Sch., Oxford; Univ. of Sheffield (BSc Hons 1971); Linacre Coll., Oxford (DPhil 1975). CBiol 1990; FRSB (FSB 1990); FCSFS 2013. SSO, Home Office Forensic Sci. Service, 1974–86; Founder and Sen. Partner, Forensic Access, 1986–97; Founder and Chief Exec., Forensic Alliance Ltd, 1997–2005; Chief Exec., LGC Forensics (incorp. Forensic Alliance Ltd), 2005–10; Forensic Sci. Dir, Forensic Access, 2018– (Chief Exec., 2013–18). Hon. DCL Northumbria, 2008; Hon. DSc: Nottingham Trent, 2011; Sheffield, 2017. Publications: When the Dogs Don't Bark, 2019; articles in learned and gen. pubns on forensic sci., esp. its use and misuse within UK criminal justice system. Recreations: opera and theatre, gardening, natural history, travelling. Address: Axiom International Ltd, Pound Court, Pound Street, Newbury, Berks RG14 6AA. T: (01235) 537006. E: angela.gallop@axiom-international-ltd.com.

**GALLOP, Prof. Hon. Geoffrey (Ian),** AC 2008; DPhil; Professor and Director, Graduate School of Government, University of Sydney, 2006, now Emeritus Professor; b 27 Sept. 1951; s of Douglas and Eunice Gallop; m 1st, 1975, Beverley Jones (d 2009); two s; 2nd, 2010, Ingrid van Beek. Educ: Univ. of Western Australia (BEc); Murdoch Univ. (MPhil); St John's and Nuffield Colls, Oxford (MA, DPhil). Res. Fellow, Nuffield Coll., Oxford, 1979–81; Lectr in Social and Political Theory, Murdoch Univ., 1981–86. MLA (ALP) Victoria Park, WA, 1986–2006; Minister: for Educn, and Parly and Electoral Reform, 1990–91; for Fuel and Energy, Microecon. Reform, Parly and Electoral Reform, and Assisting the Treas., 1991–93; Leader of the Opposition, WA, 1996–2001; Premier of WA, 2001–06. Dep. Chm., Council of Australian Govts Reform Council, 2007–11. Chm., Australian Awards Bd, 2011–13. FIPAA. Hon. DLitt: Murdoch, 2006; WA, 2012.

*Publications:* (ed) Pigs' Meat: selected writings of Thomas Spence, 1982; A State of Reform: essays for a better future, 1998; Politics, Society, Self, 2012. *Recreations:* swimming, cricket, football. *Address:* Graduate School of Government, University of Sydney, Sydney, NSW 2006, Australia. *Clubs:* Swan Districts Football, West Coast Eagles.

**GALLOWAY,** 13th Earl of, *cr* 1623; **Randolph Keith Reginald Stewart;** Lord Garlies, 1607; Bt 1627, 1687; Baron Stewart of Garlies (GB), 1796; *b* 14 Oct. 1928; *s* of 12th Earl of Galloway, and Philippa Fendall (*d* 1974), *d* of late Jacob Wendell, New York; *S* father, 1978; *m* 1975, Mrs Lily May Budge, DLJ (*d* 1999), *y d* of late Andrew Miller, Duns, Berwickshire. *Educ:* Harrow. KLJ. *Heir: cousin* Andrew Clyde Stewart [*b* 13 March 1949; *m* 1st, 1977, Sara (marr. diss. 2001), *o d* of Brig. Patrick Pollock; one *s* two *d*; 2nd, 2008, Christine Merrick Andersson]. *Address:* Castle Douglas, Kirkcudbrightshire.

**GALLOWAY, Bishop of, (RC),** since 2015; **Rt Rev. William Nolan;** *b* Motherwell, 26 Jan. 1954; *s* of late William and Catherine Nolan. *Educ:* St Vincent's Coll., Langbank; St Mary's Coll., Blairs; Pontifical Scots Coll., Rome; Gregorian Univ. (STL 1978). Ordained priest, 1977; Assistant Priest: Our Lady of Lourdes, E Kilbride, 1978–80; St David's Plains, 1980–83; Vice-Rector, Scots Coll., Rome, 1983–90; Asst Priest, St Bridget's, Baillieston, 1990–94; Parish Priest, Our Lady of Lourdes, E Kilbride, 1994–2015; Administrator, St John Ogilvie Parish, Blantyre, 2013–15; Vicar Gen., Dio. of Motherwell, 2014–15. *Address:* Diocesan and Pastoral Office, Candida Casa, 8 Corsehill Road, Ayr KA7 2ST.

**GALLOWAY, Alexander Kippen,** CVO 2006; Clerk of the Privy Council, 1998–2006; *b* 29 April 1952; *s* of late Alexander Kippen Galloway and Vera Eleanor Galloway; *m* 1st, 1973, Elaine Margaret Watkinson (marr. diss. 2005); three *s*; 2nd, 2006, Suzanne Lesley Phillips. *Educ:* Birkenhead Sch.; Jesus Coll., Oxford (MA Lit.Hum.); LLB Hons Open Univ. 2006. Department of the Environment: Exec. Officer, 1974; Principal, 1982; Private Sec. to Chancellor of Duchy of Lancaster, 1982–84, to Paymaster Gen., 1982–83 and 1984–85; Secretariat, Cabinet Office, 1992–93; Asst Sec., DoE, 1994–98. CEO, Soc. for the Envmt, 2012–14. Mem., Editl Bd, Sustain mag., 2013–14. Member: Architects' Registration Bd, 2007–13 (Chm., Investigations Cttee, 2008–13); Professional Regulation Exec. Cttee (formerly Affairs Bd), Inst. and Faculty of Actuaries (formerly Actuarial Profession), 2007–12; Council, IoD, 2007–13; Notaries Qualifications Bd, 2017–. Formerly Trustee, Projects in Partnership (Chm., 1999–2004); Trustee, Southwark Charities, 2008–12. Advr, Assoc. of Lord Lieutenants, 2007–. Pres., London Br., Oxford Univ. Soc., 2007–. Clerk, Co. of Glaziers and Painters of Glass, 2007–12 (Master, 2014–15). Juror, Court Leet of the King's Manor, Southwark, 2008– (Foreman, 2011–12). FRSA 2002. Hon. FSE 2004. *Recreations:* playing the cello, choral singing, ski-ing. *Address:* 19 Frythe Close, Kenilworth, Warwickshire CV8 2SY. *T:* (01926) 777569. *Clubs:* City Livery, Scribes, Royal Over-Seas League.

**GALLOWAY, Prof. David Malcolm,** PhD; FBPsS; Professor of Education, Durham University, 1992–2001, now Emeritus (Head of School of Education, 1993–2000); *b* 5 July 1942; *s* of late Malcolm Ashby Galloway and Joan Dorah Frances Galloway (née Slater); *m* 1971, Christina Mary King; two *s* one *d*. *Educ:* St Edmund Hall, Oxford (BA Psychol., Phil. and Physiol. 1970; MA 1974); UCL (MSc Educnl Psychol. 1972); Sheffield City Poly. (PhD 1980). FBPsS 1983. Educnl Psychologist and Sen. Educnl Psychologist, Sheffield LEA, 1972–79; Sen. Lectr, Victoria Univ. of Wellington, NZ, 1980–83; Lectr, UC Cardiff, 1983–87; Lectr and Reader in Educnl Res., Lancaster Univ., 1987–91. Chm., Assoc. for Child Psychology and Psychiatry, 1999–2001. *Publications:* books include: Schools and Persistent Absentees, 1985; (with C. Goodwin) The Education of Disturbing Children: pupils with learning and adjustment difficulties, 1987; (with A. Edwards) Primary School Teaching and Educational Psychology, 1991; (jtly) The Assessment of Special Educational Needs: whose problem?, 1994; (jtly) Motivating the Difficult to Teach, 1998; (jtly) Academies and Educational Reform, 2010; numerous articles in acad. and professional jls. *Recreations:* bee-keeping, fell search and mountain rescue (Chm., Kirkby Stephen Mountain Rescue Team, 2002–07). *Address:* Crosby Mill Cottage, Smardale, Kirkby Stephen, Cumbria CA17 4HQ.

**GALLOWAY, George;** *b* 16 Aug. 1954; *s* of George and Sheila Galloway; *m* 1st, 1979, Elaine Fyffe (marr. diss. 1999); one *d*; 2nd, Dr Amineh Abu-Zayyad (marr. diss. 2009); one *s* by Rima Husseini; *m* 2012, Putri Gayatri Pertiwi; one *d*. *Educ:* Charleston Primary Sch.; Harris Acad., Dundee. Engrg worker, 1973; organiser, Labour Party, 1977; Gen. Sec., War on Want, 1983–87. MP Glasgow, Hillhead, 1987–97, Glasgow Kelvin, 1997–2005, Bethnal Green and Bow, 2005–10 (Lab, 1987–2003, Ind Lab, 2003–04, Respect, 2004–10); contested (Respect) Poplar and Limehouse, 2010; MP (Respect) Bradford W, March 2012–2015; contested (Respect) same seat, 2015. Contested: (Respect) London reg., EP elections, 2004; (Ind) Manchester Gorton, 2017. HQA (Pakistan), 1990; HPK (Pakistan), 1995. *Publications:* (jtly) Downfall: the Ceausescus and the Romanian revolution, 1991; I'm Not the Only One, 2004; Fidel Castro Handbook, 2007. *Recreations:* boxing, football, films, music.

**GALLOWAY, Peter George,** CBE 2006; Rector, Trinity Academy, Edinburgh, 1983–2008; *b* 21 March 1944; *s* of John and Mary Galloway; *m* 1971, Elizabeth Taylor; one *d*. *Educ:* Buckhaven High Sch.; Heriot-Watt Univ. (Dip Commerce 1966; BA 1970); Moray House Coll. Asst Rector, Royal High Sch., Edinburgh, 1976–80; Depute Head, James Gillespie's High, Edinburgh, 1980–83. Chm., Partnership Planning Gp, Enterprise in Educn, 2004–; Member: UK Council for European Educn, 1995–2000; Determined to Succeed Gp, 2001; Smith Gp, 2005–. Dir, Schools Enterprise Scotland Ltd, 2003–05. FRSA. *Recreations:* all sports, particularly Rugby, cricket and football as a spectator, golf as a player, travel, cooking. *Address:* 32 Bramdean Rise, Braids, Edinburgh EH10 6JR. *T:* (0131) 447 3070. *E:* petergallowaycbe@hotmail.co.uk. *Clubs:* Mortonhall Golf, Trinity Academicals Rugby (Edinburgh).

**GALLOWAY, Rev. Canon Dr Peter John,** OBE 1996; Chaplain of the Queen's Chapel of the Savoy and of the Royal Victorian Order, 2008–19; Secretary for Church Livings, Duchy of Lancaster, 2008–19; Deputy Priest in Ordinary to the Queen, 2016–19; Canon, Chapels Royal, 2017–19, now Canon Emeritus; *b* 19 July 1954; *s* of late Henry John Galloway and Mary Selina (née Beshaw); civil partnership 2008, Michael Russell Stewart Turner. *Educ:* Westminster City Sch.; Goldsmiths' Coll., Univ. of London (BA 1976); King's Coll., London (PhD 1987); St Stephen's House, Oxford. Ordained deacon, 1983; priest, 1984; Curate: St John's Wood, 1983–86; St Giles-in-the-Fields, 1986–90; Priest-in-charge, 1990–95, Vicar, 1995–2008, Emmanuel Church, W Hampstead; Warden of Readers, London Episcopal Area, 1987–92; Area Dean, N Camden, 2002–07; Surrogate, 2006–19. Member: London Dio. Synod, 1997–2000; London Dio. Adv. Cttee, 2007–13. St John Ambulance: Asst Dir-Gen., 1985–91; Dep. Dir-Gen., 1991–99; Chm., Nat. Publications Cttee, 1988–95; Order of St John: Mem., Chapter Gen., 1996–99; Mem., Priory of England Chapter, 1999–2013; Sub Dean, Priory of England, 1999–2007; Registrar, 2007–16. Mem., Lord Chancellor's Adv. Cttee, City of London, 1994–2000 and 2005–11 (Vice Chm., 2008–11), Central and S London, 2012–13. London University: Mem. Council, 1999–2008; Vice Chm. Convocation, 1999–2003 (Acting Chm., 2001–03); Chm., Convocation Trust, 2005–12 (Trustee, 2003–16); Mem. Council, Goldsmiths' Coll., 1993–99 (Hon. Fellow, 1999); Chm., Goldsmiths' Soc., 1997–2007 (Vice-Chm., 1991–97); Mem. Council, Heythrop Coll., 2006–14. Hon. Prof. in Politics and Hist., Brunel Univ., 2008–. Gov., Soho Parish Sch., 1989–91; Chm. of Governors, Emmanuel Sch., W Hampstead, 1990–2008; Gov., St Olave's and St Saviour's GS, 2009–17 (Vice Chm., 2012–13; Chm., 2013–17); Mem., Ct of Govs, St Olave's and St Saviour's Schs Foundn, 2014–17. Trustee, St Gabriel's Trust, 2001–04. Provost (formerly Chaplain), Imperial Soc. of Knights Bachelor, 2006–; Chaplain to HRH the Princess Royal as Master, Butchers' Co., 2010–11. Freeman, City of London, 1995. JP: City of London, 1989–2011 (Dep. Chm., 2000, Chm., 2001–04, Bench); Central London, 2012–19. Dep. Chm., 2003, Chm., 2004, Gtr London Bench Chairmen's Forum. FSA 2000. Hon. DLitt Brunel, 2009. KStJ 1997. Meritorious Service Medal, Orders and Medals Res. Soc., 2013. Officer, Order of the Crown (Romania), 2013. *Publications:* The Order of St Patrick 1783–1983, 1983; Henry Falconar Barclay Mackay, 1983; (with Christopher Rawll) Good and Faithful Servants, 1988; The Cathedrals of Ireland, 1992; The Order of the British Empire, 1996, 2nd edn 2017; (jtly) Royal Service, 1996; The Most Illustrious Order, 1999; A Passionate Humility: Frederick Oakeley and the Oxford movement, 1999; The Cathedrals of Scotland, 2000; The Order of St Michael and St George, 2000, 2nd edn 2018; Companions of Honour, 2002; The Order of the Bath, 2006; The Order of the Thistle, 2009; The Queen's Chapel of the Savoy, 2009, 2nd edn 2017; Exalted, Eminent and Imperial, Honours of the British Raj, 2014; The Royal Victorian Order, 2016. *Recreations:* reading, writing, book collecting, solitude. *Clubs:* Athenæum, Beefsteak.

**GALLOWAY, Rachel;** HM Diplomatic Service; Ambassador to Macedonia, since 2018; *b* Manchester, 1976; *d* of Malcolm Edis and Hilary Edis; *m* 2010, Thomas James Galloway, OBE; one *s* one *d*. *Educ:* Manchester High Sch. for Girls; Univ. of Leeds (BA Political Sci.). First Sec., Washington, 2002–06; Diplomatic Advr to Helmand Task Force, 2006; Dep. Hd, Internat. Orgns Dept, FCO, 2010–12; Hd, Neighbourhoods Team, UK Perm. Repn to EU, Brussels, 2012–15; Chair, Mashrek-Maghreb Wkg Gp, Eur. External Action Service, 2015–17. *Recreations:* enjoy reading (science fiction in particular), travelling and cooking Indian food, exploring the world and its cultures with my family is a privilege and a joy. *Address:* c/o Foreign and Commonwealth Office, King Charles Street, SW1A 2AH.

**GALLOWAY, Prof. Tamara Susan,** OBE 2019; PhD; Professor of Ecotoxicology, University of Exeter, since 2007; Honorary Chair, University of Exeter Medical School, since 2007; *b* Bognor Regis, 6 Feb. 1963; *d* of Anatole Scobie and Wendy Scobie; *m* (marr. diss. 2015); three *s*. *Educ:* Bishopbriggs High Sch., Glasgow; Univ. of Glasgow (BSc Hons Biochem. 1979); Univ. of Edinburgh (PhD Biochem. 1983). Proj. Leader, Clin. Reagents Res. and Develt, Amersham Internat. plc, 1986–90; pt-time Res. Asst to Prof. Peter Mitchell, FRS, Glynn Res. Inst., 1991–92; Sen. Lectr, 1997–2005, Reader, 2005–07, in Biochem., Univ. of Plymouth. Expert Mem., UK Govt Hazardous Substances Adv. Cttee, 2015–. *Publications:* approx. 200 scientific articles and book chapters on envmtl pollution and human health. *Recreations:* swimming, shopping for clothes, hanging about with friends, cooking, worrying about things. *Address:* College of Life and Environmental Sciences, University of Exeter, Exeter EX4 4QD. *T:* (01392) 263436. *E:* t.s.galloway@exeter.ac.uk.

**GALSWORTHY, Sir Anthony (Charles),** KCMG 1999 (CMG 1985); HM Diplomatic Service, retired; Ambassador to the People's Republic of China, 1997–2002; *b* 20 Dec. 1944; *s* of Sir Arthur Norman Galsworthy, KCMG, and Margaret Agnes Galsworthy (née Hiscocks); *m* 1970, Jan Dawson-Grove; one *s* one *d*. *Educ:* St Paul's Sch.; Corpus Christi Coll., Cambridge (MA). FCO, 1966–67; Hong Kong (language training), 1967–69; Peking, 1970–72; FCO, 1972–77; Rome, 1977–81; Counsellor, Peking 1981–84; Head of Hong Kong Dept, FCO, 1984–86; Principal Private Sec. to Sec. of State for Foreign and Commonwealth Affairs, 1986–88; seconded to RIIA, 1988–89; Sen. British Rep., Sino-British Jt Liaison Gp, Hong Kong, 1989–93; Chief of Assessments Staff, Cabinet Office, 1993–95; Dep. Under Sec. of State, FCO, 1995–97. Scientific Associate, Natural Hist. Mus., 2001–. Member Council: British Trust for Ornithology, 2002–06; Wildfowl and Wetlands Trust, 2002–09. Advr, Standard Chartered Bank, 2002–14; Director: Bekaert SA, 2004–14; WTT Consulting, 2009–19. Dir, Earthwatch (Europe), 2002–06. Hon. Prof., Kunming Inst. of Botany, Chinese Acad. of Scis. Hon. Fellow, Royal Botanic Gdns, Edinburgh, 2001. *Publications:* (jtly) The Genus Eupithecia in China, 2013. *Recreations:* ornithology, entomology, wildlife.

**GALSWORTHY, (Arthur) Michael (Johnstone),** CVO 2002; CBE 1999; Chairman, Trewithen Estates Management Co., since 1979; Vice Lord-Lieutenant, Cornwall, 2001–14; *b* 10 April 1944; *s* of Sir John Galsworthy, KCVO, CMG and late Jennifer Ruth Johnstone; *m* 1st, 1972, Charlotte Helena Prudence Roberts (*d* 1989); one *s* one *d*; 2nd, 1991, Sarah Christian Durnford; one *s* one *d*. *Educ:* Radley; St Andrews Univ. (MA Hons). International Harvester Corp., 1967–69; English China Clays PLC, 1970–82; Man. Dir, Hawkins Wright Associates, 1982–86. Local Adv. Dir, Barclays Bank, 1987–98. Mem., Prince of Wales Council, 1985–2002; Dir, CoSIRA, 1985–88; a Develt Comr, 1987–92; Trustee, Rural Housing Trust, 1986–92; Chairman: Cornwall Rural Housing Assoc., 1985–95; Royal Cornwall Hosps NHS Trust, 1991–93; Chm., In Pursuit of Excellence Partnership for Cornwall, 1994–2000. Chm., Cornwall Co. Playing Fields, 1978–96; Dir, Woodard Corp. (W Region), 1983–87. Vice Pres., Royal Cornwall Agricl Assoc., 1987–. FRAgS 2007; FZS 2008. Mem., Court of Assts, Goldsmiths' Co., 1998– (Prime Warden, 2010–11). Chm. Council, Order of St John for Cornwall, 1995–99. DL Cornwall, 1993; High Sheriff, Cornwall, 1994. *Publications:* In Pursuit of Excellence: testimonial of business in Cornwall, 1994; The IPE Business Journal, 1996; The IPE Green Book Testimonial, 1997; A Wealth of Talent: the best of crafts in Cornwall, 1998. *Recreations:* gardening, fishing, shooting, walking. *Address:* Trewithen, Grampound Road, near Truro, Cornwall TR2 4DD. *T:* (01726) 882418. *Clubs:* Brooks's, Farmers.

**GALTON, Bernard John;** Director General, Workforce and Organisational Development, NHS Wales, 2013–14; *b* 5 July 1956; *s* of Roy and Kathleen Galton; *m* 1978, Susan Fox; two *s*. *Educ:* City of Bath Boys' Sch. Ministry of Defence, 1973–2004: Dir, HR Policy, 1996–98; HR Dir, Defence Aviation Repair Agency, 1998–2004; Dir, HR Gp, Welsh Assembly Govt, 2004–09; Dir Gen. People, Places and Corporate Services, Welsh Assembly Govt, later Welsh Govt, 2009–13. Strategic Advr, Sapienti, 2014; Associate, GreenPark Worldwide, 2015–17. Non-executive Director: Royal Nat. Hosp. for Rheumatic Diseases, 2014–15; Capita Property and Infrastructure, 2015–17. Chartered FCIPD (FCIPD 2001); Mem., BPsS. *Recreations:* reading, travelling, gym, good food and wine, family.

**GALVIN, William;** Group Chief Executive, Universities Superannuation Scheme, since 2013; *b* Waterford, Ireland, 1968; *m* 2010, Clemence Bourdariat; two *d*. *Educ:* Univ. of Limerick (BA 1989); University Coll. Cork (Postgrad. Dip. 1995); Univ. of Manchester (MBA 2001). IBM (UK), 2001–06: Strategy consultant, IBM Consulting; strategy and mktg, IBM Global Services; pensions protection policy, DWP, 2006–08; Exec. Dir for Strategic Develt, 2008–10, CEO, 2011–13, Pensions Regulator. Non-executive Director: Pensions Adv. Service, 2010–13; Solicitors Regulation Authy, 2011–15; Mem. Bd, Eur. Insce and Occupational Pensions Authy, 2010–13. Gov., Pensions Policy Inst., 2010–. *Address:* Universities Superannuation Scheme, Royal Liver Building, Liverpool L3 1PY.

**GALWAY,** 13th Viscount *cr* 1727; **John Philip Monckton;** Baron Killard, 1727; oarsman; *b* Saint Boniface, Manitoba, 8 April 1952; *s* of 12th Viscount Galway and Fiona Margaret (née Taylor); *S* father, 2017; *m* 1st, 1980, Deborah Kathleen Holmes (marr. diss. 1992); 2nd,

2002, Tracey Jean Black; one s two d. *Educ:* Univ. of W Ontario (MA). Rower: Canadian Nat. Team, 1974–84; Olympic Games 1976 (coxless fours); winner, Bronze Medal, Olympic Games 1984 (coxless quad sculls); World Rowing Championship 1975 (coxed eight), 1977 (coxless fours), 1983 (quad sculls). Vice Pres., High Performance, Canadian rowing team, 2005–12. Vice Pres., Scepter Corp., Toronto, 2006–16. *Recreations:* Masters rowing and golf.

GALWAY, Sir James, Kt 2001; OBE 1977; FRCM 1983; fluteplayer; *b* 8 Dec. 1939; *s* of James Galway and Ethel Stewart Clarke; *m* 1st, 1965; one s; 2nd, 1972; one s twin d; 3rd, 1984, Jeanne Cinnante. *Educ:* St Paul's Sch., and Mountcollyer Secondary Modern Sch., Belfast; RCM, and Guildhall Sch. of Music, London; Conservatoire National Supérieur de Musique, Paris. First post in wind band of Royal Shakespeare Theatre, Stratford-upon-Avon; later worked with Sadler's Wells Orch., Royal Opera House Orch. and BBC Symphony Orch.; Principal Flute, London Symphony Orch., 1966, Royal Philharmonic Orch., 1967–69; Principal Solo Flute, Berlin Philharmonic Orch., 1969–75; international soloist, 1975–. Principal Guest Conductor, London Mozart Players, 1999–. Recordings of works by C. P. E. Bach, J. S. Bach, Beethoven, Corigliano, Debussy, Franck, Handel, Khachaturian, Mancini, Mozart, Nielsen, Prokoviev, Reicha, Reincke, Rodrigo, Schubert, Stamitz, Telemann and Vivaldi; also albums of flute showpieces, Australian, Irish and Japanese collections. Grand Prix du Disque, 1976, 1989. Hon. FGSM 2003. Hon. MA Open, 1979; Hon. DMus: QUB, 1979; New England Conservatory of Music, 1980; St Andrews, 2003. Officier des Arts et des Lettres (France), 1987. *Publications:* James Galway: an autobiography, 1978; Flute (Menuhin Music Guide), 1982; James Galway's Music in Time, 1983 (TV series, 1983); Masterclass: performance editions of great flute literature, 1987; Flute Studies, 2003; (with Linda Bridges) The Man with the Golden Flute: Sir James, a Celtic minstrel, 2009. *Recreations:* music, walking, swimming, films, theatre, TV, chess, backgammon, computing, talking to people.

GALWAY AND KILMACDUAGH, Bishop of, (RC), since 2017; Most Rev. Brendan Kelly; *b* Loughrea, Co. Galway, 20 May 1946; *s* of Seán Kelly and Annie Kelly (*née* Monahan). *Educ:* Craughwell Nat. Sch.; St Mary's Coll., Galway; St Patrick's Coll., Maynooth (BA 1967; BD 1970); University Coll., Galway (DipEd 1973). Ordained priest, 1971; Teacher, Coláiste Éinde, Galway, 1972–80; Teacher, 1980–86, Principal, 1986–95, Our Lady's Coll., Gort, Co. Galway; Parish Priest: Lisdoonvarna, Co. Clare, 1996–2003; Spiddal, Co. Galway, 2003–08; Bishop of Achonry, (RC), 2008–17. *Address:* Diocesan Office, The Cathedral, Galway, Ireland. *T:* (91) 563566. *E:* bishop@galwaydiocese.ie.

GAMBACCINI, Paul Matthew; broadcaster, since 1973; *b* New York, 2 April 1949; *s* of Mario and Dorothy Gambaccini. *Educ:* Dartmouth Coll., USA; University Coll., Oxford (MA PPE). British corresp., Rolling Stone mag., 1970–78; presenter: BBC Radio One, 1973–86 and 1990–93; BBC Radio Four, 1974–; Classic FM, 1992–2008; BBC Radio Three, 1995–96; BBC Radio Two, 1998–; television: The Old Grey Whistle Test, 1978–85; Top of the Pops; The Other Side of the Tracks, 1983–85; TV-AM, 1983–92; Television's Greatest Hits, 1992–93; GMTV, 1992–94. Presenter: Ivor Novello Awards, 1988–; Sony Radio Awards, 1999–2008; Parly Jazz Awards, 2005–12. News Internat. Vis. Prof. of Broadcasting Media, Oxford Univ., 2009. Prince's Trust Ambassador, 2009–. Philanthropist of Year, Nat. Charity Fundraisers, 1995; Sony Awards for Music Broadcaster, 2003, Music Documentary, 2004, Career Achievement, 2007. Winner, Celebrity Mastermind, BBC TV, 2010. *Publications:* (jtly) Guinness Book of British Hit Singles, 1977, 10th edn 1996; (jtly) Guinness Book of British Hit Albums, 1982, 6th edn 1994; Radio Boy, 1986; (jtly) Television's Greatest Hits, 1993; Love Letters, 1996; Love, Paul Gambaccini, 2015. *Recreations:* film and theatre, softball (Inaugural Inductee, British Softball Federation Hall of Fame, 2007). *Address:* 1225 The Whitehouse Apartments, 9 Belvedere Road, SE1 8YW. *T:* (020) 7401 6753. *E:* paulgambaccini@hotmail.com.

GAMBETTA, Prof. Diego, PhD; FBA 2000; Carlo Alberto Chair, Collegio Carlo Alberto, Turin, since 2019; Official Fellow, Nuffield College, Oxford, 2003–17, now Emeritus; *b* 30 Jan. 1952; *s* of Carlo Gambetta and Giovanna (*née* Giavelli); *m* 1992, Dr Valeria Pizzini; one s one d. *Educ:* Chieri, Turin; Univ. of Turin (BA Philosophy); King's Coll., Cambridge (PhD 1983). Civil servant, Regl Admin, Piedmont, Italy, 1978–84; Jun. Res. Fellow, 1984–88, Sen. Res. Fellow, 1988–91, King's Coll., Cambridge; University of Oxford: Fellow, St Anne's Coll. and Lectr in Sociology, 1991–95 (ad hominem Reader, 1993); Reader in Sociology, 1995–2002; Prof. of Sociology, 2002–18, on leave as Prof. of Social Theory, Eur. Univ. Inst., Florence, 2012–18; Fellow, All Souls Coll., Oxford, 1995–2003. Vis. Prof. in Social Orgn, Grad. Sch. of Business and Dept of Sociol., Univ. of Chicago, 1994; Inaugural Fellow, Italian Acad. for Advanced Studies, Columbia Univ., 1996–97; Vis. Prof., Sciences Po, Paris, 2005, 2008; Guest Lectr, Collège de France, Paris, 2007; Internat. Scholar, Humanities Center and Freeman Spogli Inst., Stanford Univ., 2010. *Publications:* Were they pushed or did they jump?: individual decision mechanisms in education, 1987 (trans. Italian 1990), 2nd edn 1996; (ed) Trust: making and breaking co-operative relations, 1988 (trans. Italian 1989); The Sicilian mafia: the business of private protection (Premio Iglesias), 1993 (trans. Italian, 1992, German, 1994, Spanish, 2007, Polish, 2009), 2nd edn 1996 (Premio Borsellino, 2003); (with S. Warner) La retorica della riforma: fine del sistema proporzionale in Italia, 1994; (ed) Making Sense of Suicide Missions, 2005; (with H. Hamill) Streetwise: how taxi drivers establish the trustworthiness of their customers, 2005; Codes of the Underworld: how criminals communicate, 2009; (with S. Hertog) Engineers of Jihad: the curious connection between violent extremism and education, 2016; contribs to anthologies and social scientific jls. *Recreations:* mountaineering, ski-ing, yoga, cinema. *Address:* Nuffield College, Oxford OX1 1NF; Collegio Carlo Alberto, Piazza Vincenzo Arbarello 8, 10122 Turin, Italy.

GAMBLE, Alan James; an Upper Tribunal Judge (Administrative Appeals Chamber) (formerly Social Security and Child Support Commissioner), 2008–16, fee-paid, since 2016; *b* Glasgow, 29 April 1951; *s* of Frank Gamble and Nancy Gamble (*née* Johnston); *m* 1977, Elizabeth Rodger Waugh; two s one d. *Educ:* High Sch. of Glasgow; Univ. of Glasgow (LLB Hons); Harvard Law Sch. (LLM). Advocate, 1978; Lectr, 1976–86, Sen. Lectr, 1986–93, in Private Law, Univ. of Glasgow; District Chm., Appeal Tribunals, 1993–2008; Dep. Social Security and Child Support Comr, 1994–2008; Convener, Mental Health Tribunal for Scotland, 2005–; Dep. Social Security and Child Support Comr for NI, 2011–. *Publications:* (contrib.) Legal Issues in Medicine, 1981; (contrib.) The Law of Property in Scotland, 1996; (ed) Obligations in Context, 2000; articles on legal topics. *Recreations:* reading, hill walking. *Address:* Upper Tribunal (Administrative Appeals), George House, 126 George Street, Edinburgh EH2 4HH.

GAMBLE, Prof. Andrew Michael, PhD; FBA 2000; FAcSS; Professor of Politics, University of Cambridge, 2007–14, now Emeritus; Fellow of Queens' College, Cambridge, 2007–14, now Emeritus; Professor of Politics, University of Sheffield, since 2014; *b* 15 Aug. 1947; *s* of Marcus Elkington Gamble and Joan (*née* Westall); *m* 1974, Christine Jennifer Rodway; one s two d. *Educ:* Brighton Coll.; Queen's Coll., Cambridge (BA Econs 1968); Univ. of Durham (MA Pol Theory 1969); Gonville and Caius Coll., Cambridge (PhD Social and Pol Scis 1975). University of Sheffield: Lectr in Politics, 1973–82; Reader, 1982–86; Prof. of Politics, 1986–2006; Pro-Vice-Chancellor, 1994–98; Dir, Pol Economy Res. Centre, 1999–2004; Leverhulme Res. Fellow, 2004–07. Visiting Professor: Univ. of Kobe, 1990; Univ. of Hitotsubashi, 1992; Univ. of Chuo, 1994; ANU, 2005. Mem. Exec., 1988–91, Vice-Chair, 1989–91, Political Studies Assoc. Joint Editor: New Political Economy, 1996–2008; Political Qly, 1997–2012. FRSA 1999; FAcSS (AcSS 2002). Mitchell Prize, 1977; Sir Isaiah Berlin Prize for Lifetime Contrib. to Pol Studies, Pol Studies Assoc., 2005. *Publications:* (jtly) From Alienation to Surplus Value (Isaac Deutscher Meml Prize), 1972; The Conservative Nation, 1974 (new edn 2014); (jtly) Capitalism in Crisis, 1976; Britain in Decline, 1981, 4th edn 1994; An Introduction to Modern Social and Political Thought, 1981; (ed jtly) Developments in British Politics, vol. 1, 1983, vol. 2, 1986, vol. 3, 1990, vol. 4, 1993, vol. 5, 1997, vol. 6, 2000, vol. 7, 2003; (jtly) The British Party System and Economic Policy, 1984; (ed jtly) The Social Economy and the Democratic State, 1987; The Free Economy and the Strong State, 1988, 2nd edn 1994; (ed jtly) Thatcher's Law, 1989; Hayek: the iron cage of liberty, 1996; (ed jtly) Regionalism and World Order, 1996; (ed jtly) Stakeholder Capitalism, 1997; (ed jtly) Fundamentals in British Politics, 1999; (ed jtly) Marxism and Social Science, 1999; (ed jtly) The New Social Democracy, 1999; Politics and Fate, 2000; (ed jtly) The Political Economy of the Company, 2000; Between Europe and America: the future of British politics, 2003 (W. J. M. Mackenzie Prize, Pol Studies Assoc., 2005); (ed jtly) Restating the State, 2004; The Spectre at the Feast, 2009; Crisis without end?: the unravelling of western prosperity, 2014; Can the Welfare State Survive?, 2016; Open Left: the future of progressive politics, 2018; (ed jtly) Rethinking Democracy, 2019; Politics: why it matters, 2019; articles in learned jls. *Recreations:* music, growing tomatoes. *Address:* Department of Politics, University of Sheffield, Sheffield S10 2TN.
*See also* C. S. Gamble.

GAMBLE, Dr Christine Elizabeth; Director, Royal Institute of International Affairs, 1998–2001; *b* 1950; *d* of late Albert Edward Gamble and Kathleen Laura (*née* Wallis); *m* 1989, Edward Barry Antony Craxton. *Educ:* Royal Holloway Coll., London Univ. (BA 1st Cl. Hons; PhD 1977). English-French Cultural Orgn, 1974–75; British Embassy, Moscow, 1975–76; with British Council, 1977–98: New Delhi, 1977–79; Stratford-on-Avon, 1979–80; Harare, 1980–82; Regl Officer for Soviet Union in London, 1982–85; Dep. Dir, Athens, 1985–87; Dir General's Dept, 1988–90; Head, Project Pursuit Dept and Dir, Chancellor's Financial Sector Scheme for Former Soviet Union, 1991–92; Dir, Visitors' Dept, 1992–93; Gen. Manager, Country Services Gp, 1993–95 and Hd, European Series, 1994–96; Cultural Counsellor, Paris and Dir, France, 1996–98. Co. Sec., Ind. Football Commn, 2002–05; Consultant on equality and diversity issues, 2005–10. Dir, Japan 21st Century Gp, 1999–2005; Mem., Franco-British Council, 2000–06. Order of Rio Branco (Brazil), 2004. *Recreations:* collecting wine, music, theatre. *Address:* 25 Abbey Street, Faversham ME13 7BE.

GAMBLE, Prof. Clive Stephen, PhD; FBA 2000; FSA; Professor of Archaeology, University of Southampton, 2011–16, now Emeritus; *b* 10 March 1951; *s* of Marcus Elkington Gamble and Joan Gamble (*née* Westall); *m* 1981, Dr Elaine Lisk Morris. *Educ:* Brighton Coll.; Jesus Coll., Cambridge (BA 1972, MA 1975; PhD 1978). FSA 1981; MCIfA (MIFA 1987). Department of Archaeology, University of Southampton: exptl officer, 1975; Lectr, 1976–86; Sen. Lectr, 1986–90; Reader, 1990–95; Prof. of Archaeol., 1995–2004; British Acad. Res. Reader, 2000–02; Dir, Centre for Archaeol. of Human Origins, 1999–2004; Prof. of Geog., Royal Holloway, Univ. of London, 2004–11. Pres., RAI, 2011–14. Trustee, BM, 2010–18. DSc London. *Publications:* The Palaeolithic Settlement of Europe, 1986; Timewalkers: the prehistory of global colonisation, 1993; (with C. Stringer) In Search of the Neanderthals, 1993; The Palaeolithic Societies of Europe, 1999; Archaeology: the basics, 2001; Origins and Revolutions, 2007; Settling the Earth, 2013; Thinking Big, 2014. *Recreations:* cats, cricket, gardening. *Address:* Department of Archaeology, University of Southampton, Highfield, Southampton SO17 1BF.
*See also* A. M. Gamble.

GAMBLE, Sir David (Hugh Norman), 6th Bt cr 1897, of Windlehurst, St Helens, Co. Palatine of Lancashire; *b* 1 July 1966; *s* of Sir David Gamble, 5th Bt and of Dawn Adrienne, *d* of late David Hugh Gittins; *S* father, 1984. *Educ:* Shiplake College, Henley-on-Thames. Heir: cousin Hugh Robert George Gamble [*b* 3 March 1946; *m* 1989, Rebecca Jane, *d* of Lt Comdr David Odell, RN; one s one d]. *Address:* 6 Coombe Hill, Keinton Mandeville, Somerton, Somerset TA11 6DQ. *T:* (01458) 223964.

GAMBLE, Richard Arthur; non-executive Director: Highway Insurance Group (formerly Highway Insurance Holdings) plc, 2003–08 (Executive Chairman, 2006–07; non-executive Chairman, 2007–08); Equity Syndicate Management, 2011–13; *b* 19 Sept. 1939; *s* of late Arthur Gamble and of Grace Emily Gamble (*née* Little); *m* 1966, Elizabeth Ann, *d* of Edward Godwin-Atkyns; two s. *Educ:* Raynes Park Co. Grammar Sch. FCA 1962. Articled clerk, W. J. Gilbert & Co., London, 1957–62; Asst Manager, Turquand Youngs & Co., 1962–66; Dir and Co. Sec., Lee Davy Gp Ltd, 1966–68; Dir and Sec., Hamilton Smith, Lloyd's Brokers, 1968–70; Finance Dir, Lowndes Lambert Internat., Lloyd's Brokers, 1970–76; European Finance Dir, Data100/Northern Telecom Systems, 1976–80; Finance Dir, McDonnell Douglas Inf. Systems and Dir, McDonnell Douglas UK, 1980–84; Dep. Chief Financial Officer, British Airways, 1984–89; Royal Insurance Holdings PLC: Gp Finance Dir, 1989–91; Gp Chief Operating Officer, 1991; Gp Chief Exec., 1992–96; Gp Chief Exec., Royal & Sun Alliance Insurance Gp plc, 1996–97. Non-executive Chm., Denne Gp Ltd, 2001–03 (Advr, 1999–2001); non-executive Director: Mutual and Federal, 1989–97; Excel Airways Gp plc, 2003–05. Mem. Bd, ABI, 1994–96; Chm., Policy Holders Protection Bd, 1994–98. Mem., Adv. Cttee on Business in the Envmt and Chm., Financial Services Working Gp, 1993–96. Mem., Educnl Nat. Leadership Team, BITC, 1995–97. Trustee, Crimestoppers, 1995–; Pres., GB Wheelchair Basketball Assoc., 1997–; Gov., RSC, 1997–2002. CCMI (CIMgt 1992). *Recreations:* all sport, particularly golf, walking with dogs, theatre, family. *Address:* 77 St John's Road, Penn, High Wycombe, Bucks HP10 8HU. *T:* (01494) 815103. *Clubs:* Beaconsfield Golf; Falmouth Rugby Football (Life Vice Pres.); Falmouth Cricket (Vice Pres.).

GAMBLES, Dr Ian Christopher; Chief Executive Officer (formerly Director, England), Forestry Commission, since 2013; *b* Crosby, 17 Oct. 1962; *s* of Robert Henry Gambles and Hanna Hermana Gambles; *m* 2011, Helen Adlard; two s one d and two step d. *Educ:* Merchant Taylors' Sch., Crosby; Balliol Coll., Oxford (BA Hons Ancient and Modern Hist. 1983); Georgetown Univ. (MSc Foreign Service 1988); Princeton Univ. (PhD Politics 1991). FCMA 2000. Grad. trainee, Shell UK Ltd, 1984–86; Res. Associate, Internat. Inst. for Strategic Studies, 1988–89; HM Treasury: Principal (sovereign debt mgt and co-ordination of Budget), 1991–94; Principal (defence expenditure control), 1995–97; Vis. Fellow, Budapest Univ. of Econs, 1994–95; Principal Consultant, KPMG Consulting, 1997–2001; Sen. Manager, Deloitte Consulting, 2001–02; Dir, Frontline Consultants, 2002–03; Man. Dir, Enodian Ltd, 2003–09; Director: Infrastructure Planning Commn, 2009–12; Nat. Infrastructure, Planning Inspectorate, 2012–13. *Publications:* Making the Business Case, 2009. *Recreations:* fell-walking, Real Tennis, gardening, chess. *Address:* Forestry Commission, 620 Bristol Business Park, Coldharbour Lane, Bristol BS16 1EJ. *T:* 0300 067 4061. *E:* ian.gambles@forestrycommission.gov.uk.

**GAMBLIN, Dr Steven John,** FRS 2011; FMedSci; Director of Science Operations, Crick Institute, since 2013; *b* 7 Jan. 1962; *s* of Anthony Edward Gamblin and late Pamela Joy Gamblin; *m* 1996, Priscilla J. C. Meigh; two *s* one *d. Educ:* Univ. of Bristol (BSc Biochem. 1983; PhD 1986). Post-doctoral researcher: Bristol Univ., 1988–90; Harvard Univ., 1990–94; National Institute for Medical Research: Prog. Leader, Div. of Protein Structure, 1994–2005; Jt Hd, Div. of Molecular Structure, 2005–15; Dir of Res., 2011–15. Mem., EMBO, FMedSci 2008. Feldberg Prize, Feldberg Foundn, 2012. *Publications:* contribs to scientific jls incl. Nature. *Recreations:* gardening, history, music. *Address:* Francis Crick Institute, 1 Midland Road, NW1 1AT.

**GAMBLING, Prof. (William) Alex(ander),** PhD, DSc; FRS 1983; FREng; Founder and Director, Optoelectronics Research Centre, University of Southampton, 1989–95; *b* 11 Oct. 1926; *s* of George Alexander Gambling and Muriel Clara Gambling; *m* 1st, 1952, Margaret Pooley (marr. diss. 1994); one *s* two *d*; 2nd, 1994, Barbara Colleen O'Neil. *Educ:* Univ. of Bristol (BSc, Alfred Fry Prize, DSc); Univ. of Liverpool (PhD). FIERE 1964; CEng, Hon. FIET (FIEE 1967); FREng (FEng 1979); FHKAES 2000. Lectr in Electric Power Engrg, Univ. of Liverpool, 1950–55; National Res. Council Fellow, Univ. of BC, 1955–57; Univ. of Southampton: Lectr, Sen. Lectr, and Reader, 1957–64; Prof. of Electronics, 1964–80; Dean of Engrg and Applied Science, 1972–75; Hd of Prof, 1974–79; BT Prof. of Optical Communication, 1980–95; Royal Soc. Kan Tong Po Prof. and Dir, Optoelectronics Res. Centre, City Univ., Hong Kong, 1996–2001. Dir, York Ltd, 1980–97. Vis. Professor: Univ. of Colo, USA, 1966–67; Bhabha Atomic Res. Centre, India, 1970; Osaka Univ., Japan, 1977; City Univ. of Hong Kong, 1995; Hon. Professor: Huazhong Univ. of Sci. and Technol., Wuhan, China, 1986–; Beijing Univ. of Posts and Telecommunications, 1987–; Shanghai Univ., 1991–; Shandong Univ., 1999–; Hon. Dir, Beijing Optical Fibre Inst., 1987–. Member: Electronics Res. Council, 1977–80 (Mem., Optics and Infra-Red Cttee, 1965–69 and 1974–80); Board, Council of Engrg Instns, 1974–79; National Electronics Council, 1977–78, 1984–95; Technol. Sub-Cttee of UGC, 1973–83; British Nat. Cttee for Radio Science, 1978–87; Nat. Adv. Bd for Local Authority Higher Educn, Engrg Working Gp, 1982–84; Engineering Council, 1983–88; British Nat. Cttee for Internat. Engineering Affairs, 1984–88; Council, Royal Acad. of Engrg, 1989–92; Chairman: Commn D, Internat. Union of Radio Science, 1984–87 (Vice-Chm., 1981–84); Nat. DTI/SERC Optoelectronics Cttee, 1988–91. Pres., IERE, 1977–78 (Hon. Fellow 1983); Vice Pres., Hong Kong Acad. of Engrg Scis, 2004–08. Selby Fellow, Australian Acad. of Science, 1982; For. Mem., Polish Acad. of Scis, 1985. Freeman, City of London, 1987; Liveryman, Worshipful Co. of Engrs, 1988. Dr *hc* Univ. Politécnica de Madrid, 1994; Hon. DSc: Aston, 1995; Southampton, 2005. Hon. DEng Bristol, 1999. Bulgin Premium, IERE, 1961, Lord Rutherford Premium, IERE, 1964, Electronics Div. Premium, IEE, 1976 and 1978, Oliver Lodge Premium, IEE, 1981, Heinrich Hertz Premium, IERE, 1981, for research papers; J. J. Thomson Medal, IEE, 1982, Faraday Medal, IEE, 1983, Churchill Medal, Soc. of Engineers, 1984 and Simms Medal, Soc. of Engineers, 1989, for research innovation and leadership; Academic Enterprise Award, 1982; Micro-optics Award, Japan, 1989; Dennis Gabor Award, Internat. Soc. for Optical Engrg, USA, 1990; Rank Prize for Optoelectronics, 1991; Medal and Prize, Foundn for Computer and Communications Promotion, Japan, 1993; Mountbatten Medal, Nat. Electronics Council, 1993; James Alfred Ewing Medal, ICE/Royal Soc., 2002. *Publications:* 300 papers on electronics and optical fibre communications. *Recreations:* music, reading.

**GAMBON, Sir Michael (John),** Kt 1998; CBE 1990; actor; *b* 19 Oct. 1940; *s* of Edward and Mary Gambon; *m* 1962, Anne Miller; one *s*; two *s* by Philippa Hart. *Educ:* St Aloysius School for Boys, Somers Town, London. Served 7 year apprenticeship in engineering; first appeared on stage with Edwards/MácLiammoir Co., Dublin, 1962; Nat. Theatre, Old Vic, 1963–67; Birmingham Rep. and other provincial theatres, 1967–69 (title rôles incl. Othello, Macbeth, Coriolanus); RSC Aldwych, 1970–71; Norman Conquests, Globe, 1974; Otherwise Engaged, Queen's, 1976; Just Between Ourselves, Queen's 1977; Alice's Boys, Savoy, 1978; King Lear and Antony and Cleopatra (title rôles), RSC Stratford and Barbican, 1982–83; Old Times, Haymarket, 1985; Uncle Vanya, Vaudeville, 1988; Veterans Day, Haymarket, 1989; Man of the Moment, Globe, 1990; Othello and Taking Steps, Scarborough, 1990; Tom and Clem, Aldwych, 1997; The Unexpected Man, Barbican Pit, transf. Duchess, 1998; Juno and the Paycock, Gaiety, Dublin, 1999; Cressida, Albery, 2000; The Caretaker, Comedy (Variety Club Best Actor, Critics' Circle Best Actor), 2000; A Number, Royal Court, 2002; Endgame, Albery, 2004; Eh Joe, Duke of York's, 2006, Royal Lyceum, 2013; No Man's Land, Duke of York's, 2008; Krapp's Last Tape, Duchess, 2010; All That Fall, Jermyn Street Th., 2012; National Theatre: Galileo, 1980 (London Theatre Critics' Award, Best Actor); Betrayal, 1980; Tales From Hollywood, 1980; Chorus of Disapproval, 1985 (Olivier Award, Best Comedy Performance); Tons of Money, 1986; A View from the Bridge, 1987, transf. Aldwych (Best Actor, Evening Standard Awards, Olivier Awards, and Plays and Players London Theatre Critics' Awards; Best Stage Actor, Variety Club Awards); A Small Family Business, 1987; Mountain Language, 1988; Skylight, transf. Wyndhams, then NY, and Volpone (Best Actor, Evening Standard Awards), 1995; Henry IV, Parts 1 and 2, 2005. *Television* includes: The Singing Detective, 1986 (BAFTA Award, Best Actor, 1987); Maigret, 1992, 1993; Faith, 1994; Wives and Daughters, 1999 (BAFTA Award, Best Actor, 2000); Longitude, 2000 (BAFTA Award, Best Actor, 2001); Perfect Strangers, 2001 (BAFTA Award, Best Actor, 2002); The Lost Prince, 2003; Angels in America, 2004; Cranford, 2007; Emma, 2009; Page Eight, 2011; Restless, 2012; Quirke, 2014; Fortitude, 2015; The Casual Vacancy, 2015; Churchill's Secret, 2016; The Hollow Crown: The Wars of the Roses, 2016; Fearless, 2017; Little Women, 2017. *Films* include: The Cook, The Thief, His Wife and Her Lover, The Heat of the Day, Paris by Night, 1989; A Dry White Season, 1990; Mobsters, Toys, 1992; The Browning Version, 1993; A Man of No Importance, Midnight in Moscow, 1994; The Innocent Sleep, All Our Fault, 1995; Mary Reilly, Two Deaths, Nothing Personal, The Gambler, 1996; The Wings of the Dove, Dancing at Lughnasa, 1997; Plunkett and Macleane, 1999; The Last September, Sleepy Hollow, The Insider, 2000; End Game, High Heels and Low Lifes, 2001; Gosford Park, Charlotte Gray, Ali G Indahouse, Path to War, 2002; The Actors, 2003; Sylvia, Being Julia, Layer Cake, Open Range, Harry Potter and the Prisoner of Azkaban, Sky Captain and the World of Tomorrow, 2004; The Life Aquatic with Steve Zissou, Harry Potter and the Goblet of Fire, 2005; Amazing Grace, 2006; The Good Shepherd, Harry Potter and the Order of the Phoenix, 2007; Harry Potter and the Half-Blood Prince, 2009; The Book of Eli, Harry Potter and the Deathly Hallows, Pt 1, 2010, Pt 2, 2011; The King's Speech, 2011; Quartet, 2013; Dad's Army, 2016; Mad to be Normal, Victoria and Abdul, 2017; King of Thieves, 2018; Judy, 2019. Trustee, Royal Armouries, 1995. Liveryman, Gunmakers' Co. Hon. DLitt Southampton, 2002. *Recreations:* flying, gun collecting, clock making. *Address:* Independent Talent Group Ltd, 40 Whitfield Street, W1T 2RH. *Club:* Garrick.

**GAME, Amanda, (Mrs A. O. E. Raven);** independent curator and producer, since 2008; Co-Founder, Consulting Lead Director, 2008–10, IC: Innovative Craft; *b* 22 Aug. 1958; *d* of John Game and Margaret Newman Game (*née* Smith); *m* 1987, Andrew Owen Earle Raven, OBE (*d* 2005). *Educ:* Open Univ. (BA 1st Cl. Hons Humanities Art Hist. and Lit.); Royal Coll. of Arts (MPhil 2016). Asst, Oxford Gall., 1984–86; Scottish Gallery, Edinburgh: Manager for Contemporary Craft, 1986–95; Dir of Applied Art, 1995–2007. Curator, Jewellery Moves, 1997–99, Res. Associate, 1998–, Nat. Mus of Scotland. Crafts Advr, Scottish Arts Council, 1995–2001; Advisor: Inches Carr Trust, Edinburgh, 1999–; Goldsmiths' Trust, Edinburgh, 2002–. Associate, PALlabs, 2013–15. Mem., Modern Plate Cttee, Goldsmiths' Hall, 2009–. Founder Trustee, 2008–, Chm., 2010–16, Andrew Raven Trust. Trustee, Nat. Life Stories, British Liby, 2017–. Freeman, 1995, Liveryman, 2007, Goldsmiths' Co. Chair, Judging Panel, Jerwood Applied Arts Prize, Textiles, 1997; Judge: Young Designer Silversmith Award, Goldsmiths' Hall, 1994–2004; Leonardo Prize, 2004. *Publications:* Jewellery Moves, 1998, 3rd edn 2001; (contrib.) Silver from Scotland, 2008; Contemporary British Crafts: the Goodison Gift to the Fitzwilliam Museum, 2016; (ed) Notes From Morvern: ten years of the Andrew Raven Trust 2007–2017, 2017. *Recreations:* hill-walking, classical music, opera, literature, film, gardens, architecture. *E:* amandaraven2005@yahoo.co.uk.

**GAMMAGE, Jayne Agneta;** see Franklyn, J. A.

**GAMMELL, Sir William Benjamin Bowring, (Sir Bill),** Kt 2006; Chairman, Cairn Energy PLC, 2011–14 (Chief Executive, 1989–2011); *b* 29 Dec. 1952; *s* of late James Gilbert Sidney Gammell and Patricia Bowring Gammell (*née* Toms). *Educ:* Stirling Univ. (BA Econ). Founded Cairn Energy Mgt, 1980, Man. Dir, 1980–89. Director: Scottish Inst. of Sport, 1998–2008; Artemis Aim VCT Trust, 2001–08; Figured Ltd, 2014–; Chairman: Winning Scotland Foundn (formerly Scottish Inst. of Sport Foundn), 2006–; Genius Foods, 2012–; Lumity Life, 2017–. Dir, Glasgow 2014, 2009–14. FRSE 2017. Hon. DBA: Napier, 2005; Robert Gordon, 2011; DUniv Stirling, 2006; Hon. DEng Heriot Watt, 2007. *Recreations:* Rugby (Scotland Rugby Internat., 1977–78), squash, football, golf, ski-ing. *Club:* Golf House (Elie, Fife).

**GAMMIE, Malcolm James,** CBE 2005; QC 2002; *b* 18 Feb. 1951; *s* of Maj. James Ian Gammie, MC, and Florence Mary Gammie (*née* Wiggs); *m* 1974, Rosalind Anne Rowe; one *s* three *d. Educ:* Edge Grove Sch., Aldenham; Merchant Taylors' Sch.; Sidney Sussex Coll., Cambridge (MA). Linklaters & Paines: articled clerk, 1973–75; solicitor, Tax Dept, 1975–78 and 1985–87; Partner, 1987–, Tax Dept, CBI, 1978–79; Director: Nat. Tax Office, Thomson McLintock & Co., 1979–84; Nat. Tax Services, KMG Thomson McLintock, 1984–85; called to the Bar, Middle Temple, 1997, Bencher, 2010; in practice as barrister, 1997–. Dep. Special Comr and pt-time VAT and Duties Tribunal Chm., 2002–. Vis. Professorial Fellow, Centre for Commercial Law Studies, QMW, 1997–; Res. Fellow, Inst. for Fiscal Studies, 1997–; Unilever Prof. of Internat. Business Law, Leiden Univ., 1998; Visiting Professor: of Tax Law, LSE, 2000–; of Internat. Tax Law, Sydney Univ., 2000 and 2002. Editor: Law and Tax Rev., 1982–88; Land Taxation, 1985–; Consulting Ed., Butterworth's Tax Handbook, 1994–2004. Cabinet Office: Member: Taxation Deregulation Gp, 1993–97; Fiscal Studies Wkg Party Adv. Council on Sci. and Technol., 1993; Mem., 1994–97, Res. Dir, 1997–2014, Tax Law Rev. Cttee; Mem., Special Cttee of Tax Law Consultative Bodies, Taxation Cttee, IOD, 1987–97. Chartered Institute of Taxation: Mem. Council, 1985–2001; Chm., Capital Taxes Wkg Party, 1986–92; Chm., Exec. Cttee, 1991–97. London Chamber of Commerce and Industry: Mem., 1976–; Mem. Council, 1989–92; Chm., Taxation Cttee, 1989–92. Chm., Revenue Law Cttee, Law Soc., 1996–97; Mem., Soc. for Advanced Legal Studies, 1997–. Mem., Perm. Scientific Cttee, Internat. Fiscal Assoc., 1998–2008 (Vice-Chm., British Br. Cttee). FRSA 1993. *Publications:* (with S. Ball) Taxation Publishing, Tax on Company Reorganisations, 1980, 2nd edn 1982; Tax Strategy for Companies, 1981, 3rd edn 1986; (with D. Williams) Stock Relief, 1981; (with D. Williams) Tax Focus on Interest and Discounts, 1983; Tax Strategy for Directors, Executives and Employees, 1983, 2nd edn 1985; (jtly) Whiteman on Capital Gains Tax, 1988; The Process of Tax Reform in the United Kingdom, 1990. *Recreations:* music, church architecture. *Address:* (chambers) 1 Essex Court, Temple, EC4Y 9AR. *T:* (020) 7583 2000, *Fax:* (020) 7583 0118. *E:* mgammie@oeclaw.co.uk.

**GAMON, Maj.-Gen. John Anthony,** CBE 2003; Special Project Officer Deputy Chief of Defence Staff (Health), 2005–06; *b* 13 March 1946; *s* of James Davidson Gamon and Dorothy Gamon (*née* Radford); *m* 1968, Mary Patricia Medicke; one *s* one *d. Educ:* Penlan Multilateral Sch., Swansea; Royal Dental Hosp., London (BDS 1969); Eastman Dental Inst., London (MSc 1978). MGDSRCS 1982; DRD RCSEd 1983. Gen. clinical appts, Army Dental Service, 1970–92; Deputy Director: Defence Dental Services, 1993–96; Army Dental Service, 1996–97; Director: Army Dental Service, 1997–2001; Clinical Services, 1997–99; Corporate Develt, 1999–2001, Defence Dental Agency; Dir Gen., Defence Dental Services and Chief Exec., Defence Dental Agency, 2001–05. QHDS, 1997–2006. Pres., British Soc. for Gen. Dental Surgery, 2001–02. Chm., Thames Valley Crimestoppers, 2008–12. Sec., English Fly Fishing Assoc., 2012–. FInstD 2002. *Recreations:* fly fishing, hill walking, gardening, reading. *Address:* 1 Bushmead Close, Whitchurch, Aylesbury, Bucks HP22 4SH. *Club:* Naval and Military.

**GANABA, Rt Rev. Elisey Ilia;** see Hague and Netherlands, Archbishop of The, (Russian Orthodox).

**GANDEE, Jane Sara;** Headmistress, St Swithun's School, Winchester, since 2010; *b* Welwyn Garden City, 12 May 1968; *d* of John Gandee and Sara, (Sally), Gandee; *m* 1998, Richard Morgan; one *s* two *d. Educ:* Presdales Sch.; Girton Coll., Cambridge (BA French and Spanish 1990); Open Univ. (PGCE). Accountant, 1991–93; Teacher (French and Spanish): Lord Wandsworth, Hants, 1993–95; Oakham Sch., 1995–97; Hd of Langs, Queenswood, 1997–2005; Dir of Studies, City of London Sch. for Girls, 2005–10. Gov., Twyford Sch., 2011–16. *Recreations:* running, reading, Latin America, being irritated by female stereotyping. *Address:* St Swithun's School, Alresford Road, Winchester, Hants SO21 1HA. *E:* headmistress@stswithuns.com.

**GANDER, Ryan,** OBE 2017; artist; *b* Chester, 21 May 1976; *s* of Ian Gander and Frances Gander; *m* 2010, Rebecca May Marston; two *d. Educ:* Manchester Metropolitan Univ. (BA Hons 1st Cl. Interactive Art 1999). Post-Graduate Fine Art Res. Participant, Jan van Eyck Akademie, Maastricht, 1999–2000; Post-Graduate Fine Art Participant, Rijksakademie van Beeldende Kunsten, Amsterdam, 2001–02. *Solo exhibitions* include: Internat. 3, Manchester, 2002; Stedelijk Mus. Bureau, Amsterdam, 2003, 2007; STORE, London, 2003, 2005, 2007, 2008; Annet Gellink Gall., Amsterdam, 2004, 2005, 2006, 2009, 2011, 2013, Basel, 2005, 2006; La Gallerie dans ma Poche, Leeds/London, 2004; Cornerhouse, Manchester, 2004; Museo d'Arte Moderna/Galleria d'Arte Maggiore, Bologna, 2006; Museum Moderner Kunst, Vienna, 2006, 2007; Whitechapel East Wing, 2006; CCA Wattis Inst. for Contemp. Arts, San Francisco, 2007, 2012; Daiwa Press Viewing Room, Hiroshima, 2007, 2012; Taro Nasu Gall., Tokyo, 2007, 2008, 2010, 2011, 2012, 2013; Ikon Gall., Birmingham, 2008; S London Gall., 2008; Frieze Projects, Frieze Art Fair, London, 2009; Picture This, Bristol, 2009; Lisson Gall., London, 2010, 2012, 2015, NY, 2016; Dazaifu Tenmangu, Fukuoka, 2011, 2017; Artangel, London, 2011; Ingleby Gall., Edinburgh, 2011; David Risley Gall., Copenhagen, 2012, 2015; Mostyn, Llandudno, 2013; Manchester City Gall., Manchester, 2014; 2 Willow Road, London, 2014; Centre for Contemp. Art, Derry, 2014; Australian Centre for Contemp. Art, Melbourne, 2015; Nat. Mus. of Osaka, 2017. Internat. Fellow, Arts Council of England, 2001–03; Cocheme Fellow, Byam Shaw Sch. of Art, London, 2004. Hon. DArts Manchester Metropolitan, 2015. Prix de Rome for Sculpture, Netherlands, 2003; Baloise Art Prize, 2006; ABN AMRO Art Prize, 2006; DENA Foundn Art Award, 2007; Paul Hamlyn Award, 2008; Zurich Art Prize, Haus Konstruktiv, 2009.

**GANDHI, Gopalkrishna;** Governor of West Bengal, India, 2004–09; b 22 April 1945; s of Devadas Mohandas Gandhi and Lakshmi Rajagopalachari; m Tara Ananth; two d. Educ: St Stephen's Coll., Delhi Univ. (BA Hons 1964; MA English Lit 1966). Member, Indian Administrative Service, 1968–92: various positions, Tamil Nadu, 1969–77; First Sec., Asst High Commn of India, Kandy, Sri Lanka, 1978–82; Dir of Handlooms and Textiles, Govt of Tamil Nadu, 1982–83; Sec. to Governor of Tamil Nadu, 1983–85; Sec. to Vice-Pres. of India, 1985–87; Jt Sec. to Pres. of India, 1987–92; voluntary retirement, 1992; Minister (Culture) and Dir, Nehru Centre, London, 1992–96; High Comr in S Africa, 1996–97; Sec. to Pres. of India, 1997–2000; High Comr in Sri Lanka, 2000–02; Ambassador to Norway, 2002–04. Chairman: Kalakshetra Foundn, Chennai, 2011–14; Indian Inst. of Advanced Studies, 2012–14. Sen. Fellow, Centre for Public Affairs and Critical Theory, New Delhi, 2014–15. Hon. Distinguished Prof., Indian Inst. of Technol. Madras, 2011–; Distinguished Prof., Ashoka Univ., 2015–. Hon. LLD Natal, 1999; Hon. DLitt: Peradeniya, Kandy, 2001; Calcutta, 2019. Lal Bahadur Shastri Award, Lal Bahadur Shastri Inst. of Management, 2016; Sarvepalli Radhakrishnan Award, Univ. of Mysore, 2016. Publications: Saranam (novel), 1985, reprinted as Refuge, 1987; Dara Shukoh (play), 1993; (ed) The Oxford Gandhi, 2008; (ed) A Frank Friendship, 2008; Of a Certain Age: twenty life sketches, 2012; (ed) My Dear Bapu: letters from Rajagopalachari to Gandhi, 2012; Abolishing the Death Penalty, 2016; translations: Hindustani, Seth, A Suitable Boy, 1998; English, Tirukkural, 2015. Clubs: India International Centre (New Delhi); Chennai International Centre (Chennai); Madras Boat.

**GANDHI, Sonia;** MP (Congress) Raebareli, UP, Lok Sabha, 2004–March 2006 and since May 2006 (MP for Amethi, 1999–2004); Chair, United Progressive Alliance, since 2004; President, Indian National Congress Party, 1998–2017; b Italy, 9 Dec. 1947; adopted Indian nationality, 1983; d of Stefano and Paola Maino; m 1968, Rajiv Gandhi (d 1991); one s one d. Educ: language sch., Cambridge; Art restoration course, Nat. Gall. of Modern Art, New Delhi. Pres., Rajiv Gandhi Foundn. Mem., Congress Party, 1997–. Leader of the Opposition, Lok Sabha, 1999–2004. Publications: (ed) Freedom's Daughter, 1989; (ed) Two Alone, Two Together, 1992; Rajiv, 1992; Rajiv's World, 1994. Address: 10 Janpath, New Delhi 110011, India; All India Congress Committee, 24 Akbar Road, New Delhi 110011, India.

**GANDY, David James;** model; b London; s of Christopher and Brenda Gandy. Educ: Billericay Sch.; Gloucestershire Univ. Modelling contracts with: Dolce & Gabbana, 2006–, incl. Light Blue fragrance campaign, 2007, Light Blue 2, 2009; Martini, 2011; M&S, 2012; magazine covers include: V Man, by Mario Testino, 2008; L'Optimum, GQ, 2011. Creator, David Gandy Men's Style Guide app, 2010. Designer, underwear and nightwear collection with Marks and Spencer, 2014. Fashion Ambassador, Comic Relief, 2012. Face of Today Award, Shortlist, 2011. Relevant publication: David by Dolce & Gabbana, 2011. Recreations: car racing, ski-ing. T: (Monsta PR) 07958 458733. E: charl@monsta.biz.

**GANDY, David Stewart,** CB 1989; OBE 1981; Consultant, Pannone and Partners, solicitors, since 1993; Deputy Director of Public Prosecutions and Chief Executive, Crown Prosecution Service, 1987–93; b 19 Sept. 1932; s of Percy Gandy and Elizabeth Mary (née Fox); m 1956, Mabel Sheldon; one s one d. Educ: Manchester Grammar Sch.; Manchester Univ. Nat. Service, Intell. Corps (Germany and Austria), 1954–56. Admitted Solicitor, 1954; Asst Solicitor, Town Clerk, Manchester, 1956–59; Chief Prosecuting Solicitor: Manchester, 1959–68; Manchester and Salford, 1968–74; Gtr Manchester, 1974–85; Head of Field Management, Crown Prosecution Service, 1985–87; Acting DPP, Oct. 1991–May 1992. Mem., Home Office Assessment Consultancy Unit, 1993–2005. Mem. Council, Criminal Law Solicitors Assoc., 1992–2001. Lect. tour on English Criminal Justice System, for Amer. Bar Assoc., USA and Canada, 1976; Lecturer: UN Asia and FE Inst. for Prevention of Crime and Treatment of Offenders, Tokyo, 1990, 1995; Internat. Congress of Criminal Lawyers on Penal Reform, La Plata, 1995. Law Society: Mem., Criminal Law Standing Cttee, 1969–97 (Vice Chm., 1995–96); Mem., Council, 1984–96; Prosecuting Solicitors' Society of England and Wales: Mem., Exec. Council, 1966–85; Pres., 1976–78; Chm., Heads of Office, 1982–83; President: Manchester Law Soc., 1980–81; Manchester and Dist Medico-Legal Soc., 1982–84; Manchester Trainee Lawyers Gp, 1982–84. Non-exec. Dir, Mancunian Community Health NHS Trust, 1993–98. Mem. Council, Order of St John, 1978–85. Recreations: cricket, theatre, bridge, walking. Address: The Ridgeway, Broad Lane, Hale, Altrincham, Cheshire WA15 0DD.

**GANE, Barrie Charles,** CMG 1988; OBE 1978; HM Diplomatic Service, retired; Director Group Research, Group 4 Securitas, 1993–2000; b 19 Sept. 1935; s of Charles Ernest Gane and Margaret Gane; m 1974, Jennifer Anne Pitt; two d of former marriage. Educ: King Edward's School, Birmingham; Corpus Christi College, Cambridge. MA. Foreign Office, 1960; served Vientiane, Kuching and Warsaw; First Sec., Kampala, 1967; FCO, 1970; First Sec., later Counsellor, seconded to HQ British Forces, Hong Kong, 1977; Counsellor, FCO, 1982–92. Recreations: walking, reading. Club: Brooks's.

**GANE, Michael,** DPhil, MA; economic and environmental consultant; b 29 July 1927; s of late Rudolf E. Gane and Helen Gane; m 1954, Madge Stewart Taylor; one d. Educ: Colyton Grammar Sch., Devon; Edinburgh Univ. (BSc Forestry 1948); London Univ. (BSc Econ 1963); Oxford Univ. (DPhil, MA 1967). Asst Conservator of Forests, Tanganyika, 1948–62; Sen. Research Officer, Commonwealth Forestry Inst., Oxford, 1963–69; Dir, Project Planning Centre for Developing Countries, Bradford Univ., 1969–74; Dir, England, Nature Conservancy Council, 1974–81. Publications: Forest Strategy, 2007; various contribs to scientific and technical jls. Recreations: natural history, gardening. Address: Coast Watchers Cottage, 6 Avalanche Road, Southwell, Portland, Dorset DT5 2DJ.

**GANELLIN, (Charon) Robin,** PhD, DSc; FRS 1986; CSci; CChem, FRSC; Smith Kline and French Professor of Medicinal Chemistry, University College London, 1986–2002, now Emeritus; b 25 Jan. 1934; s of Leon Ganellin and Beila Cluer; m 1st, 1956, Tamara Greene (d 1997); one s one d; 2nd, 2003, Dr Monique Garbarg (née Lehmann). Educ: Harrow County Grammar School for Boys; Queen Mary Coll., London Univ. (BSc, PhD, DSc; Fellow, QMW, 1992). FRSC 1968; CChem 1976; CSci 2003. Res. Associate, MIT, 1960; Res. chemist, then Dept Hd in Medicinal Chem., Smith Kline & French Labs Ltd, 1958–59, 1961–75; Smith Kline & French Research Ltd: Dir, Histamine Res., 1975–80; Vice-President: Research, 1980–84; Chem. Res., 1984–86. Hon. Lectr, Dept of Pharmacol., UCL, 1975–86; Hon. Prof. of Medicinal Chem., Univ. of Kent at Canterbury, 1979–89. Co-inventor, cimetidine (Tagamet), 1975, and pitolisant (Wakix), 2001. Tilden Lectr and Medal, 1982, Adrien Albert Lectr and Medal, 1999, RSC. Pres., Section on Medicinal Chemistry, 2000–01, Chm., Subcttee on Medicinal Chem. and Drug Develt, IUPAC, 2002–12 (Emeritus Fellow, Chem. and Human Health Div. VII, IUPAC, 2014); Chm., Soc. for Drug Res., 1985–87; Hon. Member: Soc. Española de Quimica Terapeutica, 1982; European Histamine Res. Soc., 2007; Corresp. Academician, Real Academia Nacional de Farmacia, Spain, 2006. Hon. DSc Aston, 1995. Medicinal Chem. Award, RSC, 1977; Prix Charles Mentzer, Soc. de Chimie Therap., 1978; Div. of Medicinal Chem. Award, ACS, 1980; Messel Medal, SCI, 1988; Award for Drug Discovery, Soc. for Drug Res., 1989; USA Nat. Inventors' Hall of Fame, 1990; Nauta Prize for Pharmacochem., European Fedn for Medicinal Chem., 2004; Pratesi Gold Medal, Medicinal Chem. Div., Italian Chem. Soc., 2006; ACS Div. of Medicinal Chem. Hall of Fame, 2007; RSC—Biol and Medicinal Chem. Sector Hall of Fame, 2019. Publications: Pharmacology of Histamine Receptors, 1982; Frontiers in Histamine Research, 1985; Dictionary of Drugs, 1990; (jtly) Medicinal Chemistry, 1993; Dictionary of Pharmacological Agents, 1997; (with J. Fischer) Analogue-based Drug Discovery, 2006, vol. II, 2010, vol. III, 2013; Practical Studies in Medicinal Chemistry, 2007; (ed jtly) Introduction to Biological and Small Molecule Drug Research and Development, 2013; res. papers and reviews in various jls, incl. Jl Med. Chem., Jl Chem. Soc., Brit. Jl Pharmacol. Recreations: music, sailing, walking. Address: Department of Chemistry, University College London, 20 Gordon Street, WC1H 0AJ.

**GANI, Prof. David,** DPhil; CChem, FRSC; FRSE; Music Producer, Dave Am I Recordings, since 2018; Deputy Principal, University of Strathclyde, 2009–12; Chief Executive, Glasgow City of Science, 2011–13 (on secondment, 2011–12); b 29 Sept. 1957; one s two d. Educ: Sussex Univ. (BSc; DPhil 1983). Technician, Wellcome Res. Labs, 1974–76; Southampton University: Royal Soc. Res. Fellow and Lectr in Organic Chem., 1983–89; Sen. Lectr, 1989–90; St Andrews University: Prof. of Chemistry, 1990–98; Purdie Prof., and Res. Dir, Sch. of Chemistry, 1997–98; Dir, Centre for Biomolecular Sci, 1995–98; Prof. of Organic Chem., Birmingham Univ., 1998–2001 (Hon. Prof. of Organic Chem., 2001–09); Dir of Res. Policy, Scottish Funding Councils for Further and Higher Educn, later Dir of Res. Policy and Strategy, SFC, 2002–09. Mem., Strategy Bd, BBSRC, 1997–2002. Trustee and Governor, CRAC Ltd, 2011–18. Prog. Dir, UK-Gulf States Policy Dialogue on Res. and Innovation, UK Govt-British Council, 2010–12. Chm., Council for Doctoral Educn, Eur. Univs Assoc., 2011–12; Exec. Chair, ScotCHEM, 2010–13. Publications: (jtly) Enzymic Catalysis, 1991; over 150 articles and patents on organic and medicinal chemistry. Address: CRAC Ltd, 22 Signet Court, Swanns Road, Cambridge CB5 8LA.

**GANT, Andrew John,** PhD; composer; Organist, Choirmaster and Composer, Chapels Royal, 2000–13; b 6 Aug. 1963; s of John Gant and Vivien Gant (née Christian); m 1992, Prof. Katherine Jane Willis, qv; two s one d. Educ: Radley Coll.; St John's Coll., Cambridge (Choral Schol.; BA 1984; MA 1994); Royal Acad. of Music (MMus 1993; ARAM 2003); PhD Goldsmiths Coll., London 2000. Lay Vicar, Westminster Abbey, 1988–90; Dir of Music in Chapel, Selwyn Coll., Cambridge, 1993–98; Organist and Master of Choir, Royal Military Chapel, Wellington Barracks, 1997–2000. Tutor in Music, Univ. of Oxford, 1998–. Compositions include: May We Borrow Your Husband (opera), 1999; (with Andrew Motion) A Hymn for the Golden Jubilee, 2002; The Vision of Piers Ploughman (oratorio), 2002; A Good-Night (anthem), 2002. Mem. (Lib Dem) Oxford CC, 2014–. Publications: Christmas Carols, 2014; O Sing Unto The Lord: a history of English church music, 2015. Recreations: golf, walking, cycling. Address: 55 Middle Way, Summertown, Oxford OX2 7LE. T: (01865) 558841. E: andrew.gant@btopenworld.com.

**GANT, Diana Jillian;** Headmistress, Mount School, York, 2001–09; b 25 April 1948; d of John Edward Wakeham Scutt and Lucy Helen Scutt; m 1969, Rev. Canon Brian Leonard Gant; two d. Educ: Harrow Co. Grammar Sch. for Girls; King's Coll. London (BD Hons 1970); Christ Ch Coll., Canterbury (PGCE 1973). Various teaching posts, 1973–84; Hd of Religious Studies, King's Sch., Worcester, 1984–89; Hd of Careers and Dep. Hd of 6th Form, Tonbridge GS for Girls, 1989–95; Dep. Headmistress, Norwich High Sch. for Girls (GDST), 1995–2000. Governor: York St John Univ. (formerly Coll., then UC), 2005–14; Univ. of Worcester, 2015–. Recreations: walking, cooking, reading. Address: 122 Henwick Road, Worcester WR2 5PB. E: dianajgant@gmail.com.

**GANT, John,** CB 2003; Chairman, NHS Leicestershire County and Rutland (formerly Leicestershire County and Rutland Primary Care Trust), 2006–10; b 25 Feb. 1944; s of William and Barbara Gant; m 1967, Annette Sonia Cobb; two s. Educ: Univ. of Newcastle upon Tyne (BA Hons French and German). Inland Revenue: Inspector of Taxes, 1966; Dist Inspector, 1972–74; Head Office Adviser, 1974–77; Dist Inspector, 1977–81; Group Controller, 1981–83; Asst Dir, Ops, 1983–88; Regl Controller, 1988–90; Dep. Dir, Ops, 1990–92; Dir of Human Resources, 1992–2000; Dir of Finance, 2000–03. Mem., Audit Cttee, Statistics Commn, 2004–08. Chm., Melton, Rutland and Harborough PCT, 2003–06. Recreations: opera, ballet, theatre, travel, horse racing, importing and enjoying wine. Address: PO Box 9378, Melton Mowbray LE13 9DT.

**GANT, Katherine Jane;** see Willis, K. J.

**GAO XINGJIAN;** writer, artist and film maker; b Ganzhou, Jiangxi Province, China, 4 Jan. 1940. Formerly translator: China Reconstructs mag.; Chinese Writers' Assoc. Left China, 1987; now a French citizen. Solo and group exhibns and works in public collections in Europe, Asia and USA. Films include: Silhouette/Shadow, 2003; After the Flood, 2009; Requiem for Beauty, 2013. Nobel Prize for Literature, 2000. Chevalier de l'Ordre des Arts et des Lettres (France), 1992. Publications: A Preliminary Discussion of the Art of Modern Fiction, 1981; A Pigeon Called Red Beak, 1985; In Search of a Modern Form of Dramatic Representation, 1987; Gao Xingjian: aesthetics and creation, 2012; L'Art d'un homme libre, 2017; novels: Soul Mountain, 1999; One Man's Bible, 2002; stories: Buying a Fishing Rod for My Father, 2004; plays: Signal Alarm, 1982; Bus Stop, 1983; Wild Man, 1985; Collected Plays, 1985; The Other Shore, 1986; Fugitives; Summer Rain in Peking; articles in jls.

**GAPES, Michael John;** MP for Ilford South, since 1992 (Lab and Co-op, 1992–2019; Ind Gp for Change (formerly Change UK), since 2019); b 4 Sept. 1952; s of late Frank William Gapes and of Emily Florence Gapes (née Jackson). Educ: Staples Road Infants' Sch., Loughton; Manford County Primary Sch., Chigwell; Buckhurst Hill County High Sch., Essex; Fitzwilliam Coll., Cambridge (MA Hons Econs 1975); Middlesex Polytechnic (Dip. Indust. Relations and Trade Union Studies 1976). VSO teacher, Swaziland, 1971–72; Sec., Cambridge Students' Union, 1973–74; Chm., Nat. Orgn of Labour Students, 1976–77. Admin. Officer, Middlesex Hosp., 1977; Nat. Student Organiser, Lab. Party, 1977–80; Res. Officer, Internat. Dept, Lab. Party, 1980–88; Sen. Internat. Officer, Lab. Party, 1988–92. Contested (Lab) Ilford North, 1983. PPS to Minister of State: NI Office, 1997–99; Home Office, 2001–02. Member: Foreign Affairs Select Cttee, 1992–97, 2010– (Chm., 2005–10); Defence Select Cttee, 1999–2001, 2003–05; Treas., 2010–13, Vice Chm., 2013–, British Gp, IPU; Chairman: UN All Party Parly Gp, 1997–2001, 2015–; All Party Crossrail Gp, 2005–; Vice-Chm., All Party Parly Gp against Anti-Semitism, 1992–2005; Member: All Party Pakistan Gp, 1998; All Party Gp for the Tamils, 2009; Co-Chm., All Party EU Gp, 2010–12; Chm., PLP Children and Families' Cttee, 1994–95; Vice-Chm., PLP Defence Cttee, 1992–95 and 1996–97. Dep. Chm., Labour Friends of Israel, 1997–2005; Member: Labour Nat. Policy Forum, 1998–2005; Labour Friends of India, 1999–2019, of Palestine and the ME, 2009–19, of the Czech Republic, 2012–19; Labour ME Council, 2002–05. Mem., NATO Parly Assembly, 2002–05, 2010–. Chm., Westminster Foundn for Democracy, 2002–05. Member: Unite the Union; Co-operative Party. Member, Council: RIIA, 1996–99; VSO, 1997–2011. Vice Pres., Valentines Park Conservationists, 1998–2010; Member: Friends of Valentines Mansion, 2009–; Friends of Ilford Hosp. Chapel, 2000–. Publications: co-author of books on defence policy; Labour Party and Fabian Society pamphlets. Recreations: blues and jazz music, supporting West Ham United FC. Address: House of Commons, SW1A 0AA.

**GAPPER, Nicola Ann;** see Mackintosh, N. A.

**GARB, Prof. Tamar,** PhD; FBA 2014; Durning Lawrence Professor in the History of Art, since 2001, and Director, Institute of Advanced Studies, University College London. *Educ:* Univ. of Cape Town (BA Art 1978); Inst. of Educn, Univ. of London (MA Art Educn 1980); Courtauld Inst. of Art (MA Art Hist. 1982; PhD 1991). Lectr, Courtauld Inst. of Art, 1988; University College London: Lectr, 1989–95; Reader, 1995–2001. Curator of exhibns incl. Figures and Fictions: Contemporary South African Photography, V&A, 2011. *Publications:* Women Impressionists, 1986; Sisters of the Brush, 1994; (with K. Adler) Berthe Morisot, 1995; Bodies of Modernity: figure and flesh in fin de siècle France, 1998; The Unquiet Image: the paintings of Vivienne Koorland, 1998; The Painted Face: portraits of women in France, 1814–1914, 2007; The Body in Time: figures of femininity in late nineteenth-century France, 2008. *Address:* Department of History of Art, University College London, Gower Street, WC1E 6BT.

**GARBETT, Mark Edward;** Headteacher, Latymer School, 2005–15; *b* 14 May 1957; *s* of Edward and Mary Garbett; two *d*. *Educ:* Tividale Sch.; Selwyn Coll., Cambridge (BA Maths 1978; PGCE); Open Univ. (MEd). NPQH. Hd of Maths and Housemaster, Framlingham Coll., 1986–91; Hd of Maths and ICT, Royal Belfast Academical Instn, 1991–97; Dep. Head, Skegness GS, 1997–2000; Head, Stretford GS, 2000–05. *Recreations:* Solent sailing, running, playing piano, tennis.

**GARBUTT, Graham Bernard;** Chief Executive, Commission for Rural Communities, 2006–09; Visiting Professor of Governance and Development, University of the West of England, since 2010; *b* 16 June 1947; *s* of Alfred Garbutt and Rhoda Garbutt (*née* Jones); *m* 1986, Lyda Patricia Jadresić, MD; one *s* two *d*. *Educ:* Grove Sch., Market Drayton; Univ. of Bath (BSc 1970; BArch (1st cl.) 1972); Univ. of Sheffield (MA Town and Regl Planning 1974). Urban Renewal Co-ordinator, Haringey BC, 1974–80; Policy and Prog. Planning Officer, Hackney BC, 1980–87; Dir, S Canning Town and Custom House Project, Newham BC, 1987–90; Chief Exec., Gloucester CC, 1990–2001; Regl Dir, Govt Office for W Midlands, ODPM, 2001–05 (Chairman: Eur. Prog. Monitoring Cttee, 2001–05; Regl Housing Bd, 2004–05; Regl Resilience Forum, 2004–05); Chief Exec., Countryside Agency, 2005–06. Planning and housing consultant, Nigeria, 1976–77. Vis. Lectr, AA Grad. Sch., London, 1976–82. England rep., 2002–, Pres., 2004–05, European Assoc. of State Territorial Reps; Advr to OECD territorial review of Chile, 2008–09; Vice-Pres. and UK Rep., Entretiens Universitaires Réguliers pour l'Administration en Europe univs network, 2011–. Ind. Chm., Cheltenham Develt Task Force, 2010–; Chm., Ind. Inquiry into Cotswold Water Park, 2011–12; Chair, Neighbourhood Develt Plan steering gp, Tewkesbury Parishes, 2014–17. Patron, Friends of CAB, Cheltenham, 2010–12. *Recreations:* family, stone and wood sculpture, visual arts, architecture, travel, garden. *Address:* University of the West of England, Faculty of Environment and Technology, Frenchay Campus, Coldharbour Lane, Bristol BS16 1QY. *E:* graham.garbutt@uwe.ac.uk.

**GARDAM, Jane Mary,** OBE 2009; novelist; *d* of William Pearson, Coatham Sch., Redcar and Kathleen Mary Pearson (*née* Helm); *m* 1954, David Hill Gardam, QC (*d* 2010); two *s* (one *d* decd). *Educ:* Saltburn High Sch. for Girls; Bedford Coll., London Univ. Red Cross Travelling Librarian, Hospital Libraries, 1951; Sub-Editor, Weldon's Ladies Jl, 1952; Asst Literary Editor, Time and Tide, 1952–54. FRSL 1976. Hon. DLitt: Teesside, 2003; Royal Holloway, 2010. Heywood Hill Award for lifetime's contrib. to enjoyment of books, 2000. *Publications:* A Long Way From Verona, 1971 (Phoenix Award, Children's Literature Assoc., 1991); The Summer After The Funeral, 1973; Bilgewater, 1977; God on the Rocks, 1978 (Prix Baudelaire, 1989; televised, 1992); The Hollow Land (Whitbread Literary Award), 1981; Bridget and William, 1981; Horse, 1982; Kit, 1983; Crusoe's Daughter, 1985; Kit in Boots, 1986; Swan, 1987; Through the Doll's House Door, 1987; The Queen of the Tambourine (Whitbread Novel Award), 1991; Faith Fox, 1996; Tufty Bear, 1996; The Green Man, 1998; The Flight of the Maidens, 2000; Old Filth, 2004; The Man in the Wooden Hat, 2009; Last Friends, 2013; *non-fiction:* The Iron Coast, 1994; *short stories:* A Few Fair Days, 1971; Black Faces, White Faces (David Higham Award, Winifred Holtby Award), 1975; The Sidmouth Letters, 1980; The Pangs of Love, 1983 (Katherine Mansfield Award, 1984); Showing the Flag, 1989; Going into a Dark House, 1994; Missing the Midnight, 1997; The People on Privilege Hill, 2007; The Stories, 2014. *Address:* Haven House, 29 Harnet Street, Sandwich, Kent CT13 9ES. *Club:* PEN.

*See also* T. D. Gardam.

**GARDAM, Timothy David;** Chief Executive, Nuffield Foundation, since 2016; *b* 14 Jan. 1956; *s* of David Hill Gardam, QC and of Jane Mary Gardam, *qv*; *m* 1982, Kim Scott Walwyn (*d* 2002); one *d*; one *d* with Prof. Helen Wenda Small, *qv*. *Educ:* Westminster Sch.; Gonville and Caius Coll., Cambridge (MA). Joined BBC as trainee researcher, 1977; Asst Producer, Nationwide, 1977–79; Producer, Newsnight, 1979–82; Executive Producer: Timewatch, 1982–85; Bookmark, 1984–85; Dep. Editor, Election Programmes, 1985–87; Editor: Panorama, 1987–90; Newsnight, 1990–93; Hd, Weekly Programmes, BBC News and Current Affairs, 1993–96; Controller, News, Current Affairs and Documentaries, Channel Five, 1996–98; Dir of Programmes, 1998–2002, Dir of Television, 2002–03, Channel 4; Principal, St Anne's Coll., Oxford, 2014–16. Non-exec. Dir, OFCOM, 2008–15 (Chm., Content Bd, 2012–15). University of Oxford: Chm., Reuters Inst. for Study of Journalism, 2006–16; Chm., Admissions Exec., 2009–11. Dir, Oxford Playhouse, 2005–10. Chm., Voltaire Foundn, 2005–09. Chair, Which? (Consumers' Assoc.), 2015–. *Recreations:* history, gardens. *Address:* Nuffield Foundation, 28 Bedford Square, WC1B 3JS.

**GARDEN,** family name of **Baroness Garden of Frognal**.

**GARDEN OF FROGNAL,** Baroness *cr* 2007 (Life Peer), of Hampstead, in the London Borough of Camden; **Susan Elizabeth Garden;** PC 2015; *b* 22 Feb. 1944; *d* of late Henry George Button, author, and Edith Margaret Heslop; *m* 1965, Timothy Garden (later Baron Garden (Life Peer), KCB) (*d* 2007); two *d*. *Educ:* Westonbirt Sch., Glos; St Hilda's Coll., Oxford (BA 1965; MA 1982). Secondary sch. teacher in UK and Germany; City and Guilds of London Institute, 1988–2008: Manager, 1990–2000; consultant, 2000–08. Chm., ASM, St Hilda's Coll., Oxford, 1996–2000; Trustee, Oxford Univ. Soc., 2001–08 (Vice-Chm., 2005–08). Contested (Lib Dem) Finchley and Golders Green, 2005. Lib Dem Spokesman on univs and skills, H of L, 2009–10; government spokesman: DCMS (sport, Olympics, media), DfE, BIS (higher educn), 2010–12; BIS (HE and Skills), DfE, MoD, 2012–13; women and equalities, educn, DEFRA, 2014–15; a Baroness in Waiting (Govt Whip), 2010–13 and 2014–15; a Dep. Speaker, 2015–. Pres., Camden Lib Dems, 2008–. Mem., Co. of World Traders, 2008– (Master, 2008–09). Mem. Council, Air League, 2012–. Dir, UK-Japan 21st Century Gp, 2013–. CAB Advr, 1982–87; Pres., Relate, Central Middx, 1997–2002; SSAFA Caseworker, 2001–05; Vice-Pres., War Widows Assoc., 2014–. Patron, Hampstead Counselling Service, 2009–. Vice-Pres., C&G, 2018–. Fellow, Birkbeck, Univ. of London, 2019. FRSA 1993; FCGI 2010. Hon. FCIL 2012. *Address:* House of Lords, SW1A 0PW. *E:* gardens@parliament.uk, sue.garden@blueyonder.co.uk. *Clubs:* National Liberal, Royal Air Force.

**GARDEN, Ian Harrison;** barrister in private practice, 1989–2012; *b* 18 June 1961; *s* of late Norman Harrison Garden and Jean Elizabeth Garden; *m* 1986, Alexandra Helen Grounds; two *s*. *Educ:* Sedbergh Sch.; UC Wales, Aberystwyth (LLB Hons 1982). Dep. Chancellor, Dio. of Sheffield, 1999–2013. Mem., Gen. Synod, C of E, 1995–2005 (Member: Legislative Cttee, 1996–2000; Legal Adv. Commn, 2001–11); Member: Bishop's Council and Standing Cttee, Dio. of Blackburn, 1996–2004; Crown Appts, then Crown Nominations, Commn, 1997–2005; Archbishops' Council, 2000–05; C of E Appts Cttee, 2001–05; Dio. of Blackburn Vacancy-in-See Cttee, 2001–15 (Chm., 2001–10). Lay Canon, Blackburn Cathedral, 2003–. Member, Appeals Tribunal Panels, 1996–2001: Pastoral Measure (1983); Incumbents (Vacation of Benefices) Measure (1977); Ordination of Women (Financial Provisions) Measure (1993). Director: Walsingham Coll. Trust Assoc., 1999–2013; Walsingham Coll. (Yorks Properties) Ltd, 2001–14; Mem. Bd Dirs, Manchester Camerata Ltd, 2003–09. Guardian, Shrine of Our Lady of Walsingham, 1996–2013. Gov., Quainton Hall Sch., Harrow, 1999–2001. *Recreations:* orchestral and choral conducting, organ playing, driving classic cars on the continent, golf. *Address:* Old Church Cottage, 29 Church Road, Rufford, near Ormskirk, Lancs L40 1TA. *T:* (01704) 821303.

**GARDEN, James;** *see* Garden, O. J.

**GARDEN, Malcolm;** Sheriff of Grampian, Highland and Islands at Aberdeen, 2008–17; *b* 7 Aug. 1952; *s* of George Garden and Phillippa Mary Hills or Garden; *m* 1984, Sandra Moles; two *s* one *d*. *Educ:* Robert Gordon's Coll., Aberdeen; Univ. of Aberdeen (LLB). NP 1976. Apprentice, then Asst Solicitor, Watt and Cumine, Aberdeen, 1973–76; Asst Solicitor, 1976–79, Partner, 1979–2001, Clark-Wallace, Aberdeen; Temp. Sheriff, 1994–99; Sheriff (pt-time), 2000–01; Sheriff, Grampian Highland and Islands at Peterhead, 2001–08. Tutor (pt-time), Univ. of Aberdeen, 1980–85. Mem., Aberdeen and NE Legal Aid Cttee, 1984–86; Reporter to Scottish Legal Aid Bd, 1986–96. Member: Law Soc. of Scotland, 1976–; Soc. of Advocates, Aberdeen, 1978–. *Recreations:* family, golf, football, tennis.

**GARDEN, Prof. (Olivier) James,** CBE 2014; MD; FRCSEd, FRCPEd, FRSE; Regius Professor of Clinical Surgery, 2000–18, Director of Edinburgh Surgery Online Programmes (formerly Masters in Surgical Sciences), since 2007, and Dean International, since 2016, University of Edinburgh; Surgeon to the Queen in Scotland, 2004–18; *b* 13 Nov. 1953; *s* of late James Garden, OBE and Marguerite Marie Jeanne Garden (*née* Vourch); *m* 1977, Amanda Gillian Merrills; one *s* one *d*. *Educ:* Lanark Grammar Sch.; Univ. of Edinburgh (BSc 1974; MB ChB 1977; MD 1988). FRCSGlas 1981; FRCSEd 1994; FRCPEd 2003; FRSE 2013. Lectr in Surgery, Univ. of Glasgow, 1985; Chef de Clinique, Univ. de Paris-Sud, 1986–88; University of Edinburgh: Sen. Lectr in Surgery, 1988–98; Prof. of Hepatobiliary Surgery, 1998–2000; Head: Dept of Clin. and Surgical Scis, 1999–2003; Sch. of Clin. Scis and Community Health, 2003–06. Hon. Consultant Surgeon: Royal Infirmary of Edinburgh, 1988–2018; and Head, Scottish Liver Transplant Unit, 1992–2006. Ext. Examr, univs incl. Glasgow, Newcastle, Bristol, Hong Kong, Dublin, Oxford, Singapore, Malaysia. Member: James IV Assoc. of Surgeons, 1996– (Hon. Sec., 1999–2018; Vice Pres., 2018–20); Assoc. Upper Gastrointestinal Surgeons, 1996– (Pres., 2002–04); Internat. Hepato-Pancreato-Biliary Assoc., 1998–2006 (Pres., 2012–14); Pres., Internat. Surgical Gp, 2016–17. Chm., British Jl of Surgery Soc. Ltd, 2012–19 (Co. Sec., 2003–12). Ed. in Chief, HPB, 2009–18. Vice Chm., Edinburgh World Heritage Trust, 2015–. Hon. Mem., Amer. Surgical Assoc., 2010. Hon. FRACS 2007; Hon. FRCSCan 2008; Hon. FACS 2014; Hon. FRCS 2014; Hon. FCSHK 2015; Hon. FRCSI 2015. Hon. DSc Glasgow, 2019. *Publications:* Principles and Practice of Surgical Laparoscopy, 1994; Intraoperative and Laparoscopic Ultrasonography, 1995; Color Atlas of Surgical Diagnosis, 1995; A Companion to Specialist Surgical Practice (7 vols), 1997, 6th edn 2018; Liver Metastasis: biology, diagnosis and treatment, 1998; Principles and Practice of Surgery, 2000, 7th edn 2018; General Surgery: principles and international practice (2 vols), 2009; numerous contribs to surgical and gastroenterological jls. *Recreations:* ski-ing, golf, food, wine, arts, heritage. *Address:* 22 Moston Terrace, Edinburgh EH9 2DE. *T:* (0131) 667 3715. *Club:* New (Edinburgh).

**GARDINER OF KIMBLE,** Baron *cr* 2010 (Life Peer), of Kimble in the County of Buckinghamshire; **John Eric Gardiner;** Parliamentary Under-Secretary of State, Department for Environment, Food and Rural Affairs, since 2016; *b* London, 17 March 1956; *s* of Anthony Ernest Fiddes Gardiner and Heather Joan Gardiner (*née* Robarts); *m* 2004, Olivia Mirabel, sculptor, *e d* of Sir Richard Musgrave, 7th Bt. *Educ:* Uppingham Sch.; Royal Holloway Coll., Univ. of London (BA Mod. History and Politics). Farmer; Partner, C. M. Robarts and Son, 1992–. Countryside Alliance: Dir, Political Affairs, 1995–2004; Dep. Chief Exec., 2004–10; Bd Mem. and Exec. Dir, 2010–12. Chm., FACE (Fedn of Assocs for Hunting and Conservation) (UK), 1998–2012; Treas. Gen., FACE (Europe), 2000–12. Private Sec. to Chm., Cons. Party, 1989–95. A Lord in Waiting (Govt Whip), 2012–15; H of L Spokesperson for DCMS, 2012–15; for DEFRA, 2015–16; H of L Whip for Cabinet Office and DECC, 2012–15; Captain of the Yeoman of the Guard (Dep. Chief Whip, H of L), 2015–16. Mem., Select Cttee on HIV and Aids in UK, 2011. Cons. Party Whip, 2011–12; Cons. Dep. Chief Whip, 2013–15. Chm., Vale of Aylesbury with Garth and S Berks Hunt, 1992–2006. Pres., Bucks Agricl Assoc., 2007. *Recreations:* hunting, gardening. *Address:* House of Lords, SW1A 0PW. *E:* gardinerj@parliament.uk. *Club:* Pratt's.

**GARDINER, Barry Strachan;** MP (Lab) Brent North, since 1997; *b* 10 March 1957; *s* of late John Flannegan Gardiner and Sylvia Jean Strachan; *m* 1979, Caroline Anne Smith; three *s* one *d*. *Educ:* Haileybury; St Andrews Univ. (MA Hons). Corpus Christi Coll., Cambridge. ACII. Scottish Sec., SCM, 1979–81. John F. Kennedy Schol., Harvard Univ., 1983; General Average Adjuster, 1987–97. Parliamentary Under-Secretary of State: NI Office, 2004–05; DTI, 2005–06; DEFRA, 2006–07. Prime Minister's Special Envoy for Forests, 2007–08; Leader of Opposition's Special Envoy for Climate Change and the Envmt, 2010–13; Shadow Minister for Natural Envmt, 2013–15, for Energy and Climate Change, 2015–16; Shadow Sec. of State for Energy and Climate Change, 2016; Shadow Minister for Internat. Climate Change, 2016–17; Shadow Sec. of State for Internat. Trade, 2016–. Vice Pres., Europe, GLOBE Internat. AISBL. *Publications:* articles in Philosophical Qly, Science, Nature, Climate Change, Lloyd's List, Insurance Internat. *Recreations:* music, bird watching, hill walking. *Address:* House of Commons, SW1A 0AA.

**GARDINER, Elizabeth Anne Finlay,** CB 2013; First Parliamentary Counsel, and Permanent Secretary of the Government in Parliament Group, Cabinet Office, since 2015; *b* 19 March 1966; *m* 1990, Alan Gardiner; one *s* one *d*. *Educ:* Edinburgh Univ. (LLB 1987; DLP). Admitted as solicitor, Scotland, 1990, England and Wales, 1991; Asst Parly Counsel, 1991–95; Sen. Asst Parly Counsel, 1995–2000; Dep. Parly Counsel, 2000–03; Parly Counsel, 2003–15. Hon. Bencher, Lincoln's Inn, 2018. *Address:* Office of the Parliamentary Counsel, Cabinet Office, 1 Horse Guards Road, SW1A 2HQ. *T:* (020) 7276 6541.

**GARDINER, George;** Director General, 2007, Head of Delivery for Land and Maritime, 2008–11, Intelligence Surveillance Target Acquisition and Reconnaissance Capability, Ministry of Defence; *b* 25 Oct. 1955; *s* of George Gardiner and Isabella Colquhoun Gardiner; *m* 1981, Colleen May Holbrow; three *d*. *Educ:* Paisley Grammar Sch. MoD, 1974–2011: Asst Dir, Above Water Secretariat, 1991–92; Principal (Finance and Secretariat), Military Communications Systems, 1992–94; jsdc (No. 17), 1994; Asst Dir, Commercial Policy, 1996–98; Hd, Secretariat Smart Procurement Implementation Team, 1999; Dir, Commercial Policy, 2000; Support Dir IJ, 2002–04; Dir, Information Systems, 2004–06. *Recreations:* creating electronic music, shooting, fly fishing. *Address:* Ashperton, Herefordshire HR8 2SW. *E:* gardiner.g@btinternet.com.

**GARDINER, Sir John Eliot**, Kt 1998; CBE 1990; conductor; Founder and Artistic Director, English Baroque Soloists, Monteverdi Choir, and Orchestre Révolutionnaire et Romantique; *b* 20 April 1943; *s* of Rolf Gardiner and late Marabel Gardiner (*née* Hodgkin); *m* 1st, 1972, Cherryl ffoulkes (marr. diss. 1980); 2nd, 1981, Elizabeth Suzanne Wilcock (marr. diss. 1997); three *d*; 3rd, 2001, Isabella de Sabata. *Educ:* Pinewood Sch.; Bryanston Sch.; King's Coll., Cambridge (MA History; Hon. Fellow 2015); King's Coll., London (Certif. of Advanced Studies in Music, 1966; Hon. FKC 1992). French Govt Scholarship to study in Paris and Fontainebleau with Nadia Boulanger, 1966–68. Founded: Monteverdi Choir, following performance of Monteverdi's Vespers of 1610, King's Coll. Chapel, Cambridge, 1964; Monteverdi Orchestra, 1968; English Baroque Soloists (period instruments), 1978; Orchestre Révolutionnaire et Romantique, 1989. Guest Conductor (opera): Sadler's Wells; Royal Opera House, Covent Garden; Glyndebourne; La Scala, Milan; La Fenice, Venice; Zurich; Guest Conductor (symphonic): LSO; LPO; Philharmonia; Vienna Phil.; Czech Phil.; Orch. Nat. de France; Concertgebouw; Dresden Staatskapelle; Bavarian Radio SO; Gewandhaus; Boston SO; Cleveland Orch., Pittsburgh. Principal Conductor: CBC Vancouver Orchestra, 1980–83; NDR SO, Hamburg, 1991–94; Music Dir, Opéra de Lyon Orch., 1983–88 (Chef fondateur, 1988). Artistic Director: Göttingen Handel Fest., 1981–90; Veneto Music Fest., 1986; Anima Mundi, Pisa, 2016–18. Vis. Fellow, Peterhouse, Cambridge, 2008–09; (first) C. Wolff Dist. Vis. Scholar, Music Dept, Harvard Univ., 2015. Pres., Bach-Archive, Leipzig, 2014–18. Hon. FRAM 1992; Hon. FBA 2015; Hon. FRCM 2017. DUniv Univ. Lumière Lyon, 1987; Hon. Dr: New England Conservatory of Music, Boston, 2005; Ecole Pratique des Hautes Etudes, Paris, 2018; Hon. Dr Musicol. Pavia, 2006; Hon. DMus: St Andrews, 2014; Cambridge, 2015; KCL, 2018. Numerous awards include: Grand Prix du Disque; Deutscher Schallplattenpreis; Edison Awards; Gramophone Record of the Year, 1991, 2005; Gramophone Artist of the Year, 1994; La Medalla internacional, Complutense Univ. of Madrid, 2001; Léonie Sonnings Prize, Denmark, 2005; Bach-Medaille, City of Leipzig, 2005; RAM and Kohn Foundn Bach Prize, 2008; Gramophone Special Achievement Award, 2010; Harvard Glee Club Medal, 2015; Premier Prix, Prix des Muses, Fondation Singer-Polignac, 2015; Classic Prague Award, 2016; Gold Medal, Musicians' Co., 2019. Internat. Ambassador of Czech Music 2017. Commandeur, Ordre des Arts et des Lettres (France), 1997 (Officier, 1988); Verdienstkreuz, 1st Class (Germany), 2005; Chevalier, Légion d'Honneur (France), 2010. *Publications:* Music in the Castle of Heaven: a portrait of Johann Sebastian Bach, 2013. *Recreations:* organic farming, forestry. *Address:* c/o Intermusica Artists' Management Ltd, 9 Kingsway, WC2B 6XF.

**GARDINER, Prof. John Graham**, PhD; FIET; FREng; Professor of Electronic Engineering, 1986–94, and Dean of Engineering and Physical Sciences, 1996–2002, University of Bradford; Director, Wireless Technologies CIC, since 2006; *b* 24 May 1939; *s* of William Clement Gardiner and Ellen (*née* Adey); *m* 1962, Sheila Joyce Andrews; one *s* two *d*. *Educ:* Univ. of Birmingham (BSc 1st Cl. Hons; PhD 1964). FIET (FIEE 1988); FREng (FEng 1994). Software designer, Racal Res. Ltd, 1966–68; University of Bradford: Lectr, 1968–72; Sen Lectr, 1972–78; Reader, 1978–86; Hd, Dept of Electronic and Electrical Engrg, 1994–96. Hon. Pres., British Royal Univ., Kurdistan, 2009–. SMIEE 1995; FRSA 1997. *Publications:* (with J. D. Parsons) Mobile Communication Systems, 1989; (with B. West) Personal Communication Systems and Technologies, 1995. *Recreation:* music. *Address:* 1 Queen's Drive Lane, Ilkley, W Yorks LS29 9QS. *T:* (01943) 609581.

**GARDINER, John Ralph;** QC 1982; *b* 28 Feb. 1946; *s* of late Cyril Ralph Gardiner and Mary Gardiner (*née* Garibaldi); *m* 1976, Pascal Mary Issard-Davies; one *d*. *Educ:* Bancroft's Sch., Woodford; Fitzwilliam Coll., Cambridge (BA (Law Tripos), MA, LLM). Called to the Bar, Middle Temple, 1968 (Harmsworth Entrance Scholar and Harmsworth Law Scholar; Bencher, 1992); practice at the Bar, 1970–; Mem., Senate of Inns of Court and Bar, 1982–86 (Treasurer, 1985–86); Chm., Taxation and Retirement Benefits Cttee, Bar Council, 1982–85. FRSA 2001. *Publications:* contributor to Pinson on Revenue Law, 6th to 15th (1982) edns. *Recreations:* tennis, horse racing. *Address:* 11 New Square, Lincoln's Inn, WC2A 3QB. *T:* (020) 7242 3981; Admiral's House, Admiral's Walk, Hampstead, NW3 6RS. *T:* (020) 7435 0597.

**GARDINER, Juliet;** writer and historian; *b* 24 June 1943; *d* of Charles and Dorothy Wells; *m* 1st, 1961, George Arthur Gardiner (later Sir George Gardiner) (marr. diss. 1980; he *d* 2002); two *s* one *d*; 2nd, 1990, Henry Horwitz. *Educ:* Berkhamsted Sch. for Girls; University Coll. London (BA 1st Cl. Hons Hist.). Ed., History Today, 1981–85; Acad. Dir, then Publisher, Weidenfeld & Nicolson, 1985–89; Middlesex University: Principal Lectr, 1992–97; Acad. Chair, Communication, Cultural and Media Studies, 1997–2000; Hd, Publishing Studies, Oxford Brookes Univ., 2000–01. Res. Fellow, Inst. Histl Res., Univ. of London, 1979–81; Hon. Res. Fellow, IAS, Univ. of Edinburgh, 2006; Hon. Vis. Prof. Sch. of Arts, Middlesex Univ., 2004–07. Member: Mgt Cttee, Soc. of Authors, 2011–14; Academic Adv. Panel, Nat. Army Mus., 2014–. Trustee, History Today, 1998–. Historical adviser: Atonement (film), 2006; Upstairs Downstairs (BBC TV), 2010; Turn Back Time - The High Street (BBC TV), 2010; Turn Back Time - The Family (BBC TV), 2012; Mr Selfridge (ITV). Occasional presenter, Night Waves, BBC Radio 3; writer and presenter: A History of the Future, 2012, Presenting the Past, 2013, BBC Radio 4. Orwell Fellow, 2017. *Publications:* Over Here: GIs in wartime Britain 1942–45, 1992; The World Within: the Brontës at Haworth, 1992; (ed) Women's Voices: the new woman 1880–1914, 1993; Picture Post Women, 1994; (ed) The History Today Companion to British History, 1995; Oscar Wilde: a life in letters, writings and wit, 1995; Queen Victoria, 1997; From the Bomb to the Beatles: the changing face of post-war Britain 1945–65, 1999; The Penguin Dictionary of British History, 2000; The History Today Who's Who in British History, 2000; The 1940s House, 2000; The Edwardian Country House, 2002; Wartime: Britain 1939–1945, 2004; The Children's War, 2005; The Animals' War, 2006; War on the Home Front, 2007; The Thirties: an intimate history, 2010; The Blitz: the British under attack, 2010; Memories of Britain Past, 2011; (contrib.) Hackney: an uncommon history, 2012; Joining the Dots, 2017. *Recreation:* London. *E:* juliet@julietgardiner.com.

**GARDINER, Air Vice-Marshal Martyn John,** OBE 1987; FRAeS; non-executive Director, Singleton Birch Group Ltd, since 2013; *b* 13 June 1946; *s* of late John Glen Gardiner and Edith Eleanor Gardiner (*née* Howley); *m* 1971, Anne Dunlop Thom; two *s* one *d*. *Educ:* Frimley and Camberley Grammar Sch.; Southampton Univ. (BScEng (Hons) Aeronautics and Astronautics 1967). FRAeS 2000. Flying and staff appointments include: Coll. of Air Warfare, 1969–71; No 99 Sqdn, Brize Norton, 1971–75; Dept of Air Warfare, Gen. Duties Aero-Systems Course, 1976; No 72 Sqdn, Odiham, 1977–80; HQ 2 Armd Div., Germany, 1980–82; RAF Staff Coll., Bracknell, 1983; OC 32 Sqdn, RAF Northolt, 1984–87; HQ STC, 1987–88; Defence Policy and Commitments Staffs, MoD, 1988–91; OC RAF Northolt, 1991–93; SASO, HQ 38 Gp, 1994–96; COS Reaction Force Air Staff Kalkar, 1996–98; Dep. Comdr, Combined Air Ops Centre 4, Messstetten, 1998–2001; Mil. Advr to High Rep. for Bosnia and Herzegovina, 2001–02. Non-executive Director: Singleton Birch Ltd, 2013–; Estuary TV, 2014–16. Chairman: NE Lincs Aircrew Assoc., 2004–; Louth RAFA, 2004–10. Dir, Grimsby Inst. Corp., 2004–13; Dir and Trustee, Katherine Martin Charitable Trust, 2006–; Chm. of Govs, Duke of Kent Sch., Ewhurst, 2002–08; Chm., Alexander Duckham Meml Schs Trust, 2004–17. *Recreations:* golf, ski-ing, walking, Rugby-watching. *Address:* Heronsbrook, Stewton Lane, Louth, Lincolnshire LN11 8SB. *Club:* Royal Air Force.

**GARDINER, Victor Alec,** OBE 1977; Director and General Manager, London Weekend Television, 1971–87; *b* 9 Aug. 1929; *m*; one *s* two *d*. *Educ:* Whitgift Middle Sch., Croydon; City and Guilds (radio and telecommunications). Techn. Asst, GPO Engrg, 1947–49; RAF Nat. Service, 1949–51; BBC Sound Radio Engr, 1951–53; BBC TV Cameraman, 1953–55; Rediffusion TV Sen. Cameraman, 1955–61; Malta TV Trng Man., 1961–62; Head of Studio Prodn, Rediffusion TV, 1962–67; Man. Dir, GPA Productions, 1967–69; Production Controller, London Weekend Television, 1969–71; Director: LWT (Hldgs) Ltd, 1976–87; London Weekend Services Ltd, 1976–87; Richard Price Television Associates, 1981–87; Chairman: Dynamic Technology Ltd, 1972–87; Standard Music Ltd, 1972–87; LWT Internat., 1981–87. Mem., Royal Television Soc., 1970– (Vice-Chm. Council, 1974–75; Chm. Papers Cttee, 1975; Chm. Council, 1976–77; Fellow, 1977). *Recreations:* Big Band music, travelling, sound and video constructions, cycling.

**GARDNER,** family name of **Baroness Gardner of Parkes.**

**GARDNER OF PARKES,** Baroness *cr* 1981 (Life Peer), of Southgate, Greater London, and of Parkes, NSW; **(Rachel) Trixie (Anne) Gardner,** AM 2003; JP; dental surgeon; Chairman, Plan International (UK) Ltd, 1990–2003; *b* Parkes, NSW, Australia, 17 July 1927; eighth *c* of late Hon. J. J. Gregory McGirr and Rachel McGirr, OBE, LC; *m* 1956, Kevin Anthony Gardner (*d* 2007), *o s* of late George and Rita Gardner, Sydney, Australia; three *d*. *Educ:* Monte Sant Angelo Coll., N Sydney; East Sydney Technical Coll.; Univ. of Sydney (BDS 1954; Hon. Fellow 2005). Cordon Bleu de Paris, Diplôme 1956. Came to UK, 1954. Member: Westminster City Council, 1968–78 (Lady Mayoress, 1987–88); GLC, for Havering, 1970–73, for Enfield-Southgate, 1977–86. Contested (C) Blackburn, 1970; N Cornwall, Feb. 1974. House of Lords: a Dep. Speaker, 1999–2002; Dep. Chm. of Cttees, 1999–2002. Chm., Royal Free Hampstead NHS Trust, 1994–97; Vice-Chm., NE Thames RHA, 1990–94; Member: Inner London Exec. Council, NHS, 1966–71; Standing Dental Adv. Cttee for England and Wales, 1968–76; Westminster, Kensington and Chelsea Area Health Authority, 1974–82; Industrial Tribunal Panel for London, 1974–97; N Thames Gas Consumer Council, 1980–82; Dept of Employment's Adv. Cttee on Women's Employment, 1980–88; Britain–Australia Bicentennial Cttee, 1984–88; London Electricity Bd, 1984–90. British Chm., European Union of Women, 1978–82; UK Rep., UN Status of Women Commn, 1982–88. Director: Gateway Building Soc., 1987–88; Woolwich Building Soc., 1988–93. Chm., Suzy Lamplugh Trust, 1993–97. Governor: Eastman Dental Hosp., 1971–80; Nat. Heart Hosp., 1974–90. Fellow, Sancta Sophia Coll., Univ. of Sydney, 2011. Hon. Pres., War Widows Assoc. of GB, 1984–87; Hon. Vice-Pres., Women's Sect., RBL, 2000–06. JP North Westminster, 1971. DUniv Middlesex, 1997. Award for Internat. Achievement, 2010, UK Alumni Assoc. Lifetime Achievement Award, 2018, Univ. of Sydney. *Recreations:* gardening, reading, travel, needlework. *Address:* House of Lords, SW1A 0PW.

*See also Hon. S. L. Joiner.*

**GARDNER, Caroline Jane;** Auditor General for Scotland, since 2012; *b* London, 1 May 1963; *d* of Dennis and Pauline Bradley; *m* 1989, Edward Paul Gardner. *Educ:* Univ. of Aston (BSc Combined Hons 1985); Warwick Business Sch. (MBA 1995); Open Univ. (BA 1st Cl. Hons English Lit. 2006). CIPFA 1988; FT Non-exec. Dir Dip. 2012. Trainee accountant, Wolverhampton MBC, 1985–88; Special Projects Officer, District Audit, 1988–92; Sen. Manager, Audit Commn, 1992–95; Dir, Health and Social Work Studies, Accounts Commn, 1995–2000; Audit Scotland: Dep. Auditor Gen., 2000–10; Controller of Audit, 2004–10; Chief Financial Officer, Turks and Caicos Is Govt, 2010–11; Ind. Consultant in Public Financial Mgt, 2011–12. Mem. Bd, Public Service Audit Appointments, 2014–. Pres., CIPFA, 2006–07. Mem., Internat. Ethics Standards Bd for Accountants, 2010–15. *Address:* Audit Scotland, 4th Floor, 102 West Port, Edinburgh EH3 9DN. *T:* (0131) 625 1617. *E:* cgardner@audit-scotland.gov.uk.

**GARDNER, Charlotte Ann;** *see* Roberts, C. A.

**GARDNER, Christopher James Ellis;** QC 1994; Chief Justice of the Falkland Islands, South Sandwich, South Georgia, British Antarctic Territory and British Indian Ocean Territory, 2007–15; *b* 6 April 1945; *s* of James Charles Gardner and Phillis May Gardner (*née* Wilkinson); *m* 1972, Arlene Sellers; one *s* one *d*. *Educ:* Rossall Sch., Lancs; Fitzwilliam Coll., Cambridge (MA). Called to the Bar, Gray's Inn, 1968; a Recorder, 1993–2018; Chief Justice, Turks and Caicos Islands, 2004–07. FCIArb 1999; Chartered Arbitrator, 2003; Accredited Mediator, 2000. Fellow, Soc. for Advanced Legal Studies, 1999; FRSocMed 2000; FCJEI 2013. *Recreations:* theatre, ballet, bell ringing, cooking curries. *Address:* Old Rose Cottage, Cheriton, Hants SO24 0QA. *Clubs:* Garrick; Dartmouth Yacht; Royal Dart Yacht.

**GARDNER, Vice Adm. Christopher Reginald Summers,** CBE 2017; FCILT; Chief of Materiel (Ships), since 2019; *b* Hong Kong, 10 Oct. 1962; *s* of James Donald and Margaret Gardner; *m* 1993, Teresa Heather Edgecombe; one *s* one *d*. *Educ:* Eastbourne Coll.; Warwick Univ. (LLB 1984); Cranfield Univ. (Dip. Prog. and Project Mgt 2015). FCILT 2013; DipFM 1992; Dip Inst. of Dirs 2014. Joined RN as Logistics Officer (Submarines), 1984; appointments include: HMS Tireless, 1988–91; HMS Sirius, 1992–93; HMS Endurance, 1993–94; Comdr Submarine Sea Trng, 1994–96; RNSC 1996; Staff of Flag Officer Submarines, 1996–97; Military Asst, Dir-Gen. Fleet Support and Ops and Plans, 1997–99; Exec. Asst, FOST, 1999–2001; HMS Ark Royal, 2001–03; Defence Procurement Agency, 2003–05; Exec. Asst C-in-C Fleet, 2005–06; Ministry of Defence: Dep. Hd of Capability for Expeditionary Logistics and Sustainment, 2007–10; Hd, Capability Improvement, 2010–12; Hd, Comd Intelligent Customer Capability, 2012–14; ACOS Ships, Fleet HQ, 2014–15; Chief Naval Logistics Officer, 2015–18; ACNS (Ships), 2015–19. Gov., Royal Sch., 2016–18. Commodore, Royal Naval Sailing Assoc., 2018–. *Recreation:* sailing (RYA Yachtmaster Offshore). *Club:* Naval.

**GARDNER, Prof. David Pierpont,** PhD; President, The William and Flora Hewlett Foundation, 1993–99; President, University of California, 1983–92; Professor of Education, University of California at Berkeley, 1983–92; *b* 24 March 1933; *s* of Reed S. Gardner and Margaret (*née* Pierpont); *m* 1st, 1958, Elizabeth Fuhriman (*d* 1991); four *d*; 2nd, 1995, Sheila S. Rodgers. *Educ:* Brigham Young Univ. (BS 1955); Univ. of Calif, Berkeley (MA 1959, PhD 1966). Dir, Calif Alumni Foundn, Calif Alumni Assoc., Univ. of Calif, Berkeley, 1962–64. University of California, Santa Barbara: Asst Prof. of Higher Educn, 1964–69; Associate Prof. of Higher Educn, 1969–70; Prof. of Higher Educn (on leave), 1971–73; Asst to the Chancellor, 1964–67; Asst Chancellor, 1967–69; Vice Chancellor and Exec. Asst, 1969–70; Vice Pres., Univ. of Calif, 1971–73; Pres., and Prof. of Higher Educn, Univ. of Utah, 1973–83, Pres. Emeritus, 1985. Chm., Nat. Commn on Excellence in Educn, 1981–83. Vis. Fellow, Clare Hall, Univ. of Cambridge, 1979 (Hon. Fellow, 2002). Fellow, Nat. Acad. of Public Administration; Member: Amer. Philosophical Soc.; Nat. Acad. of Educn. Chm., J. Paul Getty Trust, 2000–04. Trustee, Tanner Lectures on Human Values, 1975–2004. Fulbright 40th Anniversary Distinguished Fellow, Japan, 1986; Fellow, Amer. Acad. of Arts and Scis, 1986. Hon. LLD: Univ. of The Pacific, 1983; Nevada, Las Vegas,

1984; Westminster Coll., 1987; Brown, 1989; Notre Dame, 1989; Hon. DH Brigham Young, 1981; Hon. DLitt Utah, 1983; Hon. HHD Utah State, 1987; Hon. Dr Bordeaux II, 1988; Hon. DHL Internat. Christian Univ. Benjamin P. Cheney Medal, Eastern Washington Univ., 1984; James Bryant Conant Award, Educn Commn of the States, 1985; Hall of Fame Award, Calif. Sch. Bd Res. Foundn, 1988. Chevalier, Légion d'Honneur (France), 1985; Knight Commander, Order of Merit (Germany), 1992. *Publications*: The California Oath Controversy, 1967; Earning My Degree: memoirs of an American university president, 2005; contrib. articles to professional jls. *Address*: (office) Center for Studies in Higher Education, 771 Evans Hall, University of California, Berkeley, CA 94720–4650, USA.

**GARDNER, Douglas Frank;** Chairman, Industrial Realisation plc, since 2000; *b* 20 Dec. 1943; *s* of late Ernest Frank Gardner and Mary Gardner; *m* 1978, Adèle (*née* Alexander); one *s* two *d*. *Educ*: Woolverstone Hall; College of Estate Management, London Univ. (BSc). FRICS. Chief Exec., Properties Div., Tarmac plc, 1976–83; Man. Dir, 1983–93, Chm., 1993–2000, Brixton Estate plc. Chairman: Industrial Develt Partnership, 2000–07; GPT Halverton Trust (formerly Halverton REIM LLP), 2004–08; Director: Invesco UK Property Income Trust, 2004–16; Hirco plc, 2006–11; Invista Real Estate Investment Mgt plc, 2010–12; Prime plc, 2010–11; Schooner Park Crossways Ltd, 2017–. Mem., Investment Cttee, Eur. Industrial Property Fund, 2001–04. Chm., Bd of Govs, Nuffield Hospitals, subseq. Nuffield Health, 2001–09 (Gov., 1995–2009). Mem. Council, RCM, 2014–; Dir, Associated Bd of Royal Schs of Music, 2014–. *Recreations*: tennis, theatre. *Address*: Flat 10 Stavordale Lodge, 10–12 Melbury Road, W14 8WL.

**GARDNER, Sir Edmund Thomas Peter B.;** see Bruce-Gardner.

**GARDNER, Edward James,** OBE 2012; conductor; Music Director, English National Opera, 2007–15; Principal Guest Conductor, City of Birmingham Symphony Orchestra, since 2010; Chief Conductor, Bergen Philharmonic Orchestra, since 2015 (Principal Guest Conductor, 2013–15); *b* Gloucester, 22 Nov. 1974; *s* of Kingsley and Helen Gardner; one *s*. *Educ*: Eton; King's Coll., Cambridge (BA 1996); Royal Acad. of Music. Asst to Music Dir, Hallé Orch., 2000–03; Founder, Hallé Youth Orch., 2002; Musical Dir, Glyndebourne Touring Opera, 2004–07. Débuts: Paris Opera, 2004; BBC SO, 2005; Metropolitan Opera, NY, 2010; La Scala, Milan, 2011; Lyric Opera, Chicago, 2016; San Francisco Symphony, 2018; NY Philharmonic, 2018; has worked with orchestras incl. NHK SO, Mahler Chamber Orch., Bamberg SO, Netherlands Radio Philharmonic, Philharmonia, LPO, Orch. of the Age of Enlightenment, Royal Concertgebouw, Deutsches SO Berlin, Orchestre Philharmonique de Radio France, Accademia Nazionale di Santa Cecilia, Orchestra Filarmonica della Scala, Czech Philharmonic, Swedish Radio Orch., Danish Nat. Symphony, Gothenberg Symphony, Rotterdam Philharmonic, Royal Scottish Nat. Orch., New York Philharmonic, Chicago SO, US Nat. SO, Seattle Symphony, Minnesota Orch., Leipzig Gewandhaus, WDR Sinfonieorchester, Finnish Radio Orch., Orchestra Sinfonica Nacionale RAI, Torino, Orchestre de la Suisse Romande, Frankfurt Radio SO, Boston SO, Toronto SO, Montreal SO, Houston SO. Conductor, Last Night of the Proms, 2011; Conductor, First Night of the Proms, 2017. *Address*: c/o Askonas Holt, 15 Fetter Lane, EC4A 1BW.

**GARDNER, Francis Rolleston,** OBE 2005; BBC Security Correspondent, since 2002; *b* 31 July 1961; *s* of Robert Neil Gardner and Grace Rolleston Gardner; *m* 1997, Amanda Jane Pearson; two *d*. *Educ*: Marlborough Coll.; Exeter Univ. (BA Hons Arabic and Islamic Studies 1984). Marketing Manager, Gulf Exports, 1984–86; Trading and Sales, Saudi Internat. Bank, 1986–90; Dir, Robert Fleming, 1990–95; joined BBC News, 1995: World TV, 1995–97; Gulf Corresp., 1997–99; ME Corresp., 1999–2002. Dist. Vis. Prof. of 2015, USC. Platoon Comdr 4th (V) Bn, RGJ, 1984–90. FRGS 2006. Hon. LLD: Staffordshire, 2006; Nottingham, 2006; Exeter, 2007; East Anglia, 2009; Open, 2009; London, 2013; Aberdeen, 2017. Person of the Year, Press Gazette, 2005; El Mundo Internat. Journalism Prize, 2006; McWhirter Award for Bravery, 2006; Zayed Medal for Journalism, UAE, 2007; AIM Ability Media Internat. Award, 2009; Master Wheelrights' Award, 2011; Journalist of the Year, Eur. Diversity Awards, 2011; David Crystal Trophy for contribn to langs, 2018. *Publications*: Blood and Sand, 2006; Far Horizons, 2009; Crisis, 2016; Ultimatum, 2018. *Recreations*: ski-ing (Pres., Ski Club of GB, 2011–17; Patron, Disability Snowsport UK, 2018–), scuba diving, birdwatching, rifle shooting. *Address*: BBC News Centre, Portland Place, W1A 1AA. *Clubs*: Rifles Officers London, Ivy.

**GARDNER, James Jesse,** CVO 1995; CBE 1986; DL; consultant, since 1986; Chairman, OFWAT National Consumer Council, 1993–98; *b* 7 April 1932; *s* of James and Elizabeth Rubina Gardner; *m* 1st, 1955, Diana Sotheran (*d* 1999); three *s* one *d*; 2nd, 2002, Joan Adamson. *Educ*: Kirkham Grammar Sch.; Victoria Univ., Manchester (LLB). Nat. Service, 1955–57. Articled to Town Clerk, Preston, 1952–55; Legal Asst, Preston Co. Borough Council, 1955; Crosby Borough Council: Asst Solicitor, 1957–59; Chief Asst Solicitor, 1959–61; Chief Asst Solicitor, Warrington Co. Borough Council, 1961–65; Stockton-on-Tees Borough Council: Dep. Town Clerk, 1966; Town Clerk, 1966–68; Asst Town Clerk, Teesside Co. Borough Council, 1968; Associate Town Clerk and Solicitor, London Borough of Greenwich, 1968–69; Town Clerk and Chief Exec. Officer, Co. Borough of Sunderland, 1970–73; Chief Exec., Tyne and Wear CC, 1973–86; Chm., Tyne and Wear PTE, 1983–86. Chief Exec., Northern Develt Co. Ltd, 1986–87; Chairman: Sunderland DHA, 1988–90; Northumbrian Water Customer Services Cttee, 1990–2001; North East Television, 1991–92; Dir, Birtley Enterprise Action Management (BEAM) Ltd, 1989–93; Sec., Northern Region Councils Assoc., 1986. Clerk to Lieutenancy, Tyne and Wear, 1974–91. Dir, Garrod Pitkin (1986) Ltd, 1991–93. Chairman: Prince's Trust Trustees, 1986–94; Prince's Trust and Royal Jubilee Trust Management Bd, 1989–93 (former Chm., Northumbria Cttee, Royal Jubilee and Prince's Trusts); Prince's Trust Events Ltd, 1987–94; Director: Threshold (formerly Prince's Trust Training & Employment Ltd), 1991–95 (Chm., 1992); NE Civic Trust, 1986–92. Chairman: Century Radio, 1993–2000; St Benedict's Hospice, Sunderland, 1993–2008; Royalty Theatre, 2001–05; Trustee: Tyne Tees Telethon Trust, 1988–91; Great North Air Ambulance Service Appeal, 1991–95. DL Tyne and Wear, 1976. FRSA 1976; CCMI (CIMgt 1987). Hon. Fellow, Sunderland Polytechnic, 1986. *Recreations*: golf, music, theatre, food and drink. *Address*: Wayside, 121 Queen Alexandra Road, Sunderland, Tyne and Wear SR2 9HR.

**GARDNER, (James) Piers,** barrister; *b* 26 March 1954; *s* of Michael Clement Gardner and Brigitte Elsa Gardner (*née* Ekrut); *m* 1978, Penelope Helen Chloros; three *s* one *d*. *Educ*: Bryanston Sch.; Brasenose Coll., Oxford (MA Jurisp. 1st Class). Solicitor of the Supreme Court, 1979–2000; called to the Bar, Gray's Inn, 2000. Articled and in private practice as solicitor, with Stephenson Harwood, London, 1977–80; Secretariat, European Commn of Human Rights, Council of Europe, Strasbourg, 1980–87; Exec. Dir, 1987–89, Dir, 1989–2000, British Inst. of Internat. and Comparative Law. *Recreations*: foreign property, arguing. *Address*: Monckton Chambers, 1–2 Raymond Buildings, Gray's Inn, WC1R 5NR. *T*: (020) 7405 7211.

**GARDNER, Julie Anne;** see Etchingham, J. A.

**GARDNER, Prof. Margaret Elaine,** AO 2007; President and Vice-Chancellor, Monash University, since 2014; *b* Sydney; *d* of Donald Maxwell and Gwendoline Gardner; *m* Prof. (Conrad) Glyn Davis, *qv*; one *s* one *d*. *Educ*: Univ. of Sydney (BEc Hons; PhD 1984). Pro Vice-Chancellor (Equity), 1994–96, Pro Vice-Chancellor (Business/Equity), 1996–2000, Griffith Univ.; Dep. Vice-Chancellor (Academic), Univ. of Queensland, 2000–05; Vice-Chancellor and Pres., RMIT, 2005–14. Chair, Universities Australia, 2017–. Dir, Infrastructure Victoria, 2016–. Pres., Museums Bd Victoria, 2008–16. GAICD, 2004. DUniv Griffith, 2005. *Address*: Office of the Vice-Chancellor, Monash University, Wellington Road, Clayton, Vic 3800, Australia. *T*: (3) 99029851. *E*: Margaret.Gardner@monash.edu. *Club*: Lyceum (Melbourne).

**GARDNER, Ven. Paul Douglas,** PhD; Senior Minister, Christ Church Presbyterian Church, Atlanta, Georgia, 2005–17; *b* 28 May 1950; *s* of late Rev. David Gardner and Dr Joy M. Gardner; *m* 1971, Sharon Anne Bickford; two *s* one *d*. *Educ*: Leeds Grammar Sch.; KCL (BA 1972, AKC 1972); Reformed Theol Seminary, USA (MDiv 1979); Ridley Hall, Cambridge; Sidney Sussex Coll., Cambridge (PhD 1989). Company dir, 1972–77. Ordained deacon, 1980, priest, 1981; Curate, St Martin's, Cambridge, 1980–83; Lectr in NT and Acad. Registrar, Oak Hill Theol Coll., 1983–90; Vicar, St John the Baptist, Hartford, Cheshire, 1990–2003; Archdeacon of Exeter, 2003–05. RD, Middlewich, 1994–99. *Publications*: The Gifts of God and the Authentication of a Christian, 1994, repr. 2017; The Complete Who's Who in the Bible, 1995; (ed and contrib.) New International Encyclopedia of Bible Characters, 1995, 4th edn 2002; Focus on the Bible series: 2 Peter and Jude, 1998, new edn as 1 Peter, 2 Peter and Jude, 2012; Revelation, 2001; Ephesians, 2006; 1 Corinthians (Zondervan Exegetical Commentary), 2018. *Recreations*: alpine walking, ski-ing, writing, photography. *Address*: 30 Archibald Road, Exeter EX1 1SA.

**GARDNER, Prof. Philippa Anne,** PhD; FBCS; Professor of Theoretical Computer Science, Imperial College London, since 2009; *b* Exeter, 29 June 1965; *d* of Kenneth Leslie Gardner and Pamela Joyce Gardner; partner, 2012, William Thomas Pike. *Educ*: St Hugh's Coll., Oxford (MA Maths); Univ. of Bristol (MSc Logic and Computation); Univ. of Edinburgh (PhD Theoretical Computer Sci. 1992). FBCS 2009. Postdoctoral Fellow, Univ. of Edinburgh, 1992–97; Teaching Fellow and Dir of Studies, St John's Coll., Cambridge, 1997–2000; EPSRC Advanced Fellow, Univ. of Cambridge and Imperial Coll. London, 1997–2001; Imperial College London: Lectr, 2000–04; Sen. Lectr, 2004–06; Microsoft Res. and RAEng Sen. Res. Fellow, 2005–10; Reader, 2006–09; Dir, Res. Instn on Automated Prog. Analysis and Verification, 2013–16; Dir, Res. Instn on Verified Trustworthy Software Systems, 2017–. *Publications*: contribs to jls on analysis and verification, programming languages and theoretical computer sci. *Recreation*: classical singing. *Address*: Department of Computing, 180 Queen's Gate, South Kensington Campus, Imperial College London, SW7 2AZ.

**GARDNER, Piers;** see Gardner, J. P.

**GARDNER, Sir Richard (Lavenham),** Kt 2005; PhD; FRS 1979; Royal Society Edward Penley Abraham Research Professor, Department of Zoology, University of Oxford, 2003–08, now Academic Visitor, Sir William Dunn School of Pathology; Student of Christ Church, Oxford, 1974–2008, now Emeritus; *b* 10 June 1943; *s* of late Allan Constant and Eileen May Gardner; *m* 1968, Wendy Joy Cresswell; one *s*. *Educ*: St John's Sch., Leatherhead; North East Surrey Coll. of Technology; St Catharine's Coll., Cambridge (BA 1st Cl. Hons Physiol., 1966; MA; PhD 1971; Hon. Fellow, 2008). Res. Asst, Physiological Lab., Cambridge, 1970–73; Oxford University: Lectr in Developmental and Reproductive Biology, Dept of Zoology, 1973–77; Res. Student, Christ Church, 1974–77; Royal Soc. Henry Dale Res. Prof., Dept of Zool., 1978–2003; Hon. Dir, ICRF Develtl Biol. Unit, 1986–96. Associate, and Hon. Vis. Prof., Dept of Biol., Univ. of York, 2007–16. Ind. Mem., ABRC, 1990–93. Pres., Inst. Biol., 2006–08. Chm., Animals in Science Educn Trust, 2009–; Trustee, Edwards and Steptoe Res. Trust, 2010–. Patrick Steptoe Meml Lect., British Fertility Soc., 2015. Hon. ScD Cambridge, 2012. Scientific Medal, Zoological Soc. of London, 1977; March of Dimes Prize in Develtl Biology, 1999; Royal Medal, Royal Soc., 2001; Albert Brachet Prize, Royal Acad. of Belgium, 2004; Waddington Medal, British Soc. for Develtl Biology, 2018. *Publications*: contribs to Jl of Embryology and Experimental Morphology, Nature, Jl of Cell Science, and various other jls and symposia. *Recreations*: ornithology, music, sailing, painting, gardening.

**GARDNER, Dr Rita Ann Moden,** CBE 2003; Chief Executive, Academy of Social Sciences, since 2019; *b* 10 Nov. 1955; *d* of John William Gardner and Evelyn Gardner (*née* Moden); partner, 1982, Dr Martin Eugene Frost. *Educ*: Huntingdon Grammar Sch.; Hinchingbrooke Sch.; University Coll. London (BSc 1st cl. Hons Geog.); Wolfson Coll., Oxford (DPhil 1981). Lectr in Physical Geog., St Catherine's Coll., Oxford, 1978–79; Lectr in Geog., KCL, 1979–94; Dir, Envmtl Sci. Unit and Reader in Envmtl Sci., QMW, 1994–96. Dir and Sec., RGS (with the IBG), 1996–2018. Advr to Schools Minister, DFES, then DCSF, 2006–09; Member: Archives Task Force, DCMS, 2002–03; Geography Advisors Gp, DfE, 2011–13; Working Gp on Open Access to Scholarly Publishing, BIS, 2011–13. Non-exec. Dir, British Antarctic Survey, 2011–14. Member, Council: ALPSP, 2008–11; Acad. of Social Scis, 2013–18. Co-Chair, Exhibition Road Cultural Gp, 2004–09; Trustee: WWF-UK, 2000–04; World Conservation Monitoring Centre, 2008–11. Ed., Geographical Jl, 1989–93. Hon. Sec., RGS, 1991–96. Hon. Fellow, QMUL, 2004. Hon. DSc Southampton, 2004; Hon. D Gloucester, 2004. Busk Medal, RGS, 1995; Ronald F. Abler Distinguished Service Honor, Assoc. of Amer. Geographers, 2015; Gold Medal, RSGS, 2016. *Publications*: Landscape in England and Wales, 1981, 2nd edn 1994; Mega-geomorphology, 1981; Land Shapes, 1986; numerous academic papers in learned jls specialising in geomorphology, physical geog., sedimentology and Quaternary envmtl change. *Recreations*: restoration of historic vernacular buildings, contemporary architecture and furniture, gardening, travel, good food and wine, dance.

**GARDNER, Sir Roy Alan,** Kt 2002; FCCA; Senior Independent Director, Mainstream Renewable Power Ltd, since 2017 (non-executive Director, since 2008; Chairman, 2011–17); Chairman, Serco Group plc, since 2015; *b* 20 Aug. 1945; *s* of Roy Thomas Gardner and Iris Joan Gardner; *m* 1969, Carol Ann Barker; one *s* two *d*. *Educ*: Strode's Sch., Egham. FCCA 1980. Works Acct, later Concorde Project Acct, BAC Ltd, 1963–75; Chief Acct, Asst Finance Dir, then Finance Dir, Marconi Space & Defence Systems, 1975–84; Finance Dir, Marconi Co. Ltd, 1984–85; STC plc: Finance Dir, 1986–89; Dir, 1986–91; Man. Dir, STC Communications Ltd, 1989–91; Chief Operating Officer, Northern Telecom Europe Ltd, 1991–92; Man. Dir, GEC-Marconi Ltd, 1992–94; Dir, GEC plc, 1994; Exec. Dir, British Gas plc, 1994–97; Chief Exec., Centrica plc, 1997–2006. Chairman: Manchester United plc, 2002–05 (non-exec. Dir, 1999–2005); Compass Gp PLC, 2006–14 (non-exec. Dir, 2005–14); Plymouth Argyle FC, 2009–10; Connaught plc, 2010; EnServe Gp Ltd (formerly Spice Ltd), 2010–14; non-executive Director: Laporte plc, 1997–2001; Willis Gp Hldgs Ltd, 2006–16; William Hill plc, 2014–18. Sen. Advr, Credit Suisse, 2006–18. Chairman: Employers' Forum on Disability, 2000–03; Modern Apprenticeship Task Force, 2002–05; Apprentices Ambassadors Network UK, 2006–14; British Olympic Appeal for Beijing Games 2008, 2007–08. Mem., Council for Ind. and Higher Educn, 1996–99. Chm., Adv. Bd, Energy Futures Lab, Imperial Coll., 2007–12. Member Council: RUSI, 1992–96; Brunel Univ., 1998–2001. Pres., Carers UK (formerly

Carers Nat. Assoc.), 1998–2014. Trustee, Develt Trust, 1997–2017. Mem. Bd, Enemy Within appeal, Combat Stress, 2010–. Chm., Bd of Govs, St Albans Sch., 2018–. CCMI; FCGI; FRSA 1995. *Recreations:* golf, running. *Address:* Serco Group plc, Serco House, 16 Bartley Wood Business Park, Bartley Way, Hook, Hants RG27 9UY. *Clubs:* Brooks's, Annabel's, Mark's, Harry's Bar, 5 Hertford Street, George.

**GARDNER, Sally Ann Collins;** author of books for children and young people, since 2005; *b* Birmingham, 2 Oct. 1953; *d* of Sir Edward Lucas Gardner, QC and Her Honour Noreen Margaret, (Nina), Lowry; *m* 1981, Adrian Corry (marr. diss. 1999); one *s* two *d*. *Educ:* Central St Martins (BA Hons Theatre 1975). Theatre designer, 1975–88; illustrator, 1989–2005. *Publications:* illustrator: Robert and the Giant, 1990; Suzi, Sam, George & Alice, 1993; Gynormous!: the ultimate book of giants, 1996; Hello? Is Anybody There?, 1997 (Norwegian edn as Hallo? Er det noen her?, 1996); The Real Fairy Storybook, 1998; Polly's Running Away Book, 2000; Polly's Absolutely Worst Birthday Ever, 2001; Polly's Really Secret Diary, 2002; *writer and illustrator:* The Little Nut Tree, 1993; My Little Princess, 1994; Playtime Rhymes, 1995; A Book of Princesses, 1997; The Strongest Girl in the World, 1999; The Fairy Catalogue: everything you need to know to make a fairy tale, 2000; The Smallest Girl Ever, 2000; The Boy Who Could Fly, 2001; The Glass Heart: a tale of three princesses, 2001; Mama, Don't Go Out Tonight, 2002; The Invisible Boy, 2002; Boolar's Big Day Out, 2003; Fairy Shopping, 2003; The Boy with the Magic Numbers, 2003; The Countess's Calamity, 2003; The Boy with the Lightning Feet, 2006; *writer:* I, Coriander, 2005 (Nestlé Smarties Book Prize, Booktrust); Lucy Willow, 2006; The Red Necklace: a story of the French Revolution, 2007; The Silver Blade, 2008; The Double Shadow, 2011; Maggot Moon, 2012 (Carnegie Medal, CILIP); Wings & Co: Operation Bunny: the fairy detective agency's first case, 2012, Three Pickled Herrings, 2012, The Vanishing of Billy Buckle, 2013; Tinder, 2013; The Matchbox Mysteries, 2014; The Door That Led to Where, 2015; My Side of the Diamond, 2017; Mr Tiger, Betsy and the Blue, 2018. *Recreations:* walking the dog, searching for peace and quiet. *Address:* c/o Orion Children's Books/Indigo, Carmelite House, 50 Victoria Embankment, EC4Y 0DZ; c/o Hot Key Books Ltd, 10 Northburgh Street, EC1V 0AT. *Club:* Union.

**GARDYNE, Lucinda Emma Kate B.;** *see* Bruce-Gardyne.

**GAREL-JONES,** family name of **Baron Garel-Jones**.

**GAREL-JONES,** Baron *cr* 1997 (Life Peer), of Watford in the co. of Hertfordshire; **William Armand Thomas Tristan Garel-Jones;** PC 1992; Managing Director, 1999–2008, Senior Advisor, 2009–17, UBS Investment Bank (formerly Warburg Dillon Read); *b* 28 Feb. 1941; *s* of Bernard Garel-Jones and Meriel Garel-Jones (*née* Williams); *m* 1966, Catalina (*née* Garrigues); four *s* one *d*. *Educ:* The King's Sch., Canterbury. Principal, Language Sch., Madrid, Spain, 1960–70; Merchant Banker, 1970–97; worked for Cons. Party, 1974–79 (Personal Asst to Party Chm., 1978–79). Contested (C): Caernarvon, Feb. 1974; Watford, Oct. 1974. MP (C) Watford, 1979–97. PPS to Minister of State, CSD, 1981; Asst Govt Whip, 1982–83; a Lord Comr of HM Treasury, 1983–86; Vice-Chamberlain of HM Household, 1986–88; Comptroller of HM Household, 1988–89; Treasurer of HM Household and Dep. Chief Whip, 1989–90; Minister of State, FCO, 1990–93. *Recreation:* collecting books. *Address:* House of Lords, SW1A 0PW.

**GARFORTH, Prof. Christopher James,** PhD; Professor of Agricultural Extension and Rural Development, University of Reading, 1995–2013, now Emeritus; *b* Hull, 15 Nov. 1950; *s* of Francis William Garforth and Francesca Mary Garforth; *m* 1971, Sally Boyes; three *d*. *Educ:* Hymers Coll., Hull; Queens' Coll., Cambridge (BA Classics and Land Econ. 1972; PhD 1977). Sen. Res. Officer, Newcastle upon Tyne CC, 1975–77; Action Res. Officer, Min. of Agric., Botswana, 1977–80; Lectr, 1980–87, Sen. Lectr, 1987–95, Univ. of Reading. Chm., Tropical Agric. Assoc., 2008–12; Mem., Develt Studies Assoc., 1990–. *Publications:* contrib. papers to internat. jls. *Recreations:* walking, music, allotment gardening, mountain biking. *Address:* Pear Tree Cottage, Wrench Green, Hackness, Scarborough YO13 9AB. *T:* (01723) 882159, 07730 532746. *E:* chrisgarforth@btinternet.com.

**GARGAN, Nicholas James;** independent consultant, since 2015; *b* York, 7 Dec. 1966; *s* of Anthony Patrick and Jean Anne Gargan. *Educ:* Bar Grammar Sch., York; Univ. of Leicester (BA Hons French and Politics 1988). Leicestershire Constabulary: Police Constable, 1988–91; Sergeant, 1991–93; Inspector, 1993–95; on secondment to the Nat. Criminal Intelligence Service (Interpol), 1995–98; Chief Inspector, 1998–2001; Detective Superintendent, 2001–03; Chief Superintendent, E Area Comdr, 2003–06; Asst Chief Constable, Thames Valley Police, 2006–09; Dep. CEO, 2010, Chief Constable and Chief Exec., 2010–13, Nat. Policing Improvement Agency; Chief Constable, Avon and Somerset Constabulary, 2013–15. *Recreations:* running, cycling, watching Leicester City FC, opera.

**GARLAND, Gary John Richard;** Tribunal Judge and President, Valuation Tribunal for England, since 2016; *b* Cleadon, 26 Aug. 1958; *s* of William Garland and Evelyn Garland. *Educ:* Northumbria Univ. (LLB), Inns of Court Sch. of Law; Queen Margaret Univ.; Regent's Coll. (Qualified Mediator). Called to the Bar, Inner Temple, 1989; barrister, 1989; Special Casework Lawyer, CPS, 1998; Internat. Prosecutor, UN Mission in Kosovo, 1999–2000; Trial Attorney, Internat. Criminal Tribunal for former Yugoslavia, 2000–03; an Asylum Support Adjudicator, 2001–03; Comr, IPCC, 2003–10; a Dep. Dist Judge, 2005–; Dep. Chief Legal Ombudsman for England and Wales, 2010. Mem., Bar Council, 1993–2000. *Recreation:* life and its living. *Address:* Valuation Tribunal for England, 120 Leman Street, E1 8EU. *T:* (020) 7480 1400. *E:* president@vts.gsi.gov.uk.

**GARLAND, Nicholas Withycombe,** OBE 1998; Political Cartoonist, The Daily Telegraph, 1966–86 and 1991–2011; *b* 1 Sept. 1935; *s* of Tom and Peggy Garland; *m* 1st, 1964, Harriet Crittall (marr. diss. 1968); 2nd, 1969, Caroline Beatrice (marr. diss. 1994), *d* of Sir Peter Medawar, OM, CH, CBE, FRS; three *s* one *d*; 3rd, 1995, Priscilla Roth (*née* Brandchaft). *Educ:* Slade School of Fine Art. Worked in theatre as stage man. and dir, 1958–64; Political Cartoonist: New Statesman, 1971–78; The Independent, 1986–91; drew regularly for The Spectator, 1979–95; with Barry Humphries created and drew comic strip, Barry McKenzie, in Private Eye. *Publications:* (illustrated) Horatius, by T. B. Macaulay, 1977; An Indian Journal, 1983; Twenty Years of Cartoons by Garland, 1984; Travels with my Sketchbook, 1987; Not Many Dead, 1990; (illustrated) The Coma, by Alex Garland, 2004; I Wish..., 2007. *E:* nicholasgarland@blueyonder.co.uk.

**GARLAND, Sir Patrick (Neville),** Kt 1985; a Judge of the High Court, Queen's Bench Division, 1985–2002; Senior Trial Judge, England and Wales, 2000–02; *b* 22 July 1929; *s* of Frank Neville Garland and Marjorie Garland; *m* 1955, Jane Elizabeth Bird (*d* 2017); two *s* one *d*. *Educ:* Uppingham Sch. (Scholar); Sidney Sussex Coll., Cambridge (Exhibnr and Prizeman; MA, LLM; Hon. Fellow, 1991). Called to the Bar, Middle Temple, 1953, Bencher, 1979. Asst Recorder, Norwich, 1971; a Recorder, 1972–85; QC 1972; Dep. High Court Judge, 1981–85; a Judge of the Employment Appeal Tribunal, 1986–95; Presiding Judge, SE Circuit, 1989–93. Mem., Judges' Council, 1993–94. President: Central Probation Council (formerly Central Council of Probation Cttees), 1986–2001; Technol. and Construction Bar Assoc., 1985–2002; Mem., Parole Bd, 1988–91 (Vice-Chm., 1989–91). *Publications:* articles in legal and technical jls. *Recreations:* shooting, gardening, industrial archaeology. *Address:* 9 Ranulf Road, NW2 2BT. *Clubs:* Savage, Royal Over-Seas League; Norfolk (Norwich); Cumberland Lawn Tennis.

**GARLAND, Prof. Peter Bryan,** CBE 1999; PhD; FRSE; Professor of Biochemistry, Institute of Cancer Research, University of London, 1992–99, now Emeritus Professor (Chief Executive, 1989–99); *b* 31 Jan. 1934; *s* of Frederick George Garland and Molly Kate Jones; *m* 1959, Ann Bathurst; one *s* two *d*. *Educ:* Hardye's Sch., Dorchester; Downing Coll., Cambridge (BA 1st Class Hons in Physical Anthropol., 1955; BChir 1958, MB 1959; PhD 1964); King's Coll. Hosp. Med. Sch. (Burney Yeo Schol.). MRC Res. Schol., Chem. Pathol. Dept, KCH Med. Sch., and Biochem. Dept, UCL, 1959–61; British Insulin Manufacturers' Fellow, Biochem. Dept, Cambridge Univ., 1961–64; Lectr, 1964–68, Reader, 1969–70 in Biochem., Bristol Univ.; Prof. of Biochem., Dundee Univ., 1970–84; Principal Scientist and Hd, Biosciences Div., Unilever Research, 1984–87; Dir of Research, Amersham Internat., 1987–89. Vis. Prof., Johnson Res. Foundn, Philadelphia, 1967–69; Vis. Fellow, ANU, 1983. Member: MRC, 1980–84 (Chm., Cell Biol.-Disorders Bd, 1980–82); EMBO, 1981; CRC Scientific Policy Cttee, 1985–92. Director: CRC Technology Ltd, 1988–96 (Chm., 1988–91); CAT plc, 1990–2004 (Chm., 1995–2004). FRSE 1977. Hon. Fellow, UCL, 1999. Hon. LLD Dundee, 1990; Hon. DSc London, 2012. Colworth Medal, Biochem. Soc., 1970. *Publications:* numerous articles in biochemistry and biophysics. *Recreations:* sport (athletics blue, Cambridge, 1954–55), travel, reading, cinema, theatre.

**GARLAND, Peter Leslie,** CB 2002; Director, Health and Social Care (Northern), Department of Health, 2002–03; *b* 21 Sept. 1946; *s* of Leslie and Stella Garland; *m* 1979, Janet Rosemary Prescott; three *d*. *Educ:* Bristol Cathedral Sch.; Manchester Univ. Joined DHSS, 1974; Asst Sec. 1989; Under Sec. and Dep. Dir of Finance, 1993–99, Regl Dir, Northern and Yorks Reg., 1999–2002, NHS Exec., DoH. *Recreations:* family, gardening. *Address:* 140 Curly Hill, Ilkley, W Yorks LS29 0DS.

**GARLAND, Hon. Sir (Ransley) Victor,** KBE 1982; High Commissioner for Australia in the United Kingdom, 1981–83; *b* 5 May 1934; *m* 1960, Lynette Jamieson, BMus (Melb.); one *s* one *d* (and one *s* decd). *Educ:* Univ. of Western Australia. BA(Econ); FCA. Practised as Chartered Accountant, 1958–70. Director: Prudential Corp., 1984–93; Mitchell Cotts PLC, 1984–86; Govett Funds Inc., 1991–2000 (Pres., 1997–2000). MP for Curtin, Australian Federal Parliament, 1969–81; Minister for Supply, 1971–72; Executive Councillor, 1971–; Minister Asstg Treasurer, 1972; Chief Opposition Whip, 1974–75; Minister for Special Trade Representations, also Minister Asstg Minister for Trade and Resources, 1977–79; Minister for Veterans' Affairs, 1977–78; Minister for Business and Consumer Affairs, 1979–80. Govt Representative Minister: at Commonwealth Ministerial Meeting for Common Fund, London, 1978; at Ministerial Meetings of ESCAP, New Delhi, 1978; Minister representing Treas., at Ministerial Meeting of OECD, Paris, 1978; Leader, Aust. Delegn to UNCTAD V and Chm. Commonwealth Delegns to UNCTAD V, Manila, 1979; attended, with Premier, Commonwealth Heads of Govt meeting, Lusaka, 1979. Parly Adviser, Aust. Mission to UN Gen. Assembly, New York, 1973; Chairman: House of Reps Expenditure Cttee, 1976–77; Govt Members' Treasury Cttee, 1977. Director: Henderson Far East Income Trust PLC, 1984–2006 (Chm., 1990–2006); Throgmorton Trust PLC, 1985–2006; Signet Gp, 1991–92; Nelson Hurst PLC, 1993–94; Fidelity Asian Values PLC, 1996–2010 (Chm., 2000–10). Vice-Chm., South Bank Bd (RFH Complex), 1985–2000; Dir, South Bank Foundn, 1996–2001. Councillor, UK, Royal Commonwealth Society for the Blind, 1988. Freeman, City of London, 1982. *Recreations:* music (chorister, St George's Cathedral, 1942–46), reading, writing, travel.

**GARLAND-THOMAS, Jane Elizabeth; Her Honour Judge Garland-Thomas;** a Circuit Judge, since 2014; *b* Swansea, 15 July 1956; *d* of Griffith Thomas Mepham David and Barbara Doris David; *m* 1st, 1979, William Paul Garland-Thomas (marr. diss. 1996); one *s* one *d*; 2nd, 1999, Jason Paul Thomas. *Educ:* Glanmor Girls' Grammar Sch., Swansea; Bishop Gore Comp. Sch., Swansea; Univ. of Bristol (LLB Hons 1977); Swansea Univ. (BA Hons Ancient Hist. 2009). Admitted solicitor, 1980; solicitor, 1980–2001; a Dep. Dist Judge, 1999–2001; Dist Judge, 2001–14. *Recreations:* walking, ancient history, cooking, reading, travelling. *Address:* Swansea Civil Justice Centre, Caravella House, Quay West, Quay Parade, Swansea SA1 1SP. *T:* (01792) 485800, *Fax:* (01792) 485810.

**GARLICK, Rev. Preb. Kathleen Beatrice, (Kay);** DL; Chaplain to the Queen, 2011–19; *b* 26 Feb. 1949; *d* of Arthur and Beatrice Harris; *m* 1973, Dr Peter Garlick; one *s* three *d*. *Educ:* Prendergast Grammar Sch.; Leeds Univ. (BA Hons Music); Birmingham Univ. (PGCE); Gloucester Sch. for Ministry. Music teacher, Kidbrooke Comprehensive Sch., 1973–75; mother and housewife, 1975–87; ordained deacon, 1990, priest, 1994; NSM, Birch Gp of parishes, Hereford dio., 1990–96; Chaplain, Hereford Sixth Form Coll., 1996–2002; Rector, Wormelow Hundred Benefice, 2002–09; Cathedral Chaplain, Hereford Cathedral, 2009–13. Member: Gen. Synod of C of E, 1995–2010 (Chair, Business Cttee, 2006–10); Archbishop's Council, 2006–10. DL Herefordshire, 2013. *Recreations:* playing and singing Early Music (Medieval and Renaissance), directing choirs and persuading and encouraging even the least confident to sing. *Address:* Birch Lodge, Much Birch, Herefordshire HR2 8HT. *T:* (01981) 540666. *E:* kaygarlick@hotmail.com.

**GARLICK, Paul Richard;** QC 1996; a Recorder, since 1997; *b* 14 Aug. 1952; *s* of late Arthur Garlick and of Dorothy Garlick (*née* Allan). *Educ:* Liverpool Univ. (LLB 1973). Called to the Bar, Middle Temple, 1974, Bencher, 2005; Standing Counsel to HM Customs and Excise, 1990–96; Asst Recorder, 1993–97. Internat. Judge, War Crimes Chamber of State Court of Bosnia and Herzegovina, 2005–06. Co-Founder, Cerno Solutions, 2015–. Trustee, Redress, 2004–09. Mem., Justice, 2005–. *Recreations:* music, cooking, walking, travel.

**GARLING, David John Haldane, (Ben),** ScD; Reader in Mathematical Analysis, Cambridge University, 1978–99, now Emeritus; Fellow of St John's College, Cambridge, since 1963; *b* 26 July 1937; *s* of Leslie Ernest Garling and Frances Margaret Garling; *m* 1963, Anthea Mary Eileen Dixon; two *s* one *d*. *Educ:* Highgate Sch.; St John's Coll., Cambridge (BA, MA, PhD; ScD 1978). Cambridge University: Asst Lectr, 1963–64; Lectr, 1964–78; Head of Dept of Pure Maths and Math. Stats, 1984–91; Pro-Proctor, 1995–96, Sen. Proctor, 1996–97, Dep. Proctor, 1997–98; Tutor, 1971–78, Pres., 1987–91, St John's Coll. Mem., SERC Mathematics Cttee, 1983–86. Exec. Sec., London Mathematical Soc., 1998–2002 (Mem. Council, 1986–88 and 1995–98; Meetings and Membership Sec., 1995–98). *Publications:* A Course in Galois Theory, 1987; Inequalities, 2007; Clifford Algebras, 2011; A Course in Mathematical Analysis, 3 vols, 2013–14; papers in sci. jls. *Address:* St John's College, Cambridge CB2 1TP. *T:* (01223) 338600.

**GARMOYLE, Viscount; Hugh Sebastian Frederick Cairns;** non-executive Chairman, Saltus Investment Managers, since 2014; *b* 26 March 1965; *s* and *heir* of Earl Cairns, *qv*; *m* 1991, Juliet, *d* of Andrew Eustace Palmer, *qv*; one *s* two *d*. *Educ:* Eton; Edinburgh Univ. (MA Hons); London Coll. of Law. With Freshfields, solicitors, 1990–94; Partner, 1999–2001, Man. Dir, 2002–08, Cazenove, stockbrokers, subseq. JPMorgan Cazenove; Partner, Venrex Investment Mgt, 2009–14. Non-executive Director: Hampden Agencies Ltd, 2010–; Hampden Capital Ltd, 2010–; Devonshire Homes (Bracken) Ltd, 2010–16;

RateSetter, 2011–17; Red Savannah, 2011– (non-exec. Chm., 2012–); Pigeon Capital Mgt, 2018–; non-exec. Chm., Cromwell Place Gall. Building, 2017–. *Heir: s* Hon. Oliver David Andrew Cairns, *b* 7 March 1993.

**GARNER, Alan,** OBE 2001; FSA, FRSL; author; *b* 17 Oct. 1934; *s* of Colin and Marjorie Garner; *m* 1st, 1956, Ann Cook; one *s* two *d*; 2nd, 1972, Griselda Greaves; one *s* one *d*. *Educ:* Alderley Edge Council Sch.; Manchester Grammar Sch.; Magdalen Coll., Oxford. Writer and presenter, documentary films: Places and Things, 1978; Images, 1981 (First Prize, Chicago Internat. Film Fest.). Vis. Prof., Sch. of Applied Scis, Univ. of Huddersfield, 2012. Mem. Internat. Editl Bd, Detskaya Literatura Publishers, Moscow, 1991–. Co-Founder, Blackden Trust, 2004. Garner Lect., Jodrell Bank Discovery Centre, 2015. FSA 2007; FRSL 2012. Hon. DLitt: Warwick, 2010; Salford, 2011; Manchester Metropolitan, 2013; DUniv Huddersfield, 2012. Karl Edward Wagner Special Award, British Fantasy Soc., 2003; World Fantasy Lifetime Award, World Fantasy Convention, Toronto, 2012. *Publications:* The Weirdstone of Brisingamen, 1960 (Lewis Carroll Shelf Award, USA, 1970); The Moon of Gomrath, 1963; Elidor, 1965; Holly from the Bongs, 1966; The Old Man of Mow, 1967; The Owl Service, 1967 (Library Assoc. Carnegie Medal 1967, Guardian Award 1968); The Hamish Hamilton Book of Goblins, 1969; Red Shift, 1973 (with John Mackenzie, filmed 1978); (with Albin Trowski) The Breadhorse, 1975; The Guizer, 1975; The Stone Book, 1976 (Phoenix Award, Children's Lit. Assoc. of Amer., 1996); Tom Fobble's Day, 1977; Granny Reardun, 1977; The Aimer Gate, 1978; Fairy Tales of Gold, 1979; The Lad of the Gad, 1980; Alan Garner's Book of British Fairy Tales, 1984; A Bag of Moonshine, 1986; Jack and the Beanstalk, 1992; Once Upon a Time, 1993; Strandloper, 1996; The Voice That Thunders, 1997; The Little Red Hen, 1997; The Well of the Wind, 1998; Grey Wolf, Prince Jack and the Firebird, 1998; Approach to the Edge, 1998; Thursbitch, 2003; By Seven Firs and Goldenstone, 2010; Collected Folk Tales, 2011; Boneland, 2012; (with Mark Edmonds) The Beauty Things, 2016; The Common Dean, 2016; Where Shall We Run To?, 2018; *plays:* Lamaload, 1978; Lurga Lom, 1980; To Kill a King, 1980; Sally Water, 1982; The Keeper, 1983; Out of the Dark, 2015; *dance drama:* The Green Mist, 1970; *libretti:* The Bellybag, 1971 (music by Richard Morris); Potter Thompson, 1972 (music by Gordon Crosse); Lord Flame, 1995. *Recreation:* work. *Address:* Blackden, Cheshire CW4 8BY.

**GARNER, Prof. (Christopher) David,** PhD; FRS 1997; CChem, FRSC; Professor of Biological Inorganic Chemistry, University of Nottingham, 1999–2010, now Emeritus; *b* 9 Nov. 1941; *s* of Richard Norman Garner and Chrystabel (*née* Potts); *m* 1968, Pamela Eva Kershaw; one *s* one *d*. *Educ:* Cheadle Hulme Warehousemen & Clerk's Orphans' Sch.; Nottingham Univ. (BSc 1st Cl. Hons Chem. 1963; PhD 1966). CChem 1982; FRSC 1982. Post-doctoral Res. Fellow, CIT, 1966–67; ICI Res. Fellow, Univ. of Nottingham, 1967–68; University of Manchester: Lectr in Chemistry, 1968–78; Sen. Lectr, 1978–84; Prof. of Inorganic Chemistry, 1984–99; Hd of Chemistry, 1988–96; Mem. Court, 1995–99; Mem. Council, 1996–99. Vis. Prof., Univ. of Lausanne, 1977; Frontiers in Chem. Res. Vis. Prof., Texas A&M Univ., 1987; Visiting Professor: Strasbourg Univ., 1990–92; Univ. of Florence, 1995; Univ. of Arizona, 1998; Sydney Univ., 2000; Wilsmore Fellow, Univ. of Melbourne, 1994; Bye Fellow and Fellow, Robinson Coll., Cambridge, 1997. Chm., Metbio Prog., ESF, 1994–98. Royal Society of Chemistry: Pres., Dalton Div., 2001–04; Mem. Council, 2005–11; Pres., 2008–10; Tilden Medal, 1985; Chatt Lectr, 1999; Inorganic Biochem. Award, 2002; Ludwig Mond Lectr, 2007–08. Founding Pres., Soc. Biol Inorganic Chem., 1996–98; Royal Society: Mem., 1998–2001, 2010–11, 2016–17, Chm., 2017–19, Sectional Cttee 3; Member: Hooke Cttee, 2011–17; Publg Bd, 2011–17; Editl Bd, Biographical Memoirs of Fellows of Royal Soc., 2016–; Editl Bd, Phil. Trans A, 2017– (Chm., 2011–18). Mem., Danish Internat. Rev. Panel in field of Chem., 2014–17. Mem., Ramsay Trust Adv. Council, 2011–. Hon. Fellow, Chinese Chemical Soc., 2011. Elder, URC, Bramhall, and Chm., Develt Gp, 1990–98. Ed.–in-Chief, RSC Metallobiol. textbook series, 2012–. *Publications:* over 400 original res. papers and reviews, primarily concerned with roles of transition metals in biological systems and develt of chemical analogues for selected transition metal centres which occur in nature. *Recreations:* spending time with family and friends, attending theatre, dining out, listening to classical music and popular music of 1960s and 1970s. *Address:* School of Chemistry, Nottingham University, Nottingham NG7 2RD. *T:* (0115) 921 2711.

**GARNER, John Donald,** CMG 1988; CVO 1991 (LVO 1979); HM Diplomatic Service, retired; *b* 15 April 1931; *s* of late Ronald Garner and Doris Ethel Garner (*née* Norton); *m* Karen Maria Conway; two *d*. *Educ:* Trinity Grammar Sch., N22. Royal Navy, National Service, 1949–51. Foreign Office, 1952–55; Third Secretary: Seoul, 1955; Bangkok, 1957; Foreign Office, 1959–63; Second Secretary: Benghazi and Tripoli, 1963–67; Sydney, 1967–69; First Sec., Tel Aviv, 1969–73; FCO, 1973–76; NDC 1976; Dep. High Commissioner, Lilongwe, 1977–80; Chargé d'affaires, Kabul, 1981–84; High Comr, The Gambia, 1984–87; Consul-Gen., Houston, 1988–91. Rep. of Sec. of State for Foreign and Commonwealth Affairs, 1996–2011. *Recreation:* golf. *Address:* 30 The Green, N14 6EN. *T:* (020) 8882 6808. *Club:* South Herts Golf.

**GARNER, His Honour Michael Scott;** a Circuit Judge, 1988–2004; *b* 10 April 1939; *s* of William Garner and Doris Mary (*née* Scott); *m* 1st, 1964, Sheila Margaret (*d* 1981) (*née* Garland); one *s* one *d*; 2nd, 1982, Margaret Anne (*née* Senior). *Educ:* Huddersfield Coll.; Manchester Univ. (LLB). Admitted Solicitor, 1965. Asst Recorder, 1978–85; a Recorder, 1985–88. *Recreations:* reading, walking, gardening, motoring, cooking.

**GARNER, Rosamund;** Headteacher, Newport Girls' High School, 2011–17; *b* Wolverhampton, 17 March 1958; *d* of Kenneth and Jean Hodgkiss; *m* 1981, Kevin Garner; two *c*. *Educ:* Highfields Sch.; Wolverhampton Univ. (BA Hons Humanities); W Midlands Coll. (PGCE); Nottingham Univ. (MBA Public Services (Educn)). NPQH. Queen Mary's High Sch., 1980–2011. *Recreations:* walking, gardening, skiing, family. *Club:* Lansdowne.

**GARNETT, Ven. David Christopher;** Archdeacon of Chesterfield, 1996–2009, now Archdeacon Emeritus; Priest-in-charge, Beeley and Edensor, 2007–12; *b* 26 Sept. 1945; *s* of Douglas and Audrey Garnett; *m* 1974, Susanne Crawford; two *s*. *Educ:* Giggleswick Sch.; Nottingham Univ. (BA Hons); Fitzwilliam Coll., Cambridge (BA Hons); Westcott House, Cambridge; MA Cantab. Curate of Cottingham, E Yorks, 1969–72; Chaplain, Fellow, Tutor, Selwyn Coll. and Pastoral Advr, Newnham Coll., Cambridge, 1972–77; Rector of Patterdale and Diocesan Dir of Ordinands, Carlisle, 1977–80; Vicar of Heald Green, Dio. Chester and Chaplain, St Ann's Hospice, 1980–87; Rector of Christleton and Chm., Bishop's Theol Adv. Gp, 1987–92; Team Rector, Ellesmere Port, 1992–96; Canon of Derby Cathedral, 1996–2009, now Canon Emeritus. Mem. Gen. Synod, 1990–96, 2000–05. Chaplain, Chatsworth, 2008–13. Mem. Council, Derby Univ., 2004–12 (Chm., Chaplaincy Council, 1996–2013). Member: Poultry Club of GB (Hon. Chaplain, 2018–); 2cv Club; Cambridge Soc. *Recreations:* clarinet playing, dog training, gardening, poultry breeding, theological exploration.

**GARNETT, Adm. Sir Ian (David Graham),** KCB 1998; Commandant, Royal College of Defence Studies, 2005–08; *b* 27 Sept. 1944; *s* of late Capt. Ian Graham Hartt Garnett, DSC, RN and Barbara Anne Langrishe (*née* Hackett); *m* 1973, Charlotte Mary Anderson; one *s* two *d*. *Educ:* Canford Sch.; BRNC, Dartmouth. Entered RN, 1962; Lt 1967; flying trng, 1968–69; HMS Hermes, 814 Sqdn, 1969–70; Loan Service, RAN, 1971–72; HMS Tiger, 826 Sqdn, 1973–74; Warfare Officer, 1974–76; HMS Blake, Sen. Pilot, 820 Sqdn, 1977–78; Dep. Dir, JMOTS, 1978–80; in comd, HMS Amazon, 1981–82; RN staff course, 1983; Asst Dir, Operational Requirements, 1983–86; Captain Fourth Frigate Sqdn (HMS Active), 1986–88; RN Presentation Team, 1988–89; Dir Operational Requirements, 1989–92; FO Naval Aviation, 1993–95; Dep. SACLANT, 1995–98; Chief of Jt Ops, MoD, 1999–2001; COS SHAPE, 2001–04. Chm., Chatham Historic Dockyard Trust, 2005–16; Mem., Commonwealth War Graves Commn, 2006–11 (Vice-Chm., 2008–11). Mem., Fleet Air Arm Officers Assoc., 1992–. *Recreation:* my family and other matters. *Address:* Haslemere, Surrey. *Club:* Royal Navy of 1765 and 1785.

**GARNETT, Dame Julia Charity;** *see* Cleverdon, Dame J. C.

**GARNETT, Kevin Mitchell;** QC 1991; *b* 22 June 1950; *s* of Frank Raymond Garnett and Cynthia Ruby Eberstein; *m* 1980, Susan Jane Louise (*née* Diboll); one *s*. *Educ:* Bradfield Coll., Berks; University Coll., Oxford (MA). Called to the Bar, Middle Temple, 1975; Bencher, Lincoln's Inn, 2000. Asst Recorder, 1996–2000; Recorder, 2000–05; a Dep. High Court Judge, 2000–05; Legal Mem., Bds of Appeal, 2005–15, Enlarged Bd of Appeal, 2010–15, Eur. Patent Office. Vice-Chm., Cartoon Art Trust, 1994–2005. *Publications:* (ed jtly) Williams, Mortimer and Sunnucks on Executors, Administrators and Probate, 16th edn 1982, 17th edn 1993; (ed jtly) Copinger and Skone James on Copyright, 13th edn 1991 to 16th edn 2010, (consulting ed.) 17th edn 2016; (contrib.) Copyright and Free Speech, 2005; (jtly) Moral Rights, 2010, 2nd edn 2016. *Recreations:* singing, mountain walking, tennis. *Club:* Travellers.

**GARNHAM, Diana Anjoli;** Director (formerly Consultant), RDBInsight, since 2015; Chief Executive, Science Council, 2006–15; *b* 17 Nov. 1954; *d* of George Leslie John Garnham and Monisha Vida (*née* Mander); *m* 2003, Rodney Stewart Buse. *Educ:* Christ's Hosp., Hertford; Lady Margaret Sch., London; Univ. of Leicester (BSocSc (Politics)); King's Coll. London (MA War Studies); University Coll. of Wales, Aberystwyth. Admin. Sec., Council on Christian Approaches to Defence and Disarmament, 1983–87; Association of Medical Research Charities: Exec. Officer, 1987–89; Asst Sec.-Gen., 1989–91; Gen. Sec., then Chief Exec., AMRC, 1991–2005. Member: BBC Appeals Cttee, 1992–98; Bd, Groundwork Southwark, 1995–2002; NHS Standing Cttee (formerly Adv. Gp) on Consumer Involvement in NHS R&D, 1997–2002; Chief Scientist Cttee, Scottish Exec., 1999–2005; COPUS, Royal Soc., 2001–03; HEFCE Res. Strategy Cttee, 2003–06; Panel, UK Stem Cell Initiative, 2005; Nat. Adv. Gp, UK Resource Centre for Women in SET, 2006–10; Forensic Sci. Occupational Cttee, 2006–08; Nat. Scis Cttee, UK Nat. Commn for UNESCO, 2006–11; Chairman: Mgt Bd, Coalition for Med. Progress, 2003–05; Sci. for Careers Expert Gp, DIUS, then BIS, 2009–11; Mem., Technician Council, 2010–14; Ind. Mem., CITB, 2015– (Chair, Audit and Risk Cttee, 2015–). Member: Adv. Cttee, Inst. of Psychiatry, 2003–08; Council, Nottingham Univ., 2003–11; Corp. of South Coast Coll. Hastings, 2012–18; Corp. of E Sussex Coll. Gp, 2018–; Co. and Council of Christ's Hosp., 2018–; Vice-Chm., Alumni Giving Cttee, 2011–17, Alumni Adv. Gp, 2017–, KCL. Trustee: Sense about Science, 2003–19; Internat. Spinal Res. Trust, 2008–11; Mem., Bd, Benevolent Soc. of Blues, 2000–13 (Dep. Chm., 2009–13); Patron, Cae Dai Trust, 2008–. Hon. DLaws Leicester, 2013; Hon. DSc Brighton, 2017. *Recreations:* family, friends, music, needlecraft, travel, gardening. *Address:* Marchmont, Friars Hill, Guestling, E Sussex TN35 4HJ. *T:* (01424) 813046. *E:* dianagarnham@rdbinsight.co.uk.

**GARNHAM, Hon. Sir Neil Stephen,** Kt 2015; **Hon. Mr Justice Garnham;** a Judge of the High Court, Queen's Bench Division, since 2015; Presiding Judge, Western Circuit, since 2019; *b* 11 Feb. 1959; *s* of Geoffrey Arthur Garnham and Cynthia Avril Rose Garnham; *m* 1991, Gillian Mary Shaw; two *s*. *Educ:* Ipswich Sch.; Peterhouse, Cambridge (MA). Called to the Bar, Middle Temple, 1982, Bencher, 2008; a Jun. Counsel to the Crown, 1995–2001; QC 2001; a Recorder, 2001–15; a Dep. High Court Judge, 2008–15. *Address:* Royal Courts of Justice, Strand, WC2A 2LL. *T:* (020) 7947 6331.

**GARNIER,** family name of **Baron Garnier.**

**GARNIER,** Baron *cr* 2018 (Life Peer), of Harborough in the County of Leicestershire; **Edward Henry Garnier,** Kt 2012; PC 2013; QC 1995; *b* 26 Oct. 1952; *s* of late Col William d'Arcy Garnier and Hon. Lavender Hyacinth (*née* de Grey); *m* 1982, Anna Caroline Mellows; two *s* one *d*. *Educ:* Wellington Coll.; Jesus Coll., Oxford (BA, MA). Called to the Bar: Middle Temple, 1976, Bencher, 2001; NI, 2010, Bencher, 2010–12; Asst Recorder, 1998–2000; a Recorder, 2000–15. Vice-Pres., Hemsworth Assoc., 1987–. Contested: Wandsworth BC by-election, 1984; Tooting ILEA election, 1986; (C) Hemsworth, Gen. Election, 1987. MP (C) Harborough, 1992–2017. PPS to Ministers of State, FCO, 1994–95; PPS to Attorney General and to Solicitor General, 1995–97, and to Chancellor of the Duchy of Lancaster, 1996–97; Opposition spokesman, Lord Chancellor's Dept, 1997–99; Shadow Attorney-Gen., 1999–2001; Shadow Minister: for Home Affairs, 2005–07; for Justice, 2007–09; Shadow Attorney-Gen., 2009–10; Solicitor Gen., 2010–12. Member: Home Affairs Select Cttee, 1992–95; Jt Cttee on Human Rights, 2014–15; Sec., Cons. Foreign Affairs Cttee, 1992–94. Mem., Exec. Cttee, 1922 Cttee, 2001–05. Member: Howard League Commn on Sex in Prison, 2013–15; Adv. Bd, Samaritans, 2013–18; Trustee, Prison Reform Trust, 2015–. Patron: Unlock, 2008–; Ridley Eye Foundn, 2011–. UK Election Observer: Kenya, 1992; Bosnia, 1996. Vis. Parly Fellow, St Antony's Coll., Oxford, 1996–97. Mem. Bd, Great Britain-China Centre, 1998–2010; Trustee, China-Oxford Scholarship Fund, 2006–10, 2015–. Mem., Leics and Rutland Cttee, 1992–2010, Legal and Parly Cttee, 1994–2000, CLA. Freeman, City of London, 2015. *Publications:* (contrib.) Halsbury's Laws of England, 4th edn, 1985; (contrib.) Bearing the Standard, 1991; (contrib.) Facing the Future, 1993; (contrib.) Lissack and Horlick on Bribery, 2nd edn 2014. *Recreations:* cricket, shooting, opera. *Address:* 4 Pump Court, Temple, EC4Y 7AN. *Clubs:* White's, Pratt's, Beefsteak; Vincent's (Oxford).

**GARNIER, Jean-Pierre,** Hon. KBE 2008; PhD; Chief Executive, GlaxoSmithKline, 2000–08; *b* 31 Oct. 1947; *m* Danyele; three *d*. *Educ:* Univ. of Louis Pasteur, France (MS, PhD); Stanford Univ., Calif (Fulbright Scholar; MBA 1974). Schering Plough: Gen. Manager of overseas subsidiaries, 1975–83; Sen. Dir of Mktg, 1983–84, Vice-Pres. of Mktg, 1984–85, Sen. Vice-Pres. and Gen. Manager for Sales and Mktg, 1987–88, Pres., 1989–90, US Pharmaceutical Products Div.; SmithKline Beecham: Pres., pharmaceutical business in N America, 1990–93; Exec. Dir, 1992–2000; Exec. Vice-Pres., 1993–94, Chm., 1994–95, Pharmaceuticals; Chief Operating Officer, 1995–2000; Chief Exec., 2000; Chief Exec., Pierre Fabre Group, 2008–10. Chm., Carmat, 2018–; Dir, United Technologies Corp., 1997–. Mem., Adv. Bd, Dubai Internat. Capital, 2008. Officier de la Légion d'Honneur (France), 2007 (Chevalier, 1997).

**GARNIER, Rear-Adm. Sir John,** KCVO 1990 (LVO 1965); CBE 1982; Extra Equerry to the Queen, since 1988; *b* 10 March 1934; *s* of Rev. Thomas Vernon Garnier and Helen Stenhouse; *m* 1966, Joanna Jane Cadbury; two *s* one *d*. *Educ:* Berkhamsted School; Britannia Royal Naval College. Joined RN 1950; served HM Yacht Britannia, 1956–57; HMS Tyne (Suez Operation) 1956; qualified navigation specialist, 1959; Naval Equerry to HM Queen, 1962–65; Comd HMS Dundas, 1968–69; Directorate of Naval Ops and Trade, 1969–71; Comd HMS Minerva, 1972–73; Defence Policy Staff, 1973–75; HMS Intrepid, 1976; Asst Dir, Naval Manpower Planning, 1976–78; RCDS 1979; Comd HMS London, 1980–81;

Dir, Naval Ops and Trade, 1982–84; Commodore Amphibious Warfare, 1985; Flag Officer Royal Yachts, 1985–90. Private Sec. and Comptroller to HRH Princess Alexandra, 1991–95. Younger Brother of Trinity House, 1974. Mem., Council, Shipwrecked Fishermen and Mariners' Royal Benevolent Soc., 1996–2004. Gov., Sherborne Sch. for Girls, 1985–2004. Freeman of City of London, 1982. *Recreations:* sailing, golf, gardening, opera. *Address:* Bembury Farm, Thornford, Sherborne, Dorset DT9 6QF.

**GARNIER, Mark Robert Timothy**; MP (C) Wyre Forest, since 2010; *b* London, 26 Feb. 1963; *s* of Peter Garnier and Patricia Garnier (*née* Dowden); *m* 2001, Caroline Louise Joyce; two *s* one *d. Educ:* Charterhouse. Associate Director: W. I. Carr (Overseas Ltd), 1982–86; Swiss Bank Corp. Internat., 1986–88; Man. Dir, S China Securities (UK) Ltd, 1988–95; Exec. Dir, Daiwa (Europe Ltd), 1995–96; Associate Director: L. C. F. Edmond de Rothschild Securities, 1996–97; Bear Stearns, 1998; Dir, Meilen Asset Mgt, 1999–2005; Partner: CGR Capital LLP, 2006–08; Severn-Capital LLP, 2008–14. Parly Under-Sec. of State, DIT, 2016–18. Member: Treasury Select Cttee, 2010–16; Finance Select Cttee, 2015–16; Parly Commn on Banking Standards, 2012–13. Prime Ministerial Trade Envoy to Burma, Brunei, Thailand, 2016–. FCSI (FSI 2007). Mem. Ct, Coachmakers' Co., 2003. *Recreations:* historic motor sport and aviation, target rifle shooting, photography, ski-ing. *Address:* House of Commons, SW1A 0AA. *T:* (020) 7219 7198. *E:* mark.garnier.mp@parliament.uk. *Clubs:* Royal Automobile; North London Rifle.

**GARNOCK, Viscount; William James Lindesay-Bethune;** *b* 30 Dec. 1990; *s* and heir of Earl of Lindsay, *qv.*

**GARNON, Tudor Mansel**; Employment Judge (formerly Chairman of Employment Tribunals), Newcastle Region, since 2002; *b* 19 Oct. 1953; *s* of David Carey Garnon and Marian Garnon; *m* 1976, Jean Davina Hewet; one *d. Educ:* Trinity Hall, Cambridge (MA). Admitted as solicitor, 1978; Partner, Richard Reed and Co., Solicitors, 1980–92; sole practitioner, Garnon and Co., 1993–99; Partner, McArdles, Solicitors, 2000–01; Chm., Employment Tribunals, London NW, 2001–02. *Recreation:* various sports. *Address:* 139 Priors Grange, High Pittington, Durham DH6 1DF. *T:* (0191) 372 0367.

**GARNSEY, Prof. Peter David Arthur,** FBA 1993; Professor of the History of Classical Antiquity, University of Cambridge, 1997–2006, now Emeritus; Fellow of Jesus College, Cambridge, 1974–2006, now Emeritus; *b* 22 Oct. 1938; *m* 1967, Elizabeth Franklin; one *s* two *d. Educ:* Sydney Univ. (BA); Rhodes Scholar, 1961; MA 1967, DPhil 1967, Oxon; PhD Cantab 1974. Jun. Fellow, University Coll., Oxford, 1964–67; Asst, then Associate, Prof., Univ. of Calif, Berkeley, 1967–73; Cambridge University: Lectr, 1974–90; Reader in Ancient History, 1990–97; Dir of Res., 2006–07. Hon. FAHA 2001. *Publications:* Social Status and Legal Privilege in the Roman Empire, 1970; (ed jtly) Imperialism in the Ancient World, 1978; (ed jtly) Trade and Famine in Classical Antiquity, 1983; (ed) Nonslave Labour in the Graeco-Roman World, 1980; (jtly) Early Principate: Augustus to Trajan, 1982; (ed jtly) Trade in the Ancient Economy, 1983; (jtly) Roman Empire: economy, society and culture, 1987; Famine and Food Supply in the Graeco-Roman World, 1988; (ed) Food, Health and Culture in Classical Antiquity, 1989; Ideas of Slavery from Aristotle to Augustine, 1996; (ed jtly) Hellenistic Constructs: essays in culture, history and historiography, 1997; (ed jtly) Cambridge Ancient History XIII: the Late Empire AD325–425, 1998; Cities, Peasants and Food in Classical Antiquity, 1998; Food and Society in Classical Antiquity, 1999; (ed jtly) Cambridge Ancient History XI: the High Empire AD70–192, 2000; (jtly) The Evolution of the Late Antique World, 2001; (jtly) Lactantius, Divine Institutes (trans. with introduction and notes), 2003; (ed jtly) Cambridge Ancient History XII: the crisis of empire AD193–337, 2005; Thinking about Property: from antiquity to the age of revolution, 2007. *Address:* Jesus College, Cambridge CB5 8BL.

**GARRAD, Dr Andrew Douglas,** CBE 2017; CEng, FREng; FIMechE; Member, Supervisory Board, DNV GL Energy, 2013–16; Chairman, GL Garrad Hassan, 2012–13 (President, 2009–12); *b* Braunston, Northants, 8 Nov. 1953; *s* of John Douglas Garrad and Mary Ann Garrad; *m* 1982, Emma Balfour; one *s* three *d. Educ:* Marlborough Coll., Wilts; New Coll., Oxford (BA Engrg Sci. 1974; Hon. Fellow 2014); Univ. of Exeter (PhD 1979). CEng 1982; FIMechE 2006. Man. Dir, Garrad Hassan Gp Ltd, 1984–2009; merged with Germanischer Lloyd AS, to become GL Garrad Hassan, 2009. Chm., British Wind Energy Assoc., 1994; Board Member: Eur. Wind Energy Assoc., 1999–2015 (Pres., 2013–15); Global Wind Energy Council, 2005–15. Chm., Bristol European Green Capital 2015, 2014–16. Mem. Council, Univ. of Bristol, 2012–16. Trustee, Centre for Sustainable Energy, 2005–18. Exec. Prod., film, Waiting for You, 2015. FEI 2005; FRAeS 2007; FREng 2011. Hon. DEng: Bristol, 2009; Exeter, 2018. Mem., Soc. of Merchant Venturers, 2007–. Poul la Cour Prize, Eur. Wind Energy Assoc., 2006; AIOLOS Prize, Hellenic Wind Energy Assoc., 2015. *Publications:* Wind Energy Conversion Systems, 1990; Wind Energy: the facts, 2004. *Recreations:* farming, mathematics. *E:* andrew.garrad@garradbalfour.com.

**GARRARD, Rt Rev. Richard;** an Hon. Assistant Bishop: Diocese of Europe, since 2001; Diocese of Norwich, since 2003; Hon. Assisting Bishop, American Episcopal Convocation of Churches, since 2001; *b* 24 May 1937; *s* of Charles John Garrard and Marjorie Louise (*née* Pow); *m* 1961, Elizabeth Ann Sewell; one *s* one *d. Educ:* Northampton Grammar Sch.; King's Coll., Univ. of London (BD, AKC). Ordained deacon, 1961, priest, 1962; Assistant Curate: St Mary's, Woolwich, 1961–66; Great St Mary's, Cambridge, 1966–68; Chaplain/Lectr, Keswick Hall Coll. of Educn, Norwich, 1968–74; Principal, Church Army Training Coll., 1974–79; Canon Chancellor, Southwark Cathedral and Dir of Training, dio. of Southwark, 1979–87; Canon Residentiary, St James's Cathedral, Bury St Edmunds and Advr for Clergy Training, dio. of St Edmundsbury and Ipswich, 1987–91; Archdeacon of Sudbury, 1991–94; Suffragan Bp of Penrith, 1994–2001; Dir, Anglican Centre in Rome, and Archbp of Canterbury's Rep. to the Holy See, 2001–03. *Publications:* Lent with St Mark, 1992; A Time to Pray, 1993; Love on the Cross, 1995. *Recreations:* cats, crosswords, Italy, the fells. *Address:* 26 Carol Close, Stoke Holy Cross, Norwich, Norfolk NR14 8NN.

**GARRARD, Susan Björg;** Senior Vice President of Global Communications, 2011–18, and of Sustainable Business Development, 2014–18, Unilever; *b* Birmingham, 30 Aug. 1960; *d* of George Robert Anderson and Evelyn Björg Anderson; *m* 1988, Dr Martin Peyton Garrard. *Educ:* Malvern Girls' Coll. Dept of Energy, 1979–86; Young & Rubicam, 1986–91; Director: Abbott Mead Vickers, 1991–2001; Fishburn Hedges, 2001–07; Communications Dir, 2007–09, Gp Dir., Communications and Customer Strategy, 2009–10, DWP. Member: British Dressage; British Horse Soc. *Recreations:* dressage, dog walking, cooking, reading. *Club:* Women in Advertising and Communications London.

**GARRATT, Hilary Mary,** CBE 2018; RGN, RHV; Director of Nursing, NHS England, since 2012 and Deputy Chief Nurse for England, since 2015; *b* Oldham, 1963; *d* of John Crawford and Carmen Crawford; *m* 1989, Stephen Joseph Garratt; one *s* two *d. Educ:* Manchester Metropolitan Univ. (BSc Hons 1st Cl. 1993; PGCE 1994); Manchester Univ. Business Sch. (MA 2008). RGN 1986; RHV 1989. Intensive care nurse, 1987; Health Visitor, 1989; Associate Dir Nursing, 1993; Dir Nursing, 2007; Chief Operating Officer, 2008; Dir Commng, 2010; Dep. Chief Exec., 2010. Mem., Rotary Club, Worsley. *Recreations:* travel, voluntary work, exercise, friends and family. *Address:* 21 Drywood Avenue, Worsley, Greater Manchester M28 2QA. *T:* (0161) 794 7791. *E:* hilary.garratt@nhs.net.

**GARRÉ, Philomene Korinna Kornelia S.;** *see* Magers, P. K. K.

**GARRETA, Caroline;** *see* Dinenage, C.

**GARRETT, Sir Anthony (Peter),** Kt 1997; CBE 1992; General Secretary, Association of British Dispensing Opticians, since 1999; *b* Jersey, 28 Nov. 1952; *m* 1st, 1974 (marr. diss. 1985); twin *d*; 2nd, 1989, Jane Wight Scott; two *d. Educ:* Canterbury Tech. High Sch. for Boys. Conservative Party Organisation, 1971–98: Constituency Agent, Rochester and Chatham, 1973–79; Cons. Central Office, 1979–98: SE Area Office, 1979–86; Asst Dir, Campaigning, 1986–92; Dir of Campaigning, 1992–98; Mem., Cons. Bd of Mgt, 1993–98. Pres., Cons. Agents' Benevolent Fund, 1992–98 and 2014– (Trustee, 2001–); Trustee, Cons. Agents' Superannuation Fund, 1992–98, 2016–. *Recreations:* cricket, travel. *Address:* c/o Association of British Dispensing Opticians, 199 Gloucester Terrace, W2 6HX. *Clubs:* Carlton (Trustee); Kent CC (Life Mem.).

**GARRETT, Charles Edmund,** OBE 2019; HM Diplomatic Service; Ambassador to the Kyrgyz Republic, since 2019; *b* Helsinki, 16 April 1963; *s* of Terence Garrett, *qv*; *m* 1991, Véronique Barnes; three *s* two *d. Educ:* Winchester Coll.; Sch. of Slavonic and E European Studies, Univ. of London (BA Hons Russian Studies). With Barclays Bank Internat., 1985–87; entered FCO, 1987; Econ. Relns Dept, FCO, 1987–88; Sino-British Jt Liaison Gp, Hong Kong, 1988–89 and 1990–93; Third Sec., Nicosia, 1989; Hong Kong Dept, FCO, 1993–95; Head: Balkans Team, UK Know How Fund, FCO, 1995–97; Political and Public Affairs, Berne, 1997–2001; Dep. Hd, Central Eur. Dept, FCO, 2001–03; Hd, EU Enlargement Team, FCO, 2003–05; Dep. Dir, British Trade and Cultural Office, Taipei, 2005–09; Strategic Finance Team, FCO, 2009–10; on secondment as: Hd, Internat. Relns, LOCOG, 2010–12; Foreign Affairs Liaison, Queen Elizabeth Diamond Jubilee Trust, 2012–14; Ambassador to Macedonia, 2014–18. *Recreations:* mountaineering, cycling. *Address:* c/o Foreign and Commonwealth Office, King Charles Street, SW1A 2AH. *E:* cegarrett33@gmail.com.

**GARRETT, Godfrey John,** OBE 1982; HM Diplomatic Service, retired; consultant on Central and Eastern Europe, 1996–2015, and on Global Conflict Prevention Policy to HM Government, 2004–06; *b* 24 July 1937; *s* of Thomas and May Garrett; *m* 1963, Elisabeth Margaret Hall; four *s* one *d. Educ:* Dulwich Coll.; Cambridge Univ. (MA). Joined FO, 1961; Third Sec., Leopoldville (later Kinshasa), 1963; Second Sec. (Commercial), Prague, 1965; FCO, 1968; First Sec., Buenos Aires, 1971; FCO, 1973; First Sec., later Counsellor, Stockholm, 1981; Counsellor: Bonn, 1983; FCO, 1988; E Berlin, 1990; Prague, 1990–92; FCO, 1992–93; Head of UK Delegn to EC Monitoring Mission, Zagreb, 1993–94; Hd, OSCE Mission to Ukraine, 1995. Consultant, Control Risks Group Ltd, 1996–98. Order of the Northern Star, Sweden, 1983. *Recreations:* all outdoor activities, especially ski-ing; travel, gardening, languages. *Address:* White Cottage, Henley, Haslemere, Surrey GU27 3HQ. *T:* (01428) 652172; Mains of Glenlochy, Bridge of Brown, Tomintoul, Ballindalloch, Banff AB37 9HR. *T:* (01807) 580257.

**GARRETT, Maj.-Gen. Henry Edmund Melvill Lennox,** CBE 1975; *b* 31 Jan. 1924; *s* of John Edmund Garrett and Mary Garrett; *m* 1973, Rachel Ann Beadon; one step *s* one step *d. Educ:* Wellington Coll.; Clare Coll., Cambridge (MA). Commnd 1944; psc 1956; DAAG, HQ BAOR, 1957–60; US Armed Forces Staff Coll., 1960; OC 7 Field Sqdn RE, 1961–63; GSO2 WO, 1963–65; CO 35 Engr Regt, 1965–68; Col GS MoD, 1968–69; Comdr 12 Engr Bde, 1969–71; RCDS, 1972; Chief of Staff HQ N Ireland, 1972–75; Maj.-Gen. i/c Administration, HQ UKLF, 1975–76; Vice Adjutant General, MoD, 1976–78; Dir of Security (Army), MoD, 1978–89. Chm., Forces Help Soc. and Lord Roberts Workshops, 1991–96; Vice-President: SSAFA, 1991–96; SSAFA/Forces Help, 1997–2013; Lady Grover's Hosp. Fund for Officers' Families, 2002–. Col Comdt RE, 1982–90. Chm., RE Assoc., 1989–93. Chm. Governors, Royal Soldiers' Daughters Sch., 1983–86. *Recreations:* reading, walking. *Address:* c/o National Westminster Bank, Bradford Market Street, 1 Market Street, Bradford, W Yorks BD1 1EG. *Club:* Army and Navy.

**GARRETT, Lesley,** CBE 2002; FRAM; Principal Soprano, English National Opera, 1984–98; *b* 10 April 1955; *d* of Derek Arthur Garrett and Margaret Garrett (*née* Wall); *m* 1991; one *s* one *d. Educ:* Thorne Grammar Sch.; Royal Acad. of Music (FRAM 1995); Nat. Opera Studio (Post-grad.). Winner, Kathleen Ferrier Meml Competition, 1979. Performed with WNO, Opera North and at Wexford and Buxton Fests and Glyndebourne; joined ENO, 1984; début with Royal Opera, 1997; has appeared in opera houses in Geneva, São Paulo, Boboli Gdns, Florence, Bolshoi Theatre, Moscow and Kirov Theatre, St Petersburg; major roles include: Susanna in Marriage of Figaro; Despina in Così Fan Tutte; Musetta in La Bohème; Jenny in The Rise and Fall of The City of Mahaggony; Atalanta in Xerxes; Zerlinda in Don Giovanni; Yum-Yum in The Mikado; Adèle in Die Fledermaus; Oscar in A Masked Ball; Dalinda in Ariodante; Rose in Street Scene; Bella in A Midsummer Marriage; Eurydice in Orpheus and Eurydice; Rosina in The Barber of Seville; Elle in La Voix Humaine; title rôles in The Cunning Little Vixen, La Belle Vivette, and The Merry Widow; Mother Superior in The Sound of Music; Nettie in Carousel; Val in Pleasure; concert hall appearances in UK and abroad include: Royal Variety Performance, 1993, Last Night of the Proms, Royal Albert Hall, Royal Fest. Hall, Centre Pompidou, Paris; numerous recordings and TV and radio appearances. Hon. DArts Plymouth, 1995. Best selling classical artist, Gramophone award, 1996. *Recreation:* watching cricket. *Address:* The Music Partnership Ltd, 58 Howe Drive, Beaconsfield, Bucks HP9 2BD.

**GARRETT, Lucy Margaret;** QC 2018; *b* Manchester, 23 Oct. 1976; *d* of Roger Garrett and Carole Garrett. *Educ:* Univ. of Manchester (BA Hons Eng. Lang. and Lit. 1998); Manchester Metropolitan Univ. (DipLaw 2000); Inns of Court Sch. of Law (BVC 2001). Called to the Bar, Gray's Inn, 2001; in practice as a barrister, 2 Temple Gardens, 2001–04, Keating Chambers, 2004–, specialising in construction and energy disputes. *Recreations:* literature, theatre, having adventures. *Address:* Keating Chambers, 15 Essex Street, WC2R 3AA. *T:* (020) 7544 2600. *E:* lgarrett@keatingchambers.com.

**GARRETT, Mark William;** FIMechE, FREng; Chief Operating Officer, Ricardo plc, since 2009; *b* Newcastle upon Tyne, 27 Sept. 1962; *s* of Anthony David Garrett, CBE and Monica Blanche Garrett; *m* 1985, Melanie Finch; three *d. Educ:* Uppingham Sch.; Univ. of Bristol (BSc Hons Mech. Engrg). FIMechE 2012; FREng 2017. Various engrg posts, incl. Powertrain Manager, New Mini, Rover Gp, 1984–88; Ricardo plc: Manager, Gasoline Engines, 1998–2003; Global Product Gp Dir, 2003–07; Gp Engrg and Products Dir, 2007–09. *Recreations:* living for Jesus, walking, gardening, grandparenting. *Address:* Lancasters Barn, West End Lane, Henfield, W Sussex BN5 9RB. *T:* 07879 697759. *E:* markwgarrett27@gmail.com.

**GARRETT, Terence,** CMG 1990; CBE 1967; Assistant Secretary (International Affairs), Royal Society, 1991–94; *b* 27 Sept. 1929; *e s* of late Percy Herbert Garrett and Gladys Annie Garrett (*née* Budd); *m* 1960, Grace Elizabeth Bridgman Braund, *yr d* of Rev. Basil Kelly Braund; two *s* three *d. Educ:* Alleyn's Sch.; Gonville and Caius Coll., Cambridge (Scholar; 1st Cl. Hons, Mathematics). Instructor Lieut RN, 1952–55. Lecturer, Ewell County Technical Coll., 1955–56; Sen. Lectr, RMCS, Shrivenham, 1957–62; Counsellor (Sci. and Technol.), Moscow, 1962–66 and 1970–74; Programmes Analysis Unit, Min. of Technology, 1967–70; Internat. Technological Collaboration Unit, Dept of Trade,

1974–76; Sec. to Bd of Governors and to Gen. Conf. of Internat. Atomic Energy Agency, Vienna, 1976–78; Counsellor (Science and Technology), Bonn, 1978–82; DCSO, Research and Technology Policy Div., DTI, 1982–87; Counsellor (Sci. and Technol.), Moscow, 1987–91. *Recreation:* travel. *Address:* Lime Tree Farmhouse, Chilton, Didcot, Oxon OX11 0SW. *Club:* Hawks (Cambridge).
*See also* C. E. Garrett.

**GARRICK, Sir Ronald**, Kt 1994; CBE 1986; DL; FREng; FRSE; Deputy Chairman, HBOS plc, 2003–09 (Director, 2001–09); *b* 21 Aug. 1940; *s* of Thomas Garrick and Anne (*née* McKay); *m* 1965, Janet Elizabeth Taylor Lind; two *s* one *d*. *Educ:* Royal College of Science and Technology, Glasgow; Glasgow University (BSc MechEng, 1st cl. hons). FIMechE; FREng (FEng 1984); FRSE 1992. Joined G. & J. Weir Ltd, 1962; Weir Pumps: Dir, Industrial Div., 1973; Dir Production Div., 1976; Managing Dir, 1981; Dir, 1981, Man. Dir and Chief Exec., 1982–99, Chm., 1999–2002, Weir Group. Vis. Prof., Dept of Mech. Engrg, Univ. of Strathclyde, 1991–96. Member: Scottish Council, CBI, 1982–90; Gen. Convocation, 1985–96, Court, 1990–96, Univ. of Strathclyde; Restrictive Practices Court, 1986–96; Offshore Industry Adv. Bd, 1989–97; Scottish Economic Council, 1989–98; Scottish Business Forum, 1998–99; Dep. Chm., Scottish Enterprise Bd, 1991–96; Dearing Cttee of Inquiry into Higher Educn, 1996–97 (Chm., Scottish Cttee). Non-executive Director: Supervisory Bd, NEL, 1989–92; Strathclyde Graduate Business Sch., 1990–96; Scottish Power PLC, 1992–99; Shell UK Ltd, 1993–98; Bank of Scotland, 2000–01. DL Renfrewshire, 1996. DUniv: Paisley, 1993; Strathclyde, 1994; Hon. DEng Glasgow, 1998. *Recreations:* golf, reading. *Address:* 14 Roddinghead Road, Giffnock, Glasgow G46 6TJ.

**GARRIDO, Damian Robin Leon**; QC 2015; a Recorder, since 2012; a Deputy High Court Judge, since 2016; *b* Manchester, 7 June 1969; *s* of Robin John Garrido and Karen Margaret Garrido; *m* 2015, Lucy Joanna Watts. *Educ:* Manchester Grammar Sch.; Univ. of Kent at Canterbury (BA Hons); City Univ., London (DipLaw); Inns of Court Sch. of Law. Called to the Bar, Middle Temple, 1993; in practice as barrister, specialising in family law, 1994–. *Publications:* Relocation: a practical guide, 2013, 2nd edn 2016. *Recreations:* motor racing, ski-ing, politics. *Address:* 2 Harcourt Buildings, Temple, EC4Y 9DB. *T:* (020) 7353 6961. *E:* clerks@harcourtchambers.co.uk.

**GARROD, Martin James**; Headmaster, King Edward VI Camp Hill School for Boys, since 2014; *b* London, 29 Nov. 1957; *s* of Arthur and Jean Garrod; *m* 1980, Dilys Hawker; two *s* one *d*. *Educ:* Merchant Taylors' Sch., Northwood; Peterhouse, Cambridge (BA Engrg Scis 1979; MA 1984); Bristol Univ. (PGCE 1992). CEng; MICE 1987–2009; NPQH 2005. Civil engr, S Africa, UK, Japan, Hong Kong, 1980–91; Teacher of Maths, Handsworth GS, Birmingham, 1993–97; Hd of Maths, King Edward VI Aston Sch., Birmingham, 1997–2003; Dep. Hd, King Edward VI Camp Hill Sch. for Boys, 2003–14. *Recreations:* walking, swimming, paragliding, reading, family. *Address:* King Edward VI Camp Hill School for Boys, Vicarage Road, Kings Heath, Birmingham B14 7QJ. *Club:* Lansdowne.

**GARSIDE, Bernhard Herbert**; HM Diplomatic Service; Ambassador to El Salvador, 2015–19; *b* Germany, 21 Jan. 1962; *s* of Capt. Roy B. Garside and Gertrud Hedwig Garside (Blome); *m* 1989, Jennifer Susan Yard; one *s* two *d*. *Educ:* Chase Bridge Jun. Sch., Whitton; St Joseph's Coll., Dumfries; Univ. of Glasgow (MA Politics, German, Philos.). Joined FCO, 1983; Consul, Havana, 1999–2002; Consul-Gen., Amsterdam, 2003–07; First Sec., Migration, Khartoum, 2007–08; FCO, 2008–11; Dep. Hd of Mission, Algiers, 2011–14. *Recreations:* diving, golf, shooting, cinema, gardening. *Address:* c/o Foreign and Commonwealth Office, King Charles Street, SW1A 2AH.

**GARSIDE, Charles Alexander**; Chairman, The Verry Goode Group, public relations; Assistant Editor, Daily Mail, 2006–19 (Managing Editor, 2004–06); *b* 9 April 1951; *s* of John Robert Garside and Florence Garside (*née* Wilson); *m* 1st, 1972, Shirley May Reynolds (marr. diss.); 2nd, 1984, Carole Anne Short (marr. diss.); one *s* one *d*; 3rd, 2010, Gail Graham. *Educ:* Queen Elizabeth's Grammar Sch., Blackburn; Harris Coll., Preston. News Editor, London Evening News, 1979–80; News Editor, 1981–85, Asst Editor, 1986, Evening Standard; Dep. News Editor, The Times, 1987; Dep. Editor, Sunday Express, 1988–89; Asst Editor, The Times, 1989–90; Dep. Editor, 1991–92, Editor and Gen. Manager, 1992–94, Editor in Chief, 1994–97, The European. Man. Dir, 649 Service Ltd, 1997–2006. Proprietor, Miller Howe Hotel and Restaurant, Windermere, 1998–2006. *Recreations:* fly fishing, theatres, classic cars. *Address:* The Verry Goode Group, 11 Billing Street, Chelsea, SW10 9UR. *T:* (020) 7352 7173. *E:* charles@verrygoodegroup.com.

**GARSIDE, Charles Roger**; QC 1993; a Recorder, since 1994; *b* 13 Aug. 1948; *s* of Richard Murray Garside and Jane Garside (*née* Boby); *m* 1973, Sophie Shem-Tov; two *s* one *d*. *Educ:* Tonbridge Sch. Called to the Bar, Gray's Inn, 1971. Mem., Manchester Pedestrian Club, 1993–. *Recreations:* gardening, cricket, Rugby. *Address:* 9 St John Street, Manchester M3 4DN. *T:* (0161) 955 9000. *Clubs:* Lancashire County Cricket; Manchester Pedestrian.

**GARSIDE, Prof. John**, CBE 2005; PhD, DSc(Eng); FREng, FIChemE; Professor of Chemical Engineering, 1982–2004, now Emeritus, and Principal and Vice-Chancellor, 2000–04, University of Manchester Institute of Science and Technology; *b* 9 Oct. 1941; *s* of Eric and Ada Garside; *m* 1965, Patricia Louise Holtom; one *s* one *d*. *Educ:* Christ's Coll., Finchley; University Coll. London (BSc(Eng), PhD, DSc(Eng); Fellow, 1994). FIChemE 1986; FREng (FEng 1988). ICI Agricl Div., 1966–69; Lectr, later Reader, UCL, 1969–81; Vice-Principal, UMIST, 1985–87. Vis. Prof., Iowa State Univ., 1976–77. Mem., various cttees and Engrg Bd, SERC, 1989–93. Institution of Chemical Engineers: Mem. Council, 1992–; Pres., 1994–95. Exec. Vice-Pres., EFCE, 2006–09. Dep. Pro-Chancellor, Lancaster Univ., 2014–19. *Publications:* (ed) Advances in Industrial Crystallization, 1991; Precipitation: basic principles and industrial application, 1992; From Molecules to Crystallizers, 2000; papers in Chem. Engrg Sci., Trans IChemE, Amer. Instn Chem. Engrs, Jl Crystal Growth, etc. *Recreations:* music, sailing, gardening. *Address:* Bryham House, Low Knipe, Askham, Penrith CA10 2PU.

**GARSIDE, Roger Ramsay**; Executive Chairman, GMA Capital Markets Ltd (formerly Garside, Miller Associates), advisers to emerging financial markets, 1990–2000; *b* 29 March 1938; *s* of late Captain F. R. Garside, CBE, RN and Mrs Peggie Garside; *m* 1st, 1969, Evelyne Guérin (marr. diss. 2001); three *d*; 2nd, 2004, Mariota Rosanna Theresa, *d* of Keith and Oonagh Kinross. *Educ:* Eton; Clare Coll., Cambridge (BA Eng Lit, MA); Sloan Fellow in Management, Massachusetts Inst. of Technology. 2nd Lieut, 6th Gurkha Rifles, 1958–59; entered HM Foreign Service, 1962; served, Rangoon, 1964–65; Mandarin Chinese Lang. Student, Hong Kong, 1965–67; Second Secretary, Peking, 1968–70; FCO, 1970–71, resigned 1971; World Bank, 1972–74; rejoined Foreign Service, 1975; served FCO, 1975; First Sec., Peking, 1976–79; on leave of absence, as Vis. Professor of East Asian Studies, US Naval Postgrad. Sch., Monterey, Calif, 1979–80; Dep. Head, Planning Staff, FCO, 1980–81; seconded, HM Treasury, 1981–82; Financial and Commercial Counsellor, Paris, 1982–87, resigned 1987; Dir, Public Affairs, Internat. Stock Exchange of UK and Rep. of Ireland (now London Stock Exchange), 1987–90. *Publications:* Coming Alive: China after Mao, 1981. *Recreations:* studying contemporary China, writing, walking. *Club:* Reform.

**GARTH, Andrew John**; HM Diplomatic Service; Ambassador to Slovakia, since 2014; *b* Bradford, 28 Sept. 1969; one *s* two *d*. *Educ:* Tong Sch. Entered FCO, 1988; Attaché, Warsaw, 1990–92; SE Asia/Far East Floater, 1992–95; Desk Officer (Asia Policy), FCO, 1995–97; Turkey Desk, UKTI, 1997–99; Sci. and Technol. Officer, Taipei, 1999–2002; on secondment to S Yorks Internat. Trade Centre, 2003–04; First Sec. (Trade Develt), Bucharest, 2004–07; Head: Political and Econ. Section, Bangkok, 2008; EU Enlargement and Pre-Accession Team, FCO, 2008–10; Commercial Develt Unit, UKTI, 2010–14. *Recreations:* football, hiking, golf. *Address:* c/o Foreign and Commonwealth Office, King Charles Street, SW1A 2AH. *E:* Andy.Garth@fco.gov.uk.

**GARTHWAITE, Sir (William) Mark (Charles)**, 3rd Bt *cr* 1919, of Durham; Director, Willis Ltd (formerly Willis Faber), Lloyds Brokers, 1997–2009; *b* 4 Nov. 1946; *s* of Sir William Francis Cuthbert Garthwaite, 2nd Bt, DSC and Bar and his 2nd wife, Patricia Beatrice Eden (*née* Neate); *S* father, 1993; *m* 1979, Victoria Lisette Hohler, *e d* of Gen. Sir Harry Tuzo, GCB, OBE, MC; one *s* two *d*. *Educ:* Dragon Sch.; Gordonstoun; Univ. of Pennsylvania (Wharton Sch.; BSc Econ.). Seascope Insurance Services, Lloyds Brokers, 1970–87 (Man. Dir, 1980–87); Brandram and Garthwaite Ltd, 1987–88; Director: Regis Low Ltd, Lloyds Brokers, 1988–92; Steel Burrill Jones Ltd, Lloyds Brokers, 1992–97. Chm., London Market Insurance Brokers Cttee Marine, 2000–02. *Recreations:* sailing, ski-ing, trekking. *Heir:* *s* William Tuzo Garthwaite [*b* 14 May 1982; *m* 2015, Rebecca Dove]. *Club:* Royal Yacht Squadron.

**GARTON ASH, Prof. Timothy John**, CMG 2000; writer; Professor of European Studies, University of Oxford, since 2004; Fellow, since 1989, Isaiah Berlin Professorial Fellow, since 2006, St Antony's College, Oxford; *b* 12 July 1955; *s* of late John Garton Ash and Lorna (*née* Freke); *m* 1982, Danuta Maria Brudnik; two *s*. *Educ:* Sherborne; Exeter Coll., Oxford (BA 1st Cl. Hons Mod. Hist., MA); St Antony's Coll., Oxford; Free Univ., W Berlin; Humboldt Univ., E Berlin. Foreign Editor, Spectator, 1984–90; editl writer on Central Europe, The Times, 1984–86; Fellow, Woodrow Wilson Center, Washington, 1986–87; columnist: Independent, 1988–90; Guardian, 2002–; Dir, European Studies Centre, St Antony's Coll., Oxford, 2001–06; Sen. Fellow, Hoover Instn, Stanford Univ., 2001–. Gov., Westminster Foundn for Democracy, 1992–2000. FRSA; FRHistS; FRSL; Fellow: Berlin-Brandenburg Acad. of Scis, European Acad. of Scis; Institut für die Wissenschaften vom Menschen, Vienna. Hon. DLitt: St Andrews, 2004; Sheffield Hallam, 2005; Leuven, 2011. Commentator of Year, What the Papers Say awards, 1989; David Watt Meml Prize, RTZ, 1990; Premio Napoli, 1995; OSCE Prize for Journalism and Democracy, 1998; George Orwell Prize, 2006; Médaille Charlemagne pour les Médias Européens, 2013; Brücke Prize, Görlitz-Zgorzelec, 2016; Theodor Heuss Prize, 2017; Charlemagne Prize, 2017; Karl Hermann Flach Prize, 2017. Order of Merit (Poland), 1992; Bundesverdienstkreuz (FRG), 1995; Order of Merit (Czech Republic), 2003. *Publications:* 'Und willst Du nicht mein Bruder sein …' Die DDR heute, 1981; The Polish Revolution: Solidarity, 1983, 3rd edn 1999 (Somerset Maugham Award, 1984); The Uses of Adversity, 1989, 2nd edn 1991 (Prix Européen de l'Essai, 1989); We the People, 1990, 2nd edn 1999; In Europe's Name: Germany and the divided continent, 1993; The File: a personal history, 1997; History of the Present, 1999, 2nd edn 2000; Free World, 2004; Facts are Subversive: political writing from a decade without a name, 2009; Free Speech: ten principles for a connected world, 2016. *Address:* St Antony's College, Oxford OX2 6JF. *T:* (01865) 274474, *Fax:* (01865) 274478.

**GARTRY, David Stanley**, MD; FCOptom, FRCS, FRCOphth; Consultant Ophthalmic Surgeon, Moorfields Eye Hospital, London, since 1995 (Director, Refractive Surgical Service, 2007–13); *b* 23 June 1956; *s* of Stanley and Phyllis Gartry; *m* 1980, Lily Giacoman; three *s*. *Educ:* Glasgow Coll. of Technol. (BSc 1st Cl. Hons Optometry 1978); University Coll. London (Suckling Prize in Neuroanatomy, 1981; Duke-Elder undergrad. prize in Ophthalmol., 1983; MB BS 1984); DO 1988; MD London 1995. FCOptom 1979 (Hon. Life FCOptom); FRCS 1988; FRCOphth 1988. Sen. Lectr, UCL, 1995–. Discourse Lectr, Royal Instn, 1995; Vis. Lectr, 1997–2006, Vis. Prof., 2006–, City Univ.; Vis. Prof., Glasgow Caledonian Univ., 2010–. External Examiner: City Univ., 2006; Anglia Ruskin Univ., 2008–; Examr, RCOphth. Mem., Ophthalmic Technol. Assessment Panel, Amer. Acad. of Ophthalmol., 2010–13. First surgeon in UK to perform laser refractive surgery, 1989. Pres., British Soc. for Refractive Surgery, 1999–2002. Hon. DSc Glasgow Caledonian, 2010. Master's (SMC), Colebrook and Porter Prizes, BOA, 1979; Iris Fund Triennial Award, 1995; Honor Award, Amer. Acad. Ophthalmol., 1999. *Publications:* Excimer Lasers in Ophthalmology, 1997; Cataract Surgery, 2003; (jtly) Corneal Surgery: essential techniques, 2013; numerous scientific contribs and book chapters. *Recreations:* formerly enthusiastic squash player (quite good, Middlesex ranked, Cumberland Cup), guitar (not bad), piano (poor!), Ferrari enthusiast! *Address:* Moorfields Eye Hospital, 162 City Road, EC1V 2PD. *T:* (020) 7490 7222; Wimpole Street Eye Clinic, 46 Wimpole Street, W1G 8SD; The London Clinic, 20 Devonshire Place, W1G 6BW. *E:* david@gartry.com. *Club:* Cumberland Lawn Tennis and Squash.

**GARTSIDE, Timothy James**; Executive Head, Hamblin Education Trust, since 2018; *b* Rochdale, Lancs, 21 Jan. 1961; *s* of John Gartside and Mary Gartside; *m* 1984, Hilary Robb; two *s* one *d*. *Educ:* Hulme Grammar Sch. for Boys, Oldham; Univ. of Edinburgh (MA Hons); Univ. of Sheffield (PGCE); Inst. of Educn, Univ. of London (NPQH). Teacher of History and Politics, Hulme Grammar Sch., 1984–89; Hd of History, Wisbech Grammar Sch., 1989–95; Hd of History and Politics, Newcastle under Lyme Sch., 1995–98; Dep. Hd, Westcliff High Sch., 1998–2003; Head Master, Altrincham Grammar Sch. for Boys, 2003–18. *Recreations:* family and friends, history, reading, cycling, supporting Rochdale AFC, camping. *Address:* Hamblin Education Trust, Marlborough Road, Bowdon, Altrincham WA14 2RS. *T:* (0161) 928 0858, *Fax:* (0161) 924 3888.

**GARVAGH, 6th Baron** *cr* 1818; **Spencer George Stratford de Redcliffe Canning**; *b* 12 Feb. 1953; *s* of 5th Baron Garvagh and Christine Edith Canning (*née* Cooper); *S* father, 2013; *m* 1979 Julia Margery Morison Bye (*d* 2009), *er d* of Col F. C. E. Bye; one *s* two *d*. *Educ:* Cranleigh; Univ. of London (Dip. Surveying). MRICS. Founded Asset Plus One Ltd, 1999. Liveryman, Ironmongers' Co. (Master, 2018–). *Heir:* *s* Hon. Stratford George Edward de Redcliffe Canning, *b* 7 Feb. 1990.

**GARVEY, Angela Josepha, (Mrs J. G. Daly)**, FRCPE; Lord-Lieutenant of Londonderry, since 2013; *b* Armagh, NI, 1 June 1953; *d* of James Edward Garvey and Mary Elizabeth Garvey (*née* Savage); *m* 1984, John Gerard Daly; two *s* two *d*. *Educ:* Our Lady's Grammar Sch., Newry, Co. Down; Queen's Univ. Belfast (BCh BAO 1977). MRCPE 1982, FRCPE 1995; FRCP 2000–19. Various posts, jun. doctor trng, 1977–86; Med. Dir, NI Hospice, Belfast, 1986–87; career break, 1987–98; Consultant, NI Hospice, 1998–2000; Consultant in Palliative Medicine, Western Health and Social Care Trust, Londonderry, 2000–13. Specialist Advr on end of life care, Care Quality Commn, 2014–17. *Publications:* contrib. articles to peer-reviewed jls on aspects of palliative medicine and evidence-based guidelines for lymphoedema. *Recreations:* walking, Irish art and literature, Gaelic games. *Address:* 9 Coolafinny Road, Eglinton, Co. Londonderry, Northern Ireland BT47 3PG. *T:* 07739 072627. *E:* a.daly489@btinternet.com.

**GARVEY, Arnold James**; Editor, Horse and Hound, 1995–2001; *b* 7 Aug. 1946; *s* of late James Adamson Garvey and Esme Muriel (*née* Noble); *m* 1st, 1969, Kathleen Gordon (marr. diss. 1996); two *d*; 2nd, 1997, Marta-Lisà Conversi; two *s* one *d*. *Educ*: Bramston, Witham, Essex; Braintree Coll., Essex. Joined Horse and Hound, as sub-editor, 1971: Dep. Ed., 1987–94; Actg Ed., 1994–95. *Recreations*: horse riding, theatre, walking. *Address*: Via Maremmana Inferiore 378, Villanova di Guidonia, 00012 Rome, Italy.

**GARVIE, Wayne Fernley**, PhD; President, International Production, Sony Pictures Television, since 2017 (Chief Creative Officer, 2012–17); *b* Plymouth, 9 Sept. 1963; *s* of George Garvie and Frances Garvie; two *d*. *Educ*: Woodbridge Sch.; Univ. of Kent at Canterbury (BA Hons 1st Cl.); Univ. of Sheffield (PhD Econ. and Social Hist. 1989). Granada Television: producer, 1988–96; Dir of Broadcasting, 1996–98; BBC: Hd, Entertainment and Features, 1998–2002; Hd, Entertainment Gp, 2002–06; Man. Dir, Content and Prodn, BBC Worldwide, 2006–10; Man. Dir, Internat. Prodn, All3Media, 2011–12. Chm., RTS, 2008–12. Trustee, People's History Mus., 2007–. Hon. DLitt Kent, 2017. *Recreations*: football, British history, life in all its messy glory. *Address*: Sony Pictures Television, 25 Golden Square, W1F 9LU. *E*: wayne_garvie@spe.sony.com. *Clubs*: Reform, Soho House.

**GARWOOD, Air Marshal Sir Richard (Frank)**, KBE 2017 (CBE 2002); CB 2010; DFC 1991; non-executive Chairman, Accident Investigation Branches, Department for Transport, since 2018; *b* 10 Jan. 1959; *s* of Sidney Richard Garwood and Queenie Blanche May Garwood (*née* Bradfield); *m* 1981, Susan Ann Trendell; one *s*. *Educ*: Smithdon High Sch., Hunstanton; Norfolk Coll. of Arts and Technol.; King's Coll. London (MA Defence Studies). Pilot, RAF, grad. RAF Coll., Cranwell, 1979; Fighter Reconnaissance pilot, 41 (Fighter) Sqdn, 1982–85; Instructor pilot, 234 Sqdn, RAF Brawdy, 1985–87; exchange pilot, USAF, 1987–90; Flight Comdr, No II (AC) Sqdn, 1990–93; Staff Officer, Operational Requirements, MoD, 1993–96; Army Comd and Staff Coll., 1995; OC II (AC) Sqdn, 1996–98; SO, PJHQ, Northwood, 1998–2000; CO, RAF Marham, 2000–02; rcds 2003; HQ 1Gp, 2003–04; HQ 1 Gp SO, Dir of Air Staff, 2004–07; CDS Liaison Officer to US Chm. of Jt Chiefs of Staff, 2007; AOC 22 (Trng) Gp, 2007–09; COS (Ops), 2009–10, Dep. C-in-C (Ops), 2010–12, Dep. Comdr (Ops), 2012–13, HQ Air Comd; Mem. for Ops, Air Force Bd, Defence Council, 2012–13; Director General: Mil. Aviation Authy, 2013–15; Defence Safety Authy, 2015–17. *Recreations*: game fishing, shooting. *Club*: Royal Air Force.

**GASCOIGNE, (Arthur) Bamber**, CBE 2018; author and broadcaster; Editor-in-Chief, www.historyworld.net, since 2000; *b* 24 Jan. 1935; *s* of late Derick Gascoigne and Midi (*née* O'Neill); *m* 1965, Christina Ditchburn. *Educ*: Eton; Magdalene Coll., Cambridge (Hon. Fellow, 1996). Commonwealth Fund Fellow, Yale, 1958–59. Theatre Critic, Spectator, 1961–63, and Observer, 1963–64; Co-editor, Theatre Notebook, 1968–74. Founded Saint Helena Press, 1977; Chm., Ackermann Publishing, 1981–85; Co-founder and Chm., HistoryWorld, 2000. Trustee: Nat. Gall., 1988–95; Tate Gall., 1993–95; Chm., Friends of Covent Garden, 1991–95; Member: Bd of Dirs, Royal Opera House, Covent Garden, 1988–95; Council, Nat. Trust, 1989–94. Owner, West Horsley Place, Surrey, 2014– (home of Grange Park Opera from 2017). Sandars Lectr in Bibliography, Cambridge, 1993–94. FRSL 1976. *Theatre*: Share My Lettuce, London, 1957–58; Leda Had a Little Swan, New York, 1968; The Feydeau Farce Festival of Nineteen Nine, Greenwich, 1972; Big in Brazil, Old Vic, 1984. *Television*: presenter of: University Challenge, (weekly) 1962–87; Cinema, 1964; (also author) The Christians, 1977; Victorian Values, 1987; Man and Music, 1987–89; The Great Moghuls, 1990; Brother Felix and the Virgin Saint, 1992; deviser and presenter of Connoisseur, 1988–89; author of: The Four Freedoms, 1962; Dig This Rhubarb, 1963; The Auction Game, 1968. *Publications*: (many with photographs or watercolour illustrations by Christina Gascoigne): Twentieth Century Drama, 1962; World Theatre, 1968; The Great Moghuls, 1971; Murgatreud's Empire, 1972; The Heyday, 1973; The Treasures and Dynasties of China, 1973; Ticker Khan, 1974; The Christians, 1977; Images of Richmond, 1978; Images of Twickenham, 1981; Why the Rope went Tight, 1981; Fearless Freddy's Magic Wish, 1982; Fearless Freddy's Sunken Treasure, 1982; Quest for the Golden Hare, 1983; Cod Streuth, 1986; How to Identify Prints, 1986; Amazing Facts, 1988; Encyclopedia of Britain, 1993; Milestones in Colour Printing, 1997; HistoryWorld's Pocket History series: The First World War, 2010; The Second World War, 2010; Science, Ancient World to 1800, 2011; Maya, Aztecs, Incas and Conquistadors, 2011; Napoleon Bonaparte, 2011. *Address*: Saint Helena Terrace, Richmond, Surrey TW9 1NR.

**GASCOYNE-CECIL**, family name of **Marquess of Salisbury**.

**GASH, Haydon Boyd W.**; see Warren-Gash.

**GASKEL GRIFFITHS, Natasha Rachel**; see Rees, N. R.

**GASKELL, Dr Colin Simister**, CBE 1988; FREng; Chairman, Ferranti Technologies Ltd, 2000–05; *b* 19 May 1937; *s* of James and Carrie Gaskell; *m* 1961, Jill (*née* Haward); one *s* one *d*. *Educ*: Manchester Grammar Sch.; Manchester Univ. (BSc); St Edmund Hall, Oxford (DPhil). CEng, FREng (FEng 1989); FIET (Hon. Treas., IEE, 1996–99). Research Fellow, Oxford Univ., 1960–61; Central Electricity Res. Labs, 1961–62; Microwave Associates, 1962–67; Chief Engineer, Microwave Div., Marconi Instruments 1967–71; Technical Dir, Herbert Controls, 1971–74; Marconi Instruments: Technical Management, 1974–77; Technical Dir, 1977–79; Man. Dir, 1979–90; Gp Man. Dir, 1990–96, Chief Exec., 1996–97, 600 Group plc; Chm., Telemetrix plc, 1997–2003. *Recreations*: reading, walking, theatre, family pursuits.

**GASKELL, His Honour Joseph William**; a Circuit Judge, 1996–2015; *b* 5 June 1947; *s* of Joseph Gerald Gaskell and Maureen Elizabeth Jane Gaskell (*née* Thomas); *m* 1970, Rowena Gillian Case; one *s* one *d*. *Educ*: Harrow Sch.; Clare Coll., Cambridge. Called to the Bar, Inner Temple, 1970; in private practice, Cardiff, 1971–96; Asst Recorder, 1990; Recorder, 1993–96; Asst Parly Boundary Comr, 1994. Mem., Parole Bd, 2010–13. *Recreations*: the arts, sailing, dog walking. *Clubs*: Cardiff and County; Penarth Yacht; Cardiff Bay Yacht.

**GASKELL, Karen Maria**; see Facey, K. M.

**GASKELL, Prof. Simon James**, PhD; FRSC; President and Principal (formerly Principal), Queen Mary University of London, 2009–17; *b* Lancs, 2 May 1950; *s* of Leo Gaskell and Olive Gaskell (*née* Bennett); *m* 1974, Deirdre Jane Ellison; one *s* one *d*. *Educ*: Haberdashers' Aske's Elstree Sch.; Univ. of Bristol (BSc Chem.; PhD 1974). FRSC 1991. Res. Scientist, Tenovus Inst. for Cancer Res., Univ. of Wales Coll. of Medicine, 1977–86; Prof. of Exptl Medicine, Baylor Coll. of Medicine, Houston, Texas, 1987–93; Prof. of Mass Spectrometry, UMIST, then Univ. of Manchester, 1993–2009; Vice-Pres. for Res., Univ. of Manchester, 2006–09. Chair: HE Statistics Agency, 2012–17; Quality Assurance Agency for HE. *Publications*: Mass Spectrometry in Biomedical Research, 1986; contrib. articles to biochem. and analytical sci. res. jls. *Recreations*: theatre, physical exercise.

**GASKELL, Vincent**; Executive Director for New Service Implementation and Communications and Marketing, Identity and Passport Service, 2009–10; *b* 17 June 1952; *s* of late John Rigby Gaskell and Eilleen Winnifred Gaskell; *m* 1972, Anne Frances Neil; one *s* two *d*. *Educ*: W Park Grammar Sch., St Helens; Salford Univ.; Open Univ. (BA). Area Dir, Benefits Agency, 1994–96; Prog. Dir, DSS, 1996–99; Mem. Bd, CSA, 1999–2003; Chief Exec., Criminal Records Bureau, 2003–09. Mem., Agency Chief Executives Assoc., 2005–. *Recreations*: mountaineering, mountain biking. *T*: 07917 115140. *E*: vincegaskell@gmail.com. *Club*: Pannal Wheelers.

**GASKIN, John Martin**; Director, Escrick Education Associates, 2010–14; *b* 27 Jan. 1951; *s* of Les and Gwen Gaskin; *m* 1980, Rosemary (marr. diss. 2005); two *d*; *m* 2005, Jean Samuel. *Educ*: City Coll. of Educn, Sheffield (CertEd); Sheffield City Poly. (BEd Hons); Univ. of Sheffield (AdvDipEd). Headteacher: Swavesey Primary Sch., Cambs, 1984–86; Concord Middle Sch., Sheffield, 1986–89; Advr, 1989–92, Chief Advr, 1992–95, Hd, Educn Services, 1995–97, Barnsley LEA; HM Inspector of Schs, 1997–98; City Educn Officer, Portsmouth LEA, 1998–2002; Dir of Educn and Lifelong Learning, Bristol CC, 2002–04; Dir, Learning Services, Prospects Services, 2004–05; Man. Dir, Education Bradford, 2005–09. *Recreations*: late comer to running, fishing, but not often enough, wondering why and concentrating on why not!

**GASPARINI, Robert Lincoln**; Partner, President and Managing Director, Monticello Partners LLC, since 2003; Operating Partner, Compass Partners International, since 2011; *b* 22 Oct. 1950; *s* of late Baron Carlo Gasparini, sometime Italian Ambassador to Nato, and Gloria Gasparini, *d* of Marquis A. Ferrante di Ruffano and Virginia MacVeagh; *m* 1979, Marilyn Varnell Murphy; one *s*. *Educ*: French Baccalaureate, Brussels; Univ. of Rome (BA Pol Scis); Columbia Univ. (MBA 1977). Product Mgt, Colgate Palmolive, NY, 1977–79; Management Consultant: Booz Allen & Hamilton, London, 1979–83; Strategy Res. Associates, London, 1983–85; Man. Dir, European Ops, Fort Howard Corp., London, 1985–88; Williams plc: Man. Dir, Europe, Paris, 1988–91; Man. Dir, Consumer & Building Products, NY, 1992–94; Man. Dir, Global Systems & Services, NY, 1994–2000; Main Bd Dir, 1999–2000; CEO, Chubb plc, 2000–03; Chm., CEO and Pres., Drake Beam Morin Inc., 2007–11. Dir, Compass Partners Internat. *Recreations*: tennis, sailing, cinema. *Address*: 164 Kirby Lane, Rye, New York, NY 10580, USA. *T*: (914) 9672865. *Club*: La Caccia (Rome).

**GASS, Dame Elizabeth (Periam Acland Hood)**, DCVO 2014; JP; Lord-Lieutenant of Somerset, 1998–2015 (Vice Lord-Lieutenant, 1996–98); *b* 2 March 1940; *d* of late Hon. John Acland-Hood, barrister, *yr s* of 1st Baron St Audries, PC and of Dr Phyllis Acland-Hood (*née* Hallett); *m* 1975, Sir Michael Gass, KCMG (*d* 1983). *Educ*: Cheltenham Ladies' Coll.; Girton Coll., Cambridge (MA). Somerset County Council: Member, 1985–97; Chm., Exmoor Nat. Park Cttee, 1989–93; Vice-Chm., Social Services Cttee, 1989–93. Dir, Avalon NHS Trust, 1993–96. Comr, English Heritage, 1995–2001. Member: Rail Users' Consultative Cttee for Western England, 1992–99; Nat. Trust Wessex Cttee, 1994–2002; Nat. Exec. Cttee, CLA, 1998–2003; Wessex Cttee, HHA, 1998–; Wells Cathedral Council, 2004–; Trustee, Bishop's Palace, Wells, 2015–. Member, Council: Cheltenham Ladies' Coll., 1992–2001; Bath Univ., 1999–2002. Trustee, West of England Sch. for Children with Little or no Sight, 1996–2008. Pres., Royal Bath and W of England Soc., 2002–03; Patron, Pres. and Mem. of many Somerset charitable orgns. High Sheriff 1994, DL 1995, JP 1996, Somerset. *Recreations*: gardening, music, archaeology. *Address*: Fairfield, Stogursey, Bridgwater, Somerset TA5 1PU. *T*: (01278) 732251, *Fax*: (01278) 732277.

**GASS, James Ronald**, CMG 1989; Consultant, European Economic Commission, since 1989; *b* 25 March 1924; *s* of Harold Amos Gass and Cherry (*née* Taylor); *m* 1950, Colette Alice Jeanne Lejeune; two *s* one *d*. *Educ*: Birkenhead Park High Sch.; Liverpool Univ. (BA Hons); Nuffield and Balliol Colls, Oxford. Flight Lieut Pilot, RAF, service in US, India and Burma, 1942–46. PSO, DSIR Intelligence Div., 1951–57; Special Asst to Chm., Task Force on Western Scientific Co-operation, NATO, Paris, 1957; OEEC, subsequently OECD, Paris: Head of Div., Scientific and Tech. Personnel, 1958–61; Dep. Dir for Scientific Affairs, 1961–68; Director: Centre for Educnl Res. and Innovation, 1968–89; Social Affairs, Manpower and Educn, 1974–89; retired 1989. *Recreations*: restoration of antiques, gymnastics, philosophy. *Address*: 2 avenue du Vert Bois, Ville d'Avray, 92410 Paris, France. *T*: 0965201546.

**GASS, Sir Simon (Lawrance)**, KCMG 2011 (CMG 1998); CVO 1999; HM Diplomatic Service, retired; Chairman, Joint Intelligence Committee, since 2019; *b* 2 Nov. 1956; *s* of late Geoffrey Gass and of Brenda Gass (*née* Lawrance); *m* 1980, Marianne Enid Stott; two *s* one *d*. *Educ*: Eltham Coll.; Reading Univ. (LLB 1977). Joined FCO, 1977; Lagos, 1979–83; Athens, 1984–87; FCO, 1987–90; Asst Private Sec. to Foreign Sec., 1990–92; Rome, 1992–95; Counsellor, FCO, 1995–98; Dep. High Comr, S Africa, 1998–2001; Dir, Resources, then Finance, FCO, 2001–04; Ambassador to Greece, 2004–09; Ambassador to Iran, 2009–11; NATO Sen. Civilian Rep. in Afghanistan, 2011–12; UK Special Rep. for Afghanistan and Pakistan, 2013–15; Political Dir, FCO, 2013–16. Comdt, RDCS, 2018–19. Formerly Chief Operating Officer, Commonwealth Secretariat.

**GASSON, (Gordon) Barry**, OBE 1985; RSA; Principal, Barry Gasson, Architects; biodynamic farmer, France; *b* 27 Aug. 1935; *s* of late Gladys Godfrey (previously Gasson; *née* Byrne) and Stanley Gasson; *m* Rosemary Mulligan; one *s* two *d*. *Educ*: Solihull Sch.; Birmingham Sch. of Architecture (Dip. Arch. 1958); RIBA (Owen Jones Student); Columbia Univ., NY (MS 1961); Q. W. Boese English Speaking Fellowship; MA Cantab 1963. ARIAS, RIBA. Lectr, Univ. of Cambridge, 1963–73; visiting critic: University Coll., Dublin, 1969–72; California State Poly., 1969; Mackintosh Sch. of Arch., 1978–85; Edinburgh Coll. of Art, 1986–92; Vis. Prof., Univ. of Manchester, 1987–95. Former Mem., Royal Fine Art Commn for Scotland. Assessor, Civic Trust Awards, RIBA student medals, nat. competitions; Chm., RIBA regional awards. Designed galleries for Burrell Collection, Glasgow (won in open comp., 1972); awards: Stone Fedn, 1983; Arch. Design; RA Premier Arch., 1984; Museum of the Year; British Tourist Trophy; Sotheby Fine Art; Services in Building; Civic Trust; Eternit Internat., 1985; RIBA 1986; RSA Gold Medal, 1983; World Biennale of Arch. Gold Medal, 1987. *Publications*: contrib. to The Burrell Collection, 1983.

**GASTON, Prof. John Stanley Hill**, PhD; FRCP, FMedSci; Professor of Rheumatology, University of Cambridge, 1995–2015, now Emeritus; Fellow, St Edmund's College, Cambridge, since 2000; *b* 24 June 1952; *s* of John Gaston, CBE and Elizabeth Gaston (*née* Gordon); *m* 1975, Christine Mary Arthur; one *s* one *d*. *Educ*: Royal Belfast Academical Instn; Lincoln Coll., Oxford (MA); Oxford Univ. Med. Sch. (BM BCh); Univ. of Bristol (PhD 1983). FRCP 1995. SHO, then Registrar posts at Hammersmith Hosp., Bristol Hosps and Torbay, 1977–80; Sir Michael Sobell Cancer Res. Fellow, Univ. of Bristol, 1980–83; MRC Travelling Fellowship, Stanford Univ. Med. Centre, 1983–85; University of Birmingham: MRC Res. Trng Fellow, 1985–87; Wellcome Sen. Res. Fellow in Clinical Sci., 1987–92; Sen. Lectr, then Reader in Rheumatology, 1992–95. Hon. Consultant in Rheumatology, S Birmingham HA, 1987–95. FMedSci 2001. *Publications*: papers on immunology and immunological aspects of rheumatic diseases. *Recreations*: music, reading biographies. *Address*: University of Cambridge School of Clinical Medicine, Box 157, Level 5, Addenbrooke's Hospital, Hills Road, Cambridge CB2 0QQ. *T*: 07884 186139. *E*: jshg2@medschl.cam.ac.uk; 6 Parsonage Court, Whittlesford, Cambs CB22 4PH.

**GASTON, Prof. Kevin John,** DPhil; Professor of Biodiversity and Conservation, University of Exeter, since 2011; *b* 5 Nov. 1964; *s* of Mervyn John and Ann Grace Gaston; *m* 1987, Sian Roberts; one *d. Educ:* Tunbridge Wells Tech. High Sch.; Univ. of Sheffield (BSc 1986); Univ. of York (DPhil 1989). Department of Entomology, Natural History Museum, London: Jun. Res. Fellow, 1989–91; Sen. Res. Fellow, 1991–93; Principal Res. Fellow, 1993–94; Hon. Res. Fellow, 1999–2005; Royal Soc. Univ. Res. Fellow, Dept of Biol., Imperial Coll., London, 1994–95; Royal Soc. Univ. Res. Fellow, Dept of Animal and Plant Scis, 1995–2002, Prof. of Biodiversity and Conservation, 2000–11, Univ. of Sheffield; Royal Soc. Wolfson Res. Merit Award, 2006–11. Prof. Extraordinary in Zool., Univ. of Stellenbosch, 2002–14; Fellow, Wissenschaftskolleg zu Berlin, 2017–18. MAE 2011. Hon. Dr Aristotle Univ. of Thessaloniki, 2017. Recognition of Professional Excellence Prize, 1999, Terrestrial Ecology Prize, 2017, Internat. Ecology Inst.; Marsh Award in Ecology, British Ecological Soc., 2013. *Publications:* Perspectives on Insect Conservation (ed jtly), 1993; Rarity, 1994; (ed) Biodiversity: a biology of numbers and difference, 1996; (ed jtly) The Biology of Rarity: causes and consequences of rare-common differences, 1987; (jtly) Biodiversity: an introduction, 1998, 2nd edn 2004; (jtly) Physiological Diversity and its Ecological Implications, 1999; (jtly) Pattern and Process in Macroecology, 2000; The Structure and Dynamics of Geographic Ranges, 2003; (ed jtly) Macroecology: concepts and consequences, 2003; (jtly) Gough Island: a natural history, 2005; (jtly) Endemic plants of the Altai mountain country, 2008; (ed) Urban Ecology, 2010; over 500 sci. papers in peer-reviewed jls. *Recreations:* kayaking, natural history, travel. *Address:* Environment and Sustainability Institute, University of Exeter, Cornwall Campus, Penryn, Cornwall TR10 9FE.

**GASZTOWICZ, Steven;** QC 2009; a Recorder, since 2009; a Deputy High Court Judge, since 2019; *b* Blackpool, 22 July 1959; *s* of Lucjan and Edna Gasztowicz; *m* 1994, Sally Louise Barnett; one *s* one *d. Educ:* Univ. of Nottingham (LLB Hons 1980). Called to the Bar, Gray's Inn, 1981; barrister specialising in land law, admin. and planning matters, and contract and commercial litigation. Trustee, Leicester GS, 2009– (Chm., 2019–). *Publications:* Scamell and Gasztowicz on Land Covenants, 2018. *Recreations:* art, swimming, books (collecting and reading), equestrian events (watching), wine (learning about, collecting and enjoying). *Address:* Cornerstone Barristers, 2–3 Gray's Inn Square, WC1R 5JH. *T:* (020) 7242 4986, *Fax:* (020) 7405 1166. *E:* sg@cornerstonebarristers.com. *Club:* Guards Polo.

**GATEHOUSE, Graham Gould;** Director, Orchard Lane Initiatives Ltd, 1995–2010; *b* 17 July 1935; *s* of G. and G. M. Gatehouse; *m* 1st, 1960, Gillian M. Newell (marr. diss. 2012); two *s* one *d*; 2nd, 2013, Wanda M. Kwilecka; one *d. Educ:* Crewkerne Sch., Somerset; Exeter Univ., Devon (DSA); London School of Economics (Dip. Mental Health). Served Royal Artillery, 1954–56. Somerset County Council, 1957–67; Worcestershire CC, 1967–70; Norfolk CC, 1970–73; West Sussex CC, 1973–81; Dir of Social Services, Surrey CC, 1981–95. Ed., TA13, 2014–18. FRSA 1987. *Recreations:* Rugby football, cricket, theatre. *Address:* 6 Millbrook Court, Prigg Lane, South Petherton, Som TA13 5ED.

**GATENBY, Michael Richard Brock,** FCA; Vice Chairman, Charterhouse Bank Ltd, 1989–95; *b* 5 Oct. 1944; *s* of Arthur Duncan Gatenby and Dora Ethel (*née* Brock); *m* 1990, Lesley Ann Harding; two step *s. Educ:* Haileybury; Trinity Hall, Cambridge (BA 1966). ACA 1970. With Peat Marwick Mitchell, 1966–71; Hill Samuel & Co. Ltd, 1971–85 (Dir, 1975–85); Charterhouse Bank Ltd, 1985–95: Man. Dir, 1986–89; Director: Staveley Industries plc, 1980–96; Bridport plc, 1980–99; Scholl plc, 1996–98; Philip Harris plc, 1996–97; SGB Gp plc, 1997–2000; Protherics (formerly Proteus International) plc, 1997–2004; Powell Duffryn plc, 1997–2000; Tarmac plc, 1999–2000; SRS Technology Gp plc, 2002–06; Porvair plc, 2002–13; Johnson Service Gp plc, 2002–10; Cobra Biomanufacturing plc, 2003–10; Chm., Alliance Pharma plc, 2004–15. *Recreations:* golf, skiing. *Address:* Norfolk House, Chiswick Mall, W4 2PS. *T:* (020) 8994 4600.

**GATES, Hon. Robert M.;** Secretary of Defense, USA, 2006–11; *b* Kansas, 25 Sept. 1943; *m* Becky; two *c. Educ:* Coll. of William and Mary (BA 1965); Indiana Univ. (MA History, 1966); Georgetown Univ. (PhD Russian and Soviet History, 1974). Joined CIA, 1966; intelligence analyst; Asst Nat. Intell. Officer for Strategic Programs; staff, Nat. Security Council, 1974–79; rejoined CIA, 1979: admin. posts; Nat. Intell. Officer for Soviet Union; Dep. Dir for Intell., 1982–86; Chm., Nat. Intell. Council, 1983–86; Dep. Dir, 1986–89, Actg Dir, 1986–87, Dir, 1991–93, Central Intelligence; Asst to the President, and Dep. for Nat. Security Affairs, Nat. Security Council, 1986–91. Pres., Texas A&M Univ., 2002–06; Chancellor, Coll. of William & Mary, 2011–. Pres., Boy Scouts of America, 2014–16. Presidential Citizens Medal; Nat. Intell. Distinguished Service Medal; Distinguished Intell. Medal, CIA; Intell. Medal of Merit; Arthur S. Flemming Award; Presidential Medal of Freedom (USA), 2011. *Publications:* From the Shadows, 1996; Duty: memoirs of a Secretary at war, 2014; A Passion for Leadership: lessons on change and reform from fifty years of public service, 2016. *Address:* c/o 1000 Pentagon, Washington, DC 20301, USA.

**GATES, Ven. Simon Philip;** Archdeacon of Lambeth, since 2013; *b* Bromley, 12 July 1960; *s* of Michael and Ann Gates; *m* 1996, Helen Rosalind Shepherd; one *s* two *d. Educ:* Univ. of St Andrews (MA Classical Studies 1982); Durham Univ. (BA Theol. 1986). Ordained deacon, 1987, priest, 1988; Asst Curate, St John, Southall Green, 1987–91; Associate Minister, St Andrews, Kowloon, Hong Kong, 1991–95; Vicar: St Stephen, Clapham Park, 1996–2006; St Thomas with St Stephen, Telford Park, 2006–13; Area Dean, Lambeth South, 2006–13; Priest-in-charge, St Andrew and St Michael, Stockwell, 2016. *Recreations:* gardening, hill-walking, cooking. *Address:* 7 Hoadly Road, Streatham, SW16 1AE. *T:* (020) 8545 2440, *Fax:* (020) 8545 2441. *E:* simon.gates@southwark.anglican.org.

**GATES, William Henry,** III, Hon. KBE 2004; Technology Adviser, Microsoft Corp., since 2014 (Chairman, 1976–2014); Co-Founder and Co-Chair, Bill & Melinda Gates Foundation (formerly William H. Gates Foundation), since 1994; *b* 28 Oct. 1955; *s* of William Henry and Mary Maxwell Gates; *m* 1994, Melinda French (Hon. DBE 2013); one *s* two *d. Educ:* Lakeside High Sch., Seattle; Harvard Univ. Co-founder, Micro Soft, later Microsoft Corp., 1975; Chief Software Architect, 2000–08. (Jtly) Presidential Medal of Freedom (USA), 2016. *Publications:* The Road Ahead, 1995; (with C. Hemingway) Business @ the Speed of Thought: using a digital nervous system, 1999. *Address:* Microsoft Corp., 1 Microsoft Way, Redmond, WA 98052–8300, USA.

**GATFORD, Ven. Ian;** Archdeacon of Derby, 1993–2005; *b* 15 June 1940; *s* of Frederick Ernest and Chrissie Lilian Gatford; *m* 1965, Anne Maire (*née* Whitehead); one *s* three *d. Educ:* King's Coll. London (AKC 1965); St Boniface Coll., Warminster. Management Trainee, Taylor Woodrow Gp, 1959–62; Accounts and Admin, Farr's (Construction) Ltd, 1965–66; ordained deacon 1967, priest 1968; Curate, St Mary, Clifton, Nottingham, 1967–71; Team Vicar, Holy Trinity, Clifton, 1971–75; Vicar, St Martin, Sherwood, 1975–84; Canon Residentiary, Derby Cathedral, 1984–2000; Sub-Provost, Derby Cathedral, 1990–93. Presenter of weekly help-line programmes, BBC Radio Nottingham, 1972–84; presenter of religious affairs programmes, BBC Radio Derby, 1984–93; Chairman: BBC Local Adv. Council, 1998–2001; Derbys Area Cttee, RSCM, 2007–13. *Recreations:* playing the piano, classical music, German and French literature and conversation, walking, cycling and cycle training with Cycle Derby 2006–08. *Address:* 9 Poplar Nook, Derby DE22 2DW.

**GATHERCOLE, Prof. Susan Elizabeth,** OBE 2016; PhD; FBA 2014; MRC Research Professor, University of Cambridge; Director, MRC Cognition and Brain Sciences Unit, Cambridge, 2011–18. *Educ:* York Univ. (BSc Psychol.); City Univ., London (PhD). Postdoctoral res., Oxford Univ., 1982–84; jun. scientist, MRC Applied Psychol. Unit, 1984–88; Lectr, Lancaster Univ., 1988–93; Reader, 1993–95, Prof. of Psychol., 1995–2001, Bristol Univ.; Professor of Psychology: Durham Univ., 2001–06; Univ. of York, 2006–11. Spearman Medal, 1989, President's Award, 2007, BPsS. *Publications:* (ed jtly) Theories of Memory, 1993; (with A. D. Baddeley) Working Memory and Language: essays in cognitive psychology, 1993; (ed with R. McCarthy) Memory Tests and Techniques, 1994; (ed) Models of Short-Term Memory, 1996; (ed jtly) Theories of Memory II, 1998; (ed) Short-term and Working Memory, 2001; (with T. P. Alloway) Working Memory in Neurodevelopmental Conditions, 2006; Working Memory and Learning: a practical guide for teachers, 2008; contribs to jls incl. Jl Child Psychol. Psychiatry, Child Neuropsychol., Jl Exptl Child Psychol., Develtl Sci., Jl Speech, Lang. and Hearing Res., Memory, Qly Jl Exptl Psychol. *Address:* MRC Cognition and Brain Sciences Unit, University of Cambridge, 15 Chaucer Road, Cambridge CB2 7EF.

**GATHORNE-HARDY,** family name of **Earl of Cranbrook**.

**GATRELL, Prof. Peter William,** PhD; FBA 2019; FRHistS; FAcSS; Professor of Economic History, University of Manchester, since 1996; *b* Edgware, Middx, 4 June 1950; *s* of Anthony William Derry Gatrell and Mary Elizabeth Gatrell (*née* Braidley); *m* 1974, Jane Shoenberg; one *s* one *d. Educ:* Haberdashers' Aske's Sch., Elstree; Gonville and Caius Coll., Cambridge (BA 1st Cl. Pts 1 and 2 Hist. Tripos 1971; MA 1975); PhD Cantab 1979. FRHistS 2016. British Council Res. Exchange Student, Kiev State Univ., 1973–74; Temp. Lectr in Econ. Hist., UEA, 1976; University of Manchester: Lectr in Econ. Hist., 1976–79; Sen. Lectr, 1989–96; Hd, Sch. of Hist. and Classics, 1997–2002. British Acad. Res. Reader, 1995–97. Chair, Sub-Panel 27 in Area Studies, REF 2014, and Mem., Main Panel D (Humanities), 2010–14, HEFCE; Member: Sub-Panel 50 (Eur. Studies), 2004–08, RAE 2008; Postgrad. Peer Rev. Panel 4 (Medieval and Modern Hist.), AHRC, 2004–07; Res. Grants Bd, ESRC, 2005–09. FAcSS 2011. *Publications:* The Tsarist Economy, 1850–1917, 1986 (trans. Italian, 1992); Government, Industry and Rearmament in Russia, 1900–1914: the last argument of Tsarism, 1994; A Whole Empire Walking: refugees in Russia during the First World War, 1999 (Wayne S. Vucinich Prize, Assoc. Slavic Studies, E Eur. and Eurasian Studies, 2000; Alexander Nove Prize, British Assoc. Slavonic and E Eur. Studies, 2001); (ed with N. P. Baron) Homelands: war, population and statehood in Eastern Europe and Russia, 1918–1924, 2004; Russia's First World War: a social and economic history, 2005; (ed with N. P. Baron) Warlands: population resettlement and state reconstruction in the Soviet-East European borderlands, 1945–1950, 2009; Free World? The Campaign to Save the World's Refugees, 1956–1963, 2011; The Making of the Modern Refugee, 2013; (ed with L. Zhvanko) Europe on the Move: refugees in the era of the Great War, 1912–1923, 2017; The Unsettling of Europe: the great migration, 1945 to the present, 2019; contrib. articles to learned jls and books. *Recreations:* listening to Radio 3, concert going, cinema, being with family and friends. *Address:* Department of History, University of Manchester, Oxford Road, Manchester M13 9PL. *E:* Peter.gatrell@manchester.ac.uk.

**GATT, Colin,** CMG 1993; Director, Managed Projects, Commonwealth Development Corporation, 1989–94; *b* 16 Aug. 1934; *s* of late William John Sim Gatt and Margaret Whyte-Hepburn; *m* 1st, 1957, Sheena Carstairs (*d* 1996); one *s* one *d* (and one *s* decd); 2nd, 1998, Susan Tessa Jennifer (*née* Lewis-Antill). *Educ:* state schs in Scotland. Engineer, 1955–71: manager, gen. manager and consultant, agricl businesses in Africa and Asia; Commonwealth Development Corporation, 1971–94: managed businesses in third world countries in Asia, Africa and Pacific regions, 1971–88. Independence Medal (Solomon Is), 1978. *Recreations:* reading, golf, wine, basic survival cookery. *Club:* Oxfordshire Golf (Thame).

**GATT, Ian Andrew;** QC 2002; a Recorder of the Crown Court, 2000–17; Partner, Stewarts Law LLP, since 2017; *b* 21 April 1963; *s* of John Alexander Gatt and Marie Gatt; *m* 1987, Nicola Jane Gatt (*née* Cherry); one *s* two *d. Educ:* Hertford Coll., Oxford (BA (Hons) Jurisprudence 1st cl.). Called to the Bar, Lincoln's Inn, 1985; Partner, Herbert Smith, later Herbert Smith Freehills LLP, 2005–16. *Publications:* (jtly) Arlidge and Parry on Fraud, 2nd edn, 1996; (with John Bowers) Procedure in Courts and Tribunals, 2nd edn 2000. *Recreations:* family, friends, Rugby, cars, Apostrophe Chambers, drumming. *Address:* Stewarts Law LLP, 5 New Street Square, EC4A 3BF. *T:* (020) 7822 8000. *Club:* Goodwood Road Racing.

**GATTI, Daniele;** conductor; Chief Conductor, Royal Concertgebouw Orchestra, Amsterdam, 2016–18; *b* Milan, 6 Nov. 1961. *Educ:* Milan Conservatory. Founder and Music Dir, Stradivari Chamber Orch., 1986–92; débuts: La Scala, Milan, 1987–88; in USA with American Symphony Orch., Carnegie Hall, NY, 1990; Covent Gdn, 1992; Metropolitan Opera, NY, 1994–95; with RPO, 1994; with NY Philharmonic, 1995; Bayreuth Fest., 2008; Music Dir, Accad. di Santa Cecilia, Rome, 1992–97; Principal Guest Conductor, Covent Gdn, 1994–96; Music Director: RPO, 1996–2009; Teatro Communale, Bologna, 1997–2007; Orch. Nat. de France, 2008–16; Principal Conductor, Zurich Opera, 2009–12; has worked with leading opera cos incl. Vienna State Opera, La Scala, Munich State Opera; has conducted leading internat. orchestras incl. New York Philharmonic, Boston Symphony, Wiener Philharmoniker, Royal Concertgebouw, Bayerischer Rundfunk, Chicago Symphony, LPO. Has toured extensively and made numerous recordings. Chevalier de la Légion d'Honneur (France), 2016. *Recreations:* reading, walking, football, chess. *Address:* CAMI Music LLC, 1500 Broadway, New York, NY 10036, USA.

**GATTING, Michael William,** OBE 1987; Director, Mike Gatting Ltd, since 2018; Member, Executive Board, Middlesex County Cricket Club, since 2015; *b* 6 June 1957; *s* of William Alfred Gatting and Vera Mavis Gatting; *m* 1980, Elaine Mabbott; two *s. Educ:* John Kelly Boys' High Sch. Middlesex County Cricket team, 1975–98: début, 1975; county cap, 1977; Captain, 1988–97; retired from 1st XI, 1998; scored 77 hundreds, 8 double hundreds, 1000 runs in a season 17 times; highest score 258, 1984; also took 129 wickets and 393 catches. Test début, 1977; England Captain, 1986–88; overseas tours with England: NZ and Pakistan, 1977–78, 1983–84; W Indies, 1980–81, 1985–86; India and Sri Lanka, 1981–82, 1992–93; India, 1984–85; Australia, 1986–87; Australia and NZ, 1987–88; Australia, 1994–95; also, World Cup, 1987–88, *v* India, Pakistan, Australia and NZ; scored ten Test centuries; highest score 207, 1984–85. England A team coach, Australia tour, 1996–97, Kenya and Sri Lanka tour, 1997–98; Dir of Coaching, Middx CCC, 1998–2000; Manager: England Under 19 team, NZ tour, 1999; England A team, NZ tour, 1999. Mem., Selection Panel, ECB, 1997–99. Man. Dir, Cricket Partnerships, England and Wales Cricket Bd, 2007–18. Dir, Ashwell Leisure Group, 2001–03. President: Lord's Taverners, 2003–06 (Trustee); MCC, 2013–14. Hon. Dr Middlesex. Freedom, London Borough of Enfield, 2003. *Publications:* Limited Overs, 1986; Triumph in Australia, 1987; Leading from the Front, 1988. *Recreations:* golf, swimming, reading, music. *Address:* c/o Middlesex County Cricket Club, Lord's Cricket Ground, St John's Wood Road, NW8 8QN.

**GATTY, Trevor Thomas,** OBE 1974; HM Diplomatic Service, retired; international business consultant, arbitrator and mediator; *b* 8 June 1930; *s* of Thomas Alfred Gatty and Lillian Gatty (*née* Wood); *m* 1st, 1956, Jemima Bowman (marr. diss. 1983); two *s* one *d*; 2nd, 1989, Myrna Saturn; one step *s* one step *d*. *Educ*: King Edward's Sch., Birmingham. Served Army, 1948–50, 2/Lieut Royal Warwickshire Regt, later Lieut Royal Fusiliers (TA), 1950–53. Foreign Office, 1950; Vice-Consul, Leopoldville, 1954; FO, 1958–61; Second (later First) Sec., Bangkok, 1961–64; Consul, San Francisco, 1965–66; Commercial Consul, San Francisco, 1967–68; FCO, 1968–73; Commercial Consul, Zürich, 1973–75; FCO, 1975–76; Counsellor (Diplomatic Service Inspector), 1977–80; Head, Migration and Visa Dept, FCO, 1980–81; Consul-General, Atlanta, 1981–85. Protocol Advr, Atlanta Organising Cttee for Olympic Games, 1996; Co-founder and Bd Mem., Internat. Soc. of Protocol and Etiquette Professionals, 2002–. Hon. British Consul for N Carolina, 1994–2001. *Address*: 229 North Poplar Street (#15), Charlotte, NC 28202, USA. *T*: (704) 3381372, (UK) (020) 7993 6587. *E*: ttgatty@gmail.com. *Club*: Royal Over-Seas League.

**GATWARD, (Anthony) James;** Chairman: North Close Holdings Ltd, since 2016; Shape Up Fitness (Bournemouth) Ltd, since 2016; Shape Up Studios Ltd, 2011–17; *b* 4 March 1938; *s* of George James Gatward and Lillian Georgina (*née* Strutton); *m* 1969, Isobel Anne Stuart Black, actress; three *d*. *Educ*: George Gascoigne Sch., Walthamstow; South West Essex Technical Coll. and Sch. of Art (drama course). Entered TV industry, 1957; freelance drama producer/director: Canada and USA, 1959–65; BBC and most ITV cos, 1966–70; partner in prodn co., acting as Exec. Prod. and often Dir of many internat. co-prodns in UK, Ceylon, Australia and Germany, 1970–78; instigated and led preparation of application for S and SE England television franchise, 1979–80 (awarded Dec. 1980); Man. Dir, 1979–84, Chief Exec., 1984–91, Television South, subseq. TVS Entertainment PLC; Dep. Chm. and Chief Exec., 1984–90, Chm., 1990–91, TVS Television; Chief Exec., 1993–96, Chm., 1996–2000, Complete Media Mgt Ltd; Chm., Digital Television Network Ltd, 1996–99; Dep. Chm., Premium TV Ltd, 2000–03. Director: Southstar, Scottish and Global TV, 1971–78; Ind. TV Publications Ltd, 1982–88; Oracle Teletext Ltd, 1982–88; Solent Cablevision Ltd, 1983–89; Channel 4 TV Co., 1984–89; Ind. TV News Ltd, 1986–91; Super Channel Ltd, 1986–88; ITV Super Channel Ltd, 1986–89; Chm., TVS Production, 1984–89; Chm. and Chief Exec., TVS N American Hldgs, 1988–91; Pres., Telso Communications Inc., 1987–90; Chairman: Telso Communications Ltd, 1987–91; Telso Overseas Ltd, 1987–91; Midem Orgn SA, 1987–89; MTM Entertainment Inc., 1988–91 (Chief Exec. Officer, 1989–91); Redgrave Theatre, 1995–98. Member: Council, Operation Raleigh; Court of the Mary Rose. Pres., SE Agricl Soc., 1992; Governor, S of England Agricl Soc. *Recreations*: sailing, music. *Club*: Royal Thames Yacht.

**GAU, John Glen Mackay,** CBE 1989; former independent television producer; Managing Director, 1981–88, Chief Executive, 1990–2002, John Gau Productions; *b* 25 March 1940; *s* of late Cullis William Gau and Nan Munro; *m* 1966, Susan Tebbs; two *s*. *Educ*: Haileybury and ISC; Trinity Hall, Cambridge; Univ. of Wisconsin. BBC TV: Asst Film Ed., 1963; Current Affairs Producer, 24 Hours, Panorama, 1965–72; Dep. Ed., Midweek, 1973–74; Ed., Nationwide, 1975–78; Head of Current Affairs Progs, 1978–81; Dep. Chief Exec. and Dir of Progs, British Satellite Broadcasting, 1988–90. Dir, Channel 4, 1984–88. Chm., Ind. Programme Producers' Assoc., 1983–86. FRTS 1986 (Chm. Council, 1986–88; Hon. Sec., 1993–2002; Gold Medal, 2003). *Publications*: (jtly) Soldiers, 1985; Lights, Camera, Action!, 1995. *Address*: 15 St Albans Mansion, Kensington Court Place, W8 5QH. *T*: (020) 7937 4033. *E*: johngau@hotmail.com.

**GAUCK, Joachim,** Hon. GCB 2015; President, Federal Republic of Germany, 2012–17; *b* Rostock, 24 Jan. 1940. Mem. (Alliance 90), GDR Parlt, 1990. Federal Comr, Files of State Security Service of former GDR, 1991–2000.

**GAUKE, Rt Hon. David (Michael);** PC 2016; MP for South West Hertfordshire, since 2005 (C, 2005–19; Ind, since 2019); *b* 8 Oct. 1971; *s* of Jim Gauke and Susan Gauke (now Hall); *m* 2000, Rachel Katherine Rank; three *s*. *Educ*: Northgate High Sch., Ipswich; St Edmund Hall, Oxford; Chester Coll. of Law. Trainee solicitor and solicitor, Richards Butler, 1995–98; admitted, 1997; solicitor, Macfarlanes, 1999–2005. Exchequer Sec., 2010–14, Financial Sec., 2014–16, HM Treasury; Chief Sec. to the Treasury, 2016–17; Sec. of State for Work and Pensions, 2017–18; Lord Chancellor and Sec. of State for Justice, 2018–19. Bencher, Middle Temple, 2018. *Recreations*: cricket, football, walking, reading, family. *Address*: House of Commons, SW1A 0AA. *T*: (020) 7219 3000. *E*: david@davidgauke.com. *Clubs*: Rickmansworth Conservative; Tring Conservative.

**GAULD, Josephine Lucy Louisa;** HM Diplomatic Service; Ambassador to Côte d'Ivoire, since 2016; *b* London, 19 Jan. 1973; *d* of Bryan Gauld and Deborah Gauld; one *d*. *Educ*: Univ. of Leeds (BA Italian and Philos. 1996); London Sch. of Econs and Political Sci. (MSc Develt Mgt 2002); École Nationale d'Administration (diplôme d'administration publique 2016); Université Paris I Panthéon-Sorbonne (Masters La Politique Publique en Europe 2016). British Council, London, 1998–2002; entered FCO, 2002; Desk Officer, EU Dept, FCO, 2002–03; Second Sec., Kinshasa, 2004–07; First Sec., Abidjan, 2007–09; Hd, South Caucasus Section, FCO, 2009–12; Dep. Hd, Political Section, Abuja, 2012–14; on secondment to study at École Nationale d'Administration, 2014–16. *Recreation*: riding horses. *Address*: British Embassy, Cocody Ambassades, Abidjan, Côte d'Ivoire.

**GAULT, David Hamilton;** Executive Chairman, Gallic Management Co. Ltd, 1974–93; *b* 9 April 1928; *s* of Leslie Hamilton Gault and Iris Hilda Gordon Young; *m* 1950, Felicity Jane Gribble (*d* 2017); three *s* two *d*. *Educ*: Fettes Coll., Edinburgh. Nat. Service, commnd in RA, 1946–48; Clerk, C. H. Rugg & Co. Ltd, Shipbrokers, 1948–52; H. Clarkson & Co. Ltd, Shipbrokers: Man. 1952–56; Dir 1956–62; Jt Man. Dir 1962–72; Gp Man. Dir, Shipping Industrial Holdings Ltd, 1972–74; Chm., Jebsen (UK) Ltd, 1962–81; Chm., Seabridge Shipping Ltd, 1965–73. *Recreations*: gardening, walking. *Address*: Kent House, East Harting, near Petersfield, Hants GU31 5LS. *T*: (01730) 825206. *Club*: Boodle's.

**GAULT, David Thomas,** FRCS; Consultant Plastic Surgeon, The Portland Hospital, since 2006; Founder: London Centre for Ear Reconstruction, Portland Hospital, 2006; EarPerfect Centres of Excellence, 2015; *b* 21 March 1954; *s* of William and Irene Mabel Bebe Gault; *m* 1989, Debra Hastings-Nield; two *s* two *d*. *Educ*: Edinburgh Univ. (MB ChB 1977). FRCS 1982. MRC French Exchange Fellow, 1987; Craniofacial Fellow, Hôpital des Enfants Malades, Paris, 1987; Sen. Registrar, Plastic Surgery, St Thomas' Hosp., Gt Ormond St Hosp. for Sick Children and Royal Marsden Hosp., 1988–91; Consultant Plastic Surgeon: Mt Vernon Hosp., 1991–2006; Gt Ormond St Hosp. for Sick Children, 2000–06; Consultant: Bishops Wood Hosp., 1991–; Wellington Hosp., 1992–. Hon. Sen. Lectr, UCL, 1999–; Vis. Prof., Chinese Univ. of Hong Kong, 2004–05. Ethicon Foundn Travelling Schol., 1987; Wellington Foundn Schol., 1989; BAPS Travelling Bursary, 1990. Developer, Ear Buddies, 1990. *Publications*: contribs to books and articles on laser and plastic surgery, particularly on ear reconstruction and depilation laser treatment. *Recreations*: rowing, painting, sculpting, planting. *Address*: The Portland Hospital, Great Portland Street, W1W 5AH. *T*: (020) 3393 1103. *Club*: Cliveden (Taplow).

**GAULT, Michael,** OBE 2008; pistol shooter; Test and Measuring Equipment Controller, Ministry of Defence, 1997–2014; *b* 2 May 1954; *s* of Elizabeth Gault; *m* 1974, Janet Mary Manning; one *s* two *d*. *Educ*: St Bede's Jun. Sch.; St Newman's Sch., Carlisle. RAF, 1969–96: trained as electronics technician, RAF Cosford; served with 29 Sqn (Lightnings), 57 Sqn (Victors), 14 and 20 Sqns (Jaguars). Pistol shooter: British Champion, annually, 1992–96, 1998–99, and 2001–12; Commonwealth Games medals: Victoria, 1994: Gold, Free Pistol; Silver, Men's 25m Centre Fire Pistol; Bronze, Free Pistol pairs (with P. Leatherdale); Kuala Lumpur, 1998: Gold: Free Pistol; Free Pistol pairs (with N. Baxter); Men's 10m Air Pistol; 10m Air Pistol pairs (with N. Baxter); Manchester, 2002: Gold: Men's 10m Air Pistol; Men's 50m Pistol; Men's 10m Air Pistol pairs (with N. Baxter); Bronze, Men's 25m Standard Pistol; Melbourne, 2006: Gold, Men's 25m Standard Pistol; Silver: Men's 10m Air Pistol pairs (with N. Baxter); Men's 50m Pistol; Bronze, 50m Pistol pairs (with N. Baxter); New Delhi, 2010: Silver, Men's Air Pistol pairs (with N. Baxter); Bronze, Men's 25m Standard Pistol pairs (with I. Ubhi); Glasgow, 2014: Bronze, Air Pistol. Hon. Life Member: London and Middlesex Rifle Assoc.; Norwich City Pistol and Rifle Club; British Pistol Club; Holt and District Rifle and Pistol Club (Hon. Life Pres.); Nat. Small-bore Rifle Assoc. (Gold Medal, 2006); Blackburn Rifle and Pistol Club; Civil Service Sports Council Target Shooting Assoc.; Life Vice-Pres., Co. of Lancaster Small-Bore Target Shooting Assoc., 2012. Dereham Citizen of the Year, 2006–07. Civil Service Sportsman of the Year, 2006; Sportsperson of the Year, Eastern Daily Press, 2007; Lifetime Achievement Award, BBC Eastern, 2007. RAF Long Service and Good Conduct Medal, 1987; Lifetime Achievement Award, Pride in Breckland Awards, 2011. *Recreations*: qualified as a Regional Pistol Coach, green bowling, doing jobs on my wife's many lists, now a grandad with five grandchildren to play with. *E*: m.gault51@btinternet.com.

**GAULTER, Derek Vivian,** CBE 1978; Chairman, Construction Industry Training Board, 1985–90; *b* 10 Dec. 1924; *s* of late Jack Rudolf Gaulter, MC and Muriel Gaulter (*née* Westworth); *m* 1st, 1949, Edith Irene Shackleton (*d* 1996); one *s* three *d*; 2nd, 2000, Marion Bowker (marr. diss. 2009). *Educ*: Denstone College; Peterhouse, Cambridge (MA). RNVR, Sub Lieut MTBs/Minesweepers, 1943–46. Lord Justice Holker Sen. Scholarship, Gray's Inn; called to the Bar, Gray's Inn, 1949; Common Law Bar, Manchester, 1950–55. Federation of Civil Engineering Contractors: Legal Sec., General Sec., Dep. Dir Gen., 1955–67; Dir Gen., 1967–86. Trustee, Woodland Trust, 1995–2000. *Recreations*: gardening, travel, opera. *Address*: 4 Abbotts Lea Cottages, Worthy Road, Winchester SO23 7HB.

**GAULTIER, Jean Paul;** fashion designer; *b* 24 April 1952; *s* of Paul Gaultier and Solange Gaultier (*née* Garrabe). *Educ*: Lycée, Arcueil, Paris. Assistant to Pierre Cardin, 1970; founder, Jean Paul Gaultier SA, 1978; Artistic Dir, Hermès, 2004–10. Début collection, 1976; first collection for men, 1984, Junior Gaultier, 1988; first perfume, 1993; designer of haute couture, 1997–. Designed costumes: for ballet, Le Défilé de Régine Chopinot, 1985; for films: The Cook, the Thief, His Wife and her Lover, 1989; Kika, 1994; La Cité des Enfants Perdus, 1995; The Fifth Element, 1996; Bad Education, 2004; The Skin I Live In, 2011; for Madonna's Blond Ambition tour, 1990; for Kylie Minogue. Chevalier des Arts et des Lettres (France); Chevalier de la Légion d'Honneur (France). *Address*: Jean Paul Gaultier SA, 325 rue Saint-Martin, 75003 Paris, France.

**GAUMOND, Most Rev. Mgr André;** Archbishop of Sherbrooke, (RC), 1996–2011, now Emeritus; *b* 3 June 1936. *Educ*: Ste Anne de la Pocatière, PQ (BA); St Paul's Seminary, Ottawa (LTh); Institut Catholique, Paris (LPh). Teacher of Philosophy: Ste Anne de la Pocatière, 1966–69; Coll. d'Enseignement Général et Professionnel de la Pocatière, 1969–80; Parish Priest, St Pamphile and St Omer, PQ, 1980–85; Bishop of Ste Anne de la Pocatière, 1985–95; Coadjutor Archbishop of Sherbrooke, 1995–96. *Recreation*: golf.

**GAUNT, Jonathan Robert;** QC 1991; a Deputy High Court Judge, 2002–17; *b* 3 Nov. 1947; *s* of late Dr Brian Gaunt and Dr Mary Gaunt (*née* Hudson); *m* 1975, Lynn Dennis; one *d*. *Educ*: St Peter's Coll.; Radley; University Coll., Oxford (BA). Called to the Bar, Lincoln's Inn, 1972, Bencher, 1998. Jt Head, Falcon Chambers, 1993–2017. *Publications*: (ed) Halsbury's Laws of England, Vol. 27, 4th edn 1981, rev. 1994; (ed) Gale on Easements, 16th edn 1996 to 20th edn 2017. *Recreations*: golf, sailing. *Address*: Falcon Chambers, Falcon Court, EC4Y 1AA. *T*: (020) 7353 2484.

**GAUNT, Maj. Gen. Mark Jarvis,** CB 2017; Director Support, Army Headquarters, 2015–19; *b* Beverley, E Yorks, 24 Dec. 1965; *s* of late Edwin Gaunt and Ida Gaunt; *m* 1991, Catherine Alice Humphrey; two *d*. *Educ*: Beverley Grammar Sch.; Welbeck Coll.; Royal Mil. Acad. Sandhurst; Royal Mil. Coll. of Sci. (MSc 1997); King's Coll. London (MA); Saïd Business Sch., Univ. of Oxford. Commnd REME, 1985; Platoon Comd 14 Berlin Field Workshop, 1984–86; NI Regt AAC, 1990–93; BEME 24 Airmobile Bde, 1993–95; Army Tech. Support Agency, 1995–96; Defence Technol. Course, 1997; acsc 1998; SO2 Prog. Directorate Equipment Capability Direct Battlefield Engagement, 1998–2000; Co. Comd 3 Bn REME, 2000–02; Dep. COS BRITFOR, Bosnia, 2002; MA to Dep. Supreme Allied Comdr Transformation, 2003–05; CO 1 Bn REME, 2005–07; Div. Dir Intermediate Comd and Staff Course (Land), 2007–08; Future Rapid Effects System Integrated Project Team, 2008; Prog. Support Function Hd of Capability Ground Manoeuvre, 2008–10; Comdr Equipment Capability, Afghanistan, 2010–11; Hd, Soldier System Prog., Defence Equipment and Support, 2011–13; Dir Equipment, Army HQ, 2013–15. *Recreations*: motorsport, running, hiking, squash.

**GAUNTLETT, Jeremy John;** SC (SA) 1989; QC 2017; Member: Financial Markets Tribunal of Dubai, since 2013; Shanghai International Arbitration Court, since 2013; *b* Salisbury, Southern Rhodesia, 10 Nov. 1950; *s* of Chief Insp. John Gauntlett, British South Africa Police and Frances Gauntlett (*née* Hopkins); *m* (marr. diss.); three *d*. *Educ*: Baines Sch., Bulawayo; Northlea Sch., Bulawayo; Sixth Form Coll., Bulawayo; Univ. of Stellenbosch (Beit Scholar; BA LLB 1973); New Coll., Oxford (Rhodes Scholar). Called to the Bar: Cape, 1976 (Pres., 1997–99); Johannesburg, 1990; Gray's Inn, 1993, Bencher, Middle Temple, 2010; sessional Judge of Appeal, Lesotho, 1995–2010. Chm., Gen. Council, Bar of SA, 1999–2001; Mem., Council, IBA, 1999–2001; Founding Vice-Pres., Bar, Internat. Criminal Court, 2001–02. Mem., Law Reform Commn of SA, 1996–2010. Mem., Council, Univ. of Cape Town, 1995–2016. Mem., Internat. Acad. of Trial Lawyers, 2011. *Recreations*: swimming, reading, walking, wine. *Address*: Brick Court Chambers, 7–8 Essex Street, WC2R 3LD. *T*: (020) 7379 3550. *E*: jeremy.gauntlett@brickcourt.co.uk.

**GAUTEL, Prof. Mathias Sebastian,** MD PhD; FMedSci; Professor of Molecular Cardiology, since 2002, British Heart Foundation Professor of Molecular Cardiology, since 2008, and Head, School of Basic and Medical Biosciences, since 2017, King's College London; *b* Karlsruhe, Germany, 31 March 1963; *s* of Peter and Uta Gautel; *m* 1992, Dr Gudrun Kunst; two *s* one *d*. *Educ*: Fichte-Gymnasium, Karlsruhe; Heidelberg Univ. (MD *summa cum laude* 1991; accreditation as med. doctor 1993; MD PhD 1998). Habilitation Fellow, German Res. Foundn, and Vis. Gp Leader, Structl Biol. Div., EMBL Heidelberg, 1996–98; Heisenberg Fellow and Gp Leader, Max-Planck-Inst. for Molecular Physiol., Dept of Physical Biochem., Dortmund, 1999–2002; Hd, Muscle Signalling Section, 2003, Hd, 2016–18, Randall Div. for Cell and Molecular Biophysics, KCL. Ed.-in-Chief, Jl Muscle Res. and Cell Motility, 2010–. FMedSci 2010. Outstanding Investigator Award, Internat. Soc. for Heart Res., 2009. *Publications*: contribs to learned jls, incl. Nature, Science, Cell, Proc. NAS (USA), EMBO Jl.

*Recreations:* family, sport diving (BSAC dive leader and assistant club instructor), art, theatre and opera, antiquity. *Address:* Randall Centre for Cell and Molecular Biophysics, King's College London, New Hunt's House, Guy's Campus, 18–20 Newcomen Street, SE1 1UL. *T:* (020) 7848 6434. *E:* mathias.gautel@kcl.ac.uk.

**GAVAGHAN, Jill;** *see* Greenfield, J.

**GAVASKAR, Sunil Manohar;** Padma Bhushan; cricketer; business executive; Chairman, Cricket Committee, International Cricket Council, 2000–08; Commissioner, T20 Mumbai League, since 2018; *b* 10 July 1949; *s* of Manohar Keshav Gavaskar and Meenal Manohar Gavaskar; *m* 1974, Marshniel Mehrotra; one *s*. *Educ:* St Xavier's High Sch.; St Xavier's Coll.; Bombay Univ. (BA). Represented India in cricket, 1971–88; Captain, Indian Team, 1978, 1979–80, 1980–82 and 1984–85; made 10,122 runs, incl. 34 centuries, in 125 Test matches; passed world records for no of runs in Test matches, 1983, and no of Test centuries, 1984; first batsman to score over 10,000 Test runs, 1987. Sheriff of Mumbai, 1994–95. *Publications:* Sunny Days, 1976; Idols, 1983; Runs 'n Ruins, 1984; One-day Wonders, 1985. *Clubs:* Cricket Club of India, Bombay Gymkhana.

**GAVENTA, Sarah Elizabeth;** Director, Illuminated River Foundation, since 2016; *b* Kent, 1964; *d* of Joseph Gaventa and Eve Gaventa (*née* Roberts); *m* 2005, Dominic Papa; one *s*. *Educ:* University Coll. London (1st yr at Courtauld Inst. of Art; BA Art Hist.); Royal Coll. of Art (MA Design Hist.). Co-Founder and Dir, Scarlet Projects, 2000–06; Dir, CABE Space, 2006–11; Associate, Rogers Stirk Harbour and Partners, 2012–14; Founding Dir, Made Public, 2014–. Curator, Out There: Our Post War Public Art, Historic England, Somerset House, 2016. Freeman, City of London, 2019. Hon. FLI 2011; Hon. FRIBA 2019. *Publications:* Concrete Design, 2001; New Public Spaces, 2006. *Recreations:* brutalism, bollards and beautiful concrete, searching for the perfect gin, landscape and comfortable high heels, loves mid century modern design and late century friends and family, LFC fan. *E:* sgaventa@yahoo.com, sarah.gaventa@illuminatedriver.london. *Club:* Groucho.

**GAVIN, (Alexander) Rupert;** Executive Chairman, Incidental Colman, since 1996; Chief Executive, Odeon and UCI Cinema Group, 2005–14; *b* 1 Oct. 1954; *s* of late David Maitland Gavin and Helen Gavin (who *m* 1991, Sir Hugh Hambling, 3rd Bt); *m* 1991, Ellen Janet Miller; two *d*. *Educ:* Magdalene Coll., Cambridge (BA Hons 1975; MA). Dir and Partner, Sharps Advertising, 1981–85; Dir, Saatchi & Saatchi Gp, 1985–87; Dep. Man. Dir, Dixons Stores Gp, 1987–94; Man. Dir, Consumer Div., British Telecom, 1994–98; Chm. and Chief Exec., BBC Worldwide, 1998–2004; Chm., Contender Entertainment Gp, 2004–06; Chief Exec., Kingdom Media, 2005–06 (Dir, 2004–06). Director: Ambassador Theatre Gp, 1999–2009; Soc. of London Th., 2018–; The Living Room Cinema, 2018–; non-executive Director: Virgin Mobile, 2004–06; Wyevale Garden Centre Gp, 2014–; Countrywide plc, 2014–. Chairman: Historic Royal Palaces, 2015–; Arts and Media Honours Cttee, 2016–. Liveryman, Grocers' Co., 1986–; Mem., Ct of Assts, Grocers' Co., 2010– (Master, 2017–18). FRTS 2005 (Vice-Pres., 1997–2006). *Recreations:* theatre producing, writing, gardening. *Clubs:* Royal Automobile, Thirty.

**GAVRON, Lady; Katharine Susan Gavron, (Kate),** PhD; Chair: Carcanet Press Ltd, since 1989; Folio Society, since 2015; Folio Holdings Ltd, since 2015; *b* 19 Jan. 1955; *d* of His Honour (Maurice John) Peter Macnair and of Vickie Macnair; *m* 1st, 1975, Gerrard Gardiner (marr. diss. 1982); 2nd, 1989, Robert Gavron (Baron Gavron, CBE) (*d* 2015). *Educ:* Francis Holland Sch.; London Sch. of Econs (BSc; PhD 1997). William Heinemann Ltd, 1974–88 (Dir, 1984–88); Director: Secker & Warburg Ltd, 1984–88; Virago Press Ltd, 1994–96; Folio Hldgs Ltd, 2009–; Granta Publications, 2016–. Dir, Mutual Aid Centre, 1996–2005; Trustee and Research Fellow: Inst. Community Studies, 1992–2005; Young Foundn, 2005–09. Trustee: Robert Gavron Charitable Trust, 1990–; Runnymede Trust, 1997–2009; The Poetry Archive, 2001–08; Ballet Boyz (formerly George Piper Dances), 2001–; Helen Hamlyn Trust, 2001–; Reprieve, 2010–16; Highgate Internat. Chamber Music Festival, 2016–. *Publications:* (with G. Dench and T. Flower) Young at Eighty: the prolific public life of Michael Young, 1995; (with G. Dench and M. Young) The New East End: kinship, race and conflict, 2006. *Address:* c/o The Folio Society, Clove Building, 4 Maguire Street, SE1 2NQ.

**GAVRON, Felicia Nicolette, (Nicky);** Member (Lab), London Assembly, Greater London Authority, since 2000 (Member for Enfield and Haringey, 2000–04); Deputy Mayor of London, 2000–03 and 2004–08; *d* of Clayton English Coates and Elisabet Charlotta Horstmeyer; *m* 1967, Robert Gavron (Baron Gavron, CBE) (marr. diss. 1987; he *d* 2015); two *d*. *Educ:* Worcester Girls' Grammar Sch.; Courtauld Inst. Lectr, Camberwell Sch. of Art and St Martin's Sch. of Art. Mem. (Lab) Haringey BC, 1986–2002 (Chm., Develt Control, Planning Tech. and Envmtl Services Cttees). Mem., London Planning Adv. Cttee, 1989–97 and 1998–2000 (Dep. Chm., 1989–94; Chm., 1994–97 and 1998–2000; Leader, Lab Gp, 1989–2000); Local Government Association: Chm., 1997–99, Vice Chm., 1999–2000, Planning Cttee; Mem., Policy and Strategy Cttee, and Envmt and Regeneration Bd, 1997–2000; Chm., Reforming Local Planning, 1997–2002; Member: Exec., GLAA, 1986–92 (Vice Chm., London Arts Bd, 1992–2000); ALA, 1988–94 (Vice Chm., Envmtl Services Cttee); AMA, 1988–96 (Mem., Urban Policy Cttee; Vice Chm., Develt and Transport Cttee, 1995–96); SE Regl Planning Conf., 1989–2001 (Leader, Lab Gp, 1993–97; Vice Chm., 1997–2000); London Res. Centre Cttee, 1992–2000; Assoc. of London Govt, 1994–2000 (Mem., Envmt Cttee); London Pride Partnership, 1994–97 (Convener, Arts and Culture Gp; Co-Vice Chm., London Pride Housing Initiative; Co-Chm., London Pride Waste Action Prog., 1995–97); Bd, London First, 1995–2000. Chm., Children and Young People's Strategy Gp, GLA, 2000–02; Chm. and Dep. Chm. (alternate years), Planning and Housing Cttee, London Assembly, 2008; Mayor of London's lead on London Plan and Strategic Planning, 2000–08, on Climate Change, 2004–08. Convener and Chairman: Land Use and Transport Interaction Working Gp, 1996–99; Brownfield Policy and Implementation Gp, 1997–98; Chairman: Nat. Planning Forum, 1999–2002; Commn for Integrated Transport, 1999–2002; Mayor's London Hydrogen Partnership, 2004–08; Dep. Chm., Mayor's London Climate Change Agency, 2004–08; Vice Chm., Global Urban Develt, 2010–; Member: Thames Adv. Gp, 1994–97; Sounding Bd on Design, DoE, subseq. DETR, 1997–99; Metropolitan Police Authy, 2000–08; Sustainable Develt Commn, 2001–03; Internat. Adv. Bd, Rotterdam, 2009–; Advr, Urban Task Force, 1998–2000; Hon. Advr, Jt US-China Collaboration on Clean Energy, 2010–; Chief Project Advr, Economics of Green Cities, 2011–17. Co-Founder and, C40 (formerly C20) Large Cities Climate Change Leadership Gp, 2005. Founding Trustee, Jackson's Lane Community Centre, 1975. Hon. FRIBA 2001. Hon. Dr London Guildhall, 2001. *Address:* Greater London Authority, City Hall, More London, Queen's Walk, SE1 2AA.

**GAW, Alistair Edward;** Executive Director, Communities and Families, City of Edinburgh Council, since 2015; *b* Glasgow, 12 July 1961; *s* of John Gaw and Mary Gaw (*née* Syme); *m* 2009, Jacqueline McRae; two *d*. *Educ:* Jordanhill Sch., Glasgow; Univ. of Edinburgh (MA Hons 1983; DipSW 1986); Napier Univ. (MBA 2000). Local authy social worker, 1988–92, Sen. Social Worker, 1992–96, Lothian Region; Social Work Manager, W Lothian Council, 1996–2000; Social Work Inspector, Scottish Govt, 2001–04; Depute Chief Inspector, Social Work Inspection Agency, 2004–07; Hd of Service, Children and Families and Criminal Justice Social Work, Fife Council, 2007–11; Hd, Children's Services, City of Edinburgh Council, 2011–15. *Recreations:* hillwalking, swimming, garden, music. *Address:* City of Edinburgh Council, Waverley Court, East Market Street, Edinburgh EH8 8BG. *T:* (0131) 469 3001. *E:* alistair.gaw@edinburgh.gov.uk.

**GAWN, Ryan Marshall;** Deployable Civilian Expert, Stabilisation Unit, UK Government, since 2009; Co-founder and Director, Stratagem International, since 2011; Global Director, LEGO Foundation, since 2018; *b* Belfast, 6 April 1979; *s* of Richard Gawn and Iris Gawn (*née* Marshall); *m* 2014, Anna Wansbrough-Jones; one *s* one *d*. *Educ:* Stirling Univ. (BA 1st Cl. Hons Politics 2001); Univ. of Salvador, Buenos Aires (MA Internat. Relns 2007). Ed., Santiago News Rev., Santiago, Chile, 2003; Business Develt Manager, Procter & Gamble UK, 2003–04; Pol Admin. Officer, Strategic Planning Unit, Exec. Office of Sec.-Gen., UN, NY, 2005; Internat. Ext. Relns Coordinator, Save the Children UK, 2006–09; Regl Manager, Peace Dividend Trust, 2009–10; Dir, Penn Schoen Berland, 2010–11; Strategic Communications Advr, FCO, 2011–12, Strategic Campaigns Advr, DFID, 2012–13, British High Commn, Pakistan; Head of Internat. Communications, ActionAid Internat., 2013–17. Member: Council, RIIA, 2008–16; Adv. Panel, NI Foundn, 2008–; Transatlantic Network, British Council, 2008–14; Adv. Bd, British German Forum, Wilton Park, 2013–; Adv. Gp, British Council, 2015–; Council, PRCA, 2019–. Hon. Sec., 2007, Hon. Treas., 2008–09, UN Assoc. Arthur D. Tripp Meml Schol., Pennsylvania, 2001–02, World Peace Fellow, Buenos Aires, 2004–06, Rotary Internat.; Salzburg Global Seminar Fellow, Salzburg, 2007. *Publications:* contribs to jls incl. New Statesman, Diplomatic Courier, Guardian, Foreign Policy Mag., Public Affairs News, PR Week, Strategic Analysis, Irish Pol Studies, Peace and Conflict Rev., Internat. Affairs Forum. *Recreations:* Rugby, squash, tennis, polo, sailing, theatre, travel. *Address:* Stratagem International, Carnegie Building, 121 Donegall Road, Belfast BT12 5JL. *T:* (028) 9087 2800, *Fax:* (028) 9087 2801. *E:* ryan@stratagemint.com.

**GAY, Mark Edward;** Partner, Solesbury Gay, since 2016; *b* London, 25 June 1962; *s* of Eamon and Hannah Gay; *m* 1997, Susan Elizabeth Holmes; two *d*. *Educ:* Clapham Coll., London; Lady Margaret Hall, Oxford (BA Juris. 1984). Trainee solicitor, 1985–88, Associate, 1988–91, Linklaters & Paines; Associate, 1991–95, Partner, 1995–99, Herbert Smith; Partner, Denton Hall, 1999; Solicitor Advocate, 2007; Partner and Head, Sports Gp, DLA Piper LLP, 2005–11; Partner, Burges Salmon LLP, 2011–15. Mem., Internat. Court, Federation Internationale d'Automobile, 2017. *Recreations:* chauffeuring my children, fine wine, Buffy the Vampire Slayer. *Address:* Solesbury Gay, 9 Disraeli Road, Putney, SW15 2DR. *Club:* Richmond Football.

**GAYMER, Dame Janet (Marion),** DBE 2010 (CBE 2004); Commissioner for Public Appointments, 2006–10; a Civil Service Commissioner, 2006–10; *b* 11 July 1947; *d* of late Ronald Frank Craddock and Marion Clara Craddock (*née* Stringer); *m* 1971, John Michael Gaymer; two *d*. *Educ:* Nuneaton High Sch. for Girls; St Hilda's Coll., Oxford (MA Jurisprudence; Hon. Fellow 2002); LSE (LLM). Simmons & Simmons: admitted solicitor, 1973; Head, Employment Law Dept, 1973–2001; Partner, 1977–2001; Sen. Partner, 2001–06. Chm., Employment Tribunal System Taskforce, 2001–02 and 2003–06; Member: Justice Cttee, Industrial Tribunals, 1987; Council, ACAS, 1995–2001; Steering Bd, Employment Tribunals Service, 2001–06; Bd, Financial Ombudsman Service, 2011–13; Ind. Mem., Speaker's Cttee, Ind. Parly Standards Authy, 2011–16; non-executive Member: Mgt Bd, H of C, 2013–15 (Actg Chm., 2014–15); H of C Commn, 2016–18 (Actg non-exec. Mem., 2015–16); Chairman: Admin Estimate Audit and Risk Assurance (formerly Audit) Cttee, H of C, 2013–18; Members Estimate Audit Cttee, H of C, 2013–18. Chairman: Employment Law Sub Cttee, City of London Law Soc., 1987; Employment Law Cttee, Law Soc., 1993–96; Founder Chm. and Life Vice-Pres., Employment Lawyers Assoc., 1993; Founder Chm. and Hon. Chm., European Employment Lawyers Assoc., 1998; Mem., Exec. Bd, 1995–2003, Council, 1995–2016, Justice. Member: Bd, RSC, 1999–2006; Bd, Internat. Women of Excellence, 2005–15; Co-Chm., Consultation Steering Panel, Legal Educn and Training Rev., 2010–13; Chair, CEO Network, Winmark Europe, 2014–15. Mem., Adv. Bd, Excello Law Ltd, 2013–19; Mem. Adv. Panel, Ind. Review of Legal Services Regulation, 2019–. Member Editorial Advisory Board: Sweet & Maxwell's Encyclopedia of Employment Law, 1987; Tolley's Health and Safety at Work, 1995–2006. Patron: Assoc. of Women Solicitors, 2000–13; City Women's Network, 2006–13. Hon. Vis. Prof., Faculty of Mgt, Cass Business Sch., 2008. Hon. QC 2008; Hon. Bencher, Gray's Inn, 2012. Hon. LLD: Nottingham, 2004; College of Law, 2009; Westminster, 2013; BPP Univ., 2013; DUniv Surrey, 2006. The Times Woman of Achievement in the Law Award, 1997; Lifetime Achievement Award, City of London Law Soc., 2006; Lifetime Achievement Award, Europe Women in Business Law Awards, 2012; Lifetime Achievement Award, Law Soc., 2018. *Publications:* The Employment Relationship, 2001. *Recreations:* watercolour painting, music, theatre, opera, swimming. *Address:* The Nutcracker House, Effingham Common Road, Effingham, Surrey KT24 5JG. *T:* and *Fax:* (01372) 452639. *E:* janet@janetgaymer.com. *Club:* Athenæum.

**GAYOOM, Maumoon Abdul,** Hon. GCMG 1997; President and Commander-in-Chief of the Armed Forces and of the Police, Republic of Maldives, 1978–2008; Co-Founder and Chairman, The Maumoon Foundation, since 2010; *b* 29 Dec. 1937; *s* of late Abdul Gayoom Ibrahim and Khadeeja Moosa; *m* 1969, Nasreena Ibrahim; two *s* twin *d*. *Educ:* Al-Azhar Univ., Cairo. Res. Asst, Amer. Univ. of Cairo, 1967–69; Lectr in Islamic Studies and Philosophy, Abdullahi Bayero Coll., Ahmadu Bello Univ., 1969–71; teacher, Aminiya Sch., 1971–72; Manager, Govt Shipping Dept, 1972–73; writer and translator, President's Office, 1972–74; Under-Sec., Telecommunications Dept, 1974; Special Under-Sec., Office of the Prime Minister, 1974–75; Dep. Ambassador to Sri Lanka, 1975–76; Under-Sec., Dept of External Affairs, 1976; Dep. Minister of Transport, 1976; Perm. Rep. to UN, 1976–77; Minister of Transport, 1977–78; Governor, Maldives Monetary Authy, 1981–2004; Minister: of Defence and Nat. Security, 1982–2004; of Finance, 1989–93; of Finance and Treasury, 1993–2004. Numerous hon. degrees. *Publications:* The Maldives: a nation in peril, 1998. *Recreations:* reading, poetry, astronomy, calligraphy, photography, badminton, cricket.

**GAZDAR, Prof. Gerald James Michael;** Professor of Computational Linguistics, University of Sussex, 1985–2002, now Emeritus; *b* 24 Feb. 1950; *s* of John and Kathleen Gazdar. *Educ:* Heath Mount; Bradfield Coll.; Univ. of East Anglia (BA Phil with Econ); Reading Univ. (MA Linguistics, PhD). Sussex University: Lectr 1975–80; Reader 1980–85; Dean, Sch. of Cognitive and Computing Scis, 1988–93. Fellow, Center for Advanced Study in the Behavioral Sciences, Stanford Univ., California, 1984–85. Vis. Prof., Univ. of Brighton, 2007–. FBA 1988–2002. *Publications:* (with Klein, Pullum) A Bibliography of Contemporary Linguistic Research, 1978; Pragmatics, 1979; (with Klein, Pullum) Order, Concord, and Constituency, 1983; (with Klein, Pullum, Sag) Generalized Phrase Structure Grammar, 1985; (with Coates, Deuchar, Lyons) New Horizons in Linguistics II, 1987; (with Franz, Osborne, Evans) Natural Language Processing in the 1980s, 1987; (with Mellish) Natural Language Processing in Prolog, An Introduction to Computational Linguistics, 1989; Natural Language Processing in LISP, An Introduction to Computational Linguistics, 1989; Natural Language Processing in POP-11, An Introduction to Computational Linguistics, 1989. *Address:* Department of Informatics, University of Sussex, Brighton BN1 9QH. *T:* (01273) 678030.

**GAZZARD, Prof. Brian George,** CBE 2011; FRCP; Clinical Research Director, HIV Unit, Chelsea and Westminster Hospital, since 1978; Professor of HIV Medicine, Imperial College, University of London, since 1998; *b* 4 April 1946; *s* of Edward George Gazzard and Elizabeth (*née* Hill); *m*; four *s*. *Educ*: Queens' Coll., Cambridge (MA); King's Coll. Hosp., London (MD 1976). FRCP 1983. Senior Registrar: Liver Unit, KCH, 1974–76; Gastroenterology Unit, St Bartholomew's Hosp., 1976–78; Consultant Physician, Westminster and St Stephen's Hosps, 1978–. Prin. UK Investigator, various collaborative AIDS studies incl. MRC Delta Trial, 1978–. *Publications*: Treatment of Peptic Ulcer, 1989; Common Symptoms in Gastroenterology, 1990; Gastroenterological Manifestations in AIDS Patients, 1992. *Recreation*: gardening. *Address*: The Old Rectory, Down Street, Dummer, Hants RG25 2AD.

**GAZZARD, Michael John;** Managing Director, Tee to Green Marketing, since 1997; Founder: British Homes Awards, 2007; The Manser Medal; *b* Bournemouth, 20 June 1949; *s* of Kenneth Howard and Nancy Campbell Gazzard; *m* 1993, Brenda Porth; one *s* one *d*. *Educ*: Oakham Sch., Rutland; Enfield Coll. of Technol. (BA Hons Business Studies); City Univ. London (MSc Mgt Scis). VW Mktg Manager, Volkswagen (GB) Ltd, 1974–78; Area Sales Manager, 1978–81, Audi Mktg Manager, 1981–83, V. A. G. UK Ltd; Dir, Mktg Ops, 1983–94, Corporate Affairs, 1994–95, Toyota (GB) Ltd; Sen. Exec., Sales and Mktg, Europe, Rolls-Royce Internat. SA, 1995–97. Hon. FRIBA 2011. *Publications*: Design: the key to a better place, 2007, 10th edn 2017. *Recreations*: golf, tennis, squash. *Address*: Whistlers, Little Cranmore Lane, West Horsley, Surrey KT24 6HZ. *T*: (01483) 286895. *E*: mike@teetogreen.com. *Clubs*: Old Oakhamian; Clandon Regis Golf, Effingham Golf.

**GBOWEE, Leymah Roberta;** Liberian peace activist, social worker and women's rights advocate; Founder and President, Gbowee Peace Foundation Africa, since 2012; *b* Liberia; two *s* three *d* and one adopted *d*. *Educ*: Eastern Mennonite Univ., Va, USA (MA Conflict Transformation 2007). Case worker and counsellor for refugees, Ministry of Health Displaced Shelter, Liberia, 1995–96; volunteer, Trauma Healing and Reconciliation Prog., 1998–2003; Founding Mem. and Liberian Prog. Co-ordinator, Women in Peacebuilding Network, W Africa Network for Peacebuilding, 2001–05 (spokesperson, Women of Liberia Mass Action for Peace); Co-founder, 2006, Regl Consultant, 2006–07, and Executive Dir, 2007–13, Women Peace and Security Network Africa. Comr Designate, Liberia Truth and Reconciliation Commn, 2004–05. Oxfam Global Ambassador, 2013–. Dist. Fellow in Social Justice, Barnard Coll., Columbia Univ., 2013–14. Member: African Women Leaders' Network for Reproductive Health and Family Planning; G7 Gender Equality Adv. Council, 2018–. Member, Board of Directors: Nobel Women's Initiative; Peacejam Foundn. Hon. LLD: Rhodes, SA; Alberta, Canada; Dr *hc* Speciality Mgt and Conflict Resolution, Poly. Univ., Mozambique. Blue Ribbon for Peace Award, Kennedy Sch. of Govt, Harvard Univ., 2007; Gruber Prize for Women's Rights, Gruber Foundn, 2009; John F. Kennedy Profile in Courage Award, 2009; (jtly) Nobel Prize for Peace, 2011. *Publications*: (with C. Mithers) Mighty Be Our Powers (memoir), 2011. *Address*: Gbowee Peace Foundation Africa, 123 ABC Street, Monrovia, Liberia.

**GEAKE, His Honour Jonathan Richard Barr;** a Circuit Judge, Northern Circuit, 1994–2012; *b* 27 May 1946; *s* of late Michael and Margaret Geake; *m* 1978, Sally Louise Dines; three *s*. *Educ*: Sherborne Sch.; Fitzwilliam Coll., Cambridge (BA). Called to the Bar, Inner Temple, 1969; practised on Northern Circuit; a Recorder, 1989; Standing Counsel for Customs & Excise, 1989. *Recreations*: golf and various other sporting activities, gardening. *Clubs*: Knutsford Golf, St Enodoc Golf; Alderley Edge Cricket.

**GEAR, Alan,** MBE 2003; author; *b* 12 June 1949; *s* of Harold Archibald Gear and Nora Esme Gear; *m* 1971, Jacqueline Anne Parker (*see* J. A. Gear). *Educ*: University Coll. of Wales, Swansea (BSc Hons 1970, MSc Civil Engrg 1971). Graduate Engr, West Glamorgan Water Bd, 1971–74; Deputy Dir, 1974–85, Chief Exec., 1985–2003, Henry Doubleday Res. Assoc. Mem., Adv. Cttee on Organic Standards, DEFRA, 2003–05. Hon. MRHS 2006. *Publications*: The Organic Food Guide, 1983, repr. as The New Organic Food Guide, 1986; (ed jtly) Thorsons Organic Consumer Guide, 1990; *contributions to*: Thorsons Organic Wine Guide, 1991; A Future for the Land: organic practice from a global perspective, 1992; Environmental Issues and the Food Industry, 1994, 2nd edn 1999; (with Jackie Gear) Organic Gardening: the whole story, 2009; (with Jackie Gear) Organic Vegetable and Fruit Growing and Preserving Month by Month, 2011. *Recreations*: listening to classical music, reading, gardening, model-making. *Address*: 12 Queens Gardens, Hunstanton, Norfolk PE36 6HD. *T*: (01485) 532219.

**GEAR, Jacqueline Anne,** MBE 2003; author; *b* 18 Dec. 1949; *d* of Stephen Edward Parker and Phyllis Mary Parker; *m* 1971, Alan Gear, *qv*. *Educ*: University Coll. of Wales, Swansea (BSc Hons Zoology 1971). Biologist, Gower RDC, 1971–74; Dir, Analytical Res., Henry Doubleday Res. Assoc., 1974–80; R&D Manager, F. H. Nash Ltd, 1981–84; Exec. Dir, Henry Doubleday Res. Assoc., 1985–2003. Hon. MRHS 2006. *Publications*: (jtly) Ryton Gardens Recipe Book, 1988; (jtly) Thorsons Organic Consumer Guide, 1990; (jtly) Thorsons Organic Wine Guide, 1991; (jtly) Organic Gardening: your questions answered, 1993; (jtly) The Chilli and Pepper Cookbook, 1995; (contrib.) Encyclopaedia of Organic Gardening, 2001; (with Alan Gear) Organic Gardening: the whole story, 2009; (with Alan Gear) Organic Vegetable and Fruit Growing and Preserving Month by Month, 2011. *Recreations*: classical music, reading, cooking, walking, the countryside. *Address*: 12 Queens Gardens, Hunstanton, Norfolk PE36 6HD. *T*: (01485) 532219.

**GEARING, Matthew Peter;** QC 2014; Partner, Hong Kong Office, since 2005, and Global Co-Head, International Arbitration Group, since 2013, Allen & Overy; *b* Croydon, 6 July 1972; *s* of Peter and Susan Gearing; *m* 1999, Katherine Brigg; two *s*. *Educ*: New Coll., Oxford (BA Hons Juris 1993); Coll. of Law, Chester. Admitted as solicitor: England and Wales, 1997; Hong Kong, 2001. Trainee solicitor, Slaughter & May, 1995–97; Solicitor, Allen & Overy, 1997–. Member, Panel of Arbitrators: Singapore Internat. Arbitration Centre, 2009–; Hong Kong Internat. Arbitration Centre, 2010–; Kuala Lumpur Regl Centre for Arbitration, 2013–. Hong Kong International Arbitration Centre: Mem. Council, 2008–; Mem., Exec. Cttee, 2014–; Chm., 2017–; London Court of International Arbitration: Co-Chm., Young Internat. Arbitration Gp, 2005–09; Vice-Pres., Asia Pacific Users' Council, 2013–. *Publications*: (jtly) Russell on Arbitration, 23rd edn 2007 to 24th edn 2015. *Recreations*: sailing, running, walking. *Address*: 9th Floor, Three Exchange Square, Central, Hong Kong. *T*: 29747000, *Fax*: 30880088; One Bishops Square, E1 6AD. *T*: (020) 3088 0000, *Fax*: (020) 3088 0088. *Club*: Royal Hong Kong Yacht.

**GEARTY, Prof. Conor Anthony,** PhD; FBA 2010; Professor of Human Rights Law, London School of Economics, since 2002; barrister; *b* Dublin, 4 Nov. 1957; *s* of Enda and Margot Gearty; *m* 1986, Diane Wales (*d* 2011); one *s* three *d*. *Educ*: Castleknock Coll.; University Coll. Dublin (BCL 1978); Wolfson Coll., Cambridge (LLB 1980); Emmanuel Coll., Cambridge (PhD 1986). Fellow, Emmanuel Coll., Cambridge, 1983–90; King's College London: Sen. Lectr, 1990–93; Reader, 1993–95; Prof. of Human Rights Law, 1995–2002; Dir, Centre for Study of Human Rights, 2002–09, Dir, Inst. of Public Affairs, 2013–17, LSE. Called to the Bar, Middle Temple, 1995; in practice as barrister, Matrix Chambers, 2000–. MRIA 2016. *Publications*: (with K. D. Ewing) Freedom Under Thatcher, 1990; Terror, 1991; (ed with A. Tomkins) Understanding Human Rights, 1995; (ed) Terrorism, 1996; The Future of Terrorism, 1997; (with K. D. Ewing) The Struggle for Civil Liberties, 2000; Principles of Human Rights Adjudication, 2004; Can Human Rights Survive?, 2006; Civil Liberties, 2007; Selected Essays, 2008; (with V. Mantouvalou) Debating Social Rights, 2011; The Rights' Future, 2010; (with C. Douzinas) Cambridge Companion to Human Rights Law, 2012; Liberty and Security, 2013; (with C. Douzinas) The Meanings of Rights, 2014; On Fantasy Island: Britain, Strasbourg and human rights, 2016. *Recreations*: tennis, reading, learning Italian. *Address*: London School of Economics, Houghton Street, WC2A 2AE. *T*: (020) 7849 4643. *E*: c.a.gearty@lse.ac.uk. *W*: www.conorgearty.com, www.twitter.com/conorgearty.

**GEATER, Sara;** Chief Operating Officer, All3Media, since 2015; *b* Coventry, 18 March 1955; *d* of Jack and late Patricia Geater; civil partnership 2007, Felicity Milton; one *s* one *d*. *Educ*: Farnham Common CP Sch.; Beaconsfield High Sch.; Leamington Coll. for Girls; City of London Poly.; Holborn Law Sch. (LLB). Called to the Bar, Middle Temple, 1998. CEDR Accredited Mediator, 2006. Prodn Accountant, LWT, 1977–84; producer, Business as Usual (film), 1985; line producer, Mr Pye (film), 1986; Head: of Production, Drama and Film, Channel 4, 1987–97; of Production, HAL/Miramax, 1997–98; of Film and TV, Avalon, 1998–2000; Dir, Rights and Business Affairs, BBC, 2000–04; Hd, Commercial Affairs, Channel 4, 2004–07; Chief Operating Officer, 2007–10, Chief Exec., 2010–14, talkbackThames, later FremantleMedia UK; Chm., Emerald Films, 2014. Chm., Women in Film and TV, 1994–97. Chairman: BAFTA Prodns, 2007–15; Pact, 2014–15, 2017–; Commercial Cttee, BAFTA, 2016–. Trustee, Debate Mate, 2016–. Gov., London Film Sch., 2007. Mem., RTS. FRSA 2006. *Recreations*: family, golf, friends, theatre, travelling. *Clubs*: Groucho, Soho House, Ivy.

**GEDDES,** family name of **Baron Geddes**.

**GEDDES,** 3rd Baron *cr* 1942; **Euan Michael Ross Geddes;** Company Director, since 1964; *b* 3 Sept. 1937; *s* of 2nd Baron Geddes, KBE, and Enid Mary, Lady Geddes (*d* 1999), *d* of late Clarence H. Butler; *S* father, 1975; *m* 1st, 1966, Gillian (*d* 1995), *d* of late William Arthur Butler; one *s* one *d*; 2nd, 1996, Susan Margaret Hunter, *d* of late George Harold Carter. *Educ*: Rugby; Gonville and Caius Coll., Cambridge (MA 1964); Harvard Business School. Elected Mem., H of L, 1999; a Dep. Speaker, 2000–; Mem., Procedure Cttee, 2002–07. Treas., Assoc. of Cons. Peers, 2000–. *Recreations*: golf, bridge, music, gardening, shooting. *Heir*: *s* Hon. James George Neil Geddes [*b* 10 Sept. 1969; *m* 2004, Alice Arabella Alexander; three *s*]. *Address*: House of Lords, SW1A 0PW. *T*: (020) 7219 4633. *Clubs*: Brooks's; Hong Kong (Hong Kong); Noblemen and Gentlemen's Catch; Hong Kong Golf.

**GEDDES, Prof. Alexander MacIntosh, (Alasdair),** CBE 1996; FRCP, FRCPE, FRCPath, FFPH, FMedSci; Professor of Infection, 1991–99, and Deputy Dean, Faculty of Medicine and Dentistry, 1994–99, University of Birmingham (Professor of Infectious Diseases, 1982–91; Associate Dean, 1999–2002); *b* 14 May 1934; *s* of Angus and Isabella Geddes; *m* 1984, Angela Lewis; two *s*. *Educ*: Fortrose Acad.; Univ. of Edinburgh (MB ChB). FRCPE 1971; FRCP 1981; FRCPath 1995; FFPH (FFPHM 1998). Served RAMC, Captain, 1958–60. Med. Registrar, Aberdeen Hosps, 1961–63; Sen. Registrar, City Hosp. and Royal Infirmary, Edinburgh, 1963–67; Cons. Phys., E Birmingham Hosp., 1967–91; Hon. Cons. Phys., S Birmingham Health Dist, 1991–99. Examiner: MRCP (UK), 1972–99; Final MB, Univs of Birmingham, Glasgow, London, Sheffield, 1975–99. Forbes Vis. Fellow, Fairfield Hosp., Melbourne, Aust., 1988; Sir Edward Finch Vis. Prof., Univ. of Sheffield, 1989. Chairman: Sub-Cttee on Communicable and Trop. Diseases, Jt Cttee on Higher Med. Trng, 1984–94; Isolation Beds Working Party, DoH, 1989–95; Member: Birmingham AHA, 1977–81; Health Educn Authority, 1987–98; Sub-Cttee on Efficacy and Adverse Reactions, Cttee on Safety of Medicines, 1978–85; DHSS Expert Adv. Gp on AIDS, 1985–92; DoH (formerly DHSS) Jt Cttee on Vaccination and Immunization, 1986–95; Trop. Med. Res. Bd, MRC, 1984–88; Ministerial Inquiry into the Public Health Function, 1985–87; DoH Cttee on Safety of Medicines, 1993–96; Consultant Advr in Infectious Diseases, DoH, 1990–94; Civilian Consultant, Infectious Diseases and Tropical Medicine, RN, 1991–. Non-exec. Dir, City Hosp. NHS Trust, 1999–. Chm., Brit. Soc. for Antimicrobial Therapy, 1982–85; Chm., Communicable and Tropical Diseases Cttee, 1983–93, Censor, 1987–89, RCP; Mem., Assoc. of Physicians of GB and Ire., 1976–; President: Internat. Soc. for Infectious Diseases, 1994–96; 21st Internat. Chemotherapy Congress, 1999. Lectures: Honyman-Gillespie, Univ. of Edinburgh, 1975; Public, Univ. of Warwick, 1980; Davidson, RCPE, 1981; Watson-Smith, 1988; Lister, RCPE, 1990. FMedSci 2000. Garrod Medal, Brit. Soc. for Antimicrobial Chemotherapy, 1999; Umezawa Medal, Internat. Soc. for Chemotherapy, 2015. Chm., Editorial Bd, Jl of Antimicrobial Therapy, 1975–85; Ed.-in-Chief, Internat. Jl of Antimicrobial Agents, 2005–15. *Publications*: (ed) Control of Hospital Infection, 1975, 5th edn 2000; (ed) Recent Advances in Infection, 1975, 3rd edn 1988; (contrib.) Davidson, Principles and Practice of Medicine, 16th edn 1991, 17th edn 1995; (contrib.) Kumar and Clark, Clinical Medicine, 6th edn 2005; (contrib.) Grayson et al, The Use of Antibiotics, 6th edn 2010, 7th edn 2017; papers on infectious diseases, immunology, antibiotic therapy and epidemiology in learned jls. *Recreations*: gardening, literature, history of science. *Address*: 34 The Crescent, Solihull, West Midlands B91 1JR. *T*: (0121) 705 8844, *Fax*: (0121) 705 2314. *E*: a.m.geddes@bham.ac.uk. *Club*: Athenæum.

**GEDDES, Prof. Duncan Mackay,** CBE 2012; MD, FRCP; Professor of Respiratory Medicine, Imperial College School of Medicine, since 1996; Consultant Physician, Royal Brompton Hospital, 1978–2007, now Honorary Consultant; *b* 6 Jan. 1942; *s* of Sir Reay Geddes, KBE and Lady Geddes (Imogen, *d* of late Captain Hay Matthey); *m* 1968, Donatella Flaccomio Nardi Dei (*d* 2018); two *s* one *d*. *Educ*: Eton Coll.; Magdalene Coll., Cambridge (MA); Westminster Hosp. Med. Sch. (MB, BS 1971; MD 1978). FRCP 1982. Hon. Consultant: Royal London Hosp., 1982–2007; Royal Marsden Hosp., 1990–2007; Civilian Consultant in chest disease to the Army and Navy, 1986–2007. Director: Finsbury Worldwide Pharmaceutical Trust, 1995–2012; SR Pharma plc, 2000–02; India Pharma Fund, 2005–09. Chm. Council, Nat. Asthma Campaign, 1996–2003. Mem., Med. Adv. Bd, Transgene, France, 1997–2002. Pres., British Thoracic Soc., 2000–01 (Vice-Pres., 1999–2000). Trustee: Garfield Weston Trust for Res. into Heart Surgery, 2005–; Paintings in Hospitals, 2008–13; Royal Brompton and Harefield Hosps Charity, 2013–; All Saints Farnborough Supporters, 2014–18. Vice Chm., Linari Classic Internat. Music Fest., 2014–16. *Publications*: Practical Medicine, 1976; Airways Obstruction, 1981; Respiratory Medicine, 1990; Cystic Fibrosis, 1995; numerous papers in med. and scientific jls. *Recreations*: tennis, golf, painting, cabinet making. *Address*: 57 Addison Avenue, W11 4QU. *Clubs*: Boodle's, Queen's; Denham Golf.

**GEDDES, Prof. John Richard,** MD; FRCPsych; Professor of Epidemiological Psychiatry, since 2002, and Head, Department of Psychiatry, since 2011, University of Oxford; *b* 28 Oct. 1961; *s* of late William Watt Geddes and of Carol Geddes (*née* Blomerley). *Educ*: Manchester Grammar Sch.; Leeds Univ. (MB ChB 1985; MD 1994). FRCPsych 2000. Registrar, Sheffield Hosps, 1986–90; Sen. Registrar, Royal Edinburgh Hosp., 1990–95; Clinical Lectr, Dept of Psychiatry, Univ. of Oxford, 1995. Hon. Consultant Psychiatrist, 1995–, Dir of Res. and Develt and Associate Medical Dir, 2012–, Oxford NHS Foundn Trust. Sen. Investigator, NIHR, 2012–; Dir, NIHR Oxford Cognitive Health Clinical Research Facility, 2012–; Dir, NIHR Oxford Health Biomed. Res. Centre, 2017–. Hon. Fellow, Amer. Coll. of Psychiatrists, 2008. *Publications*: (jtly) Psychiatry, 2nd edn 1999, 5th edn 2017; (jtly) Lecture Notes on Psychiatry, 8th edn 1998, 10th edn 2010; (jtly) New Oxford Textbook of Psychiatry, 2nd edn 2009, 3rd edn 2019; papers in gen. and specialist med. jls on psychiatry, mood disorders, research syntheses, therapeutic discovery. *Address:* Department of Psychiatry, University of Oxford, Warneford Hospital, Oxford OX3 7JX. *T:* (01865) 226451, *Fax:* (01865) 618202. *E:* john.geddes@psych.ox.ac.uk.

**GEDDES, Keith Taylor,** CBE 1998; Policy Director, Pagoda Porter Novelli (formerly P. S. Communication Consultants, then Pagoda PR) Ltd, since 1999; *b* 8 Aug. 1952. *Educ:* Galashiels Acad.; Edinburgh Univ. (BEd 1975); Moray House Coll. of Educn (Cert. in Youth and Community work 1977); Heriot-Watt Univ. (Dip. in Housing 1986). Worker, Shelter Housing Aid (Scotland), 1977–84. Lothian Regional Council: Mem. (Lab), 1982–96; Chair, Educn Cttee, 1987–90; Leader, Labour Gp, 1990–96; Leader, City of Edinburgh Council, 1995–99. Bd Mem., Accounts Commn, 2002–08. Sen. Vice Pres., 1994–96, Pres., 1996–99, COSLA. Chairman: Greenspace Scotland, 2003–09; Central Scotland Green Network Trust (formerly Central Scotland Green Network), 2010–. Contested (Lab) Tweeddale, Ettrick and Lauderdale, 2001. Dep. Chm. Bd, Scottish Natural Heritage, 2005–10 (Mem., 2001–10). *Recreations:* hill walking, golf, cricket, film. *Address:* 12 Woodmill Terrace, Dunfermline, Fife KY11 4SR. *T:* (01383) 623947.

**GEDDES, Michael Dawson;** Executive Director, Milton Keynes Economic Partnership, 1995–2003; *b* 9 March 1944; *s* of late David Geddes and Audrey Geddes; *m* 1966, Leslie Rose Webb; two *s. Educ:* Sherborne Sch., Dorset; Univ. of BC (Goldsmith's Exhibitioner) (BA). Cranfield Institute of Technology: Admin. Asst, 1968–71; Planning Officer, 1971–77; Develt and Estates Officer, 1977–83; Financial Controller, RMCS, 1983–84; Sec., Ashridge (Bonar Law Meml) Trust; Dir, Admin, Ashridge Management Coll. and Dir, Ashridge subsids, 1984–90; Chief Exec., Recruitment and Assessment Services Agency, 1990–95; Civil Service Comr, 1990–97. Gov., Tring Park Sch. for the Performing Arts (formerly Arts Educnl Sch., Tring), 2006– (Chm., 2009–). *Publications:* (with W. Briner and C. Hastings) Project Leadership, 1990; Making Public Private Partnerships Work, 2005; papers on resource allocation in univs and on project management. *Recreations:* golf, bridge. *Address:* 2 Tidbury Close, Woburn Sands, Milton Keynes MK17 8QW. *T:* (01908) 282830.

**GEDDES, Paul Robert;** Chief Executive Officer, QA, since 2019; *b* Redhill, 4 June 1969; *s* of Keith Geddes, OBE and Anne Geddes; *m* 1994, Fiona Slater; two *d. Educ:* Wilson's Sch., Wallington; St Peter's Coll., Oxford (MA Hons PPE). Brand Manager to Mktg Manager, UK Cosmetics, Procter & Gamble, 1990–97; Hd of Mktg, Superdrug Stores plc, 1997–99; Mktg and Develt Dir, Comet Gp plc, 1999–2001; Mktg Dir, Argos, 2001–04; joined RBS Group, 2004: Man. Dir, Mktg and Strategy, Retail Banking, 2004–06; CEO, UK Retail Banking (NatWest and RBS), 2006–09; Chief Exec., RBS Insurance Gp Ltd, then Direct Line Gp plc, 2009–19. Member: Bd, ABI, 2011–; Practitioner Panel, FSA, 2011–15. Non-exec. Dir, Channel 4, 2016–. *Recreations:* playing the violin, travel, family. *Address:* QA, Rath House, 55–65 Uxbridge Road, Slough SL1 1SG.

**GEDNEY, Maj. Gen. Felix Geoffrey,** OBE 2007; Deputy Commanding General III (United States) Corps, 2017–19; *b* Chainhurst, Kent, 18 Nov. 1966; *s* of Roger Gedney and Lynette Edwards (*née* Fuller); *m* 1997, Polly Sansome; three *s. Educ:* Sutton Valence Sch.; Durham Univ. (BSc Engrg); RMA Sandhurst; RMCS (MSc Defence Technol.). Troop Leader, King's Royal Hussars, then Platoon Comdr, Royal Green Jackets, 1990–93; Co. Comdr, then Sqdn Comdr, 1996–2002; CO Royal Scots Dragoon Guards, 2006–08; Dep. Comdg Gen. 1st (US) Infantry Div., 2011–13; rcds, 2013–14; Brigadier Army Staff, 2015–17. QCVS 2013. *Recreations:* equitation, off road motorcycling, cabinet making.

**GEE, Claire Louise;** *see* Lawrence, C. L.

**GEE, David Charles Laycock;** Senior Advisor, Science, Policy, Emerging Issues (formerly Co-ordinator, Emerging Issues and Scientific Liaison), European Environment Agency, Copenhagen, 1995–2013; *b* 18 April 1947; *s* of Charles Laycock Gee and Theresa Gee (*née* Garrick); *m* 1974, Vivienne Taylor Gee; four *d. Educ:* Thomas Linacre and Wigan Grammar Schs; York Univ. (BA Politics). MIOSH 1985. Res. Dept, AUEW, 1970–73; Educn Service, TUC, 1973–78; Nat. Health/Safety Officer, GMB, 1978–88; Occupational/Environmental Cons., 1988–89; Campaign Co-ordinator, 1989–90, Dir, 1990–91, Friends of the Earth; Partner, WBMG Envmtl Communications, 1992–94. Vis. Fellow, Inst. of Envmt, Health and Societies, Brunel Univ., 2014–. Fellow, Collegium Ramazzini, Italy, 1984; FRSA 1990. *Publications:* (with John Cox and Dave Leon) Cancer and Work, 1982; (with Lesley Doyal et al) Cancer in Britain, 1983; Eco-nomic Tax Reform: a primer, 1994; (with Penny Allen and Christophe Bonazzi) Metaphors for Change: partnerships, tools and civic action for sustainability, 2001; *contributions to:* Radiation and Health—Biological Effects of Low Level Exposure to Ionising Radiation, 1987; Transport and Health, ed Fletcher and McMichael, 1995; Ecotaxation, ed O'Riordan, 1997; The Market and the Environment, ed Sterner, 1999; The Daily Globe: environmental change, the public and the media, ed Smith, 2000; Late Lessons from Early Warnings, vol 1: the precautionary principle 1896–2000, 2001, vol. 2: science, precaution, innovation, 2013; The Politics of Scientific Advice, ed Lentsch and Weingart, 2011; pubns for EEA, MSF and GMB on scientific uncertainty, ecological tax reform, anticipatory res., evaluating evidence. *Recreations:* family, swimming, tennis, yoga, entertaining, theatre, music. *Address:* 24 Broomwood Road, SW11 6HT.

**GEE, His Honour David Stephenson;** a Circuit Judge, 1992–2007; a Deputy Circuit Judge, 2007–14; *b* 16 Dec. 1944; *s* of William and Marianne Gee; *m* 1972, Susan Margaret Hiley; two *s* two *d. Educ:* William Hulme's Grammar Sch., Manchester; Leeds Univ. (LLB Hons). Admitted Solicitor, 1970; Registrar, Manchester County Court and Dist Registry, 1982–90; Dist Judge, 1991–92; a Recorder of the Crown Court, 1991; Designated Family Judge: Blackburn Care Centre, 1994–2005; Lancs, 2005–07. Chairman: Selcare (Greater Manchester) Trust, 1989–95; Rhodes Foundn Scholarship Trust, 1989–2005. Adv. Editor, Atkins' Court Forms, 1989–2003; Editor, Butterworth's Family Law Service, 1990–98. *Recreations:* music, walking, reading, travelling. *Address:* c/o Regional Director, Manchester Civil and Family Justice Centre, 1 Bridge Street West, Manchester M60 9DJ.

**GEE, James;** Head of Forensic and Counter Fraud Services, Crowe Clark Whitehill LLP, since 2016; Visiting Professor and Chair, Centre for Counter Fraud Studies, University of Portsmouth, since 2010; *b* 1 Oct. 1957; *m* 1992, Lesley Ann White. *Educ:* London Sch. of Econs (BSc Econs 1978); CPE Law 1995. Civil servant, 1978–90; Counter Fraud Manager, London Boroughs of: Islington, 1990–94; Haringey, 1994–96; Lambeth, 1996–98. Advr to Social Security Select Cttee, H of C, 1995–97; Counter Fraud Advr to Minister of State for Welfare Reform, 1997–98; Dir, Counter Fraud Services, DoH, 1998–2002; Chief Exec., NHS Counter Fraud and Security Mgt Service, 2003–06; Dir of Fraud Services, KPMG, 2007–08; Director of Counter Fraud Services: MacIntyre Hudson LLP, 2009–10; BDO LLP, 2010–14; Partner and Head, Forensic and Counter Fraud Services, PKF Littlejohn LLP, 2014–16. Hon. Mem., CIPFA. *Publications:* (with Mark Button) Countering Fraud for Competitive Advantage, 2013; (jtly) The Accredited Counter Fraud Specialist Handbook, 2015. *Recreations:* military history, gardening, tennis. *Address:* Crowe Clark Whitehill LLP, St Bride's House, 10 Salisbury Square, EC4Y 8EH. *Club:* Manchester United Football.

**GEE, Dr Maggie Mary,** OBE 2012; FRSL; writer; Professor of Creative Writing, Bath Spa University, since 2012; Vice President, Royal Society of Literature, since 2008 (Chair, 2004–08); *b* 2 Nov. 1948; *d* of Victor Gee and Aileen Gee (*née* Church); *m* 1983, Nicholas Rankin; one *d. Educ:* Somerville Coll., Oxford (BA, MA, MLitt); Wolverhampton Polytech. (PhD 1980). FRSL 1994. Writing Fellow, UEA, 1982; Northern Arts Writer-in-Residence, 1996. Vis. Fellow, Sussex Univ., 1986–; Hawthornden Fellow, 1989, 2002, 2009, 2014, 2015; Vis. Prof., Sheffield Hallam Univ., 2006–09. Mem., Govt PLR Cttee, 1999–2006; non-exec. Dir, ALCS, 2015–. Member: Council, RSL, 1999–2008; Mgt Cttee, Soc. of Authors, 1991–94. Judge, Booker Prize, 1989. FEA. Best of Young British Novelists, Granta, 1982. *Publications:* Dying in Other Words, 1981, 3rd edn 1993; The Burning Book, 1983, 2nd edn 1993; Light Years, 1985, 3rd edn 2004; Grace, 1988; Where Are the Snows, 1991, 2nd edn 2006; Lost Children, 1994; The Ice People, 1998, 3rd edn 2008; The White Family, 2002; The Flood, 2004; My Cleaner, 2005; The Blue: short stories, 2006; (ed with Bernardine Evaristo) NW15: anthology of new writing, 2007; My Driver, 2009; My Animal Life (memoir), 2010; Virginia Woolf in Manhattan, 2014; Blood, 2019; (contrib.) Kiss and Part (short stories), 2019. *Recreations:* music, walking, film, theatre, looking at pictures, dancing.

**GEE, Mark Norman K.;** *see* Kemp-Gee.

**GEE, Nigel Ian,** RDI 2007; FREng; Managing Director, BMT Nigel Gee and Associates, 2003–06 (Founder and Managing Director, Nigel Gee and Associates, 1986–2003); *b* 30 July 1947; *s* of Saville and Betty Gee; *m* 1969, Susan Margaret Campbell Stewart; one *s* one *d. Educ:* Univ. of Newcastle upon Tyne (BSc Hons (Naval Architecture) 1969). CEng 1974, FREng 2006; FRINA 1993. Engrg Manager, Hovermarine, 1976–79; Sen. Lectr in Naval Architecture, Southampton Inst., 1979–83; Technical Gen. Manager, Vosper Hovermarine, 1983–86. Innovator-in-residence, Curtin Univ. of Technol., Perth, WA, 2008–09. Pres., RINA, 2004–07. Trustee, Charity Care of Destitute Children in India, 2009–. FRSA 2008. Hon. DEng Southampton Solent, 2005. *Publications:* 21 papers on fast ships and boats for a variety of worldwide confs. *Recreations:* cruising under sail, painting, solving Araucaria, tennis. *Address:* Ashlake Farmhouse, Ashlake Farm Lane, Wootton Bridge, Ryde, Isle of Wight PO33 4LF. *E:* nigelgee@btopenworld.com. *Clubs:* Royal Victoria Yacht; Ryde Lawn Tennis.

**GEE, Richard;** a Circuit Judge, 1991–99; *b* 25 July 1942; *s* of John and Marie Gee; *m* 1st, 1965; three *s*; 2nd, 1995, Mrs Marilyn Gross. *Educ:* Kilburn Grammar School; University College London (LLB Hons). Admitted Solicitor, 1966; Assistant Recorder, 1983; Recorder, 1988. Mem., Main Board, Judicial Studies Board, 1988–93 (Mem., Ethnic Minorities Adv. Cttee, 1991–93). *Recreations:* golf, the arts.

**GEE, Ruth;** Director of Strategic Human Resources, INTO University Partnerships, 2012–14; *b* 21 May 1948; *d* of late George Gaskin and Florence Ann Gaskin; *m* 1972 (marr. diss. 2003); one *s* one *d. Educ:* Stoneraise Primary Sch., Cumbria; Whitehouse Sch., Brampton, Cumbria; Manchester Polytech. (London Univ. ext. BA Gen. Arts); Newcastle upon Tyne Univ. (Postgrad. DipEd). Teacher of English in comprehensive schs, 1970–80; Asst Dir, Polytech. of N London, 1986–89; Dir/Chief Exec., Edgehill Coll. of Higher Educn, 1989–93; Chief Executive: Assoc. for Colls, 1993–96; British Trng Internat., 1997–2000; British Council: Educn Manager, London, 2000–03; Director: Hong Kong, 2003–09; India and Sri Lanka, 2009–10. Dir, Geelinks Ltd, 2011–12. Mem. (Lab) Hackney LBC, 1978–86. Co-opted Mem., 1980, Mem., 1981–86, ILEA (Dep. Leader, 1983–86). Non-executive posts: Basic Skills Agency, 1993–2003; Consumers' Assoc., 1996–2003. Mem., Hong Kong Women's Commn, 2006–08. *Recreations:* health farm addict, art gallery and exhibition enthusiast. *Address:* Flat 1, 39 Canonbury Park North, N1 2JU.

**GEE, Steven Mark;** QC 1993; a Recorder, since 2000; *b* 24 Aug. 1953; *yr s* of Dr Sidney Gee and Dr Hilda Elman; *m* 1999, Meryll Emilie Bacri; two *s. Educ:* Tonbridge Sch.; Brasenose Coll., Oxford (Open Scholar; MA 1st Cl. Hons Jurisprudence; Gibbs Prize for Law). Called to the Bar, Middle Temple, 1975 (Inns of Court Prize, Harmsworth Scholar); admitted NY Bar, 1999. Standing Jun. Counsel, ECGD, DTI, 1986–93. *Publications:* Mareva Injunctions and Anton Piller Relief, 1995, 4th edn 1998; Commercial Injunctions, 5th edn, 2004, 6th edn, 2016. *Recreations:* marathon running, bridge. *Address:* Monckton Chambers, 1 & 2 Raymond Buildings, Gray's Inn, WC1R 5NR. *Club:* MCC.

**GEEKIE, Charles Nairn;** QC 2006; a Recorder, since 2006; a Deputy High Court Judge, since 2016; *b* 7 Feb. 1962; *s* of David Nairn Geekie and Gillian Mary Geekie (*née* Dind); *m* 1993, Geeta Manglani; one *s* one *d. Educ:* Hawford Lodge; Malvern Coll.; Bristol Univ. (LLB). Called to the Bar, Inner Temple, 1985; in practice as barrister, 1985–, specialising in family law; Jt Hd of Chambers, 2013–. *Recreations:* cycling, hill walking, theatre. *Address:* 1GC Family Law, 10 Lincoln's Inn Fields, WC2A 3BP. *T:* (020) 7797 7900. *E:* geekie@1gc.com.

**GEER, Katherine Emma;** *see* Smith, K. E.

**GEERING, Ian Walter;** QC 1991. *Educ:* Bedford Sch.; Univ. of Edinburgh (BVMS). Called to the Bar, Inner Temple, 1974. *Recreations:* walking, reading, sailing, photography.

**GEERING, Rev. Prof. Sir Lloyd (George),** ONZ 2007; GNZM 2009 (PCNZM 2001); CBE 1989; Foundation Professor of Religious Studies, Victoria University of Wellington, 1971–84, now Professor Emeritus; *b* 26 Feb. 1918; *s* of George Frederick Thomas Geering and Alice Geering; *m* 1st, 1943, Nancy McKenzie (*d* 1949); one *s* one *d*; 2nd, 1951, Elaine Parker (*d* 2001); one *d*; 3rd, 2004, Shirley White. *Educ:* Univ. of Otago (MA 1st Cl. Hons Maths; BD Hons OT); Melbourne Coll. of Divinity. Presbyterian Parish Minister, 1943–55; Professor of Old Testament: Emmanuel Coll., Brisbane, 1956–59; Theol Hall, Knox Coll., Dunedin, 1960–71 (Principal, 1963–71). Hon. DD Otago, 1976. *Publications:* God in the New World, 1968; Resurrection: a symbol of hope, 1971; Faith's New Age, 1981; In the World Today, 1988; Tomorrow's God, 1994; The World to Come, 1999; Christianity without God, 2002; Every Moment Must Be Lived, 2003; Wrestling with God, 2006; Coming Back to Earth, 2009; Such is Life!, 2010; From the Big Bang to God, 2013; Reimagining God: the faith journey of a modern heretic, 2014; On Me Bike: cycling round New Zealand eighty years ago, 2015; Portholes to the Past: reflections on the early 20th century, 2016; Witness to Change: reflections on reaching 100, 2018. *Address:* A50 Bob Scott Retirement Village, 29 North Street, Petone, Lower Hutt 5012, New Zealand.

**GEFFEN, Charles Slade Henry;** Senior Of Counsel, Gibson, Dunn & Crutcher, London, since 2019 (Chair, Corporate Practice, 2014–19); *b* London, 19 Sept. 1959; *s* of Ernest, (Bill), Geffen and Bridget Geffen; *m* 1986, Rosemary Anne Valder; three *s* one *d. Educ:* Leicester Univ. (LLB). Admitted solicitor, 1984. Ashurst LLP: joined, 1982; corporate lawyer; Partner, 1991–2014; Mem. Bd, 1998–2013; Hd, Private Equity, 1999–2008; Sen. Partner, 2009–13. Non-exec. Dir, Marathon Asset Mgt, 2019–. Trustee: Inst. of Cancer Res., 2014–; City Year UK, 2014–. Mem. Council, Univ. of Surrey, 2019–. *Address:* Gibson, Dunn & Crutcher, Telephone House, 2–4 Temple Avenue, EC4Y 0HB. *T:* (020) 7071 4225. *E:* cgeffen@gibsondunn.com.

**GEHRELS, Jürgen Carlos,** Hon. KBE 1997; non-executive Chairman, Siemens Holdings plc, 1998–2007 (Chief Executive, 1986–98); *b* 24 July 1935; *s* of Dr Hans Gehrels and Ursula (*née* da Rocha); *m* 1963, Sigrid Kausch; one *s* one *d*. *Educ:* Technical Univs, Berlin and Munich (Dipl. Ing.). Siemens AG, Germany, 1965–79; Pres., General Numeric Corp., Chicago, USA, 1979–82; Dir, Factory Automation, Siemens AG, Germany, 1982–86. Chairman: Siemens Communication Systems Ltd, 1986–92; Siemens Financial Services Ltd, 1988–92; Siemens Controls Ltd, 1990–98; Siemens-Nixdorf Inf. Systems Ltd, 1990–98; Director: Siemens Domestic Appliances Ltd, 1987–98; Comparex Ltd, 1988–92; Alfred Engelmann Ltd, 1989–98; Plessey UK, 1989–98; Plessey Overseas, 1989–98; Siemens Business Communication Systems Ltd, 1996–98; non-executive Director: Nammo AS, Norway, 1989–2003; Management Engineers, Germany, 1997–2006; Plus Plan (UK) Ltd, 2001–03. Pres., German-British Chamber of Industry and Commerce in UK, 1997–2002 (Chm., 1992–97). Gov., Henley Mgt Coll., 1998–2003. FIET (FIEE 1991). FRSA 1993. *Recreations:* golf, gardening, architecture. *Address:* Al Ruscello, Via Panoramica 49, 22010 Piano Di, Porlezza, Italy. *Club:* Reform.

**GEHRIG, Kim;** Director, Somesuch, since 2011; *b* Sydney, 8 Oct. 1976; *d* of David Gehrig and June Gehrig; *m* 2009, Rhodri Thomas; two *c*. *Educ:* Central St Martins (BA Hons Graphic Design). Art Dir, Mother Advertising, 2000–09; Dir, Academy Films, 2008–11. *Recreations:* family, cinema, swimming, walking, theatre, art. *E:* kim.gehrig@me.com. *Club:* Shoreditch House.

**GEHRY, Frank Owen,** CC 2002; architect; Principal, Gehry Partners LLP (formerly Frank O. Gehry & Associates), since 1962; *b* Toronto, 28 Feb. 1929; *s* of late Irving and Thelma Gehry; *m* 1975, Berta Aguilera; two *s*, and one *d* (and one *d* decd) by a previous marriage. *Educ:* Univ. of Southern Calif (BArch 1954); Grad. Sch. of Design, Harvard Univ. Designer, 1953–54, Planning, Design and Project Dir, 1958–61, Victor Gruen Associates, LA; Project Designer and Planner, Pereira & Luckman, LA, 1957–58. Projects include: Loyola Law Sch., 1981–84; Calif Aerospace Mus., 1984; Inf. and Computer Sci./Engrg Res. Lab., Univ. of Calif, Irvine, 1986–88; Centre for Visual Arts, Univ. of Toledo, 1992; Frederick R. Weisman Art Mus., Minneapolis, 1993; American Centre, Paris, 1994; Vitra Internat. HQ, Basel, 1994; EMR Communication and Tech. Centre, Bad Oeynhausen, Germany, 1995; Nationale Nederlanden bldg, Prague, 1996; Guggenheim Mus., Bilbao, 1997; Experience Music Project, Seattle, 2000; Weatherhead Sch. of Mgt, Case Western Reserve Univ., 2001; Walt Disney Concert Hall, LA, 2003; Maggie's Cancer Care Centre, Ninewells Hosp., Dundee, 2003 (Royal Fine Art Commn Trust Bldg of Year, 2004); Jay Pritzker Pavilion, Chicago, 2004; IAC Building, NY, 2007; Serpentine Gall. Pavilion, Kensington, 2008; New York by Gehry, NY, 2011; Louis Vuitton Foundn, Paris, 2013; Biomuseo, Panama City, 2014; Pierre Boulez Concert Hall, Berlin, 2017. Charlotte Davenport Prof. of Architecture, Yale Univ., 1982, 1985, 1987–89; Eliot Noyes Prof. of Design, Harvard Univ., 1984. FAIA 1974. Hon. RA 1998. Prizes include: Arnold W. Brunner Meml Prize in Architecture, 1983; Gold Medal, RIBA, 2000; Presidential Medal of Freedom (USA), 2016. *Publications:* (with Thomas Hines) Franklin D. Israel: buildings and projects, 1992; (with L. William Zahner) Architectural Metals: a guide to selection, specification and performance, 1995; Individual Imagination and Cultural Conservatism, 1995.

**GEIDT,** family name of **Baron Geidt**.

**GEIDT, Baron** *cr* 2017 (Life Peer), of Crobeg in the County of Ross and Cromarty; **Christopher Geidt,** GCB 2018 (KCB 2014); GCVO 2017 (KCVO 2011; CVO 2007); OBE 1997; QSO 2018; PC 2007; Permanent Lord in Waiting to The Queen, since 2019; *b* 17 Aug. 1961; *m* Emma, *d* of Baron Neill of Bladen, QC; two *c*. *Educ:* Dragon Sch., Oxford; Trinity Coll., Glenalmond; King's Coll. London (FKC 2011); Trinity Hall, Cambridge; Magdalen Coll., Oxford (Hon. Fellow, 2016). RMA Sandhurst (invalided), 1982–83; small business, 1983–86; RUSI, 1987–90; Commnd Intelligence Corps, 1987–94; FCO (Sarajevo, Brussels, Geneva), 1994–2001; Asst Private Sec. to The Queen, 2002–05, Dep. Private Sec., 2005–07; Private Sec. to The Queen and Keeper of The Queen's Archives, 2007–17. Hon. Bencher, Middle Temple, 2013. Chm., King's Coll. London, 2016–.

**GEIM, Sir Andre (Konstantin),** Kt 2012; FRS 2007; Royal Society 2010 Anniversary Research Professor, since 2010, Regius Professor of Physics, since 2013, and Director, Manchester Centre for Mesoscience and Nanotechnology, since 2003, University of Manchester; *b* 21 Oct. 1958. *Educ:* Moscow Phys-Tech. Univ. (MSc 1982); Inst. of Solid State Physics, Moscow (PhD Physics 1987). Research Scientist: Russian Acad., 1987–90; Univs of Copenhagen, Bath, and Nottingham, 1990–94; Associate Prof., Nijmegen Univ., Netherlands, 1994–2000; Prof. of Physics, 2001–13, Langworthy Prof. of Physics, 2007–13, Manchester Univ.; EPSRC Sen. Res. Fellow, 2007–10. Ig Nobel Prize for levitation, 2000; Mott Medal and Prize, Inst. Physics, 2007; Europhysics Prize, European Phys. Soc., 2008; Körber Prize, Körber Foundn, 2009; J. J. Carty Award, US NAS, 2010; (jtly) Nobel Prize in Physics, 2010; Hughes Medal, Royal Soc., 2010; Niels Bohr Medal, Denmark, 2011; Copley Medal, Royal Soc., 2013. Kt Comdr, Order of the Lion (Netherlands), 2010. *Recreation:* hiking in high mountains.

**GEISSENDORFER, Lilli;** Director, Jerwood Charitable Foundation, since 2018; *b* London, 6 Sept. 1982; *d* of Hans W. Geissendorfer and Jane Geissendorfer; *m* Ossie Hirst; two *d*. *Educ:* German Sch., London; Lady Eleanor Hollis Sch.; Trinity Hall, Cambridge (BA 1st Cl. Social and Political Scis); Goldsmiths, Univ. of London (MA Dist. Social Res.). Co-founding Producer, Hightide (th. fest.), 2007; Commercial Manager, Arcola Th., 2008–10; Relationship Manager, Arts Council England, 2010–12; Gen. Manager and Producer, Almeida Th., 2012–17. Member, Board: Real Circumstance, 2008–; Fuel, 2012–. *Recreations:* swimming, cycling, campaigning, feminism, breastfeeding support. *Address:* Jerwood Charitable Foundation, 171 Union Street, SE1 0LU. *E:* info@jerwoodcharitablefoundation.org.

**GEKOSKI, Dr Richard Abraham;** writer, dealer in rare books and manuscripts, broadcaster and publisher; *b* St Louis, Mo, USA, 25 Aug. 1944; *s* of Bernard Gekoski and Edith Gekoski (*née* Kornblueh); *m* 1st, 1969, Barbara Pettifer (marr. diss. 2000); one *s* one *d*; 2nd, 2004, Belinda Jane Kitchin. *Educ:* Huntington High Sch., NY; Univ. of Pennsylvania (BA *summa cum laude* 1966); Merton Coll., Oxford (BPhil English 1968; DPhil English 1972). English Department, University of Warwick: Lectr, 1971–83; Sen. Lectr in English, 1983–84; Chm., Faculty of Arts, 1978–82; Founder: R. A. Gekoski Rare Books and Manuscripts, 1982; Sixth Chamber Press, 1983; (with T. G. Rosenthal) Bridgewater Press, 1998. Writer and presenter, series, Rare Books, Rare People, 1999–2009, Lost, Stolen or Shredded, 2006–09, BBC Radio 4. Tutor, Arvon Foundn Creative Non-fiction course, 2009–; Mem., Arvon Foundn Develt Bd, 2008–; Trustee, English PEN, 2010–13 (Curator, charity auction, First Editions, Second Thoughts, 2013; Hon. Vice-Pres., 2014). Judge, Man Booker Prize, 2005; Chm. Judges, Man Booker Internat. Prize, 2009–11; Mem., Man Booker Internat. Prize e-Council, 2013–. Columnist, Finger on the Page, online Guardian, 2010–14. Participant in internat. literary festivals. Creative writing teacher, Spread the Word, 2013–15. *Publications:* Joseph Conrad: the moral world of the novelist, 1978; (with P. A. Grogan) William Golding: a bibliography, 1994; Staying Up: a fan behind the scenes in the Premiership, 1998; Tolkien's Gown and Other Stories of Great Authors and Rare Books, 2004; Outside of a Dog: a bibliomemoir, 2009; Lost, Stolen or Shredded: stories of missing works of art and literature, 2013; Darke (novel), 2017; A Long Island Story (novel), 2018; contrib. articles and reviews to books, jls and newspapers on topics related to books. *Recreations:* watching sport unless it involves a horse or water, golf, travelling, buying pictures and antiques, doing up houses, reading thrillers. *Address:* Joiners Hall, 56 St Ann Street, Salisbury SP1 2DX. *T:* 07831 875202. *E:* rick.gekoski@gmail.com. *W:* www.gekoski.com.

**GELDOF, Bob,** Hon. KBE 1986; singer; songwriter; initiator and organiser, Band Aid, Live Aid, Live 8 and Sport Aid fund-raising events; *b* Dublin, 5 Oct. 1951; *m* 1st, 1986, Paula Yates (marr. diss. 1996; she *d* 2000); two *d* (and one *d* decd); 2nd, 2015, Jeanne Marine. *Educ:* Blackrock Coll. Sometime journalist: Georgia Straight, Vancouver; New Musical Express; Melody Maker. Jt Founder, Boomtown Rats, rock band, 1975; *albums:* Boomtown Rats: Boomtown Rats, 1977; A Tonic for the Troups, 1978; The Fine Art of Surfacing, 1979; Mondo Bongo, 1980; V Deep, 1982; In the Long Grass, 1984; Loudmouth, 1994; solo: Deep in the Heart of Nowhere, 1986; The Vegetarians of Love, 1990; The Happy Club, 1992; Sex, Age and Death, 2001; How to Compose Popular Songs That Will Sell, 2011. Acted in films: Pink Floyd—The Wall, 1982; Number One, 1985. Organised Band Aid, 1984, to record Do They Know It's Christmas, sales from which raised £8 million for famine relief in Ethiopia; organised simultaneous Live Aid concerts in London and Philadelphia to raise £50 million, 1985; organised Sport Aid to raise further £18 million, 1986. Chm., Band Aid Trust, 1985–; Founder, Live Aid Foundn, USA, 1985–; Co-founder and non-exec. Dir, Ten Alps plc, 1999–. Freeman: Borough of Swale, 1985; Newcastle. Hon. MA Kent, 1985; Hon. DSc(Econ) London, 1987; Hon. DPh Ghent; Hon. DLitt Limerick, 2019. TV film: The Price of Progress, 1987. Awards include: UN World Hunger Award, FAO Medal; EEC Gold Medal; Irish Peace Prize; music awards include: Ivor Novello (four times); Brit Award for Outstanding Contribution to Music, 2005; several gold and platinum discs. Order of Two Niles (Sudan); Cavalier, Order of Leopold II (Belgium). *Publications:* Is That It? (autobiog.), 1986; Geldof in Africa, 2005.

**GELL, Ven. Dr Anne Elizabeth;** Archdeacon of Wells and Residentiary Canon, Wells Cathedral, since 2017; *b* 1963. *Educ:* St Hugh's Coll., Oxford (BA Maths 1985); Royal Free Hosp. Sch. of Medicine (MB BS); Univ. of Surrey (BA 2001); Southern Theol Educn and Trng Scheme. Ordained deacon, 2001, priest, 2002; Curate, All Saints, Headley, 2001–05; Vicar, St Peter, Wrecclesham, 2005–17; Area Dean, Farnham, 2010–17. Hon. Canon, Guildford Cathedral, 2013–17. *Address:* 6 The Liberty, Wells, Som BA5 2SU. *T:* (01749) 685147.

**GELLER, Laurence Stephen,** CBE 2012; Chairman: Geller Capital Partners, since 2014; Innovative Aged Care, since 2015; *b* Middx, 22 Nov. 1947; *s* of Harold and Ruth Geller; *m* (marr. diss.); one *s* two *d*. *Educ:* Orange Hill Grammar Sch.; Ealing Tech. Coll. (Nat. Dip. in Hotel Mgt). Dir, Grand Metropolitan Hotels, 1971–76; Sen. Vice Pres., Holiday Inns, Inc., 1976–81; Exec. Vice Pres. and Chief Operating Officer, Hyatt Develt Corp., 1985–89; Chm. and CEO, Geller & Co., 1989–97; Pres. and CEO, Strategic Hotels & Resorts, Chicago, Ill, 1997–2012. Non-exec. Dir, Michels & Taylor, 2013–. Chancellor, Univ. of W London, 2011–. Chm., Bd of Trustees, Internat. Churchill Soc. (formerly Churchill Centre), 2007–. *Publications:* Do Not Disturb, 2006; The Last Resort, 2012. *Recreations:* marathon running, multi-national philanthropic and civic activities.

**GELLETLY, Prof. William,** OBE 1993; PhD; CPhys, FInstP; Professor of Physics, University of Surrey, 1993–2009, now Emeritus; *b* Edinburgh, 11 Dec. 1939; *s* of William Gelletly and Agnes Gelletly; *m* 1965, Alexandra Bain. *Educ:* Broughton Sen. Secondary Sch.; Univ. of Edinburgh (BSc 1st Cl. 1961; PhD 1965). Asst Lectr, Univ. of Edinburgh, 1964–65; Fellow, Chalk River Nuclear Labs, 1965–67; Associate Scientist, Brookhaven Nat. Lab., 1967–70; Lectr, 1970–78, Sen. Lectr, 1978–93, Univ. of Manchester. Hd, Nuclear Structure Facility, SERC, 1988–93; Mem. Bd, NRPB, 1997–2005; non-exec. Dir, HPA, 2005–13. *Publications:* approx. 300 articles in learned jls. *Recreations:* history, golf, theatre, music, reading. *Address:* Physics Department, University of Surrey, Stag Hill, Guildford, Surrey GU2 7XH. *T:* (01483) 682733. *E:* w.gelletly@surrey.ac.uk.

**GELLING, Donald James,** CBE 2002; Member of the Legislative Council, Isle of Man, 2002–06; Chief Minister, Isle of Man, 1996–2001 and 2004–06; *b* 5 July 1938; *s* of John Cyril Gelling and Gladys Gelling (*née* Maddrell); *m* 1960, Joan Frances Kelly; three *s* one *d*. *Educ:* Santon Primary Sch.; Murrays Road Junior; Douglas High Sch. for Boys. Comr, Santon Parish, 1961–86. MHK, 1986–2002; Minister: of Agriculture and Fisheries, 1987–89; of the Treasury, 1989–96. Chairman, Insce and Pensions Authy, 2002. Mem., British-Irish Council, 2004. Captain of the Parish, Santon, 2002–. Mem., Isle of Man Past Rotarians Club. *Recreations:* golf, DIY. *Address:* Grenaugh Beg, Harbour Road, Santon, Isle of Man IM4 1HF. *T:* (01624) 823482, *Fax:* (01624) 827178. *Club:* Castletown Golf.

**GELLING, William John,** OBE 2013; HM Diplomatic Service; Head of Caribbean and Southern Oceans Overseas Territories Department, Foreign and Commonwealth Office, since 2018; *b* Pembury, Kent, 30 Dec. 1977; *s* of John Gelling and Bridget Gelling; *m* 2013, Lucy Elizabeth Barker. *Educ:* Tonbridge Sch.; Univ. of Edinburgh (MA Hons Econs and Politics 2000); Univ. of Pennsylvania. Joined FCO, 2001; G8 Desk Officer, FCO, 2001–02; Urdu lang. trng, 2002–03; Second Sec. (Pol), Islamabad, 2003–06; First Sec. (Pol and Mil.), Baghdad, 2006–07; Hd, Iran Nuclear Section, FCO, 2008–10; Private Sec. to Sec. of State for Foreign Affairs, FCO, 2010–13; High Comr to Rwanda and Ambassador (non-resident) to Burundi, 2014–18. *Recreations:* walking, singing. *Address:* c/o Foreign and Commonwealth Office, King Charles Street, SW1A 2AH. *T:* (020) 7008 1000. *E:* william.gelling@fco.gov.uk.

**GEM, Dr Richard David Harvey,** OBE 2002; FSA; Secretary, Cathedrals Fabric Commission for England, 1991–2002; *b* 10 Jan. 1945. *Educ:* Eastbourne Coll.; Peterhouse, Cambridge (MA, PhD). Inspector of Ancient Monuments, DoE, 1970–80; Res. Officer, Council for Care of Churches, 1981–88; Dep. Sec., then Sec., Cathedrals Adv. Commn for England, subseq. Cathedrals Fabric Commn for England, 1988–91. Mem., RCHM, 1987–99. President: British Archaeol Assoc., 1983–89; Soc. for Church Archaeol., 2006–12; Bucks Archaeol Soc., 2008–19. *Publications:* Studies in English Pre-Romanesque and Romanesque Architecture, 2004; numerous papers on early medieval architecture in British and foreign learned jls. *Recreations:* gardening, theatre, music, foreign travel, philosophy and theology. *Address:* The Upper Flat, The Bothy, Mentmore, Leighton Buzzard, Beds LU7 0QG.

**GEMMELL, Alan,** OBE 2016; Chief Executive, Commonwealth Enterprise and Investment Council, since 2018; *b* Irvine, Ayrshire, 6 April 1978; *s* of Stan Gemmell and Lynn Telfer (*née* Scott); *m* 2015, Damien Lee Stirk. *Educ:* Irvine Royal Acad.; Jun. Sch., Royal Scottish Acad. of Music; Glasgow Univ. (LLB). Nat. Coordinator, Scottish Youth Parliament, 2001–02; Home Office: Presenting Officer, 2002–03; Private Sec. to Perm. Sec., 2003–05; Asst Dir, for Econ. Migration, 2005–06; Desk Officer, COBRA and preventing extremism, Defence and Overseas Secretariat, Cabinet Office, 2006–07; British Council: Hd, Ext. Relns, 2007–11; Dir, São Paulo, 2011; Dep. Dir, Mexico, 2011–12; Dir, Israel, 2012–16; Dir, British Council Gp, India and Minister (Cultural Affairs) British High Commn, India, 2016–18. Founder and Dir, fiveFilms4freedom, 2015–. FRAS; FRSA.

*Recreations:* ballet, contemporary dance, theatre and opera, playing piano, reading, running, writing, imagining we have a dog. *Address:* Commonwealth Enterprise and Investment Council, Marlborough House, Pall Mall, SW1Y 5HX.

**GEMMELL, Campbell;** *see* Gemmell, J. C.

**GEMMELL, Gavin John Norman,** CBE 1998; CA; Director, Archangel Informal Investments, 2001–16 (Chairman, 2008–14); *b* 7 Sept. 1941; *s* of late Gilbert A. S. Gemmell and Dorothy M. Gemmell; *m* 1967, Kathleen Fiona Drysdale; one *s* one *d* (and one *d* decd). *Educ:* George Watson's Coll., Edinburgh. CA 1964. Baillie Gifford & Co., 1964–2002: investment trainee, 1964–67; Partner, 1967; Partner, Pension Funds, 1973–89; Sen. Partner, 1998–2001. Chairman: Scottish Widows, 2002–07 (Dep. Chm., 1995–2002); Gyne Ideas, 2006–10; Mpathy Medical Devices, 2007–10; Net Things, 2014–18; non-executive Director: Scottish Enterprise Edinburgh and Lothian, 1995–2003; Scottish Financial Enterprise, 1998–2002; Lloyds TSB Gp, 2002–07; Flexitricity, 2009–14; Ateeda, 2014–17. Trustee, Nat. Galls of Scotland, 1999–2007. Chm., Standing Cttee, Scottish Episcopal Ch, 1997–2002. Chm. Ct, Heriot-Watt Univ., 2002–08. Non-exec. Dir, St Mary's Music Sch., Edinburgh, 2010–18. DUniv Heriot-Watt, 2009. *Recreations:* golf, foreign travel. *E:* gavingemmell@blueyonder.co.uk. *Clubs:* Hon. Co. of Edinburgh Golfers (Muirfield); Gullane Golf.

**GEMMELL, Prof. (James) Campbell,** PhD; consultant on environment protection, leadership, strategy and mediation, since 2014; Professor of Environment Research, Policy, Regulation and Governance, University of Glasgow, since 2015; *b* 24 Jan. 1959; *s* of late James Stewart Gemmell and Agnes Campbell Little; *m* 1992, Avril Gold. *Educ:* High Sch. of Stirling; Univ. of Aberdeen (BSc 1st cl. Hons; PhD 1985); MA Oxon 1985. Res. Lectr in Glaciol., Christ Church, Oxford, 1985–89; Exec., Scottish Develt Agency, Glasgow, 1988–90; Sen. Consultant, Ecotec Res. and Consulting Ltd, 1990–91; Policy Manager, then Strategist, Scottish Enterprise, 1991–94; Chief Exec., Central Scotland Countryside Trust, 1994–2001; Dir, Strategic Planning, 2001–03, Chief Exec., 2003–11, SEPA; Chief Exec., Envmt Protection Authy S Australia, 2012–14. Chm., Dounreay Particles Adv. Gp, 2001–03. Mem., Minister's Rural Focus Gp, Scottish Office, 1992–96; Dep. Chair, UK Cttee on Radioactive Waste Mgt, 2016– (Acting Chair, 2017–18). Chm., Landwise, and Mem. Gp Bd, Wise, 1999–2001. Hon. Prof., Univ. of Glasgow, 2007–; Adjunct Prof., Centre for Environmental Risk and Remediation, Univ. of S Australia, 2013–; Hon. Prof., Faculty of Natural Scis, Univ. of Stirling, 2016–; Vis. Prof. of Envmtl Regulation, Sch. of Law, Univ. of Strathclyde, 2018–. Consultant, World Bank Gp, 2018–. Mem. Court, Univ. of Stirling, 2010–12; non-exec. Dir, Scottish Agricultural Coll., 2011–12. Advr to Scottish Govt; Chair, Post-Brexit Envmtl Governance Gp; Chair, Review of Air Pollution Strategy for Scotland, 2018–19. Mediator, 2014–. Life FRSA 2008. *Publications:* (contrib.) Environmental Enforcement Networks, 2015; (contrib.) Environmental Crime and Collaborative State Intervention, 2016; earth science papers in environmental risk and regulation, water policy, and glaciol. and glacial geomorphology (winner, Wiley Earth Sci. Paper, 1991) in jls incl. Sustainability Jl, Risk Mgt Jl, Statistica, etc. *Recreations:* eating fine seafood and drinking fine beverages, combined, if possible, with leisure time in Australia, Scotland, Spain and New Zealand; passionate about Norway, Belgian beers, education and writing. *E:* campbell.gemmell@btinternet.com, campbell.gemmell@glasgow.ac.uk, campbell@canopus-scotland.com.

**GEMMELL, Roderick,** OBE 2002; HM Diplomatic Service, retired; *b* 19 Aug. 1950; *s* of Matthew and Ethel Gemmell; *m* 1975, Janet Bruce Mitchell; one *d*. *Educ:* Craigbank Secondary Sch., Glasgow. PO Savings Bank, 1966; joined FCO, 1967; Bahrain, 1971–72; Washington, 1972–74; The Hague, 1975–79; FCO, 1979–82; Mbabane, 1982–84; Stockholm, 1984–87; Second Sec. (Commercial/Econ), Ankara, 1987–91; Second Sec., FCO, 1991–94; First Sec. (Mgt), Kampala, 1994–97; First Sec. (Consular/Immigration), then Dir of Entry Clearance, Lagos, 1998–2002; High Comr, Bahamas, 2003–05. *Recreations:* travel, reading, bowling. *E:* gemmellrj@ntlworld.com. *Club:* Rutherglen Bowling.

**GENDERS, Rev. Nigel Mark;** Chief Education Officer, Church of England, since 2014; *b* St Albans, 1965; *s* of Derek and Audrey Genders; *m* 1989, Sarah Hewitt; one *s* two *d*. *Educ:* Oak Hill Theol Coll. (BA Hons Theol. 1992); Canterbury Christ Church Univ. (MA Educn 2015). Quality Assurance Manager, Royal Mail, 1986–89; ordained deacon, 1992, priest, 1993; Curate: New Malden and Coombe, 1992–96; Enfield, 1996–98; Priest-in-charge: Eastry Benefice, 1998–2003; Woodnesborough and Staple, 2003–08; Minister to Sandwich Secondary Schs, 2006–08; Area Dean of Sandwich, 2006–08; Dir of Educn, Dio. of Canterbury, 2008–12; Hd of Sch. Policy, C of E, 2012–14. *Address:* Church House, Great Smith Street, SW1P 3AZ. *T:* (020) 7898 1500. *E:* nigel.genders@churchofengland.org.

**GENN, Dame Hazel (Gillian),** DBE 2006 (CBE 2000); LLD; FBA 2000; Professor of Socio-Legal Studies, since 1994, Co-Director, Judicial Institute, since 2010, and Founding Director, UCL Centre for Access to Justice, since 2013, University College London (Dean, Faculty of Laws, 2008–17); *b* 17 March 1949; *d* of Lionel Isaac Genn and Dorothy Rebecca Genn; *m* 1973, Daniel David Appleby; one *s* one *d*. *Educ:* Univ. of Hull (BA Hons 1971); CNAA (LLB 1985); Univ. of London (LLD 1992). Res. Asst, Cambridge Inst. of Criminology, 1972–74; Sen. Res. Officer, Oxford Univ. Centre for Socio-Legal Studies, 1974–85; Lectr, 1985–88, Reader, 1988–91, Prof. and Head of Law Dept, 1991–94, Queen Mary and Westfield Coll., London Univ. Member: Cttee on Standards in Public Life, 2003–07; Judicial Appts Commn, 2006–12; Chair, Judicial Sub-Cttee, Sen. Salaries Rev. Bd, 2013–16. Hon. QC 2006; Hon. Bencher, Gray's Inn, 2008. Chair, Holberg Prize Cttee, 2018–. *Publications:* Surveying Victims, 1978; Hard Bargaining, 1987; Personal Injury Compensation: how much is enough?, 1994; Mediation in Action, 1999; Paths to Justice, 1999; Paths to Justice Scotland, 2001; Tribunals for Diverse Users, 2006; Twisting Arms, 2007; Judging Civil Justice: Hamlyn lectures, 2008. *Recreations:* music, walking, spending time with my family. *Address:* Faculty of Laws, University College London, Bentham House, Endsleigh Gardens, WC1H 0EG. *T:* (020) 3108 8335.

**GENT, Sir Christopher (Charles),** Kt 2001; Chairman, ConvaTec plc, 2016–19; *b* 10 May 1948; *s* of late Charles Arthur Gent and of Kathleen Dorothy Gent; *m* 1st, Lynda Marion Tobin (marr. diss. 1999); two *d*; 2nd, 1999, Kate Elisabeth Lock; two *s*. *Educ:* Archbishop Tenison's Grammar Sch. With Nat West Bank, 1967–71; Schroder Computer Services, 1971–79; Man. Dir, Baric Computing Services, 1979–84; Dir, Network Services Div., ICL, 1983–84; Man. Dir, Vodafone, 1985–97; Dir, Racal Telecom plc, 1988–91; Dir, 1991–97, Chief Exec., 1997–2003, Vodafone Gp plc; Chm., Supervisory Bd, Vodafone AG. Chm., GlaxoSmithKline, 2005–15; Mem. Bd Reps, Verizon Wireless Partnership; non-executive Director: China Mobile (Hong Kong) Ltd; Lehman Brothers Holdings Inc., 2003–08; Ferrari SpA; Sen. Advr, Bain & Co Inc., 2004–16; Mem., Internat. Adv. Bd, Hakluyt, 2015–. Vice-Pres., Computer Services Assoc., 1984. Nat. Chm., Young Conservatives, 1977–79. *Recreations:* family, cricket, politics, horseracing. *Clubs:* Carlton, MCC; Royal Ascot Racing; Lord's Taverners.

**GENT, (John) David (Wright),** FIMI; Director General, Retail Motor Industry Federation, 1985–95; *b* 25 April 1935; *s* of late Reginald Philip Gent and Stella Eva Parker; *m* 1970, Anne Elaine Hanson. *Educ:* Lancing Coll. Admitted a Solicitor, 1959. Joined Soc. of Motor Manufacturers as Legal Advr, 1961; Asst Sec., 1964; Sec., 1965; Dep. Dir, 1971–80; joined Lucas Industries as Gen. Man., Lucas Service UK, 1981; Gp PR Man., 1982–83; Dir, British Road Fedn, 1983–84. Director: DC Cook Hldgs, 1995–2001; Autofil Properties Ltd, 2002–05. Member: Road Transport ITB, 1985–91; Vehicle Security Installation Bd, 1994–95. FRSA 1995. Freeman, City of London, 1985; Liveryman, Coach Makers and Coach Harness Makers' Co., 1985. *Recreation:* gardening. *Address:* 44 Ursula Street, SW11 3DW. *T:* (020) 7228 8126.

**GENTLE, Sally Claire W.;** *see* Woodward Gentle.

**GENTLEMAN, David (William),** RDI 1970; artist and designer; *b* 11 March 1930; *s* of late Tom and Winifred Gentleman; *m* 1st, 1953, Rosalind Dease (marr. diss. 1966; she *d* 1997); one *d*; 2nd, 1968, Susan, *d* of late George Ewart Evans; two *d* one *s*. *Educ:* Hertford Grammar Sch.; St Albans Sch. of Art; Royal College of Art. Work includes: painting in watercolour, lithography, wood engraving, illustration and graphic design; commissions include Eleanor Cross mural designs for Charing Cross underground station, 1979; illustrations for many publishers; postage stamps for Royal Mail, including, 1962–: Shakespeare, Churchill, Darwin, Ely Cathedral, Abbotsbury Swans, Millennium, etc; coins for Royal Mint: Entente Cordiale, 2004; Slave Trade Abolition, 2007; posters for London Transport, National Trust, and Stop the War Coalition; symbols for British Steel, Bodleian Library, etc. Solo exhibitions: at Mercury Gallery: watercolours of: India, 1970; S Carolina, 1973; Kenya and Zanzibar, 1976; Pacific, 1981; Britain, 1982; London, 1985; British coastline, 1988; Paris, 1991; India, 1994; Italy, 1997; City of London, 2000; watercolours and designs, RCA, 2002; watercolours, Fine Art Soc., 2004 (retrospective), 2007, 2010, 2012, 2014. Editions of lithographs and screenprints of architecture and landscape, 1967–2008. Work in public collections incl. Tate Gall., V&A, BM, Fitzwilliam Mus., and Nat. Maritime Mus., and also in private collections. Member: Nat. Trust Properties Cttee, 1985–2005; Alliance Graphique Internat.; Council, Artists' Gen. Benevolent Instn. Master of Faculty, RDI, 1989–91. Hon. Fellow, RCA, 1981; Hon. FRIBA 1996. Prince Philip Designers Prize, Design Council, 2007. *Publications:* author and illustrator: Design in Miniature, 1972; David Gentleman's Britain, 1982; David Gentleman's London, 1985; A Special Relationship, 1987; David Gentleman's Coastline, 1988; David Gentleman's Paris, 1991; David Gentleman's India, 1994; David Gentleman's Italy, 1997; The Wood Engravings of David Gentleman, 2000; Artwork, 2002; London, You're Beautiful—An Artist's Year, 2012; In the Country, 2014; *for children:* Fenella in Greece, 1967; Fenella in Spain, 1967; Fenella in Ireland, 1967; Fenella in the South of France, 1967; *illustrator:* Plats du Jour, 1957; Bridges on the Backs, 1961; Swiss Family Robinson, 1963 (USA); The Shepherd's Calendar, 1964; Poems of John Keats, 1966 (USA); The Pattern Under the Plough, 1966; covers for New Penguin Shakespeare, 1968–78; The Jungle Book, 1968 (USA); Robin Hood, 1977 (USA); The Dancing Tigers, 1979; Westminster Abbey, 1987; The Illustrated Poems of John Betjeman, 1995; Inwards where all the battle is, 1997; The Key Keeper, 2001; Ask the Fellows Who Cut the Hay, 2010; Edward Thomas: selected poems, 2017; War to End All Wars, 2018; *illustrator and editor:* The Crooked Scythe, 1993; *relevant publication:* David Gentleman: Design, by Brian Webb and Peyton Skipwith, 2009. *Address:* 25 Gloucester Crescent, NW1 7DL. *T:* (020) 7485 8824. *E:* david@davidgentleman.com. *W:* www.davidgentleman.com.

**GEOGHEGAN, Hugh;** a Judge of the Supreme Court of Ireland, 2000–10; *b* 16 May 1938; *s* of late Hon. James Geoghegan (a Judge of the Supreme Court of Ireland, 1936–50) and Eileen Geoghegan (*née* Murphy); *m* 1981, Mary Finlay Geoghegan, Judge of Supreme Court of Ireland, *d* of late Thomas Aloysius Finlay; one *s* two *d*. *Educ:* Clongowes Wood Coll.; University Coll., Dublin (BCL, LLB). Called to the Bar: King's Inns, 1962 (Bencher, 1992); Middle Temple, 1975 (Bencher, 2006); Inn of Court of NI, 1989; Sen. Counsel 1977; Judge of High Court of Ireland, 1992–2000. Arbitrator of Public Service staff claims, 1984–92. Chm., Barristers Professional Conduct Appeals Bd, 2010–16; former Ind. Appeals Comr, Royal Coll. of Surgeons Ireland. Former Mem., Bar Council. Former Mem. Council, Royal Victoria Eye and Ear Hosp., Dublin. Mem. Council, Irish Legal Hist. Soc. Gov., Clongowes Wood Coll., 1995–2002. *Recreations:* history, genealogy, music. *Address:* Carne Lodge, Cowper Gardens, Dublin 6, Ireland. *Clubs:* Kildare Street and University, Royal Dublin Society, Fitzwilliam Lawn Tennis (Dublin).

**GEOGHEGAN, Michael Francis,** CBE 2003; Group Chief Executive, HSBC Holdings plc, 2006–10 (an Executive Director, 2004–10); Chairman, The Hongkong and Shanghai Banking Corporation Ltd, 2010; *b* 4 Oct. 1953; *m*; two *s*. Joined HSBC Gp, 1973; Pres. and CEO, HSBC Bank Brazil S.A. - Banco Múltiplo, HSBC Investment Bank Brazil S.A. and HSBC Seguros S.A., 1997–2003; Chief Exec., HSBC Bank plc, 2004–06 (Dep. Chm., 2006–10). Dir, HSBC N America Hldgs Inc., 2006–10; Chm. and Dir, HSBC Bank Canada, 2007–10; Dir, HSBC Latin America Hldgs (UK) Ltd, 2008–10. Chm., Young Enterprise UK, 2004–09.

**GEORGE;** *see* Lloyd George and Lloyd-George.

**GEORGE;** *see* Passmore, G.

**GEORGE, Andrew Henry;** researcher and writer; Director, Cornwall Community Land Trust, since 2015; *b* Mullion, Cornwall, 2 Dec. 1958; *s* of late Reginald Hugh George and of Diana May (*née* Petherick); *m* 1987, Jill Elizabeth, *d* of late William and Margery Marshall; one *s* one *d*. *Educ:* Helston Grammar (subseq. Comprehensive) Sch.; Sussex Univ. (BA); University Coll., Oxford (MSc). Rural Officer, Notts Rural Community Council, 1981–84; housing, farming and charity work, Notts, Devon and Cornwall, 1984–89; Dep. Dir, Cornwall Rural Community Council, 1989–97. Contested (Lib Dem) St Ives, 1992. MP (Lib Dem) St Ives, 1997–2015; contested (Lib Dem) same seat, 2015, 2017. Lib Dem spokesman: on fisheries, 1997–2005; on disabilities, 2000–01; on rural affairs, 2002–05; on internat. develt, 2005–06; PPS to Leader of Lib Dem Party, 2001–02. Chm., Lib Dem Parly DEFRA/DECC Team, 2010–12. *Publications:* The Natives are Revolting Down in the Cornwall Theme Park, 1986; (jtly) Cornwall at the Crossroads, 1989; A Vision of Cornwall (Cornwall Blind Assoc.), 1995; A view from the bottom left hand corner, 2002; (contrib) The Alternative: towards a new progressive politics, 2015; housing and planning pubns and res. reports. *Recreations:* football, Rugby, cricket, gardening, cycling, walking, singing, poetry, running, rowing. *Address:* 1 Riviere Cottages, Hayle, Cornwall TR27 5AA. *T:* (01736) 757070. *Clubs:* Penzance and Newlyn Rugby, Leedstown Cricket, Hayle Rugby (Vice-Pres.), Hayle Runners.

**GEORGE, Andrew James;** QC 2015; *b* London, 11 Dec. 1973; *s* of James George and Mary George; *m* 2003, Sara Phillp; one *s* one *d*. *Educ:* Windsor Boys' Sch.; St Catherine's Coll., Oxford (BA Eng. Lang. and Lit.); City Univ. (DipLaw). Called to the Bar, Gray's Inn, 1997; in practice as a barrister, specialising in commercial law, esp. financial services, Blackstone Chambers, 1997–. Chm., Trustees, Spitalfields City Farm, 2009–17. *Publications:* Milk Round, 2015. *Recreations:* poetry, theatre, city farming. *Address:* Blackstone Chambers, Blackstone House, Temple, EC4Y 9BW. *E:* andrewgeorge@blackstonechambers.com.

**GEORGE, Prof. Andrew John Timothy**, MBE 2017; PhD, DSc; FRCPath; Professor of Immunology and Deputy Vice Chancellor (Education and International), Brunel University London, 2013–18, now Emeritus; Director, Consultant and Coach, AJTG Ltd, since 2018; *b* Hong Kong, 12 May 1963; *s* of Timothy John Burr George, *qv*; *m* 1992, Dr Catherine Elizabeth Urch; one *s* one *d*. *Educ*: Clifton Coll., Bristol; Trinity Coll., Cambridge (BA 1984; MA 1995); Univ. of Southampton (PhD 1987); Imperial Coll. London (DSc 2012). MRCPath 1999, FRCPath 2005; FRSB (FSB 2011). Beit Meml Fellow, Univ. of Southampton, 1987–90; Res. Fellow, NIH, Md, 1990–92; Royal Postgraduate Medical School, subseq. part of Imperial College London: Lectr, 1992–96; Sen. Lectr, 1996–99; Reader in Molecular Immunol., 1999–2002; Prof. of Molecular Immunol., 2002–13; Director: Grad. Sch. of Life Scis and Medicine, 2010–11; Sch. of Professional Develt, 2010–13; Grad. Sch., 2011–13; Imperial Coll. Health Partners, 2014–18 (interim Chair, 2018–). Chair, Health Scis Acad., 2015–18. Hon. Reader, 2002–05, Hon. Prof., 2005–13, Inst. of Ophthalmol., UCL; Visiting Professor: Flinders Univ., Adelaide, 2005; W China Sch. of Medicine, Sichuan Univ., 2018–; Hon. Prof., Hubei Univ. of Medicine, 2013. Mem., Clin. Trials Biologicals and Vaccines Expert Adv. Gp (formerly Clin. Trials Expert Adv. Gp), MHRA, 2007–17; Chair: Nat. Res. Ethics Advrs' Panel, 2009–17; Gene Therapy Adv. Cttee, 2012. Mem., 1998–2000, Chm., 2000–10, Res. Ethics Cttee, Hammersmith, Queen Charlotte's and Chelsea and Acton Hosps; Mem. Council, British Soc. for Immunol., 2007–10; Trustee: Action Med. Res., 2008–15 (Mem., 2005–08, Chm., 2008–12, Scientific Adv. Panel); Epilepsy Soc., 2018–. Non-exec. Dir, NHS Health Res. Authy, 2019–. Dir, West London Business, 2017–19. Governor: Richmond and Hillcroft (formerly Richmond) Adult Community Coll., 2011–; John Hampden Grammar Sch., 2014–. FRSA 2006; FHEA 2007. Member, Editorial Board: Jl of Immunological Methods, 1996–2008 (Section Ed., 1999–2003); Transplantation, 2000–14; Trends in Immunology, 2007–11; Section Ed., Expert Opinion on Therapeutic Patents, 1996–2000. *Publications*: Diagnostic and Therapeutic Antibodies (with C. E. Urch), 2000; articles on immunol., transplantation and cancer res. in jls and books. *Recreations*: gardening, theatre, family. *Address*: 29 The Avenue, Twickenham, Middx TW1 1QU. *T*: (020) 8892 1859. *E*: andrew@ajtg.co.uk.

**GEORGE, Andrew Neil**; HM Diplomatic Service, retired; Governor of Anguilla, 2006–09; *b* 9 Oct. 1952; *s* of Walter George and late Madeleine George (*née* Lacey); *m* 1977, Watanalak Chaovieng; one *s* one *d*. *Educ*: Royal High Sch., Edinburgh; Univ. of Edinburgh (MA Politics and Modern History 1974). Entered HM Diplomatic Service, 1974; W Africa Dept, FCO, and Third Sec., Chad, 1974–75; SOAS, London Univ., 1975–76; Third, subseq. Second, Sec., Bangkok, 1976–80; S America Dept, 1980–81, W Africa Dept, 1981–82, Perm. Under-Sec.'s Dept, 1982–84, FCO; First Sec., Canberra, 1984–88; First Sec. and Head of Chancery, Bangkok, 1988–92; Republic of Ireland Dept, 1993–94, Eastern Dept, 1994–95, Non-Proliferation Dept, 1995–98, FCO; Ambassador to Paraguay, 1998–2001; Counsellor (Commercial), Jakarta, 2002; Asst Dir, Health and Welfare, HR Directorate, FCO, 2003–06. *Recreations*: reading, watching football. *Address*: c/o Foreign and Commonwealth Office, King Charles Street, SW1A 2AH.

**GEORGE, Prof. Andrew Robert**, PhD; FBA 2006; Professor of Babylonian, School of Oriental and African Studies, University of London, since 2000; *b* 3 July 1955; *s* of Eric and Frances George; *m* 1996, Junko Taniguchi; three *s*. *Educ*: Christ's Hosp., Horsham; Univ. of Birmingham (BA; PhD 1985). School of Oriental and African Studies, University of London: Lectr in Ancient Near Eastern Studies, 1985–94; Reader in Assyriology, 1994–2000. Hon. Res. Fellow, 1995–98, Hon. Lectr, 1998–2002, Hon. Prof., 2002, Inst. of Archaeol., UCL. Vis. Prof., Univ. of Heidelberg, 2000. Mem., Inst. for Advanced Study, Princeton, 2004–05. Res. Associate, Rikkyo Univ., Tokyo, 2009. Jt Ed., Iraq jl, 1994–2011. *Publications*: Babylonian Topographical Texts, 1992; House Most High: the temples of Ancient Mesopotamia, 1993, 2nd edn 2004; The Epic of Gilgamesh: a new translation, 1999, 3rd edn 2003; The Babylonian Gilgamesh Epic: introduction, critical edition and cuneiform texts, 2003, 2nd edn 2004; Babylonian Literary Texts in the Schøyen Collection, 2009; Cuneiform Royal Inscriptions and Related Texts in the Schøyen Collection, 2011; Babylonian Divinatory Texts Chiefly in the Schøyen Collection, 2013; Mesopotamian Incantations in the Schøyen Collection, 2016; Old Babylonian Texts in the Schøyen Collection, Part 1, 2018. *Recreation*: Assyriology. *Address*: School of Oriental and African Studies, University of London, Russell Square, WC1H 0XG. *T*: (020) 7898 4335. *E*: ag5@soas.ac.uk.

**GEORGE, Rt Hon. Bruce Thomas**; PC 2001; *b* 1 June 1942; *m* 1992, Lisa Toelle. *Educ*: Mountain Ash Grammar Sch.; UCW Swansea (Hon. Fellow, 2001); Univ. of Warwick. BA Politics Wales 1964, MA Warwick 1968. Asst Lectr in Social Studies, Glamorgan Polytechnic, 1964–66; Lectr in Politics, Manchester Polytechnic, 1968–70; Senior Lectr, Birmingham Polytechnic, 1970–74. Vis. Lectr, Univ. of Essex, 1985–86; Vis. Prof., Univ. of Portsmouth, 2009–. MP (Lab) Walsall S, Feb. 1974–2010. Member: Select Cttee on Violence in the Family; Select Cttee on Defence, 1979–2005 (Chm., 1997–2005); Chm., All Party Parly Maritime Gp. Mem., NATO Parly Assembly (formerly North Atlantic Assembly), 1981–2010 (Chm., Mediterranean Special Gp). OSCE Parliamentary Assembly: Mem., 1992–2010; Gen. Rapporteur, 1992–95; Chm., 1996–99; Vice Pres., 1999–2002; Pres., 2002–04; Pres. Emeritus, 2004–06; Hd, Election Observation Missions, Office of Democratic Instns and Human Rights, OSCE. Member: RIIA; IISS; RUSI (Mem. Council); Vice Pres., Security Inst., 2010–. Hon. Pres., Internat. Professional Security Assoc., 2013–. Hon. Advr, Royal British Legion, 1997. Co-founder, Sec., House of Commons FC. Fellow, Parliament and Industry Trust, 1977–78. Ed., Jane's NATO Handbook, 1988–91. Freedom of Walsall BC, 2011. Order of Honour (Georgia), 2011; Civilian Medal for contrib to OSCE mission, OSCE, Vienna, 2012. *Publications*: numerous books and articles on defence and foreign affairs. *Recreations*: Association football, private security and democratization, student of American Indians, eating Indian food. *E*: brucetgeorge@gmail.com.

**GEORGE, Sir Charles (Frederick)**, Kt 1998; MD; FRCP, FFPM; Chairman, Stroke Association, 2009–13; Emeritus Professor of Clinical Pharmacology, University of Southampton, since 1999; *b* 3 April 1941; *s* of William and Evelyn George; *m* 1969, Rosemary Moore (marr. diss. 1973). *Educ*: Univ. of Birmingham Med. Sch. (BSc 1962; MB ChB 1965; MD 1974). MRCP 1968; FRCP 1978; FFPM 1989. Med. Registrar, United Birmingham Hosps, 1967–69; Hammersmith Hospital, London: Med. Registrar, 1969–71; Sen. Registrar, 1971–73; University of Southampton: Sen. Lectr, 1973–75; Prof. of Clinical Pharmacology, 1975–99; Dean, Faculty of Medicine, Health and Biol Scis, 1993–98; Med. Dir, BHF, 1999–2004; Chm., Bd of Sci. and Educn, BMA, 2005–09. Non-exec. Chm., Fulcrum Pharma plc, 2008–09; non-exec. Dir, BMJ Publishing Gp, 2006–08. Pres., BMA, 2004–05. Founder FMedSci 1998. FRSA 1993; FESC 2000, Emeritus FESC 2005; Hon. FFPH 2004; Hon. FBPhS (Hon. FBPharmacolS 2006). Hon. DSc: Birmingham, 2003; Leicester, 2007; Hon. DM Southampton, 2004. Gold Medal, BMA, 2010. *Publications*: Topics in Clinical Pharmacology, 1980; (ed) Presystemic Drug Metabolism, 1982; (ed) Clinical Pharmacology and Therapeutics, vol. 1, 1982; (ed) Drug Therapy in the Elderly, 1998. *Recreations*: music, walking. *Address*: 15 Westgate Street, Southampton SO14 2AY.

**GEORGE, Charles Richard**; QC 1992; a Recorder, 1997–2017; Dean, Arches Court of Canterbury and Auditor, Chancery Court of York, since 2009; a Deputy High Court Judge, 2010–17; *b* 8 June 1945; *s* of Hugh Shaw George, CIE and Joan George (*née* Stokes); *m* 1976, Joyce Tehmina Barnard; two *d*. *Educ*: Bradfield Coll.; Magdalen Coll., Oxford (MA 1st Cl. Hons Modern History); Corpus Christi Coll., Cambridge. Asst Master, Eton Coll., 1967–72; called to the Bar, Inner Temple, 1974, Bencher, 2001; an Asst Recorder, 1994–97. Chancellor, Dio. of Southwark, 1996–2009; Mem., Legal Adv. Commn, Gen. Synod of C of E, 2003–18. Mem., Council, St Stephen's House, Oxford, 1999–2012. Hon. Fellow, Centre of Eur. Law, KCL, and Vis. Lectr in EU Envmtl Law, KCL, 2007–15. Chm., Sevenoaks Conservation Council, 2014–; Vice Chm., Sevenoaks Soc., 2018–. *Publications*: The Stuarts: an age of experiment, 1973. *Recreations*: architecture, travel. *Address*: Church Field, 2 Oak Lane, Sevenoaks, Kent TN13 1NF. *T*: (01732) 451875; Francis Taylor Building, Inner Temple, EC4Y 7BY. *T*: (020) 7353 8415. *Club*: Garrick.

**GEORGE, Prof. Danielle Amanda**, MBE 2016; PhD; FIET; Professor of Radio Frequency Engineering, since 2014 and Vice Dean, Faculty of Science and Engineering, since 2013, University of Manchester; *b* Newcastle upon Tyne, 27 Jan. 1976; *d* of Daniel Kettle and Sandra Kettle; *m* 2008, Richard George; one *d*. *Educ*: Kenton Comp. Sch., Newcastle upon Tyne; Univ. of Liverpool (BSc Hons Astrophysics); Victoria Univ. of Manchester (MSc Radio Astronomy); Univ. of Manchester Inst. of Sci. and Technol. (PhD Electrical Engrg 2006). Engr, then Sen. Engr, Jodrell Bank Centre for Astrophysics, 1999–2006; Lectr in Electronic Engrg, Univ. of Manchester, 2006–14. Vice Pres., IET, 2017–. Christmas Lectr, Royal Instn of GB, 2014. Television co-presenter: Televisions Opening Night: How the Box was Born, 2016; Hyper Evolution: Rise of the Robots, 2017; The Search for a New Earth, 2017. Mem., Bd of Govs, Univ. of Manchester, 2016–; Trustee/Gov., Oldham Sixth Form Coll., 2018–. FIET 2017. Rooke Medal, RAEng, 2016; Sir Harold Hartley Medal, Inst. of Measurement and Control, 2017; Michael Faraday Medal, Royal Soc., 2018. *Publications*: contribs to IEEE Trans. on Microwave Theory and Techniques, Astronomy & Astrophysics. *Recreations*: music, sport, tinkering, creator of Manchester Robot Orchestra. *Address*: University of Manchester, Sackville Street Building, Manchester M13 9PL. *T*: (0161) 306 4796. *E*: danielle.george@manchester.ac.uk; c/o Jo Sarsby Management Ltd, 154 Cheltenham Road, Bristol BS6 5RL.

**GEORGE, Hywel**, CMG 1968; OBE 1963; Fellow, Churchill College, Cambridge, since 1971 (Bursar, 1972–90); *b* 10 May 1924; *s* of Rev. W. M. George and Catherine M. George; *m* 1955, Edith Pirchl; three *d*. *Educ*: Llanelli Grammar Sch.; UCW Aberystwyth; Pembroke Coll., Cambridge; SOAS, London. MA Cantab 1971. RAF, 1943–46. Cadet, Colonial Admin. Service, N Borneo, 1949–52; District Officer, 1952–58; Secretariat, 1959–62; Resident, Sabah, Malaysia, 1963–66; Administrator, 1967–69, Governor, 1969–70, St Vincent; Administrator, British Virgin Is, 1971. Mem. Court and Council, Univ. of Wales, Bangor, 1999–2007. Panglima Darjah Kinabalu (with title of Datuk), Sabah, 1964; JMN, Malaysia, 1966. CStJ 1969. *Address*: 46 St Margaret's Road, Girton, Cambridge CB3 0LT. *T*: (01223) 563766; Tu Hwnt ir Afon, The Close, Llanfairfechan LL33 0AG. *T*: (01248) 681509.

**GEORGE, Jane Elizabeth; Her Honour Judge George**; a Circuit Judge, since 2014; *b* Redhill, Surrey, 1959; *d* of Maurice and Margaret Peterson; *m* 1984, Charles George; two *s*. *Educ*: Girton Coll., Cambridge (BA Law 1981). Admitted Solicitor, 1984; Partner, Rothera-Dowson Solicitors, Nottingham, 1990–2006; Pres. (pt-time), Mental Health Rev. Tribunal, 1996–2006; a Dep. Dist Judge, 1998–2006; a Dist Judge, 2007–14. Dep. Diocesan Registrar, Dio. of Southwell and Nottingham, 1996–2006. Founder Mem., Assoc. of Road Transport Lawyers, 1995. *Recreations*: gardening, walking, cricket, reading, theatre, cinema. *Address*: Leicester County Court, 90 Wellington Street, Leicester LE1 6HJ. *E*: HHJ.jane.george@ejudiciary.net.

**GEORGE, Prof. Kenneth Desmond**; Professor of Economics, 1988–98, now Emeritus, and Pro Vice-Chancellor (formerly Vice-Principal), 1993–98, University of Wales Swansea (formerly University College of Swansea); *b* 11 Jan. 1937; *s* of Horace Avory George and Dorothy Margaret (*née* Hughes); *m* 1959, Elizabeth Vida (*née* Harries); two *s* one *d*. *Educ*: Ystalyfera Grammar Sch.; University Coll. of Wales, Aberystwyth (MA). Res. Asst, then Lectr in Econs, Univ. of Western Australia, 1959–63; Lectr in Econs, University Coll. of N Wales, Bangor, 1963–64; Univ. Asst Lectr, Univ. of Cambridge, 1964–66, Univ. Lectr, 1966–73; Fellow and Dir of Studies in Econs, Sidney Sussex Coll., Cambridge, 1965–73; Prof. and Head of Dept of Econs, 1973–88, and Dep. Principal, 1980–83, UC, Cardiff; Head of Dept of Economics, 1988–95 and Dean, Faculty of Econ. and Soc. Studies, 1992–93, UC Swansea. Vis. Prof., McMaster Univ., 1970–71. Part-time Mem., Monopolies and Mergers Commn, 1978–86; Member: Ind. panel on public appointments, Welsh Office, 1996–2000; Parly Boundary Commn for Wales, 1998–2006. Editor, Jl of Industrial Economics, 1970–83; Mem. Adv. Bd, Antitrust Law and Econs Rev., 1988–92. *Publications*: Productivity in Distribution, 1966; Productivity and Capital Expenditure in Retailing, 1968; Industrial Organisation, 1971, 4th edn (with C. Joll and E. Lynk), 1992; (with T. S. Ward) The Structure of Industry in the EEC, 1975; (ed with C. Joll) Competition Policy in the UK and EEC, 1975; (with J. Shorey) The Allocation of Resources, 1978; (ed with L. Mainwaring) The Welsh Economy, 1988; articles in Econ. Jl, Oxford Econ. Papers, Aust. Econ. Papers, Jl Indust. Econs, Rev. of Econs and Stats, Oxford Bull., Scottish Jl Polit. Econ., and British Jl Indust. Relations. *Recreations*: walking, music.

**GEORGE, Dame (Lesley) Anne**; *see* Glover, Dame L. A.

**GEORGE, Lindsey Ruth; Her Honour Judge Lindsey George**; a Circuit Judge, since 2018; *b* Liverpool, 14 Aug. 1962; *m* 1986, Mike Roderick; one *s* one *d*. *Educ*: Ashcombe Sch., Dorking; Univ. of Durham (BA); Coll. of Law. Solicitor, 1987–2010; a District Judge, 2010–18. *Recreations*: family, holidays, walking, dogs.

**GEORGE, Michael**; freelance classical singer, bass-baritone; *b* 10 Aug. 1950; *s* of late John James George and Elizabeth (*née* Holmes, now Clayton); *m* 1972, Julie Elizabeth Kennard; one *s* two *d*. *Educ*: King's Coll. Choir Sch., Cambridge; Oakham Sch.; Royal Coll. of Music (ARCM Hons). Opera appearances with ENO, Buxton Opera and Scottish Opera incl. Fidelio, Semele and Orfeo, and St John Passion. Has performed in concerts worldwide and worked with leading conductors. Numerous recordings incl. Dream of Gerontius, The Creation, St Matthew Passion, Messiah, complete sacred works of Purcell. *Recreations*: golf, dog walking. *Club*: Royal Mid-Surrey Golf.

**GEORGE, Paul**; Executive Director, Corporate Governance and Reporting, Financial Reporting Council, since 2016; *b* Dartford, 19 Dec. 1960; *s* of late Derek John George and Jeannette George; *m* 1991, Phillipa Jane Brown; two *s* one *d*. *Educ*: Langtree Sch., Woodcote; Orpington Sixth Form Coll.; Warwick Univ. (BSc Hons Accountancy and Financial Analysis). ACA 1986. With KPMG, 1982–99 (Partner, 1995–99); Main Bd Dir, Mgt Consulting Gp plc, 2000–03; Dir, Professional Oversight Bd, 2004–11, Exec. Dir, Conduct Div., 2011–16, Bd Mem., 2012–18, Financial Reporting Council. Non-exec. Dir and Chair, Audit Cttee, Belvoir Lettings plc, 2018–. Gov., Alleyn's Sch., 2006–13. Trustee, Dulwich Estates, 2003–08. *Recreations*: golf, squash, cricket, Rugby, football, theatre.

*Address:* Financial Reporting Council, 8th Floor, 125 London Wall, EC2Y 5AS. *T:* (020) 7492 2300. *E:* p.george@frc.org.uk. *Clubs:* Dulwich and Sydenham Hill Golf, Dulwich Squash.

**GEORGE, Phillip Anthony;** Chairman, Arts Council of Wales, since 2016; *b* Rhondda Valley, 2 April 1950; *s* of William George and Blodwen George; *m* 1979, Ceri Davies; one *s* two *d. Educ:* Rhondda Co. Grammar Sch.; Christ Church, Oxford (BA 1971); Avery Hill Coll., Univ. of London (PGCE 1974). English teacher, Bassaleg and Olchfa Schs, 1974–81; BBC Wales: radio producer, 1982–86; TV producer, 1986–91; Exec. Producer, 1991–97; Hd, Arts, Music and Features, 1997–2000; Creative Dir, Green Bay Media, 2001–16. Founder Chair, Nat. Th. Wales, 2007–16. Advr to Creative Economy Proj., Cardiff Univ., 2014–17. Hon. Fellow, Cardiff Univ., 2017. DUniv Glamorgan, 2010. *Recreations:* wide range of arts, singing, theology. *Address:* Arts Council of Wales, Bute Place, Cardiff CF10 5AL. *T:* (029) 2044 1348. *E:* phil.george@arts.wales.

**GEORGE, Russell Ian;** Member (C) Montgomeryshire, National Assembly for Wales, since 2011; *b* Welshpool, Montgomeryshire, 27 April 1974; *s* of Richard Thomas George and Janet Elizabeth George (*née* Haynes). *Educ:* Clatter Co. Primary Sch.; Caersws Co. Primary Sch.; Newtown High Sch.; Coleg Powys; Univ. of Glamorgan (HNC Business and Finance 1994); Univ. of Central England (BA Hons Information and Media Studies 1999). Mem. (C) Powys CC, 2008– (Bd Mem., 2008–11). Shadow Minister for Envmt and Sustainable Develt, 2011–14, for Agriculture and Rural Affairs, 2014–16, for Economy and Infrastructure, 2016–, Nat. Assembly for Wales. *Recreations:* walking, cycling, member of Hope Church, Newtown, Powys. *Address:* National Assembly for Wales, Cardiff Bay, Cardiff CF99 1NA. *T:* 0300 200 7206. *E:* Russell.George@assembly.wales.

**GEORGE, Ruth Stephanie Nicole;** MP (Lab) High Peak, since 2017; four *c.* Political Officer, USDAW, 1999–2017. Mem., Work and Pensions Cttee, H of C, 2017–. *Address:* House of Commons, SW1A 0AA.

**GEORGE, Simon Ian;** Executive Director of Finance and Commercial Services, Norfolk County Council, since 2015; *b* Norwich, 18 Jan. 1972; *s* of Ian and Hazel George; *m* 2014, Teresa Muscat; one *s. Educ:* Acle High Sch., Norfolk; Univ. of Nottingham (BA Econs). Gen. Accountant, Mobil North Sea Ltd, 1994–95; Finance Manager: BBC Policy and Planning, 1995–96; BBC News Multimedia, 1996–97; BBC Radio Five Live, 1997–99; Head of Finance: BBC News Resources, 1999–2004; BBC TV News, 2004–05; Special Projects, BBC News, 2003–05; Director: Corporate Finance and Audit, Ealing LBC, 2005–13; Finance and Assurance, Harrow LBC, 2013–15. Trustee: Break, 2004–15 (Chm., 2012–15); Nancy Oldfield Trust, 2017–. CIMA 1995. *Recreations:* family, sailing, walking. *Address:* Norfolk County Council, County Hall, Martineau Lane, Norwich, Norfolk NR1 2DH. *T:* 0344 800 8020. *E:* simon.george@norfolk.gov.uk. *Club:* Norfolk (Norwich).

**GEORGE, Prof. Stephen Alan;** Professor, Department of Politics, University of Sheffield, 1994–2004, now Emeritus; *b* 14 Oct. 1949; *s* of Arthur George and Florence Lilian George (*née* Jefferson); *m* 1970, Linda Margaret Booth; one *s* one *d. Educ:* Univ. of Leicester (BA 1st cl. Hons Social Scis 1971; MPhil 1974). Res. Asst in European Affairs, Huddersfield Poly., 1971–72; Lectr, 1973–90, Sen. Lectr, 1991–92, Reader, 1992–94, in Politics, Univ. of Sheffield. Chair, Univ. Assoc. for Contemporary European Studies, 1996–2000. Dir, S Yorks Neighbourhood Watch Assoc., 2007–10. *Publications:* Politics and Policy in the European Community, 1985, 3rd edn, as Politics and Policy in the European Union, 1996; An Awkward Partner: Britain in the European Community, 1990, 3rd edn 1998; (jtly) Politics in the European Union, 2001, 4th edn 2015. *Recreations:* walking, reading history, poetry and novels. *Address:* 33 St Quentin Drive, Bradway, Sheffield S17 4PN. *T:* (0114) 236 4564.

**GEORGE, Timothy John Burr,** CMG 1991; HM Diplomatic Service, retired; *b* 14 July 1937; *s* of late Brig. J. B. George, late RAMC and M. Brenda George (*née* Harrison); *m* 1962, Richenda Mary, *d* of late Alan Reed, FRIBA and Ann Reed (*née* Rowntree); one *s* two *d. Educ:* Aldenham Sch.; Christ's Coll., Cambridge (MA). National Service, 2nd Lieut RA, 1956–58; Cambridge Univ., 1958. FCO, 1961; 3rd Secretary: Hong Kong, 1962; Peking, 1963; 2nd, later 1st Sec., FCO, 1966; 1st Sec. (Economic), New Delhi, 1969; Asst Political Adviser, Hong Kong, 1972; Asst European Integration Dept (Internal), FCO, 1974; Counsellor and Head of Chancery, Peking, 1978–80; Res. Associate, IISS, 1980–81; Counsellor and Hd of Chancery, UK Perm. Delegn to OECD, 1982–86; Hd, Republic of Ireland Dept, FCO, 1986–90; Ambassador to Nepal, 1990–95; FCO, 1996–99. Mem. Bd, CARE Internat. UK, 1998–2004. Gov., Ogbourne Sch., 2004–10, 2012–14 (Chm., 2006–08). Reader/Lay Minister, C of E, 2002–. *Publications:* (jtly) Security in Southern Asia, 1984. *Address:* 7 Jonathan Court, Windmill Road, W4 1SA.
See also A. J. T. George.

**GEORGE, His Honour William;** a Circuit Judge, 1995–2012; *b* 28 Sept. 1944; *s* of William Henry George and Elizabeth George; *m* 1973, Susan Isabel Pennington; two *d. Educ:* Herbert Strutt Grammar Sch.; Victoria Univ. of Manchester (LLB, LLM). Called to the Bar, Lincoln's Inn (Mansfield Scholar), 1968, Bencher, 2003; Chancery Bar, Liverpool, 1968–95; Head, Chancery Chambers, Liverpool, 1985–95; Asst Recorder, 1990–93; Recorder, 1993–95. Chm., Northern Chancery Bar Assoc., 1992–94. *Recreations:* history (military history and the American Civil War), contemporary British art, gardening, watching Rugby. *Address:* Queen Elizabeth II Law Courts, Derby Square, Liverpool L2 1XA. *Club:* Athenæum (Liverpool).

**GEORGE, Prof. William David,** CBE 2008; FRCS; Regius Professor of Surgery, University of Glasgow, 1999–2006 (Professor of Surgery, 1981–99), now Honorary Professor, Faculty of Medicine; *b* 22 March 1943; *s* of William Abel George and Peggy Eileen George; *m* 1st, 1967, Helen Marie (*née* Moran) (*d* 1986); one *s* three *d;* 2nd, 1990, Pauline (*née* Mooney). *Educ:* Reading Blue Coat Sch.; Henley Grammar Sch.; Univ. of London (MB, BS 1966; MS 1977). FRCS 1970. Jun. surgical jobs, 1966–71; Registrar in Surgery, Royal Postgrad. Med. Sch., 1971–73; Lectr in Surg., Univ. of Manchester, 1973–77; Sen. Lectr in Surg., Univ. of Liverpool, 1977–81. *Publications:* articles in BMJ, Lancet, British Jl of Surg. *Recreations:* veteran rowing, fishing, squash. *Club:* Clyde Amateur Rowing (Glasgow).

**GEORGIEVA, Kristalina;** Managing Director, International Monetary Fund, since 2019; *b* Sofia, Bulgaria, 13 Aug. 1953; *m;* one *c. Educ:* Univ. of National and World Economy, Sofia (MA Pol Econ. and Sociol. 1976; PhD Economic Scis 1986). Harvard Business Sch. (Corp. Finance Cert. Prog. 1997; World Bank Exec. Develt Prog. 1998). Asst Prof./Associate Prof., Dept of Econs, Univ. of Nat. and World Economy, Sofia, 1977–93; Res. Fellow, Dept of Econs, LSE, 1987–88; Consultant, Environomics and Merser Mgt Consulting, Inc., 1992; World Bank Group: Envmtl Economist, then Sen. Envmtl Economist, Envmt Div., Europe and Central Asia, 1993–97; Sector Manager, Envmt, 1997–98, Sector Dir, Envmt and Social Develt, 1998–99, E Asia and Pacific Reg.; Dir, Envmt Dept, 2000–04; Dir and Resident Rep., Russian Fedn, Moscow, 2004–07; Dir, Strategy and Ops, Sustainable Develt, 2007–08; Vice Pres. and Corporate Sec., 2008–10. Mem., 2010–17, Vice-Pres., 2014–17, European Commn. Chief Exec., World Bank Gp, 2017–19. Visiting Professor: Univ. of South Pacific, Fiji, 1991; ANU, 1991; Vis. Scholar, Special Prog. in Urban Studies, MIT, 1991–92. Member Board of Trustees: Inst. for Sustainable Communities, 2003–05; LEAD Internat., 2003–09; Univ. of Nat. and World Economy, Sofia, 2009–13. Mem., China Council for Internat. Cooperation on Envmt and Develt, 2012–. European of the Year and European Comr of the Year, European Voice, 2010. *Publications:* textbook on microeconomics; over 100 papers. *Address:* International Monetary Fund, 700 19th Street, NW, Washington, DC 20431, USA.

**GEORGY, Orla;** see Guerin, O.

**GERADA, Clare, (Lady Wessely),** MBE 2000; FRCP, FRCGP, FRCPsych; Chair of Council, Royal College of General Practitioners, 2010–13; *b* Nigeria, 8 Nov. 1959; *d* of Dr Anthony Gerada and Josephine Gerada; *m* 1988, Simon Charles Wessely (see Sir Simon Wessely); two *s. Educ:* Peterborough Co. Girls Comprehensive Sch.; University Coll. London (MB BS 1983); PGCE (Merit). MRCPsych 1988, FRCPsych 2012; MRCGP 1995, FRCGP 2000; FRCP 2008. GP Partner, Hurley Gp, 1992–; Med. Dir, Practitioner Health Prog., 2008–. Chair, N Lambeth Practice Based Commng Gp, 2006–09. Nat. Order of Merit Award (Malta), 2012. *Recreations:* running, secret love of knitting. *Address:* c/o Royal College of General Practitioners, 30 Euston Square, NW1 2FB. *T:* (020) 3188 7410.

**GERALD, Diana Judith;** Chief Executive Officer, Book Trust, since 2015; *b* London, 26 Nov. 1968; *d* of Norman and Pauline Gerald; partner, Sir John Oliver Kingman, *qv;* one *d. Educ:* Brighton and Hove High Sch.; Watford Girls' Grammar Sch.; Balliol Coll., Oxford (BA Hons). Dep. Chief Exec., 2007–09, Actg Chief Exec., 2009–10, GDST; Project Lead, Young Foundn (pt-time), 2010–12; Chief Operating Officer, Ark Schs, 2012–15. Trustee: South African Youth Educn for Sustainability; Mohn Westlake Foundn.

**GERALD, Nigel Mortimer; His Honour Judge Gerald;** a Circuit Judge, since 2009; *b* Guildford, 2 Jan. 1959; *s* of Terry John Gerald and Stella Mortimer Gerald; partner, Katie Jane Young; two *d. Educ:* Highfield Sch.; Oundle Sch.; University Coll. London (LLB 1982). Called to the Bar, Gray's Inn, 1985; Recorder, 2004–09; a Judge of the Upper Tribunal (Lands Chamber) (formerly Chm., Residential Property Tribunal Service), 2006–; a Judge of the First-tier Tribunal (Charity) (formerly Chm., Charity Tribunal), 2008–. *Recreations:* opera, theatre, films, yoga.

**GERARD,** family name of **Baron Gerard**.

**GERARD,** 5th Baron *cr* 1876; **Anthony Robert Hugo Gerard;** Bt 1611; *b* 3 Dec. 1949; *er s* of Maj. Rupert Charles Frederick Gerard, MBE (*ggs* of 1st Baron), and of Huguette Reiss-Brian; *S* cousin, 1992; *m* 1976, Kathleen (marr. diss. 1997), *e d* of Dr Bernard Ryan, New York; two *s. Educ:* Harvard. Mem., Investment Cttee, Azimuth Investment Mgt LLC; Man. Mem., Gerard Partners LLC; former Chm., SupplyPro Inc. Sen. Advr to Chm. and CEO, New York Private Bank and Trust. Director: Nicklaus Cos; Miura Golf; GolfLogix. Former Mem., Adv. Council, Conservation Trust of Puerto Rico. Former Trustee, Cardigan Mountain Sch. Former Dir and Sec., Wellness Foundn of E Hampton. *Heir: s* Hon. Rupert Bernard Charles Gerard, *b* 17 Dec. 1981. *Address:* PO Box 2308, East Hampton, NY 11937, USA.

**GERE, Richard Tiffany;** actor; Founder and Director, Healing the Divide Foundation, since 2001; *b* 31 Aug. 1949; *s* of Homer and Doris Gere; *m* 1st, 1991, Cindy Crawford (marr. diss. 1995); 2nd, 2002, Carey Lowell (marr. diss. 2016); one *s;* 3rd, 2018, Alejandra Silva; one *s. Educ:* Univ. of Massachusetts. Played trumpet, piano, guitar and bass and composed music with various gps; stage performances: with Provincetown Playhouse, Seattle Rep. Theatre; Richard Farina, Long Time Coming and Long Time Gone, Back Bog Beat Bait, off-Broadway; Soon, Habeas Corpus and Grease on Broadway; A Midsummer Night's Dream, Lincoln Center; Taming of the Shrew, Young Vic, London; Bent, on Broadway (Theatre World Award); *films* include: Report to the Commissioner, 1975; Baby Blue Marine, 1976; Looking for Mr Goodbar, 1977; Days of Heaven, Blood Brothers, 1978; Yanks, American Gigolo, 1979; An Officer and a Gentleman, 1982; Breathless, Beyond the Limit, 1983; The Cotton Club, 1984; King David, 1985; Power, No Mercy, 1986; Miles From Home, 1989; Pretty Woman, Internal Affairs, 1990; Rhapsody in August, 1991; Final Analysis, 1992; Mr Jones, Sommersby, 1993; And the Band Played On, Intersection, 1994; First Knight, 1995; Primal Fear, 1996; The Jackal, Red Corner, 1998; The Runaway Bride, 1999; Autumn in New York, Dr T and the Women, 2000; The Mothman Prophecies, Unfaithful, Chicago, 2002; Shall We Dance?, 2005; Bee Season, 2006; The Hoax, I'm Not There, 2007; Nights in Rodanthe, 2008; Amelia, 2009; Brooklyn's Finest, 2010; Arbitrage, 2012; The Second Best Exotic Marigold Hotel, The Benefactor, 2015; Time Out of Mind, 2016; Norman, The Dinner, 2017; *television series:* MotherFatherSon, 2019. Founding Chm. and Pres., Tibet House, NY; Founder, Gere Foundn, 1991. Eleanor Roosevelt Humanitarian Award, 2000; Marian Anderson Award, 2007. *Publications:* Pilgrim, 1997. *Address:* c/o William Morris Endeavor Entertainment LLC, 9601 Wilshire Boulevard, Beverly Hills, CA 90210, USA.

**GERGAUD, Perdita Mary;** see Hunt, P. M.

**GERGIEV, Valery Abesalovich;** Artistic Director and Principal Conductor, Mariinsky (formerly Kirov) Opera, since 1988; Director, Mariinsky Theatre, St Petersburg, since 1996; Music Director, Munich Philharmonic Orchestra, since 2015; *b* Moscow, 2 May 1953. *Educ:* studied conducting under Ilya Musin, Rimsky-Korsakov Conservatory, Leningrad. Asst Conductor, Kirov Opera, 1977–88 (début, War and Peace, 1978); Chief Conductor, Armenian State Orch., 1981–85; has appeared with numerous major internat. orchs, incl. Bayerische Rundfunk, Berlin Philharmonic, Boston SO, LPO, BBC Symphony, Philharmonia, NY Philharmonic, Vienna Philharmonic; tours with Kirov Opera. Principal Conductor: Rotterdam Philharmonic Orch., 1995–2008; LSO, 2007–15; Principal Guest Conductor, Metropolitan Opera, NY, 1997–2008; Artistic Director: Stars of the White Nights Fest., St Petersburg, 1993–; Rotterdam Philharmonic/Gergiev/Philips Fest., 1996–; Director and Founder: Mikkeli Internat. Fest., Finland, 1992–; Peace to the Caucasus Fest., 1996–; Red Sea Internat. Music Fest., Eilat, Israel, 1996–. Has made numerous recordings. Winner, Herbert von Karajan Conductors Competition, Berlin; Dmitri Shostakovich Award; Golden Mask Award; People's Artist of Russia. *Address:* c/o Columbia Artists, 5 Columbus Circle, 1790 Broadway, New York, NY 10019-1412, USA.

**GERHAHER, Dr Christian;** operatic and classical concert singer - baritone; *b* Straubing, Germany, 24 July 1969; *s* of Dr Franz Gerhaher and Elisabeth Gerhaher; *m* 2002, Barbara Hacker; two *s* one *d. Educ:* Johannes Turmair Gymnasium, Straubing; Ludwig Maximilians Univ., Munich (MD 2000). Singer, theatre in Würzburg, 1998–2000; freelance singer, 2002–. Prof., 2002–07, Hon. Prof., 2008, Acad. of Music, Munich. Has made numerous recordings. Member: Bayerische Akademie der Schönen Künste, 2012–; Akademie der Künste, Berlin, 2015–. Outstanding Achievement in Opera, Olivier Awards, 2011. Kammersänger, Bavaria, 2015; Mem., Maximilian Order of Sci. and Art, Bavaria, 2014. *Publications:* Halb Worte sind's, halb Melodie, 2015. *Address:* Künstlersekretariat am Gasteig, Montgelasstraße 2, 81679 Munich, Germany. *T:* 8944488792. *E:* verena.vetter@ks-gasteig.de. *Club:* Rotary (Munich).

**GERHOLD, Dorian James**, FRHistS, FSA; historian; Secretary, House of Commons Commission, 2008–12; *b* 7 March 1957; *s* of late Peter Kenneth Gerhold and Nancy Melinda Gerhold (*née* Jones); *m* 2013, Elisabeth Partridge. *Educ:* King's Coll. Sch., Wimbledon; Merton Coll., Oxford (MA Hist.); DLitt Oxon 2016. Clerk, House of Commons, 1978–2012: Energy Cttee, 1989–92; Trade and Industry Cttee, 1992–96; Table Office, 1996–2000; Eur. Scrutiny Cttee, 2000–05; Hd, Scrutiny Unit, 2005–06; Principal Clerk, Select Cttees, 2006–08. Presidential Advr, Parly Assembly of Council of Europe, 2001–04. Hon. Res. Fellow, Roehampton Univ., 2005–08. Member: Cttee, Southern History Soc., 2013–; Council, London Topographical Soc., 2016–; Mus. and Heritage Gp, Battersea Arts Centre, 2016–18. Chm., Transport Hist. Res. Trust, 1997–2000; Trustee: Wandsworth Mus. Co., 2007–16; County History Trust, 2013–. FRHistS 1996; FSA 2006. Fellow, Industry and Parlt Trust. Mem. Edit Bd, Jl Transport Hist., 1992–2015. *Publications:* Road Transport Before the Railways: Russell's London flying waggons, 1993; (with T. Barker) The Rise and Rise of Road Transport 1700–1990, 1993, 2nd edn 1995; (ed) Putney and Roehampton Past, 1994; (ed) Road Transport in the Horse-drawn Era, 1996; Wandsworth Past, 1998; Westminster Hall, 1999; Carriers and Coachmasters: trade and travel before the turnpikes, 2005 (Transport Book of the Year, 2007); The Putney Debates 1647, 2007; Bristol's Stage Coaches, 2012; London Plotted: plans of London buildings c.1450–1720, 2016; articles in jls. *Recreations:* travel, walking, tennis. *Address:* 19 Montserrat Road, SW15 2LD.

**GERKEN, Ian**, LVO 1992; HM Diplomatic Service, retired; Ambassador to Ecuador, 2000–03; *b* 1 Dec. 1943; *s* of late Alfred Gerken and Esther Mary (*née* Chesworth); *m* 1976, Susana Drucker; two *s*, and one step *d*. *Educ:* Liverpool Collegiate. Entered Foreign Office, 1962: served in Budapest, 1965; Buenos Aires, 1966–68; FCO, 1968–71; Caracas, 1971–75; FCO, 1975–79; Lima, 1979–84; UN Gen. Assembly, 1984; FCO, 1985–88; Dep. High Comr, Valletta, 1988–92; Counsellor and Dep. Head, Perm. Under Sec.'s Dept, FCO, 1992–95; Ambassador to El Salvador, 1995–99.

**GERKEN, Vice-Adm. Sir Robert (William Frank)**, KCB 1986; CBE 1975; Royal Navy, retired 1987; *b* 11 June 1932; *s* of Francis Sydney and Gladys Gerken; *m* 1st, 1966, Christine Stephenson (*d* 1981); two *d*; 2nd, 1983, Mrs Ann Fermor. *Educ:* Chigwell Sch.; Royal Naval Coll., Dartmouth. Cadet, HMS Devonshire, 1950–51; Midshipman: HMS Ocean, 1951–52; HMS Morecambe Bay, 1952; Sub-Lieut, Royal Naval Coll., Greenwich, 1953; Sea service as Lieut and Lt-Comdr, 1953–66; RN Staff Course, 1967; in command HMS Yarmouth, 1968–69; Commander Sea Training, 1970–71; Naval Staff, 1972–73; in command: Sixth Frigate Sqdn, 1974–75; HMS Raleigh, 1976–77; Captain of the Fleet, 1978–81; Flag Officer Second Flotilla, 1981–83; Dir Gen., Naval Manpower and Trng, 1983–85; Flag Officer Plymouth, Port Admiral Devonport, Comdr Central Sub Area Eastern Atlantic, Comdr Plymouth Sub Area Channel, 1985–87. Chm., Plymouth Develt Corp., 1993–96; Dir, 1988–2001, Chm., 1994–2001, Corps of Commissionaires. Chm., China Fleet Trust (formerly China Fleet Club (UK) Charitable Trust), 1987–2013. President: British Korean Veterans' Assoc. (Devon and Cornwall), 1986–2014; Plymouth Lifeboat, RNLI, 1988–2007; SSAFA (formerly SSAFA Forces Help) Plymouth Br., 1998–2016. Governor, Chigwell Sch., 1987–2000. DL Devon, 1995. Hon. DSc Plymouth, 1993. *Recreations:* travel and family. *Address:* 22 Custom House Lane, Plymouth, Devon PL1 3TG. *T:* (01752) 665104. *Club:* Royal Western Yacht (Cdre, 1993–97).

**GERMAN**, family name of **Baron German**.

**GERMAN, Baron** *cr* 2010 (Life Peer), of Llanfrechfa in the County Borough of Torfaen; **Michael James German**, OBE 1996; *b* 8 May 1945; *s* of Arthur Ronald German and Molly German; *m* 1970 (marr. diss. 1996); two *d*; *m* 2006, Veronica Watkins. *Educ:* St Mary's Coll., London (CertEd 1966); BA Open Univ. 1972; Bristol Poly. (Postgrad. Dip. in Educn Mgt 1973). Primary sch. teacher, 1966–67; Secondary sch. teacher, Mostyn High Sch., 1967–70; Head of Music: Lady Mary High Sch., Cardiff, 1970–86; Corpus Christi High Sch., Cardiff, 1986–91; Dir, European Div., Welsh Jt Educn Cttee, 1991–99. Mem., Cardiff CC, 1983–96 (Jt Leader, 1987–91); Leader, Liberal Democrats, 1983–96). National Assembly for Wales: Mem. (Lib Dem) S Wales East, 1999–2010; Sec., subseq. Minister, for Econ. Develt, 2000–01; Dep. First Minister, 2000–01 and 2002–03; Minister for Rural Develt and Wales Abroad, 2002–03; Chairman: Legislation Cttee, 1999–2000; Sustainability Cttee, 2009–10; Leader: Liberal Democrats, 1999–2008; Welsh Liberal Democrats, 2007–08. Co-Chair, Lib Dem Parly Cttee for Work and Pensions, H of L, 2010–15; Mem., Adv. Cttee on Business Appts, 2014–. Treas., Liberal Democrats, 2015–. Chm., Anglo-Azerbaijani Soc.; President: Dolen Cymru, Wales-Lesotho Link, 2008–; Monmouth, Brecon and Abergavenny Canals Trust, 2011–. Vice Chm., Parliament Choir, 2013–. *Publications:* articles in political and educnl jls. *Recreations:* music, travel. *Address:* Hycona, Crown Road, Llanfrechfa, Cwmbran NP44 8UF. *T:* (01633) 870075; House of Lords, SW1A 0PW. *T:* (020) 7219 6942.

**GERMAN, Lt-Col David John Keeling**, TD 1972; JP; Vice Lord-Lieutenant of Staffordshire, 1995–2007; *b* 25 May 1932; *s* of Col Guy German, DSO and Rosemary German (*née* Keeling), MBE; *m* 1961, Anita Blanche Jupp (*d* 2015); one *s* one *d*. *Educ:* Winchester; RMA, Sandhurst. Served Grenadier Guards, 1952–59; Keeling & Walker Ltd, Stoke on Trent, Chem. Mfrs, 1959–90, Man. Dir, 1974–90. Served Staffs Yeomanry, 1960–70, commanded QO Mercian Yeomanry, 1972–75. Founder and Curator, Mus. of Staffs Yeomanry, 1993–2017. Freeman, City of London, 1983. JP 1972, DL 1979, High Sheriff 1982–83, Staffs. *Recreations:* yachting, military history, France. *Address:* Ridgecombe, Penton Grafton, Andover SP11 0RR. *Clubs:* Army and Navy; Royal Yacht Squadron; Household Division Yacht (Cdre, 1993–98).

**GERMOND, Rt Rev. Brian Charles**; Bishop of Johannesburg, 2000–13; *b* 21 Jan. 1947; *s* of Charles Alfred Germond and Dorothy Eileen Germond (*née* Impey); *m* 1971, Susan Patricia Strong; one *s* two *d*. *Educ:* King Edward VII Sch.; Univ. of SA (BA); St Paul's Theol Coll. (DipTh); Univ. of London (BD); McCormack Seminary (DMin). Ordained deacon, 1976, priest, 1977; Curate, St Martin-in-the-Veld, Johannesburg, 1976–80; Rector: St Barnabas Lichtenburg, St Andrews, Lichtenburg, and St John's, Zeerust, 1980–85; St Martin-in-the-Veld, 1987–2000; Archdeacon of Rosebank, 1989–2000. *Recreations:* birdwatching, woodworking. *Address:* c/o PO Box 1131, Johannesburg 2000, RSA. *T:* (011) 3368724.

**GERMOND, (Catherine) Siân**; *see* Maddrell, C. S.

**GEROSA, Peter Norman**; Trustee, Tree Council, 1991–2003 (Secretary, 1983–91); *b* 1 Nov. 1928; *s* of late Enrico Cecil and Olive Doris Gerosa; *m* 1955, Dorothy Eleanor Griffin; two *d*. *Educ:* Whitgift Sch.; London Univ. (Birkbeck). BA (Hons) 1st Cl., Classics. Civil Service, 1945–82; Foreign Office, 1945; Home Office, 1949; HM Customs and Excise, 1953; Min. of Transport, 1966; DoE, 1970; Under Secretary: DoE, 1972; Dept of Transport, 1977; Dir of Rural Affairs, DoE, 1981–82. *Recreation:* walking. *Address:* Sunnyside, 2 Chart Lane, Reigate, Surrey RH2 7BW.

**GERRARD, Ven. David Keith Robin**; Archdeacon of Wandsworth, 1989–2004, now Emeritus; *b* 15 June 1939; *s* of Eric Henry and Doris Jane Gerrard; *m* 1963, Jennifer Mary Hartley; two *s* two *d*. *Educ:* Royal Grammar School, Guildford; St Edmund Hall, Oxford (BA); Lincoln Theol Coll. Curate: St Olave, Woodberry Down, N16, 1963–66; St Mary, Primrose Hill, NW3, 1966–69; Vicar: St Paul, Lorrimore Square, SE17, 1969–79; St Andrew and St Mark, Surbiton, Surrey, 1979–89; RD of Kingston upon Thames, 1983–88. *Publications:* (co-author) Urban Ghetto, 1976. *Recreations:* embroidery, Proust, Yorkshire, statistics. *Address:* 15 Woodbourne Drive, Claygate, Surrey KT10 0DR. *T:* (01372) 467295. *E:* david.gerrard@btinternet.com.

**GERRARD, Neil Francis**; *b* 3 July 1942; *m* 1968, Marian Fitzgerald (marr. diss. 1983); two *s*. *Educ:* Manchester Grammar Sch.; Wadham Coll., Oxford (BA Hons); Chelsea Coll., London (MEd). Teacher, Queen Elizabeth's Sch., Barnet, 1965–68; Lectr in Computing, Hackney Coll., 1968–92. Mem. (Lab) Waltham Forest BC, 1973–90 (Leader of Council, 1986–90). Contested (Lab) Chingford, 1979. MP (Lab) Walthamstow, 1992–2010.

**GERRARD, Peter Noël**, CBE 1991; General Counsel, London Stock Exchange, 1991–94; *b* 19 May 1930; *oc* of Sir Denis Gerrard and of Hilda Goodwin (*née* Jones, who *m* 2nd, Sir Joseph Cantley, OBE); *m* 1957, Prudence Lipson-Ward; one *s* two *d*. *Educ:* Rugby; Christ Church, Oxford (MA). 2nd Lieut, XII Royal Lancers, Malaya, 1953–54. Solicitor, 1959; Partner, Lovell, White & King, 1960, Sen. Partner, 1980–88; Sen. Partner, Lovell White Durrant, 1988–91. Member: Bd of Banking Supervision, 1990–2001; City Capital Markets Cttee, 1974–91. Member: Council, Law Society, 1972–82; Bd, Inst. of Advanced Legal Studies, 1985–96; Council, St George's Hosp. Med. Sch., 1982–94. *Recreations:* music, walking (restricted). *Address:* Pightle Cottage, Ashdon, Saffron Walden, Essex CB10 2HG. *T:* (01799) 584374.

**GERRIE, Malcolm**; Chief Executive, Whizz Kid Entertainment, since 2006; *b* Newcastle upon Tyne, 9 May 1950; *s* of Athelstan Ross Gerrie and Evelyn Gerrie (*née* Nesbitt); three *s*. *Educ:* Durham Univ. (BA); Sunderland Univ. (BEd). Schoolteacher, 1971–76; researcher and producer, Tyne Tees TV, 1976–87; Dir, 1988, Man. Dir, 1988–2006, Initial Film & TV. Hon. DArts Sunderland, 2006. *Recreations:* anything ending in '…ing'. *Address:* Whizz Kid Entertainment, 4 Kingly Street, W1B 5PE. *T:* (020) 7440 2550, *Fax:* (020) 7440 2599. *Clubs:* Royal Automobile, Groucho, Soho House, Bureau, Ivy.

**GERRISH, Prof. Catherine Anne**, PhD; CBE 2014; FRCN; Professor of Nursing Research, University of Sheffield and Sheffield Teaching Hospitals NHS Foundation Trust, 2011–16, now Emeritus; *b* Stourbridge, 10 April 1955; *d* of Arthur Walker and Gudrun Walker; *m* 1986, Paul Gerrish. *Educ:* Stourbridge Co. High Sch. for Girls; Welsh Nat. Sch. of Medicine, Univ. of Wales (Bachelor of Nursing 1977); Univ. of Manchester (MSc 1986); Univ. of Nottingham (PhD 1998). RN 1977; Specialist Practitioner Dist Nursing 1977; RM 1979; FRCN 2014. Nursing Sister, Kalene Hosp., Zambia, 1978; Student Midwife, Univ. Hosp. of Wales, 1978–79; Staff Nurse, Singleton Hosp., 1979–81; Sister, Northern Gen. Hosp., 1981–84; Nurse Tutor, Sheffield Sch. of Nursing, 1984–89; Sen. Lectr, 1989–90, Principal Lectr, 1990–92, Univ. of Huddersfield; Asst Dir, Bradford and Airedale Coll. of Health, 1992–95; Sen. Res. Fellow, Sheffield Hallam Univ., 1995–2000; Reader in Nursing Practice Develt, 2000–02, Prof. of Nursing Practice Develt, 2002–06, Univ. of Sheffield and Northern Gen. Hosp. NHS Trust; Res. Prof. in Nursing, Sheffield Hallam Univ. and Sheffield Teaching Hosps NHS Foundn Trust, 2006–11. Adjunct Prof., Karolinska Inst., 2006–14; Hon. Prof., Univ. of Sheffield, 2009–11; Vis. Sen. Acad. Scholar, Univ. of British Columbia, 2013. Chm., Res. Soc., RCN, 2002–10. Trustee, Gen. Nursing Council Trust for Eng. and Wales, 2011–. *Publications:* Nursing in a Multi-ethnic Society, 2006; The Research Process in Nursing, 5th edn 2006 to 7th edn 2015; approx. 150 articles in learned jls. *Recreations:* cycle touring, walking, gardening, needlework, theatre. *Address:* School of Nursing and Midwifery, University of Sheffield, Barber House Annexe, 3a Clarkehouse Road, Sheffield S10 2LA. *T:* (0114) 222 2030. *E:* kate.gerrish@sheffield.ac.uk.

**GERRY, Prof. Felicity Ruth**; QC 2014; *b* Hornchurch, 11 March 1968; *d* of Robin Gerry and Edith Tyler; *m* 1999; one *s* one *d* and one step *s*. *Educ:* Manning Girls Sch., Nottingham; Kingston Univ. (LLB Hons 1993); Charles Darwin Univ. (Grad. Cert. in Univ. Teaching and Learning 2017); Western Sydney Univ. (LLM (Internat. Govt) 2018; Dean's Medal). Called to the Bar, Middle Temple, 1994; admitted to practice: Australia, 2015; Hong Kong (ad hoc), 2016; Gibraltar (ad hoc), 2017. Legal media commentator, 2008–. Lectr in Law, 2013–15, Sen. Lectr in Law, 2015–18, Adjunct Fellow, 2018–, Charles Darwin Univ.; Adjunct Fellow, Western Sydney Univ., 2017–; Prof. of Legal Practice, Deakin Univ., 2018–. Member: Public Affairs Cttee, Bar Council, 2012–13; Legal Practitioners Disciplinary Tribunal, NT, Australia, 2017–. Member: Bd, Halsbury's Law Exchange, 2012–; Mgt Cttee, Advocates' Gateway, 2014–; Making Justice Work Campaign, 2017. Legal Personality of the Year, Solicitors Journal 160th Anniversary Awards, 2016. *Publications:* The Sexual Offences Handbook, 2010, 2nd edn 2014; (contrib.) Addressing Vulnerability in Justice Systems, 2016; (contrib.) Human Trafficking: emerging legal issues and applications, 2017; (contrib.) Trans-Atlantic Data Privacy Relations as a Challenge for Democracy, 2017; (contrib.) Human Trafficking and Modern Slavery: law and practice, 2018; (contrib.) Access to Justice for Vulnerable People, 2018; (contrib.) Vulnerable People in the Criminal Justice System, 2018; (contrib.) Research Handbook on Feminist Engagement with International Law, 2019; contribs to academic jls and legal press. *Recreations:* horses, vintage jewellery, Twitter @felicitygerry. *Address:* Carmelite Chambers, 9 Carmelite Street, EC4Y 0DR. *T:* (020) 7936 6300. *E:* fgerryqc@carmelitechambers.co.uk. *W:* www.felicitygerry.com.

**GERSHON, Sir Peter (Oliver)**, Kt 2004; CBE 2000; FREng; Chairman: Tate & Lyle plc, 2009–17; National Grid plc, since 2012; Aircraft Alliance Management Board, since 2014; Join Dementia Research, since 2017; Dreadnought Submarine Alliance, since 2018; *b* 10 Jan. 1947; *s* of late Alfred Joseph Gershon and Gerta Gershon; *m* 1971, Eileen Elizabeth Walker; one *s* two *d*. *Educ:* Reigate Grammar Sch.; Churchill Coll., Cambridge (MA). FIEE 1998, Hon. FIET (Hon. FIEE 2005); FRAeS 2000; FCIPS 2000; FREng 2001. Joined ICL, 1969; Mem. Mgt Bd, and Dir of Network Systems, 1985; Managing Director: STC Telecommunications Ltd, 1987–90; GPT Ltd, 1990–94; Marconi Electronic Systems Ltd, 1994–99; Chief Operating Officer, BAE Systems, 1999–2000; Chief Exec., Office of Govt Commerce, 2000–04; Chairman: Symbian Ltd, 2004–08; General Healthcare Gp, 2006–12; Premier Farnell plc, 2005–11; Vertex Data Sciences, 2007–. Mem. Ct and Council, Imperial Coll., London, 2002–10. CCMI (CIMgt 1996); FBCS 2005. Hon. Fellow: Cardiff Univ., 2007; Imperial Coll. London, 2011. Hon. DTech Kingston, 2005. *Publications:* Review of Civil Procurement in Central Government, 1999; Independent Review of Public Sector Efficiency, 2004; Independent Review of Royal Family and Ministerial Air Travel, 2006; Review of the Australian Government's Use of Information and Communication Technology, 2008. *Recreations:* cycling, reading, swimming, theatre. *T:* 07971 139650.

**GERSHUNY, Prof. Jonathan Israel**, CBE 2017; DPhil; FBA 2002; FAcSS; Professor of Economic Sociology, University College London, since 2019; Director, ESRC Centre for Time Use Research, University College London (formerly at University of Oxford), since 2012; *b* 16 Sept. 1949; *s* of Charles and Cynthia Gershuny; *m* 1974, Esther Gershuny; one *s* one *d*. *Educ:* Loughborough Univ. (BSc Econs and Politics 1971); Strathclyde Univ. (MSc 1972); Sussex Univ. (DPhil 1977). Res. Officer, Dept of Transport Technology, Loughborough Univ., 1973–74; Science Policy Research Unit, Sussex University: Fellow, 1974–81; Sen. Fellow, 1981–84; Vis. Professorial Fellow, 1986–91; on secondment as pt-time Res. Fellow, Res. Unit on Ethnic Relations, Univ. of Bristol, 1978–79; University of Bath: Prof. of Sociology, 1984–89; Head: Sociology and Social Policy Gp, 1984–88; Sch. of Social Scis, 1988–89; Univ. Lectr, Dept of Social and Admin. Studies, and Fellow of Nuffield Coll., Univ. of Oxford, 1990–93; Prof. of Econ. Sociology and Dir, ESRC Res. Centre on Micro-social Change, subseq. Inst. for Social and Econ. Res., Univ. of Essex, 1993–2006; Prof. of Sociology, 2006–11, Hd, Dept of Sociology, 2008–09, Prof. of Econ. Sociology, 2012–19, Univ. of Oxford; Fellow, St Hugh's Coll., Oxford, 2006–11; Sen. Res. Fellow, Nuffield Coll., Oxford, 2012. Chm., Sect. S4 (Sociol., Demography, Social Stats), British Acad., 2006–09. FAcSS (AcSS 2011). Silver Medal, Market Res. Soc., 1986. *Publications*: After Industrial Society?, 1978 (trans. German, 1981, Italian, 1985); Social Innovation and the Division of Labour, 1983 (trans. Swedish 1986); (with I. D. Miles) The New Service Economy, 1983 (trans. Japanese 1983, Spanish 1988); (ed jtly) Time Use Studies World Wide, 1991; L'innovazione Sociale: tempo, produzione e consumi, 1993; (jtly) Changing Households, 1994; (ed jtly) The Social and Political Economy of the Household, 1994; Changing Times: the social and political economy of post industrial society, 2000; (ed jtly) Seven Years in the Lives of British Households, 2000; (ed jtly) Information and Communication Technologies in Society, 2007. *Recreations*: classical music, travel. *Address*: Centre for Time Use Research, 55 Gordon Square, Bloomsbury, WC1H 0NU. *E*: j.gershuny@ucl.ac.uk.

**GERSON, John Henry Cary,** CMG 1999; Head of Government and Political Affairs, BP plc, 2007–12 (Group Political Adviser, 2000–07); *b* 25 April 1945; *s* of late Henry and of Benedicta Joan Gerson; *m* 1968, Mary Alison, *d* of late George Ewart Evans; one *s* one *d*. *Educ*: Bradfield; King's Coll., Cambridge (MA). HM Diplomatic Service, 1968–99: Third Sec., FCO, 1968; language student, Hong Kong, 1969–71; Second Secretary: Singapore, 1971–73; FCO, 1973–74; First Sec. and HM Consul, Peking, 1974–77; First Sec., FCO, 1978; on loan to Home CS, 1978–79; First Sec., later Counsellor, FCO, 1979–87; Counsellor, Hong Kong, 1987–92; Vis. Fellow, Princeton Univ., 1992; Counsellor, FCO, 1992–99. Mem. Bd, Handeni Gold, 2012. Mem. Simuri Tribe, Manokwari, Irian Jaya, 2001. *Recreations*: ornithology, sinology, literature. *Club*: Athenæum.

**GERSTENBERG, Frank Eric,** MA; Principal, George Watson's College, Edinburgh, 1985–2001; *b* 23 Feb. 1941; *s* of late Eric Gustav Gerstenberg and Janie Willis Gerstenberg; *m* 1966, Valerie Myra (*née* MacLellan); one *s* twin *d*. *Educ*: Trinity College, Glenalmond; Clare College, Cambridge (MA); Inst. of Education, Univ. of London (PGCE). Asst History Teacher, Kelly Coll., Tavistock, 1963–67; Housemaster and Head of History, Millfield School, 1967–74; Headmaster, Oswestry School, 1974–85. Chm. of Govs, Glenalmond Coll., 2005–11; Governor: Compass Sch., Haddington, 2007–15; Loretto Sch., 2012–16. Elder, Ch of Scotland. *Recreations*: ski-ing, golf, visiting scattered children throughout the world. *Address*: 9 Waverley North, East Links Road, Gullane, East Lothian EH31 2AF. *Clubs*: Royal Scots (Edinburgh); Luffness New Golf, Royal Dornoch Golf.

**GERSTLE, Prof. (C.) Andrew,** PhD; FBA 2015; Professor of Japanese Studies, School of Oriental and African Studies, University of London, since 1993; *b* 18 June 1951. *Educ*: Columbia Univ. (BA 1973); Waseda Univ., Tokyo (MA 1979); Harvard Univ. (PhD 1980). Lectr, 1980–89, Prof. of Japanese, 1989–93, ANU; Dir, AHRC (formerly AHRB) Centre for Asian and African Studies, SOAS, 2000–05. Guest Curator: Kabuki Heroes on the Osaka Stage 1780–1830 (special exhibn), BM, 2005; Shunga: Sex and Pleasure in Japanese Art (special exhibn), BM, 2013. *Publications*: Circles of Fantasy: convention in the plays of Chikamatsu, 1986, 2nd edn 1996; (ed) Eighteenth Century Japan: culture and society, 1989; (with K. Inobe and W. Malm) Theatre as Music: the Bunraku play 'Mt Imo and Mt Se: An Exemplary Tale of Womanly Virtue', 1990; (ed with A. Milner) Recovering the Orient: artists, scholars, appropriations, 1994; Chikamatsu: five late plays, 2001; Kabuki Heroes on the Osaka Stage 1780–1830, 2005; Edo onna no shungabon (Erotic parodies of Japanese conduct books), 2011; (ed) Shunga: sex and pleasure in Japanese Art, 2013. *Address*: School of Oriental and African Studies, University of London, Russell Square, WC1H 0XG. *E*: ag4@soas.ac.uk.

**GERSTNER, Louis Vincent,** Jr; Hon. KBE 2001; Chairman, 2003–08, Senior Advisor, 2008–16, Carlyle Group; *b* NY, 1 March 1942. *Educ*: Dartmouth Coll. (BA Engrg 1963); Harvard Business Sch. (MBA 1965). Dir, McKinsey & Co., Inc., 1965–78; Pres., American Express Co., 1978–89; Chairman and Chief Executive Officer: RJR Nabisco Inc., 1989–93; IBM, 1993–2002. Director: NY Times Co., 1986–97; Bristol-Myers Squibb Co. Dir, Japan Soc., 1992–. Founder and Chm., Teaching Commn, 2003–06. Chm., Bd of Dirs, Broad Inst., 2013–; Vice Chm., American Mus. of Natural Hist. Mem. Bd, Lincoln Center for Performing Arts, 1984–2002. Chm. Bd, Gerstner Sloan Kettering Grad. Sch. of Biomed. Scis, 2014–; Mem. Bd, Memorial Sloan Kettering Cancer Center, 1998–. Mem., Nat. Acad. of Engrg, USA, 1999. Fellow, American Acad. of Arts and Scis, 2000. *Publications*: Re-inventing Education: entrepreneurship in America's public schools (jtly), 1994; Who Says Elephants Can't Dance: inside IBM's historic turnaround, 2002.

**GERVAIS, Most Rev. Marcel;** Archbishop of Ottawa, (RC), 1989–2007, now Archbishop Emeritus; *b* 21 Sept. 1931; *s* of Frédéric Pierre Gervais and Marie-Louise Beaudry. *Educ*: St Peter's Seminary, London, Ont.; Angelicum Athenæum Pontifical Inst., Rome; Pontifical Biblical Inst., Rome; Ecole Biblique et Archéologique Française de Jérusalem. Ordained priest, 1958; Prof. of Sacred Scriptures, St Peter's Seminary, London, 1962–76; Dir of Divine Word Internat. Centre of Religious Educn, London, 1974–80; Auxiliary Bishop of London, Ontario, 1980–85; Bishop of Sault Sainte-Marie, 1985–89; Coadjutor Archbishop of Ottawa, June–Sept. 1989. Pres., Canadian Conf. of Catholic Bishops, 1991–93. *Address*: 1243 Kilborn Place, Ottawa, ON K1H 6K9, Canada.

**GERVAIS, Ricky Dene;** comedian, actor, director, producer and author; *b* Reading, 25 June 1961; *s* of late Jerry and Eva Gervais; partner, Jane Fallon. *Educ*: Ashmead Comprehensive Sch., Reading; University Coll. London (BA Hons Philosophy). With Xfm, until 1998; *television*: actor: The 11 O'Clock Show, 1998; (also writer with Stephen Merchant) Meet Ricky Gervais, 2000; (also writer, dir and exec. prod. with S. Merchant): The Office, 2001–03 (British Comedy Awards, 2002, 2004; RTS Award, 2002; BAFTA Awards, 2001, 2002, 2003; Golden Globe Awards, 2004; Emmy Award, 2006); Extras, 2005–07 (BAFTA Awards, 2005, 2006, 2007; Emmy Award, 2007; British Comedy Award, 2008; Golden Globe Award, 2008); Life's Too Short, 2011; writer: Stromberg, 2004; Le bureau, 2006; writer and exec. prod., with S. Merchant, The Office (US version), 2005–09; one episode, The Simpsons, 2006; executive producer: The Ricky Gervais Show, 2010–11; An Idiot Abroad, 2010; An Idiot Abroad 2, 2011; An Idiot Abroad 3, 2012; actor, writer, director and executive producer: Derek, 2012, 2014; After Life, 2019; *films*: actor: Dog Eat Dog, 2001; For Your Consideration, Night at the Museum, 2006; Stardust, 2007; Ghost Town, 2008; Night at the Museum: Battle of the Smithsonian, 2009; (also co-writer and dir) The Invention of Lying, 2009; (also co-writer, dir and exec. prod.) Cemetery Junction, 2010; Muppets Most Wanted, 2014; Night at the Museum: Secret of the Tomb, 2014; (also writer and dir) David Brent: Life on the Road, 2016. Stand-up comedy shows: Ricky Gervais Live: Animals, 2003; Politics, 2004; Fame, 2007; Out of England, 2008; Science, 2009–10; Out of England 2, 2010; David Brent and the Foregone Conclusion, 2013; Special Correspondents (also writer and dir), 2016; Humanity, 2017; SuperNature, 2019. *Publications*: with Rob Steen: Flanimals, 2004; More Flanimals, 2005; Flanimals of the Deep, 2006 (Galaxy British Book Award, 2007); Day of the Bletching, 2007; Flanimals Pop Up, 2009; with Stephen Merchant: The Office, Series 1, 2002; The Office, Series 2, 2003; Extras, 2006; The World of Karl Pilkington, 2006; David Brent Songbook, 2016. *Address*: c/o United Agents Ltd, 12–26 Lexington Street, W1F 0LE.

**GERVIS MEYRICK;** *see* Meyrick.

**GERY, Laura W.;** *see* Wade-Gery.

**GESTETNER, Jonathan;** Chairman, Marlborough Rare Books Ltd, since 1990; *b* 11 March 1940; *s* of late Sigmund Gestetner and Henny Gestetner, OBE; *m* 1965, Jacqueline Margaret Strasmore; two *s* one *d*. *Educ*: Bryanston Sch.; Massachusetts Institute of Technology (BScMechEngrg). Joined Gestetner Ltd, 1962; Jt Chm., Gestetner Hldgs PLC, 1972–87; Director: DRS, USA, 1987–89; Klein Associates, USA, 1987–90. Member: Executive Council, Engineering Employers' London Assoc., 1972–77 (Vice-Pres., 1975–77); Maplin Development Authority, 1973–74; SSRC, 1979–82; Dir, Centre for Policy Studies, 1982–96. Mem., Exec. Cttee, British ORT, 1967–89 (Chm., 1986–89); Vice Pres., World ORT Union, 1987–. Member: Educnl Council, MIT, 1973–; Vis. Cttee, Cambridge Univ. Liby, 2009–; Liby Cttee, Oxford Centre for Hebrew and Jewish Studies (formerly Yarnton Centre for Postgrad. Hebrew Studies), 2009–. Trustee, Jewish Mus., 2000–. *Recreations*: the visual arts, Real tennis. *Clubs*: Brooks's, MCC; Grolier (New York).

**GETHIN, Sir Richard (Joseph St Lawrence),** 10th Bt *cr* 1665, of Gethinsgrott, Cork; civil engineer, retired; *b* 29 Sept. 1949; *s* of Sir Richard Patrick St Lawrence Gethin, 9th Bt and of Fara, *y d* of late J. H. Bartlett; *S* father, 1988; *m* 1974, Jacqueline Torfrida, *d* of Comdr David Cox; three *d*. *Educ*: The Oratory School; RMA Sandhurst; RMCS Shrivenham; Cranfield Inst. of Technology (BSc(Eng), MSc). Joined first unit, 1971; served in Germany and UK; retd in rank of Major, 1990. Community Liaison Mgr, Crossrail and Thames Tideway, 2011–16. *Recreations*: gardening, woodwork. *Heir*: *cousin* Antony Michael Gethin [*b* 10 Jan. 1939; *m* 1965, Vanse, *d* of late Col C. D. Barlow, OBE, KSLI; two *s* one *d*].

**GETHINS, Stephen Patrick;** MP (SNP) Fife North East, since 2015; *b* Glasgow, 28 March 1976; *s* of James Gethins and Rhona Gethins; *m* 2013, Anya Hart Dyke; one *s* one *d*. *Educ*: Perth Acad.; Univ. of Dundee (LLB Hons); Univ. of Kent (MA Res.). EU Cttee of the Regions, 2005–07; Scotland Europa, 2007–09; Special Advr to First Minister, Scottish Govt, 2009–13; Chm., Adv. Bd, Scottish Global Forum, 2013–15. SNP spokesperson for Europe, 2015–17, for Internat. Affairs and Europe, 2017–. Mem., Foreign Affairs Select Cttee, 2015–. *Address*: House of Commons, SW1A 0AA. *T*: (020) 7219 5671. *E*: stephen.gethins.mp@parliament.uk. *Club*: Dundee United Football.

**GETTY, Mark Harris,** Hon. KBE 2015; Chairman, Getty Images Inc., 1995–2015 and since 2018; Chairman of Council, British School at Rome, since 2018 (Trustee, since 2015); *b* 9 July 1960; *s* of Sir (John) Paul Getty, KBE and of Gail Harris Getty; *m* 1982, Domitilla Lante Harding (marr. diss. 2011); three *s*; one *d* by Caterina Nahberg. *Educ*: Taunton Sch.; St Catherine's Coll., Oxford (BA). Kidder, Peabody, Inc., 1984–88; Hambros Bank, 1990–93; Getty Images Inc., 1994–2015. Mem., Sutton Place Managers LLP, 2004–. Chm., John Wisden & Co., 2006–08. Trustee, Nat. Gall., 2001–15 (Chm. Trustees, 2008–15).

**GETZLER, Lucia Helen;** *see* Zedner, L. H.

**GEUSS, Prof. Raymond,** PhD; FBA 2011; Professor of Philosophy, University of Cambridge, 2007–14, now Emeritus; *b* Evansville, Indiana, 10 Dec. 1946; *s* of Raymond Geuss and Helen Geuss; *m* 1st, 1987, Heda Šegvić (marr. diss. 1994); 2nd, 2010, Hilary Gaskin. *Educ*: Devon Prep. Sch., Penn; Columbia Univ. (BA *summa cum laude* 1966; PhD 1971). Heidelberg, 1971–73; Assistant Professor of Philosophy: Columbia Univ., 1973–76; Princeton Univ., 1976–79; Associate Prof. of Philos., Univ. of Chicago, 1979–83; Associate Prof., 1983–86, Prof., 1986–87, of Philos., Princeton Univ.; Prof. of Philos., 1987–91, Prof. of Political Sci., 1991–93, Columbia Univ.; University of Cambridge: Lectr, Faculty of Social and Pol Scis, 1993–97, Faculty of Philos., 1997–2000; Reader in Philos., 2000–07. Visiting appointments: Bielefeld, 1981; Hamburg, 1986, 1989; Yale, 1990–91; Freiburg, 1992; Frankfurt, 1992, 1999. Fellow, Wissenschaftskolleg zu Berlin, 1982–83. *Publications*: The Idea of a Critical Theory, 1981; History and Illusion in Politics, 2001; Public Goods, Private Goods, 2001; Outside Ethics, 2005; Philosophy and Real Politics, 2008; Politics and the Imagination, 2010; A World Without Why, 2014; Reality and its Dreams, 2016; Changing the Subject, 2017. *Address*: Faculty of Philosophy, University of Cambridge, Sidgwick Avenue, Cambridge CB3 9DA. *T*: (01223) 335090, *Fax*: (01223) 335091.

**GHAFFUR, Tarique,** CBE 2004; QPM 2001; Chairman, CSD Global (UK) Ltd, 2009; Senior Security Consultant, Global Knowledge Lab, since 2018; *b* 8 June 1955; *m* 1990, Shehla (*née* Aslam); one *s* one *d*. *Educ*: Uganda; Manchester Poly. (BA); Keele Univ. (MA). Greater Manchester Police: uniform and CID posts, 1974–78; Sergeant, 1978; Inspector, 1982; Chief Inspector, 1988; Superintendent, Leics Constabulary, 1989–96; Asst Chief Constable, Lancs Constabulary, 1996–99; Dep. Chief Constable, Police Inf. Technol. Orgn, 1999; a Dep. Asst Comr, 1999–2001, an Asst Comr, 2001–08, Hd of Central Ops and Olympics Security, 2006–08, Metropolitan Police; Director: Specialist Crime, 2003–08; Policing Inst. Abu Dhabi Police, 2012–13. *Publications*: articles on crime, diversity, security and IT.

**GHAHRAMANI, Prof. Zoubin,** PhD; FRS 2015; Professor of Information Engineering, University of Cambridge, since 2006; Fellow, St John's College, Cambridge, since 2009; Chief Scientist, Uber, since 2017; *b* 8 Feb. 1970; *s* of Ghahraman Ghahramani and Manijeh Dabiri. *Educ*: American Sch. of Madrid, Spain; Univ. of Pennsylvania (BA Cognitive Sci. 1990; BSE Computer Sci. 1990); Massachusetts Inst. of Technol. (PhD 1995). Postdoctoral Fellow, Univ. of Toronto, 1995–98; Lectr, Gatsby Unit, 1998–2003, Reader, 2003–06, Adjunct Faculty, Gatsby Unit, 2006–, UCL. Associate Res. Prof., Carnegie Mellon Univ., 2003–12. Cambridge Liaison Dir, Alan Turing Inst., 2015–17. *Publications*: (ed) Advances in Neural Information Processing Systems, 2002, 2013, 2014; 10th International Workshop on Artificial Intelligence and Statistics, 2005; (ed) Proceedings of the International Conference on Machine Learning, 2007; contrib. to Science, Nature, Jl Machine Learning Res., Phil. Trans, Royal Soc. B, Neural Computation, Bioinformatics. *Address*: Department of Engineering, University of Cambridge, Trumpington Street, Cambridge CB2 1PZ. *E*: zoubin@eng.cam.ac.uk.

**GHALY, Karim Raouf George;** QC 2017; *b* Cairo, 30 June 1977; *s* of Raouf George Ghaly and Francine Sourial; *m* 2017, Georgina Sylvia Wolfe. *Educ*: Bolton Sch.; St Edmund Hall, Oxford (BA Juris.). Called to the Bar, Inner Temple, 2001; in practice as a barrister, 2004–. *Publications*: (with Sean Wilken) The Law of Waiver, Variation and Estoppel, 3rd edn 2012. *Recreations*: family, friends, snowboarding, travel. *Address*: 39 Essex Chambers, 81 Chancery Lane, WC2A 1DD. *T*: (020) 7832 1111. *E*: karim.ghaly@39essex.com.

**GHANI, Prof. Azra Catherine Hilary,** PhD; FMedSci; Professor in Infectious Disease Epidemiology, Imperial College London, since 2007; *b* Loughborough, 28 Feb. 1971; *d* of Feroz Ghani and Hilary Ghani (*née* McKee); *m* 2000, Sagar Dave; two *s*. *Educ*: Newnham Coll., Cambridge (BA 1992); Univ. of Southampton (MSc 1993); Imperial Coll. London (PhD 1997). Res. Asst, St Mary's Med. Sch., 1993–96; Wellcome Res. Fellow in

Mathematical Biol., Univ. of Oxford, 1997–2001; Jun. Res. Fellow, St Cross Coll., Oxford, 1999–2001; Royal Soc. Dorothy Hodgkin Fellow, Imperial Coll. London, 2001–05; Reader in Infectious Disease Modelling, LSHTM, 2005–07. FMedSci 2017. *Publications:* 190 articles in peer-reviewed jls. *Recreations:* music (violin), travel. *Address:* Department of Infectious Disease Epidemiology, Imperial College London, Norfolk Place, W2 1PG. *T:* (020) 7594 5764. *E:* a.ghani@imperial.ac.uk.

**GHANI, Nusrat;** MP (C) Wealden, since 2015; Parliamentary Under-Secretary of State (Minister for Maritime and Shipping and Minister for HS2), Department for Transport, since 2018; a Lord Commissioner of HM Treasury (Government Whip), since 2019; *d* of Abdul Ghani and Farzand Begum; *m* 2002, David Wheeldon; one *d*. *Educ:* Bordesley Green Girls' Sch.; Cadbury Sixth Form Coll.; Univ. of Central England; Univ. of Leeds (MA Internat. Relns). Age UK; Breakthrough Breast Cancer; BBC World Service and BBC World Service Trust. An Asst Govt Whip, 2018–19. Member: Home Affairs Select Cttee, 2015–17; Armed Forces Bill Cttee, 2015; Foreign Affairs Cttee, 2017–18; Speaker's Cttee on Electoral Commn, 2017–; Chairman, All Party Parliamentary Group: on Ageing and Older People, 2015–17; on Eye Health and Visual Impairment, 2015–17; Member, All Party Parliamentary Group: on Domestic Violence, 2015–17; on Women in Parlt, 2015–17. Contested (C) Birmingham Ladywood, 2010. *Recreations:* ski-ing, sailing, travel, walking on Ashdown Forest. *Address:* House of Commons, SW1A 0AA. *E:* nusrat.ghani.mp@parliament.uk.

**GHAZAL, Prof. Peter,** PhD; FMedSci; Sêr Cymru II Professor of Systems Medicine, School of Medicine, Cardiff University, since 2017; *b* Brighton, 21 Aug. 1961; *s* of George Sabah Elias Ghazal and Jean Ghazal; *m* 1985, Jacqueline Ann Bernklow; one *s* one *d*. *Educ:* Shoreham Grammar Sch.; Univ. of Wales, Bangor (BSc Jt Hons Biochem. and Marine Scis 1982); Univ. of Edinburgh (PhD Genetics 1985). Fellow, NIH, Bethesda, 1986–88; Asst Prof., 1990–95, Associate Prof., 1995–2000, Scripps Res. Inst., Calif; University of Edinburgh: Reader, 2000–01; Prof. of Molecular Genetics and Biomedicine, 2001–17; Dir, Scottish Centre for Genomic Technol. and Informatics, 2001–07; Associate Dir, Centre for Synthetic and Systems Biol., Coll. of Sci. and Engrg, 2007–12; Hd, Div., Pathway Medicine, Sch. of Biomed. Scis, Med. Sch., 2007–13. Co-founder and non-executive Director: Arrayjet Ltd, 2001–06; Lab901 Ltd, 2002–07; Fios Genomics Ltd, 2008–. Hon. Prof., Scripps Res. Inst., 2001–11. Scholar, Leukemia Soc. of Amer., 1993–98. FMedSci 2015. Associate Ed., Virology, 1996–2000. *Publications:* contrib. chapters in books; over 250 articles in learned jls; 9 patents. *Recreation:* sailing. *Address:* Systems Immunity Research Institute, Division of Infection and Immunity, School of Medicine, Cardiff University CF14 4XN. *T:* (029) 2074 4430. *E:* ghazalp@cardiff.ac.uk. *Club:* Royal Gourock Yacht.

**GHEBREYESUS, Tedros A.;** *see* Adhanom Ghebreyesus, T.

**GHEORGHIU, Angela;** soprano; *b* 1965; *m* 1st, 1988, Andrei Gheorghiu (marr. diss.); 2nd, 1996, Roberto Alagna, *qv* (marr. diss. 2013); one step *d*. *Educ:* Bucharest Acad. Débuts: Nat. Opera, Cluj, 1990; Royal Opera, Covent Garden, 1992; Vienna State Opera, 1992; Metropolitan Opera, NY, 1993. Rôles include: Mimi in La Bohème; Violetta in La Traviata; Micaela in Carmen; title rôle in Turandot; Adina in L'elisir d'amore; Juliette in Roméo et Juliette; Amelia in Simon Boccanegra; Marguerite in Faust; title rôle in Adriana Lecouvreur; title rôle in Tosca. Film, Tosca, 2002. Performs worldwide and has made numerous recordings. *Address:* c/o Royal Opera House, Covent Garden, WC2E 9DD; c/o Alexander Gerdanovits, Seenstrasse 28a, 9081 Reifnitz, Austria. *E:* agerdanovits@gmx.net.

**GHOSE, Katie Sushila Ratna;** Chief Executive, Women's Aid, 2017–19; *b* Shoreham-by-Sea, Sussex, 13 July 1970; *d* of late Toon Ghose and of Daphne Ghose (now Wall); partner, Andrew Jonathan Gilbert Harrop, *qv*; one *d*. *Educ:* Boundstone Community Coll.; Brighton, Hove and Sussex Sixth Form Coll.; Somerville Coll., Oxford (BA Hons Law 1991); Univ. of Calif, Riverside (MA Pol Sci. 1992); Council of Legal Educn; Birkbeck, Univ. of London (Dip. Mgt (Merit) 2002). Parly researcher to Greville Janner, QC, MP, 1992–94; Parly Officer, NACAB, 1994–95; called to the bar, Middle Temple, 1996; barrister, 1 Pump Court Chambers, London, 1997–99; Campaigns Manager, Child Accident Prevention Trust, 2000–01; Parly Officer, 2001–03, Campaigns and Parly Manager, 2003–05, Age Concern England; Dir, British Inst. of Human Rights, 2005–10; Chief Exec., Electoral Reform Soc., 2010–17. Mem., Ind. Asylum Commn, 2006–08. Chair: Asylum Aid, 1997–99; Bail for Immigration Detainees, 2002–04; Yes to Fairer Votes, 2010–11. Mem. Council, Univ. of Sussex, 2015–. Trustee and Co. Sec., Stonewall, 2005–11; Trustee: Fair Vote, 2011–17; St George's House, Windsor Castle, 2019–. *Publications:* Beyond the Courtroom: a lawyer's guide to campaigning, 2005. *Recreations:* hiking, piano, table tennis. *E:* katiesghose@gmail.com. *W:* www.twitter.com/katieghose.

**GHOSH, Dame Helen Frances,** DCB 2008; Master, Balliol College, Oxford, since 2018; *b* 21 Feb. 1956; *d* of William and Eileen Kirkby; *m* 1979, Peter Robin Ghosh; one *s* one *d*. *Educ:* St Hugh's Coll., Oxford (BA (Mod. Hist.) 1976); Hertford Coll., Oxford (MLitt (6th century Italian Hist.) 1980). Admin. trainee, DoE, 1979; variety of posts in local govt finance, housing, urban regeneration, 1979–95, inc. Prin. Private Sec. to Minister of State for Housing, 1986–88; Dep. Dir, Efficiency Unit, Cabinet Office, 1995–97; Dir of Regeneration for E London, Govt Office for London, 1997–99; Dir Children's Gp, DSS, subseq. DWP, 1999–2001; Dir Gen., Machinery of Govt Secretariat, Cabinet Office, 2001–03; Dir Gen. for Corporate Services, 2003–05, and a Comr, 2003–05, Bd of Inland Revenue, later HM Revenue and Customs; Permanent Secretary: DEFRA, 2005–10; Home Office, 2011–12; Dir-Gen., Nat. Trust, 2012–18. Bencher, Middle Temple, 2018. *Publications:* (contrib.) Boethius: his life, thought and influence, 1981. *Recreations:* family life, ballet, gardening. *Address:* Balliol College, Oxford OX1 3BJ.

**GHOSH, (Indranil) Julian,** DPhil; QC 2006; QC (Scot.) 2010. *Educ:* Univ. of Edinburgh (LLB); London Sch. of Econs (LLM); Birkbeck Coll., London (MA); St Edmund Hall, Oxford (DPhil). Called to the Bar, Lincoln's Inn, 1993; a Dep. Judge, Tax, First-tier and Upper Tribunal, 2009– (a Dep. Special Comr, 2002–09). Sen. Vis. Fellow, Queen Mary and Westfield Coll., London, 1994–2006; Bye-Fellow, Peterhouse, Cambridge, 2016–. *Publications:* Taxation of Loan Relationships and Derivatives, 1996–2017; Principles of the Internal Market and Direct Taxation, 2007. *Recreations:* music, chess, fencing, cricket. *Address:* Pump Court Tax Chambers, 16 Bedford Row, WC1R 4EF. *Clubs:* Athenæum, Lansdowne, Two Brydges; New (Edinburgh); Hawks' (Cambridge).

**GHOSH, Shaks,** CBE 2015; Chief Executive, Clore Social Leadership Programme, since 2015; *b* 17 Jan. 1957; *d* of Samir Ghosh and Maria Rheinhold. *Educ:* Frank Anthony Public Sch.; Calcutta Univ. (BA 1st cl. Hons Geog. 1978); Salford Univ. (MSc Urban Studies 1980). Urban Renewal Officer, Leicester CC, 1980–84; Improvement Officer, Islington LBC, 1984–86; Supported Housing Officer, Community Housing Assoc., Camden and Westminster, 1986–89; Asst Dir, Centrepoint, 1989–92; Supported Housing Manager, NFHA, 1992–94; Head of London Region, Nat. Housing Fedn, 1994–97; Chief Executive: Crisis, 1997–2006; Private Equity Foundn, 2007–13. *Recreations:* gardening, travel, current affairs.

**GHOSN, Carlos,** Hon. KBE 2007; Chief Executive, 2005–19, and Chairman, 2009–19, Renault (Co-Chairman, 2005–09); Chairman: Nissan Motor Co. Ltd, 2008–18 (President, 2000–17; Chief Executive Officer, 2001–17; Co-Chairman, 2003–08); Mitsubishi Motors, 2016–18; *b* Brazil, 9 March 1954; *s* of late Jorges Ghosn and of Rose Ghosn; *m* 1985, Rita (marr. diss.); one *s* three *d*; *m* 2016, Carole. *Educ:* Ecole Polytechnique, Paris (engrg degree 1974); Ecole des Mines de Paris (engrg degree 1978). Michelin: joined, 1978; Plant Manager, Le Puy Plant, France, 1981–84; Hd, R&D for industrial tyres, 1984; Chief Op. Officer, S Amer. Ops, Brazil, 1985–90; Chm. and CEO, N America, 1990–96; Exec. Vice Pres., Renault, 1996–99; Chief Op. Officer, Nissan Motor Co. Ltd, 1999–2001. Mem. Bd of Dirs, Alcoa. Internat. FREng 2013. Légion d'Honneur (France), 2002; Ordem de Rio Branco (Brazil), 2002; Medal of Blue Ribbon, Emperor of Japan, 2004. *Publications:* Renaissance (autobiog.), 2001; Shift: inside Nissan's historic revival (autobiog.), 2005. *Recreations:* swimming, playing tennis, reading, playing contract bridge.

**GIACHARDI, Dr David John,** FRSC; Secretary General and Chief Executive, Royal Society of Chemistry, 2000–06; *b* 17 May 1948; *o s* of Thomas and Kathleen Giachardi; *m* 1971, Helen Margaret Fraser; one *d*. *Educ:* Watford Boys' Grammar Sch.; Merton Coll., Oxford (BA Chem. 1971); St John's Coll., Oxford (MA, DPhil 1974). FRSC 1990. Boston Consulting Group, 1975–79; Courtaulds, 1979–98: Dir of Research, 1982–94; Exec. Dir, 1987–98; Human Resources Dir, 1994–98; Dir of Policy and Assoc. Affairs, EEF, 1998–2000. Member: Nat. Commn on Educn, 1991–93; European Science and Technology Assembly, 1994–97; EPSRC, 1994–99; Quality Assurance Cttee, HEFCE, 1999–2003; Vice-Chm., Industrial R&D Adv. Cttee to Commn for EC, 1991–94. Chm. Adv. Council, ASE, 1996–2001 (Pres., 1994); Mem. Council, Royal Instn of GB, 1995–98 (Chm., 1997–98). Court Asst, Horners' Co., 2012– (Master, 2019). *Address:* Laburnum, Cheverells Green, Markyate, St Albans, Herts AL3 8RN. *Club:* Oxford and Cambridge.

**GIAEVER, Prof. Ivar;** Institute Professor, Physics Department, Rensselaer Polytechnic Institute, Troy, New York, 1988–2005, now Emeritus; Professor-at-large, University of Oslo, Norway, 1988–2009; Chief Technical Officer, Applied BioPhysics, since 2008; *b* 5 April 1929; *s* of John A. Giaever and Gudrun (*née* Skaarud); *m* 1952, Inger Skramstad; one *s* three *d*. *Educ:* Norwegian Inst. of Tech.; Rensselaer Polytechnical Inst. ME 1952; PhD 1964. Norwegian Army, 1952–53; Norwegian Patent Office, 1953–54; Canadian General Electric, 1954–56; General Electric, 1956–58; Staff Mem., Gen. Electric R&D Center, 1958–88. Member: Nat. Acad. of Sciences; Nat. Acad. of Engineering; Amer. Acad. of Arts and Scis; Norwegian Acad. of Scis; Norwegian Acad. of Technology; Norwegian Profl Engrs; Swedish Acad. of Engrg. Hon. DSc: Trondheim, 1973; RPI, 1974; Union Coll., 1974; Clarkson, Potsdam, NY, 1983; Hon. DEng, Michigan Tech. Univ., 1976; Hon. DPhys: Oslo, 1976; State Univ. of NY, 1984. Oliver E. Buckley Prize, 1964; Nobel Prize for Physics, 1973; Zworykin Award, 1974; Onsager Medal, Norwegian Univ. of Sci. and Technol., 2003; Gunnerus Medal, Royal Norwegian Soc. of Sci. and Letters, 2010. *Publications:* contrib. Physical Review, Jl Immunology. *Recreations:* ski-ing, tennis, camping, hiking. *Address:* Applied BioPhysics, 185 Jordan Road, Troy, NY 12180, USA. *T:* (518) 8806860, *Fax:* (518) 8806865. *E:* giaever@biophysics.com.

**GIBB, Andrea;** *see* Gomes da Silva, A.

**GIBB, Andrew Thomas Fotheringham;** Partner, 1975–2012, Chairman, 1996–2005, Consultant, 2012–14, Balfour and Manson, Solicitors, Edinburgh; President, Law Society of Scotland, 1990–91; *b* 17 Aug. 1947; *s* of Thomas Fotheringham Gibb and Isabel Gow McKenzie or Gibb; *m* 1971, Mrs Patricia Anne Eggo or Gibb; two *s*. *Educ:* Perth Acad.; Edinburgh Univ. (LLB Hons). Temporary Sheriff, 1989–99. Member: Lothian and Borders Legal Aid Cttee, 1977–84; Legal Aid Central Cttee, 1984–86; Council, Law Soc. of Scotland, 1981–94. Chm. Management Cttee, Lothian Allellon Soc., 1984–97 (Mem., Bd of Govs, 1984–2001). Accredited family law specialist; accredited collaborative lawyer. Trustee, Family Mediation Lothian, 2012–. Mem. Bd, Birthlink, 2012– (Chm., 2015–). Session Clerk, St Ninian's Church, Corstorphine, Edinburgh. Mem., Corstorphine Rotary Club, 2005– (Pres., 2015–16). *Recreations:* music, church organist, golf. *Address:* 39 Braehead Road, Edinburgh EH4 6BD. *Clubs:* New (Edinburgh); Royal Burgess Golfing Soc.

**GIBB, Fionna;** HM Diplomatic Service; Ambassador to Belarus, 2016–19. Joined FCO, 1990; Desk Officer, FCO, 1990–92; Vice Consul, Berlin, 1992–95; Team Leader, Kyiv, 1995–98; Asst Private Sec., Minister's Private Office, FCO, 1999–2001; Hd of Section, Envmt Policy Dept, FCO, 2001–03; Team Leader, Counter Proliferation Dept, FCO, 2003–05; Hd of Section, Counter Terrorism Dept, FCO, 2005–08; Dep. Consul-Gen., Basra, 2008–09; Deputy Head of Mission: Sana'a, 2010–12; Somalia, 2012; Dep. Hd, Projects Task Force, FCO, 2012–15. *Address:* c/o Foreign and Commonwealth Office, King Charles Street, SW1A 2AH.

**GIBB, Frances Rebecca;** Legal Editor, The Times, 1999–2019; *b* 24 Feb. 1951; *d* of late Matthew Gibb and of Bettina Mary Gibb (*née* Dawson); *m* 1978, Joseph Cahill (*d* 2009); three *s*. *Educ:* St Margaret's Sch., Bushey; Univ. of E Anglia (BA 1st Cl. Hons English). News researcher, Visnews, 1973; reporter, THES, 1974–78; Art Sales corresp., Daily Telegraph, 1978–80; The Times: reporter, 1980–82; Legal Corresp., 1982–99. Vis. Prof., QMC, 2003. Gov., King's College Sch., Wimbledon, 2002–17. MUniv Open, 2000. *Recreations:* my family, gardening, theatre. *Club:* Reform.

**GIBB, Dame Moira,** DBE 2012 (CBE 2001); Chair: City Lit, since 2013; Skills for Care, since 2014; *d* of James Bogan and Catherine Bogan (*née* McTaggart); *m* 1990, Henry Blythe; one *s*. *Educ:* Glasgow Univ. (MA); Edinburgh Univ. (Dip. Soc. Admin; CQSW); Univ. of Newcastle upon Tyne (PQCCC). Social worker and teacher, 1970–80; Lectr, Preston Polytech., 1980–81; Child Care Inspector, Surrey CC, 1981–84; Asst Dir, London Bor. of Ealing, 1984–88; Royal Borough of Kensington and Chelsea: Dep. Dir, 1988–91, Dir, 1991–2000, Social Services; Exec. Dir, Housing and Social Services, 2000–03; Chief Exec., London Bor. of Camden, 2003–11. Non-exec. Mem., UK Statistics Authy, 2008–; a Civil Service Comr, 2012–16; non-exec. Dir, NHS Commng Bd, then NHS England, 2012; Chair, Nat. Statistician's Data Ethics Adv. Cttee, 2018–. Chair: Social Work Task Force, 2009; Social Work Reform Bd, 2010–13. Pres., Assoc. of Dirs of Social Services, 2000–01. Governor: Our Lady of Victories Sch., SW15, 1996–2004; Coram Family, 2002–05. Mem. Council, Reading Univ., 2013–16. Dir, London Marathon, 2005–11. FCGI 2011. Hon. DCL UEA, 2012; Hon. DSc Kingston, 2013. *Recreations:* walking, running, detective fiction.

**GIBB, Rt Hon. Nicolas (John);** PC 2016; MP (C) Bognor Regis and Littlehampton, since 1997; Minister of State, Department for Education, 2010–12 and since 2014; *b* 3 Sept. 1960; *s* of late John McLean Gibb and Eileen Mavern Gibb; *m* 2015, Michael George Edward Simmonds, *qv*. *Educ:* Maidstone Grammar Sch.; Roundhay Sch., Leeds; Thornes House Sch., Wakefield; Univ. of Durham (BA Hons). ACA 1987. Chartered Accountant, KPMG, 1984–97. Opposition spokesman: on HM Treasury, 1998–99; on trade and industry, 1999–2001; on education, 2005–10. Member: Social Security Select Cttee, 1997–98; Public Accounts Cttee, 2001–03; Educn and Skills Select Cttee, 2003–05. Contested (C): Stoke-on-Trent Central, 1992; Rotherham, May 1994. *Address:* House of Commons, SW1A 0AA.

**GIBBENS, Nigel Paul,** CBE 2016; Chief Veterinary Officer, Department for Environment, Food and Rural Affairs, 2008–18; *b* Dover, 1 March 1958; *s* of Francis Bernard Gibbens and Pauline Carol Gibbens; *m* 1981, Jane Stirling. *Educ:* Royal Veterinary Coll. (BVetMed); Edinburgh Univ. (MSc Tropical Vet. Medicine 1984). Gen. vet. practice in Alfreton, Derbys, 1981–83; Govt vet. services in Belize, 1985–88, Yemen, 1988–90; Vet. Field Service, MAFF, Winchester, 1990–96; veterinary posts in Animal Health and Welfare Policy Gp, MAFF, 1996–2002; Department for Environment, Food and Rural Affairs: Head: Internat. Animal Health Div., 2002–04; BSE and Animal By-products Div., 2005–06; Animal Welfare Div., 2006–07; Internat. Relns Core Team, Food and Farming Gp, 2007–08. Hon. Prof., RVC, 2009–. *Recreations:* walking, cycling, gardening, travel.

**GIBBINGS, Sir Peter (Walter),** Kt 1989; Chairman, Radio Authority, 1995–99; *b* 25 March 1929; *s* of late Walter White Gibbings and Margaret Russell Gibbings (*née* Torrance); *m* 1st, Elspeth Felicia Macintosh; two *d*; 2nd, Hon. Louise Barbara, *d* of 2nd Viscount Lambert, TD; one *s*. *Educ:* Rugby; Wadham Coll., Oxford. Called to the Bar, Middle Temple, 1953. Served in 9th Queen's Royal Lancers, 1951–52. The Observer, 1960–67 (Deputy Manager and Dir, 1965–67); Man. Dir, Guardian Newspapers Ltd, 1967–73; Dir, Manchester Guardian and Evening News Ltd, 1967–73; Chm., Guardian and Manchester Evening News plc, 1973–88; Anglia Television Gp: Dir, 1981–94; Dep. Chm., 1986–88; Chm., 1988–94. Director: Press Assoc. Ltd, 1982–88 (Chm., 1986–87); Reuters Holdings PLC, 1984–88; The Economist, 1987–99; Rothschild Trust Corp. Ltd, 1989–96; Council, UEA, 1989–96. Mem., Press Council, 1970–74; Pres., CPU, 1989–91. *Recreations:* fishing, music. *Address:* 9 Physic Place, SW3 4HQ.

**GIBBON, Anthony David;** Founding Partner, BH2 (formerly BH2, then GM Real Estate), since 1994; *b* 11 Aug. 1965; *s* of Thomas David Gibbon and Iris Patricia Gibbon; *m*; two *s* three *d*. *Educ:* Gable Hall Co. Secondary Sch., Corringham; South Bank Poly. Junior positions: Prudential Portfolio Managers, 1981–86; Bates Richards & Co., 1986–88; Partner, Lambert Smith Hampton, 1988–94. *Publications:* numerous articles in jls. *Recreations:* boxing, football, ski-ing, golf, theatre. *Address:* BH2, 6–7–8 Tokenhouse Yard, EC2R 7AS. *T:* (020) 7600 5000, 07770 721002. *E:* lisad@bh2.co.uk.

**GIBBON, Gary;** Political Editor, Channel 4 News, since 2005; *b* 15 March 1965; *s* of Robert Philip Gibbon and Elizabeth Mary Gibbon (*née* Harries); *m* 1994, Laura Kate Pulay; two *s*. *Educ:* John Lyon Sch., Harrow; Balliol Coll., Oxford (BA). Researcher, Viewpoint Productions, 1987–89; Producer, BBC Business Breakfast, 1989–90; Political Prod., 1990–94, Political Corresp., 1994–2005, Channel 4 News. Home News Award, RTS, 2006; Political Broadcaster of the Year Award, Political Studies Assoc., 2008; Specialist Journalist of the Year, RTS, 2010. *Publications:* Breaking Point: the UK referendum on the EU and its aftermath, 2016. *Address:* c/o Channel 4 News, Parliamentary Press Gallery, House of Commons, SW1A 0AA. *T:* (020) 7430 4990. *E:* gary.gibbon@itn.co.uk.

**GIBBON, Michael Neil;** QC 2011; *b* Berkeley, Glos, 14 Nov. 1964; *s* of Bill and Lynne Gibbon; *m* 1991, Amanda, *d* of David Harold Owen Owen, *qv*; two *s* two *d*. *Educ:* Conyers Sch., Yarm; Uppingham Sch. (Sixth Form Schol.); Magdalen Coll., Oxford (Exhibnr and Academical Clerk; BA 1st Cl. Mod. Hist. 1986); King's Coll., Cambridge (Choral Volunteer; MPhil Internat. Relns 1987); City of London Poly. (CPE 1992). Called to the Bar, Gray's Inn, 1993. Investment banker, BZW, 1987–91; in practice as a barrister, specialising in chancery, commercial and revenue law, 1995–; Mem., Attorney Gen.'s Panel of Jun. Counsel to the Crown, 1999–2011. Gov., King's College Sch., Cambridge, 2010–. Mem. Council, Hon. Soc. of Cymmrodorion, 2016–. An Ed., Civil Procedure (The White Book), 2003–18. *Publications:* articles in Montgomeryshire Collections and in various legal pubns. *Recreations:* family, choral singing, Cyfeiliog local history. *Address:* Maitland Chambers, 7 Stone Buildings, Lincoln's Inn, WC2A 3SZ. *T:* (020) 7406 1200, *Fax:* (020) 7406 1300. *E:* mgibbon@maitlandchambers.com. *Club:* Reform.

**GIBBONS, Brian Joseph,** FRCGP; Member (Lab) Aberavon, National Assembly for Wales, 1999–2011; *b* 25 Aug. 1950. *Educ:* National Univ. of Ireland (MB BCh, BAO 1974). DRCOG 1979; Cert. FPA 1979; MRCGP 1980, FRCGP 1995. Jun. hosp. doctor, Galway, Roscommon and Sheffield, 1974–76; Calderdale GP Vocation Trng Scheme, 1977–80; GP, Blaengwynfi, 1980–99. Sec., W Glamorgan/Morgannwg LMC, 1994–99. National Assembly for Wales: Dep. Minister for Health and Social Services, 2000–03, for Economic Develt and Transport, 2003–05; Minister for Health and Social Services, 2005–07, for the Econ. and Transport, 2007, for Social Justice and Local Govt, 2007–09. Dir, Gwynfi Community Co-operative Ltd, 2013–. Chm. and Dir, Gwynfi Miners Community Hall, 2013–; Mem., Central Council, Socialist Health Assoc. UK, 2015–; Trustee, Wales Refugee Council, 2017–. Vice-President: Port Talbot Little Th.; Roger Chilcott Music in the Community; South Wales Miners Mus. *Club:* Gwynfi Social and Athletic.

**GIBBONS, Prof. Gary William,** PhD; FRS 1999; Professor of Theoretical Physics, University of Cambridge, 1997–2013, now Emeritus; Fellow of Trinity College, Cambridge, since 2002; *b* 1 July 1946; *s* of Archibald Gibbons and Bertha Gibbons (*née* Bunn); *m* 1972, Christine Howden; two *s*. *Educ:* Purley County Grammar Sch.; St Catharine's Coll., Cambridge (BA 1968; MA 1972); Clare Coll., Cambridge (PhD 1973). University of Cambridge: Lectr in Maths, 1980–90; Reader in Theoretical Physics, 1990–97. *Publications:* (with S. W. Hawking) Euclidean Quantum Gravity, 1993. *Recreations:* listening to music, looking at paintings. *Address:* 52 Hurst Park Avenue, Cambridge CB4 2AE. *T:* (01223) 363036.

**GIBBONS, Giles Christopher;** Founder and Chief Executive Officer, Good Business Ltd, since 1996; *b* Woking, Surrey, 18 Nov. 1969; *s* of Richard Gibbons and Susan Gibbons (now Gill); *m* 1996, Laura Jackson; two *s* one *d*. Marketing, Cadbury, 1989–90; Director: Saatchi & Saatchi Advertising, 1990–95; M & C Saatchi, 1995–97. Dir, Shift Design (formerly We Are What We Do), 2001–. Founder, Sustainable Restaurant Assoc., 2009–. Dir, Paraorchestra, 2012–. Fellow, Wellington Coll. 2009. *Publications:* Good Business: your world needs you, 2002; The Economist Book of Brands and Branding, 2007. *Recreations:* cooking and eating, running, opera. *Address:* Good Business Ltd, 25 Gerrard Street, W1D 6JL. *T:* (020) 7494 0565. *E:* giles@goodbusiness.co.uk.

**GIBBONS, Jeremy Stewart;** QC 1995; a Recorder, since 1993; *b* 15 July 1949; *s* of Geoffrey Gibbons and Rosemary Gibbons (*née* Stewart); *m* 1st, 1974, Mary Mercia Bradley; two *s* one *d* (and one *d* decd); 2nd, 1998, Sarah Valerie Jenkins. *Educ:* Oakmount Sch., Southampton; St Edward's Sch., Oxford. Called to the Bar, Gray's Inn, 1973; Asst Recorder, 1989–93. *Recreations:* cooking, gardening, ski-ing, carpentry. *Address:* 20 Carlton Crescent, Southampton SO15 2ET.

**GIBBONS, Ven. Kenneth Harry;** Archdeacon of Lancaster, 1981–97, now Emeritus; *b* 24 Dec. 1931; *s* of Harry and Phyllis Gibbons; *m* 1962, Margaret Ann Tomlinson; two *s*. *Educ:* Blackpool and Chesterfield Grammar Schools; Manchester Univ. (BSc); Cuddesdon Coll., Oxford. RAF, 1952–54. Ordained, 1956; Assistant Curate of Fleetwood, 1956–60; Secretary for Student Christian Movement in Schools, 1960–62; Senior Curate, St Martin-in-the-Fields, Westminster, 1962–65; Vicar of St Edward, New Addington, 1965–70; Vicar of Portsea, 1970–81; RD of Portsmouth, 1973–79; Priest-in-charge of Weeton, 1981–85; Vicar, St Michael's-on-Wyre, 1985–97; Diocesan Dir of Ordinands, Blackburn, 1982–90; Priest i/c, St Magnus the Martyr, Lower Thames St with St Margaret, Fish St, and St Michael, Crooked Lane, 1997–2003, St Clement, Eastcheap, 1999–2007, City of London. Acting Chaplain to HM Forces, 1981–85. *Address:* 15 The Oaks, Kings Meadow, Taunton, Somerset TA1 2QX; (01823) 271140.

**GIBBONS, Michael Gordon,** MBE 2002; PhD; Director, Science and Technology Policy Research, University of Sussex, 2004–06; Secretary General, Association of Commonwealth Universities, 1996–2004; *b* 15 April 1939; *m* 1968, Gillian Monks; one *s* one *d*. *Educ:* Concordia Univ., Montreal (BSc Maths and Physics); McGill Univ., Montreal (BEng); Queen's Univ., Ont (MSc Radio Astronomy); Manchester Univ. (PhD 1967). Department of Science and Technology Policy, University of Manchester: Lectr, 1967–72; Sen. Lectr, 1972–75; Prof., 1975–92; Hd of Dept, 1975–92; Dir, Univ./UMIST Pollution Res. Unit, 1979–86; Chm. and Founding Dir, Policy Res. in Engrg, Sci. and Technol., 1979–92; Dir, Res., Exploitation and Develt, Vice-Chancellor's Office, 1984–92; University of Sussex: Dean, Grad. Sch. and Dir, Science Policy Res. Unit, 1992–96; Mem., Senate and Mgt Cttee, 1992–96; Mem., Court and Council, 1994–96; Hon. Prof., 1994. Visiting Professor: Univ. of Montreal, 1976 and 1977–81; Univ. of Calif, Berkeley, 1992. Chm., Marinetech NW, 1981–91. Special Advr, H of C Sci. and Technol. Cttee, 1993–. Mem. Council, ESRC, 1997–2001 (Mem., 1994–97, Chm., 1997–2001, Res. Priorities Bd). Consultant, Cttee of Sci. and Technol. Policy, OECD, Paris, 1979–. Founding Bd Mem., Quest Univ., Canada (Chm., Bd of Govs, 2006–09); Cttee Mem., Nat. Centres of Excellence in Res. (Canada), 2010–17. Fellow, Royal Swedish Acad. of Engrg Scis, 2000. Member, Editorial Board: Technovation, 1984–; Prometheus, 1992–. Hon. LLD: Ghana, 1999; Concordia, 2004; DUniv Surrey, 2005. Golden Jubilee Medal (Canada), 2002. *Publications:* (jtly) Wealth from Knowledge, 1972; (jtly) Future of University Research, 1981; (ed jtly) Science Studies Today, 1983; (jtly) New Forms of Communication and Collaboration between Universities and Industry, 1985; (jtly) Post-Innovation Performance: technological development and competition, 1986; (with L. Georghiou) The Evaluation of Research: a synthesis of current practice, 1987; (jtly) The New Production of Knowledge: the dynamics of science and research in contemporary societies, 1994; (jtly) Re-Thinking Science: knowledge and the public in an age of uncertainty, 2001; contrib. numerous papers and articles on science policy. *Address:* 24 Fletsand Road, Wilmslow, Cheshire SK9 2AB.

**GIBBONS, Michael John Stanley,** CBE 2015 (OBE 2008); FEI; Chairman, Regulatory Policy Committee, 2009–17; Chairman, Elexon Ltd, since 2013; *b* Barnehurst, Kent, 9 Feb. 1948; *s* of Stanley Edward Gibbons and Olive Ethel Florence Gibbons (*née* Toms); partner, Joanne Ottley; one *s* two *d*. *Educ:* Chislehurst and Sidcup Grammar Sch. for Boys; Downing Coll., Cambridge (BA 1970). FEI 2011. Marketing mgt positions, USA and Belgium, 1970–85, Energy Policy and Purchasing Manager, 1985–91, ICI Ltd; Dir, Fuel Policy and Purchasing, and Dir, UK Communications, Powergen plc, 1991–2002. Chm., Carbon Capture and Storage Assoc., 2013–17. *Recreations:* playing, squash, tennis, golf, watching opera, Rugby. *Address:* Elexon Ltd, 350 Euston Road, NW1 3AW. *T:* (020) 7380 4150. *E:* michael.gibbon@elexon.co.uk. *Club:* Oxford and Cambridge.

**GIBBONS, Prof. Simon,** PhD; FRSC, FLS; Professor of Medicinal Phytochemistry, University College London, since 2012; *b* Gosport, 13 June 1966; *s* of Brian and Gillian Gibbons. *Educ:* Britannia Royal Naval Coll., Dartmouth; Kingston Poly. (BSc Hons Applied Chemistry 1989; BP Prize); Strathclyde Univ. (PhD 1994). CChem 1995; CSci 2004; FRSC 2005. Asst Prof. of Pharmaceutical Chem., Kuwait Univ., 1997; School of Pharmacy, University of London: Lectr in Pharmacognosy, 1999; teacher, 2002; Sen. Lectr in Phytochem., 2004; Reader in Phytochem., 2005; Prof. of Medicinal Phytochem., 2007–12. Adjunct Prof., Universiti Kebangsaan Malaysia, 2013–15. Member: Adv. Council on Misuse of Drugs, Home Office, 2010–18 (Chm., Novel Psychoactive Substances Work Gp, 2011–18); Herbal Medicines Adv. Cttee, Medicines and Healthcare Regulatory Products Agency, 2010–12; British Pharmacopoeia Expert Work Gp on Herbal Medicines, 2015–16; Medicinal Cannabis Work Gp, Home Office, 2018–. Pres., Phytochem. Soc. of Europe, 2012–14 (Vice Pres. 2010–12, 2014–16). Fellow, Prince of Wales' Foundn for Integrated Health, 2009–10. Mem., Governing Council, Coll. of Medicine, 2010– (Vice-Chm., Scientific Adv. Council, 2010–). Founding Ed.-in-Chief, Phytochemistry Letters, 2008–; Co-Ed., Progress in the Chem. of Organic Natural Products, 2015– (Mem., Editl Bd, 2009–); Member, Editorial Board: Phytotherapy Res., 2005–; Planta Medica, 2009–18; Phytochem. Reviews, 2009–; Fitoterapia, 2009–; Chinese Jl Natural Medicines, 2009–; Natural Product Reports, 2010–16; Phytochem. Analysis, 2010–; Natural Products and Bioprospecting, 2017–; Jl of Natural Products, 2018–; Scientia Pharmaceutica, 2010–. FLS 1995. Richard J. Cannell Biodiversity Award Lect., 2013. Pierre Fabre Prize for Phytochem., Phytochem. Soc. of Europe, 2005; Vice-Chancellor's Seminar Award, Tshwane Univ. of Technol., 2010; Pharmanex Prize for Phytochem., Phytochem. Soc. of Europe, 2012. *Publications:* (jtly) Fundamentals of Pharmacognosy and Phytotherapy, 2004, 3rd edn 2018; over 200 contribs to papers on phytochemistry, structure elucidation and biol evaluation of Novel Psychoactive Substances (NPS; 'Legal Highs'), and antibacterials from natural sources and bacterial resistance modifying agents. *Recreations:* ski-ing, drinking red wine, real ale and schnapps, eating steak, holidays in Austria, fishing, walking in the Cotswolds. *Address:* Research Department of Pharmaceutical and Biological Chemistry, UCL School of Pharmacy, 29–39 Brunswick Square, WC1N 1AX. *T:* (020) 7753 5913, *Fax:* (020) 7753 5964. *E:* anabasis@mail.com.

**GIBBONS, Sir William Edward Doran,** 9th Bt *cr* 1752; JP; cruise and ferry consultant, since 2013; Director: Passenger Shipping Association, 1994–2013; Discover Ferries, 2013–18; Membership Director, European Cruise Council, 2011–13 (Marketing Director, 2004–11); *b* 13 Jan. 1948; *s* of Sir John Edward Gibbons, 8th Bt, and of Mersa Wentworth, *y d* of late Major Edward Baynton Grove Foster; *S* father, 1982; *m* 1st, 1972, Patricia Geraldine Archer (marr. diss. 2004), *d* of Roland Archer Howse; one *s* one *d*; 2nd, 2004, Maggie Moone. *Educ:* Pangbourne; RNC Dartmouth; Bristol Univ. (BSc); Southampton Univ. Management Sch. (MBA 1996). Asst Shipping and Port Manager, Sealink UK, Parkeston Quay, 1979–82; Service Manager (Anglo-Dutch), Sealink UK Ltd, 1982–85; Ferry Line Manager (Harwich-Hook), 1985–87, Gen. Manager, IoW Services, 1987–90, Sealink British Ferries. Transport and management consultant, 1990–94. Poole Harbour Comr, 2016–. Chm., Council of Travel and Tourism, 1996–2001 (Vice Chm., 1995–96); Mem. Bd, Duty Free Confedn, 1996–2000. Non-exec. Mem., IoW DHA, 1990–94. Mem., Manningtree Parish Council, 1981–87 (Chm., 1985–87). Mem. Cttee, Poundbury Residents Assoc., 2014– (Chm., 2017–). JP: Portsmouth, 1990–94; Westminster Div., Inner London, 1994–2011 (Probation Liaison Justice, 1998–2006); Dorset, 2011–18. Freeman, 2008, Liveryman, 2011, Shipwrights' Co.; Younger Brother, Trinity House, 2011. *Recreations:* opera, Dorset cottage. *Heir: s* Charles William Edwin Gibbons, *b* 28 Jan. 1983. *Address:* 3 St John Way, Dorchester, Dorset DT1 2FG.

**GIBBS,** family name of **Barons Aldenham** and **Wraxall**.

**GIBBS, Alexander;** Manager, Policy and Operations, World Bank Group, since 2013; *b* Leicester, 22 April 1964; *s* of Michael John Gibbs and Pamela Jesse Gibbs; *m* 1986, Sonja Elizabeth Grueter; one *s* two *d*. *Educ:* Charterhouse Sch.; Wadham Coll., Oxford (BA PPE);

London Sch. of Econs (MSc Econs 1988). HM Treasury, 1985–: Econ. Advr, Public Services, 1985–87, Internat., 1988–90, Macroecon. Forecast, 1990–91; First Sec. (Econ.), British Embassy, Washington, 1991–95; Private Sec. to Chancellor of the Exchequer, 1995–97; Head: Internat. Instns, 1997–2000; Tax Policy, 2000–02; Econ. Counsellor, Washington, 2002–07; Exec. Dir for UK, IMF, and Minister (Economic), Washington, 2007–13. *Recreations:* music, baseball. *Address:* World Bank, 1818 H Street NW, Washington, DC 20433, USA. *T:* (202) 7631700. *E:* alexgibbs@mac.com.

**GIBBS, Barbara Lynn;** education consultant, since 2006; Head Teacher, British School in The Netherlands, 2001–06; *b* 8 Nov. 1945; *d* of William Newill and Mabel Till; *m* 1967, John Colin Gibbs; two *d*. *Educ:* Bromley Grammar Sch. for Girls; Univ. of Hull (BSc Hons Chem.); Univ. of E Anglia (MA; PGCE). Teaching and lecturing, mainly on chem. and maths, in various educnl estabts in Yorks, Notts, Norfolk and Barnet, 1967–86; Sen. Teacher, Henrietta Barnett Sch., 1986–90; Vice Principal, Havering Sixth Form Coll., 1990–94; Head Teacher, Newstead Wood Sch. for Girls, 1994–2001. OFSTED Inspector, 1998–2002; Strategic Dir, Prospects Educn Services, 1999–2001; ISI Inspector, 2003–; NPQH tutor. Millennium Awards Fellow, for work on osteoporosis educn in schools, 2000–. Vice Pres., Gerrards Cross Cons. Assoc., 2018– (Chm., 2015–18). Member (C): S Bucks DC, 2015– (Cabinet Mem. for Resources, 2017–); Bucks CC, 2017–. Gov., Beaconsfield High Sch., 2014. FRSA 1994 (Life Fellow). *Recreations:* music, literature, travel, swimming, Rugby Union, bridge. *Clubs:* Royal Air Force; Royal Scots (Edinburgh); Stoke Park; Rotary (Misbourne Matins).

**GIBBS, Georgina Emma; Her Honour Judge Sharkey;** a Circuit Judge, since 2019; *b* Doncaster, 1977; *d* of John Richard Gibbs and Anna Maria Gibbs (*née* Hora'nska); *m* 2010, Paul James Sharkey; one *s* one *d*. *Educ:* Hayfield Sch., Auckley, Doncaster; Univ. of Warwick (LLB with French Law). Called to the Bar, Gray's Inn, 2000; Assistant Coroner: S Yorks E, 2016; Kent, 2017. Barrister Panel Mem., Bar Tribunals and Adjudication Service, 2012–18. Jun., 2010–11, Recorder, 2011–13, Cttee, South Eastern Circuit. *Recreations:* travel, exercise, film/cinema.

**GIBBS, Dame Jennifer (Barbara),** DNZM 2009 (CNZM 2002); Member of Council, Creative New Zealand, since 2016; *b* Lower Hutt, NZ, 14 Sept. 1940; *d* of Ross Digby Gore and Barbara Mary Gore (*née* Standish); *m* 1961, Alan Timothy Gibbs (marr. diss. 1997); one *s* three *d*. *Educ:* Victoria Univ. of Wellington (BA 1961); Canterbury Univ. (MA Hons Hist. 1962). Jun. Lectr, Dept of Hist., Victoria Univ., 1962 and 1966–67; has travelled extensively and been involved in wide range of community, health, educnl and arts activities. Comr for NZ at Venice Biennale, 2001 and 2003. Member: Council, Auckland Univ., 1975–95 and 2000–08 (Pro-Chancellor, 1984 and 2004); Univ. Med. Sch. Admission Cttee, 1983–95; Founding Mem., Auckland Med. Sch. Foundn, 1993–. Founder and Chair: Patrons of Auckland Art Gall., 1986–; Auckland Contemporary Art Trust, 1993–; Dep. Chair, Regl Facilities Auckland, 2012–18; Patron and Founding Trustee, Auckland Univ. Foundn Appeal Cttee, 1996–; Founding Trustee: NZ Arts Foundn, 1999–2005; Auckland Art Gall. Foundn, 2001–; Founding Bd Mem., NZ Opera Co., 1999–2005. Mem., Ministerial Task Force on Philanthropy, 2009. Invited Member: Internat. Council, MOMA, NY, 1989–; Internat. Council, Asia Soc., NY, 2001–. Comr for NZ, Venice Biennale, 2019. Fellow, Univ. of Auckland, 1995. Hon. DLitt Auckland, 2008. *Recreations:* art - looking and collecting, reading, opera, travel, walking poodles, food and wine. *Address:* 31 Paritai Drive, Orakei, Auckland 1071, New Zealand. *E:* jennygibbs@xtra.co.nz.

**GIBBS, Rt Rev. Dr Jonathan Robert;** see Huddersfield, Area Bishop of.

**GIBBS, Marion Olive,** CBE 2012; Headmistress, James Allen's Girls' School, Dulwich, 1994–2015; Co-Founder and Co-Director, Southwark Schools Learning Partnership, 2003–15; *b* 16 Sept. 1951; *d* of Harry Norman Smith and Olive Mabel (*née* Lewis). *Educ:* Pate's Grammar Sch. for Girls, Cheltenham; Bristol Univ. (BA 1st cl. Hons Classics 1973; PGCE 1974; MLitt 1981). Assistant Mistress: City of Worcester Girls' Grammar Sch., 1974–76; Chailey Comprehensive Sch., 1977; Hd of Sixth Form, Dir of Studies and Hd of Classics, Burgess Hill Sch. for Girls, 1977–89; Hd of Sixth Form and Classics, Haberdashers' Aske's Girls' Sch., Elstree, 1989–91; HMI of Schools, 1992–94. Tutor, Open Univ., 1979–91. Co. Mem., Ind. Schs' Inspectorate, 2016–18. Member Council: Classical Assoc., 1984–87, 1995–98 (Hon. Jt Sec., 1989–92); Hellenic Soc., 1997–2000, 2008–11; Chm. Council, JACT, 2001–04. Columnist, SecEd, 2004–15. Trustee: Dulwich Picture Gall., 1999–2002, 2008–11; Arvon Foundn, 2008–16; Charleston Trust, 2017–; Classics for All, 2019–; Member: Educn Cttee, Woodward Trust, 2015–; Charter Sch. Educn Trust, 2015–16, 2019–. FRSA 1997. *Publications:* Greek Tragedy: an introduction, 1989; (contrib.) Two Sectors, One Purpose, 2002; (contrib.) The Teaching of Classics, 2003; (contrib.) Heads: leading schools in the 21st century, 2007. *Recreations:* music, gardening, drama, keeping informed about the developing world.

**GIBBS, Patrick Michael Evan;** QC 2006; *b* 24 April 1962; *s* of late Michael Edmund Hubert Gibbs and of Helen Antonia Gibbs; *m* 1989, Catherine Clare Barroll; one *s* one *d*. *Educ:* Eton; Christ Church, Oxford; City Univ. Called to the Bar, Middle Temple, 1986. *Address:* 3 Raymond Buildings, Gray's Inn, WC1R 5BH.

**GIBBS, Dr Richard John;** healthcare management consultant, since 2002; Chief Executive, Kingston and Richmond (formerly Kingston and Esher) Health Authority, 1990–2002; *b* 15 May 1943; *s* of Leslie and Mary Gibbs; *m* 1968, Laura Wanda Olasmi; one *d*. *Educ:* Merchant Taylors' Sch., Northwood; Pembroke Coll., Cambridge (BA 1965). Warwick Univ. (PhD 1974). Teacher, City of London Sch. for Boys, 1965; Scientific Officer, Home Office, 1968; Sen. Scientific Officer, 1970, PSO, 1972, DHSS; Res. Schol., Internat. Inst. for Applied Systems Analysis, Austria, 1977; SPSO, DHSS, 1978; Central Policy Review Staff, 1980; Dir of Operational Res. (DCSO), 1982, CSO, 1985, DHSS; Under Sec. and Dir of Stats and Management, DHSS, then DoH, 1986–90. Vis. Prof., UCL, 1985. Non-exec. Dir, Southwark PCT, 2007–13 (Vice Chair, 2010–13); Vice Chair, Southwark Clinical Commissioning Gp, 2013–. *Publications:* contribs to Jl of ORS. *Recreations:* windsurfing, cooking. *E:* rjgibbs@ntlworld.com.

**GIBBS, Hon. Sir Richard (John Hedley),** Kt 2000; a Judge of the High Court of Justice, Queen's Bench Division, 2000–08; Presiding Judge, Midland Circuit, 2004–07; *b* 2 Sept. 1941; *s* of late Brian Conaway Gibbs and Mabel Joan Gibbs; *m* 1965, Janet (*née* Whittall); one *s* two *d* (and one *d* decd). *Educ:* Oundle Sch.; Trinity Hall, Cambridge (MA). Called to the Bar, Inner Temple, 1965, Bencher, 2000; a Recorder, 1981–90; QC 1984; a Circuit Judge, 1990–2000. Chm. Council, Lincoln Cathedral, 2008–14. *Address:* 12 The Redlands, Manor Road, Sidmouth, Devon EX10 8RT.

**GIBLIN, Dr John Daniel;** Keeper, World Cultures, National Museums Scotland, since 2018; *b* Isle of Wight, 29 Oct. 1978; *s* of Daniel John Giblin and Sylvia Anne Giblin; *m* 2016, Charlotte Elizabeth Cross. *Educ:* University College London (BA Hons Archaeol. 2000; MA African Archaeol. 2003; PhD Archaeol. 2010). Post-Doctoral Res. Fellow, Univ. of Gothenburg, 2011–12; Lectr, Critical Heritage Studies, Univ. of Western Sydney, 2012–14; Hd, Africa Section, BM, 2014–18. Hon. Lectr, Inst. of Archaeol., UCL, 2014–. *Publications:* (ed) The Ethics of Archaeological Practice in Africa, 2014; South Africa: the art of a nation, 2016; over 20 chapters and articles in jls incl. African Archaeol Rev., Internat. Jl of Heritage Studies, Azania: Archaeol Res. in Africa, Conservation and Mgt of Archaeol Sites, Jl of Heritage and Society, Jl of Conflict Archaeol. *Recreations:* marathon running, cooking. *Address:* National Museums Scotland, Chambers Street, Edinburgh EH1 1JF. *T:* (0131) 247 4363. *E:* j.giblin@nms.ac.uk.

**GIBRALTAR, Dean of;** *no new appointment at time of going to press.*

**GIBRALTAR, Archdeacon of;** *no new appointment at time of going to press.*

**GIBRALTAR IN EUROPE, Bishop of,** since 2014; **Rt Rev. Dr Robert Neil Innes;** *b* Wolverhampton, 1959; *s* of Frank Innes and Christine Innes; *m* 1985, Helen Alexandra Bennett; one *s* three *d*. *Educ:* Royal Grammar Sch., Guildford; King's Coll., Cambridge (BA Engrg 1982); Cranmer Hall, St John's Coll., Durham (BA Theol. 1991); Durham Univ. (PhD Theol. 1995). Engrg Trainee, Central Electricity Generating Bd, 1979–83; Consultant, later Manager, Arthur Andersen Mgt Consultants, 1983–89; ordination trng and theol res., 1989–95; ordained deacon, 1995, priest, 1996; Lectr, Systematic Theology, St John's Coll., Durham, 1995–99; Curate, Sherburn, Pittington and Shadforth, 1997–99; Vicar, Belmont, 1999–2005; Chancellor and Sen. Chaplain, Pro-Cathedral of Holy Trinity, Brussels, 2005–14; a Chaplain to the Queen, 2012–14. Pres., Central Cttee, Anglican Church in Belgium, 2007–14. Pres., Council, St John's Coll., Durham, 2019–. Chm., Grove Bks Ltd, 1999–2014. *Publications:* God at Work, 1994; Personality Indicators and the Spiritual Life, 1996; Medical Vocation and Generation X, 1997; Discourses of the Self, 1999; Augustine and the Journey to Wholeness, 2004; Clergy in a Complex Age, 2016. *Recreations:* walking, tennis, fine Belgian food and beer. *Address:* (office) 47 rue Capitaine Crespel - box 49, 1050 Brussels, Belgium. *T:* (2) 2137480. *E:* bishop.europe@churchofengland.org.

**GIBRALTAR IN EUROPE, Suffragan Bishop of,** since 2002; **Rt Rev. David Hamid;** *b* 18 June 1955; *s* of Ebrahim Hamid and Patricia (*née* Smith); *m* 1978, Colleen Gwen Moore; two *s*. *Educ:* Nelson High Sch., Burlington, Canada; McMaster Univ. (BSc Hons); Univ. of Trinity Coll., Toronto (MDiv 1981). Ordained deacon, 1981, priest, 1982; Asst Curate, St Christopher's, Burlington, 1981–83; Rector, St John's, Burlington, 1983–87; Mission Co-ordinator for Latin Amer. and Caribbean, Anglican Ch of Canada, 1987–96; Dir, Ecumenical Affairs and Studies, ACC, 1996–2002. Canon, Santo Domingo, 1992–. Hon. Asst Bishop, Dio. of Rochester, 2003–11. Archbishop of Canterbury's Rep. for Muslim-led Interfaith Initiatives, 2008–13. Member: Faith and Order Adv. Gp, C of E, 1996–2002; Anglican-Old Catholic Internat. Co-ordinating Council, 2005– (Co-Sec., 1999–2002); Porvoo Panel, C of E, 2005– (Chm., 2009–); Co-Sec., Internat. Anglican-Baptist Conversations, 2000–02; Consultant: Jt Working Gp, WCC and RC Ch, 1998–2004; Internat. Anglican-RC Commn for Unity and Mission, 2002– (Anglican Co-chair, 2012–); Porvoo Ch Leaders' Consultations, 2006, 2010, 2014. Secretary: Metropolitical Council, Cuba, 1987–96; Inter Anglican Theol Doctrinal Commn, 2000–02; Inter Anglican Standing Cttee on Ecumenical Relns, 2000–02; Co-Secretary: ARCIC, 1996–2002; Internat. Commn of Anglican Orthodox Theol Dialogue, 1996–2002; Anglican-Lutheran Internat. Working Gp, 1999–2002. Trustee, CTBI, 2013–. Gov., Anglican Centre in Rome, 2014–. Treasurer: Anglican Council of N America and Caribbean, 1983–87; Canadian Interch Cttee on Human Rights in Latin America, 1987–96. Mem. Council, USPG, 2002–. Mem., Adv. Gp, Older People Residing Abroad, 2007–13. Hon. DD Trinity Coll., Univ. of Toronto, 2005. *Publications:* (contrib.) Beyond Colonial Anglicanism: the Anglican Communion in the Twenty-First Century, ed I. Douglas, 2001; contrib. to Ecclesiastical Law Jl, Unité des Chrétiens, Internationale Kirchliche Zeitschrift, Collectanea Scientifica Compostellana. *Recreations:* music, languages, history, travel. *Address:* Diocese in Europe, 14 Tufton Street, SW1P 3QZ. *T:* (020) 7898 1160, *Fax:* (020) 7898 1166. *E:* david.hamid@churchofengland.org. *W:* www.eurobishop.blogspot.com. *Club:* Army and Navy.

**GIBSON,** family name of **Baron Ashbourne.**

**GIBSON, Bryony;** *see* Gibson, J. B.

**GIBSON, His Honour Charles Andrew Hamilton;** a Circuit Judge, 1996–2010; *b* 9 July 1941; *s* of late Rev. Preb. Leslie Andrew Gibson and Kathleen Anne Frances Gibson; *m* 1969, Susan Judith Rowntree; two *d*. *Educ:* Sherborne Prep. Sch.; Sherborne Sch.; Hertford Coll., Oxford (MA). Called to the Bar, Lincoln's Inn, 1966; practised at the Bar, 1966–96; Asst Recorder, 1987–91; a Recorder, 1991–96. Mem., Mental Health Review Tribunal (Restricted Patients Panel), 2002–12. Chm., Southwark Diocesan Pastoral Cttee, 1993–2003. Vice Pres., Hertford Soc., 2012– (Chm., 2004–12). *Publications:* (with Prof. M. R. A. Hollis) Surveying Buildings, 1983, 5th edn 2005; The Winetasters, 2013. *Recreations:* music, theatre, wine, researching family history. *Club:* Oxford and Cambridge.

**GIBSON, Charles Anthony Warneford;** QC 2001; a Recorder, since 2001; *b* 25 Sept. 1960; *s* of Philip Gaythorne Gibson and Margaret Elizabeth (*née* Mellotte, now Sim); *m* 1989, Mary Ann Frances, *e d* of Sir John Albert Leigh Morgan, KCMG; three *s* one *d*. *Educ:* Wellington Coll.; Durham Univ. (BA Hons Classics); Dip. Law, Central London. Called to the Bar, Inner Temple, 1984, Bencher, 2008. Hd of Chambers, 2007–. *Recreations:* family, sport, ballet, boxing, theatre, food, comedy. *Address:* 2 Harcourt Buildings, Temple, EC4Y 9DB. *T:* (020) 7583 9020.

**GIBSON, Christopher Allen Wood;** QC 1995; a Recorder, 2002–16; *b* 5 July 1953; *s* of Rt Hon. Sir Ralph Brian Gibson and Ann Gibson; *m* 1984, Alarys Mary Calvert Eaton; two *d*. *Educ:* St Paul's Sch.; Brasenose Coll., Oxford. FCIArb 1992. Called to the Bar, Middle Temple, 1976, Bencher, 2003. *Recreations:* Whitstable, motorcycles, family. *Address:* Outer Temple Chambers, The Outer Temple, 222 Strand, WC2R 1BA. *T:* (020) 7353 6381.

**GIBSON, Rev. Sir Christopher (Herbert),** 4th Bt *cr* 1931, of Linconia, Argentina, and of Faccombe, Southampton; CP; *b* 17 July 1948; *o s* of Sir Christopher Herbert Gibson, 3rd Bt and Lilian Lake Young, *d* of Dr George Byron Young; *S* father, 1994, but his name does not appear on the Official Roll of the Baronetage. Ordained priest, 1975. *Heir:* cousin Robert Herbert Gibson [*b* 21 Dec. 1966; *m* 1992, Catherine Grace, *d* of E. W. Pugh; three *s* one *d*].

**GIBSON, Christopher Jeremy Patrick;** Associate, Templar Executives, since 2018; *b* Kent, 15 Oct. 1963; *s* of Brian Leslie Gibson and Jenefer Anne Gibson; *m* 1990, Natasha Caroline Quinn; two *s* one *d*. *Educ:* Maidstone Grammar Sch.; North East London Poly. Lead Surveyor, Geophysical Services Inc., 1984–88; Technol. Manager, Saudi American Bank, 1988–95; Citigroup: Vice Pres., Citibank, 1995–2005; Sen. Vice Pres., 2005–11; Dir, eCrime, 2011–13; Dir CERT-UK (UK Nat. Computer Emergency Response Team), 2013–16; Chief Information and Security Officer, Close Brothers, 2016–18; Chief Information Security Officer, Orwell Gp, 2018–19. Mem. Bd, Internat. Forum of Incident Response and Security Teams, 2004–14 (Chief Financial Officer, 2005–10; Pres., 2011–13). *Recreations:* sailing, reading, theatre, music, loud shirts. *Address:* Templar Executives, 83 Victoria Street, Westminster, SW1H 0HW.

**GIBSON, Dr Christopher John;** Head, National School of Healthcare Science, 2014–16; *b* Malta, 16 Nov. 1956; *s* of Walter and Audrey Gibson; *m* 1981, Yvonne Johnson; one *s* one *d. Educ:* Emmanuel Coll., Cambridge (BA Natural Scis 1977); Univ. of Aberdeen (MSc Med. Physics 1978); Univ. of Durham (PhD Med. Imaging 1988). CSci 2002; FIPEM 2002. Med. Physicist, Northern Regl HA, Durham, 1981–95; Director: N Wales Med. Physics, 1995–2002; Med. Physics, Oxford Radcliffe Hosps NHS Trust, 2002–11; Scientific Dir, NHS S of England (Central), 2011–14; Professional Lead for Physical Scis, and Dep. Hd, Nat. Sch. of Healthcare Sci., 2011–14. Non-exec. Dir, United Lincs NHS Trust, 2017–. Chair, Cttee on Med. Aspects of Radiation in the Envmt, 2015–. Pres., Inst. of Physics and Engrg in Medicine, 2010–11. *Recreations:* music, sailing, natural history. *E:* chris.gibson@nhs.net.

**GIBSON, David,** CB 1997; *b* 8 Sept. 1939; *s* of Frank Edward Gibson and Nora Jessie Gibson (*née* Gurnhill); *m* 1963, Roberta Alexandra (*née* McMaster); one *s* two *d. Educ:* King Edward VI Grammar Sch., Retford. FCCA. GPO, 1958–63; MAFF, 1963–68; Belfast City Council, 1968–72; Dept of Commerce, NI, 1972–82; Dir of Accountancy Services, 1982–85, Asst Sec., 1985–87, Under Sec., then Dep. Sec., 1987–99, Dept of Economic Develt, NI; Dep. Chm., NI Sci. Park Foundn, 1999–2002; Sec., NI in Europe, 2002–04. Pres., Irish Region, Assoc. of Chartered Certified Accountants, 1982–83. Trustee, The Bytes Project, 2000–05. *Recreations:* reading, music, walking. *Address:* 14 Bramble Grange, Newtownabbey, Co. Antrim BT37 0XH. *T:* (028) 9086 2237.

**GIBSON, Dennis;** *see* Gibson, R. D.

**GIBSON, Lt-Col Edgar Matheson, (Gary),** MBE 1986; TD 1975; DL; self-employed artist - painting and sculpture, since 1990; Vice Lord-Lieutenant of Orkney, 2007–11; *b* Kirkwall, Orkney, 1 Nov. 1934; *s* of James Edgar Gibson and Margaret Johnston Gibson (*née* Matheson); *m* 1960, Jean McCarrick; two *s* two *d. Educ:* Kirkwall Grammar Sch.; Gray's Coll. of Art, Aberdeen (DA 1957); Teachers' Training Coll., Aberdeen. National Service, Army, 1958–60. Principal Art Master, 1974–88, Asst Headmaster, 1988–90, Kirkwall Grammar Sch. Examiner in Higher Art and Design, Scottish Cert. of Educn Examn Bd, Dalkeith, 1978–93. Mem., Orkney Health Bd, 1991–99. TA and TAVR, Lovat Scouts (Lt-Col), 1961–85, JSLO, Orkney, 1980–85; Cadet Comdt, Orkney Lovat Scouts ACF, 1979–86; Hon. Col, Orkney Lovat Scouts, 1986–2004; Chm., N Area Highland TAVRA, 1987–93. Pres., Orkney Br., SSAFA, 1997–2013 (Chm., 1990–97). Mem., Selection Cttee, 1983–91, County Co-ordinator, 1991–93, Operation Raleigh. Chm., St Magnus Cathedral Fair, 1982–2004; Hon. President: Soc. of Friends of St Magnus Cathedral, 1994–; Orkney Craftsmen's Guild, 1997–2002 (Chm., 1962–82); Preservation Cttee, Italian POW Chapel, 2015– (Mem., 1976–; Chm., 2006–15). DL Orkney, 1976. Hon. Sheriff, Grampian, Highland and Is, 1992–. *Recreations:* ba playing (old Norse game), whisky tasting. *Address:* Transcona, New Scapa Road, Kirkwall, Orkney KW15 1BN. *T:* (01856) 872849. *Club:* Highland and Lowland Brigades'.

**GIBSON, Ven. (George) Granville;** Archdeacon of Auckland, Diocese of Durham, 1993–2001, Archdeacon Emeritus, 2001–16; *b* 28 May 1936; *s* of late George Henry and Jessie Gibson (*née* Farrand); *m* 1958, Edna (*née* Jackson) (*d* 2016); two *s* one *d* (and one *s* decd). *Educ:* Queen Elizabeth Grammar Sch., Wakefield; Barnsley Coll. of Technology; Cuddesdon Coll., Oxford. Mining Surveyor, NCB, 1952–62; Field Officer, The Boys' Brigade, 1962–69. Ordained deacon, 1971, priest, 1972; Curate, St Paul, Cullercoats, 1971–73; Team Vicar, Cramlington, 1973–77; Vicar, St Clare, Newton Aycliffe, 1977–85; Rector of Bishopwearmouth and RD of Wearmouth, 1985–93; Hon. Canon of Durham, 1988–2001, Emeritus, 2001–16; Interim Priest, St James the Great, Darlington, 2012–14. Proctor in Convocation, 1980–2000; Church Comr, 1991–98 (Mem., Bd of Govs, 1993–98). Stavrofor, Romanian Orthodox Church, 1997–. Mem., Archbishop of Canterbury's Romania Liaison Gp, 1994–2015. Trustee, Church Urban Fund, 1991–2003. Chm. Govs, St Aidan's (formerly Eastbourne) C of E Acad., Darlington, 2007–11 (Gov., 2011–14). *Recreations:* gardening, cactus plants, cookery, grandchildren. *Address:* 15 Worsley Park, Darlington DL3 8SF. *T:* (01325) 462526. *E:* gib65@aol.com.

**GIBSON, Prof. (Gerald) John,** MD; FRCP, FRCPE; FERS; Professor of Respiratory Medicine, University of Newcastle upon Tyne, 1993–2009, now Emeritus; Consultant Physician (Respiratory Medicine), Freeman Hospital, Newcastle upon Tyne, 1978–2009; *b* 3 April 1944; *s* of Maurice Gibson and Margaret Gibson (*née* Cronin); *m* 1977, Dr Mary Teresa Cunningham; three *s. Educ:* St Michael's Coll., Leeds; Guy's Hosp. Med. Sch., Univ. of London (BSc 1st Class Hons Physiol. 1965; MB BS Hons 1968; MD 1976). FRCP 1982; FRCPE 2000. Hse Physician, Guy's Hosp., 1968; Hse Surgeon, Leeds Gen. Infirmary, 1969; Resident Physician, McMaster Univ., Ont, 1970–71; Registrar and Sen. Registrar, Hammersmith Hosp. and RPMS, 1971–77. Mem. Council, RCP, 2000–03; President: Brit. Thoracic Soc., 2004–05 (Hon. Sec., 1986–88; Chm., 1997–99); Eur. Respiratory Soc., 2002–03. FERS 2014. British Thoracic Soc. Medal, 2012. *Publications:* Clinical Tests of Respiratory Function, 1984, 3rd edn 2009; Respiratory Medicine, 1990, 3rd edn 2003; contrib. papers on several aspects of respiratory medicine, sleep apnoea and clinical respiratory physiology. *Recreations:* photography, opera and singers. *E:* john.gibson@ncl.ac.uk.

**GIBSON, Ven. Granville;** *see* Gibson, Ven. G. G.

**GIBSON, Ian,** PhD; Journalist, Evening News, Norwich, 2009–13; *b* 26 Sept. 1938; *s* of late William and Winifred Gibson; *m* 1977, Elizabeth Frances (*née* Lubbock); two *d. Educ:* Dumfries Acad.; Edinburgh Univ. (BSc, PhD). MIBiol 2000; CBiol 2000. Indiana Univ., 1963–64; Univ. of Washington, 1964–65. Lectr, 1968–71, Sen. Lectr, and Dean, Sch. of Biol Scis, 1991–97, Hon. Prof., 2003, UEA. Vis. Prof., MIT, 2012; Lectr, Univs of Cambridge, Hull, Durham, UEA, Salford, Nottingham, Inst. of Physics, UCL and Imperial Coll. London, 2009–14. Contested (Lab) Norwich N, 1992; MP (Lab) Norwich N, 1997–June 2009. Chm., Select Cttee on Sci. and Technol., 2001–05. Chairman: Parly OST, 1998–2001; All Party Parly Gp on Cancer, 1998–2009; All Party Parly Gp on Cuba, 2004–09; All Party Parly Writers Gp, 2008–09. Non-exec. Dir, Stem Cell Foundn, 2005–09; Director, Eur. Cervical Cancer Assoc., 2010–; Community Telemedicine, 2010–15. Chairman: Nanotechnology Task Force; UK Brain Tumour Consortium, 2011–12. Jt Manager, Parly football squad, 1999–2005. Governor: Hellesdon High Sch., 1992–97; Sprowston High Sch., 1995–97 (Chm.); Parkside Sch., Norwich, 2011–15. President: Newton's Apple Charity, 2007–; Norfolk Carers Forum, 2007–17; UN Assoc. (Norwich), 2009–; Norwich City Power Chair Football, 2009–; Norwich Palestine Solidarity Campaign, 2015–; Wymondham FC, 2016–; Norfolk Assoc. of Local Councils, 2017–; Chair and Trustee, Silver Road Community Centre, Norwich, 2009–17; Trustee, UEA Students' Union, 2017–. Mem., Nat. Exec., ASTMS, 1972–92. Hon. Fellow: British Sci. Assoc., 2005; Wellcome Trust, 2015. Trustee, Children with Leukaemia, 2009–11. Hon. DCL UEA, 2011. Macmillan Cancer Relief Champion, 2003; E-Politix Health Champion, 2003–05; Parly Award, Royal Soc. Chemistry, 2004; Backbencher of Year, House mag., 2004. *Publications:* Anti-sense Technology, 1997; (with D. Turner) Best when we are Labour?, 2011; (with E. Sherriffs) Science, Politics, …and ME, 2017. *Recreations:* football coaching, watching, listening and questioning.

**GIBSON, Sir Ian,** Kt 1999; CBE 1990; FInstP; Chairman: Norbrook Laboratories Ltd, since 2016; Trinity Mirror plc, 2006–12; William Morrison Supermarkets plc, 2008–15 (Deputy Chairman 2007–08); *b* 1 Feb. 1947; *s* of Charley Gibson and Kate Gibson (*née* Hare); *m* 1st, 1969, Joy Musker (marr. diss. 1985); two *d*; 2nd, 1988, Susan Wilson (marr. diss. 2009); one *s*; 3rd, 2010, Jane Blackburn. *Educ:* UMIST (BSc Physics 1969). FInstP 1999. Ford Motor Co. and Ford Werke AG: various posts in industrial relns and gen. mgt, 1969–79; General Manager: Halewood Ops, 1979–82; Saarlouis, 1982–83; Nissan Motor Manufacturing: Dir, 1984–2000; Dep. Man. Dir, 1987–89; Man. Dir, 1989–98; Chm., UK, 1999–2000; Vice-Pres., 1994–98, Pres., 1999–2000, Nissan Europe; Sen. Vice-Pres., Nissan Motor Co. Ltd and Supervisory Bd Mem., Nissan Europe NV, 2000–01. Dep. Chm., ASDA plc, 1994–99; non-exec. Dir, 2001–05, Dep. Chm., 2003–04, Chm., 2004–05, BPB plc. Mem. Court, Bank of England, 1999–2004. Non-executive Director: GKN plc, 2002–07; Northern Rock plc, 2002–08; Greggs plc, 2006–08. Mem., Public Interest Body, PricewaterhouseCoopers LLP, 2010–14, 2015–. CCMI (CBIM 1990; Gold Medal, 2001). Hon. DBA: Sunderland Poly., 1990; York St John, 2014. Mensforth Gold Medal, IEE, 1998. *Recreations:* sailing and working on my boat, reading. *Club:* Royal Automobile.

**GIBSON, (Jennifer) Bryony;** Vice Lord-Lieutenant of Northumberland, since 2016; *b* London, 30 July 1946; *d* of Timothy and Veronica Ellis; *m* 1966, Anthony Gair Gibson; four *s. Educ:* Queen's Gate Sch., London. Mem. (C), Northumberland CC, 1998–2008. High Sheriff Northumberland, 2003. *Address:* High Juniper, Hexham, Northumberland NE46 1SN. *E:* bryony.g@btinternet.com.

**GIBSON, John;** *see* Gibson, G. J.

**GIBSON, Jonathan Hedley; His Honour Judge Jonathan Gibson;** a Circuit Judge, since 2008; *b* Harrogate, 30 March 1960; *s* of Hedley and Margaret Gibson; *m* 1984, Helen Downs; one *s* one *d. Educ:* Harrogate Grammar Sch.; Univ. of Nottingham (LLB 1981); Inns of Court Sch. of Law. Called to the Bar, Gray's Inn, 1982; Barrister, Broadway House Chambers, Bradford, 1982–2008; Asst Recorder, 1999–2000; Recorder, 2000–08. Legal Mem., Mental Health Rev. Tribunal, 2002–. Legal Assessor, GMC, 2002–08. *Recreations:* Church activities, reading. *Address:* Preston Combined Court Centre, The Law Courts, Ring Way, Preston, Lancs PR1 2LL.

**GIBSON, Kenneth James;** Member (SNP) Cunninghame North, Scottish Parliament, since 2007; *b* Paisley, 8 Sept. 1961; *s* of Kenneth George Gibson and Iris Gibson; *m* 1st, 1989, Lynda Dorothy Payne (marr. diss. 2006); two *s* one *d*; 2nd, 2007, Patricia Duffy (*see* P. Gibson). *Educ:* Bellahouston Acad., Glasgow; Univ. of Stirling (BA Econs). Member (SNP): Glasgow DC, 1992–96; Glasgow CC, 1995–99 (Leader of Opposition, 1998–99). Scottish Parliament: MSP (SNP) Glasgow, 1999–2003; Shadow Minister for Local Govt, 1999–2001, for Social Justice, Housing, Urban Regeneration and Planning, 2001–03; Mem., Local Govt Cttee, 1999–2001, 2002; Deputy Convenor: Social Justice Cttee, 2001–03; Local Govt and Communities Cttee, 2007–08 (Mem., 2016–); Educn, Lifelong Learning and Culture Cttee, 2008–11; Convenor, Finance Cttee, 2011–16; contested (SNP) Glasgow, Pollok, 2003. Mem., SNP Nat. Exec. Cttee, 1997–99. *Recreations:* cinema, theatre, swimming, classical history. *Address:* Scottish Parliament, Edinburgh EH99 1SP; (constituency office) 15 Main Street, Dalry KA24 5DL.

**GIBSON, Leigh,** OBE 2012; Director, USA, British Council, and Cultural Counsellor, British Embassy, Washington, since 2016; *b* Ramsgate, 23 Sept. 1956; *d* of Donald Spain and Freda Spain; *m* 1981, Nigel Roy Gibson; two *s. Educ:* Dover Grammar Sch. for Girls; St Hugh's Coll., Oxford (BA Hons). Tutor (pt-time), Univ. of Hong Kong, 1980–83; British Council: Director: Ops, Hong Kong, 1994–99; Arts, HQ, 2004–07; for Content and Prog., Shanghai World Expo, 2007–10; UK Now, China, 2010–13; UK-Russia Year of Culture, 2013–14; Festivals and Seasons, 2014–16. *Recreations:* hiking, running, travel, reading, cinema. *Address:* British Embassy, 3100 Massachusetts Avenue, Washington, DC 20008, USA. *E:* leigh.gibson@britishcouncil.org. *Clubs:* Royal Hong Kong Yacht; Hong Kong Cricket.

**GIBSON, Mark,** CB 2005; Chief Executive, Whitehall and Industry Group, 2009–15; *b* 2 Jan. 1953; *m* 1981, Jane Norma Lindley (*d* 2007); *m* 2013, Rachel Jenkinson. *Educ:* University Coll., Oxford (BA 1974); London Business Sch. (MSc). Entered Department of Trade and Industry, 1974: Dep. Project Manager, Next Steps team, Cabinet Office, 1990–92; Asst Sec. Competitiveness Unit, 1992–94; Principal Private Sec. to Pres., BoT, and Dep. Prime Minister, 1994–97; Dir, British Trade Internat., 1997–2000; Director General: Enterprise and Innovation, DTI, 2000–02; Business Gp, later Enterprise and Business Gp, DTI, later BERR, 2002–09. Non-exec. Dir, Centre for Process Innovation, 2015–.

**GIBSON, Rt Rev. Mary I.;** *see* Irwin-Gibson.

**GIBSON, Mel Columcille Gerard,** AO 1997; actor, director and producer; *b* Peekskill, NY, 3 Jan. 1956; *s* of Hutton Gibson and late Anne Gibson; *m* 1980, Robyn Moore; six *s* one *d* (incl. twin *s*); one *d* by Oksana Grigorieva. *Educ:* Nat. Inst. of Dramatic Art, Univ. of NSW. Joined State Theatre Co. of SA, 1977; theatre includes: Waiting for Godot, Sydney, 1979; Death of a Salesman, Nimrod Th., Sydney, 1982; No Names, No Pack Drill; Romeo and Juliet. Co-founder and Partner, Icon Entertainment Internat., 1989–. *Films include:* Summer City, 1977; Mad Max, Tim, 1979; The Z Men, 1980; Gallipoli, Mad Max 2: The Road Warrior, 1981; The Year of Living Dangerously, 1982; The Bounty, The River, Mrs Soffell, 1984; Mad Max: Beyond Thunderdome, 1985; Lethal Weapon, 1987; Tequila Sunrise, 1988; Lethal Weapon 2, 1989; Bird on a Wire, Air America, 1990; Hamlet, 1991; Lethal Weapon 3, Forever Young, 1992; The Man Without a Face (also dir), 1993; Maverick, 1994; Braveheart (also dir and co-prod.), 1995 (Academy, Golden Globe and BAFTA Awards for best dir, 1996); Ransom, 1997; Conspiracy Theory, 1997; Lethal Weapon 4, 1998; Payback, 1999; The Million Dollar Hotel, The Patriot, 2000; What Women Want, 2001; We Were Soldiers, Signs, 2002; The Singing Detective (also prod.), 2004; Edge of Darkness, 2010; The Beaver, 2011; Dark Shadows, 2012; Machete Kills, 2013; The Expendables 3, 2014; Blood Father, 2016; Daddy's Home 2, 2017; Dragged Across Concrete, 2019; dir, prod. and writer, The Passion of the Christ, 2004; dir and prod., Apocalypto, 2007; dir, Hacksaw Ridge, 2017. *Address:* c/o Shanahan Management Pty Ltd, PO Box 1509, Darlinghurst, NSW 1300, Australia.

**GIBSON, Air Vice-Marshal Michael John,** CB 1994; OBE 1979; FRAeS; Head of Aviation Regulation Enforcement, Civil Aviation Authority, 1996–99; *b* 2 Jan. 1939; *m* 1961, Dorothy Russell; one *s* one *d. Educ:* Imperial Coll., London (BSc); Selwyn Coll., Cambridge; National Defense Univ., Washington, DC. ACGI; FRAeS. Commnd RAFVR, 1959; commnd RAF, 1961; various appointments as fighter pilot and instructor; Personal Air Sec. to Air Force Minister, 1972–73; Officer Commanding: 45 Sqdn (Hunter), 1974–76; 20 Sqdn (Jaguar), 1976–79; RAF Brawdy, 1982–84; RAF Stanley, 1984–85; Air Officer Plans, HQ Strike Comd, 1987–88; Dir, Airspace Policy, 1988–91, Dir Gen. of Policy and Plans, 1991–94, Head of Mgt Support Unit, 1994–96, NATS. *Recreation:* music (singing and church organ playing). *Address:* 12 Watling Street, Radlett, Herts WD7 7NH. *Club:* Royal Air Force.

**GIBSON, Patricia;** MP (SNP) North Ayrshire and Arran, since 2015; *b* 12 May 1968; *d* of James Duffy and Eileen (*née* Doherty); *m* 2007, Kenneth James Gibson, *qv*. *Educ:* Univ. of Glasgow (MA 1991). Teacher of English, St Ninians High Sch., Giffnock, until 2015. Mem. (SNP), Glasgow CC, 2007–15. *Address:* House of Commons, SW1A 0AA.

**GIBSON, Paul Alexander;** Founder, 1973, Partner, 1973–2001, later Consultant, Sidell Gibson Partnership, Architects; *b* 11 Oct. 1941; *s* of Wing-Comdr Leslie Gibson and Betty Gibson (later Betty Stephens); *m* 1969, Julia Atkinson. *Educ:* Kingswood Sch., Bath; King's Coll., London; Canterbury Sch. of Architecture; Regent Street Polytechnic Sch. of Architecture (DipArch 1968). Worked for Farrell Grimshaw Partnership, 1968–69; Lectr, North Dakota State Univ., 1969; worked for Foster Associates, 1970–73. 3 RIBA awards, Good Housing, 1986; won open competition for redevelt of Grand Buildings, Trafalgar Square, 1986; won competition for redevelt of Winchester Barracks, 1988; expansion of Jewel House, HM Tower of London, 1992–94; Woolgate House, Northgate House and Governor's House, City of London, 1996–2001. Judge, Nat. Stone Awards, 2004–10. *Recreations:* printmaking, etching and photography.

**GIBSON, Rt Hon. Sir Peter (Leslie),** Kt 1981; PC 1993; a Lord Justice of Appeal, 1993–2005; Intelligence Services Commissioner, 2006–10; *b* 10 June 1934; *s* of late Harold Leslie Gibson and Martha Lucy Gibson (*née* Diercking); *m* 1968, Katharine Mary Beatrice Hadow, PhD (*d* 2002); two *s* one *d*. *Educ:* Malvern Coll.; Worcester Coll., Oxford (Scholar; Hon. Fellow, 1993). 2nd Lieut RA, 1953–55 (National Service). Called to the Bar, Inner Temple, 1960; Bencher, Lincoln's Inn, 1975; Treas., Lincoln's Inn, 1996. 2nd Jun. Counsel to Inland Revenue (Chancery), 1970–72; Jun. Counsel to the Treasury (Chancery), 1972–81; a Judge of the High Court of Justice, Chancery Div., 1981–93. A Judge of the Employment Appeal Tribunal, 1984–86. A Judge of Qatar Financial Centre Civil and Commercial Court, 2007–15. Chairman: Law Commn, 1990–92; Trust Law Cttee, 2004–12; Detainee Inquiry, 2010–12. Conducted Omagh Bombing Intelligence Review, 2008. *Address: c/o* Royal Courts of Justice, Strand, WC2A 2LL.

**GIBSON, Prof. (Robert) Dennis,** AO 2002; PhD, DSc; FTS, FAICD; Member, Board of Governors, Torrens University, Adelaide, since 2013; *b* 13 April 1942; *m*; one *s* two *d*; *m* 1994, Catherin Bull. *Educ:* Hull Univ. (BSc Hons); Newcastle upon Tyne Univ. (MSc, PhD); DSc CNAA 1987. FAIM 1982; FTS 1993. Asst Lectr, Maths Dept, Univ. of Newcastle upon Tyne, 1966–67; Scientific Officer, Culham Plasma Lab., UKAEA, 1967–68; Lectr in Maths, Univ. of Newcastle upon Tyne, 1968–69; Sen. Lectr, Maths and Statistics, Teesside Polytechnic, 1969–77; Head, Dept of Maths, Stats and Computing (later Sch. of Maths, Stats and Computing), Newcastle upon Tyne Polytechnic, 1977–82; Queensland Institute of Technology: Dep. Dir then Actg Dir, 1982–83; Dir, 1983–88; first Vice-Chancellor, Qld Univ. of Technol., 1989–2003, now Emeritus Prof.; Chancellor: RMIT, 2003–10; INTI Internat. Univ., Kuala Lumpur, 2011–12. Mem., 1988–92, Dep. Chm., 1991–92, Aust. Res. Council; Chm., Grad. Careers Council of Aust., 2000–06. Chairman: M & MD Pty Ltd, 2003–09; RDDT Pty Ltd, 2007–10. Academic Advr, Laureate Educn Inc., 2010–. Mem. Council, 2005–10, Professorial Fellow, 2010–, Bond Univ.; Mem. Bd of Govs, St Thomas Univ., Osaka, 2011–13. FAICD 1995. DUniv: Southern Qld, 1999; Qld Univ. of Technol., 2003; Hon. DSc Hull, 2016. *Publications:* numerous research papers on various aspects of mathematical modelling. *Recreations:* jogging, cricket. *Club:* Brisbane.

**GIBSON, Robert McKay;** Member (SNP) Caithness, Sutherland and Ross, Scottish Parliament, 2011–16 (Highlands and Islands, 2003–11); *b* 16 Oct. 1945; *s* of John and Elsie Gibson; partner, Dr Eleanor Roberta Scott, *qv*. *Educ:* Dundee Univ. (MA Hons Modern Hist.); Dundee Coll. of Educn (DipEd 1973; Secondary Teaching Dip. 1973). Teacher, Geog. and Modern Studies, 1973–74, Asst Principal Teacher of Guidance, 1974–77, Invergordon Acad.; Principal Teacher of Guidance, Alness Acad., 1977–95; writer and researcher, 1995–2003. Vice-Pres., Brittany Scotland Assoc., 2005–; Hon. Pres., Kilt Soc. of France, 2006–. *Publications:* The Promised Land, 1974; Highland Clearances Trail, 1983, new edn 2006; Toppling the Duke: outrage on Ben Bhraggie, 1996; Plaids and Bandanas, 2003; Highland Cowboys, 2010. *Recreations:* traditional music singer, organic gardener, hill walker, traveller. *Address:* Tir Nan Oran, 8 Culcairn Road, Evanton, Ross-shire IV16 9YT. *T:* (01349) 830388. *E:* robgibson273@btinternet.com.

**GIBSON, Robert Winnington,** CMG 2011; HM Diplomatic Service, retired; Foreign Secretary's Special Representative, since 2019; *b* Neath, W Glamorgan, 7 Feb. 1956; *s* of Peter Winnington Gibson and Olive May Gibson (*née* Taylor). *Educ:* Dyffryn Sch., Port Talbot; University Coll., London (BSc Hons Zool. 1978). Entered HM Diplomatic Service, 1978; Desk Officer, Eur. Integration Dept, FCO, 1978–79; ME Centre for Arabic Studies, 1979–80; Vice Consul, Jeddah, 1981–84; Second Secretary: UK Representation, Brussels, 1984–85; (Chancery), Govt of Spain, 1986–89; Head: Peacekeeping and Finance Section, UN Dept, FCO, 1989–93; Saudi Arabian and Gulf Section, ME Dept, FCO, 1993–95; First Sec., UK Delegn to OECD, Paris, 1995–99; Dep. Hd, Whitehall Liaison Dept, FCO, 1999–2001; Dep. High Comr and Commercial Counsellor, Dhaka, 2002–05; Dep. Hd of Mission, Baghdad, 2006–07 (Iraq Medal, 2007); Dep. High Comr, Karachi, and Dir, UK Trade and Investment, Pakistan, 2008–11; High Comr, Bangladesh, 2011–15; High Comr, Barbados and Eastern Caribbean States, and Ambassador, Organisation of Eastern Caribbean States and CARICOM, 2016–17. *Recreations:* music, reading, food and travel.

**GIBSON, Roy;** aerospace consultant, since 1980; Director General, British National Space Centre, 1985–87; *b* 4 July 1924; *s* of Fred and Jessie Gibson; *m* 1st, 1946, Jean Fallowes (marr. diss. 1971); one *s* one *d*; 2nd, 1971, Inga Elgerus (*d* 2009); 3rd, 2014, Christiane Glarmet. *Educ:* Chorlton Grammar Sch.; Wadham College, Oxford; SOAS. Malayan Civil Service, 1948–58; Health and Safety Br., UKAEA, 1958–66; European Space Research Orgn, 1967–75 (Dir of Admin, 1970–75); Dir Gen., European Space Agency, 1975–80. DSC (Kedah, Malaysia), 1953; Das Grosse Silberne Ehrenzeichen mit Stern (Austria), 1977. *Publications:* Space, 1992; Recollections, 2011; numerous articles in aerospace technical jls. *Recreations:* music, bridge, chess, walking. *Address:* 1 Grande Rue, 39190 Beaufort, France. *T:* (3) 84257838.

**GIBSON, Prof. Simon John,** CBE 2018 (OBE 1999); DSc; Chief Executive, Wesley Clover, since 2001; *b* Rochford, 1 March 1958; *s* of John Arthur Gibson, MBE and Sheila Ann Gibson; *m* Susan Mary Grobecker; three *s* one *d*. *Educ:* King John Sch.; Massachusetts Inst. of Technol. (Advanced Cert. for Execs); Swansea Univ. (DSc 2015). Product Mktg Manager, Mitel Corp., 1983–86; Vice Pres., Mktg, Newbridge Networks Corp., 1987–93; Pres. and CEO, Ubiquity Software Corp., 1994–2001. Founder and Chm., Alacrity Foundn, 2012–. Vis. Prof., Univ. of S Wales, 2010–; Hon. Prof., Swansea Univ., 2014–. Mem., Econ. Res. Adv. Panel, Welsh Assembly Govt, 2003–11. Mem., Consumer Panel, 2003–08, Mem., Nat. Adv. Cttee for Wales, 2008–14, Ofcom. Co-Founder and Dir, Wales Electronic Forum, 1996–2007. Chair: Digital Wales Bd, 2010–15; ReNewport Regeneration Taskforce, 2013–; MIT Regl Entrepreneurship Acceleration Prog. Wales Bd, 2015–17; Innovation Point, 2015–19. Non-executive Director: Celtic Manor Resort, 2001–; Welsh Develt Agency, 2001–06; IQE plc, 2003–17; Talkative, 2018–; Hutsix, 2018–. Cardiff University: Mem. Council, 2006–14; Mem., Adv. Bd, Business Sch., 2010–; Chm., Innovation Oversight Bd, 2014–; Regent, Harris Manchester Coll., Oxford, 2002–; Patron, Employability Acad., Swansea Univ., 2013–. Fellow: Univ. of S Wales, 2013; Cardiff Univ., 2016. Trustee/Dir, British Deer Soc., 2016–. *Recreations:* family, flyfishing, UK deer. *Address:* The Manor House, Celtic Manor Resort, Newport, S Wales NP18 1HQ. *T:* (01633) 410383, *Fax:* (01633) 410384. *E:* simon@wesleyclover.com. *Club:* Athenæum.

**GIBSON, Prof. Susan Elizabeth,** OBE 2013; DPhil; Professor of Chemistry, Imperial College, London, since 2003; *b* 3 Nov. 1960; *d* of late Arnold Sutcliffe Thomas and of Kathleen Thomas; *m* 1994, Vernon Charles Gibson, *qv*; one *s* one *d*. *Educ:* Darwen Vale High Sch.; Sidney Sussex Coll., Cambridge (BA 1981); New Coll., Oxford (DPhil 1984). Lecturer: Univ. of Warwick, 1985–90; ICSTM, London, 1990–99; Daniell Prof. of Chemistry, KCL, 1999–2003. Mem. Council, EPSRC, 2003–06. Pres., Organic Chemistry Div., RSC, 2007–10. Rosalind Franklin Award, Royal Soc., 2003–04. *Publications:* Organic Synthesis: the roles of boron and silicon, 1991; more than 130 articles in learned jls. *Recreations:* hill-walking, sailing. *Address:* Department of Chemistry, Imperial College, London, South Kensington Campus, SW7 2AZ. *T:* (020) 7594 1140. *E:* s.gibson@imperial.ac.uk.

**GIBSON, Prof. Vernon Charles,** CB 2017; DPhil; FRS 2004; Chief Scientific Adviser, Ministry of Defence, 2012–16; *b* 15 Nov. 1958; *s* of Dennis Charles Gibson and Pamela Gibson (*née* Lambley); *m* 1994, Susan Elizabeth Thomas (see S. E. Gibson); one *s* one *d*. *Educ:* Huntingtower Rd County Primary Sch.; King's Sch., Grantham; Univ. of Sheffield (R. D. Haworth Medal, 1980; BSc); Balliol Coll., Oxford (DPhil 1984). Lectr in Inorganic Chem., 1986–93, Prof. of Chem., 1993–95, Univ. of Durham; Imperial College London: Prof. of Polymer Synthesis and Catalysis, 1995–98; Sir Geoffrey Wilkinson Chair of Chem., 1998–2001; Sir Edward Frankland BP Prof. of Inorganic Chem., 2001–08; Visiting Prof., 2008–; Chief Chemist, BP plc, 2008–12. Hon. DSc Sheffield, 2010. Royal Society of Chemistry: BP Chemicals Young Univ. Lectr Award, 1990–93; Sir Edward Frankland Prize Fellowship, 1992–93; Corday-Morgan Medal and Prize, 1993–94; Monsanto Organometallic Chemistry Award, 1999; Joseph Chatt Lectr, 2001–02; Tilden Lectr, 2004–05. *Publications:* numerous book chapters; approx. 300 papers in learned jls and 30 published patents. *Recreations:* jogging around Hyde Park and Kensington Gardens, fell-walking, ski-ing, history. *Club:* Athenæum.

**GIBSON-CRAIG-CARMICHAEL, Sir David Peter William,** 15th Bt *cr* 1702 (Gibson Carmichael) and 8th Bt *cr* 1831; *b* 21 July 1946; *s* of Sir Archibald Henry William Gibson-Craig-Carmichael, 14th Bt and Rosemary Anita (*d* 1979), *d* of George Duncan Crew, Santiago, Chile; *S* father, 1969; *m* 1973, Patricia, *d* of Marcos Skarnic, Santiago, Chile; two *s* two *d*. *Educ:* Queen's Univ., Canada (BSc Hons Geology, 1971). *Heir: s* Peter William Gibson-Craig-Carmichael, *b* 29 Dec. 1975.

**GIBSON FLEMING, James Randolf;** Vice Lord-Lieutenant of Dorset, since 2006; *b* 27 July 1958; *s* of late Maj. William H. Gibson Fleming and Selina Littlehales Gibson Fleming (*née* Baker); *m* 1986, Fiona Lucy Don; two *s* one *d*. *Educ:* Eton; RMA Sandhurst; RAC Cirencester. SSC, Royal Hussars, PWO, 1977–81; served NI and W Berlin. Partner/dir, farming, property and asset mgt firms/cos, 1981–; Chief Exec., Hanford plc, 1987–93. Chairman: CLA Game Fair Bd, 1992–97; Talbot Project, 2013–. Partner, www.wessexinternet.com, 2011– (Chm., 2011–). Trustee: Talbot Village Trust, 1991–; Cancercare Dorset, 1994–2004 (Chm., 2000–04); Joseph Weld and Trimar Hospice and Cancercare Dorset, 2004–06 (Vice-Chm., 2004–06); Devonshire and Dorset Military Museums Charity, 2012–18. Pres., Queen's Own Dorset Yeomanry Assoc., 2010–. DL Dorset, 2005. Hon. DBA Bournemouth, 2017. *Recreations:* field sports, flying, ski-ing, holidaying on Isle of Mull. *Address:* Ranston, Blandford, Dorset DT11 8PU. *Clubs:* Cavalry and Guards, Royal Air Squadron, MCC, Shikar, Pratt's.

**GIBSON-SMITH, Christopher Shaw,** CBE 2011; PhD; Chairman: London Stock Exchange Group (formerly London Stock Exchange), 2003–15; JRP (formerly Partnership Assurance), since 2013; *b* 8 Sept. 1945; *s* of late John Gibson-Smith and Winifred Agnes Gibson-Smith; *m* 1969, Marjorie Hadwin Reed; two *d*. *Educ:* Durham Univ. (BSc Geol); Newcastle Univ. (PhD Geochem. 1970); Stanford Univ. (MSc Business Sci). Joined BP, 1970; CEO Europe, BP Exploration, 1992–95; Chief Operating Officer, BP Chemicals, 1995–97; Gp Man. Dir, BP, 1997–2001. Chm., NATS, 2001–05. Non-executive Director: Lloyds TSB, 2000–2005; Powergen, 2000–01; Chm., British Land plc, 2006–12. Hon. Fellow, UCD, 2006. *Recreations:* art, music, opera, ski-ing, golf, tennis. *Address:* Apt 5.01, The Knightsbridge, 199 Knightsbridge, SW7 1RH.

**GIDDEN, Mark Robert;** Master of the Administrative Court, Queen's Bench Division, since 2012; *b* Reading, 5 Oct. 1964; *s* of late Michael John Gidden and of Patricia Gidden; *m* 1986 (marr. diss. 2013); three *s* one *d*. *Educ:* Univ. of Birmingham (LLB). Admitted solicitor, 1991; solicitor, Govt Legal Service, 1991–2012, a Dir, Legal Services, DWP, 2010–11. *Recreations:* being outdoors, moving about, meeting people, abundant fruit and veg, 'thin places' away from technological excess; avoid disappointment - do not follow me on Twitter. *Address:* Administrative Court, Royal Courts of Justice, Strand, WC2A 2LL. *T:* (020) 7947 6003. *E:* master.gidden@hmcts.x.gsi.gov.uk.

**GIDDENS,** Baron *cr* 2004 (Life Peer), of Southgate in the London Borough of Enfield; **Anthony Giddens,** PhD; Director, London School of Economics, 1997–2003, now Emeritus; *b* 18 Jan. 1938; *s* of T. G. Giddens; *m* 1963, Jane M. Ellwood. *Educ:* Hull Univ. (BA); LSE (MA); MA 1970, PhD 1974, Cantab. Cambridge University: Lectr in Sociology, subseq. Reader, 1969–85; Prof. of Sociology, Faculty of Econs and Politics, 1985–96; Fellow, King's Coll., 1969–96. Reith Lectr, BBC, 1999. *Publications:* Capitalism and Modern Social Theory, 1971; (ed) Sociology of Suicide, 1972; Politics and Sociology in the Thought of Max Weber, 1972; (ed and trans) Emile Durkheim: Selected Writings, 1972; (ed) Positivism and Sociology, 1974; New Rules of Sociological Method, 1976; Studies in Social and Political Theory, 1976; Central Problems in Social Theory, 1979; Class Structure of the Advanced Societies, 2nd edn 1981; Contemporary Critique of Historical Materialism: vol. 1, Power, Property and State, 1981, vol. 2, Nation, State and Violence, 1985; (jtly) Classes, Power and Conflict, 1982; Profiles and Critiques in Social Theory, 1983; (ed jtly) Social Class and the Division of Labour, 1983; Constitution of Society, 1984; Durkheim, 1985; Sociology: a brief but critical introduction, 1986; Social Theory and Modern Sociology, 1987; (ed jtly) Social Theory Today, 1987; Sociology, 1989, 7th edn (with P. W. Sutton) 2013; The Consequences of Modernity, 1990; Modernity and Self-Identity, 1991; The Transformation of Intimacy, 1992; Beyond Left and Right, 1994; In Defence of Sociology, 1996; The Third Way, 1998, 2nd edn 2010; Runaway World (Reith Lectures), 1999; (with Will Hutton) On the Edge: living with global capitalism, 2000; The Third Way and its Critics, 2000; Europe in the Global Age, 2007; Over to You Mr Brown: how Labour can win again, 2007; The Politics of Climate Change, 2009, 2nd edn 2011; Turbulent and Mighty Continent: what future for Europe?, 2013; (with P. W. Sutton) Essential Concepts in Sociology, 2014. *Recreations:* theatre, cinema, playing tennis, supporting Tottenham Hotspur. *Address:* House of Lords, SW1A 0PW.

**GIDDINGS, Anthony Edward Buckland,** MD; FRCS; Consultant Surgeon in General and Vascular Surgery, Guy's, King's and St Thomas' Hospitals, 1997–2004; *b* 8 Feb. 1939; *s* of Edward Walter Giddings and Doris Margaret Giddings; *m* 1966, Maureen Ann Williams; one *s* one *d*. *Educ:* Cathedral Sch., Bristol; Univ. of Bristol (MB ChB 1966; MD

1978). FRCS 1971. Consultant Surgeon, Royal Surrey Co. Hosp., 1979–97. Non-exec. Dir, Nat. Clinical Assessment Authy, 2001–05. MRCS Course Dir, St Thomas' Hosp., 2003–05. Founding Pres., Assoc. of Surgeons in Training, 1976; President: Sect. of Surgery, RSM, 1994; Assoc. of Surgeons of GB and Ireland, 1997–98; Dir, James IV Assoc. of Surgeons Inc., 1998–2001; Chairman: Specialist Adv. Cttee in Gen. Surgery, 1998–2001; Fedn of Surgical Specialist Assocs, 1998–2001; Mem. Council, RCS, 2001–07. Hunterian Prof., RCS, 1978; James IV Assoc. of Surgeons Inc. Travelling Fellow, 1979; Visiting Professor: Univ. of Texas, 1980; Oregon Health Scis Univ., 1996; Lectures: A. B. Mitchell, QUB, 1996; Moynihan, RCS, 2007. Work on med. perf. and assessment, Nat. Clinical Assessment Authy, GMC and RCS, 1997–2007; work on orgn of surgical services, NHS Modernization Agency and DoH, 2001–08; clinical ress. and educn and trng develt in safety and leadership for surgeons, 1997–2008; Surgical Adviser: Performance Support Team, DoH, 2006–08; Nat. Clinical Adv. Team, DoH, 2007–15; Healthcare Commn, 2008–09; Specialist Advr, Parly Health Cttee, 2008–09; Mem., Surgical Adv. Gp, John Radcliffe Hosp., 2009–10; Chairman: Alliance for Safety of Patients, RCS, 2006–09; Clin. Reference Gp, NW sector surgical proj., Manchester, 2014–15. Founding Co-Organiser, Risky Business Confs, 2006–18. Distinguished Fellow, Soc. for Vascular Surgery, 1999. Mem., Editl Bd, British Jl of Surgery, 1994–2000. *Publications:* contrib. papers and book chapters on surgical science, the safety of patients and the orgn of surgical services. *Recreations:* theatre, music. *Address:* 6 Fairway, Guildford, Surrey GU1 2XG. *T:* (01483) 561826. *E:* tonygiddings@btinternet.com. *Club:* Royal Automobile.

**GIDDINGS, Dr Philip James;** Senior Lecturer in Politics, 1998–2011, and Head, School of Politics and International Relations (formerly School of Sociology, Politics and International Relations), 2006–11, University of Reading; occasional lecturer on politics and church affairs; *b* 5 April 1946; *s* of Albert Edward Robert Giddings and Irene Trustrail Giddings (*née* Dunstan); *m* 1st, 1970, Margaret Anne Mulrenan (*d* 1978); one *d*; 2nd, 1979, Myfanwy Hughes (*d* 2015); one *s*. *Educ:* Sir Thomas Rich's Sch., Gloucester; Worcester Coll., Oxford (BA Hons PPE); Nuffield Coll., Oxford (DPhil 1970). Lectr in Public Admin, Univ. of Exeter, 1970–72; Lectr in Politics, Reading Univ., 1972–98. Member: Crown Appointments Commn, 1992–97; Archbishops' Council, 1999–2015 (Chairman: Church and World Div., 1999–2002; Mission and Public Affairs Div., 2003–11). Mem., Gen. Synod of C of E, 1985–2015 (Vice-Chm., 1995–2000, 2006–10, Chm., 2010–15, House of Laity; Dep. Chm., Legislative Cttee, 2005–10); Lay Vice-Pres., Oxford Diocesan Synod, 1988–2000. Convenor and Chair of Trustees, Anglican Mainstream UK, 2003–14. Mem. Council and Trustee, Wycliffe Hall, Oxford, 2011–. Trustee, Oxford Centre for Religion and Politics, 2014–18. *Publications:* Marketing Boards and Ministers, 1974; Parliamentary Accountability, 1995; (with G. Drewry) Westminster and Europe, 1996; (with R. Gregory) Righting Wrongs: the ombudsman in six continents, 2000; (with R. Gregory) The Ombudsman, the Citizen and Parliament, 2002; Britain in the European Union, 2004; The Future of Parliament, 2005; (ed with M. Rush) The Palgrave Review of British Politics 2005, 2006; (ed with M. Rush) The Palgrave Review of British Politics 2006, 2007; (ed with M. Rush) When Gordon Took the Helm: the Palgrave review of British politics 2007–08, 2008; (with M. Rush) Parliamentary Socialisation: learning the ropes or determining behaviour?, 2011; (with M. Down, E. Sugden and G. Tuckwell) Talking About Dying, 2017. *Recreations:* light gardening, short walks. *Address:* 5 Clifton Park Road, Caversham, Reading, Berks RG4 7PD. *T:* (0118) 954 3892.

**GIDLEY, Sandra Julia;** *b* 26 March 1957; *d* of Frank Henry and Maud Ellen Rawson; *m* 1979, William Arthur Gidley; one *s* one *d*. *Educ:* Eggars Grammar Sch., Alton; AFCENT Internat., Brunssum, Netherlands; Windsor Girls' Sch., Hamm, Germany; Bath Univ. (BPharm). MRPharmS 1979, FRPharmS 2008. Pharmacist, Cheltenham, 1979–80; Pharmacy Manager, Gloucester, then Cheltenham, 1980–82; locum pharmacist, 1982–92; Pharmacy Manager: Safeway, 1992–99; Tesco, 1999–2000. Chair, English Pharmacy Bd, Royal Pharmaceutical Soc., 2015–. Mem. (Lib Dem) Test Valley BC, 1995–2003; Mayor of Romsey, 1997–98. MP (Lib Dem) Romsey, May 2000–2010; contested (Lib Dem) Romsey and Southampton N, 2010. Lib Dem spokesman for women, 2002–06, for older people, 2003–06, for health, 2006–10. Trustee, Beadworkers Guild. *Recreations:* food, lampworking, beading. *Address:* 15 Sycamore Close, Romsey, Hants SO51 5SB.

**GIDOOMAL, Balram, (Ram),** CBE 1998; Chairman: Winning Communications Partnership Ltd, since 1992; Allia (formerly Citylife Ltd), since 2005; Traidcraft plc, Traidcraft Exchange, since 2011; Cotton Connect Ltd, since 2016; *b* 23 Dec. 1950; *s* of late Gagandas Gidoomal and Vasanti Gidoomal; *m* 1976, Sunita Shivdasani; two *s* one *d*. *Educ:* Aga Khan Sch., Mombasa; Christopher Wren Sch., London; Imperial Coll., London (BSc Hons Physics; Fellow, 2010). ARCS 1972. Inlaks Group: Dep. Gp Chief Exec., Head Office, France, then Geneva, 1978–85; UK Gp Chief Exec. and Vice Chm., 1985–92. Non-executive Director: Amsphere Ltd, 2006–19 (Chairman: Audit and Remuneration Cttee, 2006–17); Nirmaan Bharati SAAVS, 2007–09; Dulas Ltd, 2014–17 (Chm., 2015–17); non-exec. Adv. Bd Mem., Six Senses BVI, 2007–09. Board Member: Covent Gdn Mkt Authy, 1998–2004; English Partnerships, 2000–03; Think London (formerly London First Centre), 2001–09; Postmaster.net, 2003–06; Dir, Far Pavilions Ltd, 1998–2008. Member: Better Regulation Task Force, Cabinet Office, 1997–2002; Complaints Audit Cttee, UK Border Agency (formerly Immigration Nationality Directorate, then Border and Immigration Agency), Home Office, 2006–08; Bd, Food Standards Agency, 2014–18 (Audit, Risk and Assurance Cttee, 2015–18); Bd, Parly Health Services Ombudsman, 2018– (Audit and Risk Cttee, 2018–; Remuneration and Nominations Cttee, 2018–); Adv. Bd, BAO Systems, 2018–. Mem., Royal Mail Stamp Adv. Cttee, 2002–11. Mem., Nat. Leadership Team and Chm., London Exec., Race for Opportunity, 1993–99; Founder Chm., Business Links London South, 1995–98; Director: Business Links-Nat. Accreditation Adv. Bd, 1995–2000; Business Links London, 1995–98 (Chm., CEO's Gp, 1996–98); Mem., SRI Adv. Cttee, Hendersons Global Investments, 2004–10. Patron, Small Business Bureau, 1998–. Mem. Council, Britain in Europe, 1999–2005. Chm., S Asian Develt Partnership, 1991–. Vis. Prof., Middx Univ., 2001–14. Chairman: Office of Ind. Adjudicator for Higher Educn, 2009–16; Eur. Network of Ombudsmen in Higher Educn, 2013–16; Stewardship Services (UKET) Ltd, 2016–19; Member: Council, RSA, 1993–2002, 2004–08 (Trustee, 1999–2002); Council, Inst. of Employment Studies, 2001–10 (Bd Mem., 2003–10). Chairman: Christmas Cracker Trust, 1989–2000; London Community Foundn, 2001–03; London Sustainability Exchange, 2001–07. Leader, Christian Peoples Alliance, 2001–04; Pres., Nat. Information Forum, 2003–08; Vice President: Leprosy Mission, 1999–; Livability (formerly Shaftesbury Soc.), 2003–; Employee Ownership Assoc., 2009–. Member: Adv. Bd for ethics in the workplace, 2002–06, Adv. Bd, 2009–, Inst. of Business Ethics (Hon. Vice Pres., 2015–); Adv. Council for Clinical Excellence Awards, 2004–06; Adv. Council, Friends of the Elderly, 2003–08; Internat. Health Partners, 2006–11; Internat. Justice Mission, 2008–14; External Relns Gp, Water UK, 2009–16; External Mem., Audit and Risk Cttee, Equality and Human Rights Commn, 2010–14. Gov., Health Foundn (formerly PPP Medical Healthcare Trust, subseq. PPP Foundn), 2000–05. Trustee: Inst. of Citizenship, 2000–05; Employability Forum, 2000–09 (Chm., 2003–09); Timebank, 2001–04; Forum for the Future, 2001–11; Trng for Life, 2001–04; Care for Children Trust, 2011–13. Mem. Ct of Govs, Luton Univ., 2001–08; Gov. and Mem., Ct and Council, Imperial Coll. London, 2002–09 (Chairman: Res. Ethics Cttee, 2006–09; Student Trustee Bd, 2007–09); Lay Mem. Council, St George's, Univ. of London (formerly St George's Hosp. Med. Sch.), 2002–09 (Vice-Chm., 2007–09; Chairman: Estates Project Bd, 2006–08; Audit Cttee, 2006–09). Governor: James Allen's Girls' Sch., Dulwich, 1997–2002; King's Coll. Sch., Wimbledon, 1998–2011. Freeman, City of London, 1997; Liveryman, Co. of Inf. Technologists, 2003–14 (Mem., 1998–2014; Mem., Court of Assistants, 2003–05). CCMI (CIMgt 2001; Mem. Bd of Companions, 2002–11); FRSA 1993; FCGI 2008; FIC 2010. Hon. Mem., Faculty of Divinity, Cambridge Univ., 1998–. Dehejia Fellow, Sidwell Friends Sch., Washington, DC, 2008. Hon. LLD Bristol, 2002; Hon. DLitt Nottingham Trent, 2003; DUniv Middlesex, 2003. *Publications:* Sari 'n' Chips, 1993; Karma 'n' Chips, 1994; Chapatis for Tea, 1994; Lions, Princesses and Gurus, 1996; The UK Maharajahs, 1997; Hinduism: a way of life, 1997; Building on Success: the South Asian contribution to UK competitiveness, 1997; (jtly) How Would Jesus Vote?, 2001; The British and How to Deal With Them: doing business with Britain's ethnic communities, 2001; various reports and lectures. *Recreations:* music, current affairs, swimming. *Address:* 9 Tudor Close, Cheam, Sutton, Surrey SM3 8QS.

**GIELGUD, Maina;** free-lance ballerina; ballet producer; guest répétiteur; *b* 14 Jan. 1945; *d* of late Lewis Gielgud and Elisabeth Grussner, (stage name, Zita Sutton). *Educ:* BEPC (French). Ballet du Marquis de Cuevas, 1962–63; Ballet Classique de France, 1965–67; Ballet du XXème Siècle, Maurice Béjart, 1967–72; London Festival Ballet, 1972–77; Royal Ballet, 1977–78; free-lance, 1978–; rehearsal director, London City Ballet, 1981–82; Artistic Dir, Australian Ballet, 1983–96; Dir, Royal Danish Ballet, Copenhagen, 1997–99; Artistic Associate, Houston Ballet, 2003–05; Artistic Advisor: Hungarian Nat. Ballet, 2015–; Anton Dolin Foundn, Berlin, 2017–. Guest Répétiteur and Artistic Advisor: English National Ballet; Tokyo Ballet; Béjart Ballet, Lausanne; Ballet du Rhin; Boston Ballet; Munich Ballet; Paris Opera Ballet; Australian Ballet; guest teacher and coach: WA Ballet, 2014; Qld Ballet, 2014, 2015; Australian Ballet, 2014, 2015; Ellison Ballet, NY, 2014, 2015; Tokyo Ballet, 2015; American Ballet Th., 2015; Royal Ballet, Finnish Nat. Ballet, Queensland Ballet, Royal Ballet Sch., 2016–18. Hon. AO 1991. Staged: Don Quixote, Australian Ballet, 1984, Royal Danish Ballet, 1998, Boston Ballet, 2011; (also prod.) Giselle, Australian Ballet, 1984, 2015 and 2018, Boston Ballet, 2002, Ballet du Rhin, 2003, Houston Ballet, 2005; Song of a Wayfarer, Australian Ballet, 1985, Nat. Ballet of Canada, 2011; Suite en Blanc, Australian Ballet, 1984, Houston Ballet, 2005, Hong Kong Ballet, 2008, English Nat. Ballet, 2011–12, San Francisco Ballet, 2013; (also prod., with additional choreography) The Sleeping Beauty, Australian Ballet, 1985, Joburg Ballet, 2019; Four Last Songs, Paris Opera, 2007; Les Sylphides, English Nat. Ballet, 2011; Spectre de la Rose, English Nat. Ballet, 2011; Coppelia, Australian Conservatoire of Ballet, 2015; restaged Manon, Hungarian Nat. Ballet, 2016; Variations for 4, Ellison Ballet and Accademia Teatro alla Scala, Milan, 2017; Pas de Quatre, New Nat. Ballet of Japan, 2017. Choreographed: Storm, Ellison Ballet, NY, 2018; Cinderella, Goh Ballet, Vancouver, 2018. Mem. Jury, Helsinki Competition, 2016. *Address:* 1/9 Stirling Court, 3 Marshall Street, W1F 9BD. *T:* (020) 7734 6612, 07595 249338.

**GIEVE, Sir (Edward) John (Watson),** KCB 2005 (CB 1999); Chairman of Trustees, Nesta (formerly National Endowment for Science, Technology and the Arts), since 2016 (non-executive Director, 2011; Trustee, since 2012); Chairman, Homerton University Hospital NHS Foundation Trust, since 2019 (non-executive Director, since 2011; Deputy Chairman, 2016–19); *b* 20 Feb. 1950; *s* of late David Watson Gieve, OBE and Susan Gieve; *m* 1972, Katherine Vereker; two *s*. *Educ:* Charterhouse; New Coll., Oxford (BA PPE, BPhil). Dept of Employment, 1974–78; HM Treasury: Principal, Industrial Policy Div., 1979–81; Energy Div., 1981–82; Private Sec., 1982–84; Investment Controller, Investors in Industry, 1984–86 (on secondment); Public Expenditure Survey Div., 1986–88; Press Sec., 1988–89; Principal Private Sec. to Chancellor of the Exchequer, 1989–91; Under Sec., Banking Gp, 1991–94; Dep. Dir, then Dir, Budget and Public Finances, 1994–98; Dir, then Man. Dir, Public Services, 1998–2001; Man. Dir, Finance, Regulation and Industry, 2001; Permanent Under-Sec. of State, Home Office, 2001–05; Dep. Gov., Bank of England, 2006–09. Chm., VocaLink, 2009–17 (Ind. Dir, 2017–); Independent Director: CLS Gp Hldgs, 2012–; Morgan Stanley Internat., 2012–15. Chm., Clore Social Leadership Prog., 2010–14. Vis. Prof., UCL, 2012–17. *Recreations:* golf (playing), football (watching).

**GIFFARD, Sir (Charles) Sydney (Rycroft),** KCMG 1984 (CMG 1976); HM Diplomatic Service, retired; *b* 30 Oct. 1926; *s* of Walter Giffard and Minna Giffard (*née* Cotton); *m* 1st, 1951, Wendy Vidal (marr. diss. 1976); one *s* one *d*; 2nd, 1976, Hazel Roberts, OBE. *Educ:* Repton Sch.; Wadham Coll., Oxford (Hon. Fellow, 1991). Served in Japan, 1952; Foreign Office, 1957; Berne, 1961; Tokyo, 1964; Counsellor, FCO, 1968; Royal Coll. of Defence Studies, 1971; Counsellor, Tel Aviv, 1972; Minister in Tokyo, 1975–80; Ambassador to Switzerland, 1980–82; Dep. Under-Sec. of State, FCO, 1982–84; Ambassador to Japan, 1984–86. Grand Cordon, Order of the Rising Sun (Japan), 2003. *Publications:* Japan Among the Powers 1890–1990, 1994; (ed) Guns, Kites and Horses, 2003. *Address:* Flat 2, Hays Park, Sedgehill, Shaftesbury, Dorset SP7 9JR. *Club:* Lansdowne.

**GIFFARD, John William,** CBE 2003; QPM 1997; DL; Chief Constable, Staffordshire Police, 1996–2006; *b* 25 March 1952; *s* of late Peter Richard de Longueville Giffard and of (Mary) Roana (Borwick) Giffard; *m* 1978, Crescent Vail; two *s*. *Educ:* Eton; Univ. of Southampton (BA Hons 1973). With Staffordshire Police, 1973–91: Grad. Entrant 1973; Chief Supt, 1991; Asst Chief Constable, N Yorks Police, 1991–96. Mem. Court, Drapers' Co., 2007– (Master, 2015–16). DL Staffs, 1999. *Recreations:* cricket, shooting, bridge. *Address:* Chillington Hall, Codsall Wood, Wolverhampton WV8 1RE. *T:* (01902) 850236. *Clubs:* MCC, I Zingari; Staffs Gents Cricket, Yorks Gents Cricket.

**GIFFARD, Sir Sydney;** see Giffard, Sir C. S. R.

**GIFFORD,** family name of **Baron Gifford.**

**GIFFORD, 6th Baron** *cr* 1824; **Anthony Maurice Gifford;** QC 1982; Barrister at Law, practising since 1966; Attorney-at-Law, Jamaica, since 1990; *b* 1 May 1940; *s* of 5th Baron Gifford and Lady Gifford (*née* Margaret Allen) (*d* 1990), Sydney, NSW; *S* father, 1961; *m* 1st, 1965, Katherine Ann (marr. diss. 1988), *o d* of Dr Mundy; one *s* one *d*; 2nd, 1988, Elean Roslyn (marr. diss. 1998), *d* of Bishop David Thomas, Kingston, Jamaica; one *d*; 3rd, 1998, Tina Natalia Goulbourne, Kingston, Jamaica. *Educ:* Winchester Coll. (scholar); King's Coll., Cambridge (scholar; BA 1961). Student at Middle Temple, 1959–62, called to the Bar, 1962. Sen. Partner, Gifford Thompson & Shields (formerly Gifford Thompson & Bright), Jamaica, 1991–. Chairman: Cttee for Freedom in Mozambique, Angola and Guiné, 1968–75; Mozambique Angola Cttee, 1982–90; Mem., Nat. Cttee on Reparations, Jamaica, 2009–15; Mem., Nat. Council on Reparation, Jamaica, 2016–. Chairman: N Kensington Neighbourhood Law Centre, 1974–77 (Hon. Sec., 1970–74); Legal Action Gp, 1978–83; Vice-Chm., Defence and Aid Fund (UK), 1983–94. Pres., Cttee for Human Rights, Grenada, 1987–; Vice-Pres., Haldane Soc. of Socialist Lawyers, 1986–. Chairman: Broadwater Farm Inquiry, 1986; Liverpool 8 Inquiry, 1988–89. *Publications:* Where's the Justice?, 1986; The Passionate Advocate, 2007. *Heir:* s Hon. Thomas Adam Gifford, *b* 1 Dec. 1967. *Address:* 122–126 Tower Street, Kingston, Jamaica. *T:* 922 6056, *Fax:* 967 0225. *E:* anthonymgifford@gmail.com; Doughty Street Chambers, 53–54 Doughty Street, WC1N 2LS. *T:* (020) 7404 1313. *E:* a.gifford@doughtystreet.co.uk.

**GIFFORD, Andrew Graham;** Partner, Gifford & Partners, 2002; adviser to British record industry, since 1982; *b* 3 Feb. 1953; *s* of Charles Henry Pearson Gifford, OBE and Laetitia Gifford (*née* Lyell), MBE; *m* 1990, Charlotte Montrésor; four *s*. *Educ*: Bedales; Edinburgh Univ. (BSc). Personal Assistant: to Rt Hon. David Steel, MP, 1975–76; office of Leader of Liberal Party, 1976–80; ran election tours for Leader of Liberal Party, 1979, and of Lib Dem Party, 1983 and 1987. Founder Partner and Chief Exec., GJW Govt Relns, 1980–2002; Founder Director: 4th Estate Publishing, 1983–2000; Heritage Oil & Gas, 1989–95; Director: Fleming Mid Cap Investment Trust, 1994–2005; Second London American Growth, 1997; Moneyweek mag., 2000–02. Founder Chm., Assoc. of Professional Political Consultants, 1989–95. Hon. Treas., Green Alliance, 1990–2002. *Publications*: Handbook of World Development, 1985. *Recreations*: fishing, shooting. *Clubs*: Beefsteak; New (Edinburgh).

**GIFFORD, Michael John;** HM Diplomatic Service; Ambassador to Kazakhstan, since 2018; *b* 2 April 1961; *s* of Henry Gifford and Gladys Mary Gifford (*née* Culverhouse); *m* 1986, Patricia Anne Owen; one *s* one *d*. *Educ*: Hastings Grammar Sch. Entered FCO, 1981; Arabic lang. trng, SOAS, 1982–83; Third Sec. (Commercial), Abu Dhabi, 1983–87; Second Sec. (Chancery), Oslo, 1988–90; on loan to Secretariat-Gen., EC, Brussels, 1990; Second, later First, Sec., FCO, 1991–93; First Secretary: (Econ.), Riyadh, 1993–97; FCO, 1997–2000; Counsellor and Dep. Hd of Mission, Cairo, 2001–04; Ambassador, Yemen, 2004–07; Counsellor, FCO, 2007–12; Ambassador to Democratic People's Republic of Korea, 2012–15; Russian Lang. Trng, FCO, 2016–17. *Recreations*: reading, family. *Address*: c/o Foreign and Commonwealth Office, King Charles Street, SW1A 2AH.

**GIFFORD, Sir (Michael) Roger,** Kt 2014; UK Senior Banker, SEB, since 2017; Chairman, UK Green Finance Taskforce, since 2017; Lord Mayor of London, 2012–13; *b* St Andrews, Scotland, 3 Aug. 1955; *s* of late Douglas John and Hazel Mary Gifford; *m* 1st, 1983, Jane Lunzer (marr. diss. 2004); three *s* one *d* (and one *d* decd); 2nd, 2008, Clare Taylor. *Educ*: Sedbergh; Trinity Coll., Oxford (MA Hons). SG Warburg & Co. Ltd, 1978–82; SEB: Corp. Finance, then Primary Debt, later Equity Capital Markets, Enskilda Securities, 1982–90; Hd, Debt Capital Markets, 1990–93; Hd, London Br., 1992–94; Hd, Tokyo Br., 1994–99; UK Country Mgr, then UK Country Hd, 2000–17. Chairman: Swedish Chamber of Commerce UK, 2003–07; Assoc. of Foreign Banks UK, 2007–11; City of London Green Finance Initiative, 2016–. Alderman, Cordwainer Ward, 2004–; Sheriff, City of London, 2008–09. Liveryman: Co. of Musicians, 2005– (Master, 2016–17); Co. of Internat. Bankers, 2005– (Master 2011); Co. of Cordwainers, 2013–; Mem., Guild of PR Practitioners, 2007–. Trustee: St Paul's Cath. Foundn, 2006–; St Paul's Cath. Choir Sch., 2006–12; Barbican Centre Trust, 2014–; Co-Exist House, 2014–; Governor: Summer Fields Sch., Oxford, 2001–07; King Edward's Sch., Witley, 2005–15; Sedbergh Sch., 2015–. Chairman: English Chamber Orch. and Music Soc., 2001–; From Sweden Fest., 2004–06; Sibelius and Beyond Fest., 2007; Tenebrae Choir, 2011–; City Music Foundn, 2012–. Hon. DSc City, 2013; Hon. LLD St Andrews, 2014. Comdr, Order of Polar Star (Sweden), 2007; Comdr, Order of the Lion (Finland), 2011; Knight, Order of Dannebrog (Denmark), 2017. *Recreations*: chamber music, singing, walking. *Address*: Ware House, Lyme Regis DT7 3RH; 40 Inverness Street, NW1 7HB. *E*: roger.gifford@seb.co.uk. *Club*: Garrick.

**GIL-ROBLES GIL-DELGADO, José María;** Member, European Parliament, 1989–2004 (President, 1997–99); *b* 17 June 1935; *m* 1963, Magdalena Casanueva (*d* 1999); *m* 2001, Rosario Gil-Delgado. *Educ*: Univ. of Deusto; Univ. of Salamanca. Legal Advr, Spanish Parlt, 1958; barrister, Madrid, Barcelona, Bilbao and Salamanca, 1959; Lectr in Law, Univ. of Complutense, 1959; Comité Director, Fedn of Christian Democrats, Spain, 1972. European Parliament: Pres., Institutional Affairs Cttee, 1991; Vice-Pres., 1994. President: European Movt Internat., 1999–2005 (Hon. Pres.); European Parlt Former Mems Assoc., 2006–09; Jean Monnet Foundn, Lausanne, 2005–14 (Jean Monnet European Foundn, 2009–14). Mem., Royal Acad. of Econ. and Financial Scis, Barcelona. Freeman, City of Salamanca, 1998. Hon. Fellow, Catholic Univ. of Chile, 1998. Dr *hc* State Inst. for Internat. Relations, Moscow, 1998. Robert Schuman Medal; Gold Medal, City of Athens; Order of Francisco Morazán (Central American Parlt), 1997; Silver Medal of Galicia, 2000. Medalla del Mérito Agrícola (Spain); Grand Cross, Order of Isabel la Católica (Spain), 2000; Order of European Merit (Spain), 2006; Medal of the Republic (Uruguay), 1998; Grand Cross: Order of Merit (Chile), 1998; Order of Liberator San Martin (Argentina), 1998; Order Antonio José de Irizarri (Guatemala), 1999; Officer, Legion of Honour (France), 2000. *Publications*: Derecho de huelga, 1961; Commentarios a la ley de arrendamientos rústicos, 1981; Legislación agraria básica, 1986; Control y autonomías, 1986; Los derechos del europeo, 1993; Los Parlamentos de Europa y el Parlamento Europeo, 1997; Pasión por Europa, 2002. *Recreations*: reading, golf.

**GILBERD, Rt Rev. Bruce Carlyle,** CNZM 2002; Bishop of Auckland, 1985–94; Chaplain, King's School, Remuera, 1997–2000; retired; *b* 22 April 1938; *s* of Carlyle Bond Gilberd and Dorothy Annie Gilberd; *m* 1963, Patricia Molly Tanton; two *s* one *d*. *Educ*: King's College, Auckland; Auckland Univ. (BSc); St John's Coll., Auckland (LTh Hons, STh). Deacon 1962, priest 1963, Auckland; Assistant Curate: Devonport, 1962–64; Ponsonby and Grey Lynn, 1965; Panmure, 1965–68; Vicar of Avondale, 1968–71; trainee Industrial Chaplain, Tees-side Industrial Mission, and Asst Curate of Egglescliffe, 1971–73; visited industrial missions in UK and Europe; Director, Interchurch Trade and Industrial Mission, Wellington, 1973–79; founding Mem., Wellington Industrial Relations Soc.; Hon. Asst Curate, Lower Hutt 1973–77, Waiwhetu 1977–79; Lectr, St John's Coll., Auckland, 1980–85; Priest-in-charge, Albany Greenhithe Mission Dist, 1995, St Thomas, Tamaki, 1996, dio. of Auckland. Pres., Christian Res. Assoc., Aotearoa, NZ, 1996–2000; Vice-Pres., Home and Family Soc., 1986–. Mem. Gen. Synod, NZ. Has travelled widely in UK, Europe, China, USA, S Africa and Pacific. NZ Commemorative Medal, 1990. *Publications*: (ed) Christian Ministry: a definition, 1984; (with Richard Whitfield) Taproots for Transformation, 2006; Future Focus, 2007; Life - is there more?, 2011; Guarding Paaku Bay, 2012; Ka the Falcon, 2014; Two Prayers for Today, 2018. *Recreations*: fishing, travel, reading, writing, golf. *Address*: 81 Manaia Road, Tairua, 3508, New Zealand.

**GILBERT;** *see* Proesch, G.

**GILBERT OF PANTEG,** Baron *cr* 2015 (Life Peer), of Panteg in the County of Monmouthshire; **Stephen Gilbert.** Political Sec. to the Prime Minister, 2010–15; Dep. Chm., Cons. Party, 2015. Mem., Electoral Commn, 2018–.

**GILBERT, Prof. Fiona Jane,** FRCR, FRCPE, FRCPGlas; Professor of Radiology, and Head, Department of Radiology, University of Cambridge, since 2011; *b* Edinburgh, 1 May 1956; *d* of Dr John Knight Davidson and Edith Elizabeth Davidson; *m* 1982, Martin James Gilbert, *qv*; one *s* two *d*. *Educ*: Hutchesons' Girls' Grammar Sch., Glasgow; Univ. of Glasgow (MB ChB 1982); Univ. of Aberdeen (DMRD 1984). MRCP 1981; FRCR 1986; FRCPGlas 1991; FRCPE 1994. Consultant Radiologist, Aberdeen Royal Infirmary, 1989–96; University of Aberdeen: Hon. Sen. Lectr, 1989–96; Prof. of Radiol. and Hd, Dept of Radiol., 1996–2006; Hd, Imaging Res. Prog., 2006–11; Clin. Dir, NE Scotland Breast Screening Prog., 1989–2001. Chairman: RCR Breast Gp, 2009–11; Academic Cttee, RCR, 2010. Mem. Bd, Royal Scottish Nat. Orch., 2002–08. Gov., Robert Gordon's Coll., Aberdeen, 1998–2011. *Publications*: articles in New England Jl of Medicine,

Lancet Oncol., Health Technol. Assessment. *Recreations*: ski-ing, sailing, classical music. *Address*: Department of Radiology, University of Cambridge, Box 218, Level 5, Addenbrooke's Hospital, Hills Road, Cambridge CB2 0QQ. *T*: (01223) 336890, *Fax*: (01223) 330915.

**GILBERT, His Honour Francis Humphrey Shubrick;** QC 1992; a Circuit Judge, 2001–16; *b* 25 Jan. 1946; *s* of late Comdr Walter Raleigh Gilbert, RN, DL, Compton Castle, Devon and Joan Mary Boileau Gilbert; *m* 1975, Sarah Marian Kaye, *d* of late Col Douglas Kaye, DSO, DL, Brinkley Hall, Newmarket; one *s* two *d*. *Educ*: Stowe; Trinity Coll., Dublin (MA). Called to the Bar, Lincoln's Inn, 1970, Bencher, 2000. A Recorder, 1994–2001; Hd of Chambers, 1995–2001; Res. Judge, Plymouth Crown Court, 2006–12; Recorder of Exeter, 2012–16. Devon County Councillor, 1977–85. Pres., Pegasus Club, 2001. *Recreations*: sailing, shooting and gardening.

**GILBERT, Prof. (Geoffrey) Nigel,** CBE 2016; PhD, ScD; CEng, FREng; FAcSS; FBCS; Professor of Sociology, 1991–2016, and Distinguished Professor of Computational Social Science, since 2019, University of Surrey; *b* Birmingham, 21 March 1950; *s* of Geoffrey Alan Gilbert and Lilo Maria Gilbert (*née* Czigler); *m* 2018, Lu Yang; two *d*. *Educ*: King Edward's Sch., Birmingham; Emmanuel Coll., Cambridge (Exhibnr and IBM Schol.; BA Engrg Tripos 1971); PhD 1976, ScD 2003, Cantab. CEng 1990. Lectr in Sociol., Univ. of York, 1974–76; University of Surrey: Lectr in Sociol., 1976–84; Reader in Sociol., 1984–91; Pro Vice-Chancellor, 1997–2005; Dir, Inst. of Advanced Studies, 2004–. Mem., UKRI-ESRC, 2017–. Dir, CECAN Ltd, 2018–. FBCS 1997; FREng 1999; FAcSS 2000; FRSA 2004. *Publications*: Modelling Society: an introduction to loglinear analysis for social researchers, 1981; (ed with P. Abell) Accounts and Action, 1983; (with M. Mulkay) Opening Pandora's Box: sociological analysis of scientists' discourse, 1984 (trans. Russian and Japanese); (ed with C. Heath) Social Action and Artificial Intelligence, 1985; (ed jtly) Computers and Conversation, 1991; (ed with S. Arber) Women and Working Lives: divisions and change, 1991; (ed jtly) Fordism and Flexibility: divisions and change, 1991 (trans. Japanese); (ed) Researching Social Life, 1992, 4th edn (with P. Stoneman), 2015; Analyzing Tabular Data: loglinear and logistic models for social researchers, 1993; (ed with J. Doran) Simulating Societies: the computer simulation of social phenomena, 1994; (ed with B. Conte) Artificial Societies: the computer simulation of social life, 1995; (ed with A. F. Monk) Perspectives on HCI: diverse approaches, 1995; (ed jtly) Social Science Microsimulation, 1996; (jtly) Humans, Computers and Wizards: studying human (simulated) computer interaction, 1997; (ed with P. Ahrweiler) Computer Simulations in Science and Technology Studies, 1998; (ed jtly) Multi-agent Systems and Agent-based Simulation, 1998; (with K. G. Troitzsch) Simulation for the Social Scientist, 1999, 2nd edn 2005 (trans. Russian, Japanese and Spanish); (ed jtly) Tools and Techniques for Social Science Simulation, 2000; (with J. Fielding) Understanding Social Statistics, 2000, 2nd edn 2005; (ed with S. Dresner) The Dynamics of European Science and Technology Policies, 2001; (ed) From Postgraduate to Social Scientist: a guide to key skills, 2006; Agent Based Models, 2008, 2nd edn 2019; (ed) Computational Social Science, 4 vols, 2010; (with G. Deffuant) Viability and Resilience of Complex Systems: concepts, methods and case studies from ecology and society, 2011; (with C. Eisenbroich) Modelling Norms, 2013; (ed jtly) Simulating Knowledge Dynamics in Innovation Networks, 2014; (with C. Watts) Simulating Innovation: computer-based tools for rethinking innovation, 2014; (with L. Hamill) Agent-Based Modelling in Economics, 2016; (jtly) Joining Complexity Science and Social Simulation for Innovation Policy, 2016; (jtly) Social Dimensions of Organised Crime, 2016; contribs to Amer. Jl Sociol., Amer. Behavioral Scientist. *Recreations*: family, writing computer software. *Address*: University of Surrey, Guildford, Surrey GU2 7XH. *T*: (01483) 300800. *E*: n.gilbert@surrey.ac.uk.

**GILBERT, Rt Rev. Hugh;** *see* Aberdeen, Bishop of, (RC).

**GILBERT, Ian Grant;** Under Secretary, International Relations Division, Department of Health and Social Security, 1979–85; retired; *b* Kikuyu, Kenya, 18 June 1925; *s* of Captain Alexander Grant Gilbert, DCM, indust. missionary, Lossiemouth and Kenya, and Marion Patrick Cruickshank; *m* 1st, 1960, Heather Margaret Donald, PhD (*d* 1999) (biographer of Lord Mount Stephen), *y d* of Rev. Francis Cantlie and Mary Donald, Lumphanan, Aberdeenshire; 2nd, 2001, Mrs Shirley Ann Parr. *Educ*: Fordyce Acad., Banffshire; Royal High Sch. of Edinburgh; Univ. of Edinburgh (MA 1950). Served HM Forces (Captain Indian Artillery), 1943–47. Entered Home Civil Service as Asst Principal and joined Min. of National Insurance, 1950; Private Sec. to Perm. Sec., 1953, and to Parly Sec., 1955; Principal, Min. of Pensions and Nat. Insce, 1956; seconded to HM Treasury, 1962–66; Asst Sec., Min. of Social Security (later DHSS), 1967; Head of War and Civilian Disabled Branches, DHSS, 1974–79. UK Member: Social Security, Health and Social Affairs Cttees, Council of Europe, Strasbourg, 1979–85; EEC Adv. Cttee on Social Security for Migrant Workers, Brussels, 1979–85; UK Delegate, Governing Body, Internat. Soc. Security Assoc., Geneva, 1979–85; Mem., UK Delegn to World Health Assembly, Geneva, 1983–84; Clerk/Advr to Select Cttee on European Legislation, House of Commons, 1987–90. Hon. Treasurer, Presbytery of England (Church of Scotland), 1965–77; Session Clerk, Crown Court Ch. of Scotland, Covent Garden, 1975–80. A Ch. of Scotland Mem., The Churches Main Cttee, 1986–2002. Chm., Caledonian Christian Club, 1984–86. Clerk to Govs, St Gregory's Sch., Marnhull, 1991–2002. *Recreations*: keeping half-an-acre in good heart, local and natural history, choral singing, France. *Address*: Wellpark, Moorside, Sturminster Newton, Dorset DT10 1HJ. *T*: (01258) 820306.

**GILBERT, Air Chief Marshal Sir Joseph (Alfred),** KCB 1985 (CB 1983); CBE 1974; Deputy Commander-in-Chief, Allied Forces Central Europe, 1986–89; retired; *b* 15 June 1931; *s* of late Ernest and Mildred Gilbert; *m* 1955, Betty, *yr d* of late William and Eva Lishman; two *d*. *Educ*: William Hulme's Sch., Manchester; Univ. of Leeds (BA Hons, Econ. and Pol Science; Hon. LLD 1989). Commnd into RAF, 1952; Fighter Sqdns, 1953–61; Air Secretary's Dept, 1961–63; RAF Staff Coll., 1964; CO 92 (Lightning) Sqdn, 1965–67; jssc 1968; Sec., Defence Policy Staff, and Asst Dir of Defence Policy, 1968–71; CO, RAF Coltishall, 1971–73; RCDS, 1974; Dir of Forward Policy (RAF), 1975; ACAS (Policy), MoD, 1975–77; AOC 38 Group, 1977–80; ACDS (Policy), 1980–82; Asst Chief of Staff (Policy), SHAPE, 1983–84; Dep. C-in-C, RAF Strike Command, 1984–86. Vice Chm., Commonwealth War Graves Commn, 1993–98 (Comr, 1991–98); Trustee, Imperial War Mus., 1997–2002. Life Vice-Pres., RAFA, 1995. *Publications*: articles in defence jls. *Recreations*: grandchildren, Rugby, strategic affairs. *Address*: 56 Shackleton Place, Bath Road, Devizes, Wilts SN10 2GZ. *Club*: Royal Air Force.

**GILBERT, Martin James,** CA; Vice-Chairman, Standard Life Aberdeen, since 2019 (Co-Chief Executive, 2017–19); *b* 13 July 1955; *m* 1982, Prof. Fiona Jane Davidson (*see* F. J. Gilbert); one *s* two *d*. *Educ*: Robert Gordon's Coll.; Aberdeen Univ. (MA, LLB). CA 1983. Deloitte Haskins & Sells, 1978–82; Brander & Cruickshank, 1982–83; Chief Exec., Aberdeen Asset Management, 1991–2017; Director: Aberdeen Asian Smaller Co. Investment Trust, 1995–; Aberdeen Global, 1998; Aberdeen Asia Pacific Income Fund, 2000. Non-executive Director: FirstBus, then FirstGroup, 1995–2013 (non-exec. Chm., 2000–13); Sky (formerly BSkyB), 2011–18 (Dep. Chm., 2016–18); Glencore, 2017–. Chm., Prudential Regulation Authy Practitioner Panel, 2013–; Member: Internat. Adv. Panel, Monetary Authy of Singapore, 2013; Financial Services Trade and Investment Bd,

2013–15. Jun. Vice-Pres., ICAS, 2002–03. FRSE 2017. *Recreations:* golf, ski-ing, sailing. *Address:* Standard Life Aberdeen, Standard Life House, 30 Lothian Road, Edinburgh EH1 2DH. *Clubs:* Royal Thames Yacht; Gordonians Hockey (Aberdeen); Leander; Royal & Ancient Golf (St Andrews); Royal Aberdeen Golf; Wimbledon Golf; Royal Selangor Golf; Deeside Golf; Loch Lomond Golf.

**GILBERT, Nigel;** *see* Gilbert, G. N.

**GILBERT, Penny Xenia;** Partner, Powell Gilbert LLP, since 2007; *b* W Bromwich, 7 Jan. 1960; *d* of Raymond and Madge Gilbert; *m* 1991, Dr John Whittaker; one *s* one *d*. *Educ:* Colfox Sch., Bridport, Dorset; Brasenose Coll., Oxford (BA Biochem. 1982; DPhil Molecular Biol. 1987); Coll. of Law, London; Bristol Univ. (Dip. Intellectual Property Law and Practice 1993). Departmental Demonstrator, Sir William Dunn Sch. of Pathology, Univ. of Oxford, 1985–86. Admitted as solicitor, 1991; Bristows: tech. asst, 1986–87; articled clerk, 1989–91; solicitor, 1991–97; Partner, 1997–2007. Accredited Mediator, 2004; Solicitor Advocate, 2005. Tutor, Dip. in Intellectual Property Law and Practice, Univ. of Oxford. Mem., Wkg Gp on Unjustified Threats, Law Commn, 2013–15. European Patent Lawyers Association: Mem., Bd of Dirs, 2009–16; Pres., 2015–16; Mem., Adv. Bd, 2016–. Mem., Academic Adv. Bd, Eur. Patent Acad., Eur. Patent Office, 2016–18. Mem. Cttee, Brasenose Soc., 2016– (Vice Pres., 2016–17; Pres., 2017–18). *Publications:* case reports and articles in relation to patent law and life sciences. *Recreations:* family, art, reading, travel, garden. *Address:* Powell Gilbert LLP, 85 Fleet Street, EC4Y 1AE. *T:* (020) 3040 8000, *Fax:* (020) 3040 8001. *E:* penny.gilbert@powellgilbert.com.

**GILBERT, Rev. Canon Roger Geoffrey;** Rector of Falmouth, 1986–2002; Chaplain to the Queen, 1995–2002; *b* 18 June 1937; *s* of Geoffrey and Ruth Gilbert; *m* 1965, Marie-Pascale (*née* Berthelot); three *d*. *Educ:* Truro Secondary Modern Sch. for Boys; St Peter's Coll., Birmingham; King's Coll. London (BD; AKC); St Augustine's Coll., Canterbury. RAF, 1957–59. Asst Master, Hinchley Wood Sch., 1963–67; ordained deacon, 1970, priest, 1971; Asst Curate, Walton-on-Thames, 1970–74; Licensed to Officiate, Dio. of Europe, 1973–; Rector, St Mabyn with Helland, 1974–81; Priest-in-charge, Madron with Morvah, 1981–86. Hon. Canon of Truro Cathedral, 1994–2002, now Emeritus; Rural Dean of Carnmarth South, 1994–2000. Fellow, Woodard Corp., 1988–2002. *Recreations:* travel, Cornish-Breton history and culture, post-Impressionist painters, antiques, books. *Address:* 2 rue de Plouzon, 22690 Pleudihen-sur-Rance, Brittany, France. *T:* (2) 96882869.

**GILBERT, Stephen;** *b* Truro, 6 Nov. 1976. *Educ:* Fowey Community Sch.; St Austell Coll.; Univ. of Wales, Aberystwyth (BSc Econ Internat. Politics); London Sch. of Econs and Pol Sci. (MSc Internat. Relns). Parly asst to Lembit Öpik, MP, 1998; res. and media asst to Robin Teverson, MEP, 1998–99; Account Exec., PPS, 2000–02; Public Affairs Manager: IMA, 2002–04; Fidelity Investments, 2004–05; Account Manager, Deborah Clark Associates, 2005–07. Member (Lib Dem): Restormel BC, 1998–2002; Haringey LBC, 2002–06. MP (Lib Dem) St Austell and Newquay, 2010–15; contested (Lib Dem) same seat, 2015. Mem., Communities and Local Govt Select Cttee, 2010–12; PPS to Sec. of State for Energy and Climate Change, 2012–13.

**GILBERT, Prof. Walter;** Carl M. Loeb University Professor, Department of Molecular and Cellular Biology (formerly of Cellular and Developmental Biology), Harvard University, 1987–2001, now Carl M. Loeb Professor Emeritus; Joint Founder and Vice Chairman, Myriad Genetics Inc., since 1992; Partner, BioVentures Investors; *b* Boston, 21 March 1932; *s* of Richard V. Gilbert and Emma (*née* Cohen); *m* 1953, Celia Stone; one *s* one *d*. *Educ:* Harvard Coll. (AB *summa cum laude* Chem. and Phys., 1953); Harvard Univ. (AM Phys., 1954); Cambridge Univ. (PhD Maths, 1957). National Science Foundn pre-doctoral Fellow, Harvard Univ. and Cambridge Univ., 1953–57, post-doctoral Fellow in Phys., Harvard, 1957–58; Harvard University: Asst Prof. in Phys., 1959–64; Associate Prof. of Biophys., 1964–68; Prof. of Biochem., 1968–72; Amer. Cancer Soc. Prof. of Molecular Biology, 1972–81; H. H. Timken Prof. of Science, 1986–87. Jt Founder, 1978, and Dir, 1978–84, Biogen NV (Chm. and Principal Exec. Officer, 1981–84). Guggenheim Fellow, Paris, 1968–69. Member: Amer. Acad. of Arts and Sciences, 1968; National Acad. of Sciences, 1976; Amer. Phys. Soc.; Amer. Soc. of Biol Chemists; Foreign Mem., Royal Soc., 1987–. Hon. DSc: Chicago, 1978; Columbia, 1978; Rochester, 1979; Yeshiva, 1981; Tulane, 2011. Many prizes and awards, incl. (jtly) Nobel Prize for Chemistry, 1980. *Publications:* chapters, articles and papers on theoretical physics and molecular biology, and catalogues and work on photographic art. *Address:* BioVentures Investors, 70 Walnut Street # 302, Wellesley, MA 02481, USA; 15 Gray Gardens West, Cambridge, MA 02138, USA. *T:* (617) 5157212. *W:* wallygilbert.com.

**GILBERTSON, Barry Gordon;** Chairman, City of Bath UNESCO World Heritage Site, since 2017; President, Royal Institution of Chartered Surveyors, 2004–05; *b* 6 June 1951; *s* of Bertram David Gilbertson and Joan Marion Ivy Gilbertson (*née* Gordon); *m* 1974, Yvonne Gunning; one *s*. *Educ:* Westcliff High Sch. for Boys; Coll. of Estate Management. FRICS 1974; ACIArb 1976; Registered Property (formerly Fixed Charge) Receiver 1999–2011; Counselor of Real Estate 2000–17. Partner, Butler & Hatch Waterman, 1983–86; Dir, Cherrydeal Ltd, 1986–87; Man. Dir, Claridge Gp, 1988–91; Nat. Property Advr, Coopers & Lybrand, 1992–96; Partner, PricewaterhouseCoopers, 1996–2011; Principal, Barry Gilbertson Consultancy, 2011–17. Mem., Bank of England Property Forum, 2003–11. Ind. non-exec. Dir and Trustee, Granite REIT (formerly MI Develts Inc., then Granite Real Estate Inc.), 2011–17 (Chm., Real Estate Investment Cttee, 2012–13; Chm., Compensation Cttee, 2014–16; Chm., Corporate Governance and Nomination Cttee, 2016–17); Independent non-executive Director: RONA Inc., 2013–15; Custodian REIT plc, 2014– (Sen. Ind. Dir, 2014–; Chm., Mgt Engagement Cttee, 2014–; Chm., Remuneration Cttee, 2018–); Ind. non-exec. Chm., convert Immobilien Invest SE, 2015–16. Non-exec. Consultant, Knight Frank LLP, 2011–12. Mem., UN Real Estate Adv. Gp, 2000–05 (Chm., Valuation Cttee, 2003–05). Fellow: Property Consultants Soc., 1987; Non-Administrative Receivers Assoc., 1995–2016 (Founding Chm., 1995–96); Internat. Real Estate Fedn, 2003 (Mem., 2002–05); Founding Dep. Chm., World Assoc. of Valuation Orgns, 2002–04. Internat. Associate Ed., Counselors of Real Estate, 2006–08. Trustee, Coll. of Estate Mgt, 2006–14 (Chm., Internat. Adv. Gp, 2008–11; Chm., Business Adv. Gp, 2011–13). Visiting Professor: of Architecture and Built Envmt, Univ. of Northumbria, 2003–; of Real Estate and Land Mgt, Royal Agricultural Univ., 2014–. Gov., Mem. Council and Court, Univ. of Bath, 2014– (Mem., Fire Safety Rev. Panel, 2017–18; Chm., Remuneration Cttee, 2018–). Governor: Sidney Street Primary Sch., Folkestone, 1987–90; Westcliff High Sch. for Boys, 2007–08. Mem., Nat. Scout Adv. Bd, Scout Assoc., 1983–87. Dir, Cranmer Court Tenants (Chelsea) Ltd, 2006–12. Chm., Bath World Heritage Enhancement Fund, 2017–; Mem., World Heritage UK, 2017–; Chm., Circus Area Residents' Assoc., 2016–; Mem., Fedn of Bath Residents' Assocs, 2016–19 (Mem. Exec., 2017–19); Trustee: Bath Preservation Trust, 2016–17 (Mem., Mus and Educn Cttee, 2016–17; Mem., Architecture and Planning Cttee, 2015–17; Chm., Historic Vaults Gp, 2015–17); F. G. Cooke Charity, 2016–18. Hon. Surveyor, St John's Foundn, Established 1174, 2016–18. Trustee, Fulham FC Supporters Trust, 2012–14. FICPD 1998; MInstD 1983; FRSA 2009. Hon. Member: Assoc. of S African Quantity Surveyors, 2005; S African Council for Quantity Surveying Profession, 2005; Assoc. of Valuers in Romania, 2006; Assoc. of Property and Fixed Charge Receivers,

2010. Mem., MENSA, 1976–; Folkestone Junior Chamber of Commerce, 1975–85 (Pres., 1979; SE Regl Chm., 1985). Pres., Rotary Clube of Folkestone, 2003 (Mem., 1990–2004); Mem., Committee Club, 2002– (Hon. Sec., 2008–18); Chm., Property & Finance Gp, 2010–15. Freeman, City of London, 1996; Liveryman, Co. of Chartered Surveyors, 1996–2016. *Publications:* Vision for Valuation, 2004; RICS Presidential Nuggets, 2007; (jtly) Design Economics and Sustainability, 2015; (jtly) Making Changes: a guide for owners of listed buildings in England, 2017; travelogues and book reviews; contrib. articles to learned jls in UK and abroad. *Recreations:* family and friends, jogging, black and white digital photography, Fulham Football Club, Bath Rugby Club, the arts and architecture (especially Georgian), fun, oh, and of course, The Archers! *Address:* 12 Gay Street, Bath, Somerset BA1 2PH. *T:* 07710 073456. *E:* barry@barrygilbertson.com.

**GILBERTSON, Prof. David Dennis;** Emeritus Professor, University of Wales, since 1998; *b* Stratford, London, 1 Sept. 1945; *s* of late Thomas Gilbertson and of Ivy Florence Joyce Gilbertson; *m* 1970, Barbara Mary Mitchell; one *s* two *d*. *Educ:* South West Ham Tech. Sch.; Univ. of Lancaster (BA Hons 1968); Univ. of Exeter (PGCE 1969); Univ. of Bristol (PhD 1974; DSc 1991). FGS 1983. Teacher, Pretoria Sch., London, 1964–65; Res. Asst in Geology, Univ. of Bristol, 1969–71; Lectr in Geography, Plymouth Poly., 1971–74, Univ. of Adelaide, 1974–77; Sheffield University: Lectr, 1977–85; Sen. Lectr, 1985–88; Reader, 1988–92; Prof., and Hd of Res. Sch. of Archaeology and Archaeol Scis, 1992–94; Prof. of Physical Geography, Inst. of Geography and Earth Scis, and Dir, Inst. of Earth Studies, 1994–97, Univ. of Wales, Aberystwyth, 1994–98; Prof. of Envmtl Science, Nene Centre for Res., UC Northampton, 1998–2000; Hd, Sch. of Conservation Scis, Bournemouth Univ., 2000–02. Vis. Prof. and Fulbright Schol., Univ. of Arizona, 1981–82; Munro Lectr, Edinburgh Univ., 1999; Dist. Vis. Schol., Adelaide Univ., 1999; Visiting Professor: Univ. of Plymouth, 2001–; Bournemouth Univ., 2015–. Co-Director: UNESCO Libyan Valleys Archaeol Survey, 1988–96; Wadi Faynan Survey, Jordan, 1994–2007; Niah Caves Proj., Borneo, 1998–; Chm., Univ. of Wales Subject Panel for Envmtl Studies, 1996–98. Jt Founder and Associate Ed., Applied Geography, 1981–88; Sen. UK Ed., 1992–98, Ed. Emeritus, 2009, Jl of Archaeol Sci. J. R. Wiseman Prize, Archaeol Inst. of Amer., 2001. *Publications:* (jtly) The Pleistocene Succession at Kenn, Somerset, 1978; (jtly) In the Shadow of Extinction, 1984; Late Quaternary Environments and Man in Holderness, 1984; (jtly) Practical Ecology, 1985; (jtly) The Chronology and Environment of Early Man: a new framework, 1985; (jtly) Farming the Desert: the UNESCO Libyan Valley survey, 1996; (jtly) The Outer Hebrides: the last 14000 years, 1996; (ed jtly) The Archaeology of Drylands: living on the margins, 2000; The Human Use of Caves in Island and Peninsula South East Asia, 2005; Archaeology and Desertification, 2007; contribs to books, and papers in learned jls. *Recreations:* walking, railways—large and small, West Ham United, the Teign Estuary. *Address:* c/o School of Geography, Earth and Environmental Sciences, University of Plymouth, Drake Circus, Plymouth PL4 8AA. *E:* dave.gilbertson@plymouth.ac.uk.

**GILBERTSON, David Stuart;** Chairman: Compliance Online (formerly Gambling Compliance), since 2012; Concerto Group, 2015–17; Communisis plc, since 2017; *b* 21 Sept. 1956; *s* of Donald Stuart Gilbertson and Jocelyn Mary Gilbertson (*née* Sim); *m* 1991, Danielle Donougher; one *s* one *d*. *Educ:* Trinity Hall, Cambridge (BA 1978). Editl and mgt posts with Metal Bulletin, Reuters and Reed Elsevier; joined LLP, 1987: Ed., Lloyd's List, 1987–94; Dir, 1992–96; Chief Exec., 1997–98; Chief Exec., 1998–2004, Man. Dir, 2004–07, Informa Gp plc; Chief Executive: Informa plc, 2007–08; EMAP plc, 2008–11. Chairman: MLex Mkt Intelligence, 2012–15; Briefing Media Ltd, 2013–15; non-exec. Dir, Sigaria, 2012–14; Sen. Ind. Dir, Tarsus Gp, 2014–. Chairman: Green Power Conferences, 2012–; Old St Labs, 2014–. Business Gov., City and Islington Coll., 2011–17. FRSA. *Recreations:* sport, especially football.

**GILBERTSON, Ven. Dr Michael Robert;** Archdeacon of Chester, since 2010; *b* Stockport, 18 Aug. 1961; *s* of late John and Beryl Gilbertson; *m* 1985, Jenny Gates; two *s*. *Educ:* Stockport Grammar Sch.; New Coll., Oxford (BA Hons 1982; MA 1992); St John's Coll., Durham (BA Hons 1993; PhD 1997). Department of Trade and Industry: Admin trainee, 1982–84; Higher Exec. Officer (Develt), Regl Policy Div. and Cabinet Office, 1984–85; Private Sec. to Sec. of State for Trade and Industry, 1985–87; Principal, Eur. Policy Div., 1987–89, Radiocommunications Agency, 1989–91; ordained deacon, 1997, priest, 1998; Curate, St Matthew's, Surbiton, 1997–2000; Vicar, All Saints, Stranton, Hartlepool, 2000–10; Area Dean of Hartlepool, 2002–10. Non-residentiary Canon, Durham Cathedral, 2008–10; Mem. of Chapter, Chester Cathedral, 2017–. Mem., Gen. Synod, C of E, 2015–. Trustee, Melanesian Mission UK, 2017–. Dir, Grove Bks Ltd, 1997–2000; Ed., Anvil, 1998–2003. *Publications:* God and History in the Book of Revelation: New Testament studies in dialogue with Pannenberg and Moltmann, 2003. *Recreations:* music, watching sport, hill-walking, cooking. *Address:* c/o Church House, 5500 Daresbury Park, Daresbury, Cheshire WA4 4GE. *T:* (01928) 718834.

**GILBEY,** family name of **Baron Vaux of Harrowden**.

**GILBEY, Sir (Walter) Gavin,** 4th Bt *cr* 1893, of Elsenham Hall, Essex; *b* 14 April 1949; *s* of Sir (Walter) Derek Gilbey, 3rd Bt and of Elizabeth Mary, *d* of Col K. G. Campbell; *s* father, 1991, but his name does not yet appear on the Official Roll of the Baronetage; *m* 1st, 1980, Mary (marr. diss. 1984), *d* of late William E. E. Pacetti; 2nd, 1984, Anna (marr. diss. 1995), *d* of Edmund Prosser; one adopted *s*. *Educ:* Eton. Director: Gilbey's Internat. Inc.; Great British Food Inc. *Clubs:* Army and Navy; Royal Dornoch Golf.

**GILCHRIST, Andrew Charles;** National Education Officer, Rail, Maritime and Transport Union, since 2010; *b* 5 Dec. 1960; *s* of late Edward Gilchrist and of Shirley Gilchrist; *m* 1985, Loretta Borman; one *s* one *d*. *Educ:* Bedford Modern Sch. Bedfordshire Fire Service, 1979–96; Mem., Exec. Council, 1993–2000, Nat. Officer, 1996–2000, Gen. Sec., 2000–05, Fire Bde Union; UK Co-ordinator: Service Employees Internat. Union, 2006–08; Internat. Brotherhood Teamsters, 2006–08; Project Manager, 2008, Internat. Progs Co-ordinator, 2009–10, Unite. Mem., Gen. Council, TUC 2000–05 (Mem., Exec. Cttee, 2004–05). *Recreations:* global politics, classical history, aquariums, Luton Town FC. *E:* painewon@msn.com.

**GILCHRIST, Maj. Gen. Peter,** CB 2004; non-executive Chairman, Enterprise Control Systems Ltd, since 2012; Director, Synergie Global Ltd, since 2012; *b* 28 Feb. 1952; *s* of late Col David A. Gilchrist and Rosemary Gilchrist (*née* Drewe); *m* 1981, Sarah-Jane Poyntz; one *s* one *d*. *Educ:* Marlborough Coll.; Sandhurst. Commnd Royal Tank Regiment, 1972; Troop Leader, 3RTR, Germany and NI, 1972–76; aic 1977; Schools Gunnery Instructor, Lulworth, 1978–80; Ops Officer and Adjutant, 3RTR, 1980–82; Div. II, Army Staff Course (psc†), 1983–84; COS, 20th Armd Bde, 1985–87; Comdr, Ind. Recce Sqn, Cyprus, 1986; Sqn Comdr (Challenger), 3RTR, 1988; Mil. Sec.'s Staff, 1989; Directing Staff, RMCS, 1990–93; CO, 1 RTR, 1993–95; HCSC, 1996; Dep. DOR (Armour and Combat Support Vehicles), 1996–98; Prog. Dir, Armd Systems, MoD PE, 1998–2000; Exec. Dir, 2000–04, Tech. Dir, 2004, Defence Procurement Agency, and Master Gen. of the Ordnance; Dep. Comdr Combined Forces Comd, Afghanistan, 2004–05; Defence Attaché, Washington, and Hd, British Defence Staff, USA, 2005–08; retd 2009. Col Comdt, RAC, 2000–04; Dep. Col Comdt, RTR, 2000–08. Non-executive Director: DERA Facilities Bd, 2000–01; DSTL, 2001–04; Push Technology Ltd, 2009–18; Ricardo plc, 2010– (Sen.

Ind. Dir, 2015–; Chm., Remuneration Cttee, 2013–); Chm., Electranet Gp Ltd, 2010–12. Chm., Tank Mus., 2010–18. Bronze Star Medal (USA), 2006. *Recreations:* sailing, ski-ing, field sports, gardening, DIY. *Address:* Chapel Cottage, Netherhope Lane, Tidenham, Chepstow, Mon NP16 7JD. *Club:* Army and Navy.

GILCHRIST, Prof. Roberta Lynn, DPhil; FSA; FBA 2008; Professor of Archaeology, since 1996, and Research Dean, since 2016, University of Reading; *b* 28 June 1965; *d* of John James Gilchrist and Gail Ann Foreman (*née* Campbell); *m* 2000, Dr John Miles Preston. *Educ:* Univ. of York (BA 1986; DPhil 1990). MCIfA (MIFA 1990). Lectr, UEA, 1990–95; Archaeologist, Norwich Cathedral, 1993–2005. Ed., World Archaeol., 1997–2006; Mem., Editl Bd, Social Archaeol., 1999–. Acad. Advr, Mus. of London Archaeol. Service, 1991–2015. TV presenter, Down to Earth, 1991–92. Member: Adv. Bd for Redundant Churches, 1998–2001; Ancient Monuments Adv. Cttee, English Heritage, 1998–2001. Member: Churches Cttee, Council for British Archaeol., 1989–95; Archaeol. Section Cttee, 2009–11, Pubns Cttee, 2010–16, British Acad.; Council: Soc. for Medieval Archaeol., 1990–93 (Pres., 2004–07); Inst. of Field Archaeol., 1992–98; British Archaeol Assoc., 1995–98; Soc. of Antiquaries of London, 2007–10 (Mem., Res. Cttee, 2008–11). Trustee: Glastonbury Abbey, 2009–; Antiquity, 2016–. Keeley Fellow, Wadham Coll., Oxford, 2008–09. Hon. Fellow, Jesus Coll., Cambridge, 2018. FSA 2002. Martyn Jope Prize, Soc. for Medieval Archaeol., 2008; Archaeologist of the Year, Current Archaeology Awards, 2016. *Publications:* Gender and Material Culture: the archaeology of religious women, 1994; Contemplation and Action: the other monasticism, 1995; Gender and Archaeology: contesting the past, 1999; Norwich Cathedral Close: the evolution of the English cathedral landscape, 2005 (Outstanding Acad. Title Award, Choice, 2007); (with B. Sloane) Requiem: the medieval monastic cemetery in Britain, 2005 (Scholarly Pubn Award, British Archaeol Awards, 2006); Medieval Life: archaeology and the life course, 2012; (with C. Green) Glastonbury Abbey: archaeological investigations, 1904–1979, 2015; contrib. articles to World Archaeol., Antiquity, Medieval Archaeol., Archaeol Jl, Jl British Archaeol Assoc., Annual Rev. of Anthropology. *Recreations:* singing, walking, gardening, cats, travel, food and wine. *Address:* Department of Archaeology, University of Reading, Whiteknights, Reading RG6 6AB. *T:* (0118) 931 6381, *Fax:* (0118) 931 6718. *E:* r.l.gilchrist@reading.ac.uk.

GILCHRIST, Susan; Chair, Global Clients, Brunswick Group, since 2018; *b* London, 26 May 1966; *d* of Robert David Gilchrist and Constance May Gilchrist (*née* Hodgson); *m* 2007, Andrew Roberts, *qv*; one step *s* one step *d*. *Educ:* Millfield Sch.; King's Coll., London (BA 1st Cl. Hons Eng. Lang. and Lit. 1987; FKC 2014). Mgt Consultant, Bain & Co., 1987–91; journalist: Mail on Sunday, 1991–93; The Times, 1993–95; Brunswick Group: Associate Partner, 1995–96; Partner, 1996–2005; Sen. Partner, London, 2005–10; US Man. Partner, 2010–12; Gp Chief Exec., 2012–18. Gov. (pt-time), Southbank Centre, 2008– (Chm., 2016–); Mem. Bd, Old Vic, 2015. Mem., London Campaign Bd, KCL, 2015–. *Recreations:* music, art, theatre, literature, women in business. *Address:* Brunswick Group, 16 Lincoln's Inn Fields, WC2A 3ED. *T:* (020) 7404 5959. *E:* sgilchrist@brunswickgroup.com.

GILCHRIST, William Alexander; Sheriff of Tayside, Central and Fife at Stirling, since 2006; *b* 15 Nov. 1951; *s* of William Gilchrist and Helen Lang Gilchrist (*née* Thomson). *Educ:* Stirling High Sch.; Edinburgh Univ. (LLB). Admitted solicitor, 1976; Crown Office and Procurator Fiscal Service, 1976–2006: Regl Procurator Fiscal, N Strathclyde, 1998–2002; Dep. Crown Agent, 2002–05; Area Procurator Fiscal, Lothian and Borders, 2005–06. Mem., Sentencing Commn, 2003–07. *Recreations:* tennis, ski-ing. *Address:* Sheriff's Chambers, Sheriff Court House, Viewfield Place, Stirling FK8 1NH. *T:* (01786) 462191. *E:* sheriffwagilchrist@scotcourts.gov.uk.

GILDEA, Prof. Robert Nigel, DPhil; FRHistS; FBA 2010; Professor of Modern History, University of Oxford, and Fellow, Worcester College, Oxford, since 2006; *b* 12 Sept. 1952; *s* of late Denis and Hazel Gildea; *m* 1987, Lucy Jean Lloyd; two *s* two *d*. *Educ:* Merton Coll., Oxford (BA, MA); St Antony's Coll., Oxford; St John's Coll., Oxford (DPhil 1978). FRHistS 1986. Jun. Res. Fellow, St John's Coll., Oxford, 1976–78; Lectr in Hist., KCL, 1978–79; University of Oxford: CUF Lectr in Modern Hist., 1979–96; Reader in Modern Hist., 1996–2002; Prof. of Modern French Hist., 2002–06; Fellow and Tutor in Modern Hist., Merton Coll., 1979–2006. Élie Halévy Vis. Prof., Inst. d'Etudes Politiques, Paris, 1999–2000. Chevalier, Ordre des Palmes Académiques (France), 1997. *Publications:* Education in Provincial France 1800–1914: a study of three departments, 1983; Barricades and Borders: Europe 1800–1914, 1987, 3rd edn 2002; The Third Republic from 1870 to 1914, 1988; The Past in French History, 1994; France since 1945, 1996, 2nd edn 2002 (Enid McLeod Prize, Franco-British Soc.); Marianne in Chains: in search of the German Occupation (Wolfson Hist. Prize), 2002; (ed jtly) Surviving Hitler and Mussolini: daily life in Occupied Europe, 2006; Children of the Revolution, 2008; (ed jtly) Writing Contemporary History, 2008; (ed jtly) Europe's 1968: voices of revolt, 2013; Fighters in the Shadows: a new history of the French Resistance, 2015; Empires of the Mind: the colonial past and the politics of the present, 2019. *Recreations:* walking, swimming, music, theatre, cooking, Oxford United. *Address:* Worcester College, Oxford OX1 2HB. *T:* (01865) 278348, *Fax:* (01865) 278303.

GILDERNEW, Michelle; MP (SF) Fermanagh and South Tyrone, since 2017; *m* Jimmy; two *s* one *d*. *Educ:* Univ. of Ulster. Press Officer, Sinn Féin, 1997. Mem. (SF) Fermanagh and S Tyrone, NI Assembly, 1998–July 2012 and 2016–17; Minister for Agriculture and Rural Develt, NI, 2007–11; Dep. Chm., Social Develt Cttee, 1999–2002, Mem., Centre Cttee, 2000–02, NI Assembly. MP (SF) Fermanagh and S Tyrone, 2001–15; contested (SF) same seat, 2015.

GILES, Alan James, OBE 2018; Senior Independent Director, Perpetual Income & Growth Investment Trust plc, since 2015; *b* 4 June 1954; *s* of Ronald Arthur Giles and Christine Joyce Giles; *m* 1978, Gillian Margaret Rosser; two *d*. *Educ:* Merton Coll., Oxford (MA Physics); Graduate Sch. of Business, Stanford Univ. (MSc Mgt). Various buying roles, Boots the Chemists, 1975–82; Retail Develt Manager, 1982–84, Gen. Manager (Books), 1985–87, W. H. Smith; Ops and Develt Manager, Do It All, 1988–92; Managing Dir, Waterstone's, 1993–98; CEO, HMV Gp plc, 1998–2006; Chm., Fat Face, 2006–13. Sen. Ind. Dir, CMA, 2013–19. Non-executive Director: Somerfield plc, 1993–2004; Wilson Bowden plc, 2004–07; Rentokil Initial plc, 2006–17; OFT, 2007–14. *Recreations:* cycling, watching soccer.

GILES, Bill; see Giles, W. G.

GILES, Christopher Thomas; Economics Editor, Financial Times, since 2004; *b* 9 Nov. 1969; *s* of Gerald David Norman Giles and Rotraud Ursula Giles; *m* 2000, Katie Anne Roden; two *d*. *Educ:* Jesus Coll., Cambridge (BA 1991); Birkbeck Coll., London (MSc). Sen. Res. Economist, Inst. for Fiscal Studies, 1991–98; econs reporter, BBC, 1998–2000; Leader Writer, Financial Times, 2000–04. Royal Statistical Soc. Prize for Excellence in Journalism, 2008; Business Journalist of the Year, Press Gazette British Journalism Awards, 2012; Sen. Financial Journalist Prize, Wincott Awards, 2014. *Recreations:* family, cycling, marathon running, theatre. *Address:* Financial Times, Bracken House, 1 Friday Street, EC4M 9BT. *T:* (020) 7873 4315, *Fax:* (020) 7873 3083. *E:* chris.giles@ft.com. *Clubs:* Tuesday, Political Economy.

GILES, Frank Thomas Robertson; Editor, The Sunday Times, 1981–83 (Deputy Editor, 1967–81); *b* 31 July 1919; *s* of late Col F. L. N. Giles, DSO, OBE, and Mrs Giles; *m* 1946, Lady Katharine Pamela Sackville (*d* 2010), *o d* of 9th Earl De La Warr and Countess De La Warr; one *s* one *d* (and one *d* decd). *Educ:* Wellington Coll.; Brasenose Coll., Oxford (Open Scholarship in History; MA 1946). ADC to Governor of Bermuda, 1939–42; Directorate of Mil. Ops, WO, 1942–45; temp. mem. of HM Foreign Service, 1945–46 (Private Sec. to Ernest Bevin; Mem. of Sir Archibald Clark Kerr's mission to Java); joined editorial staff of The Times, 1946; Asst Correspondent, Paris, 1947; Chief Corresp., Rome, 1950–53, Paris, 1953–60; Foreign Editor, Sunday Times, 1961–77; Dir, Times Newspapers Ltd, 1981–85. Lectures: tours, USA, 1975, FRG, 1984; Gritti, Venice, 1985. Chm., Library Cttee, Britain-Russia Centre, 1993–99. Chm., Painshill Park Trust, 1985–96; Mem., Governing Body, British Inst. of Florence, 1986–2001; Governor: Wellington Coll., 1965–89; Sevenoaks Sch., 1967–92. *Publications:* A Prince of Journalists: the life and times of de Blowitz, 1962; Sundry Times (autobiog.), 1986; The Locust Years: the story of the Fourth French Republic 1946–1958, 1991 (Franco-British Soc. award); (ed) Corfu, the Garden Isle, 1994; Napoleon Bonaparte, England's Prisoner, 2001. *Recreations:* going to the opera; collecting, talking about, consuming the vintage wines of Bordeaux and Burgundy. *Address:* 42 Blomfield Road, W9 2PF; Bunns Cottage, Lye Green, Crowborough, East Sussex TN6 1UY. *Clubs:* Brooks's, Beefsteak.

GILES, Hugh Peter; Partner, Capsticks LLP, since 2018; *b* 25 Jan. 1964; *s* of late Peter Giles and of Mary Giles (*née* Cope); *m* 1997, Karen Duke; one *s* one *d*. *Educ:* Brentwood Sch.; Univ. of Nottingham (BA 1986). Admitted solicitor, 1991; Legal Adviser's Br., Home Office, 1991–99; Legal Secretariat to the Law Officers, 1999–2001; team leader, Treasury Solicitor's Dept, 2001–03; a legal dir, DTI, 2003–06; Dir, Legal Services Gp, DTI, subseq. BERR, 2006–08; Hd, Litigation and Employment Gp, then Litigation Gp, Treasury Solicitor's Dept, 2008–12; Dir of Legal Services, Metropolitan Police Service, 2012–17. *Recreations:* cricket, running, Tottenham Hotspur. *Club:* Reform.

GILES, Roy Curtis, MA; Administrative Consultant, Busoga Trust, 1991–2011; Head Master, Highgate School, 1974–89; *b* 6 Dec. 1932; *s* of Herbert Henry Giles and Dorothy Alexandra Potter; *m* 1963, Christine von Alten; two *s* one *d*. *Educ:* Queen Elizabeth's Sch., Barnet; Jesus Coll., Cambridge (Open Scholar). Asst Master, Dean Close Sch., 1956–60; Lektor, Hamburg Univ., 1960–63; Asst Master, Eton Coll., 1963–74, Head of Modern Languages, 1970–74. Educnl Selector, ABM (formerly ACCM), 1979–92; Mem., House of Bishops' Panel on Marriage Educn, 1983–89. Mem., Council of Management, Vernon Educnl Trust (formerly Davies's Educn Services), 1975–2005; Governor: The Hall, Hampstead, 1976–89; Channing Sch., 1977–89. *Recreations:* music, theatre, Central Europe. *Address:* Chattan Court, Woodbury Lane, Axminster, Devon EX13 5TL. *T:* (01297) 33720.

GILES, William George, (Bill Giles), OBE 1995; Chairman, The Weather People Ltd, 1998–2011; *b* 18 Nov. 1939; *s* of Albert William George Giles and Florence Ellen Christina Giles; *m* 1st, 1961, Eileen Myrtle Lake (marr. diss. 1991); one *s* one *d*; 2nd, 1993, Patricia Maureen Stafford. *Educ:* Queen Elizabeth's Sch., Crediton; Bristol Coll. of Sci. and Technol.; Meteorological Office Coll. Meteorological Office, 1959; radio broadcaster, 1972; television broadcaster, 1975; Head, BBC Weather Centre, 1983–2000. Chm., Thame Bowls Club, 2011, 2018; Dir, Thame Sports Club. Patron, Iain Rennie Hospice at Home, 2007–. Prix des Scientifiques, Fest. Internat. de Météo, Paris, 1994. *Publications:* Weather Observations, 1978; The Story of Weather, 1990; (with John Teather) A Climate of Change, 2016. *Recreations:* gardening, golf, One Man Weather Show, after dinner speaker. *Address:* 73 Lower Icknield Way, Chinnor, Oxon OX39 4EA.

GILHOOLY, John, OBE 2013; Artistic and Executive Director, Wigmore Hall, since 2005 (Executive Director, 2000–05); *b* 15 Aug. 1973; *s* of Owen Gilhooly and Helena (*née* Conway). *Educ:* University Coll., Dublin (BA Hons). Administrator, University Coll., Dublin, 1994–97; Manager, Harrogate Internat. Centre, 1997–2000. Chm., Kohn Foundn Internat. Song Competition, 2006–; Trustee, London Internat. String Quartet Competition, 2006–. Chm., Royal Philharmonic Soc., 2010– (Hon. Sec.), 2007–10). Trustee: The Opera Group, 2007–; London Music Masters, 2009–; Internat. Musicians Seminar, Prussia Cove, 2015–; Chm., Mahogany Opera Gp, 2014–. Patron: Irish Heritage, 2010–; Cavatina Chamber Music Trust, 2010–; Restoration of Corpus Christi Maiden Lane, 2011–; Chopin Soc., 2018; Leeds Lieder, 2018; Wimbledon Fest., 2018. Chair: jury, Cardiff Singer of the World Song Prize, 2019; Young Musician Award, Royal Dublin Soc., 2019. Hon. FRAM 2006; Hon. RCM 2012; Hon. FGS 2015; Hon. Fellow, Royal Irish Acad. of Music, 2016. Knight, Order of the White Rose (Finland), 2015; Order of Federal Republic of Germany, 2015; Knight, Order of the Star of Italy, 2017; Austrian Cross of Honour for Sci. and Arts, 2017; Cobbett Medal for Chamber Music, Musicians' Co., 2019; Heidelberg Fest. Award, 2019. *Address:* Wigmore Hall, 36 Wigmore Street, W1U 2BP. *E:* jgilhooly@wigmore-hall.org.uk.

GILHOOLY, John Francis, CB 2005; Chief Executive, Office of the Parliamentary Counsel, 2000–08; Associate Research Fellow, Institute of Advanced Legal Studies, University of London, 2007–14; occasional lecturer; *b* 26 April 1945; *s* of Francis Gilhooly and Sarah Gilhooly (*née* Gavigan); *m* 1971, Gillian Marie (*née* Cunningham); two *s* two *d*. *Educ:* Clapham Coll. Grammar Sch. (RC); King's Coll., Cambridge (BA Econ 1970). Clerical Officer, then Exec. Officer, ODM, 1965–70; Econ. Asst, then Sen. Econ. Asst, ODA, 1970–74; Econ. Adviser, Royal Commn on the Distribution of Income and Wealth, 1974–78; HM Treasury: Econ. Adviser, then Principal, 1978–84; Asst Sec. Pay Policy, Tax Policy, Gen. Expenditure Policy, Training Review, 1984–92; Asst Dir (on loan), Capital Allowances Policy, Tax Law Rewrite, Inland Revenue, 1992–96; Mgt Advr, Office of Parly Counsel, 1996–99. Trustee, Croydon Bor. Neighbourhood Watch Assoc., 2017–. FRSA 2004. *Recreations:* reading, walking, family, friends. *Club:* Civil Service.

GILL, Rt Hon. Lord; Brian Gill; PC 2002; Lord Justice General of Scotland and Lord President of the Court of Session, 2012–15; *b* 25 Feb. 1942; *s* of Thomas and Mary Gill, Glasgow; *m* 1969, Catherine Fox; five *s* one *d*. *Educ:* St Aloysius' Coll., Glasgow; Glasgow Univ. (MA 1962, LLB 1964); Edinburgh Univ. (PhD 1975). Asst Lectr, 1964–65, Lectr, 1965–69 and 1972–77, Faculty of Law, Edinburgh Univ.; Advocate, 1967; Advocate Depute, 1977–79; Standing Junior Counsel: Foreign and Commonwealth Office (Scotland), 1974–77; Home Office (Scotland), 1979–81; Scottish Education Dept, 1979–81; QC (Scot.) 1981; a Senator of the Coll. of Justice in Scotland, 1994–2015; Lord Justice Clerk and Pres., Second Div., Court of Session, 2001–12. Chairman: Scottish Law Commn, 1996–2001; Scottish Civil Courts Review, 2007–09. Called to the Bar, Lincoln's Inn, 1991, Hon. Bencher, 2002. Keeper of the Advocates' Library, 1987–94. Dep. Chm., Copyright Tribunal, 1989–94. Vice-Pres., RSAMD, later Royal Conservatoire of Scotland, 2006– (Chm., 1999–2006); Chm., RSCM, 2010–18. FRSAMD 2002; FRSE 2004. Hon. LLD: Glasgow, 1998; Strathclyde, 2003; St Andrews, 2006; Edinburgh, 2007; Abertay, 2008; Hon. DAcad RSAMD, 2006. KSG 2011. *Publications:* The Law of Agricultural Holdings in Scotland, 1982, 4th edn as Agricultural Tenancies, 2016; (ed) Scottish Planning Encyclopedia, 1996; articles in legal jls. *Recreation:* church music. *E:* lord.bgill@gmail.com. *Clubs:* Athenæum, MCC.

**GILL, Prof. Aisha K.**, PhD; CBE 2017; Professor of Criminology, University of Roehampton, since 2015; *b* Derby, 30 April 1970; *d* of Surinder Kaur. *Educ:* Univ. of Essex (MA (Dist.) Sociol Res. Methods 1998; PhD Sociol. 2002). Teaching Asst (Sociol. and Criminology, Dept of Sociol., Univ. of Essex, 1999–2002; Sen. Lectr in Criminology, 2003–11, Reader in Criminology, 2011–15, Dept of Social Scis, Univ. of Roehampton. FRSA. *Publications:* (jtly) Violence Against South Asian Women: issues for policy and practice, 2010; (jtly) Forced Marriage: introducing a social justice and human rights perspective, 2011; (jtly) 'Honour' Killing and Violence: theory, policy and practice, 2014; (jtly) 'Honour'-based Violence: experiences and counter strategies in Iraqi Kurdistan and the UK Kurdish diaspora, 2015; articles in learned jls. *Address:* Department of Social Sciences, University of Roehampton, 80 Roehampton Lane, SW15 5SL. *T:* (020) 8392 3893. *E:* a.gill@roehampton.ac.uk.

**GILL, Brian;** *see* Gill, Rt Hon. Lord.

**GILL, Charan Singh**, MBE 1998; Chairman, Harlequin Leisure Investments Ltd, since 2005; *b* 8 Dec. 1954; *s* of Mehar Singh Gill and Bhajan Kaur Gill; *m* 1974, Parminder Kaur Brar; one *s* four *d*. Engr, Yarrows Shipbuilder, 1969–79; restaurant manager, 1979–83; Asst Manager of insce co., 1983–86; insurance salesman, 1986–89; Man. Dir, Harlequin Leisure Gp, 1989–2005. Vice-Chm., Entrepreneurial Exchange, 2005–. Chm., Glasgow Restaurateurs Assoc., 2005–. Hon. Dr Paisley, 2004; DUniv Glasgow, 2010. *Recreations:* bhangra music, charity work. *Address:* Harlequin Leisure Investments Ltd, 1287 Argyle Street, Glasgow G3 8TL. *T:* (0141) 334 4633. *E:* charangillmbe@yahoo.com.

**GILL, Prof. Christopher John**, PhD; Professor of Ancient Thought, University of Exeter, 1997–2013, now Emeritus; *b* 2 May 1946; *s* of Ross and Phyllis Gill; *m* 1981, Karen Ann Brown (*d* 2010); four *s*. *Educ:* Cowbridge Grammar Sch., Glamorgan; St John's Coll., Cambridge (BA 1967, MA 1971); Yale Univ. (PhD 1970). Teaching asst, 1967–70, Instructor, 1970–71, Yale Univ.; Lectr, Univ. of Bristol, 1971–72; Lectr, 1972–83, Sen. Lectr, 1983–89, UCW, Aberystwyth; Sen. Lectr, 1989–94, Reader, 1994–97, Univ. of Exeter. Res. Fellow, Nat. Humanities Center, USA, 1981–82; Leverhulme Maj. Res. Fellow, 2003–06; Leverhulme Emeritus Fellow, 2014–16. *Publications:* Plato: the Atlantis story, 1980; (ed) The Person and the Human Mind: issues in ancient and modern philosophy, 1990; Greek Thought, 1995; Personality in Greek Epic, Tragedy and Philosophy: the self in dialogue, 1996; Plato, the Symposium, 1999; (ed) Virtue, Norms, and Objectivity: issues in ancient and modern ethics, 2005; The Structured Self in Hellenistic and Roman Thought, 2006; Naturalistic Psychology in Galen and Stoicism, 2010; Marcus Aurelius, Meditations Books 1–6 (trans. with introdn and commentary), 2013; Plato's Atlantis Story: text, translation and commentary, 2017; co-ed vols of essays. *Recreations:* swimming, hill-walking, listening to 16th century choral music. *Address:* Department of Classics and Ancient History, University of Exeter, Exeter EX4 4RJ. *E:* C.J.Gill@exeter.ac.uk.

**GILL, Christopher John Fred**, RD 1971; retired butcher and farmer; Hon. President, Freedom Association Ltd, 2007–17 (Hon. Chairman, 2001–07); *b* 28 Oct. 1936; *m* 1960, Patricia M. (*née* Greenway); one *s* two *d*. *Educ:* Shrewsbury School. Chm., F. A. Gill Ltd, 1968–2006. Councillor, Wolverhampton BC, 1965–72. MP (C) Ludlow, 1987–2001. Member: Agriculture Select Cttee, 1989–95; Welsh Affairs Select Cttee, 1996–97. Vice Chairman: Cons. European Affairs Cttee, 1989–91 (Sec., 1988–89); Cons. Agric. Cttee, 1991–94 (Sec., 1990–91); Pres., Midlands W European Cons. Council, 1984–85. Member: Exec., 1922 Cttee, 1997–99; Council of Europe, 1997–99. Contested (UK Ind) Ludlow, 2010. *Publications:* Whips' Nightmare, 2003; Cracking the Whip, 2012. *Address:* Talbot Court, Bridgnorth, Shropshire WV16 5BR.

**GILL, Devinder Kaur;** a Judge of the Upper Tribunal (Immigration and Asylum Chamber) (formerly a Vice President, Immigration Appeal Tribunal, later a Senior Immigration Judge, Asylum and Immigration Tribunal), since 2003; a Recorder, since 2004; a Deputy Judge of the High Court, since 2013. *Educ:* Univ. of London (LLB ext. 1983); Wolfson Coll., Cambridge (LLM 1985). Called to the Bar, Middle Temple, 1984; In-house Counsel, Emerging Mkts, various banks incl. Singer & Friedlander, Samuel Montagu and HSBC, 1986–94; In-house Gp Legal Advr, Finance, 1996–97; Legal Consultant, Emerging Mkts, 1997–2000. Adjudicator, Immigration Appellate Authy, 1995–2003. *Recreations:* theatre, gardening, music, reading, walking.

**GILL, (Evelyn) Margaret**, OBE 2011; PhD; FRSE; Professor of Integrated Land Use, University of Aberdeen, since 2006, on secondment (part-time) as Senior Research Fellow, Department for International Development, 2009–16, and as Chair, Independent Science and Partnership Council, Consultative Group on International Agricultural Research, since 2014 (Member, 2011–14); *b* 10 Jan. 1951; *d* of late William Alexander Morrison Gill and Eveline Elizabeth Gill (*née* Duthie). *Educ:* Univ. of Edinburgh (BSc Hons Agricl Sci.); Massey Univ., New Zealand (PhD); Open Univ. (BA Maths). Researcher, Grassland Res. Inst., AFRC, 1976–89; Researcher, 1989–94, Dir of Res., 1994–96, Natural Resources Inst., ODA; Chief Exec., Natural Resources Internat. Ltd, 1996–2000; Chief Exec. and Dir of Res., Macaulay Land Use Res. Inst., 2000–05. Chief Scientific Advr, Scottish Govt (formerly Exec.) Envmt and Rural Affairs, 2006–11. Hon. Prof., Univ. of Aberdeen, 2001. FRSE 2003. *Recreations:* hill-walking, classical music. *E:* m.gill@abdn.ac.uk.

**GILL, (George) Malcolm**, FCIB; Head, Banking Department, Bank for International Settlements, 1995–99 (Deputy Head, 1991–95); *b* 23 May 1934; *s* of late Thomas Woodman Gill and Alice Muriel Gill (*née* Le Grice); *m* 1966, Monica Kennedy Brooks; one *s* one *d*. *Educ:* Cambridgeshire High Sch.; Sidney Sussex Coll., Cambridge (MA). Entered Bank of England, 1957: seconded to UK Treasury Delegation, Washington DC, 1966–68; Private Sec. to Governor, 1970–72; Asst Chief Cashier, 1975; seconded to HM Treasury, 1977–80; Chief Manager, Banking and Credit Markets, 1980–82; Head of Foreign Exchange Div., 1982–88; Asst Dir, 1987–88; Chief of the Banking Dept and Chief Cashier, 1988–91. *Recreations:* reading, gardening, music.

**GILL, Guy Serle G.;** *see* Goodwin-Gill.

**GILL, Jack**, CB 1984; Chief Executive (formerly Secretary), Export Credits Guarantee Department, 1983–87; Executive Director (part-time), Government Relations, BICC plc, 1987–91; *b* 20 Feb. 1930; *s* of Jack and Elizabeth Gill; *m* 1954, Alma Dorothy; three *d*. *Educ:* Bolton Sch. Export Credits Guarantee Department: Clerical Officer, 1946; Principal, 1962; Asst Sec., 1970; Asst Sec., DTI, 1972–75; Export Credits Guarantee Department: Under Sec., 1975–79; Principal Finance Officer, 1978–79; Sec., Monopolies and Mergers Commn, 1979–81; Dep. Sec., and Dir of Industrial Develt Unit, DoI, 1981–83. Mem., BOTB, 1981–87. Consultant: NEI Power Projects Ltd, 1987–90; British Aerospace plc, 1987–89; CBI Council, 1988–91 (Chm., Public Procurement Contact Gp, 1990–91; Mem., Overseas Cttee, 1990–91). National Service, REME, 1948–50. *Recreations:* music (Bass, St Paul's Cath. Sunday Evening and Special Service Choirs, 1951–60), chess; occasional crossword setter for The Listener. *Address:* 9 Ridley Road, Warlingham, Surrey CR6 9LR. *T:* (01883) 622688.

**GILL, John William;** Editor, Times Higher Education, since 2012; *b* Cambridge, 15 Dec. 1980; *s* of Andrew Gill and Chloe Gill. *Educ:* Netherhall Sch., Cambridge; Hills Road Sixth Form Coll., Cambridge; Univ. of Nottingham (BA Hons Hist.). Reporter, then Crime Reporter, Cambridge Evening News, 2003–07; Times Higher Education: reporter, 2007–08; Dep. News Editor, 2008; News Editor, 2008–12. *Address:* Times Higher Education, 26 Red Lion Square, WC1R 4HQ. *T:* (020) 3194 3077. *E:* john.gill@timeshighereducation.com.

**GILL, Judith Ann Elizabeth;** QC 2009; FCIArb; *b* Shepperton, 30 Sept. 1959; *d* of Desmond and Valerie Leighton; *m* 1984, Clifford William Gill; one *s* one *d*. *Educ:* Henley Grammar Sch.; S Oxfordshire Tech. Coll.; Worcester Coll., Oxford (MA Juris.); Queen Mary and Westfield Coll., Univ. of London (Dip. Internat. Commercial Arbitration). Admitted solicitor, 1985; Allen & Overy LLP: Asst Solicitor, 1985–92; Partner, London, 1992–2015; Partner, Singapore, 2015–18; Arbitration Mem., 20 Essex Street Chambers, Singapore, 2018–. Pres., London Court of Internat. Arbitration, 2016–19 (Dir, 1998–; Mem. Court, 2003–08); Dir, American Arbitration Assoc., 2009–. Fellow, Inst. Advanced Legal Studies, 1998. FCIArb 1999. *Publications:* (jtly) Russell on Arbitration, 21st edn 1997 to 24th edn 2015; (ed and contrib.) State Entities in International Arbitration, 2008; contribs to Jl Internat. Arbitration, Transnat. Dispute Mgt, Internat. Business Litigation and Arbitration, Global Arbitration Rev., Internat. Arbitration Law Rev. *Recreations:* yachting, ski-ing. *Address:* Maxwell Chambers, #02–09 32 Maxwell Road, Singapore 069115.

**GILL, Malcolm;** *see* Gill, G. M.

**GILL, Margaret;** *see* Gill, E. M.

**GILL, Nathan Lee;** Member for Wales, European Parliament, since 2014 (UK Ind, 2014–18; Ind, 2018–19; Brexit, since 2019); *b* Kingston upon Hull, 6 July 1973; *s* of Michael R. and Elaine Gill; *m* 2002, Jana Lyn King; three *s* four *d*. *Educ:* Ysgol David Hughes, Menai Bridge; Coleg Menai, Bangor. England London Mission, 1991–93; Man. Dir, Community Careline Services, Hull and E Yorks, 1996–2000; Man. Dir, Gill Enterprises Yorkshire Ltd, 2000–05; Campaign Manager, UKIP Wales, 2009; PA to John Bufton, MEP, 2009–14. National Assembly for Wales: contested (UK Ind) Ynys Môn, Aug. 2013; Mem. for N Wales, 2016–17 (UK Ind, 2016; Ind, 2016–17). Leader, UKIP Wales, 2014–16. Mem., European Adv. Gp, Welsh Govt, 2016–. Mem. Bd, Centre for Welsh Studies, 2017–. *Recreations:* reading, history, gardening. *Address:* 29 Ponc Y Fron, Llangefni, Anglesey LL77 7NY. *T:* (01248) 723580. *E:* nathangill1@aol.com. *Club:* Gadfly.

**GILL, Neena**, CBE 2017; Member (Lab) West Midlands Region, European Parliament, 1999–2009 and since 2014; *b* 24 Dec. 1956; *d* of late Jasmer S. Gill and of Birjinder K. Gill; *m* 1982, Dr John Towner (marr. diss. 2009); one *s*. *Educ:* Liverpool Poly.; London Business Sch. (BA Hons); Chartered Inst. of Housing (postgrad. dip. Public Sector Mgt). Admin. Officer, Ealing LBC, 1981–83; Principal Housing Officer, UK Housing Trust, 1983–86; Chief Executive: ASRA Greater London Housing Assoc., 1986–90; Newlon Housing Gp, 1990–99. Chair, S Asia Delegn, 2004–07, India Delegn, 2007–09, EP. Man. Dir, Public Affairs, Wrigglesworth Consultancy, 2009–10; Vice Pres., Corporate Affairs, Europe and Asia Pacific, SAS Inc., 2010–14. Member: Transatlantic Policy Network; Eur. Energy Foundn; Pres., Friends of Nepal; Patron, Friends of India. FRSA. Pravasi Bharatiya Samman Award (India), 2017. *Recreations:* hill walking, football, minor bird watching, cinema, opera. *Address:* European Parliament, Rue Wiertz, 1047 Brussels, Belgium.

**GILL, Parmjit Singh;** information management consultant; Member (Lib Dem), Leicester City Council, 2003–11; *b* 20 Dec. 1966; *s* of Mohinder Singh Gill and Gurdev Kaur Gill; *m* 2006, Juliet; one *s* one *d*. *Educ:* Univ. of East London (BSc Hons Biochem. 1992); Univ. of Leicester (MSc Security Mgt and IT 1995). Inf. Mgt and Security Consultant, Leicester CC, 1999–2003; Inf. Security Manager, Charnwood BC, 2003–04; information consultant, 2005–. Contested (Lib Dem) Leicester S, 2005. MP (Lib Dem) Leicester S, July 2004–2005; contested (Lib Dem) same seat, 2005, 2010. *Address:* 17 Scholars Walk, London Road, Stoneygate, Leicester LE2 1RR.

**GILL, Peter**, OBE 1980; FRWCMD; dramatic author; Associate Director, Royal National Theatre, 1989–97; *b* Cardiff, 7 Sept. 1939; *s* of George John Gill and Margaret Mary Browne. *Educ:* St Illtyd's Coll., Cardiff. FRWCMD (FWCMD 1992). Associate Dir, Royal Court Theatre, 1970–72; Dir, 1976–80, Associate Dir, 1980, Riverside Studios, Hammersmith; Dir, Royal Nat. Theatre Studio, 1984–90. Productions include: *Royal Court:* A Collier's Friday Night, 1965; The Local Stigmatic, A Provincial Life, 1966 (for Nat. Th. Wales, Sherman Cymru, Cardiff, 2012); A Soldier's Fortune, The Daughter-in-law, Crimes of Passion, 1967; The Widowing of Mrs Holroyd, 1968; Life Price, Over Gardens Out, The Sleepers' Den, 1969; The Duchess of Malfi, 1971; Crete & Sergeant Pepper, 1972; The Merry-go-round, 1973; Small Change, The Fool, 1976; The York Realist, 2002; *Riverside Studios:* As You Like It, 1976; Small Change, 1977; The Cherry Orchard (own version), The Changeling, 1978; Measure for Measure, 1979; Julius Caesar, 1980; Scrape off the Black, 1980; Hens, for Sky Arts TV, 2010; *Royal National Theatre:* A Month in the Country, Don Juan, Scrape off the Black, Much Ado about Nothing, 1981; Danton's Death, Major Barbara, 1982; Kick for Touch, Tales from Hollywood, Antigone (co-dir), 1983; Venice Preserv'd, Fool for Love (transf. Lyric), 1984; The Murderers, As I Lay Dying (also adapted), A Twist of Lemon, In the Blue, Bouncing, Up for None, The Garden of England (co-dir), 1985; Mean Tears, 1987; Mrs Klein, 1988 (transf. Apollo, 1989); Juno and the Paycock, 1989; Cardiff East (also wrote), 1997; Friendly Fire, 1999; Luther, 2001; Scenes from the Big Picture, 2003; The Voysey Inheritance, 2006; *other London theatres:* O'Flaherty VC, Mermaid, 1966; The Way of the World, Lyric, Hammersmith, 1992; Uncle Vanya, Tricycle, 1995; Tongue of a Bird, Almeida, 1997; Certain Young Men, Almeida, 1999; Speed the Plow, New Ambassadors, 2000; Days of Wine and Roses, Donmar, 2005; George Dillon, Comedy Th., 2006; Gaslight, Old Vic, 2007; The Importance of Being Earnest, Vaudeville, 2008; Aliens, Bush Th., 2010; Versailles (also wrote), Donmar Warehouse, 2014; As Good a Time As Any (also wrote), Print Room at Coronet, 2015; *other theatres:* Another Door Closed, Th. Royal, Bath, 2009; The Breath of Life, Sheffield Th., 2011; *Royal Shakespeare Co.:* Twelfth Night, 1974; New England, 1994; A Patriot for Me, 1995; Romeo and Juliet, transf. Albery, 2004; has also produced plays by Shakespeare and modern writers at Nottingham, Edinburgh and in Canada, Germany, Switzerland and USA; *music theatre and opera* includes: Down By the Green Wood Side (co-dir), Bow Down (co-dir), Queen Elizabeth Hall, 1987; Marriage of Figaro, Opera North, 1987; *television* productions include: Grace, 1972; Girl, 1973; A Matter of Taste, Fugitive, 1974; Hitting Town, 1976; *radio* productions include: The Look Across the Eyes, 2001; Lovely Evening, 2001. *Publications:* Apprenticeship, 2008; plays: The Sleepers' Den, 1965; Over Gardens Out, 1969; Small Change, 1976; Small Change, Kick for Touch, 1985; In the Blue, Mean Tears, 1987; Cherry Orchard, 1996; The Look Across the Eyes, 1997; Cardiff East, 1997; Certain Young Men, 1999; The Seagull, 2000; The York Realist, 2001; Original Sin, 2002; The Look Across the Eyes, 2002; Lovely Evening, 2002; Another Door Closed, 2009. *Address:* c/o Casarotto Ramsay & Associates, Waverley House, 7–12 Noel Street, W1F 8GQ.

**GILL, Preet Kaur**; MP (Lab Co-op) Birmingham Edgbaston, since 2017; *b* Birmingham, 21 Nov. 1972; *d* of late Daljit Singh Shergill and of Kuldeep Kaur Shergill; *m* 2009, Sureash Singh Chopra; two *d*. *Educ:* Univ. of East London (1st Cl. Hons Sociol. with Social Work). Social worker, Waltham Forest and Birmingham, specialising in child protection; Children's Services Manager, Birmingham, 2000–17. Mem. (Lab), Sandwell Council, 2012– (Cabinet Mem., Public Health and Protection, 2016–17). Shadow Minister for Internat. Develt, 2018–. Mem., Home Affairs Cttee, H of C, 2017–. *Address:* House of Commons, SW1A 0AA. *T:* (020) 7219 2879. *E:* Preet.Gill.mp@parliament.uk. *W:* www.twitter.com/preetkgillmp.

**GILL, Sir Robin (Denys)**, KCVO 2010 (CVO 1993); Founder and Chairman of Executive, 1990–2010 and Chairman, 2002–10, Royal Anniversary Trust; Founder and Chairman, The Queen's Anniversary Prizes for Higher and Further Education, 1993–2010; *b* 7 Oct. 1927; *s* of Thomas Henry Gill and Marjorie Mary (*née* Butler); *m* 1st, 1951, Mary Hope Alexander (*d* 1986); three *s*; 2nd, 1991, Denise Spencer Waterhouse. *Educ:* Dulwich Coll.; Brasenose Coll., Oxford (MA; Hon. Fellow, 2005). Unilever plc, 1949–54; British Internat. Paper Ltd, 1954–59; Founder and Man. Dir, Border TV Ltd, 1960–64; Man. Dir, ATV Corp. Ltd, 1964–69; Chairman: ITCA, 1966–67; ITN, 1968–69; 1970 Trust Ltd, 1970–93; Ansvar Insce Co. Ltd, 1975–98; Standard Ind. Trust Ltd, 1970–81; various internat. private equity funds; Director: Reed Paper Gp Ltd, 1970–75; Hewlett Packard Ltd, 1975–92; Yarrow Plc, 1979–88; Baring Hambrecht Alpine Ltd, 1986–98; SD-Scicon plc, 1988–90. Member: Nat. Adv. Bd for Higher Educn; Oxford Univ. Appts Cttee; Vis. Cttee, RCA; Cttee, Royal Family Film, 1968–70. Pres., Brasenose Soc., 1995–96. Hon. DLitt Loughborough, 2010. *Recreations:* golf, sport, travel, art collecting, new projects. *Address:* PO Box 1, East Horsley, Surrey KT24 6RE. *T:* (01483) 285290. *Clubs:* Vincent's (Oxford); St George's Hill Golf; Free Foresters Cricket.

**GILL, Rev. Prof. Robin Morton**, PhD; Professor of Applied Theology, University of Kent, 2011–13, now Emeritus (Michael Ramsey Professor of Modern Theology, University of Kent at Canterbury, later University of Kent, 1992–2011); Non-Stipendiary Minister, Hollingbourne and Hucking, with Leeds and Broomfield, Diocese of Canterbury, 2003–14; *b* 18 July 1944; *s* of Alan Morton Gill and Mary Grace (*née* Hammond); *m* 1967, Jennifer Margaret Sheppard; one *s* one *d*. *Educ:* Westminster Sch.; King's Coll., London (BD 1966; PhD 1969); Birmingham Univ. (MSocSc 1972). Deacon, 1968; priest, 1969; Curate, Rugby St Andrews, 1968–71; Lectr, Newton Theol Coll., PNG, 1971–72; Edinburgh University: Lectr in Christian Ethics, 1972–86; Associate Dean, Faculty of Theol., 1985–88; Sen. Lectr, 1986–88; William Leech Res. Prof. in Applied Theol., Newcastle Univ., 1988–92. Priest-in-charge: St Philip, Edinburgh, 1972–75; Ford with Etal, Northumberland, 1975–87; St Mary, Coldstream, 1987–92; Area Dean, N Downs, Dio. of Canterbury, 2002–09; Acting Dean, Holy Trinity Cathedral, Gibraltar, 2017–. Canon Theologian, Dio. in Europe, Gibraltar, 2012–. Hon. Provincial Canon, Canterbury Cathedral, 1992–. Editor, Theology, 2014–. *Publications:* The Social Context of Theology, 1975; Theology and Social Structure, 1977; Faith in Christ, 1978; Prophecy and Praxis, 1981; The Cross Against the Bomb, 1984; A Textbook of Christian Ethics, 1985, 4th edn 2014; Theology and Sociology, 1987, 2nd edn 1995; Beyond Decline, 1988; Competing Convictions, 1989; Christian Ethics in Secular Worlds, 1991; Gifts of Love, 1991; Moral Communities, 1992; The Myth of the Empty Church, 1993; A Vision for Growth, 1994; Readings in Modern Theology, 1995; (with Lorna Kendall) Michael Ramsey as Theologian, 1995; (with Derek Burke) Strategic Church Leadership, 1996; Moral Leadership in a Postmodern Age, 1997; Euthanasia and the Churches, 1998; Churchgoing and Christian Ethics, 1999; (ed) The Cambridge Companion to Christian Ethics, 2000, 2nd edn 2011; (ed jtly) The New Dictionary of Pastoral Studies, 2002; A Sense of Grace, 2004; Health Care and Christian Ethics, 2006; (ed) Reflecting Theologically on AIDS, 2007; A Bit Like Jesus, 2009; New Challenges for Christians: from test-tube babies to euthanasia, 2010; Sociological Theology, vol. 1, Theology in a Social Context, 2012, vol. 2, Theology Shaped by Society, 2012, vol. 3, Society Shaped by Theology, 2013; Moral Passion and Christian Ethics, 2017. *Recreations:* running churches, playing the trumpet. *E:* r.gill@kent.ac.uk.

**GILL, Stuart William**, OBE 2016; HM Diplomatic Service; High Commissioner to Malta, since 2016; *b* 6 Aug. 1958; *s* of William and Isabella Gill; *m* 1982, Maggie Denby; two *d*. *Educ:* Univ. of Kent (BA Politics and Govt 1980). DTI, 1980–94, incl. Asst Private Sec. to Minister of State, and Private Sec. to Parly Under Sec. of State; joined FCO, 1994; First Sec., and Hd, Inward Investment, Chicago, 1994–98; First Sec., and Hd of Section, UK Repn to EU, Brussels, 1998–2002; Hd of Section, EU-Asia and EU-US, Europe Directorate, 2002–06, Dep. Hd, Far Eastern Gp, Asia Pacific Directorate, 2006–08, FCO; Consul-General, Melbourne, 2008–12; Ambassador to Iceland, 2012–16. *Publications:* Blood in the Sea: HMS Dunedin and the Enigma Code, 2003. *Address:* c/o Foreign and Commonwealth Office, King Charles Street, SW1A 2AH.

**GILLAM, Sir Patrick (John)**, Kt 1998; Chairman, Asia House, 2003–05; Board Mentor, Career Management International; *b* 15 April 1933; *s* of late Cyril B. Gillam and Mary J. Gillam; *m* 1963, Diana Echlin; one *s* one *d*. *Educ:* London School of Economics (BA Hons History; Hon. Fellow, 1999). Foreign Office, 1956–57; British Petroleum Co. Ltd, 1957–91; Vice-Pres., BP North America Inc., 1971–74; General Manager, Supply Dept, 1974–78; Dir, BP International Ltd (formerly BP Trading Ltd), 1978–82; Man. Dir, BP, 1981–91; Chairman: BP Shipping Ltd, 1987–88; BP Minerals Internat. Ltd/Selection Trust Ltd, 1982–89; BP Coal Ltd, 1986–88; BP Coal Inc., 1988–90; BP America Inc., 1989–91; BP Nutrition, 1989–91; BP Oil International, 1990–91. Chairman: Booker Tate Ltd, 1991–93; Standard Chartered PLC, 1993–2003 (Dir, 1988–2003; Dep. Chm., 1991–93); Asda Gp, 1991–96; Royal & Sun Alliance Insurance Gp, 1997–2003. Chm., ICC UK, 1989–98; Mem. Exec. Bd, ICC Worldwide, 1991–98; Dir, Commercial Union, 1991–96. Mem., Court of Governors, LSE, 1989–2010, now Emeritus Governor; Trustee, Queen Elizabeth's Foundn for Disabled Develt Trust, 1984–2003. *Recreation:* gardening. *Address:* 3 St Leonard's Terrace, SW3 4QA.

**GILLAN, Rt Hon. Dame Cheryl (Elise Kendall)**, DBE 2018; PC 2010; MP (C) Chesham and Amersham, since 1992; *b* 21 April 1952; *d* of Major Adam Mitchell Gillan and Mona Elsie Gillan (*née* Freeman); *m* 1985, John Coates Leeming (*d* 2019). *Educ:* Cheltenham Ladies' Coll.; Coll. of Law. FCIM DipM. International Management Group, 1976–84; British Film Year, 1984–86; Ernst & Young, 1986–91; Dir, Kidsons Impey, 1991–93. PPS to Lord Privy Seal, 1994–95; Parly Under-Sec. of State, DFEE, 1995–97; Opposition frontbench spokesman: on trade and industry, 1997–98; on foreign and commonwealth affairs and overseas develt, 1998–2001; on home affairs, 2003–05; an Opposition Whip, 2001–03; Shadow Sec. of State for Wales, 2005–10; Sec. of State for Wales, 2010–12. Mem., Select Cttee on Public Admin, 2014–15, on Public Admin and Constitutional Affairs, 2015–; Mem., Panel of Chairs, 2015–. Mem. Bd, Cons. Party, 2018–. Chm., Bow Group, 1987; Vice Chm., 1922 Cttee, 2015–; Mem., Speaker's Cttee, Ind. Parly Standards Authy, 2015–. Asst Chair, Internat. Democratic Union, 2018–. Member: Exec. Cttee, UK Br., Commonwealth Parly Assoc., 1998– (UK Rep., British Islands and Mediterranean Reg., 1994–2004; Internat. Treas. 2004–06); Parly Assoc., NATO, 2003–05; Parly Assembly, Council of Europe, 2013–; Freeman, City of London, 1991; Liveryman, Marketors' Co., 1991. *Recreations:* golf, music, gardening, animals. *Address:* House of Commons, SW1A 0AA. *T:* (020) 7219 3000. *Club:* Royal Automobile.

**GILLAN, Prof. Michael John**, DPhil; Professor of Physics, University College London, 1998–2009, now Emeritus; *b* Birmingham, 3 Jan. 1944; *s* of Robert Urquhart Gillan and Margaret Jennings Gillan; *m* 1st, 1969, Mary Torrenza Paterson (*d* 1998); two *s* one *d*; 2nd, 2009, Hilary Jane Wigmore. *Educ:* Christ Church, Oxford (BA Physics 1965; DPhil Theoretical Physics 1968). SSO, Theoretical Physics Div., AERE Harwell, 1970–88; Prof. of Theoretical Physics, Univ. of Keele, 1988–98. Chm., Thomas Young Centre, London Centre for Theory and Simulation of Materials, 2009–11. Dirac Medal and Prize, Inst. of Physics, 2006. *Publications:* approx. 250 articles in learned jls. *Recreations:* languages, music, travel, photography.

**GILLARD, Hon. Julia Eileen**, AC 2017; MP (ALP) Lalor, Victoria, 1998–2013; Prime Minister of Australia, 2010–13; Chair: Global Partnership for Education, since 2014; Global Institute for Women's Leadership, King's College London, since 2018; *b* Barry, Wales, 29 Sept. 1961; *d* of John Oliver and Moira Gillard; partner, Tim Mathieson. *Educ:* Unley High Sch., SA; Univ. of Adelaide; Univ. of Melbourne (BA, LLB). Pres., Australian Union of Students. Solicitor, 1987–95, Partner, 1990–95, Slater & Gordon; COS to Leader of the Opposition, Vic, 1995–98. Shadow Minister: for Popn and Immigration, 2001–03; for Reconciliation and Indigenous Affairs, 2003; for Health, 2003–06; for Employment and Industrial Relns, 2006–07; for Social Inclusion, 2006–07; Dep. Manager, 2003, Manager, 2003–06, of Opposition Business, House of Reps; Dep. Leader of the Opposition, 2006–07; Minister for Educn, for Employment and Workplace Relns and for Social Inclusion, 2007–10; Dep. Prime Minister, 2007–10. Dep. Leader, 2007–10, Leader, 2010–13, ALP. Hon. Vis. Prof., Univ. of Adelaide, 2013–; Vis. Prof., Policy Inst. and Menzies Centre for Australian Studies, KCL, 2016–; Sen. Fellow, Brookings Instn, 2013–. Chair, beyondblue, 2017– (Dir, 2014–). *Publications:* My Story, 2014.

**GILLEN, Rt Hon. Sir John**, Kt 1999; PC 2014; a Lord Justice of Appeal, Supreme Court of Judicature, Northern Ireland, 2014–17; *b* 18 Nov. 1947; *s* of John Gillen and Susan Letitia Gillen; *m* 1976, Claire; two *d*. *Educ:* Methodist Coll., Belfast; The Queen's Coll., Oxford (BA 1969; BL). Called to the Bar, Gray's Inn, 1970; Barrister, 1970–83; QC (NI) 1983–99; a Judge of the High Court of Justice, NI, 1999–2014. *Recreations:* reading, music, sports.

**GILLESPIE, Dr Alan Raymond**, CBE 2003; Chairman, Economic and Social Research Council, 2009–18; *b* 31 July 1950; *s* of Charles Gillespie and Doreen Gillespie (*née* Murtagh); *m* 1st, 1973, (Georgina) Ruth Milne (*d* 2011); one *s* one *d*; 2nd, 2014, Caroline Sainsot. *Educ:* Grosvenor High Sch., Belfast; Clare Coll., Cambridge (BA 1972; MA 1973; PhD 1977; Hon. Fellow 2007). Citicorp International Bank Ltd, London and Geneva, 1976–86; Goldman Sachs & Co., NY, 1986–87; Goldman Sachs International, London, 1987–99 (Partner and Man. Dir, 1990–99); Chief Exec., CDC Gp plc, 1999–2002; Chm., Ulster Bank Gp, 2001–08. Non-executive Director: Elan Corp. plc, 1996–2007; United Business Media plc, 2007–17; Old Mutual plc, 2010–18; Contour Global plc, 2017–. Chm., Internat. Finance Facility for Immunization, 2005–12. Chm., NI IDB, 1998–2002; Member: NI Econ. Strategy Steering Gp, 1998–99; NI Econ. Council, 1999–2001. Pres., European Develt Finance Instns, 2001–02. Member: Adv. Bd, Judge Inst. of Mgt Studies, Univ. of Cambridge, 1996–2003; Adv. Council, Prince's Trust, 1999–2002. Chm., Univ. Challenge Fund, NI, 1999–2007. DUniv Ulster, 2001; Hon. LLD QUB, 2005. *Recreations:* golf, tennis, ski-ing. *Address:* 25 First Street, SW3 2LB. *Club:* Wisley Golf.

**GILLESPIE, Edward William**, OBE 2015; Lord-Lieutenant of Gloucestershire, since 2018; *b* Guildford, Surrey, 31 July 1952; *s* of Kenneth Josling Gillespie and Elizabeth Florence Gillespie; *m* 1978, Alyson Margaret; one *s* two *d*. *Educ:* Tonbridge Sch.; Univ. of York (BA Hons). Man. Dir, Cheltenham Racecourse, 1980–2012. Chair, Trustees, Summerfield Charitable Trust, 2010–19. Chair: Everyman Th., Cheltenham, 2000–10; Cheltenham Music Fest., 2013–. *Publications:* (with Robin Oakley) Sixty Years of Jump Racing, 2017. *Recreations:* cricket, theatre, music. *Address:* Gloucestershire Lieutenancy, Shire Hall, Westgate Street, Gloucester GL1 2TG. *E:* edward.gillespie@gloucestershire.gov.uk. *Club:* Jockey.

**GILLESPIE, Prof. Iain Erskine**, MD, MSc, FRCS; Professor of Surgery, University of Manchester, 1970–92 (Dean of Medical School, 1983–86); *b* 4 Sept. 1931; *s* of John Gillespie and Flora McQuarie; *m* 1957, Mary Muriel McIntyre; one *s* one *d*. *Educ:* Hillhead High Sch., Glasgow; Univ. of Glasgow. MB ChB, 1953; MD (Hons) 1963; MSc Manchester 1974; FRCSE 1959; FRCS 1963; FRCSGlas 1970. Series of progressive surgical appts in Univs of Glasgow, Sheffield, Glasgow (again), 1953–70. Nat. service, RAMC, 1954–56; MRC grantee, 1956–58; US Postdoctoral Research Fellow, Los Angeles, 1961–62; Titular Prof. of Surgery, Univ. of Glasgow, 1969. Vis. Prof. in USA, Canada, S America, Kenya, S Africa, Australia and New Zealand. Member: Cttee of Surgical Res. Socs. of GB and Ireland, 1975–; Medical Sub-Cttee, UGC, 1975–86; Univs and Polytechnics Grants Cttee, Hong Kong, 1984–89. Non-exec. Mem., Central Manchester HA, 1991–94. President: Manchester Med. Soc., 1994–95; Manchester Lit. and Phil Soc., 1999–2001 (Mem. Council, 1995–98); Manchester Luncheon Club, 2005–07. *Publications:* jt editor and contributor to several surgical and gastroenterological books; numerous articles in various med. jls of GB, USA, Europe. *Recreation:* golf. *Address:* 27 Athol Road, Bramhall, Cheshire SK7 1BR. *T:* (0161) 439 2811.

**GILLESPIE, Ian**; District Judge (Magistrates' Courts) (formerly Stipendiary Magistrate), West Midlands Area, 1991–2015; West Midlands Member, Council of District Judges (Magistrates' Courts), 2005–15; Family Court Judge, 2014–15; *b* 8 Oct. 1945; *s* of James Alexander and Margaret Cicely Gillespie; *m* 1974, Diana Mary Stevens. *Educ:* King Henry VIII Sch., Coventry. Admitted Solicitor of Supreme Court, 1973; Partner, Brindley Twist Tafft & James, Solicitors, Coventry, 1974–91; Actg Stipendiary Magistrate, Wolverhampton, 1989–91. *Recreations:* walking, theatre, music, ballet, reading (especially British Naval history), kitchen gardening, baking hand-crafted bread. *E:* ian.gillespie45@icloud.com.

**GILLESPIE, Jonathan William James**, MA; Headmaster, St Albans School, since 2014; *b* 6 Dec. 1966; *s* of J. J. M. Gillespie and P. D. Gillespie; *m* 1992, Caroline Hotchkiss; two *s*. *Educ:* Bedford Modern Sch.; Selwyn Coll., Cambridge (BA Hons 1989; PGCE 1990; MA 1992). Asst Master, Highgate Sch., London, 1990–97; Hd of Modern Langs, 1997–2001, Housemaster, Moredun House, 2001–06, Fettes Coll., Edinburgh; Head Master, Lancing Coll., 2006–14. FRSA. *Recreations:* Highland bagpipe, hockey, golf, cricket, hillwalking. *Address:* St Albans School, Abbey Gateway, St Albans, Herts AL3 4HB. *T:* (01727) 515085, *Fax:* (01727) 843447. *E:* hm@st-albans-school.org.uk.

**GILLESPIE, Robert Andrew Joseph**; Partner, Evercore Partners Inc., 2009–10; Director-General, Takeover Panel, 2010–13; *b* Nottingham, 14 April 1955; *s* of late John Robert Gillespie and Honora Margaret Littlefair; *m* 1st, Carolyn Sarah Powell (separated 2006; marr. diss. 2013); three *d*; 2nd, 2015, Elena Elizabeth Angeliki Papazoglou. *Educ:* Nottingham High Sch.; Univ. of Durham (BA Hons Econs 1977). ACA. Price Waterhouse,

1977–81; S. G. Warburg, subseq. SBC Warburg 1981–97: Dir, 1987–97; Hd, Eur. Investment Banking, 1995–97; UBS Investment Bank, 1997–2008: Jt Hd, Global Investment Banking, 1999–2005; Chief Exec., Europe, Middle East and Africa, 2004–06; Vice Chm., 2005–08. Ind. Dir, Ashurst LLP, 2013–; non-executive Director: Royal Bank of Scotland, 2013–; Citizens Financial Gp Inc., 2014–15. Chm., Somerset House Trust, 2006–15. Chm., The Boat Race Company Ltd, 2009–. Mem., Stop Organised Abuse Bd, NSPCC, 2003–12; Vice Pres., Save the Children, 2004–10. Mem. Council, Durham Univ., 2007–18 (Chm., 2012–18). *Recreations:* cycling, sailing, shooting, golf, rowing, reading. *Address:* c/o RBS Group plc, 280 Bishopsgate, EC2M 4RB. *E:* gillespieraj@msn.com. *Clubs:* Oriental; Leander.

**GILLESPIE, Prof. Ronald James,** CM 2007; PhD, DSc; FRS 1977; FRSC; FRSC (UK); FCIC; Professor of Chemistry, McMaster University, Hamilton, Ont, 1960–88, now Emeritus; *b* London, England, 21 Aug. 1924; Canadian citizen; *s* of James A. Gillespie and Miriam G. (*née* Kirk); *m* 1950, Madge Ena Garner; two *d*. *Educ:* London Univ. (BSc 1945, PhD 1949, DSc 1957). FRSC 1965; FCIC 1960; FRIC; Mem., Amer. Chem. Soc. Asst Lectr, Dept of Chemistry, 1948–50, Lectr, 1950–58, UCL; Commonwealth Fund Fellow, Brown Univ., RI, USA, 1953–54; McMaster University: Associate Prof., Dept of Chem., 1958–60; Prof., 1960–62; Chm., Dept of Chem., 1962–65. Professeur Associé, l'Univ. des Sciences et Techniques de Languedoc, Montpellier, 1972–73; Visiting Professor: Univ. of Geneva, 1976; Univ. of Göttingen, 1978. Nyholm Lectr, RSC, 1979. Faraday Soc. Hon. LLD: Dalhousie Univ., 1988; Concordia Univ., 1988; Dr *hc* Montpellier, 1991; Hon. DSc: McMaster, 1993; Lethbridge, 2007. Medals: Ramsay, UCL, 1949; Harrison Meml, Chem. Soc., 1954; Canadian Centennial, 1967; Chem. Inst. of Canada, 1977; Silver Jubilee, 1978; Henry Marshall Tory, Royal Soc. of Canada, 1983. Awards: Noranda, Chem. Inst. of Canada, 1966 (for inorganic chem.); Amer. Chem. Soc. N-Eastern Reg., 1971 (in phys. chem.); Manufg Chemists Assoc. Coll. Chem. Teacher, 1972; Amer. Chem. Soc., 1973 (for distinguished service in advancement of inorganic chem.), 1980 (for creative work in fluorine chem.); Chem. Inst. of Canada/Union Carbide, 1976 (for chemical educn); Izaak Walton Killam Meml, Canada Council (for outstanding contrib. to advancement of res. in chemistry), 1987. *Publications:* Molecular Geometry, 1972 (London; German and Russian trans, 1975); (jtly) Chemistry, 1986, 2nd edn, 1989; The VSEPR Model of Molecular Geometry, 1990 (trans. Russian, 1992; Italian, 1994); (jtly) Atoms, Molecules and Reactions: an introduction to chemistry, 1994; (jtly) The Chemical Bond and Molecular Geometry: from Lewis to electron densities, 2001; papers in Jl Amer. Chem. Soc., Canadian Jl of Chem., and Inorganic Chem. *Recreations:* swimming, walking, reading, chess. *Address:* Department of Chemistry, McMaster University, Hamilton, ON L8S 4M1, Canada. *T:* (905) 6336042.

**GILLESPIE, Simon Maxwell,** OBE 2019; Chief Executive, British Heart Foundation, 2013–19; *b* Bromley, 17 Nov. 1959; *s* of Gordon Maxwell Gillespie and Margaret Cecilia Gillespie; *m* 1989, Dr Rosemary James. *Educ:* Corpus Christi Coll., Cambridge (BA 1981; MA 1984; MPhil 1994); Henley Mgt Coll. (MBA 1994). Served RN, 1977–2000: CO, HMS Sheffield; Mil. Asst to Minister for the Armed Forces. Dir of Ops, Charity Commn, 2000–04; Hd of Ops, Healthcare Commn, 2004–06; Chief Exec., Multiple Sclerosis Soc., 2006–13. Pres., European Heart Network, 2014–19. *Recreations:* hill-walking, jogging, recreational golf.

**GILLESPIE, Prof. Vincent Anthony,** DPhil; FBA 2013; FSA, FRHistS, FEA; J. R. R. Tolkien Professor of English Literature and Language (formerly J. R. R. Tolkien Professor of Medieval English Literature and Language), University of Oxford, and Fellow of Lady Margaret Hall, Oxford, since 2004; *b* 11 Feb. 1954; *s* of George Anthony Gillespie and Florence Doreen Gillespie (*née* Preston); *m* 1979, Margaret, (Peggy), Powell; two *s*. *Educ:* St Edward's Coll., Liverpool; Keble Coll., Oxford (BA, MA; DPhil 1981; Hon. Fellow, 2014). Lectr in English, Univ. of Reading, 1977–80; University of Oxford: Lectr in English, 1980–98; Reader, 1998–2004; Fellow and Tutor in English, St Anne's Coll., 1980–2004 (Hon. Fellow, 2004). Distinguished Vis. Prof. of Medieval Studies, Univ. of Calif, Berkeley, 2009–10; William Evans Fellow, Univ. of Otago, 2013. John Coffin Meml Lect. in Palaeography, Univ. of London, 2009; Medieval Studies Lect., Univ. of York, 2014; Etienne Gilson Lect., Pontifical Inst. of Mediaeval Studies, Toronto, 2016; Chaucer Lect., Univ. of Kent, 2018; Inaugural A. I. Doyle Meml Lect., Univ. of Durham, 2019. FRHistS 2003; FEA 2003; FSA 2004. *Publications:* (jtly) The English Medieval Book, 2001; Syon Abbey, 2002; (ed jtly) The Cambridge Companion to Medieval English Mysticism, 2011; (ed jtly) After Arundel: religious writing in fifteenth-century England, 2011; Looking in Holy Books, 2012; (ed jtly) Probable Truth: editing medieval texts from Britain in the twenty-first century, 2013; (ed jtly) A Companion to the Early Printed Book in Britain, 1476–1558, 2014; articles in learned jls and collaborative books. *Recreations:* theatre, wine, music, retired double-bass player. *Address:* Lady Margaret Hall, Oxford OX2 6QA. *E:* vincent.gillespie@ell.ox.ac.uk.

**GILLETT, Rt Rev. David Keith;** Bishop Suffragan of Bolton, 1999–2008; an Honorary Assistant Bishop, since 2008, and Interfaith Adviser, since 2010, Diocese of Norwich; *b* 25 Jan. 1945; *s* of Norman and Kathleen Gillett; *m* 1988, Valerie Shannon (*d* 2013). *Educ:* Leeds Univ. (BA Theol. 1st cl. 1965; MPhil 1968). Curate, St Luke's, Watford, 1968–71; Northern Sec., Pathfinders and Church Youth Fellowship's Assoc., 1971–74; Lectr, St John's Coll., Nottingham, 1974–79; Co-Leader, Christian Renewal Centre for Reconciliation, NI, 1979–82; Vicar of St Hugh's, Luton, 1982–88; Principal, Trinity Theol Coll., Bristol, 1988–99. Mem., Gen. Synod of C of E, 1985–88, 1990–99. Vice Pres., Christian Muslim Forum, 2012–. Trustee, Council of Christians and Jews, 2011–17. Hon. Canon of Bristol Cathedral, 1991–99. *Publications:* Learning in the Local Congregation, 1979; The Darkness where God is, 1983; Trust and Obey, 1993; (ed jtly) Treasure in the Field: the Archbishops' Companion to the Decade of Evangelism, 1993; co-author and contributor to various books and reference works. *Recreations:* photography, gardening, travel, especially visiting friends and former students around the world. *Address:* 10 Burton Close, Diss, Norfolk IP22 4YJ. *T:* (01379) 640309, 07891 001533. *E:* dkgillett@btinternet.com.

**GILLETT, Sir Nicholas (Danvers Penrose),** 3rd Bt *cr* 1959, of Bassishaw Ward, City of London; Product Director - High Energy Systems, Astrophysics Inc., USA, since 2013; *b* S Kensington, London, 24 Sept. 1955; *er s* of Sir Robin Danvers Penrose Gillett, 2nd Bt, GBE, RD and Elizabeth Marion Grace, *e d* of late John Findlay, JP; *S* father, 2009; *m* 1st, 1987, Haylie Brooks (marr. diss. 1997); 2nd, 2017, Cecilia Elizabeth Weiss. *Educ:* Pangbourne Coll.; Imperial Coll., London (BSc Hons Physics 1977). ARCS. Trials Engr, then Product Assurance Manager, Project Manager, Business Develt Manager, British Aerospace, Filton, 1977–91; EU Exec. Trng Prog., Japan, 1991–92; Project Manager and Business Develt Manager, British Aerospace, Stevenage, 1993–96; Dir, Technology Sales, EG&G Astrophysics, Bristol, 1997–98; Dir, Technical Mktg, Cargo Products, EG&G Astrophysics, USA, 1999–2002; Dir, Engrg Applications, 2003–04; Dir, Technical Mktg - Cargo Systems, 2005–09, Product Manager - Cargo Imaging Systems, 2009–12, L-3 Communications Security & Detection Systems, USA. *Recreations:* photography, diving, running, 360 video, 3D printing. *Heir: b* Christopher John Gillett [*b* 16 May 1958; *m* 1st, 1984, Julia Anne Holmes (marr. diss. 1996); one *s* one *d*; 2nd, 1996, Lucy Marie Schaufer]. *Address:* 1507 7th Street #47, Santa Monica, CA 90401, USA. *T:* (424) 2418117. *E:* mail@nick-g.com.

**GILLETT, Sarah,** CMG 2009; CVO 2009 (MVO 1986); HM Diplomatic Service, retired; Ambassador to Norway, 2014–18; *b* 21 July 1956; *d* of Sir Michael Cavenagh Gillett, KBE, CMG and Margaret Gillett. *Educ:* St Anthony's Leweston, Sherborne; Aberdeen Univ. (MA Hons). Joined HM Diplomatic Service, 1976: Third Sec., Washington, 1984–87; Third, later Second, Sec., Paris, 1987–90; on secondment to ODA, 1990–91; Central Eur. Dept, FCO, 1991–92; Vice-Consul (Inward Investment), Los Angeles, 1992–94; SE Asia Dept, FCO, 1994–97; First Sec., Brasilia, 1997–99; Counsellor and Dep. Head of Mission, Brasilia, 1999–2001; Consul-Gen., Montreal, 2002–05; Vice-Marshal of the Diplomatic Corps, and Dir of Protocol, FCO, 2006–09; Ambassador to Switzerland and (non-resident) to Liechtenstein, 2009–13. *Recreation:* outdoor exercise.

**GILLFORD, Lord;** John Maximillian Meade; *b* 28 Jan. 1998; *s* and heir of Earl of Clanwilliam, *qv*.

**GILLHAM, Geoffrey Charles;** HM Diplomatic Service, retired; consultant; author; *b* 1 June 1954; *s* of Peter George Gee Gillham and Alison Mary (*née* Jackman); *m* 1991, Nicola Mary Brewer (*see* Dame N. M. Brewer); one *s* one *d*. *Educ:* UWIST (BScEcon). Joined FCO, 1981: Second Sec., Caracas, 1983–85; on loan to Cabinet Office, 1986–88; FCO, 1988–89; First Secretary: Madrid, 1989–91; UK Delegn, OECD, Paris, 1991–95; First Sec., later Counsellor, FCO, 1995–98; Counsellor, New Delhi, 1998–2001; Hd, S European Dept, FCO, 2001–03; Asst Dir, EU (Mediterranean), FCO, 2003–04; Hd, Estate Strategy Unit, later Dir, Estates, FCO, 2004–08. Sec., UK-India Round Table, 2008–11; S Africa, 2009–13. Ind. Mem., Lord Chancellor's Adv. Cttee, Central and S London, 2014–. *Publications:* Burn Before Reading: undiplomatic tales (collected short stories), 2014; The Farm of the Monks, 2017. *Recreations:* music, travel, writing, sailing.

**GILLHAM, Dame Nicola Mary;** *see* Brewer, Dame N. M.

**GILLIAM, Terry;** animator, actor, writer; film director, since 1968; *b* Minneapolis, USA, 22 Nov. 1940; *s* of James H. and Beatrice Gilliam; *m* 1973, Maggie Weston; one *s* two *d*. *Educ:* Occidental Coll., LA, Calif. *Television:* resident cartoonist, We Have Ways of Making You Laugh, 1968; animator: Do Not Adjust Your Set, 1968–69; (also actor and co-writer), Monty Python's Flying Circus, 1969–74 and 1979; The Marty Feldman Comedy Machine, 1971–72; The Do-It-Yourself Film Animation, 1974; presenter, The Last Machine, 1995; *films:* co-writer, actor and animator: And Now For Something Completely Different, 1971; (also co-dir) Monty Python and the Holy Grail, 1974; Monty Python's Life of Brian, 1979; Monty Python Live at the Hollywood Bowl, 1982; Monty Python's The Meaning of Life, 1983; (animator, writer) The Miracle of Flight, 1974; (writer, dir) Jabberwocky, 1977; (co-writer, prod., dir) Time Bandits, 1981; (co-writer, dir) Brazil, 1985; (co-writer, dir) The Adventures of Baron Münchhausen, 1989; (dir) The Fisher King, 1991; (dir) Twelve Monkeys, 1996; (co-writer, dir) Fear and Loathing in Las Vegas, 1998; Lost in La Mancha, 2002; (co-writer, dir) The Brothers Grimm, 2005; (co-writer, dir) Tideland, 2005; (co-writer, prod., dir) The Imaginarium of Doctor Parnassus, 2009; (writer, dir) The Wholly Family, 2011; (dir) The Zero Theorem, 2013; (actor) Jupiter Ascending, 2015; *opera:* (dir) The Damnation of Faust, ENO, 2011; Benvenuto Cellini, ENO, 2014; *live show:* Monty Python Live at the Hollywood Bowl, 1980; Monty Python Live (Mostly), 02 Arena, 2014. Public art installation, Past People of Potsdamer Platz, Potsdamer Platz, Berlin, 2006. Fellow, BAFTA, 2009. Hon. DFA Occidental Coll., 1987; Hon. Dr: RCA, 1989; Nat. Univ. of Drama and Cinematography, Bucharest, 2013; Hon. DA Wimbledon Sch. of Arts, 2004. Chevalier, Order of Arts and Letters (France), 2013. *Publications:* Animations of Mortality, 1978; Time Bandits, 1981; (jtly) The Adventures of Baron Münchhausen, 1989; Fear and Loathing in Las Vegas: not the screenplay, 1998; Gilliam on Gilliam, 1999; Dark Knights and Holy Fools, 1999; Gilliamesque, 2015; *contributed to:* Monty Python's Big Red Book, 1971; The Brand New Monty Python Book, 1973, Monty Python and the Holy Grail, 1977; Monty Python's Life of Brian, 1979; Monty Python's The Meaning of Life, 1983; The Pythons Autobiography by The Pythons, 2003. *Recreations:* too busy. *Address:* c/o The Casaratto Co., Waverley House, 7–12 Noel Street, W1F 8GQ.

**GILLIBRAND, Philip Martin Mangnall;** District Judge (Magistrates' Courts), Hampshire, 2005–17 (Inner London, 2001–05); Deputy District Judge, since 2017; *b* 28 June 1951; *s* of late Frank Ivor Croft Gillibrand, Chorley, Lancs and Marjorie Joyce Gillibrand (*née* Golding); *m* 1979, Felicity Alexandra Augusta Priefert; one *s* one *d*. *Educ:* Reading Blue Coat Sch. (Aldsworth's Hosp.); Poly. of Central London (LLB Hons London (ext.) 1974). Called to the Bar, Gray's Inn, 1975; in practice at the Bar, London and on Western Circuit, 1975–2000: Bristol, 1982–93; Winchester, 1993–2000; Dep. Stipendiary Magistrate, Leicester, 1997–2000; Prison Adjudicator, 2004–11, 2016–; Diversity and Community Relns Judge, 2011–15. Mem., Family Proceedings and Youth Court Panels, 2001–17; Chm., Judicial Complaints Panel, 2009–15. Parish Councillor, Crawley, Hants, 1998–2013. Pres., Old Blues Assoc., 2015–17. *Recreations:* classic and historic motoring (Mem., Brooklands Trust; E-Type register correspondent, Jaguar Drivers' Club, 2012–16), motor racing (Mem., Mini Seven Racing Club; Steward, RAC Motor Sports Assoc., 2015–), reading from 19th and early 20th century; music (Mem., Elgar Soc.), campanology, the countryside, family life. *Address:* c/o Chief Magistrate's Office, Westminster Magistrates' Court, 181 Marylebone Road, NW1 5BR.

**GILLIBRAND, Sydney,** CBE 1991; FREng; Chairman, TAG Aviation (UK) Ltd, since 1998; Director, TAG Aviation (Holdings) SA, since 2001; *b* 2 June 1934; *s* of Sydney and Maud Gillibrand; *m* 1960, Angela Ellen Williams; three *s* (and one *s* decd). *Educ:* Preston Grammar Sch.; Harris Coll., Preston; College of Aeronautics, Cranfield (MSc). FRAeS 1975 (Hon. FRAeS 1994); FREng (FEng 1987). English Electric: apprentice, Preston, 1950; Chief Stress Engr, 1966; Works Man., Preston, 1974; Special Dir, BAC (Preston) Ltd, 1974; Dir of Manufacturing, Mil. Aircraft Div., 1977; British Aerospace Aircraft Group: Div. Prodn Dir, Warton, 1978; Dep. Man. Dir, Warton Div., and Bd Mem., Aircraft Gp, 1981; Div. Man. Dir, Kingston/Brough Div., 1983, Weybridge Div., 1984; British Aerospace PLC: Man. Dir, Civil Aircraft Div., 1986; Dir, 1987–95; Vice-Chm., 1991–95; Sen. Corporate Advr, 1995–99; Chairman: British Aerospace (Commercial Aircraft) Ltd, 1988–89; Aerospace Companies, 1989–92. Chm., AMEC plc, 1997–2004 (Dir, 1995–2004); Director: ICL plc, 1996–2002; Messier-Dowty Internat. Ltd, 1998–2003; Powergen, 1999–2002. Pres., SBAC, 1990–91. Hon. FIIE 2000. CCMI. Silver Medal, RAeS, 1981; James Watt Gold Medal, IMechE, 1997. *Recreation:* golf.

**GILLICK, Liam;** artist; *b* Aylesbury, 1964; *s* of G. V. T. Gillick and G. L. Gillick; *m* 1998, Sarah Dunbar Morris (marr. diss. 2013); three *s*. *Educ:* Goldsmiths' Coll., Univ. of London (BA Hons). Lectr, Goldsmiths' Coll., Univ. of London, 1994–97; Adjunct Professor: Columbia Univ., NY, 1997–2015; Bard Coll., Annandale-on-Hudson, 2007–. Exhibitions include: Whitechapel Gall., 2002; Mus. of Contemporary Art, Chicago, 2009. Work in permanent collections incl. Tate, MOMA, NY, Guggenheim, Centre Pompidou. Actor, Exhibition (film), 2014. *Publications:* Erasmus is Late, 1995; Discussion Island/Big Conference Centre, 1997; Five or Six, 2000; Literally No Place, 2002; Proxemics: selected writings, 1988–2004, 2005; (ed jtly) Factories in the Snow, 2006; All Books, 2009; Industry and Intelligence: contemporary art since 1820, 2016. *Recreations:* motorsports, agricultural history, early socialist literature. *Address:* c/o Maureen Paley, 21 Herald Street, E2 6JT. *T:* (020) 7729 4112.

**GILLIES, Crawford Scott;** Chairman, Edrington Group Ltd, since 2017; *b* Edinburgh, 1 May 1956; *s* of Robert and Netta Gillies; *m* 1978, Alison Farquhar; three *s*. *Educ:* Perth Acad.; Univ. of Edinburgh (LLB); Harvard Business Sch. (MBA). ACA 1980. Accountant, Peat, Marwick, Mitchell, 1977–80; Bain & Co.: Consultant, 1983–86; Manager, 1986–88; Partner, 1988–2005; Man. Partner UK, 1996–2000; Man. Dir, Europe, 2001–05. Non-executive Chairman: Control Risks Gp Hldgs Ltd, 2006–17; Hammonds LLP, 2006–09; non-executive Director: Standard Life plc, 2007–16; Mitie Gp plc, 2012–15; Barclays, 2014–; Sen. Ind. Dir, SSE, 2015–. Chm., Scottish Enterprise, 2009–15. FRSE 2018. *Recreations:* Rugby, golf, football, trees. *E:* cg@crawfordgillies.co.uk. *Club:* Caledonian.

**GILLIES, Prof. Malcolm George William,** AM 2013; PhD, DMus; Vice-Chancellor and Chief Executive, London Metropolitan University, 2010–14, now Emeritus Professor; *b* 23 Dec. 1954; *s* of Frank Douglas Gillies and Beatrice Mary Belle Gillies (*née* Copeman); *m* 2008, Dr David Pear. *Educ:* Royal Coll. of Music; Australian National Univ. (BA 1978); Univ. of Queensland (DipEd 1978); Clare Coll., Cambridge (BA 1980; MA 1984); King's Coll. London (MMus 1981); Univ. of London (PhD 1987); Univ. of Melbourne (DMus 2004). Tutor, Lectr, then Sen. Lectr in Music, Univ. of Melbourne, 1981–92; Prof. of Music, 1992–99, Dean of Music, 1992–97, Univ. of Queensland; Exec. Dean and Pro-Vice-Chancellor, Univ. of Adelaide, 1999–2001; Australian National University: Dep. Vice-Chancellor (Educn), 2002–06; Vice-Pres. (Develt), 2006–07; Emeritus Prof., 2015; Vice-Chancellor and Pres., 2007–09, and Prof. of Music, 2007–10, City Univ. London. Vis. Prof., Mathias Corvinus Collegium, Budapest, 2012–; Vis. Prof., 2015–18, Sen. Res. Fellow, 2018–, KCL. President: Australian Acad. of Humanities, 1998–2001; Nat. Acads Forum, 1998–2002; Australian Council for the Humanities, Arts and Soc. Scis, 2004–06; Chm., Nat. Scholarly Communications Forum, 2001–07; Vice-Chm., 2008–09, Chm., 2010–14, London Higher. Member Council: Gresham Coll., 2009–10; Specialist Schs and Academies Trust, 2010; Mem., Foundn Bd, Nyenrode Business Univ., Netherlands, 2010–17. Ed., Studies in Musical Genesis, Structure and Interpretation, 1997–. FLCM 1973; FAHA 1993; FACE 2006; FInstD 2014; Fellow, Qld Acad. of Arts and Scis, 2015. *Publications:* Bartók in Britain: a guided tour, 1989; Notation and Tonal Structure in Bartók's Later Works, 1989; Bartók Remembered, 1990 (German edn, 1991; Spanish edn, 2004); (ed) Halsey Stevens, The Life and Music of Béla Bartók, 3rd edn 1993; (ed) The Bartók Companion, 1993; (ed with David Pear) The All-Round Man: selected letters of Percy Grainger 1914–1961, 1994; (ed) Northern Exposures, 1997; (ed jtly) Grainger On Music, 1999; (with David Pear) Portrait of Percy Grainger, 2002; (ed jtly) Self-Portrait of Percy Grainger, 2006; Bartók Connections, 2007; (jtly) Open Knowledge Institutions: reinventing universities, 2018. *Recreations:* swimming, arts, the 1890s. *Address:* 1501/2 Marcus Clarke Street, Canberra City, ACT 2601, Australia.

**GILLIES, Prof. Norman Neil Nicolson,** OBE 2003; independent consultant, since 2012; *b* Stenscholl, Isle of Skye, 1 March 1947; *s* of Angus and Peggy Gillies; *m* 1977, Jean Brown Nixon; one *s* two *d*. *Educ:* Portree High Sch.; Ross Hall Scottish Hotel Sch.; Glasgow Coll. of Technol. (Cert. Accounting); Open Univ. (BA). Asst to Owner, Flodigarry Hotel, Isle of Skye, 1969–75; Admin. Manager, Allscott (CES) Ltd, 1975–83; Coll. Sec., 1983–86, Dir, 1986–2008, Sabhal Mòr Ostaig (Nat. Centre for Gaelic Lang. and Culture); Develt Dir, Clan Donald Lands Trust, 2009–11. Hon. Prof., Contemporary Highland Studies, Univ. of Aberdeen, 2002; Emeritus Prof., Univ. of Highlands and Islands, 2010. Gov., Royal Conservatoire of Scotland, 2010–. *Recreations:* reading, television, walking, films. *Address:* Innis Ard, Ardvasar, Sleat, Isle of Skye IV45 8RU. *T:* (01471) 844281. *E:* tormod281@btinternet.com.

**GILLIES, Prof. Pamela A.,** CBE 2013; PhD; FFPH; Principal and Vice-Chancellor, Glasgow Caledonian University, since 2006; *b* Dundee, 13 Feb. 1953. *Educ:* Univ. of Aberdeen (BSc Physiol.; PGCE; MEd); Univ. of Nottingham (MMedSci 1978; PhD Epidemiol. 1986). FFPH 2002. Posts in Sheffield evaluating health promotion initiatives, 1978–84; University of Nottingham, 1984–2006: Lectr in Public Health Medicine, then Prof. of Public Health Medicine; Pro Vice-Chancellor, 2001–06; Exec. Dir of Res., Health Educn Authy for England (on secondment), 1996–99. Abbott Fellow for AIDS Res., San Francisco, 1988; Harkness Fellow, Vis. Scholar and Vis. Prof. in Health and Human Rights, Cabot House, Harvard, 1992–93. Mem., Global Prog. on AIDS, WHO, Geneva, 1989–90. Chair: Glasgow Task Force, 2010–; Glasgow Health Commn. Member: Bd, Scottish Inst. for Excellence in Social Work Educn, 2006–08; W Regl Adv. Bd, Scottish Enterprise; Bioscis Wkg Gp on Public Health, Nuffield Inst.; Grameen Scotland Foudn, 2012–18; Global Adv. Council, African Leadership Coll. Trustee: British Council, 2008–14; Saltire Foundn; Founding Trustee, Robert F. Kennedy Human Rights UK, 2018–. FAcSS (AcSS 2005). FRSA; FRSE 2015. Hon. FRCPSGlas 2007. Hon. DSc Aberdeen, 2016. *Publications:* contribs to acad. jls and to Govt reports. *Address:* Office of the Vice-Chancellor, Glasgow Caledonian University, Britannia Building, City Campus, Cowcaddens Road, Glasgow G4 0BA.

**GILLIES, Rt Rev. Robert Arthur;** Bishop of Aberdeen and Orkney, 2007–16; *b* 21 Oct. 1951; *s* of Duncan and Vera Gillies; *m* 1976, Katherine Elizabeth Greening Tucker; three *s* (and one *s* decd). *Educ:* Univ. of Edinburgh (BD Hons 1978); Univ. of St Andrews (PhD 1991). Medical Lab. Technician, 1968–72; ordained deacon, 1977, priest, 1978; Curate, Christ Church, Falkirk, 1977–80; Curate, Christ Church, Edinburgh and Chaplain, Napier Coll., 1980–84; Chaplain, Univ. of Dundee, 1984–90; Rector, St Andrews Episcopal Church, St Andrews, 1991–2007; Synod Clerk, 2005–07, Dean, 2007, Dio. of St Andrews, Dunkeld and Dunblane. Hon. Lectr in Philosophy, Univ. of Dundee, 1985–94. *Publications:* A Way for Healing, 1995; Informing Faith, 1996; Healing Broader and Deeper, 1998; New Language of Faith, 2001; Where Earth and Heaven Meet, 2005; Sounds Before the Cross, 2007; Three Days in Holy Week, 2014; Approaching the Cross, 2017; Guilt and Forgiveness: a study in the thought and personality of Paul Ricoeur, 2019. *Recreations:* climbing Scotland's mountains, travelling England's canals, supporting Grimsby Town FC at a distance, watching ice hockey at close range. *Address:* 4 Kilrymont Place, St Andrews, Fife KY16 8DH. *E:* ragillies1@gmail.com.

**GILLIGAN, Andrew Paul;** Senior Correspondent, Sunday Times, since 2016; *b* London, 22 Nov. 1968; *s* of Kevin and Ann Gilligan. *Educ:* Grey Court Sch., Richmond; Kingston Coll. of Further Educn; St John's Coll., Cambridge. Defence corresp., Sunday Telegraph, 1995–99; Defence and Diplomatic corresp., Today Prog., BBC News, 1999–2004; reporter and columnist, London Evening Standard, 2004–09; London Ed., Telegraph Media Gp, 2009–16. Cycling Comr for London, GLA, 2013–16. *Recreation:* cycling. *Address:* Sunday Times, The News Building, 1 London Bridge Street, SE1 9GF.

**GILLIGAN, Prof. Christopher Aidan,** CBE 2015; DPhil, ScD; Professor of Mathematical Biology, University of Cambridge, since 1999 (Deputy Head, 2008–09, Head, 2009–13, School of Biological Sciences); Fellow, King's College, Cambridge, since 1988; *b* 9 Jan. 1953; *s* of William Christopher Gilligan and Kathleen Mary Gilligan (*née* Doyle); *m* 1974, Joan Flood; one *s* three *d*. *Educ:* St Mary's Coll., Crosby; Keble Coll., Oxford (BA 1974; MA 1978); Wolfson Coll., Oxford (DPhil 1978); Univ. of Cambridge (ScD 1999). University of Cambridge: Univ. Demonstrator, 1977; Lectr, Dept of Applied Biol., 1982–89, Dept of Plant Scis, 1989–95; Reader in Mathematical Biol., 1995–99; Royal Soc. Leverhulme Trust Sen. Res. Fellow, 1998–99; BBSRC Professorial Fellow, Dept of Plant Scis, 2004–10. King's College, Cambridge: Tutor, 1988–94; Mem. Coll. Council, 1988–91; Dir of Studies in Natural Sci., 1990–2004; Mem. Electors, 1995–98. Vis. Prof., Dept of Botany and Plant Pathol., Colorado State Univ., 1982. Chair: Sci. Adv. Council, DEFRA, 2011–14; Bd, Cambridge Prog. for Sustainability Leadership, 2011–16; JNCC, 2014–. Member: Council, Nat. Inst. Agricl Botany, 1985–91; Governing Body, Silsoe Res. Inst., 1998–2006; Council, BBSRC, 2003–09 (Mem., Strategy Bd, 2005–09); Adv. Cttee on Forest Res., Forestry Commn, 2006–09; Chairman: BBSRC Crop Sci. Review, 2003–04; Commn of Evaluation on Plant Health and Envmt, Institut Nat. de la Recherche Agronomique, France, 2003; Adviser on agricl systems research: Scottish Exec. Envmt and Rural Affairs Dept, 1998–2003; Institut Nat. de la Recherche Agronomique, 2003–05. Pres., British Soc. for Plant Pathol., 2001. Fisher Lectr, Rothamsted Res., 2009; R. W. Holley Lectr, Cornell Univ., 2011. Fellow, Royal Statistical Soc., 1995; Rothamsted Fellow, 1998–2015; Hon. Fellow, Amer. Phytopathol. Soc., 2005. Trustee, Natural Hist. Mus., 2011–19. *Publications:* (ed) Mathematical Modelling of Crop Disease, 1985; numerous articles on botanical epidemiol. and modelling in biol. and mathematical biol. jls. *Recreations:* family, running, reading, travel. *Address:* Department of Plant Sciences, University of Cambridge, Downing Street, Cambridge CB2 3EA. *T:* (01223) 333900. *E:* cag1@cam.ac.uk.

**GILLILAND, David;** see Gilliland, His Honour J. A. D.

**GILLILAND, His Honour (James Andrew) David;** QC 1984; a Circuit Judge, 1992–2007; a Judge, Technology and Construction Court, 2000–07; an Arbitrator, since 2007; *b* 29 Dec. 1937; *s* of James Albin Gilliland and Mary Gilliland (*née* Gray); *m* 1961, Elsie McCully; two *s*. *Educ:* Campbell College; Queen's University Belfast. LLB (1st Class Hons) 1960. Called to the Bar, Gray's Inn, 1964 (Holt Scholar, Atkin Scholar, Macaskie Scholar); Lectr in Law, Manchester University, 1960–72; a Recorder, 1989–92. *Recreations:* music, opera, stamp collecting. *Address:* Kings Chambers, 36 Young Street, Manchester M3 3FT. *T:* (0161) 832 9082. *Club:* Athenæum (Liverpool).

**GILLILAND, Jennifer, (Mrs David Gilliland);** see Johnston, J.

**GILLINGHAM, Prof. John Bennett,** FBA 2007; historian; Professor of History, London School of Economics and Political Science, 1995–98, now Emeritus; *b* 3 Aug. 1940; *s* of Arthur Gillingham and Irene Gillingham; *m* 1966, June Guy (marr. diss. 1978); two *d*. *Educ:* Rottingdean Primary Sch.; Brighton, Hove and Sussex Grammar Sch.; Queen's Coll., Oxford (BA Hons Modern Hist.; BPhil Medieval Hist.). Laming Travelling Fellow, Queen's Coll., Oxford, 1963–65; Lectr, then Sen. Lectr, LSE, 1965–95. Dir, Battle Conf. on Anglo-Norman Studies, 2000–04; Ed., Anglo-Norman Studies, 2000–04. *Publications:* Cromwell: portrait of a soldier, 1976; Richard the Lionheart, 1978, 2nd edn 1989 (trans. German, French; Prix Guillaume le Conquérant, 1997); The Wars of the Roses, 1981 (trans. Hungarian); (ed with Malcolm Falkus) Historical Atlas of Britain, 1981 (trans. Japanese); The Angevin Empire, 1984, 2nd edn 2001; (ed) Richard III: a medieval kingship, 1993; Richard Coeur de Lion: kingship, chivalry and war in the twelfth century, 1994; Richard I, 1999, 2nd edn 2001 (trans. Spanish); The English in the Twelfth Century, 2000; (with Ralph Griffiths) Medieval Britain: a very short introduction, 2000 (trans. Chinese); Medieval Kingdoms, 2001; (with Danny Danziger) 1215 The Year of Magna Carta, 2003; Conquests, Catastrophe and Recovery: Britain and Ireland 1066–1485, 2014; William II: the Red King, 2015. *Recreation:* walking.

**GILLINGS, Ven. Richard John;** Archdeacon of Macclesfield, 1994–2010, now Archdeacon Emeritus; Priest, St Columba's, Grantown-on-Spey, and St John's Rothiemurchus, Diocese of Moray, since 2011; *b* 17 Sept. 1945; *s* of John Albert Gillings and Constance Ford Gillings; *m* 1972, Kathryn Mary Hill; two *s* two *d*. *Educ:* Sale GS; St Chad's Coll., Durham (BA, Dip Biblical Studies); Lincoln Theol Coll. Ordained deacon 1970, priest 1971; Curate, St George's, Altrincham, 1970–75; Priest i/c, then Rector, St Thomas', Stockport, 1975–83, and Priest i/c, St Peter's, Stockport, 1978–83; Rector, Birkenhead Priory, 1983–93; Vicar, Bramhall, 1993–2005. RD, Birkenhead, 1985–93; Hon. Canon, Chester Cathedral, 1992–94. Mem., Gen. Synod, 1980–2005. *Recreations:* music, cinema, theatre, railways. *Address:* Culvardie, Desher Road, Boat of Garten, Inverness-shire PH24 3BN.

**GILLINGWATER, Richard Dunnell,** CBE 2008; Chairman: Janus Henderson (formerly Henderson Group), since 2013; SSE plc, since 2015; *b* 21 July 1956; *s* of Malcolm and Olive Gillingwater; *m* 1981, Helen Margaret Leighton Davies; one *s* three *d*. *Educ:* Chesterfield Grammar Sch.; St Edmund Hall, Oxford (MA Jurisprudence); Inst. for Mgt Develt, Lausanne (MBA). Articled Clerk, Lovell, White and King, Solicitors, 1978–80; admitted solicitor, 1980; with Kleinwort Benson Ltd, 1980–90 (Dir, 1990); Barclays De Zoete Wedd: Dir, Corporate Finance, 1990–92; Man. Dir, 1992; Jt Hd, Global Corporate Finance, 1995–98; Jt Dep. Hd, 1998–2001, Chm., 2001–03, European Investment Banking, Credit Suisse First Boston; Chief Exec., 2003–06, Chm., 2006–07, Shareholder Exec., Cabinet Office; Dean, Cass Business Sch., City Univ., 2007–12. Chairman: Faber Music, 2002–07; CDC, 2009–13; non-executive Director: Kidde, 2004–05; QinetiQ, 2004–06; Tomkins, 2005–10; P&O, 2005–06; Debenhams, 2006–09; SSE (formerly Scottish and Southern Energy), 2007–; Hiscox, 2010–15; Helical Bar, 2012–18; Wm Morrison Supermarkets plc, 2013–15; Sen. Ind. Dir, Whitbread plc, 2018–; Mem., Adv. Council, City UK, 2010–16. Mem., Prime Minister's Business Council, 2018–. Trustee, British Council, 2012–14. Chm., Malcolm Arnold Fest., 2010–. Mem., Adv. Bd, St Edmund Hall, Oxford, 2004–10; Pro-Chancellor, Open Univ., 2014–18. Chevalier de l'Ordre des Palmes Académiques (France), 2012. Hon. DSc City. Hon. Fellow, ACT. *Recreations:* music, reading, walking, travelling.

**GILLINSON, Sir Clive (Daniel),** Kt 2005; CBE 1998; Executive and Artistic Director, Carnegie Hall, New York, since 2005; *b* 7 March 1946; *s* of Stanley Gillinson and Regina Schein; *m* 1979, Penelope Morsley (marr. diss. 2018); one *s* two *d*; *m* 2018, Anya Deutsch. *Educ:* Frensham Heights Sch.; Queen Mary Coll., London; Royal Acad. of Music (Recital Dip., May Mukle Prize). Mem., Cello Section, LSO, 1970–84. Jt owner, Clive Daniel Antiques, 1978–86. Founding Partner, Masterprize, 1997. Chm., Assoc. of British Orchestras, 1992–95; Gov. and Mem. Exec. Cttee, NYO of GB, 1995–2004; Man. Dir, LSO, 1984–2005. *Recreations:* tennis, ski-ing, reading, theatre, cinema, carpentry. *Address:* Carnegie Hall, 881 7th Avenue, New York, NY 10019–3210, USA.

**GILLION, Rt Rev. (Alan) Robert;** Bishop of Riverina, 2014–18; Hon. Assistant Bishop, Diocese of Lincoln, since 2018; *b* Docking, Norfolk, 7 Sept. 1951; *s* of Arthur and Barbara Gillion; *m* 1974, Janine Ellis; two *s*. *Educ:* Norwich Sch.; New Coll. of Speech and Drama; London Univ. (Dip. in Dramatic Art; DipEd); Salisbury and Wells Theol Coll. (DipTh). LRAM 1973. Actor and theatre dir, 1970–81; ordained deacon, 1983, priest, 1984; Curate, East Dereham, 1983–86; Team Vicar, Richmond, Surrey, 1986–90; Priest-in-charge, Discovery Bay Church, Hong Kong, 1990–98; Bishop of Kensington's Officer for Evangelism, 1998–2001; Vicar, St Simon Zelotes and St Saviour, London, 2001–08; Area Dean of Chelsea, 2004–11; Rector, Holy Trinity and St Saviour, Upper Chelsea, 2008–14.

Chaplain: St John's Cathedral, Hong Kong, 1990–98; Shek Pik Prison, Hong Kong, 1990–98; Exec. Sec. for Religious Broadcasting, Hong Kong Christian Council, 1990–98. Chaplain to Harrods, 2004–14; Sen. Chaplain, Actors Church Union, 2006–13. Trustee, Bible Reading Fellowship, 2008–14. Freelance broadcaster, BBC, 1998–2014; contrib. to New Daylights, 1998–2005. *Recreations:* family, theatre, sport, golf, tennis. *Address:* 7 Peachwood Close, Grantham NG31 8QP. *T:* 07465 696419. *E:* robgillion@hotmail.com.

**GILLMAN, Derek Anthony;** Distinguished Teaching Professor, Art History and Museum Leadership, Antoinette Westphal College of Media Arts and Design, since 2016, and Senior Adviser to President for University Collections, Drexel University, since 2018 (Distinguished Visiting Professor, 2014–16); *b* 7 Dec. 1952; *s* of Abraham Gillman and Esther Gillman; *m* 1987, Yael Joanna Hirsch; one *s* two *d*. *Educ*: Clifton Coll., Bristol; Magdalen Coll., Oxford (MA); Beijing Langs Inst.; Univ. of E Anglia (LLM). Chinese specialist, Christie's Auctioneers, London, 1977–81; Res. Asst, Dept of Oriental Antiquities, BM, 1981–85; Keeper, Sainsbury Centre for Visual Arts, UEA, 1985–95; Dep. Dir, Internat. Art and Collection Mgt, 1995–96, Curatorial and Educn Services, 1996–99, Nat. Gall. of Victoria; Exec. Dir and Provost, 1999–2000, Pres. and Edna S. Tuttleman Dir, 2001–06, Pennsylvania Acad. of Fine Arts; Exec. Dir and Pres., Barnes Foundn, 2006–13; Chm., Impressionist and Modern Art, and Sen. Vice Pres., Christie's, 2015–16. Sen. Fellow, Melbourne Inst. of Asian Langs and Socs, 1998–2003; Consulting Scholar, Asian Sect., Penn Mus., 2009–; Marina Kellen French Dist. Visitor, Amer. Acad. in Berlin, 2013. *Publications:* The Idea of Cultural Heritage, 2006, 2nd edn 2010 (Chinese edn 2018); contrib. to exhibn catalogues; articles and reviews for Art, Antiquity and Law, SOAS Bull., Buddhist Forum, Apollo, Orientations, Trans Oriental Ceramic Soc. *Recreations:* reading, drawing. *Address:* Antoinette Westphal College of Media Arts and Design, Drexel University, 3501 Market Street, Philadelphia, PA 19104, USA.

**GILLON, John Christopher M.;** *see* Moore-Gillon.

**GILLON, Karen Macdonald;** Associate Secretary, Guild team, Church of Scotland, since 2016; *b* 18 Aug. 1967; *d* of Edith Turnbull (*née* Macdonald); *m* 1999, James Gillon; two *s* one *d*. *Educ*: Jedburgh Grammar Sch.; Birmingham Univ. (Cert. Youth and Community Work 1991). Project Worker, Terminal One youth project, Blantyre, 1991–94; Community Educn Worker, N Lanarkshire Council, 1994–97; PA to Rt Hon. Helen Liddell, MP, 1997–99. Project Coordinator, Douglas St Brides Community Centre, 2012–14; Local Develt Worker, World Mission Council, Church of Scotland, 2014–16. Mem. (Lab) Clydesdale, Scottish Parlt, 1999–2011; contested (Lab) same seat, 2011. *Recreations:* sport, cooking, flower arranging, music.

**GILLON, Prof. Raanan Evelyn Zvi,** FRCP; Professor of Medical Ethics, School of Medicine, Imperial College, London, 1995–99, now Emeritus (Visiting Professor, 1989–94); part-time general practitioner, 1974–2002; NHS Senior Partner, Imperial College Medical Partnership, 1991–2002; *b* Jerusalem, 15 April 1941; *s* of late Diana Gillon and Meir Gillon; *m* 1966, Angela Spear; one *d*. *Educ*: Christ's Hospital; University College London (MB BS 1964); Christ Church, Oxford; Birkbeck College London (BA Phil 1st cl. Hons 1979; philosophy prize). MRCP 1974, FRCP 1988. Medical journalism, 1964–71 (Ed., Medical Tribune); part-time GP, part-time philosophy student then teacher, 1974–2006; Dir, Imperial Coll. Health Service, 1982–95; Dir of Teaching in Medical Ethics (for MA course), KCL, 1986–89. Vis. Prof. in Med. Ethics, KCL, 1988–91. Chm., Imperial Coll. Ethics Cttee, 1984–93. Member: BMA, 1964– (Pres., 2019–June 2020); Mem., 1998–, Vice-Chm., 2002–06, Ethics Cttee); Archbp of Canterbury's Adv. Gp on Med. Ethics, 1999–2006. Mem. Governing Body and Trustee, 1989–, Chm., 2000–11, a Vice Pres., 2011–13, Pres., 2013–, Inst. of Medical Ethics; Pres., Health Care Ethics Forum, 2005–13. Trustee, London Nightline, 2002–. Mem. Ct of Govs, Christ's Hosp., 2007–. Ed., Jl of Med. Ethics, 1980–2001. FRSocMed 1966; Fellow, Hastings Center, USA, 2005. Hon. RCM 1986. Hon. DSc Oxon, 2006. Henry Beecher Award, Hastings Center, USA, 1999; Millennium Award, Norwegian Univ. of Sci and Tech., 2001. *Publications:* Philosophical Medical Ethics, 1986 (13 reprints); (Sen. Ed. and contrib.) Principles of Health Care Ethics, 1994; numerous papers on medical ethics. *Recreations:* enjoying the company of wife and daughter, thinking and writing about medical ethics; reading moral philosophy and, intermittently, thrillers and novels, mostly recommended by Angela; previously playing (blowing?) own trumpet, or rather, Uncle Peter's trumpet, kindly lent in 1954 and bequested to me by his executor, cousin Stephen; now singing in a small a cappella choir, occasional ski-ing, swimming, active walks on a golf course; regular cooking, winetasting, arguing and good company. *Address:* 42 Brynmaer Road, SW11 4EW. *T:* (020) 7622 1450.

**GILMORE, Brian Terence,** CB 1992; *b* 25 May 1937; *s* of late John Henry Gilmore and of Edith Alice Gilmore; *m* 1962, Rosalind Edith Jean Fraser (*see* R. E. J. Gilmore). *Educ*: Wolverhampton Grammar Sch.; Christ Church, Oxford (Passmore-Edwards Prize, 1956; BA Lit. Hum.; MA 1961). CRO and Diplomatic Service Admin Office, 1958–65: Private Sec. to Perm. Sec., 1960–61, to Parly Under Sec., 1961–62; Asst Private Sec. to Sec. of State, 1962–64; British Embassy, Washington, 1965–68; Min. of Technology and DTI, 1968–72: Private Sec. to Minister of State, Industry, 1969–70, and to Lord Privy Seal and Leader of the House of Lords, 1971–72; CSD, 1972–81; Under Sec., 1979; Principal, CS Coll., 1979–81; HM Treasury, 1981–88; Principal Estabt Officer and Principal Finance Officer, 1982–84; Dep. Sec., Office of Minister for CS, Cabinet Office, 1988–92; Dep. Sec., DSS, 1992–94. Chairman: PYBT (E London), 1996–2000; Bart's and the London NHS Trust, 1999–2000. Vice-Pres., Soc. for Promotion of Hellenic Studies, 2000–. *Recreations:* music, walking, Greece. *Address:* 3 Clarendon Mews, W2 2NR. *Club:* Athenæum (Chm., 2000–03; Trustee, 2006–15).

**GILMORE, Eamon;** Special Representative for Human Rights, European Union, since 2019; *b* Caltra, Co. Galway, 24 April 1955; *s* of John Gilmore and Celia Concannon; *m* Carol Hanney; two *s* one *d*. *Educ*: Garbally Coll., Ballinasloe, Galway; University Coll., Galway (BA Psychol.). Pres., Union of Students in Ireland, 1976–78. Trade union organiser, Irish Transport and Gen. Workers' Union, 1978–89. Mem., Dublin CC, 1985–2003. Mem. of the Dáil (TD) for Dún Laoghaire, 1989–2016 (Workers', 1989–92, Democratic Left, 1992–99, Lab, 1999–2016); Tánaiste (Dep. Prime Minister) and Minister for Foreign Affairs and Trade, Ireland, 2011–14; Leader, Irish Labour Party, 2007–14; Special Envoy for Peace Process in Colombia, EU, 2015–19. Adjunct Prof. Sch. of Law and Governance, Dublin City Univ., 2016–; George Soros Vis. Practitioner Chair, Sch. of Public Policy, Central European Univ., Budapest, 2017. Hon. DLaws, NUI Galway, 2016. Officier, Légion d'Honneur (France), 2016. *Publications:* Leading Lights: people who've inspired me, 2010; Inside the Room: the untold story of Ireland's Crisis Government, 2015. *Recreations:* sport, family, cooking. *T:* (086) 7947624. *E:* eamon.gilmore@eeas.europa.eu. *W:* www.gilmore.ie.

**GILMORE, Prof. Gerard Francis,** PhD, ScD; FRS 2013; FRAS, FInstP; Professor of Experimental Philosophy, University of Cambridge, since 2000; *b* Timaru, NZ, 7 Nov. 1951; *s* of Joseph and Eva Gilmore; *m* 1975, Annette Mary Connolly; one *s* one *d*. *Educ*: St Bede's Coll., Christchurch, NZ; Canterbury Univ., NZ (BSc 1st Cl. Hons 1973; PhD 1979); Clare Hall, Cambridge (MA; ScD 2002). FInstP 2000; FRAS 2009. Sen. Res. Fellow, Royal Observatory, Edinburgh, 1979–84; University of Cambridge: Advanced Res. Fellow, 1984–89; Royal Soc. Smithson Fellow, 1987–91; Fellow, King's Coll., 1987–91; John Couch Adams Astronomer, 1989–95; Reader in Astrophysics, 1995–2000; Dep. Dir, Inst. of Astronomy, 1996–2006. UK Principal Investigator, ESA Gaia mission, 2000–; Co-ordinator, Opticon, 2002–. Mem. Council, Eur. Southern Observatory, 2002–07; Member, Advisory Board: Iran Nat. Observatory, 2007–; Aarhus Univ., 2013–. MAE 2004. Hon. Fellow, Royal Astronomical Soc. of NZ, 2016; Hon. FRSNZ 2017. *Publications:* (ed jtly) The Galaxy, 1987; (jtly) The Milky Way as a Galaxy, 1989; (ed jtly) Baryonic Dark Matter, 1990; (ed jtly) Galactic and Solar System Optical Astrometry, 1994; (ed jtly) Stellar Populations, 1994; (ed jtly) Stellar Initial Mass Function, 1998; contrib. scientific articles. *Recreations:* sport, visiting historical sites, being a good dad, cooking, thinking, weighing galaxies, watching Shaun the Sheep, gnomes. *Address:* Institute of Astronomy, University of Cambridge, Madingley Road, Cambridge CB3 0HA. *T:* (01223) 337506. *E:* gil@ast.cam.ac.uk.

**GILMORE, Sir Ian (Thomas),** Kt 2010; MD; FRCP; Consultant Physician, Royal Liverpool Hospital, 1980–2011, now Honorary Consultant Physician; Professor of Medicine, University of Liverpool, since 1999; *b* 25 Sept. 1946; *s* of James M. and Jean M. Gilmore; *m* 1975, Hilary Elizabeth Douglas; two *s* one *d*. *Educ*: Royal Grammar Sch., Newcastle upon Tyne; King's Coll., Cambridge (BA 1968; MB BChir 1971; MD 1979); St Thomas' Hosp., London. FRCP 1985. MRC Trng Fellow, St Thomas' Hosp., 1976–77; MRC Travelling Fellow, Univ. of Calif, San Diego, 1979–80. Chair, Liverpool Health Partners, 2011–18. President: RCP, 2006–10; British Gastroenterology Soc., 2012–14; Alcohol Concern, 2014–17. Chm., Alcohol Health Alliance, 2007–. *Publications:* (ed) Gastrointestinal Emergencies, 1992; contrib. original articles, chapters and invited reviews on gastrointestinal and liver diseases. *Recreations:* golf, travel. *Address:* Liverpool Health Partners, University of Liverpool, 1st Floor, Liverpool Science Park, 131 Mount Pleasant, Liverpool L3 5TF. *Clubs:* Artists (Liverpool); Royal Liverpool Golf (Captain, 2018).

**GILMORE, Margaret, (Mrs Eamonn Matthews);** writer, broadcaster and counter-terrorism analyst; *b* 9 Feb. 1956; *d* of late Rev. Canon Norman and Barbara Gilmore; *m* 1993, Eamonn Matthews; one *s*. *Educ*: North London Collegiate Sch., Middlesex; Westfield Coll., London (BA Hons English). Reporter: Kensington Post, 1977–79; Independent Radio News, 1979–84; BBC N Ireland, 1984–85; Newsnight, BBC, 1986–89; This Week, ITV, 1989–92; Panorama, BBC, 1993–95; news corresp., 1995–97, envmt corresp., 1997–2000, home and legal affairs corresp., 2000–07, BBC. Member: Bd, Food Standards Agency, 2008–14; HFEA, 2015– (Dep. Chair, 2016–). Asst Comr, Boundary Commn for England, 2016–18. Sen. Associate Fellow, RUSI, 2014–18 (Associate Fellow, 2007–09; Sen. Res. Fellow, 2009–14). *Publications:* (with A. Hayman) The Terrorist Hunters, 2009. *Recreations:* travel, football (supporting Reading FC), music. *Address:* c/o Knight Ayton Management, 29 Gloucester Place, W1U 8HX. *E:* MargaretGilmore@btinternet.com. *W:* www.MargaretGilmore.com.

**GILMORE, Rosalind Edith Jean, (Mrs B. T. Gilmore),** CB 1995; Independent Director, Prudential Regulation Authority, Bank of England, 2013–14; *b* 23 March 1937; *oc* of Sir Robert Brown Fraser, OBE, and Betty Fraser; *m* 1962, Brian Terence Gilmore, *qv*. *Educ*: King Alfred Sch.; University Coll. London (BA; Hon. Fellow (Fellow, 1989)); Newnham Coll., Cambridge (BA, MA; Associate Fellow, 1986–95, Hon. Fellow, 1995). Asst Principal, HM Treasury, 1960–65; IBRD, 1966–67; Principal, HM Treasury, 1968–73; Prin. Pvte Sec. to Chancellor of Duchy of Lancaster, Cabinet Office, 1974; HM Treasury: Asst Sec., 1975–80; Press Sec. and Hd of Inf., 1980–82; Gen. Man., Corporate Planning, Dunlop Ltd, 1982–83; Dir of Marketing, Nat. Girobank, 1983–86; Directing Fellow, St George's House, Windsor Castle, 1986–89; re-instated, HM Treasury, and seconded to Bldg Socs Commn, 1989; Dep. Chm., 1989–91, Chm. (First Comr), 1991–94, Bldg Socs Commn; Chief Registrar of Friendly Socs, 1991–94; Industrial Assurance Comr, 1991–94; Dir of Regulation, Lloyd's of London, 1995; Dir, Zurich Financial Services AG, 1998–2007. Chairman: Arrow Broadcasting, 1994–97; Homeowners Friendly Soc., 1996–98; Director: Mercantile Gp plc, 1986–89; London and Manchester Gp plc, 1986–89; BAT Industries, 1996–98; TU Fund Managers, 2000–06; Cons. Man., FI Gp plc, 1987–89. Mem., SIB, 1993–96; Comr, Nat. Lottery Commn, 2000–02. Director: Leadership Foundn, Washington, 1997– (Chm., 2005–07); Internat. Women's Forum, 2005–07 (Vice Pres., 1997–2001). Member: Board: Opera North, 1993–97; Moorfields Eye Hosp. NHS Trust, 1994–2000; Council, RCM, 1997–2007; Court, Cranfield Univ., 1992– (Mem. Adv. Bd, Sch. of Mgt, 2010–; Vis. Fellow, 2013–); Adv. Bd, Winton Centre for Financial History, 2011–. FRSA 1985; CCMI (CIMgt 1992); Hon. RCM 2009. *Publications:* Mutuality for the Twenty-first Century, 1998. *Recreations:* swimming (Half Blue, Cambridge Univ.), music, languages. *Address:* 3 Clarendon Mews, W2 2NR. *Club:* Athenæum.

**GILMORE, Sheila;** *b* Aberdeen, 1 Oct. 1949; *d* of Harry Hawthorne and Elizabeth McDonald; *m* 1969, Brian Gilmore; three *s* one *d*. *Educ*: Univ. of Kent (Hist. and Pols 1970); Univ. of Edinburgh (LBB 1977). Teacher, 1971–73; family lawyer, 1977–2001. Mem., Edinburgh CC, 1991–2007 (Housing Convenor, 1999–2007). MP (Lab) Edinburgh E, 2010–15; contested (Lab) same seat, 2015. *Recreations:* cycling, reading.

**GILMOUR, Lt-Col Colin Edward,** MBE 2001; Vice Lord-Lieutenant of Sutherland, since 2017; *b* Petty, Inverness-shire, 18 Oct. 1946; *s* of Col Sir Allan Macdonald Gilmour, KCVO, OBE, MC and Jean Gilmour; *m* 1971, Caroline Bourne; two *d*. *Educ*: Winchester Coll.; RMA, Sandhurst. Commnd Queen's Own Highlanders (Seaforth and Camerons), 1967; Regtl and staff appts, 1968–89; i/c 2nd 51st Highland Volunteers, 1989–91; on staff, MoD, 1992–96; SO, Perm. Jt HQ Northwood, 1996–2001. Chm., Northern Area Highland Reserve Forces and Cadets, 2008–12. DL Sutherland, 2003. *Recreations:* hill walking, fishing, gardening. *Address:* Shenaval, Altass, Lairg, Sutherland IV27 4EU.

**GILMOUR, David Jon,** CBE 2003; singer, guitarist and songwriter; *b* Cambridge, 6 March 1946; *s* of Douglas Gilmour and Sylvia Gilmour (*née* Wilson); *m* 1st, 1975, Virginia, (Ginger), Hasenbein (marr. diss.); one *s* three *d*; 2nd, 1994, Polly Samson, *qv*; two *s* one *d* and one step *s*. *Educ*: Perse Sch. for Boys; Cambridgeshire Coll. of Arts and Technol. Joined Pink Floyd, 1968; albums include: A Saucerful of Secrets, 1968; Atom Heart Mother, 1970; Meddle, 1971; Obscured by Clouds, 1972; The Dark Side of the Moon, 1973; Wish You Were Here, 1975; Animals, 1977; The Wall, 1979; The Final Cut, 1983; A Momentary Lapse of Reason, 1987; The Division Bell, 1994; The Endless River, 2014; solo albums: David Gilmour, 1978; About Face, 1984; On an Island, 2006; Live in Gdansk, 2008; Rattle that Lock, 2015; Live At Pompeii, 2017. Ivor Novello Award for Lifetime Achievement, 2008. *Address:* c/o One Fifteen, 1 Globe House, Middle Lane Mews, N8 8PN.

**GILMOUR, Sir David (Robert),** 4th Bt *cr* 1926; writer; *b* 14 Nov. 1952; *er s* of Lord Gilmour of Craigmillar, PC (Life Peer) and of Lady Caroline Gilmour (*née* Montagu-Douglas-Scott); *S* to father's Btcy, 2007; *m* 1975, Sarah Anne, *d* of late M. H. G. Bradstock; one *s* three *d*. *Educ*: Eton; Balliol Coll., Oxford (BA Hons). FRSL 1990. Dep. Ed., 1979–81, Contributing Ed., 1981–85, Middle East International; Res. Fellow, St Antony's Coll., Oxford, 1996–97; Sen. Res. Associate, Balliol Coll., Oxford 2011–13. Chm., CPRE Cherwell Dist, 2018–. *Publications:* Dispossessed: the ordeal of the Palestinians, 1980; Lebanon: the fractured country, 1983, 3rd edn 1987; The Transformation of Spain: from Franco to the constitutional monarchy, 1985; The Last Leopard: a life of Giuseppe di Lampedusa, 1988 (Marsh Biography Award, 1989), 5th edn 2007; The Hungry

Generations, 1991; Cities of Spain, 1992; Curzon, 1994 (Duff Cooper Prize, 1995), 2nd edn 2003; (ed) The French and their Revolution, 1998; (ed) Paris and Elsewhere, 1998; The Long Recessional: the Imperial life of Rudyard Kipling, 2002 (Elizabeth Longford Prize for Historical Biography, 2003); The Ruling Caste: Imperial lives in the Victorian Raj, 2005; The Pursuit of Italy: a history of a land, its regions and their peoples, 2011; The British in India: three centuries of ambition and experience, 2018. *Recreations:* gardening, baking, cricket, opera. *Heir: s* Alexander Ian Michael Gilmour, *b* 19 Feb. 1980. *Address:* The Barn House, Alkerton, Oxon OX15 6NL. *Clubs:* Brooks's, Grillions.

**GILMOUR, Sir (John) Nicholas,** 5th Bt *cr* 1897, of Lundin and Montrave, co. Fife; *b* 15 Dec. 1970; *s* of Sir John Gilmour, 4th Bt and of Valerie Jardine Gilmour (*née* Russell); *S* father, 2013; *m* 1996, Airin Thamrin; two *s. Heir: s* John Edward Arief Gilmour, *b* 23 July 2001. *Address:* Montrave House, Leven, Fife KY8 5NY.

**GILMOUR, His Honour Nigel Benjamin Douglas;** QC 1990; a Circuit Judge, 2000–13; *b* 21 Nov. 1947; *s* of late Benjamin Waterfall Gilmour and Barbara Mary Gilmour (subseq. Mrs E. Harborow); *m* 1972, Isobel Anne, *d* of E. Harborow; two *d. Educ:* Tettenhall Coll., Staffordshire; Liverpool Univ. (LLB Hons). Called to the Bar, Inner Temple, 1970; an Asst Recorder, 1984–90; a Recorder, 1990–2000. *Recreations:* wine, food.

**GILMOUR, Polly;** *see* Samson, P.

**GILMOUR, Dr Roger Hugh,** FIFST; consultant, 2008–10; *b* 24 March 1942; *s* of late William Gilmour and Elizabeth Gilmour; *m* 1968, Margaret Jean Chisholm; one *s* one *d. Educ:* Ross High Sch.; Edinburgh Univ. (BSc); Heriot-Watt Univ. (PhD 1969). FIFST 1989. Griffith Laboratories: Canada, 1969; UK/Internat., 1970–79; Pres., USA, 1979–83; CEO Agricl Genetics Co. Ltd, 1983–93; Business Develt Dir, Centre for Applied Microbiol. and Res., 1994–96; Chief Exec., Microbiol Res. Authy, and Centre for Applied Microbiol. and Res., 1996–2003; Dir, Business Div. and Porton Down site, HPA, 2003–04; Dir, 2004–07, Consultant, 2007–09, Centre for Emergency Preparedness and Response, HPA. Dir, MRC Collaborative Centre, 1992–99. Chm., NMT Gp plc, 1998–2004; Dir, Syntaxin Ltd, 2005–07. Trustee, SCI, 2012–15. Mem. Council, Univ. of Third Age, Cambridge, 2012–15. *Recreations:* walking, ski-ing, gardening, cycling, photography. *Address:* Pentlands, Kearsey Court, Charlbury, Chipping Norton OX7 3BF. *Club:* Farmers.

**GILMOUR, Soutra;** theatre designer, since 1995; *b* London; *d* of Angus and Ruth Gilmour; one *s. Educ:* Wimbledon Sch. of Art (BA 1st Cl. Theatre Design). Theatre designs, 1999–, incl. for Gate Th., London, Glasgow Citizens, Royal Court, Almeida, Old Vic, Young Vic, Traverse, Donmar, Wiltons Music Hall, NT (Cottesloe, Lyttleton, Olivier), Royal Opera Hse, RSC, Palace, Comedy, Vaudeville and Apollo theatres; productions include: Hair, Gate Th., 2005; The Caretaker, Crucible, 2006; The Pride, Royal Court, 2008; Piaf, Donmar, transf. Vaudeville, 2008; The Lover and the Collection, Comedy, 2008; Three Days of Rain, Apollo, 2009; Inadmissible Evidence, Donmar, 2011; Antigone, Olivier, 2012 (Evening Standard Award for Best Design, 2012); The Commitments, Palace Th., 2013; Macbeth, 2013, Richard III, 2014, Transformed@Trafalgar Studios; Urinetown, St James Th., transf. Apollo, 2014; Assassins, Menier Chocolate Factory, 2014; Bull, Young Vic, 2015; The Ruling Class, 2015, The Homecoming, 2015, The Maids, 2016, Trafalgar Studios; Reasons to be Happy, Hampstead Th., 2016; Dr Faustus, Duke of York's Th., 2016; Twelfth Night, NT, 2017; Guys and Dolls, Royal Exchange, 2017; Strictly Ballroom, Piccadilly Th., 2018; The Country Wife, Minerva Th., Chichester, 2018; The Turn of the Screw, Open Air Th., Regent's Park, 2018; Pinter One to Pinter Seven, 2018–19, Betrayal, 2019, Harold Pinter Th.; Breaking the Waves, King's Th., Edinburgh, 2019. *Recreations:* bookbinding, architectural walks, photographing the urban fabric, London, amateur gardening. *W:* www.soutragilmour.com.

**GILROY, Elizabeth Patricia, (Patsy);** Lord-Lieutenant, Stewartry of Kirkcudbright, since 2018; *b* Kirkcudbright, 9 March 1954; *d* of George MacGill and Elizabeth MacGill; *m* 1974, James Carey Gilroy (*d* 2014); one *d* (one *s* decd). *Educ:* Mount Sch., York; Chelsea Coll., Eastbourne. Partner in farm, 1976–. Mem., Dumfries and Galloway Council, 1999–2018 (Convener, 2007–12). Hon. Vice Pres., Army Cadet Force League (West Lowland), 2019–. *Recreations:* tennis, bridge, travelling to East Africa, swimming. *Address:* East Kirkcarswell, Dundrennan, Kirkcudbright DG6 4QW. *T:* (01557) 500249. *E:* patsy.gilroy@gmail.com.

**GILROY, Linda;** *b* 19 July 1949; *d* of late William Jarvie and Gwendoline Jarvie (*née* Gray); *m* 1987, Bernard Gilroy. *Educ:* Edinburgh Univ. (MA Hons History 1971); Strathclyde Univ. (Postgrad. Secl Dip. 1972); MITSA (Dip. in Consumer Affairs 1990). Dep. Dir, Age Concern Scotland, 1972–79; Regl Sec., subseq. Regl Manager, SW Office, Gas Consumers' Council, 1977–97. MP (Lab and Co-op) Plymouth Sutton, 1997–2010; contested (Lab and Co-op) Plymouth, Sutton and Devonport, 2010. PPS to Minister of State for Local Govt, Dept of Transport, Local Govt and the Regions, 2000–05, for Sci. and Innovation, 2008–10. Mem., Defence Select Cttee, 2005–10. Hon. DBus Plymouth, 2011. *Recreations:* swimming, walking, keep fit. *E:* gilroyl@hotmail.co.uk.

**GILROY, Patsy;** *see* Gilroy, E. P.

**GILROY, Paul;** QC 2006; barrister; *b* 1 May 1962; *s* of George Gilroy and Joan Gilroy (*née* McConnell); two *s* one *d. Educ:* Hutchesons' Grammar Sch., Glasgow; Univ. of Dundee (LLB Hons 1984). Called to the Bar, Gray's Inn, 1985; in practice as a barrister, 1985–, specialising in employment, sport, professional discipline and public inquiries. Attorney General's Provincial Panel, 2000–; an Employment Judge (pt-time) (formerly a Chm. (pt-time), Employment Tribunals), 2000–. Chairperson's list, Sport Resolutions (UK) Panel (formerly Sports Dispute Resolution Panel), 2007–; Specialist Mem., Judicial Panel, 2007–, Mem., Appeal Panel, 2008–, FA. *Recreations:* ski-ing, Manchester United FC, travel. *Address:* 9 St John Street, Manchester M3 4DN. *T:* (0161) 955 9000, *Fax:* (0161) 955 9001. *E:* paul.gilroy@9sjs.com; Littleton Chambers, 3 King's Bench Walk North, EC4Y 7HR. *T:* (020) 7797 8600, *Fax:* (020) 7797 8699. *E:* pg@littletonchambers.co.uk.

**GILROY, Prof. Paul,** FBA 2014; Professor of American and English Literature, King's College London, since 2012; *b* 16 Feb. 1956; *s* of late Patrick Gilroy and Beryl Gilroy. *Educ:* University Coll. Sch.; Univ. of Sussex (BA American Studies 1978); Univ. of Birmingham (PhD). Prof. of Cultural Studies and Sociol., Goldsmiths Coll., 1995–99; Charlotte Marian Saden Prof. of African American Studies and Sociol., Yale Univ., 1999–2005; Giddens Prof. of Social Theory, LSE, 2005–12. FRSL 2016. Holberg Prize (Norway), 2019. *Publications:* There Ain't No Black in the Union Jack, 1987; The Black Atlantic: modernity and double consciousness, 1993; Small Acts: thoughts on the politics of black cultures, 1993; Against Race: imagining political culture beyond the color line, 2000; Between Camps: nations, culture and the allure of race, 2000; (ed jtly) Without Guarantees: essays in honour of Stuart Hall, 2000; After Empire, 2004; Black Britain: a photographic history, 2007; Darker than Blue: on the moral economies of Black Atlantic culture; (ed with Rosi Braidotti) Conflicting Humanities, 2016. *Address:* Department of English, King's College London, Virginia Woolf Building, 22 Kingsway, WC2B 6LE.

**GILSENAN, Prof. Michael Dermot Cole;** David B. Kriser Professor of Middle Eastern Studies and Anthropology, New York University, since 1995 (Director, Kevorkian Center for Near Eastern Studies, 2007–15); *b* 6 Feb. 1940; *s* of Michael Eugene Cole Gilsenan and Joyce Russell Horn. *Educ:* Eastbourne Grammar Sch.; Oxford Univ. BA (Oriental Studies), Dip. Anth., MA, DPhil (Soc. Anthropology). Research Fellow, Amer. Univ. in Cairo, 1964–66; Research studentship, St Antony's Coll., Oxford, 1966–67; Research Fellow, Harvard Middle East Center, 1967–68; Asst Prof., Dept of Anthropology, UCLA, 1968–70; Research Lectr, Univ. of Manchester, 1970–73; Associate Fellow, St Antony's Coll., Oxford, 1970–73; Lectr, 1973–78, Reader, 1978–83, Dept of Anthropology, University College London; Mem., Sch. of Social Sci., Inst. for Advanced Study, Princeton, 1979–80; Khalid bin Abdullah al Saud Prof. for study of contemp. Arab world, and Fellow of Magdalen Coll., Oxford Univ., 1984–95, Emeritus Fellow, 1995. Anthrop. field work, Egypt, 1964–66, Lebanon, 1971–72, Java and Singapore, 1999–2000, Singapore, 2000–, Malaysia, 2001–02, 2003–05. Carnegie Corp. Scholar, 2003–05. Mem. Editl Bd, History and Anthropology and Ethnos, Arabian Humanities, Comparative Studies in S Asia, Africa and Middle East, and formerly of Past and Present, Man, and Internat. Jl of Middle Eastern Studies; Mem. Editl Bd, Jl of Royal Anthropol Soc., 2016–; Series Editor, Society and Culture in the Modern Middle East, 1987–96. *Publications:* Saint and Sufi in Modern Egypt, 1973; Recognizing Islam, 1982; Lords of the Lebanese Marches, 1996. *Recreations:* music, theatre, being elsewhere. *Address:* Department of Middle Eastern and Islamic Studies, New York University, 50 Washington Square South, New York, NY 10012–1073, USA.

**GILSON, Michael;** Head of Communications, Adur and Worthing Councils, since 2017; *b* 1 March 1963; *s* of Kenneth and Janet Gilson; *m* 1988, Susan Hunt; two *s. Educ:* Temple Secondary Sch., Strood, Kent; Poly. of Wales (BA Hons Communication Studies). With local newspapers, Kent, 1985–88; travel in Peru, 1988–89; News Ed., Hull Daily Mail, 1989–94; Night Ed., Western Mail, 1994–96; Editor: Peterborough Evening Telegraph, 1996–2000; The News, Portsmouth, 2000–06; The Scotsman, 2006–09; Belfast Telegraph, 2009–15; Gp Editor, Newsquest Sussex, and Editor, The Argus, 2015–16. Associate Fellow, Sch. of Media, Film and Music, Univ. of Sussex, 2017–. Mem., Code Cttee, Press Complaints Commn, 2004–09. Dir, Regulatory Funding Co., 2014–17. Mem., Johnston Press Editl Rev. Gp, 2003–09. *Publications:* (contrib.) Last Words?: how can journalism survive the decline of print?, 2016; (contrib.) Brexit, Trump and the Media, 2017. *Recreations:* football (player and sons' team coach), tennis, S American travel, trying to interest anyone in obscure 80's indie group, Orange Juice.

**GILSON, Prof. Simon Ashley,** PhD; Agnelli-Serena Professor of Italian, University of Oxford, since 2018; Fellow, Magdalen College, Oxford, since 2018; *b* Newcastle-under-Lyme, 4 Aug. 1968; *s* of Alan and Joan Gilson; *m* 1995, Julie Herbert; two *d. Educ:* Leeds Univ. (BA Modern Langs 1991); St John's Coll., Cambridge (PhD 1995). Lectr in Italian, Leeds Univ., 1998–99; Warwick University: Lectr in Italian, 1999–2004; Sen. Lectr in Italian, 2004–05; Reader in Italian, 2005–10; Prof. of Italian, 2010–17; Chair: Sub-faculty of Modern Langs, 2012–14; Arts Faculty, 2015–17. *Publications:* Medieval Optics and Theories of Light in the Works of Dante, 2000; Dante and Renaissance Florence, 2005; Reading Dante in Renaissance Italy: Florence, Venice and the divine poet, 2016. *Recreations:* squash, walking, family. *Address:* Faculty of Medieval and Modern Languages, University of Oxford, 41 and 47 Wellington Square, Oxford OX1 2JF. *T:* (01865) 270750. *E:* simon.gilson@mod-langs.ox.ac.uk.

**GILVARY, Dr Brian;** Group Chief Financial Officer and Director, BP plc, since 2012; *b* Liverpool, 12 Feb. 1962; *s* of John and Gladys Gilvary; *m* 1988, Jo Roycroft; two *s. Educ:* Univ. of Sheffield (BSc Maths 1983); Univ. of Manchester (MSc Maths; PhD Maths 1986). Upstream Technol., BP Res., Sunbury, 1986–90; Strategy and Planning, Europe, BP Europe, Brussels, 1990–95; Hd, North Sea Crude Oil Trading, 1995–96, Oil Products Trading, 1996–97, BP Internat. Ltd; Hd, Oil Products Trading, BP America, NY, 1997–98; Commercial Vice Pres., Amoco Natural Gas Liquids, BP America, Chicago, 1999–2000; BP plc: COS, 2000–01, Vice Pres. Strategy, 2001, Downstream; Exec. Asst to CEO, 2001–02; Mem. Exec. Cttee and Chief Financial Officer, Refining and Mktg, 2002–05; Mem. Exec. Cttee, Gas, Power and Renewables, 2005–09; CEO, Internat. Supply and Trading, BP Internat. Ltd, 2005–09; Dep. Chief Financial Officer, BP plc, 2010–11. Dir, TNK-BP, Moscow, 2003–05 and 2010–13. Non-executive Director: Air Liquide, 2016–; Royal Navy, 2017–. Vis. Prof., Manchester Univ., 2013–. Advr, Business in the Community Prince of Wales' Initiatives, Farmers' Mktg, Hill Farming and Supporting local economy, community and heritage, 2007–09; Ext. Advr to Dir Gen. (Spending and Finance), HM Treasury Financial Mgt Rev. Bd, 2014–17. Mem. Bd, Francis Crick Inst., 2018–. Chm., 100 Gp. Freeman, Tallow Chandlers' Co., 2013. Hon. DSc Sheffield, 2018. Award for Best Young Researcher, Tallow Chandlers, 1990. *Recreations:* swimming, cycling, running, football, Rugby, Speakers for School charity. *Address:* BP plc, 1 St James's Square, SW1Y 4PD. *Club:* Royal Automobile.

**GIMBLETT, (Catherine) Margaret (Alexandra Forbes);** Sheriff of North Strathclyde at Dunoon, 1999–2005; part-time Sheriff, 2005–09; *b* 24 Sept. 1939; *d* of Alexander Forbes Hendry and Margaret Hendry (*née* Whitehead); *m* 1965, Iain McNicol Gimblett; one *s* one *d. Educ:* St Leonard's Sch., St Andrews; Edinburgh Univ. (MA); Glasgow Univ. Sec. and PA, Humphreys & Glasgow Ltd, London, 1960–63; Staff Manager, John Lewis Partnership, London, 1963–67; Partner, Alexander Hendry & Son, subseq. Russel & Aitken, Denny, Solicitors, 1972–95; admitted solicitor, 1974; Temp. Sheriff, 1992–95; Sheriff, Glasgow and Strathkelvin, 1995–99. Churchill Fellowship, 1986. *Recreations:* gardening, walking, people, travelling.

**GIMZEWSKI, Prof. James Kazimierz,** PhD; FRS 2009; FREng, FInstP; Professor of Chemistry, since 2001, Director, Nano and Pico Characterization Core Facility, California NanoSystems Institute, since 2003, and Scientific Director, Art|Sci Center, since 2005, University of California, Los Angeles; Satellite Director and Principal Investigator, National Institute for Materials Science and International Centre for Materials Nanoarchitectronics, Japan, since 2008. *Educ:* Univ. of Strathclyde (BS 1974; PhD 1977). FInstP 1995; FREng 2001. Post-doctoral Research Fellow: Oregon State Univ., 1977–79; Inst. of Inorganic Chem., Univ. of Zurich, 1979–83; Gp Leader, IBM Zurich Res. Lab., 1983–2001. Prof. of Physics, Univ. of Bristol, 2013–15. PhD *hc* Univ. de la Méditerranée, Aix-Marseille II, 2008; Hon. DSc Strathclyde, 2010. *Publications:* articles in jls. *Address:* Department of Chemistry and Biochemistry, University of California, Los Angeles, Charles E. Young Drive East, Los Angeles, CA 90095–1569, USA.

**GINGRICH, Newton Leroy, (Newt);** Chief Executive Officer, Gingrich Group, 1999–2011; Chairman, Gingrich 360, since 2019; *b* 17 June 1943; *s* of late Robert Bruce Gingrich and of Kathleen (*née* Daugherty); *m* 1st, 1962, Jacqueline Battley (marr. diss. 1981); two *d*; 2nd, 1981, Marianne Ginther (marr. diss. 2000); 3rd, 2000, Callista Bisek. *Educ:* Emory Univ. (BA). Tulane Univ. (MA; PhD 1971). Taught history, W Georgia Coll., Carrollton, 1970–78; Mem. from 6th Dist of Georgia, US Congress, 1979–99 (Republican Whip, 1989–94); Speaker, US House of Representatives, 1995–99. Founder, Center for Health Transformation, 2003. Gen. Chm., American Solutions for Winning the Future, 2007–11. *Publications:* (jtly) Window of Opportunity: a blueprint for the future, 1984; (jtly) 1945, 1995; To Renew America, 1995; Lessons Learned the Hard Way, 1998; (jtly) Saving

Lives and Saving Money, 2006; Winning the Future: a 21st contract with America, 2006; Rediscovering God in America, 2006; (with Nancy Desmond) The Art of Transformation, 2006; (with T. L. Maple) A Contract with the Earth, 2007; Real Change: from the world that fails to the world that works, 2008; A Nation Like No Other, 2011; To Save America, 2011; Breakout, 2013; Understanding Trump, 2017; Trump's America: the truth about our nation's great comeback, 2018; *novels* (with William Forstchen): Grant Comes East, 2004; Gettysburg, 2004; Never Call Retreat, 2007; Pearl Harbor: a novel of December the 8th, 2007; Days of Infamy, 2008; (with P. Earley) Duplicity, 2015; Collusion, 2019.

**GINNEVER, John Anthony;** Director of Education, Leisure and Libraries, East Riding of Yorkshire, 1995–2002; *b* 24 June 1948; *s* of George Edward Ginnever and Olive Ginnever; *m* 1971, Wendy Marian Brown; one *s* one *d*. *Educ:* Hatfield Coll., Durham Univ. (BSc Hons 1970; PGCE 1971); Newcastle Univ. (MEd 1977). Teacher, 1971–77; Education Officer: Leeds MBC, 1978–82; Bucks CC, 1982–87; N Yorks CC, 1987–89; Dep. Dir of Educn, Newcastle MBC, 1989–95. Chm., Yorks and Humber Regl Adv. Cttee, Duke of Edinburgh's Award, 1998–2009; Member: Cttee, RSPB Richmondshire and Hambleton Local Gp, 2009–; Mgt Gp, Foxglove Covert Local Nature Reserve, 2010–. *Recreations:* birdwatching, hill walking, globetrotting, volunteering.

**GINSBURG, Ruth Bader;** Associate Justice of the Supreme Court of the United States, since 1993; *b* 15 March 1933; *d* of Nathan Bader and Celia Amster Bader; *m* 1954, Martin D. Ginsburg (*d* 2010); one *s* one *d*. *Educ:* James Madison High Sch., Brooklyn; Cornell Univ. (BA Hons 1954); Harvard Law Sch.; Columbia Law Sch. (Kent Scholar; LLB, JD 1959). Clerk, Southern Dist, NY, 1959–61; Columbia Law Sch. Project on Internat. Procedure, 1961–63; Professor: Rutgers Univ. Sch. of Law, 1963–72; Columbia Law Sch., 1972–80; Circuit Judge, Court of Appeals for Dist of Columbia, 1980–93. American Civil Liberties Union: Gen. Counsel, 1973–80; Nat. Board, 1974–80; Counsel to Women's Rights Project, 1972–80. Fellow: Amer. Bar Foundn, 1978– (Exec. Cttee and Sec., 1979–89); Amer. Acad. of Arts and Scis, 1982– (Mem. Council, Foreign Relations, 1975–). *Publications:* (with A. Bruzelius) Civil Procedure in Sweden, 1965; (with A. Bruzelius) Swedish Code of Judicial Procedure, 1968; (jtly) Text, Cases and Materials on Sex-Based Discrimination, 1974, Supp. 1978; numerous contribs to learned jls. *Address:* Supreme Court, 1 First Street NE, Washington, DC 20543, USA.

**GIORDANO, Sir Richard (Vincent),** KBE 1989; Chairman, BG Group plc, 2000–03 (Chairman, BG (formerly British Gas) plc, 1994–2000); *b* March 1934; *s* of late Vincent Giordano and of Cynthia Giordano (*née* Cardetta); granted British citizenship, 2002; *m* 1st, 1956 (marr. diss. 1993); one *s* two *d*; 2nd, 2000, Susan Ware (*d* 2001); 3rd, 2002, Marguerite Rule Johnstone. *Educ:* Harvard Coll., Cambridge, Mass, USA (BA); Columbia Univ. Law Sch. (LLB). Shearman & Sterling, 1959; Airco, Inc., 1963–78: Gp Vice Pres., 1967; Gp Pres. and Chief Operating Officer, 1971; Chief Exec. Officer, Airco, Inc., 1978; Chief Exec. Officer, BOC Gp, 1979–91; Chm., BOC, 1985–92, 1994–96; Grand Metropolitan plc: Bd Mem., 1985–97; Dep. Chm., 1991–97. Mem., CEGB, 1982–92; part-time Board Member: Rio Tinto plc (formerly RTZ Corp.), 1992–2005 (Dep. Chm., 2000–05); Georgia Pacific Corp., Atlanta, Ga, 1984–; Reuters, 1991–94; non-executive Director: Lucas Industries, 1993–94; Nat. Power. Hon. Fellow, London Business Sch., 1994. Hon. Dr of Commercial Science, St John's Univ., 1975; Hon. LLD Bath, 1998. *Recreations:* ocean sailing, tennis. *Clubs:* The Links, New York Yacht (New York).

**GIORGIONE, Bethan Heulwen;** *see* Gray, B. H.

**GIOSERANO, Richard Stephen; His Honour Judge Gioserano;** a Circuit Judge, since 2016; *b* Leeds, 8 Oct. 1968. *Educ:* St Michael's Coll., Leeds; Newcastle Univ. (LLB Hons Law 1990). Called to the Bar, Gray's Inn, 1992; in criminal practice as a barrister, 6 Park Square, Leeds, 1993–2016; a Recorder, 2012–16.

**GIPPS, Prof. Caroline Victoria,** PhD; Vice Chancellor, University of Wolverhampton, 2005–11; *b* 2 Feb. 1948; *d* of John Stephen Davis and Adriaantje de Baat; *m* 1970, Dr Jonathan Henry William Gipps, *qv*; two *s*. *Educ:* St Winifred's Sch. for Girls, Llanfairfechan; Univ. of Bristol (BSc Psychol 1968); Inst. of Education, London (MSc 1973, PhD Psychol of Educn 1980). Primary sch. teacher, 1968–70; Researcher: Nat. Foundn for Educnl Res., 1970–74; Nat. Children's Bureau, London, 1975–77; Teaching Asst, Psychol. Dept, Univ. of British Columbia, 1977–79; Institute of Education, London: Researcher, Lectr and Reader, 1980–94; Nuffield Res. Fellow, 1992; Hd, Curriculum Studies Dept, 1993–94; Prof. of Educn, 1994–2000; Dean of Res., 1994–99; Dep. Vice Chancellor, Kingston Univ., 2000–05. Pres., British Educnl Res. Assoc., 1992; Member: Panel for Educn, 1996 RAE; Steering Cttee, ESRC Teaching and Learning Res. Prog., 1999–2004; Adv. Cttee, Staff and Educn Develt Assoc., 2002–05; Gen. Teaching Council for England, 2003–05; Ext. Cttee on Examination Standards, QCA, 2003–05; Adv. Cttee, Thomas Coram Res. Unit, Inst. of Educn, London, 2004–11; ESRC Strategic Res. Bd, 2005–08; Advr, Wingate Foundn Scholarships, 1995–2012. Mem. Bd, Kingston Univ., 2012–19. Trustee, Buttle UK, 2012– (Chair, 2016–). AcSS 2001. Hon. LLD Bristol 2010. *Publications:* (jtly) Language Proficiency in the Multiracial Junior School: a comparative study, 1975; (jtly) Combined Nursery Centres, 1981; (jtly) Testing Children: standardised testing in Local Education Authorities and schools, 1983; (jtly) Warnock's 18%: children with special needs in the primary school, 1987; Beyond Testing: towards a theory of educational assessment, 1994 (Japanese edn 2001), reissued 2012; (with P. Murphy) A Fair Test?: assessment, achievement and equity, 1994 (Standing Council for Studies in Educn prize for best educnl book); Intuition or Evidence?: teachers and national assessment of seven year olds, 1995; (ed with P. Murphy) Equity in the Classroom: towards effective pedagogy for girls and boys, 1996; (with G. Stobart) Assessment: a teachers' guide to the issues, 3rd edn 1997; (jtly) What Makes a Good Primary School Teacher?, 2000, reissued 2016. *Recreations:* sailing, seabathing, Handel opera, Mozart. *Address:* 2 Beech Close, SW15 4HW. *T:* (020) 8789 4306. *Clubs:* Athenæum; Trearddur Bay Sailing.

*See also* Sir P. J. Davis.

**GIPPS, Dr Jonathan Henry William,** OBE 2000; Director, Bristol Zoo Gardens, and Bristol, Clifton and West of England Zoological Society Ltd, 2001–10; *b* 7 July 1947; *s* of late Capt. Louis H. F. P. Gipps, RN and Molly Joyce Gipps; *m* 1970, Caroline Victoria Davis (*see* C. V. Gipps); two *s*. *Educ:* Imperial Coll., Univ. of London (BSc Zool. 1973); Royal Holloway Coll., Univ. of London (PhD 1977). RN, 1966–70. Post-doctoral Research Fellow, Univ. of British Columbia, 1977–79; Lectr in Biology, Univ. of Bath, 1980–81; Res. Fellow, RHBNC, 1981–84; Educn Officer, Computer Centre, Kingston Poly., 1984–87; London Zoo: Curator of Mammals, 1987–91; General Curator, 1991–93; Dir, 1993–2001. Co-keeper, Giant Panda Internat. Studbook, 1988–2010. Member, Council: UK Fedn of Zoos, subseq. British and Irish Assoc. of Zoos and Aquariums, 1995–2010 (Hon. Treas., 1998–2001); European Assoc. of Zoos and Aquaria, 1999–2006 (Chm., Conservation Cttee, 2002–06); World Assoc. of Zoos and Aquariums, 2005–10 (Chm., Conservation Cttee, 2002–10); Chm., Adv. Bd, 2009–, Chm., Global Conservation Network, 2010–, Conservation Planning (formerly Breeding) Specialist Gp, IUCN. Pres., Anchor Soc., Bristol, 2010–11. Chm. Trustees, Bristol Natural Hist. Consortium, 2006–11; Trustee: Internat. Species Inf. System, 2000–05; SS Great Britain Trust, 2007–12; St George's, Bristol, 2010–18; Early Opera Co., 2011– (Chm., 2012–); La Nuova Musica, 2011–17. Freeman, Musicians' Co., 2019–. FRSA 1998. Hon. DSc: Kingston, 1993; Bristol, 2011. *Publications:* (ed jtly) The Ecology of Woodland Rodents, 1981; (ed) Beyond Captive Breeding: re-introducing endangered mammals to the wild, 1989. *Recreations:* baroque opera and early music, species conservation and conservation planning, fly fishing, making jewellery, sailing, ski-ing, cooking, travelling.

**GIRDWOOD, David Greenshields;** DL; Rector, St Columba's School, Kilmacolm, 2002–17; *b* 14 Oct. 1957; *s* of Alexander and Margaret Girdwood; *m* 1985, Lisa Greig; two *d*. *Educ:* St Andrews Univ. (BSc 1978); Jordanhill Coll. of Educn, Glasgow (PGCE 1979); Stirling Univ. (MEd 1985); Scottish Qualification for Headship, 2001. Teacher of Chemistry, 1979–85, Asst Hd of Science, 1985–87, Lornshill Acad., Alloa; Principal Teacher of Chemistry and Hd of Scis, 1987–96, Hd of Upper Sch., 1996–2002, Stewart's Melville Coll., Edinburgh. Associate Assessor, HM Inspectorate of Educn, 1999–2002. Member: Erskine Stewart's Melville Governing Council, 2006–; Scottish Strategic Adv. Cttee, Duke of Edinburgh's Award, 2010–13. Gov., Lomond Sch., 2016–. DL Renfrewshire, 2009. *Recreations:* family activities, walking.

**GIRET, Joseph John Bela Leslie;** QC 2010; *b* Paddington, London, 30 Sept. 1954; *s* of Joseph and Elizabeth Giret; *m* 2006, Magdalena Szajtek; one *s* one *d*. *Educ:* St Marylebone Grammar Sch.; Warwick Univ. (LLB). Inns of Court Sch. of Law. Called to the Bar, Gray's Inn, 1985; in practice at Common Law Bar, specialising in civil law, commercial and business, regulatory and sport. Freeman, City of London, 2006; Mem., Co. of Watermen and Lightermen, 2006. Mem., British Jun. Decathlon Squad, 1972. *Recreations:* opera, especially at Glyndebourne and Royal Opera House, Rugby (3 England caps and Captain Middx and London Counties at schoolboy level), sailing (qualified Yacht Master Ocean, 1988; has sailed across Atlantic twice), fair-weather sculling on River Thames, dedicated cyclist and follower of Tour de France, historic Formula single seater and sports car events (held International Racing Drivers Licence). *Address:* near Wargrave, Berks.

**GIRI, Anu;** Head of Business and Operations, BFI Festivals, since 2019; *b* Hyderabad, India, 11 Feb. 1968; *d* of Dr Ganjeti Yada Giri and Dr Arcot Kishori; *m* 2004, Paul Martindale; two *d*. *Educ:* King's High Sch. for Girls, Warwick; Liverpool Poly. (BA Hons Drama and Sociol. 1990); Birkbeck Coll., Univ. of London (Dip. Mgt 2001). Presenter, Network East, BBC2, 1992–93; Projects Asst, Dance 4, 1992–93; Administrator, Claire Russ Ensemble and Chitralekha and Co., 1993–94; Educn Manager, Birmingham Royal Ballet, 1994–97; Gen. Manager, Shobana Jeyasingh Dance Co., 1997–2000; Sen. Dance Officer, 2000–03, Hd of Dance, 2003–10, Arts Council England; Co-Dir, English Nat. Ballet Sch., 2010–15; Exec. Dir, Dance Umbrella, 2014–19. Chair, Aakash Odedra Co., 2016–; Member, Board: Rambert, 2010–; One Dance UK, 2016–. *Recreations:* film, dance, theatre, literature. *Address:* 47 Bective Road, Putney, SW15 2QA. *T:* (020) 8870 6679, 07989 404428. *E:* anugiri11@hotmail.com.

**GIRLING, (John) Anthony;** President of the Law Society, 1996–97; *b* 21 Aug. 1943; *s* of James William Girling, OBE and Annie Doris (*née* Reeves); *m* 1965, Lynne Margaret Davis; one *s* one *d*. *Educ:* Tonbridge Sch.; Guildford Coll. of Law. Admitted Solicitor, 1966; Girlings, Solicitors: Partner, 1968; Man. Partner, 1982–96; Chm., 1997–2000; Consultant, 2000–09. Hon. Sec., 1974–80, Pres., 1980–81, Kent Law Soc.; Mem. for Kent, Council of Law Soc., 1980–99. Hon. Sen. Mem., Darwin Coll., Univ. of Kent, 1984. Fellow, Inst. of Advanced Legal Studies, Univ. of London, 1997–2009. Hon. LLD Kent, 1998. *Publications:* contrib. to Law Soc. Gazette and other legal jls. *Recreations:* golf, ski-ing, the countryside. *Address:* Los Almendros 30, Urb. Los Arqueros, 29679 Benhavis, Malaga, Spain. *Clubs:* Canterbury Golf; El Paraíso Golf.

**GIRLING, Julie McCulloch;** Member for South West England and Gibraltar, European Parliament, 2009–19 (C, 2009–17; Ind, 2017–19); *b* London, 21 Dec. 1956; *m* 1981, Warren Glyn Girling; one *s*. *Educ:* Twickenham Co. Grammar Sch.; Liverpool Univ. (BA Hist. and Politics 1979). Grad. trainee, Ford Motor Co., 1979–82; Buyer and Merchandise Controller, Argos Catalogue Gp, 1982–88; Mktg Manager, Dixons Stores Gp, 1988–90; Marketing and Buying Manager: Boots, 1991; Halfords, until 1993; freelance trainer, 1995–2009. Member (C): Cotswold DC, 1999–2009 (Leader, 2003–06); Glos CC, 2000–09.

**GIROLAMI, Prof. Mark,** PhD; FRSE; Sir Kirby Laing Professor of Civil Engineering, University of Cambridge, since 2019; *b* Irvine, Scotland, 29 Oct. 1963; *s* of Santino Girolami and Maria Girolami. *Educ:* Univ. of Glasgow (BSc); Univ. of Paisley (PhD 1998). Engineer, IBM UK, 1985–94; Univ. of Paisley, 1997–2004; Prof. of Computing, Univ. of Glasgow, 2004–10; Professor of Statistics: UCL, 2010–14; Univ. of Warwick, 2015–16; Prof. of Stats, and Lloyds Register Foundn-RAEng Res. Prof. in Data Centric Engrg, Imperial Coll. London, 2016–19. Prog. Dir, Alan Turing Inst., 2015–. FRSE 2011. *Publications:* A First Course in Machine Learning, 2011, 2nd edn 2017. *Recreations:* cycling, fine dining. *Address:* Department of Engineering, University of Cambridge, Trumpington Street, Cambridge CB2 1PZ. *E:* mgirolami@turing.ac.uk. *Club:* Athenæum.

**GIROLAMI, Sir Paul,** Kt 1988; Chief Executive, 1980–86, and Chairman, 1985–94, Glaxo Holdings; *b* 25 Jan. 1926; *m* 1952, Christabel Mary Gwynne Lewis (*d* 2009); two *s* one *d*. *Educ:* London School of Economics (Hon. Fellow, 1989); FREconS; FIMC 1990. Chantrey & Button, Chartered Accountants, 1950–54; Coopers & Lybrand, Chartered Accountants, 1954–65; Glaxo Holdings: Financial Controller, 1965; Finance Director, 1968. Director: Inner London Board of National Westminster Bank, 1974–89; Credito Italiano Internat. UK, 1990–93; Forte plc, 1992–96; UIS France, 1994–. Member: Bd of Dirs, Amer. Chamber of Commerce (UK), 1983–; CBI Council, 1986–93; Appeal Cttee, ICA, 1987–; Stock Exchange Listed Cos Adv. Cttee, 1987–92. Chm., Senate for Chartered Accountants in Business, 1990–2000. Chm. Council, Goldsmiths' Coll., Univ. of London, 1994–2003; Mem. Open Univ. Vis. Cttee, 1987–89. Gov., NIESR, 1992–. Freeman, City of London; Liveryman, Goldsmiths' Co., 1980– (Mem., Ct of Assistants, 1986–; Prime Warden, 1995–96); Mem., Soc. of Apothecaries, 1993–. Hon. FCGI 1994; FCMI (FBIM 1986); FRSA 1986. Hon. DSc: Aston, 1990; Trieste, 1991; Sunderland, 1991; Bradford, 1993; Hon. LLD: Singapore, 1993; Warwick, 1996; Hon. DBA Strathclyde, 1993. Centenary Medal, UK SCI, 1992; Centenary Award, UK Founding Socs, 1992. Grand Cross, Order of the Holy Sepulchre, 1994. Grande Ufficiale, Ordine al Merito della Repubblica Italiana, 1987; Cavaliere al Merito del Lavoro, Italy, 1991; Insignia of the Order of the Rising Sun, Japan, 1991; Public Service Star, Singapore, 2000. *Recreations:* reading, music.

*See also* P. J. Girolami.

**GIROLAMI, Paul Julian;** QC 2002; barrister; *b* 5 Dec. 1959; *s* of Sir Paul Girolami, *qv*; *m* 1991, Deborah Bookman; one *s* two *d*. *Educ:* St Paul's Sch., London; Corpus Christi Coll., Cambridge. Called to the Bar, Middle Temple, 1983; Jun. Counsel to the Crown, Chancery, 1991–2000; a Dep. High Court Judge, 2006–. Freeman, City of London; Liveryman, Goldsmiths' Co. *Address:* Maitland Chambers, 7 Stone Buildings, Lincoln's Inn, WC2A 3SZ. *T:* (020) 7406 1200, *Fax:* (020) 7406 1300. *E:* clerks@maitlandchambers.com.

**GIROUARD, Mark,** PhD; FRSL; writer and architectural historian; Slade Professor of Fine Art, University of Oxford, 1975–76; *b* 7 Oct. 1931; *s* of late Richard D. Girouard and Lady Blanche Girouard; *m* 1970, Dorothy N. Dorf; one *d*. *Educ:* Ampleforth; Christ Church,

Oxford (MA); Courtauld Inst. of Art (PhD); Bartlett Sch., UCL (BSc, Dip. Arc). Staff of Country Life, 1958–66; studied architecture, Bartlett Sch., UCL, 1966–71; staff of Architectural Review, 1971–75. George Lurcy Vis. Prof., Columbia Univ., NY, 1987. Member: Council, Victorian Soc., 1979 (Founder Mem. 1958; Mem. Cttee, 1958–66); Royal Fine Art Commn, 1972–96; Royal Commn on Historical Monuments (England), 1976–81; Historic Buildings Council (England), 1978–84; Commn for Historic Buildings and Monuments, 1984–90 (Mem., Buildings Adv. Cttee, 1984–86; Mem., Historic Areas Adv. Cttee, 1985–89; Mem., Historic Bldgs Cttee, 1988–90); Council, Spitalfields Historic Buildings Trust, 1983–2003 (Chm., 1977–83); Trustee, Architecture Foundn, 1992–99. Mem., Adv. Council, Paul Mellon Centre for Studies in British Art, 1990–96. Hon. Student, Christ Ch, Oxford, 2002. FSA 1986; FRSL 2012. Hon. FRIBA, 1980. Hon. DLitt: Leicester, 1982; Buckingham, 1991. *Publications:* Robert Smythson and the Architecture of the Elizabethan Era, 1966, 2nd edn, Robert Smythson and the Elizabethan Country House, 1983; The Victorian Country House, 1971, 2nd edn 1979; Victorian Pubs, 1975, 2nd edn 1984; (jtly) Spirit of the Age, 1975 (based on BBC TV series); Sweetness and Light: the 'Queen Anne' movement 1860–1900, 1977; Life in the English Country House, 1978 (Duff Cooper Meml Prize; W. H. Smith Award, 1979); Historic Houses of Britain, 1979; Alfred Waterhouse and the Natural History Museum, 1981; The Return to Camelot: chivalry and the English gentleman, 1981; Cities and People, 1985; A Country House Companion, 1987; The English Town, 1990; Town and Country, 1992; Windsor: the most romantic castle, 1993; Big Jim: the life and work of James Stirling, 1998; Life in the French Country House, 2000; Elizabethan Architecture: its rise and fall, 1540–1640, 2009; Enthusiasms, 2011; Friendships, 2017; articles in Country Life, Architect. Rev., Listener. *Address:* 35 Colville Road, W11 2BT.

**GIRVAN, Rt Hon. Sir (Frederick) Paul,** Kt 1995; PC 2007; a Lord Justice of Appeal, Supreme Court of Judicature, Northern Ireland, 2007–15; *b* 20 Oct. 1948; *s* of Robert Frederick Girvan and Martha Elizabeth (*née* Barron); *m* 1974, Karen Elizabeth Joyce (MBE 2013); two *s* one *d*. *Educ:* Belfast Royal Acad.; Clare Coll., Cambridge (BA); Queen's Univ., Belfast; Gray's Inn. Called to the Bar: NI, 1971; Inner Bar (NI), 1982; Jun. Crown Counsel, NI, 1979–82; Justice of the High Court, NI, 1995–2007. Chancellor, Archdio. of Armagh, 1999–. Chairman: Council of Law Reporting for NI, 1994–2001; Law Reform Adv. Cttee for NI, 1997–2004 (Mem., 1994–2004). Hon. Bencher, Gray's Inn, 1999. *Recreations:* badminton, walking, swimming, reading, modern languages, gardening, cooking, golf, painting.

**GIRVAN, Paul;** MP (DemU) South Antrim, since 2017; *b* 6 July 1963; *m* Mandy Burrows; one *s* one *d*. Mem. (DemU) S Antrim, NI Assembly, 2003–07 and 2010–17. Northern Ireland Assembly: Private Sec., Office of First Minister and Dep. First Minister, 2011–16; Member: Finance and Personnel Cttee, 2010–16 (Chm.); Public Accounts Cttee, 2011–16. Mem. (DemU), Newtownabbey BC, 1997–2013 (Mayor, 2002–04). Mem., Transport Cttee, H of C, 2017–. *Address:* House of Commons, SW1A 0AA.

**GISBOROUGH,** 3rd Baron *cr* 1917; **Thomas Richard John Long Chaloner;** Lord-Lieutenant of Cleveland, 1981–96; Lieutenant of North Yorkshire, 1996–2001; *b* 1 July 1927; *s* of 2nd Baron and Esther Isabella Madeleine (*d* 1970), *yr d* of late Charles O. Hall, Eddlethorpe; *S* father, 1951; *m* 1960, Shane, *e d* of late Sidney Newton, London, and *gd* of Sir Louis Newton, 1st Bt; two *s*. *Educ:* Eton; Royal Agricultural Coll. 16th/5th Lancers, 1948–52; Captain Northumberland Hussars, 1955–61; Lt-Col Green Howards (Territorials), 1967–69. Mem., Rural Develt Commn, 1985–89. CC NR Yorks, 1964–74, Cleveland, 1974–77. Hon. Col, Cleveland County Army Cadet Force, 1981–92. President: British Ski Fedn, 1985–90; Assoc. of Professional Foresters, 1998–2001. DL N Riding of Yorks and Cleveland, 1973; JP Langbaurgh East, 1981–94. KStJ 1981. *Recreations:* shooting, fishing, tennis, bridge, piano. *Heir: s* Hon. Thomas Peregrine Long Chaloner [*b* 17 Jan. 1961; *m* 1992, Karen, *o d* of Alan Thomas]. *Address:* Gisborough House, Guisborough, Cleveland TS14 6PT. *T:* (01287) 632002, 07717 411110.

**GISBY, Jonathan Hugh;** Managing Director, WildBrain, since 2018; *b* Salisbury, 27 May 1968; *s* of John Gisby and Rosalie Gisby (*née* Uwins); *m* 1996, Kate Wilson; two *s* one *d*. *Educ:* Exeter Coll., Oxford (BA Hons Mod. Hist. 1990); Johns Hopkins SAIS, Bologna (Dip. Internat. Relns 1991); Harvard Univ. (MBA 1996). Sen. Advr, Corporate Strategy, BBC, 1997–99; Man. Dir, Portals, Freeserve plc, 1999–2004; Man. Dir, Yahoo UK, 2004–06; Vice Pres. Media, Yahoo Europe, 2005–07; Dir, Future Media and Technol., Channel 4, 2007–10; Exec. Vice Pres. Business Develt, Magine.com, 2012–15; Hd of Europe, Vevo, 2016–18. Mem. Bd, Artichoke Prodns, 2009–17; Chair, British Screen Adv. Council, 2016–. *Recreation:* adventures.

**GISBY, Robin William,** CEng, FIET; Chairman, London North Eastern Railway, since 2018; *b* Chatham, Kent, 19 Sept. 1956; *s* of John and Rosalie Gisby; *m* 1978, Jill Oliver; two *s* two *d*. *Educ:* Bishop Wordsworth's Sch., Salisbury; Magdalen Coll., Oxford (MA Engrg Sci.); Manchester Business Sch. (MBA). CEng 1982; FIET 2017. Chloride Gp plc, 1980–82; Arthur D Little Ltd, 1984–87; GKN plc, 1987–90; Charterail, 1990–92; Brown & Tawse plc, 1993–97; Railtrack plc, then Network Rail, 1997–2015, Man. Dir, Network Ops, 2011–15; Chm., Tomorrow's Engrs Prog. Bd, 2015–18; Mem. Bd, Railway Delivery Bd, 2018–. Chm., Navigator Terminals, 2017–. Non-exec. Dir, Defence Infrastructure Orgn, 2018–. *Address:* 16 Herondale Avenue, SW18 3JL. *T:* 07860 760663. *E:* robin.gisby@riverbourneadvisory.co.uk.
See also J. H. Gisby.

**GISCARD d'ESTAING, Valéry;** Grand Croix de la Légion d'Honneur; Croix de Guerre (1939–45); Member, Académie Française, 2003; President of the French Republic, 1974–81; Member, Constitutional Council, since 1981; President and Co-Founder, Re-Imagine Europa, since 2018; *b* Coblence, 2 Feb. 1926; *s* of late Edmond Giscard d'Estaing and May Bardoux; *m* 1952, Anne-Aymone de Brantes; two *s* two *d*. *Educ:* Lycée Janson-de-Sailly, Paris; Ecole Polytechnique; Ecole Nationale d'Administration. Inspection of Finances: Deputy, 1952; Inspector, 1954; Dep. Dir, Cabinet of Président du Conseil, June–Dec. 1954. Elected Deputy for Puy-de-Dôme, 1956; re-elected for Clermont N and SW, Nov. 1958, Nov.–Dec. 1962, March 1967, June 1968, March 1973, 1984, 1986 and 1988–89; Deputy for Puy-de-Dôme, 1993–2002; Sec. of State for Finance, 1959; Minister of Finance, Jan.–April 1962; Minister of Finance and Economic Affairs, April–Nov. 1962 and Dec. 1962–Jan. 1966; Minister of Economy and Finance, 1969–74. Pres., Nat. Fedn of Ind. Republicans, 1966–73 (also a Founder); Pres., comm. des finances de l'économie générale et du plan de l'Assemblée nationale, 1967–68; Chm., Commn of Foreign Affairs, Nat. Assembly, 1987–89, 1993–97. Mem., Eur. Parlt, 1989–93. President: Conseil Régional d'Auvergne, 1986–2004; Eur. Movt Internat., 1989–97; Council of Eur. Municipalities and Regions, 1997–2004; European Convention, 2001–03. Mayor of Chamalières, 1967–74. Deleg. to Assembly of UN, 1956, 1957, 1958. Mem., Real Acad. de Ciencias Económicas y Financieras, Spain, 1995–. Nansen Medal, UNHCR, 1979; Gold Medal, Jean Monnet Foundn, 2001; Karl Prize, Aachen, 2003. *Publications:* Démocratie Française, 1976 (Towards a New Democracy, 1977); 2 Français sur 3, 1984; Le Pouvoir et la Vie (memoirs), 1988; L'Affrontement, 1991; Le Passage (novel), 1994; Dans 5 ans l'an 2000, 1995; La princesse et le président (novel), 2009. *Clubs:* Polo (Paris); Union Interalliée.

**GISSING, Jason;** Co-Founder, and Director, 2000–14, Ocado.com (Chief Financial and Marketing Officer, 2000–09; Commercial Director, 2011–14); *b* UK, 25 Oct. 1970; *s* of Graham and Mikiko Gissing; *m* 2002, Katinka, *d* of late Arne Naess; two *s* two *d*. *Educ:* Oundle Sch., Northants; Worcester Coll., Oxford (BA Juris.). Goldman Sachs, 1992–2000. *Recreations:* tennis, ski-ing, football, yoga, history, the environment. *Clubs:* Queen's, Campden Hill Lawn Tennis, 5 Hertford Street.

**GITTINGS, (Harold) John;** writer and script editor; *b* 3 Sept. 1947; *s* of Harold William Gittings and Doris Marjorie Gittings (*née* Whiting); *m* 1st, 1988, Andrea (*née* Fisher) (*d* 1995); 2nd, 2002, Barbara (*née* Lowenstein). *Educ:* Duke of York's Royal Military School, Dover. ACIS. Beecham Group, 1971–73; Peat Marwick Mitchell, Hong Kong, 1973–74; N. M. Rothschild & Sons, 1974–81; Continental Bank, 1981–82; Target Group, 1982–85; Man. Dir, Touche Remnant & Co., 1986–90; Chm., Greenfield Marketing, subseq. Greenfield Gp, 1992–96; Dir, Meltemi Entertainment Ltd, 1996–2000. *Recreations:* travel, collecting, film. *Address:* 27 Cambridge Road, Hove BN3 1DE.

**GITTINS, Timothy James; His Honour Judge Gittins;** a Circuit Judge, since 2015; *b* Hexham, Northumberland, 11 Jan. 1968; *s* of Allan and Margaret Gittins; *m* 1993, Sally Conway; one *s* one *d*. *Educ:* Ponteland Co. High Sch.; Manchester Univ. (LLB Hons 1989). Called to the Bar, Middle Temple, 1990; in practice at the Bar, Trinity Chambers, Newcastle upon Tyne, 1990–2015; a Recorder, 2008–15. Trustee, Adm. Lord Collingwood Soc., 2015–. Vice Chm. Govs, St Bartholomew's C of E Primary Sch., 2008–. Dep. Chancellor, Dio. of Durham, 2019–. *Recreations:* cycling, ski-ing, history, watching Rugby. *Address:* Newcastle upon Tyne Combined Court Centre, Quayside, Newcastle upon Tyne NE1 3LA. *T:* (0191) 201 2000. *E:* HHJ.Timothy.Gittins@ejudiciary.net.

**GIUDICE, Hon. Geoffrey Michael,** AO 2010; Judge of the Federal Court, Australia, 1997–2012; Consultant, Ashurst Australia, since 2013; *b* 16 Dec. 1947; *s* of Rupert Emanuel Giudice and Emily Muriel Giudice; *m* 1970, Beth Hayden; three *s* one *d*. *Educ:* Xavier Coll., Melbourne; Univ. of Melbourne (BA 1970; LLB). Res. Officer, Hosp. Employees Union, 1971; IR Manager, Myer Emporium Ltd, 1972–78; Partner, Moule Hamilton and Derham, solicitors, 1979–84; Barrister, Victoria Bar, 1984–97. Pres., Fair Work Australia (formerly Australian Industrial Relns Commn), 1997–2012. Hon. Professorial Fellow, Univ. of Melbourne, 2012–. Chm., Ind. Review Panel, Gambling Regulation Act (Vic), 2016–; Chair, Catholic Professional Standards Ltd, 2016–; Mem., Australian Football League Tribunal, 2015–. *Recreations:* tennis, bridge. *Address:* Ashurst Australia, 181 William Street, Melbourne, Vic 3000, Australia. *Clubs:* Athenæum (Melbourne); Melbourne Cricket, Victoria Racing.

**GIULIANI, Rudolph William,** Hon. KBE 2001; Mayor, City of New York, 1994–2001; *b* 28 May 1944; *m* 1984; one *s* one *d*. *Educ:* Manhattan Coll. (AB); New York Univ. (JD). Legal Clerk to US Dist Court Judge, NYC, 1968–70; Asst Attorney, S Dist, NY, 1970–73; Exec. Asst Attorney, Dept of Justice, 1973–75; Associate Dep. Attorney Gen., 1975–77; with Patterson, Belknap, Webb and Tyler, 1977–81; Associate Attorney Gen., 1981–83; US Attorney, US Dist Court, S Dist, NY, 1983–89; with White & Case, 1989–90; with Anderson Kill Olick & Oshinsky PC, 1990–93; Founder, Chm. and Chief Exec., Giuliani Partners, 2002; Partner, Bracewell & Giuliani, 2005–16; Chm., Cybersecurity, Privacy and Crisis Mgt Practice, and Sen. Advr to Exec. Chm., Greenberg Traurig LLP, 2016–18. Republican Candidate for Mayor, NY, 1989. *Publications:* Leadership, 2002.

**GIUSSANI, Bruno;** Global Curator, TED, since 2018 (European Director, TED and Curator, TEDGlobal, 2005–17); *b* Faido, Switzerland, 26 April 1964. *Educ:* Univ. of Geneva (Econ. and Social Scis 1989). Political Editor, 1992–93, Technol. Editor, 1994–97, l'Hebdo mag.; Cybertimes columnist, New York Times, 1996–2000; Hd, Online Strategy, WEF, 1998–2000; Eur. Editor, Industry Standard mag., 2000–01; Dir, Innovation, 3G Mobile, 2002; Knight Fellow, Stanford Univ., 2003–04. Producer and Host, Forum des 100, 2005–15. Chm., Geneva Internat. Film Fest. on Human Rights, 2017–. Vice-Chm., Tinext, 2001–. *Publications:* ROAM: making sense of the wireless internet, 2001. *W:* www.giussani.com.

**GLADDEN, Prof. Lynn Faith,** CBE 2009 (OBE 2001); PhD; FRS 2004; FREng; Shell Professor of Chemical Engineering, University of Cambridge, since 2004; Fellow, Trinity College, Cambridge, since 1999; Executive Chair, Engineering and Physical Sciences Research Council, since 2018; *b* 30 July 1961; *d* of John Montague Gladden and Sheila Faith (*née* Deverell); partner, Prof. Paul Alexander, *qv*. *Educ:* Heathfield Sch., Harrow; Univ. of Bristol (BSc 1st cl. Hons (Chemical Physics) 1982); Keble Coll., Oxford (PGCE 1983); Trinity Coll., Cambridge (PhD 1987). FIChemE 1996; FRSC 2000; FInstP 2003. Pickering Res. Fellow, Royal Soc., 1986; University of Cambridge: Asst Lectr, 1987–91, Lectr, 1991–95; Reader in Process Engrg Sci., 1995–99; Prof. of Chem. Engrg Sci., 1999–2004; Hd, Dept of Chem. Engrg, later Chem. Engrg and Biotechnol., 2006–10; Pro-Vice-Chancellor for Res., 2010–15. Miller Vis. Prof., Univ. of Calif., Berkeley, 1996; Hon. Prof., Beijing Univ. of Chem. Technol., 2010–. Member: Royal Soc./Royal Acad. of Engrg Adv. Gp to NPL, 2003–15; EPSRC, 2006–12; Council, Royal Soc., 2006–08. Comr, Royal Commn for Exhibn of 1851, 2010–. Non-executive Director: IP Gp plc, 2014–; British Land plc, 2015–. FREng 2003. Mem., NAE, 2015. Beilby Medal, Inst. of Materials, Minerals and Mining, RSC, and Soc. of Chem. Industry, 1995; Tilden Lect. and Silver Medal, RSC, 2001; Bakerian Medal and Lect., Royal Soc., 2014. *Recreations:* reading, walking, wine, modern art. *Address:* Jasmine Cottage, 79 Green End, Landbeach, Cambridge CB25 9FD. *T:* (01223) 334762, *Fax:* (01223) 334796. *E:* lfg1@cam.ac.uk.

**GLADSTONE, Sir Charles (Angus),** 8th Bt *cr* 1846; *b* Worthing, 11 April 1964; *s* of Sir (Erskine) William Gladstone, 7th Bt, KG and of Rosamund Anne Gladstone; *S* father 2018; *m* 1988, Caroline Mali, *d* of Sir Derek Morison David Thomas, *qv*; two *s* four *d*. *Educ:* Eton Coll.; Worcester Coll., Oxford (MA). Music publisher, Warner Chappell Music; retailer, Pedlars and Hawarden Estate Farm Shop; restaurateur, The Glynne Arms, Hawarden; festival founder, land owner. *Publications:* (jtly) Pedlars' Guide to the Great Outdoors, 2012; Family Guide to the Great Outdoors, 2013. *Recreations:* pop music, podcasting, literature, running, walking, shooting, photography, family. *Heir: s* Jack William Gladstone [*b* 28 July 1989; *m* 2016, Reyhan Akyildiz]. *Address:* Hawarden Castle, Deeside, Flintshire CH5 3BP. *E:* caglstone@me.com; Glen Dye Lodge, Strachan, Kincardineshire AB31 6LT. *Clubs:* Conduit; Liverpool Football.

**GLADSTONE, David Arthur Steuart,** CMG 1988; HM Diplomatic Service, retired; *b* 1 April 1935; *s* of late Thomas Steuart Gladstone and Muriel Irene Heron Gladstone; *m* 1961, April (*née* Brunner); one *s* one *d*. *Educ:* Eton; Christ Church, Oxford (MA History). National Service, 1954–56; Oxford Univ., 1956–59. Annan, Dexter & Co. (Chartered Accountants), 1959–60; FO, 1960; MECAS, Lebanon, 1960–62; Bahrain, 1962–63; FO, 1963–65; Bonn, 1965–69; FCO, 1969–72; Cairo, 1972–75; British Mil. Govt, Berlin, 1976–79; Head of Western European Dept, FCO, 1979–82; Consul-Gen., Marseilles, 1983–87; High Comr, Colombo, 1987–91; Chargé d'Affaires *ai*, Kiev, 1992. Dir, SANE, 2002–. *Publications:* What shall we do with the Crown Prerogative?, 1998; A Sri Lankan Tempest, 2017. *Recreations:* music, theatre, cinema, dreaming, landscape gardening. *Address:* 1 Mountfort Terrace, N1 1JJ.

**GLADSTONE, Emma Ace;** Artistic Director and Chief Executive, Dance Umbrella, since 2013; *b* London, 12 Nov. 1960; *d* of Tim Gladstone and Caroline Gladstone; *m* 2004, Barnaby Stone; one *d*, and one step *s* one step *d. Educ:* Camden Sch. for Girls; Manchester Univ. (BA Hist. 1984); Laban Dance Centre (Postgrad. Cert. 1985; Advanced Performance Course 1986). Freelance dancer with Arlene Philips, 1977–79, Lea Anderson, 1989–97; Co-Founder and Dir, Adventures in Motion Pictures, 1986–89; Associate Dir, The Place Th., 1997–2003; Artistic Programmer and Producer, Sadler's Wells, 2005–13. Artistic Dir, Rolex Mentor Protégé Arts Weekend, 2013. Mem. Adv. Bd, Family Arts Campaign, 2012–17. Chair, Siobhan Davies Dance, 2017–. Mentoring, talks and adv. work incl. Prakriti Excellence in Contemporary Dance Awards, India; Korea Internat. Modern Dance Competition, S Korea; IntegrART, Switzerland; Draft Works, Royal Opera House; Arts Cross, Beijing Dance Acad.; British Council, Chile. Hon. Fellow, Trinity Laban Conservatoire of Music and Dance, 2014. *Recreations:* Dartmoor, wild swimming, surfing badly. *Address:* Dance Umbrella, Somerset House, West Wing, Strand, WC2R 1LA. *T:* (020) 7257 9380. *E:* emmag@danceumbrella.co.uk.

**GLADSTONE, Jessica Catherine;** Partner, Clifford Chance LLP, since 2015; *b* Beverley, 1978; *d* of Rex Hartley Pogson and Marion Avril Pogson; *m* 2008, Paul Gladstone; one *d. Educ:* Rugby High Grammar Sch. for Girls; Balliol Coll., Oxford (BA Juris. 1999); Sidney Sussex Coll., Cambridge (LLM 2000); Nottingham Law Sch. (Legal Practice Course 2001). Linklaters, 2002–07; Legal Advrs, FCO, 2007–10; Debevoise & Plimpton LLP, 2010–15. Appeals, UN Internat. Criminal Tribunal for Rwanda, 2004. Founding Dir, Advocates for Internat. Develt, 2005–; Chair, Rule of Law Expertise UK, 2015–. *Recreations:* music, theatre, dance, wildlife, travel. *Address:* Clifford Chance LLP, 10 Upper Bank Street, E14 5JJ. *T:* (020) 7006 1000. *E:* jessica.gladstone@cliffordchance.com.

**GLADWIN, Rt Rev. John Warren;** Bishop of Chelmsford, 2003–09; Honorary Assistant Bishop, Diocese of St Albans, since 2010; *b* 30 May 1942; *s* of Thomas Valentine and Muriel Joan Gladwin; *m* 1981, Lydia Elizabeth Adam (*d* 2018). *Educ:* Hertford Grammar School; Churchill Coll., Cambridge (BA History and Theology, MA 1969); St John's Coll., Durham (Dip. Theol). Asst Curate, St John the Baptist Parish Church, Kirkheaton, Huddersfield, 1967–71; Tutor, St John's Coll., Durham and Hon. Chaplain to Students, St Nicholas Church, Durham, 1971–77; Director, Shaftesbury Project on Christian Involvement in Society, 1977–82; Secretary, Gen. Synod Board for Social Responsibility, 1982–88; Prebendary, St Paul's Cathedral, 1984–88; Provost of Sheffield, 1988–94; Bishop of Guildford, 1994–2003. Mem., Gen. Synod of C of E, 1990–2009. Jt Pres., Church Nat. Housing Coalition, 1997–2006; Chm. Bd, Christian Aid, 1998–2008; Chair, Citizens Advice, 2009–15. Trustee, St Albans Old People's Trust, 2017–. Hon. DTh Anglia Ruskin, 2009. *Publications:* God's People in God's World, 1979; The Good of the People, 1988; Love and Liberty, 1998. *Recreations:* gardening, travel, beekeeping. *Address:* 131a Marford Road, Wheathampstead, Herts AL4 8NH. *T:* (01582) 834223.

**GLAISTER, Lesley Gillian,** FRSL; writer; *b* 4 Oct. 1956; *d* of Leonard Oliver Richard Glaister and Maureen Jillian Glaister (*née* Crowley); three *s*; *m* 2001, Andrew Greig. *Educ:* Open Univ. (BA 1st Cl. Hons Humanities); Univ. of Sheffield (MA Socio-Legal Studies). Adult Educn Tutor (pt-time), Sheffield, 1982–90; Lectr (pt-time), for MA in Writing, Sheffield Hallam Univ., 1993–2011. Writer-in-Residence: Cheltenham Fest. of Literature, and Univ. of Gloucester, 2002–03; Univ. of Edinburgh, 2008–11; Lectr, Univ. of St Andrews, 2011–. FRSL 1994. Author of the Year, Yorkshire Post, 1994. *Play:* Bird Calls, Crucible Th., Sheffield, 2003. *Publications:* Honour Thy Father (Somerset Maugham Award, Betty Trask Award), 1990; Trick or Treat, 1991; Digging to Australia, 1992; Limestone and Clay, 1993; Partial Eclipse, 1994; The Private Parts of Women, 1996; Easy Peasy, 1997; Sheer Blue Bliss, 1999; Now You See Me, 2001; As Far As You Can Go, 2004; Nina Todd Has Gone, 2007; Chosen, 2010; Little Egypt, 2014 (Jerwood Fiction Uncovered Prize, 2014); Visiting the Animal (poetry), 2015; The Squeeze, 2017; Aphra's Child (for young adults), 2018. *Recreations:* walking, yoga, theatre, cinema, knitting, crochet, playing the ukulele. *Address:* 8 Greenbank Loan, Edinburgh EH10 5SH; Pentland View, Stromness, Orkney KW16 3JW.

**GLAISTER, Prof. Stephen,** CBE 1998; PhD; Professor of Transport and Infrastructure, Department of Civil and Environmental Engineering, 1998–2009, now Emeritus, and Chairman, Railway Technology Strategy Centre, since 2009 (Director, 1998–2009), Imperial College, London; Director, RAC Foundation, 2008–15; Chair, Office of Rail and Road, 2016–18; *b* 21 June 1946; *s* of Kenneth Goodall Glaister and Mary Glaister (*née* Jones); *m* 1977, Alison Sarah Linning; one *s. Educ:* Univ. of Essex (BA 1967); LSE (MSc 1968; PhD 1976). Lectr in Econs, 1969–78, Cassel Reader, 1978–98, LSE. Member, Board: LRT, 1984–93; Transport for London, 2000–. Co-chair, Transport Safety Commn, 2013–. Advisor: DfT (various dates); Rail Regulator, 1994–2001. Trustee, Rees Jeffreys Road Fund, 1979–. *Publications:* Mathematical Methods for Economists, 1972, 3rd edn 1984; Fundamentals of Transport Economics, 1981; Urban Public Transport Subsidies, 1982; (with C. M. Mulley) Public Control of the Bus and Coach Industry, 1983; (jtly) Application of Social Cost Benefit Analysis to London Transport Policies, 1983; (with Tony Travers) Meeting the Transport Needs of the City, 1993; (with Tony Travers) New Directions for British Railways?: the political economy of privatisation and regulation, 1993; (with R. Layard) Cost Benefit Analysis, 1994; (with Tony Travers) Tolls and Shadow Tolls, 1994; (with Tony Travers) An Infrastructure Fund for London, 1994; (jtly) London Bus Tendering, 1995; (jtly) London's Size and Diversity: the advantages in a competitive world, 1996; (with Dan Graham) Who Spends What on Motoring in the UK?, 1996; (jtly) Transport Policy in Britain, 1998; (jtly) Getting Partnerships Going: public private partnerships in transport, 2000; (with T. Grayling) A New Fares Contract for London, 2000; (jtly) Capital Asset: London's healthy contribution to jobs and services, 2000; (with Dan Graham) The Effect of Fuel Prices on Motorists, 2000; (jtly) A Reassessment of the Economic Case for CrossRail, 2001; (jtly) Streets Ahead: safe and liveable streets for children, 2002; (with T. Travers) Treasurehouse and Powerhouse, 2004; (with D. Graham) Pricing Our Roads: vision and reality, 2004; (with D. Graham) National Road Pricing: is it fair and practical?, 2006; (jtly) Roads and Reality, 2007; (contrib.) Road Pricing: technologies, economics and acceptability, 2018; numerous articles in learned jls. *Recreation:* playing the oboe. *Address:* 39 Huntingdon Street, N1 1BP. *T:* (020) 7609 1401. *E:* s.glaister@imperial.ac.uk.

**GLAISYER, Ven. Hugh;** Archdeacon of Lewes and Hastings, 1991–97, Archdeacon Emeritus, since 2007; *b* 20 Jan. 1930; *s* of Rev. Canon Hugh Glaisyer and Edith Glaisyer; *m* 1962, Alison Marion Heap; one *s* two *d. Educ:* Tonbridge Sch.; Oriel Coll., Oxford (MA 2nd cl. Hon. Mods, 2nd Cl. Theol.); St Stephen's House, Oxford. FO, RAF, 1954. Ordained, Manchester, 1956; Curate: St Augustine's, Tonge Moor, Bolton, 1956–62; Sidcup, 1962–64; Vicar, Christ Church, Milton-next-Gravesend, 1964–81; RD, Gravesend, 1974–81; Vicar, Hove, 1981–91; RD, Hove, 1982–91; Canon of Chichester Cathedral, 1982–91. *Recreations:* British shorthair cats, gardening. *Address:* Florence Villa, Hangleton Lane, Ferring, W Sussex BN12 6PP. *T:* (01903) 244688.

**GLANCY, Robert Peter;** QC 1997; a Recorder, since 1999; a Judge of the First Tier Tribunal (Mental Health) (formerly a President, Mental Health Review Tribunal), since 1999; *b* 25 March 1950; *s* of Dr Cecil Jacob Glancy, JP and Anita Glancy; *m* 1976, Linda Simons; one *s* two *d. Educ:* Manchester Grammar Sch.; St John's Coll., Cambridge (MA). Called to the Bar, Middle Temple, 1972, Bencher, 2007; in practice at the Bar, 1973–; Asst Recorder, 1993–99. *Publications:* (jtly) The Personal Injury Handbook. *Recreations:* theatre, cinema, reading, watching Manchester United. *Address:* 26 Litchfield Way, Hampstead Garden Suburb, NW11 6NJ. *T:* (020) 8933 1938.

**GLANUSK,** 5th Baron *cr* 1899; **Christopher Russell Bailey,** TD 1977; Bt 1852; *b* 18 March 1942; *o s* of 4th Baron Glanusk and Lorna Dorothy (*d* 1997), *o d* of Capt. E. C. H. N. Andrews, MBE, RA; *S* father, 1997; *m* 1974, Frances Elizabeth, *o d* of Air Chief Marshal Sir Douglas Charles Lowe, GCB, DFC, AFC; one *s* one *d. Educ:* Summer Fields, Oxford; Eton Coll.; Clare Coll., Cambridge (BA 1964). Design Engr, English Electric Leo Ltd, 1964–66; Product Mkting Manager, Ferranti Ltd, 1966–78; Internat. Product Manager, Bestobell Mobrey Ltd, 1978–83; Sales Engr, STC Telecommunication Ltd, 1984–86; General Manager: Autocar Equipment Ltd, 1986–97; Woolfram Research Europe Ltd, 1997–98. Territorial Army: Captain, Berks Yeo. Signal Sqdn, 1967–76, Cheshire Yeo. Signal Sqdn, 1976–79; Maj., HQ2 Signal Bde, 1979–83. *Heir: s* Hon. Charles Henry Bailey [*b* 12 Aug. 1976; *m* 2009, Silvie Zamazalová]. *Address:* 51 Chertsey Road, Chobham, Surrey GU24 8PD.

**GLANVILLE, Brian Lester;** author and journalist since 1949; *b* 24 Sept. 1931; *s* of James Arthur Glanville and Florence Glanville (*née* Manches); *m* 1959, Elizabeth Pamela de Boer (*née* Manasse) (*d* 2016), *d* of Fritz Manasse and Grace Manasse (*née* Howden); two *s* two *d. Educ:* Newlands Sch.; Charterhouse. Literary Advr, Bodley Head, 1958–62; Sunday Times (football correspondent), 1958–92; sports columnist, 1960–66; The People (sports columnist), 1992–96; The Times (football writer), 1996–98; Sunday Times, 1998–. *Publications:* The Reluctant Dictator, 1952; Henry Sows the Wind, 1954; Soccer Nemesis, 1955; Along the Arno, 1956; The Bankrupts, 1958; After Rome, Africa, 1959; A Bad Streak, 1961; Diamond, 1962; (ed) The Footballer's Companion, 1962; The Director's Wife, 1963; The Rise of Gerry Logan, 1963; The King of Hackney Marshes, 1965; A Second Home, 1965; A Roman Marriage, 1966; The Artist Type, 1967; The Olympian, 1969; A Cry of Crickets, 1970; The Financiers, 1972; The History of the World Cup, 1973; The Thing He Loves, 1973; The Comic, 1974; The Dying of the Light, 1976; Never Look Back, 1980; (jtly) Underneath The Arches (musical), 1981; A Visit to the Villa (play), 1981; Kissing America, 1985; Love is Not Love, 1985; (ed) The Joy of Football, 1986; The Catacomb, 1988; Champions of Europe, 1991; Story of the World Cup, 1993; Football Memories, 1999; Dictators, 2001; The Arsenal Stadium History, 2006; England's Managers, 2007; For Club and Country, 2008; The Real Arsenal, 2009; The Man Behind the Goal, 2015; *juvenile:* Goalkeepers are Different (novel), 1971; Target Man (novel), 1978; The Puffin Book of Football, 1978; The Puffin Book of Tennis, 1981. *Address:* 160 Holland Park Avenue, W11 4UH. *T:* (020) 7603 6908.
*See also J. Glanville.*

**GLANVILLE, Josephine;** freelance journalist, since 2017; Director, English PEN, 2012–17; *b* London, 1 Sept. 1963; *d* of Brian Lester Glanville, *qv. Educ:* Worcester Coll., Oxford (1st Cl. Hon. Mods Classics 1985); School of Oriental and African Studies, Univ. of London (BA 1st Cl. Hons Hebrew 1995). Freelance journalist and teacher, 1985–91; freelance journalist, 1995–98; Producer, BBC Current Affairs, 1998–2006; Ed., Index on Censorship, 2006–12. Amnesty Media Award, 2008. *Publications:* (ed) Qissat, 2006. *Recreations:* hill walking, reading, music. *E:* joglanville@gmail.com.

**GLANVILLE, Philippa Jane,** OBE 2015; FSA; Academic Director (formerly Director), Waddesdon Manor, Buckinghamshire, 1999–2003; *b* 16 Aug. 1943; *d* of late Wilfred Henry Fox-Robinson and Jane Mary (*née* Home); *m* 1968, Dr Gordon Harris Glanville; two *s. Educ:* Talbot Heath, Bournemouth; Girton Coll., Cambridge (MA Hist.); University Coll. London (Archives Admin). FSA 1968. Tudor and Stuart Curator, London Mus., 1966–72; Hd, Tudor and Stuart Dept, Mus. of London, 1972–80; Victoria and Albert Museum: Asst Keeper, Metalwork Dept, 1980–89; Curator, 1989–96, Chief Curator, 1996–99, Metalwork, Silver and Jewellery Dept. Consultant Curator, Gilbert Collection, 2001–03; Sen. Res. Fellow, 2004–07; Guest Curator, Nat. Archives, Drink: a History, 2006; Curatorial Advr, Harley Foundn, 2005–14. Member: Council for Care of Churches, 1997–2001; Westminster Abbey Fabric Commn, 1998–2017; Arts Council, Nat. Museums of Wales, 2002–11. Trustee: Bishopsland Educnl Trust, 2003–12; Geffrye Mus., 2005–14; Art Fund, 2011–; Library and Mus. of Freemasonry, 2017–; Vice-Pres., NADFAS, 2009–; Mem., Reviewing Cttee on Export of Works of Art, 2010–18. Mem. Cttee, Court Dining Res. Gp, 1989–; contributor, Henry VIII inventory project, 1992–. Associate Fellow, Univ. of Warwick, 2003–06. Liveryman, Co. of Goldsmiths, 1991–; Master, Co. of Art Scholars, 2011–12. Mem., Editl Bd, Apollo, 2004–11. *Publications:* London in Maps, 1972; Silver in England, 1987; Silver in Tudor and Early Stuart England, 1990; (with J. Goldsborough) Women Silversmiths 1685–1845, 1991; (ed and contrib.) Silver, 1996, 2nd edn 1999; (ed with Hilary Young and contrib.) Elegant Eating, 2002; (contrib.) City Merchants and the Arts 1670–1720, 2004; (contrib.) East Anglian Silver 1550–1750, 2004; (contrib.) Britannia and Muscovy, 2006; (contrib.) Feeding Desire, 2006; The Art of Drinking, 2007; (contrib.) Quand Versailles était meublé, 2007; (contrib.) Treasures of the Church, 2008; Dinner with a Duke: decoding food and drink at Welbeck Abbey 1695–1914, 2010; (contrib.) Gold Power and Allure, 2012; contrib. articles in Antiquaries Jl, Burlington Mag., Silver Society Jl, Country Life, World of Interiors, etc, and in exhibn catalogues.

**GLASBY, John Hamilton;** Treasurer, Devon and Cornwall Police Authority, 1993–2009; *b* 29 March 1950; *s* of James Ronald Glasby and Lucie Lillian Glasby (*née* Baxter); *m* 1st, 1971 (marr. diss. 1989); two *s* one *d*; 2nd, 2003, Vivienne Amanda Lloyd. *Educ:* Univ. of Sheffield (BA); Univ. of Birmingham (MSocSc); Liverpool Poly. Mem., CIPFA, 1982. Lectr in Econs, Univ. of E Anglia, 1972–73; Economist: Central Lancs New Town, 1973–76; Shropshire CC, 1976–82; Asst Dir of Finance, Dudley Metropolitan Borough, 1982–84; Devon County Council: Dep. Co. Treas., 1984–93; Co. Treas., 1993–96; Dir of Resources, 1996–2000. Treasurer: Dartmoor Nat. Park Authy, 1997–2000; Devon Fire Authy, 1998–2000. Trustee, Devon Community Foundn, 2010–17. *Recreation:* amateur author.

**GLASCOCK, Prof. John Leslie,** PhD; Professor of Real Estate Finance, and Director, Center for Real Estate and Urban Economic Studies, University of Connecticut, since 2011; *b* 2 Jan. 1950; *s* of Leslie Albert Glascock and Clara Jean Glascock; *m* 1961, Linda Diane Brown; one *s* three *d. Educ:* Tennessee Technol Univ. (BSc (Business Admin (Econs)) 1971); Stetson Univ. (MBA 1974); Virginia Poly. Inst. and State Univ. (MEc 1978); Univ. of N Texas (PhD (Finance) 1984). Louisiana Real Estate Commn Endowed Chair of Real Estate and Prof. of Finance, 1988–96, Interim Dean, 1994–95, Orso Coll. of Business Admin, Louisiana State Univ.; Prof. of Finance and Real Estate and Hd, Dept of Finance, Sch. of Business Admin, Univ. of Connecticut, 1996–98; Oliver T. Carr Dist. Prof. of Real Estate Finance, Sch. of Business and Public Mgt, 1998–2003, Associate Dean for Res. and Doctoral Progs, 2001–03, George Washington Univ.; Grosvenor Prof. of Real Estate Finance, Univ. of Cambridge, and Fellow, Pembroke Coll., Cambridge, 2003–09; West Shell Prof. of Real Estate Finance, and Dir, Real Estate Center, Univ. of Cincinnati, 2009–11. Sec.-Treas., Amer. Real Estate and Urban Econs Assoc., 1993; Pres., Southwest Finance Assoc., 1996–97; Bd Mem., Asian Real Estate Soc., 1999–. Member Editorial

Board: Jl of Real Estate Finance and Econs, 1992– (Special Issue Ed., March 2000); Jl of Real Estate Practice and Educn, 1998–. *Publications:* over 50 refereed articles in jls and numerous reports and monographs. *Recreations:* travel, reading. *Address:* School of Business, University of Connecticut, 2100 Hillside Road, U1041RE, Storrs, CT 06269, USA.

**GLASER, Dr Daniel Eduard;** Director of Science Gallery London, King's College London, 2013–18; *b* 1 April 1968; *s* of Denis Victor Glaser and Danya Ruth Glaser (*née* Samson); *m* 1996, Nathalie Claire Bloomberg; three *d. Educ:* George Eliot Jun. Sch.; Jews' Free Sch.; Westminster Sch.; Trinity Coll., Cambridge (BA Pt 1 Pure Maths, Pt 2 English Lit 1990); Sussex Univ. (MSc Knowledge Based Systems 1991); Weizmann Inst., Rehovot, Israel (PhD Neurobiol. 1999). University College London: Res. Fellow, Inst. of Ophthalmol., 1999–2000; Sen. Res. Fellow, Inst. of Cognitive Neurosci., 2000–06; Hon. Sen. Res. Fellow, 2006–; Develt Manager, 2006–07, Hd of Special Projects, Public Engagement, later Hd of Engaging Science, 2007–13, Wellcome Trust. Scientist in Residence, ICA, 2001–02; Chair, London Café Scientifique, 2002–. Presenter, Under Laboratory Conditions, BBC TV, 2006. Columnist, Observer Mag., 2016–17; Guardian podcast, A Neuroscientist Explains, 2017–. Mem., Camden Cycling Campaign, 2000–. A Judge, Man Booker Prize, 2014. Churchill Fellow, 2019. NESTA Cultural Leadership Award, Nassau, Bahamas, 2005. *Publications:* Trust Me I'm a Scientist, 2004; contrib. scientific papers on visual cortex, brain imaging techniques and effect of experience on vision. *Recreations:* fatherhood, restaurants, berating motorists, egosurfing.

**GLASER, Milton;** graphic designer; *b* 26 June 1929; *s* of Eugene and Eleanor Glaser; *m* 1957, Shirley Girton. *Educ:* High Sch. of Music and Art, NY; Cooper Union Art Sch., NY; Acad. of Fine Arts, Bologna (Fulbright Schol.). Joint Founder: Pushpin Studios, 1954; New York mag., 1968 (Pres. and Design Dir, 1968–77); WBMG, pubn design co., 1983; Milton Glaser Inc., 1974; *projects* include: 600 foot mural, New Federal Office Building, Indianapolis, 1974; Observation Deck and Perm. Exhibn, Twin Towers, World Trade Center, NY, 1975; Sesame Place, Pennsylvania, 1981–83; Grand Union Co. architecture, interiors and packaging; Internat. AIDS symbol and poster, WHO, 1987; Trattoria dell'Arte, NY, 1988; New York Unearthed mus., 1990; *solo exhibitions* include: MOMA, NY, 1975; Centre Georges Pompidou, Paris, 1977; Lincoln Center Gall., NY, 1981; Posters, Vicenza Mus., 1989; Art Inst. of Boston, 1995; *work in public collections* including: MOMA, NY; Israel Mus., Jerusalem; Nat. Archive, Smithsonian Instn, Washington; Cooper Hewitt Nat. Design Mus., NY. Member: Bd, Sch. of Visual Arts, NY, 1961–; Bd of Dirs, Cooper Union, NY; Amer. Inst. of Graphic Arts. Gold Medal, Soc. of Illustrators; St Gauden's Medal, Cooper Union; Prix Savignac, Urban Art Internat. and UNESCO, 1996; Honors Award, AIA, 1992; Lifetime Achievement Award, Cooper Hewitt Nat. Design Mus., 2004; Nat. Medal of Arts, USA, 2010. *Address:* Milton Glaser Inc., 207 East 32nd Street, New York, NY 10016, USA. *T:* (212) 8893161, *Fax:* (212) 2134072. *E:* studio@miltonglaser.com.

**GLASGOW, 10th Earl of,** *cr* 1703; **Patrick Robin Archibald Boyle;** DL; Lord Boyle, 1699; Viscount of Kelburn, 1703; Baron Fairlie (UK), 1897; television director/producer; *b* 30 July 1939; *s* of 9th Earl of Glasgow, CB, DSC, and Dorothea, *o d* of Sir Archibald Lyle, 2nd Bt; *S* father, 1984; *m* 1975, Isabel Mary James; one *s* one *d. Educ:* Eton; Paris Univ. National Service in Navy; Sub-Lt, RNR, 1959–60. Worked in Associated Rediffusion Television, 1961; worked at various times for Woodfall Film Productions, Asst on Film Productions, 1962–64; Asst Dir in film industry, 1962–67; producer/director of documentary films, Yorkshire TV, 1968–70; freelance film producer, 1971–, making network television documentaries for BBC Yorkshire Television, ATV and Scottish Television. Formed Kelburn Country Centre, May 1977, opening Kelburn estate and gardens in Ayrshire to the public. Elected Mem. (Lib Dem), H of L, Jan. 2005. DL Ayrshire and Arran, 1995. *Recreations:* theatre and performing arts, railways. *Heir: s* David Michael Douglas Boyle, *b* 15 Oct. 1978. *Address:* Kelburn, Fairlie, Ayrshire KA29 0BE. *T:* (01475) 568204; (office) South Offices, Kelburn Estate, Fairlie, Ayrshire KA29 0BE. *T:* (01475) 568685.

**GLASGOW, Archbishop of, (RC),** since 2012; **Most Rev. Philip Tartaglia,** STD; *b* 11 Jan. 1951; *s* of Guido and Annita Tartaglia. *Educ:* St Mungo's Acad., Glasgow; St Vincent's Coll., Langbank; St Mary's Coll., Blairs; Pontifical Scots Coll., Rome; Pontifical Gregorian Univ., Rome (PhB; STD 1980). Ordained priest, 1975; Dean of Studies, Pontifical Scots Coll., Rome, 1978–79; Asst Priest, Our Lady of Lourdes, Cardonald, 1980–81; Lectr, 1981–83, Dir of Studies, 1983–85, St Peter's Coll., Newlands, Glasgow; Vice-Rector, 1985–87, Rector, 1987–93, Chesters Coll., Bearsden, Glasgow; Asst Priest, St Patrick's, Dumbarton, 1993–95; Parish Priest, St Mary's, Duntocher, 1995–2004; Rector, Pontifical Scots Coll., Rome, 2004–05; Bishop of Paisley, (RC), 2005–12. *Address:* c/o Curial Offices, 196 Clyde Street, Glasgow G1 4JY.

**GLASGOW, (St Mary's Cathedral), Provost of;** *see* Holdsworth, Very Rev. K.

**GLASGOW, Edwin John,** CBE 1998; QC 1987; *b* 3 Aug. 1945; *s* of late Richard Edwin, (Dick), Glasgow and Diana Geraldine Mary Glasgow (*née* Markby); *m* 1967, Janet Coleman; one *s* one *d. Educ:* St Joseph's Coll., Ipswich; University Coll. London (LLB; Fellow, 2004–16). Called to the Bar, Gray's Inn, 1969, Bencher, 1994. Pres., Internat. Tribunal, Fedn Internat. de l'Automobile, 2011– (Vice-Pres., Court of Appeal, 2009–14). Judge, Qatar Financial Regulatory Authy, 2015–. Chm., Stafford Corporate Consulting, 2001–15. Chairman: Financial Reporting Review Panel, 1992–97; Advocacy Trng (formerly Teaching) Council, 2005–08 (Fellow, 2009–); Singapore Internat. Mediation Centre, 2014–; Sport Resolutions UK, 2016–; Mem., Singapore Internat. Arbitration Centre, 2014– (Chm., 2014–16); Pres., Internat. Advocacy Trng Council, 2011–15. Member: Adv. Council, Public Concern at Work, 2001– (Trustee, 1994–); Le Demi-Siècle de Londres, 2002–. Chm., Bentham Club, UCL, 2000–14; Trustee: Mary Glasgow Language Trust, 1978–2014 (Chm., 1984–2014); London Opera Players, 1985–2008. FCIL 2010; FCIArb 2012. *Recreations:* family, friends, France, music. *Address:* 39 Essex Chambers, 81 Chancery Lane, WC2A 1DD. *T:* (020) 7832 1111; Copper Hall, Watts Road, Thames Ditton, Surrey KT7 0BX; Entrechaux, Vaucluse, France. *Clubs:* Garrick, Royal Automobile (Chm. Stewards, 2005–); Harlequins FC (Chm. Trustees, 1995–2004); Thames Ditton Cricket (Vice-Pres., 2001–).
*See also* O. E. J. Glasgow.

**GLASGOW, Oliver Edwin James;** QC 2016; Senior Treasury Counsel, Central Criminal Court, since 2016; *b* Roehampton, 6 Jan. 1972; *s* of Edwin John Glasgow, *qv*; *m* 2003, Rachel Celia Mortimer; two *s* one *d. Educ:* King's College Sch., Wimbledon; St Hugh's Coll., Oxford (BA 1994). Called to the Bar, Middle Temple, 1995; Jun. Treasury Counsel, 2009–15. Trustee, Kalisher Trust, 2010–. *Recreations:* swimming, cycling, running. *Address:* 2 Hare Court, Temple, EC4Y 7BH. *T:* (020) 7353 5324. *E:* oliverglasgowqc@2harecourt.com.

**GLASGOW AND GALLOWAY, Bishop of;** *no new appointment at time of going to press.*

**GLASGOW AND GALLOWAY, Dean of;** *see* Barcroft, Very Rev. I. D.

**GLASHOW, Prof. Sheldon Lee,** PhD; Metcalf Professor of Mathematics and Science, Boston University, since 2000; Higgins Professor of Physics, Harvard University, 1979–2000, now Emeritus (Professor of Physics, 1966–84); *b* 5 Dec. 1932; *s* of Lewis and Bella Glashow; *m* 1972, Joan (*née* Alexander); three *s* one *d. Educ:* Cornell Univ. (AB); Harvard Univ. (AM, PhD). National Science Foundn Fellow, Copenhagen and Geneva, 1958–60; Res. Fellow, Calif Inst. of Technol., 1960–61; Asst Prof., Stanford Univ., 1961–62; Associate Prof., Univ. of Calif at Berkeley, 1962–66. Visiting Professor: CERN, 1968; Marseille, 1971; MIT, 1974 and 1980; Boston Univ., 1983; Univ. Schol., Texas A&M Univ., 1983–86. Consultant, Brookhaven Nat. Lab., 1966–80; Affiliated Senior Scientist, Univ. of Houston, 1983–96. Pres., Sakharov Internat. Cttee, Washington, 1980–85. Hon. DSc: Yeshiva, 1978; Aix-Marseille, 1982. Nobel Prize for Physics (jtly), 1979. *Publications:* (jtly) Interactions, 1988; The Charm of Physics, 1990; From Alchemy to Quarks, 1994; articles in learned jls. *Recreations:* scuba diving, tennis. *Address:* Physics Research Building, Boston University, 3 Cummington Mall, Boston, MA 02215, USA; 30 Prescott Street, Brookline, MA 02446, USA.

**GLASMAN,** family name of **Baron Glasman**.

**GLASMAN, Baron** *cr* 2011 (Life Peer), of Stoke Newington and of Stamford Hill in the London Borough of Hackney; **Maurice Mark Glasman,** PhD; Reader in Political Theory, London Metropolitan University, since 2011; *b* Walthamstow, London, 8 March 1961; *s* of Coleman Glasman and Rivie Glasman (*née* Pressberg); *m* Catherine Green; two *s* one *d. Educ:* Clapton Jewish Day Sch.; J. F. S. Comprehensive Sch.; St Catharine's Coll., Cambridge (BA Modern Hist. 1982; MA 1986); York Univ. (MA Political Philos. 1987); European Univ. Inst. (PhD 1995). Sen. Lectr in Political Theory, London Guildhall Univ., later London Metropolitan Univ., 1995–2011. *Publications:* Unnecessary Suffering, 1996. *Recreations:* Tottenham Hotspur FC, writing songs, playing jazz trumpet. *Address:* House of Lords, SW1A 0PW. *T:* 07795 283810. *E:* glasmanm@parliament.uk.

**GLASS, Patricia;** *b* Esh Winning, Co. Durham; *m* Bob Glass; two *s.* Assistant Director of Education: Sunderland, 2004–06; Greenwich, 2006–08; Govt Advr on SEN for Yorks and Humber Reg., 2009–10. MP (Lab) NW Durham, 2010–17. Shadow Minister for Educn, 2015, for Foreign and Commonwealth Affairs, 2016; Shadow Sec. of State for Educn, 2016; Shadow Minister for Transport, 2016–17. Mem., Educn Select Cttee, 2010–15. Mem., Lanchester Parish Council, 2007.

**GLASS, Philip;** American composer and performer; *b* 31 Jan. 1937; *s* of Benjamin Glass and Ida Glass (*née* Gouline); *m* 1st, JoAnne Akalaitis; one *s* one *d;* 2nd, Luba Burtyk; 3rd, Candy Jernigan; 4th, Holly Critchlow; two *s. Educ:* Peabody Conservatory; Univ. of Chicago; Juilliard Sch. of Music. Has worked as a taxi-driver, plumber and furniture mover. Composer-in-Residence, Pittsburgh Public Schs, 1962–64; studied with Nadia Boulanger, Paris, 1964–66; Musical Dir, Mabou Mines Co., 1965–74; Founder: Philip Glass Ensemble, 1968; record companies: Chatham Square Productions, 1972; Point Music, 1991; music publishers: Dunvagen, Inc., 1982. *Compositions include: operas:* Einstein on the Beach, 1976; Satyagraha, 1980; The Photographer, 1982; The Civil Wars, 1984; Akhnaten, 1984; The Juniper Tree, 1986; The Making of the Representative for Planet 8, 1986; The Fall of the House of Usher, 1988; 1000 Airplanes on the Roof, 1988; The Hydrogen Jukebox, 1990; White Raven, 1991; The Voyage, 1992; Orphée, 1993; La Belle et la Bête, 1994; Les Enfants Terribles, 1996; Monsters of Grace, 1998; In the Penal Colony, 2000; Galileo Galilei, 2002; Appomattox, 2007; The Perfect American, 2013; The Trial, 2014; Akhnaten, 2016; *film scores:* Koyaanisqatsi, 1982; Mishima (Cannes Special Jury Prize), 1985; Powaqqatsi, 1987; The Thin Blue Line, 1989; Hamburger Hill, 1989; Mindwalk, 1990; A Brief History of Time, 1991; Anima Mundi, 1991; Candyman, 1992; Compassion in Exile, 1992; Candyman II, 1995; Jenipapo, 1995; Secret Agent, 1995; Bent, 1998; Kundun, 1998; The Truman Show (Golden Globe award for best score), 1998; Dracula, 1998; Naqoyqatsi, 2001; The Man in the Bath, 2001; Notes, 2001; Passage, 2001; Diaspora, 2001; The Hours, 2003; Taking Lives, 2004; Secret Windows, 2004; Notes on a Scandal, 2007; Icarus at the Edge of Time, 2010; Visitors, 2017; Jane, 2017; *theatre music:* Endgame, 1984; Cymbeline, 1989; (with Foday Musa Suso) The Screens, 1990; Henry IV, 1992; Woyzeck (Drama Desk Award), 1992; The Mysteries & What's So Funny?, 1992; The Elephant Man, 2002; King Lear, 2019; *dance music:* In the Upper Room, 1986; Witches of Venice, 1995; *instrumental works:* String Quartet no 1, 1966; Piece in the Shape of a Square, 1967; Strung Out, 1969; Music in Similar Motion, 1969; Music in Fifths, 1969; Music with Changing Parts, 1970; Music in Twelve Parts, 1974; Another Look at Harmony, 1974; North Star, 1977; Modern Love Waltz, 1979; Dance nos 1–5, 1979; Company, 1983; String Quartet no 2, 1983; String Quartet no 3 (Mishima), 1985; Songs from Liquid Days, 1986; Violin Concerto, 1987; The Light, 1987; Itaipu, 1988; Canyon, 1988; String Quartet no 4 (Buczak), 1989; Solo Piano, 1989; (with Ravi Shankar) Passages, 1990; String Quartet no 5, 1991; Symphony no 1 (Low), 1992; Mato Grosso, 1992; Symphony no 2, 1994, no 3, 1995; Symphony no 4 (Heroes), 1996; Symphony no 5 (Requiem, Bardo and Nirmanakaya), 1999; Concerto Fantasy, 2000; Concerto for Cello and Orchestra, 2001; Symphony no 6 (Plutonian Ode), 2001; Voices for Organ, Didgeridoo and Narrator, 2001; Dancissimo, 2001; Symphony no 7 (Toltec), 2005; Symphony no 8, 2005; Second Violin Concerto, 2010; Symphony no 9, 2011; Symphony no 10, 2012; String Quartet no 6, 2013; String Quartet no 7, 2014; Symphony no 11, 2016; Piano Concerto no 3, 2017; String Quartet no 8, 2018; Piano Quintet (Annunciation), 2018; Passacaglia for Solo Piano (Distant Figure), 2018; Symphony no 12 (Lodger), 2019; Tao of Glass, 2019. Numerous awards and prizes, including: Benjamin Award, 1961; Fulbright Award, 1966–67; Praemium Imperiale, Japan, 2012; Nat. Medal of Arts (USA), 2015; Glenn Gould Prize, 2016; Kennedy Center Honor (USA), 2018. Officer, Order of Arts and Letters (France), 1995. *Publications:* Music by Philip Glass, ed R. T. Jones, 1987; Words Without Music: a memoir, 2015. *Address:* c/o Dunvagen Music Publishers, 40 Exchange Place, Suite 1906, New York, NY 10005, USA.

**GLASSBROOK, Karen Margaret;** *see* Steyn, K. M.

**GLASSCOCK, John Lewis,** FCIS; Director, British Aerospace PLC, 1982–87; *b* 12 July 1928; *s* of Edgar Henry and Maude Allison Glasscock; *m* 1959, Anne Doreen Baker; two *s. Educ:* Tiffin Sch.; University Coll. London (BA Hons). Served Royal Air Force, 1950–53. Joined Hawker Aircraft Ltd, 1953, Asst Sec., 1956, Commercial Man., 1961; Hawker Siddeley Aviation Ltd: Divl Commercial Man., 1964; Dir and Gen. Man. (Kingston), 1965–77; British Aerospace Aircraft Group: Admin. Dir, 1978; Commercial Dir, 1979; Man. Dir (Military), 1981; BAe PLC: Dep. Chief Exec., Aircraft Gp, and Man. Dir, Civil Aircraft Div., 1982–85; Commercial Dir, 1986–87. Mem. Supervisory Bd, Airbus Industrie, 1983–85. Mem. Council, SBAC, 1979–87. *Recreation:* golf. *Address:* The Apple Shaw, St Nicholas Hill, Leatherhead, Surrey KT22 8NE. *Club:* Royal Automobile.

**GLASSON, Jonathan Joseph;** QC 2013; *b* Newport, 15 Feb. 1965; *s* of Bernard and Glythyn Glasson; civil partnership 2006, *m* 2015, Jamie Lake. *Educ:* Maidstone Grammar Sch.; New Coll., Oxford (MA). Admitted Solicitor (Hons), 1995; called to the Bar, Middle Temple, 1996; in practice as barrister, 1996–. *Publications:* (Contrib. Ed.) Butterworth's Personal Injury Litigation Service, 2005–; (with J. B. Knowles) Blackstone's Guide to the Coroners and Justice Act 2009, 2010. *Recreations:* reading, theatre, enjoying the North Norfolk coast. *Address:* Matrix Chambers, Griffin Building, Gray's Inn, WC1R 5LN. *T:* (020) 7404 3447. *E:* jonathanglasson@matrixlaw.co.uk.

**GLASTONBURY, Virginia**; Partner, since 1988, and Practice Group Leader, Real Estate UK Practice, since 2014, Dentons UK and Middle East LLP (formerly Denton Hall, later Denton Wilde Sapte, then SNR Denton UK), Solicitors; *b* 25 Feb. 1957; *d* of Rt Hon. Sir Frank Cooper, GCB, CMG, PC and Peggie Cooper; *m* 1980, Richard Glastonbury; one step *s*. *Educ*: Bromley High Sch.; LMH, Oxford (BA (Modern Hist.) 1978). Admitted solicitor, 1982; Managing Partner, Denton Hall, 1999–2000; Man. Partner UK, 2000–02, Chief Exec., 2002–05, Denton Wilde Sapte. FRSA 2003. *Recreations*: grandchildren, motor racing, travel. *Address*: Dentons UK and Middle East LLP, One Fleet Place, EC4M 7WS. *E*: virginia.glastonbury@dentons.com.
*See also M. Cooper.*

**GLAZEBROOK, Rosie Pema**; Commissioner, Civil Service Commission, since 2017; Chair, Publishers' Licensing Services, since 2019; Co-Chair, Copyright Licensing Agency, since 2019; *b* Welwyn, 1 Dec. 1968; *d* of Sir Simon Alexander Bowes Lyon, *qv*; *m* 1996, David Glazebrook; three *d*. *Educ*: St Catherine's Coll., Oxford (BA Chem. 1991; MA). UK/Export Sales Manager: Macmillan Press Ltd, 1992–96; Oxford University Press (Academic), 1996–98; Mktg Manager, Times Newspapers, then Publisher, News International Enterprises, 1998–2001; Commercial Dir, Dr Foster Ltd, 2001–04. Nonexec. Dir, NHS Hammersmith and Fulham, 2004–13. Food Standards Agency: Lay Mem., Cttees on Carcinogens and Mutagens in Food and Consumer Products, 2004–13; Consumer Mem., Adv. Cttee on Microbiol Safety of Food, 2007–16. NHS Research Ethics Committee: Mem., Central London, 2007–12; Chm., Camden and Kings Cross, 2013–; Mem. Bd, Human Tissue Authy, 2010–16; Ext. Review Mem., Clwyd-Hart NHS Complaints Rev., 2013; non-exec. Bd Mem., Public Health England, 2014–17; Member, Board: Gen. Optical Council, 2015–; Food Standards Agency, 2016–19. Trustee: Book Aid Internat., 2011–; Bhutan Soc. Trust Fund, 2012–. Membership Sec., Bhutan Soc. of UK, 2011–. *Recreations*: travel, growing vegetables, entertaining. *E*: rosieglazebrook@outlook.com.

**GLAZEBROOK, Hon. Dame Susan (Gwynfa Mary)**, DNZM 2014; a Judge of the Supreme Court of New Zealand, since 2012; *b* 1956; *d* of Harry Glazebrook and Megan Glazebrook; *m* 1992, Greg Kane; two *s*. *Educ*: Univ. of Auckland (BA 1975; MA 1st Cl. Hons 1978; LLB Hons 1980; Dip. Business (Finance) 1994); St Antony's Coll., Oxford (DPhil 1985). Jun. Lectr in Hist., Univ. of Auckland, 1976–79; Interpreter, Rouen, France, 1981–83; Res. Asst and Tutor, Univ. of Auckland, 1984; Partner, Simpson Grierson, Auckland, 1985–2000; a Judge of the High Court of NZ, 2000–02; a Judge of the Court of Appeal of NZ, 2002–12. Member: Bd of Trustees, Nat. Provident Fund, 1989–2000; Bd, South Auckland Health, 1993–2000. Pres., Inter-Pacific Bar Assoc., 1998. Mem., Adv. Council of Jurists, Asia Pacific Forum of Nat. Human Rights Instns, 2002–10. Chm., Inst. of Judicial Studies, NZ, 2007–12. International Association of Women Judges: Mem. Bd, 2006–08, 2012–16; Vice-Pres., 2016–18; Pres. Elect, 2018–20. *Publications*: The New Zealand Accrual Regime, 1989, 2nd edn 1999; numerous articles in jls incl. Victoria Univ. of Wellington Law Rev. and Otago Law Rev. *Recreations*: photography, cinema, music, theatre, reading, yoga, tramping, travel, family. *Address*: Supreme Court of New Zealand, 85 Lambton Quay, Wellington, New Zealand. *T*: (4) 9188222, *Fax*: (4) 9188495. *E*: Justice.Glazebrook@courts.govt.nz. *Club*: Wellington (Wellington).

**GLEAN, Sir Carlyle (Arnold)**, GCMG 2008; Governor-General of Grenada, 2008–13; *b* St George's, 11 Feb. 1932; *s* of George Glean and Olive McBurnie; *m* 1955, Norma DeCoteau; one *s* five *d* (and one *d* decd). *Educ*: Grenada Teachers' Coll.; Univ. of Calgary (BEd 1970; MA (Ed) 1973); Univ. of East Anglia (MA (Ed) 1982). Primary sch. teacher, 1947–56, 1960–63, 1965–66, primary sch. principal, 1963–64, 1967; Grenada Teachers' College: Lectr, 1970–74; Principal, 1974–76; Lectr, Faculty of Educn, Univ. of the West Indies, 1976–86; educnl consultant, 1986–89. Minister of Educn, 1990–95; Senator, 1995–98. Asst Chief Examiner, Social Studies, Caribbean Exam. Council, 1979–84; Member: Conservation Educn Cttee, 1978–81; CARICOM Wkg Party on Family Life Educn, 1988–89. Volunteer teacher, Skills Trng Centre for Youth, New Life Orgn, 1995–2003; Chm., Mgt Cttee, Hillsview Home for the Elderly, 1997–2007. Founder, Camerhogne Foundn (Grenada) Inc., 2009. *Publications*: articles in Caribbean Jl of Educn, Bulletin of Eastern Caribbean Affairs, Curriculum and Caribbean Secondary and Primary Social Studies series. *Recreation*: walking. *Address*: St Dominic Street, Gouyave, Grenada. *E*: patogg@spiceisle.com.

**GLEAVE, Sarah Ann Boyd**; *see* Pinch, S. A. B.

**GLEDHILL, Andreas Nikolaus**; QC 2015; *b* London, 21 April 1967. *Educ*: Christ's Coll., Cambridge (BA 1988; MA). Called to the Bar, Middle Temple, 1992; in practice as barrister, 1992–. *Address*: Blackstone Chambers, Temple, EC4Y 9BW.

**GLEDHILL, Anthony John**; GC 1967; Divisional Auditor, NWS plc, 1993–97; cruise lecturer, since 2009; *b* 10 March 1938; *s* of Harold Victor and Marjorie Edith Gledhill; *m* 1958, Marie Lilian Hughes; one *s* one *d*. *Educ*: Doncaster Technical High Sch., Yorks. Accounts Clerk, Officers' Mess, RAF Bruggen, Germany, 1953–56. Metropolitan Police: Cadet, 1956–57; Police Constable, 1957–75; Detective Sergeant, 1976–87; Investigator, PO Investigation Dept, 1987–88. Vice Chm., Victoria Cross and George Cross Assoc., 2014– (Treas., 2000–14). *Recreations*: golf, bowls, DIY.

**GLEDHILL, Prof. John E.**, FBA 2010; FAcSS; Max Gluckman Professor of Social Anthropology, University of Manchester, now Emeritus. *Educ*: University of Oxford (BA PPE). Sen. Lectr, then Reader, Dept of Anthropology, UCL; University of Manchester: Prof. of Social Anthropology, 1996; Hd of Dept, 1997–2001; former Co-Dir, Centre for Latin American and Caribbean Studies. Chm., Assoc. of Social Anthropologists of UK and Commonwealth, 2005–09; Vice Pres., Internat. Union of Anthropological and Ethnological Scis, 2009–13. FAcSS (AcSS 2001). *Publications*: (ed jtly) State and Society: the emergence and development of social hierarchy and political centralization, 1988; Casi Nada: a study of agrarian reform in the homeland of Cardenismo, 1991; Neoliberalism, Transnationalization and Rural Poverty, 1995; Power and Its Disguises: anthropological perspectives on politics, 2000; (ed with Patience A. Schell) New Approaches to Resistance in Brazil and Mexico, 2012; The New War on the Poor: the production of insecurity in Latin America, 2015; (ed) World Anthropologies in Practice: situated perspectives, global knowledge, 2016; La cara oculta de la inseguridad en México, 2017; (ed jtly) Disputas em torno do espaço urbano: processos de [re]produção/construção e apropriação da cidade, 2017.

**GLEDHILL, Rt Rev. Jonathan Michael**; Bishop of Lichfield, 2003–15; *b* 15 Feb. 1949; *s* of A. Gavan Gledhill and Susan M. (*née* Roberts); *m* 1971, S. Jane Street, PhD; one *s* one *d*. *Educ*: Keele Univ. (BA Hons 1972); Bristol Univ. (MA 1975); Trinity Coll., Bristol (BCTS 1975). Ordained deacon, 1975, priest, 1976; Curate, All Saints, Marple, Gtr Manchester, 1975–78; Priest-in-charge, St George's, Folkestone, 1978–83; Vicar, St Mary Bredin, Canterbury, 1983–96; Bp Suffragan of Southampton, 1996–2003. RD, Canterbury, 1988–94; Hon. Canon, Canterbury Cathedral, 1992–96. Tutor, Canterbury Sch. of Ministry, then SE Inst. for Theol Studies, 1983–96. Member: Gen. Synod, 1995–96; Meissen Commn, 1993–97; C of E Sen. Appts Gp, 2009–13. Chm., Nat. Coll. of Evangelists, 1998–2010. Link Bishop, Old Catholic Churches of Union of Utrecht, 1998–2014. Entered H of L, 2009. DUniv Keele, 2007. *Publications*: Leading a Local Church in the Age of the Spirit, 2003. *Recreations*: sailing, ski-ing.

**GLEDHILL, Michael Geoffrey James**; QC 2001; **His Honour Judge Gledhill**; a Circuit Judge, since 2008; *b* 28 Dec. 1954; *s* of Geoffrey Gledhill and L. Barbara Gledhill (*née* Haigh); *m* 1988, Elizabeth Ann Miller Gordon. *Educ*: Christ Church, Oxford (MA Juris.). Called to the Bar, Middle Temple, 1976, Bencher, 2007; Asst Recorder, 1995–98; Recorder, 1998–2008; Hd of Chambers, 2 Dyers Buildings, 2002–08. Dep. Chancellor, Dio. of Salisbury, 2007–15. *Address*: Southwark Crown Court, 1 English Grounds, SE1 2HU.

**GLEDHILL, Orlando John**; QC 2017; *b* Hamburg, Germany, 28 Feb. 1971; *s* of Hugh Gledhill and Anne Gledhill; *m* 2005, Rosalind Jayne Phelps, *qv*; three *s*. *Educ*: Upper Canada Coll., Toronto; Queen's Univ., Kingston, Ont (BA Hons 1992); Corpus Christi Coll., Oxford (MPhil 1994); City Univ., London (DipLaw 1997); Inns of Court Sch. of Law (BVC 1998). Called to the Bar, Inner Temple, 1998; in practice as a barrister, specialising in commercial law, One Essex Court, 1999–. *Recreation*: dinghy sailing. *Address*: One Essex Court, Temple, EC4Y 9AR. *T*: (020) 7583 2000, *Fax*: (020) 7583 0118. *E*: ogledhill@oeclaw.co.uk.

**GLEDHILL, Rosalind Jayne**; *see* Phelps, R. J.

**GLEDHILL, Ruth**; Online Editor, The Tablet, since 2017; *b* 15 Dec. 1959; *d* of late Rev. Peter Gledhill and Bridget Mary Gledhill (*née* Rathbone), Anglesey, N Wales; *m* 1st, 1989, John Edward Stammers (marr. diss. 1994); 2nd, 1996, Andrew Daniels (marr. diss. 2003); 3rd, 2006, Alan Lewis Duder Franks, *qv*; one *s*. *Educ*: Thomas Alleyne's GS, Uttoxeter; London Coll. of Printing (HND); Birkbeck Coll., London (Cert. Religious Studies); Goldsmith's, Univ. of London (MA Digital Journalism). With Uttoxeter Advertiser news service, 1980–81; Australasian Printer, Sydney, 1981–82; indentured, Birmingham Post & Mail, 1982–84; Industrial corresp., Birmingham Post, 1984; gen. news reporter and feature writer, Daily Mail, 1984–87; The Times: Home News Reporter, 1987–90; Religion Correspondent, 1990–2014; columnist, At Your Service, 1993–2002; also writer on dance sport for sports pages, 1997–2002; occasional corresp. on religion and new technology for Interface, 1998–2001; News Reporter, The Tablet, 2014; Contrib. Ed., 2014–17, Ed., 2017, Christian Today. Columnist, Church of England Newspaper. Guest presenter: Good Worship Guide, Yorks TV, 1996; ITV Sunday Worship, 1999. Vis. Lectr, Sch. of Journalism, City Univ., 2008–. Member: IJA Commn on Rise of Neo-Fascism, 1993; BBC Governors' Independent Advice Panel: Religious Programmes, 1998. Mem., London Rotary, 1997–. Andrew Cross Award for Religious Journalism, 2005. Blog: ArticlesofFaith. *Publications*: (jtly) Birmingham is Not a Boring City, 1984; (ed and introd.) The Times Book of Best Sermons, annually 1995–2001; At A Service Near You, 1996; (ed) The Times Book of Prayers, 1997. *Recreation*: photography. *T*: 07880 505806. *W*: www.ruthgledhill.com, www.twitter.com/ruthiegledhill.

**GLEDITSCH, Prof. Kristian Skrede**, PhD; Regius Professor of Political Science, University of Essex, since 2018; *b* Oslo, Norway, 9 Oct. 1971; *s* of Nils Petter Gleditsch and Kari Skrede; *m* 2002, Prof. Theodora-Ismene Gizelis. *Educ*: Univ. of Oslo (MA Soc. Scis 1993); Univ. of Colorado (PhD Political Sci. 1999). Lectr in Social Sci. Methodology, Univ. of Glasgow, 1999–2001; Asst Prof. of Political Sci., UCSD, 2001–05; Reader, 2005–07, Prof., 2007–17, Dept of Govt, Univ. of Essex. Res. Associate, Peace Res. Inst. Oslo, 2003–. Vis. Prof., Univ. of Konstanz, 2015–. *Publications*: All International Politics is Local: the diffusion of conflict, integration and democratization, 2002; (with Michael D. Ward) Spatial Regression Models, 2008, 2nd edn 2018; (jtly) Inequality, Grievances and Civil War, 2013; over 60 articles in scholarly jls. *Recreations*: running, hiking, cross-country ski-ing. *Address*: Department of Government, University of Essex, Colchester CO4 3SQ. *T*: (01206) 872517. *E*: ksg@essex.ac.uk. *W*: www.ksgleditsch.com. *Club*: Great Bentley Running.

**GLEES, Ann Margaret**; *see* Jefferson, A. M.

**GLEESON, Hon. (Anthony) Murray**, AC 1992 (AO 1986); Chief Justice of Australia, 1998–2008; *b* 30 Aug. 1938; *s* of Leo John Gleeson and Rachel Alice Gleeson; *m* 1965, Robyn Paterson; one *s* three *d*. *Educ*: St Joseph's Coll., Hunters Hill; Univ. of Sydney (BA, LLB). Called to the NSW Bar, 1963; QC 1974. Tutor in Law, St Paul's Coll., Sydney Univ., 1963–65; Part-time Lectr in Company Law, Sydney Univ., 1965–74. Chief Justice of NSW, 1988–98; Lt-Gov., NSW, 1989–98. Non-perm. Judge, HK Court of Final Appeal, 2009–. President: Judicial Commn, NSW, 1988–98; Australian Assoc. of Constit. Law, 2009–15. Mem., Perm. Court of Arbitration, 1999–2009. Mem. Council, NSW Bar Assoc., 1979–85 (Pres., 1984 and 1985). Hon. Bencher, Middle Temple, 1989. Patron, Chartered Inst. of Arbitrators (Australia) Ltd, 2009–. Hon. LLD Sydney, 1999; DUniv: Griffith, 2001; Aust. Catholic Univ., 2005. *Recreations*: tennis, golf. *Address*: Level 17, 115 Pitt Street, Sydney, NSW 2000, Australia. *Club*: Australian (Sydney).

**GLEESON, Dermot James**; non-executive Chairman, M. J. Gleeson Group plc, since 2005 (Executive Chairman, 1998–2005); *b* 5 Sept. 1949; *s* of late Patrick Joseph Gleeson and Margaret Mary Gleeson (*née* Higgins); *m* 1980, Rosalind Mary Catherine Moorhead; one *s* one *d*. *Educ*: Downside; Fitzwilliam Coll., Cambridge (MA). Conservative Res. Dept, 1974–77 (Dir, 1979); Mem., Cabinet of C. Tugendhat, EC, 1977–79; EEC Rep., Brussels, Midland Bank, 1979–81; Dep. Man. Dir, 1982–88, Chief Exec., 1988–98, M. J. Gleeson Gp plc. Chm., Major Contractors Gp, 2003–05. Mem. Bd, Housing Corp., 1986–92; Dir, CITB, 1996–2002. A Gov., BBC, 2000–06; Trustee, BBC Trust, 2007–08. Trustee: Inst. of Cancer Res., 2006–11; Fitzwilliam Mus. Develt Trust, 2006–08. Chm. of Govs, Rydes Hill Prep. Sch., 2015–19; Gov., Downside Sch., 2015–17. *Recreations*: studying the history of political thought, family life - especially on the Outer Hebrides. *Address*: Hook Farm, White Hart Lane, Wood Street Village, Guildford, Surrey GU3 3EA. *Clubs*: Beefsteak (Chm., 2004–07), Royal Automobile, Brooks's.

**GLEESON, Judith Amanda Jane**; a Judge of the Upper Tribunal (Immigration and Asylum Chamber) (formerly a Vice President, Immigration Appeal Tribunal, later Senior Immigration Judge, Asylum and Immigration Tribunal), since 2002; *b* 24 Aug. 1955; *d* of late Derek Young Coomber and Jennifer Isabel Coomber (*née* Strudwick); *m* 1980, Donald Frank Gleeson (marr. diss. 2010); one *s*. *Educ*: Univ. Libre de Bruxelles (Wiener Anspach Schol.; Cert. Civil Law and Eur. Community Law 1976); Lady Margaret Hall, Oxford (MA Jurisprudence 1977); Coll. of Law. Articled Linklaters & Paines, 1978–80; Solicitor, 1981; Hedleys Solicitors, 1981–95; an Employment Judge (formerly a Chm., Employment Tribunals), 1993–2009; Immigration Adjudicator, 1995–2002. Vis. Industrial Fellow, Faculty of Business and Law, Kingston Univ., 1993–. *Recreations*: world and silent films, blues and jazz. *Address*: Upper Tribunal (Immigration and Asylum Chamber), Field House, 15–25 Bream's Buildings, EC4A 1DZ. *Club*: Athenæum.

**GLEESON, Hon. Murray**; *see* Gleeson, Hon. A. M.

**GLEITZMAN, Morris**; author; Australian Children's Laureate, 2018–19; *b* 9 Jan. 1953; *s* of Philip and Pamela Gleitzman; *m* 1974, Christine McCaul (marr. diss. 1994); one *s* one *d*. *Publications*: The Other Facts of Life, 1985; Two Weeks with the Queen, 1990; Second Childhood, 1990; Misery Guts, 1991; Worry Warts, 1991; Blabber Mouth, 1992; Sticky Beak, 1993; Puppy Fat, 1994; Belly Flop, 1996; Water Wings, 1996; (with P. Jennings) Wicked!, 1997; Bumface, 1998; Gift of the Gab, 1999; Toad Rage, 1999; (with P. Jennings) Deadly!, 2000; Adults Only, 2001; Toad Heaven, 2001; Boy Overboard, 2002; Teacher's Pet, 2003; Toad Away, 2003; Girl Underground, 2004; Worm Story, 2004; Once, 2005; Aristotle's Nostril, 2005; Doubting Thomas, 2006; Give Peas a Chance, 2007; Then, 2008; Toad Surprise, 2008; Grace, 2009; Now, 2010; Too Small To Fail, 2011; Pizza Cake, 2011; After, 2012; Extra Time, 2013; Loyal Creatures, 2014; Soon, 2015; Toad Delight, 2016; Snot Chocolate, 2016; Maybe, 2017; Help Around the House, 2018; Funny Stories, 2018. *Address*: c/o Penguin Books (Australia), 707 Collins Street, Melbourne, Vic 3008, Australia. *T*: (3) 98112400. *E*: morris@morrisgleitzman.com.

**GLEN, John Philip**; MP (C) Salisbury, since 2010; Economic Secretary to HM Treasury, since 2018; *b* Bath, 1 April 1974; *s* of Philip Glen and Thalia Glen (*née* Mitchenere); *m* 2008, Emma Caroline O'Brien (*née* Stephens); one step *s* one step *d*. *Educ*: King Edward's Sch., Bath (Hd Boy); Mansfield Coll., Oxford (BA Mod. Hist. 1996; Pres. JCR 1995); Judge Inst., Univ. of Cambridge (MBA 2003); King's Coll., London (MA Internat. Security and Strategy, RCDS, 2015). Accounts Asst, Fleet Support Gp, Chippenham, 1992–93; Parly Researcher to Gary Streeter, MP and Michael Bates, MP, 1996–97; Strategy Consultant, Accenture, 1997–2004, on secondment to Hd, Political Section, Conservative Res. Dept, 2000–01; Dep. Dir, 2004–05, Dir, 2005–06, Conservative Res. Dept; Sen. Advr to Global Hd of Strategy, Accenture, 2006–10. PPS to Sec. of State for Communities and Local Govt, 2012–15, to Sec. of State for Business, Innovation and Skills, 2015–16, to Chancellor of Exchequer, 2016–17; Parly Under-Sec. of State, DCMS, 2017–18. Member: Defence Select Cttee, 2010–12; Cttee on Arms Exports, 2010–12; Downing St Policy Bd, 2014–15; Work and Pensions Select Cttee, 2015–16. JP Westminster, 2006–11. *Publications*: (contrib.) There is Such a Thing as Society, 2002. *Recreations*: family, church, eating out, travel, squash. *Address*: (office) Morrison Hall, 12 Brown Street, Salisbury, Wilts SP1 1HE; House of Commons, SW1A 0AA. *T*: (020) 7219 3000. *E*: john.glen.mp@parliament.uk.

**GLEN, Marlyn Laing**; Member (Lab) Scotland North East, Scottish Parliament, 2003–11; *b* 30 Sept. 1951; *d* of Stewart and Rita Mitchell; *m* 1974, Neil Glen (*d* 2004); one *s* one *d*. *Educ*: Kirkton High Sch., Dundee; St Andrews Univ. (MA Hons); Dundee Univ. (DipEd; Dip Special Ed); Open Univ. (BA Hons; BSc Hons). Teacher, English, Stanley Park Comp. Sch., 1974–76, Belmont Acad., 1976–77; Asst Prin. Teacher of English, Ravenspark Acad., Irvine, 1977–82; Teacher of English and Learning Support (pt-time), Ravenspark Acad. and Auchenharvie Acad., Stevenston, 1982–90; Sen. Teacher, Craigie High Sch., Dundee, 1991–97; Principal Teacher, Support for Learning, Baldragon Acad., Dundee, 1997–2003. Chair, CAB, Dundee, 2015–16. Trustee, One World Centre, Dundee, 2012–. *Recreations*: music, theatre, literature, yoga, gardening.

**GLENAPP, Viscount; Fergus James Kenneth Mackay**; *b* 9 July 1979; *s* and heir of 4th Earl of Inchcape, *qv*; *m* 2010, Rebecca Margaret, *d* of Charles Jackson; one *s* one *d*. *Educ*: Radley Coll.; Edinburgh Univ. (MA); BPP Sch. of Law (CPE; BVC); Imperial Coll. London (MBA). *Heir*: *s* Hon. Alexander David James Mackay, *b* 19 Aug. 2017. *Address*: 40 Richford Street, W6 7HP.

**GLENARTHUR**, 4th Baron *cr* 1918; **Simon Mark Arthur**; Bt 1903; *b* 7 Oct. 1944; *s* of 3rd Baron Glenarthur, OBE, and Margaret (*d* 1993), *d* of late Captain H. J. J. Howie; *S* father, 1976; *m* 1969, Susan, *yr d* of Comdr Hubert Wyndham Barry, RN; one *s* one *d*. *Educ*: Eton. Commissioned 10th Royal Hussars (PWO), 1963; ADC to High Comr, Aden, 1964–65; Captain 1970; Major 1975; retired 1975; Royal Hussars (PWO), TA, 1976–80. British Airways Helicopters Captain, 1976–82. A Lord in Waiting (Govt Whip), 1982–83; Parly Under Sec. of State, DHSS, 1983–85, Home Office, 1985–86; Minister of State: Scottish Office, 1986–87; FCO, 1987–89; elected Mem., H of L, 1999. Sen. Exec., 1989–96, Consultant, 1996–99, Hanson PLC; Dep. Chm., Hanson Pacific Ltd, 1994–96; Director: Aberdeen and Texas Corporate Finance Ltd, 1977–82; The Lewis Gp, 1993–95; Whirlybird Services Ltd, 1995–2004; Millennium Chemicals Inc., 1996–2004; Medical Defence Union Ltd, 2002–06; Audax Trading Ltd, subseq. Audax Global SARL, 2003– (Consultant, 2001–03); Chm., British European Aviation Ltd, 2015–. Consultant: BAe PLC, 1989–99; Chevron UK Ltd, 1994–97; Imperial Tobacco Gp, 1996–98. Chm., St Mary's Hosp., Paddington, NHS Trust, 1991–98 (Special Trustee, St Mary's Hosp., 1991–2000). Chm., Eur. Helicopter Assoc., 1996–2003; Dep. Chm., Internat. Fedn of Helicopter Assocs, 1996–97 and 2000–04 (Chm., 1997–2000); Pres., British Helicopter Assoc. (formerly Adv. Bd), 2004– (Chm., 1992–2004). Pres., Nat. Council for Civil Protection, 1991–2003; Mem. Council, Air League, 1994–2009; Mem., Nat. Employers Liaison Cttee for Britain's Reserve Forces, 1996–2002; Chm., Nat. Employer Adv. Bd for Britain's Reserve Forces, 2002–09. Scottish Patron, Butler Trust, 1994–2014; Trustee, RCO, 2014– (Chm., Trustee Council, 2017–). Governor: Nuffield Nursing Homes Trust, then Nuffield Hosps, later Nuffield Health, 2000–09; King Edward VII Hosp. (Sister Agnes), 2010–13 (Mem. Council and Trustee, 2011–13; Chm. Council, 2012–13); Sutton's Hosp. in Charterhouse, 2011–19; Comr, Royal Hosp., Chelsea, 2001–07. Former Capt., Queen's Body Guard for Scotland (Royal Co. of Archers). FCILT until 2011 (FCIT 1999; MCIT 1979); FRAeS 1992–2011. Liveryman, GAPAN, 1996–2011. DL Aberdeenshire, 1988. *Recreations*: field sports, gardening, choral singing, organ-playing, barometers. *Heir*: *s* Hon. Edward Alexander Arthur, *b* 9 April 1973. *Address*: Northbrae Farmhouse, Crathes, Banchory, Kincardineshire AB31 6JQ. *Club*: Cavalry and Guards.

**GLENCONNER**, 4th Baron *cr* 1911; **Cody Charles Edward Tennant**; Bt 1885; *b* 2 Feb. 1994; *o s* of Hon. Charles Edward Pevensey Tennant (*d* 1996), and of Sheilagh, *y d* of Matthew Raymond Walker Scott; *S* grandfather, 2010. *Educ*: Edinburgh Acad.; Aberdeen Univ. (MA Hons); Univ. of Law (GDL). *Heir*: cousin Euan Lovell Tennant [*b* 22 July 1983; *m* 2011, Helen Clare, *d* of Paul Cross; one *s*].

**GLENDAY, Craig Douglas**; Editor-in-Chief, Guinness World Records, since 2002; *b* Dundee, 31 May 1973; *s* of Douglas and Sylvia Glenday. *Educ*: Balerno Primary Sch.; Powrie Primary Sch.; Craigie High Sch., Dundee; Royal Scottish Acad. of Music and Drama Jun. Sch., Glasgow; Napier Univ., Edinburgh (BA Publishing). Ed., Marshall Cavendish Publishing Ltd, 1992–97; Sen. Ed., Midsummer Books, 1997–2000; Producer: Trinity Mirror Digital Media, 2000–01; iVillage, 2001–02; publisher, Sondheim The Magazine, 2012–. Reviewer, Musical Th. Rev. mag., 2014–. Producer, Hey, Old Friends!, Th. Royal, Drury Lane, 2015. Trustee, Stephen Sondheim Soc., 2014– (Chm., 2015–); Producer, Student Performer of the Year competition, 2015–). *Publications*: UFO Investigator's Handbook, 1999; Vampire Hunter's Notebook, 2003; (ed) Guinness World Records, annually, 2006–; (ed) Guinness World Records Gamer's Edition, annually, 2008–; (ed) Blockbusters, 2016. *Recreations*: member, The Infamous Grouse band (drummer) and London Metropolitan Brass (percussionist), theatre, script writing. *Address*: Guinness World Records, South Quay Plaza 3, South Quay Building, 189 Marsh Wall, E14 9SH. *T*: (020) 7891 4500, *Fax*: (020) 7891 4501. *E*: craig.glenday@guinnessworldrecords.com.

**GLENDEVON**, 3rd Baron *cr* 1964, of Midhope, Co. Linlithgow; **Jonathan Charles Hope**; *b* 23 April 1952; *yr s* of 1st Baron Glendevon and Elizabeth Mary (*d* 1998), *d* of (William) Somerset Maugham, CH; *S* brother, 2009.

**GLENDINNING, Hon. Victoria, (Hon. Mrs O'Sullivan)**, CBE 1998; FRSL; author and journalist, since 1969; *b* 23 April 1937; *d* of Baron Seebohm, TD and Evangeline, *d* of Sir Gerald Hurst, QC; *m* 1st, 1958, Prof. (Oliver) Nigel (Valentine) Glendinning (marr. diss. 1981; he *d* 2013); four *s*; 2nd, 1982, Terence de Vere White (*d* 1994); 3rd, 1996, Kevin (Patrick) O'Sullivan. *Educ*: St Mary's Sch., Wantage; Millfield Sch.; Somerville Coll., Oxford (MA Mod. Langs); Hon. Fellow, 2004); Southampton Univ. (Dip. in Social Admin). Part-time teaching, 1960–69; part-time psychiatric social work, 1970–73; Editorial Asst, TLS, 1974–78. Trustee, Booker Prize Foundn, 2010–18. FRSL 1982 (Vice-Pres., RSL, 2000–); Vice-Pres., English Centre, PEN, 2003 (Pres., 2001–03). Hon. DLitt: Southampton, 1994; Ulster, 1995; Dublin, 1995; York, 2000. *Publications*: A Suppressed Cry, 1969, re-published 2013; Elizabeth Bowen: portrait of a writer, 1977; Edith Sitwell: a unicorn among lions, 1981, repr. 2013; Vita: a biography of V. Sackville-West, 1983, republd 2018; Rebecca West: a life, 1987; The Grown-Ups (novel), 1989; Hertfordshire, 1989; Trollope, 1992; Electricity (novel), 1995; (ed with M. Glendinning) Sons and Mothers, 1996; Jonathan Swift, 1998; Flight (novel), 2002; Leonard Woolf: a life, 2006; (ed) Love's Civil War, 2008; Raffles and the Golden Opportunity, 2012; The Butcher's Daughter (novel), 2018; reviews and articles in newspapers and magazines in Britain, Ireland and USA. *Address*: c/o David Higham Associates, 7th Floor, Waverley House, 7–12 Noel Street, W1F 8GQ. *Club*: Athenæum.

**GLENDONBROOK**, Baron *cr* 2011 (Life Peer), of Bowdon in the County of Cheshire; **Michael David Bishop**, Kt 1991; CBE 1986; Chairman of Trustees, The Michael Bishop Foundation, since 1989; Chairman: British Midland Plc (formerly Airlines of Britain Holdings Plc), 1978–2009; British Regional Air Lines Group Plc, and Manx Airlines, 1982–2001; Glendonbrook Foundation (Australia), since 2012; *b* 10 Feb. 1942; *s* of Clive Leonard Bishop. *Educ*: Mill Hill School. Joined: Mercury Airlines, Manchester, 1963; British Midland Airways, 1964; Director: Airtours plc, 1987–2001 (Dep. Chm., 1996–2001); Williams Plc, 1993–2000. Member: E Midlands Electricity Bd, 1980–83; E Midlands Reg. Bd, Central Television, 1981–89; Dep. Chm., 1991–93, Chm., 1993–97, Channel 4 Television Corp. Non-exec. Dir, Kidde plc, 2000–02. Chm., D'Oyly Carte Opera Trust Ltd, 1989–2008. Trustee and Dir, Friends in the UK, Royal Flying Doctor Service of Australia, 2005–14. Hon. Mem., Royal Soc. of Musicians of GB, 1989. *Address*: House of Lords, SW1A 0PW. *Clubs*: Brooks's; Australian (Sydney).

**GLENDYNE**, 4th Baron *cr* 1922; **John Nivison**; Bt 1914; *b* 18 Aug. 1960; *o s* of 3rd Baron Glendyne and Elizabeth, *y d* of Sir Cecil Armitage, CBE; *S* father, 2008. *Educ*: Harrow Sch.

**GLENFIELD, Rt Rev. Ferran**; see Kilmore, Elphin and Ardagh, Bishop of.

**GLENISTER, Philip Haywood**; actor, television presenter and producer; *b* Harrow Weald, London, 10 Feb. 1963; *s* of John and Joan Glenister; *m* 2006, Beth Goddard; two *d*. *Educ*: Hatch End High Sch.; Harrow Weald Sixth Form Coll. *Theatre* includes: A Free Country, Tricycle, 1990; Romeo and Juliet, Lyceum, Edinburgh, 1991; Beautiful Thing, 1993, Crossing the Equator, 1995, Bush; Translations, Abbey, Dublin, 1996; The Feast of Snails, Lyric, 2002; This House, RNT, 2012; *television* includes: Frontiers, 1996; My Wonderful Life, 1996–97; Have Your Cake and Eat It, 1997; Vanity Fair, 1998; Roger Roger, 1998–2003; Clocking Off, 2000–02; State of Play, 2003; Island at War, 2004; Vincent, 2005; Life on Mars, 2006–07; Cranford, 2007; Ashes to Ashes, 2008–10; Demons, 2009; Hidden, 2011; Mad Dogs, 2011–13; Treasure Island, 2012; From There to Here, 2013; Big School, 2013–14; (presenter) Love of Cars, 2014; Prey, 2015; The Hollow Crown, Outcast, The Level, 2016; Living the Dream, 2017–19; *films* include: I.D., 1995; The Other Boleyn Girl, Calendar Girls, 2003; Kingdom of Heaven, 2005; You Will Meet a Tall Dark Stranger, 2010; Bel Ami, 2012. Patron: Momentum; Shooting Star Chase. Mem., BAFTA. *Publications*: Things Ain't What They Used To Be, 2007. *Recreations*: golf, red wine, sleeping. *Address*: c/o ARG, 4A Exmoor Street, W10 6BD. *Clubs*: Richmond Golf, Stage Golf Soc.

**GLENN, Sir Owen (George)**, KNZM 2013 (ONZM 2008); Executive Chairman and Owner, OTS Logistics Group, 1978–2011; Founder, Glenn Family Foundation, since 1984; *b* Calcutta, 19 Feb. 1940; *s* of Owen Arthur Glenn and Decima Irene Glenn; one *s* five *d*. *Educ*: Mt Roskill Grammar Sch.; Harvard Business Sch. (OPM 1990). With Trans-Tasman Airways, 1963–64; estabd McGregor Squire Air Services, 1969–75; consulting, 1975; estabd Pacific Forwarding, 1975–78; Founder: Direct Container Lines, 1978; NACA Logistics, 1981. Hon. LLD Auckland, 2012. *Publications*: Make a Difference, 2011. *Recreations*: hockey, Rugby, Rugby League, golf, cricket, philanthropy. *Address*: 314/121 Customs Street West, Auckland 1010, New Zealand; 1/17 Gladeswood Gardens, Double Bay, NSW 2028, Australia. *T*: (2) 9362 9096; Vale Levu, Molololailai, Fiji Islands. *T*: (1) 3103847043.

**GLENN, Paul Anthony**; DL; **His Honour Judge Glenn**; a Circuit Judge, since 2004; *b* 14 Sept. 1957; *m* 1985, Diane Burgess; two *s*. *Educ*: Liverpool Univ. (LLB Hons 1979). Called to the Bar, Gray's Inn, 1983; Magistrates' Court Service, 1980–85; County Prosecuting Solicitor's Office, Cheshire, 1985–86; CPS, 1986–90; in practice as a barrister, 1990–2004; a Recorder, 2000–04. Hon. Recorder, Stoke-on-Trent, 2008. DL Staffs, 2017. *Recreations*: sport, avid supporter of Stoke City FC and enjoys watching Rugby and cricket. *Address*: Stoke-on-Trent Combined Court, Bethesda Street, Hanley, Stoke-on-Trent ST1 3BP. *T*: (01782) 854000.

**GLENNERSTER, Prof. Howard**, FBA 2002; FAcSS; Co-Director, 1997–2007, Associate, since 2008, Centre for Analysis of Social Exclusion, and Professor of Social Administration, 1984–2001, now Professor Emeritus, London School of Economics; *b* 4 Oct. 1936; *s* of John Howard Glennerster and Charlotte Nellie Glennerster; *m* 1962, Ann Dunbar Craine; one *s* one *d*. *Educ*: Pixmore Secondary Modern Sch., Letchworth; Letchworth Grammar Sch.; Wadham Coll., Oxford (BA PPE). Res. Asst, Labour Party Res. Dept, 1959–64; London School of Economics: Res. Officer, Higher Educn Res. Unit, 1964–68; Lectr in Social Admin, 1968–79; Reader, 1979–84; Chm., Suntory and Toyota Internat. Centres for Econs and Related Disciplines, 1994–2000; Hon. Fellow, 2005. Vis. Prof. or acad. visitor, Brookings Instn, 1972, 1996, 2000, Univs of Berkeley, Calif, 1982, Washington State, 1982 and Chicago, 1989. Mem., Sec. of State for Health's Adv. Cttee on Resource Allocation, 1997–2010; Specialist Advr to H of L Cttee on Public Services and Demographic Change, 2012–13. Director: Basic Skills Agency, 1997–2007; Mgt Cttee, King's Fund, 2002–07. FAcSS (AcSS 2000); FRSA 1995. *Publications*: Social Service Budgets and Social Policy, 1974; Planning for Priority Groups, 1983; Paying for Welfare, 1984, 3rd edn 1997; Implementing GP Fundholding, 1994; British Social Policy since 1945, 1995, 3rd edn 2007; The State of Welfare: the economics of social spending, 1998; Understanding the Finance of Welfare, 2003, 3rd edn 2017; Wealth in the UK: distribution, accumulation, and policy, 2013; contrib. numerous papers on econs of social policy to acad. jls. *Recreations*: walking, bird-watching, gardening, tending an allotment, watching cricket, enjoying grandchildren. *Address*: London School of Economics, Houghton Street, WC2A 2AE. *E*: h.glennerster@lse.ac.uk. *Club*: Middlesex CC.

**GLENNIE, Rt Hon. Lord; Angus James Scott Glennie;** PC 2016; a Senator of the College of Justice in Scotland, since 2005; farmer; *b* 3 Dec. 1950; *yr s* of late Robert Nigel Forbes Glennie and Barbara Scott (*née* Nicoll); *m* 1981, Patricia Jean Phelan, *er d* of His Honour Andrew Phelan; three *s* one *d*. *Educ*: Sherborne Sch.; Trinity Hall, Cambridge (MA Hons). Called to the Bar, Lincoln's Inn, 1974, Bencher, 2007; QC 1991; admitted to Faculty of Advocates, 1992; QC (Scot.) 1998. *Recreations*: sailing, ski-ing, Real tennis. *Address*: Parliament House, Parliament Square, Edinburgh EH1 1RQ.

**GLENNIE, Dame Evelyn (Elizabeth Ann),** CH 2017; DBE 2007 (OBE 1993); FRAM, FRCM; musician, motivational speaker, jewellery designer, composer; *b* 19 July 1965; *d* of Isobel and Arthur Glennie. *Educ*: Ellon Acad., Aberdeenshire; Royal Academy of Music (GRSM Hons, LRAM, ARAM; FRAM 1992; Queen's Commendation Prize); FRCM 1991. Shell Gold Medal, 1984; Leonardo da Vinci Prize, 1987; début, Wigmore Hall, 1986; soloist in Europe, Asia, N and S America, Russia and Middle East; percussion and timpani concertos specially written; TV and radio presenting; numerous recordings and awards. Headline artist, London 2012 Olympic Games. Hon. Fellow, Homerton Coll., Cambridge, 2016. Hon. DMus: Aberdeen, 1991; Bristol, 1995; Portsmouth, 1995; Leicester, Surrey, 1997; Belfast, Essex, Durham, 1998; Cambridge, 2010; Robert Gordon, 2016; Royal Conservatoire Scotland, 2017; Hon. DLitt: Warwick, 1993; Loughborough, 1995. Grammy Award, 1989, 2002, 2014; Polar Music Prize, 2015; Andrew Fletcher of Saltoun Award for Outstanding Contribn to Arts and Humanities, Saltire Soc., 2016. *Publications*: Good Vibrations (autobiog.), 1990. *Recreations*: reading, walking, cycling, antiques, metal detecting. *Address*: 6 Ramsay Court, Hinchingbrooke Business Park, Huntingdon, Cambs PE29 6FY. *T*: (01480) 459279. *W*: www.evelyn.co.uk.

**GLENNIE, Robert McDougall;** Chief Executive, NewGalexy Partners Ltd, since 2008; Joint Chief Executive, ContractPod Technologies Ltd (formerly NewGalexy Services Ltd), since 2012; *b* 4 April 1951. *Educ*: Jordanhill Coll. Sch., Glasgow; Univ. of Strathclyde (LLB). FCIS 2000 (MCIS). Admitted Solicitor, 1978. Joined McGrigor Donald, subseq. McGrigors, 1976; Partner, 1980–2002; Managing Partner of London Office, 1989–96; Sen. Partner, 2000–02; Chief Exec., KLegal Internat., 2002–04; Principal, Robert Glennie Legal Consulting, 2004–; Sen. Advr, Restructuring and Recovery, Pinsent Masons LLP (formerly McGrigors), 2010–13. Mem., Law Soc. of Scotland, 1977–. *Recreations*: hillwalking, cinema, travel, ayurvedic medicine and therapies. *Address*: ContractPod Technologies Ltd, Savoy Tower, 9th Floor, 77 Renfrew Street, Glasgow G2 3BZ. *T*: (0141) 280 1600.

**GLENNY, Kirsty;** *see* Lang, K.

**GLENNY, Misha;** journalist and historian; *b* 25 April 1958; *s* of late Michael V. G. Glenny and of Juliet Sydenham (*née* Crum); *m* 1987, Snezana Curcic (marr. diss. 2001); one *s* (one *d* decd); *m* 2006, Kirsty Lang, *qv*; one *s*. *Educ*: Bristol Univ. (BA Drama); Charles Univ., Prague. Rights editor, Verso publishing house, London, 1983–86; Central Europe Correspondent (based in Vienna): The Guardian, 1986–89; BBC World Service, 1989–93. Vis. Prof., Columbia Univ., NYC, 2012. Hon. Dr Hist. American Univ. in Bulgaria. Sony Special Award for Broadcasting, 1993; American Overseas Pressclub Award for Best Book on Foreign Affairs, 1993; Information Security Journalist of the Year, BT Information Security Journalism Awards, 2011. *Publications*: The Rebirth of History: Eastern Europe in the age of democracy, 1990, 2nd edn 1993; The Fall of Yugoslavia, 1992, 2nd edn 1993; The Balkans 1804–1999: nationalism, war and the great powers, 1999; McMafia: crime without frontiers, 2008 (televised, 2018); DarkMarket: cyberthieves, cybercops and you, 2011; Nemesis: one man and the battle for Rio, 2015. *Address*: 138 Percy Road, W12 9QL.

**GLENNY, Rt Rev. Olivia Josephine;** *see* Graham, Rt Rev. O. J.

**GLENNY, Dr Robert Joseph Ervine,** CEng, FIMMM; Consultant to UK Government, industry, and European Economic Community, 1983–2006; *b* 14 May 1923; *s* of late Robert and Elizabeth Rachel Glenny; *m* 1947, Joan Phillips Reid; one *s* one *d*. *Educ*: Methodist Coll., Belfast; QUB (BSc Chemistry); London Univ. (BSc Metallurgy, PhD). CEng, 1979; FIMMM (FIM 1958). Res. Metallurgist, English Electric Co. Ltd, Stafford, 1943–47; National Gas Turbine Establishment, 1947–70; Materials Dept, 1947–66; Head of Materials Dept, 1966–70; Supt, Div. of Materials Applications, National Physical Lab., 1970–73; Head of Materials Dept, RAE, 1973–79; Group Head of Aerodynamics, Structures and Materials Depts, RAE, 1979–83. *Publications*: research and review papers on materials science and technology, mainly related to gas turbines, in ARC (R&M series) and in Internat. Metallurgical Rev. *Recreations*: reading, gardening, walking. *Address*: 77 Gally Hill Road, Fleet, Hants GU52 6RU. *T*: (01252) 615877.

**GLENSER, Peter Heath;** QC 2018; *b* London, 26 Aug. 1963; *s* of Oscar Eric Glenser and Heather Wanda Glenser; *m* 2001, Fiona Margaret McMillan; one *d*. *Educ*: Dulwich Coll.; Southampton Univ. (LLB Hons); Inns of Court Sch. of Law (BVC). Called to the Bar, Inner Temple, 1993; in practice as barrister, specialising in criminal, military, licensing and rural regulatory, 1993–. Chm., British Assoc. of Shooting and Conservation, 2016– (Mem. Council, 2009–). *Recreations*: stalking, shooting, ski-ing, cooking, military history, family, dogs, travel. *Address*: 9 Bedford Row, WC1R 4AZ. *T*: (020) 7489 2727. *Club*: Cavalry and Guards.

**GLENTON, Anthony Arthur Edward,** CBE 2000 (MBE mil. 1982); TD 1972 (bars 1980, 1986, 1992); FCA; Senior Partner, Ryecroft Glenton, Chartered Accountants, Newcastle, since 1967; Director, 1988–2005, Chairman, 1994–2005, Port of Tyne Authority; Vice Lord-Lieutenant of Northumberland, 2013–16; *b* 21 March 1943; *s* of late Lt-Col Eric Cecil Glenton, Gosforth, Newcastle, and of Joan Lydia Glenton (*née* Taylor); *m* 1972, Caroline Ann, *d* of Maurice George Meade-King; one *s* one *d*. *Educ*: Merchiston Castle Sch., Edinburgh. FCA 1965. Chm., Charles W. Taylor & Son Ltd, Iron Founders, S Shields, 1995–2003; Dir, Newcastle Bldg Soc., 1987–2008 (Chm., 1992–97). Joined Royal Artillery, Territorial Army, 1961: Lieut Col 1984; CO 101 (Northumbrian) Field Regt RA (V), 1984–86; Col 1986; Dep. Comdr, 15 Inf. Bde, 1986–89; ADC to the Queen, 1987–89; TA Advr to GOC Eastern Dist, 1989–94; Hon. Col, 101 (Northumbrian) Regt RA (V), 2005–10. Chairman: N of England RFCA, 1999–2003 (Vice Chm., 1995–99); Northumberland Br., SSAFA (formerly SSAFA Forces Help), 1989–; Newcastle Cathedral Council, 2012–. Freeman, City of London, 1981; Liveryman, Co. of Chartered Accountants of England and Wales, 1981. DL Northumberland, 1993. *Recreations*: shooting, sailing, contemporary art. *Address*: Whinbank, Rothbury, Northumberland NE65 7YJ. *T*: (01669) 620361; Palace Hill Cottage, St Cuthbert's Square, Holy Island of Lindisfarne, Northumberland TD15 2SP. *T*: (01289) 389312; Ryecroft Glenton, 32 Portland Terrace, Newcastle upon Tyne NE2 1QP. *T*: (0191) 281 1292. *Club*: Army and Navy.

**GLENTORAN,** 3rd Baron *cr* 1939, of Ballyalolly, Co. Down; **Thomas Robin Valerian Dixon,** CBE 1992 (MBE 1969); DL; Bt 1903; *b* 21 April 1935; *er s* of 2nd Baron Glentoran, KBE, PC; *S* father, 1995; *m* 1959, Rona, *d* of Captain G. C. Colville; three *s*; *m* 1990, Margaret Rainey. *Educ*: Eton. Man. Dir, Redland (NI) Ltd, 1971–92. Mem., Millennium Fund Commn, 1994–2005. Elected Mem., H of L, 1999–2018; front bench opposition spokesman, H of L, on NI, 1999–2010, on sport, 2005–06, on Olympics, 2007–10, on Wales, 2007–10. Non-executive Director: NHBC, 2001–07; BetonSports plc, 2004–07. Comr, Irish Light House Service, 1996–2010. Olympic Gold Medal for two-man bobsleigh, 1964. President: British Bobsleigh Assoc., 2012–; British Shooting Sports Council (former Chm.); Chm., Skiing with Heroes. DL Antrim, 1995. *Recreations*: sailing, golf. *Heir*: *s* Hon. Daniel George Dixon [*b* 26 July 1959; *m* 1983, Leslie Hope Brooke; two *s*]. *Address*: Drumadarragh House, Ballyclare, Co. Antrim BT39 0TA. *Clubs*: Boodle's; Royal Yacht Squadron.

**GLENVILLE, Dr Marilyn,** CPsychol; nutritionist, since 1982; *b* London, 13 Aug. 1952; *d* of John and Margaret Eaton; *m* 1981, Kriss Glenville; two *s* one *d*. *Educ*: Highbury Hill High Sch., London; Avery Hill Coll., London Univ. (BEd); Leeds Univ. (MA); Darwin Coll., Cambridge (PhD 1980). CPsychol 1990. Mem. Council, Food and Health Forum, RSocMed, 2001– (Pres., 2007–09). Mem., Nutrition Soc., 2001–. Patron, Daisy Network, 2004–. FRSocMed 1999; Associate Fellow, BPsS, 2014–. *Publications*: (contrib.) Response to Stress, 1979; Natural Alternatives to HRT, 1997; Natural Alternatives to Dieting, 1999, 2019; Natural Alternatives to HRT Cookbook, 2000, re-issued as Healthy Eating for the Menopause, 2004; Natural Solutions to Infertility, 2000; Nutritional Health Handbook for Women, 2001; Natural Solutions to PMS, 2002; Osteoporosis - the silent epidemic, 2005; Fat Around the Middle, 2006; (contrib.) An Atlas of Endometriosis, 3rd edn, 2007; Getting Pregnancy Faster, 2008; Natural Health Bible for Women, 2010; Natural Solutions to Menopause, 2011; Natural Solutions to PCOS, 2012; Natural Solutions to IBS, 2013; Natural Alternatives to Sugar, 2016; Natural Solutions for Dementia and Alzheimer's, 2017; contribs to jls incl. Sleep, Chronobiologia, Ergonomics, Current Opinion in Obstetrics and Gynaecology. *Recreations*: walking, reading, tennis, dancing. *Address*: Dr Marilyn Glenville Clinic, 14 St Johns Road, Tunbridge Wells, Kent TN4 9NP. *T*: (01892) 515905, *Fax*: (01892) 515914. *E*: health@marilynglenville.com.

**GLERAWLY, Viscount; Michael Stephen Annesley;** IT consultant; *b* 26 July 1957; *er s* and *heir* of Earl Annesley, *qv*; *m* 1st, 1983, Angela, *d* of David Matthews (marr. diss. 2000); one *s* one *d* (twins); 2nd, 2004, Karen Lesley Coolman, *d* of Ronald Fuller. *Educ*: Burford Grammar Sch. Man. Dir, Mikrotek Solutions Ltd, 1996–. *Recreation*: classic motorcycle racing. *Heir*: *s* Hon. Michael David Annesley, *b* 28 Jan. 1984.

**GLESTER, John William;** Managing Director (formerly Principal), John Glester Consultancy Services, since 1996; Consultant Director, Colliers CRE, since 2010; *b* 8 Sept. 1946; *o s* of late George Ernest Glester and Maude Emily Glester; *m* 1970, Ann Gleave Taylor (*d* 1998); two *s*. *Educ*: Plaistow Grammar Sch.; Reading Univ. (BA Hons); Open Univ. (Dip. Eur. Studies). Joined Civil Service 1968; served DEA, DoE and Merseyside Task Force; Regl Controller, NW, DoE, 1985–88; Chief Exec., Central Manchester Develt Corp., 1988–96; Trust Fund Adminr, Lord Mayor of Manchester's Emergency Appeal Fund, 1996–98; Dir (Regl Strategy), NW Regl Develt Agency, 1999–2000. Principal Associate (formerly Associate Dir), Locum Consulting, 2006–12. Chairman: Castlefield Management Co., 1992–2002; Castlefield Heritage Trust, 1996–2003; Hallogen Ltd (Bridgewater Hall), 1998–2004 (Dir, 1995–98); Ancoats Bldgs Preservation Trust, 2001–07 (Trustee, 2001–07); Commissions in the Environment, 2002–04; Urban Experience Ltd, 2002–04; Merseyside Housing Market Renewal, 2003–11; Manchester Salford Trafford NHS LIFT, 2003–07; Bolton, Rochdale and Heywood Middleton NHS LIFT, 2007–12; Heritage Works, 2007–; non-exec. Dir, Langtree Gp plc, 1999–2001; Consultant: Lloyds Metal Group plc, 1997–98; Dunlop Heywood, 1998–99; Valley and Vale Properties plc, 1998–2000. Chm., Network Space Consultative Cttee, 1999–2001. Director: Salford Phoenix, 1987–95; Manchester Arts Fest., 1989–93; Manchester 2000, 1992–94; Manchester City of Drama, 1992–94; Manchester Concert Hall Ltd, 1994–2004; Patterson Inst. for Cancer Res., 2001–03. Dep. Chair, Manchester Olympic Bid Cttee, 1990–93; Consultant, Commonwealth Games 2002, 2000–02. *Recreations*: cricket, football (West Ham United in particular), golf, music, theatre, cooking. *E*: johnglester27@gmail.com.

**GLICK, Ian Bernard;** QC 1987; a Recorder, 2000–06; *b* 18 July 1948; *s* of late Dr Louis Glick and Phyllis Esty Glick; *m* 1986, Roxane Eban; three *s*. *Educ*: Bradford Grammar School; Balliol College, Oxford (MA, BCL). President, Oxford Union Society, 1968. Called to the Bar, Inner Temple, 1970, Bencher, 1997. Junior Counsel to the Crown, Common Law, 1985–87; Standing Junior Counsel to DTI in Export Credit Cases, 1985–87. Chm., Commercial Bar Assoc., 1997–99. *Address*: 1 Essex Court, Temple, EC4Y 9AR.

**GLICKSMAN, Brian Leslie,** CB 2005; Treasury Officer of Accounts, HM Treasury, 2000–05; *b* 14 Dec. 1945; *s* of Henry and Kitty Glicksman; *m* 1971, Jackie Strachan; two *d*. *Educ*: Ealing Grammar Sch.; New Coll., Oxford (BA Maths); Warwick Univ. (MSc Mgt Sci. and OR). OR Scientist, CSD, 1969; Principal, DoE, 1976; Asst Dir, PSA, 1984; Sec. Royal Commn on Envmtl Pollution, 1987; Divl Manager, DoE, 1992. Mem., Audit Cttee, Office of Govt Commerce, 2001–07. Trustee, 2Care, 2004–11 (Vice-Chm., 2006–07; Chm., 2007–11). Trustee, 2Care Staff Pension Scheme, 2004–. Hon. Treas., CS Sports Council, 2006–17. Treas., SW London br., Urostomy Assoc., 2017–. Chm., Phoenix Concert Band, 2008–. *Publications*: contrib. to Canadian Parly Rev. *Address*: 18 Worcester Road, Sutton, Surrey SM2 6PG.

**GLINDON, Mary;** MP (Lab) North Tyneside, since 2010; *b* 13 Jan. 1957; *d* of Margaret and Cecil Mulgrove; *m* 2000, Raymond Glindon; one *d* and one step *s* one step *d*. *Educ*: Sacred Heart Grammar Sch., Fenham; Newcastle upon Tyne Poly. (BSc Sociol. 1979). Clerical officer, CS, 1980–85; adminr, local govt, 1987–88; adminr/community develt manager, Centre for Unemployment, 1988–2004; Adminr, NHS call centre, 2005; trainee dispenser, NHS, 2005–06; travel sales advr, call centre, 2006; sales asst in department store, 2006–08; Admin Officer, DWP and Child Maintenance and Enforcement Commn, 2008–10. Mem. (Lab) N Tyneside Council, 1995–2010 (Mayor, 1999–2000). Shadow Minister for Farming and Rural Communities, 2016–17. Member: Envmt, Food and Rural Affairs Select Cttee, 2010–15; Transport Select Cttee, 2015–16. *Address*: House of Commons, SW1A 0AA.

**GLOAG, Dame Ann Heron,** DBE 2019 (OBE 2004); Director, Stagecoach Group (formerly Holdings) plc, since 1986 (Managing Director, 1986–94; Executive Director, 1986–2000); *b* 10 Dec. 1942; *d* of late Iain and Catherine Souter; *m* 1st, 1965, Robin N. Gloag (*d* 2007); one *d* (one *s* decd); 2nd, 1990, David McCleary. *Educ*: Caledonian Road Primary School; Perth High School. Trainee Nurse, Bridge of Earn Hosp., Perth, 1960–65; Ward Sister, Devonshire Royal Hosp., Buxton, 1965–69; Theatre Sister, Bridge of Earn Hosp., 1969–80; Founding Partner, Gloagtrotter, re-named Stagecoach Express Services, 1980–83; Co-Director, Stagecoach Ltd, 1983–86 (acquired parts of National Bus Co., 1987 and 1989 and Scottish Bus Group, 1991). Hon. Dr: Paisley, 1994; Napier, 1995; Dundee, 2014. Scottish Marketing Woman of the Year, Scottish Univs, 1989; UK Businesswoman of the Year, Veuve Cliquot and Inst. of Dirs, 1989–90; Susan B. Anthony Humanitarian of the Year Award, 2009; Eleanor Roosevelt Award for Outstanding Achievement, 2011. Order of the Star of Africa, 2009. *Recreations*: family, travel, charity support. *Address*: Stagecoach Group, 10 Dunkeld Road, Perth PH1 5TW.
*See also* Sir B. Souter.

**GLOBE, Hon. Sir Henry (Brian),** Kt 2011; a Judge of the High Court of Justice, Queen's Bench Division, 2011–17; a Judicial Commissioner, since 2017; *b* 18 June 1949; *o s* of late Theodore Montague Globe and of Irene Rita Globe; *m* 1972, Estelle Levin; two *d*. *Educ*:

Liverpool Coll.; Birmingham Univ. (LLB Hons). Called to the Bar, Middle Temple, 1972, Bencher, 2005; in practice on Northern Circuit, 1972–2003 (Junior, 1974; Treas., 2001–03); Standing Counsel to: DSS, 1985–94; HM Customs and Excise, 1992–94; Asst Recorder, 1987–90; a Recorder, 1991–2003; QC 1994; a Circuit Judge, then a Sen. Circuit Judge, 2003–11; Presiding Judge, North Eastern Circuit, 2013–16. Hon. Recorder, Liverpool, 2003–11. Member: Bar Council, 2001–03; Criminal Cttee, Judicial Studies Bd, 2001–05; Criminal Justice Council, 2004–10; Sentencing Council, 2010–15. Governor: King David Primary Sch., Liverpool, 1979–2001; King David High Sch., Liverpool, 1985–2000 (Chm., 1990–2000); Foundn Mem., Liverpool Coll., 2003–. Trustee, King David Foundn, 2001–13. Hon. Fellow, Liverpool John Moores Univ., 2013; Hon. LLD Liverpool, 2015. *Recreations:* tennis, bridge, cycling. *E:* sir.henry.globe@ejudiciary.net.

**GLOCER, Thomas Henry;** Chief Executive Officer, Thomson Reuters (formerly Reuters Group plc), 2001–12; *b* NYC, 8 Oct. 1959; *s* of Walter Glocer and Ursula Glocer (*née* Goodman); *m* 1988, Maarit Leso; one *s* one *d*. *Educ:* Columbia Coll. (BA *summa cum laude* 1981); Yale Law Sch. (JD 1984). Mergers and acquisitions lawyer, Davis Polk and Wardwell, NY, Paris and Tokyo, 1985–93; joined Reuters, 1993: mem., Legal Dept, Gen. Counsel, Reuters America Inc., NYC, 1993–96; Exec. Vice-Pres., Reuters America Inc. and CEO, Reuters Latin America, 1996–98; Chief Executive Officer: Reuters business in the Americas, 1998–2001; Reuters Inf., 2000–01. Director: NYC Investment Fund, 1999–2003 (Mem., Exec. Cttee); Instinet Corp., 2000–05. Mem., Adv. Bd, Singapore Monetary Authy, 2001–05. Director: Merck & Co., 2007–; Council on Foreign Relns, 2011–16; K2 Intelligence, 2013–; Morgan Stanley, 2013– (Ind. Lead Dir, 2017–). Member: Corporate Council, Whitney Mus. of American Art, 2000–03; Corporate Adv. Gp, Tate Britain, 2005–08. Author of computer software, incl. (jtly) Coney Island: a game of discovery, 1983. NY Hall of Sci. Award, 2000; John Jay Alumni Award, 2001. *Recreations:* tennis, windsurfing, ski-ing.

**GLOSTER, Rt Hon. Dame Elizabeth,** DBE 2004; PC 2013; a Lady Justice of Appeal, 2013–18; Vice-President, Court of Appeal (Civil Division), 2016–18; international commercial arbitrator, since 2018; *b* 5 June 1949; *d* of late Peter Gloster and Betty Gloster (*née* Read); *m* 1st, 1973, Stanley Eric Brodie, *qv* (marr. diss. 2005); one *s* one *d*; 2nd, 2008, Sir Oliver Popplewell, *qv*. *Educ:* Roedean Sch., Brighton; Girton Coll., Cambridge (BA Hons; Hon. Fellow 2011). Called to the Bar, Inner Temple, 1971, Bencher 1992; QC 1989; a Judge of the Courts of Appeal of Jersey and Guernsey, 1993–2004; a Recorder, 1995–2004; a Judge of the High Ct of Justice, QBD (Commercial Ct), 2004–13; Judge in Charge of Commercial Court, 2010–12. A Judge (pt-time), Abu Dhabi Global Markets Courts, 2018–; a Justice of the Court of Appeal of Bermuda (pt-time), 2019–. Mem., panel of Counsel who appear for DTI in company matters, 1982–89. Mem. Bd (non-exec.), CAA, 1992–93. Patron, CIArb, London Br., 2012–. Hon. Fellow, Harris Manchester Coll., Oxford, 2016. Freeman, Arbitrators' Co., 2019–. *Address:* One Essex Court, Temple EC4Y 9AR. *T:* (020) 7583 2000.

**GLOUCESTER, Bishop of,** since 2015; **Rt Rev. Rachel Treweek;** *b* 4 Feb. 1963; *d* of Robert Steven Montgomery and Marian Montgomery; *m* 2006, Guy Matthew Treweek. *Educ:* Univ. of Reading (BA Linguistics and Lang. Pathol. (Speech Therapy) 1985); Wycliffe Hall, Oxford (BTh 1994). Paediatric Speech and Language Therapist, Hampstead Health Authority, 1985–91: Hampstead Child Develt Team, 1987–89; Manager for Therapists in Health Centres, Bloomsbury, Hampstead and Islington, 1989–91. Ordained deacon, 1994, priest, 1995; Curate, 1994–97, Associate Vicar, 1997–99, St George's, Tufnell Park; Vicar, St James-the-Less, Bethnal Green, 1999–2006; Archdeacon of Northolt, 2006–11; Archdeacon of Hackney, 2011–15. Mem., Gen. Synod, 2011–. Entered H of L, 2015. *Address:* 2 College Green, Gloucester GL1 2LR.

**GLOUCESTER, Dean of;** *see* Lake, Very Rev. S. D.

**GLOUCESTER, Archdeacon of;** *see* Dawson, Ven. H. J.

**GLOVER, Dame Anne;** *see* Glover, Dame L. A.

**GLOVER, Anne Margaret,** CBE 2006; Co-Founder and Chief Executive Officer, Amadeus Capital Partners Ltd, since 1997; *b* 6 Feb. 1954; *d* of John and Mary Glover. *Educ:* Clare Coll., Cambridge (BA 1st Cl. Metallurgy and Materials Sci. 1976); Yale Sch. of Mgt (MPPM 1978). Sen. Tech. Associate, Bell Telephone Labs, Murray Hill, 1977; Cummins Engine Company: Asst to Vice Pres., Affiliated Enterprises, 1978–79; Rod Line Foreman, 1979–80; Engine Order Mgt Consultant, NY, 1980–81; Customer Services Team Advr, NY, 1981–83; Bain & Co., Boston: Consultant, 1983–85; Sen. Consultant, 1985–86; Manager, 1986–88; Asst Dir, Apax Partners & Co. Ventures, London, 1989–93; Chief Op. Officer, Virtuality Gp plc, Leicester, 1994–95; Founder and non-exec. Dir, Calderstone Capital, 1996–97. Mem. Bd, Glysure Ltd, 2008–; non-executive Director: Future Cities Catapult, 2015–18; Court, Bank of England, 2018–. Chm., British Venture Capital Assoc., 2004–05; Chm., Eur. Private Equity and Venture Capital Assoc., 2014–15. Non-exec. Dir, Technol. Strategy Bd, 2005–12; Mem., Council for Sci. and Technol., 2014–. Mem., Investment Cttee, Yale Univ., 2019–. Hon. FREng 2008. *Address:* Amadeus Capital Partners Ltd, 130 Jermyn Street, SW1Y 4UR. *T:* (020) 7024 6900, *Fax:* (020) 7024 6999. *E:* aglover@amadeuscapital.com.

**GLOVER, Dame Audrey (Frances),** DBE 2004; CMG 1997; barrister; Leader, UK Delegation to UN Human Rights Commission, 1998–2003; *d* of Robert John Victor Lush and Frances Lucy de la Roche; *m* 1971, Edward Charles Glover, *qv*; two *s* two *d* (and one *s* decd). *Educ:* St Anne's Coll., Sanderstead, Surrey; King's Coll. London (LLB Hons). Called to the Bar, Gray's Inn, 1961; LCD, 1965–67; HM Diplomatic Service, 1967–97: joined Foreign Office, as Asst Legal Advr, 1967; Asst (Temp.), Attorney Gen's Dept, Australia, 1972–73; Advr on British Law, Liby of Congress, Washington, 1974–77; Legal Advr (Asst), FCO, 1978–85; Legal Advr, British Mil. Govt, Berlin, 1985–89; Legal Counsellor, FCO, and UK Agent to EC and Ct of Human Rights, 1990–94; Dir (with rank of Ambassador), OSCE Office of Democratic Instns and Human Rights, Warsaw, 1994–97. Sen. Advr to Coalition Provisional Authy, Iraq and to Iraqi Minister of Human Rights, 2004–06. Head, OSCE Election Observation Mission: Belarus, 2004; Kazakhstan, 2005; former Yugoslav Republic of Macedonia, 2006, 2017; Ukraine, 2007; Italy, 2008; USA, 2008; Albania, 2009; Georgia, 2010; Azerbaijan, 2010; Slovenia, 2011; Ukraine, 2012; Mongolia, 2013; Hungary, 2014; Bulgaria, 2014; Albania, 2015; Spain, 2015; Mongolia, 2016; USA, 2016; Italy, 2018; Turkey, 2018; Co-Leader, Carter Center Election Missions: Tunisia, 2014; Guyana, 2015. Expert, Inst. of Stabilization and Transformation, 2013–; Mem., UN Mediation Roster, 2014–. Member, Advisory Board: British Inst. of Human Rights, 2004–; Gender Aspects of Peace and Security, 2011–; Chm., Internat. Adv. Council, LINKS, 1999–; Mem. Bd, Electoral Reform Internat. Services, 2005–; Rep., Nat. Democratic Inst., Georgia, 2018. Trustee, Prison Reform Trust, 2006–; Chair of Trustees, Foreign Policy Centre, 2018–. *Recreations:* collecting paintings, sailing, travelling, theatre. *Address:* The Oak House, Thornham, Norfolk PE36 6LY. *Club:* Brancaster Staithe Sailing (Norfolk).

**GLOVER, Prof. Beverley Jane,** PhD; FLS; Professor of Plant Systematics and Evolution, University of Cambridge, since 2013; Director, Cambridge University Botanic Garden, since 2013; Fellow, Queens' College, Cambridge, since 1996; *b* Ely, 7 March 1972; *d* of Michael Glover and Margaret Glover (*née* Smith); *m* 2003, Stuart Nigel Bridge, *qv*; one *s* one *d*. *Educ:* Perth High Sch.; Univ. of St Andrews (BSc Plant and Envmtl Biol. 1993); John Innes Centre and Univ. of E Anglia (PhD 1997). Res. Fellow, Queens' Coll., Cambridge, 1996–99; University of Cambridge: Lectr, 1999–2005; Sen. Lectr, 2005–10; Reader, 2010–13; Admissions Tutor (Sci.), 2001–07; Dir of Studies, 2007–13. Member: Council, Eur. Soc. for Evolutionary Develtl Biol., 2010–; Botanical Soc. of America, 2009–; British Soc. for Develtl Biol., 2011–; Council, Systematics Assoc., 2014–. Trustee: Royal Botanic Garden Edinburgh, 2015–. FLS 2010. Bicentenary Medal, Linnean Soc., 2010; William Bate Hardy Prize, Cambridge Philosophical Soc., 2010. *Publications:* Understanding Flowers and Flowering: an integrated approach, 2007, 2nd edn 2014 (Marsh Book of Year Award, British Ecol Soc., 2009); contrib. papers on plant develt, evolution and function to scientific jls. *Recreations:* family, local community, reading, swimming in the sea. *Address:* University of Cambridge Botanic Garden, Brookside, Cambridge CB2 1JE. *T:* (01223) 333938. *E:* bjg26@cam.ac.uk.

**GLOVER, Rev. Canon David Charles;** Rector, Holy Trinity, Washington, since 2007 (Priest-in-charge, 2005–07); a Chaplain to the Queen, since 2017; *b* Birkenhead, 25 Feb. 1966; *s* of Geoffrey Glover and Eveline Glover; *m* 1989, Emma Catharine Howard; one *s* two *d*. *Educ:* South Cantley High Sch.; Doncaster Grammar Sch.; Hallcross Comp. Sch., Doncaster; St John's Coll., Durham (BA Hons Theol. 1987); St John's Coll., Cambridge (MPhil Dogmatic Theol. 1990); Ridley Hall Theol Coll., Cambridge; Durham Univ. (Advanced Dip. in Counselling 1995). Ordained deacon, 1990, priest, 1991; Asst Curate, Wash upon Dearne, 1990–92; Chaplain, Hatfield Coll., Durham Univ., 1992–99; Priest-in-charge, 1995–2000, Rector, 2000–05, St Margaret, Durham; Area Dean: Chester le Street, 2008–18; Chester le Street and Houghton, 2018–. Non-res. Canon, Durham Cathedral, 2011–. *Publications:* (contrib.) Liturgy in Dialogue, 1993. *Recreations:* music (singing in Newcastle upon Tyne Bach Choir), attending classical concerts, walking, recreational sports, theatre, film. *Address:* 27 Wroxton, Washington, Tyne and Wear NE38 7NU. *T:* 07886 289311. *E:* davidglover1966@gmail.com.

**GLOVER, Prof. David Moore,** PhD; ScD; FRS 2009; FRSE; Arthur Balfour Professor of Genetics, University of Cambridge, 1999–2015, now Director of Research (Head, Department of Genetics, 1999–2004); Fellow, Fitzwilliam College, Cambridge, since 2004; Director, Cancer Research UK (formerly Cancer Research Campaign) Cell Cycle Genetics Group, since 1989; Wellcome Investigator, since 2016; *b* 28 March 1948; *s* of Charles David Glover and Olivia Glover; *m* 2000, Magdalena Zernicka (*see* M. Zernicka-Goetz). *Educ:* Broadway Tech. Grammar Sch., Barnsley; Fitzwilliam Coll., Cambridge (BA 2nd Cl. Biochem.); ICRF and UCL (PhD 1972); ScD Cantab 2016. FRSE 1992. Damon Runyon Cancer Res. Foundn Fellow, Stanford Univ., Calif, 1972–75; Imperial College, London: Lectr in Biochem., 1975–81; Sen. Lectr in Biochem., 1981–83; Reader in Molecular Genetics, 1983–86; Prof. of Molecular Genetics, 1986–89; Hd, Dept of Biochem., 1988–89; Prof. of Molecular Genetics, Dept of Biochem., 1989–92, Dept of Anatomy and Physiol., 1992–99, Univ. of Dundee. Jt Dir, 1979–86, Dir, 1986–89, CRC Eukaryotic Molecular Genetics Gp. Chief Scientist, Cyclacel Ltd, 1999–2009. Mem., EMBO, 1978. *Publications:* Genetic Engineering: cloning DNA, 1980; Gene Cloning: the mechanics of DNA manipulation, 1984; DNA Cloning: a practical approach (3 vols), 1985, 2nd edn (jtly with B. D. Hames) 1995; (with C. J. Hutchison) The Cell Cycle, 1995; (with S. Endow) Dynamics of Cell Division, 1998; contrib. over 250 scientific papers. *Recreations:* music, reading, walking. *Address:* University of Cambridge, Department of Genetics, Downing Street, Cambridge CB2 3EH. *T:* (01223) 333988.

**GLOVER, Edward Charles,** CMG 2003; MVO 1976; HM Diplomatic Service, retired; author, since 2013; *b* 4 March 1943; *s* of Edward and Mary Glover; *m* 1971, Audrey Frances Lush (*see* Dame A. F. Glover); two *s* two *d* (and one *s* decd). *Educ:* Goudhurst Sch. for Boys; Birkbeck Coll., London (BA Hons Hist., MPhil Hist.). Joined FO from BoT, 1967: Private Sec. to High Comr, Australia, 1971–73; Washington, 1973–77; Sec. to UK Delegn to UN Law of Sea Conf., 1978–80; on secondment to Guinness Peat Gp, 1981–83; Sect. Hd, Arms Control and Disarmament Dept, FCO, 1983–85; Senate Liaison Officer, BMG, Berlin, 1985–89; Dep. Hd, Near East and N Africa Dept, FCO, 1989–91; Hd, Mgt Rev. Staff, FCO, 1991–94; Dep. Hd of Mission and Consul-Gen., Brussels, 1994–98; High Comr to Guyana and Amb. to Suriname, 1998–2002; Quality and Efficiency Unit, FCO, 2002–03. Short term expert on Macedonia, Public Admin Internat., 2003–05; Adviser: on Foreign Affairs to Coalition Provisional Authy, Iraq, 2004; to Minister of Foreign Affairs, Iraq, 2004–05; on consular and visa matters to Foreign Minister, Bahamas, 2006; Associate Consultant, DFID Support: to Office of Prime Minister, Kosovo, 2006–07; to Min. of Foreign Affairs, Sierra Leone, 2008. Chm., Bd of Trustees, Iwokrama Internat. Centre for Rainforest Conservation and Develt, 2005–12; Trustee, Size of Wales, 2013–. Associate Fellow, Centre for Caribbean Studies, Univ. of Warwick, 2003–; Associate Consultant, Public Admin Internat., 2009–13; Chair, Univ. of Warwick Caribbean Scholarships Cttee, 2016–. Mem., RIIA, 1969–. Dir (Communication), FCO Assoc., 2015– (Mem. Cttee, 2011–13; Vice Chm., 2017–). Chm., NW Norfolk DFAS, 2003–06; Mem. Bd of Mgt, King's Lynn Preservation Trust, 2002–. Mem., Hakluyt Soc., 2003–14. *Publications: novels:* The Music Book, 2014; Fortune's Sonata, 2015; A Motif of Seasons, 2016; The Executioner's House, 2017; The Lute Player, 2018; contrib. articles in jls on climate change. *Recreations:* writing, tennis, reading, water-colour painting, ran 2014 London Marathon. *Address:* The Oak House, Thornham, Norfolk PE36 6LY. *E:* edward.glover@btopenworld.com. *Club:* Brooks's.

**GLOVER, Prof. (Edward William) Nigel,** PhD; FRS 2013; Professor of Physics, since 2002, and Head, Department of Physics, since 2017, Durham University; *b* Sunderland, 20 June 1961; *s* of late John Edward Glover and Iris Rebecca Glover (*née* Anderson); *m* Prof. Anne Taormina; one *s* one *d*. *Educ:* Downing Coll., Cambridge (BA 1982); Durham Univ. (PhD 1985). Research at: Univ. of Cambridge, 1985–87; CERN, Geneva, 1987–89; Fermi Nat. Accelerator Lab., Batavia, Ill, 1989–91; Durham University: Lectr, 1991–96; Reader, 1996–2002; Dir, Inst. for Particle Physics Phenomenology, 2005–10. PPARC Sen. Fellow, 2003–06. *Publications:* contribs to jls incl. Physical Rev. Letters, Jl High Energy Physics. *Address:* Department of Physics, Durham University, Science Laboratories, South Road, Durham DH1 3LE.

**GLOVER, Rt Rev. (Elistan) Patrick;** Bishop of the Diocese of the Free State (formerly Bishop of Bloemfontein), 1997–2012; an Assistant Bishop, Diocese of George, South Africa, since 2013; *b* 1 Feb. 1944; *s* of Rev. Chirho Glover and Sylvia Glover; *m* 1971, Kirsteen Marjorie Bain; two *s* two *d*. *Educ:* King Edward VII High Sch., Johannesburg; Rhodes Univ. (BA); Keble Coll., Oxford (BA Theol 1968; MA 1978); St Paul's Theol Coll., Grahamstown. Deacon 1969, priest 1970; Curate: St Peter's Church, Krugersdorp, 1969–71; St Martin's-in-Veld, Johannesburg, 1971–74; Rector: St Catherine's, Johannesburg, 1975–83; St George's, Johannesburg, 1983–86; Dean of Bloemfontein, 1987–94; Suffragan Bishop of Bloemfontein, 1994–97; Dean, Province of the Anglican

Church of S Africa, 2009–12. *Recreations:* squash, jogging, cycling, tennis, ballroom dancing. *Address:* Shusanyana, 18 Sunninghill Road, Hunters Estate, Knysna 6511, Western Cape, South Africa.

**GLOVER, Fiona Susannah Grace;** Presenter, The Listening Project, and Generations Apart, since 2010, and Shared Experience, since 2013, BBC Radio 4; *b* 27 Feb. 1969; *d* of William and Priscilla Glover; partner, Rick Jones; one *s* one *d*. *Educ:* Prince's Mead Sch., Winchester; St Swithun's Sch., Winchester; Univ. of Kent (BA Hons Classical Hist. and Philosophy). Trainee reporter scheme, BBC, 1993; presenter: Gtr London Radio Breakfast Show, 1994–95; Travel Show, BBC 2, 1995–97; Five Live, BBC Radio, 1997–2003; Radio 4: Broadcasting House, 2004–06; Travellers' Tree, 2006–07; Saturday Live, 2006–10. Columnist, Waitrose Weekend, 2009–. Mem. Bd, Sound Women, 2010–15. Chair of Judges, Orange Prize, 2009. *Publications:* Travels with My Radio, 2000; (contrib.) Journey to the Sea, 2005; (contrib.) Modern Manners Defined, 2012. *Recreations:* cooking, domesticity, world wide radio. *Address:* c/o BBC Radio 4, W1A 1AA. *Club:* Shoreditch House.

**GLOVER, Prof. Jane Alison,** CBE 2003; DPhil; FRCM; conductor; Director of Opera (formerly Artistic Director of Opera), Royal Academy of Music, 2009–16; Professor, University of London, since 2010; Music Director, Music of the Baroque, Chicago, since 2002; *b* 13 May 1949; *d* of late Robert and Jean Glover. *Educ:* Monmouth School for Girls; St Hugh's Coll., Oxford (BA, MA, DPhil; Hon. Fellow, 1991). FRCM 1993. Oxford University: Junior Research Fellow, 1973–75, Sen. Res. Fellow, 1982–91, St Hugh's Coll.; Lecturer in Music: St Hugh's Coll., 1976–84; St Anne's Coll., 1976–80; Pembroke Coll., 1979–84; elected to OU Faculty of Music, 1979. Professional conducting début at Wexford Festival, 1975; thereafter, operas and concerts for: BBC; Glyndebourne (Musical Dir, Touring Opera, 1982–85); Royal Op. House, Covent Garden (début, 1988); ENO (début, 1989); Teatro la Fenice, Venice; Royal Danish Opera; Glimmerglass Opera, NY; Australian Opera; Chicago Opera; Berlin Staatsoper; London SO; London Philharmonic Orch.; Philharmonia Orch.; Royal Philharmonic Orch.; English Chamber Orch.; BBC SO; BBC Welsh SO; Scottish Nat. Orch.; Bournemouth SO; Toronto SO; Houston SO; St Louis SO; San Francisco SO; Philadelphia Orch.; Metropolitan Opera; Cleveland Orch.; NY Philharmonic Orch.; Houston Grand Opera; Washington Nat. Opera; and many others in Italy, Holland, Denmark, China, Hong Kong, Austria, Germany, France, Belgium, Australia, NZ, etc; Artistic Dir, London Mozart Players, 1984–91; Principal Conductor: London Choral Soc., 1983–99; Huddersfield Choral Soc., 1989–96. A Gov., BBC, 1990–95. Radio and television documentaries and series, and presentation for BBC and LWT, esp. Orchestra, 1983, Mozart, 1985, Opera House, 1995, Musical Dynasties, 2000. Governor, RAM, 1985–90. Hon. RAM 2014. Hon. DMus: Exeter, 1986; London, 1992; City, 1994; Glasgow, 1997; Hon. DLitt: Loughborough, 1988; Bradford, 1992; Brunel, 1996; DUniv Open, 1988; Hon. DMus CNAA, 1991. ABSA/Daily Telegraph Arts Award, 1990. *Publications:* Cavalli, 1978; Mozart's Women, 2005; Handel in London, 2018; contribs to: The New Monteverdi Companion, 1986; Monteverdi 'Orfeo' handbook, 1986; articles in Music and Letters, Proc. of Royal Musical Assoc., Musical Times, The Listener, TLS, Early Music, Opera, and others; many recordings. *Recreations:* theatre, skiing, walking. *Address:* c/o Music International, 13 Ardilaun Road, N5 2QR. *T:* (020) 7359 5183.

**GLOVER, Julian Wyatt,** CBE 2013; actor; *b* 27 March 1935; *s* of late (Claude) Gordon Glover and Honor Ellen Morgan (*née* Wyatt); *m* 1st, 1957, Eileen Atkins (now Dame Eileen Atkins, *qv*) (marr. diss. 1966); 2nd, 1968, Isla Blair; one *s*. *Educ:* St Paul's Sch., Hammersmith; Alleyn's Sch., Dulwich. Full-time actor, 1956–; *theatre includes:* Royal Shakespeare Co.: Coriolanus, Henry VI, 1977; Henry IV, pts I and II, 1991–92 (best supporting actor, Olivier award, 1993); Julius Caesar, Romeo and Juliet, Stratford, transf. Barbican, 1995–96; All My Sons, Palace, Watford, 1992; Cyrano de Bergerac, Haymarket, 1992–93; An Inspector Calls, Aldwych, 1993–94; Chips With Everything, RNT, 1996–97; Prayers of Sherkin, Old Vic, 1997; Waiting for Godot, Piccadilly, 1998; Phèdre, Britannicus, Albery, 1998; A Penny for a Song, Whitehall, 1999; The Tempest, Nuffield, 2000; In Praise of Love, UK tour, 2001; King Lear, Shakespeare's Globe, 2001; Macbeth, Albery, 2003; Taking Sides, UK tour, 2003–04; Galileo's Daughter (Peter Hall Co.), 2004; The Dresser, UK tour, 2004, Duke of York's, 2005; Richard II, The Soldier's Tale, Old Vic, 2005; The Voyesy Inheritance, NT, 2006; Shadowlands, Salisbury Playhouse, 2007; The President's Holiday, Hampstead, 2008; Oliver, Theatre Royal, 2008–10; Maurice's Jubilee, The Pleasance, Edinburgh, 2012, UK tour, 2013; The Scottsboro Boys, Young Vic, 2013, transf. Garrick Th., 2014; Richard II, Barbican and Brooklyn Acad. of Music, 2016; Julius Caesar, Bristol Old Vic, 2017; The Night of the Iguana, Noël Coward Th., 2019; Dir, Hamlet, Norwich Playhouse, 1996; *films include:* Tom Jones, 1963; I Was Happy Here, 1965; The Empire Strikes Back, 1980; For Your Eyes Only, 1981; The Fourth Protocol, Cry Freedom, 1987; Indiana Jones and the Last Crusade, 1989; Treasure Island, 1990; King Ralph, 1991; Vatel, 2000; Two Men Went to War, Harry Potter and the Chamber of Secrets, 2002; Troy, 2004; The Young Victoria, 2009; Battle for Britain, 2010; The Timber, 2012; *television includes:* Cover Her Face, 1985; The Chief, 1990; Born and Bred, 2002; In Search of Shakespeare, 2003; Waking the Dead, 2004; Trial and Retribution, 2005; The Impressionists, 2006; Michael Wood on Beowulf, 2008; Silent Witness, 2010; Game of Thrones, 2011–15; Spies of Warsaw, 2013; Holby City, 2014; Grantchester, 2017; Black Earth Rising, 2018. *Publications:* Beowulf, 1987. *Address:* c/o Conway Van Gelder Grant Ltd, 8–12 Broadwick Street, W1F 8HW.

**GLOVER, Prof. Keith,** FRS 1993; FIEEE; FREng, FInstMC; Professor of Engineering, 1989–2013, now Emeritus, and Director of Research (part-time), 2015–18, University of Cambridge; Fellow, Sidney Sussex College, Cambridge, 1976–2013, now Emeritus; *b* 23 April 1946; *s* of William Frank Glover and Helen Ruby Glover (*née* Higgs); *m* 1970, Jean Elizabeth Priestley; one *s* one *d*. *Educ:* Dartford Grammar Sch., Kent; Imperial College London (BSc(Eng)); MIT (PhD). FIEEE 1993; FInstMC 1999. Development engineer, Marconi Co., 1967–69; Kennedy Meml Scholar, MIT, 1969–71; Asst Prof. of Electrical Engineering, Univ. of S California, 1973–76; Department of Engineering, University of Cambridge: Lectr, 1976–87; Reader in Control Engineering, 1987–89; Head of Inf. Engrg Div., 1993–2001; Head of Dept, 2002–09. Non-exec. Dir, Sagentia Gp plc, 2011–15. FREng 2000. Control Systems Award, IEEE, 2001. *Publications:* (with D. C. McFarlane) Robust Controller Design using Normalized Coprime Factor Plant Descriptions, 1989; (with D. Mustafa) Minimum Entropy H-infinity Control, 1990; (jtly) Robust and Optimal Control, 1996; contribs to control and systems jls. *Address:* Department of Engineering, Trumpington Street, Cambridge CB2 1PZ.

**GLOVER, Dame (Lesley) Anne,** DBE 2015 (CBE 2009); FRS 2016; FRSE; President, Royal Society of Edinburgh, since 2018; Special Adviser to the Principal and Vice-Chancellor, University of Strathclyde, since 2018; *b* 19 April 1956; *d* of Wesley and Mary Johnstone Glover; *m* 1996, Ian George. *Educ:* Dundee High Sch.; Edinburgh Univ. (BSc 1st Cl. Hons Biochem. 1978); King's Coll., Cambridge (MPhil 1979, PhD 1981). University of Aberdeen: Lectr in Biochem., 1983–94; Sen. Lectr, 1994–98; Reader in Molecular and Cell Biol., 1998–2001; Prof. of Molecular and Cell Biol., 2001–18; Vice-Principal for Ext. Affairs, 2015–18. Chief Scientific Advr for Scotland, 2006–11; Chief Scientific Advr to Pres., EC, 2012–14. Mem., NERC, 2001–11. Chair: UK Collaborative on Devel. Scis, 2009–11; Carnegie Trust for the Universities of Scotland, 2015–; Industrial Biotechnol. Innovation Centre, 2018–. Mem. Council, Soc. of Gen. Microbiol., 1995–98. Member, Board: Scottish Enterprise, 2015–; Offshore Renewable Energy Catapult, 2016–; Collaborative for Applied Biosci. Internat., 2016–. Trustee, African Agriculture Technol. Foundn, 2015–. Patron, Humanists UK (formerly British Humanist Soc.), 2016–; Ambassador, Orgn for Women in Sci. for the Developing World, 2017–; Fellow, Amer. Acad. of Microbiol., 1995; FRSE 2005; FRSA 2009. *Publications:* book chapters; numerous reviewed contribs to learned jls; invited reviews and conf. abstracts; opinion pieces. *Recreations:* sailing, reading. *Address:* University of Strathclyde, Royal College Building, 204 George Street, Glasgow G1 1XW.

**GLOVER, Magdalena;** *see* Zernicka-Goetz.

**GLOVER, Nigel;** *see* Glover, E. W. N.

**GLOVER, Rt Rev. Patrick;** *see* Glover, Rt Rev. E. P.

**GLOVER, Rebecca Ruth;** Principal, Surbiton High School, since 2018; *b* Huddersfield, 11 April 1967; *d* of Nicholas Hartley Couch and Susan Couch (*née* Tweed); *m* 1990, John Nicholas Glover; one *s* one *d*. *Educ:* Rishworth Sch.; Univ. of Leeds (BEd Hons). NPQH 2007. Hd of Girls Physical Educn, Hymers Coll., 1996–2000; Dir, Sixth Form, Roundwood Park Sch., 2000–02; Dep. Headteacher, Tadcaster Grammar Sch., 2002–14; Headteacher, Hull Collegiate Sch., 2014–18. *Recreations:* marathon running, tennis. *Address:* Laburnum Cottage, The Green, Green Hammerton, York YO26 8BQ. *T:* 07983 106293. *E:* rebecca.glover@surbitonhigh.com. *Club:* East India.

**GLOVER, Richard Michael;** QC 2009; *b* Woking, 12 Dec. 1961; *s* of William James Glover, QC and of Rosemary Glover; *m* 1988, Caroline Elizabeth de Rougemont; two *d*. *Educ:* Harrow; Gonville and Caius Coll., Cambridge (BA Hons 1983). Called to the Bar, Inner Temple, 1984. *Publications:* (ed) Ryde on Rating and the Council Tax. *Recreations:* books, theatre, music, horse racing and other things of beauty. *Address:* Francis Taylor Building, Temple, EC4Y 7BY. *T:* (020) 7353 8415. *E:* richard.glover@ftb.eu.com.

**GLOVER, Stephen Charles Morton;** journalist; *b* 13 Jan. 1952; *s* of Rev. Prebendary John Morton Glover and Helen Ruth Glover (*née* Jones); *m* 1982, Celia Elizabeth (*née* Montague); two *s*. *Educ:* Shrewsbury Sch.; Mansfield Coll., Oxford (MA). Daily Telegraph, 1978–85: leader writer and feature writer, 1978–85; parly sketch writer, 1979–81; Independent: Co-Founder, 1986; Foreign Editor, 1986–89; Editor, The Independent on Sunday, 1990–91; Associate Editor, Evening Standard, 1992–95; Columnist: Daily Telegraph, 1996–98; Spectator, 1996–2005; Daily Mail, 1998–; Independent, 2005–12; Oldie mag., 2014–. Dir, Newspaper Publishing, 1986–92. Vis. Prof. of Journalism, St Andrews Univ., 1992. *Publications:* Paper Dreams, 1993; (ed) Secrets of the Press, 1999; Splash! (novel), 2017. *Address:* c/o Aitken Alexander Associates, 291 Gray's Inn Road, WC1X 8EB.

**GLOVER, Hon. Sir Victor (Joseph Patrick),** Kt 1989; GOSK 1992; legal consultant; Chief Justice, Mauritius, 1988–94; *b* 5 Nov. 1932; *s* of Joseph George Harold Glover and Mary Catherine (*née* Reddy); *m* 1960, Marie Cecile Ginette Gauthier; two *s*. *Educ:* Collège du St Esprit; Royal Coll., Mauritius; Jesus Coll., Oxford (BA (Hons) Jurisprudence). Called to the Bar, Middle Temple, 1957. District Magistrate, 1962; Crown Counsel, 1964; Sen. Crown Counsel, 1966; Prin. Crown Counsel, 1970; Parly Counsel, 1972; Puisne Judge, 1976; Sen. Puisne Judge, 1982. Actg Governor General, July 1988, May 1989, June 1990 and Feb. 1991; Actg Pres. of the Republic, 1992. Chm., Tertiary Educn Commn, 1988–97; Pres., ESU, 1993–2007, now Patron. Hon. Prof. of Civil Law, Univ. of Mauritius, 1986. Hon. Bencher, Middle Temple, 1991. *Publications:* Abstract of Decisions of Supreme Court of Mauritius 1966–1981, 1982, Supplement 1982–1986, 1987; The Law of Seychelles through the Cases, 1999; The New Mauritius Digest, 2000. *Recreations:* reading, swimming, bridge. *Address:* River Court, Saint Denis Street, Port Louis, Mauritius. *Clubs:* Oxford Union Society; Oxford University Boat.

**GLOVER, Prof. Vivette Ann Susan,** PhD, DSc; Professor of Perinatal Psychobiology, Imperial College London, since 2000; *b* 9 Oct. 1942; *d* of William Fownes Luttrell and Marguerite Luttrell; *m* 1966, Jonathan Glover; two *s* one *d* (and one *d* decd). *Educ:* St Paul's Girls' Sch. (Foundn Schol.); Somerville Coll., Oxford (MA); University Coll. London (PhD 1970; DSc 1990). Res. Assistant, Chemistry Dept, UCL, 1971–76; Res. Biochemist, 1976–81, Clinical Biochemist, 1981–98, Queen Charlotte's Hosp., London; Reader in Perinatal Psychobiol., ICSTM, 1998–2000. Adjunct Prof., Univ. of Rochester, USA, 2004–. Hon. Sen. Lectr, Inst. of Psychiatry, London, 1994. Adviser: Early Intervention Foundn; NSPCC; Best Beginnings. Biometric Lead, A Better Start. Marcé Soc. Medal, 2004; John Cox Medal, 2016; Award for Res. into Pregnancy and Infant Mental Health, Parent Infant Partnership UK, 2017. *Publications:* over 450 articles and contribs to jls incl. Nature, Lancet, BMJ. *Recreations:* cycling (to Soho and in English counties), reading novels, opera, football. *Address:* 3 Chalcot Square, NW1 8YB. *T:* (020) 7586 5312. *E:* v.glover@imperial.ac.uk.

**GLUCK, Malcolm Richard;** author and broadcaster; *b* Hornchurch, Essex, 23 Jan. 1942; *s* of late Harry Gluck and Ivy Gluck (*née* Messer); *m* 1st, 1969, Marilyn Janet Day (marr. diss. 1976); one *s* by Patricia Wellington; 2nd, 1984, Susan Ashley (marr. diss. 2003); one *s* one *d*. *Educ:* Drury Falls Sch., Hornchurch; Watford Coll. of Art. Lathe operator, Rotary Hoes Ltd, 1957; apprentice, Ford Motor Co., 1957–60; trainee salesman, Kingsland Shoes Ltd, 1960; poet, 1960–61; office boy, Stratford East Waste Paper Mill, cost clerk, Hackney Springs & Screws, clerk, Spillers Petfoods, Asst to Domestic Superintendent, Mile End Hosp., 1961; jun. sec., Motor Agents Assoc., 1961–62; trainee copywriter, S. H. Benson, 1963; copywriter: Press & General Publicity, 1963–64; Arks Publicity, 1964–65; Streets Advertising, 1965; Mclaren Dunkley Friedlander, 1965–66; Doyle Dane Bernbach: copywriter, London, 1966–69; Sen. Copywriter, NY, 1969; Gp Hd/Associate Dir, London, 1970–71; Copy Chief, 1971–73; Co-proprietor, Sales Dir and games developer, Intellect Games Ltd, 1973–75; Creative Dir, Drakes Jarvis Walsh & Gluck Ltd, 1973–75; script writer and contrib., Punch mag., 1976; Consultant Creative Dir, Pincus Vidler Arthur Fitzgerald, 1976–77; Dir and Sen. Copywriter, Abbott Mead Davies Vickers, 1977–80; Sen. Copywriter, Collet Dickenson Pearce, 1980–84; Dir, Ogilvy & Mather, 1984–85; Exec. Creative Dir, Lintas, 1986–88; Creative Dir, Priestley Marin-Guzman & Gluck, 1989–92; Wine Writer, Superplonk column, 1989–2004, Wine Corresp., 1996, The Guardian; Publisher, Adze Mag., 1992; Consultant Wine Editor, Sainsbury's Mag., 1993–2001; Wine Editor, Cosmopolitan mag., 1995–96; Co-proprietor, Superplonk Online Ltd, 2000–07. Presenter: Gluck, Gluck, Gluck, BBC TV, 1996. Compiler and presenter, Vintage Classics, Deutsche Grammophon, 1996. Over 200 advertising awards from Designers and Art Dirs Assoc., British Advertising Film Awards, British Creative Circle and overseas, 1966–92. *Publications:* Superplonk, (annually) 1991–2005; (with Anthony Worrall Thompson) Supernosh, 1993; Gluck's Guide to High Street Wine, 1995; Gluck on High, 1996; Gluck, Gluck, Gluck, 1996; Summerplonk, 1997, 1998; Streetplonk (annually), 1997–2000; The Sensational Liquid: Gluck's guide to wine tasting, 1999; Wine Matters: why water just won't do, 2003; (contrib.) New Media Language, 2003; Superplonk: the top one thousand, 2004; Supergrub, 2005; (with Mark Hix) The Simple Art of Matching Food and Wine,

2005; Malcolm Gluck's Brave New World, 2006; The Great Wine Swindle, 2008; Chateau Lafite 1953 and Other Stories, 2010; Five Tons of Jam: the poetry of John Orland, 2010; contrib. articles for Amateur Photographer, Punch, Guardian, Independent, Sunday Express, City Limits, Jl of ESU, Cosmopolitan, Living Well, Travel Spirit, Condé Nast Traveller and Hello! *Recreations:* reading fiction, occult research, wine, food. *E:* malcolm.gluck@gmail.com.

**GLUCKMAN, Sir Peter (David),** ONZ 2015; KNZM 2009 (DCNZM 2008; CNZM 1997); DSc; FRACP, FRCPCH, FMedSci; FRS 2001; FRSNZ; Director, Liggins Institute, University of Auckland, 2001–09, now Director Emeritus and University Distinguished Professor; New Zealand Prime Minister's Chief Scientific Advisor, 2009–18; *b* 8 Feb. 1949; *s* of Laurie Kalman Gluckman and Ann Jocelyn Gluckman (née Klippel); *m* 1970, Judith Lucy Nathan; one *s* one *d. Educ:* Univ. of Otago (MB ChB); Univ. of Auckland (MMedSci, DSc); Univ. of Calif, San Francisco. FRSNZ 1988; FRCPCH 2004. Res. Fellow, Univ. of Auckland, 1973–76; Res. Fellow, 1976–78, Asst Prof., 1978–80, Dept of Paediatrics, Univ. of Calif, San Francisco; University of Auckland: Sen. Res. Fellow, 1980–88, Prof. and Chair, 1988–92, Dept of Paediatrics; Dean, Faculty of Med. and Health Scis, 1992–2001. FMedSci 2006. Hon. DSc Otago, 2014. *Publications:* contrib. numerous papers to scientific jls relating to fetal physiology, neurosci., endocrinology of growth and evolutionary medicine; numerous articles and commentaries on sci. diplomacy and sci. for policy. *Recreations:* travel, nature photography. *Address:* Liggins Institute, University of Auckland, Private Bag 92019, Auckland 1142, New Zealand. *T:* (office) (9) 9236318. *Club:* Northern (Auckland).

**GLUCKSMANN, Dame Margaret Myfanwy Wood;** see Booth, Dame Margaret.

**GLUCKSMANN, Prof. Miriam Anne,** PhD; FBA 2005; FAcSS; Professor of Sociology, University of Essex, 1996–2015, now Emeritus; Visiting Professor of Sociology, London School of Economics and Political Science, since 2015; *b* 8 April 1946; *d* of late Alfred Glucksmann, MD and Ilse Lasnitzki-Glucksmann, MD, PhD, DSc; partner, Prof. Mark Harvey. *Educ:* Perse Sch. for Girls, Cambridge; London Sch. of Econs and Political Sci. (BA, PhD 1972). Lecturer in Sociology: Brunel Univ., 1970–71; Univ. of Leicester, 1971–73; Sen. Lectr in Sociol., South Bank Poly., 1973–91; Sen. Lectr in Sociol., 1991–92, Reader in Sociol., 1992–96, Dept of Sociol., Univ. of Essex. ESRC Professorial Fellowship 2004–07; Eur. Res. Council Advanced Investigator Grant, 2010–13. FAcSS (AcSS 2012). Hon. DSocSci Stockholm, 2011. *Publications:* Structuralist Analysis in Contemporary Social Thought, 1974, 2nd edn 2014; (as Ruth Cavendish) Women on the Line, 1982, 2nd edn 2009; Women Assemble: women workers and the new industries in inter-war Britain, 1990; Cottons and Casuals: the gendered organisation of labour in time and space, 2000; The New Sociology of Work, 2005; Household Recycling and Consumption Work, 2015. *Address:* Department of Sociology, University of Essex, Wivenhoe Park, Colchester CO4 3SQ.

**GLYN,** family name of **Baron Wolverton.**

**GLYN, Caspar Hilary Gordon;** QC 2012; a Recorder, since 2018; *b* London, 6 Aug. 1969; *s* of James and Lucinda Glyn; *m* 1997, Christine Agnew, qv; two *s* one *d. Educ:* Ludgrove Sch.; Eton; Manchester Univ. (LLB Hons 1991). Called to the Bar, Inner Temple, 1992; in practice as barrister, 1992–. Chair, Industrial Law Soc., 2013–15 (Vice Chair, 2011–13). *Publications:* (jtly) Sweet & Maxwell's Small Claims Practice, 1999; (jtly) The Personal Injury Handbook, 2nd edn 2001; (jtly) Bullen & Leake Precedents and Pleading, 17th edn 2011. *Recreations:* contrarian, auditioning for an obituary in the Daily Mail, Chelsea season ticket holder. *Address:* Cloisters, 1 Pump Court, Temple, EC4Y 7AA. *T:* (020) 7827 4052. *E:* cg@cloisters.com.

**GLYN, Christine;** see Agnew, C.

**GLYN, Sir Richard (Lindsay),** 10th Bt cr 1759, and 6th Bt cr 1800; *b* 3 Aug. 1943; *s* of Sir Richard Hamilton Glyn, 9th and 5th Bt, OBE, TD, and Lyndsay Mary (*d* 1971), *d* of T. H. Baker; *S* father, 1980; *m* 1970, Carolyn Ann Williams (marr. diss. 1979); one *s* one *d. Educ:* Eton. Co-Founder: Ashton Farm, 1976; High Lea Sch., 1982; Founder: Gaunts House Centre, 1989; Richard Glyn Foundn, 1995; Honeybrook Victorian Farm & Country Park, 2002. *Recreation:* tennis. *Heir: s* Richard Rufus Francis Glyn [*b* 8 Jan. 1971; *m* Zoe Auriel Marsden; two *s*]. *Address:* Gaunts House, Wimborne, Dorset BH21 4JQ.

**GLYNN, Faith Helen;** see Wainwright, F. H.

**GLYNN, Prof. Ian Michael,** MD, PhD, FRS 1970; FRCP; Professor of Physiology, University of Cambridge, 1986–95, now Emeritus; Fellow, Trinity College, since 1955 (Vice-Master, 1980–86); *b* 3 June 1928; 2nd *s* of late Hyman and Charlotte Glynn; *m* 1958, Jenifer Muriel, 2nd *d* of Ellis and Muriel Franklin; one *s* two *d. Educ:* City of London Sch.; Trinity Coll., Cambridge; University Coll. Hosp. 1st cl. in Pts I and II of Nat. Sci. Tripos; BA (Cantab) 1949; MB, BChir, 1952; MD 1970; FRCP 1987. House Phys., Central Middx Hosp., 1952–53; MRC Scholar at Physiol. Lab., Cambridge; PhD 1956. Nat. Service in RAF Med. Br., 1956–57. Cambridge University: Res. Fellow, 1955–59, Staff Fellow and Dir of Med. Studies, 1961–73, Trinity Coll.; Univ. Demonstrator in Physiology, 1958–63; Lecturer, 1963–70; Reader, 1970–75; Prof. Membrane Physiology, 1975–86. Vis. Prof., Yale Univ., 1969. Member: MRC, 1976–80 (Chm., Physiological Systems and Disorders Bd, 1976–78); Council, Royal Soc., 1979–81, 1991–92; AFRC (formerly ARC), 1981–86. Chm., Editorial Bd, Jl of Physiology, 1968–70. Hon. Foreign Mem., Amer. Acad. of Arts and Scis, 1984. Hon. MD Aarhus, 1988. *Publications:* (with J. C. Ellory) The Sodium Pump, 1985; An Anatomy of Thought: the origin and machinery of the mind, 1999; (with J. M. Glynn) The Life and Death of Smallpox, 2004; Elegance in Science: the beauty of simplicity, 2010; scientific papers dealing with transport of ions across living membranes, mostly in Jl of Physiology. *Address:* Trinity College, Cambridge CB2 1TQ; Daylesford, Conduit Head Road, Cambridge CB3 0EY. *T:* (01223) 353079.

**GLYNN, Joanna Elizabeth;** QC 2002; *d* of Geraint David Vernet Glynn and Virginia Browell; *m* 1995, Christopher Tehrani; one *s*. Called to the Bar, Middle Temple, 1983; Bencher, 2011; in practice, specialising in professional regulatory work and related criminal litigation. Asst Recorder, 1997–2000; Recorder, 2000–13. Contrib. Ed., Archbold Criminal Pleading Evidence and Practice, annual edns 1995–2006. *Publications:* (jtly) Fitness to Practise: health care regulatory law, principle and process, 2005; (jtly) The Regulation of Healthcare Professionals: law, principle and process, 2012.

**GLYNN, Lucy Alexandra;** see Davies, L. A.

**GOAD, Dame Sarah (Jane Frances),** DCVO 2012; JP; Lord-Lieutenant of Surrey, 1997–2015; *b* 23 Aug. 1940; *er d* of Uvedale Lambert and late Diana (née Grey) and step *d* of Melanie Grant Lambert, Denver, Colo; *m* 1961, Timothy Francis Goad, DL; two *s* one *d. Educ:* St Mary's, Wantage. Worked for Faber & Faber, 1959–70; Dir, Tilburstow Farms Co. Ltd, 1963–70; Partner, Lambert Farmers, 1970–94. JP Surrey, 1974; Dep. Chm., Family Panel, 1992–97; Mem., Surrey Magistrates' Soc., 1987–93. Trustee: St Mark's Foundn, 1971–; Love Walk (home for disabled), 1984–98 (Chm. Trustees, 1989–93); Surrey Care Trust, 1987–97 (Chm. Trustees, 1995–97); Chevening Estate, 2001–12. Chm., Southwark Cathedral Council, 2000–08; Lay Canon, Southwark Cathedral, 2004–15, now Hon. Lay Canon Emeritus. Pres., SE Reserve Forces' and Cadets' Assoc., 2006–11. Governor: local C of E sch., 1970–90; Hazelwood Sch., 1979–84. Patron, Yvonne Arnaud Theatre, 2004–15. Hon. Fellow, RHUL, 2013. DStJ 1997. *Recreations:* books, buildings, arts. *Address:* South Park, Bletchingley, Surrey RH1 4NE.

**GOAD, Tina Gail;** see Cook, T. G.

**GOATER, Very Rev. Catherine;** see Ogle, Very Rev. C.

**GOBBO, Hon. Sir James (Augustine),** AC 1993; Kt 1982; CVO 2000; Chairman, National Library of Australia, 2001–10; Commissioner for Italy, Victoria, 2001–06; *b* 22 March 1931; *s* of Antonio Gobbo and Regina Gobbo (née Tosetto); *m* 1957, Shirley Lewis; two *s* three *d. Educ:* Xavier Coll., Kew, Victoria; Melbourne Univ. (BA Hons); Magdalen Coll., Oxford Univ. (Rhodes Scholar for Victoria, 1951; MA; Pres., OUBC, 1955; Mem., winning Boat Race Crew, 1954, 1955). Called to the Bar, Gray's Inn, London, 1956; Barrister and Solicitor, Victoria, Aust., 1956; signed Roll of Counsel, Victorian Bar, 1957; QC 1971; Supreme Court Judge, Victoria, 1978–94; Lt Gov., 1995–97, Governor, 1997–2000, of Victoria. Ind. Lectr in Evidence, Univ. of Melbourne, 1963–68. Comr, Victorian Law Reform Commn, 1985–88. Chairman: Aust. Refugee Council, 1977; Multicultural Taskforce for Aust. Bicentenary, 1982–84; Reference Gp into Public Liby Funding, 1987; Aust. Multicultural Affairs Council, 1987–91; Aust. Bicentennial Multicultural Foundn, 1988–97, 2001–; Palladio Foundn, 1989–97; Aust. Banking Industry Ombudsman Council, 1994–97; Electricity Industry Ombudsman Council, 1995–97; Council, Order of Australia, 2001–09 (Mem., 1982–92); Nat. Cttee of the Ageing, 2002–; Mercy Private Hosp., Melbourne, 1977–87 (Mem. Bd, Mercy Maternity Hosp., 1972–91); Caritas Christi Hospice, 1986–97; Order of Malta Hospice Home Care, 1986–97; Italian Historical Soc. of Vic, 1980–97. Member: Immigration Reform Gp, 1959–64; Aust. Inst. of Multicultural Affairs, 1979–86; Nat. Population Council, 1983–87; Victorian Health Promotion Foundn, 1989–97; Victorian Community Foundn, 1992–97; Nat. Adv. Cttee, Centenary of Fedn, 1994; Newman Coll. Council, 1970–85; Italo-Australian Educn Foundn, 1974–97; Palladio Trust, Univ. of Melbourne, 1989–97; Cttee, Italian Australian Foundn (formerly Italian Services Inst.), 1993–97, 2001–18 (Pres., 2018–); Bd of Govs, Ian Potter Foundn, 2001–; Bd of Govs, CEDA, 2004–10; Bd, Monash Inst. for Study of Global Movts, 2005–10; Bd, St Vincent's Foundn, 2006; Bd, Internat. Specialised Skills Inst., 2010– (Chm., 1994–97); Pres., CO-AS-IT, 1979–84, 1986–94. Trustee: Victorian Opera Foundn, 1983–97; WWF, Australia, 1991–97. Vice-Pres., Aust. Assoc. of SMO Malta, 1984–87 and 2001–15, Pres., 1987–97; Pres., Scout Assoc. of Victoria, 1987–97. Fellow, Rockefeller Foundn, Bellagio, 1994. Hon. Fellow Aust. Inst. of Valuers, 1985; Hon. Life Member: Aust. Inst. of Architects, 1997; Nat. Gall., Vic, 1999. Hon. LLD Monash, 1995; Hon. Dr Aust. Catholic Univ., 1996; Hon. Dr Jurisp. Bologna, 1998; Hon. LLD Melbourne, 2000. GCSG 2003. Commendatore, 1973, Grand Cross, 1998, Order of Merit, Republic of Italy; Kt Grand Cross, SMO Malta, 1982. *Publications:* (ed) Cross on Evidence (Australian edn), 1970–1978; Something to Declare: a memoir, 2010; various papers. *Address:* 8/25 Douglas Street, Toorak, Vic 3142, Australia. *T:* (3) 98266115.

**GOBBY, Clive John;** Director, South Africa and Regional Director, Southern Africa, British Council, 2000–03; *b* 2 June 1947; *m* 1978, Margaret Ann Edwards. *Educ:* Bective Secondary Mod. Sch., Northampton; Northampton GS; Leicester Univ. (BA 1968). Joined British Council, 1982; Dep. Manager, Enterprises, 1992–96; Network Manager, Grant in Aid Services, 1996; Dir, Turkey, 1997–2000. *Recreations:* walking, net surfing, dog training.

**GOBLE, Prof. Carole Anne,** CBE 2014; FREng; FBCS; Professor of Computer Science, University of Manchester, since 2000; *b* Maidstone, 10 April 1961; *d* of George Goble and Barbara Goble; *m* 2003, Ian Cottam. *Educ:* Maidstone Sch. for Girls; Univ. of Manchester (BSc Hons 1st Cl. Computing and Inf. Systems 1982). FBCS 2002. University of Manchester: Lectr, 1985–95; Sen. Lectr, 1995–2000. Mem., BBSRC, 2013. *Publications:* over 250 articles in learned jls and confs in computer sci. and bioinformatics. *Recreations:* shopping, dining, music festivals. *Address:* School of Computer Science, University of Manchester, Kilburn Building, Oxford Road, Manchester M13 9PL. *E:* carole.goble@manchester.ac.uk.

**GODARD, Jean-Luc;** French film director; *b* 3 Dec. 1930; *s* of Paul Godard and Odile Godard (née Monad); *m* 1st, 1961, Anna Karina (marr. diss.); 2nd, 1967, Anne Wiazemsky (*d* 2017). *Educ:* Collège de Nyon; Lycée Buffon; Faculté de Lettres, Paris. Former journalist and film critic: La Gazette du cinéma; Les Cahiers du cinéma. Mem., Conseil supérieur de la langue française, 1989. *Films include:* A bout de souffle, 1959 (prix Jean Vigo, 1960; Best Dir Award, Berlin Fest., 1960); Le Petit Soldat, 1960; Une femme est une femme, 1961 (Special Prize, Berlin Fest.); Les sept péchés capitaux, 1961; Vivre sa vie, 1962 (Special Prize, Venice Fest.); Les Carabiniers, 1963; Les plus belles escroqueries du Monde, 1963; Le Mépris, 1963; Paris vu par…, 1964; Une femme mariée, 1964; Alphaville, 1965; Pierrot le fou, 1965; Masculin-Féminin, 1966; Made in USA, 1966; Deux ou trois choses que je sais d'elle, 1966; La Chinoise, 1967 (Special Prize, Venice Fest.); Week-end, 1967; Loin du Vietnam, 1967; La Contestation, 1970; Ici et ailleurs, 1976; (jtly) Tout va bien, 1972; Moi je, 1974; Comment ça va?, 1975; Sauve qui peut, 1980; Passion, 1982; Prénom Carmen, 1983 (Golden Lion, Venice Fest.); Je vous salue Marie, 1985; Détective, 1985; Soigne ta droite, 1987; Le Roi Lear, 1987; Nouvelle vague, 1990; Hélas pour moi, 1993; JLG/JLG, 1995; For Ever Mozart, 1996; Eloge de l'amour, 2001; Notre Musique, 2005; Film Socialisme, 2010; Goodbye to Language, 2014. Hon. Academy Award, 2011. Chevalier de l'ordre national du Mérite. *Publications:* Introduction à une véritable histoire du cinéma.

**GODBER, John Harry,** OBE 2018; playwright, since 1981; *b* 18 May 1956; *s* of Harry Godber and Dorothy (née Deakin); *m* 1993, Jane Thornton; two *d. Educ:* Leeds Univ. (CertEd, BEd Hons, MA, MPhil). School teacher, 1979–83; writing for TV, 1981–; Artistic Dir, Hull Truck Theatre Co., 1984–2010; Creative Dir, John Godber Co., Theatre Royal Wakefield, 2013–. Prof. of Contemporary Theatre, Liverpool Hope Univ., 2004–. *Plays include:* Up 'N' Under, 1984 (filmed, 1997); Bouncers, 1986; Teechers, 1987; On the Piste, 1993; April in Paris, 1994; Passion Killers, 1994; Shakers: the musical, 1994; Lucky Sods, 1995; Weekend Breaks, 1997; Perfect Pitch, 1998; Unleashed, 1998; It started with a Kiss, 1998; Thick as a Brick, 1999 (filmed, 2004); On a Night Like This, 1999; Departures, 2001; Reunion, 2002; Screaming Blue Murder, 2003; Black Tie and Tails, 2003; Fly Me to the Moon, 2004; Beef and Yorkshire Pudding, 2004; Going Dutch, 2004; Wrestling Mad, 2005; Crown Prince, 2007; Horrid Henry - Live and Horrid!, 2008; The Debt Collectors, 2011; (with Jane Thornton) Lost & Found, 2012; Muddy Cows, 2013; This Might Hurt, 2016; The Empty Nester's Club, 2017; Scary Bikers, 2019; television series, Thunder Road (also filmed), 2002; television film, Oddsquad, 2005. Sunday Times Play-writing Award, 1981; Olivier Award for Comedy of Year, 1984. Hon. DLitt: Hull, 1988; Humberside, 1997. *Publications:* Up 'N' Under, 1985; Bouncers, 1986; John Godber: 5 plays, 1989; On the Piste, 1991; April in Paris, 1992; Blood Sweat and Tears, 1995; Lucky Sods, 1995; Passion Killers, 1995; Gym and Tonic, 1996; John Godber Plays: vols 1 and 2, 2001, vol. 3, 2003. *Recreations:* keep fit, reading, theatre, cinema, opera.

**GODDARD OF STOCKPORT,** Baron cr 2014 (Life Peer), of Stockport in the County of Greater Manchester; **David Goddard.** Mem. (Lib Dem) Stockport MC, 1990–2012 and 2014–18 (Leader, 2007–12). Former Mem., Greater Manchester Police Authy; former non-exec. Dir, Manchester Internat. Airport. Vice Chair: Exec. Bd, Assoc. of Gtr Manchester Authorities, 2007–12; Gtr Manchester Combined Authy, 2007–; Envmt Comr for Gtr Manchester, 2008–12; Bd Mem., Gtr Manchester Enterprise Partnership, 2011–12. *W*: www.twitter.com/GoddardLord.

**GODDARD, Prof. Andrew Francis,** MD; FRCP; Consultant Gastroenterologist, Royal Derby Hospital, since 2002; President, Royal College of Physicians, since 2018 (Registrar, 2014–18); *b* Plymouth, 8 Nov. 1967; *m* 1994, Nicola; one *s* one *d*. *Educ*: City of London Freemen's Sch.; St John's Coll., Cambridge (BA 1988; BChir 1990, MB 1991; MD 1997). MRCP 1993, FRCP 2005. Prof., Univ. of Nottingham. Director: Derbys Bowel Cancer Screening Prog., 2007–18; IBD Registry Ltd, 2018–. *Recreations*: cycling, golf. *Address*: Royal College of Physicians, 11 St Andrews Place, Regent's Park, NW1 4LE. *T*: (020) 3075 1234. *E*: andrew.goddard@rcplondon.ac.uk. *Club*: Borth and Ynyslas Golf.

**GODDARD, Andrew Stephen;** QC 2003; *b* 5 Oct. 1959; *s* of Lt Col C. E. Goddard and Kathleen Goddard; one *s* two *d*. *Educ*: St John's Sch., Billericay; Chelmsford Coll. of Further Educn; Univ. of Sussex (BA 1st Cl. Hons Law); Inns of Court Sch. of Law. Called to the Bar, Inner Temple, 1985 (QE II Major Schol. 1984; Poland Prize 1985); barrister, specialising in internat. construction disputes, 1987–. *Recreations*: child rearing, peace and quiet. *Address*: 1 Atkin Building, Gray's Inn, WC1R 5AT. *T*: (020) 7404 0102, *Fax*: (020) 7405 7456. *E*: agoddard@atkinchambers.com.

**GODDARD, Prof. John Burgess,** OBE 1986; Henry Daysh Professor of Regional Development Studies, University of Newcastle upon Tyne, 1975–2008, now Emeritus (Deputy Vice-Chancellor, 2001–08; Leverhulme Emeritus Fellow, 2008–10; Special Advisor to Vice Chancellor and President, 2017–18); *b* 5 Aug. 1943; *s* of Burgess Goddard and Molly Goddard (*née* Bridge); *m* 1966, Janet Patricia (*née* Peddle); one *s* two *d*. *Educ*: Latymer Upper Sch.; University Coll. London (BA; Hon. Fellow, 2010); LSE (PhD). Lectr, LSE, 1968–75; Leverhulme Fellow, Univ. of Lund, 1974; University of Newcastle: Hon. Dir, Centre for Urban and Regional Develt Studies, 1978–98; Dean, Faculty of Law, Envmt and Social Scis, 1994–98; Pro Vice-Chancellor, 1998–2001. Dir, ESRC Prog. on Inf. and Communications Technol., 1992–93. Vis. Fellow, NESTA, 2008–09. Advr, Trade and Industry Select Cttee, H of C, 1994–95. Chairman: Assoc. of Dirs of Res. Centres in Social Sciences, 1991–98; Assoc. of Res. Centres in the Social Scis, 1998–99. Member: Northern Economic Planning Council, 1976–79; Human Geography Cttee, SSRC, 1976–80; Bd, Port of Tyne Authority, 1990–93; Bd, Tyne and Wear Sub-Regl Partnership, 2005–08; Bd, Newcastle City Centre Partnership, 2008–09; Lead Expert Gp, Foresight Project on Land Use Futures, 2008–10; Newcastle City Futures Develt Gp, 2015–; Dir, Newcastle NE1 Ltd, 2009–18; Vice Chair, Civic Univ. Commn, UPP Foundn, 2017–19; Trustee: Newcastle Together, 2013–; Newcastle Cathedral, 2015–. Chairman: NE Reg. Cttee, Community Fund, 2003–04; Voluntary and Community Sector Cttee, Big Lottery Fund, 2005–06. European Commission: Mem., Smart Specialisation Platform Mirror Gp, 2014–; Chair, Adv. Gp on Widening Participation and Spreading Excellence in Horizon 2020, 2015–18; Mem., Horizon 2020 Adv. Gp on Science With and For Society, 2015–18; Mem., Smart Specialisation and Sci. and Innovation Adv. Gp, BIS, subseq. BEIS, 2016–. Member: Newcastle Cathedral Council, 2012–; Council, Acad. of Social Scis, 2013–; Bd, Campaign for Social Scis, 2014–. Chm. Trustees, Tyne Rowing Club, 2016–. Governor, University of Northumbria at Newcastle (formerly Newcastle upon Tyne Poly.), 1989–98, Editor, Regional Studies, 1980–85; Member, Editorial Board: Jl of Higher Educn Policy and Mgt, 2008–10; 21st Century Society, 2008–. FAcSS (AcSS 2003). FRSA 1992; Fellow, Acad. Europaea, 2015. Victoria Medal, RGS, 1992. Lord Dearing Lifetime Achievement Award for Higher Educn, 2012. *Publications*: Office Linkages and Location, 1973; Office Location in Urban and Regional Development, 1975; The Urban and Regional Transformation of Britain, 1983; Technological Change, Industrial Restructuring and Regional Development, 1986; Urban Regeneration in a Changing Economy, 1992; (with Paul Vallance) The University and the City, 2013; (jtly) The Civic University: the policy and leadership challenges, 2016; articles in professional jls. *Club*: Athenæum.

**GODDARD, Rt Rev. John William;** Bishop Suffragan of Burnley, 2000–14; an Honorary Assistant Bishop: Diocese of Manchester, since 2015; Diocese of Liverpool, since 2015; Diocese of Blackburn, since 2017; *b* 8 Sept. 1947; *s* of Rev. Canon William and Anna Elizabeth Goddard; *m* 1970, Vivienne Selby; two *s*. *Educ*: Durham Univ. (BA Hons Theol 1969; DipTh 1970). Ordained deacon, 1970, priest, 1971; Curate: St John, Southbank, 1970–74; Cayton with Eastfield, 1974–75; Vicar: Ascension, Middlesbrough, 1975–82; All Saints, Middlesbrough, 1982–88; RD, Middlesbrough, 1981–87; Canon and Prebend, York Minster, 1987–88, now Canon Emeritus; Vice-Principal, Edin. Theol Coll., 1988–92; Team Rector, Ribbleton, 1992–2000. *Recreations*: restoring old houses and working with wood, narrow boating, restoring Morris Minor. *Address*: 39 Kearsley Avenue, Tarleton, Preston PR4 6BP. *T*: (01772) 812532, 07779 786114.

**GODDARD, Jonathan Rupert;** dancer, movement director and choreographer; *b* Chertsey, 12 Dec. 1979; *s* of John David Goddard and Louise Janet Goddard. *Educ*: Rambert Sch. of Ballet and Contemporary Dance (Dip. Dance). Dancer: Scottish Dance Th., 1999–2002; Richard Alston Dance Co., 2002–09; Rambert Dance Co., 2009–12; New Movement Collective, 2009–; Goddard Nixon, 2010–13; Mark Bruce Co., 2013–16; Headspace Dance, 2014–16; Yorke Dance Proj., 2014–15; movement director: NT, 2013–16; RSC, 2014. *Address*: 1A Trumpington Road, E7 9EH. *E*: mail@jonathangoddard.com.

**GODDARD, Katherine Lesley;** QC 2019; *b* Sheffield, 17 July 1963; *d* of Charles Michael Goddard and Una Kathleen Goddard. *Educ*: Hull High Sch. for Girls; Univ. of Keele (BSocSc). Called to the Bar, Inner Temple, 1987; in practice as a barrister: Figtree Lane Chambers, Sheffield, 1987–90; Bank House Chambers, Sheffield, 1990–, Hd of Chambers, 2017–. *Recreations*: show horses and land management, music, art history, literature. *Address*: Bank House Chambers, 3 Hartshead, Sheffield S1 2EL.

**GODDARD, Hon. Dame Lowell (Patria),** DNZM 2014; QC (NZ) 1988; a Judge of the High Court of New Zealand, 1995–2015; *b* Auckland, 25 Nov. 1948; *d* of Pat Vaughan Goddard and Janet Frances Goddard (*née* Collinson); *m* 1992, Christopher John Hodson, QC. *Educ*: Diocesan High Sch., Auckland; Auckland Univ. (LLB 1975). Called to the Bar, NZ, 1975; in practice as barrister, 1977–89; Dep. Solicitor-Gen. for NZ, 1990–95. Chair: Ind. Police Conduct Authy, 2007–12; Ind. Panel Inquiry into Child Sexual Abuse, UK, 2015–16. Expert Mem., UN Subcttee on Prevention of Torture, 2010–16. Commemoration Medal (NZ), 1990; Suffrage Medal (NZ), 1994. *Recreations*: equestrian sport, thoroughbred racing and breeding, ski-ing, landscape and garden design. *Address*: High Court of New Zealand, PO Box 1091, Wellington 6140, New Zealand. *Club*: Wellington (Wellington, NZ).

**GODDARD, Prof. Peter,** CBE 2002; ScD; FRS 1989; Professor, Institute for Advanced Study, Princeton, 2012–16, now Emeritus (Director, 2004–12); Fellow, St John's College, Cambridge, 1975–94 and since 2004 (Master, 1994–2004); *b* 3 Sept. 1945; *s* of Herbert Charles Goddard and Rosina Sarah Goddard (*née* Waite); *m* 1968, Helen Barbara Ross; one *s* one *d*. *Educ*: Emanuel Sch., London; Trinity Coll., Cambridge (BA 1966; MA, PhD 1971; Hon. Fellow, 2009); ScD Cantab 1996. FInstP 1990. Res. Fellow, Trinity Coll., Cambridge, 1969–73; Vis. Scientist, CERN, Geneva, 1970–72, 1978; Lectr in Applied Maths, Univ. of Durham, 1972–74; Mem., Inst. for Advanced Study, Princeton, NJ, 1974, 1988; Cambridge University: Asst Lectr 1975–76; Lectr 1976–89; Reader in Mathematical Physics, 1989–92; Prof. of Theoretical Physics, 1992–2004; Dep. Dir, Isaac Newton Inst. for Mathematical Scis, 1991–94 (Sen. Fellow, 1994–2010; Hon. Fellow, 2011); Mem., Univ. Council, 2000–03; St John's College: Lectr in Maths 1975–91; Tutor 1980–87; Sen. Tutor 1983–87. Vis. Prof. of Maths and Physics, Univ. of Virginia, 1983; SERC Vis. Fellow, Imperial Coll., 1987. Mem., Inst. for Theoretical Physics, Univ. of California, Santa Barbara, 1986, 1990. Pres., LMS, 2002–03. Chm., Univ. of Cambridge Local Exams Syndicate, 1998–2003. Governor: Berkhamsted Schs, 1985–96; Emanuel Sch., 1992–2003; Shrewsbury Sch., 1994–2003; Hills Road Sixth Form Coll., Cambridge, 1999–2003 (Chm., 2001–03). Hon. Fellow, TCD, 1995. Dirac Medal and Prize, Internat. Centre for Theoretical Physics, Trieste, 1997. *Publications*: articles on elementary particle physics and mathematical physics in sci. jls. *Recreations*: informal flower arranging, mathematical physics, idle thought. *Address*: Institute for Advanced Study, Einstein Drive, Princeton, NJ 08540, USA. *T*: (609) 7348335.

**GODDARD, Roy;** independent business consultant, since 1988; Member, Independent Television Commission, 1991–97; *b* 21 Feb. 1939; *s* of Roy Benjamin Goddard and Emma Annie Coronation (*née* Beckett); *m* 1961, Sally Anne Pain; one *s* one *d*. *Educ*: Henry Thornton Grammar Sch.; Regent Street Polytechnic. Cummins Engine Co., 1964–68; Partner, Alexander Hughes & Associates, executive search consultants, 1968–70; Founder, Goddard Kay Rogers & Associates, 1970–88. Chm., Network Gp of Cos, 1992–98; Mem. Adv. Bd, Private Equity Div., Mercury Asset Mgt, 1997–2000; Director: Hg Capital LLP (formerly Mercury Private Equity), 2001–11; Hg Investment Mgt, 2002–07; Hg Pooled Mgt, 2002–11. Member: IBA, 1990–91; GMC, 1994–99. Home Office selection panel appointee, Sussex Police Authy, 1994–2000; Ind. Assessor, Legal Aid Bd, 1996–98. Hon. Vice Pres., Dyslexia Inst., 1997–2014 (Chm., 1990–96). Freeman, City of London, 1981; Liveryman, Co. of Glaziers and Painters of Glass, 1981–. *Recreations*: water gardening, reading, eating, cinema, theatre. *Address*: Newells, Brighton Road, Lower Beeding, West Sussex RH13 6NQ. *T*: (01403) 891110.

**GODDARD, Suzanne Hazel Read;** QC 2008; **Her Honour Judge Goddard;** a Circuit Judge, since 2015; *b* Manchester, 26 Sept. 1963; *d* of Geoffrey St John Lister Goddard and Phyllis Mary Goddard; *m* 1994, Richard Harrison Bevan. *Educ*: Dinas Bran Comp. Sch., Llangollen; Wrekin Coll., Wellington; Univ. of Manchester (LLB Hons 1985). Called to the Bar, Gray's Inn, 1986; Lincoln House Chambers, 1986–2015; Jun., N Circuit, 1989; a Recorder, 2002–15. *Recreations*: walking, ski-ing, theatre, cricket (Pres., Gentlemen Gardener's Cricket Club, 2008–).

**GODDEN, Charles Henry,** CBE 1982; HM Diplomatic Service, retired; Governor (formerly HM Commissioner), Anguilla, 1978–83; *b* 19 Nov. 1922; *s* of late Charles Edward Godden and Catherine Alice Godden (*née* Roe); *m* 1943, Florence Louise Williams; two *d*. *Educ*: Tweeddale Sch., Carshalton; Morley Coll., Westminster. Served Army, 1941–46. Colonial Office, 1950–66 (seconded British Honduras, 1961–64: Perm. Sec., External Affairs; Dep. Chief Sec.; Clerk of Executive Council); FCO, 1966–: First Sec., 1968; Asst Private Sec. to Sec. of State for Colonies; Private Secretary: to Minister of State, FCO, 1967–70; to Parly Under Sec. of State, 1970; First Sec. (Commercial), Helsinki, 1971–75; First Sec., Belize, 1975–76; Dep. High Comr and Head of Chancery, Kingston, 1976–78. *Publications*: Trespassers Forgiven: memoirs of imperial service in an age of independence, 2009. *Recreations*: cricket, walking, reading. *Address*: Stoneleigh, Blackboys, Sussex TN22 5JL. *T*: (01825) 890410. *Club*: MCC.

**GODDEN, Prof. Malcolm Reginald,** PhD; FBA 2009; Rawlinson and Bosworth Professor of Anglo-Saxon, University of Oxford, 1991–2012; Fellow of Pembroke College, Oxford, 1991–2012; *b* 9 Oct. 1945. *Educ*: Devizes Grammar Sch.; Barton Peveril Sch., Eastleigh; Pembroke Coll., Cambridge (BA 1966; MA, PhD 1970). Res. Fellow, Pembroke Coll., Cambridge, 1969–72; Asst Prof., Cornell Univ., 1970–71; Lectr in English, Liverpool Univ., 1972–75; Univ. Lectr in English, and Fellow, Exeter Coll., Oxford, 1976–91. Exec. Editor, Anglo-Saxon England, 1989–2012. *Publications*: Ælfric's Catholic Homilies, (ed) second series, 1979, (ed jtly) first series, 1997, introduction, commentary and glossary, 2000 (Gollancz Prize, British Acad., 2001); The Making of Piers Plowman, 1990; (ed jtly) The Cambridge Companion to Old English Literature, 1991; (ed jtly) Anglo-Saxon England, vol. 27, 1999; (ed jtly) The Old English Boethius, 2009; (ed and trans.) The Old English History of the World: an Anglo-Saxon rewriting of Orosius, 2016; contribs to Anglia, English Studies, Anglo-Saxon England, Rev. of English Studies.

**GODDEN, Tony Richard Hillier,** CB 1975; Secretary, Scottish Development Department, 1980–87, retired; *b* 13 Nov. 1927; *o s* of late Richard Godden and Gladys Eleanor Godden; *m* 1953, Marjorie Florence Snell; one *s* one *d* (and one *d* decd). *Educ*: Barnstaple Grammar Sch.; London Sch. of Economics (BSc (Econ.) 1st cl.). Commissioned, RAF Education Branch, 1950. Entered Colonial Office as Asst Principal, 1951; Private Sec. to Parly Under-Sec. of State, 1954–55; Principal, 1956; Cabinet Office, 1957–59; transferred to Scottish Home Dept, 1961; Asst Sec., Scottish Development Dept, 1964; Under-Sec., 1969; Sec., Scottish Economic Planning Dept, 1973–80. Member: Council on Tribunals, 1988–94; Ancient Monuments Board for Scotland, 1990–95. Sec., Friends of Royal Scottish Acad., 1987–2000. *Address*: Byways, Kiln Lane, Stokenham, Kingsbridge TQ7 2SQ. *T*: (01548) 580319.

**GODFRAY, Sir (Hugh) Charles (Jonathan),** Kt 2017; CBE 2011; PhD; FRS 2001; Professor of Population Biology and Director, Oxford Martin School, University of Oxford, since 2018; Fellow of Balliol College, Oxford, since 2018; *b* 27 Oct. 1958; *s* of Hugh and Annette Godfray; *m* 1992, Caroline Essil Margaret Elmslie. *Educ*: Millfield Sch., Som; St Peter's Coll., Oxford (MA; Hon. Fellow, 2001); Imperial Coll., London (PhD 1983). NERC Postdoctoral Fellow, Dept of Biol., Imperial Coll., London Univ., 1982–85; Demonstrator in Ecol., Dept of Zool., Univ. of Oxford, 1985–87; Imperial College, London University: Lectr, 1987–92, Reader, 1992–95, Dept of Biol Scis; Prof. of Evolutionary Biol., 1995–2006; Dir, NERC Centre for Population Biol., 1999–2006; Head, Div. of Biol., 2005–06; Hope Prof. of Zoology (Entomology), and Fellow of Jesus Coll., Univ. of Oxford, 2006–18. Mem., NERC, 2008–15. Chm., BIS (formerly DIUS) Lead Expert Gp, Foresight Future of Food and Farming Project, 2009–11; Dir, Oxford Martin Prog. on Future of Food, 2012–; Chair, Sci. Adv. Council, DEFRA, 2015–; Chair, Bovine TB Strategy Rev., DEFRA, 2018. Pres., British Ecol Soc., 2009–11 (Hon. Mem., 2016). Hon. Fellow, Nat. Hist. Mus., 2002–. Hon. Fellow, Royal Entomological Soc., 2017. Trustee, Royal Botanic Gdns, Kew, 2004–10; Trustee Dir, Rothamsted Research, 2012–. MAE 2012. For. Mem., American Acad. of Arts and Scis, 2009. Scientific Medal, 1994, Frink Medal, 2010, Zool. Soc.; Linnean Medal, Linnean Soc., 2011. *Publications*: Parasitoids, 1994; scientific papers in population biology and food security. *Recreations*: natural history, gardening, opera, walking. *Address*: Oxford Martin School, University of Oxford, 34 Broad Street, Oxford OX1 3BD.

**GODFRAY, Timothy Edmund;** Executive Chairman, Booksellers Association Group, since 2018 (Chief Executive, Booksellers Association of UK and Ireland, 1984–2018); *b* Kingston-upon-Thames, 13 Nov. 1950; *s* of Verden and Sylvia Godfray; *m* 1974, Elizabeth

Gent; three *s* one *d*. *Educ:* Wellington Coll., Crowthorne; Kingston Poly. Bookseller, Regency Bookshop, 1970–72; Trade Practice Exec., Booksellers Assoc., 1972–84. *Recreations:* family, running, walking, playing piano and guitar, reading. *Address:* 58 Ormond Avenue, Hampton, Middx TW12 2RX. *E:* tgodfray@aol.com. *Club:* Lensbury (Teddington).

**GODFREY, Daniel Charles;** Founder and Chief Executive, The People's Trust, since 2015; *b* 30 June 1961; *s* of late Gerald Michael Godfrey, CBE; *m* 1994, Frederiki Androulla Perewiznyk; three *s* one *d*. *Educ:* Westminster Sch.; Victoria Univ. of Manchester (BA Hons Econs). Life Insp., UK Provident, 1982–85; Mktg Manager, Schroders, 1985–88; Project Manager, Mercury Asset Mgt, 1988–90; Mktg Manager, Laurentian Life, 1990–91; Proprietor, The Sharper Image, 1991–94; Mktg Dir, Flemings, 1994–98; Dir Gen., Assoc. of Investment Trust Cos, later Assoc. of Investment Cos, 1998–2009; Communications Dir, Phoenix Gp Hldgs (formerly Pearl Gp), 2009–12; Chief Exec., Investment Assoc. (formerly Investment Mgt Assoc.), 2012–15. Chm., Personal Finance Education Gp, 2000–03. Mem., Adv. Bd, Ethical Capitalism Gp, 2014–; non-executive Director: Investor Forum, 2014–17; Big Issue Invest Fund Mgt Ltd, 2015–; Digital Moneybox, 2016–; Positive Peace Capital, 2018–; Mem., Ind. Governance Cttee, Legal & General, 2017–; Sen. Advr, Hermes Investment Mgt, 2018–. Member: ICA, 1987–; IoD, 2001–; Internat. Bankers' Co. (formerly Guild of Internat. Bankers), 2001–. *Recreations:* theatre, cinema, travel, food, football. *E:* daniel@coburglodge.com.

**GODFREY, David Warren,** CBE 2017; Chairman: Nomura Europe Holdings plc, since 2015; Nomura International plc, since 2016; Nomura Bank International plc, since 2017; Nomura Banque France; *b* Halifax, W Yorks, 22 Sept. 1950; *s* of Kenneth and Beryl Godfrey; *m* 2009, Theresa Froehlich; one *s* two *d*. *Educ:* Heath Grammar Sch., Halifax; Nottingham Univ. (BA Hons 1972). J. P. Morgan, 1994–2002; Mem., Exec. Bd, Swiss Re, 2002–09; Hd, Wholesale Risk, Lloyds Banking Gp, 2009–11; Chief Risk Officer, Pension Insce Corp., 2012–13; CEO, UK Export Finance, 2013–15 (non-exec. Dir, 2005–13). Non-exec. Dir, Charity Bank Ltd, 2013–; Chm., Wellesley Gp Investors Ltd, 2015–. *Recreation:* classic cars. *Address:* 63 Cloudesley Road, N1 0EL. *T:* (020) 7913 9297, 07810 756442. *E:* dwgodfrey51@aol.com.

**GODFREY, Rt Rev. (Harold) William;** Bishop of Peru, 1998–2016, now Emeritus; Vicar of Lastingham with Appleton-Le-Moors, Rosedale and Cropton, since 2017 (Honorary Priest-in-Charge, 2016–17); *b* 21 April 1948; *s* of Charles Robert Godfrey and Irene Eva Godfrey (*née* Kirk); *m* 1968, Judith Moya (*née* Fenton); one *s* two *d*. *Educ:* Chesterfield School; King's Coll., Univ. of London (AKC; Jelf Medal); St Augustine's Coll., Canterbury. VSO, Isfahan, Iran, 1966–67; Asst Curate, Warsop with Sookholme, Diocese of Southwell, 1972–75; Team Vicar of St Peter and St Paul, Hucknall Torkard, 1975–86; Bishop of Southwell's Ecumenical Officer, 1981–82; Rector of Montevideo, 1986–87; Archdeacon of Montevideo, 1986–87; Asst Bishop of Argentina and Uruguay, 1987–88; Bishop of Uruguay, 1988–98; Asst Presiding Bishop, Prov. of S America (formerly Prov. of Southern Cone of America), 1989–95, 2010–13. Benedictine Oblate, Elmore Abbey, then Salisbury Abbey, 2008–. Consultant for Confessional Affairs, Min. of Justice, Peru, 2004–16; President: Bible Soc. of Peru, 2003–06; Interconfessional Cttee of Peru, 2004–09; Pres. (formerly Co-Pres.), Interreligious Cttee of Peru, 2009–16. Member: Anglican Consultative Council, 2009–; Anglican Witness (formerly Core Gp), Evangelism and Ch Growth Initiative, Anglican Communion, 2009–16. Founder: Instituto Teológico Anglicano del Uruguay, 1990; Seminario Diocesano Santos Agustín, 2000; Founder and Pres., Comunión–Perú NGO, 2005. Member: Jesus Caritas Fraternity, 1974–86; USPG Mission, 1986–2013. Hon. DD: Nashotah Hse, USA, 2008; Univ. of South, Sewanee, USA, 2017. *Publications:* Santa Eucaristía, Rito Anglicano. *Address:* The Vicarage, Anserdale Lane, Lastingham, N Yorks YO62 6TN. *E:* hwgodfrey@gmail.com.

**GODFREY, Howard Anthony;** QC 1991; a Recorder, 1992–2005; *b* 17 Aug. 1946; *s* of late Emanuel and Amy Godfrey; *m* 1972, Barbara Ellinger; two *s*. *Educ:* William Ellis Sch.; LSE (LLB). Asst Lectr in Law, Univ. of Canterbury, NZ, 1969. Called to the Bar, Middle Temple, 1970 (Bencher, 2004), *ad eundem* Inner Temple, 1984; part-time Tutor, Law Dept, LSE, 1970–72; practising on SE Circuit, 1972–; called to the Bar, Turks and Caicos Is, 1996. Fellow, Soc. for Advanced Legal Studies, 1998. *Recreations:* wine and food, travel, humour, film and theatre, boating. *Address:* 2 Bedford Row, WC1R 4BU. *T:* (020) 7440 8888, *Fax:* (020) 7242 1738. *E:* hgodfrey@2bedfordrow.co.uk. *Clubs:* MCC; Royal Corinthian Yacht.

**GODFREY, James Eric,** OBE 2002; FRAgS; Director: R. J. & A. E. Godfrey, since 1974; Elsham Linc Ltd, since 2006; Searby Farming Co., since 2016; *b* Lincs, 25 April 1953; *s* of Arthur Eric Godfrey and Etheldreda Godfrey (*née* Cadas); *m* 1975, Janet Barclay; two *s* one *d*. *Educ:* Epsom Coll.; Univ. of Reading (BSc 1974). FRAgS 2000. Director, Am. Sentry Farming Gp plc, subseq. Willisham Gp plc, 1997–2002. Director: Fen Peas Ltd, 1991–2013; Dream Direct Gp plc, 2002–06. Chairman: Potato Mktg Bd, 1992–93 (Mem., 1988–97); Sustainable Agric. and Food Innovation Platform, Innovate UK (formerly Technol. Strategy Bd), 2010–16; Commercial Farmers Gp, 2013–16 (Mem., 2003–); Mem., BBSRC, 2009–15; non-exec. Dir, Rural Payments Agency, 2010–13. Dir, Lincs Rural Support Network, 2009–19. Mem. Council, Humberside TEC, 1995–2000. Mem. Council, RASE, 1993– (Hon. Vice Pres., 2014–17; Mem., Awards Council, 2018–; Hon. Pres., 2018–19). Chairman: Internat. Potato Centre, Peru, 2003–08 (Trustee, 2000–08); Alliance of 15 Consultative Gp on Internat. Agricl Res. Centres, USA, 2006–07; Investment Cttee, Ceres, 2018–. Member: Ct, Univ. of Reading, 2008–; Steering Gp, Farming Futures (formerly Centre for Excellence in UK Farming), 2012–17; Agri Food Technology Council (formerly Agri Tech Strategy), 2013–18; Lincoln Inst. for Agri-Food Technol., Univ. of Lincoln, 2016–; Ext. Adv. Bd, Future Food Beacon of Excellence, Univ. of Nottingham, 2019–. Trustee, Nat. Inst. of Agricultural Botany, 2012– (Chm., 2016–). Governor: Scottish Crop Res. Inst., 1991–2003 (Chm., 1999–2003); Roslin Res. Inst., 2006–08; Trustee, Internat. Rice Res. Inst., 2013– (Chm., 2016–). Mem., Barbados Nat. Trust. FInstD 2004. Hon. DSc Reading, 2007. World Potato Congress Award, 2006; British Potato Council Award, 2008; RASE Nat. Agriculture Award, 2015. *Recreations:* tennis, bridge, reading, travel. *Address:* Lautus Place, Silver Street, Barrow upon Humber, N Lincs DN19 7DN. *T:* (01469) 531521. *E:* Jim.Godfrey@godfrey.uk.com. *Clubs:* Farmers; Barbados Yacht.

**GODFREY, Dr Malcolm Paul Weston,** CBE 1986; Chairman, Public Health Laboratory Service Board, 1989–96; *b* 11 Aug. 1926; *s* of late Harry Godfrey and Rose Godfrey; *m* 1955, Barbara Goldstein; one *s* one *d* (and one *d* decd). *Educ:* Hertford Grammar Sch.; King's Coll., London Univ. (FKC 2000); KCH Med. Sch. (MB, BS (Hons and Univ. Medal) 1950); MRCP 1955, FRCP 1972. Hosp. posts at KCH, Nat. Heart and Brompton Hosps; RAF Med. Br., 1952–54; Fellow in Med. and Asst Physician (Fulbright Scholar), Johns Hopkins Hosp., USA, 1957–58; MRC Headquarters Staff, 1960–74: MO, 1960; Sen. MO, 1964; Principal MO, 1970; Sen. Principal MO, 1974; Dean, Royal Postgrad. Med. Sch., 1974–83 (Mem. Council, 1974–83, 1988–96; Chm., Audit Cttee, 1995–96; Hon. Fellow, 1985); Second Sec., MRC, 1983–88. University of London: Member: Senate, 1980–83; Court, 1981–83; Chm., Jt Med. Adv. Cttee, 1979–82. Mem., Faculty Bd of Clinical Medicine, Univ. of Cambridge, 1988–89. Chm., Brit. Council Med. Adv. Cttee, 1985–90; Member: Sci. Adv. Panel CIBA Foundn, 1974–91; Ealing, Hammersmith and Hounslow AHA(T), 1975–80; NW Thames RHA, 1980–83, 1985–88; Hammersmith SHA, 1982–83; Sec. of State's Adv. Gp on London Health Services, 1980–81; GMC, 1979–81. Lay Mem., Professional Standards Dept, Gen. Council of the Bar, 1990–95. Consultant Advr, WHO Human Reproduction Programme, 1979–90; Scientific Advr, Foulkes Foundn, 1983–89. Member, Council: Charing Cross Hosp. Med. Sch., 1975–80; St Mary's Hosp. Med. Sch., 1983–88; Royal Free Hosp. Sch. of Medicine, 1991–96; KCL, 1997–2001; Mem., Governing Body, BPMF, 1974–89; Chm., Council of Governors, UMDS of Guy's and St Thomas' Hosps, 1996–98 (Mem., 1990–96; Trustee, UMDS, 1998–2009); Mem., Special Trustees, Hammersmith Hosp., 1975–83. Pres., KCL Assoc., 2002–04 (Vice-Pres., 2000–02). Trustee, Florence Nightingale Fund, 1996–. Mem., Soc. of Scholars, Johns Hopkins Univ., USA, 2000. Gov., Quintin Kynaston Sch., 2000–03. Liveryman, Goldsmiths' Co., 1984– (Mem., Charity Cttee, 1998–2006); Mem. Court of Assts, Soc. of Apothecaries, 1979–94 (Master, 1989–90; Assistant Emeritus, 1995–). JP Wimbledon, 1972–92 (Chm. of the Bench and of Merton Magistrates' Courts Cttee, 1988–90 (Dep. Chm., 1987); Chm., Juvenile Panel, 1983–87). QHP, 1987–90. FRSA, 1989–92. Hon. Fellow, ICSM, 1999. *Publications:* contrib. med. jls on cardiac and respiratory disorders. *Recreations:* theatre, art galleries, reading. *Address:* 23 Bentinck Close, 76–82 Prince Albert Road, NW8 7RY. *T:* (020) 3638 0196.

**GODFREY, Very Rev. Nigel Philip;** Dean of Sodor and Man, since 2011; Vicar, West Coast, since 2012; Leader, West Mission Partnership, since 2012; *b* Douglas, Isle of Man, 25 April 1951. *Educ:* King William's Coll.; Bristol Poly. (Dip. Town Planning 1973); Ripon Coll., Cuddesdon (BA 1978); MA 1984); London Guildhall Univ. (MBA 2000); King's Coll. London (MSc 2009). MRTPI 1976. Ordained deacon, 1979, priest, 1980; Asst Curate, St John the Divine, Kennington, 1979–89; Vicar, Christ Church, Brixton Road, 1989–2001; Principal, Ordained Local Ministry Training Scheme, Dio. of Southwark, 2001–07; Chaplain, Southwark Cathedral, 2002–07; Vicar and Vice-Dean, St German's Cathedral, 2007–11; Dir of Vocation and Training, Dio. of Sodor and Man, 2010–. Leader, Community of Christ the Servant, Christ Ch, Brixton, 1984–93. *Publications:* (ed with H. Morgan) Approaches to Prayer: a resource book for groups and individuals, 1991; (contrib.) Here to Stay: ordained local ministry in the Church of England, 2006. *Recreation:* landscape architecture. *Address:* The Deanery, Albany Road, Peel, Isle of Man IM5 1JS. *T:* (01624) 844830.

**GODFREY, Sarah;** see Radclyffe, S.

**GODFREY, Rt Rev. William;** see Godfrey, Rt Rev. H. W.

**GODFREY, William Thomas;** Chief Executive, Newport City Council, since 2013; *b* Darlington, Co. Durham, 1 April 1965; *s* of late Howard Godfrey and of Pat Godfrey; *m* 2002, Karen Arnott; one *s*. *Educ:* Richmond Sch., N Yorks; Univ. of Hull (BA Hons Politics and Sociol.); Univ. of Durham (MA Business Admin). CIPFA. Dir of Resources, Welsh LGA, 2002–03; Chief Exec., E Hants DC, 2003–09; Strategic Dir (Resources), then Strategic Dir (Corporate Services), Bristol CC, 2009–12. *Recreations:* walking, supporting Swansea City FC, reading modern history and political biographies, trying to keep up with my son's knowledge of technology. *Address:* Newport City Council, Civic Centre, Newport, South Wales NP20 4UR. *T:* (01633) 217925. *E:* will.godfrey@newport.gov.uk.

**GODLEY,** family name of **Baron Kilbracken.**

**GODSAL, Brig. David Hugh,** MBE 1984; Vice Lord-Lieutenant of Somerset, since 2018; *b* Whitchurch, Shropshire, 24 Dec. 1947; *s* of Major Philip Godsal and Pamela Godsal; *m* 1971, Tamsin Edge-Partington; two *s* one *d*. *Educ:* Eton Coll.; RMA Sandhurst; Univ. of Exeter (BA Hons). Royal Green Jackets, 1969–2002: CO 1st Bn RGJ, 1986–89; Comdr 2 Bde and Dep. Constable, Dover Castle, 1995–98. SW Regl Dir Fundraising, Army Benevolent Fund, 2002–07. Pres., Somerset, RBL, 2008–15. Trustee: RFEA, 2002–16; Sir Oswald Stoll Foundn, 2013–18. Co. Col, Somerset, the Rifles, 2008–17. DL Somerset, 2012. *Recreations:* shooting, walking, classical music, churchwarden. *Address:* Edbrooke House, Winsford, Minehead, Somerset TA24 7AE. *T:* (01643) 851239. *E:* dgodsal@aol.com.

**GODSAL, Lady Elizabeth Cameron,** MBE 2002; Vice Lord-Lieutenant of Berkshire, 2005–10; *b* 10 April 1939; *d* of 8th Earl of Courtown, OBE, TD and late Christina Margaret (*née* Cameron); *m* 1962, Alan Anthony Colleton Godsal (*d* 2011); one *s* two *d*. Comr, St John Ambulance, Berks, 1983–90; Chief Pres., St John Ambulance, 1990–96; Pres., St John Fellowship, 1996–2008. Mem., Indep. Monitoring Bd, HM YOI, Reading, 1993–2006 (Chm., 2000–03). High Sheriff, 1990–91, DL 1994, Berks. High Steward, Wokingham, 1992–2018. Patron and Pres., numerous orgns. GCStJ 2009. *Address:* Queen's Arbour, Hungerford Lane, Twyford, Berks RG10 0LZ. *T:* (0118) 932 0956.

**GODSIFF, Roger Duncan;** MP (Lab) Birmingham Hall Green, since 2010 (Birmingham, Small Heath, 1992–97; Birmingham Sparkbrook and Small Heath, 1997–2010); *b* 28 June 1946; *s* of late George and of Gladys Godsiff; *m* 1977, Julia Brenda Morris; one *s* one *d*. *Educ:* Catford Comprehensive Sch. Bank clerk, 1965–70; political officer, APEX, 1970–90; senior research officer, GMB, 1990–92. Mem. (Lab) Lewisham BC, 1971–90 (Mayor, 1977). Contested (Lab) Birmingham, Yardley, 1983. Chm., British-Japanese Parly Gp, 1994–. Chm., Charlton Athletic Charitable Trust, 2004–. Gold and Silver Star, Order of Rising Sun (Japan), 2014. *Recreations:* sport - particularly football and cricket, listening to music, spending time with family. *Address:* House of Commons, SW1A 0AA. *Clubs:* Rowley Regis Labour; Charlton Athletic Supporters.

**GODSMARK, Nigel Graham,** QC 2001; **His Honour Judge Godsmark;** a Circuit Judge, since 2012; Designated Civil Judge for Nottinghamshire, Derbyshire and Lincolnshire, since 2013; *b* 8 Dec. 1954; *s* of Derek and Betty Godsmark; *m* 1982, Priscilla Howitt; one *s* two *d*. *Educ:* Queen Mary's Grammar Sch., Basingstoke; Univ. of Nottingham (LLB 1978). Called to the Bar, Gray's Inn, 1979; Asst Recorder, 1998–2000; Recorder, 2000–12. Hon. Prof. of Law, Univ. of Nottingham, 2009. *Recreations:* sport (Rugby, cricket, sailing, ski-ing), wine, family. *Address:* Nottingham County Court, 60 Canal Street, Nottingham NG1 7EJ.

**GODSON, Anthony;** HM Diplomatic Service, retired; government records sensitivity reviewer, since 2012; *b* 1 Feb. 1948; *s* of late Percival Lawrence Godson and Kathleen Elizabeth Godson (*née* Jennings); *m* 1977, Maryan Jane Margaret (*née* Hurst). Joined FCO, 1968; Attaché, Bucharest, 1970–72; Third Sec., Jakarta, 1972–76; Private Sec. to High Comr, Canberra, 1976–79; FCO, 1980–81; Second, later First, Sec., UKMIS to UN, NY, 1982–86; First Secretary: Kinshasa, 1987; FCO, 1988–89; Dep. Hd of Mission, Bucharest, 1990–92; UKMIS to UN, Geneva, 1992–95; FCO, 1996–97; Counsellor, later Dep. Hd of Mission and Consul Gen., Jakarta, 1998–2002; FCO, 2002–04; High Comr to Mauritius and Ambassador (non-res.) to Comoros, 2004–07. Exec. Dir, Prospect Burma, 2007–10. *Recreations:* tennis, ski-ing, walking, classical music, reading, photography.

**GODSON, Rory James;** Managing Partner, Powerscourt, since 2004; *b* Dublin, 2 Nov. 1962; *s* of Noel Anthony Godson and Bini Godson; *m* 1990, Hilary Hynes; three *s* one *d*. *Educ:* Rockwell Coll.; Dublin Inst. of Technol. (Cert. Journalism). Business and Finance mag., Dublin, then sports and business journalist, Sunday Tribune, 1985–90; Ed., Dublin

Tribune, 1990–92; News Ed., Sunday Tribune, then Business Ed. and Chief Correspondent, Sunday Independent, 1992–95; Dep. Ed., Sunday Tribune, 1995; Ireland Ed., 1996–2000, Business Ed., 2000–02, Sunday Times; Dir, Corporate Affairs, Goldman Sachs Internat., 2003. *Address:* Powerscourt, 1 Tudor Street, EC4Y 0AH. *T:* (020) 7250 1446. *E:* rory.godson@powerscourt-group.com. *Clubs:* Soho House; Lansdowne Football (Dublin).

**GODWIN, Joseph;** Director, BBC Academy, since 2015, and BBC Midlands, since 2016 (Director, BBC Birmingham, 2015–16); *b* Leamington Spa, 7 July 1964; *s* of Stanley Godwin and Zena Godwin. *Educ:* Trinity Sch., Leamington Spa; Univ. of Manchester (BA Hons Hist. 1985). BBC: regl news, BBC Southampton, 1986; trainee, Children's Progs Dept, 1989; prod., Blue Peter, 1995–97; Ed., BBC Children's Presentation, 1997–2000; Hd, Original Prodn, Nickelodeon UK, 2000–05; BBC Children's: Hd of Entertainment, 2005–08; Hd of News, Factual and Entertainment, 2008–09; Dir, 2009–14. Member: BAFTA, 2002–; Adv. Panel on Children's Viewing, BBFC, 2004–. Trustee: Nat. Museums Liverpool, 2012–15; CBSO, 2016–. *Recreations:* photography, CBSO concerts, making bread, travelling. *Address:* BBC Birmingham, The Mailbox, Birmingham B1 1RF.

**GODWIN, William George Henry;** QC 2017; *b* Singapore, 8 April 1957; *s* of Antony P. Godwin and Queenie P. Godwin; *m* 1981, Jane Teresa Geering; three *s* one *d*. *Educ:* University Coll. London (BA Philos. 1978); Oriel Coll., Oxford (Maj. State Student; BPhil 1980; DPhil 1984). Called to the Bar, Middle Temple (Benefactors' Sen. Law Scholar), 1986; in practice as a barrister specialising in commercial and construction law, 1986–. Mem. Bd, GB China Centre, 2014–. *Recreations:* bee keeping, walking, music, reading. *Address:* 3 Hare Court, Temple, EC4Y 7BJ. *T:* (020) 7415 7800. *E:* williamgodwin@3harecourt.com.

**GOEDERT, Michel,** MD, PhD; FRS 2000; Member of Scientific Staff, since 1984, Programme Leader, since 1987, and Head, Division of Neurobiology, 2007–16 (Joint Head, 2003–07), Medical Research Council Laboratory of Molecular Biology, Cambridge; *b* 22 May 1954; *s* of Pierre Goedert and Dr Marie-Antoinette Goedert (*née* Bové); partner, Prof. Maria Grazia Spillantini, *qv*; one *s*. *Educ:* Athénée, Luxembourg; Univ. of Basel (MD 1980); Trinity Coll., Cambridge (PhD 1984). Hon. Prof., Univ. of Cambridge, 2014. Mem., EMBO, 1997. FMedSci 2006. 1st Prize, Eur. Contest for Young Scientists and Inventors, 1973; Metropolitan Life Foundn Award for Med. Res., 1996; Potamkin Prize, Amer. Acad. Neurol., 1998; Prix Lions, Luxembourg, 2002; Eur. Grand Prix for Res., Foundn for Res. on Alzheimer's Disease, Paris, 2014; Brain Prize, Copenhagen, 2018. *Publications:* contrib. res. papers and reviews to scientific jls. *Recreations:* reading and writing, football. *Address:* MRC Laboratory of Molecular Biology, Francis Crick Avenue, Cambridge CB2 0QH. *T:* (01223) 267056.

**GOEHR, Prof. Alexander;** composer; Professor of Music, and Fellow of Trinity Hall, University of Cambridge, 1976–99, now Emeritus Professor and Fellow; *b* 10 Aug. 1932; *s* of Walter and Laelia Goehr. *Educ:* Berkhamsted; Royal Manchester Coll. of Music; Paris Conservatoire. Lectr, Morley Coll., 1955–57; Music Asst, BBC, 1960–67; Winston Churchill Trust Fellowship, 1968; Composer-in-residence, New England Conservatory, Boston, Mass, 1968–69; Associate Professor of Music, Yale University, 1969–70; West Riding Prof. of Music, Leeds Univ., 1971–76. Artistic Dir, Leeds Festival, 1975; Vis. Prof., Peking Conservatoire of Music, 1980. Reith Lectr, BBC, 1987. Mem., Bd of Dirs, Royal Opera House, 1982–84. Hon. Vice-Pres., SPNM, 1983–. Hon. Prof., Beijing Central Conservatory. Hon. Mem., Amer. Acad. and Inst. of Arts and Letters. Hon. FRMCM; Hon. FRAM 1975; Hon. FRNCM 1980; Hon. FRCM 1981. Hon. DMus: Southampton, 1973; Manchester, 1990; Nottingham, 1994; Siena, 1998; Cambridge, 2000. *Compositions include:* Songs of Babel, 1951; Fantasia Op. 4, 1954; String Quartet No. 1, 1957; La Belle Dame Sans Merci (ballet), 1958; Suite Op. 11, 1961; Hecuba's Lament, 1961; A Little Cantata of Proverbs, 1962; Concerto Op. 13, 1962; Little Symphony, 1963; Pastorals, 1965; Piano Trio, 1966; String Quartet No. 2, 1967; Romanza, 1968; Paraphrase, 1969; Symphony in One Movement, 1970; Concerto for Eleven, 1970; Concerto Op. 33, 1972; Chaconne for Wind, 1974; Lyric Pieces, 1974; Metamorphosis/Dance, 1974; String Quartet No. 3, 1976; Fugue on the notes of the Fourth Psalm, 1976; Romanza on the notes of the Fourth Psalm, 1977; Chaconne for Organ, 1979; Sinfonia, 1979; Kafka Fragments, 1979; Deux Etudes, 1981; Sonata, 1984; …a musical offering (JSB 1985), 1985; Symphony with Chaconne, 1986; …in real time, 1989; Still Lands, 1990; Bach Variations, 1990; Piano Quintet, 2000; …second musical offering (GFH 2001), 2001; Symmetry Disorders Reach, 2003; Marching to Carcassonne, 2003; Since Brass, no Stone…, 2008; TurmMusik, 2010; When Adam Fell, 2011; Largo Siciliano, 2012; between the Lines, 2014; After the Waking, 2017; *vocal:* The Deluge, 1958; Sutter's Gold, 1960; Virtutes, 1963; Arden Must Die (opera), 1966; Triptych (Naboth's Vineyard, 1968; Shadowplay, 1970; Sonata about Jerusalem, 1970); Psalm IV, 1976; Babylon the Great is Fallen, 1979; The Law of the Quadrille, 1979; Behold the Sun, 1981; Behold the Sun (opera), 1984; Eve Dreams in Paradise, 1988; Sing Ariel, 1990; The Death of Moses, 1992; Colossos or Panic, 1993; Arianna (opera), 1995; Schlussgesang, 1997; Kantan and Damask Drum (opera), 1999; Promised End (opera), 2010. *Address:* c/o Schott Music, 48 Great Marlborough Street, W1F 7BB.

**GOERNE, Matthias;** baritone; *b* Weimar, Germany, 31 March 1967. *Educ:* Studied under Prof. Beyer at Leipzig, Elizabeth Schwarzkopf and Dietrich Fischer-Dieskau. Début with Leipzig Radio SO; performances with Berlin Phil. Orch., Concentus Musicus, Concertgebouw; recitals in London, Amsterdam, Paris, Leipzig, Cologne and New York. Opera appearances include: Dresden Opera, and Komische Oper, Berlin, 1993; débuts, as Papageno, Salzburg Fest., 1997, Metropolitan Opera, NY, 1998; title rôle in Wozzeck, Zürich, 1999. Numerous recordings. Gramophone Award; Diapason d'Or; Echo Prize, Germany; Cecilia Award, Belgium. *Address:* c/o Michael Kocyan Artists Management, Alt-Moabit 104A, 10559 Berlin, Germany.

**GOFF, Hon. Philip Bruce,** CNZM 2017; Mayor of Auckland, since 2016; *b* 22 June 1953; *s* of Bruce Charles Goff and Elaine Loyola Goff; *m* 1979, Mary Ellen Moriarty; two *s* one *d*. *Educ:* Univ. of Auckland (MA 1st Cl. Hons); Nuffield Coll., Oxford. MP (Lab): Roskill, 1981–90 and 1993–96; New Lynn, 1996–99; Roskill, 1999–2016. Cabinet Minister: for Housing, Employment and Envmt, 1984–87; for Employment, Tourism, Youth Affairs and Associate Educn, 1987–89; for Educn, 1989–90; of Justice, and of For. Affairs and Trade, 1999–2005; of Pacific Is. Affairs, 2002–07; for Disarmament and Arms Control, 2005–08; of Defence and of Trade, 2005–08; Leader of the Opposition, 2008–11. Lab. spokesperson for defence, veterans' affairs, disarmament, ethnic communities and Auckland issues, 2014–16. *Recreations:* motorbike riding, sport, gardening. *Address:* Auckland Council, Private Bag 92300, Victoria Street West, Auckland 1142, New Zealand.

**GOFF, Sir Robert (William Davis-),** 4th Bt *cr* 1905; Director, O'Connor & Co., Art Dealers and Property Investment Co.; *b* 12 Sept. 1955; *s* of Sir Ernest William Davis-Goff, 3rd Bt, and of Alice Cynthia Davis-Goff (*née* Woodhouse); *S* father, 1980; *m* 1978, Nathalie Sheelagh, *d* of Terence Chadwick; three *s* one *d*. *Educ:* Cheltenham College, Glos. *Recreations:* shooting, ski-ing, motorcycling. *Heir: s* William Nathaniel Davis-Goff, *b* 20 April 1980. *Address:* Eairy Moar Farm, Glen Helen, Isle of Man IM4 3NP.

**GOFFE, Judith Ann,** FCA; independent business consultant, since 1991; *b* 6 March 1953; *d* of Albert Edward Goffe and Jennie Lucia Goffe (*née* Da Costa); *m* 1992, Peter Alexander Rose; one *s*. *Educ:* Immaculate Conception High Sch., Kingston, Jamaica; Reading Univ. (BSc 1976). Chartered Accountant, 1981; FCA 1991. Investment Dir, 3i Group plc, 1984–91. Director: Moorfields Eye Hosp. Trust, 1994–2004; Monitor (Ind. Regulator of NHS Foundn Trusts), 1994–2012. Mem., ITC, 1994–2003. Trustee, King's Fund, 2008–12. FRSA 1994. *Recreations:* collecting contemporary ceramics and jewellery, design, travel, family, food.

**GOFFEE, Prof. Robert Edward,** PhD; Professor of Organisational Behaviour, London Business School, 1994–2013, now Emeritus; *b* Ilford, 18 April 1952; *s* of Edward William Goffee and Rose Elizabeth Goffee; *m* 1978, Victoria Julie Marriott; one *s* one *d*. *Educ:* Univ. of Kent (BA 1973; PhD 1978). Res. Officer, Sch. of Mgt, Univ. of Bath, 1976–78; Res. Fellow, Faculty of Social Scis, Univ. of Kent, 1978–81; Lectr in Mgt Studies, Faculty of Human Studies, Univ. of Surrey, 1981–83; London Business School: Lectr, 1983–87, Sen. Lectr, 1988–90, in Organisational Behaviour; Associate Prof. of Organisational Behaviour, 1990–94; Subject Area Chm., Organisational Behaviour, 1995–98; Dir, Innovation Exchange, 1997–2003; Faculty Advr, Exec. Educn, 1999–2001; Dep. Dean (Exec. Educn), 2001–04; Faculty Dir for Exec. Educn, 2004–06. Vis. Prof. of Organisational Behaviour, Australian Graduate Sch. of Mgt, Univ. of NSW, 1995, 2007. FRSA 1997. Series Ed., Organisational Behaviour and Mgt, 1989–96; Man. Ed., 2001–04, Contrib. Ed., 2004–, Business Strategy Rev. (Mem., Editl Bd, 1992–94); Member, Editorial Board: M@n@gement, 2005–10; Leadership, 2006–12. *Publications:* with R. Scase: The Real World of the Small Business Owner, 1980, 2nd edn 1989; The Entrepreneurial Middle Class, 1982; Women in Charge, 1985; (ed) Entrepreneurship in Europe: the social processes, 1987; Reluctant Managers, 1989; Corporate Realities: the dynamics of organisations - large and small, 1995; with G. Jones: The Character of a Corporation, 1998, 2nd edn 2003; Why Should Anyone be Led by You?, 2006, rev. edn 2015; Clever: leading your smartest, most creative people, 2009; Why Should Anyone Work Here?, 2015; (ed jtly) Career Frontiers: new conceptions of working lives, 2000; articles in learned jls. *Recreations:* family, walking, good food and wine, football (supporting West Ham). *Address:* London Business School, Regent's Park, NW1 4SA. *T:* (020) 7000 7000. *E:* rgoffee@london.edu.

**GOH CHOK TONG;** Senior Minister, Prime Minister's Office, Singapore, 2004–11, now Emeritus; Senior Adviser, Monetary Authority of Singapore, since 2011 (Chairman, 2004–11); *b* 20 May 1941; *m* Tan Choo Leng; one *s* one *d* (twins). *Educ:* Raffles Instn; Univ. of Singapore (1st cl. Hons Econs); Williams Coll., USA. Admin. Service, Singapore Govt, 1964–69; Neptune Orient Lines, 1969–77. MP for Marine Parade, 1976–; Sen. Minister of State for Finance, 1977–79; Minister: for Trade and Industry, 1979–81; for Health, 1981–85; for Defence, 1981–91; First Dep. Prime Minister, 1985–90; Prime Minister, 1990–2004. People's Action Party: Mem., Central Exec. Cttee, 1979; First Organising Sec., 1979; Second Asst Sec. Gen., 1979–84; Asst Sec. Gen., 1984–89; First Asst Sec. Gen., 1989–92; Sec. Gen., 1992–2004. Formerly Chairman: Singapore Labour Foundn; NTUC Income, NTUC Fairprice. Medal of Honour, NTUC, 1987. *Recreations:* golf, tennis. *Address:* c/o Prime Minister's Office, Orchard Road, Istana Annexe, Istana, Singapore 238823.

**GOLANT, Farah R.;** *see* Ramzan Golant.

**GOLD,** family name of **Baron Gold**.

**GOLD,** Baron *cr* 2011 (Life Peer), of Westcliff-on-Sea in the County of Essex; **David Laurence Gold;** Principal: David Gold & Associates LLP, since 2011; Gold Collins Associates, since 2018; *b* 1 March 1951; *s* of Michael Gold and Betty Gold; *m* 1978, Sharon Levy; two *s* one *d*. *Educ:* Westcliff High Sch. for Boys; London Sch. of Econs (LLB). Admitted Solicitor, 1975; Herbert Smith: Partner, 1983–2011; Head of Litigation, 2003–05; Senior Partner, 2005–10; Sen. Litigation Partner, 2010–11. Pres., Southend and Westcliff Hebrew Congregation, 1997–2006. CEDR Accredited Mediator, 2010–. Monitor, BAE Systems plc, 2010–13; Leader of governance review, Rolls-Royce plc, 2013–19. Chm., Disciplinary Cttee, Conservative Party, 2010–12; Mem., EU Justice Cttee, H of L, 2017–18; Mem., Bribery Act 2010 Select Cttee, H of L, 2018–19. Chm., Proven Ltd, 2013–14; UK Chm., ESCP Europe Business Sch., 2018–. Sen. Advr, G3, 2014–18. Dir, C5 Hldgs, 2015–; Member: Investment Cttee, Balance Legal Capital, 2016–; Ind. Compliance Review Panel, Airbus, 2017–. Gov., LSE, 2009– (Mem., Finance Cttee, 2010–16). Freeman: Solicitors' Co., 1977; City of London, 2010. *Recreations:* theatre, cinema, bridge, travel, family. *Address:* (office) 3 Fitzhardinge Street, W1H 6EF. *T:* (020) 3535 8989. *E:* David.Gold@davidgoldassociates.com.

**GOLD, Jacqueline,** CBE 2016; Chief Executive: Ann Summers, since 1993; Knickerbox, since 2000; *b* 16 July 1960; *d* of David Gold and late Beryl Gold; *m* 1st, 1980, Tony D'Silva (marr. diss. 1990); 2nd, Daniel Cunningham; one *d*. Royal Doulton, 1979; joined Gold Gp as wages clerk, 1979; launched Ann Summers Party Plan, 1981; acquired Knickerbox, 2000. Business Communicator of the Year, British Assoc. of Communications in Business, 2004; Inspirational Women's Award, 2012; Female Entrepreneur of the Year, TiE Awards, 2013. *Publications:* Good Vibrations (autobiog.), 1995; A Woman's Courage (autobiog.), 2007. *Recreations:* travelling, watching football, partying, shopping. *Address:* Gold Group House, Godstone Road, Whyteleafe, Surrey CR3 0GG. *T:* (01883) 629629. *E:* shelley@pha-media.com.

**GOLD, Jeremy Spencer;** QC 2003; **His Honour Judge Gold;** a Circuit Judge, since 2009; *b* 15 July 1955; *s* of late Alfred Gold and Ruby Caroline Gold; *m* 1976, Joanne Driver. *Educ:* Brighton, Hove and Sussex Grammar Sch.; Univ. of Kent at Canterbury (BA Hons). Called to the Bar, Middle Temple, 1977; in practice as barrister specialising in criminal work, 1977–2009; Recorder, 2000–09. *Recreations:* walking football, theatre, good food, good company. *Address:* Lewes Crown Court, High Street, Lewes BN7 1YB.

**GOLD, John (Joseph Manson);** Public Relations Consultant, 1979–90, retired; Manager of Public Relations, Hong Kong Mass Transit Railway (construction phase), 1975–79; *b* 2 Aug. 1925; *m* 1953, Berta Cordeiro; one *d*. *Educ:* Clayesmore Sch., Dorset. Yorkshire Evening News, 1944–47; London Evening News, 1947–52; Australian Associated Press (New York), 1952–55; New York Corresp., London Evening News, 1955–66; Editor, London Evening News, 1967–72; Dir, Harmsworth Publications Ltd, 1967–73. Free-lance writer and lectr, Far East, 1973–75.

**GOLD, Murray Jonathan;** writer and freelance composer; *b* Portsmouth, 28 Feb. 1969; *s* of Lenny and Suzanne Gold. *Educ:* Corpus Christi Coll., Cambridge (BA Hons Hist. 1991). Composer: for *films:* Beautiful Creatures, Wild About Harry, 2000; Miranda, 2002; Kiss of Life, 2003; Alien Autopsy, Mischief Night, 2006; Death at a Funeral, I Want Candy, 2007; for *television:* Vanity Fair, 1998; Queer As Folk, 1999 (RTS Award for Best Original Score); Randall & Hopkirk (Deceased), 2000–01; Clocking Off, 2000–02; Shameless, 2004–13; Casanova, 2005; Dr Who, 2005–17; Torchwood, 2006–11; Sarah Jane Adventures, 2007–11; The Devil's Whore, 2008; Single Father, 2010; Scott & Bailey, 2011–13; Last Tango in Halifax, 2012, 2016; The Musketeers, 2014; A Very English Scandal, 2018; writer: *plays:* Resolution, Battersea Arts Centre, 1994; 50 Revolutions, Whitehall, 2000;

Electricity, Radio 3, 2000, W Yorkshire Playhouse, 2004 (Imison Award for Best New Radio Play, Soc. of Authors, 2002); radio play, Kafka the Musical, 2011 (Tinniswood Award for Best Original Radio Drama, Soc. of Authors, 2013); Snow White, Sadler's Wells and Northern Stage, Newcastle, 2016.

**GOLD, Nicholas Roger;** b 11 Dec. 1951; s of Rev. (Guy) Alastair Whitmore Gold, TD, MA and Elizabeth Gold, JP; m 1983, Laura Arnold-Brown (marr. diss. 2005); one s two d. Educ: Felsted Sch.; Univ. of Kent; Coll. of Law. ACA 1977, FCA 1982. Chartered accountant, Touche Ross & Co., 1973–76; admitted solicitor, 1979; solicitor, Freshfields, 1977–86; Man. Dir, ING Bank NV (formerly Baring Bros and Co.), 1986–2008. Beach café proprietor, Winking Prawn brasserie, Salcombe, 1994–. Director: BlackRock Income and Growth Investment Trust plc (formerly British Portfolio Trust plc), 2008–; Cobra Mist Ltd, 2015–; Adviser: Pottinger Co. Pty (Sydney), 2009–; Edmond de Rothschild Ltd (London), 2011–14. Member: Council, RADA, 2003–14; Bd, RADA Enterprises Ltd, 2012–; Bd, Prince's Foundn for Integrated Health, 2004–08. Gov., Downe House Sch., 2008–17. Lighthouse Keeper, Orford Ness, 2013–. Recreations: the arts, portraiture, painting, drawing, sailing, country pursuits, tennis, travel, especially in India. Address: 14 Northumberland Place, W2 5BS; Avocets, Quay Street, Orford IP12 2NU. E: nicholasgold@aol.com. Clubs: Garrick, Hurlingham; Orford Sailing.

**GOLDACRE, Dr Ben Michael,** MBE 2018; author; Senior Clinical Research Fellow, University of Oxford, since 2015; Research Fellow, London School of Hygiene and Tropical Medicine, since 2010; columnist, The Guardian, since 2003; b London, 1974; s of Michael Goldacre and Susan Goldacre. Educ: Church Cowley St James, Oxford; Temple Cowley St James, Oxford; Magdalen College Sch., Oxford; Magdalen Coll., Oxford (BA 1st Cl. Hons Physiol Scis 1995); King's Coll. London (MA Philos. 1997); University Coll. London (MB BS 2000); London Sch. of Hygiene and Tropical Medicine (MSc Epidemiol. 2010). MRCPsych 2005. Res. Fellow, Univ. of Milan, 1996; NHS, 2000–07; Research Fellow: KCL, 2008; Nuffield Coll., Oxford, 2009. Chair, HealthTech Adv. Bd, DoH, 2018–. Publications: Bad Science, 2008; Bad Pharma: how drug companies mislead doctors and harm patients, 2012; I Think You'll Find It's a Bit More Complicated Than That, 2014; Do Statins Work?: the battle for perfect evidence-based medicine, 2019. Recreations: analogue modular synthesisers, blogging, abandoned buildings. Address: c/o Sarah Ballard, United Agents, 12–26 Lexington Street, W1F 0LE. T: (020) 3214 0800. E: ben@badscience.net.

**GOLDBERG, David Gerard;** QC 1987; b 12 Aug. 1947; s of late Arthur Goldberg and of Sylvia Goldberg; m 1981, Alison Ninette Lunzer (marr. diss. 2003); one s one d. Educ: Plymouth Coll.; London School of Economics (LLB, LLM). Called to the Bar, Lincoln's Inn, 1971, Bencher, 1997; practice at Revenue Bar, 1972–. Chm. Trustees, Surgical Workshop for Anatomical Prosection, 1994–. Publications: (jtly) Introduction to Company Law, 1971, 4th edn 1987; (jtly) The Law of Partnership Taxation, 1976, 2nd edn 1979; various articles and notes in legal periodicals mainly concerning taxation and company law. Recreations: reading, writing letters, thinking. Address: Gray's Inn Tax Chambers, 36 Queen Street, EC4R 1BN. T: (020) 7242 2642.

**GOLDBERG, Sir David (Paul Brandes),** Kt 1996; DM; FRCP, FRCPsych; Professor of Psychiatry, 1993–99, and Director of Research and Development, 1993–99, Institute of Psychiatry, University of London, now Professor Emeritus; b 28 Jan. 1934; s of Paul Goldberg and Ruby Dora Goldberg; m 1966, Ilfra Joy Pink; one s three d. Educ: William Ellis Sch., London; Hertford Coll., Oxford (MA 1956; DM 1970; Hon. Fellow 2002); St Thomas' Hosp.; Manchester Univ. (MSc 1974). FRCPsych 1974; FRCP 1976. Trained at Maudsley Hosp., 1962–69; Sen. Lectr, 1969–72, Prof., 1972–92, Univ. of Manchester. Visiting Professor: Medical Univ. of S Carolina, 1978–79; Univ. of WA, 1986. Non-exec. Chm., Psychiatry Res. Trust. Founder FMedSci 1998; FKC. Hon. FRSocMed 2008. Lifetime Achievement Award, RCPsych, 2009. Publications: Mental Illness in the Community: the pathway to psychiatric care, 1981; Common Mental Disorders: a biosocial model, 1991; Psychiatric Illness in Medical Practice, 1992; (with I. Goodyer) The Origins and Course of Common Mental Disorders, 2005; 350 papers. Recreations: walking, talking, travelling. Address: Institute of Psychiatry, Psychology and Neuroscience, King's College London, De Crespigny Park, SE5 8AF.

**GOLDBERG, Jonathan Jacob;** QC 1989; a Recorder, 1993–2013; b 13 Nov. 1947; s of late Rabbi Dr and Mrs P. Selvin Goldberg; m 1st, 1980, Alexis Jane (marr. diss. 1991), e d of late Sir George Henry Martin, CBE; one s one d; 2nd, 2009, Mrs Regina Skyer, of New York. Educ: Manchester Grammar Sch.; Trinity Hall, Cambridge (MA, LLM). Called to the Bar, Middle Temple, 1971; Member, NY State Bar, 1985; Asst Recorder, 1988–93. Pres., Tribunal, Zionist Fedn of UK, 2017–. Recreations: music, cinema, wine, travel. Address: North Square Chambers, PO Box 61360, N6 6DH. E: jg@goldbergqc.com.

**GOLDBERG, Pamela Jill,** OBE 2013; Chief Executive, Breast Cancer Campaign, 1995–2011; Chairman, Institute of Health Visiting, since 2016; b 1945; d of late Jack and Norma Wolfowitz; m 1964, John Martin Goldberg; one s one d. Educ: Kingsmead Coll. for Girls, Johannesburg. Dir, Nordene Galls, S Africa, 1974–79; Talentmark Ltd, 1979–81; Res. Co-ordinator, Stephen Rose and Partners Ltd, 1981–88; London Partner, Lared Gp, 1988–95. Non-exec. Dir, Barnet FHSA, 1994–96. Mem., Human Tissue Authy, 2008–14. Mem. Council and Vice-Chm., AMRC, 1999–2004. Trustee, Moorfields Eye Charity, 2011–14. Liveryman, Needlemakers' Co., 1987– (Master, 2011–12). FRSA. Recreations: food, family, friends. T: 07973 195870. E: pamelajgoldberg@gmail.com.

**GOLDBLATT, Prof. David,** PhD; FRCP, FRCPCH; Consultant Paediatric Immunologist, since 1995, and Director, Clinical Research and Development, since 2004, Great Ormond Street Hospital for Children (Director, NIHR Biomedical Research Centre, 2007–17); Professor of Vaccinology, since 2003, and Deputy Director (NHS Translation), since 2014, UCL Great Ormond Street Institute of Child Health (formerly Institute of Child Health), University College London; Senior Investigator, National Institute for Health Research, since 2012; b 16 March 1960; s of Samuel Goldblatt and Betty (née Kramer); m 1994, Isobel Beatrice Pemberton; one s two d. Educ: Univ. of Cape Town (MB ChB); Univ. of London (PhD 1991). FRCPCH 2001; FRCP 2006. Trng as paediatrician and immunologist, Red Cross Children's Hosp., Cape Town, Queen Elizabeth Children's Hosp., Hackney, and Gt Ormond St Hosp. for Sick Children, 1983–95. Publications: (contrib.) Oxford Textbook of Medicine, 6th edn 2016; (contrib.) Oxford Handbook of Tropical Medicine, 2nd edn 2005; (contrib.) Harrisons Principles and Practice of Internal Medicine, 18th edn 2011, 20th edn 2016; contrib. numerous papers to learned jls incl. Lancet and BMJ. Address: Great Ormond Street Institute of Child Health, University College London, 30 Guilford Street, WC1N 1EH. T: (020) 7905 2886, Fax: (020) 7905 2882. E: d.goldblatt@ucl.ac.uk. Club: Arsenal Football.

**GOLDBLATT, Simon;** QC 1972. Called to the Bar, Gray's Inn, 1953 (Bencher, 1982). Address: 39 Essex Chambers, 81 Chancery Lane, WC2A 1DD.

**GOLDEN, Maurice Charles;** Member (C) Scotland West, Scottish Parliament, since 2016; b Dundee, 12 Jan. 1980. Educ: Univ. of Dundee (MA Hons Econs 2001; MPhil Urban and Cultural Histories 2004; LLM Envmtl Law 2005). Res. Fellow, Univ. of Dundee, 2004–05; Campaign Manager, Waste Aware Scotland, 2005–09; Transmission Policy Manager, Ofgem, 2009–11; Circular Econ. Prog. Manager, Zero Waste Scotland, 2011–16. Scottish Parliament: Shadow Cabinet Sec. for the Envmt, Climate Change and Land Reform, 2016; Spokesperson for Low Carbon Economy. Recreations: current affairs, football. Address: Scottish Parliament, Edinburgh EH99 1SP. E: maurice.golden.msp@parliament.scot.

**GOLDFRAPP, Alison E. M.;** singer, songwriter and producer; b Enfield, Middx, 13 May 1966; d of Nicholas John Goldfrapp and Isabella Patricia Goldfrapp (née Barge). Educ: Middlesex Univ. (BA Hons Fine Art). Formed Goldfrapp music duo (with Will Gregory), 1999; albums: Felt Mountain, 2000; Black Cherry, 2002; Supernature, 2005; Seventh Tree, 2008; Head First, 2010; Tales of Us, 2013; Silver Eye, 2017. Recreations: photography, travelling, wild swimming, reading, cooking, film and cinema. Address: c/o Fascination Management, First Floor, 6 South Hill Park, NW3 2SB. T: (020) 7986 6457. E: peter@fascinationmanagement.com.

**GOLDHILL, Flora Taylor,** CBE 2007; Director for Children, Families and Communities (formerly Maternity, and Health Inequalities, then Children, Families and Social Inclusion), Department of Health, 2012–16. Educ: Morgan Academy, Dundee; Edinburgh Univ. (MA Hons). Civil Servant, DHSS and DoH, 1977–90; Chief Exec., HFEA, 1991–96; Department of Health: Head, Policy Mgt Unit, 1996–98; Dir of Personnel, 1999–2001; Dir, Chief Nursing Officer's Directorate, 2001–07; Dir, Workforce Directorate, 2007–10; acting Dir-Gen., Corporate Develt, 2010–12. Governor: Canonbury Primary Sch., 1994–2005 (Vice-Chm., 1996–2003); Islington Arts and Media Sch., 2012– (Chair, 2013–). Recreations: family, friends, walking, horse riding, theatre.

**GOLDHILL, Prof. Simon David,** PhD; FBA 2016; Professor of Greek, University of Cambridge, since 2002 (Director, Centre for Research in Arts, Social Sciences and Humanities, 2011–18); Fellow, King's College, Cambridge, since 1982 (Director of Studies in Classics, 1990–2013); b London, 17 March 1957; s of Michael and Pamela Goldhill; m 1983, Shoshana Shira Rosenfeld; one s one d. Educ: University Coll. Sch., London; King's Coll., Cambridge (BA 1st Cl. 1978; Chancellor's Medal; MA 1982; PhD 1982). Kennedy Fellow, Harvard, 1978–79; Jun. Res. Fellow, 1982–85, Lectr, 1985–88, King's Coll., Cambridge; Lectr, 1988–98, Reader, 1998–2002, John Harvard Prof. in Humanities, 2013–18, Univ. of Cambridge. Old Dominion Prof. of Classics, Princeton Univ., 2007; Schaffner Prof., Chicago Univ., 2009; Webster Prof., Stanford Univ., 2013. Martin Lectr, Oberlin Coll., 2010; Onassis Lectr, Onassis Foundn, 2011–12. Dir, Cambridge Victorian Studies Gp, 2006–11. Chm., Eur. Res. Council Panel, 2009–13; Mem., AHRC, 2015–; Member, Board: Consortium of Humanities Centres and Institutes, 2016–; Rachel Carson Centre, Munich, 2017–. Pres., Network of Insts of Advanced Study, 2015–. Foreign Sec., British Acad., 2019–. Fellow, Amer. Acad. Arts and Scis, 2009. Publications: Language, Sexuality, Narrative: the Oresteia, 1984; Reading Greek Tragedy, 1986, 14th repr. 2012; Poet's Voice, 1991, repr. 1999; Aeschylus' Oresteia, 1992, 2nd edn 2002 (trans. Greek 2006; trans. Chinese 2018); (with R. Osborne) Art and Text in Ancient Greece, 1994; Foucault's Virginity, 1995; (with R. Osborne) Performance Culture and the Democratic City, 1999; Being Greek under Rome, 2001; Who Needs Greek?, 2002 (trans. Greek 2004); The Invention of Prose, 2002; Love, Sex and Tragedy, 2004 (trans. Greek 2004, Portuguese 2005, Turkish 2008, Dutch 2010, Chinese 2014); The Temple of Jerusalem, 2004 (trans. Hungarian, Greek, 2006, Portuguese 2007, Russian, Bulgarian 2008, Italian, 2009, Chinese 2012); Jerusalem, City of Longing, 2008 (Gold Medal, Ind. Publishers Book Awards); The End of Dialogue in Antiquity, 2009; Victorian Culture and Classical Antiquity, 2012 (Robert Lowry Patten Award, Rice Univ., 2012); Freud's Couch, Scott's Buttocks, Brontë's Grave, 2012; Sophocles and the Language of Tragedy, 2013 (Runciman Book Prize, Anglo-Hellenic League); The Buried Life of Things, 2015; A Very Queer Family Indeed, 2016. Recreations: food, theatre, sport. Address: King's College, Cambridge CB2 1ST. E: sdg1001@cam.ac.uk.

**GOLDIE,** Baroness cr 2013 (Life Peer), of Bishopton in the County of Renfrewshire; **Annabel MacNicoll Goldie;** DL; Minister of State, Ministry of Defence, since 2019; b 27 Feb. 1950; d of Alexander MacIntosh Goldie and Margaret MacNicoll Goldie. Educ: Greenock Acad.; Strathclyde Univ. (LLB; Hon. Fellow 2004). Admitted Solicitor, 1974; Notary Public, 1978–2007. Apprentice Solicitor, McClure Naismith Brodie & Co., Glasgow, 1971–73; Asst Solicitor, Haddow & McLay, Glasgow, subseq. Dickson, Haddow & Co., 1973–77; Partner, Dickson, Haddow & Co., subseq Donaldson, Alexander, Russell & Haddow, 1978–2006. Scottish Parliament: Mem. (C) Scotland W, 1999–2016; Dep. Convener, Enterprise and Lifelong Learning Cttee, 1999–2003; Convener, Justice 2 Cttee, 2003–06. A Baroness in Waiting (Govt Whip), 2016–19. Scottish Conservative and Unionist Party: Vice-Chm., 1992–95; Dep. Chm., 1995–97 and 1997–98; Chm., 1997; Dep. Leader, 1998–2005; Leader, 2005–11. Dir, Prince's Scottish Youth Business Trust, 1995–2010. Mem., Adv. Bd, W Scotland Salvation Army. Mem., Charing Cross Rotary Club, Glasgow. DL Renfrew, 1993. Hon. FRIAS 2014. Recreations: gardening badly, walking happily, watching birds usually uncomprehendingly, listening to classical music enthusiastically, if not knowledgeably.

**GOLDIN, Prof. Ian Andrew,** DPhil; Professor of Globalisation and Development, since 2011, and Director, Oxford Martin Programme on Technological and Economic Change, since 2017, University of Oxford; Professorial Fellow, Balliol College, Oxford, since 2006; b Pretoria, SA, 3 March 1955; s of Harry Goldin and Alice Goldin (née Widrich); m 1992, Theresa Webber; one s one d. Educ: Univ. of Cape Town (BSc, BA Hons 1977); London Sch. of Econs (MSc 1979); Univ. of Oxford (DPhil 1983; MA 2007); INSEAD France (AMP 1999). Vis. Prof. and Actg Hd, Econs Dept, Univ. of Cape Town, 1980–81; Tutor in Econs, St Peter's Coll., Oxford, 1982–83; Commodities Analyst, Landell Mills Commodities Ltd, London and NY, 1984–88; Res. Dir of Progs, Develt Centre, OECD, Paris, 1988–92; Principal Economist: Country Ops, World Bank (IBRD), Washington, 1992–95; EBRD, London, 1995–96; Chief Exec. and Man. Dir, Develt Bank of SA, Johannesburg, 1996–2001; Dir, Develt Policy, 2001–03, Vice Pres., 2003–06, World Bank, Washington; Dir, James Martin 21st Century Sch., then Oxford Martin Sch., Univ. of Oxford, 2006–16. Chair of Trustees, CORE Economics Educn. Presenter, BBC series: After the Crash, 2018; Will AI Kill Development?, 2019. Chevalier de l'Ordre Nationale du Mérite (France), 2000. Publications: Making Race: the economics and politics of coloured identity in South Africa, 1987; (with Gervasio Castro de Rezende) Economic Crisis: lessons from Brazil, 1990 (trans. French and Portuguese); (ed with Odin Knudsen) Trade Liberalization: implications for developing countries, 1990 (trans. French); (with Dominique van der Mensbrugghe) Trade Liberalisation: what's at stake?, 1992 (trans. French, Chinese and Indonesian); (ed with L. Alan Winters) Open Economies, 1992; (with Gervasio Castro de Rezende) Crescimento numa Economia em Crise, 1993 (trans. English); (jtly) Trade Liberalization: global economic implications, 1993 (trans. French and Chinese); (ed jtly) Modelling Economy-wide Reforms, 1994 (trans. French); (ed) Economic Reform, Trade and Agricultural Development, 1994; (ed with L. Alan Winters) The Economies of Sustainable Development, 1995; (jtly) The Case for Aid, 2002; (with Kenneth Reinert) Globalisation for Development: trade, finance, aid, migration and policy, 2006, new edn 2007 (trans. Spanish, Chinese, French); Exceptional People: how migration shaped our world and will define our future, 2011 (trans. Greek); Globalisation for Development: meeting new challenges, 2012; Divided Nations: why global governance is failing and what we can do about it, 2013; The Butterfly Defect: how globalisation creates systematic risk, and what we can do about it, 2014; (ed) Is the Planet Full?, 2014; Age of Discovery: navigating the storms of our second renaissance, 2017; The Pursuit of Development: economic growth, social change and ideas, 2016; Development: a very short introduction, 2018. *Recreations:* music, cycling, ski-ing, scuba, hiking, triathlon, running. *Address:* Oxford Martin School, University of Oxford, Old Indian Institute, 34 Broad Street, Oxford OX1 3BD. *T:* (01865) 287430. *E:* info@oxfordmartin.ox.ac.uk.

**GOLDING,** Baroness *cr* 2001 (Life Peer), of Newcastle-under-Lyme in the County of Staffordshire; **Llinos Golding;** *b* 21 March 1933; *d* of Rt Hon. Ness Edwards, MP and Elina Victoria Edwards; *m* 1st, 1957, Dr John Roland Lewis; one *s* two *d*; 2nd, 1980, John Golding (*d* 1999). *Educ:* Caerphilly Girls' Grammar Sch.; Cardiff Royal Infirmary Sch. of Radiography. Mem., Soc. of Radiographers. Worked as a radiographer at various times; Assistant to John Golding, MP, 1972–86. MP (Lab) Newcastle-under-Lyme, July 1986–2001. An Opposition Whip, 1987–92; opposition spokesman: on social security, 1992–95; on children and the family, 1993–95; on agric., fisheries and food, 1995–97. Mem., Select Cttee on Culture, Media and Sport, 1997–2001. Former Chm., All Party Parly Gp on Children; Joint Chairman: All Party Parly Gp on Homeless, 1989–99; All Party Parly Gp on Drugs Misuse, until 1998; All Party Parly Gp on Racing and Gaming Gp, 2006–; former Treas., All Party Parly Gp on Racing and Bloodstock. Admin. Steward, BBB of C, 2004–18 (Hon. Steward, 2018–). Member: BBC Gen. Adv. Council, 1988–91; Commonwealth War Graves Commn, 1992–2003. Chm., Angling Cttee, Countryside Alliance, 2004–. Chairman: Second Chance, children's charity, 2000–; Citizen Card, 2001–18. Former Mem., Dist Manpower Services Cttee; Mem., N Staffs DHA, 1983–87. Sec., Newcastle (Dist) Trades Council, 1976–87. *Address:* House of Lords, SW1A 0PW.

**GOLDING, Lois Patricia, (Peaches),** OBE 2009; Lord-Lieutenant of the City and County of Bristol, since 2017; *b* Spartanburg, SC, USA, 13 Dec. 1953; *d* of Dr Charlie Brady Hauser and Lois Elizabeth Hauser; *m* 1981, Robert Roy Golding; one *s. Educ:* R. J. Reynolds High Sch., Winston-Salem, NC; Univ. of North Carolina, Chapel Hill (Biology Degree 1976). Owner Manager, Peaches Golding Mktg and Communications, 1992–; Business in the Community, 1994–2011: Consultant; Dep. Dir, Race for Opportunity Campaign; SW Regl Dir; Dir, Special Projects; Principal Consultant, then non-exec. Consultant, Moon Consulting Ltd, 2012–. Non-exec. Dir, Western Trng and Enterprise Council, 1992–2000; Mem., Gen. Chiropractic Council, 1996–2004 (Chair: Health Cttee; Communications Strategy Wkg Gp); Mem., Ethnic Minority Business Forum, DTI, 2004–06; Home Office Rep., Avon and Somerset Police Authy, 2000–08. Non-exec. Dir, 1992–2001, Dir, Local Adv. Bd, 2001–06, GWR (West) Ltd. Non-exec. Dir, ITV West of England and Wales, 1997–2006; Chair: Viewer Adv. Panel, ITV West Country west opt, 2003–17; Regl Adv. Cttee, ITV West east opt, 2003–11. Non-executive Director: N Bristol NHS Hosp. Trust, 2004–10; Avon and Wilts Mental Health Partnership NHS Trust, 2013–16. Ind. Chair, Bristol Water Customer Challenge Panel, 2016–. Trustee, SS Great Britain Trust, 2011–. Ind. Mem., Bd of Govs, UWE, 1992–2000. MCIM 1995. Hon. MBA, 2010, DUniv, 2017, UWE. *Recreations:* gardening, photography, needlework, learning Italian. *Address:* Charlton, Abbots Leigh Road, Leigh Woods, Bristol BS8 3PX. *T:* (0117) 973 5920. *E:* peaches@gopeaches.co.uk. *W:* www.lordltbristol.org.uk.

**GOLDING, Michael Redvers,** OBE 2007; professional yachtsman, since 1992; Managing Director, Mike Golding Yacht Racing Ltd, since 2001; yachting consultant, coach, speaker and writer, since 2012; *b* 27 Aug. 1960; *s* of Jack Golding and late Margaret Golding; *m* 2002, Andrea Bacon; one *s. Educ:* Reading Blue Coat Sch., Sonning; Windsor and Eton Coll. Fire Officer, Royal Berks Fire and Rescue Service, 1979–92; professional yachtsman: skipper, British Steel Challenge, 2nd place, 1992–93; skipper, British Admiral's Cup Team, 1995; winner: BT Global Challenge Round the World Race, 1996–97; Défi Atlantique, 2003; Transat, 2004; Internat. Monohull Open Cl. Assoc. World Champion, 2004–05, 2005–06; Forum Internat. de la Course Océanique World Champion, 2005–06; competitor: 7 consecutive Transat Jacques Vabre races, 1999–2011; 4 Vendée Globe non-stop solo circumnavigations, incl. 7th place, 2000–01 (dismasted day 1, restarted 8 days after main fleet), 3rd place, 2004–05, 6th place, 2012–13 (first person to complete 3 Vendée Globe circumnavigations, 2013); first non-stop solo in both directions round the world, 2001; *world records:* non-stop solo round the world E to W (125 days), 1993–94; single-handed, non-stop circumnavigation W to E against prevailing winds and currents, 1994–2001; fastest single-handed transatlantic crossing Plymouth to Boston (12 days 15 hours), 2004; fastest single-handed monohull crossing of Indian Ocean (14 days 24hrs 1 min.), 2004; fastest single-handed monohull crossing of S Pacific Ocean (16 days 5hrs 26 mins), 2005. Mem., Oceanic Events Cttee, 2012–, Chm., Sustainability Commn, 2017–, World Sailing. Silver Medal, Royal Humane Soc., 2007; Emile Robin Award, Shipwrecked Mariners' Soc., 2008. *Publications:* No Law No God, 1993; Racing Skipper, 1999. *Recreations:* travel, ski-ing, mountain biking, cars. *Address:* Mike Golding Yacht Racing Ltd, 24 Shore Road, Warsash, Hants SO31 9FU. *T:* (01489) 557960. *E:* info@mikegolding.com. *Clubs:* Royal London Yacht (Hon. Mem.), Little Ship (Hon. Mem.); Pres., 2017–); Royal Southampton Yacht (Hon. Mem.); Corinthian Yacht (Boston, Mass) (Hon. Mem.).

**GOLDING, Peaches;** *see* Golding, L. P.

**GOLDING, Sarah;** Chief Executive Officer and Partner, The & Partnership London (formerly CHI & Partners), since 2002; *b* Blackburn, 27 April 1971; *d* of Peter Gold and Jeanne Bishop; *m* 2009, David Golding; one *s* one *d. Educ:* Queen Elizabeth's Grammar Sch., Blackburn; New Hall, Cambridge (MA French and German). With Lowe Howard-Spink, 1994–2002 (Mem. Bd, 1999–2002; New Business Dir, 2001–02). Non-exec. Dir, Cru Kafe, 2015–. Trustee, Adopt a Better Way, 2012–14. Mem., Christmas Cttee, Gt Ormond St Hosp., 2014–. Member: WACL, 2004–; Council, IPA, 2011– (Pres., 2017–19); Mktg Gp of GB, 2014–. *Recreations:* Game of Thrones, holidays, just started ski-ing. *Address:* The & Partnership London, Charlotte Building, 17 Gresse Street, Evelyn Yard, W1T 1QL. *T:* (020) 7462 8500, *Fax:* (020) 7462 8501. *Club:* Soho House.

**GOLDING, Ven. Simon Jefferies,** CBE 2002; Hon. Priest, Diocese of Leeds (formerly West Yorkshire and the Dales), since 2014; *b* 30 March 1946; *s* of late George William Golding and Gladys Joyce Golding (*née* Henstridge); *m* 1968, Anne Reynolds; one *s* one *d. Educ:* HMS Conway Merchant Navy Cadet Sch.; Brasted Place Coll.; Lincoln Theol Coll. Navigating Officer, MN, and Lieut (X) RNR, 1963–69; ordained deacon 1974, priest 1975; Curate, St Cuthbert, Wilton, 1974–77; Chaplain, Royal Navy, 1977–2002; Chaplain of the Fleet, 1997–98; Archdeacon for RN and Principal Anglican Chaplain (Naval), 1998–2002; Dir Gen., Naval Chaplaincy Service and Chaplain of the Fleet, 2000–02. QHC 1997–2002; Hon. Canon, Gibraltar Cathedral, 1998–2002. Diocese of Ripon and Leeds: Hon. Priest, 2003–14; Convenor, Ministerial Rev. Scheme, 2003–08; Advr, Non-Stipendiary Ministry, 2008–11; Associate Minister, E Richmond Team Ministry, 2011–14; Hon. Chaplain to High Sheriff, of Co. Durham, 2014–15, of N Yorks, 2017–18. Lay Advr, N Yorks Multi Agency Public Protection Arrangements, 2005–12. Mem., Gen. Council, Royal Nat. Mission to Deep-Sea Fishermen, 2007–. *Address:* Arlanza, Hornby Road, Appleton Wiske, Northallerton DL6 2AF. *T:* (01609) 881185.

**GOLDING, Terence Edward,** OBE 1992; FCA; Chief Executive, National Exhibition Centre, Birmingham, 1978–95; Deputy Chairman, Earls Court and Olympia Ltd, 1995–99; *b* 7 April 1932; *s* of Sydney Richard Golding and Elsie Golding; *m* 1955, Sheila Jean (*née* Francis); one *s* one *d. Educ:* Harrow County Grammar Sch. FCA 1967. Earls Court Ltd (Exhibition Hall Proprietors): Chief Accountant, 1960; Co. Sec., 1965; Financial Dir, 1972; Financial Dir, Olympia Ltd, and Earls Court & Olympia Ltd, 1973; Commercial Dir, Earls Court & Olympia Group of Cos, 1975; Chief Exec., Internat. Convention Centre, Birmingham, 1990–95; Dir, Alexandra Palace Trading Ltd, 2000–10; Chm., Expocentric plc, 2000–02. Member: Exhibition Liaison Cttee, 1979–97; Nat. Assoc. of Exhibn Hallowners, 1988–97. Director: British Exhibitions Promotion Council, 1981–83; Birmingham Convention and Visitor Bureau, 1981–93; Heart of England Tourist Bd, 1984–91; Central England, TEC, 1990–92; Birmingham Marketing Partnership, 1993–95; Chm., Exhibn Industry Fedn, 1995–97; Exhibition Venues Assoc., 1997–99. Hon. Mem. Council, Birmingham Chamber of Industry and Commerce, 1990–95. Midlander of the Year, 1990. *Recreation:* following sport. *Address:* 11 East Close, Barton on Sea, Hants BH25 7QE. *T:* (01425) 613503.

**GOLDINGAY, Rev. Prof. John Edgar,** PhD; Professor of Old Testament Studies, Fuller Theological Seminary, Pasadena, since 1997; *b* 20 June 1942; *s* of Edgar Charles and Ada Irene Goldingay; *m* 1st, 1967, Ann Elizabeth Wilson (*d* 2009); two *s*; 2nd, 2010, Kathleen Susan Scott. *Educ:* King Edward's School, Birmingham; Keble Coll., Oxford (BA); Nottingham University (PhD). Ordained deacon 1966, priest 1967; Asst Curate, Christ Church, Finchley, 1966–69; St John's College, Nottingham: Lectr, 1970–75; Dir of Acad. Studies, 1976–79; Registrar, 1979–85; Vice-Principal, 1985–88; Principal, 1988–97. DD Lambeth, 1997. *Publications:* Songs from a Strange Land, 1978; Approaches to Old Testament Interpretation, 1981; Theological Diversity and the Authority of the Old Testament, 1987; Daniel, 1989; (ed) Signs, Wonders and Healing, 1989; Models for Scripture, 1994; Models for the Interpretation of Scripture, 1995; (ed) Atonement Today, 1995; After Eating the Apricot, 1996; To The Usual Suspects, 1998; Men Behaving Badly, 2000; Isaiah, 2001; Walk On, 2002; Old Testament Theology, vol. 1, 2003, vol. 2, 2006, vol. 3, 2009; The Message of Isaiah 40–55, 2005; Isaiah 40–55, 2 vols, 2006; Psalms vol. 1, 2006, vol. 2, 2007, vol. 3, 2008; (ed) Uprooting and Planting, 2007; (with P. J. Scalise) Minor Prophets II, 2009; Genesis, 2 vols, 2010; Exodus and Leviticus, 2010; Numbers and Deuteronomy, 2010; Key Questions about Christian Faith, 2010; Joshua, Judges and Ruth, 2011; 1 and 2 Samuel, 2011; Remembering Ann, 2011; 1 and 2 Kings, 2011; Key Questions about Interpretation, 2011; 1 and 2 Chronicles, 2012; Ezra, Nehemiah, and Esther, 2012; Job, 2013; Isaiah 56–66, 2013; Psalms Part 1, 2013; Psalms Part 2, 2014; The Theology of the Book of Isaiah, 2014; Isaiah, 2015; Proverbs, Ecclesiastes, and Song of Songs, 2014; Do We Need the New Testament?, 2015; Jeremiah, 2015; An Introduction to the Old Testament, 2015; Lamentations and Ezekiel, 2016; Daniel and the Twelve Prophets, 2016; Biblical Theology, 2016; Reading Jesus's Bible, 2017; The Bible for Everyone, 2018; Old Testament Ethics, 2019. *Address:* 4 Mill Stream House, Norfolk Street, Oxford OX1 1EB. *E:* johngold@fuller.edu.

**GOLDINGHAM, Claire Louise Margaret W.;** *see* Wills-Goldingham.

**GOLDMAN, Antony John,** CB 1995; Director General, Civil Aviation, Department of the Environment, Transport and the Regions, 1996–99; *b* 28 Feb. 1940; *s* of Sir Samuel Goldman, KCB and step *s* of late Patricia Goldman (*née* Hodges); *m* 1964, Anne Rosemary Lane; three *s. Educ:* Marlborough College; Peterhouse, Cambridge (BA). International Computers Ltd, 1961–73; entered Civil Service, DoE, 1973; Private Sec. to Sec. of State for Transport, 1976–78; Asst Sec., 1977; seconded to HM Treasury, 1981–83; Under Sec., 1984. Non-exec. Dir, Hugh Baird & Sons, 1985–86. Chm., Eur. Air Traffic Control Harmonisation and Integration Prog., 1994–99; Vice-Pres., Eur. Civil Aviation Conf., 1997–99; Pres., Eurocontrol Council, 1998–99. Special Advr to H of L Select Cttee on Europe, 2001. Trustee, Watts Gall., 2004–17. Hon. CRAeS 1997. Eur. Regl Airlines Award, 1993. *Recreations:* music, writing doggerel.

**GOLDMAN, Prof. Lawrence Neil,** PhD; FRHistS; Professor of History, Institute of Historical Research, School of Advanced Study, University of London, since 2014 (Director, 2014–17); Senior Research Fellow, St Peter's College, Oxford, since 2014; *b* 17 June 1957; *s* of Basil Benjamin Goldman and Hilda Hannah Goldman (*née* Schmerkin); *m* 1985, Madeleine Jean McDonald; two *s* one *d. Educ:* Haberdashers' Aske's Sch., Elstree; Jesus Coll., Cambridge (BA 1979); Trinity Coll., Cambridge (PhD 2003); Yale Univ. FRHistS 2002. Harkness Fellow, Commonwealth Fund of NY, 1979–80; Res. Fellow, Trinity Coll., Cambridge, 1982–85; Lectr in Hist. and Politics, Dept for Continuing Educn, Univ. of Oxford, 1985–90; Fellow and Tutor in Modern History, St Peter's Coll., Oxford, 1990–2014. Dist. Fellow, Rothermere Amer. Inst., Univ. of Oxford, 2014–. Vis. Prof., Univ. of S Carolina, 1994; Vis. Fellow, Humanities Res. Centre, 2006, Dept of Hist., 2012, ANU. Assessor, Univ. of Oxford, 2000–01; External Mem., Cambridge History Faculty review, 2011. Member: Adv. Council, Warburg Inst., 2014–17; Council, N Amer. Conf. on British Studies, 2014–17. Pres., Thames and Solent Dist, WEA, 2002–04. Governor: NLCS, 2006–11; Haberdashers' Aske's Schs, Elstree, 2011–. Hon. Fellow, Historical Assoc., 2015–. Editor: Oxford Dictionary of National Biography, 2004–14; Oxford Historical Monographs, 2009–14; Historical Research, 2014–17. *Publications:* (ed) The Blind Victorian: Henry Fawcett and British Liberalism, 1989; Dons and Workers: Oxford and adult education since 1850, 1995; Science, Reform and Politics in Victorian Britain: the Social Science Association 1857–1886, 2002; (ed with P. Ghosh) Politics and Culture in Victorian Britain: essays in memory of Colin Matthew, 2006; (ed) The Federalist, 2008; The Life of R. H. Tawney: socialism and history, 2013; (ed with J. Pellew) Dethroning Historical Reputations: universities, museums and the commemoration of benefactors, 2018; (ed) Welfare and Social Policy in Britain since 1870, 2019; contribs to learned jls incl. English Histl Rev., Past and Present, Histl Jl. *Recreations:* walking, swimming, gardening, cricket, Suffolk. *Address:* Gun Hill House, Gun Hill, Southwold, Suffolk IP18 6HF. *T:* (01502) 724715. *E:* lawrence.goldman@spc.ox.ac.uk; Flat 316, The Latitude, 130 Clapham Common Southside, SW9 9DX. *T:* (020) 8772 8305. *Club:* Southwold Sailors' Reading Room.

**GOLDMARK, Peter Carl,** Jr; Director, Climate and Air Program, Environmental Defense, 2003–10; independent consultant and columnist, 2011–18; *b* 2 Dec. 1940; *m* 1964, Aliette Misson; three *d. Educ:* Harvard Univ. (BA Govt *magna cum laude* with Highest Hons 1962; Phi Beta Kappa). History teacher, Putney Sch., Vermont, 1962–64; US Office of Econ. Opportunity, Washington, 1965–66; City of New York: Exec. Asst to Dir of Budget, 1966–68; Asst Budget Dir for Prog. Planning and Analysis, 1968–70; Exec. Asst to Mayor and COS, 1970–71; Sec. of Human Services, Commonwealth of Massachusetts, 1971–74; Dir of Budget, State of NY, 1975–77; Exec. Dir, Port Authy of NY and NJ, 1977–85; Sen. Vice Pres., Times Mirror Co., 1985–88; Pres., Rockefeller Foundn, 1988–97; Chm. and CEO, Internat. Herald Tribune, 1998–2003. Hon. Dr: New Sch., NY; Pratt Inst., NY. Chevalier, Légion d'Honneur (France), 2003.

**GOLDREIN, Iain Saville;** QC 1997; a Recorder, since 1999; a Deputy High Court Judge, since 2008; Panel Deemster, Isle of Man, since 2012; *b* 10 Aug. 1952; *s* of Neville Clive Goldrein, *qv*; *m* 1980, Margaret de Haas, *qv*; one *s* one *d. Educ:* Merchant Taylors' Sch.,

Crosby; RAF Flying Scholarship; Hebrew Univ., Jerusalem; Pembroke Coll., Cambridge (exhibnr, Ziegler Prize for Law; Cambridge Squire Schol. for Law). Called to the Bar, Inner Temple, 1975 (Duke of Edinburgh Scholarship); Dep. Head, No 7 Harrington Street Chambers, Liverpool, 2003–12 (Jt Hd, 1989–2003); Asst Recorder, 1995–99. Mem., Mental Health Review Tribunal, 1999–2002. Vis. Prof., Nottingham Law Sch., 1991 (Hon. Prof., 2017); Mem., Internat. Adv. Bd, Centre for Islamic Finance, 2014–, Vis. Prof. in Law and Genetics, 2016–, Bolton Univ. Mediator: Acad. of Experts, 1992 (Companion, 1992); Commercial, 2009, Family, 2010, ADR Gp. Member: Council, Internat. Inst. of Experts, Hong Kong, 2010–; Adv. Bd, Centre for Opposition Studies, 2012–; Adv. Bd, Belief in Mediation and Arbitration, 2012–; Steering Bd and Trustee, Cornerstone Foundn for vulnerable children, Liverpool CC, 2015– (Chair, 2017–); Bd of Deputies of British Jews, 2018–. Mayoral Comr for City of Liverpool (Envmtl Sustainability), 2013–15. Hon. Advr, Faith in the Future. FRSA 1992. Jt Ed.-in-Chief, Genetics Law Monitor, 2000–02; Ed., In Brief, 2006–11; Adv. Ed., Hong Kong White Book, 2012, 2015; Internat. Adv. Ed., Malaysian White Book, 2013–18; Consulting Ed., Commercial Litigation in Hong Kong: a practical guide, 2013. Hon. DLaws Bolton, 2014. *Publications:* Personal Injury Litigation: practice and precedents, 1985; (with Clyde & Co.) Ship Sale and Purchase: law and technique 1985, 6th edn (with M. Hannaford and P. Turner) 2012; (with K. H. P. Wilkinson) Commercial Litigation: pre-emptive remedies, 1987, 4th edn (with Sir Robin Jacob and P. M. Kershaw) 2003, internat. edn (with sub-editors) 2005, 2nd internat. edn 2011; with Sir J. Jacob: (ed) Bullen and Leake and Jacob's Precedents of Pleadings, 13th edn 1990; Pleadings, Principles and Practice, 1990; (ed jtly) Insurance Disputes (loose-leaf), 1999–2003, hardback edn 2004, 3rd edn (with sub-editors) 2012; (ed jtly) Civil Court Practice, 1999–2013; (jtly) Human Rights and Judicial Review: case studies in context, 2001; (supervisory ed.) Hong Kong Bullen and Leake and Jacob's Precedents of Pleadings, 2013; with M. de Haas: Property Distribution on Divorce, 1983, 2nd edn 1985; Butterworths Personal Injury Litigation Service, 1988–; Structured Settlements, 1993, 2nd edn 1997; Medical Negligence: cost effective case management, 1997; (also ed jtly) Personal Injury Major Claims Handling: cost effective case management, 2000; (with L. J. Ryder) Child Case Management Practice, 2009, 2nd edn (with sub-editors) 2012, 3rd edn 2018; Media Access to the Family Courts, 2009; (ed jtly) Hong Kong Mediation Handbook, 2010; Privacy Injunctions and the Media: a practice manual, 2012. *Recreations:* Classical Hebrew, history, English legal history, new ideas, anything aeronautical or nautical, classical motor vehicles. *Address:* 7 Harrington Street Chambers, Liverpool L2 9YH. *T:* (0151) 242 0707.

**GOLDREIN, Margaret Ruth;** *see* de Haas, M. R.

**GOLDREIN, Neville Clive,** CBE 1991; Senior Partner, Goldrein & Co., 1953–85; Consultant, Deacon Goldrein Green, Solicitors, 1985–92; *b* 28 Aug. 1924; *s* of Saville and Nina Goldrein; *m* 1949, Dr Sonia Sumner, MB, BS Dunelm (*d* 2016); one *s* one *d. Educ:* Hymers Coll., Hull; Pembroke Coll., Cambridge (MA). Served Army: commnd E Yorks Regt; served East Africa Comd (Captain). Admitted Solicitor of the Supreme Court, 1949; former Dep. Circuit Judge. Mem., Crosby Bor. Council, 1957–71; Mayor of Crosby, 1966–67, Dep. Mayor, 1967–68; Mem., Lancs CC, 1965–74; Merseyside County Council: Mem., 1973–86; Dep. Leader, Cons. Gp, 1974–77; Vice-Chm. of Council, 1977–80; Leader, 1980–81; Leader, Cons. Gp, 1981–86. Chm., Crosby Constituency Cons. Assoc., 1986–89. Area Vice-Pres., Sefton, St John Ambulance, 1980–87 (Chm., S Sefton Div., 1975–87); Member: NW Econ. Planning Council, 1966–72; Bd of Deputies of British Jews, 1966–85, 1992–2001; Council, Liverpool Univ., 1977–81; Council, Merseyside Chamber of Commerce, 1987 (Chairman: Envmt and Energy Cttee, 1993–2006; Rivers Cttee, 1990–93; Police Liaison Cttee, 1994–2003; Mem., Arts and Culture Cttee, 2006; Hon. Life Mem., 2006–); Regl Affairs Cttee, British Assoc. of Chambers of Commerce, 1993–97. Director: Merseyside Economic Develt Co. Ltd, 1981–87; Merseyside Waste Derived Fuels Ltd, 1983–86. Vice-Pres., Crosby Mencap, 1967–2011; Chm., Crosby Hall Residential Trust Appeal, 1989–91. Chm., Liverpool Royal Court Theatre Foundn, 1994–2005; Trustee, Liverpool Inst. for Performing Arts, 2008 (Mem. Council, 2005–08). Governor, Merchant Taylors' Sch., Crosby, 1965–74. *Publications:* Life is Too Serious to be Taken Seriously (autobiog.), 2010. *Recreations:* videography, photography, music, freelance journalism, travel.
*See also* I. S. Goldrein.

**GOLDRING, Jeremy Edward;** QC 2013; *b* London, 22 April 1971; *s* of Rt Hon. Sir John Bernard Goldring, *qv* and Wendy Margaret Lancaster Goldring, *qv*; *m* 1997, Elizabeth Geren; one *d. Educ:* Oakham Sch.; Pembroke Coll., Oxford (BA, MA); Yale Univ. (MA; Henry Fellow). Called to the Bar, Lincoln's Inn, 1996; in practice as barrister, 1996–. *Recreations:* ski-ing, books. *Address:* 3–4 South Square, Gray's Inn, WC1R 5HP. *T:* (020) 7696 9900, *Fax:* (020) 7696 9911.

**GOLDRING, Rt Hon. Sir John (Bernard),** Kt 1999; PC 2008; a Lord Justice of Appeal, 2008–14; Senior Presiding Judge of England and Wales, 2010–12 (Deputy Senior Presiding Judge, 2008–09); President, Court of Appeal, Cayman Islands, since 2016; *b* 9 Nov. 1944; *s* of Joseph and Marianne Goldring; *m* 1970, Wendy Margaret Lancaster Bennett (see W. M. L. Goldring); two *s. Educ:* Wyggeston Grammar Sch.; Exeter Univ. (LLB). Called to the Bar, Lincoln's Inn, 1969, Bencher, 1996 (Treas., 2016–17). QC 1987; a Recorder, 1987–99; a Dep. Sen. Judge, Sovereign Base Areas, Cyprus, 1991–99; a Dep. High Court Judge, 1996–99; a Judge of the Courts of Appeal of Jersey and Guernsey, 1998–99; a Judge of the High Court of Justice, QBD, 1999–2008; a Presiding Judge, Midland Circuit, 2002–05; a Judge, Court of Appeal, Gibraltar, 2016. Asst Dep. Coroner for Hillsborough Inquests, 2012–16. Comr, Judicial Appts Commn, 2006–08. Intelligence Services Comr, 2017; Dep. Investigatory Powers Comr, 2017–. Hon. LLD: Leicester, 2012; Exeter, 2015. *Recreations:* gardening, ski-ing. *Address:* Honourable Society of Lincoln's Inn, The Treasury Office, Lincoln's Inn, WC2A 3TL. *Club:* Athenæum.
*See also* J. E. Goldring.

**GOLDRING, Mark Ian,** CBE 2008; Chief Executive, Oxfam GB, 2013–19; *b* 8 March 1957; *s* of Stephen and Pamela Goldring; *m* 1989, Rachel Carnegie; one *s* one *d. Educ:* Keble Coll., Oxford (BA Law 1979); LSE (MSc Social Policy and Planning in Developing Countries 1989). VSO Volunteer Teacher, Sarawak, 1979–81; Legal Researcher, Linklaters & Paines, 1982; Field Officer, Caribbean, 1983–85, Field Dir, Bhutan, 1985–88, VSO; UNDP Asst Rep., 1990–91, Oxfam Country Rep., 1991–94, Bangladesh; DFID Social Develt Advr, Pacific, 1994–95; VSO Overseas Dir, 1995–99; Chief Executive: VSO, 1999–2008; Mencap, 2008–13. Chairman: Revolving Doors Agency, 2002–05; Learning Disability Coalition, 2010–12; British Overseas Aid Gp, 2016–18; Steering Cttee for Humanitarian Response, 2018–19; Member: Nat. Programme Bd, DoH, 2009–13; NHS Futures Forum, 2011–12; Foreign Sec.'s Human Rights Adv. Gp, 2013–15; Marks and Spencer Sustainability Adv. Bd, 2013–19; Inter Agency Steering Cttee, 2017–19; Advr, Winterbourne View Rev. Team, 2011–12. Trustee: Accenture Develt Partnership, 2002–08; African Med. and Res. Foundn UK, 2008–13 (Vice-Chm., 2009–13); Bangladesh Rural Advancement Cttee (BRAC), 2009–13; Humanitarian Leadership Acad., 2015–18. Chm., Thames Ditton Island (Maintenance and Service) Ltd, 2012–14. *Recreations:* cycling, Rugby, river life. *E:* mark.goldring@yahoo.co.uk.

**GOLDRING, Mary Sheila,** OBE 1987; economist; presenter, Goldring Audit, Channel 4, 1992, 1993, 1994, 1995. *Educ:* Our Lady's Priory, Sussex; Lady Margaret Hall, Oxford (PPE). Air and Science correspondent, 1949–74, Business editor, 1966–74, Economist Newspaper; economist and broadcaster, 1974–; *television:* presenter: Analysis, BBC, 1977–87; Answering Back, Channel 4 interviews, 1989–91. Trustee, Science Museum, 1987–97. Fawley Foundn Lect., 1992. CRAeS 1995. Hon. DLitt UWE, 1994. Blue Circle Award for industrial journalism, 1979; Sony Radio Award for best current affairs programme (Analysis: Post-Recession Britain), 1985; Industrial Journalist Award, Industrial Soc., 1985; Outstanding Personal Contribution to Radio, Broadcasting Press Guild, 1986; Harold Wincott Award for Broadcasting, 1991; Industrial Journalist of the Year, Industrial Soc. and BP, 1991, 1995. *Publications:* Economics of Atomic Energy, 1957. *Recreation:* shopping.

**GOLDRING, Wendy Margaret Lancaster, (Lady Goldring);** Vice Lord-Lieutenant of Rutland, 2006–18; *b* 10 July 1946; *d* of Ralph and Margaret Bennett; *m* 1970, John Bernard Goldring (*see* Rt Hon. Sir J. B. Goldring); two *s. Educ:* Farrington's Sch., Chislehurst; Univ. of Exeter (BA). Mem., Bd of Visitors, HMP Ashwell, 1984–92. Member: E Midlands Cttee, Nat. Lottery Charities Bd, 1995–99; County Bd, Prince's Trust, 2002–09. Trustee, Uppingham Sch., 2000–09. Pres., League of Friends, Rutland Meml Hosp., 2000–; Vice-Chm., Voluntary Action Rutland, 2001–12. JP Rutland, 1984–2012 (Chm. Bench, 1996–99); High Sheriff, 1999–2000, DL 2005, Rutland. *Recreations:* travel, gardening, history of art and architecture, reading. *Address:* c/o Lieutenancy Office, Catmose, Oakham, Rutland LE15 6HP.
*See also* J. E. Goldring.

**GOLDSACK, His Honour Alan Raymond;** QC 1990; a Circuit Judge, 1994–2013; a Senior Circuit Judge, 2002–13; *b* 13 June 1947; *s* of Raymond Frederick Goldsack, MBE and Mildred Agnes Goldsack (*née* Jones); *m* 1971, Christine Marion Clarke; three *s* one *d. Educ:* Hastings Grammar School; Leicester Univ. (LLB). Called to the Bar, Gray's Inn, 1970, Bencher, 2003; a Recorder, 1988–94. Hon. Recorder, Sheffield, 2002–13. Mem., Parole Bd, 2009–19. DL S Yorks, 2009–17. *Recreations:* gardening, walking. *Address:* 21 Pollard Way, St Elphin's Park, Darley Dale, Matlock DE4 2RU.

**GOLDSCHMIED, Marco Lorenzo Sinnott,** PPRIBA; Chairman, Thames Wharf Studios Ltd, 1984–2010; Managing Director, Rogers Architects Ltd, 1984–2004; Director, SPARK, 2011–16; *b* 28 March 1944; *s* of Guido Rodolfo Goldschmied and Elinor Violet (*née* Sinnott); *m* 1969, Andrea Halvorsen; four *s* one *d. Educ:* Architectural Assoc. (AA Dip. 1969); Reading Univ. (MSc 1986). RIBA 1971. Associate Partner, Piano & Rogers, 1971–77; Founder Partner, Rogers Partnership, 1977–84; Vice-Pres., Richard Rogers Japan KK, 1988–2004. Teacher: AA, 1971; Glasgow Sch. of Art, 1999; Lectr, RIBA, 1981–99 (Pres., 1999–2001). Mem., Architects Registration Bd, 1997–2000 (Mem., European Adv. Gp, 1998–2000); Trustee, Architectural Assoc., 1991–93; Chm., European Awards, 1996–99, Educn Review, 1998–99, C4 Stirling Prize, 2001, Chm., S and SE regions Awards, 2012–, RIBA. Royal Academy Summer Exhibitor, 2000. *Projects* include: Lloyd's HQ, City of London, 1978 (Civic Trust Award, 1987; RIBA Award, 1988); Fleetguard Manufg and Distribn Centre, Quimper, France, 1979–81; Inmos Microprocessor Factory, Newport, 1982 (British Steel Design Award, 1982; RIBA Award, 1983); PA Technology Res. Centre, Princeton, 1983; Linn-Sondek HQ, Glasgow, 1985 (RIBA Award); Billingsgate Mkt Restoration and Conversion, 1988 (Civic Trust Award, 1989); Reuters Computer Centre, London, 1988 (RIBA Award, 1990); Pumping Station, Victoria Docks, 1989; Terminal 5, Heathrow, 1990 (RIBA Award 2007); Channel 4 HQ, 1994 (RIBA Award, and RFAC Award, 1995); European Court of Human Rights, Strasbourg, 1995; Learning Resource Centre, Thames Valley Univ., 1996 (RIBA Award, 1998); Europier Passenger Terminal, Heathrow, 1996 (RIBA Award, and British Steel Award, 1997); Bordeaux Law Courts, 1998; Lloyd's Register of Shipping HQ, 1999; Daiwa Europe Office, 1999; 88 Wood Street, London, 1999 (RIBA Award, 2000); Millennium Dome, Greenwich, 1999; Offices and Laboratories, Gifu, Japan, 1999; Montevetro Apartments, London (RIBA Award, 2000); Nat. Assembly of Wales, Cardiff, 2001; 16 Ha Masterplan, News Internat., 2004; The Albany Th., Deptford. Chair: Appeal for Care of Victims of Torture, Med. Foundn, 1999–2001; Leadership Gp, Amnesty Internat., 2003–05; Trustee, Marco Goldschmied Foundn, 1998– (Sponsor: Stephen Lawrence RIBA Award, 1998–; RIBA Stirling Prize, 2009). Patron, Stephen Lawrence Trust, 2004–. TV and radio interviews. Hon. Mem., AIA. Hon. FRSA. *Publications:* (jtly) Architecture 98, 1998; articles in jls. *Recreations:* twentieth century European history, etymology, ski-ing.

**GOLDSMITH,** family name of **Baron Goldsmith.**

**GOLDSMITH,** Baron *cr* 1999 (Life Peer), of Allerton in the county of Merseyside; **Peter Henry Goldsmith;** PC 2002; QC 1987; Chair of European and Asian Litigation (formerly European Chair of Litigation), since 2007, and Co-Managing Partner, since 2014, Debevoise & Plimpton LLP; *b* 5 Jan. 1950; *s* of late Sydney Elland Goldsmith, solicitor, and of Myra Nurick; *m* 1974, Joy; three *s* one *d. Educ:* Quarry Bank High Sch., Liverpool; Gonville and Caius Coll., Cambridge (Sen. Schol., Tapp Postgrad. Schol., Schuldham Plate, 1968–71; MA); UCL (LLM 1972; Fellow 2002). Called to the Bar, Gray's Inn (Birkenhead Schol.), 1972, Bencher, 1994; Avocat, Barreau de Paris, 1997; a Jun. Counsel to the Crown, Common Law, 1985–87; a Recorder, 1989–; HM Attorney Gen., 2001–07. Chairman: Bar Council, 1995 (Chairman: Legal Services Cttee, 1992–94; Internat. Relations Cttee, 1996); Bar Pro Bono Unit, 1996–2001 (Pres., 2001–); Financial Reporting Review Panel, 1997–99 (Mem., 1995–97); Mem. Council, 1996–2001, Co-Chm., Human Rights Inst., 1998–2001, Internat. Bar Assoc. Personal Rep. of Prime Minister to Convention to draft EU Charter of Fundamental Rights, 1999–2000. Member: Jt Human Rights Select Cttee, 2001; Constitution Select Cttee, 2011–15. Member: Council, Public Concern at Work, 1995–2001; Exec. Cttee, GB-China Centre, 1997–2001; Adv. Bd, Cambridge Centre for Commercial and Corporate Law, 1998–; Council, Internat. Law Section, ABA, 2008–; Bd, Rule of Law Initiative, 2010–; Council, Hong Kong Internat. Arbitration Centre, 2012– (Vice-Chm., 2013–). Chm., Access to Justice Foundn, 2009–. Non-exec. Dir, Westfield Gp, 2008–17. Fellow, American Law Inst., 1997. Hon. LLD Univ. of Law, 2014. *Publications:* (contrib.) Common Law, Common Bond; articles in nat., internat. and legal press and jls. *Address:* House of Lords, SW1A 0PW; Debevoise & Plimpton LLP, 65 Gresham Street, EC2V 7NQ.

**GOLDSMITH, Alexander Benedict Hayum;** Director: Cavamont Holdings (formerly Cavamont Investment Advisers) Ltd, since 1998; Yetro Ltd, since 2001; *b* 10 Dec. 1960; *s* of late Edward René David Goldsmith and of Gillian Marion (*née* Pretty); *m* 1990, Louisa Kate Slack; two *s* one *d. Educ:* Westminster Sch.; Jesus Coll., Cambridge (MA Social Anthropol. 1986). Researcher and fundraiser for Survival Internat., 1986; Publisher and Editor, Envmt Digest, 1987–90; Editor: Geographical Magazine, 1991–94; People and Places in Peril series, 1995; Green Futures mag., 1996–98; Dir, Book Runner Ltd, 1999–2003. Chm., Weeding Technologies Ltd, 2011–13. Trustee: Ecology Trust, 2004–06; Cancer Prevention and Educn Soc. (formerly Cancer Prevention Soc.), 2000–05. FRGS 2002. *Recreations:* sailing, walking, ski-ing. *Clubs:* Groucho; Travellers (Paris).

**GOLDSMITH, Alexander Kinglake, (Alick);** HM Diplomatic Service, retired; *b* 16 Jan. 1938; *s* of Maj.-Gen. Robert Frederick Kinglake Goldsmith, CB, CBE and Brenda (*née* Bartlett); *m* 1971, Deirdre Stafford; one *s* one *d*. *Educ:* Sherborne; Trinity Coll., Oxford (MA Modern History). National Service, 1956–58 (DCLI and Queen's Own Nigeria Regt). Asst Principal, CRO, 1961; Hindi student, SOAS, 1962; Third Sec., New Delhi, 1963; FCO, 1967; First Sec. (Inf.), Wellington, NZ, 1971; FCO, 1975; Head of Chancery, E Berlin, 1978; FCO, 1980; Hd of Commonwealth Co-ordination Dept, FCO, 1982; seconded to Hong Kong Govt, 1984; Consul-Gen., Hamburg, 1986–90. Dir, Export Gp for the Constructional Industries, 1991–2001. *Recreations:* walking, swimming. *Address:* c/o Lloyds Bank, Butler Place, SW1H 0PR. *Club:* Royal Automobile.

**GOLDSMITH, Benjamin James;** Founding Partner, WHEB Asset Management, since 2002; Founder, Menhaden Capital Plc, 2015; Chief Executive Officer, Menhaden Capital Management LLP, since 2015; *b* London, 28 Oct. 1980; *s* of late Sir James Michael Goldsmith and of Lady Annabel Goldsmith (formerly Lady Annabel Vane Tempest Stewart); *m* 1st, 2003, Kate Emma Rothschild (marr. diss. 2013); two *s* (one *d* decd); 2nd, 2014, Jemima, *d* of Edward David Brynmor Jones, *qv*. *Educ:* Eton. Non-exec. Dir, DEFRA, 2018–. Chm., Conservative Envmt Network, 2013–; Member, Advisory Board: JMG Foundn; Envmtl Funders Network. Trustee, Children's Investment Fund Foundn. *Recreations:* cricket, the natural world, backgammon. *Address:* 14 Curzon Street, W1J 5HN. *E:* ben.goldsmith@menhaden.com. *Clubs:* Brooks's, 5 Hertford Street, Bath and Racquets.
*See also* F. Z. R. Goldsmith.

**GOLDSMITH, Rt Rev. Dr Christopher David;** Director, Ministry Division, Archbishops' Council, since 2019; *b* 1954; *m* Ellen. *Educ:* Dartford Grammar Sch.; York Univ. (BA 1976; DPhil 1979); N Thames Ministerial Trng Course. Worked in oil and gas industry; ordained deacon, 2000, priest, 2001; non-stipendiary Minister, Pitsea with Nevendon, Essex, 2000–04; Vicar, Christ Church, Warley and St Mary the Virgin, Gt Warley, Essex, 2004–13; Warden of the Readers, Dio. of Truro, 2013–19; Bishop Suffragan of St Germans, 2013–19. *Address:* Church House, Great Smith Street, SW1P 3AZ.

**GOLDSMITH, Frank Zacharias Robin, (Zac);** MP (C) Richmond Park, 2010–Oct. 2016 and since 2017; Minister of State, Department for Environment, Food and Rural Affairs and Department for International Development, since 2019; *b* Westminster, 20 Jan. 1975; *s* of late Sir James Michael Goldsmith and of Lady Annabel Goldsmith (formerly Lady Annabel Vane Tempest Stewart); *m* 1st, 1999, Sheherazade Ventura-Bentley (marr. diss. 2012); one *s* two *d*; 2nd, 2013, Alice Miranda Rothschild; one *s* two *d*. *Educ:* Hawtreys; Eton Coll.; Internat. Honours Programme, Boston. Worked with Redefining Progress, San Francisco, 1994–95; joined Internat. Soc. for Ecology and Culture, 1995–97, based in Calif, Bristol and Ladakh, India (ran tourist educn prog. in Ladakh for part of time), later Assoc. Dir; Ed., 1997–2007, Dir, 2007–12, The Ecologist mag. Resigned as MP (C) Richmond Park, Oct. 2016; contested (Ind) same seat, Dec. 2016. Parly Under-Sec. of State, DEFRA and DFID, 2019. Mem., Envmtl Audit Cttee, 2010–16, 2017–. Co-founder, FARM, 2002. Dir, Ecosystems Ltd. Mem. Adv. Bd, JMG Foundn; Trustee: Royal Parks Foundn; Rainforest Foundn UK; Aspinall Foundn; Countryside Restoration Trust; Pres., Nat. Gardens Scheme, 2006–10. Speeches at numerous venues incl. Schumacher Meml Lects, Oxford Union, colls, schs and Think Tanks in UK. (Jtly) Beacon Prize for Young Philanthropist of the Year, 2003; Internat. Envmtl Leadership Award, Global Green USA, 2004. *Publications:* The Constant Economy: how to create a stable society, 2009; contrib. newspapers incl. The Times, Sunday Times, Daily Mail, Mail on Sunday, Independent, Guardian, Observer, Standard, Express, Daily Telegraph, Tribune and many regl newspapers; over 50 articles for The Ecologist; articles for other magazines incl. Country Life (contrib. and ed special edn, Dec. 2002), Big Issue, New Statesman, Spectator, Week, Global Agenda 2003, Geographical, Tatler and Vanity Fair. *Address:* House of Commons, SW1A 0AA. *Club:* Travellers.
*See also* B. J. Goldsmith.

**GOLDSMITH, Harvey Anthony,** CBE 1996; Managing Director, Artist Promotion Management (formerly Artiste Management Productions) Ltd, since 1973; *b* 4 March 1946; *s* of Sydney and Minnie Goldsmith; *m* 1971, Diana Gorman; one *s*. *Educ:* Christ's Coll.; Brighton Coll. of Technol. Partner, Big O Posters, 1966–67; organised first free open-air concert in Parliament Hill Fields, 1968; (with Michael Alfandary) opened Round House, Camden Town, 1968; Crystal Palace Gdn Party series of concerts, 1969–72; merged with John Smith Entertainments, 1970; formed Harvey Goldsmith Entertainments (rock tours promotions co.), 1976; acquired Allied Entertainments Gp (rock concert promotions co.), 1984; (with Mark McCormack) formed Classical Productions (to produce operas), 1986; Man. Dir, TBA Entertainment Corp. (Europe) Ltd, 2000–04. Promoter and producer of pop, rock and classical musical events, including: *concerts:* Bruce Springsteen; The Rolling Stones; Elton John; The Who; Pink Floyd; Led Zeppelin reunion, 2007; *opera:* Aida, 1698 and 1998, Carmen, 1989, Tosca, 1991, Earls Court; Pavarotti at Wembley, 1986; Pavarotti in the Park, 1991; The Three Tenors, 1996; Pavarotti World Tour, 2005; Salute Petra: Pavarotti tribute concert, 2008. Producer: Live Aid, 1985; Net Aid, 2000; Live 8, 2005; Executive Producer: Nokia New Year's Eve, 2006; Live Earth - SOS, 2007. Manager, Jeff Beck, 2008–13. Chm., Ignition Internat., 2006–09. Dir, British Red Cross Events Ltd, 2000–03; Member: London Tourist Bd, 1994–2002 (Dir, 1993–2003); Prague Heritage Fund, 1994–2002; Mayor's Adv. Gp on Tourism, 2003. Chairman: Nat. Music Fest., 1991; Concert Promoters' Bd, 1994–99; Foundn and Bd, British Music Experience, 2007–; Editorial Intelligence, 2016–; Harley House, 2017–; YMU Gp, 2018–; Nvisible, 2019–; Co-Chm., President's Club, 1994–2014; Vice-Chm., Action Mgt Bd, Prince's Trust, 1993–2000; Trustee: Band Aid, 1985–; Live Aid, 1985–; Royal Opera House, 1995–2001; Vice-President: REACT, 1989–; Music Users' Council, 1994–; Mem., Communications Panel, BRCS, 1992–. Patron, Teenage Cancer Trust, 2006–. Hon. DArts Brighton, 2012. Freedom, City of London, 2011. Lifetime Achievement Award, Nat. Outdoor Events Assoc., 2009; Internat. Music Person of the Year, Musexpo, 2010. Chevalier des Arts et Lettres (France), 2006. *Recreation:* golf. *T:* (020) 7224 1992. *Clubs:* Royal Automobile, Home House; Century (NY); Vale de Lobo Golf.

**GOLDSMITH, Jonathan Philip;** Secretary-General, Council of Bars and Law Societies of Europe, 2002–15 (Consultant, 2015); independent consultant, since 2016; *b* 22 Aug. 1953; *s* of Hans and Gisela Goldsmith; *m* 1978, Hermione St John Smith; two *d*. *Educ:* Trinity Coll., Oxford. Solicitor; Citizens Advice Bureaux: Advr, 1978–80; Community Lawyer, 1980–86; Law Society: Dep. Hd, Communications, 1986–95; Dir, Internat., 1995–2001.

**GOLDSMITH, Philip;** Director (observation of the Earth and its environment), European Space Agency, Paris, 1985–93; *b* 16 April 1930; *s* of late Stanley Thomas Goldsmith and Ida Goldsmith (*née* Rawlinson); *m* 1st, 1952, Daphne (*d* 1983), *d* of William Webb; two *s* two *d*; 2nd, 1990, Gail Lorraine. *Educ:* Almondbury Grammar Sch.; Pembroke Coll., Oxford (MA). Meteorologist with the Meteorological Office, 1947–54, incl. National Service, RAF, 1948–50; Research Scientist, AERE Harwell, 1957–67; Meteorological Office: Asst Director (Cloud Physics Research), 1967–76; Dep. Director (Physical Research), 1976–82; Dir (Res.), 1982–85. President: Royal Meteorological Society, 1980–82; Internat. Commn on Atmospheric Chem. and Global Pollution, 1979–83. *Publications:* articles in scientific jls mainly on atmospheric physics and chemistry and space research related to associated environmental concerns. *Recreations:* golf, gardening, antiques, old cars. *Address:* 17 Mill Street, Sidmouth, Devon EX10 8DW.

**GOLDSMITH, Thomas;** Clerk, Foreign Affairs Committee, House of Commons, since 2018; *b* London, 28 Nov. 1974; *s* of late Thomas Henry Goldsmith and Catherine Mary Goldsmith (*née* Peak). *Educ:* Ilford Co. High Sch. for Boys; Univ. of York (BA Hons). House of Commons: a clerk, 1996–; Table Office Clerk, 2006–08; Clerk: Energy and Climate Change Cttee, 2009–10; Justice Cttee, 2010–12; Hd, Office of the Chief Exec., 2013–15; Sec., H of C Commn and Hd, Governance Office, 2015–16; Principal Clerk, Cttee Office, H of C, 2016–18. *Recreation:* jazz. *Address:* House of Commons, SW1A 0AA. *E:* goldsmitht@parliament.uk.

**GOLDSMITH, Walter Kenneth,** FCA; Chairman, Estates & Management Ltd, 2006–18; *b* 19 Jan. 1938; *s* of late Lionel and of Phoebe Goldsmith; *m* 1961, Rosemary Adele, *d* of Joseph and Hannah Salter; two *s* two *d*. *Educ:* Merchant Taylors' School. Admitted Inst. of Chartered Accountants, 1960; Manager, Mann Judd & Co., 1964; joined Black & Decker Ltd, 1966: Dir of Investment, Finance and Administration, Europe, 1967; Gen. Man., 1970; Man. Dir, 1974; Chief Executive and European Dir, 1975; Black & Decker USA, 1976–79: Corporate Vice-Pres. and Pres. Pacific Internat. Operations; Dir Gen., Inst. of Dirs, 1979–84; Chm., Korn/Ferry International Ltd, 1984–86; Gp Planning and Marketing Dir, Trusthouse Forte plc, 1985–87; Chm., Food from Britain, 1987–90; Chm., British Food & Farming Ltd (Dep. Chm., 1990). Chairman: Ansoll Estates Ltd, 1989–98; Trident, later Flying Flowers, Ltd, 1990–99; Royal Stafford Tableware Ltd, 1997–2002; Asite plc, 2009– (Dep. Chm., 2001–09); Energy Technique plc, 2011–16; Dep. Chm., MICE Gp, 1994–95; Director: Bank Leumi (UK) plc, 1984–2013; Trusthouse Forte Inc., 1985–87; The Winning Streak Ltd, 1985–2000; Isys plc (Dep. Chm.), 1987–99; CLS Group, 1992–2000; Chambers & Newman, 1994–2000; Betterware, 1995–97 (Chm., 1990–97); Fitness First plc, 1997–2003; Guiton Gp plc, 1998–2003; SCS Upholstery plc, 1998–2005; Visonic, 2004–10; KBH Media Ltd, 2005–17 (Chm.); Mercury Gp plc, 2006–09; Mem. Adv. Bd, Kalchas, 1990–97; Advisor to: Rotch Property Gp, 1996–2011; Consensus Business Gp, 2006–. Member: English Tourist Board, 1982–84; BTA, 1984–86; Vice-Pres., British Overseas Trade Gp for Israel, 1992–2000 (Chm., 1987–91). Mem., Develt Adv. Bd, SOAS, 2009–13. Treas., Leo Baeck Coll., 1987–89; Chm., Jewish Music Inst., 2003–08 (Vice Pres., 2008–). Council Mem., RASE, 1988–95. Trustee, Israel Diaspora Trust, 1982–92; Chm., Grange Hospice Project, 1994–99. FRSA; CCMI. Liveryman, Worshipful Co. of Chartered Accountants in England and Wales, 1985. Free Enterprise Award, Aims for Industry, 1984. *Publications:* (with D. Clutterbuck): The Winning Streak, 1984; The Winning Streak Workout Book, 1985; The Winning Streak: Mark 2, 1997; (with Berry Ritchie) The New Elite, 1987. *Recreations:* music, travel. *Address:* 35 Park Lane, W1K 1RB.

**GOLDSMITH, Zac;** *see* Goldsmith, F. Z. R.

**GOLDSPRING, Paul;** a District Judge (Magistrates' Courts), since 2013; *b* Greenwich, London, 11 Oct. 1971; *s* of Anthony George Goldspring and Maureen Ann Goldspring; *m* 1999, Joanne Naomi Jayne; two *s*. *Educ:* Eaglesfield Sch.; Univ. of Hertfordshire (LLB Hons 1993); Univ. of Cambridge (Dip. Legal Skills 1995). Admitted solicitor, 1997; a Dep. District Judge (Magistrates' Courts), 2009–13. *Recreations:* cricket, golf, football, jazz, wine. *Address:* Westminster Magistrates' Court, 181 Marylebone Road, NW1 5RB.

**GOLDSTAUB, His Honour Anthony;** QC 1992; a Circuit Judge, 2004–16; *b* 26 May 1949; *er s* of late Henry Goldstaub, engineer, and of Hilda (*née* Bendix); *m* 1st, 1982 (marr. diss. 1989); two *s*; 2nd, 1993, Moira Pooley; one *d*. *Educ:* Highgate Sch.; Nottingham Univ. (LLB 1971). Called to the Bar, Middle Temple, 1972; an Asst Recorder, 1995–98; a Recorder, 1999–2004. A Pres., Mental Health Review Tribunals, 2002–12.

**GOLDSTAUB, Jane Hilary, (Mrs T. C. Goldstaub);** *see* Procter, J. H.

**GOLDSTEIN, Alfred,** CBE 1977; FREng; consulting engineer, 1951–93; Senior Partner, Travers Morgan & Partners, 1972–85; Chairman, Travers Morgan Group, 1985–87; *b* 9 Oct. 1926; *s* of late Sigmund and Regina Goldstein; *m* 1959, Anne Milford, *d* of late Col R. A. M. Tweedy and Maureen Evans, and step *d* of Hubert Evans; two *s*. *Educ:* Rotherham Grammar Sch.; Imperial Coll., Univ. of London. BSc (Eng); ACGI 1946; DIC. FICE 1959; FIStructE 1959; FCIHT (FIHE 1959); FREng (FEng 1979); FCGI 1984. Partner, R. Travers Morgan & Partners, 1951; early projects include: Oxford Univ. Parks Footbridge, 1949 (Grade II listed 1998); Bournemouth Bus Garage, 1950 (Grade II listed 1999); Winthorpe Bridge, Newark, 1962 (Grade II★ listed 1998); responsible for planning, design and supervision of construction of major road and bridge projects and for planning and transport studies, incl. M23, Belfast Transportation Plan, Clifton Bridge, Nottingham, Elizabeth Bridge, Cambridge, Itchen Bridge, Southampton. Transport Consultant to Govt SE Jt Planning Team for SE Regional Plan; in charge London Docklands Redevelopment Study; Cost Benefit Study for 2nd Sydney Airport for Govt of Australia; Mem. Cttee on Review of Railway Finances, 1982; UK full mem., EC Article 83 Cttee (Transport), 1982–85; TRRL Visitor on Transport Res. and Safety, 1983–87. Member: Building Research Bd, subseq. Adv. Cttee on Building Research, 1963–66; Civil Engrg EDC on Contracting in Civil Engrg since Banwell, 1965–67; Baroness Sharp's Adv. Cttee on Urban Transport Manpower Study, 1967–69; Commn of Inquiry on Third London Airport, 1968–70; Urban Motorways Cttee, 1969–72; Genesys Bd, 1969–74; Chairman: DoE and Dept of Transport Planning and Transport Res. Adv. Council, 1973–79; DoE Environmental Bd, 1975–78; Mem., TRRL Adv. Cttee on Transport, 1974–80; Mem. Bd, Coll. of Estate Management, Reading Univ., 1979–92. *Publications:* papers and lectures, including: Criteria for the Siting of Major Airports, 4th World Airports Conf., 1973; Highways and Community Response, 9th Rees Jeffreys Triennial Lecture, RTPI, 1975; Environment and the Economic Use of Energy, (Plenary Paper, Hong Kong Transport Conf., 1982); Decision-taking under Uncertainty in the Roads Sector, PIARC Sydney, 1983; Investment in Transport (Keynote address, CIT Conf., 1983); Buses: social enterprise and business (main paper, 9th annual conf., Bus and Coach Council, 1983); Public Road Transport: a time for change (Keynote address, 6th Aust. passenger trans. conf., 1985); Private Enterprise and Highways (Nat. Res. Council conf., Baltimore, 1986); The Expert and the Public: local values and national choice (Florida Univ.), 1987; Travel in London: is chaos inevitable? (LRT), 1989. *Recreations:* carpentry, music, bridge. *Club:* Athenæum.

**GOLDSTEIN, Prof. Harvey,** FBA 1996; Professor of Social Statistics, University of Bristol, since 2005; *b* 30 Oct. 1939; *s* of Jack and Millicent Goldstein; *m* 1970, Barbara Collinge; one *s*. *Educ:* Oakthorpe Primary Sch., London; Hendon Grammar Sch.; Manchester Univ. (BSc Hons); University College London (Dip. Stats). Lectr in Statistics, Inst. of Child Health, 1964–71; Head of Statistics Section, Nat. Children's Bureau, 1971–76; Prof. of Statistical Methods, Inst. of Educn, Univ. of London, 1977–2005. *Publications:* (jtly) From Birth to Seven, 1972; (jtly) Assessment of Skeletal Maturity and Prediction of Adult Height, 1976; The Design and Analysis of Longitudinal Studies, 1979; (with C. Gipps) Monitoring Children, 1983; Multilevel Statistical Models, 1987, 4th edn 2011; (with T. Lewis) Assessment, 1996; (with A. Leyland) Multilevel Modelling of Health

Statistics, 2001; (jtly) Measuring Success: league tables in the public sector, 2012. *Recreations:* playing the flute, walking, cycling, tennis. *Address:* Graduate School of Education, University of Bristol, Bristol BS8 1JA.

**GOLDSTEIN, Janet Mary;** *see* Ainley, J. M.

**GOLDSTEIN, Prof. Joseph Leonard;** physician, genetics educator; Paul J. Thomas Professor of Medicine, and Chairman, Department of Molecular Genetics, since 1977, Regental Professor, since 1985, Julie and Louis A. Beecherl Distinguished Chair in Biomedical Science, University of Texas Southwestern Medical (formerly Health Science) Center at Dallas (Member of Faculty, since 1972); *b* 18 April 1940; *s* of Isadore E. and Fannie A. Goldstein. *Educ:* Washington and Lee University (BS); Univ. of Texas Health Science Center at Dallas (MD). Intern, then Resident in Medicine, Mass Gen. Hosp., Boston, 1966–88; clinical associate, NIH, 1968–70; Postdoctoral Fellow, Univ. of Washington, Seattle, 1970–72. Harvey Soc. Lecture, Rockefeller Univ., 1977. Member: Sci. Rev. Bd, Howard Hughes Med. Inst., 1978–84, Med. Adv. Bd, 1985–90 (Chm., 1995–2002; Trustee, 2002–); Bd of Dirs, Passano Foundn, 1985–; Sci. Adv. Bd, Welch Foundn, 1986–; Bd of Consultants, Meml Sloan-Kettering Cancer Center, 1992–; Bd of Trustees, Rockefeller Univ., 1994–; Bd of Govs, Scripps Res. Inst., 1996–; Bd of Sci. Advrs, Van Andel Res. Inst., 1996–; Sci. Adv. Ctee, Mass Gen. Hosp., 2005–; Bd of Dirs, Albert and Mary Lasker Foundn, 2007– (Chm., Awards Jury, 1996–). Fellow, Salk Inst., 1983–94. Member, editorial board: Jl Clin. Investigation, 1977–82; Annual Review of Genetics, 1980–85; Arteriosclerosis, 1981–87; Jl Biol Chemistry, 1981–85; Cell, 1983–; Science, 1985–98; Genomics, 1988–; Mol. Biol. of the Cell, 1992–97; Proc. Nat. Acad. Scis, 1992–. Member: Nat. Acad. of Scis (Lounsbery Award, 1979); Amer. Acad. of Arts and Scis, and other bodies; Foreign Mem., Royal Soc., 1991. Hon. DSc: Chicago, 1982; Rensselaer Polytechnic Inst., 1982; Washington and Lee, 1986; Paris-Sud, 1988; Buenos Aires, 1990; Southern Methodist, 1993; Miami, 1996; Rockefeller, 2001; Albany Med. Coll., 2004. Numerous awards from scientific instns, incl. Pfizer Award in Enzyme Chemistry, Amer. Chem. Soc., 1976; award in biol and med. scis, NY Acad. Scis, 1981; Albert Lasker Award in Basic Science (with Michael Brown), 1985; Nobel Prize (with Michael Brown) for Physiology or Medicine, 1985; Amer. Coll. of Physicians Award, 1986; US Nat. Medal of Science, 1988; Distinguished Alumni Award, NIH, 1991; Warren Alpert Foundn Prize, Harvard Med. Sch., 2000; Albany Med. Center Prize in Med. and Biomed. Res., 2003; Distinguished Scientist Award, American Heart Assoc., 2003; Woodrow Wilson Award for Public Service, 2005; Builders of Sci. Award, Research!America, 2007. *Publications:* (jtly) The Metabolic Basis of Inherited Diseases, 5th edn 1983; papers on genetics educn and science subjects. *Address:* Department of Molecular Genetics, University of Texas Southwestern Medical Center at Dallas, 5323 Harry Hines Boulevard, Dallas, TX 75390–8548, USA; 3831 Turtle Creek Boulevard, Apt 22–B, TX 75219–4480, USA.

**GOLDSTEIN, Dr Michael,** CBE 1997; FRSC; higher education consultant, since 2004; author; *b* 1 May 1939; *s* of Sarah and Jacob Goldstein; *m* 1st, 1962, Janet Sandra Skevington (marr. diss. 2009); one *s*; 2nd, 2016, Cyrrhian Lucia Macrae. *Educ:* Hackney Downs Grammar School; Northern Polytechnic, London. BSc, PhD, DSc; CChem. Lectr, sen. lectr, principal lectr, Polytechnic of N London, 1963–73; Head of Dept of Chemistry, 1974–83 and Dean of Faculty of Science, 1979–83, Sheffield City Polytechnic; Dep. Dir, Coventry Lanchester Polytechnic, 1983–87; Dir, Coventry Polytechnic, 1987–92; Vice-Chancellor, Coventry Univ., 1992–2004. Mem., cttees and bds, CNAA, 1975–93, incl. Chm., CNAA Chem. Bd, 1978–84; Dep. Chm., Polys and Colls Admissions System, 1989–94; Member: UCAS, 1993–2001 (Dep. Chm., 1995–97; Chm., 1997–2001); Univs and Colls Employers Assoc., 1994–2001. Director: Coventry and Warwicks TEC, 1992–97; City Centre Co. (Coventry) Ltd, 1997–2002 (Vice-Chm., 1999–2002); Coventry and Warwicks Chamber of Commerce, Trng and Enterprise, 1997–2001; CV One Ltd, 2002–08 (Dep. Chm., 2004–08); ContinYou Ltd, 2003–10; Chairman: Creative Partnerships Coventry, 2004–08; Heist Enterprises Ltd, 2004–06; Cre8us, 2008–10. Member: Adv. Cttee, Coventry Common Purpose, 1989–2004; Coventry is making it, 1992–95; Coventry and Warwicks LSC, 2001–07; Mgt Bd, Foundn Degree Forward, 2006–10. Non-exec. Dir, Coventry and Warwicks Partnership NHS Trust, 2006–11 (Chm., 2010–11). Member: RSC Council, 1983–86, 1993–99; other RSC cttees, 1975–99 (Pres., Educn Div., 1993–95; Chm., Educn and Quals Bd, 1995–99); Chairman: Council for Registration of Forensic Practitioners, 2005–08; Higher Educn Develt Gp, States of Jersey, 2005–08; Mem., Skills Bd, States of Jersey, 2008–15. Panel Mem., Judicial Appts Commn, 2012–19; Mem., HMP Ind. Monitoring Bd, 2012– (Ind. Interviewer, 2016–). Trustee, Community Educn Develt Centre, 1996–2003. Emeritus Gov., Solihull Coll., 2012–. Hon. FCGI 1994. Hon. Fellow, Univ. of Worcester, 1998. Hon. DSc Warwick, 2003. Ambassadors' Award, City of Coventry, 2004. *Publications:* (jtly) Three Lives in Education: reflections of an Anglo-Jewish Family, 2011; (jtly) John Hibbs: his journey by bus, coach and train, 2015; Shalom, Jack: a celebration of the life of Sergeant Jacob 'Jack' Goldstein, RAFVR, 2018; contribs to sci. jls and periodicals, chapters in review books. *Recreations:* Coventry City FC, exercise, collector of classic Rupert items. *Address:* 78 Whitehouse Drive, Lichfield, Staffs WS13 8FE. *T:* (01543) 418063.

**GOLDSTEIN, Nathan Harold;** a Judge of the Upper Tribunal (Immigration and Asylum Chamber) (formerly a Vice President, Immigration Appeal Tribunal, later a Senior Immigration Judge, Asylum and Immigration Tribunal), 2003–16; *b* 21 Sept. 1944; *s* of Joseph and Fay Goldstein; *m* 1988, Shelley Katrina Sofier; one *s* two *d. Educ:* Carmel Coll.; Hasmonean Grammar Sch.; Coll. of Law. Admitted solicitor, 1987; Equity Partner, Nelsons Solicitors, 1988–95. Immigration Adjudicator (pt-time), 1996–97; Special Adjudicator (pt-time), 1997–99; Immigration Adjudicator, 1999–2003; Legal Mem., Special Immigration Appeals Commn, 2005–16; an Investigating Judge and Mem., Review Bodies, 2006–16. Mem., Law Soc., 1987–. Mem., Knightsbridge Speakers Club, 1983–2004. *Publications:* papers on immigration matters. *Recreations:* family, cinema, theatre, jazz, football (lifelong Arsenal supporter), my grandchildren, reading (incl. subscribing to endless magazines which I never throw away).

**GOLDSTEIN, Prof. Raymond Ethan,** PhD; FRS 2013; FInstP; Schlumberger Professor of Complex Physical Systems, University of Cambridge, since 2006; Fellow, Churchill College, Cambridge, since 2007. *Educ:* Massachusetts Inst. of Technol. (SB Physics and Chem. 1983); Cornell Univ. (MSc Physics 1986; PhD Physics 1988). FInstP 2009; FIMA 2010. Fannie and John Hertz Foundn Grad. Fellow, Cornell Univ., 1983–88; Vis. Scientist, Service de Physique Théorique, Centre d'Etudes Nucléaires de Saclay, Gif-sur-Yvette, France, 1988; Postdoctoral Res., James Franck and Enrico Fermi Insts, Univ. of Chicago, 1988–91; Asst Prof. of Physics, Princeton Univ., 1991–96; University of Arizona: Associate Prof. of Physics and Applied Maths, 1996–2002; Prof. of Physics and Applied Maths, 2002–10. Alfred P. Sloan Res. Fellow, Princeton Univ., 1992–96; NSF Presidential Faculty Fellow, Princeton Univ. and Univ. of Arizona, 1993–98. Fellow, Amer. Physical Soc., 2003. William Hopkins Prize, Cambridge Philosophical Soc., 2011; (jtly) Ig Nobel Prize in Physics, 2012; G. K. Batchelor Prize, 2016. *Publications:* contribs to jls incl. Procs NAS, Physical Rev. Letters, Jl Fluid Mechanics. *Address:* Department of Applied Mathematics and Theoretical Physics, Centre for Mathematical Sciences, Wilberforce Road, Cambridge CB3 0WA.

**GOLDSTEIN-JACKSON, Kevin Grierson;** JP; writer; poet; artist; company director; *b* 1946; *s* of H. G. and W. M. E. Jackson; *m* 1975, Jenny Mei Leng, *e d* of Ufong Ng, Malaysia; two *d. Educ:* Reading Univ. (BA Phil. and Sociol.); Southampton Univ. (MPhil Law). Staff Relations Dept, London Transport (Railways), 1966; Scottish Widows Pension & Life Assurance Soc., 1967; Prog. Organizer, Southern TV, 1970–73; Asst Prod., HK-TVB, Hong Kong, 1973; freelance writer/TV prod., 1973–75; Head of Film, Dhofar Region TV Service, Sultanate of Oman, 1975–76; Founder and Dir, Thames Valley Radio, 1974–77; Asst to Head of Drama, Anglia TV, 1977–81; Founder, TSW-Television South West: Programme Controller and Dir of Progs, 1981–85; Jt Man. Dir, 1981–82; Chief Exec., 1982–85. Gov., Lilliput First Sch., Poole, 1988–93. FRSA 1978; FInstD 1982; FRGS 1989. Freeman, City of London, 1996. JP Poole, 1990. *Publications:* 19 books, including: The Right Joke for the Right Occasion, 1973; Encyclopaedia of Ridiculous Facts, 1975; Experiments with Everyday Objects, 1976; Things to make with Everyday Objects, 1978; Magic with Everyday Objects, 1979; Dictionary of Essential Quotations, 1983; Jokes for Telling, 1986; Share Millions, 1989; The Public Speaker's Joke Book, 1991; The Astute Private Investor, 1994; Quick Quips, 2002; First Flutter, 2017; contrib. financial and gen. pubns. *Recreations:* writing, TV, films, music, walking, philosophical and sociological investigation, haiku.

**GOLDSTONE, Prof. Anthony Howard,** CBE 2008; FRCP, FRCPE; FRCPath; Professor, Department of Haematology, University College London, since 1999; Director of Services, North London Cancer Network, 2000–09; Chairman, Royal National Orthopaedic Hospital NHS Trust, since 2011; *b* 13 Sept. 1944; *s* of Norman Goldstone and Edith Goldstone; *m* 1970, Jennifer Anne Krantz; one *s* one *d. Educ:* Bolton Sch.; St John's Coll., Oxford (BM BCh 1968; MA); University Coll. Hosp. Med. Sch. (Fellow, UCL, 1993). FRCPE 1979; FRCP 1983; FRCPath 1987. Sen. House Officer, Gastrointestinal Unit, Western General Infirmary, Edinburgh, 1969–70; Sen. Registrar in Haematology, Addenbrooke's Hosp., Cambridge, 1973–76; University College Hospital, London: Consultant Haematologist, 1976–2011, now Hon. Consultant Haematologist; Dir, Bone Marrow Transplantation, 1979–2000; Postgrad. Dean, UCH Med. Sch., 1984–87; Chm., UCH Med. Cttee, 1986–88; Med. Dir, 1992–2000, and Dir, Clinical Haematology and Cancer Services, 1997–2000, UCL Hosps NHS Trust. Chm., NE Thames Regl Haematologists, 1988–90. Mem. Bd, European Gp for Bone Marrow Transplantation, 1990–98; Nat. Co-ordinator, UK Adult Leukaemia Trials, 1987–2006. President: British Soc. for Blood and Bone Marrow Transplantation, 1999–2000; British Soc. for Haematology, 2000–01. Lifetime Achievement Award, UCLH NHS Foundn Trust, 2013. *Publications:* (jtly) Leukaemias, Lymphomas and Allied Disorders, 1976; Examination Haematology, 1977; (jtly) Synopsis of Haematology, 1983; Low Grade Lymphoma, 2005; 350 papers on leukaemia, lymphoma, myeloma and stem cell transplantation. *Recreations:* cuddling grandchildren, shouting at the dog, driving fast cars, still waiting for Manchester City to win Champions League. *Address:* 5th Floor, University College Hospital Macmillan Cancer Centre, Huntley Street, WC1E 6AG; 67 Loom Lane, Radlett, Herts WD7 8NX.

**GOLDSTONE, David Joseph,** CBE 2010; Chairman and Chief Executive, Regalian Properties Plc, 1970–2001; *b* 21 Feb. 1929; *s* of Solomon Goldstone and Rebecca Goldstone (née Degotts); *m* 1957, Cynthia (née Easton); one *s* two *d. Educ:* Dynevor Secondary Sch., Swansea; London School of Economics and Political Science (LLB Hons; Hon. Fellow, 1995). Admitted Solicitor (Hons), 1955. Legal practice, 1955–66. Mem., Capital Adv. Gp (formerly Strategic Capital Investment Panel), Welsh Assembly Govt, 2008–12. Dir, Swansea Sound Commercial Radio Ltd, 1974–96; Special Adviser (Estates) and Hon. Vice-Pres., Wales Millennium Centre Ltd, 2006–15 (Dir, 1998–2006). Mem., London First (formerly London Forum), 1993–97. Member Council: WNO, 1984–89; Royal Albert Hall, 1999–2006 (Hon. Vice Pres., 2007–). Mem., Court of Govs, LSE, 1985–2009, now Emeritus Gov.; Dep. Chm., Council, London Univ., 2002–06 (Mem., 1994–2006). Mem. Court, 1999–2005, Chm., 2001–05, Hon. Vice-Pres., 2006–, Coram Family. Adviser (Estates): Welsh Rugby Union, 2008–16; Ind. Advr to Minister for Business, Enterprise, Technol. and Sci., Welsh Govt, 2008–15. Hon. Vice Pres., London Welsh Male Voice Choir, 2007–. Trustee, Civil Liberties Trust, 1999–15. *Recreations:* family, reading, sport. *Address:* Flat 4 Grosvenor Hill Court, 15 Bourdon Street, W1K 3PX. *Clubs:* Lansdowne, Bath & Racquets.

**GOLDSTONE, David Julian;** QC 2006; *b* 30 July 1962; *s* of Leslie and Barbara Goldstone; *m* 1991, Ruby Azhar; three *d. Educ:* Haberdashers' Aske's, Elstree; Emmanuel Coll., Cambridge (MA Law); New Coll., Oxford (BCL). Called to the Bar, Middle Temple, 1986; in practice at the Bar, 1989–: Queen Elizabeth Bldg, 1989–2002; Quadrant Chambers, 2002–. First Standing Counsel to the Admiralty, 1999–2006. Lectr (pt-time), LSE and KCL, 1985–88. *Recreations:* classical liberalism (Founding Mem., Soc. of liberal Lawyers, 2006), gardening, especially Mediterranean and sub-tropical plants, chess, Chelsea FC, off piste ski-ing. *Address:* Quadrant Chambers, 10 Fleet Street, EC4Y 1AU. *T:* (020) 7583 4444, *Fax:* (020) 7583 4455. *E:* david.goldstone@quadrantchambers.com.

**GOLDSTONE, David Lionel Alexander,** CBE 2013; Chief Operating Officer, Ministry of Defence, since 2017; *b* Manchester, 9 July 1962; *s* of His Honour Peter Walter Goldstone and of Patricia Goldstone; *m* 1990, Jenny Parry; three *s. Educ:* Haberdashers' Aske's Sch.; Hertford Coll., Oxford (BA PPE 1984); Univ. of Leicester (PGCE 1985). CIPFA 1990. Teacher of Politics, Econs and History, Whitgift Sch., 1985–86; Public Sector Audit Trainee, Audit Commn, 1986–89; Public Sector Auditor, then Financial Manager, Price Waterhouse, 1989–97 (on secondment to Private Finance Panel, 1995–97); Private Finance Taskforce, HM Treasury, 1997–2000; Partnerships UK, 2000–07: on secondment as Chief Exec., Partnerships for Health, 2000–01; Finance Dir, 2001–07; on secondment as Chief Exec., Partnerships for Schs, 2004–05; Finance and Prog. Dir, Govt Olympic Exec., DCMS, 2007–12; Chief Finance Officer, TfL, 2013–14; Chief Exec., London Legacy Develt Corp., 2014–17. Mem. Bd, Sport England, 2013–17. *Recreations:* running, supporting my children's sports, going out with friends.

**GOLDSTONE, Prof. Jeffrey,** PhD; FRS 1977; Professor of Physics, Massachusetts Institute of Technology, 1977–2004, now Emeritus (Cecil and Ida Green Professor in Physics, 1983–2004; Director, Center for Theoretical Physics, 1983–89); *b* 3 Sept. 1933; *s* of Hyman Goldstone and Sophia Goldstone; *m* 1980, Roberta Gordon; one *s. Educ:* Manchester Grammar Sch.; Trinity Coll., Cambridge (MA 1956, PhD 1958). Trinity Coll., Cambridge: Entrance Scholar, 1951; Res. Fellow, 1956; Staff Fellow, 1962; Hon. Fellow, 2000; Cambridge University: Lectr, 1961; Reader in Math. Physics, 1976. Vis. appointments: Institut for Teoretisk Fysik, Copenhagen; CERN, Geneva; Harvard Univ.; MIT; Inst. for Theoretical Physics, Santa Barbara; Stanford Linear Accelerator Center; Lab. de Physique Théorique, L'Ecole Normale Supérieure, Paris; Università di Roma I. Smith's Prize, Cambridge Univ., 1955; Dannie Heineman Prize, Amer. Phys. Soc., 1981; Guthrie Medal, Inst. of Physics, 1983; Dirac Medal, Internat. Centre for Theoretical Physics, 1991. *Publications:* articles in learned jls. *Address:* Department of Physics, (6–407) Massachusetts Institute of Technology, Cambridge, MA 02139, USA. *T:* (office) (617) 2536263. *E:* goldston@mit.edu.

**GOLDSTONE, His Honour Leonard Clement**; QC 1993; a Circuit Judge, 2002–19; a Senior Circuit Judge, and Resident Judge, Liverpool, 2011–19; *b* 20 April 1949; *s* of Maurice and Maree Goldstone; *m* 1972, Vanessa, *yr d* of late Donald Forster, CBE three *s*. *Educ*: Manchester Grammar Sch.; Churchill Coll., Cambridge (BA). Called to the Bar, Middle Temple, 1971, Bencher, 2004; a Recorder, 1992–2002. Pres., Mental Health Review Tribunal (Restricted Cases), 1999–2004. Treas., Northern Circuit, 1998–2001. Hon. Recorder, Liverpool, 2011–19. Hon. Fellow in Law, Liverpool John Moores Univ., 2016. *Recreations*: golf, bridge, music, theatre. *Clubs*: Dunham Forest Golf and Country (Altrincham); Athenaeum (Liverpool).

**GOLDSWORTHY, Andrew Charles, (Andy)**, OBE 2000; artist and sculptor; *b* 25 July 1956; *s* of Frederick Goldsworthy and Muriel Goldsworthy (*née* Stangar); *m* 1982, Judith Gregson (marr. diss. 2006); three *s* two *d*. *Educ*: Harrogate Secondary Mod. Sch.; Harrogate High Sch.; Bradford Coll. of Art; Lancashire Poly. Based in SW Scotland, has worked in many different countries, 1978–. Hon. Fellow, Central Lancashire Univ., 1995. Hon. MA Bradford, 1993; Hon. DLit Glasgow, 2005. *Publications*: Touching North, 1989; Leaves, 1989; Hand to Earth, 1990; Andy Goldsworthy, 1990; Snow and Ice Drawings, 1992; Two Autumns, 1993; Stone, 1994; Black Stones—Red Pools, 1995; Wood, 1996; Cairns, 1997; Andy Goldsworthy (Arches), 1998; Arch, 1999; Wall, 2000; Time, 2000; Midsummer Snowballs, 2001; Refuges D'Art, 2002; Passage, 2004; Enclosure, 2007; Ephemeral Works, 2015. *Address*: c/o Galerie Lelong, 528 West 26th Street, New York, NY 10001, USA.

**GOLDSWORTHY, Julia Anne**; Special Adviser, PwC, since 2014; Director of Strategy, West Midlands Combined Authority, since 2017; *b* 10 Sept. 1978; *d* of Edward Douglas Goldsworthy and Margaret Joan Goldsworthy; *m* 2012, Christopher Church. *Educ*: Fitzwilliam Coll., Cambridge (BA Hist. 2000); Daiichi Univ. of Econs, Japan (Japanese Exchange Schol.); Birkbeck Coll., London (Postgrad. Cert. Econs 2002). Res. asst to Matthew Taylor, MP, 2001; Sen. Educn/Econ. Advr to Lib Dems, 2003; Res. Advr, Truro Coll. Business Centre, 2004; Regeneration Officer, Carrick DC, 2004–05. MP (Lib Dem) Falmouth and Camborne, 2005–10; contested (Lib Dem) Camborne and Redruth, 2010, 2015. Special Advr to Chief Sec. to the Treasury, 2010–14; Sen. Policy Advr, Hanover Communications, 2014–15. FRSA. *Recreations*: pilot gig rowing, music (piano and clarinet).

**GOLDSWORTHY, Most Rev. Kay Maree**; *see* Perth (Australia), Archbishop of.

**GOLDTHORPE, John Harry**, CBE 2002; FBA 1984; Official Fellow, Nuffield College, Oxford, 1969–2002, now Emeritus; Distinguished Senior Research Fellow, Department of Social Policy and Intervention, University of Oxford, 2012–15; *b* 27 May 1935; *s* of Harry Goldthorpe and Lilian Eliza Goldthorpe; *m* 1963, Rhiannon Esyllt (*née* Harry); one *s* one *d*. *Educ*: Wath-upon-Dearne Grammar School; University College London (BA Hons 1st Class Mod. Hist.); LSE. MA Cantab; MA Oxon. Asst Lectr, Dept of Sociology, Univ. of Leicester, 1957–60; Fellow of King's College, Cambridge, 1960–69; Asst Lectr and Lectr, Faculty of Economics and Politics, Cambridge, 1962–69. Vis. Prof. of Sociol., Cornell Univ., 2003–06; Vis. Professorial Fellow, Centre for Longitudinal Studies, Inst. of Educn, Univ. of London, 2009–12. Lectures: Fuller, Univ. of Essex, 1979; Marshall, Univ. of Southampton, 1989; Aubert, Oslo Univ., 1993; Geary, Econ. and Social Res. Inst., Dublin, 1998; Cummings, McGill Univ., Montreal, 2001; First Sociol., British Acad., 2015. MAE 1988. For. Mem., Royal Swedish Acad. of Scis, 2001. Hon. Fellow: Eur. Acad. of Sociol., 2012; Royal Statistical Soc., 2016. Hon. FilDr Stockholm Univ., 1990. (Jtly) Polanyi Prize, Hungarian Sociol Assoc., 2010. *Publications*: (with David Lockwood and others): The Affluent Worker: industrial attitudes and behaviour, 1968; The Affluent Worker: political attitudes and behaviour, 1968; The Affluent Worker in the Class Structure, 1969; (with Keith Hope) The Social Grading of Occupations, 1974; (with Fred Hirsch) The Political Economy of Inflation, 1978; Social Mobility and Class Structure in Modern Britain, 1980, 2nd edn 1987; Order and Conflict in Contemporary Capitalism, 1984; (with Hermann Strasser) Die Analyse Sozialer Ungleichheit, 1985; (contrib.) John H. Goldthorpe: consensus and controversy (ed Clark, Modgil and Modgil), 1990; (with Robert Erikson) The Constant Flux: a study of class mobility in industrial societies, 1992; (with Christopher Whelan) The Development of Industrial Society in Ireland, 1992; Causation, Statistics and Sociology, 1999; On Sociology, 2000, 2nd edn, 2 vols, 2007; (with Catherine Bunting and others) From Indifference to Enthusiasm: patterns of arts attendance in England, 2008; Sociology as a Population Science, 2016; (with Erzsebet Bukodi) Social Mobility and Education in Britain: research, policy and politics, 2018; papers in Acta Sociologica, American Jl of Sociology, American Sociological Rev., British Jl of Sociology, Comparative Soc. Res., Cultural Trends, Sociological Review, Sociology, European Jl of Sociology, European Sociological Rev., European Economic Rev., Jl of Economic Perspectives, Proc. NAS, National Institute Economic Rev., Poetics, Rationality and Society, Res. in Social Stratification and Mobility, Sociological Methods and Res., Sociologie du Travail, Rev. Française de Sociologie, Jl of Royal Statistical Soc., Quantity and Quality, European Societies, Longitudinal and Life-Course Studies, Jl of Social Policy. *Recreations*: bird watching, cryptic crosswords. *Address*: 32 Leckford Road, Oxford OX2 6HX. *T*: (01865) 556602.

**GOLDWAG, Wanda**; Chair, Office of Legal Complaints, since 2017; *b* England, 1954; *m* 2013, Catherine Worboyes. *Educ*: London Sch. of Econs and Political Sci. (BSc Econ). Advr, Smedvig Venture Capital, 2000–. Chair, Financial Services Consumer Panel, 2019–; Interim Chair, LEASE, 2019–; Mem., QC Appointments Panel, 2016–. Non-exec. Dir, Royal Free London NHS Foundn Trust, 2017–. *Address*: Smedvig Venture Capital, Ryger House, 11 Arlington Street, SW1A 1RD. *T*: (020) 7451 2100.

**GOLOMBOK, Prof. Susan Esther**, PhD; FBA 2019; Professor of Family Research, and Director of Centre for Family Research, University of Cambridge, since 2006; Fellow, Newnham College, Cambridge, since 2006; *b* 11 Aug. 1954; *d* of Bennie and Kitty Golombok; *m* 1999, Prof. John Neville Rust, *qv*; one *s*. *Educ*: Hutcheson's Girls' Sch.; Univ. of Glasgow (BSc Hons 1976); Inst. of Educn, Univ. of London (MSc Child Develt 1977; PhD 1982). London University Institute of Psychiatry: Res. Psychologist, 1977–83; Lectr in Psychology, 1983–86; City University: Lectr, 1987–89; Sen. Lectr, 1989–90; Dir, Family and Child Psychology Res. Centre, 1989–2005; Reader, 1990–92; Prof. of Psychology, 1992–2005. Trustee: Laura Ashley Foundn, 1998–2014; One Plus One, 2005–13. Freeman, City of London, 1986. *Publications*: (with Valerie Curran) Bottling It Up, 1985; (with John Rust) Modern Psychometrics, 1989, 3rd edn 2009; (with Robyn Fivush) Gender Development, 1994; (with Fiona Tasker) Growing Up in a Lesbian Family, 1997; Parenting: what really counts?, 2000; Modern Families: parents and children in new family forms, 2015; contribs to sci. jls. *Recreations*: reading, cinema, cooking, moving house. *Address*: Howe House, Huntingdon Road, Cambridge CB3 0LX. *T*: (01223) 277797.

**GOMBRICH, Prof. Richard Francis**; Boden Professor of Sanskrit, Oxford University, 1976–2004; Fellow of Balliol College, Oxford, 1976–2004, now Emeritus Fellow; Academic Director, 2004–09 and since 2011, Founder-President, since 2008, and Chair, since 2009, Oxford Centre for Buddhist Studies; *b* 17 July 1937; *s* of Sir Ernst Hans Josef Gombrich, OM, CBE, FBA; *m* 1st, 1964, Dorothea Amanda Friedrich (marr. diss. 1984); one *s* one *d*; 2nd, 1985, Sanjukta Gupta. *Educ*: Magdalen Coll., Oxford (MA, DPhil); Harvard Univ. (AM). Univ. Lectr in Sanskrit and Pali, Oxford Univ., 1965–76; Fellow of Wolfson Coll., 1966–76, Emeritus Fellow, 1977. Stewart Fellow, Princeton Univ., 1986–87. President: Pali Text Soc., 1994–2002 (Hon. Sec., 1982–94); UK Assoc. of Buddhist Studies, 2007– (Chair, 2006–13); Hon. Life Mem., Internat. Assoc. of Buddhist Studies, 2008. Editor: Clay Sanskrit Library, 2004–08; Jl of Oxford Centre for Buddhist Studies, 2011–. Hon. Fellow, Internat. Assoc. of Buddhist Studies, 2008–. Hon. DLitt Kalyani Univ., West Bengal, 1991; Hon. DEd De Montfort, 1996; Vacaspati, Tirupati Univ., 1997. S. C. Chakraborty Medal, Asiatic Soc., Calcutta, 1993; Univ. Medal, Warsaw Univ., 1997. Sri Lanka Ranjana (Sri Lanka), 1994. *Publications*: Precept and Practice: traditional Buddhism in the rural highlands of Ceylon, 1971, 2nd edn, as Buddhist Precept and Practice, 1991; (with Margaret Cone) The Perfect Generosity of Prince Vessantara, 1977, 2nd edn 2011; On being Sanskritic, 1978; (ed with Heinz Bechert) The World of Buddhism, 1984; Theravada Buddhism: a social history from ancient Benares to modern Colombo, 1988, 2nd edn 2006; (with G. Obeyesekere) Buddhism Transformed, 1988; How Buddhism Began, 1996, 2nd edn 2006; What the Buddha Thought, 2009, new edn 2013; Buddhism and Pali, 2018; contribs to oriental and anthropological journals. *Recreations*: singing, photography. *Address*: Oxford Centre for Buddhist Studies, Wolfson College, Linton Road, Oxford OX2 6UD.

**GOMERSALL, Sir Stephen (John)**, KCMG 2000 (CMG 1997); HM Diplomatic Service, retired; Deputy Chairman, Hitachi Europe and Advisor to Chief Executive Officer, Hitachi Ltd; *b* 17 Jan. 1948; *s* of Harry Raymond Gomersall and Helen Gomersall; *m* 1975 (marr. diss. 2006); two *s* one *d*. *Educ*: Forest Sch., Snaresbrook; Queens' Coll., Cambridge (Mod. Langs, MA); Stanford Univ., Calif (MA 1970). Entered HM Diplomatic Service, 1970; Tokyo, 1972–77; Rhodesia Dept, FCO, 1977–79; Private Sec. to Lord Privy Seal, 1979–82; Washington, 1982–85; Econ. Counsellor, Tokyo, 1986–90; Head of Security Policy Dept, FCO, 1990–94; Dep. Perm. Rep., UK Mission to UN, 1994–98; Dir, Internat. Security, FCO, 1998–99; Ambassador to Japan, 1999–2004. Chief Exec. for Europe, 2004–11, Gp Chm. for Europe and Mem. Bd, 2011, Hitachi Ltd. Dir, JP Morgan Japanese Investment Trust. Mem., Adv. Council, LSO, 2005–; Mem., Monteverdi Choir and Orchestras, 2019–. Hon. DLitt Sheffield, 2009. Grand Cordon, Order of Rising Sun (Japan), 2015. *Recreations*: music, golf, composing silly songs. *Address*: Hitachi Europe Ltd, Whitebrook Park, Lower Cookham Road, Maidenhead SL6 8YA. *T*: (01628) 585000. *E*: stephen.gomersall@hitachi-eu.com; 24 Windsor Court, Moscow Road, W2 4SN.

**GOMES DA SILVA, Andrea**; Executive Director, Markets and Mergers, Competition and Markets Authority, since 2018; *b* Kettering, Northants, 27 Sept. 1972; *d* of Dr Luiz E. Gomes da Silva and Anthea Blackhurst Gomes da Silva (*née* Blackhurst); *m* 2004, Graham Gibb; one *s*. *Educ*: Malvern Girls' Coll.; Exeter Coll., Oxford (BA 1st Cl. Hons Modern Langs); Birkbeck Coll., London (MA Latin American Studies). Trainee Solicitor, 1997–99, Associate, 1999–2001, Slaughter and May; Associate, 2001–08, Partner, 2008–15, Freshfields Bruckhaus Deringer; Sen. Legal Dir, Mkts and Mergers, CMA, 2015–18. *Recreations*: pilates, travel, reading, good food and wine. *Address*: Competition and Markets Authority, The Cabot, 25 Cabot Square, E14 4QA. *E*: andrea.gomesdasilva@cma.gov.uk.

**GOMEZ, Most Rev. Drexel Wellington**, CMG 1994; Assistant Bishop of the Bahamas and the Turks and Caicos Islands, since 2009; Associate Priest, St Agnes, New Providence, since 2009; *b* Jan. 1937; *s* of late Rueben and Wealthy Gomez; *m* Carrol Gomez; four *c*. *Educ*: Codrington Coll., Barbados (DipTh 1957); Durham Univ. (BA 1959). Ordained 1959; parochial work, Bahamas, 1962–64; Tutor, Codrington Coll., 1964–68; Sec. and Treas., dio. of Bahamas, 1970–72; Bishop of Barbados, 1972–93; Asst Bishop, dio. of Bahamas, 1993–95; Bishop of Bahamas and Turks and Caicos Is (formerly Nassau and Bahamas), 1995–2008; Archbishop of the WI, 1998–2008. *Address*: c/o PO Box N–7107, Nassau, Bahamas.

**GOMEZ, Jill, (Countess of Northesk)**; opera and concert singer; *b* New Amsterdam, British Guiana; *d* of late Albert Clyde Gómez de Machado de Calderón and Denise Price Denham; *m* 2010, Earl of Northesk, (Dr Patrick Carnegy), *qv*. *Educ*: St Joseph's Convent, Port of Spain, Trinidad, WI; St Maur's Convent, Weybridge; Royal Academy of Music (FRAM 1986); Guildhall School of Music, London. Operatic début as Adina in L'Elisir d'Amore with Glyndebourne Touring Opera, 1968 (after winning John Christie Award), then Mélisande, Glyndebourne Fest. Opera, 1969, and has subseq. sung leading rôles, incl. Calisto, 1970, Anne Trulove in The Rake's Progress, 1975, and Helena in A Midsummer Night's Dream, 1984; Royal Opera House début, 1970, creating role of Flora in Tippett's The Knot Garden, subseq. rôles incl. Tytania in A Midsummer Night's Dream, and Lauretta in Gianni Schicchi; rôles include: The Governess in The Turn of the Screw, Ilia in Idomeneo, English Opera Gp; The Governess in The Turn of the Screw, ENO; Jenifer in The Midsummer Marriage, WNO, 1976; with Scottish Opera: Pamina, Fiordiligi, The Countess in Figaro; Elizabeth in Elegy for Young Lovers; Anne Trulove; Leïla in Les Pêcheurs de Perles, 1984; with Kent Opera: Tatiana in Eugene Onegin, 1977; Violetta in La Traviata, 1979; Amyntas in Il Re Pastore, 1987; Donna Anna in Don Giovanni, 1988; created rôle of the Countess in Thea Musgrave's Voice of Ariadne, Aldeburgh, 1974; created title rôle in William Alwyn's Miss Julie for radio, 1977; title rôle BBC world première, Prokofiev's Maddalena, 1979; created rôle of Duchess, Adès' Powder Her Face, Cheltenham Fest. and Almeida Th., 1995; other rôles incl. Donna Elvira (Ludwigsburg), 1978, Cinna in Mozart's Lucio Silla (Zurich), 1981, Cleopatra in Giulio Cesare, Donna Anna (Frankfurt), Teresa in Benvenuto Cellini (Lyon), title rôle in Massenet's Thaïs (Wexford), Blanche in Dialogues des Carmélites (Hildesheim), Desdemona in Otello (London); première of Eighth Book of Madrigals, Monteverdi Fest., Zürich Opera, 1979. Also recitalist, progs incl. A Spanish Songbook, Night and Day (cabaret), Fortunes of Love and War, 1998 and A Bouquet from the Pleasure Gardens, Cambridge Spring Concerts, 2007; concert repertoire includes Rameau, Bach (Passions and cantatas), Handel (Messiah, cantatas and oratorios), Haydn's Creation and Seasons, Mozart's Requiem and concert arias, Beethoven's Ninth and Egmont, Berlioz's Nuits d'Eté, Brahms's Requiem, Fauré's Requiem, Ravel's Shéhérazade, Falla's Three-Cornered Hat, Mahler's Second, Fourth and Eighth Symphonies, Strauss's Four Last Songs, Britten's Les Illuminations, Spring Symphony and War Requiem, Tippett's A Child of Our Time, Messiaen's Poèmes pour Mi, Webern op. 13 and 14 songs, and Schubert songs orch. Webern. Commissioned Cantiga: the song of Inés de Castro (dramatic scena for soprano and orch.) from David Matthews (world première, BBC Prom., 1988). Concerts and recitals in Austria, Belgium, France, Germany, Holland, Hong Kong, Italy, Scandinavia, Spain, Switzerland, Thailand, West Indies, UK and USA; masterclasses incl. Britten Pears Sch., Aldeburgh, Darlington Summer Sch., Trin. Coll. of Music, Southern TV; festival appearances incl. Aix-en-Provence, Aldeburgh, Bath, Bergen, Cheltenham, Edinburgh, Flanders, Florence, Hong Kong, Lausanne, Naantali, Prague, Singapore, Spoleto, Versailles, and BBC Prom. concerts. Recordings incl. three solo recitals (French, Spanish, and Mozart songs, with John Constable), Monteverdi's Vespro della Beata Vergine 1610, Ravel's Poèmes de Mallarmé, Handel's Admeto, Acis and Galatea, Ode on St Cecilia's Day, Elvira in Don Giovanni, Fauré's Pelléas et Mélisande, Rameau's La Danse, Hippolyte et Aricie, Britten's Les Illuminations, Peter Grimes, Canteloube's Songs of the Auvergne, Villa Lobos' Bachianas Brasileiras no 5, Samuel Barber's Knoxville—Summer of 1915, Cabaret Classics (with John Constable), South of the Border (...Down Mexico Way), A Spanish Songbook (with John Constable), Tippett's A Child of Our Time; première recordings: David Matthew's Cantiga: the Song of Inés de Castro, Mahler's Seven Early Songs (with David and Colin

**GÓMEZ PICKERING, Diego,** Hon. KCVO 2015; Consul General of Mexico in New York, 2016–18; *b* Mexico City, 6 Nov. 1977; *s* of Diego Gómez Soler and Patricia Pickering Chouza. *Educ:* Instituto Tecnológico Autónomo de México, Mexico City (BA Internat. Affairs); Columbia Univ. (Master Internat. Affairs). Protocol Officer, Mexican Pavilion, World Expo Hanover, 2000; freelance producer and reporter, Mexico City Bureau, CNN, 2001; Res. Fellow, Centro de Estudios Juan Marinello, Havana, 2001; Res. Fellow, Indian Inst. of Mass Communication, New Delhi, 2002; Consultant, UNESCO Global Alliance for Cultural Diversity, Paris, 2004; Consultant, Solana Consultores, Mexico City, 2005; Political, Cultural and Press Attaché, Embassy of Mexico, Kenya, 2006–07; Communications Consultant, UNRWA, Damascus, 2008–11; Foreign Press Officer, Presidential Office, Mexico City, 2012–13; Ambassador of Mexico to UK, 2013–16. Internat. Writers Award, Internat. Commn of Writers, 2014. *Publications:* La foto del recuerdo, 2006; Thursdays in Nairobi, 2010; La Primavera de Damasco, 2013. *Recreations:* tennis, cinema, hiking, cycling, travel, languages. *Clubs:* Royal Automobile, Athenæum, Groucho, Caledonian, Naval and Military, Harry's Bar, Mosimann, St Marks.

**GOMPERTZ, (Arthur John) Jeremy;** QC 1988; *b* 16 Oct. 1937; *s* of late Col Arthur William Bean Gompertz and Muriel Annie Gompertz (*née* Smith). *Educ:* Beaumont Coll.; Trinity Coll., Cambridge (MA). Called to the Bar, Gray's Inn, 1962, Bencher, 1997; in practice, South East Circuit, 1963–2009; a Recorder, 1987–2002. Counsel for: Metropolitan Police, Stephen Lawrence Inquiry, 1998; Kelly family, Hutton Inquiry, 2003; Humberside Police, Bichard (Soham) Inquiry, 2004. Chm., Mental Health Review Tribunal, 1993–2010. Member: Jockey Club Security and Investigations Cttee, 2002–05; Council, Racehorse Owners' Assoc., 2007–15; Disciplinary Rev. Gp, British Horseracing Authy, 2013–. *Recreations:* racing and breeding, travel, ski-ing. *Address:* 5 Essex Court, Temple, EC4Y 9AH. *T:* (020) 7410 2000.

**GOMPERTZ, William Edward;** Arts Editor, BBC, since 2009; *b* Tenterden, Kent, 25 Aug. 1965; *s* of Dr Hugh Gompertz, OBE and Frances Gompertz; *m* 1995, Kate Anderson; three *s* one *d*. *Educ:* Bedford Sch. Stage hand, Sadler's Wells, 1987–88; runner, Moving Picture Co., 1988–89; Co-Founder, Shots mag., 1990–96; Founder, Purple House, 1996–2002; Dir, Communications, 2002–06, Media, 2006–09, Tate. Mem. Bd, Nat. Campaign for the Arts, 2006–09. Hon. Fellow, Harris Manchester Coll., Oxford. *Publications:* What Are You Looking At?, 2012; Think Like an Artist, 2015. *E:* will.gompertz@bbc.co.uk. *Club:* Army and Navy.

**GONZÁLEZ MÁRQUEZ, Felipe;** Member for Madrid, 1977–2000, for Seville, 2000–04, Congress of Deputies; Prime Minister of Spain and President, Council of Ministers, 1982–96; *b* 5 March 1942; *s* of Felipe González and Juana Márquez; *m* 1969, Carmen Romero Lopez; two *s* one *d*; *m* 2012, Mar García Vaquero. *Educ:* Univ. of Seville (Law degree); Univ. of Louvain. Opened first labour law office, Seville, 1966; Spanish Socialist Party (PSOE), 1964–: Mem., Seville Provincial Cttee, 1965–69; Mem., Nat. Cttee, 1969–70; Mem., Exec. Bd, 1970; First Sec., 1974–79, resigned; re-elected, 1979; Sec.-Gen., 1974–97. Former Chm., Socialist Parly Group. Rep., OSCE and EU for Federal Republic of Yugoslavia, 1996–98; Extraordinary Ambassador and Plenipotentiary, Bi-Centenary of Independence of Ibero-American Republics, 2007–11; Pres., Cttee of the Wise, European Council, 2007–10. Co-Chm., Global Progress Council (formerly Fundación Socialismo XXI, then Global Progress Foundn), 1978–2009; Pres., Felipe González Foundn, 2013–. Pres., Cttee for Participation, Doñana Nature Reserve, 2009–12. Member: Club de Madrid; Iberoamérica Forum; Círculo de Montevideo Foundn; Real Instituto Elcano. Hon. Member: Jean Monnet Assoc.; Club de Roma; European Democratic Forum; Patron: Fundación Alternativas; Fundación Barenboim-Said. Hon. Dr: Louvain, 1995; Toulouse, 1998; Tel Aviv, 2005. Charlemagne Prize, 1993; Charles V Award, Yuste Eur. Acad. Foundn, 2000; Distinguished Leadership Award for Public Service in Americas, The Dialogue, 2015; I Beato Arnulfo Romero Prize, 2016; Co-existence Prize, Manuel Broseta Foundn, 2017; City of Athens Democracy Award, 2017. Grand Cross: Order of Military Merit (Spain), 1984; Order of Christ (Portugal), 1984; Order of José Martí (Cuba), 1986; Order of Isabel the Catholic (Spain), 1996; Order of Merit (Austria), 1997; Order of Quetzal (Colombia), 2004. *Publications:* What is Socialism?, 1976; PSOE, 1977; An Ethical Style: conversations with Victor Márquez Reviriego, 1982; The Future Is Not What It Was, 2001; Memories of the Future: reflections on the present, 2003; (ed) Ibero-America 2020: challenges from the crisis, 2009; My Idea of Europe, 2010; Can We Still Reach an Understanding?, 2011; In Search of Answers: leadership in times of crisis, 2013; Who's in Charge Here?: the global crisis of representative democracy, 2017. *Address:* Felipe González Foundation, Fuenterrabia 2, 28014 Madrid, Spain. *W:* www.felipegonzalez.es.

**GONZÁLEZ-PÁRAMO, Dr José Manuel;** Professor of Economics, Universidad Complutense, Madrid, since 1988; *b* Madrid, 9 Aug. 1958. *Educ:* Univ. Complutense, Madrid (Econs degree 1980; PhD Econs 1985); Columbia Univ., New York (MA Econs 1983; MPhil Econs 1984; PhD Econs 1986). Universidad Complutense, Madrid: Res. Asst and Teaching Fellow, 1980–82; Associate Prof. of Econs, 1985–88; Hd, Public Finance Dept, 1986–94. Econ. Advr, Min. of Econ. and Finance, 1985–87; Banco de España: Sen. Econ. Advr, 1989–94; Gov., 1994–2004; Mem., Exec. Bd, 1998–2004; Mem., Exec. Bd, European Central Bank, 2004–12; Mem., Exec. Bd, Banco Bilbao Vizcaya Argentaria, 2013– (Chief Officer, Global Econs, Regulation and Public Affairs; Chm., Internat. Adv. Bd). Europe Chair, TransAtlantic Business Council (formerly TransAtlantic Business Dialogue), 2016–. Advisory posts include: World Bank, Washington, 1984, 1989, 2000–02; Internat. Develt Bank, Argentina, 1998; EC, 1989, 1993; Spanish govt agencies, 1985–2004. Prof., World Bank Inst., 2001–02; Vis. Prof., Econs, IESE Business Sch., Univ. of Navarra, 2012–. Vice-Chm., Fundación Consejo España. Member: Eur. Acad. Scis and Arts, 2000–; Real Academia de Ciencias Morales y Políticas, 2015–. Hon. Dr Malaga. Charles V Medal, German-Spanish Chamber of Commerce; Premio Institut D'Estudis Financers a la Excelencia Financiera; Premio Círculo de Empresarios. *Publications:* (jtly) The Spanish Financial System, 1982; (ed jtly) Argentina: tax policy for stabilization and economic recovery, 1990; (jtly) Public Management, 1997; Costs and Benefits of Fiscal Discipline: the budget stability law in perspective, 2001; (jtly) Taxation of Savings Products in Europe, 2001; (with B. Moreno-Dodson) The Role of the State and Economic Consequences of Alternative Forms of Public Expenditures Financing, 2003; (jtly) Public Economics, 2004; numerous contribs to books and to jls on monetary and financial policy and fiscal and structural policies. *E:* officegonzalezparamo@gmail.com.

**GONZI, Hon. Dr Lawrence,** KUOM 2004; Prime Minister of Malta, 2004–13; *b* 1 July 1953; *s* of Louis and Inez Gonzi; *m* 1977, Catherine Callus; two *s* one *d*. *Educ:* Univ. of Malta (LLD 1975). Practised law, 1975–88. Mem., Prisons Bd, 1987–88; Chairman: Pharmacy Board, 1987–88; Nat. Commn for Mental Health Reform, 1987–94 and 1994–96; Nat. Commn for Persons with Disabilities, 1987–94 (Pres., 1994–96); Electoral System (Revision) Commn, 1994–95. Chm., Bd of Dirs, Mizzi Orgn, 1989–97. Speaker, House of Reps, 1988–92 and 1992–96; elected to House of Reps, from 2nd Dist, 1996; Opposition Party Whip, Sec. to Parly Gp and Shadow Minister for Social Policy, 1996–98; Minister for Social Policy and Leader, House of Reps, 1998–99, Dep. Prime Minister, 1999–2004, Minister of Finance, 2004–08. Sec.-Gen., 1997–98, Dep. Leader, 1999–2004, Nationalist Party. Gen. Pres., Malta Catholic Action Movement, 1976–86.

**GOOBY, Peter Frederick T.;** *see* Taylor-Gooby.

**GOOCH, Anthony John;** HM Diplomatic Service, retired; Deputy High Commissioner and Economic and Commercial Counsellor, Singapore, 1997–2000; freelance writer, researcher and consultant on competition issues, since 2014; *b* 28 Nov. 1941; *s* of John Edgar Gooch and Mary Elizabeth (*née* Bricknell); *m* 1966, Jennifer Jane Harrison (*d* 1984); one *d*; *m* 1988, Cynthia Lee Barlow. *Educ:* Latymer Upper Sch.; St Catharine's Coll., Cambridge (BA Hist.); Open Univ. (MA 2002). Pubns Editor, Europa Pubns, 1964–70; joined FCO, 1970: attachment to SEATO, Bangkok, 1972–74; Second, later First, Sec., FCO, 1974–80; First Secretary: (Economic), Stockholm, 1980–83; (Labour), Pretoria, 1984–88; FCO, 1988–92; (Commercial), Warsaw, 1992–96; Dir, Trade Promotion, and Consul-Gen., Warsaw, 1996–97. Inquiry Sec., later Manager (panellist), Competition Commn, 2002–14. *Recreations:* tennis, gardening, theatre, cinema. *Address:* 22 Trinity Place, Windsor, Berks SL4 3AT. *Club:* Windsor Lawn Tennis.

**GOOCH, Brig. Sir Arthur (Brian Sherlock Heywood),** 14th Bt *cr* 1746, of Benacre Hall, Suffolk; *b* 1 June 1937; *s* of late Col Brian Sherlock Gooch, DSO, TD and Monica Mary (*née* Heywood); *S* cousin, 2008; *m* 1963, Sarah Diana Rowena Perceval, JP; two *d*. *Educ:* Eton; RMA Sandhurst. Comdg The Life Guards, 1978–81. Hon. Col, Kent and Co. of London Yeomanry (Sharpshooters), 1992–99. DL Wilts 1998. *Recreation:* fishing. *Heir:* *b* Thomas Sherlock Heywood Gooch [*b* 12 Nov. 1943; *m* 1971, Elizabeth Clarice Joan Peyton; one *s* one *d*]. *Address:* Manor Farmhouse, Chitterne, Wilts BA12 0LG. *Club:* Army and Navy.

**GOOCH, Graham Alan,** OBE 1991; DL; Batting Coach, England cricket team, 2009–14; *b* 23 July 1953; *s* of late Alfred and of Rose Gooch; *m* 1976, Brenda Daniels; three *d* (incl. twins). *Educ:* Leytonstone. Batsman and bowler; first played for Essex CCC, 1973, Captain, 1986–94, retired, 1997; Member, England Test team, 1975–82 and 1986–Jan. 1995 (retired); played in S Africa, 1982; Captain of England, July 1988 and Sept. 1989–1993; 333 against India, highest score by a Test captain, 1990; 20 Test centuries; record no of runs (8900) in English Test cricket, 1995. England A team manager, Kenya and Sri Lanka tour, 1997–98; Manager, England Test tour, Australia, 1998–99. Chief Coach, 2001–05, Batting Coach, 2005–11, Essex CCC. Mem., Selection Panel, ECB, 1997–99. DL Essex, 2009. Hon. DArts E London, 2011. *Publications:* Batting, 1980; (with Alan Lee) My Cricket Diary 1981, 1982; (with Alan Lee) Out of the Wilderness, 1985; Testing Times (autobiog.), 1991; (with Frank Keating) Gooch: My Autobiography, 1995. *Address:* c/o England and Wales Cricket Board, Lord's Cricket Ground, NW8 8QZ.

**GOOCH, Prof. John,** PhD; FRHistS; Professor of International History, Leeds University, 1992–2010; *b* 25 Aug. 1945; *s* of George Gooch and Doris Evelyn (*née* Mottram); *m* 1967, Catherine Ann Staley; one *s* one *d*. *Educ:* Brockenhurst County High Sch.; King's Coll., Univ. of London (BA Hons History, class 1, 1966; PhD War Studies 1969). FRHistS 1975. Asst Lectr in History, 1966–67, Asst Lectr in War Studies, 1969, KCL; University of Lancaster: Lectr in History, 1969–81; Sen. Lectr, 1981–84; Reader in History, 1984–88; Prof. of History, 1988–92. Sec. of the Navy Sen. Res. Fellow, US Naval War Coll., 1985–86; Vis. Prof. of Military and Naval History, Yale Univ., 1988; Associate Fellow, Davenport Coll., Yale, 1988. Chm. of Council, Army Records Soc., 1983–2000; Vice-Pres., RHistS, 1990–94. Editor, Jl of Strategic Studies, 1978–2006; Gen. Editor, Internat. Relations of the Great Powers; Member of Editorial Board: European History Qly; Diplomacy and Statecraft; Terrorism and Small Wars; Security Studies; War in History. Premio Internazionale di Cultura, Città di Anghiari, 1983. Kt, Order of Vila Viçosa (Portugal), 1991; Cavaliere dell'Ordine della Stella della Solidarietà Italiana (Italy), 2010. *Publications:* The Plans of War: the general staff and British military strategy *c*. 1900–1916, 1974; Armies in Europe, 1980; The Prospect of War: studies in British defence policy 1847–1942, 1981; Politicians and Defence: studies in the formulation of British defence policy 1847–1970, 1981; Strategy and the Social Sciences, 1981; Military Deception and Strategic Surprise, 1982; Soldati e Borghesi nell'Europa Moderna, 1982; Army, State and Society in Italy 1870–1915, 1989 (trans. Italian); Decisive Campaigns of the Second World War, 1989; (with Eliot A. Cohen) Military Misfortunes: the anatomy of failure in war, 1990; Airpower: theory and practice, 1995; The Boer War: direction, experience and image, 2000; Mussolini and his Generals: the armed forces and fascist foreign policy, 1922–1940, 2007; The Italian Army and the First World War, 2014. *Recreation:* Italian food and wine. *Address:* Wellfield House, 15 Rutland Avenue, Matlock, Derbyshire DE4 3GQ. *T:* (01629) 593527.

**GOOCH, Sir Miles (Peter),** 6th Bt *cr* 1866, of Clewer Park, Berkshire; *b* 3 Feb. 1963; *s* of Sir Trevor Sherlock Gooch, 5th Bt and Denys Anne (*née* Venables); *S* father, 2003; *m* 2000, Louise Alicia Spiret; three *d*. *Educ:* Victoria Coll., Jersey; Preston Poly. (BEng). *Heir:* kinsman John Daniel Gooch, VRD [*b* 9 Dec. 1935; *m* 1972, Ann Patricia Lubbock; two *d*].

**GOOD, Anthony Bruton Meyrick,** OBE 2014; FCIPR; Group Chairman: Cox & Kings Ltd (formerly Cox and Kings (India) Ltd, later Cox & Kings Ltd), since 1975 (Director, since 1971); Flagship Group Ltd (formerly Millbank), 1994–2011; *b* 18 April 1933; *s* of Meyrick George Bruton Good and Amy Millicent Trussell; *m* (marr. diss.); one *d* (and one *d* decd); *m* 2010, Dr Iris Shafir. *Educ:* Felsted Sch. Mgt Trainee, Distillers Gp, 1950–52; Editorial Asst, Temple Press Ltd, 1952–55; PRO, Silver City Airways, 1955–60; Founder Chm., Good Relations Gp plc, 1961–88; Chairman: Good Relations (India) Ltd, 1988–; Good Consultancy Ltd, 1988–; Tulip Star Hotels Ltd, 1989–; Outright Marketing and Distribution Ltd, 1999–2014; Outright Communication Ltd, 2008–15; I-Connections Ltd, 2007–; Obento Ltd, 2004–13; Benney Watches plc, 2007–13; Director: Nutrahealth plc, 2005–15 (Chm., 2011–15); DQ Entertainment plc, 2008–13. Dir, UK India Business Council, 2005–15 (Chm., India, 2009–13). FCIPR (FIPR 1975); FInstD 1994, Hon. Life FInstD 2012. *Recreations:* travel, reading, theatre. *Address:* Flat 83, Whitelands House, Cheltenham Terrace, SW3 4QZ. *Club:* Royal Automobile.

**GOOD, Diana Frances;** Commissioner, Independent Commission for Aid Impact, 2011–15; Chair, Mary Ward Settlement and Mary Ward Legal Centre, 2008–16; *b* 16 July 1956; *d* of Michael and Valerie Hope; *m* 1981, Alexander Good; four *d*. *Educ:* Croydon High Sch., GPDST; St Anne's Coll., Oxford (BA Juris.); Chester Coll. of Law; Univ. of Aix-en-Provence (Dip. Etudes Supérieures). Admitted solicitor, 1981; a Recorder, 2001–11; joined Linklaters, 1979: Litigation Partner, 1988–2008; Litigation Partner, Brussels, 1989–92; Member: Finance and Policy Cttee, 1993–96; Diversity Cttee, 2000–08; Internat. Bd, 2001–04. Specialist Advr, Internat. Develt Cttee, H of C, 2015–. Member, Advisory Board, Advocates for Internat. Develt, 2007–11; Global Governance Advr, Camfed, 2018–. Trustee: British Inst. Internat. and Comparative Law, 2000–08; Access to Justice Foundn, 2008–12; Conciliation Resources, 2016–; Queen's Commonwealth Trust, 2017–. Mem. Bd, Red Shift Theatre Co., 2002–15. *Recreations:* holidays/travelling, theatre and cinema, cycling, including 450 miles in NW Vietnam for Medical Foundation for Victims of Torture, reading and discussion with Book Club members.

**GOOD, Sir John James Griffen, (Sir Ian),** Kt 2008; CBE 1992; CA; Chairman, Edrington Group, 1994–2013 (Director, 1979–2013); *b* Renfrewshire. CA 1967. Price Waterhouse, 1967–69; joined Edrington Holdings Ltd, 1969: Man. Dir, Robertson and Baxter Ltd; Chief Exec., 1989–2004. Former Chm., Scottish Industrial Develt Adv. Bd. Chairman: Hamilton Park Racecourse; Scottish Racing Mktg Ltd. Non-exec. Dir, Horserace Totalisator Bd, 2006–08. Former Chm., Robertson Trust. Former Chm., Scotch Whisky Assoc. Dep. Sen. Steward, Jockey Club (Mem., 2005–; Steward, 2007–). Trustee, Racing Foundation, 2012 (Chm., 2016–17).

**GOOD, Rt Rev. Kenneth Raymond;** Bishop of Derry and Raphoe, 2002–19; *b* 1 Nov. 1952; *s* of (William Thomas) Raymond Good and Jean Beryl (*née* Hewson); *m* 1977, Mary Knox; two *s* one *d*. *Educ*: Dublin Univ. (BA 1974); Nottingham Univ. (BA Theol., 1976); NUI (HDipEd 1981, MEd 1984). Ordained deacon, 1977, priest, 1978; Curate, Willowfield Parish, Belfast, 1977–79; Chaplain and Hd of Religious Educn, Ashton Comprehensive Sch., Cork, 1979–84; Rector: Dunganstown Union, dio. Glendalough, 1984–90; Shankill Parish, Lurgan, 1990–2002; Archdeacon of Dromore, 1997–2002. *Publications*: A Heart for the Unchurched, 1996. *Recreations*: golf, swimming, opera. *Address*: 15 Woodhall, Moira, Craigavon BT67 0NG. *E*: krgoodhome@btinternet.com.

**GOOD, Ven. Kenneth Roy;** Archdeacon of Richmond, 1993–2006, now Emeritus; *b* 28 Sept. 1941; *s* of Isaac Edward Good and Florence Helen Good (*née* White); *m* 1970, Joan Thérèse Bennett; one *s* one *d*. *Educ*: Stamford Sch.; King's Coll., London (BD 1966; AKC). Ordained deacon 1967, priest 1968; Asst Curate, St Peter, Stockton on Tees, 1967–70; Missions to Seamen: Port Chaplain, Antwerp, 1970–74, Kobe, 1974–79; Asst Gen. Sec., 1979–85; Vicar of Nunthorpe, 1985–93; RD of Stokesley, 1989–93. Hon. Canon, Kobe, 1985. *Recreations*: reading, rotary. *Address*: 18 Fox Howe, Coulby Newham, Middlesbrough TS8 0RU.

**GOODACRE, Peter Eliot,** RD 1979, with clasp 1991; DL; chartered surveyor; Principal, College of Estate Management, Reading, 1992–2007, Hon. Fellow, 2007; *b* 4 Nov. 1945; *s* of late Edward Leslie Goodacre and of Cicely May (*née* Elliott); *m* 1971, Brita Christina Forsling; one *d* (and one *d* decd). *Educ*: Kingston Grammar Sch.; Coll. of Estate Management; Loughborough Univ. of Technology (MSc). FRICS 1980. Commnd RNR, 1965; Lt Comdr, 1979. In private practice, 1966–69; Lecturer: Coll. of Estate Mgt, 1970–73; Univ. of Reading, 1973–78, Sen. Lectr 1978–83; Vice-Principal, Coll. of Estate Mgt, 1984–92. Mem., Gen. Council, RICS, 1986–2009 (Vice-Pres., 2005–08, Sen. Vice-Pres., 2007–08, Pres., 2008–09); Vice-Chm., 1997–98, Pres., 1998–99, Quantity Surveyors' Divl Council). Mem., Gtr London RFCA (Chm., Works and Bldgs Sub-Cttee, 1997–2003). Chm., James Butcher Housing Assoc., 2006–10; Member: Bd, Southern Housing Assoc., 2006–10; NHBC Council, 2009–14; Bd, Central and Cecil Housing Trust, 2013–15. Non-exec. Dir, Thames Valley Strategic Health Authy, 2004–06. Trustee: Harold Samuel Educn Trusts, 1992–; Guy Bigwood Trust, 2007–09; Sonning Volunteer Fire Brigade Trust, 2010–; Vice Patron, Commonwealth Housing Trust, 2010–. Pres., Berks, St John Ambulance, 2010–14. Chairman: Friends of St Andrew's Ch, Sonning, 2010–14 (Trustee, 2014–); Sonning Volunteer Fire Bde Trust, 2015–. FCIOB 1999. Freeman, City of London, 1994; Liveryman, Chartered Surveyors' Co., 1995–. DL Berks, 2011. *Publications*: Formula Method of Price Adjustment for Building Contracts, 1978, 2nd edn 1987; Cost Factors of Dimensional Co-ordination, 1981; Worked Examples in Quantity Surveying Measurement, 1982. *Recreations*: family, home and garden, visiting Sweden. *Address*: Kingsmead, West Drive, Sonning, Berks RG4 6GE. *T*: (0118) 969 2422. *Clubs*: Athenæum (Mem., Gen. Cttee, 2009–12), MCC; Phyllis Court (Henley).

**GOODALE, Prof. Melvyn Alan,** PhD; FRS 2013; FRSC 2001; Canada Research Chair in Visual Neuroscience, since 2001, and Founding Director, Brain and Mind Institute, since 2005, University of Western Ontario; *b* Leigh-on-Sea, Essex, 22 Jan. 1943; *s* of Lawrence and Alice Goodale; *m* 1982, Joan Finegan; one *s* two *d*. *Educ*: Univ. of Alberta (BA Psychol. 1963); Univ. of Calgary (MA 1966); Univ. of Western Ontario (PhD Psychol. 1969). Postdoctoral Fellow, Univ. of Oxford, 1969–71; Lectr, Univ. of St Andrews, 1971–77; Associate Prof., 1977–83, Prof., 1983–, Univ. of Western Ont. Hon. Fellow, Durham Univ., 2003. *Publications*: (with A. D. Milner) The Visual Brain in Action, 1995, 2nd edn 2006; (with A. D. Milner) Sight Unseen: an exploration of conscious and unconscious vision, 2004, 2nd edn 2013; contrib. papers to jls. *Recreations*: walking, cinema, bicycling, hiking, travel. *Address*: Brain and Mind Institute, Western Interdisciplinary Research Building, University of Western Ontario, London, ON N6A 5B7, Canada. *T*: 5196612070, *Fax*: 5196613613. *E*: mgoodale@uwo.ca.

**GOODALL, Caroline Mary Helen;** *b* Dewsbury, 22 May 1955; *d* of late Peter Goodall, CBE, TD and Sonja Jeanne Goodall; *m* 1983, Vesey John Munnings Hill. *Educ*: Queen Ethelburga's Sch., Harrogate; Newnham Coll., Cambridge (BA 1977); Harvard Business Sch. (MA). Admitted solicitor; Herbert Smith, later Herbert Smith Freehills LLP: Partner, 1987–2009; Global Hd, Corporate Practice, 2000–05; Consultant and Sen. Advr, 2009–17. Non-executive Director: SVG Capital plc, 2010–14; Grant Thornton LLP, 2010–17; Next plc, 2013–19. Associate Fellow, Newnham Coll., Cambridge, 2003–08. Trustee, Woodland Trust, 2009–12; Trustee and Chm. Audit Cttee, Nat. Trust, 2012–18 (Mem., Council, 2010–16). MInstD 2008–16. FRSA. *Recreations*: tennis, walking, sailing, theatre, classical music. *E*: cmhg@cmhgoodall.com. *Clubs*: Roehampton, Athenæum; Brancaster Staithe Sailing.

**GOODALL, Howard Lindsay,** CBE 2011; composer and broadcaster; *b* 26 May 1958; *s* of Geoffrey and Marion Goodall. *Educ*: New College Sch.; Stowe Sch.; Lord Williams' Sch., Thame; Christ Church, Oxford (MA 1979). ARCO 1975. Freelance composer, 1976–. Nat. Ambassador for Singing, 2007–11. *TV and film themes/scores* include: Blackadder; Red Dwarf; The Vicar of Dibley; The Thin Blue Line; 2.4 Children; Mr Bean; Rowan Atkinson in Revue; Q.I.; The Catherine Tate Show; *compositions* include: The Hired Man, 1984 (Ivor Novello Award for best musical, 1985); Girlfriends, 1987; Days of Hope, 1990; Silas Marner, 1993; Missa Aedis Christi, 1993; Marlborough Canticles, 1995; In Memoriam Anne Frank, 1995; The Kissing-Dance, 1998; We are the Burning Fire, 1998; The Dreaming, 2001; O Lord God of Time and Eternity, 2003; The Gathering Storm, 2003; Jason and the Argonauts, 2004; A Winter's Tale, 2005; Mr Bean's Holiday, 2007; Two Cities, 2006; Winter Lullabies, 2007; Eternal Light: a requiem, 2008 (Composer of the Year, Classical Brit Awards, 2009); Enchanted Voices: the beatitudes, 2009; Into the Storm, 2009; The Seasons, 2009; Love Story, 2010; Rigaudon for Diamond Jubilee, 2012; Sure of the Sky - Des Himmels sicher, commnd to be performed at St Symphorien Mil. Cemetery, 2014; (musical) Bend it Like Beckham, 2015; Invictus: a passion, 2018. Presenter: BBC: Choir of the Year, 1990–2002; The Story of Music, 2013; Channel Four: Howard Goodall's Organ Works (RTS Award for best original title music), 1997; Four Goes to Glyndebourne, 1997–98; Howard Goodall's Big Bangs, 2000 (BAFTA Award, Huw Weldon Award for Arts, Religion, Hist. and Sci., Peabody Award for Mass Journalism and Communication, IMZ TV Award for Best Documentary); Howard Goodall's Great Dates, 2002; Howard Goodall's Twentieth Century Greats, 2004; How Music Works, 2006; Sgt Pepper's Musical Revolution with Howard Goodall, 2017. Hon. DMus Bishop Grosseteste UC, 2006; Hon. DArts Bolton, 2008. Gold Badge, BACS, 2006; Making Music Sir Charles Grove Prize for Outstanding Contribn to British Music, 2007. *Publications*: The Story of Music, 2013. *Address*: c/o Caroline Chignell, PBJ Management, 22 Rathbone Street, W1T 1LG. *T*: (020) 7287 1112, *Fax*: (020) 7287 1191. *E*: PA@howardgoodall.info. *W*: www.howardgoodall.co.uk.

**GOODALL, Dame Jane;** *see* Goodall, Dame V. J.

**GOODALL, Rt Rev. Jonathan Michael;** *see* Ebbsfleet, Bishop Suffragan of.

**GOODALL, Rt Rev. Lindsay;** *see* Urwin, Rt Rev. L. G.

**GOODALL, Patrick John;** QC 2014; a Recorder, since 2018; *b* Bury St Edmunds, 1 Jan. 1971; *s* of Robert Christopher Goodall and Bridget Anne Goodall (*née* Sadlier); *m* 1999, Emily Kate Bainbridge; one *s* three *d*. *Educ*: St Joseph's Coll., Ipswich (Hd of Sch.); Univ. of Southampton (LLB); Brasenose Coll., Oxford (BCL). Admitted solicitor, 1997; Freshfields, 1995–97; called to the Bar, Inner Temple, 1998, Bencher, 2018; in practice as barrister, specialising in commercial law, 1998–; Jun. Counsel to the Crown (A Panel), 2011–14. *Publications*: (ed jtly) Commercial Court Procedure, 2001; (contrib.) Bullen and Leake and Jacob's Precedents of Pleadings, 2001, 18th edn 2016; (contrib.) Law of Bank Payments, 2004, 5th edn 2018; (contrib.) The Law of Privilege, 2006, 3rd edn 2018. *Recreations*: family, cinema, Isles of Scilly. *Address*: Fountain Court Chambers, Fountain Court, Temple, EC4Y 9DH. *T*: (020) 7583 3335, *Fax*: (020) 7353 0329. *Club*: Royal Automobile.

**GOODALL, Air Marshal Sir Roderick Harvey,** KBE 2001 (CBE 1990); CB 1999; AFC 1981, Bar 1987; Chief of Staff, Component Command Air North, NATO, 1999–2003; *b* 19 Jan. 1947; *s* of late Leonard George Harvey Goodall and Muriel Goodall; *m* 1973, Elizabeth Susan Haines; two *d*. *Educ*: Elizabeth Coll., Guernsey; RAF Coll., Cranwell. FRAeS 1997–2015. Commissioned 1968; served Bahrain, UK and Germany, to 1981; RAF Staff Coll., 1981; PMC Barnwood, 1982; OC 16 Sqn, Laarbruch, 1983–85; MoD, 1986–87; Station Comdr, RAF Bruggen, 1987–89; RCDS 1990; Station Comdr, RAF Detachment, Bahrain, 1990; Dir, Air Offensive and Air Force Ops, MoD, 1991–93; AOC No 2 Gp, 1994–96; COS Perm. Jt HQ, 1996–98; Leader, RAF Officers Branch Structure Review Team, 1998–99. Pres., RAF Golf Assoc., 1995–2003. Trustee, Lloyds TSB Foundn for the Channel Isles, 2005–11. *Recreations*: golf, photography, family. *Address*: c/o Lloyds Bank, 2 North Gate, Sleaford, Lincs NG34 7BL. *Club*: Royal Air Force.

**GOODALL, Prof. Roger Morgan,** PhD; FIMechE, FREng; Professor of Control Systems Engineering, Loughborough University, since 1994 (part-time, since 2017); Professor of Control, Institute of Railway Research, University of Huddersfield, since 2013 (part-time, since 2016); *b* Finchley, 7 May 1946; *s* of Philip Morgan and Gwynedd Marie Goodall; *m* 1987, Lesley Allison Page; one *s* three *d*. *Educ*: Ashville Coll., Harrogate; Peterhouse, Cambridge (BA 1968); Loughborough Univ. (PhD 1989). FIET (FIEE 1992); FIMechE 1995; FREng 2007. Jun. Engr, GEC-AEI Electronics Ltd, 1968–70; PSO, British Rail Res., Derby, 1970–82; Lectr, 1982–87, Sen. Lectr, 1987–94, Electronic & Electrical Engrg Dept, Loughborough Univ. Chm., UK Automatic Control Council, 2005–08. Member: Rolls-Royce Electrical Controls Systems and Electronics (formerly Electrical and Controls) Adv. Bd, 2003–13; Eur. Rail Res. Adv. Council, 2003–; Railway Tech. Strategy Leadership Gp (formerly Railway Tech. Strategy Adv. Gp), 2007–12; Scientific and Tech. Adv. Bd, Austrian Centre of Competence in Mechatronics, 2008–12. Vice-Pres., IFAC, 2008–14. Chm., Railway Div., IMechE, 2009–10 (Vice-Chm., 2005–09). James Watt Internat. Gold Medal, IMechE, 2011. *Publications*: Digital Control, 1991; contrib. learned jls incl. Proc. IEE, Proc. IMechE, Vehicle System Dynamics, Trans IEEE. *Recreations*: skiing, snowboarding, long walks with dogs, GPS gadgets, dining out, grandchildren. *Address*: Wolfson School of Mechanical, Electrical and Manufacturing Engineering, Loughborough University, Ashby Road, Loughborough, Leics LE11 3TU. *E*: R.M.Goodall@lboro.ac.uk.

**GOODALL, Dame (Valerie) Jane,** DBE 2003 (CBE 1995); PhD; Scientific Director, Gombe Wildlife Research Institute, Tanzania, since 1967; *b* 3 April 1934; *er d* of Mortimer Herbert Morris-Goodall and Vanne Morris-Goodall (*née* Joseph); *m* 1st, 1964, Baron Hugo van Lawick (marr. diss. 1974); one *s*; 2nd, 1975, Hon. Derek Bryceson, Tanzanian MP (*d* 1980). *Educ*: Uplands Sch., Bournemouth; Cambridge Univ. (PhD 1965). Sec., Oxford Univ., 1952; worked as asst to Louis and Mary Leakey, Olduvai Gorge, 1957; engaged in res. into behaviour of chimpanzees, Gombe Stream Game Reserve, now Gombe Nat. Park, 1960–; res. in social behaviour of Spotted Hyena, Ngorongoro, 1968–69; dir. res. on behaviour of Olive Baboon, Gombe, 1972–82. Vis. Prof., Dept of Psychiatry and Program of Human Biology, Stanford Univ., 1971–75; Hon. Vis. Prof. in Zoology, Dar es Salaam Univ., 1973–; A. D. White Prof.-at-Large, Cornell Univ., 1996–. Vice-Pres., Animal Welfare Inst., BVA, 1987–; Mem. Adv. Bd, Albert Schweitzer Inst. for the Humanities, 1991–; Patron, Voiceless (Australia); Trustee, Jane Goodall Insts in UK, USA and Canada, and member of many other conservation and wildlife socs and foundns. Documentary films for television on research with chimpanzees incl. Fifi's Boys, BBC, 1995. Hon. FRAI 1991. UN Messenger for Peace, 2002–. Many hon. degrees. Numerous awards and prizes including: Franklin Burr Award for contrib. to Science, 1963, 1964, Centennial Award, 1988, Hubbard Medal, 1995, Nat. Geographic Soc.; Conservation Award, NY Zool Soc., 1974; Gold Medal, Soc. of Women Geographers, 1990; Kyoto Prize, 1990; Edinburgh Medal, 1991; Silver Medal, Zool Soc. of London, 1996; 60th Anniversary Medal, UNESCO, 2006. *Publications*: My Friends the Wild Chimpanzees, 1967; (with H. van Lawick) Innocent Killers, 1970; In the Shadow of Man, 1971; The Chimpanzees of Gombe: patterns of behaviour, 1986; Through A Window: 30 years observing the Gombe chimpanzees, 1990; (with Dale Peterson) Visions of Caliban, 1993; Jane Goodall: with love, 1994; Reason for Hope (autobiog.), 1999; (jtly) Hope for Animals and their World: how endangered species are being rescued from the brink, 2010; (with Gail Hudson) Seeds of Hope: wisdom and wonder from the world of plants, 2013; contribs to learned jls; *for children*: (with H. van Lawick) Grub: the bush baby, 1972; My Life with the Chimpanzees, 1988; The Chimpanzee Family Book, 1989; Jane Goodall's Animal World: chimps, 1989; Animal Family Series, 1991; The Eagle and the Wren, 2000. *Address*: Jane Goodall Institute UK, Suite 2, M Shed, Bath Road, Lymington, Hants SO41 3YL. *E*: info@janegoodall.org.uk. *Club*: Explorers (New York).

**GOODBODY, Clarissa Mary;** *see* Farr, C. M.

**GOODBY, Prof. John William,** PhD; FRS 2011; CChem, FRSC; Professor of Materials Chemistry, University of York, 2005–16, now Emeritus; Director, Kingston Chemicals Ltd, since 2000. *Educ*: Univ. of Hull (BSc Chem. 1974; PhD Organic Chem. 1977; DSc Chem. 1988). CChem 1979; FRSC 1989. AT&T Bell Labs, USA, 1979–88; University of Hull: STC-Thorn EMI Industrial Reader, 1988–90; Prof. and Hd of Organic Chemistry, 1990–2004; Hd, Dept of Chem., 1999–2001. Member, Editorial Board: Jl Liquid Crystals, 1989–; Jl Materials Chem., 1991–. Chair, British Liquid Crystal Soc., 2003–05 (Vice-Chair, 2000–03, 2005–06); Pres., Internat. Liquid Crystal Soc., 2000–04 (Vice-Pres., 1996–2000; Hon. Mem., 2010). Fellow: World Technol. Network, 2004; World Innovation Foundn, 2005. Hon. ScD TCD, 2002; Hon. DSc Inst. Nat. des Scis Appliquées, Lyon, 2015. GW Gray Medal, British Liquid Crystal Soc., 1996; Tilden Medal and Lectr, 2002, Interdisciplinary Award, 2007, Derek Birchall Medal, 2013, RSC; AkzoNobel UK Sci.

Prize, 2014; Freedericksz Medal, Russian Liquid Crystal Soc., 2016; Royal Medal, Royal Soc., 2016; Pierre Gilles de Gennes Prize, Internat. Liquid Crystal Soc., 2018. *Publications*: (jtly) Smectic Liquid Crystals, 1984; (contrib.) Ferroelectric Liquid Crystals: principles, properties and applications, 1991; (Co-ed) The Handbook of Liquid Crystals, 4 vols, 1998, (Sen. Ed.) 2nd edn as The New Handbooks of Liquid Crystals, 8 vols, 2014; contribs to scientific jls incl. Jl Materials Chem., Jl Structural Chem., Liquid Crystal, Physics Rev. E, Jl Amer. Chem. Soc. *Address*: Department of Chemistry, University of York, Heslington, York YO10 5DD.

GOODCHILD, David Lionel Napier, CMG 1986; a Director, Directorate-General of External Relations, Commission of the European Communities, 1985–86; *b* 20 July 1935; *s* of Hugh N. Goodchild and Beryl C. M. Goodchild. *Educ*: Eton College; King's College, Cambridge (MA). Joined Foreign Office, 1958; served Tehran, NATO (Paris), and FO, 1959–70; Dep. Political Adviser, British Mil. Govt, Berlin, 1970–72; transferred to EEC, Brussels, 1973; Head of Division, 1973, Principal Counsellor then Director, 1979–86. *Address*: Linden, Hall Road, Lavenham, Sudbury, Suffolk CO10 9QU. *T*: (01787) 248339.

GOODCHILD, Marianne, (Mrs Trevor Goodchild); *see* Rigge, M.

GOODCHILD, Peter Robert Edward; writer and film producer; *b* 18 Aug. 1939; *s* of Douglas Richard Geoffrey Goodchild, MBE and Lottie May Goodchild; *m* 1968, Penelope Jane, *d* of Dr William and Gwendoline Pointon-Dick; two *d*. *Educ*: Aldenham Sch., Elstree; St John's College, Oxford (MA). CChem, FRSC 1979. General trainee, BBC, 1963; BBC TV: Producer, Horizon, 1965–69, Editor, 1969–76; Editor, Special Features, 1977–80; Head, Science Features Dept, 1980–84; Head, Plays Dept, 1984–89; Exec. Producer, BBC Films, 1989–92. Producer, Television: The March, 1990; Trust Me, 1991; Adam Bede, 1992, Black Easter, 1994 (Gold Award, Chicago Film Fest., 1996); King of Chaos, 1998. Director: Screen Partners, 1992–94; Stone City Films, 1995–98; Green Umbrella Films, 1998–2005. Vis. Lectr, Nat. Film and TV Sch., 1995–2001. Pres., Dunchideock Treacle Mines, 2000–. Radio plays: Chicago Conspiracy Trial, 1993 (Gold Award, NY Radio Fest., 1995); Nuremberg, 1995; In the Name of Security, 1998; Lockerbie on Trial, 2001; The Putney Debates, 2002; The Real Dr Strangelove, 2006; stage plays: The Great Tennessee Monkey Trial, US tours, 2005–09; The Real Dr Strangelove, US tours, 2010–11. SFTA Mullard Award, for Horizon, 1967, 1968, 1969; BAFTA Awards: best factual series, for Horizon, 1972, 1974; best drama series, Marie Curie, 1977, Oppenheimer, 1980; Italia Prize for best factual prog., for Horizon, 1973, 1975. *Publications*: J. Robert Oppenheimer: 'shatterer of worlds', 1980; Edward Teller: the real Dr Strangelove, 2004. *Recreations*: music, painting, rowing. *Address*: Dunchideock House, Dunchideock, Exeter, Devon EX2 9TS. *Club*: Oxford and Cambridge.

GOODE, Cary; *see* Goode, P. C. A.

GOODE, Charles Barrington, AC 2001; Chairman, Flagstaff Partners, since 2009; *b* 26 Aug. 1938; *s* of Charles Thomas Goode and Jean Florence (*née* Robertson); *m* 1987, Cornelia Masters (*née* Ladd; former wife of Baron Baillieu, *qv*); one step *s*. *Educ*: Univ. of Melbourne (BCom Hons); Columbia Univ., NY (MBA). Joined Potter Partners, 1961: Partner, 1969; Sen. Partner, 1980–86; Chm., Potter Partners Gp Ltd, 1987–89. Chairman: Australian United Investment Co. Ltd, 1990–; Diversified United Investment Ltd, 1991–; Australia and New Zealand Banking Gp, 1995–2009 (Dir, 1991–2009); Woodside Petroleum Ltd, 1999–2007 (Dir, 1988–2007); Director: Pacific Dunlop Ltd, 1987–99; Qld Investment Corp. Ltd, 1991–99; CSR Ltd, 1993–2000; Singapore Airlines Ltd, 1999–2006. Chm., Ian Potter Foundn Ltd, 1994–. Member: Melbourne Cttee, Ludwig Inst. for Cancer Res., 1981–92; Exec. Cttee, Anti-Cancer Council of Victoria, 1981–84; Cttee of Mgt, Royal Victorian Eye and Ear Hosp., 1982–86; Chm., Howard Florey Inst. Exptl Physiol. and Medicine, 1997–2004. Pres., Inst. Public Affairs, 1984–93. Member of Council: Monash Univ., 1980–85 (Trustee, Monash Univ. Foundn, 1983–85); Australian Ballet Sch., 1980–86. Hon. LLD: Melbourne, 2001; Monash, 2002. Centenary Medal, 2003. *Recreations*: golf, reading. *Address*: 801/6 Victoria Street, St Kilda, Vic 3182, Australia. *T*: (3) 95348585, *Fax*: (3) 95341019. *Clubs*: Melbourne; Frankston Golf.

GOODE, Dr David Anthony, FLS; ecologist; Head of Environment, Greater London Authority, 2000–04; *b* 16 Jan. 1941; *s* of Rev. William Aubrey Goode and Vera Goode (*née* Parkinson); *m* 1966, Diana Lamble (*d* 2008); one *s* one *d*. *Educ*: Queen's Sch., Mönchen Gladbach, Germany; Malet Lambert High Sch., Hull; Univ. of Hull (BSc Sp. Hons Geol. 1963; PhD Botany 1970); University Coll. London (Postgrad. Dip. Conservation 1964). MIEEM 1991, FCIEEM (FIEEM 2002) (Pres., 1994–97; Patron, 2010–); CEnv 2005. Peatland Officer, 1967–69, Hd, Peatland Ecology, 1969–73, Nature Conservancy; PSO, 1973–76, Asst Chief Scientist, 1976–82, NCC; Sen. Ecologist, GLC, 1982–86; Dir, London Ecology Unit, 1986–2000. Vis. Prof., UCL, 1994–; Hon. Prof., E China Normal Univ., Shanghai, 1996–2000. Brian Walker Lect., Green Coll., Oxford, 2003. Member: Envmt Panel, C of E Bd for Social Responsibility, 1983–92; Terrestrial Life Scis Grants Panel, 1984–87; Expert Rev. Gp on Urban Envmtl Sci., 1993–94, NERC; UK-Man and the Biosphere Urban Forum, 1987– (Vice Chm., 1990–94; Fellow, 2010); Adv. Cttee, Envmtl Law Foundn, 1991–2000; RHS Sci. and Horticulture Cttee, 1994–2002; UK Biodiversity Action Plan Steering Gp, 1994–95 (Chm., Public Awareness Gp, 1994–95); UK Agenda 21 Steering Gp, 1995–2000; UK Biodiversity Gp, 1996–2001 (Chm., Local Issues Gp, 1996–98); New Renaissance Gp, 1996–2002; Adv. Cttee, Darwin Initiative for Survival of the Species, 2000–06; UK Local Sustainability Gp, 2001–02; RHS Conservation and Envmt Cttee, 2001–11; England Biodiversity Gp, 2003–11 (Chm., Urban Gp, 2003–11); IUCN Task Force on Cities and Protected Areas, 2004–; Panel, UK Sustainable Develt, 2006–11; Adv. Bd, London Nat. Park City, 2017. Member Board: Field Studies Council Exec., 1979–85; London Ecology Centre Trust, 1985–91; Think Green Campaign, 1985–91; Dir, Nat. Forest Co., 1998–2004; Chairman: Trust for Urban Ecology, 1987–91 (Pres., 1991–94); London Biodiversity Partnership, 1997–2004; Vice-Chm., 1991–92, Chm., 1992–94, Vice-Pres., 2002–06, Tree Council. Vice-Pres., British Assoc. Nature Conservationists, 1981–85; President: Reigate Soc., 1995–2000; Ecology and Conservation Studies Soc., 1999–2001; Biol Scis Section, BAAS, 2000; Bath Natural History Soc., 2018–. Advr, Landscape and Arts Network, 2001–11. Mem., British Ecol Soc., 1964– (Mem. Council, 1977–80 and 1988–92). FLS 1981 (Mem. Council, 1983–86); FRSA 1999. Heidelberg Award for Envmtl Excellence, 1999; Chartered Inst. of Ecol. and Envmtl Mgt Medal, 2015. *Publications*: Wild in London, 1986; (ed jtly) Ecology and Design in Landscape, 1986; (ed jtly) Routledge Handbook of Urban Ecology, 2011; Nature in Towns and Cities, 2014; contrib. numerous scientific papers and articles on envmtl topics. *Recreations*: photography, music, theatre, walking, ornithology, exploring the natural world. *Address*: Eastergate, 37a Lyncombe Hill, Bath BA2 4PQ. *Club*: Athenæum.

GOODE, (Penelope) Cary (Anne); freelance garden designer, since 1992; *b* 5 Dec. 1947; *d* of Ernest Edgar Spink and Rachel Atcherly Spink; *m* 1987, Richard Nicholas Goode. *Educ*: Westwing Sch. Royal Ascot Enclosure Office, 1971; MoD, 1973; Manager, retail business, 1978; Domestic and Social Sec., RCOG, 1980; Educn Administrator, British Heart Foundn, 1982; Dir, Asthma Res. Council, later Nat. Asthma Campaign, 1988–92. *Recreations*: gardening, vintage cars, dogs. *Address*: Rhodds Farm, Lyonshall, Hereford HR5 3LW. *T*: (01544) 340120.

GOODE, Sir Royston Miles, (Sir Roy), Kt 2000; CBE 1994 (OBE 1972); QC 1990; FBA 1988; Norton Rose Professor of English Law, Oxford University, 1990–98, now Emeritus Professor; Fellow, St John's College, Oxford, 1990–98, now Emeritus Fellow; *b* 6 April 1933; *s* of Samuel and Bloom Goode; *m* 1964, Catherine Anne Rueff; one *d*. *Educ*: Highgate School. LLB London, 1954; LLD London, 1976; DCL Oxon 2005. Admitted Solicitor, 1955. Partner, Victor Mishcon & Co., solicitors, 1966–71, Consultant 1971–88. Called to the Bar, Inner Temple, 1988; Hon. Bencher, 1992. Queen Mary College, University of London: Prof. of Law, 1971–73; Head of Dept and Dean of Faculty of Laws, 1976–80; Crowther Prof. of Credit and Commercial Law, 1973–89; Dir and Founder, Centre for Commercial Law Studies, 1980–89. Vis. Prof., Melbourne, 1975; Aust. Commonwealth Vis. Fellow, 1975. Chairman: Advertising Adv. Cttee, IBA, 1976–80; Pension Law Rev. Cttee, 1992–93; Member: Cttee on Consumer Credit, 1968–71; Monopolies and Mergers Commn, 1981–86; Deptl Cttee on Arbitration Law, DTI, 1986–; Governing Council, Internat. Inst. for Unification of Private Law, 1988–2003; Council of the Banking Ombudsman, 1989–92. Justice: Mem. Council, 1975; Chm. Exec. Cttee, 1994–96 (Vice-Chm., 1988–94); Mem., Council of Mgt, British Inst. of Internat. and Comparative Law, 1982. Hon. President: Centre for Commercial Law Studies, 1990–; Oxford Inst. of Legal Practice, 1994–96. Editor, Consumer Credit Law and Practice (looseleaf), 1999–. Hon. Fellow, QMW (Fellow, 1991). FRSA 1990. Hon. DSc (Econ) London, 1996; Hon. LLD: UEA, 2003; Coll. of Law, 2011. *Publications*: Hire-Purchase Law and Practice, 1962, 2nd edn 1970, with Supplement 1975; The Hire-Purchase Act 1964, 1964; (with J. S. Ziegel) Hire-Purchase and Conditional Sale: a Comparative Survey of Commonwealth and American Law, 1965; Introduction to the Consumer Credit Act, 1974; (ed) Consumer Credit Legislation, 1977, reissued as Consumer Credit Law and Practice (looseleaf), 1999; Consumer Credit, 1978; Commercial Law, 1982, 3rd edn 2004; Legal Problems of Credit and Security, 1982, 3rd edn 2003; Payment Obligations in Commercial and Financial Transactions, 1983; Proprietary Rights and Insolvency in Sales Transactions, 1985, 2nd edn 1989; Principles of Corporate Insolvency Law, 1990, 4th edn 2011; Convention on International Interests in Mobile Equipment and Protocol Thereto on Matters Specific to Aircraft Equipment: official commentary, 2002, 4th edn 2019; (jtly) Transnational Commercial Law, 2007, 2nd edn 2015; Convention on International Interests in Mobile Equipment and Luxembourg Protocol Thereto on Matters Specific to Railway Rolling Stock: official commentary, 2008, 2nd edn 2014; (jtly) Guide to ICC Uniform Rules for Demand Guarantees, 2011; Convention on International Interests in Mobile Equipment and Protocol Thereto on Matters Specific to Space Assets: official commentary, 2013. *Recreations*: chess, reading, walking, browsing in bookshops. *Address*: c/o St John's College, Oxford OX1 3JP; 42 St John Street, Oxford OX1 2LH. *Club*: Reform.

GOODENOUGH, Sir Anthony (Michael), KCMG 1997 (CMG 1990); HM Diplomatic Service, retired; High Commissioner to Canada, 1996–2000; *b* 5 July 1941; *s* of Rear-Adm. Michael Grant Goodenough, CBE, DSO, and Nancy, *d* of Sir Ransford Slater, GCMG, CBE; *m* 1967, Veronica Mary, *d* of Col Peter Pender-Cudlip, LVO; two *s* one *d*. *Educ*: Wellington Coll.; New Coll., Oxford (MA 1980). Voluntary Service Overseas, Sarawak, 1963–64; Foreign Office, 1964; Athens, 1967; Private Secretary to Parliamentary Under Secretary, 1971, and Minister of State, FCO, 1972; Paris, 1974; FCO, 1977; Counsellor on secondment to Cabinet Office, 1980; Hd of Chancery, Islamabad, 1982; Hd, Personnel Policy Dept, FCO, 1986–89; High Comr, Ghana and Ambassador (non-resident), Togo, 1989–92; Asst Under-Sec. of State (Africa and Commonwealth), FCO, 1992–95. Sec.-Gen., Order of St John, 2000–03. Governor: Goodenough Coll. for Overseas Graduates, 2000–12; Wellington Coll., 2002–10 (Vice-Pres., 2004–10). *Recreations*: family, travel, reading, writing. *Address*: The Old House, North Cheriton, Templecombe, Somerset BA8 0AE.

GOODENOUGH, Prof. John Bannister; Virginia H. Cockrell Centennial Professor of Engineering, University of Texas at Austin, since 1986; *b* 25 July 1922; *s* of Erwin Ramsdell Goodenough and Helen Lewis Goodenough; *m* 1951, Irene Johnston Wiseman. *Educ*: Yale Univ. (AB, Maths); Univ. of Chicago (MS, PhD, Physics). Meteorologist, US Army Air Force, 1942–48; Research Engr, Westinghouse Corp., 1951–52; Research Physicist (Leader, Electronic Materials Gp), Lincoln Laboratory, MIT, 1952–76; Prof. and Hd of Inorganic Chemistry Laboratory, Oxford Univ., 1976–86. Member: Nat. Acad. of Engrg, 1976–; Presidential Commn on Superconductivity, 1989–90; Nat. Acad. of Sci., USA, 2012; Nat. Acad. of Inventors, USA, 2016. Foreign Associate: Acad. of Scis, Institut de France, 1992; Acad. de Ciencias Exactas, Físicas y Naturales, Spain, 2003. Foreign Mem., Royal Soc., 2010. Dr *hc*: Bordeaux, 1967; Santiago de Compostela, 2002; Iona, 2018. Von Hippel Award, Materials Res. Soc., 1989; Sen. Res. Award, Amer. Soc. of Engrg Educn, 1990; Univ. of Pennsylvania Medal for Dist. Achievement, 1996; John Bardeen Award, Minerals, Metals & Materials Soc., 1997; Olim Palladium Award, Electrochem. Soc., 1999; Japan Prize, Sci. and Technol. Foundn of Japan, 2001; Enrico Fermi Award, US Dept of Energy, 2009; Nat. Medal of Sci., USA, 2011; Charles Stark Draper Prize for Engrg, NAE, 2014; Eric and Sheila Samson Prime Minister's Prize for Innovation in Alt. Fuels for Transportation, 2015; Benjamin Franklin Medal in Chemistry, Franklin Inst., 2018. Associate Editor: Materials Research Bulletin, 1966–; Jl Solid State Chemistry, 1969–; Structure and Bonding, 1978–; Solid State Ionics, 1980–94; Superconductor Science and Technology, 1987–; Jl of Materials Chem., 1990–95; Chem. of Materials, 1990–; Co-editor, International Series of Monographs on Chemistry, 1979–86; Member Executive, Editorial Board: Jl of Applied Electrochem., 1983–88; European Jl of Solid State and Inorganic Chem., 1992–. *Publications*: Magnetism and the Chemical Bond, 1963; Les oxydes des métaux de transition, 1973; Witness to Grace, 2008; (with K. Huang) Solid Oxide Fuel Cell Technology: principles, performance and operations, 2009; numerous research papers in learned jls. *Recreations*: walking, travel. *Address*: Texas Materials Institute, University of Texas at Austin, ETC 9.102, Austin, TX 78712, USA. *T*: (512) 4711646.

GOODENOUGH, Sir William (McLernon), 3rd Bt *cr* 1943, of Broadwell and Filkins, co. Oxford; Group Executive Chairman, Design Bridge Ltd, since 2002; *b* 5 Aug. 1954; *o s* of Sir Richard Edmund Goodenough, 2nd Bt and Jane Isobel Goodenough (*d* 1998); *S* father, 1996; *m* 1st, 1982, Louise Elizabeth Ortmans (marr. diss. 1998); one *s* two *d*; 2nd, 2002, Delia Mary, *d* of David Curzon-Price. *Educ*: Stanbridge Earls Sch.; Southampton Univ. Designer, 1980–83, Dir, 1984–87, Allied International Designers Ltd; Man. Dir, Allied International Designers (Singapore), 1983–86; Founding Partner and Man. Dir, 1986, Jt Man. Dir and Sales Dir, 1987–2002, Design Bridge Ltd. Gov., Goodenough Coll., London, 2011–. *Recreations*: fishing, shooting, painting. *Heir*: *s* Samuel William Hector Goodenough, *b* 11 June 1992. *Address*: Beck Hall, Billingford, East Dereham, Norfolk NR20 4QZ. *Clubs*: Allsorts, Boodle's, Pratt's.

GOODER, Rev. Canon Dr Paula R.; Canon Chancellor, St Paul's Cathedral, since 2019; *b* Manchester, 1969; *d* of Martin Lee Gooder and Margaret Carol Gooder; *m* 1998, Peter Babington; two *d*. *Educ*: Fallowfield C of E Secondary Sch., Manchester; Loreto Sixth Form Coll., Manchester; Worcester Coll., Oxford (MA Oxon 1st cl. 1992); Queen's Coll., Oxford (DPhil 1998). Lectr in Old Testament Studies, Ripon Coll., Cuddeson, 1995–2001; Lectr in New Testament Studies, Queen's Foundn for Ecumenical Theol Educn, Birmingham, 2001–07; freelance writer and lectr, 2007–14; Theologian-in-Residence,

Bible Soc., 2014–17; Dir of Mission, Learning and Develt, Dio. of Birmingham, 2017–18. Hon. Sen. Lectr, St Andrews Univ.; Hon. Res. Fellow, Durham Univ.; Hon. Fellow, St Chad's Coll., Durham. Six Preacher, Canterbury Cathedral; Canon Theologian, Birmingham Cathedral. *Publications:* (contrib.) Oxford Dictionary of the Christian Church, 3rd edn 1997; Exploring New Testament Greek: a way in, 2004; (contrib.) Paths to Unity: explorations in ecumenical method, 2005; Searching for Meaning: an introduction to interpreting the New Testament, 2008; (contrib.) The Diaconal Church: beyond the mould of Christendom, 2008; (contrib.) The Anglican Communion and Homosexuality, 2008; Heaven, 2011; Body, 2016; Phoebe: a story, 2018; The Spirit of the Christian Year series: The Meaning is in the Waiting, 2008; This Risen Existence, 2009; Everyday God, 2012; Let Me Go There, 2016; Biblical Exploration Series: Journey to the Empty Tomb, 2014; Journey to the Manger, 2015; contrib. articles in jls incl. Transmission, Sojourners Mag, New Blackfriars, Modern Believing, Priest and People. *Address:* The Chapter House, St Paul's Churchyard, EC4M 8AD.

**GOODERHAM, Peter Olaf,** CMG 2007; PhD; UK Permanent Representative to Office of the United Nations and other international organisations, Geneva, 2008–12; *b* 29 July 1954; *s* of Leonard Eric Gooderham and Gerd Gooderham; *m* 1985, Carol Anne Ward. *Educ:* Univ. of Newcastle (BA Hons); Univ. of Bristol (PhD 1981). Res. Fellow, Centre for Russian and E European Studies, Univ. of Birmingham, 1981–83; joined FCO, 1983; Falkland Is Dept, FCO, 1983–85; Second, later First, Sec., UK Delegn to NATO, Brussels, 1985–87; First Secretary: W Africa Dept, FCO, 1987–90; Riyadh, 1990–93; Dep. Hd, Security Policy Dept, FCO, 1993–96; Counsellor (Econ. and Social), UK Mission to UN, NY, 1996–99; Counsellor (Pol and Mil.), Washington, 1999–2003; UK Rep. to Pol and Security Cttee, EU, and UK Perm. Rep. to WEU, Brussels (with rank of Ambassador), 2003–04; Dir, Middle E and N Africa, FCO, 2004–07; Internat. Dir, MoJ, 2012; Sen. Dir, RCDS, 2013–14; Dir, Internat. Chamber of Commerce (UK), 2014–15; Sen. Directing Staff, RCDS, 2015–17, 2018–19. *Recreations:* travel, cinema, swimming.

**GOODEY, Felicity Margaret Sue,** CBE 2001; DL; consultant on media and urban regeneration; Chairman, Buxton International Festival, since 2015; *b* 25 July 1949; *d* of Henry Ernest Arthur and Susan Elsie Goodey; *m* 1973, John R. Marsh; two *s*. *Educ:* St Austell Grammar Sch.; St Hugh's Coll., Oxford (BA Hons Hist. Oxon 1971). Graduate trainee and reporter, World at One, BBC Radio, 1971–85; Northern Corresp., 1974–75, Northern Industrial Corresp., 1975–85, BBC TV; Presenter, 1987–99: File on Four, Punters, Sunday Programme, R4; Northwest Tonight, Northwestminster, BBC TV; owner and manager, Felicity Goodey & Associates, 1989–98; Director, Precise Communications, 1998–2004; Interim Chief Exec., Mediacity:UK, 2006–07. Chairman: The Lowry, 1994–2004 (Pres., 2004–); Lowry Operational & Develt Cos, 1994–2002; founder and non-exec. Dir, Excellence Northwest, 1993–2003; Bd Mem., Going for Green, 1994–98; Chairman: Cultural Consortium NW, 1999–2004; NW Tourism Forum, later Tourism NW England, 2004–11; Central Salford Urban Regeneration Co., 2005–11; University Hosp. of S Manchester NHS Foundn Trust, 2008–15; non-executive Director: Sustainability Northwest, 1994–98; Manchester Commonwealth Games Ltd, 1997–2002; Northwest Agency, 1998–2002; Manchester Chamber of Commerce and Industry, 1999–2005 (Pres., 2001–02); Nord Anglia plc, 1999–2007; Gtr Manchester Chamber of Commerce and Industry, 2005–. Dir, Unique Communications Gp, 2004–07. Member: Private Investment Commn Northern Way, 2007–10; Panel, Regl Growth Fund, 2011–. Mem., AHRB, subseq. AHRC, 2003–07. Member Council: Salford Univ., 2006–12; Manchester Univ., 2008–. Member: Adv. Bd, Manchester Business Sch., 2008–; Bd, Royal Northern Sch. of Music, 2014–. Hon. Vice Pres., Northwest Riding for Disabled, 1978–; Trustee, Friends of Rosie (children's cancer res.), 1992–; Pres., Cheshire Wildlife Trust, 2011–; Hon. Col 207 (Manchester) Field Hosp. (V), 2009–14. Gov., Manchester Grammar Sch., 1994–2008. DL Greater Manchester, 1998. Hon. Fellow, Bolton Inst., 2002; Hon. FRIBA 2005. Hon. DLitt: Salford, 1996; Manchester Metropolitan, 2000; Hon. LLD Manchester, 2003. *Recreations:* the family, theatre, opera. *Address:* Buxton Festival, 3 The Square, Buxton, Derbys SK17 6AZ. *E:* felicity.goodey@buxtonfestival.co.uk.

**GOODFELLOW, Giles William Jeremy;** QC 2003; *b* 14 Nov. 1960; *s* of late Keith Frank Goodfellow, QC and Rosalind Erica Goodfellow, sometime Moderator, Gen. Assembly of URC; *m* 1990, Dr Maha Rosa Saif; three *s*. *Educ:* Harrow Sch.; Trinity Coll., Cambridge (MA; Henry Arthur Hollond Studentship; Capt., Univ. Boxing Team); Univ. of Virginia Law Sch. (LLM). Called to the Bar, Middle Temple, 1983 (Harmsworth Schol.), Bencher, 2016. Mem., Pump Court Tax Chambers, 1985–. Gov., John Lyon Foundn, 2012–; Chm. of Govs, John Lyon Sch., 2015–. *Publications:* (jtly) Inheritance Tax Planning, 1986; (jtly) Financial Provision and Taxation on Divorce, 1989. *Recreations:* field sports, sailing, exercising and being exercised by children. *Address:* Pump Court Tax Chambers, 16 Bedford Row, WC1R 4EF. *T:* (020) 7414 8080, *Fax:* (020) 7414 8099. *E:* clerks@pumptax.com. *Club:* Hawks (Cambridge).

**GOODFELLOW, Dame Julia (Mary),** DBE 2010 (CBE 2001); PhD; FMedSci; FRSB, FInstP; President, Royal Society of Biology, since 2018; Chair, Public Health England, since 2018; *b* 1 July 1951; *d* of late Gerald Lansdall and Brenda Lansdall; *m* 1972, Peter Neville Goodfellow, *qv*; one *s* one *d*. *Educ:* Woking Co. Sch. for Girls; Reigate Co. Sch. for Girls; Univ. of Bristol (BSc Physics); Open Univ. (PhD Biophysics 1975). FRSB (FIBiol 2000); FInstP 2002. NATO Res. Fellow, Stanford Univ., 1976–78; Birkbeck College, University of London: Res. Fellow, 1979–83; Lectr, then Sen. Lectr and Reader, 1983–95; Prof. of Biomolecular Sci., 1995–2001; Chm., Dept of Crystallography, 1996–2001; Vice-Master, 1998–2001; Hon. Fellow, 2005; Chief Exec. and Dep. Chm., BBSRC, 2002–07 (Mem., 1997–2007); Vice-Chancellor, Univ. of Kent, 2007–17. Wellcome Trust Res. Leave Fellow, 1990–93. Chm., Wellcome Trust Molecular and Cell Panel, 1995–98. Member: CCLRC, 2000–04; RURAL Council, 2003–07; NESTA, 2005–09; SE Sci., Technol. and Engrg Adv. Cttee, 2005–; HEFCE Res. and Innovation Adv. Bd, 2008–; STFC, 2011–; Council for Sci. and Technol., 2011–. Member Governing Body: St Paul's Girls Sch., 2001–08; Acad. Med. Scis, 2002–05. Pres., Univs UK, 2015–17. Trustee: STEMNET, 2008–11; John Innes Foundn, 2008–12; East Malling Trust, 2008–14; Daphne Jackson Trust, 2008–14; Inst. for Res. in Schs, 2015–. Chm., British Sci. Assoc., 2009–14. Hon. Fellow (Hon. Fellow, BAAS, 2008); Hon. Fellow, Biochem. Soc., 2014. FRSA; FMedSci 2001. Hon. DSc: Strathclyde, 2002; Bristol, 2002; Durham, 2005; Manchester, 2009; London, 2009; Kent, 2018; DU Essex, 2004; Hon. DVSc Edinburgh, 2005. *Publications:* (ed) Molecular Dynamics: applications in molecular biology, 1990; (ed) Computer Modelling in Molecular Biology, 1992; (ed) Computer Simulation in Molecular Biology, 1995; numerous contribs to learned jls. *Recreations:* reading, family, theatre, tapestry. *E:* j.m.goodfellow@kent.ac.uk.

**GOODFELLOW, Michael Robert,** PhD; Director, Goodfellow Consulting Ltd, 2007–17; Divisional Managing Director, QinetiQ plc (formerly Defence Evaluation and Research Agency, Ministry of Defence), 1998–2007; *b* 7 Aug. 1948; *s* of Henry Goodfellow, MBE and Eileen Goodfellow (née Muff); *m* 1972, Karon Elizabeth Taylor; one *s* one *d*. *Educ:* St Bartholomew's Grammar Sch., Newbury; Imperial Coll., London (BSc 1st Cl. Hons Theoretical Physics 1970; ARCS 1970; DIC 1974; PhD 1974); Univ. of Surrey (MSc Dist. Econs 2013). Cert. IoD 2015; Dip. IoD 2015. CEng, FIET (FIEE 1988); FInstP 1999. Student Asst, Rutherford High Energy Lab., 1967; Res. Student, UKAEA, 1970–73; Sen. Analyst, Scicon Ltd, BP Gp, 1973–76; PSO, Systems Analysis Res. Unit, Depts of the Envmt and Transport, 1976–79; project manager, then staff manager, subseq. business gp manager, Sema Gp plc, 1979–95 (on secondment as Commercial Dir, DRA, 1992); Commercial Dir, DRA, MoD, 1995–98. Director, 1987–91: Yard Ltd; Sema Scientific Ltd; Dowty-Sema Ltd; Stephen Howe Ltd; VSEL-CAP Ltd; CAP-DBE Ltd; non-executive Director: Army Base Repair Orgn, MoD, 1998–2005; Met Office, 2007–13. Mem. Council, RUSI, 2006–. University of Surrey: Mem., Audit and Assce Cttee, 2014– (Chm., 2016–); Chm., Health and Safety Cttee, 2014–; Mem. Council, 2016–. Chm., Mgt Cttee, Surrey and NE Hants Industrial Mission, 1998–2004. Gov., Holy Trinity Sch., Guildford, 1989–97 (Chm., Finance Cttee). Mem., IAM. FCMI (FIMgt 1998); CDir 2016; FInstD 2016. *Recreations:* walking, gardening. *E:* mike@goodfellows.org.uk.

**GOODFELLOW, Prof. Peter Neville,** DPhil; FRS 1992; Scientific Advisor, Abingworth LLP, since 2008; *b* 4 Aug. 1951; *s* of Bernard Clifford Roy Goodfellow and Doreen Olga (née Berry); *m* 1972, Julia Mary Lansdall (see Dame J. M. Goodfellow); one *s* one *d*. *Educ:* Bristol Univ. (BSc 1st Cl. Hons 1972); Oxford Univ. (DPhil 1975). MRC Postdoctoral Fellow, Oxford Univ., 1975–76; Stanford University: Jane Coffin Childs Postdoctoral Fellow, 1976–78; Amer. Cancer Soc. Sen. Fellow, 1978–79; Imperial Cancer Research Fund: Staff Scientist, 1979–83; Sen. Scientist, 1983–86; Principal Scientist, 1986–92; Arthur Balfour Prof. of Genetics, Cambridge Univ., 1992–96; Sen. Vice Pres., Biopharmaceuticals and Neuroscis, then Discovery, SmithKline Beecham Pharmaceuticals, 1996–2001; Sen. Vice Pres., Discovery Res., GlaxoSmithKline, 2001–06. Visiting Professor: Birkbeck, Univ. of London, 1996–; UCL, 2000–; Bristol Univ., 2005–; Univ. of Kent, 2008–; Rockefeller Univ., NY, 2008; Dr Mok Hing-Liu Vis. Prof., Hong Kong Univ., 2009–14. Member: Bd, Prosensa BV, 2009–14; Bd, Gensight Biologicals, 2014–; Chm., Bd, GammaDelta Therapeutics, 2016–. Trustee and Mem. Council, Inst. of Cancer Res., 2007–14. Founder FMedSci 1998. Hon. DSc Bristol, 2002. *Publications:* (ed) Genetic analysis of the cell surface in Receptors and Recognition, Vol. 16, 1984; (ed jtly) The Mammalian Y Chromosome: molecular search for the sex determining gene, 1987; (ed) Cystic Fibrosis, 1989; (ed jtly) Molecular genetics of muscle disease, 1989; (ed jtly) Sex determination and the Y chromosome, 1991; (ed jtly) Mammalian Genetics, 1992; numerous reviews and contribs to learned jls. *Recreations:* soccer, science, sex. *Address:* Abingworth LLP, 38 Jermyn Street, SW1Y 6DN.

**GOODHART, Lady; Celia McClare Goodhart;** Principal, Queen's College, Harley Street, London, 1991–99; *b* 25 July 1939; *er d* of 2nd Baron Hemingford and Elizabeth (née Clark) (*d* 1979); *m* 1966, William Howard Goodhart (Baron Goodhart, QC) (*d* 2017); one *s* two *d*. *Educ:* St Michael's, Limpsfield; St Hilda's Coll., Oxford (MA; Hon. Fellow 1989). HM Civil Service, MAFF, seconded to Treasury, 1960–66; Hist. Tutor, Queen's Coll., London and Westminster Tutors, 1966–81. Contested: (SDP) Kettering, 1983; (SDP Liberal Alliance) Kettering, 1987; (SDP) Northants (for European Parlt), 1984. Chairman: SDP Envmt Policy Gp, 1985–87; Women for Social Democracy, 1986–88; Member: SDP Nat. and Policy Cttees, 1984–88; Liberal Democrats Fed. Exec. Cttee, 1988–90; Pres., E Midlands Liberal Democrats, 1988–91. Chm., Family Planning Assoc., 1999–2005. Member: Elizabeth Nuffield Educnl Fund, 1972–82; St Bartholomew's Hosp. Ethical Cttee, 1974–86; Lindop Cttee on Data Protection, 1976–78; Nat. Gas Consumer Councils, 1979–82 (also Chm., N Thames Gas Consumer Council); Women's Nat. Commn, 1986–89; Code Monitoring Cttee for Mkting of Infant Formulae in UK, 1986–90; Med. Audit Cttee, RCP, 1989–92; Council, GSA, 1997–99 (Sec., 1994–96, Chm., 1996–99, London Reg.); Council, Goldsmiths, Univ. of London, 2003–10 (Hon. Fellow 2010). President: Schoolmistresses and Governesses Benevolent Instn, 1991–2008; London Marriage Guidance Council, 1990–95; Chm., Youth Clubs, UK, 1988–91 (Vice-Pres., 1991–); Mem., First Forum (formerly Forum UK) (Chm., 2001–03). Gov., Compton Verney, 2006–15. Chm. Bd Trustees, Oxford Univ. Soc. (formerly Oxford Soc.), 1996–2004; Trustee: CPRE, 1987–91; Oxford Univ. Nuffield Medical Benefaction, 1988–96; Childline, 1999–2004; Mem. Bd, Dignity in Dying, 2007–13. FRSA 1989. Hon. FCGI 2003. Distinguished Friend, Oxford Univ., 2001. *Recreations:* sociability, bridge, tapestry. *Address:* 11 Clarence Terrace, NW1 4RD. *T:* (020) 7262 1319. *Club:* Reform.
See also H. T. Moggridge.

**GOODHART, Prof. Charles Albert Eric,** CBE 1997; PhD; FBA 1990; Norman Sosnow Professor of Banking and Finance, London School of Economics and Political Science, 1985–2002, now Emeritus; Joint Founder, 1987, Deputy Director, 1987–2005, and Member, since 2005, Financial Markets Group, London School of Economics; *b* 23 Oct. 1936; *s* of late Prof. Arthur Lehman Goodhart, Hon. KBE, QC, FBA, and Cecily (née Carter); *m* 1960, Margaret, (Miffy), Ann Smith; one *s* three *d*. *Educ:* Eton; Trinity Coll., Cambridge (scholar; 1st Cl. Hons Econs Tripos); Harvard Grad. Sch. of Arts and Sciences (PhD 1963). National Service, 1955–57 (2nd Lieut KRRC). Prize Fellowship in Econs, Trinity Coll., Cambridge, 1963; Asst Lectr in Econs, Cambridge Univ., 1963–64; Econ. Adviser, DEA, 1965–67; Lectr in Monetary Econs, LSE, 1967–69; Bank of England: Adviser with particular reference to monetary policy, 1969–80; a Chief Adviser, 1980–85; External Mem., Monetary Policy Cttee, 1997–2000. Mem., Adv. Cttee, Hong Kong Exchange Fund, 1990–97. Hon. Fellow, LSE, 2006. *Publications:* The New York Money Market and the Finance of Trade 1900–13, 1968; The Business of Banking 1891–1914, 1972; Money, Information and Uncertainty, 1975, 2nd edn 1989; Monetary Theory and Practice: the UK experience, 1984; The Evolution of Central Banks, 1985, rev. edn 1988; (ed jtly) The Operation and Regulation of Financial Markets, 1987; (ed) EMU and ESCB after Maastricht, 1992; (jtly) The Future of Central Banking, 1994; The Central Bank and the Financial System, 1995; (ed) The Emerging Framework of Financial Regulation, 1998; (jtly) Financial Regulation: why, how and where now?, 1998; (ed) Which Lender of Last Resort for Europe, 2000; (jtly) The Foreign Exchange Market, 2000; (ed jtly) Regulating Financial Services and Markets in the 21st Century, 2001; (ed jtly) Financial Crises, Contagion, and the Lender of Last Resort, 2002; (jtly) House Prices and the Macroeconomy, 2007; The Regulatory Response to the Financial Crisis, 2009; (jtly) Geneva Report on The Fundamental Principles of Financial Regulation, 2009; The Basel Committee on Banking Supervision, 2011; (jtly) Financial Stability in Practice: towards an uncertain future, 2012; (jtly) The Challenges of Financial Stability: a new model and its applications, 2012; articles in econ. jls and papers contrib. to econ. books. *Recreation:* keeping sheep. *Address:* Financial Markets Group, London School of Economics and Political Science, Houghton Street, WC2A 2AE. *T:* (020) 7955 7555.

**GOODHART, David Forbes;** Founder Editor, Prospect Magazine, 1995–2011; Director, Integration Hub and Head, Demography Unit, Policy Exchange, since 2016; *b* 12 Sept. 1956; *s* of Sir Philip Carter Goodhart and Valerie Goodhart (née Winant); *m* 1990, Lucy Rosamond Kellaway; two *s* two *d*. *Educ:* Eton Coll.; York Univ. (BA 1st Cl. Hist./Politics 1979). Reporter, Yorkshire Evening Press, 1979–82; journalist, Financial Times, 1982–94 (incl. labour reporter, City reporter, Lex columnist, corresp. in Germany and employment ed.); Dir, Demos, 2011–14. FRSA. *Publications:* (with Patrick Wintour) Eddie Shah and the Newspaper Revolution, 1986; The Reshaping of the German Social Market, 1994; Progressive Nationalism: citizenship and the Left, 2006; The British Dream, 2013; The

Road to Somewhere: the populist revolt and the future of politics, 2017. *Recreations:* football, cricket, singing. *Address:* 6c Willow Road, NW3 1TH. *T:* (020) 7340 2650. *E:* davidgood52@icloud.com. *Clubs:* Academy, Groucho.

GOODHART, Sir Robert (Anthony Gordon), 4th Bt *cr* 1911; Medical Practitioner, retired; *b* 15 Dec. 1948; *s* of Sir John Gordon Goodhart, 3rd Bt, FRCGP, and of Margaret Mary Eileen, *d* of late Morgan Morgan; *S* father, 1979; *m* 1972, Kathleen Ellen, (Caitlin), *d* of late Rev. A. D. MacRae; two *s* two *d*. *Educ:* Rugby; Guy's Hospital Medical School, London Univ. MB BS (Lond.), MRCS, LRCP, MRCGP, DObstRCOG. Qualification, 1972. *Recreation:* sailing. *Heir: s* Martin Andrew Goodhart, *b* 9 Sept. 1974.

GOODHEW, David William; Head, Latymer Upper School, since 2012; *b* London, 1971; *m* 2012, Dr C. Haines; two *s*. *Educ:* Cardinal Vaughan Meml Sch.; Corpus Christi Coll., Oxford (BA 1st Cl. Lit.Hum. 1993; MA 1996); Univ. of Nottingham (PGCE Classics 1994). Teacher of Classics: Bancroft's Sch., 1994–98; Eton Coll., 1998–2000; Hd of Classics, Bristol GS, 2000–05; Dir of Studies, Arnold Sch., 2005–08; Dep. Headmaster, Durham Sch., 2008–12. Governor: Glendower Prep. Sch., 2013–; Dauntsey's Sch., 2014–. *Recreations:* cycling, classical music (violin). *Address:* Latymer Upper School, King Street, Hammersmith, W6 9LR. *T:* 0845 6385991, *Fax:* (020) 8748 5212. *E:* head@latymer-upper.org. *Clubs:* East India, Lansdowne.

GOODHEW, Duncan Alexander, MBE 1983; Director: Limelight Sports Ltd (formerly LEA Events & Marketing Group), since 1997; Premier Education Group plc (formerly Premier Sports Holdings), since 2006; *b* 27 May 1957; *s* of late Donald Frederick Goodhew and of Dolores Perle Goodhew (*née* Venn); *m* 1984, Anne Patterson; one *s* one *d*. *Educ:* Millfield Sch.; North Carolina State Univ. (BA Business Mgt 1979). International swimmer, 1976–80; Captain, England and GB squads, 1978–80; competitions: Montreal Olympic Games, 1976; Commonwealth Games, 1978 (Silver Medal: 100m breast stroke; 200m breast stroke; 4×100 medley); World Championships, 1978 (Bronze Medal, 4×100 medley relay); Moscow Olympic Games, 1980 (Gold Medal, 100m breast stroke; Bronze Medal, 4×100 medley relay); Mem., 2-man and 4-man Bobsleigh teams, European Championships, 1981. Ambassador, Team GB. Pres., Swimathon, 1987–; Vice President: Dyslexia Action, 1994–; Youth Sport Trust, 1995–. Chm., Millfield Foundn. Patron: Disability Sport, England; Sparks; Cranial Facial Support Unit; James Powell Trust. Hon. Citizen, N Carolina. Royal Humane Soc. Award, 2001. *Publications:* Sink or Swim (with Victoria Hislop), 2001; contrib. Financial Times. *Recreations:* sport (including squash, aerobics, cycling), photography, cooking.

GOODHEW, Most Rev. Richard Henry, (Harry), AO 2001; Archbishop of Sydney and Metropolitan of New South Wales, 1993–2001; *b* 19 March 1931; *s* of Baden Powell Richard Goodhew and Christina Delgarno Goodhew (*née* Fraser); *m* 1958, Pamela (*née* Coughlan); two *s* two *d*. *Educ:* Univ. of Wollongong (MA Hons; DLitt *hc*, 1993); Moore Theol Coll. (ThL 2nd cl. Hons, Diploma 2nd cl. Hons). Ordained 1958; Curate, St Matthew's, Bondi, NSW, 1958; Curate-in-charge, St Bede's, Beverly Hills, NSW, 1959–63; with Bush Church Aid, Ceduna, SA, 1963–66; Rector: St Paul's, Carlingford, NSW, 1966–71; St Stephen's, Coorparoo, Qld, 1971–76; Rector and Senior Canon, St Michael's Cathedral, Wollongong, 1976–79; Archdeacon of Wollongong and Camden, 1979–82; Bishop of Wollongong, Asst Bishop in dio. of Sydney, 1982–93. *Recreations:* walking, reading, swimming. *Address:* 239 Gipps Road, Keiraville, NSW 2500, Australia. *T:* (2) 42253332.

GOODIER, Gareth John; Chief Executive Officer, Abu Dhabi Health Services Company, since 2018; *b* 5 Aug. 1951; *s* of Eric and Lilian Goodier; *m* 1st, 1970, Zena Edwards (marr. diss. 1976); 2nd, 1988, Georgina Hickling (marr. diss. 2003); one *s* one *d*; 3rd, 2004, Lynette Katherine Isabella Morero (*d* 2004); 4th, 2013, Joanne Pickard. *Educ:* Sheffield University Med. Sch. (MB ChB 1974); Univ. of NSW (Masters Health Admin 1993). FAFPHM 1990; FRACMA 1995 (Bernard Nicholson Prize, 1995). Regional Director: Kimberley Health Reg., 1989–91; Peninsula and Torres Strait Regl HA, 1991–93; Chief Executive Officer: Women's and Children's Health Service, WA, 1993–98; Royal Perth Hosp., 1998–2001; Royal Brompton and Harefield NHS Trust, 2003–04; North West London Strategic HA, 2004–06; Cambridge Univ. Hosps NHS Foundn Trust, 2006–12; Melbourne Health, 2012–16. Exec. Chair, Melbourne Biomedical Precinct, 2016–18. Consultant, World Bank projects in Lebanon and Kuwait, 2001–03. Hon. Adv. Prof., Shanghai Jiao Tong Univ. Sch. of Medicine, 2015. Hon. DSc (Health) Anglia Ruskin, 2009. *Recreations:* art, art history, history, design/architecture, football, current affairs, travel, movies.

GOODIN, David Nigel; His Honour Judge Goodin; a Circuit Judge, since 2003; *b* 31 March 1953; *s* of Nigel Robin Fyson Goodin and Diana Goodin (*née* Luard); *m* 1st, 1993 (marr. diss. 2003); two *s*; 2nd, 2010, Catherine Mary, *d* of James Maurice Robson; one step *s* one step *d*. *Educ:* King's Sch., Ely; Coll. of Law. Admitted solicitor, 1980; Higher Courts Advocate, 1995; articled to Norton, Rose, Botterell & Roche, London; in practice as solicitor, Newmarket, Bury St Edmunds and Ipswich, 1980–2003; Founder, Saunders Goodin Riddleston, 2000; Asst Recorder, 1996–2000; Recorder, 2000–03; Resident Judge, Ipswich Crown Court, 2009–17. Mem., Funding Revw. Cttee, Legal Services Commn, 1995–2003. Chm., Local Duty Solicitor Cttee, 1987–95. *Recreation:* family and friends. *Address:* The Crown Court, 1 Russell Road, Ipswich IP1 2AG.

GOODING, Mark, OBE 2011; HM Diplomatic Service; Director for European Union (Future Partnership), Foreign and Commonwealth Office, since 2018; *b* Guildford, 17 Dec. 1974; *s* of Air Vice Marshal Keith Horace Gooding, CB, OBE and of Jean Gooding; civil partnership 2005, Dr Christopher McCormick. *Educ:* Royal Grammar Sch., Guildford; Lady Margaret Hall, Oxford (MA Modern Langs). Teacher, British Sch. in Colombo, Sri Lanka, 1996–98; Equinox Gp Pharma Consultancy, 1998–99; entered FCO, 1999; Mandarin lang. trng, 2000–02; Consul, Shanghai, 2002–04; Hd, EU Budget Team, FCO, 2004–06; Private Sec. to Foreign Sec., 2006–08; Dep. High Comr, Sri Lanka and the Maldives, 2008–11; Ambassador to Cambodia, 2011–14; Minister Counsellor (Pol), Beijing, 2014–17; Dep. Dir for Europe, FCO, 2017–18. *Recreations:* music, travel, running, swimming. *Address:* Foreign and Commonwealth Office, King Charles Street, SW1A 2AH.

GOODING, Nigel Alexander, CBE 2019; Deputy Director, EU Fisheries Policy and Negotiations, Department for Environment, Food and Rural Affairs, since 2018; *b* 18 March 1956; *s* of Alexander Albert Gooding and Pearl Evelyn Gooding; *m* 1978, Anne Teresa Redwood; two *s* one *d*. *Educ:* Spencer Park Secondary Sch. Ministry of Agriculture, Fisheries and Food, 1974–2001: Policy Advr on Vet. Medicines, 1985–89, on Animal Health, zoonoses, 1989–92; Co-ordination of UK Presidency of EU, 1992; Head of Policy Br., UK Fisheries Enforcement, 1993; Chief Inspector of Fisheries, Eng. and Wales, DEFRA, 2003–05; Chief Exec., Marine and Fisheries Agency, 2005–10; Hd of Marine Biodiversity, 2010–15, Head of Sea Fisheries and Conservation, 2015, Marine Prog., Dep. Dir, EU and Internat. Fisheries, 2016–18, DEFRA. UK Comr, Internat. Whaling Commn, 2010–16. *Recreations:* football, golf, reading, theatre, music, walking. *Address:* Department for Environment, Food and Rural Affairs, 2 Marsham Street, SW1P 4DF.

GOODING, Richard Ernest, OBE 2006; Chief Executive Officer, London City Airport, 1996–2012 (non-executive Director, since 2012); freelance aviation consultant, since 2012; *b* Halesworth, 9 Oct. 1947; *s* late Frank Gooding and Gladys Gooding; one *d*. *Educ:* Leiston Grammar Sch.; Slough Technical Coll. CMILT (MCIT 1994). British European Airways, later British Airways, 1966–81: joined as apprentice, 1966; Sales Econs Officer; Activity Analyst; Ramp Supt; Overseas Area Manager; Ops Dir, Manchester Airport, 1981–86; Man. Dir, Oglen Allied Aviation Services, 1986–91; CEO, London Luton Airport, 1991–96. Non-exec. Dir, High Speed One, 2012–. Chm., Newham Homes, 2007–11. Hon. MBA LMU, 2003; Hon. DBA UEL, 2000. *Recreations:* charity, music, theatre. *T:* (01728) 747186. *E:* richard@goodingobe.com.
*See also* V. F. Gooding.

GOODING, Stephen Leonard, CB 2016; Director, RAC Foundation, since 2015; *b* 20 Nov. 1960; *s* of Leonard Armstrong Gooding and Margaret Jane Gooding (*née* Horan); *m* 1985, Bernadette Kearns; two *s*. *Educ:* Colfe's Sch., Lee; Univ. of Durham (BA Hons Politics 1982). Brebner, Allen & Trapp (chartered accountants), 1982; PSA, DoE, 1983; Dept of Transport, 1987; Private Secretary: to Minister for Roads and Traffic, 1988; to Minister for Public Transport, 1989–91; Principal, 1991–97, Asst Sec., 1997–2000, Dept of Transport, subseq. DETR; Sec., CS Mgt Bd, Cabinet Office, 2000–01; Dir, Office of the Rail Regulator, 2001–04; Dir, Road Perf. and Strategy, then Roads and Road Pricing, 2004–08, Dir Gen., Motoring and Freight Services, then Domestic, later Roads, Traffic and Local, 2009–15, DfT. *Recreations:* motorcycles, film, cookery, early, baroque and heavy rock music. *Address:* c/o RAC Foundation, 89–91 Pall Mall, SW1Y 5HS. *T:* (020) 7747 3489. *E:* steve.gooding@racfoundation.org.

GOODING, Valerie Frances, CBE 2002; Chairman, Aviva UK Insurance, since 2018; *b* 14 May 1950; *d* of Frank and Gladys Gooding; *m* 1986, Crawford Macdonald; two *s*. *Educ:* Leiston GS, Suffolk; Univ. of Warwick (BA Hons 1971); Kingston Univ. (Dip. Mgt Studies 1981). British Airways, 1973–96; Man. Dir, UK, 1996–98, CEO, 1998–2008, BUPA. Chm., Premier Farnell, 2011–16; non-executive Director: Standard Chartered plc, 2005–13; J. Sainsbury plc, 2007–11; BBC, 2008–11; Home Office, 2011–14; Vodafone plc, 2014– (Sen. Ind. Dir, 2017–); TUI AG (formerly TUI Travel plc), 2014–. Dir, Lawn Tennis Assoc., 2005–13; Chm., Lawn Tennis Assoc. Trust, 2014–18. Trustee: British Mus., 2004–11; Rose Theatre, Kingston upon Thames, 2009–11; Historic Royal Palaces, 2013–16; English Nat. Ballet, 2014–; Royal Botanic Gdns, Kew, 2014–. Hon. DBA: Bournemouth, 1999; Middlesex, 2007; Hon. DSc Cranfield, 2009; Hon. DLaws Warwick, 2009. *Recreations:* tennis, theatre, travel, keeping fit, family life. *Club:* Athenæum.
*See also* R. E. Gooding.

GOODISON, Sir Nicholas (Proctor), Kt 1982; Chairman: Stock Exchange, 1976–88; TSB Group, 1989–95; Courtauld Institute of Art, 1982–2002 (Governor, 2002–09); National Art Collections Fund, 1986–2002; *b* 16 May 1934; *s* of Edmund Harold Goodison and Eileen Mary Carrington (*née* Proctor); *m* 1960, Judith Abel Smith; one *s* two *d*. *Educ:* Marlborough Coll.; King's Coll., Cambridge (Scholar; BA Classics 1958, MA; PhD Architecture and History of Art, 1981; Hon. Fellow, 2002). H. E. Goodison & Co., later Quilter Goodison, 1958–88: Partner, 1962; Chm., 1975–88; Chm., TSB Bank plc, 1989–2000; Dep. Chm., Lloyds TSB Gp plc, 1995–2000. Director: Ottoman Bank, 1986–92; Banque Paribas (Luxembourg) SA, 1986–88; Banque Paribas Capital Markets Ltd, 1986–88; Gen. Accident, 1987–95; British Steel, later Corus Gp plc, 1989–2002 (Dep. Chm., 1993–99). Mem. Council, Stock Exchange, 1968–88; President: Internat. Fedn of Stock Exchanges, 1985–86; British Bankers' Assoc., 1991–96; Vice Pres., Chartered Inst. of Bankers, 1989–2000 (FCIB 1989); Member: Panel on Takeovers and Mergers, 1976–88; Council of Securities Industry, 1978–85; Securities Assoc., 1986–88. Mem. Council, Industrial Soc., 1976–2000; Chairman: Crafts Council, 1997–2005; Burlington Magazine Ltd, 2002–07 (Dir, 1975–2007); Burlington Magazine Foundn, 2002–07 (Trustee, 1975–); Dir, ENO, 1977–98 (Vice-Chm., 1980–98); Trustee: ENO Trust, 1979–; Kathleen Ferrier Meml Scholarship Fund, 1987–; Nat. Heritage Meml Fund, 1988–97. Leader, Goodison Review, 2003 (report, Securing the Best for our Museums: Private Giving and Government Support for HM Treasury, published 2004). Mem., Royal Commn on the Long Term Care of the Elderly, 1997–99; Trustee, 2002–15, Chm., 2003–15, Advr, 2015–, Nat. Life Story Collection. Hon. Keeper of Furniture, Fitzwilliam Museum, Cambridge; President: Furniture History Soc., 1990– (Hon. Treas., 1970–90); Antiquarian Horological Soc., 1986–93; Walpole Soc., 2007–. Chm., Review Steering Gp, Nat. Record of Achievement, 1996–97; Pres., Heads, Teachers and Industry, 1999–2002; Member: Adv. Bd, Judge Inst. of Mgt Studies, 1999–2003; FEFCE, 2000–01. Governor, Marlborough Coll., 1981–97. CCMI; FSA, FRSA, Sen. FRCA; Hon. Fellow RA, 1987; Hon. FRIBA 1992; Hon. FBA 2004; Hon. FCGI, 2007. Hon. DLitt: City, 1985; London, 2003; Hon. LLD Exeter, 1989; Hon. DSc Aston, 1994; Hon. DArt De Montfort, 1998; Hon. DCL Northumbria, 1999. CINOA Prize for lifetime achievement in arts, 2004; Robinson Medal, V&A Mus., 2007. Chevalier, Légion d'Honneur, 1990. *Publications:* English Barometers 1680–1860, 1968, 2nd edn 1977; Ormolu: The Work of Matthew Boulton, 1974, rev. edn as Matthew Boulton: Ormolu, 2002; (ed jtly) Hotspur: eighty years of antiques dealing, 2004; These Fragments, 2005; many papers and articles. *Recreations:* history of art, music, opera, walking. *Address:* PO Box 2512, W1A 5ZP. *Clubs:* Athenæum, Beefsteak, Brooks's.

GOODLAD, family name of Baron Goodlad.

GOODLAD, Baron *cr* 2005 (Life Peer), of Lincoln in the County of Lincolnshire; Alastair Robertson Goodlad, KCMG 1997; PC 1992; High Commissioner to Australia, 2000–05; *b* 4 July 1943; *y s* of late Dr John Goodlad and Isabel (*née* Sinclair); *m* 1968, Cecilia Barbara, 2nd *d* of late Col Richard Hurst and Lady Barbara Hurst; two *s*. *Educ:* Marlborough Coll.; King's Coll., Cambridge (MA, LLB). Contested (C) Crewe Div., 1970; MP (C) Northwich, Feb. 1974–1983, Eddisbury, 1983–99. An Asst Govt Whip, 1981–82; a Lord Commissioner of HM Treasury, 1982–84; Parly Under-Sec. of State, Dept of Energy, 1984–87; Comptroller of HM Household, 1989–90; Dep. Govt Chief Whip and Treasurer, HM Household, 1990–92; Minister of State, FCO, 1992–95; Parly Sec. to HM Treasury and Govt Chief Whip, 1995–97; Opposition frontbench spokesman on internat. develt, 1997–98. Chairman, H of L Select Cttees: on the Constitution, 2007–10; on Merits of Statutory Instruments, 2010–15; Mem., H of L Select Cttee on Communications, 2017–; Mem., H of L Standing Orders Cttee (Private Bills), 2017–. *Address:* House of Lords, SW1A 0PW. *Clubs:* Brooks's, Beefsteak, Pratt's.

GOODLAND, Judith Mary; Head Mistress, Wycombe Abbey School, 1989–98; *b* 26 May 1938; *d* of Rolf Thornton Ferro and Joan (*née* O'Hanlon); *m* 1961, A. T. Goodland (marr. diss.); one *s* two *d*. *Educ:* Howell's Sch., Denbigh; Bristol Univ. (BA Hons). Charlotte Mason Coll., Ambleside (Cert Ed). Head, Modern Languages Dept, Cartmel Priory C of E Comprehensive Sch., 1968–72; Casterton Sch., Kirkby Lonsdale, 1980–83; Headmistress, St George's Sch., Ascot, 1983–88. Trustee, Bendrigg Trust, 2007–16 (Chm., 2011–14). Chm., U3A South Lakes, 2014–16 (Vice-Chm., 2012–14). FRSA 1994. *Recreations:* bridge, quilting, table tennis, bird watching. *Address:* 10 Starnthwaite Ghyll, Crosthwaite, Kendal, Cumbria LA8 8JN.

**GOODMAN, Catherine Anne,** LVO 2014; artist; Co-Founder and Artistic Director, Royal Drawing School (formerly Prince's Drawing School), since 2000; *b* London, 22 April 1961; *d* of Philip Goodman and Sonia Goodman. *Educ*: Queen's Coll., London; Camberwell Sch. of Arts and Crafts, London (Art Foundn; BA Fine Art Painting 1984); Royal Acad. Schs, London (Postgrad. Dip. 1987). Professional artist working in London and India, 1987–; Hd, Fine Art, Prince of Wales's Inst. for Architecture, 1992–2000. Gold Medal, RA, 1987; First Prize, BP Portrait Award, 2002. *Recreations*: walking, yoga. *Address*: Royal Drawing School, 19–22 Charlotte Road, EC2A 3SG. *T*: (020) 7613 8568. *E*: goodman-studio@royaldrawingschool.org.

**GOODMAN, Elinor Mary;** freelance journalist; *b* 11 Oct. 1946; *d* of Edward Weston Goodman and Pamela Longbottom. *Educ*: private schools, secretarial college. Financial Times: Consumer Affairs Corresp., 1971–78; Political Corresp., 1978–82; Channel Four News: Political Corresp., 1982–88; Political Ed., 1988–2005. Chm., Affordable Rural Housing Commn, 2005–06. Mem. Bd, Commn for Rural Communities, 2006–12. Assessor, Leveson Inquiry into culture, practice and ethics of the press, 2011–. *Recreations*: riding, walking.

**GOODMAN, Helen Catherine;** MP (Lab) Bishop Auckland, since 2005; *b* 2 Jan. 1958; *d* of Alan Goodman and Hanne Goodman; *m* 1988, Charles; two *c*. *Educ*: Lady Manners Sch., Bakewell; Somerville Coll., Oxford (BA 1979). HM Treasury, 1980–97, latterly Hd of Strategy Unit; Advr to Prime Minister of Czechoslovakia, 1990; Dir, Commn on Future of Multi Ethnic Britain, 1998; Hd of Strategy, Children's Soc., 1998–2002; Chief Exec., Nat. Assoc. of Toy and Leisure Libraries, 2002–05. Parly Sec., Office of the Leader of the H of C, 2007–08; Parly Under-Sec. of State, DWP, 2009–10. Shadow Minister: for Justice, 2010–11; for Culture, 2011–14; for Work and Pensions, 2014–15. Member: Treasury Select Cttee, 2015–17; Public Accounts Cttee, 2005–07; Procedure Cttee, 2011–14, 2016–. *Address*: House of Commons, SW1A 0AA. *T*: (020) 7219 4346. *E*: goodmanh@parliament.uk.

**GOODMAN, Prof. John Francis Bradshaw,** CBE 1995; PhD; CCIPD; Frank Thomas Professor of Industrial Relations, University of Manchester Institute of Science and Technology, 1975–2002 (Vice-Principal, 1979–81); *b* 2 Aug. 1940; *s* of Edwin and Amy Goodman; *m* 1967, Elizabeth Mary Towns; one *s* one *d*. *Educ*: Chesterfield Grammar Sch.; London Sch. of Economics (BSc Econ); MSc Manchester; PhD Nottingham. Personnel Officer, Ford Motor Co. Ltd, 1962–64; Lectr in Industrial Econs, Univ. of Nottingham, 1964–69; Industrial Relations Adviser, NBPI, 1969–70; Sen. Lectr in Industrial Relations, Univ. of Manchester, 1970–74; Chm., Manchester Sch. of Management, UMIST, 1977–79, 1986–94. Vis. Professor: Univ. of WA, 1981, 1984; McMaster Univ., 1985; Univ. of Auckland, 1996. Pres., British Univs Industrial Relations Assoc., 1983–86. Member: Council, ACAS, 1987–98; Training Bd, 1991–97, Council, 1993–97, ESRC. Dep. Chm., Central Arbitration Cttee, 1998–2011; Chairman: Professional Football Negotiating and Consultative Cttee, 2000–19; Police Arbitration Tribunal, 2003–14. *Publications*: Shop Stewards in British Industry, 1969; Shop Stewards, 1973; Rulemaking and Industrial Peace, 1977; Ideology and Shop-floor Industrial Relations, 1981; Employment Relations in Industrial Society, 1984; Unfair Dismissal Law and Employment Practice, 1985; New Developments in Employee Involvement, 1992; Industrial Tribunals and Workplace Disciplinary Procedures, 1998; contribs to British Jl of Industrial Relations, ILR, Industrial Relations Jl, Jl of Management Studies, Personnel Management, etc. *Recreations*: hill walking (compleat Munroist, 1997), football, ornithology, golf. *Address*: 2 Pott Hall, Pott Shrigley, Macclesfield, Cheshire SK10 5RT. *T*: (01625) 572480.

**GOODMAN, Prof. Martin David,** DPhil, DLitt; FBA 1996; Professor of Jewish Studies, Oxford University, since 1996; Fellow of Wolfson College, Oxford, since 1991 (Viceregent, 2012–14); Fellow, Oxford Centre for Hebrew and Jewish Studies, since 1986 (President, 2014–18); *b* 1 Aug. 1953; *s* of late Cyril Joshua Goodman and Ruth (*née* Sabel); *m* 1976, Sarah Jane Lock; two *s* two *d*. *Educ*: Rugby; Trinity Coll., Oxford (MA; DPhil 1980; DLitt 2009; Hon. Fellow 2010). Kaye Jun. Res. Fellow, Oxford Centre for Postgrad. Hebrew Studies, 1976–77; Lectr in Ancient Hist., Birmingham Univ., 1977–86; Oxford University: Sen. Res. Fellow, St Cross Coll., 1986–91; Lectr in Roman Hist., Christ Church, Oxford, 1988–; Reader in Jewish Studies, 1991–96. Fellow, Inst. for Advanced Studies, Hebrew Univ. of Jerusalem, 1993. Pres., British Assoc. for Jewish Studies, 1995. Jt Ed., Jl of Jewish Studies, 1995–99; Ed., Jl of Roman Studies, 2000–03. Hon. DLitt Southampton, 2015. *Publications*: State and Society in Roman Galilee, 1983, 2nd edn 2000; (trans. with Sarah Goodman) Johann Reuchlin, On the Art of the Kabbalah, 1983; (ed jtly) E. Schürer, The History of the Jewish People in the Age of Jesus Christ, vol. 3, pt 1 1986, pt 2 1987; The Ruling Class of Judaea, 1987; (with G. Vermes) The Essenes according to the Classical Sources, 1989; Mission and Conversion, 1994; The Roman World 44BC–AD180, 1997, 2nd edn 2012; (ed) Jews in a Graeco-Roman World, 1998; (ed jtly) Apologetics in the Roman Empire, 1999; (ed jtly) Representations of Empire: Rome and the Mediterranean world, 2002; (ed) The Oxford Handbook of Jewish Studies, 2002; Judaism in the Roman World: collected essays, 2007; Rome and Jerusalem: the clash of ancient civilizations, 2007; (ed jtly) Abraham, the Nations, and the Hagarites: Jewish, Christian and Islamic perspectives on kinship with Abraham, 2010; (ed jtly) Rabbinic Texts and the History of Late-Roman Palestine, 2010; (jtly) Toleration within Judaism, 2013; (jtly) Josephus, The Jewish War, 2017; A History of Judaism, 2017; Josephus's The Jewish War: a biography, 2019. *Address*: Clarendon Institute, Walton Street, Oxford OX1 2HG.
*See also Prof. R. J. Goodman.*

**GOODMAN, Michael Jack,** MA, PhD; Social Security Commissioner (formerly National Insurance Commissioner), 1979–98, and Child Support Commissioner, 1993–98, Deputy Commissioner, 1999–2002; *b* 3 Oct. 1931; *s* of Vivian Roy Goodman and Muriel Olive Goodman; *m* 1958, Susan Kerkham Wherry; two *s* one *d*. *Educ*: Sudbury Grammar Sch., Suffolk; Corpus Christi Coll., Oxford (MA). PhD Manchester. Solicitor. Lectr, Gibson & Weldon, 1957; solicitor, Lincoln, 1958–60; Lectr, Law Society's Sch., 1961–63; Lectr, then Sen. Lectr in Law, Manchester Univ., 1964–70; Prof. of Law, Durham Univ., 1971–76; Perm. Chm. of Indust. Tribunals, Newcastle upon Tyne, 1976–79. Gen. Editor, Encyclopedia of Health and Safety at Work, 1974–2016. *Publications*: Industrial Tribunals' Procedure, 1976, 3rd edn 1985; Health and Safety at Work: law and practice, 1988; contrib. Mod. Law Rev., and Conveyancer. *Recreations*: amateur radio (licence holder), National Trust volunteering.

**GOODMAN, Paul Alexander Cyril;** Editor, Conservative Home, since 2013; *b* 17 Nov. 1959; *s* of Abel Goodman and Irene Goodman (*née* Rubens); *m* 1999, Fiona Gill; one *s*. *Educ*: Cranleigh Sch., Surrey; York Univ. (BA Hons Eng. Lit). Exec., Extel Consultancy, 1985–86; Res. Asst to Rt Hon. Tom King, MP, 1985–87; Mem., Public Unit, Westminster CC, 1987–88; Novice, Quarr Abbey, 1988–90; Home Affairs Ed., Catholic Herald, 1991–92; Leader Writer, Daily Telegraph, 1992; reporter, Sunday Telegraph, 1992–95; Comment Ed., Daily Telegraph, 1995–2001. MP (C) Wycombe, 2001–10. Shadow Minister: for Work and Pensions, 2003–05; for Childcare, HM Treasury, 2005–07; DCLG, 2007–09. Member, Select Committee: on Work and Pensions, 2001–05; on Deregulation and Regulatory Reform, 2001–03.

**GOODMAN, Perry;** Director (Industry and Regions), The Engineering Council, 1990–92; *b* 26 Nov. 1932; *s* of Cyril Goodman and Anne (*née* Rosen); *m* 1958, Marcia Ann (*née* Morris) (*d* 2016); one *s* one *d*. *Educ*: Haberdashers' Aske's Hampstead Sch.; University Coll., London (BSc); Open Univ. (MSc). MIMMM (MICeram 1964). 2nd Lieut, Royal Corps of Signals, 1955–57; Jt Head, Chemistry Res. Lab., then Project Leader, Morgan Crucible Co. Ltd, 1957–64; Sen. Scientific Officer, DSIR, 1964–65; Principal Scientific Officer, Process Plant Br., Min. of Technology, 1965–67; 1st Sec. (Scientific), 1968–70, Counsellor (Scientific), 1970–74, British Embassy, Paris; Research Gp, DoI, 1974–79; Hd, Policy and Perspectives Unit, DoI, 1980–81; Department of Trade and Industry: Hd, Design Policy/Technical Adv. Services for Industry, 1981–86; Hd, Electrical Engrg Br., 1986–90. Mem. Bd, Northern Engrg Centre, 1990–92. FRSA 1986. *Recreations*: travel, walking, conversation. *Address*: 118 Westbourne Terrace Mews, W2 6QG. *T*: (020) 7262 0925.

**GOODMAN, Prof. Roger James,** DPhil; Nissan Professor of Modern Japanese Studies, since 2003, and Pro-Vice-Chancellor, since 2017, University of Oxford; Fellow, since 1993, and Warden, since 2017, St Antony's College, Oxford (Acting Warden, 2006–07); *b* 26 May 1960; *s* of late Cyril Joshua Goodman and Ruth (*née* Sabel); partner, Carolyn Joy Dodd; two *s* one *d*. *Educ*: Rugby; King Edward VI Grammar Sch., Chelmsford; Univ. of Durham (BA 1981); St Antony's Coll., Oxford (DPhil 1987). Nissan Jun. Res. Fellow in Social Anthropol. of Japan, St Antony's Coll., Oxford, 1985–88; Lectr, Japan-Europe Ind. Res. Centre, Imperial Coll., Univ. of London, 1988–89; Reader in Japanese Studies, Dept of Sociol., Univ. of Essex, 1989–93; Lectr in Social Anthropol. of Japan, 1993–2003, Head, Social Sciences Division, 2008–17, Univ. of Oxford. Oxford University: Assessor, 1997–98; Chair, Japan Foundn Endowment Cttee, 1999–2006. Pres., Acad. of Social Scis, Jan. 2020– (Chair, Council, 2015–20). *Publications*: Japan's International Youth: the emergence of a new class of schoolchildren, 1990; (ed jtly) Ideology and Practice in Modern Japan, 1992; (ed jtly) Case Studies on Human Rights in Japan, 1996; (ed jtly) The East Asian Welfare Model: welfare orientalism and the state, 1998; Children of the Japanese State: the changing role of child protection institutions in contemporary Japan, 2000; (ed) Family and Social Policy in Japan: anthropological approaches, 2002; (ed jtly) Can the Japanese Reform Their Education System?, 2003; (ed jtly) Global Japan: the experience of Japan's new minorities and overseas communities, 2003; (ed jtly) The Big Bang in Japanese Higher Education: the 2004 reforms and the dynamics of change, 2005; (ed jtly) Ageing in Asia, 2007; (ed jtly) A Sociology of Japanese Youth: from returnees to NEETs, 2012; (ed jtly) Higher Education and the State: changing relationships in Europe and East Asia, 2013. *Recreation*: hockey coach. *Address*: Nissan Institute of Japanese Studies, 27 Winchester Road, Oxford OX2 6NA. *T*: (01865) 274576. *E*: roger.goodman@nissan.ox.ac.uk.
*See also Prof. M. D. Goodman.*

**GOODMAN, Roy Peter,** FRCO; conductor; violinist; Principal Guest Conductor, English Chamber Orchestra, 2004–15; *b* 26 Jan. 1951; *s* of Peter and Mary Sheena Goodman; *m* 1st, 1970, Gillian Dey (marr. diss. 1992); two *s* one *d*; 2nd, 1992, Sally Jackson (marr. diss. 1999). *Educ*: King's Coll., Cambridge (chorister); Royal Coll. of Music; Berkshire Coll. of Educn. ARCO 1968, FRCO 1970; ARCM 1976. Head of Music: Alfred Sutton Boys' Sch., Reading, 1971–74; Bulmershe Comprehensive Sch., Reading, 1974–76; Sen. String Tutor, Berks, 1976–78; Dir of Music, Univ. of Kent, Canterbury, 1986–87; Dir, Early Music, RAM, 1987–89. Founder and Dir, Brandenburg Consort, 1975–2001; Co-Founder and Co-Dir, Parley of Instruments, 1979–86; Musical Dir, European Union Baroque Orch., 1988–2003, now Emeritus; Principal Conductor: Hanover Band, 1986–94; Umeå Symphony Orchestra and Swedish Northern Opera, 1994–99; Manitoba Chamber Orch., Winnipeg, 1999–2005; Holland Symfonia, Amsterdam, 2003–06; Principal Guest Conductor: Västerås Sinfonietta, Sweden, 1995–2011; Auckland Philharmonia, NZ, 2007–11. Hon. FRCM 2005. Hon. DMus Hull, 2002. *Recreations*: squash, sailing, ski-ing, cycling, hiking, caravanning. *Address*: 38 Blackbrook Road, Newark, Notts NG24 2ST. *E*: roy@roygoodman.com.

**GOODMAN, Rupert Andrew Woodward,** FRGS; DL; Chairman and Founder, FIRST, since 1985; *b* Kidderminster, 17 April 1963; *s* of Nigel and late Rachel Goodman (*née* Woodward); *m* 1991, Pamela Jane Blount; one *s* two *d*. *Educ*: Eton Coll.; Trinity Coll., Cambridge (BA Hons 1985). Founder, Responsible Capitalism Initiative, 2000–. Chairman: World Petroleum, 2000–; World Energy Insight, 2010–; Elmbridge Partners, 2014–. Vice Pres., FFI, 2011–. Mem., Develt Bd, Artes Mundi, 2009–. Founder Director: Equilibrium Gulf, 2014–; Equilibrium Global, 2014–. Dir, New Waves Solutions, 2016–. Mem., Internat. Dendrol. Soc., 2008–. Founder Trustee, 2002–, Chm., 2013–, British Kazakh Soc.; Trustee, Nat. Botanic Gdns of Wales, 2005–08; Dep. Chm. and Trustee, Prince's Trust Internat., 2016–. DL Gtr London, 2012. Freeman, City of London, 2013. FRGS 1992. Metropolitan Police Comr's Award, 2012. *Publications*: (ed) The Critical Decade, 2003; (ed) The 21st Century: a view from the South, 2005; (ed with Baron Cormack) Responsible Capitalism: essays on morality, ethics and business, vol. 1, 2009, vol. 2, 2017; (ed) Leadership Perspectives, 2015; (ed) Celebrating 200 Years Together, 2017; contrib. articles to jls. *Recreations*: hill walking, country pursuits, dendrology, sport, international affairs, Led Zeppelin. *Address*: c/o FIRST, 6 Vigo Street, Mayfair, W1S 3HF. *T*: (020) 7440 3550, *Fax*: (020) 7440 3544. *Clubs*: Hawks, Brooks's, Pitt; Pitt (Cambridge); Achilles.

**GOODNOW, Prof. Christopher Carl,** PhD; FRS 2009; FAA; Bill and Patricia Ritchie Foundation Professor, NH&MRC Australia Fellow, and Head, Division of Immunogenomics, since 2015, and Executive Director, since 2018, Garvan Institute of Medical Research (Deputy Director, 2015–18); Adjunct Professor, John Curtin School of Medical Research, Australian National University, since 2015; *b* Hong Kong, 19 Sept. 1959. *Educ*: Univ. of Sydney (BVSc Hons, BSc (Vet) Hons 1984; Univ. Medal 1984). Vis. Student and Res. Asst. Stanford Univ. Med. Sch., 1985; NH&MRC Biomed. Scholar, Walter and Eliza Hall Inst., 1985; NH&MRC Biomed. Scholar, 1986–89, Medical Foundn Postdoctoral Fellow, 1989–90, Clinical Immunology Res. Centre, Univ. of Sydney; Asst Investigator, Howard Hughes Med. Inst. and Asst Prof. of Microbiol. and Immunol., Stanford Univ. Med. Sch., 1990–97; John Curtin School of Medical Research, Australian National University: Prof. of Immunol. and Genetics, 1997–2014; Dir, Med. Genome Centre, 1997–2007; Founder Dir, Australian Phenomics Facility and ACRF Med. Genome Centre, 1997–2006; Hd, Div. of Genetics and Immunol., 2007–14. Founder and Chief Scientific Officer, Phenomix Corp. Searle Scholar, 1992–95. Pres., Australasian Soc. for Immunology, 2015–16. *Publications*: articles in jls. *Address*: Garvan Institute of Medical Research, 384 Victoria Street, Darlinghurst, Sydney, NSW 2010, Australia.

**GOODSELL, (John) Andrew;** non-executive Chairman, Saga plc, 2015–18 (Executive Chairman, Saga Group Ltd, 2007–15); *b* 4 Jan. 1959; *s* of John Leonard Goodsell and Pamela Doris Goodsell; *m* 1st, 1983, Claire Hornsby (marr. diss.); one *s* one *d*; 2nd, 1999, Virginia Hubert; one *s* two *d*. *Educ*: West Kent Coll. Norwich Winterthur Reinsurance Co. Ltd, 1978–87; Lloyds of London, 1987–92; Saga Group Ltd: Business Develt Manager, 1992–95; Business Develt Dir, 1995–99; Chief Exec., Saga Services and Saga Investment Direct, 1999–2001; Dep. Gp Chief Exec., 2001–04; Gp Chief Exec., 2004–07; Exec.

Chm., AA Ltd, 2007–14. Chm., Fundraising Bd, Age UK, 2009–17. Patron, Rotherfield St Martin, 2013–. Hon. Fellow, Harris Manchester Coll., Oxford, 2002. *Recreations:* cooking, ski-ing, sailing.

**GOODSHIP, Prof. Allen Edward,** PhD; Professor of Orthopaedic Sciences, Royal Veterinary College, London, and the Institute of Orthopaedics, 1996–2011, now Emeritus, and Professorial Research Associate in Orthopaedic Science, Institute of Musculoskeletal Science, 2012–14, University College London; Director and Head, Centre for Comparative and Clinical Anatomy, Vesalius Clinical Training Centre, 2012–15, Professorial Research Associate, Department of Physics and Bio-Engineering, 2015–17, Hon. Professor, 2015, Emeritus Professor, 2017, University of Bristol; *b* 1 Feb. 1949; *m* 1975, Dawn Taylor; two *d. Educ:* Reigate Grammar Sch.; Sch. of Vet. Sci., Univ. of Bristol (BVSc 1972; PhD 1977). MRCVS 1972. Res. Asst, RCVS Trust Fund Scholar, 1972–74; University of Bristol: Temp. Lectr in Vet. Anatomy, 1974–76; Res. Asst, Horserace Betting Levy Bd, 1976–78, Lectr, 1978–88, Dept of Anatomy; Reader in Vet. Anatomy, 1988; Prof. of Comparative Biomed. Scis, 1988–96 (Vis. Prof., 1996–); Hd, Dept of Anatomy, 1992–96; Dir, Inst. of Orthopaedics and Musculoskeletal Sci., UCL, 2009–11; Chm., Bd of Dirs, Vesalius Clin. Trng Centre, Univ. of Bristol, 2015–16. Acad. Associate, QMW, 1996–; Convenor, Cell and Molecular Path. Res. Centre, Royal Nat. Orthopaedic Hosp. Trust, 1999–2003. Vis. Prof., Univ. of Guelph, 1989–; D. L. T. Smith Vis. Scientist, Univ. of Saskatoon, 1989–; Vis. Prof. of Pathol., Univ. of Adelaide, 2006–11. Trustee, Silsoe Res. Inst., 2002–06; Director: Stanmore Implants Worldwide, 2000–08; Bristol Zoo Enterprises Ltd; Consultant: Orthopaedic Div., Johnson & Johnson (DePuy); Res. Centre, Smith & Nephew Gp; Co-inventor, VetCell. Vice Pres. and Univ. Rep. to Council, and Chm., Welfare and Res. Adv. Bd, Bristol & SW Zool Soc.; Member: Med. Adv. Bd, General Orthopaedics, Boston; Adv. Bd, MRC. Member: Orthopaedic Res. Soc., USA (Mem. Prog. Cttee, 1997–98); British Vet. Zool Soc.; Anatomical Soc. of GB and Ire.; President: Internat. Soc. for Fracture Repair, 1994–96 (Chm. Memship Cttee, 1994–); British Orthopaedic Res. Soc., 2009–. Scientific Ed., Res. in Vet. Sci.; former Mem., Editl Adv. Bd, Clinical Materials; Member Editorial Board: Jl of Orthopaedic Trauma (Dep. Ed.); Equine & Comparative Exercise Physiology; Asst Ed., Equine Vet. Jl. Companion Fellow, British Orthopaedic Assoc. Hon. Mem., Uruguay Orthopaedic Assoc., 1994–. Prof. W. M. Mitchell Meml Fund Award, RCVS, 1976; Gary Hampson Meml Prize for Orthopaedic Res., 1984; Edwin Walker Prize, IMechE, 1988; Clinical Biomechanics Award, European Soc. of Biomechanics, 1990; Prize for Spinal Res., AcroMed, 1992; Medal, Nat. Back Pain Assoc., 1994; Open Award, Equine Vet. Jl, 1995; Scheering Plough Animal Health Vet. Achievement Award, Animal Health Trust, 2001; Meggers Award, Soc. for Applied Spectroscopy, 2006. *Publications:* (ed jtly) European Biomechanics: proceedings of the 6th meeting of the European Society of Biomechanics, 1988; book chapters and many articles in learned jls. *Recreations:* sailing, walking, gardening, vintage motorcycle restoration. *Address:* Department of Medical Physics and Biomedical Engineering, Institute of Orthopaedics and Musculoskeletal Science, University College London, Royal National Orthopaedic Hospital Trust, Brockley Hill, Stanmore, Middx HA7 4LP. *T:* (020) 8909 5532, *Fax:* (020) 8954 8560.

**GOODSMAN, James Melville,** CBE 1993; Managing Director, 1995–97, Chairman, 1997–2002, Michael Fraser Associates Ltd; Director, Michael Fraser & Co. Ltd, 1997–2002; *b* 6 Feb. 1947; *s* of late James K. Goodsman and Euphemia Goodsman, Elgin, Moray; *m* 1990, Victoria, *y d* of late Col Philip Smitherman and Rosemary Smitherman, CBE. *Educ:* Elgin Academy. Joined Cons. Party organisation, 1966; Agent: to Rt Hon. Betty Harvie Anderson, 1970–74; to Rt Hon. Maurice Macmillan, 1974–80; Conservative Central Office: Dep. Agent, NW Area, 1980–84; Asst Dir (Community Affairs), 1984–90; Head, Community and Legal Affairs, May–Sept. 1990; Dir, Cons. Party in Scotland, 1990–93. Director: ICP Ltd, 1997–2001; Capitalize Ltd, 2001–02. Hon. Sec., One Nation Forum, 1986–90. Mem., Edinburgh Morayshire Club (Chm., 1996). *Publications:* contribs to Cons. party and community relations papers. *Recreation:* church music. *Address:* Le Bourg, 61170 Coulognes-sur-Sarthe, France. *E:* james.goodsman@orange.fr.

**GOODSON, Sir Alan (Reginald),** 4th Bt *cr* 1922, of Waddeton Court, Co. Devon; farmer; *b* Kelso, Roxburghshire, 15 May 1960; *s* of Sir Mark Weston Lassam Goodson, 3rd Bt and Barbara Mary Constantine Goodson (née Andrews); *S* father, 2015; *m* 1990, Melanie Jayne Lodder; one *s* one *d. Educ:* Ampleforth Coll.; Edinburgh Univ. (MA Hons English Lit.). *Recreations:* field sports, literary research. Heir: *s* Hugh Mark Edwin Goodson, *b* 31 May 1993. *Address:* Marlefield House, Kelso, Roxburghshire TD5 8ED. *T:* (01573) 440 506. *E:* alan.goodson@virgin.net.

**GOODSON, Prof. Ivor Frederick,** DPhil; Professor of Learning Theory, Education Research Centre, University of Brighton, since 2004; *b* 30 Sept. 1943; *s* of Frederick G. J. Goodson and Lily W. Goodson; *m* 1975, Mary L. Nuttall; one *s. Educ:* Forest Grammar Sch.; University Coll. London (BSc Econ); Inst. of Educn, Univ. of London; London Sch. of Econs; DPhil Sussex 1979. University of Sussex: Res. Fellow, 1975–78; Dir, Eur. Schools Unit, 1978–85; University of Western Ontario: Prof., Faculty of Educn, Faculty of Grad. Studies and Centre for Theory and Criticism, 1986–96; Dir, Educnl Res. Unit, 1989–96; Hon. Prof. of Sociol., 1993–98; Prof. of Educn, Sch. of Educn and Professional Develt, UEA, 1996–2004. Founding Ed. and Man. Ed., Jl Educn Policy, 1986–. Frederica Warner Schol., 1991–96, Susan B. Anthony Scholar in Residence and Prof., 1996–2001, Margaret Warner Grad. Sch. of Educn and Professional Develt, Univ. of Rochester, NY; Vis. Internat. Guest Scientist, Max Planck Inst. of Human Develt and Educn, Berlin, 1994; J. Woodrow Wilson Vis. Prof., Oppenheimer Foundn, Univ. of Witwatersrand, SA, 1996; Visiting Professor: Sch. of Educn, Univ. of Exeter, 2001–04; Centre for Educnl Innovation, Univ. of Sussex, 2002–03; STINT Foundn Prof., Uppsala Univ., Sweden, 2003–10; Res. Associate, Von Hügel Inst., St Edmund's Coll., Cambridge, 2004–12; Catalan Res. Prof., Univ. of Barcelona, 2005; Joss Owen Chair of Education, Univ. of Plymouth, 2007–11; Sen. Vis. Fellow, Guerrand-Hermès Foundn for Peace, 2008–; Internat. Res. Prof., Univ. of Tallinn, 2012–19. Mem., Consultative Cttee, Educn Res. Centre, 2002–15, Chm., Consultative Cttee, Faculty of Social Sci., 2015, Univ. of Minho, Portugal; Mem., Selection Cttee, Wellbeing in Social Contexts, Nat. Centre of Competence in Res., 2004–; CORE Societal Challenges Panel Expert, Fonds Nat. de la Recherche, Luxembourg, 2013–. Life Fellow, RSA, 2009. Dist. Vis. Professorial Award, Japanese Soc. for Promotion of Sci., Univ. of Tokyo, 1993. *Publications:* School Subjects and Curriculum Change, 1983, 3rd edn 1993; The Making of Curriculum: collected essays, 1988, 2nd edn 1995; Biography, Identity and Schooling, 1991; Through the Schoolhouse Door, 1993; Studying Curriculum: cases and methods, 1994; Currículo: teoria e história (Brazil), 1995, 3rd edn 1999; Historia del Curriculum (Spain), 1995; Att Starka Lararnas Roster: sex essaer om lararforskning och lararforskarsamarbete (Sweden), 1996; The Changing Curriculum: studies in social construction, 1997; Studying School Subjects, 1997; Subject Knowledge: readings for the study of school subjects, 1998; Das Schulfach als Handlungsrahmen: vergleichende Untersuchung zur Geschichte und Funktion der Schulfächer (Germany), 1999; La Crisis del Cambio Curricular (Spain), 2000; (with P. Sikes) Life History Research in Educational Settings: learning from lives, 2001; The Birth of Environmental Education (China), 2001; (jtly) Cyber Spaces/Social Spaces: culture clash in computerised classrooms, 2002; Estudio del Curriculum: casos y métodos (Argentina), 2003; Professional Knowledge, Professional Lives: studies in education and change, 2003; Learning Curriculum and Life Politics: selected works, 2005; Professional Knowledge, Professional Lives (China), 2007; Professionel Viden. Professionelt Liv (Denmark), 2007; (ed jtly) Education, Globalisation and New Times, 2007; Políticas do Conhecimento: vida e trabalho docente entre saberes e instituições, 2007; Investigating the Teacher's Life and Work, 2008 (Chinese edn 2014); As Políticas de Currículo e de Escolarização, 2008; Developing Professional Knowledge about Teachers, 2009; (jtly) Narrative Learning, 2010; Through the Schoolhouse Door, 2010; (jtly) Professional Knowledge and Educational Restructuring in Europe, 2011; (jtly) Narrative Pedagogy, 2011; Improving Learning Through the Lifecourse, 2011; Life Politics: conversations about education and culture, 2011; (jtly) The Life History of a School, 2011; (ed jtly) Explorations in Narrative Research, 2012; Developing Narrative Theory: life histories and personal representation, 2013; The Politics of Curriculum and Schooling, Chinese edn 2014; Curriculum, Personal Narrative and the Social Future, 2014; (with S. Gill) Critical Narrative as Pedagogy, 2014; (contrib. jtly) European and Latin American Higher Education Between Mirrors, 2014; Narrativas em Educação: a vida e a voz dos Professores (Portugal), 2015; (with T. Rudd) Negotiating Neoliberalism: developing alternative educational visions, 2017; (ed jtly) The Routledge International Handbook on Narrative and Life History, 2017; contribs to learned jls incl. Jl Hist. of Educn Society, Power and Educn. *Recreations:* tennis, walking and birdwatching, jazz and rhythm and blues, Brighton and Hove FC supporter. *Address:* Education Research Centre, Room B323, Checkland Building, University of Brighton, Falmer, Brighton BN1 9PH. *T:* (01273) 644560.

**GOODSON, Michael John;** Assistant Auditor General, National Audit Office, 1984–93; *b* 4 Aug. 1937; *s* of late Herbert Edward William Goodson and Doris Maud Goodson; *m* 1958, Susan Elizabeth (née Higley) (*d* 2015); one *s* one *d. Educ:* King Henry VIII Sch., Coventry. Joined Exchequer and Audit Dept, 1955; Asst Auditor, 1955; Auditor, 1965; Private Sec. to Comptroller and Auditor Gen., 1967–70; Sen. Auditor, 1970; Health Service Ombudsman (on secondment), 1973–76; Chief Auditor, Exchequer and Audit Dept, 1976; Dep. Dir of Audit, 1978; Dir of Audit, 1981. *Recreations:* ornithology, model engineering, indoor and outdoor bowls. *Address:* 2 Bayley Mead, St John's Road, Boxmoor, Herts HP1 1US. *T:* (01442) 242611.

**GOODSON-WICKES, Dr Charles;** DL; consulting physician, company director, business consultant; *b* 7 Nov. 1945; *s* of late Ian Goodson Wickes, FRCP, Consultant Paediatrician and farmer, of Stock Harvard, Essex and Monica Goodson-Wickes; *m* 1974, Judith Amanda Hopkinson, *d* of late Comdr John Hopkinson, RN, JP, of Sutton Grange, near Stamford, Lincs; two *s. Educ:* Charterhouse; St Bartholomew's Hosp. (MB BS 1970). Called to the Bar, Inner Temple, 1972. Ho. Physician, Addenbrooke's Hosp., Cambridge, 1972; Surgeon-Capt., The Life Guards, 1973–77 (served BAOR, N Ireland, Cyprus); Silver Stick MO, Hsehold Cavalry, 1977; RARO, 1977–2000; re-enlisted as Lt-Col, 1991, for Gulf Campaign (served S Arabia, Iraq, Kuwait, with HQ 7 Armoured Bde). Clin. Asst, St Bart's Hosp., 1977–80; Consulting Phys., BUPA, 1977–86; Occupational Phys., 1980–94; formerly Med. advr to Barclays Bank, RTZ, McKinsey, Christie's, British Alcan, Collins, Meat & Livestock Commn etc; UK Advr, Norwegian Directorate of Health, 1983–94; Chm., Appeals Bd, Asbestos Licensing Regulations, 1982–87; Member: Med. Adv. Cttee, Industrial Soc., 1981–87; Fitness Adv. Panel, Inst. of Dirs, 1982–84; Council, Inst. for the Study of the Americas, Univ. of London, 2010–12. Director: Medarc Ltd, 1981–; Thomas Greg and Sons Ltd, 1992– (Chm., 2011–); Nestor Healthcare Gp plc, 1993–99; Gyrus Gp plc, 1997–2007; RICS Business Develt Bd, 2010–14; Ecohydra Technologies Ltd, 2014–, and other internat. cos. Publisher, Beaumont Fox, 2014–. Contested (C) Islington Central, 1979. MP (C) Wimbledon, 1987–97; contested (C) same seat, 1997. Vice-Pres., Islington South and Finsbury Cons. Assoc., 1982–97. PPS to Minister of State for Housing and Planning, DoE, 1992–94, to Financial Sec. to HM Treasury, 1994–95, to Sec. of State for Transport, 1995–96. Mem., Select Cttee on Members' Interests, 1992–94; Vice-Chm., Constitutional Affairs Cttee, 1990–91; Sec., Arts and Heritage Cttee, 1990–92; Vice Chm., Defence Cttee, 1991–92; Mem., Jt Cttee, Consolidation of Bills, 1987–92; Founder Chm., All Party, British-Colombian Gp, 1995–97; Vice Chm., All Party British-Russian Gp, 1993–97; Treas., All Party British Chinese Gp, 1992–97. Fellow, Industry and Parlt Trust, 1991; Patron, Hansard Soc., 2003–. Vice Chm., Cons. Foreign and Commonwealth Council, 1997–2011. Dir Gen., Canning Hse, 2010–12. Treas., Dr Ian Goodson Wickes Fund for Handicapped Children, 1979–88; Vice-Pres., Combat Stress (formerly Ex-Services Mental Welfare Soc.), 1990–; Founder Chm., Countryside Alliance, 1997–99 (Patron, 2003–; Chm., 1994–98, Mem., Public Affairs Cttee, 1980–87, British Field Sports Soc.); Chm., 1997–98, Chief Exec., 1998–2007, London Playing Fields Soc., later Foundn; Chm., Rural Trust, 1999–2014; Mem., London Sports Bd, 2000–03 (Chm., Envmt Cttee, 2001–03); Vice-Pres., Gt Bustard Gp, 2008–. Chm., Islington/City Ring, 2018–. Governor, Highbury Grove Sch., 1977–85. Pte, The Parachute Regt (TA), 1963–65; Mem. HAC, 2013. Founder Chm., Essex Kit Cat Club, 1965. Freeman, City of London, 2014. DL Gtr London, 1999; Rep. DL Islington, 2011. *Publications:* The New Corruption, 1984; (contrib.) Another Country, 1999. *Recreations:* hunting, shooting, Real tennis, gardening, travel, history. *Address:* Watergate House, Bulford, Wilts SP4 9DY. *T:* (01980) 632344; 37 St James's Place, SW1A 1NS. *T:* (020) 7629 0981. *Clubs:* Boodle's, Pratt's, MCC (Mem. Cttee, 2019–).

**GOODWAY, Russell;** Member (Lab), County Council of the City and County of Cardiff, since 1995; Chief Executive, Community Pharmacy Wales, since 2009; *b* 23 Dec. 1955; *s* of Russell Donald Goodway and Barbara Mary Goodway (née Vizard); *m* 1979, Susan Yvonne Witchard; one *s. Educ:* Barry Boys' Comprehensive Sch.; University Coll., Swansea (BA Econs and Politics 1977). Partner, Keane Goodway & Co., Accountants, 1988–2000. Dep. Chm., Millennium Stadium plc, 1996–2004; Chief Exec., Cardiff Chamber of Commerce and Industry, 2005–07; Business Develt Dir, Paramount Office Interiors Ltd, 2008–09. Bd Mem., Cardiff Bay Develt Corp., 1993–2000. Member: Porthkerry Community Council, 1977–82 (Chm., 1980–81); Rhoose Community Council, 1982–87 (Chm., 1985–86); S Glamorgan County Council: Mem., 1985–96; Chm., Property Services Cttee, 1988–89; Chm., Finance Cttee, 1989–92; Leader, and Chm. Policy Cttee, 1992–96; Dep. Chm., 1992–93; County Council of City and County of Cardiff: first Leader of the Council, 1995–2004, Exec. Leader, 2002–04; Chairman: Policy Cttee, 1995–99; Council's Cabinet, 1999–2004; Lord Mayor of Cardiff, 1999–2003; Cabinet Member: for Finance, Business and Local Economy, 2012–13; for Finance and Econ. Develt, 2013–14; for Investment and Develt, 2017–. Dep. Chm., Assembly of Welsh Counties, 1994–96. Chm., Millennium Stadium Charitable Trust, 2009–. OStJ 2004. *Recreations:* sport, especially Rugby and tennis, reading political biographies, music. *Address:* Singleton, 82 Colcot Road, Barry CF62 8HP. *T:* (01446) 749976.

**GOODWILL, Rt Hon. Robert;** PC 2018; MP (C) Scarborough and Whitby, since 2005; *b* 31 Dec. 1956; *s* of late Robert W. Goodwill and Joan Goodwill; *m* 1987, Maureen (née Short); two *s* one *d. Educ:* Bootham Sch., York; Univ. of Newcastle upon Tyne (BSc Hons Agriculture). Farmer, 1979–. Contested (C): Redcar, 1992; NW Leics, 1997; Cleveland and Richmond, 1994, Yorks S, May 1998, EP elecns. MEP (C) Yorks and the Humber Reg., 1999–2004; Dep. Cons. Leader, EP, 2003–04. Opposition Whip, 2006–07; Shadow Transport Minister, 2007–10; an Asst Govt Whip, 2010–11; Govt Pairing Whip, 2011–13;

a Lord Comr of HM Treasury (Govt Whip), 2012–13; Parly Under-Sec. of State, 2013–15, Minister of State, 2015–16, DfT; Minister of State: Home Office, 2016–17; DFE, 2017–18; DEFRA, 2019. *Recreations*: steam ploughing, travel, languages. *Address*: Southwood Farm, Terrington, York YO60 6QB. *T*: (01653) 648459; (constituency office) 6 Albemarle Crescent, Scarborough, N Yorks YO11 1XS. *E*: robert.goodwill.mp@parliament.uk.

**GOODWIN, Christine, (Mrs Richard Goodwin);** *see* Edzard, C.

**GOODWIN, Daisy Georgia, (Mrs Marcus Wilford);** television producer, novelist and screenwriter; *b* London, 19 Dec. 1961; *d* of Richard Goodwin and late Jocasta Innes; *m* 1988, Marcus Wilford; two d. *Educ*: Westminster Sch.; Trinity Coll., Cambridge (BA Hist. 1983); Columbia Univ. (Harkness Fellow). Producer, BBC, 1985–98; programmes include: Homefront, Bookworm; Editl Dir, Talkback Thames, 1998–2005; programmes include: Grand Designs, Property Ladder, The Apprentice; Founder and CEO, Silver River Prodns, 2005–14; programmes include: The Supersizers, Pulling, Off By Heart, Hidden Talent, Shakespeare Off By Heart, If Walls Could Talk - an intimate history of the home; The Big Allotment Challenge, 2014. Presenter, Essential Poems, BBC, 2003–. Writer and creator, Victoria, ITV, 2016–. Chair: Poetry Book Soc., 2003–07; Women Taking Action. Trustee, London Library, 2018. FRSA. *Publications*: Silver River: memoir, 2007; My Last Duchess (novel), 2010; The Fortune Hunter (novel), 2014; edited: The Nation's Favourite Love Poems, 1997; 101 Poems to Save Your Life, 1998; 101 Poems to Get You Through Day and Night, 1999; Essential Poems to Fall in Love With, 2003; Poems for Life, 2004; Victoria (novel), 2016. *Recreations*: collecting books with Daisy in the title, avoiding meetings, quilting, making marmalade, reading poetry and classic crime, collecting Victoriana, tapestry.

**GOODWIN, Dr Elizabeth Jane,** OBE 2015; Senior Fellow, and Director, Food Loss and Waste, World Resources Institute, Washington, DC, since 2016; Chair, London Waste and Recycling Board, since 2017; *b* London, 6 June 1961; *d* of late David Goodwin and of Anna Goodwin (*née* Stretch, now Fitter); *m* 2011, Bruce Eggeling. *Educ*: Chichester High Sch. for Girls; University Coll. London (BSc 1st Cl.); Univ. of Exeter (PhD 1986). Technical Manager, ICI, 1986–92; Zeneca: Envmtl Advr, 1992–99; Envmtl Manager, 1999–2000; Eur. Envmtl Advr, 2000–01; Dir of Materials, 2001–07, CEO, 2007–16, Waste and Resources Action Prog. (WRAP). Chm., Strategic Adv. Gp, Plastics Res. and Innovation Fund, 2018–. Hon. FSE 2013. Hon. DSc Cranfield, 2010. *Recreations*: running, walking, crosswords, sudokus, bridge, opera.

**GOODWIN, Frederick Anderson;** Chief Executive, Royal Bank of Scotland Group plc, 2000–08 (Deputy Group Chief Executive, 1998–2000); Senior Adviser, RMJM, 2009–11; *b* 17 Aug. 1958; *s* of Frederick Anderson Goodwin and Marylyn Marshall Goodwin (*née* Mackintosh). *Educ*: Paisley GS; Univ. of Glasgow (LLB). CA 1983; FCIBS 1996; FCIB 2002. Joined Touche Ross & Co., 1979, Partner, 1988–95; Dep. Chief Exec., 1995, Chief Exec., 1996–98, Clydesdale Bank PLC; Chief Exec., Yorkshire Bank, 1997–98. Director: Bank of China, 2006–08; ABN AMRO, 2007–08. Dir, Scottish Business Achievement Award Trust, 2001–03. Chairman: Prince's Trust, Scotland, 1999–2003; Prince's Trust, 2003–09. DUniv: Paisley, 2001; Glasgow, 2002; Hon. LLD St Andrews, 2004. *Recreations*: restoring cars, golf.

**GOODWIN, Prof. Graham Clifford,** PhD; FRS 2002; FIEEE, FAA, FTSE; Professor of Electrical Engineering, 1983, now Emeritus Laureate Professor, and Director, ARC Centre for Complex Dynamic Systems and Control, 2007–11, now Academic Researcher, University of Newcastle, New South Wales; *b* NSW, 20 April 1945; *s* of C. H. R. F. Goodwin; *m* 1967, Rosslyn Mackintosh; one *s* one d. *Educ*: Broken Hill High Sch.; Univ. of NSW (BSc 1964; BE 1966; PhD 1970). Lectr, Imperial Coll., Univ. of London, 1971–74; University of Newcastle, New South Wales: Lectr, 1974–75, Sen. Lectr, 1976, Associate Prof., 1977–83, Dept of Electrical Engrg; Hd, Dept of Electrical and Computer Engrg, 1979–84; Dir, Centre for Industrial Control Sci., 1988–96; Dean, Faculty of Engrg, 1994–96; Dir, Centre for Integrated Dynamics and Control, 1997–2001; ARC Fedn Fellow, 2002–06; Res. Dir, ARC Centre for Complex Dynamic Systems and Control, 2002–07. *Publications*: (jtly) Control Theory, 1970; (jtly) Dynamic System Identification, 1977; (jtly) Adaptive Filtering, Prediction and Control, 1984; (jtly) Digital Estimation and Control, 1990; (ed jtly) Adaptive Control Filtering and Signal Processing, 1994; (jtly) Sampling in Digital Signal Processing and Control, 1996; (jtly) Fundamental Limitations in Filtering and Control, 1996; (jtly) Control System Design, 2000; (jtly) Constrained Control and Estimation, 2003; chapters in books and articles in learned jls. *Address*: School of Electrical Engineering and Computer Science, University of Newcastle, University Drive, Callaghan, NSW 2308, Australia.

**GOODWIN, Prof. Guy Manning,** DPhil; FRCPsych, FMedSci; W. A. Handley Professor of Psychiatry, and Head, Department of Psychiatry, University of Oxford, 1996–2014, now Emeritus; Fellow of Merton College, Oxford, 1996–2014, now Emeritus; *b* 8 Nov. 1947; *s* of Kenneth M. Goodwin and Constance (*née* Hudson); *m* 1971, Philippa Catherine Georgeson; two d. *Educ*: Manchester GS; Exeter Coll., Oxford (open schol.; MA); Wolfson Coll., Oxford (Grad. Schol.; DPhil 1972); Magdalen Coll., Oxford (MB BCh 1978). FRCPE 1995–2000; FRCPsych 1995. Scholar, MRC, 1968–71; Fellow, Magdalen Coll., Oxford, 1971–76; House Physician, Nuffield Dept of Clin. Medicine, Oxford and House Surgeon, Horton Gen. Hosp., Banbury, 1978–79; Sen. House Officer, Nat. Hosp., Queen Sq., and Professorial Unit, Brompton Hosp., 1979–80; Registrar, Rotational Trng Scheme in Psychiatry, Oxford, 1980–83; MRC Clin. Trng Fellow, and Lectr, MRC Clin. Pharmacol. Unit, Oxford, 1983–86; MRC Clin. Scientist, Hon. Consultant Psychiatrist and Hon. Sen. Lectr, Edinburgh Univ., 1986–95; Prof. of Psychiatry, Edinburgh Univ., 1995–96. Res. Associate, Univ. of Washington, Seattle, 1972–74; Hobson Meml Schol., Oxford, 1975. Sen. Investigator, NIHR, 2011–17; Investigator, Thomson Reuters, 2017–. Mem., Neuroscis and Mental Health Grants and Fellowships Cttee, Wellcome Trust, 1992–97. Pres., British Assoc. for Psychopharmacol., 2002–04 (Mem. Council, 1993–97); Pres., Eur. Coll. of Neuropsychopharmacol., 2013–16. FMedSci 2006. *Publications*: contrib. learned jls on neurophysiol., neuropharmacol. and psychiatry. *Recreations*: football and opera passively, hillwalking actively. *Address*: Department of Psychiatry, Warneford Hospital, Oxford OX3 7JX.

**GOODWIN, Jonathan,** OBE 2018; Partner and Head of Merchant Banking, Alvarium Merchant Banking, since 2019; *b* London, 12 Nov. 1972; *s* of Philip Goodwin and Ann Goodwin-Rooze; *m* 2011, Hon. Flora, *d* of Baron Hesketh, *qv*; five *s* one d. *Educ*: Charterhouse Sch.; Univ. of Nottingham (BA Geog.). Associate, Apax Partners, 1995–97; Man. Dir, Talk Radio, 1997; Gp Man. Dir, Wireless Gp plc, 1998–2000; Co-Founder, LongAcre Partners, 2000–07; Founder, Lepe Partners, 2011–19. Co-Founder: Founders Forum, 2005–; PROfounders Capital, 2010–. *Recreations*: shooting, sailing (J/109 class Cowes Week winner, 2012, 2013), tennis. *Address*: Alvarium Merchant Banking, 10 Old Burlington Street, W1S 3AG. *E*: sarah.jones@alvariuminvestments.com. *Clubs*: Queen's, Royal Yacht Squadron.

**GOODWIN, Katrina Noelle;** Drue Heinz Curator, since 2010, and Head of Architecture, since 2014, Royal Academy of Arts; *b* Sydney, Australia, 28 Oct. 1977; *d* of Clive Benson Goodwin and Jenny Joy Goodwin. *Educ*: Univ. of Sydney (BSc Arch. 1998; BArch 1st Cl. Hons 2002). Architecture Prog. Co-ordinator, 2003–05, Architecture Prog. Curator, 2005–10, Royal Acad. of Arts. Curator: Sensing Spaces: Architecture Re-imagined, Royal Acad. of Arts, 2014; Inside Heatherwick Studio, British Council Asia, 2015–17. Member: Adv. Bd, London Fest. of Architecture, 2017; Bd, Mayfair Art Weekend, 2017–. Mem., Editl Bd, Architectural Design, 2015–. Hon. FRIBA 2016. *Publications*: Dandelion: the making of the UK Pavilion at Shanghai World Expo 2010, 2011. *Recreations*: sailing, outdoor adventures, theatre, festivals. *Address*: Royal Academy of Arts, Burlington House, Piccadilly, W1J 0BD. *T*: (020) 7300 8000. *E*: kate.goodwin@royalacademy.org.uk.

**GOODWIN, Michael;** QC 2019; a Deputy District Judge, since 2012; *b* London, 1971; *m* Natalie; one *s* one d. *Educ*: Univ. of Leeds (BSc Psychol.); City Univ., London (DipLaw); Inns of Court Sch. of Law. Called to the Bar, Inner Temple, 1996; in practice as a barrister, specialising in business crime and serious organised crime. Mem. Cttee, South Eastern Circuit, 2017–. Mem., Social Mobility Cttee, Criminal Bar Assoc., 2017–. *Address*: Red Lion Chambers, 18 Red Lion Court, EC4A 3EB. *T*: (020) 7520 6000. *E*: michael.goodwin@18rlc.co.uk.

**GOODWIN, Dr Neil,** CBE 2007; photographer, since 2016; Chair, Aintree University Hospitals NHS Foundation Trust, since 2014; Independent Chair, Central and Eastern Cheshire Partnership Board, since 2018; *b* 1 March 1951; *s* of James and Dorothy Goodwin; *m* 1980, Sian Elizabeth Mary Holliday (marr. diss. 1992); two *s*; *m* 2006, Chris Hannah; one step *s* one step d. *Educ*: North Salford County Secondary Sch.; London Business Sch. (MBA); Manchester Business Sch. (PhD). FHSM, later FIHM, 1990–2014; CIHM, 2006–13. NHS mgt posts, London, Manchester, Liverpool, Southport, Bromsgrove, Hertfordshire, 1969–85; General Manager, Central Middlesex Hosp., 1985–88; Chief Executive: St Mary's Hosp., subseq. St Mary's Hosp. NHS Trust, 1988–94; Manchester HA, 1994–2002; Chief Exec., Gtr Manchester Strategic HA, 2002–06. Vis. Prof. of Leadership Studies, Univ. of Manchester, 2004–15, Durham Univ., 2006–14, UCL, 2009–14. Dir, GoodwinHannah Ltd, 2006–14. Project Dir, UCL Partners Academic Health Science Partnership, 2008–09. Interim Dir, Nuffield Trust, 2007–08. Advisor: E. C. Harris LLP, 2006–08; Pinsent Masons, 2007–08; CHKS, 2007–12; Bd, Channel 3 Gp, 2015–16. Chair, Onward Homes Ltd (formerly Symphony Housing Gp), 2015–. Chair: London Cancer Alliance, 2012–16; Healthcare Support (Newcastle) Ltd, 2014–16; Ind. Chair, Caring Together Prog. Bd, NHS Eastern Cheshire, 2016–17; Chair, Liverpool Health Partners, 2018– (Interim Chair, 2017–18). Non-exec. Dir, UK Transplant Authy, 2000–05. Member: Orgnl Audit Council and Accreditation Cttee, King's Fund Coll., 1993–2000; Manchester TEC Investors in People accreditation panel, 1995–99; Cabinet Office review of public sector leadership, 2000; Scientific Cttee, 2000–05, Bd, 2005–09, Eur. Health Mgt Assoc. Mem. Court, Manchester Univ., 2003–05. Advr, Serco Health, 2009–10. Editorial Adviser: British Jl of Health Care Mgt, 1998–2014; Jl of Mgt in Medicine, 1999–2014; Leadership in Health Services, 2008–14. MCMI (MBIM 1982), FCMI 2008. *Publications*: Leadership in Healthcare: a European perspective, 2005; (contrib.) Perspectives in Public Health, 2006; (contrib.) Health Care Management, 2006; academic papers and articles on corporate failure, public sector leadership, the contextual challenges of leadership, customer care in hosps, leadership develt needs of chief execs and public health professionals, and internat. healthcare. *Recreation*: Friend of Lloyd George Museum. *Address*: The Old School, Windmill Lane, Preston on the Hill, Cheshire WA4 4AZ. *E*: neil@goodwinhannah.co.uk. *W*: www.neilgoodwinphotography.org.

**GOODWIN, Nicholas Alexander John;** QC 2014; a Recorder, since 2009; a Deputy High Court Judge, since 2016; *b* London, 10 Nov. 1970; *s* of Frank and Mary Rose Goodwin; *m* 2006, Alison Marshall; one d. *Educ*: King's Sch., Canterbury; Oriel Coll., Oxford (MA English Lit.). Called to the Bar, Inner Temple, 1995; in practice as barrister, specialising in family law; Head, Harcourt Chambers, 2018–. *Recreations*: music, mountaineering. *Address*: Harcourt Chambers, 2 Harcourt Buildings, Temple, EC4Y 9DB. *T*: (020) 7353 6961. *E*: ngoodwin@harcourtchambers.co.uk.

**GOODWIN, Paul;** Artistic Director and Principal Conductor, Carmel Bach Festival, since 2011; Principal Guest Conductor, Cappella Aquileia, since 2016; *b* 2 Sept. 1956; *s* of Norman and Audrey Goodwin; *m* 1995, Helen Gough; two *s* one d. *Educ*: City of London Sch.; Univ. of Nottingham (BMus); Hochschule für Musik, Wien (Postgrad. Dip.); Guildhall Sch. of Music and Drama (Postgrad. Dip.). Chorister, Temple Ch Choir, London. Principal and solo oboist, English Consort, King's Consort, and London Classical Players, 1985–97; Prof. of Baroque Oboe, RCM, 1986–96; Musical Director: London Oboe band, 1985–97; Royal Coll. of Music baroque orch., 1993–99; Dartington Early Opera, 1995–2001; Associate Conductor, Acad. of Ancient Music, 1996–2008; Principal Guest Conductor, English Chamber Orch., 1997–2003; regular guest conductor in Europe incl. Bayerischer Rundfunk, Munich and all major German radio orchs, Nat. Orchs of Belgium, Spain, Poland, Hungary; in USA incl. Philadelphia Orch., Nat. SO Washington, San Francisco, Seattle SO; in UK incl. Scottish Chamber Orch., Scottish Nat. Orch., Hallé, CBSO, BBC SO; opera productions incl. Le Nozze di Figaro and Die Zauberflöte, Opera de Oviedo and Opera North, Iphigénie en Tauride, Komische Oper Berlin; Idomeneo, Graz Opera; Orlando, Scottish Opera, Flanders Opera, Opera Australia, Jeptha, Welsh Nat. Opera. Handel Hon. Prize, City of Halle, 2007. *Recreations*: sailing, racquet sports.

**GOODWIN, Dr Philip Paul;** Chief Executive Officer, Voluntary Service Overseas International, since 2015; *b* 15 Feb. 1965; *s* of Dennis Paul Goodwin and Wendy Goodwin; *m* 1999, Annette Schwalbe; one *s* one d. *Educ*: Univ. of Reading (BSc Agricl Econs); Wye Coll., Univ. of London (MSc Rural Resource and Envmtl Policy; PhD Cultural Geog.). Professional musician and songwriter, 1989–93; volunteer, UNA Internat. Service, Mali, 1998; Res. Officer, ODI, 1999; British Council: Director: Develt Services, Pakistan, 1999–2002; Uganda, 2002–04; Regional Director: East and West Africa, 2004–08; Sub-Saharan Africa, 2008–09; Global Prog. Leader, Creative and Knowledge Economy, 2009–10; CEO, TREE AID, 2010–15. Non-exec. Dir, Internat. Civil Soc. Centre, 2015–17, 2019–. Pres., VSO USA, 2017–; non-exec. Dir, VSO Netherlands, 2018–. Vice-Chair, Internat. Forum for Volunteering in Develt, 2015–; Trustee, RNLI, 2018–. *Publications*: (with Tony Page) From Hippos to Gazelles: how leaders create leaders, 2008; contrib. refereed articles to Trans IBG, Society and Space: Envmt and Planning D, Jl Rural Studies. *Recreations*: songwriting, making records, my garden, making chutney and jam. *Address*: c/o VSO International, 100 London Road, Kingston upon Thames KT2 6QJ.

**GOODWIN, Prof. Phillip Bramley,** PhD; Professor of Transport Policy, Centre for Transport and Society, University of the West of England, 2005–12, now Emeritus Professor; *b* 6 March 1944; *s* of Dennis and Joan Goodwin; *m* 1966, Margaret Livesey (separated); one d. *Educ*: Henry Thornton Grammar Sch.; UCL (BSc Econs 1965; PhD Civil Engrg 1973). FCILT, FCIHT. Res. Asst, LRD Ltd, 1965–66; Res., UCL, 1966–74; Transport Planner, GLC, 1974–79; Dep. Dir, 1979–81, Dir, and Reader, 1981–95, Transport Studies Unit, Univ. of Oxford; Prof. of Transport Policy and Dir, ESRC Transport Studies Unit, UCL, 1996–2004, now Emeritus Prof. Mem., Standing Adv. Cttee on Trunk Road Assessment, 1979–2000; Chm., Ind. Adv. Panel for Transport White Paper, 1997–98. Non-exec. Dir, Dover Harbour Bd, 1989–2005. Distinguished Contrib. Award, Instn of Highways and Transportation, 1998. Founding Ed., Transport Policy, 1993; Ed.-in-chief, Jl Transportation Res. (A) Policy & Practice, 2005–10. *Publications*:

Subsidised Public Transport and the Demand for Travel, 1983; Long Distance Transportation, 1983; (jtly) Transport and the Environment, 1991; (jtly) Trunk Roads and the Generation of Traffic, 1994; Car Dependence, 1995; (jtly) Transport and the Economy, 1999; approx. 200 articles in learned jls, conf. papers, and contribs to books on transport policy and travel behaviour. *Recreation:* Isla de el Hierro. *E:* philinelh@yahoo.com.

**GOODWIN, Rain;** *see* Newton-Smith, R.

**GOODWIN-GILL, Prof. Guy Serle,** DPhil; Professor of International Refugee Law, University of Oxford, 1998–2014, now Emeritus; Senior Research Fellow, All Souls College, Oxford, 2002–14, now Emeritus; Professor of Law, University of New South Wales, Sydney, since 2017 (Acting Director, Kaldor Centre for International Refugee Law, 2017–18); *b* Ealing, 25 Dec. 1946; *s* of Walter Booth Goodwin and Josephine Esther Goodwin (*née* Brown) and step *s* of Ian Arthur Gill; *m* 1991, Sharon Anne Rusu. *Educ:* Mill Hill Sch.; Wadham Coll., Oxford (BA Juris. 1968; MA; DPhil 1974). Called to the Bar, Inner Temple, 1971; Lectr, 1971–74, Sen. Lectr, 1974–76, Coll. of Law, London; Legal Advr, UNHCR, UK, Australia and Geneva, 1976–88; Vis. Prof., Osgoode Hall Law Sch., 1988; Vis. Prof., 1988–89, Prof. of Law, 1989–97, Carleton Univ., Ottawa; Prof. of Asylum Law (pt-time), Univ. of Amsterdam, 1994–99; Rubin Dir of Res., Inst. of Eur. Studies, Oxford Univ., 1997–2002; in practice at the Bar, Blackstone Chambers, 2000–18; Vis. Prof., Académie de droit humanitaire, Geneva, 2008–11; Julius Stone Vis. Fellow, Faculty of Law, Univ. of NSW, 2010; Dir, Hague Acad. of Internat. Law, Centre for Res. and Studies, 2010; W. J. Ganshof van der Meersch Chair, Univ. Libre de Bruxelles, 2010–11; Hon. Sen. Fellow, Melbourne Law Sch., 2015–; Vis. Professorial Fellow, Univ. of NSW, 2015–16; Hon. Associate, Refugee Studies Centre, Oxford, 2015–. Founding Ed. and Ed.-in-Chief, Internat. Jl Refugee Law, 1988–2001. Pres., Refugee and Migrant Justice (formerly Refugee Legal Centre), 1997–2010. Mem. Council, Overseas Develt Inst., 2007–13. Pres., Media Appeals Bd of Kosovo, 2000–03. Order of Independence (Jordan), 2007. *Publications:* International Law and the Movement of Persons Between States, 1978; The Refugee in International Law, 1983, 3rd edn with J. McAdam, 2007; Free and Fair Elections, 1994, 2nd edn 2006; (with I. Cohn) Child Soldiers, 1994; (ed with S. Talmon and contrib.) The Reality of International Law: essays in honour of Ian Brownlie, 1997; Codes of Conduct for Elections, 1998; (ed with I. Brownlie) Basic Documents on Human Rights, 4th edn 2002, 6th edn 2010; Toleranz in einem Zeitalter der Ungewißheit/ Tolerance in an Age of Uncertainty, 2002; (ed with H. Lambert and contrib.) The Limits of Transnational Law, 2010; (ed with P. Weckel and contrib.) Protection des migrants et des réfugiés au XXIe siècle: aspects de droit international/Migration and Refugee Protection in the 21st Century: international legal aspects, 2015. *Recreations:* music, cooking, gardening, cats, cycling. *Address:* All Souls College, Oxford OX1 4AL.

**GOODY, Juliet Constance Wyatt, (Lady Goody);** *see* Mitchell, J. C. W.

**GOODYEAR, Charles Waterhouse, (Chip);** non-executive Chairman, Metallum Holding SA, since 2014; *b* 18 Jan. 1958; *s* of Charles and Linda Goodyear; *m* 1992, Elizabeth Dabezies; one *s* one *d. Educ:* Yale Univ. (BSc Geol., Geophys 1980); Wharton Sch. of Finance, Univ. of Pennsylvania (MBA 1983). Kidder, Peabody & Co.: Associate, 1983–85; Asst Vice Pres., 1985–86; Vice Pres., 1986–89; Freeport-McMoRan, Inc.: Vice Pres., Corporate Finance, 1989–93; Sen. Vice Pres. and Chief Investment Officer, 1993–95; Exec. Vice Pres. and Chief Financial Officer, 1995–97; Pres., Goodyear Capital Corp., 1997–99; Chief Financial Officer, BHP Ltd, 1999–2001; Exec. Dir and Chief Develt Officer, 2001–03, CEO, 2003–07, BHP Billiton. Non-exec. Dir, Anadarko Petroleum Corp., 2012–15. Trustee: Yale Univ., 2011–; Nat. World War II Mus., New Orleans, 2014–. Chm., BHP Foundn, 2019–. *Recreations:* bicycling, ski-ing, fishing.

**GOODYER, Prof. Ian Michael,** OBE 2018; MD; FRCPsych, FMedSci; Foundation Professor of Child and Adolescent Psychiatry, Cambridge University, 1992–2017, now Emeritus; Fellow of Wolfson College, Cambridge, 1993–2017, now Emeritus; *b* 2 Nov. 1949; *s* of Mark and Belle Goodyer; *m* 1979, Jane Elizabeth Akister; one *s* one *d. Educ:* University College London; St George's Hosp.; Oxford Univ.; Newcastle Univ.; Brown Univ. MB BS, MD London; MRCPsych 1976, FRCPsych 1990; DCH 1978. Sen. Lectr, Child/Adolescent Psych. and Consultant, Univ. of Manchester and Salford HA, 1983–87; Cambridge University: Foundn Lectr in Child Psych., 1987–92; Head, Developmental Psych. Section, 1992–. FMedSci 1999. *Publications:* Life Experiences, Development and Child Psychopathology, 1991; The Depressed Child and Adolescent: developmental and clinical perspectives, 1995, 2nd edn 2000; Unipolar Depression: a lifespan perspective, 2003; (with David Goldberg) The Origins and Course of Common Mental Disorders, 2005; (jtly) Social Cognition and Developmental Psychopathology, 2008; contribs to learned jls. *Recreations:* keeping fit, guitar. *Address:* Developmental Psychiatry Section, Douglas House, 18 Trumpington Road, Cambridge CB2 8AH. *T:* (01223) 746066.

**GOOLAMALI, Nina Soraya;** QC 2017; *b* Newcastle upon Tyne, 11 Feb. 1973; *d* of Saleem Karim Goolamali, MD, FRCP and late Alma Maria Goolamali, SRN, SCM. *Educ:* St Helen's Sch., Northwood; Lady Margaret Hall, Oxford (BA Juris. 1994); King's Coll. London (Dip. Sports Law 2007). Called to the Bar, Middle Temple, 1995 (Harmsworth Law Schol.); in practice as a barrister, 2 Temple Gardens, 1995–; Advocacy Trainer, Middle Temple, 2007–. Dir, Bar Mutual Indemnity Fund, 2014–; Mem., Pro Bono Legal Service, Sport Resolutions UK, 2015–. Mem., Editl Bd, LawInSport, 2014–. *Publications:* (ed jtly) A Practical Guide to Maternity and Parental Rights, 2nd edn 2005. *Recreations:* family, friends, food. *Address:* 2 Temple Gardens, Temple, EC4Y 9AY. *T:* (020) 7822 1200, *Fax:* (020) 7822 1300. *E:* ngoolamaliqc@2tg.co.uk.

**GOOLD, Sir George William,** 8th Bt *cr* 1801, of Old Court, Cork; *b* 25 March 1950; *o s* of Sir George Leonard Goold, 7th Bt of Joy Cecelia Goold (now Joy, Lady Goold); *S* father, 1997; *m* 1973, Julie Ann Crack; two *s. Heir: s* George Leonard Powell Goold [*b* 1 Dec. 1975; *m* 1999, Kirsty Ann Ling (marr. diss. 2014); one *s* one *d*]. *Address:* PO Box 176, Woollahra, NSW 1350, Australia. *T:* (2) 408421159.

**GOOLEY, Michael David William,** CBE 2007; FRGS; Founder and Chairman, Trailfinders Ltd, since 1970; *b* 13 Oct. 1936; *s* of late Denis David Gooley and Lennie Frances May Gooley (*née* Woodward); *m* 1st, 1961, Veronica Georgina Broad (marr. diss. 1970); two *d*; 2nd, 1971, Hilary Eila (marr. diss. 1981; she *d* 1993), *d* of Sir Paul Mallinson, 3rd Bt; one *s* one *d*; 3rd, 1983, Bernadette Mary Woodward (marr. diss. 1997); 4th, 2000, Fiona Kathleen Leslie. *Educ:* St John's Beaumont Prep. Sch.; St George's, Weybridge; RMA Sandhurst. Enlisted Regular Army, 1955: commnd 2nd Lieut, S Staffs Regt, 1956; joined 22 SAS, 1958; served Malaya and Arabian Peninsula; Adjt, 21 SAS, 1961–63; 1st Bn Staffords, 1963; served Kenya; 2nd tour, 22 SAS, 1964; served Malay Peninsula, Borneo and S Arabia; retd 1965. Mil. Advr to Royalist Yemini Army, 1965–69. Leader, expedition Trans Africa, 1971. Founder Trustee, Mike Gooley Trailfinders Charity, 1995. FInstD 1978; FRGS 1996. Hon. Life FRSA 2005. Patron, Prostate Cancer Charity, 1998–. Trustee, Special Forces Club, 1996–2007. *Publications:* Trans Africa Route Report, 1972. *Recreations:* travel, aviation, pragmatic entrepreneurialism, wining and dining, supporting Ealing Trailfinders RFC. *Address:* (office) 9 Abingdon Road, W8 6AH. *Club:* Special Forces.

**GOOSE, Duncan;** Founder and Chief Executive Officer, Global Ethics Group, since 2004; *b* Edinburgh, 1968; *s* of Dr David Goose and Joy Goose; *m* 2009, Dr Marta Boffito; one *s* one *d. Educ:* Wisbech Grammar Sch.; Framlingham Coll.; Coventry Poly. (HND Business Studies 1987). Business Develt Dir, Black Cat, 1994–98; global motorcycle odyssey (sabbatical), 1998–2000; Business Develt Dir, JWT, 2000–04. Launched: One Water, 2004; Global Investment Fund for Water, 2015–; One for Money, 2015–. Trustee: One Foundn, 2005–12; Coventry Univ., 2009–11; John Lewis Foundn, 2010–12. Hon. Mem., Path North, 2007–. Hon. DBA Sunderland, 2009. *Recreations:* motorbiking, travel, charitable causes, paragliding, painting, cookery. *Address:* Global Ethics Ltd, 13–17 Princes Road, Richmond, Surrey TW10 6DQ. *E:* duncan@global-ethics.com.

**GOOSE, Hon. Sir Julian (Nicholas),** Kt 2017; **Hon. Mr Justice Goose;** a Judge of the High Court, Queen's Bench Division, since 2017; *b* 26 July 1961; *s* of Alan Charles Goose and Pauline Jean Goose; *m* 1987, Susan Frances Rose Bulmer; two *s* one *d. Educ:* Birkdale Sch.; Silverdale Sch.; Leeds Univ. (LLB Hons). Called to the Bar, Lincoln's Inn, 1984, Bencher, 2009. Junior, NE Circuit, 1992; Recorder 1998–2013; QC 2002; Hd of Zenith Chambers, 2004–13; a Sen. Circuit Judge and Resident Judge, Sheffield Combined Court Centre, 2013–17; Hon. Recorder of Sheffield, 2013–17. Member: Advocacy Trng Council, 2004–14 (Vice Chm., 2012–14); Sentencing Council, 2014–. *Recreations:* golf, friends, family. *Address:* Royal Courts of Justice, Strand, WC2A 2LL. *Club:* Alwoodley Golf.

**GOOSE, Margaret Elizabeth,** OBE 2004; Vice President, Stroke Association, since 2006 (Chief Executive, 1997–2004); *b* 10 Oct. 1945; *d* of late Leonard Charles Goose and Gladys Muriel Goose (*née* Smith). *Educ:* Blyth Sch., Norwich; Newnham Coll., Cambridge (BA 1967; MA 1971). FHSM 1991. Gen. mgt in hosps and health authorities, 1967–82; Chief Exec., N Beds HA, 1982–92; Hd of Health and Mgt Develt Div., Nuffield Inst. for Health, Univ. of Leeds, 1993–97. Lay Mem., Council, RCP, 2004–08 (Chm., Patient and Carer Involvement Steering Gp, 2004–08; Trustee, 2008–12). Gov., Health Foundn, 2007–16; Mem., DoH Nat. Quality Bd, 2009–14. Trustee, Beds, Cambs, Northants, and Peterborough Wildlife Trust, 2005–14 (Vice-Chm., 2009–14). Pres., IHSM, 1989–90. Hon. MFPHM 1998. Hon. FRCP 2008. *Recreations:* walking, travel, theatre, music, friends.

**GOOSEY, Michael William,** PhD; FRSC; sustainable bioenergy and industrial biotechnology research and development consultant, 2010–18; *b* Northampton, 18 Nov. 1955; *s* of Donald Joseph Goosey and Doris Edith Mary Goosey (*née* Line); *m* 1981, Elizabeth Ann Curtis; two *s* one *d. Educ:* Raunds Secondary Sch.; Univ. of Birmingham (BSc Hons Biochem. 1978; PhD Biochem. 1981). CChem 1997; FRSC 2007. Parkinson's Disease Res. Fellow, 1981–82; Sen. Res. Scientist, Dow Chemical Co. Ltd, King's Lynn and Letcombe Regis, 1982–88; Shell: Gp Leader, Sittingbourne Res. Centre, 1988–94, Resource and Prog. Manager, Analysis and Measurement Dept, Thornton Res. Centre, 1994–99, Shell Research Ltd; Business Gp Manager, Analytical Shell Global Solutions and Stanlow Oil and Petrochemicals Refinery, 1999–2005; Global Analytical Technol. Manager, Shell Global Solutions, 2005–07; Global Innovation Biodomain Technol. Manager, 2007–10. Member: Neurosci. Initiative Bd, SERC, 1989–93; Steering Gp, Industrial Biotechnol. Innovation and Growth Team (report to govt on Maximising UK Opportunities from Industrial Biotechnol. in a Low Carbon Econ.), 2009; Council, BBSRC, 2011–18; Ind. Adv. Gp on Energy, Doctoral Trng Alliance, University Alliance, 2016–18. Mem., Industrial Bd, Diamond Synchrotron Radiation Source, Oxford, 2005–07. Non-exec. Dir, Biosyntha Technol. Ltd, 2012–16 (Chm., 2013–16); Mem., Adv. Bd, Algenuity, 2012–18. Hon. Prof. of Sustainable Bioenergy, Univ. of Nottingham, 2011–17. Mem., Editl Bd, Pesticide Sci. Jl, 1991–93. *Publications:* (ed jtly) Biochemistry of Cell Walls and Membranes in Fungi, 1989; papers on insect and fungal biochemical subjects. *Recreations:* woodland and wildlife conservation, fly fishing, gardening in Madeira. *Address:* Cherry Tree Cottage, The Orchard, Worthenbury, near Wrexham LL13 0BF. *T:* (01948) 770516. *E:* mikegoosey@hotmail.com.

**GOPALAN, Coluthur,** MD, DSc; FRCP, FRCPE; FRS 1987; President, Nutrition Foundation of India, New Delhi, since 1979; *b* 29 Nov. 1918; *s* of C. Doraiswami Iyengar and Mrs Pattammal; *m* 1940, Seetha Gopalan; one *s* one *d* (and one *s* decd). *Educ:* Univ. of Madras (MD 1945); Univ. of London (PhD, DSc). Fellow, Acad. of Med. Scis, India, 1961; FIASc 1964; FNA 1966. Dir, Nat. Inst. of Nutrition, Hyderabad, 1960–74; Dir-Gen., Indian Council of Med. Res., New Delhi, 1975–79. Hon. DSc: Banares Hindu, 1982. Padma Bhushan (India), 2003. *Publications:* Nutritive Value of Indian Foods, 1966; Nutrition and Health Care, 1984; Use of Growth Charts for Promoting Child Nutrition: a review of global experience, 1985; Combating Undernutrition: basic issues and practical approaches, 1987; Nutrition Problems and Programmes in South East Asia, 1987; Nutrition in Developmental Transition in South East Asia, 1992; Recent Trends in Nutrition, 1993; Towards Better Nutrition: problems and policies, 1993; Nutrition Research in South East Asia: the emerging agenda for the future, 1994; over 200 contribs to sci. jls; chapters on specific topics to several books on nutrition in internat. pubns on nutrition. *Recreation:* music. *Address:* Nutrition Foundation of India, C-13, Qutab Institutional Area, New Delhi 110016, India. *T:* (11) 6857814, 6965410; 39 Landon Road, Kilpauk, Chennai 600010, India. *Club:* India International Centre (New Delhi).

**GORAI, Rt Rev. Dinesh Chandra;** Bishop of Calcutta, 1982–99; *b* 15 Jan. 1934; *m* Binapani; two *c. Educ:* Calcutta Univ. (BA 1956). Serampore Theological Coll. (BD 1959). Ordained, 1962; Methodist Minister in Calcutta/Barrackpore, 1968–70; first Bishop, Church of N India Diocese of Barrackpore, 1970–82; Dep. Moderator, 1980, Moderator, 1983–86, Church of N India. Hon. DD: Bethel Coll., 1985; Serampore Coll., 1991. *Publications:* Society at the Cross Road, 1968; (ed) Transfer of Vision: a leadership development programme for the Church of North India 1983–1986, 1984; New Horizons in Christian Ministry, 1993. *Address:* Binapani Villa, 28 Mahatma Gandhi Road, Keorapukur M., Calcutta 700 082, India.

**GORARD, Anthony John;** *b* 15 July 1927; *s* of William James and Rose Mary Gorard; *m* 1954, Barbara Kathleen Hampton; one *s* three *d. Educ:* Ealing Grammar School. Chartered Accountant, 1951; Manufacturing Industry, 1952–58; Anglia Television Ltd, 1959–67, Executive Director and Member of Management Cttee; Managing Director, HTV Ltd, 1967–78; Chief Exec., HTV Gp Ltd, 1976–78; Director: Independent Television Publications Ltd, 1967–78; Independent Television News Ltd, 1973–78; Chief Exec., Cardiff Broadcasting Co. Ltd, 1979–81; Consultant, Mitchell Beazley Television, 1982–83; hotel proprietor, 1983–87; restaurant owner, 1987–94. Chm., British Regional Television Association, 1970–71. *Recreations:* gardening, pottery, rambling. *Address:* 18 Turners Avenue, Tenterden, Kent TN30 6QL. *T:* (01580) 764449.

**GORASIA, Charu;** Director General, Capabilities and Resources, Home Office, since 2018; *b* Mumbai, 30 April; *d* of Navinchandra Waghami and Sheela Waghami; *m* 1997, Sachhin Gorasia; one *s. Educ:* BSc Life Sci. and Biochem.; MSc Biochem. ACMA. Dir, Finance, IT, Estates and Commercial, UKTI, 2012–14; Gp Finance Dir, BIS, 2014–18; Dir Gen., Finance, Commercial and Estates, DWP, 2018. *Recreations:* gym, yoga, travelling. *Address:* Home Office, 2 Marsham Street, Westminster, SW1P 4DF. *T:* (020) 7035 6045.

**GORBACHEV, Mikhail Sergeyevich**; President: International Foundation for Socio-Economic and Political Studies (Gorbachev Foundation), since 1992; Green Cross International, since 1993; Executive President of the Soviet Union, 1990–91; *b* 2 March 1931; *m* 1953, Raisa Gorbacheva (*d* 1999); one *d*. *Educ*: Moscow State Univ. (law graduate); Stavropol Agric. Inst. Machine operator, 1946; joined CPSU 1952; First Sec., Stavropol Komsomol City Cttee, 1956–58, later Dep. Head of Propaganda; 2nd, later 1st Sec., Komsomol Territorial Cttee, 1958–62; Party Organizer, Stavropol Territorial Production Bd of Collective and State Farms, 1962; Head, Dept of party bodies, CPSU Territorial Cttee, 1963–66; 1st Sec., Stavropol City Party Cttee, 1966–68; 2nd Sec., 1968–70, 1st Sec., 1970–78, Stavropol Territorial CPSU Cttee; Central Committee, Communist Party of Soviet Union: Mem., 1971–91; Sec., with responsibility for agric., 1978–85; Alternate Mem., 1979–80, then Mem., Political Bureau; Gen. Sec., 1985–91. Deputy, Supreme Soviet: USSR, 1970–89 (Chm., Foreign Affairs Commn of the Soviet of the Union, 1984–85; Mem., 1985–88, Chm., 1988–89, Presidium); RSFSR, 1980–90; Deputy, Congress of Peoples' Deps, USSR, 1989; Chm., Supreme Soviet, USSR, 1989–90. Freeman of Aberdeen, 1993. Hon. Citizen of Berlin, 1992. Nobel Peace Prize, 1990; Ronald Reagan Freedom Award, 1992. Orders of Lenin, of Red Banner of Labour, Badge of Honour. *Publications*: A Time for Peace, 1985; The Coming Century of Peace, 1986; Speeches and Writings (7 vols), 1986–90; Peace has no Alternative, 1986; Moratorium, 1986; Perestroika: new thinking for our country and the world, 1987; The August Coup, 1991; December, 1991; My Stand, 1992; The Years of Hard Decisions, 1993; Life and Reforms, 1995 (UK edn, Memoirs, 1996); Reflections on the Past and Future, 1998; Alone With Myself, 2012; The New Russia, 2016. *Address*: (office) 39 Leningradsky Prospekt bdg14, Moscow 125167, Russia. *T*: (095) 9439990, *Fax*: (095) 9439594.

**GORDHAN, Pravin Jamnadas**; MP (ANC), South Africa, since 2014; Minister of Public Enterprises, since 2018; *b* Durban, 12 April 1949; *s* of Jamnadas Gordhan and Rumba Gordhan; *m* 1990, Vanitha Raju; two *d*. *Educ*: Sastri Coll., Durban; Univ. of Durban Westville (Bachelor of Pharmacy 1973). Organised and led student movement and civic structures during 1970s and 1980s; pharmacist, King Edward VII Hosp., Durban, 1974–81. Chm., multi-party talks, Convention for a Democratic SA, 1990; Co-Chm., Transitional Exec. Council, 1991–94. MP (ANC), SA, 1994–98; Chm., Constitutional Cttee, 1996–98. Dep. Comr, 1998–99, Comr, 1999–2009, SA Revenue Service; Minister of Finance, 2009–14, 2015–17; Minister of Cooperative Governance and Traditional Affairs, 2014–15. Chairman: World Customs Orgn, 2000–06; Forum on Tax Admin, OECD, 2008–09. Hon. Dr Commerce South Africa, 2007; Hon. Dr Law Cape Town, 2007; DTech (Business Admin) Free State Central Univ. of Technol., 2009. Comdr, Order of the Crown (Belgium), 2002. *Recreations*: reading, gym, walks.

**GORDIEVSKY, Oleg Antonovich**, CMG 2007; writer on political affairs; lecturer; *b* Moscow, 10 Oct. 1938; *s* of Anton Lavrentyevich Gordievsky and Olga Nikolayevna Gordievsky; *m* (marr. diss.); two *d*. *Educ*: Inst. of Internat. Relations, Moscow (Bachelor Internat. Relns). Dep. Hd of Station, Copenhagen, 1974–78, Actg Hd of Station, London, 1984–85, KGB; Secret Agent, SIS, 1974–85; arrested by KGB, evacuated to Moscow and subseq. escaped back to UK, 1985. Hon. DLitt Buckingham, 2005. *Publications*: (with C. Andrew) KGB: the inside story of its foreign operations from Lenin to Gorbachev, 1990; (with C. Andrew) Instructions from the Centre, 1991; (with C. Andrew) More Instructions from the Centre, 1992; Next Stop Execution, 1995; (with I. Rogatchi) Opaque Mirror, 1997; (with J. Andersen) De Rode Spioner, 2002; contrib. internat. and political magazines. *Recreations*: cycling, collection of dictionaries of Germanic languages. *Address*: c/o A. M. Heath & Co. Ltd, 6 Warwick Court, WC1R 5DJ. *T*: and *Fax*: (01483) 417481. *E*: navole1@aol.com.

**GORDON**, family name of **Marquess of Huntly** and of **Baron Gordon of Strathblane**.

**GORDON OF STRATHBLANE**, Baron *cr* 1997 (Life Peer), of Deil's Craig in Stirling; **James Stuart Gordon**, CBE 1984; Chairman, Scottish Radio Holdings, 1996–2005; *b* 17 May 1936; *s* of James Gordon and Elsie (*née* Riach); *m* 1971, Margaret Anne Stevenson; two *s* one *d*. *Educ*: St Aloysius' Coll., Glasgow; Glasgow Univ. (MA Hons). Political Editor, STV, 1965–73; Man. Dir, Radio Clyde, 1973–96; Chief Exec., Radio Clyde Hldgs, subseq. Scottish Radio Hldgs, 1991–96. Chairman: Scottish Exhibn Centre, 1983–89; Scottish Tourist Bd, 1998–2001 (Mem., 1997–98); Rajar, 2003–06; Vice-Chm., Melody Radio, 1991–97; Member: Scottish Develt Agency, 1981–90; Scottish Adv. Bd, BP, 1990–2003; Director: Clydeport Hldgs, 1992–98; Johnston Press plc, 1996–2007; Active Capital (formerly AIM) Trust plc, 1996–2009. Chm., Adv. Gp on Listed Sporting Events, 1997–98; Member: Cttee of Inquiry into Teachers' Pay and Conditions, 1986; Cttee to Review Funding of BBC, 1999. Trustee: John Smith Meml Trust, 1994–2007; Nat. Galls of Scotland, 1998–2002. Chm., Glasgow Common Purpose, 1995–97. Mem. Court, Univ. of Glasgow, 1984–91. Hon. DLitt Glasgow Caledonian, 1994; DUniv Glasgow, 1998. *Recreations*: ski-ing, walking, genealogy. *Address*: Deil's Craig, Strathblane, Glasgow G63 9ET. *T*: 07711 223149. *Clubs*: New (Edinburgh); Glasgow Art (Glasgow); Prestwick Golf.

**GORDON, Alexander Mark; His Honour Judge Gordon**; a Circuit Judge, since 2018; *b* London, 1966; *s* of Edward Gordon and Gillian Gordon; partner, Ruth; two *s*. *Educ*: Nottingham High Sch.; Univ. of Manchester (LLB Hons); Coll. of Law, London. Admitted solicitor, 1990; Solicitor, Berwin Leighton, subseq. Berwin Leighton Paisner, 1990, Partner, 1997–2010; a Recorder, 2010–18. *Recreations*: family, walking, cooking, growing veg, Nottingham Forest, exercising kids and cat.

**GORDON, Very Rev. Canon Alexander Ronald**; Chaplain, Holy Trinity, Geneva, since 2014; *b* 16 Dec. 1949; *s* of Alexander Donald and Norah May Gordon; *m* 1979, Geraldine Worrall; one *s* two *d*. *Educ*: Nottingham Univ. (BPharm 1971); Leeds Univ. (DipTh 1976); Coll. of the Resurrection, Mirfield. MRPharmS 1972. Ordained deacon, 1977, priest, 1978; Asst Curate, St Michael and All Angels, Headingley, 1977–80; Asst Priest, St Peter and St Paul, Fareham, 1980–83; Vicar, St John Baptist, Cudworth, 1983–85; *locum tenens*, St Andrew, Tain, 1985–87; Priest-in-charge, Lairg, Dornoch and Brora, 1987–2001; Diocesan Dir of Ordinands, Dio. Moray, Ross and Caithness, 1990–2001; Canon, St Andrew's Cathedral, Inverness, 1995–2001 (Hon. Canon, 2001–); Chaplain, St Alban, Strasbourg, 2001–05; Asst Dir of Ordinands, Dio. Gibraltar in Europe, 2004–05; Provost, St Andrew's Cathedral, Inverness, 2005–14. Associate Staff Mem., Church and Soc. Commn, Conf. of European Chs, 2004–. *Recreations*: music, travel, hill walking, reading detective and spy fiction, trying to get my computer to do what I want it to do, photography. *Address*: 84 rue de Montbrillant, 1202 Geneva, Switzerland. *T*: 227343817. *E*: canonalexgordon@holytrinitygeneva.org, canonalexgordon@outlook.com.

**GORDON, Sir Andrew Cosmo Lewis D.**; *see* Duff Gordon.

**GORDON, Boyd**; Fisheries Secretary, Department of Agriculture and Fisheries for Scotland, 1982–86; *b* 18 Sept. 1926; *er s* of David Gordon and Isabella (*née* Leishman); *m* 1951, Elizabeth Mabel (*née* Smith); two *d*. *Educ*: Musselburgh Grammar School. Following military service with the Royal Scots, joined the Civil Service, initially with Min. of Labour, then Inland Revenue; Department of Agriculture and Fisheries for Scotland: joined, 1953; Principal, Salmon and Freshwater Fisheries Administration and Fisheries R&D, 1962–73; Asst Secretary, Agriculture Economic Policy, EEC Co-ordination and Agriculture Marketing, 1973–82. *Recreations*: family and church affairs, gardening, sport of all kinds, reading, playing and writing Scottish fiddle music. *Address*: 87 Duddingston Road, Edinburgh EH15 1SP. *Club*: Civil Service.

**GORDON, Brian William**, OBE 1974; HM Diplomatic Service, 1949–81, retired; Commercial Counsellor, Caracas, 1980–81; *b* 24 Oct. 1926; *s* of William and Doris Margaret Gordon; *m* 1951, Sheila Graham Young (*d* 2016); two *s* one *d*. *Educ*: Tynemouth Grammar School. HM Forces (Lieut in IA), 1944–47; joined HM Foreign Service (now Diplomatic Service), 1949; served in: Saigon; Libya; Second Sec. in Ethiopia, 1954–58 and in Peru, 1959–61; HM Consul: Leopoldville, Congo, 1962–64; New York, 1965–67; Puerto Rico, 1967–69; Consul-General, Bilbao, 1969–73; Asst Head, Trade Relations and Export Dept, FCO, 1974–77; Dep. Consul-Gen., Los Angeles, 1977–80. *Recreation*: walking. *Address*: 5 Primlea Court, Corbridge, Northumberland NE45 5ES.
*See also* I. W. Gordon.

**GORDON, Charles**; Managing Director, Charlie Gordon Associates Ltd, since 2012; *b* 28 Oct. 1951; *m* 1st; two *s*; 2nd, Emma; one *s*. *Educ*: St Mungo's Acad., Glasgow. Member (Lab): Strathclyde Regl Council, 1987–96; Glasgow CC, 1995–2005 (Dep. Leader, 1997–99; Leader, 1999–2005). Mem. (Lab) Glasgow Cathcart, Scottish Parlt, Sept. 2005–2011; contested (Lab) same seat, 2011. Non-exec. Dir, Hampden Park Ltd, 2001–11. Chm., Develt Bd, Paddle Steamer Waverley, 2011–12.

**GORDON, His Honour (Cosmo) Gerald (Maitland)**; a Circuit Judge, 1990–2017; a Senior Circuit Judge, Central Criminal Court, 1994–2017; *b* 26 March 1945; *s* of John Kenneth Maitland Gordon, CBE and Erica Martia Clayton-East; *m* 1973, Vanessa Maria Juliet Maxine Reilly-Morrison, LLB, AKC, barrister; two *s*. *Educ*: Eton. Called to the Bar, Middle Temple, 1966, Bencher, 2003. Asst Recorder, 1982–86; Recorder, 1986–90. Royal Borough of Kensington and Chelsea: Mem. Council, 1971–90; Chm., Works Cttee, 1978–80; Chm., Town Planning Cttee, 1988; Dep. Leader, 1982–88; Mayor, 1989–90. Chairman: Edwardes Square Scarsdale and Abingdon Assoc., 1990–2002; Westway Develt Trust (formerly N Kensington Amenity Trust), 1992–2002. Liveryman, Merchant Taylors' Co., 1995–. *Club*: Garrick.

**GORDON, Prof. David**, FRCP, FMedSci; President, World Federation for Medical Education, since 2015; Professor of Medicine, University of Manchester, 1999–2008, now Emeritus; *b* 23 Feb. 1947; *s* of late Lawrence Gordon and Pattie Gordon (*née* Wood); *m* Dr C. Louise Jones; three *s* one *d*. *Educ*: Whitgift Sch.; Magdalene Coll., Cambridge (BA 1967, MA 1971; MB BChir 1970); Westminster Med. Sch. MRCP 1972, FRCP 1989. Clin. appts, Leicester and Cambridge, 1970–72; St Mary's Hospital Medical School: Res. Fellow, 1972–74; Lectr in Medicine, 1974–80; Sen. Lectr in Medicine, 1980–83; Hon. Sen. Lectr in Medicine, 1983–94; Hon. Cons. Physician, St Mary's Hosp., London, 1980–94; Wellcome Trust: Asst Dir, 1983–89; Prog. Dir, 1989–98; Dir of Special Initiatives, 1998–99; University of Manchester: Dean, Faculty of Medicine, Dentistry, Nursing and Pharmacy, Victoria Univ. of Manchester, then Faculty of Med. and Human Scis, 1999–2006; Vice-Pres., 2004–08. Hon. Consultant Physician, Manchester Royal Infirmary, Salford Royal Hosps and S Manchester Univ. Hosps, 1999–2006. Visiting Professor: Univ. of Copenhagen, 2007–; QMUL, 2008–11; State Medical and Pharmaceutical Univ., Chişinău, Moldova, 2009–; Kazakh Nat. Medical Univ., Almaty, 2014–. Consultant, Health Sector Reform Project, Min. of Health, Azerbaijan, 2010. Dir of several technol. transfer and biotech. cos, 2002–06. Member: Res. Sub-Gp, Task Force on Support of R&D in NHS, 1994; Academic Wkg Gp, HEFCE-CVCP-SCOP Cttee on Post Grad. Educn, 1995; Indep. Task Force on Clin. Academic Careers, CVCP, 1996–97; Res. Cttee, HEFCE, 1998–99; Chief Scientist Cttee, Scottish Office DoH, 1997–99; Pres., Assoc. of Med. Schs in Europe, 2004–14; Chm., Council of Heads of Medical Schs, 2003–06; Dep. Chm., ORPHEUS, 2005–10. Hon. Life Mem., St John Ambulance Assoc., 1983. FMedSci 1999. Hon. Dr Tbilisi State Med. Univ., 2019. *Publications*: papers, reviews, etc on biomed. res., sci. policy, med. educn and other subjects in learned jls. *Recreations*: music (cello), books, food, finding out what is going on. *Address*: World Federation for Medical Education, 13A chemin du Levant, 01210 Ferney-Voltaire, France. *E*: president@wfme.org. *Club*: Garrick.

**GORDON, David Sorrell**; Principal, Gordon Advisory, LLC, since 2008; *b* 11 Sept. 1941; *s* of late Sholom and Tania Gordon; *m* 1st, 1963, Enid Albagli (marr. diss. 1969); 2nd, 1974, Maggi McCormick; two *s*. *Educ*: Clifton College; Balliol College, Oxford (PPE, BA 1963); LSE; Advanced Management Program, Harvard Business Sch. FCA. Articles with Thomson McLintock, 1965–68; The Economist: editorial staff, 1968–78; Production and Develt Dir, 1978–81; Gp Chief Exec., Economist Newspaper Ltd, 1981–93; Chief Exec., ITN, 1993–95; Sec., Royal Acad. of Arts, 1996–2002; CEO and Dir, Milwaukee Art Mus., Wisconsin, 2002–08. Director: Financial Times, 1983–93; eFinancial News, 1999–2006 (Chm., 2001–06); Profile Books, 1996–; DHI Gp (formerly Dice Holdings, Inc.), 2006–17. Dir, South Bank Bd, 1986–96; a Governor, BFI, 1983–91. Chm., Contemporary Art Soc., 1991–98; Trustee: Tate Gall., 1993–98; Architecture Foundn, 1993–2002; Architecture Assoc. Foundn, 1995–98; Assoc. of Art Mus. Dirs, 2006–08; Amer. Folk Art Mus., 2013–; Wende Mus. of Cold War, 2014–. Pres., Sierra Madre Playhouse, 2017–. Friends Council, Avery Architectural and Fine Arts Library, 2011–. Gov., LSE, 1990–2000. *Publications*: (with Fred Hirsch) Newspaper Money, 1975. *Recreation*: hiking. *Address*: 460 Fairview Avenue, Sierra Madre, CA 91024, USA. *E*: david@gordonadvisory.com. *Club*: Garrick.

**GORDON, Sir Donald**, Kt 2005; Founder, Liberty International PLC (formerly TransAtlantic Holdings) (Chairman, 1981–2005; Life President, 2005–10; Life President, Intu Properties plc (formerly Capital Shopping Centres PLC) and Capital and Counties PLC, since 2010); *b* 24 June 1930; *s* of Nathan and Sheila Gordon; *m* 1958, Peggy Cowan (*d* 2014); two *s* one *d*. *Educ*: King Edward VII Sch., Johannesburg. CA (SA). Partner, Kessel Feinstein, 1955–57; Founder, Chm. and CEO, 1957–99, now Hon. Life Pres., Liberty Life Assoc. of Africa Ltd, subseq. Liberty Gp Ltd; Chairman: Liberty Hldgs, SA, 1968–99; Liberty Investors Ltd, 1971–99; Guardian Nat. Insce Co. Ltd, 1980–99; Capital & Counties (UK), 1982–2005; Continental & Industrial Trust, 1986–93; Capital Shopping Centres plc, 1994–2005; Deputy Chairman: Standard Bank Investment Corp., 1979–99; Premier Gp Ltd, 1983–96; SAB Miller plc, 1989–99; Beverage & Consumer Industry Hldgs, 1989–99; Sun Life Corp., UK, 1992–95. Director: Guardbank Mgt Corp. Ltd, 1969–99; Guardian Royal Exchange Assurance (UK), 1971–94; Charter Life Insce Co. Ltd, 1985–99; GFSA Hldgs, 1990–94. Hon. DEconSc Witwatersrand, 1991; Hon. DCom Pretoria, 2005. Business Man of Year Award, Financial Mail (SA), 1965; Sunday Times (SA) Businessman of the Year, 1969; Special Award for Lifetime Achievement, Entrepreneur of the Year Awards, 2000; (UK) Top 100 Lifetime Achievement Award, Sunday Times (SA), 2004. *Recreations*: opera, ballet. *Address*: Intu Properties plc, 40 Broadway, SW1H 0BT. *T*: (020) 7960 1200, *Fax*: (020) 7960 1333.

**GORDON, Douglas Lamont**; artist; *b* Glasgow, 20 Sept. 1966; *s* of James Gordon and Mary Clements Gordon (*née* MacDougall). *Educ*: Glasgow Sch. of Art (BA Hons 1st cl. 1988); Slade Sch. of Art (Postgrad. Res. Dip. 1990). Former Vis. Prof. and John Florent Stone Fellow, Edinburgh Coll. of Art; Vis. Prof. of Fine Art, Glasgow Sch. of Art, Glasgow Univ., 1999–. Works in video, film, photography and sculpture include: List of Names; Something between My Mouth and Your Ear; 24 Hour Psycho, 1993; Hysterical; The

Confessions of a Justified Sinner; Between Darkness and Light, 1997; Feature Film, 1999; Play Dead, Real Time, 2003; The Vanity of Allegory, Berlin, 2005; Zidane: a 21st century portrait, 2006; I Had Nowhere To Go, 2016. *Exhibitions* include: Lisson Gall., 1993, 1995 (solo), 1998, 2000; Hayward Gall., 1996, 1997, 2002; MOMA, Oxford, 1996; 10th Sydney Biennale, 1996; Venice Biennale (Premio 2000), 1997; Tate Liverpool, 2000; Sheep and Goats, Musée d'Art Moderne de la Ville de Paris, 2000; Mus. of Contemp. Art, LA, 2001; Van Abbemuseum, Eindhoven, 2003; Hirshhorn Mus. and Sculpture Garden, Washington, DC, 2004; The Vanity of Allegory, Deutsche Guggenheim Mus., Berlin, 2005; Mus. Morsbrich, Leverkusen, 2006; Timeline, MOMA, New York, 2006; Superhumanatural (solo), Nat. Galls of Scotland, 2006; Between Darkness and Light (solo), Kunstmuseum, Wolfsburg, 2007; Mus. of Contemp. Art, Chicago, 2007; Kunsthaus Bregenz, 2007; San Francisco MOMA, 2007; Timeline (solo), Museo de Arte Latinoamericano de Buenos Aires, 2007; Palais de Papes, Avignon, 2008; Pergamon Mus., Berlin, 2008; Où se trouvent les clefs?, La Collection Lambert en Avignon, 2008; Galerie Eva Presenhuber, Zürich, 2009; DVIR Gall., Israel, 2009; blood, sweat, tears, DOX, Prague, 2009; Art and the Sublime (solo), TATE Britain, 2010; Museum fuer Moderne Kunst, Frankfurt, 2011; K.364, Gagosian Gall., London, 2011; Phantom, Yvon Lambert Gall., Paris, 2011; Mus. of Contemp. Art, LA, 2012; Galerie Niels Borch Jensen, Berlin, 2012; Douglas Gordon: Left Is Right and Right Is Wrong…, Inst. of Modern Art, Brisbane, 2012; Maestros, Mead Gall., Warwick, 2012; Schafstall Bisdorf, Bisdorf, 2012; Akademie der Künste, Berlin, 2012; Douglas Gordon: The End of Civilisation, Gagosian Gall., NY, 2012; Sharpening Fantasy (solo), 2012, Blain|Southern, Berlin, 2013; I am also… Douglas Gordon (solo), Tel Aviv Mus., Tel Aviv, 2013; Galerie Eva Presenhuber (solo), Zurich, 2013, 2016; Mus. Folkwang, Essen, 2013; NY Armory on Park (solo), NY, 2014; Neck of the Woods, Manchester Internat. Fest., 2015; Gagosian Gall., Geneva (solo), 2016; Gagosian Gall., NY, 2017. Mem., Akademie der Künste, Berlin, 2018. Corresp. FRSE 2018. Turner Prize, 1996; Hugo Boss Prize, 1998; Central Kunstpreis, Kölnischer Kunstverein, 1998; Lord Provost's Award, Glasgow City Council, 1998; Roswitha Haftmann Prize, 2008; Käthe-Kollwitz Prize, Akademie der Künste, Berlin, 2012; Efebo d'Oro Prize, Res. Centre for Film and Narrative Palermo, 2016. Comdr, Order of Arts and Letters (France), 2012. *Address:* Lost But Found, 21 Woodlands Terrace, Glasgow G3 6DF; olddognewtricks GmbH, Kurfürstenstrasse 14, 10785 Berlin, Germany.

**GORDON, Eileen;** *b* 22 Oct. 1946; *d* of late Charles Leatt and Margaret Rose Leatt; *m* 1969, Tony Gordon (*d* 2005); one *s* one *d*. *Educ:* Harold Hill Grammar Sch.; Shoreditch Comp. Sch.; Westminster Coll., Oxford (CertEd). Teacher; Asst to Tony Banks, MP, 1990–97. MP (Lab) Romford, 1997–2001. Contested (Lab) Romford, 1992 and 2001. Member: Broadcasting Select Cttee, 1998–2001; Health Select Cttee, 1999–2001.

**GORDON, François;** *see* Gordon, J. F.

**GORDON, His Honour Gerald;** *see* Gordon, His Honour C. G. M.

**GORDON, Sir Gerald (Henry),** Kt 2000; CBE 1995; QC (Scot.) 1972; LLD; Sheriff of Glasgow and Strathkelvin, 1978–99; Temporary Judge of Court of Session and High Court of Justiciary, 1992–2004; Member, Scottish Criminal Cases Review Commission, 1999–2009; *b* 17 June 1929; *er s* of Simon Gordon and Rebecca Gordon (*née* Bulbin), Glasgow; *m* 1957, Marjorie Joseph (*d* 1996), *yr d* of Isaac and Aimée Joseph (*née* Strump), Glasgow; one *s* two *d*. *Educ:* Queen's Park Senior Secondary Sch., Glasgow; Univ. of Glasgow (MA (1st cl. Hons Philosophy with English Literature) 1950; LLB (Distinction) 1953; PhD 1960); LLD Edinburgh 1968. National Service, RASC, 1953–55 (Staff-Sgt, Army Legal Aid, BAOR, 1955). Admitted Scottish Bar 1953; practice at Scottish Bar, 1953, 1956–59; Faulds Fellow, Univ. of Glasgow, 1956–59. Procurator Fiscal Depute, Edinburgh, 1960–65. University of Edinburgh: Sen. Lectr, 1965; Personal Prof. of Criminal Law, 1969–72; Head of Dept of Criminal Law and Criminology, 1965–72; Prof. of Scots Law, 1972–76; Dean of Faculty of Law, 1970–73; Vis. Prof., 2000–03. Sheriff of S Strathclyde, Dumfries and Galloway at Hamilton, 1976–77. Commonwealth Vis. Fellow and Vis. Res. Fellow, Centre of Criminology, Univ. of Toronto, 1974–75. Temporary Sheriff, 1973–76. Member: Interdepartmental Cttee on Scottish Criminal Procedure, 1970–77; Cttee on Appeals Criteria and Alleged Miscarriages of Justice Procedures, 1995–96. Hon. FRSE 2002. Hon. LLD: Glasgow, 1993; Aberdeen, 2003; Edinburgh, 2011. *Publications:* The Criminal Law of Scotland, 1967, 2nd edn 1978; (ed) Renton and Brown's Criminal Procedure, 4th edn 1972, to 6th edn 1996; (ed) Scottish Criminal Case Reports, 1981–; various articles. *Recreations:* Jewish studies, coffee conversation, crosswords.

**GORDON, Gillian Hunter;** *see* Jones, G. H.

**GORDON, Hannah Campbell Grant;** actress; *b* 9 April 1941; *d* of William Munro Gordon and Hannah Grant Gordon; *m* 1st, 1970, Norman Warwick (*d* 1994); one *s*; 2nd, 2009, Robert Lampitt. *Educ:* St Denis School for Girls, Edinburgh; Glasgow Univ. (Cert. Dramatic Studies); College of Dramatic Art, Glasgow (Dip. in speech and drama). FRSAMD 1980. Hon. DLitt Glasgow, 1993. Winner, James Bridie Gold Medal, Royal Coll. of Music and Dramatic Art, Glasgow, 1962. *Stage:* Dundee Rep., Glasgow Citizens Theatre, Belgrade Theatre, Coventry, Ipswich, Windsor; Can You Hear me at the Back, Piccadilly, 1979; The Killing Game, Apollo, 1980; The Jeweller's Shop, Westminster, 1982; The Country Girl, Apollo, 1983; Light Up the Sky, Old Vic, 1985; Mary Stuart, Edinburgh Fest., 1987; Shirley Valentine, Duke of York's, 1989; Hidden Laughter, Vaudeville, 1991; An Ideal Husband, Globe, 1992; The Aspern Papers, Wyndham's, 1996; My Fair Lady, Th. Royal, 2003, nat. tour, 2003–04; *television:* 1st TV appearance, Johnson Over Jordan, 1965; Great Expectations, 1969; Middlemarch, 1969; My Wife Next Door, 1972; Upstairs, Downstairs, 1976; Telford's Change, 1979; Goodbye Mr Kent, 1983; Gardener's Calendar, 1986; My Family and Other Animals, 1987; The Day after the Fair, 1987; Joint Account, 1989; Midsomer Murders, 1999; One Foot in the Grave (final episode), 2000; Moving On, 2010; Hustle, 2011; Unforgotten, 2015; presenter, Watercolour Challenge, 1998–2001; *films:* Spring and Port Wine, 1970; The Elephant Man, 1979; Made of Honour, 2008; numerous radio plays, recorded books and poetry and music recitals. *Recreations:* gardening, cooking, walking. *Address:* c/o Conway Van Gelder Grant Ltd, 8–12 Broadwick Street, W1F 8HW.

**GORDON, Iain James,** PhD; CBiol; FRSB; FRSE; Deputy Vice-Chancellor, Division of Tropical Environments and Societies, James Cook University, since 2015; *b* Chester, 18 Oct. 1959; *s* of James William and Gillian Ann Gordon; *m* (marr. diss.); one *s* one *d* (and one *s* decd). *Educ:* Robert Gordon's Coll., Aberdeen; Univ. of Aberdeen (BSc Zool.); King's Coll., Cambridge (PhD Zool. 1986). CBiol 1983; FRSB (FIBiol 2003); FRSE 2012. Research Assistant: Large Animal Res. Gp, Dept of Zool., Univ. of Cambridge (red deer distrib. in Highlands of Scotland), 1986; Conservation Monitoring Centre, Cambridge (Biosphere Reserves Project), 1986; Res. Consultant, Zool Soc. of London (Scimitar-horned Oryx reintrod. project), 1986–96; Res. Associate, Station Biologique de la Tour du Valat, Carmargue, France, 1987–88; Res. Scientist, Macaulay Land Use Res. Inst., Aberdeen (Hd, prog. on ecol. of grazed ecosystems), 1988–2003; Officer-in-Charge, CSIRO Davies Lab., Townsville, 2003–10; Theme Leader, Bldg Resilient Biodiversity Assets, Canberra, 2009–10; CEO and Dir, James Hutton Inst., 2010–15. Dir, Centre of Expertise for Climate Change, 2011–15. Adjunct Associate Prof., Univ. of Qld, 2004; Adjunct Professor: Sch. of Tropical Biol., James Cook Univ., Australia, 2005; Sch. of Maths and Geospatial Scis, Royal Melbourne Inst. of Technol. Univ., 2005; ANU, 2010. Hon. Prof., Univ. of Aberdeen, 2000. Fellow, N American Acad. of Arts and Scis, 1996. Graduate, Australian Rural Leadership Prog. and Fellow, Australian Rural Leadership Foundn, 2007; GAICD 2017. Hon. Fellow, Univ. of Edinburgh, 1994. Hon. DSc Abertay, 2013. *Publications:* (ed with R. Rubino) Grazing Behaviour of Goats and Sheep, 1994; (with A. M. Sibbald) Tracking Animals with GPS, 2001; (ed with H. H. T. Prins) The Ecology of Grazing and Browsing, 2008; (ed) The Vicuna: the theory and practice of community based wildlife management, 2008; (ed with H. H. T. Prins) Invasion Biology and Ecological Theory, 2014; (ed with H. H. T. Prins and G. Squires) Food Production and Nature Conservation: conflicts and solutions, 2016; (ed with H. H. T. Prins) The Ecology of Browsing and Grazing II, 2019; contrib. book chapters; contribs to learned jls incl. Jl Applied Ecol., Jl Zool., Oecologia, Functional Ecol., Animal Behaviour, Small Ruminant Res. *Recreations:* golf, book clubs, motorbike riding, collecting antique inkwells, collecting signed first edition science books, bee keeping, making bookmarks. *Address:* James Cook University, Townsville, Qld 4811, Australia. *E:* iain.gordon@jcu.edu.au. *Club:* Royal Over-Seas League.

**GORDON, Ian William;** Director, Service Policy and Planning, Scottish Executive Health Department, 2003–06; *b* 27 Dec. 1952; *s* of Brian William Gordon, *qv*; *m* 1979, Alison Margaret Bunting; two *s*. *Educ:* Strathallan Sch., Perth; Downing Coll., Cambridge (BA). Joined Civil Service, 1975; Dept of Energy, 1975–81; Scottish Office, 1981–99; Industry, 1981–85; Finance, 1985–86; Educn, 1986–90; Agriculture, 1990–93; Fisheries, 1993–99 (Fisheries Sec., 1995–99); Head of Dept, Scotland Office, 1999–2002. Non-exec. Dir, Cumbria PCT, 2007–13 (Chair, 2011–13); Chm., N Cumbria Univ. Hosp. Trust, 2013–14.

**GORDON, Isabel;** *see* Allende, I.

**GORDON, Maj.-Gen. James Charles Mellish,** CBE 1992; Chairman, Victory Services Association, 2008–16 (Trustee, 2005–16); *b* 3 Aug. 1941; *s* of Brig. Leonard Henry Gordon and Joyce Evelyn Mary Gordon (*née* Gurdon); *m* 1964, Rosemary Stella Kincaid; two *s* one *d*. *Educ:* Tonbridge Sch.; RMA Sandhurst. Commissioned RA 1961; served in UK, Germany, Singapore; RMCS, Shrivenham, 1972; Staff Coll., Camberley, 1973; MoD, 1974–75; Comdr, D Batt., RHA, UK and BAOR, 1976–78; MA to MGO, MoD, 1978–80; CO 45 Field Regt RA, BAOR, 1980–83; Col, ASD1, MoD, 1983–86; CRA 4th Armoured Div., BAOR, 1986–89; Dir, Mil. Ops, MoD, 1989–91; COS, HQ UKLF, 1991–94. Dir Gen., Assoc. of Train Operating Cos, 1994–99 (Director: Rail Settlement Plan Ltd; Rail Staff Travel Ltd; Nat. Rail Enquiry Service); Gen. Sec., Officers' Pensions Soc., later Forces Pension Soc., 2000–07; Dir, FPS Investment Co. Ltd, 2000–07; Man. Trustee, FPS Widows' Fund, 2000–07. FCILT (FCIT 1994–99); Corporate Fellow, Industry and Parlt Trust, 1998. Mem. Council Officers' Assoc., 2000–08. Trustee: Haig Homes, 2003–09; Tall Ships Youth Trust, 2012–16. Chm., Woodard Schs Corp., 2010; Governor: Oakwood Sch., 2010–11; St Andrew's Sch., Woking, 2015– (Chm., 2017–). *Recreations:* sailing, music, theatre, travel. *Club:* Victory Services.

**GORDON, Maj. Gen. James Henry,** CB 2013; CBE 2006 (MBE 1991); Chief Executive, Council of Reserve Forces' and Cadets' Association, since 2016; Gentleman Usher of the Scarlet Rod, Order of the Bath, since 2018; *b* London, 4 Dec. 1957; *s* of late Graeme and Kirsten Gordon; *m* 1996, Fiona Fairbairn; three *s*. *Educ:* Trinity Coll., Glenalmond; RMA Sandhurst; Staff Coll. CO 2nd Bn, RGJ, 1995–98; Dep. Asst COS Operational Support PJHQ, 1998–2001; Comdr, British Forces, Falkland Is, 2002–03; COS, HQ NI, 2003–05; Dep. Comdr, Multinational Security Transition Comd, Iraq, 2006; Dir Personal Services (Army), 2006–08; i/c British Forces Cyprus and Administrator Sovereign Base Areas, 2008–10; Sen. British Loan Service Officer Oman, 2011–14. Queen's Body Guard for Scotland (Royal Co. of Archers), 2001–. Officer, Legion of Merit (USA), 2015. *Recreations:* field sports, ski-ing, sailing. *Club:* Boodle's.

**GORDON, Jane-Anne Mary E.;** *see* Evans-Gordon.

**GORDON, (Jean) François,** CMG 1999; CVO 2007; consultant and policy adviser, since 2013; European Strategy Adviser, Kent Police, 2009–13; *b* 16 April 1953; *s* of late Michael Colin Gordon and of Jeanine Marie Gordon (*née* Parizet); *m* 1977, Elaine Daniel; two *d*. *Educ:* Queen's Coll., Oxford (BA Hons Jurisprudence 1974); Université d'Aix et Marseille (Diplôme d'Etudes Supérieures 1975). Articled clerk, Ingledew Brown, 1975–78; admitted solicitor, 1979; joined HM Diplomatic Service, 1979: EU Dept, FCO, 1979–81; Second, later First Sec., Luanda, 1981–83; First Secretary: UK Delegn to UN Conf. on Disarmament, Geneva, 1983–88; UN Dept, FCO, 1988–90; (Political), Nairobi, 1990–92; Africa Dept (Southern), FCO, 1992–95; Dep. Hd, Drugs, Internat. Crime and Terrorism Dept, FCO, 1995–96; Hd, Drugs and Internat. Crime Dept, FCO, 1996; Ambassador to Algeria, 1996–99; RCDS, 2000; Ambassador to Côte d'Ivoire, and (non-resident) to Niger, Liberia and Burkina Faso, 2001–04; High Commissioner, Uganda, 2005–08. *Recreations:* reading, gardening, vintage cars, target shooting, watching African wildlife. *Club:* Alvis Owner.

**GORDON, John Alexander,** CB 1995; CEng; FRAeS; Partner, Gordon Consulting, since 1999; *b* 7 Nov. 1940; *s* of John and Eleanor Gordon; *m* 1962, Dyanne Calder; two *d*. *Educ:* RAF Colls, Henlow and Cranwell. CEng, MIMechE; FRAeS 1990. Engr Br., RAF, 1958–70; Ministry of Defence, Procurement Executive, 1970–95: mil. aircraft procurement, Dir Gen. Aircraft 1; projects incl. Harrier, Jaguar, Tornado and Eurofighter; Gen. Manager, NATO Eurofighter and Tornado Mgt Agency, 1996–99; Compliance Officer for Merger Undertakings, BAE Systems, 1999–2007. RAeS British Gold Medal, 1997. *Recreation:* carriage driving.

**GORDON, Josephine;** *see* Dobrin, J.

**GORDON, Kate;** *see* Gordon, V. K.

**GORDON, Kate Gillian;** *see* Storey, K. G.

**GORDON, Sir Lionel Eldred Peter S.;** *see* Smith-Gordon.

**GORDON, Dr Lyndall Felicity,** FRSL; writer; Senior Research Fellow, St Hilda's College, Oxford, since 1995; *b* 4 Nov. 1941; *d* of Harry Louis Getz and Rhoda Stella Getz (*née* Press); *m* 1963, Prof. Siamon Gordon, *qv*; two *d*. *Educ:* Univ. of Cape Town (BA Hons); Columbia Univ., NY (PhD 1973). Rhodes Vis. Fellow, St Hilda's Coll., Oxford, 1973–75; Asst Prof., Columbia Univ., NY, 1975–76; Lectr, Jesus Coll., Oxford, 1977–84; Fellow and Tutor, St Hilda's Coll., and CUF Lectr, Oxford Univ., 1984–95. FRSL 2003. *Publications:* Virginia Woolf: a writer's life, 1984, 4th edn 2006; Shared Lives, 1992, 2nd edn 2005; Charlotte Brontë: a passionate life, 1994, 2nd edn 2008; A Private Life of Henry James, 1998, reissued as Henry James: his women and his art, 2012; T. S. Eliot: an imperfect life, 1998, reissued as The Imperfect Life of T. S. Eliot, 2012; Mary Wollstonecraft: a new genus, 2005 (US edn and UK pbk edn as Vindication: a life of Mary Wollstonecraft); Lives Like Loaded Guns: Emily Dickinson and her family's feuds, 2010; Divided Lives: dreams of a mother and daughter, 2014; Outsiders: five women writers who changed the world, 2017. *Recreation:* reading. *Address:* St Hilda's College, Oxford OX4 1DY.

**GORDON, Pamela Joan**; Chief Executive, City of Sheffield Metropolitan District, 1989–97; *b* 13 Feb. 1936; *d* of Frederick Edward Bantick and Violet Elizabeth Bantick; *m* 1st, 1959, Wallace Henry Gordon (*d* 1980); two *s*; 2nd, 1997, Peter Charles Hoad. *Educ*: Richmond (Surrey) Grammar School for Girls; St Hilda's Coll., Oxford (MA). Variety of posts with ILEA, GLC and LCC, 1957–81; Greater London Council: Asst Dir Gen., 1981–83; Dep. Dir of Industry and Employment, 1983–85; Chief Exec., London Bor. of Hackney, 1985–89. Member: Adv. Cttee, Constitution Unit, 1995–97; Local Govt Commn for England, 1998–2002; Indep. Panel of Assessors for Public Appts, 1999–2007; Electoral Commn, 2001–07 (Chm., Boundary Cttee for England, 2002–07). Chm., Borders Exec. Cttee, Relationships Scotland, 2011–18 (Chm., Nat. Bd, 2012–15). Pres., SOLACE, 1996–97. Gov., Sheffield Hallam Univ., 1995–2003. Hon. Fellow, Inst. of Local Govt Studies, Birmingham Univ., 1990. Columnist, Local Government Chronicle. *Publications*: (as Pamela Gordon Hoad) The Devil's Stain (novel), 2016; The Angel's Wing (novel), 2016; The Cherub's Smile (novel), 2017; The Martyr's Scorn (novel), 2018; The Prophet's Grief (novel), 2019; short stories and articles in various jls. *Recreations*: opera, theatre, foreign travel.

**GORDON, Richard John Francis**; QC 1994; a Recorder, since 2000; *b* 26 Nov. 1948; *s* of John Bernard Basil Gordon and Winifred Josephine (*née* Keenan); *m* 1975, Jane Belinda Lucey; two *s*. *Educ*: St Benedict's Sch., Ealing; Christ Church, Oxford (Open Schol.; MA); University Coll. London (LLM). Called to the Bar, Middle Temple, 1972, Bencher, 2003. Sen. Lectr in Admin. Law, KCL, 1991–93. Visiting Professor of Law: UCL, 1994–; Chinese Univ. of Hong Kong, 2008–11; Hong Kong Univ., 2012–. Member: Exec. Cttee, Admin. Law Bar Assoc., 1991; Adv. Bd, Constitution Soc. UK, 2010–. Trustee: Internat. Sen. Lawyers Project, 2013–; African Commercial Law Foundn, 2015–. Editor-in-Chief, Administrative Court (formerly Crown Office) Digest, 1989–. *Publications*: The Law Relating to Mobile Homes and Caravans, 1978, 2nd edn 1985; Judicial Review: law and procedure, 1985, 2nd edn 1996; Crown Office Proceedings, 1990; Community Care Assessments, 1993, 2nd edn 1996; Human Rights in the United Kingdom, 1996; Judicial Review and Crown Office Practice, 2000; Judicial Review and the Human Rights Act, 2000; The Strasbourg Cases: leading cases from the European Human Rights Reports, 2001; (ed) Judicial Review in the New Millennium, 2003; EC Law in Judicial Review, 2006, 2nd edn 2014; Repairing British Politics: a blueprint for constitutional change, 2010; (with J. Mok) Judicial Review in Hong Kong, 2nd edn 2014; contrib. to numerous legal jls on admin. law. *Recreations*: reading, writing. *Address*: Brick Court Chambers, 7–8 Essex Street, WC2R 3LD. *T*: (020) 7379 3550. *Club*: MCC.

**GORDON, Robert Anthony Eagleson**, CMG 1999; OBE 1983; HM Diplomatic Service, retired; Chairman, Prospect Burma, 2011–18; *b* 9 Feb. 1952; *s* of late Major Cyril Vivian Eagleson, MC, RE and Clara Renata Romana Gordon (*née* Duse); *m* 1978, Pamela Jane Taylor; two *s* two *d*. *Educ*: King's Sch., Canterbury; Magdalen Coll., Oxford (MA Modern Langs). FCO 1973; Second Sec., Warsaw, 1975–77; First Sec., Santiago, 1978–83; FCO, 1983–87; First Sec., UK Deleg. to OECD, Paris, 1987–92; Counsellor and Dep. Head of Mission, Warsaw, 1992–95; Ambassador to Burma (Union of Myanmar), 1995–99; Head, SE Asia Dept, FCO, 1999–2003; Ambassador to the Socialist Republic of Vietnam, 2003–07. Dir, VinaLand, 2009–11. Pres., Britain-Burma Soc., 2011–.

**GORDON, Maj. Gen. Robert Duncan Seaton**, CMG 2005; CBE 1994; Founder and Managing Director, RG Consulting Ltd, international peace and security operations and UN senior leadership training for peacekeeping, since 2006; *b* 23 Nov. 1950; *s* of Col Jack Gordon and Joan Gordon (*née* Seaton); *m* 1979, Virginia Brown, Toronto; two *s*. *Educ*: Wellington Coll.; St Catharine's Coll., Cambridge (BA Hons Modern Hist. 1974; MA 1978). Commnd 17th/21st Lancers, 1970; Army Staff Coll., 1982; COS, 4th Armoured Bde, 1983–84; MA (Lt-Col) to C-in-C BAOR/COMNORTHAG, 1987–90; CO 17th/21st Lancers, 1990–92; Sec. to Chiefs of Staff Cttee, MoD, 1992–94 (Col); Brig. 1993; HCSC 1994; Comdr, 19th Mechanized Bde, 1994–96; rcds 1996; DPR (Army), 1997–99; Maj.-Gen. 1999; GOC 2nd Div. in York, 1999–2000; GOC 2nd Div. in Edinburgh, and Gov. of Edinburgh Castle, 2000–02; Force Comdr, UN Mission in Ethiopia and Eritrea, 2002–04; retd 2005; Consultant to UN Peacekeeping, 2005–; Senior Adviser to: Challenges for Peace Forum, 2008–; Pearson Peacekeeping Centre of Canada, 2009–13; UNDP Iraq for Security Sector Reform, 2013–16. Mem. Bd, Peace Ops Trng Inst., Va, USA, 2014–18. Col Comdt, RAVC, 2001–07. Trustee, Kohima Educnl Trust, 2006–16 (Pres., 2019–). Chm., Bulford and Tidworth Garrison Shoot, 2019–. QCVS 1995. *Recreations*: history, offshore sailing, game shooting, international travel. *Address*: The Old Manor, Milton Road, Pewsey, Wilts SN9 5JJ. *E*: rds.gordon@btinternet.com. *Club*: Cavalry and Guards.

**GORDON, Sir Robert James**, 10th Bt *cr* 1706, of Afton and Earlston, Kirkcudbrightshire; farmer, since 1958; *b* 17 Aug. 1932; *s* of Sir John Charles Gordon, 9th Bt and of Marion, *d* of late James B. Wright; *S* father, 1982; *m* 1976, Helen Julia Weston Perry. *Educ*: Barker College, Sydney; North Sydney Boys' High School; Wagga Agricultural Coll., Wagga Wagga, NSW (Wagga Dip. of Agric., Hons I and Dux). *Recreations*: tennis, ski-ing, swimming. *Heir*: none. *Address*: 126 Earlstoun Road, Guyra, NSW 2365, Australia. *T*: (2) 67791343.

**GORDON, Prof. Robert Patterson**, PhD, LittD; FBA 2011; Regius Professor of Hebrew, Cambridge University, 1995–2012, now Professor Emeritus; Fellow, St Catharine's College, Cambridge, 1995–2012, now Emeritus Fellow; Foundation Member, Trinity College, Cambridge, 1995–2012; *b* 9 Nov. 1945; *s* of Robert Gordon and Eveline (*née* Shilliday); *m* 1970, Helen Ruth Lyttle; two *s* one *d*. *Educ*: Methodist Coll., Belfast; St Catharine's Coll., Cambridge (Jarrett Schol. in Oriental Studies, 1966; John Stewart of Rannoch Hebrew Schol., 1966; BA 1st Cl. Hons Oriental Studies 1968; Bender Hebrew Prize, 1968; Sen. Schol., 1968; Tyrwhitt Scholarship and Mason Hebrew Prize, 1969; MA 1972; PhD 1973; LittD 2001). Asst Lectr in Hebrew and Semitic Langs, 1969–70, Lectr, 1970–79, Glasgow Univ.; Cambridge University: Lectr in Divinity, 1979–95; Fellow, St Edmund's Coll., 1985–89 (Tutor, 1986–89); Univ. Preacher, 1999. Lectures include: McManis, Wheaton, 1990; Macbride Sermon, Oxford Univ., 2000; Didsbury, Manchester, 2001; 11th Annual Biblical Studies, Samford Univ., Alabama, 2004; Second Annual Conf. for Church and Acad. Lectures, Brisbane, 2010; Tisley Annual, Motherwell, 2017. Sec., Internat. Orgn for Study of OT, 2001–04; Pres., SOTS, 2003. Mem., Carrickfergus Gasworks Preservation Soc. Trustee, Spalding Trust, 2013–. Review Ed., Vetus Testamentum, 1998–2010; Ed., Hebrew Bible and its Versions, monograph series, 2001–15. *Publications*: 1 and 2 Samuel, 1984 (Chinese edn 2002); 1 and 2 Samuel: a commentary, 1986, repr. 2004; (ed jtly) The Targum of the Minor Prophets, 1989; Studies in the Targum to the Twelve Prophets, 1994; (ed jtly) Wisdom in Ancient Israel, 1995; (ed) The Place is too Small for Us: the Israelite prophets in recent scholarship, 1995; (Consulting Ed.) New International Dictionary of Old Testament Theology and Exegesis, 1997; (ed) The Old Testament in Syriac: Chronicles, 1998; Hebrews: a new biblical commentary, 2000, 2nd edn, 2008; Holy Land, Holy City, 2004; (ed jtly) The Old Testament in its World, 2005; Hebrew Bible and Ancient Versions, 2006; (ed) The God of Israel, 2007; (ed jtly) Thus Speaks Ishtar of Arbela: prophecy in Israel, Assyria, and Egypt in the Neo-Assyrian period, 2013; (ed jtly) Leshon Limmudim: essays on the language and literature of the Hebrew Bible in honour of A. A. Macintosh, 2013; Genesis 1–11 in its Ancient Context, 2015; The Syriac Peshitta Bible with English Translation: Chronicles, 2019; contrib. to learned jls incl. Jl Jewish Studies, Jewish Qly Rev., Jl Semitic Studies, Jl for Study of OT, Jl Theol Studies, Revue de Qumran, Vetus Testamentum, and to various composite vols. *Recreations*: walking, otopianistics, local history (N Ireland). *Address*: St Catharine's College, Cambridge CB2 1RL. *Club*: National.

**GORDON, Prof. Robert Samuel Clive**, PhD; FBA 2015; Serena Professor of Italian, University of Cambridge, since 2012; Fellow of Gonville and Caius College, Cambridge, since 1998; *b* London, 13 March 1966; *s* of Lionel Lawrence Gordon and Jillian May Gordon; *m* 2001, Barbara Placido; two *s*. *Educ*: King's College Sch., Wimbledon; Pembroke Coll., Oxford (BA Hons); St John's Coll., Cambridge (PhD 1993). Lectr, Univ. of Oxford, and Fellow, Pembroke Coll., Oxford, 1990–97; Lectr, 1998–2001, Sen. Lectr, 2001–06, Reader, 2006–11, Prof., 2011–12, Univ. of Cambridge. *Publications*: (ed) Ignazio Silone, Fontamara, 1994; Pasolini: forms of subjectivity, 1996; (ed) Primo Levi, The Voice of Memory, 2000; Primo Levi's Ordinary Virtues: from testimony to ethics, 2001; A Difficult Modernity, 2005; (ed) Culture, Censorship and the State in Twentieth-Century Italy, 2005; (ed) Leonardo De Benedetti and Primo Levi, Auschwitz Report, 2006; (ed) The Cambridge Companion to Primo Levi, 2007; Bicycle Thieves, 2008; Sfacciata Fortuna, 2010; The Holocaust in Italian Culture, 2012; (ed) Holocaust Intersections, 2013; (ed) Holocaust Intersections in 21st-Century Europe, 2016. *Address*: Gonville and Caius College, Cambridge CB2 1TA. *E*: rscg1@cam.ac.uk.

**GORDON, Robert Smith Benzie**, CB 2000; Chair, Bethany Christian Trust, since 2009; executive coach and change consultant, since 2011; Associate, Kynesis, since 2011; *b* 7 Nov. 1950; *s* of William Gladstone Gordon and Helen Watt Gordon (*née* Benzie); *m* 1976, Joyce Ruth Cordiner; two *s* two *d*. *Educ*: Univ. of Aberdeen (MA Hons Italian Studies). Admin. trainee, Scottish Office, 1973–78; Principal, Scottish Develt Dept, 1979–85; Asst Sec., 1984; Principal Private Sec. to Sec. of State for Scotland, 1985–87; Dept of Agriculture and Fisheries for Scotland, 1987–90; Scottish Office, later Scottish Executive, then Scottish Government: Mgt Orgn and Industrial Relns, 1990–91; Dir of Admin. Services, 1991–97; Under Sec., 1993; Head of Constitution Gp, 1997–98; Dep. Sec., 1998; Hd of Exec. Secretariat, 1999–2001; Hd of Finance and Central Services Dept, 2001–02; Chief Exec., Crown Office and Procurator Fiscal Service, 2002–04; Hd of Legal and Parly Services, 2002–10, and Hd of Justice Dept, later Dir-Gen. of Justice and Communities, 2004–10. Convenor, Standing Cttee, Gen. Synod of Scottish Episcopal Ch, 2015–. Chm., Audit and Accountability Cttee, Police Investigation and Rev. Comr, 2016–19. Chm., Safe Families for Children Scotland, 2015–18. Dir, Inspiring Scotland, 2008–16. Chair, Resources Gp, St Paul's and St George's Church, Edinburgh, 2011–15. Warden, Incorporation of Goldsmiths, City of Edinburgh, 2000–17. *Address*: c/o Bethany Christian Trust, 65 Bonnington Road, Edinburgh EH6 5JQ.

**GORDON, Ronald Dingwall**; Chairman, John Gordon & Son Ltd, since 2000; Vice Lord-Lieutenant of Nairnshire, 1999–2011; *b* 13 Nov. 1936; *s* of Ronald James Robertson Gordon and Mary Isabella Cardno Gordon; *m* 1961, Elizabeth Ancell Gordon; two *s* one *d*. *Educ*: Nairn Acad. Nat. Service, RAF, 1955–57. Joined John Gordon & Son, 1957; jt partner with father, 1961; sole trader, 1965–85; Man. Dir, 1985–2000. Dir, Nairn Museum Ltd, 2014–. DL Nairnshire, 1991. *Recreations*: golf, fishing, gardening. *Address*: Achareidh House, Nairn IV12 4UD. *T*: (01667) 452130. *Clubs*: Royal and Ancient Golf, Royal Dornoch Golf, Nairn Golf (Capt., 1980–82; Vice Pres., 2000–05; Pres., 2006–).

**GORDON, Shirley Denise**; *see* Rogers, S. D.

**GORDON, Prof. Siamon**, PhD; FRS 2007; Glaxo-Wellcome Professor of Cellular Pathology, Oxford University, 1991–2008, now Emeritus (Professor of Cellular Pathology, 1989–91); Fellow, Exeter College, Oxford, 1976–2006, now Emeritus Fellow; *b* 29 April 1938; *s* of Jonah and Liebe Gordon; *m* 1963, Lyndall Felicity Getz (*see* L. F. Gordon); two *d*. *Educ*: South African Coll. Sch., Cape Town; Univ. of Cape Town (MB ChB 1961); Rockefeller Univ. (PhD 1971). Res. Asst, Wright-Fleming Inst., St Mary's, London, 1964–65; Rockefeller University, NY: Res. Associate, 1965–71; Asst Prof. of Cellular Immunology, 1971–76; Adjunct Associate Prof., 1976–; Reader in Exptl Pathology, Sir Wm Dunn Sch. of Pathology, Univ. of Oxford, 1976–89, Actg Hd of Dept, 1989–90, 2000–01. University of Oxford: Chairman: Physiol Scis Bd, 1984–86; Search Cttee, E. P. Abraham Bldg, 1999–2003; Member: General Bd, 1989–92; Med. Scis Div., 2000–03. Member: Lister Scientific Adv. Cttee, 1987–92; Scientific Adv. Cttee, Inst. of Infection, Immunity and Molecular Medicine, Univ. of Cape Town, 2003– (Chm., 2003–08, 2013–). Special Fellow and Scholar, Leukaemia Soc. of America, 1971–76; Vis. Scientist, Genetics, Oxford Univ., 1974–75; Vis. Scholar, NIH, Bethesda, USA, 2009–10. FMedSci 2003. Hon. Mem., Amer. Assoc. of Immunologists, 2004. Hon. DSc Cape Town, 2003. Marie T. Bonazinga Award, Soc. of Leukocyte Biol., 2003. *Publications*: contribs to jls of exptl medicine, immunology, cell biology, AIDS educn in Southern Africa. *Recreations*: reading biography, medical history. *Address*: c/o Sir William Dunn School of Pathology, South Parks Road, Oxford OX1 3RE.

**GORDON, (Vera) Kate, (Mrs E. W. Gordon)**, CB 1999; Chair, Queen Elizabeth Hospital NHS Foundation Trust, King's Lynn, 2007–13; *b* 8 Oct. 1944; *d* of late Kenneth Timms and Elsie Timms (*née* Cussans); *m* 1977, Ernest William Gordon (*d* 2018); one step *d*. *Educ*: Queen Anne Grammar School, York; St Hilda's College, Oxford (PPE Hons). Economic Asst, NEDO, 1966–70; Ministry of Agriculture, Fisheries and Food, 1970; Asst Private Sec. to Minister of Agric., 1974–75; seconded to European Secretariat of Cabinet Office, 1976–79; Principal Private Sec. to Minister of Agric., 1980–82; Asst Sec. responsible for marketing policy, MAFF, 1982–84; Counsellor, Paris, seconded to HM Diplomatic Service, 1984–88; Asst Sec. and Head of Sugar and Oilseeds Div., MAFF, 1988–89; Under Sec., Arable Crops Gp, MAFF, 1989–90; Minister (Agriculture), Office of the UK Perm. Rep., Brussels, 1990–95; Principal Finance Officer, MAFF, 1995–96; Dep. Sec., Agriculture, Crops and Commodities, later Agriculture and Food Industry, MAFF, 1996–2001; Policy Dir, Health and Safety Exec., 2001–04. Member: Basic Skills Agency, 2004–07; Flagship Housing Gp (formerly Peddars Way Housing Assoc.), 2004–13; Passenger Focus (formerly Rail Passengers' Council), 2005–09. Ordre du Mérite Agricole (France), 1988. *Address*: Holly House, 62A London Street, Swaffham, Norfolk PE37 7DJ. *T*: (01760) 723034; 42 The Foreshore, SE8 3AG. *T*: (020) 8691 0823.

**GORDON BANKS, Matthew Richard William**; Director, International Institute for Strategic Affairs, since 2015 (Director, Middle East and South Asia, 2014–15); *b* 21 June 1961; *s* of Harry and Audrey Banks; *m* 1992, Jane, *d* of Michael Miller; one *s* one *d*. *Educ*: private; Sheffield City Polytechnic (BA Hons History and Econs); RMA Sandhurst; Donald Harrison Sch. of Business, SE Missouri State Univ., USA (MBA 2001). 1st Bn, 51st Highland Vols, 1979–81; Commnd, The Gordon Highlanders, 1981–83; War Disablement Pension, 1983. Barclays Bank, 1984–88; Private Sec. to Cecil Franks, MP, 1988–89. Dir, and Sen. Advr on ME Affairs, LBJ Ltd, 1989–. Mem., Wirral BC, 1984–90 (Chairman: Schs Cttee, 1985–86; Works Cttee, 1986–87). Contested (C) Manchester Central, 1987; MP (C) Southport, 1992–97; contested (C) same seat, 1997. PPS, DoE, 1996–97. Mem., Select Cttee on Transport, 1992–97; Chm., Anglo-Venezuela Parly Gp, 1993–97; Sec., Anglo-UAE Parly Gp, 1993–97. Advr, Jt Security Industry Council, 2002–06; Sen. Advr, Middle East and SE Asia, Advanced Res. Assessment Gp, Defence Acad., MoD, 2006–10; Dir, Internat. Relns and Public Affairs, Inst. of Islamic Strategic and Socio-Political Affairs,

2010–14; Advr, Internat. Inst. for Security Services, 2007–09; Foreign and Policy Advr to Tim Farron, MP, 2015–16. Mem. (C) Cotswold DC, 2001–04 (Chm., Overview and Scrutiny Cttee). FRGS 1983. *Recreations:* walking, travel, reading, flying, fishing. *Address:* Gordon Castle, Fochabers, Morayshire IV32 7PQ; The Green, Charlbury, Oxon OX7 3QB. *Club:* Caledonian.

**GORDON CLARK, (Elizabeth) Jane;** artist, sculptor; Founder/Designer, Ornamenta Ltd, since 1987; *m* 1981, Sam Gordon Clark. *Educ:* Ruskin Sch. of Art, Oxford. Consultant, Fine Art Develt plc, 1968–77; Founder/Designer: Davan Wetton Design, 1977–2008. Solo exhibition, Hothouse Flowers: The Gallery at Oxo, 2003; The Orangery, Holland Park, 2006; The Exhibition Gallery, SW7, 2007; sculptures: Grange Festival, 2018, Henley Festival, 2019. Trustee, V&A Mus., 2000–08 (Mem. Develt Adv. Bd, 2011–16); Chm., Friends of the V&A, 1994–2001; Member: Bd, V&A Enterprises, 2005–08; Cttee, Theatre Mus., 2003–06. Trustee, Heatherley Sch. of Fine Art, 2016–. Mem., British Interior Design Assoc., 2003. Freeman, Painter Stainers' Co., 1981. *Publications:* Paper Magic, 1991; Italian Style, 1999; Wallpaper in Decoration, 2001. *Club:* Chelsea Arts.

**GORDON CLARK, Robert Michael;** Executive Chairman, London Communications Agency, since 2010 (Managing Director and Chairman, 1999–2010); *b* Derby, 8 May 1961; *s* of Rev. John Gordon Clark and late Jennifer Gordon Clark; *m* 1985, Lisa, *d* of Sir Michael John Day, *qv*; two *d. Educ:* St John's Sch., Leatherhead; Southampton Univ. (LLB Hons). Marketing Manager: Matthew Clark & Sons Ltd, 1983–89; CCA Galleries, 1989–90; Hd of Public Affairs, London Arts Bd, 1990–93; Dir of Communications, 1993–97, Dep. CEO, 1997–99, London First. Dir, Shannon & Clark Prodns Ltd, 2008–11. Non-exec. Dir, Hayes Davidson, 1999–2010. Chm., Mayor's Thames Fest., London, 2013– (Trustee, 2006–13). Presenter, The Business, LBC Radio, 1999–2002. Gov., St John's Sch., Leatherhead, 1996–2011. *Recreations:* cricket (Vice Pres., HAC CC), theatre (Questors Th., Ealing), singing. *Address:* London Communications Agency, 8th Floor, Berkshire House, 168–173 High Holborn, WC1V 7AA. *T:* (020) 7612 8480. *E:* rgc@londoncommunications.co.uk.

**GORDON CUMMING, Sir Alexander Penrose, (Sir Alastair),** 7th Bt *cr* 1804, of Altyre, Forres; *b* 15 April 1954; *s* of Sir William Gordon Cumming, 6th Bt and of Elisabeth Gordon Cumming (*née* Hinde); *S* father, 2002; *m* 1991, Louisa Clifton-Brown; two *s* one *d. Educ:* Ludgrove; Harrow. Insurance broker, 1976–95; Penrose Forbes Ltd, 1995–2000; Consultant, R. K. Harrison, 2000–14. *Recreation:* all country pursuits. *Heir: s* William Gordon Cumming, *b* 4 April 1993. *Address:* Altyre House, Forres, Morayshire IV36 2SH. *T:* (01309) 673774, *Fax:* (01309) 672270. *Clubs:* Turf, Pratt's; Shikar.

**GORDON LENNOX,** family name of **Duke of Richmond**.

**GORDON-MacLEOD, David Scott;** HM Diplomatic Service, retired; Chargé d'Affaires, Monrovia, Liberia, 2012–13; *b* 4 May 1948; *s* of Adam Denys Gordon-MacLeod and Margaret Rae Gordon-MacLeod (*née* Miller); *m* 1988, Adrienne Felicia Maria Atkins (marr. diss. 2013); two *s* two *d. Educ:* St Peter's Coll., Oxford (exhibitioner; BA); Carleton Univ., Canada (MA); Sarajevo Univ. (Dip. Islamic Studies). ODA, 1973–78; Mbabane, 1978–83; Second, later First Sec., Arms Control and Disarmament Dept, FCO, 1983–87; Dep. Hd of Mission, Maputo, 1987–91; First Sec., Equatorial Africa Dept, FCO, 1991–92; Hd of Missile Technol., Defence Dept, FCO, 1992–94; Dep. Hd of Mission, Bogotá, 1995–97; Dir, EU and Econ. Affairs, Athens, 1998–2003; High Comr to Papua New Guinea, 2003–07; Manager, FCO Global Response Centre, 2007; Dep. Ambassador, Bosnia and Herzegovina, 2009–10. Sensitivity Reviewer, FCO, 2014–; Deployable Civilian Expert on conflict resolution and stabilisation, Stabilisation Unit, FCO, 2014–; Foreign Sec.'s Special Rep. for VIP Arrivals and Departures, FCO, 2019–; Election Observer, EU and OSCE, 2014–. Ext. Marker, Dept of Internat. Security and Develt, MSc prog., Leicester Univ., 2014–18. Business Corresp., Supply Finder (global business website), 2016–. FRGS 1975. *Recreations:* family, travel, environmental issues, climbing, tennis, writing.

**GORDON-SAKER, Andrew Stephen;** Senior Costs Judge of England and Wales, since 2014; *b* 4 Oct. 1958; *s* of Vincent Gordon-Saker and Gwendoline (*née* Remmers); *m* 1985, Liza Helen Marle (*see* L. H. Gordon-Saker); one *s* one *d. Educ:* Stonyhurst Coll.; Univ. of E Anglia (LLB). Called to the Bar, Middle Temple, 1981; in practice, SE Circuit, 1982–2003. Dep. Taxing Master of Supreme Court, 1994–2003; Master of the Sen. (formerly Supreme) Courts Costs Office, 2003–14. Costs Officer, Supreme Court, 2010–. Mem., Cambridge Legal Aid Area Cttee, 1995–2003. Mem. (C) Camden LBC, 1982–86. Trustee, Jimmy's Night Shelter, Cambridge, 2000–03. Mem., Sen. Editl Bd, Civil Procedure (The White Book), 2015–. *Publications:* (ed) Butterworths Costs Service, 2006–17; (contrib.) Civil Procedure (The White Book), 2012–. *Recreations:* gardening, construction. *Address:* Royal Courts of Justice, Strand, WC2A 2LL. *Club:* Trumpington Bridge.

**GORDON-SAKER, Liza Helen; Her Honour Judge Gordon-Saker;** a Circuit Judge, since 2014; *b* London, 30 Nov. 1959; *d* of William James Marle and Doreen Maud Marle; *m* 1985, Andrew Stephen Gordon-Saker, *qv*; one *s* one *d. Educ:* Farringtons Sch., Chislehurst; Univ. of E Anglia (LLB). Called to the Bar, Gray's Inn, 1982; in practice, SE Circuit, 1983–2009; Dep. Dist Judge, 2006–09; Dist Judge, Principal Registry of Family Div., 2010–14. Mem., Family Justice Council, 2013–15. Dir, Bar Mutual Indemnity Fund, 1988–2002. Parish Councillor, 1998–2007. Trustee, Jimmy's Night Shelter, Cambridge, 2004–10. Chm., Univ. of E Anglia Soc. (Alumni Assoc.), 1985–88. Freeman, City of London, 1984. *Publications:* (contrib.) Atkin's Court Forms, 2011–16. *Recreations:* golf, bridge, The Archers. *Address:* Cambridge County Court, 197 East Road, Cambridge CB1 1BA. *Club:* Trumpington Bridge (Chair, 2014–16).

**GORDON-SMITH, Prof. Edward Colin,** FRCP, FRCPE, FRCPath, FMedSci; Professor of Haematology, St George's, University of London (formerly St George's Hospital Medical School, London), 1987–2003, now Emeritus; *b* 26 June 1938; *s* of late Gordon John Gordon-Smith and Valentine (*née* Waddington); *m* 1968, Moira Phelan; two *s. Educ:* Oakham Sch.; Epsom Coll.; Exeter Coll., Oxford (MA, BSc, BM BCh); Westminster Med. Sch., London (MSc). FRCP 1978; FRCPath 1987; FRCPE 1999. House Officer, Westminster Hosp., 1964; Sen. House Officer, Nuffield Dept of Medicine, Radcliffe Infirmary, Oxford, 1966; Lectr in Neurology, Churchill Hosp., Oxford, 1966–67; Registrar in Haematology, Hammersmith Hosp., 1968–69; MRC Clinical Trng Fellow, RPMS Metabolic Unit, Oxford, 1970–71; Sen. Lectr 1972–83, Reader 1983–86, RPMS. Editor, Brit. Jl of Haematology, 1983–86. President: European Bone Marrow Transplant Gp, 1980; Internat. Soc. Exptl Haematology, 1990–92; British Soc. for Haematology, 1995; Vice-Pres., RCPath, 1996–99. Founder FMedSci 1998. Order of Prasidda Prabala Gorkha-Dakshin Bahu (2nd class), Nepal, 1984. *Publications:* papers on aplastic anaemia, bone marrow transplantation, inherited bone marrow disorders, culture of human bone marrow and drug induced blood disorders. *Recreations:* golf, music, gardening, arguing with the wireless. *Address:* 35 Park Road, Chiswick, W4 3EY. *T:* (020) 8994 2112, *Fax:* (020) 8995 6631. *Club:* Royal Society of Medicine.

**GORE;** *see* Ormsby Gore.

**GORE,** family name of **Earl of Arran**.

**GORE, Albert Arnold,** Jr; Chairman, Current TV (formerly INdTV), 2004–12; Founding Partner and Chairman, Generation Investment Management, since 2004; *b* 31 March 1948; *s* of late Albert and Pauline Gore; *m* 1970, Mary Elizabeth, (Tipper), Aitcheson; one *s* three *d. Educ:* Harvard and Vanderbilt Univs. Served US Army in Vietnam, 1969–71. Reporter and editorial writer, The Tennessean, 1971–76; livestock farmer, 1971–. Democrat; Mem., US House of Representatives, 1977–85; Mem. for Tennessee, US Senate, 1985–92; Chm., US Senate Delegn to Earth Summit, Rio de Janeiro, 1992; Vice-President of USA, 1993–2001; Presidential cand., US elections, 2000. Dir, Apple, 2003–; Sen. Advr, Google, 2001–09. Visiting Professor: Fisk Univ., 2001; Middle Tenn State Univ., 2001; UCLA, 2001. (Jtly) Nobel Peace Prize, 2007. *Publications:* Earth in the Balance: ecology and the human spirit, 1992; (with Tipper Gore): Joined at the Heart: the transformation of the American family, 2002; The Spirit of Family (photographs), 2002; An Inconvenient Truth: the crisis of global warming, 2007; The Assault on Reason, 2007; Our Choice: a plan to solve the climate crisis, 2009; The Future: six drivers of global change, 2013.

**GORE, Allan Peter;** QC 2003; **His Honour Judge Gore;** a Circuit Judge, since 2010; a Senior Circuit Judge, since 2011; Designated Civil Judge for Devon and Cornwall, since 2018; *b* 25 Aug. 1951; *s* of Gerry and Hansi Gore; *m* 1981 (marr. diss.); three *d*; *m* 2016, Alison Taylor. *Educ:* Trinity Hall, Cambridge (MA 1973; LLB 1st class 1974). Called to the Bar, Middle Temple, 1977; in practice, specialising in personal injury (particularly asbestos and other industrial disease), clinical negligence and related legal negligence litigation; Recorder, 2000–10; Designated Civil Judge: for Liverpool, 2010–13; for Manchester, 2013–18. Pres., Assoc. of Personal Injury Lawyers, 2005–06. Mem., Editl Bd, Jl of Personal Injury Law, 2006–08. *Publications:* (ed jtly) Occupational Illness Litigation; contributions to: Personal Injury Pleadings, ed by Patrick Curran, 2001, 5th edn, 2014; Personal Injury Handbook, 2001; Butterworths Personal Injury Litigation Service; Butterworths Civil Court Precedents; Cordery on Legal Services; Jordan's Civil Court Service. *Recreations:* travel, sport, music, cooking. *Address:* Exeter Combined Court Centre, Southernhay Gardens, Exeter EX1 1UH.

**GORE, Sir Hugh (Frederick Corbet),** 15th Bt *cr* 1622 (Ire.), of Magherabegg, Co. Donegal; *b* Goondiwindi, Qld, 31 Dec. 1934; *s* of late Frederick Dundas Corbet Gore and Ella Maud, *d* of Charles Sydney Jones; *S* cousin, 2008; *m* 1963, Jennifer Mary Copp; one *s* two *d. Educ:* Church of England Grammar Sch., Brisbane; Univ. of Sydney. Qantas Airways Ltd: Traffic Handling, 1957–61; Ops Planning, 1961–68; Computer Systems Develt, 1968–90 (latterly Strategic Planning Manager, Systems Develt). *Recreations:* bridge, bushwalking. *Heir: s* Timothy Milton Corbet Gore [*b* 26 Nov. 1969; *m* 2009, Aya Tokito]. *Address:* 7 Romney Road, St Ives, Sydney, NSW 2075, Australia. *Clubs:* Australian, Union University and Schools, Australasian Pioneers', Tripe, Royal Automobile of Australia (Sydney).

**GORE, Michael Edward John,** CVO 1994; CBE 1991; HM Diplomatic Service, retired; Governor, Cayman Islands, 1992–95; *b* 20 Sept. 1935; *s* of late John Gore and Elsa Gore (*née* Dillon); *m* 1957, Monica Shellish; two *d* (and one *d* decd). *Educ:* Xaverian College, Brighton. Reporter, Portsmouth Evening News, 1952–55; Captain, Army Gen. List, 1955–59; Air Ministry, Dep. Comd. Inf. Officer, Cyprus and Aden, 1959–63; CRO, later FCO, 1963; served Jesselton, 1963–66, FCO, 1966–67, Seoul, 1967–71, Montevideo, 1971–74; First Sec., Banjul, 1974–78; FCO, 1978–81; Nairobi, 1981–84; Dep. High Comr, Lilongwe, 1984–87; Ambassador to Liberia, 1988–90; High Comr to the Bahamas, 1991–92. Mem., UK Dependent, then UK Overseas, Territories Conservation Forum, 1996–; Chm., Wider Caribbean Working Gp, 1997–2006. Member: Nature Photographers Portfolio, 1979– (Pres., 2001–13); Zool Photographic Club, 1992– (Pres., 2013–15). Hon. Vice Pres., Birdlife Cyprus, 2003–. Patron, Humanists UK (formerly British Humanist Assoc.), 2011–. FRPS. *Publications:* The Birds of Korea (with Pyong-Oh Won), 1971; Las Aves del Uruguay (with A. R. M. Gepp), 1978; Birds of the Gambia, 1981, 2nd edn 1991; On Safari in Kenya: a pictorial guide to the national parks and reserves, 1984, 2nd edn, 2007; papers on birds and conservation; wild-life photographs in books and magazines. *Recreations:* ornithology, wildlife photography, fishing. *Address:* 5 St Mary's Close, Fetcham, Surrey KT22 9HE. *W:* www.wildlife-photography.net.

**GORE, Prof. Van Jonathan,** CBE 2014; Vice-Chancellor, Southampton Solent University, 2007–14; *b* Birmingham; *s* of John and Daisy Gore; *m* Jill Helen; two *d. Educ:* Univ. of Sheffield (BA Hons Hist. and Politics; MA Modern British Politics). Sheffield Polytechnic, subseq. Sheffield Hallam University, 1972–2001: Prof. of Quality Mgt; Sen. Academic, Cultural Studies; Special Policy Advr to Vice-Chancellor; Sen. Vice-Principal, Southampton Inst., 2001–05; Dep. Vice-Chancellor, Southampton Solent Univ., 2005–07. *Recreations:* music, books, gardening, table tennis.

**GORE-BOOTH, Sir Josslyn (Henry Robert),** 9th Bt *cr* 1760 (Ire.), of Artarman, Sligo; *b* 5 Oct. 1950; *o s* of Sir Angus Gore-Booth, 8th Bt and Hon. Rosemary Myra Vane, *o d* of 10th Baron Barnard, CMG, OBE, MC, TD; *S* father, 1996; *m* 1980, Jane Mary, *o d* of Rt Hon. Sir Roualeyn Hovell-Thurlow-Cumming-Bruce; two *d. Educ:* Eton Coll.; Balliol Coll., Oxford (BA); Insead (MBA). Dir, Kiln Cotesworth Corporate Capital Fund plc, 1993–97. Chm., Herriot Hospice Homecare, 2007–13. Treas., Georgian Gp, 2015–. Patron: living of Sacred Trinity, Salford; Herriot Hospice Homecare, 2014–. *Recreations:* cooking, shooting. *Heir:* cousin (Paul Wyatt) Julian Gore-Booth [*b* 29 July 1968; *m* 1999, Amanda Marie McConnell; one *s* one *d*]. *Address:* Home Farm, Hartforth, Gilling West, Richmond, N Yorkshire DL10 5JS.

**GORE-LANGTON;** *see* Temple-Gore-Langton, family name of Earl Temple of Stowe.

**GORE-RANDALL, Philip Allan,** FCA; Chairman, Forensic Risk Alliance, since 2017; *b* 16 Dec. 1952; *s* of late Alec Albert Gore-Randall and Joyce Margaret Gore-Randall; *m* 1984, Prof. Alison Elizabeth While; two *s. Educ:* Merchant Taylors' Sch., Northwood; University Coll., Oxford (MA 1975). FCA 1978. Arthur Andersen, subseq. Andersen, 1975–2002: Partner, 1986–2002; UK Man. Partner, Assurance and Business Advisory, 1995–97, Man. Partner, Assurance and Business Advisory, Europe, Africa, Middle East and India, 1996–97; UK Managing Partner, 1997–2001; Man. Partner, Global Ops, 2001–02; Chm. and CEO, Aon Risk Services, 2004–05; Dir, Aon Ltd, 2004–07; Chief Operating Officer, Aon UK, 2006–07; Chief Operating Officer and Dir, HBOS plc and Bank of Scotland plc, 2007–09. Mem., Exec. Cttee, RAK Economic Zone (formerly RAK Free Trade Zone and RAK Investment Authy), 2015–. Chairman: Envmtl Resources Mgt Ltd, 2010–11; Fircroft Engrg Services Hldgs Ltd, 2013–; Alvarez and Marsal, Corporate Performance Europe, 2013–; Equiom Hldgs Ltd, 2014–19. Non-executive Director: Compass Mgt Consulting Gp Hldgs Ltd, 2007–11; esure Ltd, 2009–10; Topaz Energy and Marine PLC, 2011– (Chm., Audit Cttee, 2013–); Ind. Mem., Internat. Exec. Cttee, Lovells, 2007–08; Advisor: Renaissance Services SAOG, 2011–13; RAK Ceramics PSC, 2014–; Chm., Audit and Compliance (formerly Ops) Cttee, Chm., Compensation Cttee, and non-exec. Mem., Exec. Cttee, Samena Capital, 2013–; Dir and Chm., Exec. Cttee, RAK Logistics Pte Ltd, 2016–. *Recreations:* classical music/opera, good food, travel. *Club:* Vincent's (Oxford).

*See also Baron Randall of Uxbridge.*

**GORELL**, 5th Baron cr 1909, of Brampton, co. Derby; **John Picton Gorell Barnes**; Principal, Gorell Barnes, chartered surveyors, since 2009; b 29 July 1959; s of Hon. Ronald Alexander Henry Barnes, yr s of 3rd Baron, and Gillian Picton Barnes; S uncle, 2007; one s one d. Educ: Mount House Sch., Tavistock; N Staffordshire Poly. (BSc Est. Mgt 1983). Assoc. Dir, Lambert Smith Hampton, 1984–89; Man. Dir, Barnes Noble Edwards, chartered surveyors, 1993–2009. Patron: Nat. Army Mus.; Chrysalis Foundn. Freeman, City of London, 1987. Upper Warden, Weavers' Co., 2014–15. Recreations: sailing, gun dog training, Stoke City FC, walking football. Heir: s Hon. Oliver Gorell Barnes, b 4 April 1993. E: john@gorellbarnes.com.

**GORHAM, Ian David**; Chief Executive Officer, Hargreaves Lansdown plc, 2010–17 (Chief Operating Officer, 2009–10). Educ: Castle Rushen High Sch., I of M; Warwick Univ. (BSc Econs 1993). ACA 1996. Dir, Deloitte UK LLP, 1993–2003; Partner and Hd of UK Financial Services, Grant Thornton UK LLP, 2003–09. Recreations: golf, fitness. Club: Clevedon Golf.

**GORHAM, Rt Rev. Karen Marisa**; see Sherborne, Bishop Suffragan of.

**GORHAM, Martin Edwin**, OBE 2005; Director: Gorham Consulting, since 2017; Gorham Partnership Ltd, 2007–13; Douglas-Gorham Partnership Ltd, 2008–15; b 18 June 1947; s of Clifford Edwin Gorham and Florence Ada Gorham; m 1st, 1968, Jean McNaughton Kerr (marr. diss. 1998); 2nd, 1998, Sally Ann Stevens (née Fletcher); one step d. Educ: Buckhurst Hill County High Sch.; Queen Mary Coll., Univ. of London (BA Hons History 1968). MHSM, DipHSM 1973. NHS Mgt Trainee, 1968; Deputy Hospital Secretary: Scarborough Gen. Hosp., 1970–72; Doncaster Royal Infirmary, 1972–75; Hosp. Manager, Northern Gen. Hosp., Sheffield, 1975–83; Dep. Dist Gen. Manager, Newcastle HA, 1983–86; Gen. Manager, Norfolk and Norwich Hosp., 1986–90; Dep. Regl Gen. Manager, SW Thames RHA, 1990–92; Chief Exec., London Ambulance Service, 1992–96; Dir of Projects, S Thames Regl Office, NHS Exec., DoH, 1996–98; Chief Executive: Nat. Blood Authy, 1998–2005; NHS Blood and Transplant, 2005–07. Pres., European Blood Alliance, 2001–07 (Hon. Pres., 2014–). Trustee, Princess Royal Trust for Carers, 2001–06; Mem. Bd, Foundn of the Internat. Soc. of Blood Transfusion, 2012–. Recreations: travel, music, books, art, food and wine, gardening, cricket (Essex CC), football (West Ham). Address: 20 Grange Road, Bishop's Stortford, Herts CM23 5NQ. T: (01279) 501876. Club: Royal Society of Medicine.

**GORHAM, Robin Stuart**; HM Diplomatic Service, retired; Lecturer, University of East Anglia, since 2011; b 15 Feb. 1939; s of Stuart Gorham and Dorothy Gorham (née Stevens); m 1st, 1966, Barbara Fechner (marr. diss. 1991); three d; 2nd, 1992, Joanna Bradbury (marr. diss. 2004). Educ: Sutton Manor High Sch.; Oriel Coll., Oxford (MA). CRO, 1961–62; Ottawa, 1962–64; Centre for Econ. Studies, 1964–65; Bonn, 1965–66; Central European Dept, FCO, 1967–69; First Secretary: (External Affairs and Defence) and Dep. Hd of Chancery, Tokyo, 1970–74; (Commercial and Develt), Accra, 1974–77; ME Dept, FCO, 1977–79; Hd of Chancery, Helsinki, 1980–83; Counsellor and Dep. High Comr, Lusaka, 1983–86; rcds, 1987; Hd, W Indian and Atlantic Dept, FCO, 1988–91; Dep. Hd of Mission, Lagos, 1991–94; Head of Protocol Dept and Asst Marshal of Diplomatic Corps, FCO, 1994–98. Recreations: fox-hunting, tall ship sailing, Himalayan trekking. Address: The Arch, Thornham Hall Stables, Thornham Magna, Eye, Suffolk IP23 8HA. T: (01379) 783938; L'Oreneta, Barri d'Amunt, 66150 Corsavy, France. T: (4) 68834094.

**GORICK, Ven. Martin Charles William**; Archdeacon of Oxford, since 2013; b Liverpool, 23 June 1962; s of David Gorick and Janet Gorick; m 1985, Katharine Bentley; one s two d. Educ: West Bridgford Comp. Sch.; Selwyn Coll., Cambridge (BA 1984; MA 1988). Ordained deacon, 1987, priest, 1988; Curate, Birtley, 1987–91; Domestic Chaplain to Bishop of Oxford, 1991–94; Vicar, Smethwick, 1994–2001; Area Dean, Warley, 1997–2001; Vicar, Stratford-upon-Avon, 2001–13. Publications: (ed) Shakespeare's Church: a parish for the world, 2010; Eight Hundred Years: ten lifetimes, 2013. Recreations: family, walking, bird-watching, theatre, gardening. Address: Archdeacon's Lodging, Christ Church, Oxford OX1 1DP.

**GORING, (Richard) Harry**; farmer, Findon Park Farm; Vice Lord-Lieutenant of West Sussex, since 2014; b 10 Sept. 1949; s of Lt Col John Goring, CBE and Lady Hersey Margaret Goring (née Boyle); m 1972, Penelope Ann Broadbent; three s three d. Educ: Eton; RAC, Cirencester. Manager, 1975–97, owner, 1987–, Wiston Estate; estabd Wiston Estate Winery, 2006. Former Member, Council: CLA (Chm., Sussex Br.); NT (Chm., SE Reg.). High Sheriff, 1993–94, DL 1994, W Sussex. Address: Wiston Estate Office, Wiston Park, Steyning, W Sussex BN44 3DD.

**GORING, Sir William (Burton Nigel)**, 13th Bt cr 1627; Member of London Stock Exchange, 1963; b 21 June 1933; s of Major Frederick Yelverton Goring (d 1938) (6th s of 11th Bt) and Freda Margaret (d 1993), o d of N. V. Ainsworth; S uncle, Sir Forster Gurney Goring, 12th Bt, 1956; m 1st, 1960, Hon. Caroline Thellusson (marr. diss. 1993; she d 2010), d of 8th Baron Rendlesham and of Mrs Patrick Barthropp; 2nd, 1993, Mrs Judith Rachel Walton Morison (d 1995), d of Rev. R. J. W. Morris, OBE; 3rd, 1998, Mrs Stephanie Bullock, d of George Carter, DFC. Educ: Wellington; RMA Sandhurst. Lieut, The Royal Sussex Regt. Master, Co. of Woolmen, 2000–01. Recreation: bridge. Heir: kinsman Richard Harry Goring [b 10 Sept. 1949; m 1972, Penelope Ann, d of J. K. Broadbent; three s three d]. Address: c/o Quilter Cheviot, One Kingsway, WC2B 6AN. Club: Hurlingham.

**GORMALLY, Michael Anthony Peter Thomas**; Headmaster, The Cardinal Vaughan Memorial School, Kensington, 1997–2010; b 30 Jan. 1956; s of Charles Gormally and Frances Edna Gormally. Educ: Inst. of Education, Univ. of London (BA Hons French). ACP 1986. Cardinal Vaughan Memorial School, 1981–2010: Asst Master, 1981–84; Hd, Modern Langs, 1984–90; Sen. Master, 1990–95; Dep. Headmaster, 1995–97. FRSA 1998. Recreations: reading, playing the piano, cooking. Address: c/o Cardinal Vaughan Memorial School, 89 Addison Road, W14 8BZ.

**GORMAN, Christopher Nicoll**; Partner, Linklaters & Paines, Solicitors, 1972–97 (Managing Partner, 1991–95); b 29 Aug. 1939; s of late James Gorman and Louise Barbara (née Rackham); m 1967, Anne Beech (d 1996); one s one d. Educ: Royal Liberty Sch., Romford; St Catharine's Coll., Cambridge (MA, LLM). Admitted Solicitor, 1965. Publications: (ed) Nelson's Tables of Company Procedure, 6th edn 1975 to 8th edn 1983; (ed) Westby Nunn's Company Secretarial Handbook, 7th edn 1977 to 11th edn 1992. Recreations: books and bookshops, outdoor activity, unfinished business. Clubs: Athenæum, Royal Automobile.

**GORMAN, Gayle**; HM Chief Inspector of Education, Scotland, and Chief Executive, Education Scotland, since 2017; b Glasgow, 12 April 1970; d of William McK. Gorman and Margaret Gorman (née Jardine); m 1995, Thomas Hill. Educ: Jordanhill Coll., Glasgow Univ. (BEd (Merit)); Homerton Coll., Cambridge (Advanced Dip. Lang. and Lit. (Dist.)). Roles in education, teaching and leadership; Dir, Intensifying Support Prog., DfES, 2001–03; Sen. Regl Advr, Nat. Strategies, 2003–08, Sen. Dir, Nat. Strategies, 2008–12, DfES, then DCSF; Dir of Learning, Cambs CC, 2010–13; Dir, Educn, Culture and Sport, 2013–14, of Educn and Children's Services, 2014–17, Aberdeen CC; Northern Alliance Regl Improvement Lead, 2016–18. Trustee, Gordon Cook Foundn, 2015– (Chm., 2018–). Recreations: children's literature, reading, spending time travelling. Address: Education Scotland, Optima Building, 58 Robertson Street, Glasgow G2 8DU. T: (0131) 244 3000. E: Gayle.Gorman@educationscotland.gov.scot.

**GORMAN, Justin**; Chief Executive Officer and Creative Director, Man Alive Entertainment, since 2016; b Bromley, Kent, 25 April 1972; s of John Gorman and Sue Gorman; m 1999, Emily Tudor; two d. Educ: Goldsmith's Coll., Univ. of London (BA Hons Drama and Theatre Arts 1993). Researcher: Action Time, 1995–97; Hat Trick Prodns, 1996–97; BBC TV, 1997–98; Granada TV, 1999–2001; Executive Producer: Princess Prodns, 2001–05; Objective Prodns, 2005–10, prodns incl. Derren Brown, The Cube; Hd of Entertainment, Channel 4, 2010–15. Recreations: theatre, film, marathon running, drumming. T: 07940 797579. E: justingorman@mac.com.

**GORMAN, Prof. Neil Thomson**, PhD; FRCVS; DL; Vice-Chancellor, Nottingham Trent University, 2003–14; b 10 Sept. 1950; s of George Stewart Gorman and Madge Isobella Gorman; m 1975, Susan Mary (née Smith); one s one d. Educ: Univ. of Liverpool (BVSc 1974); Wolfson Coll., Cambridge (PhD 1977; Hon. Fellow, 2006). MRCVS 1974, FRCVS 1980. Asst Prof., Univ. of Florida, 1980–84; Lectr in Clinical Vet. Medicine, Univ. of Cambridge, 1984–87; Prof. of Vet. Surgery, Univ. of Glasgow, 1987–93; Hd of Res., Waltham, 1993–97; European Dir of R&D, 1997, Vice-Pres. of R&D, 1997–99, Mars Europe; Vice-Pres. of R&D, Masterfoods Europe, 2000–01; Global Dir, Sci. and Technol. Platforms, Mars Inc., 2001–03. President: British Small Animal Vet. Assoc., 1992–93; RCVS, 1997–98. Diplomate: American Coll. of Vet. Internal Medicine, 1988; Eur. Coll. of Vet. Internal Medicine, 2005. DL Notts, 2007. Hon. DVMS Glasgow, 2004; Hon. DVSc Liverpool, 2006; Hon. DVetMed RVC, 2012. FRSA. Publications: Advances in Veterinary Immunology, vol. 1 1983, vol. 2 1985; Contemporary Issues in Small Animal Medicine, 1986; Clinical Veterinary Immunology, 1988, 2nd edn 1990; Basic and Applied Chemotherapy, 1992; Canine Medicine and Therapeutics, 1998; 150 scientific articles. Recreations: sport, golf, opera, ballet.

**GORMANSTON**, 17th Viscount cr 1478; **Jenico Nicholas Dudley Preston**; Baron Gormanston (Ire.), 1365; Baron Gormanston (UK), 1868; Premier Viscount of Ireland; b 19 Nov. 1939; s of 16th Viscount and Pamela (who m 2nd, 1943, M. B. O'Connor, Irish Guards; he d 1961, she d 1975), o d of late Capt. Dudley Hanly, and Lady Marjorie Heath (by her 1st marriage); S father, who was officially presumed killed in action, France, 9 June 1940; m 1st, 1974, Eva Antoine Landzianowska (d 1984); two s; 2nd, 1997, Lucy Arabella, former wife of David Grenfell and d of Edward Fox, qv and of Tracy Reed. Educ: Downside. Heir: s Hon. Jenico Francis Tara Preston [b 30 April 1974; m 2015, Kelly Catherine Reade; one s]. Address: 27A Ifield Road, SW10 9AZ.

**GORMLEY, Sir Antony (Mark David)**, Kt 2014; OBE 1998; RA 2003; sculptor; b London, 30 Aug. 1950; s of Arthur John Constantine Gormley and Elspeth Gormley (née Brauninger); m 1980, Vicken Parsons; two s one d. Educ: Trinity Coll., Cambridge (BA Hist. of Art; Hon. Fellow 2003); Central Sch. of Art, London; Goldsmiths' Sch. of Art, London (BA Fine Art; Hon. Fellow, Goldsmiths Coll., 1998); Slade Sch. of Fine Art (Boise travelling scholar, 1979). Mem., Arts Council England (formerly Arts Council of England), 1998–. Trustee: Baltic Centre for Contemp. Art, 2004–07; British Mus., 2007–15. Numerous solo exhibitions in Europe, America, Japan and Australia, 1980–, including: Whitechapel Art Gall., 1981; Louisiana Mus. of Modern Art, Denmark, 1989; American Field, US touring exhibn, 1991; Recent Iron Works, LA, 1992; Tate Gall., Liverpool, 1993; European Field, touring exhibn, 1993–95; Irish Mus. of Modern Art, Dublin, 1994; Lost Subject, White Cube, London, 1994; Escultura, Portugal, 1994; Field for the British Isles, GB tour, 1994–95, Hayward Gall., 1996, Gt Court Gall., BM, 2002 and Yorks Sculpture Park, 2005; Kohji Ogura Gall., Nagoya, 1995; Drawings, San Antonio, USA, 1995; Critical Mass, Vienna, 1995, RA, 1998; New Work, Sarajevo, 1996; Inside the Inside, Brussels, 1996; Arts 04, St Rémy de Provence, France, 1996; Still Moving, retrospective tour, Japan, 1996–97, Long Mus., Shanghai, 2017; Drawings 1990–94, Ind. Art Space, London, 1996; Cuxhaven, and Total Strangers, Cologne, 1997; Neue Skulpturen, Cologne, 1998; Insiders, Brussels, 1999; Intimate Relations, Ontario and Cologne, 1999; European Field, Malmö, 1999; Quantum Clouds, Paris, 2000; Asian Field, China tour, 2003, ICA Singapore, Sydney Biennial, 2006; Baltic Centre, Gateshead, 2003; Clearing, White Cube, London, 2004; Display, Tate Britain, 2004; New Works, Sean Kelly Gall., NY, 2005; Certain Made Places, Tokyo, 2005; Inside Australia, Melbourne, 2005; Altered States, Naples, 2006; Breathing Room, Paris, 2006; Blind Light, Hayward Gallery, Sean Kelly Gall., NY, 2007; Bodies in Space, Berlin, 2007; Feeling Material, Berlin, 2007; Ataxia, Melbourne, 2007; Firmament, White Cube, London, 2008; Acts, States, Times, Perspectives, Copenhagen, 2008; Another Singularity, Gall. Andersson Sandström, Sweden, 2008; Lot, Guernsey, 2008; Drawings 1981–2008, Galerie Ropac, Paris, 2008; Between You and Me, Kunsthal Rotterdam, Musée d'Art Moderne St Etienne, 2008; Antony Gormley, Museo de Arte Contemporáneo, Monterrey, Mexico, 2008; One and Other, Fourth Plinth, Trafalgar Square, 2009; Test Sites, White Cube, London, 2010; Event Horizon, Madison Sq. Art, NY, 2010; Memes, Melbourne, 2011; Flare II, Salisbury Cath., 2011; For the Time Being, Galerie Ropac, Paris, 2011; Two States, Harewood House, Yorks, 2011; Still Standing, State Hermitage Mus., St Petersburg, 2011; Space Station and other Instruments, Galleria Continua Le Moulin, France, 2011; Model, White Cube, London, 2012; Horizon Field Hamburg, Deichtorhallen, Hamburg, 2012; Vessel, Galleria Continua, San Gimignano, 2012; Still Being, Centro Cultural Banco do Brasil, Rio de Janeiro, 2012; Bodyspace, Sean Kelly Gall., NY, 2012; according to a given mean, Xavier Hufkens, Brussels, 2013; Meter, Galerie Thaddeus Ropac, Salzburg, 2013; State and Conditions, White Cube, Hong Kong, 2014; Human, Forte di Belvedere, Florence, 2015; Cast, Alan Cristea Gall., 2016; Fit, White Cube, London, 2016; Living Room, Xavier Hufkens, Brussels, 2017; Co-ordinate, Galleria Continua, San Gimignano, 2017; Being, Art Hall Foundn, Schloss Derneberg, 2017; Critical Mass and Expansion Field, Changsha Mus. of Art, 2017; Subject, Kettle's Yard, Cambridge, 2018; Earth Body, Galerie Thaddeus Ropac, Salzburg, 2018; Rooting the Synapse, White Cube, Hong Kong, 2018; Stand, Philadelphia Mus. of Art, USA, 2019; Essere, Uffizi Gall., Florence, 2019; RA, 2019; group exhibitions include: British Sculpture in the 20th Century, Whitechapel Art Gall., 1981; Biennale de Venezia, Venice, 1982 and 1986; An Internat. Survey of Recent Painting and Sculpture, Mus. of Modern Art, NY, 1984; Documenta 8, Kassel, 1987; Avant-garde in the Eighties, LA Co. Mus. of Art, 1987; Starlit Waters, Tate Gall., Liverpool, 1988; GB-USSR, Kiev, Moscow, 1990; British Art Now, touring Japan, 1990; Arte Amazonas, Rio de Janeiro, 1992, Berlin, 1993, Dresden, 1993, Aachen, 1993; From Beyond the Pale, Irish Mus. of Modern Art, Dublin, 1994; Un Siècle de Sculpture anglaise, Jeu de Paume, Paris, 1996; Malmö, Sweden, 1996; Sydney, Lisbon and Knislinge, Sweden, 1998; Presence, Liverpool, 1999; Trialogo, Rome, 2000; Tate Liverpool, 2004; Millennium Galls, Sheffield, 2005; Figure/Sculpture, Vienna, 2005; Henry Moore - Epoch and Echo, Künzelsau, Germany, 2005; Zero Degrees, Sadler's Wells, 2005; Space: Now & Then, Fundament Foundn, Tilburg, 2005; To the Human Future, Mito Contemporary Art Center, Japan, 2006; Asian Field, Sydney Biennale, 2006; 60 Years of Sculpture, Arts Council Collection, Yorks Sculpture Park, 2006; Turner Prize: a retrospective, Tate Britain, 2007; Reflection, Pinchuk Art Centre, Kiev, 2007; Fourth Plinth Proposals, Nat. Gall., 2008; Gravity:

Ernesto Esposito Collection, Spain, 2008; Genesis - The Art of Creation, Bern, Switzerland, 2008; Locked In, Luxembourg, 2008; History in the Making, Mori Art Mus., Tokyo, 2008; En Perspective, Giacometti, Musée des Beaux-Arts de Caen, 2008; Kivik Art 08, Kivik Art Centre, Sweden, 2008; Statuephilia, British Mus., 2008; Earth: Art of a Changing World, RA, 2009; Visceral Bodies, Vancouver Art Gall., 2010; XIV Internat. Sculpture Biennale of Carrara, Italy, 2010; A Serpentine Gesture and Other Prophecies, 49 Nord 6 Est Frac Lorraine, Metz, France, 2011; TRA: Edge of Becoming, Palazzo Fortuny, Venice, 2011; Summer Exhibn, Royal Acad. of Arts, 2011; Arte Torna Arte, Galleria dell'Accademia, Florence, 2012; Last Days of Pompeii, Getty Villa, Calif, 2012; Unlimited Bodies, Paris, 2012; Uncommon Ground, UK tour, 2013; Body and Void: Echoes of Henry Moore, Perry Green, 2014; Walk Through British Art, Tate Britain, 2015; From Life, Royal Acad. of Arts, 2017; A National Treasure: Fred Meijer, his Collection and Legacy, Frederik Meijer Gardens and Sculpture Park, USA, 2019; work in private and public collections worldwide, including: Tate Gall., London; Scottish Gall. of Modern Art, Edinburgh; Jesus Coll., Cambridge; Art Gall. of NSW, Sydney; Louisiana Mus., Denmark; Israel Mus., Jerusalem; Sapporo Sculpture Park, Hokkaido, Japan; Mus. of Contemporary Art, LA; MIT; Uffizi Gall., Florence; sculpture in public places: Out of the Dark, Kassel, Germany, 1987; Open Space, Rennes, France, 1993; Iron Man, Birmingham, 1994; Havmann, mo I Rana, Norway, 1995; Angel of the North, Gateshead, 1998 (Civic Trust Award, 2000); Quantum Cloud, Greenwich, 2000; Sound II, Winchester Cathedral, 2001; Planets, British Library, 2002; Inside Australia, Lake Ballard, Australia, 2003; Broken Column, Stavanger, Norway, 2003; Fai Spazio, Poggibonsi, Italy, 2004; Another Place, Crosby Beach, Liverpool, 2005; You, Roundhouse, London, 2006; Resolution, Shoe Lane, London, 2007; Event Horizon, S Bank, London, 2007; NY, 2010; Flare II, St Paul's Cathedral, 2010; Exposure, Edinburgh, 2010; 6 Times, Edinburgh, 2010; Horizon Field, Austria, 2010–12; Transport, Canterbury Cathedral, 2011; Sculpture in the City, London, 2013; Chord, MIT, Cambridge, USA, 2015. FRSA 2000. Hon. FRIBA 2001. Hon. doctorates incl. Sunderland, 1998; UCE, 1998; Open, 2001; Cambridge, 2003; Newcastle upon Tyne, 2004; Teesside, 2004; Liverpool, 2006; UCL, 2006. Turner Prize, 1994; South Bank Award, 1999; Bernard Heiliger Award for Sculpture, 2007; Praemium Imperiale (Japan), 2013.
*See also Sir P. B. Gormley.*

**GORMLEY, Sir (Paul) Brendan,** KCMG 2014; MBE 2001; international relief and development consultant, since 2012; Chairman, Communicating with Disaster Affected Communities Network, 2013–19; *b* 2 Sept. 1947; *s* of Arthur John Constantine Gormley and Elspeth Gormley; *m* 1974, Sally Henderson; two *s* one *d*. *Educ*: Strasbourg Univ. (Bacc. en Théologie); Trinity Coll., Cambridge (BA Social and Pol Scis 1973). OXFAM: Country Dir, Niger, 1976–78; Regl Dir, W Africa, 1978–83; Country Dir, Egypt, 1983–85; Asst to Overseas Dir, Evaluation Officer, Area Co-ordinator for Africa (N), HQ based, 1985–91; Africa Dir, 1991–2000; Chief Exec., Disasters Emergency Cttee, 2000–12. Lead Expert, Risk and Horizon Scanning Expert Gp, Govt Office for Sci., 2012–; Mem., Ind. Rev. Panel, Internat. Non-Govtl Orgns Accountability Charter, Berlin, 2013–14; Chm., Accountable Now (formerly Internat. Non-Govtl Orgns Accountability Charter Co.), 2014–19. Mem. Council, ODI, 2012–14. Trustee: Noel Buxton Trust, 2002–; One World Broadcasting Trust, 2004–16; Age Internat., 2012–18. FRSA 2012. *Publications:* (contrib.) Indigenous Knowledge System and Development, ed David Brokenshaw, 1980. *Recreations:* sailing, golf. *Address:* Foxburrow Barn, Hailey, Witney, Oxon OX29 9UH. *T:* (01993) 773592. *E:* gormley.dec@btinternet.com.
*See also Sir A. M. D. Gormley.*

**GORMLEY, Philip Michael Christopher,** QPM 2013; HM Inspector of Constabulary and Inspector of Fire & Rescue Authorities, since 2018; *b* Redhill, Surrey, 8 March 1963; *s* of Bernard John and Barbara Mary Gormley; *m* 1998, Claire Louise Stevens; one *d*. *Educ:* John Fisher Grammar Sch., Purley; Univ. of Gloucestershire (BA English and Hist.); Fitzwilliam Coll., Cambridge (Postgrad. Dip.). Comdr, Metropolitan Police, 2003–07; Dep. Chief Constable, W Midlands Police, 2007–10; Chief Constable, Norfolk Constabulary, 2010–13; Dep. Dir Gen., Nat. Crime Agency, 2013–15; Chief Constable, Police Scotland, 2016–18. *Recreations:* fly fishing, cycling, walking. *Clubs:* New, Royal Scots (Edinburgh).

**GORMLY, Allan Graham,** CMG 2005; CBE 1991; Chairman, BPB plc (formerly BPB Industries), 1997–2004 (Deputy Chairman, 1996–97; Director, 1995–2004); *b* 18 Dec. 1937; *s* of William Gormly and Christina Swinton Flockhart Arnot; *m* 1962, Vera Margaret Grant; one *s* one *d*. *Educ:* Paisley Grammar School. CA. Peat Marwick Mitchell & Co., 1955–61; Rootes Group, 1961–65; John Brown PLC, 1965–68; Brownlee & Co. Ltd, 1968–70; John Brown PLC, 1970: Finance Director, John Brown Engineering Ltd, 1970–77; Director, Planning and Control, John Brown PLC, 1977–80; Dep. Chairman, John Brown Engineers and Constructors Ltd, 1980–83; Gp Man. Dir, John Brown PLC, 1983–92; Chief Exec., Trafalgar House, 1992–94 (Dir, 1986–95); Dir, 1990–96, Dep. Chm., 1992–94, Chm., 1994–96, Royal Insce Hldgs; Dir and Dep. Chm., Royal & Sun Alliance, 1996–98. Chm., Q-One Biotech Ltd, 1999–2003; Director: Brixton Estates, subseq. Brixton plc, 1994–2003 (Chm., 2000–03); European Capital Co., 1996–2000; Bank of Scotland, 1997–2001. Chm., Overseas Projects Bd, 1988–91; Dep. Chm., Export Guarantees Adv. Council, 1990–92; Member: BOTB, 1988–92; Review Body on Top Salaries, 1990–92; FCO Bd of Mgt, 2000–04. *Recreations:* golf, music. *Address:* 56 North Park, Gerrards Cross, Bucks SL9 8JR.

**GORRINGE, Christopher John,** CBE 1999; Chief Executive, All England Lawn Tennis and Croquet Club, Wimbledon, 1983–2005; *b* 13 Dec. 1945; *s* of late Maurice Sydney William Gorringe and Hilda Joyce Gorringe; *m* 1976, Jennifer Mary Chamberlain; two *d*. *Educ:* Bradfield Coll., Berks; Royal Agricl Coll., Cirencester. MRICS. Asst Land Agent, Iveagh Trustees Ltd (Guinness family), 1968–73; Asst Sec., 1973–79, Sec., 1979–83, All England Lawn Tennis and Croquet Club. Hon. Fellow, Roehampton Univ. (formerly Univ. of Surrey, Roehampton), 1998. *Publications:* Holding Court, 2009. *Recreations:* lawn tennis, golf. *Clubs:* All England Lawn Tennis and Croquet, International Lawn Tennis of GB, Queen's, St George's Hill Lawn Tennis, Rye Lawn Tennis (Pres.), Jesters.

**GORRINGE, Rev. Prof. Timothy Jervis;** St Luke's Professor of Theological Studies, University of Exeter, 1998–2013; *b* 12 Aug. 1946; *s* of R. C. and M. V. Gorringe; *m* 1st, 1972, Carol (*née* James) (*d* 2004); one *s* two *d*; 2nd, 2008, Gill (*née* Westcott). *Educ:* St Edmund Hall, Oxford (BA 1969); Univ. of Leeds (MPhil 1975); DD (Oxon) 2008. Ordained deacon, 1972, priest, 1973; Curate, St Matthew's, Chapel Allerton, 1972–75; Chaplain, Wadham Coll., Oxford, 1975–78; Lectr, Tamil Nadu Theol Seminary, India, 1979–86; Chaplain, Fellow and Tutor in Theol., St John's Coll., Oxford, 1986–95; Reader in Contextual Theol., Univ. of St Andrews, 1995–98. *Publications:* Redeeming Time, 1986; Discerning Spirit, 1990; God's Theatre: a theology of Providence, 1991; Capital and the Kingdom: theological ethics and economic order, 1994; Alan Ecclestone: priest as revolutionary, 1994; God's Just Vengeance: crime, violence and the rhetoric of salvation, 1996; The Sign of Love: reflections on the Eucharist, 1997; Karl Barth: against hegemony, 1999; The Education of Desire, 2001; A Theology of the Built Environment, 2002; Furthering Humanity: a theology of culture, 2004; Crime, 2004; Harvest: food, farming and the churches, 2006; The Common Good and the Global Emergency, 2011; Earthly Visions: theology and the challenges of art, 2011; (jtly) Transition Movement for Churches: a prophetic imperative for today, 2013; The World Made Otherwise, 2018. *Recreations:* bee keeping, wine-making, vegetable gardening, folk music, smallholding. *Address:* Venbridge House, Cheriton Bishop, Devon EX6 6HD. *T:* (01647) 24789. *E:* T.J.Gorringe@exeter.ac.uk.

**GORT,** 9th Viscount *cr* 1816 (Ire.); **Foley Robert Standish Prendergast Vereker;** Baron Kiltarton 1810; photographer; *b* 24 Oct. 1951; *er s* of 8th Viscount Gort and Bettine Mary Mackenzie, *d* of Godfrey Greene; *S* father, 1995; *m* 1st, 1979, Julie Denise Jones (marr. diss. 1984); 2nd, 1991, Sharon Quayle; one *s* one *d*. *Educ:* Harrow. *Recreation:* golf. *Heir: s* Robert Foley Prendergast Vereker, *b* 5 April 1993. *Address:* 9 Arbory Road, Castletown, Isle of Man IM9 1NA. *T:* (01624) 822295.

**GOSCHEN,** family name of **Viscount Goschen**.

**GOSCHEN,** 4th Viscount *cr* 1900; **Giles John Harry Goschen;** with Korn/Ferry International, since 2005; *b* 16 Nov. 1965; *s* of 3rd Viscount Goschen, KBE, and Alvin Moyana Lesley, *yr d* of late Harry England, Durban, Natal; *S* father, 1977; *m* 1991, Sarah Penelope, *d* of late Alan Horsnail; one *s* two *d*. *Educ:* Eton. A Lord in Waiting (Govt Whip), 1992–94; Parly Under-Sec. of State, Dept of Transport, 1994–97; elected Mem., H of L, 1999. With Deutsche Bank, 1997–2000; Dir, Barchester Advisory, 2000–02. *Heir: s* Hon. Alexander John Edward Goschen, *b* 5 Oct. 2001.

**GOSCHEN, Sir Edward (Alexander),** 4th Bt *cr* 1916 of Beacon Lodge, Highcliffe, co. Southampton; *b* 13 March 1949; *s* of Sir Edward Goschen, 3rd Bt, DSO and Cynthia, *d* of Rt Hon. Sir Alexander Cadogan, OM, GCMG, KCB, PC; *S* father, 2001; *m* 1976, Louise Annette (*d* 2006), *d* of Lt-Col R. F. L. Chance, MC and Lady Ava Chance; one *d*. *Educ:* Eton. *Heir:* cousin Sebastian Bernard Goschen, *b* 1 Jan. 1959.

**GOSDEN, Prof. Christine Margaret,** PhD; FRCPath; Professor of Medical Genetics, University of Liverpool, 1993; *b* 25 April 1945; *d* of George G. H. Ford and Helena P. S. Ford; *m* 1971, Dr John Gosden. *Educ:* Univ. of Edinburgh (BSc Hons; PhD 1971). MRCPath, FRCPath. Res. Fellow, Univ. of Edinburgh, 1971–73; Mem., MRC Sen. Scientific Staff, MRC Human Genetics Unit, Western Gen. Hosp., Edinburgh, 1973–93; Vis. Prof. in Human Genetics, Harris Birthright Centre for Fetal Medicine, and Dept of Obstetrics and Gynaecology, King's Coll. Hosp. Sch. of Medicine and Dentistry, 1987–93; Hon. Consultant, Liverpool Women's Hosp., 1993. Mem., HFEA, 1996. Researcher, scriptwriter, co-presenter, etc of films (incl. contrib. to TV series Dispatches (Saddam's Secret Time Bomb) and 60 Minutes, 1998) and author of articles on med. effects of chemical and biological weapons use. *Publications:* (jtly) Is My Baby All Right?, 1994; numerous scientific papers, articles and contribs to books on human genetics, fetal medicine, mental illness, childhood and adult cancers and med. effects of chemical and biological weapons. *Recreations:* campaigner for human rights, whalewatching, alpine gardening, organ and harpsichord music, modern poetry.

**GOSDEN, Prof. Christopher Hugh,** PhD; FBA 2005; FAHA; Professor of European Archaeology, University of Oxford, since 2006; Fellow, Keble College, Oxford, since 2006; *b* 6 Sept. 1955; *s* of Hugh and Margaret Gosden; *m* 1992, Jane Kaye; one *s* one *d*. *Educ:* Univ. of Sheffield (BA 1977; PhD 1983). Vis. Fellow, ANU, 1984–85; Lectr, then Sen. Lectr, Dept of Archaeol., La Trobe Univ., Melbourne, 1986–93; Oxford University: Lectr, 1994–2004, Prof. of Archaeology, 2004–06, Hd, 2004–07, Sch. of Archaeol.; Curator, Pitt Rivers Museum, 1994–2006; Fellow, St Cross Coll., 1994–2006. Trustee, BM, 2018–. FAHA 2016. *Publications:* Social Being and Time: an archaeological perspective, 1994; Archaeology and Anthropology: a changing relationship, 1999; (with J. Hather) The Prehistory of Food, 1999; (with C. Knowles) Collecting Colonialism: material culture and colonial change in Papua New Guinea, 2001; Prehistory: a very short introduction, 2003; Archaeology and Colonialism, 2004; (with F. Larson) Knowing Things: exploring the collections of the Pitt Rivers Museum, 2007; (with D. Garrow) Technology of Enchantment, 2012; papers and monographs. *Recreations:* reading, running, travel. *Address:* School of Archaeology, 34 Beaumont Street, Oxford OX1 2PG. *T:* (01865) 278240, *Fax:* (01865) 278254. *E:* chris.gosden@arch.ox.ac.uk.

**GOSDEN, John Harry Martin,** OBE 2017; racehorse trainer; *b* 30 March 1951; *s* of late John Montague Gosden and Peggie Gosden; *m* 1982, Rachel Dene Serena Hood; two *s* two *d*. *Educ:* Eastbourne Coll.; Emmanuel Coll., Cambridge (MA; athletics blue, 1970–73). Member: Cambridge Univ. Athletics Team, 1970; British Under-23 Rowing Squad, 1973. Assistant trainer to: Noel Murless, 1974–76; Vincent O'Brien, 1976–77; trainer, USA, 1979–88: trained 8 State champions, Calif, 3 Eclipse Award winners; in top 10 US trainers throughout 1980s; England, 1989–: by 2015, over 3000 UK winners (fastest 1000 winners trained in UK); over 300 Group Stakes winners, incl. Derby (Benny the Dip, 1997, Golden Horn, 2015), St Leger, English and French 1000 Guineas, Prix de l'Arc de Triomphe, Breeders' Cup Turf; winners trained include: Shantou, 1996, Lucarno, 2007, Arctic Cosmos, 2010, Masked Marvel, 2011, St Leger; Raven's Pass, Breeders' Cup Classic, 2008; two-year-old Breeders' Cup winners, Donativum, 2008, Pounced, 2009; Dar Re Mi, Dubai Sheema Classic, 2010; Debussy, Arlington Million, 2010; Duncan, Irish St Leger, 2011; Nathaniel, King George & Queen Elizabeth Diamond Stakes, 2011; Eclipse Stakes, 2012; Great Heavens, Irish Oaks, 2012; Fallen for You, Coronation Stakes, 2012; The Fugue, Irish Champion Stakes, 2013, Yorkshire Oaks, 2013, Prince of Wales Stakes, 2014; Seek Again, Hollywood Derby, 2013; Elusive Kate, Falmouth Stakes and Prix Rothschild, 2013; Champion Miler, Kingman, 2014; Champion Classic Filly, Taghrooda, Epsom Oaks, King George & Queen Elizabeth Diamond Stakes, 2014; Star of Seville, Prix de Diane, 2015; Jack Hobbs, Irish Derby, 2015; Golden Horn, Derby, Eclipse Stakes, Irish Champion Stakes, Prix de l'Arc de Triomphe, 2015; Journey, British Champions Fillies and Mares Stakes, 2016; Enable, Epsom Oaks, Irish Oaks, King George & Queen Elizabeth Diamond Stakes, Yorkshire Oaks, Prix de l'Arc de Triomphe, 2017, 2018, Breeders' Cup Turf, 2018; Jack Hobbs, Dubai Sheema Classic, 2017; Cracksman, Champion Stakes, 2017, 2018 (Jt World Champion, 2018); Stradivarius, Goodwood Cup, 2017, 2018, Ascot Gold Cup, Million Bonus Stayer, 2018; Persuasive, Queen Elizabeth II Stakes, 2017; Roaring Lion, Eclipse Stakes, Juddmonte Internat. Stakes, Irish Champion Stakes, Queen Elizabeth II Stakes, 2018; Too Darn Hot, Dewhurst Stakes, 2018; leading trainer at Royal Ascot, 6 winners, 2012; champion flat racing trainer, 2012, 2015, 2018. Trustee, Horatio's Garden, 2016–; Patron, Spinal Res. Trust, 1992–. *Recreations:* opera, polo, ski-ing, environmental issues. *Address:* Clarehaven Stables, Bury Road, Newmarket, Suffolk CB8 7BY.

**GOSDEN, Prof. Roger Gordon;** Professor, and Director of Research in Reproductive Biology, Weill Medical College, Cornell University, 2004–10; Owner and Director, Jamestowne Bookworks LLC, Williamsburg, Virginia, since 2012; *b* 23 Sept. 1948; *s* of Gordon Conrad Jason Gosden and Peggy (*née* Butcher); *m* 1st, 1971, Carole Ann Walsh (marr. diss. 2003); two *s*; 2nd, 2004, Lucinda Leigh Veeck. *Educ:* Bristol Univ. (BSc); Darwin Coll., Cambridge (PhD 1974); Edinburgh Univ. (DSc 1989). CBiol, FRSB (FIBiol 1987). MRC Fellow, Physiological Lab., Cambridge, 1973–74, 1975–76; Population Council Fellow, Duke Univ., N Carolina, 1974–75; Lectr and Sen. Lectr and Dep. Head, Dept of Physiol., Edinburgh Univ. Med. Sch., 1976–94; Prof. of Reproductive Biol., Leeds Univ., 1994–99; Hon. Consultant, Leeds Gen. Infirmary and St James's Univ. Hosp., Leeds, 1994–99; Res. Dir, Dept of Obstetrics and Gynecology, McGill Univ., Montreal,

1999–2001; The Howard and Georgeanna Jones Prof. of Reproductive Med., and Scientific Dir, Jones Inst. for Reproductive Med., Eastern Virginia Med. Sch., 2001–04. Guest Scientist: Univ. of Southern California, 1979, 1980, 1981, 1987; Univ. of Naples, 1989; Visiting Professor: Univ. of Washington, Seattle, 1999; Univ. of Leeds, 1999–2003; Sun Yat-Sen Univ. (Guangzhou), China, 2005–08; Adjunct Prof., McGill Univ., 2001–08; Visiting Scholar, Coll. of William and Mary, Va, 2017–. Scientific conf. organiser. Mem., Bd of Prison Visitors, Wetherby, 1996–99. Elder, Church of Scotland, 1982–. FRSA 1996. Occasional broadcasts. *Publications:* Biology of Menopause, 1985; Cheating Time, 1996; Transplantation of Ovarian and Testicular Tissues, 1996; Designer Babies, 1999; (ed jtly) Biology and Pathology of the Oocyte, 2003, 2nd edn 2013; (ed jtly) Preservation of Fertility, 2004; (ed with P. Walker) A Surgeon's Story: the autobiography of Robert T. Morris, 2013; A Biologist in Paradise, 2017; Letters from a Biologist in Paradise, 2019; Let There Be Life: an intimate portrait of Robert Edwards and his IVF revolution, 2019; technical articles and contribs to popular press. *Recreations:* Virginia Master Naturalist, creative writing, science writing and publishing. *Address:* Shire House, 107 Paddock Lane, Williamsburg, VA 23188, USA. *W:* http://rogergosden.com.

**GOSFORD,** 7th Earl of, *cr* 1806; **Charles David Nicholas Alexander John Sparrow Acheson;** Bt (NS) 1628; Baron Gosford 1776; Viscount Gosford 1785; Baron Worlingham (UK) 1835; Baron Acheson (UK) 1847; *b* 13 July 1942; *o s* of 6th Earl of Gosford, OBE, and Francesca Augusta (*d* 2009), *er d* of Francesco Cagiati, New York; *S* father, 1966; *m* 1983, Lynnette Redmond. *Educ:* Harrow; Byam Shaw Sch. of drawing and painting; Royal Academy Schs. Chm., Artists Union, 1976–80; Mem. Visual Arts Panel, Greater London Arts Assoc., 1976–77; Council Member, British Copyright Council, 1977–80. Represented by: Barry Stern Gall., Sydney; Phillip Bacon Galls, Brisbane; Solander Gall., Canberra; Von Bertouch Gall., Newcastle, NSW. *Heir:* cousin Hon. Nicholas Hope Carter [*b* 29 Oct. 1957; *m* 1983, Patricia, *d* of James Beckford, Jacksonville Beach, Florida; one *s* one *d*].

**GOSKIRK, (William) Ian (Macdonald),** CBE 1986; Partner, Coopers & Lybrand Deloitte, 1990–92; *b* 2 March 1932; *s* of William Goskirk and Flora Macdonald; *m* 1969, Hope Ann Knaizuk; one *d*. *Educ:* Carlisle Grammar Sch.; Queen's Coll., Oxford (MA). Served REME, 1950–52. Shell Internat. Petroleum, 1956–74; Anschutz Corp., 1974–76; BNOC, 1976–85; Man. Dir, BNOC Trading, 1980–82; Chief Exec., BNOC, 1982–85; Dir, Coopers & Lybrand Associates, 1986–90. *Recreation:* gardening.

**GOSLING, Allan Gladstone;** Sales Director, PSA Projects, Property Services Agency, Department of the Environment, 1991–92, retired (Operational Director, 1990–91); Consultant to TBV Consult, 1992–95; *b* 4 July 1933; *s* of late Gladstone Gosling and of Elizabeth Gosling (*née* Ward); *m* 1961, Janet Pamela (*née* Gosling) (*d* 2015); one *s* one *d*. *Educ:* Kirkham Grammar Sch.; Birmingham Sch. of Architecture. DipArch; RIBA 1961; FRIAS 1988 (RIAS 1984); FFB 1991. Asst Architect, Lancs County Council, 1950–54; Birmingham Sch. of Architecture, 1954–57; Surman Kelly Surman, Architects, 1957–59; Royal Artillery, 1959–61; Army Works Organisation, 1961–63; Min. of Housing R&D Group, 1963–68; Suptg Architect, Birmingham Regional Office, Min. of Housing, 1968–72; Regional Works Officer, NW Region, PSA, 1972–76; Midland Regional Dir, PSA, 1976–83; Dir, Scottish Services, PSA, 1983–90. *Recreations:* walking, gardening, watercolour painting, DIY. *Address:* 11 The Moorlands, Four Oaks Park, Sutton Coldfield, West Midlands B74 2RF.

**GOSLING, Sir Donald,** KCVO 2004; Kt 1976; Joint Chairman, National Car Parks Ltd (formerly Central Car Parks), 1950–98; Chairman, Palmer & Harvey Ltd, since 1967; *b* 2 March 1929; *s* of Maisie Jordan; *m* 1959, Elizabeth Shauna (marr. diss. 1988), *d* of Dr Peter Ingram and Lecky Ingram; three *s*. Joined RN, 1944; served Mediterranean, HMS Leander. Mem., Council of Management, White Ensign Assoc. Ltd, 1970– (Chm., 1978–83; Vice Pres., 1983–93; Pres., 1993–); Mem., Exec. Cttee, Imperial Soc. of Kts Bachelor, 1977– (Hon. Dep. Kt Principal, 2007–). Chm., Berkeley Square Ball Trust, 1982–; Trustee: Fleet Air Arm Museum, Yeovilton, 1974–2000 (Chm., Mountbatten Meml Hall Appeals Cttee, 1980); RYA Seamanship Foundn, 1981–; Vice Pres., Seafarers UK (formerly King George's Fund for Sailors), 1993–; Patron: Submarine Meml Appeal, 1978–; HMS Ark Royal Welfare Trust, 1986–. Hon. Capt., 1993, Hon. Cdre, 2005, Hon. Rear Adm., 2009, Vice Adm. of the UK, 2012, Hon. Vice Adm., 2015, RNR. Younger Brother, Trinity House, 1998. Pres., TS Saumarez Sea Cadets, 1989–. Freeman, City of London, 1979; Hon. Freeman, Shipwrights' Co., 2007–. Mem., Grand Order of Water Rats, 1999. Hon. Dr Maritime Studies Southampton Solent, 2014. KJStJ 2009. *Recreations:* swimming, sailing, shooting. *Address:* (office) 21 Bryanston Street, Marble Arch, W1H 7PR. *T:* (020) 7499 7050. *Clubs:* Royal Thames Yacht, Royal London Yacht, Royal Naval Sailing Association, Thames Sailing, Royal Yacht Squadron; Saints and Sinners.

**GOSLING, Jonathan Vincent Ronald; His Honour Judge Gosling;** a Circuit Judge, since 2009; *b* Codsall, 28 April 1957; *s* of Gerard and Eileen Gosling; *m* 1987, Suzanne Kidson; two *s*. *Educ:* Ampleforth; Univ. of Wolverhampton (BA Law). Called to the Bar, Middle Temple, 1980; Standing Counsel, UK Register of Canine Behavourists, 1993–2009; Actg Stipendiary Magistrate, 1997–2004; Recorder, 2000–09. *Recreations:* calligraphy, classic cars, game shooting, smallholding. *Address:* c/o Stafford Combined Court, Victoria Square, Stafford ST16 2QQ. *T:* (01785) 610730.

**GOSLING, Justin Cyril Bertrand;** Principal, St Edmund Hall, Oxford, 1982–96; *b* 26 April 1930; *s* of Vincent and Dorothy Gosling; *m* 1958, Margaret Clayton; two *s* two *d*. *Educ:* Ampleforth Coll.; Wadham Coll., Oxford (BPhil, MA). Univ. of Oxford: Fereday Fellow, St John's Coll., 1955–58; Lectr in Philosophy, Pembroke Coll. and Wadham Coll., 1958–60; Fellow in Philosophy, St Edmund Hall, 1960–82; Sen. Proctor, 1977–78. Barclay Acheson Prof., Macalester Coll., Minnesota, 1964; Vis. Res. Fellow, ANU, Canberra, 1970 (Pro-Vice-Chancellor, 1989–95). *Publications:* Pleasure and Desire, 1969; Plato, 1973; (ed) Plato, Philebus, 1975; (with C. C. W. Taylor) The Greeks on Pleasure, 1982; Weakness of the Will, 1990; The Jackdaw in the Jacaranda, 2008; articles in Mind, Phil Rev. and Proc. Aristotelian Soc. *Recreations:* gardening, intaglio printing, recorder music. *Address:* 124 Caldecott Road, Abingdon, Oxon OX14 5EP.

**GOSLING, Prof. (Leonard) Morris,** PhD; CBiol, FRSB; Professor of Animal Behaviour, University of Newcastle, 1999–2008, now Emeritus; *b* 22 Jan. 1943; *s* of William Richard Gosling and Marian (*née* Morris); *m* 1977, Dr Marion Petrie; two *d*. *Educ:* Wymondham Coll., Norfolk; Queen Mary Coll., London (BSc Zool. 1965); University Coll., Nairobi (PhD 1975). CBiol, FRSB (FIBiol 1989). Ministry of Agriculture, Fisheries and Food: SSO, Coypu Res. Lab., 1970–73; PSO, Mammal Ecology Gp, 1974–85; SPSO, Central Science Lab., 1986–93; Dir of Sci., Zool Soc. of London and Dir, Inst. of Zool., 1993–99. Hon. Lectr, UEA, 1978–81; Vis. Prof., UCL, 1994–99. Leader, Mt Zebra Project, Namibia Nature Foundn 2005–. Member, Council: Mammal Soc., 1982–85; Assoc. for Study of Animal Behaviour, 1988–90 (Sec., Ethical Cttee, 1991–94); Royal Vet. Coll., 1994–99; Mem., Mgt Cttee, UCL Centre for Ecology and Evolution, 1995–99. *Publications:* (ed with M. Dawkins) Ethics in Research on Animal Behaviour, 1992; (ed with W. J. Sutherland) Behaviour and Conservation, 2000; numerous articles in learned jls and books on population biol. and behavioural ecology. *Recreations:* ditching, drawing, birdwatching, formerly Rugby. *Address:* School of Natural and Environmental Sciences, University of Newcastle, Newcastle upon Tyne NE1 7RU. *E:* l.m.gosling@ncl.ac.uk.

**GOSNELL, Mark; His Honour Judge Gosnell;** a Senior Circuit Judge, since 2010; Designated Civil Judge for Leeds and North Yorkshire, since 2010, and for Bradford Group of Courts, since 2012; *b* Hyde, Cheshire, 23 Sept. 1957; *s* of Peter and Shirley Gosnell; *m* 2009, Sarah Jane Pritchard; one *s* one *d*. *Educ:* St Mary's Coll., Blackburn; Christ's Coll., Cambridge (BA 1978). Admitted Solicitor, 1981; Solicitor, Woodcocks, 1981–98; Dist Judge, 1998–2010; Recorder, 2005–10. *Recreations:* watching Burnley Football Club, playing guitar. *Address:* Leeds Combined Court Centre, Oxford Row, Leeds LS1 3BG. *T:* (0113) 306 2740. *E:* HHJ.Mark.Gosnell@ejudiciary.net. *Club:* Kimberley (Bacup).

**GOSS, Hon. Sir James Richard William;** Kt 2014; **Hon. Mr Justice Goss;** a Judge of the High Court, Queen's Bench Division, since 2014; *b* 12 May 1953; *s* of His Honour Judge William Alan Belcher Goss and of Yvonne Goss; *m* 1982; two *s* three *d*. *Educ:* Charterhouse; University Coll., Durham (BA). Called to the Bar, Inner Temple, 1975, Bencher, 2002; Recorder, 1994–2009; QC 1997; Circuit Judge, 2009–11; Senior Circuit Judge and Hon. Recorder of Newcastle upon Tyne, 2011–14; Presiding Judge, North Eastern Circuit, 2016–. Vis. Fellow, Law Sch., Durham Univ., 2018. *Address:* Royal Courts of Justice, Strand, WC2A 2LL.

**GOSS-CUSTARD, Rakhi;** non-executive Director: Rightmove plc, since 2014; Kingfisher plc, since 2016; Schroders plc, since 2017; *b* Connecticut, 9 April 1974; *d* of Kishor Parekh and Pushpa Parekh; *m* 2006, Daniel Goss-Custard; one *s* one *d*. *Educ:* Univ. of Pennsylvania (BA Mktg and Communications and Sociol. 1996). Associate, Oliver Wyman, 1996–2000; Product Manager, TomTom, 2000–01; Amazon: Sen. Product Manager, UK Books, 2002–04; Gp Product Manager, UK Media Demand, 2004–06; Dir, UK Entertainment Demand, 2006–07; Dir, UK Music and DVD, 2007–09; Consultant Advr, Zappos, 2009–10; Dir, UK Hardlines, 2010–13; Dir, UK Media, 2013–14. Owner, Stanlake Park Wine Estate, 2013–. Gov., Lambrook Prep. Sch., 2019–. Mem., Pilgrims Soc. *Recreations:* walking, reading, family. *Address:* The Manor House, Stanlake Park, Twyford RG10 0BN. *T:* 07891 880132. *E:* rakhip@gmail.com.

**GOSSCHALK, His Honour Joseph Bernard;** a Circuit Judge, 1991–2007; *b* 27 Aug. 1936; *s* of late Lionel Samuel Gosschalk and of Johanna (*née* Lion); *m* 1973, Ruth Sandra Jarvis; two *d*. *Educ:* East Ham Grammar Sch.; Magdalen Coll., Oxford (MA Jurisprudence). Called to the Bar, Gray's Inn, 1961; Asst Recorder, 1983–87; Head of Chambers, Francis Taylor Bldg, Temple, EC4, 1983–91; a Recorder, SE Circuit, 1987–91. *Recreations:* theatre, reading, foreign travel.

**GOSTIN, Prof. Lawrence,** DJur; O'Neill Professor of Global Health Law, Georgetown University Law Center, since 1994, Faculty Director, O'Neill Institute for National and Global Health Law, since 2005, and University Professor, since 2012, Georgetown University; Professor of Health Policy, Johns Hopkins School of Public Health (formerly Hygiene and Public Health), since 1994; Director, World Health Organization Collaborating Center on Public Health Law and Human Rights, since 2006; *b* 19 Oct. 1949; *s* of Joseph and Sylvia Gostin; *m* 1977, Jean Catherine Allison; two *s*. *Educ:* State Univ. of New York, Brockport (BA Psychology); Duke Univ. (DJur 1974). Dir of Forensics and Debate, Duke Univ., 1973–74; Fulbright Fellow, Social Res. Unit, Univ. of London, 1974–75; Legal Dir, MIND (Nat. Assoc. for Mental Health), 1975–83; Gen. Sec., NCCL, 1983–85; Harvard University: Sen. Fellow of Health Law, 1985–86; Lectr, 1986–87; Adjunct Prof. in Health Law, Sch. of Public Health, 1988–94; Exec. Dir, Amer. Soc. of Law and Medicine, 1986–94. Legal Counsel in series of cases before Eur. Commn and Eur. Court of Human Rights, 1974–. Vis. Prof., Sch. of Social Policy, McMaster Univ., 1978–79; Vis. Fellow in Law and Psychiatry, Centre for Criminological Res., Oxford Univ., 1982–83. Chm., Advocacy Alliance, 1981–83; Member: National Cttee, UN Internat. Year for Disabled People, 1981; Legal Affairs Cttee, Internat. League of Socs for Mentally Handicapped People, 1980–; Cttee of Experts, Internat. Commn of Jurists to draft UN Human Rights Declarations, 1982–; Adv. Council, Interights, 1984–; AE Trust, 1984–85; WHO Expert Cttee on Guidelines on the Treatment of Drug and Alcohol Dependent Persons, 1985; WHO Steering Cttee, Internat. Ethical Guidelines for Human Population Res., 1990–; Nat. Bd of Dirs, Amer. Civil Liberties Union, 1986– (Mem. Exec. Cttee, 1988–); Nat. Cancer Adv. Bd, Nat. Cancer Inst., US, 2017–. Mem., Inst. of Medicine, NAS, 2000. FRSPH, 2013–. Western European and UK Editor, Internat. Jl of Law and Psychiatry, 1978–81; Exec. Ed., Amer. Jl of Law and Medicine, 1986–; Ed.-in-chief, Jl of Law, Medicine and Health Care, 1986–; Global Health Ed., Jl of Amer. Med. Assoc., 2018–. Hon. LLD: SUNY, 1994; Sydney, 2012; Hon. SJD Sydney, 2014. Rosemary Delbridge Meml Award for most outstanding contribution to social policy, 1983; Lifetime Achievement Award, APHA, 2015. *Publications:* A Human Condition: vol. 1, 1975; vol. 2, 1977; A Practical Guide to Mental Health Law, 1983; The Court of Protection, 1983; (ed) Secure Provision: a review of special services for mentally ill and handicapped people in England and Wales, 1985; Mental Health Services: law and practice, 1986; Human Rights in Mental Health: an international report for the World Federation for Mental Health, 1988; Civil Liberties in Conflict, 1988; Surrogate Motherhood: politics and privacy, 1990; AIDS and the Health Care System, 1990; Implementing the Americans with Disabilities Act: rights and responsibilities of all Americans, 1993; Rights of Persons who are HIV Positive, 1996; Human Rights and Public Health in the AIDS Pandemic, 1997; Public Health Law: power, duty, restraint, 2000, 3rd edn 2016; Public Health Law and Ethics: a reader, 2002, 3rd edn 2017; The Human Rights of Persons with Intellectual Disabilities: different but equal, 2003; The AIDS Pandemic: complacency, injustice and unfulfilled expectations, 2004; Public Health Ethics, 2007; Biosecurity in the Global Age, 2008; Principles of Mental Health Law and Policy, 2010; Global Health Law, 2014; (ed) Human Rights in Global Health: rights-based governance in a globalizing world, 2018; articles in learned jls. *Recreations:* family outings, walking on the mountains and fells of the Lake District. *Address:* Georgetown University Law Center, 600 New Jersey Avenue NW, Washington, DC 20001–2075, USA. *T:* (202) 6629373.

**GOSWAMI, Prof. Usha Claire,** DPhil; FBA 2013; Professor of Cognitive Developmental Neuroscience, Department of Psychology (formerly Department of Experimental Psychology), University of Cambridge, since 2010 (Professor of Education, 2003–10); Fellow, St John's College, Cambridge, 1990–97 and since 2003; *b* 21 Feb. 1960; *d* of late Roshan Lal Goswami and of Elisabeth Irene Goswami (*née* Zenner); *m* 1995, Mark Thomson (marr. diss. 2004); one *d*. *Educ:* St John's Coll., Oxford (BA Hons Exptl Psychol.; DPhil Psychol.); Univ. of London Inst. of Educn (PGCE Primary Educn). Res. Fellow, Merton Coll., Oxford, 1986–87 and 1988–89; Harkness Fellow, Univ. of Illinois, 1987–88; Lectr in Exptl Psychol., Univ. of Cambridge, 1990–97; Prof. of Cognitive Develtl Psychol., UCL, 1997–2002. Leverhulme Major Res. Fellow, 2009–11. AcSS 2004; FRSA; Fellow, Assoc. for Psychol Sci., 2009. *Publications:* (with P. Bryant) Phonological Skills and Learning to Read, 1990; Analogical Reasoning in Children, 1992; Cognition in Children, 1997; (ed) Blackwell Handbook of Childhood Cognitive Development, 2002, 2nd edn, 2010; (ed) Cognitive Development, 2007; Cognitive Development: the learning brain, 2008; (ed jtly) Mental Capital and Wellbeing, 2009; Child Psychology: a very short introduction, 2014; contrib. papers to scientific jls. *Recreations:* enjoying my daughter, travel, reading. *Address:* St John's College, Cambridge CB2 1TP. *T:* (01223) 338600, *Fax:* (01223) 337720. *E:* ucg10@cam.ac.uk.

**GOTO, Prof. John Philip**; artist; Professor of Fine Art, University of Derby, 2003–13, now Emeritus; b Stockport, 11 Feb. 1949; s of late Bernard Glithero and Catherine Glithero (née Craig); changed name by Deed Poll to Goto; m 1st, 1972, Linda Gowan (marr. diss. 1985); two d; 2nd, 1992, Celia Agnes Farrelly. Educ: Windsor Grammar Sch.; Berkshire Coll. of Art; St Martin's Sch. of Art (BA Hons Fine Art (Painting)); Ecole de Louis Lumière, Paris and Acad. of Performing Arts, Prague (British Council Schol. in Photography). Lectr, Oxford Brookes Univ., 1981–99. Visiting Lecturer: Poly. of Central London, 1979–87; Ruskin Sch. of Drawing and Fine Art, Univ. of Oxford, 1987–2002, and numerous art schs in UK and abroad. Artist Fellow, Girton Coll. and Kettle's Yard, Univ. of Cambridge, 1988–89; Artist-in-Residence, NPG, 1999–2000. Panellist, 1986–89, Vice Chair, 1989–90, Visual Arts Panel, Southern Arts Assoc.; Adv. Panellist, John Hansard Gall., Univ. of Southampton, 1991–96. Solo exhibitions include: Goto, Photographs 1971–81, Photographers' Gall., London, 1981; Goto, Photographs 1975–83, PPS Galerie Gundlac, Hamburg, ULUV Gall., Prague, Moravian Gall., Bruno and tour of Spain, 1983–85; Sites of Passage, Ashmolean Mus., Oxford, 1988; Terezin, Raab Gall., Berlin, John Hansard Gall., Univ. of Southampton, Cornerhouse Gall., Manchester, 1989; The Atomic Yard, Kettle's Yard, Cambridge, Raab Gall., London, 1990–91; The Scar, Benjamin Rhodes Gall., London, Manchester City Art Mus. and Gall., 1993; John Goto 94, touring Russia, 1994; The Framer's Collection, Portfolio Gall., Edinburgh, 1997; The Commissar of Space, MOMA, Oxford, 1998; NPG 2000, Photoworks, NPG, 1999; Capital Arcade, Andrew Mummery Gall., London, 2000; Loss of Face, Tate Britain, London, 2002–03; High Summer, British Acad., 2005–09; John Goto's New World Circus, Gallery On, Seoul, 2006; Green and Pleasant Land, 2008, Sweet Augmentations, 2013, Galerie Dominique Fiat, Paris; Mosaic, Edinburgh Printmakers Gall., 2011; Jazz, 2011, Three Series, 2014, Gallery On, Seoul; Dreams of Jelly Roll, Freud Mus., 2012; John Goto's High Summer, Yale Center for British Art, New Haven, 2018; group exhibitions include: Summer Show 4, 1977, Blasphemies, Ecstasies, Cries, 1989, Serpentine Gall.; The Third Meaning, MOMA, Oxford, Painting/Photography, Richard de Marco Gall., Edinburgh, 1986; Romantic Visions, Camden Arts Centre, 1988; Photographic Art in Britain 1945–1989, Barbican Gall., 1989; John Moores Exhibition 18, Walker Art Gall., Liverpool (prizewinner), 1993; After Auschwitz, RFH and tour, Pretext: Heteronyms, Rear Window, London, 1995; Modern Times 3, Hasselblad Center, Goteborg, 2000; Trade, Fotomus., Winterthur, Netherlands Fotoinst., Rotterdam, 2001–02; Sight Seeing, Graz, 2003; Collage, Bloomberg Space, London, 2004; Experimentieren, Inst. Cervantes, Berlin, 2005; Fotofestiwal, Lodz, 2009; Abstracts, f5.6 Galerie, Munich, 2011; Imagine Earth, Hangaram Art Mus., Seoul, 2011; (curator and exhibitor) An Uncommon Past, New Media Gall., Sichuan Fine Art Inst., Chongqing, China, 2012; Medusa Caravage, Palais de Tokyo, Paris, 2013; Before the Deluge: apocalyptic floodscapes from John Martin to John Goto, 1789 to now, Yale Centre for British Art, New Haven, USA, 2019; Paris-Londres: music migrations (1962–89), Musée de L'histoire de L'immigration, Paris, 2019; work in collections includes: Arts Council of GB, Australian Nat. Gall., V&A Mus., MOMA, Valencia, Univ. of Warwick, Univ. of Sussex, St Anne's Coll., Oxford, Deutsche Bank, British Govt Art Collection, British Art Centre, Yale, NPG, British Acad., Chongqing Art Mus., China. Recreations: jazz, architecture, history, film, good cuisine. Address: Galerie Dominique Fiat, 16 Rue Coutures St Gervais, 75003 Paris, France. E: johngoto@who.net. W: www.johngoto.org.uk.

**GOTO, Midori**; violinist; b Osaka, Japan, 25 Oct. 1971; d of Setsu Goto. Educ: Professional Children's Sch., New York; Juilliard Sch. of Music, New York; New York Univ. (BA 2000; MA Psychol. 2005). Début with New York Philharmonic Orch., 1982; concert and recital appearances worldwide. Numerous recordings. Founder: Midori & Friends Foundn, 1992; Partners in Performance, 2003; Orchestra Residencies Program, 2004; Music Sharing, 2004. Jascha Heifetz Chair in Violin, Thornton Sch. of Music, Univ. of S Calif, 2006–. UN Messenger of Peace, 2007. Fellow, American Acad. of Arts and Scis, 2012. Hon. DMus Yale, 2012. Japanese Govt Artist of the Year, 1988; Avery Fisher Prize, 2001; Deutsche Schallplattenpreis, 2002, 2003; Kennedy Center Gold Medal, 2010; Award of Merit for Achievement in Performing Arts, Assoc. Performing Arts Presenters, 2015. Publications: Einfach Midori (memoir), 2004. Address: c/o Intermusica, 9 Kingsway, WC2B 6XF.

**GOTT, Haydn**; a District Judge (Magistrates' Courts) (formerly Metropolitan Stipendiary Magistrate), 1992–2011; b 29 April 1946; s of Alan Gott and Delia Mary Gott (née Pugh); m 1975, Brigid Mary Kane (marr. diss. 2002); one s one d; m 2004, Susan Valerie Green, qv. Educ: Manchester Grammar Sch.; Oxford Univ. (MA). Admitted solicitor, 1972; Partner, Alexander & Partners, solicitors, 1975–92. Legal Mem., Mental Health Review Tribunal, 1986–. Recreations: sport, music. Club: Ronnie Scott's.

**GOTT, Paul Andrew**; QC 2012; b Essex, 1967; s of Prof. Geoffrey Gott and Hilary Gott; m 1991, Judith Ann Lee; three d. Educ: Marple Hall Comprehensive Sch.; Downing Coll., Cambridge (BA Law 1989); Brasenose Coll., Oxford (BCL 1990). Called to the Bar, Lincoln's Inn, 1991; in practice as a barrister, specialising in employment law and commercial law, especially industrial disputes; Jun. Counsel to the Crown, 1999–2012. Mem., Standards Bd for England, 2006–12. Recreations: family, numismatics, collecting (especially tat), Shuna, presents from Margate. Address: Fountain Court Chambers, Temple, EC4Y 9DH. T: (020) 7583 3335.

**GOTT, Richard Willoughby**; journalist; Literary Editor, The Guardian, 1992–94; b 28 Oct. 1938; s of Arthur Gott and Mary Moon; m 1st, 1966, Ann Zammit (marr. diss. 1981); one adopted s one adopted d; 2nd, 1985, Vivien Ashley. Educ: Winchester Coll.; Corpus Christi Coll., Oxford (MA). Res. Asst, RIIA, 1962–65; Leader Writer, Guardian, 1964–66; Res. Fellow, Inst. de Estudios Internacionales, Univ. of Chile, 1966–69; Foreign Editor, Tanzanian Standard, Dar es Salaam, 1970–71; Third World corresp., New Statesman, 1971–72; The Guardian: Latin American corresp., 1972–76; Foreign News Editor, 1977–78; Features Editor, 1978–89; Asst Editor, 1988–94. Editor, Pelican Latin American Library, 1969–78; Dir, Latin American Newsletters, 1973–79. Contested (Ind.) North Hull, by-election 1966. Order of Francisco Miranda, 1st cl. (Venezuela), 2002. Publications: The Appeasers (with Martin Gilbert), 1963; Guerrilla Movements in Latin America, 1970; Land Without Evil: Utopian journeys across the South American watershed, 1993; In the Shadow of the Liberator: Hugo Chavez and the transformation of Venezuela, 2000; Cuba: a new history, 2004; Britain's Empire: resistance, repression and revolt, 2011. Recreation: travelling. Address: 88 Ledbury Road, W11 2AH. T: (020) 7229 5467.

**GOTT, Susan Valerie**; see Green, S. V.

**GÖTTGENS, Prof. Berthold**, DPhil; Professor of Molecular Haematology, University of Cambridge, since 2011; b Mechernich, Germany, 25 March 1966; s of Hans-Peter and Marlene Göttgens; m 1994, Euphemia Mutasa; two d. Educ: Hermann Josef Kolleg Steinfeld (Abitur 1985); Univ. of Tübingen (Dip. Biochem. 1992); Linacre Coll., Oxford (DPhil 1994). University of Cambridge: Res. Associate, 1994–2000; Sen. Res. Associate, 2000–02; Leukaemia Res. Fund Lectr, 2003–06; Sen. Lectr, 2006–07; Reader in Molecular Haematol., 2007–11. Pres., Internat. Soc. for Experimental Haematology, 2018–19. Publications: contrib. res. articles on gene regulatory control of normal and leukaemic blood stem cells. Recreations: accomplished violinist, enjoying spending time with family. Address: Department of Haematology, University of Cambridge, Cambridge CB2 0XY. T: (01223) 336829, Fax: (01223) 762670. E: bg200@cam.ac.uk.

**GOTTLIEB, Anthony John**; author and journalist; b 26 May 1956; s of Felix Gottlieb and Jutta Gottlieb; m 1989, Miranda Seymour (marr. diss. 2005). Educ: John Lyon Sch., Harrow-on-the-Hill; Gonville and Caius Coll., Cambridge (MA Philos. 1979); University Coll. London. The Economist, 1984–2006: Science Ed., 1988–91; Surveys Ed., 1991–94; Exec. Ed., 1997–2006. Vis. Fellow, 2013–14, Fellow, 2017–19, All Souls Coll., Oxford. Ivan Boesky Fellow, Harvard Univ., 1986. Publications: Socrates, 1997; The Dream of Reason: a history of Western philosophy, 2000; The Dream of Enlightenment, 2016. Recreations: music, reading. Address: 60 West 57th Street, New York, NY 10019, USA.

**GOTTLIEB, Robert Adams**; dance and book critic; Editor-in-Chief, The New Yorker, 1987–92; b 29 April 1931; s of Charles and Martha Gottlieb; m 1st, 1952, Muriel Higgins (marr. diss. 1965); one s; 2nd, 1969, Maria Tucci; one s one d. Educ: Columbia Coll., NY; Cambridge Univ. Simon & Schuster, publishers, 1955–68 (final positions, Editor-in-Chief and Vice-Pres.); Pres. and Editor-in-Chief, Alfred A. Knopf, publishers, 1968–87. Pres., Louis B. Mayer Foundn. Publications: Reading Jazz, 1996; (jtly) Reading Lyrics, 2000; George Balanchine: the ballet maker, 2004; Sarah: the life of Sarah Bernhardt, 2010; Great Expectations: the sons and daughters of Charles Dickens, 2012; Avid Reader, 2016; (essays) Near-Death Experiences… and Others, 2018. Recreations: ballet, classic film, shopping.

**GOTTLOB, Prof. Georg**, PhD; FRS 2010; Professor of Informatics, University of Oxford, since 2012; Fellow, St John's College, Oxford, since 2012; b Vienna, 30 June 1956; m Dr Laura Carlotta; one s one d. Educ: Univ. of Technol., Vienna (Dipl Ing 1979; Dr phil 1981); Univ. of Oxford (MA). Italian Nat. Res. Council, Genoa; University of Technology, Vienna: Professor of Computer Sci., 1988–2006; Dir, Christian Doppler Laboratory for Expert Systems, 1989–96; Adjunct Prof., 2006–; Prof. of Computing Sci., Univ. of Oxford, 2006–11; Fellow, St Anne's Coll., Oxford, 2006–11 (Hon. Fellow, 2012). McKay Prof., Univ. of Calif, Berkeley, 1999. Co-Founder: Lixto Corp.; Wrapidity, 2015; Founding Mem., Oxford-Man Inst. of Quantitative Finance, 2007–. Member: Austrian Acad. of Scis; German Acad. of Scis Leopoldina; MAE. Wittgenstein Award, Austrian Nat. Sci. Fund. Hon. Dr: Klagenfurt, 2016; Calabria, 2017. Ada Lovelace Medal, BCS Acad. of Computing, 2017. Publications: (jtly) Hypertree Width and Related Hypergraph Invariants, 2007; (jtly) A Backtracking-based Algorithm for Computing Hypertree-Decompositions, 2007; (jtly) A General Datalog-based Framework for Tractable Query Answering Over Ontologies, 2010. Address: Department of Computer Science, University of Oxford, Wolfson Building, Parks Road, Oxford OX1 3QD.

**GOTTS, Andrew James**, MBE 2012; photographer, since 1991; Director, Dr Gotts Ltd, since 2013; b Erpingham, Norfolk, 9 Feb. 1971; s of Ivor Gotts and Enid Gotts. Educ: Norfolk Coll. of Arts and Technol. (BTEC Nat. Dip. Design Photography 1991); Univ. of Wolverhampton (HND Photography 1994); De Montfort Univ. (MA Photography 2007). Creative Dir, Ark, 2000–02. Pres., British Inst. of Professional Photographers, 2011–12. Ambassador for UK Now, China, 2012. Exhibitions include: Degrees, Getty Gall., London, 2005, Film Mus., Potsdam, 2006; Selected Works, Savoy Hotel, 2006–; Behind the Mask, Somerset House, Lowry, 2014, Williamson Gall., Munro Gall., 2015; Unseen, Flemings Mayfair, 2015; Herrick Gall., 2017, The Showroom Presents, London, 2017, Chelsea Design Centre, 2018; Save the Arctic, K11 Art Mus., Shanghai, 2017; Fame, Box Galleries, London, 2018; Get a Life, Laforet Mus., Tokyo, 2018; Andy Gotts: Photography, Flo Peters Gall., Hamburg, 2018. Hon. DArts De Montfort, 2011. Publications: Degrees, 2005; iCons, 2014; Monty Python Live, 2014; Save the Arctic: Vivienne Westwood, 2014; Behind the Mask, 2015. Recreations: film, theatre, art galleries, travelling, champagne. Address: Dr Gotts Ltd, 7–8 Park Place, SW1A 1LP. T: 0845 045 0078. E: info@andygotts.com.

**GOUCHER, Mark Terence**; independent theatrical producer, since 1987; Chief Executive, Everyman Theatre, Cheltenham, since 2017; b Redhill, Surrey, 29 Aug. 1965; s of Terence and Barbara Goucher; partner, 1994, Andrew Mackie. Educ: St John's Church Sch.; Warlingham Secondary Sch.; Univ. of Leeds (BA Drama and Media). Produced first show, Edinburgh Fringe, 1987, West End, 1991; West End productions include: Kit and the Widow, Vaudeville, 1991; Steven Berkoff, Garrick, 1993; The Complete Works of Shakespeare (abridged), 1996, The Complete History of America (abridged), 1996, The Bible - the Complete Word of God (abridged), 2003, Reduced Shakespeare Co., Criterion; Trainspotting, Queen's, Whitehall, 1995; Jackie Clune and Graham Norton, Arts, 1995; Fever Pitch, Arts, 1996; Shopping and F***ing, Gielgud, Queen's, 1997; Issey Ogata, Lyric, 1998; Rent - The Musical, Prince of Wales, 1999; Holy Mothers, Last Dance at Dum Dum, Ambassadors, 1999; Fame - The Musical, Victoria Palace, Cambridge, Aldwych, 1999–2005; Frantic Assembly, 2000, Ambassadors; Dolly West's Kitchen, Old Vic, 2000; The Snowman, Peacock, 2000–; Vagina Monologues, New Ambassadors, 2001, Arts, 2002, Wyndhams, 2005; Elaine Stritch at Liberty, Old Vic, 2002; The Anniversary, Garrick, 2005; Amajuba, Criterion, 2005; High Society, Shaftesbury, 2005; Footloose - The Musical, Novello, 2006; Whipping it Up, New Ambassadors, 2007; Shout! - The Musical, Arts, 2007; Dickens Unplugged, Comedy, 2008; Yes, Prime Minister, Gielgud, Apollo, Trafalgar Studios, 2010–12; Crazy for You, Novello, 2011; Slava's Snowshow, Royal Festival Hall, 2012; A Chorus Line, Palladium, 2013; Jeeves and Wooster, Duke of York's, 2013; Taken at Midnight, Minerva, Chichester, 2014, Theatre Royal Haymarket, 2015; The King's Speech, UK tour, 2015; The Dresser, Duke of York's, 2016; Million Dollar Quartet, UK tour, 2016–17, RFH, 2017; The Miser, Garrick, 2017; Hairspray, UK tour, 2017–18; The Height of the Storm, Wyndham's, 2018; touring productions include: Single Spies, Oh What A Lovely War, Pygmalion, Bette and Joan Jus' Like That, The Wedding Singer - The Musical, Stones in His Pockets. Member: SOLT, 2004– (Mem. Bd, 2012–18); Bd, League of Ind. Producers, 2012–17. Recreation: I ride with the Cotswold. Address: c/o Mark Goucher Productions Ltd, 19 Garrick Street, WC2E 9AX. E: mark@markgoucher.com. Clubs: Groucho, Century, Garrick.

**GOUDIE**, family name of **Baroness Goudie**.

**GOUDIE, Baroness** cr 1998 (Life Peer), of Roundwood in the London Borough of Brent; **Mary Teresa Goudie**; strategic and management consultant, since 1998; b 2 Sept. 1946; d of Martin Brick and Hannah Brick (née Foley); m 1969, Thomas James Cooper Goudie, qv; two s. Educ: Our Lady of the Visitation; Our Lady of St Anselm. Asst Dir, Brent Peoples' Housing Assoc., 1977–80; Sec. and Organiser, Labour Solidarity Campaign, 1980–84; Director: The Hansard Soc., 1985–89; The House Magazine, 1989–90; Public Affairs Dir, WWF, 1990–95; public affairs consultant, 1995–98. Mem. (Lab) Brent LBC, 1971–78. Vice Chm., Labour Peers, 2001–03. Vice Chairman: All-Party Parly Equality Gp; All-Party Gp on Global Educn; Member: Select Cttee on Sexual Violence in Conflict; Finance Cttee, H of L. UK Dir, Centre for Talent Innovation, 2012–. Chair, Women Leaders' Council to Fight Human Trafficking, UN, 2007–; Founding Mem., 30% Club, 2010–; Member: Global Adv. Bd, WEConnect Internat., 2012–; Exec. and Bd of Dirs, Vital Voices Global Partnership; Adv. Bd, Centre for Women, Peace and Security, LSE; Adv. Bd, Women's Forum; Adv. Bd, Gender Action for Peace and Security; Advr, Georgetown Inst. for Women, Peace and Security. Ambassador, Internat. Centre for Res. on Women. Trustee:

E-Hibri Charitable Foundn, 2012–; Share Gift. Patron, Community Foundn of NI, 2000–. Hon. LLD Napier, 1999. Global Power Award, Center for Women Policy Studies, 2010. *Publications:* various articles. *Recreations:* family, gardening, travelling, art, food and wine, reading. *Address:* (office) 11 Groom Place, SW1X 7BA. *T:* (020) 7245 9181, *Fax:* (020) 7235 9879. *W:* www.baronessgoudie.com, www.twitter.com/BaronessGoudie.
*See also W. M. P. Goudie.*

GOUDIE, Prof. Andrew Shaw; Professor of Geography, University of Oxford, 1984–2003, now Emeritus; *b* 21 Aug. 1945; *s* of late William and Mary Goudie; *m* 1987, Heather (*née* Viles); two *d*. *Educ:* Dean Close Sch., Cheltenham; Trinity Hall, Cambridge. BA, PhD Cantab; MA, DSc 2002, Oxon. Oxford University: Departmental Demonstrator, 1970–76; Univ. Lectr, 1976–84; Head: Dept of Geography, 1984–94; Sch. of Geography and the Envmt, 2002–03; Fellow, Hertford Coll., 1976–2003 (Hon. Fellow, 2003); Pro-Vice-Chancellor, 1995–97; Head of Develt Prog., 1995–97; Master, St Cross Coll., 2003–11, now Hon. Fellow; Dir, China Centre, 2011–13. Hon. Secretary: British Geomorphological Res. Gp, 1977–80 (Chm., 1988–89); RGS, 1981–88; Member: Council, Inst. of British Geographers, 1980–83; British Nat. Cttee for Geography, 1982–87. Dep. Leader: Internat. Karakoram Project, 1980; Kora Project, 1983. President: Geographical Assoc., 1993–94; Section E, BAAS, 1995–96; Internat. Assoc. of Geomorphologists, 2005– (Vice-Pres., 2005; Hon. Fellow, 2013); British Inst. in Eastern Africa, 2011–16. Fellow, British Soc. for Geomorphology, 2014. Cuthbert Peek award, RGS, 1975; Geographic Soc. of Chicago Publication award, 1982; Founder's Medal, RGS, 1991; Mungo Park Medal, RSGS, 1991; Medal, Royal Belgian Acad., 2002; Farouk El-Baz Prize for Desert Res., Geol Soc. of America, 2007; David Linton Award, British Soc. for Geomorphology, 2009. *Publications:* Duricrusts of Tropical and Sub-tropical Landscapes, 1973; Environmental Change, 1976, 3rd edn 1992; The Warm Desert Environment, 1977; The Prehistory and Palaeogeography of the Great Indian Desert, 1978; Desert Geomorphology, 1980; The Human Impact, 1981, 8th edn 2018; Geomorphological Techniques, 1981, 3rd edn 1990; The Atlas of Swaziland, 1983; Chemical Sediments and Geomorphology, 1983; The Nature of the Environment, 1984, 4th edn 2001; (jtly) Discovering Landscape in England and Wales, 1985; The Encyclopædic Dictionary of Physical Geography, 1985, 3rd edn 2000; (jtly) Landshapes, 1989; The Geomorphology of England and Wales, 1990; Techniques for Desert Reclamation, 1990; Climate, 1997; Great Warm Deserts of the World, 2002; Encyclopedia of Geomorphology, 2004; Desert Dust in the Global System, 2006; Global Environments through the Quaternary, 2007, 2nd edn 2013; Wheels across the Desert, 2008; The Oxford Companion to Global Change, 2009; Geomorphological Hazards and Disaster Prevention, 2010; Handbook of Geomorphology, 2011; Arid and Semi-Arid Geomorphology, 2013; Landscapes and Landforms of Namibia, 2014; Geomorphology in the Anthropocene, 2016; Great Desert Explorers, 2016; contribs to learned jls. *Recreations:* bush life, old records, old books. *Address:* St Cross College, St Giles, Oxford OX1 3LZ. *Clubs:* Geographical; Gilbert (Oxford).
*See also T. J. C. Goudie.*

GOUDIE, Andrew William, CB 2011; PhD; FRSE; Chief Economic Adviser, 1999–2011, and Director-General of Economy (formerly Head, Finance and Central Services Department), 2003–11, Scottish Government (formerly Scottish Office, then Scottish Executive); Special Adviser to the Principal, and Visiting Professor, University of Strathclyde, Glasgow, since 2011; *b* 3 March 1955; *s* of Britton Goudie and Joan Goudie; *m* 1978, Christine Lynne Hurley; two *s* two *d*. *Educ:* Queens' Coll., Cambridge (Wrenbury Schol.; BA Econs, MA; PhD 1992); Open Univ. (BA Maths and Stats). FRSE 2005. University of Cambridge: Research Officer, Dept of Applied Econs, 1978–85; Res. Fellow, Queens' Coll., 1981–83; Fellow and Dir of Studies, Robinson Coll., 1983–85; Sen. Economist, World Bank, Washington, 1985–90; Sen. Economic Advr, Scottish Office, 1990–95; Principal Economist, OECD Develt Centre, Paris, 1995–96; Chief Economist, DFID (formerly ODA), 1996–99. Mem., Adv. Gp, Oxfam Scotland, 2010–; Dir, Scotland Malawi Partnership, 2013–. Hon. DLitt Strathclyde, 2003. *Publications:* articles in learned jls, incl. Econ. Jl, Jl Royal Statistical Soc., Economica, Scottish Jl Political Economy. *Address:* University of Strathclyde, 16 Richmond Street, Glasgow G1 1XQ. *T:* (0141) 552 4400.

GOUDIE, Martin; *see* Goudie, W. M. P.

GOUDIE, (Thomas) James (Cooper); QC 1984; a Recorder, 1986–2008; a Deputy High Court Judge (Queen's Bench Division), 1995–2017; *b* 2 June 1942; *s* of late William Cooper Goudie and Mary Isobel Goudie; *m* 1969, Mary Teresa Brick (*see* Baroness Goudie); two *s*. *Educ:* Dean Close Sch.; London School of Economics (LLB Hons). FCIArb 1991. Solicitor, 1966–70; called to the Bar, Inner Temple, 1970 (Bencher, 1991). A Dep. Chm., 2000–12, Pres., 2007–12, Information Tribunal (for nat. security appeals). Chairman: Law Reform Cttee, Gen. Council of the Bar, 1995–96; Administrative Law Bar Assoc., 1994–96; Soc. of Labour Lawyers, 1994–99; Bar European Gp, 2001–03. Contested (Lab) Brent North, Feb. and Oct. 1974; Leader of Brent Council, 1977–78. Gov., LSE, 2001–15, now Emeritus. *Publications:* (ed jtly and contrib.) Judicial Review, 1992, 6th edn 2017; (ed with P. Elias, and contrib.) Butterworths Local Government Law, 1998; (ed jtly and contrib.) Local Authorities and the Human Rights Act 1998, 1999. *Address:* 11 King's Bench Walk, Temple, EC4Y 7EQ. *T:* (020) 7583 0610.
*See also A. S. Goudie, W. M. P. Goudie.*

GOUDIE, (William) Martin (Philip); QC 2017; a Recorder, since 2019; *b* London, 5 July 1973; *s* of (Thomas) James (Cooper) Goudie, *qv* and Baroness Goudie, *qv*; partner, Dr Vanessa Elliott; one *d*. *Educ:* Marlborough Coll.; Univ. of Exeter (LLB LAW 1994); Inns of Court Sch. of Law (BVC 1996). Called to the Bar: Inner Temple, 1996, Bencher 2019; NI, 2016; in practice as a barrister, specialising in nat. security, crime and professional discipline, Charter Chambers, 1996– (Treas., 2014–); Attorney Gen.'s Panel of Special Advocates, 2005–. Pegasus Scholar, Crown Law Office, Wellington, NZ, 1999. Mem., Bar Liaison Cttee, Inner Temple, 2002–14. *Address:* Charter Chambers, 33 John Street, WC1N 2AT. *Club:* London Scottish Football (Head of Discipline, 2009–).

GOUGH, family name of Viscount Gough.

GOUGH, 5th Viscount *cr* 1849, of Goojerat, of the Punjaub, and Limerick; Shane Hugh Maryon Gough; Bt 1842; Baron Gough 1846; Irish Guards, 1961–67; *b* 26 Aug. 1941; *o s* of 4th Viscount Gough and Margaretta Elizabeth (*d* 1977), *o d* of Sir Spencer Maryon-Wilson, 11th Bt; *S* father, 1951. *Educ:* Abberley Hall, Worcs; Winchester Coll. Mem. Queen's Bodyguard for Scotland, Royal Company of Archers. Member: Exec. Council, RNIB; Scottish Lifeboat Council, RNLI. FRGS. *Heir:* none. *Address:* Keppoch Estate Office, Strathpeffer, Ross-shire IV14 9AD. *T:* (01997) 421224; 17 Stanhope Gardens, SW7 5RQ. *Clubs:* Pratt's, White's, MCC.

GOUGH, Rear-Adm. Andrew Bankes, CB 2000; Secretary-General, Order of St John, 2003–12; *b* 22 June 1947; *s* of late Gilbert Bankes Gough and Pauline Gough; *m* 1971, Susanne Jensen, Copenhagen; two *s*. *Educ:* Bridgnorth Grammar Sch.; Britannia Royal Naval Coll. Joined RN, 1965; flying tours, 1970–76; i/c, HMS Bronington, 1976–78; 824 Naval Air Sqdn, 1978–80; i/c, 737 Naval Air Sqdn, 1980–81; SS Uganda, Falklands Task Force, 1982; HMS Glamorgan, 1982–84; JSDC, 1985; MoD, 1985–87; in command HM Ships: Broadsword, 1987–88; Beaver, 1988; Brave, 1988–89; RCDS, 1990; MoD, 1991–93; Dep. UK Mil. Rep. to NATO, 1993–96; Comdr, Standing Naval Force, Atlantic, 1996–97; ACOS (Policy/Requirements), Supreme HQ Allied Powers in Europe, 1997–2000. Dep. Chief Exec., 2000–02, Man. Dir, 2003, Affinitas Ltd; Man. Dir, AFFAS Ltd, 2003. Chm., SSAFA Somerset, 2015–. KStJ 2004. *Recreations:* military history, Bordeaux wine.

GOUGH, Prof. Douglas Owen, PhD; FRS 1997; Professor of Theoretical Astrophysics, University of Cambridge, 1993–2008, now Emeritus; Leverhulme Emeritus Fellow, Institute of Astronomy, Cambridge, 2008–11 and 2016–18 (Director, 1999–2004); Fellow, Churchill College, Cambridge, since 1972; *b* 8 Feb. 1941; *s* of Owen Albert John Gough and Doris May Gough (*née* Camera); *m* 1965, Rosanne Penelope Shaw; two *s* two *d*. *Educ:* Hackney Downs Sch.; St John's Coll., Cambridge (BA 1962; MA 1966; PhD 1966). CPhys 1997. Res. Associate, Jt Inst. for Lab. Astrophysics, Univ. of Colo, 1966–67; Nat. Acad. of Scis Sen. Postdoctoral Resident Res. Associate, Inst. for Space Studies, NY, 1967–69; Vis. Mem., Courant Inst. of Mathematical Scis, NYU, 1967–69; University of Cambridge: Mem., Grad. Staff, Inst. of Theoretical Astronomy, 1969–73; Lectr in Astronomy and Applied Maths, 1973–85; Reader in Astrophysics, 1985–93; Dep. Dir, Inst. of Astronomy, 1993–99. Astronome Titulaire Associé des Observatoires de France, 1977; SRC Sen. Fellow, 1978–83; Prof. Associé, Univ. de Toulouse, 1984–85; Academic Forum Lectr, Savitribai Phule Pune Univ., India, 1985; Hon. Prof. of Astronomy, QMW, Univ. of London, later QMUL, 1986–2009; Fellow Adjoint, Jt Inst. for Lab. Astrophysics, Boulder, Colo, 1986–; Scientific Co-ordinator, Inst. for Theoretical Physics, Univ. of Calif, Santa Barbara, 1990; Vis. Prof., 1996–2010, Consulting Prof., 2010–15, Sen. Res. Associate, 2016–17, Adjunct Prof., 2018–, Stanford Univ.; Vis. Fellow, S African Astronomical Observatory, 2004–10; Associé de recherche, CNRS, Observatoire de Paris-Meudon, 2005–06; Vis. Fellow, 2005, Invitation Fellow, 2005, 2012, Japan Soc. for the Promotion of Sci.; Vis. Scientist, High Altitude Observatory, Boulder, Colo, 2014–; Distinguished Vis. Prof., Univ. of Mumbai, 2015; Homi Bhabha Lectr, Tata Inst. for Fundamental Res., Mumbai, 2015; Vis. Scientist Fellow, Centro de Astrofísica da Universidade do Porto, 2017. Lectures: James Arthur, Harvard, 1982; Sir Joseph Larmor, Cambridge Philosophical Soc., 1988; Wernher von Braun, Marshall Space Flight Center, 1991; Morris Loeb, Harvard, 1993; Halley, Oxford Univ., 1996; Bishop, Columbia Univ., 1996; Coloquios BBV, Inst. de Astrofisica de Canarias, Spain, 1996; R. J. Tayler Meml, RAS, 2000; Colloquium Ehrenfestii, Instituut Lorentz, 2003; Vainu Bappu, Indian Inst. of Astrophysics, 2008. Member, Editorial Board: Solar Physics, 1983–2004; Fundamentals of Cosmic Physics, 1985–93; Inverse Problems, 1997–2003; Advr, Encyclopedia of Astronomy and Astrophysics, Inst. of Physics, 1997–2000. FInstP 1997; Fellow, Nat. Astronomical Observatory of Japan, Tokyo, 2014. For. Mem., Royal Danish Acad. of Scis and Letters, 1998. William Hopkins Prize, Cambridge Philosophical Soc., 1984; George Ellery Hale Prize, Amer. Astronomical Soc., 1994; Eddington Medal, 2000, Gold Medal, 2010, RAS; Pioneer to Life of the Nation, 2003. Mousquetaire d'Armagnac, 2001. *Publications:* mainly res. papers and reviews in scientific jls. *Recreations:* cooking, listening to music, hiking. *Address:* Institute of Astronomy, Madingley Road, Cambridge CB3 0HA. *T:* (01223) 337548.

GOUGH, Rev. Canon Flora Jane Louise; *see* Winfield, Rev. Canon F. J. L.

GOUGH, Janet, MA; *b* 1 Aug. 1940; *d* of Clifford Gough and Sarah (*née* Allen). *Educ:* Ludlow High Sch.; Newnham Coll., Cambridge (BA Hons and MA). St Paul's Girls' Sch., 1964–71; Manchester Grammar Sch., 1972; Worcester High Sch. for Girls, 1973; St Paul's Girls' Sch., 1973–98, High Mistress, 1993–98. Governor: Dulwich Coll., 1999–2008; Oundle Sch., 2002–12; Ludlow Coll., 2009–11. *Recreations:* book collecting, architecture, music. *Address:* 58 Corve Street, Ludlow, Shropshire SY8 1DU.

GOUGH, Janet Frances, (Mrs Jim Lloyd), OBE 2017; architectural historian, lecturer, commissioning editor and senior heritage consultant specialising in historic churches; *b* London, 3 Sept. 1961; *d* of Geoffrey and Caryl Gough (*née* Howard); *m* 2001, Jim Lloyd; one *s* one *d*. *Educ:* St Margaret's, Bushey; Haileybury Coll.; Emmanuel Coll., Cambridge (Entrance Exhibnr; BA Hist. and Hist. of Art 1983; MA). ACA 1989. Art for Offices, 1984; KPMG, 1985–89; Charterhouse Bank, 1989–91; Sotheby's, 1991–2000, Dir, 1995–2000; Acting Dir, Prince of Wales's Phoenix Trust (UK Building Preservation Trust), 2001–02; V&A tours and Janet Gough Architectural Tours, 2002–08; Dir, Cathedral and Church Bldgs Div., Archbishop's Council, C of E, Sec., Church Bldgs Council and Sec., Cathedrals Fabric Commn for England, 2008–16. Mem., World War One Centenary Cathedral Fabric Repairs Expert Panel, DCMS, 2014–. Trustee: Fulham Palace Trust, 1997–2011; Churches Conservation Trust, 1998–2005; Friends of V&A, 2013–17; Priory of England and The Islands of the Order of St John, 2017–. Gov., Haileybury Coll., 2016–. *Publications:* Director's Choice: the Cathedrals of the Church of England, 2015; Director's Choice: the churches of the Church of England, 2017. *Recreations:* history, art, museums, historic churches, community engagement, collecting, the great outdoors, my family (incl. dog and cat), entertaining. *E:* janet@janet-gough.com. *W:* www.janet-gough.com, www.twitter.com/Gough_Janet. *Clubs:* House of St Barnabas, Lansdowne; Northeast Harbor Fleet (Mount Desert Island, Maine); Campden Hill Lawn Tennis Club.

GOUGH, Ven. Jonathan Robin Blanning; Archdeacon of Richmond and Craven, since 2019; *b* 11 May 1962; *s* of Alec Robin Blanning Gough and Margaret Gough (*née* Elliston); *m* 1985, Rev. Canon Flora Jane Louise Winfield, *qv*. *Educ:* Exeter Sch.; St David's UC, Lampeter (BA Hons 1983); St Stephen's House, Oxford; Westminster Coll., Oxford (MTh 1996). Ordained deacon, 1985, priest, 1986; Assistant Curate: Braunton, 1985–86; Matson, 1986–89; Royal Army Chaplains' Department, 1989–2001: served: NI, 1990–92 and 2000–01; Bosnia (UN Protection Force), 1993–94 and 1995, (NATO Stabilisation Force), 1997; Kosovo (NATO Kosovo Force), 1999–2000; Archbishop of Canterbury's Sec. for Ecumenism, 2001–05; Royal Army Chaplains' Dept, 2005–19; Sen. Chaplain British Forces, Afghanistan, 2008; Chaplain, RMA Sandhurst, 2009–11; Dep. Asst Chaplain Gen., 2011–17; Asst Chaplain Gen., 2017–19. Hon. Canon: Holy Trinity Cathedral, Gibraltar, 2013; St Paul's Cathedral, Nicosia, 2006–. FRSA 2017. *Recreations:* music, history, country pursuits.

GOUGH, Judith Margaret; *see* Carlisle, J. M.

GOUGH, Judith Mary, CMG 2018; FCMA; HM Diplomatic Service; Ambassador to Sweden, since 2019; *b* Amersham, 8 Nov. 1972; *d* of Richard and Mary Gough; civil partnership 2011, Nerantzoula, (Julia), Kleiousi; two *s*. *Educ:* Univ. of Nottingham (BA Jt Hons German and Russian 1995); King's Coll. London (MA War in Modern World 2012). CGMA. Audit trainee, 1995–96, Asst, later Sen. Consultant, Mgt Consultancy Services, 1996–2001, Ernst & Young; entered FCO, 2001; Gibraltar Desk, 2001–02, Hd, Albania, former Yugoslav Rep. of Macedonia and Balkans Strategic Policy Team, Eastern Adriatic Dept, 2002–04, FCO; Political Counsellor, Seoul, 2004–07; Dep. Dir, Corporate Services Prog., 2007–08; Dep. Hd, Security Policy Gp, 2008–10; Ambassador to Georgia, 2010–12; Dir, Eastern Europe and Central Asia Directorate, FCO, 2013–14; lang. trng, 2014–15;

Ambassador to Ukraine, 2015–19. FCMA 2015 (Mem., CIMA 1999). *Recreations:* climbing mountains, cycling, collecting maps, talking, playing with dinosaurs. *Address:* c/o Foreign and Commonwealth Office, King Charles Street, SW1A 2AH.

GOUGH, Ven. Martyn John, QHC 2018; Chaplain of the Fleet and Archdeacon of the Royal Navy, since 2018; *b* Aberdare, Glamorgan, 21 April 1966; *s* of Ronald John Gough and Stella Darby Gough; *m* 2004, Amanda Jane Paterson; one *s* one *d*. *Educ:* Aberdare Boys' Grammar Sch.; Univ. of Cardiff (BTh 1987); Univ. of Oxford (PGC); Univ. of Wales, Lampeter (MA 2005). Ordained deacon, 1990, priest, 1991; Chaplain, Varese Italy and European Res. Centre, 1995–98; RN Chaplain (varying ships), 1998–2014; Sen. Chaplain, Afghanistan, 2013–14; Dep. Chaplain of the Fleet, 2014–17. Mem., RCDS, 2017–. Chaplain, RN Assoc. *Publications:* contribs to jls. *Recreations:* figurative mid-century art, music. *Address:* Naval Chaplaincy Service, Navy Command HQ, Leach Building, Whale Island, Portsmouth PO2 8BY. *T:* (023) 9262 5055, 07887 594946. *E:* martyn.gough656@mod.gov.uk, martyngough@yahoo.com. *Club:* Naval and Military.

GOUGH, Michael Charles, CEng, FIET, FBCS; Founder and Chief Engineer, MG Guitars, since 2015; *b* 21 May 1960; *s* of Cyril John Gough and Evelyn Rose Gough; *m* 1982, Lesley Irene Baglee; three *s*. *Educ:* Univ. of Liverpool (BSc Hons Computational and Statistical Sci. 1981; MSc Computer Sci. 1987). CITP 2002; CEng 2006; FIET 2006; FBCS 2006; Univ. of Chester (Church Colls Cert. 2009). Computer software engr, Fraser Williams, 1981–87; Project Manager, CAP Gp Plc, 1987–89; IT Dir, CERT Plc, 1989–91; Dir, Technol. Strategy, SEMA Gp Plc, 1991–2000; Chief Exec., National Computing Centre, 2000–08; Hewlett Packard Enterprise Services (formerly Electronic Data Systems): Hd, Information Assce, UK Public Sector, 2008–11; Prog. Leader, 2009–11; Delivery Assce Dir, Application Services EMEA, 2011–14. Director: Dynamic Systems Develt Method Consortium, 1997–2003; AIRTO, 2000–03. Mem., Exec. Cttee, BCS, 2013–15. MInstD 1996. *Recreations:* music: teaching, playing and composing, photography, theology, the Methodist Church.

GOUGH, Prof. Michael John, FRCS; Professor of Vascular Surgery, University of Leeds, 2009–17, now Emeritus; *b* Birmingham, 18 Feb. 1952; *s* of Henry John Gough and Kathleen June Gough; *m* 1974, Moira Cockerham; two *s* one *d*. *Educ:* Teignmouth Grammar Sch.; Leeds University Sch. of Medicine (MB ChB 1975; ChM 1984). FRCS 1980. Surgical Registrar, Royal Free Hosp., London, 1980–82; Sen. Surgical Registrar, Yorks RHA, 1982–86; Consultant Surgeon, Bradford Hosps, 1986–90; Consultant Vascular Surgeon, Leeds Teaching Hospitals NHS Trust, 1990–2017; Hd, Sch. of Surgery, Yorks and Humber Postgrad. and Dental Deanery, 2009–17. President: Vascular Soc. (formerly Vascular Surgical Soc.) of GB and Ire., 2007–08 (Mem., 1986–); Moynihan Chirurgical Club, 2009–10 (Mem., 1995–); Member: Assoc. of Surgeons of GB and Ire., 1986–; Eur. Soc. for Vascular Surgery, 1986–. Mem., Court of Examiners (Gen. Surgery), FRCS Intercollegiate Exams Bd, 2002–07. Associate Ed. and Mem. Editl Bd, Eur. Jl of Vascular and Endovascular Surgery, 2009–14. *Publications:* over 100 articles in learned jls incl. Lancet, BMJ, Brit. Jl of Surgery, Jl of Vascular Surgery, Eur. Jl of Vascular and Endovascular Surgery, Stroke, Radiology, New Eng. Jl of Med. *Recreations:* golf, tennis, sailing, ski-ing, fly fishing, photography, family, anything outdoors. *Address:* Laurel Cottage, Gilstead Lane, Gilstead, Bingley BD16 3LN.

GOUGH, Piers William, CBE 1998; RA 2001; RIBA; architect; Partner, CZWG Architects, since 1975; *b* 24 April 1946; *s* of late Peter Gough and Daphne Mary Unwin Banks; *m* 1991, Rosemary Elaine Fosbrooke Bates (marr. diss. 2009). *Educ:* Uppingham Sch., Rutland; Architectural Assoc. Sch. of Architecture. Principal works: Phillips West 2, Bayswater, 1976; Lutyens Exhibn, Hayward Gall., 1982; Cochrane Sq., Glasgow, 1987–94; China Wharf, 1988; The Circle, 1990, Bermondsey; Craft, Design and Technol. Bldg, 1988, two boarding houses, 1994, Bryanston Sch.; Street-Porter House, 1988, 1–10 Summers St, 1994, Clerkenwell; Crown St Regeneration Proj., Gorbals, 1991–2004; Westbourne Grove Public Lavatories, 1993; Brindleyplace Café, Birmingham, 1994–97; Bankside Lofts, Southwark, 1994–99; 19th and 20th century galls, 1995–96, Regency galls, 2003, Nat. Portrait Gall.; Soho Lofts, Wardour Street, 1995; Leonardo Centre, Uppingham Sch., 1995; The Glass Building, Camden, 1996–99; Camden Wharf, Camden Lock, 1996–2002; Green Bridge, Mile End Park, 1997–2000; Westferry Studios, Isle of Dogs, 1999–2000; Bankside Central, 2000–02; Allen Jones' Studio, Ledwell, 2000–01; Samworths' Boarding House, Uppingham Sch., 2000–01; Site A, Edinburgh Park, 2000–01; Tunnel Wharf, Rotherhithe, 2001; Fulham Island Site, 2001–02; Ladbroke Green, 2002–; Arsenal Masterplan project, 2002–; Queen Elizabeth Square and Crown Street Corner, Gorbals, 2003–04; Saved Exhibn, Hayward Gall., 2003–04; Fortune Green, 2003–10; Maggie's Centre, Nottingham, 2003–11; Brewery Square, Dorchester, 2003–; Steedman St, SE17, 2006; Bling Bling Building, Liverpool, 2006; Islington Sq., 2006–; One Lansdowne Rd, Croydon, 2008–; Canada Water Library, 2008–11. Commissioner: English Heritage, 2000–07 (Mem., London Adv. Cttee, 1995–2003; Mem., Urban Panel, 1999–2003); CABE, 2007–11. Pres., AA, 1995–97 (Mem. Council, 1970–72, 1991–99; Trustee, 1999–2007). Trustee, Artangel, 1994–2004. Television: (co-writer and presenter) The Shock of the Old (series), Channel 4, 2000. Hon. Fellow, Queen Mary, Univ. of London, 2001. DUniv Middlesex, 1999. *Publications:* English Extremists, 1988. *Recreation:* swimming. *Address:* CZWG Architects LLP, 17 Bowling Green Lane, EC1R 0QB. *T:* (020) 7253 2523, *Fax:* (020) 7250 0594. *E:* piersgough@czwgarchitects.co.uk.

GOUGH, Rachel Mary; *see* Sandby-Thomas, R. M.

GOULBORN, Caroline Barbara; a District Judge (Magistrates' Courts), 2004–14; *b* 9 Sept. 1949; *d* of Sydney Aubrey Goulborn and Peggy Goulborn (*née* Millhouse). *Educ:* Wycombe High Sch.; Trent Polytech. (BA Hons (Law) 1978). Admitted solicitor, 1981; Assistant Solicitor: Huntsmans, Nottingham, 1981–84; Nelsons, Nottingham, 1985–88; Sen. Partner, Fletcher's Solicitors, 1989–2004. *Recreations:* long-distance Wycombe Wanderers supporter, Sutton Bonington Cricket Club (Vice Pres.), reading, foreign travel.

GOULD, family name of **Baronesses Gould of Potternewton** and **Rebuck**.

GOULD OF POTTERNEWTON, Baroness *cr* 1993 (Life Peer), of Leeds in the Metropolitan County of West Yorkshire; **Joyce Brenda Gould**; a Deputy Speaker, House of Lords, 2002–12; *b* 29 Oct. 1932; *d* of Sydney and Fanny Manson; *m* 1952, Kevin Gould (*d* 2017); one *d*. *Educ:* Cowper Street Primary Sch.; Roundhay High Sch. for Girls; Bradford Technical Coll. Dispenser, 1952–65; Labour Party: Mem., 1951–; Asst Regional Organiser, 1969–75; Asst Nat. Agent and Chief Women's Officer, 1975–85; Dir of Organisation, 1985–93. Mem., H of L, 1993–2019. Opposition spokesperson on women's affairs, 1995–97; a Baroness in Waiting (Govt Whip), 1997–98. Chm., All Party Parly Gp on Pro-Choice, 1995–2018. Member: Council of Europe, 1993–96 (Ldr, Delegn to UN Conf. on Women, Beijing, 1995); WEU, 1993–96; CPA, 1998–; IPU, 1998–; Fellow, Parlt and Industry Trust. Mem., Ind. Commn on Voting Systems, 1998–; Vice-Chm., Hansard Soc., 2002–06. Chairman: Ind. Adv. Cttee for Sexual Health and HIV, 2003–11; Women's Nat. Commn, 2008–11 (Interim Chm., 2007–08). Sec., Nat. Jt Cttee of Working Women's Orgns, 1975–85; Vice-Pres., Socialist Internat. Women, 1978–86. President: BEA, 1998–2007; FPA, 1999–; Brighton and Hove Fabian Soc., 2001–; Straight Talking, 2007–. Chm., Mary MacArthur Holiday Trust, 1994–2007 (Pres., 2007–); Pres., Martin Fisher Foundn, 2017–. Patron: FORWARD, 1996–; Brighton and Hove Women's Centre, 2000–16; Yorks MESMAC, 2008–; HIV Sport, 2010–; Sussex Beacon, 2011–; Vice Patron, Impact's 30th Anniv. Appeal, 2008; Trustee: Age UK, Brighton and Hove, 2011–15; Hangleton & Knoll Project, 2018–. Mem., Univ. of Third Age. Hon. FFSRH (Hon. FFFP 2006); Hon. Fellow, British Assoc. for Sexual Health and HIV, 2007. Hon. Dr: Brighton; Birmingham City; Greenwich. Health Champion, Charity Champion Awards, 2007. *Publications:* (ed) Women and Health, 1979; Witchfinder General: a political odyssey, 2016; No Ordinary Woman: a memoir of Jo Richardson MP, 2018; pamphlets on feminism, socialism and sexism, women's right to work, and on violence in society; articles and reports on women's rights and welfare. *Recreations:* relaxing, sport as a spectator, theatre, cinema, reading. *Address:* 58 Hangleton Way, Hove BN3 8EQ.

GOULD, Dr Alexander Paul, FMedSci; Senior Group Leader, Francis Crick Institute, since 2015; *b* 29 Jan. 1964; *s* of Dr Arthur Gould and Mrs Jean Alison Firth (*née* Brighton); *m* 2015, Dr Caroline Vincent. *Educ:* Burleigh Community Coll., Loughborough; King's Coll., Cambridge (BA Hons Natural Scis 1986; MA 1990; PhD Develtl Biol. 1990). Wellcome Trust Res. Associate, Univ. of Cambridge, 1990–91; Jun. Res. Fellow, King's Coll., Cambridge, 1991–95; MRC National Institute for Medical Research: Beit Meml Fellow, 1992–95; MRC Trng Fellow, 1995–97; Gp Leader, 1998–2012; Hd, Div. of Physiol. and Metabolism, 2012–15. Mem., EMBO, 2008–. Wellcome Trust: Mem., Molecules, Genes and Cells Funding Cttee, 2007–11; Mem., Peer Rev. Coll., 2012–16; Sir Henry Dale Fellowship Interview Cttee, 2017–. Member: British Soc. for Develtl Biol., 1987; Genetics Soc. of America, 1990; Biochem. Soc., 1998. Member: Editl Adv. Bd, Develt, 2013–; Editl Bd, PLOS Biol., 2015–. FMedSci 2013. Francis Perch Bedford Prize for Zool., King's Coll., Cambridge, 1986; Hooke Medal, British Soc. for Cell Biol., 2011; Wellcome Trust Sen. Investigator Award, 2015. *Publications:* contrib. articles and reviews to learned jls, incl. Nature, Cell. *Recreations:* keeping fit, gastronomy, travelling, wildlife. *Address:* Francis Crick Institute, 1 Midland Road, NW1 1AT. *E:* Alex.Gould@crick.ac.uk.

GOULD, Andrew Frederick James; Chairman, BG-Group plc, 2012–15; *b* Walton-on-Thames, 17 Dec. 1946; *s* of James McIntosh Gould and Joan Vivien Gould (*née* Wilson); *m* 1974, Sylvie de Thesut; one *s* two *d*; *m* 2015, Catherine Hughes. *Educ:* W Buckland Sch., Barnstaple, Devon; Univ. of Wales Coll. of Cardiff (BA Hons). CA 1969. Schlumberger: financial and mgt positions, Asia, USA and Europe, 1975–2003; Chm. and CEO, 2003–11. Member, Board of Directors: Saudi Aramco, 2013–; BJ Services, 2017–; Chm., Adv. Bd, Kayrros, 2016–. Mem., Prime Minister's Council for Sci. and Technol., 2004–07. Member: Adv. Bd, King Fahd Univ. Petroleum and Minerals, Dhahran, Saudi Arabia, 2007–; Bd of Trustees, King Abdullah Univ. for Sci. and Technol., Jeddah, Saudi Arabia, 2009–. *Recreation:* fly fishing.
*See also* D. J. Gould.

GOULD, Bryan Charles, CNZM 2005; Vice-Chancellor, Waikato University, New Zealand, 1994–2004; Chair, National Centre for Tertiary Teaching Excellence, since 2007; *b* 11 Feb. 1939; *s* of Charles Terence Gould and Elsie May Driller; *m* 1967, Gillian Anne Harrigan; one *s* one *d*. *Educ:* Auckland Univ. (BA, LLM); Balliol Coll., Oxford (MA, BCL). HM Diplomatic Service: FO, 1964–66; HM Embassy, Brussels, 1966–68; Fellow and Tutor in Law, Worcester Coll., Oxford, 1968–74. MP (Lab): Southampton Test, Oct. 1974–1979; Dagenham, 1983–94; an opposition spokesman on trade, 1983–86, on economy and party campaigns, 1986–87, on Trade and Industry, 1987–89, on the environment, 1989–92, on national heritage, 1992 (Mem. of Shadow Cabinet, 1986–92). Presenter/Reporter, TV Eye, Thames Television, 1979–83. Chm., Eastern Bay Primary Health Alliance, 2011–. Chm., Foundn for Res., Sci. and Technol., 2008–11. Hon. Dr Waikato, 2006. *Publications:* Monetarism or Prosperity?, 1981; Socialism and Freedom, 1985; A Future for Socialism, 1989; Goodbye to All That (memoirs), 1995; The Democracy Sham, 2006; Rescuing The New Zealand Economy, 2008; Myths, Politicians and Money, 2013. *Recreations:* gardening, food, wine. *Address:* 239 Ohiwa Beach Road, Opotiki, New Zealand.

GOULD, David John, CB 2004; defence, programme management, government and industry consultant, since 2015; *b* 9 April 1949; *s* of James McIntosh Gould and Joan Vivienne Gould; *m* 1st, 1973; two *s* one *d*; 2nd, 2001, Christine Lake. *Educ:* West Buckland Sch., Barnstaple; Univ. of Sussex (Hons, French and European Studies). Joined MoD Naval Weapons Dept, 1973; Materiel Finance (Air), 1978; NATO Defence College, 1980; MoD (Air), 1981; UK Delegn to NATO, 1983; Asst Sec., Materiel Finance (Air), 1987; Head of Resources and Programmes (Air), 1990; Assistant Under-Secretary of State: (Supply and Orgn) (Air), 1992; Policy, 1993; seconded to Cabinet Office, 1993–95; Asst Under-Sec. of State, Fleet Support, 1995–99; Dir Gen., Finance and Business Plans, Defence Logistics Orgn, MoD, 1999–2000; Dep. Chief Exec., Defence Procurement Agency, 2000–07; Chief Operating Officer, Defence Equipment and Support, MoD, 2007–08; Gen. Manager, Submarines, Dept of Defence, Australia, 2012–15. Non-exec. Dir, Vega Consulting Services Ltd, 2009–10; Exec. Chm., Selex Systems Integration Ltd, 2010–12. Silver Jubilee Medal, 1977. *Recreations:* fitness, Bath Rugby, fly fishing (Avon and tributaries), music, especially opera and lieder.
*See also* A. F. J. Gould.

GOULD, Edward John Humphrey, MA; FRGS; Master, Marlborough College, 1993–2004; *b* Lewes, Sussex, 31 Oct. 1943; *s* of Roland and Ruth Gould; *m* 1970, Jennifer Jane, *d* of I. H. Lamb; two *d*. *Educ:* St Edward's Sch., Oxford; St Edmund Hall, Oxford (BA 1966, MA 1970, DipEd 1967). FRGS 1974. Harrow School, 1967–83: Asst Master, 1967–83; Head, Geography Dept, 1974–79; Housemaster, 1979–83; Headmaster, Felsted Sch., 1983–93. Chm., ISC, 2006–07 (Mem., Council, and Policy Cttee (Chm., 2000), 2000–02); Member: Ind. Schs Curriculum Cttee, 1985–92 (Chm., 1990–92); Bd, QCA, 2002–07; Bd, United Learning Trust, 2004–14 (Chm., 2010–14); Bd, ESU, 2004–11 (Dep. Chm., 2005–11); Nat. Council for Educnl Excellence, 2007–10. Chairman: ISIS East, 1989–93; HMC, 2002. Governor: St Edward's Sch., Oxford, 2003–11; Harrow Sch., 2004–16; Norwich Sch., 2004–16; Gresham's Sch., 2013–19; Chm., Harrow Internat. Schs Ltd, 2009–. JP Essex, 1989–93. *Recreations:* Rugby (Oxford Blue, 1963–66), swimming (Half Blue, 1965), rowing (rep. GB, 1967), music, golf, sailing. *Address:* Brette Cottage, Cross Lane, Brancaster, Norfolk PE31 8AE. *Clubs:* East India, Devonshire, Sports and Public Schools; Vincent's (Oxford).

GOULD, Jane Elizabeth; *see* Cannon, J. E.

GOULD, Matthew Steven, CMG 2014; MBE 1998; Chief Executive Officer, NHSX, since 2019; *b* 20 Aug. 1971; *s* of Sidney and Jean Gould; *m* 2009, Celia Jane Leaberry; two *d*. *Educ:* Orley Farm Sch., Harrow; St Paul's Sch., Barnes; Peterhouse, Cambridge (BA Theol. 1993). Teacher, Nyarukunda Secondary Sch., Zimbabwe, 1989–90; entered FCO, 1993; Manila, 1994–97; Speech Writer to Foreign Sec., 1997–99; Dep. Hd, Consular Div., FCO, 1999–2001; Political Counsellor, Islamabad, 2002–03; Dep. Hd of Mission, Tehran, 2003–05; Counsellor (Foreign and Security Policy), Washington, 2005–07; Pvte Sec. for For. Affairs to Prime Minister (on secondment), 2007; Principal Private Sec. to Sec. of State for Foreign and Commonwealth Affairs, 2007–10; Ambassador to Israel, 2010–15; Dir,

Cyber Security and Inf. Assurance, Cabinet Office (on secondment), 2015–16; Dir, EU Referendum Unit, 2016; Dir Gen. for Digital and Media, DCMS, 2016–19. *Recreations:* horse-riding, ski-ing, films, cats and dogs, curry.

**GOULD, Patricia,** CBE 1978; RRC 1972; Matron-in-Chief, Queen Alexandra's Royal Naval Nursing Service, 1976–80; *b* 27 May 1924; *d* of Arthur Wellesley Gould. *Educ:* Marist Convent, Paignton. Lewisham Gen. Hosp., SRN, 1945; Hackney Hosp., CMB Pt I, 1946; entered QARNNS, as Nursing Sister, 1948; accepted for permanent service, 1954; Matron, 1966; Principal Matron, 1970; Principal Matron Naval Hosps, 1975. QHNS 1976–80. OStJ (Comdr Sister), 1977. *Recreations:* gardening, photography.

**GOULD, Peter John Walter;** Owner/Director, Gould Advisory Services Ltd, 2007–12; Chief Executive, Northamptonshire County Council, 2000–07; Clerk to Lord-Lieutenant of Northamptonshire, 2000–07; *b* 10 Feb. 1953; *s* of Morris Edwin Gould and Hilda Annette Gould; *m* 1977, June Lesley Sutton; one *s. Educ:* Yeovil Sch., Som; NE London Poly. (BScSoc, London Univ.). Res. Fellow, Sch. for Independent Study, NE London Poly., 1976; London Borough of Lambeth, 1977–98: Hd of Strategy, 1995; Dir of Personnel, 1996–98; Corporate Dir, Middlesbrough Unitary Council, 1998–2000. Chair, 78 Derngate Trust, 2008–14. Mem., Eye Town Council, 2014–. FRSA 2007. *Recreations:* music, opera, flute, cooking, literature, social history, woodcarving. *Address:* Brome Park Farm, Brome Avenue, Eye, Suffolk IP23 7HW.

**GOULD, Richard;** Chief Executive, Surrey County Cricket Club, since 2011; *b* London, 14 March 1970; *s* of Bobby and Margery Gould; *m* 1993, Rebecca Yelland; two *d. Educ:* Bristol Grammar Sch.; Royal Mil. Acad., Sandhurst; Army Staff Coll. Jun. Div. and Cranfield Univ.; Harvard Business Sch. (AMP). Served RTR, 1990–2001 (retd as Major). Commercial Dir, Bristol City FC, 2001–05; CEO, Somerset CCC, 2005–11. Trustee, Addaction, 2017–. *Recreations:* cycling, shooting, Left Bank wines. *Address:* Treetops House, Hare Lane, Buckland St Mary, Som TA20 3JT. *T:* (01823) 480592. *E:* rgould@surreycricket.com.

**GOULD, Robert;** JP; DL; Member, Glasgow City Council, 1994–2003 (Leader, 1994–97); *b* 8 Feb. 1935; *s* of James and Elizabeth Gould; *m* 1953, Helen Wire; two *s* two *d. Educ:* Albert Secondary Sch. Formerly with BR. Entered local government, 1970: Glasgow Corp., 1970–74; Mem., Strathclyde Regl Council, 1974–96 (Leader, 1992–96). JP Glasgow; DL Glasgow, 1997. *Recreations:* all sports (spectator), hill-walking. *Address:* Flat 6D, 15 Eccles Street, Springburn, Glasgow G22 6BJ. *T:* (0141) 558 6438.

**GOULD, Prof. Warwick Leslie;** Professor of English Literature, University of London, 1995–2013, now Emeritus; Founder Director, Institute of English Studies, School of Advanced Study, University of London, 1999–2013, now Senior Research Fellow; *b* 7 April 1947; *s* of Leslie William Gould and Fedora Gould (*née* Green). *Educ:* Brisbane Grammar Sch.; Univ. of Queensland (BA 1st Cl. Hons English Language and Lit. 1969). Royal Holloway College, then Royal Holloway and Bedford New College, University of London: Lectr in English Language and Lit., 1973–86; Sen. Lectr, 1986–91; Reader in English Lit., 1991–95; British Acad. Res. Reader, 1992–94; Prof., 1995–; Dep. Prog. Dir, 1994–97, Prog. Dir, 1997–99, Centre for English Studies, Sch. of Advanced Study, Univ. of London; Dep. Dean, 2000–03, Mem., Bd, 2011–13, Sch. of Advanced Study. Acting Dir, Inst. of Commonwealth Studies, 2009. University of London: Member: Senate, 1990–94; Academic Council, 1990–94; Academic Cttee, 1994–2000; Council, 1995–2000 and 2002–09. FRSL 1997; FRSA 1998; FEA 1999. Cecil Oldman Meml Medal for Bibliography and Textual Criticism, Leeds Univ., 1993; British Acad. Pres.'s Medal, 2012. Editor, Yeats Annual, 1983–. *Publications:* (jtly) Joachim of Fiore and the Myth of the Eternal Evangel, 1987, 2nd edn, as Joachim of Fiore and the Myth of the Eternal Evangel in the Nineteenth and Twentieth Centuries, 2001; (ed jtly) The Secret Rose: stories by W. B. Yeats, 1981, 2nd edn 1992; (ed jtly) The Collected Letters of W. B. Yeats, Vol. II 1896–1990, 1997; (jtly) Gioacchino da Fiore e il mito dell'Evangelo eterno nella cultura europea, 2000; (ed jtly) Mythologies by W. B. Yeats, 2005; (ed) The Living Stream: essays in memory of A. Norman Jeffares, 2013; (ed jtly) Yeats's Mask, 2013; (ed) Yeats's Legacies, 2018. *Recreation:* book collecting. *Address:* Institute of English Studies, Room 260, Senate House, Malet Street, WC1E 7HU. *T:* (020) 7862 8673, *Fax:* (020) 7862 8720. *E:* warwick.gould@sas.ac.uk.

**GOULDBOURNE, Rev. Dr Ruth Mary Boyd;** Minister, Grove Lane Baptist Church, Cheadle Hulme, since 2018; *b* 5 July 1961; *d* of Derek Boyd Murray and Giles Watson Murray; *m* 1984, Ian Duncan Gouldbourne. *Educ:* Drummond High Sch., Edinburgh; St Andrews Univ. (MA 1983); King's Coll. London (BD 1986; MA Shakespearean Studies 2017); Royal Holloway and Bedford New Coll., Univ. of London (PhD 2000); Bristol Univ. (Postgrad. Dip. Counselling 2004). Baptist Minister, Bunyan Meeting Free Ch, 1988–95; Tutor, Bristol Baptist Coll., 1995–2006; Co-Minister, Bloomsbury Central Baptist Ch, 2006–18. *Publications:* Reinventing the Wheel: women and ministry in English Baptist history, 1997; The Flesh and the Feminine: gender and theology in the writings of Caspar Schwenckfeld, 2007; (jtly) On Being the Church, 2008; (ed jtly) Questions of Identity: studies in honour of Brian Haymes, 2011; articles in jls. *Recreations:* reading, live theatre, wine, cross-stitch, dolls house building, being bemused at being in Who's Who. *Address:* Grove Lane Baptist Church, Pingate Lane South, Cheadle Hulme, Cheadle, Cheshire SK8 7NP.

**GOULDEN, Sir (Peter) John,** GCMG 2001 (KCMG 1996; CMG 1989); PhD; HM Diplomatic Service, retired; *b* 21 Feb. 1941; *s* of George Herbert Goulden and Doris Goulden; *m* 1962, Diana Margaret Elizabeth Waite; one *s* one *d. Educ:* King Edward VII Sch., Sheffield; Queen's Coll., Oxford (BA 1st Cl. Hons History, 1962); Durham Univ. (PhD Music 2013). HM Diplomatic Service, 1962–2001: Ankara, 1963–67; Manila, 1969–70; Dublin, 1976–79; Head of Personnel Services Dept, 1980–82; Head of News Dept, FCO, 1982–84; Counsellor and Hd of Chancery, Office of the UK Permt Rep. to EEC, Brussels, 1984–87; Asst Under-Sec. of State, FCO, 1988–92; Ambassador to Turkey, 1992–95; Ambassador and UK Perm. Rep. to N Atlantic Council and to Perm. Council of WEU, 1995–2001. *Recreations:* music, theatre, opera, family.

**GOULDER, Catharine Anne O.;** *see* Otton-Goulder.

**GOULDING, Jeremy Wynne Ruthven,** MA; Headmaster, Shrewsbury School, 2001–10; *b* 29 Aug. 1950; *s* of Denis Arthur and Doreen Daphne Goulding; *m* 1974, Isobel Mary Fisher; two *s* two *d. Educ:* Becket Sch., Nottingham; Magdalen Coll., Oxford (MA, PGCE). Asst Master and Head of Divinity, Abingdon Sch., 1974–78; Head of Divinity, 1978–83, and Housemaster, Oldham's Hall, 1983–89, Shrewsbury Sch.; Headmaster: Prior Park Coll., 1989–96; Haberdashers' Aske's Sch., 1996–2001. Freeman, 2001, Liveryman, 2012–, Haberdashers' Co. *Recreations:* music-making, hill-walking. *Address:* 2 Chalford Lane, Chipping Norton, Oxon OX7 5GG.

**GOULDING, Rt Rev. June;** *see* Llandaff, Bishop of.

**GOULDING, Sir Lingard;** *see* Goulding, Sir W. L. W.

**GOULDING, Paul Anthony;** QC 2000; *b* 24 May 1960; second *s* of Byron and Audrey Goulding; *m* 1984, June Osborne (*see* Bishop of Llandaff); one *s* one *d. Educ:* Latymer Sch.; St Edmund Hall, Oxford (BA 1st Cl. Jurisprudence 1981; BCL 1982; MA). Tutor in Law, St Edmund Hall, Oxford, 1982–84; called to the Bar, Middle Temple, 1984, Bencher, 2011; practising barrister, 1985–. Chm., 1998–2000, Vice-Pres., 2000–04, Employment Lawyers Assoc.; Member: Mgt Cttee, Bar Pro Bono Unit, 2000–03; Mgt Bd, European Employment Lawyers Assoc., 2001–05; Specialist Mem., FA Judicial Panel, 2008–. *Publications:* European Employment Law and the UK, 2001; Employee Competition: covenants, confidentiality, and garden leave, 2007, 3rd edn 2016. *Recreations:* football, Rugby, golf, opera. *Address:* Blackstone Chambers, Blackstone House, Temple, EC4Y 9BW. *T:* (020) 7583 1770. *Club:* Reform.

**GOULDING, Sir (William) Lingard (Walter),** 4th Bt *cr* 1904; Headmaster of Headfort Preparatory School, 1977–2000; *b* 11 July 1940; *s* of Sir (William) Basil Goulding, 3rd Bt, and Valerie Hamilton (Senator, Seanad Éireann), *o d* of 1st Viscount Monckton of Brenchley, PC, GCVO, KCMG, MC, QC; S father, 1982, but his name does not appear on the Official Roll of the Baronetage. *Educ:* Ludgrove; Winchester College; Trinity College, Dublin (BA, HDipEd). Computer studies for Zinc Corporation and Sulphide Corporation, Conzinc Rio Tinto of Australia, 1963–66; Systems Analyst, Goulding Fertilisers Ltd, 1966–67; Manager and European Sales Officer for Rionore, modern Irish jewellery company, 1968–69; Racing Driver, formulae 5000, 3 and 2, 1967–71; Assistant Master: Brook House School, 1970–74; Headfort School (IAPS prep. school), 1974–76. Jr coach and curator, Goodwood Cricket Club, Adelaide, 2005–; teacher and cricket coach, St Peter's, Adelaide, 2007–12; coach, Christian Brothers Coll., Adelaide, 2013–. *Publications:* Your Children are not Your Children: the story of Headfort School, 2012. *Recreations:* squash, cricket, running, bicycling, tennis, music, reading, computers. *Heir: b* Timothy Adam Goulding [*b* 15 May 1945; *m* 1971, Patricia Mohan]. *Address:* The Habitaunce, Headfort Estate, Kells, Co. Meath, Ireland. *T:* (46) 49952.

**GOULDSBROUGH, Catherine Mary;** *see* Newman, C. M.

**GOULTY, Alan Fletcher,** CMG 1998; HM Diplomatic Service, retired; Ambassador to Tunisia, 2004–08; *b* 2 July 1947; *s* of late Anthony Edmund Rivers Goulty and Maisie Oliphant Goulty (*née* Stein); *m* 1983, Lillian Craig Harris, OBE; one *s* by former marr. *Educ:* Bootham School, York; Corpus Christi College, Oxford (MA 1972). FCO 1968; MECAS, 1969–71; Beirut, 1971–72; Khartoum, 1972–75; FCO, 1975–77; Cabinet Office, 1977–80; Washington, 1981–85; FCO, 1985–90; Counsellor, 1987; Head of Near East and N Africa Dept, 1987–90; Dep. Head of Mission, Cairo, 1990–95; Ambassador to Sudan, 1995–99; Fellow, Weatherhead Center for Internat. Affairs, Harvard Univ., 1999–2000; Dir, Middle East and N Africa, FCO, 2000–02; UK Special Rep. for Sudan, 2002–04, for Darfur, 2005–06. Sen. Scholar, 2009–13, Global Fellow, 2013–, Woodrow Wilson Internat. Center for Scholars, Washington, DC; Adjunct Prof., Georgetown Univ., 2010–11. Cross of St Augustine, Lambeth, 2002. Grand Cordon du Wissam Alaouite (Morocco), 1987. *Recreations:* Real tennis, chess, bird-watching, gardening. *Clubs:* Travellers, Royal Over-Seas League, MCC.

**GOURDAULT-MONTAGNE, Maurice,** Hon. CMG 2004; Hon. LVO 1992; Secretary General, Ministry of Foreign Affairs, France, since 2017; *b* Paris, 16 Nov. 1953; *s* of Col Jean Gourdault-Montagne and Colette Nelly Bastide; *m* 1st, 1980, Soline de Courrèges d'Agnos (marr. diss. 2011); two *s* three *d,* 2nd, 2017, Amanda Galsworthy. *Educ:* Institut d'Études Politiques, Paris (MA 1975); Faculté de Droit, Paris II (MA 1976); Institut Nat. des Langues et Civilisations Orientales (MA 1977; Dip. Hindi and Urdu 1977). Joined Min. of Foreign Affairs, 1978; Indian Desk, 1978–81; First Sec., New Delhi, 1981–83; Pvte Sec. to Sec. Gen., 1983–86; Advr to Foreign Minister for Parlt and Press, 1986–88; Counsellor, Bonn, 1988–91; Dep., then Actg Spokesman, Min. of Foreign Affairs, 1991–93; Dep. Principal Sec. to the Foreign Minister, 1993–95; Principal Sec., Head of Prime Minister's Office, 1995–97; Ambassador to Japan, 1998–2002; Sen. Diplomatic Advr to President of France and G8 Sherpa, 2002–07; Ambassador: to the Court of St James's, 2007–11; to Germany, 2011–14; of France to China, 2014–17. Director: EDF, 2017–; Orano, 2017–. Chevalier de l'Ordre national du Mérite, 1998; Officier de la Légion d'Honneur, 2010. *Recreations:* music (opera), history, linguistics, hiking and mountaineering. *Address:* (office) 37 Quai d'Orsay, 75007 Paris, France.

**GOURGEON, Pierre-Henri;** President, 1998–2011 and Chief Executive Officer, 2009–11, Air France (Chief Operating Officer, 1998–2008); President and Chief Executive Officer, Air France-KLM, 2009–11 (Deputy Chief Executive Officer, 2004–08); *b* 28 April 1946; *s* of Henri Gourgeon and Hélène (*née* Deiziani); *m* 1969, Mireille Blanc; one *s* one *d. Educ:* Lycée Gautier à Alger, Algeria; Lycée Louis-le-Grand, Paris; Ecole polytechnique, Paris; Ecole nationale supérieure de l'aéronautique; California Inst. of Technol. (MSc). Fighter pilot, French Air Force; engrg posts in aeronautical tech. and prodn depts, MoD, 1971–81; Mem., Prime Minister's staff, 1981–83; Special Tech. Advr to Minister of Labour and Vocational Trng, 1984; Vice-Pres. i/c mil. progs, Soc. nationale d'études et de constructions de moteurs d'avions, 1985–88; Special Advr to Minister of Transport, Equipt and Housing, 1988–90; Dir Gen., Civil Aviation Authorities, 1990–93; Pres., Eur. Civil Aviation Conf., 1993; Air France Group, 1993–2011: Chairman: and CEO, Servair Gp, 1993–96; and CEO, Esterel, 1996–97; Amadeus Internat., 1997–2002; Exec. Vice-Pres. for Corporate Develt and Internat. Affairs, 1997–98. Officier: Ordre national du Mérite; de la Légion d'honneur. *Recreations:* flying, ski-ing.

**GOURGEY, Alan;** QC 2003; *b* 27 Oct. 1961; *s* of Zaki and Vilma Gourgey; *m* 1987, Rosalynd Samuels; two *s* one *d. Educ:* Epsom Coll.; Bristol Univ. (LLB Hons); Inns of Court Sch. of Law. Called to the Bar, Lincoln's Inn, 1984; in practice, specialising in commercial litigation. *Recreations:* 5-a-side football, golf, Daf Yomi, my family. *Address:* Wilberforce Chambers, 8 New Square, Lincoln's Inn, WC2A 3QP.

**GOURIET, Gerald William;** QC 2006; *b* 31 March 1947; *s* of Geoffrey George Gouriet, CBE and Anne Wallace (*née* Campbell). *Educ:* Royal Coll. of Music (BMus). Called to the Bar, Inner Temple, 1974; in practice at the Bar, 1974–; writing film music, Hollywood, 1991–99: Madame Sousatzka, 1988; A Question of Attribution, 1992; The Innocent, 1994; The Substitute, 1996. Liveryman, Distillers' Co., 2017–. *Publications:* (ed jtly) Paterson's Licensing Acts, 2011–; (ed jtly) Smith & Monkcom: the law of gambling, 4th edn 2017. *Recreations:* music, film, theatre. *Address:* Francis Taylor Building, Inner Temple, EC4Y 7BY. *Club:* Travellers.

**GOURLAY, Robert Martin, (Robin);** Chairman, awg (formerly Anglian Water) plc, 1994–2003; *b* 21 April 1939; *s* of late Cleland Gourlay and Janice (*née* Martin); *m* 1971, Rosemary Puckle Cooper; one *s* two *d. Educ:* Sedbergh Sch.; St Andrews Univ. (BSc). Joined BP, 1958: Gen. Manager, BP of Greece, 1970–74; European Finance and Planning Co-ordinator, 1975–77; Asst Gen. Manager, Corporate Planning, 1978–79; Gen. Manager, Public Affairs, 1979–83; BP Australia: Dir, Refining and Marketing, 1983–86; Chief Exec., 1986–90; Chm., BP PNG, 1986–90; Dir, BP NZ, 1988–90; Chief Exec., BP Nutrition, 1990–94. Chairman: Rugby Gp plc, 1994–2000 (non-exec. Dir, 1994–96); Fundamental Data, 2000–08; Director: Beazer Gp (formerly Beazer Homes) plc, 1995–2001; Astec (BSR) plc, 1996–99. Bd Mem., Australia Staff Coll., Mt Eliza, 1986–90; Chm., BITC,

Victoria, 1988–90. Mem. Council, WaterAid, 1995–2002; Chm., Meath Epilepsy Trust, 2004–14. Gov., Sedbergh Sch., 2002–09. *Recreations:* music, gardening, tennis, Greece and Greek affairs. *Club:* Boodle's.

**GOURLEY, Prof. Brenda Mary;** company director and higher education consultant; Vice-Chancellor and President, Open University, 2002–09; *b* 1 Dec. 1943; *d* of William and Irene Elliott; *m* 1966, James Ednie Gourley; three *s* one *d*. *Educ:* Univ. of Witwatersrand (Cert. Theory of Accountancy); Univ. of S Africa (MBL). Professional Chartered Accountant; Dep. Vice-Chancellor, 1988–93, Vice-Chancellor and Principal, 1994–2001, Univ. of Natal. Non-exec. Dir, SAGE Publications, 2006–11; Ind. non-exec. Dir, AdvTech Ltd, 2008–; Dir, Internat. Assoc. for Digital Publishing, 2009–17. Member: Bd, ACU, 1997–2009 (Chm., 1996–97, 2007–09); Bd, Internat. Assoc. of Univs, 2000–08; Unesco Bd of Educn, 2005–06; Bd, Talloires Network, 2007–13 (Mem., Steering Cttee, 2005–11); Bd, Nat. Inst. of Adult Continuing Educn, 2009–11; Council, Univ. of Brighton, 2011–15; Bd, City and Guilds Inst., 2011–15. Trustee, Royal Anniversary Trust, 2011–16; Trustee, Council for Educn in Commonwealth, 2013–15 (Chair, 2013–15). Gov., Univ. of the World, 2012–15 (Chair, 2012–15). FCGI 2008; FRSA 2016. Hon. Fellow: Open Univ. of Israel, 2008; Commonwealth of Learning, 2008; Open Univ., 2011; Hon. LLD Nottingham, 1997; Hon. DHL Richmond, Amer. Internat. Univ. in London, 2004; Hon. DEd: Abertay Dundee, 2004; Witwatersrand, 2013; Hon. DPhil: Allama Iqbal, 2007; SA, 2011; Gloucestershire, 2011; Hon. Dr: Québec à Montreal, 2007; Open Univ. of Netherlands, 2009; Open Univ. of Catalonia, 2011; Hon. DCom Pretoria, 2008. Symon's Medal, Assoc. of Commonwealth Univs, 2008; Ind. Prize of Excellence, Internat. Council for Distance Educn, 2008; UK Internat. Public Servant of the Year and Outstanding Achiever of the Year, Women in Public Life Initiative, 2009; Outstanding Educator Award, Univ. of S Africa, 2014. *Publications:* Dancing with History: a cautionary tale, 2010; (contrib.) Turning the University Upside Down: actions for the future, 2011; (contrib.) Higher Education and Civic Engagement, 2012; (contrib.) Open and Distance Education, 2013; (contrib.) Reflections of South African University Leaders 1981 to 2014, 2016; (contrib.) Just and Lasting Change, 2016; contrib. The Independent, THES, Univ. World News, etc. *Recreations:* reading, writing, public speaking, gardening. *Address:* 88 Wayland Avenue, Brighton, E Sussex BN1 5JN. *T:* (01273) 509791. *W:* brendagourley.com.

**GOVE, Rt Hon. Michael (Andrew);** PC 2010; MP (C) Surrey Heath, since 2005; Chancellor of the Duchy of Lancaster, since 2019; *b* 26 Aug. 1967; *s* of Ernest and Christine Gove; *m* 2001, Sarah Vine; one *s* one *d*. *Educ:* Robert Gordon's Coll., Aberdeen; Lady Margaret Hall, Oxford (BA). Reporter, Aberdeen Press and Jl, 1989; researcher/reporter, Scottish TV, 1990–91; reporter, BBC News and Current Affairs, 1991–95; editor, 1995–2005, writer, 1995–2010, columnist, 2016–17, The Times. Sec. of State for Educn, 2010–14; Parly Sec. to HM Treasury (Govt Chief Whip), 2014–15; Lord Chancellor and Sec. of State for Justice, 2015–16; Sec. of State for Envmt, Food and Rural Affairs, 2017–19. *Publications:* Michael Portillo, 1995; The Price of Peace: a study of the Northern Ireland peace process, 2000; Celsius 7/7, 2006. *Address:* House of Commons, SW1A 0AA. *T:* (020) 7219 3000.

**GOVENDER, Very Rev. Rogers Morgan,** MBE 2019; Dean of Manchester, since 2006; *b* 29 June 1960; *s* of Joseph and Sheila Govender; *m* 1985, Celia; one *s* one *d*. *Educ:* St Paul's Coll., Grahamstown, RSA (DipTh 1985); Univ. of Natal (BTh 1997). Ordained deacon, 1985, priest, 1986; Curate, Christ Church, Overport, S Africa, 1985–87; Rector: St Mary's, Greyville, Durban, SA, 1988–93; St Matthew's, Hayfields, Pietermaritzburg, 1993–97; Archdeacon, Pietermaritzburg, 1997–99; Rector, St Thomas, Berea, Durban, 1999–2000; Priest-in-charge, Christ Church, Didsbury, Manchester, 2000–06; Area Dean, Withington, 2003–06. *Recreations:* fishing, walking, reading, listening to music (esp. rock, classical and folk). *Address:* 1 Booth-Clibborn Court, Park Lane, Salford M7 4PJ. *T:* (0161) 833 2220. *E:* dean@manchestercathedral.org.

**GOVENDIR, Ian John;** business coach, since 2006; Founder, 2009, and Chief Executive Officer, since 2014, Aids Orphan UK Trust (Chairman, 2009–14); *b* 5 April 1960; *s* of Philip Govendir and Eve Karis Govendir (née Cohen). *Educ:* City of London Poly. (HND (Dist.) Business and Finance); Univ. of Lancaster (MA Mktg). MCIM 1990; MInstF 1992. Asst Product Manager, then Showroom Manager, Sony UK Ltd, 1979–83; Direct Marketing Manager, Bull Computers, 1988–92; Head of Direct Marketing/Fundraising, BRCS, 1992–94; Chief Exec., British Lung Foundn, 1994–96; marketing and fundraising consultant, Ian Govendir Marketing, 1997–2000; Marketing Manager, Jewish Care, 2000–02; Chief Exec., Complementary Health Trust, 2002–03; Head of Fundraising, Carers UK, 2003–04; on sabbatical, travelling the world, Sri Lanka tsunami relief, 2004–05; life coach, 2006–; Hd of Big Gifts and Legacies, then of Develt, National Deaf Children's Soc. and Deaf Child Worldwide, 2007–09; Hd of Individual Giving, ABF The Soldiers' Charity, 2010. Hon. Vis. Prof., Guildhall Sch. of Business and Law, London Metropolitan Univ., 2015–; part-time Lectr in Marketing, London Guildhall Univ., 1992–95; Fellow, and Lectr in strategic mkting and voluntary sector mgt, MSc prog., South Bank Univ., 2007–. Member: CSCLeaders progs, 2015–; New London Synagogue Council, 2016–19; Emerging Leaders Dialogue, 2017– (Mem. Bd, 2018–). Sec., UK Coalition Trust, 1996–97; Member, Board: Cara, 2007– (Treas., 2011–12; Chm., 2012–); Home Live Art, 2009–12; Riverhouse Trust, 2018–; Trustee: Jewish AIDS Trust, 1998–2003; Stop Aids, 2000–15; UK Consortium on AIDS and Internat. Develt, 2011–; Royal Commonwealth Soc., 2012–15. Interim Dir, Commonwealth Business Council, 2013. FRSA 1996. Halifax Giving Extra Award, 2015. *Recreations:* leadership development in the Commonwealth, swimming, travel, cooking, gardening, preservation of national heritage, such as National Trust, architecture old and new, effect of religions on society, Middle Eastern politics, digital photography, interested in what is happening with the fight against AIDS and involved with a number of grass roots orgns. *E:* ian@aidsorphan.net

**GOVETT, William John Romaine;** *b* 11 Aug. 1937; *s* of John Romaine Govett and Angela Mostyn (née Pritchard); *m* 1st, Mary Hays; two *s* one *d*; 2nd, Penelope Irwin; one *d*; 3rd, 1994, Jacqueline de Brabant. *Educ:* Sandroyd; Gordonstoun. National Service, commnd Royal Scots Greys, 1956–58. Joined John Govett & Co. Ltd, 1961; Chm., 1974–86; Dep. Chm., 1986–90. Director: Legal & General Gp, 1972–96; Govett Oriental Investment Trust, 1972–98; Govett Strategic Investment Trust, 1975–98; Scottish Eastern Investment Trust, 1977–98; Govett Amer. Smaller Cos Trust (formerly Govett Atlantic Investment Trust), 1979–98; Union Jack Oil Co., 1981–94; 3i (formerly Investors in Industry), 1984–98; Coal Investment Nominees NCB Pension Fund, 1985–96; Ranger Oil (UK), 1988–95; Ranger Oil (N Sea), 1995–97; Halifax Financial Services (Hldgs), 1998–2002; Halifax Life, 1998–2002; Halifax Unit Trust Mgt, 1998–2002; Halifax Fund Mgt, 1998–2002; Insight Investment Mgt (formerly Clerical and Medical Investment Mgt) Ltd, 2002–09. Chairman: Hungarian Investment Co., 1990–98; 3i Smaller Quoted Cos Trust, 1996–2006; Govett Mexican Horizons Investment Co. Ltd, 1991–96. Advr, Mineworkers' Pension Scheme, 1996–2003. Trustee: NACF, 1985–2008; Tate Gall., 1988–93. *Recreations:* modern art, fishing.

**GOW, David James,** CBE 2014; FREng; Head, Smart Services, NHS Lothian, 2009–15; *b* Dumfries, 15 Jan. 1957; *s* of James Gow and Effie Gow; *m* 2004, Janet Brunton. *Educ:* Annan Acad., Dumfriesshire; Univ. of Edinburgh (BSc Hons); Queen Margaret Univ. (Postgrad. Dip.). CEng 1995; CSci 2004; FIPEM 2009; FREng 2010. Develt Engr, Electro-Optics Gp, Ferranti, Scotland, 1980–81; Res. Associate, Univ. of Edinburgh, 1981–84; NHS Lothian, 1984–: Dir, Rehabilitation Engrg Services, 1993–2009; on pt-time secondment as CEO, Touch Emas Ltd, 2002–04, Dir of Res. and Technol., Touch Bionics, 2004–09. FRSA. Hon. DSc Edinburgh, 2018. MacRobert Award, RAEng, 2008. *Publications:* papers in various jls and patents. *Recreations:* football (watching, videoing and archiving Queen of the South Football Club), cricket, music. *Address:* 33 Fox Spring Rise, Edinburgh EH10 6NE. *T:* (0131) 445 2450. *E:* David.Gow@blueyonder.co.uk.

**GOW, Dame Jane;** *see* Whiteley, Dame J. E.

**GOW, John Stobie,** PhD; CChem, FRSC; FRSE 1978; Secretary-General, Royal Society of Chemistry, 1986–93; *b* 12 April 1933; *s* of David Gow and Jeannie Gow; *m* 1955, Elizabeth Henderson; three *s*. *Educ:* Alloa Acad.; Univ. of St Andrews (BSc, PhD). Res. Chemist, ICI, Billingham, 1958; Prodn Man., Chem. Co. of Malaysia, 1966–68; ICI: Res. Man., Agric. Div., 1968–72; Gen. Man. (Catalysts), Agric. Div., 1972–74; Res. Dir, Organics, 1974–79; Dep. Chm., Organics, 1979–84; Man. Dir, Speciality Chemicals, 1984–86. Assessor, SERC, 1988–94; Sec., CSTI, 1995–2001; Chief Exec., Sci. Council, 2001–02; Dir, Sci., Engrg and Manufacturing Technol. Assoc., 2002–05. FRSA 1980. *Publications:* papers and patents in Fertilizer Technology and Biotechnology. *Recreations:* choral music, golf. *Address:* 19 Longcroft Avenue, Harpenden, Herts AL5 2RD. *T:* (01582) 764889.

**GOW, Prof. Neil Andrew Robert,** PhD; FRS 2016; FRSB; FMedSci; FRSE; Deputy Vice-Chancellor for Research and Impact, University of Exeter, since 2018; *b* Tezpur, India, 30 Nov. 1957; *s* of Ian Douglas Gow and Rosalie Mallet Gow; *m* 2006, Dr Gillian Christine Auld; three *s* two *d*. *Educ:* Newport-on-Tay Primary Sch.; Madras Coll., St Andrews; Perth Acad.; Edinburgh Univ. (BSc 1st Cl. Hons Microbiol. 1979); Aberdeen Univ. (PhD 1983). University of Aberdeen: Lectr in Microbiol., 1983–90; Sen. Lectr, 1990–93; Reader, 1993–95; Prof. of Microbiol., Coll. of Life Scis and Medicine, 1995–2018. President: British Mycological Soc., 2001–03; Internat. Soc. of Human and Animal Mycol., 2012–15; Microbiol. Soc., 2016–18. FRSB (FSB 2000); FRSE 2001; Fellow, Amer. Acad. of Microbiol.; FMedSci 2015. Hon. DSc Kent, 2018. *Publications:* contribs to learned jls incl. Microbiol., Current Opinion in Microbiol., Jl Bacteriol., Trends in Microbiol., Nature, Molecular Microbiol., Jl Clin. Investigation, Jl Clin. Microbiol., Proc. NAS, Infection and Immunity. *Recreation:* fly fishing. *Address:* University of Exeter, Prince of Wales Road, Exeter EX4 4SB.

**GOW, Roderick Charles,** OBE 2002; Founder, Canongate Partners Ltd, since 2011; *b* 9 Sept. 1947; *s* of Gen. Sir (James) Michael Gow, GCB and Jane Emily Gow (née Scott); *m* 1st, 1977, Anne Bayart (*d* 2000); two *s*; 2nd, 2001, April Sgro Riddle. *Educ:* Winchester Coll.; Trinity Coll., Cambridge (BA 1970, MA 1972). ACIB 1982. Capt., Scots Guards, NW Germany, NI and Belgium, 1966–78; ADC to Chm., Mil. Cttee, NATO, Brussels, 1975–77; Instructor, RMA, Sandhurst, 1977–78. Barclays Bank, London and NY, 1978–83 (Vice-Pres., to 1983); Russell Reynolds Associates, London, 1983–91 (Man. Dir, UK, then Man. Dir, Internat., 1986–91); Chief Exec., GKR Gp, London, 1991–93, NY, 1993–95; Exec. Vice Pres. and Co-Hd, Global Financial Services Practice, NY, LAI Worldwide, later TMP, 1995–2000; Chm., Americas, later Dep. Chm., Worldwide, Amrop Internat., 1995–99; Odgers, Ray & Berndtson: London Dir, 2000–02; Chm. Bd, Practice and Financial Services Practice, 2000–02; Founder and Chm. of Gow & Partners Gp, later Gow & Partners World Team, 2002–09; Chief Exec., Asia House, 2010–11; Chm. and Founder, Asia Scotland Inst., 2012–. Chm., Adv. Bd, Positive Moves Consulting (UK) Ltd, 011–12; Vice-Chm., Cubitt Consulting, 2011–16. Chm., Action Resource Centre, 1991–93. Chm., British American Chamber of Commerce of NY and London, 1999–2001; Chm., Pres. and Vice-Pres., British American Business Council, 2001–03; Mem. Bd, British American Business, 2006. Chm. and Founder, Asia Scotland Inst., 2012–; Mem. Bd, Oceana Energy UK Ltd, 2016–; Mem., Internat. Adv. Bd, Ethics Metrics, 2015–. Mem., Adv. Council, Prince of Wales Business Trust, 2002–03. Mem., Business Adv. Council, Saïd Business Sch., Oxford Univ., 2006–15. Mem. Council, Brookings Instn, 2008–09. Member: Adv. Council, LSO (Co-Chm., Amer. Foundn), 2001–09; Adv. Bd, Welsh Nat. Opera, 2012–14; Chm., Commonwealth Youth Orch., 2011–12. Mem., Guild of Internat. Bankers, 2001–09. FIPD; FRSA. Fellow, Foreign Policy Assoc., 1994–2000. Mem., Royal Co. of Archers, Queen's Bodyguard for Scotland, 1982–. *Recreations:* shooting, sailing, music, reading. *E:* roddy.gow@canongatepartners.com. *Clubs:* Brooks's, Pratt's, Cavalry and Guards; New (Edinburgh); Indian Harbor Yacht (Greenwich, CT).

**GOWAN, David John,** CMG 2005; HM Diplomatic Service, retired; *b* 11 Feb. 1949; *s* of late Prof. Ivor Lyn Gowan and of Gwendoline Alice Gowan (née Pearce); *m* 1975, Marna Irene Williams; two *s*. *Educ:* Nottingham High Sch.; Ardwyn Grammar Sch., Aberystwyth; Balliol Coll., Oxford (MA Eng. Lang. and Lit.). Asst Principal, MoD, 1970–73; Home CS, 1973–75; joined HM Diplomatic Service, 1975: Second Sec., FCO, 1975–76; Russian lang. trng, 1976–77; Second, then First Sec., Moscow, 1977–80; First Sec., FCO, 1981–85; Hd of Chancery and Consul, Brasilia, 1985–88; on secondment to Cabinet Office, 1988–89; Asst Hd, Soviet Dept, FCO, 1989–90; on secondment, as Counsellor, Cabinet Office, 1990–91; Counsellor (Commercial and Know How Fund), Moscow, 1992–95; Counsellor and Dep. Hd of Mission, Helsinki, 1995–99; Counsellor, FCO, 1999; Sen. Associate Mem., St Antony's Coll., Oxford, 1999–2000; Minister, Moscow, 2000–03; Ambassador to Serbia and Montenegro, 2003–06. Guest Mem., St Antony's Coll., Oxford, 2007–10; Hon. Sen. Res. Fellow, Univ. of Birmingham, 2008–11. Chm., Russian Booker Cttee, 2012–15. Mem. Council, Keston Inst., 2009–. Mem., Bishop's Council, 2007–18, Synod, 2008–18, Dio. in Europe. *Publications:* How the EU Can Help Russia, 2000. *Recreations:* reading, walking, travel, music, theatre. *Address:* 8 Blackmore Road, Malvern, Worcs WR14 1QX. *T:* (01684) 565707. *Club:* Athenæum.

**GOWANS, Sir James (Learmonth),** Kt 1982; CBE 1971; FRCP 1975; FRS 1963; Secretary General, Human Frontier Science Programme, Strasbourg, 1989–93; Secretary, Medical Research Council, 1977–87; *b* 7 May 1924; *s* of John Gowans and Selma Josefina Ljung; *m* 1956, Moyra Leatham; one *s* two *d*. *Educ:* Whitgift Middle Sch., Croydon; King's Coll. Hosp. Med. Sch. (Med. Relief, Belsen, 1945; MB BS (Hons) 1947; Fellow, 1979); Lincoln Coll., Oxford (BA (1st cl. Hons Physiology) 1948; MA; DPhil 1953; Hon. Fellow, 1984). MRC Exchange Scholar, Pasteur Institute, Paris, 1952–53; Research Fellow, Exeter Coll., Oxford, 1955–60 (Hon. Fellow, 1983–); Fellow, St Catherine's Coll., Oxford, 1961–87 (Hon. Fellow, 1987); Henry Dale Res. Prof. of Royal Society, 1962–77; Hon. Dir, MRC Cellular Immunology Unit, 1963–77; Dir, 1980–86, Sen. Sci. Advr, 1988–90, Celltech Ltd. Consultant: WHO Global Prog. on AIDS, 1987–88; 3i plc, 1988–92. Member: MRC, 1965–69; Adv. Bd for Res. Councils, 1977–87; Director: Charing Cross Sunley Res. Centre, 1989–91; European Initiative for Communicators of Science, Munich, 1995–99. Royal Society: Mem. Council and a Vice-Pres., 1973–75; Assessor to MRC, 1973–75. Member: Governing Council, Internat. Agency for Res. on Cancer, Lyon, 1980–87; Sci. Cttee, Fondation Louis Jeantet de Médicine, Geneva, 1984–87; Council, St Christopher's Hospice, 1987–98; Res. Progs Adv. Cttee, Nat. MS Soc., NY, 1988–90;

Awards Assembly, Gen. Motors Cancer Res. Foundn, NY, 1988–90; Scientific Advr, Motor Neurone Disease Assoc., 1992–2002; Chm., Scientific Adv. Cttee, Lister Inst. of Preventive Medicine, 1994–97. Non-exec. Dir, Tavistock and Portman NHS Trust, 1994–97. Delegate, OUP, 1971–77. Trustee, Spinal Muscular Atrophy Trust, 2006–. FRSA 1994. Founder FMedSci 1998. Vis. Prof., NY Univ. Sch. of Med., 1967; Lectures: Harvey, NY, 1968; William Withering, Birmingham, 1970; Foundation, RCPath, 1970; Dunham, Harvard, 1971; Bayne-Jones, Johns Hopkins, 1973; Langdon Brown, RCP, 1980; Harveian Orator, RCP, 1987. Foreign Associate, Nat. Acad. of Scis, USA, 1985. Mem., Academia Europaea, 1991. Hon. Member: Amer. Assoc. of Immunologists; Soc. of Leukocyte Biol. Hon. ScD Yale, 1966; Hon. DSc: Chicago, 1971; Birmingham, 1978; Rochester, NY, 1987; Hon. MD: Edinburgh, 1979; Sheffield, 2000; Hon. DM Southampton, 1987; Hon. LLD Glasgow, 1988. Gairdner Foundn Award, Toronto, 1968; Paul Ehrlich Ludwig-Darmstaedter Prize, Frankfurt, 1974; Royal Medal, Royal Society, 1976; Feldberg Foundn Award, 1979; Wolf Prize in Medicine, Wolf Foundn, Israel, 1980; Medawar Prize, 1990; Galen Medal, Soc. of Apothecaries, 1991. *Publications:* articles in scientific journals. *Address:* 75 Cumnor Hill, Oxford OX2 9HX. *T:* (01865) 862304.

**GOWANS, James Palmer;** JP; DL; Lord Provost of Dundee and Lord-Lieutenant of the City of Dundee, 1980–84; *b* 15 Sept. 1930; *s* of Charles Gowans and Sarah Gowans (*née* Palmer); *m* 1950, Davina Barnett (*d* 2003); one *s* three *d* (and one *s* one *d* decd). *Educ:* Rockwell Secondary School, Dundee. With National Cash Register Co., Dundee, 1956–94. Elected to Dundee DC, May 1974; Mem., Dundee City Council, 1975–92. JP 1977; DL Dundee 1984. *Recreations:* golf, motoring. *Address:* 41 Dalmahoy Drive, Dundee DD2 3UT. *T:* (01382) 84918.

**GOWAR, Martyn Christopher;** Senior Counsel, McDermott Will & Emery UK LLP, 2014–15 (Partner, 2009–14); *b* Cheam, Surrey, 11 July 1946; *s* of Thomas Welch Gowar and Maude Annie Gowar (*née* Bower); *m* 1971, Susan Mary Scotchmer; three *s*. *Educ:* King's Coll. Sch., Wimbledon; Magdalen Coll., Oxford (MA). ATII 1976, CTA (Fellow) (FTII 1981). Lawrence Graham & Co.: articled clerk, 1967; admitted as solicitor, 1970; Partner, 1973–2006; Sen. Partner, 1997–2002; Consultant, 2006–08; Consultant, Penningtons, 2008–09. Academician, 1986, Vice Pres. (Europe), 2008–17, Internat. Acad. of Estate and Trust Law; Mem., Internat. Cttee, Soc. of Trusts and Estate Practitioners, 1996–; Mem., Exec. Cttee, Inst. of Advanced Legal Studies, 1998–2015. Chm., Succession Sub-cttee, Chartered Institute of Taxation, 2009–15; Mem., Estates Business Gp, 1997–. Internat. Fellow, Amer. Coll. of Trusts and Estate Counsel, 2011–. Gov., St Paul's Cathedral Sch., 1998–2014. Chm., Ashley Family Foundn, 2010– (Trustee, 1995–); Mem., Addington Soc., 1990–. Liveryman: Glaziers' Co., 1979–; Tax Advrs' Co., 2007–. Mem., Lord's Taverners, 1988–. FRSA 1995. *Publications:* (contrib.) Trusts in Prime Jurisdictions, 2010; contribs to Soc. of Trusts and Estate Practitioners Jl, Spear's Wealth Mag. *Recreations:* golf, cricket, gardening. *Address:* Church Farm, Westbrook Hill, Elstead, Godalming, Surrey GU8 6LQ. *E:* mcgowar@btinternet.com. *Clubs:* Naval and Military, MCC; Hankley Common Golf, Rye Golf, London Solicitors' Golfing Society.

**GOWAR, Prof. Norman William;** Chairman, Office of the Independent Adjudicator for Higher Education, 2003–09; Principal, Royal Holloway (Royal Holloway and Bedford New College), University of London, 1990–2000; Professor Emeritus, University of London, since 2000; *b* 7 Dec. 1940; *s* of Harold James and Constance Dawson-Gowar; *m* 1st, 1963, Diane May Parker (marr. diss.); one *s* one *d*; 2nd, 1981, Prof. Judith Margaret Greene, *d* of Lord Gordon-Walker, PC, CH. *Educ:* Sir George Monoux Grammar Sch.; City Univ. (BSc, MPhil). FIMA. English Electric Co., 1963; Lectr in Maths, City Univ., 1963; Open University: Lectr and Sen. Lectr, 1969; Prof. of Mathematics, 1983; Dir, Centre for Maths Educn, 1983; Pro-Vice-Chancellor, 1977–81; Dep. Vice-Chancellor, 1985–90; Dir, Open Coll., 1986. Vis. Fellow, Keble Coll., Oxford, 1972. Member, Council: CNAA, 1979–83; NCET, 1986–91 (Chm., Trng Cttee); Mem. Bd, CVCP, 1998–2000; Mem., Fulbright Commn, 2001–05. Chm. and Dir, Open Univ. Educational Enterprises Ltd, 1988–90. Dir, Surrey TEC, 1991–93. Mem., London Math. Soc. Governor: South Bank Univ. (formerly Polytechnic), 1992–95; UCS, 1993–2000; Rugby Sch., 1994–2004; Middlesex Univ., 2000–04; Sussex Univ., 2004–08. Mem. Council, IMA, 1993–96. FRSA. Hon. Fellow, Royal Holloway, Univ. of London, 2002. Hon. DSc City, 1994; DUniv Open, 2001. *Publications:* Mathematics for Technology: a new approach, 1968; Basic Mathematical Structures, vol. 1, 1973, vol. 2, 1974; Fourier Series, 1974; Invitation to Mathematics, 1980; articles and TV series. *Address:* 1 Prior Bolton Street, N1 2NX.

**GOWDY, David Clive,** CB 2001; Permanent Secretary, Department of Health, Social Services and Public Safety, Northern Ireland, 1997–2005; *b* 27 Nov. 1946; *s* of Samuel David Gowdy and Eileen Gowdy (*née* Porter); *m* 1973, Linda Doreen Traub; two *d*. *Educ:* Royal Belfast Academical Instn; Queen's Univ. Belfast (BA, MSc). Min. of Finance, NI, 1970; N Ireland Office, 1976; Exec. Dir, Industrial Develt Bd for NI 1985; Under Sec., Dept of Econ. Develt, NI, 1987; Under Sec., Dept of Health and Social Services, NI, 1990; Dir of Personnel, NICS, 1994. Vis. Prof., Univ. of Ulster, 2006–13. Chm., Unlocking Potential Project, Volunteer Now, 2009–14; Member: Bd, Belfast Charitable Soc., 2006– (Chm., 2010–13); Regl Cttee, Nat. Trust, 2008–10. *Recreations:* study and exercise. *Address:* Bangor, Co. Down.

**GOWER;** *see* Leveson Gower.

**GOWER, David Ivon,** OBE 1992; broadcaster and journalist; *b* 1 April 1957; *s* of Richard Hallam Gower and Sylvia Mary Gower (*née* Ford); *m* 1992, Thorunn Ruth Nash; two *d*. *Educ:* King's Sch., Canterbury; University Coll., London. Professional cricketer, 1975–93; Leicestershire, 1975–89; Hampshire, 1990–93; 117 Test matches for England, 1978–92; 8,231 Test runs (3rd highest for England), incl. 18 centuries; captained England 32 times, 1984–86, 1989; retired from 1st class cricket, Nov. 1993. PR consultant (cricket sponsorship), Nat. Westminster Bank, 1993–2000. BBC Cricket Commentator, 1994–99; Presenter: Gower's Cricket Monthly, BBC TV, 1995–98; David Gower's Cricket Weekly, BBC Radio 5, 1995–98; Internat. Cricket, Sky Sports, 1999–2019; panel mem., They Think It's All Over, BBC TV, 1996–2003. Columnist, Sunday Times, 2002–14. Hon. MA: Southampton Inst. (Nottingham Trent Univ.), 1993; Loughborough, 1994; Hon. DSc Winchester, 2010; Hon. DLitt De Montfort, 2014. Hon. Blue, Heriot-Watt Univ. *Publications:* With Time to Spare, 1979; Heroes and Contemporaries, 1983; A Right Ambition, 1986; On the Rack, 1990; Gower, The Autobiography, 1992; An Endangered Species, 2013; David Gower's 50 Greatest Cricketers of All Time, 2015. *Recreations:* ski-ing, safari, Cresta Run, tennis. *Address:* c/o EBP, 44 Maiden Lane, WC2E 7LN. *Clubs:* East India, MCC (Mem. Cttee, 2000–03); Garrick, Groucho; St Moritz Tobogganing.

**GOWER, Rear Adm. John Howard James,** CB 2014; OBE 1998; Assistant Chief of Defence Staff, Nuclear and Chemical, Biological, 2011–14; Director, Mimir Consulting Ltd, since 2016; *b* Carshalton, 28 July 1960; *s* of late Howard Gower and of Josephine Gower (*née* Smart); *m* 1986, Diana Steven; two *s* one *d*. *Educ:* Solihull Sch.; Salford Univ. (BSc Electrical Engrg Sci. 1982). Joined RN, 1978; sea-going career, 1978–97; Submarine Commands: HMS Unicorn, 1992–94; HMS Trafalgar, 1995–97; Ministry of Defence: Naval Ops, 1997–99 (Comdr); Naval Staff, 1999–2002 (Captain); Asst Naval Attaché to USA, 2002–05; Divl Dir, Staff Coll., 2005–06; Dir Underwater Capability, MoD, 2006–08 (Cdre); Chemical, Biological, Radiological and Nuclear Policy, MoD, 2008–11. Chm., Lady Grover's Fund. *Recreations:* poetry, cycling, theatre. *Club:* Royal Navy of 1765 and 1785.

**GOWER, Peter John de Peauly;** QC 2006; **His Honour Judge Gower;** a Circuit Judge, since 2012; *b* 30 Nov. 1960; *s* of His Honour John Hugh Gower, QC; *m* 1993, Emma Clout; two *s*. *Educ:* Lancing Coll.; Christ Church, Oxford (Classics Schol.; MA Juris.). Called to the Bar, Lincoln's Inn, 1985; in practice specialising in criminal and regulatory law; a Recorder, 2002–12. Standing Counsel to BIS (formerly DTI, later BERR), 1991–2006. Chm., Kent Bar Mess, 2007–10. *Recreations:* spending time with the family, reading, walking, gardening, horses, fishing. *Address:* Croydon Crown Court, The Law Courts, Altyre Road, Croydon, Surrey CR9 5AB.

**GOWER ISAAC, Anthony John;** *see* Isaac.

**GOWERS, Andrew;** Global Head of Corporate Affairs, Trafigura, 2013–18; *b* 19 Oct. 1957; *s* of Michael and Anne Gowers; *m* 1982, Finola Clarke; one *s* one *d*. *Educ:* Trinity Sch., Croydon; Gonville and Caius Coll., Cambridge (MA 1980). Reuters: London, Brussels and Zurich, 1980–83; Financial Times, 1983–2005: on foreign staff, 1983–84; Agric. Corresp., 1984–85; Commodities Ed., 1985–87; ME Ed., 1987–90; Features Ed., 1990–92; Foreign Ed., 1992–94; Dep. Ed., 1994–97; Actg Ed., 1997–98; Ed.-in-Chief, FT Deutschland, 1998–2001; Ed., 2001–05; Global Co-Hd of Communications, Mkting and Brand Mgt, Lehman Brothers, 2006–08; Hd, External Relns, London Business Sch., 2008–09; Hd of Media Relns, BP plc, 2009–10; Dir, External Relns, Assoc. for Financial Mkts in Europe, 2011–13. Leader, Gowers Review of Intellectual Property, HM Treasury, 2006; Mem., Digital Britain Steering Bd, 2008–09. *Publications:* Arafat: the biography, 1990; Investing in Change: the reform of Europe's financial markets, 2012. *Recreations:* theatre, food, wine, tennis, film, music.

**GOWERS, Prof. Emily Joanna,** PhD; FBA 2019; Professor of Latin Literature, University of Cambridge, since 2016; Fellow of St John's College, Cambridge, since 2002; *b* Oxford, 27 Sept. 1963; *d* of Sir Keith Vivian Thomas, *qv*; *m* 1988, Sir (William) Timothy Gowers, *qv* (marr. diss. 2007); two *s* one *d*. *Educ:* Oxford High Sch.; Trinity Coll., Cambridge (BA Classics 1985; PhD 1990). Title A Fellow, Trinity Coll., Cambridge, 1988–91; Lectr in Latin, UCL, 1991–93; Lectr, Dept of Classics, Princeton Univ., 2000–02; University of Cambridge: Lectr in Classics, 2002–09; Sen. Lectr, 2009–13; Reader, 2013–16. Vis. Prof. and Webster Dist. Lectr, Stanford Univ., 2011; Vis. Prof., Princeton Univ., 2014. Leverhulme Major Res. Fellowship, 2014–16. MAE 2013. *Publications:* The Loaded Table, 1993 (Premio Langhe Ceretto, 1994); (ed with William Fitzgerald) Ennius Perennis, 2007; Horace Satires Book I, 2012. *Recreations:* food, travel, swimming, 20th-century British art. *Address:* St John's College, Cambridge CB2 1TP. *T:* (01223) 338600. *E:* eg235@cam.ac.uk.

**GOWERS, Sir (William) Timothy,** Kt 2012; PhD; FRS 1999; Rouse Ball Professor of Mathematics, University of Cambridge, since 1998; Fellow of Trinity College, Cambridge, since 1995; Royal Society 2010 Anniversary Research Professor, since 2010; *b* 20 Nov. 1963; *s* of late William Patrick Gowers and of Caroline Molesworth Gowers; *m* 1988, Emily Joanna Thomas (*see* E. J. Gowers) (marr. diss. 2007); two *s* one *d*; *m* 2008, Julie, *d* of Alain and Sylvie Barrau; one *s* one *d*. *Educ:* Eton Coll.; Trinity Coll., Cambridge (BA; PhD 1990). Res. Fellow, Trinity Coll., Cambridge, 1989–93; Lectr, 1991–94, Reader, 1994–95, UCL; Lectr, Univ. of Cambridge, 1995–98. Hon. Fellow, UCL, 1999. Hon. DSc St Andrews, 2013. European Mathematical Soc. Prize, 1996; Fields Medal, 1998; Stefan Banach Medal, Polish Acad. of Scis, 2011; Sylvester Medal, Royal Soc., 2016. *Publications:* Mathematics: a very short introduction, 2002; (ed) The Princeton Companion to Mathematics, 2008; contrib. papers in mathematical jls. *Recreation:* jazz piano. *Address:* Department of Pure Mathematics and Mathematical Statistics, Centre for Mathematical Sciences, Wilberforce Road, Cambridge CB3 0WB. *T:* (01223) 337999.

**GOWING, Nicholas Keith, (Nik);** Main Presenter, BBC World News, BBC News, 2000–14 (Presenter, 1996–2000); Visiting Professor: King's College London, since 2014; Nanyang Technological University, Singapore, 2016–19; *b* 13 Jan. 1951; *s* of Donald James Graham Gowing and Margaret Mary Gowing (*née* Elliott); *m* 1982, Judith Wastall Venables; one *s* one *d*. *Educ:* Latymer Upper Sch.; Simon Langton Grammar Sch., Canterbury. Reporter, Evening Chronicle, Newcastle upon Tyne, 1973–74; Presenter and Reporter, Granada TV, 1974–78; joined ITN, 1978; Rome Corresp., 1979; Eastern Europe Corresp., Warsaw, 1980–83; Foreign Affairs Corresp., 1983–87, Diplomatic Corresp., 1987–89, Diplomatic Editor, 1989–96, Channel 4 News; presenter, World Debates, 1999–, Dateline London, 1999–2012, The Hub, 2010–12, BBC. Fellow, Shorenstein Center, J. F. Kennedy Sch., Harvard Univ., 1994; Vis. Fellow, Keele Univ., 1998–. Dir, Think Unthink Ltd, 2017–. Consultant: Carnegie Commn on Preventing Deadly Conflict, 1996–97; on Wars and Information Mgt, EC Humanitarian Office, 1997–98. Vice Chair and Gov., Westminster Foundn for Democracy, 1996–2005; Governor: British Assoc. for Central and Eastern Europe, 1996–2008; Ditchley Foundn, 2000–; Member: IISS 1990; Council, 1998–2004, Exec. Council, 2000–02, RIIA; Adv. Council, Wilton Park, 1998–2012; Adv. Bd, Birmingham Univ. Centre for Studies in Security and Diplomacy, 1999–2011; Cttee, Project on Justice in Times of Transition, 1999–; Steering Cttee, Konigswinter Conf., 1999–; Exec. Cttee and Council, 2005–, Adv. Council, 2011–16, Trustee, 2016–, RUSI; Council, ODI, 2007–14; Cttee, Rory Peck Trust, 1996–2014; Trustee, Liddell Hart Archive, KCL, 2004–. Member, Board: Hay Fest., 2005–18; Hay Fest. Foundn, 2019–. Fellow, Reuters Inst., Oxford Univ., 2008–09. Hon. DLitt Exeter, 2012; Hon. LLD Bristol, 2015. *Publications:* The Wire, 1988; The Loop, 1993; Skyful of Lies and Black Swans, 2009; Thinking the Unthinkable, 2018. *Recreations:* cycling, ski-ing, authorship, lecturing, chairing conferences. *Club:* Savile.

**GOWLETT, Prof. John Anthony Jamys,** PhD; FBA 2017; FSA, FRAI; Professor of Archaeology and Evolutionary Anthropology, University of Liverpool, since 2000; *b* Douglas, I of M, 1 June 1950; *s* of James A. and Kathleen Gowlett. *Educ:* King's Sch., Chester; Corpus Christi Coll., Cambridge (BA Archaeol. and Anthropol. 1972; MA 1976; PhD 1980). Lectr in Archaeol., Univ. of Khartoum, Sudan, 1974–77; Interuniv. Council Vis. Lectr, Univ. of Ibadan, Nigeria, 1979; Sen. Archaeologist, Radiocarbon Accelerator Unit, Res. Lab. for Archaeol. and Hist. of Art, Univ. of Oxford, 1980–87; Sen. Lectr, 1987–94, Reader, 1994–2000, Dept of Archaeol., Univ. of Liverpool. Co-Dir, British Acad. Centenary Res. Project, Lucy to Lang., Archaeol. of the Social Brain, 2003–11. Chm., Bd of Examrs in Forensic Anthropol., RAI, 2014–. FSA 1988; FRAI 2011. *Publications:* Ascent to Civilization: the archaeology of early humans, 1984, 2nd edn 1993 (trans. Spanish 1999); (ed jtly) Social Brain and Distributed Mind, 2010; (ed jtly) Lucy to Language: the benchmark papers, 2014; (jtly) Thinking Big, 2014; contribs to professional jls incl. Nature, Science, Scientific American, Philosophical Trans Royal Soc., World Archaeol., Antiquity. *Recreations:* dog walking, drawing, taking photographs. *Address:* Department of Archaeology, Classics and Egyptology, HLC, 12 Abercromby Square, University of Liverpool, Liverpool L69 3BX. *E:* Gowlett@liverpool.ac.uk.

**GOWRIE, 2nd Earl of,** *cr* 1945; **Alexander Patrick Greysteil Hore-Ruthven;** PC 1984; Baron Ruthven of Gowrie, 1919; Baron Gowrie, 1935; Viscount Ruthven of Canberra, 1945; Chairman, The Magdi Yacoub Institute (formerly Harefield Research Foundation), since 2003; Director, Sotheby's Holdings Inc., 1985–98 (Chairman, Sotheby's London, 1987–94); *b* Dublin, 26 Nov. 1939; *er s* of late Capt. Hon. Alexander Hardinge Patrick Hore-Ruthven, Rifle Bde (killed in action, 1942), and Pamela Margaret (as Viscountess Ruthven of Canberra, she *m* 1952, Major Derek Cooper, MC, The Life Guards), 2nd *d* of late Rev. A. H. Fletcher; *S* grandfather, 1955; *m* 1st, 1962, Xandra Bingley (marr. diss. 1973); one *s*; 2nd, 1974, Adelheid Gräfin von der Schulenburg, *y d* of late Fritz-Dietlof, Graf von der Schulenburg. *Educ:* Eton; Balliol Coll., Oxford. Visiting Lectr, State Univ. of New York at Buffalo, 1963–64; Tutor, Harvard Univ., 1965–68; Lectr in English and American Literature, UCL, 1969–72. Fine Art consultant, 1974–79. Provost, RCA, 1986–95. Chm., Arts Council of England, 1994–98. Chairman: The Really Useful Gp, 1985–90; Development Securities, 1995–99; Fine Art Gp, 2002–. A Conservative Whip, 1971–72; Parly Rep. to UN, 1971; a Lord in Waiting (Govt Whip), 1972–74; Opposition Spokesman on Economic Affairs, 1974–79; Minister of State: Dept of Employment, 1979–81; NI Office, 1981–83 (Dep. to Sec. of State); Privy Council Office (Management and Personnel), 1983–84; Minister for the Arts, 1983–85; Chancellor, Duchy of Lancaster, 1984–85. FRSL 2003. Freeman, City of London, 1976. Picasso Medal, UNESCO, 1996. *Publications:* A Postcard from Don Giovanni, 1972; (jtly) The Genius of British Painting, 1975; (jtly) The Conservative Opportunity, 1976; (jtly) Derek Hill: an appreciation, 1987; The Domino Hymn: poems from Harefield, 2005; Third Day: new and selected poems, 2008; The Italian Visitor and Other Poems, 2013; Collected Poems, 2014. *Recreation:* Wales. *Heir: s* Viscount Ruthven of Canberra, *qv*. *Address:* The Magdi Yacoub Institute, Heart Science Centre, Harefield, Middlesex UB9 6JH.

See also Hon. M. W. M. K. H. Ruthven.

**GOY, David John Lister;** QC 1991; *b* 11 May 1949; *s* of late Rev. Leslie Goy and Joan Goy; *m* 1970, Jennifer Anne Symington; three *s*. *Educ:* Haberdashers' Aske's School, Elstree; King's College London. Called to the Bar, Middle Temple, 1973, Bencher, 2007. Chm., Revenue Bar Assoc., 2005–08. *Publications:* VAT on Property, 1989, 2nd edn 1993. *Recreations:* golf and other sports. *Address:* East Horsley, Surrey.

**GOYMER, His Honour Andrew Alfred;** a Circuit Judge, 1999–2017; a Deputy Circuit Judge, since 2017; *b* 28 July 1947; *s* of late Richard Kirby Goymer and Betty Eileen Goymer (*née* Thompson); *m* 1972, Diana Mary, *d* of late Robert Harry Shipway, MBE and Sheila Mary Shipway; one *s* one *d*. *Educ:* Dulwich Coll.; Pembroke Coll., Oxford (Hull Schol., MA). Called to the Bar, Gray's Inn, 1970 (Gerald Moody Entrance Schol., Holker Sen. Exhibnr, Arden Atkin and Mould Prizeman); practised, S Eastern Circuit, 1972–99; admitted to NSW Bar, 1988; Asst Recorder, 1987–91; Recorder, 1991–99. Mem. Cttee, 2009–17, 2018–, Asst Sec., 2012–17, Chm., Criminal Sub-Cttee, 2014–17, Council of HM Circuit Judges. Mem., Forensic Sci. Adv. Council, 2007–14. *Address:* c/o Southwark Crown Court, 1 English Grounds, SE1 2HU. *T:* (020) 7522 7200; 6 Pump Court, Temple, EC4Y 7AR. *T:* (020) 7797 8400.

**GOZNEY, Sir Richard Hugh Turton,** KCMG 2006 (CMG 1993); CVO 2009; HM Diplomatic Service, retired; Lieutenant Governor, Isle of Man, since 2016; *b* 21 July 1951; *s* of Thomas Leonard Gozney and Elizabeth Margaret Lilian Gozney (*née* Gardiner); *m* 1982, Diana Edwina Baird; two *s*. *Educ:* Magdalen Coll. Sch., Oxford; St Edmund Hall, Oxford (BA Hons Geol. 1973). Teacher, Tom Mboya Rusinga Secondary Sch., Kenya, 1970; joined FO, 1973; Jakarta, 1974–78; Buenos Aires, 1978–81; FCO, 1981–84; Hd of Chancery, Madrid, 1984–88; Asst Private Sec., later Private Sec., to Foreign Sec., FCO, 1989–93; High Comr, Swaziland, 1993–96; Head of Security Policy Dept, FCO, 1996–97; Chief of Assessments Staff, Jt Intelligence Orgn, Cabinet Office, 1998–2000; Ambassador, Indonesia, 2000–04; High Comr, Nigeria, 2004–07, and Ambassador (non-resident) to Benin, 2005–07, and to Equatorial Guinea, 2006–07; Gov. and C-in-C, Bermuda, 2007–12. Strategic Advr, Green Park Worldwide, 2014–; Sen. Advr, Africa and Asia, Guardian Global Resources, 2014–16. Non-exec. Dir, Asia Resource Minerals plc, 2013–15. Vice-Chm., Bermuda Soc., 2012–16. Trustee, Orangutan Foundn, 2014–. KStJ 2010. *Publications:* Gibraltar and the EC, 1993; Birds on the Abuja Golf Course, 2007. *Recreations:* bird-watching, walking, sailing, gardening. *Address:* Government House, Isle of Man IM3 1RR.

**GRAAFF, Sir De Villiers,** 4th Bt *cr* 1911, of Cape Town; Managing Director, Degrendel Wines (Pty) Ltd, since 2015; *b* Cape Town, 16 July 1970; *s* of Sir David de Villiers Graaff, 3rd Bt and of Winifred Sally Melinda Graaff (*née* Williams); *S* father, 2015; *m* 2000, Gaedry Laurian Kriel; three *s* one *d*. *Educ:* Diocesan Coll., Cape Town; Univ. of Stellenbosch (BAgricAdmin); Univ. of Colorado. Director: Graaff Fruit, 1995–; Delecta Fruit, 2000–; Waitrose Foundation, 2007–; Graaffs Trust, 1995–; Milnerton Estates, 2015–. *Recreations:* golf, fishing. *Heir: s* David Peter Berkeley de Villiers Graaff, *b* 1 Feb. 2003. *Address:* Degrendel Estate, Plattekloof Road, Panorama, 7500 Western Cape, South Africa. *T:* 5586280, *Fax:* 5586280. *E:* devilliers@degrendel.co.za.

**GRABBE, Dr Heather Mary Claire;** Director, Open Society European Policy Institute (formerly Open Society Institute - Brussels), since 2009; *b* Pasadena, Calif, 30 Aug. 1970; *m* 1994, Prof. Andrew Ian Wilson, *qv* (marr. diss.); two *d*. *Educ:* Somerville Coll., Oxford (BA Hons PPE 1991); Univ. of Birmingham (PhD 2002). Res. Fellow, Eur. Prog., RIIA, 1996–97; Dep. Dir, Centre for Eur. Reform, 2000–04; Sen. Advr to EU Enlargement Comr, Olli Rehn, 2004–09. Vis. Fellow, Eur. Inst., LSE, 2004–. Member: Eur. Council on Foreign Relns, 2008–; Adv. Bd, Centre for Eur. Reform, 2011–17. Mem., Sen. Common Room, St Antony's Coll., Oxford 2004–. *Publications:* The EU's Transformative Power: Europeanisation through conditionality in Central and Eastern Europe, 2006; contrib. Jl Eur. Public Policy, Hommes & Migrations, Internat. Politik, Jl Common Mkt Studies Annual Rev., Internat. Spectator. *Address:* Open Society European Policy Institute, Rue du Trône 130, 1050 Brussels, Belgium. *T:* (2) 5054646, *Fax:* (2) 5024646. *E:* heather.grabbe@opensocietyfoundations.org.

**GRABIEC, Stephanie Ann;** *see* Sirr, S. A.

**GRABINER,** family name of **Baron Grabiner.**

**GRABINER, Baron** *cr* 1999 (Life Peer), of Aldwych in the City of Westminster; **Anthony Stephen Grabiner;** QC 1981; Master of Clare College, Cambridge, since 2014; *b* 21 March 1945; *e s* of late Ralph Grabiner and Freda Grabiner (*née* Cohen); *m* 1983, Jane, *e d* of late Dr Benjamin Portnoy, TD, JP, MD, PhD, FRCP, Hale, Cheshire; three *s* one *d*. *Educ:* Central Foundn Boys' Grammar Sch., London, EC2; LSE, Univ. of London (LLB 1st Cl. Hons 1966, LLM with Distinction 1967; Hon. Fellow, 2009). Lincoln's Inn: Hardwicke Scholar, 1966; called to the Bar, 1968; Droop Scholar, 1968; Bencher, 1989; Treas., 2013–14. Standing Jun. Counsel to Dept of Trade, Export Credits Guarantee Dept, 1976–81; Jun. Counsel to the Crown, 1978–81; a Recorder, 1990–99. Mem., Financial Markets Law Cttee, Bank of England, 2002–06. Non-executive Director: Next plc, 2002; Goldman Sachs Internat., 2015–; non-exec. Chm., Arcadia Gp, 2002–17. Chm., Ct of Govs, LSE, 1998–2007 (Mem., 1991–; Vice-Chm., 1993–98); Pres., Univ. of Law, 2015–. Mem., Bd of Mgt, Surrey CCC, 2011–. Gov., St Paul's Boys' Sch., 2015–. *Publications:* (ed jtly) Sutton and Shannon on Contracts, 7th edn 1970; contrib. Banking Documents, to Encyclopedia of Forms and Precedents, 5th edn, 1986. *Recreations:* theatre, golf. *Address:* One Essex Court, Temple, EC4Y 9AR. *T:* (020) 7583 2000. *E:* agrabiner@oeclaw.co.uk; Master's Lodge, Clare College, Cambridge CB2 1TL. *T:* (01223) 333207. *E:* asg43@cam.ac.uk. *Clubs:* Garrick, MCC.

**GRABINER, Michael,** CBE 2012; Partner, Portland Place Advisers LLP, 2012–17; *b* 21 Aug. 1950; *s* of Henry Grabiner and Renée (*née* Geller); *m* 1976, Jane Olivia Harris; three *s* one *d*. *Educ:* St Albans Sch.; King's Coll., Cambridge (MA Econ; Pres., Students' Union, 1972–73). Joined Post Office, 1973: Personal Asst to Man. Dir, Telecommunications, 1976–78; London Business Sch. (Sloan Prog.), 1980–81; British Telecommunications: Controller, Commercial Finance Divl HQ, 1982–84; Dep. Dir, Mktg, 1984–85; General Manager: Northern London Dist, 1985–88; City of London Dist, 1988–90; Director: Quality and Orgn, 1990–92; Global Customer Service, Business Communications Div., 1992–94; BT Europe, 1994–95; Chief Executive: Energis Communications Ltd, then Energis plc, 1996–2001; Partner, Apax Partners, 2002–09. Director: BT Telecommunications SA Spain, 1994–95; VIAG InterKom Germany, 1994–95; Telenordia Sweden, 1994–95; Albacom Italy, 1994–95; Chairman: Planet Online, 1998–2000; Spectrum Strategy Consultants, 2003–07; Partnerships for Schs, 2005–11; non-executive Director: Littlewoods plc, 1998–2002; Emblaze Systems, 2000–05; Chelsfield plc, 2002–04; Synetrix Hldgs Ltd, 2004–09; Telewest Global Inc., 2004–06; Tim Hellas Telecommunications SA, 2005–06; Bezeq, 2006–10; Pelephone, 2008–10. Mem. (Lab) Brent BC, 1978–82 (Chm., Develt Cttee, 1980–82). Dir, E London Partnership, 1994–95; non-exec. Dir, Centre for Effective Dispute Resolution, 2012–17. Treas., Reform Synagogues of GB, 2002–05. Chairman: UK Jewish Film Fest., 2004–06; UK Movt for Reform Judaism, 2005–08; ResponseAbility, 2009–11; World Union for Progressive Judaism, 2011–15 (Mem., Exec. Bd, 2007–; Vice Chm., 2009–11); Mem., Jewish Leadership Council, 2005–08. Trustee, Jewish Community Secondary Sch., 2008–16 (Chm. of Govs, 2009–13). Freeman, City of London, 1995; Mem., Co. of Inf. Technologists, 1995. *E:* mike@grabiner.net.

See also S. Grabiner.

**GRABINER, Stephen;** Chairman, Jewish Chronicle newspaper, since 2013; Partner, Grabiner LLP, since 2011; *b* 30 Sept. 1958; *s* of Henry and Renée Grabiner (*née* Geller); *m* 1984, Miriam Loebl; two *s* one *d*. *Educ:* Univ. of Sheffield (BA 1981); Manchester Business Sch. (MBA 1983). Mgt Consultant, Coopers and Lybrand, 1983–86; Telegraph plc: Mktg Dir, 1986–93; Dep. Man. Dir, 1993–94; Man. Dir, 1994–96; Exec. Dir, UK Consumer Publishing, United News and Media plc, 1996–98; Chief Exec., ONdigital, 1998–99; Partner, and Hd of Media and London Office, Apax Partners, 1999–2010. Ind. Nat. Dir, Times Newspaper Hldgs Ltd, 2012–; Dir, Cloverhawk Ltd, 1996–. Trustee: Blue Thread, 2009–; Timewise Foundn, 2012–17. *Recreations:* family, philanthropy, community. *E:* stephen@grabiner.com.

See also M. Grabiner.

**GRACE, Clive Lester,** OBE 2013; DPhil; Chairman, UK Shared Business Services Ltd (formerly Research Councils UK Shared Services Centre Ltd), 2007–15; *b* 5 Aug. 1950; *s* of Henri Hyams Grace and Mary Madeline Grace; *m* 1982, Vivienne Robins (now V. Robins-Grace); one *s* two *d*. *Educ:* Univ. of Birmingham (BSocSc 1971); Univ. of Calif (MA Govt 1972); Wolfson Coll., Oxford (DPhil Law and Sociol. 1984); Open Univ. (Professional Dip. in Mgt). Solicitor of the Supreme Court, 1981. Hd of Legal Br., ILEA, 1987–89; Dir of Law and Admin, London Bor. of Southwark, 1989–95; Chief Exec., Torfaen CBC, 1995–2003; Dir-Gen., Audit Commn in Wales, 2003–05; Dep. Auditor Gen. for Wales, 2004–05. Chairman: Internat. Panel, CIPFA, 2006–09; Local Better Regulation Office, 2007–12; BT Wales Bd (formerly Wales Adv. Forum, BT), 2009– (Mem., 2000–); Observer Mem., Financial Reporting Council, 2004–07. Non-exec. Chm., Supporta plc, 2007–10; non-exec. Dir, Nominet, 2008–15; Co-Founder and Dir, UK Research and Consultancy Services Ltd, 2013–; Dir, Public Sector Audit Appointments Ltd, 2015–. Mem., Corporate Governance Cttee (Health and Social Services), Welsh Assembly Govt, later Welsh Govt, 2009–13. Mem., Local Govt Knowledge Navigator Team, 2013–15. Hon. Secretary: SOLACE, 1998–2002; SOLACE Foundn, 1998–2014 (Chm., SOLACE Foundn Imprint, 2005–14). Mem., Morristours, 2005–. Hon. Res. Fellow, Cardiff Business Sch., 2005–. *Publications:* Sociological Inquiry and Legal Phenomena, 1979; Social Workers, Children and the Law, 1986; (ed) Civil Service Reform: experiences of the United Kingdom, India, South Africa, and Nepal, 2012. *Recreations:* ski-ing, walking, golf. *E:* clivegrace@hotmail.com. *Club:* Reform.

**GRACEY, Howard,** OBE 1998; FIA, FIAA, FPMI; consulting actuary; Senior Partner, R. Watson and Sons, 1993–95 (Partner, 1970–95); *b* 21 Feb. 1935; *s* of late Charles Douglas Gracey and Margaret Gertrude (*née* Heggie); *m* 1960, Pamela Jean Bradshaw; one *s* two *d*. *Educ:* Birkenhead Sch. FIA 1959; FIAA 1982; FPMI 1977; ASA 1978–2018. National Service, 1960–61 (2nd Lieut). Royal Insurance Co., 1953–69. Church Comr, 1978–95; Member: Gen. Synod of C of E, 1970–97; C of E Pensions Bd, 1970–97 (Chm., 1980–97); Archbishops' Commn on orgn of C of E; Treasurer, S Amer. Missionary Soc., 1975–93 (Chm., 1994–2004); Pres., Pensions Management Inst., 1983–85; Chm., Assoc. of Consulting Actuaries, 1991–93. Mem. Council, St John's Coll., Nottingham, 1998–2003. *Recreations:* fell-walking, photography. *Address:* Loughrigg, Guildford Road, Fetcham, Surrey KT22 9DY.

**GRACIAS, His Eminence Cardinal Oswald;** *see* Bombay, Archbishop of, (RC).

**GRACIE, Carrie;** Presenter, BBC News Channel, 2000–14 and since 2018; *b* Manama, Bahrain, 1962; *d* of David Gracie and Judith Grace (*née* Gomm); *m* (marr. diss.); one *s* one *d*. *Educ:* Aberdeen Grammar Sch.; Hertford Coll., Oxford (BA PPE 1984); Univ. of Westminster (BA Mandarin Chinese); Middlesex Univ. (Dip. Interactive Media). Founder Manager, White Cottage Restaurant, Aboyne, 1981; teacher of English: Chongqing Univ., 1985–86; Yantai Univ., 1986; Dir, Oxford Experience, 1986–87; BBC: prodn trainee, 1987–89; current affairs producer, World Service, 1989–91; Beijing reporter, 1991–95; Beijing corresp., 1997–99; Presenter: BBC World Service, 1999–2000; The Interview, BBC, 2003–09; China Editor, BBC News, 2014–18. Nick Clarke Award for best single interview, BBC, 2008; Peabody Award, 2008, Emmy Award for business reporting, 2009, for White Horse Village reports. *Publications:* Equal: a story of women, men and money, 2019. *Recreations:* hanging out with friends and family, reading, walking, theatre, cinema. *Address:* c/o BBC News, Broadcasting House, Portland Place, W1A 1AA.

**GRADE,** family name of **Baron Grade of Yarmouth.**

**GRADE OF YARMOUTH, Baron** *cr* 2011 (Life Peer), of Yarmouth in the County of Isle of Wight; **Michael Ian Grade,** CBE 1998; Director, GradeLinnit Company Ltd, since 2010; Chairman, Infinity Creative Media, since 2015; *b* 8 March 1943; *s* of Leslie Grade and *g s* of Olga Winogradski; *m* 1st, 1967, Penelope Jane (*née* Levinson) (marr. diss. 1981); one *s* one *d*; 2nd, 1982, Hon. Sarah Lawson (marr. diss. 1991), *y d* of 5th Baron Burnham; 3rd, 1998, Francesca Mary (*née* Leahy); one *s*. *Educ:* St Dunstan's Coll., London. Daily Mirror: Trainee Journalist, 1960; Sports Columnist, 1964–66; Theatrical Agent, Grade Organisation, 1966; joined London Management and Representation, 1969, Jt Man. Dir until 1973; London Weekend Television: Dep. Controller of Programmes (Entertainment), 1973; Dir of Programmes and Mem. Bd, 1977–81; Pres., Embassy Television, 1981–84;

Controller, BBC1, 1984–86; Dir of Programmes, BBC TV, 1986–87; Chief Exec., Channel Four, 1988–97; First Leisure Corporation: Dir, 1991–2000; non-exec. Chm., 1995–97; Chm., 1997–98; Chief Exec., 1997–2000; Exec. Chm. and Chief Exec., ITV, 2007–09. Chair, Charity Fundraising Regulator, 2016–18. Chairman: VCI plc, 1995–98; Pinewood Studios, later Pinewood-Shepperton plc, 2000–16 (Sen. Ind. Consultant, 2017–18); Octopus Publishing Gp, 2000–01; Hemscott plc, 2000–06; Bd of Govs, BBC, 2004–06; James Grant Gp, 2010–12; Ocado, 2006–13; Reach4Entertainment Enterprises plc, 2017–; Gate Ventures plc, 2017– (Dep. Chm., 2015–17); Director: ITN, 1989–93; Delfont Macintosh Theatres Ltd, 1994–99; Charlton Athletic FC, 1997–2008; New Millennium Experience Co., 1997–2001; Camelot Gp, 2000–04 (Chm., 2002–04); Reel Enterprises Ltd, 2002–04; SMG, 2003–04; Television Corp., 2003–04; WRG Gp, 2011–15. Chm. Develt Council, RNT, 1997–2004; Member: Council, LAMDA, 1981–93; Council, RADA, 1996–2004; Council, BAFTA, 1981–82, 1986–88 (Vice-Pres., 2004–); 300 Group; Milton Cttee; British Screen Adv. Council, 1986–97; Council, Cinema and Television Benevolent Fund, 1993–2004; Council, Royal Albert Hall, 1997–2004. Chm., Heathrow Expansion Adv. Bd, Arora Gp, 2018–. Chm., Wkg Gp, Fear of Crime, 1989; Member: Nat. Commn of Inquiry into Prevention of Child Abuse, 1994–96; Panel on Fair Access to the Professions, 2009; Chm., Index on Censorship, 2000–04; Lay Mem., Press Complaints Commn, 2011–14. Non-executive Director: PRS, 2015–17; Ben Ainslie Racing Ltd, 2015–18; One Media IP Gp plc, 2018–. President: TV and Radio Industries Club, 1987–88; Newspaper Press Fund, 1988–89; Entertainment Charities Fund, 1994–; Vice-Pres., Children's Film Unit, 1993–97; Director: Open Coll., 1989–97; Cities in Schools, 1991–96; Gate Theatre, Dublin, 1990–2004; Internat. Council, Nat. Acad. of Television Arts and Scis, 1991–97; Jewish Film Foundn, 1997–99. Chm., Nat. Media Mus., Bradford, 2012–19. Trustee: Science Mus. Gp (formerly Nat. Mus. of Sci. and Industry), 2011–19; Band Aid; Samaritans, 2013–17; Dep. Chm., Soc. of Stars, 1995–; Hon. Treas., Stars Organisation for Spastics, 1986–92; Chm., Ecotonian Sports Fund, 2017–. FRTS 1991 (Pres., 1995–97); Fellow, BAFTA, 1994. Hon. Prof., Thames Valley Univ., 1994. Hon. LLD Nottingham, 1997. *Publications:* It Seemed Like a Good Idea at the Time (autobiog.), 1999. *Recreations:* entertainment, sailing. *Address:* House of Lords, SW1A 0PW. *Clubs:* Royal Thames Yacht; Royal Yacht Squadron.

**GRADIN, Anita Ingegerd**; Chairperson, Swedish Council for Working Life and Social Research, 2000–06; *b* 12 Aug. 1933; *d* of Ossian Gradin and Alfhild Gradin; *m* Bertil Kersfelt; one *d*. *Educ:* Grad. Fr. Sch. of Social Work and Public Admin, Stockholm. Journalist in various newspapers, 1950–63; Mem., Social Welfare Planning Cttee, Stockholm, 1963–67; MP, 1968–92; posts include: Chairperson: Council, Cttee on Educn and Financial Affairs; Cttee on Migration, Refugees and Democracy, Council of Europe; Cabinet Minister for Migration and Equality between Women and Men, 1982–86; Minister for Foreign Trade and Eur. Affairs, 1986–91; Swedish Ambassador to Austria, Slovenia and UN, 1992–95; Mem., Commn of EC, 1995–99. Vice-Chairperson, Nat. Fedn of Social Democratic Women, 1975–92; Vice-Pres., Socialist Internat., 1983–92; Pres., Socialist Internat. Women, 1986–92. Member: Bd, Stockholm Sch. of Econs, 2001–; Bd, Center for Gender Medicine, Karolinska Inst., 2002–. FD *hc* Umeå, 2002. Pro Merito Medal, Council of Europe, 1982; Wizo Woman of the Year Award, 1986; Marisa Bellizario European Prize, Italy, 1998; King's Medal, Royal Order of Seraphim, Sweden, 1998. Cavalieri di Gran Croce (Italy), 1991; Order of Merit (Austria) 1995; European of the Year, Swedish Pan-Europa Orgn, 2007. *Recreations:* swimming, walking in the woods, stamps, fishing. *Address:* Fleminggatan 85, 11245 Stockholm, Sweden. *E:* gradin.kersfelt@telia.com.

**GRADY, Prof. Monica Mary, (Mrs I. Wright)**, CBE 2012; PhD; Professor of Planetary and Space Sciences, Open University, since 2005 (Head, Department of Physical Sciences, 2011–15); *b* 15 July 1958; *d* of James and Mary Grady; *m* 1986, Prof. Ian Peter Wright, *qv*; one *s*. *Educ:* Notre Dame Grammar Sch., Leeds; Durham Univ. (BSc); Cambridge Univ. (PhD). Natural History Museum: researcher in meteorites, 1991–97; Hd, Div. of Petrology and Meteoritics, 1997–2005. Hon. Reader in Meteoritics, 2000–04, Hon. Prof., 2004, UCL. Christmas Lectures, Royal Instn, 2003. Coke Medal, Geol Soc., 2016. *Publications:* (ed jtly) Meteorites: their flux with time and impact effects, 1998; The Catalogue of Meteorites, 5th edn 2000; Search for Life, 2001; (with S. S. Russell) Meteorites, 2002; A Voyage in Space and Time, 2003; contrib. numerous papers to peer-reviewed jls. *Recreations:* reading, gardening, crossword puzzles. *Address:* School of Physical Sciences, Open University, Walton Hall, Milton Keynes MK7 6AA. *T:* (01908) 659251. *E:* monica.grady@open.ac.uk.

**GRADY, Patrick John**; MP (SNP) Glasgow North, since 2015; *b* Edinburgh, 5 Feb. 1980. *Educ:* Inverness Royal Acad.; Univ. of Strathclyde (BA Hons Hist.). Scottish Churches world exchange volunteer, St Peter's Secondary Sch., Mzuzu, Malawi, 2004–05; Countryside Campaign Manager, Ramblers' Assoc., 2006–07; Parly Asst to James Hepburn, MSP and Aileen Campbell, MSP, 2007–11; Advocacy Manager, Scottish Catholic Internat. Aid Fund, 2011–15. SNP Spokesperson on Internat. Develt, 2015–17; SNP Chief Whip 2017–. Mem., Procedure Cttee, 2015–17, Cttee of Selection, 2017–, H of C. Nat. Sec., SNP, 2012–16. Exec. Mem., CPA UK, 2015–19; Mem. Bd, Westminster Foundn for Democracy, 2017–. Contested (SNP) Glasgow N, 2010. *Address:* House of Commons, SW1A 0AA. *E:* patrick.grady.mp@parliament.uk.

**GRAEF, Roger Arthur**, OBE 2006; writer, director and producer of films; criminologist; broadcaster; Chief Executive: Films of Record, 1979–2016; Roger Graef Productions, since 2016; *b* NYC, 18 April 1936; UK citizen, 1995; *m* 1st, 1971, Karen Bergemann (marr. diss. 1983); one *s* one *d*; 2nd, 1986, Susan Mary Richards. *Educ:* Horace Mann Sch., NYC; Putney Sch., Vermont; Harvard Univ. (BA Hons). Directed, USA, 26 plays and operas including: Brother to Dragons, The Disenchanted, Two for the Seesaw, A Raisin in the Sun, The Underpants, Titus Andronicus, The Tempest, The Mother of Us All; also directed CBS television; Observer/Dir, Actors Studio, NYC, 1958–62; resident in England, 1962–; Director, London: Period of Adjustment (Royal Court, Wyndham's); Afternoon Men (Arts); has written, produced and/or directed more than 160 films; *films for television include:* One of Them is Brett, The Life and Times of John Huston, Esq., 1965; (Series Producer) 13-part Who Is series, 1966–67 (dir. films on Pierre Boulez, Jacques Lipchitz, Walter Gropius, Maurice Béjart); Günter Grass' Berlin, 1965; Why Save Florence?, 1968; In the Name of Allah, 1970; The Space between Words, 1971–72; A Law in the Making, 1973; Inside the Brussels HQ, 1975; Is This the Way to Save our Cities?, 1975; Arena: Save Britain's Heritage, 1976; Decision series: British Steel, etc, 1976–77, British Communism, 1978 (Royal Television Soc. Award); Pleasure at Her Majesty's, 1976; The Mermaid's Frolics, 1977; The Secret Policeman's Ball, 1977–78; Police series, 1980–82 (BAFTA Award; Eur. TV Critics Award); Police: Operation Carter, 1981–82; Nagging Doubt, 1984; The Fifty-Minute Hour, 1984; Maybe Baby, 1985; Comic Relief, 1986; Closing Ranks, 1987; The Secret Life of the Soviet Union, 1990; Turning the Screws, 1993; Look at the State We're In, 1995; In Search of Law and Order (UK), 1995; Breaking the Cycle, 1996 (British Social Services Award); In Search of Law and Order (USA), 1998; Witness: Keeping it in the Family, 1998; The Siege of Scotland Yard, 1999; Race Against Crime, 1999; Masters of the Universe, 1999; Police, 2001; executive producer: Inside Story; Looks That Kill, Who's Your Father, 2000; Breaking the Rules; Not Black and White, 2001; Who Cares for Granny?, Who Cares for Gary?, 2003; Chinatown, Feltham Sings (BAFTA Award), Rail Cops, RailCops 2, Welcome to Potters Bar, The Protectors, Storyville: Who am I Now?, Secrets of the Iraq War, Who Killed PC Blakelock?, 2004; Murder Blues, Classroom Chaos, What Killed My Dad?, Malaria: Fever Road/The Vaccine Challenge (One World Award), What Future for Kurt? (Panorama), Classroom Chaos, 2005; Artistic Convictions; This World: Blood and Land, Property to Die For, Potters Bar: Search for the Truth, Rape on Trial (Panorama), When Cops Kill (Panorama), 2006; Hold Me Tight, Let Me Go, 2007; Race for the Beach, The Burning Season, 2007; Searching for Madeline, Was Crippen Innocent?, 2008; May Contain Nuts (Panorama), Remember the Secret Policeman's Ball, The Millionaire and the Murder Mansion, The Truth about Crime, Dispatches: Ready for a Riot, The Child Protectors (Panorama), 2009; Requiem for Detroit (Grierson Award), Great Ormond Street, Kids in Care (Panorama Special) (RTS Award), Storyville: The Trouble with Pirates, 2010; Storyville: Amnesty! When They Are All Free, Dispatches: Medical Devices, The Truth About Adoption (Panorama Special), First Cut: Sex, Lies and Parkinsons, 2011; September Mourning, 2012; Brett: a life with no arms, 2015; Monty Python: The Meaning of Live, 2015; Storyville: The Confession, 2016 (Storyville); The Trouble with Being 100, 2017; producer/director, Police 2001, 2001; Series Editor: Inside Europe, 1977–78; Signals, 1988–89; *radio includes:* Living Dangerously, 1993; The Illusion of Information, 2000. Mem., Develt Control Review (Dobry Cttee), Chm., Study Gp on Public Participation in Planning, and Mem., Cttee on Control of Demolition, DoE, 1974–76; Member: Commn on Child and Adolescent Mental Health, 1997–98; Prince's Trust Wkg Party on surviving damage in childhood, 1997–98; Fulbright Commn, 2000–03 (Chm., Police Scholarships Cttee, 1999–2003); RIBA Commn on New Housing; Advr, Oxford Probation Studies Unit, 1997–99; Social Affairs Advr, Paul Hamlyn Foundn, 1999–2014; Member: Council, ICA, 1970–82; Founder ICA Architectural Forum Council, BAFTA, 1976–77; Bd, Channel Four, 1980–85; Governor, BFI, 1974–78. Adviser on broadcasting to Brandt Commn, 1979–80; Media Advisor: Collins Publishing, 1983–88; London Transport (Mem. Bd, LTE, 1976–79; co-designer, new London Bus Map). Part-time Tutor, AA Sch. of Architecture, 1973–75. Pres., Signals Internat. Trust, 1990–94; Trustee: Koestler Trust for Prisoners' Art, 1995– (Patron); Butler Trust, 1997–2001; Divert Trust, 1999–2000; Music at Plush, 2012–. Chm., Youth Advocate Prog. UK, 2002–05. Chairman: Book Aid, 1991; Théâtre de Complicité, 1991–; Bd Mem., Photographers' Gall., 2003. Member: Collège Analytique de Securité Urbaine, 1993–98; British Soc. of Criminology. Visiting Professor: Broadcast Media, Oxford Univ., 1999–2000; Univ. of London, 2001–02; Mannheim Centre for the Study of Criminology and Criminal Justice, LSE (formerly Vis. Fellow); Bournemouth Univ. Media Sch. FRTS 1996; Fellow, BAFTA, 2004. Hon. FRIBA 2014. Lifetime Achievement Award: Sheffield Internat. Documentary Fest., 2014; Aldeburgh Documentary Fest., 2016. *Publications:* Talking Blues, 1989; Living Dangerously, 1992; Why Restorative Justice?, 2000; contrib. Daily Telegraph, The Times (media columnist, 1992–94), Sunday Telegraph, Observer, Daily Mail, Mail on Sunday, Evening Standard, Police Review, The Independent, Guardian, Sunday Times, Independent on Sunday. *Recreations:* tennis, flute, photography, theatre, Dorset. *Address:* 72 Westbourne Park Villas, W2 5EB. *T:* (020) 7727 7868. *Club:* Groucho.

**GRAF, (Charles) Philip**, CBE 2003; Chairman, Gambling Commission, 2011–16; *b* 18 Oct. 1946; *s* of Charles Henry Graf and Florence (*née* Mulholland); *m* 1st, 1970, Freda Mary Bain (marr. diss. 2003); three *d*; 2nd, 2004, Kirstan Anne Marnane. *Educ:* Methodist Coll., Belfast; Carlmont High Sch., Calif; Clare Coll., Cambridge (MA). Circulation Mktg Controller, Thomson Regl Newspapers, 1978–83; Asst Man. Dir, Liverpool Daily Post and Echo, 1983–85; Chief Exec., Trinity Paper and Packaging, 1986–90; Corporate Develt Dir, 1990–93, Chief Exec., 1993–99, Trinity plc; Chief Exec., Trinity Mirror plc, 1999–2002. Dir, TDG plc, 2003–07; Partner, Praesta Partners LLP, 2005–10. Chairman: Press Standards Bd of Finance, 2004–05; Broadband Stakeholders Gp, 2005; Dep. Chm., Ofcom, 2006–11 (Chm., Content Bd, 2006–11). Dir, Archant Ltd, 2006–09. Chair: Educn Develt Trust (formerly CfBT Educn Trust), 2011–; Nursing and Midwifery Council, 2018–. Trustee, Crisis, 2004–13. *Recreations:* reading, opera, watching Rugby, soccer and cricket, theatre.

**GRAF, Prof. Hans-Friedrich**, PhD, DSc; Professor of Environmental Systems Analysis, University of Cambridge, 2003–16, now Emeritus; Fellow of Clare Hall, Cambridge, 2003–16, now Emeritus; Visiting Fellow, Chinese Academy of Sciences; *b* 6 Jan. 1950; *s* of Dr Hans and Ilse Graf; *m* 1997, Dr Marie-Luise Waguer-Kuschfeldt; two *d*. *Educ:* Humboldt Univ., Berlin (MSc Met. 1974; PhD Met. 1979; Habilitation Dr *scientiae naturalis*, 1989). Scientific Asst, Humboldt Univ., Berlin, 1974–78; Industrial Meteorologist, Kombinat Kraftwerksanlagenbau, Berlin, 1978–79; Scientific Asst, Meteorol Inst., Humboldt Univ., Berlin, 1979–90; Sen. Scientist, Max-Planck-Inst. for Meteorol., Hamburg, 1991–2003. Suehring Medal, Deutsche Meteorologische Gesellschaft, 1989, 2015. *Publications:* more than 160 book chapters and papers in jls. *Address:* Hermann-Foege-Weg 14a, 37073 Goettingen, Germany.

**GRAF, Philip**; see Graf, C. P.

**GRAF, Stefanie**; German tennis player, 1982–99; Founder, and Chairman, Children for Tomorrow, since 1998; *b* 14 June 1969; *d* of late Peter and Heidi Graf; *m* 2001, André Agassi, *qv*; one *s* one *d*. Has won 107 singles titles, including 22 Grand Slam titles: French Open, 1987–88, 1993, 1995–96, 1999; Australian Open, 1988–90, 1994; Wimbledon, 1988–89, 1991–93, 1995–96; US Open, 1988–89, 1993, 1995–96. Olympic Gold Medal, Seoul, 1988; Olympic Silver Medal, Barcelona, 1992; Olympic Order, 1999. *Publications:* (jtly) Wege zum Erfolg, 1999. *Address:* Stefanie Graf Marketing, Gartenstrasse 1, 68723 Schwetzingen, Germany.

**GRAFEN, Prof. Alan**, DPhil; FRS 2011; Professor of Theoretical Biology, University of Oxford, since 1999; Fellow, St John's College, Oxford, since 1999; *b* 1956; *m* 1998, Prof. Elizabeth Anne Fallaize, PhD (*d* 2009). *Educ:* Univ. of Oxford (BA Exptl Psychol. 1977; MPhil Econs 1979; DPhil Zool. 1983). Lectr in Quantitative Methods in Biol., Univ. of Oxford. Trustee, Oxford Playhouse, 2010–. *Publications:* (contrib.) Reproductive Success, 1988; (ed) Evolution and its Influence, 1989; (contrib.) Behavioural Ecology, 3rd edn 1991; (contrib.) Phylogenies and the Comparative Method in Animal Behaviour, 1996; (with R. Hails) Modern Statistics for the Life Sciences, 2002; (ed with M. Ridley) Richard Dawkins: how a scientist changed the way we think, 2006; contribs to jls incl. Animal Behaviour, Nature, Jl Theoretical Biol., Parasitol., Proc. Royal Soc., Science, Jl Evolutionary Biol. *Address:* Department of Zoology, South Parks Road, Oxford OX1 3PS.

**GRAFF, Laurence**, OBE 2013; Founder and Chairman, Graff Diamonds Holdings, since 1960; *b* 13 June 1938; *s* of Harry Graff and Rebecca Graff (*née* Segal); *m* 1962, Anne-Marie Bessiere; two *s* one *d*. *Educ:* St George's Sch., E London. Jeweller apprentice, Hatton Garden, 1953; founded Graff Diamonds, 1960; opened first major retail store in Knightsbridge, 1974; other stores incl. Bond St, London, NY, Monte Carlo, Courchevel, Geneva, Hong Kong, China and Japan. Mem., European Adv. Bd, Christies, 2014–. Member: Internat. Council, Tate, 2004–; Exec. Cttee, Internat. Dir's Council, Guggenheim Mus., 2005–; Internat. Council, Berggruen Mus., Berlin, 2009–; Internat. Bd of Trustees, Mus. of Contemporary Art, LA, 2010–; Bd of Govs, Tel Aviv Mus. of Art, 2010–. Queen's Award to Industry, 1973; Queen's Award for Export Achievement, 1977,

1994; Queen's Award for Enterprise, 2006, 2014. *Recreations:* collector of contemporary and modern art, ski-ing, sailing. *Address:* Graff Diamonds Ltd, 28–29 Albemarle Street, W1S 4JA. *Clubs:* Annabel's, Harry's Bar, George, Mark's, Arts, 5 Hertford Street.

**GRAFTON,** 12th Duke of, *cr* 1675; **Henry Oliver Charles FitzRoy;** Earl of Euston, Viscount Ipswich, Baron Sudbury 1672; *b* 6 April 1978; *s* of Earl of Euston (*d* 2009) and of Countess of Euston; *S* grandfather, 2011; *m* 2010, Olivia Margaret Hogarth, *d* of Simon Sladen; one *s. Educ:* Harrow Sch.; Edinburgh Univ.; RAC, Cirencester. Music business mgt, FBMM, and radio host, Nashville, Tenn, 2002–04; merchandise co-ordinator, Rolling Stones tour, A Bigger Bang, 2005–06. *Heir: s* Earl of Euston, *qv.*

**GRAFTON, Fortune, Duchess of; (Ann) Fortune FitzRoy,** GCVO 1980 (DCVO 1970; CVO 1965); Mistress of The Robes to the Queen, since 1967; *o d* of Captain Eric Smith, MC, LLD, Lower Ashfold, Slaugham; *m* 1946, Earl of Euston, later 11th Duke of Grafton, KG (*d* 2011); one *s* three *d* (and one *s* decd). Lady of the Bedchamber to the Queen, 1953–66. SRCN Great Ormond Street, 1945; Mem. Bd of Governors, The Hospital for Sick Children, Great Ormond Street, 1952–66; Patron, Nurses' League. President: W Suffolk Mission to the Deaf; W Suffolk Decorative and Fine Arts Soc.; Bury St Edmunds Br., BHF; National Vice Pres., Royal British Legion Women's Section, 2003 (Vice Pres., Suffolk Br., 1970–2009); Vice Pres., Trinity Hospice, later Royal Trinity Hospice, Clapham Common, 1951–. Governor: Felixstowe Coll.; Riddlesworth Hall. Patron: Relate, W Suffolk; Guildhall String Ensemble; Clarence River Historical Soc., Grafton, NSW. JP County of London, 1949, W Suffolk, 1970–95. *Address:* 14 Whitelands House, Cheltenham Terrace, SW3 4QX.
See also Jeremy F. E. Smith.

**GRAFTON, NSW, Bishop of,** since 2018; **Rt Rev. Dr Murray Alexander Harvey;** *b* Brisbane, 8 Oct. 1963; *s* of Norman and Jean Harvey; *m* 1996, Leanne; one *s* one *d. Educ:* Univ. of Queensland (BA Hons Psychol. 1985); St Francis Theol Coll., Qld (BTh 1991); Deakin Univ. (DHSc 2003). Ordained deacon, 1991, priest, 1992; Priest-in-charge, St George's, Tamborine Mountain, Qld, 1995–2001; Vicar, Pinchbeck, Dio. of Lincoln, 2001–11; Rector, St Mark's, Clayfield, Qld, 2011–18; Residentiary Canon, St John's Cathedral, Brisbane, 2014–18. Chaplain, Britain-Australia Soc., Cambridge, 2001–11. Chair of Govs, Pinchbeck East C of E Primary Sch., 2001–10; Dir, Sch. Council, St Margaret's Anglican Girls Sch., Brisbane, 2011–18. *Recreations:* Rugby, travel, walking, cycling. *Address:* Bishop's Registry, 50 Victoria Street, Grafton, NSW 2460, Australia. *E:* bishop@graftondiocese.org.au. *Clubs:* Univ. of Queensland Rugby; Spalding Rugby (Vice-Pres., 2002–11).

**GRAFTON-GREEN, Patrick;** Chairman, Simkins LLP (formerly Senior Partner, Michael Simkins LLP), since 2006; *b* 30 March 1943; *s* of George Grafton-Green and Brigid Anna Grafton-Green (*née* Maxwell); *m* 1982, Deborah Susan Goodchild; two *s* two *d. Educ:* Ampleforth Coll., York; Wadham Coll., Oxford (MA 1965). Joined Theodore Goddard, later Addleshaw Goddard, solicitors, 1966; qualif. as solicitor, 1969; Partner, 1973–2006; Head, Media and Communications Dept, 1993–2006; Sen. Partner, 1997–2003; Chm., 2003–06. *Recreations:* cricket, music, theatre. *Address:* Simkins LLP, Lynton House, 7–12 Tavistock Square, WC1H 9LT. *T:* (020) 7874 5634. *Club:* MCC.

**GRAHAM,** family name of **Duke of Montrose** and **Baron Graham of Edmonton**.

**GRAHAM, Marquis of; James Alexander Norman Graham;** *b* 16 Aug. 1973; *s* and heir of Duke of Montrose, *qv; m* 2004, Cecilia, *d* of late Francesco Manfredi. *Educ:* Eton; Univ. of Edinburgh (BSc); Univ. of Cape Town (MSc). *Address:* Auchmar, Drymen, Glasgow G63 0AG.

**GRAHAM OF EDMONTON,** Baron *cr* 1983 (Life Peer), of Edmonton in Greater London; **Thomas Edward Graham;** PC 1998; *b* 26 March 1925; *m* 1950, Margaret (*d* 2005), *d* of Frederick Golding; two *s. Educ:* elementary sch.; WEA Co-operative College; BA Open Univ., 1976. Newcastle-on-Tyne Co-operative Soc., 1939–52; Organiser, British Fedn of Young Co-operators, 1952–53; Educn Sec., Enfield Highway Co-operative Soc., 1953–62; Sec., Co-operative Union Southern Section, 1962–67; Nat. Sec., Co-operative Party, 1967–74. Mem. and Leader, Enfield Council, 1961–68. Contested (Lab) Enfield W, 1966; MP (Lab and Co-op) Enfield, Edmonton, Feb. 1974–1983; contested (Lab) Edmonton, 1983. PPS to Minister of State, Dept of Prices and Consumer Protection, 1974–76; a Lord Comr of HM Treasury, 1976–79; Opposition spokesman on the environment, 1980–83; Opposition Chief Whip, H of L, 1990–97. Chm., Labour Peers' Gp, 1997–2000. FCMI. *Address:* 2 Clerks Piece, Loughton, Essex IG10 1NR.

**GRAHAM, Alastair Carew;** Head Master, Mill Hill School, 1979–92; *b* 23 July 1932; *s* of Col J. A. Graham and Mrs Graham (*née* Carew-Hunt); *m* 1969, Penelope Rachel Barth (*née* Beaumont); two *d. Educ:* Winchester Coll.; Gonville and Caius Coll., Cambridge (1st Cl. Mod. and Med. Langs). Served 1st Bn Argyll and Sutherland Highlanders, 1951–53. Foy, Morgan & Co. (City), 1956–58; Asst Master, 1958–70, House Master, 1970–79, Eton. *Recreations:* education, European travel, DFAS theatre and opera, music listening. *Address:* Apartment 7, Lawnswood Court, Wellington Square, Cheltenham, Glos GL50 4AB.

**GRAHAM, Alexander;** television producer; Joint Chief Executive, Two Cities Television Ltd, since 2016; Chief Executive, Wall to Wall Media, 1997–2013; *b* 28 Oct. 1953; *s* of Alexander and Jean Graham; *m* 2000, Maeve Haran; one *s* two *d. Educ:* West Coats Primary Sch., Cambuslang; Hamilton Acad.; Glasgow Univ. (MA Hons English Lit. and Sociol.); City Univ. (Dip. Journalism). Reporter, Bradford Telegraph and Argus, 1978–79; researcher and producer, LWT, 1979–83; Editor, Diverse Reports, 1983–86, Media Show, 1987–91, Channel 4; Jt Man. Dir, Wall to Wall Media, 1991–97; Executive Producer: Baby It's You, 1993; Our Boy, 1997; A Rather English Marriage, 1998; The 1900 House, 1999; The 1940s House, 2001; Edwardian Country House, 2003; New Tricks, 2002–13; Who Do You Think You Are?, 2004–13; Who Do You Think You Are? (USA), 2007–17. Chair, Red Sky Prodns, 2017–. Vis. Fellow, Bournemouth Media Sch., 2004–10; Vis. Prof., Univ. of Lincoln, 2011–. Producers Association for Cinema and Television: Mem. Council, 1991–2008; Vice Chm., 1995–96 and 1999–2000; Chair, 2006–07. Chair, Media Literary Task Force, 2009. Chair, Sheffield Internat. Documentary Fest., 2011–. Chair: The Space, 2014–15; The Scott Trust, 2016– (non-exec. Dir, 2013–16). Trustee, The Creative Society (formerly New Deal of the Mind), 2010–16. Ambassador, ActionAid, 2010–. Mem. Bd, Hampstead Th., 2011–17. FRSA 2004; FRTS 2006. Hon. DArts City, 2009. Grierson Trustees' Award, British Documentary Awards, 2014; Outstanding Contribn to Broadcasting, British Acad. Scotland Awards, 2014; Gold Medal, RTS, 2016. *Recreations:* cooking, walking, guitar, piano, Arsenal FC, single malt whisky. *T:* 07940 965104. *E:* alex@bigeck.com. *Club:* Reform.

**GRAHAM, Sir Alexander (Michael),** GBE 1990; JP; Lord Mayor of London, 1990–91; *b* 27 Sept. 1938; *s* of Dr Walter Graham and Suzanne Graham (*née* Simon); *m* 1964, Carolyn, *d* of Lt-Col Alan Wolryche Stansfeld, MBE; three *d. Educ:* Fyvie Village Sch.; Hall Sch., Hampstead; St Paul's Sch. National Service, 1957–59; commnd Gordon Highlanders; TA 1959–67; Chm., Nat. Employers Liaison Cttee for TA and Reserve Forces, 1992–97. Joined Norman Frizzell & Partners Ltd, 1957: Dir, 1967–93; Man. Dir, 1973–90; Dep. Chm., 1990–93; Underwriting Member of Lloyd's, 1978–2000; Director: Folgate Insce Co. Ltd, 1975–2001, 2004–05 (Chm., 1995–2001); Folgate Partnership Ltd, 2002–05; Chairman: FirstCity Insce Brokers, 1993–98; Employment Conditions Abroad Internat. Ltd, 1993–2005 (Dir, 1992–93); Euclidian plc, 1994–2001. Mercers' Co.: Liveryman, 1971–; Mem., Ct of Assistants, 1980; Master, 1983–84; Mem., Ct of Common Council, City of London, 1978–79; Alderman for Ward of Queenhithe, 1979–2004; Pres., Queenhithe Ward Club, 1979–2004. Sheriff, City of London, 1986–87; HM Lieut, City of London, 1989–2004. Hon. Liveryman, Co. of Chartered Secretaries and Administrators, 1992; Hon. Freeman: Insurers' Co., 1992; Merchant Adventurers of York, 1983. President: CS Motoring Assoc., 1993–2006; British Insurance Law Assoc., 1994–96; Vice-Pres., Insurance Inst. of London, 1978–. Governor: Hall Sch., Hampstead, 1975–93; Christ's Hosp. Sch., 1979–2004; King Edward's Sch., Whitley, 1979–2004; St Paul's Sch., 1980–93, 2003–09 (Chm., 2004–09; Vice Pres., 1988–2000, Dep. Pres., 2000–01, Pres., 2001–03, Old Pauline Club; Chm., Gen. Charitable Trust, 1997–2004); St Paul's Girls' Sch., 1980–93, 2004–09; City of London Boys' Sch., 1983–85; City of London Girls' Sch., 1992–95; Mem. Council, Gresham Coll., 1983–93; Trustee, Morden College, 1988–2013 (Chm., 1995–2013); Chancellor, City Univ., 1990–91; Mem. Court, Univ. of Herts, 2006–. Trustee: United Response, 1988–2002 (Chm., 1993–2002); Lord Mayor's 800th Anniversary Trust, 1989–2000; Temple Bar Trust, 1992–2004; Vice Pres., 1992–, and Hon. Life Mem., 1993, Macmillan Cancer Relief (formerly Cancer Relief Macmillan Fund); Vice Pres., Garden House Hospice, 1992–2016; Hon. Mem., Ct, HAC, 1979–2004; Member, Executive Committee: Army Benevolent Fund, 1991–98; Fedn of London Youth Clubs, 1991–95; Chm. Council, Order of St John, Herts, 1993–2001; Mem., Royal Soc. of St George, 1981–; Vice Pres., Royal Soc. of St George, Herts Br., 1999–. Vice Pres., Herts Agricl Show, 1996–2015. Mem., Adv. Council, Herts Community Foundn, 2008–. Gentlemen Usher of the Purple Rod, Order of the British Empire, 2000–13. FCII 1964; FBIIBA 1967; FCIS 1990; FInstD 1975; CCMI (CBIM 1991); FRSA 1980. JP City of London, 1979. Hon. Keeper of the Quaich, 1992; Commandeur de l'Ordre du Tastevin, 1985; Vigneron d'Honneur et Bourgeois de St Emilion, 1999. Hon. DCL City, 1990; Hon. DLitt Herts, 2016. KStJ 1990. Silver Medal, City of Helsinki, 1990; Medal, City of Santiago, 1991. Order of Wissam Alouite (Morocco), 1987; Grand Cross Order of Merit (Chile), 1991. *Recreations:* wine, calligraphy, genealogy, music, reading, silver, bridge, golf, swimming, avoiding gardening. *Address:* 33a High Street, Whitwell, Hitchin, Herts SG4 8AJ. *T:* and *Fax:* (01438) 871223. *Clubs:* Garrick, City Livery; Royal Worlington and Newmarket Golf, Mid Herts Golf, Lloyd's Golf (Capt. 1994, Pres., 1996).
See also Lt-Gen. Sir P. W. Graham.

**GRAHAM, Sir Alistair;** *see* Graham, Sir J. A.

**GRAHAM, Rt Rev. Andrew Alexander Kenny;** an Hon. Assistant Bishop, Diocese of Carlisle, since 1997; *b* 7 Aug. 1929; *o s* of late Andrew Harrison and Magdalene Graham; unmarried. *Educ:* Tonbridge Sch.; St John's Coll., Oxford (Hon. Fellow, 1986); Ely Theological College. Curate of Hove Parish Church, 1955–58; Chaplain and Lectr in Theology, Worcester Coll., Oxford, 1958–70; Fellow and Tutor, 1960–70, Hon. Fellow, 1981; Warden of Lincoln Theological Coll., 1970–77; Canon and Prebendary of Lincoln Cathedral, 1970–77; Bishop Suffragan of Bedford, 1977–81; Bishop of Newcastle, 1981–97. Chairman: ACCM, 1984–87; Doctrine Commn, 1987–95. DD Lambeth, 1995; Hon. DCL Northumbria, 1997. *Address:* Fell End, Butterwick, Penrith, Cumbria CA10 2QQ. *T:* (01931) 713147. *Club:* Oxford and Cambridge.

**GRAHAM, Lt Gen. Andrew John Noble,** CB 2011; CBE 2002 (MBE 1993); Chairman, Waves Training Solutions Ltd, since 2016; Managing Partner, Larbert Partnership Ltd, since 2011; *b* 21 Oct. 1956; *er s* and heir of Sir John (Alexander Noble) Graham, Bt, *qv*; *m* 1984, Susie Mary Bridget, *er d* of Rear Adm. John Patrick Bruce O'Riordan, *qv*; one *s* three *d. Educ:* Eton Coll.; Trinity Coll., Cambridge (MA). Commnd Argyll and Sutherland Highlanders, 1979; served in UK, NI, Hong Kong, Cyprus, S Georgia, MoD, 1979–88; acsc 1988; 1 Argyll and Sutherland Highlanders, Germany, 1989–90; MoD, 1990–92; Directing Staff, Army Staff Coll., 1992–95; CO, 1st Bn, Argyll and Sutherland Highlanders (Princess Louise's), 1995–97; Comdr, 3rd Inf. Bde, 1999–2001; Dir, Army Resources and Plans, MoD, 2001–03; Dep. Comdg Gen., Multinat. Corps, Iraq, 2004; Director General: Army Trng and Recruiting, subseq. Army Recruiting and Trng Div., 2004–07; Defence Academy of the UK, 2008–11. Hd of Doctrine and Strategic Analysis, Gen. Dynamics UK, 2011–13; Exec. Dir, British Exploring Soc., 2014–16. Non-exec. Dir, DWP, 2015–19 (Mem., 2013–19, Chair, 2015–19, Audit and Risk Assurance Cttee). Colonel: Argyll and Sutherland Highlanders (Princess Louise's), 2000–06; Royal Regt of Scotland, 2007–14; Col Comdt, The Infantry, 2013–. Brig., Queen's Body Guard for Scotland (Royal Company of Archers), 2012–. Trustee, Combat Stress, 2012–19 (Chair, 2013–19). Pres., ACFA, 2013–. Officer, Legion of Merit (USA), 2006. *Recreations:* piping, outdoor sports, destructive gardening, travel/history reading, hobby smallholding, beekeeping.

**GRAHAM, Andrew Winston Mawdsley;** Master, Balliol College, Oxford, 2001–11 (Hon. Fellow, 2011); Acting Warden, Rhodes House, Oxford, 2012–13; Executive Chair, Europaeum, since 2017 (Chairman, Academic Council, since 2006); *b* 20 June 1942; *s* of late Winston Mawdsley Graham, OBE, FRSL; *m* 1970, Peggotty Fawssett. *Educ:* Charterhouse; St Edmund Hall, Oxford (MA (PPE); Hon. Fellow, 2002). Economic Assistant: NEDO, 1964; Dept of Economic Affairs, 1964–66; Asst to Economic Adviser to the Cabinet, 1966–68; Economic Adviser to Prime Minister, 1968–69; Balliol College, Oxford: Fellow, 1969–2001; Tutor in Econs, 1969; Estates Bursar, 1978; Investment Bursar, 1979–83; Vice Master, 1988 and 1992–94; Acting Master, 1997–2001; Policy Adviser to Prime Minister (on leave of absence from Balliol), 1974–75; Economic Advr to Shadow Chancellor of Exchequer, 1988–92, to Leader of the Opposition, 1992–94. Tutor, Oxford Univ. Business Summer Sch., 1971, 1972, 1973 and 1976; Acting Dir, Oxford Internet Inst., 2002 (Chm., Adv. Bd, 2001–11; Mem., Adv. Bd, 2011–12; Sen. Fellow, 2011–). Vis. Researcher, SE Asian Central Banks Res. and Trng Centre, Malaysia, 1984; Vis. Fellow, Griffith Univ., Brisbane, 1984; Vis. Scholar, MIT, and Vis. Fellow, Center for Eur. Studies, Harvard, 1994; Sen. Fellow, Gorbachev Foundn of N America, 1999–. Founder Mem., Editl Bd, Liby of Political Economy, 1982–. Member: Council of Mgt, Templeton Coll., Oxford, 1990–95; Council, Oxford Univ., 2006–10. Member: Wilson Cttee to Review the Functioning of Financial Institutions, 1977–80; Economics Cttee, SSRC, 1978–80; British Transport Docks Bd, 1979–82; Chm., St James Gp (Economic Forecasting), 1982–84, 1985–92. Mem., ILO/Jobs and Skills Prog. for Africa (JASPA) Mission to Ethiopia, 1982; Hd, Queen Elizabeth House/Food Studies Gp team assisting Govt of Republic of Zambia, 1984. Consultant: BBC, 1989–92; Mammoth Screen, 2014–; Mem. Bd, Channel Four Television Ltd, 1998–2005. Member: Media Adv. Cttee, IPPR, 1994–97; Adv. Bd, Ind. Social Res. Foundn, 2009–17. Trustee: Foundn for Information Policy Res., 1998–2000; Esmée Fairbairn Foundn, 2003–05; Rhodes Trust, 2013–16; Reprieve, 2015–; Dir, Scott Trust Ltd, 2005–16. Hon. DCL Oxford, 2003. *Publications:* (ed) Government and Economies in the Postwar Period, 1990; (jtly) Broadcasting, Society and Policy in the Multimedia Age, 1997. *Recreation:* windsurfing on every possible occasion. *Address:* 8 Leckford Place, Oxford OX2 6JB.

**GRAHAM, Anne Silvia, (Anne, Lady Graham);** Chairman, South Cumbria Health Authority, 1988–94; *b* 1 Aug. 1934; *o d* of late Benjamin Arthur Garcia and Constance Rosa (*née* Journeaux). *Educ:* Francis Holland Sch., SW1; LSE (LLB). Called to the Bar, Inner

Temple, 1958; Yarborough-Anderson Scholar, 1959. Joined Min. of Housing and Local Govt, 1960; Dep. Legal Advr, DoE, 1978–86. Mem. Court, Lancaster Univ., 1993–2006. *Recreations:* gardening, arts, music.

**GRAHAM, Anthony James;** QC (Scot.) 2017; *b* Glasgow, 8 Sept. 1971; *s* of Kevin Graham and Josephine Gordon. *Educ:* St Aloysius' Coll., Glasgow; Univ. of Glasgow (LLB 1992; DipLP 1993). Trainee solicitor, David G. Hogg, 1993–95; solicitor, McAfee Solicitors, 1995–2001; in practice as Advocate, 2002–; Advocate Depute (*ad hoc*), 2007–. KHS 2014. *Recreations:* sailing, hill walking, classic cars, motoring, Jack Russell Terriers, provoking political discussion. *Address:* 25 Boclair Road, Bishopbriggs, Glasgow G64 2NB. *T:* (0141) 772 6214, 07976 951906, *Fax:* (0141) 772 9617. *E:* tonygraham1994@aol.com. *Club:* Allan Glen's School (Glasgow).

**GRAHAM, Anthony Ronald,** CEng; FREng, FRINA; Chief Operating Officer, Cammell Laird, since 2019 (Director, since 2017); *b* Omagh, Co. Tyrone, 13 Aug. 1962; *s* of Ronald George Graham and Bridie Graham; *m* 1993, Catherine Tuck; one *s* one *d*. *Educ:* Bath Tech. Coll. (MoD apprenticeship; Higher Technician Cert. Shipbuilding 1984); Univ. of Glasgow (BEng 1st Cl. Naval Architecture and Ocean Engrg 1987); University Coll. London (MSc Naval Architecture and Marine Engrg 1988; Submarine Design Dip. 1988); Univ. of W of England (MBA 1997). FRINA 2002; FREng 2016. Ministry of Defence: Mil. Exchange Officer in Canada, 1997–2000; Hd, Ship Safety Mgt Office, 2000–03; Team Leader: Battlefield Infrastructure Integrated Project, 2003–05; Landing Ship Dock (Auxiliary) Integrated Project, 2005–07; Mil. Afloat Reach and Sustainability Integrated Project, 2007–08; Dir, Afloat Support, 2008; Hd, Capital Ships, 2008–11; Dir, Ships, Defence Equipment and Support, 2011–15. Dir, Bluewater Portfolio, 2015–. Hd, RCNC, 2011–. Fellow, Internat. Centre for Complex Proj. Mgt, 2015. *Recreation:* enjoying life with family and friends. *Address:* 9 Vayre Close, Chipping Sodbury, Bristol BS37 6NT. *T:* 07983 513840. *E:* tonyrgraham@blueyonder.co.uk.

**GRAHAM, (Arthur) William;** JP; Member (C) South Wales East, National Assembly for Wales, 1999–2016; *b* 18 Nov. 1949; *s* of late William Douglas Graham and of Eleanor Mary Scott (*née* Searle); *m* 1981, Elizabeth Hannah, *d* of late Joshua Griffiths; one *s* two *d*. *Educ:* Blackfriars; Coll. of Estate Mgt, London. FRICS 1974. Principal, Graham & Co., Chartered Surveyors, 1970–. Newport Harbour Comr, 1990–2005 (Chm., 2001). Member: Gwent CC, 1985–89; Newport County BC, subseq. CC, 1988–2004 (Leader, Conservative Gp, 1992–2004). National Assembly for Wales: Chief Whip, Cons. Gp, 2001–14; opposition spokesman on local govt and housing, 2001–03, on social justice, 2003–07; Shadow Leader of the House, 2007–14; Shadow Minister for Social Services, 2012–14, for Business, Enterprise and Skills, 2014–16; Chairman: Educn Cttee, 1999–2001; Constitutional Cttee, 2009–11; Enterprise and Business Cttee, 2014–16; First Comr for Assembly Resources, 2007–11. Gov., Rougemont Sch. Trust, 1991–2005 (Chm., 2002–05). Founder Mem., Aelwydd Housing Assoc., 1988–98. Trustee, Stow Park Community Centre, 2010–16. JP Newport, 1979. *Recreations:* breeder of pedigree Suffolk sheep, foreign travel. *Address:* The Volland, Lower Machen, Newport NP10 8GY. *T:* (01633) 440419. *Club:* Carlton.

**GRAHAM, Charles Robert Stephen;** QC 2003; *b* 1 April 1961; *s* of Major (Cosmo) Stephen Graham and Mary Graham; *m* 1991, Jane Lindsay; three *s*. *Educ:* Ludgrove Sch., Wokingham; Wellington Coll., Crowthorne; University Coll., Oxford (1st cl. Greats (Lit. Hum.) 1984); City Univ. (Dip Law 1985). Called to the Bar, Middle Temple, 1986; in practice, specialising in commercial law; Mem., SE Circuit. *Address:* One Essex Court, Temple, EC4Y 9AR. *T:* (020) 7583 2000, *Fax:* (020) 7583 0118. *E:* cgraham@oeclaw.co.uk.

**GRAHAM, Prof. Christopher Forbes,** DPhil; FRS 1981; Professor of Animal Development, and Professorial Fellow, St Catherine's College, University of Oxford, 1985–2007, now Professor Emeritus; *b* 23 Sept. 1940. *Educ:* St Edmund Hall, Oxford (BA 1963); DPhil Oxon 1966. Formerly Junior Beit Memorial Fellow in Med. Research, Sir William Dunn Sch. of Pathology. Lectr, Zoology Dept, Oxford Univ., 1970–85. Member: Brit. Soc. Cell Biology; Brit. Soc. for Developmental Biology; Soc. for Experimental Biology; Genetical Soc. *Publications:* The Developmental Biology of Plants and Animals, 1976, new edn as Developmental Control in Plants and Animals, 1984. *Address:* Department of Zoology, University of Oxford, South Parks Road, Oxford OX1 3PS.

**GRAHAM, Christopher Sidney Matthew;** Chair, Foxhill House and Woodlands, Diocese of Chester, since 2019; *b* 21 Sept. 1950; *s* of late David Maurice Graham and Rosemary West Graham; *m* 1st, 1985, Christine Harland (*née* McLean) (marr. diss. 2008); 2nd, 2010, Mary Elizabeth Shevaun Crockett. *Educ:* Canterbury Cathedral Choir Sch.; St Edward's Sch., Oxford (Music Scholar); Univ. of Liverpool (Pres., Guild of Undergrads, 1971–72; BA Hons Hist. 1973). BBC News Trainee, 1973–75; Producer: General Talks, Radio, BBC Manchester, 1976–78; Television Current Affairs, BBC, Lime Grove, 1979–87; A Week in Politics, Channel 4, 1987–88; Dep. Editor, The Money Prog., BBC, 1988–89; Asst Editor, 1989–90, Man. Editor, 1990–93, BBC Television News; Man. Editor, BBC News Progs, 1994–95; Sec., BBC, 1996–99; Dir Gen., Advertising Standards Authy, 2000–09; Information Comr, 2009–16; Chair, Capacity: The Public Services Lab LLP, 2017–19. Chm., European Advertising Standards Alliance, 2003–05. Vice-Chair, Article 29 Wkg Party of Eur. data protection authorities, 2012–14. Non-exec. Dir, Electoral Reform Services Ltd, 2001–09, 2017–18 (Sen. Ind. non-exec. Dir, 2017–18). Lay Mem., Bar Standards Bd, 2006–09. Vice Pres., Council, Univ. of Liverpool, 2016–19. Mem. (L), Liverpool City Council, 1971–74. Contested (L) Wilts N, 1983, 1987. *Recreations:* music, travel, history. *Address:* 9 Leigh Road, Hale, Altrincham, Cheshire WA15 9BG.

**GRAHAM, Prof. Daniel Joseph,** PhD; Professor of Statistical Modelling, Imperial College London, since 2013; *b* Glasgow, 6 March 1970; *s* of Daniel and Rita Graham; *m* 2004, Holly; two *s* two *d*. *Educ:* St Aloysius Coll., Glasgow; Univ. of Strathclyde (BA 1st Cl. Hons); London Sch. of Econs and Polit. Sci. (PhD); Imperial Coll. London (PhD). Imperial College London: Res. Associate, Dept of Computing, 1997–99; Res. Fellow, 1999–2007, Reader, 2007–13, Dept of Civil Engrg. *Publications:* (with S. Glaister) Pricing Our Roads, 2004; (with S. Glaister) National Road Pricing, 2006; contrib. papers to jls. *Recreations:* cycling, guitar, Glasgow Celtic. *Address:* Department of Civil Engineering, Imperial College London, South Kensington Campus, SW7 2AZ. *T:* (020) 7594 6088. *E:* d.j.graham@imperial.ac.uk.

**GRAHAM, David;** *see* Graham, S. D.

**GRAHAM, Rt Hon. Sir Douglas (Arthur Montrose),** KNZM 1999; PC 1998; Minister of Justice, 1990–97, Minister in charge of Treaty of Waitangi Negotiations, 1991–99, and Attorney General, 1997–99, New Zealand; *b* 12 Jan. 1942; *s* of late Robert James Alister Graham and Patricia Kennedy Graham; *m* 1966, Beverley Virginia Cordell; two *s* one *d*. *Educ:* Southwell Preparatory Sch.; Auckland GS; Auckland Univ. (BL 1965). Barrister and solicitor, 1968–84; Sen. Partner, Graham & Co., Solicitors, 1972–84. MP (N) New Zealand, 1984–99, for Remuera, 1984–96; Minister of Cultural Affairs, and of Disarmament and Arms Control, 1990–96. Hon. Dr Waikato, 1998. *Publications:* Trick or Treaty?, 1997. *Recreations:* music, gardening. *Address:* 3A Martin Avenue, Remuera, Auckland, New Zealand. *T:* (9) 5242921.

**GRAHAM, Duncan Gilmour,** CBE 1987; Senior Partner, Duncan Graham Consultants, 1991–2001; *b* 20 Aug. 1936; *s* of Robert Gilmour Graham and Lilias Turnbull Graham (*née* Watson); *m* 1st, 1962, Margaret Gray Graham (*née* Cairns) (marr. diss. 1991); two *s* one *d*; 2nd, 1991, Wendy Margaret Wallace (*d* 2012). *Educ:* Hutchesons', Glasgow; Univ. of Glasgow (MA (Hons) History); Jordanhill Coll. of Education (Teachers' Secondary Cert.). Teacher of History: Whitehill Sec. Sch., Glasgow, 1959–62; Hutcheson's, Glasgow, 1962–65; Lectr in Social Studies, Craigie Coll. of Educn, Ayr, 1965–68; Asst Dir of Educn, Renfrewshire, 1968–70; Sen. Depute Dir of Educn, Renfrewshire, 1970–74, Strathclyde Regl Council, 1974–79; Advr to COSLA and Scottish Teachers' Salaries Cttee, 1974–79; County Educn Officer, Suffolk, 1979–87; Chief Exec., Humberside CC, 1987–88; Chm. and Chief Exec., Nat. Curriculum Council, 1988–91. Advr to ACC, 1982–88; Mem., Burnham Cttee, 1983–87 and of ACAS Ind. Panel, 1986. Sec., Co. Educn Officers Soc., 1985–87; Chm., Assoc. of Educn Officers, 1985; Project Dir, DES Teacher Appraisal Study, 1985–86; Chm., Nat. Steering Gp on Teacher Appraisal, 1987–90. Member: BBC North Adv. Council, 1988–91; Lincs and Humberside Arts Council, 1988–91; Yorks and Humberside Arts, 1991–94; Council of Nat. Foundn for Educnl Res., 1984, and 1989–90; Exec. Council, Industrial Soc., 1988–90; Chm., Nat. Mathematics Wkg Gp, 1988. Mem. Exec., Caravan Club, 1997–2000. Chairman: Eden Rivers Trust, 2000–03; Cumbria Local Access Forum, 2003–10, England Access Forum, 2008–11; Fellrunner Village Bus, 2004–08; Youth Work in Cumbria Partnership, 2005–08. Trustee, S Tynedale Rly, 2013–14. FRSA 1981. *Publications:* Those Having Torches, 1985; In the Light of Torches, 1986; Sense, Nonsense and the National Curriculum, 1992; A Lesson For Us All, 1992; Sunset on the Clyde, 1993, 3rd edn 2005; The Education Racket, 1996; Visiting Distilleries, 2001, 2nd edn 2003; many articles in nat. press and educn and local govt jls. *Recreations:* garden railways, walking, fly-fishing, cycling, bowling. *Address:* 37 Pele Court, Friargate, Penrith, Cumbria CA11 7XT. *T:* (01768) 864997.

**GRAHAM, Elizabeth;** Director of Education, London Borough of Enfield, 1994–2003; *b* 25 Jan. 1951. *Educ:* Knightswood Secondary Sch., Glasgow; Edinburgh Univ. (MA History); Moray House Coll. of Educn, Edinburgh (PGCE). Teacher, Stirlingshire CC, 1971–73; Head of Dept, Waltham Forest LBC, 1973–81; Professional Asst, Haringey LBC, 1982–84; Asst Educn Officer, Enfield LBC, 1984–89; Asst Dir of Educn, Redbridge LBC, 1989–94. Dir, Forest Acad. Trust, 2011–13. *Recreations:* cats, the crusades.

**GRAHAM, George;** Manager, Tottenham Hotspur Football Club, 1998–2001; *b* Scotland, 30 Nov. 1944; *m* 1998, Sue Schmidt. Professional football player, 1962–77: Aston Villa, 1962–64; Chelsea, 1964–66 (League Cup, 1965); Arsenal, 1966–72 (League and FA Cups, 1971); Manchester United, 1972–74; Portsmouth, 1974–76; Crystal Palace, 1976–77; twelve Scotland caps; coach: Queen's Park Rangers, 1977; Crystal Palace, 1977–82; Manager: Millwall, 1982–86; Arsenal, 1986–95 (League Cup, 1987, 1993; League Champions, 1989, 1991; FA Cup, 1993; European Cup Winners' Cup, 1994); Leeds, 1996–98; Tottenham Hotspur, 1998–2001 (League Cup, 1999).

**GRAHAM, (George) Ronald (Gibson),** CBE 1986; Partner, 1968–2000, Senior Partner, Maclay, Murray & Spens, Solicitors, Glasgow, Edinburgh, Aberdeen and London; *b* 15 Oct. 1939; *o s* of James Gibson Graham, MD, and Elizabeth Waddell; *m* 1965, Mirren Elizabeth Carnegie; three *s*. *Educ:* Glasgow Academy; Loretto Sch., Musselburgh; Oriel Coll., Oxford (MA); Glasgow Univ. (LLB). Director: Scottish Widows' Fund and Life Assce Soc., 1984–2000; Scottish Widows Bank PLC, 1995–2002; Second Scottish National Trust plc, 2002–04. Co-ordinator of Diploma in Legal Practice, 1979–83; Clerk to Gen. Council, Glasgow Univ., 1990–96, Mem. Ct, 1996–2004. Mem. Council, 1977–89, Pres., 1984–85, Law Soc. of Scotland. Gov., Jordanhill Coll. of Educn, Glasgow, 1991–93; Chm. of Govs, Loretto Sch., 2004–07. *Recreations:* fishing, golf, swimming, walking. *Address:* Carse of South Coldoch, Gargunnock, by Stirling FK8 3DF. *T:* (01786) 860397.

**GRAHAM, Gordon;** *see* Graham, L. G.

**GRAHAM, Prof. Ian Alexander,** PhD; FRS 2016; Weston Professor of Biochemical Genetics, Centre for Novel Agricultural Products, University of York, since 1999; *b* Castlederg, NI, 13 June 1963; *s* of Robert William George Graham and (Edith) Eileen Elizabeth Graham; *m* 1989, Deborah Catherine Boal; two *s*. *Educ:* Langfield Primary Sch.; Castlederg Secondary Sch.; Omagh Acad.; Queen's Univ., Belfast (BSc 1st Cl. Hons Botany and Genetics 1986); Univ. of Edinburgh (PhD Plant Molecular Biol. 1989). Postdoctoral scientist, Dept of Plant Scis, Univ. of Oxford, 1990–93; Lectr, 1993–98, Sen. Lectr, 1998–99, Univ. of Glasgow; SERC-NATO Res. Fellow, Carnegie Instn of Washington, Dept of Plant Biol., Stanford Univ., Calif, 1994; University of York: Dep. Dir, 2003–08, Dir, 2008–13, Centre for Novel Agricl Products; Hd, Dept of Biol., 2014–18. Mem., UKRI-BBSRC, 2018–. Dir, BioYork, 2018–. *Publications:* articles in jls. *Recreations:* cycling, reading, travelling. *Address:* Department of Biology, University of York, Wentworth Way, York YO10 5DD. *T:* (01904) 328750. *E:* ian.graham@york.ac.uk.

**GRAHAM, Ian David; His Honour Judge Graham;** a Circuit Judge, since 2008; *b* Alnwick, 9 May 1955; *s* of late David Graham and Elsie Graham. *Educ:* Duke's Sch., Alnwick; Christ Church, Oxford (Open Exhibnr; BA Hons Juris. 1977; MA 1981). Called to the Bar, Middle Temple, 1978 (Harmsworth Exhibnr; Astbury Scholar); barrister, NE Circuit, 1979–2008; Recorder, 2000–08. *Recreations:* listening to music, travelling in Europe. *Address:* Basildon Crown Court, The Gore, Basildon, Essex SS14 2BU. *Clubs:* National Liberal, Northumbria (Chm., 2013–).

**GRAHAM, Sir James Bellingham,** 11th Bt *cr* 1662; *b* 8 Oct. 1940; *e s* of Sir Richard Bellingham Graham, 10th Bt, OBE, and Beatrice, OBE (*d* 1992), *d* of Michael Hamilton-Spencer-Smith, DSO, MC; *S* father, 1982; *m* 1986, Halina, *d* of Major Wiktor Grubert, soldier and diplomat and Eleonora Grubert. *Educ:* Eton College; Christ Church, Oxford. Researcher in fine and decorative arts, Cecil Higgins Mus. and Art Gall., Bedford, 1980–96; Curator (with Halina Graham), Norton Conyers and its collections, 1996–. *Publications:* Guide to Norton Conyers, 1976, revised 2018; (with Halina Graham) Cecil Higgins, Collector Extraordinary, 1983; (with Halina Graham) A Guide to the Cecil Higgins Museum and Art Gallery, 1987; reviews of art exhibitions. *Recreations:* travel, visiting historic houses and museums. *Address:* Norton Conyers, Wath, near Ripon, N Yorks HG4 5EQ. *T:* (01765) 640333.

**GRAHAM, Sir James (Fergus Surtees),** 7th Bt *cr* 1783, of Netherby, Cumberland; farmer; *b* 29 July 1946; *s* of Sir Charles Graham, 6th Bt and Isabel Susan Anne, *d* of Major R. L. Surtees, OBE; *S* father, 1997; *m* 1975, Serena Jane, *yr d* of Ronald Frank Kershaw; one *s* two *d*. *Educ:* Milton Abbey; Royal Agricl Coll., Cirencester. Lloyd's Reinsurance Broker, 1969–90. *Heir:* *s* Robert Charles Thomas Graham, *b* 19 July 1985. *Address:* Crofthead, Longtown, Cumbria CA6 5PA. *T:* (01228) 791262.

**GRAHAM, James Lowery,** OBE 1991; DL; Deputy Chairman, Border Television Ltd, Carlisle, 2001–06; *b* 29 Oct. 1932; *s* of William and Elizabeth Graham; *m* 1984, Ann Routledge; two *d* by previous marr. *Educ:* Whitehaven Grammar School. Journalist, North

West Evening Mail, Barrow, 1955–62; News Editor, Border Television, 1962–67; Producer, BBC, Leeds, 1967–70; BBC: Regional News Editor, North, 1970–75; Regional Television Manager, North East, 1975–80; Head of Secretariat, Broadcasting House, 1980–82; Border Television plc: Man. Dir., 1982–96; Dep. Chm., 1990–96; CEO and Chm., 1996–98; non-exec. Chm., 1999–2001. Sec., BBC Central Music Adv. Council, 1981–82; Jt Sec., Broadcasters' Audience Res. Bd, 1980–82. Dir, Ind. Television Publications, 1982–89. Chairman: Independent Television Facilities Centre Ltd, 1987–2007; Beat 106 FM, Glasgow, 2001–05; Director: Oracle Teletext, 1988–93; Radio Borders, 1989–93; Radio SW Scotland, 1989–93 (Chm., 1990–93); Bay Radio Ltd, 1992–94; Central Scotland Radio, 1993–95; Century (formerly North East) Radio, 1993–2000; Border Radio Holdings, 1999–2000; Century Radio 105, 1998–2000; Sunderland City Radio, 1998–2003; Reliance Security Gp plc, 1999–2002. Pres., Prix Italia, 1998–2002, now Hon. Life Pres. (ITVA rep., 1987–2011). Dir, Educnl Broadcasting Services Trust, 1992–2008. Ombudsman, GM-TV, London, 2008–10. Member: BAFTA; Internat. Council, Nat. Acad. of Television Arts and Scis, NY, 1999–2011 (ITVA rep.); European Movement; Co-operative Internationale de Recherche et d'Action en Matière de Communication (European Producers). Governor: Newcastle Polytechnic, 1975–80; Cumbria Inst. of Art (formerly Coll. of Art and Design), 1995–2007; Mem. Court, Univ. of Central Lancs, 2006–. DL Cumbria 2000–10. FRSA 1987. FRTS 1994. Hon. Fellow: Univ. of Central Lancs, 2001; Univ. of Cumbria, 2012. Hon. DCL Northumbria, 1999. News Film Award, RTS, 1975; European Flag of Honour, Council of Europe, 1980; Beffroi d'Or, Lille (European regional broadcasting award), 1983; RTS Regl Broadcasting Award, 1989. *Publications*: Whistler Rhymes (poetry), 1998. *Recreations*: hill walking, skiing, cycling. *Address*: Carlisle, Cumbria; Whistler, BC, Canada. *Club*: Groucho.

**GRAHAM, Sir James (Thompson),** Kt 1990; CMG 1986; farmer, since 1946; Director, 1979–89, Chairman, 1982–89, New Zealand Dairy Board, retired; *b* 6 May 1929; *s* of Harold Graham and Florence Cicely Graham; *m* 1955, Ina Isabelle Low (*d* 2002); one *s* two *d*; *m* 2005, Robin. *Educ*: New Plymouth Boys' High Sch. Dir, NZ Co-op Dairy Co., 1974–89 (Chm., 1979–82). *Recreations*: golf, tennis, bowls. *Address*: 12A Sunbrae Grove, Mount Maunganui, Tauranga 3116, New Zealand. *T*: (75) 754043.

**GRAHAM, Janice Joanne, (Mrs Anthony Woolley);** Artistic Director, English Sinfonia, since 2005 (Leader, since 1995); Leader, English National Opera Orchestra, since 2007; *b* Watford, 21 April 1968; *d* of John and Jean Graham; *m* 1996, Anthony Woolley; one *s* one *d*. *Educ*: Purcell Sch.; Guildhall Sch. (AGSM Dist.; ARCM Hons); Juilliard Sch., NY (Adv. Cert.). Principal 2nd, 1993–95, Asst Leader, 1995–2000, LSO; Leader, BBC Nat. Orch. of Wales, 1997–2002; Guest Leader: LPO; RPO; Royal Opera Hse; BBC SO; BBC Philharmonic Orch.; BBC Scottish Orch.; CBSO; Bournemouth SO; RTE SO. Professor: RCM, 1995–2009; GSM, 2009–. Has made recordings. Gov., Purcell Sch., 2001–. Winner, Shell/LSO Competition, 1990. *Recreations*: family, sailing. *Address*: 1 Causton Road, Highgate, N6 5ES. *E*: Janice.Woolley@me.com.

**GRAHAM, Sir John (Alexander Noble),** 4th Bt *cr* 1906, of Larbert; GCMG 1986 (KCMG 1979 CMG 1972); HM Diplomatic Service, retired; Registrar, Order of Saint Michael and Saint George, 1987–2001; Director, Ditchley Foundation, 1987–92; *b* 15 July 1926; *s* of Sir John Reginald Noble Graham, 3rd Bt, VC, OBE and Rachel Septima (*d* 1984), *d* of Col Sir Alexander Sprot, 1st and last Bt; *S* father, 1980; *m* 1st, 1956, Marygold Ellinor Gabrielle Austin (*d* 1991); two *s* one *d*; 2nd, 1992, Jane, widow of Christopher Howells. *Educ*: Eton Coll. (scholar); Trinity Coll., Cambridge (scholar). Army, 1944–47; Cambridge, 1948–50; HM Foreign Service, 1950; Middle East Centre for Arab Studies, 1951; Third Secretary, Bahrain 1951, Kuwait 1952, Amman 1953; Asst Private Sec. to Sec. of State for Foreign Affairs, 1954–57; First Sec., Belgrade, 1957–60, Benghazi, 1960–61; FO 1961–66; Counsellor and Head of Chancery, Kuwait, 1966–69; Principal Private Sec. to Foreign and Commonwealth Sec., 1969–72; Cllr (later Minister) and Head of Chancery, Washington, 1972–74; Ambassador to Iraq, 1974–77; Dep. Under-Sec. of State, FCO, 1977–79; Ambassador to Iran, 1979–80; Deputy Under-Sec. of State, FCO, 1980–82; Ambassador and UK Permanent Representative to NATO, Brussels, 1982–86. Hon. Air Cdre, RAuxAF Regt, 1990–2001. *Publications*: Ditchley Park: the house and the foundation, 1996. *Heir*: *s* Lt Gen. Andrew John Noble Graham, qv. *Address*: Salisbury Place, Church Street, Shipton under Wychwood, Oxon OX7 6BP. *Club*: Army and Navy.

**GRAHAM, Sir (John) Alistair,** Kt 2000; Chairman, PhonePayplus, the Premium Rate Services Regulator (formerly Independent Committee for the Supervision of Standards of the Telephone Information Services), 2008–12; Lay Member, Queen's Counsel Selection Panel for England and Wales, 2011–15; *b* 6 Aug. 1942; *s* of late Robert Graham and Dorothy Graham; *m* 1967, Dorothy Jean Wallace; one *s* one *d*. *Educ*: Royal Grammar Sch., Newcastle upon Tyne. FCIPD (FITD 1989; FIPM 1989). Clerical Asst, St George's Hosp., Morpeth, 1961; Admin. Trainee, Northern Regional Hosp. Bd, 1963; Higher Clerical Officer, Royal Sussex County Hosp., Brighton, 1964; Legal Dept, TGWU, 1965; The Civil and Public Services Association: Asst Sec., 1966; Asst Gen. Sec., 1975; Dep. Gen. Sec. 1976; Gen. Sec., 1982–86; Chief Executive: Industrial Soc., 1986–91; Calderdale & Kirklees TEC, 1991–96; Leeds TEC, 1996–2000; Chairman: Police Complaints Authy, 2000–04; W Yorks Strategic HA, 2002–03; Northern and Yorks Regl Comr, NHS Appts Commn, 2003–04; British Transport Police Authy, 2004–08; Mem., British Transport Police Cttee, 2004; Mem., 2003–07, Chm., 2004–07, Ctee on Standards in Public Life. Chm., Shareholders' Trust FI Group, 1991–97. Vis. Fellow, Nuffield Coll., Oxford, 1984–92; Vis. Prof., Mgt Sch., Imperial Coll., London Univ., 1989–91. External assessor, teacher trng courses, Univ. of Huddersfield, 1993–96. Chairman: BBC S and E Regl Adv. Council, 1987–90; Training and Develt Lead Body, 1989–94; Member: Personnel Lead Body, 1991–94; BBC Educn Broadcasting Council, 1991–97; Restrictive Practices Court, 1993–99; Bd, Univ. of Huddersfield Trng and Quality Services Certification Div., 1993–96; Overview Gp on producing standards for Teachers, Teacher Trng Agency, 1996–97; Employment Appeal Tribunal, 2003–12; Lay Mem., Fitness to Practise Cttee, General Optical Council, 2005–15. Lay Observer, Council of Chartered Inst. of Taxation, 2011–15. Non-exec. Dir, Mgt Bd, Information Comr's Office, 2004–09. Mem., TUC Gen. Council, 1982–84, 1985–86. Mem., 1988–97, Chm., Staff Cttee, 1991–97, OU Council. Trustee, Duke of Edinburgh Study Conf., 1989–92. Mem., Work, Income and Social Policy Cttee, Joseph Rowntree Foundn, 1997–2000. Vice-Pres., Opera North, 2002– (Bd Mem., 1989–2002, Chm. Finance Cttee, 1996–97); Mem. Mgt Cttee, Huddersfield Contemp. Music Fest., 1992–97; Chm., Yorks Youth and Music, 1995–97. Assessor, Guildford and Woolwich Inquiry, 1990–94; Chm., Parades Commn for NI, 1997–2000. Contested (Lab) Brighton Pavilion, 1966. DUniv: Open, 1999; Bradford, 2006. *Recreations*: music, theatre, Durham CCC (non-exec. dir, 2007–16).

**GRAHAM, Prof. (John) Michael (Russell),** PhD; FREng; Professor of Unsteady Aerodynamics, Imperial College, University of London, since 1990; *b* 26 April 1942; *s* of George Desmond Graham and Evelyn Ann Graham (*née* Russell); *m* 1966, Philippa Gabrielle Freeman; one *s* one *d*. *Educ*: Epsom Coll., Surrey; Clare Coll., Cambridge (BA Maths, MA); Imperial Coll., Univ. of London (PhD Aeronautical Engrg). Lectr, 1970–90, Head of Dept of Aeronautics, 1999–2003, Imperial Coll., Univ. of London. FRAeS 1999;

FCGI 2000; FREng 2006; FRINA 2007. *Recreations*: walking, climbing, grandchildren. *Address*: Department of Aeronautics, Imperial College, SW7 2AZ. *E*: m.graham@imperial.ac.uk.

**GRAHAM, Sir John (Moodie),** 2nd Bt *cr* 1964; Director, Kinnegar Inns Ltd, since 1981; Chairman, John Graham (Dromore) Ltd, 1966–83; *b* 3 April 1938; *s* of Sir Clarence Graham, 1st Bt, MICE, and Margaret Christina Moodie (*d* 1954); *S* father, 1966; *m* 1970, Valerie Rosemary (marr. diss. 1983), *d* of late Frank Gill, Belfast; three *d*; civil partnership 2006, David Galway. *Educ*: Trinity Coll., Glenalmond; Queen's Univ., Belfast. BSc, Civil Engineering, 1961. Joined family firm of John Graham (Dromore) Ltd, Building and Civil Engineering Contractors, on graduating from University. Director: Electrical Supplies Ltd, 1967–83; Concrete (NI) Ltd, 1967–83; Ulster Quarries Ltd; Graham (Contracts) Ltd, 1971–83; Fieldhouse Plant (NI) Ltd, 1976–83. Chm., Concrete Soc., NI, 1972–74; Senior Vice-Pres., Concrete Soc., 1980; Pres., Northern Ireland Leukaemia Research Fund, 1967. Mem., Lloyd's, 1977–2004. *Recreations*: sailing, photography.

**GRAHAM, John Strathie;** Chief Executive, Historic Scotland, 2004–09; *b* 27 May 1950; *s* of Sir Norman William Graham, CB and of Catherine Mary Graham (*née* Strathie); *m* 1979, Anne Janet Stenhouse; two *s* one *d*. *Educ*: Edinburgh Academy; Corpus Christi College, Oxford (BA Lit. Hum.). Joined Scottish Office, 1972; Private Sec. to Minister of State, 1975–76; Industrial Develt and Electricity Divs, 1976–82; Private Sec. to Sec. of State, 1983–85; Asst Sec., Planning and Finance Divs, 1985–91; Under Sec. (Local Govt), Envmt Dept, 1991–96; Prin. Finance Officer, 1996–98; Sec. and Head, Scottish Office Agric., Envmt and Fisheries Dept, then Scottish Exec. Rural Affairs Dept, subseq. Scottish Exec. Envmt and Rural Affairs Dept, 1998–2004. *Recreations*: music, hillwalking.

**GRAHAM, Rev. Prof. (Lawrence) Gordon,** PhD; FRSE; Henry Luce III Professor of Philosophy and the Arts, Princeton Theological Seminary, 2006–18, now Emeritus; Director, Princeton Center for the Study of Scottish Philosophy, 2007–18; *b* 15 July 1949; *s* of William Moore Graham and Hyacinth Elizabeth (*née* Donald); *m* 1971; one *s* one *d*; *m* 2003; one *s* one *d*. *Educ*: Univ. of St Andrews (MA); Univ. of Durham (MA; PhD 1975). FRSE 1999. University of St Andrews: Lectr in Moral Philosophy, 1975–88; Reader, 1988–95; Dir of Music, 1991–95; Regius Prof. of Moral Philosophy, Univ. of Aberdeen, 1996–2005; Stanton Lectr, Univ. of Cambridge, 2005. Adjunct Prof. of Sacred Music, Westminster Choir Coll., Rider Univ., 2010–12. Ordained deacon, 2005, priest, 2006, Scottish Episcopal Church. Sec., Scots Philosophical Club, 1987–2001. Founding Trustee, Soko Fund, 2003–; Founding Dir, Edinburgh Sacred Arts Foundn, 2018–. Founding Editor: Jl of Scottish Philosophy, 2004–18; Kuyper Center Rev., 2010–15. *Publications*: Historical Explanation Reconsidered, 1983; Politics in its Place, 1986; Contemporary Social Philosophy, 1988, 4th edn 1995; The Idea of Christian Charity, 1990; Living the Good Life, 1990, 2nd edn 1994; The Shape of the Past, 1997; Ethics and International Relations, 1997, 2nd edn 2008; Philosophy of the Arts, 1997, 3rd edn 2005; The Internet: a philosophical inquiry, 1999; Evil and Christian Ethics, 2000; Genes: a philosophical inquiry, 2002; The Case Against the Democratic State, 2002; Universities: the recovery of an idea, 2002, 2nd edn 2008; Eight Theories of Ethics, 2004; The Institution of Intellectual Values, 2005; The Re-enchantment of the World, 2007; Theories of Ethics, 2011; Wittgenstein and Natural Religion, 2014; (ed) Scottish Philosophy in the 19th and 20th centuries, 2015; Philosophy, Art and Religion: understanding faith and creativity, 2017. *Recreations*: music, walking, cookery.

**GRAHAM, Luke Patrick;** MP (C) Ochil and South Perthshire, since 2017; *b* 1985. Accountant. Finance Officer, Sheffield Union; Central Finance, Tesco plc, until 2012; Tough Mudder, 2012–14; Marks and Spencer plc, 2014; co-founder, Tech and the Beancounters Ltd, 2016. Mem., Public Accounts Cttee, H of C, 2017–. *Address*: House of Commons, SW1A 0AA.

**GRAHAM, Michael;** see Graham, J. M. R.

**GRAHAM, Rt Rev. Olivia Josephine;** see Reading, Area Bishop of.

**GRAHAM, Sir Peter,** KCB 1993 (CB 1982); QC 1990; First Parliamentary Counsel, 1991–94; *b* 7 Jan. 1934; *o s* of late Alderman Douglas Graham, CBE, Huddersfield, and Ena May (*née* Jackson); *m* 1st, Judith Mary Dunbar; two *s*; 2nd, Anne Silvia Garcia; 3rd, Janet, *o d* of late Capt. William Eric Walker, TD, Mayfield, Sussex. *Educ*: St Bees Sch., Cumberland (scholar); St John's Coll., Cambridge (scholar, 1st cl. Law Tripos, MA, LLM, McMahon Law Studentship). Served as pilot in Fleet Air Arm, 1952–55, Lieut, RNR. Called to the Bar, Gray's Inn, 1958 (Holker Exhibn; H. C. Richards Prize, Ecclesiastical Law; Bencher, 1992), Lincoln's Inn, 1982; joined Parliamentary Counsel Office, 1959; Parly Counsel, 1972–86; with Law Commn, 1979–81; Second Parly Counsel, 1987–91. External Examr (Legislation), Univ. of Edinburgh, 1977–81; Consultant: in Legislative Drafting, Office of Attorney-Gen., Dublin, 1994–96; to Hassans (formerly J. A. Hassan & Partners), Gibraltar, 1997–2016; for specific legislative projects incl. Brunei, Hong Kong, Maldives, Malta, Mauritius, Sri Lanka, SA. Mem., Tax Law Review Cttee, Inst. of Fiscal Studies, 1994–2006. Mem., Council, Huddersfield Univ., 1992–96. Hon. Legal Adviser, Historic Vehicle Clubs Cttee, 1967–86. *Recreations*: amateur dramatics, restoring and enjoying vintage and classic cars, la bonne cuisine, playing keyboards. *Address*: Le Petit Château, La Vallette, 87190 Magnac Laval, France. *Club*: Sette of Odd Volumes.

**GRAHAM, Dr Peter John;** Director, Change Programme, Health and Safety Executive, 2002–03 (Board Member, 1994–2003); *b* 16 Sept. 1943; *s* of late John Graham and Judy Graham; *m* 1968, Janice Head; three *s*. *Educ*: St Joseph's Coll., Stoke-on-Trent; Liverpool Univ. (BSc; PhD Maths 1968). DTI, 1969–79; 1st Sec., UK Perm. Repn, Brussels, 1979–82; DTI, 1982–84; Dept of Employment, 1984–88; Health and Safety Executive: Hazardous Substances Div., 1988–91; General Policy Br., 1991–93; Offshore Safety Div., 1993–94; Dir, Health, 1994–99; Dir, Strategy and Analytical Support, 1999–2002. Lay Mem. Bd, Faculty of Occupational Medicine, 2005–11. Chm., Centre 33, St Albans, 2003–12.
*See also P. T. Graham.*

**GRAHAM, Lt-Gen. Sir Peter (Walter),** KCB 1991; CBE 1981 (OBE 1978; MBE 1972); GOC Scotland and Governor of Edinburgh Castle, 1991–93, retired; *b* 14 March 1937; *s* of Dr Walter Graham and Suzanne Graham (*née* Simon); *m* 1963, Alison Mary, MB ChB, MRCGP, *d* of D. B. Morren, TD; three *s*. *Educ*: Fyvie Village School, Aberdeenshire; Hall Sch., Hampstead; St Paul's Sch.; RMA Sandhurst; psc (Aust), ocds (Can). Commissioned, The Gordon Highlanders, 1956; regtl appts, Dover, BAOR, Scotland, Kenya, 1957–62; HQ Highland Bde, 1962–63; Adjt, 1 Gordons, Kenya, Scotland, Borneo (despatches), 1963–66; Staff Capt., HQ (1 Br) Corps, 1966–67; Aust. Staff Coll., 1968; Co. Comdr, 1 Gordons, BAOR, 1969–70; Bde Maj., 39 Inf. Bde, Ulster, 1970–72; 2nd i/c 1 Gordons, Scotland, Ulster, Singapore, 1972–74; MA to Adjt-Gen., MoD, 1974–75; CO 1 Gordons, Scotland, Ulster, Chester, 1976–78; COS HQ 3rd Armd Div., BAOR, 1978–82; Comdr UDR, 1982–84 (despatches); Nat. Defence Coll., Canada, 1984–85; Dep. Mil. Sec., MoD, 1985–87; GOC Eastern Dist, 1987–89; Comdt, RMA Sandhurst, 1989–91. Col, The Gordon Highlanders, 1986–94; Col Comdt, The Scottish Div., 1991–93. Mem., Royal Company of Archers, Queen's Body Guard for Scotland, 1986–. Chm., Gordon

Highlanders Regtl Trust Fund, 1986–2004; Chm., Regtl Mus. Mgt Cttee, 1993–2003, Vice Patron, 2009–, The Gordon Highlanders Mus.; Pres., Gordon Highlanders London Assoc., 2009–. Mem., NE Scotland Co-ordination Cttee, Better Together, 2012–14. Vice Pres., Old Pauline Club, 2016–. Hon. Firemaster, Grampian Fire and Rescue Service, 2010–13. Burgess of Guild, City of Aberdeen, 1994. Hon. DLitt Robert Gordon Univ., Aberdeen, 1996. *Publications*: (with Pipe Major B. MacRae) The Gordon Highlanders Pipe Music Collection, Vol. 1, 1983, 3rd edn 1986, Vol. 2, 1985; (contrib.) John Baynes, Soldiers of Scotland, 1988; contrib. to Jl of RUSI. *Recreations*: military history, hill walking, reading, pipe music, amusing grandchildren, gardening under wife's directions. *Address*: c/o Gordon Highlanders Museum, Viewfield Road, Aberdeen AB15 7XH.
*See also* Sir A. M. Graham.

**GRAHAM, Prof. Philip Jeremy;** Professor of Child Psychiatry, Institute of Child Health, London University, 1975–94, now Emeritus; *b* 3 Sept. 1932; *s* of Jacob Rackham Graham and Pauline Graham; *m* 1960, Nori (*née* Burawoy); two *s* one *d*. *Educ*: Perse Sch., Cambridge; Cambridge Univ. (MA); University Coll. Hosp., London. FRCP 1973; FRCPsych 1972. Consultant Psychiatrist: Maudsley Hosp., London, 1966–68; Hosp. for Sick Children, Great Ormond Street, London, 1968–74; Dean, Inst. of Child Health, London Univ., 1985–90; Prof. of Child Psychiatry, Univ. of Oslo, 1994–2000; Lectr, Dept of Develtl Psychiatry, Univ. of Cambridge, 1994–2000; Sen. Mem., Wolfson Coll., Cambridge, 1994–2002. Chairman: Nat. Children's Bureau, 1994–2000 (Chm., Child Policy Rev. Gp, 1987–89); Assoc. of Child Psychol. and Psychiatry, 2002–04. Vice-Chair, Dignity and Dying, 2011– (Mem. Bd, 2010–). President: European Soc. for Child and Adolescent Psychiatry, 1987–91; Psychiatry Section, RSM, 1994–95; Vice-Pres., RCPsych, 1996–98. Obituaries Ed., BJPsych Bulletin, 2014–. Community Gov., Woodside High Sch., Haringey, 2009–. Hon. FRCPCH 1993; Hon. FRCPsych 2004. *Publications*: A Neuropsychiatric Study in Childhood (jtly), 1970; (ed) Epidemiological Approaches to Child Psychiatry, 1977; (jtly) Child Psychiatry: a developmental approach, 1986, 4th edn 2007; (jtly) So Young, So Sad, So Listen, 1995, 2nd edn 2005; (ed) Cognitive Behaviour Therapy for Children and Families, 1998, 3rd edn 2012; The End of Adolescence, 2004; Susan Isaacs: freeing the minds of children, 2008; Where There Is No Child Psychiatrist, 2012; Men and Sex: a script approach, 2017; The Ages of Desire, 2018; various publications on child and adolescent psychiatry. *Recreations*: walking, chess. *Address*: 36 St Alban's Road, NW5 1RD.

**GRAHAM, Philip Thomas;** Chief Executive, National Infrastructure Commission, since 2015; *b* Welwyn Garden City, 7 June 1973; *s* of Dr Peter John Graham, *qv*; *m* 2010, Suzanne Turnock; one *s*. *Educ*: Nicholas Breakspear Sch., St Albans; Univ. of Sheffield (BA Hons French and Philos. 1996); Birkbeck, Univ. of London (MSc Public Policy and Mgt 2009). Dir, Brute Farce Theatre Co., 1996–2000; Policy Advr, DETR, subseq. DTLR, then DfT, 2000–06; Department for Transport: Hd, Strategy Unit, 2006–07; Deputy Director: Threats and Contingencies, 2007–09; High Speed Rail Strategy, 2010–12; Hd, Secretariat, Airports Commn, 2012–15. Chm., Trustees, New Diorama Th., 2010–. *Recreations*: indie music, fringe theatre, road cycling. *Address*: National Infrastructure Commission, Finlaison House, 15–17 Furnival Street, EC4A 1AB. *T*: (020) 7270 3000. *E*: enquiries@nic.gsi.gov.uk.

**GRAHAM, Sir Ralph Stuart,** 14th Bt *cr* 1629 (NS), of Esk, Cumberland; *b* 5 Nov. 1950; *s* of Sir Ralph Wolfe Graham, 13th Bt and of Geraldine, *d* of Austin Velour; S father, 1988, but his name does not appear on the Official Roll of the Baronetage; *m* 1st, 1972, Roxanne (*d* 1978), *d* of Mrs Lovette Gurzan; 2nd, 1979, Deena Vandergrift; one adopted *s*. *Heir: b* Robert Bruce Graham [*b* 14 Nov. 1953; *m* 1974, Denise, *d* of T. Juranich; two *s*].

**GRAHAM, Richard;** MP (C) Gloucester, since 2010; *b* Reading, 4 April 1958; *s* of Robin and Judith Graham; *m* 1989, Anthea Knaggs; two *s* one *d*. *Educ*: Eton Coll.; Christ Church, Oxford (BA Hist. 1979); Investment Mgt Cert. 1998. Airline Manager, Cathay Pacific Airways and John Swire & Sons, 1980–86; HM Diplomatic Service, 1986–93: First Sec., Nairobi, Peking; Trade Comr, China, and Consul, Macau, 1989–92; Chief Rep. in China, Barings plc, 1993–95; Dir, ING Barings, 1995–97; Dir and Hd, Instnl Business, Baring Asset Mgt, 1997–2010. Director: Greater China Fund Inc., 1994–2004; Care 4 Children, 1999–2001; Chm., British Chamber of Commerce, Shanghai, 1995–97. Prime Minister's Trade Envoy to Indonesia, ASEAN Econ. Community, Malaysia and Philippines, 2012–. Mem. (C) Cotswold DC, 2003–07. Contested (C) SW England, EP, 2004. PPS to Minister of State, FCO, 2010–14. Member: Work and Pensions Select Cttee, 2010, 2015–17; Cttee on Exiting the EU, 2017–; Chm., All Party Parly China Gp, 2010–; Founder Chm., All Party Parly Commonwealth Gp, 2012–13. Chm., Westminster Foundn for Democracy, 2018–. Chm., Gloucester Hist. Trust, 2018–. *Recreations*: playing cricket, tennis and squash, watching Gloucester Rugby, walking or cycling anywhere. *Address*: House of Commons, SW1A 0AA. *T*: (020) 7219 7077. *E*: richard.graham.mp@parliament.uk. *Clubs*: MCC, Lords and Commons Cricket, Gloucester Cricket.

**GRAHAM, Robert Martin;** Chief Executive, British United Provident Association, 1984–91; *b* 20 Sept. 1930; *s* of Francis P. Graham and Margaret M. Graham (*née* Broderick); *m* 1959, Eileen (*née* Hoey); two *s* two *d*. *Educ*: Dublin; ACII. Hibernian Fire and General Insurance Co. Ltd, 1948–57; Voluntary Health Insurance Board, 1957–82 (to Chief Exec.); Dep. Chief Exec., BUPA, 1982–84. Chm., Board of Management, Marah Hosp., 1972–82; Pres., Internat. Fedn of Voluntary Health Service Funds, 1988–90 (Dep. Pres., 1986–88); Vice-Pres., Assoc. Internationale de la Mutualité, 1990– (Mem. Bd of Govs, 1978–91); Mem., Central Council, Federated Voluntary Hosps, Ireland, 1978–82. *Address*: 39 Garratts Lane, Banstead, Surrey SM7 2ED. *Clubs*: Royal Automobile, Rotary Club of London.

**GRAHAM, Ronald;** *see* Graham, G. R. G.

**GRAHAM, Dr Ronald Cairns,** CBE 1992; General Manager, Tayside Health Board, 1985–93 (Chief Administrative Medical Officer, 1973–85); *b* 8 Oct. 1931; *s* of Thomas Graham and Helen Cairns; *m* 1959, Christine Fraser Osborne; two *s* one *d*. *Educ*: Airdrie Acad.; Glasgow Univ. MB, ChB Glasgow 1956; DipSocMed Edin. 1968; FFCM 1973; FRCPE 1983. West of Scotland; house jobs, gen. practice and geriatric med., 1956–62; Dep. Med. Supt, Edin. Royal Infirmary, 1962–65; Asst Sen. Admin. MO, SE Regional Hosp. Bd, 1965–69; Dep. and then Sen. Admin. MO, Eastern Regional Hosp. Bd, 1969–73. Mem. Court, Univ. of Dundee, 1994–2003. *Recreations*: fishing, bowling. *Address*: 34 Dalgleish Road, Dundee DD4 7JT. *T*: (01382) 455426.

**GRAHAM, Prof. Stephen Douglas Nelson,** PhD; FBA 2019; Professor of Cities and Society, University of Newcastle, since 2010; *b* Tynemouth, 26 Feb. 1965; *s* of David and Doreen Graham; *m* 1997, Annette Kearney; two *s*. *Educ*: Univ. of Southampton (BSc Hons Geog.); Univ. of Newcastle upon Tyne (MPhil Urban Planning); Univ. of Manchester (PhD Sci. and Technol. Policy 1995). Planning Officer, Sheffield CC, 1989–92; Lectr, 1992–97, Reader, 1997–2000, Prof., 2000–04, Sch. of Architecture, Planning and Landscape, Univ. of Newcastle upon Tyne; Prof. of Human Geog., Univ. of Durham, 2004–10. Vis. Prof. of Urban Planning, MIT, 1999–2000. *Publications*: (with S. Marvin) Telecommunications and the City, 1996; (with S. Marvin) Splintering Urbanism, 2001; Cities, War and Terrorism, 2004; The Cybercities Reader, 2004; Disrupted Cities, 2009; Cities Under Siege: the new military urbanism, 2010; Vertical: the politics of up and down, 2014; (with C. McFarlane) Infrastructural Lives, 2014; Vertical: the city from satellites to bunkers, 2016. *Recreations*: cycling, hill walking, cinema, rock music concerts, history writings. *Address*: School of Architecture, Planning and Landscape, University of Newcastle, Newcastle upon Tyne NE1 7RU. *T*: (0191) 222 8579, *Fax*: (0191) 222 6115. *E*: steve.graham@ncl.ac.uk.

**GRAHAM, (Stewart) David;** QC 1977; Partner, Cork Gully, 1985–92; *b* 27 Feb. 1934; *s* of late Lewis Graham and of Gertrude Graham; *m* 1959, Corinne Carmona (*d* 2009); two *d*. *Educ*: Leeds Grammar Sch.; St Edmund Hall, Oxford (MA, BCL). Called to the Bar, Middle Temple, 1957; Harmsworth Law Scholar, 1958. Mem. Council, Justice, 1976–96 (Chm., Cttee on Protection of Small Investor, 1989–92; Chm., Cttee on Insolvency, 1993–94); Mem., Insolvency Rules Adv. Cttee, 1984–86; Chm., Law, Parly and Gen. Purposes Cttee, Bd of Deputies of British Jews, 1983–88. Ind. Mem. Council, The Insurance Ombudsman Bureau, 1993–2001; Associate Mem., British and Irish (formerly UK) Ombudsman Assoc., 1994–. Vis. Fellow, Centre for Commercial Law, QMW, London, 1992–; Vis. Prof., Faculty of Business, Centre for Insolvency Law and Policy, Kingston Univ., 2004–. Member Committee: Stanmore Soc., 2001–; Harrow Heritage Trust, 2002–. Chm. Editorial Bd, Insolvency Intelligence, 1988–94. FRSA 1995. *Publications*: (ed jtly) Williams and Muir Hunter on Bankruptcy, 18th edn 1968, 19th edn 1979; (contrib.) Longman's Insolvency, 1986; (contrib.) Muir Hunter on Personal Insolvency, 2002; (contrib.) Oxford DNB, 2005; (ed) legal textbooks; contrib. Internat. Insolvency Review. *Recreations*: biography, music, drama, travel, history of insolvency. *Address*: 6 Grosvenor Lodge, Dennis Lane, Stanmore, Middx HA7 4JE.

**GRAHAM, Susan Alesta;** mezzo soprano; *b* 23 July 1960; *d* of Floyd Ben Graham and Betty Fort. *Educ*: Midland Lee High Sch.; Texas Technical Univ.; Manhattan Sch. of Music. Opera début in Vanessa, St Louis, 1988. Regular performances with NY Metropolitan Opera, 1991–, and at Salzburg Fest.; other appearances include: Royal Opera, 1994–; WNO, 1994–; Glyndebourne; Vienna State Opera; La Scala; Paris Opéra, etc. Rôles include: title rôle, Chérubin; Octavian in Der Rosenkavalier; Dorabella in Così fan tutte; Cherubino in Le Nozze di Figaro; title rôle, Arianna; title rôle, Iphigénie en Tauride; Charlotte in Werther; title rôle, Béatrice et Bénédict; Marguerite in La damnation de Faust; title rôle in world première of Monteverdi's Arianna; Composer in Ariadne auf Naxos; Donna Elvira in Don Giovanni; Sycorax in The Enchanted Island; Countess Geschwitz in Lulu; *theatre*: The King and I, Théâtre du Châtelet, Paris, 2014. Numerous recitals and recordings. Metropolitan Opera Nat. Council Award, 1988.

**GRAHAM, Teresa Colomba,** CBE 2008 (OBE 1998); business and government advisor, since 2003; Member, Office of Tax Simplification, HM Revenue and Customs, since 2009; *b* Newcastle upon Tyne, 8 March 1956; *d* of Albert Rea and Anna Rea (*née* Mastroianni). *Educ*: Univ. of Newcastle upon Tyne (BA Eng. Linguistics 1977). FCA 1982. Price Waterhouse, 1977–90; Baker Tilly, 1990–2003. Chm., Salix Finance, 2004–; non-exec. Dir, British Business Bank, 2014–. Seconded to Enterprise and Deregulation Unit, 1986–87; Mem., Deregulation Adv. Panel, 1988–90; Dep. Chm., Better Regulation Task Force, subseq. Better Regulation Commn, 1997–2007 (Chm. gp on report Better Routes to Redress, 2004; Chm. Subgp on report Regulation—Less is More, 2005); leader: independent review of Small Firms Loan Guarantee, 2003–04 (Graham Review of Small Firms Loan Guarantee, 2004); independent review of Pre-packaged Administrations, 2014; Chm., Admin. Burdens Adv. Bd, HMRC, 2006–. Ind. Regulator, RICS, 2007–09. Mem. Council, Newcastle Univ., 2015–. *Recreations*: walking, travelling, reading, cinema, art. *Address*: Upper Maisonette, 9 Eccleston Square, SW1V 1NP. *T*: 07767 486486, *Fax*: (020) 7630 6264. *E*: teresa@teresagraham.co.uk.

**GRAHAM, Thomas;** *b* 5 Dec. 1943; *m* Joan Bagley; two *s*. Engineer with Rolls-Royce, 1965–78; Office Manager, Robertson and Ross, solicitors, 1982–87. Mem., Strathclyde Reg. Council, 1978–87. MP Renfrew and Inverclyde, 1987–97, Renfrewshire, 1997–2001 (Lab 1987–98, Ind. 1998–2001). *Address*: 265 Gilmartin Road, Linwood, Paisley PA3 3SU.

**GRAHAM, William;** *see* Graham, A. W.

**GRAHAM, Hon. William Carvel,** CM 2014; PC (Can) 2002; QC (Can.); MP (Liberal) Toronto Centre (formerly Rosedale, then Toronto Centre-Rosedale), Canada, 1993–2007; *b* 17 March 1939; *s* of Francis Ronald Graham and Helen Payne Graham (*née* White); *m* 1962, Catherine Elizabeth Curry; one *s* one *d*. *Educ*: Univ. of Toronto (BA 1961; LLB 1964); Univ. of Paris (DJur 1970). Barrister and solicitor, Fasken and Calvin, 1967–80, Partner, 1983; Prof. of Law, 1980–94, and Dir, Centre for Internat. Studies, 1986–88, Univ. of Toronto. Minister of Foreign Affairs, 2002–04, of Nat. Defence, 2004–06; Leader of the Opposition, 2006; Interim Leader, Liberal Party of Canada, 2006. Chancellor, Trinity Coll., Univ. of Toronto, 2007–. Chair: Atlantic Council of Canada, 2007–13; Canadian Internat. Council, 2013– (Co-Vice Chair, 2007–13). Hon. Col, Gov. Gen.'s Horse Guards, 2011– (Hon. Lt-Col, 2008–11). Hon. LLD Royal Mil. Coll. of Canada, 2010; Doctoral Ring, Univ. of Siena, 2010. Chevalier, Legion of Honour (France), 1984; Chevalier, Order of the Pléiade (France), 1999. *Publications*: contrib. to books and jls on internat. trade law and public internat. law. *Address*: 151 Bloor Street West, Suite 610, Toronto, ON M5S 1S4, Canada.

**GRAHAM, Prof. William George,** PhD; FInstP; Professor of Physics, Queen's University Belfast, 1995–2009, now Emeritus and Hon. Research Professor; *b* Belfast, 11 June 1949; *s* of Albert and Hazel Graham; *m* 1987, Bernadette Hannigan; two *s*. *Educ*: Annadale Grammar Sch., Belfast; Queen's Univ., Belfast (BSc 1971; PhD 1974). FInstP 1987. Scientist, Lawrence Berkeley Lab., USA, 1974–79; Lectr, Univ. of Ulster, 1979–88; Queen's University, Belfast: Lectr, 1988–90; Reader, 1990–95; Dir, Internat. Centre for Exptl Physics, 2001–05; Dir, Centre for Plasma Physics, 2006–12. Ed. in Chief, Plasma Sources Sci. and Technol., 2014– (Associate Ed., 2007–13). Fellow, APS, 1996. MRIA 2006. Hon. Prof., Univ. of Bucharest, 2004. Von Engel and Franklin Prize in Plasma Physics, Internat. Conf. on Phenomena in Ionised Gases, 2013. *Publications*: over 150 articles in physics jls. *Recreations*: hiking, ski-ing, travelling, blues and rock music, beer. *Address*: Centre for Plasma Physics, Queen's University Belfast, Belfast BT7 1NN. *T*: (028) 9097 3564.

**GRAHAM, Yvonne Georgette;** Headmistress, Clifton High School, Bristol, 1996–97; *b* 31 Aug. 1943; *d* of J. van Gorkom and M. E. van Gorkom-Pas; *m* 1967, Lt-Col I. G. Graham, RE (retd) (*d* 2008); two *s*. *Educ*: Alexander Hegius-Gymnasium-Deventer; Amsterdam Univ. (MA); London Univ. Various teaching posts in England, Germany and Holland, 1965–90; Headmistress, Lavant House Sch., Chichester, 1990–95. *Recreations*: reading, travel, theatre, music. *Address*: 20 Stanton Drive, Chichester, West Sussex PO19 5QN. *T*: (01243) 528111.

**GRAHAM-CAMPBELL, Prof. James Alastair,** FBA 2001; FSA, FSAScot; FRHistS; Professor of Medieval Archaeology, University of London, at University College, 1991–2002, now Emeritus; *b* 7 Feb. 1947; *s* of David John Graham-Campbell and Joan Sybil Graham-Campbell (*née* Maclean); *m* 2017, Otelo Miranda Fabião. *Educ*: Eton Coll.; Trinity Coll., Cambridge (MA, PhD); Bergen Univ.; Oslo Univ.; UCL. FSA 1977. Asst Lectr in Archaeology, UC Dublin, 1971–73; University College London: Lectr, 1973–82;

Reader in Medieval Archaeology, 1982–91; Fellow, 2003. Vis. Prof., Univ. of Minnesota, 1981; British Acad. Res. Reader, 1988–90; O'Donnell Lectr, Univ. of Wales, 1989; Crabtree Orator, UCL, 1990; Rhind Lectr, Soc. of Antiquaries of Scotland, 1996; Special Prof. of Viking Studies, Nottingham Univ., 2003–12; Hon. Prof., Aarhus Univ., 2004–11. Mem., Ancient Monuments Adv. Cttee, English Heritage, 1992–97. Sec., Soc. for Medieval Archaeology, 1976–82 (Hon. Vice-Pres., 2001–). *Publications:* Viking Artefacts, 1980; The Viking World, 1980, 4th edn 2013; (jtly) The Vikings, 1980; (ed) Cultural Atlas of the Viking World, 1994; The Viking-Age Gold and Silver of Scotland, 1995; (jtly) Vikings in Scotland: an archaeological survey, 1998; (ed with G. Williams) Silver Economy in the Viking Age, 2007; (ed with M. Valor) The Archaeology of Medieval Europe, Vol. 1, 2007; (ed with M. Ryan) Anglo-Saxon/Irish Relations before the Vikings, 2009; (ed with R. Philpott) The Huxley Viking Hoard: Scandinavian settlement in the North West, 2009; (ed jtly) Silver Economies, Monetisation and Society in Scandinavia AD 800–1100, 2011; The Cuerdale Hoard and Related Viking-Age Silver and Gold from Britain and Ireland in the British Museum, 2012; Viking Art, 2013; numerous articles in learned jls. *Recreations:* cooking, gardening. *Address:* Institute of Archaeology (UCL), 31–34 Gordon Square, WC1H 0PY.

GRAHAM-DIXON, **Andrew Michael**; writer and presenter on the visual arts, BBC Television, since 1992; *b* 26 Dec. 1960; *s* of Anthony Philip Graham-Dixon, QC and Margaret Suzanne Graham-Dixon; *m* 1985, Sabine Marie-Pascale Tilly (marr. diss. 2016); one *s* two *d*; *m* 2018, Jill Mason; one *s*. *Educ:* Westminster Sch.; Christ Church, Oxford (MA 1st Cl. English); Courtauld Inst. Chief Art Critic, 1986–97, Chief Arts Feature Writer, 1997–99, The Independent; Chief Arts Feature Writer, Sunday Telegraph Mag., 1999–2004. Presenter, The Culture Show, BBC TV, 2010–. Television series include: A History of British Art, 1996; Renaissance, 1999; The Secret of Drawing, 2006; Art of Eternity, 2007; Art of Spain, 2008; The Art of Russia, 2009; Art of Germany, 2010; The High Art in the Low Countries, 2013; Art of China, 2014; Art of Gothic, 2014; Secrets of the Mona Lisa, 2015; The Art of Scandinavia, 2016; The Art of France, 2017; Art, Passion and Power, 2018; with Giorgio Locatelli: Sicily Unpacked, 2012; Italy Unpacked, 2013–15; Rome Unpacked, 2017. BP Arts Journalist of Year, 1988, 1989, 1990; Hawthornden Prize for Art Criticism, 1991; 1st Prize, Reportage Section, Montreal Internat. Fest. of Films, 1994. *Publications:* Howard Hodgkin: paintings, 1994; A History of British Art, 1996; Paper Museum: writings about paintings, mostly, 1996; Renaissance, 1999; In the Picture: the year through art, 2003; Michelangelo and the Sistine Chapel, 2008; Caravaggio: a life sacred and profane, 2010. *Recreations:* golf, horse-racing. *Club:* Reform.

GRAHAM-HALL, **John,** (John Leonard Hall); operatic tenor (freelance); *b* Pinner, 23 Nov. 1955; *s* of Leonard Hall and Betty Hall; *m* 1990, Helen Williams; two *d*. *Educ:* Malvern Coll.; King's Coll., Cambridge (BA 1977; MA 1981); Royal Coll. of Music. Major roles include: title role in Albert Herring, Glyndebourne, 1985–90, Royal Opera House, 1989; Kudrjas in Katya Kabanova, Glyndebourne, 1988, 1990; Aschenbach in Death in Venice, Glyndebourne on Tour, 1989, Monnaie Brussels, 2009, La Scala Milan, 2011, ENO 2013; Eisenstein in Die Fledermaus, Scottish Opera, 1989, Glyndebourne on Tour, 2006; title role in Perela, world première, Paris Bastille, 2003; Michel in Juliette, Paris Bastille, 2006; Podesta in Finta Giardiniera, Salzburg Fest., 2006; title role in Adventures of Mr Broucek, Opera North, 2009, Scottish Opera, 2010; title role in Peter Grimes, La Scala, Milan, 2012, Opéra de Nice, 2015; Shuisky in Boris Godunov, Toulouse, 2014, Royal Opera House, 2016; Zivny in Osud, Stuttgart, 2012–13, Opera North, 2017; Kaufmann in Jakob Lenz, Stuttgart, 2014, Brussels Monnaie, 2015, Berliner Staatsoper, 2017; Aron in Moses und Aron, Paris, 2015, Madrid, 2016; company principal, ENO, 1997–2003, then freelance: roles include: Herod in Salome, 1998, 2005; Sylvester in Silver Tassie, 2000; Alwa in Lulu, 2002; Mime in Ring of the Nibelung, 2002–04; Danilo, 2008; Mayor in Albert Herring, Opera North, 2002, Glyndebourne, 2008, Toulouse, 2013; Basilio in Nozze de Figaro, NY Metropolitan and Aix-en-Provence, 2012, Glyndebourne, 2016; Valzacchi in Rosenkavalier and Triquet, Onegin Metropolitan, 2013; Teapot, Arithmetic and Frog in L'Enfant et Les Sortilèges, Opera North, 2017, Carciere and Inquisitor in Il Prigioniero, Monnaie and Stuttgart, 2018; M Taupe in Capriccio, Madrid, 2019. Other roles include: Sellem in Rake's Progress; Monostatos in Magic Flute; Bob Boles in Peter Grimes; Tikhon in Katya Kabanova; Tanzmeister in Ariadne auf Naxos; Lysander and Flute in Midsummer Night's Dream. Trustee, ENO Benevolent Fund, 1998–2019 (Chm., 2004–08). Numerous recordings, 1986–. *Recreations:* theatre, cooking, bridge. *Address:* c/o Musichall UK, Oast House, Crouch's Farm, Hollow Lane, E Hoathly, E Sussex BN8 6QX. *T:* (01825) 840437. *E:* jgraham.hall@btinternet.com.

GRAHAM-HARRISON, **Catherine,** (Lady Warren), OBE 2010; adviser and mentor; *b* London, 11 Jan. 1949; *d* of Francis Laurence Theodore Graham-Harrison, CB and Carol Mary St John Graham-Harrison, *d* of Sir Francis Stewart, CIE; *m* 1994, Hon. Sir Nicholas Roger Warren, *qv*; two step *s* one step *d*. *Educ:* North London Collegiate Sch.; St Anne's Coll., Oxford (BA Mod. Hist. 1970). Dep. Dir, New Islington and Hackney Housing Assoc., 1978–83; Vice Pres., Citibank, 1983–92; Dir, Paul Hamlyn Foundn, 1992–94. Member, Board: Heritage Lottery Fund, 2002–08; Nat. Heritage Meml Fund, 2002–08; Natural England, 2009–14; Mem., Architectural Panel, 2009–12 (Chair, 2012–16), Commercial Gp, 2016–, Nat. Trust; Chair and Trustee, Policy Cttee, CPRE, 2016–. Chair, Nat. Forest Company, 2011–16. Trustee: Joseph Rowntree Foundn, 1998–2006; Womankind Worldwide, 2001–05 (Chm., 2001–05); Foundling Mus., 2008–09; Gov., Coram, 2005–09. *Recreations:* built and natural heritage, arts, walking, gardening. *E:* Catherine@cghassociates.co.uk.
See also R. M. Graham-Harrison.

GRAHAM-HARRISON, **Robert Montagu**, CMG 2003; Director, British Development Co-operation Office, New Delhi, 1997–2003; *b* 16 Feb. 1943; *s* of Francis Laurence Theodore Graham-Harrison, CB and Carol Mary St John, *d* of Sir Francis Stewart, CIE; *m* 1977, Kathleen Patricia, *d* of John and Mary Gladys Maher; two *d*. *Educ:* Eton Coll.; Magdalen Coll., Oxford. VSO India, 1965; GLC, 1966; Min. of Overseas Development, later Overseas Development Administration, then Dept for Internat. Develt, 1967–2003; World Bank, Washington, 1971–73; Private Sec. to Minister for Overseas Development, 1978; Asst Sec., ODA, 1979; Hd, British Develt Div. in E Africa, Nairobi, 1982–86; Hd, E Asia Dept, ODA, 1986–89; Alternate Exec. Dir, World Bank, Washington, 1989–92; UK Exec. Dir, EBRD, 1992–97. Sen. Clerk, H of L, 2003–08. Mem., Remuneration Cttee, EBRD, 2012–18. Trustee: CASA Social Care, 2003–12; EveryChild, 2006–16; Blenheim CDP, 2012–15; PlaNet Finance UK, 2011–14. Mem., Internat. Cttee, Leonard Cheshire Disability, 2006–09. Chm., DFID Alumni Assoc., 2007–13. Ambassador, Paintings in Hospitals, 2007–11. Mem. Cttee, Wine Soc., 2010–13. *Recreations:* hill walking, travel, tennis. *Address:* 122 St George's Avenue, N7 0AH.
See also C. Graham-Harrison.

GRAHAM-DMOON, **Sir Peter Wilfred Giles**; *see* Moon.

GRAHAM-SMITH, **Sir Francis**; *see* Smith.

GRAHAM-TOLER, family name of **Earl of Norbury**.

GRAHAME, **Angela Thomson**; QC (Scot.) 2009; barrister; *b* Edinburgh, 8 April 1968; *d* of late Joseph Scott Grahame and of Norma Grahame (*née* Thomson); *m* 2004, Kenneth Wilson Cloggie (separated 2017); one *d*. *Educ:* Leith Acad.; Univ. of Aberdeen (LLB Hons, DipLP). Admitted solicitor, 1993; admitted to Faculty of Advocates, 1995 (Vice Dean, 2016–); Advocate Depute, 2003–05; Sen. Advocate Depute, 2005–07; called to the Bar, Middle Temple, 2019. Legal Mem., Police Appeals Tribunal, Scotland, 2013– (Chair, 2018). FCIArb 2018. *Publications:* (contrib. with D. R. Parratt) World Arbitration Reporter, 2nd edn 2018; (contrib.) Women Pioneers in Dispute Resolution, 2nd edn 2018; contribs Juridical Rev., Scottish Law Agents Gazette, Reparation Law Bulletin, Jl of Enforcement of Arbitration Awards. *Recreation:* reading murder mysteries. *Address:* Advocates' Library, Parliament House, Edinburgh EH1 1RF. *T:* (0131) 226 5071.

GRAHAME, **Christine**; Member (SNP) Midlothian South, Tweeddale and Lauderdale, Scottish Parliament, since 2011 (South Scotland, 1999–2011); Deputy Presiding Officer, Scottish Parliament, since 2016; *b* 9 Sept. 1944; *d* of Christie and Margaret Grahame; *m* (marr. diss.); two *s*. *Educ:* Edinburgh Univ. (MA 1966; DipEd 1967; LLB 1984; DipLP 1985). Schoolteacher, secondary schs, 1967–80; solicitor, 1986–99. Shadow Minister for Social Justice, Scottish Exec., 2004–07. Scottish Parliament: Convenor: Cross Party Gp, Borders Rail; Justice Cttee I, 2001–03; Health Cttee, 2003–04; Health and Sport Cttee, 2007–11; Justice Cttee, 2011–16; Policing sub-cttee; Cross Party Gp, Animal Welfare. *Recreations:* cats, trad jazz, and additionally gardening and drinking malt, not necessarily at the same time. *Address:* Scottish Parliament, Edinburgh EH99 1SP. *T:* (0131) 348 5729.

GRAINGE, **Sir Lucian (Charles)**, Kt 2016; CBE 2010; Chairman and Chief Executive Officer, Universal Music Group, since 2011 (Co-Chief Executive Officer, 2010–11); *b* London, 29 Feb. 1960; *s* of Cecil and Marion Grainge; *m* 2002, Caroline Lewis; one *s* one *d* and one step *d*. *Educ:* Queen Elizabeth Grammar Sch., Barnet, London. Hd, Creative Dept, April Music/CBS UK, 1979–82; Dir and Gen. Manager, RCA Music UK, 1982–85; A&R Dir, MCA UK, 1985–86; Man. Dir, PolyGram Music Publishing UK, 1986–93; Gen. Manager, A&R and Business Affairs, 1993–97, Man. Dir, 1997–99, Polydor Records UK; Dep. Chm., 1999–2001, Chm. and Chief Exec., 2001–05, Universal Music UK; Chm. and Chief Exec., Universal Music Gp Internat., 2005–10. Member, Board: Internat. Fedn of Phonographic Industry, 2005–; Music Industry Trusts' Award, Vivendi 2008, 2010–12; Activision Blizzard, 2011–13. Member, Board of Directors: Northwestern Univ., 2012–; DreamWorks, 2013–; Lionsgate, 2016–. UK Trade Ambassador for global and media entertainment, 2012–16. Trustee, American Friends of Royal Foundn of the Duke and Duchess of Cambridge (formerly of the Duke and Duchess of Cambridge and Prince Harry, then the Duke and Duchess of Sussex), 2011–. Hon. DMus Berklee Coll. of Music, 2016; Hon. Dr, Northeastern, 2017. Music Industry Trusts' Award, 2008; Humanitarian Award, Foundn for Ethnic Understanding, 2013; President's Merit Award, Recording Acad., 2014; Spirit of Life Award, City of Hope, 2015; Empowerment Award, Variety, 2016; Media Person of Year, Cannes Lions Internat. Fest. of Creativity, 2017; Songwriters Hall of Fame, 2018; PTTOW! Icon Award, 2018. Officier des Arts et des Lettres (France), 2011. *Recreations:* soccer, automobiles. *Address:* Universal Music Group, 2220 Colorado Avenue, Santa Monica, CA 90404, USA. *T:* (310) 8651823, *Fax:* (310) 8653230.

GRAINGER, **His Honour Ian David**; a Circuit Judge, 2009–19; *b* Kingston upon Hull, 1 Aug. 1956; *s* of David Grainger and Edna Grainger (*née* Rudrum). *Educ:* Tynemouth High Sch.; Tynemouth Coll.; University Coll., Oxford (MA Juris. 1981); London Univ. (BA Italian (ext.) 2001); University Coll. London (MA Italian Studies 2003). Called to the Bar, Inner Temple, 1978, Bencher, 2008; in commercial practice, 1979–2009; a Recorder, 2003–09. Mem. Council and Chair, Audit Cttee, Roehampton Univ., 2003–09; Mem., Bd of Trustees, Univ. of London, 2008–14. Vice Chm., British-Italian Soc., 2007–09. *Publications:* (with M. Fealy) An Introduction to the New Civil Procedure Rules, 1999, 2nd edn as The Civil Procedure Rules in Action, 2000. *Recreations:* Italy and all things Italian, classical music, reading, walking.

GRAINGER, **Ian Richard Peregrine L.**; *see* Liddell-Grainger.

GRAINGER, **John Andrew**, CMG 2005; HM Diplomatic Service, retired; Deputy Legal Adviser, Foreign and Commonwealth Office, 2003–14; *b* 27 Aug. 1957; *m* 1998, Katherine Veronica Bregou (*d* 2011); one *s*. Called to the Bar, Lincoln's Inn, 1981. Joined HM Diplomatic Service, 1984; Asst Legal Advr, FCO, 1984–89; First Sec. (Legal Advr), BMG Berlin, 1989–91; Asst Legal Advr, FCO, 1991–94; Legal Counsellor: FCO, 1994–97; UK Mission to UN, NY, 1997–2001; FCO, 2001–03.

GRAINGER, **Stephen**, MBE 2007; Rugby Development Director, Rugby Football Union, since 2011; *b* Saltburn-by-the-Sea, 5 March 1966; *s* of Malcolm and Patricia Grainger; *m* 1989, Julie Tack; two *d*. *Educ:* Saltscar Sch., Redcar; Sir William Turner's Sixth Form Coll., Redcar; Leeds Poly. (BA Hons). Athletics Manager, Mansfield DC, 1987–89; Principal Officer (Sport), Notts CC, 1989–92; various posts with Nat. Coaching Foundn, 1992–95; Youth Sport Trust: Implementation Dir, 1995–99; Man. Dir, 1999–2004; Chief Exec., 2004–11. *Recreations:* track and field athletics, road running, ski-ing, travel. *Address:* Rugby Football Union, Rugby House, Twickenham Stadium, 200 Whitton Road, Twickenham, Middx TW2 7BA. *E:* stevegrainger@rfu.com.

GRAMMENOS, **Prof. Constantinos Theophilos**, Hon. CBE 2008 (Hon. OBE 1994); Comdr, Order of Phoenix 2013; DSc; Founding Chairman, Costas Grammenos Centre (formerly Centre, then International Centre) for Shipping, Trade and Finance, since 1984, and Professor of Shipping, Trade and Finance, since 1986 (Lloyd's Register Foundation Chair in Shipping, Trade and Finance, since 2007), Cass Business School, City, University of London (formerly City University Business School, then Cass Business School, City University); *b* 23 Feb. 1944; *s* of late Commander Theophilos C. Grammenos and Argyro (*née* Spanakos); *m* 1972, Anna C. Papadimitriou; one *s*. *Educ:* Third State Sch. of Athens; Panteion Univ. (BA); Univ. of Wales (MSc); City University (DSc). National Service, Greek Navy, 1968–70. Nat. Bank of Greece, 1962–74 (shipping finance expert, head office, 1972–74); independent researcher and advr, 1977–82; Vis. Prof., 1982–86, Actg Dean, 2000, Dep. Dean, Cass Undergrad. Sch., 2004–10, Cass Business Sch., City Univ. (formerly City Univ. Business Sch.); Pro Vice-Chancellor, City Univ., London, 1998–2011. Visiting Professor: World Maritime Univ., Malmö, 1990–95; Univ. of Antwerp, 2000–. Founding Pres., Man. Cttee, Internat. Hellenic Univ., Thessaloniki, 2006–18. Founding Chm., 1999–, City of London Biennial Meeting; Pres., Internat. Assoc. of Maritime Economists, 1998–2002; Member: Bd of Dirs, Alexander S. Onassis Public Benefit Foundn, 1995– (Dep. Pres., 2017–); American Bureau of Shipping, 1996–; Baltic Exchange, 1997–. Mem., Bd of Govs (Educn), Baltic and Internat. Maritime Council, 1995–2001. Mem., Bd of Trustees, Inst. of Marine Engineers Meml Trust, 2000–12; Maritime 2050 Experts Panel, 2018–. Vice Chm., Maria Tsakos Foundn, 2011–. Freeman, City of London, 2000; Liveryman, Shipwrights' Co., 2002–. Hon. FIMarEST 2008; Hon. FICS 2016. Archon of Ecumenical Patriarchate of Constantinople, 1994. FRSA 1996; FCIB 2004. Hon. Fellow, Univ. of Bangor, 2017. Seatrade Personality of the Year, 1998; Greek Shipping Leadership Award, Capital Link, 2017; Lifetime Achievement Award, Lloyd's List Global Awards, 2018. *Publications:* Bank Finance for Ship Purchase, 1979; (ed) The Handbook of Maritime

Economics and Business, 2002, 2nd edn 2010; papers on shipping finance in acad. jls. *Recreations:* music, walking, cooking. *Address:* Cass Business School, City, University of London, 106 Bunhill Row, EC1Y 8TZ. *T:* (020) 7040 8670. *Club:* Travellers.

**GRAN, Maurice Bernard**; scriptwriter, since 1978; *b* 26 Oct. 1949; *s* of Mark and Deborah Gran; *m* 1994, Carol James; one *s* one *d*. *Educ:* William Ellis Sch., London; University Coll. London (BSc Internat. Relations 1971). Mgt trainee, Dept of Employment, 1971; Manager, Tottenham Employment Exchange, 1974–76; marketing develt advr, 1976–78, Manager, London Employment Intelligence Unit, 1978–80, Dept of Employment. Co-Founder and Company Dir, Alomo Productions, 1988–2001. With Laurence Marks, scriptwriter, 1980–: main *television* credits: Shine on Harvey Moon, 1982–85, 1995; The New Statesman, 1987–91 (BAFTA Award, Best Comedy, 1990); Birds of a Feather, 1989–98 and 2014–17; Love Hurts, 1991–93; Goodnight Sweetheart, 1993–99, (special) 2016; Mosley, 1997; *radio:* My Blue Heaven, 2006; Dr Freud Will See You Now, Mr Hitler, 2007; My Blue Wedding, 2007; Von Ribbentrop's Watch, 2008; Grey Expectations, 2009; Love Me Do, 2012; *stage:* Playing God, Stephen Joseph Th., Scarborough, 2005; The New Statesman – Episode 2006, nat. tour, 2006–07; Dreamboats and Petticoats (musical), nat. tour, then Savoy, 2009, transf. Playhouse, 2010, nat. tours, 2010–12 and 2013–14, Wyndham's, 2012, nat. tour, 2017; Von Ribbentrop's Watch, nat. tour, 2010; Save the Last Dance for Me (musical), nat. tours, 2012–13, 2016; Dreamboats and Miniskirts (musical), nat. tour, 2014–15; Love Me Do, Watford Palace, 2014. Mem., BAFTA, 1992– (Councillor, 1994–95). BAFTA Writers Award, 1992. *Publications:* with Laurence Marks: Holding the Fort, 1981; The New Statesman Scripts, 1992; Dorien's Diary, 1993; Shine on Harvey Moon, 1995. *Recreations:* watching football, theatre, film. *Address:* 61 Gratton Road, Cheltenham GL50 2BZ. *Club:* Savile.

**GRANARD, 10th Earl of**, *cr* 1684 (Ire.); **Peter Arthur Edward Hastings Forbes;** Bt (NS) 1628; Viscount Granard, Baron Clanehugh (Ire.), 1675; Baron Granard (UK), 1806; *b* 15 March 1957; *s* of Hon. John Forbes (*d* 1982), *yr s* of 8th Earl, and of Joan, *d* of A. Edward Smith; *S* uncle, 1992; *m* 1980, Noreen Mitchell; three *s* one *d*. *Heir: s* Viscount Forbes, *qv*. *Address:* Strathallan Cliff House, Strathallan Road, Onchan, Isle of Man IM3 1NN.

**GRANATT, Michael Stephen Dreese**, CB 2001; Director (formerly Partner), Luther Pendragon, 2004–14; Chair, Emergency Aid, 2014–17; *b* 27 April 1950; *s* of Arthur Maurice Granatt and Denise Sylvia Granatt (*née* Dreese); *m* 1974, Jane Veronica Bray; one *s* three *d*. *Educ:* Westminster City Sch.; Queen Mary Coll., London. Sub-ed., subseq. Dep. Chief Sub-ed., Kent & Sussex Courier, 1973–77; Prodn Ed., Industrial Relns Services, 1977–79; Asst Ed., Dept of Employment, 1979–81; Press Officer, Home Office, 1981–83; Sen. Press Officer, 1983–85, Chief Press Officer, 1985–86, Hd of Inf., 1986–89, Dept of Energy; Dir, Public Affairs and Internal Communication, Metropolitan Police Service, 1989–92; Director of Communication: DoE, 1992–94; Home Office, 1995–98; Hd of Profession, Govt Inf. Service, subseq. Govt Inf. and Communication Service, 1997–2003 (Dir-Gen., 2002–03); also Hd of Civil Contingencies Secretariat, Cabinet Office, 2001–02. Vis. Prof., Univ. of Westminster, 2003–06; Sen. Res. Fellow, Inst. for Security and Resilience Studies, UCL, 2011–18. Chairman: London Emergency Press Officers' Gp, 1989–92; Nat. Industries Press Officers' Gp, 1992–94; Media Emergency Forum, 1996–2003; UK Press Card Authy, 2004–. Chair, Community Resilience, 2012–14. Bd Mem., Sci. Media Centre, Royal Instn, 2004–11. Co-ordinator: Club of Venice, 2003–14; Kent County Raynet, 2018– (Controller, 2014–18); Trustee, Kent County Raynet charity, 2018– (Chm., 2018–). Gov., Mary Hare Schs, 2004–17 (Chm. Govs, 2010–17). FCIPR (FIPR 2000). Master, City of London Guild of Public Relns Practitioners, 2005–06. *Publications:* (contrib.) Disasters and the Media, 1999; contrib. Jl Communication Mgt, Internat. Jl Emergency. *Recreations:* amateur radio (Mem., W Kent Amateur Radio Soc. (Chm., 2016–19)), walking the dogs, photography, reading science fiction. *E:* mike.granatt@blueyonder.co.uk.

**GRANBY, Marquis of; Charles John Montague Manners;** *b* 3 July 1999; *s* and *heir* of Duke of Rutland, *qv*.

**GRAND, Stephen Lewis**, OBE 2000; independent scientist and writer, since 1999; *b* 12 Feb. 1958; *s* of Dennis and Jean Grand; *m* 1979, Ann Nicholson (marr. diss. 2007); one *s*. *Educ:* self-taught. Sen. Programmer, Millennium Ltd, 1993–96; Dir of Technology, Cyberlife Technology Ltd, 1996–99; Dir, Cyberlife Research Ltd, 1999–. NESTA Fellow, 2002–03. Hon. Fellow: Cognitive Sci., Univ. of Sussex, 1997–99; Psychology, Univ. of Cardiff, 2001–04; Biomimetics, Univ. of Bath, 2002–04; Res. Fellow, Inst. of Creative Technologies, De Montfort Univ., 2006–07. DUniv Open, 2008. *Publications:* Creation: life and how to make it, 2000; Growing Up With Lucy: how to build an android in twenty easy steps, 2003. *Recreation:* work! *E:* steve@cyberlife-research.com.

**GRANDAGE, Michael**, CBE 2011; theatre director and producer; *b* 2 May 1962. *Educ:* Humphry Davy Grammar Sch., Cornwall; Central Sch. of Speech and Drama, London (Hon. Fellow). Theatre director, 1995–; Associate Dir, Crucible Th., Sheffield, 2000–05; Artistic Dir, Donmar Warehouse, London, 2002–12. Pres., Royal Central Sch. of Speech and Drama (formerly Central Sch. of Speech and Drama), 2010–. Vis. Prof., Falmouth Univ. (formerly University Coll., Falmouth), 2009–18. Productions include: Crucible Theatre, Sheffield: What the Butler Saw, 1997; Twelfth Night, 1998; The Country Wife, As You Like It, transf. Lyric, Hammersmith (Best Director award, Evening Standard, Critics' Circle; award for theatre, South Bank Show), 2000; Edward II, Don Juan, 2001; Richard III, The Tempest, transf. Old Vic, 2002; A Midsummer Night's Dream, 2003; Suddenly Last Summer, 2004; Don Carlos, 2004, transf. Gielgud Th., 2005 (Best Director award, Evening Standard, 2005); Almeida Theatre: The Doctor's Dilemma, 1998; The Jew of Malta, 1999; Donmar Warehouse: Good, 1999; Passion Play, transf. Comedy Th. (Best Director award, Evening Standard, Critics' Circle); Merrily We Roll Along (Best Director award, Critics' Circle); Olivier Award for Best New Musical), 2000; Privates on Parade, 2001; The Vortex, 2002; Caligula (Olivier Award for Best Dir, 2004), After Miss Julie, 2003; Henry IV, Grand Hotel (Olivier Award for Outstanding Musical; Best Director award, Evening Standard, 2005), 2004; Guys and Dolls (at Piccadilly Th.), The Wild Duck, 2005 (Best Director award, Critics' Circle, 2005); The Cut, 2006; Frost/Nixon, 2006, transf. Gielgud, 2006, NY, 2007; John Gabriel Borkman, 2007; Othello, 2007 (Best Director award, Evening Standard, 2008); The Chalk Garden (Best Director award, Evening Standard, 2008), Ivanov, Twelfth Night (at Wyndham's Th.), 2008; Madame de Sade (at Wyndham's Th.), 2009; Hamlet (at Wyndham's Th.), transf. NY, 2009; Red, 2009, transf. NY, 2010 (Tony Award); King Lear, 2010 (Jt Best Director award, Critics' Circle); Luise Miller, 2011; Richard II, 2011; Michael Grandage Company: Noël Coward Theatre: Privates on Parade, 2012; Peter and Alice, 2013; The Cripple of Inishmaan, 2013, transf. NY, 2014; A Midsummer Night's Dream, 2013; Henry V, 2013; Photograph 51, 2015; The Lieutenant of Inishmore, 2018; Dawn French: 30 Million Minutes, solo UK tour and Vaudeville Th., 2014; Hughie, NY, 2016; Red, Wyndham's Th., 2018; other productions: Evita, Adelphi Th., 2006, transf. NY, 2012; Danton's Death, NT, 2010; Frozen, NY, 2018; opera: Billy Budd, Glyndebourne, 2010, 2013; Madama Butterfly, Houston, 2010; Don Giovanni, Met. Opera, NY, 2011; Le nozze di Figaro, Glyndebourne, 2012, 2013, 2016; film, Genius, 2016. DUniv: Sheffield Hallam, 2002; Sheffield, 2004; London, 2014. *Address:* Michael Grandage Company, Fourth Floor, Wyndham's Theatre, Charing Cross Road, WC2H 0DA. *T:* (020) 3582 7210. *E:* mg@michaelgrandagecompany.com.

**GRANDI, Filippo Achille Maria;** United Nations High Commissioner for Refugees, since 2016; *b* Milan, 30 March 1957; *s* of Antonio Grandi and Maria Matilde Rosa. *Educ:* State Univ., Milan (BA Modern Hist.); Gregorian Univ., Rome (BA Philosophy). Dep. Special Rep. of UN Sec.-Gen. in Afghanistan, 2004–05; Dep. Comr-Gen. for Palestine Refugees in Near East, 2005–10, Comr-Gen., 2010–14, UNWRA. Hon. Dr Coventry. *Publications:* Rifugi e Ritorni, 2017. *Address:* UN High Commissioner for Refugees, 94 Rue de Montbrillant, 1202 Geneva, Switzerland. *T:* (22) 7398111, *Fax:* (22) 7397377. *E:* grandi@unhcr.org.

**GRANGE, Edward Stephen;** Partner, Corker Binning, since 2015; *b* King's Lynn, Jan. 1980; *s* of Stephen Grange and Carole Grange; *m* 2013, Natalie Smith; one *s*. *Educ:* Univ. of Wales, Bangor (BA Criminol. and Criminal Justice); BPP Law Sch., London (GDL 2004; LPC 2005). Sonn Macmillan Walker: trainee solicitor, 2005–07; Solicitor, 2007–12; Sen. Associate, Hodge Jones & Allen, 2012–15. *Publications:* (jtly) Extradition Law: a practitioner's guide, 2013, 2nd edn 2015. *Recreation:* tennis. *Address:* Corker Binning, The Cursitor Building, 38 Chancery Lane, WC2A 1EN. *T:* (020) 7353 6000. *E:* eg@corkerbinning.com.

**GRANGE, Katherine Elizabeth, (Mrs Charles Cory-Wright)**; QC 2017; *b* Nottingham, 21 Sept. 1975; *d* of Robert Andrew Grange and Josephine Mary Grange; *m* 2005, Charles Cory-Wright; two *s*. *Educ:* Ellis Guildford Sch., Nottingham; High Pavement Sixth Form Coll.; Queens' Coll., Cambridge (BA Law 1994; MA 1997). Called to the Bar, Middle Temple, 1998; Mem., Attorney Gen.'s A-Panel of Counsel, 2012–17. *Recreations:* theatre, swimming, school governor. *Address:* 39 Essex Chambers, 81 Chancery Lane, WC2A 1DD. *T:* (020) 7832 1111. *E:* Kate.grange@39essex.com.

**GRANGE, Sir Kenneth Henry**, Kt 2013; CBE 1984; RDI, FCSD; product designer; in private practice, since 1958; *b* 17 July 1929; *s* of Harry Alfred Grange and Hilda Gladys (*née* Long). *Educ:* London. Technical Illustrator, RE, 1948–50; Design Asst, Arcon Chartered Architects, 1948; Bronek Katz & Vaughn, 1950–51; Gordon Bowyer & Partners, 1951–54; Jack Howe & Partners, 1954–58; Founding Partner, Pentagram Design, 1972–91. Retrospective exhibn, Kenneth Grange: Making Britain Modern, Design Mus., 2011. Pres., CSD, 1987–88; Master of Faculty, RDI, 1985–87. RDI 1969; FCSD (FSIAD 1959). Hon. Prof., Heriot-Watt, 1987. Hon. Dr RCA, 1985; DUniv: Heriot-Watt, 1986; De Montfort, 1998; Staffs, 1998; Open, 2003. 10 Design Council Awards; Duke of Edinburgh Award for Elegant Design, 1963; Prince Philip Designers Prize, 2001. *Recreations:* memories of tennis, ski-ing. *Address:* 53 Christchurch Hill, NW3 1LG.

**GRANGER, John;** Headmaster, Bournemouth School, 1996–2009; *b* Heston, Middx, 5 Aug. 1949; *s* of Raymond and Mary Jane, (Jenny), Granger; *m* 1974, Heather Pyatt; two *d*. *Educ:* Spring Grove Grammar Sch.; Atlantic Coll.; Univ. of Hull (BSc Hons Applied Physics; PGCE). Sci. teacher, Plymstock Sch., 1973–74; Hd of Physics, 1977–87, Hd of Sci., 1987–96, Dep. Headmaster, 1991–96, Torquay Boys' GS, 1974–96. FRSA. *Recreations:* keeping fit, being with the family, music.

**GRANGER, Richard;** Director General, NHS Information Technology, and Chief Executive Officer, NHS Connecting for Health, Department of Health, 2002–08; *b* April 1965; *m* 1998, Gabrielle Virag; one *s* two *d*. *Educ:* Univ. of Bristol (BSc Hons (Geol.) 1987). Geologist, Geoservices SA, Singapore and Australia, 1987–89; Andersen Consulting, 1989–96 (Manager, 1993–96); Prog. Dir, Electronic Data Systems, 1996–98; Partner, Deloitte & Touche, 1998–2002. Hon. DSc City, 2006. *Publications:* articles on electronic govt and electronic health. *Recreations:* family, cycling, walking, books. *Clubs:* Reform, Ronnie Scott's; Cycle Touring.

**GRANT;** *see* Lyall Grant.

**GRANT,** family name of **Earl of Dysart** and **Baron Strathspey**.

**GRANT, Andrew Robert;** educational consultant, since 2014; Headmaster, St Albans School, 1993–2014; *b* Rochford, 29 April 1953; *s* of Walter Frank Grant and Joan Grant (*née* Bartram); *m* 1977, Hilary Sheena Kerr (*née* Charlton); two *s*. *Educ:* Southend High Sch.; Corpus Christi Coll., Cambridge (Open Exhibn; BA Hons English 1975; MA 1979; PGCE 1976). Asst Master, Merchant Taylors' Sch., Northwood, 1976–83; Hd of English, Whitgift Sch., Croydon, 1983–90; Second Master, Royal Grammar Sch., Guildford, 1990–93. Chm., HMC, 2009–10 (Chm., London Div., 2006–07); Director: ISC, 2009–11; Minerva Educn, 2014–18 (non-exec. Principal, Secondary Schs, 2015–18); Member: HMC/GSA Educn and Academic Policy Cttee, 2000– (Chm., 2002–05); Jt Assocs Curriculum Gp, 2000–06; Tomlinson 14–19 Rev. Assessment Gp, 2003–05; QCA 14–19 Adv. Gp, 2004–06; HMC/GSA Univs Cttee, 2005–08; Ind. State Schs Partnership Forum, DCSF, 2006–08. Mem. Court, Univ. of Hertfordshire, 2006–14; Governor: Colfe's Sch., 2012–16; Norwich Sch., 2013–; St Mary's Sch., Cambridge, 2014–. FRSA. *Recreations:* theatre, literature, music, cycling, squash, sailing. *E:* abbotwulsin@icloud.com. *Clubs:* East India; Hawks (Cambridge).

**GRANT, Andrew Steven**, RDI 2012; landscape architect; Founder and Director, Grant Associates, since 1996; *b* Withernsea, 29 Oct. 1958; *s* of Peter and Joyce Grant; *m* 2010, Caroline Ambrose; two *d*, two *s* by a previous marriage. *Educ:* Edinburgh Coll. of Art, Heriot Watt Univ. (BA Hons Landscape Architecture 1982). CMLI 1992. Landscape architect, Ash Gulf, Doha, 1983–86; Associate, Nicholas Pearson Associates, 1986–95. Vis. Prof., Univ. of Sheffield, 2013. Hon. FRIBA 2010. *Address:* Grant Associates, 22 Milk Street, Bath BA1 1UT. *T:* (01225) 332664. *E:* ag@grant-associates.uk.

**GRANT, Andrew Young;** Chief Operating Officer (formerly Principal), Grant Leisure Group, 1982–2005; Chief Executive Officer, Grant Leisure Inc., since 2005; Chairman, Real Live Leisure Co. Ltd, 1998–2007; *b* 8 April 1946; *s* of Marshall Grant and Marilyn Greene (*née* Phillips); *m*: 1st, 1969, Dietra (marr. diss.); one *d*; 2nd, 1973, Lindy Lang (marr. diss.); one *d*; 3rd, 2005, Debra Gould (marr. diss. 2013). *Educ:* Univ. of Oregon (BSc). Personnel Manager, Universal Studios Tour, Universal City, Calif, 1967–69; Dir of Personnel, Busch Gardens, LA, 1969–71, Ops Dir, 1971–73; Gen. Manager, Squaw Valley Ski Resort, 1973–74; Gen. Manager, Busch Gardens, 1974–76; Dir, Economic Research Associates, LA, 1976–79; Dep. Dir, Zoological Soc., San Diego, 1979–83; Dir, Leeds Castle Enterprises, 1983–88; Director: Granada Studios Tour, 1987–90; Grant Leisure Developments, 1987–; Blackpool Zoo, 2003–; Man. Dir, Zoo Operations Ltd, Zoological Soc., 1988–91; Principal, Internat. Spirit Develt Corp. Ltd (formerly Internat. Spirit Management Co.), 1995–. Member: Internat. Assoc. of Amusement Parks and Attractions, 1975–; Tourism Soc., 1988–; Tourism and Leisure Industries Sector Gp, NEDC, 1990–; Urban Land Inst., 1998–. Member Board: Montecito YMCA, 2006–; Channel Islands YMCA, 2010–; Mem. Adv. Bd, Devereux Foundn, Calif, 2013–. *Publications:* Nearly Human: the gorilla's guide to good living, 2007; Rain Forest Wisdom, 2013. *Recreations:* swimming, fishing, golf. *Address:* 1511 Bath Street #5, Santa Barbara, CA 93101, USA. *E:* andy@grant-leisure.com.

**GRANT, Ann**; Vice Chairman, Africa, Standard Chartered Capital Markets Ltd, 2005–14; *b* 13 Aug. 1948. *Educ*: Univ. of Sussex; SOAS, Univ. of London (MSc 1971). Joined FCO, 1971; Calcutta, 1973–75; Dept of Energy, 1976–79; Head of Chancery and Consul, Maputo, 1981–84; First Sec. (Energy), Office of UK Perm. Rep. to EU, Brussels, 1987–89, resigned; Communications Dir, Oxfam, 1989–91; rejoined FCO, 1991; Counsellor (Econ. and Social Affairs), UK Mission to UN, NY, 1992–96; Counsellor, FCO, 1996–98; Dir, African Dept, FCO, 1998–2000; High Comr, South Africa, 2000–05. Non-exec. Dir, Tullow Oil plc, 2009–17 (Sen. Ind. Dir, 2014–17). Member, Council: ODI, 2012–; LSHTM, 2013–. Trustee: UK Disasters Emergency Cttee, 2006–14; Rift Valley Inst., 2013–. Chair, Serious Music Trust, 2012–.

**GRANT, Ann Catherine**; *see* Cormack, A. C.

**GRANT of Monymusk, Sir Archibald**, 13th Bt *cr* 1705; *b* 2 Sept. 1954; *e s* of Captain Sir Francis Cullen Grant, 12th Bt, and of Lady Grant (Jean Margherita, *d* of Captain Humphrey Douglas Tollemache, RN), who *m* 2nd, 2nd Baron Tweedsmuir, CBE, CD; *S* father, 1966; *m* 1st, 1982, Barbara Elizabeth (marr. diss. 2009), *e d* of A. G. D. Forbes, Druminnor Castle, Rhynie, Aberdeenshire; two *d*; 2nd, 2012, Fiona Mary Julia, *e d* of Sir Duncan Alexander Grant of Dalvey, 13th Bt. *Address*: House of Monymusk, Aberdeenshire AB51 7HL. *T*: (01467) 651220.

*See also* Sir P. A. B. Grant of Dalvey, Bt.

**GRANT, Prof. (Barbara) Rosemary**, PhD; FRS 2007; Senior Research Scholar, since 1997, with rank of Professor, 1997–2008, now Emeritus, Department of Ecology and Evolutionary Biology, Princeton University (Research Scholar and Lecturer, 1985–96); *b* Arnside, Cumbria, 8 Oct. 1936; *m* 1962, Peter Raymond Grant, *qv*; two *d*. *Educ*: Edinburgh Univ. (BSc Hons 1960); Uppsala Univ. – Sweden (PhD 1985). Research Associate: Univ. of BC, 1960–64; Yale Univ., 1964–65; McGill Univ., 1973–77; Univ. of Michigan, 1977–85. Vis. Prof., Univ. of Zurich, 2002, 2003. Mem., Amer. Acad. Arts and Scis, 1997; For. Mem., NAS, 2008. Hon. DSc Toronto, 2017. Darwin Medal, Royal Soc., 2002; Darwin-Wallace Medal, Linnean Soc., 2009; with P. R. Grant: Balzan Prize for Population Biol., Internat. Balzan Prize Foundn, 2005; Kyoto Prize, Inamori Foundn, 2009; Royal Medal, Royal Soc., 2017; Frontiers of Knowledge Award, BBVA Foundn, 2018. *Publications*: (with P. R. Grant) Evolutionary Dynamics of a Natural Population: the large cactus finch of the Galapagos, 1989; (with P. R. Grant) How and Why Species Multiply: the radiation of Darwin's finches, 2008; (ed with P. R. Grant) In Search of the Causes of Evolution: from field observations to mechanisms, 2010; 40 Years of Evolution, 2014; contribs to jls incl. Proc. NAS, Oecologia (Berlin), Ecology, Evolution, Proc. Royal Soc. London, Biol Conservation, Science, Nature. *Address*: Department of Ecology and Evolutionary Biology, Princeton University, Princeton, NJ 08544–1003, USA. *E*: rgrant@princeton.edu.

**GRANT, Bill**; MP (C) Ayr, Carrick and Cumnock, since 2017; *m* Agnes; two *d*. Firefighter, Strathclyde Fire and Rescue Service; retd as Dep. Comdr. Mem. (C), S Ayrshire Council, 2007–17. Mem., Sci. and Technol. Cttee, H of C, 2017–. Contested (C) Ayr, Carrick and Cumnock, 2010. JP Ayr. *Address*: House of Commons, SW1A 0AA.

**GRANT, Charles Peter**, CMG 2013; Co-founder, 1995, and Director, since 1998, Centre for European Reform; *b* 9 Oct. 1958; *s* of Peter Forbes Grant and Elizabeth Ann Grant (*née* Shirreff). *Educ*: Selwyn Coll., Cambridge (BA Hons Hist. 1980); Grenoble Univ. (Dip. French). Journalist, Euromoney, 1981–86; joined The Economist, 1986; financial journalist, 1986–89; Brussels corresp., 1989–93; home news, 1993–94; Defence Ed., 1994–98. Dir and Trustee, British Council, 2002–08; Trustee and Mem. Council of Mgt, Ditchley Foundn, 2013–. Mem. Bd, Moscow Sch. of Civic Educn (formerly Moscow Sch. of Pol Studies), 2002–. Chevalier, Ordre Nat. du Mérite (France), 2004; Bene Merito Medal (Poland), 2015; Star of Italy (Italy), 2015. *Publications*: Delors: inside the house that Jacques built, 1994; Can Britain Lead in Europe?, 1998; EU 2010: an optimistic vision of the future, 2000; Transatlantic Rift: how to bring the two sides together, 2003; What Happens if Britain Votes No?, 2005; Europe's Blurred Boundaries: rethinking enlargement and neighbourhood policy, 2006; European Choices for Gordon Brown, 2007; Preparing for the Multipolar World: European foreign and security policy in 2020, 2007; Can Europe and China Shape a New World Order?, 2008; Is Europe Doomed to Fail as a Power?, 2009; Cameron's Europe: can the Conservatives achieve their EU objectives? 2009; Russia, China and Global Governance, 2012; (jtly) How to Build a Modern EU, 2013. *Recreations*: classical music, hill-walking. *Address*: Centre for European Reform, 14 Great College Street, SW1P 3RX. *T*: (020) 7233 1199, *Fax*: (020) 7233 1117. *E*: charles@cer.eu. *Club*: Reform.

**GRANT, Sir David**, Kt 2016; CBE 1997; PhD; CEng, FREng, FIET; FLSW; Chair, National Physical Laboratory, since 2015; *b* 12 Sept. 1947; *s* of Edmund Grant and Isobel Scorer Grant (*née* Rutherford); *m* 1974, Helen Joyce Rutter; one *s* one *d*. *Educ*: Univ. of Durham (PhD 1974). CEng 1975; FIET (FIEE 1984); FREng (FEng 1997). Reyrolle Parsons Gp, 1966–77; United Technologies Corp., 1977–84; Gp Technical Dir, Dowty Gp, 1984–91; Technical Dir, GEC, then Marconi plc, 1991–2001; Vice-Chancellor, Cardiff Univ., 2001–12. Non-exec. Dir, DSTL, 2012–18; Senior Independent Director: IQE plc, 2012–; Renishaw plc, 2012–. Member: EPSRC, 2001–06; UK Technol. Strategy Bd, later Innovate UK, 2007–14 (Interim CEO, 2015). Vice-Pres., RAEng, 2007–12; Chair, STEMNET, 2012–18. FLSW 2011. Hon. Fellow, Wolfson Coll., Cambridge, 2000. Mensforth Internat. Gold Medal, IEE, 1996. *Address*: Cardiff University, Main Building, Park Place, Cardiff CF10 3AT.

**GRANT, Helen**; MP (C) Maidstone and the Weald, since 2010; *b* London, 28 Sept. 1961; *d* of Dr Julius Okuboye and Dr Gladys Spedding (*née* Butler); *m* 1991, Simon Julian Grant; two *s*. *Educ*: St Aidan's Sch., Carlisle; Trinity Sch., Carlisle; Univ. of Hull (LLB Hons); Guildford Coll. of Law (solicitors finals). Articled clerk, Cartmell Mawson and Maine, Carlisle; admitted solicitor, 1988; Clinical Negligence Solicitor, Hempsons, London, 1987–88; Equity Partner, Fayers & Co., S Wimbledon, 1988–94; Founder and Sen. Partner, Grants Solicitors LLP, 1996–. Non-exec. Dir, Croydon NHS PCT, 2005–07. Member: Family Div., Social Justice Policy Gp, 2006–08; Family Law Reform Commn, 2007–09; Centre for Social Justice; Equality and Diversity Cttee, Law Soc., 2008–09. Parliamentary Under-Secretary of State: (Women and Equalities), MoJ, 2012–13; (Women, Equalities, Sport and Tourism), DCMS, 2013–15. Mem., Justice Select Cttee, 2010–11; Vice Chm., Army Div., All Party Parly Gp for Armed Forces, 2010; Chair, All Party Parly Gp for Channel 4 Television, 2018–. Chair, Govt Apprenticeship Nat. Diversity Network, 2017–; Vice Chair (Communities), Conservative Party, 2018–. Trustee, Social Mobility Foundn, 2016–; Pres., Bd of Trustees, Maidstone Museums' Foundn, 2008–18; Patron, Women in Racing, 2016–; Hon. Vice-Pres., Maidstone MENCAP Trust, 2010–19. Hon. MInstRE 2010. *Publications*: contrib. to reports for Social Justice Policy Gp, Centre for Social Justice. *Recreations*: tennis, cinema, major sporting events, family life. *Address*: House of Commons, SW1A 0AA. *T*: (020) 7219 7107. *E*: helen.grant.mp@parliament.uk.

**GRANT, Helen Louise**; *see* Munn, H. L.

**GRANT, Hugh John Mungo**; actor; *b* 9 Sept. 1960; *s* of James Murray Grant and late Fynvola Susan Grant (*née* Maclean); one *s* one *d* by Tinglan Hong; *m* 2018, Anna Eberstein; three *c*. *Educ*: Latymer Upper Sch., Hammersmith; New Coll., Oxford (BA). Began career in theatre performing in Jockeys of Norfolk (written with Chris Lang and Andy Taylor); actor in theatre, TV and films; co-founder, 1994, and producer for Simian Films. *Films include*: White Mischief, Maurice (Best Actor, jtly with James Wilby, Venice Film Fest.), 1987; Lair of the White Worm, La Nuit Bengali, 1988; Impromptu, 1989; Bitter Moon, 1992; Remains of the Day, 1993; Four Weddings and a Funeral (Golden Globe Award, BAFTA Award, Evening Standard Peter Sellers Award for Comedy, 1995), Sirens, 1994; The Englishman Who Went Up a Hill but Came Down a Mountain, Nine Months, An Awfully Big Adventure, Sense and Sensibility, 1995; Restoration, 1996; Notting Hill, 1999 (Evening Standard Peter Sellers Award for Comedy, Empire Film Awards Best British Actor, 2000); Small Time Crooks, 2000; Bridget Jones's Diary, 2001 (Evening Standard Peter Sellers Award for Comedy, 2002); About A Boy, 2002 (Empire Film Awards Best British Actor, London Critics' Circle Film Awards Best British Actor, 2003); Two Weeks Notice, Love Actually, 2003; Bridget Jones: The Edge of Reason, 2004; American Dreamz, 2006; Music and Lyrics, 2007; Did You Hear About the Morgans?, 2010; Cloud Atlas, 2013; The Rewrite, 2014; The Man from U.N.C.L.E., 2015; Florence Foster Jenkins, 2016; Paddington 2, 2017; Simian Films productions: Extreme Measures, 1996; Mickey Blue Eyes, 1998. *Television includes*: A Very English Scandal, 2018. Mem. Bd, Hacked Off. Patron: Fynvola Foundn; Pancreatic Cancer Action; DIPEx. Ambassador Marie Curie Cancer Care.

**GRANT, Sir Ian (David)**, Kt 2010; CBE 1988; DL; Chairman, Scottish Exhibition Centre Ltd, 2002–13 (Director, since 1998; Deputy Chairman, 2001–02); *b* Dundee, 28 July 1943; *s* of late Alan H. B. Grant and Florence O. Grant; *m* 1968, Eileen May Louisa Yule; three *d*. *Educ*: Strathallan Sch.; East of Scotland College of Agriculture (Dip.). Vice Pres. 1981–84, Pres. 1984–90, National Farmers' Union of Scotland; Mem., Scottish Council, CBI, 1984–96; Crown Estate Comr for Scotland, 1996–2009; First Crown Estate Comr, later Chm., The Crown Estate, 2002–09. Mem. Bd, 1988–90, Chm., 1990–98, Scottish Tourist Bd; Mem. Bd, BTA, 1990–98. Director: East of Scotland Farmers Ltd, 1978–2002; Clydesdale Bank PLC, 1989–97; NFU Mutual Insce Soc. Ltd, 1990–2008 (Dep. Chm., 2003–08); Scottish and Southern Energy plc (formerly Scottish Hydro Electric PLC), 1992–2003 (Dep. Chm., 2000–03); Chm., Cairngorms Partnership, 1998–2003. Vice Pres., Royal Smithfield Club, 1996. Trustee: NFU Mutual Charitable Trust, 2009–16; Queen Elizabeth Castle of Mey Trust, 2010–18. Hon. Dir, RHASS, 2014–19. FRAgS 1987. DL Perth and Kinross, 2011. Hon. DBA Napier, 1999. *Recreations*: travel, gardening, reading, music. *Address*: Leal House, Loyal Road, Alyth PH11 8JQ.

**GRANT, (Ian) Nicholas**; Chief Executive Officer, Mediatrack Research Ltd, 2007–18 (Managing Director, 1992–2002, Chairman, 2002, Mediatrack); *b* 24 March 1948; *s* of late Hugo and Cara Grant; *m* 1977, Rosalind Louise Pipe; one *s* one *d*. *Educ*: Univ. of London (LLB); Univ. of Warwick (MA, Industrial Relns). Confederation of Health Service Employees: Research Officer, 1972–74; Head of Research and Public Relations, 1974–82; Dir of Communications, Labour Party, 1982–85; Public Affairs Advr, Mirror Group Newspapers and Maxwell Communication Corp., 1985–89. Pres., Internat. Assoc. for the Measurement and Evaluation of Communication (formerly Assoc. of Media Evaluation Cos, then Assoc. for Measurement and Evaluation of Communication), 2011–13 (Dep. Chm., 1997–2005; Chm., 2005–10). Dir, Locus Breadalbane Ltd, 2016–. Chairman: Breadalbane Heritage Soc., 2017–; Scottish Crannog Centre and Scottish Trust for Underwater Archaeology, 2019–. Member: Council, London Borough of Lambeth, 1978–84; Lambeth, Southwark and Lewisham AHA, 1978–82; W Lambeth DHA, 1982–83. Contested (Lab) Reigate, 1979. FCIPR 2010. FRSA 2013. Hon. MRSocMed 2014. *Publications*: contrib. to: Economics of Prosperity, ed D. Blake and P. Ormerod, 1980; Political Communications: the general election campaign of 1983, ed I. Crewe and M. Harrop, 1985. *Recreations*: walking, reading, photography, cartography. *Address*: Tigh na Clachan, Fearnan, Perthshire PH15 2PF.

**GRANT, Prof. Ian Philip**, DPhil; FRS 1992; CMath; FIMA, FRAS, FInstP; Professor of Mathematical Physics, University of Oxford, 1992–98, now Emeritus Professor; Tutorial Fellow in Mathematics, Pembroke College, Oxford, 1969–98, now Emeritus Fellow; Visiting Professor, Department of Applied Mathematics and Theoretical Physics, University of Cambridge, since 2013; *b* 15 Dec. 1930; *er s* of Harold Hyman Grant and Isabella Henrietta Ornstien; *m* 1958, Beryl Cohen; two *s*. *Educ*: St Albans Sch., Herts; Wadham Coll., Oxford (Open Scholar 1948; MA; DPhil 1954). FInstP (FPhysS 1955); FIMA 1965; CMath 1990. SSO, 1957–61, PSO, 1961–64, UKAEA, Aldermaston; Res. Fellow, Atlas Computer Lab., SRC, 1964–69; Lectr in Maths, 1969–90, Reader in Mathematical Physics, 1990–92, Oxford Univ.; Res. Fellow in Maths, 1964–69, Actg Master, 1984–85, Pembroke Coll., Oxford. Visiting Professor: McGill Univ., 1976; Abo Akademi, Finland, 1977; Inst. de Fisica, Univ. Nacional Autónoma de México, 1981; Imperial Coll., London, 2001–08. Nat. Service, Royal Signals, 1995–96. Chair, Oxford Synagogue and Jewish Centre, 1985–2004. Governor: Royal Grammar Sch., High Wycombe, 1981–99; St Paul's Schs, 1993–2001. *Publications*: Relativistic Quantum Theory of Atoms and Molecules, 2006; papers in learned jls on relativistic quantum theory in atomic and molecular physics, and on radiative transfer theory in astrophysics and atmospheric science. *Recreations*: walking, music, theatre-going. *Address*: Mathematical Institute, University of Oxford, Andrew Wiles Building, Radcliffe Observatory Quarter, Woodstock Road, Oxford OX2 6GG. *E*: ipg@maths.ox.ac.uk, ipg21@damtp.cam.ac.uk; Apt 46 Abbeyfield Girton Green, Wellbrook Way, Girton, Cambridge CB3 0GQ. *T*: (01223) 276364.

**GRANT, Janet**; *see* Thompson, J.

**GRANT, Sir John Douglas Kelso**, KCMG 2005 (CMG 1999); HM Diplomatic Service, retired; *b* 17 Oct. 1954; *s* of Douglas Marr Kelso Grant and Audrey Stevenson Grant (*née* Law); *m* 1983, Anna Maria Lindvall; one *s* two *d*. *Educ*: Edinburgh Acad.; St Catharine's Coll., Cambridge (BA 1976). HM Diplomatic Service: W African Dept, FCO, 1976; Stockholm, 1977–80; Russian lang. trng, 1980–81; Moscow, 1982–84; Morgan Grenfell and Co. Ltd, 1985–86; Press Office, FCO, 1986–89; UK Permt Repn to EU, 1989–93 (Press Spokesman, later External Relns) and 1994–97 (Counsellor, External Relns); European Secretariat, Cabinet Office, 1993–94; Principal Private Sec. to Sec. of State for Foreign and Commonwealth Affairs, 1997–99; Ambassador to Sweden, 1999–2003; UK Permanent Rep. to EU, Brussels, 2003–07. Pres., BHP Billiton Europe, 2007–09; Exec. Vice-Pres., Policy and Corporate Affairs, BG Gp plc, 2009–15; Vice-Pres., Anadarko Petroleum Corp., 2016–. *Recreations*: cross-country ski-ing, walking. *Address*: 54a Fairholme Road, W14 9JY.

**GRANT, John Stephen**; author; business consultant, since 1999; social entrepreneur; *b* Hythe, Kent, 8 Nov. 1964; *s* of Paul and Ursula Grant; one *s*. *Educ*: Emmanuel Coll., Cambridge (BA Hons Natural Scis 1987); Birkbeck Coll., London (MSc Psychodynamics of Infant Develt 2002). Account Rep., J. Walter Thomson, 1987–89; Account Planner, BMP DDB Needham, 1989–94; Planning Dir, Chiat Day, 1994–95; Co-founder, St Luke's Communications, 1995–99; Founder and Proprietor, TheJohnGrant, 1999–. Associate: Demos, 2007–09; Forum for the Future, 2008–12. Non-executive Director: Onzo Ltd, 2007–11; Ecoinomy Ltd, 2009–14. FRSA 2009. *Publications*: The New Marketing

Manifesto, 1999; After Image, 2002; The Brand Innovation Manifesto, 2006; The Green Marketing Manifesto, 2007; Coopportunity, 2010; Made With, 2013; Better, 2018. *Recreations:* reading, music, cinema, social campaigns. *E:* thejohngrant@btinternet.com.

**GRANT, Julia Catherine;** Chief Executive, Pro Bono Economics, since 2016; a Forestry Commissioner, Forestry Commission, since 2016 (Chair, Audit, Risk and Assurance Committee, since 2016); *b* Emsworth, Hants, 28 Sept. 1960; *d* of Captain Malcolm E. Trussler and late Mary Trussler; *m* 1992, Clive Grant; three *d. Educ:* Portsmouth High Sch.; Havant Coll.; St Hilda's Coll., Oxford (MA PPE); London Business Sch. (MBA). Graduate trainee, Barclays Bank Internat., 1982–84; A.T. Kearney Mgt Consultants, 1984–86; Sen. Consultant, Touche Ross Mgt Consultants, 1986–89; Gp Business Develt Manager, Lloyds Abbey Life, Lloyds Bank, 1989–91; Principal, PwC Consulting, 1991–97; Chief Executive: Surrey Community Action, 1999–2004; Nat. Gardens Scheme, 2004–10; Chief Exec. and Portfolio Dir, Impetus Private Equity Foundn, 2011–16. Mem., AHRC, 2015–. Member: Adv. Bd, Big Society Capital, 2013–16; Impact Investment Cttee, British Venture Capital Assoc., 2015–. Mem. Council and Mem., Audit Cttee, LSC Surrey, 2002–05. Trustee: Shelter, 1987–98 (Mem., Audit Cttee); Surrey Community Foundn, 2014–17; Educn Develt Trust, 2017–. *Recreations:* sailing, tennis, music, landscape and heritage. *Address:* Pro Bono Economics, Clarence Centre, 6 St George's Circus, SE1 6FE. *T:* (020) 3632 2668. *E:* julia.grant@probonoeconomics.com.

**GRANT, Keith Wallace;** Dean, Faculty of Design, Kingston University (formerly Polytechnic), 1988–99; *b* 30 June 1934; *s* of Randolph and Sylvia Grant; *m* 1968, Deanne Bergsma; one *s* one *d. Educ:* Trinity Coll., Glenalmond; Clare Coll., Cambridge (MA). Account Exec., W. S. Crawford Ltd, 1958–62; General Manager: Covent Garden Opera Co., later Royal Opera, 1962–73; English Opera Group, 1962–73; Sec., Royal Soc. of Arts, 1973–77; Dir, Design Council, 1977–88. Called to the Bar, Middle Temple, 2001. Member: Adv. Council, V&A Mus., 1977–83; PO Stamp Adv. Cttee, 1978–89; Exec. Bd, Internat. Council of Socs of Industrial Design, 1983–87; Chm., Nat. Lead Body for Design, 1995–98. Chm., English Music Theatre Co., 1979–92; Mem., Management Cttee, Park Lane Gp, 1988–95; Sec., Peter Pears Award for Singers, 1988–95. Governor: Central Sch. of Art and Design, 1974–77; Birmingham Polytechnic, 1981–86; Edinburgh Coll. of Art, 1982–86; Mem. Ct, Brunel Univ., 1985–89. Hon. Prof., Heriot-Watt Univ., 1987. Hon. Fellow, Birmingham Univ. (formerly Birmingham Poly., later Univ. of Central England), 1988. Hon. FCSD (Hon. FSIAD, 1983). *Recreations:* music, gardening, voluntary work for the Royal Botanic Gardens, Kew. *Address:* 43 St Dunstan's Road, W6 8RE. *Club:* Garrick.

**GRANT, Kenneth Isaac;** a District Judge (Magistrates' Courts) (formerly Metropolitan Stipendiary Magistrate), 1999–2019; *b* 14 Nov. 1951; *s* of late Samuel Grant and Mercia Grant; *m* 1980, Irene Whilton; one *s* one *d. Educ:* Haberdashers' Aske's Sch., Elstree; Univ. of Sussex (BA); Coll. of Law. Admitted Solicitor, 1977; Solicitor, Darlington & Parkinson, 1977–99, Sen. Partner, 1990–99. Chm., Area Cttee, Legal Aid Bd, 1994–99 (Chm., Area 14 Regional Cttee, 1997–99). *Recreations:* theatre, opera. *Club:* Hurlingham.

**GRANT, Rev. Canon Malcolm Etheridge;** Priest Associate, All Saints', Leighton Buzzard, since 2009; *b* 6 Aug. 1944; *s* of Donald Etheridge Grant and Nellie Florence May Grant (*née* Tuffey); *m* 1984, Katrina Russell Nuttall (*née* Dunnett); one *s* one *d. Educ:* Dunfermline High School; Univ. of Edinburgh (Bruce of Grangehill Bursar, 1962); BSc (Hons Chemistry); BD (Hons New Testament); Divinity Fellowship, 1969); Edinburgh Theological College. Deacon 1969, priest 1970; Assistant Curate: St Mary's Cathedral, Glasgow, 1969–72; St Wulfram's, Grantham (in charge of Church of the Epiphany, Earlesfield), 1972; Team Vicar of Earlesfield, Grantham, 1972–78; Priest-in-charge, St Ninian's, Invergordon, 1978–81; Examining Chaplain to Bishop of Moray, Ross and Caithness, 1979–81; Provost and Rector: St Mary's Cathedral, Glasgow, 1981–91; St Andrew's Cathedral, Inverness, 1991–2002 (Hon. Canon, 2002–); Rector, St Paul's, Strathnairn, and Priest i/c, St Mary's-in-the-Fields, Culloden, 1991–97. Vicar of Eaton Bray with Edlesborough, Dio. St Albans, 2002–09; RD of Dunstable, 2004–09; permission to officiate, Dio. St Albans, 2009, Dio. Oxford, 2009–19. Member, Highland Regional Council Education Cttee, 1979–81. Trustee: Scottish Churches Architectural Heritage Trust, 1991–2011; Beds and Herts Historic Churches Trust, 2018–. *Address:* 13 Rock Lane, Leighton Buzzard, Beds LU7 2QQ. *T:* (01525) 372771. *E:* mandkgrant@btinternet.com.

**GRANT, Sir Malcolm (John),** Kt 2013; CBE 2003; LLD; FAcSS; Chairman, NHS England (formerly NHS Commissioning Board), 2011–18; Chancellor, University of York, since 2015; *b* 29 Nov. 1947; *s* of Francis William Grant and Vera Jessica Grant; *m* 1974, Christine (*née* Endersbee); two *s* one *d. Educ:* Waitaki Boys' High Sch., NZ; Univ. of Otago (LLB 1970; LLM 1973; LLD 1986). Called to the Bar, Middle Temple, 1998, Bencher, 2004. Lectr, subseq. Sen. Lectr in Law, Southampton Univ., 1972–86; University College London: Sen. Lectr in Law, 1986–88; Prof. of Law, and Vice-Dean, Faculty of Laws, 1988–91; Cambridge University: Prof. of Land Economy, 1991–2003; Pro-Vice-Chancellor, 2002–03; Fellow of Clare Coll., 1991–2016, Hon. Fellow, 2016; Provost and Pres., UCL, 2003–13. Chairman: Local Govt Commn for England, 1996–2002 (Mem., 1992–2002; Dep. Chm., 1995–96); Ind. Panel on Remuneration of Councillors in London, 1999–2004; Agric. and Envmt Biotechnol. Commn, 2000–05; Steering Bd for Nat. Public Debate on Genetic Modification, 2002–03; Member: ESRC, 2008–12; Bd, HEFCE, 2008–14. British Business Ambassador, 2008–18; Chm., Governing Bd, Sainsbury Wellcome Centre for Neural Circuits and Behaviour, UCL, 2017–. Dir, Genomics England Ltd, 2014–18. Mem., 2000–08, Chm., 2004–08, Standards Cttee, GLA. Chairman: Russell Gp, 2006–09; PLuS Alliance, 2017–; Governor: London Business Sch., 2003–13; Royal Instn, 2006–09; Hon. Gov., Ditchley Foundn, 2019– (Gov., 2002–19; Mem., Council of Mgt, 2003–11); Member: Internat. Council, Free Univ. of Berlin, 2006–12; Univ. Grants Cttee, Hong Kong, 2008–15; Higher Educn Adv. Council, Russian Fedn, 2013–; Internat. Adv. Bd, Moscow Inst. of Physics and Technol., 2013–; Sen. Strategy Advr, Arizona State Univ., 2015–. Pres., Council for the Assistance of At-Risk Academics, 2013–. Trustee, Somerset Hse, 2014–. Patron: New London Orch., 2005–; UK Envmtl Law Assoc., 2006–; Envmtl Law Foundn, 2010–. Hon. MRTPI 1993 (Hon. Life Mem., 2014); Hon. MRICS 1995. FAcSS (AcSS 2000). Hon. FRCP 2016. Hon. Life Fellow, Selwyn Coll., Dunedin, NZ, 2013; Montgomery Fellow, Dartmouth Coll., USA, 2014. Hon. LLD: Otago, 2006; UCL, 2013; Cambridge, 2017. Gen. Editor, Encyclopedia of Planning Law and Practice, 1981–2005 (Consultant Editor, 2005–); Consultant Editor, Encyclopedia of Environmental Law, 1993–. Officier, Ordre National du Mérite (France), 2004. *Publications:* Planning Law Handbook, 1981; Urban Planning Law, 1982, 2nd Suppl. 1990; Rate Capping and the Law, 1985, 2nd edn 1986; Permitted Development, 1989, 2nd edn 1996; (ed jtly) Concise Lexicon of Environmental Terms, 1995; Singapore Planning Law, 1999. Environmental Court Report, 2000. *Recreations:* opera, woodlands, forestry management, grandchildren, organ music.

**GRANT, Margaret;** *see* Exley, M.

**GRANT, (Martin Alistair) Piers; His Honour Judge Grant;** a County Court Judge (peripatetic), Northern Ireland, since 2005; *b* 1 April 1950; *s* of Ranald and Maureen Grant; *m* 1977, Siobhan Bell; three *d. Educ:* Queen's Univ., Belfast (LLB Hons 1974). Called to the Bar, 1975; Dep. County Court Judge, 1992–2005. *Recreations:* travel, reading, family, tennis, golf. *Address:* c/o Royal Courts of Justice, Chichester Street, Belfast BT1 3JF. *Clubs:* Army and Navy; Royal Belfast Golf.

**GRANT, Martin James;** Chief Executive Officer, Park Resorts, 2007–08; *b* 29 June 1949; *s* of James and Barbara Grant; *m* 1979, Helena Kay; two *s. Educ:* King Henry VIII, Coventry; Nottingham Univ. (BSc). Marks and Spencer, 1971–74; Grand Metropolitan, 1974–79; Holt Lloyd, 1979–82; Imperial Foods, 1982–83; Whitbread & Co. plc, 1983–90; Allied Lyons, subseq. Allied Domecq, 1990–98: Managing Director: Ansells Ltd, 1990–95; Allied Domecq Leisure, 1995–98; Chief Executive: Vaux Gp, 1998–99; Inn Partnerships, 1999–2002; RoadChef Motorways Hldgs, 2004–07. Mem. Council, Aqa Education, 2012. Fellow, Mktg Soc., 1995; Chm., BII, 2007–12 (Treas., 2000–07; CBII 2003). *Recreations:* military music, military history.

**GRANT, Martin Macdonald,** PhD; FREng; Executive Vice President, Engineering and Consulting, Oil and Gas, SNC-Lavalin, since 2018 (Chief Executive Officer, Energy, Atkins plc, 2012–17); *b* Inverness, 23 Dec. 1958; *s* of Alistair Grant and Patricia Grant; *m* 1988, Shona Robertson; one *d. Educ:* George Heriot's Sch., Edinburgh; Univ. of Edinburgh (BSc 1st Cl. Hons Mech. Engrg 1980); City Univ. (PhD Fluid Mechanics 1984). FREng 2012. Atkins plc: Consultant Engr, 1984–97; Managing Director: Oil and Gas, 1997–2008; Energy, 2008–12. Trustee, Royal Acad. of Engrg, 2018–. *Recreations:* golf, football, Land Rovers, learning French. *Address:* Atkins, member of SNC-Lavalin Group, Nova North, 11 Bressenden Place, SW1E 5BY. *T:* (020) 7121 2000. *E:* martin.grant@atkinsglobal.com.

**GRANT, Dame Mavis,** DBE 1999; Headteacher, Canning Street Primary School, Newcastle upon Tyne, 1999–2008; *b* 1 Feb. 1948; *d* of Joseph S. Edgar and Edna M. Edgar (*née* Hewson); *m* 1970, Roger M. Grant. *Educ:* Northumberland Coll. of Educn (CertEd and Cert. Advanced Educn Studies). Teaching in primary schools, Herts, Northumberland and Newcastle upon Tyne, 1969–2008: Dep. Headteacher, Cowgate Primary Sch., Newcastle upon Tyne, 1978–84; Headteacher, Mary Trevelyan Primary Sch., Newcastle upon Tyne, 1984–99. *Recreations:* reading, theatre, travel, dining out.

**GRANT, Michael John,** CEng, FICE, FCT; Partner, Aaronite Partners Ltd, since 2006; *s* of Michael George Grant and Zena Grant; *m* 1979, Maureen Hampson; one *s* two *d. Educ:* North East London Poly. (BSc Hons Civil Engrg); City Univ. Business Sch., London (MBA Finance); Harvard Business Sch. (AMP). Trainee engr, Sir Alexander Gibb & Partners Consulting Engrs, 1971–72; Civil Engineer: DoE, 1972–78; BRB, 1978–84; Financial Analyst, Laing & Cruikshank (Stock Brokers), 1985–86; Dir of Corporate Finance and Gp Treas., Eurotunnel plc, 1987–98; Property Dir, Railtrack, 1998–99; Chief Exec., Strategic Rail Authy, 1999–2001; Franchising Dir, OPRAF, 1999–2001; Dir, Cable & Wireless, 2003–06; Chm., Cable & Wireless USA, 2003–06; Strategic Advr, UK Houses of Parlt, 2006–07; Chief Restructuring Officer, Deutsche Woolworth, 2007–09; Investment Dar (Kuwait), 2009–11; Ind. Exec., Energy City Qatar, 2011–12; Chief Restructuring Officer, 2011–14, Gp CEO, 2014–16, Al Jaber Gp (Abu Dhabi). Director: Eurotunnel Finance & Services, 1987–98; Broadgate Plaza, 1998–99; Railtrack Develts, 1999; BRB, 1999; Seadrill Ltd, 2016–; non-executive Director: Liverpool Vision, 1999–2003; Great Eastern Telecommunications, Cayman Islands, 2004–06; Monaco Telecom, 2004–05; Mobile One, Singapore, 2004–06; Torexretail plc, 2007. Advr, Bd, Mushrif Contracting Kuwait, 2016–; Mem., Adv. Bd Dubai, City Univ., 2016–. Mem., Inst. for Turnaround. *Recreations:* travel, live music, sport. *Club:* Reform.

**GRANT, Nicholas;** *see* Grant, I. N.

**GRANT of Dalvey, Sir Patrick Alexander Benedict,** 14th Bt *cr* 1688 (NS); Chieftain of Clan Donnachy, (Donnachaidh); Managing Director, Grants of Dalvey Ltd, since 1988; *b* 5 Feb. 1953; *e s* of Sir Duncan Alexander Grant, 13th Bt, and Joan Penelope (*d* 1991), *o d* of Captain Sir Denzil Cope, 14th Bt; *S* father, 1961; *m* 1981, Dr Carolyn Elizabeth Highet, MB ChB, DRCOG, MRCGP (marr. diss. 2005), *d* of Dr John Highet, Glasgow; two *s*; *m* 2017, Helen Jane Dickinson (*née* Ramsay). *Educ:* St Conleth's Coll., Dublin; The Abbey Sch., Fort Augustus; Univ. of Glasgow (LLB 1981). Former deer-stalker, inshore fisherman. *Recreations:* professional competing piper, deerstalking, shooting. *Heir: s* Duncan Archibald Ludovic Grant, *b* 19 April 1982. *Address:* Tomintoul House, Flichity, Invernessshire IV2 6XD. *Club:* New (Edinburgh).

**GRANT, Patrick James;** fashion designer and tailor; Director, Norton & Sons, since 2005; Creative Director: E. Tautz, since 2008; Hammond & Co., since 2012; Director of Social Enterprise, Community Clothing, since 2016; *b* Edinburgh, 1 May 1972; *s* of James Gilbert Turner Grant and Susan Grant (*née* Fitzearle). *Educ:* Univ. of Leeds (BEng Materials Sci. and Engrg); Saïd Business Sch., Oxford Univ. (MBA 2005). Hon. Prof., Sch. of Business and Society, Glasgow Caledonian Univ., 2014. Judge: Great British Sewing Bee, BBC TV, 2013–16, 2019–; Village of the Year, Channel 4 TV, 2018. Co-Chair, Prince of Wales's charity Future Textiles, 2018–. Hon. DLitt Heriot-Watt, Sch. of Textiles and Design, 2017. *Publications:* Original Man, 2014. *Address:* c/o Norton & Sons, 16 Savile Row, W1S 3PL. *T:* (020) 7437 0829. *E:* patrick@etautz.com.

**GRANT, Prof. Patrick Spencer,** DPhil; FREng; Vesuvius (formerly Cookson) Professor of Materials, since 2004, Head, Department of Materials, since 2015, and Pro-Vice-Chancellor (Research), since 2018, University of Oxford; Fellow, St Catherine's College, Oxford, since 2004; *b* 24 Feb. 1966; *s* of Richard Arthur Grant and Ann Dorothy Grant (*née* Reynolds); *m* 1999, Dr Zena Louise Forster; two *s* one *d. Educ:* Univ. of Nottingham (BEng Metallurgy and Materials Sci. 1987); St Edmund Hall, Oxford (DPhil Materials 1991). University of Oxford: Department of Materials: Res. Asst, 1990–92; SERC Postdoctoral Fellow, 1992–94; Royal Soc. Res. Fellow, 1994–2002; Lectr, 2002–04; Dir, Oxford Centre for Advanced Materials and Composites, 1999–2004; Jun. Res. Fellow, Jesus Coll., 1993–95; Sen. Res. Fellow, Linacre Coll., 1995–2004. Dir, Faraday Advance, 2000–07. FREng 2010. *Publications:* papers on process-microstructure relationships and modelling of materials processing. *Recreations:* running, guitar. *Address:* Department of Materials, Oxford University, Parks Road, Oxford OX1 3PH. *T:* (01865) 283763, *Fax:* (01865) 848785. *E:* patrick.grant@materials.ox.ac.uk.

**GRANT, Sir Paul (Joseph Patrick),** Kt 2009; DL; Education Adviser, since 2017, and Executive Mentor, since 2014, Premier League; Consultant Headteacher, since 2017; *b* Liverpool, 16 May 1957; *s* of late Thomas Grant and Teresa Grant (*née* Walsh); *m* 1996, Deniece Jones; three *d. Educ:* Salesian Coll., Bootle; Hull Univ. (BA Hons Hist. 1978; Hon. Fellow 2011); Durham Univ. (PGCE 1979); Inst. of Educn, London Univ. (MA Educnl Mgt 1996). Teacher of history, Whitby Sch., 1979–87, exchange teacher, Australia, 1986; Hd of Hist., 1987–90, Hd of Year, 1989–90, Saint Bonaventures Sch.; Hd of Humanities and Sch. Professional Tutor, Robert Clack Sch., 1990–97; Headteacher, Robert Clack Sch., 1997–2017. Vis. Prof. of Educn, Anglia Ruskin Univ., 2012–; Consultant, Coventry Univ., 2019–. Member: Educn Bd, BITC, 2003–; Nat. Adv. Gp for History in the Curriculum, 2010–12; Educn Adv. Gp, FA Premier League, 2013–; England FA Educn Advr, 2017–. Mem., Senate Council, Hull Univ., 2014–17; Chair, Hull Univ. Alumni, 2014–. Nat. Leader of Educn, 2014. Freedom of Bor. of Barking and Dagenham, 2009. DL Gtr London, 2009. Hon. LLD Hull, 2011. *Publications:* Changing Times (with Kieran

Costello), 1990. *Recreations:* family life, music (popular to classical), hill walking, holidaying in France, reading (historical novels), sports (particularly Everton and Liverpool FC and Lancashire CC). *Address:* 35 Rutland Road, Wanstead, E11 2DY. *E:* pgrant100@btinternet.com.

**GRANT, Peter;** MP (SNP) Glenrothes, since 2015.

**GRANT, Peter David;** Senior Fellow, Agulhas Applied Knowledge, since 2010; *b* 31 May 1958; *s* of late Desmond John Noel Grant and of Judith Mary Grant; *m* 1985, Stella Elizabeth Lucy Flower; one *s* one *d*. *Educ:* King Edward VI Sch., Birmingham; St John's Coll., Cambridge (BA (Econs) 1980; MA); LSE (MSc Econs). Economist, Govt of Malawi (ODI Fellow), 1980–82; Consultant, Coopers & Lybrand Associates, 1983–86; Pricing Strategy Manager, British Telecom Internat., 1986–90; Overseas Development Administration, later Department for International Development: Economist, India, 1990–92; First Sec. (Econ.), Dhaka, 1992–96; Head: Internat. Econs Dept, 1996–98; Econ. Policy and Res. Dept, 1998–2000; Asia Policy Dept, and Dep. Dir, Asia, 2000–02; Dir, Internat., 2002–05; Internat. Dir, Tearfund, 2005–10; Co-Dir, Restored, 2010–18. Vis. Prof. in Internat. Develt Econs, Richmond Univ., 2014–. Co-Chm., OECD/DAC Poverty Reduction Network, 1999–2001. Mem., Council, Evangelical Alliance, 2008–14. *Publications:* Poor No More, 2008; The Ascent, 2017. *Recreations:* theology, travel, running. *Address:* Agulhas Applied Knowledge, 10E Branch Place, N1 5PH. *T:* 0333 700 0770. *E:* peter@agulhas.co.uk.

**GRANT, Prof. Peter John,** MD; FRCP, FRCPE, FESC, FMedSci; Professor of Medicine, since 2000, and Head, Division of Cardiovascular and Diabetes Research, since 1999, University of Leeds; Honorary Consultant Physician and Diabetologist, Leeds Acute NHS Trust, since 1989; *b* Brighton, 29 July 1952; *s* of John Grant and Joan Grant; *m* 1996, Penny Rice; two *s*, and two step *d*. *Educ:* Univ. of Bristol (MB ChB 1976; MD 1987); FRCP 1995; FRCPE 2003. FESC 2010. Médecin Asst Boursier, Central Hosp., Univ. Vaudois, Lausanne, 1988–89; University of Leeds: Sen. Lectr in Medicine, 1989–96; Prof. of Molecular Vascular Medicine, 1996–2000; Dir of Res., Faculty of Medicine and Health, 2000–04; Dir, Leeds Inst. of Genetics, Health and Therapeutics, 2004–05; Lead, Units of Assessments 1–3, 2001, Unit of Assessments 1, 2008, RAE. Co-Chm., EASD/ESC working party on cardiovascular risk, 2010–. FMedSci 2012. Ed.-in-Chief, Diabetes and Vascular Disease Res., 2004–. *Publications:* over 200 articles in scientific jls incl. Lancet, Circulation, Blood and Diabetes. *Recreations:* tennis, golf, music, walking. *Address:* Division of Cardiovascular and Diabetes Research, LIGHT Laboratories, Clarendon Way, University of Leeds, Leeds LS2 9JT. *T:* (0113) 343 7721, *Fax:* (0113) 343 7738. *E:* p.j.grant@leeds.ac.uk. *Clubs:* Sandmoor Golf, Alwoodley Golf.

**GRANT, Prof. Peter Mitchell,** OBE 2009; PhD; FRSE; FREng, FIEEE; Regius Professor of Engineering, University of Edinburgh, 2007–09, now Emeritus; *b* 20 June 1944; *s* of George Mitchell Grant and late Isobel Margaret (*née* Wilkinson); *m* 1974, Marjory Renz; two *d*. *Educ:* Heriot-Watt Univ. (BSc 1966); Univ. of Edinburgh (PhD 1975). FIET (FIEE 1988); FIEEE 1996; FRSE 1997; FREng 1997. Develt Engr, Plessey Co., 1966–70; Sen. Applications Engr, Hughes Microelectronics Ltd, 1970–71; University of Edinburgh: Res. Fellow, 1971–76; Lectr, 1976–82; Reader, 1982–87; Prof. of Electronic Signal Processing, 1987–2007; Hd, Dept of Electronics and Electrical Engrg, 1999–2002; Hd, Sch. of Engrg and Electronics, 2002–08. Vis. Prof., Stanford Univ., 1977–78; Vis. Staff Mem., MIT Lincoln Laboratory, 1985–86. Pres., European Assoc. for Signal Speech and Image Processing, 2000–02. Hon. DEng: Heriot-Watt, 2006; Napier, 2007. Faraday Medal, IEE, 2004. *Publications:* Digital Communications, 1998, 3rd edn 2009; Digital Signal Processing, 1999, 2nd edn 2003. *Address:* School of Engineering, University of Edinburgh, The King's Buildings, Mayfield Road, Edinburgh EH9 3JL. *Fax:* (0131) 650 6554. *E:* Peter.Grant@ed.ac.uk.

**GRANT, Prof. Peter Raymond,** FRS 1987; FRSCan 2003; Class of 1877 Professor of Zoology, Princeton University, 1989–2008, now Emeritus; *b* 26 Oct. 1936; *s* of late Frederick Thomas Charles and Mavis Irene Grant (later Matchett); *m* 1962, (Barbara) Rosemary Matchett (*see* Prof. B. R. Grant); two *d*. *Educ:* Whitgift Sch.; Selwyn Coll., Cambridge (BA Hons; Hon. Fellow, 2018); Univ. of British Columbia (PhD). Seessel-Anonymous Postdoctoral Fellow in Biology Dept of Yale Univ., 1964–65; Asst Prof. 1965–68, Associate Prof. 1968–73, Prof. 1973–78, McGill Univ.; Prof., Univ. of Michigan, 1977–85; Prof. of Biology, Princeton Univ., 1985–89. FLS 1986. Hon. PhD: Uppsala, 1986; Zürich, 2008; Hon. DSc: McGill, 2000; San Francisco, Quito, 2005; Ohio Wesleyan, 2012; Toronto, 2017. With B. R. Grant: Balzan Prize for Population Biol., Internat. Balzan Prize Foundn, 2005; Kyoto Prize, Inamori Foundn, 2009; Royal Medal, Royal Soc., 2017; Frontiers of Knowledge Award, BBVA Foundn, 2018. *Publications:* Ecology and Evolution of Darwin's Finches, 1986, 2nd ed 1999; with B. R. Grant: Evolutionary Dynamics of a Natural Population, 1989 (Wildlife Soc. Publication Award, 1991); How and Why Species Multiply, 2008; (ed) In Search of the Causes of Evolution: from field observations to mechanisms, 2010; 40 Years of Evolution, 2014; contribs to Science, Nature, Proc. Royal Society, Proc. Nat. Acad. of Scis (USA), etc. *Recreations:* walking, tennis, music. *Address:* Department of Ecology and Evolutionary Biology, Princeton University, Princeton, NJ 08544–1003, USA. *T:* (609) 2585156.

**GRANT, Piers;** *see* Grant, M. A. P.

**GRANT, Rhoda;** Member (Lab) Highlands and Islands, Scottish Parliament, 1999–2003 and since 2007; *b* 26 June 1963; *d* of Donald and Morag MacCuish; *m* 1989, (Christopher) Mark Grant. *Educ:* Open Univ. (BSc Hons Social Sci.). Administrator: Highland Regl Council, 1987–93; UNISON, 1993–99. Contested (Lab) Inverness E, Nairn and Lochaber, Scottish Parlt, 2003. Founder, Positive Politics, political advice consultancy, 2003. *Address:* Scottish Parliament, Edinburgh EH99 1SP.

**GRANT, Richard E.;** actor and writer; *b* 5 May 1957; *né* Richard Grant Esterhuysen; *m* 1986, Joan Washington; one *d*. *Educ:* Waterford-Kamhlaba, Swaziland; Univ. of Cape Town (BA English). *Films:* Withnail and I, 1986; How to Get Ahead in Advertising, 1988; Warlock, Killing Dad, Henry and June, 1989; LA Story, The Player, Hudson Hawk, 1990; Dracula, The Age of Innocence, 1991; Jack and Sarah, 1993; Prêt-à-Porter, 1994; Twelfth Night, Portrait of a Lady, 1995; Serpent's Kiss, 1996; Keep the Aspidistra Flying, 1997; Cold Light of Day, All for Love, The Match, 1998; Little Vampire, 1999; Gosford Park, 2002; Monsieur Napoleon, Bright Young Things, 2003; Tooth, Colour Me Kubrick, 2004; (writer and dir) Wah-Wah, Penelope, 2006; Filth and Wisdom, 2008; The Nutcracker, Love Hurts, 2009; Jackboots on Whitehall, Cuckoo, Foster, 2010; First Night, Last Fashion Show, Horrid Henry, Iron Lady, Kim and Kinderella, Zambezia, 2011; Dom Hemingway, 2013; Queen and Country, 2015; Jackie, Logan, Their Finest, The Hitman's Bodyguard, 2017; The Nutcracker and the Four Realms, 2018; Can You Ever Forgive Me?, 2019; *television:* Trial and Retribution, Scarlet Pimpernel, 1999; Young Sherlock Holmes, Hildegarde, 2000; Hound of the Baskervilles, 2002; Above and Beyond, 2005; Miss Marple: Nemesis, Dalziel and Pascoe, 2006; Mumbai Calling, 2008; The History of Safari, 2010; The Crimson Petal and the White, Rab C. Nesbitt, Rev, 2011; The Fear, 2012; Hotel Secrets, 2012, 2014; Dr Who, 2012–13; Girls, 2014; Downton Abbey, 2014; Wellington: the Iron Duke Unmasked, 2015; Jekyll and Hyde, 2015; Hang Ups, 2018; *theatre:* The Play What I Wrote, Wyndhams, 2002; Otherwise Engaged, Criterion, 2005; My Fair Lady, Sydney Opera, 2008; God of Carnage, nat. tour, 2009; My Fair Lady, Lyric Opera House, Chicago, 2017. *Publications:* With-Nails: film diaries, 1996; By Design: Hollywood novel, 1998; Wah-Wah: film diaries, 2006. *Recreation:* scuba diving. *Address:* c/o ARG, 4a Exmoor Street, W10 6BD. *T:* (020) 7436 6400.

**GRANT, Dr Richard Sturge;** Chairman, Arts Council of New Zealand, 2013–17; *b* 3 Nov. 1945; *s* of Sydney Wallace Grant and Eva Grant; *m* 1973, Cherrilyn Gaye Turnbull; two *d*. *Educ:* Victoria Univ. of Wellington (MA Hons); Univ. de Clermont-Ferrand (Dr d'Univ.). Department of External Affairs, Wellington, 1968; French Govt Scholar, 1968–70; NZ Embassy, Paris, 1971–75; Min. of Foreign Affairs, 1976–78; Counsellor and Dep. Head of Mission, Vienna, 1978–81; Consul-Gen., Noumea, 1982–85; Head, European Div., Min. of Foreign Affairs, 1985–86; Consul-Gen., Sydney, 1987–90; Ambassador, Bonn, 1990–94; Dir, Australia Div., Min. of Foreign Affairs, 1994–97; High Comr for NZ in the UK, 1997–99; Ambassador for NZ in France, 1999–2002; Dep. Sec., Min. of Foreign Affairs and Trade, NZ, 2002–04; High Comr for NZ in Singapore, 2004–08; Exec. Dir, Asia New Zealand Foundn, 2008–12. Visiting Scholar: John F. Kennedy Sch. of Govt, Harvard Univ., 1999; Oxford Internet Inst., Oxford Univ., 2004. *Recreations:* tennis, cricket, reading.

**GRANT, His Honour Rodney Arandall;** a Circuit Judge, 1995–2011; *b* 8 May 1944; *s* of Thomas and Olive Grant; *m* 2007, Catherine Jane Grimshaw. *Educ:* Leeds Grammar Sch.; Trinity Coll., Oxford (Minor Scholar; MA Mod. Langs). Called to the Bar, Inner Temple, 1970; NE Circuit, 1970–95; Head of Chambers, 1992–95; a Recorder, 1993–95. Mem., Adv. Panel, Rugby Football League, 2005–. *Recreations:* cookery, travel, jazz, reading, music. *Address:* c/o Circuit Administrator, 17th Floor, West Riding House, Albion Street, Leeds LS1 5AA.

**GRANT, Rosemary;** *see* Grant, B. R.

**GRANT, Lt-Gen. Sir Scott (Carnegie),** KCB 1999 (CB 1995); Chief Royal Engineer, 1999–2004; *b* 28 Sept. 1944; *s* of Maurice and Margaret Wotherspoon Gibb Grant; *m* 1973, Catharine Susan Pawsey; one *s* one *d*. *Educ:* Ray's Sch., Pontefract; RMA Sandhurst; Clare Coll., Cambridge (MA). Commissioned Royal Engineers, 1965; Regtl duty Aden, Sharjah, BAOR and UK, 1965–73; Instructor, RMA, 1973–74; student, Staff Coll., 1975–76; MoD, 1977–78; Sqn Comdr, BAOR, 1979–80; Instructor, Staff Coll., 1981–82; CO 26 Engineer Regt, 1982–84; MoD, 1985; SHAPE, 1986–87; Comdr, 33 Armoured Brigade, 1988–89; RCDS 1990; Army Member, Prospect Team, 1991; Dir Gen. of Army Trng, 1991–93; Team Leader, Army Command Structure Review, 1993; GOC, UK Support Comd (Germany), 1994–95; Comdt, RCDS, 1996–98; QMG, 1998–2000. Col, The Queen's Lancashire Regt, 1993–99; Colonel Commandant: King's Div., 1997–2001; RE, 1997–2004. Dir, Customer Support, 2001–04, Vice-Pres., Ops, 2004–07, Thales UK; non-exec. Dir, NAAFI, 2001–07 (Dep. Chm., 2006–07). *Recreations:* 20th Century art and literature, British orchids. *Clubs:* Army and Navy; Hawks (Cambridge).

**GRANT, Prof. Seth Garran Niels,** FMedSci; FRSE; Professor of Molecular Neuroscience, University of Edinburgh, since 2000; *b* Newcastle, Australia, 17 Feb. 1959; *m* Marguerite; two *d*. *Educ:* Knox Grammar Sch., Sydney, Australia; Univ. of Sydney (BSc Med. (Dist.) 1980; MB BS 1st Cl. Hons 1984). Scientist: Dept of Physiol., Univ. of Sydney, 1979; Royal Free Hosp., London, 1981, 1983; Resident MO, Royal Prince Alfred Hosp., Sydney, 1984; Postdoctoral Fellow, Cold Spring Harbor Lab., NY, 1985–89; Associate Res. Scientist, Howard Hughes Med. Inst., Columbia Univ., NY, 1989–92; Res. Scientist, NY State Psychiatric Inst., Columbia Univ., 1992–94; Sen. Scientist and Reader, Centre for Genome Res., 1994–2000, Dir, Centre for Neurosci., 1997–2002, Univ. of Edinburgh; Principal Investigator, Wellcome Trust Sanger Inst., Cambridge, 2003–11. John Cade Vis. Prof., Melbourne Univ., 2005; Vis. Prof., Univ. of Cambridge, 2007–; Hon. Prof., Florey Inst. for Neurosci. and Mental Health, Melbourne Univ., 2012–. Dir, Genes to Cognition Internat. Consortium, 2002–. MAE 2018. FRSE 2011; FMedSci 2015. Herbert Wilkinson Prize for Anatomy, John Irvine Hunter Prize for Medicine and Anatomy, Univ. of Sydney, 1977; Kenneth B. Meyer Award, Australia, 2014; Dist. Investigator Award, IBANGS, 2019; European Jl of Neurosci. Award, Fedn of Neurosci., 2020. *Publications:* contribs to jls incl. Nature, Science, Cell, Nature Neurosci., Neuron. *Address:* Centre for Clinical Brain Sciences, University of Edinburgh, Chancellor's Building, 49 Little France Crescent, Edinburgh EH16 4SB.

**GRANT, Sharon Margaret,** OBE 2014; consumer, service user and complaints specialist; *b* 28 Oct. 1952; *d* of Philip Arthur Lawrence and Margaret Theresa Lawrence; *m* 1998, Bernard Alexander Montgomery Grant, MP (*d* 2000). *Educ:* Tonbridge Girls' Grammar Sch.; Univ. of Birmingham (BSocSci Social Admin 1974, MSocSci Comparative Social Policy 1984). Campaigner on consumer and social equality issues, 1975–; Sen Lectr in Social Policy, Hatfield Polytechnic, 1977–87; Tutor and Examiner, Open Univ., 1984–87; Parly Sec. to late Bernie Grant, MP, 1987–2000; Chairman: Commn for Patient and Public Involvement in Health, 2003–08; London TravelWatch, 2008–12. Health Policy Advr to Rt Hon. Ann Clwyd, MP, 2013–. Food Standards Agency: Mem., Adv. Cttee on Consumer Engagement, 2007–13; Mem., Food Hygiene Regulation Steering Cttee, 2013–18. Councillor, London Bor. of Haringey, 1984–90. Founder and Sec., Bernie Grant Trust, 2000–; Director: Bernie Grant Centre Partnership Ltd, 2002–; Public Voice CIC, 2014– (Chm., 2014–). Mem. Bd, Dignity in Dying, 2008–11. Trustee and Dir, Consumers' Assoc., 2018–. Chairman: Haringey CAB, 2008–15; Healthwatch Haringey, 2013–. Member: Haringey Panel, post-riot enquiry, 2011–13; Ind. Adv. Gp, Metropolitan Police, Haringey, 2015–. *Recreations:* gardening, gym, travel, walking. *Club:* Conduit.

**GRANT, Theresa Noeleen;** Chief Executive, Northamptonshire County Council, since 2018; *b* Wexford, Ire., 18 Dec. 1961; *d* of James Black and Kathleen Black; partner, 1997, Richard Guy. *Educ:* Presentation Convent, Wexford; Manchester Metropolitan Univ. (MBA 2002). County Develt Officer, Wexford CC, 1978–96; Manchester CC, 1996–2009, on secondment as Villages Gen. Manager, Commonwealth Games, 2000–02; Dir of Transformation, 2002–09; Dep. Chief Exec., 2009–11, Chief Exec., 2011–18, Trafford MBC. Non-exec. Dir, John Laing Infrastructure Fund Ltd, 2016–18. Ambassador for Hallé Orch., 2018– (non-exec. Dir, 2012–18). Trustee, Irish Diaspora Foundn, 2004–18. *Recreations:* cycling, reading. *Address:* Northamptonshire County Council, One Angel Square, Angel Street, Northampton NN1 1ED. *T:* (01604) 365434. *E:* tgrant@northamptonshire.gov.uk.

**GRANT, Thomas Paul Wentworth;** QC 2013; *b* Colchester, 14 Aug. 1969; *s* of Neville James Henry Grant and Jane Wentworth Grant (*née* Gibbons); *m* 1999, Hester Xanthe Jane, *d* of Rt Hon. Sir Anthony James Denys McCowan, PC; one *s* two *d*. *Educ:* Colchester Royal Grammar Sch.; Univ. of Bristol (BA 1st Cl. Hons); City Univ. (DipLaw (Dist.)). Called to the Bar, Middle Temple, 1993; in practice as a barrister, 1994–, specialising in commercial chancery, fraud, property, professional negligence litigation. *Publications:* (Jt Gen. Ed.) Lender Claims, 2010; (contrib.) Solicitors' Negligence and Liability, 2012; Jeremy Hutchinson's Case Histories, 2015; (Jt Gen. Ed.) Civil Fraud: law, practice and procedure, 2018; Court Number One: the Old Bailey trials that defined modern Britain,

2019. *Recreations:* legal history, acting at The Old Bailey, gossip, hill-running, the 1890s. *Address:* Maitland Chambers, 7 Stone Buildings, Lincoln's Inn, WC2A 3SZ. *T:* (020) 7406 1200. *E:* tgrant@maitlandchambers.com. *Clubs:* Garrick, Beefsteak, Two Brydges.

**GRANT PETERKIN, Maj. Gen. (Anthony) Peter,** CB 2003; OBE 1990; Serjeant at Arms, House of Commons, 2005–07; *b* 6 July 1947; *s* of late Brig. James Grant Peterkin, DSO and Dorothea Grant Peterkin; *m* 1974, Joanna, *d* of Sir Brian Walter Mark Young; one *s* one *d*. *Educ:* Ampleforth; RMA Sandhurst; Durham Univ. (BA 1971); Madras Univ. (MSc 1980). Commnd Queen's Own Highlanders; ADC to CGS, 1973–74; Indian Staff Coll., 1980; Australian JSSC, 1986; CO, 1st Bn, 1987–89; MA to Mil. Sec., 1989–91; MA, UN Observer Mission, Iraq and Kuwait, 1991; Comdr, 24 Airmobile Bde, 1993–94; rcds, 1995; Dep. Mil. Sec., 1996–98; Sen. Directing Staff, RCDS, 1999; Man. Dir, OSCE Mission, Kosovo, April–Sept. 1999; GOC 5th Div., 2000; Mil. Sec., 2000–03. Chm., ACF, 2005–08. Chm., Global Vetting, 2009–10. Chairman: Saigon Children's Charity, 2000–07; Highlanders' Mus., Fort George, 2009–18; Bee House Educn Saigon, 2010–. Chm. Trustees, Queen's Own Highlanders, 2009–. *Recreations:* travelling in Indochina, football, Scottish Victorian art. *Address:* Grange Hall, Forres, Moray IV36 2TR. *Club:* Army and Navy (Chm., 2018–).

**GRANT-SUTTIE, Sir James (Edward);** *see* Suttie.

**GRANTCHESTER,** 3rd Baron *cr* 1953; **Christopher John Suenson-Taylor;** *b* 8 April 1951; *e s* (twin) of 2nd Baron Grantchester, CBE, QC and Betty, *er d* of Sir John Moores, CBE; *S* father, 1995; *m* 1973, Jacqueline (marr. diss.), *d* of Dr Leo Jaffé; two *s* two *d*. *Educ:* Winchester; LSE (BSc Econ). Elected Mem., H of L, 2003; an Opposition Whip, 2010–15; Labour spokesperson for DEFRA, 2013–15, for DECC, 2015–. *Heir: s* Hon. Jesse David Suenson-Taylor, *b* 6 June 1977. *Address:* Lower House Farm, Back Coole Lane, Audlem, Crewe, Cheshire CW3 0ER.

**GRANTHAM, Bishop Suffragan of,** since 2015; **Rt Rev. Nicholas Alan Chamberlain;** *b* Chiswick, 25 Nov. 1963; *s* of Alan Roger and Pauline Chamberlain. *Educ:* Christleton Co. High Sch., Chester; St Chad's Coll., Durham (BA 1985; PhD 1991); Univ. of Edinburgh (BD 1991). Ordained deacon, 1991, priest, 1992; Curate, St Mary's, Cockerton, Darlington, 1991–94; Curate, then Team Vicar, Gt Aycliffe, 1994–98; Priest-in-charge, St Barnabas, Burnmoor, and Officer for POT/CME, 1998–2006; Vicar, St George and St Hilda, Jesmond, 2006–15. *Recreations:* running, cycling, reading, good food. *Address:* Edward King House, Minster Yard, Lincoln LN2 1PU. *Club:* Northern Counties.

**GRANTLEY,** 8th Baron *cr* 1782; **Richard William Brinsley Norton;** Baron of Markenfield 1782; a Director, Project and Export Finance, HSBC Bank plc (formerly HSBC Investment Bank), 1997–2005; *b* 30 Jan. 1956; *er s* of 7th Baron Grantley, MC and of Lady Deirdre Freda Mary Hare (who *m* 2001, Ian Bayley Curteis, *qv*), *e d* of Earl of Listowel, GCMG, PC; *S* father, 1995. *Educ:* Ampleforth Coll.; New Coll., Oxford (Open Schol. in Maths; BA (Law), MA). Pres., Oxford Union Soc., 1976. Cons. Res. Dept, 1977–81; Morgan Grenfell & Co. Ltd, 1981–97; Dir, Morgan Grenfell Internat., 1994–97. Contested (C) Wentworth, 1983. Councillor, RBK&C, 1982–86. Leader, UKIP, H of L, 1997. Kt SMO Malta, 1981. *Recreations:* bridge, smoking. *Heir: b* Hon. Francis John Hilary Norton [*b* 30 Sept. 1960; *m* 2004, Eva, *d* of Mr and Mrs Elemér Figder, Budapest]. *Address:* 8 Halsey Street, SW3 2QH. *T:* (home) (020) 7589 7531. *Club:* Pratt's.

**GRANVILLE,** 6th Earl *cr* 1833; **Granville George Fergus Leveson Gower;** Viscount Granville 1815; Baron Leveson 1833; *b* 10 Sept. 1959; *s* of 5th Earl Granville, MC and Doon Aileen (*née* Plunket); *S* father, 1996; *m* 1997, Anne, *o d* of Bernard Topping; one *s* two *d*. *Heir: s* Lord Leveson, *qv*. *Address:* Callernish, Lochmaddy, Isle of N Uist, Western Isles HS6 5BZ.

**GRANVILLE-CHAPMAN, Gen. Sir Timothy (John),** GBE 2007 (CBE 1991); KCB 2001; Master Gunner, St James's Park, 2008–17; Director, Defence and National Rehabilitation Centre Programme, since 2009; *b* 5 Jan. 1947; *s* of Guy Granville-Chapman and Elsa Granville-Chapman (*née* Campbell); *m* 1971, Elizabeth Stevens; one *s* one *d*. *Educ:* Charterhouse; Christ's Coll., Cambridge (BA Law 1968; MA 1972). VSO, Tanzania, 1965. Commissioned RA, 1968; regtl duties, 1968–77; Staff Coll., 1978–79; MA to Comdr, 1st BR Corps, 1980–82; CO 1st Regt RHA, 1985–88; Higher Command and Staff Course, 1988; Mil. Doctrine Author, 1988; Policy Staff, MoD, 1989–90; Comdr 12th Armd Bde, 1990–93; Dir, Army Staff Duties, MoD, 1994; ACGS, MoD, 1994–96; Comdt, Jt Services Comd and Staff Coll., 1997–99; Adjutant Gen., 2000–03; C-in-C Land Comd, 2003–05; Vice Chief of the Defence Staff, 2005–09; ADC Gen. to the Queen, 2003–09. Col, Dorset Yeomanry, 1997–2008; Pres. and Col Comdt, HAC, 2003–10. Gov., Harrow Sch., 1997–2009. Hon. FKC 2010. *Recreations:* sailing, some country pursuits, architecture, clocks. *Address:* Artillery House, Royal Artillery Barracks, Larkhill, Salisbury, Wilts SP4 8QT.

**GRANZIOL, Dr Markus Johannes;** non-executive Chairman, Eurex, 2002–06 (non-executive Director, 1997–2006); *b* 21 Jan. 1952; *m* Manuela Fornera; one *s* three *d*. *Educ:* Univ. of Zurich (MA Econs; PhD Econs 1980). University of Zurich: res. analyst, Inst. for Empirical Res. in Econs, 1976–85; Lectr in Macroecons and Financial Theory, Dept of Juris. and Pol Sci., 1978–90; COS, Dept III, Swiss Nat. Bank, Zurich, 1985–87; Swiss Bank Corporation, 1987–98: Man. Dir and Hd, Securities Dept, 1987–94; Man. Dir, Hong Kong and Global Hd, Equities Business, 1994–95; Jt Global Hd, Equities Business, SBC Warburg, 1995–96 (also Mem. Exec. Bd and Investment Banking Bd); Gen. Manager and Mem., Gp Exec. Bd, 1996–98; Global Hd, Equities and Fixed Income, Warburg Dillon Read, 1998–99; CEO, 1999–2001, Chm., 2000–02, UBS Warburg; Mem., Gp Exec. Bd, UBS AG, 1999–2002. Non-exec. Mem. Bd, Zurich Financial Services, 2002–04; Incentive Asset Mgt, 2005. Vis. Schol., Grad. Sch. of Business Admin, Univ. of Chicago, 1981–82. *Publications:* contribs to scientific jls. *Recreations:* sports, piano.

**GRASSIE, Colin Steuart;** Chairman, Scottish Rugby Union, since 2017; *b* Glasgow, 9 June 1961; *s* of Alexander Grassie and Lilias Grassie; *m* 1991, Jorie Allen; four *s*. *Educ:* Fettes Coll., Edinburgh; Girton Coll., Cambridge (BA Law 1983; Barbara Bodichon Foundn Fellow). Grad. trainee, Samuel Montagu and Kleinwort Benson, 1983–86; J. P. Morgan and Co.: Trader of Fixed Income, Tokyo, 1986–91; Hd, Non US Fixed Income Sales USA, 1991–93; Hd, Fixed Income Sales Asia, Singapore, 1993–95; Deutsche Bank: Hd, Fixed Income Sales Asia Pacific, 1995–97; Hd, Fixed Income Sales Europe, 1997–2000; Hd, Global Mkts, Europe, 2003–05; Chief Executive Officer: Deutsche Bank Asia Pacific, 2005–09; Deutsche Bank UK, 2009–15. Vice Chm., Assoc. for Financial Mkts in Europe, 2003–05; Mem. Bd, Internat. Capital Mkt Assoc., Practitioner Panel, FCA. Chm., Trustees, Fettes Coll., Edinburgh. *Recreations:* triathlete, Ironman, Rugby. *Clubs:* Caledonian; Shek O Country (Hong Kong).

**GRATTAN-BELLEW, Sir Henry Charles,** 5th Bt *cr* 1838; *b* 12 May 1933; *s* of Lt-Col Sir Charles Christopher Grattan-Bellew, 4th Bt, MC, KRRC and Maureen Peyton, *niece* and adopted *d* of late Sir Thomas Segrave, Shenfield, Essex; *S* father, 1948; *m* 1st, 1956, Naomi Ellis (marr. diss. 1966; she *d* 2000); 2nd, 1967, Gillian Hulley (marr. diss. 1973; she *d* 2011); one *s* one *d*; 3rd, 1978, Elzabé Amy (*née* Body) (marr. diss. 1993), *widow* of John Westerveld, Pretoria, Tvl, SA. *Educ:* St Gerard's, Bray, Co. Wicklow; Ampleforth Coll., York. Publisher: Horse and Hound, SA, and Sustagen Supersport, 1977. Sports administrator, leading radio and TV commentator, hotelier, thoroughbred breeder and owner, author. *Publications:* A Pinch of Saltee, 2003; Sundown Safari, 2005; Mountbellew-Moylough: a pictorial memoir, 2010. *Heir: s* Patrick Charles Grattan-Bellew [*b* 7 Dec. 1971; *m* 2000, Liezel Wallis]. *Address:* 16 Ard Lorcain, Stillorgan, Co. Dublin, Ireland.

**GRATTON, Paul;** Director, SDL Surveying Ltd (formerly Direct Valuations Ltd), since 1989; Executive Chairman, SDL Group Services (formerly Shepherd Direct Ltd), since 2007; *b* 10 Nov. 1959; *s* of Robert and Audrey Gratton; *m* 1997, Elizabeth; three *s*. *Educ:* Nottingham High Sch. Various posts incl. mgt posts, Midland Bank plc, 1978–89; Financial Services Dir, First Direct, 1989–96; Ops Dir, Prudential Banking, 1996–98; Chief Operating Officer, Prudential Banking plc/Egg plc, 1998–2000; Dep. Chief Exec., 2000–01, CEO, 2001–06, Egg plc; Executive Chairman: Artilium (formerly Future Internet Technologies) plc, 2006–07 (non-exec. Dir, 2007–08); moneyQuest Mortgage Brokers. 2008–15. Non-exec. Dir, borro Ltd, 2010.

**GRATWICKE, Charles James Phillip; His Honour Judge Gratwicke;** a Circuit Judge, since 2003; Resident Judge, Chelmsford Crown Court, since 2012; *b* 25 July 1951; *s* of Phillip and Maeve Gratwicke; *m* 1981, Jane Vivien Meyer; two *s* one *d*. *Educ:* Franciscan Coll., Buckingham; St John's Coll., Southsea; Leeds Univ. (LLB Hons). Called to the Bar, Middle Temple, 1974; in practice as barrister, 1974–2003; a Recorder, 1998–2003; Hon. Recorder of Chelmsford, 2013–. Part-time Chairman, Disciplinary Committee: Potato Mktg Bd, 1990–2003; MMB, 1991–96. Hon. LLD BPP, 2016. *Recreations:* long distance walking, sailing, maritime matters, marine painting, London in all its forms and history, foreign travel, writing novels. *Address:* The Crown Court, New Street, Chelmsford, Essex CM1 1EL. *Clubs:* National Liberal; Seven Seas; Essex.

**GRAVENEY, David Anthony,** OBE 2006; Vice President, Professional Cricketers' Association, since 2003 (General Secretary, subseq. Chief Executive, 1994–2003); *b* 2 Jan. 1953; *s* of Ken Graveney and late Jeanne Graveney; *m* 1978, Julie Anne Smith Marriott; one *s* one *d*. *Educ:* Millfield Sch., Somerset. Gloucestershire CCC, 1972–90, Captain 1981–88; Somerset CCC, 1991; Durham CCC, 1992–94, Captain 1992–93. Treasurer, Professional Cricketers' Assoc., 1979–94. Manager: England cricket team, South Africa tour, 1990; England A team, Australia tour, 1996; England cricket team, One-Day series, Australia, 1998–99, and World Cup, 1999; Selector, England cricket team, 1995–96, Chm. of Selectors, 1997–2008; Nat. Performance Manager, ECB, 2008–. Mem., Exec. Bd, Gloucestershire CCC, 2013–16. *Recreations:* golf, watching Rugby. *Address:* 6 Southover Close, Westbury-on-Trym, Bristol BS9 3NG.

**GRAVES,** family name of **Baron Graves**.

**GRAVES,** 10th Baron *cr* 1794 (Ire.); **Timothy Evelyn Graves;** *b* 27 March 1960; *s* of 9th Baron Graves and of Marjorie Ann (*née* Holder), OAM; *S* father, 2002. *Heir:* none.

**GRAVES, Christopher James Mitchell;** Director, Tudor Trust, since 1986 (Project Officer, 1985–86); *b* 6 April 1956; *s* of Desmond James Turner Graves and late Mary Kathleen Graves, OBE (*née* Mitchell); *m* 1986, Amanda Patricia Mayhew; one *s* two *d*. *Educ:* Westminster Sch.; Queens' Coll., Cambridge (BA 1978, MA 1981, DipArch 1981). RIBA 1983. Architect, Trehearne, Norman, Preston & Partners, 1981–85. *Recreations:* watercolours, opera, singing, watching a failing football team. *Address:* Tudor Trust, 7 Ladbroke Grove, W11 3BD. *T:* (020) 7727 8522.

**GRAVES, Monica Irmela;** *see* Fogarty, M. I.

**GRAVES, Rev. Dr Peter Charles;** Minister, Wesley Methodist Church, Cambridge, and Methodist Chaplain to the Universities in Cambridge, 2000–08; *b* 23 March 1943; *s* of Walter and Eileen Graves; *m* 1976, Patricia Mary Campbell; two *s* one *d*. *Educ:* Handsworth Theol Coll., Birmingham; Union Theol Seminary, Virginia (ThM, DMin); London Univ. (Cert Ed). Minister: Enfield Circuit (St John's, Goffs Oak), 1968–69; Highgate Circuit (Holly Park), 1969–72; Chaplain and Associate Lectr, Enfield Coll. of Technol., 1969–72; Chaplain and Sen. Lectr, 1972–77, Sen. Chaplain and Hd of Student Welfare, 1977–79, Middlesex Poly.; Minister: Epsom, 1979–89; Cullercoats, 1989–95; Superintendent Minister, Methodist Central Hall, Westminster, 1995–2000. Interim Sen. Minister, Centenary Utd Methodist Church, Winston-Salem, N Carolina, 2009–11; Interim Minister, Histon Methodist Church, Cambridge, 2014–15. Methodist Tutor, North East Ordination Course, 1990–95; Tutor, Wesley Study Centre, Cranmer Hall, Durham, 1992–95; Chaplain to Methodist MPs and Leader, Methodist Parly Fellowship, 1995–2000. Finch Lectr, High Point Univ., NC, USA, 1997. Vice Pres., Bible Soc., 1998–2008. Chm. Judges, Times Preacher of the Year Award, 1998–2000. Broadcaster, Premier Radio, London, 1997–2008. *Publications:* Living and Praying the Lord's Prayer, 2002; contrib. New Daylight, 1997–2005. *Recreations:* travel, theatre, family life. *Address:* Old Ness Farm, Ness Road, Burwell, Cambridge CB25 0DB.

**GRAVES, Rupert;** actor; *b* Weston-super-Mare, 30 June 1963; *m* 2001, Susie Lewis; three *s* two *d*. *Educ:* Wyvern Comp. Sch. Early career in a circus; London theatrical début, King's Head, Islington; film actor, 1986–. *Theatre includes:* Torch Song Trilogy, Albery, 1985; The Importance of Being Earnest; Candida, 1988; 'Tis Pity She's a Whore, NT, 1988; A Madhouse in Goa, Lyric, Hammersmith, 1989; Les Enfants du Paradis, Barbican, 1996; Hurlyburly, Old Vic, transf. Queen's, 1997; The Iceman Cometh, Almeida, 1998; Closer, NY, 1999; The Caretaker, Comedy, 2000; The Elephant Man, NY, 2002; Dumb Show, Royal Court, 2004; The Exonerated, Riverside Studios, 2006; Pinter Five, Harold Pinter Th., 2018. *Films include:* A Room with a View, 1986; Maurice, 1987; A Handful of Dust, 1988; Where Angels Fear to Tread, 1991; Damage, 1992; The Madness of King George, 1994; Different for Girls, 1996; Intimate Relations, Mrs Dalloway, 1997; All My Loved Ones, 1999; Extreme Ops, 2003; Rag Tale, 2005; V for Vendetta, 2005; Intervention, 2006; Death at a Funeral, 2006; The Waiting Room, 2008; Made in Dagenham, 2010; Bone in the Throat, 2015; Swimming with Men, 2018; Horrible Histories: The Movie, 2019. *Television includes:* Fortunes of War, 1987; Open Fire, 1994; The Tenant of Wildfell Hall, 1996; Blonde Bombshell, 1999; The Forsyte Saga, 2002; Charles II: The Power and the Passion, 2003; Clapham Junction, The Dinner Party, 2007; God on Trial, 2008; Garrow's Law, 2009–11; Single Father, 2010; Sherlock (4 series), 2010–17; Case Sensitive, 2011; Scott & Bailey, 2011; Secret State, 2012; The White Queen, 2013; Turks & Caicos, Salting the Battlefield, 2014; Last Tango in Halifax, 2014; The Family, 2016. *Address:* c/o United Agents, 12–26 Lexington Street, W1F 0LE.

**GRAY;** *see* Pereira Gray.

**GRAY,** 23rd Lord *cr* 1445; **Andrew Godfrey Diarmid Stuart Campbell-Gray;** *b* 3 Sept. 1964; *s* of 22nd Lord Gray and Patricia Margaret (*née* Alexander); *S* father, 2003; *m* 1993, Hon. Lucy, *y d* of 2nd Baron Elton, *qv*; one *s* one *d*. *Heir: s* Master of Gray, *qv*.

**GRAY, Master of;** Hon. **Alexander Godfrey Edward Diarmid Campbell-Gray;** *b* 7 Oct. 1996; *s* and *heir* of Lord Gray, *qv*.

**GRAY, Alasdair James**; self-employed verbal and pictorial artist; b 28 Dec. 1934; s of Alexander Gray and Amy (née Fleming); m 1st, 1961, Inge Sørensen (marr. diss.); one s; 2nd, 1991, Morag McAlpine (d 2014). Educ: Glasgow Sch. of Art (Scottish Educn Dept Dip. in mural painting and design); Jordanhill Teachers' Trng Coll. (CertEd). Part-time teacher and painter, 1958–62; theatrical scene painter, 1962–63; social security scrounger, 1963–64; painter and playwright, 1965–76 (8 one-man exhibns, two retrospective; 17 TV and radio plays broadcast; 4 plays staged); Glasgow's official artist-recorder for People's Palace local history mus., 1977; Writer-in-Residence, 1977–79, Consulting Prof. of Creative Writing, 2001–03, Glasgow Univ.; mural decorator, Oran Mór, Glasgow, 2003; one-man show, Talbot Rice Gall., Edinburgh, 2010; exhibition: Alasdair Gray: City Recorder, Gall. of Modern Art, Glasgow, 2011; Spheres of Influence I, Gall. of Modern Art, Glasgow, 2015. Collections of paintings owned by: Collins Gall., Strathclyde Univ.; People's Palace local history mus., Glasgow Green; Hunterian Gall., Glasgow Univ.; personal archives lodged with Nat. Liby of Scotland, Edinburgh. Publications: novels: Lanark, 1981; 1982 Janine, 1984; The Fall of Kelvin Walker, 1985; Something Leather, 1990; McGrotty and Ludmilla, 1990; Poor Things, 1992; A History Maker, 1994; Old Men in Love, 2007; short story collections: Unlikely Stories Mostly, 1983; (with J. Kelman and A. Owens) Lean Tales, 1985; Ten Tales Tall and True, 1993; Mavis Belfrage, 1996; The Ends of Our Tethers: thirteen sorry stories, 2003; Every Short Story 1952–2012, 2012; poetry: Old Negatives, 1989; Sixteen Occasional Poems, 2000; Collected Verse, 2010; Hell: Dante's Divine Comedy Part One: decorated and Englished in prosaic verse, 2018; Guts Minced with Oatmeal: ten late poems, 2018; plays: Working Legs (a play for people without them), 1997; Fleck (verse comedy), 2008; A Gray Play Book, 2009 (collection of plays); non-fiction: Saltire Self-Portrait no 4 (autobiog.), 1989; (ed) The Book of Prefaces, 2000; A Short Survey of Classic Scots Writing, 2001; A Life in Pictures, 2010; Some of Me and Others: a life in prose (autobiog.), 2014; polemics: Why Scots Should Rule Scotland, 1992; Why Scots Should Rule Scotland, 1997; (with A. Tomkins) How We Should Rule Ourselves, 2005; Independence, 2014.

**GRAY, Sir Bernard Peter**, Kt 2015; Executive Chairman, Time Inc. (UK) Ltd, since 2018; b Redhill, Surrey, 6 Sept. 1960; s of Peter and Angela Gray; m 2010, Kathryn Anne Rowbotham; one d. Educ: Hitchin Boys Sch.; Hertford Coll., Oxford (MA Hons). Investment banker, Bankers Trust and Chase Manhattan, 1983–88; FT Group, 1988–97: Dep. Editor, Investors Chronicle, 1989–92; Lex Columnist, FT, 1992–94; Defence Correspondent, FT, 1994–97; Special Advr to Sec. of State for Defence, 1997–99; Strategy Dir, UBM, 1999–2001; CEO, CMP Information, 2001–05; CEO, then Chm., TSL Educn, 2005–11; Chief of Defence Materiel, MoD, 2011–15. Owner, Pole Star Strategy Ltd, 2015–; owner and Exec. Chm., New Scientist Ltd, 2017–. Non-exec. Dir, Cable & Wireless plc, 2003–06; Sen. Advr, McKinsey & Co., 2017–. Publications: Beginners' Guide to Investment, 1991, 2nd edn 1993. Recreations: cinema, opera, motor sport. Clubs: h, Ivy.

**GRAY, Bethan Heulwen**; Creative Director, Bethan Gray Design, since 2009; b Cardiff, 14 March 1976; d of Michael Gray and Teleri Gray (née Jarman); m 2010, Massimo Giorgione; one s. Educ: Glantaf Sch., Cardiff; Coll. of Higher Educn, Gwent (Dip. Foundn Studies Art and Design); De Montfort Univ., Leicester (BA Hons Three Dimensional Design specialising in Furniture Design). Hd, Furniture Design, Habitat, 2000–09. Lectr, Central Saint Martins, 2011–13. Trends Consultant, Stylus Media Gp, 2011–13. Hon. Fellow, Cardiff Metropolitan Univ. New Designers Award, Habitat Innovation Awards, 1998; Best in Kitchen Award, 2005, Best British Designer, 2013, Best British Designer for Tableware, 2018, ELLE Decoration British Design Awards. Recreations: yoga, travelling, gardening. Address: Bethan Gray Design, 116 Great Western Studios, 65 Alfred Road, W2 5EU. T: (020) 3214 3150. E: info@bethangray.com.

**GRAY, Brian James**; Chair, Audit Committee: European Council, since 2018; Fusion For Energy, since 2018; ITER, since 2018; b Wellington, India, 12 March 1946; s of John Alan Gray and Doreen Nelly Gray (née Service); m 1967, Gillian Anne Lydon (marr. diss. 2004); one s two d; partner, Christina Borchmann; one s one d. Educ: Woking Grammar Sch. FCA 1973. Audit manager, London and Zambia, Deloitte, Haskins and Sells, 1973–78; Auditor, Eur. Court of Auditors, 1978–91; European Commission: Hd, audit of CAP, 1992–99; Dir, Regl Fund resources, 1999–2002; Chief Financial Officer, 2003–09; Dir-Gen., Internal Audit Service, and Internal Auditor, 2009–12. Consultant on accounting and audit in internat. public sector, 2012–17. Publications: articles in accounting and auditing jls. Recreations: horse-riding, ski-ing, bridge, snooker, defending the European Union. Address: Avenue des Chalets 5, 1180 Brussels, Belgium. T: 47 7284891. E: briangray2012@gmail.com.

**GRAY, Bryan Mark**, CBE 2009 (MBE 2001); DL; Pro Chancellor, Lancaster University, 2003–13; Director: Westmorland Ltd, 2005–18 (Chairman, 2005–17); Chapel Beck Ltd, since 2018; b 23 June 1953; s of late Clifford Benjamin Gray and June Mary Gray; m 1976, Lydia Ann Wallbridge; three s. Educ: Wath-upon-Dearne Grammar Sch.; Univ. of York (BA (Chemistry) 1974). Joined ICI, 1974; commercial appointments: Sales Office, Birmingham; ICI Petrochemicals and Plastics Div., Wilton; ICI Films and ICI Advanced Materials, Welwyn Garden City; Man. Dir, EVC Compounds Ltd, 1989–93; Commercial Dir, 1993, Chief Exec., 1994–2000, Baxi Partnership; Dep. Chm., Baxi Gp Ltd, 2000–04; Chm., Baxi Technologies, 2001–08. Chairman: Urban Splash Hotels, 2006–09; Peel Media Gp Ltd, 2008–11; non-exec. Dir, United Utilities Water plc, 2008–09. Chm., NW Develt Agency, 2002–09. Chairman: NW Reg., CBI, 2000–02; Central Heating Inf. Council, 2000–03; Mem., LSC, 2004–09. Pres., Soc. of British Gas Industries, 2000–01; Vice President: European Heating Industries Assoc., 2002–04; Micropower Council, 2005–08. Founder Chm., Nat. Football Mus., 1995–2001; Board Member: NW Cultural Consortium, 2003–08; Liverpool Culture Co. Ltd, 2003–09; Adv. Bd, Nat. Rlwy Mus., 2011–18; Trustee, Nat. Mus. Liverpool, 2004–12; Mem., Lake Dist Nat. Park Authy, 2006–14. Chairman: Churches Trust in Cumbria, 2008–15; Lowther Castle and Gardens Trust, 2008–; Cumbria County History Trust, 2010–; Cumbria Bldgs Preservation Trust, 2012–; Settle Carlisle Line Assoc., 2014–; Settle and Carlisle Rlwy Trust, 2017–. Chm., Preston Post Grad. Med. Centre, 1996–2004; Gov., Univ. of Central Lancashire, 1999–2002. Hon. Prof., Dept of Built Envmt, Univ. of Nottingham, 2003–. Vice Patron, Deafway, 2002–13. Reader, C of E, various dios, 1981– (Carlisle Dio., 2009–); Lay Canon and Mem. Chapter, Carlisle Cathedral, 2014–. FRSA. DL 2002–10, High Sheriff, 2003–04, Lancs; DL Cumbria, 2010. Hon. LLD Lancaster, 2018. Recreations: heritage, Midland Railway, scrapbooks, Preston North End. Address: c/o Westmorland Ltd, Tebay, Cumbria CA10 3SB. E: bryangray@bryangray.co.uk. Club: Preston North End Football (Chm., 1994–2001, Vice Pres., 2001–).

**GRAY, Charles**; see Gray, J. C. R.

**GRAY, Hon. Sir Charles (Antony St John)**, Kt 1998; a Judge of the High Court, Queen's Bench Division, 1998–2008; b 6 July 1942; s of late Charles Herbert Gray and Catherine Margaret Gray; m 1st, 1968, Rosalind Macleod Whinney (marr. diss. 1990); one s one d; 2nd, 1995, Susan Astor (née Eveleigh) (d 1997); 3rd, 2001, Cynthia Elizabeth Selby. Educ: Winchester; Trinity College, Oxford (scholar; Hon. Fellow 2003). Called to the Bar, Lincoln's Inn, 1966, Bencher, 1991; QC 1984; a Recorder, 1990–98; arbitrator/mediator, 2008–16. Comr, Royal Court of Jersey, 2011–16. Recreations: travel, music, tennis, ski-ing, gardening. Address: Hunter's Rise, 15 Leydene Park, East Meon, Hants GU32 1HF. Club: Brooks's.

**GRAY, Sir Charles (Ireland)**, Kt 2007; CBE 1994; JP; Member, North Lanarkshire Council, 1995–2007 (Chairman, Education Committee, 1995–2007); b 25 Jan. 1929; s of Timothy Gray and Janet (née Brown); m 1952, Catherine Creighton Gray; three s two d. Educ: Coatbridge. Dept of Public Affairs, Scotrail, 1946; Mem. (later Chm.), Lanark DC, 1958–64; Mem., Lanark CC, 1964–75; founder Mem., 1975–96, first Vice-Convener, and Leader, 1986–92, Strathclyde Regl Council. Leader, UK delegn to Euro Cttee of the Regions, 1994–98. Pres., Convention of Scottish Local Authorities, 1992–94. Member: Scottish Exhibn and Conf. Centre, 1986–91; Scottish Enterprise Bd, 1990–93. Trustee, AgeScotland, 2007–12. FEIS 2005. JP Strathclyde, 1970. Recreations: music, reading, politics. Address: 9 Moray Place, Chryston G69 9LZ. T: (0141) 779 2962.

**GRAY, Christopher Mark**, FRCO; Director of Music, Truro Cathedral, since 2008; b Bangor, NI, 2 June 1978; s of Denis and Anne Gray. Educ: Pembroke Coll., Univ. of Cambridge (BA 1999); Royal Coll. of Music (Dip. 2000). FRCO 2005. Organ Scholar, Guildford Cathedral, 1999–2000; Asst Dir of Music, Truro Cathedral, 2000–08. Recreation: surfing. Address: Truro Cathedral, The Old Cathedral School, Truro, Cornwall TR1 2FQ. T: (01872) 276782. E: christophergray@trurocathedral.org.uk.

**GRAY, David**; see Gray, J. N. D.

**GRAY, David John**; Chairman, Eversheds International, 2009–13; Pro-Chancellor and Chair of Council, University of Leeds, since 2013; b 9 Jan. 1955; s of Allan and Vena Gray; m 1984, Julie Sergeant. Educ: Magdalene Coll., Cambridge (BA (Law) 1976; MA). Admitted solicitor, 1979; Equity Partner, Hepworth and Chadwick, 1982; Eversheds: Hd of Corporate, Leeds and Manchester, 1995–98; Dep. Managing Partner, Leeds and Manchester, and Head of Corporate, 1998–2000; Managing Partner, Leeds and Manchester, 2000–03; Managing Partner, later CEO, 2003–09. Non-exec. Dir, DWF plc, 2013–18; Consultant, Eversheds-Sutherland, 2018–. Recreations: golf, National Hunt racing, football. Address: University of Leeds, Leeds LS2 9JT. Clubs: Alwoodley Golf; Ganton Golf; Liverpool Football.

**GRAY, Rev. Canon Dr Donald Clifford**, CBE 1998; TD 1970; Canon of Westminster and Rector of St Margaret's, Westminster Abbey, 1987–98, Canon Emeritus, since 1998; Chaplain to the Queen, 1982–2000; Chaplain to the Speaker, House of Commons, 1987–98; b 21 July 1930; s of Henry Hackett Gray and Constance Muriel Gray; m 1955, Joyce (née Jackson) (d 2010); one s two d. Educ: Newton Heath Technical High Sch.; King's Coll., London and Warminster (AKC); Univ. of Liverpool (MPhil); Univ. of Manchester (PhD). Curate, Leigh Parish Church, 1956–60; Vicar: St Peter's, Westleigh, 1960–67; All Saints', Elton, Bury, 1967–74; Rector of Liverpool, 1974–87; RD of Liverpool, 1975–81; Canon Diocesan of Liverpool, 1982–87. Proctor-in-Convocation for Manchester, 1964–74; Mem., Gen. Synod, 1980–87. President: Soc. for Liturgical Study, 1998– (Chm., 1978–84); Societas Liturgica, 1987–89 (Treas., 1981–87); Mem., Liturgical Commn, 1968–86; Chm., Jt Liturgical Gp, 1989–94 (Mem., 1969–96; Sec., 1980–89); Mem., Cathedrals Fabric Commn, 1991–96. Chairman: Liverpool Luncheon Club, 1981–82; Alcuin Club, 1987–2015 (Vice Pres., 2015–). CF (TA), 1958–67; CF (T&AVR), 1967–77; QHC, 1974–77. FRHistS 1988; FSA 2007. KStJ 2003. Publications: (contrib.) Worship and the Child, 1975; (contrib.) Getting the Liturgy Right, 1982; (contrib.) Liturgy Reshaped, 1982; (ed) Holy Week Services, 1983; Earth and Altar, 1986; (ed) The Word in Season, 1988; (contrib.) Towards Liturgy 2000, 1989; (contrib.) Liturgy for a New Century, 1990; Chaplain to Mr Speaker, 1991; Ronald Jasper: his life, his work and the ASB, 1997; (contrib.) They Shaped Our Worship, 1998; All Majesty and Power: royal prayers, 2000; Percy Dearmer, 2000; Memorial Services, 2002; (contrib.) Liturgy in a Postmodern World, 2003; (contrib.) St Paul's: the Cathedral Church of London, 2004; (contrib.) Oxford DNB, 2004; (contrib.) Strengthen For Service, 2005; (contrib.) Liturgical Renewal as a Way to Christian Unity, 2005; The 1927–28 Prayer Book Crisis, part i, 2005, part ii, 2006; (contrib.) The Oxford Handbook of English Literature & Theology, 2007; (contrib.) The Collect in the Reformed Tradition, 2010. Recreations: watching cricket, reading modern poetry. Address: 3 Barn Hill Mews, Stamford, Lincs PE9 2GN. T: (01780) 765024. Clubs: Army and Navy; Athenæum (Pres., 1983–84), Artists' (Liverpool).

**GRAY, George Thomas Alexander**, CB 2018; First Legislative Counsel for Northern Ireland, 1996–2012; b 20 Jan. 1949; s of George Gray and Eveline Gray; m 1985, Mary Louise Gray; two s. Educ: Annadale Grammar Sch., Belfast; The Queen's University of Belfast (LLB 1st Cl. Hons). Called to the Bar of N Ireland; Draftsman, 1971–88, Second Legislative Counsel, 1988–96, Office of the Legislative Counsel for NI. Recreation: cricket.

**GRAY, (Hamish) Martin (Vincent)**; Chairman: The Evolution Group plc, 2005–11; National Savings & Investments, 2009–11 (Director, 2005–11); b 8 June 1946; s of Kenneth Dunwell Gray and Helen McGeorge Gray; m; two s; m 2nd, 1992, Alison Margaret Wells. Educ: Cockburn High Sch., Leeds; Harvard Business Sch. (AMP 1987). FCIB. Appts with National Westminster Bank, 1963–99; Head of Group Planning, Business Develt Div., 1986–88; Asst Gen. Manager, Group Develt, 1988–89; Gen. Manager, UK Branch Business, 1990–92; Chief Exec., UK Br. Business, later NatWest UK, 1992–98; Exec. Dir, Retail and Commercial Businesses and Main Bd Dir, 1993–99. Mem., Global Bd, Mastercard Inc., 1993–96; Dir, Visa Europe, 1996–99. Chm., Mktg Adv. Cttee, England and Wales Cricket Bd, 2000–03. Recreations: walking, gardening, cricket. Address: Wethered Park, Marlow, Bucks SL7 2BH.

**GRAY, Prof. Hanna Holborn**, PhD; President, University of Chicago, 1978–93, now President Emeritus (Harry Pratt Judson Distinguished Service Professor of History, 1993–2000, now Emeritus); b 25 Oct. 1930; d of Hajo and Annemarie Holborn; m 1954, Charles Montgomery Gray (d 2011). Educ: Bryn Mawr Coll., Pa (BA); Univ. of Oxford (Fulbright Schol.); Univ. of Harvard (PhD). Instructor, Bryn Mawr Coll., 1953–54; Harvard University: Teaching Fellow, 1955–57, Instr, 1957–59, Asst Prof., 1959–60, Vis. Lectr, 1963–64; Asst Prof., Univ. of Chicago, 1961–64, Associate Prof., 1964–72; Dean and Prof., Northwestern, Evanston, Ill, 1972–74; Provost, and Prof. of History, Yale Univ., 1974–78, Acting Pres., 1977–78. Hon. degrees include: LHD: Duke, 1982; Brandeis, 1983; Amer. Coll. of Greece, 1986; Univ. of Chicago, 1996; LLD: Dartmouth Coll., Yale, 1978; Brown, 1979; Rochester, Notre Dame, 1980; Michigan, 1981; Princeton, 1982; Georgetown, 1983; Columbia, 1987; Toronto, 1991; Harvard, 1995; DLaws Pontifical Inst. of Mediaeval Studies, Toronto, 2005; DLitt: Oxford, 1979; Washington, 1985; DSc: Rockefeller, 2010; Cold Spring Harbor, 2015. Charles Frankel Prize, 1993; Jefferson Medal, Amer. Philosophical Soc., 1993; Centennial Medal, Harvard Univ., 1994; Dist. Service Award in Educn, Inst. of Internat. Educn, 1994; Fritz Redlich Dist. Alumni Award, Internat. Inst. of Educn, 2004; Gold Medal, Nat. Inst. of Social Scis, 2006; Newberry Liby Award, Chicago, 2006; Chicago History Maker Award, Chicago Hist. Mus., 2008. Medal of Liberty (USA), 1986; Presidential Medal of Freedom (USA), 1991. Publications: ed (with Charles M. Gray) Jl Modern History, 1965–70; Searching for Utopia, 2011; An Academic

Life, 2018; articles in professional jls. *Address:* (office) 1126 E 59th Street, Chicago, IL 60601, USA. *T:* (630) 3997200. *Clubs:* Quadrangle (Chicago); Cosmopolitan (New York City).

**GRAY, Huon Hamilton,** CBE 2019; MD; FRCP; MACC; FESC; National Clinical Director for Heart Disease, NHS England, 2013–19; *b* Liverpool, 6 Oct. 1954; *s* of late Tom Douglas, (Tony), Gray and of Kathleen Elizabeth Craig Gray; *m* 2004, Marion Slevin; two *s. Educ:* Shrewsbury Sch.; St Thomas's Hosp. Med. Sch., Univ. of London (MB BS 1977; MD 1986). FRCP 1994; FESC 1997; FACC 1999, MACC 2018. Consultant Cardiologist, Univ. Hosp. of Southampton, 1989–. Dep. Nat. Clin. Dir for Heart Disease, DoH, 2007–13. Hon. Civilian Clin. Advr to Army, 2008–16. Hon. Professor: QMUL, 2010–; UCL, 2012–. Pres., British Cardiac Soc., 2003–05. Trustee, Amer. Coll. of Cardiol., 2012–16. Trustee, Wessex Heartbeat, 1990–2012. *Publications:* over 150 articles in jls on cardiol. and health service delivery. *Recreations:* wine appreciation, ski-ing, sailing. *Address:* c/o Wessex Cardiology, Spire Southampton Hospital, Southampton SO16 6UY. *T:* (023) 8076 4333. *E:* huon@mac.com. *Clubs:* Royal Over-Seas League, 67 Pall Mall.

**GRAY, Iain Cumming;** Member (Lab) East Lothian, Scottish Parliament, since 2007; *b* Edinburgh, 7 June 1957; *s* of Robert and Catherina Gray; *m* 1997, Gillianne (née McCormack); one *d*, and two step *d. Educ:* Inverness Royal Acad.; Edinburgh Univ. (BSc Hons). Physics teacher: Gracemount High Sch., Edin., 1978–82; Escola Agrária, Chokwe, Mozambique, 1982–83; Inveralmond High Sch., Livingston, 1983–86; Campaigns Manager, OXFAM, Scotland, 1986–99. MSP (Lab) Edinburgh Pentlands, 1999–2003; contested same seat, 2003; Scottish Executive: Deputy Minister: for Community Care, 1999–2000; for Justice, 2000–01; Minister: for Social Justice, 2001–02; for Enterprise, Transport and Lifelong Learning, 2002–03. Leader, Scottish Labour Party, 2008–11. Special Advr to Sec. of State for Scotland, 2003–07. *Recreations:* football (season ticket, Hibernian FC), reading, hill-walking. *Address:* Scottish Parliament, Edinburgh EH99 1SP.

**GRAY, Prof. Iain Gilmour,** CBE 2014; CEng, FREng; FRAeS; FRSE; Professor and Director, Aerospace, Cranfield University, since 2015; *b* Manchester, 22 March 1957; *s* of Alexander William and Mary Bulloch Gray; *m* 1980, Rhona May Gammack; three *s* one *d. Educ:* Aberdeen Grammar Sch.; Aberdeen Univ. (BSc Eng. Hons); Southampton Univ. (MPhil). CEng 1985; FRAeS 1998; FREng 2008. Engr, British Aerospace, 1979–2007, Man. Dir, Airbus UK, 2004–07; Chief Exec., Technol. Strategy Bd, later Innovate UK, 2007–14. Non-exec. Dir, Versarien, 2016–. Member, Board: SEMTA (formerly Sector Skills Council for Sci., Engrg and Manuf. Technols), 2005–17; EngineeringUK (formerly Engrg and Technol. Bd), 2008–14; Vice Pres., Royal Acad. of Engrg, 2017–. Gov., UWE, 2006–14; Mem. Council, City Univ. London, 2013–19. Chm., Bristol Aero Collection Trust, 2012–. Mem., Co. of Engrs, 2008. FRSE 2011 (Vice Pres., 2016–19). Hon. Fellow, Cardiff Univ., 2012. Hon. DEng: Bath, 2005; Bristol, 2006; Exeter 2012; UWE, 2017; Hon. DSc: Aberdeen, 2007; Aston, 2011. Gold Medal, RAeS, 2007. *Recreations:* walking, ski-ing, stamp collecting, friends and family, travelling. *Address:* Cranfield University, Aerospace Building 83, Cranfield, Beds MK43 0AL. *T:* (01234) 750111. *E:* I.gray@cranfield.ac.uk.

**GRAY, Irene Elizabeth;** Director, IreneGray.co.uk, since 2012; executive coach, since 2014; *b* 1 Oct. 1954; *d* of Bernard and Eileen Rowlinson; *m* 1984, George Scott (marr. diss.); two *s*; *m* 2009, Malcolm Gray. *Educ:* S Manchester HA (RN); Nottingham Univ. (MSc). Level 7 coach, ILM. Ward Sister, 1976–83, Dep. Dir of Nursing, 1983–86, Withington Hosp., Manchester; Director of Nursing: Christie Hosp., Manchester, 1986–94; Leicester Royal Infirmary, 1994–99; Regl Dir of Nursing, W Midlands NHS Exec., 1999–2001; Dir of Nursing, Guy's Hosp. and St Thomas' Hosp., 2001–04; CEO, Nurse Dirs Assoc. UK, 2004–05; Dir of Nursing, Surrey and Sussex Healthcare NHS Trust, 2005–08; Chief Operating Officer, University Hosps of Bristol NHS Foundn Trust, 2008–10; Dir of Care, Southern Cross Healthcare plc, 2010–11; Interim Dir of Nursing, 2012–13, Professional Advr, 2013–, Weston Area Health NHS Trust. Non-exec. Dir, Forest Healthcare, 2014–; Sen. Associate, IMD Consulting, 2012–17. Vis. Prof. of Nursing, De Montfort Univ., 1992–2003; Hon. Professor of Nursing: Wolverhampton Univ., 2000–; South Bank Univ., 2002–; KCL, 2002–. Trustee and Dir, Royal Hosp. for Neurol Diseases, 2001–07; Trustee, Future Care Capital, 2017–. *Publications:* (with W. Bishop) Challenges in Clinical Practice, 2000. *Recreations:* gardening, keep fit, reading for relaxation. *Address:* The Old Vicarage, 2 Queens Road, Weston-super-Mare, N Som BS23 2LG. *E:* irene@irenegray.co.uk.

**GRAY, (James Northey) David;** Principal, Brummana High School, Beirut, Lebanon, since 2019; *b* 30 April 1955; *s* of Baron Gray of Contin, PC; *m* (marr. diss.); one *s* two *d*; *m* 2009, Marie-Helene Gray. *Educ:* Fettes Coll.; Univ. of Bristol (BA Hons; PGCE). English teacher, Henbury Sch., Bristol, 1978–80; Partner, Key Lang. Sch., Athens, 1980–85; teacher, English and Modern Greek, Dulwich Coll., 1985–88; Hd of English, Leeds GS, 1988–92; Headmaster, Pocklington Sch., E Yorks, 1992–2000; Principal, Erskine Stewart's Melville Schs (Stewart's Melville (formerly Daniel Stewart's and Melville's) Coll. and Mary Erskine Sch.), Edinburgh, 2000–18. *Recreations:* cricket, golf, cross-country running, music, Anglo-Saxon literature, Balkan current affairs. *E:* principal@bhs.edu.lb.

**GRAY, James Whiteside;** MP (C) North Wiltshire, since 1997; *b* 7 Nov. 1954; *s* of Very Rev. John Rodger Gray, VRD, sometime Moderator, Gen. Assembly of C of S, and of Dr Sheila Gray (née Whiteside); *m* 1st, 1980, Sarah Ann Beale (marr. diss. 2007); two *s* one *d*; 2nd, 2009, Philippa Gay Mayo (née Keeble); one step *s* two step *d. Educ:* Hillhead Primary Sch., Glasgow; Glasgow High Sch.; Glasgow Univ. (MA Hons); Christ Church, Oxford. Grad. mgt trainee, P&O, 1977–78; Shipbroker, Anderson Hughes & Co., 1978–84; Mem., Baltic Exchange, 1978–91, 1997–; Dir, Baltic Futures Exchange, 1989–91; Man. Dir, GNI Freight Futures, 1985–92; Special Advr to Sec. of State, DoE, 1992–95; Dir, Westminster Strategy Ltd, 1995–97. Dep. Chm., Wandsworth Tooting Cons. Assoc., 1994–96. Contested (C) Ross, Cromarty and Skye, 1992. An Opposition Whip, 2000–01; Opposition front bench spokesman on defence, 2001–02, on countryside, 2002–05; Shadow Sec. of State for Scotland, 2005. Member, Select Committee: on Envmtl Affairs, 1997–2000; on DEFRA, 2007–10; on Finance and Services, 2010–13; on Procedure, 2010–15; on Defence, 2013–17 (Chm., Sub-Cttee on Defence in Arctic, 2016); on Admin, 2015–17; Mem., Jt Cttee on Nat. Security, 2017–. Jt Chm., All-Party Minerals Gp, 1997–2001 and 2009–15; Chairman: All-Party Multiple Sclerosis Gp, 2004–11; All-Party Parly Gp for the Army, 2004–10; All-Party Parly Gp for Armed Forces, 2010–; All-Party Parly Gp for Polar Regions, 2015– (Vice-Chm., 2012); All-Party Parly Gp on Mongolia, 2016–17; Vice-Chm., All-Party Parly Gp on Deafness, 2004–07; Mem., Speaker's Panel of Chairmen, 2010–; Chm., Cons. Rural Action Gp, 2003–05; Cons. Defence and Foreign Affairs Policy Gp, 2006–07. Chm., 1922 Defence Cttee, 2018–. Mem., UK Delegn to Council of Europe and WEU, 2007–08, to NATO Parly Assembly, 2015–. Chm., Horse and Pony Taxation Cttee, 1999–2002. Trustee, Armed Forces Parly Trust (formerly Scheme), 2013– (Chm., 2013–) (Graduate, 1997–98, Post-grad. Scheme, 2001, Advanced Post-grad., 2010; rcds, 2003); Vis. Parly Fellow, St Antony's Coll., Oxford, 2005–06. Convenor, Poles Apart Conf., RUSI, 2013. Mem., Cons. Party Bd for SW, 2010–. Served HAC (TA), 1977–84 (Mem., Court of Assts, 2002–07); Vice-Pres., HAC Saddle Club. Vice-Chm., Charitable Properties Assoc., 2002–10; President: Chippenham Br., Multiple Sclerosis Soc., 2000–06 (Patron, Devizes Br., 2007–); Assoc. of British Riding Schs, 2001–16; Consultant, British Horse Industry Confedn, 1999–2002. Patron: Mutual Support, 2006–16; Operation Christmas Box, 2017–. Freeman, City of London, 1982. Younger Brother, Trinity House, 2017–. *Publications:* Financial Risk Management in the Shipping Industry, 1985; Futures and Options for Shipping, 1987 (Lloyds of London Book Prize); Shipping Futures, 1990; Crown vs Parliament: who decides on going to war? (thesis), 2003; Poles Apart, 2013; (with M. Lomas) Who Takes Britain to War?, 2014; Full English Brexit, 2018. *Recreations:* countryside, riding horses, English local history, Polar regions. *Address:* House of Commons, SW1A 0AA. *T:* (020) 7219 6237. *Clubs:* Pratt's; Chippenham Constitutional (Pres., 1999–); Royal Wootton Bassett Conservative.

*See also* J. C. R. Gray.

**GRAY, Sir (John Armstrong) Muir,** Kt 2005; CBE 1998; MD; FRCP, FRCPSGlas; FFPH; Director, National Knowledge Service, NHS (formerly Director of Clinical Knowledge, Process and Safety, Department of Health), 2004–13; Director, Better Value Healthcare Ltd, since 2007; *b* 21 June 1944; *yr s* of late John Gray and Nancie Gray (née Armstrong); *m* 1974, Jacqueline Elizabeth Rosenthal; two *d. Educ:* Jordanhill Coll. Sch.; Univ. of Glasgow (MB, ChB 1969; MD 1981); Univ. of Bristol (DPH 1973). FFPH (FFPHM 1984); MRCGP 1985; FRCPSGlas 1989; FRCP 1993. House surgeon, Western Infirmary, Glasgow, 1966–70; Sen. House Officer, Aberdeen, 1970–71; SMO, City of Oxford, 1972–74; Public Health Specialist, Oxfordshire HA, 1974–91; Dir, Health Policy and Public Health, Oxford RHA, 1991–94; Dir of R&D, Anglia and Oxford RHA, then Anglia and Oxford Regl Office, NHS Exec., DoH, 1994–98; Dir, Inst. of Health Scis, Univ. of Oxford, 1999–2002; Chief Knowledge Officer, NHS, until 2013. Fellow, Green Coll., Oxford, 1984–94, Fellow Emeritus, 1994. Co-ordinator: Nat. Breast Cancer Screening Prog., 1988–91; Nat. Cervical Screening Prog., 1988–94; Programmes Dir, UK Nat. Screening Cttee, 1995–2008. Dir, National Campaign for Walking; Campaign for Greener Healthcare. Advr, WHO, 1984–91. Hon. DSc: UEA 1998; City 2006. *Publications:* Man Against Disease, 1979; Take Care of Your Elderly Relative, 1980; Football Injuries, 1981; Prevention of Diseases in the Elderly, 1985; Evidence Based Healthcare, 1996, 3rd edn 2007; The Resourceful Patient, 2002; How to get Better Value Healthcare, 2008; Dr Gray's Walking Cure, 2009; Sod 70!: the guide to living well, 2015; articles in med., epidemiology and public health jls. *Recreations:* reading, linguistics, combating the effects of biological ageing. *Address:* 59 Lakeside, Oxford OX2 8JQ. *T:* (01865) 554066.

**GRAY, (John) Charles (Rodger),** CMG 2003; LVO 2013; HM Diplomatic Service, retired; HM Marshal of the Diplomatic Corps, 2008–14; Adviser, Ministry of Presidential Affairs, United Arab Emirates, since 2018; *b* 12 March 1953; *s* of Very Rev. John Rodger Gray, VRD, sometime Moderator, Gen. Assembly of C of S, and of Dr Sheila M. Gray (née Whiteside); *m* 1988, Anne-Marie Lucienne Suzanne, *d* of Marquis and Marquise de Dax d'Axat, Paris; three *s. Educ:* High Sch. of Glasgow; Glasgow Univ. (MA). Entered HM Diplomatic Service, 1974; W Africa Dept, FCO, 1974; Polish lang. trng, 1975; Third, later Second, Sec., Warsaw, 1976–79; Eastern European and Soviet Dept, FCO, 1979–83; First Sec., UK Delegn, OECD, Paris, 1983–87; Seconded Assessments Staff, Cabinet Office, 1987–89; Foreign and Commonwealth Office: Deputy Head: Central African Dept, 1989; Central European Dept, 1989–92; Hd, Eastern Adriatic Dept, 1992–93; Counsellor and Hd of Chancery, Jakarta, 1993–96; Fellow, Centre for Internat. Affairs, Harvard Univ., 1996–97; Counsellor, Washington, 1997–2001; attached Counter Terrorism Policy Dept, FCO, 2001–02; Hd, ME Dept, FCO, 2002–04; Iran Coordinator, FCO, 2004–05; Ambassador to Morocco, 2005–08. Consultant: Prime Minister's Office, Govt of Hungary, 2014–15; FCO, 2018. Lectr, Barcelona Inst. of Internat. Affairs, 2014. Trustee, Anglo-Jordanian Soc., 2015–18. *Recreation:* history. *Address:* Flat 23, Drayton Court, Drayton Gardens, SW10 9RH. *E:* jcrgray53@gmail.com. *Club:* New (Edinburgh).

*See also* J. W. Gray.

**GRAY, Prof. John Clinton,** PhD; Professor of Plant Molecular Biology, University of Cambridge, 1996–2011, now Emeritus; Fellow, Robinson College, Cambridge, since 1977; *b* 9 April 1946; *s* of William John Gray and Edith Grace Gray (née Tooke); *m* 1971, Julia Hodgetts; one *s* one *d. Educ:* Sir Joseph Williamson's Mathematical Sch., Rochester; Simon Langton Grammar Sch., Canterbury; Univ. of Birmingham (BSc 1967; PhD 1970); MA Cantab 1977. Res. Fellow, Univ. of Birmingham, 1970–73; Res. Biochemist, UCLA, 1973–75; University of Cambridge: SRC Res. Fellow, 1975–76; Demonstrator, 1976–80; Lectr, 1980–90; Reader in Plant Molecular Biol., 1990–96; Hd, Dept of Plant Scis, 2003–09. Nuffield Foundn Sci. Res. Fellow, 1983–84; Royal Soc. Leverhulme Trust Res. Fellow, 1991–92. Non-exec. Dir, Horticulture Res. Internat., 1997–2003. Member: SERC Biol Scis Cttee, 1990–93; EMBO, 1994–; Council, Sainsbury Lab., 1999–2008. Plant Sci. Advr, Gatsby Charitable Foundn, 1996–2008. Trustee, Sci. and Plants for Schs, 1991–2008. Mem., Midlands Assoc. of Mountaineers, 1967–. *Publications:* (ed with R. J. Ellis) Ribulose Bisphosphate Carboxylase-Oxygenase, 1986; (ed with D. L. Hallahan) Plant Trichomes, 2000; papers in scientific and philatelic jls. *Recreations:* growing plants, family history, philately. *Address:* 47 Barrons Way, Comberton, Cambridge CB23 7EQ. *T:* (01223) 263325.

**GRAY, Prof. John Michael,** DPhil; FBA 2000; Professor of Education, 2001–15, now Emeritus, and Chairman of Board, Faculty of Education, 2008–13, University of Cambridge; Fellow, 2001–15, now Emeritus, and Vice-Principal, 2009–14, Homerton College, Cambridge; *b* 25 March 1948; *s* of Ronald Gray and Patricia Gray (née Martin); *m* 1st, 1977, Susan Lendrum (marr. diss. 1985); one *d*; 2nd, 2005, Prof. Jean Rudduck (*d* 2007); 3rd, 2012, Dr Margaret Challis. *Educ:* Exeter Coll., Oxford (BA); Harvard Univ. (EdM); Sussex Univ. (PGCE, DPhil 1976). Asst to Dir, Shelter, 1966–67; Res. Asst, Harvard Univ., 1970–72; teacher, ILEA, 1974–75; Res. Fellow, Edinburgh Univ., 1975–79; Sheffield University: Lectr, 1979–84; Reader, 1984–86; Prof., 1987–93; Jt Dir, Qualitative and Quantitative Studies in Educn Res. Gp, 1988–93; Res. Co-ordinator Social Scis, 1989–93; Dir of Res., Homerton Coll., Cambridge, 1994–2001; Syndic, Cambridge Assessment, 2001–13. Vis. Prof., Inst. of Educn, Univ. of London, 1996–2000. Mem., Res. Adv. Cttee, DfES, 2002–06; Specialist Advr, Children, Schs and Families Select Cttee, 2009–10. Mem. Cttees, 1985–2009, Chm., Wkg Party on Future of Educnl Res., 1992, ESRC. Mem. Bd and Chm., Res. Cttee, TTA, 1997–2000; Chairman: Standards Cttee, Oxford, Cambridge and RSA Exams Bd, 2001–13; Section S4, British Acad., 2012–15. Mem., Royal Soc./British Acad. Enquiry into Educnl Res., 2016–18. *Publications:* jointly: Reconstructions of Secondary Education, 1983; Elton Enquiry into School Discipline, 1989; National Youth Cohort Study of England and Wales (1988–94), Good School, Bad School, 1995; Merging Traditions, 1996; Inspecting Schools, 1996; Gender and Educational Performance, 1998; Improving Schools, 1999; Quality and Equity in European Education, 2004; Schools on the Edge, 2006; The Supportive School, 2011. *Address:* Homerton College, Cambridge CB2 8PH. *T:* (01223) 767600.

**GRAY, Prof. John Nicholas,** DPhil; Professor of European Thought, London School of Economics and Political Science, 1998–2007; Emeritus Professor, University of London, since 2008; *b* 17 April 1948; *s* of Nicholas Chatt Wardle Gray and Joan Gray (née Bushby); *m* 1988, Mieko Kawai. *Educ:* South Shields Grammar-Technical Sch. for Boys; Exeter Coll., Oxford (BA Hons 1971; MA 1976; DPhil 1978). Lectr in Political Theory, Univ. of Essex, 1973–76; Fellow and Tutor in Politics, Jesus Coll., Oxford, 1976–98; Prof. of

Politics, Univ. of Oxford, 1996–98. Vis Prof. in Govt, Harvard Univ., 1986; Olmsted Vis. Prof. in Social Philosophy, Yale Univ., 1994. DUniv Open, 2006. Nonino Prize to a Master of Our Time, 2017. *Publications:* Mill on Liberty: a defence, 1983, 2nd edn 1996; Hayek on Liberty, 1984, 3rd edn 1998; Liberalism, 1986, 2nd edn 1995; Liberalisms: essays in political philosophy, 1989; Post-liberalism: studies in political thought, 1993; Beyond the New Right: markets, government and the common culture, 1993; Enlightenment's Wake: politics and culture at the close of the modern age, 1995; Isaiah Berlin, 1995; Endgames: questions in late modern political thought, 1997; Voltaire and Enlightenment, 1998; False Dawn: the delusions of global capitalism, 1998, 3rd edn 2002; Two Faces of Liberalism, 2000; Straw Dogs: thoughts on humans and other animals, 2002; Al Qaeda and What It Means To Be Modern, 2003, 2nd edn 2007; Heresies: against progress and other illusions, 2004; (contrib.) The Political Theory of John Gray, 2007; Black Mass: apocalyptic religion and the death of Utopia, 2007 (Notable Book Award, Lannan Foundn, 2008); Gray's Anatomy: selected writings, 2009, enlarged 2nd edn 2016; The Immortalization Commission: science and the strange quest to cheat death, 2011; The Silence of Animals: on progress and other modern myths, 2013; Isaiah Berlin: an interpretation of his thought, 2013; The Soul of the Marionette: a short inquiry into human freedom, 2015; Seven Types of Atheism, 2018. *Recreations:* reading, films, music. *Address:* c/o Tracy Bohan, The Wylie Agency, 17 Bedford Square, WC1B 3JA. *E:* tbohan@wylieagency.co.uk.

**GRAY, Jonathan;** Editor, since 2008, and Creative Director, since 2010, Dancing Times; *b* Newport, S Wales, 3 May 1967; *s* of Douglas John Gray and Judith Gray (*née* Wilson); civil partnership 2006, Robin Francis. *Educ:* Royal Ballet Sch., London; Wycliffe Secondary Sch., Leicester; Wyggeston Collegiate Sixth Form Coll., Leicester; Leicester Poly. (Foundn Cert. Art and Design); Wimbledon Sch. of Art (BA Hons Theatre Design). Archive Asst, 1990–95, Asst Curator, 1995–2005, Theatre Mus.; Associate Ed., Dancing Times, 2005–08. Member: Critics' Circle, 2007– (Mem., Cttee, Nat. Dance Awards, 2015–); Costume Soc., 2010–. Trustee: Dance Teachers' Benevolent Fund, 2012–15; Voices of British Ballet, 2014–. Member, Judging Panel: Choreog. Prize, West London Sch. of Dance, 2015–; Knights of Illuminations Awards, 2016–17. *Publications:* (with Dr J. Fowler) Unleashing Britain: theatre gets real 1955–1964, 2005; contrib. articles to FT and The Guardian; prog. notes and articles for Royal Ballet, Birmingham Royal Ballet and Ballet Black. *Recreations:* travel, theatre, opera, particular interest in historical costume. *Address:* c/o Dancing Times, 36 Battersea Square, SW11 3RA. *T:* (020) 7250 3006. *E:* jonathan@dancing-times.co.uk.

**GRAY, Kenneth Walter,** CBE 1992; PhD; FREng; FInstP, FIET; Chairman, Gorilla TV, 2011–14; *b* 20 March 1939; *s* of late Robert W. Gray and Ruby M. Gray; *m* 1st, 1962, Jill Henderson (marr. diss. 2006); two *s* one *d*; 2nd, 2010, Jean Woodley. *Educ:* Blue Coat Sch.; Univ. of Wales (BSc, PhD). FInstP 1991; FIET (FIEE 1992); FREng (FEng 1996). Research on magnetic resonance, as Nat. Res. Council of Canada post-doctoral Fellow, Univ. of British Columbia, Vancouver, 1963–65; research on semiconductor devices and on radiometry, N American Rockwell Science Center, Thousand Oaks, Calif, 1965–70; research on devices and systems at Royal Signals and Radar Estabt, 1971; Supt Solid State Physics and Devices Div., 1976; Head of Physics Group, 1979; RCDS 1981; Royal Signals and Radar Establishment: CSO, MoD, Dep. Dir (Applied Physics), 1982–84; Under Sec., Dep. Dir (Information Systems), 1984; Dir of Res., 1984–86, Technical Dir, 1986–96, THORN EMI plc; Technical Dir, EMI Group plc, Aug.–Dec. 1996; Exec. Chm., Thorn Software, 1987–89; Technical Dir, Thorn Security and Electronics, 1991–93; Man. Dir, Thorn Transaction, 1993–96. Chairman: Scipher plc, 1996–2004; London Biofuels, 2006–08; Ocean Blue Software, 2006–08; DGTL Products, 2008–11; non-exec. Dir, British Steel, 1995–99. Visiting Research Fellow: Univ. of Newcastle, 1972–74; Univ. of Leeds, 1976–90; Vis. Prof., Univ. of Nottingham, 1986–96. Member: DTI Innovation Adv. Bd, 1988–93; SERC, 1991–94; Technology Foresight Steering Cttee, OST, 1993–97; HEFCW, 1996–2002. Hon. DSc Nottingham Trent, 1998. *Publications:* over 30 scientific and technical papers in various learned jls. *Recreations:* bird-watching, theatre, gardening.

**GRAY, Kevin Adrian;** a District Judge (Magistrates' Courts), Devon and Cornwall, 2011–16; *b* 12 Oct. 1947; *s* of Kenneth Thomas Gray and Gladys Gray; *m* 1st, 1971 (marr. diss.); one *s* one *d*; 2nd, 2005, Anita Poole. *Educ:* Portsmouth Southern Grammar Sch.; Kingston Poly. (LLB Hons). Police Officer, Portsmouth City Police, later Hampshire Constabulary, 1964–71; admitted Solicitor, 1976; Sen. Partner, Gray Purdue & Co., 1977–90; sole practitioner, 1990–92; Partner, Gregsons, 1993–94; Acting Metropolitan Stipendiary Magistrate, 1993–95; Stipendiary Magistrate, then District Judge (Magistrates' Courts), Essex, 1995–2011; Dir of Continuation Trng, 2008–12; a Dep. Dist Judge (Magistrates' Courts), 2016–17. *Recreation:* enjoying family and good friendships.

**GRAY, Prof. Kevin John,** PhD, LLD, DCL; FBA 1999; Professor of Law, University of Cambridge, 1993–2011, now Emeritus; Fellow, Trinity College, Cambridge, 1981–90 and since 1993 (Dean, 2004–05 and 2006–15); *b* 23 July 1951; *s* of late Bryce Holmes Gray, Belfast, and Priscilla Margaret Gray (*née* McCullough), Lisburn; *m* 1996, Susan Francis (*d* 2014). *Educ:* Trinity Hall, Cambridge (BA 1972 (1st Cl. Law Tripos Parts I and II); MA, PhD 1976; Yorke Prize, 1977; LLD 1991); DCL Oxford, 1994. Called to the Bar, Middle Temple, 1993, Bencher, 2014. University of Cambridge: Jt Coll. Lectr, Queens' and Trinity Colls, 1975–77; Fellow, Queens' Coll., 1975–81; Asst Lectr and Lectr in Law, 1978–90; Univ. Advocate, 1986–88; Res. Fellow, ANU, 1990; Drapers' Prof. of Law, QMW, Univ. of London, 1991–93. Vis. Fellow, ANU, 1979, 1989, 1998, 2005–06; Sen. Vis. Res. Fellow, St John's Coll., Oxford, 1993–94; Leverhulme Trust Major Res. Fellow, 2008–11; Prof. of Law, Nat. Univ. of Singapore, 2008–16; Visiting Professor: Grad. Sch. of Law, Univ. of Osaka, 2001; Univ. of NSW, 2003; Univ. of Stellenbosch, 2005 and 2008; Univ. of Tasmania, 2006; Nat. Univ. of Singapore, 2006, 2007. Dist. Gifford Lect., Univ. of Hawaii, 2010; Dist. Visiting Mentor, ANU, 2015. Associate Mem., Acad. Internat. de Droit Comparé, 1995; Overseas Res. Fellow, Nat. Res. Foundn of SA, 2005; Hon. Academic Mem., Property Bar Assoc., 2016. Member: Access, Conservation and Envmt Cttee (formerly Access and Conservation Cttee), British Mountaineering Council, 2002–06; AHRC (formerly AHRB) Peer Rev. Coll., 2004–07. Fellow, Stellenbosch Inst. for Advanced Study, 2009–. Jun. and sen. internat. athlete, 1968–69. *Publications:* Reallocation of Property on Divorce, 1977; Elements of Land Law, 1987, 5th edn (with S. F. Gray) 2009; (with S. F. Gray) Land Law, 1999, 7th edn 2011; other books and articles on law, legal theory, human rights, and the envmt. *Recreations:* mountaineering, rock climbing, wild country, old churches. *Address:* Trinity College, Cambridge CB2 1TQ. *T:* (01223) 338497.

**GRAY, Linda Esther, (Mrs Peter McCrorie);** retired as opera singer, now teaching; *b* 29 May 1948; *d* of James and Esther Gray; *m* 1971, Peter McCrorie; one *d*. *Educ:* Greenock Academy; Royal Scottish Academy of Music and Drama. Cinzano Scholarship, 1969; Goldsmith Schol., 1970; James Caird Schol., 1971; Kathleen Ferrier Award, 1972; Christie Award, 1972. London Opera Centre, 1969–71; Glyndebourne Festival Opera, 1972–75; Scottish Opera, 1974–79; Welsh Opera, 1980; English National Opera, 1979; American début, 1981; Royal Opera House: Sieglinde, 1982; Fidelio, 1983. Records: Tristan und Isolde, 1981; Wagner's Die Feen, 1983. Principal rôles: Isolde, Sieglinde, Kundry (Wagner); Tosca (Puccini); Fidelio (Beethoven). *Publications:* A Life Behind Curtains (autobiog.), 2007; (with Caroline Finlayson) Can We All Sing?, 2007; Dame Eva Turner: a life on the high Cs, 2011; Sing! Don't Drown, 2018. *Recreations:* cooking, swimming. *Address:* 35 Green Lane, New Malden, Surrey KT3 5BX.

**GRAY, Lindsay;** *see* Gray, Peter Lindsay.

**GRAY, Martin;** *see* Gray, H. M. V.

**GRAY, Ven. Martin Clifford;** Archdeacon of Lynn, 1999–2009, now Emeritus; Interim Archdeacon of Stow and Lindsey, 2015; *b* 19 Jan. 1944; *s* of John Oscar Gray and Lilian Annie Bertha Gray; *m* 1966, Pauline Jean Loader; three *s*. *Educ:* West Ham Coll. of Technology (DipChemEng; AWHCT 1967); Westcott House, Cambridge. Process Engineer, May & Baker, Norwich, 1968–70; Process Engr, Plant Supt, Project Manager, 1970–78, Dow Chemical, Kings Lynn, Norfolk and Bilbao, Spain. Deacon 1980, priest 1981; Asst Curate, St Faith's, Gaywood, Kings Lynn, 1980–84; Vicar, St Peter's, Sheringham, 1984–94; Rector, Lowestoft St Margaret Team Ministry, Suffolk, 1994–99. *Recreations:* golf, hill-walking. *Address:* 11 Cann's Lane, Hethersett, Norwich NR9 3JE. *E:* mandpgray11@btinternet.com.

**GRAY, Morag Graham,** MBE 2005; *b* 12 Oct. 1962; *d* of Bill and Mary Chalmers; *m* 1st, 1993, Nigel Gray (marr. diss. 1998); 2nd, 2012, Angus Crichton-Miller. *Educ:* Lanark Grammar Sch.; Univ. of Strathclyde (BA 1983). Product Manager, British Telecom, 1983–88; Clerk of the Course, Scottish Racing, 1988–90; Planning Exec., 1990–97, Racing Dir, 1997–2000, Racecourse Assoc.; Chief Exec., Hamilton Park Racecourse, 2000–04; Dir, Racecourse Assoc., 2002–04. Ind. Dir, British Horseracing Authy, 2007–14. Trustee: Racing to School, 2009–; Racing Welfare, 2013–; Chair, Racing Together. *Recreations:* horseracing, Scottish Rugby, fitness, food. *E:* Moraggray@crichton-miller.scot.

**GRAY, Sir Muir;** *see* Gray, Sir J. A. M.

**GRAY, Muriel Janet, (Mrs H. Barbour);** presenter, broadcaster and author; *b* 30 Aug. 1958; *d* of Adam and Elizabeth Gray; *m* 1991, Hamish Barbour; two *s* one *d*. *Educ:* Glasgow Sch. of Art (BA Hons Graphic Design). Asst Hd of Design, Mus. of Antiquities, Edinburgh, 1980–83; presenter and broadcaster, 1982–: *television* includes: The Tube, The Media Show, Design Awards, Art is Dead, The Munro Show, The Snow Show; *radio* includes: Start the Week, Whatever Gets You Through, various progs for Radio Scotland; newspaper and magazine columnist, including: Time Out, Sunday Mirror, Sunday Correspondent, Scotland on Sunday, Sunday Herald. Rector, Edinburgh Univ., 1988–91. Founder and Man. Dir, Gallus Besom Prodns, 1987. Dir, Ideal World and IWC Prodns, 1990–2005. Trustee, British Mus., 2016–. Chair, Bd of Govs, Glasgow Sch. of Art, 2013–. FRSE 2018. *Publications:* The First Fifty, 1991; The Trickster, 1994; Furnace, 1997; The Ancient, 2001; Kelvingrove: portal to the world, 2006. *Recreations:* growing trees, mountaineering, chess, snow boarding, horror cinema. *Address:* IWC Media, St George's Studios, 93–97 St George's Road, Glasgow G3 6JA. *T:* (0141) 353 3222, *Fax:* (0141) 353 3221.

**GRAY, Neil Charles;** MP (SNP) Airdrie and Shotts, since 2015; *b* Orkney Isles, 16 March 1986; *m* Karlie; one *d*. *Educ:* Kirkwall Grammar Sch.; Stirling Univ. (BA 1st Cl. Hons Politics and Journalism 2008). Contract producer and reporter, BBC Radio Orkney, 2003–08; press and res. intern, SNP, Scottish Parlt, 2008; work in office of Alex Neil, MSP, 2008–15, Office Manager, 2011–15. SNP spokesperson for Fair Work and Employment, 2015–17, for Social Justice, 2017–18. Mem., Finance Cttee, H of C, 2015–. *Address:* House of Commons, SW1A 0AA.

**GRAY, Paul Alexander;** Director General, Health and Social Care, Scottish Government, 2013–19; Chief Executive, NHS Scotland, 2013–19; *b* Edinburgh, 17 Aug. 1962; *s* of Robert Gray and Rachel Gray; *m* 1982, Fiona Gray; one *s* two *d*. *Educ:* Linlithgow Acad. Scottish Office, later Scottish Executive, then Scottish Government: various posts, 1979–2000; Dir, Inf. and Communications Technol., 2000–03; Dir for Social Justice, 2003–05; Dir, Primary and Community Care and Dir, eHealth, 2005–07; Dir, Change and Corporate Services, 2007–09; Director General: Rural Affairs and Envmt, then Rural Affairs, Envmt and Services, 2009–11; Governance and Communities, 2011–13.

**GRAY, Paul Herbert Lucas,** DPhil; Managing Director, Public Service Solutions Ltd, since 2006; *b* 20 Jan. 1957; *s* of Alfred N. Gray and Doris J. Gray (*née* Hutchens); *m* 1st, 1982, Patricia Ann Wright (marr. diss. 2005); 2nd, 2011, Joanne Bedford; one *s*. *Educ:* Univ. of Durham (BA Hons); Univ. of Birmingham (DPhil). Lectr, 1980–84, Sen. Lectr and Asst Principal, 1984–86, Merseyside; Sen. Educn Officer, Cambs CC, 1986–90; Dep. Chief Educn Officer, Devon CC, 1990–96; Dir of Educn, Surrey CC, 1996–2006. Vis. Prof., Univ. of London, 1997–2002. Chm., QCDA (formerly QCA) Curriculum and Assessment Cttee, 1999–2003. Chm. Bd, Exeter Council for Voluntary Service, 2013–; Mem. Bd, Nat. Youth Agency, 1999–2004. Trustee: Exeter CVS, 2013–; Youth, Arts and Health Trust, 2016– (Chm., 2017–); Sentient Trust, 2017. Mem., Exeter Diocesan Bd of Educn. Director: Ventrus Multi Acad. Trust, 2015–; ACE Multi Acad. Trust, 2016–; Chm., Govs, Southbrook Sch., 2016–; Gov., Dawlish Fedn of Schs, 2017–. Freeman, City of London, 2004. FRSA 1997. *Recreations:* sport, music, literature, sailing, extreme charity fundraising events, wide-ranging voluntary work. *Address:* 36 Bartholomew Street West, Exeter EX4 3BN.

**GRAY, Paul Richard Charles,** CB 2000; Executive Coach, Praesta Partners LLP, since 2008; Chairman, Social Security Advisory Committee, 2011–18; *b* 2 Aug. 1948; *s* of Rev. Sidney Gray and Ina (*née* Maxey); *m* 1972, Lynda Elsie Braby; two *s*. *Educ:* Wyggeston Boys' Sch., Leicester; LSE (BSc Econ 1969). Dept of Econ. Affairs, 1969; HM Treasury, 1969–77; with Booker McConnell Ltd, 1977–79; HM Treasury: Principal, 1979–83; Asst Sec., 1984–87; Econ. Affairs Private Sec. to Prime Minister, 1988–90; Under Sec., Monetary Gp, 1990–93; Dir, Personnel and Support Services, 1994–95; Dir, Budget and Public Finances, 1995–98; Hd of Policy Gp, DSS, 1998–99; Gp Dir, Children, Pensioners and Disabled, DSS, subseq. DWP, 1999–2001; Man. Dir, Pensions and Disability, 2001–04; Second Permanent Sec., 2002, DWP; Dep. Chm., 2004–06, Chm., 2006–07, HMRC. Dir (non-exec.), Laing Management Ltd, 1993–95. *Recreations:* family, walking, sport, gardening, travel.

**GRAY, Paul Shapter,** FRSC; consultant on climate change and environment; Director, Environment, Climate and Marine Science and Technology Research Programmes, European Commission, 1992–97; *b* 18 Sept. 1932; *s* of Frederick Archibald and Vera Emma Gray; *m* 1958, Diane Lillian Platt (*d* 2017); one *s* one *d* (and one *s* decd). *Educ:* St Chad's Coll., Wolverhampton; Birmingham Univ. (BSc Hons; MSc). FRSC (FRIC 1967). Chief Chemist, Midland Tar Distillers, 1954–57; Sen. Research Fellow, Ministry of Power, 1957–59; Head of Div., Reactor Chemistry, UKAEA, Winfrith, 1959–63; Ops Controller, OECD DRAGON (high temp. gas cooled reactor expt), 1963–73; European Commission, 1973–97: Dep. Head of Div., Elimination of Technical Barriers to Trade, 1977–81; Head of Service, Wood, Paper and Construction Industries, 1981–83; Head of Div., Food Law and Food Trade, 1983–91; Advr for industrial aspects of biotechnology, 1991–92. Sci. Advr, European Assoc. for Global Ocean Observing System, 1996–2001; Mem., Sci. Cttee, Royal Inst. for sustainable mgt of natural resources and promotion of clean technols, Belgium, 1997–2010; Royal Society of Chemistry: Member: Council, 2004–05; Prof. Affairs Bd, 2005–07; Pres., Belgium Section, 2005–09. Vis. Prof., Human Ecol., Vrije Universiteit Brussel, 2002–10. Hon. DSc Birmingham, 1999. Mem., St Nicholas, Alcester PCC, 2012–18. *Publications:* jointly: Radionuclides in the Food Chain, 1988; Chernobyl, 1991;

EU Committees as Influential Policymakers, 1998; International Handbook on Food Safety, 1999; numerous pubns in scientific and economic jls. *Recreations:* music, singing, sailing, playwriting, gardening.

**GRAY, Peter Francis**; Chairman, Berkeley Capital Ltd, since 2009; *b* 7 Jan. 1937; *s* of Rev. George Francis Selby Gray; *m* 1978, Fiona Bristol; two *s*. *Educ:* Marlborough; Trinity College, Cambridge. MA; FCA. Served Royal Fusiliers, attached 4th Kings African Rifles, Uganda, 1956–58. HM Foreign Service, 1963–64; SG Warburg & Co., 1964–66; Cooper Brothers & Co., 1966–69; Samuel Montagu & Co., 1970–77; Head of Investment Div., Crown Agents for Oversea Govts & Admins, 1977–83; Man. Dir, Touche Remnant & Co., 1983–87; Dep. Chm., Assoc. of Investment Trust Cos, 1985–87. Chairman: Exmoor Dual Investment Trust plc, 1988–98; Aberdeen Lloyd's Insurance Trust plc, 1993–98; Finsbury Income and Growth Investment Trust plc, 1993–2004; Supervisory Bd, Postbank and Savings Bank Corp. (Hungary), 1998; Close Finsbury Euro-Tech Trust plc, 2000–06; Hampden Capital plc, 2001–07; New Europe Property Investments plc, 2007–09; Anglo Japanese Investment Corp. plc, 2006–12; KB Re Ltd, 2010–15; Director: TR Industrial and General Trust plc, 1984–88; New Zealand Investment Trust plc, 1988–2003; Gartmore Value Investments plc, 1989–94; Gartmore Distribution Trust plc, 1993–2002; F&C Private Equity Trust plc, 1994–2002; Graphite Enterprise Trust plc, 2002–09; UTI India Pharma Fund, 2005–10; Farida (Europe) Ltd, 2008–18. Member, Advisory Board: Mellenthin Corporate Finance, 2004–; Al Farida Investments, 2007–15; OMFIF, 2013–. *Recreations:* literature, music. *Address:* 26 Ursula Street, SW11 3DW; Berkeley Capital Ltd, 42 Berkeley Square, W1J 5AW. *Club:* Brooks's.

**GRAY, Peter Leigh**; Chairman and Chief Executive Officer, John Smith & Son Group Ltd, since 2001; *b* Hants, 3 Nov. 1967; *s* of Robert Frank Gray and Patricia Rosemary Leigh Gray; *m* 1995, Lesley Adams; one *s* two *d*. *Educ:* Salisbury Coll. (OND Construction Technol. 1986); Southampton Coll. (HND Construction Mgt 1988). Mgt trainee, Lovell Construction, 1986–88; Dir, BMBC Ltd, 1989–99; Ops Dir, Coutts Information Services Ltd, 2000–01. Gov., Ringwood Jun. Sch., 2000–08. *Recreations:* ski-ing, motorsport, Rugby, shooting, flying, sailing, diving (general adventurer). *Address:* JS Group Ltd, Ash House, Headlands Business Park, Ringwood, Hants BH24 3PB. *T:* (01425) 485935. *E:* Peter.gray@johnsmith.co.uk.

**GRAY, (Peter) Lindsay**; consultant, adviser and mediator (education, music and charities), since 2012; Director, Royal School of Church Music, 2008–12, now Emeritus; *b* Nottingham, 22 July 1953; *s* of Harold Geoffrey Gray and Mairi Gray (*née* Hay); *m* 1980, Caroline Susan Bick; two *d*. *Educ:* Nottingham High Sch.; King's Coll., Cambridge (BA 1974; Choral Schol.; MA); Durham Univ. (PGCE 1975); ARCO (Dip. 1971). Dir of Music, Grenville Coll., Bideford, 1975–79; Asst Dir of Music, Magdalen College Sch., Oxford, 1979–80; Director of Music: Queen's Coll., Taunton, 1980–86; Cheltenham Coll., 1986–92; Headmaster: Brightlands Sch., Newnham-on-Severn, 1992–94; Cathedral Sch., Llandaff, Cardiff, 1994–2008. Conductor, Bottisham Choral Soc., 1973–74; Organist and Choirmaster: St John's, Neville's Cross, 1974–75; St Peter's, Peterston-super-Ely, 1999–2006, 2014–16; Dir, Somerset Youth Choir, 1984–86; Director and Founder: Llandaff Cathedral Girl Choristers, 1995–2000, 2002–04; Caritas Choir and Consort, 2013–. Trustee, Woodard Academies Trust, 2013–14; Chair of Trustees, 2 Wish Upon a Star, 2015–19. Gov., Peterston-super-Ely Sch., 2013–17; Mem. Council, Clifton Coll., 2014–16. FRSCM 2013. Hon. FGCM 2016. *Recreations:* cricket, golf, table tennis, singing, choir directing, organ, rural and coastal walking, socialising, Indian food. *T:* 07823 325844. *E:* plgray227@gmail.com. *Clubs:* Mitres Cricket (Llandaff); Peterston-super-Ely Table Tennis (Vale of Glamorgan).

**GRAY, Phillip**; Chief Executive, Chartered Society of Physiotherapy, 1998–2014; *b* 30 April 1949; *s* of Paul and Sally Gray; *m* 1979, Pauline Tierney; two *s* three *d*. *Educ:* Liverpool Poly. (grad. IPM 1970); UC, Cardiff (BSc Econs 1st Cl. Hons 1976; Pres., Students' Union, 1976–77); LSE (MSc Industrial Relations 1978). Personnel Officer, Plessey Electronics, Liverpool, 1968–73; Dir of Industrial Relations, Chartered Soc. of Physiotherapy, 1978–90; Dir of Labour Relations, RCN, 1990–98. Trustee, Arthritis and Musculoskeletal Alliance (Chm., 2013). Member: NHS Workforce Develt Bd; NHS Older People's Services Taskforce; Primary Care Alliance Exec.; Allied Health Professions Fedn. Hon. FCSP. *Recreations:* squash, walking, football, poetry, collecting books, family and five children.

**GRAY, Richard Dennis**; proprietor, Hillrise Stonework (formerly Hillrise Walls), since 2007; *b* 19 Sept. 1951; *s* of John Dennis and Betty Gray; *m* 1976, Cherry Elizabeth Allen; two *s*. *Educ:* Carre's Grammar Sch.; Bristol Univ. (BA Hist. and Hist. of Art); Manchester Univ. (Museum Studies). AMA. Asst Keeper and Keeper, Manchester City Art Galls, 1974–89; Director: Manchester City Art Galls, 1989–98; Compton Verney, 1998–2005; Consultant Dir, NE Inst., Newcastle upon Tyne, 2005–10. Member: English Ceramic Circle, 1976–; Glass Circle, 1981–; Cttee, Glass Assoc., 1983–87; Cttee, Northern Ceramic Soc., 1986–89; NW Museums Service Adv. Panel, 1988–98 (Mem., Bd of Management, 1994–98); W Midlands Mus. Policy Forum, 2004–. Ind. Assessor, Reviewing Cttee on Export of Works of Art; Ext. Examr, Manchester Polytechnic, 1989–92. Trustee: Spode Mus., 1989–; Rekonstruktsiya Trust, 1991–93. Professional Mem., Dry Stone Walling Assoc. of GB, 2010–. Dry Stone Walling Instructor, Cotswold Conservation Bd, 2017–. Silver Gilt Medal (with Christine Cottrell) for Conceptual Garden, RHS Hampton Court Palace Flower Show, 2012. *Publications:* The History of Porcelain, Chapter 1, 1982; catalogues and inventories, Manchester Art Galleries; articles and book reviews for arts jls. *Recreations:* music, fishing, walking. *Address:* 35 Park Street, Bladon, Woodstock, Oxon OX20 1RW.

**GRAY, Prof. Richard John**, PhD; FBA 1993; Professor of Literature, University of Essex, 1990–2015, now Emeritus; *b* 5 Jan. 1944; *s* of George Ernest Gray and Helen Gray; *m* 1st, 1965, Joyce Mary Gray (marr. diss. 1991); one *s* one *d*; 2nd, 1991, Sheona Catherine Binnie; one *s* one *d*. *Educ:* St Catharine's Coll., Cambridge (BA MA, PhD). Res Schol., St Catharine's Coll., Cambridge, 1966–67; Harkness Fellow, for res. in US Univs, 1967–69; Lectr, Sen. Lectr and Reader in Literature, Univ. of Essex, 1969–90. Robert E. McNair Vis. Prof. in Southern Studies, Univ. of South Carolina, 1993; Barbara Lester Methvin Vis. Dist. Prof. of Southern Studies, Univ. of Georgia, 2009. Lectures: Eccles Centre, BL, 2004; Sarah Toyphena Phillips, British Acad., 2005; Lamar, USA, 2006; Fullbrook, Bristol, 2008; Methvin, Univ. of Georgia, 2009; De La Warr Pavilion, 2010. Leverhulme Emeritus Res. Fellow, 2016–18. Editor, Jl of Amer. Studies, 1997–2001. Research awards of: Amer. Philos. Soc., 1979; Internat. Communications Agency, 1981; Humanities Res. Bd, 1995, 1998; AHRB, 1997, 2000; British Acad., 2006. *Publications:* American Verse of the Nineteenth Century, 1973; American Poetry of the Twentieth Century, 1976; The Literature of Memory: modern writers of the American South, 1977; Robert Penn Warren: essays, 1980; American Fiction: new readings, 1983; Writing the South: ideas of an American region (C. Hugh Holman Award, Soc. for Study of Southern Lit.), 1986, 2nd edn 1997; American Poetry of the Twentieth Century, 1990; (ed) The Complete Poems of Edgar Allan Poe, 1993; The Life of William Faulkner: a critical biography, 1994; (ed) Selected Poems of Edgar Allan Poe, 1996; Southern Aberrations: writers of the American South and the problems of regionalism, 2000; Companion to the Literature and Culture of the American South, 2004; A History of American Literature, 2004, rev. edn 2011; A Web of Words: the great dialogue of Southern literature, 2007; Transatlantic Exchanges: the South in Europe - Europe in the American South, 2007; A Brief History of American Literature, 2011; After the Fall: American literature since 9/11, 2011; A History of American Poetry, 2014. *Recreations:* running, tennis, wine tasting, cycling, cinema, travel, walking, music. *Address:* Department of Literature, University of Essex, Wivenhoe Park, Colchester, Essex CO4 3SQ. *T:* (01206) 872590.

**GRAY, Hon. Sir Robert McDowall, (Sir Robin)**, Kt 1994; *b* 2 July 1931; *s* of Adam Gray and Elsie McDowall; *m* 1957, Mary Thomson (*d* 1981); one *s* two *d*. *Educ:* George Watson's Boys' Coll., Edinburgh. Served 4th/7th Royal Dragoon Guards, 1949–51; immigrated to NZ, as farm labourer, 1952; purchased farm, 1956; entered politics, 1978; MP (Nat.) Clutha, 1978–96; Whip, 1985, Sen. Whip, 1987; Speaker, NZ House of Reps, 1990–93; Minister of State, Associate Minister of For. Affairs and Trade, 1993–96. Chm., Parly Service Commn, 1990–93.

**GRAY, Robin**; Member, Parliamentary Boundary Commission for England, 1999–2009; management consultant, since 1993; *b* 16 April 1944; *s* of late Robert George and Jeannie Gray; *m* 1971, Kathleen Rosemary Kuhn; two *d*. *Educ:* Woking County Grammar Sch. for Boys; London Univ. (BA Hons). UKAEA, 1962–64; HM Treasury, 1964–70; Asst Sec. to Crowther Cttee on Consumer Credit, 1968–70; Min. of Housing and Local Govt, subseq. DoE, 1970–92; seconded to Water Resources Bd, 1973–75, to W Sussex CC, 1982–83; Sec., London and Metropolitan Govt Staff Commn, 1984–86; PSA, 1986–92; Under Sec., 1988–92; Dir of Civil Projects, 1988–89; Dir, Marketing and Planning, 1990–92; Internat. Dir, 1991–92; Business Develt Dir, PSA Projects Ltd, 1992–93. Mem., Local Govt Commn for England, 1996–2002; Dep. Electoral Comr and Mem., Boundary Cttee for England, 2002–08. Chm., Hampshire Govs Assoc., 2002–; Mem., Hampshire Schs Forum, 2002–. Governor: Oak Farm Community Sch., 1994–2011; The Connaught Sch., 2006–17; Samuel Cody Specialist Sports Coll., 2013–; Member, Interim Executive Board: Andover C of E Primary Sch., 2011–13; Cove Secondary Sch., 2014–. *Recreations:* cricket, walking and other outdoor activities, talking.

**GRAY, Hon. Robin (Trevor)**, BAgrSc; farmer, since 2005; Chairman, Botanical Resources Australia Pty Ltd, 1996–2011; *b* 1 March 1940; *s* of late Rev. W. J. Gray; *m* 1965, Judith, *d* of late A. G. Boyd; two *s* one *d*. *Educ:* Box Hill High Sch.; Dookie Agricl Coll., Melbourne Univ. Tech. 1961–65 (in UK, 1964); agricl consultant, Colac, Vic, 1965, Launceston, Tas, 1965–76; pt-time Lectr in Agricl Econs, Univ. of Tasmania, 1970–76. MHA (L) for Wilmot, Tas, 1976–85, for Lyons, 1985–95; Dep. Leader of the Opposition, Tasmania, 1979–81; Leader of the Opposition, 1981–82 and 1989–91; Premier of Tasmania and Treasurer, 1982–89; Minister: for Racing and Gaming, 1982–84; for Energy, 1982–88; for Forests, 1984–86; for State Develt, 1984–89; for Small Business, 1986–89; for Status of Women, 1989; for Antarctic Affairs, 1989; for Science and Technology, 1989; for Primary Industry, Fisheries and Energy, 1992–95; for the TT-Line, 1993–95. Partner, Evers Gray Consultants, 1996–2004. Director: Evergreen Olive Oil Pty Ltd, 1995–2000; Gunns Ltd, 1996–2010; Fujii Tasmania Pty Ltd, 1996–2000; AMC Search Ltd, 1996–2011; Agribusiness Project Mgt Pty Ltd, 1999–2012; Gunns Plantations Ltd, 2009–11. Trustee, Tasmanian Wool Museum, 1996–. *Address:* 11 Beech Road, Launceston, Tas 7250, Australia.

**GRAY, Victor William**, MBE 2010; Director, Rothschild Archive, 1993–2004; *b* 27 Oct. 1946; *s* of William Albert Gray and Eva Thirza (*née* Bint); *m* 1967, Jennifer Anne Whittle (*d* 2016); one *s* one *d*. *Educ:* King's Coll., Cambridge (BA Hons Eng., MA). County Archivist, Essex, 1978–93. Chm., Nat. Council on Archives, 1996–2001; Member: Lord Chancellor's Adv. Council on Public Records, 1992–98; Royal Commn on Historical Manuscripts, 2000–03; Bd, MLA (formerly Resource: Council for Museums, Archives and Libraries), 2000–04. Pres., Soc. of Archivists, 2005–08 (Chm., 1989–91); Chm., Suffolk Records Soc., 2013– (Vice Chm., 2012–13). Sen. Vis. Res. Fellow, Univ. of Suffolk, 2015–. FSA 2007. DU Essex, 1993. Ellis Prize for dist. contribs to archival theory and practice, Soc. of Archivists, 2002. *Publications:* Bookmen: London: 250 years of Sotheran bookselling, 2011; numerous articles on archives for prof. jls, esp. Jl of Soc. of Archivists. *Recreations:* reading, walking, collecting dictionaries. *Address:* 8A Station Road, Halesworth, Suffolk IP19 8BZ. *T:* (01986) 872437. *E:* VicGray8a@gmail.com.

**GRAY, Sir William (Hume)**, 3rd Bt *cr* 1917; Director: Eggleston Hall Ltd; William Gray Associates; *b* 26 July 1955; *s* of William Talbot Gray (*d* 1971) (*er s* of 2nd Bt), and of Rosemarie Hume Gray, *d* of Air Cdre Charles Hume Elliott-Smith; *S* grandfather, 1978; *m* 1984, Catherine Victoria Willoughby (marr. diss. 1998), *d* of late John Naylor and of Mrs Jerram, Wadebridge, Cornwall; one *s* two *d*; *m* 2001, Juliet Rachel, *d* of Mr and Mrs D. J. Jackson, Headlam, Co. Durham; one *s* one *d*. *Educ:* Aysgarth School, Bedale, Yorks; Eton College; Polytechnic of Central London BA (Hons) Architecture; DipArch; RIBA. High Sheriff, Durham, 1998–99. *Recreation:* sport. *Heir: s* William John Cresswell Gray, *b* 24 Aug. 1986. *Address:* Egglestone Hall, Barnard Castle, Co. Durham DL12 0AG. *T:* (01833) 650316.

**GRAYDON, Air Chief Marshal Sir Michael (James)**, GCB 1993 (KCB 1989); CBE 1984; FRAeS; *b* 24 Oct. 1938; *s* of James Julian Graydon and Rita Mary Alkan; *m* 1963, Margaret Elizabeth Clark. *Educ:* Wycliffe Coll.; RAF Coll., Cranwell. Qualified Flying Instructor No 1 FTS, Linton-on-Ouse, 1960–62; No 56 Sqn, 1962–64; No 226 OCU, 1965–67 (Queen's Commendation); Flight Comd, No 56 Sqn, 1967–69; RAF Staff Coll., Bracknell, 1970; PSO to Dep. C-in-C Allied Forces Central Region, Brunssum, 1971–73; Operations, Joint Warfare, MoD, 1973–75; NDC, Latimer, 1976; OC No 11 Sqn, Binbrook, 1977–79; MA to CDS, MoD, 1979–81; OC RAF Leuchars, 1981–83; OC RAF Stanley, Falkland Is, 1983; RCDS, 1984; SASO 11 Gp, Bentley Priory, 1985–86; ACOS Policy, SHAPE, 1986–89; AOC-in-C, RAF Support Comd, 1989–91; AOC-in-C, RAF Strike Comd, and C-in-C, UK Air Forces, 1991–92; CAS, and Air ADC to the Queen, 1992–97. Chm., Symbiotics, 2005–15. Non-exec. Dir, Thales plc, 1999–2011; Mil. Advr, Cassidian, 2008–15. Vice-Patron, Air Cadet Council, 1999–2018; Pres., Battle of Britain Meml Trust, 1999–2016. Chm., Air Sqdn, 2005–10. Mem. Council, Church Schs Co., 1997– (Dep. Chm., 2003–11); Governor: Wycliffe Coll., 1986– (Vice-Chm., 1992–2011); Vice Pres., 2011–16); Sutton's Hosp. in Charterhouse, 1998–2018 (Chm., 2006–18); ESU, 2012–18 (Chm., Lincs Br., 2003–); Chm., United Learning, 2012–15. FRAeS 1993. Freeman, City of London, 1995; Liveryman, Hon. Co. of Air Pilots (formerly GAPAN), 1996–. Mem., Authors Gp, UK Nat. Defence Assoc., 2008–. *Publications:* contrib. to professional jls; contrib. articles to The Times, Telegraph, FT, Mail on Sunday and Independent on Sunday. *Recreations:* golf, flying, reading. *Address:* c/o Lloyds Bank, Cox and King's Branch, 8–10 Waterloo Place, SW1Y 4BE. *Clubs:* Royal Air Force; Royal & Ancient Golf (St Andrews).

**GRAYLING, Prof. Anthony Clifford**, CBE 2017; DPhil; FRSL; Master, New College of the Humanities, since 2011; *b* 3 April 1949; *s* of Henry Clifford Grayling and Ursula Adelaide Burns; *m* 1970, Gabrielle Yvonne Smyth (marr. diss. 1979); one *s* one *d*; *m* 2012, Katie Hickman (marr. diss. 2017); one *d*. *Educ:* Sussex Univ. (BA Hons 1971, MA 1976); London Univ. (BA Hons ext. 1975); Magdalen Coll., Oxford (DPhil 1981). Lectr in Philosophy, St Anne's Coll., Oxford, 1983–91; Lectr in Philosophy, 1991–99, Reader, 1999–2005, Prof. of Philosophy, 2005–11, Birkbeck Coll., Univ. of London.

Supernumerary Fellow, St Anne's Coll., Oxford, 1991–; Vis. Prof., Univ. of Tokyo, 1998. A Judge, Man Booker Prize, 2003, Chm. Judges, 2014. FRSA 2004; FRSL 2007. *Publications:* An Introduction to Philosophical Logic, 1982, 3rd edn 1997; The Refutation of Scepticism, 1985; Berkeley: the central arguments, 1986; Wittgenstein, 1988; (jtly, as Li Xiao Jun) The Long March to the Fourth of June, 1990; (with S. Whitfield) A Literary Companion to China, 1994; (ed) Philosophy, vol. 1, A Guide Through the Subject, 1995, vol. 2, Further Through the Subject, 1998; Russell, 1996; Moral Values, 1997; The Quarrel of the Age: the life and times of William Hazlitt, 2000; The Meaning of Things, 2001; The Reason of Things, 2002; What is Good?, 2003; The Mystery of Things, 2003; (ed) Robert Herrick: lyrics of love and desire, 2003; The Heart of Things, 2005; Descartes, 2005; Among the Dead Cities, 2006; The Form of Things, 2006; Against All Gods, 2007; Truth, Meaning and Reality, 2007; Towards the Light, 2007; The Choice of Hercules, 2007; Scepticism and the Possibility of Knowledge, 2008; Ideas That Matter, 2009; Liberty in the Age of Terror, 2009; To Set Prometheus Free, 2009; Thinking of Answers, 2010; The Good Book: a secular Bible, 2011; The God Argument: the case against religion and for humanism, 2013; Friendship, 2013; The Challenge of Things: thinking through troubled times, 2015; The Age of Genius: the seventeenth century and the birth of the modern mind, 2016; War: an enquiry, 2017; Democracy and its Crisis, 2017; The History of Philosophy, 2019. *Clubs:* Athenæum, Groucho, Garrick.

**GRAYLING, Rt Hon. Christopher (Stephen);** PC 2010; MP (C) Epsom and Ewell, since 2001; *b* 1 April 1962; *s* of John Terence Grayling and Elizabeth Grayling; *m* 1987, Susan Dillistone; one *s* one *d*. *Educ:* Royal Grammar Sch., High Wycombe; Sidney Sussex Coll., Cambridge (MA Hist.). BBC News producer, 1985–88; producer and editor, Business Daily, Channel 4, 1988–91; Commissioning Editor, BBC Select, 1991–93; Dir, Charterhouse Prodns, 1993; Div. Dir, Workhouse Ltd, 1993–95; Dir, SSVC Gp, 1995–97; Change Consultant and Eur. Mktg Dir, Burson-Marsteller, 1997–2001. An Opposition Whip, 2002; Opposition front bench spokesman on health, 2002–03, on higher and further educn, 2003–05; Shadow Leader, H of C, 2005; Shadow Secretary of State: for Transport, 2005–07; for Work and Pensions, 2007–09; Shadow Home Sec., 2009–10; Minister of State, DWP, 2010–12; Lord Chancellor and Sec. of State for Justice, 2012–15; Leader of the H of C and Lord President of the Council, 2015–16; Sec. of State for Transport, 2016–19. Trustee, NPG, 2015–16. *Publications:* The Bridgewater Heritage, 1984; A Land Fit for Heroes, 1985; The Story of Joseph Holt, 1985, 2nd edn 1999; (jtly) Just Another Star, 1988. *Recreations:* football, cricket. *Address:* House of Commons, SW1A 0AA. *T:* (020) 7219 8194.

**GRAYSON, David Roger,** CBE 1999 (OBE 1994); Professor of Corporate Responsibility and Director, Doughty Centre for Corporate Responsibility, Cranfield School of Management, 2007–17, now Emeritus; Chairman, Institute of Business Ethics, since 2019; *b* 26 May 1955; *s* of late Henry Eric Fitton Grayson and Patricia Grayson (*née* Clayton). *Educ:* Mount St Mary's Coll.; Downing Coll., Cambridge (MA Law); Free Univ. of Brussels (Wiener Anspach Schol.); MA 1978); Newcastle Univ. (MBA 1985). Brand Mgt, Procter and Gamble, 1978–80; Co-Founder and Dir, Project NE, 1980–86; Jt Man. Dir, Prince's Youth Business Trust, 1986–87; Business in the Community, 1987–2007: Jt Man. Dir, resp. for ops and staff, 1989–92; Man. Dir, Business Strategy Gp, 1992–95; Dir, 1995–2007. Principal, BLU, 2001–06. Visiting Fellow: Sch. of Mgt, Imperial Coll., 1998–2007; Teesside Business Sch., 2004–07; Vis. Prof., London Guildhall Univ., 2000–03; Vis. Sen. Fellow, Kennedy Sch. of Govt, Harvard, 2006–10. Chairman: Business Link Nat. Assessment Panel, DTI, 1993–97; Business Link Nat. Accreditation Bd, 1996–2000; Nat. Disability Council, 1996–2000; UK Small Business Consortium, 2002–10; UnLtd Ageing Challenge Cttee, 2010–12; Member: Bd, Strategic Rail Authority (formerly BRB), 2000–05; SustainAbility Faculty, 2008–10; Corporate Responsibility Adv. Panel, Camelot, 2008–19; Editl Bd, Ethical Corp., 2009–14, 2016–; Faculty, Forward Inst., 2016–; Circle of Advrs, Business Fights Poverty, 2016–. Chm. Judges, UK Capital Enterprise, 2005–06. Ambassador, Nat. AIDS Trust, 2000–; Trustee: Prince of Wales Innovation Trust, 1989–; AbilityNet, 2000–02; Responsibility in Gambling Trust, 2004–08; Chm., Housing 21, 2006–11. Gov., Lilian Baylis Sch., Lambeth, 2000–05. Trustee, Carers UK, 2012– (Chm., 2013–). Patron, SCOPE, 2003–10. FRSA 1991. Hon. LLD London South Bank, 2005. Contrib. Ed., Corporate Citizenship Briefing, 2008–13. *Publications:* (contrib.) Mastering Enterprise, 1996; (contrib.) What If..., 2000; (with A. Hodges) Everybody's Business: managing risks and opportunities in today's global society, 2001; Corporate Social Opportunity, 2004; (contrib.) Entrepreneurship: a catalyst for urban regeneration, 2004; (contrib.) Sustainable Enterprise, 2004; (contrib.) The Accountable Corporation, 2005; (ed jtly) Cranfield on Corporate Sustainability, 2012; (with J. Nelson) Corporate Responsibility Coalitions: the past, present and future of alliances for sustainable capitalism, 2013; (with M. McLaren and H. Spitzeck) Social Intrapreneurism and all that Jazz, 2014; (contrib.) International Human Resource Management, 2016; Take Care: how to be a great employer for working carers, 2017; (contrib.) Managing Sustainable Business, 2018; (jtly) All In: the future of business leadership, 2018; (contrib.) Incorporating Sustainability in Management Education: an interdisciplinary approach, 2019. *Recreations:* scuba diving, travel; happiest in, on or underwater, preferably in warm climates. *Address:* Institute of Business Ethics, 24 Greencoat Place, SW1P 1BE. *E:* David@DavidGrayson.net. *W:* www.DavidGrayson.net, www.twitter.com/DavidGrayson_. *Club:* Royal Automobile.

**GRAYSON, Sir Jeremy (Brian Vincent),** 5th Bt *cr* 1922, of Ravenspoint, Co. Anglesey; *b* 30 Jan. 1933; *s* of Brian Harrington Grayson (*d* 1989), 3rd *s* of 1st Bt and of Sofia Maria (*née* Buchanan); *S* uncle, 1991; *m* 1958, Sara Mary, *d* of C. F. Upton; three *s* three *d* (and one *d* decd). *Educ:* Downside. Retired photographer. *Heir: s* Simon Jeremy Grayson, *b* 12 July 1959.

**GRAZIANO da SILVA, José,** PhD; Director General, Food and Agriculture Organization of the United Nations, 2012–19; *b* 17 Nov. 1949; *m* Paola Ligasacchi; two *c*. *Educ:* Univ. of São Paulo (Bachelor's degree Agronomy; Master's degree Rural Econs and Sociol.); State Univ. of Campinas (PhD Econs); University Coll. London (Latin Amer. Studies); Univ. of Calif, Santa Cruz (Envmtl Studies). State University of Campinas: teaching, from 1978; Prof.; Chair, Master's and Doctoral Prog. in Econ. Develt and Envmt, Inst. of Econs; co-ordinated formulation of 'Zero Hunger' Prog. (Fome Zero), Brazil, 2001; Extraordinary Minister of Food Security and the Fight against Hunger, 2003; Regl Rep. for Latin America and Caribbean and Asst Dir-Gen., UNFAO, 2006–11. *Publications:* over 25 books on rural develt, food security and agrarian econs.

**GREANEY, Paul Richard;** QC 2010; a Recorder, since 2016; *b* Halifax, W Yorks, 5 April 1970; *s* of Patrick Greaney and Anne Lesley Greaney (*née* Filby, now Phillips); *m* 1st, 2003, Pauline Mary Healy (marr. diss. 2006); one *d*; 2nd, 2009, Selina Ruth Cranidge; one *s* one *d*. *Educ:* Bradford Grammar Sch.; Durham Univ. (BA Hons Law 1992); Inns of Court Sch. of Law. Called to the Bar, Inner Temple, 1993, Bencher, 2016; in practice as barrister, specialising in criminal and regulatory law, inquiries and inquests, Leeds and London. *Address:* New Park Court Chambers, 16 Park Place, Leeds LS1 2SJ.

**GREATOREX, Barbara;** Headteacher, Wallington High School for Girls, 2002–12; *b* 11 March 1951; *d* of Benjamin John Jackson and Millicent Claire Jackson; two *s* one *d*. *Educ:* Warwick Univ. (BSc Hons); York Univ. (PGCE); Open Univ. (MA). Sen. Teacher, Joseph Rowntree Sch., 1995–97; Dep. Headteacher, Wolverhampton Girls' High Sch., 1997–2002. Master Practitioner, Neuro-Linguistic Programming, 2009–11. *Recreations:* birdwatching, reading, travelling.

**GREATOREX, Raymond Edward,** FCA; Executive Chairman, Baker Tilly, 2002–06; *b* 28 May 1940; *s* of late Percy Edward and Lilian Alice Greatorex; *m* 1982, Barbara Anne (*née* Booth); one *d*. *Educ:* Westcliff High Sch.; Lewes Co. Grammar Sch. FCA 1975. Sydenham, Snowden Nicholson & Co., chartered accountants, subseq. Sydenham & Co.: Articled Clerk, 1959; Partner, 1970; firm merged into Hodgson Harris, 1980, Hodgson Impey, 1985, Kidsons Impey, 1990, and merged with Baker Tilly, 2002; Mem., Nat. Exec. and Regl Man. Partner, Southern England, 1990–94; Chm., HLB Internat., 1994–99; Nat. Managing Partner, HLB Kidsons, 2000–02. Liveryman and Freeman, City of London; Liverymen, Farriers' Co. (Master, 2002–03). *Recreations:* race horse owner, cricket and football (watching), gardening, travelling, reading, especially autobiographies. *Address:* Beeches Brook, Strood Green, Wisborough Green, Billingshurst, W Sussex RH14 0HP. *T:* (01403) 700796. *Clubs:* East India, MCC.

**GREATREX, Neil;** National President and General Secretary, Union of Democratic Mineworkers, 1993–2009; *b* 1 April 1951; *s* of late John Edward and Joyce Irene Greatrex; *m* 1972, Sheila Waterhouse; two *d*. *Educ:* Greenwood Drive Jun. Sch.; Mowlands Intermediate Sch.; Ashfield Comprehensive Sch. Bentinck Colliery, 1965–85. National Union of Mineworkers: Cttee Mem., 1970–74; Branch Treas., 1974–80; Branch Pres., 1980–85; full-time Area Official, 1985–86; Union of Democratic Mineworkers: Area Pres., 1986–88; Nat. Vice-Pres., 1988–93. *Recreations:* Do It Yourself, shooting.

**GREATREX, Thomas James;** Chief Executive, Nuclear Industry Association, since 2016; *b* Ashford, Kent, 30 Sept. 1974; *s* of Simon Greatrex and Brenda Greatrex; *m* 2003, Laura Orrock; two *d*. *Educ:* Judd Sch., Tonbridge; London Sch. of Econs and Pol Sci. (BSc Econs, Govt and Law 1996). Parly Asst, Opposition Whips' Office, 1996–97; Special Advr to Chief Whip, 1997–98, to Minister of Agric., Fisheries and Food, 1998–99; regl organiser, GMB, 1999–2004; Hd, Policy and Public Affairs, E Dunbartonshire Council, 2004–06; Dir, Corporate Affairs, NHS 24, 2006–07; Special Advr to Sec. of State for Scotland, 2007–10. MP (Lab Co-op) Rutherglen and Hamilton W, 2010–15; contested (Lab Co-op) same seat, 2015. Mem., Fulham Supporters' Trust. *Recreations:* football (Fulham FC), cinema. *Address:* Nuclear Industry Association, 5th Floor, Tower House, 10 Southampton Street, WC2E 7HA. *E:* tom.greatrex@niauk.org. *Club:* Blantyre Miners Welfare.

**GREAVES,** family name of **Baron Greaves**.

**GREAVES, Baron** *cr* 2000 (Life Peer), of Pendle in the county of Lancashire; **Anthony Robert Greaves;** *b* 27 July 1942; *s* of Geoffrey Greaves and Moyra Greaves (*née* Brookes); *m* 1968, Heather Ann (*née* Baxter); two *d*. *Educ:* Queen Elizabeth GS, Wakefield; Hertford Coll., Oxford (BA Hons Geog.). Teacher/Lectr, 1968–74; Organising Sec., Assoc. of Liberal Councillors, 1977–85; Man. Dir, Hebden Royd Publications Ltd, (Lib Dem publications), 1985–90; second-hand book dealer, Liber Books, 1992–. Member: (L) Colne BC, 1971–74; (L then Lib Dem): Pendle BC, 1973–92, 1994–98, 2004–; Lancs CC, 1973–97. Contested: (L) Nelson and Colne, Feb. and Oct. 1974; (Lib Dem) Pendle, 1997. Vice President: LGA 2011–16; Open Spaces Soc. *Publications:* (with Rachael Pitchford) Merger: the inside story, 1988. *Recreations:* climbing, mountain/hill walking, wild flowers, cycling, politics. *Address:* 3 Hartington Street, Winewall, Colne, Lancashire BB8 8DB. *T:* (01282) 864346, 07760 196752, *T:* (office) (020) 7219 8620. *E:* greavesa@parliament.uk. *W:* www.liberallord.com.

**GREAVES, James Peter, (Jimmy);** TV broadcaster, since 1983; football correspondent, The Sunday People (formerly The People); *b* 20 Feb. 1940; *s* of James and Mary Greaves; *m* Irene Barden; two *s* two *d* (and one *s* decd). *Educ:* Kingswood Sch., Hainault. Professional footballer (inside forward), 1957; played for: Chelsea, 1957–61; AC Milan, 1961; Tottenham Hotspur, 1961–70 (FA Cup wins, 1962, 1967); West Ham, 1970–71; scored record 357 goals in First Division, 55 goals in FA Cup ties; played 57 times for England (scored 44 goals). Football correspondent, The Sun. *Publications* include: Greavsie (autobiog.), 2003; (with N. Giller): This one's on me, 1981; It's a funny old life, 1990; The Heart of the Game, 2005. *Address:* c/o Sports Department, The Sunday People, 1 Canada Square, Canary Wharf, E14 5AP.

**GREAVES, Jeffrey;** HM Diplomatic Service, retired; Consul General, Alexandria, 1978–81; *b* 10 Dec. 1926; *s* of Willie and Emily Greaves; *m* 1949, Joyce Mary Farrer; one *s* one *d*. *Educ:* Pudsey Grammar Sch. Served RN, 1945–48. Joined HM Foreign Service, 1948; FO, 1948; Benghazi, 1951; Vice Consul, Tehran, 1953; ME Centre for Arab Studies, 1955; Second Sec. and Vice Consul, Paris, 1960; Vice Consul, Muscat, 1962; Second Sec. and Consul, Athens, 1965; Second Sec. (Commercial), Cairo, 1968; First Sec. and Consul, Muscat, 1970; First Sec. (Com.), Bangkok, 1972; FCO, 1976. *Address:* 17 Queens Drive, Pudsey LS28 7HL. *T:* (0113) 257 7238.

**GREAVES, Rt Rev. Jeremy David;** an Assistant Bishop, Diocese of Brisbane (Bishop for the Northern Region), since 2017; *b* Kingsbury, UK, 7 Sept. 1969; *s* of late Robert John Ley Greaves and of Elizabeth Anne Greaves (*née* Baddeley); *m* 1996, Josephine Helen Keynes; one *s* two *d*. *Educ:* Flinders Univ. (BTh 1997). Ordained deacon, 1997, priest, 1998; Asst Curate: St John's, Salisbury, 1997–98; Christ Church, N Adelaide, 1999–2000; Rector: St Michael and All Angels, Ceduna, 2000–04; St Paul's, Katherine, 2004–07; Dean, Christ Church Cathedral, Darwin, 2007–13; Adminr, Dio. of Northern Territory, 2010–13; Rector, St Mark's, Buderim, 2014–17; Archdeacon, Sunshine Coast, 2015–17. Chair: Anglicare Willochra, 2003–04; Future Summit Leadership Award, 2005–07. Chaplain, Police, Fire and Emergency Services, 2006–07; Police Chaplain, Darwin, 2009–13. Vincent Fairfax Fellow, 1999–2000. KStJ 2016. *Address:* GPO Box 421, Brisbane, Qld 4001, Australia. *T:* (4) 28315763. *E:* jgreaves@anglicanchurchsq.org.au.

**GREAVES, Prof. Malcolm Watson,** MD, PhD; FRCP; Consultant Dermatologist, St John's Institute of Dermatology, St Thomas' Hospital, 2007–16; Consultant in Dermatology and Allergy, London Allergy Clinic, 2007–16; *b* 11 Nov. 1933; *s* of Donald Watson Greaves and Kathleen Evelyn Greaves; *m* 1964, Evelyn Yeo; one *s* one *d*. *Educ:* Epsom College; Charing Cross Med. Sch. MD, PhD London. MRC Clinical Res. Fellow, UCL, 1963–66; Reader in Dermatology, Univ. of Newcastle upon Tyne, 1966–75; Prof. of Dermatology, Univ. of London, 1975–99, now Emeritus; Dean, St John's Inst. of Dermatology, UMDS of Guy's and St Thomas' Hosps, 1989–95. Prof. of Dermatology, Nat. Univ. of Malaysia, 2001–02. Sen. Consultant in Dermatology, Singapore Gen. Hosp., 2003–05; Sen. Consultant Dermatologist, Singapore Nat. Skin Centre, 2005–07; Clinical Prof., Faculty of Medicine, Nat. Univ. of Singapore, 2006–07. Chm., Scientific Cttee and Trustee, Skin Disease Res. Fund, 1980–96; Mem., Cttee on Safety of Medicines, DHSS, 1982–89. President: European Soc. for Dermatol Research, 1984; Sect. of Dermatol., RSM, 1996; Chm., Therapy and Audit Cttee, British Assoc. of Dermatologists, 1994–96. Prog. Dir, American Acad. of Dermatol., 1998–2001. Dean, Internat. Faculty, Regl Conf. on Dermatol., Malaysia, 2010. Internat. Hon. Mem., Amer. Dermatol. Assoc., 1987; Hon. Member: Amer. Soc. for Investigative Dermatol., 1989; Malaysian Dermatol Assoc., 1995; British Assoc. of Dermatologists, 2000; Eur. Soc. for Dermatol Res., 2000. Mem.

Management Bd Exec., UMDS, 1990–95; Mem. Governing Body, Sch. of Pharmacy, Univ. of London, 1990–95. FAMS 2005. Sir Archibald Gray Gold Medal, British Assoc. of Dermatologists, 1998; Leo Von Zumbusch Gold Medal, Univ. München, 1998; Cert. of Appreciation, Internat. Cttee of Dermatol., 2001; Dist. Sci. Achievement Award, Eur. Acad. of Allergy and Clin. Immunology, 2002; Dist. Res. Award, Eur. Acad. of Dermatol. and Venereol., 2005; Dist. Res. Award, World Allergy Orgn, 2007; Dist. Academic Achievement Award, Amer. Skin Foundn, 2010; Medal for Contribs to Dermatol Res., British Soc. for Investigative Dermatol., 2012. *Publications*: Pharmacology of the Skin, Vol. I, Pharmacology of Skin Systems and Autocoids in Normal and Inflamed Skin, 1989; Vol. II, Methods, Absorption, Metabolism, Toxicity, Drugs and Diseases, 1989; (ed) Urticaria and Angioedema, 2004, 2nd edn 2009; Itch: basic mechanisms and therapy, 2004; contrib. Immunol. and Allergy Clinics of N America. *Address*: 4 Randalls Close, Wrestlingworth, Beds SG19 2BZ.

**GREAVES, Mary;** *see* Bownes, M.

**GREAVES, Sir Melvyn Francis, (Sir Mel),** Kt 2019; FRS 2003; Chairman, Section of Haemato-Oncology, since 2006, and Founding Director, Centre for Evolution and Cancer, since 2013, Institute of Cancer Research; *b* 12 Sept. 1941; *s* of Edward and Violet Greaves; *m* 1966, Josephine Pank; one *s* one *d*. *Educ*: City of Norwich Grammar Sch.; University Coll. London; Middlesex Hosp. Med. Sch. BSc, PhD London. FRCPath 1997. Vis Scientist, Karolinska Inst., Stockholm, 1968–69; Res. Fellow, Nat. Inst. for Med. Res., London, 1969–72; Res. Scientist, Dept of Zoology, UCL, 1972–76; Hd, Membrane Immunology Dept, Imperial Cancer Res. Fund, 1976–84; Dir, Leukaemia Res. Fund Centre, Inst. of Cancer Res., London, 1984–2005. Hon. MRCP 1987. FMedSci 1999. Paul Martini Prize (Germany), 1977; Peter Debye Prize (Holland), 1981; King Faisal Internat. Prize for Medicine, 1988; José Carreras Prize (Europe), 2001; Lifetime Achievement Award, CRUK, 2015; Royal Medal, Royal Soc., 2017. *Publications*: T and B Lymphocytes, 1973; Cellular Recognition, 1975; Atlas of Blood Cells, 1981, 2nd edn 1988; Monoclonal Antibodies to Receptors, 1984; Cancer: the evolutionary legacy, 2000; White Blood: personal journeys with childhood leukaemia, 2008; The Making of You, 2017; contribs to bio-med. jls. *Recreations*: music, cooking, photography, natural history, being grandad. *Address*: Institute of Cancer Research, Sutton, Surrey SM2 5NG.

**GREEN,** family name of **Barons Green of Deddington** and **Green of Hurstpierpoint**.

**GREEN OF DEDDINGTON,** Baron *cr* 2014 (Life Peer), of Deddington in the County of Oxfordshire; **Andrew Fleming Green,** KCMG 1998 (CMG 1991); HM Diplomatic Service, retired; Founder Chairman, Migrationwatch UK, since 2001; *b* 6 Aug. 1941; *s* of late Gp Captain J. H. Green, RAF, and Beatrice Mary (*née* Bowditch); *m* 1968, C. Jane Churchill; one *s* one *d*. *Educ*: Haileybury and ISC; Magdalene Coll., Cambridge (MA). Served as 2nd Lieut, RGJ, 1962–65; joined HM Diplomatic Service, 1965; Middle East Centre for Arab Studies, 1966–68; Aden, 1968–69; Asst Political Agent, Abu Dhabi, 1970–71; First Secretary, FCO, 1972–74; Private Sec. to Minister of State, FCO, 1975, and to Parliamentary Under Sec. of State, 1976; First Secretary, UK Delegn to OECD, Paris, 1977–79; First Sec., FCO, 1980–81; Counsellor, Washington, 1982–85; Counsellor, Hd of Chancery and Consul Gen., Riyadh, 1985–88; Counsellor, FCO, 1988–90; Ambassador to Syria, 1991–94; Asst Under-Sec. of State (Middle East), FCO, 1994–96; Ambassador to Saudi Arabia, 1996–2000. Chm., Med. Aid for Palestinians, 2002–04; Trustee, Christian Solidarity Worldwide, 2002–14. *Recreations*: tennis, bridge.

**GREEN OF HURSTPIERPOINT,** Baron *cr* 2010 (Life Peer), of Hurstpierpoint in the County of West Sussex; **Stephen Keith Green;** *b* 7 Nov. 1948; *s* of late Dudley Keith Green and Dorothy Rosamund Mary Green; *m* 1971, Janian Joy; two *d*. *Educ*: Lancing Coll.; Exeter Coll., Oxford (BA PPE); MIT (MSc Pol Sci.). ODA, FCO, 1971–77; McKinsey & Co. Inc., 1977–82; Hong Kong & Shanghai Banking Corp. Ltd, 1982–92; HSBC Hldgs plc, 1993–2010: Exec. Dir, Investment Banking and Markets, 1998–2003; Gp Chief Exec., 2003–06; Gp Chm., 2006–10. Dir, HSBC Bank plc, 1995–2010 (Chm., 2005–10). Dep. Pres., CBI, 2010. Minister of State (Minister for Trade and Investment), BIS and FCO, 2011–13. Chairman: Trustees, Natural History Mus., 2014–; Asia House, 2017–; Pres., Inst. of Export and Internat. Trade, 2017–. Ordained deacon 1987; priest 1988. *Publications*: Serving God? Serving Mammon?, 1996; Good Value: reflections on money, morality and an uncertain world, 2009; Reluctant Meister, 2014; The European Identity, 2015; Brexit and the British, 2017. *Recreations*: opera, art, European literature, walking. *Address*: House of Lords, SW1A 0PW. *Club*: Athenæum.

**GREEN, Sir Albert A.;** *see* Aynsley-Green.

**GREEN, Sir Allan (David),** KCB 1991; QC 1987; *b* 1 March 1935; *s* of late Lionel and Irene Green; *m* 1st, 1967, Eva (*d* 1993), *yr d* of Prof. Artur Attman and Elsa Attman, Gothenburg, Sweden; one *s* one *d*; 2nd, 2004, Anna, *er d* of late Lemuel Harries and Muriel Harries, Gower. *Educ*: Charterhouse; St Catharine's Coll., Cambridge (Open Exhibnr, MA). Served RN, 1953–55. Called to the Bar, Inner Temple, 1959, Bencher, 1985; Jun. Prosecuting Counsel to the Crown, Central Criminal Court, 1977, Sen. Prosecuting Counsel, 1979, First Senior Prosecuting Counsel, 1985; a Recorder, 1979–87; DPP and Hd of Crown Prosecution Service, 1987–91. Mem., Gen. Council of the Bar, 1992. *Recreations*: music, especially opera, admiring calligraphy. *Address*: c/o 2 Hare Court, Temple, EC4Y 7BH. *Club*: Garrick.

**GREEN, Andrew Curtis;** farmer and horticulturalist, since 1960; *b* 28 March 1936; *s* of Christopher Green and Marjorie (*née* Bennett); *m* 1966, Julia Margaret (*née* Davidson); two *s*. *Educ*: Charterhouse; Magdalene Coll., Cambridge. MA (Nat. Scis), Dip. of Agriculture. Commnd RNVR, 1954–56. Farm management, 1960–67; founded Greens of Soham farming and horticultural business, 1967; Director: Elsoms Spalding Seed Co., 1982–2009; Spearhead Internat. Ltd, 1999–2011; Chm., Hassy Ltd, 1983–89. Mem., AFRC, 1984–88. Mem., E England Regl Cttee, NT, 2005–11. Founder, Kingfishers Bridge Wetland Creation Project, 1995. FLS 1978; Hon. FIHort 1986 (Industrial Mem. Council, 1988–94); FRAgS 1995. MInstD 1985. Extra Mem., Court of Skinners' Co., 1994–96. *Recreations*: wildlife conservation, sailing, ski-ing, fishing, shooting. *Address*: Mill House, Tower Road, Burnham Overy Staithe, Kings Lynn, Norfolk PE31 8JB. *Clubs*: Sloane, Farmers; Hawks (Cambridge); Cambridge Univ. Cruising; Brancaster Staithe Sailing; Burnham Overy Staithe Sailing.

*See also* P. C. Green.

**GREEN, Andrew James;** Chairman, IG Group, 2014–19; *b* England, 7 Sept. 1955; two *s* one *d*; *m* 2014, Susan Elizabeth Jukes. *Educ*: King Edward's Sch., Edgbaston; Leeds Univ. (BSc Hons Chem. Engrg 1976). Sales and mktg, Shell, 1976–83; Consultant, Deloitte, Haskin & Sells, 1984–86; Bd Mem., BT, 1986–2007; CEO, Logica, 2008–12; Chairman: Dockon Inc., 2012; NP Gp, 2013–; Connected Digital Catapult, 2013–. Non-executive Director: ARM Hldgs, 2011; Avanti Communications, 2014–. Pres., UK Space, 2009–. Liveryman, Information Technologists' Co., 2011–. FRSA. *Recreations*: scuba diving, cricket, whisky and wine. *Address*: 24 The Wallpaper Apartments, 142 Offord Road, N1 1NS. *T*: 07802 243885. *E*: agreen8@mac.com.

**GREEN, Andrew James Dominic;** QC 2010; *b* London, 8 Nov. 1965; *s* of Barry and Marilyn Green; *m* 1994, Jennifer Hirschl; one *s* one *d*. *Educ*: Eton Coll.; London Sch. of Econs (LLB). Called to the Bar, Inner Temple, 1988; in practice as barrister, specialising in commercial and financial services law, Blackstone Chambers, 1988–. Author, Report of FSA's enforcement actions following failure of HBOS, FCA and Prudential Regulation Authy, 2015; Specialist Advr to Treasury Select Cttee, 2016– (jt author, Maxwellisation Report, 2016). *Recreation*: involved in running charity Just1Life. *Address*: Blackstone Chambers, Blackstone House, Temple, EC4Y 9BW. *T*: (020) 7583 1770. *Clubs*: Athenæum, Garrick.

**GREEN, Andrew Michael Walter;** Librarian, National Library of Wales, 1998–2013; *b* 30 Sept. 1952; *s* of Harry Green and Ellen Martha Kennedy Green (*née* Allan); *m* 1980, Carys Evans; two *d*. *Educ*: Hoylandswaine Primary Sch.; Queen Elizabeth Grammar Sch., Wakefield; Gonville and Caius Coll., Cambridge (BA 1973; MA 1975; Wace Medal for Classical Archaeology 1973); Coll. of Librarianship, Wales (Dip. Librarianship 1975). MCLIP (ALA 1977). Asst Librarian, UC, Cardiff, 1975–88; Arts and Social Studies Librarian, UWCC, 1988–89; Sub-Librarian (Services and Collection Develt), Univ. of Sheffield, 1989–92; Librarian, 1992–95, Dir of Library and Information Services, 1996–98, UC, Swansea. Vice-Chm., 2000–02, Chm., 2002–04, SCONUL. Chair, Coleg Cymraeg Cenedlaethol, 2014–17 (Hon. Fellow, 2019). Pres., Royal Instn of S Wales, 2018–. FLSW 2013. Hon. Fellow: Univ. of Wales, Swansea, 2001; NE Wales Inst. of Higher Educn, 2003; Univ. of Wales, Lampeter, 2006; Hon. FCLIP 2015. Mem., Gorsedd Beirdd Ynys Prydein, 2009. Hon. DLitt Wales, 2013; Hon. PhD Open, 2015. *Publications*: In the Chair: how to guide groups and manage meetings, 2014; Wales in 100 Objects, 2018; Can Gwrthrych Cymru, 2018; numerous articles on library and information studies; weekly blog (gwallter.com). *Recreations*: running, cycling, walking, music, looking out of windows. *Address*: 30 Caswell Drive, Caswell, Swansea SA3 4RJ. *T*: (01792) 361260.

**GREEN, Ann Margaret,** CBE 2010; Pro-Chancellor and Chairman, Governing Board, York St John University, since 2011; *b* Chester, 28 March 1951; *d* of John Britton and Margaret Britton (*née* Constable); *m* 2016, Trevor Duncan Berry. *Educ*: Southport High Sch. for Girls. Nationwide Bldg Soc., 1969–77; Partner, commercial and business insce brokers, 1977–83; Northern Dir, Stock Exchange, 1983–85; Dir, Allied Provincial Securities, 1986–91; Northern Dir, Industrial Soc., 1992–96; self-employed business consultant, 1996–. Non-executive Director: Stag Security Services Ltd, 2006–12; DCMS, 2009–11. Chairman: Hadrian's Wall Heritage Ltd, 2006–15; York Th. Royal Trust, 2014–; York Guildhall Orch., 2016–. Trustee, Royal Armouries, 1998–2011 (Chm., 2003–11). *Recreations*: heritage, museums, art, theatre, driving, opera. *Address*: 89 Postern Close, Bishops Wharf, York YO23 1JF. *T*: 07702 213013. *E*: annmargaretgreen@gmail.com.

**GREEN, Anthony Eric Sandall,** RA 1977 (ARA 1971); NEAC 2002; Member, London Group, 1964; artist (painter); *b* 30 Sept. 1939; *s* of late Frederick Sandall Green and Marie Madeleine (*née* Dupont); *m* 1961, Mary Louise Cozens-Walker; two *d*. *Educ*: Highgate Sch., London; Slade Sch. of Fine Art, University Coll. London (Fellow, UCL, 1991). Henry Tonks Prize for drawing, Slade Sch., 1960; French Govt Schol., Paris, 1960; Gulbenkian Purchase Award, 1963; Harkness Fellowship, in USA, 1967–69. Trustee, RA, 2000–08. Has exhibited in: London, New York, Haarlem, Rotterdam, Stuttgart, Hanover, Helsingborg, Malmö, Tokyo, Brussels, W Berlin, Chicago and Sydney. Paintings in various public collections, including: Tate Gallery; Metropolitan Mus. of Art, N York; Mus. of Fine Art, Boston, USA; Nat. Mus. of Wales; Gulbenkian Foundn; Arts Council of GB; British Council; Victoria and Albert Mus.; Contemporary Art Soc.; Wolfson Coll., Cambridge; Frans Hals Mus., Holland; Boymans-van Beuningen Mus., Holland; Ulster Mus., Belfast; Ikeda and Niigata Mus., Setagaya Art Mus., Metropolitan, Tokyo; Hiroshima; Fukuoka. Featured Artist, RA Summer Exhibn, 2003. Hon. RBA 1998; Hon. ROI 2004. Hon. Fellow, Wolfson Coll., Cambridge, 2015. DUniv Buckingham, 2011. Exhibit of the Year award, RA, 1977. *Publications*: A Green Part of the World, 1984; *relevant publication*: Anthony Green: painting life, by Martin Bailey, 2017. *Recreations*: travelling, family life. *Address*: Mole End, 40 High Street, Little Eversden, Cambridge CB23 1HE. *T*: (01223) 262292, *Fax*: (01223) 265656.

**GREEN, Prof. Anthony Richard,** PhD; FRCP, FRCPath, FMedSci; Professor of Haemato-Oncology, since 1999, and Head, Department of Haematology, since 2000, University of Cambridge; Chair, Department of Haematology, Addenbrooke's Hospital, since 2000; Director, Cambridge Stem Cell Institute, since 2016; *b* 13 Oct. 1955; *s* of John Richard Green and Jeanne Dorothy Green; *m* 1984, Sarah Frances Rann; one *s* two *d*. *Educ*: Highgate Sch.; Queens' Coll., Cambridge; University Coll. Hosp., London (PhD 1987). FRCP 1995; FRCPath 1997. Jun. hosp. posts, London, 1980–84; Clinical Res. Fellow, ICRF, 1984–87; Lectr in Haematology, Univ. Hosp. of Wales, Cardiff, 1987–89; CRC Hamilton Fairley Travelling Fellow, Walter & Eliza Hall Inst., Melbourne, 1989–91; Wellcome Trust Sen. Clinical Fellow, Dept of Haematology, Cambridge Univ., 1991–99. Pres., Eur. Hematol. Assoc., 2015–17. FMedSci 2001. *Recreations*: family, friends, hill walking, scuba diving, photography. *Address*: Wellcome-MRC Cambridge Stem Cell Institute, Jeffrey Cheah Biomedical Centre, Cambridge Biomedical Campus, University of Cambridge, Puddicombe Way, Cambridge CB2 0AW.

**GREEN, Arthur;** Senior Partner, Grant Thornton, 1986–88, retired; President, Institute of Chartered Accountants in England and Wales, 1987–88; *b* 15 June 1928; *s* of Arthur Henry and Elizabeth Burns Green; *m* 1952, Sylvia Myatt; one *s* one *d*. *Educ*: Liverpool Collegiate. FCA. Qualified Chartered Accountant, 1950; Partner, Bryce Hanmer & Co., Liverpool, 1954 (merged Thornton Baker; later Grant Thornton); Nat. Managing Partner, Thornton Baker, 1975–84; Chm. and Man. Dir, Grant Thornton International, 1984–85. Vice-Pres., 1985–86, Dep. Pres., 1986–87, ICA. *Recreations*: bridge, theatre. *Address*: Up Yonder, Herbert Road, Salcombe, Devon TQ8 8HP. *T*: (01548) 842075.

**GREEN, Prof. Ben Joseph,** PhD; FRS 2010; Waynflete Professor of Pure Mathematics, University of Oxford, since 2013; Fellow, Magdalen College, Oxford, since 2013; *b* 27 Feb. 1977; *s* of late Robert Norman Green and of Judith Mary Green; *m* 2014, Dr Yvonne Lee; two *s*. *Educ*: Trinity Coll., Cambridge (BA Hons Maths 1998, MA 2001; PhD 2003). Res. Fellow, Trinity Coll., Cambridge, 2001–05; Prof. of Pure Maths, Univ. of Bristol, 2005–06; Herchel Smith Prof. of Pure Maths, Univ. of Cambridge, 2006–13; Fellow, Trinity Coll., Cambridge, 2006–13. *Publications*: contrib. learned jls. *Recreations*: orienteering, hill-walking, jazz. *Address*: Mathematical Institute, University of Oxford, Andrew Wiles Building, Radcliffe Observatory Quarter, Woodstock Road, Oxford OX2 6GG. *E*: Ben.green@maths.ox.ac.uk.

**GREEN, Brian Russell;** QC 1997; *b* 25 July 1956; *s* of late Bertram Green and Dora Green (*née* Rinsler); *m* 1994, Yvonne Mammon; one *s* one *d*, and two step *d*. *Educ*: Ilford County High Sch. for Boys; St Edmund Hall, Oxford (BA, BCL). Called to the Bar, Middle Temple, 1980; Mem., Lincoln's Inn, 1991. *Recreations*: travel, hill-walking, ski-ing, the arts. *Address*: Wilberforce Chambers, 8 New Square, Lincoln's Inn, WC2A 3QP. *T*: (020) 7306 0102. *Club*: Athenæum.

**GREEN, Prof. Brynmor Hugh,** OBE 1995; Sir Cyril Kleinwort Professor of Countryside Management, University of London, Wye College, 1987–96, now Professor Emeritus; *b* 14 Jan. 1941; *s* of Albert Walter Green and Margaret Afona Green (*née* Griffiths); *m* 1965, Jean Armstrong; two *s. Educ:* Dartford Grammar Sch.; Univ. of Nottingham (BSc 1st Cl. Hons Botany, PhD Plant Ecol.). Lectr in Plant Ecology, Dept of Botany, Univ. of Manchester, 1965–68; Dep. Regl Officer (SE) 1968–69, Regl Officer (SE) 1969–75, Nature Conservancy Council; Lectr and Sen. Lectr, Wye Coll., 1975–87. Chm., Council of Europe Wkg Party on Flora, Fauna and Landscapes, 1971–73. Mem., England Cttee, Nature Conservancy Council, 1983–90; a Countryside Comr, 1984–93. Vice-Pres., Kent Wildlife Trust, 2002–. Churchill Fellow, 1999. *Publications:* Countryside Conservation: landscape ecology, planning and management, 1981, 3rd edn 1996; (jtly) The Diversion of Land: conservation in a period of farming contraction, 1990; (jtly) The Changing Role of the Common Agricultural Policy: the future of farming in Europe, 1991; (jtly) Threatened Landscapes: conserving cultural environments, 2001; Natural Kent: an introduction to the habitats, wildlife and wild places of the county, 2008; numerous chapters in books, conf. reports, sci. jls. *Recreations:* golf, watercolour sketching, bird-watching. *Address:* Heatherbank, 49 Brockhill Road, Saltwood, Hythe, Kent CT21 4AF. *T:* (01303) 261093.

**GREEN, Charlotte Rosamund;** freelance writer and broadcaster, since 2013; continuity announcer and newsreader, BBC Radio 4, 1985–2013; *b* 4 May 1956; *y d* of Geoffrey Hugh Green, CB and of Ruth Hazel (*née* Mercy). *Educ:* Haberdashers' Aske's Sch. for Girls; Univ. of Kent at Canterbury (BA Hons Eng. and American Lit.). Joined BBC as studio manager, 1978; newsreader, BBC Radio 4, 1986–2013; regular participant in The News Quiz, 1987–2013; producer and presenter, Morning has Broken, BBC Radio 4, 1986–91; presenter, News Speak, BBC World Service, 1999; narrator, Music in Camera, BBC TV, 1989; presenter, Charlotte Green's Great Composers, 2013, Charlotte Green's Culture Club, 2013–17, Classic FM; reader of classified football results, Sports Report, BBC Radio 5 Live, 2013–; quotations reader, Quote Unquote, BBC Radio 4, 2014–. Trustee, Univ. of Kent Develt Trust, 2003–10. Judge, BBC Frank Gillard Annual Local Radio Awards, 2000–02. DUniv Kent, 2013. Most Attractive Female Voice on the Radio award, Radio Times, 2002; Roberts Radio Special Award for Excellence in Broadcasting, 2009; Radio Broadcaster of the Year Award, Broadcasting Press Guild, 2013; inducted into Radio Acad. Hall of Fame, 2013. *Publications:* The News is Read (autobiog.), 2014. *Recreations:* theatre, books, art, music, laughing with friends, supporting Tottenham Hotspur FC, gardening. *Address:* c/o Excellent Talent, Grand Union Studios, 332 Ladbroke Grove, W10 5AD. *T:* 0845 210 0111.

**GREEN, Chris;** MP (C) Bolton West, since 2015; *b* 12 Aug. 1973. Engr, mass spectrometry industry. Contested (C) Manchester Withington, 2010. Member: Sci. and Technol. Select Cttee, 2015–17; Work and Pensions Select Cttee, 2017–18; Home Affairs Select Cttee, 2018–. *Address:* House of Commons, SW1A 0AA.

**GREEN, Christopher Edward Wastie,** MA; FCILT; non-executive Director, Heathrow Express, 2013–18; *b* 7 Sept. 1943; *s* of James Wastie Green and Margarita Mensing; *m* 1966, Waltraud Mitzie Petzold; one *s* one *d. Educ:* St Paul's School, London; Oriel College, Oxford. MA Mod. Hist. British Rail: Management Trainee, 1965–67; served Birmingham, Nottingham, Hull, Wimbledon; Passenger Operating Manager, HQ, 1979–80; Chief Operating Manager, Scotland, 1980–83; Dep. Gen. Manager, Scotland, 1983–84; Gen. Manager, Scottish Region, 1984–86; Dir, Network SouthEast, 1986–91; Managing Director: InterCity, 1992–94; ScotRail, 1994–95; Chief Exec. and Comr, English Heritage, 1995–96; Director: Gibb Rail Ltd, 1996–99; Gibb Ltd, 1996–99; Chief Exec., Virgin Trains, 1999–2004; Dir, 1999–2004, Chm., 2004–05, Virgin Rail Gp. Director: Eurotunnel, 1995–2004; Connex Rail, 1998–99. Chm., Rail Forum, 2004–07. Non-executive Director: Network Rail, 2005–10; W Herts Hosp. NHS Trust, 2010–13; Dover Harbour Bd, 2010–14. Chm., Expert Adv. Panel, Crossrail, 2013–; Ind. Advr to Thameslink, Crossrail and InterCity Express projects. Mem., Regl Council, CBI, 1986. President: Railway Study Assoc., 1989–90, 1997–98; Railway Convalescent Homes, 2002–; Vice Pres., CIT, 1988; Mem., Railway Heritage Trust Adv. Panel, 2003–. Mem. Adv. Bd, Cranfield Univ. Logistics and Transportation Centre, 1996–2002; Trustee, Royal Liverpool Phil. Orch., 2004–08. Hon. DBA IMCB, 2002; DUniv UCE, 2002. *Recreations:* music, reading, walking, canals, architecture. *Address:* 14 Meadway, Berkhamsted, Herts HP4 2PN. *T:* (01442) 862978, 07788 924258. *E:* chrisgreen0709@gmail.com.

**GREEN, Prof. Christopher Kenneth,** PhD; FBA 1999; Professor of History of Art, Courtauld Institute of Art, 1991–2008, now Emeritus; *b* 1943; *m* Charlotte Sebag-Montefiore; one *s* one *d. Educ:* Christ's Coll., Cambridge (BA 1966); London Univ. (MA); PhD. Courtauld Institute of Art: successively Asst Lectr, Lectr, and Reader in History of Art; Curator, Juan Gris exhibn, Whitechapel Gall., 1992; Curator, Roger Fry exhibn, Courtauld, 1999; Co-curator, Henri Rousseau exhibn, Tate Modern, Paris and Washington, 2005; Curator, Picasso exhibn, Barcelona, 2008; Co-curator, Modern Antiquity exhibn, J. Paul Getty Museum, LA, 2011; Co-curator, Mondrian/Nicholson exhibn, Courtauld, 2012. Leverhulme Res. Fellow, 1997–98. Trustee, Nat. Museums Liverpool, 2001–10. *Publications:* Léger and the Avant-Garde, 1976; Cubism and its Enemies, 1987; (jtly) Juan Gris, 1992; European Avant-Gardes, 1995; One Man Show (novel), 1995; (ed) Art Made Modern: Roger Fry's vision of art, 1999; Art in France 1900–1940, 2000; Picasso: architecture and vertigo, 2005; (ed) Modern Antiquity: Picasso, de Chirico, Léger, Picabia, 2011; (ed) Mondrian/Nicholson: in parallel, 2012; exhibn catalogues. *Recreation:* finding calm.

**GREEN, Colin Raymond;** Chairman, Hermes Group Pension Scheme, 2002–13; *b* 16 April 1949; *s* of Gerald and Maisie Green; *m* 1975, Hazel Ruth Lateman; one *s* one *d. Educ:* Hampton Grammar Sch.; LSE (LLB Hons); Coll. of Law; WUJS Post-grad. Inst., Israel. Solicitor, 1973; Paisner & Co., 1971–74; Partner, Clintons, 1975–77; Solicitor's Office, Post Office, 1977; British Telecommunications: Solicitor's Office, 1981; Head, Privatisation Div., 1982–84; Head, M&A Div., 1984–85; Dir, Commercial Dept, 1985–89; Solicitor, 1989–94; Chief Legal Adviser, 1989–99; Secretary, 1994–2002; Mem. Exec. Cttee, 1996–2002; Gp Commercial Dir, 1999–2002. Trustee, BT Pension Scheme, 1994–2002. Chm., BT Telecomunicacoes SA, 2001–02; Director: Vio (Worldwide) Ltd, 1998–2001; Airtel SA, 1999–2001; Radware Inc., 2009–10; Sen. non-exec. Dir, ECI Telecom Inc., 2002–07. Chm., Shalom Nursery Ltd, 2007–09. Dir, Centre for Dispute Resolution, 1995–2000. Chm., Green Aid, 2004–. Trustee: Nightingale Hammerson (formerly Nightingale House), 2003–; Refugee Action Kingston, 2013–. Voluntary Advr, Citizen's Advice Kingston, 2002–. *Recreations:* music (playing and composing), walking, reading, theatre, football. *Address:* PO Box 771, Edgware HA8 4QW. *T:* 07447 066569.

**GREEN, Rt Hon. Damian (Howard),** PC 2012; MP (C) Ashford, since 1997; *b* 17 Jan. 1956; *s* of late Howard and Audrey Green; *m* 1988, Alicia Collinson; two *d. Educ:* Reading Sch.; Balliol Coll., Oxford (MA 1st cl. Hons. PPE). Producer, BBC Financial Unit, 1980–82; Business Producer, Channel 4 News, 1982–84; Business News Ed., The Times, 1984–85; Business Ed., Channel 4 News, 1985–87; Presenter and City Ed., Business Daily prog., Channel 4, 1987–92; Prime Minister's Policy Unit, 1992–94; Public Affairs Advr, 1994–97. Opposition spokesman: on employment and higher educn; 1998–99; on the envmt, 1999–2001; Shadow Educn Sec., 2001–03; Shadow Transport Sec., 2003–04; Shadow Minister for Immigration, 2005–10; Minister of State: (Minister for Immigration), Home Office, 2010–12; (Minister for Policing, Criminal Justice and Victims), Home Office and MoJ, 2012–14; Sec. of State for Work and Pensions, 2016–17; First Sec. of State and Minister for the Cabinet Office, 2017. Chairman: European Mainstream Gp, 2014–16; All-Party BBC Gp, 2015–16, Longevity Gp, 2019–; Mem., European Scrutiny Cttee, 2015–16. Mem. Bd, Britain Stronger in Europe, 2015–16. Contested (C) Brent E, 1992. Trustee, Communities Develt Foundn, 1997–2001; Vice-Chm., John Smith Meml Trust, 2004–10. *Publications:* ITN Budget Factbook, annually 1984–86; A Better BBC, 1990; Communities in the Countryside, 1995; The Four Failures of the New Deal, 1998; Better Learning, 2002; More Than Markets, 2003; (with David Davis) Controlling Economic Migration, 2006. *Recreations:* cricket, football, opera, cinema. *Address:* House of Commons, SW1A 0AA. *T:* (020) 7219 3000.

**GREEN, Sir David;** *see* Green, Sir G. D.

**GREEN, David,** FCA; Managing Director, C. Hoare & Co., 2015–19; *b* London, 27 July 1956; *s* of Joseph Charles and Florence May Green; *m* 1998, Stephanie Linda Smith; one *s* one *d. Educ:* Harvard Business Sch. (AMP). FCA 1990. Trained as accountant, Price Bailey; Consultant, then Manager, KPMG, 1985–87; Finance Dir, Midland do Brasil, then Sen. Manager, Corporate Finance and Capital Markets, later Sen. Manager, Gp Planning, Midland Bank, subseq. HSBC, 1987–93; Dir of Planning, Trustee Savings Bank, 1993–95; Hd of Financial Strategy, BBC, then Finance Dir, later CEO, BBC Resources, 1995–2002; Chief Financial Officer, 2003–12, Dep. CEO, 2012–15, C. Hoare & Co. Ind. non-exec. Dir, Bank of Cyprus (UK), 2012–19. FInstD 2010. *Recreations:* travel, photography, reading. *Address:* Parsonage Farm, Wimbish, Saffron Walden, Essex CB10 2UZ. *T:* (01799) 598174. *E:* neergd.56@gmail.com.

**GREEN, David Charles,** CBE 2001; *b* 3 June 1943; *s* of Phillip and Eileen Green; *m* 1969, Anne Patricia Ward; one *s* one *d. Educ:* Latymer Upper Sch. Exec. Officer, Traders Road Transport Assoc., 1966–71; Freight Transport Association: Regl Controller, 1971–87; Exec. Dir, 1987–93; Dir-Gen., 1993–2000; Exec. Vice-Pres., 2001–03. Pres., Internat. Road Transport Union, 1995–2001. *Publications:* numerous articles and reports on freight transport and logistics. *Recreations:* golf, cricket, modern political history.

**GREEN, David George,** PhD; Director, Civitas: Institute for the Study of Civil Society, since 2000; *b* 24 Jan. 1951; *s* of George Green and Kathleen Mary (*née* Ellis); *m* 1980, Catherine Walker; one *s* one *d. Educ:* Newcastle upon Tyne Univ. (BA Hons 1973; PhD 1980). Pt-time Lectr, Newcastle upon Tyne Poly., 1974–81; Res. Fellow, ANU, 1981–83; Res. Fellow, 1984–86, Dir, Health and Welfare Unit, 1986–2000, Inst. of Economic Affairs. Mem. (Lab), Newcastle upon Tyne CC, 1975–81. *Publications:* Power and Party in an English City, 1981; Mutual Aid or Welfare State, 1984; Working Class Patients and the Medical Establishment, 1985; Challenge to the NHS, 1986; The New Right, 1987; Everyone a Private Patient, 1988; Reinventing Civil Society, 1993; Community without Politics, 1996; From Welfare State to Civil Society, 1996; Benefit Dependency, 1998; An End to Welfare Rights, 1999; Delay, Denial and Dilution, 2000; Stakeholder Health Insurance, 2000; Health Care in France and Germany, 2001; Crime and Civil Society, 2005; We're (Nearly) All Victims Now!, 2007; Individualists Who Co-operate, 2009; Prosperity with Principles, 2010; The Demise of the Free State, 2014; Democratic Civilisation or Judicial Supremacy?, 2016; Inclusive Capitalism: how we can make independence work for everyone, 2017. *Recreation:* walking. *Address:* Civitas, 55 Tufton Street, Westminster, SW1P 3QL.

**GREEN, Prof. David Headley,** AM 2006; FRS 1991; FAA; Director, Research School of Earth Sciences, Australian National University, 1994–2001, now Professor Emeritus (Honorary Research Professor, 2002–08); Honorary Research Professor and Professor Emeritus, University of Tasmania, since 2008; *b* 29 Feb. 1936; *s* of Ronald Horace Green and Josephine May Headley; *m* 1959, Helen Mary McIntyre; three *s* three *d. Educ:* Univ. of Tasmania (BSc Hons 1957; MSc 1959; DSc 1988); Univ. of Cambridge (PhD 1962). Geologist, Bureau of Mineral Resources, Geology and Geophysics, Canberra, 1957–59; Postgrad. Scholarship, Royal Commn for Exhibn of 1851, 1959–62; Research School of Earth Sciences, Australian National University: Res. Fellow, 1962–65; Fellow, 1965–68; Sen. Fellow, 1968–74; Professorial Fellow, 1974–76; Prof. of Geology, Univ. of Tasmania, 1977–93. Chief Science Advr, Dept of Arts, Sport, Envmt, Tourism and Territories, 1991–93. FAA 1974. For. Mem., Russian Acad. of Scis, 2003. Fellow, Amer. Geophysical Union, 2004. Hon. Fellow: Eur. Union of Geoscis, 1985; Geol Soc. of America, 1986; Mineralogical Soc., 2004. Hon. DLitt Tasmania, 1994. Hallimond Lect., Mineralogical Soc., 1996. Edgeworth David Medal, Royal Soc., NSW, 1968; Stillwell Medal, Geol Soc. of Australia, 1977; Mawson Medal, 1982, Jaeger Medal, 1990, Aust. Acad. of Sci.; A. G. Werner Medaille, Deutsche Mineralogische Ges., 1998; Murchison Medal, Geol Soc., 2000; Humboldt Research Prize, 2001; Centenary Medal (Australia), 2002; Internat. Gold Medal, Geol Soc. of Japan, 2007; Gold Medal, Internat. Mineralogical Assoc., 2012. *Publications:* numerous articles in fields of petrology, experimental petrology and geochemistry, in learned jls. *Recreation:* music. *Address:* School of Earth Sciences, University of Tasmania, Private Bag 79, Hobart, Tas 7001, Australia. *T:* (3) 62262814, (4) 08005538. *E:* david.h.green@utas.edu.au.

**GREEN, Sir David John Mark,** Kt 2018; CB 2011; QC 2000; Senior Consultant, Slaughter and May, since 2018; Director, Serious Fraud Office, 2012–18; *b* 8 March 1954; *s* of John Geoffrey Green and Margaret Rowena Green (*née* Millican); *m* 1980, Kate Sharkey; one *s* two *d. Educ:* Christ's Hosp., Horsham; St Catharine's Coll., Cambridge (MA Hons). Defence Intelligence Staff, MoD, 1975–78; called to the Bar, Inner Temple, 1979, Bencher, 2008; practising barrister, 1979–2004, 2011–12; an Asst Recorder, 1995–2000; Recorder, 2000–; Director: Revenue and Customs (formerly Customs and Excise) Prosecutions Office, 2004–10; Central Fraud Gp, CPS, 2010–11. Liveryman, Co. of Gardeners, 2000– (Master, 2017–18). *Recreations:* walking, gardening, cooking, Fornasetti. *Club:* Garrick.

*See also* G. S. Green.

**GREEN, Prof. David Mino Allen,** CBE 2019; Vice Chancellor and Chief Executive, and Professor of Economics, University of Worcester (formerly University College Worcester), since 2003; *b* 12 Aug. 1952; *s* of Prof. Mino Green, *qv*; *m* 1999, Catherine Nicole Mortimore; two *d. Educ:* Westminster Sch.; St John's Coll., Cambridge (MA, BA Econs 1973). Res./Campaigns Officer, Shelter (Scotland), 1973–74; Founder, Welfare Rights Service, Harlow DC, Essex, 1975–77; Economist, Imres Ltd, 1977–79; South Bank Polytechnic, then South Bank University: Lectr, 1979–84; Sen. Lectr, 1984–89; Principal Lectr and Hd of Econs, 1989–94; Jt Hd of Sch., Business Sch., 1994–98; Prof. of Econs, and Dean of Leeds Business Sch., Leeds Metropolitan Univ., 1998–2001; Pro Vice Chancellor, Thames Valley Univ., 2001–02. Bd Mem., Teaching and Develt Agency for Schs, 2006–12; Mem., Adv. Cttee on Degree Awarding Powers, QAA, 2010–; Chm., Univs W Midlands (formerly W Midlands Higher Educn Assoc.), 2010–11). Chm., Worcester Alliance, 2005–; Member, Board: Worcester Cathedral Council, 2010–; Worcs Local Econ. Partnership, 2011–12. Trustee, Worcester Warriors RFC Community Foundn, 2011–. Pride of Worcs award, Worcs Ambassadors, 2006. *Publications:* Banking and Financial Stability in Central Europe, 2002; contrib. articles to econ. and socio-econ. learned jls; contrib. articles on higher educn policy and issues to UK and US press and broadcast media. *Recreations:* family life, cooking, cricket, tennis, reading, travelling, ski-ing. *Address:* Vice Chancellor's Office, University of Worcester, St John's Campus, Henwick Grove, Worcester WR2 6AJ. *T:* (01905) 855123, *Fax:* (01905) 424638. *E:* vc@worc.ac.uk. *Clubs:* Hurlingham; Worcestershire County Cricket (Mem. Bd, 2010–).

**GREEN, Prof. Diana Margaret, (Mrs J. W. Davy),** CBE 2007; PhD; DL; leadership, organisational development and change management consultant; Founder and Director, Diana Green Consultancy Ltd, 2008–12; *b* 10 April 1943; *d* of Charles Edward Harris and Joan Harris (née Beresford); *m* 1st, 1967, Neville A. Green (marr. diss. 1979); 2nd, 2011, John William Davy. *Educ:* South Park High Sch. for Girls, Lincoln; Reading Univ.; Queen Mary Coll., London (BSc Econ.); London Sch. of Econs (PhD Econ. 1976). HM CS, 1969–76; Lectr, Sen. Lectr and Actg Hd, Dept of Politics and Govt, City of London Poly., 1976–83; University of Central England: Hd of Dept, 1984–87; Asst Dir, 1987–92; Pro Vice-Chancellor, 1992–98; Vice-Chancellor, Sheffield Hallam Univ., 1998–2007. Consultant (part-time), DTI, 1976–81. Key Associate: Leadership Foundn for Higher Educn, 2008–11 (Mem., 2003–07); Active Human Capital Ltd, 2008–11. Member: Quality Assessment Cttee, HEFCE, 1992–96; Higher Educn Innovation Fund Expert Gp, HEFCE/DTI, 2001–07; Better Regulation Stakeholder Gp, DfES, 2003–05; Chm., SRHE, 1998–99. Member: Black Country Develt Corp., 1992–94; Alexandra NHS Healthcare Trust, 1996–98. Member: W Midlands Regl Council, CBI, 1994–98; W Midlands Council, IoD, 2008–12; Birmingham Chamber of Commerce and Industry, 2008–12. Founder Dir, Midlands Excellence, 1996–99; Director: Phoenix Sports UK, 1997–2000; Sheffield TEC, 1998–2001; Sheffield Industrial Mus. Trust, 1998–2002; Sheffield First for Investment, 1999–2002; Sheffield One, 2000–07; UUK, 2001–07; Creative Sheffield, 2006–07; Centre for Cities, 2006–09; non-exec. Dir, Mid Staffordshire NHS Foundn Trust, 2009–11. Trustee: Sheffield Galls and Museums Trust, 2000–08; AGORA, Forum for Culture and Educn, 2007–08; Flying Scholarships for Disabled People Trust, 2007–12; Kings World Trust for Children, 2013–18. Gov., London Film Sch., 2016– (Acting Chair, 2017–18; Vice Chair, 2018–). Hon. Co. of Air Pilots (formerly GAPAN): Trustee, Air Safety Trust, 2006–13; Dir, 9 Warwick Court Ltd, 2009–; Chm., Envmt Cttee, 2010–13. Former Mem. Council, All Party Parly Univ. Gp (now Hon. Mem.). Member: E Surrey Business Club, 2012– (Mem. Cttee, 2014–); Limpsfield Common Local Cttee, NT London and SE Region, 2014–19. Chm., Greensands Place Ltd, 2015–. Churchwarden, St Andrew's Ch, Limpsfield Chart, 2017–. Mem., British Women Pilots Assoc., 1998 (Mem. Cttee, 2015–16). MRIN 2014–19. FRSA. DUniv Sheffield Hallam, 2007. Freeman, City of London, 1998; Freeman, 2005, Liveryman, 2008, GAPAN (Mem., Court of Assts, 2009–15); Freeman, Guild of Educators, 2008–11. DL W Midlands, 2008. *Publications:* articles, chapters, books and reports on industrial change and quality in higher education; contrib. to THES; articles on aspects of aviation in Air Pilot (formerly Guild News). *Recreations:* flying light aircraft, music, art, theatre, film.

**GREEN, Ven. Duncan Jamie;** Archdeacon of Northolt, 2013–19; *b* 30 April 1952; *m* 1975, Janet Mary Orpin; one *s* two *d*. *Educ:* Salisbury and Wells Theol Coll. Sales Dir, Agricultural Engrg firm, Surrey; ordained deacon, 1984, priest, 1985; Asst Curate, Holy Cross, Uckfield, 1984–87; Diocesan Youth Officer, Dio. of Chelmsford, 1987–96; Warden and Chaplain, St Mark's Coll. Res. Youth Centre, Audley End, 1993–96; Team Rector, 1996–2007, Rural Dean, 2000–07, Saffron Walden; C of E Olympic and Paralympic Co-ordinator, 2007–13 (seconded to LOCOG as Faith Advr and Hd, Multi-Chaplaincy Services). Hon. Canon, Chelmsford Cath., 2003–13.

**GREEN, Edward Maurice;** DL; Director, Green & Frederick Ltd, since 1998; Trustee, National Galleries of Scotland, since 2014; *b* London, 19 Aug. 1952; *s* of late Joseph Green and of Toby Green (later Lawson); *m* 1994, (Elizabeth) Maryla (Helen) Chojecki; one *s*. *Educ:* Haberdashers' Aske's Sch.; Univ. of Strathclyde (BA Hotel and Catering Mgt). Collingwood of Conduit St, 1975–83, Dir, 1977–83; Man. Dir, Mappin & Webb Ltd, 1985–91; Dep. Chm., Garrard the Crown Jewellers, 1986–91; Pres., Asprey United States, 1991–95. FGA 1977 (Diamond Grading Assoc. 1978). DL Edinburgh, 2016. *Recreations:* ski-ing, opera, family, art, antiques. *Address:* Innerwick, Ellersly Road, Murrayfield, Edinburgh EH12 6HZ. *T:* (office) (020) 3544 6440. *E:* edwardmgreen@me.com. *Club:* New (Edinburgh).

**GREEN, Felicity, (Mrs Geoffrey Hill),** OBE 2012; fashion journalist; *b* Dagenham, 26 June 1926; *d* of Emanuel and Annie Green; *m* 1952, Geoffrey Hill. *Educ:* Clarks Coll., Ilford; Pitmans Coll., Forest Gate (Shorthand Cert.). Fashion Ed., Woman and Beauty mag., 1951–53; Exec. Ed., and est. Press and PR dept, Crawfords Advertising, London, 1953–55; Mirror Group Newspapers, 1955–77: Associate Ed., Women's Ed., and Fashion Ed., Women's Sunday Mirror, later Sunday Pictorial, 1955–60; Associate Ed., Women's Ed., and Fashion Ed., 1960–73, Press and Publicity Dir, 1973–77, Daily Mirror; Man. Dir, Vidal Sassoon Europe, and Exec. Vice Pres., Vidal Sassoon Internat., 1977–79; Associate Ed., and consultant, Daily Express, 1980–84; Contributing Ed., Working Woman mag., 1984–87; Sen. Lectr, Fashion Journalism and Promotion, BA degree course, St Martin's Sch. of Art, London, 1984–90; Editl and Mktg Consultant, Daily Telegraph Gp, 1986–96; Creative Consultant, Redwood Gp, 1987–2013 (incl. Launch Ed., Marks & Spencer Mag. and Editl Consultant, Harvey Nichols Mag.); Editl Consultant, Express Newspapers, 1996–99; Editl and Launch Consultant, ONdigital Ind. Television listings mag., ON7, 1998–2001; Teaching Mentor, Fashion Journalism and Communication, BA and MA courses, Central St Martin's, 2014–17. Mem. Bd, Nat. Film Finance Corp., 1972–77. Member: Cttee, Media Soc.; Internat. Women's Forum, 1995–2016; BSME, 2002–03. Mem. Cttee, Hugh Cudlipp Trust, 2004–14. Hon. Fellow, Univ. of the Arts, 2014. Women's Page Journalist of Year, Nat. Press Awards, Internat. Publishing Corp., 1970; Mark Boxer Award for Outstanding Contribn to Journalism, BSME, 1991; Press Gazette Hall of Fame, 2005. *Publications:* (ed jtly) Colour by Quant, 1984; (ed jtly) Jean Muir: beyond fashion, 2007; Sex, Sense and Nonsense: Felicity Green on the 60's fashion scene, 2014. *Recreations:* cinema, reading magazines, books and newspapers, visiting museums and art galleries, going to authors' talks. *Address:* 78 Nottingham Terrace, York Gate, NW1 4QE. *T:* (020) 7486 3405.

**GREEN, Dr Frank Alan,** CEng, FIMMM; Principal, Charing Green Associates, since 1983; non-executive Director: 2 GC Active Management Ltd, since 2000; Somerset Health Authority, 2001–02; *b* 29 Oct. 1931; *s* of Frank Green and Winifred Hilda (née Payne); *m* 1957, Pauline Eleanor Tayler (*d* 2014); one *s* one *d* (and one *d* decd). *Educ:* Mercers' Sch., London; Univ. of London (BSc, PhD); Univ. of Exeter (MA 2002). CEng 1980; FIMMM (FIM 1978). UKAEA, 1956–57; various appts, Glacier Metal Co. Ltd (Associated Engrg Gp), 1957–65; Technical Dir, Alta Fricción SA, Mexico City, 1965–68; Manufg Dir, Stewart Warner Corp., 1968–72; Marketing Develt Manager, Calor Gp, 1972–74; Manufg Dir, 1974–77, Man. Dir, 1977–81, British Twin Disc Ltd; Industrial Advr (Under-Sec.), DTI, 1981–84. Director: Gen. Technology Systems (Scandinavia), 1989–91; Gen. Technology Systems (Portuguesa), 1989–91; Principal Consultant, General Technology Systems Ltd, 1984–90. Dir, Anglo-Mexican Chamber of Commerce, Mexico City, 1966–68. Member of Council: Inst. of Metals, 1990–91; Inst. of Materials, 1992–94; Chm., W of England Metals and Materials Assoc., 1999–2000. BUniv Surrey, 2011. *Publications:* contrib. technical, medical ethical, historical and managerial books and jls in UK and Mexico. *Recreations:* military history, charity work. *Address:* Lynedale, Green Lane, Milford, Godalming, Surrey GU8 5BG.

**GREEN, Prof. Gary George Reginald,** DPhil; Director and Chief Technology Officer: Croton Healthcare, since 2017; York Instruments Ltd, since 2017; Professor of Neuroimaging, and Director, York Neuroimaging Centre, University of York, 2004–16, now Emeritus Professor; *b* 27 May 1951; *s* of Harry Clifford Green and Iris Ellen Green (née Asser); *m* 1981, Rose Hilton; one *s* one *d*. *Educ:* Burnt Mill Comp. Sch., Harlow; Hertford Coll., Oxford (MA 1979; DPhil 1976; BM BCh 1979). E. P. Abrahams Fellow, Hertford Coll., Oxford, 1978–80; University of Newcastle upon Tyne: Lectr, 1980–95; Reader, 1995–2004; Dir, Inst. of Neuroscience, 2003–04; Co-Dir, Centre for Hyperpolarisation in Magnetic Resonance, Univ. of York, 2013–17. Chm., Am Systems Ltd, 1987–95; Dir, YNI Ltd, 2004–15. Mem. Court, RCS, 1994–2000. Vice-Chm., Wellcome Trust Neurosci. and Mental Health Cttee, 2004 (Mem., 2000–04). Trustee, Jesmond Swimming Pool, 2002–04. *Publications:* articles on neurosci., non-linear dynamics, child language and neurological problems in learned jls. *Recreations:* making my wife laugh, gardening, swimming. *Address:* Sycamore Barn, Langwith Lane, Heslington, York YO10 5EJ. *T:* (01904) 567958. *E:* ggrgreen@gmail.com.

**GREEN, Geoffrey Stephen;** Chairman, Financial Reporting Review Panel, Financial Reporting Council, since 2015; *b* 3 Sept. 1949; *s* of John Geoffrey Green and Margaret Rowena Green (née Millican); *m* 1982, Sarah Charlton Chesshire; three *s*. *Educ:* Forest Sch.; St Catharine's Coll., Cambridge (MA). Admitted Solicitor, 1975. Ashurst Morris Crisp, later Ashurst LLP: Solicitor, 1975–2013; Partner, 1983–2013; Sen. Partner, 1998–2008; Man. Partner, 2009–13. Non-exec. Dir, Vedanta Resources plc, 2012–. *Recreations:* golf, tennis, hiking. *Address:* c/o Financial Reporting Review Panel, Financial Reporting Council, 8th Floor, 125 London Wall, EC2Y 5AS.

*See also Sir D. J. M. Green.*

**GREEN, Gerard Nicholas Valentine;** Chairman, HCP Infrastructure UK Ltd (formerly Health Care Projects Ltd) 2010–12 (Executive Director, 1997; Chief Executive, 1999–2010); *b* 6 Aug. 1950; *s* of James Arnold Green and Margarathe Ella Green; *m* 1977, Maralyn Ann Ranger; one *s* one *d*. *Educ:* Highgate Sch.; University Coll., London (BA); Univ. of Warwick (MA); Birkbeck Coll., London (MA). AHSM. Nat. admin. trainee, 1974–75; Dep. Hosp. Sec., St George's Hosp., SW17, 1975–77; Asst Sector Administrator, Cane Hill Hosp., Surrey, 1977–79; Sector Administrator, Farnborough Hosp., Kent, 1979–82; Administrator, KCH, 1982–84; Chief Exec. Officer, Tabuk Military Hosp., Saudi Arabia, 1984–87; Dist Gen. Man., Bromley HA, 1987–89; Regl Gen. Man., SE Thames RHA, 1989–94; Chief Exec., Royal Hosps NHS Trust, 1994–97. Dir, HCP (Defence Projects) Ltd, 2001–08. Non-exec. Dir, Meridian Hosp. Co., 2000–05; Chairman: Derby Healthcare plc, 2003–06; Central Nottinghamshire Hosps plc, 2005–07; HCP (Canada) Ltd, 2006–12; ISL Health (Victoria) Ltd, 2008–11; ISL Health (Fort St John), 2009–11. Mem., UKCC, 1993–98. FRSA 1989. *Recreations:* travel, reading, wine. *Club:* Reform.

**GREEN, Sir (Gregory) David,** KCMG 2004 (CMG 1999); CVO 2018; Director-General, British Council, 1999–2007; *b* 2 Dec. 1948; *s* of Thomas Dixon Green and Mary Mabella Green (née Walley); *m* 1977, Corinne Butler; three *d*. *Educ:* Leys Sch., Cambridge; Keswick Hall Coll. of Educn, Norwich (Cert Ed); Trinity Hall, Cambridge (BEd). Volunteer, VSO, Pakistan, 1967–68; teaching, Conisborough and Rotherham, 1972–76; Dir, Children's Relief Internat., 1976–79; Save the Children Fund: Staff Develt and Trng Officer, 1979; Dep. Dir of Personnel, 1982; Dir of Personnel, 1983–88; Dep. Dir-Gen., 1988–90; Dir, VSO, 1990–99. Dir and Council Mem., Council for Colony Holidays for School-children, 1970–80; Mem. Council, VSO, 2000–08. Member: Laurence Olivier Awards Panel, 1984–85; Council, English Stage Co., 2005–; Bd, Finnish Inst., 2015–. Chm., Prince's Sch. of Traditional Arts, 2008–18. Governor: Univ. of the Arts London, 2007–17; ESU, 2008–10. Chair: Dartington Hall Trust, 2008–15; Soumik Datta Arts, 2012–; Chm. and Trustee, Dash Arts, 2010–16; Trustee: Africa's Voices Foundn, 2015–; Prince's Foundn, 2018–. FRGS 1991. Freeman, City of London, 2006. Freeman, City of Freetown, Sierra Leone, 2004. *Publications:* Chorus, 1977; Drawing on Experience, 2011. *Recreations:* theatre, music, painting.

**GREEN, Hon. Sir Guy (Stephen Montague),** AC 1994; KBE 1982; CVO 2000; Governor of Tasmania, 1995–2003; *b* 26 July 1937; *s* of Clement Francis Montague Green and Beryl Margaret Jenour Green; *m* 1963, Rosslyn Mary Marshall; two *s* two *d*. *Educ:* Launceston Church Grammar Sch.; Univ. of Tasmania. Alfred Houston Schol. (Philosophy) 1958; LLB (Hons) 1960. Admitted to Bar of Tasmania, 1960; Partner, Ritchie & Parker Alfred Green & Co. (Launceston), 1963–71; Magistrate 1971–73; Chief Justice of Tasmania, 1973–95; University of Tasmania: Mem., Faculty of Law, 1974–85; Chancellor, 1985–95. Lieut-Gov., Tasmania, 1982–95; Adminr, Commonwealth of Australia, May–Aug. 2003. Pres., Tasmanian Bar Assoc., 1968–70; Chm., Council of Law Reporting, 1978–85; Dep. Chm., Australian Inst. of Judicial Admin, 1986–88. Chm., Tasmanian Cttee, Duke of Edinburgh's Award Scheme in Australia, 1975–80; Dir, Winston Churchill Meml Trust, 1975–85 (Dep. Nat. Chm., 1980–85; Chm. Tasmanian Regional Cttee, 1975–80); Chairman: Bd, Ten Days on the Island, 2003–15; Trustees, Tasmanian Mus. and Art Gall., 2004–15; Tim Hawkins Meml Scholarship Cttee, 2004–. Chairman: Internat. Antarctic Inst., 2006–15 (Chm. Steering Cttee, 2004–06); Organising Cttee, Internat. Forums on Sub Antarctic, 2006, 2009, 2011. Member: Bd, Menzies Foundn, 2005–12 (Chm., 2008–12); Menzies Res. Inst., 2005–12; Trustee and Mem., Foundn Council, Constitution Educn Fund Australia, 2004–08. Advr, Arts and Culture Centre, Beijing Normal Univ./Hong Kong Baptist Univ. United Internat. Coll., 2010–; Hon. Pres., Tianjin Modern Vocational Technol. Coll., China, 2012–. Pres., Tasmanian Br., Australia China Business Council, 2014–17. Nat. Pres., Order of Australia Assoc., 2004–07. St John Ambulance, Australia: Pres., Tasmanian Council, 1984–92; Priory Exec. Officer, 1984–91; Chancellor, 1991–95; Dep. Prior, 1995–2003. Hon. Antarctic Ambassador for Tasmania, 2005–. Hon. Prof., Antarctic Climate and Ecosystems Co-operative Res. Centre, Univ. of Tasmania, 2005–. Hon. LLD Tasmania, 1996. KStJ 1985. *Address:* Hobart, Tas, Australia. *Club:* Tasmanian (Hobart).

**GREEN, Harriet,** OBE 2010; Head, Asia Pacific, IBM, since 2018 (Vice President and General Manager, 2015–17); *b* 12 Dec. 1961; *d* of late Dermot Green and of Nerys Allen; *m* 2004, Graham Clarkson; two step *c*. *Educ:* Univ. of London (BA Hons Medieval Hist. 1983); London Sch. of Econs (Business Psychol. 1985); Harvard Business Sch.; Aspen Inst.; Ashridge Mgt Coll. Man. Dir, Macro Gp, 1985–94; Arrow Electronics Inc.: Vice Pres., Eur. Mktg, 1994–96; Pres., Arrow N Europe and Africa, and Corp. Vice Pres., 1996–2000; Pres., Arrow CMS, N America, 2000–01; Hd, Global Strategy and New Business Develt, 2002; Pres., Asia Pacific, 2002–06; CEO, Premier Farnell plc, 2006–12; CEO, Thomas Cook Gp plc, 2012–14. Non-executive Director: Emerson, 2008–15; BAE Systems, 2010–. Former Mem., Young Presidents Assoc. *Recreations:* yoga, reading, theatre, hiking, horse-riding, cycling.

**GREEN, Henrietta-Jane;** food writer, since 1977; broadcaster; company director, since 1987; food consultant, since 1989; *b* 27 Oct. 1948; *d* of Aubrey and Valerie Green. *Educ:* Sarum Hall Prep. Sch.; Queen's Coll., Harley St; Royal Acad. of Dramatic Art (Dip. Stage

Mgt). Free-lance journalist, broadcaster and consultant; Consultancy Dir, Henrietta Green Associates, 2012–. Founder, FoodLoversBritain.com, and organiser of FoodLovers' Fairs; involved with the introduction of Farmers' Markets in the UK and develt of local and regl strategy for Waitrose; launched consumer mkt at Borough Mkt. Mem., London Food Bd, 2004–08; Partner, Independent Hotel Show (annual), 2012–. Trustee, Jane Grigson Trust. *Publications*: Fine Flavoured Food, 1978; The Marinade Cookbook, 1978; RAC Food Routes, 1988; 10 Minute Cuisine, 1991; The Festive Food of England, 1991; Henrietta Green's New Country Kitchen, 1992; A Glorious Harvest, 1994; Fresh From the Garden, 1994; Henrietta Green's Food Lovers' Guide to Britain, 1994, 1996; British Food Finds, 1997; The Food Lovers' Christmas, 1997; Henrietta's Home Cooking, 1997; Recipes from an English Country Garden, 1998; Henrietta Green's Farmers' Market Cookbook, 2001. *Recreations*: walking, talking, shopping, playing with my dog, eating, movies, looking at gardens, gardening, looking at buildings, bird-watching. *Address*: Flat A, 40 Warrington Crescent, W9 1EL. *Club*: Groucho.

**GREEN, Ian Richard;** Chief Executive, Terrence Higgins Trust, since 2016; *b* Hayes, Middx, 21 Sept. 1965; *s* of Eric John Green and Brenda May Green; *m* 2015, Paul Day. *Educ*: Coll. of Ripon and York St John (BA). YMCA: Housing Manager, Ealing, 1989–92; CEO, London City, 1992–98; Regl Dir, London, 1998–2001; Chief Exec., London SW, 2001–08, England, 2008–13; Mem., Exec. Team, World Alliance of YMCAs, 2013–16. Chm., Ealing Hosp. NHS Trust, 2008–13; Mem. Bd, W Hampshire NHS CCG, 2013–17. Vice Chm., Wandle Housing Assoc., 2013–. Chm., Disciplinary Cttee, RCVS, 2014–. FCMI; FRSA. Mem. (C), Ealing LBC, 1990–2010. JP Hounslow, 1994–2010. *Recreations*: theatre, travel, walking with two wayward labradors. *Address*: Terrence Higgins Trust, 314–320 Gray's Inn Road, WC1X 8DP. *T*: (020) 7812 1855. *E*: ian.green@tht.org.uk.

**GREEN, Ven. John,** CB 2010; Archdeacon of Coventry, and Archdeacon Pastor, Diocese of Coventry, 2012–17; Associate Minister, St Mary Magdalen's, Coventry, 2014–17; *b* 14 Aug. 1953; *s* of Albert Frederick and Lilian Green; *m* 1977, Janette Silvester; two *s*. *Educ*: S W Ham Co. Tech. Sch.; NE London Poly. (Grad. Inst. Physics); Lincoln Theol Coll. (BCS 1983). Project engr, Thorn Lighting Ltd, 1974–80 (Sen. Engr, 1977–80); ordained deacon 1983, priest 1984; Curate: St Michael and All Angels, W Watford, 1983–86; St Stephen's, St Albans, 1986–91; Chaplain, RN, 1991–2010: HMS Sultan, 1991–92; 3rd Destroyer Sqdn, 1992–93; HM Naval Base, Portsmouth, 1993–94; HMS Excellent, 1994–95; Minor Warfare Vessel Flotilla, 1996–98; Staff Chaplain to Chaplain of the Fleet, 1998–2001; HMS Ark Royal, 2001–03; HMS Collingwood, 2003–06; Dir Gen., Naval Chaplaincy Service, Chaplain of the Fleet and Archdeacon for RN, 2006–10. Chair: Coventry and Warks Br., RSCM, 2014–17; Dio. of Coventry Multi Acad. Trust, 2015–17. QHC 2006–10. *Recreations*: music, inland waterways and boating, physical sciences and astronomy, photography, amateur radio (callsign M0ACN). *E*: venjgreen@yahoo.co.uk.

**GREEN, John Edward,** PhD; FREng, FRAeS, FAIAA; Chief Executive, 1988–95, Consultant and Chief Scientist, 1995–2013, Aircraft Research Association Ltd; *b* 26 Aug. 1937; *s* of John Green and Ellen Green (*née* O'Dowd); *m* 1959, Gillian (*née* Jackson); one *s* one *d*. *Educ*: Birkenhead Inst. Grammar Sch.; St John's Coll., Cambridge (Scholar; BA 1959; MA 1963; PhD 1966). CEng 1972; FRAeS 1978. Student Apprentice, Bristol Aircraft Ltd, 1956; De Havilland Engine Co., 1959–61; Royal Aircraft Establishment, 1964–81: Head of Transonic/Supersonic Wind Tunnel Div., 1971; Head of Propulsion Div., 1973; Head of Noise Div., 1974; Head of Aerodynamics Dept, 1978–81; Dir, Project Time and Cost Analysis, MoD (PE), 1981–84; Minister-Counsellor Defence Equipment, and Dep. Head of British Defence Staff, Washington, 1984–85; Dep. Dir (Aircraft), RAE, 1985–87. Vis. Prof., Cranfield Univ., 1996–2004. President: Internat. Council of Aeronautical Scis, 1996–98 (Mem. Council, 1986–2000; Chm., Prog. Cttee, 1992–96; Life Mem., 2002; Hon. Fellow, 2008); RAeS, 1996–97 (Mem. Council, 1986–2000; Vice Pres., 1992–95; Hon. Treas., 1992–96; Mem., Exec. Cttee, Greener by Design Gp, 2000–); Mem. Council, AIRTO, 1988–95. Corresp., L'Académie de l'Air et de l'Espace, 2010. Mem. Court, Cranfield Univ. (formerly Cranfield Inst. of Technol.), 1988–2008 (Mem. Council, 1995–2005). Royal Aeronautical Society: Goldstein Lectr, 1991; Busk Prize, 1992; de Havilland Lectr, 2000; Westland Prize, 2002; Templer Lectr, 2004; Lanchester Lectr, 2005; Wilbur and Orville Wright Lectr, 2006; Hodgson Prize, 2005; Gold Award, 2005; J. D. North Lectr, 2008; R. K. Pierson Lectr, 2008. FREng (FEng 1994); FAIAA 1999. Maurice Roy Medal, Internat. Council of Aeronautical Scis, 2006. *Publications*: contribs to books and learned jls, chiefly on fluid mechanics, aerodynamics and envmtl impact of aviation. *Recreations*: music, mountain walking (Munroist, 1994). *Address*: 1 Leighton Street, Woburn, Beds MK17 9PJ. *T*: (01525) 290631.

**GREEN, John Louis;** Chairman, Merchant John East Securities plc (formerly Merchant Securities), 2006–12; *b* 2 March 1945; *s* of Stanley and Rose Green; *m* 1972, Kathleen Whelan; three *s* one *d*. *Educ*: Merchant Taylors' Sch., Northwood; Oriel Coll., Oxford (MA). FCA 1970. Price Waterhouse & Co., 1966–69; Kleinwort Benson, 1969–70; McAnally Montgomery & Co., 1970–79; James Capel, 1979–92; HSBC Investment Bank, 1992–96, Man. Dir, HSBC-Capel UK, 1995–96; Chief Exec., James Capel Investment Mgt, 1996–98. Chairman: Principal Investment Mgt, 2000–08; Inventive Leisure plc, 2000–06; IBG plc, 2008–09; Huntress Group, 2008–09. Dir various cos, 1999–2012. *Recreations*: golf, opera, reading. *Address*: Croft House, Cobham, Surrey KT11 2QR. *T*: (01372) 842951. *Clubs*: Royal Automobile; Effingham Golf.

**GREEN, Dr John Timothy;** Chair, Astins Ltd, since 2011; *b* 1 Jan. 1944; *s* of Thomas Albert Green and Joan (*née* Chamberlain); *m* 1985, Susan Mary Shattock; one *s*. *Educ*: King Edward's Five Ways Sch., Birmingham; Queens' Coll., Cambridge (BA 1966; MA 1970; PhD Maths 1970). Queens' College, Cambridge: Bye Fellow, 1970–72; Fellow, 1972–93; Lectr in Maths, 1972–93; Dean of Coll., 1972–77; Tutor, 1977–80; Sen. Tutor, 1980–93; Life Fellow, 1993; Chief Exec., RSocMed, 1993–96; Dir, Historic Properties (London), English Heritage, 1997–98; Sec., Faculty of Medicine, 1998–2004, Chief Co-ordinating Officer, 2004–10, Imperial Coll. London. Chair, Alexander Street Press, 2009–16; Director: S Leics Garages Ltd, 1985–95; Pennant Hotels Ltd, 1987–95; RSM Press Ltd, 1993–96; Chadwyck-Healey Ltd, 1997–99; Kennedy Inst. of Rheumatology, 1999–2010; NW London Hosps Trust, 2001–10; Imperial Coll. Bioincubator Ltd, 2004–07; MyAction Ltd, 2009–10; Careers Information Services Ltd, 2009–10; myChoice Data Systems Ltd, 2009–16; Ind. Dir, 3i plc, 1996–2007. Member: CBI Professions Wkg Gp, 1995–96; London First Medicine, 1995–96. Recruitment Advr, FCO, 1992–99. Dir, Assoc. of Research Managers and Administrators, 2008–10. Trustee: Harpur Trust, Bedford, 1984–87; Project Hope, 1995–2001 (Vice-Chm., 1998–2001). Governor: Hills Rd Sixth Form Coll., Cambridge, 1993–98; Perse Sch., Cambridge, 2001–09. *Publications*: contrib. Jl Fluid Mechanics and others. *Recreations*: opera, music, fell-walking. *Address*: Queens' College, Cambridge CB3 9ET.

**GREEN, Katherine Anne, (Kate),** OBE 2005; MP (Lab) Stretford and Urmston, since 2010; *b* 2 May 1960; *d* of Maurice Green and Jessie Craig Green (*née* Bruce); *m* 1985, Richard Duncan Mabb (marr. diss. 2006). *Educ*: Currie High Sch., Midlothian; Univ. of Edinburgh (LLB Hons 1982). Barclays Bank, 1982–97; Whitehall and Industry Gp Secondee to Home Office, 1997–99; Dir, NCOPF, 2000–04; Chief Exec., Child Poverty Action Gp, 2004–09. Member: Lord Chancellor's Adv. Cttee, City of London, 2001–09; Nat. Employment Panel, 2001–07; London Child Poverty Commn, 2006–09; Greater Manchester Poverty Commn, 2012–13. Shadow Minister: for Equalities, 2011–13; for Disabled People, 2013–15; for Women and Equalities, 2015–16; Chair, H of C Cttee on Standards, 2018–, on Privileges, 2018–. Dir, Project Fresh Start, 2001–03. Trustee: Family and Parenting (formerly Nat. Family and Parenting) Inst., 2000–07 (Treas., 2006–07); Avenues Youth Project, 2000–05; Inst. for Fiscal Studies, 2004–09; Friends Provident Foundn, 2007–09; Webb Meml Trust, 2011–18. Chm., Fabian Soc., 2017–18. JP City of London, 1993–2009. *Recreations*: theatre, swimming. *Address*: House of Commons, SW1A 0AA. *T*: (020) 7219 7162. *E*: kate.green.mp@parliament.uk.

**GREEN, Prof. Laura Elizabeth,** OBE 2017; FRSB; Pro-Vice-Chancellor, and Head, College of Life and Environmental Sciences, University of Birmingham, since 2018; *b* Ongar, Essex, 13 April 1964; *d* of Trevor and June McCann; *m* 1988, Martin Green; one *s* two *d*. *Educ*: Loughton Co. High Sch.; King's High Sch., Warwick; Univ. of Bristol (BVSc 1987; PhD 1992); London Sch. of Hygiene and Tropical Medicine (MSc Epidemiol. 1990). MRCVS 1987; FRSB 2015. Asst in mixed vet. practices, Warwickshire and Bucks, 1987–88; Wellcome Trust Schol. (Epidemiol.), LSHTM and Bristol Univ., 1988–92; post-doctoral Res. Fellow, MAFF, 1993; Lectr, Dept of Clin. Veterinary Sci., Univ. of Bristol, 1993–99; University of Warwick: Lectr, 1999–2001, Sen. Lectr, 2001–04, Reader, 2004–05, Dept of Biol Scis; Prof., 2005–18, Hd, 2014–17, Sch. of Life Scis; Dep. Pro Vice Chancellor, Interdisciplinary Res. and Impact, 2017–18. Mem., UKRI-BBSRC, 2018– (Chair, Agric. and Food Security Strategy Adv. Panel, 2018–). Mem., Sci. Adv. Council, Food Standards Agency, 2017–. *Publications*: contrib. peer-reviewed res. pubns. *Recreations*: walking, travelling, gardening, reading, ballet, theatre. *Address*: University of Birmingham, College of Life and Environmental Sciences, Birmingham B15 2TT. *E*: l.e.green.1@bham.ac.uk.

**GREEN, Rt Rev. Dr Laurence Alexander, (Laurie);** Area Bishop of Bradwell, 1993–2011; Hon. Assistant Bishop: Diocese of Chichester, since 2011; Diocese of Rochester, since 2018; *b* 26 Dec. 1945; *s* of Leonard Alexander and Laura Elizabeth Green; *m* 1969, J. Victoria Bussell; two *d*. *Educ*: King's Coll. London (BD Hons, AKC); New York Theological Seminary, NY State Univ. (STM, DMin); St Augustine's Coll., Canterbury. Curate, St Mark, Kingstanding, Birmingham, 1970–73; Vicar, St Chad, Erdington, Birmingham, 1973–83; Industrial Chaplain, British Steel Corp., 1975–83; Lectr in Urban Studies, Urban Theol. Unit, Sheffield, 1976–82; Principal, Aston Training Scheme, 1983–89; Hon. Curate, Holy Trinity, Birchfield, Handsworth, 1983–89; Team Rector, All Saints, Poplar, 1989–93; Tutor in Urban Theology, Sheffield Univ., 1989–93. Chair: Nat. Estate Churches Network, 1996–2016; Friends of the Poor in S India, 2007–. Episcopal Visitor, Malling Abbey, Kent, 2011–. *Publications*: Power to the Powerless, 1987; (jtly) A Thing Called Aston (ed Todd), 1987; Let's Do Theology, 1989, (ed) rev. edn 2009 (trans. Mandarin Chinese, 2012); God in the Inner City, 1993; (jtly) God in the City, 1995; (contrib.) Urban Christ, 1997; (contrib.) Gospel from the City, 1997; (jtly) A Reader in Urban Theology, 1998; The Impact of the Global: an urban theology, 2001 (trans. Japanese, Spanish, Tamil, Portuguese); Urban Ministry and the Kingdom of God, 2003; Building Utopia, 2008; (jtly) Crossover City, 2010; Blessed are the Poor?, 2015; contrib. St George's Windsor Review, Theology. *Recreations*: folk, jazz and classical guitar (recorded CD, Songs For You, 2018), DIY. *Address*: 86 Belle Hill, Bexhill-on-Sea TN40 2AP. *E*: mail@lauriegreen.org. *W*: www.lauriegreen.org.

**GREEN, Prof. Leslie,** DPhil; Professor of the Philosophy of Law, University of Oxford, since 2007; Fellow of Balliol College, Oxford, since 2007; *b* Bridge of Weir, Scotland, 27 Nov. 1956; *s* of Robert Frederick Green and Elizabeth Laird Mackie; *m* 1980, Prof. Denise Réaume. *Educ*: Queen's Univ., Kingston, Ont (BA 1978); Nuffield Coll., Oxford (MPhil 1980; DPhil 1984). Darby Fellow and Tutor in Pol Theory, Lincoln Coll., Oxford, 1983–85; Prof. of Law and Philos., Osgoode Hall Law Sch., York Univ., Toronto, 1986–2006; Prof. of Law and Distinguished Fellow, Queen's Univ., Canada, 2010–. Visiting Professor: Boalt Hall Sch. of Law, Univ. of Calif, Berkeley, 1995; Sch. of Law, Univ. of Texas, Austin, 2002–06; Hauser Global Law Sch. Prog., NY Univ. Sch. of Law, 2007; Univ. of Chicago Law Sch., 2009; Vis. Fellow, Centre for Law and Philos., Columbia Law Sch., NY, 2003. Jt Ed., Oxford Studies in the Philosophy of Law. *Publications*: The Authority of the State, 1988; Law and the Community, 1989; Kelsen Revisited, 2013; articles in jls incl. Oxford Jl of Legal Studies, Legal Theory, Michigan Law Rev., NYU Law Rev., Philos. Qly, Jl of Pol Philos., Canadian Jl of Law and Jurisprudence, Osgoode Hall Law Jl, Ethics, Current Legal Problems, etc. *Recreation*: music. *Address*: Balliol College, Oxford OX1 3BJ. *T*: (01865) 277777. *E*: leslie.green@law.ox.ac.uk.

**GREEN, Lucinda Jane,** MBE 1978; three-day event rider; *b* 7 Nov. 1953; *d* of Maj.-Gen. George Erroll Prior-Palmer, CB, DSO and Lady Doreen Hersey Winifred Prior-Palmer; *m* 1981, David (marr. diss. 1992), *s* of Burrington Green, Brisbane; one *s* one *d*. *Educ*: St Mary's, Wantage; Idbury Manor, Oxon. Member of winning Junior European Team, 1971; Winner, 3 Day Events: Badminton Horse Trials Championships, 1973, 1976, 1977, 1979, 1983, 1984; Burghley, 1977, 1981; Individual European Championships, 1975, 1977; World Championship, 1982; Member: Olympic Team, Montreal, 1976, Los Angeles, 1984; European Championship Team: Luhmühlen, W Germany 1975 (team Silver Medallist and individual Gold Medallist); Burghley, 1977 (team Gold Medallist), 1985 (team Gold Medallist), 1987 (team Gold Medallist); European Team, 1979, 1983 (team and individual Silver Medallist); Alternative Olympic Team, 1980; World Championship Team: Kentucky, 1978; Luhmühlen, W Germany, 1982 (team and individual Gold Medallist). Co-presenter, Horses, Channel 4, 1987; Commentator: BBC, Badminton, 1987–2005; BBC, Olympic Games, 1988, 1996, Channel 7, Australia, Olympic Games, 1992, 1996, 2000 and 2004; Channel 9, Australia, Olympic Games, 2012; Presenter, Rural Rides, Meridian TV, 1997 and 1998. Selector, British three-day event teams, 2002–08; cross-country coach worldwide; cross-country consultant coach for Austria and Shanghai. Editorial Consultant, Eventing, 1989–92. Contrib., various equestrian mags. *Publications*: Up, Up and Away, 1978; Four Square, 1980; Regal Realm, 1983; Cross-Country Riding, 1986, 2nd edn 1995; The Young Rider, 1993. *Recreations*: driving, ski-ing, scuba diving, stalking, travelling abroad. *Address*: The Tree House, Appleshaw, Andover SP11 9BS.

**GREEN, Prof. Sir Malcolm,** Kt 2007; DM; FRCP; Vice Principal, Faculty of Medicine, 1997–2006, and Head of National Heart and Lung Institute, 2001–06, Imperial College of Science, Technology and Medicine; Professor of Respiratory Medicine, Imperial College, 1998–2006, now Professor Emeritus; Consultant Physician, Royal Brompton Hospital (formerly Brompton Hospital), 1975–2006; *b* 25 Jan. 1942; *s* of late James Bisdee Malcolm Green and Frances Marjorie Lois Green; *m* 1971, Julieta Caroline Preston (*d* 2018); two *s* two *d* (and one *d* decd). *Educ*: Charterhouse Sch. (Foundn Scholar); Trinity Coll., Oxford (Exhibnr; BA 1963; BSc 1965; MA, BM, BCh 1967; DM 1978; Hon. Fellow, 2011); St Thomas's Hosp. Med. Sch. (Scholar). FRCP 1980 (MRCP 1970). Jun. appts, St Thomas' and Brompton Hosps, 1968–71; Lectr, Dept of Medicine, St Thomas' Hosp., 1971–74; Radcliffe Travelling Fellow, Harvard University Med. Sch., 1971–73; Sen. Registrar, Westminster and Brompton Hosps, 1974–75; Consultant Physician and Physician i/c Chest Dept, St Bartholomew's Hosp., 1975–86; Dean, Nat. Heart and Lung Inst., 1988–90 (Mem., Cttee of Management, 1988–95); Dir, BPMF, 1991–96; Campus Dean, St Mary's Hosp., 1997–2001. Member: Supraregl Services Adv. Cttee, 1991–96; NHS Taskforce on

Res. (Culyer Cttee), 1993–94; Health of the Nation Wider Health Wkg Gp, 1991–97; NHS Central R&D Cttee, 1995–2002 (Chm., 1999); NHS Exec. Bd, 1999; Chairman: NHS R&D Bd, 1999; NHS London Leading for Health, 2010–11; acting Dir, R&D for NHS, 1999. Chm., Exec. Cttee and Nat. Council, British Lung Foundn, 1984–94 (Pres. and Chm., Council, 1994–2001); Chm. Acad. Steering Gp, BPMF, 1989–90; Member, Committees of Management, Institutes of Child Health, Psychiatry, Neurology, Ophthalmology, Cancer Research, Dental Surgery, and RPMS, 1991–96. Member: Bd of Govs, Nat. Heart and Chest Hosps, 1988–90; Senate, 1998–2004, Council, 1997–2005, Imperial Coll., London. Chm., London Medicine, 1996–2000; Member: Bd, London First Centre, 1996–99; London First, 2000–02; Adv. Bd, Medtel, 2006–08; Adv. Bd, Westover (formerly Brompton Cross) Clinic, 2006–10; Adv. Bd, Greenbrook Healthcare, 2008–18. Non-executive Director: St Mary's NHS Trust, 1997–2001; Royal Brompton and Harefield Hosps, 2001–06. Trustee: Heart Disease and Diabetes Res. Trust, 1988–2003; Fledgeling Charity Funds, 1993–98; Nat. Heart and Lung Foundn, 2000–; Chm., Medikidz Foundn, 2010–17. Treasurer, 1977–85, Pres., 1992–2001, United Hosps Sailing Club. FMedSci 2000. Hon. Fellow, European Respiratory Soc., 2014. Hon. Dr Nat. and Kapodistrian Univ. of Athens, 2017. *Publications:* chapters and articles in med. books and jls on gen. medicine, respiratory medicine and respiratory physiology. *Recreations:* sailing, ski-ing. *E:* malcolm@malcolmgreen.net. *Clubs:* Royal Thames Yacht; Itchenor Sailing (Commodore, 2006–09); Bosham Sailing; Royal Yacht Squadron; Imperial Poona Yacht (Hon. Sec., 1985–2010).

**GREEN, Prof. Malcolm Leslie Hodder**, PhD; FRS 1985; CChem, FRSC; Professor of Inorganic Chemistry, 1989–2003, now Emeritus, and Head of Department, Inorganic Chemistry Laboratory, 1988–2003, University of Oxford; Fellow of St Catherine's College, Oxford, 1988–2003, now Emeritus; *b* 16 April 1936; *s* of late Leslie Ernest Green, MD and Sheila Ethel (*née* Hodder); *m* 1965, Jennifer Clare Bilham; two *s* one *d. Educ:* Denstone Coll.; Acton Technical Coll. (BSc); Imperial Coll. of Science and Technol., London Univ. (DIC, PhD 1958); MA Cantab; MA Oxon. CChem, FRSC 1981. Asst Lectr in Inorganic Chem., Univ. of Cambridge, 1960–63; Fellow of Corpus Christi Coll., Cambridge, 1961–63; University of Oxford: Septcentenary Fellow and Tutor in Inorganic Chem., Balliol Coll., 1963–88, now Emeritus Fellow; Deptl Demonstrator, 1963; Lectr, 1965–88; British Gas Royal Soc. Sen. Res. Fellow, 1979–86. A. P. Sloan Vis. Prof., Harvard Univ. 1973; Sherman Fairchild Vis. Scholar, CIT, 1981. Tilden Lectr and Prize, RSC, 1982; Debye Lectr, Cornell Univ., 1985; Sir Edward Frankland Prize Lectr, 1988; Ernest H. Swift Lectr, CIT, 1998. A Founder and Dir, Oxford Catalysts Gp Plc, 2006–08. Dr *hc* Universidade Técnica de Lisboa, 1996; Hon. DSc Warwick, 2014. Corday-Morgan Medal and Prize in Inorganic Chem., Chemical Soc., 1974; Medal for Transition Metal Chem., Chemical Soc., 1978; Award for Inorganic Chem., ACS, 1982; RSC Award for Organometallic Chem., 1986; Karl-Ziegler Prize, Ges. Deutscher Chemiker, 1992; Davy Medal, Royal Soc., 1995; Award for Organometallic Chem., ACS, 1997; Sir Geoffrey Wilkinson Medal, RSC, 1999; European Prize for Organometallic Chem., 2015. *Publications:* Organometallic Compounds: Vol. II, The Transition Elements, 1968; (with G. E. Coates, P. Powell and K. Wade) Principles of Organometallic Chemistry, 1968. *Address:* St Catherine's College, Oxford OX1 3UJ.

**GREEN, Malcolm Robert**, DPhil; Member, City of Glasgow Council, 1995–2007; Lecturer in Roman History, University of Glasgow, 1967–98; *b* 4 Jan. 1943; *m* 1971; one *s* two *d. Educ:* Wyggeston Boys' School, Leicester; Magdalen College, Oxford. MA, DPhil. Member: Glasgow Corp., 1973–75; Strathclyde Regional Council, 1975–96 (Chairman: Educn Cttee, 1982–90; Envmt Sub-Cttee, 1990–94; Racial Equality Sub-Cttee, 1994–96); Chm., Educn Cttee, 1996–99, Chief Whip, subseq. Business Manager, 1999–2005, City of Glasgow Council. Chairman: Educn Cttee, Convention of Scottish Local Authorities, 1978–90; Management Side, Scottish Jt Negotiating Cttees for Teaching Staff in Sch. and Further Educn, 1977–90; Nat. Cttee for In-Service Training of Teachers, 1977–86; Scottish Cttee for Staff Develt in Educn, 1987–91. Chair, Scottish Alliance of Regl Equality Councils, 2012–; Vice-Chair, W of Scotland Regl Equality Council, 2010–. Commissioner, Manpower Services Commn, 1983–85. *Recreation:* talking politics. *Address:* 4A Hughenden Gardens, Glasgow G12 9XW. *T:* (0141) 339 2007.

**GREEN, Margaret Beryl;** *see* Clunies Ross, M. B.

**GREEN, Air Vice-Marshal Mark Colin**, CBE 2005; Senior Programme Manager, 2014–19, and Director, Strategy and Business Development, 2016–19, Lockheed Martin; *b* London, 10 May 1959; *s* of Leslie and Sylvia Green; *m* 2001, Jane Louise Trant; one *s* one *d. Educ:* Imperial Coll. London (BSc Hons Aeronautical Engrg). Joined RAF, 1977; Stn Comdr, RAF Valley, 2003–05; Team Leader, Jt Combat Aircraft Integrated Project, 2005–09; Dir, Flying Trng, 2009–10; AOC 22 (Trng) Gp, 2010–11; Dir, Inf. Superiority, 2011–12, Dir, 2012–14, MoD. Adm. and Trustee, RAF Sailing Assoc., 2011–14. *Recreations:* sailing, ski-ing, running, cycling.

**GREEN, Martin**, OBE 2012; Chief Executive, Care England, since 2004; *b* Birmingham, 10 Nov. 1959; *s* of late Ronald George Green and Margaret Winifred Green. *Educ:* King Edward VI Sch., Morpeth; Northumbria Univ. (BSc Hons Sociol.). Chief Executive: Age Concern Greenwich, 1984–87; Action for Dysphasic Adults Speakability, 1987–90; Project Dir, Uganda Cooperative Alliance Kampala, Uganda, 1990–92; Chief Executive: Age Concern Wandsworth, 1992–94; Age Concern Lambeth, 1994–99; Counsel and Care, 1999–2004. DoH, subseq. DHSC Ind. Sector Dementia Champion, 2011–. Vis. Prof., Social Care, Bucks New Univ., 2012–. Chm., Internat. Longevity Centre UK, 2011–. Trustee: Nat. AIDS Trust, 2010–; Ind. Age, 2013–. FInstLM 2005; FIAM 2006; FIPEM 2008; FRSA. *Recreations:* theatre, cinema, travel. *Address:* Care England, 40 Artillery Lane, E1 7LS. *E:* mgreen@careengland.org.uk. *Club:* National Liberal.

**GREEN, Prof. Martin Andrew**, AM 2012; PhD, DEng; FRS 2013; Director, Australian Centre for Advanced Photovoltaics, since 2013, and Scientia Professor, since 1999, UNSW Sydney (formerly University of New South Wales); *b* Brisbane, 20 July 1948; *s* of Eric William Green and Gwendolyn Lorraine Green (*née* Horsfall); *m* 1970, Judith Frances Smith; one *s* one *d. Educ:* Univ. of Queensland (BEng 1970; MEng Sc 1971); McMaster Univ., Canada (PhD 1974); Univ. of New South Wales (DEng 2010). Grad. engr, AWA Microelectronics, Sydney, 1969–70; Lectr, 1974–78, Sen. Lectr, 1978–82, Univ. of NSW; res. scientist, Hitachi Central Res. Labs, Tokyo, 1977; Associate Prof., 1982–86, Prof., 1996–98, Univ. of NSW; Res. Dir, Pacific Solar Pty Ltd, 1995–2004. Dir, CSG Solar AG, 2004–10. Visiting Professor: Katholieke Univ., Leuven, Belgium, 1977; Huazhong Univ. of Sci. and Technol., Wuhan, China, 1984; Vis. Consultant, Solar Energy Res. Inst., Golden, USA, 1981. Hon. DSc McMaster, 2010. *Publications:* Solar Cells: operating principles, technology and system application, 1982; High Efficiency Silicon Solar Cells, 1987; (jtly) Applied Photovoltaics, 1993, 3rd edn 2012; Silicon Solar Cells: advanced principles and practice, 1995; Power to the People, 2000; Third Generation Photovoltaics, 2003. *Recreations:* travel, family, jogging, bicycle touring. *Address:* School of Photovoltaic and Renewable Energy Engineering, UNSW Sydney, NSW 2052, Australia. *T:* (2) 93854018. *Club:* Bronte Surf (Sydney) (Hon. Vice Pres., 1990).

**GREEN, Martin Keith**, CBE 2018; Chief Creative Officer, Commonwealth Games Birmingham 2022, since 2019; executive producer in arts and events industry, since 1997; Chair, Middle Child Theatre Company, since 2018; *b* Billericay, 30 Sept. 1971; *s* of Derek Green and Margaret Green. *Educ:* Univ. of Plymouth (BA Hons Theatre Arts and Performance Studies 1994); Univ. of Leeds (MA (dist.) Theatre Studies 1996). Various PR and events roles, 1997–2000; Public Affairs Manager, ITV, 2000–02; Hd, Events for London, Mayor's Office, 2002–07; Dir, Events, O2, 2007; Hd of Ceremonies, London 2012 Olympic and Paralympic Games, 2007–12; major events and exec. producer, 2012–14; CEO and Dir, Hull UK City of Culture 2017, 2014–18. Advr to Tokyo 2020 Olympic and Paralympic Games, 2016–. Hon. DLitt Hull, 2018. *Recreations:* site specific theatre, contemporary architecture, cooking, LGBTQ advocacy. *Address:* c/o Middle Child Theatre, Darley's, Porter Street, Hull HU1 2JE. *T:* (01482) 221857. *E:* martinkgreen@gmail.com. *Club:* House of St Barnabas.

**GREEN, Matthew Roger;** Director, Green Planning Studio Ltd, since 2014; *b* 12 April 1970; *s* of Roger Hector Green and Pamela Gillian Green. *Educ:* Birmingham Univ. (BA (Hons) Medieval Studies). Sales and Marketing Manager, Plaskit Ltd, 1991–96; self employed, working in timber products and PR sectors, 1996–2003; Planning Consultant, Green Planning Solutions, 2005–07; Sen. Partner, Green Planning Solutions LLP, 2007–14. Contested (Lib Dem) Wolverhampton SW, 1997; MP (Lib Dem) Ludlow, 2001–05; contested (Lib Dem) same seat, 2005. *Recreations:* cricket, mountaineering. *Address:* (office) Unit D, Lunesdale, Upton Magna Business Park, Shrewsbury SY4 4TT. *E:* matthew.green@gpsltd.co.uk. *Club:* Liberal.

**GREEN, Michael;** *see* Green, N. M.

**GREEN, Michael Anthony;** QC 2009; a Deputy High Court Judge, since 2018; *b* London, 23 Oct. 1964; *s* of late Jeffrey Isaac Green and of Susan Henrietta Green (*née* Bush); *m* 1991, Giselle Serena Finlay; one *s* two *d. Educ:* University Coll. Sch., Hampstead; Jesus Coll., Cambridge (BA 1986; MA 1990). Called to the Bar, Lincoln's Inn, 1987; in practice as barrister, 1988–, specialising in commercial, company and insolvency law; Acting High Court Judge, Commercial Div., Eastern Caribbean Supreme Court, 2019. Mem., Attorney Gen.'s A Panel of Counsel, 1997–2008. Inspector for Insider Dealing Inquiry, DTI, 1997. Mem., Ind. Monitoring Bd, HM Prison Wormwood Scrubs, 2008. *Recreations:* ski-ing, squash, cricket, Manchester United, 20th century classical music. *Address:* Fountain Court Chambers, Temple, EC4Y 9DH. *T:* (020) 7583 3335, *Fax:* (020) 7353 0329. *E:* mg@fountaincourt.co.uk.

**GREEN, Prof. Michael Boris**, FRS 1989; Lucasian Professor of Mathematics, University of Cambridge, 2009–13, now Emeritus; Fellow of Clare Hall, Cambridge, 1993–2010, now Hon. Fellow; *b* 22 May 1946; *s* of late Absalom and Genia Green; *m* 2005, Prof. Joanna Chataway; one *d. Educ:* Churchill Coll., Cambridge (BA, PhD; Rayleigh Prize 1969; Hon. Fellow 2010). Res. Fellow, Inst. for Advanced Study, Princeton, NJ, 1970–72; Fellowships in Cambridge, 1972–77; SERC Advanced Fellow, Oxford, 1977–79; Lectr, Queen Mary Coll., London Univ., 1979–85; Prof. of Physics, QMC, later QMW, 1985–93; John Humphrey Plummer Prof. of Theoretical Physics, Univ. of Cambridge, 1993–2009. Vis. Associate, Caltech, Pasadena, for periods during 1981–85; Nuffield Science Fellowship, 1984–86; SERC Sen. Fellowship, 1986–91. Vis. Prof., Physics Dept, QMUL. Hon. FInstP 2013. Hon. DSc QMUL, 2004. Maxwell Medal and Prize, 1987, Dirac Medal and Prize, 2004, Inst. of Physics; Hopkins Prize, Cambridge Philosophical Soc., 1987; Dirac Medal, Internat. Centre for Theoretical Physics, Trieste, 1989; Dannie Heinemann Prize, APS, 2002; Naylor Prize, London Math. Soc., 2008; Fundamental Physics Prize, 2014. *Publications:* Superstring Theory, vols I and II (with J. H. Schwarz and E. Witten), 1987; many contribs to physics and mathematics jls. *Address:* Department of Applied Mathematics and Theoretical Physics, University of Cambridge, Cambridge CB3 0WA.

**GREEN, Michael John;** Controller, BBC Radio 4, 1986–96; Deputy Managing Director, BBC Network Radio, 1993–96; *b* 28 May 1941; *s* of David Green and Kathleen (*née* Swann); *m* 1965, Christine Margaret Constance Gibson; one *s* one *d. Educ:* Repton Sch.; Barnsley Grammar Sch.; New Coll., Oxford (BA Modern Langs). Swiss Broadcasting Corp., 1964–65; Sheffield Star, 1965–67; Producer, BBC Radio Sheffield, 1967–70; Documentary Producer, BBC Manchester, 1970–77; Editor, File on Four, 1977; Head of Network Radio, Manchester, 1978–86. Chm., Radio Acad., 1990–95. Mem., NCC, 1997–2001. *Recreations:* France, cinema, collecting glass.

**GREEN, Michael Philip;** psychoanalytic psychotherapist; *s* of Cyril and Irene Green; *m* 1st, 1972, Hon. Janet Frances Wolfson (*see* Hon. Dame J. F. W. de Botton) (marr. diss. 1989); two *d*; 2nd, 1990, Theresa Mary Buckmaster (*see* T. M. Green); three *s* one *d. Educ:* Haberdashers' Aske's School; Univ. of Wales (MA); Advanced Dip. Integrative Psychotherapy. Co-Founder and Dir, Tangent Industries Ltd, 1968–. Chairman: Carlton Communications Plc, 1983–2004 (Chief Exec., 1983–91); Carlton Television Ltd, 1991–94; Tangent Communications plc, 2012–; Director: GMTV Ltd, 1992–2004; Reuters Holdings PLC, 1992–99; ITN, 1993–2004 (Chm., 1993–95); Getty Communications plc, 1997–98. Founder, Tangent Charitable Trust, 1984; Chm., The Media Trust, 1997–2006. Trustee, Sainsbury Centre for Mental Health, 2001–05. Mem., British Assoc. for Counselling and Psychotherapy, 2010–. UKCP registered. Hon. DLitt City, 1999. *Recreations:* reading, bridge. *Address:* 21 South Street, W1K 2XB. *T:* (020) 7663 6464. *Club:* Portland.

**GREEN, Prof. Mino**, FIET; Professor of Electrical Device Science, Electrical Engineering, 1983–92, now Emeritus, Senior Research Fellow, since 1992, Imperial College of Science and Technology; Founder and Chief Scientist, Nexeon Ltd, since 2006; *b* 10 March 1927; *s* of Alexander and Elizabeth Green; *m* 1951, Diana Mary Allen (*d* 2012); one *s* one *d. Educ:* Dulwich Coll.; University Coll., Durham Univ. (BSc, PhD, DSc). Group Leader: Solid State Res., Lincoln Laboratory, MIT, 1951–55; Res., Zenith Radio Corp., USA, 1956–60; Associate Dir, Electrochemistry Lab., Univ. of Pennsylvania, 1960–62; Man. Dir, Zenith Radio Research Corp. (UK) Ltd, 1962–72; Lectr, then Reader, Elec. Engrg Dept, Imperial Coll. of Science and Technology, 1972–83. Imperial Coll. Medal, 2015. *Publications:* Solid State Surface Science, vols I, II and III (ed), 1969–73; many pubns (and many patents) on various aspects of semiconductor and optical device science and of nano-science and technol. *Recreations:* walking, art appreciation. *Address:* 55 Gerard Road, SW13 9QH. *T:* (020) 8748 8689. *Club:* Hurlingham.
*See also* D. M. A. Green.

**GREEN, Miranda Jane A.;** *see* Aldhouse-Green.

**GREEN, Rt Hon. Sir Nicholas (Nigel)**, Kt 2013; PC 2018; PhD; **Rt Hon. Lord Justice Green**; a Lord Justice of Appeal, since 2018; Chair, Law Commission of England and Wales, since 2018; *b* 15 Oct. 1958; *s* of John Reginald Green and Pauline Barbara Green; *m* 1990, Fiona Clare Cramb; one *s* one *d. Educ:* King Edward VI Sch., Camp Hill, Birmingham; Univ. of Leicester (LLB 1980); Univ. of Toronto (LLM 1981); Univ. of Southampton (PhD 1985). Lectr in Law, Univ. of Southampton, 1981–85; pt-time Lectr in Law, UCL, 1985–87; called to the Bar, Inner Temple, 1986 (Bencher, 2002; Exec. Cttee, 2003–06); in practice at the Bar, 1986–2013; QC 1998; a Recorder, 2004–13; Jt Hd of

Chambers, Brick Court Chambers, 2011–13; a Judge of the High Ct of Justice, QBD, 2013–18; Presiding Judge, SE Circuit, 2017–18. *Chm.*, Bar European Gp, 1999–2001; Bar Council of England and Wales: Vice Chm., Internat. Relns Cttee, 2000–02; Chm., European Cttee, 2003–05; Chm., Legal Services Cttee, 2006–08; Mem., Gen. Mgt Cttee, 2002–10; Vice Chm., 2009; Chm., 2010; Chm., Advocacy Trng Council, 2011–16. UK Perm. Rep. of CCBE to European Court of Justice, Court of First Instance and EFTA Court, 2000–02. Vis. Prof. of Law, Univ. of Durham, 2000–07; Hon. Prof. of Law, Univ. of Leicester, 2005–. Mem., BMA Bd of Sci. Ref. Gp on Drugs of Dependence, 2011–12. *Publications:* Commercial Agreements and Competition Law: practice and procedure in the UK and EEC, 1986, 2nd edn (jtly) 1997; (jtly) The Legal Foundations of the Single European Market, 1991; (ed jtly) Competition Litigation, 2009; over 50 articles in legal jls worldwide. *Recreations:* family, swimming (former international, 1976–77), collecting Victorian watercolours. *Address:* Royal Courts of Justice, Strand, WC2A 2LL.

**GREEN, Dr (Norman) Michael,** FRS 1981; affiliated to scientific research staff, Francis Crick Institute, since 2015 (affiliated to Department of Mathematical Biology, National Institute for Medical Research, 1992–2015); *b* 6 April 1926; *s* of Ernest Green and Hilda Margaret Carter; *m* 1953, Iro Paulina Moschouti; two *s* one *d*. *Educ:* Dragon Sch., Oxford; Clifton Coll., Bristol; Magdalen Coll., Oxford (BA; Athletics Blue, Cross Country Blue); UCH Med. Sch., London (PhD). Res. Student, Univ. of Washington, Seattle, 1951–53; Lectr in Biochemistry, Univ. of Sheffield, 1953–55; Res. Fellow and Lectr in Chem. Pathol., St Mary's Hosp. Med. Sch., London, 1956–62; Vis. Scientist, NIH, Maryland, 1962–64; Res. Staff, Divs of Biochem. and Protein Structure, NIMR, 1964–91. *Publications:* research papers on the structure of proteins and of membranes, in scientific jls. *Recreations:* mountain climbing, geometry. *Address:* 57 Hale Lane, Mill Hill, NW7 3PS.

**GREEN, Patrick Curtis;** QC 2012; *b* Cambridge, 1967; *s* of Andrew Curtis Green, *qv*; *m* 2001, Trisha Leigh Little; one *s* two *d*. *Educ:* Haileybury Coll. (Exhibnr); Magdalene Coll., Cambridge (BA Law 1989). 2nd Lieut, RM SSLC, 1985–86. Called to the Bar, Middle Temple, 1990; in practice as barrister, 1990–, specialising in fields of commercial and employment law and judicial review. Vis. Fellow, LSE, 2005–. Director: ResoLex Ltd, 2000–; ResoLex Hldgs, 2003–; Habeas Film Co., 2011–. *Publications:* The Manual of Employment Appeals, 2008. *Recreations:* Real tennis, tennis, ski-ing, sailing, shooting, art, music, film, theatre and comedy. *Address:* Henderson Chambers, 2 Harcourt Buildings, Temple, EC4Y 9DB. *T:* (020) 7583 9020. *E:* clerks@hendersonchambers.co.uk. *Club:* Brooks's.

**GREEN, Patrick G.;** *see* Grafton-Green.

**GREEN, Dame Pauline,** DBE 2003; President, International Co-operative Alliance, 2009–15; *b* 8 Dec. 1948; *d* of late Bertram Wiltshire and of Lucy Wiltshire; *m* 1971, Paul Adam Green (marr. diss. 2003); one *s* one *d*. *Educ:* John Kelly Secondary Modern Sch. for Girls, Brent; Kilburn Poly.; Open Univ. (BA); London School of Economics (MSc). Sec., 1981, Chair, 1983, Chipping Barnet Labour Party. MEP (Lab): London N, 1989–99; London Reg., 1999; Leader: European PLP, 1993–94; Gp of Pty of Eur. Socialists, 1994–99; Chief Exec., Co-operative Union Ltd, later Co-operatives UK, 2000–09. Contested (Lab) Arkley ward, Barnet Council elecns, 1986. Parly Asst, Co-operative Movement, 1986–89. Pres., Co-operative Congress, 1997; Vice Pres., Socialist International, 1994. Mem., NEC, Labour Party, 1998–99. Mem., USDAW. *Recreations:* music, swimming.

**GREEN, Prof. Peter James,** PhD; FRS 2003; Professorial Research Fellow, University of Bristol, since 2011 (Professor of Statistics, 1989–2011, now Emeritus); Distinguished Professor, University of Technology, Sydney, since 2011; *b* 28 April 1950; *s* of late Frank Green and Joyce (*née* Walder); *m* 1984, Elizabeth Jane Bennett; two *d*. *Educ:* Solihull Sch.; Pembroke Coll., Oxford (BA 1971, MA); Univ. of Sheffield (MSc; PhD 1976). CStat 2000. Lectr in Stats, Univ. of Bath, 1974–78; Lectr, then Sen. Lectr in Stats, Univ. of Durham, 1978–89; Henry Overton Wills Prof. of Maths, Univ. of Bristol, 2003–11. Various vis. appts at foreign univs, 1979–. Pres., Royal Statistical Soc., 2001–03. FIMS 1991. Fellow, Internat. Soc. for Bayesian Analysis, 2016. Guy Medals, Bronze, 1987 and Silver, 1999, Royal Statistical Soc.; Royal Soc. Wolfson Res. Merit Award, 2006. *Publications:* (with B. Silverman) Nonparametric Regression and Generalized Linear Models, 1994; (ed with S. Richardson and N. L. Hjort) Highly Structured Stochastic Systems, 2003; contrib. numerous papers to learned jls. *Recreations:* biking, mountains, running. *Address:* School of Mathematics, University of Bristol, Bristol BS8 1TW. *T:* (0117) 928 7967. *E:* P.J.Green@bristol.ac.uk.

**GREEN, Prof. Peter Morris;** author and translator, since 1953; Professor of Classics, University of Texas at Austin, 1972–97 (James R. Dougherty Jr Centennial Professor of Classics, 1982–84, 1985–97), now Emeritus; Adjunct Professor of Classics, University of Iowa, since 1998; *b* 22 Dec. 1924; *oc* of late Arthur Green, CBE, MC, LLB, and Olive Slaughter; *m* 1st, 1951, Lalage Isobel Pulvertaft (marr. diss.); two *s* one *d*; 2nd, 1975, Carin Margreta (*d* 2015), *y d* of late G. N. Christensen, Saratoga, USA. *Educ:* Charterhouse; Trinity Coll., Cambridge. Served in RAFVR, 1943–47: overseas tour in Burma Comd, 1944–46. 1st Cl. Hons, Pts I and II, Classical Tripos, 1949–50; MA and PhD Cantab 1954; Craven Schol. and Student, 1950; Dir of Studies in Classics, 1951–52; Fiction Critic, London Daily Telegraph, 1953–63; Literary Adviser, The Bodley Head, 1957–58; Cons. Editor, Hodder and Stoughton, 1960–63; Television Critic, The Listener, 1961–63; Film Critic, John o'London's, 1961–63; Mem. Book Soc. Cttee, 1959–63. Former Mem. of selection cttees for literary prizes: Heinemann Award, John Llewellyn Rhys, W. H. Smith £1000 Award for Literature. Translator of numerous works from French, Italian, Latin, and classical and modern Greek, including books by Simone de Beauvoir, Fosco Maraini, Joseph Kessel, Yannis Ritsos. FRSL 1956; Mem. Council, Royal Society of Literature, 1958–63 (resigned on emigration). In 1963 resigned all positions and emigrated to Greece as full-time writer (1963–71). Visiting Professor of Classics: Univ. of Texas, 1971–72; UCLA, 1976; Mellon Prof. of Humanities, Tulane Univ., 1986; Vis. Prof. of History, Univ. of Iowa, 1997–98; Sen. Fellow for independent study and res., National Endowment for the Humanities, 1983–84; Vis. Res. Fellow and Writer-in-Residence, Princeton Univ., 2001; King Charles II Dist. Vis. Prof. in Classics and Ancient Hist., 2004, Whichard Dist. Vis. Prof. in the Humanities, 2006, 2009, E Carolina Univ. Editor, Syllecta Classica, 1999–2009, 2013–17. *Publications:* The Expanding Eye, 1953; Achilles His Armour, 1955; Cat in Gloves (pseud. Denis Delaney), 1956; The Sword of Pleasure (W. H. Heinemann Award for Literature), 1957; Kenneth Grahame 1859–1932: A Study of his Life, Work and Times, 1959; Essays in Antiquity, 1960; Habeas Corpus and other stories, 1962; Look at the Romans, 1963; The Laughter of Aphrodite, 1965, repr. 1993; Juvenal: The Sixteen Satires (trans.), 1967, 3rd edn 1998; Armada from Athens: The Failure of the Sicilian Expedition 415–413 BC, 1970; Alexander the Great: a biography, 1970; The Year of Salamis 480–479 BC, 1971, rev. as The Greco-Persian Wars, 1996; The Shadow of the Parthenon, 1972; The Parthenon, 1973; A Concise History of Ancient Greece, 1973; Alexander of Macedon 356–323 BC: a historical biography, 1974, repr. 1991; Ovid: The Erotic Poems (trans.), 1982; Beyond the Wild Wood: the world of Kenneth Grahame, 1982; Medium and Message Reconsidered: the changing functions of classical translation, 1986; Classical Bearings: interpreting ancient history and culture, 1989; Alexander to Actium: the historical evolution of the Hellenistic Age, 1990, rev. edn 1993; (ed) Hellenistic History and Culture, 1993; Yannis Ritsos: The Fourth Dimension (trans.), 1993; Ovid: The Poems of Exile (trans.), 1994, rev. edn 2005; Apollonios Rhodios: The Argonautika (trans. and commentary), 1997; From Ikaria to the Stars, 2004; The Poems of Catullus (trans.), 2005; Diodorus Siculus Bks 11–12.37.1: Greek History 480–431 BCE the alternative version, 2006; Alexander the Great and the Hellenistic Age: a short history, 2007; Diodorus Siculus, The Persian Wars to the Fall of Athens: books 11–14.34 (480–401 BCE) (trans.), 2010; Homer's Iliad (trans.), 2015; Homer's Odyssey (trans.), 2018. *Recreations:* reading poetry and fiction, keeping in touch with old friends, avoiding urban life, listening to chamber music. *Address:* 1268 Chamberlain Drive, Iowa City, IA 52240–2922, USA. *T:* (319) 6213710. *E:* peter-green-1@uiowa.edu. *Club:* Savile.

**GREEN, Peter Richard Austin;** Head Master, Rugby School, since 2014; *b* Dumfries, Scotland, 8 Dec. 1964; *s* of Louis and Margaret Green; *m* 1990, Brenda O'Connor; one *s* one *d*. *Educ:* St Joseph's Coll., Dumfries; Edinburgh Univ. (MA Hons 1986); St Andrew's Coll. (PGCE, Cert. RE 1987). Teacher of Geography, St Olave's and St Saviour's Grammar Sch., 1987–89; Teacher of Geography and i/c Rugby, Strathallan Sch., 1989–95; Housemaster, Hd of Geography and i/c Rugby, Uppingham Sch., 1996–2002; Second Master, Ampleforth Coll., 2002–07; Headmaster, Ardingly Coll., 2007–14. Vice Chair, Woodard Heads Assoc., 2011–14. Gov., Belhaven Hill Prep. Sch., 2003–11. Mem., Ampleforth Soc.; St Joseph's Past Pupils. *Recreations:* Rugby, opera, wine tasting, family, theatre, school governor, Church. *Address:* Rugby School, Rugby CV22 5EH. *T:* (01788) 556217, *Fax:* (01788) 578635. *E:* head@rugbyschool.net. *Clubs:* Lansdowne, East India, Oriental.

**GREEN, Sir Philip,** Kt 2006; retail executive; *b* 15 March 1952; *m* 1990, Cristina; one *s* one *d*. Took over family property company, 1973; bought: Jean Jeanie, 1985 (sold to Lee Cooper, 1986); Owen Owen, 1994; Olympus Sports, 1995 (merged with Sports Division, 1996; sold to JJB Sports, 1998); Mark One, 1996; Shoe Express, 1997 (sold, 1998); Sears (incl. Miss Selfridge, Wallis, Warehouse, Freemans), 1999; Bhs, 2000 (sold, 2015); Arcadia (incl. Top Shop, Dorothy Perkins, Evans, Burton), 2002; Chm. and Chief Exec., Amber Day, 1988–92. *Address:* Taveta Investments Ltd, Colegrave House, 70 Berners Street, W1T 3NL.

**GREEN, Philip Nevill,** CBE 2014; non-executive Chairman: BakerCorp. Inc., 2011–17; Sentebale, 2011–18; *b* 12 May 1953; *s* of Harry Green and Sheila Saveker (*née* Emery); *m* 1977, Judy Rippon; two *d*. *Educ:* UC of Swansea, Wales (BA Hons); London Business Sch. (MBA). DHL: Regl Dir, Northern Europe, 1990–94; Chief Operating Officer, Europe and Africa, 1994–99; Divl CEO, 1999–2001, Chief Operating Officer, 2001–03, Reuters Gp Plc; Chief Executive: Royal P&O Nedlloyd, 2003–06; United Utilities plc, 2006–11. Sen. Ind. Dir, 2011–14, Chm., 2014–18, Carillion plc; Sen. Ind. Dir, Saga plc, 2014–17. Adviser to Prime Minister on Corporate Responsibility, 2011–17. Trustee, Philharmonia Orch., 2002–14; Chm., Bible Soc., 2012–15. Patron, Hope Through Action, 2007–. *Recreations:* walking, cricket, Africa, wine, music. *Clubs:* Royal Automobile, MCC.

**GREEN, Rodney Alan Rupert,** CBE 2015; Prior of England and the Islands, Order of St John, and Chairman, St John Ambulance, 2010–16; *b* 7 Feb. 1953; *s* of Timothy Green and Mercy Green (*née* Mathison); *m* 1975, Helen Frances Benjamin; two *s*. *Educ:* Christ's Hosp., Horsham; Emmanuel Coll., Cambridge (MA 1974). Greater London Council: cttee clerk, Dir-Gen.'s Dept, 1974–76; Scientific Br. Staffing Officer, 1976–78; Surrey County Council: Head, Teaching Personnel Section 1978–82; Principal: Schools, 1982–84; Special Needs, 1984–87; Asst Co. Educn Officer, 1987–91; Asst Chief Exec., W Glamorgan CC, 1991–96; Chief Exec., Leicester CC, 1996–2008. Director: Leics TEC, 1998–2001; Nat. Space Centre, 1998–2006; Leicester Regeneration Co., 2001–06; Leicestershire Cares, 2001–08; Member: Adv. Panel on Beacon Scheme, 2005–08; Inst. of Community Cohesion, 2006–08; Migration Impacts Forum, 2007–08. Trustee, A Rocha Internat., 2010–. Non-exec. Dir, British Waterways, 2009–12. Hon. LLD De Montfort, 2003. KStJ 2010. *Publications:* 90,000 Hours: managing the world of work, 2002. *Recreations:* films, theatre, travel, Leicester Tigers Rugby, swimming, Biblical studies, feasting.

**GREEN, Prof. Roger,** FRCP; Professor of Physiology, University of Manchester, 1981–2005, now Professor Emeritus; *b* 9 Feb. 1942; *s* of Donald Victor and Joyce Green; *m* 1965, Rita Mavis; one *s* two *d*. *Educ:* Univ. of Sheffield (MB ChB 1965); Univ. of Manchester (MSc 1981). FRCP 2002. House Officer posts, Sheffield Royal Hosp., 1965–66; University of Manchester: Asst Lectr, Lectr, Sen. Lectr, then Reader in Physiol., 1966–81; Dean: Undergrad. Med. Studies, 1993–97; Medical Sch., 1997–2003. Hon. DSc: St Andrews, 2004; Keele, 2004; Hon. MD Internat. Med. Univ. Malaysia, 2012. *Publications:* contribs to physiological jls. *Recreation:* brass bands. *Address:* 105 Heaton Park Road, Manchester M9 0QQ. *T:* (0161) 795 9983.

**GREEN, Samuel;** QC 2015; a Recorder, since 2018; *b* Ballymena, NI, 30 Dec. 1975; *s* of Rev. Norman Green and Mildred Green (*née* Bond); *m* Anne; one *d*. *Educ:* Trinity Coll., Cambridge (BA 1997). Called to the Bar: Lincoln's Inn, 1998; NI, 2007; in practice as a barrister, 1998–. *Recreations:* cycling, boxing, keeping fit, legal biography, wine. *Address:* St Pauls Chambers, Leeds LS1 5JF.

**GREEN, Simon Antony;** Head, BT Sport, since 2012; *b* Wivenhoe, Essex, 13 Nov. 1964; *s* of Roy Edward and Margaret Rosaline Green; *m* 2014, Anthea Frances Hartridge; two *s* one *d*. *Educ:* Wing Co. Secondary Sch.; Leicester Univ. (BSc Hons Engrg (Civil) 1987). On sabbatical, Australia, 1989; Accountant, 1990–94; Ops Manager, 1994–97, Sky Sports; Sen. Vice Pres., Ops, Fox Sports LA, 1997–99; Gen. Manager, Sky Sports Ventures, Sky Sports, 1999–2005; Channels Hd, Setanta Sports, 2005–09; Man. Dir (pt-time), Box Nation, 2009–12; Commercial Contractor (pt-time), FA, 2009–12. Non-exec. Dir, Opta Sports Data, 2005–12. Mem., BAFTA, 2014–. *Recreations:* football, tennis, walking, kids, my wife, cycling. *Address:* Stoneacre, Tylers Green, Cuckfield, Haywards Heath, W Sussex RH17 5DZ. *T:* (01444) 410790, 07725 811622. *E:* greensimon@mac.com. *Clubs:* Soho House, Number 20.

**GREEN, Susan Valerie;** District Judge (Magistrates' Courts), since 2001; *b* 1 Nov. 1954; *d* of Nat Green and Ettie Green (*née* Blacker); *m* 2004, Haydn Gott, *qv*. *Educ:* Birmingham Univ. (LLB); Coll. of Law, Guildford. Admitted solicitor, 1981; J. P. Malnick and Co., subsequently Malnick & Rance: articled clerk, 1979–81; Asst Solicitor, 1981–82; Partner, 1982–98; Consultant, Traymans, 1998–2000. Legal Mem. and Pres., Mental Health Review Tribunal, then Tribunal Judge, First-tier Tribunal (Mental Health), 2003–; Designated District Judge, S London LJA. Formerly Sec. and Pres., NE London Law Soc.; Pres., London Criminal Courts Solicitors' Assoc., 1998–99. *Recreations:* sports, cookery, travel, theatre, dance. *Address:* c/o Camberwell Green Magistrates' Court, D'Eynsford Street, SE5 7UP. *T:* (020) 7805 9802.

**GREEN, Terence Anthony;** Chief Executive, Clothing, Tesco, 2006–10; retail consultant, since 2011; *b* 9 Oct. 1951; *s* of Henry Green and Nora Green (*née* Sayers); *m* 1981, Geraldine A. Daniels (marr. diss. 1996); one *s* two *d*; one *d* by Vanessa Field. *Educ:* Liverpool Univ. (BSc Maths; BSc (Hons) Maths, Computer Sci. and Stats). Exec. Dir, Burton Gp plc, 1992–98; Chief Executive: Debenhams, 1992–98; Topshop and Top Man, 1995–98;

Debenhams plc, 1998–2000 (Debenhams demerged from Burton Gp, 1998); Bhs Ltd, 2000–02; Allders, 2003–05. Non-exec. Dir, First Choice Holidays plc, 1997. FRSA 1997. Hon. DA Hertfordshire, 2010. *Recreations:* food, opera, reading, collecting art and fine wines, writing, painting, algorithm trading for private fund.

**GREEN, Theresa Mary,** CBE 2008; Chairman, Moorfields Eye Hospital NHS Foundation Trust, since 2016; *b* 29 July 1964; *d* of Richard Buckmaster and Jacqueline Buckmaster (*née* Leche); *m* 1990, Michael Philip Green, *qv*; three *s* one *d*. *Educ:* Putney High Sch.; Lady Margaret Hall, Oxford (MA); City Univ. (LLB 1993). Called to the Bar, Middle Temple, 1994, Bencher, 2018. Head of Corporate Communications, Carlton Communications Plc, 1986–90. Chm., Royal Marsden NHS Foundn Trust (formerly NHS Trust), 1998–2010; non-executive Director: Royal Berkshire and Battle Hosps NHS Trust, 1994–98; Barts Health NHS Trust, 2013–14; Pets at Home plc, 2014–. Member: Res. Ethics Cttee, Royal Marsden Hosp., 1994–98 (Chm., 1996); Bd of Trustees, Inst. of Cancer Res., 1998–2010; Assoc. Mem., BUPA, 2013– (Mem., Medical Adv. Panel, 2013–); Mem. Adv. Bd, Healthcare UK, 2017–18. Trustee: Nat. Portrait Gall., 1999–2002; Royal Botanic Gardens, Kew, 2011–14; Royal Foundn of the Duke and Duchess of Cambridge (formerly of Prince William, later of the Duke and Duchess of Cambridge and Prince Harry, then the Duke and Duchess of Sussex), 2011–. Hon. LLD City, 2018.

**GREEN-ARMYTAGE, John McDonald;** Chairman, JZ International Ltd, since 1996; *b* 6 June 1945; *s* of John Whitla Green-Armytage and Elizabeth McDonald Green-Armytage; *m* 1977, Susan Rosemary Le Messurier; one *s* three *d*. *Educ:* McGill Univ., Montreal (BA (Econs) 1966); Columbia Univ., NY (MBA 1970). Joined N. M. Rothschild & Sons Ltd, 1970, exec. Dir, 1977–82, non-exec. Dir, 1988–97; Man. Dir, Guthrie Corp. plc, 1982–88; Jt Chm. and CEO, Kelt Energy plc, 1990–91; William Baird plc: non-exec. Dir, 1992–94; CEO, 1995–96; Dep. Chm., 1996. Non-exec. Chm., AMEC plc, 2004–11 (non-exec. Dir, 1996–2011); Chm., Star Capital Partners Ltd, 2001–17. *Recreations:* country pursuits, polo, sailing. *Address:* JZ International Ltd, 17a Curzon Street, W1J 5HS. *Clubs:* Brooks's, Turf; Guards Polo.

**GREEN-PRICE, Sir Robert (John),** 5th Bt *cr* 1874; landowner; Assistant Professor of English, Chiba University of Commerce, 1982–97; *b* 22 Oct. 1940; *o s* of Sir John Green-Price, 4th Bt, and Irene Marion (*d* 1954), *d* of Major Sir (Ernest) Guy Lloyd, 1st Bt, DSO; *S* father, 1964. *Educ:* Shrewsbury. Army Officer, 1961–69; Captain, RCT, retd. ADC to Governor of Bermuda, 1969–72. Lectr in English, Teikyo Univ., 1975–82. Part-time Lecturer: Keio Univ., 1977–97; Waseda Univ., 1986–97; Guest Lectr, NHK Radio, 1978–83. *Heir: cousin* Simon Richard Green-Price, *b* 10 May 1964.

**GREENALL,** family name of **Baron Daresbury**.

**GREENAWAY, Sir David,** Kt 2014; DL; Vice Chancellor, 2008–17, and Professor of Economics, 1987–2017, University of Nottingham, now Emeritus Vice-Chancellor and Professor; *b* 20 March 1952; *s* of David and Agnes Greenaway; *m* 1975, Susan Elizabeth Hallam; two *s*. *Educ:* Henry Mellish Grammar Sch.; Liverpool Poly. (BSc London ext. 1974); Liverpool Univ. (MCom 1975); DLitt Nottingham 1997. Lectr in Econs, Leicester Poly., 1975–78; University of Buckingham: Lectr, 1978–83; Sen. Lectr, 1983–85; Reader, 1985–86; Prof. of Econs, 1986–87; Pro-Vice-Chancellor, Univ. of Nottingham, 1994–2001, 2004–08. Non-executive Director: Nottingham HA, 1994–98; Queen's Med. Centre, Nottingham Univ. Hosp. NHS Trust, 2001–04. Member: Council, 1990–97, Exec., 1991–97, REconS; Acad. Adv. Council, IEA, 1991–2004; Technology Foresight Steering Gp, 1994–95; Council, ESRC, 1997–2001; Armed Forces Pay Review Body, 1997– (Chm., 2004–10); Sen. Salaries Rev. Body, 2004–10; Asia Task Force, 2010–; Chair, Panel for Econs and Econometrics, RAE, HEFCE, 2001 and 2008 (Vice Chair, 1996). Chair: Ind. Review of Postgrad. Med. Educn and Trng, 2012–13; Bd of Trustees, CASE Europe, 2013–17; Russell Gp of Univs, 2015–17. Adviser: UNIDO, 1983; World Bank, 1986, 1988; GATT, 1986; DTI, 1994; UNECE, 1994; Commonwealth Secretariat, 1997; Asian Develt Bank, 1997; Caribbean Regl Negotiating Machinery, 2000; Dept for Transport, 2003–04. Gov., NIESR, 1995– (Mem. Council, 2018–). Mem. Council, Univ. of Cambridge, 2017–. Chair, British Malaysia Soc., 2016–. FRSA 1994; AcSS 2000. Hon. Fellow, Liverpool John Moores Univ., 2012. Hon. Col, E Midlands Univs OTC, 2013–17. Hon. Citizen, City of Ningbo, China, 2012; Hon. Freeman, City of Nottingham, 2017. DL Notts, 2009. Hon. LLD: Liverpool, 2016; Western Ontario, 2017; Nottingham, 2019; Hon. DSc Glasgow Caledonian, 2017. Dato Paduka Mahkota Perak (Malaysia), 2017. *Publications:* International Trade Policy, 1983; (jtly) Economics of Intra-Industry Trade, 1986; (jtly) Imperfect Competition and International Trade, 1986; Companion to Contemporary Economic Thought, 1991; (jtly) Evaluating Trade Policy in Developing Countries, 1993; (jtly) Economics of Commodity Markets, 1999; Globalisation and Labour Markets, 2000; Adjusting to Globalisation, 2005; (ed jtly) China and the World Economy, 2010; Palgrave Handbook of International Trade, 2011; (ed jtly) The Globalization of Higher Education, 2012; (ed jtly) The Business Growth Benefits of Higher Education, 2014; papers in learned jls. *Recreations:* golf, tennis, football, wine, reading, cycling.

**GREENAWAY, Peter,** CBE 2007; film director, painter and writer; Professor of Cinema Studies, European Graduate School, Saas-Fee, Switzerland; *b* 5 April 1942; *m*; two *d*. *Educ:* Forest Sch.; Walthamstow Coll. of Art. Film Editor, Central Office of Information, 1965–76. Maker of short films, 1966–, of feature length films, 1978–. *Exhibitions:* Lord's Gall., 1964; The Physical Self, Rotterdam, 1991; 100 Objects to Represent the World, Acad. of Fine Arts, Vienna, 1992; Flying Out of this World, Louvre, 1992; Watching Water, Venice, 1993; Some Organising Principles, Swansea, 1993; The Audience of Macon, Cardiff, 1993; The Stairs, Geneva, 1994, Munich, 1995; Spellbound, London, 1996; Flying Over Water, Barcelona, 1997; *one-man shows:* Canterbury, 1989; Carcassone, Paris, 1989; NY, Melbourne, Liège, Tokyo, Fukoa, Munich, Copenhagen, Oddense, Brussels, 1990; Brentford, Dublin, 1991; Bremen, NY, 1992; Tempe, Ariz, and Salzburg, 1994; Biel-Bienne, Switzerland, New York, and Munich, 1995; Milan, Ghent, and Thessaloniki, 1996; Manchester, 1998; Edinburgh, 1999; *group shows* include: Freezeframe, Lamont Gall., 1996; The Director's Eye, Mus. of Modern Art, Oxford, 1996. *Films:* (writer and director): Train, 1966; Tree, 1966; Five Postcards from Capital Cities, 1967; Revolution, 1967; Intervals, 1969; Erosion, 1971; H is for House, 1973; Windows, 1975; Water Wrackets, 1975; Goole by Numbers, 1976; Dear Phone, 1977; 1–1Co, 1978; A Walk Through H, 1978; Vertical Features Remake, 1978; The Falls, 1980 (Special Award, BFI); Act of God, 1981 (Best short film, Melbourne Film Fest.); Zandra Rhodes, 1981; The Draughtsman's Contract, 1982; Four American Composers, 1983; Making a Splash, 1984; (jtly) A TV Dante-Canto V, 1984; Inside Rooms—The Bathroom, 1985; A Zed and Two Noughts, 1985; The Belly of an Architect, 1986; Fear of Drowning, 1988; Drowning by Numbers, 1988 (Prize for Best Artistic Contribution, Cannes Film Fest.); The Cook, the Thief, his Wife and her Lover, 1989; Prospero's Books, 1990; M is for Man, Music, Mozart, 1991; Rosa, 1992; Darwin, 1992; The Baby of Macon, 1993; The Stairs, Geneva, 1994; The Pillow Book, 1996; The Bridge, 1996; 8½ Women, 1999; Nightwatching, 2007; Goltzius and the Pelican Company, 2012; Eisenstein in Guanajuato, 2016; *operas:* Rosa: a Horse Drama, 1994; Writing to Vermeer, 1999. Officier de l'Ordre des Arts et des Lettres (France), 1998. *Publications:* The Falls, 1993; filmscripts and exhibn catalogues.

**GREENAWAY, Sir Thomas Edward Burdick,** 4th Bt *cr* 1933, of Coombe, Surrey; Partner, Greenaway Mosaics LLP, since 2007; *b* Tunbridge Wells, Kent, 3 April 1985; *s* of Sir John Michael Burdick Greenaway, 3rd Bt and Susan Greenaway (*née* Birch); *S* father, 2015. *Educ:* Cothill House; Stowe Sch.; Chippendale Sch. of Furniture. *Recreations:* ski-ing, water ski-ing, tennis, walking, golf. *Heir: cousin* Michael Philip Greenaway [*b* 14 Dec. 1949; *m* 1978, Alison Robyn Cohen; one *s* two *d*]. *Address:* Lois Weedon House, Weedon Lois, Towcester, Northants NN12 8PJ. *T:* (01327) 860472. *E:* thomas@greenawaymosaics.com.

**GREENBERG, Daniel Isaac;** Counsel for Domestic Legislation, House of Commons, since 2016; *b* 5 Sept. 1965; *s* of Dr Morris Greenberg and Dr Gillian Greenberg; *m* 1988, Julia Sharon Becker; two *s* two *d*. *Educ:* Trinity Coll., Cambridge (BA); Inns of Court Sch. of Law. Legal Advr, Lord Chancellor's Dept, 1988–91; Asst Parly Counsel, 1991–95; Sen. Asst Parly Counsel, 1995–99; Dep. Parly Counsel, 1999–2003; Parly Counsel, 2003–08, pt-time, 2009–10; Parly Counsel (pt-time), Berwin Leighton Paisner LLP, 2010–16. Gen. Editor, Annotated Statutes (formerly Technical Annotations), Westlaw UK, 2008–; Editor in Chief, Statute Law Review, 2012–. *Publications:* (ed) Stroud's Judicial Dictionary, 6th edn 2000 to 9th edn 2016; (ed) Craies on Legislation, 9th edn 2008 to 11th edn 2016; How to Become Jewish (and Why Not To), 2009; (ed) Jowitt's Dictionary of English Law, 3rd edn 2010 to 4th edn 2015; Laying Down the Law, 2011. *Recreations:* teaching Jewish law and philosophy, reading. *Address:* 74 North End Road, NW11 7SY. *T:* 07950 491512. *E:* dgreenberg@hotmail.co.uk.

**GREENBERG, Joanna Elishever Gabrielle;** QC 1994; **Her Honour Judge Greenberg;** a Circuit Judge, since 2014; *b* 28 Nov. 1950; *d* of Ivan Marion Greenberg and Doris Rosalie Greenberg (*née* Sandground). *Educ:* Brondesbury and Kilburn High Sch. for Girls; King's Coll. London (LLB, AKC). Called to the Bar, Gray's Inn, 1972, Bencher, 2002; an Asst Recorder, 1992–95; a Recorder, 1995–2014. Approved Counsel for Internat. Criminal Court, 2007; Approved Lead Counsel for Special Tribunal for Lebanon, 2009. Chm., Police Appeals Tribunals, 1997–2014. *Address:* Wood Green Crown Court, Woodall House, Lordship Lane, N22 5LF.

**GREENBURGH, Matthew Steven;** Vice Chairman and Senior Vice President, Merrill Lynch & Co., Inc., 2008–10; *b* London, 6 March 1961; *s* of Raymond Greenburgh and Virginia Greenburgh (*née* Rothman); *m* 1990, Helen Elisabeth Payne; one *s* one *d*. *Educ:* Westminster Sch.; Worcester Coll., Oxford (BA Hons Philos. and Econs). Barclays Merchant Bank/BZW, 1983–87; Enskilda Securities, 1987–91; Baring Brothers, 1991–98, Dir, 1995–98; Merrill Lynch, 1998–2010: Co-Head, Global Financial Instns Gp, 2001–06; Vice Chm., Global Investment Banking, 2006–08. *Recreations:* arboriculture, puericulture, culture.

**GREENE, Jamie Gillan;** Member (C) Scotland West, Scottish Parliament, since 2016; *b* Greenock, 19 March 1980; *s* of James Gillan Greene and Cathleen Ann Hanley. *Educ:* James Watt Coll. Director: Business Develt, Viacom Internat., 2011–15; Seachange Internat., 2015–16. *Recreations:* sailing, ski-ing, silversmithing, wine, travel. *Address:* Scottish Parliament, Edinburgh EH99 1SP. *T:* (0131) 348 6137. *E:* jamie.greene.msp@parliament.scot.

**GREENE, Jenny, (Mrs Michael Boys-Greene);** Editor, Country Life, 1986–93, retired; *b* 9 Feb. 1937; *d* of Captain James Wilson Greene and Mary Emily Greene; *m* 1971, John Gilbert (marr. diss. 1987); *m* 1994, Michael Boys-Greene. *Educ:* Rochelle Sch., Cork; Trinity Coll., Dublin; Univ. of Montpellier, France. Researcher, Campbell-Johnson Ltd, 1963–64; Account-Exec., Central News, 1964–65; Account-Exec., Pemberton Advertising, 1965–66; Publicity Exec., Revlon, 1966–71; Beauty Editor, Woman's Own, 1971–75; Features Writer and Theatre Critic, Manchester Evening News, 1975–77; Asst Editor, Woman's Own, 1977–78; Editor: Homes and Gardens, 1978–86; A La Carte, 1984–85; columnist, Today, 1985–87. Contrib., Country Life and Gardens Illustrated, 1998–. *Recreations:* gardening, trying to entertain the French. *Address:* 21 rue de Grissais, 85200 Fontenay-le-Comte, France.

**GREENE, Maurice Alan; His Honour Judge Maurice Greene;** a Circuit Judge, since 2012; *b* Salford, 19 April 1960; *s* of late Jack Greene and Freda Greene; *m* 1986, Amanda Ashe; two *d*. *Educ:* Prestwich Jewish Day Sch.; Stand Grammar Sch., Whitefield; Liverpool Poly. (BA Hons Law); Leicester Univ. (Postgrad. Dip Criminal Justice Studies). Called to the Bar, Inner Temple, 1982; in practice as barrister, specialising in crime and regulatory work, Sheffield, 1982–91, Manchester, 1991–2012; a Dep. Dist Judge (Magistrates' Courts), 1999–2012; a Recorder, 2002–12; Liaison Judge, Tameside Magistrates' Court, 2013–16, Greater Manchester Magistrates, 2016–; Tribunal Judge, Health Educn and Social Care, Mental Health Tribunal, Restricted Patients Panel, 2018–. *Recreations:* English and European political history, sport, dog walking. *Address:* Manchester Crown Court, Minshull Street, Manchester M1 3FS. *T:* (0161) 954 7500. *E:* enquiries@manchesterminshullstreet.crowncourt.gsi.gov.uk.

**GREENE, His Honour Peter Livesey;** a Circuit Judge, 2011–17; a Deputy High Court Judge, 2012–17; *b* 21 June 1947; *s* of late George Greene, MBE and Nell Greene; *m* 1986, Linda Rowell; three *d*. *Educ:* Bemrose Grammar Sch., Derby; Manchester Coll. of Commerce (LLB); Guildford Coll. of Law. Admitted solicitor, 1972; Sen. Partner, Greene D'sa, 1977–94; Greene Deavin, 1994–2001, Solicitors, Leicester; Dep. Dist Judge, 1999–2004, Dist Judge, 2004–11, Principal Registry of Family Div.; Designated Family Judge for Cambridge and Peterborough, 2012–16. *Recreations:* hill walking, music, theatre.

**GREENER, Sir Anthony (Armitage),** Kt 1999; Chairman, Minton Trust, since 2006; *b* 26 May 1940; *s* of William and Diana Marianne Greener; *m* 1st, 1974, Min Ogilvie (marr. diss. 2016); one *s* one *d*; 2nd, 2016, Audrey Paterson. *Educ:* Marlborough Coll. FCMA. Marketing Manager, Thames Board Mills, 1969; Retail Controller 1972, Dir 1974, Alfred Dunhill Ltd; Man. Dir, Alfred Dunhill Ltd, subseq. Dunhill Holdings plc, 1975; Man. Dir, United Distillers, 1987–92, Chm., 1996–97; Guinness PLC: Dir, 1986–97; Jt Man. Dir, 1989–91; Chief Exec., 1992–97; Chm., 1993–97; Jt Chm., 1997–98, Chm., 1998–2000, Diageo plc; Dep. Chm., British Telecommunications plc, 2001–06; Chm., University for Industry Ltd, 2000–04. Director: Louis Vuitton Moët Hennessy, 1989–97; Reed International, 1990–98; Reed Elsevier, 1993–98; Nautor's Swan, 2009–12. Chm., QCA, 2002–08; Board Member: United Learning Trust, 2005–17; Williams Sonoma, 2007–; WNS Global Services, 2007–16. Chm., St Giles Trust, 2008–17. *Recreations:* ski-ing, sailing. *E:* greenera@mintontrust.com. *Clubs:* Royal Ocean Racing; Royal Yacht Squadron (Cowes).

**GREENER, George Pallister,** CBE 2005; PhD; FCIWEM; Chairman, Kellen Investments Ltd, 2006–14; *b* 14 July 1945; *m* 1969, Rosemary Orchard; one *s*. *Educ:* Newcastle upon Tyne Univ. (BSc Hons 1966); PhD Southampton 1969. Joined Mars Gp, 1971; Man. Dir, Mars UK, 1986–91; Dir, BAT Industries, 1991–96; Chief Exec., BAT UK Financial Services, 1993–96; Chm. and Chief Exec., Allied Dunbar Assurance, 1991–96; Chairman: Eagle Star Hldgs, 1993–96; Threadneedle Asset Mgt, 1994–96; Chief Exec., Hillsdown Hldgs, 1996–98; Chairman: Swallow Gp, 1999–2000; British Waterways, 1999–2005; Big Food (formerly Iceland) Group plc, 2001–05; SHA for London, 2006–08. Non-executive Director: Reckitt & Coleman, subseq. Reckitt Benckiser, 1996–2006; J. P. Morgan

American Investment (formerly Fleming American Investment) Trust, 1999–2008. Chm., HEROS (homing of ex-racehorses charity), 2008–12 (Patron, 2012–). Mem. Ct, Univ. of Newcastle upon Tyne, 2005–07. FRSA. *Recreations:* piano playing, horses.

**GREENER, Very Rev. Jonathan Desmond Francis;** Dean of Exeter, since 2017; *b* 9 March 1961; *s* of Desmond Walter Kingsley Greener and Maureen Frances (*née* Murden); *m* 2006, Pamela Green. *Educ:* Reigate Grammar Sch.; Trinity Coll., Cambridge (BA 1983, MA 1987); Coll. of the Resurrection, Mirfield. Sales and Export Manager, A & M Hearing Ltd, 1984–89. Ordained deacon, 1991, priest, 1992; Asst Curate, Holy Trinity with St Matthew, Southwark, 1991–94; Bp of Truro's Domestic Chaplain, 1994–96; Vicar, Ch of the Good Shepherd, Brighton, 1996–2003; Archdeacon of Pontefract, 2003–07; Dean of Wakefield, 2007–17. Co-ordinator, Archbp of Canterbury's Romania Liaison Gp, 1993–2006; Chm., Nat. Archdeacons' Forum, 2007. A Church Comr, 2011–18. Chair of Sponsors, Trinity Acad. Halifax, 2007–17. *Publications:* (contrib.) The Fire and the Clay, 1993. *Recreations:* France, icons, ski-ing, photography. *Address:* c/o Cathedral Offices, 1 The Cloisters, Exeter EX1 1HS. *T:* (01392) 255573. *E:* jonathan.greener@exeter-cathedral.org.uk.

**GREENFIELD,** Baroness *cr* 2001 (Life Peer), of Ot Moor in the County of Oxfordshire; **Susan Adele Greenfield,** CBE 2000; DPhil; Professor of Pharmacology, Oxford University, 1996–2013; Senior Research Fellow, Lincoln College, Oxford, 1999–2018 (Fellow, 1985–99); Hon. Research Fellow, St Hilda's College, Oxford, since 1999; Founder and Chief Executive Officer, Neuro-Bio Ltd, since 2014 (Chief Scientific Officer, 2013–14); *b* 1 Oct. 1950; *d* of Reginald Myer Greenfield and Doris Margaret Winifred Greenfield; *m* 1991, Peter William Atkins, *qv* (marr. diss. 2003). *Educ:* Godolphin and Latymer Sch. for Girls; St Hilda's Coll., Oxford (BA Hons Exp. Psychol. 1973; MA 1978; DPhil 1977; Hon. Fellow, 1999). Dame Catherine Fulford Sen. Scholarship, St Hugh's Coll., Oxford, 1974; MRC Training Fellow, Univ. Lab. of Physiol., Oxford, 1977–81; Collège de France, Paris; Royal Soc. Study Visit Award, 1978; MRC-INSERM French Exchange Fellow, 1979–80; Oxford University: Jun. Res. Fellow, Green Coll., 1981–84; Lectr in Synaptic Pharmacol., 1985–96. Hon. Dir, Royal Institution, 1998–2010. Co-founder: Synaptica Ltd, 1997; BrainBoost Ltd, 2002. Gresham Prof. of Physic, Gresham Coll., 1995–99; Vis. Fellow, Inst. of Neuroscience, La Jolla, USA, 1995; Vis. Dist. Scholar, Queen's Univ., Belfast, 1996. Adelaide Thinker in Residence, 2004–06; Chancellor, Heriot-Watt Univ., 2006–12. Mem., Nat. Adv. Cttee on Cultural and Creative Educn, 1998–; Pres., ASE, 2000; Vice-Pres., Assoc. of Women in Sci. and Engrg, 2001. Trustee, Science Mus., 1998–2003. Non-executive Director: Britech Foundn Ltd, 2002–06; Oxford Inspires Ltd, 2002–05; Israel Britain Business Council, 2002; Young Foresight Ltd, 2003; Bank Leumi (UK), 2003–06; Cherwell Capital plc, 2004–06; Enkephala Ltd, 2005–. Presenter, Brain Story, BBC 2, 2000. Dimbleby Lectr, 1999. FRSE 2007; Fellow: Australian Davos Connection, 2007; Sci. Mus., 2010. Hon. Fellow, Cardiff Univ., 2000. Hon. FRCP 2000; Hon. Fellow, Inst. of Risk Mgt, 2012. 32 hon. degrees. Michael Faraday Award, Royal Soc., 1998; Woman of Distinction, Jewish Care, 1998; Hon. Australian of Year, 2006; Sci. and Technol. Award, British Inspiration Awards, 2010; Australian Soc. for Med. Res. Medal, 2010. Chevalier, Légion d'Honneur (France), 2003. *Publications:* (ed with C. B. Blakemore) Mindwaves, 1987; (with G. Ferry) Journey to the Centers of the Brain, 1994; Journey to the Centers of the Mind, 1995; (ed) The Human Mind Explained, 1996; The Human Brain: a guided tour, 1997; (ed) Brain Power, 2000; Private Life of the Brain, 2000; Brain Story, 2000; Tomorrow's People, 2003; ID: the quest for identity in the 21st Century, 2008; You And Me: the neuroscience of identity, 2011; 2121: a tale from the next century, 2013; Mind Change: how digital technologies are leaving their mark on our brains, 2014; A Day in the Life of the Brain, 2016; approx. 200 papers in learned jls. *Recreations:* squash, dance. *Address:* Lincoln College, Turl Street, Oxford OX1 3DR. *T:* (01235) 420084. *W:* www.susangreenfield.com. *Club:* h.

**GREENFIELD, Andrew,** PhD; Programme Leader, Medical Research Council Harwell Institute, since 1996; *b* Essex, 15 April 1963; *s* of John Greenfield and Joyce Greenfield (*née* Fitt); *m* 1994, Eila Watson; two *s*. *Educ:* Bedfords Park Comp. Sch.; St John's Coll., Cambridge (BA); St Mary's Hosp. Med. Sch., London (PhD); Birkbeck Coll., Univ. of London (MA). FRSB 2015. Postdoctoral Researcher, Inst. for Molecular Bioscis, Univ. of Queensland, 1992–96. Member: HFEA, 2009–18; Nuffield Council on Bioethics, 2014–. *Publications:* over 85 articles in scientific jls. *Recreations:* youth football, STEM ambassador (outreach), music, philosophy. *Address:* Mammalian Genetics Unit, Medical Research Council Harwell Institute, Oxon OX11 0RD. *T:* (01235) 841126. *E:* a.greenfield@har.mrc.ac.uk.

**GREENFIELD, Howard;** *see* Greenfield, R. H.

**GREENFIELD, Jill, (Mrs Jonathan Gavaghan);** Partner, and Head, Serious Injury Sector, Fieldfisher LLP, since 2005; *b* Fegg Hayes, Stoke-on-Trent, 7 Sept. 1968; *d* of Frederick Greenfield and Ellen Groves; *m* 2005, Jonathan Gavaghan; one *s*. *Educ:* St Peter's C of E High Sch., Penkhull, Stoke-on-Trent; Liverpool Univ. (LLB Hons). Admitted as solicitor, 1993. Brabner Holden, 1991–94; Elliots and Co., 1994–96; Betesh Fox, 1996–97; Reynolds Porter Chamberlain, 1997–2005. Treas., Assoc. of Personal Injury Lawyers, 2018–. *Recreations:* drawing, travel, friends and family. *Address:* Fieldfisher LLP, Riverbank House, 2 Swan Lane, EC4R 3TT. *T:* (020) 7861 4557. *E:* jill.greenfield@fieldfisher.com. *Club:* Royal Automobile.

**GREENFIELD, Peter Charles;** a District Judge (Magistrates' Courts), since 2012; *b* Hitchin, Herts, 1 Nov. 1961; *s* of late Lawrence Greenfield and Elisabeth Greenfield (*née* Dyke); *m* 1991, Alyson Lyndsey Florence; three *d*. *Educ:* Kingston Univ. (BA Hons Law 1984); Inns of Court Sch. of Law. Called to the Bar, Middle Temple, 1989; Crown Prosecutor, Hants and Dorset, 1990–93; producer/presenter, BBC North/British Forces Broadcasting Service, 1993–97; in practice as barrister, Kings Bench Chambers, Bournemouth, 1997–2012; a Dep. Dist Judge (Magistrates' Courts), 2010–12. Mem., Lord Chancellor's Adv. Cttee, Hants, 2006–12. Mem., Ind. Monitoring Bd, HMP Winchester, 2006–11. Mem. (C), New Forest DC, 1999–2012 (Cabinet Mem. for Housing, 2000–07). *Recreations:* fly fishing, sport, astronomy, family, cricket, golf. *Address:* West Hampshire Magistrates' Court, Southampton Court House, 100 The Avenue, Southampton SO17 1EY. *E:* djmc.peter.greenfield@ejudiciary.net. *Clubs:* Naval, Savage.

**GREENFIELD, (Robert) Howard,** FCA; Project Director, British Gas plc, 1990, retired; *b* 4 Feb. 1927; *s* of James Oswald Greenfield and Doris Burt Greenfield; *m* 1951, Joyce Hedley Wells; one *s* one *d*. *Educ:* Rutherford Coll., Newcastle upon Tyne. FCA 1953. Northern Gas Board, 1956–74; Northern Gas: Dir of Customer Service, 1974; Dir of Marketing, 1976; Dep. Chm., 1977; Chm., N Eastern Reg., 1982–85; Regl Chm., British Gas, N Western, 1985–89. OStJ 1988.

**GREENGROSS,** family name of **Baroness Greengross.**

**GREENGROSS,** Baroness *cr* 2000 (Life Peer), of Notting Hill in the Royal Borough of Kensington and Chelsea; **Sally Greengross,** OBE 1993; Chief Executive, International Longevity Centre UK, since 2004 (Chairman, 2000–04); Vice-President, Age Concern England, 2002–09 (Director, then Director General, 1987–2000); *b* 29 June 1935; *m* 1959, Sir Alan David Greengross (*d* 2018); one *s* three *d*. *Educ:* Brighton and Hove High Sch.; LSE. Formerly linguist, executive in industry, lectr and researcher; Asst Dir, 1977–82, Dep. Dir, 1982–87, Age Concern England. Secretary General: Internat. Fedn on Ageing, 1982–87 (Vice-Pres. (Europe), 1987–2001); Eurolink Age, 1989–2001. Jt Chm. Bd, Age Concern Inst. of Gerontology, KCL, 1987–2000. Mem. Bd, Britain in Europe, 1999–2006; House of Lords: Member: Sub-Cttee F, Select Cttee on EU, 2000–03, Sub-Cttee G, 2004–07; Intergenerational Fairness and Provision Cttee, 2018–; Chair, All Party Gp on Corporate Social Responsibility, on Intergenerational Futures, on Continence Care; Chair, All Party Parly Gp on Dementia; Vice Chair, All Party Gp on Ageing and Older People, 2001–10; Treas., All Party Gp on Equalities. Chm., Experience Corps, 2001–05. Vice-Pres., LGA, 2001–. Independent Member: UN Network on Ageing, 1983–2000; WHO Network on Ageing, 1983–2000; Mem., OFCOM Adv. Gp on Older and Disabled People, 2004–06. Member: HelpAge Internat., 2000–07; Adv. Council, Internat. Assoc. of Homes and Services for the Ageing, 2002–. Mem., Equality and Human Rights Commn, 2006–12. Former Member: Inner London Juvenile Court Panel; Management Bd, Hanover Housing Gp. Gov., Pensions Policy Inst., 2002– (Pres., 2004–); Adviser: Internat. Centre for Health and Soc., UCL, 2000–; Good Corp., 2000–07; Merck Inst. of Ageing and Health, 2001–05; Chm. Adv. Cttee, English Longitudinal Study on Ageing, UCL, 2000–; Co-Chair, Alliance for Health and the Future, 2003–08. Patron: Action on Elder Abuse, 1999–; Groundwork Foundn, 1999–; Pennell Initiative, 1999–; Sheffield Inst. for Studies on Ageing, 1999–; Care and Repair England, 1999–; Ransackers, 2006–; Global Ambassador, Help Age Internat., 2007–; Trustee, Help Age Internat. Sri Lanka, 2008–. Hon. Pres., Women for Europe, 1999–. FRSPH (FRSH 1994); FRSA 1994. Hon. FIA 2001. Hon. FRSocMed. Hon. DLitt: Ulster, 1994; Brunel, 2002; Keele, 2004; DUniv: Kingston, 1996; Open, 2002; Leeds Metropolitan, 2002; Hon. LLD Exeter, 2000; Newcastle. UK Woman of Europe Award, EC, 1990. *Publications:* (ed) Ageing: an adventure in living, 1985; (ed) The Law and Vulnerable Elderly People, 1986; (jtly) Living, Loving and Ageing, 1989; and others on ageing issues and social policy. *Recreations:* countryside, music. *Address:* House of Lords, SW1A 0PW. *T:* (020) 7219 5494. *Clubs:* Reform, Hurlingham, Royal Society of Medicine.

**GREENHALGH, Prof. Christine Anne,** PhD; Professor of Applied Economics, University of Oxford, 2008–09, now Emeritus; Fellow and Tutor in Economics, St Peter's College, Oxford, 1979–2009, now Emeritus Fellow; *b* Crayford, Kent, 16 May 1946; *d* of late John Graham and Vera Graham (*née* Hammond); *m* 1967, Dr Peter Greenhalgh; one *s* one *d*. *Educ:* London Sch. of Econs (BSc 1st Cl. Econs 1967; MSc 1968); Princeton Univ. (PhD 1978). Lecturer: Univ. of Cape Coast, Ghana, 1968–70; Univ. of Ghana, Legon, 1971–72; Univ. of Southampton, 1975–79; University of Oxford: Lectr, 1979–96; Reader in Econs, 1996–2008. Vis. Associate Prof., London Business Sch., 2000–01; Res. Associate, Intellectual Property Res. Inst. of Australia, Univ. of Melbourne, 2004–12; Vis. Schol., Stanford Inst. Econ. Policy Res., 2007; Departmental Guest, Industrial Relns Section, Princeton Univ., 2011; Adjunct Prof., Centre for Transformative Innovation, Faculty of Business and Law, Swinburne Univ. of Technol., Australia, 2015–18. Hon. Professorial Fellow, Melbourne Inst. for Applied Econ. and Social Res., 2012–16. *Publications:* (ed jtly) The Causes of Unemployment, 1984; (with M. Rogers) Innovation, Intellectual Property and Economic Growth, 2010; contrib. articles to learned jls on labour econs, innovation and intellectual property; reports to UK Intellectual Property Office on small firms and intellectual property. *Recreations:* travel, concerts. *Address:* 4 The Green, Cuddesdon, Oxford OX44 9JZ. *T:* (01865) 873643. *E:* christine.greenhalgh@spc.ox.ac.uk.

**GREENHALGH, Colin Ayton,** CBE 2003 (OBE 1997); DL; MA; Principal, Hills Road Sixth Form College, Cambridge, 1984–2002; Vice Chairman, 2002–10, and Senior Independent Director, 2006–10, Cambridge University Hospitals NHS Foundation Trust (formerly Addenbrooke's NHS Trust) (non-executive Director, 2001–02); *b* 11 Aug. 1941; *s* of Robert Ayton Greenhalgh and Ethel Mary Henderson (*née* Cattermole); *m* 1966, Vivienne Christine Grocock, MSc, PhD; one *s* two *d*. *Educ:* Gateway Sch., Leicester; St John's Coll., Cambridge (MA); Univ. of Nottingham (PGCE). Teacher of Hist., Bradford Grammar Sch., 1964–70; Hd of Hist., Hd of Upper Sch. and Dep. Hd, Bulmershe Sch., Reading, 1970–76; Dep. Hd and Second Master, St Bartholomew's Sch., Newbury, 1976–84. Non-exec. Dir, Cambs HA, 2000–01. Mem., Cambs LEA Inspectorate, 1991–92; Further Education Funding Council: Mem., Eastern Regl Cttee, 1993–98, Quality Assessment Cttee, 1997–2001; Registered Inspector, 1998–2001; Board Member: Learning and Skills Develt Agency (formerly Further Educn Develt Agency), 1999–2003; Further Educn Cttee, SHA, 1998–2002; Mem., Appeals Panel, 2000–, Malpractice Panel for Internat. Exams, 2004–, Univ. of Cambridge and RSA Exams Bd. Registered OFSTED Inspector, 2001–10; educnl consultant, 2002–. Cambridgeshire Association of Secondary Heads: Sec., 1988–89; Chm., 1989–90. Mem., Univ. of Cambridge Sports Centre Appeal Cttee, 2003–05. Trustee, Cambridge Centre for Sixth Form Studies, 2002–08; Chm. of Trustees, Addenbrooke's Recreational and Develt Trust, 2004–09. Governor: Stapleford Primary Sch., 1992–2007; Grammar Sch. at Leeds, 2005–14; Comberton Village Coll., 2013–; Long Rd Sixth Form Coll., 2013–; Trustee and Dir, CAM Acad. Trust (formerly Comberton Acad. Trust), 2014–. Patron, Romsey Mill, Cambridge, 2004–. Hon. Sen. Mem., Wolfson Coll., Cambridge, 1990–. Hon. Fellow, Anglia Poly. Univ., 2002. St John's College, Cambridge: Ambassador, Johnian Soc., 2017– (Sec., 1992–99 and 2013; Chm., 1999–2012; Vice Pres., 2014; Pres., 2015); Obituaries Ed., The Eagle, 2015–; Fellow Commoner, 2018–; Mem., Rotary Club, Cambridge, 1988–. Lay Chair, Parochial Ch Council, St Clement's, Cambridge, 2017–18. Mem., Stapleford Parish Council, 1996–2002, 2019–. DL Cambs, 1998. *Recreations:* family (children Rebecca, Jonathan and Elizabeth and eight grandchildren), churches and country houses, cinema, collecting books, sport, travel, Venice. *Address:* 9 Finch's Close, Stapleford, Cambridge CB22 5BL. *Clubs:* MCC; Hawks; Rotary (Cambridge); Cambridge University Cricket; Leicestershire County Cricket; Jack Frost Cricket.

**GREENHALGH, Prof. Douglas Anthony,** PhD; CEng, CPhys, FInstP, FIES; Executive Dean and Pro-Vice Chancellor, School of Engineering and Built Environment, Glasgow Caledonian University, 2011–14; collaborative research on combustion, fuels and laser diagnostics, Technical University of Berlin and Imperial College London; *b* Manchester, 26 Sept. 1951; *s* of William Douglas and Josephine Greenhalgh; *m* (marr. diss. 1996); two *s*. *Educ:* William Harvey Grammar Sch., Folkestone; Univ. of Newcastle upon Tyne (BSc; PhD 1977). CPhys 1983; CEng 2001; FInstP 2001. Res. Fellow, Southampton Univ., 1976–78; Govt Scientist, UKAEA Harwell, 1979–89; Prof. and Hd of Dept, Cranfield Univ., 1989–2007; Hd, Sch. of Engrg and Physical Scis, Heriot-Watt Univ., 2007–11. Consultant, Rolls-Royce 1971 plc, 1998–2001. Director: CIM Ltd, 2003–07; iSLI Ltd, 2008–11. Ind. Mem., UK Defence Sci. Adv. Council, 2008–. UK Rep. and Vice-Chair, Exec. Cttee, Task Leaders Gp on Energy Conservation and Emissions Reduction in Combustion, Internat. Energy Agency, 2004–. Dir, Beds Golf Club, 2006–07. FHEA; FIES 2013. *Publications:* contrib. book chapters on laser diagnostics and papers to jls; two patents. *Recreations:* golf, walking, gastronomy and wine. *Clubs:* New Golf (St Andrews), Luffness New Golf, Dunbar Golf.

**GREENHALGH, Prof. Patricia Mary, (Trisha), (Mrs Fraser Macfarlane),** OBE 2001; MD; FRCP, FRCGP; FMedSci; Professor of Primary Health Care Sciences, University of Oxford, since 2015; *b* Newcastle-under-Lyme, 11 March 1959; *d* of Daniel

Joseph Greenhalgh and Audrey Mary Greenhalgh; m 1987, Fraser Macfarlane; two s. Educ: Folkestone Grammar Sch.; Clare Coll., Cambridge (BA 1980; MD Diabetes and Endocrinol. 1995); University Coll., Oxford (BM BCh 1983); University Coll. London (MBA 2015). MRCP 1986, FRCP 1998; MRCGP 1990, FRCGP 2000; FRSB (FSB 2011); FFPH 2012; FMedSci 2014. University College London: Lectr, 1992–96; Sen. Lectr, 1996–2001; Prof., 2001–10; Queen Mary University of London: Prof. of Primary Health Care, 2010–14; Dean for Res. Impact, 2013–14. Mem., Health Cttee on Ethical Aspects of Pandemic Flu, DoH, 2008–14. Dep. Chair, Main Panel for Medicine, UK REF, 2010–14. Mem. Council, RCGP, 2011–17. *Publications:* How to Read a Paper: the basics of evidence-based medicine, 1997, 6th edn 2019; Primary Health Care: theory and practice, 2007; What Seems to be the Trouble?: stories in illness and health care, 2007; The Complete Guide to Breast Cancer, 2018.

**GREENHALGH, Paul;** Director, Sainsbury Centre for Visual Arts, University of East Anglia, since 2010; b 21 Oct. 1955; s of William Greenhalgh and Marie Joan Greenhalgh; m 1981 (marr. diss.); two s. Educ: Bolton Smithills Grammar Sch.; Univ. of Reading (BA); Courtauld Inst., Univ. of London (MA). Lectr, Cardiff Inst., 1980–87; Dep. Curator of Ceramics and Glass, V&A Mus., 1988–92; Tutor in Art History, RCA, 1990–92; Hd of Art History, Camberwell Coll. of Arts, 1992–94; Hd of Res., V&A Mus., 1994–2000; Curator, Art Nouveau 1890–1914 exhibn, V&A and Nat. Gall. of Art, Washington, 2000, Metropolitan Mus., Tokyo, 2001; Pres., NSCAD Univ. (formerly Nova Scotia Coll. of Art and Design), 2001–06; Dir and Pres., Corcoran Gall. of Art and Coll. of Art and Design, Washington, 2006–10. Vis. Prof., Brighton Univ., 2009–; Prof. of Art History, UEA, 2011–. Academic Editor, Manchester Univ. Press, 1989–. Chair, Cttee for Art, Design and Art History, REF 2014, 2012–15; Chair, Art Adv. Cttee, Edinburgh Univ., 2012–; Arts Consultant, BBC, 2012–. Member: Crafts Council Educn Cttee, 1992–; Adv. Council, Winston Churchill Meml Trust, 2016–. Hon. Fellow, Res. Dept, V&A Mus., 2001. FRSA 2017. Hon. PhD Brighton, 2007; Hon. DLitt Brighton. *Publications:* Ephemeral Vistas: great exhibitions, expositions universelles and world's fairs 1850–1939, 1988; (ed) Modernism in Design, 1990; Quotations and Sources on Design and the Decorative Arts 1800–1990, 1993; (ed) Art Nouveau 1890–1914, 2000; The Essential Art Nouveau, 2000; The Persistence of Craft, 2002; The Modern Ideal: the rise and collapse of idealism in the visual arts from the enlightenment to postmodernism, 2005; Fair World: a history of expositions from London to Shanghai 1851–2010, 2011; L'Art Nouveau: les artistes de la vie moderne, 2013. *Recreations:* running, football. *Address:* Sainsbury Centre for Visual Arts, University of East Anglia, Norwich NR4 7TJ. T: (01603) 592467. E: p.greenhalgh@uea.ac.uk.

**GREENHALGH, Prof. Roger Malcolm,** FRCS; Emeritus Professor of Surgery and Head of Imperial College of Science, Technology and Medicine Vascular Research Group at Charing Cross Hospital, since 2006; Hon. Consultant Surgeon, Charing Cross Hospital, since 1976; b 6 Feb. 1941; s of John Greenhalgh and Phyllis Poynton; m 1964, Karin Maria Gross; one s one d. Educ: Clare Coll., Cambridge; St Thomas' Hosp., London. BA 1963, BChir 1966, MB, MA 1967, MChir 1974, MD 1983 (Cantab); FRCS 1971. Ho. Surg., 1967, Casualty Officer, 1968, St Thomas' Hosp.; Sen. Ho. Officer, Hammersmith Hosp., 1969; Registrar in Surgery, Essex County Hosp., Colchester, 1970–72; Lectr and Sen. Registrar in Surgery, St Bartholomew's Hosp., 1972–76; Sen. Lectr in Surgery, Charing Cross Hosp., 1976–81; Head of Dept of Surgery, 1981–84, Prof. of Surgery, 1982–2006, Chm. of Dept of Surgery, 1989–97, Dean, 1993–97, Charing Cross Hosp. Med. Sch., later Charing Cross and Westminster Med. Sch.; Clinical Dir, 1994–98, Chief of Vascular Surgical Service, 1998–2002, Hammersmith Hosps NHS Trust; Head of Dept of Vascular Surgery, Div. of Surgery, Anaesthetics and Intensive Care, Imperial Coll. London, 1997–2006. Chm., Eur. Examining Bd, Surgery Qualification, 1995–2002; President: Surgery sect., EU of Medical Specialities, 1998–2002; Eur. Bd of Surgery, 2002–06; Eur. Fedn of Surgical Specialties, UEMS, 2004–08. Sometime examiner, Univs of Cambridge, London, Edinburgh, Bristol, Leicester, UCD, Southampton, Birmingham, Hong Kong. Chairman: Charing Cross Internat. Symposium, 1978–; Liaison Cttee, Bioengrg Centre, Roehampton, London, 1985–88; Riverside Med. Council, 1992–93; Member: Scientific Cttee on Tobacco and Health (formerly Ind. Scientific Enquiry into Smoking and Health), 1979–; Coll. of Experts, MRC, 2002–; CMO's Scientific Cttee on Tobacco and Health, 2004–; Abdominal Aortic Aneurysm Nat. Screening Prog. Adv. Gp (formerly Wkg Party), 2004–; DoH, then DHSC Mem., NICE approval cttee for endovascular aneurysm repair, 2008–11. Vice-President: Section of Surgery, RSM, 1986–89; BRCS, 1992–; Sec. Gen. and Chm. Exec. Cttee, Assoc. of Internat. Vascular Surgeons, 1982–2005; Chm. Dirs and Trustees, European Soc. for Vascular Surgery, 1987–2006 (Mem. Council, 1987–93); Mem. Council, Assoc. of Surgeons of GB and Ireland, 1993–2008; Pres., Vascular Soc. of GB and Ire., 1999–2000. Hon. Life Pres., Eur. Bd of Vascular Surgery, 2004. Hon. FRCSE (ad eundem) 1999; Hon. FRCSI 2007; Hon. FRACS 2018; Hon. Fellow, British Soc. of Interventional Radiol., 2006; Hon. Member: S African Vascular Surgical Soc., 1989; Canadian Vascular Soc., 1991; Polish Surgical Soc., 1991; German Vascular Soc., 1992; Hellenic Surgical Soc., 1992; Eur. Soc. for Vascular Surgery, 1993 (Dist. Person's Award, 2002); Brazilian Angiology Soc., 1993; Hellenic Vascular Surg. Soc., 1995; Mediterranean League of Vascular Surgeons, 1996; Soc. for Vascular Surgery, 2003 (Corresp. Mem., 1991); Austrian Vascular Soc., 2002; Swiss Vascular Soc., 2003; Eur. Venous Forum, 2007; Internat. Union of Angiol., 2008; Soc. of Clinical Vascular Surgeons, 2011. Moynihan Fellow of Assoc. of Surgeons, 1975; Hunterian Prof., RCS, 1980; Protem Prof., Brigham Hosp., Harvard Med. Sch., 1984; Boone Powell Prof., Baylor Dallas Med. Sch., 1984; Hunter Sweeney Prof., Duke Univ., 1991; Mannick Vis. Prof., Harvard Univ., 1996. Sir Peter Freyer Lect., Univ. of Galway, 1995; Scott Heron Lect., QUB, 1999; Michael van Vloten Lect., Eindhoven, 2003. Hon. Dr: Warsaw Med. Acad., 2003; Athens Univ., 2004. Hon. Citizen, Kranidi, Greece, 2006; Lifetime Achievement Award, Vascular and Endovascular Surgery, Arizona Heart Inst. and Miami Heart Inst., 2011; Lifetime Achievement Award, Soc. for Vascular Surgery, 2018. Chm. Editl Bd, European Jl of Vascular Surgery, 1987–2003; Mem. Editl Bd, Annals of Surgery, 1991–; Ed., Vascular News, 1998–. *Publications:* Progress in Stroke Research, 1, 1979; Smoking and Arterial Disease, 1981; Hormones and Vascular Disease, 1981; Femoro-distal bypass, 1981; Extra-Anatomic and Secondary Arterial Reconstruction, 1982; Progress in Stroke Research, 2, 1983; Vascular Surgical Techniques, 1984, 2nd edn 1989, 3rd edn as Vascular and Endovascular Surgical Techniques, 1994, 4th edn 2001; Diagnostic Techniques and Assessment Procedures in Vascular Surgery, 1985; Vascular Surgery: issues in current practice, 1986; Indications in Vascular Surgery, 1988; Limb Salvage and Amputations for Vascular Disease, 1988; The Cause and Management of Aneurysms, 1990; The Maintenance of Arterial Reconstruction, 1991; Vascular Surgical Emergencies, 1992; Surgery for Stroke, 1993; Vascular Imaging for Surgeons, 1995; Trials and Tribulations of Vascular Surgery, 1996; Clinical Surgery, 1996; Inflammatory and thrombotic problems in vascular surgery, 1997; Indications in Vascular and Endovascular Surgery, 1998; The Durability of Vascular and Endovascular Surgery, 1999; Vascular and Endovascular Opportunities, 2000; The evidence for vascular and endovascular reconstruction, 2002; Vascular and Endovascular Controversies, 2003; Vascular and Endovascular Challenges, 2004; Towards Vascular and Endovascular Consensus, 2005; More Vascular and Endovascular Controversies, 2006; More Vascular and Endovascular Challenges, 2007; More Vascular and Endovascular Consensus, 2008; Vascular and Endovascular Controversies Update, 2009, 2012, 2015, 2018; Vascular and Endovascular Challenges Update, 2010, 2013, 2016, 2019; Vascular and Endovascular Consensus Update, 2011, 2014, 2017; Born to be a Surgeon, 2011; Vascular and Endovascular Controversies, 2012. *Recreations:* tennis, ski-ing, swimming, music. *Address:* 271 Sheen Lane, East Sheen, SW14 8RN. T: (020) 8878 1110. *Club:* Garrick.

**GREENHALGH, Trisha;** see Greenhalgh, P. M.

**GREENHILL,** family name of **Baron Greenhill.**

**GREENHILL, 3rd Baron** cr 1950, of Townhead; **Malcolm Greenhill;** retired from Ministry of Defence; b 5 May 1924; s of 1st Baron Greenhill, OBE and Ida, d of late Mark Goodman; S brother, 1989. Educ: Kelvinside Acad., Glasgow; Glasgow Univ. (BSc). CPA. Ministries of Aircraft Production and Supply, 1944–54; UK Scientific Mission, Washington DC, USA, 1950–51; UKAEA, 1954–73; MoD, 1973–89. *Recreation:* gardening. *Club:* Civil Service.

**GREENHOUGH, Kathleen;** see Soriano, K.

**GREENING, Rt Hon. Justine;** PC 2011; MP for Putney, since 2005 (C, 2005–19; Ind, since 2019); b 30 April 1969. Educ: Oakwood Comprehensive Sch., Rotherham; Thomas Rotherham Coll.; Univ. of Southampton (BSc 1990); London Business Sch. (MBA 2000). ACA 1995. Audit Asst, Price Waterhouse, 1991–94; Audit Asst Manager, Revisuisse Price Waterhouse, 1995–96; Finance Manager, SmithKline Beecham, 1996–2001; Business Strategy Manager, GlaxoSmithKline, 2001–02; Sales and Mktg Finance Manager, Centrica, 2002–05. Econ. Sec., HM Treasury, 2010–11; Sec. of State for Transport, 2011–12, for Internat. Devel., 2012–16, for Educn, 2016–18; Minister for Women and Equalities, 2016–18. Mem. (C), Epping Town Council, 1999. Contested (C) Ealing, Acton and Shepherd's Bush, 2001. *Address:* (office) 3 Summerstown, SW17 0BQ; House of Commons, SW1A 0AA. W: www.justinegreening.co.uk.

**GREENISH, Rear Adm. Philip Duncan,** CBE 2003; CEng, FIET; Chairman, Council, University of Southampton, since 2018; Chief Executive, Royal Academy of Engineering, 2003–17; b Sept. 1951; s of late Comdr Geoffrey Harold Greenish, OBE, RN and Alice Greenish (née Thierens); m 1972, Wendy Midmer; two s one d. Educ: Cheltenham Coll.; Durham Univ. (BSc Hons Engrg Sci.). CEng 1989; FIET (FIEE 2001). Captain Weapon Trials and Acceptance, 1992–94; MA to Chief of Defence Procurement, 1994–96; rcds 1997; Director: Operational Requirements (Sea Systems), 1997–99; Equipment Capability (Above Water Battlespace), 1999–2000; COS (Corporate Develt) to C-in-C Fleet, 2000–02; COS (Support) to C-in-C Fleet, 2002–03. ADC to the Queen, 1997–2000. Member: CCLRC, 2005–07; STFC, 2007–11; EngineeringUK (formerly Engrg and Technology Bd), 2007–17. Mem. Council, Southampton Univ., 2011– (Vice Chm., 2017–18). Trustee: Daphne Jackson Trust, 2004–14; Sci. Media Centre, 2011–15. Hon. FREng 2018. DUniv Huddersfield, 2017. *Recreations:* tennis, golf, ski-ing, music, gardening. *Address:* c/o Office of the President and Vice Chancellor, University of Southampton SO17 1BJ.
See also S. Greenish.

**GREENISH, Simon,** MBE 2013; Chief Executive Officer and Director, Bletchley Park Trust, 2006–12, Consultant, since 2012; b 11 Oct. 1949; s of late Comdr Geoffrey Harrold Greenish, OBE, RN and Alice Greenish (née Thierens); m 1986, Gillian (née Wilkinson); two d. Educ: Durham Univ. (BSc Hons Eng. Sci. 1971). CEng, MICE 1975. Engr, N Beds BC, 1971–80; Prin. Engr, CAA, 1980–95; Develt Manager, 1995–2004, Dir of Collections, 2004–06, RAF Mus. Hon. DSc Bedfordshire, 2012. *Recreation:* music. *Address:* Cartref, Grange Road, Felmersham, Beds MK43 7EU. T: (01234) 782559. E: simongreenish@btinternet.com.
See also Rear Adm. P. D. Greenish.

**GREENLAW, Lavinia,** FRSL; writer; b London, 30 July 1962. Educ: Kingston Univ. (BA Hons Modern Arts); London Coll. of Printing (Postgrad. Dip.); Courtauld Inst. (MA). FRSL 2014. Pubns Ed., Imperial Coll. of Sci. and Technol., 1985–86; Desk Ed., Allison & Busby, 1986–87; Man. Ed., Earthscan Pubns, 1988–90; Literature Co-ordinator, RFH, 1990–92; Principal Literature Officer, London Arts, 1992–94; Vis. Lectr, 2001, Sen. Lectr, 2002–07, Goldsmiths Coll., Univ. of London; Prof. of Creative Writing, UEA, 2007–13. Vis. Prof., KCL, 2015–16; Samuel Fischer Guest Prof., Freie Univ., Berlin, 2017. Artistic Advr, 14–18 Now, 2013–. Writer and dir, film, The Sea is an Edge and an Ending, 2016. Artist-in-residence: Sci. Mus., 1994–95; RSocMed, 2004; Calouste Gulbenkian Foundn, 2004. British Council Fellow in Writing, Amherst Coll., Mass, 1995. NESTA Fellow, 2000–03; Wellcome Engagement Fellow, 2013–15. Trustee, RSL, 2014–. Chm., Poetry Soc., 2000–04. *Publications: poetry:* The Cost of Getting Lost in Space, 1991; Love from a Foreign City, 1992; Night Photograph, 1993; A World Where News Travelled Slowly, 1997; Minsk, 2003; The Casual Perfect, 2011; A Double Sorrow: Troilus and Criseyde, 2014; The Built Moment, 2019; *novels:* Mary George of Allnorthover, 2001 (Prix du Premier Roman Etranger, 2003); An Irresponsible Age, 2006; In the City of Love's Sleep, 2018; *non-fiction:* (with G. F. Miller) Thoughts of a Night Sea, 2003; The Importance of Music to Girls, 2007; Questions of Travel: William Morris in Iceland, 2011; The Idea of Elsewhere, 2018. *Address:* c/o The Wylie Agency, 17 Bedford Square, WC1B 3JA. T: (020) 7908 5900. E: mail@wylieagency.co.uk.

**GREENO, Edward Patrick;** Partner, Quinn Emanuel Urquhart & Sullivan LLP, since 2013; b Walton-on-Thames, 10 May 1958; s of Edward Greeno and Brenda Greeno; m 1987, Fleur van Roosmalen (marr. diss. 2015); two s one d. Educ: Cranleigh Sch.; King's Coll., London (LLB). Admitted solicitor, 1983; Herbert Smith, later Herbert Smith Freehills, 1981–2013: Partner, Litigation and Arbitration Div., 1989–2013; Recruitment Partner, 1993–97; Mem., Partnership Council, 2002–06; Solicitor Advocate, 2006. Mem., Editl Bd, Commercial Dispute Resolution, 2011–16. *Recreations:* sailing, golf, music, Rugby, ski-ing, family. *Address:* Quinn Emanuel Urquhart & Sullivan LLP, 1 Fleet Place, EC4M 7RA. T: (020) 7653 2030. E: tedgreeno@quinnemanuel.com. *Clubs:* Athenæum, Kandahar, 606 Jazz; St George's Hill Tennis, St George's Hill Golf; Harlequin Football.

**GREENOAK, Francesca;** writer; Alexander Teacher: in private practice, since 1999; Tring Park School for the Performing Arts (formerly Arts Educational School), since 2000; b 6 Sept. 1946; d of Francis Buchanan Greenoak and Alice Lavinia (née Marston); m 1981, John Kilpatrick; one s one d. Educ: St Mary's Convent Grammar Sch., Woodford Green; Univ. of Essex (BA Hons); Alexander Re-Educn Centre, Stoke Mandeville. Book Club Associates, 1968; Editor: George Harrap, 1970; Penguin Educn, Penguin Books, 1972; Chameleon Publishing Co-operative, 1974; Gardening Correspondent: She mag., 1978–80; The Times, 1986–94; Gardens Ed., Good Housekeeping, 1993–96; Express Saturday, 1997–99. Member: Garden History Soc., 1999–2009 (Mem. Council, 1999–2002; Ed., Garden History Soc. News, 1999–2002); Mem., Educn and Pubns Cttee, 2000–02); Soc. of Teachers of the Alexander Technique, 1999– (Mem. Council, 2000–05; Dir, 2005–09; Mem., Pubns Cttee, 2000–13). Chair and Founder Trustee, Hardings Wood Trust, 2002–. Editor, Alexander Jl, 2002–09. Leverhulme Res. Award, to study cultural and natural history of churchyards, 1995. *Publications:* Trees, 1976; Guide to Wildflowers, 1977; What Right Have You Got?, 1977; Alone, 1978; Heath and Moorland, 1979; All The Birds of the Air, 1979, 2nd edn as British Birds: their folklore, names and literature, 1997; Forgotten Fruit, 1983; (with R. Mabey) Back to the Roots, 1983; God's Acre, 1985, 2nd edn as Wildlife in Churchyards, 1993; (ed) Journals of Gilbert White, 3 vols, 1989; Glorious Gardens, 1989; Fruit and Vegetable Gardens, 1990; Water in Small Gardens, 1996, 2nd edn as Water Features for Small Gardens, 2002; Natural Style for Gardens, 1998, 2nd edn as The Natural Garden, 2001; Gardens of the National Trust for Scotland, 2005; Hardings Wood, 2009; The Alexander Album: a century of Alexander pupils, 2014. *Recreations:* literature, gardening, botany, music, dance, education and science. *Address:* 3–4 Wood Row, Wigginton, Tring, Herts HP23 6HS. *W:* www.fgreenoak.co.uk.

**GREENOCK, Lord; Alan George Cathcart;** Director, Spring Garden Eggs Ltd, since 2011; *b* 16 March 1986; *s* and *heir* of Earl Cathcart, *qv*; *m* 2015, Camilla Petronel, *o d* of Col Sir Alexander Malcolm, Bt, *qv*. *Educ:* Stowe. *Address:* Gateley Hall, North Elmham, Dereham, Norfolk NR20 5EF.

**GREENSHIELDS, Robert McLaren;** HM Diplomatic Service, retired; Counsellor, Foreign and Commonwealth Office, 1985–88; *b* 27 July 1933; *s* of late Brig. James Greenshields, MC, TD, and Mrs James Greenshields; *m* 1960, Jean Alison Anderson; one *s* two *d*. *Educ:* Edinburgh Academy; Lincoln Coll., Oxford (MA Hons); Open Univ. (Dip. German 2009). National Service, 2nd Lieut Highland Light Infantry, 1952–54. District Officer, Tanganyika, HMOCS, 1958–61; Asst Master and Housemaster, Gordonstoun Sch., 1962–68; HM Diplomatic Service, 1969–88. Chm., Berwickshire Br., Cons. Party, 2014–15. *Recreations:* ornithology, conservation, politics.

**GREENSLADE, Ellison Edroy,** QPM 2015; High Commissioner for the Bahamas to the Court of St James's, since 2017; *b* Nassau, 24 May 1961; *s* of Thomas Greenslade and Elva Greenslade (*née* Moncur); *m* 1984, Kimberley Morley; four *s* one *d*. *Educ:* S. C. McPherson Jun. High Sch., Nassau; Govt High Sch., Nassau; Coll. of the Bahamas (Associate's degree Business Admin); Univ. of Leicester (Postgrad. Cert. Police Mgt); Univ. of Miami (MBA Hons 1997). Royal Bahamas Police Force, 1979–2017: Asst Comr of Police, Freeport, Grand Bahama, 2000–07; Sen. Asst Comr of Police, Nassau, 2007; on secondment with Royal Canadian Mounted Police, 2008; Actg Dep. Comr of Police, 2009; Comr of Police, 2010–17. Pres., Assoc. of Caribbean Comrs of Police, 2010–13; Internat. Vice-Pres., IACP, 2017–18 (Mem., Exec. Cttee, 2015–17); Mem., Bd of Govs of Commonwealth, 2017– (Chm., Exec. Cttee, 2019–June 2020). Hon. DHumLit Sojourner-Douglas Coll., Baltimore, 2011. Meritorious Award, 2000, Medal for Long Service and Good Conduct, 2000, Medal for Gallantry, 2017, Royal Bahamas Police Force. *Recreations:* playing guitar, horseback riding. *Address:* High Commission for the Commonwealth of the Bahamas, 10 Chesterfield Street, W1J 5JL. *T:* (020) 7408 4488, *Fax:* (020) 7499 9937. *E:* information@bahamashclondon.net.

**GREENSLADE, Roy;** freelance journalist, broadcaster and author, since 1992 (blogger, 2006–17); Hon. Visiting Professor, City, University of London (formerly City University), 2003–17; *b* 31 Dec. 1946; *s* of Ernest Frederick William Greenslade and Joan Olive (*née* Stocking); *m* 1984, Noreen Anna Taylor (*née* McElhone); one step *s* one step *d*. *Educ:* Dagenham County High Sch.; Sussex Univ. (BA Hons) Politics, 1979). Trainee journalist, Barking Advertiser, 1964–66; Sub-Editor: Lancashire Evening Telegraph, 1966–67; Daily Mail, 1967–69; The Sun, 1969–71; researching and writing book, 1973–75; Daily Star, 1979–80; Daily Express, 1980–81; Daily Star, 1981; Asst Editor, The Sun, 1981–87; Man. Editor, Sunday Times, 1987–90; Editor, Daily Mirror, 1990–91; Consultant Editor, Today and Sunday Times, 1991. Columnist: Observer, 1996; Guardian, 1996–2005, 2018–; Daily Telegraph, 2005–06; Evening Standard, 2006–16; blogger, Guardian, 2006–17. Dir, Impact Books, 1993–98. Presenter: Mediumwave, Radio 4, 1995–96; Britain Talks Back, TV, 1996–97. Mem. Bd, British Journalism Review, 1994–2016. FRSA 2004. Hon. DLitt Brighton, 1999. *Publications:* Goodbye to the Working Class, 1975; Maxwell's Fall, 1992; Press Gang, 2003. *Recreations:* reading, gardening. *Address:* Brighton BN2 1GA; Ballyarr House, Ramelton, Co. Donegal, Ireland.

**GREENSMITH, (Thomas) Andrew (Lewis); His Honour Judge Greensmith;** a Circuit Judge, since 2018; *b* Chesterfield, 13 Oct. 1959; *s* of Thomas William Greensmith and Margaret Raine Greensmith; *m* 2009, Sarah Louise Halliwell; one *s* one *d*. *Educ:* Lancaster Royal Grammar Sch.; Lancaster Univ. Admitted solicitor, 1986; a District Judge, 2011–18. Chm., Resolution, 2006. *Address:* Liverpool Civil and Family Court, 35 Vernon Street, Liverpool L2 2BX. *E:* HHJ.Andrew.Greensmith@ejudiciary.net. *Club:* Royal Over-Seas League.

**GREENSPAN, Alan,** Hon. KBE 2002; President, Greenspan Associates LLC, since 2006; Chairman, Board of Governors of the Federal Reserve System, USA, 1987–2006; *b* 6 March 1926; *o s* of late Herbert Greenspan and Rose (*née* Goldsmith); *m* 1997, Andrea Mitchell. *Educ:* New York Univ. (BS 1948; MA 1950; PhD 1977). Pres., 1954–74 and 1977–87, Townsend-Greenspan & Co., NY. Director: Trans World Financial Co., 1962–74; Dreyfus Fund, 1970–74; Gen. Cable Corp., 1973–74, 1977–78; Sun Chemical Corp., 1973–74; Gen. Foods Corp., 1977–85; J. P. Morgan & Co., 1977–87; Mobil Corp., 1977–87; Capital Cities/ABC, 1978–87; ALCOA, 1978–87; ADP, 1980–87. Consultant to Council of Economic Advisers, 1970–74, to US Treasury, 1971–74, to Fed. Reserve Board, 1971–74; Chairman: Council of Economic Advisers, 1974–77; Nat. Commn on Social Security Reform, 1981–83; Dir, Council on Foreign Relations; Presidential Commn on Financial Structure and Regulation, 1971, on an All-Volunteer Armed Force, 1971; Member: President's Econ. Policy Adv. Board, 1981–87; President's Foreign Intell. Adv. Board, 1983–85. Hon. degrees from Edinburgh, Harvard, Leuven, Pennsylvania and Yale univs. Jefferson Award, 1976; William Butler Meml Award, 1977; US Presidential Medal of Freedom, 2005. Commander, French Legion of Honour, 2003. *Publications:* The Age of Turbulence, 2007; The Map and the Territory: risk, human nature, and the future of forecasting, 2013; (with A. Wooldridge) Capitalism in America: a history, 2018. *Address:* (office) 1133 Connecticut Avenue NW, Suite 810, Washington, DC 20036, USA.

**GREENSTOCK, Sir Jeremy (Quentin),** GCMG 2003 (KCMG 1998; CMG 1991); HM Diplomatic Service, retired; King of Arms, Most Distinguished Order of St Michael and St George, 2007–19; Chairman, Gatehouse Advisory Partners Ltd, since 2010; *b* 27 July 1943; *s* of late John Wilfrid Greenstock and Ruth Margaret Logan; *m* 1969, Anne Derryn Ashford Hodges; one *s* two *d*. *Educ:* Harrow Sch.; Worcester Coll., Oxford (MA Lit. Hum.; Hon. Fellow, 2006). Asst Master, Eton Coll., 1966–69; entered HM Diplomatic Service, 1969; MECAS, 1970–72; Dubai, 1972–74; Private Sec. to the Ambassador, Washington, 1974–78; FCO, 1978–83 (Planning Staff, Personnel Ops Dept, N East and N African Dept); Counsellor (Commercial), Jedda, 1983–85; Riyadh, 1985–86; Hd of Chancery, Paris, 1987–90; Asst Under-Sec. of State, FCO, 1990–93; Minister, Washington, 1994–95; Dep. Under Sec. of State, FCO, 1995; Pol Dir, FCO, 1996–98; UK Perm. Rep. to UN, 1998–2003; UK Special Envoy for Iraq, 2003–04. Dir, Ditchley Foundn, 2004–10. Chm., UN Assoc.-UK, 2011–16. Special Advr, BP Gp, 2004–10; Chm., Lambert Energy Advisory Ltd, 2012– (non-exec. Dir, 2010–); non-exec. Dir, De La Rue plc, 2005–13. Member: Adv. Gp, UN Develt Fund for Women, 2005–09; Internat. Adv. Gp, Brookings Instn, 2007–09; Nat. Security Commn, IPPR, 2007–09; Council, RIIA, 2011–18; BASIC Trident Commn, 2012–14; Special Consultant, Forward Thinking, 2006–. Trustee, Internat. Rescue Cttee (UK), 2006–12. Mem. Adv. Council, Oxford Philomusica Orchestra, 2007–11. Gov. London Business Sch., 2005–07. Hon. FKC 2006. *Publications:* Iraq: the cost of war, 2016. *Recreations:* family, travel/wildlife, golf, ski-ing, watching sport, music/theatre. *Address:* 3 Cornwall Gardens, SW7 4AJ.

**GREENTREE, (William Wayne) Chris;** Chief Executive, LASMO Group plc, 1982–93; *b* 6 April 1935; *s* of J. Murray and Grace M. Greentree; *m* 1st, 1956, Patricia Ann Hugo (marr. diss. 1990); three *d* (and two *d* decd); 2nd, 1990, Hilary J. Wilson; one *d*. *Educ:* Moose Jaw Technical High Sch., Saskatoon; Univ. of Alberta (BSc Hons, PEng). Joined Shell Canada, 1957: technical and managerial appts, onshore and offshore exploration; Ranger Oil London, 1972–79: Man. Dir, 1976; Mapco Inc. USA: Sen. Vice Pres. Exploration and Production, 1979–82. Chm., Bd of Govs, Internat. Sch. São Lourenço, Algarve, 2005–12. Ordre National du Mérite (Gabon), 1987. *Recreation:* golf.

**GREENWAY,** family name of **Baron Greenway**.

**GREENWAY, 4th Baron** *cr* 1927; **Ambrose Charles Drexel Greenway;** Bt 1919; marine photographer and author; *b* 21 May 1941; *s* of 3rd Baron Greenway and Cordelia Mary, *d* of late Major Humfrey Campbell Stephen; *S* father, 1975; *m* 1985, Mrs Rosalynne Schenk. *Educ:* Winchester. Chairman: Marine Soc., 1994–2000; Sail Trng Assoc., subseq. Tall Ships Youth Trust, 2001–03; World Ship Trust, 2003–14. Elected Mem., H of L, 1999. Jt Chm., All-Party Ports and Maritime Gp, 2010–. Elder Brother, Trinity House, 2007–. *Publications:* Soviet Merchant Ships, 1976; Comecon Merchant Ships, 1978; A Century of Cross Channel Passenger Ferries, 1980; A Century of North Sea Passenger Steamers, 1986; Cargo Liners, 2009; Ferries and Short Sea Passenger Ships, 2013. *Recreations:* ocean racing and cruising, swimming. *Heir:* nephew Nicholas Greenway, *b* 6 Dec. 1988. *Address:* c/o House of Lords, SW1A 0PW. *Club:* House of Lords Yacht.

**GREENWAY, Prof. Diana Eleanor,** PhD; FBA 2001; Professor of Medieval History, University of London, 1998–2003; Hon. Fellow, Institute of Historical Research, University of London, since 2004; *b* 1937; *d* of Charles and Winifred Greenway. *Educ:* Aylesbury Grammar Sch.; Girton Coll., Cambridge (Capt., Univ. Women's Cricket, 1958–59; BA Hist. 1959; MA 1963; PhD 1967). Asst Archivist, Lambeth Palace Liby, 1963–64; University of London: Ed., Fasti Ecclesiae Anglicanae 1066–1300 (11 vols, 1968–2011), at Inst. of Historical Res., 1964–2003; teaching hist. and palaeography, 1966–97; Reader in Medieval Hist., 1993–98. Founder and Chair, Univ. of London Palaeography and Diplomatic Teachers' Gp, 1993–98. Gen. Ed., Oxford Medieval Texts, 1974–97. Literary Dir, RHistS, 1982–87. Dir, Summer Insts in Palaeography, Newberry Liby, Chicago, 1985, 1990 and 1994. British Rep., Assembly of Repertorium Fontium Historiae Medii Aevi, 1993–2003. Freeman, City of London, 2011. *Publications:* Charters of the Honour of Mowbray 1107–91, 1972; (ed jtly) Early Yorkshire Families, 1973; (ed jtly) Richard fitzNigel: Dialogus de Scaccario, 1983; (ed jtly) Tradition and Change: essays in honour of Marjorie Chibnall, 1985; (ed jtly) Handbook of British Chronology, 1986; (jtly) The Chronicle of Jocelin of Brakelond, 1989; Henry, Archdeacon of Huntingdon: Historia Anglorum, 1996; (ed jtly) The Book of the Foundation of Walden Monastery, 1999; Saint Osmund, Bishop of Salisbury 1078 to 1099, 1999; Henry of Huntingdon: The History of the English People 1000–1154, 2002; contrib. articles to learned jls. *Recreations:* birdwatching, dragonflies.

**GREENWAY, Harry;** *b* 4 Oct. 1934; *s* of John Kenneth Greenway and Violet Adelaide (*née* Bell); *m* 1969, Carol Elizabeth Helena, *e d* of late Major John Robert Thomas Hooper, barrister at law and Metropolitan Stipendiary Magistrate, and Dorinda Hooper (*née* de Courcy Ireland); one *s* two *d*. *Educ:* Warwick Sch.; College of St Mark and St John, London; Univ. of Caen, Normandy. Assistant Master, Millbank Sch., 1957–60; successively, Head of English Dept, Sen. Housemaster, Sen. Master, Acting Dep. Head, Sir William Collins Sch., 1960–72; Dep. Headmaster, Sedgehill Sch. (Comprehensive for 2,000 plus pupils), 1972–79. Contested (C) Stepney, 1970, Stepney and Poplar, Feb. and Oct. 1974; MP (C) Ealing North, 1979–97; contested (C) same seat, 1997. Vice-Chm., Greater London Cons. Members, 1981–97; Chairman: All Party Adult Educn Cttee, 1979–97; All Party Parly Friends of Cycling, 1987–95; Member: Parly Select Cttee on Educn, Science and the Arts, 1979–92; Parly Select Cttee on Employment, 1992–95, on Educn and Employment, 1995–97; Vice-Chairman: Cons. Parly Educn Cttee, 1983–87 (Sec., 1981); Cons. Parly Sports Cttee, 1990–97 (Sec., 1986–90); Parly Sec., Cons. National Adv. Cttee on Educn, 1981–94; Sec., Cons. Parly Arts and Heritage Cttee, 1986–87. Parly Sec., Cons. Nat. Educn Soc., 1995–97 (Dep. Pres., 1998–); Chm., Mauritius Parly Gp, 1983–97. Led All Party Parly Delegn to Sri Lanka, 1985, to Gibraltar, 1989, to Zaire, 1990. Pres., Cons. Trade Unionist Teachers, 1982–83; Chm., Educn Cttee, British-Atlantic Cttee, 1971–85; Open University: Mem. Council, 1981–99; Audit Cttee, 1997–99; Grievance Cttee, 1998–99; Mem., Educn Cttee, NACRO, 1985–88. President: Age Concern, Greenford, Northolt and Perivale, 1980–; Ealing Youth Choir, 1985–; Nat. Equine Welfare Council, 1990–; Assoc. of British Riding Schs, 1993–2003; Spencer Hockey Club, 2000–03; Ealing N Cons. Assoc., 2012–; Mem. Council, British Horse Soc., 1973–97 (Trustee, 1998–2006); Mem. Bd of Govs, Horse Rangers Assoc., 2000–02; Founder Trustee, The Greater London Equestrian Centres Trust Ltd; Trustee, Teenage Cancer Trust, 1991–2007. Vice-Pres., Greenford Br., RBL, 1977–. Chm., National Prayer Breakfast, 1995. Freeman: City of London, 1986; London Bor. of Ealing, 2008; Liveryman, Farriers' Co., 1986–2006. DUniv Open, 2001. Award of Merit, 1980, President's Award, 2006, Sefton Award, 2007, British Horse Soc. Kt Comdr's Cross, Order of Merit (Poland), 1998. *Publications:* Adventure in the Saddle, 1971; (ed and compiled) Electing to Bat: tales of glory and disaster from the Palace of Westminster, 1996; regular contributor to educnl and equestrian jls. *Recreations:* riding (Asst Instructor, BHS, 1966), ski-ing, choral music, hockey (Vice-Pres., England Schoolboys' Hockey Assoc.; Founder, Lords and Commons Hockey Club), tennis, cricket, parliamentary parachutist. *Address:* 64 Cambridge Street, Westminster, SW1V 4QQ. *Clubs:* National, MCC, Middlesex CC, Lord's Taverners, Ski Club of Gt Britain; Worcs CC.

**GREENWAY, John Robert;** *b* 15 Feb. 1946; *s* of Thomas William and Kathleen Greenway; *m* 1st, 1974, Sylvia Ann Gant (marr. diss. 2006); two *s* one *d*; 2nd, 2008, Johanna ten Kate. *Educ:* Sir John Deane's Grammar School, Northwich; London College of Law. Midland Bank, 1964; Metropolitan Police, 1965–69; Equitable Life Assurance Soc., 1970–71; National Provident Instn, 1971–72; own firm of insurance brokers, J. R. Greenway, subseq. Greenway Middleton, & Co. Ltd, York, then Greenway Smart and Cook Ltd, later Smart and Cook Ltd, now part of Bluefin Gp, 1972–2010. Treasurer, Ryedale Cons. Assoc., 1984–86; Mem., North Yorks CC, 1985–87; Vice-Chm., N Yorks Police Authy, 1986–87. MP (C) Ryedale, 1987–2010. PPS to Minister of State, MAFF, 1991–92; Opposition front bench spokesman on home affairs, 1997–2000, on sport and tourism, 2000–03. Mem., Home Affairs Select Cttee, 1987–97. Chm., Jt Scrutiny Cttee, Draft Gambling Bill, 2003–05; Sec., Cons. backbench Health Cttee, 1988–91; Vice-Chairman: Cons. backbench Agricl Cttee, 1989–97; All Party Football Cttee, 1989–2010; Chairman: All Party Racing and Bloodstock Cttee, 1993–97; All Party Insce and Financial Services Gp, 1992–2010 (Sec., 1991–92); Jt Chm., All Party Opera Gp, 1994–2010. Elected rep. to Council of Europe, 2005–10 (Chm., Rules Cttee, 2008–10; Chm., Migration Cttee, 2010–); Mem., Assembly of WEU, 2005–10. Dir, Responsibility in Gambling Trust, 2006–10. Pres., Inst. of Insce Brokers, 1987–2011; Chm., Fedn of Insce and Investment

Intermediary Assocs, 1998–2001; Mem., Insce Brokers Registration Council, 1991–2001. Pres., The Insurance Charities, 2014–15 (Dep. Pres., 2012–14; Vice Chm., 2016–18; Chm., 2018–). *Recreations:* opera, football (Pres., York City FC, 1989–2003), wine, travel, home in France.

**GREENWELL, (Arthur) Jeffrey,** CBE 1991; DL; Chief Executive, Northamptonshire County Council, 1973–96; Independent Adjudicator, Department for Communities and Local Government (formerly Department of the Environment, Transport and the Regions, later Department for Transport, Local Government and the Regions, then Office of the Deputy Prime Minister), 1998–2008; *b* 1 Aug. 1931; *s* of late George Greenwell and of Kate Mary Greenwell (*née* Fleming), Durham; *m* 1958, Margaret Rosemary, *d* of late Sidney David Barnard; one *s* two *d*. *Educ:* Durham Sch.; University Coll., Oxford (MA). FCIS. Solicitor (Hons). Nat. Service, RHA, 1950–51. Articled to Town Clerk, Newcastle upon Tyne, 1955–58; law tutor, Gibson & Weldon, 1958–59; Asst Solicitor, Birmingham Corp., 1959–61; Hants County Council: Asst Solicitor, 1961–64; Asst Clerk, 1964–67; Dep. Clerk of Council, Dep. Clerk of the Peace and Dep. Clerk, Hants River Authy, 1967–73; Clerk of Northants Lieutenancy, 1977–96. Chm., Assoc. of Co. Chief Execs, 1993–94 (Hon. Sec., 1980–84); Hon. Sec., SOLACE, 1984–88 (Pres., 1991–92); President: CIS, 1989; Northants Assoc. of Local Councils, 1974–96. Chm., Home Office Gp on Juvenile Crime, 1987. Vice-Pres., Internat. City Management Assoc., 1990–92; Chm., Northants ACRE, 1998–2002; Vice-Chm., Northants CPRE, 2002–08. Trustee, Central Festival Opera. Gov., UC, Northampton, 1998–2002. Freeman, City of London, 1989 (Pres., Aldgate Ward Club, 2008–09); Liveryman, Chartered Secretaries' and Administrators' Co. (Master, 2005–06). DL Northants, 1996. Freeman, City of Durham, 1992. *Recreations:* bridge, travel, local history, going to meetings. *Address:* 2 Hillside Way, Northampton NN3 3AW. *T:* (01604) 401858.

**GREENWELL, Sir Edward (Bernard),** 4th Bt *cr* 1906; DL; farmer, since 1975; *b* 10 June 1948; *s* of Sir Peter McClintock Greenwell, 3rd Bt, TD, and Henrietta (who *m* 1985, Hugh Kenneth Haig), 2nd *d* of late Peter and Lady Alexandra Haig-Thomas; *S* father, 1978; *m* 1st, 1974, Sarah Louise Gore-Anley (*d* 2010); one *s* three *d*; 2nd, 2015, Clare, *widow* of Edward Mann. *Educ:* Eton; Nottingham University (BSc); Cranfield Institute of Technology (MBA). Pres., CLA, 2001–03. DL, 1988, High Sheriff, 2013–14, Suffolk. *Heir: s* Alexander Bernard Peter Greenwell, *b* 11 May 1987. *Address:* Gedgrave Hall, Woodbridge, Suffolk IP12 2BX. *T:* (01394) 450440. *Club:* Turf.

**GREENWELL, Jeffrey;** *see* Greenwell, A. J.

**GREENWELL, Joseph,** CBE 2011; DL; Chairman, Ford of Britain, 2009–13; *b* Portsmouth, 8 May 1951; *s* of Joseph and Eileen Joyce Florence Greenwell; *m* 1979, Anne Carson; three *d* (one *s* decd). *Educ:* Purbrook Grammar Sch.; Univ. of East Anglia (BA Hons English and American Lit. 1973). Grad. trainee, British Leyland, 1973–82; Jaguar Cars: Mktg Res. Manager, 1983–84; Product Strategy Manager, 1984–88; Public Affairs Manager, 1988–93; Dir, Overseas Sales, 1993–96; Dir, Public Affairs, 1996–99; Public and Govt Affairs Dir, Ford of Europe, 1999–2001; Global Vice Pres., Mktg, Ford Motor Co., USA, 2001–03; Chm. and CEO, Jaguar Land Rover, 2003–05; Vice Pres., Govt Affairs, Ford of Europe, 2005–09. Hon. Pres., SMMT, 2009–10. Pres., BEN, 2006–13. Trustee, Nat. Motor Mus., 2009–13. DL Warwicks, 2011. *Recreations:* golf, classic cars, football, tennis, walking, theatre, music, family, history and art history. *Address:* Field House, The Pound, Harbury, Warwicks CV33 9HH. *E:* joegreenwell2003@yahoo.co.uk. *Clubs:* Athenæum, Royal Automobile; Warwick Boat; Leamington and County Golf, Stratford upon Avon Golf.

**GREENWOOD, His Honour Alan Eliezer;** a Circuit Judge, 2000–17; *b* 5 June 1947; *s* of Rabbi Hans Isaac Grunewald and Martha Grunewald; *m* 1975, Naomi (*née* Ohayon); two *s* one *d*. *Educ:* University Coll., London (LLB Hons). Called to the Bar, Middle Temple, 1970; in practice at the Bar, 1971–2000. *Recreations:* travel, film, theatre, football, tennis, skiing, swimming, cycling.

**GREENWOOD, Brian John;** Partner, Clyde & Co. LLP, since 2016; *b* Dorking, 15 April 1950; *s* of Ronald Greenwood and Marianne Louise Greenwood (*née* Weiss); *m* 1978, Julia Le Messurier; four *s* one *d*. *Educ:* Forest Sch.; Univ. of Southampton (LLB). Articled clerk, City of Westminster, 1974–76; admitted as solicitor, 1976; Chief Solicitor, Beds CC, 1981–85; Partner, Planning and Envmtl Law Gp, Norton Rose, 1988–2010; Partner, Planning and Envmtl Law, Osborne Clarke, 2010–16. Pres., City of London Law Soc., 2004. Master, Solicitors' Co., 2004; Liveryman, Gardeners' Co., 2006–. Vice Chm., Pavenham Parish Council, 2015. FRSA. *Publications:* (principal author and Gen. Ed.) Butterworths Planning Law Encyclopaedia, 1990; (contrib.) Environmental Regulation and Economic Growth, 1994; (ed) Butterworths Planning Law Handbook, 1995, 5th edn 2000. *Recreations:* classical music, violin, sport. *Address:* Clyde & Co. LLP, St Botolph Building, 138 Houndsditch, EC3A 7AR. *T:* (020) 7876 6140. *E:* Brian.Greenwood@clydeco.com.

**GREENWOOD, Sir Christopher (John),** GBE 2018; Kt 2009; CMG 2002; QC 1999; a Judge of the Iran-United States Claims Tribunal, since 2018; international arbitrator; *b* 12 May 1955; *o s* of late Murray Guy Greenwood and Diana Maureen (*née* Barron); *m* 1978, Susan Anthea, *d* of late Geoffrey and Patricia Longbotham; two *d*. *Educ:* Wellingborough Sch.; Magdalene Coll., Cambridge (BA Law 1st Cl. Hons; LLB Internat. Law 1st Cl. Hons; McNair Schol. 1976, Whewell Schol. 1977, in Internat. Law). Pres., Cambridge Union Soc., 1976. Called to the Bar, Middle Temple, 1978, Bencher, 2003; Fellow, Magdalene Coll., Cambridge, 1978–96 (Hon. Fellow, 2009); Asst Lectr in Law, 1981–84, Lectr, 1984–96, Univ. of Cambridge; Prof. of Internat. Law, LSE, 1996–2009; Judge, Internat. Court of Justice, 2009–18. Mem., Panel of Arbitrators: Law of the Sea Convention, 1998–; ICSID, 2004–. Vice-Pres., British Inst. of Internat. and Comparative Law, 2012–. Hon. Fellow, Lauterpacht Centre for Internat. Law, 2009–; Associate, Institut de droit internat., 2015–. Gov., Ditchley Foundn, 2001–. Jt Editor, International Law Reports, 1990–. *Publications:* Essays on War in International Law, 2006; contrib. articles in Brit. Year Book of Internat. Law, Internat. and Comparative Law Qly, Modern Law Rev. and other legal jls. *Recreations:* political biography, the novels of Anthony Trollope, walking. *Address:* c/o Essex Court Chambers, 24 Lincoln's Inn Fields, WC2A 3EG. *T:* (020) 7813 8000. *E:* CGreenwood@arbitratorsinternational.com. *Clubs:* Athenæum, Oxford and Cambridge; Haagsche, de Witte Society (The Hague).

**GREENWOOD, Prof. Geoffrey Wilson,** PhD, DMet; FRS 1992; FInstP, FIMMM, FREng; Professor of Metallurgy, University of Sheffield, 1966–94, now Emeritus; *b* 3 Feb. 1929; *s* of Richard Albert Greenwood and Martha Alice (*née* Wilson); *m* 1954, Nancy Cole; two *s* one *d*. *Educ:* Grange Grammar Sch., Bradford; Univ. of Sheffield (BSc, PhD, DMet). FInstP 1966; FIMMM (FIM 1966); FREng (FEng 1990). SO and SSO, UKAEA, Harwell, 1953–60; Head, Fuel Materials Section, Berkeley Nuclear Labs, CEGB, 1960–65; Res. Manager, Scis Div., Electricity Council Res. Centre, 1965–66. Pro-Vice-Chancellor, Univ. of Sheffield, 1979–83. L. B. Pfeil Prize, Inst. Metals and Iron and Steel Inst., 1972; Rosenhain Medal, Metals Soc., 1975; Griffith Medal, Inst. of Materials, 1995. *Publications:* contribs to Metallurgy, Materials Science, Physics and Engrg. *Recreations:* music, variety of outdoor activities. *Address:* Department of Materials Science and Engineering, University of Sheffield, Sir Robert Hadfield Building, Mappin Street, Sheffield S1 3JD. *T:* (0114) 222 5517; 26 Stumperlowe Hall Road, Sheffield S10 3QS. *T:* (0114) 230 3565.

**GREENWOOD, Helen Mary;** *see* Megarry, H. M.

**GREENWOOD, Jeffrey Michael;** Senior Partner, Nabarro Nathanson, 1987–95; *b* 21 April 1935; *s* of Arthur Greenwood and Ada Greenwood (*née* Gordon); *m* 1964, Naomi Grahame; three *s* one *d*. *Educ:* Raine's Foundation Sch.; LSE; Downing Coll., Cambridge (MA, LLM). Admitted solicitor 1960; Partner, Nabarro Nathanson, 1963–95, Consultant, 1995–2001. Dir, Bank Leumi (UK), 1990–2005; Chairman: Wigmore Property Investment Trust, 1996–2004; Stow Securities, 1997–2007; Dep. Chm., Jewish Chronicle, 1994–2005. Chm., CCETSW, 1993–98. Chairman: Jewish Welfare Bd, 1986–90; Jewish Care, 1990; Council Member: Jewish Historical Soc. of England, 1993–2017; Anglo Israel Assoc., 2010–; Hampstead Garden Suburb Trust (Law Soc. Appointee), 1984–87; Trustee, Policy Res. Inst. for Ageing and Ethnicity, 2000–09. Founder Mem., Campaign Cttee, ProHelp. *Publications:* articles in learned jls. *Recreations:* conversing with grandchildren, swimming, literature, travel. *E:* jeff@thegreenwoods.org.

**GREENWOOD, Dr Jeremy John Denis,** CBE 2008; Director, British Trust for Ornithology, 1988–2007 (Hon. Research Fellow, 2007); *b* 7 Sept. 1942; *s* of Denis Greenwood and Phyllis Marjorie Greenwood (*née* Leat); *m* 1971, Cynthia Anne Jones; two *d*. *Educ:* Royal Grammar Sch., Worcester; St Catherine's Coll., Oxford (BA 1964); Univ. of Manchester (PhD 1972). MRSB (CBiol, MIBiol 1990), FRSB 2015. Dundee University: Asst Lectr in Zoology, 1967–70; Lectr in Biol Scis, 1970–87; University of East Anglia: Hon. Lectr, 1994–98; Hon. Reader, 1998–2002; Hon. Prof., 2002–08; Hon. Professor: Univ. of Birmingham, 2003–; Univ. of St Andrews, 2007–. Vis. Prof. in Animal Ecology, Univ. of Khartoum, 1976. Natural Environment Research Council: Workshop on Grey Seal Population Biol., 1979–84; Special Cttee on Seals, 1986–96, 2008–13; Terrestrial Life Scis Cttee, 1988–91; Data Adv. Gp, 2000–01. Mem., Scottish Govt Wildlife Penalties Rev. Gp, 2014–15. Chairman: Exec. Cttee, European Bird Census Council, 1992–98; Scientific and Tech. Adv. Gp, Langholm Demonstration Project, 2007–11 (Mem., 2007–15); Member: Council, RSPB, 1983–88; Adv. Cttee on Birds, NCC, 1988–91; Envmtl Res. Cttee, British Agrochem. Assoc., 1988–93; Grants Cttee, Internat. Council for Bird Preservation, British Section, 1988–92; Council, British Ornith. Union, 1989–93; Sci. Adv. Cttee, Wildfowl & Wetlands Trust, 1989–92; Professional Affairs Cttee, Inst. of Ecology and Envmtl Management, 1991–93; Scottish Wildlife Trust Conservation Cttee, 2007–13; Natural Envmt Panel (formerly Nature Conservation Panel), NT, 2007–13; Vice Pres., 2003–05, Pres., 2005–09, Eur. Ornithologists' Union. Director: West Palaearctic Birds Ltd, 1990–2000; BB 2000 Ltd, 2001–13. Pres., Scottish Ornithologists' Club, 1987. Hon. DSc Birmingham, 2007. Trustee, British Birds Charitable Trust, 2001–16. Editor, Bird Study, 1984–87; Member, Editorial Board: Heredity, 1988–92; Biol Conservation, 2001–08. *Publications:* (ed jtly) Joint Biological Expedition to North East Greenland 1974, 1978; (ed jtly) Birds as Monitors of Environmental Change, 1993; papers in learned jls; chapters in books. *Recreations:* birdwatching, walking, gardening. *Address:* Centre for Research into Ecological and Environmental Modelling, University of St Andrews, Fife KY16 9LZ.

**GREENWOOD, Lilian Rachel;** MP (Lab) Nottingham South, since 2010; *b* Bolton, Lancs, 26 March 1966; *d* of Harry Greenwood and Patricia Greenwood; three *d*; *m* 2008, Ravi Subramanian. *Educ:* Canon Slade Sch., Bolton; St Catharine's Coll., Cambridge (BA Hons 1987); South Bank Poly. (MSc). Research Officer: LACSAB, 1988–89; Civil and Public Services Assoc., 1989–92; Trainee Regl Officer, NUPE, 1992–93; UNISON: Regl Organiser, 1993–98; Regl Educn Officer, 1998–2002; Regl Manager, 2002–10. Shadow Sec. of State for Transport, 2015–16. Chm., Select Cttee on Transport, 2017–. *Recreations:* running, walking, cycling, cinema. *Address:* (office) 12 Regent Street, Nottingham NG1 5BQ. *T:* (0115) 711 7000; House of Commons, SW1A 0AA. *E:* lilian.greenwood.mp@parliament.uk.

**GREENWOOD, Margaret;** MP (Lab) Wirral West, since 2015; *b* 14 March 1959. Teacher of English in secondary schs, further educn colleges and adult educn centres, Liverpool and Wirral; teacher of literacy to adult learners and adults with special needs; travel writer; website consultant. Shadow Minister, 2016–18, Shadow Sec. of State, 2018–, for Work and Pensions. *Address:* House of Commons, SW1A 0AA.

**GREENWOOD, Michael Peter;** independent producer, broadcaster and media consultant, since 2010; Director, Wakewood Productions, since 2017; *b* Leicester, 26 Feb. 1959; *s* of Peter Greenwood and Petronella Greenwood (*née* Bontenbal); *m* 1995, Elizabeth Havern. *Educ:* Wyggeston Boys' Grammar Sch., Leicester; Downing Coll., Cambridge (BA Eng. Lit. 1981). Producer and presenter, BBC local radio, 1983–86; producer, then chief producer, BBC network radio, 1987–94; producer, BBC Music and Arts TV, 1994–95; Commissioning Exec. and Exec. Producer, BBC Educn, 1996–2002; Commissioning Exec., Culture Online, DCMS, 2002–07; Dir, Digital, Creative and Cultural Skills, 2008–09. Trustee, Woodland Trust, 2012–. Gov., Rhodes Avenue Prim. Sch., 2008–. BP Arts Journalism Award, 1990. *Recreations:* arts, history and archaeology, independent travel, restoring a Connemara cottage and garden, walking in woods, enthusiastic if incompetent angling. *Address:* Woodland Trust, Kempton Way, Grantham, Lincs NG31 6LL. *T:* 07880 717584. *E:* mpgreenwood@btinternet.com.

**GREER, Adrian,** CMG 2004; Chief Operating Officer, British Council, 2012–19; *b* 26 April 1957; *s* of David Smith Greer and Christine Greer (*née* Dawson); *m* 1985, (Mary) Diana Cuddy; one *s* three *d*. *Educ:* Queen Mary's Grammar Sch., Walsall; St Andrews Univ. (MA Eng. Lang. and Lit.). CPFA 1984, FCPFA. Auditor, Nat. Audit Office, 1979–84; joined British Council, 1984; Finance Develt Office, 1984–85; Finance Manager, Japan, 1985–88; Finance Project Manager, 1988–89, Chief Accountant, 1989–91, London; Director: Lesotho and Swaziland, 1991–93; Zambia, 1993–96; Europe (Develt and Trng Services), 1996–98; Asia and Americas (Develt and Trng Services), 1998–2000; Cultural Counsellor and Dir, Russia, 2000–04; Dir of Learning, Creativity and Society, 2004–07; Regl Dir, E Asia, 2007–11; Dir, Global Network, 2011–12. Mem., Marshall Aid Commemoration Commn, 2019–. Chancellor's Assessor and Mem. Court, Univ. of St Andrews, 2016–. FRSA. *Recreations:* travel, swimming, running, reading. *Address:* 33 Rollscourt Avenue, SE24 0EA. *E:* adrian.greer@sky.com.

*See also* K. Greer.

**GREER, Bonnie,** OBE 2010; writer; *b* Chicago, 16 Nov. 1948; *d* of late Ben Greer and of Willie Mae Greer; naturalised British citizen, 1997; *m* 1993, David Hutchins, solicitor. *Educ:* DePaul Univ., Chicago (BA Hist. 1974). Studied playwriting: with David Mamet, St Nicholas Th., Chicago, 1975–76; with Elia Kazan, Actors Studio, NYC, 1982–86; Arts Council Playwright in Residence: Soho Th., 1990; Black Th. Co-op., 1992. Plays include: 1919, 1977; Diary of a Slave Girl, 1984; Roadhouse, 1985; Zebra Days, 1989; Dancing on Black Water, 1996; Ella, Meet Marilyn, 2006; Equiano, Esclave, Maitre, Survivant, 2006; The Hotel Cerise, 2016; opera, Yes, 2011; radio plays include Marilyn and Ella Backstage at the Mocambo, 2005, and various adaptations and translations; television: White Men Are Cracking Up, 1996; Reflecting Skin (also co-producer), 2004. Critic, Late Review and Newsnight Review, BBC2, 1998–2005. Chancellor, Kingston Univ., 2013–. Member: Bd,

Serpentine Gall., 2013–; Adv. Cttee, 2013–, Cultural Cttee, 2013–, First World War Centenary. Trustee, BM, 2005–09 (Dep. Chm., 2005–13). Mem., Acad. and Artistic Bd, and Mem. Council, 2009–, RADA. Judge: Orange Prize, 2000; Samuel Johnson Prize, 2003; Whitbread First Novel Prize, 2003; Best Play, Sony Radio Awards, 2010. FRSA 2003. DuNouy Prize for Playwriting, Phoenix Th., NYC, 1979; Verity Bargate Award, 1992. *Publications*: So Very English (short stories), 1989; Hanging By Her Teeth (novel), 1994; How Maxine Learned To Like Her Legs (short stories), 1995; (contrib.) Black Plays Three, 1995; Entropy (novel), 2009; Obama Music (memoir), 2009; Langston Hughes, 2011; A Parallel Life, 2014. *Recreations:* reading popular books on theoretical maths esp. Prime Number Theory and the Riemann Hypothesis, collecting studio jewellery, listening and dancing to jazz, soul and funk music, the gym. *Address:* c/o Judith Antell, The Antell Agency, Peckhams, Knowle Lane, Lewes, E Sussex BN8 6PR. *T:* 07736 063726. *E:* judith@theantellagency.co.uk. *Club:* Union.

**GREER, Prof. Germaine,** PhD; FRSL; writer and broadcaster; Professor of English and Comparative Studies, Warwick University, 1998–2003; *b* Melbourne, 29 Jan. 1939. *Educ:* Melbourne Univ. (BA 1959); Sydney Univ. (MA 1962); Commonwealth Scholarship, 1964; Cambridge Univ. (PhD 1967). Sen. Tutor in English, Sydney Univ., 1963–64; Asst Lectr, then Lectr in English, Warwick Univ., 1967–72; Lectr, American Program Bureau, 1973–78; Prof. of Modern Letters, Univ. of Tulsa, 1980–83; Founder Director: Tulsa Centre for Studies in Women's Literature, 1981; Friends of Gondwana Rainforest, 2011–; Special Lectr and Unofficial Fellow, Newnham Coll., Cambridge, 1989–98. Vis. Prof., Univ. of Tulsa, 1979. Proprietor, Stump Cross Books, 1988–. FRSL 2016. *Publications:* The Female Eunuch, 1970; The Obstacle Race: the fortunes of women painters and their work, 1979; Sex and Destiny: the politics of human fertility, 1984; Shakespeare, 1986; The Madwoman's Underclothes: selected journalism, 1986; (ed jtly) Kissing the Rod: an anthology of 17th century women's verse, 1988; Daddy, We Hardly Knew You, 1989 (J. R. Ackerly Prize; Premio Internazionale Mondello); (ed) The Uncollected Verse of Aphra Behn, 1989; The Change: women, ageing and the menopause, 1991, rev. edn 2019; Slipshod Sibyls: recognition, rejection and the woman poet, 1995; (ed jtly) The Surviving Works of Anne Wharton, 1997; The Whole Woman, 1999; (ed) 101 Poems by 101 Women, 2001; The Boy, 2003; (ed) Poems for Gardeners, 2003; Whitefella Jump Up: the shortest way to nationhood, 2004; Shakespeare's Wife, 2007; White Beech: the rainforest years, 2014; On Rape, 2018; contribs to Journalist. *Address:* c/o Aitken Alexander Associates Ltd, 291 Gray's Inn Road, WC1X 8QJ.

**GREER, Prof. Ian Andrew,** MD; FRCP, FRCPE, FRCPGlas, FRCPI, FRCOG, FFSRH, FCCP; FMedSci; President and Vice Chancellor, Queen's University Belfast, since 2018. *Educ:* Univ. of Glasgow (MB ChB 1980; MD 1986). MRCP 1984, FRCP 2001; MRCOG 1987, FRCOG 1999; FRCPGlas 1994; FRCPE 1999; FRCPI 2006; MFFP 1994, FFSRH (FFFP 2008); FCCP 2011. Registrar in Medicine, Glasgow Royal Infirmary, 1983–85; Lectr in Obstetrics and Gynaecol., Univ. of Edinburgh, 1987–90; Clinical Res. Scientist, MRC Reproductive Biol. Unit, Edinburgh, 1990–91; Glasgow University: Muirhead Prof., 1991–2000; Regius Prof., 2000–06; Head, Dept of Obstetrics and Gynaecology, 1991–2006; Depute Dean, 2003–06; Dean, Hull York Med. Sch., 2007–10; Exec. Pro-Vice-Chancellor, 2010–15, Provost, 2013–15, Faculty of Health and Life Scis, Univ. of Liverpool; Vice Pres., Dean, Faculty of Med. and Human Scis, subseq. Biology, Medicine and Health, and Dir, Manchester Academic Health Sci. Centre, Univ. of Manchester, 2015–18. Chair, Northern Health Sci. Alliance, 2013–18. FMedSci 2006. *Publications:* (jtly) Haemostasis and Thrombosis in Obstetrics and Gynaecology, 1992; Venous Thromboembolism in Obstetrics and Gynaecology, in Baillière's Clinical Obstetrics and Gynaecology, 1997; (jtly) Mosby's Colour Atlas and Text of Obstetrics and Gynaecology, 2000; (with A. J. Thomson) Antenatal Disorders for the MRCOG, 2000; Pregnancy: the inside guide, 2003; Venous Thrombosis in Women, 2003; (jtly) Problem-based Obstetrics and Gynaecology, 2003; (jtly) The Menopause in Practice, 2003; (jtly) Practical Obstetric Haematology, 2005; (jtly) Preterm Labour, 2005; Fertility and Conception, 2007; (jtly) Women's Vascular Health, 2007; (jtly) Maternal Medicine, 2007; (jtly) Textbook of Periconceptional Medicine, 2009; contrib. numerous res. papers and rev. articles on haemostasis and thrombosis, medical disorders in pregnancy and labour and preterm labour. *Address:* Vice Chancellor's Office, Queen's University Belfast, University Road, Belfast, N Ireland BT7 1NN.

**GREER, Kenneth;** independent education consultant, since 2014; *b* 21 Nov. 1953; *s* of David Smith Greer and Christine Greer (*née* Dawson); *m* 1st, 1977, Lorna Margaret Murray (*d* 2001); two *s*; 2nd, 2008, Belinda Margaret Sheehan. *Educ:* St Edmund's Coll., Ware; Univ. of St Andrews (MA Hons English Lang. and Lit.); Moray House Coll. (PGCE); Open Univ. (MA Educn). Teacher: Lanark GS, 1976–78; Whitburn Acad., 1978–80; Buckhaven High Sch., 1980–84; Dunfermline High Sch., 1984–90; Advr in English, Grampian Reg., 1990–94; HM Inspector of Schs, 1994–2003; Sen. Educn Manager, 2003–05, Exec. Dir (Educn), 2005–14, Fife Council. Sen. Advr, Abu Dhabi Educn Council, 2014–15. Vice-Pres., Assoc. of Dirs of Educn in Scotland, 2011–13. Trustee, Link Community Develt, Scotland, 2007–16. *Recreations:* running, ski-ing, reading. *Address:* Four Seasons Place, 8 Finance Street, Hong Kong. *T:* 64119614.

See also A. Greer.

**GREGG, Hilary;** *see* Manley, H.

**GREGG, Prof. Paul James,** MD; FRCS; Professor of Orthopaedic Surgical Science, University of Durham, since 2000; Consultant Orthopaedic Surgeon, South Tees Acute Hospitals NHS Trust, 2000–12, now Emeritus Consultant Orthopaedic Surgeon; *b* 26 Nov. 1945; *s* of George Ernest Gregg and Hebe Elizabeth Gregg; *m* 1977, Jennifer Hall; one *d*. *Educ:* St Peter's Sch., York; Med. Sch., Univ. of Newcastle upon Tyne (MB BS 1969; MD 1977). FRCS 1974; FRCSE *ad hominem* 1998. House Physician and House Surgeon, Royal Victoria Infirmary, Newcastle upon Tyne, 1969–70; surgical trng, Newcastle upon Tyne hosps, 1971–74; University of Newcastle upon Tyne: Demonstrator in Anatomy, 1970–71; Sen. Res. Associate, MRC Decompression Sickness Res. Team, 1976–77; Lectr in Orthopaedic Surgery, 1979–83; Sen. Registrar in Orthopaedic Surgery, N Reg. Trng Prog., 1977–79; Clin. Res. Fellow, Massachusetts Gen. Hosp., 1982–83; Sen. Lectr in Orthopaedic Surgery, Univ. of Edinburgh, 1983–85; Foundation Prof. of Orthopaedic Surgery, Univ. of Leicester, 1985–97; Prof. of Trauma and Orthopaedic Surgery, Univ. of Newcastle upon Tyne, 1997–2000. Pres., British Orthopaedic Assoc., 2002–03. *Publications:* Fractures and Dislocations: principles of management, 1995; contribs to books; more than 140 scientific papers. *Recreations:* walking, golf. *Address:* Upper Loads Farm, Upper Loads, Holymoorside, Derbys S42 7HP.

**GREGG, Paul Richard;** Chairman, Apollo Cinemas, 2003–07; *b* 2 Oct. 1941; *m* 1970, Anita Kim, (Nita), Grehan (*d* 2010); two *s* one *d*. *Educ:* Hull Nautical Coll. ABC Cinema Gp, 1961–65; Star Gp of Cinemas, 1965–67; Pressed Steel Fisher Ltd, 1967–70; Entertainment Dir, Rover Motor Co., 1968–70; Entertainment and Tourist Manager, Southport DC, 1970–77; Chm., Apollo Leisure Gp plc, 1978–2001. Mem., Variety Club of GB (former Pres.; Chief Barker, 1991). *Recreation:* theatre.

**GREGOR, Anna, (Mrs Neil Magee),** CBE 2005; FRCPE, FRCR; Consultant Oncologist, Lothian Health Board, 1997–2008; *b* Prague, 13 Aug. 1948; *d* of Dr and Mrs J. Drachovsky; *m* 1983, Neil Magee; two *s*. *Educ:* Academic Grammar Sch., Prague; Faculty of Medicine, Charles Univ., Prague; Royal Free Sch. of Medicine, Univ. of London. LRCP, MRCS 1973, MRCP 1975; FRCR 1981; FRCPE 1993. Postgrad. trng, Brompton Hosps, Cardiothoracic Inst. and Royal Marsden Hosps, London, 1974–80; Lectr in Clinical Oncology, Univ. of Edinburgh, 1980–83; Consultant Oncologist, Beatson Oncol. Centre, Glasgow, 1983–87; Sen. Lectr, Univ. of Edinburgh, 1987–97; Clin. Dir, SE Scotland Cancer Network, 2001–08; Lead Cancer Clinician for Scotland, 2001–06. Trustee, Nat. Museums of Scotland, 2009–17. *Publications:* Lung Cancer: recent results, 1989; Oxford Textbook of Oncology, 1995; Comprehensive Textbook of Thoracic Oncology, 1999; contribs to jls incl. Clin. Oncol., BMJ, Thorax, Annals NY Acad. Sci., Clin. Radiol. *Recreations:* friends, music, food and wine. *E:* annagregor@doctors.net.uk. *Club:* New (Edinburgh).

**GREGORIADIS, Prof. Gregory,** PhD, DSc; Member, Scientific Advisory Board, Xenetic Biosciences plc (formerly Lipoxen plc), since 1998 (Founder, Director of Research and Board Member, 1998–2015); Professor and Head, Centre for Drug Delivery Research, School of Pharmacy, University of London, 1990–2001, now Professor Emeritus; *b* 27 Feb. 1934; *s* of late Christos Gregoriadis and Athina Sakellariou; *m* 1968, Susan Byron-Brown; one *s* one *d*. *Educ:* Univ. of Athens (BSc 1958); McGill Univ. (MSc 1966; PhD 1968); DSc London 2002. Research Fellow: Albert Einstein Coll. of Medicine, 1968–70; Royal Free Hosp. Sch. of Medicine, 1970–72; Sen. Scientist, MRC, 1972–93. Pres., Internat. Liposome Soc., 2003–. Fellow: Amer. Assoc. of Pharmaceutical Scientists, 1998; Acad. of Pharmaceutical Scientists, 2008; Controlled Release Soc., 2010. 15 NATO Scientific Affairs Div. awards, 1980–98; Founder's Award, Controlled Release Soc., 1994; Bangham Award, 1995, Founders Award, 2010, Liposome Res. Days Inc.; Lifetime Achievement Award, Jl of Drug Targeting, 2008. *Publications:* (ed) Drug Carriers in Biology and Medicine, 1979; (ed jtly) Liposomes in Biology and Medicine, 1980; (ed jtly) Targeting of Drugs, 1982, 10th edn 2000; (ed) Liposome Technology, 1984, 3rd edn 2007; (ed) Liposomes as Drug Carriers: recent trends and progress, 1988; (ed jtly) Vaccines, 1989, 5th edn 1997; Still the Cicadas Sing (novel), 2014; over 300 papers on drug and vaccine targeting. *Recreations:* creative writing, history and philosophy of Ancient Athens, politics. *Address:* Crantock, Kewferry Hill, Rickmansworth Road, Northwood, Middx HA6 2RQ.

**GREGOROWSKI, Rt Rev. Christopher John;** an Assistant Bishop of Cape Town (Bishop of Table Bay), 1998–2005; *b* 19 Feb. 1940; *s* of William Victor Gregorowski and Doris Alice Gregorowski (*née* Skinner); *m* 1964, Margaret Merle Perold; two *d* (and one *d* decd). *Educ:* Diocesan Coll., Rondebosch, S Africa; Univ. of Cape Town (BA, MA); Birmingham Univ. (DPS); Cuddesdon Coll., Oxford. Ordained deacon 1963, priest 1964, Anglican Church of Southern Africa (formerly Church of Province of S Africa); Rector: St Cuthbert's, Tsolo, 1968–74; St Thomas, Rondebosch, 1974–86; All Saints, Somerset West, 1986–98. Member: Friends of the Opera: Contemplative Outreach, Western Cape. *Publications:* Why a Donkey was Chosen, 1975; The Bible for Little Children, 1982; Fly, Eagle, Fly!, 1982, 2nd edn 2000; Angelo at the Waterfront, 2008; Bill Davis, Sculptor: his life and work, 2010. *Recreations:* marathon running, reading, walking, ornithology. *Address:* 15 Starke Road, Bergvliet, 7945, South Africa. *T:* (21) 7125136. *Clubs:* Owl, Western Province Cricket, Spartan Harriers Athletic (Cape Town).

**GREGORY, Prof. Alan,** FCMA; artist; Professor of Corporate Finance, University of Exeter, 1997–2016, now Emeritus; *b* Mountain Ash, S Wales, 19 March 1954; *s* of William Raymond and late Margaret Mary Gregory; *m* 2007, Julie May Whittaker. *Educ:* St Bartholomew's Grammar Sch., Newbury; London Sch. of Econs and Pol Sci. (MSc Accounting and Finance 1983). FCMA 1986. Management Accountant: British Rail, 1974–76; Green Shield Stamps, 1977; Lectr, South West London Coll., 1977–78; Senior Lecturer in Accounting: Luton Coll. of Higher Educn, 1978–83; Brighton Poly., 1983–86; Principal Lectr in Accounting and Fin., City of London Poly., 1986–89; Lectr in Accounting and Fin., Univ. of Exeter, 1989–95; Professor: of Accounting, Univ. of Glasgow, 1995–96; of Business, Univ. of Wales, Aberystwyth, 1996–97. Man. Dir, AGRF Ltd, 2013–. Mem., Competition, 2002–10. *Publications:* Valuing Companies, 1992; Strategic Valuation of Companies, 2000, 2nd edn 2002; (ed jtly) Recent Advances in Mergers and Acquisitions, vol. 1, 2000, vol. 2, 2003; contribs to peer-reviewed jls incl. Econ. Jl, Jl Business Finance & Accounting, Accounting and Business Res., British Jl Mgt, Jl Business Ethics, British Accounting Rev. *Recreations:* painting, sailing, running, ski-ing. *Address:* Xfi Centre, Streatham Campus, University of Exeter, Exeter EX4 4ST. *E:* a.gregory@exeter.ac.uk.

**GREGORY, Alan Thomas,** CBE 1984; Director, Willis Corroon (formerly Willis Faber) plc, 1987–97; *b* 13 Oct. 1925; *s* of Lloyd Thomas Gregory and Florence Abbott; *m* 1st, 1952, Pamela Douglas Scott (*d* 1986); one *s* two *d*; 2nd, 1988, Mrs Marion Newth (*née* Nash), JP (*d* 2007). *Educ:* Dulwich Coll.; St John's Coll., Cambridge (Classics). Directed into coal mining, coal face worker, 1944; Min. of Power, 1948; JSSC 1957; Chm., NATO Petroleum Planning Cttee, 1967–70; joined British Petroleum, 1971; Gen. Manager, BP Italiana, 1972–73; Dir, Govt and Public Affairs, 1975–85, and Dir, UK and Ireland Region, 1980–85, British Petroleum Co.; Chm., BP Oil Ltd, 1981–85; Director: BP Chemicals International Ltd, 1981–85; National Home Loans Corp., 1985–91. Governor, Queen Mary Coll., London Univ., 1981–87. President, Inst. of Petroleum, 1982–84. Univ. Comr, 1988–95. Churchwarden, St Mary's, Stoke D'Abernon, 1990–92. *Recreations:* books, gardening, theatre. *Address:* 10 Summerhays, Cobham, Surrey KT11 2HQ. *T:* (01932) 864457. *Club:* Travellers.

**GREGORY, Rear-Adm. Alexander Michael,** OBE 1987; Lord-Lieutenant of Dunbartonshire, since 2008; *b* 15 Dec. 1945; *s* of Vice-Adm. Sir (George) David (Archibald) Gregory, KBE, CB, DSO and Florence Eve Patricia Gregory (*née* Hill); *m* 1970, Jean Charlotte Muir; four *d*. *Educ:* Marlborough; BRNC Dartmouth. Served HM Ships Albion, Aisne, Narwhale, Otter, Warspite, Courageous, Odin (Australia), Finwhale (i/c), Repulse 1965–80; Staff, US 3rd Fleet, Hawaii, 1980–82; HMS Renown (i/c), 1982–85; Comdr 10th SM Sqdn and HMS Resolution (i/c), 1985–86; Jt Services Defence Coll., 1987; Naval Warfare, MoD, 1987–88; HMS Cumberland (i/c), 1988–91; Captain, 10th Submarine Sqdn, 1991–93; Naval Staff Duties, MoD, 1993–94; Naval Attaché, Washington, 1994–97; Flag Officer, Scotland, Northern England and NI, 1997–2000. Chief Executive: Mechanical and Metal Trades Confedn, 2001–04; Energy Industries Council, 2004–07. Dir, Mercy Corps Scotland, 2007–. Pres., Highland RFCA, 2012–. Lt, Queen's Body Guard for Scotland, Royal Company of Archers. *Recreations:* fishing, ski-ing, gardening.

**GREGORY, Lt Gen. Sir Andrew (Richard),** KBE 2016; CB 2010; Controller, SSAFA, since 2016; *b* 19 Nov. 1957; *s* of Lt Col Richard B. Gregory and Alison Gregory (*née* Egerton); *m* 1986, Sally Ann Sheard; two *s*. *Educ:* Malsis Sch.; Sedbergh Sch.; St John's Coll., Cambridge (BA Eng 1979; MA 1982). Graduate trainee/shift foreman, Metal Box Co. Ltd, 1975–81; Army: jun. officer appts, UK, NI and Germany, 1982–97; CO, 1st Regt RHA, UK and Bosnia, 1997–2000; Dir, Army Jun. Div., JSCSC, 2000–02; Comdr, RA and Dep. Comdr, 1st (UK) Armoured Div., Germany and Iraq, 2002–04; ACOS Comd and Battlespace Mgt, HQ Land Comd, 2004–06; Team Leader, HQ Land Comd and HQ Adjt Gen. Co-location Study, 2006–08; Dir Gen. Personnel and Dir Gen. Service Conditions (Army), MoD, 2008–11; Military Secretary, 2011–13; Chief of Defence People (formerly Personnel), 2013–16. Master Gunner, St James's Park, 2017–. Hon. Colonel: 106 (Yeomanry) Regt RA (V), 2008–15; 1st Regt RHA, 2012–17. Gov., Sedbergh Sch., 2016–. Trustee, On Course Foundn, 2016–. Mem., Wheelwrights' Co. *Recreations:* golf, ski-ing, being educated in art and theatre by my wife, walking an energetic black labrador.

**GREGORY, Rt Rev. Clive Malcolm;** *see* Wolverhampton, Area Bishop of.

**GREGORY, Conal Robert;** wine consultant and financial journalist; *b* 11 March 1947; *s* of Patrick George Murray Gregory and Marjorie Rose Gregory; *m* 1971, Helen Jennifer Craggs; one *s* one *d*. *Educ:* King's College Sch., Wimbledon; Univ. of Sheffield (BA Hons Mod. Hist. and Pol Theory and Instns, 1968). Master of Wine by examination, Vintners' Co., 1979. Manager, Saccone & Speed Vintage Cellar Club, 1971–73; Wine Buyer, Reckitt & Colman, 1973–77; Editor, Internat. Wine and Food Soc.'s Jl, 1980–83; Dir, Standard Fireworks Ltd, 1987–92; Chm., Internat. Wine and Spirit Competition Ltd, 1997–98; Dir, Jackson Prentice Ltd, 1999–2004. Norfolk County Councillor, Thorpe Div., 1977–81; Vice-Pres., Norwich Jun. Chamber of Commerce, 1975–76; Mem., E Anglia Tourist Bd, 1979–81. Chairman: Norwich N Cons. Assoc., 1980–82; Norwich CPC, 1978–81; Vice-Chm., Eastern Area CPC, 1980–83; Member: Cons. Eastern Area Agric. Cttee, 1975–79; Cons. Provincial Council, Eastern Area, 1978–83; Chm. and Founder, Bow Gp of E Anglia, 1975–82; Nat. Vice-Chm., Bow Gp, 1976–77. MP (C) York, 1983–92. Hon. Treas., British/Cyprus CPA Gp, 1987–92; Sec., UK-Manx Parly Gp, 1987–92; Chm., Cons. Parly Food and Drinks Industries Cttee, 1989–92 (Vice-Chm., 1985–89); Vice-Chairman: Cons. Parly Tourism Cttee, 1985–92; Cons. Parly Transport Cttee, 1987–89 and 1990–92 (Sec., 1983–87); All Party Parly Hospice Gp, 1990–92; All Party Parly Tourism Cttee, 1991–92 (Sec., 1983–91); Mem. Cttee, British Atlantic Gp of Young Politicians, 1983–92 (Chm., 1988–89; Pres., 1989–92); Pres., York Young Conservatives, 1982–93; Vice-Pres., York Br., UNA, 1983–92. Parliamentary Consultant: The Market Res. Soc., 1984–91; Consort Hotels Ltd, 1984–91; Consultant: Andry Montgomery Ltd, 1979–97; Jackson Nugent Vintners Ltd, 1997–. Fellow, Industry and Parlt Trust, 1984–87. Private Member's Bills on consumer safety, 1985, on smoke alarms, 1991, on cheque fraud, 1992. Member: Wymondham Abbey PCC, 1982–83; Humbleyard Deanery Synod, 1982–83; High Steward's Cttee, York Minster Fund, 1983–89; York Archaeol Trust, 1983–; York Georgian Soc., 1982–92, 2002–; York Civic Trust, 1982–92, 2007–18; 20th/21st Century British Art Fair Council, 1992–; ESU, 1994–2014; Gideons Internat., 2017–. Governor, Heartsease Sch., Norwich, 1977–83; Member, Court of Governors: Univ. of Sheffield, 1981–90; Univ. of York, 1983–92; Univ. of Hull, 1983–92. Patron, Selby Abbot's Sixth Heritage Trust, 2015–. Sen. Judge, Internat. Wine Challenge, 2003–17. Wine Corresp., Catering Times, 1979–83. Personal Finance Regional Journalist of the Year: Bradford & Bingley, 2007; BIBA, 2007, 2009; Assoc. of Investment Cos, 2008, 2012, 2016, 2018; Headlinemoney Award, 2015. *Publications:* (with W. Knock) Beers of Britain, 1975; (with R. A. Adley) A Policy for Tourism?, 1977; A Caterer's Guide to Drinks, 1979; (with M. Shersby and A. McCurley) Food for a Healthy Britain, 1987; (contrib.) The Dictionary of Art, 1996; The Cognac Companion, 1997; contribs to The Times, Scotsman, Yorkshire Post, etc. *Address:* c/o Jackson Nugent Vintners Ltd, 30 Homefield Road, Wimbledon Village, SW19 4QF.

**GREGORY, David St John Thomas;** Chairman, Scottish Aquaculture Innovation Centre, since 2018; *b* London, 27 Aug. 1953; *s* of Francis Gregory and Margaret Gregory; *m* 1975, Susan Barker; two *s* one *d*. *Educ:* Brunel Univ. (BTech Hons Applied Chem. 1975); North London Coll. (Dip. Envmtl Health 1978); Slough Coll. (Dip. Mgt Studies 1981). FIFST 2002; CSci 2004. Tech. Dir (Foods), Marks & Spencer plc, 1983–2009. Chairman: Assured Food Standards Ltd, 2009–15; Acoura Ltd, 2015–18; non-executive Director: 2 Sisters Food Gp, Boparan Hldgs Ltd, 2010–; BRC Trading Ltd, 2012–16. Mem., BBSRC, 2010–18. Chm., Trustees, Brit. Nutrition Foundn, 2012–15 (Vice Chm., 2007–12); Trustee, Inst. of Food Res., Norwich, 2006–15. Pres., Inst. of Food Sci. and Technol., 2017–. Vis. Prof., Centre for Food Security, Univ. of Reading, 2010–. *Recreations:* fine food and wine, cycling, photography, family. *E:* dstgregory@googlemail.com.

**GREGORY, Janice;** Member (Lab) Ogmore, National Assembly for Wales, 1999–2016; *b* 10 Jan. 1955; *d* of Sir Raymond Powell, MP and of Marion Grace (*née* Evans); *m* 1977, Michael Gregory; two *d*. Parly Asst to Sir Raymond Powell, MP, 1991–99. National Assembly for Wales: Chair: Social Justice and Regeneration Cttee, 2003–07; Communities and Culture Cttee, 2007–09; Govt Chief Whip, 2009–16. Member: USDAW, 1979; Fabian Soc., 1980; Co-op. Party, 1980; Unite the Union (TGWU, 1997; Amicus, 2002).

**GREGORY, Prof. Kenneth John,** CBE 2007; PhD, DSc; CGeog; FBSG; Warden, Goldsmiths' College, University of London, 1992–98, now Professor Emeritus and Hon. Fellow; *b* 23 March 1938; *s* of Frederick Arthur Gregory and Marion Gregory; *m* Margaret Christine Wilmot; one *s* two *d*. *Educ:* University College London (BSc Special 1959; PhD 1962; DSc 1982; Fellow 1999). University of Exeter: Lectr in Geography, 1962–72; Reader in Physical Geography, 1972–76; University of Southampton: Prof. of Geography, 1976–92; Head of Geography Dept, 1978–83; Dean of Science, 1984–87; Dep. Vice-Chancellor, 1988–92; Vis. Prof., 1998–. Hon. Res. Fellow, UCL, 1993–; Hon. Prof., Univ. of Birmingham, 1997–2008; Leverhulme Emeritus Fellow, 1998–2001. Vis. Lectr, Univ. of New England, NSW, 1975; Distinguished Visiting Professor, 1987: Univ. Kebangsaan; Arizona State Univ.; Snyder Lectr, Univ. of Toronto, 1990. President: Commn on Global Continental Palaeohydrology, Internat. Assoc. on Union for Quaternary Res., 1999–2004 (Vice-Pres., 1992); British Soc. for Geomorphology, 2009–14. Trustee, Horniman Mus. and Gardens, 1997–2003. Gov., Southampton Solent Univ. (formerly Southampton Inst.), 1998–2007 (Vice Chm., Bd of Govs, 1999–2007); Mem. Council, Brunel Univ., 2010–18 (Dep. Chm., 2015–18). For. Mem., Polish Acad. of Arts and Scis, 1995. Freeman, City of London, 1997; Liveryman, Goldsmiths' Co., 1998– (Freeman, 1997; Mem., Educn Cttee, 1999–2006). FBSG 2013. Hon. Fellow, Goldsmiths' Coll., 1998. Hon. FRGS 2015. Hon. DSc: Southampton, 1997; Greenwich, 1997; Brunel, 2019; DUniv Southampton Solent, 2008. Back Award, 1980, Founder's Medal, 1993, RGS; Linton Award, British Geomorphological Res. Gp, 1999; Scottish Geographical Medal, RSGS, 2000. *Publications:* (with A. H. Shorter and W. L. D. Ravenhill) Southwest England, 1969; (with D. E. Walling) Drainage Basin Form and Process, 1973; (jtly) An Advanced Geography of the British Isles, 1974; (with E. Derbyshire and J. R. Hails) Geomorphological Processes, 1979; The Yellow River, 1980; The Nature of Physical Geography, 1985 (trans. Russian and Portuguese); (ed jtly) The Encyclopedic Dictionary of Physical Geography, 1985; (ed) Energetics of Physical Environment, 1987; (ed jtly) Human Activity and Environmental Processes, 1987; (ed jtly) Palaeohydrology in Practice, 1987; (ed jtly) Horizons in Physical Geography, 1988; (ed) The Earth's Natural Forces, 1990; (ed) The Guinness Guide to the Restless Earth, 1991; (ed jtly) Temperate Palaeohydrology, 1991; (ed jtly) Global Continental Palaeohydrology, 1995; (ed jtly) Global Continental Changes: the context of palaeohydrology, 1996; (ed jtly) Evaluating Teacher Quality in High Education, 1996; (ed) Geological Conservation Review Fluvial Geomorphology of Great Britain, 1997; (ed jtly) Palaeohydrology and Environmental Change, 1998; The Changing Nature of Physical Geography, 2000; (ed jtly) Palaeohydrology: understanding global change, 2003; (with P. W. Downs) River Channel Management, 2004; (ed) Physical Geography, 4 vols, 2005; (jtly) Environmental Sciences: a student's companion, 2008; The Earth's Land Surface, 2010; (ed jtly) The Sage Handbook of Geomorphology, 2011; (with J. Lewin) Basics of Geomorphology: the key concepts, 2014. *Recreations:* travel, gardening, reading. *Address:* 9 Poltimore Road, Guildford, Surrey GU2 7PT. *E:* k.j.gregory@ntlworld.com.

**GREGORY, Sir Michael (John),** Kt 2011; CBE 2003; FREng; Professor, Head, Manufacturing and Management Division, Department of Engineering, 1995–2015, and Founding Head, Institute for Manufacturing, University of Cambridge, 1998–2015; Fellow, Churchill College, Cambridge, 1985–2015, now Emeritus. *Educ:* MA Cantab. Lectr, Engrg Dept, then Prof. of Manufg Engrg, 1995–2015, Univ. of Cambridge; Exec. Dir, Cambridge MIT Inst., 2005–08. Springer Vis. Prof., Univ. of Calif, Berkeley, 2008–09. Chair, Babbage Policy Forum, 2015–. Pres., Cambridge Soc. for Application of Res., 2017–. Trustee, Royal Acad. of Engrg, 2013–17. FREng 2011. *Address:* Churchill College, Cambridge CB3 0DS.

**GREGORY, Prof. Peter John,** PhD; FRSB, FRASE, FCIHort; Professor of Global Food Security, University of Reading, 2011–16, now Emeritus; Research Advisor, Crops for the Future, Malaysia, since 2016; *b* 19 July 1951; *s* of Joseph Henry Gregory and June Rosamond Gregory; *m* 1973, Jane Sandra Crump; two *s*. *Educ:* Chatham House Grammar Sch.; Univ. of Reading (BSc Soil Sci.); Univ. of Nottingham (PhD Soil Sci. 1977). FRSB (FIBiol 1994). Lectr, Univ. of Reading, 1980–89; Principal Res. Scientist, CSIRO Div. of Plant Industry, Australia, 1990–93; University of Reading: Prof. of Soil Sci., 1994–2005; Pro-Vice-Chancellor, 1998–2003, 2004–05; Dir, Scottish Crop Res. Inst., 2005–11; Chief Exec., East Malling Research, 2011–15. Vis. Scientist, Forschungszentrum, Julich, 2016–18. Chair, Global Envmtl Change and Food Systems, 2001–06. Chairman: UK Adv. Cttee on Novel Foods and Processes, 2009–; Sci. Cttee, RHS, 2010– (Mem. Council, 2010–); Recommended List Bd, Agric. and Hort. Develt Bd Cereals and Oilseeds, 2014–; Jt Chm., TempAg Internat. Res. Prog., 2014–17; Member: Scottish Sci. Adv. Council, 2010–11; Nutrition Cttee Rank Prize Funds, 2011–. Pres., Internat. Soc. of Root Res., 2009–18. Hon. Res. Fellow, Rothamsted Res., 2013–16. FRASE 2004; FCIHort 2014; ARAgS 2015. *Publications:* (ed jtly) Root Development and Function, 1987; (ed jtly) Soils in the Urban Environment, 1991; (ed jtly) Crop Production on Duplex Soils, 1992; (ed jtly) Land Resources: on the edge of the Malthusian precipice?, 1997; (ed jtly) Science in the Garden, 2002, 3rd edn 2016; Plant Roots: growth, activity and interactions with soil, 2006; (ed jtly) Soil Conditions and Plant Growth, 2013; (ed jtly) Climate Change Impact and Adaptation in Agricultural Systems, 2014; numerous scientific papers on soil/plant interactions in learned jls and books. *Recreations:* gardening, folk dancing, fishing. *Address:* School of Agriculture, Policy and Development, University of Reading, Reading RG6 6AR.

**GREGORY, Peter Joseph John; His Honour Judge Peter Gregory;** a Circuit Judge, since 2015; a Judge, Court of Protection, since 2017; *b* Belfast, 18 Sept. 1958; *s* of Patrick Brian Gregory and Sheila Gregory (*née* Kennedy); *m* 1982, Jennifer Jones; four *s* one *d*. *Educ:* St MacNissi's Coll., Garron Tower; Univ. of Manchester (LLB Hons 1981). Called to the Bar, Gray's Inn, 1982; a Recorder, 2002–15; Jun. Treasury Counsel (Civil), 2007–15. *Publications:* (contrib.) Occupational Illness Litigation, 2002. *Recreations:* football, music, reading, beer. *Address:* Liverpool Civil and Family Court, 35 Vernon Street, Liverpool L2 2BX. *T:* (0151) 296 2200.

**GREGORY, Peter Roland;** JP; Director, Personnel, Management and Business Services, subsequently Personnel and Accommodation, National Assembly for Wales, 2000–03; *b* 7 Oct. 1946; *s* of Tom and Ruby Gregory; *m* 1978, Frances Margaret Hogan (marr. diss. 2016); *m* 2018, Jean Elizabeth Brading. *Educ:* Sexey's Grammar Sch., Blackford, Som; University College Swansea (BA Hons 1968); Manchester Univ. (PhD 1972). Joined Welsh Office, 1971; Private Sec. to Perm. Sec., 1974–75; Principal, 1976; Asst Sec., 1982; Under Sec., Transport, Planning and Envmt Gp, 1990–94; Dir, Health Dept, 1994–99; Dir, NHS Wales, 1999–2000. JP Somerset, 2006. *Recreations:* walking, theatre, music. *Address:* 6 Tanyard, Broadway, Ilminster, Somerset TA19 9JT.

**GREGORY, His Honour Philip John;** a Circuit Judge, 2004–19; *b* 13 Jan. 1953; *s* of late John Godfrey Gregory and Winifred Gregory; *m* 1st, 1979, Deborah Ann (*née* Lane) (*d* 2012); one *s* two *d*; 2nd, 2013, Rosemary (*née* Young). *Educ:* Moseley Grammar Sch., Birmingham; Pembroke Coll., Oxford (MA). Called to the Bar, Middle Temple, 1975; in practice as barrister, specialising in personal injury, 1975–2004; Asst Recorder, 1998–2000, Recorder, 2000–04. *Recreations:* golf, tennis, reading.

**GREGORY, Philip William,** MBE 2008; Chairman, United Bristol Healthcare NHS Trust, 1998–2006; *b* 30 Sept. 1947; *s* of late Thomas Douglas Gregory and Winifred (*née* Brooks); partner, Rosemary Clarke. *Educ:* Beaminster Comprehensive Sch., Dorset; Southampton Coll. of Technology (Dip. Municipal Admin). Regl Official, NALGO, 1974–82; SW Regl Sec., TUC, 1982–93. Member: Dorset AHA, 1974–79; Somerset AHA, 1979–91. Member Board: South West Electricity, 1985–89; Bristol Develt Corp., 1988–96; DTI Develt Bd for SW, 1988–97; SW Regl Chm., Nat. Training Awards, 1993–97; Chm., Community Foundn Network, 1995–2000; Member: Employment Tribunal, 1975–; Bristol Initiative, 1989–2006. Mem. (Lab Co-op), Lockleaze Ward, Bristol CC, 1992–99. Treas., Lockleaze Neighbourhood Trust, 1996–2006. Sec., Brixham CC, 2012–. Vice Chm. Govs, Torbay Sch., 2013–17; Chm. Govs, Brunel Acad., 2018–. *Recreations:* gardening, walking, watching cricket (Somerset), scoring for cricket team (Brixham). *Address:* 2 Oxford Lane, Brixham, Devon TQ5 8PP.

**GREGORY, Dr Philippa;** author; *b* 9 Jan. 1954; *d* of Arthur Gregory and Elaine Gregory (*née* Wedd); *m* Anthony Mason; one *s* one *d*. *Educ:* Univ. of Sussex (BA 1979); Univ. of Edinburgh (MLitt; PhD 1984). Newspaper journalist, 1971–75; BBC Radio journalist, 1975–; book reviewer, TV presenter, broadcaster and playwright, 1986–. Founder, Gardens for The Gambia, 1993. *Publications:* Wideacre, 1986; The Favoured Child, 1988; Meridon, 1990; Mrs Hartley and the Growth Centre, 1991; The Wise Woman, 1992; Fallen Skies, 1994; The Little House, 1995; A Respectable Trade, 1997 (televised); Earthly Joys, 1999; Virgin Earth, 2000; The Other Boleyn Girl, 2001 (televised 2003, filmed 2008); The Queen's Fool, 2003; The Virgin's Lover, 2004; The Constant Princess, 2005; The Boleyn Inheritance, 2006; The Other Queen, 2008; The White Queen, 2009 (televised, 2013); The Red Queen, 2010; The Lady of the Rivers, 2011; (jtly) The Women of the Cousins' War, 2011; Changeling, 2012; The Kingmaker's Daughter, 2012; Stormbringers, 2013; The White Princess, 2013; The King's Curse, 2014; The Taming of the Queen, 2015; Three Sisters, Three Queens, 2016; The Last Tudor, 2017; Dark Tracks, 2018; Tidelands, 2019. *Recreations:* child-raising (2 children, 5 step-children), riding, gardening, ski-ing, hiking, loafing. *Address:* c/o Levon Publishing Ltd, 20 Harcourt Street, Dublin 2, DO2 PF99, Ireland.

**GREGORY, Richard John,** OBE 2004; Senior Advisor, CYGB plc, since 2017; Hon. Yorkshire Bank Chair, since 2017 (Yorkshire Bank Chair, 2004–17); *b* 18 Aug. 1954; *s* of John and Joan Gregory. Trainee, Doncaster Gazette, 1972–75; gen. reporter, Doncaster Evening Post, 1976; labour corresp. and industrial corresp., Sheffield Morning Telegraph, 1977–79; News Ed., Granada TV, 1979–81; Yorkshire Television: News Ed., 1981–82;

Producer, 1982–84; Ed., Calendar, 1984–89; Hd of News, 1989–92; Controller, 1992–93; Dir, Regl Progs, 1993–95; Dir of Broadcasting, 1995; Man. Dir, Broadcasting, Yorkshire Tyne Tees, 1996–97; Man. Dir, 1997–2002. Non-executive Director: Yorkshire Bank, 2000–17; Clydesdale Bank plc, 2000–17 (Sen. Ind. Dir and Chair, Risk Cttee, 2012–17); Imagesound plc, 2002–10 (Chm., 2002–05; Sen. Ind. non-exec. Dir, 2005–); Sheffield University Enterprises Ltd, 2005–07; Chm., Together Personal Finance Ltd, 2019–. Member: Bd, BITC, 2001–08 (Chm., Yorks and Humber Regl Leadership Team, 2001–08); Yorkshire Forward (formerly Yorks and Humber Regl Develt Agency), 1998–2004 (Dep. Chm., 1999–2004); Chairman: Yorks Initiative, 1997–2001; Yorkshire Innovation (formerly Yorkshire Science), 2006–11; Science City York, 2007–13; Chair, Yorks Internat. Business Convention, 1999–2003. Chair, Chesterfield Royal Hosp. NHS Foundn Trust, 2006–15; Interim Chm., Derbyshire Healthcare NHS Foundn Trust, 2015–16; Mem. Bd, Foundn Trust Network, 2010–13; Mem., Strategic Adv. Bd, NHS Leadership Acad., 2013–15. Mem., Yorkshire Culture (formerly Yorks Regl Cultural Consortium), 2000–04. Mem. Council, Inst. for Employment Studies, 2003–05. Chm., Sheffield Hallam Univ., 1999–2003 (Gov., 1992–2003). Trustee Dir, Sheffield Galls and Mus Trust, 2002–08. Hon. DLit: Bradford, 1999; Sheffield Hallam, 2003. *Recreations:* Peak District, Kefalonia.

**GREGORY, Roger Michael;** Deputy Receiver for the Metropolitan Police, 1989–94, retired; *b* 1 June 1939; *s* of Walter James Gregory and Catherine Emma Gregory (*née* Regan); *m* 1961, Johanna Margaret O'Rourke; five *s* two *d*; partner, Lorraine Maureen Curry. *Educ:* Gillingham (Kent) Grammar Sch.; Univ. of Herts (BA Hons 2006). Joined Metropolitan Police Civil Staff, 1957; Hd of Operations, Police National Computer Unit, 1976; Dep. Dir of Finance, Metropolitan Police, 1981; Dir of Computing, Metropolitan Police, 1983. *Recreations:* cricket, bridge, gentle gardening. *Address:* Willow Lodge, Poplar Close, Leighton Buzzard, Beds LU7 3BS.

**GREGORY-HOOD, Peter Charles Freeman;** HM Diplomatic Service, retired; *b* 12 Dec. 1943; *s* of late Col A. M. H. Gregory-Hood, OBE, MC and Diana, *d* of Sir John Gilmour, 2nd Bt (she *m* 2nd, Sir John Beith, KCMG); *m* 1966, Camilla Bethell (*d* 2006); three *d. Educ:* Summerfields, St Leonard's; Eton Coll.; Aix-en-Provence Univ.; Trinity Coll., Cambridge (BA Econs and Sociol.); Univ. of Buckingham (MA Biography 2003). Joined FCO, 1965: Third Sec., Dakar, 1967–69; Third, later Second Sec., Tel Aviv, 1969–71; First Secretary: FCO, 1972–76; (Commercial), Paris, 1976–80; FCO, 1980–86; (Inf.), New Delhi, 1986–90; Counsellor and Consul-Gen., Casablanca, 1990–95; Dep. High Comr, Colombo, 1995–98. *Recreations:* tennis, golf, swimming, theatre. *Address:* Loxley Hall, Loxley, Warwick CV35 9JP. *Clubs:* White's, Royal Over-Seas League; Rotary (Stratford-upon-Avon); Tadmarton Heath Golf.

**GREGSON, Charles Henry;** Chairman, Art UK (formerly Public Catalogue Foundation), since 2011 (Trustee, 2002–11); *b* 7 June 1947; *s* of Geoffrey and Anne Gregson; *m* 1972, Caroline Blake; two *s. Educ:* Harrow; Trinity Hall, Cambridge (MA). Solicitor; Clifford-Turner & Co., 1970–74; Gp Solicitor and Company Sec., Mills & Allen Internat. plc, later MAI plc, subseq. United Business Media, 1974–77, Dir, 1984–2007; Chief Executive: Shepperton Studios Ltd, 1975–79; Harlow Butler/Garban Gp, 1980–98; exec. Chm., 1998–2001, non-exec. Chm., 2001–, NEX Gp plc (formerly Garban plc, then Garban-Intercapital plc, subseq. ICAP plc); CEO, 2005–09, Chm., 2010–18, PR Newswire. Non-executive Director: International Personal Finance plc, 2007–12; Caledonia Investments plc, 2009–; Non Standard Finance plc, 2015– (Chm., 2017–); Chairman: CPPGroup plc (formerly CPP plc), 2010–14; St James's Place plc, 2011–13 (Dir, 2010–13). *Recreations:* deerstalking, gardening, National Hunt racing. *Address:* Hope House, The Haven, Billingshurst RH14 9BN. *T:* (01403) 822066. *Club:* Turf.

**GREGSON, David John;** Chairman, Lawn Tennis Association, 2013–18; *b* Walton-on-Thames, 28 June 1956; *s* of Bill and Rosalind Gregson; *m* 1987, Renée Cambier van Nooten; one *s* two *d. Educ:* Edinburgh Acad.; St Catharine's Coll., Cambridge (BA Hons Natural Scis 1978); Manchester Business Sch. (MBA 1983). Prodn Controller, Metal Box (Wrexham), 1979–81; Venture Capital Fund Manager, Dartington & Co., 1983–85; Dir, Globe Investment Trust, 1985–90; Phoenix Equity Partners: Co-founder, 1991; Chair, 2001–12; Sen. Advr, 2012–13. Chairman: Precise Media Gp, 2006–14; Karma Gp, 2015–16; Dir, Letts Filofax, 2007–13. Adviser, Carter Review: of Legal Aid, 2006; of Prison Service in England and Wales, 2008. Chair, Mayor's 2012 Olympic Legacy Bd of Advrs, 2008–09; Dir, Olympic Park Legacy Co., later London Legacy Develt Corp., 2009–. Member: Assoc. of British Sch., Netherlands, 2008–15; Adv. Bd (formerly Steering Bd Cttee), Apeldoorn: British-Dutch Dialogue, 2010–; Green Investment Bank Adv. Gp, 2011–12; Adv. Bd, Educn Endowment Foundn, 2011–15. Chair, Jane Goodall Inst. (UK), 2002–06. Chm., Crime Reduction Initiatives, 2010–15; Trustee: WWF-UK, 2006–12; Climate Gp, 2006–11; Advr, Sutton Trust, 2006–. *Recreations:* tennis, golf, ski-ing, family. *Clubs:* Lansdowne, Mosimann's; Royal Wimbledon Golf, Koninklijke Haagsche Golf and Country; Haagsche Lawn Tennis Leimonias.

**GREGSON, Prof. Edward;** composer; Principal, Royal Northern College of Music, Manchester, 1996–2008; *b* 23 July 1945; *s* of Edward Gregson and May Elizabeth (*née* Eaves); *m* 1967, Susan Carole Smith; two *s. Educ:* Manchester Central Grammar Sch.; Royal Academy of Music (GRSM, LRAM); Goldsmiths' Coll., Univ. of London (BMus Hons). Lectr in Music, Rachel McMillan Coll., London, 1970–76; Sen. Lectr, 1976–89, Reader, 1989–94, and Prof. of Music, 1994–96, Goldsmiths' Coll., Univ. of London. Composer in Assoc., Black Dyke Band, 2016; Composer in Residence, Presteign Fest., 2017. Hon. Prof. of Music, Univ. of Manchester, 1996. Mem., Music Industry Forum, DCMS, 1998–2001; Bd Mem., Cultural Consortium Northwest, 2003–04; Chm., Conservatoires UK, 2004–08. Vice-Chm., Composers' Guild, 1976–78; Chm., Assoc. of Professional Composers, 1989–91; Director: PRS, 1995–2010, 2012–; Associated Bd of Royal Schs of Music, 1996–2008; Hallé Orch., 1998–2006. Gov. and Feoffee, Chetham's Sch. of Music, 1996–. Trustee: Nat. Foundn for Youth Music, 1999–2003; PRS Foundn, 2009–. Companion, RNCM, 2008. Fellow: Dartington Coll. of Arts, 1997; Leeds Coll. of Music, 2008. FRAM 1990; FRNCM 1998; Hon. FLCM 1999; FRCM 2000. Hon. DMus: Sunderland, 1996; Lancaster, 2006; Manchester, 2008; Chester, 2009; Hon. DArts Manchester Metropolitan, 2003; DUniv UCE, 2007. *Compositions include:* Oboe Sonata, 1965; Brass Quintet, 1967; Music for Chamber Orchestra, 1968; Horn Concerto, 1971; Essay for Brass Band, 1971; Tuba Concerto, 1976; Music for the York Cycle of Mystery Plays, 1976 and 1980; Connotations for Brass Band, 1977; Metamorphoses, 1979; Trombone Concerto, 1979; Trumpet Concerto, 1983; Piano Sonata in one movement, 1983; Contrasts for orchestra, 1983, revised 2001 as Contrasts—a concerto for orch.; Dances and Arias, 1984; Festivo, 1985; Missa Brevis Pacem, 1988; RSC History Play Cycles: Plantagenets Trilogy, 1988–89; Henry IV Parts 1 and 2, 1990–91; Celebration, 1991; Of Men and Mountains, 1991; The Sword and the Crown, 1991; Blazon, 1992; Clarinet Concerto, 1994; Concerto for Piano and Wind, 1995; The Kings Go Forth, 1996; Stepping Out, 1996; A Welcome Ode, 1997; …And the Seven Trumpets, 1998; Three Matisse Impressions, 1998; The Dance, forever the Dance, 1999; Violin Concerto, 2000; The Trumpets of the Angels, 2000, new performing edn 2016; An Age of Kings, 2004; Shadow of Paradise, for Oboe and Percussion, 2005; Saxophone Concerto, 2006; A Song for Chris - concerto for cello and chamber orchestra, 2007; Rococo Variations, 2008; Goddess, for string orchestra, 2009; Aztec Dances for recorder (or flute) and piano, 2010; Dream Song for large orch., 2010; Tributes for clarinet and piano, 2010; An Album for my Friends (piano), 2011; Triptych for solo violin, 2011; Symphony in two movements for brass band, 2012; Of Distant Memories (for brass band), 2013; Concerto for flute and ensemble, 2013; Three John Donne Settings for choir, 2013; String Quartet, 2014; Symphony in two movements (for symphonic brass and percussion), 2015; Cornet Concerto, 2016; Four Etudes (for brass band), 2016; Le Jardin à Giverny (cor anglais and string quartet), 2016; The Sad Tale of Barbara Allen (for upper voices and piano, and for SATB and piano), 2017; String Quartet no 2, 2017; Blow, blow, thou Winter Wind (SATB), 2017; Fanfare for a New Era (symphonic brass and percussion), 2017; Euphonium Concerto, 2018; The Salamander and the Moonraker (An Adventure Story in Music for narrator, children's choir and orchestra), 2018; Music of the Angels (symphonic brass and percussion), 2019; A Vision of Paradise (oboe concerto), 2020; The World Rejoicing (brass band), 2020; commns from orchestras incl. English Chamber, Bournemouth Symphony, Royal Liverpool, Halle and BBC Philharmonic; many broadcasts (mainly BBC Radio 3) and recordings. *Publications:* (contrib.) Composers on the Nine, 2011; music articles in professional jls incl. Musical Opinion, BBC Music Mag., Classical Music, Brass Band World. *Recreations:* walking, wine, watching sport. *Address:* c/o Novello Publishing Ltd, 14/15 Berners Street, W1T 3LJ. *E:* promotion@musicsales.co.uk. *W:* www.edwardgregson.com.

**GREGSON, Sir Peter (John),** Kt 2011; FREng, FIAE; Chief Executive and Vice-Chancellor, Cranfield University, since 2013; *b* 3 Nov. 1957; *s* of late Howard Davenport Gregson and of Susan Katharine Gregson (*née* Lunn); *m* 1983, Rachael Kathleen McClaughry; three *d. Educ:* Imperial Coll., London (BSc Eng 1980 (Bessemer Medal); PhD 1983 (Matthey Prize, 2000)). CEng 1983, FREng 2000; FIMMM (FIM 1998); FIEI 2005; MRIA 2007; FIAE 2007; CCMI 2007. University of Southampton: Lectr in Engrg Materials, 1983–90; Sen. Lectr, 1990–92; Reader, 1992–95; Prof. of Aerospace Materials, 1995–2004; Hd, Engrg Materials, 1995–99; Dir of Res., Faculty of Engrg and Applied Sci., 1993–99; Dep. Hd, Sch. of Engrg Scis, 1999–2000; Dep. Vice-Chancellor, 2000–04; Pres. and Vice-Chancellor, QUB, 2004–13. Academic Director: Luxfer Advanced Technol. Centre, 1999–2001; Defence and Aerospace Res. Partnership in Advanced Metallic Airframes, 1999–2004; DePuy Internat. Univ. Technol. Partnership, 2000–04. Director: Southampton Innovations Ltd, 2000–04; Southampton Asset Mgt Ltd, 2000–04; Photonic Innovations Ltd, 2000–04; Univ. of Southampton Hldgs Ltd, 2000–04; SULIS Innovations, 2002–04; NI Sci. Park, 2004–13; QUBIS Ltd, 2004–13; QUB Bookshop, 2004–13; Rolls Royce Gp plc, 2007–12; Cranfield Ventures Ltd, 2013–; Chm., SETsquared, 2002–04. Sen. Res. Fellow, DERA, 1997–2001; Consultant: Johnson & Johnson/DePuy Internat., 1986–2004; Alcan Internat., 1989–93; Lockheed Martin UK, 2016–18. Mem., DTI/OST Materials Foresight Panel, 1997–99. Mem. Council, CCLRC, 2003–07. Institute of Materials: Chairman: Alloy Design Cttee, 1991–92; Metals Sci. Cttee, 1992–93; Materials Strategy Commn, 1997–99; Milton Keynes Futures 2050 Commn, 2015–16. Mem. Council, Royal Acad. Engrg, 2005–08. EPSRC: Member: Structural Materials Coll., 1994–2005; Engrg Rev. Panel, 1999; User Panel, 2005–07; Chm., Postgrad. Trng Prog. Panel, 2000. Dir, ACU, 2010–14; Sen. Advr, Chongqing Acad. of Sci. and Technol., 2011–. Trustee: Southampton Univ. Develt Trust, 2000–04; Wessex Med. Trust, 2001–04; Windsor Leadership Trust, 2002–. Associate Ed., Jl Materials Letters, 1990–2004. Chm., St Albans Internat. Organ Fest., 2016–18. FCGI 2006. DL Belfast 2007–13. Hon. DSc: Bengal Engrg and Science Univ., 2008; NUI, 2008; Southampton, 2009; Soka, 2010; QUB, 2014. Donald Julius Groen Prize, IMechE, 1994; Rosenhain Medal and Prize, Inst. Materials, 1996; Flax Trust Award, 2010. *Publications:* numerous scientific papers in learned jls, on engrg performance of aerospace materials and computational and experimental modelling of load bearing med. devices. *Recreations:* opera, gardening, tennis, sailing. *Address:* Cranfield University, Cranfield, Beds MK43 0AL. *T:* (01234) 754014. *Club:* Athenæum.

**GREIDER, Prof. Carol W,** PhD; Daniel Nathans Professor and Director, Department of Molecular Biology and Genetics, since 2003, and Professor of Oncology, since 2001, Johns Hopkins University School of Medicine; *b* San Diego, Calif, 15 April 1961; *d* of Kenneth Randolph Greider and Jean Foley Greider; *m* (marr. diss.); one *s* one *d. Educ:* Univ. of California, Santa Barbara (Regents Scholar 1981; BA Biol. 1983); Univ. of California, Berkeley (PhD Molecular Biol. 1987). Cold Spring Harbor Fellow, 1988–90; Cold Spring Harbor Laboratory: Asst Investigator, 1990–92; Associate Investigator, 1992–94; Investigator, 1994–97; Johns Hopkins University School of Medicine: Associate Prof. of Molecular Biol. and Genetics, 1997–99; Prof. of Molecular Biol. and Genetics, 1999–2003. Member: Inst. of Medicine, 2010–; Royal Acad. of Medicine of Catalonia, 2012–; Alpha Omega Honor Med. Soc., 2013–. MNAS 2003; FAAAS 2003; Fellow: Amer. Acad. of Arts and Scis, 2003; Amer. Acad. of Microbiol. 2004. (Jtly) Wiley Prize in Biomed. Scis, Wiley Foundn, 2006; Dickson Prize in Medicine, Univ. of Pittsburgh, 2007; (jtly) Paul Ehrlich and Ludwig Darmstaedter Prize, 2009; (jtly) Nobel Prize in Physiology or Medicine, 2009. *Publications:* (jtly) Molecular Biology: principles of genome function, 2010; contrib. chapters in books; articles in learned jls. *Address:* Department of Molecular Biology and Genetics, Johns Hopkins University School of Medicine, 603 PCTB, 725 N. Wolfe Street, Baltimore, MD 21205, USA. *T:* (410) 6146506, *Fax:* (410) 9550831. *E:* cgreider@jhmi.edu.

**GREIG, Geordie Carron;** Editor, Daily Mail, since 2018; Director: Mail Newspapers, since 2012; London Evening Standard and Independent Print Ltd, since 2012; *b* 16 Dec. 1960; *s* of Sir (Henry Louis) Carron Greig, KCVO, CBE and of Monica Kathleen Greig; *m* 1995, Kathryn Elizabeth Terry; one *s* twin *d. Educ:* Eton Coll.; St Peter's Coll., Oxford (MA English Lit. and Lang.). Reporter: South East London and Kentish Mercury, 1981–83; Daily Mail, 1984–85; Today, 1985–87; Sunday Times: Reporter, 1987–89; Arts Corresp., 1989–91; NY Corresp., 1991–95; Literary Editor, 1995–99; Editor: Tatler, 1999–2009; London Evening Standard (formerly Evening Standard), 2009–10; Edtl Dir, London Evening Standard, Independent, Independent on Sunday and i, 2010–12; Ed., Mail on Sunday, 2012–18. Trustee: Raisa Gorbachev Foundn, 2006–12; Friends of Nat. Libraries, 2013– (Chm., 2018–); Quintessentially Foundn, 2016–. FRSA 2005. *Publications:* Louis and the Prince, 1999; Breakfast with Lucian, 2013. *Address:* Daily Mail, Northcliffe House, 2 Derry Street, W8 5TT.

**GREIG, Kenneth Muir,** PhD; Head Master, Brighton College Al Ain, UAE, since 2016; *b* 30 March 1960; *s* of Walter and Margaret Greig; *m* 1st, 1987, Josephine Claire Berenice Taylor (marr. diss. 2017); one *s* one *d*; 2nd, 2018, Hacer Gülru Kutluk. *Educ:* George Heriot's Sch., Edinburgh; Worcester Coll., Oxford (BA 1981, MA); Univ. of Edinburgh (PhD 1984). Exploration geologist, BP, 1984–87; Maths Teacher and Housemaster, Christ's Hosp., 1987–93; Hd of Maths and Dir of Studies, Dollar Acad., 1993–2000; Headmaster, Pangbourne Coll., 2000–05; Rector, Hutchesons' Grammar Sch., Glasgow, 2005–16. *Recreations:* natural history, beachcombing, sea fishing, music, watching sport. *Address:* Brighton College Al Ain, PO Box 101110, Al Ain, United Arab Emirates. *E:* headmaster@brightoncollegealain.ae.

**GREIG, Lesley Gillian;** *see* Glaister, L. G.

**GREINER, Hon. Nicholas Frank, (Nick),** AC 1994; Federal President, Liberal Party, 2017–19; Chairman, QBE Asia-Pacific, 2017–19; *b* 27 April 1947; *s* of Nicholas and Clare Greiner; *m* 1970, Kathryn Callaghan (AO 2001) (separated); one *s* one *d. Educ:* St Ignatius

Coll., Riverview; Sydney Univ. (BEc Hons); Harvard Univ. (MBA High Dist.). Asst Vice-Pres., Boise Cascade Corp., USA, 1970–71; NSW Dir and Chief Exec., White River Corp., 1972–80; Chm., Harper & Row (Australasia), 1977–83. Chairman: Baulderstone Hornibrook, 1993–2004; United Utilities Australia Pty Ltd (formerly North West Water), 1993–2010; Natwest Markets, 1993–97 (Dir, 1992–98); IAMA (formerly SBS-IAMA) Ltd, 1994–2000; W. D. & H. O. Wills, 1996–99 (Dir, 1995–99); British American Tobacco Australasia, 1999–2004; BMC Media, 1999–2002; Nuance Australia, 2001–16; Bilfinger Berger Australia Pty Ltd, 2003–10; Bradken Resources Pty Ltd, 2004–15 (Dir, 2002–04); Healthcare Australia Ltd, 2006–10; BlueStar Print Gp, 2007–12; QBE LMI (formerly PMI), 2008–11 (Dir, 2007–08); Citigroup Australia, 2008–11; QBE Australia/NZ and Asia-Pacific, 2011–16; QBE Emerging Markets, 2015–17; Australian Adv. Bd, Rothschild Global Financial Adv., 2011–; Adv. Bd, Degremont and SAS Gp of Cos, Australia/NZ, 2011–15; Rearden Capital, 2014–16; Adv. Bd, Crosby Textor, 2014–. Co-Chair, Ausflag Ltd, 1996–2000; Deputy Chairman: Stockland Trust Property Gp, 1992–2010; Coles Myer, 1995–96 (Dir, 1992–2000); Castle Harlan Australian Mezzanine Pty Ltd, 2000– (Chm., 2018–); Accolade Wines, 2017–18 (Chm., 2013–17). Director: Australian Vintage Pty Ltd (formerly Brian McGuigan Wines, subseq. McGuigan Simeon Wines), 1992–2008; QBE Inscce Gp, 1992–2007; Blue Freeway, 2006–09; SGSP (Aust.) Assets Pty Ltd, 2015–; Consultant: Clayton Utz, 1992–2004; Citigroup, 1997–2008; Deloitte Touche Tohmatsu, 1999–2004; Advr, BDO Australia, 2015–16. Prof., Macquarie Grad. Sch. of Management, 1992–2004. Director: Harvard Business Sch. Alumni Assoc. Bd., 2005–08; Harvard Business Sch. Asia-Pacific Adv. Bd, 2011–; Chm., SMART Infrastructure Facility, Univ. of Wollongong 2009–11. Chm., Australian Subscription Television and Radio Assoc., 2003–08. MP (L) Ku-ring-gai, NSW, 1980–92; Shadow Minister for Urban Affairs, June 1981; Shadow Treasurer, and Shadow Minister for Housing and Co-operatives, Oct. 1981; Leader of State Opposition, 1983–88; Shadow Treasurer, and Shadow Minister for Ethnic Affairs, 1983; Premier, Treasurer, and Minister for Ethnic and Aboriginal Affairs, NSW Coalition Govt, 1988–92. Chm., Infrastructure NSW, 2011–13. Mem., GST Distribution Review Panel, Australian Govt, 2011–12. Chm., European-Australian Business Council, 2015–19 (Mem., Corporate Council, 2002–13; Dir, 2013–). Gov., CEDA, 2005–. Director: Sydney Organising Cttee for Olympic Games, 1993–2000; S Sydney Rugby League Club, 2003–06, now Life Mem. President: Squash Australia, 1998–2000; Soccer Australia, 1996–99. Life Fellow, Australian Inst. of Co. Dirs; Hon. Fellow, CPA Australia; Life Mem., State Council, NSW Div., Liberal Party, 2012–. Centenary Medal (Australia), 2000. *Recreations:* walking, ski-ing, theatre, opera, spectator sports.

**GRENDER**, Baroness *cr* 2013 (Life Peer), of Kingston upon Thames, in the London Borough of Kingston upon Thames; **Rosalind Mary, (Olly) Grender**, MBE 1996; *b* 19 Aug. 1962. Res. and Policy Officer to Leader of Liberal Democrats, 1989–92; Communications Director: Lib Dem Party, 1992–95; Shelter, 1995–2000; Sen. Consultant, LLM Communications, 2000–02; Dep. Dir of Communications for Govt, 2011–12. *Address:* House of Lords, SW1A 0PW.

**GRENFELL**, family name of **Baron Grenfell**.

**GRENFELL**, 3rd Baron *cr* 1902; **Julian Pascoe Francis St Leger Grenfell**; Baron Grenfell of Kilvey (Life Peer) 2000; *b* 23 May 1935; *o s* of 2nd Baron Grenfell, CBE, TD, and of Elizabeth Sarah Polk, *o d* of late Captain Hon. Alfred Shaughnessy, Montreal, Canada; *S* father, 1976; *m* 1st, 1961, Loretta Maria Reali (marr. diss. 1970), Florence; one *d*; 2nd, 1970, Gabrielle Raab (marr. diss. 1987), Berlin; two *d*; 3rd, 1987, Mrs Elisabeth Porter (marr. diss. 1992), Washington, DC; 4th, 1993, Mrs Dagmar Langbehn Debreil, *yr d* of late Dr Carl Langbehn, Berlin. *Educ:* Eton; King's Coll., Cambridge. BA (Hons), President of the Union, Cambridge, 1959. 2 Lieut, KRRC (60th Rifles), 1954–56; Captain, Queen's Royal Rifles, TA, 1963; Programme Asst, ATV Ltd, 1960–61; frequent appearances and occasional scripts, for ATV religious broadcasting and current affairs series, 1960–64. Joined World Bank, Washington, DC, 1965; Chief of Information and Public Affairs for World Bank Group in Europe, 1970; Dep. Dir, European Office, 1973; Special rep. of World Bank to UN, 1974–81; Special Advr, 1983–87, Sen. Advr, 1987–90; Head of Ext. Affairs, European Office, 1990–95; Sen. Advr, European Office, 1995, retired. UK Delegn to Parly Assemblies of Council of Europe and WEU, 1997–99. A Dep. Speaker, H of L, 2002–08; Chm., Econ. and Financial Subcttee, H of L Select Cttee on EU, 1999 and 2001–02; Principal Dep. Chm. of Cttees and Chm., Select Cttee on EU, 2002–08; retired from H of L, 2014. Pres., Anglo-Belgian Soc. of the UK, 2006–14. Chevalier de la Légion d'Honneur (France), 2005; Médaille d'Honneur du Senat (France), 2008; Comdr, Cross of the Order of Merit (Germany), 2008; Comdr, Order of the Crown (Belgium), 2009; High Order of Merit (Croatia), 2010. *Publications:* novels: Margot, 1984; The Gazelle, 2004; The Widow of Honfleur, 2016. *Recreation:* European history. *Heir: cousin* Richard Arthur St Leger Grenfell [*b* 4 Nov. 1966; *m* 1995, Sally Marie Halstead; one *s*]. *Address:* 24 rue Chaptal, 75009 Paris, France. *Club:* Royal Green Jackets.

**GRENFELL, Andrée, (Mrs David Milman)**; Director, Mossplum Pty Ltd, since 1995; *b* 14 Jan. 1940; *d* of Stephen Grenfell (writer) and Sybil Grenfell; *m* 1st, 1972, Roy Warden; two step *s*; 2nd, 1984, David Milman; two step *s*. *Educ:* privately. Graduate Diploma in Agric., Hawkesbury Agricl Coll., 1989. Man. Dir, Elizabeth Arden Ltd, UK, 1974–76; Pres., Glemby Internat., UK and Europe, 1976–80; Sen. Vice Pres., Glemby Internat., USA, 1976–80. Chm., Kelly Burrell & Jones, 1988–91; Director: Harvey Nichols Knightsbridge, 1972–74; Peter Robinson Ltd, 1968–72; Milman Internat. Aust., 1990–2003; Non-executive Director: NAAFI, 1981–83; Prince of Wales Res. Inst., Sydney, 1994–2004. Mem. Council, Inst. of Dirs, 1976; FCMI (FBIM 1977). Mem., Cercle des Amis de la Veuve. Business Woman of the Year, FT, 1979. *Recreations:* riding, dressage, swimming, yoga. *Address:* 3/1 Rosemount Avenue, Woollahra, NSW 2025, Australia. *T:* (2) 93275964.

**GRENFELL, Prof. Bryan Thomas**, OBE 2002; DPhil; FRS 2004; Kathryn Briger and Sarah Fenton Professor of Ecology, Evolutionary Biology and Public Affairs, Princeton University, since 2009; *b* 7 Dec. 1954; *s* of Bryan and Gwenda Grenfell; *m* 1996, Catherine Williams. *Educ:* Imperial Coll., London (BSc; ARCS); Univ. of York (MSc; DPhil 1981). Res. Fellow, Dept of Biol., Imperial Coll., London, 1981–86; Lectr, Dept of Animal and Plant Scis, Univ. of Sheffield, 1986–90; Department of Zoology, University of Cambridge: Lectr, 1990–98; Reader, 1998–2002; Prof. of Population Biol., 2002–04; Fellow, Girton Coll., Cambridge, 2001–04; Alumni Prof. of Biol., Pennsylvania State Univ., 2004–09. Mem., Bd of Govs, Wellcome Trust, 2014–. *Publications:* (ed with A. P. Dobson) Ecology of Infectious Diseases in Natural Populations, 1995; numerous papers in learned jls. *Recreations:* cooking, reading, hiking. *Address:* 211 Eno Hall, Princeton University, Princeton, NJ 08544, USA. *T:* (609) 9240308.

**GRENFELL, (Jeremy) Gibson**; QC 1994; a Recorder, since 1992; *b* 13 Dec. 1945; *s* of late Edward Gerald James Grenfell and of June (*née* Hunkin). *Educ:* Falmouth Grammar Sch.; Fitzwilliam Coll., Cambridge (Open Exhibnr, MA). Called to the Bar, Middle Temple, 1969 (Harmsworth Schol.; Bencher, 2003). *Address:* c/o 6KBW, 21 College Hill, EC4R 2RP. *T:* (020) 3301 0910.

**GRENFELL, Rt Rev. Joanne Woolway**; *see* Stepney, Area Bishop of.

**GRENFELL, Dr Michael Paul**; Executive Director, Enforcement, Competition and Markets Authority, since 2015; *b* London, 17 Feb. 1963; *s* of Dr Joseph Grenfell and late Eva Hanna Grenfell; *m* 2006, Sally Sweiry; two *s*. *Educ:* Haberdashers' Aske's Sch., Elstree; Peterhouse, Cambridge (BA Hons Hist. and Law 1985); London Sch. of Econs and Political Sci. (PhD Political Thought 1991). Admitted solicitor, 1988; Associate, Linklaters, 1988–91; Associate, 1991–98, Partner, 1998–2013, Norton Rose, later Norton Rose Fulbright; Sen. Dir, Sector Regulation, CMA, 2014–15. *Publications:* (with Martin Coleman) The Competition Act 1998: law and practice, 1999; (contrib.) The Philosophy, Politics and Religion of British Democracy: Maurice Cowling and conservatism, 2010. *Recreations:* current affairs, history, travel, good conversation. *Address:* Competition and Markets Authority, The Cabot, 25 Cabot Square, E14 4QA. *E:* michael.grenfell@cma.gov.uk.

**GRENFELL, His Honour Simon Pascoe**; commercial, civil and community mediator, since 2011; a Circuit Judge, 1992–2010; Senior Circuit Judge, 2002–10; a Deputy Circuit Judge, 2010–14; *b* 10 July 1942; *s* of late Osborne Pascoe Grenfell and Margaret Grenfell; *m* 1974, Ruth De Jersey Harvard; one *s* three *d*. *Educ:* Fettes College; Emmanuel College, Cambridge (MA). Called to the Bar, Gray's Inn, 1965; practice on NE Circuit; a Recorder, 1985–92; Designated Civil Judge: Bradford Group of Courts, 1998–2000; Leeds Group of Courts, 2000–10. Accredited mediator, 2011; Mediation and Trng Alternatives, RICS, 2011; Member: Assoc. of Northern Mediators, 2011–; ARCH Resolution, 2012–; Civil Mediation Council Registered Mediator, 2016–; Associate Practitioner, Restorative Justice Council, 2019–. Chancellor, Dio. of Ripon and Leeds (formerly Dio. of Ripon), 1992–2014. Chair of Trustees, Craven and Harrogate Dists, Citizens Advice, 2016–. Liveryman, Vintners' Co., 1965. *Recreations:* music, sailing and messing about in boats, coarse gardening, online information, walking, travelling, good food and wine, young grandchildren.

**GRENIER, Rear-Adm. Peter Francis, (Frank)**, CB 1989; self-employed glass engraver; *b* 27 Aug. 1934; *s* of late Dr F. W. H. Grenier and Mrs M. Grenier; *m* 1957, Jane Susan Bradshaw; two *s* one *d* (and one *s* decd). *Educ:* Montpelier School, Paignton; Blundell's School, Tiverton. Entered RN (Special Entry), 1952; Midshipman, Mediterranean Fleet, 1953; commissioned, 1955; joined Submarine service, 1956; 1st command (HMS Ambush), 1965; final command (HMS Liverpool), 1982; Chief of Staff to C-in-C Naval Home Command, 1985–87; FO Submarines, and Comdr Submarine Forces E Atlantic, 1987–89. Defence Advr, H of C Defence Cttee, 1991–98. Vice-Pres., Royal Naval FA, 1988–. Chm. of Govs, Blundell's Sch., 1991–96 (Gov., 1986–96). FGE 2009 (AFGE 1998). *Recreations:* family, sketching and painting, golf. *Address:* 2 Grange Cottages, North Cadbury, Yeovil, Somerset BA22 7BY. *T:* (01963) 440176. *W:* www.frankgrenier.co.uk. *Club:* Army and Navy.

**GRENVILLE**; *see* Freeman-Grenville, family name of Lady Kinloss.

**GRENVILLE, Dr Jane Clare**, OBE 2014; FSA; freelance consultant in historic buildings archaeology and conservation, since 2015; *b* 17 June 1958; *d* of Henry William Grenville and Helen Caroline Grenville (*née* Westmacott). *Educ:* Girton Coll., Cambridge (BA Hons Archaeol. and Anthropol., MA 1983); Univ. of York (PhD 2005). MCIfA (MIFA 1993); IHBC 1996; FSA 2002. Caseworker, Listed Buildings Resurvey for Yorkshire and Humberside, 1984–87; Res. Officer, Chester Rows Res. Project, 1987–88; Historic Buildings Officer, Council for British Archaeol., 1988–91; University of York: Lectr, 1991–2000; Sen. Lectr in Archaeol., 2000–07; Hd, Dept of Archaeol., 2001–06; Actg Vice-Chancellor, 2013; Pro-Vice-Chancellor for Students, 2007–15; Dep. Vice Chancellor, 2012–15; Hon. Res. Fellow, Dept of Archaeol., 2015–. Comr, English Heritage, 2001–08. Trustee: York Civic Trust, 2006–; York Museums Trust, 2008–11; Chm. Trustees, Council for British Archaeol., 2013–16. Mem., Fabric Adv. Cttee, York Minster, 2016–. *Publications:* Medieval Housing, 1997; Managing the Historic Rural Landscape, 1999. *Recreations:* dogs, walking, reading, yoga. *Address:* University of York, King's Manor, York YO1 7EP. *T:* (01904) 323903. *E:* jane.grenville@york.ac.uk.

**GRETTON**, family name of **Baron Gretton**.

**GRETTON**, 4th Baron *cr* 1944, of Stapleford; **John Lysander Gretton**; *b* 17 April 1975; *s* of 3rd Baron Gretton and of Jennifer Ann (*see* Jennifer, Lady Gretton); *S* father, 1989; *m* 2006, Sarah Elizabeth Anne, *er d* of Alfred Attard; one *s* two *d*. *Educ:* Shrewsbury; RAC Cirencester. Dir and Partner, Gretton Bergius (formerly Griffiths Bergius), independent home search agents, 2007–; Partner, Stapleford Farms and Stapleford Estate, 2009–. *Heir:* s Hon. John Frederick Bruce Gretton, *b* 9 June 2008.

**GRETTON, Jennifer, Lady; Jennifer Ann Gretton**, DCVO 2017; JP; Lord-Lieutenant of Leicestershire, 2003–18; owner, Stapleford Estate; *b* 14 June 1943; *o d* of Edmund Sandford Moore and Emily Joan Moore; *m* 1970, Hon. John Henrik Gretton (later 3rd Baron Gretton; *he d* 1989); one *s* one *d*. *Educ:* York Coll. for Girls. Member: Leics and Rutland CLA Cttee, 1989–2012; Envmt and Water Cttee, CLA, 1994–98. President: Melton Mowbray & District Model Engrg Soc., 1989–; Rural Community Council (Leics and Rutland), 1994–; Leics Orgn for the Relief of Suffering, 1999–; St John Council, Leics, 2003–18; Leics and Rutland Cttee, Army Benevolent Fund, 2003–; Leics and Rutland Br., SSAFA, 2008–; Vice-President: Scout Council, Leics, 2003–18; E Midlands RFCA, 2003– (Pres., Leics and Rutland County Cttee, 2003–); Leics and Rutland Branch, Magistrates' Assoc., 2004–; Co. Vice Pres., Leicester, Leics and Rutland, Girlguiding, 2011–18. Member: Cttee, Somerby PCC, 1991–; Leics Cathedral Council, 2003–12. Patron: Heart of the Nat. Forest Foundn, 2003–; Leics and Rutland Wildlife Trusts, 2004–; Laura Centre, 2008–; Friends of Leicester Cathedral, 2011–; Radio Leicester Applause Charity, 2011–; Soft Touch Arts, 2013–; Co. Patron, Leics and Rutland, RBL, 2006–. DL 2001, JP 2003, Leics. *Recreations:* sport, music, all aspects of steam. *T:* (01664) 454607.
*See also* Baron Gretton.

**GRETTON, Prof. George Lidderdale**, WS; Lord President Reid Professor of Law, University of Edinburgh, 1994–2016, now Professor Emeritus; a Scottish Law Commissioner, 2006–11; *b* 10 Nov. 1950; *s* of David Foster Gretton and Patience Mary Gretton (*née* Lidderdale); *m* 1976, Helen Jessica Morgan; two *s* one *d*. *Educ:* King Edward's Sch., Birmingham; Univ. of Durham (BA); Univ. of Edinburgh (LLB). WS 1980. Lectr, Sen. Lectr, and Reader, Univ. of Edinburgh, 1981–94. FRSE 2002. *Publications:* The Law of Inhibition and Adjudication, 1996; (with K. Reid) Conveyancing (2005), 2005; contribs to books, and jls incl. Edinburgh Law Rev., Scots Law Times, Jl Business Law, Eur. Rev. of Private Law; *festschrift:* Nothing So Practical as a Good Theory, ed by A. J. M. Steven, R. G. Anderson and J. MacLeod. *Address:* University of Edinburgh, School of Law, Old College, South Bridge, Edinburgh EH8 9YL. *E:* G.Gretton@ed.ac.uk.

**GRETTON, Vice. Adm. Michael Peter**, CB 1998; CVO 2005; Associate, 2020 Delivery, since 2012; Chairman, Winchester and Eastleigh Healthcare NHS Trust, 2007–12; *b* 14 March 1946; *s* of Vice Adm. Sir Peter Gretton, KCB, DSO, OBE, DSC, MA and late Dorothy (*née* Du Vivier); *m* 1973, Stephanie O'Neill; one *s* three *d*. *Educ:* Ampleforth Coll.; BRNC Dartmouth; Trinity Coll., Oxford (BA PPE; MA). Joined RN, 1963; served HMS Torquay, Tiger, Rothesay, Ark Royal and Bacchante; commanded: HMS Bossington,

1972–73; HMS Ambuscade, 1977–80; RCDS, 1987; commanded: HMS Invincible, 1988–90; NATO Standing Naval Force Atlantic, 1990–91; Dir of Naval Staff Duties, MoD, 1991–93; comd UK Task Force and NATO Anti-Submarine Warfare Striking Force, 1993–94; Rep. of SACLANT in Europe, 1994–98. Dir, Duke of Edinburgh's Award, 1998–2005; World Challenge Ltd, 2005–07. Chm., Youth Options (formerly Hants and IoW Youth Options), 2007–18. Governor: St Edward's Sch., Oxford, 1985–2008; Farleigh Sch., Red Rice, 1992–2004; St Mary's Sch., Shaftesbury, 1998–2008. Pres., RN RFU, 1993–95. Mem. Council, Tall Ships Youth Trust (formerly Sail Training Assoc.), 1999–2010. Chm., Battle of the Atlantic Meml, 2004–18. FNI 1994. *Recreations:* Real Tennis, sightseeing, listening to music. *Clubs:* Naval (Pres., 2005–13); I Zingari.

**GREVILLE**, family name of **Earl of Warwick**.

**GREWAL, Harnam Singh**, CBE 1990; ED 1976; Secretary for the Civil Service, Government Secretariat, Hong Kong, 1987–90, retired; *b* 5 Dec. 1937; *s* of late Joginder Singh Grewal and Ajaib Kaur; *m* 1973, Shiv Pal Kaur Chima; one *s* one *d. Educ:* Sir Ellis Kadoorie Sch.; King's Coll., Univ. of Hong Kong (BA Hons 1959; DipEd 1960); Pembroke Coll., Cambridge Univ. (BA 1962; MA 1974). Asst Educn Officer, Hong Kong, 1962; Admin. Officer, 1964; Dist Officer, Tai Po, 1970; Dep. Dir of Urban Services, New Territories, 1976; Dep. Sec. for CS, 1980; Comr of Customs and Excise, 1984; Sec. for Transport, 1986. Royal Hong Kong Regt (The Volunteers), 1963–84, Major (retd); Hon. Col, 1987–90. *Recreation:* lawn bowls. *Address:* 3495 Cadboro Bay Road, Victoria, BC V8R 5K7, Canada.

**GREY;** *see* De Grey.

**GREY**, family name of **Earl Grey**.

**GREY, 7th Earl** *cr* 1806; **Philip Kent Grey;** Bt 1746; Baron Grey, 1801; Viscount Howick, 1806; *b* 11 May 1940; *s* of Albert Harry George Campbell Grey (*d* 1942) and Vera Helen Louise Grey (*née* Harding); *S* brother, 2013; *m* 1968, Ann Catherine, *y d* of Cecil Applegate; one *s* one *d. Heir: s* Alexander Edward Grey, Viscount Howick, *b* 20 Dec. 1968.

**GREY OF CODNOR**, 6th Baron *cr* 1397 (in abeyance 1496–1989); **Richard Henry Cornwall-Legh;** *b* 14 May 1936; *s* of 5th Baron Grey of Codnor, CBE and Dorothy (*d* 1993), *er d* of J. W. Scott; *S* father, 1996; *m* 1974, Joanna Storm, 7th *d* of Sir Kenelm Cayley, 10th Bt; three *s* one *d. Educ:* Stowe. High Sheriff, 1993, DL 1995, Cheshire. *Heir: s* Hon. Richard Stephen Cayley Cornwall-Legh [*b* 24 March 1976; *m* 2005, Annie Helen, *y d* of Frederick Riches; two *s* one *d* (of whom one *s* one *d* are twins)]. *Address:* Greys End, Knutsford, Cheshire WA16 0QS. *Clubs:* Boodle's, MCC.

**GREY de WILTON, Viscount;** Julian Francis Martin Grosvenor; *b* 8 June 1959; *s* of Earl of Wilton, *qv; m* 1987, Danielle (marr. diss. 1989), sixth *d* of Theo Rossi, Sydney, Australia; one *s* (*b* 2006).

**GREY, Sir Anthony (Dysart)**, 7th Bt *cr* 1814; former Inspector, Department of Industrial Affairs, Government of Western Australia; *b* 19 Oct. 1949; *s* of Edward Elton Grey (*d* 1962) (*o s* of 6th Bt) and of Nancy, *d* of late Francis John Meagher, Perth, WA; *S* grandfather, 1974; *m* 1970 (marr. diss.); *m* 1993, Alison Turner; one *s* three *d. Educ:* Guildford Grammar School, WA. *Recreations:* fishing, painting. *Heir: s* Thomas Jasper Grey, *b* 30 April 1998. *Address:* 86 Kingsway Gardens, 38 Kings Park Road, W Perth, WA 6005, Australia.

**GREY, Dame Beryl (Elizabeth),** CH 2017; DBE 1988 (CBE 1973); a Director, Royal Opera House, 1999–2003; Prima Ballerina, Sadler's Wells Ballet, now Royal Ballet, 1941–57; Artistic Director, London Festival Ballet, 1968–79; *b* London, 11 June 1927; *d* of late Arthur Ernest Groom; *m* 1950, Dr Sven Gustav Svenson (*d* 2008); one *s. Educ:* Dame Alice Owen's Girls' Sch., London. Professional training: Madeline Sharp Sch., Sadler's Wells Sch. (Schol.), de Vos Sch. Début Sadler's Wells Co., 1941, with leading Ballerina rôles following same year in Les Sylphides, The Gods Go A'Begging, Le Lac des Cygnes, Act II, Comus. First full-length ballet, Le Lac des Cygnes on 15th birthday, 1942. Has appeared since in leading rôles of many ballets including: Sleeping Beauty, Giselle, Sylvia, Checkmate, Ballet Imperial, Donald of the Burthens, Homage, Birthday Offering, The Lady and the Fool. Film: The Black Swan (3 Dimensional Ballet Film), 1952. Left Royal Ballet, Covent Garden, Spring 1957, to become free-lance ballerina. Regular guest appearances with Royal Ballet at Covent Garden and on European, African, American and Far Eastern Tours. Guest Artist, London's Festival Ballet in London and abroad, 1958–64. First Western ballerina to appear with Bolshoi Ballet: Moscow, Leningrad, Kiev, Tiflis, 1957–58; First Western ballerina to dance with Chinese Ballet Co. in Peking and Shanghai, 1964. Engagements and tours abroad include: Central and S America, Mexico, Rhodesia and S Africa, Canada, NZ, Lebanon, Germany, Norway, Sweden, Denmark, Finland, Belgium, Holland, France, Switzerland, Italy, Portugal, Austria, Czechoslovakia, Poland, Rumania; Producer: Sleeping Beauty, 1967; Swan Lake, 1972, London Fest. Ballet; Giselle, Western Australia Ballet, 1984, 1986; Sleeping Beauty, Royal Swedish Ballet, Stockholm, 1985, 2002. Regular television and broadcasts in England and abroad; concert narrator. Dir-Gen., Arts Educational Trust and Teacher Trng Coll., 1966–68. Vice-Pres., Royal Acad. of Dancing, 1980– (Exec. Mem., 1982–89); Pres., Dance Council of Wales, 1981–2004; Life Pres., ISTD, 2002– (FISTD 1960; Mem. Council, 1966–91; Chm., 1984–91; Pres., 1991–2001; ISTD Imperial Award for Outstanding Service, 1987, Lifetime Achievement Award, 2004); Mem. Bd, BRB, 1995–99; Council for Dance Education and Training: Mem. Council, 1984–96; Mem. Exec., 1995–96; Patron, 2011–. Trustee: London City Ballet, 1978–92; Adeline Genée Theatre, 1982–90; Royal Ballet Benevolent Fund, 1982– (Chm. Trustees, 1992–2011; Patron, 2011–); Dance Critics Circle, 2005–11 (Patron, 2005–); Vice Chm., Dance Teachers Benevolent Fund, 1984–2004 (Trustee, 1981–2004; Pres., 2012–15); President: Keep Fit Assoc., 1992–93; E Grinstead Operatic Soc., 1986–2009; English Nat. Ballet, 2005–; British Ballet Orgn, 2010–; Vice-President: Music Therapy Charity, 1980–; British Fedn of Music Festivals, 1985–; London Ballet Circle, 2001–. Governor: Dame Alice Owens Girls' Sch., London, 1960–71; Frances Mary Buss Foundn, 1963–72; Royal Ballet Cos, 1993–2002 (Vice Chm. Govs, 1995–2002). Patron: Lisa Ullman Travelling Scholarship Fund, 1986–; British Sch. of Osteopathy, 1987–; Benesh Inst. of Choreology, 1988–; Dancers' Career Develt (formerly Dancers' Resettlement Trust), 1988–; Nature Cure Clinic, 1988–2005; Tanya Bayona Princess Poutiatine Acad. of Ballet, Malta, 1988–2005; Language of Dance Centre, 1990–; Friends of Sadler's Wells Theatre, 1991–; Pro-Dogs, 1991–2005; Osteopathic Centre for Children, 1992–; Furlong Research Foundn, 1993– (Trustee, 2005–09); AMBER Trust, 1995–; Theatre Design Trust, 1995–; Legat Foundn, 1998–; Sussex Opera and Ballet Soc., 2001–; Discs, 2005– (Trustee, 1993–2005); Early Dance Circle, 2007–; German Shepherd Dog Rescue, 2010–; Internat. Dance Teachers Assoc., 2011–; Gielgud Acad., 2012–; Rosche, 2014–; Vice-Patron, BASE, 2010–. Hon. DMus: Leicester, 1970; Univ. of London, 1996; Hon. DLitt: City, 1974; Buckingham, 1993; Hon. DEd CNAA, 1989; Hon. DArt: Bedford, 2010; Bath, 2018. Queen Elizabeth II Coronation Award, Royal Acad. of Dancing, 1995; Critics' Circle Award for Service to Dance, 2002; Lifetime Achievement Carl Alan Award, Internat. Dance Teachers' Assoc., 2010; De Valois Award for Outstanding Achievement, Critics' Circle, 2016. *Publications:* Red Curtain Up, 1958; Through the Bamboo Curtain, 1965; My Favourite Ballet Stories, 1981; For the Love of Dance (autobiog.), 2017; *relevant publications:* biographical studies (by Gordon Anthony), 1952, (by Pigeon Crowle), 1952; Beryl Grey, Dancers of Today (by Hugh Fisher), 1955; Beryl Grey, a biography (by David Gillard), 1977. *Recreations:* music, opera, reading, swimming. *Address:* Pen-Bré, Beaconsfield Road, Chelwood Gate, E Sussex RH17 7LF.

**GREY, Prof. Clare Philomena,** DPhil; FRS 2011; Geoffrey Moorhouse Gibson Professor of Chemistry, University of Cambridge, since 2009; Fellow, Pembroke College, Cambridge, since 2011; Adjunct Professor, Department of Chemistry, State University of New York at Stony Brook, since 2015 (Professor, 2001–15). *Educ:* Christ Church, Oxford (BA 1st Cl. Hons Chem. 1987; DPhil 1991). Res. Fellow, Balliol Coll., Oxford, 1990–91; Royal Soc. Postdoctoral Fellow, Univ. of Nijmegen, 1991–92; Vis. Scientist, DuPont CR&D, 1992–94; Stony Brook University: Asst Prof., 1994–97, Associate Prof., 1997–2001, Dept of Chemistry; Associate Dir, NSF Center for Envmtl Molecular Sci., 2002–07. John Jeyes Award, RSC, 2010; Kavli Medal and Lect., 2011, Davy Prize, 2014, Royal Soc. *Publications:* contribs to jls incl. Nature Materials, Jl Amer. Chem. Soc., Chem. Materials, Science. *Address:* Department of Chemistry, University of Cambridge, Lensfield Road, Cambridge CB2 1EW.

**GREY, John Egerton,** CB 1980; Clerk Assistant and Clerk of Public Bills, House of Lords, 1974–88; *b* 8 Feb. 1929; *s* of late John and Nancy Grey; *m* 1961, Patricia Hanna (*d* 2007); two adopted *s. Educ:* Dragon Sch., Oxford; Blundell's; Brasenose Coll., Oxford. MA, BCL. Called to the Bar, Inner Temple, 1954; practised at Chancery Bar, 1954–59. Clerk in Parliament Office, House of Lords, 1959–88. Adviser, Colchester CAB, 1989–99. *Recreation:* gardening. *Address:* 51 St Peters Road, West Mersea, Colchester, Essex CO5 8LL. *T:* (01206) 383007. *Clubs:* Arts; West Mersea Yacht.

**GREY, Maj.-Gen. John St John,** CB 1987; *b* 6 June 1934; *s* of late Major Donald John Grey, RM and Doris Mary Grey (*née* Beavan); *m* 1958, Elisabeth Ann (*née* Langley); one *s* one *d. Educ:* Christ's Hospital. rcds, ndc, psc(M), osc(US). Commissioned 2/Lt 1952; Commando service, Malta, Egypt, Cyprus, 1955–64; Cruiser HMS Lion as OC RM, 1964–65; Instructor, Army Sch. of Infantry, 1967–69; US Marine Corps, 1970–71; Commando service, 1972–76; Commanded 45 Cdo Gp (incl. tours in N Ireland and Arctic Norway), 1976–78; Mil. Sec. and Col Ops/Plans, MoD, 1979–84; Maj.-Gen. Commando Forces, 1984–87; RM COS, 1987–88, retired. Clerk, Pewterers' Co., 1988–96. Col Comdt RM, 1995–98. Pres., SSAFA, Devon, 1993–2007. President: Exeter and Dist, ESU, 2010–13 (Mem. Council, 2000–10); Topsham br., RBL, 2007–12. Chm. of Trustees, Northcott Devon Foundn, 2010–. *Recreations:* sailing, walking. *Address:* c/o Lloyds Bank plc, Teignmouth Branch, PO Box 99, BX1 1LT. *Clubs:* Army and Navy; Royal Naval Sailing Association (Portsmouth); Royal Marines Sailing.

**GREY, Nicholas;** Chief Executive Officer, Grey Technology Ltd, since 2001; *b* Bromsgrove, 12 July 1968; *s* of George Grey and Mary Grey; *m* 2005, Louise Gleave; three *s* one *d*. Vax Ltd, 1989–2001: Lab technician; Design Engr; Sen. Design Engr; Design Manager; Engr Manager; Managing Dir. *Recreations:* surfing, low-level sky diving. *Address:* Gtech, Brindley Road, Worcester WR4 9FB. *T:* (01905) 345891.

**GREY, Robin Douglas;** QC 1979; a Recorder of the Crown Court, 1979–99; *b* 23 May 1931; *s* of Dr Francis Temple Grey, MA, MB, and Eglantine Grey; *m* 1st, 1972, Berenice Anna Wheatley (marr. diss.); one *s* one *d;* 2nd, 1993, Mrs Annick Regnault. *Educ:* Summer Fields Prep. Sch., Oxford; Eastbourne Coll.; London Univ. (LLB Hons). Called to the Bar, Gray's Inn, 1957. Crown Counsel, Colonial Legal Service, Aden, 1959–63 (Actg Registrar Gen. and Actg Attorney Gen. for short periods); practising barrister, 1963–2015; Dep. Circuit Judge, 1977. FCO Consultant to Govt of Russian Fedn, 1993–96; led FCO team to Moscow on Jury Trials, 1993. Chm., Home Office Police Appeals Tribunals, 1990–2006; Legal Assessor to GMC, 1995–; Legal Advr to GDC, 2010–15; Legal Assessor for HCPC, 2012–15. Appeal Chm., British Equestrian Fedn, 2010–. Member: Internat. Bar Assoc., 1994; Cttee, Criminal Bar Assoc., 1990–93 (Chm., Internat. Sub-Cttee, 1993); Cttee, European Criminal Bar Assoc., 1998–; British Acad. of Forensic Sciences. *Recreations:* walking, reading, theatre, fishing, six grandsons. *Address:* 184 Bromyard House, Bromyard Avenue, W3 7BN. *T:* (020) 8740 7709. *Club:* Hurlingham.

**GREY-THOMPSON**, family name of **Baroness Grey-Thompson**.

**GREY-THOMPSON, Baroness** *cr* 2010 (Life Peer), of Eaglescliffe in the County of Durham; **Carys Davina, (Tanni) Grey-Thompson,** DBE 2005 (OBE 2000; MBE 1993); wheelchair athlete; Board Member: Transport for London, since 2008; London Legacy Development Corporation; Chairman, UK Active, since 2015; *b* 26 July 1969; *d* of Peter Alexander Harvey Grey and Sulwen Davina Grey (*née* Jones); *m* 1999, Dr (Robert) Ian George Thompson; one *d. Educ:* Loughborough Univ. (BA Hons Politics & Admin 1991). Develt Officer, UK Athletics, 1996–2000. Member Council: Sports Council for Wales, 1996–2002; UK Sport, 1998–2003; Dep. Chm., UK Lottery Sports Fund, 1998–2002; Vice Chm., Sports Adv. Gp, LOCOG, 2007–13. Mem., BBC Bd, 2017–. Member Board: Winston Churchill Meml Trust, 2006–; V, 2006–14. Has represented GB at 100m–800m distances, 1987–2007: competitor: Paralympics, 1988, 1992, 1996, 2000 and 2004 (winner 16 medals, incl. 11 Gold Medals); Olympics, 1992 and 1996 (in exhibn 800m), 2000, 2004; World Championships (winner 11 medals, incl. 5 Gold Medals); has broken over 30 world records; winner, London Marathon, 1992, 1994, 1996, 1998, 2001, 2002. Pro-Vice-Chancellor, Staffordshire Univ., 2004–14; Chancellor, Northumbria Univ., 2015–. Hon. Fellow: UWCC, 1997; UWIC, Swansea Univ., Coll. of Ripon and York St John, 2001; John Moores Univ., Liverpool, 2004. Hon. MA Loughborough, 1994; Hon. Dr Sport Staffordshire, 1998; Hon. DBA Southampton, 1998; Hon. MSc Manchester Metropolitan, 1998; DUniv: Surrey, 2000; Open, 2004; Sheffield Hallam, 2005; Hon. Master Teesside, 2001; Hon. DTech Loughborough, 2001; Hon. Dr: Leeds Metropolitan, 2001; Wales, 2002; Oxford Brookes, 2005; Glasgow, 2015; Hon. LLD: Exeter, 2003; Heriot-Watt, 2004; Leicester, 2005; Hon. DCL Newcastle, 2005; Hon. DLaws Bath, 2010; Hon. DSc: Hull, 2006, Greenwich, 2013; Oxford, 2013. *Publications:* Seize the Day (autobiog.), 2001; Aim High, 2007. *Address:* c/o Benchmark Sport, 23/24 Henrietta Street, Covent Garden, WC2E 8ND. *T:* (020) 7240 7799, *Fax:* (020) 7240 7703.

**GREY-WILSON, Christopher,** PhD; VMH 2008; Editor, Alpine Garden Society, 1990–2011; *b* 28 Sept. 1944; *s* of late Vyvyan William Grey-Wilson and Jean Grey-Wilson (*née* Parsley); *m* 1978, Christine Mary Dent; one *d. Educ:* Churston Ferrers Grammar Sch.; Wye Coll., Univ. of London (BSc Hort. 1967); Reading Univ. (PhD 1976). Botanist (PSO), Royal Botanic Gardens, Kew, 1968–90. Vice-Chairman: RHS Jt Rock Gdn Plant Cttee, 2017– (Chm., 2009–17); RHS Bursaries Cttee, 2000–17; RHS Awards Cttee, 2018–. Editor: Curtis's Botanical Magazine, incl. Kew Magazine, 1983–89; The New Plantsman, subseq. The Plantsman, 2001–05. Botanical Scientific expeditions: Iran and Afghanistan, 1971; Nepal, 1973, 1978, 1989; Kenya and Tanzania, 1976, 1979; Sri Lanka, 1978; W China, 1987, 1994. *Publications:* The Alpine Flowers of Britain and Europe, 1979, 2nd edn 1995; Impatiens of Africa, 1980; (jtly) Bulbs, 1981; (jtly) Gardening on Walls, 1983; The Genus Cyclamen, 1988; The Genus Dionysia, 1989; The Illustrated Flora of Britain and Northern Europe, 1989; A Manual of Alpine and Rock Garden Plants, 1989; Poppies, 1993, 2nd edn 2000; Mediterranean Wild Flowers, 1993; The Alpine Garden, 1994; (jtly) Gardening with Climbers, 1997; Cyclamen, 1997, 2nd edn 2002; Clematis: the genus,

2000; How to Identify Wild Flowers, 2000; Alpines: the new plant library, 2001; Wildflowers of Britain and Northern Europe, 2003; The Rock Garden Plant Primer, 2009; A Field Guide to the Bulbs of Greece, 2010; (jtly) Flowers of Western China, 2011; Pasqueflowers, the Genus Pulsatilla, 2014; The Genus Meconopsis: blue poppies and their relatives, 2014; (ed) Meconopsis for Gardeners, 2017; A Plant-hunter in Afghanistan, 2019; numerous scientific papers in Kew Bulletin, gen. papers in The Garden, Bull. of Alpine Garden Soc., The Alpine Gardener, Gardens News, The Plantsman and The New Plantsman. *Recreations:* gardening, walking, drawing, photography, listening to classical music. *Address:* Honeysuckle Cottage, The Green, Redgrave, Suffolk IP22 1RR.

**GRIBBIN, John Richard,** PhD; writer; Visiting Fellow in Astronomy, University of Sussex, since 1993; *b* 19 March 1946; *s* of William James Gribbin and Lilla (*née* Reed); *m* 1966, Mary Murray; two *s*. *Educ:* Univ. of Sussex (BSc Physics 1966; MSc Astronomy 1967); Wolfson Coll., Cambridge (PhD Astrophysics 1971). Asst Editor, Nature, 1970–75; Vis. Fellow, Sci. Policy Res. Unit, 1975–78; Physics Consultant, New Scientist, 1978–98. FRAS 1972; FRMetS 1985; FRSL 1999; FRSA. Lifetime Achievement Award, Assoc. of British Sci. Writers, 2009. *Publications:* (jtly) The Jupiter Effect, 1974; Our Changing Climate, 1975; Forecasts, Famines and Freezes, 1976; Galaxy Formation, 1976; Astronomy for the Amateur, 1976; Our Changing Universe, 1976; Our Changing Planet, 1977; White Holes, 1977; (ed and contrib.) Climatic Change, 1978; The Climatic Threat, 1978 (US edn as What's Wrong with our Weather?); This Shaking Earth, 1978; Timewarps, 1979; Climate and Mankind, 1979; Weather Force, 1979; (jtly) The Sixth Winter (novel), 1979; Future Worlds, 1979; The Strangest Star, 1980 (US edn as The Death of the Sun); Carbon Dioxide, Climate and Man, 1981; Genesis, 1981; (jtly) The Jupiter Effect Reconsidered, 1982; (ed and contrib.) Cosmology Today, 1982; (jtly) The Weather Book, 1982; (jtly) The Monkey Puzzle, 1982; Brother Esau (novel), 1982; Future Weather, 1982; Beyond the Jupiter Effect, 1983; Spacewarps, 1983; (jtly) The Redundant Male, 1984; In Search of Schrödinger's Cat, 1984; In Search of the Double Helix, 1985; (ed and contrib.) The Breathing Planet, 1986; In Search of the Big Bang, 1986, rev. edn 1998; The Omega Point, 1987; The Hole in the Sky, 1988; (jtly) Double Planet (novel), 1991; Father to the Man (novel), 1989; (jtly) Cosmic Coincidences, 1989; (jtly) Winds of Change, 1989; Hothouse Earth, 1990; (jtly) The Cartoon History of Time, 1990; Blinded by the Light, 1991; (jtly) Reunion (novel), 1991; (jtly) Ragnarok, 1991; (jtly) The Matter Myth, 1991; (jtly) Stephen Hawking, 1992; In Search of the Edge of Time, 1992 (US edn as Unveiling the Edge of Time); Innervisions, 1993; In the Beginning, 1993; (jtly) Albert Einstein, 1993; Schrödinger's Kittens and the Search for Reality, 1995; (jtly) Darwin, 1995; (jtly) Origins, 1997; Cosmology, 1998; Watching the Universe, 1998 (US edn as The Case of the Missing Neutrinos); In Search of SUSY, 1998 (US edn as The Search for the Superstrings); (jtly) Empire of the Sun, 1998; (ed and contrib.) A Brief History of Science, 1998; The Birth of Time, 1999; The Little Book of Science, 1999; Dalla scimmia all'universo, 1999; Get a Grip on the New Physics, 1999; (jtly) Deep Space, 1999; (jtly) The First Chimpanzee, 2001; Space, 2001; (jtly) XTL, 2001; (jtly) The Mating Game, 2001; Science: a history, 2002; Quantum Physics, 2002; The Fellowship, 2005; The Origins of the Future, 2006; The Universe: a biography, 2007; Not Fade Away: the life and music of Buddy Holly, 2009; Timeswitch (novel), 2009; In Search of the Multiverse, 2010; The Alice Encounter (novel), 2010; The Reason Why, 2011; From Here to Infinity, 2011; (jtly) Planet Earth, 2012; Erwin Schrödinger and the Quantum Revolution, 2012; Computing with Quantum Cats, 2013; 13.8: the quest to find the true age of the universe and the theory of everything, 2015; Einstein's Masterwork: 1915 and the general theory of relativity, 2016; *with Mary Gribbin:* Weather, 1985; The One Per Cent Advantage, 1988; Children of the Ice, 1990; Too Hot to Handle?: the greenhouse effect, 1992; Being Human, 1993; Time and Space, 1994; Companion to the Cosmos, 1996; Fire on Earth, 1996; Watching the Weather, 1996; Richard Feynman, 1997; Time and the Universe, 1997; Curie, Halley, Newton, Darwin, Faraday, Galileo, and Einstein, all in In 90 Minutes series, 1997; Q is for Quantum, 1998; Almost Everyone's Guide to Science, 1998; Chaos and Uncertainty, 1999; Stardust, 2000; Ice Age, 2001; Big Numbers, 2003; How Far is Up?, 2003; FitzRoy, 2003; The Science of Philip Pullman's His Dark Materials, 2003; Deep Simplicity, 2004; Inventing the Future, 2004; Annus Mirabilis: Einstein in 1905, 2005; Flower Hunters, 2008; He Knew He Was Right: the irrepressible life of James Lovelock and Gaia, 2009; Know About Planets, 2009; Know About Stars, 2009; Know About Moons, 2009; Science: a history in 100 experiments, 2016; In the Shadow of a Giant, 2017. *Recreations:* watching Kent CCC, collecting vinyl 45 rpm records, travel, cooking, songwriting. *Address:* Astronomy Group, University of Sussex, Falmer, Brighton BN1 9RH. *E:* j.r.gribbin@sussex.ac.uk.

**GRIBBLE, Prof. Fiona Mary,** DPhil; FRCPath; FMedSci; Professor of Endocrine Physiology, University of Cambridge, since 2012; *b* Guildford, Surrey, 12 June 1965; *d* of Donald and Mary Gribble; *m* 1999, Frank Reimann; one *s* three *d*. *Educ:* Alton Convent; Alton Sixth Form Coll.; Churchill Coll., Cambridge (BA Natural and Med. Scis 1986); Univ. of Oxford (BM BCh 1990; DPhil 1997). MRCP 1993; FRCPath 2008. SHO, Gen. Medicine, Oxford Radcliffe Hosps, 1991–93; MRC Clin. Trng Fellow, 1994–97; Wellcome Trust Advanced Fellow, 1998–2003; Wellcome Trust Sen. Res. Fellow, 2003–15; Wellcome Trust Investigator, 2015–. Hon. Consultant in Clinical Biochem., Addenbrooke's Hosp., 2005–. FMedSci 2015. *Address:* Wellcome-MRC Institute of Metabolic Science, Addenbrooke's Hospital, Cambridge CB2 0QQ. *T:* (01223) 336746. *E:* fmg23@cam.ac.uk.

**GRIBBON, Deborah,** PhD; Interim Deputy Director for Collections, Education, and Performing Arts, Cleveland Museum of Art, 2013–16; *b* 11 June 1948; *d* of late Daniel M. and Jane Gribbon; *m* 1976, Dr Winston Alt; two *d*. *Educ:* Wellesley Coll., Mass (BA Art Hist. 1970); Harvard Univ. (MA Fine Arts 1972; PhD 1982). Teaching Fellow, Dept of Fine Arts, Harvard Univ., 1972–74; Curator, Isabella Stewart Gardner Mus., 1976–84; Instructor, Extension Sch., Harvard Univ., 1982–84; J. Paul Getty Museum: Asst Dir, 1984–87; Associate Dir for Curatorial Affairs, 1987–91; Associate Dir and Chief Curator, 1991–98; Dep. Dir and Chief Curator, 1998–2000; Dir, 2000–04; Interim Dir, Cleveland Mus. of Art, 2009–10. Vice Pres., J. Paul Getty Trust, 2000–04. Mem. Bd, Courtauld Inst., 2001–04. Mem., Internat. Women's Forum, 2003–. Phi Beta Kappa, 1970. *Publications:* Sculpture in the Isabella Stewart Gardner Museum, 1978; (with J. Walsh) The J. Paul Getty Museum and its Collections: a museum for a new century, 1997; contrib. articles to Apollo, Burlington Mag. and Connoisseur.

**GRIBBON, Edward John;** Under Secretary, Board of Inland Revenue, 1991–2000; Director, Compliance Division, 1996–2000; *b* 10 July 1943; *s* of late Henry Derwent Gribbon and Dorothy Gribbon (*née* Boyd); *m* 1968, Margaret Nanette Flanagan; one *s* two *d*. *Educ:* Coleraine Academical Instn; Univ. of London (LLB). FCA. Qualified as Chartered Accountant, 1965; joined Inland Revenue as HM Inspector of Taxes, 1966; HM Principal Inspector of Taxes, 1981; Dep. Dir of Operations, 1989–90; Dir, Business Profits Div., 1991–96. JP N and E Herts (formerly N Herts), 2002–13. Gov., N Herts Coll., 2004–10. *Recreations:* family, photography, local church, ornithology, philately.

**GRICE, Ian Michael;** *b* 2 May 1953; *s* of James Frederick and late Joan Grice; *m* Patricia; two *d*. *Educ:* Royal Grammar Sch., High Wycombe; Loughborough Univ. (BSc Hons Civil Engrg). MICE. Engineer: John Laing plc, 1974–76; Mowlem plc, 1976–79; Kier plc, 1979–81; Mowlem plc, 1981–95; Alfred McAlpine plc, 1995–2008, Gp Chief Exec., 2003–08; Chm., Pims Gp, 2008–10; Partner, Newby Mgt UK Ltd (Chm., 2010–11). *Recreations:* golf, shooting, watching football, walking.

**GRICE, Joseph William;** Chairman, Group of Economic Experts, Office for National Statistics, since 2016; *b* Tamworth, Staffs, 25 July 1952; *s* of Stanley John Grice and Emily Grice; *m* 1976, Deborah Mary Wicks; two *s* one *d*. *Educ:* Worcester Coll., Oxford (BA PPE 1972); Univ. of Chicago (AM Econs 1976). Economist, HM Treasury, 1972–81; Asst Dir, Baring Brothers & Co Ltd, 1981–84; HM Treasury: Hd of Monetary and Exchange Rate Policy, 1986–90; Hd of Health Spending, 1991–95; Dir, Macroeconomic Policy, 1996–2000; Chief Economist and Dir, Public Services, 2000–03; Office for National Statistics: Executive Director: Atkinson Review of Measurement of Public Sector Output, 2004–05; Social and Public Sector Analysis and Reporting, 2006–08; Chief Economist and Exec. Dir, Economic, Labour Mkt and Social Analysis, 2008–12; Exec. Dir and Chief Economist, 2012–16; Actg Chief Economist, DfT, 2012–13. Dep. Hd, Govt Econ. Service, 2000–05; Mem., Adv. Bd, UK Secure Data Service, 2010–11; Mem., ONS Bd, UK Stats Authy, 2014. Chm., Wkg Party on Macroeconomic and Structural Policy Issues, OECD, 2002–12. Chairman: EU Econ. Policy Cttee, 2005–08; EU Cttee on Monetary, Financial and Balance of Payments Stats, 2013–15; Mem., EU Council of Econ. and Finance Ministers, 2005–08. Mem. Adv. Council, Green Growth Knowledge Forum, 2012–; Co-Chm., Green Growth Knowledge Platform/MAVA Foundn project on Natural Capital, 2017–. Mem. Adv. Bd, Wales Inst. for Social and Econ. Res. Data and Methods, 2010–; Mem. Council, REconS, 2011–17. Treas., First Richmond Scout Gp, 1988–2000. *Publications:* Microeconomic Reform in Britain (with Ed Balls and Gus O'Donnell), 2004; various articles in learned jls. *Recreations:* swimming, theatre, ballet. *Address:* Office for National Statistics, Government Buildings, Cardiff Road, Newport NP10 8XG. *E:* joe.grice@ons.gov.uk.

**GRICE, Sir Paul (Edward),** Kt 2016; Clerk and Chief Executive, Scottish Parliament, since 1999; *b* 13 Oct. 1961; *s* of Kenneth William Grice and Maureen (*née* Power); *m* 1987, Elaine Rosie; two *d*. *Educ:* Archbishop Holgate's Sch., York; York Coll. of Arts and Technol.; Univ. of Stirling (BSc Econs and Envmtl Sci.). Dept of Transport, 1985–87; DoE, 1987–92; Scottish Office, Edinburgh, 1992–99: Head of Housing and Urban Regeneration Br., 1992–95; Head of Mgt and Change Unit, 1995–97; Head of Division, Constitution Group: Referendum, Scotland Bill, 1997–98; Dir of Implementation, 1998–99. Mem., ESRC, 2009–15. Member: Ct, Univ. of Stirling, 2005–13; Council, IFS, 2019–. FRSE 2017. Hon. FRIAS 2006. Trustee, Bank of Scotland Foundn, 2011–. Mem. Council, Edinburgh Internat. Fest., 2013–. *Recreations:* reading, theatre, triathlons. *Address:* Scottish Parliament, Holyrood, Edinburgh EH99 1SP. *T:* (0131) 348 5255.

**GRIDLEY,** family name of **Baron Gridley**.

**GRIDLEY,** 3rd Baron *cr* 1955; **Richard David Arnold Gridley;** Chief Executive Officer, InterGrid Property Services, since 2014; *b* 22 Aug. 1956; *o s* of 2nd Baron Gridley and Edna Lesley, *e d* of Richard Wheen; *S* father, 1996; *m* 1st, 1979, Amanda Mackenzie (marr. diss. 1983); 2nd, 1983, Suzanne Elizabeth Hughes (marr. diss.); one *s* one *d*; 3rd, 2008, Marie Hooper; three *s*. *Educ:* Monkton Combe; Portsmouth Polytech.; Univ. of Brighton (BA). Project manager, construction industry, 1980–92; Sen. Lectr in Leisure and Tourism, and Inf. Technol., subseq. in Travel and Tourism, and Teaching Mentor, South Downs Coll. of Further Educn, 1995–2014. Gov., Morelands Primary Sch., 2017–. Patron, Care for the Wild Internat., 1996–2014. *Address:* Little Hollow, 94 The Dale, Widley, Hants PO7 5DF. *E:* lordgrid@yahoo.co.uk.

**GRIEF, Alison Sarah;** QC 2015; a Recorder, since 2012; *b* Kent, 5 Nov. 1966; *d* of William Kenneth and Sheila Grief; *m* 2001, Martin King; two *s*. *Educ:* Middlesex Poly. (LLB Hons 1988). Called to the Bar, Inner Temple, 1990; in practice as barrister, specialising in family law (children), 1990–; Assistant Coroner: Mid-Kent and Medway, 2008; Herts, 2012. *Address:* 4 Paper Buildings, Temple, EC4Y 7EX. *E:* ag@4pb.com.

**GRIERSON, Prof. Donald,** OBE 2000; PhD, DSc; FRS 2000; FRSB; Professor of Plant Physiology, Nottingham University, 1986–2008, now Emeritus; Guang Biao Professor, Zhejiang University, China, since 2011; *b* 1 Oct. 1945; *s* of John Harvey Grierson and Margaret (*née* Head); *m* 1965, Elizabeth Carole Judson; two *s* two *d*. *Educ:* Univ. of E Anglia (BSc 1967); Univ. of Edinburgh (Ellis Prize in Physiol. 1970; PhD 1971); DSc Nottingham 1999. FRSB (FIBiol 1985). Plant Physiologist, British Sugar Corp. Res. Lab., Norwich, 1967–68; University of Nottingham: Asst Lectr in Plant Physiol., 1971–74; Lectr, 1974–82; Nuffield Foundn Sci. Res. Fellow, 1981–82; Reader, 1982–86; Head: Dept of Physiol. and Envmtl Sci., 1988–91 and 1992–94; Plant Sci. Section, 1988–97; Plant Sci. Div., 1997–2002; Sch. of Biosciences, 2000–02; Pro-Vice-Chancellor for Res. and Industry, 2003–07. EMBO Res. Fellow, Genetics Dept, Univ. of Tubingen, 1975–76; Vis. Prof., Shanxi Agricl Univ., 2014–. Chm., Sainsbury Lab. Council, 2000–04. Foreign Mem., Chinese Acad. of Engrg, 2017. Hon. DSc l'Institut Nat. Polytechnique de Toulouse, 2000. Res. Medal, RASE, 1990; Da Bei Nong Internat. Biotechnol. Prize, Beijing, 2015. *Publications:* (with S. N. Covey) Plant Molecular Biology, 1984, 2nd edn 1988 (English, Mandarin Chinese and Spanish edns); edited: (with H. Smith) The Molecular Biology of Plant Development, 1982; (with H. Thomas) Developmental Mutants in Higher Plants, 1987; (with G. W. Lycett) Genetic Engineering of Crop Plants, 1990; (with G. W. Lycett and G. A. Tucker) Mechanisms and Applications of Gene Silencing, 1996; Plant Biotechnology, vol. I, 1991, vol. II, 1991, vol. III, 1993; contrib. numerous refereed scientific papers and articles. *Recreations:* walking, boating, gardening, snorkelling. *Address:* Plant and Crop Sciences Division, School of Biosciences, University of Nottingham, Sutton Bonington Campus, Loughborough LE12 5RD. *T:* (0115) 951 6333.

**GRIESE, Sister Carol,** CHN; Religious Sister since 1970; *b* 26 Sept. 1945; *d* of Gwendoline and Donald Griese. *Educ:* Merrywood Grammar School, Bristol; King's College London (BA Hons English 1968); Clare Hall, Cambridge (Cert. Theol. 1970). Member, Community of the Holy Name, 1970–; Lay Rep. of Religious in General Synod, 1980–95. Mem., Crown Appointments Commn, 1990–92. *Recreations:* reading, walking. *Address:* Convent of the Holy Name, Morley Road, Oakwood, Derby DE21 4TB. *T:* (01332) 671716.

**GRIEVE, Alan Thomas,** CBE 2003; Chairman, Jerwood Foundation, since 1991; *b* 22 Jan. 1928; *s* of late Lewis Miller Grieve and Doris Lilian (*née* Amner); *m* 1st, 1957, Anne, *d* of Dr Lawrence Dulake (marr. diss. 1971); two *s* one *d*; 2nd, 1971, Karen Louise, *d* of late Michael de Sivrac Dunn; one *s* one *d*. *Educ:* Aldenham; Trinity Hall, Cambridge (MA, LLM). Nat. Service, 2nd Lieut, 14/20 King's Hussars; Capt., City of London Yeo., TA. Admitted solicitor, 1953; Senior Partner: Taylor & Humbert, 1979–82; Taylor Garrett, 1982–88; Consultant: Taylor Joynson Garrett, 1988–2002; Taylor Wessing, 2002–09. Director: Baggeridge Brick plc, 1964–2003; Wilson Bowden plc, 1993–96; Jerwood Space Ltd, 1999–2015; Jerwood Ltd (formerly Jerwood Gall. Ltd), 2011–, and other cos; Chm., Reliance Resources Ltd, 1978–97. Mem., Educnl Assets Bd, 1988–90. Chm., Racehorse Owners Award, 1978–99. Mem. Council, Royal Court Th., 2000–. Dir, Med. Insce Agency Charity, 1992–98; Trustee: Hereford Mappa Mundi Trustee Co. Ltd, 1998–2011; RCP, 2007–10 (Mem., F and GP Bd, 1986–92); Alan and Karen Grieve Charitable Trust.

Pres., Trinity Hall Assoc., Cambridge, 2001–03. Vice Cdre, Sea Cadets Assoc., 2001–. Patron, Brendoncare for the Elderly, 1993–; Ambassador, Samaritans, 1999–. Hon. FTCL 2002; Hon. FRCP 2002. *Publications:* Purchase Tax, 1958; Jerwood: the Foundation and the Founders, 2009. *Recreations:* performing and visual arts, country life, collecting. *Address:* (office) 7 St Stephen's Mews, W2 5QZ. *T:* (020) 7792 1410, *Fax:* (020) 7792 1539; Cleefold, Stoke Lodge Farm, Clee Downton, Ludlow, Salop SY8 3EG. *T:* (01584) 823212. *Clubs:* Boodle's; Hawks (Cambridge).

**GRIEVE, Rt Hon. Dominic (Charles Roberts);** PC 2010; QC 2008; MP for Beaconsfield, since 1997 (C, 1997–2019; Ind, since 2019); *b* Lambeth, London, 24 May 1956; *s* of William Percival Grieve, QC and Evelyn Grieve (*née* Mijouain); *m* 1990, Caroline Hutton; two *s*. *Educ:* Westminster Sch.; Magdalen Coll., Oxford (MA Modern History); Poly. of Central London. Called to the Bar, Middle Temple, 1980, Bencher, 2004. Mem., Hammersmith and Fulham LBC, 1982–86. Contested (C) Norwood, 1987. Opposition front bench spokesman: for Scotland and on constitutional affairs, 1999–2001; on home affairs, 2001–03; on community cohesion, 2003–08; Shadow Attorney Gen., 2003–09; Shadow Home Sec., 2008–09; Shadow Sec. of State for Justice, 2009–10; Attorney Gen., 2010–14. Member: Jt Select Cttee on Statutory Instruments, 1997–2001; Select Cttee on Envmtl Audit, 1997–2001; Intelligence and Security Cttee, 2015–. Chm. Res. Cttee, 1992–95, Chm. Exec. Cttee, 2006–08, Finance and Gen. Purposes Cttee, 2006–08, Soc. of Cons. Lawyers. Member: Council, Justice, 1997– (Vice Chair); Franco-British Soc., 1997–2010 (Pres., 2011–); Luxembourg Soc., 1997–; Franco-British Council, 2010– (Vice Chm., 2011–). Hon. Recorder, Royal Bor. of Kingston-upon-Thames, 2012–. Lay visitor, police stations, 1990–96. Mem., London Dio. Synod, C of E, 1995–2001. Gov., 2010–, Mem. Council of Mgt, 2018–, Ditchley Foundn. Trustee, Oxford Centre for Islamic Studies, 2018–. *Recreations:* mountaineering, ski-ing, scuba diving, fell walking, travel, architecture. *Address:* House of Commons, SW1A 0AA. *T:* (020) 7219 6220; Temple Garden Chambers, 1 Harcourt Buildings, Temple, EC4Y 9DA. *T:* (020) 7353 0407. *Club:* Garrick.

**GRIEVE, Elizabeth Elaine;** Vice Lord-Lieutenant of Orkney, since 2019; *b* Aberdeen, 21 Feb. 1958; *d* of James Arnold Grieve and Elizabeth Anne May Grieve (*née* Groat). *Educ:* Kirkwall Grammar Sch.; Aberdeen Coll. of Educn (DipCE 1978); Univ. of Glasgow (MEd 1993). Teacher, Papdale Primary Sch., 1978–79; Glaitness Primary Sch., 1979–84; Asst Hd Teacher, Papdale Primary Sch., 1984–88; Hd Teacher, Stromness Primary Sch., 1988–98; Asst Dir, Educn, 1998–2005, Asst Chief Exec. and Dir, Corporate Services, 2005–11, Orkney Islands Council. Chair, Orkney Folk Fest., 2011–. DL Orkney, 2018. *Recreations:* music, travel, film, local history and culture. *Address:* Borgarnes, Finstown, Orkney KW17 2ET. *T:* (01856) 761736, 07715 547702. *E:* elainegrieve@yahoo.com.

**GRIEVE, James Robert;** theatre director; *b* Ashford, Kent, 28 July 1979; *s* of Robert Grieve and Linda Grieve. *Educ:* Harvey Grammar Sch., Folkestone; Univ. of Sheffield (BA Hons Eng. Lit. 2001). Reporter, Kent Regl Newspapers, 1997–98; freelance journalist, 1998–2001; JustGiving: Content Editor, 2001–02; Mktg Manager, 2003–05. Co-Founder and Artistic Dir, nabokov, 2001–10; Associate Dir, Bush Th., 2007–10; Jt Artistic Dir, Paines Plough, 2010–19. Productions include: Love, Love, Love, 2010–12; Jumpers for Goalposts, 2013–14; Translations, 2014; The Angry Brigade, 2014–15; Les Misérables, Wermland Opera, 2016–17; The Assassination of Katie Hopkins, 2018. *Recreations:* theatre, books, travel, restaurants, golf, Folkestone Invicta FC. *Address:* c/o Lily Williams, Curtis Brown Group Ltd, Haymarket House, 28–29 Haymarket, SW1Y 4SP. *T:* (020) 7393 4400. *E:* lily@curtisbrown.co.uk.

**GRIEVE, Michael Robertson Crichton,** QC 1998; **His Honour Judge Grieve;** a Circuit Judge, since 2011; *b* 12 Aug. 1951; *s* of Hon. Lord Grieve, VRD and Lorna St John Grieve, *y d* of late Engineer Rear-Adm. E. P. St J. Benn, CB; *m* 1983, Nadine Hilary Dyer; one *s*. *Educ:* Edinburgh Acad.; Sedbergh Sch.; New Coll., Oxford (BA PPE 1st cl. Hons 1972). Called to the Bar, Middle Temple, 1975, Bencher, 2008; in practice at the Bar, 1975–2011; Asst Recorder, 1998–2000; Recorder, 2000–11. *Recreations:* playing and watching football, tennis, music. *Address:* Southwark Crown Court, 1 English Grounds, SE1 2HU. *Club:* Queen's Park Rangers Football.

**GRIEVES, David,** CBE 1988; Vice Chairman, British Steel plc, 1991–94; Chairman, BSC Industry plc, 1995–98 (Deputy Chairman, 1980–95); *b* 10 Jan. 1933; *s* of Joseph and Isabel Grieves; *m* 1960, Evelyn Muriel Attwater; two *s*. *Educ:* Durham Univ. BSc, PhD. Graduate apprentice, United Steel cos, 1957; Labour Manager, Appleby Frodingham Steel Co., 1962; British Steel Corporation: Manager, Industrial Relations, S Wales Group, 1967; Gen. Man., Stocksbridge and Tinsley Park Works, 1971; Personnel Dir, Special Steels Div., 1973; Dir, Indust. Relations, 1975; Man. Dir, Personnel and Social Policy, 1977; Dir, BSC, later British Steel plc, 1983. Chairman: Avesta Sheffield, 1992–94; Xansa plc pension funds, 1995–2004. Mem. (non-exec.), Post Office, 1990–98. Mem., Employment Appeal Tribunal, 1983–2003. *Address:* 6 Collens Road, Harpenden, Herts AL5 2AJ. *T:* (01582) 259081.

**GRIFFEE, Andrew John;** writer; communications, broadcasting and projects consultant, since 2013; owner, Griff Consultancy Ltd, since 2014; *b* 25 Aug. 1961; *s* of John William Griffee and Kathleen Sandra Griffee; *m* 1988, Helen Caroline Emery; one *s* one *d*. *Educ:* Duke of York's Royal Military Sch., Dover; Highbury Coll. of Technol. (NCTJ Proficiency 1981); Univ. of Manchester (BA 1st cl. Hons 1986); Stanford Univ. (Exec. Develt Prog. 2001). Reporter: Poole and Dorset Herald, 1982–86; Northern Echo, 1986–87; Bath Evening Chronicle, 1987–89; Asst News Editor, BBC Bristol, 1989–92; Editor, News and Current Affairs, 1992–96, Head of Regl and Local Progs, 1996–99, BBC South; Controller, BBC English Regions, 1999–2008; Editl Dir, then Dir, W1 Project, BBC, 2008–13; Partner, Marquis Media Partners LLP, 2015–18. Member: Crime Writers' Assoc.; Soc. of Authors. *Publications:* The Abberley Space Rocket, 2016; Canal Pushers, 2019. *Recreations:* keeping Oxford Sandy and Black pigs, border terriers, Mark 1 Triumph Spitfire, hiring narrowboats. *Address:* Vinney Hill, Kingswood, Stanford Bridge, Worcs WR6 6SB.

**GRIFFIN, Avril;** *see* MacRory, A.

**GRIFFIN, Brian;** photographer; *b* Birmingham, 13 April 1948; *s* of James Henry Griffin and Edith Griffin; *m* 2003, Brynja Sverrisdottir; one *s* one *d*. *Educ:* Manchester Poly. (Dip. Photography; Dip. Associateship of Manchester). Freelance photographer and film maker, 1972–. Vis. Prof. of Photography, Univ. of Derby, 2013–. Hon. FRPS. DUniv Birmingham City, 2014. *Publications:* Copyright, 1978; Power, 1980; 'Y', 1983; Open, 1986; Portraits, 1987; Work, 1988; Influences, 2005; The Black Kingdom, 2013; Himmelstrasse, 2015; Gig, 2017; POP, 2017; Spud, 2018; England 1970's, 2018; Moscow 1974, 2018. *Recreations:* cycling, speedway racing. *Address:* Flat 11, Canada Wharf, 255 Rotherhithe Street, SE16 5ES. *T:* (020) 7394 7447, 07836 687166. *E:* brian@briangriffin.co.uk.

**GRIFFIN, Prof. George Edward,** CBE 2018; PhD, DSc; FRCP, FRCPI, FMedSci; Professor of Infectious Diseases and Medicine, St George's, University of London (formerly St George's Hospital Medical School), 1992–2013, now Emeritus (Chairman, Department of Cellular and Molecular Medicine, 2003–10; Vice Principal for Research, 2004–10); *b* 27 Feb. 1947; *s* of Herbert Griffin and Enid Mary Griffin (*née* Borril); *m* 1972, Daphne Joan Haylor (*d* 1998), Romford; two *s* one *d*. *Educ:* Malet Lambert Grammar Sch., Kingston upon Hull; King's Coll., London (BSc); St George's Hosp. Med. Sch. (MB BS; DSc); Univ. of Hull (PhD 1974); Harvard Univ. (Harkness Fellow). MRCP 1979, FRCP 1988; FRCPI 2009. Registrar and Tutor in Medicine, RPMS, 1977–78; St George's Hospital Medical School: Lectr in Medicine, 1978–82; Wellcome Trust Sen. Lectr, 1982–90; Dir, Wellcome Trust Clinical Tropical Unit, 1994–99; Chm., Dept of Internal Medicine, 1994–95; Hon. Cons. Physician, St George's Hosp., 1988–. Vis. Prof. of Medicine, Univ. of Michigan, 1992–. Chairman: Adv. Cttee on Dangerous Pathogens, DoH, 2005–14 (Mem., 1994–98); Ind. Cttee investigating E. Coli O157 outbreak in Surrey, 2009; Prion Risk Mgt Gp, DoH, 2011–17; TSE Risk Cttee, 2012–; Chair: Cttee Rev. of Highest Level Microbiological Containment Facilities in UK, 2008; Cttee on Common Regulatory Regulations for Contained Use of Pathogens, 2009–10; Enteric Disease Cttees (Global Enteric Multicenter Study, Malnutrition and Enteric Disease), Bill and Melinda Gates Foundn, 2013–18; Expert Advr, H of L Select Cttee on Fighting Infection, 2002–03. Wellcome Trust: Member: Infection and Immunity Panel, 1989–94; Tropical Interest Gp, 1991–94; Internat. Interest Gp, 1991–; Medical Research Council: Chm., Cttee for Develt and Implementation of Vaccines, 1994–; Member: Physiological Medicine and Infection Bd, 1994–; AIDS Vaccine Cttee, 1995–2010; HIV Virucidal Cttee, 1995–99; Bd, PHLS, 1995–2002; Adv. Bd, Public Health England, 2015–. Founder FMedSci 1998 (Vice Pres. (Internat.), 2013–18). *Publications:* scientific and clinical papers relating to pathogenesis of infection, vaccines. *Recreations:* walking, gardening, music. *Address:* 8 Buxton Drive, New Malden, Surrey KT3 3UZ. *T:* (020) 8949 4953. *Clubs:* Royal Automobile, MCC, Kennels.

**GRIFFIN, Dr Ian Paul;** JP; Director, Otago Museum, Dunedin, New Zealand, since 2013; *b* St Mary Cray, Orpington, Kent, 22 Jan. 1966; *s* of late Barry Paul Griffin and Carole Anne Griffin (*née* Armstrong); *m* 1990, Maria Anna Dunphy; one *s* two *d*. *Educ:* St Olave's Sch., Orpington; University Coll. London (BSc 1st Cl. Hons Astronomy 1987); Univ. of London (PhD Astrophys 1991). Director: Armagh Planetarium, Armagh, NI, 1990–94; Astronaut Meml Planetarium and Observatory, Cocoa, Fla, 1994–99; Auckland Observatory, NZ, 1999–2001; Hd, Office of Public Outreach, NASA Space Telescope Sci. Inst., Baltimore, Md, 2001–04; Dir, Mus. of Sci. and Industry, Manchester, 2004–07; CEO, Oxford Trust, 2008–13. Chm., UK Assoc. of Sci. and Discovery Centres, 2011–13. Hon. Fellow, Dept of Physics, Univ. of Otago, 2013. JP NZ, 2018. Prime Minister's Sci. Media Communication Prize (NZ), 2015. *Publications:* contrib. papers to scientific jls. *Recreations:* stargazing, panoramic photography, playing Aunt Sally. *Address:* c/o Otago Museum, 419 Great King Street, PO Box 6202, Dunedin 9059, New Zealand. *T:* 34747471. *E:* ian.griffin@otagomuseum.nz. *Club:* Explorers (New York) (Internat. Fellow).

**GRIFFIN, Prof. James Patrick,** DPhil; White's Professor of Moral Philosophy, University of Oxford, 1996–2000; Fellow, Corpus Christi College, Oxford, 1996–2000, now Emeritus Fellow; *b* 8 July 1933; *s* of Gerald Joseph Griffin and Catherine Griffin (*née* Noonan); *m* 1966, Catherine Maulde von Halban (*d* 1993); one *s* one *d*. *Educ:* Choate Sch., Wallingford, Conn; Yale Univ. (BA 1955); Oxford Univ. (DPhil 1960; MA 1963). University of Oxford: Rhodes Schol., Corpus Christi Coll., 1955–58; Sen. Schol., St Antony's Coll., 1958–60; Lectr, Christ Church, 1960–66; Fellow and Tutor in Philosophy, Keble Coll., 1966–96 (Hon. Fellow, 1996); Lectr in Philosophy, 1964–90; Radcliffe Fellow, 1982–84; Reader, 1990–96. Visiting Professor: Univ. of Wisconsin, 1970, 1978; Univ. of Santiago de Compostela, 1988, 1995; Gtr Philadelphia Philosophy Consortium, 1989; ITAM, Mexico, 1994; UNAM, Mexico, 1995, etc; Adjunct Prof., Centre for Applied Philosophy and Public Ethics, Canberra, 2002–; Dist. Vis. Prof., Rutgers Univ., 2002–; Tang Chun-I Vis. Prof., Chinese Univ. of Hong Kong, 2010. Medal, Nat. Educn Commn, Poland, 1992. Hon. DFil Santiago de Compostela, 2003. Order of Diego de Losada (Venezuela), 1999. *Publications:* Wittgenstein's Logical Atomism, 1964, repr. 1997; Well-Being: its meaning, measurement and moral importance, 1986; (jtly) Values, Conflict and the Environment, 1989, 2nd edn 1996; Value Judgement: improving our ethical beliefs, 1996; On Human Rights, 2008; (contrib.) Griffin on Human Rights, 2014; What Can Philosophy Contribute to Ethics?, 2015; articles in philosophical jls. *Recreations:* eating, drinking. *Address:* 10 Northmoor Road, Oxford OX2 6UP. *T:* (01865) 554130. *Club:* Oxford and Cambridge.

*See also* N. J. *Griffin*.

**GRIFFIN, Janet Mary, (Mrs Paul Griffin);** *see* Turner, Janet M.

**GRIFFIN, Prof. Jasper,** FBA 1986; Professor of Classical Literature, and Public Orator, Oxford University, 1992–2004; Fellow and Tutor in Classics, Balliol College, Oxford, 1963–2004; *b* 29 May 1937; *s* of Frederick William Griffin and Constance Irene Griffin (*née* Cordwell); *m* 1960, Miriam Tamara Dressler (*d* 2018); three *d*. *Educ:* Christ's Hospital; Balliol College, Oxford (1st Cl. Hon. Mods 1958; 1st Cl. Lit. Hum. 1960; Hertford Scholar 1958; Ireland Scholar 1958). Jackson Fellow, Harvard Univ., 1960–61; Oxford University: Dyson Research Fellow, Balliol Coll., 1961–63; Reader in Classical Lit., 1990–92. T. S. Eliot Meml Lectr, Univ. of Kent at Canterbury, 1984. *Publications:* Homer on Life and Death, 1980; Homer, 1980; Snobs, 1982; Latin Poets and Roman Life, 1985; The Mirror of Myth, 1986; (ed with J. Boardman and O. Murray) The Oxford History of the Classical World, 1986; Virgil, 1986; Homer, The Odyssey, 1987; Homer, Iliad ix, 1995. *Address:* Balliol College, Oxford OX1 3BJ. *T:* (01865) 559507.

**GRIFFIN, Dr John Parry,** BSc, PhD, MB, BS; FRCP, FRCPath; Director, Asklepieion (formerly John Griffin Associates) Ltd, since 1994; *b* 21 May 1938; *o s* of late David J. Griffin and Phyllis M. Griffin; *m* 1962, Margaret, *o d* of late Frank Cooper and Catherine Cooper; one *s* two *d*. *Educ:* Howardian High Sch., Cardiff; London Hosp. Medical Coll. Lethby and Buxton Prizes, 1958; BSc (1st Cl. Hons) 1959; PhD 1961; George Riddoch Prize in Neurology, 1962; MB BS 1964; LRCP, MRCS 1964; MRCP 1980, FRCP 1990; FRCPath 1986 (MRCPath 1982); FFPM 1989. Ho. Surg., Poplar Hosp., 1964; Ho. Phys., King George V Hosp., Ilford, 1964; Ho. Phys., London Hosp. Med. Unit, and Ho. Surg., London Hosp. Accident and Orthopaedic Dept, 1964–65; Lectr in Physiology, King's Coll., London, 1965–67; Head of Clinical Research, 3M Riker Labs (formerly Riker Labs), 1967–71; SMO, Medicines Div., 1971–76; PMO, Medicines Div., and Medical Assessor, Cttee on Safety of Medicines, 1976–77; SPMO and Professional Head of Medicines Div., DHSS, 1977–84; Med. Assessor, Medicines Commn, 1977–84; Dir, Assoc. of the British Pharmaceutical Industry, 1984–94. Hon. Clinical Asst, Royal Brompton Hosp., 1969–75; Hon. Consultant, Lister Hosp., Stevenage, 1973–94. Consultant, CDEE, MoD, 1976–94. Faculty Mem., Scripps Med. Res. Center, San Diego, 1997–98; Vis. Prof., Univ. of Surrey, 2000–05. Mem., Jt Formulary Cttee for British Nat. Formulary, 1978–84; UK Rep., EEC Cttee on Proprietary Med. Products; Chairman: Cttee on Prop. Med. Products Working Party on Safety Requirements, 1977–84; ICH Working Party on Safety Requirements, 1987–94. Mem. Bd, Faculty of Pharmaceutical Med., RCP, 1993–2005 (Chm., Bd of Examiners, 1997–2003; Mem., Fellowship Cttee, 1998–2005; Acad. Registrar, 2003–06). Ed. in Chief, Adverse Reactions and Toxicology Reviews, 1990–2003. FRSocMed. Thomas Young Lectr and Gold Medallist, St George's Hosp. Med. Sch., 1992. Commemorative Medal, Faculty of Pharm. Med., 2005. *Publications:* (jtly) Iatrogenic Diseases, 1972, 3rd edn 1985; (jtly) Manual of Adverse Drug Interactions, 1975, 5th edn

1997; (jtly) Drug Induced Emergencies, 1980; Medicines: research, regulation and risk, 1989, 2nd edn 1992; International Medicines Regulations, 1989; (jtly) The Textbook of Pharmaceutical Medicine, 1993, 7th edn 2013; Regulation of Medicinal Products, 2003; numerous articles in sci. and med. jls, mainly on aspects of neurophysiology, clinical pharmacology, toxicology and pharmacoeconomics. *Recreations:* gardening, local history. *Address:* Quartermans, Digswell Lane, Digswell, Herts AL6 0SP. *E:* johnparry38@sky.com.

**GRIFFIN, Keith Broadwell,** DPhil; Distinguished Professor of Economics, University of California, Riverside, 1988–2004, now Emeritus Distinguished Professor (Chairman, Department of Economics, 1988–93); *b* 6 Nov. 1938; *s* of Marcus Samuel Griffin and Elaine Ann Broadwell; *m* 1956, Dixie Beth Griffin; two *d*. *Educ:* Williams Coll., Williamstown, Mass (BA; Hon. DLitt, 1980); Balliol Coll., Oxford (BPhil, DPhil). Fellow and Tutor in Econs, Magdalen Coll., Oxford, 1965–76, Fellow by special election, 1977–79; Warden, Queen Elizabeth House, Oxford, 1978–79 (Actg Warden, 1973 and 1977–78); Dir, Inst. of Commonwealth Studies, Oxford, 1978–79 (Actg Dir, 1973 and 1977–78); Pres., Magdalen Coll., Oxford, 1979–88. Chief, Rural and Urban Employment Policies Br., ILO, 1975–76; Vis. Prof., Inst. of Econs and Planning, Univ. of Chile, 1962–63 and 1964–65; Dist. Vis. Prof., Amer. Univ. in Cairo, 2001; Vis. Fellow, Oxford Centre for Islamic Studies, 1998. Consultant: ILO, 1974, 1982, 1994, 1996, 1997; Internat. Bank for Reconstruction and Develt, 1973; UN Res. Inst. for Social Develt, 1971–72; FAO, 1963–64, 1967, 1978; Inter-Amer. Cttee for Alliance for Progress, 1968; US Agency for Internat. Develt, 1966; UNDP, 1989, 1991–98, 2001–02, 2004. Res. Advr, Pakistan Inst. of Develt Econs, 1965, 1970; Sen. Advr, OECD Develt Centre, Paris, 1986–88; Economic Advr, Govt of Bolivia, 1989–91. Member: Council, UN Univ., 1986–92; UN Cttee for Develt Planning, 1987–94; Chm., UN Res. Inst. for Social Develt, 1988–95. Mem., World Commn on Culture and Develt, 1994–95. Pres., Develt Studies Assoc., 1978–80. FAAAS 1997. *Publications:* (with Ricardo ffrench-Davis) Comercio Internacional y Políticas de Desarrollo Económico, 1967; Underdevelopment in Spanish America, 1969; (with John Enos) Planning Development, 1970; (ed) Financing Development in Latin America, 1971; (ed with Azizur Rahman Khan) Growth and Inequality in Pakistan, 1972; The Political Economy of Agrarian Change, 1974, 2nd edn 1979; (ed with E. A. G. Robinson) The Economic Development of Bangladesh, 1974; Land Concentration and Rural Poverty, 1976, 2nd edn 1981; International Inequality and National Poverty, 1978; (with Ashwani Saith) Growth and Equality in Rural China, 1981; (with Jeffrey James) The Transition to Egalitarian Development, 1981; (ed) Institutional Reform and Economic Development in the Chinese Countryside, 1984; World Hunger and the World Economy, 1987; Alternative Strategies for Economic Development, 1989; (ed with John Knight) Human Development and the International Development Strategy for the 1990s, 1990; (ed) The Economy of Ethiopia, 1992; (ed with Zhao Renwei) The Distribution of Income in China, 1993; (with Terry McKinley) Implementing a Human Development Strategy, 1994; (ed) Poverty and the Transition to a Market Economy in Mongolia, 1995; Studies in Globalization and Economic Transitions, 1996; (ed) Social Policy and Economic Transformation in Uzbekistan, 1996; (ed) Economic Reform in Vietnam, 1998; Studies in Development Strategy and Systemic Transformation, 2000; (ed) Poverty Reduction in Mongolia, 2003. *Recreation:* travel.

**GRIFFIN, Kenneth James,** OBE 1970; Deputy Chairman, Ugland International, 1993–2000; *b* 1 Aug. 1928; *s* of late Albert Griffin and Catherine (*née* Sullivan); *m* 1951, Doreen Cicely Simon (*d* 1992); one *s* one *d* (and one *s* decd). *Educ:* Dynevor Grammar Sch., Swansea; Swansea Technical College. Area Sec., ETU, 1960; Dist Sec., Confedn of Ship Building Engrg Unions, 1961; Sec., Craftsmen Cttee (Steel), 1961; Mem., Welsh Council, 1968; Mem., Crowther Commn on Constitution (Wales), 1969; Joint Sec., No 8 Joint Industrial Council Electrical Supply Industry, 1969; Industrial Adviser, DTI, 1971–72; Co-ordinator of Industrial Advisers, DTI, 1972–74; Special Adviser, Sec. of State for Industry, 1974; part-time Mem., NCB, 1973–82; a Dep. Chm., British Shipbuilders, 1977–83; Chm., Blackwall Engrg, 1983–85; Member: Suppl. Benefits Commn, 1968–80; Solicitors Disciplinary Tribunal, 1982–2002; Tribunal, Inst. of Legal Execs, 1992–2008. Chm., Network Housing Assoc., 1991–97; Vice-Chm., UK Housing Trust, 1989; Mem. Bd, Housing Corp., 1995–2002; Exec. Advr, Mobile Training, 1989–90. *Recreations:* golf, music, reading. *Address:* 214 Cyncoed Road, Cyncoed, Cardiff CF23 6RS. *T:* (029) 2075 2184. *Club:* Reform.

**GRIFFIN, Liam;** Vice Chairman, Addison Lee Ltd, since 2015; *b* Barnet, 9 March 1973; *s* of John Griffin and Janet Griffin; *m* Clare; three *s*. *Educ:* Loughborough Univ. (BSc Econs and Politics). Ops Dir, 2002–05, Man. Dir, 2005–13, CEO, 2013–15, Addison Lee Ltd. *Recreations:* motor racing, golf. *Address:* Addison Lee Ltd, 35–37 William Road, NW1 3ER. *T:* (020) 7387 8888. *E:* mel.bartram@addisonlee.com.

**GRIFFIN, Prof. Matthew Joseph,** PhD; Professor, since 2001 and Head, Astronomy Instrumentation Group, School of Physics and Astronomy, since 2019, Cardiff University (Head, School of Physics and Astronomy, 2014–18); *b* Dublin, 25 July 1954; *s* of Matthew Griffin and Eileen Griffin; *m* 1991, Melanie Tuke; two *s* one *d*. *Educ:* University Coll. Dublin (BE Electrical 1976); Queen Mary Coll., Univ. of London (MSc Astrophysics 1980; PhD Physics 1985). FInstP 2012. Electronics Engr, Standard Telephones and Cables, 1976–80; Queen Mary College, subseq. Queen Mary and Westfield College, University of London: Postdoctoral Res. Associate, 1983–89; Lectr in Astrophyiscs, 1989–95; Reader in Astrophysics, 1995–2000; Prof. of Astrophysics, 2000–01; Cardiff University: Dep. Hd, Sch. of Physics and Astronomy and Dir, Res., 2006–14. Chairman: UK Next Generation Space Telescope Adv. Gp, 2001–02; Space Sci. Adv. Cttee, PPARC, 2002–06 (Mem., 2000–02); Sci. Bd, STFC, 2012–14 (Mem., 2007–09; Dep. Chm., 2010–12); Mgt Bd, Athena Prog., UK Space Agency, 2018–; Mem., REF2021 Physics Panel, 2018–. Member: ESA Herschel Sci. Team, 1998–2017; ESA SPICA Sci. Study Team, 2018–; Chm., Bd, James Clerk Maxwell Telescope, 2011–12 (Dep. Chm., 2009–11). FLSW 2012; FRAS 2017. Hon. Dr Aix-Marseille, 2018. Jackson-Gwilt Medal, RAS, 2013. *Publications:* over 450 scientific articles in jls. *Recreations:* reading, cinema, football, golf. *Address:* School of Physics and Astronomy, Cardiff University, Queen's Building, The Parade, Cardiff CF24 3AA. *T:* (029) 2087 4203. *E:* matt.griffin@astro.cf.ac.uk.

**GRIFFIN, Michael;** see Griffin, S. M.

**GRIFFIN, Nicholas John;** Member (BNP) North West Region, European Parliament, 2009–14; *b* Barnet, 1 March 1959; *s* of Edgar Griffin and Jean Griffin; *m* 1985, Jacquelene Cook; one *s* three *d*. *Educ:* Downing Coll., Cambridge (BA Hons Law 1980; boxing blue). Former agricl engr, builder, forestry worker. Editor, Spearhead, 1996–99. Leader, 1999–2014, Pres., 2014, BNP. Contested (BNP): Barking, 2010; NW Reg., EP, 2014. Mem., Editl Bd, Nationalism Today, 1980–89. *Recreations:* walking, reading, cooking, annoying liberals.

**GRIFFIN, Nicholas John;** QC 2012; *b* Oxford, 14 Feb. 1968; *s* of Prof. James Patrick Griffin, *qv*; *m* 2001, Julia Zagrodnik; one *d*. *Educ:* Univ. of Bristol (LLB Hons Eur. Legal Studies). Called to the Bar: Inner Temple, 1992, Bencher, 2019; NI, 2011. Assistant Commissioner: Boundary Commn for England, 2011–12; to Dist Electoral Areas Comr for NI, 2013. Mem., Security Vetting Appeals Panel, 2017–. Bd Mem., UK Anti-Doping, 2017–. Trustee, Anti-Slavery Internat., 2015–. *Address:* QEB Hollis Whiteman, 1–2 Laurence Pountney Hill, EC4R 0EU.

**GRIFFIN, Robert;** Headmaster, Exeter School, since 2003; *b* 17 June 1962; *s* of Paschal and Patricia Griffin; *m* 1989, Allison White; one *s* one *d*. *Educ:* Wallington High Sch. for Boys; Christ Church, Oxford (MA 1st Cl. Mod. Langs 1985; Arteaga prize); Univ. of York (PGCE Mod. Langs 1989). Asst Master, Markham Coll., Lima, 1986–88; Asst Master and Hd of Mod. Langs, Haileybury, Hertford, 1989–98; Second Master, Royal Grammar Sch., Guildford, 1998–2003. Chm., SW Div., HMC, 2010–11. Gov., Truro Sch., 2017–. *Recreations:* cycling, walking on Dartmoor, the works of García Márquez and Neruda, visiting National Trust properties. *Address:* Exeter School, Victoria Park Road, Exeter, Devon EX2 4NS. *T:* (01392) 273679. *E:* headmaster@exeterschool.org.uk.

**GRIFFIN, Prof. (Selwyn) Michael,** OBE 2013; MD; FRCS; Professor of Surgery, University of Newcastle upon Tyne, since 1999; Consultant Surgeon, Newcastle upon Tyne Hospitals NHS Trust, since 1998; Head, Northern Oesophagogastric Cancer Unit, Royal Victoria Infirmary, Newcastle upon Tyne, since 1990; President, Royal College of Surgeons of Edinburgh, since 2018; *b* Newcastle upon Tyne, 7 Feb. 1955; *s* of late Selwyn Griffin and Joan Campbell Griffin (*née* Dickinson); *m*; one *s* two *d*. *Educ:* Fettes Coll., Edinburgh; Univ. of Newcastle upon Tyne (MB BS 1978; MD 1989). FRCS 1983. Sen. Registrar in Surgery, northern reg.; Consultant Surgeon: to Newcastle Gen. Hosp., 1990–98; to Royal Victoria Infirmary, 1998–2019. Mem. Bd, Intercollegiate Examinations, 2010–; Chairman: Intercollegiate Bd of Gen. Surgery, 2013–16; Jt Cttee of Intermediate Examinations, 2017–19; Jt Colleges Surgical Fellowship Examinations, 2017–19; external examr at univs incl. Edinburgh, Trinity Coll., Dublin, Hong Kong, Cambridge, Malaysia, W Indies, Southern Calif, Nottingham and London. Member: N of England Surgical Soc., 1990– (Pres., 2008–09); Assoc. of Upper Gastrointestinal Surgeons of GB and Ire., 1996– (Pres., 2004–06); European Soc. of Diseases for the Oesophagus, 2000– (Pres., 2011–13); James IV Assoc. of Surgeons, 2000– (Vice Pres., 2011–14); Internat. Soc. for Diseases of the Oesophagus, 2000–; Moynihan Chirurgical, 2000– (Pres., 2015–16). Mem. Council, RCSEd, 2009–. FFSTEd 2016. Hon. FCSHK 1995; Hon. FRCSEd 1997; Hon. FRCSGlas 2015; Hon. FRCSI 2016. Ed., Diseases of the Oesophagus, 2009–. *Publications:* (ed jtly) Oesophagogastric Surgery: a companion to specialist surgical practice, 1997, 6th edn 2018; over 350 articles in med. and surgical jls incl. BMJ, Brit. Jl Surgery. *Recreations:* Rugby Union, cricket, football, fine wine. *Address:* The Beehive, Hartburn, Morpeth NE61 4JB. *T:* (01352) 271635. *E:* smgriffin@rcsed.ac.uk.

**GRIFFIN, Theresa Mary;** Member (Lab) North West Region, European Parliament, since 2014; *b* Coventry, 11 Dec. 1962. *Educ:* Bishop Ullathorne Comprehensive Sch.; Lancaster Univ. (BA 1st Cl.; MA). Worked in community theatre; Dir of Communications and Res., North West Arts; Regl Organiser, UNISON, 2009–14. Former Mem. (Lab) Liverpool CC. Mem., NW Political Cttee, UNITE. *Address:* European Parliament, 60 Rue Wiertz, 1047 Brussels, Belgium; (office) Unit 303, Vanilla Factory, 39 Fleet Street, Liverpool L1 4AR.

**GRIFFINS, Roy Jason,** CB 2003; Chairman, London City Airport, 2007–17; *b* 8 May 1946; *s* of Manuel Griffins and Betty Griffins; *m* 1984, Margaret Alison Redfern; one *d*. *Educ:* Blackpool Grammar Sch.; Bristol Univ. (BA). Barclays Bank Foreign Branches, 1967–68; Systems Analyst, Internat. Computers Ltd, 1968–70; Sen. Systems Analyst, with BBC, 1970–74; Copywriter, Krohn Advertising, Montreal, 1975–76; Principal, Wildlife Conservation, DoE, 1976–77; First Sec. (Envmt), UK Representation to EC, Brussels (on secondment), 1978–80; Sec. to Third London Airport Inquiry, DoE, 1981–83; Department of Transport: Principal (Aviation), then Head, Airports Policy, 1984–87; Principal Private Sec. to Sec. of State for Transport, 1987–89; Counsellor, Washington (on secondment), 1990–93; Asst Sec., Channel Tunnel Rail Link, Dept of Transport, 1993–96; Dir, Railways, DETR, 1996–99; Dir-Gen., Civil Aviation, DETR, subseq. DTLR, then DfT, 1999–2004; UK Public Affairs Dir, Eurotunnel, 2004; Dir-Gen., Airports Council Internat. for Europe, 2004–06; Head, UK Delegn to Channel Tunnel Intergovernmental Commn, 2006–12. Mem., Franco-British Council, 2006–16 (Treas., 2010–16). Non-executive Director: London Ambulance Service, 2006–14 (Vice-Chair, 2010–14); NHS Blood and Transplant, 2012–18. Gov., King's Cross Acad., 2018–. Chevalier, Légion d'Honneur (France), 2017. *Recreations:* tennis, France, films, food. *Address:* 55 Tapestry, Canal Reach, N1C 4AZ. *Club:* Reform.

**GRIFFITH, Rev. (Arthur) Leonard;** Lecturer in Homiletics, Wycliffe College, Toronto, 1977–87, retired; *b* 20 March 1920; *s* of Thomas Griffiths and Sarah Jane Taylor; *m* 1947, Anne Merelie Cayford; two *d*. *Educ:* Public and High Schs, Brockville, Ont; McGill Univ., Montreal (BA, McGill, 1942); United Theological Coll., Montreal (BD 1945; Hon. DD 1962); Mansfield Coll., Oxford, England, 1957–58. Ordained in The United Church of Canada, 1945; Minister: United Church, Arden, Ont, 1945–47; Trinity United Church, Grimsby, Ont, 1947–50; Chalmers United Church, Ottawa, Ont, 1950–60; The City Temple, London, 1960–66; Deer Park United Church, Toronto, 1966–75; ordained in Anglican Church 1976; Minister, St Paul's Church, Bloor St, Toronto, 1975–85 (Hon. Asst, 1995). Hon. DD Wycliffe Coll., Toronto, 1985. *Publications:* The Roman Letter Today, 1959; God and His People, 1960; Beneath The Cross of Jesus, 1961; What is a Christian?, 1962; Barriers to Christian Belief, 1962; A Pilgrimage to the Holy Land, 1962; The Eternal Legacy, 1963; Pathways to Happiness, 1964; God's Time and Ours, 1964; The Crucial Encounter, 1965; This is Living!, 1966; God in Man's Experience, 1968; Illusions of our Culture, 1969; The Need to Preach, 1971; Hang on to the Lord's Prayer, 1973; We Have This Ministry, 1973; Ephesians: a positive affirmation, 1975; Gospel Characters, 1976; Reactions to God, 1979; Take Hold of the Treasure, 1980; From Sunday to Sunday, 1987. *Recreations:* music, drama, travelling, adult education, bridge.

**GRIFFITH, Martin Peter W.;** see Wyn Griffith.

**GRIFFITH, Nia Rhiannon;** MP (Lab) Llanelli, since 2005; *b* 4 Dec. 1956; *d* of Prof. T. Gwynfor Griffith and Dr Rhiannon Griffith (*née* Howell); *m* (marr. diss.). *Educ:* Univ. of Oxford (BA 1st cl. Hons Mod. Foreign Langs 1979); UCNW, Bangor (PGCE 1980). Language teacher: Oldham, 1981–83; Queen Elizabeth Cambria Sch., Carmarthen, 1983–85; Hd of Langs Faculty, Gowerton Comp. Sch., Swansea, 1986–92; Advr and Schs Inspector, Estyn, 1992–97; Hd of Langs, Morriston Comp. Sch., Swansea, 1997–2005. Mem. (Lab), Carmarthen Town Council, 1987–99 (Sheriff, 1998; Dep. Mayor, 1998). Shadow Minister for Business, Innovation and Skills, 2010–11, for Wales, 2011–15; Shadow Sec. of State for Wales, 2015–16, for Defence, 2016–. *Publications:* Ciao! Book 2: a textbook for teaching Italian, 1990; 100 Ideas for Teaching Languages, 2005. *Address:* (office) 43 Pottery Street, Llanelli SA15 1SU; House of Commons, SW1A 0AA.

**GRIFFITH, Prof. Rachel Susan,** CBE 2015; PhD; FBA 2009; Professor of Economics, University of Manchester, since 2010; Research Director, Institute for Fiscal Studies, since 2016 (Deputy Research Director, 2006–16); *b* Ithaca, NY, 16 May 1963; *d* of Joe H. Griffith and Patricia Jean Griffith (*née* Jeffries); *m* 2000, James Banks. *Educ:* Univ. of Massachusetts (BSc); City of London Poly. (MSc Econometrics and Forecasting 1991); Keele Univ. (PhD 1999). Hd of Res., EIRIS Services Ltd, London, 1986–93; Lectr (pt-time), City of London Poly., 1991–93; Institute for Fiscal Studies: Sen. Res. Economist,

**GRIFFITH-JONES**; 1993–97; Dir, Productivity and Innovation Res., 1997–2002; Dep. Dir, 2002–06; Sen. Economist, Competition Commn, 2001–02; Prof. of Econs, UCL, 2003–10. Res. Associate, Centre for Econ. Policy Res., London, 1999– . President: Eur. Econ. Assoc., 2015; REconS, 2019– (Mem., Exec. Cttee, 2005–11). Dep. Chair, HEFCE REF 2014 sub-panel 18, 2011–14; Mem., ESRC, 2018– . Fellow, Econometric Soc., 2016. Bd Mem., 2002–11, Dir, 2006–11, Rev. of Econ. Studies; Man. Ed., Econ. Jl, 2011–14. *Publications:* (with P. Aghion) Competition and Growth, 2005; contribs to learned jls incl. Amer. Econ. Rev., Qly Jl of Econs, Rev. of Econ. Studies, Econ. Jl, Rev. of Econs and Stats, Jl of the Eur. Econ. Assoc., Jl of Public Econs, Fiscal Studies, Oxford Rev. of Econ. Policy. *Recreations:* running, cycling, hiking. *Address:* Institute for Fiscal Studies, 7 Ridgemount Street, WC1E 7AE.

**GRIFFITH-JONES, David Eric;** QC 2000; **His Honour Judge David Griffith-Jones;** a Circuit Judge, since 2007; Resident Judge and Honorary Recorder for Maidstone, since 2018; *b* Nairobi, 7 March 1953; *s* of Sir Eric Newton Griffith-Jones, KBE, CMG, QC and Mary Patricia Griffith-Jones; *m* 1st, 1978, Deborah Judith Laidlaw Mockeridge (marr. diss. 1983); 2nd, 1984, Virginia Ann Meredith Brown; two *s* one *d*. *Educ:* Marlborough Coll.; Bristol Univ. (LLB 1974). FCIArb 1991. Called to the Bar, Middle Temple, 1975; Asst Recorder, 1992–97; Recorder, 1997–2007. Asst Boundary Comr, 2000– . Part-time Pres., Mental Health Review Tribunal, 2002–08; a Tribunal Judge, First-tier Tribunal (Health, Educn and Social Care Chamber) Mental Health, 2009– ; Judicial Mem., Parole Bd, 2009–14. Member: Sports Disputes Resolution Panel, 2000– ; Panel of Sports Arbitrators, CIArb, 2002– ; Chairman: Drugs Appeal Tribunal, ICC Champions Trophy, 2004; ICC Johnny Walker Series, 2005; ICC Under-19 World Cup, 2006; World Cup, 2007; Appeals Cttee, LTA, 2004–06. CIArb accredited mediator, 2003. *Publications:* Law and the Business of Sport, 1997; (contrib.) Sport: law and practice, 2003, 3rd edn 2014. *Recreations:* sport, woodturning, skydiving, blues harmonica. *Address:* Maidstone Combined Court Centre, The Law Courts, Barker Road, Maidstone, Kent ME16 8EQ. *Clubs:* Sevenoaks Rugby Football, Falconhurst Cricket, Royal Ashdown Forest Golf.

**GRIFFITH-JONES, John Guthrie;** DL; Chairman, StepChange Debt Charity, since 2019; *b* 11 May 1954; *s* of Mervyn Griffith-Jones and Joan (*née* Baker); *m* 1990, Cathryn Mary Stone; one *s* one *d*. *Educ:* Eton; Trinity Hall, Cambridge (BA 1975). Peat Marwick Mitchell, subseq. KPMG: joined 1975; Partner, Corporate Finance, 1987–2002; Chief Exec., 2002–06, Chm and Sen. Partner, KPMG UK, 2006–12; Chm., Europe, Middle East, Africa and India Region, 2008–12. Non-exec. Dir and Dep. Chm., FSA, 2012–13; Chm., FCA, 2013–18. Served TA, Royal Green Jackets, 1975–90. Liveryman, Co. of Skinners, 1997– . DL Essex, 2019. *Recreations:* tennis, bridge.

**GRIFFITH-JONES, His Honour Richard Haydn;** a Circuit Judge, 1999–2017; Resident Judge, Coventry and Warwick Crown Court, 2011–17; *b* 29 June 1951; *s* of Wyn and Mary Griffith-Jones; *m* 1974, Susan Hale; three *s* one *d*. *Educ:* Solihull Sch.; Leeds Univ. (LLB Hons). Called to the Bar, Middle Temple, 1974; a Recorder, 1994–99. Liaison Judge to Birmingham Magistrates and Sutton Coldfield Magistrates, 2006–10. Hon. Recorder of Coventry, 2011–17. *Publications:* contrib. to Law Qly Rev. *Recreations:* poultry keeping, watching Association football.

**GRIFFITH-JONES, Rev. Robin Guthrie,** DLitt; FSA; Master of The Temple, Temple Church, since 1999; *b* 29 May 1956; *s* of Mervyn and Joan Griffith-Jones. *Educ:* Westminster; New Coll., Oxford (MA); Westcott House; Christ's Coll., Cambridge (MA); King's Coll. London (DLitt 2014). Christie's (English Drawings and Watercolours), 1978–84; ordained deacon, 1989, priest, 1990; Curate, St Jude, Cantril Farm and Stockbridge Village, Liverpool, 1989–92; Chaplain: Lincoln Coll., Oxford, 1992–99; to Lord Mayor of London, 2002–03. Vis. Lectr, 2008–12, Sen. Lectr, 2012– , KCL. *Publications:* The Four Witnesses, 2000; The Gospel according to St Paul, 2004; The Da Vinci Code and the Secrets of the Temple, 2006; Mary Magdalene, 2008; (ed jtly) The Temple Church, 2010; (ed) Islam and English Law, 2013; (ed jtly) Magna Carta, Religion and the Rule of Law, 2015; (ed jtly) Tomb and Temple: re-imagining the sacred buildings of Jerusalem, 2018. *Address:* Master's House, Temple, EC4Y 7BB. *T:* (020) 7353 8559. *Clubs:* Athenæum, Pratt's.

**GRIFFITH WILLIAMS, Hon. Sir John,** Kt 2007; a Judge of the High Court of Justice, Queen's Bench Division, 2007–14; President and Lay Judge, Provincial Court of Church in Wales, since 2007; Commissioner, Special Immigration Appeals Commission, since 2014; Judicial Commissioner, Investigatory Powers Commission, since 2017; *b* 20 Dec. 1944; *s* of Griffith John Williams, TD and Alison Williams; *m* 1971, Mair Tasker Watkins, *d* of Rt Hon. Sir Tasker Watkins, VC, GBE, PC; two *d*. *Educ:* King's School, Bruton; The Queen's College, Oxford (BA; Hon. Fellow 2014). Served 4th Bn, RWF (TA), 1965–68; Welsh Volunteers (TAVR), 1968–71 (Lieut). Called to the Bar, Gray's Inn, 1968, Bencher, 1994; a Recorder, 1984–2000; QC 1985; a Dep. High Court Judge, 1993–2000; a Circuit Judge, 2000–01; a Sen. Circuit Judge and Hon. Recorder of Cardiff, 2001–07; a Presiding Judge, Wales Circuit, 2010–13; Dep. High Court Judge, 2015– . Mem., Criminal Injuries Compensation Bd, 1999–2000. Mem., Bar Council, 1990–93; Leader, Wales and Chester Circuit, 1996–98 (Treas., 1993–95). Asst Comr, Boundary Commn for Wales, 1994–2000. Chancellor, dio. of Llandaff, 1999–2016 (Dep. Chancellor, 1996–99). Hon. Fellow, Cardiff Univ., 2008. Hon. LLD S Wales, 2013. *Recreation:* golf. *Address:* c/o Royal Courts of Justice, Strand, WC2A 2LL. *Clubs:* Cardiff and County (Cardiff); Royal Porthcawl Golf.

**GRIFFITHS,** family name of **Barons Griffiths of Burry Port** and **Griffiths of Fforestfach**.

**GRIFFITHS OF BURRY PORT,** Baron *cr* 2004 (Life Peer), of Pembrey and Burry Port in the County of Dyfed; **Rev. Dr Leslie John Griffiths;** Superintendent Minister, Wesley's Chapel, 1996–2017; President of the Methodist Conference, 1994–95; *b* 15 Feb. 1942; *s* of late Sidney and Olwen Griffiths; *m* 1969, Margaret, *d* of Alfred and Kathleen Rhodes; two *s* one *d*. *Educ:* Llanelli Grammar Sch.; Univ. of Wales (BA); Univ. of Cambridge (MA); Univ. of London (PhD). Junior Res. Fellow, University Coll. of S Wales and Monmouthshire, Cardiff, 1963; Asst Lectr in English, St David's Coll., Lampeter, 1964–67; trained for Methodist Ministry, Wesley Ho., Cambridge, 1967–70; Asst Minister, Wesley Church, Cambridge, 1969–70; Petit Goâve Circuit, Haïti, 1970–71; Port-au-Prince Circuit and Asst Headmaster, Nouveau Collège Bird, 1971–74; Minister, Reading Circuit, 1974–77; Superintendent Minister: Cap Haïtien Circuit, Haïti, 1977–80; Wanstead and Woodford Circuit, 1980–86; W London Mission, 1986–91; Finchley and Hendon Circuit, 1991–96. Hon. Canon, St Paul's Cathedral, 2000–17, now Emeritus Canon (Mem. Council, 2000– ). Opposition Spokesperson for DCMS, 2017– , for Wales, 2017– , H of L; Mem., Ecclesiastical Cttee, 2010–17; Vice Chair, All Party Parly Gp on Haiti, 2010– , on Cambodia, 2011– . Trustee: Addiction Recovery Foundn, 1989–2004; Sir Halley Stewart Trust, 1999–2013; Art and Christianity Enquiry, 1999–2008; One World Trust, 2008–11; Mem., Bd of Dirs, The Abraham Path, Harvard Univ., 2009–11. Dir, Birnbeck Housing Assoc., 1992–96. Gov., Bd of Christian Aid, 1990–98 (Chm., Africa and ME Cttee, 1991–95); Chm., Bd of Govs, Southlands Coll., 1997–2003; Mem. Council, Univ. of Surrey Roehampton (formerly Roehampton Inst.), 1997–2003; Gov. and Trustee, Central Foundn Schs of London, 2000– (Vice Chm., Central Foundn Schs Trust, 2009–11; Chm. of Trustees, 2011– ); Trustee, Wesley House, Cambridge, 2002–04 (Chm., F and GP Cttee, 2002–04). Chairman: Methodist Church's European Reference Gp, 1996–99; Churches Adv. Council on Local Broadcasting, 1996–2000; Coll. of Preachers, 2004–11; Methodist Church Heritage Cttee, 2008–11. Pres., Boys' Brigade, 2011– . FLSW 2012. Hon. Fellow: Sarum Coll., 2001; Sion Coll., 2002; Cardiff Univ., 2005; St David's Coll., Lampeter, 2006; Harris Manchester Coll., Oxford, 2015. DUniv Oxford Brookes, 2016; Hon. DMin Evansville, 2016. Mem., Order of Christopher Columbus (Dominican Republic), 2011. KCSJ 1989. *Publications:* A History of Haïtian Methodism, 1991; Letters Home, 1995; The Aristide Factor, 1997; Touching the Pulse: worship and our diverse world, 1998; Voices from the Desert, 2002; (with J. Potter) World Without End?, 2007; View from the Edge (autobiog.), 2010. *Recreation:* fun and fellowship spiced with occasional moments of solitude. *Address:* 26 Stroud Road, Woodside, Croydon, SE25 5DR. *Club:* Graduate Centre (Cambridge).

**GRIFFITHS OF FFORESTFACH,** Baron *cr* 1991 (Life Peer), of Fforestfach in the county of West Glamorgan; **Brian Griffiths;** Vice Chairman, Goldman Sachs (Europe), since 1991; *b* 27 Dec. 1941; *s* of Ivor Winston Griffiths and Phyllis Mary Griffiths (*née* Morgan); *m* 1965, Rachel Jane Jones; one *s* two *d*. *Educ:* Dynevor Grammar School; London School of Economics, Univ. of London. (BSc(Econ), MSc(Econ)). Assistant Lecturer in Economics, LSE, 1965–68, Lecturer in Economics, 1968–76; City University: Prof. of Banking and Internat. Finance, 1977–85; Dir, Centre for Banking and Internat. Finance, 1977–82; Dean, Business Sch., 1982–85; Head of Prime Minister's Policy Unit, 1985–90. Vis. Prof., Univ. of Rochester, USA, 1972–73; Prof. of Ethics, Gresham Coll., 1984–87; Dir, Bank of England, 1984–86 (Mem., Panel of Academic Consultants, 1977–86). Director: Herman Miller, 1991–2012; Times Newspapers, 1991– ; HTV (Wales), 1991–93; Servicemaster, 1992–2007; Telewest, 1994–98; English, Welsh and Scottish Railway, 1996–2007; Goldman Sachs Internat., 2007–17; Internat. Advr, Goldman Sachs, 1991– . Chairman: Trillium, 1998–2008; Westminster Health Care, 1999–2002. Chairman: Centre for Policy Studies, 1991–2000; Sch. Exams and Assessment Council, 1991–93; Trustees, Lambeth Fund, 1997–2009. Fellow: Trinity Coll., Carmarthen, 1997; Swansea Inst. of HE, 2003; Sarum Coll., 2006; Univ. of Wales, Swansea, 2006. Hon. Senator, Univ. of St Gallen, Switzerland. Hon. DSc City, 1999; Hon. DSc(Econ) Wales, 2004. *Publications:* Is Revolution Change? (ed and contrib.), 1972; Mexican Monetary Policy and Economic Development, 1972; Invisible Barriers to Invisible Trade, 1975; Inflation: the price of prosperity, 1976; (ed with G. E. Wood) Monetary Targets, 1980; The Creation of Wealth, 1984; (ed with G. E. Wood) Monetarism in the United Kingdom, 1984; Morality and the Market Place, 1989. *Address:* c/o House of Lords, SW1A 0PW. *Club:* Garrick.

**GRIFFITHS, (Albert) John;** Member (Lab) Newport East, National Assembly for Wales, since 1999; *b* 19 Dec. 1956; *s* of Albert John Griffiths and Hannah Griffiths (*née* O'Connor); *m* 1978, Alison Kim Hopkins; two *s*. *Educ:* UC, Cardiff (LLB Hons Law); Dip. in Social Studies, 1996. Lectr in Further Educn and Higher Educn, 1988–89; Production Exec., 1989–90; solicitor, 1990–99. National Assembly for Wales: Dep. Minister for Economic Develt, 2001–03, for Health and Social Care, 2003–07, for Educn, Lifelong Learning and Skills (formerly for Skills), 2007–10; Counsel Gen. and Leader of Legislative Prog., 2010–11; Minister for Envmt and Sustainable Develt, 2011–13, for Culture and Sport, 2013–14. Chm., All Party Gp on Internat. Develt, 2004– , on Sport, 2004– . *Recreations:* cricket, tennis, running, circuit training, reading, travel. *Address:* National Assembly for Wales, Cardiff Bay, Cardiff CF99 1NA. *T:* 0300 200 7122; (office) Suite 5, Seventh Floor, Clarence House, Clarence Place, Newport NP19 7AA. *T:* (01633) 222302.

**GRIFFITHS, Alun Brynmor,** MW; International Director, Vats Liquor Chain Store Management Co. Ltd, Beijing, since 2013; *b* 29 Dec. 1953; *s* of Islwyn ap Ifan Griffiths and Olwen Enid Griffiths; *m* 1981, Helen Mary Hayes; two *s*. *Educ:* Glyn Grammar Sch., Epsom; University Coll. of Wales, Aberystwyth (BA Hons French). MW 1991. Manager: Stones of Belgravia, wine merchants, 1976–81; Butlers Wine Bar, London, 1981–83; Sales Exec., Enotria Wines, London, 1983–85; Admin. Manager, Fields Wine Merchants, London, 1985–87; Wine buyer: Fortnum & Mason, 1987–92; Harrods, 1992–94; Gen. Manager Heathrow, 1994–96, Wine Dir, 1996–2012, Berry Bros & Rudd Ltd. Hospitalier de Pomerol, 1989; Jurade de St Emilion, 1990; Comdr de Bontemps du Médoc et du Graves, 1992; Chevalier du Tastevin, 2001; Ordre des Coteaux de Champagne, 2016. *Recreations:* squash, horse-racing, food and wine, walking, tennis. *E:* alun.griffiths@vatsliquor.com.

**GRIFFITHS, Andrew James;** MP (C) Burton, since 2010; *b* Wolverhampton, 19 Oct. 1970; *s* of Robert Griffiths and Harriet Griffiths (*née* Du'Rose); *m* 2013, Kate Kniveton; one *d*. *Educ:* High Arcal Sch., Sedgley. Worked for family engrg business; Halifax plc, until 1999; Advr to Cons. MEPs, 1999–2004; Chief of Staff: to Shadow Sec. of State for Envmt and Transport, 2004, for Family, 2004–05, for Culture, Media and Sport, 2005–07, for Community and Local Govt, 2007–09; to Chm., Cons. Party, 2009–10; Sec. to Bd, Cons. Party, 2009–10. Contested (C) Dudley N, 2001. PPS to Brandon Lewis, MP, 2015–16, to Rt Hon. Mark Francois, MP, 2015–16; a Lord Comr of HM Treasury (Govt Whip), 2016–18; Parly Under-Sec. of State, BEIS, 2018. *Recreations:* supporting British brewing industry, football, cricket. *Address:* (office) Gothard House, 9 St Paul's Square, Burton on Trent, Staffs DE14 2EF. *T:* (01283) 568894. *E:* andrew.griffiths.mp@parliament.uk. *Clubs:* Uttoxeter British Legion; Rolleston Working Men's.

**GRIFFITHS, Antony Vaughan,** FBA 2000; Keeper, Department of Prints and Drawings, British Museum, 1991–2011; *b* 28 July 1951; *s* of late Richard Cerdin Griffiths and Pamela de Grave Griffiths (*née* Hetherington). *Educ:* Highgate Sch.; Christ Church, Oxford (BA); Courtauld Inst. of Art, London Univ. (MA). Joined Dept of Prints and Drawings, BM, 1976, as Asst Keeper; Dep. Keeper, 1981–91. Slade Prof. of Fine Art, Univ. of Oxford, 2014–15. Chm., Print Quarterly Pubns, 2001– . Chm., Walpole Soc., 2013– . Trustee: Art Fund, 2011– ; Henry Moore Foundn, 2014– . *Publications:* Prints and Printmaking, 1980, 2nd edn 1996; (with Reginald Williams) The Department of Prints and Drawings in the British Museum: a user's guide, 1987; (with Frances Carey) German Printmaking in the Age of Goethe, 1994; The Print in Stuart Britain, 1998; Prints for Books: book illustration in France 1760–1800, 2004; The Print before Photography, 2016; British Museum exhibn catalogues; contribs to learned jls, esp. Print Qly. *Address:* 1 Highbury Hill, N5 1SU.

**GRIFFITHS, Prof. Christopher Ernest Maitland,** OBE 2018; MD; FRCP, FMedSci; Foundation Professor of Dermatology, University of Manchester, since 1994 (Head, School of Translational Medicine, 2007–08; Associate Dean for Research, Faculty of Medical and Human Sciences, 2008–10; Director, Manchester Academic Health Science Centre, 2010–11); *b* Dudley, 14 June 1954; *s* of Sir (Ernest) Roy Griffiths and of Winifred Griffiths; *m* 1992, Dr Tamara Wang; two *d*. *Educ:* Dulwich Coll.; St Thomas' Hosp. Med. Sch., Univ. of London (BSc 1st Cl. Hons 1976; MB BS 1979; MD 1991). FRCP 1995; FRCPath 2002; FRCPE 2011. Jun. hosp. doctor posts, London, 1979–85; Wellcome Trust Clin. Res. Trng Fellow, St Mary's Hosp. Med. Sch., London, 1985–87; Sen. Res. Fellow, then Asst Prof. of Dermatol., Univ. of Michigan, 1987–93; Hon. Consultant Dermatologist, Salford Royal NHS Foundn Trust, and Hd, Gtr Manchester Dermatol. Centre, 1994– . Non-exec. Dir, University Hosp. of S Manchester NHS Foundn Trust, 2008–10. Sen. Investigator, NIHR, 2011–19 (Emeritus, 2019). Dir, Global Psoriasis Atlas, 2017– . President: British Assoc. of Dermatologists, 2004–05; European Dermatology Forum, 2010–11 (Pro Meritis, 2018);

Mem., Exec. Bd, Internat. League of Dermatological Socs, 2011–; Sec./Treas., 2017–19, Pres., 2019–, Eur. Soc. for Dermatological Res. Co-founder and Hon. Sec., Internat. Psoriasis Council, 2004–13 (Pres., 2014–16). MAE 2015. FMedSci 2011. Sir Archibald Gray Medal, British Assoc. of Dermatologists, 2015; Medal, British Soc. for Investigative Dermatol., 2019. *Publications:* (ed jtly) Rook's Textbook of Dermatology, 7th edn 2004 to 9th edn (Ed. in Chief) 2016; contrib. Lancet, New England Jl Medicine, BMJ and specialist dermatology jls on psoriasis, ageing skin and brain-skin interaction. *Recreations:* natural history, gardening, distance running, viticulture on a Welsh hillside. *Address:* Dermatology Centre, Barnes Building, Salford Royal Hospital, Manchester M6 8HD. *T:* (0161) 206 4392, *Fax:* (0161) 206 1095. *E:* Christopher.Griffiths@manchester.ac.uk. *Clubs:* Athenæum, Royal Automobile.

**GRIFFITHS, Hon. Clive Edward,** AO 1997; JP; consultant and company director, since 2001; Agent-General for Western Australia, 1997–2001; *b* Perth, WA, 20 Nov. 1928; *s* of T. E. Griffiths and D. M. Beattie; *m* 1st, 1949, Myrtle Holtham (marr. diss. 1995; she *d* 1996); one *d*; 2nd, 1995, Norma Marie Paonessa. *Educ:* Fremantle Boys' High Sch.; Kalgoorlie Sch. of Mines. Electrical Engineer and Contractor, 1953–66. City Councillor, S Perth, 1962–66; MLC (L), WA, 1965–97 (Pres., 1977–97); Parly Sec., Lib Party and Jt Govt Parties, 1974–77; Regl Rep. for Australia and Pacific Region, 1988–90, Chm., Exec. Cttee, 1990–93, Commonwealth Parly Assoc. JP W Australia, 1983. *Recreations:* sailing, football, cricket. *Address:* PO Box 412, Melville, WA 6956, Australia. *T:* (8) 932 99039. *E:* haigroad@iinet.net.au. *Club:* Shelley Sailing.

**GRIFFITHS, Courtenay Delsdue McVay;** QC 1998; a Recorder, 2000–14; *b* 10 Oct. 1955; *s* of Wrenford Dacosta Griffiths and Adelaide Tamonda Griffiths; *m* 1985, Angela Maria Hill; three *s. Educ:* Bablake Sch., Coventry; LSE, London Univ. (LLB Hons 1979). Called to the Bar, Gray's Inn, 1980, Bencher, 2002; Legal Asst, GLC Police Cttee, 1980–84; Revson Fellow, Urban Legal Studies Prog., City Coll., CUNY, 1984–85; in practice at the Bar, 1985–; an Asst Recorder, 1999–2000; Head of Chambers, Garden Court Chambers, 2002–11. Hon. Lectr in Law, KCL, 1987–. Hon. PhD: Leeds Metropolitan, 2005; Coventry, 2005; Kent. *Recreations:* swimming, music (reggae and soul), watching Liverpool FC.

**GRIFFITHS, David Hubert;** Clerk/Adviser, House of Commons European Scrutiny Committee (formerly Select Committee on European Legislation), 1998–2016; *b* 24 Dec. 1940; *s* of late Hubert Griffiths and Margaret Joan Waldron; *m* Mary Abbott; one *s* one *d. Educ:* Kingswood School, Bath; St Catharine's College, Cambridge (MA). Joined Ministry of Agriculture, Fisheries and Food as Asst Principal, 1963; Principal, 1968; Asst Secretary, 1975; Under Secretary, 1982–97; Hd, European Communities Gp, 1982–83; Fisheries Sec., 1983–87; Hd, Food, Drink and Marketing Policy Gp, 1987–90; Dir of Establishments, 1990–94; Hd, Arable Crops and Horticulture Gp, 1995–97. Non-exec. Dir, ICI (Paints Div.), 1985–87. *Recreations:* cooking, music.

**GRIFFITHS, His Honour David Laurence;** a Circuit Judge, 1989–2009; *b* 3 Aug. 1944; *s* of late Edward Laurence Griffiths and of Mary Middleton Pudge; *m* 1971, Sally Hollis; four *d. Educ:* Christ's Hospital; Jesus College, Oxford (MA). Called to the Bar, Lincoln's Inn, 1967; Asst Recorder, 1981; Recorder, 1985. *Recreations:* walking, cycling, watching Rugby and cricket, opera, history, classical music.

**GRIFFITHS, Prof. Dorothy Seymour,** OBE 2010; Professor of Human Resource Management, Imperial College London, 2002–17, now Emeritus (Dean, Imperial College Business School, 2012–13); Provost's Envoy for Gender Equality, 2014–17); Chair, Central and North West London NHS Foundation Trust, since 2014; *b* London, 26 May 1947; *d* of Henry Griffiths and Jackie Griffiths (*née* Broderick). *Educ:* Enfield Coll. of Technol.; London Univ. (BSc Sociol. (ext.) 1968); Univ. of Bath (MSc 1970). Imperial College London: Res. Asst, 1969–72; Lectr in Sociol., 1972–87; Sen. Lectr in Sociol., 1987–2001; Dep. Principal and Hd of Progs, Imperial Coll. Business Sch., 2001–12. Non-exec. Dir, 2000–13, Sen. Ind. Dir, 2009–13, Central and NW London NHS Foundn Trust. Chair, Feminist Rev. Trust, 2003–. Governor: Salisbury Sch., 2007–11 (Chm. Govs, 2011–16); Queens Park Community Sch., 2008–16. *Recreations:* work, cats, tennis when knees permit, watching sport, house in Cyprus, progressive politics. *Address:* 46 Wrentham Avenue, Kensal Rise, NW10 3HA. *T:* 07771 742058. *E:* d.griffiths@imperial.ac.uk.

**GRIFFITHS, Elaine Mary, (Mrs P. Doyle),** FRCS, FRCSEd; consultant in medico-legal practice, since 1994; Consultant Cardiac Surgeon, Liverpool Heart and Chest Hospital NHS Foundation Trust (formerly Cardiothoracic Centre Liverpool), 1993–2013; *b* 15 Jan. 1955; *d* of Hedley and Kathleen Griffiths; *m* 2000, Dr Peter Doyle; two step *d. Educ:* Bullers Wood Sch., Chislehurst; King's College Med. Sch., London (MB BS 1979; AKC 1979). FRCS 1985; FRCSEd 1985. Cardiothoracic surgical trng, Southampton, Royal Brompton, Harefield and St George's Hosps. Hon. Dir, Cardiothoracic Studies, Univ. of Liverpool Med. Sch., 1994–2012. Member: DoH Ext. Ref. Gp for Nat. Service Framework for Coronary Heart Disease, 1998–2000; Welsh NHS Ext. Ref. Gp, Welsh Nat. Service Framework for Coronary Heart Disease, 1999–2002; Doctors' Forum, DoH, 2002–04; Med. Devices Adv. Gp, H of C, 2005–07. Royal College of Surgeons of England: Consultant Appts Assessor, 1998–2012; Regl Rep., Women in Surgical Trng Scheme, 2005–09; Mem. Council, RCSE, 2006–17 (Equality and Diversity Lead, 2012–17; Mem., Policy Cttee, 2015–18); Chm., Flexible Careers Cttee, Acad. of Med. Royal Colls. Lectr on patient level costing, 2010–12. Member: Exec., Soc. of Cardiothoracic Surgeons of GB and Ire., 1997–2000; Amer. Soc. of Women in Cardiothoracic Surgery, 1996–. Mem., BMA. Founder Mem. and Advr, Heart of Mersey and Cheshire Charity, 2002–15. *Recreations:* foreign travel, walking, ski-ing, golf, gardening, ancient coins and netsuke, my menagerie of pets: Koi carp, tropical fish, dog and cat. *T:* 07802 448017. *E:* elainegriffiths@doctors.org.uk.

**GRIFFITHS, Prof. Gillian Margaret,** PhD; FRS 2013; FMedSci; Professor of Immunology and Cell Biology, since 2007, and Director, Cambridge Institute for Medical Research, since 2012, University of Cambridge; Fellow, King's College, Cambridge, since 2007; *d* of Charles Stephen Griffiths and Marjorie Sybil Griffiths (*née* Sweaney); *m* 1995, Prof. James Frederick Kaufman; two *s. Educ:* University Coll. London; Darwin Coll. and King's Coll., Cambridge (PhD 1984). Post-doctoral Fellow, Stanford Univ., 1985–90; Scientific Mem., Basel Inst. for Immunol., 1990–95; Wellcome Trust Senior Fellow: MRC Lab. for Molecular Cell Biol., UCL, 1995–97; Sir William Dunn Sch. of Pathology, Univ. of Oxford, 1997–2007. Mem., Editl bd, Jl Cell Biol. Mem., EMBO 2006. FMedSci 2015. *Publications:* contribs to jls incl. Nature, Science, Immunity, Proc. NAS, Current Biol., Jl Cell Biol. *Address:* Cambridge Institute for Medical Research, Wellcome-MRC Building, Cambridge Biomedical Campus, Hills Road, Cambridge CB2 0XY.

**GRIFFITHS, Harold Morris;** Assistant Secretary, HM Treasury, 1978–86; *b* 17 March 1926; *s* of Rt Hon. James Griffiths, CH; *m* 1st, 1951, Gwyneth Lethby (*d* 1966); three *s* one *d*; 2nd, 1966, Elaine Burge (*née* Walsh); two *s. Educ:* Llanelly Grammar Sch.; London Sch. of Economics. Editorial Staff: Glasgow Herald, 1949–55; Guardian, 1955–67; Information Division, HM Treasury: Deputy Head, 1967–68, Head, 1968–72; Asst Sec., HM Treasury, 1972–75; Counsellor (Economic), Washington, 1975–78. *Address:* The Old Coach House, Park Road, Hampton Hill, Middx TW12 1HR. *T:* (020) 8979 1214.

**GRIFFITHS, Howard;** Command Secretary, RAF Logistics Command, 1994–98; *b* 20 Sept. 1938; *s* of Bernard and Olive Griffiths; *m* 1963, Dorothy Foster (*née* Todd) (*d* 2011); one *s* one *d. Educ:* London School of Economics (BScEcon, MScEcon). Ministry of Defence: Research Officer, 1963–69; Principal, Army Dept, 1970–72; Central Staffs, 1972–76; Asst Secretary, Head of Civilian Faculty, National Defence Coll., 1976–78; Procurement Executive, 1978–80; Deputy and Counsellor (Defence), UK Delegn, Mutual and Balanced Force Reductions (Negotiations), Vienna, 1980–84; Asst Sec., Office of Management and Budget, 1984–86; Asst Sec. and Head of Defence Arms Control Unit, 1986–88; Asst Under Sec. of State (Policy), 1988–91; Fellow, Center for Internat. Affairs, Harvard Univ., 1991–92; Assistant Under Secretary of State: (Ordnance), 1992; (Supply and Orgn) (Air), 1993–94.
*See also* L. *Griffiths.*

**GRIFFITHS, Prof. Hugh Duncan,** OBE 2019; PhD, DSc(Eng); FIET, FREng, FIEEE; Thales/Royal Academy of Engineering Professor of RF Sensors, University College London, since 2009; *b* Bournemouth, 22 March 1956; *s* of Gordon Griffiths and Morag Griffiths; *m* 1989, Morag Kirkwood; two *d. Educ:* Hardye's Sch., Dorchester; Keble Coll., Oxford (MA Phys 1978); University Coll. London (PhD 1986; DSc(Eng) 2000). FIET 1995; FREng 1997; FIEEE 1999. Admiralty Underwater Weapons Establishment, 1975; University College London: Lectr, 1985–93; Prof., 1993–2009; Hd, Dept of Electronic and Electrical Engrg, 2001–06; Principal, Defence Coll. of Mgt and Technol., Shrivenham, 2006–08. Chairman: Campaign for Sci. and Engrg, 2006–14; Defence Sci. Expert Cttee, MoD, 2017–. Gov. and Chair Bd of Trustees, Thomas Hardye Sch., Dorchester, 2011–. Freeman, City of London, 2003; Liveryman, Engineers' Co., 2003. A. F. Harvey Prize, IET, 2013; Dennis J. Picard Medal, IEEE, 2017. *Publications:* (jtly) Modern Antennas, 1997; (ed jtly) Advances in Bistatic Radar, 2007; (ed jtly) Radar Automatic Target Recognition and Non-Cooperative Target Recognition, 2013; (ed jtly) Introduction to Airborne Radar, 2014; (jtly) An Introduction to Passive Radar, 2017; (ed jtly) Biologically Inspired Radar and Sonar: lessons from nature, 2017; (ed jtly) Novel Radar Techniques and Applications, 2 vols, 2017; over 100 articles in learned jls. *Recreations:* horticulture, fish, military history, food and wine, most sports. *Address:* Department of Electronic and Electrical Engineering, University College London, Gower Street, WC1E 6BT. *T:* (020) 7679 3966. *E:* h.griffiths@ucl.ac.uk. *Club:* MG Owners.

**GRIFFITHS, Ian Ward;** Group Finance Director, 2008–18, and Chief Operating Officer, 2017–18, ITV plc; *b* St Asaph, N Wales, 26 Sept. 1966; *s* of Glyn and Dorothy Griffiths; *m* 1996, Alison Barbara. *Educ:* Flint High Sch.; Rydal Sch., Colwyn Bay; Fitzwilliam Coll., Cambridge (BA 1988; MA). ACA 1991. Audit and Corporate Finance, Ernst & Young, Cambridge, 1988–94; finance rôles, 1994–2005, Gp Finance Dir, 2005–08, Emap plc. Non-exec. Dir, DS Smith plc, 2014–18. *Recreations:* football, photography, philately, walking.

**GRIFFITHS, Jane Patricia;** Teacher, Arkon Educational Institute, Khujand, Tajikistan, since 2019; *b* 17 April 1954; *d* of late John Griffiths and of Patricia Griffiths (*née* Thomas); *m* 1st, 1975, Ralph Spearpoint (marr. diss. 1994); one *s* one *d*; 2nd, 1999, Andrew Tattersall (marr. diss. 2018). *Educ:* Univ. of Durham (BA Hons Russian). GCHQ linguist, 1977–84; Editor, BBC Monitoring, 1984–97. Mem. (Lab), Reading BC, 1989–99. MP (Lab) Reading E, 1997–2005. Languages teacher, Riga, Latvia and E London, 2006–07; Legal Editor, Eur. Court of Human Rights, Strasbourg, 2007–19 (on sabbatical leave teaching English in Phnom Penh, 2016–18). *Publications:* (with John Newman) Bushido, 1988; The One (political memoir), 2008; Priors Gardens (novel), 2012. *Recreations:* travel, language learning. *Address:* Ozodi 2–15, Khujand, Soghd, Tajikistan.

**GRIFFITHS, Joan,** MBE 2010; Depute Lord Provost of the City of Edinburgh, since 2017; *b* Edinburgh, 16 Aug. 1949; *d* of John Morrison and Jane Morrison; *m* 1974, Thomas Barclay Griffiths; two *s. Educ:* Ainslie Park Secondary Sch.; Open Univ. Member (Lab): Lothian Regl Council, 1986–96; Midlothian Council, 1996–2014; Mem. (Scot. Lab and Co-op), Edinburgh CC, 2012–. *Recreations:* reading, football (spectator), dressmaking, walking dog, spending time with grandchildren. *Address:* City of Edinburgh Council, City Chambers, High Street, Edinburgh EH1 1YJ. *T:* (0131) 529 4019. *E:* joan.griffiths@edinburgh.gov.uk.

**GRIFFITHS, John;** *see* Griffiths, Albert J.

**GRIFFITHS, John Calvert,** CMG 1983; QC 1972; SC (Hong Kong) 1997; *b* 16 Jan. 1931; *s* of Oswald Hardy Griffiths and Christina Flora Griffiths (*née* Littlejohn); *m* 1958, Jessamy, er *d* of Prof. G. P. Crowden and Jean Crowden; three *d*; *m* 1999, Marie Charlotte Biddulph. *Educ:* St Peter's Sch., York (scholar); Emmanuel Coll., Cambridge (sen. exhibnr) (BA 1st Cl. Hons 1955; MA 1960). Called to the Bar, Middle Temple, 1956 (Bencher, 1983), Hong Kong, 1979; a Recorder, 1972–90. Attorney-General of Hong Kong, 1979–83; Mem. Exec. and Legislative Councils, and Chm. Hong Kong Law Reform Commn, 1979–83. Chm., Telecommns (Competition Provisions) Appeal Bd, HK, 2000–07; Mem., Competition Policy Rev. Cttee, 2005–07. Member: Exec. Cttee, General Council of the Bar, 1967–71, 1983–89 (Treas., 1987); Senate of Inns of Court and the Bar, 1984–86 (Mem., Exec. Cttee, 1973–77); Nat. Council of Social Service, 1974–79; Greater London CAB Exec. Cttee, 1978–79; (co-opted) Develt and Special Projects Cttee, 1977–79; Court, Hong Kong Univ., 1980–84; Exec. Cttee, Prince Philip Cambridge Scholarships, 1980–84. Chm., Middle Temple Soc. (Hong Kong), 2000. Trustee, Pearson-Young African Educn Trust. Lieutenant, RE, 1949–50 (Nat. Service). *Recreations:* fishing, reading, gardening. *Clubs:* Flyfishers'; Hong Kong, Foreign Correspondents', Hong Kong Jockey (Hong Kong).

**GRIFFITHS, John Charles,** FLS; JP; writer; *b* 19 April 1934; *s* of Sir Percival Griffiths, KBE, CIE; *m* 1st, 1956, Ann Timms (marr. diss.); four *s*; 2nd, 1983, Carole Jane Mellor (marr. diss.); one *d. Educ:* Uppingham; Peterhouse, Cambridge (MA). Exec. Dir, Nat. Extension Coll., 1965–68; Dep. General Manager, Press Association, 1968–70; PR adviser, British Gas, 1970–74; Chm., MSG Public Relations, 1974–78; Chm. and founder, The Arts Channel, 1983–89; Chairman: Minerva Arts Channel, 1989–98; Minerva Vision, 1989–2009. Chairman: National League of Young Liberals, 1962–64 (Mem., Nat. Exec., 1964–66); Assoc. of Liberals in Small Business and Self Employed, 1980; Pres., Liberal Party, 1982–83. Contested (L): Ludlow, 1964; Wanstead and Woodford, 1966; Bedford, Feb. 1974, Oct. 1974. Develt Dir, Bardsey Island Trust, 1992–96. Chm. Govs, Llangynidr Sch., 1993–95. Trustee, Nat. Asthma Campaign, subseq. Asthma UK, 2002–12 (Vice Chm., 2009–12). FLS 2005. JP Cardiff, 1960. *Publications:* The Survivors, 1964; Afghanistan, 1967; Modern Iceland, 1969; Three Tomorrows, 1980; The Science of Winning Squash, 1981; Afghanistan: key to a continent, 1981; The Queen of Spades, 1983; Flashpoint Afghanistan, 1986; The Third Man: the life and times of William Murdoch, 1992; Nimbus, 1994; Fathercare, 1997; Imperial Call, 1997; Afghanistan: a history of conflict, 2001; Hostage, 2003; Tea, 2006; Afghanistan: land of conflict and beauty, 2009, 2nd edn 2011. *Recreations:* conversation, reading, music, walking. *Address:* Cotswold Suite, 9 Beaufort Arms Court, Agincourt Square, Monmouth NP25 3UA.

**GRIFFITHS, John Pankhurst,** RIBA; Clerk to the Worshipful Company: of Chartered Architects, 1995–2000; of Tylers and Bricklayers, 1996–97; *b* 27 Sept. 1930; *s* of late William Bramwell Griffiths and Ethel Doris Griffiths (*née* Pankhurst); *m* 1959, Helen Elizabeth (*née* Tasker); two *s* one *d*. *Educ*: Torquay Grammar School; King George V School, Southport; School of Architecture, Manchester Univ. Dip Arch. Resident architect, Northern Nigeria, for Maxwell Fry, 1956–58; staff architect, Granada Television, 1959; Founder and first Dir, Manchester Building Centre, 1959–65; Head of Tech. Inf., Min. of Public Buildings and Works, later DoE, 1965–77; formed Building Conservation Assoc. later Building Conservation Trust, 1977, Dir, 1979–93. Mem. Bd of Mgt, Surrey Historic Bldgs Trust, 1996–2000; Trustee, Tylers and Bricklayers Craft Trust, 1993–96. Pres., Rye Conservation Soc., 2018–. *Publications*: articles in tech. and prof. jls. *Recreations*: looking at buildings, writing, speaking, cooking. *Address*: 19 Watchbell Street, Rye, E Sussex TN31 7HB.

**GRIFFITHS, (John) Peter (Gwynne);** QC 1995; a Recorder, since 1991; *b* 9 Dec. 1945; *m* 1st (marr. diss.); four *c*; *m* 2nd; two *c*. *Educ*: Bristol Univ. (Civil Engrg); UWIST (LLB Hons). Work in oil exploration industry, 1968–70; called to the Bar, Gray's Inn, 1970; Asst Recorder, 1987–91. Mem. Welsh Arts Council, then Arts Council of Wales, 1992; Chm., Visual Arts Bd for Wales; Vice-Pres., Cywaith Cymru (formerly Welsh Sculpture Trust). *Publications*: (ed jtly) Injuries at Work, 1996. *Recreations*: angling, sailing, ski-ing, the arts. *Address*: 2 Bedford Row, WC1R 4BU. *T*: (020) 7440 8888.

**GRIFFITHS, Lawrence;** a Recorder of the Crown Court, 1972–93; *b* 16 Aug. 1933; *s* of Bernard Griffiths, CBE and Olive Emily Griffiths (*née* Stokes); *m* 1st, 1959, Josephine Ann (*née* Cook), JP (*d* 2012); one *s* two *d*; 2nd, 2016, Sheila (*née* Jones). *Educ*: Gowerton Grammar Sch.; Christ's Coll., Cambridge (MA). Called to the Bar, Inner Temple, 1957; practised Swansea, 1958–99; Mem. Wales and Chester Circuit; Prosecuting Counsel to Inland Revenue for Wales and Chester Circuit, 1969–93; Standing Counsel to HM Customs and Excise for Wales and Chester Circuit, 1989–93. Mem., Mental Health Review Tribunal for Wales, 1970–91. *Recreations*: wine, walking, travel by sea, snooker. *Address*: 26 Hillside Crescent, Uplands, Swansea SA2 0RD; (chambers) Iscoed Chambers, 86 St Helens Road, Swansea SA1 4BQ. *T*: (01792) 652988. *Club*: Bristol Channel Yacht (Swansea) (Chm., 2006–13).
See also H. *Griffiths*.

**GRIFFITHS, Lesley;** *see* Griffiths, S. L.

**GRIFFITHS, Dame Marianne (Elizabeth),** DBE 2019; Chief Executive: Western Sussex Hospitals NHS Foundation Trust, since 2009; Brighton and Sussex University Hospitals NHS Trust, since 2017; *b* Limerick, Ireland, 17 May 1960; *d* of Thomas O'Regan and Philomena O'Regan; one *s* one *d*; *m* 2009, John Dixon. *Educ*: Salesian Convent Sch., Limerick; Univ. of Exeter (BA 1st Cl. Hons Psychol. 1989). Chartered Accountant 1992. Nurse trng, 1978–82; trng, KPMG, 1989–91; Provider Lead, Devon Social Services, 1993–97; Hd, Commissioning, Social Services, West Sussex, 1997–2001; Dir, Strategic Develt, West Sussex HA, 2001–02; Dir, Strategic Develt, 2002–05, Chief Exec., 2005–06, Kent and Medway Strategic HA; Dep. Chief Exec. and Dir of Commng and Delivery, NHS South East Coast, 2006–08; Chief Exec., Royal West Sussex Trust, 2009. Hon. DSc Brighton, 2019; Hon. Dr Public Service Mgt, Chichester, 2019. Chief Exec. of the Year, Health Service Jl, 2016. *Recreations*: walking, wine, bridge.

**GRIFFITHS, Hon. Sir Martin (Alexander),** Kt 2019; **Hon. Mr Justice Griffiths;** a Judge of the High Court, Queen's Bench Division, since 2019; *b* 27 April 1962; *s* of late Roy Arnold Griffiths and Susan Reay Gail Griffiths (*née* Landon); *m* 1995, Susan Jane Burden, barrister, *oc* of Kenneth John Burden; two *s* one *d*. *Educ*: City of London Sch. (Temple Chorister; John Carpenter Schol.); New Coll., Oxford (Open Schol.; BA 1st Cl. Hons Modern Hist. and Modern Langs 1984; MA 1988); City Univ. (Dip. Law 1985); Inns of Court Sch. of Law. Called to the Bar, Inner Temple, 1986 (Duke of Edinburgh Schol., Horace Avory Schol., Inner Temple Award), Bencher, 2013; in practice at the Bar, 1986–2019; QC 2006; Recorder, 2009–19; Dep. High Court Judge, 2016–19. Volunteer, Waterloo Legal Advice Service, 1988–93; Trustee and Mem., Mgt Cttee, N Kensington Law Centre, 2007–09; Chm., Professional Conduct Sub-Cttee, London Maritime Arbitrators Assoc., 2007–; Mem. Cttee, Employment Law Bar Assoc., 2008–15. Mem., Bar Council, 2008–15. Sponsor: New Coll., Oxford Burden Griffiths Awards, 2001–; Brenda Landon Pye Portrait Prize, Chelsea Coll. of Art, 2006–13. Dep. Chancellor, Dio. of Peterborough, 2017–. *Publications*: (contrib.) Mortimore on Company Directors, 2009, 3rd edn 2017; (contrib.) International Employment Disputes, 2020. *Recreations*: laughter, music, exercise and thought. *Address*: Royal Courts of Justice, Strand, WC2A 2LL. *Clubs*: Travellers, House of St Barnabas.

**GRIFFITHS, Sir Michael,** Kt 2014; education consultant, SMG Education Ltd, since 2014; Headmaster, Northampton School for Boys, 2001–14; *b* Wednesfield, Wolverhampton, 23 Sept. 1951; *s* of David Wesley Griffiths and Muriel Griffiths (*née* Belfield); *m* 1984, Kathryn Margaret Simister; two *s*. *Educ*: Wolverhampton Grammar Sch.; Univ. of York (BA Biochem.); Univ. of Sussex (PGCE). NPQH 1999. Teacher of Science: Highfields Sch., Wolverhampton, 1974–86; Moreton Community Coll., Wolverhampton, 1986–89; Sen. Lectr in Sci. Educn, Sheffield City Poly., 1989–91; Sci. Advr, Sefton LEA, 1991–93; Dep. Headteacher, Northampton Sch. for Boys, 1993–99; Headmaster, Wallingford Sch., Oxford, 1999–2001. Ofsted Inspector, 1993–2005. Pres., Assoc. of Sch. and Coll. Leaders, 2012–13 (Mem. Council, 2006–16; Hon. Life Mem., 2014). Chair, Adv. (formerly Steering) Gp, STEM Learning (formerly Nat. STEM Learning Centre and Network), 2014–; Mem., Headteacher Bd for NW London and S Central, 2014–17. Member, Council: UCAS, 2013–16; AQA, 2014–. Gov., Northampton Internat. Acad., 2016–18; Dir, St Dominic's Sch., Brewood, 2016–. Trustee, Northants Music and Performing Arts Trust, 2014–18; Mem., Windsor Acads Trust, 2017–. FRSA 2007. *Recreations*: supporting Wolverhampton Wanderers FC, music, travel, politics, education, Broadway Golf Club, Stratford Symphony Orchestra, Stratford Concert Band, Shades on Black (jazz ensemble). *E*: sir.michael.griffiths@btinternet.com. *Clubs*: East India; Old Wulfrunians, Old Northamptonians.

**GRIFFITHS, Sir Michael N.;** *see* Norton-Griffiths.

**GRIFFITHS, Nicholas Mark;** HM Diplomatic Service; Ambassador to Mali, 2010–12, and to Niger, 2011–12; *b* St Asaph, 20 Nov. 1958; *s* of late Bernard Parry Griffiths and of Jennifer Ann Griffiths (*née* Northall). *Educ*: Monmouth Sch.; Southampton Univ. (LLB). Admitted as solicitor, 1984; entered FCO, 1985; Second Secretary: Moscow, 1988–90; Arms Control and Disarmament Dept, 1990–93; S Asian Dept, 1993–96; First Secretary: UK Delegn, OECD, Paris, 1996–2001; Aviation, Maritime and Energy Dept, 2001–05; Dep. Ambassador to Sweden, 2005–10. *Recreations*: sport, travel. *Address*: c/o Foreign and Commonwealth Office, King Charles Street, SW1A 2AH.

**GRIFFITHS, Nigel;** Chairman: Queen's Hall, Edinburgh, since 2014; Enforce Technology; *b* 20 May 1955; *s* of late Lionel and Elizabeth Griffiths; *m* 1979, Sally, *d* of Hugh and Sally McLaughlin. *Educ*: Hawick High Sch.; Edinburgh Univ. (MA 1977). Joined Labour Party, 1970. City of Edinburgh: District Councillor, 1980–87 (Chm., Housing Cttee); Member: Edinburgh Festival Council, 1984–87; Edinburgh Health Council, 1982–87; Wester Hailes Sch. Council, 1981. MP (Lab) Edinburgh S, 1987–2010. Opposition Whip, 1987–89; Opposition front bench spokesman on consumer affairs, 1989–97; Parly Under-Sec. of State, 1997–98, Parly Under-Sec. of State (Minister for Construction, and for Enterprise), 2001–05, DTI; Parly Sec., Privy Council Office, and Dep. Leader, H of C, 2005–07. Chair, Open Door Dementia Action, Edinburgh, 2010–; Dir, Parly Outreach Trust, 2017–. Advr, Cambio Healthcare Systems and Investcorp (formerly Cambio Health Services), Sweden, 2017–. Vice Pres., Inst. of Trading Standards Admin, 1994. Co-founder, Big Issue (Scotland), 1995; Co-Chair, Scottish Kosovo Refugee Appeal, 1999–. Founding Patron, Capital Credit Union, 1989–. Member: War on Want, SEAD, Amnesty Internat., Anti-apartheid, Friends of the Earth, Nat. Trust, Ramblers' Assoc. *Publications*: Guide to Council Housing in Edinburgh, 1981; Council Housing on the Point of Collapse, 1982; Welfare Rights Survey, 1981; 300 Gains from our Labour Government, 2007; various welfare rights guides. *Recreations*: squash, travel, theatre and music, badminton, hill walking and rock climbing, art and architecture, reading, politics, helicopter pilot, classic car restoration. *Address*: 30 McLaren Road, Edinburgh EH9 2BN. *T*: (0131) 667 1947.

**GRIFFITHS, Paul;** Vice Lord-Lieutenant of Greater Manchester, since 2017; Co-Founder, 1996 and Chairman, since 1999, Monastery of St Francis and Gorton Trust; *b* Manchester, 28 May 1953; *s* of John Griffiths and Agnes Mary Griffiths (*née* Heaney); *m* 1995, Elaine Christine Geldard; one *d*. *Educ*: St Francis Secondary Sch., Gorton. Retail Manager, Technical Advisory, Danish Agri Producers, 1970–82; Product Manager, Danepak, 1985–89; Trading Controller, 1989–91, Business Unit Dir, 1991–96, ASDA HQ; Gp Sales and Mktg Dir, Tulip Internat., 1995–96; Man. Dir, Food Gp, United Co-op, 1996–2003; Chief Exec., Interlink Foods plc, 2003–06. Dir, Consultancy, Griffiths Mrkt, 2009–10; Head-hunter, Robinson Keane, 2013–14. Chm., Provision Trade Fedn, 1991–96; Adv. Bd, BITC, 1996–2003. Trustee: Manchester Guardian Soc. Charitable Trust, 2014; High Sheriff Police Trust, 2016–. Greater Manchester: DL 2003; High Sheriff 2013. Hon. Dr Bolton, 2014. *Recreations*: family, football, motor racing, piloting helicopters. *Address*: The Monastery, Gorton, Manchester M12 5WF. *T*: (0161) 223 3211. *E*: paul.griffiths@themonastery.co.uk.

**GRIFFITHS, Paul Anthony,** OBE 2014; writer; Music Critic of The New Yorker, 1992–96; *b* 24 Nov. 1947; *s* of Fred Griffiths and Jeanne Veronica (*née* George); *m* 1st, 1977; two *s*; 2nd, 1998, Anne Kathryn West. *Educ*: King Edward's Sch., Birmingham; Lincoln Coll., Oxford (BA, MSc). Area Editor for Grove's Dictionary of Music and Musicians, 6th edn, 1973–76; Asst Music Critic, 1979–82, Music Critic, 1982–92, The Times. Fellow, Amer. Acad. of Arts and Scis, 2011. Chevalier, Ordre des Arts et des Lettres (France), 2002. *Publications*: A Concise History of Modern Music, 1978; Boulez, 1978; A Guide to Electronic Music, 1979; Modern Music, 1980; Cage, 1981; Igor Stravinsky: The Rake's Progress, 1982; Peter Maxwell Davies, 1982; The String Quartet, 1983; György Ligeti, 1983, 2nd edn 1997; Bartók, 1984; Olivier Messiaen, 1985; New Sounds, New Personalities, 1985; The Thames & Hudson Encyclopaedia of 20th-Century Music, 1986; Stravinsky, 1992; Modern Music and After, 1995, 2nd edn 2010; The Sea on Fire: Jean Barraqué, 2003; The Penguin Companion to Classical Music, 2004 (repr. as The New Penguin Dictionary of Music, 2006); The Substance of Things Heard: writings about music, 2005; A Concise History of Western Music, 2006; *fiction*: Myself and Marco Polo, 1989; The Lay of Sir Tristram, 1991; let me tell you, 2008; The Tilted Cup, 2013; so this is it, 2019; *libretti*: The Jewel Box, 1991; Marco Polo, 1996; What Next?, 1999; The General, 2007; Let Me Tell You, 2013. *Recreation*: swimming. *Address*: Disgwylfa 2, Manorbier SA70 7TE.

**GRIFFITHS, Prof. Paul David,** MD; Professor of Virology, UCL Medical School (formerly Royal Free Hospital School of Medicine, then Royal Free and University College Medical School), since 1989; *b* 30 Jan. 1953; *s* of George Griffiths and Jean Beckett (formerly Griffiths, *née* Pring); *m* 1979, Brenda Louise Attenborough; three *s*. *Educ*: St Bartholomew's Hosp. Med. Coll., Univ. of London (BSc 1974; MB BS Hons 1977; MD 1982); DSc (Med) London, 1995. FRCPath 1996. Lawrence Postgrad. Res. Schol., 1979; Lectr, Bart's Med. Coll., 1979–82; Fogarty Internat. Scholar, NIH, USA, 1980–81; Royal Free Hospital School of Medicine, London University: Sen. Lectr in Virology, 1982–86; Reader, 1986–87; Chm., Univ. Div. of Pathology and Communicable Diseases, 1991–95. William Julius Mickle Fellow, London Univ., 1991. Lectures: Richard Clemens Meml, Washington DC, 2007; Charles Alford Meml, Univ. of Alabama, 2016; Gertrude Elion Meml, Internat. Soc. for Antiviral Res., 2018. Member: UK med. socs; Internat. AIDS Soc.; Fellow, Amer. Soc. for Microbiol., 2003. Editor, Reviews in Medical Virology, 1990–. Ian Howat Prize in Med. Microbiol., 1975, Wheelwright Prize for Paediatrics, 1977, St Bartholomew's Hosp. Med. Coll.; Wellcome Award, European Gp for Rapid Viral Diagnosis, 1988; Garrod Medal, British Soc. for Antimicrobial Chemotherapy, 2001. *Publications*: The Stealth Virus, 2012; Gut Feeling, 2014; Lenti, 2017; Five Eyes, 2019; papers on viruses, HIV/AIDS, herpes viruses and cytomegalovirus. *Recreations*: family, music, viruses, bridge. *Address*: Centre for Virology, UCL Medical School, Rowland Hill Street, Hampstead, NW3 2PF. *T*: (020) 7794 0500, ext. 33210.

**GRIFFITHS, Paul Dennis,** CMG 2015; Chief Executive Officer, Dubai Airports, since 2007; *b* London, 16 Oct. 1957; *s* of Dennis Frederick Griffiths and Jean Griffiths; *m* 2001, Joanna Marsh; two *s* one *d* (and one *s* decd). *Educ*: Richard Hale Sch., Hertford. LRAM 1981; ARCM 1982; FRCO 1984; FRAeS 2011. Manager, Mktg and Res., Reed Publishing, 1980–85; Mktg and Planning Manager, Dragonair Hong Kong, 1985–89; Man. Dir, Trinity Aviation Systems, 1989–91; Executive Director: Virgin Atlantic Airways, 1991–2002; Virgin Rail Gp, 2002–04; Chm. and Man. Dir, Gatwick Airport Ltd, 2004–07. Chm., Bd of Trustees, 2000–07, Vice Pres., 2007–, RCO. Organist, Guildford Cath. Singers, 2003–. Trustee, St Albans Cathedral Trust, 2001–07. Hon. PhD Middlesex, 2015. *Recreations*: music, motorsports, theatre, cycling, collecting motorcycles and model trains, commissioning pipe organs. *Address*: Dubai Airports, Dubai International Airport Building, PO Box 2525, Dubai, United Arab Emirates. *T*: (4) 2162727, *Fax*: (4) 2244074. *E*: paul.griffiths@dubaiairports.ae. *Clubs*: Royal Automobile, Home House; Capital (Dubai).

**GRIFFITHS, Rev. Paula Whitmore Llewellyn;** Associate Priest, Saffron Walden and Villages (formerly Saffron Walden) Team Ministry, since 2013 (Assistant Curate, 2009–13); Priest, St Botolph's Hadstock, since 2014; *b* 30 June 1949; *d* of Rev. John Whitmore Griffiths and Evelyn Doreen Griffiths (*née* Pearson); *m* 1st, 1971 (marr. diss. 1978); two *d*; 2nd, 2006, Roger John Mance. *Educ*: S Hampstead High Sch. (GPDST); Lady Margaret Hall, Oxford (BA (Mod. Hist.) 1971; MA 1975); Westcott House, Cambridge (Cert. Christian Theology, 2009). Departments of the Environment and Transport, 1972 and 1976–92: Principal, 1982; posts incl. Hd, branches in Planning Land Use Policy Directorate, 1983–87, and Heritage Sponsorship Div., 1987–92; English Heritage, 1992–2002: Head: SE Team, 1993–94; Anglia Team, 1994–99; Asst Regl Dir, E of England Region, 1999–2002. Hd, Cathedral and Church Buildings Div. (Secretary: Council for Care of Churches; Cathedrals Fabric Commn for England), Archbishops' Council, 2002–07; ordained deacon, 2009, priest, 2010. Priest, St John's, Little Walden, 2012–17. FRSA 1985. *Publications*: articles in conservation and church jls. *Recreations*: travel, walking, poetry, travel writing. *Address*: Greatford Cottage, Stocking Green, Radwinter, Saffron Walden, Essex CB10 2SS.

**GRIFFITHS, Peter;** see Griffiths, J. P. G.

**GRIFFITHS, Peter Anthony,** CBE 2013; Chairman: Queen Victoria Hospital NHS Foundation Trust, 2005–15; Foundation Trust Network, 2010–13 (Trustee, 2007–08); Vice Chairman, 2008–10); President, Institute of Health Service Managers, 1995–96 (Chairman, 1994–95)); *b* 19 May 1945; *m* 1966, Margaret Harris; two *s*. *Educ:* Swansea Technical Coll. Regl admin. trainee, Welsh Hosp. Bd, Cardiff Royal Inf., 1963–66; nat. admin. trainee, Birmingham Reg./Nuffield Centre, Leeds, 1966–69; Dep. Hosp. Sec., E Birmingham HMC, 1969–71; Dep. Dist Administrator, Hosp. Sec., Southampton and SW Hampshire Health Dist (Teaching), 1971–76; Dist Administrator, Medway Health Dist, 1976–81; Actg Area Administrator, Kent AHA, 1981–82; Dist Administrator, 1982–84, Dist Gen. Man., 1984–88, Lewisham and N Southwark HA; Regl Gen. Manager, SE Thames RHA, 1988–89; Dep. Chief Exec., NHS Management Exec. for England, 1990–91; Chief Exec., Guy's and Lewisham NHS Trust, 1991–94; Dep. Chief Exec., King's Fund, 1994–97; Chief Exec., The Health Quality Service, 1997–2004. Non-exec. Dir, Sussex Downs and Weald PCT, 2002–05. Chm., NHS Pensioners' Trust, 2005– (Trustee, 2002–); Trustee, 2010–, non-exec. Mem., Corporate Bd, 2010–, NHS Confederation. *Recreation:* golf.

**GRIFFITHS, Prof. Peter Denham,** CBE 1990; MD, FRCPath, FRCPE; Professor of Biochemical Medicine 1968–89, and Dean, Faculty of Medicine and Dentistry, 1985–89, University of Dundee (Vice-Principal, 1979–85); Hon. Consultant Clinical Chemist, Tayside Health Board, 1966–89; *b* 16 June 1927; *s* of Bernard Millar Griffiths and Florence Marion Fletcher; *m* 1949, Joy Burgess; three *s* one *d*. *Educ:* King Edward VI Sch., Southampton; Guy's Hosp. Med. Sch., Univ. of London (BSc 1st Cl. Hons, MD). LRCP, MRCS; FRCPath 1978; FRCPE 1998. Served RN, 1946–49. Jun. Lectr in Physiol., Guy's Hosp. Med. Sch., 1957–58; Registrar, then Sen. Registrar in Clin. Path., Guy's and Lewisham Hosps, London, 1958–64; Consultant Pathologist, Harlow Gp of Hosps, Essex, 1964–66; Sen. Lectr in Clin. Chemistry, Univ. of St Andrews and subseq. Univ. of Dundee, 1966–68. Pres., Assoc. of Clin. Biochemists, UK, 1987–89 (Chm. Council, 1973–76); Member: Tayside Health Bd, 1977–85; GMC, 1986–93; various cttees of SHHD and DHSS, 1969–98. Dir, Drug Development (Scotland), 1982–89. Dir, Dundee Rep. Theatre, 1977–90. FCMI; FRSA. Consulting Editor, Clinica Chimica Acta, 1986–96 (Mem. Editl Bd, 1976; Jt Editor-in-Chief, 1979–85). *Publications:* contrib. scientific and med. jls (pathology, clin. chemistry, computing). *Recreations:* music, gardening, walking. *Address:* 52 Albany Road, West Ferry, Dundee DD5 1NW. *T:* (01382) 776772.

**GRIFFITHS, Peter John;** higher education management consultant, since 2000; *b* 19 April 1944; *s* of Ronald Hugh Griffiths and Emily Vera (*née* Cockshutt); *m* 1968, Lesley Florence (*née* Palmer) (marr. diss. 1993); two *d*. *Educ:* Battersea Grammar Sch.; Univ. of Leicester (BA Classics); McMaster Univ. (MA Classics). University of London: Asst to Principal, 1968–70; Asst Sec. to Cttee of Enquiry into governance of the university, 1970–72; Special Duties Officer, Vice-Chancellor's and Principal's Office, 1972–78; Dep. Head, Legal and Gen. Div., Court Dept, 1978–82; Asst Clerk of the Court, 1982–85; Dep. Clerk of the Court, 1985–87; Clerk of the Court, 1987–91; Dir of Resources and Planning, 1991–93; Sec. and Chief Admin. Officer, Charing Cross and Westminster Med. Sch., 1993–97; Dep. Sec., Imperial Coll. Sch. of Medicine, 1997–2000. *Recreation:* choral singing. *Address:* Upland House, Upland Road, Sutton, Surrey SM2 5HW. *T:* (020) 8643 3599.

**GRIFFITHS, Prof. Ralph Alan,** OBE 2005; PhD; DLitt; FRHistS; FLSW; Professor of Medieval History, University of Wales, Swansea, 1982–2002, now Emeritus; Emeritus Leverhulme Fellow, 2003–05; *b* 4 Nov. 1937; *er s* of Thomas Rowland Griffiths and Marion Lovin Griffiths (*née* Jones). *Educ:* Lewis Sch., Pengam, Gwent; Univ. of Bristol (BA 1959, PhD 1963; DLitt 1983). FRHistS 1966. Research Asst, Bd of Celtic Studies, Univ. of Wales, 1961–64; University of Wales, Swansea: Asst Lectr, 1964–66; Lectr, 1966–71; Sen. Lectr, 1971–78; Reader, 1978–82; Dean of Admissions, 1990–2002; Pro-Vice-Chancellor, 1998–2002. Visiting Professor: Dalhousie Univ., Canada, 1964; Ohio Univ., 1977, 1981; Haverford Coll., USA, 1977, 1981; Lectures: James Ford in English Hist., Univ. of Oxford, 1993; Sir John Rhys, British Acad., 2001; Stenton, Reading Univ., 2001; Virgoe, UEA, 2003; Bond, St George's Chapel, Windsor, 2006. Member: Royal Commn on Ancient and Historical Monuments (Wales), 1990–2009 (Chm., 1999–2009); Hist. and Archaeol Panel, Humanities Res. Bd, 1994–96; Adv. Council on Public Records, 1996–2001; Adv. Council, Inst. of Histl Res., 1996–2003 (Hon. Fellow, 2005). Member, Council: RHistS, 1987–91 (Vice-Pres., 1992–96; Hon. Vice-Pres., 2003–); Royal Instn, S Wales, 2004–09. Hon. Sec., Glamorgan Co. History Trust, 1974–2002; Trustee, Glamorgan-Gwent Archaeol Trust, 1985–98; President: S Wales Record Soc., 1994–97, 2004–07, 2013–16; Histl Assoc., Swansea, 2011–15. FLSW 2011. Hon. Fellow, Histl Assoc., 2011. *Publications:* The Principality of Wales in the Later Middle Ages, I: South Wales 1277–1536, 1972, 2nd edn 2018; The Reign of King Henry VI, 1981, 2nd edn 1998; (with R. S. Thomas) The Making of the Tudor Dynasty, 1985, 2nd rev. edn 2013; (with J. Cannon) The Oxford Illustrated History of the British Monarchy, 1988, 2nd edn 1998; King and Country: England and Wales in the Fifteenth Century, 1990; Sir Rhys ap Thomas and his Family, 1993, rev. edn 2014; Conquerors and Conquered in Medieval Wales, 1994; (with J. Gillingham) Medieval Britain: a very short history, 2000 (trans. Chinese 2006); (ed) The Fourteenth and Fifteenth Centuries, 2003 (trans. Japanese 2010); The Household Book of Sir Edward Don, 2004; (Gen. Ed.) Gwent County History, (5 vols), 2004–13; (with J. E. Law) Rawdon Brown and the Anglo-Venetian Relationship, 2005; (ed jtly) Gwent County History II: age of the marcher lords, 2008; In Conversation with Napoleon Bonaparte: J. H. Vivian's visit to the island of Elba, 2008; (ed jtly) Hidden Histories: discovering the heritage of Wales, 2008; (ed jtly) Wales and the Welsh in the Middle Ages, 2011; contrib. to books and learned jls. *Recreations:* music, painting, Shakespeare.

**GRIFFITHS, Richard Anthony;** Senior Partner, Farrer & Co., 1993–2000; *b* 30 Oct. 1936; *s* of Howel Harris Griffiths and Rena Kelford Griffiths; *m* 1st, 1964, Sarah Janet Williams (*d* 1964); 2nd, 1970, Sheila Mary Wallace; two *d*. *Educ:* Denstone Coll.; Trinity Coll., Cambridge (MA). Admitted Solicitor, 1963; Partner, Farrer & Co., 1966–2000. Dir, London Cremation Co. plc, 2000–. Life Trustee, Sir John Soane's Mus., 1994–2014 (Chm., 1997–2008). Mem. Council, ICRF, 1997–2002. Founder Mem., Resolution (formerly Solicitors Family Law Assoc.), 1982–2000. FRSA. *Recreations:* golf, fishing, theatre, travel. *Address:* Wintergreen House, North Entrance, Saxmundham, Suffolk IP17 1AP. *Clubs:* Garrick; Aldeburgh Golf.

**GRIFFITHS, Richard Perronet,** RIBA; Founding Director, Richard Griffiths Architects, 1993; *b* 21 Feb. 1954; *s* of Richard Cerdin Griffiths and Pamela Griffiths (*née* Hetherington); *m* 1985, Penelope Roskell; one *s* one *d*. *Educ:* Highgate Sch.; Trinity Hall, Cambridge (BA 1976, DipArch); Architectural Assoc. (Grad. Dip. Conservation). RIBA 1983; AABC. Worked with Frederick Burn, Christophe Grillet and Julian Harrap before setting up Richard Griffiths Architects, 1993. Major projects include: Lambeth Palace, 1998; Sutton House (NT), 1999–2003; St Pancras Hotel, 2003; Freston Tower (Landmark Trust), 2002–05; Burghley House, 2002–06; Kenilworth Castle (English Heritage), 2005; Clissold House, 2013; Tynbee Hall, 2015. Cathedral Architect: Southwark Cathedral, 1997–2012; St Albans Abbey, 2000–17; Russian Orthodox Cathedral, London. Member: Cttee, SPAB, 1993–99; Awards Panel, RIBA, 2004–12. Trustee, Churches Conservation Trust, 2000–06.

*Publications:* articles in ASCHB Trans, SPAB News, Architects' Jl, Building Design. *Recreation:* music (bassoon). *Address:* c/o Richard Griffiths Architects, 5 Maidstone Mews, 72/76 Borough High Street, SE1 1GN. *T:* (020) 7357 8788. *E:* richard@rgarchitects.com.

**GRIFFITHS, Robert;** see Griffiths, W. R.

**GRIFFITHS, Prof. Robert Charles,** PhD; FRS 2010; FIMS; Professor of Mathematical Genetics, University of Oxford, 2000–11, now Emeritus; Fellow, Lady Margaret Hall, Oxford, 1998–2011, now Emeritus; Adjunct Professor, Monash University, since 2018; *b* Wagga Wagga, Australia, 17 July 1944; *s* of Noel Charles Griffiths and Evelyn Eunice Griffiths; *m* 1977, Yvonne Joy Fripp; one *s* one *d* (and one *s* from previous marriage decd). *Educ:* Yanco Agricl High Sch.; Univ. of Sydney (BSc Hons 1967; PhD 1970). FIMS 1993. Lectr, Dept of Stats, Macquarie Univ., 1970–73; Department of Mathematics, Monash University: Lectr, 1973–79; Sen. Lectr, 1979–88; Reader, 1989–98; Univ. Lectr, Dept of Stats, Univ. of Oxford, 1998–2011. *Publications:* about 110 articles on mathematical genetics in Theoretical Population Biology, Applied Probability and other jls. *Recreations:* photography, music, walking, cycling, yoga, life drawing. *Address:* 10 Tyrol Court, Doncaster East, Vic 3108, Australia. *E:* griffiths.bob@gmail.com.

**GRIFFITHS, Prof. Roderic Keith,** CBE 2000; Professor of Public Health Practice, University of Birmingham, since 1990; President, Faculty of Public Health Medicine, Royal Colleges of Physicians of the UK, 2004–07; *b* 12 April 1945; *s* of Tom and Olwen Griffiths; *m* 1st, 1967, Margaret Ash (marr. diss. 1993); one *s* two *d*; 2nd, 1995, Lois Parker. *Educ:* Birmingham Univ. (BSc, MB ChB 1969); Univ. of Gloucestershire (MA Creative and Critical Writing 2015). Lectr in Anatomy, 1970, in Social Medicine, 1978, Birmingham Univ.; GP in Birmingham, 1975; Dir of Public Health, Central Birmingham HA, 1982; Regl Dir of Public Health, W Midlands, DoH (formerly W Midlands RHA), 1993–2004. Chm., Assoc. of CHCs England and Wales, 1979–81. Mem:, Birmingham Lunar Soc., 1992–. *Publications:* A Rag Doll Falling (novel), 2010; Aimless Fear (novel), 2013; articles on stress in bones, and public health. *Recreations:* ski-ing, pottery, sailing very occasionally, creative writing. *E:* rod.griff@gmail.com.

**GRIFFITHS, Sarah-Jane;** a District Judge (Magistrates' Courts), since 2016; *b* Chester, 15 March 1975; *d* of Robert Anthony Griffiths and Barbara Anne Griffiths; partner, Hugh Michael Burr. *Educ:* Queen's Sch., Chester; Univ. of Newcastle upon Tyne (LLB Hons 1996); Inns of Court Sch. of Law (Bar Vocational Course). Qualified Lawyer Transfer Test, 2010; Higher Court (Criminal) Rights, 2011. Called to the Bar, Lincoln's Inn, 1998; Listing Officer, Lambeth Co. Court, 1998–2000; Court Clerk, Central Criminal Court, 2000–01; trainee legal advr, Nottingham Magistrates' Court, 2001–03; Legal Advr, HM Courts, Newcastle and Sunderland Magistrates' Courts, 2003–16; Training and Policy Lawyer, Judicial Coll., 2009–16; Fee-paid Tribunal Judge: Social Entitlement Chamber, 2013–; Immigration and Asylum Tribunal, 2014–16. *Recreations:* running, family, reading, travel, gardening. *Address:* Gateshead Magistrates' Court, Warwick Street, Gateshead NE8 1DT. *T:* (0191) 477 5821.

**GRIFFITHS, Siân Meryl, (Mrs Ian Wylie),** OBE 2000; FFPH, FRCP, FHKCCM, FHKAM; JP; independent health care consultant, 2015–17; Professor of Public Health, 2005–13, Professor Emeritus, 2014, Founding Director, Centre for Global Health, 2013, and Senior Adviser on International Academic Development, since 2013, Chinese University of Hong Kong (Director, School of Public Health and Primary Care, 2005–13); *b* 20 March 1952; *d* of late John Daniel Griffiths, FRCS and of Rosemary Marjorie Griffiths (*née* Quick); *m* 1st, 1978, Anthony Chu (marr. diss. 1986); two *d*; 2nd, 1987, Ian Martin Wylie, *qv*; one *s*. *Educ:* Felixstowe College; N London Collegiate Sch.; New Hall, Cambridge (MB BChir 1977; MA). MSc London, 1981. DRCOG 1979; FFPH (FFPHM 1991), Hon. FFPH 2011; FRCP 1998; FHKCCM 2006; FHKAM 2009. Clinical MO, KCH, 1979–80; Res. Fellow, NY, 1981; Dist MO, City and Hackney HA, 1985–87; Consultant in Public Health Medicine, Oxford RHA, 1988–90; Dir of Public Health and Health Policy, SW Thames RHA, 1990–93, Oxfordshire HA, 1994–2002; Consultant in Public Health Medicine, Oxford Radcliffe Hosps NHS Trust, 2002–05; Sen. Fellow, Oxford Inst. for Ethics and Communication in Health Care Practice, Oxford Univ., 2002–05. Hon. Sen. Clin. Lectr, 1997–2017, Hon. Vis. Sen. Res. Fellow, 2017–, Oxford Univ.; Visiting Professor: Oxford Brookes Univ., 1999–2005; Inst. of Global Health Innovation, Imperial Coll. London, 2015–; Honorary Professor: Cardiff Univ., 2008–; Guangzhou Med. Univ., 2009–. Specialist Advr, 2013–15, Specialist Advr in Trng and Educn, 2016, to Healthcare UK; Associate non-exec. Mem. Bd, Public Health England, 2014– (Chm., Global Health Cttee, 2014–); Exec. Educn Associate, Møller Centre, Churchill Coll., Cambridge Univ., 2017–. Mem., Health Policy Forum, IPPR, 1998–2000; Advr, Democratic Health Network, 1999–2001. Co-Chair, Assoc. of Public Health, 1995–99; Chairman: Pharmacy Healthlink, 2003–04; NHS Alliance Health Network, 2004–05; Centre for Health and Develt, 2013–; Oxfordshire Commn on Health Inequalities, 2015–17; Centre for Health and Develt, Stafford Univ., 2016–; Member Board: NAHAT, 1995–98; FPH (formerly FPHM), 1999–2005 (Treas., 1995–99); Vice-Pres., 2000–01; Pres., 2001–04; Chm., Internat. Cttee, 2004–05); New Opportunities Fund, 1998–2004; Postgrad. Med. Educn Trng Bd, 2003–05; HPA, 2003–05; Mem., Nat. Cancer Task Force, 2001–05; Co-Chm., Hong Kong Govt SARS Expert Review, 2003; Convenor, Task Force on concepts for health care reform, Hong Kong Govt, 2009–. Trustee: Thames Valley Partnership, 1999–2001; Gamble Aware, 2017–. Member: Adv. Cttee, Common Purpose, 1999–2003; Central Res. Ethics Adv. Gp, Unilever, 2010–15; Nat. Workforce Develt Bd, 2002–04; Nat. Cycling Strategy Bd, 2002–04; Adv. Gp on Physical Activity, 2002–04. Trustee, RSPH, 2015–. JP Hong Kong, 2011. Hon. Fellow, Cardiff Univ., 2012. Hon. DSc UWE, 2006. *Publications:* Indicators for Mental Health, 1990; Creating a Common Profile, 1990; (ed jtly) Prevention of Suicide, 1993; (ed) Perspectives in Public Health, 1999; Health of Rough Sleepers, 2002; Change and Development of Specialist Public Health Practice, 2005; New Perspectives on Public Health, 2006; Public Health and Primary Care, 2006; Routledge Handbook on Global Public Health in Asia, 2014; contribs to med. jls. *Recreations:* spending time with family, films, theatre, grandparenting. *Address:* 2 Canal Yard, Thrupp, Kidlington OX5 1JZ. *Clubs:* Athenæum; Jockey (Hong Kong).

**GRIFFITHS, Steffan Daniel Anderson;** Head Master, Norwich School, since 2011; *b* Lingfield, 22 June 1972; *s* of Brian Griffiths and Jane Griffiths; *m* 2000, Harriet Richmond; two *s* one *d*. *Educ:* Whitgift Sch., Croydon; University Coll., Oxford (BA Lit Hum; Plumptre Exhibnr 1993; Richard Blackwell Schol. 1992–94); Open Univ. (BA 1st Cl. Eng.). Assistant Master: Tonbridge Sch., 1995–99; Eton Coll., 1999–2006; Usher (Dep. Hd), Magdalen College Sch., 2006–11. Mem., Sports Sub-Cttee, HMC, 2012–. Trustee: Swifts Sports Trust, 2009– (Chm., 2014–); Royal Norfolk Agricl Assoc., 2014–; Transforming Educn in Norfolk, 2018–; Mem., Community Interest Gp, Viscount Nelson Educn Trust, 2017–; Chair, Norfolk Music HUB, 2017–. Gov., City Acad., Norwich, 2011–18. Chm., Young Norfolk Arts, 2013–. *Recreations:* theatre, birdwatching, sport (especially hockey and golf). *Address:* Norwich School, 70 The Close, Norwich NR1 4DD.

**GRIFFITHS, Stuart Mark,** OBE 2015; Programming Director, Ambassador Theatre Group, since 2015; *b* Castleford, Leeds, 23 April 1963; *s* of George Griffiths and Brenda Griffiths; *m* 2006, Daryl Back; two *d*. *Educ:* Univ. of Leicester (BA Hons 1986). Gen.

Manager, Beck Th., Hayes, London, 1987–92; Chief Executive Officer: Wycombe Swan Th., High Wycombe, 1992–2001; Birmingham Hippodrome, 2002–15. *Recreations:* theatre, dance, opera, visual arts, The Archers.

**GRIFFITHS, (Susan) Lesley;** Member (Lab) Wrexham, National Assembly for Wales, since 2007; Minister for Environment, Energy and Rural Affairs (formerly Cabinet Secretary for Environment and Rural Affairs, then Energy, Planning and Rural Affairs), since 2016; two d. Wrexham Maelor Hosp.; Constituency Asst to Ian Lucas, MP, 2001–07. Dep. Minister for Sci., Innovation and Skills, 2009–11, Minister for Health and Social Services, 2011–13, Minister for Local Govt and Govt Business, 2013–14, Minister for Communities and Tackling Poverty, 2014–16, Wales. *Address:* National Assembly for Wales, Cardiff Bay, Cardiff CF99 1NA.

**GRIFFITHS, Tania Veronica;** QC 2006; a Recorder, since 2000; b 7 Dec. 1959; d of Robert and Vera Griffiths; two s two d. *Educ:* Our Lady of Lourdes RC Primary Sch., Southport; Christ the King RC Comp. Sch., Southport; Liverpool Poly. (BA Hons Law 1981). Called to the Bar, Gray's Inn, 1982; Treasury Counsel, 2002–. *Recreations:* I love my football (Liverpool FC), my dogs and my kids (not necessarily in that order!). *Address:* Exchange Chambers, Pearl Assurance House, Derby Square, Liverpool L2 9XX. *T:* (0151) 236 7747, *Fax:* (0151) 236 3433. *E:* griffithsqc@exchangechambers.co.uk.

**GRIFFITHS, Trevor;** playwright; b 4 April 1935; s of Ernest Griffiths and Anne Connor. *Educ:* Manchester Univ. BA (Hons) Eng. Lang. and Lit. Teaching, 1957–65; Educn Officer, BBC, 1965–72. Writer's Award, BAFTA, 1981. DUniv York, 2013. *Publications:* Occupations, 1972, 3rd edn 1980; Sam Sam, 1972; The Party, 1974, 2nd edn 1978; Comedians, 1976, 2nd edn 1979; All Good Men, and Absolute Beginners, 1977; Through the Night, and Such Impossibilities, 1977; Thermidor and Apricots, 1977; (jtly) Deeds, 1978; (trans.) The Cherry Orchard, 1978; Country, 1981; Reds (screenplay), 1981 (Writers' Guild of America Best Original Screenplay Award); Oi for England, 1982; Sons and Lovers (television version), 1982; Judgement Over the Dead (television screenplays of The Last Place on Earth), 1986; Fatherland (screenplay), and Real Dreams, 1987; Collected Plays for Television, 1988; Piano, 1990; The Gulf Between Us, 1992; Hope in the Year Two, 1994; Thatcher's Children, 1994; Who Shall Be Happy…?, 1996; Collected Stage Plays, Vol. 1, 1996; Food for Ravens (screenplay), 1998 (RTS Best Regl Prog. Award; BAFTA Cymru Gwyn A. Williams Award); Camel Station, 2001; These are the Times: a life of Thomas Paine, 2005 (adapted for stage, 2009); Trevor Griffiths: theatre plays one, 2007; Trevor Griffiths: theatre plays two, 2007; Willie and Maud, 2008; Bill Brand: the screenplays, 2010; March Time, 2012. *Address:* c/o United Agents, 12–26 Lexington Street, W1F 0LE. *W:* www.trevorgriffiths.co.uk.

**GRIFFITHS, William Arthur;** Director, Acklea Homes Ltd, 2004; Chairman, Fremantle Trust, 2004–11; b 25 May 1940; s of Glyndwr and Alice Rose Griffiths; m 1963, Margaret Joan Dodd (marr. diss. 1988); two s one d. *Educ:* Owen's Sch., London; Queens' Coll., Cambridge; Univ. of Manchester. VSO, 1959–60. Probation Officer, Southampton, 1965–71; Home Office, 1971–76; Chief Probation Officer, N Ireland, 1977–84; Dir, NCVO, 1985–86; mgt consultant, 1986–95; Principal Inspector, Social Services, Bucks CC, 1995–2002; Asst Dir, Nat. Soc. for Epilepsy, 2002–04. Official Visitor, Ministry of Community Develt, Singapore, 1982 and 1985. Mem., Westminster CC, 1990–94. *Recreations:* literature, travel, horseracing.

**GRIFFITHS, (William) Robert;** QC 1993; SC (NSW) 1999; practising barrister, 6 Pump Court, since 2017; b 24 Sept. 1948; s of late (William) John Griffiths and of Megan Marjorie Griffiths (*née* Green); m 1984, Angela May Crawford; one s two d. *Educ:* Haverfordwest Grammar Sch.; St Edmund Hall, Oxford (Open Schol.; BCL, MA). Called to the Bar, Middle Temple, 1974, Bencher, 2004; Jun. Counsel to the Crown (Common Law), 1989–93; admitted as Legal Practitioner, NSW, 1998, Sen. Counsel, 1999; Special Advocate, 2004; Jt Hd of Chambers, 4/5 Gray's Inn Square, 2008–15; Hd of Mondial Chambers, 2015–17. Mem., Trade Mission to Dubai and Abu Dhabi, London Chamber of Commerce and BIS, 2014; Dir and Mem. Bd, LCCI, 2014–; Leader, LCCI Trade Mission to S Africa, 2016; Pres. London Chamber of Arbitration, 2017–. Chairman: Test Match Grounds Consortium, 1998–2002; First Class Forum Internet Working Party, 2000–02; Greyhound Regulatory Bd, 2015–17; Interim Chm., Greyhound Racing Bd of GB, 2017–18. Special Advr, Prince's Regeneration Trust, 2008–14; Legal Advr to Sec. Gen. of the Commonwealth, 2019–. Marylebone Cricket Club: Member: Cttee, 2000–01, 2001–03 (resigned re. Zimbabwe), 2006–11, 2012–15, 2016–19; Estates Sub-Cttee, 1996–2004; Cricket Cttee, 2000–04, 2008–14, 2016–18; Indoor Sch. and Coaching Sub-Cttee, 2000–10; Chairman: Laws Sub-Cttee, 2008–14; Develt Cttee, 2009–11; Ambassador on cricket tours to Singapore, Malaysia and Dubai, 2014, S Africa (Capetown, Johannesburg), 2016. Fellow, Erasmus Forum, 2018–. Freeman, City of London, 1997. *Recreations:* reading, philosophy, collecting modern first editions, British paintings, 18th and 19th century furniture; cricket (Schoolboy Cricket Internat., Wales, 1966–68; rep. Glamorgan CCC (non first-class), 1967–68, OUCC and OUCC (Authentics), 1968–72), Rugby (Schoolboy Internat., Wales, 1965–66), travel. *Address:* 6 Pump Court, EC4Y 7AR. *T:* (020) 7797 8400; Selborne Wentworth Chambers, 174 Phillip Street, Sydney, NSW 2000, Australia. *T:* (2) 92334081; Lascelles Great House, Holetown, Barbados, WI. *T:* 4321262. *Clubs:* MCC, Garrick, Lord's Taverners (Trustee, 2011–13).

**GRIFFITHS, Winston James,** OBE 2012; Chairman: Abertawe Bro Morgannwg University Local Health Board, 2009–12 (Chairman, Bro Morgannwg NHS Trust, 2005–08, Abertawe Bro Morgannwg University NHS Trust, 2008–09); Wales Council for Voluntary Action, 2006–14; b 11 Feb. 1943; s of (Rachel) Elizabeth Griffiths and (Evan) George Griffiths; m 1966, (Elizabeth) Ceri Griffiths; one s one d. *Educ:* State schools in Brecon; University College of South Wales and Monmouthshire, Cardiff. BA Hons, DipEd. Taught in Tanzania, Birmingham, Barry, Cowbridge. Non-exec. Dir, Welsh Biofuels, 2005–07. Mem., Ct of Govs, Nat. Mus. and Galls of Wales, 1998–2005. European Parliament: MEP (Lab) Wales South, 1979–89; Hon. Life Mem., 1989; a Vice Pres., 1984–87; former Chm., Parliamentarians for World Order, then Parliamentarians Global Action for Disarmament, Develt and World Reform; former Mem., delegn to S Asia. MP (Lab) Bridgend, 1987–2005. Opposition front bench spokesman on: envmtl protection, 1990–92, on education, 1992–94; on Welsh affairs, 1994–97; Parly Under-Sec. of State, Welsh Office, 1997–98. Mem., Speaker's Panel of Chairmen, 2001–05; All-Party Parliamentary Groups: Chairman: British Indonesia, 2001–05; Sierra Leone, 2004–05; Co-Chm., Street Children, 2001–05; Vice-Chm., Botswana, 2003–05; Sec., Southern Africa, 2001–05; Co-Sec., Children in Wales, 2001–05. H of C Rep., EU Convention on Charter of Fundamental Rights, 1999–2000. Member: Labour Movt for Europe (Sec., 2002); Labour Campaign for Electoral Reform. Chairman: Wales Non-Emergency Transport Services Review, 2007–10 (Interim Griffiths' Report, 2010), Non-Emergency Patient Transport Review Project, 2010–12 (Griffiths' Review Report, 2012); Wales NHS Confederation, 2010–12 (Mem., 2005–12); Task and Finish Gp, Access to Justice, 2011– (Access to Justice guidebook, 2013). Member: Rural Health Implementation Gp, Wales, 2010–12; Wales Learning Disabilities and Criminal Justice Working Gp, 2010–12. Associate Hosp. Manager, Abertawe Bro Morgannwg Univ. Health Bd, 2015–. Member: Christians on the Left (formerly Christian Socialist Movement); Amnesty International; Fabian Society; Anti-Apartheid Movement; Socialist Educn Assoc.; Socialist Health Assoc.; Exec. Bd, Internat. Islamic Christian Council for Reconciliation and Reconstruction, 2003–; Vice-Chm., British Cttee for Iran Freedom, 2003–; Chm., ABMU Health Bd, Africa Health Links, 2009–12. Trustee for Wales, Action on Hearing Loss, 2010–16, Employer-appointed Pension Trustee, 2016–, RNID. President: Kenfig Hill and Dist Male Voice Choir, 1986–; Porthcawl Choral Soc., 1993–; Cefn Cribwr Boys' and Girls' (formerly Boys') Club, 1987–2007; Boys' Brigade, Wales, 1994–2004 (Hon. Pres., 2005–). Methodist local preacher, 1966–. *Address:* Tŷ Llon, John Street, Y Graig, Cefn Cribwr, Mid Glamorgan CF32 0AB. *T:* (01656) 740526.

**GRIGG,** family name of **Baron Altrincham**.

**GRIGG, Christopher Montague;** Chief Executive, British Land Co. plc, since 2009; President, British Property Foundation, 2012–13 (Vice-President, 2011–12); b Basingstoke, 6 July 1959; s of Colin and Ann Grigg; m 1987, Fionna Stirling; one s four d. *Educ:* King Edward VI Sch., Southampton; Trinity Hall, Cambridge (BA 1st Cl. Econs 1981; MA). With Morgan Grenfell, 1981–85; Goldman Sachs International, 1985–2004: Man. Dir, 1997–2000; Partner, 2000–04; Treas., 2005–07, CEO, 2007–08, Commercial Bank, Barclays Bank plc. Non-exec. Dir, BAE Systems plc, 2013–. Mem. Exec. Bd, European Public Real Estate Assoc., 2010–. *Recreations:* military history, ski-ing, golf, supporter of England's cricket and Rugby teams. *Address:* British Land Co. plc, York House, 45 Seymour Street, W1H 7LX. *T:* (020) 7486 4466.

**GRIGG, Prof. Ronald,** PhD; FRS 1999; Professor of Medicinal Chemistry, 2000, now Emeritus (Professor of Organic Chemistry, 1989–2000), and Director, Molecular Innovation Diversity and Automated Synthesis (Midas) Centre, 1994, University of Leeds; b 1935. *Educ:* Univ. of Nottingham (PhD). Lectr, Dept of Chemistry, Univ. of Nottingham, 1965–74; Prof. of Organic Chemistry, QUB, 1974–89. Co-ordinator, Eur. Network on Cascade Combinatorial Chem., 1998. Lectures: Inaugural Schering Plough, 2008; Syngenta, 2008. Yorks Enterprise Fellow, 2009. Royal Society of Chemistry: Chm., Heterocyclic Gp, 1985–87; Heterocyclic Chemistry Medal, 1985; Tilden Medal and Lectr, 1986; Pedler Medal and Lectr, 1998; Medal for Synthesis, 2000. *Publications:* contribs to sci. jls incl. Tetrahedron, Jl of Med. Chem., Chem. Eur. Jl and Chem. Communications. *Address:* School of Chemistry, University of Leeds, Leeds LS2 9JT.

**GRIGGS, Prof. David John,** PhD; FRMetS, FTSE; Professor of Sustainable Development, 2015–18, and Director, Institute for Global Sustainable Development, 2017–18, University of Warwick, now Honorary Professor; Professor of Sustainable Development, Monash University, 2015–18, Adjunct Professor, since 2018; b 14 April 1958; s of Robert William Griggs and Barbara Griggs (*née* Musgrave); m 1982, Hillarie Jean Paston; one s one d. *Educ:* Helsby Grammar Sch. for Boys; UMIST (BSc Hons (Physics) 1979; PhD (Atmospheric Physics) 1982). Post Doctoral Fellow: Univ. of Toronto, 1982–84; UMIST, 1984–86; joined Meteorological Office, 1986: Hd, Sensor Develt, 1987–91; Internat. Manager, 1991–96; Hd, Wkg Gp I, Tech. Support Unit, Intergovtl Panel on Climate Change, 1996–2001; Dir, Hadley Centre for Climate Prediction and Res., 2001–06 and Dep. Chief Scientist, 2005–06; Dir, Govt Business, Met Office, 2006–07; Monash University: Prof. of Math. Scis, 2007–15; Dir, Monash Sustainability Inst., 2007–15. CEO, ClimateWorks, Australia, 2007–15. Gen. Sec., RMetS, 1993–96. FTSE 2011. Vilho Vaisala Award, WMO, 1992. *Publications:* co-ed and contrib., Reports of Intergovtl Panel on Climate Change, 1997, 1999, 2001; scientific papers on glaciation processes in clouds, sustainability and sustainable develt to jls incl. Nature. *Recreations:* trying to keep fit, sports, music. *Address:* Halwell Farm, Denbury, Newton Abbot, Devon TQ12 6ED. *E:* dave@griggs.me.uk.

**GRIGGS, Rt Rev. Ian Macdonald;** Bishop Suffragan of Ludlow, 1987–94; an Hon. Assistant Bishop, Diocese of Carlisle, since 1994; b 17 May 1928; s of late Donald Nicholson Griggs and Agnes Elizabeth Griggs; m 1953, Patricia Margaret Vernon-Browne; two s three d (and one s decd). *Educ:* Brentwood School; Trinity Hall, Cambridge (MA); Westcott House, Cambridge. Curate, St Cuthbert, Copnor, dio. Portsmouth, 1954–59; Domestic Chaplain to Bishop of Sheffield, 1959–64; Diocesan Youth Chaplain (part-time), 1959–64; Vicar of St Cuthbert, Fir Vale, dio. Sheffield, 1964–71; Vicar of Kidderminster, 1971–83; Hon. Canon of Worcester Cathedral, 1977–83; Archdeacon of Ludlow, 1984–87; Priest-in-Charge, St Michael, Tenbury, 1984–88. Mem., Gen. Synod of C of E, 1984–87. Chm., Churches' Council for Health and Healing, 1990–99. Governor: Bedstone Coll., 1987–93; Atlantic Coll., 1988–2002; Chm., Coll. of the Ascension, Selly Oak, 1992–94. *Address:* Rookings, Patterdale, Penrith, Cumbria CA11 0NP. *T:* (017684) 82064. *E:* iangriggs08@gmail.com.

**GRIGGS, His Honour Jeremy David;** a Circuit Judge, 1995–2010; Designated Civil Judge for Devon and Cornwall, 2006–10; a Deputy Circuit Judge, 2010–16; b 5 Feb. 1945; s of Celadon Augustine Griggs and Ethel Mary Griggs (*née* Anderson); m 1st, 1971, Wendy Anne Russell (*née* Culham) (marr. diss. 1982); two s one d; 2nd, 1985, Patricia Maynard; two step d. *Educ:* St Edward's Sch., Oxford; Magdalene Coll., Cambridge (MA); Open Univ. (BA Hons 1st cl. History). Called to the Bar, Inner Temple, 1968; Mem., Western Circuit, 1968–; a Recorder, 1990–95. Bar Rep., CCBE, 1990–94. Chm., London Choral Soc., 1986–90. *Publications:* A South African Childhood, 2006; Bishop Hugh Oldham: conservative or radical, 2019. *Recreations:* playing the piano, choral singing, walking, creating a garden. *Address:* c/o Crown and County Court, Southernhay Gardens, Exeter EX1 1UH. *Club:* Victory Services.

**GRIGOR, (William Alexander) Murray,** OBE 2012; film maker, writer and exhibition designer; Director: Viz Ltd, 1972–2015; Channel Four Television, 1995–99; b 20 June 1939; s of James McIntosh Grigor and Katharine Grigor (*née* Murray); m 1st, 1968, (Joan) Barbara Sternschein (d 1994); two d; 2nd, 2011, Carol Høgel (*née* Colburn). *Educ:* Loretto Sch.; St Andrews Univ. (BSc). Film Editor, BBC, 1963–67; Dir, Edinburgh Internat. Film Fest., 1967–72 (Hon. Fellow., 1991–94). Mem. Production Bd, BFI, 1968–72. *Films* include: Mackintosh, 1968; Space and Light, 1972; Big Banana Feet, 1975; The Architecture of Frank Lloyd Wright, 1981; Eduardo Paolozzi—Sculptor, 1986 (Rodin Prize, Paris Biennale, 1992); Carlo Scarpa, 1996; The Architecture of Alexander 'Greek' Thomson, 1999; Nineveh on the Clyde (Europa Nostra Award), 2000; The Work of Angels, 2001; (jtly) Is Mise an Teanga (I am the Tongue), 2003; Sir John Soane—British Architect—American Legacy, 2005; Infinite Space: The Architecture of John Lautner, 2008; Space and Light Revisited (two screen), 2008; Contemporary Days, 2010; Ever to Excel (documentary to mark 600th anniv. of St Andrews Univ.), 2012; Beatus—The Spanish Apocalypse, 2014; Turn End—The Home and Garden of Architect Peter Aldington (documentary celebrating 50th anniv. of house and gardens), 2017; The Cellist—The Legacy of Gregor Piatigorsky, 2018; Mackintosh Redux, 2019; television series: (jtly) Pride of Place (USA), 1986; Face of Russia (USA), 1998. *Exhibitions:* Scotch Myths, Edinburgh Fest., 1981; Scotland Creates, McLellan, Glasgow, 1990; Seeds of Change, Royal Mus. of Scotland, 1992; The Sixties, Barbican, 1992; The Unknown Genius: Alexander Greek Thomson, Glasgow 1999; John Byrne at 60, Paisley Mus. and Art Galls, 2000. UK/US Bicentennial Fellow in the Arts, 1976; Hon. FRIAS 1994; Hon. FRIBA 1999; Hon. RSA 2018. Hon. DArts Anglia Ruskin, 2010; Hon. DLitt St Andrews, 2012. Reith Award, RTS, 1990. *Publications:* (with Richard Murphy) The Architects' Architect, 1993; (with Sir Sean

Connery) Being a Scot, 2008. *Recreation:* saving Edinburgh's historic buildings, especially promoting Thomas Hamilton's Greek Revival Royal High School's conversion for St Mary's Music School which will save the Acropolis on Calton Hill from inappropriate hotel blocks. *Address:* 2 Bank Street, Inverkeithing, Fife KY11 1LR. *T:* 07769 716141. *Clubs:* Chelsea Arts; Scottish Arts (Edinburgh).

**GRIGSON, Hon. Sir Geoffrey (Douglas),** Kt 2000; a Judge of the High Court of Justice, Queen's Bench Division, 2000–09; Presiding Judge, North Eastern Circuit, 2004–05; *b* 28 Oct. 1944; *s* of Frederic Walter Grigson and Nora Marion Grigson; *m* 1967, Jay Sibbring (marr. diss. 1998); two *s* one *d. Educ:* Denstone Coll.; Selwyn Coll., Cambridge (MA). Called to the Bar, Gray's Inn, 1968; Midland and Oxford Circuit; a Recorder, 1985–89; a Circuit Judge, 1989–2000; a Permanent Judge, CCC, 1993–2000. A Dep. Sen. Judge, Sovereign Base Area, Cyprus, 1997–2000; Acting Puisne Judge, Gibraltar, 2012–14. *Recreations:* reading newspapers, walking. *Clubs:* Athenæum, Achilles.

**GRIGSON, Sophie;** freelance food writer and broadcaster, since 1983; Principal, Sophie's Cookery School, since 2012; *b* 19 June 1959; *d* of late Geoffrey Edward Harvey Grigson and Jane Grigson; *m* 1992, William Black (marr. diss. 2005; he *d* 2014); one *s* one *d. Educ:* UMIST (BSc Hons Maths). Cookery Correspondent: Evening Standard, 1986–93; Independent, 1993–94; Sunday Times Magazine, 1994–96; Restaurant Reviewer, Independent on Sunday, 1997–98. Chef: Story Mus., Oxford, 2015–16; Isis Farmhouse, Oxford, 2016–17. Presenter: television: Grow Your Greens, and, Eat Your Greens, 1993; Travels à la Carte, 1994; Sophie's Meat Course, 1995; Taste of The Times, 1997; Sophie Grigson's Herbs, 1999; Feasts for a Fiver, 1999; Sophie's Sunshine Food, 2000; Sophie's Weekends, 2003; Sophie in the Souk, 2009; Sophie Grigson on the Orient, 2010; Sophie Grigson in the Home Counties, 2011; Sophie Grigson in Thailand, 2012; radio: Curious Cooks, 1994, 1995; The Food Programme: Pears, BBC Radio 4, 2008. Trustee, Jane Grigson Trust, 1991– (Chairperson, 1993–96, 2007–08). Food Writer of the Year, Restaurateurs' Assoc. of GB, 1992; Magazine Writer of the Year, 1998, Cookery Journalist of 2001, Guild of Food Writers. *Publications:* Food For Friends, 1987; (with J. Molyneux) The Carved Angel Cookbook, 1990; Sophie's Table, 1990; Sophie Grigson's Ingredients Book, 1991; The Students' Cookbook, 1992; Eat Your Greens, 1993; (with William Black) Travels à la Carte, 1994; Sophie's Meat Course, 1995; Sophie Grigson's Taste of The Times, 1997; (with William Black) Fish, 1998; Sophie Grigson's Herbs, 1999; Feasts for a Fiver, 1999; Sunshine Food, 2000; The Complete Sophie Grigson Cookbook, 2001; My Favourite Family Recipes, 2003; Sophie's Country Kitchen, 2003; The First-Time Cook, 2004; Vegetables, 2006; Spices, 2011. *Recreations:* travel, reading, eating.

**GRILLS, Michael Geoffrey;** a Recorder of the Crown Court, 1982–2000; a District Judge, 1991–2000; *b* 23 Feb. 1937; *s* of Frank and Bessie Grills; *m* 1969, Ann Margaret Irene (née Pyle); two *d. Educ:* Lancaster Royal Grammar Sch.; Merton Coll., Oxford (MA). Admitted Solicitor, 1961; Partner with Crombie Wilkinson & Robinson, York, 1965; County Court and District Registrar, York and Harrogate District Registries, 1973–90. *Recreations:* music, tennis, golf. *Address:* Cobblestones, Skelton, York YO30 1XX. *T:* (01904) 470246.

**GRIME, Prof. (John) Philip,** PhD; FRS 1998; Director, Buxton Climate Change Impacts Laboratory, Unit of Comparative Plant Ecology, since 1989, and Professor, 1983–98, now Emeritus, University of Sheffield; *b* 30 April 1935; *s* of Robert and Gertrude Grime; *m* 1st, 1966, Jean Carol Sorensen (marr. diss. 1982); one *s*; 2nd, 2000, Sarah Margaret Buckland. *Educ:* Middleton Grammar Sch., Lancs; Sheffield Univ. (BSc; PhD 1960). Postgrad. researcher, Univ. of Sheffield, 1960–63; Ecologist, Connecticut Agricl Expt Stn, 1963–65; University of Sheffield: Res. Ecologist, Nature Conservancy Grassland Res. Unit, 1965–71; Dep. Dir, NERC Unit of Comparative Ecol., 1971–89. Vice Pres., British Ecological Soc., 1989–91. Foreign Mem., Royal Netherlands Acad. Arts and Sci., 1991; Hon. Member: Lund Ecological Soc., 1992; Ecol Soc. of America, 1998. Hon. Dr Univ. of Nijmegen, Netherlands, 1998. Marsh Award for Ecol., British Ecol Soc., 1997; Alexander von Humboldt Award, Internat. Assoc. for Vegetation Sci., 2011. *Publications:* Ecological Atlas of Grassland Plants (with P. S. Lloyd), 1973; Plant Strategies and Ecological Processes, 1979; (jtly) Comparative Plant Ecology: a functional approach to common British species, 1988; Plant Strategies, Vegetation Processes and Ecosystem Properties, 2001; numerous contribs to scientific jls. *Recreation:* league and friendly cricket. *Address:* Department of Animal and Plant Sciences, Alfred Denny Building, University of Sheffield, Western Bank, Sheffield S10 2TN; 24 Delph House Road, Crosspool, Sheffield S10 5NR. *T:* (0114) 267 1214.

**GRIME, Mark Stephen Eastburn;** QC 1987; *b* 16 March 1948; *s* of late R. T. Grime, ChM, FRCS and M. D. Grime; *m* 1973, Christine Emck; two *d. Educ:* Wrekin College; Trinity College, Oxford (Scholar; MA). FCIArb 1997. Called to the Bar, Middle Temple, 1970, Bencher, 1997; practising Northern Circuit, 1970–; Asst Recorder, 1988–90; Recorder, 1990–2003; Technol. and Construction Recorder, 1998–2003. Chairman: Disciplinary Appeal Tribunal, UMIST, 1980–2003; Northern Arbitration Assoc., 1994–98 (Mem. Council, 1990–94); Northern Circuit Med. Law Assoc., 1999–2002. *Recreations:* antiquarian horology, sailing. *Address:* Homestead Farm, Jackson's Edge, Disley, Cheshire SK12 2JR. *T:* (01663) 766976; Deans Court Chambers, 24 St John Street, Manchester M3 4DF. *T:* (0161) 214 6000.

**GRIME, Philip;** *see* Grime, J. P.

**GRIMES, Hon. Roger (Dale);** MHA (L) Exploits, 1989–2005; Premier, Newfoundland and Labrador, Canada, 2000–03; *b* 2 May 1950; *s* of late Fred and Winnie Grimes; *m* 1996, Mary Ann Lewis; one *d. Educ:* Meml Univ. of Newfoundland (BSc; BEd 1972; MEd 1988). High Sch. teacher, 1972–89. Pres., Newfoundland and Labrador Teachers' Assoc., 1985–87; Dir, Canadian Teachers' Fedn, 1985–87. Parly Asst to Premier of Newfoundland and Labrador, 1989–91; Minister: of Employment and Labour Relns, 1991–93; of Tourism, Culture and Recreation, 1993–96; of Educn, 1996–98; of Mines and Energy, 1998–99; of Health and Community Services, 2000–01; Leader of Opposition, Newfoundland and Labrador, 2003–05. Mem., Canada-Newfoundland Offshore Petroleum Bd, 2018–. *Recreations:* recreational hockey, jogging, golf, softball, reading.

**GRIMLEY, Very Rev. Robert William;** Dean of Bristol, 1997–2009, now Dean Emeritus; *b* 26 Sept. 1943; *s* of William Bracebridge Grimley and Gladys Mary (née Draper); *m* 1968, Joan Elizabeth Platt; two *s* one *d. Educ:* Derby Sch.; Christ's Coll., Cambridge (BA 1966; MA 1970); Wadham Coll., Oxford (BA 1968; Ellerton Theol Essay Prize, 1974; MA 1976); Ripon Hall, Oxford. Ordained deacon 1968, priest 1969; Asst Curate of Radlett, 1968–72; Chaplain, King Edward's Sch., Birmingham and Hon. Curate, St Mary, Moseley, 1972–84; Vicar, St George's, Edgbaston, 1984–97. Examining Chaplain to the Bishop of Birmingham, 1988–97; Bishops' Inspector of Theol Colls, 1998–2009. Chaplain to the High Sheriff of W Midlands, 1988–89. A Church Comr for England, 2006–08 (Mem., Bishoprics and Cathedrals Cttee, 2005–09). Select Preacher, Univ. of Oxford, 2013. Trustee, Bishop's Palace, Wells, 2005–06. Governor: The Queen's Coll., Birmingham, 1974–97; The Foundn of the Schs of King Edward VI in Birmingham, 1991–97; Bristol Cathedral Sch., 1997–2009; Kingswood Sch., 1998–2008; Bristol Cathedral Choir Sch., 2008–09. Hon. DLitt UWE, 2004; Hon. LLD Bristol, 2009. *Recreations:* reading, travel, languages, bread-making. *Address:* 88 Old High Street, Oxford OX3 9HW. *T:* (01865) 308219. *E:* robertgrimley88@gmail.com.

**GRIMLEY, Susan Elaine;** *see* Hartley, S. E.

**GRIMMETT, Prof. Geoffrey Richard,** DPhil, DSc, ScD; FRS 2014; Professor of Mathematical Statistics, 1992–2018, now Emeritus, and Director of Research, University of Cambridge; Master, Downing College, Cambridge, 2013–18; *b* 20 Dec. 1950; *s* of Benjamin and Patricia Grimmett; *m* 1986, Rosine Bonay; one *s. Educ:* King Edward's Sch., Birmingham; Merton Coll., Oxford (BA 1971; MSc 1972; MA, DPhil 1974); DSc (Oxon) 2010; ScD (Cantab) 2010. Jun. Res. Fellow, New Coll., and IBM Res. Fellow, Oxford Univ., 1974–76; Bristol University: Lectr, 1976–85; Reader, 1985–89; Prof. of Maths, 1989–92; Cambridge University: Dir, Statistical Lab., 1994–2000; Hd, Dept of Pure Maths and Math. Stats, 2002–07; Fellow, 1999–2013, Mem. Council, 2000–02, Churchill Coll., Cambridge. Vis. appts at Cornell Univ., Univ. of Arizona, Univ. of Rome II, Univ. of Utah, UCLA, UBC, Univ. of Paris, Univ. of Calif Berkeley, Univ. of Melbourne, etc. Managing Editor: Probability Theory and Related Fields, 2000–05; Probability Surveys, 2009–11. Public Schs Foil Champion, 1968; GB Under 20 Foil Champion, 1970; Member: GB Fencing Team, 1973–77; Olympic Foil Team, 1976. Hon. FIA 1999. *Publications:* (with D. R. Stirzaker) Probability and Random Processes, 1982, 3rd edn 2001; (with D. J. A. Welsh) Probability: an introduction, 1986, 2nd edn 2014; Percolation, 1989, 2nd edn 1999; (with D. R. Stirzaker) One Thousand Exercises in Probability, 2001; The Random-Cluster Model, 2006; Probability on Graphs, 2010, 2nd edn 2018; contrib. to learned jls. *Recreations:* mountaineering, music. *Address:* Statistical Laboratory, University of Cambridge, Wilberforce Road, Cambridge CB3 0WB. *T:* (01223) 337957. *W:* www.statslab.cam.ac.uk/~grg. *Clubs:* Alpine; Climbers'.

**GRIMMOND, Steven David;** Chief Executive, Fife Council, since 2013; *b* Dundee, 12 June 1963; *s* of David Grimmond and Freda Grimmond (née Connolly); *m* 1983, Audrey Krawec; one *s* one *d. Educ:* Craigie High Sch., Dundee; Dundee Univ. (BA Politics and Social Admin 1985; MBA 1995). Exec. Officer, DHSS, 1985–87; Sen. Housing Officer, Dundee DC, 1987–90; Prin. Officer, 1990–95, Policy Planning Manager, 1995–98, Dundee CC; Area Manager, Aberdeenshire Council, 1998–2000; Dir, Arts and Heritage, 2000–02, Leisure and Arts, 2002–05, Dundee CC; Hd, Community Services, 2005–09, Exec. Dir, 2009–13, Fife Council. Mem. Bd, Creative Scotland, 2012–16. *Recreations:* cycling, football, painting. *Address:* Fife Council, Fife House, North Street, Glenrothes, Fife KY7 5LT. *T:* 0345 155 5555, ext. 444143. *E:* steven.grimmond@fife.gov.uk. *Clubs:* West End Tennis; Royal Tay Yacht.

**GRIMSBY, Bishop Suffragan of,** since 2014; **Rt Rev. Dr David Court;** *b* Norwich, 16 Oct. 1958; *s* of Eric and Eileen Court; *m* 1984, Ann White; two *s* one *d. Educ:* Univ. of Southampton (BSc 1980; PhD 1983; PGCE 1984); Oak Hill Theol Coll. (BA 1991). Teacher of Chemistry and Physics, Prince William Sch., Oundle, Northants, 1984–88; ordained deacon, 1991, priest, 1992; Assistant Curate: St Botolph, Barton Seagrave, 1991–94; St Andrew, Kinson, 1994–97; Priest-in-charge, 1997–99, Vicar, 1999–2003, St Catherine, Mile Cross; Vicar, St Peter and St Paul, Cromer, 2003–14; Rural Dean, Repps, 2010–14. Hon. Canon, Norwich Cathedral, 2010–14. *Recreations:* family, friends, sport, reading, music, theatre, walking. *Address:* c/o The Diocese of Lincoln, Edward King House, Minster Yard, Lincoln LN2 1PU.

**GRIMSEY, Elizabeth Jon,** CBE 2002; LVO 1977; Director of Judicial Services (formerly of Policy), 2003–07, and of Corporate Diversity, 2006–07, Legal and Judicial Services Group, Ministry of Justice (formerly Department for Constitutional Affairs); *b* 31 May 1947; *d* of Archibald Charles Sermon and Betty Elaine Sermon (née Swanborough); *m* 1976, Colin Robert Grimsey (*d* 2002); one *s* one *d. Educ:* Old Palace Sch., Croydon; Univ. of Durham (BA Hons 1968); Rose Bruford Coll. of Theatre and Performance (BA Hons Univ. of Manchester 2016). Home Office: Asst Principal, 1968–73; Principal, 1973–77 and 1983–86; Head of Division: Personnel and Immigration Depts, 1986–90; Prison Service, 1990–96; Dir, Corporate Services, 1996–99, Judicial Gp, 1999–2003, LCD. Trustee, Children and Families Across Borders (formerly International Social Service (UK)), 2005–11. *Recreations:* family, reading, music, theatre going, supporting Crystal Palace FC.

**GRIMSEY, Inga Margaret Amy, (Mrs G. R. Dunn),** OBE 2017; Chairman: Saxmundham Free School, since 2012; East of England Regional Advisory Board, National Trust, since 2015; *b* 20 Oct. 1952; *d* of Robert Jessup Grimsey and Annelise Grimsey (née Albeck); *m* 2002, Geoffrey Richard Dunn. *Educ:* Gravesend Grammar Sch.; Regent Street Poly. (BA Hons (Finance) Business Studies). Man. Dir, Anonymous (fashion chain), Storehouse plc, 1983–91; Chief Exec., Ski Club of GB, 1991–96; National Trust: Man. Dir, National Trust (Enterprises), 1996–2001; Territory Dir, 2001–05; Hd, Trading, NPG, 2005–06; Dir Gen., RHS, 2006–09. Chm., E England Cttee, HLF, 2010–16. Trustee: Seckford Foundn, 2010–; Seckford Foundn Free Schs Trust, 2014–. *Recreations:* ski-ing, opera, gardening, countryside.

**GRIMSHAW, John Roland,** CBE 2008 (MBE 1996); Engineer and Director, 1981–2008, Chief Executive, 1984–2008, Sustrans; *b* 12 July 1945; partner, Sue Learner; two *s* one *d. Educ:* Gonville and Caius Coll., Cambridge (BA Engrg 1966). Engr, Taylor Woodrow, 1963–68; VSO, Uganda, 1969–70; engr, MRM (Bristol), 1971–80. Asst Hon. Engr, Cyclebag, 1977–83. Board Member: Railway Paths Ltd, 1997–2009; Cycling England, 2005–08 (Special Advr, 2008–10); John Grimshaw and Associates Ltd, 2010–. Surveyor of cycleway associated with HS2, DfT, 2014–. Trustee, Greenways and Cycleroutes Ltd, 2016–. DUniv York, 2000; Hon. Dr: Strathclyde, 2001; Bath, 2008; Hon. MSc Bristol, 2007. *Recreation:* sculpture. *Address:* 58 Bellevue Crescent, Bristol BS8 4TF.

**GRIMSHAW, Mark;** Founder and Chief Executive Officer, Blackridge Business Services, since 2017; *b* Stafford, 13 Jan. 1961; *s* of Antony John and Thelma Jean Grimshaw; *m* 1984, Nicola Jane; three *d. Educ:* Manshed Upper Sch.; RAF St Athan Tech. Sch.; INSEAD Euro-Asia Centre. Served RAF, 1979–83. Swan Nat. Car Rental Gp, 1984–89; Dir, Mercury Communications, 1990–95; Customer Service Dir, UK and Europe, and Sen. Vice Pres. for Service Delivery, Cable and Wireless, 1996–2001; Employer Services Dir, Job Centre Plus, 2002–06; Chief Operating Officer, Strategic Prog. Dir and Man. Dir, Child Support Agency, 2006–11; Chief Exec., Rural Payments Agency, 2011–17. *Recreations:* supporter of Manchester City FC, holder of Private Pilot's Licence.

**GRIMSHAW, Sir Nicholas (Thomas),** Kt 2002; CBE 1993; RA 1994; Chairman, Grimshaw Architects LLP (formerly Nicholas Grimshaw & Partners Ltd), architects, planners and industrial designers, since 1980; President, Royal Academy of Arts, 2004–11; *b* 9 Oct. 1939; *s* of Thomas Cecil Grimshaw and Hannah Joan Dearsley; *m* 1972, Lavinia, *d* of late John Russell, CBE; two *d. Educ:* Wellington College; Edinburgh College of Art; Architectural Assoc. Sch. AA Dip. Hons 1965; RIBA 1967; FCSD (FSIAD 1969); numerous prizes and scholarships. Major projects include: Channel Tunnel terminal, Waterloo (Mies van der Rohe Pavilion Award, 1994, RIBA Building of the Year Award, 1994); British Pavilion for Expo '92, Seville, Spain; Financial Times Printing Plant (Royal Fine Art Commn/Sunday Times Building of the Year Award, 1989); Pusan Internat. Rly Terminus, Korea, 1996; Zurich Airport Expansion, 1996; Regl HQ for Orange Telephones, Darlington, 1996; restoration of Paddington Stn, 1996; restoration of existing Spa and new building, Bath, 1997; Caixa Galicia Art Foundn, La Coruña, Spain, 1997; Berlin Stock Exchange and Communications Centre; British Airways Combined

Operations Centre, Heathrow; HQ for Igus GmbH, Cologne; RAC Rescue Services HQ; Satellite and Piers, Heathrow Airport; Research Centre for Rank Xerox; BMW HQ, Bracknell; Herman Miller Factory, Bath; Oxford Ice Rink; Gillingham Business Park; J. Sainsbury Superstore, Camden; Head Office and Printing Press for Western Morning News; redevelopment of Terminal One, Manchester Airport, for MA plc; teaching and res. bldg, Univ. of Surrey; head office for Mabeg GmbH, Soest (RIBA Internat. Award), 1999; Eden Project, St Austell, 2000; Exhibn Hall, Frankfurt Fair, 2000; HQ and factory for Pfeiffer Vacuum, Dortmund, 2000; Plant Sci. Centre, St Louis, USA, 2001; Nat. Space Sci. Centre, Leicester, 2001; Ijburg Bridge, Amsterdam, 2001; HQ and assembly plant for Rolls Royce, Goodwood, Sussex, 2001; NE Wing, RCA, 2001; Millennium Point, Birmingham, 2001; UCL Cancer Inst., 2001; HQ for Lloyds TSB, London, 2002; Spine House, Cologne, 2002; London Stock Exchange, 2003; KPMG Berlin HQ, 2003; Southern Cross Stn, Melbourne, 2006 (Lubetkin Award, 2007; Australian Construction Achievement Award, 2007; Victorian Industry Capability Award, 2007; Victorian Arch. Medal, Walter Burley Griffin Award for Urban Design, RAIA, 2007; William Wardle Public Arch. Award, 2007); high-speed rly stn, Bijlmer, Amsterdam, 2007 (Bldg of the Year, Royal Inst. of Dutch Architects, 2008); Brunel Award, Watford Gp, 2008); Newport City Footbridge, Wales, 2007; Experimental Media and Perf. Arts Centre for Rensselaer Poly. Inst., Albany, NY, 2007 (Structl Engrg Award, 2010); Steel Mus., Monterrey, Mexico, 2007 (Nuevo Leon Arch. Chapter 14th Arch. Biennale; Cemex Bldg Awards, 2008; AIA Honor Award for Arch., 2009; American Soc. of Landscape Architects Honor Award, 2009); New Academic Bldg for LSE, 2008 (Camden Bldg Quality Award, 2009); Front Engrg Bldg, UCL, 2008; K2 London Southbank Univ., 2009; Minerva Bldg, St Botolph's, City of London, 2010; ExCel Phase 2 Develt, 2010 (UK Commercial Property Award); Nunawading Stn, Melbourne, 2010; Newport Stn, S Wales, 2010 (Inst. of Civil Engrg Award, 2011); John Lewis Fashion Pavilion, London, 2012; Cutty Sark, Greenwich, 2012; Via Verde, NY, 2012 (Andrew J. Thomas Award for Housing, 2012); Highpoint Retail Centre, Melbourne, 2013; Stoke on Trent City Centre Bus Station, 2013; Peter Doherty Inst., Univ. of Melbourne, 2013; Queens Mus., NY, 2013; Pulkova Airport, St Petersburg, 2013; Terminal 2 Concourse B, Heathrow, 2014; Reading Station, 2014; Queens Mus., NY, 2014; Fulton Center, NY, 2014; SUEZ Energy from Waste Facility, 2015; Boldrewood Innovation Campus, Univ. of Southampton, 2015; Materials Sci. and Engrg Bldg, Univ. of NSW, 2015; 699 Bourke St, Melbourne, 2015; Univ. of Bangor Arts and Innovation Centre, 2016; Duke Univ. W Campus Union, NC, 2016; 333 George Street, Sydney, NSW, 2017; Yoox Net-a-Porter Tech Hub fit-out, UK, 2017; London Bridge Station, 2018. Pres. Council, AA, 1999–2001. Assessor for: British Construction Industry Awards; DoE; British Gas; Scottish Develt Agency; Stirling Prize, 2012. Hon. Mem., Bund Deutscher Architekten, 1997. Hon. FAIA 1995; Hon. FRIAS 2002; Hon. Fellow, Politecnico Milano, 2009. Hon. DLitt: South Bank, 1993; Heriot-Watt, 2008; Edinburgh, 2008; UCL, 2011; Hon. DSocSc Edinburgh, 2010. Awards and Commendations include: RIBA, 1975, 1978, 1980, 1983, 1986, 1989, 1990, 1991, 1994, 1995, 1999, 2001, 2002, 2003, 2004, 2008, 2009, 2013, 2014, Royal Gold Medal for Architecture, 2019; Financial Times (for Industrial Architecture), 1977, 1980, 1995; Structural Steel Design, 1969, 1977, 1980, 1989, 1993, 1994, 1995, 1999, 2000, 2001, 2002, 2003, 2007, 2013; Civic Trust, 1978, 1982, 1989, 1990, 1991, 1996, 2007, 2015, 2016; British Construction Industry Awards, 1988, 1989, 1992, 1993, 1995, 1999, 2001, 2010, 2015, 2016; Royal Fine Art Commn/Sunday Times Bldg of the Year Award, 1989, 1993, 1994, 1999, 2001, 2004; Constructa Preis for Industrial Architecture in Europe, 1990; Quaternario Foundn Internat. Award for Innovative Technol. in Architecture, 1993; AIA/London UK Chapter Design Excellence Award, 1995, 2001, 2005, AIA State Award, 2013; Nat. Heritage Arts Sponsorship Scheme Award, 1995; Design Innovation Award, 1996; British Council for Offices Award, 1996; Internat. Brunel Award, 1996; Leisure Property Award for best regeneration scheme, 2001; European Award for Aluminium in Architecture, 2001; Archtectl Practice of Year, Transport Architect of Year, World Architect of Year, Building Design Awards, 2008; Medal and Dip. for IAA Academician, Internat. Acad. Architecture, Sofia, 2012; Medal of Honor, AIA, 2015; Robert Matthew Award, CAA, 2016. *Publications:* Nicholas Grimshaw & Partners: product and process, 1988; (jtly) Architecture, Industry and Innovation: the work of Nicholas Grimshaw & Partners 1966–88, 1995; (jtly) Structure, Space & Skin: the work of Nicholas Grimshaw & Partners 1988–93, 1993; Equilibrium: the work of Nicholas Grimshaw & Partners 1993–99, 2000; Capturing the Concept: the sketchbooks of Sir Nicholas Grimshaw, CBE, PRA, from 1987 to 2007, 2009; Blue 01: water, energy and waste, 2009; Blue 02: systems and structure, 2010; Grimshaw: Architecture: the first 30 years, 2011; articles for RSA Jl. *Recreations:* sailing, tennis. *Address:* 57 Clerkenwell Road, EC1M 5NG. *T:* (020) 7291 4141.
*See also T. Traeger.*

**GRIMSTON**, family name of **Earl of Verulam** and of **Baron Grimston of Westbury**.

**GRIMSTON, Viscount; James Walter Grimston;** Portfolio Manager, Odey Asset Management LLP, since 2010; *b* 6 Jan. 1978; *s* and *heir* of Earl of Verulam, *qv*; *m* 2008, Lady Rosanagh Innes-Ker, *d* of 10th Duke of Roxburghe and Lady Jane Dawnay, *qv*; two *s* one *d*. *Educ:* Eton; St Edmund Hall, Oxford (MSc). *Heir: s* Hon. John Innes Archie Grimston, *b* 10 Aug. 2010.
*See also Countess of Verulam.*

**GRIMSTON OF WESTBURY**, 3rd Baron *cr* 1964; **Robert John Sylvester Grimston;** Bt 1952; *b* 30 April 1951; *er s* of 2nd Baron Grimston of Westbury and Hon. June Mary (*d* 2010), *d* of 5th Baron de Mauley; *S father*, 2003; *m* 1984, Emily Margaret, *d* of Major John Shirley; two *d*. *Educ:* Eton; Reading Univ. (BSc). ACA 1985. Commnd, The Royal Hussars (PWO), 1970–81 (Captain 1976). *Heir: b* Hon. Gerald Charles Walter Grimston [*b* 4 Sept. 1953; *m* 1980, Katherine Evelyn (*née* Kettle); two *s* one *d*].

**GRIMSTONE, Sir Gerald Edgar, (Sir Gerry),** Kt 2014; Chairman: Barclays Bank plc, 2018–19 (Deputy Chairman, Barclays Group plc, 2016–18); Standard Life Aberdeen, 2017–19 (Chairman, Standard Life plc, 2007–17); *b* 27 Aug. 1949; *s* of Edgar Wilfred Grimstone and Dorothy Yvonne Grimstone; *m* 1973, Hon. Janet Suenson-Taylor (marr. diss. 1995); one *s* two *d*. *Educ:* Winterbourne Primary Sch.; Whitgift Sch.; Merton Coll., Oxford (MA, MSc; Hon. Fellow, 2016). NATO-CCMS Fellow, Wolfson Coll., Oxford. Civil Service, 1972–86, Asst Sec., HM Treasury, 1984–86; J. Henry Schroder Wagg, 1986–99: Head: Internat. Finance Adv. Dept, 1992–94; Investment Banking, Asia Pacific, 1994–97; Investment Banking, N America, 1997–98; Global Vice-Chm., Investment Banking, 1998–99; Mem., Horserace Totalisator Bd, 1999–2006; Chairman: Candover Investments plc, 2006–11; Heng An Standard Life (China), 2011–; TheCityUK, 2012–15. Ind. non-exec. Dir, Deloitte LLP, 2011–. Sen. Advr, Fenchurch Advisory, 2019–. HM Treasury Operational Efficiency Prog. Advr, 2008–10; UK Business Ambassador, 2009–10; Mem. Bd, Shareholder Exec., BIS, 2009–16; Advr, 2010–, Lead non-exec. Dir and Mem., Defence Bd, 2011–, MoD; Bd Advr, Abu Dhabi Commercial Bank, 2013–; Chair, Public Service Leadership Taskforce, 2018. Member: RAF Strike Comd Bd, 2000–07; RAF Air Comd Bd, 2007. Trustee, RAF Mus., 2008–18. Hon. Gp Captain RAF 601 Sqn, 2017. *Publications:* contribs on pollution to learned jls. *Recreations:* travelling, tidying my office, my friends and family. *Clubs:* Athenæum, Royal Air Force; Hong Kong, China (Hong Kong).

**GRIMTHORPE,** 5th Baron *cr* 1886; **Edward John Beckett;** Bt 1813; *b* 20 Nov. 1954; *er s* of 4th Baron Grimthorpe, OBE and of Lady Grimthorpe (*see* Elizabeth, Lady Grimthorpe); *S father*, 2003; *m* 1st, 1992, Mrs Carey Elisabeth McEwen (marr. diss. 2009), *yr d* of Robin Graham; one *s*; 2nd, 2013, Mrs Emma Benyon (*née* Villiers). *Educ:* Harrow. Mem., Jockey Club, 2007–. Chm., York Racecourse, 2012–. *Heir: s* Hon. Harry Maximillian Beckett, *b* 28 April 1993. *Address:* Brinkley House, Brinkley, Newmarket, Suffolk CB8 0RB.

**GRIMTHORPE, Elizabeth, Lady; Elizabeth Beckett,** DCVO 1995 (CVO 1983); Lady of the Bedchamber to HM Queen Elizabeth The Queen Mother, 1973–2002; *b* 22 July 1925; 2nd *d* of 11th Earl of Scarbrough, KG, GCSI, GCIE, GCVO, PC and Katharine Isabel, Countess of Scarbrough, DCVO, K-i-H Gold Medal; *m* 1954, Hon. Christopher John Beckett, later 4th Baron Grimthorpe, OBE (*d* 2003); two *s* one *d*. *Address:* Herbert Cottage, Westow, York YO60 7NE. *T:* (01653) 618225.

**GRIMWADE, Sir Andrew (Sheppard),** Kt 1980; CBE 1977; Australian industrialist, cattle breeder, arts patron and aged care philanthropist; *b* 26 Nov. 1930; *s* of late Frederick and Gwendolen Grimwade; *m* 1st, 1959, Barbara (*d* 1990), *d* of J. B. D. Kater; one *s*; 2nd, 1994, Marsha, *d* of Hon. Dr Reginald John David Turnbull. *Educ:* Melbourne Grammar Sch.; Trinity Coll., Melbourne Univ. (Exhib. Eng.; BSc); Oriel Coll., Oxford (swimming blue; MA). FRACI, FAIM. Principal, Green Valley Cattle Co., 1959–; Man. Dir, Carba Ind. Ltd, 1960–70; Chairman: Kemtron Ltd, 1964–88; Australian Cons. Ind. Ltd, 1975–82; Founding Chm., Beolite Village Ltd, 2005–; Vice-Chm., Nat. Mutual Life Assoc., 1988–92 (Dir, 1970–92); Dep. Chm., Turoa Ski Resort Ltd, 1986–2001; Director: Commonwealth Ind. Gases Ltd, 1960–90 (Dep. Chm., 1987–90); Nat. Aust. Bank, 1965–85; IBM (Aust.) Ltd, 1971–92; Sony (Aust.) Pty Ltd, 1974–92. Member: Bd, Melbourne UP, 1996–2002; Adv. Bd, Deutscher-Menzies Pty Ltd, 1998–; Dep. Chm., Cert. Aust. Angus Beef Pty, 1996–2003. Mem., first Aust. Govt Trade Mission to China, 1973. Member: Australian Govt Remuneration Tribunal, 1974–82; Bd, Rev. of Victorian Govt Salaries and Allowances, 1980. Pres., Walter and Eliza Hall Inst. of Med. Research, 1978–92 (Mem. Bd, 1963–92; Laureate, 2007); Founding and Life Mem., Miegunyah Fund, Melbourne Univ., 1987–; Patron, Miegunyah Press. Chairman: Australian Art Exhibn Corp. (Chinese Exhibn), 1976–77; Australian Govt Official Estabts Trust, 1976–82; Trustee, Victorian Arts Centre, 1980–90; Emeritus Trustee, Nat. Gallery of Vic, 1990– (Trustee, 1964–90; Pres., 1976–90); Dep. Chm., Art Foundn of Victoria, 1976–90; Dep. Pres., Australiana Fund, 1978–82; Chm., Royal Soc. of Victoria Foundn, 2007–08. Member: Council for Order of Australia, 1975–82; Felton Bequests' Cttee, 1973– (Chm., 2004–). Hon. Life Mem., RACI; Hon. Mem., Royal Soc. of Victoria. *Publications:* Involvement: The Portraits of Clifton Pugh and Mark Strizic, 1968; (with Dr G. Vaughan) Great Philanthropists on Trial, 2006; Storied Windows: casting light on the arts, science and life in Australia 1959 to 2011, an anthology, 2011. *Recreations:* ski-ing, Australian art, limericks. *Address:* PO Box 607, Mansfield, Vic 3724, Australia.

**GRIMWOOD, Ven. Andrew Stuart;** Archdeacon of St Asaph, since 2018; *b* 1968. *Educ:* Exeter Univ. (BA 1989); St Michael's Coll., Llandaff (BD 1997). Ordained deacon, 1998, priest, 1999; Curate, St Cynwyd, Llangynwyd, 1998–2001; Priest-in-charge, Holy Trinity, Rhyl, 2001–04; Rector, All Saints, Llanllwchaiarn, 2004–13; Area Dean, Cedewain, 2008–13; Vicar, Holy Trinity, Rhyl, 2013–16; Team Vicar, Aber-Morfa Mission Area, 2017–18. *Address:* c/o The Diocesan Office, High Street, St Asaph, Denbighshire LL17 0RD.

**GRIMWOOD, Sam Jayne;** *see* Baker, Samantha J.

**GRINDLEY, Prof. Nigel David Forster,** PhD; FRS 2006; Professor of Molecular Biophysics and Biochemistry, Yale University, 1986–2012, now Professor Emeritus and Senior Research Scientist; *b* 24 Nov. 1945; *s* of Eric Edward Grindley and Evelyn Marion Grindley; *m* Catherine Mary Joyce; one *s* one *d*. *Educ:* Gonville and Caius Coll., Cambridge (BA 1967); Univ. of London (PhD 1974). Mem., Scientific Staff, Central Public Health Lab., London, 1967–73; Postdoctoral Fellow: Biol Scis, Carnegie-Mellon Univ., 1973–75; Molecular Biophysics and Biochem., Yale Univ., 1975–78; Asst Prof. of Biol Scis, Univ. of Pittsburgh, 1978–80; Yale University: Asst Prof. of Molecular Biophysics and Biochem., 1980–83, Associate Prof., 1983–86; Chm., Dept of Molecular Biophysics and Biochem., 2003–06. NATO Postdoctoral Fellow, SRC, 1974–76; Guggenheim Fellow, 1987–88; Vis. Fellow, Brasenose Coll., Oxford, 2007–08. FAAAS 2007; Fellow, Amer. Acad. of Microbiol., 2011. Ed., Molecular and Gen. Genetics, 1985–91; Member, Editorial Board: Jl Bacteriol., 1988–93; Molecular Microbiol., 1990–2003 (Mem., Edid Adv. Bd, 2005–09); Mobile DNA, 2009–13. World Health Organisation: Mem., Immunol. of Leprosy Molecular Biol. Subcttee, Geneva, 1987–90 (Mem., Steering Cttee, 1990–92); Immunol. of Mycobacterial Disease Steering Cttee, 1992–96; Mem., NIH Study Section, Microbial Physiol. and Genetics, 1988–92. Merit Award, NIH, 1991–2001. *Publications:* contrib. to learned jls. *Address:* Department of Molecular Biophysics and Biochemistry, Yale University, Bass Center, 260 Whitney Avenue, New Haven, CT 06520-8114, USA. *T:* (203) 4328991. *E:* nigel.grindley@yale.edu.

**GRINDROD, David William;** Casting Director, David Grindrod Associates, since 1998; *b* Warwick, 2 June 1952; *s* of William Grindrod and Betty Grindrod (*née* Ellis). *Educ:* Feldon Sch., Leamington Spa; London Acad. of Music and Dramatic Art. Stage manager and co. manager for various prodns in UK and overseas, incl. RSC, 1977–81, Really Useful Gp, 1991–98. Associate Artist, Old Vic Th., 2015–. Mem., Casting Dirs' Guild of UK and Ireland, 1999–. Consultant, Andrew Lloyd Webber Foundn, 2011–. Casting credits include: *films:* Phantom of the Opera, 2004; Mamma Mia! (ensemble), 2008; Nine (dancers), 2009; Beauty and the Beast, 2017; *television:* How Do You Solve a Problem Like Maria?, 2006; Any Dream Will Do, 2007; I'd Do Anything, 2008; Over the Rainbow, 2010; Superstar, 2012; The Sound of Music Live, 2015; *theatre:* all Andrew Lloyd Webber musicals; Mamma Mia! (worldwide); Matilda; Once; Chicago; Groundhog Day; Fat Friends. *Recreations:* theatre, film, music, walking. *Address:* (office) 4th Floor, Palace Theatre, Shaftesbury Avenue, W1D 5AY. *T:* (020) 7437 2506. *E:* dga@grindrodcasting.co.uk. *Clubs:* Ivy, Union.

**GRINDROD, Prof. Peter,** CBE 2005; Professor of Mathematics, University of Oxford, since 2013; *b* Oxford, 22 Nov. 1959; *s* of Alan and Alma Grindrod; *m* 1985, Dora Louise Bennett; three *s* one *d*. *Educ:* Bristol Univ. (BSc Hons Maths 1981); Dundee Univ. (PhD Maths 1984). Res. Fellow in Maths, Dundee Univ., 1983–85; Oxford University: Jun. Lectr, 1985–88, SRC Advanced Fellow in Maths, 1988–89, Mathematical Inst.; Jun. Res. Fellow, Brasenose Coll., 1985–88; Dynamical Systems Gp Leader, Intera Inf. Technologies, later QuantSci, Henley-on-Thames, 1989–98; Technical Dir, and Co-founder, Numbercraft Ltd, Oxford, 1998–2007; Prof. of Maths and its Applications, Univ. of Reading, 2007–13. Visiting Professor: in Applied Maths, Univ. of Bath, 2001–; in Applied Industrial Maths, Oxford Univ., 2005–08. Mem., User Panel, 1999– (Chm., 2000–04), Mem. Council, 2000–04, EPSRC; Mem. Council, BBSRC, 2009. Mem. Council, Inst. of Maths and its Applications, 1996 (Pres., 2006–08). Mem., Bioinformatics Cttee, Wellcome Trust, 1999–2002. *Publications:* Patterns and Waves: theory and applications of reaction-diffusion equations, 1990, 2nd edn 1995; Mathematical Underpinnings of Analytics, 2015; contrib. numerous papers to learned jls. *Recreations:* published poet, guitarist, football fan

(Manchester United). *Address:* Mathematical Institute, University of Oxford, Andrew Wiles Building, Radcliffe Observatory Quarter, Woodstock Road, Oxford OX2 6GG. *E:* peter_grindrod@hotmail.com.

**GRINLING, Jasper Gibbons,** CBE 1978; Chairman, London Jazz Radio plc, 1989–91, retired; *b* 29 Jan. 1924; *s* of late Lt-Col Antony Gibbons Grinling, MBE, MC, and Jean Dorothy Turing Grinling; *m* 1950, Jane Moulsdale; one *s* two *d*. *Educ:* Harrow (Scholar); King's Coll., Cambridge (Exhibnr, BA). Served War, 12th Lancers, 1942–46 (Captain). Joined W. & A. Gilbey Ltd, 1947, Dir 1952; Man. Dir, Gilbeys Ltd, 1964; Man. Dir, International Distillers & Vintners Ltd, 1967; Dir, North British Distillery Co. Ltd, 1968–86; Dir of Corporate Affairs, Grand Metropolitan, 1981–85, Dir of Trade Relations, 1985–86; Chm., The Apple & Pear Develt Council, 1986–89. Pres., EEC Confedn des Industries Agricoles et Alimentaires, 1976–80; Mem. Council, Scotch Whisky Assoc., 1968–86. CCMI (FBIM 1969). Chevalier, Ordre National du Mérite, France, 1983. *Publications:* The Annual Report, 1986. *Recreations:* gardening, jazz drumming, painting. *Address:* The Old Vicarage, Helions Bumpstead, near Haverhill, Suffolk CB9 7AS. *T:* (01440) 730316.

**GRINYER, Clive;** design consultant, since 2019; *b* Southampton, 29 July 1960; *s* of Tony and Hazel Grinyer; *m* 1988, Janis; two *s*. *Educ:* Highcliffe Comprehensive Sch., Dorset; Central Sch. of Art and Design (BA Hons Industrial Design). Founder, Tangerine, 1989–94; Hd, Samsung Studio, Palo Alto, Calif, then Eur. Design Hd, Samsung Electronics, 1994–98; Hd, Eur. Product Design, Fitch Design plc, 1998–99; Hd, Product Design, TAG McLaren Audio, 1999–2001; Dir, Design and Innovation, Design Council, 2001–03; Hd, Customer Experience and Design and Usability, Orange and France Telecom, 2003–08; Dir, Customer Experience, CISCO, 2008–13; Barclays: Dir, Customer Experience, 2013–16; Process Improvement Dir, 2016–17; Dir of Service Design, 2016–18; Creative Dir, New Products and Service Design, Object Tech Gp, 2018–19. Fellow, Policy Lab, Cabinet Office, 2019–. Vis. Prof., Glasgow Sch. of Art; Vis. Tutor, RCA, 2017–. Trustee: RSA, 2010–16; Policy Connect, 2012–14. *Publications:* Smart Products, 2000, 3rd edn 2005. *Recreations:* musician - guitarist, classic car owner, sailing. *Address:* 122 Dorset Road, SW19 3HD. *T:* (020) 8544 1785. *E:* clive@clivegrinyer.com.

**GRINYER, Prof. Peter Hugh;** Emeritus Professor, University of St Andrews, since 1993; *b* 3 March 1935; *s* of Sidney George and Grace Elizabeth Grinyer; *m* 1958, Sylvia Joyce Boraston; two *s*. *Educ:* E Ham Grammar Sch.; Balliol Coll., Oxford (BA, subseq. MA, PPE); LSE (PhD in Applied Economics). Unilever Sen. Managerial Trainee, 1957–59; PA to Man. Dir, E. R. Holloway Ltd, 1959–61; Lectr and Sen. Lectr, Hendon Coll. of Tech., 1961–64; Lectr, 1965–69, Sen. Lectr, 1969–72, City Univ.; Reader, 1972–74, Prof. of Business Strategy, 1974–79, City Univ. Business School; University of St Andrews: Esmée Fairbairn Prof. of Econs (Finance and Investment), 1979–93; Chm., Dept of Econs, 1979–85; Vice-Principal, 1985–87, Actg Principal; Founder and Chm., Dept of Mgt, 1987–92. Chairman: St Andrews Management Inst., 1989–96; St Andrews Strategic Management Ltd, 1989–96. Visiting Professor: Stern Sch. of Business, New York Univ., 1992, 1996–98; Imperial Coll., London, 2002–04; Erskine Fellow, Univ. of Canterbury, NZ, 1994. Member: Business and Management Studies Sub-Cttee, UGC, 1979–85; Scottish Legal Aid Bd, 1992–2000; Appeal Tribunals Panel, Competition Commn, 2000–03; Competition Appeal Tribunals, 2003–11. Founding Dir, Glenrothes Enterprise Trust, 1983–86; Director: John Brown PLC, 1984–86; Don and Low (Hldgs) Ltd (formerly Don Bros Buist), 1985–91; Ellis and Goldstein (Hldgs) PLC, 1987–88; Chm., McIlroy Coates, 1991–95. *Publications:* (with J. Wooller) Corporate Models Today, 1975, 2nd edn 1979; (with G. D. Vaughan and S. Birley) From Private to Public, 1977; (with J.-C. Spender) Turnaround: the fall and rise of Newton Chambers, 1979; (with D. G. Mayes and P. McKiernan) Sharpbenders, 1988; (with Dr Foo Check Teck) Organizing Strategy: Sun Tzu business warcraft, 1994; some 55 papers in academic jls. *Recreations:* hill walking, golf. *Address:* 60 Buchanan Gardens, St Andrews, Fife KY16 9LX. *Club:* Royal & Ancient Golf (St Andrews).

**GRISHAM, John;** author; *b* 8 Feb. 1955; *m* Renée Jones; one *s* one *d*. *Educ:* Mississippi State Univ. (BS Accounting); Univ. of Mississippi (JD 1981). Mem., Miss. Bar, 1981; Law practice, Southaven, 1981–91; Mem. (Democrat), Miss. House of Reps, 1984–90. *Publications:* The Firm, 1991; The Pelican Brief, 1992; A Time to Kill, 1992; The Client, 1993; The Chamber, 1994; The Rainmaker, 1995; The Runaway Jury, 1996; The Partner, 1997; The Street Lawyer, 1998; The Testament, 1999; The Brethren, 2000; A Painted House, 2001; The Summons, 2002; The King of Torts, 2003; Bleachers, 2003; The Last Juror, 2004; The Broker, 2005; Playing for Pizza, 2007; The Appeal, 2008; The Associate, 2009; Theodore Boone, 2010; Theodore Boone: the abduction, 2011; The Litigators, 2011; The Racketeer, 2012; Calico Joe, 2012; Gray Mountain, 2014; Rogue Lawyer, 2015; The Whistler, 2016; Camino Island, 2017; The Rooster Bar, 2017; The Reckoning, 2018; *non-fiction:* The Innocent Man, 2006 (televised, 2018). *Recreations:* reading, coaching baseball. *Address:* c/o Doubleday, 1745 Broadway, New York, NY 10019, USA.

**GRIST,** family name of **Baroness Bertin**.

**GRIST, Maj.-Gen. Robin Digby,** CB 1994; OBE 1979; Director, Gloucestershire Enterprise Ltd, 2001–11; Chairman, Quality South West Ltd, 2003–08 (Director, since 2001); *b* 21 Oct. 1940; *s* of late Lt-Col and Mrs Digby Grist; *m* 1971, Louise Littlejohn; one *s* two *d*. *Educ:* Radley Coll.; Royal Military Acad., Sandhurst. Commnd, Gloucestershire Regt, 1960; seconded to Army Air Corps, 1965–69 (despatches, 1968); CO 1st Bn Gloucestershire Regt, 1979–82; Comdr 6 Airmobile Bde, 1985–86; rcds 1987; Mil. Attaché and Comdr Brit. Army Staff, Washington, USA, 1988–89; Dir, AAC, 1989–92; Dir Gen., AGC, 1992–94. Col, The Gloucestershire Regt, 1990–94, The Royal Gloucestershire, Berkshire and Wiltshire Regt, 1994–2001. Chm., Glos Community Foundn, 2000–05. DL Gloucestershire, 1995–2002. *Publications:* Their Laurels are Green: a short history of The Royal Gloucestershire, Berkshire and Wiltshire Regiment, 1997; A Gallant County: the regiments of Gloucestershire in the Great War, 2018. *Recreations:* fishing, gardening, military history. *Address:* Cleeve Cottage, Corton, Warminster, Wilts BA12 0SZ.

**GRISWOLD, Rt Rev. Frank Tracy, III;** Presiding Bishop, Episcopal Church in the United States of America, 1998–2006; *b* 18 Sept. 1937; *s* of Frank Tracy Griswold Jr and Louisa Johnson (*née* Whitney); *m* 1965, Phoebe Wetzel; two *d*. *Educ:* Harvard Univ. (BA 1959); Gen. Theol Seminary; Oriel Coll., Oxford (BA 1962; MA 1966). Ordained deacon 1962, priest 1963; Curate, Church of the Redeemer, Bryn Mawr, Penn, 1963–67; Rector: St Andrew's, Yardley, Penn, 1967–74; St Martin-in-the-Fields, Philadelphia, 1974–85; Bishop Coadjutor of Chicago, 1985–87; Bishop of Chicago, 1987–97. Hon. DD: Gen. Theol Seminary, 1985; Seabury-Western Theol Seminary, 1985; Virginia Theological Seminary, 1999; Nashotah House, Wisconsin, 2000; Univ. of the South, 2001; Berkeley Divinity Sch., 2002; Bexley Hall, 2006; Episcopal Divinity Sch., 2006; Church Divinity Sch. of the Pacific, 2007; Hon. LHD: Episcopal Theol Seminary of the Southwest, 2004; Rikkyo, Tokyo, 2005. *E:* ftgriswold@mac.com.

**GRITTON, Susan;** soprano; Principal with English National Opera, 2000–02; *b* 31 Aug. 1965; *m* Stephen Medcalf; two *c*. *Educ:* Univ. of Oxford; Univ. of London; National Opera Studio. Major rôles include: Liù in Turandot and Micaëla in Carmen, Royal Opera, Covent Gdn; Konstanze in Die Entführung aus dem Serail, Deutsche Staatsoper and Bayerische Staatsoper; Vitellia in La Clemenza di Tito, Blanche in Dialogues des Carmelites, Bayerische Staatsoper, Munich; Elettra in Idomeneo, Netherlands Opera; Countess in Le Nozze di Figaro, ENO; Donna Anna in Don Giovanni, Opera de Montréal and Bolshoi; Ellen Orford in Peter Grimes, La Scala, Opera Australia and New Nat. Th., Tokyo; Countess Madeleine in Capriccio, Tatyana in Eugene Onegin, Grange Park Opera; Female Chorus in Rape of Lucretia, Snape Maltings; title rôles include: Theodora, Glyndebourne; Rodelinda, Bayerische Staatsoper, Munich; The Bartered Bride, Royal Opera, Covent Garden; The Cunning Little Vixen, ENO; has performed with Rome Opera, Teatro la Fenice, Venice, Th. des Champs Elysées, Paris and Mostly Mozart Fest., NY. Recitalist at Wigmore Hall (solo début, 1994), Lincoln Centre, NY, and Oxford Lieder Fest.; has performed in concert with many orchestras including BBC orchs, LSO, Orch. of the Age of Enlightenment, Berlin Philharmonic and NY Philharmonic. Has made numerous recordings. Arts Foundn Fellowship, 1994. Kathleen Ferrier Meml Prize, 1994. *Address:* c/o Askonas Holt Ltd, 15 Fetter Lane, EC4A 1BW.

**GROARKE, Ven. Nicola Jane;** Archdeacon of Dudley, since 2014; *b* London, 2 June 1962; *d* of Basil and Thelma Barnett; *m* 1986, Philip Groarke (*d* 1992). *Educ:* Univ. of Lancaster (BA Hons 1984); Ridley Hall, Cambridge (CTM 2000). Sen. Marketing Manager, Elsevier Sci. Publishers, 1985–95; Bereavement Services Co-ord., Sobell House Hospice, 1985–88; ordained deacon, 2000, priest, 2001; Curate/Associate Vicar, Ascension, Balham Hill, 2000–08; Vicar, St Stephen's, Canonbury, 2008–13. *Recreations:* running, hill-walking, cycling, gardening, entertaining. *Address:* 15 Worcester Road, Droitwich, Worcs WR9 8AA. *T:* (01905) 773301. *E:* NGroarke@cofe-worcester.org.uk.

**GROBEL, His Honour Peter Denis Alan Christian Joseph;** a Circuit Judge, 2001–14; *b* 11 Aug. 1944; *s* of Cyril Peter Grobel and Kathleen (*née* Donaghy); *m* 1975, Susan Twemlow, LRAM; three *s* one *d*. *Educ:* Mt St Mary's Coll.; University Coll. London (LLB Hons). Called to the Bar, Lincoln's Inn, 1967; in practice at common law bar, 1971–2001; a Recorder, SE Circuit, 1991–2001. Chm., Special Educnl Needs Tribunal, 1994–2001; Mem. (part-time), Parole Bd, 2016–. Chm. of Govs, St Teresa's Sch., Effingham, 2002–09.

**GROCOCK, Dr (Catherine) Anne;** Executive Director, Royal Society of Medicine, 1997–2006; *b* 7 March 1947; *d* of late Arthur Raymond Grocock and Alice Grace Grocock. *Educ:* Westonbirt Sch.; St Anne's Coll., Oxford (BA Zool. 1968; MA, DPhil 1973). University of Oxford: Deptl Demonstrator in Human Anatomy, 1973–79; Deptl Res. Asst, 1979–80 and 1982–85, and ICRF Res. Fellow, 1985–89, Dept of Human Anatomy; Lectr in Anatomy, Merton Coll., Oxford, 1977–80 and 1985–89; Bursar and Official Fellow, St Antony's Coll., Oxford, 1990–97; Asst Registrar, Univ. of Oxford, 2006–10. Chm., Reproduction Res. Inf. Services Ltd, 1988–93. Member: Defence Estates Audit Cttee, 2006–10; Veterinary Labs Agency Owners' Adv. Bd, 2007–11; Defence Storage and Distribution Agency Audit Cttee, 2008–10; Standards Cttee, Gen. Optical Council, 2010–17. Non-exec. Dir, Oxford Health NHS Foundn Trust (formerly Oxfordshire and Bucks Mental Health Trust), 2008–18. Trustee: Nat. Mus. Sci. and Industry, 1996–2006 (Chm. Audit Cttee, 1997–2006; Dep. Chm. of Trustees, 2002–06); Royal Med. Benevolent Fund, 1998–2004; Nuffield Oxford Hosp. Fund, 2001– (Chm., 2005–). Member: Court, ICSTM, 2001–06; Council, Taunton Sch., 1990–2001; Gov., Westonbirt Sch., 1991–97. Trustee, Oxford Soc., 1995–2003; Pres., ASM, St Anne's Coll., Oxford, 1997–2000. FRSA, 2000–16. *Publications:* contribs to learned jls in reproductive physiology. *Recreations:* gardens, opera, sculpture.

**GROCOTT,** family name of **Baron Grocott**.

**GROCOTT, Baron** *cr* 2001 (Life Peer), of Telford in the County of Shropshire; **Bruce Joseph Grocott;** PC 2002; Captain of the Hon. Corps of Gentleman at Arms (Government Chief Whip in the House of Lords), 2002–08; *b* 1 Nov. 1940; *s* of Reginald Grocott and Helen Grocott (*née* Stewart); *m* 1965, Sally Barbara Kay Ridgway; two *s*. *Educ:* Hemel Hempstead Grammar Sch.; Leicester and Manchester Univs. BA (Pol), MA (Econ). Admin. Officer, LCC, 1963–64; Lectr in Politics, Manchester Univ., Birmingham Polytechnic, and N Staffs Polytechnic, 1964–74. Television presenter and producer, 1979–87. Chm., Finance Cttee, Bromsgrove UDC, 1972–74. Contested (Lab): SW Herts, 1970; Lichfield and Tamworth, Feb. 1974, 1979; The Wrekin, 1983. MP (Lab): Lichfield and Tamworth, Oct. 1974–1979; The Wrekin, 1987–97; Telford, 1997–2001. Parliamentary Private Secretary: to Minister for Local Govt and Planning, 1975–76; to Minister of Agriculture, 1976–78; Dep. Shadow Leader, H of C, 1987–92; Opposition front bench spokesman on foreign affairs, 1992–93; PPS to Leader of the Opposition, 1994–97, to Prime Minister, 1997–2001; a Lord in Waiting (Govt Whip), 2001–02. Mem., Select Cttee on Nat. Heritage, 1994–95. Mem., Internat. Relns Cttee, H of L, 2016–. Chancellor, Leicester Univ., 2013–18. *Recreations:* sport, steam railways. *Address:* House of Lords, SW1A 0PW. *Club:* Trench Labour.

**GROCOTT, Susan;** QC 2008; a Recorder, since 2003; Deputy High Court Judge, Family Division, since 2010; *b* Rochdale, 30 March 1963; *d* of late Peter and Joan Grocott. *Educ:* Oulder Hill Community Sch., Rochdale; Exeter Coll., Oxford (BA). Called to the Bar, Middle Temple, 1986. *Recreations:* literature, shopping, fine dining. *Address:* Deans Court Chambers, 24 St John Street, Manchester M3 4DF. *T:* (0161) 214 6000, *Fax:* (0161) 214 6001. *E:* grocott@deanscourt.co.uk.

**GRODZINSKI, Samuel Marc;** QC 2011; a Deputy High Court Judge, since 2018; *b* London, 12 Feb. 1968; *s* of Emmanuel Grodzinski and Vera Grodzinski; *m* 1993, Marion Baker; three *s* one *d*. *Educ:* University College Sch., London; St Anne's Coll., Oxford (BA Juris.). Admitted Solicitor, 1993; Solicitor, 1993–95; called to the Bar, Middle Temple, 1996; in practice as a barrister, specialising in public law and tax law, 1996–; Mem., Attorney Gen.'s Panel of Civil Counsel, 1997–2011. *Recreations:* walking, reading, ski-ing. *Address:* Blackstone Chambers, Blackstone House, Temple, EC4Y 9BW. *T:* (020) 7583 1770. *E:* samgrodzinski@blackstonechambers.com.

**GROENING, Matthew Abram;** cartoonist; *b* Portland, Oregon, 15 Feb. 1954; *s* of late Homer Philip Groening and Margaret Ruth Groening (*née* Wiggum); *m* 1987, Deborah Lee Caplan (marr. diss. 1999); two *s*. *Educ:* Lincoln High Sch., Portland, Oregon; Evergreen State Coll. (BA 1977). Worked on LA Reader, 1979–85; cartoonist, weekly comic strip, Life in Hell, 1980–2012; creator: The Simpsons, interludes on The Tracey Ullman Show, 1987–89; TV series, The Simpsons, 1990– (also Exec. Prod.); TV series, Futurama (also Co-developer), 1999–2003, 2008–13; TV series, Disenchantment, 2018; Exec. Prod., TV film, Olive the Other Reindeer, 1999; co-writer, The Simpsons Movie, 2007. Co-founder, Life in Hell, Inc., 1985; President: Matt Groening Prodns, Inc., 1988–; Bongo Entertainment, Inc., 1993–; Founder and Publisher: Bongo Comics Gp, 1993–; Zongo Comics, 1995. *Publications:* Love is Hell, 1985; Work is Hell, 1986; School is Hell, 1987; Childhood is Hell, 1988; Greetings from Hell, 1989; Akbar and Jeff's Guide to Life, 1989; The Postcards That Ate My Brain, 1990; The Big Book of Hell, 1990; The Simpsons Xmas Book, 1990; Greetings from the Simpsons, 1990; With Love from Hell, 1991; The Simpsons Rainy Day Fun Book, 1991; The Simpsons Uncensored Family Album, 1991; The Simpsons Student Diary, 1991; How to Go to Hell, 1991; Maggie Simpson's Alphabet Book, 1991; Maggie Simpson's Counting Book, 1991; Maggie Simpson's Book of Colors and Shapes, 1991;

Maggie Simpson's Book of Animals, 1991; The Road to Hell, 1992; The Simpsons Fun in the Sun Book, 1992; Making Faces with the Simpsons, 1992; Bart Simpson's Guide to Life, 1993; The Simpsons Ultra-Jumbo Rain-Or-Shine Fun Book, 1993; Cartooning with the Simpsons, 1993; Bongo Comics Group Spectacular, 1993; Binky's Guide to Love, 1994; Simpsons Comics Extravaganza, 1994; Simpsons Comics Spectacular, 1994; Bartman: the best of the best, 1994; Simpsons Comics Simps-O-Rama, 1995; Simpsons Comics Strike Back, 1995; Simpsons Comics Wing Ding, 1997; The Huge Book of Hell, 1997; A Little Book of Hell, 2006; The Simpsons Forever - and Beyond!, 2006. *Address:* c/o Fox Broadcasting Company, PO Box 900, Beverly Hills, CA 90213, USA.

**GROGAN, John Timothy;** MP (Lab) Keighley, since 2017 (Selby, 1997–2010); *b* 24 Feb. 1961; *s* of late John Martin Grogan and Maureen Grogan (*née* Jennings). *Educ:* St Michael's Coll., Leeds; St John's Coll., Oxford (BA Hons 1982; Pres., Student Union, 1982). Asst to Leader, Wolverhampton Council, 1985–87; Communications Dir, Leeds CC, 1987–94; Press Officer, Eur. Parly Lab. Party, 1994–95; Conf. Organiser, Yorks, 1995–97. Contested (Lab): Selby, 1987, 1992; York, EP elecn, 1989. Contested (Lab) Keighley, 2015. Chairman: Mongolian British Chamber of Commerce, 2010–; Hatfield Colliery, 2013–15. *Recreations:* running, football, keen supporter of Bradford City FC and Yorks CCC. *Address:* House of Commons, SW1A 0AA. *Club:* Yorks CC.

**GRONN, Prof. Peter Christian,** PhD; Professor of Education, 2008–15, now Emeritus and Head, Faculty of Education, 2011–14, University of Cambridge; Fellow of Hughes Hall, Cambridge, 2009–14, now Quondam Fellow; *b* Melbourne, 15 Nov. 1946; *s* of Lorenz Christian Gronn and Ena Winifred Gronn; *m* 1972, Barbara Jean Reith; one *d* (and one *d* dead). *Educ:* Canterbury State Sch.; Camberwell Central Sch.; Camberwell High Sch.; Univ. of Melbourne (BA Hons 1968; DipEd 1969); Monash Univ. (BEd 1973; PhD 1979). Teacher, Educn Dept of Vic, Australia, 1970–73; Lectr in Politics, State Coll. of Vic, Burwood, 1974–79; Faculty of Education, Monash University: Lectr, 1980–84; Sen. Lectr, 1985–94; Associate Prof., 1995–2003; Prof. of Educn, 2003–07; Prof. Emeritus, 2014; Prof. of Public Service, Educnl Leadership and Mgt, Dept of Educnl Studies, Univ. of Glasgow, 2007–08. Fellow, Australian Council of Educnl Leaders, 1997. FRSA 2004. FAcSS (AcSS 2012). *Publications:* The Making of Educational Leaders, 1999; The New Work of Educational Leaders, 2003; (ed. with J. Biddulph) A University's Challenge: Cambridge's primary school for the nation, 2016; Just As I Am: a life of J. R. Darling, 2017; contrib. articles to jls, incl. Leadership Qly, Jl Educnl Admin, Australian Jl Educn, Australian Historical Studies, Human Relations. *Recreations:* reading, music, travel, walking, sport, gardening, house renovating, cycling.

**GROOM, Brian William Alfred;** writer and editorial consultant; UK Business and Employment Editor, Financial Times, 2009–14; *b* 26 April 1955; *s* of Fred and Muriel Groom; *m* 1980, Carola May Withington; one *s* one *d*. *Educ:* Manchester Grammar Sch.; Balliol Coll., Oxford (BA Hons). Journalist: Goole Times, 1976–78; Financial Times, 1978–88; Dep. Editor, 1988–94, Editor, 1994–97, Scotland on Sunday; Financial Times: British and Regl Affairs Ed., 1997–2000; Political Ed., 2000–02; Ed., European Edn, 2002–05; Ed., Comment and Analysis, 2005–09. *Recreations:* cricket and football, walking, Britain's culture and history. *Address:* Alphin House, 69 Chew Valley Road, Greenfield, Oldham OL3 7JG. *T:* (01457) 878278.

**GROOM, Maj.-Gen. John Patrick,** CB 1984; CBE 1975 (MBE 1963); Director General, Guide Dogs for the Blind Association, 1983–89; *b* Hagley, Worcs, 9 March 1929; *s* of Samuel Douglas Groom and Gertrude Groom (*née* Clinton); *m* 1951, Jane Mary Miskelly; three *d*. *Educ:* King Charles I Sch., Kidderminster; Royal Military Academy, Sandhurst. Enlisted as Sapper, Dec. 1946; commnd into RE, 1949; regimental service, N Africa, Egypt, Singapore, Malaya, UK, 1949–59; sc Camberley, 1960; War Office, 1961–63; regimental service, UK, Aden, 1963–65 (despatches); Directing Staff, Staff Coll., 1965–68; Regimental Comdr, BAOR, 1968–70; MoD, Military Operations, 1970–71; Dep. Sec., Chiefs of Staff Cttee, 1971–73; HQ Near East Land Forces, Cyprus, 1973–75; RCDS 1976; Comdr, Corps of Royal Engineers, BAOR (Brig.), 1976–79; Chief Engineer, HQ BAOR, 1979–82; Head of Army Trng Rev. Team, MoD (Army), 1982–83. Col Comdt 1983–91, Rep. Col Comdt, 1986, RE. Chairman: GDBA (Trading Co.) Ltd, 1984–89; GDBA (Recreational Services) Co. Ltd, 1986–89; (non-exec.) BKP Environmental Services Ltd, 1992–99; Dir, GDBA (Pension Fund Trustees) Ltd, 1985–89; Hon. Vice-Pres., Internat. Fedn of Guide Dog Schs, 1989–. Chm., Reach Foundn, 1993–96; Member: Adv. Bd, Talking Newspapers, 1988; Council, Oakhaven Hospice, 1992–96. Governor: Gordon's Sch., Woking, 1982–88; Sandle Manor Sch., Fordingbridge, 1984–88. Vice-Chm., Solent Protection Soc., 1994–99; Chm., Adv. Bd, Yarmouth Harbour Comrs, 1997–2002. Member: RYA, 1982–; ASA, 1982–. FCMI (FBIM 1979); FIPlantE 1976; Fellow, RSPB 1975. Freeman, City of London, 1978; Liveryman, Worshipful Co. of Plumbers, 1978–92. *Recreations:* ocean sailing, country pursuits, the environment. *Address:* Medlar House, 6 Grove Pastures, Lymington, Hants SO41 3RG. *T:* (01590) 675710. *Clubs:* Royal Ocean Racing; Royal Engineer Yacht; Royal Lymington Yacht; British Kiel Yacht (Germany) (Life Mem.); Kieler Yacht (Germany) (Hon. Mem.).

**GROOM, Michael John,** FCA; President, Institute of Chartered Accountants in England and Wales, 2001–02; *b* 18 July 1942; *s* of Thomas Rowland Groom and Eliza Groom; *m* 1966, Sheila Mary Cartwright; two *d*. *Educ:* St Chad's Grammar Sch., Wolverhampton; Cotton Coll., N Staffs. FCA 1964. Articled, Plevey & Co., Chartered Accountants, 1958–63; Sen. Clerk, Dixon Hopkinson, Chartered Accountants, 1963–65; Sec. and Dir, Thorneville Properties Ltd/Aldridge Builders Ltd, 1965–67; Manager/Partner, Camp Ravenscroft & Co., Chartered Accountants, 1967–71; in practice as chartered accountant, 1971–76, 1981–89; Partner, Tansley Witt/Binder Hamlyn, Chartered Accountants, 1976–81. Mem. Council, ICAEW, 1975–2004. Dep. Chm., Financial Reporting Council, 2001–02; Chm., CCAB, 2001–02; Mem., Takeover Panel, 2001–02. Non-exec. dir of cos; lectr and consultant on strategy formulation in the medium-sized business, the rôle of the non-exec. director, mgt and financial advice, professional practice mgt. Freeman, City of London, 1977; Liveryman, Chartered Accountants' Co., 1977 (Mem., 1994–2006, Hon. Mem., 2006, Ct of Assts); Trustee, Chartered Accountants' Livery Charity, 2004–06. Hon. DBA Wolverhampton, 2003. *Publications:* The Chartac Administration Manual, 1975; Financial Management in the Professional Office, 1977; (jtly) Cash Control in the Smaller Business, 1978; (jtly) Current Cost Accounting the Easy Way, 1980; (jtly) Budgeting and Cash Management, 1981; joint author and series editor, 1975–81: The Chartac Accounting Manual; The Chartac Auditing Manual; The Chartac Taxation Manual; The Chartac Accounting and Auditing Model File. *Recreations:* ballet, theatre, music, photography, travel, food and wine. *Address:* 14 High Meadows, Compton, Wolverhampton WV6 8PH. *T:* (01902) 753816. *Club:* Albert Lawn Tennis (Wolverhampton).

**GROOM, Hon. Raymond John,** AO 2010; barrister and solicitor; arbitrator; Chairman, Southern Cross Care (Tasmania) Inc., since 2006; *b* 3 Sept. 1944; *s* of Raymond James Groom and Eileen Margaret (*née* Waters); *m* 1967, Gillian M. Crisp; four *s* two *d*. *Educ:* schools in Tasmania and Victoria; Univ. of Melbourne (LLB 1967). Barrister and Solicitor, Supreme Court, Victoria, 1968, Tasmania, 1970; practised: Melbourne, 1968–69; Burnie, 1969–76; Partner, Hudson and Mann, Tasmania, 1969–76. Sec., Law Liby Cttee, NW Tasmania Law Soc., 1969–75; Mem. Council, Bar Assoc., Tasmania, 1974–75. MHR,  Braddon, Tasmania, 1975–84; Federal Minister for: Envmt, Housing, Community Develt, 1977–78; Housing and Construction, 1978–80; Mem., Parly Delegn to Bangladesh, India, Sri Lanka, 1978; Leader, Australian Delegn to ESCAP UN Meeting, Manila (Chm., First Session), 1979; Chm., S Pacific Commonwealth and State Housing Ministers Conf., NZ, 1980; Tasmania: MHA (L) for Denison, 1986–2001; Minister for Forests, Sea Fisheries and Mines, and Minister Assisting the Premier, 1986–89; Dep. Premier, 1988; Dep. Leader, Liberal Party, 1986–91; Shadow Attorney-General and Shadow Minister for Deregulation, 1989–91; Leader of Opposition, Shadow Treas. and Shadow Minister for Commonwealth and State Relns, 1991–92; Premier of Tasmania, 1992–96; Treas. and Minister for Economic Develt, 1992–93; Minister for State Develt and Resources, for Forests, and for Mines, 1993–96; Attorney-General, Minister for Justice, Minister for Tourism and for Workplace Standards, 1996–98; Shadow Minister: for Justice and for Tourism, 1998–99; for Industrial Relns and for Workplace Standards, 1998–2001; for Educn and Trng and for Public Sector Mgt, 1999–2001; for Consumer Affairs, for Justice and Shadow Attorney-Gen., 2001. Chm., Australian Construction Industry Council, 1979–80. Dep. Pres., Administrative Appeals Tribunal (Australia), 2004–14. Stolen Generations Assessor, Tasmania, 2007. *Recreations:* family, painting, poetry, golf, Australian Rules football. *Address:* PO Box 68, Battery Point, Tas 7004, Australia. *Clubs:* Melbourne Cricket; Royal Hobart Golf; Royal Yacht (Tasmania).

**GROOM, Ven. Susan Anne;** Archdeacon of Wilts, since 2016; *b* Wokingham, 28 March 1963; *d* of Alan Jackson and Margaret Jackson; *m* 1987, Philip Groom. *Educ:* Chosen Hill Sch., Glos; University Coll. of N Wales, Bangor (BA Hons 1985); Hughes Hall, Cambridge (MPhil 1986); London Bible Coll. (MA 1994); Open Univ. (MPhil 2000); Durham Univ. (DThMin 2016); Coll. of St Mark and St John, Plymouth (PGCTh 2005). Ordained deacon, 1996, priest, 1997. Assistant Curate: Harefield, 1996–99; Eastcote, 1999–2001; Vicar, Yiewsley, Hillingdon, 2001–07; Dir of Deanery Licensed Ministers, London, 2007–09; Priest-in-charge, Henlow and Langford, and Diocesan Dir of Ordinands, Dio. of St Albans, 2009–16. Honorary Canon: St Albans, 2014; Salisbury, 2015–. *Publications:* Linguistic Analysis of Biblical Hebrew, 2003; contrib. Anvil, Evangelical Quarterly, Anglican Theol Rev. *Recreations:* boating on the canals, swimming, reading, detective novels, Franciscan Tertiary, jigsaws. *Address:* Ramsbury Office, Church House, Crane Street, Salisbury SP1 2QB. *E:* adwilts@salisbury.anglican.org.

**GROOMBRIDGE, Rev. Jeremy Carl,** CB 2008; independent consultant and Director, LCS Services, since 2013; Assistant Priest (non-stipendiary), All Saints Church, Sanderstead, since 2018 (Curate, 2015–18); *b* Derby, 10 Oct. 1955; *s* of late Denis Groombridge and Betty Groombridge; *m* 1983, Sandra Young; three *s*. *Educ:* Spondon Park Grammar Sch.; Wilmorton Coll. Joined DHSS, 1974; Private Sec. to Sec. of State for Health and Social Security, 1988–90; Hd, Policy Develt Unit, Benefits Agency, Leeds, 1990–92; Hd, Unemployment Benefit Policy, 1992–94, Policy Manager, Jobseekers and Incentives, 1994–2001, DSS; Dir, Implementation Prog., 2002–06, Dir, 2006–11, Jobcentre Plus; Dir, Universal Credit Prog., DWP, 2011–13. Ordained deacon, 2015, priest, 2016. Chair, European Skills/Competences, Qualifications and Occupations Bd, 2011–16. Dir, Reedham Children's Trust, 2013– (Vice Chm., 2015–). Gov., Beaumont Sch., Purley, 2014– (Dep. Chm., 2018–). Mem., Scotch Malt Whisky Soc. *Recreations:* family, photography, travel, whisky, two West Highland terriers. *Address:* All Saints Church, Onslow Gardens, Sanderstead, Surrey CR2 9AB.

**GROOTENHUIS, Prof. Peter,** FREng, FIMechE; Professor of Mechanical Engineering Science, Imperial College of Science, Technology and Medicine, 1972–89, now Professor Emeritus and Senior Research Fellow; *b* 31 July 1924; *yr s* of Johannes C. Grootenhuis and Anna C. (*née* van den Bergh); *m* 1954, Sara J. Winchester, *oc* of late Major Charles C. Winchester, MC, The Royal Scots (The Royal Regt), and Margaret I. (*née* de Havilland); one *d* one *s*. *Educ:* Nederlands Lyceum, The Hague; City and Guilds College. BSc MechEng 1944, PhD, DIC, DSc London Univ.; Apprenticeship and Design Office, Bristol Aero Engine Co., 1944–46; Lectr 1949, Reader 1959, Mech. Eng. Dept, Imperial College, research in heat transfer and in dynamics; Dir, Derritron Electronics, 1969–82; Partner, Grootenhuis Allaway Associates, consultants in noise and vibration, 1970–93; Associate Mem., Ordnance Board, 1965–70; Mem. Governing Body, Imperial College, 1974–79. Freeman, City of London, 1984; Liveryman, Engineers' Co., 1985–2014. FCGI 1976; Mem., Inst. of Acoustics; Fellow, Soc. of Environmental Engineers (Pres., 1964–67); FREng (FEng 1982). *Publications:* technical papers to learned jls, and patents. *Recreations:* sailing, gardening.

**GROSE, Vice-Adm. Sir Alan,** KBE 1989; Flag Officer Plymouth, Naval Base Commander Devonport, Commander, Central Sub Area Eastern Atlantic, and Commander Plymouth Sub Area Channel, 1990–92; Group Executive, Security, De Beers Consolidated Mines Ltd, 1993–2000; *b* 24 Sept. 1937; *s* of George William Stanley Grose and Ann May Grose (*née* Stanford); *m* 1961, Gillian Ann (*née* Dryden Dymond); two *s* one *d*. *Educ:* Strode's School; Britannia Royal Naval College, Dartmouth. Served: Mediterranean and S Atlantic, 1957–63; sub-specialised in Navigation, 1964; RAN, 1964–66; Home, W Indies, Med., 1966–72; Comd, HMS Eskimo, 1973–75; Staff of C-in-C, Naval Home Command, 1975–77; MoD, 1977–79; RCDS 1980; Comd, HMS Bristol, 1981–82; RN Presentation Team, 1983–84; Comd, HMS Illustrious, 1984–86; Flag Officer, Sept. 1986; ACDS, Operational Requirements (Sea Systems), MoD, 1986–88; Flag Officer Flotilla Three and Comdr, Anti-Submarine Warfare Striking Force, 1988–90. Hon. Fellow, Liverpool John Moores Univ., 1993. *Recreations:* genealogy, opera, travel. *Address:* Flat 4, Marwell Court, Oakcroft Road, SE13 7EE; Quinta, 15 Rocklands Road, Simons Town, Cape 7975, South Africa. *E:* sagrose@mweb.co.za. *Club:* Western Province Cricket.

**GROSS, Prof. David Jonathan,** PhD; Chancellor's Chair Professor of Theoretical Physics, Kavli Institute for Theoretical Physics, University of California, Santa Barbara, since 2013 (Director, 1997–2012); Frederick W. Gluck Professor of Theoretical Physics, 2002–12); *b* 19 Feb. 1941; *s* of Bertram Meyer Gross and Nora Gross (*née* Faine); *m* 1st, 1962, Shulamith Toaff; two *d*; 2nd, 2001, Jacquelyn Savani. *Educ:* Hebrew Univ., Jerusalem (BSc 1962); Univ. of Calif, Berkeley (PhD 1966). Princeton University: Asst Prof., 1969–71; Associate Prof., 1971–73; Prof., 1973–86; Eugene Higgins Prof. of Physics, 1986–95; Thomas Jones Prof. of Math. Physics, 1995–97, now Emeritus; Prof., Univ. of Calif, Santa Barbara, 1997–. (Jtly) Nobel Prize in Physics, 2004. *Address:* Kavli Institute for Theoretical Physics, Kohn Hall, University of California, Santa Barbara, CA 93106, USA.

**GROSS, Howard Anthony,** FCA, FCCA; Founder, 1968, and Chief Executive, since 2001, Gross Klein and Gross Klein Wood; *b* Hoddesdon, Herts, 24 May 1948; *s* of late Harold Gross and Pamela Gross; *m* 1973, Beverley Teff; two *d*. *Educ:* Minchenden Sch.; City of London Coll. FCA 1971; CTA 1972; FCCA 1980. Chartered Accountant, 1968–. Chairman: (Founding) Hartley Computer User Gp, 1979–82; N London Chartered Accountants, 1984–85; Solution 6 Accounts Computer User Gp, 1998–2000. Mem., 1984–, Hon. Treas., 1990–93, Pres., 2001–02, London Soc. of Chartered Accountants; Mem. Council, 2002–, Mem., Main Bd, 2012–17, ICAEW (Chairman: Practice Cttee, 2011–12; Members Bd, 2012–16; Members and Commercial Bd, 2016–17; Mem., Editl Adv. Bd, Economia, 2012–); Chm., Soc. of Professional Accountants, 2017– (Vice Chm., 2010–17); Exec. Ed., Accountants Digest, 2001–06. Chair, Patient Participation Gp,

Temple Fortune Med. Gp, 2017– (Vice Chair, 2016–17). Chm., Heathfield Sch. Parents' Assoc., 1985–89. Freeman, City of London. *Recreations:* London Marathon (1989), jogging, football. *Address:* Gross Klein, 5 St John's Lane, EC1M 4BH. *T:* (020) 7549 1683. *E:* howard@grosskleinnet.com.

**GROSS, Prof. Mark William,** PhD; FRS 2017; Professor of Pure Mathematics, University of Cambridge, since 2013; Fellow, King's College, Cambridge, since 2016; *b* Ithaca, NY, 30 Nov. 1965; *s* of Leonard Gross and Grazyna Gross; *m* 1997, Rachel Engler. *Educ:* Cornell Univ. (BA 1984); Univ. of Calif, Berkeley (PhD 1990). Asst Prof., Univ. of Michigan, 1990–93; Asst Prof., 1993–97, Associate Prof., 1997–98, Cornell Univ.; Lectr, 1998–99, Sen. Lectr, 1999–2001, Reader, 2001–02, Prof., 2002–03, Univ. of Warwick, 1998–2004; Prof., UCSD, 2001–13. *Publications:* Tropical Geometry and Mirror Symmetry, 2011; scientific articles. *Recreation:* piano. *Address:* Department of Pure Mathematics and Mathematical Statistics, Centre for Mathematical Sciences, University of Cambridge, Wilberforce Road, Cambridge CB3 0WB. *T:* (01223) 337931, *Fax:* (01223) 765900. *E:* mgross@dpmms.cam.ac.uk.

**GROSS, Miriam Marianna, (Lady Owen);** freelance journalist, editor and teacher; *b* 12 May 1938; *d* of late Kurt May and of Wera May; *m* 1st, 1965, John Jacob Gross (marr. diss. 1988; he *d* 2011); one *s* one *d;* 2nd, 1993, Sir Geoffrey Owen, *qv. Educ:* Dartington Hall Sch.; St Anne's Coll., Oxford (MA). Observer: Dep. Lit. Editor, 1969–81; Woman's Editor, 1981–84; Arts Editor, Daily Telegraph, 1986–91; Literary Editor, Sunday Telegraph, 1991–2005; Sen. Editor, Standpoint Mag., 2008–10. Editor, Book Choice, Channel Four TV, 1986–89. Mentor, Longford Scholarship Trust, 2016–. Patron, Real Action, 2017–. Trustee, Friends of Nat. Libraries, 2018–. *Publications:* (ed) The World of George Orwell, 1971; (ed) The World of Raymond Chandler, 1976; So Why Can't They Read?, 2010; An Almost English Life: literary, and not so literary recollections, 2012. *Recreations:* painting, tennis. *Address:* 24A St Petersburgh Place, W2 4LB. *T:* (020) 7727 2291.

See also S. Gross.

**GROSS, Rt Hon. Sir Peter (Henry),** Kt 2001; PC 2010; **Rt Hon. Lord Justice Gross;** a Lord Justice of Appeal, since 2010; Lead Judge, International Relations for the Judiciary of England and Wales, since 2018; *b* 13 Feb. 1952; *s* of late Sam Lewis Gross and Fanny Alice Gross; *m* 1985, Ruth Mary Cullen; two *s. Educ:* Herzlia Sch., Cape Town; Univ. of Cape Town (BBusSc, MBusSc); Oriel Coll., Oxford (Rhodes Scholar, MA, BCL, Eldon Scholar). Called to the Bar, Gray's Inn, 1977, Bencher, 2000 (Chm., Mgt Cttee, 2018); admitted to the Bar of NSW, 1986; QC 1992; a Recorder, 1995–2001; a Judge of the High Ct, QBD, 2001–10; Presiding Judge, SE Circuit, 2004–08; Judge in Charge of Commercial Court, 2009–10; Dep. Sen. Presiding Judge of England and Wales, 2011–13; Sen. Presiding Judge of England and Wales, 2013–15. Chairman: London Common Law and Commercial Bar Assoc., 1995–97; Bar Educn and Trng Cttee, 1998–2000; Bar Internat. Relations Cttee, 2001; Judicial Security Cttee, 2009–11. Chm., Adv. Bd, Inst. of Law, City Univ., 2003–05. *Publications:* Legal Aid and its Management, 1976. *Recreations:* jogging, cricket, sailing, cross-country ski-ing. *Address:* Royal Courts of Justice, Strand, WC2A 2LL. *Club:* Oxford and Cambridge.

**GROSS, Philip John;** poet, novelist and playwright; *b* Delabole, 27 Feb. 1952; *s* of Juhan Karl Gross and Mary Jessie Alison Gross. *Educ:* Devonport High Sch. for Boys; Sussex Univ. (BA Hons English 1973); N London Poly. (DipLib 1977). Librarian, London Bor. of Croydon, 1977–84; freelance writer and educator, 1984–; Lectr, Bath Spa UC, 1990–2004; Prof. of Creative Writing, Glamorgan Univ., later Univ. of S Wales, 2004–17. FEA 2017; Fellow, Welsh Acad., 2011. Mem., Religious Soc. of Friends (Quakers). *Publications: poetry:* Familiars, 1983; The Ice Factory, 1984; Cat's Whiskers, 1987; (with S. Kantaris) The Air Mines of Mistila, 1988; The Son of the Duke of Nowhere, 1991; I.D., 1994; A Cast of Stones, 1996; The Wasting Game, 1998; Change of Address: poems 1988–98, 2001; Mappa Mundi, 2003; The Egg of Zero, 2006; The Water Table, 2009 (T. S. Eliot Prize); (with S. Denison) I Spy Pinhole Eye, 2009; Deep Field, 2011; Caves, 2013; Later, 2013; (with Valerie Coffin Price) A Fold in the River, 2015; Love Songs of Carbon, 2015; A Bright Acoustic, 2017; (with Jenny Pollak) Shadowplay; (with Lesley Saunders) A Part of the Main, 2018; *for children:* Manifold Manor, 1989; The All-Nite Cafe, 1993; Scratch City, 1995; Off Road to Everywhere, 2010; Dark Sky Park, 2018; *novels:* The Song of Gail and Fludd, 1991; Plex, 1994; The Wind Gate, 1995; Transformer, 1996; Psylicon Beach, 1998; Facetaker, 1999; Going for Stone, 2002; Marginaliens, 2003; The Lastling, 2004; The Storm Garden, 2006. *W:* www.philipgross.co.uk. *Club:* Penn.

**GROSS, Susanna, (Mrs John Preston);** Literary Editor, Mail on Sunday, since 1999; *b* 31 July 1968; *d* of late John Jacob Gross, and of Miriam Marianna Gross, *qv; m* 2005, John Preston; one *s* one *d. Educ:* Godolphin and Latymer Sch., Hammersmith; Univ. of York (BA Philosophy). Obituaries Ed., Daily Mail, 1993–96; Features Ed., Harpers & Queen, 1996–97; Dep. Ed., The Week, 1997–2000; bridge columnist, Spectator, 2000–. *Recreations:* bridge, blackjack, hiking. *Address:* 11 Luxemburg Gardens, W6 7EA; Mail on Sunday, Northcliffe House, 2 Derry Street, W8 5TS. *T:* (020) 3615 3254.

**GROSSART, Sir Angus (McFarlane McLeod),** Kt 1997; CBE 1990; DL; Managing Director, since 1969, and Chairman, Noble Grossart Ltd, Merchant Bankers, Edinburgh, since 1990; merchant banker; *b* 6 April 1937; 3rd *s* of William John White Grossart and Mary Hay Gardiner; *m* 1978, Mrs Gay Thomson; one *d. Educ:* Glasgow Acad.; Glasgow Univ. (MA 1958, LLB 1960). CA 1962; Mem., Faculty of Advocates, 1963. Practised at Scottish Bar, 1963–69. Chm., Scottish Investment Trust PLC, 1975–2003; major directorships include: Edinburgh US Tracker Trust (formerly American Trust), 1973–2007; Royal Bank of Scotland plc, 1982–2005 (Vice Chm., 1996–2005); Alexander & Alexander, 1985–97; Scottish Financial Enterprise, 1987–2001; British Petroleum Scottish Bd, 1990–2005; Trinity Mirror (formerly Mirror Gp) PLC, 1998–2007; Scottish & Newcastle plc, 1998–2008; Chairman: Scotland Internat., 1997–; Lyon and Turnbull, 2000–; Edinburgh Partners, 2006–18; Charlotte St Partners, 2014–; Deputy Chairman: Edinburgh Fund Managers PLC, 1991–2002 (Chm., 1983–91); Ronson Capital Partners, 2010–. Mem., Scottish Develt Agency, 1974–78; Dir, St Andrews Management Inst., 1990–97 (Chm. Adv. Council, 1994–97). Chm., Scottish Futures Trust, 2008–16. Chairman, Board of Trustees: National Galleries of Scotland, 1988–97 (Trustee, 1986–97); Nat. Museums Scotland, 2006–12; Trustee and Dep. Chm., Nat. Heritage Meml Fund, 1999–2005; Trustee: Heritage Lottery Fund, 1999–2005; Glasgow Life (formerly Culture and Sport Glasgow), 2007– (Dep. Chm.); High Steward of Scotland's Dumfries House Trust, 2007–16; Chm., Edinburgh Internat. Cultural Summit, 2014–. Vice Pres., Scottish Opera, 1986–93; Director: Edinburgh Internat. Film Festival, 1994–96; Friends of Royal Scottish Acad., 1989–97; Chairman: Fine Art Soc., 1998–2016; Burrell Renaissance, 2013–. Formerly: Trustee, Scottish Civic Trust; Dir, Scottish Nat. Orch.; Mem., Scottish Industrial Develt Adv. Bd. Mem., Speculative Soc. Hon. Gov., Glasgow Acad., 2000–. Hon. QC (Scot.) 2011. FRSE 1998; FSA (Scot.) 2011. DL Edinburgh, 1996. Livingstone Captain of Industry Award, 1990. Hon. FCIBS 1999; Hon. FRIAS 2016. Hon. LLD: Glasgow, 1985; Aberdeen, 2006; Hon. DBA Strathclyde, 1998; Hon. DLitt St Andrews, 2004. Lord Provost of Glasgow Award for public service, 1994; Paolozzi Gold Medal, 1997; Walpole Medal of Excellence, 2003; Nat. Museums of Scotland Gold Medal, 2012. Pushkin Medal (Russia),

2018. Formerly: Scottish Editor, British Tax Encyc., and British Tax Rev. *Recreations:* golfing (runner-up, British Youths' Golf Championship, 1957; Captain, Scottish Youths' Internat., 1956 and 1957), the applied and decorative arts, Scottish painting, Scottish castle restoration. *Address:* 48 Queen Street, Edinburgh EH2 3NR. *T:* (0131) 226 7011. *Clubs:* New, Honourable Company of Edinburgh Golfers (Edinburgh); Royal and Ancient (St Andrews).

**GROSSMAN, Loyd Daniel Gilman,** CBE 2015 (OBE 2003); FSA; broadcaster, writer; *b* Boston, Mass, 16 Sept. 1950; *s* of late David K. Grossman and Helen Katherine Grossman (née Gilman); *m* 1985, Hon. Deborah Jane (marr. diss. 2005), *d* of Baron Puttnam, *qv;* two *d. Educ:* Marblehead High Sch.; Boston Univ. (BA *cum laude*); London School of Economics (MSc Econ.); Magdalene Coll., Cambridge (MPhil; PhD 2014). Design Editor, Harpers and Queen, 1981–84; Contributing Editor: Sunday Times, 1984–86; Condé Nast Traveller, 2006–. *Television* includes: deviser or writer or presenter: Through the Keyhole, 1983–; Behind the Headlines; MasterChef, 1990–2000 (Glenfiddich Award, 1996); The Dog's Tale, 1993; Junior MasterChef, 1995–99; Off Your Trolley, 1995; Conspicuous Consumption, 1996; The World on a Plate, 1997; Loyd on Location, 1999–2001; History of British Sculpture, 2003; Build Britain, 2007; Step Up to the Plate, 2008. Presenter, Composers at Home, BBC Radio 3, 2004–. Member: Bd, mda (formerly Museum Documentation Assoc.), 1998–2001; MLA (formerly Museums, Libraries and Archives Council, subseq. Resource: Council for Mus, Archives and Libraries), 1999–2006 (Chm., Designation Challenge Fund, 2001–03); Commissioner: Museums and Galleries Commn, 1996–2000; English Heritage, 1997–2003 (Chairman: Mus. and Collections Adv. Cttee, 1997–2001; Nat. Blue Plaques Panel, 2003–06; Mus and Archives Panel, 2001–03); Royal Commn on Histl Monuments of England, 1999–2003; Chm., 2000, Co-Chm., 2001–08, Museums and Galleries Month; Chairman: Campaign for Mus, 1995–2009; The 24 Hour Mus., 2000–05; Public Monuments and Sculpture Assoc., 2001–07; Nat. Mus Liverpool, 2005–08; Churches Conservation Trust, 2007–16; Heritage Alliance, 2009–18; The Royal Parks, 2016–; Dep. Chm., Liverpool Culture Co., 2005–07; Vice-Chm., NW Regl Cultural Consortium, 2000–02; Member, Board: Culture Northwest: Cultural Consortium for England's Northwest, 2002–09 (Chm., 2004–09); Assoc. of Leading Visitor Attractions, 2013–18. President: British Assoc. of Friends of Mus, 2005–14; Arts Soc. (formerly NADFAS), 2014–. Trustee: Mus. of Sci. and Industry in Manchester, 1999–2002; St Deiniol's Liby, 2003–08 (Fellow, 2008); Gladstone's Liby, 2014–18; Warburg Charitable Trust, 2018–. Mem., Court of Govs, LSE, 1996–2009 (Mem. Council, 2003–08, Emeritus Gov., 2009); Chm., Univ. for the Creative Arts, 2008–12; Mem. Council, British Sch. at Rome, 2013–17; Dep. Chm., Royal Drawing Sch., 2014–17; Governor: Building Crafts Coll., 2014–17; Compton Verney Hse Trust, 2017–; British Inst. of Florence, 2019. Chm., Conservation Awards, 1998–2003; Chm. of Judges, Gulbenkian Prize for Mus, 2004. Chm., Better Hosp. Food Panel, NHS, 2001–06; Patron: Haslemere Educnl Mus., 2011–; Heritage Open Days, 2012–; Historic Lincoln Trust, 2012–; Cavell Nurses' Trust, 2014–17. Hon. Life Mem., Dogs Trust (formerly Nat. Canine Defence League). Mem., Internat. Dendrol. Soc., 2019. Freeman, City of London, 2011; Liveryman, Arts Scholars' Co. (formerly Co. of Arts Scholars, Dealers and Collectors), 2010– (Master, 2017–18; Dep. Master, 2018–19); Hon. Liveryman, Glaziers' Co., 2011–; Liveryman, Carpenters' Co., 2013–. Albums with The New Forbidden: Ain't Doin' Nothin', 2010 (songwriter and guitarist); Songs from the Subway, 2018; performances at various festivals, incl. Glastonbury, Vintage, Cornbury and Rebellion. Member: Piscatorial Soc., 2014–; Pilgrims. FRSA; FSAScot; FRSocMed 2004. Hon. DLitt Chester, 2007; Hon. DArts Lincoln, 2011; DUniv Essex, 2014. *Publications:* The Social History of Rock Music, 1975; Harpers and Queen Guide to London's 100 Best Restaurants, 1987; The Dog's Tale, 1993; Loyd Grossman's Italian Journey, 1994; (ed) Courvoisier's Book of the Best, 1994–96; The World on a Plate, 1997; The 125 Best Recipes Ever, 1998; Foodstuff, 2002; Benjamin West and the Struggle to be Modern, 2015; Bernini's Elephant, 2020; articles on architecture, history, design and food in newspapers and magazines. *Recreations:* fishing, scuba diving (PADI Divemaster), looking at buildings, tennis, chess, the Boston Red Sox, playing old Gibson and Gretsch guitars. *Clubs:* Brooks's, Flyfishers', Hurlingham, Chelsea Arts, Oxford and Cambridge, City Livery, Walbrook, London Sketch, Lloyd's Flyfishing Soc.

**GROSSMAN, Russell Lawrence;** Director of Communications, Office of Rail and Road, since 2015; Head of Government Internal Communications Profession, since 2014; *b* Blackpool, 7 April 1961; *s* of David Grossman and Irene Grossman; *m* 1985, Eunice Goodstone; three *s* one *d. Educ:* Arnold Sch., Blackpool; Univ. of Manchester (BSc Hons Mgt and Chem. Scis); Univ. of Salford (MSc Transport Engrg and Planning); London Metropolitan Univ. (DipPR); Royal Roads Univ. (ABC). Hd, Transport Communications, London Docklands Develt Corp., 1988–94; PR Manager, Jubilee Line Extension, London Underground, 1994–96; Sen. Consultant, Nichols Associates, 1994–97; Dir, Communications, Royal Mail, London, 1997–99; Hd, Internal Communications, BBC, 1999–2006; Hd, Internal and Change Communications, HMRC, 2006–08; Gp Dir, Communications, BERR, subseq. BIS, 2008–15. Dir, Engage for Success, 2013–. Vis. Fellow, Cass Business Sch., 2011–15. FCIM; FRSA; FCIPR. *Recreations:* family, reading, hill walking, music, cantorial arts. *Address:* Office of Rail and Road, 25 Cabot Square, E14 4QA. *T:* (020) 7282 2137. *E:* russell.grossman@hotmail.com.

**GROSVELD, Prof. Franklin Gerardus, (Frank),** PhD; FRS 1991; Professor of Cell Biology, Erasmus University, Rotterdam, since 1993; *b* 18 Aug. 1948; *m;* four *s. Educ:* Univ. of Amsterdam (MSc); McGill Univ. (PhD). Sen. Scientist, NIMR, 1982–93. *Publications:* papers on human globin genes. *Address:* Department of Cell Biology, Erasmus MC, PO Box 2040, 3000 CA Rotterdam, The Netherlands.

**GROSVENOR,** family name of **Duke of Westminster** and of **Earl of Wilton.**

**GROSVENOR, Dr Bendor Gerard Robert;** art historian; writer; *b* London, 27 Nov. 1977; *s* of Hon. Richard Alexander Grosvenor and Gabriella Grosvenor; *m* 2015, Ishbel Hall; one *d*, and two step *s. Educ:* Harrow Sch.; Univ. of East Anglia (BA Hons; DPhil); Pembroke Coll., Cambridge (MPhil). Researcher, Tony Banks, MP, 2002–04; Special Advr, Sir Hugo Swire, MP, 2004–05; Director: Historical Portraits Ltd, subseq. Philip Mould Ltd, 2005–14; Iconografie Ltd, 2014–; Iconografie Films Ltd, 2015–. Non-exec. Dir, Lyon & Turnbull Ltd, 2017–. Member: Arts Taskforce, 2005–06; Lord Chancellor's Adv. Council on Archives and Public Records, 2010–16. Presenter, television programmes, 2011–: Fake or Fortune; The Culture Show; Britain's Lost Masterpieces. *Publications:* (jtly) Crap MPs: the 40 worst Members of Parliament in history, 2009; (ed jtly) Documents on Conservative Foreign Policy, 1852–1878; articles in British Art Jl. *Recreations:* looking at paintings, war films, bedtime stories, Scotland, evangelising, challenging conventional wisdom. *E:* bendor@arthistorynews.com. *Club:* Reform.

**GROSVENOR, Lady Edwina Louise;** prison philanthropist; *b* London, 4 Nov. 1981; *d* of 6th Duke of Westminster, KG, CB, CVO, OBE, TD, CD and Natalia Ayesha Grosvenor (née Phillips); *m* 2010, Daniel Boder Snow, *s* of Peter John Snow, *qv;* one *s* two *d. Educ:* Univ. of Northumbria (BSc Criminol. and Sociol. 2005); Edith Cowan Univ., Perth. Prison reform, 2005–, work has taken her all over UK and around world visiting different models of criminal justice and examples of best practice. Advr to Bishop of Liverpool, in H of L, 2007–10; contrib. to Corston Report on Female Offenders, 2007; Mem., Adv. Bd on

Female Offenders, 2013–18; Founding investor and Trustee, Clink Restaurant chain, 2009–18; Founder, One Small Thing, 2016–; sponsor, Future Prison Project, RSA, 2016–. Mem., Adv. Bd, Centre for Criminol., Faculty of Law, Univ. of Oxford, 2012–. *Recreations:* travel, visiting and learning about prisons abroad, walking in the Himalayas. *T:* 07889 534032. *E:* catrina@tansen.org.
See also Duke of Westminster.

**GROSZ, Stephen Ernest;** Partner, 1981–2013, Senior Consultant, since 2013, Bindmans LLP (formerly Bindman & Partners), solicitors; *b* 14 April 1953; *s* of Emil, (Joe), Grosz and Therese Grosz (*née* Baer); *m* 1981, Judith Beale (marr. diss. 1995); *m* 2012, Vicki Chapman. *Educ:* William Ellis Sch.; Clare Coll., Cambridge (BA 1974); Université Libre de Bruxelles (licencié special en droit européen 1976). Joined Bindman & Partners, 1976. Significant cases include: Marshall *v* Southampton & SW Hants AHA, instrumental in changing UK law on equal rights for retirement age and for compensation for discrimination; R *v* Sec. of State for Foreign & Commonwealth Affairs ex parte World Develt Movt, in which the High Court declared unlawful aid for construction of the Pergau Dam in Malaysia; R *v* Lord Chancellor ex parte Witham, quashing changes to court fees as contrary to constitutional rights of access to the courts; R *v* MoD ex parte Lustig-Prean and Lustig-Prean & others *v* UK, concerning the rights of homosexuals & lesbians to serve in the armed forces; Abdulaziz & others *v* UK, instrumental in removing sex discrimination from the immigration rules; Silver & others *v* UK, instrumental in removing restrictions on prisoners' rights to respect for correspondence; Sutherland *v* UK, in which the European Commission of Human Rights ruled unlawful discrimination in the age of consent for gay men; R *v* Sec. of State for Home Dept, ex parte Amnesty Internat. & others, concerning disclosure of med. reports relating to extradition of Augusto Pinochet; Sahin *v* Turkey, concerning ban on headscarves in Turkish univs; Goodwin *v* UK, concerning recognition of transsexuals; Ghaidan *v* Ghodin, concerning succession rights for same-sex partners; R (David Hicks) *v* Sec. of State for Home Dept, concerning power to deny citizenship on public policy grounds; R (RJM) *v* Sec. of State for Work and Pensions, concerning discrimination against homeless people and effects of Human Rights Act 1998. Civil and commercial mediator, 2012. Gov., 1992–2004, Mem. Adv. Bd, 2004–13, British Inst. of Human Rights; Chm., Domestic Human Rights Reference Gp, 2004–08, Mem., Human Rights Cttee, 2011–15 (Chm., 2014), Law Soc.; Member: Mgt Cttee, Public Law Project, 1991–2001; Exec. Bd, Justice, 1999–2014; Council, Liberty, 2001–03; Exec. Cttee, Alliance for Lawyers at Risk, 2017–. Member Advisory Board: Judicial Review Qly, 1996–2016; Educn, Public Law and the Individual, 1996. Fellow, Bingham Centre for Rule of Law, 2013–. Member: Editl Bd, Civil Procedure, 2000–04; Strategic Bd, Navigating Brexit, 2017–. Hon. QC 2012. *Publications:* (jtly) Human Rights: the 1998 Act and the European Convention, 2000; (jtly) Human Rights: judicial protection in the United Kingdom, 2008; *contributions to:* Public Interest Law, 1986; Atkin's Court Forms, 1987; Public Interest Perspectives in Environmental Law, 1995; Judicial Rev. in the New Millennium, 2003; articles and reviews in newspapers and legal jls. *Recreations:* cycling, walking, choral singing, eating and drinking, trying to make people laugh. *Address:* (office) 236 Gray's Inn Road, WC1X 8HB. *T:* (020) 7833 4433.

**GROTE, Dr John David,** OBE 1991; Director, British Council, Egypt, 2001–05; *b* 5 Sept. 1945; *s* of Roy and Dorothy Grote; *m* 1st, 1970, Pauline Bolton (marr. diss. 1979); one *s* one *d*; 2nd, 1979, Barbara Elzbieta Orzechowska (*née* Smigielska). *Educ:* Rydens Co. Secondary Sch.; Southampton Univ. (BSc 1st Cl. Hons Maths 1967; PhD 1971). Temp. Lectr, Maths Dept, Univ. of Southampton, 1970–71; Res. Fellow, Control Theory Centre, Warwick Univ., 1971–74; British Council, 1974–2005: Sci. Advr, 1974–75; Sci. Officer, Poland, 1975–79; Staff Inspector, 1979–82; Dep. Dir, Computer Systems, 1982–83; Science Officer: Germany, 1983–86; Japan, 1987–91; Director: Hungary, 1991–96; Singapore, 1996–2000. Ext. Mem., Audit and Risk Mgt Cttee, Essex Univ., 2008–14. *Recreations:* reading, thinking, wine, walking with my wife. *Address:* Bridgeford House, 68 Belle Vue Road, Wivenhoe, Essex CO7 9LD. *E:* johngrote_99@yahoo.com.

**GROTRIAN, Sir Philip Christian Brent,** 3rd Bt *cr* 1934; *b* 26 March 1935; *s* of Robert Philip Brent Grotrian (*d* on active service, 1945) (*y s* of 1st Bt), and Elizabeth Mary, *d* of Major Herbert Hardy-Wrigley; *S* uncle, 1984; *m* 1st, 1960, Anne Isabel, *d* of Robert Sieger Whyte, Toronto; one *s*; 2nd, 1979, Sarah Frances, *d* of Reginald Harry Gale, Montreal; one *s* one *d*. *Educ:* Eton; Trinity Coll., Toronto. *Heir: s* Philip Timothy Adam Brent Grotrian, *b* 9 April 1962. *Address:* Calle Ample 2, Regencós, Gerona, Spain.

**GROUND, (Reginald) Patrick;** QC 1981; *b* 9 Aug. 1932; *s* of late Reginald Ground and Ivy Elizabeth Grace Ground (*née* Irving); *m* 1964, Caroline Dugdale (*d* 2017); three *s* one *d*. *Educ:* Beckenham and Penge County Grammar Sch.; Lycée Gay Lussac, Limoges, France; Selwyn Coll., Cambridge (Open Exhibnr; MA Mod. Langs, French and Spanish); Magdalen Coll., Oxford (MLitt, Mod. History). Inner Temple Studentship and Foster Boulton Prize, 1958; called to the Bar, Inner Temple, 1960, Bencher, 1987. National Service, RN, 1954–56: Sub-Lt RNVR; served in Mediterranean Fleet and on staff of C-in-C Mediterranean; rep. RN at hockey and lawn tennis; Lt-Comdr RNR. Worked for FO on staff of Wilton Park European Conf. Centre, 1958–60. Councillor, London Bor. of Hammersmith, 1968–71 (Chm., Cttees responsible for health and social services, 1969–71). Contested (C): Hounslow, Feltham and Heston, Feb. and Oct. 1974, and 1979; Feltham and Heston, 1992 and 1997. MP (C) Feltham and Heston, 1983–92. PPS to the Solicitor General, 1987–92. Treasurer and Pres., Oxford Univ. Cons. Assoc., 1958; Chm., Fulham Soc., 1975–96. Trustee, Daisy Trust, 1981–. *Publications:* articles on housing, security of tenure and paying for justice. *Recreations:* lawn tennis, theatre, music, sailing, travel, forestry. *Address:* 13 Ranelagh Avenue, SW6 3PJ. *T:* (020) 7736 0131. *Clubs:* Brooks's, Carlton, Queen's (Trustee, 2008–10).
See also R. W. S. Ground.

**GROUND, Richard William Scott;** QC 2016; *b* London, 26 April 1970; *s* of (Reginald) Patrick Ground, *qv*; *m* 2006, Alexandra Williams; one *s* one *d*. *Educ:* St Paul's Sch., London; St John's Coll., Cambridge (BA 1992). Called to the Bar, Inner Temple, 1994. *Publications:* (contrib.) Burnett-Hall on Environmental Law, 2nd edn 2008, 3rd edn 2012. *Recreations:* tennis, family, eating. *Address:* Cornerstone Barristers, 2–3 Gray's Inn Square, WC1R 5JH. *Clubs:* Roehampton, Hurlingham; Hawks' (Cambridge); All England Lawn Tennis and Croquet.

**GROUNDS, Dr Adrian Thomas,** FRCPsych; Hon. Research Fellow, Institute of Criminology, University of Cambridge, since 2010; Fellow, Darwin College, Cambridge, since 1987; *b* Bath, 21 Feb. 1952; *s* of Thomas and Mary Grounds; *m* 1985, Krishna Kumari Singh (marr. diss. 2017); one *s*. *Educ:* Monkton Combe Sch.; Univ. of Nottingham (BMedSci 1974; BM BS 1977; DM 1986). MRCPsych 1981, FRCPsych 1996. SHO and Registrar in Psychiatry, Maudsley Hosp., London, 1979–82; Sen. Registrar in Forensic Psychiatry, Broadmoor Hosp. and Bethlem Royal Hosp., 1982–84; Clin. Lectr in Forensic Psychiatry, Inst. of Psychiatry, 1984–87; University of Cambridge: Lectr in Forensic Psychiatry and Hon. Consultant Forensic Psychiatrist, Inst. of Criminol., 1987–2003; Sen. Lectr, 2003–10. Northern Ireland: Sentence Rev. Comr, 1998–; Life Sentence Rev. Comr, 2001–08; Parole Comr, 2008–. Mem., Adv. Cttee, Miscarriages of Justice Support Service, Royal Courts of Justice Advice Bureau, 2004–; Med. Mem., First-tier Tribunal (Mental Health), 2013–. Trustee, Prison Reform Trust, 2001–17. *Publications:* contrib. articles on forensic psychiatry and effects of miscarriages of justice. *Address:* Institute of Criminology, Sidgwick Avenue, Cambridge CB3 9DA. *T:* (01223) 335360. *E:* ag113@cam.ac.uk.

**GROVE, Sir Charles Gerald,** 5th Bt *cr* 1874; *b* 10 Dec. 1929; *s* of Walter Peel Grove (*d* 1944) (3rd *s* of 2nd Bt) and Elena Rebecca, *d* of late Felipe Crosthwaite; *S* brother, 1974, but his name does not appear on the Official Roll of the Baronetage. *Heir: b* Harold Thomas Grove, *b* 6 Dec. 1930.

**GROVE, Elliot;** Founder: Raindance Film Festival, since 1993; British Independent Film Awards, since 1998; *b* Markham, Ont; *s* of Merlin Grove and Dorothy Grove (*née* Bechtel); *m* 1980, Suzanne Ballantyne; two *d*. *Educ:* Central Tech. Sch., Toronto (Cert. Art Degree Sculpture). Founder, Raindance VRX Awards, 2017. DUniv Open, 2009. *Publications:* Raindance Writers' Lab, 2004, 2nd edn 2013; Raindance Producers' Lab, 2006, 2nd edn 2015; Beginning Filmmaking, 2009. *Recreation:* movies. *Address:* c/o Raindance, 10A Craven Street, WC2N 5PE. *T:* (020) 7930 3412. *E:* elliotgrove@raindance.org. *W:* www.twitter.com/Elliot_Grove.

**GROVE, Trevor Charles;** JP; journalist; *b* 1 Jan. 1945; *s* of Ronald and Lesley Grove; *m* 1975, Valerie Jenkins (*see* V. Grove); one *s* three *d*. *Educ:* St George's, Buenos Aires; Radley; St Edmund Hall, Oxford. Editorial Staff, Spectator, 1967–70; Leader Writer, then Features Editor, Evening Standard, 1970–78; Asst Editor, Sunday Telegraph, 1978–80; Sen. Asst Editor, Observer, 1980–83; Editor, Observer Magazine, 1983–86; Asst Editor, Daily Telegraph, 1986–89; Editor, Sunday Telegraph, 1989–92; Gp Exec. Ed. and Dep. Ed., Daily Telegraph, 1992–94; Launch Editor, El Periódico de Tucumán, Argentina, 1994; Chm., Inside Time: The Prisoners' Newspaper, 2004–. JP Haringey, 1999. Trustee, Butler Trust, 2006–14. *Publications:* (co-ed) Singlehanded, 1984; (ed) The Queen Observed, 1986; The Juryman's Tale, 1998; The Magistrate's Tale, 2002; One Dog and His Man, 2003. *Recreations:* tennis, cooking, dog-walking, grandchild-minding. *Address:* 14 Avenue Road, Highgate, N6 5DW. *T:* (020) 8348 2621.

**GROVE, Valerie;** journalist and biographer; *b* 11 May 1946; *d* of Doug Smith, cartoonist; *m* 1st, 1968, David Brynmor Jenkins (marr. diss. 1975); 2nd, 1975, Trevor Charles Grove, *qv*; one *s* three *d*. *Educ:* South Shields Grammar Sch.; Kingsbury County Grammar Sch.; Girton Coll., Cambridge (MA 1969). Evening Standard, 1968–87; Sunday Times, 1987–92; The Times, 1992–2013; The Oldie, 1992–. *Publications:* (as Valerie Jenkins) Where I Was Young, 1976; (as Valerie Grove): The Compleat Woman, 1987; Dear Dodie: the life of Dodie Smith, 1996; Laurie Lee: the well-loved stranger, 1999, rev. edn as The Life and Loves of Laurie Lee, 2014; A Voyage Round John Mortimer, 2007; So Much to Tell: the life of Kaye Webb, 2010; (ed) Grumbling at Large: selected essays of J. B. Priestley, 2016. *Recreations:* tennis, archives, litter-picking. *Address:* 14 Avenue Road, Highgate, N6 5DW. *T:* (020) 8348 2621. *E:* vgrove@dircon.co.uk.

**GROVE-WHITE, Prof. Robin Bernard;** Professor of Environment and Society, Institute for Environment, Philosophy and Public Policy, Lancaster University, 2000–05, now Emeritus; *b* 17 Feb. 1941; *s* of Charles William Grove-White and Cecile Mary Rabbidge; *m* 1st, 1970, Virginia Harriet Ironside (marr. diss.); one *s*; 2nd, 1979, Helen Elizabeth Smith; two *s* one *d*. *Educ:* Uppingham Sch.; Worcester Coll., Oxford (BA); Bangor Univ. (PhD Welsh History 2013). Freelance writer for TV, radio, press and advertising in UK, Canada and US, 1963–70; McCann-Erickson Ltd, London, 1970; Asst Secretary, 1972–80, Dir, 1981–87, CPRE; Res. Fellow, Centre for Envmtl Technol., Imperial Coll., London, 1987–89; Lancaster University: Sen. Res. Fellow, 1989–91; Dir, Centre for Study of Envmtl Change, 1991–2001. Member: Forestry Commn, 1991–98; Agric. and Envmt Biotechnology Commn, 2000–05; Standards Cttee, Anglesey CC, 2007–11. Chm., Greenpeace UK, 1997–2003; Pres., N Wales Wildlife Trust, 2010–. Chm., Inst. for Study of Welsh Estates, Bangor Univ., 2015–. High Sheriff Anglesey and Gwynedd, 2011. Hon. Fellow, Bangor Univ., 2018. Hon. DSc Bath, 2011. *Publications:* (contrib.) Politics of Physical Resources, 1975; (contrib.) Future Landscapes, 1976; (with Michael Flood) Nuclear Prospects, 1976; contribs to New Scientist, Nature, Times, Independent, and numerous academic jls. *Recreations:* walking, cricket. *Address:* Brynddu, Llanfechell, Ynys Mon LL68 0RT. *T:* (01407) 710245.

**GROVENOR, Prof. Christopher Richard Munro,** DPhil; FInstP, FIMMM; Professor of Materials, University of Oxford, since 2004; Fellow, St Anne's College, Oxford, since 1990; *b* 21 Oct. 1955; *s* of late John and Christine Grovenor; *m* 1987, Susan Ruth Ortner; two *d*. *Educ:* Marlborough Coll.; St Catherine's Coll., Oxford (MA, DPhil). FInstP 2004; FIMMM 2008. Lectr in Materials, Univ. of Oxford, 1986–. *Publications:* contribs on relationship between microstructure and properties of functional materials. *Recreations:* cricket, bassoonist. *Address:* Department of Materials, University of Oxford, 16 Parks Road, Oxford OX1 3PH. *T:* (01865) 273751. *E:* chris.grovenor@materials.ox.ac.uk.

**GROVER, Derek James Langlands,** CB 1999; consultant, 2005–11; Group Director of Distributed Learning, NHSU, Department of Health, 2004–05; *b* 26 Jan. 1949; *s* of late Donald James Grover and Mary Barbara Grover; *m* 1972, Mary Katherine Morgan; one *s*. *Educ:* Hove County Grammar Sch. for Boys; Clare Coll., Cambridge (Foundn Schol. 1970; BA Eng. Lit. 1971, MA 1975; Grene Prize 1971). Various positions, Dept of Employment, 1971–78; Cabinet Office, 1978–80; MSC, 1980–87; Training Agency: Head of Personnel, 1987–89; Dir of Youth Training, 1989; Dir of Systems and Strategy, 1989; Dir of Trng Strategy and Standards, later of Trng Strategy and Infrastructure, 1990–94; Dep. Chief Exec. and Sen. Dir of Operations, Employment Service, 1994–97; Dir of Employment and Adult Trng, DFEE, 1997–98; Dir, Skills and Lifelong Learning, then Adult Learning Gp, DfEE, then DfES, 1998–2002; Dir of Develt, NHSU, 2002–03. Chair: NIACE Enquiry on ESOL, 2005–06; Nat. ESOL Adv. Forum, 2007–11; Sheffield Assoc. for Voluntary Teaching of English, 2012–. Chm. of Govs, Broomhill Sch., Sheffield, 2009–; Gov., Norfolk Park Sch., Sheffield, 2014–18. Nat. Leader of Governance, Nat. Coll. for Teaching and Leadership, 2014–. Mem., Sheffield Diocesan Bd of Educn, 2015–. Trustee: Sheaf Learning Trust, 2015–; Sheffield SE Learning Trust, 2016–. FRSA 1991. MCIPD (MIPM 1993). *Recreations:* music, reading, walking, watching cricket. *Address:* 8 Oakbrook Road, Sheffield S11 7EA.

**GROVER, Rajiv,** MD; FRCS; Consultant Plastic Surgeon, King Edward VII Hospital, London, since 2002; President, British Association of Aesthetic Plastic Surgeons, 2012–14; *m* 1992, Nikita; two *d*. *Educ:* St Bartholomew's Medical Sch., Univ. of London (BSc 1st Cl. Hons 1986; MB BS (Triple Dist.) 1989; MD 1996). FRCS 1993 (Hallett Prize and Gold Medal); FRCS (Plast) 2000. Hse Surgeon and Hse Physician, St Bartholomew's Hosp., 1989–90; Surgical SHO rotation, University Coll. Hosp., 1991–93; RCS Res. Fellow in Plastic Surgery, 1994–96; Pan Thames Plastic Surgery Rotation, Mt Vernon Hosp., Royal Marsden Hosp. and Gt Ormond St Hosp., 1996–99; RCS Schol. in Plastic Surgery, Harvard Med. Sch., 1999; Consultant Plastic Surgeon, NW London Regl Centre, Mt Vernon Hosp., 2001–06; in private practice, Harley St, 2002–. Hunterian Prof., RCS, 1998–. *Publications:* (with B. Jones) Textbook of Facial Rejuvenation Surgery, 2008; contrib. papers on improving outcome and safety in cosmetic surgery to Amer. and British Jls of Plastic Surgery. *Recreations:* personal fitness, cycling, photography. *Address:* 94 Harley Street, W1G 7HX. *T:* (020) 7486 4301, *Fax:* (020) 7486 4327. *Club:* Arts.

**GROVES, His Honour Richard Bebb,** TD 1966; RD 1979; a Circuit Judge, 1985–2000; *b* 4 Oct. 1933; *s* of George Thomas Groves and Margaret Anne (*née* Bebb); *m* 1958, Eileen Patricia (*née* Farley); one *s* one *d*. *Educ:* Bancroft's Sch., Woodford Green, Essex; DipFrench Open, 2003. Admitted Solicitor of the Supreme Court, 1960. Partner, H. J. Smith & Co. and Richard Groves & Co., 1962–85. Dep. Circuit Judge, 1978–80; a Recorder, 1980–85. Nijmegen Medal, Royal Netherlands League for Physical Culture, 1965 and 1966. *Recreations:* Royal Naval Reserve, tennis, philately, walking, reading. *Club:* Royal Automobile.

**GROVES, Sally Hilary,** MBE 2015; consultant, since 2015; Creative Director, Schott Music Ltd, 2011–14 (Director, 2001–14); *b* Manchester, 11 March 1949; *d* of Sir Charles Barnard Groves, CBE and Hilary Hermione Groves; *m* 1st, 1971, Bruce Laidlaw (marr. diss. 1990); one *s*; 2nd, 1992, Dennis Michael Marks (*d* 2015). *Educ:* Belvedere Sch., Liverpool; Univ. of Birmingham (BMus Hons 1970). Promotions Manager: Stainer and Bell, 1970–72; Novello, 1972–74; Promotions Manager, 1974–90, Hd of Contemp. Music, 1990–2011, Schott Music Ltd. Chm., Bd of Trustees, British Music Inf. Centre, 2000–08. Member: Bd of Govs, Royal Coll. of Music, 1999–2008; Bd, Bournemouth Symphony Orch., 2000–04; Bd, Birmingham Contemporary Music Gp, 2000–04; Bd of Trustees, Sound and Music, 2000–08. Trustee: Vaughan Williams Charitable Trust, 2012– (Chm., 2015–); RVW Trust, 2014–; Listenpony, 2015–; ORA, 2016–; Nash Ensemble, 2016–; UPROAR, 2017–. Chair: Opera Ventures, 2016–; Music Libraries Trust, 2017–. Lesley Boosey Award, Royal Philharmonic Soc., 2013; Assoc. of Brit. Orchs Award, 2016; Internat. Artist Managers' Assoc. Award, 2016. *Recreations:* chamber music, theatre, grandchildren. *E:* sallygroves49@ gmail.com, sally@minervasearch.com.

**GRUBB, Prof. Andrew,** LLD; a Judge of the Upper Tribunal (Immigration and Asylum Chamber) (formerly a Senior Immigration Judge and Training Judge, Asylum and Immigration Tribunal), since 2005; a Recorder, since 2009; a Deputy High Court Judge, since 2013; *b* 24 March 1958; *s* of late Graham Grubb and of Valerie Grubb; *m* 1988, Helga Anne Moore (marr. diss. 2015); two *s* one *d*. *Educ:* Brynmawr Comprehensive Sch.; Selwyn Coll., Cambridge (BA 1st Cl. Hons 1979; MA 1983); LLD London 1998. Called to the Bar, Inner Temple, 1980 (Scarman Schol., 1980; Certificate of Honour 1980). Cambridge University: Law Fellow, Fitzwilliam Coll., 1981–90; Asst Univ. Lectr, 1984–89, Univ. Lectr, 1989–90, in Law; King's College, London: Sen. Lectr in Law, 1990–92; Reader in Med. Law, 1992–94; Prof. of Health Care Law, 1994–98; acting Dir, 1992–93, Dir, 1993–97, Centre of Med. Law and Ethics; Prof. of Med. Law, 1998–2004, Hd of Sch., 1999–2004, Cardiff Law Sch., Cardiff Univ. (Vis. Prof., 2004–09; Hon. Prof., 2009–); Trng Immigration Adjudicator, Immigration Appellate Authy, 2004–05. Visiting Professor of Law: Boston Univ. Sch. of Law, 1989; Univ. of New Mexico Sch. of Law, 1989. Member: Ethical Cttee, RCP, 1994–2004; HFEA, 1997–2003; UK Xenotransplantn Regulatory Authy, 2003–04; Nuffield Council on Bioethics, 2003–04; pt-time Immigration Adjudicator, 1996–2004; Chm., Ind. Review Panel (NHS Complaints), Wales, 1998–99. Vice Pres., Wales Medico-Legal Soc., 2000–04. Founder FMedSci 1998. Editor, Medical Law Review, 1993–2004. Ver Heyden de Lancey Medico-Legal Prize, Cambridge Univ., 1991. *Publications:* (with I. Kennedy) Medical Law: cases and materials, 1989, rev. edn, Medical Law: text with materials, 1994, 3rd edn 2000; (with D. Pearl) Blood Testing, AIDS and DNA Profiling: law and policy, 1990; (jtly) Doctors' Views on the Management and Care of Patients in Persistent Vegetative State: a UK study, 1997; (ed) Principles of Medical Law (with I. Kennedy), 1998, (consultant ed.) 4th edn 2017. *Recreations:* music and music trivia, appreciating electric guitars, tennis, the Welsh countryside, Welsh Rugby. *Address:* Upper Tribunal (Immigration and Asylum Chamber), Cardiff Civil and Family Justice Centre, 2 Park Street, Cardiff CF10 1ET. *T:* (029) 2037 6440.

**GRUBB, Hon. Dame Bobbie C.;** *see* Cheema-Grubb.

**GRUBB, Deborah Mary Hinton;** Chair: Gardner Arts Centre, 2001–07; South East Regional Arts Council, 2002–05; *b* 21 Feb. 1946; *d* of Joe Grubb and Winifred Grubb (*née* Axtell); *m* 2000, Peter Guttridge. *Educ:* Haberdashers' Aske's Sch. for Girls; UC Cardiff (BA Hons). Various posts in local govt, theatre and PR; Dir, Arts, Recreation and Tourism, Brighton and Hove CC, 1991–2000. Mem., Arts Council England (formerly Arts Council of England), 2002–05. *Recreations:* theatre, gardening, travel. *E:* deborahgrubb@ btinternet.com.

**GRUBB, Prof. Michael John,** PhD; Professor of Energy and Climate Change (formerly International Energy and Climate Change Policy), University College London, since 2014; *b* Southall, Middx, 29 Feb. 1960; *s* of Martyn Patrick and Anne Isobel Grubb; *m* 2005, Joanna Depledge; one *s* two *d*. *Educ:* King's Coll., Cambridge (BA 1982; PhD 1987). Res. Fellow, Electrical Engrg, Imperial Coll., London, 1986–88; Res. Fellow, 1988–92, Hd, Energy and Envmt Prog., 1993–98, RIIA; Prof. of Climate Change and Energy Policy, Imperial Coll., London, 1999–2001; Associate Dir of Policy, 2002–04, Chief Economist, 2005–10, Carbon Trust; Sen. Res. Associate, Cambridge Univ., 2005–14. Sen. Advr, Ofgem, 2011–16. Chm., Climate Strategies, 2007–12; Mem., UK Climate Change Cttee, 2008–11; Chair, UK Panel of Technical Experts on Electricity Market Reform, BEIS, 2016–. Lead Author, Intergovtl Panel on Climate Change: Assessment Reports II 1996, III 2001 and IV 2007; Ed.-in-Chief, Climate Policy Jl, 2000–16. *Publications:* Energy Policies and the Greenhouse Effect, vol. 1 1990, vol. 2 (ed) 1991; (ed) Emerging Energy Technologies: impacts and policy implications, 1992; The Earth Summit Agreements: a guide and assessment, 1993; Renewable Energy Strategies for Europe: vol. 1 1995, vol. 2 1997; The Kyoto Protocol: a guide and assessment, 1999; (ed jtly) A Low Carbon Electricity System for the UK: technology, economics and policy, 2008; Planetary Economics: energy, climate change and the three domains of sustainable energy development, 2014. *Recreations:* time with family; music, guitar. *Address:* UCL Institute for Sustainable Resources, Central House, 14 Upper Woburn Place, WC1H 0NN. *E:* m.grubb@ucl.ac.uk.

**GRUBB, Prof. Peter John,** PhD, ScD; Professor of Investigative Plant Ecology, Cambridge University, 2000–01, now Emeritus; Fellow, Magdalene College, Cambridge, 1960–2002, now Emeritus (President, 1991–96); *b* 9 Aug. 1935; *s* of Harold Amos Grubb and Phyllis Gertrude (*née* Hook); *m* 1965, Elizabeth Adelaide Anne, *d* of Charles Edward and Adelaide Gertrude Hall; one *s* one *d*. *Educ:* Royal Liberty Sch.; Magdalene Coll., Cambridge (Schol.; BA 1957; PhD 1962; ScD 1995). Magdalene College, Cambridge: John Stothert Bye Fellow, 1958–60; Res. Fellow, 1960; Tutor, 1963–74; Jt Dir of Studies in Natural Scis, 1980–96; Cambridge University: Demonstrator in Botany, 1961–64; Lectr, 1964–92; Reader, 1992–2000. Nuffield-Royal Soc. Bursar, Univ. of Adelaide, 1963; Hon. Res. Fellow, ANU, 1970–71; Vis. Prof., Cornell Univ., 1982, 1987; Sen. Vis. Researcher, CSIRO Tropical Forest Res. Centre, Atherton, 1992–2000; Vis. Prof., ICSTM, 1999–2007. Editor: Jl of Ecology, 1972–77; Biol Flora of British Isles, 1978–87. Jt Leader, Cambridge Expedn to Colombian Cordillera Oriental, 1957; Leader, Oxford Univ. Expedn to Ecuador, 1960. President: Brit. Ecol Soc., 1990–91 (Hon. Mem., 2001; first Award for outstanding service to the Soc., 2003); Cambridge Philosophical Soc., 1990–91. Frank Smart Prize in Botany, Cambridge Univ., 1956; Rolleston Meml Essay Prize, Oxford Univ., 1963. *Publications:* (with P. F. Stevens) Forests of Mt Kerigomna, Papua New Guinea, 1985; (ed with J. B. Whittaker) Toward a More Exact Ecology, 1989; (jtly) 100 Years of Plant Sciences in Cambridge 1904–2004, 2004; (ed with J. B. Whittaker) 100 Influential Papers, 2013; papers in ecol and botanical jls. *Recreations:* history of architecture, biographies, savouring continental cheeses. *Address:* Magdalene College, Cambridge CB3 0AG. *T:* (01223) 332109.

**GRUBBS, Prof. Robert Howard,** PhD; Victor and Elizabeth Atkins Professor of Chemistry, California Institute of Technology, Pasadena, since 1990 (Professor of Chemistry, 1978–90); *b* 27 Feb. 1942; *s* of Henry Howard Grubbs and Evelyn Faye Grubbs; *m* 1967, Helen M. O'Kane; two *s* one *d*. *Educ:* Univ. of Florida, Gainesville (BS Chem. 1963, MS Chem. 1965); Columbia Univ., NY (PhD Chem. 1968). NIH Postdoctoral Fellow, Stanford Univ., Calif, 1968–69; Asst Prof., 1969–73, Associate Prof., 1973–78, Michigan State Univ., E Lansing. MACS 1964; MNAS 1989; Fellow, Amer. Acad. of Arts and Scis, 1994; FRCS 2004. Hon. MRIA 1999; Hon. FRSC 2006; Foreign Mem., Royal Soc., 2017. Hon. Prof., Shanghai Inst. of Organic Chemistry, Chinese Acad. of Scis, 2001. Camille and Henry Dreyfus Teacher-Scholar Award, 1975; American Chemical Society Awards: Nat. Award in Organometallic Chem., 1988; Arthur C. Cope Scholar, 1990; Polymer Chemistry, 1995; Herman F. Mark Polymer Chemistry, 2000; Herbert C. Brown for Creative Res. in Synthetic Methods, 2001; Arthur C. Cope, 2002; for Creative Res. in Homogenous or Heterogeneous Catalysis, 2003; Richard C. Tolman Medal, 2003; Pauling Award Medal, 2003; Kirkwood Medal, 2005; Nagoya Univ. Medal of Organic Chemistry, 1997; Fluka Prize, Reagent of the Yr, 1998; Benjamin Franklin Medal in Chemistry, Franklin Inst., 2000; Bristol-Myers Squibb Dist. Achievement Award in Organic Synthesis, 2004; August Wilhelm von Hofmann Denkmünze, German Chem. Soc., 2005; (jtly) Nobel Prize in Chemistry, 2005; Havinga Medal, Leiden Univ., 2006. *Publications:* 495 research pubns and 106 patents issued. *Recreations:* rock climbing, walking. *Address:* Chemistry & Chemical Engineering, MC 164–30, California Institute of Technology, Pasadena, CA 91125, USA. *T:* (626) 3956003, *Fax:* (626) 5649277. *E:* rhg@caltech.edu.

**GRUBE, Claus,** Comdr, First Cl., Order of Dannebrog (Denmark), 2010; Ambassador of Denmark to the Court of St James's, 2013–17; Senior Advisor: Flint Global Ltd, London, since 2017; Seafresh Group Holding Ltd, Redditch, since 2017; AxcelFuture, Copenhagen, since 2017; *b* Copenhagen, 14 Dec. 1950; *s* of late Willy Grube and Grethe Grube Mikkelsen; *m* 2005, Susanne Fournais; one *s* two *d*. *Educ:* Copenhagen Univ. (Master in Law 1976). Dep. Judge, Min. of Justice, 1976–77; entered Danish Foreign Service, 1977; Sec., Perm. Mission to EC, Brussels, 1979–83; Hd of Section, Min. of Foreign Affairs, 1983–84; Personal Asst to State Sec. for For. Econ. Affairs, 1984–88; Counsellor (Econ. Affairs), Paris, 1988–93; Dep. Hd, 1993–94, Hd, N Gp 3rd Dept, 1994–97, Min. of Foreign Affairs; Under Sec., N Gp and Ambassador, Min. of Foreign Affairs, 1997–2000; Dep. Perm. Rep., 2000–03, Perm. Rep., 2003–09, EU, Brussels; Perm. Sec. of State, Min. of Foreign Affairs, 2009–13. Mem. Bd, Danish Theatres and Mus, 2017–. Mem., Danish Assoc. of Business Mgt. Hon. Chamberlain, Court of the Queen of Denmark, 2016–. Freedom of London, 2017. Grand Cross, Order of Phoenix (Greece), 2009; Grand Cross, Order of Lion (Finland), 2011; Comdr, Order of the Crown (Belgium); Officier, Ordre nat. du Mérite (France). *Recreations:* sailing, outdoor activities. *Address:* Toldbodhus, Brogade 8, DK5970 Aeroeskoebing, Denmark. *T:* (45) 45820033, (45) 25267500. *E:* grube.toldbodhus@gmail.com, (business) clausgrube@flint-global.com. *Clubs:* Travellers, National Liberal; Rotary International.

**GRUBEN, Baron Thierry de;** *see* de Gruben.

**GRUDER, Jeffrey Nigel;** QC 1997; *b* 18 Sept. 1954; *s* of late Bernard Gruder and Lily Gruder; *m* 1979, Gillian Vera Hyman; one *s* two *d*. *Educ:* City of London Sch.; Trinity Hall, Cambridge (MA). Called to the Bar, Middle Temple, 1977, Bencher, 2008; in practice at the Bar, 1978–. *Recreations:* reading, theatre, art. *Address:* Essex Court Chambers, 24 Lincoln's Inn Fields, WC2A 3EG. *T:* (020) 7813 8000.

**GRUMBAR, Jocelyn Atholl S.;** *see* Stuart-Grumbar.

**GRUNDY, David Stanley,** CB 1997; Commissioner for Policy and Resources, Forestry Commission, 1992–97; *b* 10 April 1943; *s* of Walter Grundy and Anne Grundy (*née* Pomfret); *m* 1965, Elizabeth Jenny Schadla Hall; one *s*. *Educ:* De La Salle Coll., Manchester; Jesus Coll., Cambridge (MA); Jesus Coll., Oxford (MPhil). Asst Principal, MOP, 1967–70; Asst Private Sec. to Minister, Min. of Technology, 1970–71; Principal, DTI, 1971–73; Economic Adviser: FCO, 1976–78; DoE, 1978–79; Chief Economic Advr, Govt of Vanuatu, 1979–81; Forestry Commission: Chief Economist, 1982–90; Comr for Finance and Admin, 1990–92. Member: Scottish Ornithologists' Club, 1997–; Scottish Wildlife Trust, 1999– (Vice Chm., 2002–08). *Publications:* (ed) The Birds of Scotland, 2007. *Recreations:* angling, bird watching, gardening, tennis. *Address:* 9 Ann Street, Edinburgh EH4 1PL. *Club:* Dean Tennis (Edinburgh).

**GRUNDY, Prof. Emily Marjata Dorothea,** PhD; FBA 2017; FAcSS; Professor of Population Science and Director, Institute for Social and Economic Research, University of Essex, since 2018; *b* 24 July 1955; *d* of late John Grundy and Dorothea Grundy (later Sheppard); *m* M. J. Murphy; one *s* one *d* (twins). *Educ:* King's Coll., Cambridge (BA (Hist.) 1976); LSHTM (MSc (Med. Demography) 1979); Univ. of London (PhD Medicine 1989). FAcSS 2016. Res. Officer, Dept of Health Care of Elderly, Univ. of Nottingham, 1981–83; Res. Fellow, Social Stats Res. Unit, City Univ., London, 1983–86; Lectr, then Reader, in Social Gerontology, KCL, 1986–98; Reader in Social Gerontology, 1998–2003, Prof. of Demographic Gerontology, 2003–12, LSHTM; Professor of Demography: Univ. of Cambridge, 2012–13; LSE, 2013–18. Chair, Population Investigation Cttee, 2015–. Pres., British Soc. for Population Studies, 2008–10. Sec. Gen. and Treas., Internat. Union for the Scientific Study of Population, 2010–14 (Mem. Council, 2014–18). *Publications:* Women's Migration, Marriage, Fertility and Divorce, 1989; (jtly) Living Well into Old Age, 1997; (ed jtly) Ageing Well: nutrition, health and social interventions, 2007; approx. 200 papers in learned jls and book chapters. *Recreations:* family and friends, cycling. *Address:* Institute for Social and Economic Research, University of Essex, Wivenhoe Park, Colchester CO3 3LG.

**GRUNDY, (James) Milton;** Founder and Chairman, The Milton Grundy Foundation (formerly Warwick Arts Trust), since 1978; *b* 13 June 1926; civil partnership 2010, Omar Afridi. *Educ:* Cowley Sch.; Sedbergh Sch.; Gonville and Caius Coll., Cambridge (MA). Called to the Bar, Inner Temple, 1954. Founder and Chm., Gemini Trust for the Arts, 1959–66; Founder Mem. and Pres., Internat. Tax Planning Assoc., 1975–; Charter Mem., Peggy Guggenheim Collection, 1980–89; Chm., Internat. Management Trust, 1986–96; Trustee: Nat. Museums and Galls of Merseyside, 1987–96; New End Theatre, Hampstead, 1994–96. *Publications:* Tax and the Family Company, 1956, 3rd edn 1966; Tax Havens, 1968, 8th edn (jtly), as Offshore Business Centres, 2008; Venice, 1971, 6th edn 2007; The World of International Tax Planning, 1984; (jtly) Asset Protection Trusts, 1990, 4th edn 2019; (with V. I. Atroshenko) Mediterranean Vernacular, 1991; Essays in International Tax Planning, 2001; More Essays in International Tax Planning, 2007; Six Fiscal Fables, 2010. *Recreation:* conversation. *Address:* Gray's Inn Tax Chambers, 36 Queen Street, EC4R 1BN. *T:* (020) 7242 2642.

**GRUNDY, Jennifer Anne**; JP; Vice Lord-Lieutenant of Merseyside, 2004–10; *b* 29 Sept. 1935; *d* of Edward and Marjorie Denton; *m* 1956, Martin Anthony Wilson Grundy (*d* 2007); one *s* four *d*. *Educ*: Huyton Coll. JP Knowsley, 1975 (Chm. Bench, 2000–03); DL Merseyside, 1989. *Recreations*: calligraphy, narrow-boating, gardening, traditional canal painting. *Address*: Stanley Cottage, 60 Roby Road, Roby, Liverpool L36 4HF. *T*: (0151) 489 1159. *E*: grundy500@tiscali.co.uk.

**GRUNDY, Rev. Canon Dr Malcolm Leslie**; Partner, Live-Wires Associates, 2009–12; *b* 22 March 1944; *s* of Arthur James Grundy and Gertrude Alice Grundy; *m* 1972, Wendy Elizabeth Gibson; one *s*. *Educ*: Sandye Place Sch., Beds; Mander Coll., Bedford; King's Coll., London (AKC 1968); Open Univ. (BA 1976); Leeds Univ. (PhD 2014). Ordained deacon 1969, priest 1970; Curate, St George's, Doncaster, 1969–72; Chaplain and Sen. Chaplain, Sheffield Industrial Mission, 1972–80; Dir of Educn, dio. of London, 1980–86; Team Rector of Huntingdon, 1986–91; Dir, Avec, 1991–94; Archdeacon of Craven, 1994–2005; Actg Dean, Bradford Cathedral, 2004–05; Dir, Foundn for Church Leadership, 2005–09. Hon. Canon of Ely, 1988–94; Canon Emeritus, Bradford, 2005. Vis. Fellow, York St John Univ., 2014–. Trustee, Women's Educn Partnership, 2015–19. Mem. Council, Retired Clergy Assoc., 2014–19 (Vice-Chm., 2015–19), Chair, York Anglo Scandinavian Soc., 2016–19. *Publications*: Light in the City, 1990; An Unholy Conspiracy, 1992; Community Work, 1995; (ed) The Parchmore Partnership, 1995; Management and Ministry, 1996; Understanding Congregations, 1998; (contrib.) Managing, Leading, Ministering, 1999; (jtly) Faith on the Way, 2000; What They Don't Teach You at Theological College, 2003; What's New in Church Leadership, 2007; Leadership and Oversight, 2011; Multi-Congregation Ministry, 2015. *Recreations*: classic cars, gardening, writing. *Address*: 11 Givendale Grove, York YO10 3QF.

**GRUNDY, Sir Mark**, Kt 2006; Executive Principal, Collegiate Academy Trust and Shireland Collegiate Academy, since 2007; *b* 19 July 1959; *s* of James and Gloria Grundy. *Educ*: Hawtonville Jun. Sch., Newark; Magnus Grammar Sch., Newark; Loughborough Univ. (MSc Human Biol. 1983). Teacher, Forest Comp. Sch., Walsall, 1983–84; Teacher, Darlaston Comp. Sch., Walsall, 1984–87; Sen. Teacher, Thorns Community Coll., Dudley, 1987–92; Dep. Headteacher, Wodensborough Community Technology Coll., Wednesbury, 1992–97; Headteacher, Shireland Lang. Coll., Smethwick, 1997–2007. Exec. Dir, George Salter High Sch., West Bromwich, 2003–11. Consultant Headteacher, DfES, 2001–03. FRSA 2007. *Recreations*: hockey, tennis, watching sport, ICT. *Address*: Shireland Collegiate Academy, Waterloo Road, Smethwick B66 4ND. *T*: (0121) 558 8086, *Fax*: (0121) 558 8377. *E*: m.grundy@collegiateacademy.org.uk.

**GRUNDY, Milton**; *see* Grundy, J. M.

**GRUNDY, Stephanie Christine**; legal consultant, legislative drafting; *b* 11 Dec. 1958; *d* of Harry Grundy and June (*née* Hazell). *Educ*: Grange Sch., Oldham; Hertford Coll., Oxford (Schol.; Gibbs Prize; MA, BCL). Called to the Bar, Middle Temple, 1983. Research Asst, Law Commn, 1985; Asst Parly Counsel, 1985–92; on secondment to Law Commn, 1988–90; Legal Advr, Treasury Solicitor's Dept, 1992–2000; Lawyer, FSA, 2000–05; consultancy services to govt depts, IMF, Shearman and Stirling, Bindman and Partners, Lord Lester of Herne Hill, MPs, and others, 2000–. *Recreations*: yoga, walking, conservation.

**GRUNENBERG, Dr Christoph**; Director, Kunsthalle Bremen, since 2011; *b* 28 Oct. 1962; *s* of Johannes and Marlis Grunenberg; *m* 1994, Gina. *Educ*: Johann Wolfgang Goethe Gymnasium, Frankfurt am Main; Courtauld Inst. of Art, Univ. of London (MA 1988; PhD 1993). Res. Asst, Nat. Gall. of Art, Washington, 1990–91; Asst Curator, Kunsthalle Basel, 1993–95; Curator, 1995–99, Actg Dir, 1997–98, Inst. of Contemporary Art, Boston; Curator, Contemporary Art, Collections Div., Tate Gall., London, 1999–2001; Dir, Tate Liverpool, 2001–11. Hon. Prof., Hochschule für Künste, Univ. of the Arts, Bremen, 2015–. *Publications*: Mark Rothko, 1991; (ed) Gothic: transmutations of horror in late twentieth century art, 1997; (ed) Enterprise: venture and process in contemporary art, 1997; (ed) FRIEZE: wall paintings by Franz Ackerman, John Armleder, Margaret Kilgallen, Sarah Morris and Alexander Scott, 1999; (ed with Victoria Pomery) Marc Quinn, 2002; (ed) Summer of Love: art of the psychedelic era, 2005; (ed with J. Harris) Summer of Love: psychedelic art, social crisis and counterculture in the 1960s, 2005; (ed with Tanya Barson) Jake and Dinos Chapman: bad art for bad people, 2006; (ed with Robert Knifton) Centre of the Creative Universe: Liverpool and the Avant-Garde, 2007; (ed with Laurence Sillars) Peter Blake: a retrospective, 2007; (ed with Lynda Morris) Picasso: peace and freedom, 2010; (ed with Darren Pih) René Magritte: the pleasure principle, 2011; (ed with Astrid Becker) Friedensreich Hundertwasser: gegen den Strich, werke 1949 bis 1970, 2012; (ed with Astrid Becker) Picasso and the Model: Sylvette, Sylvette, Sylvette, 2014; (ed with Eva Fischer-Hausdorf) Last Year in Marienbad: a film as art, 2015. *Recreations*: books, reading, music, travel. *Address*: Kunsthalle Bremen, Am Wall 207, 28195 Bremen, Germany.

**GRUNWALD, Henry Cyril**; OBE 2009; QC 1999; *b* 15 Aug. 1949; *s* of Eugen Grunwald and Hetty Grunwald (*née* Steppel); *m* 1976, Alison Appleton; two *s* two *d*. *Educ*: City of London Sch.; University Coll. London (LLB Hons; Fellow, 2006). Called to the Bar, Gray's Inn, 1972, Bencher, 2002. Pres., Bd of Deputies of British Jews, 2003–09 (Vice-Pres., 1997–2000, Sen. Vice-Pres., 2000–03); Warden, Hampstead Synagogue, 1997–2008); Chm., Jewish Leadership Council, 2003–09; Pres., World Jewish Relief, 2009–; Vice-Pres., Council of Christians and Jews, 2009–. Mem., Expert Wkg Gp on Educn, Prime Minister's Holocaust Commn, 2014–. Pres., Relate N London, 2007–09 (Trustee, 1996–2006); Vice-Chm., Holocaust Meml Day Trust, 2005–13; Chairman: Holocaust Centre, Laxton, Nottingham, 2012–; Covenant and Conversation Trust, 2013–. Chm., Shechita UK, 2003–. Patron: Interfaith Youth Trust, 2007–; Drugslone, 2011–; Jewish Heritage UK, 2013–; London Cantorial Singers, 2019–. *Recreations*: family, friends, theatre, reading, travel. *Address*: Charter Chambers, 33 John Street, WC1N 2AT. *T*: (020) 7618 4400. *Club*: Royal Automobile.

**GRYBAUSKAITĖ, Dalia**, PhD; President of Lithuania, since 2009; *b* Vilnius, 1 March 1956. *Educ*: Leningrad Univ. (degree in Econs 1983); Moscow Acad. of Public Scis (PhD 1988); Foreign Service Sch., Georgetown Univ., Washington. Hd, Dept of Sci., Inst. of Econs, 1990–91; Prog. Dir, Prime Minister's Office, Lithuania, 1991; Director: European Dept, Min. of Internat. Econ. Relns, 1991–93; Econ. Relns Dept, Min. of Foreign Affairs, 1993–94; Envoy and Minister, Lithuanian Mission to EU, Brussels, 1994–95; Minister, Lithuanian Embassy, USA, 1996–99; Deputy Minister: of Finance, 1999–2000; of Foreign Affairs, 2000–01; Minister of Finance, 2001–04; Mem., European Commn, 2004–09. *Address*: (office) S. Daukanto a. 3, Vilnius 01122, Lithuania.

**GRYLLS, Edward, (Bear)**, OBE 2019; television presenter and author; Chief Scout, Scout Association, since 2009; Chief Ambassador, World Organisation of the Scout Movement, since 2018; *b* 7 June 1974; *s* of Sir (William) Michael (John) Grylls and Sarah Grylls; *m* 2000, Shara Cannings Knight; three *s*. *Educ*: Eton Coll.; University Coll. London (BA Hons Spanish). Trooper, E Sqdn, 21 SAS Regt, 1994–99. Ascended summit of Mt Ama Dablam, 1997, summit of Mt Everest, 1998; circumnavigated UK on jetski for RNLI, 2000; crossed Arctic Ocean in open rib for Prince's Trust, 2003; highest open air dinner under hot-air balloon for Duke of Edinburgh Awards, 2005; flew above Mt Everest in powered paraglider for Global Angels, 2007. *Television* series: Channel 4: Escape to the Legion, 2005; Born Survivor, 2006–13; Wild Weekends; Mission Everest, 2008; The Island, 2014, 2015, 2016; Celebrity Island, 2017, 2018; Bear Goes Wild with Barack Obama, 2015; Discovery: Man vs Wild, 2006–; Fan vs Wild; Worst Case Scenario; Escape from Hell, 2013; Extreme Survival Caught on Camera, 2014; Breaking Point, 2015; Working the Wild; Behind the Scenes; Science of Survival; Treasure Island with Bear Grylls, 2019; ITV: Mission Survive, 2015, 2016; Great British Adventures; Bear Grylls Survival School, 2016, 2017; NBC: Get Out Alive; Running Wild, 2014, 2015, 2016, 2017, 2018; Dragon TV: Absolute Wild, 2016, 2017; Survivor Games; Face the Wild (Facebook); You vs Wild (Netflix). Ambassador, Land Rover. Bear Grylls Adventure, theme park, Birmingham, 2018. Hon. Lt Comdr, RN, 2004; Hon. Lt Col, RM Commandos, 2014. *Publications*: over 80 books incl. Facing Up, 2000; Facing the Frozen Ocean, 2004; Born Survivor, 2007; Bear Grylls' Great Outdoor Adventures, 2008; Living Wild, 2009; With Love Papa x, 2009; Mud, Sweat and Tears (autobiog.), 2011; Survival Guide to Life, 2012; To My Sons, 2012; True Grit, 2013; Extreme Food, 2014; Your Life - Train For It, 2014; Ghost Flight, 2015; Fuel for Life, 2015; Burning Angels, 2016; How to Stay Alive: the ultimate survival guide for any situation, 2017; The Devil's Sanctuary, 2017; The Hunt, 2018; Soul Fuel, 2019; *for children*: Mission Survival: Gold of the Gods, 2008; Way of the Wolf, 2008; Sands of the Scorpion, 2009; Tracks of the Tiger, 2009; Strike of the Shark, 2013; Claws of the Crocodile, 2013; Rage of the Rhino, 2014; Lair of the Leopard, 2015; Mission Raptor, 2016; Mission Typhoon, 2016; Mission Jaguar, 2016; Mission Dragon, 2016; Survival Camp, 2016; In the Jungle (colouring book), 2016; Reptiles (colouring book), 2016; Dangerous Animals, 2016; Animal Detective, 2016; Bear Grylls Extreme Planet, 2016; Dangers and Emergencies, 2017; Hiking, 2017; Dangerous Aid; Tracking, 2017; Weather Watching, 2017; Desert, 2018; Polar, 2018. *Recreations*: mountaineering, paragliding, sailing, yoga, martial arts, piano. *W*: www.beargrylls.com. *Clubs*: Special Forces, Alpine.

**GUAN MOYE**; writer, as Mo Yan; *b* Gaomi, Shandong Province, China, 2 Feb. 1955; *m* 1979, Du Qinlan; one *d*. *Educ*: Literature Dept, People's Liberation Army Arts Acad.; Beijing Lu Xun Literary Inst. (MA 1991). Cattle herder, 1966; recorder of work points for local prodn brigade, 1970–73; labourer and contract worker, Gaomi Cotton Processing Plant No 5, 1973–76; enlisted in People's Liberation Army, 1976–97 (confidential clerk and librarian; instructor of theory, then regular instructor; writer in mil. unit cultural dept); Procuratorate Daily, 1997–2007; Chinese Arts Res. Inst., 2007–13; Dir, Internat. Writing Centre, Beijing Normal Univ., 2013–. Mem., Chinese Assoc. of Writers, 1986–. Nobel Prize for Literature, 2012. *Publications*: as Mo Yan: Tou ming de hong luo bo, 1986; Hong gao liang jia zu, 1987; Bao zha, 1988; Huan le shi san zhang, 1989; Shi san bu, 1989; Tian tang suan tai zhi ge, 1989 (The Garlic Ballads, 1995); Explosions and Other Stories, 1991; Jiu guo, 1992 (The Republic of Wine: a novel, 2000); Jin fa ying er, 1993; Shi cao jia zu, 1993; Fen nu de suan tai, 1993; Huai bao xian hua di nü ren: Mo Yan xiao shuo jin zuo ji, 1993; Shen liao: Mo Yan zui xin zhong duan pian xiao shuo xuan, 1993; Zai bao zha, 1994; Dao shen piao, 1995; Feng ru fei tun, 1995 (Big Breasts and Wide Hips: a novel, 2004); Hong gao liang, 1995 (Red Sorghum, 2003) (filmed 1987); Ming ding guo, 1995; Mo Yan wen ji, 1995; Xian nü ren, 1995; Hong er duo, 1998; Shi fu yue lai yue you mo, 2000 (Shifu, You'll Do Anything for a Laugh, 2001) (filmed as Xingfu shiguang, 2000); Tan xiang xing, 2001 (Sandalwood Death: a novel, 2013); Liang xin zuo zheng, 2002; Mu zhi kao, 2003; Sishiyi pao, 2003 (Pow!, 2012); Mo Yan zhong pian xiao shuo xuan, 2004; Yu da shi yue hui, 2005; Sheng si pi lao, 2006 (Life and Death are Wearing Me Out: a novel, 2008); Wa, 2009 (Frog, 2014); Grand Ceremony, 2013. *Address*: International Writing Centre, Beijing Normal University, No 19, XinJieKouWai Street, HaiDian District, Beijing 100875, China.

**GUARENTE, Catherine Jean**; *see* May, C. J.

**GUBBAY, Hon. Anthony Roy**; SC; Chief Justice of Zimbabwe, 1990–2001; *b* 26 April 1932; *s* of Henry and Gracia Gubbay; *m* 1st, 1962, Alice Wilma Sanger (*d* 2002); two *s*; 2nd, 2006, Suzanne Lesley Cox. *Educ*: Univ. of Witwatersrand, SA (BA); Jesus Coll., Cambridge Univ. (MA, LLM; Hon. Fellow, 1992). Admitted to practice, 1957; emigrated to S Rhodesia, 1958; in private practice as advocate, Bulawayo; SC 1974; Judge: of the High Court, 1977–83; of the Supreme Court, 1983–90. Pres., Valuations Bd, 1974–77; National President: Special Court for Income Tax Appeals, 1974–77; Fiscal Court, 1974–77; Patents Tribunal, 1974–77. Chairman: Legal Practitioners' Disciplinary Tribunal, 1981–87; Law Develt Commn, 1990–2001; Judicial Service Commn, 1990–2001. Mem., Perm. Court of Arbitration, 1993–. Member: Commonwealth Reference Gp on the promotion of human rights of women and the girl child through the Judiciary, 1996–; Gruber Justice Adv. Bd, 2002–05; Patron, Commonwealth Magistrates' and Judges' Assoc., 1994–2001. Former Pres., Oxford and Cambridge Soc. of Zimbabwe; Mem., Oxford and Cambridge Soc. of Vancouver, 2013–. Hon. Bencher, Lincoln's Inn, 1997. Hon. Mem., Soc. of Legal Scholars, 2004. DU Essex, 1994; Hon. LLD: London, 2002; Witwatersrand, 2005. Peter Gruber Foundn's Annual Justice Award, 2001. Great Cross, Order of Rio Branco (Brazil), 1999. *Recreations*: reading novels and biographies, walking, gym, theatre, travel. *Address*: 2802 West One, 1408 Strathmore Mews, Vancouver, BC V6Z 3A9, Canada. *T*: (11) 6046206542. *E*: coxgub@shaw.ca.

**GUBBAY, Raymond Jonathan**, CBE 2001; impresario; Founder and Chairman (formerly Managing Director), Raymond Gubbay Ltd, 1966–2016; Director, Fiery Angel Entertainment, since 2017; *b* 2 April 1946; *s* of late David and Ida Gubbay; *m* 1972, Johanna Quirke (marr. diss. 1988); two *d*. *Educ*: University Coll. Sch., Hampstead. Concert promoter, 1966–2016: regular series of concerts at major London concert halls, including: Royal Festival Hall; Royal Albert Hall; The Barbican (*c* 1,200 concerts, 1982–); also major regl arenas and concert venues; has presented many of the world's greatest artists in concert; The Ratepayers Iolanthe, South Bank and Phoenix Theatre, 1984; The Metropolitan Mikado, South Bank, 1985; also Royal Opera prodn of Turandot, Wembley Arena, 1991; Royal Albert Hall: Centenary prodn of La Bohème, 1996; Carmen, 1997; Swan Lake, 1997; Madam Butterfly, 1998; Romeo and Juliet, 1998; Tosca, 1999; Sleeping Beauty, 2000; Aida, 2001; Cavalleria Rusticana and Pagliacci, 2003; Strictly Gershwin, 2008; The King and I, 2009; Guys and Dolls, 2018; Royal Festival Hall: D'Oyly Carte Opera Co., 1998 and 1999 (also Queen's Th., 1998–99, and Savoy Th., 2000, 2001, 2002, 2003); Follies, 2002; On Your Toes, 2003; Carmen Jones, 2007; Circus 1903, 2018; Barry Humphreys Weimar Cabaret, Barbican, 2018; Bolshoi Ballet, Th. Royal, 2001; Ute Lemper, Queen's Th., 1999, Savoy Th., 2001; Pirates of Penzance, Savoy Th., 2004; Barber of Seville, Marriage of Figaro, Savoy Opera, Savoy Th., 2004; Julie Andrews, Carmen, O2, 2010; Romeo and Juliet, Royal Ballet, O2, 2011; Peppa Pig: My First Concert, 2019; tours and seasons by various visiting ballet cos. incl. Stanislavsky Ballet, RFH, 2001, 2003, 2004; Carl Rosa Gilbert and Sullivan season, Gielgud Th., 2008; Spring Dance Season, incl. NY City Ballet, Carlos Acosta, Sylvie Guillem, Amer. Ballet Th., Cuban Nat. Ballet, Mark Morris, London Coliseum, 2008–10. Co-prod., The Moderate Soprano, Duke of York's Th., 2018. Founder, City of London Antiques and Fine Art Fair, Barbican Exhibn Halls, 1987–92. Member: Council, Corps of Army Music, 2001–09; Bd of Govs, Central Sch. of Ballet, 2010–15; Bd, RPO, 2011–; Bd, Fiery Dragons Ltd, 2011–; Bd, Mousetrap Foundn, 2013–16; Co-founder, Fiery Angel Entertainments, 2017. Trustee, Belvedere Trust, 2015–16. Hon. FRAM 1988; Hon FTCL 2000. FRSA 2001. *Recreations*: travel, art, having six grandchildren. *Address*: 8 Artillery Row, SW1P 1RZ. *E*: raymond@gubbay.org.

**GUBBAY, Dr Susan**, (Mrs A. R. Davis), FRICS; independent marine consultant working on projects for public sector, private sector, and non-governmental organisations on marine ecology, marine conservation and integrated coastal management, since 1994; *d* of Eldred Gubbay and Flora Gubbay; *m* 1986, Alan Ramsay Davis. *Educ:* Lancaster Univ. (BSc Hons Ecol.); York Univ. (DPhil Marine Ecol.). FRICS. Conservation Officer, 1984–88, Sen. Conservation Officer, 1988–94, Marine Conservation Soc. Buckland Prof. (Marine Protected Areas and Fisheries), Buckland Foundn, 1993. Specialist Advisor: to H of C Envmt Select Cttee inquiry into Coastal Zone Protection and Planning, 1991–94; to Parly Scrutiny Unit Jt Select Cttee inquiry into draft Marine Bill, 2008; Mem., Ministerial Gp reviewing EU Commn Fisheries Policy, 1995–96. Wildlife and Countryside Link: Chair: Jt Marine Wkg Gp, 1993–94; Marine Gp, 1993–96; Member: Action Plan Steering Gp, UK Biodiversity, 1994–95; Cttee, UK Marine Biodiversity, 1997–99; Council, English Nature, 1998–2004; Council, Countryside Council for Wales, 2008–13. Marine and Coastal Biol Diversity expert on Roster of Experts for Convention on Biol Diversity, 1998–. Pres., Eur. Coastal Assoc. of Sci. and Technol. (EUROCOAST), 1994–96. External Examiner: MSc Coastal and Marine Resource Mgt, Univ. of Portsmouth, 1999–2004; Marine Resource Mgt, Univ. of Aberdeen, 2001–05. FRSA 1995. *Publications:* (ed) Marine Protected Areas: principles and techniques for management, 1995; numerous contribs on marine conservation to jls, reports and popular articles. *Recreations:* the great outdoors (above and below sea level), scuba diving, natural history, clarinet, gardening, photography, travel, painting and botanical illustration.

**GUBBINS, Prof. David**, PhD; FRS 1996; CPhys, FInstP; Professor of Geophysics, University of Leeds, 1989–2009, now Emeritus; Research Associate, Institute of Geophysics and Planetary Physics, Scripps Institution of Oceanography, since 2009; Visiting Professor, University of Sydney, since 2011; *b* 31 May 1947; *s* of late Albert Edmund Gubbins and of Joyce Lucy Gubbins; *m* 1972, (Margaret) Stella McCloy; one *s* two *d*. *Educ:* King Edward VI Grammar Sch., Southampton; Trinity Coll., Cambridge (BA, PhD). CPhys, FInstP 1996. Vis. Res. Fellow, Univ. of Colorado, 1972–73; Instructor in Applied Maths, MIT, 1973–74; Asst Prof., Inst. of Geophysics and Planetary Physics, UCLA, 1974–76; Cambridge University: Res. Assistant and Sen. Assistant in Res., Dept of Geodesy and Geophysics, 1976–81; Asst Dir of Res., Dept of Earth Scis, 1981–89; Fellow of Churchill Coll., 1978–90. Fellow, Amer. Geophys. Union, 1985; Foreign Mem., Norwegian Acad. of Arts and Sci., 2005. Murchison Medal, Geol Soc., 1999; Gold Medal, RAS, 2003; John Adam Fleming Medal, Amer. Geophys. Union, 2004; Chree Medal, Inst. of Physics, 2005; Love Medal, 2007, Holmes Medal and Hon. Mem., 2009, Eur. Geoscis Union. *Publications:* Seismology and Plate Tectonics, 1990; Time Series Analysis and Inverse Theory for Geophysicists, 2004; (ed) Encyclopedia of Geomagnetism and Paleomagnetism, 2007; scientific papers. *Recreations:* sailing, swimming. *Address:* School of Earth and Environment, University of Leeds, Leeds LS2 9JT. *T:* (0113) 343 5255.

**GUBERT, Walter Alexander**; Vice Chairman, since 1988, Chairman, Europe, Middle East and Africa, since 2004, and Member, Executive Committee, since 2005, J. P. Morgan Chase & Co. (formerly J. P. Morgan); *b* Merano, Italy, 15 June 1947; *m* 1974, Caroline Espagno; two *d*. *Educ:* Univ. of Florence (Dr in Law 1970); INSEAD (MBA 1973). Joined J. P. Morgan, Paris, 1973; Hd, Capital Mkts, USA, 1981–87; Leader, J. P. Morgan Securities, EMEA and Asia, 1987–88; Hd, Global Investment Banking, 1988–2000; Sen. Exec. in London, 1989–; Dir, 1995–; Chm., JP Morgan Investment Bank, 2000–. *Recreations:* golf, piano, history, books. *Address:* J. P. Morgan, 25 Bank Street, Canary Wharf, E14 5JP. *E:* walter.gubert@jpmorgan.com.

**GUCKIAN, Dr Noel Joseph**, CVO 2010; OBE 2001; HM Diplomatic Service, retired; Ambassador to Oman, 2005–11; *b* 6 March 1955; *s* of late William Joseph Guckian and Mary Patricia Joan Guckian (*née* Kelly); *m* 1990, Lorna Ruth Warren (*d* 2012); one *s* three *d*. *Educ:* Notre Dame Internat. Sch., Rome; New Univ. of Ulster (BA Hons History 1976); UCW, Aberystwyth (MSc Econs, Internat. Politics 1977; PhD Internat. Politics 1985). FCO 1980; Arabic at SOAS, 1983–84; Jedda, 1984–87; 1st Sec., Financial, Paris, 1988; Head, British Interest Section, Tripoli, 1990; Head, Political Section, Kuwait, 1991–92; Counsellor and Dep. Head of Mission, Muscat, 1994–97; Dep. Hd of Mission and Consul-Gen., Tripoli, 1998–2002 (Hd, British Interests Sect., 1998–99, then Chargé d'Affaires *ai* on restoration of diplomatic relns, 1999); Dep. Hd of Mission, Damascus, 2002–04; Consul Gen., Northern Iraq, 2004–05. *Recreations:* fly-fishing, sailing. *Clubs:* Royal Over-Seas League, Travellers; Pin Mill Sailing.

**GUDJONSSON, Prof. Gisli Hannes**, CBE 2011; PhD; Professor of Forensic Psychology, King's College London, 2000–11, now Emeritus; *b* Reykjavik, Iceland, 26 Oct. 1947; *s* of Gudjon Gudmundsson and Thora Hannesdottir; *m* 1979, Julia Vivienne; two *d*. *Educ:* Brunel Univ. (BSc 1st Cl. Hons Social Scis 1975); Univ. of Surrey (MSc Clin. Psychol. 1977; PhD 1981). Health and Care Professions Council (formerly Health Professionals Council) registered clinical and forensic psychologist. Clin. Psychologist, West Park and Epsom Dist Hosps, 1977–79; Lectr in Psychol., 1980–86, Sen. Lectr in Psychol., 1987–93, Reader in Forensic Psychol., 1993–99, Inst. of Psychiatry, KCL. Consultant in cases for police, prosecution, Criminal Cases Rev. Commn and defence lawyers; also testimony abroad, incl. in USA, Canada, Norway, Israel and The Hague. Hon. DMed Iceland, 2001. JP Croydon, 1990–99. Lifetime Achievement Award: BPsS, 2009; Eur. Assoc. Psychol. and Law, 2012; Tom Williamson Award, Internat. Investigative Interviewing Res. Gp, 2017. *Publications:* (with H. Eysenck) The Causes and Cures of Criminality, 1989; The Psychology of Interrogations, Confessions and Testimony, 1992; The Gudjonsson Suggestibility Scales Manual, 1997; (with L. R. C. Haward) Forensic Psychology: a guide to practice, 1998; The Psychology of Interrogations and Confessions: a handbook, 2003; (ed jtly) Witness Testimony: psychological investigative and evidential perspectives, 2006; (ed jtly) Forensic Neuropsychology in Practice: a guide to assessment and legal processes, 2009; (ed jtly) Witness Testimony in Sexual Cases: evidential, investigative and scientific perspectives, 2016; The Psychology of False Confessions: forty years of science and practice, 2018. *Recreations:* walking, travelling. *Address:* Department of Psychology (PO 78), Institute of Psychiatry, Psychology and Neuroscience, King's College London, De Crespigny Park, Denmark Hill, SE5 8AF. *E:* gisli.gudjonsson@kcl.ac.uk.

**GUÉGUINOU, Jean**, Hon. GCVO 1996; Commandeur de la Légion d'Honneur (Chevalier 1991; Officier, 2003); Officier de l'Ordre du Mérite, 1995 (Chevalier, 1979); Commandeur, Ordre des Arts et des Lettres, 2007; Ambassadeur de France, 2000; Chairman, French Section, Franco British Council, 2007–10; *b* 17 Oct. 1941. *Educ:* Ecole Nationale d'Administration. Press and Inf. Dept, Min. of Foreign Affairs, Paris, 1967–69; Second Sec., London, 1969–71; Chargé de Mission, Private Office of Ministre d'Etat, Minister of Nat. Defence, 1971–73; Asst Private Sec., then Special Advr to Minister of Foreign Affairs, 1973–76; Principal Private Sec. to Minister of State resp. to Prime Minister, 1976–77; Head of Southern Africa and Indian Ocean Dept, Min. of Foreign Affairs, 1977–82; Consul Gen., Jerusalem, 1982–86; Dir of Press and Inf. Dept, Min. of Foreign Affairs, and Ministry Spokesman, 1986–90; French Ambassador: in Prague, 1990–93 (Czechoslovakia, 1990–92; Czech Republic, 1993); to UK, 1993–98; to the Holy See, 1998–2001; Ambassador and Perm. Deleg. of France to UNESCO, 2002–07. Mem. Governing Body, Agence France Presse, 1986–90. KSG 1976. *Address:* 5 avenue Montespan, 75116 Paris, France.

**GUERIN, Orla**, Hon. MBE 2005; International Correspondent, BBC News; *b* Dublin, 15 May 1966; *d* of late Patrick James Guerin and Monica Guerin; *m* 2003, Michael Georgy. *Educ:* Coll. of Commerce, Dublin (Journalism Cert. 1985); University Coll., Dublin (MA Film Studies 1999). Joined RTE, 1987, E Europe Corresp., 1990–94; BBC: joined as news corresp., 1995; S Europe Corresp., 1996–2000; ME Corresp., 2001–05; Africa Corresp., 2006–08; Pakistan Corresp., 2009–13; Egypt Corresp., 2013. DU Essex, 2002; Hon. D Dublin Inst. of Technology, 2005; Hon. DLitt Ulster, 2009; DUniv: Open, 2007; QUB, 2009. Broadcaster of the Year, London Press Club, 2002; News and Factual Award, Women in Film and TV, 2003; a Bayeux Prize for War Correspondents, 2007; David Bloom Award, Radio and TV Assoc., 2009.

**GUERNSEY, Lord**; Heneage James Daniel Finch-Knightley; *b* 29 April 1985; *s* and heir of Earl of Aylesford. *Recreations:* ski-ing, archery, field sports. *Heir: s* Hon. Alfie Charles Heneage Finch-Knightley, *b* 28 Sept. 2014. *Address:* c/o Packington Hall, Meriden, Warwickshire CV7 7HF.

**GUERNSEY, Dean of;** see Barker, Very Rev. T. R.

**GUEST;** see Haden-Guest.

**GUEST**, family name of **Viscount Wimborne**.

**GUEST, Prof. Anthony Gordon**, CBE 1989; QC 1987; FBA 1993; FCIArb; Barrister-at-Law; Professor of English Law, King's College, University of London, 1966–97; *b* 8 Feb. 1930; *o s* of late Gordon Walter Leslie Guest and Marjorie (*née* Hooper), Maidencombe, Devon; unmarried. *Educ:* Colston's Sch., Bristol; St John's Coll., Oxford (MA). Exhibnr and Casberd Schol., Oxford, 1950–54; 1st cl. Final Hon. Sch. of Jurisprudence, 1954. Bacon Schol., Gray's Inn, 1955; Barstow Law Schol., 1955; called to the Bar, Gray's Inn, 1956, Bencher, 1978. University Coll., Oxford: Lectr, 1954–55; Fellow and Prælector in Jurisprudence, 1955–65; Dean, 1963–64; Reader in Common Law to Council of Legal Educn (Inns of Court), 1967–80. Travelling Fellowship to S Africa, 1957; Mem., Lord Chancellor's Law Reform Cttee, 1963–84; Mem., Adv. Cttee on establishment of Law Faculty in University of Hong Kong, 1965; UK Deleg. to UN Commn on Internat. Trade Law, NY, Geneva and Vienna, 1968–84 and 1986–87, to UN Conf. on Limitation of Actions, 1974. Vis. Prof., Univ. of Leuven, 2004–05. Mem., Board of Athlone Press, 1968–73; Mem. Governing Body, Rugby Sch., 1968–88. FKC 1982; FCIArb 1984; FRSA 2004. Served Army and TA, 1948–50 (Lieut RA). *Publications:* (ed) Anson's Principles of the Law of Contract, 21st to 26th edns, 1959–84; Chitty on Contracts: (Asst Editor) 22nd edn 1961, 28th edn to 31st edns, 1999–2012, (Gen. Editor) 23rd to 27th edns, 1968–94; (ed) Oxford Essays in Jurisprudence, 1961; The Law of Hire-Purchase, 1966; (Gen. Editor) Benjamin's Sale of Goods, 1st to 7th edns, 1974–2006; (ed jtly) Encyclopedia of Consumer Credit, 1975; (jtly) Introduction to the Law of Credit and Security, 1978; (ed) Chalmers and Guest on Bills of Exchange, 14th edn to 17th edns, 1991–2009; Only Remember Me (anthology), 1993; The Law of Assignment, 2012–15; The Law of Treasure, 2018; articles in legal jls. *Address:* 17 Ranelagh Grove, SW1W 8PA. *T:* (020) 7730 2799. *Club:* Garrick.

**GUEST, Christopher;** see Haden-Guest, 5th Baron.

**GUEST, Claire Marie;** Co-Founder, Chief Executive and Chief Scientific Officer, Medical Detection Dogs, since 2008; *b* Sedgley, 23 Jan. 1964; *d* of John and Maureen Guest. *Educ:* Aylesbury High Sch.; University Coll. Swansea (BSc Hons Psychol.); Univ. of Warwick (MSc Psychol. by res.; Dip. Human Psychol.). Dir, Ops and Res., Hearing Dogs for Deaf People, 1990–2007; Assistance Dog Behaviour Consultant, 2008–. Hon. DSc Bedford, 2011. British Citizen Award for Health, 2015; Award for Sci. and Technol., CBI, 2016. *Publications:* Daisy's Gift, 2016; contribs to scientific peer reviewed jls. *Recreations:* dogs, countryside. *Address:* Medical Detection Dogs, Unit 3 Millfield, Greenway Business Park, Great Horwood, Milton Keynes MK17 0NP. *T:* (01296) 655888. *E:* claire.guest@medicaldetectiondogs.org.uk.

**GUEST, Prof. John Rodney**, FRS 1986; Professor of Microbiology, Sheffield University, 1981–2000, now Emeritus; *b* 27 Dec. 1935; *s* of Sidney Ramsey Guest and Dorothy Kathleen Guest (*née* Walker); *m* 1962, Barbara Margaret (*née* Dearsley); one *s* two *d*. *Educ:* Campbell College, Belfast; Leeds Univ. (BSc); Trinity Coll., Oxford Univ. (DPhil). Guinness Fellow, Oxford, 1960–62, 1965; Fulbright Scholar and Research Associate, Stanford, 1963, 1964; Sheffield University: Lectr, Sen. Lectr, Reader in Microbiology, 1965–81. SERC Special Res. Fellow, 1981–86. Marjory Stephenson Prize Lectr, Soc. Gen. Microbiol., 1992; Leeuwenhoek Lectr, Royal Soc., 1995. *Publications:* contribs to Jl of Gen. Microbiol., Biochem. Jl, Microbiol., Molec. Microbiol. *Recreations:* walking, family history, natural history, gardening, orchids, bonsai, U3A, Probus. *Address:* Department of Molecular Biology and Biotechnology, Sheffield University, Western Bank, Sheffield S10 2TN. *T:* (0114) 222 2722.

**GUEST, Megan Michelle Elaine;** see Pullum, M. M. E.

**GUEST, Melville Richard John**, OBE 2007; Chief Executive, Asia House, 1996–2002; *b* 18 Nov. 1943; *s* of late Ernest Melville Charles Guest, DFC and Katherine Mary Guest; *m* 1970, Beatriz Eugenia, (Jenny), Lopez Colombres de Velasco; four *s*. *Educ:* Rugby Sch.; Magdalen Coll., Oxford (MA Jurisprudence). HM Diplomatic Service, 1966–96: Third, later Second, Sec., Tokyo, 1967–72; Pvte Sec. to Parly Under-Sec. of State, FCO, 1973–75; First Sec., Paris, 1975–79; FCO, 1979–80; Prés.-Dir Gén., Soc. Française des Industries Lucas, 1980–85; Dir, Thomson-Lucas SA, 1980–85; Director: Franco-British Chamber of Commerce, 1980–85; Channel Tunnel Gp, 1985–86; Counsellor (Commercial), Tokyo, 1986–89; Counsellor (Political) and Consul General, Stockholm, 1990–93; Head, S Pacific Dept, 1993–94, SE Asian Dept, 1994–96, FCO. Executive Director: UK-Korea Forum for the Future, 1998–2007; UK-Japan 21st Century Gp, 2001–08; Rapporteur, UK-India Round Table, 2000–08. Sen. Adviser, Imperial Coll. London, 2005–13. Mem., Bd of Govs, Ampleforth Coll., 1989–96. Japanese Foreign Minister's Award, 2009. *E:* melvilleguest@hotmail.com. *Clubs:* Hurlingham; Vincent's (Pres., 1965–66; Chm., Vincent's 150, 2011–17; Chm. Trustees, 2017–19).

**GUETERBOCK**, family name of **Baron Berkeley**.

**GUGGENHEIM, Her Honour Anna Maeve**; QC 2001; Advocate, Royal Court of Guernsey, since 2016; Partner, Babbé LLP, Guernsey, since 2016; *b* 2 Sept. 1959; *d* of late Peter Francis Guggenheim and Maura Teresa Guggenheim (*née* McCarthy); *m* 1987, Mark Eban; one *s* one *d*. *Educ:* King Edward VI High Sch. for Girls, Edgbaston; Somerville Coll., Oxford (BA Juris. 1981). Called to the Bar, Gray's Inn, 1982; barrister, 1982–2005; a Recorder, 2002–05; a Circuit Judge, 2006–14. *Recreation:* sailing.

**GUILD, Lorna Allison;** see Drummond, L. A.

**GUILD, Rear-Adm. Nigel Charles Forbes**, CB 2003; PhD; FIET, FIMarEST, FREng, FIMA, FCGI; Chief Naval Engineer Officer, and Senior Responsible Owner (Carrier Strike), Ministry of Defence, 2003–08; *b* 9 Feb. 1949; *s* of Surg. Capt. William John Forbes Guild and Joan Elizabeth Guild (*née* Innes); *m* 1971, Felicity Jean Wilson; two *s*. *Educ:* Fernden Sch.; Bryanston Sch.; BRNC Dartmouth; Trinity Coll., Cambridge (BA); Univ. of Bristol (PhD 1979). MIEE 1980; MIMA 1980; FIMarEST 2001; FIET (FIEE 2002);

FREng 2007; FIMA 2008. Joined Royal Navy, 1966; HMS Hermes, 1972–75; Weapons Trials, 1976–78; British Underwater Test and Evaluation Centre Project, 1979–82; HMS Euryalus, 1982–84 and 1986–87; Future Projects (Naval), 1984–85; HMS Beaver, 1987–88; Staff Weapons Engr Officer to FO Sea Trng, 1988–90; MA to Chief of Defence Procurement, 1991–92; CSO (E) Surface Flotilla, 1993–95; Project Dir, PE, MoD, 1996–99; Controller of the Navy, and Exec. Dir 4, Defence Procurement Agency, MoD, 2000–03. Chm., Atlas Elektronik UK Ltd, 2009–. Chm., Engrg Council, 2011–17. FCGI 2010. Hon. DEng Bristol, 2006. *Publications:* contrib. papers on Fuzzy Logic. *Recreations:* rowing, village pantomime, steam boating. *Address:* 20 Church Street, Modbury, Devon PL21 0QR. *E:* nigel.guild@btinternet.com. *Club:* Leander (Henley on Thames).

**GUILDFORD, Bishop of,** since 2014; **Rt Rev. Andrew John Watson;** *b* Bicester, 16 July 1961; *s* of Angus Watson and Alison Watson; *m* 1986, Beverly Anne Woolcock; two *s* two *d*. *Educ:* MA Cantab 1990. Ordained deacon, 1987, priest, 1988; Curate, St Peter's, Ipsley, Redditch, 1987–91; Curate, subseq. Associate Vicar, St John's & St Peter's, Notting Hill, 1991–96; Vicar, St Stephen's, E Twickenham, 1996–2008; Area Dean of Hampton, 2003–08; Bishop Suffragan of Aston, 2008–14. *Publications:* The Fourfold Leadership of Jesus, 2008; Confidence in the Living God, 2009; The Way of the Desert, 2011; The Great Vocations Conversation, 2018. *Recreations:* piano, bassoon, singing, composing, cliff-walking, photography. *Address:* Willow Grange, Woking Road, Guildford, Surrey GU4 7QS. *T:* (01483) 590500. *E:* bishop.andrew@cofeguildford.org.uk.

**GUILDFORD, Dean of;** *see* Gwilliams, Very Rev. D. L.

**GUILFORD, 10th Earl of,** *cr* 1752; **Piers Edward Brownlow North;** Baron Guilford 1683; *b* 9 March 1971; *s* of 9th Earl of Guilford and Osyth Vere Napier, *d* of Cyril Napier Leeston Smith; *S* father, 1999; *m* 1994, Michèle Desvaux de Marigny; one *s* one *d*. *Heir: s* Lord North, *qv*. *Address:* Waldershare Park, Dover, Kent CT15 5BA. *T:* (01304) 820245.

**GUILFOYLE, Hon. Dame Margaret (Georgina Constance),** AC 2005; DBE 1980; Chair, Judicial Remuneration Tribunal, 1995–2001; Deputy Chair, Infertility Authority, 1995–2001; *b* 15 May 1926; *d* of William and Elizabeth McCartney; *m* 1952, Stanley M. L. Guilfoyle; one *s* two *d*. *Educ:* ANU (LLB 1990). FCIS; FCPA. Senator for Victoria, 1971–87; Minister: for Education, Commonwealth of Australia, 1975; for Social Security, 1975–80; for Finance, 1980–83. Dep. Chm., Mental Health Res. Inst., 1988–2001; Dir, Aust. Children's TV Foundn, 1989–2002 (Dep. Chm., 1989–2002). Mem., Infertility Treatment Authy, 1996–2003. *Recreations:* reading, gardening. *Address:* 34/2 Malmsbury Street, Kew, Vic 3101, Australia. *Club:* Lyceum (Melbourne).

**GUILLAUME, Gilbert Pierre;** Judge, International Court of Justice, 1987–2005 (President, 2000–03), now Judge *ad hoc*; *b* 4 Dec. 1930; *s* of Pierre Guillaume and Berthe (*née* Brun); *m* 1961, Marie-Anne Hidden; one *s* two *d*. *Educ:* Univ. of Paris (LLM Law and Econ.); Inst. of Political Scis, Paris (Dip.); Ecole Nat. d'Admin. Mem., Council of State, France, 1957–96; Legal Advr, Secretariat for Civil Aviation, France, 1968–79; Director of Legal Affairs: OECD, 1978–79; Ministry of Foreign Affairs, France, 1979–87. Mem., Permanent Court of Arbitration. Mem., Institut de France, 2007 (Pres., 2016). Grand Croix de la Légion d'Honneur (France) 2016. *Publications:* Terrorisme et Droit International, 1989; Les grandes crises internationales et le droit, 1994; La Cour Internationale de Justice à l'Aube du XXIᵉ Siècle, 2003; La vie internationale et le droit, 2017. *Address:* 36 rue Perronet, 92200 Neuilly-sur-Seine, France. *E:* g.ma.guillaume@orange.fr.

**GUILLE, Very Rev. John Arthur;** Dean of Southwell, 2007–14, now Dean Emeritus; *b* 21 May 1949; *s* of Arthur Leonard Guille and Winifred Maud Guille (*née* Lane); *m* 1976, Susan Stallard; one *s* two *d*. *Educ:* Guernsey GS for Boys; Christ Church Coll., Canterbury (CertEd London 1970); Salisbury and Wells Theol Coll.; BTh Southampton 1979; Univ. of Wales, Lampeter (MA 2008). Teacher of Religious Studies: Stockbridge Co. Secondary Sch., 1970–72; St Sampson's Secondary Sch., 1972–73; ordained deacon 1976, priest 1977; Curate, Chandler's Ford, 1976–80; Priest i/c, St John, Surrey Road, Bournemouth, 1980–84, Vicar, St John with St Michael, 1984–89; Rector, St André de la Pommeraye, Guernsey, 1989–99; Vice Dean, Guernsey, 1996–99; Archdeacon of Basingstoke, 1999–2000; Canon Residentiary, Winchester Cathedral, 1999–2007; Archdeacon of Winchester, 2000–07. *Publications:* A Millennium of Archdeacons, 2003. *Recreations:* walking, gardening, family history.

**GUILLEBAUD, Rev. (Jette) Margaret;** Associate Chaplain, Sarum College, 2010–13; Chaplain, Church House, Salisbury, since 2011; *b* 24 March 1948; *d* of Justin Brooke and Kirsten (*née* Møller-Larsen); *m* 1st, 1971, Robin Simon, *qv* (marr. diss. 1978); one *s* one *d*; 2nd, 1984, Hugh Guillebaud (*d* 2017). *Educ:* Wycombe Abbey Sch. (Head Girl); Exeter Univ. (BA Hons Eng.); Ripon Coll., Cuddesdon (BTh). Tutor, Oxford Sch. of English, Verona, Italy, 1971–72; Examr, Oxford Exams Bd, 1972–75; Tutor, Open Univ., 1973–75; Man. Dir, Jobline Employment Agency, 1989–91; Chairman: SW Arts, 1991–97; English Regl Arts Bds, 1993–94; Mem., Arts Council of England, 1994–97. Ordained deacon, 2005, priest, 2006. Curate, later Cathedral Asst Priest, Salisbury Cath., 2005–10. Chm., Glos Ambulance NHS Trust, 1991–93. Non-executive Director: Cheltenham Festivals Ltd, 1991–96; at Bristol (formerly Bristol 2000), 1995–2001; Harbourside Centre, Bristol, 1995–2000; South West Film Commn, 1997–2002. Mem. Bd, Salisbury Internat. Arts Festival, 2006–15. Trustee, Holburne Mus., Bath, 1997–2002. Governor: Bath Spa UC (formerly Bath Coll. of Higher Educn), 1996–98; Wyvern Coll., 2007–11; Sarum Acad., Salisbury, 2011–. Mem., Univ. of Gloucestershire Develt Adv. Bd, 2001–03. JP S Glos, 1988–98. FRSA 1992. Hon. MA UWE, 1998. *Recreations:* opera, theatre, visual arts, fishing, travel. *Address:* 178 The Close, Salisbury SP1 2EZ. *Club:* Nikæan.

**GUILLEM, Sylvie,** Hon. CBE 2003; ballet dancer; *b* Paris, 23 Feb. 1965. *Educ:* Ecole de Danse, Paris Opera. With Paris Opera, 1981–89, Etoile, 1984; with Royal Ballet Co., 1989–2006; guest artist with other cos, 1989–2015. Lead roles in: Giselle; Swan Lake; La Bayadère; Cinderella; Sleeping Beauty; Romeo and Juliet; Raymonda; Manon; Don Quixote; Marguerite and Armand; Lilac Garden; Carmen; Winter Dreams. Title role created for her in Sissi, Rudra Béjart Co.; other created roles in: In the Middle, somewhat Elevated; Le Martyre de Saint-Sebastien; Firstext; Rearray, Bye, 2011. Prod Giselle for Nat. Ballet of Finland, 1999, for La Scala, Milan, 2001. Comdr des Arts et des Lettres (France), 1988; Chevalier de la Légion d'Honneur (France), 1994; Officier de l'Ordre du Mérite (France), 1999.

**GUILLEMIN, Prof. Roger Charles Louis,** MD, PhD; Distinguished Professor, Salk Institute, La Jolla, since 1997 (Interim President, 2007–09); *b* Dijon, France, 11 Jan. 1924; (naturalized US Citizen, 1963); *s* of Raymond Guillemin and Blanche (*née* Rigollot); *m* 1952, Lucienne Jeanne Billard; one *s* five *d*. *Educ:* Univ. of Dijon (BA 1941, BSc 1942); Faculty of Medicine, Lyons (MD 1949); Univ. of Montreal (PhD 1953). Resident Intern, univ. hosps, Dijon, 1949–51; Associate Dir, then Asst Prof., Inst. of Exper. Medicine and Surgery, Univ. of Montreal, 1951–53; Prof. of Physiol. and Dir, Labs for Neuroendocrinology, Baylor Coll. of Med., Houston, 1953–70; Associate Dir, Dept of Exper. Endocrinol., Coll. de France, Paris, 1960–63; Resident Fellow and Res. Prof., and Chm., Labs for Neuroendocrinology, Salk Inst. for Biol Studies, 1970–89; Dist. Prof., Whittier Inst. for Diabetes and Endocrinology, La Jolla, 1989–94 (Dir, 1993–94). Adjunct Professor: of Physiol., Baylor Coll. of Med., 1970–; of Medicine, UCSD, 1970–94. Member: Nat. Acad. of Sciences, USA, 1974; Amer. Acad. Arts and Scis, 1976; Amer. Physiol Soc.; Endocrine Soc. (Pres., 1986); Soc. of Exptl Biol. and Medicine; Internat. Brain Res. Orgn; Internat. Soc. Res. Biol Reprodn. Foreign Associate: Acad. des Sciences, France; Acad. Nat. de Médecine, Paris; Hon. Mem., Swedish Soc. of Med. Scis; Foreign Mem., Acad. Royale de Médecine de Belgique. Mem. Club of Rome. Hon. DSc: Rochester, NY, 1976; Chicago, 1977; Manitoba, 1984; Kyung Hee Univ., Seoul, Korea, 1986; Univ. de Paris VII, 1986; Madrid, 1988; Univ. Claude Bernard, Lyon, 1989; Laval Univ., Quebec, 1990; Sherbrooke Univ., Quebec, 1997; Hon. MD: Ulm, 1978; Montreal, 1979; Univ. Libre de Bruxelles, Belgium, 1979; Turin, 1985; Barcelona, 1988; Univ. Claude Bernard, Lyon I, 1989; Laval Univ., Quebec, 1996; Hon. LMed Baylor Coll. of Med., 1978. Gairdner Internat. Award, 1974; Lasker Award, USA, 1975; Dickson Prize in Medicine, Univ. of Pittsburgh, 1976; Passano Award in Med. Sci., Passano Foundn, Inc., 1976; Schmitt Medal in Neuroscience, Neurosciences Res. Prog., MIT, 1977; National Medal of Science, USA, 1977; (jtly) Nobel Prize in Physiology or Medicine, 1977; Barren Gold Medal, USA, 1979; Dale Medal (Soc. for Endocrinology), UK, 1980; Ellen Browning Scripps Soc. Medal, Scripps Meml Hosps Foundn, San Diego, 1988; Dist. Scientist Award, Nat. Diabetes Res. Coalition, 1996. Officier, Légion d'Honneur, France, 1984. *Publications:* scientific pubns in learned jls. *Recreation:* computer art (one-man shows, Milan, 1991, Houston, 1996, Paris, 1999; jtly with sculptures by son François, Athenaeum, La Jolla, Calif, 2012). *Address:* The Salk Institute, 10010 N Torrey Pines Road, La Jolla, CA 92037–1099, USA.

**GUILLOU, Prof. Pierre John,** MD; FRCS, FMedSci; Yorkshire landscape artist; Professor of Surgery, St James's University Hospital, Leeds, 1993–2007, now Emeritus; Dean of the School of Medicine, University of Leeds, 1998–2002; *b* 30 Oct. 1945; *s* of Sarah Anne Guillou (*née* Greenfield) and Yves Guillou; *m* 1998, Patricia Katherine Ollerenshawe; one *s* one *d* from previous marriage. *Educ:* Normanton Grammar Sch.; Univ. of Leeds (BSc; MB ChB 1970; MD 1975). Leeds Gen. Infirmary and St James's Univ. Hosp., 1970–73; S Manchester Univ. Hosp., 1973–74; Surgical Registrar, Leeds Gen. Infirmary, 1974–76; Lectr in Surgery, Univ. of Leeds, 1976–79; MRC Fellow in Immunology, Hôpital Necker, Paris, 1979–80; Sen. Lectr in Surgery, Univ. of Leeds, 1980–88; Prof. of Surgery, Imperial Coll. of Sci., Technology and Medicine and Dir, Academic Surgical Unit, St Mary's Hosp., London, 1988–93. Visiting Professor: Aust. Surgical Res. Soc., 1989, 1992; Univ. of Richmond, Va, 1992; S African Surgical Res. Soc., 1993; Ethicon, Malaysia, 1995; Sir Arthur Sims Commonwealth Prof., 1996; Lectures: Crookshank, Royal Soc. of Radiologists, 1990; Smith, Univ. of WA, 1991; A. B. Mitchell, QUB, 1991; jt meeting of Royal Colls of Surgeons of India and Glasgow, Madras, 1992; G. B. Ong, also Wilson T. S. Wang Internat. Surgical Symposium on Surgical Oncology, Chinese Univ. of Hong Kong, 1992, 1994; Annual Scientific Meeting of the Royal Coll. of Surgeons of Thailand, 1993; Stanford Cade, RCS, 1994; Marjorie Budd, Univ. of Bristol, 1995; 12th Asia Pacific Cancer Conf., Singapore, 1995. Member: James IV Assoc. of Surgeons, 1992–; Eur. Surgical Assoc., 1994–. Founder FMedSci 1998. Ed., British Jl of Surgery, 1994–2003; Ed.-in-Chief, Internat. Jl of Med. Robotics and Computer-Assisted Surgery, 2003–06. *Publications:* (ed) Surgical Oncology, 1991; Clinical Surgery, 1992; numerous papers on immunology, cell biology and laparoscopic colorectal surgery in treatment of cancer. *Recreations:* fishing, semi-professional artist (oils and watercolours). *Club:* Royal Society of Medicine.

**GUINERY, Paul Trevor;** musician; broadcaster; *b* 19 Jan. 1957; *s* of Dennis William Prickett and Eileen Grace Guinery. *Educ:* St Paul's Sch.; Royal Coll. of Music (ARCM 1975); Queen's Coll., Oxford (BA 1979). Joined BBC, 1980: studio manager, 1980–85; announcer and newsreader: World Service, 1985–89; Radio 3, 1989–2002; Presenter: Your Concert Choice, 1990–92; Concert Hall, 1992–98; Sacred and Profane, 1993–98; Choral Voices, 1998; Sounding the Millennium, 1999; Choirworks, 1999–2003. Vice-Chm., Delius Soc., 2001–03; Music Advr, 2015–, Chm., 2018–, Delius Trust. *Publications:* Delius and Fenby (with Lyndon Jenkins), 2004; (with Martin Lee-Browne) Delius and his Music, 2014; articles in Delius Soc. Jl. *Recreations:* playing the piano, theatre, collecting sheet music. *Address:* 68 Cambridge Street, SW1V 4QQ.

**GUINNESS,** family name of **Earl of Iveagh** and **Baron Moyne**.

**GUINNESS, Bunny;** landscape architect, journalist and broadcaster; Director, Bunny Guinness Landscape Design Ltd, since 1986; *b* Marlborough, 16 Dec. 1955; *d* of late Sqdn Ldr Peter William Ellis, DFC and Barbara Helen Stockitt (*née* Austin); *m* 1976, Kevin Michael Rundell Guinness; one *s* one *d*. *Educ:* Bath High Sch.; Reading Univ. (BSc Hons Horticulture 1977); Birmingham City Univ. (Dip. Landscape Arch. 1981). Assistant landscape architect: Maurice Pickering Associates, 1978–80; Wimpey Gp Services, 1980–82; landscape architect, Lewisham BC, 1982–84; Regl Landscape Architect, McCarthy & Stone plc, 1984–86. Garden designer, Horatio's Garden, Midland Centre for Spinal Injuries, Robert Jones and Agnes Hunt Orthopaedic Hosp., Oswestry, 2019. Panellist, Gardeners' Question Time, BBC Radio 4, 1999–; presenter and/or contributor to TV progs, incl. Guinness in the Garden, Better Gardens, Small Town Gardens, Great Garden Challenge; (presenter) Capability Brown's Unfinished Garden, BBC4, 2016–17; gardening columnist, Saturday and Sunday Telegraph, 2003–. DUniv Birmingham City, 2009. Gold Medals, Chelsea Flower Show, 1994, 1995, 1996, 1998, 1999, 2001; Garden Writer of the Year, LSL Property Press Awards, 2014, 2015. *Publications:* Creating a Family Garden, 1996, 4th edn as Family Gardens, 2008; Garden Transformations, 1999, 2nd edn 2002; Garden Workshop, 2001; Decorative Gardening with Bunny Guinness, 2005; (with J. Knox) Garden Your Way to Health and Fitness, 2008; (with HRH the Prince of Wales) Highgrove: a garden celebrated, 2014. *Recreations:* family, including Jack Russells, extreme gardening, self sufficiency including growing, breeding and eating my own livestock and veg, cooking. *Address:* Sibberton Lodge, Thornhaugh, Peterborough, Cambs PE8 6NH. *E:* bunnyguinness@btconnect.com. *W:* www.bunnyguinness.com.

**GUINNESS, Hon. Desmond (Walter);** writer; *b* 8 Sept. 1931; *yr s* of 2nd Baron Moyne and Hon. Diana Mitford (later Hon. Lady Mosley) (*d* 2003); *m* 1st, 1954, Marie-Gabrielle von Urach (marr. diss. 1981; she *d* 1989); one *s* one *d*; 2nd, Penelope, *d* of late Graham and Teresa Cuthbertson. *Educ:* Gordonstoun; Christ Church, Oxford (MA). Founder, 1958, and Chm., 1958–91, Irish Georgian Society to work for the study of, and protection of, buildings of architectural merit in Ireland, particularly of the Georgian period. Mem., Friendly Brothers of St Patrick, 1973–. Hon. LLD TCD, 1980. *Publications:* Portrait of Dublin, 1967; Irish Houses and Castles, 1971; Mr Jefferson, Architect, 1973; Palladio, 1976; Georgian Dublin, 1980; The White House: an architectural history, 1981; Newport Preserv'd, 1982; (with Jacqueline O'Brien) Great Irish Houses and Castles, 1992; (with Jacqueline O'Brien) Dublin: a Grand Tour, 1994. *Clubs:* Chelsea Arts; Kildare Street and University, Royal Irish Automobile.

**GUINNESS, Sir John (Ralph Sidney),** Kt 1999; CB 1985; FSA; Chairman, Trinity Group Finance Ltd, 1999–2003; *b* 23 Dec. 1935; *s* of late Edward Douglas Guinness, CBE and Martha Letière (*née* Sheldon); *m* 1967, Valerie Susan North (*d* 2014); one *s* one *d* (and one *s* decd). *Educ:* Rugby Sch.; Trinity Hall, Cambridge (BA Hons History, MA Hons). Union Discount Co. Ltd, 1960–61; Overseas Develt Inst., 1961–62; joined FO, 1962;

Econ. Relations Dept, 1962–63; Third Sec., UK Mission to UN, New York, 1963–64; seconded to UN Secretariat as Special Asst to Dep. Under-Sec. and later Under-Sec. for Econ. and Social Affairs, 1964–66; FCO, 1967–69; First Sec. (Econ.), Brit. High Commn, Ottawa, 1969–72; seconded to Central Policy Rev. Staff, Cabinet Office, 1972–75; Counsellor, 1974; Alternate UK Rep. to Law of the Sea Conf., 1975–77; seconded to CPRS, 1977–79; transferred to Home Civil Service, 1980; Under-Sec., 1980–83, Dep. Sec., 1983–91, Permanent Sec., 1991–92, Dept of Energy. Chm., British Nuclear Fuels, 1992–99; Director: Guinness Mahon Hldgs, 1993–99; Ocean Gp, 1993–2000; Mithras Investment Trust, 1994–2006. Governor, Oxford Energy Inst., 1984–92. Chairman: Reviewing Cttee on Export of Works of Art, 1995–2004; Expert Panel, Heritage Lottery Fund, 2005; Expert Panel, NHMF, 2006–13. Member: E Anglia Regl Cttee, NT, 1989–94; Develt Cttee, Nat. Portrait Gall., 1994–99; Council, BITC, 1992–99; Pres. Cttee, CBI, 1997–99 (Mem. Council, 1993–97); Dir, UK-Japan 2000 Gp, 1995–99. Mem., Adv. Council, Business Div., Prince's Trust, 1999–; Trustee: Prince's Youth Business Trust, 1992–99; Royal Collection Trust, 2001–07; Nat. Maritime Mus., 2005–13; Heritage Conservation Trust, 2006–; Gov., Compton Verney House Trust, 2000–03; Mem., Eton Collections Cttee, 2009–16. Hon. Freeman, Co. of Fuellers, 1999. FSA 2005. Hon. Fellow: Mgt Sch., Lancaster Univ., 1997; Univ. of Central Lancashire, 1998. *Recreation:* iconography. *Clubs:* Brooks's, Beefsteak.

**GUINNESS, Sir Kenelm (Edward Lee)**, 5th Bt *cr* 1867, of Ashford, co. Galway; commercial pilot; *b* Washington, DC, USA, 30 Jan. 1962; *er s* of Sir Kenelm Ernest Lee Guinness, 4th Bt and of Jane Nevin Guinness (*née* Dickson); *S* father, 2011; *m* 2001, Melissa Ann Wheeley; one *s* one *d*. *Educ:* Maret Sch., Washington, DC; Embry-Riddle Aeronautical Univ., USA (BSc). Founder/operator, Bay Seaplane Service, 1988; chief pilot, Safari Air, 1999–2011. *Recreation:* yacht racing. *Heir: s* Kenelm Arthur Lee Guinness, *b* 15 Nov. 2005. *Address:* General Delivery, Hope Town, Elbow Cay, Bahamas. *T:* 6993109. *Clubs:* Cruising Club of America; Quiet Birdmen.

**GUINNESS, William Loel Seymour**; Chairman, Sibir Energy Plc, 1999–2009; *b* 28 Dec. 1939; *s* of Thomas Loel Evelyn Guinness, OBE and Lady Isabel Guinness (*née* Manners, later Throckmorton), *d* of 9th Duke of Rutland; *m* 1st, 1971, Elizabeth Lynn Day (marr. diss. 1994); two *s* one *d*; 2nd, 2003, Lucia Gomez de Parada. *Educ:* Ludgrove; Eton. Lt Irish Guards, 1959–61. Non-exec. Dir, Henry Ansbacher, 1983–93, and other cos. Mem. (C), Daventry DC, 1976–83 (Leader, 1977–83). *Recreations:* golf, photography, gardening, travelling. *Address:* Zanroc, Chemin de Ballegue 58, 1066 Epalinges, Switzerland. *T:* (21) 7843427, *Fax:* (21) 7843565. *E:* bguinness@mac.com; Bosque de Cafetos 102, Mexico City, 11700 DF, Mexico. *T:* (55) 55960108. *Clubs:* White's, Pratt's; Swinley Forest Golf; Royal West Norfolk Golf (Brancaster); Golf de Lausanne; Corviglia (St Moritz); Club de Golf Chapultepec (Mexico City).

**GUISE, Sir (Christopher) James**, 8th Bt *cr* 1783, of Highnam Court, Glos; *b* 10 July 1930; *s* of Sir Anselm William Edward Guise, 6th Bt and Nina Margaret Sophie, *d* of Sir James Augustus Grant, 1st Bt; *S* brother, 2007; *m* 1969, Mrs Carole Hoskins Benson (*née* Master); one *s* one *d*. *Educ:* Wellesley House; Stowe. Business and banking career in London and S Africa; now retired company Dir. *Recreations:* fishing, shooting, gardening. *Heir: s* Anselm Mark Guise [*b* 7 Feb. 1971; *m* (marr. diss.); *m* 2010, Sarah Whewell; one *s* one *d*]. *Address:* Weir Farm, Elmore, Glos GL2 3NS. *E:* guises@me.com. *Clubs:* Turf, Beefsteak, MCC.

**GUIVER, Rev. Fr George Paul Alfred**, CR; Superior, Community of the Resurrection, 2003–18; *b* 18 Dec. 1945; *s* of Alfred and Doris Guiver. *Educ:* St Chad's Coll., Durham (BA 1968); Cuddesdon Coll., Oxford (Cert. in Theology 1973). Ordained deacon 1973, priest 1974; Curate, Mill End and Heronsgate with West Hyde, St Albans, 1973–76; Priest-in-charge, Bishop's Frome, Castle Frome, Acton Beauchamp and Evesbatch, Hereford, 1976–82; Community of the Resurrection, 1983–; Vice-Principal, Coll. of the Resurrection, 1990–2002. Hon. Lectr, Leeds Univ., 1990–. *Publications:* Company of Voices: daily prayer and the people of God, 1988; Faith in Momentum: the distinctiveness of the church, 1990; (ed) The Fire and the Clay: the priest in today's church, 1993; Everyday God, 1994; Pursuing the Mystery: worship and daily life as presences of God, 1996; (ed) Priests in a People's Church, 2001; Vision Upon Vision: processes of change and renewal in Christian worship, 2009. *Recreations:* cycling and recycling. *Address:* Community of the Resurrection, Mirfield, W Yorks WF14 0BN. *T:* (01924) 483301, *Fax:* (01924) 490489. *E:* GGuiver@mirfield.org.uk.

**GULL, Prof. Keith**, CBE 2004; PhD; FRS 2003; Professor of Molecular Microbiology, University of Oxford, since 2002; Principal, St Edmund Hall, Oxford, 2009–18; *b* 29 May 1948; *s* of David Gull and Doris Gull (*née* Manging); *m* 1972, Dianne Hilary Leonora Elgar; one *s* one *d*. *Educ:* Queen Elizabeth Coll., Univ. of London (BSc Hons 1969, PhD 1972, Microbiology). University of Kent: Lectr, 1972–82; Sen. Lectr, 1982–84; Reader, 1984–86; Prof. of Cell Biology, 1986–89; Prof. of Molecular Biology, Univ. of Manchester, 1989–2002; Wellcome Trust Principal Res. Fellow, Univ. of Oxford, 2002–09; Sen. Res. Fellow, Lincoln Coll., Oxford, 2002–09. Vis. Sen. Scientist, Sandoz Inst., Vienna, 1978; Vis. Prof., McArdle Lab. for Cancer Res., Univ. of Wisconsin, 1982. Darwin Lectr, BAAS, 1983; Marjory Stephenson Lectr, Soc. for Gen. Microbiology, 1996. Mem., EMBO, 2010. FMedSci 1999; FRSB (FSB 2010). Biochemical Soc. Medal, 2017. *Publications:* numerous contribs to books and scientific jls. *Recreations:* fly fishing, painting. *Address:* Sir William Dunn School of Pathology, University of Oxford, South Parks Road, Oxford OX1 3RE. *T:* (01865) 285455. *E:* keith.gull@path.ox.ac.uk.

**GULL, Sir Rupert (William Cameron)**, 5th Bt *cr* 1872, of Brook Street; company director; *b* 14 July 1954; *s* of Sir Michael Swinnerton Cameron Gull, 4th Bt and Yvonne (*d* 1975), *o d* of Dr Albert Oliver Macarius Heslop, Cape Town; *S* father, 1989; *m* 1980, Gillian Lee, *d* of Robert MacFarlane; three *d*. *Educ:* Diocesan Coll., Cape Town; Cape Town Univ. *Heir:* cousin Angus William John Gull [*b* 24 Dec. 1963; *m* 1988, Jacqueline Mary, *d* of Gerald Edgar Ford; one *s* two *d* (of whom one *s* one *d* are twins)]. *Address:* 2 Harcourt Road, Claremont, Cape Town, South Africa.

**GULLAND**; *see* Milner-Gulland.

**GULLICK, His Honour Stephen John**; a Circuit Judge, 1998–2015; *b* 22 Feb. 1948; *s* of late David and Evelyn Gullick; *m* 1973, Lesley Steadman; two *s*. *Educ:* Taunton Sch.; Birmingham Univ. (LLB 1970). Called to the Bar, Gray's Inn, 1971; in practice at the Bar, 1971–98; a Recorder, 1990–98; Standing Counsel, NE Circuit, HM Customs and Excise, 1991–98; Resident Judge, Bradford Crown Court, 2001–09. Hon. Recorder, Bradford, 2002–09. *Recreations:* campanology, watching sport.

**GULLIFER, Prof. Louise Joan**, FBA 2019; Rouse Ball Professor of English Law, University of Cambridge, since 2019; Fellow of Gonville and Caius College, Cambridge, since 2019; *b* London, 8 Oct. 1960; *d* of Ralph Edwards and Joan Edwards; *m* 1987, Robert Gullifer; two *d*. *Educ:* Brighton and Hove High Sch.; Univ. of Oxford (BCL; MA). Called to the Bar, Gray's Inn, 1984; Bencher, 2013; barrister, 3 Gray's Inn Place, 1985–90; University of Oxford: Fellow in Commercial Law, Brasenose Coll., 1994–97; Fellow and Tutor in Law, Harris Manchester Coll., 1999–2019; Reader in Commercial Law, 2008–11; Prof. of Commercial Law, 2011–19. Vis. Prof. of Internat. Commercial Law, Radboud Univ., Nijmegen, 2017–20. Mem., Council, Malvern Coll., 2002–17. Hon. QC 2018. *Publications:* (jtly) The Law of Personal Property Security, 2006, 3rd edn as The Law of Security and Title-Based Financing, 2018; (ed) Goode on Legal Problems of Credit and Security, 4th edn 2008 to 6th edn, as Goode and Gullifer on Legal Problems of Credit and Security, 2017; (with J. Payne) Corporate Finance Law, 2008, 2nd edn 2015; (jtly) The Law of Personal Property, 2013; (ed jtly) Intermediation and Beyond, 2019; (with M. Dubovec) Secured Transaction Law Reform in Africa 2019. *Recreations:* music, long distance train travel, detective fiction. *Address:* Gonville and Caius College, Trinity Street, Cambridge CB2 1TA.

**GULLIFORD, Rev. Canon William Douglas FitzGerald**; Vicar, St Mark's, Regent's Park, since 2012; *b* 23 Sept. 1969; *s* of late Maurice Nicholas Gulliford and of Caroline Mary Louise Gulliford; *m* 1993, Béatrice Priscilla Marie Rambaud; three *d* (one *s* decd). *Educ:* Taunton Sch.; Richard Huish Coll., Taunton; Selwyn Coll., Cambridge (BA 1991; MA 1995); Westcott House, Cambridge. Ordained deacon, 1994, priest, 1995; Asst Curate, All Saints', Banstead, 1994–97; Asst Priest, St Paul's, Knightsbridge, 1997–2000; Vicar, Guild Church of St Dunstan-in-the-West, 2000–12; Rector, St Mary le Strand with St Clement Danes, 2002–08. Dir of Ordinands, Dio. of Europe, 2003–; Canon of Gibraltar, 2012–. Chaplain: GSMD, 1997–2001; to Bishop of London, 2000–02; Courtauld Inst. of Art, 2003–08; to Master Draper, Lady Victoria Leatham, 2012–13. Gen. Sec., Anglican & Eastern Churches Assoc., 2000–04. Hon. Chaplain to: Aldermanic Sheriff of London, 2005–06; Lord Mayor of London, 2006–07. Freedom, City of London, 2001. *Recreations:* domestic ecumenism, theatre, other people's gardening. *Address:* St Mark's Vicarage, 4 Regent's Park Road, NW1 7TX. *T:* and *Fax:* (020) 7485 6340. *E:* william.gulliford@london.anglican.org.

**GULLY**, family name of **Viscount Selby**.

**GUMBEL, Elizabeth-Anne, (Mrs Michael Wainwright)**; QC 1999; *d* of Walter and Muriel Gumbel; *m* 1984, Michael Wainwright; one *s* one *d*. *Educ:* St Paul's Girls' Sch.; Wycombe Abbey Sch.; Lady Margaret Hall, Oxford (MA). Called to the Bar, Inner Temple, 1974, Bencher, 2002. *Address:* 1 Crown Office Row, EC4Y 7HH.
*See also* Rev. N. G. P. Gumbel.

**GUMBEL, Rev. Nicholas Glyn Paul**; Vicar, Holy Trinity, Brompton, since 2005; *b* 28 April 1955; *s* of Walter and Muriel Gumbel; *m* 1978, Philippa Hislop; two *s* one *d*. *Educ:* Trinity Coll., Cambridge (BA Law 1976); Wycliffe Hall, Oxford (MA Theol. 1986). Called to the Bar, Middle Temple, 1977; in practice as barrister, 1977–83; ordained deacon, 1986, priest, 1987; Curate, Holy Trinity, Brompton, 1986–2005. Pioneer of Alpha Course (a practical introduction to Christian faith, running in over 63,000 locations in 169 countries); Alpha Chaplain, 1996–2005. Vice Pres., Tearfund, 2008–. Hon. DPhil Glos, 2007. *Publications:* Questions of Life, 1993, 7th edn 2010; Searching Issues, 1994, 8th edn 2013; How to Run the Alpha Course: telling others, 1994, 5th edn as Telling Others, 2011; A Life Worth Living, 1994, 6th edn 2010; Challenging Lifestyle, 1996, 5th edn as The Jesus Lifestyle, 2010; The Heart of Revival, 1997; 30 Days, 1999, 4th edn 2008; The Da Vinci Code: a response, 2005, 2nd edn 2006; Wilberforce: the challenge for today, 2007; Is God a Delusion?, 2008. *Address:* Holy Trinity Brompton, Brompton Road, SW7 1JA.
*See also* E.-A. Gumbel.

**GUMENDE, António**; Ambassador and Permanent Representative of the Republic of Mozambique to the United Nations, since 2011; High Commissioner to Jamaica (non-resident), since 2014; *b* Capezulo, Maputo, 1 Jan. 1961; *s* of Solomone Gumende and Macumbine Tembe; *m* 1992, Simangaliso Gatsi; one *s* three *d*. *Educ:* Sch. of Journalism, Mozambique (Dip. Journalism 1984); Nottingham Trent Univ. (Postgrad. Dip. Mgt Studies 1998; MBA 1999); Open Univ. (Dip. Econs 2004); Birkbeck Coll., London (Postgrad. Cert. Econs 2005); Centre for Financial and Mgt Studies, Sch. of Oriental and African Studies, Univ. of London (MSc Financial Econs 2010). News writer, then reporter, later Business Ed., Mozambique News Agency, Maputo, 1984–90; Staff Writer, then Business Ed., Southern African Economist, Harare, 1990–96; Man. Ed., then Business Ed., Southern African Political Economy Series, SAPES Trust, Harare, 1996–97; Exec. Ed., Southern African Res. and Documentation Centre, Maputo, 1997–2002 (Exec. Ed., Nat. Human Develt Report for Mozambique, 1998, 1999, 2000, 2001); High Comr for Mozambique in UK, 2002–11. Chair, Bd of Govs, Commonwealth Secretariat, 2006–08. Chair: Portuguese Speaking Countries Gp of Ambassadors, NY, 2012–14; S African Develt Community Gp of Ambassadors, NY, 2012–13; African Leaders Malaria Alliance Gp of Ambassadors, NY, 2013–14. Vice Pres., Gen. Assembly, UN, 2015–16; Interim Chair, Candidatures Cttee, African Gp of States to UN, 2017–. Exec. Chm., 1995–97, 2002, Chm. AGM, 2002–16, Chair, Oversight Cttee, 2016–, MediaCoop Jornalistas Associados SCRL. Correspondent: Italian News Agency, 1988–90; Southern African Economist, 1988–90; Harare Correspondent: MediaFax, Savana Independent Weekly, Mozambique, 1993–97; Lusa News Agency, Portugal, 1993–97; A Bola newspaper, Portugal, 1994–97; Channel Africa Radio, Portuguese Service, 1994–97. *Recreations:* reading with particular interest in journalism, economics, finance, management, politics and international relations, watching movies and documentaries about nature and history. *Address:* c/o Mozambique Mission to the United Nations, 420 E 50th Street, New York, NY 10022, USA. *E:* agumende15@gmail.com, originarioag@gmail.com.

**GUMLEY-MASON, Frances Jane**, MA; broadcaster and journalist; Headmistress, St Augustine's Priory, Ealing, 1995–2011; *b* 28 Jan. 1955; *o d* of late Franc Stewart Gumley and Helen Teresa (*née* McNicholas); name changed to Gumley-Mason by statutory declaration, 1995; *m* 1988, Andrew Samuel Mason (now Gumley-Mason); one *s* one *d*. *Educ:* St Augustine's Priory, Ealing; Newnham Coll., Cambridge (MA). Parly research, 1974; Braille transcriber, 1975; Catholic Herald: Editorial Assistant and Assistant Literary Editor, Dec. 1975; Literary Editor and Staff Reporter, 1976–79; Editor, 1979–81; RC Asst to Head of Religious Broadcasting, and sen. producer, religious progs, radio, and producer, religious television, 1981–88; Series Editor, Religious Programmes, C4, 1988–89; guest producer, scriptwriter and presenter, BBC World Service and Radio 4, 1989–94. Mistress of The Keys, Guild of Catholic Writers, 1983–88. ACIEA 2008. *Publications:* (as F. J. Gumley, with Brian Redhead): The Good Book, 1987; The Christian Centuries, 1989; The Pillars of Islam, 1990; Protestors for Paradise, 1993; (jtly) Discovering Turkey, 1995. *Recreations:* playing with children's toys, being a background actor for film and television. *Address:* 2 Rathgar Avenue, Ealing, W13 9PL.

**GUMMER**, family name of **Barons Chadlington** and **Deben**.

**GUMMER, Rt Hon. Benedict Michael, (Rt Hon. Ben)**; PC 2016; *b* London, 19 Feb. 1978; *s* of Baron Deben, *qv*; *m* 2014, Sarah Margaret Langford; two *s*. *Educ:* St Saviour's C of E Prim. Sch.; St John's College Sch., Cambridge; Tonbridge Sch.; Peterhouse, Cambridge (MA Hons). Company Dir, 2001–10; writer. MP (C) Ipswich, 2010–17; contested (C) same seat, 2017. Parly Under-Sec. of State, DoH, 2015–16; Minister for the Cabinet Office and Paymaster Gen., 2016–17. Sen. Advr, McKinsey & Co., 2018–. Fellow, Blavatnik Sch. of Govt, Univ. of Oxford, 2018–. *Publications:* The Scourging Angel: the black death in the British Isles, 2009. *Recreations:* music, reading, architecture. *E:* ben@bengummer.com.

**GUMMETT, Prof. Philip John,** CBE 2013; PhD; higher education consultant, since 2012; Chief Executive, Higher Education Funding Council for Wales, 2004–12; *b* 26 Oct. 1947; *s* of Rev. Philip Charles Gummett and Morfydd Ioli Gummett (*née* Brown); *m* 1969, Karen Hope Thurgood; one *s* one *d*. *Educ:* Univ. of Birmingham (BSc); Univ. of Manchester (MSc; PhD). University of Manchester: Lectr in Sci. and Technol. Policy, 1974–81; Sen. Lectr, 1981–94; Prof. of Govt and Technol. Policy, 1994–2000; Pro-Vice-Chancellor, 1997–2000; Dir, PREST (Prog. of Policy Res. in Engrg, Sci. and Technol.), Manchester, 1997–2000; Dir of Higher Educn, HEFCW, 2000–04. Advr to UK and European Parlts and EC. Trustee, Jisc, 2013–19. *Publications:* Scientists in Whitehall, 1980; (ed with J. Reppy) The Relations Between Defence and Civil Technologies, 1988; (with W. Walker) Nationalism, Internationalism and the European Defence Market, 1993; (ed) Globalisation and Public Policy, 1996; (ed with R. Bud) Cold War Hot Science: applied research in Britain's defence laboratories 1945–1990, 1999. *Recreations:* reading, walking, cycling, music, grandchildren. *E:* phil@gummett.com.

**GUMMOW, Hon. William Montague Charles,** AC 1997; Non-Permanent Judge, Hong Kong Court of Final Appeal, since 2013; *b* 9 Oct. 1942; *s* of W. C. R. Gummow and A. C. Gummow (*née* Benson). *Educ:* Sydney Grammar Sch.; Univ. of Sydney (BA 1962; LLB 1965; LLM 1970). Admitted Solicitor, Supreme Court of NSW, 1966; Partner, Allen, Allen & Hemsley, 1969–76; admitted to NSW Bar, 1976; in practice at the Bar, 1976–86; QC (NSW) 1986; Judge, Federal Court of Australia, 1986–95; Justice, High Ct of Australia, 1995–2012. Clarendon Law Lectr, Oxford Univ., 1999; WA Lee Equity Lectr, Qld Univ. of Technol., 2002; Sir Maurice Byers Lectr, NSW Bar Assoc., 2005; Prof. of Law, Univ. of Sydney and ANU, 2013–. Mem., Amer. Law Inst., 1997. Hon. LLD Sydney, 1992. *Publications:* Jacobs' Law of Trusts in Australia, 3rd edn 1971 to 6th edn (jtly) 1997; Equity: doctrines and remedies, 1975, 3rd edn (jtly) 1992; Cases and Materials on Equity and Trusts, 1975, 4th edn 1993. *E:* wmcg1@bigpond.com.au. *Club:* Australian (Sydney).

**GUNATILLAKE, Rohan Mangala;** Head of Product, NDS, NHS Education for Scotland, since 2019; *b* Kingston-upon-Thames, 15 July 1980; *s* of K. Lakdasa Gunatillake and Daya Gunatillake; *m* 2013, Lucy Robinson; one *s* one *d*. *Educ:* King's Coll. Sch., Wimbledon; University Coll., Oxford (MChem 1st Cl.). Mgt Consultant, Accenture, 2003–08; Prog. Lead, Nesta, 2008–09; Ind. Innovation Producer, 2009–15; Creator, buddhify, 2011–. Trustee, British Council, 2013–19. *Publications:* 24 Hour Mindfulness, 2015; A Very Mindful Christmas, 2015; This is Happening: redesigning mindfulness for our very modern lives, 2016; Modern Mindfulness: how to be more relaxed, focused and kind while living in a fast, digital, always-on world, 2017. *Recreations:* cooking, campervans, video games, Buddhist meditation, parenting, sleep. *Address:* 7 Park Circus Lane, Glasgow G3 6BH. *E:* rohan.gunatillake@gmail.com.

**GUNAWARDENA, Jeremy Harin Charles,** PhD; Associate Professor of Systems Biology, since 2010, Harvard Medical School, since 2010 (Director, Virtual Cell Program, Department of Systems Biology, 2004); *b* 12 Nov. 1955; *s* of late Charles Gunawardena and of Yvonne Gunawardena (*née* Weerakoon). *Educ:* Imperial Coll., London (BSc); Trinity Coll., Cambridge (MA; PhD 1983). L. E. Dickson Instr, Dept of Mathematics, Univ. of Chicago, 1981–83; Res. Fellow in Mathematics, Trinity Coll., Cambridge, 1983–87; Hewlett-Packard Laboratories: Mem., Technical Staff, 1987–2001; Dir, Basic Res. Inst. in the Mathematical Scis, 1994–2001; Vis. Scientist and Hd of Systems Biol., Bauer Center for Genomics Res., Harvard Univ., 2002–04. Vis. Schol., Dept of Computer Sci., Stanford Univ., 1992–94; Vis. Res. Fellow, Trinity Coll., Cambridge, 1995; Prof. Invitée, Ecole Normale Supérieure, Paris, 2000. Mem., EPSRC, 1999–2002. *Publications:* (ed) Idempotency, 1998. *Recreations:* tennis, cricket, classical music, flying aeroplanes. *Address:* Department of Systems Biology, Harvard Medical School, 200 Longwood Avenue, Boston, MA 02115, USA. *T:* (617) 4324839.

**GUNEWARDENA, Desmond Anthony Lalith;** Chairman and Chief Executive, D&D London (formerly Conran Restaurants), since 2006; *b* Kandy, Sri Lanka, 11 Aug. 1957; *s* of Kingsley and Muriel Gunewardena; *m* 1991, Elisabeth Pask; one *s* one *d*. *Educ:* Wimbledon Coll.; Univ. of Bristol (BSc 1978). ACA 1981. Ernst & Young, 1978–84; Heron Internat., 1984–89; Chief Exec., Conran Hldgs, 1989–2006. Non-executive Director: Fitch plc, 1994–99; Individual Restaurant Co. plc, 2005–08; Conran, 2006–. Non-executive Director: London First, 2002–; Visit London, 2005–09. FRSA 2002. *Recreations:* tennis, skiing, chess. *Address:* D&D London, 16 Kirby Street, EC1N 8TS. *T:* (020) 7716 7800.

**GUNN, Prof. John Charles,** CBE 1994; MD; FMedSci, FRCPsych; Professor of Forensic Psychiatry, Institute of Psychiatry, 1978–2002, now Emeritus; *b* 6 June 1937; *s* of late Albert Charles Gunn and Lily Hilda Edwards; *m* 1st, 1959, Celia Willis (marr. diss. 1986, she *d* 1989); one *s* one *d*; 2nd, 1989, Pamela Jane Taylor, *qv*. *Educ:* Brighton, Hove and Sussex Grammar Sch.; Reigate Grammar Sch.; Birmingham Univ. (MB ChB 1961; Acad. DPM 1966; MD 1969). MRCPsych 1971, FRCPsych 1980, Hon. FRCPsych 2010. Queen Elizabeth Hosp., Birmingham, 1961–63; Maudsley Hosp., 1963–67; Institute of Psychiatry: Res. Worker, 1967–69; Lectr, 1969–71; Sen. Lectr, 1971–75; Dir, Special Hosps Res. Unit, 1975–78. H. B. Williams Vis. Prof. to Aust. and NZ, 1985. Advisor, H of C Select Cttees on Violence in Marriage, 1975, on Prison Med. Service, 1986; Member: Home Sec's Adv. Bd on Restricted Patients, 1982–91; Royal Commn on Criminal Justice, 1991–93; Parole Bd for England and Wales, 2006–15. WHO Specialist Advisor in Forensic Psychiatry to China, 1987; Consultant, Eur. Cttee for Prevention of Torture, 1993–; Co-organiser, Ghent Gp, 2004–. Royal College of Psychiatrists: Chm., Res. Cttee, 1976–80; Dep. Chief Examr, 1993–95; Mem., Council, 1977–83, 1997–2004; Mem., Ct of Electors, 1985–91, 1993–99, 2003–04; Mem., Exec. Cttee, 1998–2004; Chm., Faculty of Forensic Psychiatry, 2000–04. Chm., Crime in Mind, 2013–. Founder FMedSci 1998. Editor, Criminal Behaviour and Mental Health, 1991–. *Publications:* Epileptics in Prison, 1977; Psychiatric Aspects of Imprisonment, 1978; Current Research in Forensic Psychiatry and Psychology, vols 1–3, 1982–85; Violence in Human Society, 1983, 2nd edn 2013; (ed with P. J. Taylor) Forensic Psychiatry: clinical, legal and ethical issues, 1993, 2nd edn 2009; 118 peer reviewed papers. *Recreations:* theatre, opera, cinema, photography, walking, living with Pamela. *E:* johncgunn@gmail.com. *Clubs:* Athenæum, Royal Society of Medicine.

**GUNN, John Humphrey;** company director and venture capitalist; Chairman, Rotala plc, since 2005; *b* 15 Jan. 1942; *s* of Francis (Bob) Gunn and Doris Gunn; *m* 1965, Renate Sigrid (*née* Boehme); two *d* (and one *d* decd). *Educ:* Sir John Deane's Grammar School, Northwich; Univ. of Nottingham (BA Hons 1964). Barclays Bank, 1964–68; Astley & Pearce, 1968–85; Chief Executive: Exco International, 1979–85; British & Commonwealth Holdings, 1986–87 and 1990 (Chm., 1987–90). Dir, John Duncan & Co., 1992–2001; Chm., Wengen Ltd, 1994–. Hon. LLD Nottingham, 1989. *Recreations:* golf, ski-ing, mountain walking, classical music, opera. *Address:* Rotala plc, Cross Quays Business Park, Hallbridge Way, Tividale, Oldbury B69 3HW. *T:* (0121) 322 2222. *Clubs:* MCC; Downhill Only (Wengen).

**GUNN, Prof. Michael John;** Vice Chancellor and Chief Executive, Staffordshire University, 2011–16; *b* Wolverhampton, 29 Dec. 1955; *s* of late Eric James Gunn and Dorothy Mary Gunn (*née* McKnight); *m* 1986, Diane Birch; two *d*. *Educ:* St George's Primary Sch., New Mills; New Mills Grammar Sch.; Chesterfield Grammar Sch.; Univ. of Manchester (LLB 1977). Lectr, then Sen. Lectr in Law, Univ. of Nottingham, 1978–93; Prof. and Hd, Sch. of Law, Univ. of Westminster, 1993–95; Prof. of Mental Health Law, De Montfort Univ., Leicester, 1995–97; Nottingham Trent University: Prof. of Law, 1997–2006; Hd of Dept; Asst Dean, then Dean, Sch. of Law; Pro Vice Chancellor and Prof., Derby Univ., 2006–10. *Publications:* Halsbury's Laws of England, 4th edn, vol. 11(1) and (2), 1990; (jtly) Smith, Bailey and Gunn on the Modern Legal System, 2nd edn 1991 to 4th edn 2002; (contrib.) Blackstone's Criminal Practice, 1991–2006; Blackstone's Guide to the Sexual Offences Act, 2003; over 100 articles, chapters and notes. *Recreations:* family, gardening, watching sport.

**GUNN, Pamela Jane;** *see* Taylor, Pamela J.

**GUNN-JOHNSON, Ven. David Allan;** Archdeacon of Barnstaple, 2003–14; *b* 2 May 1949; *s* of Sidney and Violet Winifred Johnson; *m* 1979, Susan Wells; two *d*. *Educ:* St Stephen's House, Oxford. Ordained deacon 1981, priest 1982; Assistant Curate: Oxhey, 1981–84; Cheshunt, 1984–88; Team Rector, Colyton, 1988–2003; RD, Honiton, 1990–96; Preb., Exeter Cathedral, 1999–2003. STh (Archbp's Schol. of Theol.) 1985, MA 1995, Lambeth. *Recreations:* historical research, theatre (writing, directing and performing), motorcycling. *Address:* 12 Hylton Gardens, Exeter EX4 2QE. *T:* (01392) 496877, 07921 150428. *E:* dgunnjohnson549@btinternet.com.

**GUNNELL, Prof. David John,** PhD, DSc; FFPHM, FMedSci; Professor of Epidemiology, University of Bristol, since 2003; *b* London, 17 Nov. 1960; *s* of John C. Gunnell and Rosemary P. Gunnell; *m* 1987, Gillian McLeish; two *d*. *Educ:* Univ. of Bristol (MB ChB 1984; PhD Epidemiol. 1996; DSc Epidemiol. 2009); London Sch. of Hygiene and Tropical Medicine, Univ. of London (MSc Med. Statistics (Dist.) 1997). MRCGP 1989; MFPHM 1993, FFPHM 1999. GP trng, Bristol and Weston-Super-Mare, 1986–89; gen. psychiatry trng, Bristol, 1989–91; Registrar, 1991–93, Sen. Registrar, 1993, in Public Health Medicine, Somerset HA; Lectr in Epidemiol. and Public Health, 1993–96, Consultant Sen. Lectr, Dept of Social Medicine, 1997–2003, Univ. of Bristol; Hon. Sen. Registrar, Avon HA, 1993–96; Hon. Consultant in Public Health, N Bristol NHS Trust, 1997–. Mem., Pharmacovigillance Expert Adv. Gp, Medicines and Healthcare Products Regulatory Agency, 2006–13 (Vice Chm., 2012–13). NIHR Sen. Investigator, 2007. Trustee, Samaritans, 2015–18. FHEA 2007. Res. Prize, Amer. Foundn for Suicide Prevention, 2015; Stengel Res. Award, Internat. Assoc. of Suicide Prevention, 2015. *Publications:* over 400 research articles in jls incl. Lancet, BMJ, Public Liby of Sci. Medicine, Internat. Jl of Epidemiol. *Recreations:* palaeontology, travel, walking. *Address:* Department of Population Health Sciences, University of Bristol, Canynge Hall, 39 Whatley Road, Clifton, Bristol BS8 2PS. *T:* (0117) 928 7253. *E:* d.j.gunnell@bristol.ac.uk.

**GUNNELL, Sally Jane Janet,** OBE 1998 (MBE 1993); DL; athlete, retired 1997; television presenter and motivational speaker; *b* 29 July 1966; *m* 1992, Jonathan Bigg; three *s*. *Educ:* Chigwell High School. Life Member, Essex Ladies' Club, 1978; GB Team Captain, 1992–97; 400 m hurdles wins include: Olympic Champion, 1992; World Champion, 1993; World Record Holder, 1993; European Champion, 1994; Commonwealth Champion, 1994; also Commonwealth Champion, 100 m hurdles, 1986, 1990. Mem. Bd, Sport England, 2013–16. DL W Sussex, 2011. *Publications:* Running Tall, 1994; Be Your Best, 2001. *W:* www.sallygunnell.com.

**GUNNING, Alexander Rupert;** QC 2012; *s* of Peter and Jennifer Gunning; *m* Jerusalen Vital; two *s*. *Educ:* Sherborne Sch.; King's Coll. London (LLB Hons; LLM Commercial and Corporate Law). Called to the Bar, Inner Temple, 1994; in practice as a barrister, specialising in internat. arbitration arising from disputes concerning energy-related projects. *Recreation:* Bath Rugby. *Address:* One Essex Court, Temple, EC4Y 9AR. *T:* (020) 7583 2000.

**GUNNING, Prof. Brian Edgar Scourse,** FRS 1980; FAA 1979; Professor of Plant Cell Biology, Australian National University, 1974–97, now Emeritus; *b* 29 Nov. 1934; *s* of William Gunning and Margaret Gunning (*née* Scourse); *m* 1964, Marion Sylvia Forsyth; two *s*. *Educ:* Methodist Coll., Belfast; Queen's Univ., Belfast (BSc (Hons), MSc, PhD); DSc ANU. Lecturer in Botany, 1957–65, Reader in Botany, 1965–74, Queen's Univ., Belfast. Hon. MRIA 1999. *Publications:* Ultrastructure and the Biology of Plant Cells (with Dr M. Steer), 1975; Intercellular Communication in Plants: studies on plasmodesmata (with Dr A. Robards), 1976; (with M. Steer) Plant Cell Biology, 1996; contribs to research jls. *Recreations:* hill walking, photography. *Address:* 50 Cargelligo Street, Duffy, ACT 2611, Australia. *T:* (2) 62812879.

**GUNNING, Sir Charles Theodore,** 9th Bt *cr* 1778, of Eltham, Kent; CD 1964; RCN retired; engineering consultant, Promaxis Systems Inc., Ottawa; *b* 19 June 1935; *s* of Sir Robert Gunning, 8th Bt and of Helen Nancy, *d* of Vice-Adm. Sir Theodore John Hallett, KBE, CB; *S* father, 1989; *m* 1st, 1969, Sarah (marr. diss. 1982), *d* of Col Patrick Arthur Easton; one *d*; 2nd, 1989, Linda Martin (*née* Kachmar). *Educ:* Canadian Mil. Coll.; RNEC Plymouth; Tech. Univ. of NS. PEng. Royal Commonwealth Soc. Liaison, Nat. Student Commonwealth Forum, 1979–2009; Chm., Nat. Council in Canada, Royal Commonwealth Soc., 1990–93 (Pres., Ottawa Br., 1974–76, 1979–80 and 1983; a Nat. Hon. Chm.). Silver Jubilee Medal, 1977; Golden Jubilee Medal, 2002. *Heir: b* John Robert Gunning [*b* 17 Sept. 1944; *m* 1st, 1969, Alina Tylicki (marr. diss. 1995); two *s* one *d*; 2nd, 1999, Diane Grosschmidt]. *Address:* 2940 McCarthy Road, Ottawa, ON K1V 8K6, Canada.

**GUNNYEON, William James,** CBE 2009; FRCP, FRCPE, FFOM, FRCGP; independent consultant, since 2014; Chief Medical Adviser, Director, Health and Wellbeing, and Chief Scientist, Department for Work and Pensions, 2005–14; *b* 10 June 1953; *s* of late William Campbell Gunnyeon and Muriel Gunnyeon (*née* Dunn, latterly Shearer); *m* 1975, Joan Elizabeth Moorcroft; two *s*. *Educ:* Dundee Univ. (MB ChB 1977). DIH 1984. FFOM 1994; FRCP 1999; FRCGP 2003; FFOMI 2006; FRCPE 2007. House Officer, Stirling Royal Infirmary, 1977–78; MO, RAF, 1978–83; Med. Advr, then Sen. Med. Advr, OMS Ltd, 1983–92; Principal Med. Advr, Grampian Regl Council, 1992–96; Dir, Grampian Occupational Health Service, 1996–97; Liberty Occupational Health: Dir, Occupational Health, 1997–99; Chief Exec., 1999–2000; Med. Dir, Aon, subseq. Capita, Health Solutions, 2000–05. Faculty of Occupational Medicine: Registrar, 1999–2001; Pres., 2002–05; Mem. Council, RCP, 2002–05; Member: Acad. of Med. Royal Colls, 2002–05; Specialist Trng Authy, 2002–05; Lay Mem., Gen. Osteopathic Council, 2016–. Chairman: Assoc. of Local Authy Med. Advrs, 1995–97; Instn of Occupational Safety and Health, 2016–. Gov., Glasgow Caledonian Univ., 2017–. *Publications:* (jtly) Fitness to Teach, 2000. *Recreations:* gardening, hill-walking, travel, reading, classical music. *E:* bill.gunnyeon@btopenworld.com.

**GUNSTON, Sir John (Wellesley),** 3rd Bt *cr* 1938, of Wickwar, Co. Gloucester; company director; *b* 25 July 1962; *s* of Sir Richard Gunston, 2nd Bt and of Mrs Joan Elizabeth Marie Gunston; *S* father, 1991; *m* 1990, Rosalind (marr. diss. 1998), *y d* of Edward Gordon Eliott; one *s*. *Educ:* Harrow; RMA Sandhurst. BSAP Reserve, Rhodesia, 1979–80. Commnd 1st Bn Irish Guards, 1981. Since 1983 has covered wars, revolutions and foreign travel assignments in: Afghanistan, Albania, Brazil, Burma, Colombia, Egypt, Eritrea, Israel (West Bank and Gaza), Lebanon, Liberia, South Africa, Sudan, Uganda, Ulster (esp. Derry) and also in North America, Eastern Europe and South East Asia. Dir, North-West Frontier Productions, 1995; Man. Dir, Hard News Ltd, 1998. Chm., Rory Peck Trust and Award, 1995–97. Fellow: Soc. of Authors, 1994; RSAA, 1995; FRGS 1988; FRAS 1998–2012. *Recreations:* books, biking and ballistics. *Heir:* s Richard St George Gunston, b 3 July 1992. *Clubs:* Cavalry and Guards, Special Forces.

**GUPTA, Atul;** Director: Zhaikmunai LP, since 2009; Vetra Energy, since 2012; Chairman, Seven Energy, since 2017 (Director, since 2012); b 15 Dec. 1959; s of Satya Pal Gupta and Sarmishta Gupta; m 1991, Anjali Garg, MSc; two d. *Educ:* Sidney Sussex Coll., Cambridge (BA Hons 1981; MEng Chem. Eng. 1983); Heriot-Watt Univ., Edinburgh (MEng Pet. Eng.). Charterhouse Petroleum plc, 1983–86; Petrofina SA, 1986–90; Monument Oil plc, 1990–99, Gen. Dir Turkmenistan, 1996–99; Chief Operating Officer, 1999–2006, CEO, 2006–08, Burren Energy plc; CEO, DB Petroleum, 2010–13; Dir of Investments, Essar Capital, 2013–16. Advr, Cairn India, 2017–. *Recreations:* football, cricket, art, reading.

**GUPTA, Prof. Ravindra Kumar,** PhD; FRCP, FRCPath; Professor of Clinical Microbiology, University of Cambridge, since 2019; b Sunderland, 20 Sept. 1975; s of Dr Nagendra Gupta and Pramila Gupta; m 2005, Dr Ambika Chadha; three d. *Educ:* Brentwood Sch.; Downing Coll., Cambridge (BA 1997); Worcester Coll., Oxford (BCh BM 2001); Harvard Univ. (MPH 1999); University Coll. London (PhD 2010). FRCP 2016; FRCPath 2018. House Officer, Oxford, 2001–02; Sen. House Officer, Hammersmith Hosp., 2002–04; Specialist Registrar: Guy's and St Thomas' Hosps, 2004–05; Health Protection Agency, Colindale, 2005–06; Oxford Deanery, 2006–07; Intermediate Fellow, 2011–16, Sen. Fellow, 2016–, Wellcome Trust; Professorial Res. Fellow, UCL, 2016–19. Honorary Consultant Physician: UCLH, 2012–19; Cambridge Univ. Hosps NHS Foundn Trust, 2019–. Scientific Advr, WHO HIV Drug Resistance Guidelines Gp, 2016–17; Guidelines Cttee, British HIV Assoc., 2018–19. *Publications:* articles on first evidence for HIV drug resistance increasing worldwide and on world's second HIV cure in jls incl. Lancet and Nature. *Recreations:* cycling, swimming, tennis, travelling and working in Africa. *Address:* Box 157, Level 5, Department of Medicine, University of Cambridge, Cambridge CB2 0QQ. *T:* 07500 792984. *E:* rkg20@cam.ac.uk.

**GUPTA, Prof. Sunetra,** PhD; novelist; Professor of Theoretical Epidemiology, Department of Zoology, University of Oxford, since 2006; b Calcutta, 15 March 1965; d of Dhruba and Minati Gupta; m 1994, Adrian Vivian Sinton Hill, *qv*; two d. *Educ:* Princeton Univ. (AB 1987); Univ. of London (PhD 1992). University of Oxford: Jun. Res. Fellow, Merton Coll., 1993–96; Department of Zoology: Wellcome Trust Sen. Res. Fellow, 1995–99; Reader, 1999–2006. Scientific Medal, Zool Soc. of London, 2008; Rosalind Franklin Award, Royal Soc., 2009; Doubleday Award, 2013. *Publications:* novels: Memories of Rain, 1992 (Sahitya Akademi Award, 1997); The Glassblower's Breath, 1993; Moonlight into Marzipan, 1995; A Sin of Colour, 1999 (Southern Arts UK Prize for Lit., 2000); So Good in Black, 2009; contrib. scientific articles to Science, Nature, Lancet. *Recreations:* cinema, art, gardening, architecture. *Address:* Department of Zoology, University of Oxford, Peter Medawar Building for Pathogen Research, South Parks Road, Oxford OX1 3SY. *T:* (01865) 281225. *E:* sunetra.gupta@zoo.ox.ac.uk.

**GUPTA, Teertha;** QC 2012; a Recorder, since 2009; a Deputy High Court Judge, since 2016; b London, 26 Oct. 1966; s of Tapan Kumar Gupta and Gairika Gupta; m 1st, 1995, Joy Katherine Emmett (marr. diss. 2015); two s; 2nd, 2016, Sarah Jane Benhadj; one s one d. *Educ:* Mill Hill Sch., London; Leeds Univ. (LLB Hons). Called to the Bar, Inner Temple, 1990; in practice as a barrister, specialising in internat. child law, 1990–. *Recreations:* family, playing and coaching football, following international test cricket and Rugby, reading about developments in sports law, theatre (the plays of Tanika Gupta, MBE), raising four children. *Address:* 4 Paper Buildings, Temple, EC4Y 7EX. *T:* (020) 7583 0816. *E:* clerks@4pb.com.

**GURDON,** family name of **Baron Cranworth.**

**GURDON, Sir John (Bertrand),** Kt 1995; DPhil; FRS 1971; research scientist; Chairman, Company of Biologists, Cambridge, 2001–11; Master, Magdalene College, Cambridge, 1995–2002 (Hon. Fellow, 2002); b 2 Oct. 1933; s of late W. N. Gurdon, DCM, formerly of Assington, Suffolk, and Elsie Marjorie (*née* Byass); m 1964, Jean Elizabeth Margaret Curtis; one s one d. *Educ:* Edgeborough; Eton (Fellow, 1978–93); Christ Church, Oxford (BA 1956; DPhil 1960). Beit Memorial Fellow, 1958–61; Gosney Research Fellow, Calif. Inst. Technol., 1962; Departmental Demonstrator, Dept of Zool., Oxford, 1963–64; Vis. Research Fellow, Carnegie Instn, Baltimore, 1965; Lectr, Dept of Zoology, Oxford, 1965–72; Research Student, Christ Church, 1962–72; Mem. Staff, MRC Lab. of Molecular Biology, Cambridge, 1972–83 (Hd, Cell Biology Div., 1979–83); Fellow, Churchill Coll., Cambridge, 1973–94; John Humphrey Plummer Prof. of Cell Biology, Univ. of Cambridge, 1983–2001; Chm., Wellcome Cancer Res. Campaign Inst., Cambridge, 1991–2001. Fullerian Prof. of Physiology and Comparative Anatomy, Royal Instn, 1985–91. Lectures: Harvey Soc., NY, 1973; Dunham, Harvard, 1974; Croonian, Royal Soc., 1976; Carter-Wallace, Princeton, 1978; Woodhull, Royal Instn, 1980; Florey, Aust., 1988; Fischberg Meml, Geneva, 1989; Rutherford, Royal Soc., 1996; Rodney Porter Meml, Oxford, 1999; Hitchcock, Berkeley, USA, 2006. Pres., Internat. Soc. Develt Biol., 1989–93. Gov., The Wellcome Trust, 1995–2000. Chm., Co. of Biologists, 2001–. Hon. Foreign Member: Amer. Acad. of Arts and Scis, 1978; Foreign Associate: Nat. Acad. of Sciences, USA, 1980; Belgian Royal Acad. of Scis, Letters and Fine Arts, 1984; Foreign Member: Amer. Philos. Soc., 1983; Lombardy Acad. Sci., Italy, 1989; Acad. Les Sciences, France, 1990; Inst. of Medicine, USA, 2004. Hon. Student, Christ Church, Oxford, 1985; Hon. Fellow, Churchill Coll., Cambridge, 2007. Hon. DSc: Chicago, 1978; René Descartes, Paris, 1982; Oxford, 1988; Hull, 1998; Glasgow, 2000; Cambridge, 2007; Vrije Univ. Brussels, 2009; Univ. Libre de Bruxelles, 2009; Rockefeller, 2014. Albert Brachet Prize (Belgian Royal Academy), 1968; Scientific Medal of Zoological Soc., 1968; Feldberg Foundn Award, 1975; Paul Ehrlich Award, 1977; Nessim Habif Prize, Univ. of Geneva, 1979; CIBA Medal, Biochem. Soc., 1980; Comfort Crookshank Award for Cancer Research, 1983; William Bate Hardy Prize, Cambridge Philos. Soc., 1984; Prix Charles Leopold Mayer, Acad. des Scis, France, 1984; Ross Harrison Prize, Internat. Soc. of Develtl Biologists, 1985; Royal Medal, Royal Soc., 1985; Emperor Hirohito Internat. Prize for Biology, Japan Acad., 1987; Wolf Prize in Medicine, Israel, 1989; Jan Waldenstram Medal, Swedish Oncol. Soc., 1991; Dist. Service Award, Miami, 1992; Edridge Green Medal, RCOphth, 1997; Jean Brachet Meml Prize, Internat. Soc. Differentiation, 2000; Conklin Medal, Soc. Develtl Biol., 2001; Copley Medal, Royal Soc., 2003; Rosenstiel Award, Brandeis Univ., USA, 2009; Albert Lasker Award for Basic Med. Res., Lasker Foundn, USA, 2009; (jtly) Nobel Prize in Physiology or Medicine, 2012. *Publications:* Control of Gene Expression in Animal Development, 1974; articles in scientific jls, especially on nuclear transplantation. *Recreations:* ski-ing, tennis, horticulture, Lepidoptera. *Address:* Whittlesford Grove, Whittlesford, Cambridge CB22 4NZ. *Club:* Eagle Ski.

**GURNEY, Prof. Robert James,** OBE 2001; PhD; Professor of Earth Observation Science (formerly of Physical Geography), University of Reading, 1990–2015, now Emeritus Professor; b 31 March 1951; s of James William Stratton Gurney and Jeanne Mary Gurney; m 1977, Charlotte Mary (*née* Carr); one s one d. *Educ:* King's Coll. London (BSc Hons); Univ. of Bristol (PhD). Res. Fellow, Inst. of Hydrology, 1975–80; Research Associate: NASA Goddard Space Flight Center, Maryland, 1981–82; Dept of Civil Engrg, Univ. of Maryland, 1983–84; Hd, Hydrological Scis Branch, NASA Goddard Space Flight Center, Maryland, 1984–90; University of Reading: Dir, NERC Envmtl Systems Sci. Centre, 1990–2012; Co-ordinator, Envmtl Inf., NERC, 2013–14. Chm., ReadiBus, 1993–2007. FRMetS 1970. Award and Gold Medal, Remote Sensing and Photogrammetry Soc., 2013. *Publications:* (with E. T. Engman) Remote Sensing in Hydrology, 1991; (ed jtly) Atlas of Satellite Observations Related to Global Climate Change, 1993; (with K. A. Browning) Global Energy and Water Cycles, 1999. *Recreations:* theatre, arts. *Address:* Department of Meteorology, University of Reading, Harry Pitt Building, PO Box 238, 3 Earley Gate, Reading RG6 6AL. *T:* (0118) 378 8741, *Fax:* (0118) 378 6413. *E:* r.j.gurney@reading.ac.uk.

**GURNEY, Tim,** OBE 2006; HM Diplomatic Service, retired; Deputy High Commissioner, Canberra, 2006–08; b 28 April 1955; s of Brian and Joy Gurney; m 1976, Denise Elizabeth Harker (marr. diss. 2011); one s one d. Joined FCO, 1973; Istanbul, 1976–79; Karachi, 1979–82; Montreal, 1982–85; Second Secretary: FCO, 1985–88; (Chancery/Inf.), Accra, 1988–90; Dep. Dir, British Inf. Services, NY, 1991–96; First Sec., FCO, 1996–98; Dep. Governor, Bermuda, 1998–2003; Dep. Hd of Mission, Kabul, 2003–05. Sen. Stabilisation Adviser: Nad-e Ali, Helmand, Afghanistan, 2010–11; Marjah and Khaneshin, 2011–12; Sen. Advr on civilian-military co-operation for UK Govt's Stabilisation Unit, 2012–. Dir, Triken consultancy, 2012–. *Recreations:* scuba diving instructor, soccer referee, photography. *W:* www.timsimages.uk.

**GURR, Douglas John,** PhD; Country Manager, Amazon UK, since 2016; b Leeds, 9 July 1964; s of Prof. Andrew John Gurr and Elizabeth Ann Gurr; m 1996, Lucy Makinson; one s one d. *Educ:* King's Coll., Cambridge (BA 1986; MMath (Cert. Adv. Studies in Maths Pt III 1987)); Univ. of Edinburgh (PhD 1990). Lectr, Univ. of Aarhus, 1990–91; Principal, Dept of Transport, 1992–94; Partner, McKinsey & Co., 1995–2001; Founder and CEO, Blueheath Hldgs plc, 2001–05; Exec. Bd Dir, Asda-Walmart, 2006–11; Vice-Pres., Amazon.com, 2011–14; Pres., Amazon China, 2014–16. Non-executive Director: DWP, 2016; Land Registry, 2018–. Trustee: Sci. Mus. Gp (formerly Nat. Mus. of Sci. and Industry), 2004–14 (Chm., 2010–14); Landmark Trust, 2014–; Nat. Gall., 2019–; Dep. Chm., Nat. Media Mus., 2006–11; Chm., BHF, 2015–. Mem., LMS, 2011. Fellow, Sci. Mus., 2014. *Publications:* Staying Alive Off Piste, 2012; contrib. articles in acad. jls incl. Jl of Pure and Applied Algebra, Logic in Computer Sci. and Information and Computation. *Recreations:* Ironman Triathlon, ski mountaineering including over 20 first ascents (Mem., Bob Graham 24 Hour Club #1649), museums and galleries. *Address:* Amazon UK, 1 Principal Place, Worship Street, Shoreditch, EC2A 2FA. *Clubs:* Athenæum; Calderdale.

**GURR, Dr Michael Ian;** Maypole Scientific Services, private nutrition consultancy, 1990–99; Partner, Isles of Scilly Specialist Crops, 1999–2006; b 10 April 1939; s of Henry Ormonde Gurr and Hilda Ruth Gurr; m 1963, Elizabeth Anne Mayers; two s one d. *Educ:* Dunstable Grammar Sch.; Univ. of Birmingham (BSc, PhD). Postdoctoral Fellowship, Harvard Univ., 1964–66; Unilever European Fellowship of Biochem. Soc., State Univ. of Utrecht, 1966–67; Res. Scientist, Unilever Res. Lab., Sharnbrook, Bedford, 1967–78; Hd, Department of Nutrition, Nat. Inst. for Res. in Dairying, Shinfield, Reading, 1978–85; Dir, Reading Lab. of AFRC Inst. of Food Res., 1985–86; Nutrition Consultant and Hd of Nutrition Dept, MMB, 1986–90. Chm., Isles of Scilly Wildlife Trust, 2001–05; Sec., Isles of Scilly Bat Gp, 2006–18; Mem., Jt Adv. Cttee, Isles of Scilly Area of Outstanding Beauty, 2008–10. Visiting Professor: Univ. of Reading, 1986–99; Oxford Poly., later Oxford Brookes Univ., 1990–99. Mem. Cttee, Isles of Scilly U3A, 2016– (Chm., 2017–). Chairman: Editl Bd, British Jl of Nutrition, 1988–90; Editl Adv. Bd, British Nutrition Foundn, 1994–99; Man. Ed., Nutrition Research Reviews, 1991–99. *Publications:* Lipid Biochemistry: an introduction (jtly), 1971, 6th edn as Lipids: biochemistry, biotechnology and health, 2016; Role of Fats in Food and Nutrition, 1984, 2nd edn 1992; Anthony Trafford James: a biography, 2014; numerous original pubns and reviews. *Recreations:* sailing, walking, gardening, piano playing, hand-bell ringing, nature conservation volunteer (especially studies of bats), local U3A Music Appreciation Group (Leader, 2014–). *Address:* Vale View Cottage, Maypole, St Mary's, Isles of Scilly TR21 0NU. *T:* (01720) 422224.

**GURR, Nicholas Bryan;** Director, International Security Policy, Ministry of Defence, since 2014; b Barnehurst, Kent, 1 June 1964; s of Brian and Patricia Gurr; m 1992, Susan Railton; two d. *Educ:* Bexley/Erith Tech. Sch. for Boys; Royal Coll. of Defence Studies. Joined CS, 1982; various policy posts, 1983–98, Hd of Communication Planning, 1999–2002, MoD; Mem., RCDS 2002; Dep. Chief of Assessments Staff, Cabinet Office, 2003–06; Dir, Communication Planning, 2006–07, Dir (formerly Dir Gen.) Media and Communications, 2007–11, Dep. Chief Defence Intelligence, 2011–14, MoD. *Recreations:* sport, music, travel. *Address:* Ministry of Defence, Whitehall, SW1A 2HB. *T:* (020) 7218 2505. *E:* nick.gurr665@mod.uk.

**GURR, Prof. Sarah Jane,** PhD; Professor of Food Security, University of Exeter, since 2013; b Cuckfield, Sussex, 7 May 1958; d of Denis Smith and late Marie Smith; two d. *Educ:* King's Sch., Canterbury; Imperial Coll. of Sci., Technol. and Medicine (BSc Hons 1979; ARCS 1979; PhD 1984; DIC); MA Oxon 1992. Postdoctoral Res. Fellow, Univ. of St Andrews, 1984–89; University of Oxford: Lectr, 1992–2002; Reader, 2002–04; Prof. of Molecular Plant Pathol., 2004–13; Fellow, Somerville Coll., Oxford, 1992–2013. Bd Dir, Rothamsted Res., 1999–2006. Royal Soc. Leverhulme Trust Sen. Res. Fellow, 2002–03; NESTA Fellow, 2004–07. Mem. Cttee, 2008–12, Council, 2012–18, BBSRC. Pres., British Soc. for Plant Pathol., 2009–10. Governor: King's Sch., Canterbury, 1999–2012; Stowe Sch., 2005–. Huxley Medal, RAI, 1998. *Publications:* (ed jtly) Molecular Plant Pathology, 2 vols, 1992; contrib. res. articles and papers to jls incl. Nature, Nature Climate Change, Science. *Recreations:* wine, art, reading, plants, progeny. *Address:* BioSciences, University of Exeter, Exeter EX4 4QD. *E:* s.j.gurr@exeter.ac.uk.

**GURRÍA TREVIÑO, (José) Angel;** Secretary-General, Organisation for Economic Co-operation and Development, since 2006; b Tampico, Mexico, 8 May 1950; s of Francisco José Gurría Lacroix and Carmen Treviño Humana; m 1973, Lulu Ululani Quintana Pali; one s two d. *Educ:* Univ. Nacional Autónoma de México (BA Econs); Univ. of Leeds (MA Econs). Financial analyst, Federal Power Commn, 1968–70; COS to Dep. Mayor of City of Mexico, 1970; COS to Dep. CEO, then CEO, Nafinsa (Mexico's Develt Bank); Hd, Dept of Negotiations of Foreign Loans, Nafinsa; Dep. Financial Manager, Rural Develt Fund, 1975–76; Perm. Rep. to Internat. Coffee Orgn, London, 1976–78; Treasury posts, 1978–92: Dep. Dir, Public Debt; Dir, Foreign Debt; Gen. Dir, Public Credit; Dep. Sec. for Internat. Affairs; Pres. and CEO, Bancomext (Mexico's Export/Import Bank), 1992–93, Nafinsa, 1993–94; Sec. for Internat. Affairs, Instnl Revolutionary Party (PRI), 1993–94; Minister: of Foreign Affairs Mexico, 1994–97; of Finance and Public Credit, 1998–2000. Holds numerous foreign decorations. *Publications:* Politics of External Debt, 1994; contribs on econs, debt develt and governance. *Address:* Organisation for Economic Co-operation and Development, 2 rue André Pascal, 75775 Paris Cedex 16, France. *E:* secretary.general@oecd.org.

**GURU-MURTHY, Krishnan;** presenter: Channel 4 News, since 1998; Unreported World, since 2011; b 5 April 1970; s of Krishnan and Indrani Guru-Murthy; m 2005, Lisa Jane Colles; one s one d. *Educ:* Queen Elizabeth's Grammar Sch., Blackburn; Hertford

Coll., Oxford (BA Hons PPE). BBC: presenter: Open to Question, 1988–89; East, 1989–90; presenter/reporter, Newsround, 1991–94; reporter, Newsnight, 1994–97; presenter, News 24, 1997–98; presenter: Channel 4: Powerhouse, 2001–03; News at Noon, 2003–08; Ask the Chancellors, 2010; LBC Radio: The Krishnan Guru-Murthy prog., 2003–05. Columnist: Eastern Eye, 2001–03; Metro, 2002–06. Trustee, Royal Botanic Gardens, Kew, 2018–. *Recreations:* guitar, piano, travel, cycling. *Address:* Channel 4 News, ITN, 200 Gray's Inn Road, WC1X 8XZ. *T:* (020) 7833 3000. *E:* krishnan.guru-murthy@itn.co.uk. *Clubs:* Groucho, Soho House, Ivy.

**GUSTAFSSON, Poppy,** OBE 2019; Co-Chief Executive Officer, Darktrace, since 2016; *b* UK, 24 Aug. 1982; *d* of John Prentis and Gilly Prentis; *m* 2008, Roland Joel Gustafsson; two *d*. *Educ:* Univ. of Sheffield (BSc Maths 2003). ACA 2006. Deloitte, 2004–08; Fund Accountant, Amadeus Capital Partners, 2008–09; Corporate Controller, Autonomy Corp. plc, subseq. HP Autonomy, 2009–11; Darktrace: Chief Financial Officer, 2013–16; Chief Operating Officer, 2016. *Address:* Darktrace, 1–3 Strand, Charing Cross, WC2N 5EJ. *E:* info@darktrace.com.

**GUSTERSON, Prof. Barry Austin,** PhD; FRCPath; Professor of Pathology, 2000–10, now Emeritus, Head of Forensic Medicine and Forensic Science, 2006–10, and Project Director for the Beatson Translational Research Centre, 2008–10, University of Glasgow (Chairman, Division of Cancer Sciences and Molecular Pathology, 2002–07); *b* Colchester, 24 Oct. 1946; *s* of Joseph Austin Gusterson and Doris Edith (*née* Fairweather); *m* 1972, Ann Josephine Davies; one *s* two *d*. *Educ:* St Bartholomew's Hosp., London (BSc Physiol. 1967; MB BS 1976); Royal Dental Hosp. (BDS 1972); Inst. Cancer Res. (PhD 1980). FRCPath 1995. Sen. Clinical Scientist and Cons., Ludwig Inst. Cancer Res., London, 1983–86; Cons. in Histopathol., Royal Marsden Hosp., 1984–; Prof. of Histopathol., and Chm., Sect. of Cell Biol and Exptl Pathol., Inst. of Cancer Res., London Univ., 1986–2000. Founding Dir, Toby Robins Breast Cancer Res. Centre, London, 1998. Dir, Pathology, Internat. Breast Cancer Study Gp, Berne, 1995–. Oakley Lectr, Pathological Soc. of GB and Ire., 1986. Chm., Pathology Gp, Orgn Eur. Cancer Insts, Geneva, 1992–96 (Mem., Faculty Bd, 1992–96); Mem., Faculty Bd, Eur. Soc. Mastology, Milan, 1994–. Mem., Brit. Soc. Cell Biol. *Publications:* contrib. chapters in books and numerous articles to professional jls. *Recreations:* antique English glass and furniture, gardening, walking, reading.

**GUTCH, Richard Evelyn;** Associate, Prospectus, 2008–13; *b* 17 Nov. 1946; *s* of Sir John Gutch, KCMG, OBE, and late Diana Mary Gutch (*née* Worsley); *m* 1971, Rosemary Anne Capel Pike; two *s*. *Educ:* Winchester Coll.; Gonville and Caius Coll., Cambridge (BA); University Coll. London (MPhil). Town planning posts in Camden and S Yorks, 1970–76; Sen. Lectr, Planning Unit, PCL, 1976–80; Asst to Chief Exec., Brent LBC, 1980–85; Asst Dir, NCVO, 1985–92; Chief Exec., Arthritis Care, 1992–2001; Dir for England and Strategic Progs, Community Fund, 2001–04; Chief Exec., Futurebuilders England, 2004–08. Freelance consultant, 2008–14. FRSA 1992. *Publications:* reports and booklets. *Recreations:* the arts, Venice, the Isle of Wight, walking, carpentry, gardening. *Address:* Carina, Cliff Road, Totland Bay, Isle of Wight PO39 0EH. *T:* (01983) 752180.

**GUTERRES, António Manuel de Oliveira;** Secretary-General, United Nations, since 2017; *b* 30 April 1949; *m* (wife decd); one *s* one *d*. *Educ:* Technical Univ. of Lisbon. Electrical engr; Asst Prof., Technical Univ. of Lisbon, 1973–75; Chief of Staff to Sec. of State for Industry, 1974–75. Deputy (Socialist), Portuguese Parlt, 1976–83 and 1985–93; Prime Minister of Portugal, 1995–2002. UN High Comr for Refugees, 2005–15. Mem., Commn for European Integration, 1976–79; Pres., Parly Commn for Economy and Finance, 1977–79, for Territory Admin, Local Power and Envmt, 1985–88; Strategic Develt Dir, State Investment and Participation Agency, 1984–85. Mem., Parly Assembly, Council of Europe, 1981–83. Mem., Municipal Assembly of Fundão, 1979–95 (Pres.). Portuguese Socialist Party: joined 1974; Mem., Nat. Secretariat, 1986–88; Pres., Parly Gp, 1988–91; Sec.-Gen., 1992–2001; Vice Pres., 1992–99, Pres., 1999–2005, Socialist Internat. Founder and Vice Pres., Portuguese Assoc. for Consumer Protection, 1973–74; Mem., Assoc. for Economic and Social Develt, 1970–96. *Publications:* articles in jls. *Address:* United Nations, New York, NY 10027, USA.

**GUTFREUND, Prof. Herbert,** FRS 1981; Professor of Physical Biochemistry, University of Bristol, 1972–86, now Emeritus; Scientific Member (external), Max-Planck-Institut für medizinische Forschung, Heidelberg, since 1987; Hon. Scientist, Rutherford Appleton Laboratory, Oxfordshire, 2001–09; *b* 21 Oct. 1921; *s* of late Paul Peter Gutfreund and Clara Angela Gutfreund; *m* 1958, Mary Kathelen, *er d* of late Mr and Mrs L. J. Davies, Rugby; two *s* one *d*. *Educ:* Vienna; Univ. of Cambridge (PhD). Research appts at Cambridge Univ., 1947–57; Rockefeller Fellow, Yale Univ., 1951–52; part-time Research Associate, Yale Univ., 1953–58; Principal Scientific Officer, National Inst. for Research in Dairying, Univ. of Reading, 1957–65; Visiting Professor: Univ. of California, 1965; Max Planck Inst., Göttingen, 1966–67; Reader in Biochemistry and Director of Molecular Enzymology Laboratory, Univ. of Bristol, 1967–72. Visiting appointments: Univ. of Leuven, 1972; Univ. of Adelaide, 1979; Univ. of Alberta, 1983. Part-time Scholar in Residence, NIH, Bethesda, 1986–89. Mem., EMBO, 1971. Hon. Member: British Biophysical Soc., 1990; Amer. Soc. for Biochem. and Molecular Biol., 1993; Biochemical Soc., 1996. *Publications:* An Introduction to the Study of Enzymes, 1966; Enzymes: physical principles, 1972; (ed) Chemistry of Macromolecules, 1974; (ed) Biochemical Evolution, 1981; Biothermodynamics, 1983; Kinetics for the Life Sciences, 1995; papers and reviews on many aspects of physical biochemistry. *Recreations:* mountain walking in Austria, cooking, reading general literature and philosophy of science, listening to music and all other good things in life. *Address:* Somerset House, Chilton Road, Upton, Oxon OX11 9JL. *T:* (01235) 851468. *E:* h.gutfreund@bristol.ac.uk. *Club:* Oxford and Cambridge.

**GUTHARDT, Rev. Dame Phyllis (Myra),** DBE 1993; PhD; retired Methodist minister; *b* 1 Aug. 1929; *d* of Johan Detlef Guthardt and Amelia Guthardt. *Educ:* University of New Zealand: Auckland (BA 1957); Canterbury (MA 1959); Newnham Coll., Cambridge (PhD 1963). Primary school teacher, 1950–53; Methodist theol trng, 1954–56; ordained, 1959 (first woman ordained in NZ); active ministry in Methodist and Presbyterian parishes, incl. hosp. and univ. chaplaincy, 1957–90. Pres., Methodist Ch of NZ, 1985–86; Mem. Praesidium, World Methodist Council, 1986–91. Chancellor, Univ. of Canterbury, 1999–2002 (Mem. Council, 1981–2002; Pro-Chancellor, 1992–99). Hon. Dr Waikato, 1986; Hon. LLD Canterbury, 2003. *Publications:* contrib. theol jls. *Recreations:* music, reading, gardening. *Address:* 5 Cholmondeley Lane, Governors Bay, RD1 Lyttelton 8971, New Zealand. *T:* (3) 3299675.

**GUTHRIE,** family name of **Baron Guthrie of Craigiebank.**

**GUTHRIE OF CRAIGIEBANK, Baron** *cr* 2001 (Life Peer), of Craigiebank in the City of Dundee; **Field Marshal Charles Ronald Llewelyn Guthrie,** GCB 1994 (KCB 1990); GCVO 2019 (LVO 1977); OBE 1980; DL; Chief of the Defence Staff, 1997–2001; Aide-de-Camp General to the Queen, 1993–2001; *b* 17 Nov. 1938; *s* of late Ronald Guthrie and Nina (*née* Llewelyn); *m* 1971, Catherine (OBE 2010), *er d* of late Lt Col Claude Worrall, MVO, OBE, Coldstream Guards; two *s*. *Educ:* Harrow; RMA Sandhurst. Commnd Welsh Guards, 1959; served: BAOR, Aden; 22 SAS Regt, 1965–69; psc 1972; MA (GSO2) to CGS, MoD, 1973–74; Brigade Major, Household Div., 1976–77; Comdg 1st Bn Welsh Guards, Berlin and N Ireland, 1977–80; Col GS Military Ops, MoD, 1980–82; Commander: British Forces New Hebrides, 1980; 4th Armoured Brigade, 1982–84; Chief of Staff 1st (BR) Corps, 1984–86; GOC NE Dist and Comdr 2nd Infantry Div., 1986–87; ACGS, MoD, 1987–89; Comdr 1 (BR) Corps, 1989–91; Comdr Northern Army Gp, 1992–93; C-in-C BAOR, 1992–94; CGS, 1994–97. Director: N. M. Rothschild & Sons, 2001–10; Petropavlovsk PLC (formerly Peter Hambro Mining), 2008–15; Gulf Keystone Petroleum, 2011–15. Visiting Professor: Dept of War Studies, KCL, 2002–; St Mary's Univ., Twickenham, 2017–. Col Comdt, Intelligence Corps, 1986–95; Col, The Life Guards, 1999–2019; Gold Stick to the Queen, 1999–2019; Col Comdt, SAS Regt, 2000–09. President: Army Saddle Club, 1991–96; Army LTA, 1991–99; Fedn of London Youth Clubs, 2001–; Action Research, subseq. Action Medical Research, 2001–; Army Benevolent Fund, 2002–11; Weston Spirit, 2003–12; Harrow Assoc., 2011–16. Chairman: Liddle Hart Archives, 2002–18; Hosp. of St John and St Elizabeth, 2009–19; St John's Hospice, 2009–19. Mem. Council and Trustee, IISS, 2002–18. Chancellor, Liverpool Hope Univ., 2013–. Hon. Bencher, Middle Temple, 2010. Freeman, City of London, 1988; Liveryman, Painter Stainers' Co., 1989. DL Dorset, 2007. Hon. FKC 2002. Kt, SMO Malta, 1999. Comdr, Legion of Merit (USA), 2001. *Publications:* (with Sir Michael Quinlan) Just War: the just war tradition: ethics in modern warfare, 2007. *Recreations:* tennis, opera. *Address:* PO Box 25439, SW1P 1AG. *Clubs:* White's, Beefsteak, All England Lawn Tennis.
*See also J. D. Guthrie.*

**GUTHRIE, Hannah Gillian Isabella;** *see* Duncan, H. G. I.

**GUTHRIE, James Dalglish;** QC 1993; a Recorder, since 1999; *b* 21 Feb. 1950; *s* of late Ronald Guthrie and Nina Guthrie (*née* Llewelyn); *m* 1981, Lucille Gay Page-Roberts; one *s* one *d*. *Educ:* Harrow; Worcester Coll., Oxford (BA Modern History). Called to the Bar, Inner Temple, 1975, Bencher, 2000; admitted as barrister: Turks and Caicos Is, 1995; St Lucia, 1997; St Vincent and The Grenadines, 1998; Trinidad and Tobago, 2000; St Kitts and Nevis, 2005; Grenada, 2006; Bermuda, 2007; Belize, 2008; Antigua, 2008; Cayman Is, 2014; Mauritius, 2018; The Bahamas, 2018. *Recreations:* fishing, travel, photography. *Address:* 3 Hare Court, Temple, EC4Y 7BJ. *T:* (020) 7415 7800. *Club:* Turf.
*See also Baron Guthrie of Craigiebank.*

**GUTHRIE, Sir Malcolm (Connop),** 3rd Bt *cr* 1936; *b* 16 Dec. 1942; *s* of Sir Giles Connop McEacharn Guthrie, 2nd Bt, OBE, DSC, and Rhona, *d* of late Frederic Stileman; *S* father, 1979; *m* 1967, Victoria, *o d* of late Brian Willcock; one *s* one *d*. *Educ:* Millfield. *Heir: s* Giles Malcolm Welcome Guthrie [*b* 16 Oct. 1972; *m* 2000, Susan, *e d* of Bill and Sheila Thompson]. *Address:* Brent Eleigh, Belbroughton, Stourbridge, Worcestershire DY9 0DW.

**GUTHRIE, Prof. Peter Moir,** OBE 1993; FREng, FICE; Professor of Engineering for Sustainable Development, University of Cambridge, since 2000; *b* La Paz, Bolivia, 21 Feb. 1951; *s* of William Moir Guthrie and Mary Barbara Guthrie; *m* 1979, Lorna Jane Cowcher; one *s* one *d*. *Educ:* Imperial Coll., London (BSc 1973; MSc 1976; DIC 1973). FICE 1992; FREng 1998. VSO, Kaduna, Nigeria, 1974; Engineer: Turriff Taylor, Flotta, 1975, Iran, 1976; Soil Mechanics, 1976–78; Engr, then Dir, Scott Wilson, 1978–2004. Non-exec. Dir, Buro Happold, 2009–15. Mem., Scientific Adv. Council, DEFRA, 2004–11. Founder, 1980, and Vice-Pres., RedR, 2005–, Engrs for Disaster Relief. FCGI 1995. FRSA. Hon. LLD Bristol, 1992. *Publications:* (jtly) Building Roads By Hand, 1990; contrib. papers on sustainable develt to learned jls. *Recreations:* ski-ing, tennis, golf. *Address:* Department of Engineering, University of Cambridge, Trumpington Street, Cambridge CB2 1PZ. *T:* (01223) 765627, *Fax:* (01223) 765625. *E:* pmg31@cam.ac.uk.

**GUTHRIE, Robert Bruce,** PhD; Principal, Hockerill Anglo-European College, 1996–2008; *b* 16 Jan. 1949; *s* of Robert Guthrie and Edith Guthrie (*née* Wilcock); *m* 1970, Christine Haswell; one *s* one *d*. *Educ:* Sale County Grammar Sch. for Boys; Univ. of Leeds (BSc Hons Phys 1969; PhD Ceramics 1975); Univ. of Durham (MBA Distn 1995). Teacher and House Tutor: Bedstone Coll., 1973–74; Stonyhurst Coll., 1974–79; Housemaster and Hd of Sci., Dover Coll., 1979–90; Hd, St George's Sch., Rome, 1991–94. Chm., State Boarding Schs Assoc., 2000–02. Mem. (Ind), Oakham Town Council, 2011–15. Director: Oakham Town Partnership, 2012–; Rutland and District Schs Fedn, 2016–. Chm., Govs, Harington Sch., 2014–; Gov., St George's British Internat. Sch., Rome, 2017–. *Publications:* ceramics patent and papers, 1972; contrib. to educnl books and papers. *Recreations:* Rugby (England Schools, British Universities and Yorkshire), watching Leicester Tigers and Man Utd, stationary rowing, cycling, gardening, reading short poems, travel. *Address:* 4 Catmose Park Road, Oakham, Rutland LE15 6HN. *Club:* Bishop's Stortford Hockey (Vice Pres.).

**GUTIÉRREZ, Fernando Jose,** RDI 2014; graphic designer; Director, Studio Fernando Gutiérrez, since 2006; *b* London, 1963; *s* of Fernando Gutiérrez Viejo and Laura Gomes Duarte; *m* 2006, Constance Laperche De Crozals; two *d*. *Educ:* St George's Sch., Maida Vale; London Coll. of Printing (BA Hons Graphic Design 1985). Designer and Associate, CDT Design, London, 1986–93; Sen. Designer, Summa, Barcelona, 1990–91; Co-founder, Grafica Design, Barcelona, 1993–2000; Partner, Pentagram, London, 2000–06. Mem., Alliance Graphique Internationale, 1997. FRSA. *Address:* The Old Piano Factory, 5 Charlton Kings Road, NW5 2SB.

**GUTTERIDGE, Charles Norman,** FRCP, FRCPath; Chief Clinical Information Officer, Barts Health NHS Trust, since 2013; *b* 15 March 1952; *s* of Frank and Mary Gutteridge; *m* 1976, Charlotte Lorimer; two *s*. *Educ:* Rugby Sch.; Trinity Hall, Cambridge (BA, MB BChir 1976); London Hosp. Med. Coll. FRCP 1995; FRCPath 1997. Dist MO, Soufrière Dist, St Lucia, WI, 1977–79; training posts in gen. medicine and haematology, 1980–88; Wellcome Res. Training Fellow in Haematology, 1985–88; Sen. Lectr in Haematol., and Hon. Consultant Haematologist, Newham Gen. Hosp., 1988–2002, Actg Chief Exec., 1996–97, Med. Dir, 1997–2001, Newham Healthcare NHS Trust; Med. Dir, Barts and the London NHS Trust, 2002–10; Nat. Clinical Dir for Informatics, DoH, 2010–13. *Address:* Barts Health NHS Trust, Pathology and Pharmacy Building, Royal London Hospital, 80 Newark Street, E1 2ES.

**GUTTRIDGE, Deborah Mary Hinton;** *see* Grubb, D. M. H.

**GUY, Alan James,** DPhil; FRHistS, FRAS; Director, National Army Museum, 2004–10; *b* 13 July 1950; *s* of late James Alfred Guy and Florence Elizabeth Guy (*née* Farr); *m* 1975, Vivien Ruth Wilson; one *s*. *Educ:* Keble Coll., Oxford (MA 1976; DPhil 1983). National Army Museum: Curator, Dept of Weapons, 1977–86; Special Asst to Dir, 1986–88; Asst Dir (Collections), 1988–2000; Asst Dir (Admin), 2000–04. Vis. Fellow, Wolfson Coll., Cambridge, 2010–13. FRHistS 1989; FRAS 1999. *Publications:* Oeconomy and Discipline: officership and administration in the British Army 1714–1763, 1985; Colonel Samuel Bagshawe and the Army of George II, 1990; (with P. B. Boyden) Soldiers of the Raj: the Indian Army 1660–1947, 1997; (with P. B. Boyden and M. Harding) Ashes and Blood: the British Army in South Africa 1795–1914, 1999; (with A. W. Massie) Captain L. E. Nolan, 15th Hussars: expedition to the Crimea 1854, 2010. *Recreation:* bel canto opera and their substitutes. *Club:* Travellers.

**GUY, Diana;** a Deputy Chairman, Competition Commission, 2004–10 (Member, 2001–04); *b* 27 March 1943; *d* of late Charles Stanley Eade and Vera Dorothy Eade (*née* Manwaring); *m* 1968, John Robert Clare Guy; two *s*. *Educ:* Lady Margaret Hall, Oxford

(MA Juris.). Admitted solicitor; Partner, 1973–95, Consultant, 1995–2001, Theodore Goddard. *Publications:* (with G. I. F. Leigh) The EEC and Intellectual Property, 1981. *Recreations:* reading, walking, spending time at our house in France.

**GUY, Frances Mary;** HM Diplomatic Service, retired; Gender Adviser, Regional Bureau for Arab States, United Nations Development Programme, since 2017; *b* 1 Feb. 1959; *d* of David Guy and Elizabeth Guy (*née* Hendry); *m* 1989, Guy Raybaudo (marr. diss. 2015); one *s* two *d*. *Educ:* Aberdeen Univ. (MA Hons); Johns Hopkins Univ., Bologna (Dip.); Carleton Univ., Ottawa (MA Internat. Relns). Entered FCO, 1985: lang. trng, 1987; Second Sec. (Chancery), Khartoum, 1988–91; First Secretary: FCO, 1991–95; and Hd, Pol Section, Bangkok, 1995–96; Dep. Hd of Mission, Addis Ababa, 1997–2001; Ambassador to the Yemen, 2001–04; Hd, Engaging the Islamic World Gp, FCO, 2004–06; Ambassador to Lebanon, 2006–11; Advr on ME to Sec. of State for Foreign Affairs, 2011–12; Rep., UN Women, Iraq, 2012–14; Hd, ME Reg., Christian Aid, 2014–17. Pres., British Inst. of Middle East Studies, 2013–17. Hon. DLaws Aberdeen, 2015. *Recreations:* swimming, running.

**GUY, Geoffrey William;** Founder, and Executive Chairman, GW Pharmaceuticals plc, since 1998; *b* 30 Sept. 1954; *m* 1986, Katherine Mary Husk. *Educ:* St Bartholomew's Hosp. Med. Coll., Univ. of London (BSc Pharmacol. 1976; MB BS 1979). MRCS, LRCP 1979; LMSSA 1979; Dip. Pharmaceutical Medicine, RCP, 1984. Various hosp. appts, incl. St Bartholomew's, Southampton Gen. Hosp. and New Addenbrooke's Hosp., Cambridge, 1979–81; Internat. Clin. Res. Co-ordinator, Pierre Fabre Labs, France, 1981–83; Dir, Clin. Develt, Napp Labs, 1983–85; Founder, 1985, Chief Exec., 1985–97, Ethical Hldgs Plc; Founder, 1989, Chm., 1989–97, Phytopharm Plc (floated on NASDAQ; listed on London Stock Exchange, 1996). Visiting Professor: Sch. of Sci. and Medicine, Univ. of Buckingham, 2011–; Westminster Univ. Mem. Ct of Benefactors, RSocMed, 2008–. Chm. Bd, Weldmar Hospice Care Trust, 2006–14. Hon. DSc Reading, 2016. Liveryman, Soc. of Apothecaries. Venturer of Year Award, 3i, 1997; Deloitte Dir of Year Award, Pharmaceuticals and Healthcare, 2011. *Publications:* (ed jtly) The Medicinal Uses of Cannabis and Cannabinoids, 2004; contrib. various scientific papers on drug develt, drug delivery, pharmacokinetics, narcotics, cannabis and cannabinoids; inventor on numerous patents. *Recreations:* Real tennis, boating, horse breeding. *Address:* c/o GW Pharmaceuticals plc, 1 Cavendish Place, W1G 0QF.

**GUY, Dr John Alexander;** historian, author and broadcaster; Fellow in History, Clare College, Cambridge, since 2003; *b* Warragul, Vic, Australia, 16 Jan. 1949; *s* of Frank and Marjorie Guy; *m* 2005, Julia Fox; one *s* one *d*. *Educ:* King Edward VII Sch., Lytham, Lancs; Clare Coll., Cambridge (BA 1970); Selwyn Coll., Cambridge (PhD 1973). Res. Fellow, Selwyn Coll., Cambridge, 1970–73; Asst Keeper of Public Records, PRO, 1973–78; Lectr in Modern British Hist., 1978–82, Reader in British Hist., 1982–90, Univ. of Bristol; Prof. of Modern Hist., Univ. of St Andrews, 1992–2002. Vis. Lectr, Univ. of Calif, Berkeley, 1977; John Hinkley Vis. Prof., Johns Hopkins Univ., 1990; Richard L. Turner Prof. of Humanities and Prof. of Hist., Univ. of Rochester, NY, 1990–92; Hon. Res. Prof., Univ. of St Andrews, 2002–09; Guest Prof., Yale-in-London prog., Paul Mellon Centre for Studies in British Art, London, 2012–14; Vis. Fellow, Clare Coll., Cambridge, 2002–03. Television documentaries: presenter: The King's Servant, 2001; Renaissance Secrets series, 2001; contributor: Wolsey's Lost Palace of Hampton Court, 2002; Royal Deaths and Diseases series, 2003; Tudor histl expert, Time Team, 2004, 2005, 2006; histl consultant, The Tudors, 2008; histl consultant, film, Mary Queen of Scots, 2018. *Publications:* The Cardinal's Court, 1977; The Public Career of Sir Thomas More, 1980; Law and Social Change in British History, 1984; The Court of Star Chamber and its Records to the Reign of Elizabeth I, 1985; Christopher St German on Chancery and Statute, 1985; (with A. Fox) Reassessing the Henrician Age, 1986; Tudor England, 1988; (with J. Morrill) The Tudors and Stuarts, 1992; The Reign of Elizabeth I: court and culture in the last decade, 1995; The Tudor Monarchy, 1997; Cardinal Wolsey, 1998; Politics, Law and Counsel in Tudor and Early-Stuart England, 2000; Thomas More, 2000; The Tudors: a very short introduction, 2000, 2nd edn 2013; My Heart is My Own: the life of Mary Queen of Scots, 2004 (Whitbread Biography Award); A Daughter's Love: Thomas and Margaret More, 2008 (TV adaptation 2011); Thomas Becket: warrior, priest, rebel, victim - a 900-year-old story retold, 2012; The Children of Henry VIII, 2013; Henry VIII: the quest for fame, 2014; Elizabeth: the forgotten years, 2016; Thomas More: a very brief history, 2017; Gresham's Law: the life and world of Queen Elizabeth I's banker, 2019; contrib. articles to learned histl jls. *Recreations:* opera, art, theatre, animals, watching the steamers on Lake Geneva. *Address:* Clare College, Trinity Lane, Cambridge CB2 1TL. *T:* (01223) 333237, *Fax:* (01223) 333219. *E:* jag64@cam.ac.uk.

**GUY, John Westgarth,** OBE 1986; HM Diplomatic Service, retired; Consul General, St Petersburg, 1996–2000; *b* 17 July 1941; *s* of late John Westgarth Guy and Stella (*née* Sanderson); *m* 1st, 1961, Sylvia Kathleen Stokes (*d* 2002); one *s* one *d*; 2nd, 2005, Thelma Georgina Barbieri (*née* Larter). *Educ:* Queen Mary's Sch. for Boys, Basingstoke. CRO, 1960; Karachi, 1961–63; Calcutta, 1964–67; Vice Consul, New York, 1968–70; FCO, 1970–72; Third Secretary: Moscow, 1972–73; Jakarta, 1974; Second Sec., São Paulo, 1975–77; FCO, 1977–79; DTI, 1979–80; First Secretary: Yaoundé, 1981–84; Maputo, 1984–87; FCO, 1987–91; High Comr, PNG, 1991–94; RCDS, 1995. *Recreation:* sailing. *Address:* Hampshire.

**GUY, Captain Robert Lincoln,** LVO 1980; RN; Executive Director, Universities' China Committee in London, since 2002; *b* 4 Sept. 1947; *s* of late John and Susan Guy; *m* 1981, Rosemary Ann Walker; two *d*. *Educ:* Radley Coll. Entered BRNC Dartmouth, 1966; ADC to Governor and Commander-in-Chief, Gibraltar, 1973; commanded: HMS Ashton, 1974; HMS Kedleston, 1975; HMS Sirius, 1984–85. Equerry to the Queen, 1977–80; First Lieut, HMS Antelope (sunk in action 1982), 1981–82. Lieut 1971; Lt-Comdr 1979; Comdr 1983; Captain 1991. Executive Director: Japan Soc., 1997–2007; Hong Kong Assoc. and Hong Kong Soc., 2002–17. Order of Rising Sun, Gold Rays with Rosette (Japan), 2015. *Recreations:* polo, ski-ing, shooting. *Address:* The Barn House, Lees Hill, South Warnborough, Hook, Hants RG29 1RQ. *Club:* White's.

**GUYTON, Marjorie A.;** see Allthorpe-Guyton.

**GWENLLIAN, Sian;** Member (Plaid Cymru) Arfon, National Assembly for Wales, since 2016; *b* Dolgellau, 19 June 1956; *d* of late John Arfon Hughes and of Beti Isabel Hughes; *m* 1988, Dafydd Vernon Jones (*d* 1999); three *s* one *d*. *Educ:* Ysgol Friars, Bangor; Univ. of Aberystwyth (BA Geog.); Cardiff Univ. (Postgrad. Dip. Journalism). Reporter, BBC, 1979–85; reporter and presenter, HTV, 1985–87; freelance journalist, 1987–98; Press Officer, Gwynedd Council, 1998–2005; journalist and writer, Golwg mag., 2005–12. Mem. (Plaid Cymru) Gwynedd Council, 2008–16. *Recreations:* theatre, art, walking, yoga, Welsh rock scene and culture. *Address:* Plaid Cymru, 8 Stryd y Castell, Caernarfon, Gwynedd LL55 1SE. *T:* (01286) 672076. *E:* Sian.Gwenllian@assembly.wales.

**GWILLIAM, Kenneth Mason;** Principal Transport Economist, then Economic Adviser, Transport, World Bank, Washington, 1993–2002; *b* 27 June 1937; *s* of John and Marjorie Gwilliam; *m* 1987, Sandra Wilson; two *s* by former *m*. *Educ:* Magdalen Coll., Oxford (BA 1st Cl. Hons PPE). Res. Asst, Fisons Ltd, 1960–61; Lecturer: Univ. of Nottingham, 1961–65; Univ. of E Anglia, 1965–67; Prof. of Transport Economics, Univ. of Leeds, 1967–89; Prof. of Econs of Transport and Logistics, Erasmus Univ., Rotterdam, 1989–93. Director: Nat. Bus Co., 1978–82; Yorkshire Rider, 1986–88. Editor, Jl of Transport Economics and Policy, 1977–87. *Publications:* Transport and Public Policy, 1964; Economics and Transport Policy, 1975; (jtly) Deregulating the Bus Industry, 1984; Cities on the Move, 2002; Africa's Transport Infrastructure: mainstreaming maintenance and management, 2011. *Recreations:* golf, detective fiction, cruising. *Address:* 12720 Grand Traverse Drive, Dade City, FL 33525–8230, USA.

**GWILLIAM, Michael Colin;** Planning and Transport Director, South East England Regional Assembly, 2001–06; *b* 4 Jan. 1948; *s* of late Alfred and Grace Gwilliam; *m* 1st, 1970, Mary (marr. diss. 1995); two *d*; 2nd, 1996, Janice; two step *d*. *Educ:* Keble Coll., Oxford (MA Hist.); University Coll. London (DipTP); De Montfort Univ., Leicester (DMS). Chief Planner, Leics CC, 1985–88; Co. Planning Officer, Bedfordshire CC, 1988–96; Dir, The Civic Trust, 1996–2000. Vice-Pres., County Planning Officers' Soc., 1995–96. FRSA 1989. Hon. RICS 1999. *Publications:* Sustainable Renewal of Suburban Areas, 1999; Small Town Vitality, 2000; (jtly) Abraham's Children, 2013. *Recreations:* wood carving, woodland management, supporting Palestine, fair trade.

**GWILLIAM, Robert John;** Senior Associate Solicitor, British Telecommunications PLC, 1990–96; *b* 6 Jan. 1943; *s* of Benjamin Harold Gwilliam and Dora Gwilliam; *m* 1966, Linda Mary Ellway; two *s*. *Educ:* Lydney Grammar Sch.; Nottingham Univ. (BA Hons Law); Cambridge Univ. (Dip. Criminology); College of Law. Admitted Solicitor, 1969; practised in Local Govt Prosecuting Depts, 1969–83; Chief Prosecuting Solicitor for Hampshire, 1983–86; Chief Crown Prosecutor, Crown Prosecution Service: London South/Surrey Area, 1986; Inner London Area, 1987; London and SE Regl Dir, Grade 3, 1987–89. *Recreations:* supporting Harlequins RFC, dog walking in Purbeck. *Address:* 1 The Downs, Seymer Road, Swanage, Dorset BH19 2AL.

**GWILLIAMS, Very Rev. Dianna Lynn;** Dean of Guildford, since 2013; *b* Colorado, 1957; *m* Martin; one *s* one *d* (and one *d* decd). *Educ:* California Univ. (BA 1978); King's Coll. London (MA Youth Ministry and Theol Educn 2001). Sound Engr; ordained deacon, 1992, priest, 1994; non-stipendiary Minister, St Saviour, Peckham, 1992–97; Asst Curate, 1997–99, Vicar, 1999–2013, St Barnabas, Dulwich; Area Dean, Dulwich, 2005–12; Priest-in-charge, St Saviour, Peckham, 2007–11; Dean of Women's Ministry, Dio. of Southwark, 2009–12. Chaplain, Alleyn's Foundn, 1999–2013. Hon. Canon, Southwark Cath., 2006–13. *Address:* The Deanery, Cathedral Close, Guildford GU2 7TL. *T:* (01483) 547861, *Fax:* (01483) 303350.

**GWILT, George David,** FFA; General Manager, 1979–84, Managing Director and Actuary, 1984–88, Standard Life Assurance Company; *b* 11 Nov. 1927; *s* of Richard Lloyd Gwilt and Marjory Gwilt (*née* Mair); *m* 1956, Ann Dalton Sylvester; three *s*. *Educ:* Sedbergh Sch.; St John's Coll., Cambridge (MA). FFA 1952; FBCS. Joined Standard Life Assurance Co., 1949: Asst Official, 1956; Asst Actuary, 1957; Statistician, 1962; Mechanisation Manager, 1964; Systems Manager, 1969; Dep. Pensions Manager, 1972; Pensions Actuary, 1973; Asst General Manager and Pensions Manager, 1977; Asst Gen. Man. (Finance), 1978. Dep. Chm., Associated Scottish Life Offices, 1986–88. Special Advr in Scotland, Citicorp, 1989–91; Director: Hammerson Property Investment and Develt Corp., 1979–94; Scottish Mortgage and Trust, 1983–98; European Assets Trust NV, 1979–2000; Hodgson Martin, 1989–2000. Trustee, TSB of South of Scotland, 1966–83. Member: Younger Cttee on Privacy, 1970–72; Monopolies and Mergers Commn, 1983–87. Pres., Faculty of Actuaries, 1981–83. Convener, Scottish Poetry Library, 1988–2001. *Recreation:* flute playing. *Address:* 39 Oxgangs Road, Edinburgh EH10 7BE. *T:* (0131) 445 1266. *Clubs:* Royal Air Force; New (Edinburgh).

**GWILT, Michael Peter;** Motor Risk Manager, HDI Global SE (formerly HDI-Gerling Insurance), since 2012; *b* 29 April 1957; *s* of Geoffrey and Joy Gwilt; *m* 1984, Cheryl Harrison; one *s*. *Educ:* Bishop Perowne C of E Sch., Worcester; King's Sch., Worcester. Family business, R. & G. Gwilt Engineering, 1975–82; Uniweld Ltd, 1983–84; joined Interleasing (UK) Ltd, 1984: Sales and Mktg Dir, 1988–94; Managing Director: Interleasing North, 1994–97; Cowie Interleasing, 1997; Gp Man. Dir, Arriva plc, 1998; Gp Man. Dir, Onlyfair Denmark ApS, subseq. CEO, Fleet Logistics Internat. NV, 1999–2006; Man. Dir, Europe, Drive Cam Inc., 2006–09; Sales Dir, GreenRoad, 2010–11. *Recreations:* ski-ing, travelling, theatre, house renovation.

**GWYER, Ven. Judith;** *see* Rose, Ven. K. J.

**GWYN, Alison Frances M.;** *see* Moore-Gwyn.

**GWYNEDD, Viscount;** William Alexander Lloyd George; Managing Director, Acropora Capital Ltd, since 2017; *b* 16 May 1986; *er s* and *heir* of Earl Lloyd-George of Dwyfor, *qv*. *Educ:* Eton; Sch. of Oriental and African Studies, Univ. of London.

**GWYNN, Dominic Leigh Denys;** Partner, Martin Goetze and Dominic Gwynn, Organ Builders, since 1979; *b* 18 Aug. 1953; *s* of Kenneth Leigh Maxwell Gwynn and Elisabeth (*née* Molenaar); *m* 1976, Antonia Rosamund Cordy; two *d*. *Educ:* Christ's Hosp.; St John's Coll., Oxford (BA Hons; MA). Major projects include: reconstructions: 1716 Handel organ, St Lawrence Whitchurch, Little Stanmore, 1994; 1743 organ, St Helen Bishopsgate, London, 1995; new organs: Handel House Mus., 1998; Magdalene Coll., Cambridge, 2000; reconstruction, two early Tudor organs, Early English Organ Project, 2000–01; restorations: 1829 organ, St James Bermondsey, London, 2002; 1704 Renatus Harris organ, St Botolph, Aldgate, 2006; 1969 Grant Degens and Bradbeer organ, New Coll., Oxford, 2014. *Publications:* (contrib.) Performing Purcell's Music, 1995; Historic Organ Conservation, 2001; contribs to Jl British Inst. of Organ Studies, Organ Yearbook and Organists Review. *Recreations:* choral singing, early modern church, social and cultural history. *Address:* 12 Burcott Road, Wells, Somerset BA5 2EQ. *T:* (01749) 675955, *T:* (office) (01909) 485635.

**GWYNNE, Andrew John;** MP (Lab) Denton and Reddish, since 2005; *b* 4 June 1974; *s* of Richard John Gwynne and Margaret Elisabeth Gwynne (*née* Ridgway); *m* 2003, Allison Louise Dennis; two *s* one *d*. *Educ:* Univ. of Salford (BA Hons Politics and Contemp. Hist.); NE Wales Inst. of Higher Educn (HND Business and Finance). Asst to EDS Prog. Manager, ICL, Manchester, 1990–92; Mem., Year 2000 Team, Nat. Computing Centre, 1999–2000; European Co-ordinator, office of Arlene McCarthy, MEP, 2000–01; researcher, office of Andrew Bennett, MP, 2000–05. PPS to Minister of State, Home Office, 2005–07, to Home Sec., 2007–09, to Secretary of State, Children, Schs and Families, 2009–10; Shadow Minister: of Transport, 2010–11; for Health, 2011–15; Shadow Minister without Portfolio, 2016–17; Shadow Sec. of State for Communities and Local Govt, 2017–. Co-Nat. Campaign Co-ordinator, Labour Party, 2017–. Mem. (Lab) Tameside MBC, 1996–2008. *Recreations:* history, reading, computing, spending time with family. *Address:* House of Commons, SW1A 0AA. *T:* (020) 7219 4708. *E:* gwynnea@parliament.uk; (constituency office) Town Hall, Market Street, Denton M34 2AP. *T:* (0161) 320 1504, *Fax:* (0161) 320 1503.

**GWYNNE, Emily;** *see* Maitlis, E.

**GWYNNE JONES,** family name of **Baron Chalfont**.

**GWYTHER, Christine;** Member (Lab) Carmarthen West and South Pembrokeshire, National Assembly for Wales, 1999–2007; Member, Pembrokeshire Coast National Park Authority, 2007; *b* 9 Aug. 1959; *d* of Ivor George Gwyther and Marjorie Gwyther (*née* Doidge). *Educ:* Pembroke Sch.; UC, Cardiff. Milford Haven Waterway Enterprise Zone, 1986; local govt officer, S Pembrokeshire DC, 1987–96, Pembrokeshire CC, 1996–99. National Assembly for Wales: Sec. for Agric. and Rural Develt, 1999–2000; Chm., Econ. Develt and Transport Cttee, 2003–07. Contested (Lab): Carmarthen W and S Pembs, Nat. Assembly for Wales, 2007, 2011; Carmarthen E and Dinefwr, 2010. Welsh Chair, Interreg III Prog. Monitoring Cttee, 2002. Mem., Pembrokeshire Business Club. Mem., RSPB.

**GYIMAH, Samuel Phillip;** MP for East Surrey, since 2010 (C, 2010–19; Lib Dem, since 2019); *b* Beaconsfield, Bucks, 10 Aug. 1976; *m* 2012, Dr Nicky Black. *Educ:* Achimota Secondary Sch., Ghana; Freman Coll., Herts; Somerville Coll., Oxford (BA PPE). Pres., Oxford Union, 1997. Investment Banker, Internat. Equities and Investment Banking Div., Goldman Sachs, 1999–2003; entrepreneur in trng, employment and internet sectors, 2003–10. PPS to the Prime Minister, 2012–13; a Lord Comr of HM Treasury (Govt Whip), 2013–14; Parly Sec., Cabinet Office, 2014–15; Parly Under-Sec. of State, DfE, 2014–16, MoJ, 2016–18; Minister of State (Minister for Univs and Sci.), DfE and BEIS, 2018. Chm., Bow Gp, 2007. Gov., Haverstock Sch., 2004–07. *Publications:* (ed) From the Ashes...: the future of the Conservative Party, 2005; (jtly) Beyond the Banks, 2011. *Address:* House of Commons, SW1A 0AA. *T:* (020) 7219 3504. *E:* sam@samgyimah.com.

**GYLE, Rev. Alan Gordon;** Vicar, St Paul's, Knightsbridge, since 2003 (Priest-in-charge, 2001–03); *b* Aberdeen, 27 June 1965; *s* of late Ernest Gordon Gyle and of Janet May Cochrane (*née* Cunningham). *Educ:* Univ. of Aberdeen (MA 1987); St Stephen's House, Oxford (MA 1996); Univ. of E London (MA 2008). Ordained deacon, 1992, priest, 1993; Asst Curate, Acton Green, 1992–94; Minor Canon (Succentor & Dean's Vicar), St George's Chapel, Windsor Castle, 1994–99; Chaplain: Imperial Coll. London, 1999–2004; Royal Coll. of Art, 1999–2004; Dir of Trng and Develt (Two Cities), Dio. of London, 2008–12. Examining Chaplain to the Bishop of London, 2007–17; Priest Vicar, Westminster Abbey, 2008–. Hon. Chaplain, Royal Thames Yacht Club, 2001–. Hon. Fellow, St George's House, Windsor, 1999–2001. FRSA 1999. *Recreations:* music, cookery. *Address:* The Vicarage, 32 Wilton Place, SW1X 8SH. *T:* (020) 7201 9999. *E:* alangyle@me.com. *Clubs:* Athenæum, Caledonian.

**GYLLENHAMMAR, Dr Pehr Gustaf;** Vice Chairman, Europe, Rothschild, 2003; *b* 28 April 1935; *s* of Pehr Gustaf Victor Gyllenhammar and Aina Dagny Kaplan; *m* 1959, Eva Christina (*d* 2008), *d* of Gunnar Ludvig Engellau; one *s* three *d*; *m* 2010, Christel Behrmann (marr. diss. 2013); *m* 2013, Lee Welton Croll; one *d*. *Educ:* University of Lund. LLB. Mannheimer & Zetterlöf, solicitors, 1959; Haight, Gardner, Poor & Havens, NY, 1960; Amphion Insurance Co., Gothenburg, 1961–64; Skandia Insurance Co., 1965, Exec. Vice-Pres., 1968, Pres. and Chief Exec. Officer, 1970; AB Volvo, Gothenburg, 1970, Man. Dir and Chief Exec. Officer, 1971; Chm. and Chief Exec. Officer, 1983–90, Exec. Chm. Bd of Dirs, 1990–93, Volvo; Dep. Chm., Commercial Union plc, 1997–98; Chm., CGU, subseq. CGNU, then Aviva, plc, 1998–2005. Chairman: MC European Capital (Holdings), SA, 1994–96; Lazard AB, 1999–2003; Thomson Reuters (formerly Reuters) Founders Share Co. Ltd, 1999–2012; Investment AB Kinnevik, 2004–07; Majid Al Futtaim Hldg LLC, 2004–09; Arise Windpower AB, 2007–14; Sen. Advr, Lazard Frères & Co., 1996–2003; Dir of companies in Sweden, Netherlands, UK and USA. Member: Internat. Adv. Cttee, Chase Manhattan Bank, NA, NY, 1972–95; Bd, Cttee of Common Market Automobile Constructors, 1977–91; Bd, Assoc. des Constructeurs Européens d'Automobiles, 1991–93; Bd, Fedn of Swedish Industries, 1979–93; Roundtable of European Industrialists, 1982–93; Chm., European Financial Services Round Table, 2001–06. Mem. Bd Trustees, Rockefeller Univ., NY, 1991–96; Chm. Bd Trustees, LPO, 2006. Lethaby Prof., Royal Coll. of Art, London, 1977; Mem., Royal Swedish Acad. of Engineering Scis, 1974. Hon. DM Gothenburg Univ., 1981; Hon. DTech Brunel, 1987; Hon. DEng Technical Univ., NS, 1988; Hon. DSocSc Helsinki, 1990; Hon. DEc Gothenburg, 2003. Golden Award, City of Gothenburg, 1981. Officer, Royal Order of Vasa, 1973; King's Medal, with Ribbon of Order of Seraphim, 1981; Commander: Order of Lion of Finland, 1977 (Comdr 1st Class 1986); Ordre National du Mérite, France, 1980; St Olav's Order, Norway, 1984; Légion d'honneur, France, 1987; Order of Leopold, Belgium, 1989; Kt Grand Officer, Order of Merit, Italy, 1987. *Publications:* Mot sekelskiftet på måfå (Toward the Turn of the Century, at Random), 1970; Jag tror på Sverige (I Believe in Sweden), 1973; People at Work (US), 1977; En industripolitik för människan (Industrial policy for human beings), 1979; Fortsättning följer... (To Be Continued...), 2000; Oberoende ar stark (Independence is Strong), 2014. *Recreations:* golf, music.

**GYPPS, His Honour Godfrey Howard;** a Circuit Judge, 2003–08; Designated Family Judge for the County of Essex, and Chairman, Essex Family Justice Council, 2005–08; *b* 24 March 1947; *s* of Jack and Hilda Gypps; *m* 1974, Judith Wendy Falkner; two *d*. *Educ:* Colchester Royal Grammar Sch.; Queen Mary Coll., Univ. of London (LLB Hons 1969). Admitted solicitor, 1972; on teaching staff, Coll. of Law, 1972–90; Dist Judge, 1991–2003; on secondment to staff of Hd of Civil Justice, 1998 and 2000. Vis. Fellow, Dept of Law, Univ. of Essex, 1998–. Member: Civil Procedure Rule Cttee, 1997–2001; Civil Justice Council, 2002–03. *Publications:* contribs to various legal pubns and periodicals. *Recreations:* the countryside, dogs, radio. *Address:* c/o HM Court Service, Priory Place, Chelmsford CM2 0PP. *Clubs:* Colchester Garrison Officers', Old Colcestrians.

# H

**HAAG, Jessica Margaret Poppaea;** *see* Simor, J. M. P.

**HAAKONSSEN, Prof. Knud,** Dr phil, PhD; FBA 2012; FRSE; FRHistS; Professor of Intellectual History and Director, Sussex Centre for Intellectual History, University of Sussex, 2005–11, now Professor Emeritus; Long-term Fellow, Max-Weber-Kolleg, University of Erfurt, since 2012; Professor of Intellectual History (part-time), University of St Andrews, since 2015; *b* Tingsted, Falster, Denmark, 9 July 1947; *s* of Helmer Daniel Haakonssen and Laura Eline Haakonssen; *m* 2001, Åsa Marie Söderman; one *s*. *Educ:* Nykøbing Realskole; Nykøbing Katedralskole; Univ. of Copenhagen (Cand.Art.; MA; Dr phil 1996); Univ. of Aarhus (Gold Medal in Philosophy); Univ. of Edinburgh (PhD 1978). FRHistS 2005. Sen. Tutor, Dept of Philosophy, Monash Univ., 1976–79; Lectr, Sch. of Pol Sci., Victoria Univ. of Wellington, 1979–82; Res. Fellow, Sen. Res. Fellow, Fellow, then Sen. Fellow, Hist. of Ideas Unit, Res. Sch. of Social Scis, ANU, 1982–94; Prof., Dept of Philosophy, Boston Univ., 1995–2004. Fellow, Woodrow Wilson Center, Washington, 1988. Visiting Professor: Dept of Philosophy, McGill Univ., 1992–93; Martin-Luther-Univ. Halle-Wittenberg, 2011; Torgny Segerstedt Prof., Univ. of Uppsala, 2001; Hon. Prof. of Hist., UCL, 2011–16; Lim Chong Yah Prof., 2012, Vis Prof., 2013–14, of Pol Sci., NUS; Sen. Scholar, Univ. of Bergen, 2013–14; Affiliated Prof. of Hist., Univ. of Copenhagen, 2018–. FASSA 1992; FRSE 2002; Fellow, Japan Soc. for Promotion of Sci., 2000. Corresp. Fellow, Royal Danish Acad. of Sci. and Letters, 1995. *Publications:* The Science of a Legislator, 1981 (trans. French, 1998, Japanese, 2001, Chinese, 2010); Thomas Reid on Practical Ethics, 1990, 2007; (ed jtly) A Culture of Rights: the Bill of Rights in philosophy, politics and Law, 1791 and 1991, 1991; Natural Law and Moral Philosophy: from Grotius to the Scottish Enlightenment, 1996 (trans. Chinese 2010) (ed) Enlightenment and Religion: rational dissent in eighteenth-century Britain, 1996; (ed) The Cambridge History of Eighteenth-Century Philosophy, 2 vols, 2006 (trans. Chinese 2018); (ed) Cambridge Companion to Adam Smith, 2006; (ed jtly) Northern Antiquities and National Identities: perceptions of Denmark and the North in the eighteenth century, 2008; Enlightenments and Religions, 2010; (ed jtly) David Hume, 2013; (ed jtly) Ludvig Holberg (1684–1754): learning and literature in the Nordic Enlightenment, 2017; General Editor: The Edinburgh Edition of Thomas Reid, 10 vols, 1994–; Natural Law and Enlightenment Classics, 44 vols, 2001–; *festschrift:* Philosophy, Rights and Natural Law: essays in honour of Knud Haakonssen, ed. Ian Hunter and Richard Whatmore, 2019. *Recreations:* opera, reading, hiking. *E:* k.haakonssen@gmail.com.

**HAAVISTO, Heikki Johannes;** Chairman Board of Directors, Raisio Group, 1997–2001 (Chairman, Administrative Council, 1977–96); *b* Turku, Finland, 20 Aug. 1935; *s* of Urho and Alli Haavisto; *m* 1964, Maija Rihko; three *s*. *Educ:* Univ. of Helsinki (MSc, LLM). Hd of Dept, Oy Vehnä Ab, 1963–66; Sec.-Gen., Central Union of Agricl Producers and Forest Owners, 1966–75 (Pres., 1976–94); Member, Administrative Council: Osuuskunta Metsäliitto, Helsinki, 1976–93 (Vice-Chm. and Pres., 1976–93); Central Union Co-op. Banks, Helsinki, 1985–93; Minister of For. Affairs, Finland, 1993–95. Chm., Delegn, Finnish Co-operative Pellervo, Helsinki, 1979–2001. Mem., Internat. Policy Council on Agric. and Trade, Washington, 1988–2000. Mem., Centre Party, Finland. Hon. PhD Turku; Hon. Dr Agr. & For., Hon. DVM Helsinki, 1995. *Address:* Hintsantie 2, 21200 Raisio, Finland.

**HABERFELD, Dame Gwyneth;** *see* Jones, Dame G.

**HABERMAN, Prof. Steven,** PhD, DSc; FIA; Professor of Actuarial Science, City, University of London (formerly City University London), since 1985; *b* London, 26 June 1951; *s* of Louis and Lily Haberman; *m* 1974, Mandy Brecker; one *s* two *d*. *Educ:* Trinity Coll., Cambridge (BA Maths 1972); City Univ. (PhD 1982; DSc 2000). FIA 1975. Trainee actuary, Prudential Assce Co. Ltd, 1972–74; Actuary (pt-time), Govt Actuary's Dept, 1977–97; City University: Lectr in Actuarial Sci., 1974–80; Sen. Lectr, 1980–85; Hd, Dept of Actuarial Sci. and Stats, 1987–95; Dean, Sch. of Maths, 1995–2002; Dep. Dean, 2003–12, Dean, 2012–15, Cass Business Sch. Chm., Bd of Govs, London Inst. of Banking & Finance, 2017–. Hon. PhD Haifa, 2018. *Publications:* Pensions: the problem of today and tomorrow, 1987; History of Actuarial Science, 1995; Modern Actuarial Theory and Practice, 1999, 2nd edn 2005; Actuarial Models for Disability Insurance, 1999; Modelling Longevity Dynamics for Pensions and Annuity Business, 2009. *Recreations:* theatre, cinema, opera, hiking, playing with grandchildren. *Address:* Cass Business School, 106 Bunhill Row, EC1Y 8TZ. *T:* (020) 7040 8470, *Fax:* (020) 7040 8899. *E:* S.Haberman@city.ac.uk.

**HABGOOD, Sir Anthony (John),** Kt 2018; Chairman: RELX Group (formerly Reed Elsevier), since 2009; Preqin, since 2011; *b* 8 Nov. 1946; *s* of John Michael Habgood and Margaret Diana Middleton Habgood (*née* Dalby); *m* 1974, Nancy Atkinson; two *s* one *d*. *Educ:* Gonville and Caius Coll., Cambridge (MA Econ 1972); Carnegie Mellon Univ., Pittsburgh (MS Indust. Admin 1970). Boston Consulting Gp, 1970–86: Director, 1976; Management Cttee, 1979; Exec. Cttee, 1981; Tootal Group, 1986–91: Director, 1986; Chief Exec., 1991; Chief Exec., 1991–96, Chm., 1996–2009, Bunzl plc. Chairman: Whitbread Group plc, 2005–14; Mölnlycke Health Care, 2006–07; Norwich Research Park LLP, 2013–16; Director: Geest, 1988–93; Powergen, 1993–2001; SVG Capital (formerly Schroder Ventures Internat. Investment Trust), 1995–2009; NatWest Gp, 1998–2000; Marks and Spencer, 2004–05; Norfolk and Norwich Univ. Hosp. Trust, 2006–13. Chm., Ct of Dirs, Bank of England, 2014–18. Vis. Fellow, Univ. of Oxford, 2008–. Hon. DCL East Anglia, 2016. *Recreation:* country pursuits. *Address:* RELX Group, 1–3 Strand, WC2N 5JR. *Clubs:* Brooks's, Royal Automobile; Royal Norfolk and Suffolk Yacht.

**HABGOOD, Hon. Francis John Stapylton,** QPM 2012; Chief Constable, Thames Valley Police, 2015–19; *b* Jedburgh, Scotland, 19 Nov. 1964; *s* of Baron Habgood, PC; *m* 1990, Dr Nicolette Tamsin Campbell; two *s*. *Educ:* Durham Chorister Sch.; Repton Sch.; Univ. of Newcastle upon Tyne (BSc Hons Mech. Engrg); Univ. of Cambridge (Dip. Applied Criminol.). Police Officer, W Yorks Police, 1987–2004; Asst Chief Constable, 2004–08, Dep. Chief Constable, 2008–15, Thames Valley Police. Ind. Chair: Bucks Safeguarding Children Bd, 2019–; Bucks Safeguarding Adults Bd, 2019–. Vis. Fellow, Lady Margaret Hall, Oxford, 2016–19. *Recreations:* family, gardening, DIY, walking.

**HÄCKER, Prof. Birke,** DPhil; Professor of Comparative Law, since 2016, and Director, Institute of European and Comparative Law, since 2018, University of Oxford; Fellow of Brasenose College, Oxford, since 2016; *b* 1977; *d* of Otto and Heide Häcker; *m* Dr Tobias Reker; one *d*. *Educ:* Univ. of Oxford (BA 2001; DPhil 2007); Univ. of Bonn (Dipl.-Jur. 2004); 1st and 2nd German State Examination in Law, 2004 and 2011. Examination Fellow, All Souls Coll., Oxford, 2001–08; Res. Associate, then Lectr in Law, Ludwig-Maximilians-Universität, Munich, 2009–15; Sen. Res. Fellow, Max Planck Inst. for Tax Law and Public Finance, Munich, 2011–16; Fifty-Pound Fellow, All Souls Coll., Oxford, 2011–16. Therese von Bayern Prize 2015, Ludwig-Maximilians-Universität, 2016. *Publications:* Consequences of Impaired Consent Transfers: a structural comparison of English and German law, 2009, repubd 2013; (ed jtly) Restitution of Overpaid Tax, 2013; (ed jtly) Current Issues in Succession Law, 2016; articles in learned jls and edited collections. *Address:* Brasenose College, Oxford OX1 4AJ.

**HACKER, Rt Rev. George Lanyon;** Bishop Suffragan of Penrith, 1979–94; an Honorary Assistant Bishop, Diocese of Carlisle, 1994–2018; *b* 27 Dec. 1928; *s* of Edward Sidney Hacker and Carla Lanyon; *m* 1969, June Margaret Erica Smart; one *s* one *d*. *Educ:* Kelly College, Tavistock; Exeter College, Oxford (BA 1952, MA 1956); Cuddesdon College, Oxford. Deacon 1954, priest 1955; Bristol; Curate of St Mary Redcliffe, Bristol, 1954–59; Chaplain, King's College London at St Boniface Coll., Warminster, 1959–64; Perpetual Curate, Church of the Good Shepherd, Bishopwearmouth, 1964–71; Rector of Tilehurst, Reading, 1971–79. Pres., Rural Theol. Assoc., 1989–94; Pres., Age Concern Cumbria, 1991–2007 (Chm., 1987–91); Chm., Age Concern Eden, 1994–2000; Episcopal Advr, Anglican Young People's Assoc., 1987–94. Editor, Chrism, 1996–2008. *Publications:* The Healing Stream: Catholic insights into the ministry of healing, 1998. *Recreation:* researching family history. *Address:* Keld House, Milburn, Penrith, Cumbria CA10 1TW. *T:* (01768) 361506. *E:* bishhack@outlook.com.

**HACKER, Peter Michael Stephen,** DPhil; Fellow and Tutor in Philosophy, 1966–2006, Librarian, 1986–2006, Emeritus Research Fellow, 2006–15, St John's College, Oxford, now Emeritus Fellow; Professor of Philosophy, University of Kent at Canterbury, 2013–16; *b* 15 July 1939; *s* of Emeric Hacker and Thea Hacker (*née* Mendel); *m* 1963, Sylvia Dolores Imhoff; two *s* one *d*. *Educ:* Queen's Coll., Oxford (MA; Hon. Fellow 2010); St Antony's Coll., Oxford (DPhil). Jun. Res. Fellow, Balliol Coll., Oxford, 1965–66; British Acad. Res. Reader, 1985–87; Leverhulme Res. Fellow, 1991–94. Visiting Professor: Swarthmore Coll., Pa, 1973, 1986; Univ. of Michigan, Ann Arbor, 1974; Queen's Univ., Ont, 1985; Vis. Fellow, Rockefeller Foundn, Bellagio, 2006; Vis. Sen. Res. Fellow, Univ. of Bologna, 2009. *Publications:* Insight and Illusion, 1972, 2nd edn 1986; Appearance and Reality, 1987; (ed) The Renaissance of Gravure: the art of S. W. Hayter, 1988; Wittgenstein: meaning and mind, 1990; (ed) Gravure and Grace: the engravings of Roger Vieillard, 1993; Wittgenstein: mind and will, 1996; Wittgenstein's Place in Twentieth Century Analytic Philosophy, 1996; Wittgenstein: connections and controversies, 2001; (with M. R. Bennett) Philosophical Foundations of Neuroscience, 2003; (jtly) Neuroscience and Philosophy, 2007; Human Nature: the categorial framework, 2007; (with M. R. Bennett) A History of Cognitive Neuroscience, 2008; (ed with J. R. Cottingham) Mind, Method and Morality: essays in honour of Anthony Kenny, 2009; (ed with J. Schulte) Wittgenstein: philosophical investigations, 4th edn 2009; with G. P. Baker: Wittgenstein: understanding and meaning, 1980, 2nd edn 2004; Frege: logical excavations, 1984; Language, Sense and Nonsense, 1984; Scepticism, Rules and Language, 1984; Wittgenstein: rules, grammar and necessity, 1985, 2nd edn 2009; *festschrift:* Wittgenstein and Analytic Philosophy: essays for P. M. S. Hacker, ed H.-J. Glock and J. Hyman, 2009; The Intellectual Powers: a study of human nature, 2013; Wittgenstein: comparisons and contexts, 2013; The Passions: a study of human nature, 2017. *Recreations:* art history, music. *Address:* St John's College, Oxford OX1 3JP.

**HACKER, Richard Daniel;** QC 1998; *b* 1954; *s* of Samuel Hacker and Lilli Hacker; *m* 1988, Sarah; one *d*. *Educ:* Haberdashers' Aske's Sch.; Downing Coll., Cambridge (Wiener Anspach Schol., 1976; BA Law 1976; MA 1979); Univ. Libre de Bruxelles (Licence Spéciale en Droit Européen (Distinction) 1978). Called to the Bar: Lincoln's Inn, 1977 (Hardwicke Schol.; Student of the Year Prize), ad eundem Gray's Inn, 1989; British Virgin Islands, 2003. Asst Parly Boundary Comr, 2000; Chm., Inquiry into Herts Parly Constituency Boundaries, 2000. *Recreations:* travel, food, family life. *Address:* 3–4 South Square, Gray's Inn, WC1R 5HP. *T:* (020) 7696 9900, *Fax:* (020) 7696 9911. *E:* contact@hacker.plus.com.

**HACKETT, John Wilkings,** CMG 1989; Director, Financial, Fiscal and Enterprise Affairs, Organisation for Economic Co-operation and Development, Paris, 1979–89; *b* 21 Jan. 1924; *s* of Albert and Bertha Hackett; *m* 1952, Anne-Marie Le Brun. *Educ:* LSE (BSc(Econ) 1950); Institut d'Etudes Politiques, Paris (Diplôme 1952); Univ. of Paris (Dr d'état ès sciences économiques 1957). Served RN, 1942–46. Economic research, 1952–57; OECD, 1958–89. FRSA 1986. *Publications:* Economic Planning in France (with A.-M. Hackett), 1963; L'Economie Britannique—problèmes et perspectives, 1966; (with A.-M. Hackett) The British Economy, 1967; articles on economic subjects in British and French economic jls. *Recreations:* music, painting, reading. *Address:* 48 rue de la Bienfaisance, 75008 Paris, France. *Clubs:* Royal Over-Seas League; Cercle de l'Union Interalliée (Paris).

**HACKING,** family name of **Baron Hacking**.

**HACKING,** 3rd Baron *cr* 1945, of Chorley; **Douglas David Hacking;** Bt 1938; International Arbitrator and Mediator; Solicitor of Supreme Court of England and Wales, 1977–99; Attorney and Counselor-at-Law of State of New York, since 1975; Barrister-at-law, 1963–76 and since 1999; Chartered Arbitrator, since 1999; *b* 17 April 1938; *er s* of 2nd Baron Hacking, and Daphne Violet (*d* 1998), *e d* of late R. L. Finnis; *S* father, 1971; *m* 1st, 1965, Rosemary Anne, *e d* of late Francis P. Forrest, FRCSE; two *s* one *d*; 2nd, 1982, Dr Tessa M. Hunt, MB, MRCP, FRCA, *er d* of late Roland C. C. Hunt, CMG;

three s. Educ: Aldro School, Shackleford; Charterhouse School; Clare College, Cambridge (BA 1961, MA 1968). Served in RN, 1956–58; Ordinary Seaman, 1956; Midshipman, 1957; served in HMS Ark Royal (N Atlantic), 1957; HMS Hardy (Portland) and HMS Brocklesby (Portland and Gibraltar), 1958; transferred RNR as Sub-Lt, 1958, on completion of National Service; transf. List 3 RNR, HMS President, 1961; Lieut 1962; retired RNR, 1964. Called to the Bar, Middle Temple, Nov. 1963 (Astbury and Harmsworth Scholarships). With Simpson, Thacher and Bartlett, NYC, 1975–76; with Lovell, White and King, 1976–79; Partner: Lane & Partners, 1979–81; Richards Butler, 1981–94; Sonnenscheins, 1994–99; Mem., Littleton Chambers, 2000–. Mem., H of L Select Cttee on the European Community, 1989–93, 1995–99. Chm. Steering Cttee, London Internat. Arbitration Trust, 1980–81. Trustee, Carthusian Trust, 1971–2001. Gov., Charlotte Sharman Sch., Southwark, 1996–97. Member: Amer. Bar Assoc.; Bar Assoc. of City of New York; Indian Council of Arbitration, 1997–; Swiss Arbitration Assoc., 2000–. Fellow: Singapore Inst. of Arbitrators, 2004–; Malaysian Inst. of Arbitrators, 2004–. Pres., Assoc. of Lancastrians in London, 1971–72, 1998. Apprenticed to Merchant Taylors' Co., 1955, admitted to Freedom, 1962; Freedom, City of London, 1962. FCIArb 1979. *Recreations*: reading biographies, mountain walking. *Heir*: s Hon. Douglas Francis Hacking [b 8 Aug. 1968; m 2000, Dr Jodie McVernon; two d]. *Address*: 27 West Square, Kennington, SE11 4SP. *T*: (020) 7735 4400. *E*: david.hacking@london-arbitration.com: Littleton Chambers, 3 King's Bench Walk, Temple, EC4Y 7HR. *T*: (020) 7797 8600, *Fax*: (020) 7797 8699. *E*: dhacking@littletonchambers.co.uk. *Clubs*: Reform, MCC.

**HACKING, Anthony Stephen;** QC 1983; *b* 12 Jan. 1941; *s* of late John and Joan Hacking, Warwick; *m* 1969, Carin, *d* of late Dr Svante and of Brita Holmdahl, Gothenburg; one *d* three *s*. *Educ*: Warwick Sch.; Lincoln Coll., Oxford (MA Jurisprudence). Called to the Bar, Inner Temple, 1965, Bencher, 1993; a Recorder, 1985–2006; a Dep. High Ct Judge (QBD), 1993–2001. Hd of Chambers, 1 King's Bench Walk, 1999–2005.

**HACKING, Prof. Ian MacDougall,** CC 2004; PhD; FRSC; University Professor, University of Toronto, 1991–2003, now University Professor Emeritus (Professor, Department of Philosophy, 1981–2003); Chair de philosophie et histoire des concepts scientifiques, Collège de France, 2000–06, now Professeur honoraire; *b* 18 Feb. 1936; *s* of Harold Eldridge Hacking and Margaret Elinore Hacking (*née* MacDougall); *m* 1983, Judith Baker (*d* 2014); one *s* two *d*. *Educ*: Univ. of British Columbia (BA 1956); Trinity Coll., Cambridge (BA 1958, MA 1962; PhD 1962; Hon. Fellow, 2000). Res. Fellow, Peterhouse, Cambridge, 1962–64; Asst Prof., then Associate Prof. of Philos., Univ. of British Columbia, 1964–69, seconded to Makerere UC, by External Aid, Canada, 1967–69; Univ. Lectr in Philos., Univ. of Cambridge and Fellow, Peterhouse, Cambridge, 1969–74 (Hon. Fellow, 2005); Stanford University: Fellow, Center for Advanced Study in the Behavioral Scis, 1974–75; Prof., 1975–82; Henry Waldegrave Stuart Prof. of Philos., 1981–82. FRSC 1986; Fellow Amer. Acad. of Arts and Scis, 1991; Corresp. FBA, 1995. Hon. Dr: British Columbia, 2001; Cordoba, 2007; McMaster, 2008; Toronto, 2010; Carleton, 2012. Gold Medal for Achievement in Res., Social Scis and Humanities Res. Council, Canada, 2008; Ludvig Holberg Internat. Meml Prize, 2009; Austrian Decoration of Honour for Sci. and Arts, 2012; Balzan Prize for Epistemology and Philosophy of Mind, Internat. Balzan Prize Foundn, 2014. *Publications*: Logic of Statistical Inference, 1965; A Concise Introduction to Logic, 1972; Why Does Language Matter to Philosophy?, 1975; The Emergence of Probability, 1975, 2nd edn 2006; Representing and Intervening, 1983; The Taming of Chance, 1990; Le Plus pur nominalisme: L'énigme de Goodman: 'vleu' et usages de 'vleu', 1993; Rewriting the Soul: multiple personality and the sciences of memory, 1995; Mad Travelers: reflections on the reality of transient mental illnesses, 1998; The Social Construction of What?, 1999; Probability and Inductive Logic, 2001; Historical Ontology, 2002; Why is There Philosophy of Mathematics At All?, 2014. *Recreations*: canoeing, mountain hiking. *E*: ihack@chass.utoronto.ca.

**HACKITT, Dame Judith (Elizabeth), (Dame Judith Lea),** DBE 2016 (CBE 2006); FIChemE; FCGI; FREng; Chairman, Make UK (formerly EEF Ltd), since 2016; *b* 1 Dec. 1954; *d* of Kenneth G. Hackitt and Kathleen Rhoda Hackitt (*née* Jeffcott); *m* 1977, David John Lea; two *d*. *Educ*: Queen Elizabeth Grammar Sch., Atherstone, Warwicks; Imperial Coll., London (BSc (Eng) 1975). ACGI 1972, FCGI 2008; FIChemE 2001; FREng 2010. Eur. Pigments Ops Dir, 1990–96, Gp Risk Manager, 1996–98, Elementis plc; Dir, Business and Envmt, 1998–2002, Dir Gen., 2002–06, CIA; Dir of Implementation, CEFIC, Brussels, 2006–07; Chair, HSC, later HSE, 2007–16. Non-exec. Dir, Oxon HA, 1995–98. Co-Chair, EU Chemicals Policy Strategy Gp, 2002–05. Member: Bd, Energy Saving Trust, 2009–17; Bd, High Value Manufacturing Catapult, 2014–. Non-exec. Dir, High Speed Two Ltd, 2019–. Mem. Council, IChemE, 2008–15 (Pres., 2013–14); Chm., Sci., Engrg and Manufg Technologies Alliance, 2017–. Trustee, RAEng, 2018–. *Recreations*: music (ageing rock stars), walking, ski-ing, good food and wine. *Address*: Make UK, Broadway House, Tothill Street, SW1H 9NQ. *T*: (020) 7222 7777. *E*: chair@makeuk.org, judithhackitt@hotmail.com.

**HACKLAND, Brian Anthony;** Director, Government Office Network Closure Programmes, Department for Communities and Local Government, 2010–11; *b* 3 March 1951; *s* of Alan Keith Hackland and Catherine Mary Hackland; *m* 1978, Sarah Ann Spencer, *qv*; two *s*. *Educ*: Univ. of Natal (BSc Hons Botany and Entomology 1974); Balliol Coll., Oxford (Rhodes Schol.). BA Hons Pol, Philos. and Econs 1977); DPhil Pol Sci. Oxon 1984. Parly Asst to Shadow Sec. of State for NI, 1985–88; Investigator with Local Govt Ombudsman, 1988–90; on secondment as Ombudsman, Bedfordshire CC, 1990; Department of the Environment: Team Leader, Housing Action Trusts Prog., 1991–93, Central Finance, 1993–95; Private Sec. to Minister for Local Govt, Housing and Regeneration, 1995–97; Hd, Air and Envmt Quality Div., 1997–99; Sen. Policy Advr (Envmt and Transport), Prime Minister's Policy Directorate, 1999–2001; Dir, Town and Country Planning, ODPM, 2002–05; Regl Dir, Govt Office for the E of England, 2005–08; Dir, Regl Coordination Unit and Govt Office Network, later Govt Office Network Centre and Services, DCLG, 2008–10. Dir, Eur. Regl Develt Fund, 2000–06. *Publications*: (with Gwyneth Williams) Dictionary of Contemporary Southern African Politics, 1985, repubd 2016. *Recreations*: gardening, walking, cycling.

**HACKLAND, Sarah Ann;** *see* Spencer, S. A.

**HACKNEY, Archdeacon of;** *see* Adekunle, Ven. E.

**HACKNEY, Roderick Peter,** PhD; PPRIBA; Joint Director, Kansara Hackney Ltd, architectural consultancy, since 2019 (Managing Director, Rod Hackney & Associates, 1972–2019; Co-founder and Director, Kansara Hackney Ltd, 2009–19); *b* 3 March 1942; *s* of William Hackney and Rose (*née* Morris); *m* 1964, Christine Thornton; one *s*. *Educ*: John Bright Grammar School, Llandudno; Sch. of Architecture, Manchester Univ. (BAArch 1966, MA 1969, PhD 1979). ARIBA 1969; FCIArb 1977; ASAI; FFB 1987; MCIOB 1987. Job Architect, EXPO '67, Montreal, for Monorail Stations; Housing Architect, Libyan Govt, Tripoli, 1967–68; Asst to Arne Jacobsen, Copenhagen, working on Kuwait Central Bank, 1968–71. Established: Castward Ltd, building and develt firm, 1983 (Sec., 1983–92). Royal Institute of British Architects: Pres., 1987–89; Mem. Council, 1978–84 (Vice-Pres., Public Affairs, and Overseas Affairs, 1981–83), and 1991–99 (Vice-Pres., Internat. Affairs, 1992–94); Hon. Librarian, 1998–99; Chairman: Discipline Hearings Cttee, 2001–03; Discipline Cttee, 2003–07; Mem., Conservation Cttee, 2010–; Sen. Conservation Architect, 2010–; Dir, RIBAC Cos, 1996–2001. Mem. Council, Internat. Union of Architects, 1981–85, and 1991–, First Vice-Pres., 1985–87, Pres., 1987–90. Vis. Prof., Paris, 1984; Special Prof., Nottingham Univ., 1990–; Vis. Prof., Xian Univ., China, 1999; has lectured in Europe, N and S America, Asia, Middle East, Australia and Africa. Chm., Times/RIBA Community Enterprise Scheme, 1985–89; Mem. Council, Nat. Historical Bldg Crafts Inst., 1989–; Advr on regeneration and inner city problems in Sweden, Italy, Brazil, USA, Russia, Dubai, China and Germany, 1990–; Internat. Advr, Centre for Internat. Architectl Studies, Univ. of Manchester Sch. of Architecture, 1992–; Jury Mem., overseas housing develts; Juror for internat. competitions in Netherlands and China, 1992–; Mem., Adv. Gp, UN World Habitat Awards, 2003–; Chm., UN Good Practice Awards, 2004; Pres., UN Cttee on Housing for the Elderly, 2010–; Co-Architectl Advr to Samba Bank HQ, Saudi Arabia, 2010–; deleg., UK and overseas confs. Chairman: Trustees, Inner City Trust, 1986–97; British Architectl Liby Trust, 1999–2001. President: Snowdonia (formerly Snowdonia Nat. Park) Soc., 1987–2005; N Wales Centre, NT, 1990–2008. Patron: Llandudno Mus. and Art Gall., 1988–2007; Dome Project, Buxton, 2000–07. Hon. FAIA 1988; Hon. FRAIC 1990; Hon. Fellow: United Architects of Philippines, 1988; Fedn of Colls of Architects, Mexico, 1988; Indian Inst. of Architecture, 1990; Hon. Member: Superior Council of Colls of Architects of Spain, 1987; Architectural Soc. of China, 2003. Hon. DLitt Keele, 1989. Awards and prizes include: DoE Award for Good Design in Housing (1st Prize), 1975; 1st Prize, St Ann's Hospice Arch. Comp., 1976; RICS Conservation Award, 1980; Sir Robert Matthew Prize, IUA, 1981; PA Consulting Gp Award for Innovation in Bldg Design and Construction (for Colquhoun St, Stirling), 1988; Award for work and leader of Community Arch. Movt, Charleston, USA, 1989; The Times, BITC, and Housing and Homeless Award, 1993. *Television*: Build Yourself a House, 1974; Community Architecture, 1977; BBC Omnibus, 1987; consultant, Europe by Design, BBC, 1991; The man who led an entire street to take back control, BBC, 2017; *radio*: The Listener, 1986; Third Ear, 1990; Call to Account, 1992; Woman's Hour, 1992; Common Ground, 1996. Consultant, World Architecture Review Agency, China, 1992; Advr, Habitat Center News Jl, India, 1992–. *Publications*: Highfield Hall: a community project, 1982; The Good the Bad and the Ugly, 1990, re-issue 2014; Good Golly Miss Molly (music play), 1991; The First 10 Years of Kansara Hackney, 2019; articles in UK and foreign architectural jls. *Recreations*: outdoor pursuits, walking, photography, travelling, looking at buildings, organising and speaking at conferences. *Address*: St Peter's House, Windmill Street, Macclesfield, Cheshire SK11 7HS.

**HACKSTON, Fiona C.;** *see* Clarke-Hackston.

**HACKWOOD, Ven. Paul Colin;** Executive Director, Church Urban Fund, since 2018 (Trustee, since 2005; Chair of Trustees, 2009–18; Executive Chair, 2013–18); *b* 1961; *m* Josie; two *s*. *Educ*: Bradford Coll. of Educn (DipHE 1982); Huddersfield Polytech. (BSc 1984); Birmingham Univ. (DipTh 1988); Queen's Coll., Birmingham; Bradford Business Sch. (MBA 2005). Ordained deacon, 1989, priest, 1990; Curate, Horton, 1989–93; Social Responsibility Advr, Dio. St Albans, 1993–97; Vicar, Thornbury, 1997–2005; Archdeacon of Loughborough, 2005–09; Residentiary Canon, 2007–15, Hon. Canon, 2015–, Leicester Cathedral.

**HADAWAY, Lisa;** *see* Armstrong, Lisa.

**HADDACKS, Vice-Adm. Sir Paul (Kenneth),** KCB 2000; Lieutenant-Governor, Isle of Man, 2005–11; *b* 27 Oct. 1946; *s* of late Kenneth Alexander Haddacks and of Edith Lillian Haddacks (*née* Peardon); *m* 1970, Penny Anne Robertson; one *s*. *Educ*: Plymouth Coll.; Kingswood Sch., Bath; BRNC; RN Staff Coll.; HCSC; RCDS. Joined RN 1964; commanded HM Ships: Scimitar, 1971–72; Cleopatra, 1981–82; Naiad, 1982–83; Intrepid, 1986–88; US Naval Acad., 1979–80; Asst Dir, Navy Plans, 1984–86; Dep. Dir, Naval Warfare, 1988–89; Comdr, RN Task Force, Gulf, 1990; Captain of the Fleet, 1991–94; Asst COS (Policy) to SACEUR, 1994–97; UK Mil. Rep., HQ NATO, 1997–2000; Dir, NATO Internat. Mil. Staff, 2001–04. Chm. Govs, Chichester Coll., 2014–16. Chm., Coastal Forces Heritage Trust, 2016–. KStJ 2010 (CStJ 2006). *Recreations*: family, travel.

**HADDINGTON, 14th Earl of,** *cr* 1619; **George Edmund Baldred Baillie-Hamilton;** Lord Binning 1613; Lord Binning and Byres 1619; *b* 27 Dec. 1985; *o s* of 13th Earl of Haddington and of (Susan) Jane Antonia Baillie-Hamilton (*née* Heyworth); S father, 2016. *Educ*: Eton; Glasgow Univ. *Heir*: kinsman Thomas Richard Baillie-Hamilton [*b* 29 Dec. 1948; *m* 1975, Marina Josepha Anna Sidone von Sengen und Etterlin; three *d*].

**HADDO, Earl of; George Ian Alastair Gordon;** *b* 4 May 1983; *s* and *heir* of Marquess of Aberdeen and Temair, *qv*; *m* 2009, Isabelle Anna Nancy Coaten; three *s* one *d*. *Educ*: Harrow; Oxford Brookes Univ. (BSc Hons Real Est. Mgt 2005). With Knight Frank LLP, 2005–06; Rutley Capital Partners LLP (Knight Frank Gp), 2007–09; Cording Real Estate Gp (formerly Cording Capital LLP), 2009–14; FORE Partnership, 2011–14; LJ Partnership, 2015–18; Kinrise, 2019–. *Heir*: *s* Viscount Formantine, *qv*.

**HADDON, Kenneth William,** FCA; Chairman, Axa Reinsurance UK plc, 1994–99 (Chief Executive Officer, 1987–98); *b* 30 April 1938; *s* of William Percy Haddon and Constance Margaret Haddon; *m* 1966, Jarmaine (*née* Cook); one *s* one *d*. *Educ*: Minchenden Grammar Sch. FCA 1960. Nat. Service, RAF, 1960–62. Chartered Accountant, Thomson McLintock, 1962–64; London Reinsurance Co., later Netherlands Reinsurance Gp, then NRG London Reinsurance Co.: Sec. and Accountant, 1964; various posts, 1964–82; Gen. Manager, 1983–87. Chairman: London Underwriting Centre, 1995–98, and 1999–2001; London Processing Centre, 1997–99; London Internat. Insce and Reinsce Mkt Assoc., 1997–98. FRSA. *Recreations*: golf, gardening. *Clubs*: City of London, Langbourn Ward; Brookmans Park Golf.

**HADDON-CAVE, Rt Hon. Sir Charles (Anthony),** Kt 2011; PC 2018; **Rt Hon. Lord Justice Haddon-Cave;** a Lord Justice of Appeal, since 2018; Deputy Senior Presiding Judge for England and Wales, from Jan. 2020; *b* 20 March 1956; *s* of Sir (Charles) Philip Haddon-Cave, KBE, CMG; *m* 1980, Amanda Charlotte Law; two *d*. *Educ*: King's Sch., Canterbury; Pembroke Coll., Cambridge (MA). Called to the Bar, Gray's Inn, 1978, Bencher, 2003; in practice as barrister, London and Hong Kong, 1980–2011; QC 1999; a Recorder, 2000–11; a Judge of the High Ct of Justice, QBD, 2011–18; a Presiding Judge, Midland Circuit, 2014–17. Chair, Grange Fest., Hants. *Recreations*: art, music, running. *Address*: Royal Courts of Justice, Strand, WC2A 2LL. *Club*: Garrick.

**HADDRILL, Stephen Howard;** Chief Executive, Financial Reporting Council, 2009–19; *b* 12 Jan. 1956; *s* of Albert George and Pauline Haddrill; *m* 1983, Joanne Foakes; two *s*; *m* Kate Marshall. *Educ*: Trinity Sch., Croydon; New Coll., Oxford (BA Modern Hist. and Econs). Joined Department of Energy, 1978: Private Sec. to Sec. of State, 1987–89; Asst Sec., Nuclear Power Policy, 1989–90; Mem., Governor's Central Policy Unit, Hong Kong Govt, 1991–94; Department of Trade and Industry, 1994–2005: Dep. Dir, Competitiveness Unit, 1994–98; Dir, Consumer Affairs, 1998–2000; Dir, Employment Relns, 2000–02; Dir Gen., Fair Markets, 2002–05; Dir Gen., Assoc. of British Insurers, 2005–09. *Recreations*: gardening, sailing.

**HADEN-GUEST,** family name of **Baron Haden-Guest**.

**HADEN-GUEST,** 5th Baron *cr* 1950, of Saling, Essex; **Christopher Haden-Guest;** film director, writer, actor and musician (as Christopher Guest); *b* 5 Feb. 1948; *s* of 4th Baron Haden-Guest and of Jean Haden-Guest (*née* Hindes); *S* father, 1996; *m* 1984, Jamie Lee Curtis; one *s* one *d* (both adopted). *Educ:* The Stockbridge Sch.; New York Univ. *Films:* (writer, director and actor): Waiting for Guffman, 1997; Best in Show, 2000; For Your Consideration, 2006; (writer and director): The Big Picture, 1989; Mighty Wind, 2004; (writer and actor) This is Spinal Tap, 1984; (dir) Almost Heroes, 1998; (actor): Mrs Henderson Presents, 2005; Night at the Museum 2, The Invention of Lying, 2009; (exec. prod.) Her Master's Voice (TV film), 2012; (writer, dir and prod.) Family Tree (TV series), 2013; (writer and dir) Mascots, 2016; (dir) Surviving Twin, 2018. Scriptwriter for TV and radio progs. *Recreations:* fly-fishing, ski-ing. *Heir: b* Hon. Nicholas Haden-Guest [*b* 5 May 1951; *m* 1st, 1980, Jill Denby (marr. diss. 1988); one *d*; 2nd, 1989, Pamela Rack; one *d*]. *Address:* 447 Mesa Road, Santa Monica, CA 90402, USA.

**HADFIELD, Antony;** Deputy Chairman, NHS Redditch and Bromsgrove Clinical Commissioning Group, 2013–17; Senior Partner, Hadfield Associates, 1997–2005; *b* 9 Sept. 1936; *s* of Thomas Henry Hadfield and Edna (*née* Cooke); *m* 1959, Dorothy Fay Osman; one *s*. *Educ:* Sheffield; Brighton; Middx Poly. (BA). CEng 1966; FIET (FIEE 1975). Design engr, Plessey, 1958–62; design and project engr, Metal Industries Gp, 1962–65; design engr, CEGB, 1965–67; Sen. Engr and Manager, Eastern Electricity, 1967–77; Area Manager, Yorks Electricity, 1977–79; Dir of Engrg, Midlands Electricity, 1979–85; Chief Exec. and Dep. Chm., NI Electricity (formerly NI Electricity Service), 1985–91; Man. Dir, 1991–94, Chief Exec., 1994–97, Northern Electric plc; Chief Exec., Teesside Power Ltd, 1998–2000 (Dir, 1991–97). Chairman: Northern Inf. Systems Ltd, 1994–97; NEDL Ltd, 1994–97; Northern Utility Services Ltd, 1994–97; Sovereign Exploration Ltd, 1996–97; Dep. Chm., BCN Data Systems Ltd, 1998–2000. Non-exec. Dir, NHS Worcestershire, 2008–13. Associate, PB Power Ltd, 1997–2004. Mem., Competition (formerly Monopolies and Mergers) Commn, 1998–2005. Chm., Power Div., IEE, 1992–93. Chm., BITC, Tyneside, 1993–97. CCMI (CIMgt 1987); FRSA 1993. *Recreations:* mountaineering, sailing.

**HADFIELD, Mark;** a District Judge (Magistrates' Courts), since 2005; *b* 6 July 1960; *s* of late William Hadfield and Marie Helen Hadfield; *m* 1993, Denise Ferns; one *d*. *Educ:* St Augustine's Grammar Sch., Manchester; Liverpool Poly. (BA Hons Law). Admitted solicitor, 1985; in private practice with Colin Watson Solicitors, Warrington, 1985–2005; Solicitor Advocate, 1995. *Recreations:* golf, supporting Manchester City FC. *Address:* Manchester City Magistrates' Court, Crown Square, Manchester M60 1PR.

**HADJI-ARGYRIS, Nicholas John;** *see* Argyris, N. J. H.

**HADKISS, Christopher;** Chief Executive, Animal and Plant Health Agency (formerly Animal Health and Veterinary Laboratories Agency), since 2012; *b* Erith, Kent, 28 Jan. 1960; *s* of Ronald Leonard Hadkiss and Rosemary Hadkiss; *m* 1985, Kim Denise Oram; one *s* one *d*. *Educ:* Bromley Coll. of Technol. (HNC Applied Biol. 1980); Univ. of London (BSc Hons Applied Biol. 1983). Forensic Science Service: Operational Forensic Scientist, 1979–2003; Gen. Manager, 2003–04; Regl Gen. Manager, 2004–07; Ops Dir, 2007–08; Exec. Dir, 2008–12; Advr on Forensic Sci., Home Office, 2012; Consultant Forensic Scientist, Optimal Forensics Ltd, 2012. *Publications:* contribs to Jl of Forensic Sci. Soc., Interpol Jl. *Recreations:* model engineering, motorsport racing. *Address:* Animal and Plant Health Agency, Woodham Lane, New Haw, Addlestone, Surrey KT15 3NB. *T:* (020) 8026 9519. *E:* chris.hadkiss@apha.gov.uk.

**HADLEE, Sir Richard (John),** Kt 1990; MBE 1980; promotional and public speaker; New Zealand cricketer, retired; *b* 3 July 1951; *s* of late Walter Hadlee, CBE and Lilla Hadlee; *m* 1973, Karen Ann Marsh; two *s*; *m* 1999, Dianne Taylor. *Educ:* Christchurch Boys' High Sch. Played for: Canterbury, 1972–89; Nottinghamshire (UK), 1978–87 (made 1000 runs and took 100 wickets in English season, 1984); Tasmania, 1979–80; Test début for NZ, 1973; toured: Australia, 1972–73, 1973–74, 1980–81, 1985–86; England, 1973, 1978, 1983, 1986, 1990; India, 1976, 1988; Pakistan, 1976; Sri Lanka, 1983–84, 1987; West Indies, 1984–85. Held world record of 431 Test wickets, 1990 (passed previous record of 373 in 1988). NZ Selector, 2000–08 (Chm., NZ Bd Selectors, 2001–04); Mem., Bd of Dirs, NZ Cricket, 2014–17 (Life Mem.). Patron, Sir Richard Hadlee Sports Trust, 1990–. Hon. Dr Nottingham. *Publications:* Rhythm and Swing (autobiog.), 1989; Changing Pace: a memoir, 2009. *Address:* PO Box 78061, Waimakariri 7648, New Zealand. *W:* www.hadlee.co.nz. *Club:* MCC (Hon. Life Mem.).

**HADLEY, David Allen,** CB 1991; Deputy Secretary (Agricultural Commodities, Trade and Food Production), Ministry of Agriculture, Fisheries and Food, 1993–96; *b* 18 Feb. 1936; *s* of Sydney and Gwendoline Hadley; *m* 1965, Veronica Ann Hopkins; one *s*. *Educ:* Wyggeston Grammar Sch., Leicester; Merton Coll., Oxford. MA. Joined MAFF, 1959; Asst Sec., 1971; HM Treas., 1975–78; Under Sec., 1981–87, Dep. Sec., 1987–89, MAFF; Dep. Sec., Cabinet Office, 1989–93. *Recreations:* gardening, music. *Address:* Old Mousers, Dormansland, Lingfield, Surrey RH7 6PP.

**HADLEY, Gareth Morgan;** Chairman, General Optical Council, since 2013; *b* 22 April 1951; *s* of late Ronald Hadley and Gweneth Doreen Hadley (*née* Morgan). *Educ:* Harrow Weald Grammar Sch.; University Coll. London (BSc); Henley Mgt Coll. (MA). FCIPD. Greater London Council, 1972–86; Asst to Hd of Industrial Relns, 1980–81; Head: Central Recruitment, 1981–83; craft, operative manual and fire service employee relns, 1983–86; Asst Dir of Personnel, ILEA, 1986–89; British Railways Board, 1989–97: Gp Employee Relns Manager, 1989–94; Director: Employee Relns, 1994–97; Human Resources, N and W Passenger Ops, 1994–97; Principal, Gareth Hadley Associates, 1997–99; Dir of Personnel, HM Prison Service, 1999–2006; Comr responsible for E of England and E Midlands regions, 2007–12, London, 2011–12, Appointments Commission. Chairman: British Transport Police Pension Fund, 1992–97; ScotRail Railways Ltd, 1996–97. Human Resources Advr, Nat. Offender Mgt Service, 2004–05. Dir, Skills for Justice (Justice Sector Skills Council), 2004–06. Mem., Inf. and Consultation Taskforce, 2002–04; Employee Relations Panel, 2003–08, CIPD; Member: Adv. Bd, SW London Academic Network, Inst. of Mgt and Leadership in Health, 2008–11; Ext. Adv. Bd, Centre for Better Managed Health and Social Care, Cass Business Sch., City Univ., 2010–. Vis. Fellow, Kingston Univ., 2005–. Gov., Notts Healthcare NHS Trust, 2014–17. MInstD 1997. Liveryman, Spectacle Makers' Co., 2014. *Recreations:* opera, food and drink. *Address:* General Optical Council, 10 Old Bailey, EC4M 7NG. *T:* (020) 7307 3468. *E:* ghadley@optical.org; 29 Bemish Road, Putney, SW15 1DG. *E:* gareth.hadley@lowerputney.demon.co.uk. *Club:* Savile.

**HADLEY, Graham Hunter;** economic and business management consultant, 2007–12; Member, Competition (formerly Monopolies and Mergers) Commission, 1998–2007; *b* 12 April 1944; *s* of late Dr A. L. Hadley and Mrs L. E. Hadley; *m* 1971, Lesley Ann Smith; one *s*. *Educ:* Eltham Coll., London; Jesus Coll., Cambridge (BA Hons Mod. Hist.); Harvard Business Sch. (AMP 1991). Entered Civil Service (Min. of Aviation), 1966; Dept of Energy, 1974; seconded to: Civil Service Commn, 1976–77; British Aerospace, 1980–81; Under-Sec., Dept of Energy, 1983; Sec., CEGB, 1983–90; Exec. Dir, 1990–95, and Man. Dir, Internat. Business Develt, 1992–95, National Power. Sen. Advr, Nat. Econ. Res. Associates, 1996–2007. Dir, de Havilland Aircraft Heritage Centre (formerly Mus. Trust), 1990–2010; Trustee, 2006–15, Pres., 2016–18, New Brewery Arts (formerly Cirencester Brewery Arts), Cirencester; Trustee and Dir, Humanitarian Aid and Relief Trust, 2017–. *Recreations:* include cricket, cycling, history, architecture, aviation. *Address:* 129 The Hill, Burford, Oxon OX18 4RE.

**HADLEY, Dr Tessa Jane,** FRSL; novelist and short story writer; Professor of Creative Writing, Bath Spa University, since 2012; *b* Bristol, 28 Feb. 1956; *d* of Geoffrey and Mary Nichols; *m* 1982, Eric Hadley; three *s*. *Educ:* Ashton Park Comprehensive Sch., Bristol; Clare Coll., Cambridge (BA Hons English 1978); Bath Spa Univ. (MA 1994; PhD 1997). Sen. Lectr in English and Creative Writing, Bath Spa Univ., 1997–2012. Fellow, Welsh Acad.; FRSL 2009. *Publications:* Accidents in the Home, 2002; Henry James and the Imagination of Pleasure, 2002; Everything Will Be All Right, 2004; Sunstroke and Other Stories, 2004; The Master Bedroom, 2007; The London Train, 2011; Married Love and Other Stories, 2012; Clever Girl, 2013; The Past, 2015 (Hawthornden Prize, 2016); Bad Dreams and Other Stories, 2017; Late in the Day, 2019; contrib. short stories to New Yorker. *Recreations:* reading, cinema, paintings. *Address:* Bath Spa University, Corsham Court, Corsham, Chippenham, Wilts SN13 0BZ. *E:* t.hadley@bathspa.ac.uk.

**HADOW, Rupert Nigel Pendrill, (Pen);** explorer; Director, Pen Hadow Consultancy Ltd, since 2004; *b* Perth, Scotland, 26 Feb. 1962; *s* of late Nigel Phillip Ian Hadow and of Anne Pendrill Hadow (*née* Callingham); *m* 1995, Mary Frances Nicholson (marr. diss. 2013); one *s* one *d*; *m* 2017, Venetia (*née* Cooper). *Educ:* Temple Grove Prep. Sch.; Harrow Sch.; University Coll. London (BA Hons Geog. 1984). Agent, Internat. Management Gp, 1985–88; Founder and Director: Polar Travel Co. Ltd, 1995–2004; Geo Mission Ltd, 2009–14; 90 North Unit, protecting North Pole wildlife; Dir, Arctic Mission. Expeditions: first person solo without resupply from Canada to North Geographic Pole, 2003; first Briton without resupply from continental coasts to North and South Geographic Poles, 2004. Hon. Vice-Pres., RSGS, 2009; Hon. Vice-Patron, British Exploring Soc., 2009 (Fellow, 2018). Mem., Harrow Assoc.; Pres., Old Harrovian Adventurers. FRGS. Hon. LLD Exeter, 2004; Hon. DSc Plymouth, 2009. World Technol. Award - Envmt, World Technol. Network, 2009. *Publications:* Solo: alone and unsupported to the North Pole, 2004, 4th edn 2014; Catlin Arctic Survey 2009: the story of a pioneering scientific mission to the Arctic Ocean, 2010; Catlin Survey 2009–2011: investigating the changing Arctic Ocean environment, 2013. *Recreations:* classic shrub roses, wildfowl, surfing, Rugby, cricket. *Address:* Little Orchard, Bedchester, Shaftesbury, Dorset SP7 0JU. *T:* 07970 619161. *E:* pen@penhadow.com. *Clubs:* MCC, Century.

**HADRILL, Andrew Frederic W.;** *see* Wallace-Hadrill.

**HAENDEL, Ida,** CBE 1991; violinist; *b* Poland, 15 Dec. 1928; Polish parentage; adopted British nationality. Began to play at age of 3½; amazing gift discovered when she picked up her sister's violin and started to play. Her father, a great connoisseur of music, recognised her unusual talent and abandoned his own career as an artist (painter) to devote himself to his daughter; studied at Warsaw Conservatoire and gained gold medal at age of seven; also studied with such masters as Carl Flesch and Georges Enesco. British début, Queen's Hall, with Sir Henry Wood, playing Brahms' Violin Concerto. Gave concerts for British and US troops and in factories, War of 1939–45; after War, career developed to take in North and South America, USSR and Far East, as well as Europe; has accompanied British orchestras such as London Philharmonic, BBC Symphony and English Chamber on foreign tours including Hong Kong, China, Australia and Mexico; performs with major orchestras worldwide, incl. Berlin Philharmonic, Boston Symphony, and Concertgebouw. Has performed with conductors such as Beecham, Klemperer, Szell, Celibidache, Mata, Pritchard, Rattle, Haitink, Ashkenazy; performances include appearances at BBC Prom. A major interpreter of Sibelius, Brahms and Beethoven. Concerts, Edinburgh Fest., masterclasses. Hon. DMus McGill, 2008. Huberman Prize; Sibelius Medal, Sibelius Soc. of Finland, 1982. *Publications:* Woman with Violin (autobiog.), 1970.

**HAFFENDEN, Prof. John Charles Robert,** DPhil; FBA 2007; FRSL; Senior Research Fellow, since 2009 and Principal Investigator, T. S. Eliot Research Project, 2009–14, Institute of English Studies, School of Advanced Study, University of London; *b* 19 Aug. 1945; *s* of Donald Haffenden and Sheila McCulloch Haffenden; *m* 1973, Susan Elizabeth (marr. diss. 1977). *Educ:* Trinity Coll., Dublin (MA 1970); St Peter's Coll., Oxford (DPhil 1977). Educn Officer, Oxford Prison, 1970–73; Lectr in English, Univ. of Exeter, 1973–74; University of Sheffield: Lectr, 1975; Sen. Lectr, 1985; Reader, 1988; Prof. of English Literature, 1994–2004, now Emeritus; Res. Prof., 2004–. British Acad. Res. Reader, 1989–91; Leverhulme Res. Fellow, 1995–96. Vis. Fellow Commoner, Trinity Coll., Cambridge, 1995–96; Vis. Scholar, St John's Coll., Oxford, 1997; Vis. Fellow, Magdalen Coll., Oxford, 1998. Mem., Soc. of Authors; FEA. Gen. Editor, Letters of T. S. Eliot, 2009. *Publications:* (ed) Henry's Fate and Other Poems 1967–1972 by John Berryman, 1978; John Berryman: a critical commentary, 1980; Viewpoints: poets in conversation, 1981; The Life of John Berryman, 1982; (ed) W. H. Auden: the critical heritage, 1983; Novelists in Interview, 1985; (ed) The Royal Beasts and Other Works by William Empson, 1988; (ed) Argufying: essays on literature and culture by William Empson, 1988; (ed) Essays on Renaissance Literature, vol. 1, Donne and the New Philosophy by William Empson, 1993, vol. 2, The Drama by William Empson, 1994; (ed) The Strength of Shakespeare's Shrew: essays, memoirs and reviews by William Empson, 1996; (ed) Berryman's Shakespeare, 1999; (ed) The Complete Poems of William Empson, 2000; William Empson: among the Mandarins (Award for Biog. and Autobiog., Assoc. of Amer. Publishers), 2005; William Empson: against the Christians, 2006; (ed) Selected Letters of William Empson, 2006; General Editor: Letters of T. S. Eliot, vol. 1: 1898–1922, 2009, vol. 2: 1923–1925, 2009; Editor with Valerie Eliot: Letters of T. S. Eliot, vol. 3: 1925–1928, 2012, vol. 4: 1928–1929, 2013, vol. 5: 1930–31, 2014, vol. 6: 1932–33, 2016; vol. 7: 1934–35, 2017; vol. 8: 1936–38, 2019; contrib. to periodicals incl. London Rev. of Books, Essays in Criticism and PN Rev. *Recreations:* country walking, travel, art and architecture, filleting research libraries.

**HAGARD, Dr Spencer;** international consultant in health promotion and public health, since 1989; *b* 25 Oct. 1942; *s* of Maurice (Bozzie) Markham (killed in action, 11 June 1944) and Eva Markham (*née* Mearns, subseq. Hagard) and, by adoption, of late Noel Hagard; *m* 1968, Michele Dominique, *d* of late Stanislas and Madeleine Aquarone; two *s* one *d*. *Educ:* Varndean Grammar Sch., Brighton; Univ. of St Andrews (MB ChB 1968); Univ. of Glasgow (PhD 1977); MA Cantab 1977. DPH 1972; FFPH (FFCM 1981). Jun. med. appts, Arbroath, London and Dorking; MO and Med. Supt, Kawolo Hosp., Lugazi, Uganda, 1971–72; MO, Health Dept, Glasgow, 1972–74; Trainee in Community Med., Greater Glasgow Health Bd, 1974–77; Specialist in Comm. Med., Cambs AHA, 1977–82; Dist MO, Cambridge HA, 1982–87; Chief Exec., HEA, 1987–94; Sen. Lectr, 1999–2005, Course Organiser, MSc (Health Promotion Scis), 2001–03, Hd, Health Promotion Res. Unit, 2002–04, and Distance Learning Tutor, 2007–, LSHTM. Associate Lectr, Univ. of Cambridge Sch. of Clinical Med., 1977–87; Vis. Prof., 2001–02, Thesis Evaluator, 2009–, Univ. of Bergen. Hon. Consultant, Camden PCT (formerly Camden and Islington Community Health Services Trust), 1996–2005; Consultant: WHO, 1991–; DFID, 1999–2004; World Bank, 2000–05; Health Policy Advr, Hungarian Govt, 1996–2000. National Association for the Education of Sick Children: Mem. Council, 1995–2002; Trustee, 1997–2005; Chm. of Trustees, 2000–05. Sec., Eur. Cttee for Health Promotion

Develt, 1995–2004; Mem., EU Health Policy Forum, 2006–; Mem., Bd of Trustees, Internat. Union for Health Promotion and Educn, 1991–2007 (Pres., 1996–2001; Mem., Regl Cttee for Europe, 2007–08). FRSA 1997. *Publications:* Health, Society and Medicine (with Roy Acheson), 1984; papers in BMJ and other learned jls. *Recreations:* marriage, family, studying human beings, politics, gardening, reading, photography, appreciation of art, music, sporting new dawns (Brighton & Hove Albion, Sussex CCC). *Address:* 396 Milton Road, Cambridge CB4 1SU. *T:* (01223) 563774, *Fax:* (01223) 423970. *E:* spencer@hagard.net.

**HAGART-ALEXANDER, Sir Claud;** *see* Alexander.

**HAGEN, Dakis Steven;** QC 2017; *b* Newcastle-upon-Tyne, 2 Dec. 1978; *s* of Prof. Stephen Hagen and Prof. Roulla Hagen; *m* 2012, Georgina Rose Elizabeth Cole; two *d*. *Educ:* Royal Grammar Sch., Newcastle-upon-Tyne; Peterhouse, Cambridge (MA). Called to the Bar, Lincoln's Inn, 2002; in practice as barrister, specialising in chancery litigation, 2002–. *Recreations:* music, reading history. *Address:* Serle Court, 6 New Square, Lincoln's Inn, WC2A 3QS. *T:* (020) 7242 6105. *E:* dhagen@serlecourt.co.uk.

**HAGEN, Martin John,** FCA; President, Institute of Chartered Accountants in England and Wales, 2009–10 (Deputy President, 2008–09); *b* Leeds, 20 Sept. 1951; *s* of Christopher and Nancy Hagen; *m* 1978, Hilary Channell; three *s*. *Educ:* Herringthorpe Primary Sch., Rotherham; Rotherham Grammar Sch.; Thomas Rotherham Coll.; Sheffield Poly. FCA 1973. With Knox Franklin & Co., Sheffield, 1969–73; with Spicer and Pegler, London, 1974–81, Bristol, 1981–90; Touche Ross, Bristol, 1990–93; Deloitte & Touche, Bristol, 1993–2005; Consultant, Deloitte, 2007–10. Dep. Chm., Regulatory Decisions Cttee, FSA, 2008–13 (Mem., 2005–13), Financial Conduct Authy, 2013–15. Member: Takeover Panel, 2009–10; Bd, Companies Hse, 2017–. Chm. CCAB, 2009–10. Ind. Mem., Audit and Risk Assurance Cttee, DWP, 2014–. Non-executive Director: Oxonica plc, 2006–08; South West Water Ltd, 2010–; Swallowfield plc, 2011–14. Mem. Bd, CIPFA, 2010–11. Trustee, Fleet Air Arm Mus., 2010–15. Gov., UWE, 2010–. Freeman, City of London, 2004; Liveryman, Chartered Accountants' Co., 2004. Hon. DBA UWE, 2010. *Recreations:* playing acoustic guitar, Bristol City Football Club, wine, all things French, travel. *Address:* Sunny Brae, 2 Belmont Road, Winscombe, N Somerset BS25 1LE. *Club:* East India.

**HAGERTY, William John Gell, (Bill);** writer and editor; Member, Editorial Board, British Journalism Review, since 1998 (Editor, 2002–12; Chairman, 2012–19); *b* 23 April 1939; *s* of William (Steve) Hagerty and Doris Hagerty (*née* Gell); *m* 1st, 1965, Lynda Beresford (marr. diss. 1990); one *s* one *d* (and one *d* decd); 2nd, 1991, Elizabeth Vercoe (*née* Latta); one *s*. *Educ:* Beal Grammar Sch., Ilford. Local newspapers, East London, 1955–58; RAF Nat. Service, 1958–60; local newspapers, Sunday Citizen, Daily Sketch, 1960–67; Daily Mirror, 1967–81; Sunday Mirror and Sunday People, 1981–85; Managing Editor (Features), Today, 1986; Editor, Sunday Today, 1987; Deputy Editor: Sunday Mirror, 1988–90; Daily Mirror, 1990–91; Editor, The People, 1991–92; Theatre Critic, 1993–95, Film Critic, 1994–95, Today; Theatre Critic: various pubns, 1996–2003; The Sun, 2004–09. Consultant, Tribune, 1993–2004, 2007–. Mem., BAFTA. Mem. Council, 2002–, Chm., 2011–12, Journalists' Charity (formerly Newspaper Press Fund); Dir, London Press Club, 2008–. *Publications:* Flash, Bang, Wallop! (with Kent Gavin), 1978; Read All About It, 2003; (ed with Alastair Campbell) The Alastair Campbell Diaries, vol. 1, prelude to power 1994–1997, 2010, vol. 2, power and the people 1997–99, 2011, vol. 3, power and responsibility 1999–2001, 2011, vol. 4, the pressures of power 2001–03, 2012, vol. 5, outside, inside 2003–05, 2016, vol. 6, from Blair to Brown 2005–07, 2017, vol. 7, from crash to defeat 2007–10, 2018, vol. 8, on the slide to Cameron 2010–15, 2020. *Recreations:* jazz, cricket, singing, lunch (thanks to Keith Waterhouse). *Address:* 11 Strand-on-the-Green, Chiswick, W4 3PQ. *Clubs:* Gerry's, Acts and Actors.

**HAGESTADT, John Valentine;** adviser on government reform, international investment and trade to OECD, World Bank and EU, then adviser on trade aspects of Brexit and international investment attraction, 1997–2017; *b* 11 Oct. 1938; *s* of late Leonard and Constance Hagestadt; *m* 1963, Betty Tebbs; three *d*. *Educ:* Dulwich Coll.; Worcester Coll., Oxford (BA). Asst Principal, Min. of Aviation, 1963; Principal, BoT, 1967; Nuffield Travelling Fellow, 1973–74; Asst Sec., Vehicles Div., Dept of Industry, 1976; Asst Sec., Overseas Trade Div. (Middle East and Latin America), Dept of Trade, 1980; Dir, British Trade Develt Office, NY 1982; Dir, Invest in Britain Bureau, NY, 1984–87; Head, N Amer. Br., DTI, 1987–93; Dir, Govt Office for London, 1994; Dir, Invest in Britain Bureau, DTI, 1995–96. *Address:* 7 Elm House, 50 Holmesdale Road TW11 9NE.

**HAGGAN, Nicholas Somerset;** QC 2003; a Recorder, since 2000; *b* 25 Aug. 1955; *s* of late Rev. David Anthony Haggan and of Hope Haggan; *m* 1993, Julie Carolyn Owen (*d* 2019). *Educ:* Monkton Combe Sch., Bath; Coll. of Law, London. Called to the Bar: Middle Temple, 1977; NI, 1986; in practice, specialising in crime and regulatory offences, particularly in relation to compliance issues in the field of consumer law and health and safety at work; Asst Recorder, 1997–2000. *Recreations:* running, food and wine, cooking, gardening, travel. *Address:* 12CP Barristers, 20 Carlton Crescent, Southampton, Hants SO15 2ET. *T:* (023) 8032 0320, *Fax:* (023) 8032 0321.

**HAGGARD, Prof. Mark Peregrine,** CBE 2001; PhD; FMedSci; Medical Research Council External Staff, Cambridge, 2002–08; founder Director, Medical Research Council Institute of Hearing Research, 1977–2002; *b* 26 Dec. 1942; *m* 1962, Liz (*née* Houston); two *s*. *Educ:* Edinburgh Univ. (MA Psych, 1st cl. hons); Corpus Christi Coll., Cambridge (PhD Psych 1967). Univ. Demonstrator in Experimental Psychology, Univ. of Cambridge, 1967–71; Prof. of Psychology and Head of Dept, QUB, 1971–76; sabbatical, 1975–76; Special Prof. in Audiological Scis, Nottingham Univ., 1980. Trustee, Deafness Research UK, 1986 (former Chm., Vice Pres. and Chief Scientific Advr). Founder FMedSci 1998. Hon. FRCSE 2001. *Publications:* Screening Children's Hearing, 1991; Research in the Development of Effective Services for Hearing-impaired People, 1993; contribs to learned jls. *Recreations:* ski-ing, choral music. *Club:* Royal Society of Medicine.

**HAGGARD, Prof. Patrick Neville,** PhD; FBA 2014; Professor of Cognitive Neuroscience, Institute of Cognitive Neuroscience, University College London. *Educ:* Trinity Hall, Cambridge (BA Hons 1987; PhD 1991). Harkness Fellow, Yale Univ., 1987–88; Wellcome Trust Prize Fellow, Physiol. Dept, Univ. of Oxford, and Jun. Res. Fellow, Christ Church, Oxford, 1991–94; Psychology Department, University College London: Lectr, 1995–98; Sen. Lectr, 1998–2002; Reader in Cognitive Neurosci., 2002. Leverhulme Res. Fellow, 2001–03. Chm., Steering Cttee, Study of Cognition, Adolescents and Mobile Phones, 2014–. *Publications:* (ed jtly) Hand and Brain: the neurophysiology and psychology of hand movements, 1996; (ed jtly) Sensorimotor Foundations of Higher Cognition: attention and performance, 2007; (ed jtly) Mental Processes in the Human Brain, 2008; contribs to learned jls incl. Exptl Brain Res., Jl Psychosomatic Res., Neuropsychologia, Psychol Sci., Jl Neurosci. *Address:* Institute of Cognitive Neuroscience, University College London, Alexandra House, 17 Queen Square, WC1N 3AR.

**HAGGART, Mary Elizabeth;** *see* Scholes, M. E.

**HAGGETT, Prof. Peter,** CBE 1993; FBA 1992; Professor of Urban and Regional Geography, 1966–98, now Emeritus Professor, and Acting Vice-Chancellor, 1984–85, University of Bristol; *b* 24 Jan. 1933; *s* of Charles and Elizabeth Haggett, Pawlett, Somerset; *m* 1956, Brenda Woodley; two *s* two *d*. *Educ:* Dr Morgan's Sch., Bridgwater; St Catharine's Coll., Cambridge (Exhib. and Scholar; MA 1958; PhD 1970; ScD 1985). Asst Lectr, University Coll. London, 1955–57; Demonstrator and University Lectr, Cambridge, 1957–66, and Fellow, Fitzwilliam Coll., 1963–66 (Hon. Fellow, 1994). Leverhulme Research Fellow (Brazil), 1959; Canada Council Fellow, 1977; Erskine Fellow (NZ), 1979; Res. Fellow, Res. Sch. of Pacific Studies, ANU, 1983. Visiting Professor: Berkeley; Monash; Pennsylvania State; McMaster; Toronto; Western Ontario; Wisconsin; Hill Prof., Minnesota, 1994. Provost, Inst. for Advanced Studies, Bristol Univ., 1996–99. Member, SW Economic Planning Council, 1967–72. Governor, Centre for Environmental Studies, 1975–78; Member: Council, RGS, 1972–73, 1977–80; UGC, 1985–89; Nat. Radiological Protection Bd, 1986–93; Chm., Hist. of Med. Grants Panel, Wellcome Trust, 1994–2000. Vice-Pres., British Acad., 1995–97. Hon. Fellow, Bristol Univ., 1998. Hon. Foreign Mem., Amer. Acad. of Arts and Sci., 2006; Foreign Associate, NAS, 2008. Hon. DSc: York, Canada, 1983; Durham, 1989; Copenhagen, 1999; UWE, 2004; UCL, 2008; Hon. LLD Bristol, 1986; Hon. FilDr Helsinki, 2003. Cullum Medal of American Geographical Soc., 1969; Meritorious Contribution Award, Assoc. of American Geographers, 1973; Patron's Medal, RGS, 1986; Prix Internationale de Géographie Vautrin Lud, 1991; Lauréat d'Honneur, IGU, 1992; Scottish Medal, RSGS, 1993; Anders Retzius Gold Medal, Sweden, 1994. *Publications:* Locational Analysis in Human Geography, 1965; Geography: a modern synthesis, 1972, 4th edn, 1983; The Geographer's Art, 1990; Geographical Structure of Epidemics, 2000; Geography: a global synthesis, 2001; The Quantocks, 2012; On Geography, 2020; *jointly:* (with R. J. Chorley): Models in Geography, 1967; Network Analysis in Geography, 1969; (with M. D. I. Chisholm) Regional Forecasting, 1971; (with A. D. Cliff and others): Elements of Spatial Structure, 1975; Spatial Diffusion, 1981; Spatial Aspects of Influenza Epidemics, 1986; Atlas of Disease Distributions, 1988; Atlas of AIDS, 1992; Measles: an historical geography, 1993; Deciphering Global Epidemics, 1998; Island Epidemics, 2000; World Atlas of Epidemic Diseases, 2004; Emerging Diseases: a geographical analysis, 2009; research papers on related geographical topics. *Recreations:* Somerset history, cricket. *Address:* 5 Tun Bridge Close, Chew Magna, Somerset BS40 8SU. *Club:* Oxford and Cambridge.

**HAGGETT, Stuart John,** MA; Headmaster, English School, Nicosia, 2003–09; *b* 11 April 1947; *s* of Wilfred Francis and Doreen Ada Haggett; *m* 1971, Hilary Joy Hammond; two *d*. *Educ:* Dauntsey's Sch., West Lavington, Wilts; Downing Coll., Cambridge (MA 1972); PGCE London (ext.), 1970. Canford Sch., Wimborne, Dorset, 1970–83: Head of Modern Languages, 1973–83; Housemaster, 1975–83; Second Master, King's Sch., Rochester, 1983–88; Headmaster, Birkenhead Sch., 1988–2003. *Recreations:* France (travel and culture), sport, theatre, architecture, cooking.

**HAGGIE, Dr Paul;** HM Diplomatic Service, retired; Deputy Director (Africa), Foreign and Commonwealth Office, 2001–04; *b* 30 Aug. 1949; *s* of George Henry Haggie and Eva Haggie (*née* Hawke); *m* 1979, Rev. Deborah (marr. diss. 2000; remarried 2015), *d* of Douglas Graham Frazer, CBE; one *s* one *d*. *Educ:* Royal Grammar Sch., Newcastle upon Tyne; Manchester Univ. (BA; PhD 1974). Joined HM Diplomatic Service, 1974: Second, later First Sec., Bangkok, 1976–80; First Secretary: FCO, 1980–82; Islamabad, 1982–86; FCO, 1986–89; Pretoria, 1989–93; Counsellor, FCO, 1993–94; on secondment to Cabinet Office as Sec., Requirements and Resources, 1994–96; FCO, 1996–98; Counsellor and UK Perm. Rep. to ESCAP, Bangkok, 1998–2001. Licensed Lay Minister, Dio. of Rochester, 2012–17. *Publications:* Britannia at Bay: the defence of the British Empire against Japan 1931–1941, 1981; contrib. various articles to historical jls. *Recreations:* sailing, scuba, music, history (esp. maritime). *Address:* 2 Marc Brunel Way, Historic Dockyard, Chatham, Kent ME4 4BH. *Club:* Royal Automobile.

**HAGUE OF RICHMOND,** Baron *cr* 2015 (Life Peer), of Richmond in the County of North Yorkshire; **William Jefferson Hague;** PC 1995; FRSL; Chairman, Royal United Services Institute, since 2015; *b* 26 March 1961; *s* of late Timothy Nigel Hague and Stella Hague; *m* 1997, Ffion Llywelyn Jenkins (*see* F. L. Hague). *Educ:* Wath-upon-Dearne Comprehensive School; Magdalen College, Oxford (MA); Insead (MBA). Pres., Oxford Union, 1981; Pres., Oxford Univ. Cons. Assoc., 1981. Management Consultant, McKinsey & Co., 1983–88. Political Adviser, HM Treasury, 1983. Contested (C) Wentworth, S Yorks, 1987. MP (C) Richmond, Yorks, Feb. 1989–2015. PPS to Chancellor of the Exchequer, 1990–93; Parly Under-Sec. of State, DSS, 1993–94; Minister for Social Security and Disabled People, DSS, 1994–95; Sec. of State for Wales, 1995–97; Leader, Cons. Party and Leader of the Opposition, 1997–2001; Shadow Foreign Sec., 2005–10; Sec. of State for Foreign and Commonwealth Affairs, 2010–14; First Sec. of State and Leader of the H of C, 2014–15; Prime Minister's Special Representative on Preventing Sexual Violence in Conflict, 2014–15. Vis. Prof. in Practice, Centre for Women, Peace and Security, LSE, 2016–. Chm., Internat. Adv. Gp, Linklaters LLP, 2015–; Senior Adviser: Teneo Hldgs, 2015–; Citigroup, 2017–. Director: Intercontinental Exchange Ltd, 2015–; ICE Futures Europe, 2015– (Chm., 2016–). Columnist, Daily Telegraph, 2016–. FRSL 2009. *Publications:* William Pitt the Younger, 2004 (History Book of the Year, British Book Awards, 2005); William Wilberforce, 2007. *Clubs:* Beefsteak, Carlton, Buck's, Pratt's, Budokwai, Groucho.

**HAGUE, Prof. Clifford Bertram,** OBE 2016; freelance consultant; Professor, School of the Built Environment, Heriot-Watt University, 2002–06, now Emeritus (Professor, School of Planning and Housing, Edinburgh College of Art, Heriot-Watt University, 1995–2002); *b* 22 Aug. 1944; *s* of Bertram Hague and Kathleen Mary Hague; *m* 1966, Irene Williamson; one *s* three *d*. *Educ:* Magdalene Coll., Cambridge (MA); Univ. of Manchester (DipTP). MRTPI 1973. Planning Asst, Glasgow Corp., 1968–69; Edinburgh College of Art, Heriot-Watt University: Lectr, 1969–73; Sen. Lectr, 1973–90; Head, Sch. of Planning and Housing, 1990–95. Mem., Permanent Internat. Wkg Party, European Biennial of Towns and Town Planning, 1996–2011; UK National Contact: European Spatial Planning Observation Network, 2001–06; Eur. Observation Network for Territorial Develt and Cohesion, 2008–14 (Consultant, 2012–14). Project Consultant: EU INTERREG projects: NoordXXI, 1998–2000; PIPE, 2004; Innovation Circle, 2005–06; SusSET, 2006; CoUrbit, 2006; Trans-in-Form, 2010–12; TENTacle, 2017–19; EU INTERACT project, CULTPLAN, 2007; ESPON Projects: INTERSTRAT, 2010–12; USESPON, 2012–13; ESPON on the Road, 2014; EU ERASMUS+ project, Young Eyes, 2015; Smart Cities project with British Expertise Internat., Angola, 2016–17; also UK govt projects; Chair, Internat. Adv. Bd to UN-Habitat, on Planning in Area C, West Bank of occupied Palestinian territory, 2015; Advr, UN-Habitat on Nat. Spatial Plan for Palestine, 2016. Mem. Bd, Innovation Circle Network, 2015–. Chairman: Commonwealth Expert Gp on Urbanisation, 2011; Built Envmt Forum Scotland, 2011–14; Member: Strategic Historic Envmt Forum for Scotland, 2014; Strategic Historic Envmt Operational Gp, Scotland, 2014; Chm., Cockburn Assoc. (Edinburgh Civic Trust), 2016–. Member: Jury, Internat. Urban Planning and Design Competition for the banks of Huangpu River, 2001; Internat. Jury, Detailed Construction Plan, Qingdao Olympic Sailing, 2003; Jury, planning of Olympic Central Green and Forest Park, Beijing, 2003.

Pres., RTPI, 1996–97; Pres. and CEO, 2000–06, Sec. Gen., 2006–10, Commonwealth Assoc. of Planners. Patron, Planning Aid for Scotland, 2013–. FAcSS; Fellow, Higher Educn Acad., 2004. Series Ed., RTPI Library Series, 2000–08. Centenary Medal, Technical Univ. of Brno, 2000. *Publications:* The Development of Planning Thought: a critical perspective, 1984; (ed with P. Jenkins) Place Identity, Participation and Planning, 2005; (jtly) Making Planning Work: a guide to approaches and skills, 2006; (jtly) Regional and Local Economic Development, 2011; (jtly) Leading Change: delivering the new urban agenda through urban and territorial planning, 2018; articles in Town Planning Rev., Town and Country Planning, Planning, etc. *Recreations:* Manchester United, cricket, theatre, films. *W:* www.cliffhague.com, www.twitter.com/cliffhague.

**HAGUE, Ffion Llywelyn;** author; Founder and Principal Consultant, Independent Board Evaluation, since 2008; *b* 21 Feb. 1968; *d* of (John) Emyr Jenkins, *qv*, and Myra (*née* Samuel); *m* 1997, William Jefferson Hague (*see* Baron Hague of Richmond). *Educ:* Jesus Coll., Oxford (BA English Lit. 1989); UCW, Aberystwyth (MPhil Welsh Lit. 1993). Joined CS, 1991; Private Sec. to Sec. of State for Wales, 1994–97; Dir of Policy and Planning, Arts & Business (formerly Dir of Ops, ABSA), 1997–2000; Director: Leonard Hull Internat., 2000–02; Hanson Green, 2003–08. Mem., Barclays Wealth Adv. Cttee, 2007–12. Presenter/Exec. Producer (S4C): Dwy Wraig Lloyd George, 2009; Mamwlad, 2012, 2013, 2016. Mem. Bd, British Council, 1999–2002. Mem. Adv. Council, LSO, 1998–2008; Trustee: Voices Foundn, 1998–2005; Action on Addiction, 2001–04; Outward Bound Trust, 2002–12; ENO, 2009–14. Hon. Fellow, Harris Manchester Coll., Oxford, 2010. *Publications:* The Pain and the Privilege: the women in Lloyd George's life, 2008. *Address:* BM Box 1983, London, WC1N 3XX.

*See also M. B. Antoniazzi.*

**HAGUE AND NETHERLANDS, Archbishop of The, (Russian Orthodox),** since 2017; **Rt Rev. Elisey Ilia Ganaba;** *b* St Petersburg, 1 Aug. 1962. Head, Russian Ecclesiastical Mission in Jerusalem, 2002–06; Bishop of Bogorodsk, 2006–17; Archbishop of Sourozh (Russian Orthodox), 2010–17. *Address:* Russian Orthodox Church, Obrechtstraat 9, 2517 VL Den Haag, Netherlands.

**HAHN, Carl Horst,** Dr rer. pol.; German business executive; *b* 1 July 1926; *m* 1960, Marisa Traina (*d* 2013); three *s* one *d*. Chm. Bd, Continental Gummi-Werke AG, 1973–81; Chm. Mgt Bd, Volkswagen AG, 1981–92, now Chm. Emeritus. Member, Supervisory Board: Hanseatisches Wein und Sekt Kontor, Hamburg; Perot Systems, Dallas; Member, International Advisory Board: Instituto de Empresa, Madrid; Textron Inc., Providence; Indesit Co. (formerly Merloni Electrodomestic), Fabriano. Board Member: Mayo Clinic Stiftung, Frankfurt; Global Consumer Acquisition Corp., NY; Lauder Inst., Wharton Sch., Philadelphia; Mem. Internat. Adv. Cttee, Salk Inst., La Jolla, Calif. *Address:* Hollerplatz 1, 38440 Wolfsburg, Germany. *T:* (5361) 26680, *Fax:* (5361) 266815.

**HAHN, Daniel;** writer, editor and translator; *b* London, 26 Nov. 1973; *s* of Dr Alberto Hahn and Maria Ignês Sodré. *Educ:* Westminster Sch.; Selwyn Coll., Cambridge (BA 1995); University Coll. London (MA 1997). Prog. Dir, British Centre for Literary Translation, UEA, 2010–14. Chm., Translators Assoc., 2009–11 (Mem., 2007–11 and 2016–); Mem. Council, Soc. of Authors, 2018– (Mem., 2012–18, Chm., 2014–16, Mgt Cttee). Member: Council, Shakespeare's Globe, 2005–; London Cttee, Council, Human Rights Watch, 2005–13; Adv. Bd, Public Lending Right, 2019–. Member, Board: English PEN, 2010–15 and 2017–; Pop Up Projects, 2010–15; Modern Poetry in Translation, 2012–19; Children's Bookshow, 2012– (Chm., 2016–); Member, Advisory Board: And Other Stories, 2016–; Cheltenham Lit. Fest., 2017–. Patron: Henley Literary Fest., 2011–; Little Green Pig, 2016–. Judge: Booktrust Teenage Prize, 2009; Ind. Foreign Fiction Prize, 2010; UK Literacy Assoc. Book Awards, 2012–; IMPAC Dublin Literary Award, 2015; Man Booker Internat. Prize, 2017; British Book Awards, 2018–19; Judge and Prize Founder, TA First Translation Prize, 2018–19. *Publications:* The Tower Menagerie, 2003; (ed jtly) The Ultimate Book Guide: over 600 good books for 8–12s, 2004, 2nd edn 2009 (Blue Peter Book Award, 2004); (ed jtly) The Ultimate Teen Book Guide: over 750 great books, 2006, 2nd edn 2010; (ed jtly) The Ultimate First Book Guide: over 500 great books for 0–7s, 2008; (ed jtly) The Oxford Guide to Literary Britain and Ireland, 3rd edn, 2008; Poetic Lives: Shelley, 2009; (ed) The Oxford Companion to Children's Literature, 2nd edn, 2015; (ed jtly) Lunatics, Lovers and Poets: twelve stories after Cervantes and Shakespeare, 2016; (ed) Odyssey, 2017; (ed) Quest, 2017; *translated:* José Eduardo Agualusa, The Book of Chameleons, 2006 (Independent Foreign Fiction Prize, 2007); Pelé, Pelé: the autobiography, 2006; José Eduardo Agualusa, My Father's Wives, 2009; José Luís Peixoto, The Piano Cemetery, 2010; María Dueñas, The Seamstress, 2011; Gonçalo M. Tavares, Learning to Pray in the Age of Technique, 2011; Stella Dreis, Happiness is a Watermelon on Your Head, 2012; Philippe Claudel, The Investigation, 2013; Zulmira Ribeiro Tavares, Family Heirlooms, 2014; Paulo Scott, Nowhere People, 2014; Socorro Acioli, The Head of the Saint, 2014; José Eduardo Agualusa, A General Theory of Oblivion, 2015 (Internat. Dublin Literary Award, 2017); María Elena Walsh, An Elephantasy, 2016; Roger Mello, You Can't Be Too Careful, 2017 (Mildred L. Batchelder Honor, Amer. Liby Assoc., 2018); Gabi Martínez, In the Land of Giants, 2017; Michel Laub, A Poison Apple, 2017; Grégoire Solotareff, Wolfy, 2017; Victor Dixen, Phobos trilogy, 2018–19; Julián Fuks, Resistance, 2018; Beatrice Alemagna, The Big Little Thing, 2019; José Eduardo Agualusa, The Society of Reluctant Dreamers, 2019; *translated jointly:* José Saramago, The Notebook, 2010; Eduardo Halfon, The Polish Boxer, 2012; Albert Sanchez Piñol, Victus, 2014; Corsino Fortes, Poems, 2015; Eduardo Halfon, Mourning, 2018. *Recreations:* mostly work; also proselytising for books, writers, translators; also more books. *Address:* c/o Society of Authors, 84 Drayton Gardens, SW10 9SD. *W:* www.danielhahn.co.uk.

**HAIG,** family name of **Earl Haig.**

**HAIG, 3rd Earl** *cr* 1919; **Alexander Douglas Derrick Haig;** Viscount Dawick 1919; Baron Haig 1919; 31st Laird of Bemersyde; farmer; *b* 30 June 1961; *o s* of 2nd Earl Haig, OBE and Adrienne Thérèse, *d* of Derrick Morley; *S* father, 2009; *m* 2003, Jane Hartree Risk, *widow* of Michael Risk and *d* of late Donald Grassick Crieff. *Educ:* Stowe School; Royal Agricl Coll., Cirencester. *Heir:* none. *Address:* Findas Farm, Chance Inn, Cupar, Fife KY15 5PQ. *Club:* New (Edinburgh).

**HAIG, David,** MBE 2013; actor and writer; *m* Jane Galloway; five *c. Theatre includes:* seasons with RSC, 1983, 1986; Tom and Viv, Royal Court, 1984, NY, 1985; Our Country's Good (Olivier Award for best actor in a new play), Royal Court, 1988; Berenice, RNT, 1990; Dead Funny, Vaudeville, 1994; Fair Ladies at a Game of Poem Cards, RNT, 1996; Art, Wyndham's, 1997, NY, 1998; My Boy Jack (also writer), Hampstead, 1997; House and Garden, RNT, 2000; Gasping (tour), 2000; Life x 3, Savoy, 2002; Hitchcock Blonde, Royal Court, transf. Lyric, 2003; Journey's End, Comedy, 2004; Mary Poppins, Prince Edward, 2004; Donkey's Years, Comedy, 2006; The Country Wife, Haymarket, 2007; The Sea, Haymarket, 2007; Loot, Tricycle, 2008; Yes, Prime Minister, Chichester Fest. Th., transf. Gielgud, 2010; The Madness of George III, Th. Royal, Bath, 2011, transf. Apollo, 2012; King Lear, Th. Royal, Bath, 2013; Someone Who'll Watch Over Me, Chichester, 2015; Guys and Dolls, Savoy Th., 2016; Blue/Orange, Young Vic, 2016; Rosencrantz and Guildenstern are Dead, Old Vic, 2017; Racing Demon, Th. Royal, Bath, 2017; writer, The Good Samaritan, Hampstead, 2000; writer and actor, Pressure, Royal Lyceum, Edinburgh, transf. Chichester, 2014, Park Th., 2018. *Films include:* The Moon Stallion, 1978; Dark Enemy, 1984; Morons from Outer Space, 1985; Four Weddings and a Funeral, 1994; Two Weeks Notice, 2002; Florence Foster Jenkins, 2016; Downton Abbey, 2019; *television includes:* Portrait of a Marriage, 1990; Soldier, Soldier, 1991; Love on a Branch Line, 1993; Nice Day at the Office, 1994; The Thin Blue Line (series), 1995; Keeping Mum, 1997; Talking Heads 2, 1998; Station Jim, 2001; Crime and Punishment, 2002; Hustle, 2004; My Boy Jack (also writer), 2007; Mo, 2010; Yes, Prime Minister, 2013; The Wright Way, 2013; The Witness for the Prosecution, 2016; Killing Eve, 2018. *Address:* c/o Artists Rights Agency, 4A Exmoor Street, W10 6BD.

**HAIGH, Andrew Michael;** Executive Director, Coutts & Co., 2001–16; adviser and freelance consultant; *b* Manchester, 28 Oct. 1958; *s* of Colin and Audrey Haigh. *Educ:* Hipperholme Grammar Sch.; Univ. of Hull (BA Jt Hons). Finance Dir, Internat. Businesses, NatWest, 1993–96; Chief Operating Officer, NatWest Offshore, 1996–99; Chief Corporate Officer, N America, NatWest, 1999–2000. Mem. Council, RCM, 2010–. Trustee: Chisenhale Gall., 2008–; Photographers' Gall., 2009–16. FRSA 1999. *Recreations:* visual and performing arts, gardening, cooking.

**HAIGH, Prof. Joanna Dorothy,** CBE 2013; DPhil; FRS 2013; FInstP; Professor of Atmospheric Physics, since 2001, and Co-director, Grantham Institute - Climate Change and Environment, since 2014, Imperial College London; *b* London, 7 May 1954; *d* of Adrian Haigh and Sanda Haigh; *m* 1981, Paul Julian Fouracre; one *s* two *d*. *Educ:* Hitchin Girls' Grammar Sch.; Somerville Coll., Oxford (MA Phys 1975; Hon. Fellow, 2014); Imperial Coll. London (MSc Meteorol. 1977); St Cross Coll., Oxford (DPhil Phys 1980). FInstP 2004. Post-doctoral Res. Asst, Atmospheric Phys, Univ. of Oxford, 1980–84; Imperial College London: Lectr in Remote Sensing, 1984–90; Lectr, 1990–97, Reader, 1997–2001, Atmospheric Phys; Hd, Dept of Phys, 2009–14. Pres., RMetS, 2012–14; Hon. FRMetS 2017. FCGI 2014. *Address:* Grantham Institute - Climate Change and Environment, Imperial College London, SW7 2AZ. *T:* (020) 7594 5798. *E:* j.haigh@imperial.ac.uk.

**HAIGH, Louise Margaret;** MP (Lab) Sheffield Heeley, since 2015; *b* Sheffield, 22 July 1987. *Educ:* Sheffield High Sch.; Nottingham Univ. Call centre worker; council youth services; Co-ordinator, All Party Parly Gp on Internat. Corporate Responsibility; Corporate Governance Policy Manager, Aviva plc. Shadow Minister for Cabinet Office, 2015–16, for Digital Economy, 2016–17, for Policing, 2017–. *Address:* House of Commons, SW1A 0AA.

**HAIGH, Mark Richard;** His Honour Judge **Haigh;** a Circuit Judge, since 2019; *b* Halifax, 10 Nov. 1958; *s* of Hanson Haigh and Claire Florence Haigh; *m* Ann; two *s* one *d*. *Educ:* Crossley and Porter Sch.; Univ. of Nottingham (LLB 1980). Admitted solicitor, 1983; Solicitor and Managing Partner, Wilkinson Woodward and Boococks, solicitors; a District Judge, 2006–18. *Recreations:* squash, cooking, simple DIY projects. *Address:* Manchester Civil and Family Justice Centre, Bridge Street West, Manchester M60 9DJ.

**HAILES, Timothy Russell;** JP; Managing Director, J.P. Morgan Chase & Co., since 2006; *b* Dorchester, 7 Oct. 1967; *s* of David Roger Hailes and Blenda Olive Hailes (*née* Wensley). *Educ:* Hampton Sch., Middx; Bristol Grammar Sch.; King's Coll. London (BA Hons Hist. 1990). Trainee solicitor, 1993–95, solicitor, 1995–97, Wilde Sapte; solicitor, Cadwalader Wickersham & Taft, 1997–99; J.P. Morgan Chase & Co., 1999–. City of London: Alderman, 2013–; Sheriff, 2017–18. JP Central London, 2012. Vice-Chm., Govs, King Edward's Sch., Witley, 2013–. Churchwarden, St Lawrence Jewry, 2013–. FKC 2019. Hon. LLD UWE, 2018. MStJ 2018. *Recreations:* history, military strategy, Tolkein, labrador walking, Thai food, heraldry, Freemason. *Address:* 32 Guildford Grove, Greenwich, SE10 8JT. *T:* 07801 151780. *E:* tim.hailes@btinternet.com. *Club:* City of London.

**HAILEY, Prof. John Martin,** PhD; Co-Founder, International NGO Training and Research Centre, Oxford, 1992–2012; Professor, Cass Business School, City, University of London (formerly City University London), since 2003; *b* Oxford, 31 Aug. 1952; *s* of Peter and Rowena Hailey; *m* 1995, Prof. Veronica Hope Hailey, *qv*; two *d* and three step *d*. *Educ:* Douai Abbey Sch.; Exeter Univ. (BA); City Univ. (MBA); Queensland Univ. (PhD 1990). Lectr, Univ. of S Pacific, Fiji, 1980–85; Res. Fellow, East-West Center, Hawaii, 1986–88; Lectr, Cranfield Sch. of Mgt, 1988–98; Dept Dir, Oxford Brookes Univ. Business Sch., 1998–2003. *Recreations:* dog walking, tennis, theatre, film, sailing, Bath Rugby. *Address:* Cass Business School, 106 Bunhill Row, EC1Y 8TZ. *T:* (020) 7040 8600. *E:* john.hailey.2@city.ac.uk.

**HAILEY, Nicolas James;** HM Diplomatic Service; High Commissioner to Kenya, 2015–19; *b* London, 27 Jan. 1975; *s* of Michael Hailey and Anthea Hailey (*née* Briault); *m* 2004, Caroline Cerruti; two *d*. *Educ:* Michael Hall Sch.; Peterhouse, Cambridge (BA English 1997); École nat. d'admin, Paris (MPA 2001). Joined FCO, 1997; Desk Officer, EU Dept, 1997–99; Private Sec. to Ambassador, Berlin, 2002–03; Speech-writer to Foreign Sec., 2003–05; Hd, Consular Strategy, Communications and Trng Dept, FCO, 2005–08; Counsellor, Pol and Public Affairs, Washington, 2008–12; Dep. Ambassador, Kabul, 2012–13; Dir, Africa, FCO, 2013–15. *Recreations:* music, tennis, bridge, vegetable growing. *Address:* c/o Foreign and Commonwealth Office, King Charles Street, SW1A 2AH.

**HAILEY, Veronica H.;** *see* Hope Hailey.

**HAILSHAM, 3rd Viscount** *cr* 1929, of Hailsham, co. Sussex; **Douglas Martin Hogg;** PC 1992; QC 1990; Baron 1928; Baron Hailsham of Kettlethorpe (Life Peer) 2015; *b* 5 Feb. 1945; *er s* of Baron Hailsham of Saint Marylebone (Life Peer), PC, KG, CH, FRS (who disclaimed his hereditary peerages for life, 1963); *S* father, 2001; *m* 1968, Sarah Boyd-Carpenter (*see* Baroness Hogg); one *s* one *d*. *Educ:* Eton (Oppidan Schol.); Christ Church, Oxford (Schol.; Pres., Oxford Union). Called to the Bar, Lincoln's Inn, 1968 (Kennedy Law Schol.). MP (C) Grantham, 1979–97, Sleaford and N Hykeham, 1997–2010. Mem., Agric. Select Cttees, 1979–82; PPS to Chief Sec., HM Treasury, 1982–83; an Asst Govt Whip, 1983–84; Parly Under-Sec. of State, Home Office, 1986–89; Minister of State (Minister for Industry and Enterprise), DTI, 1989–90; Minister of State, FCO, 1990–95; Minister of Agriculture, Fisheries and Food, 1995–97. *Heir: s* Hon. Quintin John Neil Martin Hogg [*b* 12 Oct. 1973; *m* 2006, Elizabeth Sophia Anne Heneage]. *Address:* House of Lords, SW1A 0PW.

*See also Hon. C. M. Hogg, Hon. Dame M. C. Hogg.*

**HAILSHAM, Viscountess;** *see* Hogg, Baroness.

**HAIN,** family name of **Baron Hain.**

**HAIN, Baron** *cr* 2015 (Life Peer), of Neath in the County of West Glamorgan; **Peter Gerald Hain;** PC 2001; *b* 16 Feb. 1950; *s* of late Walter Hain and Adelaine Hain; *m* 1st, 1975, Patricia Western (marr. diss. 2002); two *s*; 2nd, 2003, Dr Elizabeth Zaidee Haywood, *qv*. *Educ:* Queen Mary College, London (BSc Econ 1st cl. hons); Univ. of Sussex (MPhil). Brought up in S Africa, until family forced to leave in 1966, due to anti-apartheid activity, since when lived in UK. Union of Communication Workers: Asst Research Officer, 1976–87; Head of Research, 1987–91. Chm., Stop the Seventy Tour campaign, 1969–70; Nat. Chm., Young Liberals, 1971–73; Press Officer, Anti-Nazi League, 1977–80. Contested (Lab) Putney, 1983, 1987. MP (Lab) Neath, April 1991–2015. An Opposition

Whip, 1995–96; an Opposition Spokesman on employment, 1996–97; Parly Under-Sec. of State, Welsh Office, 1997–99; Minister of State, FCO, 1999–2000 and 2001–02; Minister of State, DTI, Jan.–June 2001; Sec. of State for Wales, 2002–08 and 2009–10; Leader, H of C, 2003–05; Sec. of State for NI, 2005–07, for Work and Pensions, 2007–08; Shadow Sec. of State for Wales, 2010–12. Global Govtl Advr, Ince Gordon Dadds (formerly Gordon Dadds) LLP, 2016–; Special Advr, Moti Gp, 2018–19. Non-exec. Dir, DNG Energy. Visiting Professor: Univ. of S Wales, 2014–; Wits Business Sch., Johannesburg, 2016–. Chm. Trustees, Donald Woods Foundn, 2014–. *Publications:* Don't Play with Apartheid, 1971; Community Politics, 1976; Mistaken Identity, 1976; (ed) Policing the Police, vol. I, 1978, vol. II, 1980; Neighbourhood Participation, 1980; Crisis and Future of the Left, 1980; Political Trials in Britain, 1984; Political Strikes, 1986; A Putney Plot?, 1987; The Peking Connection (novel), 1995; Ayes to the Left, 1995; Sing the Beloved Country, 1996; Mandela, 2010; Outside In, 2012; Ad & Wal, 2014; Back to the Future of Socialism, 2015; Mandela, 2018. *Recreations:* soccer, cricket, Rugby, motor racing, fan of Chelsea, Swansea FC, Ospreys and Neath RFCs, rock and folk music fan. *Address:* House of Lords, SW1A 0PW. *T:* (020) 7219 3000. *E:* peter.hain@parliament.uk. *W:* www.peterhain.org.uk. *Clubs:* Resolven Rugby; Ynysygerwn Cricket.

**HAIN, Elizabeth Zaidée, (Lady Hain);** *see* Haywood, E. Z.

**HAINER, Herbert;** Chief Executive Officer and Chairman, Executive Board, adidas AG (formerly adidas-Salomon AG), 2001–16; *b* Dingolfing, Germany, 3 June 1954; *m* Angela; two *d*. *Educ:* Univ. of Landshut (degree in Business Studies 1979). Div. Manager, Sales and Mktg Germany, Procter & Gamble GmbH, 1979–87; adidas Germany: Sales Dir Hardware (Bags, Rackets, Balls), 1987–89; Sales Dir Field (Footwear, Textiles, Hardware), 1989–91; Nat. Sales Dir, 1991–93; Man. Dir (Sales and Logistics), 1993–95; adidas AG, then adidas-Salomon AG: Sen. Vice Pres. (Sales and Logistics), Europe, Africa, Middle East Reg., 1996–97; Mem., 1997–2016, Dep. Chm., 2001, Exec. Bd. Member, Supervisory Board: Bayerische Versicherungsbank AG, Munich; Engelhorn KGaA, Mannheim; Dep. Chm. Supervisory Bd, FC Bayern München AG, Munich; Mem. Bd, Accenture Global Services Ltd, 2016–.

**HAINES, Andrew,** OBE 2016; Chief Executive, Network Rail, since 2018; *b* Merthyr Tydfil, 21 April 1964; *s* of Eric and Megan Haines; *m* 1986, Caroline Fletcher; one *s* one *d*. *Educ:* Cyfarthfa High Sch.; King's Coll. London (BA Hons Hist. 1985); Kingston Univ. (MBA 1995). South West Trains: Ops Dir, 1999–2000; Man. Dir, 2000–05; Man. Dir, Rail Div., FirstGroup, 2005–08; Chief Operating Officer, First Great Western, 2007–08; CEO, Civil Aviation Authy, 2009–18. Non-exec. Dir, Eversholt Rail Ltd, 2013–18. Chm., Balsam Family Project, 2009–. Gov., Oxford Acad., 2010–13. FIRO 2006; FCILT 2012; FRAeS 2015; FRSA. Hon. DLitt Kingston, 2013. *Recreations:* keeping fit, classical music, gardening, cooking. *Address:* Network Rail, 1 Eversholt Street, Euston, NW1 2DN.

**HAINES, Sir Andrew (Paul),** Kt 2005; MD; FRCP, FRCGP, FFPH; FMedSci; FRSB; Professor of Environmental Change and Public Health (formerly of Public Health and Primary Care), London School of Hygiene and Tropical Medicine, University of London, since 2001 (Director (formerly Dean), 2001–10); *b* 26 Feb. 1947; *s* of Charles George Thomas Haines and Lillian Emily Haines; *m* 1st, 1982, June Marie Power (marr. diss. 1987); 2nd, 1998, Dr Anita Berlin; two *s*. *Educ:* King's Coll., London (MB BS 1969; MD Epidemiology 1985; Hon. Fellow 2009). MRCP 1971, FRCP 1993; MRCGP 1976, FRCGP 1991; MFCM 1987, FFPH (FFPHM 1992; Hon. FFPH 2009); FRSB 2016. Mem. Scientific Staff, MRC Epidemiology and Med. Care Unit, 1974–87; part-time Sen. Lectr in General Practice, Middlesex Hosp. Med. Sch., 1980–84, St Mary's Hosp. Med. Sch., 1984–87; on secondment as Dir, R&D, NE Thames RHA, subseq. N Thames Reg., NHS Exec., 1993–96; Prof. of Primary Health Care, UCL, 1987–2000; Head, Dept of Primary Care and Population Scis, Royal Free and UC Med. Sch., 1998–2000. Medical Research Council: Mem., 1996–98; Mem., Strategy Bd, 2008–12; Chm., Global Health Gp, 2008–12. Chm., Health Services and Public Health Bd, 1996–98; Member: Bd, Univs UK, 2007–10 (Chm., Health and Social Care Policy Cttee, 2007–09); Scientific Adv. Cttee, AMRC, 1998–2004; Res. Strategy Cttee, Multiple Sclerosis Soc., 2010–19 (Chm., 2011–19); Scientific Adv. Gp, Climate and Clean Air Coalition, 2012–18; Res. Adv. Gp, DFID, 2012–18 (Chm., 2017–18); Scientific Adv. Gp, Global Challenges Res. Fund, 2017–; Chm., Res. Strategy Cttee, Marie Curie Cancer Care, 2014–; Co-Chairman: Develt of Knowledge Action Network for Health, Future Earth, 2016–18; Wkg Gp on climate change and health, European Academies Sci. Adv. Council, 2018–. Mem., UN Intergovernmental Panel on Climate Change, 1993–96, 1998–2001 (Rev. Ed., Health Chapter, Working Gp II, AR5, 2011–14); Consultant, 1998, Mem., Adv. Cttee on Health Res., 2004–08, WHO; Chairman: WHO Task Force on Evidence for Health Systems Strengthening, 2010–11; Scientific Adv. Panel, WHO World Health Report 2013, 2011–13. Chairman: Tropical Health Educn Trust, 2010–16; Rockefeller Foundn/Lancet Commn on Planetary Health, 2014–15 (report, 2015). Trustee: UK Biobank, 2010–16; Med. Res. Foundn, 2014–18; RSocMed, 2014–18. Founder FMedSci 1998; FRGS 2012. Hon. Fellow, UCL, 2006; Hon. Fellow, Philippines Acad. of Family Physicians, 2011. For. Associate Mem., Inst. of Medicine, USA, 2008; Hon. Mem., Nat. Acad. of Medicine, Mexico, 2012. *Publications:* (ed jtly) Climate Change and Human Health, 1996; (ed jtly) Evidence Based Practice in Primary Care, 1998; (ed jtly) Getting Research Findings into Practice, 1998; numerous articles in medical and scientific jls; ed series of articles on climate change mitigation and public health in Lancet, 2009. *Recreations:* swimming, environmental issues. *Address:* London School of Hygiene and Tropical Medicine, Keppel Street, WC1E 7HT. *T:* (020) 7927 2938.

**HAINES, Christopher John Minton;** Chairman, Harlequin Football Club, 1998–2004; *b* 14 April 1939; *m* 1967, Christine Cobbold; two *s* one *d*. *Educ:* Stowe. The Rifle Brigade, 1957–68; sugar trade, 1968–89; Chm., James Budgett & Son, 1984–89. Non-executive Director: Devonshire Arms (Bolton Abbey), 1995–2003; SPG Media (formerly Sterling Publg Gp) plc, 1996–2008 (Chm., 1996–2001). Chief Exec., The Jockey Club, 1989–93. *Recreations:* music, gardening, racing. *Club:* Turf.
    *See also* M. Haines.

**HAINES, Joseph Thomas William;** Assistant Editor, The Daily Mirror, 1984–90; Group Political Editor, Mirror Group Newspapers, 1984–90; *b* 29 Jan. 1928; *s* of Joseph and Elizabeth Haines; *m* 1955, Irene Betty Lambert; no *c*. *Educ:* Elementary Schools, Rotherhithe, SE16. Parly Correspondent, The Bulletin (Glasgow) 1954–58, Political Correspondent, 1958–60; Political Correspondent: Scottish Daily Mail, 1960–64; The Sun, 1964–68; Dep. Press Sec. to Prime Minister, Jan.–June 1969; Chief Press Sec. to Prime Minister, 1969–70 and 1974–76, and to Leader of the Opposition, 1970–74; Feature Writer, 1977–78, Chief Leader Writer, 1978–90, The Daily Mirror. Political Columnist, Today, 1994–95. Director: Mirror Gp Newspapers (1986) Ltd, 1986–92; Scottish Daily Record & Sunday Mail Ltd, 1986–92. Mem. Tonbridge UDC, 1963–69, 1971–74. Mem., Royal Commn on Legal Services, 1976–79. *Publications:* The Politics of Power, 1977; (co-editor) Malice In Wonderland, 1986; Maxwell, 1988; Glimmers of Twilight (memoir), 2003; Kick 'em Back: Wilson, Maxwell and me, 2019. *Recreations:* heresy, watching football. *Address:* 1 South Frith, London Road, Southborough, Tunbridge Wells, Kent TN4 0UQ. *T:* (01732) 365919.

**HAINES, Margaret Patricia Joyce,** FCLIP; University Librarian, Carleton University, Ottawa, 2006–14; *b* Ottawa, 28 May 1950; *d* of Ernest and Mary Haines; *m* 1st, Roderick Stewart Taylor (marr. diss. 1989); 2nd, 1991, Ian Cordery (marr. diss. 2007); one step *d*. *Educ:* Carleton Univ. (BA Psychol. 1970); Univ. of Toronto (MLS 1975). Librarian, Health Scis Educn Centre, Mohawk Coll., Hamilton, Canada, 1975–78; Dir, Liby Services, Children's Hosp. of Eastern Ontario, Ottawa, 1978–88; Associate Instructor (Inf. Sci.), Univ. of Toronto, 1988–89; Dir, Inf. Resources, Kings' Fund, London, 1989–94; NHS Liby Advr, DoH, 1995–96; Chief Exec., Liby and Inf. Commn, 1996–2000; Dir, Res. and Knowledge Mgt, NHS SE London, 2000–02; Actg Dir, Knowledge Mgt, NHS Modernisation Agency, 2002–03; Dir, Inf. Services and Systems, KCL, 2003–06. Pres., CILIP, 2004–05. Pres., Ontario Hosp. Libraries Assoc., 1987. Hon. FCLIP 2006 (FCLIP 2004). Barnard Prize, LA, 1996. *Publications:* contrib. numerous articles to liby and information jls and chapters in books, including: Health Care Librarianship and Information Work, 2nd edn 1995; (jtly) Getting Research Findings into Practice, 1998; (jtly) Challenge and Change in the Information Society, 2003. *Recreations:* gardening, travelling, reading. *Address:* 37 Shandon Avenue, Nepean, ON K2J 4E3, Canada. *T:* (613) 8259615. *E:* mpjhaines@aol.com.

**HAINES, Miranda, (Mrs Luke Taylor);** writer; Consultant Editor, Geographical magazine, 2002–05 (Editor, 1999–2002); *b* 15 Oct. 1968; *d* of Christopher Haines, *qv*; *m* 1998, Luke Taylor; one *s* one *d*. *Educ:* Manchester Coll., Oxford (BA Hons English Lit.). International Herald Tribune, 1993–96; freelance writer, London, 1996–97; Editor, Traveller magazine, 1997–98. *Publications:* (ed jtly) The Traveller's Handbook, 1998; (ed jtly) The Traveller's Health Book, 1998; (contrib.) A Pilgrimage to Mecca, 2008. *Recreation:* travelling. *Address:* 2 Souldern Road, W14 0JE.

**HAINES, Patricia, (Trish);** Chief Executive, Worcestershire County Council, 2008–14; *d* of David and Roberta Calvert; two *s*, and one step *s* three step *d*. *Educ:* Belfast Royal Acad.; Univ. of Bradford (BA Hons, CQSW 1979); Henley Mgt Coll. (MBA 1994). Case worker, Manchester Law Centre, 1979–80; Intake Social Worker, Bradford MBC, 1980–83; Fostering and Adoption Social Worker, Kirklees MBC, 1983–86; Sen. Social Worker, Bradford MBC, 1986–87; Prin. Social Worker, Social Services, Berks CC, 1987–92; Prin. Staff Officer, Suffolk Social Services, 1992–96; Asst Dir, Social Services, Hereford and Worcs CC, 1996–97; Dir of Social Services, Warwicks CC, 1997–2002; Chief Exec., Reading BC, 2002–08. Ind. Complaints Reviewer, IPSO, 2016–. Pres., SOLACE, 2008–09 (Vice-Pres., 2006–08); Chair, Age UK, Hereford and Worcs, 2015–. Lay Mem., Governing Body, S Worcs CCG, 2014–. *Recreations:* enjoying family life, exploring new possibilities in retirement.

**HAINES, Ronald William Terence,** CEng, FICE, FIStructE; Director of Construction Services, HM Prison Service, 1993–96; *b* 19 Dec. 1937; *s* of John William Haines and Mary Agnes Power; *m* 1957, Linda, *d* of Sidney and Lilian Hampton; one *s* two *d*. *Educ:* South East London Tech. Coll.; Regent Street Poly.; City Univ. MCIWEM. Design Engineer: William Harbrow & Co., 1954–56; Liverpool Reinforced Concrete Co., 1956–58; Civil and Structl Engr, Min. of Works and MPBW, 1958–67; Chief Civil and Structl Engr, Home Office, 1967–87; Dep. Dir of Works, HM Prison Service, Home Office, 1987–93. *Recreations:* organic farming, walking, theatre. *Address:* Barklye Farm, Swife Lane, Broad Oak, Heathfield, E Sussex TN21 8UR.

**HAINES, Timothy Michael;** Creative Director and Founder, Impossible Pictures Ltd, since 2002; *b* 14 Oct. 1960; *s* of Douglas and Ann Haines; *m* 1989, Clare Worgan; three *s* two *d*. *Educ:* Tonbridge Sch., Kent; University Coll. of N Wales, Bangor (BSc Hons Zool.; Hon. Fellow 2004). Medical journalist, Doctor newspaper, 1981–85; Producer: BBC Radio, 1986–88; BBC TV Sci. and Features, 1989–2001; Creative Dir, Drama, ITV, 2013–17. Creator and Producer, Walking with Dinosaurs, 1999; Executive Producer: Ballad of Big Al, 2000; Walking with Beasts, 2001; Lost World, 2001; Space Odyssey, 2004; Walking with Monsters, 2005; Ocean Odyssey, 2006; Co-creator and Executive Producer: Primeval, 2007–11; Sinbad, 2012; Beowulf, 2016; The Loch, 2017. Consultant, Walking with Dinosaurs, Live Arena Experience, 2009; Creative Dir, Dinosaurs in the Wild, 2017. *Publications:* Walking with Dinosaurs, 1999; Walking with Beasts, 2001; Space Odyssey, 2004; Complete Guide to Prehistoric Life, 2005. *Recreations:* watching film and TV, gardening, walking. *Address:* Impossible Pictures Ltd, 39 Long Acre, WC2E 9LG.

**HAINSWORTH, Prof. Sarah Victoria,** OBE 2019; PhD; CEng, FREng, CSci, FIMMM; Pro-Vice-Chancellor and Executive Dean, School of Engineering and Applied Sciences, Aston University, since 2017; *b* Leeds, 5 Oct. 1967; *d* of Ian and Joan Hainsworth; *m* 1999, Prof. Michael Edward Fitzpatrick; two *d*. *Educ:* Richmond Sch., Richmond, N Yorks; Univ. of Newcastle upon Tyne (BEng 1989; PhD 1993). MIM 2000; CEng, 2000; CSci 2005; FIMMM 2005. Postdoctoral Res. Asst, Univ. of Newcastle upon Tyne, 1992–97; University of Leicester: Lectr, 1997–2005; Sen. Lectr, 2005–08; Reader, 2008–09; Grad. Dean, 2009–16; Prof. of Materials and Forensic Engrg, 2009–17; Hd, Dept of Engrg, 2016–17. Mem., Registrants Panel, 2002–07; Dir and Trustee, 2005–07, Engrg Technol. Bd. Chm., Facilities Res. and Develt Panel, 2008–10, Mem., Physical Scis and Engrg Adv. Panel, 2012–15, STFC. Mem., Exec. Cttee, UK Council for Grad. Educn, 2010–16. Mem., Internat. Rev. Panel for Statutory Rev. of Materials Sci. and Engrg Expert Cttee of ESF, 2013. Member: Senate, Engrg Council, 2001–02; Structure of Materials Cttee, IMMM, 2009–14. Mem., Scientific Adv. Council, Helmholtz Zentrum Berlin für Materialien und Energie, 2011–. FWES 2015; FREng 2016; SFHEA 2016. Tribology Bronze Medal, IMechE, 1995; Jim Kape Meml Medal, Inst. Materials Finishing, 2007; Rosenhain Medal, IMMM, 2008; Inspiring Tech. Women (90 for 90), Women's Energy Soc., 2009; Andrew H. Payne Jr Special Achievement Award, Amer. Acad. Forensic Sci., 2015. *Publications:* (jtly) The Bones of a King: Richard III rediscovered, 2015; (ed jtly) Criminal Dismemberment: forensic and investigative analysis, 2017; contribs to forensic engrg sci, metallurgy and materials sci. jls. *Recreations:* hockey, gardening, sewing. *Address:* Aston University, Aston Triangle, Birmingham B4 7ET.

**HAIR, Kirstene;** MP (C) Angus, since 2017; *b* Brechin, Angus. *Educ:* Brechin High Sch.; Univ. of Aberdeen (MA Politics 2011). PA, Scottish Conservatives, 2012–13; Personal Sec., Wild Thyme Ltd, 2012–13; Personal Sec., 2014–15, Exec. Asst, 2016, DC Thomson, Publishers. Mem., Women and Equalities Cttee, H of C, 2017–. Contested (C) Angus S, Scottish Parlt, 2016. *Address:* House of Commons, SW1A 0AA.

**HAIRD, Susan Margaret,** CB 2007; Associate Director, Trade and Investment, IMC Worldwide, since 2017; *b* 10 Oct. 1952; *d* of late Douglas Haird and Myrah Haird; *m* 1979, David Simpson; one *s* one *d*. *Educ:* Dollar Acad.; St Andrews Univ. (MA Hons Hist. and Econs); Coll. of Europe, Bruges (Cert. and Dip. in Advanced Eur. Studies). Stage at EC, 1976; joined Department of Trade and Industry, 1976: Private Secretary: to Perm. Sec., 1978; to Parly Under-Sec., 1979; Commercial Relns and Exports Div., 1980–84; Personnel Div., 1985–89; Industrial Materials Div., 1989; Equal Opportunities Div., Cabinet Office (on loan), 1989–92; Atomic Energy Div., 1992–96; Office of Manpower Econs, 1996–99; Director: Export Control, 1999–2000; Export Control and Non-Proliferation, 2000–02; UK Gov., IAEA and UK Mem., Exec. Council, Orgn for Prohibition of Chemical Weapons, 2000–02; Dir, Human Resources and Change Mgt, DTI, 2002–04; Dep. Chief Exec., UK Trade & Investment, 2004–12; European Trade and Investment Rep. for British

Columbia, 2012–17. Dir, Canada-UK Chamber of Commerce, 2013–17; Chair, Internat. Adv. Bd, UK Lebanon Tech Hub, 2016–17; non-exec. Dir, Engrg Employers Fedn, 2012–18; Mem., Adv. Council, British Expertise, 2012–; non-exec. Dir, Newcastle Univ. London, 2018–. Lectr, Internat. Centre for Parly Studies, 2013–. *Recreations*: family, travel, swimming.

**HAIRE, William David Adams**, CB 2015; Permanent Secretary, Department for Social Development, Northern Ireland, 2010–15; *b* 14 April 1956; *s* of Prof. James Haire and Dr Margaret Haire; *m* 1984, Bronwen Jess; two *d*. *Educ*: Queens' Coll., Cambridge (BA 1979); Univ. of Ulster (MSc). Joined Dept of Manpower Services, NI, 1980; on secondment, UKRep, Brussels, 1990–93; Director: Equality and Industrial Relns, Dept of Econ. Develt, 1993–97; Internat. Mktg, Industrial Develt Bd for NI, 1997–2000; Dir, Econ. Policy Unit, 2000–02, Second Perm. Sec., 2002–04, Office of First and Dep. First Minister; Permanent Secretary: Dept for Employment and Learning, 2004–06; Dept of Educn, 2006–10. Trustee: Joseph Rowntree Foundn, 2014– (Chm., 2017–); Quaker Internat. Educn Trust, 2015– (Vice Chm., 2017–). *Recreations*: gardening, walking, reading.

**HAIRER, Prof. Martin**, Hon. KBE 2016; PhD; FRS 2014; Professor of Probability and Stochastic Analysis, Imperial College London, since 2017; *b* Geneva, 14 Nov. 1975; *s* of Ernst and Evi Hairer; *m* 2003, Xue-Mei Li. *Educ*: Univ. of Geneva (BSc Maths; MSc Physics 1998; PhD Physics 2001). Asst Prof., 2004–06, Associate Prof., 2006–09, Univ. of Warwick; Associate Prof., New York Univ., 2009–10; Prof., 2010–14, Regius Prof. of Maths, 2014–17, Univ. of Warwick. *Publications*: (with P. Friz) A Course on Rough Paths, 2014. *Address*: Mathematics Department, Imperial College London, SW7 2AZ. *E*: martin@hairer.org.

**HAITES, Prof. Neva Elizabeth**, OBE 2006; PhD; FRCPE; FRCPath; FMedSci; Professor of Medical Genetics, since 1996, and Vice-Principal for Development, since 2011, University of Aberdeen (Vice-Principal and Head of College of Life Sciences and Medicine, 2004–11); *b* 4 June 1947; *d* of Jack Kingsbury and Neva (*née* Gartside); *m* 1971, (Binnert) Roy Haites; two *d*. *Educ*: Somerville House, Brisbane; Univ. of Queensland (BSc; PhD 1974); Univ. of Aberdeen (MB ChB 1980). MRCPath 1996; FRCPE 1997. Lectr in Med. Genetics, Univ. of Aberdeen, 1986–96; Hon. Consultant Clinical Geneticist, 1991, and non-exec. Bd Mem., NHS Grampian (formerly Aberdeen Royal Hosps NHS Trust). Mem., HFEA, 2003–. FMedSci 2000; FRSE 2010. *Publications*: (ed jtly) Familial Breast and Ovarian Cancer: genetics, screening and management, 2002. *Address*: College of Life Sciences and Medicine, University of Aberdeen, Polwarth Building, Foresterhill, Aberdeen AB25 2ZD; 32 Cairn Road, Bieldside, Aberdeen AB15 9AL.

**HAITINK, Bernard**, Hon. CH 2002; Hon. KBE 1977; Commander, Order of Orange Nassau, 1988; Principal Conductor, Chicago Symphony Orchestra, 2006–10; Music Director: Royal Opera House, Covent Garden, 1987–2002; Dresden Staatskapelle, 2002–04; *b* Amsterdam, 4 March 1929. *Educ*: Amsterdam Conservatory. Studied conducting under Felix Hupke, but started his career as a violinist with the Netherlands Radio Philharmonic; in 1954 and 1955 attended annual conductors' course (org. by Netherlands Radio Union) under Ferdinand Leitner; became 2nd Conductor with Radio Union at Hilversum with co-responsibility for 4 radio orchs and conducted the Radio Philharmonic in public during the Holland Fest., in The Hague, 1956; conducted the Concertgebouw Orch., Oct. 1956; then followed guest engagements with this and other orchs in the Netherlands and elsewhere. Debut in USA, with Los Angeles Symph. Orch., 1958; 5 week season with Concertgebouw Orch., 1958–59, and toured Britain with it, 1959; apptd (with Eugen Jochum) as the Orchestra's permanent conductor, Sept. 1961; sole artistic dir and permanent conductor of the orch., 1964–88; toured Japan, USSR, USA and Europe; 1974; début at Royal Opera House, Covent Garden, 1977. London Philharmonic Orchestra: Principal Conductor, Artistic Dir, 1967–79; toured: Japan, 1969; USA, 1970, 1971, 1976; Berlin, 1972; Holland, Germany, Austria, 1973; USSR, 1975. Musical Dir, Glyndebourne Opera, 1978–88; conducted Figaro for rebuilt opera house of Glyndebourne (60th anniversary), 1994; Music Dir, EU Youth Orch., 1994–99, Conductor Laureate, 2015; Principal Guest Conductor, Boston Symph. Orch., 1995–2004, now Conductor Emeritus. Appearances at BBC Promenade Concerts and at Tanglewood, Salzburg, Edinburgh and Lucerne Festivals. Hon. RAM 1973. Hon. DMus: Oxford, 1988; Leeds, 1988; RCM, 2004. Bruckner Medal of Honour, 1970; Gold Medal, Internat. Gustav Mahler Soc., 1971; Erasmus Prize, Netherlands, 1991; Lifetime Achievement Award, Gramophone Awards, 2015. Chevalier de L'Ordre des Arts et des Lettres, 1972; Officer, Order of the Crown (Belgium), 1977; Comdr, Order of Lion (Netherlands), 2017. *Address*: c/o Askonas Holt Ltd, 15 Fetter Lane, EC4A 1BW.

**HAJDUCKI, Andrew Michael**, QC (Scot.) 1994; FSAScot; *b* London, 12 Nov. 1952; *s* of Henryk Hajducki, civil engineer, and Catherine Maxwell Moore, teacher; *m* 1st, 1980, Gayle Shepherd (marr. diss. 1998); two *s* one *d* (and one *s* decd); 2nd, 2002, Katharine Lilli Dodd. *Educ*: Dulwich Coll.; Downing Coll., Cambridge (BA 1975; MA 1979). FSAScot 1990. Called to the Bar, Gray's Inn, 1976; Advocate at Scots Bar, 1979–2017; Tutor, Edinburgh Univ., 1979–81; reporter, Session Cases, 1980; temp. Sheriff, 1987–99. Safeguarder: Lothian Reg. Children's Panel, 1987–96; Edinburgh and E Lothian Children's Panels, 1996–98; Reporter, Scottish Legal Aid Bd, 1999–; Arbitrator, Motor Insurers' Bureau (Untraced Drivers) scheme, 2000–03. Agent for Scottish Liberal Party and contested (Scottish L), local govt elections, 1979–85. Chm. of Trustees, Edinburgh Gestalt Inst., 2010–15 (Trustee, 2015–18). *Publications*: Scottish Civic Government Licensing Law, 1994, 4th edn 2016; Civil Jury Trials, 1998, 3rd edn 2017; (contrib.) Scottish Licensing Handbook, 1999; (contrib.) Renton & Brown's Statutory Offences, 1999; *railway history*: The North Berwick & Gullane Branch Lines, 1992, 2nd edn 2019; The Haddington, Macmerry & Gifford Branch Lines, 1994; The Lauder Light Railway, 1996; The St Andrews Railway, 2008; The Anstruther and St Andrews Railway, 2009; The Railways of Beckenham, 2011; The Leven and East of Fife Railway, 2013; The East Fife Central Railway, 2015; articles in Scots Law Times and other legal, local history and railway jls. *Recreations*: reading, exploring the world about us. *Address*: 16 Howard Place, Edinburgh EH3 5JZ.

**HAJI-IOANNOU, Sir Stelios**, Kt 2006; Founder, and Chairman, easyGroup, since 1998; Honorary General Consul for Republic of Cyprus in Principality of Monaco, since 2009; *b* 14 Feb. 1967; *s* of late Loucas Haji-Ioannou. *Educ*: London Sch. of Econs and Pol Sci. (BSc Econs); City of London Business Sch. (MSc Shipping, Trade and Finance). Joined Troodos Maritime, 1988; Founder: Stelmar Tankers, based in Athens and London, 1992 (floated NY Stock Exchange 2001, sold 2005); easyJet budget airline, 1995 (floated London Stock Exchange 2000) (Chm., 1995–2002; non-exec. Dir, 2005–10); easyCar, 2000; easyBus, 2004; easyHotel, 2005 (floated London Stock Exchange 2014); easyVan, 2006; easyOffice, 2007; easyGym, 2010; easyProperty, 2014; easyFoodstore, 2016; easyTennis, 2017. Founder: Cyprus Marine Envmt Protection Assoc., 1992; Stelios Philanthropic Foundn, 2006; Stelios Philanthropic Foundn (UK), 2011. Hon. Dr: Liverpool John Moores; Newcastle Business Sch.; Cranfield; Cass Business Sch. *Recreations*: yachting, philanthropy. *Address*: easyGroup Ltd, 10 Sydney Place, South Kensington, SW7 3NL.

**HAKESLEY-BROWN, Roswyn Ann**, CBE 2007; author; consultant in healthcare education, since 1996; *b* 2 Aug. 1945; *d* of Hector Redvers Hakesley; *m* 1968, Alan Graham Brown; one *s* one *d*. *Educ*: SE Staffs Co. Commercial Secondary Sch., Wednesbury; Univ. of Birmingham (Cert Ed); Open Univ. (BA Social Studies); Univ. of Warwick (MPhil Sociol.); Royal Hosp., Wolverhampton (RGN 1966); New Cross Hosp., Wolverhampton (RM 1967); London Univ. (DipN 1970). Nurse Tutor, Queen Elizabeth Hosp., Birmingham, 1973–84; Principal Lectr, Birmingham Poly., later UCE, Birmingham, 1984–96. Florence Nightingale Schol., 1995. Pres., RCN, 2000–02. Member: Refugee Healthcare Professionals' Steering Gp, DoH, 2002–06; Council, Grubb Inst., 2007–; PLAB Review Working Gp, GMC, 2012–14; Chairman: Refugee Nurses' Task Force, 2003–04; Allied Health Professionals Patients' Forum, 2009–14; Acad. of Nursing, Midwifery and Health Visiting Res. (UK), 2012. Trustee, ExtraCare Charitable Trust for Older People, 1997–2006. FRSPH (FRSH 1990). Member: Soc. of Authors, 1992; Sigma Theta Tau Internat., 1996; Honour Sch. of Nursing. World of Difference 100 Award, Internat. Alliance for Women, 2009. Commng Ed., reviewer and mem., editl bds. *Publications*: Individualised Care: the role of the ward sister, 1989; Portfolios and Profiling for Nurses, 1992, 2nd edn 1995; (with B. Hawkesley) Learning Skills, Studying Styles and Profiling, 1996; chapters, reviews, prefaces and articles. *Recreations*: antique collecting, the National Trust, partying, picnics, having fun, reading, watching films, ballet, plays, listening to classical music. *Address*: c/o Royal College of Nursing, 20 Cavendish Square, W1G 0RN.

**HAKIM, Prof. Nadey**, MD, PhD; FRCS, FRCSI, FACS; Consultant General, Transplant and Bariatric Surgeon, St Mary's Hospital and Lindo Wing, Imperial College Healthcare NHS Trust, since 2005; Consultant General Surgeon, Imperial College Healthcare NHS Trust and Harefield and Brompton Hospitals, since 2016; Professor of Transplantation Surgery, Imperial College London, since 2013 (Reader, 2010–12); Transplantation Tutor, London School of Surgery, since 2009; Max Thorek Professor of Surgery, International College of Surgeons, Chicago, since 2008; *b* 9 April 1958; *s* of Subhy Elias A. Hakim and Katy Hakim (*née* Namur); *m* 1992, Nicole Abounader; one *s* three *d*. *Educ*: René Descartes Univ., Paris (MD 1983); University Coll. London (PhD 1991). FRCSI 1987; FRCS 1988. Fellow in Surgery: Mayo Clinic, Rochester, Minn, 1987–89; Univ. of Minnesota, 1993–95; Consultant Surgeon, St Mary's Hosp., London, 1995–2005; Surgical Dir, Transplant Unit, St Mary's Hosp., London and Hammersmith Hosp., London, 1996–2015. Hon. Consultant Paediatric Transplant Surgeon, Gt Ormond St Hosp., 1996–2001; Hon. Consultant Transplant Surgeon: Royal Free Hosp., 1996–2001; Hammersmith Hosp., 1998–2005; Harefield Hosp., 2000–15; Responsible Officer, Medicare Français Two London, 2018–. Hon. Professor of Surgery: Univ. of São Paulo, 1999; Baskent Univ., Ankara, 2006–; Lima Univ., Peru, 2006–; Lyon Univ., 2007–; Belgrade Med. Sch., 2018–; Visiting Professor: Univ. of Hong Kong, 1997; Harvard Univ., 2007; Cleveland Clinic, 2011; Univ. of Louvain, 2011; Univ. of Minnesota, 2011. Editor in Chief: Internat. Surgery, 2001–11, Emeritus, 2012; Introductory Series in Medicine, Imperial Coll. Press, 2012–. First Vice-Pres., 2000–02, Pres., 2004–06, Internat. Coll. Surgeons; Vice Pres., Internat. Med. Scis Acad., 2018–. Mem. Council, RSM, 2009– (Hon. Sec., 2011–14; Pres., Transplant Sect., 2001–03; Vice Pres., 2014–16); Gov., Amer. Coll. of Surgeons, 2015–. Non-exec. Dir, Medicsight, 2003–05. Ambassador, All Party Parly Gp for Diabetes. Hon. Scientific Chm., Roads for Life, 2015–. Imperial Coll. President's Envoy, 2017–. FACS 1998; FICS 1987 (now Hon.). Internat. Fellow, Amer. Soc. for Metabolic and Bariatric Surgery, 2008. Hon. Fellow: Internat. Napoleonic Soc., 2008; Internat. Med. Scis Assoc., 2009; Assoc. of Surgeons of India, 2010; Georgian Surgical Soc., 2018. Hon. Dr: Charles Univ., Prague, 1998; Aden, 2003; Lima, 2007; Beirut Arab Univ., 2018; Bolton, 2019. Laureate, Faculty of Medicine, Paris, 1994; Prize of Excellence in Medicine, Makhzoum Foundn, 1998; J. Wesley Alexander Award for outstanding res. in transplantation, 2007. GCStJ 2010 (KStJ 1998; KCJSJ 2007); Bailiff OStJ 2010. Chevalier de la Légion d'Honneur (France), 2016. *Publications*: (jtly) Enteric Physiology of Transplanted Intestine, 1994; (ed) Introduction to Organ Transplantation, 1997; British Symposium Pancreas Transplantation, 1998; Access Surgery, 2001; joint editor: Transplantation Surgery, 2001, 2nd edn 2019; Pancreas and Islet Transplantation, 2002; History of Organ and Cell Transplantation, 2003; Hernias Update, 2005; Composite Tissue Allograft, 2005; Haemostasis in Surgery, 2005; Living Related Transplants, 2005; Surgical Complications, 2008; Artificial Organs, 2009; Pancreas, Islets and Stem Cell Transplantation for the Cure of Diabetes, 2010; Bariatric Surgery, 2011; Atlas of Transplantation, 2012; Ethics and Legal Issues in Modern Surgery, 2015; Surgery for Benign Oesophageal Disorders, 2018. *Recreations*: sculpture (sculpture of HM Queen Elizabeth in Royal Collection Trust, 2009; sculpture of Rt Hon. David Cameron exhibited at Carlton Club and Conservative HQ, 2014; replica sculpture of Michelangelo's David in Monterchi Museum, Italy, 2016; sculpture of Theresa May sitting in 10 Downing St, 2018; sculpture of Emmanuel Macron sitting at Elysée Palace, 2018; sculpture of Pope Francis at Vatican, 2018; sculpture of Prof. Roger Williams at Liver Institute unveiled by Health Secretary, 2018; sculpture of Supreme Leader Kim Jong Un, Pyongyang Internat. Mus., 2018; sculpture of John Griffin at John Griffin Institute, Northwick Park Hospital, 2019; sculpture of Sir Naim Dangoor at RSM, 2019; Baron's Prize for three-dimensional art, 2016), clarinet (ten recordings), languages. *Address*: 34 Hocroft Road, NW2 2BL.
*See also* N. S. P. I. Hakim.

**HAKIM, Naji Subhy Paul Irénée**; organist and composer; Professor of Musical Analysis, Conservatoire à Rayonnement Régional de Boulogne-Billancourt, since 1988; *b* Beirut, 31 Oct. 1955; *s* of Subhy Elias A. Hakim and Katy Hakim; *m* 1980, Marie-Bernadette Dufourcet; one *s* one *d*. *Educ*: Ecole Nationale Supérieure des Télécommunications, Paris (Ingénieur); Conservatoire National Supérieur de Musique, Paris. Organist: Basilique du Sacré-Coeur, Paris, 1985–93; Eglise de la Trinité, Paris, 1993–2008. Vis. Prof., RAM, 1993–. Mem., Consociatio Internat. Musicae Sacrae, Rome. Dr *hc* Saint-Esprit de Kaslik, Lebanon, 2002. Prix André Caplet, Académie des Beaux-Arts, 1991; first prizes at internat. organ, improvisation and composition competitions. Papal honour, Augustae crucis insigne pro Ecclesia et Pontifice, 2007. *Compositions* include: works for organ, violin, flute, oboe, guitar, trumpet; Fantasy for Piano and Orchestra, Concerto for Violin and String Orchestra, five concertos for organ, Concerto for Piano and Orchestra, Concerto for txistu (or flute or recorder) and orchestra, an oratorio, symphony, Les Noces de l'Agneau, a symphonic poem, Hymne de l'Univers, Augsburger Symphonie; three Masses; two Magnificats. *Publications*: Guide Pratique d'Analyse Musicale, 1991, 8th edn 2012; Anthologie Musicale pour l'Analyse de la Forme, 1995; The Improvisation Companion, 2000. *Address*: Conservatoire de Boulogne-Billancourt, 22 Rue de la Belle Feuille, 92100 Boulogne-Billancourt, France. *E*: mail@najihakim.com. *W*: www.najihakim.com.
*See also* N. Hakim.

**HAKIN, Dame Barbara (Ann)**, DBE 2009 (OBE 2001); National Director, Commissioning Operations (formerly Chief Operating Officer and Deputy Chief Executive), NHS England, 2013–15. *Educ*: Univ. of Leeds (MB ChB 1975). MRCP 1977; MRCGP 1980. GP, Bradford, 1980–2000; Chief Exec., Bradford S and W PCT, 2000–06; Interim Dir Gen., Commng, DoH; Dir, Primary Care Modernisation Agency; Chief Exec., E Midlands SHA, 2006–10; Nat. Man. Dir, Commng Develt, DoH, 2010–13; Interim Dep. Chief Exec. and Chief Operating Officer, NHS Commng Bd, 2013.

**HÄKKINEN, Mika;** former racing driver; Brand Ambassador and Driver Manager with Aces Management Group, since 2008; *b* Helsinki, 28 Sept. 1968; two *s* three *d.* Driver in: Go-karts, 1974–86 (five times Finnish champion); Formula Ford 1600, 1987 (Finnish, Swedish and Nordic champion); Opel Lotus Euroseries Championship, 1988; Formula 3, 1989–90 (British champion, 1990) and 2005–07; Formula 1: Lotus team, 1991–93; McLaren team, 1993–2001. Grand Prix wins: European, 1997; Australia, 1998; Brazil, 1998, 1999; Spain, 1998, 1999, 2000; Monaco, 1998; Austria, 1998, 2000; Germany, 1998; Luxembourg, 1998; Japan, 1998, 1999; Hungary, 1999, 2000; Canada, 1999; Belgium, 2000; USA, 2001; Britain, 2001; Drivers' World Champion, 1998, 1999.

**HALBERG, Sir Murray (Gordon),** ONZ 2008; Kt 1988; MBE 1961; *b* 7 July 1933; *s* of Raymond Halberg; *m* 1959, Phyllis, *d* of Alex Korff; two *s* one *d. Educ:* Avondale College. Started internat. distance running, Commonwealth Games, 1954; Commonwealth Gold Medals, 3 miles, 1958, 1962; Olympic Gold Medal, 5,000 metres, Rome, 1960; world records at 2 miles and 3 miles, 1961, participant in 4x1 mile record. Founder, Halberg Trust (to honour sporting excellence and to support children with disabilities), 1963. Blake Medal, Sir Peter Blake Trust, 2008.

**HALBERT, His Honour Derek Rowland;** a Circuit Judge, 1995–2015; *b* 25 March 1948; *s* of Ronald Halbert and Freda Mabel Halbert (*née* Impett); *m* 1972, Heather Rose Ashe; two *d. Educ:* King's Sch., Chester; Selwyn Coll., Cambridge (MA Law 1974); Open Univ. (BA Technol. 1984). Called to the Bar, Inner Temple, 1971; Mem., Wales and Chester Circuit, 1971–; a Recorder, 1991–95; Designated Civil Judge: Chester and N Wales, 2003–07; Cheshire, 2007–15. Hon. Sen. Lectr in Law, 2015–16, Vis. Prof. of Law, 2016–, Chester Univ. Hon. LLD Chester, 2012. *Recreations:* walking, tennis. *Club:* Leander (Henley).

**HALCRO JOHNSTON, James William;** Member (C) Highlands and Islands, Scottish Parliament, since 2017; *b* Oxford, 8 Oct. 1975; *s* of Hugh and Erica Halcro-Johnston. *Educ:* Radley Coll.; Univ. of Exeter (BA Hons Ancient Hist. 1998). Sales, FT, 2000–01; Recruitment Exec., Stevens & Ross, 2001–02; sabbatical, Orkney, 2002–03; Political Advr, Cons. MSPs, 2003–07; Sales Manager, 2007–14, Sales Consultant (freelance), 2014–17, Holyrood Communications. Dir, Campaign House, 2013–17. *Recreations:* Rugby, hockey, squash, history, walking. *Address:* Scottish Parliament, Edinburgh EH99 1SP. *T:* (0131) 348 6140. *E:* jamie.halcrojohnston.msp@parliament.scot. *Club:* New (Edinburgh).

**HALDANE, Prof. (Frederick) Duncan (Michael),** PhD; FRS 1996; Eugene Higgins Professor of Physics, Princeton University, since 1999 (Professor of Physics, 1990–99); *b* 14 Sept. 1951; *s* of Frederick Paterson Haldane and Ljudmila Haldane (*née* Renko); *m* 1981, Odile Marie Elisabeth Belmont; one *s* one *d. Educ:* St Paul's Sch.; Christ's Coll., Cambridge (BA 1973; MA; PhD 1978). FInstP. Physicist, Inst. Laue-Langevin, Grenoble, 1977–81; Asst Prof., Univ. of Southern California, 1981–85; Mem. Technical Staff, AT&T Bell Labs, 1985–87; Prof. of Physics, Univ. of California, San Diego, 1987–90. For. Associate, NAS, 2017. Fellow: Amer. Phys. Soc. (Oliver E. Buckley Prize in Condensed-Matter Physics, 1993); Amer. Acad. of Arts and Scis; FAAAS 2001. Dirac Medal, Internat. Centre for Theoretical Physics, 2012; (jtly) Nobel Prize in Physics, 2016. *Publications:* contribs to Jl of Physics, Physical Review and other learned jls. *Address:* 74 Maclean Circle, Princeton, NJ 08540, USA. *T:* (609) 9211531.

**HALDANE, Prof. John Joseph,** PhD; FRSE; Professor of Philosophy, since 1994, and Senior Fellow, Centre for Ethics, Philosophy and Public Affairs, since 2016, St Andrews University; J. Newton Rayzor Sr Distinguished Professor of Philosophy, Baylor University, since 2015; *b* London, 19 Feb. 1954; *s* of James Haldane and Hilda Haldane (*née* Dunne); *m* 1980, Hilda Budas; two *s* two *d. Educ:* St Aloysius Coll., Glasgow; Wimbledon Coll. of Art (BA Fine Art 1975); Inst. of Educn, Univ. of London (PGCE 1976); Birkbeck Coll., Univ. of London (BA Philosophy 1980; PhD Philosophy 1984). Art Master, St Joseph's Convent Sch., Abbey Wood, 1976–79; University of St Andrews: Lectr in Philosophy, 1983–90; Reader in Moral Philosophy, 1990–94; Dir, Centre for Ethics, Philosophy and Public Affairs, 1988–2000 and 2002–16. Royden Davis Prof. of Humanities, Georgetown Univ., 2001–02. Stanton Lectr in Philosophy and Religion, Univ. of Cambridge, 1999–2002); Gifford Fellow and Gifford Lectr, Univ. of Aberdeen, 2004–05; Sen. Fellow, Witherspoon Inst., Princeton, 2007–; McDonald Lectr, Univ. of Oxford, 2011; Remick Senior Fellow, Center for Ethics and Culture, Univ. of Notre Dame, Indiana, 2013–; Hon. Prof., Sch. of Educn, Univ. of Birmingham, 2014–. Chm., Royal Inst. of Philos., 2011–. Consultor, Pontifical Council for Culture, Vatican, 2005–15. FRSE 1995. Corresp. Member: Pontifical Acad. of St Thomas Aquinas, Vatican, 2010; Pontifical Acad. of Life, Vatican, 2015. KCHS 2011 (KHS 2004). *Publications:* (with J. J. C. Smart) Atheism and Theism, 1996, 2nd edn 2002; An Intelligent Person's Guide to Religion, 2003; Faithful Reason, 2004; Seeking Meaning and Making Sense, 2008; The Church and the World, 2008; Practical Philosophy: ethics, culture and society, 2009; Reasonable Faith, 2010; edited vols on art, educn and philosophy; contribs to jls incl. Amer. Philosophical Qly, Analysis, Jl Applied Philosophy, Jl Architecture, Jl Scottish Philosophy, Monist, New Blackfriars, Philosophical Papers, Philosophical Investigations, Philosophical Rev., Philosophy, Proc. Aristotelian Soc., Ratio, Rev. of Metaphysics, Scottish Jl Theol.; contrib. articles and reviews to Art Book, Burlington Mag., Catholic Herald, Catholic Times, First Things, Herald, Modern Painters, Scotland on Sunday, Scotsman, Sunday Herald, Tablet, The Times, TES, THE. *Recreations:* gardening, visiting art exhibitions, music. *Address:* Department of Philosophy, University of St Andrews, Fife KY16 9AL. *T:* (01334) 462488. *E:* jjh1@st-and.ac.uk. *Club:* Travellers.

**HALDENBY, Andrew John;** Director, Reform, 2005–19; *b* London, 4 Jan. 1972; *s* of Gerald Haldenby and Elizabeth Haldenby; *m* 2003, Simone Macey; one *s* one *d. Educ:* Burnham Grammar Sch.; Corpus Christi, Cambridge (BA Hons Hist. 1993); Birkbeck, Univ. of London (MSc Econs 2008). Conservative Res. Dept, 1995–97; Dir of Studies, Centre for Policy Studies, 1998–99; Dir of Communications, Business for Sterling, 2000–01; Co-founder and Dir of Res., Reform, 2001–05. *Recreations:* family, chess, reading, house music.

**HALE OF RICHMOND,** Baroness *cr* 2004 (Life Peer), of Easby in the County of North Yorkshire; **Brenda Marjorie Hale,** DBE 1994; PC 1999; a Justice, 2009–Jan. 2020, and President, 2017–Jan. 2020, Supreme Court of the United Kingdom (Deputy President, 2013–17) (a Lord of Appeal in Ordinary, 2004–09); *b* 31 Jan. 1945; *d* of Cecil Frederick Hale and Marjorie Hale (*née* Godfrey); *m* 1st, 1968, Anthony John Christopher Hoggett, *qv* (marr. diss. 1992); one *d*; 2nd, 1992, Julian Thomas Farrand, *qv. Educ:* Richmond High School for Girls, Yorks; Girton College, Cambridge (MA; Hon. Fellow, 1996). University of Manchester: Asst Lectr in Law, 1966; Lectr, 1968; Sen. Lectr, 1976; Reader, 1981; Prof., 1986–89. Vis. Prof., KCL, 1990–; Vis. Fellow, Nuffield Coll., Oxford, 1997–2005. Called to the Bar, Gray's Inn, 1969 (Vice-Treas., 2016; Treas., 2017); Barrister, Northern Circuit, 1969–72; Law Comr, 1984–93; QC 1989; an Asst Recorder, 1983–89; a Recorder, 1989–94; a Judge of the High Court, Family Div., 1994–99; Family Div. Liaison Judge for London, 1997–99; a Lord Justice of Appeal, 1999–2004. Legal Mem., Mental Health Review Tribunal for NW Region, 1979–80; Member: Council on Tribunals, 1980–84; Civil and Family Cttee, Judicial Studies Bd, 1990–94; Human Fertilisation and Embryology Authy, 1990–93. Chm., Mgt Cttee, Royal Courts of Justice Advice Bureau, 2002–03. Man. Trustee, Nuffield Foundn, 1987–2002; Gov., Centre for Policy on Ageing, 1990–93. President: Nat. Family Mediation, 1994– (Chm., Nat. Family Conciliation Council, then Nat. Assoc. of Family Mediation and Conciliation Services, 1989–93); Assoc. of Women Barristers, 1998–2005; UK Assoc. of Women Judges, 2004–; Internat. Assoc. of Women Judges, 2010–12. Chancellor, Bristol Univ., 2004–16; Visitor, Girton Coll., Cambridge, 2004–. Editor, Jl of Social Welfare Law, 1978–84. Hon. FBA 2004; Hon. FRCPsych 2007. Hon. LLD: Sheffield, 1989; London Guildhall, 1996; Manchester, 1997; Bristol, 2002; Cambridge, 2005; Hull, 2006; KCL, 2007; Oxford, 2007; City, 2007; Reading, 2007; College of Law, 2008; UWE, 2009; Huddersfield, 2009; Sussex, 2009; Georgetown, Washington, DC, 2010; Salford, 2010; Glasgow, 2011; Kent, 2011; Westminster, 2011; Liverpool, 2013; Swansea, 2014; York, 2015; LSE, 2015; Ulster, 2016; Northumbria, 2017; York St John, 2017; Bradford, 2018; Liverpool Edge Hill, 2018; DUniv: Essex, 2005; Open, 2016. *Publications:* Mental Health Law, 1976, 6th edn 2017; Parents and Children, 1977, 4th edn 1993; (jtly) The Family Law and Society: Cases and Materials, 1983, 6th edn 2008; (with S. Atkins) Women and the Law, 1984, 2018; Mental Health Law, in Halsbury's Laws of England, 4th edn 1992; From the Test Tube to the Coffin: choice and regulation in private life (Hamlyn Lectures), 1996; many contribs to legal periodicals and other texts; lectures publd on www.supremecourt.uk. *Recreations:* domesticity, drama, duplicate bridge. *Address:* (until Jan. 2020) Supreme Court of the United Kingdom, Parliament Square, SW1P 3BD. *Club:* Athenæum.

**HALE, Charles Stanley;** QC 2014; *b* Bournemouth; *s* of Roland and Sandra Hale; *m* 2006, Emily; three *d. Educ:* Winton Boys' Sch., Bournemouth; Kingston Univ. (LLB Hons); Council of Legal Educn. Called to the Bar, Middle Temple, 1992. Mem., Bar Council, 2001–13. Fellow, Internat. Acad. of Family Lawyers (formerly Internat. Acad. of Matrimonial Lawyers), 2012–. MCIArb 2016. *Publications:* (contrib.) Rayden and Jackson on Relationship Breakdown, Finance and Children, 2016; contrib. Counsel Mag. *Recreations:* sport, fine wine, food, friends and family. *Address:* 4 Paper Buildings, Temple, EC4Y 7EX. *T:* (020) 7583 0816. *E:* csh@4pb.com. *W:* www.twitter.com/twitbarrister. *Club:* Refreshers Cricket.

**HALE, Christopher George;** Partner, since 1987, and Senior Partner, since 2013, Travers Smith LLP; *b* London, 27 Sept. 1955; *s* of Alan and Sylvia Hale; *m* 2003, Stephanie Smith; three *s. Educ:* King's Coll. Sch., Wimbledon; Emmanuel Coll., Cambridge (BA Hist. 1977); Wolfson Coll., Cambridge (LLM 1983). Admitted as solicitor, 1981; Articled Clerk, 1979–81, Associate, 1981–82, Kingsley Napley; Travers Smith LLP: Associate, 1983–87; Head: Private Equity, 1996–2003; Corporate Dept, 2003–13. Gov., King's Coll. Sch., Wimbledon, 2018–. *Publications:* Private Equity: a transitional analysis, 2007, 3rd edn 2015. *Recreations:* cycling, football, Rugby, opera, theatre. *Address:* 10 Snow Hill, EC1A 2AL. *T:* (020) 7295 3263. *E:* chris.hale@traverssmith.com.

**HALE, His Honour David John;** a Circuit Judge, 1994–2013; *b* 18 June 1948; *s* of John and Kathleen Hale; *m* 1st, 1974, Lynn Thomas (*d* 1998); 2nd, 1999, Mrs Eileen Rafferty (*née* Hawthornthwaite). *Educ:* Calday Grange GS, West Kirby; Liverpool Univ. (LLB (Hons)). Called to the Bar, Gray's Inn, 1970; in practice, 1970–94.

**HALE, Prof. Geoffrey,** PhD; consultant scientist and entrepreneur, since 2011; Chairman, Native Antigen Co., since 2011; Visiting Professor, Sir William Dunn School of Pathology, University of Oxford, since 2007; *b* 2 Sept. 1953; *s* of Harold and Christine Hale; *m* 1977, Gillian Hutson; one *s* two *d. Educ:* Fitzwilliam Coll., Cambridge (MA; PhD 1977). University of Cambridge: Research Asst, Dept of Biochem., 1977–80; Sen. Res. Associate, Dept of Pathology, 1980–95; University of Oxford: Res. Lectr, Sir William Dunn Sch. of Pathol., 1995–98; Res. Dir, Therapeutic Antibody Centre, 1995–2007; Reader in Therapeutic Immunol., 1998–2000; Prof. of Therapeutic Immunol., 2000–07; Founder and CEO, BioAnalab Ltd, 2002–09; Man. Dir, 2009–10, Chief Scientist, 2010–11, Millipore Biopharma Services. *Publications:* numerous contribs on protein chemistry and therapeutic uses of monoclonal antibodies in various jls. *Recreations:* playing the piano, watching the garden grow.

**HALE, Raymond,** CPFA; County Treasurer, Leicestershire County Council, 1977–97; *b* 4 July 1936; *s* of Tom Raymond Hale and Mary Jane (*née* Higgin); *m* 1959, Ann Elvidge; one *s. Educ:* Baines Grammar Sch., Poulton-le-Fylde. Lancashire CC, 1952–54; served Royal Air Force, 1954–56; Lancashire CC, 1956–61; Nottinghamshire CC, 1961–65; Leicestershire CC, 1965–97. Treasurer: Leics Police Authy, 1977–97; Leicester Univ. Med. Sch. and Associated Leics Teaching Hosps Jt Trust (Medisearch), 1988–2018; Access Cttee for England, 1997–99; Chm., Hind Sisters Homes Charity, 1993–; Treas. and Co. Sec., Mosaic – Shaping Disability Services (formerly Leics Guild of Disabled), 1999–2015 (Vice-Chm., 1990–97). *Recreations:* Rugby, cricket, gardening. *Address:* The Stables, Main Street, Nailstone, Nuneaton, Warwicks CV13 0QB. *T:* (01530) 264174.

**HALE, Rt Rev. Stephen John;** Lead Minister, St Hilary's Network (formerly Senior Minister, St Hilary's Kew/North Balwyn), since 2009; *b* Sydney, 26 June 1955; *s* of William James and Patricia Edna Hale; *m* 1986, Karen (*née* Ellis); one *s* one *d. Educ:* Univ. of Sydney (BA 1975; DipEd 1976); Moore Theol Coll., Sydney (BTh 1983; DipArts (Theol.) 1984). Secondary teacher, NSW Dept of Educn, 1977–80; ordained deacon 1985, priest 1985, Sydney; Curate, St Paul's, Castle Hill, NSW, 1985–88; Youth Dir, dio. Melbourne, 1988–96; Vicar, St John's, Diamond Creek, Vic, 1996–2001; an Asst Bishop, Dio. of Melbourne (Bishop of the Eastern Region), 2001–09. Chm. Council, ACCESS ministries (formerly Christian Educn in Schs), 2006– (Mem. Council, 2002–); Chm., Anglican Diocesan Schs Commn, Vic, 2002–09. Chm., Arrow Leadership Aust. Inc., 1994–; Mem. Bd, Benetas Vic, 2005–07. *Recreations:* swimming, surfing, theatre, travel, tennis. *Address:* 1/38 Melrose Street, Mont Albert North, Vic 3129, Australia; St Hilary's Network, 12 John Street, Kew, Vic 3101, Australia. *T:* (3) 98167100, *Fax:* (3) 98171078. *E:* stephenh@sthils.com.

**HALE, Stephen Maynard,** OBE 2011; Chief Executive, Refugee Action, since 2015; *b* London, 5 Sept. 1971; *s* of Richard Hale and Jean Hale; *m* 2005, Zoë Parks; one *s* one *d. Educ:* Sevenoaks Sch.; Manchester Univ. (BA Econ.); Middlesex Univ. (MProf). Senior Consultant: GPC, 1997–99; ERM, 1999–2002; Special Advr, DEFRA, 2002–06; Dir, Green Alliance, 2006–10; Dep. Advocacy and Campaigns Dir, Oxfam Internat., 2010–14. Trustee: Christian Aid, 2007–10; Friends of the Earth, 2015–; Samworth Foundn, 2016–. *Recreations:* cycling, Crystal Palace Football Club. *Address:* Refugee Action, Victoria Charity Centre, Belgrave Road, SW1V 1RB. *T:* (020) 7952 1511. *E:* stephenhale@refugee-action.org.uk.

**HALES, Antony John,** CBE 2008; Chairman, Associate Board, Royal Schools of Music, since 2018; *b* 25 May 1948; *s* of Sidney Alfred Hales and Margaret Joan (*née* Wood); *m* 1975, Linda Churchlow; three *s* one *d. Educ:* Repton; Bristol Univ. (BSc Chem). With Cadbury Schweppes, 1969–79; Mkting Dir, Joshua Tetley & Son, 1979–83; Managing Director: Halls Oxford & West Brewery Co., 1983–85; Ind Coope-Taylor Walker, 1985–87; Retail Dir, Allied Breweries, 1987; Man. Dir, Ansells, 1987–89; Chief Exec., J. Lyons & Co., 1989–91; Dir, 1989–99, Chief Exec., 1991–99, Allied Lyons, then Allied Domecq; Chairman: Allied Domecq Spirits & Wine Ltd (formerly Hiram Walker Gp), 1992–99; Allied Domecq (formerly Allied Lyons) Retail, 1992–99. Director: Hyder PLC (formerly

Welsh Water), 1993–97; Aston Villa plc, 1997–2006; non-executive Director: HSBC (formerly Midland) Bank, 1994–2001; David Halsall Internat., 2000–05; Tempo Hldgs, 2000–01; Reliance Security Gp, 2001–05; SIS Hldgs, 2002–10; IPF Gp plc (formerly Provident Financial plc), 2006–19; Capital and Regional plc, 2011–; Chm., Workspace Gp plc, 2002–11. Chairman: Navy, Army, Air Force Institutes Ltd, 2001–08; NAAFI Pension Trustees, 2010–; Trustees, Greenwich Foundn, 2014–. Director: SSVC Corp., 2010–; WNO, 2010–19. Chm., Nat. Manufg Council, CBI, 1993–95. Chm., Canal and River Trust (formerly British Waterways), 2005–15. Hon. Governor, RSC, 2000–.

**HALES, Prof. Frederick David,** FREng, FIMechE, FIMA; Professor of Surface Transport, Loughborough University of Technology, 1968–93, now Professor Emeritus; *b* 19 Dec. 1930; *s* of Christina Frances and Frederick David Hales; *m* 1955, Pamela Hilary Warner (*d* 2009); one *s* one *d* (and one *d* decd). *Educ:* Kingswood Grammar Sch.; Bristol Univ. (BSc Hons Maths, PhD). Sigma Xi. Asst Chief Aerodynamicist, Bristol Aircraft, 1953–60; Group Research Head, MIRA, 1960–67; Vis. Scientist, Stevens Inst., Hoboken, 1967–68; Loughborough University: Hd of Dept of Transport Technology, 1982–89; Pro-Vice-Chancellor, 1984–85, Sen. Pro-Vice-Chancellor, 1985–87; acting Vice-Chancellor, 1987–88; Dean of Engrg, 1989–92. Mem., Tech. Adv. Council to Ford Motor Co., 1985–93; Scientific Visitor to Dept of Transport, 1986–90. FREng (FEng 1990). Hon. DSc Loughborough, 2000. *Publications:* papers on dynamics and vehicle control and stability. *Recreations:* sailing, photography, wine, wood carving, painting. *Address:* 14 Kenilworth Avenue, Loughborough, Leics LE11 4SL. *T:* (01509) 261767. *Club:* Rutland Sailing.

**HALES, Sally-Ann;** QC 2012; **Her Honour Judge Hales;** a Circuit Judge, since 2018; *b* Estevan, Canada, 18 July 1965; *d* of Peter Jeffrey Skinner and Patricia Ann Skinner (now Mrs Thomas David Hales); two *d*. *Educ:* Macclesfield Co. High Sch. for Girls; De Montfort Univ. (LLB Hons 1987). Called to the Bar, Gray's Inn, 1988, Bencher, 2016; in practice as a barrister, specialising in criminal law, 1988–2018; a Recorder, 2010–18. *Recreations:* family and friends, cooking, fine dining.

**HALFON, Rt Hon. Robert;** PC 2015; MP (C) Harlow, since 2010. *Educ:* Highgate Sch.; Exeter Univ. (BA Politics 1991; MA Russian and E Eur. Politics 1992). Formerly: res. and policy analyst to public affairs consultancies; freelance consultancy work; COS to Oliver Letwin, MP, 2001–05. Mem., Adv. Bd, Centre for Social Justice. Political Consultant to Cons. Friends of Israel, 2005–10. PPS to Chancellor of the Exchequer, 2014–15; Minister of State (Minister without Portfolio), Cabinet Office, 2015–16; Minister of State, DfE, 2016–17. Chm., Select Cttee on Education, 2017–; Member: Public Admin Select Cttee, 2010–14; Exec., 1922 Cttee, 2010–14. Dep. Chm., Cons. Party, 2015–16. Chair: Western Area Cons. Students, 1989–90; Exeter Univ. Cons. Assoc., 1989–90; Dep. Chair, Vauxhall Cons. Assoc., 1998–2000. Contested (C) Harlow, 2001, 2005. Mem. (C) Roydon PC, 2005–11. Hon. Pres., Cons. Workers and Trade Unionists, 2015–. Trustee: Harlow Employability; Parndon Mill. Formerly: Gov., Passmores Sch.; Patron: Harlow Homeless Centre; St Clare's Hospice. *Publications:* former contrib. articles to nat. newspapers. *Recreations:* reading, watches, Chelsea Football, countryside. *Address:* House of Commons, SW1A 0AA. *T:* (020) 7219 7223. *E:* halfon4harlow@roberthalfon.com.

**HALFORD, Alison Monica;** Member (L), Flintshire County Council, 2008–17; *b* 8 May 1940; *d* of William Charles Halford and Yvonne (*née* Bastien). *Educ:* Notre Dame Grammar Sch., Norwich. Metropolitan Police, 1962–83; Asst Chief Constable (most senior post for woman in UK), Merseyside Police, 1983–92. Mem. (Lab) Delyn, Nat. Assembly for Wales, 1999–2003. Flintshire County Council: Mem. (Lab), 1995–99; Member of Committees, 2008–17: Community and Housing; Planning; Audit; Mem., Hawarden Community Council, 2008–17. Mem., Cons. Party, 2006–. Gov., Hawarden High Sch., 2011–18. Police Long Service and Good Conduct Medal, 1984. Following police tapping her telephone in sex discrimination case, brought action in which Court of Human Rights ruled, 1997, that statutory warning required; resulted in introduction of Regulation of Statutory Powers Act 2000. *Publications:* No Way up the Greasy Pole (autobiog.), 1993; Leaks from the Back Benches (autobiog.), 2007. *Recreations:* birdwatching, serving the community, theatre, gardening, music, charity work.

**HALFORD, John Gordon;** Solicitor, since 2002, and Partner, since 2006, Bindmans LLP; *b* Newcastle upon Tyne, 28 May 1967; *s* of Gordon and Mary Halford. *Educ:* Abraham Darby Sch.; Marlwood Comprehensive Sch.; Essex Univ. (LLB Hons); Southampton Univ. (LLM). Manager and Legal Advr, Immigration Rights Centre, Bristol, 1990–91; Solicitor, Humberside Law Centre, 1992–96; admitted Solicitor, 1996; Project Solicitor, Public Law Project, 1998–2002. *Publications:* Butterworths' Health Services Law and Practice, 2001; contrib. articles to Judicial Rev., Legal Action. *Recreations:* spending time with my family, hill-walking, reading, film, jazz. *Address:* Bindmans LLP, 236 Gray's Inn Road, WC1X 8HB. *T:* (020) 7833 4433, *Fax:* (020) 7837 9792. *E:* j.halford@bindmans.com.

**HALFORD, Prof. Stephen Edgar,** PhD; FRS 2004; Professor of Biochemistry, University of Bristol, 1995–2011, now Emeritus; *b* 22 Sept. 1945; *s* of Walter R. Halford and Jessie M. Halford (*née* Edgar). *Educ:* Univ. of Bristol (BSc 1967; PhD 1970). Department of Biochemistry, University of Bristol: Lectr, 1976–89; Reader, 1989–95. *Publications:* numerous scientific papers. *Recreations:* turf, jazz, wine. *Address:* Department of Biochemistry, School of Medical Sciences, University of Bristol, University Walk, Bristol BS8 1TD. *E:* s.halford@bristol.ac.uk.

**HALFPENNY, Ven. Brian Norman,** CB 1990; Team Rector of the Parish of the Ridge, Redditch, 1991–2001; Hon. Assistant Priest, St Lawrence, Bourton-on-the-Water, since 2001; *b* 7 June 1936; *s* of Alfred Ernest Halfpenny and Fanny Doris Halfpenny (*née* Harman); *m* 1961, Hazel Beatrice Cross; three *d*. *Educ:* George Dixon Grammar Sch., Birmingham; St John's Coll., Oxford (BA 1960; MA 1964); Wells Theol Coll. Curate, Melksham, 1962–65; Chaplain, RAF, 1965–91; served RAF Stations Cosford, Wildenrath, Leeming, Hong Kong, Brize Norton, Halton, Akrotiri; RAF Coll., Cranwell, 1982–83; Asst Chaplain-in-Chief, Support Comd, 1983–85, Strike Comd, 1985–88; QHC 1985–91; Chaplain-in-Chief and Archdeacon, RAF, 1988–91; Priest i/c St Clement Danes, 1988–91; Canon and Prebendary, Lincoln Cathedral, 1989–91; permission to officiate, dio. Gloucester, 2001–. Co. Chaplain, RBL, Worcs, 1994–2001. Mem., Gen. Synod of C of E, 1988–91. Vice-Pres., Clergy Orphan Corp., 1988–91. Mem. Council, RAF Benevolent Fund, 1988–91; Visitor, Soldiers' and Airmen's Scripture Readers Assoc., 1988–91. *Recreations:* music, theatre, running. *Address:* 80 Roman Way, Bourton-on-the-Water, Cheltenham, Glos GL54 2EW. *T:* (01451) 821589. *Clubs:* Royal Air Force; Oxford Union Society.

**HALFPENNY, Prof. Peter John,** PhD; Professor of Sociology, University of Manchester, 1993–2010, now Emeritus; *b* Whitehaven, 1 March 1945; *s* of Arthur and Joan Halfpenny; *m* 1968, Daphne Taylorson; two *s*. *Educ:* Whitehaven Grammar Sch.; Magdalen Coll., Oxford (BA Hons Natural Sci.; MA); Univ. of Essex (MA; PhD Sociol. 1976). University of Manchester: Lectr in Sociol., 1971–83; Sen. Lectr, 1983–92; Hd, Dept of Sociol., 1993–96; Dir, Centre for Applied Social Res., 1985–2004; Dean, Faculty of Social Scis and Law, 2003–04; Hd, Sch. of Social Scis, 2003–06; Exec. Dir, Nat. Centre for e-Social Science, 2004–09; Dep. Dir, Manchester Informatics, 2007–10. Chm. Trustees, Voluntary Sector Studies Network, 2003–09. Ed., Voluntary Sector Rev., 2009–14. *Publications:* Positivism and Sociology: explaining social life, 1982, 3rd edn 2014; (ed with P. McMylor) Positivist Sociology and its Critics, 3 vols, 1994; (ed with R. Procter) Innovations in Digital Research Methods, 2015; contrib. jl articles, chapters, reports and conf. presentations. *Recreations:* computer applications, crossing disciplinary boundaries, modern literary novels, gardening. *Address:* Sociology, School of Social Sciences, University of Manchester, Manchester M13 9PL. *E:* p.halfpenny@manchester.ac.uk.

**HALIFAX, 3rd Earl of,** *cr* 1944; **Charles Edward Peter Neil Wood;** DL; Bt 1784; Viscount Halifax, 1866; Baron Irwin, 1925; Vice Lord-Lieutenant, East Riding of Yorkshire, 1996–2006; *b* 14 March 1944; *s* of 2nd Earl of Halifax and Ruth (*d* 1989), *d* of late Captain Rt Hon. Neil James Archibald Primrose, MC, sometime MP; S father, 1980; *m* 1976, Camilla, *d* of late C. F. J. Younger, DSO, TD; one *s* one *d*. *Educ:* Eton; Christ Church, Oxford. Contested (C) Dearne Valley, Feb. and Oct. 1974. High Steward of York Minster, 1988–. JP Wilton Beacon, 1986, Bridlington, 2001; DL Humberside, 1983–96, 2005. KStJ 1994. *Heir:* s Lord Irwin, qv. *Address:* Bugthorpe House, York YO41 1QG.

**HALIFAX, Archdeacon of;** see Dawtry, Ven. Dr A. F.

**HALIL, Natika Handan;** Chief Executive Officer, Family Planning Association, since 2015; *b* Hackney, London; *d* of Ahmet Halil and Cemile Halil. *Educ:* Kingsland Sch.; Kingsway Coll.; Middlesex Univ.; Birkbeck Coll., Univ. of London. Lullaby Trust, 1997–2001; Stroke Assoc., 2001–08; FPA, 2008–. *Recreations:* keen walker and reader. *Address:* Family Planning Association, 23–28 Penn Street, N1 5DL. *T:* (020) 7608 5263. *E:* natikah@fpa.org.uk.

**HALL,** family name of **Baron Hall of Birkenhead.**

**HALL OF BIRKENHEAD,** Baron *cr* 2010 (Life Peer), of Birkenhead in the County of Cheshire; **Anthony William, (Tony), Hall,** CBE 2006; Director-General, BBC, since 2013; *b* 3 March 1951; *s* of late Donald William Hall and of Mary Joyce Hall; *m* 1977, Cynthia Lesley Hall (*née* Davis); one *s* one *d*. *Educ:* King Edward's Sch., Birmingham; Birkenhead Sch., Merseyside; Keble Coll., Oxford (Exhibnr; MA). Joined BBC as News trainee, 1973; Producer: World Tonight, 1976; New York (Radio), 1977; Sen. Producer, World at One, 1978; Output Editor, Newsnight, 1980; Sen. Producer, Six O'Clock News, 1984; Asst Editor, Nine O'Clock News, 1985; Editor: News and Election '87, 1987; News and Current Affairs, BBC TV, 1988–90; Dir, 1990–93, Man. Dir, 1993–96, News and Current Affairs, BBC; Chief Exec., BBC News, 1996–2001; Exec. Dir, later Chief Exec., Royal Opera House, Covent Gdn, 2001–13. Non-exec. Dir, HM Customs and Excise, 2002–05; Dep. Chm., Channel 4, 2012 (non-exec. Dir, 2005–12). Mem., King's Healthcare Expert Reference Gp, 1995–96. Mem., Steering Cttee, Regeneration through Heritage, BITC, 1999–2000; Chairman: Strategic Skills Council, Creative and Cultural Industries, 2004–09; Music and Dance Adv. Gp, DFES, 2004–07; Member: Olympics Cultural Adv. Bd, DCMS, 2006–13; LOCOG, 2009–13 (Chm. Bd, Cultural Olympiad, 2009–13). Chm., Theatre Royal, Stratford, 2001–09 (Dir, 1999–2009). Member: Mgt Cttee, Clore Leadership Prog., 2005–11; Bd, Paul Hamlyn Foundn, 2011–. Trustee, British Council, 2008–12. Non-exec. Dir, Univ. for Industry, 2003–06. Hon. Vis. Fellow, City Univ., 1999–2000. Mem. Council, Brunel Univ., 1999–2003. Patron, Newsworld, 1999; Gov. for Media, World Econ. Forum, 2000. Mem. Cttee, Race for Opportunity, 1999–2001 (as Race Champion led BBC's campaign on diversity and race issues). Liveryman, Painter Stainers' Co., 1989–. FRTS 1994 (Chm., 1998–2000); FRSA 1997. *Publications:* King Coal: a history of the miners, 1981; Nuclear Politics, 1984; articles in various periodicals. *Recreations:* architecture, opera, ballet, walking, gardening, my family. *Address:* BBC Broadcasting House, Portland Place, W1A 1AA; House of Lords, SW1A 0PW.

**HALL, Alexandra Mary H.;** see Hall Hall.

**HALL, Andrew;** Chairman: Babington Group, since 2016; Housemark Group, since 2017; Cottsway Housing, since 2019; *b* Bournemouth, 13 June 1956; *s* of John Hall and Esther Ina Hall; *m* 1980, Susan Jacqueline Evans; two *d*. *Educ:* King Edward's Sch., Witley; St Paul's Coll., Cheltenham; Univ. of Bristol (BEd Hons). ACA 1981, FCA 1991. Ernst & Young, 1983–87; TRW Valves, 1983–87; Finance Dir, 1987–90, Man. Dir, 1990–94, Bomford Turner; Chief Exec., Eliza Tinsley Gp plc, 1994–2006; Chief Exec. and Dir, QCA, 2006–10; Chief Exec., Assessment and Qualifications Alliance, then AQA Educn, 2010–17. *Recreations:* tennis, travel, family time. *Address:* Babington Group, Babington House, Mallard Way, Derby DE24 8GX. *E:* Andrew.hall53@btinternet.com.

**HALL, Sir Andrew (James),** Kt 2013; PhD; Professor of Epidemiology, London School of Hygiene and Tropical Medicine, University of London, 2000–13; *b* 9 Feb. 1951. *Educ:* Guy's Hosp. Med. Sch., London Univ. (MB BS 1973); London Sch. of Hygiene and Tropical Medicine (MSc 1982); Southampton Univ. (PhD 1986). MRCP 1976, FRCP 1994; MFPHM 1990; FFPH 1996. Epidemiologist, Internat. Agency for Res. on Cancer, WHO, 1986–90; Sen. Lectr in Epidemiol., 1990–96, Reader in Epidemiol., 1996–2000, LSHTM. Mem., cttees of WHO, MRC and DoH. Member: Bd, PHLS, 1997–2004; Bd, HPA, 2003–13; Chm., Jt Cttee on Vaccines and Immunisation, 2006–13 (Mem., 2002–06). *Publications:* (with D. J. P. Barker) Practical Epidemiology, 2nd edn 1991; numerous contribs to scientific literature. *Recreations:* live music, cooking, gardening, Chinese brush painting. *E:* andrewjhall1@icloud.com.

**HALL, Andrew Joseph;** QC 2002; *b* 17 Feb. 1953; *s* of James Clement Hall and Jane Hall. *Educ:* Marist Coll.; Univ. of Birmingham (LLB); Inst. of Criminol., Univ. of Sheffield (MA). Admitted solicitor, 1980; in practice as solicitor, 1980–90, Partner, Hodge, Jones & Allen, London, 1982–90; called to the Bar, Gray's Inn, 1991, Bencher, 2005; in practice as barrister, 1991–. Member: Gen. Council of the Bar, 1998–; Criminal Bar Assoc., 1998– (Chm., 2006–07); Bar Human Rights Cttee, 1999–. Chm., Kalisher Scholarship Trust, 2011–14. Mem., Editl Bd, Internat. Jl Evidence and Proof, 2001–14. Hon. LLD Sheffield, 2015. *Publications:* Emergency Procedures Handbook, 1986; Criminal Justice in Crisis, 1993; Confidentiality and Mental Health, 2001; Guide to the Proceeds of Crime Act, 2002. *Recreations:* African skies, Spanish mountains. *Address:* Doughty Street Chambers, 53–54 Doughty Street, WC1N 2LS. *T:* (020) 7404 1313, *Fax:* (020) 7404 2283.

**HALL, Andrew Rotely,** OBE 1994; HM Diplomatic Service, retired; Ambassador to Nepal, 2006–10; *b* 3 May 1950; *s* of David and Sheila Hall; *m* 1973, Kathie Wright; two *d*. *Educ:* Univ. of Keele (BA Hons); Sch. of Oriental and African Studies, Univ. of London (PhD 1982). Joined HM Diplomatic Service, 1980; First Secretary: New Delhi, 1984–87; FCO, 1987–91; Dep. Hd of Mission and Consul, Kathmandu, 1991–95; FCO, 1995–2003; Dep. High Comr in Eastern India, Kolkata, 2003–06. *Club:* Tollygunge (Kolkata).

**HALL, Anthony Stewart, (Tony);** Director, Central Council for Education and Training in Social Work, 1986–97; *b* 26 Oct. 1945; *s* of Dora Rose Ellen Hall (*née* Rundle) and Albert Hall; *m* 1968, Phoebe Katharine Souster; one *s* one *d*. *Educ:* Gillingham Grammar School; London Sch. of Economics (BScSoc). Research Student, LSE, 1968–71; Lectr in Management and Organisation Studies, Nat. Inst. for Social Work, 1971–73; Lectr in Social Admin, Univ. of Bristol, 1973–78; Dir, Assoc. of British Adoption and Fostering Agencies, 1978–80; Dir and Sec., British Agencies for Adoption and Fostering, 1980–86; Dep. Man. Dir, Retirement Security Ltd, 1997. *Publications*: A Management Game for the Social Service (with J. Algie), 1974; The Point of Entry: a study of client reception in the social services, 1975; (ed) Access to Birth Records: the impact of S.26 of the Children Act 1975, 1980; (with Phoebe Hall) Part-time Social Work, 1980; (series editor) Child Care Policy and Practice, 1982–86; chapters in books and articles in professional and learned jls. *Recreations*: photography, genealogy, watching sport and old films, music, collecting British stamps and card game paraphernalia, computer games, researching and writing about the history of card games, cricket, Bob Dylan, looking after grandchildren. *Address*: 24 Church Road, Cowley, Uxbridge, Middx UB8 3NA. *T*: (01895) 470500. *E*: tony_hall@dsl.pipex.com.

**HALL, Rev. Bernard**, SJ; Spiritual Director, Infirmary of the Roman Delegation, Society of Jesus, since 2004 (Director, 2001–04); *b* 17 Oct. 1921. *Educ*: St Michael's Coll., Leeds; Heythrop Coll., Oxford. LicPhil, STL. Captain RA, 1941–46. Entered Society of Jesus, 1946; ordained priest, 1955; Provincial of the English Province, Society of Jesus, 1970–76; Rector, Collegio San Roberto Bellarmino, Rome, 1976–82 and 1989–94; English Asst to Father General, SJ, Rome, 1982–88; Superior, Jesuit Hse of Writers, Rome, 1994–2001. *Address*: Residenza di San Pietro Canisio, via dei Penitenzieri 20, 00193 Rome, Italy.

**HALL, Brian**; *see* Hall, F. B.

**HALL, Prof. Bronwyn Hughes**, PhD; Professor of Economics, University of California at Berkeley, 1999–2005, now Emerita; Professor of Economics of Technology, University of Maastricht, 2005–15; Founder and Principal, TSP International, Palo Alto, California, 1979–2012; *b* 1 March 1945; *d* of Richard Roberts Hughes and Elizabeth Flandreau Hughes; *m* 1966, Robert Ernest Hall (marr. diss. 1983); one *s* one *d*. *Educ*: Wellesley Coll., Mass (BA 1966); Stanford Univ. (PhD 1988); MA Oxon 1997. Programmer: Lawrence Berkeley Lab., Berkeley, Calif, 1963–66; Lyman Lab. of Physics, Harvard Univ., 1966–67; Lawrence Berkeley Lab., 1967–70; Sen. Programmer, Harvard Inst. of Econ. Res., 1971–77; National Bureau of Economic Research, Cambridge, Massachusetts: Res. Economist, 1977–88; Res. Associate, 1988–; Asst Prof., 1987–94, Assoc. Prof., 1994–99, Univ. of Calif, Berkeley; Internat. Res. Associate, Inst. for Fiscal Studies, London, 1995–; Prof. of Econs, and Fellow of Nuffield Coll., Oxford Univ., 1996–2001. Vis. Prof., Max Planck Inst., Munich, 2015–. Sloan Dissertation Fellow, 1985–86; Hoover Instn Nat. Fellow, 1992–93; Professorial Res. Fellow, UNU-MERIT, Netherlands, 2005–15; Vis. Res. Fellow, NIESR, 2013–. Mem., Sci. Technol. and Econ. Policy Bd, Nat. Res. Council, Washington, 1999–2005. Mem., Sigma Xi Soc., 1966. Associate Editor: Econs of Innovation and New Technol., 1994– (Mem. Editl Bd, 1989–94); Jl of Economic Behavior and Organization, 2001–07; Industrial and Corporate Change, 2009–; Mem. Adv. Bd, Internat. Finance jl, 1997–2005; Mem., Editl Bd, Res. Policy, 2006–13. *Publications*: TSP 4.3 User's Manual, 1977, rev. edn, version 5.1, 2009; TSP 4.3 Reference Manual, 1977, rev. edn, version 5.1, 2009; (ed jtly) New Frontiers in the Economics of Innovation and New Technology, 2005; (ed jtly) Handbook of Economics of Innovation, 2010; (ed jtly) Intellectual Property for Economic Development: issues and policy implications, 2013; contrib. articles to Amer. Econ. Rev., Econometrica, Jl Industrial Econs, Jl Econometrics, Brookings Papers on Econ. Activity, Econs of Innovation and New Technol., Rand Jl of Econs, Industrial and Corp. Change, Rev. of Econs and Stats, Small Business Econs Jl. *Recreations*: travel, walking, opera, painting. *Address*: Department of Economics, University of California at Berkeley, Berkeley, CA 94720, USA.

**HALL, Prof. Christine Joy**, PhD; Professor of Education, University of Nottingham, since 2008; *b* Surrey, 13 Nov. 1951; *d* of David William Lymer and Joan Ivy Lymer; *m* 1973, Peter Vincent Hall; one *s* one *d*. *Educ*: Royal Holloway Coll., Univ. of London (BA Hons English 1973); Inst. of Educn, Univ. of London (PGCE 1975); Univ. of Nottingham (MA American Studies 1987; PhD Educn 1997). Teacher of English, Hounslow Manor Sch., London and Gedling Comprehensive Sch., Nottingham, 1975–79; Hd of English, Rufford Comprehensive Sch., Nottingham, 1979–83; Tutor, Open Univ., 1984–89; University of Nottingham: Lectr in Educn, 1989–97; Sen. Lectr in Educn, 1998–2008; Hd, Sch. of Educn, 2008–14; Mem. Council, 2008–. Dir, Nottingham Univ. Samworth Acad. Trust; Mem. Bd, Nottingham Univ. Acad. of Sci. and Technol. Series Ed., Literary Land. *Publications*: (with M. Coles) Children's Reading Choices, 1998; (with P. Thomson) Place-based Methods for Researching Schools, 2016; (with P. Thomson) Inspiring School Change, 2017; text books and books for teachers; contrib. articles, chapters, reports on literacy, the arts, teaching and teacher educn. *Recreations*: talking, reading, cinema, theatre, arts, travel, playing with grandchildren. *Address*: School of Education, University of Nottingham, Jubilee Campus, Wollaton Road, Nottingham NG8 1BB. *T*: (0115) 951 4440. *E*: christine.hall@nottingham.ac.uk.

**HALL, Christopher Myles**; Editor of The Countryman, 1981–96; *b* 21 July 1932; *s* of Gilbert and Muriel Hall; *m* 1957, Jennifer Bevan Keech (marr. diss. 1980); one *s* one *d*; lives with Kate Ashbrook, *qv*. *Educ*: Berkhamsted Sch.; New Coll., Oxford (2nd cl. Hons PPE); Kellogg Coll., Oxford (MSt English Local History, with distinction, 1996). Reporter and Feature-writer, Daily Express, 1955–58; Sub-editor and Leader-writer, Daily Mirror, 1958–61; Feature-writer and Leader-writer, Daily Herald/Sun, 1961–65; Special Assistant (Information): to Minister of Overseas Develt, 1965–66; to Minister of Transport, 1966–68; Chief Information Officer, MoT, 1968; Ramblers' Association: Sec., 1969–74; Mem. Exec. Cttee, 1982–84; Vice-Chm., 1984–87; Chm., 1987–90; Pres., 1990–93; Vice-Pres., 1993–; Chm., Oxfordshire Area, 1984–87, 1994–97, 2002–07, Footpaths and Publicity Sec., 1997–98; Dir, Council for Protection of Rural England, 1974–80. Pres., The Holiday Fellowship, 1974–77; Vice-Chm., S Reg. Council of Sport and Recreation, 1976–82; Member: DoT Cttee of Inquiry into Operators' Licensing, 1977–79; Common Land Forum, 1984–86; Countryside Access Forum, Oxon CC, 2003–06; Hon. Sec., Chiltern Soc., 1965–68; Chm., Oxfordshire Local Hist. Assoc., 2001–11. Columnist, Rambling Today, 1993–96; Editor, Oxfordshire Local History, 1997–; Sub-ed., ad familiares (Jl of Friends of Classics), 2008–16. Publishing Award, British Assoc. for Local Hist., 2011. *Publications*: How to Run a Pressure Group, 1974; (jtly) The Countryside We Want, 1988; The Countryman's Yesterday, 1989; Scenes from The Countryman, 1992; contributions to: Motorways in London, 1969; No Through Road, 1975; The Countryman's Britain, 1976; Book of British Villages, 1980; Sunday Times Book of the Countryside, 1981; Walker's Britain, 1982; Britain on Backroads, 1985; Making Tracks, 1985; (with John Tookey) The Cotswolds, 1990; pamphlets; contrib. to Oxford DNB, Vole, The Countryman, New Statesman, New Scientist, The Geographical Magazine, Country Living, The Guardian, Open Space and various jls. *Recreations*: local history, walking in the countryside. *Address*: Telfer's Cottage, Turville, Henley-on-Thames RG9 6QL. *T*: (01491) 638396. *Club*: Oxford and Cambridge.

**HALL, Sir David Bernard**, 4th Bt *cr* 1919; *b* 12 May 1961; *s* of Sir John Bernard Hall, 3rd Bt and Delia Mary Hall (*née* Innes); *S* father, 2018; *m* 2013, Belinda Gyford (*née* Blundell); one *d*. *Educ*: Eton Coll.; Univ. of York. Founder: Sunlite Blinds, Stafford, 1988; Alton Blinds, 1998. *Address*: Fallowfields, Swaines Hill, Alton, Hants GU34 4DP.

**HALL, Sir David (Christopher)**, 4th Bt *cr* 1923, of Grafham, co. Surrey; *b* 30 Dec. 1937; *yr s* of Sir Frederick Henry Hall, 2nd Bt and Olwen Irene (*née* Collis); *S* brother, 2013; *m* 1st, 1962, Irene Duncan (marr. diss. 1987; she *d* 2014); one *s* one *d*; 2nd, 1991, Annie Madelaine Renée Olivier, adopted *d* of late Bottemanne Raould. *Heir*: *s* John Christopher Hall, *b* 22 May 1965. *T*: (01276) 61010, 07759 495882. *E*: david-hall@sky.com.

**HALL, Prof. Sir David (Michael Baldock)**, Kt 2003; FRCP, FRCPCH; Hon. Professor of Paediatrics, University of Cape Town, since 2007; Professor of Community Paediatrics, University of Sheffield, 1993–2005, now Emeritus; President, Royal College of Paediatrics and Child Health, 2000–03; *b* 4 Aug. 1945; *s* of Ronald Hall and Ethel Gwen Hall (*née* Baldock); *m* 1966, Susan M. Luck; two *d*. *Educ*: Reigate Grammar Sch.; St George's Hosp., London Univ. (MB BS; BSc; Univ. Gold Medal). FRCP 1986; FRCPCH 1996. SMO, Baragwanath Hosp., Johannesburg, 1973–76; Sen. Registrar, Charing Cross Hosp., 1976–78; Consultant Paediatrician, St George's Hosp., 1978–93. Hon. FRCPE 2003. Mem., Breede River Winelands Rotary Club (Pres., 2011–12). *Publications*: Health for All Children, 1989, rev. 4th edn 2006; Child Surveillance Handbook, 1990, 3rd edn 2009; Child with a Disability, 1996; contrib. numerous papers to jls, etc. *Recreations*: travel, walking, music. *Address*: Storrs House Farm, Storrs Lane, Stannington, Sheffield S6 6GY. *E*: d.hall@sheffield.ac.uk.

**HALL, Col David Stevenson**, CBE 1993; TD 1971 (and bars 1977, 1983, 1989); Chairman: Meadowcroft Management Ltd, since 1985; NHS Logistics Agency, 2000–02; *b* 29 March 1938; *s* of late Robert Hall and Maude Hall; *m* 1962, Marion Esmé Blundstone; one *s* one *d*. *Educ*: Scarborough Coll. Nat. Service, RAOC, 1956–58. Man. Dir, UDS Tailoring Ltd, 1979–81; Chm. and Man. Dir, Collier Holdings plc, 1982–85. Non-executive Director: Sharp and Law plc, 1989–90; Toye plc, 1994–95. Chairman: United Leeds Teaching Hosps NHS Trust, 1995–98; NHS Supplies, 1998–2000. Trustee, RAOC Charitable Trust, 1993–2000. RAOC (TA), 1958–93; Col, 1985–89; ADC, 1986–91; TA Col Logistics MoD/UKLF, 1989–93; Hon. Col, RAOC Specialist Units, 1991–93; Combat Services Support Group, RLC(V), 1995–2000. Freeman, City of London, 1993. *Recreations*: cricket, reading. *Address*: Courtways, Potterton Court, Barwick in Elmet, Leeds LS15 4HP. *T*: (0113) 281 3587. *Clubs*: Army and Navy (Vice-Chm., 2003–05), MCC; Yorkshire County Cricket (Chm., Archives Cttee, 2005–10; Museum Dir, 2010–16; Vice Pres., 2011–).

**HALL, Duncan**; Managing Director, Duncan Hall Associates Ltd, 1998–2016; *b* 2 Sept. 1947; *s* of Leslie and Joan Elizabeth Hall; two *s* one *d*; *m* 2004, Fiona Mary Blackwell. *Educ*: Acklam Hall Grammar Sch.; LLB Hons. Articled Clerk and Senior Legal Assistant, Wellingborough UDC, 1970–74; Corby District Council: PA to Chief Exec., 1974–75; Asst Chief Exec., 1975–78; Housing and Property Controller, 1978–79; Chief Exec., 1980–87; Chief Exec., Teesside Develt Corp., 1987–98. FRSA. *Recreations*: reading, travel, music, theatre. *Address*: Ivor House, 1 South Green, Staindrop, Darlington, Co. Durham DL2 3LD. *T*: (01833) 660077.

**HALL, Edward Peter**; theatre, film and television director; *b* 27 Nov. 1966; *s* of Sir Peter Reginald Frederick Hall, CBE and of Jacqueline Hall; *m* 2000, Issy van Randwyck; two *d*. *Educ*: Bedales Sch.; Univ. of Leeds; Mountview Theatre Sch. Associate, NT, 2004–; Associate Director: Watermill Th. Co., 2006–; Old Vic, 2006–; Founder and Artistic Dir, Propeller Th. Co., 1997–; Artistic Dir, Hampstead Th., 2010–19. Watermill Theatre productions: Othello, 1995; Propeller Theatre Co. productions include: Henry V, 1997; The Comedy of Errors, 1998; Twelfth Night, 1999; Rose Rage (adaptation of Shakespeare's Henry VI trilogy), 2001, transf. Th. Royal, Haymarket, 2002; A Midsummer Night's Dream, transf. Comedy Th., 2003; The Winter's Tale, 2005; The Taming of the Shrew, and Twelfth Night, 2006, transf. Old Vic, 2007; For Services Rendered, 2007; Merchant of Venice, 2009; Richard III, and The Comedy of Errors, 2011 (Best Touring Production, TMA Awards, 2011); Henry V, The Winter's Tale, 2012; A Midsummer Night's Dream, 2013; The Comedy of Errors, 2014; Hampstead Theatre productions: Enlightenment, 2010; Loyalty, No Naughty Bits, 2011; Chariots of Fire, 2012, transf. Gielgud Th.; Raving, 2013; Sunny Afternoon, transf. Harold Pinter Th., 2014; Wonderland, 2014; Firebird, transf. Trafalgar Studios, 2015–16; Rabbit Hole, 2016; Filthy Business, 2017; Cell Mates, 2017; The Strange Death of John Doe, 2018; I and You, 2018; Cost of Living, 2019; Jude, 2019; other productions include: Two Gentlemen of Verona, Henry V, 2000, Julius Caesar, RSC, 2001; Edmond, 2003, A Funny Thing Happened on the Way to the Forum, 2004, Once in a Lifetime, 2005, NT; A Streetcar Named Desire, Roundabout Th., NY, 2005; The Deep Blue Sea, Vaudeville, 2008; Two Men of Florence, Boston, 2009; (co-dir) Tantalus, Denver, 2000, UK tour and Barbican, 2001; The Constant Wife, Apollo, 2002; Macbeth, Albery, 2002; Calico, Duke of York's, 2004. Director: Into Exile, Dear Exile, Radio 4; Restless, BBC TV/Sundance; The Durrells, 2017; episodes of TV series, Miss Marple, Trial and Retribution, Kingdom, Spooks, Strike Back, Downton Abbey, Partners in Crime. *Publications*: Rose Rage, 2001; (ed) A Midsummer Night's Dream, 2003. *Address*: c/o Casarrotto Ramsay & Associates Ltd, Waverley House, 7–12 Noel Street, W1F 8GQ.

**HALL, Prof. Elizabeth Anne Howlett, (Lisa)**, CBE 2015; PhD; CChem, FRSC; Professor of Analytical Biotechnology, Institute of Biotechnology, since 2003, and Head, Department of Chemical Engineering and Biotechnology, since 2018, University of Cambridge; Fellow, Queens' College, Cambridge, since 1988 (Vice President, 2013–18); *b* Bromley, Kent, 28 Nov. 1952; *d* of Philip Sydney Hall and Joan Howlett; *m* 2013, Dr John Robert Saffell; one step *s* one step *d*. *Educ*: Stratford Hse Sch., Kent; Queen Mary Coll., Univ. of London (BSc Chem. 1974; PhD 1977); Queens' Coll., Cambridge (MA 1988). CChem 1983; FRSC 2005. Asst de Recherche, Univ. of Clermont, France, 1977–78; Res. Associate, Johannes Gutenberg Univ., Mainz, Germany, 1978–80; Sen. Analyst, Bernard Dyer and Partners (1948) Ltd, London, 1980–81; Res. Fellow, Nuffield Dept of Anaesthetics, Univ. of Oxford, 1981–85; University of Cambridge: New Blood Lectr, 1985–99, Reader, 1999–2003, Inst. of Biotechnol.; Dep. Hd (Res.), Dept of Chem. Engrg and Biotechnol., 2010–19. Queen Eugene Vis. Prof., Complutense Univ. of Madrid, 2005–06. Chm., Editl Bd, Analyst, 2006–10. Co-Founder and Dir, CamBridgeSens, 2008–. Mem., Diagnostics Adv. Cttee, NICE, 2010–12. Vice Pres., Analytical Div., RSC, 2006–08. Chm., Disability Snowsport UK, 1993–2018 (Pres., 2018–). Hon. DSc Chichester. *Publications*: contrib. articles to learned sci. and engrg jls. *Recreations*: ski-ing, adaptive snowsport, sailing, woodcrafts, DIY. *Address*: Queens' College, Silver Street, Cambridge CB3 9ET. *E*: lisa.hall@biotech.cam.ac.uk.

**HALL, Sir Ernest**, Kt 1993; OBE 1986; DL; pianist and composer, since 1954; property developer, since 1971; Chairman, Dean Clough Business, Arts and Education Centre, 1983–2007; *b* 19 March 1930; *s* of Ernest and Mary Elizabeth Hall; *m* 1st, 1951, June (*née* Annable) (*d* 1994); two *s* two *d*; 2nd, 1975, Sarah (*née* Wellby); one *s*. *Educ*: Bolton County Grammar Sch.; Royal Manchester Coll. of Music (ARMCM (teacher and performer) 1950–51; Royal Patron's Fund Prize for Composition, 1951). Textile manufr, 1961–71. Dep. Chm., Eureka! Children's Museum, 1989–2000; Mem., Arts Council of England (formerly of GB), 1990–97; Chm., Yorks and Humberside Arts Bd, 1991–97; Pres., Yorks Business in the Arts, 1990–; Vice-Pres., RSA, 1994–99. Trustee: Yorkshire Sculpture Park, 1989–2003; Henry Moore Foundn, 1999–2002. Founder, Camel House Concerts,

Lanzarote, 2010. Chancellor, Univ. of Huddersfield, 1996–2003. DL W Yorks, 1991. Hon. Fellow: Huddersfield Polytechnic, 1989; Leeds Polytechnic, 1991; Bolton Inst., 1994. DUniv: York, 1986; Leeds Metropolitan, 1996; Hon. DLitt Bradford, 1990; Hon. DArt Bristol Poly., 1991; Hon. LLD Leeds, 1996. Envmt Award, Business and Industry Panel, RSA, 1988; Guildhall Helping Hand, Nat. Fedn of Self-Employed and Small Businesses, 1989; Special Free Enterprise Award, Aims of Industry, 1989; Best Practice Award, BURA, 1992; Lifetime Achievement Award, Inst. for Social Inventions, 1992; Albert Medal, RSA, 1994; Montblanc de la Culture UK Award, Fondation d'Enterprise, France, 1996; Goodman Award, ABSA, 1997. *Publications:* How to be a Failure and Succeed (autobiog.), 2008. *Recreations:* gardening, art collecting, theatre, languages. *T:* (Lanzarote) (928) 834150.

**HALL, Fiona Jane,** MBE 2013; advisor on energy efficiency policy, since 2014; Member (Lib Dem) North East Region, European Parliament, 2004–14; Leader, Liberal Democrat European Parliamentary Party, 2009–14; *b* 15 July 1955; *d* of Edward and Dorothy Cutts; *m* 1975, Michael Hall (marr. diss. 2009); two *d*. *Educ:* St Hugh's Coll., Oxford (MA Mod. Langs 1976); Oxford Poly. (PGCE). Teacher in self-help sch., Naledi, Gaborone, Botswana, 1977–79; pt-time, supply teacher, tutor, 1986–95; Asst to Newcastle City Councillors, 1994–97; Press Officer to Lembit Öpik, MP and Richard Livsey, MP, 1997–99; Researcher and Organiser to Rt Hon. Alan Beith, MP, 1999–2004. *Address:* The School House, Whittingham, Alnwick, Northumberland NE66 4UP. *T:* (01665) 574383.

**HALL, (Frederick) Brian;** Master (Care and Protection), Supreme Court of Judicature of Northern Ireland, 1986–2006; *b* 2 Oct. 1934; *s* of Frederick Hall and late Mary Hall (née Kernahan); *m* 1965, Isobel Frances Deirdre Boyce; two *d*. *Educ:* Coleraine Academical Instn; Queen's Univ. Belfast (LLB). Admitted Solicitor, NI, 1958; Legal Adviser, Min. of Home Affairs, 1972; Asst Solicitor, NI Office, 1973; Dep. Dir, NI Court Service, 1979; Official Solicitor to Supreme Court, NI, 1982. Mem., Sec. of State's Cttee on County Courts and Magistrates' Courts, 1974. *Recreations:* golf, travel, reading. *Club:* Royal Belfast Golf.

**HALL, Gareth John;** consultant on consenting of major infrastructure projects, since 2016; *b* 26 June 1956; *s* of late Trevor John Grenville Hall and Margaret Gwendoline Hall (née Jones); *m* 1986, Moira Ann Llewellyn. *Educ:* Brecon Boys' Grammar Sch.; Bristol Poly. (BSc 1977); Univ. of Reading (MSc 1981); Cardiff Univ. (MBA 1989). MRICS 1980. Valuation Office, SE London, 1977–80; Defence Land Agent, Wales, MoD, 1981–91; jsdc, 1991; Welsh Development Agency: Sen. Manager on land reclamation, property and regeneration projects, 1991–97; Regl Dir, SW Wales, Strategy Develt, 1997–2004; Chief Exec., 2004–06; Dir, then Dir Gen., Dept for Enterprise, Innovation and Networks, later for Econ. and Transport, 2006–11, Welsh Assembly Govt; on secondment from Welsh Govt to promote proposed nuclear new build project and other major energy generation projects on Anglesey, 2011–15. Chm., Wales European Centre, Brussels, 2003–05. Vis. Lectr, Sch. of Planning and Geography (formerly Dept of City and Regl Planning), Cardiff Univ., 1995–. Mem., Nat. and Regl Gp, LOCOG, 1997–2011. Gov., Swansea Coll., 1998–2000. *Recreation:* sawing logs for wood burning stoves. *T:* 07764 841168. *E:* gareth@bidbenbidbont.com.

**HALL, Sir Geoffrey,** Kt 2012; General Secretary, Principals' Professional Council, 2015–18; *b* Sutton Coldfield, 26 Jan. 1951; *s* of late Leonard and Florence Hall; *m* 1976, Fionnuala Mary; one *s* one *d*. *Educ:* Bishop Vesey's Grammar Sch., Sutton Coldfield; Liverpool Univ. (BA Hons 1972); Manchester Poly. (Dip. Mgt Educn 1982). Further Educn Officer, Birmingham LEA, 1984–88; Dir of Educn, London Bor. of Bexley, 1988–93; Director: FEFC, 1993–2000; LSC, 2000–02; Dep. Chief Exec., 2002–03, Principal and Chief Exec., 2004–11, New Coll. Nottingham; Chair, Information Authy, 2011–13. *Publications:* (contrib.) British Politics Today, 1976; Managing and Changing Further Education, 1988; (contrib.) Unfinished Business in Widening Participation, 2008; (contrib.) Global Development of Community Colleges, 2008. *Recreations:* walking our two setters, current affairs, watching Rugby Union.

**HALL, Prof. George Martin,** PhD, DSc; FRCA; Foundation Professor of Anaesthesia, St George's, University of London (formerly St George's Hospital Medical School), 1992–2013, now Emeritus; *b* 14 May 1944; *s* of George Vincent Hall and Dora Hortensia Hall; *m* 1st, 1964, Marion Edith Burgin (marr. diss.); one *d*; 2nd, 2017, Dr Barbara Kennedy. *Educ:* University Coll. Hosp. Med. Sch. (MB BS 1967; PhD 1976); DSc London, 1999. FRCA 1971. Royal Postgraduate Medical School: Sen. Lectr in Anaesthesia, 1977–85; Reader, 1985–89; Prof. of Clinical Anaesthesia, 1989–92. Hunterian Prof., RCS, 1983–84. *Publications:* How to Write a Paper, 1994, 5th edn 2012; How to Survive in Anaesthesia, 1997, 5th edn 2017; Short Practice of Anaesthesia, 1997; Diabetes: emergency and hospital management, 1999; Perioperative Care of the Eye Patient, 2000; How to Present at Meetings, 2001, 3rd edn 2012; over 250 res. papers on anaesthesia and human physiology. *Recreations:* hiking, travel, supporting Staffordshire. *Address:* Department of Anaesthesia and Intensive Care Medicine, St George's, University of London, SW17 0RE. *T:* (020) 8725 2836. *Club:* Farmers.

**HALL, Rev. Canon George Rumney,** CVO 2003 (LVO 1999); Rector of the Sandringham Group of Parishes, and Domestic Chaplain to the Queen, 1987–2003; Chaplain to the Queen, 1989–2007; *b* 7 Nov. 1937; *s* of John and Deborah Hall; *m* 1965, Diana Lesley Brunning; one *s* one *d*. *Educ:* Brasted Place, Kent; Westcott House, Cambridge. Deacon 1962, priest 1963; Assistant Curate: St Philip's, Camberwell, 1962–65; Holy Trinity, Waltham Cross, 1965–67; Rector of Buckenham, Hassingham, Strumpshaw, dio. Norwich, 1967–74; Chaplain: St Andrew's Psychiatric Hosp., Norwich, 1967–72; HM Prison, Norwich, 1972–74; Vicar of Wymondham, 1974–87; RD of Humbleyard, 1986–87; Hon. Canon, Norwich Cathedral, 1987–2003, now Canon Emeritus; RD of Heacham and Rising, 1989–2001. Founder Mem., Wymondham Branch of Mind Day Centre; Mem. Bd, Cotman Housing Assoc., Norwich. *Recreations:* walking, reading, theatre, music. *Address:* Town Farm Cottage, Lynn Road, Bircham, King's Lynn, Norfolk PE31 6RJ. *T:* (01485) 576134. *E:* george_hall@btinternet.com.

**HALL, Sir Graham (Joseph),** Kt 2003; Chairman, Leeds Bradford International Airport, 2007–08; *b* 12 Oct. 1943; *s* of Herbert and Phyllis Hall; *m* 1963, Pamela Wilmot; one *s* one *d*. *Educ:* Doncaster Technical Coll.; Rotherham Coll. of Technol. (DipEE 1967); Blackburn Coll. of Technol. CEng 1977; FIET (FIEE 1988). Commercial Dir, 1984–89, Divl Dir, Energy Supply, 1989–91, Yorkshire Electricity Bd; Gp Exec. Dir, 1991–97, Gp Ops Dir, 1997, Chief Exec., 1998–2001, Yorkshire Electricity Gp plc. Chm., Regl Develt Agency for Yorkshire and the Humber (Yorkshire Forward), 1998–2003. Mem. Ct Dirs, Bank of England, 2001–07. Chm., Yorks and the Humber Regl Council, CBI, 1997–99. CCMI 2002 (FIMgt 1987). Hon. DEng Bradford, 1999. *Recreations:* gardening, golf, international travel.

**HALL, Sir Iain (Robert),** Kt 2002; education consultant; Chief Executive, Great Schools Trust (formerly Great Schools for All Children), since 2012; *b* 13 Feb. 1943; *s* of Edward and Annie Hall; three *s* from former *m*. *Educ:* Liverpool Collegiate Sch.; Liverpool Univ. (BSc). Physics teacher, Liverpool Inst., 1965–72; Hd of Sci., Brookfield Sch., Kirkby, 1972–78; Dep. Headteacher, Glenburn High Sch., Lancs, 1978–82; Headteacher: Breckfield Sch., Liverpool, 1982–91; Parrs Wood Technol. Coll., Manchester, 1991–2003. Mem., Gov. Council, Nat. Coll. of Sch. Leadership, 2002. Associate Dir, Schools Network, 2002–12. Advr, Oasis Community Learning, 2012–; Educn Advr, Oasis Academies, 2012– (Principal, Oasis Acad., Oldham, 2011–12); Leadership Advr, Teach First, 2009–12. *Publications:* Nuffield Physics, 1985; contribs to various educnl mags. *Recreations:* cooking, supporter of Liverpool FC. *E:* IainRHall@btconnect.com.

**HALL, James Douglas Ellis;** photographer, farmer and businessman; Chairman: Carbon Clear Ltd, 2011–17; Save Britain's Heritage, 2012–17; *b* 9 Oct. 1954; *s* of late (William) Douglas Hall and of (Helen) Elizabeth Hall; *m* 1980, Carol; two *d*. *Educ:* Edinburgh Acad.; Univ. of Aberdeen (MA Hons Pol Studies). Accenture, 1976–2006: UK Man. Partner, 1994–2000; Global Man. Partner, Technol. and Systems Integration, 2001–05; Chief Exec., Identity and Passport Service, 2006–10; Registrar Gen. for England and Wales, 2008–10. Commn on Public Policy and British Business, 1996–97. Mem. Court, 2011–19, Sen. Ind. Gov., 2017–19, Univ. of Aberdeen. *Recreations:* camera, rod and gun. *Address:* Barlaston Hall, Staffordshire ST12 9AT.

**HALL, Prof. James William,** PhD; FREng, FICE; Professor of Climate and Environmental Risks, University of Oxford, since 2011; Fellow of Linacre College, Oxford, since 2011; *b* Sidcup, Kent, 6 May 1968; *s* of Dr David Sunderland Hall and Gillian Mary Hall; *m* 1999, Laura Madurini; one *s* two *d*. *Educ:* Eltham Coll.; Univ. of Bristol (BEng 1st Cl. Civil Engrg 1990; PhD 1999); MA Oxon 2011. CEng 1996; MICE 1996, FICE 2005; FREng 2011. Engineer: VSO, Guyana, 1991–93; HR Wallingford, 1993–95; Lectr, 1998–2004, Reader, 2004, Univ. of Bristol; Prof., Newcastle Univ., 2004–11; Dir, Envmtl Change Inst., Univ. of Oxford, 2011–18. Dir, Oxford Infrastructure Analytics, 2017–. Mem., Adaptation Sub-Cttee, Cttee on Climate Change, 2009–19. Fellow, Royal Statistical Soc., 2004. Associate Ed., Jl of Flood Risk Mgt, 2007–17; Ed., Jl Water Resources Res., 2017–. *Publications:* Flood Risk Management in Europe, 2007; Applied Uncertainty Analysis for Flood Risk Management, 2014; The Future of National Infrastructure, 2016. *Recreation:* mountaineering. *Address:* Oxford University Centre for the Environment, South Parks Road, Oxford OX1 3QY. *T:* (01865) 275846, *Fax:* (01865) 275850. *E:* jim.hall@eci.ox.ac.uk. *Club:* Alpine.

**HALL, Janice Elizabeth, (Jan),** OBE 1996; Founding Partner, No4, since 2019; *b* 1 June 1957; *d* of John Brian Hall and late Jean Hall; one *s*. *Educ:* St Anne's Coll., Oxford (MA Hons). Mktg Manager, ICI, 1979–83; Chm. and Chief Exec., Coley Porter Bell, 1983–93; Eur. Chief Exec., GGT Gp, 1994–97; Partner: Spencer Stuart, 1997–2005; JCA Gp, 2005–16; Chm., Heidrick & Struggles/JCA Gp, 2016–18. Sen. non-exec. Dir, First Choice Holidays, 1994–2003. Hon. Prof., Warwick Business Sch., 1995–2008 (Mem., Bd, 1993–). Mem. Council, IoD, 1991–2005. Mem. Adv. Bd, Saïd Business Sch., Univ. of Oxford, 2009–17. *Publications:* Dementia Essentials, 2013.

**HALL, Jean Morag;** *see* Rankine, J. M.

**HALL, Joan Valerie,** CBE 1990; Member, Central Transport Consultative Committee, 1981–86; *b* 31 Aug. 1935; *d* of late Robert Percy Hall and Winifred Emily Umbers. *Educ:* Queen Margaret's Sch., Escrick, York; Ashridge House of Citizenship. Contested (C) Barnsley, 1964 and 1966. MP (C) Keighley, 1970–Feb. 1974; PPS to Minister of State for Agriculture, Fisheries and Food, 1972–74. Vice-Chm., Greater London Young Conservatives, 1964. Chm., Sudan Studies Soc. of UK, 1989–92. Mem. Council, Univ. of Buckingham (formerly University Coll. Buckingham), 1977–. *Address:* 7 Greenland, High Hoyland, Barnsley, South Yorks S75 4AZ.

**HALL, John;** *see* Hall, W. J.

**HALL, Sir John,** Kt 1991; DL; Chairman: Cameron Hall Developments Ltd, 1973–93; Newcastle United Football Club, 1992–97; a Director, Bank of England, 1996–98; *b* 21 March 1933; *m* Mae; one *s* one *d*. *Educ:* Bedlington Grammar Sch. Chartered surveyor. Developed MetroCentre (shopping and leisure complex), Gateshead, 1985. Mem., Millennium Commn, 1994–2000. Gordon Grand Fellow, Yale Univ., 1991. DL Co. Durham, 2007. Hon. DCL: Newcastle upon Tyne, 1988; Durham, 1995. NE Business Man of the Year, 1987. *Address:* Wynyard Hall, Billingham, Cleveland TS22 5NF.

**HALL, Ven. John Barrie;** Archdeacon of Salop, 1998–2011, now Archdeacon Emeritus; *b* 27 May 1941; *s* of Arthur Cyril Hall and Beatrice Hall (née Clark); *m* 1963, Kay Deakin; three *s*. *Educ:* Salisbury and Wells Theol Coll. Self-employed in garage and caravan sales until 1982; ordained deacon 1984, priest 1985; Curate, St Edward, Cheddleton, 1984–88; Vicar, Rocester, then Rocester and Croxden with Hollington, 1988–98. Mem., Gen. Synod of C of E, 2002–10. Hon. Canon of Lichfield Cathedral, 1999. Lichfield Diocese: Chairman: Redundant Church Users' Cttee, 2001–11; Child Protection Cttee, 2002–11; Pastoral Cttee, 2006–11; Adv. Cttee on care of churches, 2014–; Vice Chm., Bd of Finance, 2007–11. Mem., C of E Inter-Diocesan Finance Forum, 2007–11. Pres., Adv. Cttee, Telford Christian Council, 2007–11. Chairman: Shropshire Historical Churches Trust, 1998–2011; Staffs Historic Churches Trust, 2013–17. *Recreations:* reading, a little walking, most sports (now watching only), cooking, building a model railway. *Address:* 16 Mill House Drive, Cheadle, Stoke-on-Trent ST10 1XL.

**HALL, Sir John Douglas Hoste,** 15th Bt *cr* 1687 (NS), of Dunglass, Haddingtonshire; Professor of Performance Writing, Falmouth University (formerly University College Falmouth), 2010–15, Professor Emeritus, 2016; *b* 7 Jan. 1945; *s* of Sir Douglas Basil Hall, 14th Bt, KCMG and Rachel Marion Gartside-Tippinge; S father, 2004; *m* 1972, Angela Margaret, *d* of George Keys (marr. diss. 1989); two *s*. *Educ:* Dover Coll.; Gonville and Caius Coll., Cambridge (BA); Southampton Univ. (Cert Ed); Dartington Coll. of Arts, Plymouth (PhD). Dartington College of Arts, later University College Falmouth: Vice-Principal (Academic), 1990–2002; Associate Dir of Res., 2002–10. *Publications:* (poems): Between the Cities, 1968; Days, 1972; Meaning Insomnia, 1978; Malo-lactic Ferment, 1978; Couch Grass, 1978; Else Here: selected poems, 1999; Couldn't You?, 2007; The Week's Bad Groan, 2008; (with Peter Hughes) Interscriptions, 2011; Keepsache, 2013; As a Said Place, 2017; (novel) Apricot Pages, 2005; (essays): Thirteen Ways of Talking about Performance Writing, 2008; Essays on Performance Writing, Poetics and Poetry, 2013: vol. 1, On Performance Writing, with Pedagogical Sketches; vol. 2, Writings towards Writing and Reading: on Poetics, with implicated readings. *Heir:* *s* Thomas James Hall, *b* 10 Dec. 1975.

**HALL, John Leonard;** *see* Graham-Hall.

**HALL, Dr John Lewis;** Senior Fellow, National Institute of Standards and Technology, USA, Emeritus since 2004; *b* Aug. 1934; *s* of John Ernest Hall and Elizabeth Rae Hall (née Long); *m* 1958, Marilyn Charlene Robinson; two *s* one *d*. *Educ:* Carnegie Mellon Univ., Pittsburgh (BS 1956, MS 1958; PhD Physics 1961). National Bureau of Standards, later National Institute of Standards and Technology, USA: Postdoctoral Res. Associate, Washington, 1961–62; Physicist, Boulder, Colo, 1962–75; Sen. Scientist, 1975–2004; Lectr, 1997, Prof. Adjoint, 2007–, Dept of Physics, Univ. of Colorado. Adv. Prof., E China Normal Univ., Shanghai, 1995. Mem., NAS. Hon. Dr: Paris Nord, 1989; Carnegie-Mellon, 2006; Glasgow, 2007; Ohio State, 2008. (Jtly) Nobel Prize for Physics, 2005. Légion d'Honneur (France), 2004. *Publications:* (ed) Laser Spectroscopy III, 1977; 235

papers in jls; 11 US patents. *Recreations:* music, electronic hobbies, reading, travel. *Address:* JILA, University of Colorado, Boulder, CO 80309-0440, USA. *T:* (303) 4927843, *Fax:* (303) 4925235. *E:* jhall@jila.colorado.edu.

**HALL, John Peirs;** Chief Executive (formerly Managing Director), Brewin Dolphin Holdings PLC, 1987–2007; *b* 26 June 1940; *s* of Robert Noel Hall and Doreen Cecelia Hall (*née* Russell); *m* 1965, Sarah Gillian Page; three *s* (and one *s* decd). *Educ:* Stowe. Read Hurst-Brown, Stockbrokers, 1959–65; joined Wontner Renwick & Francis, 1965, which became Wontner Dolphin & Francis, 1970, then Brewin Dolphin Hldgs PLC, 1974; Partner, 1967; Chm., Mgt Cttee, 1980. Chm., Assoc. of Private Client Investment Managers and Stockbrokers, 2006–12. Founder, Soundabout charity. Freeman, City of London, 1970; Mem., Ct of Assts, Co. of Merchant Taylors, 1993– (Master, 2005–06). *Recreations:* sailing, golf, breeding British White cattle, Suffolk horse breeding, bee-keeping (Pres., South Children Beekeepers). *Address:* Chalkhouse Green Farm, Kidmore End, near Reading RG4 9AL. *T:* (0118) 972 3631. *Clubs:* City of London; Royal Yacht Squadron, Island Sailing; Huntercombe Golf.

**HALL, Very Rev. John Robert;** Dean of Westminster, 2006–19, now Dean Emeritus; Dean of the Order of the Bath, 2006–19; *b* 13 March 1949; *e s* of late Ronald John Hall, FCIB, FCIS and Katie Margaret Brock Hall (*née* Walker). *Educ:* St Dunstan's Coll.; St Chad's Coll., Durham (BA Hons Theol.; Hon. Fellow 2009); Cuddesdon Theol Coll. Head of RE, Malet Lambert High Sch., Hull, 1971–73; ordained deacon 1975, priest 1976; Curate, St John the Divine, Kennington, 1975–78; Priest-in-charge, All Saints', S Wimbledon, 1978–84; Vicar, St Peter's, Streatham, 1984–92; Dir of Educn, Dio. Blackburn, 1992–98; Residentiary Canon, Blackburn Cathedral, 1994–98, Canon Emeritus, 2000 (Hon. Canon, 1992–94, 1998–2000); Gen. Sec., C of E Bd of Educn, subseq. Chief Educn Officer, C of E, and Gen. Sec., Nat. Soc. for Promoting Religious Educn, 1998–2006; Hon. Curate, St Alban's, S Norwood, 2003–06; Hon. Pres., Coll. of St Barnabas Lingfield, 2013–; Bursalis Prebend, Chichester Cathedral, 2018–. Examng Chaplain to Bp of Southwark, 1988–92. Chm., Commn on Religious Educn, 2016–18. Member: Gen. Synod of C of E, 1984–92; C of E Bd of Educn, 1991–92; Lancs Educn Cttee, 1992–98; Council, National Soc., 1997–98; Gen. Teaching Council, 2000–04, Chm., Standards Cttee, City of Westminster, 2008–12. Chm., Fedn of Catholic Priests, 1991–94. Mem. Council, Sch. of St Mary and St Anne, Abbots Bromley, 1992–2002; Governor: St Martin's Coll., Lancaster, 1992–98; St Dunstan's Coll., 2002–11; Sutton Valence Sch., 2013–15; Chairman of Governors: Westminster Sch., 2006–19; Harris Westminster Sixth Form, 2014–19; Member, Governing Body: Urban Learning Foundn, 1998–2002; Canterbury Christ Church Univ. (formerly University Coll.), 1999–2006 (Hon. Fellow, 2007); Pro Chancellor, Roehampton Univ., 2011–18; Chair, Council, RSCM, 2019–. Trustee: St Gabriel's Trust, 1998–2006; King James Bible Trust (formerly 2011 Trust), 2008–11. Pres., Westminster Soc., 1996–19; Vice Pres., The London Soc., 2006–19. Fellow, Woodard Corp., 1992– (Mem. Bd, 2019–). FRSA 2002; FSA 2014; FCIS 2019. Hon. FCollT 2009. Hon. Liveryman, Educators' Co., 2015. Hon. Fellow, Univ. of Wales Trinity St David, 2015. Hon. DD Roehampton, 2007; Hon. DTheol Chester, 2008; Hon. DLitt: Westminster, 2014; Hull, 2016. *Publications:* (contrib.) Distinctiveness in Church Schools, 1998; (jtly) Governing and Managing Church Schools, 2nd edn 2003; Queen Elizabeth II and Her Church: Royal Service at Westminster Abbey, 2012; contrib. Church Times, TES, Parly Brief, Guardian, C of E Newspaper, Tablet, etc. *Recreations:* music, British political history. *Address:* 16 Little London, Chichester PO19 1NZ. *Clubs:* Athenæum, Beefsteak.

**HALL, John Thridgould;** education sector lawyer, 1988–2013; Chair, Education Group, Eversheds LLP, 2006–13; *b* Pinner, Middx, 23 Dec. 1948; *s* of Stanley Dennis Hall and Kathleen Joan Hall; *m* 1982, Julie Charlotte Arnold; two *s* one *d*. *Educ:* St John's Sch., Pinner; University Coll. Sch., London; Wadham Coll., Oxford (BA 1971; MA 1973). Admitted as solicitor, 1975; Asst Solicitor, 1975–78, Partner, 1978–93, Wedlake Saint; Partner, Eversheds LLP, 1994–2008. Chm., London Young Solicitors Gp, 1982–83. Mem. Bd, E-ACT, 2009–13. Mem., London Diocesan Synod, 2012–15. Member: Bd, Barnet Coll., 1992–2002; Council, RCM, 1999–2009; Bd, Lochinver Hse Sch., 2000–14; Chm., Crest Academies, London, 2009–14. Member: Internat. Adv. Council, Centre for Excellence in HE Law and Policy, Stetson Univ., Florida, 2008–16; Bd, Crosslinks, 2015–19. Hon. RCM 2010. Hon. Fellow, Brunel Univ., 2012. FRSA 1996. Church Warden and Trustee, St Paul's Ch, Hadley Wood, 2002– (Chm., Trustees, 2019–); Trustee, Barnet Mus. and Histl Soc., 2017– (Chm., Trustees, 2019–). *Publications:* (also Gen. Ed.) Purposive Governance: an annotated guidance for further education colleges, 1999, 14th edn 2013; Model Code of Conduct for Further Education Colleges, 1999, 11th edn 2013. *Recreations:* music, history, art, Mallorca, walking, family, Bible exposition. *Address:* 31 Lancaster Avenue, Hadley Wood, Barnet, Herts EN4 0EP. *T:* (020) 8440 1820, 07767 304361. *E:* johnthridhall@gmail.com.

**HALL, Dr John Tristan Dalton;** University Librarian, University of Durham, 1989–2009, now Librarian Emeritus; *b* 28 Oct. 1945; *m* 1970, Inge Lise Lindqvist; one *s* two *d*. *Educ:* Lady Lumley's Sch., Pickering; Univ. of Manchester (BA 1968; PhD 1977); MA Cantab 1989. Asst Librarian, John Rylands Univ. Library of Manchester, 1971–78; Sub-Librarian (Special Collections), Edinburgh Univ. Library, 1978–86; Dep. Librarian, Cambridge Univ. Library, 1986–89; Fellow, Darwin Coll., Cambridge, 1987–89. *Publications:* Manuscript Treasures in Edinburgh University Library: an album of illustrations, 1980; The Tounis College: an anthology of Edinburgh University student journals 1823–1923, 1985; articles and reviews in learned jls. *Recreations:* music, pottery, gardening.

**HALL, Jonathan David D.;** *see* Durham Hall.

**HALL, Maj.-Gen. Jonathan Michael Francis Cooper,** CB 1998; OBE 1987; DL; Lieutenant Governor, Royal Hospital, Chelsea, 1997–2005; *b* 10 Aug. 1944; *s* of Charles Richard Hall and Rosemary Hall (*née* Beckwith); *m* 1968, Sarah Linda Hudson; two *d*. *Educ:* Taunton Sch.; RMA Sandhurst. Commissioned 3rd Carabiniers, 1965; Staff Coll., 1977; commanded Royal Scots Dragoon Guards, 1984–86 and 12th Armd Bde, 1988–90; Higher Command and Staff Course, 1988; Mem., RCDS, 1991; Dep. Mil. Sec., MoD(A), 1992–93; DRAC, 1994; GOC Scotland, and Gov., Edinburgh Castle, 1995–97. Colonel Commandant: RAVC, 1995–2001; Scottish Div., 1995–97; Col, Royal Scots Dragoon Guards, 1998–2003. Mem., 1999–2012, Standard Bearer, 2012–14, HM Body Guard of Hon. Corps of Gentlemen-at-Arms. Trustee: RACWM Benevolent Fund, 1998–2011; VC and GC Assoc. Benevolent Fund, 2004–18; Army Mus Ogilby Trust, 2004–14; Life Mem., Sandhurst Trust, 2016. Mem., Ethical Review Process, Imperial Coll., London, 2003–09; Designated Mem., Ethics and Welfare Gp, BVA, 2007–10. Managing Consultant, Compton Fundraising Ltd, 2006–. Gov., Blind Veterans UK (formerly St Dunstan's), 2011–18. Vice President: ABF Dorset, 2008–16; Soc. of Dorset Men, 2010–14; Vice Patron, Nat. Assoc. of Almshouses 65th Anniv. Appeal, 2012–13. Mem., Sherborne Abbey PCC, 2006–16. Chm. and Mem. Council, Order of St John, Dorset, 2008–11. Gov., Taunton Sch., 2007–16 (Hon. Life Vice Pres., 2018). FCMI (FIMgt 1997). Associate Mem., Wessex Reserve Forces and Cadets Assoc., 2019–; Hon. Associate Mem., BVA, 1996; Hon. Vice Pres., Purbeck and Bovington Beagles, 2019–. Freeman, City of London, 2006; Liveryman, Farriers' Co., 2006–. DL Dorset, 2010. Kt Comdr, Order of Francis I, 2014; OStJ 1998. *Recreations:* country, music, travel. *Address:* Orchard House, Nether Compton, Sherborne, Dorset DT9 4QA. *Clubs:* Cavalry and Guards (Mem. Adv. Council; Trustee, 2007–14), MCC, Pratt's; Woodroffe's; Somerset County Cricket.

**HALL, Jonathan Rupert;** QC 2014; a Recorder, since 2012; *b* Brighton, 23 July 1971; *s* of Stephen Hall and Dr Rosemary Hall; *m* 2000, Michelle Dyson; two *s* one *d*. *Educ:* Tonbridge Sch., Kent; Christ Church, Oxford (BA English Lang. and Lit.). Called to the Bar, Inner Temple, 1994; in practice as barrister, 1994–. Ind. Reviewer of Terrorism Legislation, 2019–. *Recreations:* family, squash, novels, cycling. *Address:* 6KBW College Hill, 21 College Hill, EC4R 2RP. *T:* (020) 3301 0910. *E:* jonathan.hall@6kbw.com.

**HALL, His Honour Julian;** a Circuit Judge, 1986–2010; Resident Judge, Oxford Combined Court Centre, 2002–10; authorised to sit in the Court of Appeal (Criminal Division), 2007–10; *b* 13 Jan. 1939; *s* of late Dr Stephen Hall, FRCP and Dr Mary Hall, Boarstall Tower, Bucks; *m* 1st, 1968, M. Rosalind Perry (marr. diss. 1988); one *s* one *d*; 2nd, 1989, Ingrid Cecilia, *er d* of late Rev. Canon Ronald Lunt, MC. *Educ:* Eton (Scholar); Christ Church, Oxford (Scholar; MA); Trinity Coll., Dublin (LLB). ARCM (flute). Industrial Chemist, Shell Internat. Chemical Co., 1961–63. Called to the Bar, Gray's Inn, 1966, Bencher, 2002; in practice in Common Law Chambers on Northern Circuit, Manchester, 1966–86; Standing Prosecuting Counsel to Inland Revenue, Northern Circuit, 1985–86; a Recorder, 1982–86; Resident Judge, Northampton Combined Court Centre, 2000–02; Hon. Recorder of Oxford, 2002–10. A Judge of Appeal, Oxford Univ. Student Disciplinary Panel, 2010–. Mem., Adv. Panel, HM Prison Grendon, 2008–17. Tutor judge, Judicial Studies Bd, 1989–93. Chm., Northants Family Mediation Service, 1995–2000; Pres., Mental Health Rev. Tribunals, 1997–2011. Shrieval Remembrancer for Oxon, 2010–19. Trustee, Oxford Lieder Festival, 2012–. *Recreations:* making music, in orchestras, choirs and at home, photography, bread and jam making. *Address:* c/o Oxford Crown Court, St Aldate's, Oxford OX1 1TL.

*See also* C. E. Henderson.

**HALL, Katja Anneli;** Corporate Affairs Director, Capita plc, since 2018; *b* Sweden, 24 Sept. 1972; *d* of Kjell Klasson and Riitta Harkola; *m* 2002, Chris Hall; two *d*. *Educ:* Univ. of York (BA Hons Econs and Politics 1995); Univ. of Nottingham (MA Internat. Relns 1996). Policy Advr, Sen. Policy Advr, then Hd, Employee Relns, CBI, 1996–2002; Sen. Manager, HR Policy and Employee Relns, BBC, 2002–05; Hd, Employee Relns, 2006–08, Dir, Employment Policy, 2008–11, Chief Policy Dir, 2011–14, Dep. Dir-Gen., 2014–15, CBI; Gp Hd of Public Affairs, then Gp Gen. Manager and Gp Hd of Ext. Affairs and Sustainability, HSBC, 2015–17; Partner, Chairman Mentors Internat., 2017–18. Mem. Bd, Office for Students, 2018–. *Recreations:* ski-ing, reading. *Address:* Capita plc, 30 Berners Street, W1T 3LR.

**HALL, Sir Kenneth Octavius,** ON 2006; GCMG 2007; OJ 2004; PhD; Governor-General of Jamaica, 2006–09; Hon. Distinguished Research Fellow, University of West Indies, Mona, since 2009; *b* Lucea, Hanover, Jamaica; *m* Rheima Holding. *Educ:* Univ. of W Indies, Mona (BA 1966); Univ. of W Indies, Trinidad (Dip. Internat. Relns 1967); Queen's Univ., Ontario (MA Hist. 1967; PhD 1971). Teacher, Rusea's High Sch., Jamaica, 1961–63; Admin. Officer, Min. of Agric., Govt of Jamaica, 1966; teaching asst, Div. of Social Scis, Univ. of WI, St Augustine, Trinidad and Tobago, 1966–67; Instructor, Hist. Dept, Queen's Univ., Ontario, 1969–71; Asst Prof. of Hist., SUNY, 1971–73; Lectr, Hist. Dept, Univ. of WI, Mona, Jamaica, 1972–73; Faculty Res. Associate, Foreign and Comparative Studies, Syracuse Univ., NY, 1973–84; State University of New York: Oswego: Associate Prof. of Hist., 1973–84; Asst Provost 1982–84; Prof. of Hist., 1984–86; Central Administration, Albany: Asst Vice-Chancellor for Acad. Progs, 1984–88; Asst Provost for Acad. Progs, 1988–89; Vice Pres. for Acad. Affairs and Dean of Faculty, SUNY at Old Westbury, 1990–94; Principal, Univ. of WI, Mona, Jamaica, 1996–2006. Chancellor, University Coll. of the Caribbean, 2011–12. Caribbean Community Secretariat, Guyana: Chief, Res. and Conf. Section, 1975–76; Dir, Gen. Services and Admin, 1976–77; Dep. Sec.-Gen., 1994–96. *Publications:* (ed) Education and the Black Experience, 1979; The Group of 77: strengthening its negotiating capacity, 1979; Imperial Proconsul: Sir Hercules Robinson and South Africa, 1881 to 1889, 1980; (ed) Makers of the Twentieth Century, 1982; (with D. Benn) Globalisation: a calculus of inequality, perspectives from the South, 2000; (with D. Benn) Contending with Destiny: the Caribbean in the 21st Century, 2000; CARICOM: unity in adversity, 2000; The Caribbean Community: beyond survival, 2001; Reinventing CARICOM: the road to a new integration, 2002; Integrate or Perish!: perspectives of leaders of the integration movement 1963–1999, 1999, 2nd edn 2003; (with D. Benn) Caribbean Imperatives: regional governance and integrated development, 2005; Rex N: Rex Nettleford, selected speeches, 2006; (with D. Benn) Production Integration in CARICOM: from theory to action, 2006; (with Rheima Holding) Tourism: the driver of change in the Jamaican economy?, 2006; (ed with Myrtle Chuck-A-Sang): Integration: CARICOM's key to prosperity, 2006; CARICOM Single Market and Economy: genesis and prognosis, 2007; CARICOM Single Market and Economy: challenges, benefits prospects, 2007; Confronting Challenges, Maximising Opportunities: a new diplomacy for market access, 2007; Intervention Border and Maritime Issues in CARICOM, 2007; The Caribbean Integration Process: a people-centred approach, 2007; CARICOM Policy Options for International Engagement, 2010; contrib. chapters in books and articles in jls and papers on history and current issues in the Caribbean.

**HALL, Lee;** dramatist; *b* 20 Sept. 1966; *s* of Peter and Sylvia Hall; *m* 2003, Beeban Kidron (*see* Baroness Kidron). *Educ:* Benfield Comprehensive Sch., Newcastle; Fitzwilliam Coll., Cambridge (BA English Lit.). Writer in Residence: Live Th., Newcastle upon Tyne, 1997–98; RSC, 1998–99. *Plays:* I Luv You Jimmy Spud (radio), 1995 (Sony Award); Spoonface Steinberg (radio), 1996; The Student Prince (TV), 1996; Mr Puntila and his Man Matti (trans.), Almeida, 1997; Cooking with Elvis, Live Th., transf. Whitehall, 2000; A Servant to Two Masters, RSC at Young Vic, 2000; The Good Hope, NT, 2001; Two's Company/Child of the Snow, Bristol Old Vic, 2005; Billy Elliot—the Musical, Victoria Palace, 2005–16, NY, 2008; The Pitmen Painters, Live Th., Newcastle, 2007, RNT UK tour, 2009–10, NY, 2010; Shakespeare in Love, Noël Coward Th., 2014, UK tour, 2018; Our Ladies of Perpetual Succour, Traverse Th., Edinburgh, 2015, NT and UK tour, 2016, Duke of York, 2017; Network, NT, 2017; *films:* Billy Elliot, 2000; (with R. Curtis) War Horse, 2012; Victoria and Abdul, 2017; Rocketman, 2019; *television:* The Wind in the Willows, 2006; Toast, 2010. Hon. Dr Royal Central Sch. of Speech and Drama, 2016. *Publications:* Spoonface Steinberg and other plays, 1996; Cooking with Elvis, 1999; A Servant to Two Masters (new adaptation), 2000; Pinocchio (new adaptation), 2000; Billy Elliot (screenplay), 2001; The Good Hope (new adaptation), 2001; Plays 1, 2002; Plays 2, 2003. *Recreations:* cooking, reading, sleeping. *Address:* c/o Judy Daish Associates, 2 St Charles Place, W10 6EG.

**HALL, Lisa;** *see* Hall, E. A. H.

**HALL, Luke Anthony**; MP (C) Thornbury and Yate, since 2015; Parliamentary Under Secretary of State, Ministry of Housing, Communities and Local Government, since 2019; *b* S Glos, 8 July 1986. Shop worker, then Store Manager, Lidl, Yate; Area Manager, Farmfoods, until 2015. Member: Envmtl Audit Cttee, 2015–17; Work and Pensions Cttee, 2016–17; Petitions Cttee, 2016–17. *Address*: House of Commons, SW1A 0AA.

**HALL, Margaret Dorothy**, OBE 1973; RDI 1974; Head of Design, British Museum, 1964–2001; *b* 22 Jan. 1936; *d* of Thomas Robson Hall and Millicent (*née* Britton). *Educ*: Bromley County Grammar Sch.; Bromley College of Art; Royal College of Art (DesRCA). Design Assistant: Casson, Condor & Partners, 1960–61; Westwood Piet & Partners, 1961–63; Dennis Lennon & Partners, 1963–64; British Museum, 1964–2001: exhibitions designed include: Masterpieces of Glass, 1968; Museum of Mankind, 1970; Treasures of Tutankhamun, 1972; Nomad and City, 1976; Captain Cook in the South Seas, 1979. Designer, Manuscripts and Men, National Portrait Gallery, 1969. Chm., Gp of Designers/Interpreters in Museums, 1978–81; Mem. Council, RSA, 1984–89. FCSD (FSIAD 1975–90; MSIAD 1968) (Chm., SIAD Salaried Designers Cttee, 1979–81). Chm., Wynkyn de Worde Soc., 1982. Governor, Ravensbourne College of Art, 1973–78. FRSA 1974; FMA 1983. *Publications*: On Display: a grammar of museum exhibition design, 1987. *Club*: Double Crown (Pres., 1998).

**HALL, Prof. Martin**, PhD; Vice-Chancellor, University of Salford, 2009–15; Chairman, Jisc, 2014–15; *b* Guildford; *m* Prof. Brenda Cooper; three *c*. *Educ*: Peterhouse, Cambridge (BA 1973; PhD 1980). Worked in museums in S Africa; University of Cape Town: Res. Officer, then Associate Prof., later Prof., Dept of Archaeol., 1983–98, now Emeritus Prof.; Dir, Centre for African Studies, 1986–90; Dean, Higher Educn Develt, 1999–2002; Dep. Vice-Chancellor, 2002–09. Pres., World Archaeol Congress, 1999–2003; former Gen. Sec., S African Archaeol Soc. *Publications*: The Changing Past, 1987, 2nd edn 1990; (with C. Malherbe) Changes in the Land, 1988; The Iron Age: an illustrated dictionary of South African history, 1994; Slaves, Rings and Rubbish, 1995; Archaeology Africa, 1996; The Smuts Hall Windows, 1997; (jtly) Writing from the Edge: historical archaeology, 1999; (with R. Stefoff) Great Zimbabwe, 2006; (ed jtly) Desire Lines: memory and identity in the post-apartheid city, 2007; contribs to jls incl. Jl African Hist., S African Jl Sci., British Archaeol Reports, Annals of Natal Mus., S African Archaeol Soc., Social Dynamics, Jl Social Archaeol., Studies in Higher Educn, Histl Archaeol.

**HALL, Melanie Jane**; *see* Davies, M. J.

**HALL, Melanie Ruth**, QC 2002; *b* 29 Dec. 1959; *m* 1991, Martin Harold Hall; one *s* two *d*. *Educ*: Durham Univ. (BA). Called to the Bar, Inner Temple, 1982. Non-exec. Dir, Home Housing Ltd, 1995–99. Trustee: Somerset Hse, 2017–; The Circle, 2017–. Hon. Fellow, Durham Univ., 2018. Ed., Tax Jl, 2008–. Tax QC of Yr, Chambers and Partners, 2018–19. *Address*: Monckton Chambers, Gray's Inn, WC1R 5NR. *T*: (020) 7405 7211, *Fax*: (020) 7405 2084.

**HALL, Dr Michael George**, FRS 1993; scientific consultant, since 1991; *b* 16 Oct. 1931; *s* of George Albert Victor Hall and Mabel Hall (*née* Gittins); *m* 1964, Merete Blatz; one *s* one *d*. *Educ*: Sydney Grammar Sch.; Univ. of Sydney (BSc, BE, MEngSc, PhD). Research in Fluid Dynamics at Aerodynamics Dept, RAE, 1958–91, retired 1991; sabbatical at Dept of Mechanics, Johns Hopkins Univ., 1966–67. Founder-Director, Hall C. F. D. Ltd, 1991–2003. *Publications*: contribs on fluid dynamics to sci. and tech. jls. *Address*: 8 Dene Lane, Farnham, Surrey GU10 3PW.

**HALL, Michael Harold Webster**, FSA; Editor, Burlington Magazine, since 2017; *b* 6 July 1957; *s* of late Dr L. W. Hall and Barbara Hall. *Educ*: Cambridgeshire High Sch. for Boys; Trinity Hall, Cambridge (BA 1980); Birkbeck Coll., London (MA). Ed., Thames and Hudson, 1982–89; Country Life: architectural writer, 1989–94; architectural ed., 1994–98; Dep. Ed., 1998–2004; Ed., Apollo, 2004–10. Contrib. Ed., Visual Arts, Country Life, 2010–17. FSA 2003. Trustee: Emery Walker Trust, 1999– (Chair, 2015–); Victorian Soc., 2000–06; Marc Fitch Fund, 2007–; Mem. Cttee, William Morris Soc., 2013–. *Publications*: The English Country House: from the archives of Country Life, 1994, repr. 2001; Waddesdon Manor, 2002, 3rd edn 2012; (ed) Gothic Architecture and its Meanings 1550–1830, 2002; The Victorian Country House, 2009; George Frederick Bodley and the Later Gothic Revival in Britain and America, 2014; Treasures of the Portland Collection, 2015; Art, Passion and Power: the story of the Royal Collection, 2017; contrib. articles to Country Life, Architectural Hist., Jl Soc. of Architectural Historians, Furniture Hist., Jl British Inst. of Organ Studies, etc. *E*: mhall@burlington.org.uk.

**HALL, Michael Thomas**; *b* 20 Sept. 1952; *s* of late Thomas and Veronica Hall; *m* 1975, Lesley Evelyn Gosling; one *s*. *Educ*: Padgate Coll. of Higher Educn (Teachers' Cert. 1977); N Cheshire Coll., Victoria Univ., Manchester (BEd Hons 1987). Scientific Asst, ICI Ltd, 1969–73; teaching history and physical educn, Bolton, 1977–85; support teacher, Halton Community Assessment Team, 1985–92. Councillor, Warrington Borough Council, 1979–93: Chairman: Envmtl Health Cttee, 1981–84; Finance Sub-Cttee, 1984–85; Policy and Resources Cttee, 1985–92; Dep. Leader of Council, 1984–85, Leader 1985–92. Member, Parish Council: Great Sankey, 1979–83; Birchwood and Croft, 1983–87; Poulton with Fearnhead, 1987–93. MP (Lab) Warrington S, 1992–97, Weaver Vale, 1997–2010. PPS to Ldr of the House of Commons and Pres. of the Council, 1997–98; an Asst Govt Whip, 1998–2001; PPS to Sec. of State for Health, 2001–05, to Lord Chancellor and Sec. of State for Justice, 2008–10. Member: Modernisation Select Cttee, 1997–98; Culture, Media and Sports Select Cttee, 2005–10. Mem., Public Accounts Cttee, 1992–97; Chm., Labour Party Back Bench Educn Cttee, 1996–97. *Publications*: A Miners Pals Battalion at War (2 vols), 2015. *Recreations*: tennis, reading, cooking, dog walking, World War I.

**HALL, Nigel John**, RA 2003; sculptor; *b* 30 Aug. 1943; *s* of Herbert John Hall and Gwendoline Mary Hall (*née* Olsen); *m* 1986, Manijeh Yadegar. *Educ*: Bristol Grammar Sch.; West of England Coll. of Art; Royal Coll. of Art (MA). Harkness Fellow, USA, 1967–69; Tutor, RCA, 1971–74; Principal Lectr, Chelsea Sch. of Art, 1974–81. Ext. Examr, RCA, Goldsmiths Coll., Brighton Univ., Reading Univ., Middlesex Univ., Central Sch. of Art, W Surrey Coll. of Art. Mem. Faculty, British Sch. at Rome, 1979–83. Member: CNAA, 1975–76; Bursaries Cttee, 1975, Exhibns Cttee, 1983, Arts Council. First solo exhibn, Galerie Givaudan, Paris, 1967. *Solo exhibitions include*: Robert Elkon, NY, 1974, 1977, 1979, 1983; Annely Juda Fine Art, London, 1978, 1981, 1985, 1987, 1991, 1996, 2000, 2003, 2005, 2011, 2016; Galerie Maeght, Paris, 1981, 1983; Staatliche Kunsthalle, Baden-Baden, 1982; Nishimura Gall., Tokyo, 1980, 1984, 1988; Garry Anderson Gall., Sydney, 1987, 1990; Hans Mayer Gall., Düsseldorf, 1989, 1999; Fondation Veranneman, Kruishoutem, Belgium, 1987, 1995, 1997; Galerie Ziegler, Zurich, 1986, 1988, 1995; Park Gall., Seoul, 1997, 2000, 2005, 2008; Galerie Konstruktiv Tendens, Stockholm, 2000; Schoenthal Monastery, Switzerland, 2001; Galerie Scheffel, Bad Homburg, 2004, 2007, 2011, 2015, 2019; Kunsthalle, Mannheim, 2004; Galleri C. Hjärne, Helsingborg, 2004; Centre Cultural Contemporani Pelaires, Palma de Mallorca, 2007, 2009; Yorks Sculpture Park, 2008; Galerie Andres Thalmann, Zurich, 2010, 2012, 2014, 2018; Oklahoma City Art Center, 2010; Royal Acad., 2011; Art Space Gall., London, 2011, 2017; Churchill Coll., Cambridge, 2013; Galerie Alvaro Alcazar, Madrid, 2015, 2019; Canary Wharf, 2016; Heidelberg Sculpture Park, 2017; Artists' Lab. Series, Royal Acad., 2017; Isaac Newton Inst., Cambridge, 2017; *group exhibitions include*: Kassel, 1977; Whitechapel Gall., 1981; Tokyo Metropolitan Mus., 1982; Le Havre Mus. of Fine Art, 1988; MOMA, NY, 1993; Fogg Art Mus., Harvard Univ., 1994; Schloss Ambras, Innsbruck, 1998; British Council touring exhibn, Pakistan, S Africa, Zimbabwe, 1997–99; York City Art Gall. and tour, 2001–02; Bad Homburg, Germany, 2003; Beaufort Triennial, Ostend, 2006; Rhode Island Sch. of Design, Providence, 2011; Inst. of Contemporary Arts, Singapore, 2012; Mus. Biedermann, Donaueschingen, 2015; Henry Moore Inst., Leeds, 2016; Nat. Mus. of Art, Osaka, 2018. *Commissions*: Australian Nat. Gall., Canberra, 1982; IBM, London, 1983; Airbus Industrie, Toulouse, 1984; Mus. of Contemp. Art, Hiroshima, 1985; Olympic Park, Seoul, 1988; Clifford Chance, London, 1992; Glaxo Wellcome Res., Stevenage, 1994; NTT, Tokyo, 1996; Bank of America, London, 2003; Saïd Business Sch., Univ. of Oxford, 2005; Bank for Internat. Settlements, Basel, 2007; Kensington Acad., London, 2015. *Work in collections including*: Tate Gall.; BM; Musée Nat. d'Art Moderne, Paris; Nat. Gall., Berlin; MOMA, NY; Australian Nat. Gall., Canberra; Art Inst. of Chicago; Kunsthaus, Zurich; Tokyo Metropolitan Mus.; Musée d'Art Moderne, Brussels; Louisiana Mus., Denmark; Nat. Mus. of Art, Osaka; Mus. of Contemp. Art, Sydney; Dallas Mus. of Fine Art; Tel Aviv Mus.; Los Angeles Co. Mus.; Nat. Mus. of Contemp. Art, Seoul. Hon. DA UAL, 2017. *Relevant publications*: Nigel Hall: sculpture and works on paper, by A. Lambirth, 2008; Nigel Hall: other voices, other rooms, by A. Lambirth, 2012. *Address*: 11 Kensington Park Gardens, W11 3HD. *T*: (020) 7727 3162. *E*: nigelhallra@gmail.com.

**HALL, Patrick**; *b* 20 Oct. 1951; *m* 2004, Claudia Caggiula. *Educ*: Bedford Modern Sch.; Birmingham Univ.; Oxford Poly. Local Govt Planning Officer, Bedford, 1975–91; Bedford Town Centre Co-ordinator, 1991–97. Mem., Bedfordshire CC, 1989–97. Contested (Lab) Bedfordshire N, 1992. MP (Lab) Bedford, 1997–2010; contested (Lab) same seat, 2010, 2015.

**HALL, Sir Peter (Edward)**, KBE 1993; CMG 1987; HM Diplomatic Service, retired; *b* 26 July 1938; *s* of late Bernard Hall and Monica Hall (*née* Blackbourn); *m* 1972, Marnie Kay; one *d*. *Educ*: Portsmouth Grammar Sch.; HM Services Sch. for Linguists); Pembroke Coll., Cambridge (Scholar; 1st Cl. parts I and II, Mediaeval and Modern Langs Tripos). Foreign Office, 1961–63; 3rd Sec., Warsaw, 1963–66; 2nd Sec., New Delhi, 1966–69; FCO (European Integration Dept), 1969–72; 1st Sec., UK Permanent Representation to EEC, 1972–76; Asst Head, Financial Relations Dept, FCO, 1976–77; Counsellor, Caracas, 1977–78; Hd of British Information Services, NY, 1978–83 and Counsellor, British Embassy, Washington, 1981–83; Dir of Res., FCO, 1983–86; Under Sec., Cabinet Office, 1986–88; Vis. Schol., Stanford Univ., 1988–89; Ambassador to Yugoslavia, 1989–92; Advr to Lord Carrington, 1992, Lord Owen, 1992–93, Peace Conf. on Yugoslavia; Ambassador to Argentina, 1993–97. *Recreations*: reading (A. Powell, Byron), music (Rolling Stones, Mozart). *Address*: 13 Raby Place, Bath BA2 4EH.

**HALL, Prof. Philip**, PhD; Professor and Head, School of Mathematical Sciences, Monash University, since 2014; *b* 21 Feb. 1950; *s* of John Thomas Hall and Pamela Hall; *m* 1973, Eileen Haig; two *d*. *Educ*: Goole Grammar Sch.; Imperial Coll., London (BSc 1971; PhD 1973). Reader in Maths, Imperial Coll., London, 1984–85; Prof. of Maths, Exeter Univ., 1985–90; Beyer Prof. of Maths, Manchester Univ., 1990–96; Prof. of Applied Maths, 1996, Hd, Dept of Maths, 1998–2003, ICSTM, then Imperial Coll. London. Sen. Fellow, EPSRC, 1990–95. *Publications*: about 120 articles on fluid dynamics, mostly with relevance to aerodynamics and transition to turbulence. *Recreations*: golf, reading, theatre, travelling. *Address*: School of Mathematical Sciences, Monash University, Vic 3800, Australia.

**HALL, Philip David**; Chairman, PHA Media (formerly Phil Hall Associates), since 2005; *b* 8 Jan. 1955; *s* of Norman Philip Hall and Olive Jean Hall; *m* 1997, Marina Thomson, patent attorney; one *s* two *d*. *Educ*: Beal Grammar Sch., Ilford. Reporter: Dagenham Post, 1974–77; Ilford Recorder, 1977–80; Sub-editor: Newham Recorder, 1980–84; Weekend Magazine, 1984–85; The People: Reporter, 1985–86; Chief Reporter, 1986–89; News Editor, 1989–92; News Editor, Sunday Express, 1992–93; News of the World: Asst Editor (Features), 1993–94; Dep. Editor, 1994–95; Editor, 1995–2000; with Max Clifford Associates, 2000; Ed.-in-chief, Hello! magazine, 2001–02; Man. Dir, Contract Publg Div., Press Assoc., 2002–03; Dir of Editorial Develt, Trinity Mirror, 2003–05. Mem., Press Complaints Commn, 1998–2000, 2002–03. Member: Guild of Editors; PPA, 2001–02. *Recreations*: golf, cinema, theatre. *Address*: PHA Media, Hammer House, 117 Wardour Street, W1F 0UN. *T*: (020) 7025 1352. *Clubs*: Ivy; Stoke Park.

**HALL, Philip Ridley**, OBE 2003; HM Diplomatic Service; Consul General, Jerusalem, since 2017; *b* Chichester, 11 Oct. 1967; *s* of late J. Ridley Hall and Janette Lavinia Hall; *m* 2005, Karine; one *s* two *d*. *Educ*: Cranleigh Sch.; Gonville and Caius Coll., Cambridge (BA Law 1989); Universitaet des Saarlandes (Postgrad. Cert. Eur. Integration (Law) 1993); London Sch. of Econs and Political Sci. (Exec. Masters Public Policy 2017). Admitted solicitor; articled clerk, Herbert Smith, Solicitors, London and Brussels, 1990–92; HM Treasury, 1994–97, UK Delegn to EU, 1995–97; joined FCO, 1997; Foreign and Commonwealth Office: Hd, Middle East Peace Process Section, 1999–2001; Deputy Head: Africa Dept (Equatorial), 2001–02; Middle East Dept (Iraq), 2002–03; Hd of Div., Europ. Secretariat, Cabinet Office, 2003–06; Dep. Hd of Mission, Bucharest, 2007–08; Defence Counsellor, UK Delegn to NATO, 2008–12; Hd, Counter Proliferation Dept, 2012–14; Additional Dir, Spending Rev., 2015. *Recreations*: cycling, acting, messing about on the river (rowing/skiffing, canoeing). *Address*: British Consulate-General, 15 Ragheb Nashashibi Street, PO Box 19690, Jerusalem 97200. *T*: (2) 5414100. *E*: Philip.Hall@fco.gov.uk.

**HALL, Raymond Walter**, CBE 1993; FREng; Chief Executive, Magnox Electric plc, 1996–98; *b* 24 Sept. 1933; *s* of Alfred Henry Hall and Elsie Frieda Hall; *m* 1955, Diane Batten; one *s* three *d*. *Educ*: Portsmouth, Grays Thurrock, and Gravesend Colls of Technology. FIMechE 1981; FIET (FIEE 1983); FNucI (FINucE 1983); FREng (FEng 1993). Engineering and managerial positions, CEGB, 1975–89: Station Manager: Trawsfynydd Nuclear Power Station, 1975–77; Hinkley Point A & B Nuclear Power Stations, 1978–82; Corporate Trng Manager, 1983–85; Corporate Dir of Personnel, 1986–87; Divl Dir of Generation, 1988–89; Exec. Dir, Operations, Nuclear Electric plc, 1990–95. World Association of Nuclear Operators: Gov., Main Bd, 1993–97; Chm., Paris Centre, 1993–97; Chairman: Orgn Producteurs d'Energie Nucléaire, 1994–97; British Nuclear Industry Forum, 1997–2002 (Mem. Bd, 1996–2002). Trustee, Bristol Exploratory, 1992–2000. FRSA 1980; FCMI (FIMgt 1980); FIPD 1988. Freeman: City of London, 1996; Worshipful Co. of Engrs, 1996 (Liveryman, 1997–). *Publications*: contribs to learned jls on nuclear engrg matters. *Recreations*: music, gardening, walking, golf, travel. *Address*: Kingsthorn, Trull, Taunton, Somerset TA3 7HA. *T*: (01823) 252325. *E*: hall.r15@sky.com.

**HALL, Rev. Canon Roger John**, MBE 1999; Chaplain of the Chapel Royal of St Peter ad Vincula, HM Tower of London, since 2007; a Deputy Priest in Ordinary to the Queen, since 2007; Canon of the Chapels Royal within the Tower of London, since 2012; *b* 1 Dec. 1953; *s* of Sydney and Patricia Hall; *m* 1979, Barbara Mary Hutchinson; one *s* two *d*. *Educ*: Wolsingham Sch., Co. Durham; Lincoln Theological Coll. Ordained deacon, 1984, priest, 1985; Asst Curate, St Giles, Shrewsbury with St Eata's, Atcham, 1984–87; Regtl Chaplain, 1987–90; Brigade Sen. Chaplain, 1990–95; Amport House: Asst Warden, 1996–98;

Warden, 1998–2000; Dep. Asst Chaplain Gen., Germany, 2000–01; Sen. Chaplain, Guard's Chapel, 2001–03; Asst Chaplain Gen., 2003–07. QHC 2006–07. Mem., Forces Synod, 1993–; Dir of Ordinands, 1996–2001; Warden of Readers, 1998–. Nat. Chaplain, BLESMA, 2001–; Chaplain: MoD Main Bldg, 2007–; Gallantry Medallist's League, 2019–; Sch. Chaplain, Bacon's Acad., 2007–; Hon. Chaplain: Co. of City of London Solicitors, 2007–; Co. of Builders Merchants, 2007–; Guild of Arts Scholars, Dealers and Collectors, 2007–; Co. of Security Professionals, 2007–. Member: Family Support Working Pty, SSAFA, 1998–; Scottish Veterans Housing Assoc., 2003–; Trustee, Chapter 1 Charity (formerly Christian Alliance Housing Assoc.), 2007–. Mem., Stone Masons' Co., 2007–; Mem., Anglo-German Soc. QCVS 1995. *Recreations:* music, art, reading, travel, ski-ing, shooting, café culture. *Address:* Chaplain's Residence, HM Tower of London, EC3N 4AB. *T:* (020) 3166 6796. *E:* roger.hall@hrp.org.uk. *Club:* East India.

HALL, Ruth, CB 2004; FRCP, FRCPCH, FFPH; Director, Health Protection Agency South West, 2006–09; *b* 8 Feb. 1948; *d* of Robert and Molly Dobson; *m* 1971, William Hall; two *s* two *d*. *Educ:* Sch. of St Helen and St Katharine, Abingdon; King's Coll. Hosp. Med. Sch., London (MB BS 1970). LRCP, MRCS 1970; FFPH (FFPHM 1994); FRCPCH 1997; FRCP 2000. Med. posts in London, 1970–71, Chester, 1971–73, and N Wales, 1973–97; Dir of Public Health, N Wales HA, 1995–97; CMO, Welsh Office, then Welsh Assembly Govt, 1997–2005; Dir of Public Health, Avon, Glos and Wilts Strategic HA, 2005–06. Member: MRC, 1997–2005; Public Health Interventions Adv. Cttee, NICE, 2005–16; Future Regulatory Adv. Panel, Ofwat, 2010–13; all-Wales Partnership, Canal and River Trust, 2013–15; Bd, Glandwr Cymru (Canal and River Trust in Wales), 2015–; Council, Canal and River Trust Council, 2016–; Council, Nat. Trust, 2016–; Vice Chair, Bd of Govs, Public Policy Inst. Wales, 2013–17; Advr, Wales Centre for Public Policy, 2017–; Chair, Nat. Access Forum Wales, 2013–18; Co-Chair, Mid Wales Healthcare Collaborative, 2015–18; non-executive Director: Envmt Agency, 2005–12; Natural Resources Wales, 2012–18; Health Educn and Improvement Wales, 2018–. Career Mentor, Office of Public Appts, Cabinet Office, 2009–. Vis. Prof., Faculty of Health and Social Care, UWE, 2006–; Ext. Examiner, Univ. of Surrey, 2012. Liveryman, Apothecaries' Soc., 2009; Freeman, City of London, 2008.

HALL, Sasha; *see* Wass, S.

HALL, Simon Robert Dawson, MA; Warden of Glenalmond College, 1987–91; *b* 24 April 1938; *s* of late Wilfrid Dawson Hall and Elizabeth Helen Hall (*née* Wheeler); *m* 1961, Jennifer Harverson; two *s*. *Educ:* Tonbridge School; University College, Oxford. 2nd Lieut, 7th Royal Tank Regt, 1956–58; Asst Master, Gordonstoun School, 1961–65; Joint Headmaster, Dunrobin School, 1965–68; Haileybury: Asst Master, 1969–79; Senior Modern Languages Master, 1970–76; Housemaster, Lawrence, 1972–79; Second Master, 1976–79; Headmaster, Milton Abbey School, 1979–87. 21st SAS Regt (TA), 1958–61; Intelligence Corps (V), 1968–71. *Recreations:* reading, music, motoring, sailing, hill-walking. *Address:* 54 Tuckers Court, Richmond Village, Witney, Oxon OX28 5DG.

HALL, Prof. the Rev. Stuart George; Priest-in-Charge, St Michael's, Elie, and St John's, Pittenweem, 1990–98; Professor of Ecclesiastical History, King's College, University of London, 1978–90; *b* 7 June 1928; *s* of George Edward Hall and May Catherine Hall; *m* 1st, 1953, Brenda Mary Henderson (*d* 2016); two *s* two *d*; 2nd, 2017, Eveline Mary Elliott. *Educ:* University Coll. Sch., Hampstead; New Coll., and Ripon Hall, Oxford (BA 1952, MA 1955, BD 1973). National Service, Army, 1947–48. Deacon 1954, priest 1955; Asst Curate, Newark-on-Trent Parish Church, 1954–58; Tutor, Queen's Coll., Birmingham, 1958–62; Lectr in Theology, Univ. of Nottingham, 1962–73, Sen. Lectr, 1973–78. President: Acad. Internat. des Scis Religieuses, 2006–11; Ecclesiastical History Soc., 1997. Editor for early church material, Theologische Realenzyklopädie. *Publications:* Melito of Sardis On Pascha and fragments: (ed) texts and translations, 1979, rev. edn 2013; (contrib.) The Easter Sermons of Gregory of Nyssa, 1981; (contrib.) El "Contra Eunomium I" en la producción literaria de Gregorio de Nisa, 1988, rev. edn, 2018; Doctrine and Practice in the Early Church, 1991, 2nd edn 2005; (ed) Gregory of Nyssa, Homilies on Ecclesiastes, 1993; (ed with Averil Cameron) Eusebius, Life of Constantine, 1999; (ed jtly) Gregory of Nyssa, Homilies of the Beatitudes, 2000; Heritage and Hope: the Episcopal churches in the East Neuk of Fife 1805–2005, 2004; (ed jtly) Decoding Early Christianity: truth and legend in the Early Church, 2007; (ed jtly) Gregory of Nyssa, Contra Eunomium II, 2007, rev. edn 2014; (ed) Jesus Christ Today, 2009; contrib. to vols of Procs of Acad. Internat. des Scis Religieuses, 1986–2011; contrib. to Studies in Church History, to Cambridge History of Christianity, Cambridge Ancient History, Expository Times, Heythrop Jl, Jl of Eccles. History, Jl of Theol Studies, Religious Studies, Studia Evangelica, Studia Patristica, Theology and Theologische Realenzyklopädie. *Recreations:* gardening, choral music. *Address:* 15 High Street, Elie, Leven, Fife KY9 1BY. *T:* (01333) 330216.

HALL, Susan Margaret; *see* Standring, S. M.

HALL, Suzanne; Headmistress, Rugby High School, 1998–2006; *b* 5 Jan. 1946; *d* of John and Louise Keats; *m* 1971, Eric Lonsdale Hall; two *s*. *Educ:* Braintree Grammar Sch.; Univ. of Wales (BSc Hons Chem. 1969); Univ. of Southampton (PhD research). Cancer res., ICRF, 1966; Information Scientist, 1970; teacher, 1975; Dep. Hd, Chelmsford Co. High Sch., 1993–98. *Publications:* papers on x-ray crystallography in Jl of Chemical Soc. *Recreations:* reading, crosswords, Scrabble, gardening. *Address:* December House, 2 Highfields Meadow, East Bilney, Dereham, Norfolk NR20 4FB. *T:* (01362) 861459.

HALL, Col Thomas Armitage, CVO 1998; OBE 1966; HM Body Guard of Honourable Corps of Gentlemen at Arms, 1980–98 (Lieutenant, 1994–98); *b* 13 April 1928; *s* of Athelstan Argyle Hall and Nancy Armitage Hall (*née* Dyson); *m* 1954, Mariette Hornby; two *s* four *d*. *Educ:* Heatherdown Sch.; Eton Coll. Commissioned, 11th Hussars, 1947, Berlin; ADC to CIGS, 1952–53; Adjutant, 11 H Malayan Emergency, 1953–56 (despatches); Army Staff Coll., 1960–61; Sqdn Leader 11 H, Aden, Gulf, Kenya, Kuwait, 1961–62; Instr, RN Staff Coll., Greenwich, 1962–64; CO 11 H, Germany, 1965–66; Equerry to King of Thailand, 1966; Regtl Col, Royal Hussars, 1974–83; Advr to Crown Prince of Japan, 1983–85. Regl Dir, Lloyds Bank, 1983–85. Chm., Internat. Lang. Centres, 1971–88. High Sheriff, Oxon, 1981–82. FRSA. *Recreations:* ski-ing, shooting, travel, architecture. *Address:* Marylands Farm, Chiselhampton, Oxford OX44 7XD. *T:* (01865) 890350. *Club:* Cavalry and Guards (Chm., 1990–96; Vice Pres., 2007–13).

HALL, Thomas William; Under-Secretary, Department of Transport, 1976–79 and 1981–87; retired; *b* 8 April 1931; *s* of Thomas William and Euphemia Jane Hall; *m* 1961, Anne Rosemary Hellier Davis; two *d*. *Educ:* Hitchin Grammar Sch.; St John's Coll., Oxford (MA); King's Coll., London (MA). Asst Principal, Min. of Supply, 1954; Principal: War Office, Min. of Public Building and Works, Cabinet Office, 1958–68; Asst Sec., Min. of Public Building and Works, later DoE, 1968–76; Under Sec., Depts of Environment and Transport, 1979–81. Member: Road Traffic Law Review, 1985–88; Transport Tribunal, 1990–99. *Recreations:* literature, gardening, walking. *Address:* 43 Bridge Road, Epsom, Surrey KT17 4AN. *T:* (01372) 725900.

HALL, Veronica Jane, (Ronni); *see* Ancona, V. J.

HALL, His Honour Victor Edwin; a Circuit Judge, 1994–2013; Family Mediator and Arbitrator, Trinity Family Mediation and Arbitration, since 2013; *b* 2 March 1948; *s* of Robert Arthur Victor James Hall and Gwladys (*née* Fukes); *m* 1974, Rosemarie Berdina Jenkinson; two *s*; *m* 2009, Anita Elaine Everill. *Educ:* Univ. of Hull (LLB 1969). Lectr in Law, Kettering Tech. Coll., 1969–71; called to the Bar, Inner Temple, 1971; an Asst Recorder, 1983–88; a Recorder, 1988–94. Designated Family Judge, Leicester County Court, 1996–2003. Asst Parly Boundary Comr, 1991–93; Mem./Pres., Mental Health Review Tribunals, 1997–2003. Member: Cttee, Council of Circuit Judges, 1997–2002 (Treas., 1999–2001); Family Rules Cttee, 2001–04; Jt Course Dir, Family Seminars, 2002–03; Dir of Studies, 2004–06, Judicial Studies Bd. Lectr in Dispute Resolution, Univ. of Derby, 2014–. Mem. Adv. Cttee, Commonwealth Judicial Educn Inst., 2004–06; Sec.-Gen., 2008–11, Mem., Linguistics Prog., 2014–, European Judicial Trng Network, Brussels. Member, Board of Trustees: European Acad. of Law, Trier, 2008–; Internat. Orgn for Judicial Trng, 2009– (Mem. Bd, 2006–04; European Vice Pres., 2004–09). External Examr in Family Law, City Univ., Hong Kong, 2010– (Adjunct Prof. of Law, 2005–08). *Recreations:* sailing (and dreaming about being on the water!), cookery, fell walking, gardening, cricket.

HALL, (Wallace) John; Regional Director, DTI East (Cambridge), Department of Trade and Industry, 1989–94; *b* 5 Oct. 1934; *s* of Claude Corbett Hall and Dulcie Hall (*née* Brinkworth); *m* 1962, Janet Bowen (*d* 2010); three *d*. *Educ:* Crypt Sch., Gloucester; Hertford Grammar Sch.; Downing Coll., Cambridge (MA Classics). National Service, RAF, 1953–55. Pirelli-General Cable Works Ltd, 1958–62; Sales Manager, D. Meredew Ltd, 1962–67; Principal, Min. of Technology, 1967–70; Dept of Trade and Industry, Civil Aviation Policy, 1970–72; Consul (Commercial), São Paulo, Brazil, 1972–76; Asst Secretary, Dept of Trade, Shipping Policy, 1976–79; Counsellor (Economic), Brasilia, 1979–81; Consul-Gen., São Paulo, 1981–83; Assistant Secretary, DTI: Internat. Trade Policy, 1983–85; Overseas Trade (E Asia), 1985–89. *Recreations:* bridge, croquet, walking. *Address:* 10 Greenway, Letchworth Garden City, Herts SG6 3UG.

HALL, Dame Wendy, (Dame Wendy Chandler), DBE 2009 (CBE 2000); PhD; FRS 2009; FREng; Executive Director, Web Science Institute, since 2014, and Regius Professor of Computer Science, since 2017, University of Southampton (Professor of Computer Science, 1994–2017); *b* 25 Oct. 1952; *d* of Kenneth D. Hall and Elizabeth Hall; *m* 1980, Dr Peter E. Chandler. *Educ:* Ealing Grammar Sch. for Girls; Univ. of Southampton (BSc Maths 1974; PhD 1977); City Univ. (MSc Computer Sci. 1986). CEng 1990; FIET (FIEE 1998). Lecturer: in Engrg, Oxford Poly., 1977–78; La Sainte Union Coll. of Higher Educn, 1978–84; University of Southampton: Lectr, 1984–90, Sen. Lectr, 1990–94, Dept of Electronics and Computer Sci.; Hd, Sch. of Electronics and Computer Sci., 2002–07; Dean, Faculty of Physical and Applied Scis, subseq. Faculty of Physical Scis and Engrg, 2010–14. Kluge Chair in Technol. and Society, Library of Congress, 2016. Mem., EPSRC, 1997–2002 (Sen. Fellow, 1996–2001). Member: Prime Minister's Council for Sci. and Technol., 2004–10; Scientific Council, European Res. Council, 2005–10; Bd, British Library, 2007–15; Bd, DSTL, 2012–18; Council, Royal Soc., 2013–16; Bd, Digital Catapult, 2014–; Global Commn on Internet Governance, 2014–; Artificial Intelligence Council, 2019–; Chm., Educn Cttee, British Council, 2014–17. Co-Chm., Rev. of UK Artificial Intelligence Sector, 2017 (Hall/Pesenti Report publd 2017); UK Artificial Intelligence Skills Champion, 2018–. Non-exec. Dir, Idox plc, 2012–15. Pres., ACM, 2008–10. FBCS 1996 (Pres., 2003–04); FREng 2000 (Sen. Vice Pres., 2005–08); FCGI 2002; FACM 2011. Hon. Fellow, Cardiff Univ., 2004. Hon. DSc: Oxford Brookes; 2002; Glamorgan, 2005; Loughborough, 2008; Glasgow, 2009; QUB, 2012; Birmingham, 2012; Sussex, 2013; Hon. PhD Pretoria, 2007; Hon. LLD Dalhousie, 2012; Hon. Dr Aristotle Univ. of Thessaloniki, 2010; Hon. DSc: City, 2013; Bradford, 2015; Open, 2015; Hon. DSc(Eng) UCL, 2014. *Publications:* (jtly) Rethinking Hypermedia: the microcosm approach, 1996; (jtly) Hypermedia and the Web: an engineering approach, 1999; (jtly) A Framework for Web Science, 2006; articles in jls, conf. proceedings. *Recreations:* going to the gym and swimming, walking with my husband, particularly in the New Forest; fine wines and dining, travelling, theatre; favourite form of relaxation is reading a good book on a sunny beach or shopping! *Address:* Web Science Institute, University of Southampton, Southampton SO17 1BJ. *T:* (023) 8059 2388.

HALL, Sir William (Joseph), KCVO 2009; JP; Lord-Lieutenant of Co. Down, 1996–2009; *b* 1 Aug. 1934; *s* of late Capt. Roger Hall and Marie Hall; *m* 1964, Jennifer Mary Corbett (*d* 2008); one *s* one *d*; *m* 2012, Catharine Dorinda Okuno (*née* Clements). *Educ:* Ampleforth Coll., York. SSC, Irish Guards, 1952–56. With W. C. Pitfield & Hugh McKay, investment mgt co., then with Shell Oil, Canada, 1956–62; dir of own wine wholesale business, also sheep farmer and commercial narcissus bulb grower, 1962–90, retired. Chm., Rostrevor and Warrenpoint Bee Keepers Assoc., 2010–. Mem., Lord Chancellor's Adv. Cttee on JPs, 1975–2009 (Chm., Ards Div., 1996–2009). County Down: JP 1973; DL 1975–93; High Sheriff, 1983; Vice Lord Lieutenant, 1993–96. NI ACF, 1967–79 (Hon. Major, 1980; Pres., NI ACFA, 1999–2002); President: RFCA NI, 2000–05; Ulster Br., Irish Guards Assoc., 2009– (Chm., 1979–2009). Hon. Col, 1st Bn (NI), ACF, 2003–05. Vice Pres., RBL, NI, 2005–. KStJ 2011 (CStJ 1997), Kt Comdr, Commandery of Ards (Order of St John), 2011. *Recreations:* field sports in general, bridge, travel abroad when time allows! *Address:* The Mill House, Narrow Water, Warrenpoint, Co. Down, Northern Ireland BT34 3LW. *T:* (028) 4175 4904. *Clubs:* Army and Navy; Down Hunt (Downpatrick).

HALL HALL, Alexandra Mary, (Mrs D. C. Twining); HM Diplomatic Service; Brexit Counsellor, British Embassy, Washington, since 2018; *b* 1 Feb. 1964; *d* of late Francis Alleyne Hall Hall and Mary Hall Hall (*née* Whittaker); *m* 2002, Daniel Charles Twining; two *s*. *Educ:* Durham Univ. (BA Jt Hons Politics and Econs 1986); Sch. of Oriental and African Studies, Univ. of London (Advanced Thai); FCO Advanced Thai Dip. 1999. Entered FCO, 1986; Desk Officer, SE Asian Dept, FCO, 1987–88; Second Sec., Political and Inf. Officer, Bangkok, 1989–93; Hd, Humanitarian Section, UN Dept, FCO, 1993–95; European Secretariat, Cabinet Office (on secondment), 1995–97; Hd, ME Peace Process Section, FCO, 1997–98; First Sec. (Political), Washington, 1999–2001; Counsellor, on secondment to US State Dept, Washington, 2002–04; Hd of Human Rights, Democracy and Good Governance Gp, FCO, 2004–06; Political Counsellor, New Delhi, 2006–07; Dep. Hd of Mission, British Embassy, Bogota, 2009–11; Ambassador to Georgia, 2013–16; Sen. non-resident Fellow, Atlantic Council, 2016–18. *Recreations:* travel, tennis, ski-ing, archery, dogs, hard labour to convert a scrap of wilderness in W Virginia, USA into the American answer to Sissinghurst, Kent. *Address:* c/o Foreign and Commonwealth Office, King Charles Street, SW1A 2AH.

HALL-MATTHEWS, Rt Rev. Dr Anthony Francis Berners; Bishop of Carpentaria, 1984–96, Emeritus, 2011; Chaplain and Welfare Officer, Honourable Company of Air Pilots (formerly Guild of Air Pilots and Air Navigators), Australian Region, since 2010; *b* 14 Nov. 1940; *s* of Rev. Cecil Berners Hall and Barbara (who *m* 1944, Rt Rev. Seering John Matthews); *m* 1966, Valerie Joan Cecil; two *s* three *d*. *Educ:* Sanctuary School, Walsingham, Norfolk; Southport School, Queensland; St Francis Theol Coll., Milton, Brisbane; James Cook Univ., Qld (Graduate Dip. of Arts, 1997; PhD 2005). ThL Aust. Coll. of Theology, 1962. Asst Curate at Darwin, 1963–66; Chaplain, Carpentaria Aerial

Mission, 1966–84, and Rector of Normanton, 1966–76; Hon. Canon of Carpentaria, 1970–76; Archdeacon of Cape York Peninsula, 1976–84; Priest-in-charge of Cooktown, Dio. Carpentaria, 1976–84; Bishop Resident in Mareeba, Dio. N Qld, 1999–2000. Liaison Officer for PNG, Third Order of Soc. of St Francis (Provincial Chaplain, 2003–09). Principal, Carpentaria Consulting Services, 1997–2006. Centenary Medal (Australia), 2001. *Publications*: From Village to Mission then Community, 2004; A Remarkable Venture of Faith, 2007. *Recreations*: flying, reading, composting. *Address*: 5 Wattle Close, Yungaburra, Queensland 4884, Australia. *T*: (7) 40953188.

**HALL-SMITH, Vanessa Frances,** MBE 2009; Director, British Institute of Florence, 2004–11; *b* 30 April 1951; *d* of late Patrick Hall-Smith and Angela Hall-Smith; two *d*. *Educ*: Roedean Sch., Brighton; Univ. of Exeter (LLB); Johannes Gutenberg Univ. Mainz; Univ. d'Aix-Marseille. Called to the Bar, Inner Temple, 1976; Sec., Internat. Law Assoc., 1976–79; admitted solicitor, 1993; Partner: Simkins Partnership, Solicitors, 1996–2000; Harrison Curtis Solicitors, 2001–03. Trustee, Estorick Collection of Modern Italian Art, 2011–. Co-ed., Rivista, Mag. of British Italian Soc., 2013–18. *Publications*: (contrib. ed) Butterworths Encyclopaedia of Forms and Precedents, Advertising vol., 5th edn 1993. *Recreations*: theatre, music, cinema, cooking.

**HALLAM, Bishop of, (RC),** since 2014; **Rt Rev. Ralph Heskett,** CSSR; *b* Sunderland, 3 March 1953. Ordained priest, 1976; Superior and Dir of Missions, Redemptorist Community at Kinnoull, Perth, 1987–90; Superior, Redemptorist Community and Parish of Our Lady of the Annunciation, Bishop Eton, Liverpool, 1990–96; on sabbatical, 1996–97; Novice Master, Canterbury, 1997–99; Parish Priest, St Mary's, Clapham, 1999–2008; Bishop of Gibraltar, (RC), 2010–14. *Address*: Bishop's House, 75 Norfolk Road, Sheffield S2 2SZ.

**HALLAM, David John Alfred;** communications specialist; Managing Director, Horizon Glen Ltd, since 2003; *b* 13 June 1948; *s* of Arthur Ernest Hallam and Marjorie Ethel Hallam (née Gibbs); *m* 1988, Claire Vanstone; two *s* one *d*. *Educ*: Upton House Secondary Modern Sch., London; Univ. of Sussex (BA); Brighton Poly. (Dip. Marketing); Univ. of Birmingham (MA). Res. Asst, Sussex CC, 1971–73; Information Officer, Birmingham Social Services Dept, 1973–80; Public Relations Officer, Nat. Children's Home, 1984–89; Dir of Communications, Birmingham Heartlands and Solihull NHS Trust, 2000–02. Mem., Sandwell BC, W Midlands, 1976–79. MEP (Lab) Hereford and Shropshire, 1994–99; contested (Lab) W Midlands Reg., 1999. Mem., Agricl Cttee, 1994–99, Substitute Mem., Budget Cttee, 1997–99, Eur. Parlt; Mem., Slovak Delegn, 1995–99; Substitute Mem. of Israel Delegn and to EU African, Caribbean and Pacific Parly Assembly, 1994–99. W Midlands Rep., Nat. Members' Council, Co-op Gp, 2016–18. Contested (Lab): Solihull, 1979; Shropshire and Staffordshire, European parly elections, 1984, 1989; Hereford, 2001. MCIM; MCIPR. Mem., NUJ. Methodist local preacher. Editor, The Potter, newspaper, 1982–94. *Publications*: Eliza Asbury: her cottage and her son, 2003; One Hundred Years of Service to Newton: the history of Newton Road United Reformed (Allen Memorial) Church, 1917–2017, 2018; Taking on the Men: the first women Parliamentary candidates in the West Midlands, 2018. *T*: (0121) 429 4207. *E*: davidhallam5@aol.com. *W*: www.davidhallam.com.

**HALLAM, Jacob William;** QC 2017; a Recorder, since 2016; *b* Leicester, 4 Jan. 1973; *s* of Peter Hallam and Jennifer Hallam (née Barnett, now Evans); *m* 1999, Juliet Foster; two *d*. *Educ*: Loughborough Grammar Sch.; Corpus Christi Coll., Cambridge (MA Hons Hist.). Called to the Bar, Gray's Inn, 1996; Jun. Treasury Counsel, 2014. *Recreations*: hill walking, ski-ing, alternative music, reading historical books. *Address*: 6 KBW College Hill, 21 College Hill, EC4R 2RP. *T*: (020) 3301 0910. *E*: clerks@6kbw.com.

**HALLAM, Prof. Philip,** PhD; CEng; Vice-Chancellor and Chief Executive Officer, Arden University, since 2015; *b* Nottingham, 26 April 1964; *s* of Robert and Laura Hallam; *m* 1999, Julia Wilkinson; one *s* one *d*. *Educ*: Huddersfield Poly. (BSc Hons Electrical and Electronic Engrg 1986; PhD 1990). CEng 1992. Sen. Lectr, Huddersfield Poly., subseq. Univ. of Huddersfield, 1990–95; Principal Lectr, Manchester Metropolitan Univ., 1995–97; Hd of Div., Univ. of Northumbria, 1997–98; Prof. and Associate Dir, UCE, 1998–2001; Man. Dir, 2002–06, CEO, 2006–15, Resource Develt Internat. Ltd. *Recreations*: walking, cycling, family, theatre. *Address*: Arden University, Arden House, Middlemarch Park, Coventry CV3 4FJ. *T*: (024) 7651 5700. *E*: phallam@arden.ac.uk, phil_hallam@hotmail.com.

**HALLAM, Prof. Susan,** MBE 2015; PhD; CPsychol; Professor of Education and Music Psychology (formerly Professor of Education), Institute of Education, University of London, 2003–14, now Emerita (Dean, Faculty of Policy and Society, 2007–13); *b* Leicester, 9 April 1949; *d* of Thomas and Gwendoline Whetstone; *m* 1971, Richard John Hallam, MBE; one *s*. *Educ*: Hinckley Grammar Sch., Leics; Royal Acad. of Music (LRAM, ARAM 2006); Univ. of London (BA Psychol. (ext.)); City of Birmingham Poly. (Cert Ed); Inst. of Educn, Univ. of London (MSc, PhD 1992). CPsychol 1994. Principal 2nd violin, Midland Light Orch., 1971–77; peripatetic violin teacher: Sandwell Educn Authy, 1978–80; Oxon Local Authy, 1980–82; Thame Area Music School: Dir, 1982–88; Sen. Instrumental Teacher, 1983–88; Hd of Strings, 1988–90; Lectr in Psychol., City of Westminster Coll., 1991; Course Tutor, Open Univ., 1991–95; Lectr, then Sen. Lectr, Inst. of Educn, Univ. of London, 1991–2000; Prof. of Educn (Teaching and Learning) and Hd, Curriculum Acad. Div., Westminster Inst. of Educn, Oxford Brookes Univ., 2000–01; Institute of Education, University of London: Sen. Lectr, 2001, Reader, 2001–03, in Educn and Chair, Learning and Teaching Cttee; Hd, Sch. of Lifelong Educn and Internat. Develt, 2004–07. Subject Reviewer for Educn, 2000–01, Instnl Auditor, 2001–09, QAA. British Psychological Society: Sec., Educn Section, 1998–99; Chair, Psychol. of Educn Section, 1999–2001, 2004–06 and 2011–12; British Educational Research Association: Mem. Council, 2000–02; Treas., 2002–08; Mem., Advocacy Cttee, Internat. Soc. for Music Educn, 2006–08. Jt Ed., British Psychol Soc. Educn Section Rev., 1996–99; Ed., Psychol. of Music, 2002–07. AFBPsS 1995; FHEA 2001; FAcSS (AcSS 2003). FRSA 1996. Hon. Mem., BPsS, 2014; Hon. Lifetime Mem., Internat. Soc. for Music Educn, 2014. *Publications*: (with C. Roaf) Here Today, Here Tomorrow: helping schools to promote attendance, 1995; Improving School Attendance, 1996; Instrumental Teaching: a practical guide to better teaching and learning, 1998; (with J. Ireson) Ability Grouping in Education, 2001; (jtly) Effective Pupil Grouping in the Primary School: a practical guide, 2002; Ability Grouping in Schools: a literature review, 2002; Homework: the evidence, 2004; Music Psychology in Education, 2006; (with L. Rogers) Improving Behaviour and Attendance at School, 2008; (ed jtly) Oxford Handbook of Music Psychology, 2008, 2nd edn 2016; (ed jtly) Music Education in the 21st Century in the United Kingdom: achievements, analysis and aspirations, 2010; (with Helena Gaunt) Preparing for Success: a practical guide for young musicians, 2012; (jtly) Active Ageing with Music: supporting wellbeing in the third and fourth ages, 2014; The Power of Music, 2015; Psychology of Music (The Psychology of Everything), 2018; (with L. Rogers) Homework: the evidence, 2018; contrib. chapters to books and articles to jls. *Recreations*: reading, films, walking. *Address*: UCL Institute of Education, 20 Bedford Way, WC1H 0AL. *T*: (01908) 522850, *Fax*: (020) 7612 6632. *E*: s.hallam@ucl.ac.uk.

**HALLAM SMITH, Elizabeth Mary,** CB 2017; PhD; FSA, FRHistS; independent scholar and consultant; Director of Information Services and Librarian, House of Lords, 2006–16; *b* 5 Nov. 1950; *d* of Edwin William Lewis Hallam and Barbara Mary Hallam; *m* 1975, Terence Stephen Smith (marr. diss. 2004); one *s* one *d*. *Educ*: Bath High Sch. for Girls; Westfield Coll., London (BA Hons Hist.; PhD Hist.). FRHistS 1980; FSA 1982. Tutorial Fellow, Univ. of Reading, 1975–76; Public Record Office: Asst Keeper, 1976–88; Hd, Publishing and Publicity, 1988–94; Dir, Public Services, 1994–2003; Dir, Nat. Adv. and Public Services, National Archives, 2003–06. Chm., Nat. Council on Archives, 2005–06. Vis. Prof., Sch. of Liby, Archives and Information, UCL, 2007–12; Hon. Res. Prof., Univ. of York, 2016–; Hon. Res. Fellow, UEA, 2015–. Mem., Westminster Abbey Fabric Commn, 2009–. Chairman: Adv. Bd, Victoria County History, 2012–15; Adv. Bd, St Stephen's Chapel Westminster Proj., 2013–15; Mem., Rlwy Heritage Designation Adv. Bd, 2015–; Res. Advr, Architecture and Heritage, Houses of Parlt, 2016–. Vice Pres., Soc. of Antiquaries of London, 1998–2002; Hon. Vice Pres., Soc. of Genealogists, 1999–2014. FRSA 1999. *Publications*: Capetian France 987–1328, 1980, 2nd edn 2001 (with Judith Everard); Itinerary of Edward II and his Household, 1307–1328, 1984; Domesday Book through Nine Centuries, 1986; The Domesday Project Book, 1986; (ed) The Plantagenet Chronicles, 1986; (ed) Chronicles of the Age of Chivalry, 1987; (ed) Chronicles of the Wars of the Roses, 1988; (ed) Chronicles of the Crusades, 1989; (ed) Saints: over 200 Patron Saints for today, 1994; (ed) Gods and Goddesses, 1996; (ed with Andrew Prescott) The British Inheritance: a treasury of historic documents, 1999; Domesday Souvenir Guide, 2000; (ed with D. Bates) Domesday Book, 2001; articles on inf. sci. and hist. in learned jls. *Recreations*: travel, walking, music, gardens, historical research. *Address*: House of Commons, SW1P 3JA. *E*: hallamsmithe@parliament.uk.

**HALLATT, Rt Rev. David Marrison;** an Assistant Bishop, Diocese of Salisbury, since 2011; *b* 15 July 1937; *s* of John Vincent Hallatt and Edith Elliott Hallatt; *m* 1967, Margaret Smitton; two *s*. *Educ*: Birkenhead School; Southampton Univ. (BA Hons Geography 1959); St Catherine's Coll., Oxford (BA Theology 1962; MA 1966). Curate, St Andrew's, Maghull, Liverpool, 1963–67; Vicar, All Saints, Totley, dio. Sheffield, 1967–75; Team Rector, St James & Emmanuel, Didsbury, Manchester, 1975–89; Archdeacon of Halifax, 1989–94; Bishop Suffragan of Shrewsbury, 1994–2001; an Asst Bishop, Dio. of Sheffield, 2001–10. FRGS 2009. *Recreations*: walking, birdwatching, music, crosswords, golf. *Address*: St Nicholas Hospital, St Nicholas Road, Salisbury, Wilts SP1 2SW. *T*: (01722) 413360. *E*: david.hallatt@btopenworld.com.

**HALLCHURCH, David Thomas,** TD 1965; Chief Justice, Turks and Caicos Islands, West Indies, 1996–98; *b* 4 April 1929; *s* of Walter William Hallchurch and Marjorie Pretoria Mary Hallchurch (née Cooper); *m* 1st, 1954, Gillian Mary Jagger (marr. diss. 1972); three *s*; 2nd, 1972, Susan Kathryn Mather Brennan; one step *s* one step *d*. *Educ*: Bromsgrove Sch.; Trinity Coll., Oxford (MA Hons). Called to the Bar, Gray's Inn, 1953; Whitehead Travelling Scholarship, Canada and USA, 1953–54; practised as barrister-at-law on Midland and Oxford Circuit, 1954–60 and 1964–96; a Recorder, 1980–97. Puisne Judge, Botswana, 1986–88; Actg Chief Justice, Turks and Caicos Is, 1993. Pt-time Immigration Adjudicator, 1990–96; Asst Comr, Parly Boundary Commn for England, 1992. Legal Mem., Mental Health Review Tribunal for the West Midlands, 1979–86. Major, Staffs Yeomanry (Queen's Own Royal Regiment), TA, 1953–66. *Publications*: The Law is Not a Bore, 2008. *Recreations*: cricket, drawing (cartoons). *Address*: Neachley House, Tong, Shifnal, Shropshire TF11 8PH. *Club*: Vincent's (Oxford).

**HALLETT;** *see* Hughes-Hallett and Hughes Hallett.

**HALLETT, Anthony Philip;** Director, Consortio Security, since 2017; *b* 11 Feb. 1945; *s* of late Maurice George Hallett and Ann Halliwell Bailey; *m* 1972, Faith Mary Holland-Martin; three *s*. *Educ*: Ipswich Sch.; Britannia RN Coll. Joined RN 1963; served in HM Ships Victorious and Hermes; Flag Lieut, Hong Kong; HMS Eskimo; RNC Greenwich; BRNC, 1975–77; MoD, 1978–79; HMS Invincible, 1979–81; served C-in-C Fleet, 1982–83; HMS Illustrious, 1983–85; MoD, 1986–90; RNSC Greenwich, 1990–91; Sec. to Chief of Fleet Support, 1992–94; Captain, RN, retd 1995. Dir, CE Security, 2016–17. Rugby Football: Navy Captain, 1969; 11 caps; played for US Portsmouth, Banbury, Blackheath, Richmond, Oxfordshire, S Counties, Combined Services, Hong Kong *v* England 1971. Rugby Football Union: Mem., 1979–97; Privilege Mem., 1997–; Chm., Ground Cttee, 1979–95; Chm., Twickenham Stadium Redevelt, 1991–95; Sec., 1995–97; Chief Exec., 1997; Selector and Chm., RN RU, 1985–94. Richmond Football Club: Chm., 1991–95 and 1999–2004; Chief Exec., 1998–99; Dir, 2000–18; Pres., 2004–07. Chm., CE Facilities Services Ltd (formerly Cleanevent Gp Ltd), 2012–16. Chm., Beckford and Ashton Br., RBL, 2016–. *Recreations*: gardening (Mem., Nat. Gardens Scheme), contemporary art, cricket, Rugby (Life Mem., Richmond Rugby and RFU), field sports. *Address*: Whitcombe, Overbury, Tewkesbury GL20 7NZ. *T*: (01386) 725206. *Clubs*: Turf, East India, MCC, Lord's Taverners.

**HALLETT, Prof. Christine Margaret,** PhD; FRSE; Professor of Social Policy, 1995–2010, and Principal and Vice-Chancellor, 2004–10, University of Stirling; *b* 4 May 1949; *d* of Richard William Hallett and Gwendoline Hallett (née Owen). *Educ*: Newnham Coll., Cambridge (BA 1970); Loughborough Univ. (PhD Social Policy 1994). Civil servant, DHSS, 1970–74; research and teaching posts: Oxford Univ., 1974–76; Keele Univ., 1976–83; Univ. of WA, 1983–84; Univ. of Leicester, 1984–89; University of Stirling: Reader in Social Policy, 1989–95; Sen. Dep. Principal, 2001–03. A Civil Service Comr, 2008–13. Non-exec. Dir, Royal Bournemouth and Christchurch Hosps NHS Foundn Trust, 2015–. Trustee, UKCISA, 2007–11 (Chm., 2007–11). Mem. Bd, Bournemouth Univ. 2010–12. FRSE 2002. *Publications*: (with O. Stevenson) Child Abuse: aspects of interprofessional co-operation, 1979; The Personal Social Services in Local Government, 1982; (ed) Women and Social Services Department, 1989; (with E. Birchall) Co-ordination and Child Protection, 1992; Interagency Co-ordination in Child Protection, 1995; (with E. Birchall) Working Together in Child Protection, 1995; (ed) Women and Social Policy: an introduction, 1996; (ed jtly) Social Exclusion and Social Work, 1998; (ed jtly) Hearing the Voices of Children: social policy for a new century, 2003; monographs; contrib. learned jls. *Recreations*: golf, walking, tennis, music.

**HALLETT, Rt Hon. Dame Heather (Carol),** DBE 1999; PC 2005; **Rt Hon. Lady Justice Hallett;** a Lord Justice of Appeal, since 2005; Vice-President, Court of Appeal (Criminal Division), 2013–19; *b* 16 Dec. 1949; *d* of late Hugh Hallett, QPM and Doris Hallett; *m* 1974, Nigel Wilkinson, *qv*; two *s*. *Educ*: St Hugh's Coll., Oxford (MA; Hon. Fellow, 1999). Called to the Bar, Inner Temple, 1972, Bencher, 1993 (Treasurer, 2011); QC 1989; a Recorder, 1989–99; a Dep. High Court Judge, 1995–99; a Judge of the High Court of Justice, QBD, 1999–2005. Leader, S Eastern Circuit, 1995–97; Presiding Judge, Western Circuit, 2001–04; Vice Pres., QBD, 2012–14. Mem., Judicial Appts Commn, 2006–10 (Vice-Chm., 2007–10); Chm., Judicial College (formerly Judicial Studies Bd), 2010–14 (Mem., 2000–04); Chm., Security Vetting Appeal Panel, 2019–. Chm., Gen. Council of the Bar, 1998 (Vice Chm., 1997). Hon. LLD: Derby, 2000; UCL, 2012; Portsmouth, 2012; DUniv Open, 2004. *Recreations*: theatre, music, games. *Address*: Royal Courts of Justice, Strand, WC2A 2LL.

[Created a Baroness (Life Peer), 2019 but title not gazetted at time of going to press.]

**HALLETT, Prof. Mark Louis,** PhD; Director of Studies, Paul Mellon Centre for Studies in British Art, since 2012; *b* Worcester, 11 March 1965; *s* of Roger Hallett and Linda Hallett; *m* 2005, Lynda Murphy; one *d*. *Educ:* Tregaron Secondary Sch., Dyfed; Pembroke Coll., Cambridge (BA Hons Hist. 1986); Courtauld Inst. of Art (MA Hons Hist. of Art 1989; PhD Hist. of Art 1995). University of York: Lectr, 1994–2001, Sen. Lectr, 2001–04, Reader, 2004–06, in Hist. of Art; Prof. of History of Art, 2006–12; Hd, Dept of Hist. of Art, 2007–12. Andrew W. Mellon Fellow, Yale Univ., 1990–91. Co-Curator: Hogarth Exhibn, Musée du Louvre, Tate Britain and Caixa Forum, Barcelona, 2006–07; William Etty: art and controversy, York Art Gall., 2011–12; Joshua Reynolds: Experiments in Paint, Wallace Collection, 2015; George Shaw: A Corner of a Foreign Field, Yale Center for British Art, New Haven, 2018. Vis. Scholar, Pembroke Coll., Cambridge, 2013–14; Vis. Prof., Courtauld Inst. of Art, 2014–16. *Publications:* The Spectacle of Difference: graphic satire in the age of Hogarth, 1999; Hogarth, 2000; (ed with Jane Rendall) Eighteenth-Century York: culture, space and society, 2003; Faces in a Library: Sir Joshua Reynolds's 'Streatham Worthies', 2012; (ed jtly) Living with the Royal Academy: artistic ideals and experiences in England, 1768–1848, 2013; Reynolds: portraiture in action, 2014; (ed jtly) Court, Country, City: British art and architecture, 1660–1735, 2016; (with S. Turner) The Great Spectacle: 250 years of the Royal Academy Summer Exhibition, 2018; exhibition catalogues. *Recreations:* reading short stories and The New York Review of Books, watching films and football. *Address:* Paul Mellon Centre for Studies in British Art, 16 Bedford Square, WC1B 3JA. *T:* (020) 7580 0311. *E:* mhallett@paul-mellon-centre.ac.uk. *Club:* Athenæum.

**HALLETT, Dame Nancy Karen,** DBE 2013 (OBE 2004); Chief Executive, Homerton University Hospital NHS Foundation Trust, 1999–2012. *Educ:* City University (MSc Health Mgt 1998). Nurse trng, St Bartholomew's Hosp., 1974; Homerton University Hospital: Dir of Nursing, 1993; Dir of Service Develt, until 1999. Non-exec. Dir, The Royal Marsden, 2013–17.

**HALLETT, Rob Leonard;** Chief Executive Officer: Robomagic Live Ltd, since 2015; Robomagic 360, since 2015; Robomagic Capital, since 2015; *b* London, 9 March 1958; *s* of Vernon Harold Leonard Hallett and Alma Victoria Hallett (*née* Braham); *m* Yvette Isha Allen; one *s*. *Educ:* Holy Cross Primary Sch., Uckfield; Uckfield Sch.; Lewes Tertiary Coll. Dir, DBA Artist Agency, 1980–84; Man. Dir, Performance and Trident Studios, 1984–90; Director: Marshall Arts Ltd, 1990–2000; Mean Fiddler plc, 2000–04; Sen. Vice Pres., 2004–07, Pres., 2007–14, AEG Live; CEO, AEG Live UK, 2012–14. Member: Cttee, Julie's Bicycle, 2007–; Bd, Fund for Tolerance, Reconciliation and Peace, 2009–; Bd, Revox Internat. AG, 2012–; Bd, Tickets for Troops, 2014–. Fundraising Ambassador, Community Links, 2013–. *Recreations:* watching Chelsea FC, food, wine, not accepting universal alibi. *E:* rob@robomagiclive.com.

**HALLGARTEN, His Honour Anthony Bernard Richard;** QC 1978; a Circuit Judge, 1993–2004; Mercantile List Judge, Central London County Court, 1996–2004; arbitrator, since 2004; *b* 16 June 1937; *s* of late Fritz and Friedel Hallgarten; *m* 1962, Katherine Borchard (marr. diss. 1996); one *s* three *d*; *m* 1998, Theresa Carlson (*née* Tower). *Educ:* Merchant Taylors' Sch., Northwood; Downing Coll., Cambridge (BA). Called to the Bar, Middle Temple, 1961 (Barstow Scholar, Inns of Court, 1961); Bencher, 1987 (Reader, Lent 2006); a Recorder, 1990–93. Chm., Bar/Inns' Councils Jt Regulations Cttee, 1990–93. Mem., London Maritime Arbitrators' Assoc., 2008. Chair, Management Cttee, Camden Victim Support, 1989–93. *Recreations:* ski-ing, SW France, cycling. *Address:* 20 Essex Street, WC2R 3AL. *Clubs:* Garrick, MCC.

**HALLIDAY, Sir Alexander (Norman),** Kt 2019; PhD; FRS 2000; Professor, Department of Earth and Environmental Sciences and Director, Earth Institute, Columbia University, since 2018; *b* 11 Aug. 1952; *s* of Ronald James Rivers Halliday and Kathleen Elizabeth Halliday; *m* 1986, Christine Craig Young; two *s*. *Educ:* Univ. of Newcastle upon Tyne (BSc Hons Geol.; PhD Physics). Postdoctoral Fellow, 1976–81, Lectr, 1981–86, Scottish Univs Res. and Reactor Centre, E Kilbride; Department of Geological Sciences, University of Michigan: Associate Prof., 1986–91; Prof., 1991–98; Adjunct Prof., 1998–2000; Prof., ETH, Zürich, 1998–2004; Prof. of Geochem., 2004–18, Hd, Math., Phys. and Life Scis Div., 2007–15, Univ. of Oxford; Fellow: St Hugh's Coll., Oxford, 2004–12; Wadham Coll., Oxford, 2012–18. Member: NERC, 2004–11; Panel, UK RAE, 2005–08; Council, Royal Soc., 2011–18 (Physical Sec. and Vice-Pres., 2014–18). Trustee, Natural History Mus., 2006–. President: Geochemical Soc., 1995–97 (Fellow, 2001); European Assoc. for Geochemistry, 2007–08 (Urey Medal, 2012). Fellow, Amer. Geophysical Union, 2000 (Bowen Award, 1998; Pres. Volcanology, Geochemistry and Petrology sect., 2008–10); Foreign Associate, US Nat. Acad. of Scis, 2015. Murchison Medal, Geol Soc., 2003; Oxburgh Medal, Inst. of Measurement and Control, 2015. *Publications:* over 360 articles in sci. jls. *Recreation:* cycling. *Address:* Department of Earth and Environmental Sciences, Columbia University, Lamont-Doherty Earth Observatory, PO Box 1000, Palisades, NY 10964, USA.

**HALLIDAY, Charlotte Mary Irvine,** NEAC 1961; RWS 1976 (ARWS 1971); topographical artist; Keeper, New English Art Club, since 1989; *b* 5 Sept. 1935; *d* of late Edward Halliday, CBE, RP, RBA and Dorothy Halliday. *Educ:* Francis Holland Sch.; Royal Academy Sch. *Commissions* include: construction of the Shell Centre, 1957–59; head offices of many City banks and insurance cos, incl. Willis Faber, Nat West Tower; clubs, colleges, major ecclesiastical buildings, incl. St Paul's and Salisbury Cathedrals; numerous stately and private homes. *Publications:* (illus.) A. Stuart Gray, Edwardian Architecture, 1985; (with A. Stuart Gray) Fanlights, a visual architectural history, 1990. *Recreations:* choral singing, walking in the Downs, cats. *Address:* 36A Abercorn Place, St John's Wood, NW8 9XP. *T:* (020) 7289 1924; St Magnus Cottage, Houghton, near Arundel, W Sussex.

**HALLIDAY, Prof. Ian Gibson,** CBE 2009; PhD; FRSE, FLSW; Chief Executive, Scottish Universities Physics Alliance, 2005–09; Professor, University of Edinburgh, 2005–09, now Emeritus; *b* 5 Feb. 1940; *s* of John Alexander Halliday and Gladys (*née* Taylor); *m* 1965, Ellenor Gardiner Hervey Wilson (*d* 2016); one *s* one *d*. *Educ:* Kelso High Sch.; Perth Acad.; Edinburgh Univ. (MA 1961; MSc 1962); Clare Coll., Cambridge (PhD 1964). Instructor, Princeton Univ., 1964–66; Fellow, Christ's Coll., Cambridge, 1966–67; Imperial College, University of London: Lectr, 1967–75; Reader, 1975–90; Prof., 1990–92; University of Wales, Swansea: Prof. of Physics and Hd of Dept, 1992–98; Dean of Graduate Sch., 1993–96; Hon. Prof., 2002–; Hon. Fellow, 2005; Chief Exec., PPARC, 1998–2005. Chm., Prior Options Review of Royal Observatories, 1995. Member: PPARC, 1996–98; European Res. Adv. Bd, 2001–07; Reconfiguration and Collaboration Panel, 1998–2013, Res. Libraries Review, 2001–02, HEFCE. Member: Bd, World Premier Inst., Min. of Educn, Culture, Sports, Sci. and Technol., Japan, 1998–2015; Governing Bd, Fermi Res. Alliance, Fermi Nat. Accelerator Lab., Chicago, 2007–13; Internat. Review, Korean Nat. Res. Foundn, 2012. Pres., European Sci. Foundn, 2006–11. FLSW 2011. Hon. FInstP 2012. Hon. DSc: Edinburgh, 2005; Wales, 2006; Glasgow, 2006; Heriot Watt, 2011. *Publications:* numerous papers on theoretical particle physics in Nuclear Physics, Physics Letters. *Recreations:* catching Tweed salmon, golf, tennis. *Address:* Derwent House, Walkley Hill, Rodborough, Stroud GL5 3TX. *E:* Ian.Halliday@e-halliday.org.

**HALLIDAY, Dr John Dixon;** Rector, High School of Dundee, since 2008; *b* Wantage, 24 June 1955; *s* of Dixon and Audrey Halliday; *m* 1988, Anna Salvesen; two *s* one *d*. *Educ:* Abingdon Sch., Oxon; Univ. of Exeter (BA Hons German and Linguistics); Robinson Coll., Cambridge (PhD German and Austrian Satire 1986). Lectr in English, Univ. of Passau, Germany, 1982–85; freelance translator, Cambridge, 1985–87; Head of German, Merchiston Castle Sch., Edinburgh, 1987–91; Head of Modern Langs, 1991–95, Housemaster, 1993–96, Dir of Studies (Middle Sch.), 1996–97, Sedbergh Sch.; Headmaster, Rannoch Sch., Perthshire, 1997–2001; teacher of French and German, Dollar Acad., 2001–02; Headmaster, Albyn Sch., Aberdeen, 2002–08. Mem. Council, Scottish Rugby Union, 2016–. Gov., St Aloysius' Coll., Glasgow, 2015–. Burgess: City of Aberdeen; Guildry, Dundee. *Publications:* Karl Kraus, Franz Pfemfert and the First World war, 1986; contrib. articles on German literary hist., censorship and the GDR. *Recreations:* sport, music – viola, fiddle, singing; reading – history, politics. *Address:* High School of Dundee, Euclid Crescent, Dundee DD1 1HU. *Club:* Rotary (Dundee).

**HALLIDAY, John Frederick,** CB 1994; Deputy Under Secretary of State, Home Office, 1990–2001; *b* 19 Sept. 1942; *s* of E. Halliday; *m* 1970, Alison Burgess; four *s*. *Educ:* Whitgift School, Croydon; St John's College, Cambridge (MA). Teacher, under VSO, Aitchison College, Lahore, 1964–66; Home Office, 1966; Principal Private Sec. to Home Sec., 1980; Asst Under-Sec. of State, Home Office, 1983–87; Under Sec., DHSS, then Dept of Health, 1987–90, on secondment. *Publications:* Making Punishments Work (Govt report), 2001. *Recreations:* music, gardening, theatre.

**HALLIDAY, Norman Pryde;** Senior Principal Medical Officer (Under Secretary), Department of Health and Social Security, later Department of Health, 1977–92; *b* 28 March 1932; *s* of late James and Jessie Thomson Hunter Halliday; *m* 1st, 1953, Eleanor Smith (marr. diss. 2012); three *s* one *d*; 2nd, 2012, Eithne Keaveney; one *s* one *d*. *Educ:* Woodside, Glasgow; King's Coll., London; King's Coll. Hosp. Med. Sch. SRN 1955; MB BS, MRCS, LRCP 1964; DCH RCPGlas 1969; MBA: Warwick, 1991; Open Univ., 1992. Various posts in clinical medicine, incl. Registrar (Paediatrics), KCH, London; SMO, DHSS, 1972. Gen. Man., Eur. Dialysis and Transplant Assoc., 1994–95; Consultant Advr to Minister of Health, Saudi Arabia, 1996–2000; Consultant to UN in Abu Dhabi, 2001. Tutor: Open Univ., 1992–96; Warwick Univ., 1992–96. QHP 1990–93. *Publications:* articles on medical subjects in professional journals. *Recreations:* photography, sub aqua diving, fashion, DIY, cross-bow shooting. *Address:* Gurrs Farm, Crowborough Hill, Crowborough, E Sussex TN6 2SD. *T:* (01892) 669776.

**HALLIDAY, Rt Rev. Robert Taylor;** Bishop of Brechin, 1990–96; *b* 7 May 1932; *s* of James Halliday and Agnes Logan Halliday (*née* Scott); *m* 1960, Georgina Mabel, (Gena) (*née* Chadwin) (*d* 2013); one *d*. *Educ:* High Sch. of Glasgow; Univ. of Glasgow (MA, BD); Episcopal Theol Coll., Edinburgh. Deacon 1957; priest 1958. Assistant Curate: St Andrew's, St Andrews, 1957–60; St Margaret's, Newlands, Glasgow, 1960–63; Rector, Church of the Holy Cross, Davidson's Mains, Edinburgh, 1963–83; External Lectr in New Testament, Episcopal Theol Coll., Edin., 1963–74; Canon of St Mary's Cathedral, Edinburgh, 1973–83; Rector of St Andrew's, St Andrews, 1983–90; Tutor in Biblical Studies, Univ. of St Andrews, 1984–90; warrant, dio. of Edinburgh, 1997–. Hon. Canon, Trinity Cathedral, Davenport, Iowa, 1990. *Recreations:* walking, reading, visiting gardens, shredding appeals from Uganda. *Address:* 28 Forbes Road, Edinburgh EH10 4ED. *T:* (0131) 221 1490.

**HALLIDAY, Sandra Pauline,** CEng; Founder and Principal, Gaia Research, since 1996. *Educ:* Warwick Univ. (BSc Hons Engrg Design and Appropriate Technology); Reading Univ. (MPhil 1999). MCIBSE 1994. Research at Univs of Bath and Reading, 1986–91; Founder, then Head of Centre for Construction Ecology, BSRIA, 1990–95. Research projects incl. dementia and sustainability, passive design, construction processes, solar design, innovative building membranes, daylighting, low allergy housing, teaching, research and guidance in sustainable building design, model briefs for sustainable develt of schs, housing, communities. Royal Acad. of Engrg Vis. Prof. in Sustainable Engrg Design, Univ. of Strathclyde, 2003–08; Vis. Lectr, Energy, Envmt and Sustainable Develt Postgrad. Prog., Oslo Internat. Summer Sch., 2013–. FRSA. Hon. FRIAS 2019. *Publications:* Green Guide to the Architects' Job Book, 2000, 2nd edn 2007; Anarchi: animal architecture, 2003; Sustainable Construction, 2008, 2nd edn 2018; Indoor Air Quality and Design of Ventilation for People with Dementia, 2014; Sustainability Guide to the RIBA Plan of Work 2013, 2016; papers, articles, technical reports and conf. proceedings. *Recreations:* walking, cycling, drama, arts, music, ecology.

**HALLIGAN, Liam James;** columnist, Sunday Telegraph, since 2001; Editor-at-Large, Business New Europe, since 2013; Senior Columnist, UnHerd.com, since 2017; Panelist, CNN-Talk, since 2017; *b* 29 April 1969; *s* of Martin Thomas Halligan and Evelyn Halligan (*née* Thorp); partner, Lucy Ward; one *s* two *d*. *Educ:* John Lyon Sch., Harrow (entrance schol., head boy); Univ. of Warwick (BSc 1st Cl. Hons Econs 1991); St Antony's Coll., Oxford (MPhil Econs 1994). Economics Intern: Internat. Food Policy Res. Inst., 1991; IMF, 1992; Hd of Res., Social Mkt Foundn, 1993; Res. Economist, and author, Russian Econ. Trends, LSE, 1994–95; Moscow Reporter, The Economist, 1995–96; columnist, Moscow Times, 1995–96; Political Corresp., FT, 1996–98; Econs Corresp., Channel 4 News, 1998–2006; Econs Ed., Sunday Telegraph, 2006–07; columnist, Sunday Business, 2000–01; Financial Columnist, GQ Mag., 2007–10; Chief Economist, Prosperity Capital Mgt, 2007–13; Man. Dir, New Sparta Media, 2013–16. Founding Panellist, CNN-Talk, 2017–. Gov., John Lyon Sch., 2016–. Wincott Business Broadcaster of Year, Harold Wincott Foundn, 1999; Business Journalist of Year (Broadcast), World Leadership Forum, 2004, 2005; Business and Finance Journalist of Year, British Press Awards, 2007; Columnist of Year, Workworld, 2007. *Publications:* (with Frank Field) Europe Isn't Working, 1994; (with Gerard Lyons) Clean Brexit, 2017; contrib. numerous articles for Economist Intelligence Unit and Wall St Jl. *Recreations:* family, sailing, rowing, guitar, double bass, Saffron Walden Choral Society, football, roller-skating, film. *Address:* Bridge House, 15 Bridge Street, Saffron Walden, Essex CB10 1BT. *E:* liam.halligan@telegraph.co.uk. *Clubs:* Groucho, Leander.

**HALLIGAN, Prof. Stephen,** MD, PhD; FRCP, FRCR, FMedSci; Professor of Radiology, since 2005, Director, UCL Centre for Medical Imaging, since 2006, and Head, UCL Department of Imaging, Division of Medicine, since 2019, University College London; Honorary Consultant Radiologist, University College Hospitals, since 2005; Consultant Radiologist, The London Clinic, since 1996 (Clinical Director, 2008–18); *b* Nottingham, 2 March 1962; *s* of William Francis Halligan and Philomena Halligan (*née* Charlton); *m* 1991, Alison Jean Rutherford; two *d*. *Educ:* Becket Grammar Sch., Nottingham; Westminster Med. Sch., London (MB BS 1987); London Univ. (MD 1995); University Coll. London (PhD 2015). FRCR 1995; FRCP 2004. Jun. med. posts, Mayday Hosp., Croydon, St Bartholomew's Hosp., London and Queen Elizabeth Hosp., King's Lynn, 1987–90; Registrar, Radiol., St Bartholomew's Hosp., London, 1990–92; Res. Radiologist, St Mark's Hosp., London, 1992–94; Sen. Registrar, Radiol., University College Hosp. and Middlesex Hosp., London, 1994–96; Consultant Gastrointestinal Radiologist, St Mark's Hosp., Harrow, 1996–2005. Sen. Investigator, NIHR, 2009–12, now Emeritus. President: British Soc. of Gastrointestinal and Abdominal Radiol., 2006–08;

Eur. Soc. of Gastrointestinal and Abdominal Radiol., 2017–19 (Mem., Exec. Cttee, 2004–19); St Mark's Assoc., 2018–19. FMedSci 2017. *Publications:* more than 400 res. articles, book chapters and reviews on gastrointestinal radiol., computer-assisted detection and res. methodology for medical imaging studies. *Recreations:* music (both listening and performing), avid cook, coarse and game fishing. *Address:* UCL Centre for Medical Imaging, 2nd Floor, Charles Bell House, 43–45 Foley Street, W1W 7TS. *E:* s.halligan@ucl.ac.uk.

**HALLINAN, Mary Alethea;** *see* Parry Evans, M. A.

**HALLIWELL, Prof. (Francis) Stephen,** DPhil; FBA 2014; FRSE; Professor of Greek, since 1995, and Wardlaw Professor of Classics, since 2014, University of St Andrews; *b* Wigan, 18 Oct. 1953; *s* of Francis Halliwell and Joyce Halliwell (*née* Casey); *m* 1978, Helen Ruth Gainford (marr. diss. 2010); two *s*. *Educ:* St Francis Xavier's Coll., Liverpool; Worcester Coll., Oxford (Schol.; BA 1st Cl. Lit. Hum. 1976 (Passmore Edwards Prize 1976); DPhil 1981). Lecturer: in Classics, Jesus Coll., Oxford, 1979–80; in Classics and Drama, Westfield Coll., London, 1980–82; Fellow, Corpus Christi Coll., Cambridge, 1982–84; Birmingham University: Lectr in Classics, 1984–90; Sen. Lectr, 1990–94; Reader, 1994–95. Visiting Professor: of Classics, Chicago Univ., 1990; of Aesthetics, Univ. of Rome (Roma Tre), 1998; H. L. Hooker Dist. Vis. Prof., McMaster Univ., 2009; Chaire Cardinal Mercier, Univ. of Louvain, 2010; Townsend Vis. Prof., Cornell Univ., 2012; Vis. Faculty Fellow, Center for Ideas and Society, Univ. of Calif, Riverside, 1993; Fellow, Lorenzo Valla Foundn, 2015. FRSE 2011. *Publications:* Aristotle's Poetics, 1986, 2nd edn 1998; The Poetics of Aristotle, 1987; Plato Republic 10, 1988; Plato Republic 5, 1993; Aristotle Poetics (Loeb Classical Liby edn), 1995; Aristophanes: Birds, Lysistrata, Assembly-Women, Wealth, 1997; The Aesthetics of Mimesis, 2002 (Premio Europeo d'Estetica, Società Italiana d'Estetica, 2008); Greek Laughter, 2008 (Criticos Prize, Hellenic Soc. of London); Between Ecstasy and Truth, 2011; Aristophanes: Clouds, Women at the Thesmophoria, Frogs, 2015. *Recreation:* music. *Address:* School of Classics, University of St Andrews, St Andrews, Fife KY16 9AL. *T:* (01334) 462617. *E:* fsh@st-andrews.ac.uk.

**HALLIWELL, Mark Gareth; His Honour Judge Halliwell;** a Specialist Civil Circuit Judge, since 2018; *b* Bolton; *s* of James Halliwell and Valerie Halliwell; *m* 1994, Fiona; one *s* two *d*. *Educ:* Queen's Coll., Taunton; London Sch. of Econs and Political Sci. (BSc Econ); City Univ., London (DipLaw). Called to the Bar, Lincoln's Inn, 1985; barrister, Kings Chambers, Manchester, 1986–2018; a Recorder, 2002–18. *Publications:* Distribution on Intestacy, 1996. *Recreations:* cycling, walking, golf. *Address:* Manchester Civil Justice Centre, 1 Bridge Street West, Manchester M60 9DJ. *Club:* Hale Golf.

**HALLIWELL, Prof. Richard Edward Winter;** William Dick Professor of Veterinary Clinical Studies, Royal (Dick) School of Veterinary Studies, University of Edinburgh, 1988–2002, now Emeritus (Dean, Faculty of Veterinary Medicine, 1990–94 and 2000–02); *b* 16 June 1937; *s* of Arthur Clare Halliwell and Winifred Dorothea Goode; *m* 1963, Jenifer Helen Roper; two *d*. *Educ:* St Edward's Sch., Oxford; Gonville and Caius Coll., Cambridge (MA, VetMB, PhD); MRCVS. Jun. Fellow in Vet. Surgery, Univ. of Bristol, 1961–63; private vet. practice, London, 1963–68; Vis. Fellow in Dermatology, Univ. of Pennsylvania Sch. of Vet. Med., 1968–70; Wellcome Vet. Fellowship Univ. of Cambridge, 1970–73; Asst Prof. of Dermatology, Univ. of Pennsylvania Sch. of Vet. Med., 1973–77; Prof. and Chm., Dept of Med. Scis, Univ. of Florida Coll. of Vet. Medicine, 1977–88; Prof., Dept of Med. Microbiol., Univ. of Florida Coll. of Med., 1977–88. Part-time Prof., Sch. of Veterinary Medicine, St George's Univ., Grenada, 2008–12. UK Rep., EC Adv. Cttee on Vet. Trng, 1994–98. President: Amer. Acad. of Veterinary Allergy, 1978–80; Amer. Assoc. of Veterinary Immunologists, 1984; Amer. Coll. of Veterinary Dermatology, 1984–86; Eur. Assoc. of Estabs for Vet. Educn, 1994–98 (Hon. Life Pres., 2002); Eur. Coll. of Vet. Dermatology, 1996–98; World Congress of Vet. Dermatology Assoc., 1999–2010; Royal College of Veterinary Surgeons: Treas., 2001–02; Jun. Vice-Pres., 2002–03; Pres., 2003–04; Sen. Vice-Pres., 2004–05. FMedSci 1999. Dr *hc* Warsaw Agricl Univ., 2003. Lifetime Career Achievement Award, Eur. Coll. of Veterinary Dermatol., 2004; Internat. Award for Scientific Achievement, World Small Animal Veterinary Assoc., 2012; Schindelka Award, World Assoc. for Veterinary Dermatology, 2012. *Publications:* (with N. T. Gorman) Veterinary Clinical Immunology, 1989; (with C. von Tscharner) Advances in Veterinary Dermatology, 1990; numerous pubns in area of clin. immunology and vet. dermatology. *Recreations:* wine, music, travelling. *Address:* 2A Ainslie Place, Edinburgh EH3 6AR. *T:* (0131) 225 8765.

**HALLIWELL, Stephen;** *see* Halliwell, F. S.

**HALLS, Andrew David,** MA; Head Master, King's College School, Wimbledon, since 2008; *b* 29 Jan. 1959; *s* of Gerald and Barbara Halls; *m* 1987, Véronique Le Droff; two *d*. *Educ:* Shenley Court Sch., Birmingham; Gonville and Caius Coll., Cambridge (Schol.; BA Double 1st Cl. Hons English 1981; MA). English teacher: Chigwell Sch., 1981–84; Whitgift Sch., 1984–89; Hd of English, Bristol GS, 1989–95; Dep. Headmaster, Trinity Sch., 1995–98; Master, Magdalen Coll. Sch., 1998–2007. *Recreations:* family, reading, theatre, running. *Address:* King's College School, Wimbledon, SW19 4TT.

**HALLS, David John;** Director of Music, Salisbury Cathedral, since 2005; *b* 14 Jan. 1963; *s* of William and Sally Halls; *m* 1986, Nicola Holman; three *s* two *d* (and one *d* decd). *Educ:* Worcester Coll., Oxford (BA Hons Music 1984, MA); Winchester (PGCE 1985). FRCO 1985. Organ Scholar, Winchester Cath., 1984; Salisbury Cathedral: Asst Organist, 1985–2000; Asst Dir of Music, 2000–05. *Recreations:* reading, wine, football, cricket. *Address:* Wyndham House, 65 The Close, Salisbury SP1 2EN. *T:* (01722) 555125. *E:* d.halls@salcath.co.uk.

**HALLS, Meryl Jane;** Managing Director, Booksellers Association of the UK and Ireland Ltd, since 2018; *b* Edinburgh, 3 June 1965; *d* of Michael and Sheila Halls; *m* 1998, Douglas Schatz; one *s* one *d*. *Educ:* Galashiels Acad.; St Andrews Univ. (MA Hons English Lang. and Lit.). Conference Asst, 1989–96; Hd, Membership Services, Booksellers Assoc., 1996–2018. Member: Bd, Ind. Retailers Confedn, 2015–; Policy Bd, British Retail Consortium, 2018–; Bd, European Booksellers Fedn, 2018–. Trustee, World Book Day, 2019–. *Recreations:* reading, theatre, walking, politics. *Address:* Booksellers Association, 6 Bell Yard, WC2A 2JR. *T:* (020) 7421 4692. *E:* Meryl.halls@booksellers.org.uk.

**HALONEN, Tarja Kaarina;** President of Finland, 2000–12; Drylands Ambassador, UN Convention to Combat Desertification, since 2014; *b* Helsinki, 24 Dec. 1943; *m* (marr. diss.); one *d*; *m* 2000, Pentti Arajarvi. *Educ:* Univ. of Helsinki (ML). Lawyer, Lainvalvonta Oy, 1967–68; Social Affairs Sec. and Gen. Sec., Nat. Union of Finnish Students, 1969–70; Lawyer, Cultural Orgn of Finnish Trade Unions, 1970–74; lawyer, 1975–79. Prime Minister's Parly Sec., 1974–75; Mem., Helsinki CC, 1977–96. MP (SDP), Finland, 1979–2000; Chm., Parly Social Affairs Cttee, 1984–87; Minister, Min. of Social Affairs and Health, 1987–90; Minister: for Nordic Co-operation, 1989–91; of Justice, 1990–91; for Foreign Affairs, 1995–2000.

**HALPERN, David Anthony;** QC 2006; a Recorder, since 2009; a Deputy High Court Judge, Chancery Division, since 2013; *b* 23 May 1956; *s* of Cecil and Audrey Halpern; *m* 1981, Dr Helen Kahn; two *s* one *d*. *Educ:* St Paul's Sch., London; Magdalen Coll., Oxford (Exhibnr; MA Juris). Called to the Bar, Gray's Inn, 1978, Bencher, 2009; in practice as barrister, 1979–, specialising in commercial chancery work and professional negligence. *Publications:* (contrib.) Jackson & Powell on Professional Liability, 6th edn 2006, 7th edn 2012. *Recreations:* piano, cycling, travel, cold-water swimming. *Address:* (chambers) 4 New Square, Lincoln's Inn, WC2A 3RJ. *T:* (020) 7822 2000. *E:* d.halpern@4newsquare.com.

**HALPERN, Sir Ralph (Mark),** Kt 1986; Chairman, Halpern (formerly Halpern Associates), 1994–2005; Chairman, 1981–90, and Chief Executive, 1978–90, Burton Group plc (Managing Director, 1978); Halpern Consulting, since 1992; *b* 24 Oct. 1938; *m* (marr. diss.); one *d*; *m* 2003, Laura (marr. diss. 2007); one *s*. *Educ:* St Christopher School, Letchworth. Started career as trainee, Selfridges; joined Burton Group, 1961; founder, Top Shop, 1970. Member: President's Cttee, CBI, 1984–90; President's Cttee, Business in the Community, 1991–92; Adv. Council, Prince's Youth Business Trust, 1991. Chm., British Fashion Council, 1990–94. Formerly: Local Councillor, Surrey; Chm., E Surrey Rural Police and Community Partnership Gp. FInstD; CCMI.
*See also* J. Halpern Prince.

**HALPERN PRINCE, Jennifer Ann;** Founder and Chief Executive Officer, Halpern Ltd, since 1993; *b* Kingston Upon Thames, 16 Oct. 1968; *d* of Sir Ralph (Mark) Halpern, *qv* and Joan Halpern; *m* 2003, Ryan Prince; one *s* two *d*. *Educ:* Roedean Sch. Press Officer, Joseph, 1989–92. Founder Trustee, Access Aspiration, 2012–17, subseq. merged into Mayor's Fund for London, Trustee, 2017–; Co-Founder and Chm. Trustees, Lady Garden Foundn (Gynaecological Cancer Fund), 2014–; Mem. Bd, Accelerate-Her, 2016–. Patron, Natural Hist. Mus., 2010–. *Address:* Halpern Ltd, The Charlotte Building, 6 Evelyn Yard, W1T 1QL. *T:* (020) 7349 2500. *E:* jenny@halpern.co.uk.

**HALSALL, Hazel Anne;** *see* Blears, Rt Hon. H. A.

**HALSEY, Rev. John Walter Brooke,** 4th Bt *cr* 1920 (but uses designation Brother John Halsey); *b* 26 Dec. 1933; *s* of Sir Thomas Edgar Halsey, 3rd Bt, DSO, and of Jean Margaret Palmer, *d* of late Bertram Willes Dayrell Brooke; *S* father, 1970. *Educ:* Eton; Magdalene College, Cambridge (BA 1957). Deacon 1961, priest 1962, Diocese of York; Curate of Stocksbridge, 1961–65; Brother in Community of the Transfiguration, 1965–. *Heir:* cousin Nicholas Guy Halsey, TD [*b* 14 June 1948; *m* 1976, Viola Georgina Juliet, *d* of Maj. George Thorne, MC, DL; one *s*]. *Address:* The Hermitage, 70E Clerk Street, Loanhead, Midlothian EH20 9RG. *T:* (0131) 440 3028.

**HALSEY, Simon Patrick,** CBE 2015; FRCM; Chorus Director: City of Birmingham Symphony Orchestra Choruses, since 1983; London Symphony Orchestra, since 2012; Director, BBC Proms Youth Chorus, since 2012; Chief Conductor, Rundfunkchor Berlin, 2001–15, now Conductor Laureate; Artistic Director: Berlin Philharmonic Youth Choral Programme, since 2012; Orfeó Català Choirs, since 2016; Professor and Director of Choral Activities, University of Birmingham, since 2012; *b* 8 March 1958; *s* of Louis Arthur Owen Halsey and late Evelyn Elisabeth (*née* Calder); *m* 1st, 1986, Lucy Jane Lunt (marr. diss.); one *s* one *d*; 2nd, 2016, Wiebke Roloff. *Educ:* chorister, New Coll., Oxford; Winchester Coll.; King's Coll., Cambridge (Choral Schol.); BA 1979; MA 1983); Royal Coll. Music (Schol.). FRCM 2016. Conductor, Scottish Opera (Opera-Go-Round), 1979; Dir of Music, Univ. of Warwick, 1980–88; Principal Conductor, City of Birmingham Touring Opera, 1987–2000; Chorus Dir, De Vlaamse Opera, Antwerp, 1991–94; Founder and Artistic Dir, BBC Nat. Chorus of Wales, 1995–2000; Founding Conductor, European Voices, 1999–; Chief Conductor, Netherlands Radio Choir, 2002–08 (Chief Guest Conductor, 1995–2002); Principal Conductor, Choral Programme, Northern Sinfonia, 2004–12. Chief Guest Conductor, Sydney Philharmonia Choirs, 1997–2001; frequent Guest Conductor of choruses, Châtelet Th., Paris, 1996–, and Salzburg Fest., 1998–; Chorus Dir, Sydney Olympic Games, 2000; Artistic Adviser: Schleswig-Holstein Musik Fest. Choir, 2014–; Palau de la Música Barcelona, 2016–. Consultant Ed., Choral Prog. Series, Faber Music, 1986–, Faber Music, 1994–. Internat. Chair of Choral Conducting, RWCMD, Cardiff, 2008–14. FRWCMD 2015. Hon. Dr UCE, 2000; Hon. MA Warwick, 2007; Hon. DMus: Birmingham, 2009; Aberdeen, 2017. Recording awards include: Gramophone Record of Year, Gramophone Magazine (many); Deutsche Schallplatten Kritik Preis (many); Grammy, 2008, 2009, 2011. Queen's Medal for Music, 2015. Bundesverdienstkreuz, 1st Cl. (Germany), 2011. *Publications:* Ed., 30 vols of choral music, 1995–; Schott Master Class Chorleitung - Vom Konzept zum Konzert, 2011. *Recreations:* reading, walking. *Address:* c/o Intermusica Artists' Management, 9 Kingsway, WC2B 6XF.

**HALSTEAD, Sir Ronald,** Kt 1985; CBE 1976; Deputy Chairman, British Steel plc (formerly British Steel Corporation), 1986–94; *b* 17 May 1927; *s* of Richard and Bessie Harrison Halstead; *m* 1st, 1968, Yvonne Cecile de Monchaux (*d* 1978); two *s*; 2nd, 2000, Eugenie Susanne Stoessl (*d* 2013). *Educ:* Lancaster Royal Grammar Sch.; Queens' Coll., Cambridge (Hon. Fellow, 1985). MA, FRSC. Research Chemist, H. P. Bulmer & Co., 1948–53; Manufg Manager, Macleans Ltd, 1954–55; Factory Manager, Beecham Products Inc. (USA), 1955–60; Asst Managing Dir, Beecham Research Labs, 1960–62; Vice-Pres. (Marketing), Beecham Products Inc. (USA), 1962–64; Pres., Beecham Research Labs Inc. (USA), 1962–64; Chairman: Food and Drink Div., Beecham Group Ltd, 1964–67; Beecham Products, 1967–84; Man. Dir (Consumer Products) Beecham Gp, 1973–84; Chm. and Chief Exec., Beecham Gp, 1984–85. Dir, Otis Elevator Co. Ltd (UK), 1978–83; non-executive Director: BSC, later British Steel, 1979–94; The Burmah Oil PLC, 1983–89; Amer. Cyanamid Co. (USA), 1986–94; Davy Corp. plc, 1986–91; Gestetner Holdings PLC, 1986–95; Laurentian Financial Gp, 1991–95. Mem. Egg Re-organisation Commn, 1967–68; Pres., Incorp. Soc. of Brit. Advertisers, 1971–73; Chairman: British Nutrition Foundn, 1970–73; Knitting Sector Gp (formerly Knitting Sector Working Party), NEDO, 1978–90; Bd for Food Studies, Reading Univ., 1983–86; Garment and Textile Sector Gp, NEDO, 1991–93; CAB Internat., 1995–98; Cons. Foreign and Commonwealth Council, 1995–2016 (Pres., 2016–). Vice-Chairman: Proprietary Assoc. of GB, 1968–77; Advertising Assoc.–, 1973–81; Food and Drink Industries Council, 1973–76; Member: Council and Exec. Cttee, Food Manufrs' Fedn Inc., 1966–85 (Pres., 1974–76); Council, British Nutrition Foundn, 1967–79; Cambridge Univ. Appts Bd, 1969–73; Council, CBI, 1970–86; Council, BIM, 1972–77; Council, Univ. of Buckingham (formerly University Coll. at Buckingham), 1973–95; Council, Nat. Coll. of Food Technol., 1977–78 (Chm. Bd, 1978–83); Council, Univ. of Reading, 1978–98; AFRC, 1978–84; Council, Trade Policy Res. Centre, 1985–89; Monopolies and Mergers Commn, 1993–99 (Mem., Newspaper Panel, 1980–92); Industrial Develt Adv. Bd, 1984–93 (Chm., 1985–93); Council and Exec. Cttee, Imperial Soc. of Knights Bachelor, 1986–2002; Pres., EIA, 1991. Dir and Hon. Treas., Centre for Policy Studies, 1984–93. Trustee, Inst. of Economic Affairs, 1980–93. Governor, Ashridge Management Coll., 1970–2006 (Vice-Chm., 1977–2006); President: Nat. Advertising Benevolent Soc., 1978–80; Inst. of Packaging, 1981–82 (a Vice-Pres., 1979–81). Fellow, Marketing Soc., 1981; FCMI; FInstM; FRSA; FRSC. Hon. Fellow, Inst. of Food Sci. and Technol., 1983–84. Hon. DSc: Reading, 1982; Lancaster, 1987. *Recreations:* sailing, squash racquets, ski-ing. *Address:* 37 Edwardes Square, W8 6HH. *T:* (020) 7603 9010. *Clubs:* Athenæum, Brooks's, Hurlingham, Carlton, Royal Thames Yacht.

**HALTON, Prof. David John,** EdD; Vice Chancellor, University of Glamorgan, 2005–10, now Professor Emeritus; *b* 23 June 1949; *s* of late Kenneth Robert Depledge Halton and Margaret Alice (*née* Searle); *m* 1973, Yvonne Geneste Ambrose; three *d*. *Educ:* Beckenham and Penge Grammar Sch. for Boys; Thames Poly. (BA 1972); Roehampton Inst. (PGCE 1973); Aston Univ. (MSc 1976); Univ. of Leicester (EdD 1998). Teacher, Hurlingham Comprehensive Sch., 1973–76; Lectr, N Tyneside Coll. of Further Educn, 1977–80; Hd of Dept of Business and Marketing, Coll. for Distributive Trade, 1980–86; Dean, Business Sch., N London Poly., 1987–90; Dep. Rector, Nene Coll., Northampton, 1990–99; Dep. Vice-Chancellor, Dep. Chief Exec., and Prof. of Higher Educn, UWE, Bristol, 1999–2004, Prof. Emeritus, 2004. Chm. Council, Bristol Old Vic Th. Sch., 2012–; Mem. Bd, Conservatoire for Dance and Drama, 2012– (Interim CEO, 2014). Hon. LLD Roehampton, 2010; DUniv Glamorgan, 2011. Hon. FRWCMD 2010. *Publications:* Theories of Education Management in Practice, 1998; Pricing Toolkit for Higher Education, 2001. *Recreations:* playing blues piano, running, ornithology. *Address:* 45 High Street, Saltford, Bristol BS31 3EJ.

**HAM, Sir Christopher John,** Kt 2018; CBE 2004; DL; PhD; Chief Executive, The King's Fund, 2010–18; Professor of Health Policy and Management, University of Birmingham, 1992–2014, now Emeritus; *b* 15 May 1951; *s* of Raymond Percival Thomas Ham and Agnes Anne Ham (*née* Evans); *m* 1980, Ioanna Burnell; two *s* one *d*. *Educ:* Cardiff High Sch.; Univ. of Kent (BA MPhil); Univ. of Bristol (PhD 1983). Research Asst, Univ. of Leeds, 1975–77; Lectr in Health Policy, Univ. of Bristol, 1977–86; Fellow, King's Fund Coll. and King's Fund Inst., 1986–92; Dir, Health Services Mgt Centre, Univ. of Birmingham, 1992–2000; Policy Analyst, 2000–01, Dir, Strategy Unit, 2001–04, DoH (on secondment). Vis. Prof., Univ. of Surrey, 2009–12; Hon. Prof., LSHTM, 2011–. Sen. Associate, Nuffield Trust, 2008–10. Non-executive Director: Heart of England NHS Foundn Trust, 2007–10 (Gov., 2005–07); Royal Free London NHS Foundn Trust, 2019–; Gov., Health Foundn, 2006–10; Trustee, Canadian Health Services Res. Foundn, 2006–09; Chair, Coventry and Warwicks Sustainability and Transformation Partnership, 2019–. Advr to World Bank, WHO, Audit Commn, NAO, BMA, RCP, etc. FRSocMed; Founder FMedSci 1998. Hon. FRCP 2004; Hon. FRCGP 2008. Hon. DLitt Kent, 2012. DL W Midlands, 2013. Homenot Internat. Award, Avedis Donabedian Foundn, 2013; Peggy Leatt Award, Univ. of Toronto, 2017. *Publications:* Policy Making in the NHS, 1981; Health Policy in Britain, 1982, 6th edn 2009; (with M. J. Hill) The Policy Process in the Modern Capitalist State, 1984; Managing Health Services, 1986; (jtly) Health Check: health care reforms in an international context, 1990; The New NHS: organisation and management, 1991; (jtly) Priority Setting Processes for Healthcare, 1995; Public, Private or Community: what next for the NHS?, 1996; Management and Competition in the NHS, 1994, 2nd edn 1997; (ed) Health Care Reform, 1997; (with S. Pickard) Tragic Choices in Health Care: the case of Child B, 1998; (with A. Coulter) The Global Challenge of Health Care Rationing, 2000; The Politics of NHS Reform 1988–1997, 2000; (with S. McIver) Contested Decisions, 2000; (with G. Robert) Reasonable Rationing, 2003; (with J. Ellins) NHS Mutual, 2009; (jtly) Medical Leadership: from the dark side to centre stage, 2012. *Recreations:* sport, music, theatre, reading, travel, cycling. *E:* Chrisham01@aol.com.

**HAM, Sir David Kenneth R.;** *see* Rowe-Ham.

**HÄMÄLÄINEN-LINDFORS, Sirkka Aune-Marjatta,** DSc; Comdr, 1st Cl., Order of White Rose (Finland); Member of Supervisory Board, European Central Bank, 2014–16; *b* 8 May 1939; *m* Bo Lindfors; two *c*. *Educ:* Helsinki Sch. of Econs (DSc 1981). Economics Department, Bank of Finland: Economist, 1961–72; Head of Office, 1972–79; acting Head of Econs Dept, 1979–81; Dir, Econs Dept, Finnish Min. of Finance, 1981–82; Bank of Finland: Dir resp. for macroeconomic analysis and monetary and exchange rate policy, 1982–91; Mem. of Bd, 1991–92; Gov. and Chm. of Bd, 1992–98; Mem., Exec. Bd, European Central Bank, 1998–2003. Docent and Adjunct Prof. in Econs, Helsinki Sch. of Econs and Business Admin, 1991–2006. Member: Council, European Monetary Inst., 1992–98; Economic Council of Finland, 1992–98; Nat. Bd of Economic Defence, 1992–98; Internat. Adv. Council, CEPS, 1993–98; Bd, Foundn for Economic Educn, 1996–2007; Develt Prog. of Nat. Strategy, 1996–98; Chm., Bd of Financial Supervision Authy, 1996–97. Director: Investor AB, 2004–11; Sanoma Corp. (formerly SanomaWSOY), 2004–13; KONE Corp., 2004–15 (Vice Chm., 2004–12). Member: Bd, Finnish Nat. Theatre, 1992–98; Supervisory Bd, Finnish Cultural Foundn, 1996–2005; Chm., The Raging Roses, theatre gp, 1997–99; Chm., Finnish Nat. Opera and Ballet, 2007–16. Foreign Academician, Real Academia de Ciencias Económicas y Financieras, Spain, 2010. Hon. Dr of Econs Turku, 1995; Hon. DSc Tech. Aalto, 2014. Merit Medal, 1st Cl., Order of White Star (Estonia). *Publications:* numerous articles on economics and monetary policy.

**HAMANN, Paul;** Managing Director and Creative Director, Wild Pictures Ltd, since 2006; *b* 9 Nov. 1948; *s* of Leonard Hamann and Anita Hamann (*née* Davies); *m* 1st, 1971, Kay Allen (marr. diss. 1981); (one *d* decd); 2nd, 1981, Marilyn Wheatcroft (marr. diss. 1999; she *d* 2018); one *s* one *d*. Dir and Prod., over 50 documentaries for BBC TV, 1976–88: incl. Your Life in Their Files, Sister Genevieve, Pushers, I Call It Murder, The Survivalists, At the Edge of the Union, A Company, Transmit and be Damned, Africa's Last Colony, Phantom, Lest We Forget, The Duty Men (Best Factual Series Award, BAFTA, 1987), Fourteen Days in May (Grierson Award, BFI, 1988); Editor, BBC 1 Documentaries, 1989–93: series incl. Inside Story, Rough Justice, Children's Hospital; Head of Documentaries, 1994–97, Chair, Factual Bd, 1996–99, Head of Documentaries and Hist. and of Community Prog. Unit, 1997–2000, BBC TV; Creative Director, Factual Progs, Shine Ltd, 2000–05: progs incl. Macintyre's Millions, Warrior School, Snatched, The Day I'll Never Forget, The Death Belt, My Shakespeare with Baz Luhrmann. Exec. Prod., feature film, Bullet Boy, 2005; Creative Director: Putin's Palace, 2006; Execution of a Teenage Girl, 2007 (Amnesty Documentary of the Year, 2007); World's Tallest Man, 2007; The Slaves in the Cellar, 2008; In the Line of Fire, 2009; Holloway, 2009; Wormwood Scrubs, 2010; The Zoo, 2010, 2012, 2013; Smugglers, 2011; Strangeways, 2011; Baby Hospital, 2011; Fraud Squad, 2011, 2012, 2013, 2015; The Factory, 2011; The Real Thumbelina, 2012; Death Row Dogs, 2012; Britain's Hidden Alcoholics, 2012; Smugglers Special, 2012; Dirty Britain, 2012, 2013; Pensioners Behind Bars, 2012; Trouble Abroad, 2013; Allotment Wars, 2013; Her Majesty's Prison: Aylesbury, 2013; Brady and Hindley: Possession, 2013; Dangerous Dogs, 2014; Kids Behind Bars, 2014; Hit and Run, 2014; The Billion Dollar Chicken Shop, 2015; Trawlermen Tales, 2016; The Cruise, 2016, 2017; Her Majesty's Prison, Norwich, 2016; Mr v Mrs: Call the Mediator, 2016; The Forgotten Children, 2016; Women who Kill, 2017; Army: behind the front lines, 2017; The E-Bay Scammers, 2017; Stalkers, 2017; The Cruise, 2018, 2019; Miriam's Big American Adventure, 2018; The Funeral Murders, 2018; Harold Shipman: Doctor Death, 2018; The Trouble With Women, 2018; The Hunt for the Birmingham Bombers, 2018; How They Steal Your Bank Account, 2019; Miriam's Dead Good Adventure, 2019. Mem. Council, BAFTA, 1993–96. Chm., Reprieve, 2000–10 (Founding Trustee, 2000–16; Patron, 2016–). *Publications:* (with Peter Gillman) The Duty Men, 1987; contrib. professional jls. *Recreations:* family, theatre, opera, Italy. *T:* (020) 7428 5622. *E:* paul@wildpictures.co.uk.

**HAMBIDGE, Most Rev. Douglas Walter,** DD; Principal, St Mark's Theological College, and Assistant Bishop, Dar es Salaam, 1993–95; *b* London, England, 6 March 1927; *s* of Douglas Hambidge and Florence (*née* Driscoll); *m* 1956, Denise Colvill Lown; two *s* one *d*. *Educ:* London Univ.; London Coll. of Divinity. BD, ALCD; DD, Anglican Theol Coll. of BC, 1970. Asst Curate, St Mark's, Dalston, 1953–56; Rector: All Saints, Cassiar, BC, 1956–58; St James, Smithers, BC, 1958–64; Vicar, St Martin, Fort St John, BC, 1964–69; Canon, St Andrew's Cathedral, Caledonia, 1965–69; Bishop of Caledonia, 1969–80; Bishop of New Westminster, 1980; Archbishop of New Westminster and Metropolitan of Province of BC, 1981–93. Mem., ACC, 1987–93 (Mem., Standing Cttee, 1990–93). Pres., Missions to Seamen, 1980–93. Chancellor, Vancouver Sch. of Theology, 1999–2007 (Mem. Bd of Governors, 1980–85). *Publications:* The 'S' Word, 2009. *Address:* 1621 Golf Club Drive, Delta, BC V4M 4E6, Canada. *E:* douglashambidge@gmail.com.

**HAMBLEDEN, 5th Viscount** *cr* 1891; **William Henry Bernard Smith;** *b* 18 Nov. 1955; *e s* of 4th Viscount Hambleden and of Donna Maria Carmela Attolico di Adelfia; *S* father, 2012; *m* 1983, Sarah Suzanne Anlauf; two *d*. Heir: *b* Hon. Bernardo James Smith, *b* 17 May 1957. *Address:* The Manor House, Hambleden, Henley-on-Thames, Oxon RG9 6SG.

**HAMBLEN, Rt Hon. Lord; Nicholas Archibald Hamblen,** Kt 2008; PC 2016; a Justice of the Supreme Court of the United Kingdom, from Jan. 2020; *b* 23 Sept. 1957; *s* of Derek Ivens Archibald Hamblen, CB, OBE; *m* 1985, Kate Hayden; one *s* one *d*. *Educ:* Westminster Sch.; St John's Coll., Oxford (MA); Harvard Law Sch. (LLM). Called to the Bar, Lincoln's Inn, 1981; QC 1997; Asst Recorder, 1999–2000; Recorder, 2000–08; a Judge of the High Court, QBD, 2008–16; a Lord Justice of Appeal, 2016–20. *Address:* Supreme Court of the United Kingdom, Parliament Square, SW1P 3BD.

**HAMBLEN, Prof. David Lawrence,** CBE 2001; FRCSE, FRCS, FRCSGlas; Professor of Orthopaedic Surgery, University of Glasgow, 1972–99, now Emeritus; Hon. Consultant Orthopaedic Surgeon, 1972–2002, and Chairman, 1997–2002, Greater Glasgow Health Board; *b* 31 Aug. 1934; *s* of Reginald John Hamblen and Bessie Hamblen (*née* Williams); *m* 1968, Gillian Frances, *d* of late Edgar Leonard Bradley, OBE; one *s* two *d*. *Educ:* Roan Sch., Greenwich; Univ. of London (MB BS 1957); PhD Edinburgh 1975. FRCSE 1962; FRCS 1963; FRCSGlas 1976. Fulbright Fellow, Harvard; Fellow, Massachusetts Gen. Hosp., 1966–67; Lectr in Orthopaedics, Nuffield Orthopaedic Centre, Univ. of Oxford, 1967–68; Sen. Lectr in Orthopaedic Surgery, Univ. of Edinburgh and Hon. Consultant Orthopaedic Surgeon to SE Regl Hosp. Bd, Scotland, 1968–72. Hon. Consultant in Orthopaedic Surgery to the Army in Scotland, 1976–99. Vis. Prof., Univ. of Strathclyde (Nat. Centre for Trng and Educn in Prosthetics and Orthotics), 1981–2008. Non-exec. Dir, W Glasgow Hosps Univ. NHS Trust, 1994–97. Chm. Council, Jl of Bone and Joint Surgery, 1995–2001. Pres., British Orthopaedic Assoc., 1990–91 (Hon. Fellow, 2002); Member: British Hip Soc. (Pres., 2001–02); European Hip Soc. Mem. Council and Trustee, St Andrew's Ambulance Assoc., 1998–2014; Mem., Merchants House of Glasgow, 2009–; Strathclyde Cttee, Tenovus Scotland, 2018–. Hon. DSc: Strathclyde, 2003; Glasgow, 2003. *Publications:* (ed with J. C. Adams): Outline of Fractures, 10th edn 1992 to 12th edn 2007; Outline of Orthopaedics, 11th edn 1990 to 14th edn 2009; Young First Aider Learning Guide, 2015. *Recreations:* golf, music, reading, curling. *Address:* 3 Russell Drive, Bearsden, Glasgow G61 3BB. *T:* (0141) 942 1823. *Club:* Royal Society of Medicine.

**HAMBLEN, Nicholas Archibald;** *see* Hamblen, Rt Hon. Lord.

**HAMBLETON, Prof. Kenneth George,** FREng; Professor of Defence Engineering, University College London, 1991–2001, now Emeritus; *b* 15 Jan. 1937; *s* of George William Hambleton and Gertrude Nellie Hambleton (*née* Brighouse); *m* 1959, Glenys Patricia Smith; one *s* one *d*. *Educ:* Chesterfield Grammar Sch.; Queens' Coll., Cambridge (MA). CEng, FIET; FREng (FEng 1994). Services Electronics Res. Lab., Baldock, 1958–73; ASWE, Portsdown, 1973–81; a Dep. Dir, ASWE, 1981–82; Dir, Strategic Electronics-Radar, MoD PE, 1982–85; Asst Chief Scientific Advr (Projects and Res.), MoD, 1985–86; Dir Gen., Air Weapons and Electronic Systems, 1986–90, Air 3, 1990–91, MoD. *Publications:* numerous articles and letters in nat. and internat. physics and electronic jls. *Recreations:* chess, bridge, golf, music—especially jazz.

**HAMBLIN-BOONE, Russell John;** Chief Executive Officer, Civil Enforcement Association, since 2018; *b* Salisbury, 11 April 1967; *s* of John Hamblin and Brenda Hamblin (*née* Ford); *m* 1990, Sharon Carter; one *s* one *d*. *Educ:* Robert May's Sch., Odiham; Queen Mary's Coll., Basingstoke. Houses of Parliament: Private Office Manager, Chief Whip's Office, 1994–98; Asst Private Sec. and Parly Clerk to Law Officers, Attorney Gen.'s Chambers, 1998–99; Private Sec. to Leader of H of L and Minister for Women, 1999–2000; Hd, Public Affairs, British Retail Consortium, 2000–03; Dir, Corporate Affairs, Energy Retail Assoc., 2003–08; Hd, Communications, Finance and Leasing Assoc., 2009–12; Chief Exec., Consumer Finance Assoc., 2012–17. Chm., Governing Bd, Abbas and Templecombe Sch., 2005–. Sec., PCC, 2009–, Lay Worship Asst, 2017–, St Mary the Virgin, Abbas and Templecombe; Deanery Synod Rep., Bath and Wells Dio., 2010–. *Recreations:* angling, Southampton Football Club, Philadelphia Eagles, sharing fun, sparing time, caring for people, daring to try, wearing a smile. *Address:* Wincanton, Somerset. *E:* russellhamblinboone@gmail.com.

**HAMBLING, Sir (Herbert) Peter (Hugh),** 4th Bt *cr* 1924, of Yoxford, co. Suffolk; *b* 6 Sept. 1953; *o s* of Sir (Herbert) Hugh Hambling, 3rd Bt, and Anne Page Oswald (*d* 1990), Spokane, Washington, USA; *S* father, 2010; *m* 1991, Lorayn Louise, *d* of late Frank Joseph Koson; three *s*. *Educ:* Univ. of Washington (BSc); Von Karman Inst. (Dip.); Yale Univ. Sch. of Management (MBA). Co-Founder, and Pres., Digital Control Inc., WA. Heir: *s* Colin Hugh Hambling, *b* 1991.

**HAMBLING, Maggi,** CBE 2010 (OBE 1995); artist; *b* 23 Oct. 1945; *d* of late Harry Hambling and Marjorie Hambling (*née* Harris). *Educ:* Hadleigh Hall Sch., Suffolk; Amberfield Sch., Suffolk; Ipswich Sch. of Art; Camberwell Sch. of Art (DipAD 1967); Slade Sch. of Fine Art (HDFA 1969). Boise Travel Award, NY, 1969; first Artist in Residence, Nat. Gall., London, 1980–81; Tutor in Painting and Drawing, Morley Coll. *One-man exhibitions include:* Paintings and Drawings, Morley Gall., London, 1973; New Oil Paintings, Warehouse Gall., London 1977; Drawings and Paintings on View, Nat. Gall., 1981; Pictures of Max Wall, Nat. Portrait Gall., 1983 (and tour); Maggi Hambling, Serpentine Gall., 1987 (and tour); An Eye Through a Decade, Yale Center for British Art, Newhaven, Conn, 1991; Towards Laughter, Northern Centre for Contemporary Art, 1993–94 (and tour); Maggi Hambling, Marlborough Fine Art, London, 1996; A Matter of Life and Death, Yorkshire Sculpture Park, 1997; also exhibn, A Statue for Oscar Wilde, Nat. Portrait Gall., and Hugh Lane Gall. of Modern Art, Dublin, 1997; statue, A Conversation with Oscar Wilde, bronze and granite, Adelaide Street, London, 1998; Good Friday paintings, drawings and sculpture, Gainsborough's House, Sudbury, Suffolk, 2000, LMH, Oxford, 2001; Henrietta Moraes, Marlborough Fine Art, London, 2001; Father, Morley Gall., London, 2001; The Very Special Brew Series, Sotheby's, 2003; North Sea Painting, Aldeburgh Fest., 2003; Scallop, Aldeburgh beach, 2003; Portraits of People and the Sea, Marlborough Fine Art, 2006; No Straight Lines, Fitzwilliam Mus., Cambridge and tour, 2007; Waves Breaking, Marlborough Fine Art, 2007; Waves and Waterfalls, Abbot Hall Art Gall., Kendal, Marlborough Fine Art, London, 2008; George Always: portraits of George Melly,

Walker Art Gall., Liverpool, 2009; The Sea, Lowry, Manchester, 2009; Maggi Hambling: The Wave, Fitzwilliam Mus., Cambridge, New Sea Sculpture, Marlborough Fine Art, 2010; The Brixton Heron, 2010; The North Sea, Europe House, 2010; Wall of Water, Hermitage Mus., St Petersburg, 2013; The Winchester Tapestries, Winchester Cathedral, 2013; Walls of Water, Nat. Gall., 2014; Walls of Water: the monotypes, Marlborough Fine Art, 2014; War Requiem & Aftermath, KCL, 2015; Touch: works on paper, British Mus., 2016; Edge, Marlborough Fine Art, 2017; *participating artist*: Snap, Aldeburgh Fest., 2012, 2013; Central Acad. of Fine Arts, Beijing, 2019; *public collections include*: Arts Council; Ashmolean Mus., Oxford; Australian Nat. Gall.; Birmingham City Art Gall.; British Council; BM; Contemporary Art Soc.; Fitzwilliam Mus., Cambridge; Gulbenkian Foundn, Lisbon; Harris Mus. and Art Gall., Preston; Imperial War Mus.; Nat. Gall.; Nat. Portrait Gall.; Rugby Collection; Scottish Nat. Gall. of Modern Art, Edinburgh; Scottish Nat. Portrait Gall., Edinburgh; Southampton Art Gall.; Swindon Art Gall.; Tate Gall.; V&A Mus.; Wakefield Art Gall.; Whitworth Art Gall.; Yale Center for British Art. Hon. Fellow: New Hall, Cambridge, 2004; Univ. of the Arts, London, 2004; London South Bank Univ., 2011. *Publications*: (with John Berger) Maggi & Henrietta, 2001; (with Andrew Lambirth) Maggi Hambling: the works, 2006; The Aldeburgh Scallop, 2010; (with James Cahill) War Requiem & Aftermath, 2015; Touch: works on paper, 2016. *Recreation*: tennis. *Address*: Morley College, Westminster Bridge Road, SE1 7HT. *Club*: Chelsea Arts.

**HAMBLING, Sir Peter;** *see* Hambling, Sir H. P. H.

**HAMBLY, Christl Ann;** *see* Donnelly, C. A.

**HAMBRO, James Daryl;** Chairman: J. O. Hambro Capital Management Ltd, since 1994; James Hambro & Partners LLP, since 2010; *b* 22 March 1949; *s* of late Jocelyn Hambro, MC and Ann Silvia Hambro (*née* Muir); *m* 1981, Diana Cherry; three *d*. *Educ*: Eton College; Harvard Business Sch. Hambros Bank, 1970–85 (Exec. Dir, 1982–85); J. O. Hambro & Co., subseq. J. O. Hambro Ltd, 1986–99. Chairman: Ashtenne Hldgs, 1997–2005; ViCTory (formerly Singer & Friedlander) AIM VCT, 2000–11; Hansteen Holdings plc, 2005–15; Wiltons (St James's) Ltd, 2008– (Dir, 1992). Director: Vodafone plc, 1982–85; Primary Health Properties, 1996–2014; Capital Opportunities Trust, 1997–2003; Enterprise Capital Trust, 1997–2004; Biocompatibles Internat., 2002–03. Dep. Chm., Peabody Trust, 1998–2005; Chairman: Internat. Students' Trust, 1988–2016; Henry Smith's Charity, 2007–15; Guide Dogs for the Blind, 2015–. *Recreations*: shooting, golf, farming, painting. *Address*: James Hambro & Partners, 45 Pall Mall, SW1Y 5JG; 15 Elm Park Road, SW3 6BP; Manor Farm, Kimberley, Wymondham, Norfolk NR9 4DT. *Clubs*: White's; Royal West Norfolk.
*See also* R. N. Hambro.

**HAMBRO, Peter Charles Percival;** Founder and Chairman, Peter Hambro Ltd, since 1990; Chairman, IRC Ltd, since 2018; *b* 18 Jan. 1945; *s* of late Lt Col Everard Hambro and Mary Hambro; *m* 1968, Karen Brodrick; three *s*. *Educ*: Eton Coll. Exec. Chm., 1994–2017, Pres., 2018–, Petropavlovsk PLC (formerly Peter Hambro Mining Plc). Chm., Sundeala Ltd, 2000–. *Recreation*: painting.

**HAMBRO, Rupert Nicholas,** CBE 2014; Chairman: J O Hambro Ltd, since 1986 (Group Managing Director, 1986–94); Robinson Hambro, since 2010; Co-founder, Hambro Perks, since 2013; *b* 27 June 1943; *s* of late Jocelyn Olaf Hambro, MC and Ann Silvia (*née* Muir); *m* 1970, Mary Robinson Boyer; one *s* one *d*. *Educ*: Eton; Aix-en-Provence. Peat Marwick Mitchell & Co., 1962–64; joined Hambros Bank, 1964, Director, 1969, Dep. Chm., 1980, Chm., 1983–86; Chm., J. O. Hambro Magan Ltd, 1988–96. Director: Anglo American Corporation of South Africa, 1981–97; Chatsworth House Trust Ltd, 1982–2004; Racecourse Hldgs Trust Ltd, 1985–94; Telegraph Group Ltd (formerly Daily Telegraph PLC, then The Telegraph plc), 1986–2003; Sedgwick Group plc, 1987–92; Triton Europe plc, 1987–90; Pioneer Concrete Hldgs PLC, 1989–99; Hamleys plc, 1988–96 (Chm., 1989–94); KBC Peel Hunt Ltd (formerly Peel Hunt plc), 2000–03; Business for Sterling, 2002–07; Open Europe Ltd, 2006–07; Mem. Supervisory Bd, Bank Gutmann AG, 2000–17; Chairman: Wilton's (St James's) Ltd, 1987–2003; Mayflower Corp. Plc, 1988–2004; Internat. Adv. Bd, Montana AG, Vienna, 1988–2000; Fenchurch plc, 1993–97; CTR Group plc, 1990–97; Longshot plc, 1996–2007; Woburn Golf & Country Club Ltd, 1998–2008; Third Space Gp Ltd, 1999–2007; Jermyn Street Assoc. Ltd, 2000–03; Roland Berger & Partners Ltd, 2000–02; Walpole Cttee Ltd, 2000–05; Cazenove & Loyd Ltd, 2004–17; Lovedean Ltd, 2008–10; Sipsmith Ltd, 2009–17; Woburn Enterprises Ltd, 2008–11; Theo Fennell plc, 2009–14. Chairman: Assoc. of International Bond Dealers, 1979–82; Soc. of Merchants Trading to the Continent, 1995–2009. Mem., SE Econ. Planning Council, 1971–74. Treas., NACF, 1991–2003; Chm. Govs, Mus. of London, 1998–2005; Co. Chm., Mus. in Docklands, 2003–05; Chm. Develt Strategy Bd, ZSL, 2011–; Patron, RBS, 1997–. Chm. Council, Univ. of Bath in Swindon, 2000–07; Member, Council: Univ. of Bath, 2004–10; RCA, 2010–18. Vice-Chm., 1991–96, Dep. Pres., 2001–11, Clubs for Young People (formerly NAYC); Chairman of Trustees: Boys' Club Trust, 1991–2000; Chiswick House & Gardens Trust, 2005–11; Silver Trust, 1987–2019; Trustee, Wallace Collection, 2013–17; Mem., English Heritage Blue Plaques Panel, 2014–19; Patron, 2005–08, Pres., 2008–17, British Assoc. of Adoption and Fostering; Patron, Assoc. of British Designer Silversmiths, 2006–. Dep. Pres., Anglo-Danish Soc., 1987–. Freeman, Fishmongers' Co., 1969–; Liveryman, Goldsmiths' Co., 1994– (Mem. Ct of Assts, 1998–; Prime Warden, 2009–10). Hon. Fellow, Univ. of Bath, 1998. Walpole Award for British excellence, 2005. Knight of the Falcon (Iceland), 1986. *Recreation*: country pursuits. *Address*: Hambro Perks, 8 Greencoat Place, SW1P 1PL. *Clubs*: White's, Walbrook, Groucho; Jupiter Island (Florida).
*See also* J. D. Hambro.

**HAMEED,** Baron *cr* 2007 (Life Peer), of Hampstead in the London Borough of Camden; **Khalid Hameed,** CBE 2004; DL; Chairman, Alpha Hospital Group, 2003–16; Executive Chairman, Lucknow International Hospital, India; *s* of late Prof. M. Abdul Hameed and Rashida Abdul Hameed; *m* 1989, Dr Ghazala Hameed; two *s* two *d* and one step *s* one step *d*. *Educ*: Lucknow Univ., India (BSc; DPA; MB BS; DSc); London Univ. (DTM&H). FRCP 2006. CEO, Cromwell Hosp., London, 1990–2005. Chm., Commonwealth Youth Exchange Council, 1999–2015; Trustee, Political Council for Co-existence, 2006–; Chm., Woolf Inst., 2007–16 (Vice Pres., 2016–); Gov., Internat. Students Hall, 2007–. Vice Pres., Friends of BL, 2015–. Pres., Little Foundn, 2007–. Patron, Three Faiths Forum, 2006–. Freedom, City of London, 2011. High Sheriff, 2006–07, DL 2007, Greater London. Hon. DLitt Middlesex, 2008; Hon. DSc London Metropolitan. Sternberg Award for Interfaith Work, 2006; Ambassador of Peace Award, Universal Peace Fedn, 2007; Asian of the Year Award, 2011. *Recreations*: chess, cricket, poetry, polo, bridge. *Address*: House of Lords, SW1A 0PW. *E*: hameed@parliament.uk. *Clubs*: Athenæum, Mosimann's, MCC; Guards Polo.

**HAMER, Christopher John;** Property Ombudsman (formerly Ombudsman for Estate Agents), 2006–15; *b* 26 Dec. 1952; *s* of late Ronald and Olive Hamer; *m* 1975, Sarah Anne Preston; three *s*. *Educ*: Thornbury Grammar Sch., Glos; Dorset Inst. of Higher Educn (HNC Business Studies). HM Customs & Excise, Dover, Southampton and London, 1974–84; Private Sec. to Parly Comr for Admin, 1984–85; Mem., Mgt and Efficiency Unit, Cabinet Office, 1985–88; Dir of Services, Insurance Ombudsman Bureau, 1988–96; Gen. Manager, Personal Investment Authy Ombudsman Bureau, 1996–2000; Hd, Product Risk, HSBC Insce, 2000–06. Exec. Chm., Propertymark, 2016–. Non-exec. Dir, AgencyPro, 2015–. Pres., Mgt Bd, Jardines de Casares Malaga, 2017–. *Recreations*: motoring, travel, First and Second World Wars.

**HAMER, John Alan,** OBE 2011; education consultant; Chairman, AlphaPlus Consultancy Ltd, 2012–18 (Vice-Chairman, 2000–12); *b* Manchester, 24 Jan. 1940; *s* of Frank Hamer and Mary Hamer; *m* 1965, Rachel Hamilton; one *s* one *d*. *Educ*: Manchester Grammar Sch.; Hatfield Coll., Durham Univ. (BA Hons Mod. Hist. 1962); Pembroke Coll., Oxford (DipEd 1965); Inst. of Educn, London Univ. (Advanced Dip. Educn 1972; MA Educn 1974). Primary sch. teacher, Manchester LEA, 1962–63; Asst Teacher, Jun. High Sch., Montreal, 1963–64; Asst Teacher, 1965–67, Hd of Hist., 1967–79, Collyer's Grammar Sch., Horsham; Asst Vice Principal, Collyer's Sixth Form Coll., Horsham, 1979–83; HM Inspector of Schs, 1984–97; Educn Policy Advr, Heritage Lottery Fund, 1997–2000. Hon. Lectr (formerly Special Lectr), Sch. of Educn, Nottingham Univ., 2000–14. Educn Consultant, Council of Europe, 2000–. Trustee: Heritage Educn Trust, 2000– (Chm., 2008–); Historic Royal Palaces, 2005–11; Mem. Council, Nat. Trust, 2002–05; Educn Advr, Historic Houses Assoc., 2005–10. Governor: Farlington Sch., Horsham, 2003–14; Tanbridge House Sch., Horsham, 2003–10; Frewen Coll., Northiam, 2005–16. Mem., Warnham Parish Council, 2007–. FRSA. *Publications*: History in the Making: the twentieth century, 1980, 2nd edn 1992; contribs to various UK and Council of Europe pubns on aspects of history and heritage educn. *Recreations*: local history, travel, golf, walking. *Address*: The Banks, Bailing Hill, Warnham, W Sussex RH12 3RT. *T*: (01403) 265088, *Fax*: (01403) 259988. *E*: j.a.hamer@btinternet.com.

**HAMEROW, Prof. Helena Francisca,** DPhil; Professor of Early Medieval Archaeology, University of Oxford, since 1996; Fellow, St Cross College, Oxford, since 1996 (Vice-Master, 2005–08); *b* Madison, Wisconsin, 18 Sept. 1961; *d* of Theodore S. Hamerow and Margareta Lotter Hamerow; partner, Eric R. Brown; one *s* one *d*. *Educ*: Univ. of Wisconsin-Madison (BA Hons Anthropol. 1983); Lincoln Coll., Oxford (DPhil Archaeol. 1988). Mary Somerville Res. Fellow, Somerville Coll., Oxford, 1988–90; Lectr in Early Medieval Archaeol., Durham Univ., 1990–96. Sen. Res. Fellow, British Acad., 2006–07. Hon. Ed., 1999–2002, Vice Pres. and Mem. Council, 2012–18, Royal Archaeol Inst.; Mem. Council, Univ. of Oxford, 2016–19. Pres., Soc. for Medieval Archaeol., 2014–16. Trustee, Oxford Archaeol., 2011–. FSA 1996. *Publications*: Mucking Excavations, vol. 2, The Anglo-Saxon Settlement, 1993; Early Medieval Settlements: the archaeology of rural communities in Northwest Europe, AD 400–900, 2002; The Oxford Handbook of Anglo-Saxon Archaeology, 2011; Rural Settlements and Society in Anglo-Saxon England, 2012. *Recreations*: music, travel. *Address*: Institute of Archaeology, University of Oxford, 34–36 Beaumont Street, Oxford OX1 2PG. *T*: (01865) 278240. *E*: Helena.hamerow@arch.ox.ac.uk.

**HAMES, Christopher William;** QC 2015; a Recorder, since 2018; *b* Brentwood, Essex, 11 Jan. 1964; *s* of Peter Hames and Sheila Hames (*née* Hickman, now Markwick); *m* 1989, Megan Veronica Butler, *qv*; one *s* one *d*. *Educ*: Eastbourne Grammar Sch.; Univ. of Sheffield (LLB Hons). Called to the Bar, Inner Temple, 1987; in practice as a barrister, specialising in internat. children law and matrimonial finance, 1987–; 4 Paper Buildings, 2000–. Mem. Cttee, Child Abduction Lawyers Assoc., 2015– (Chair, 2018–). Trustee, Children and Families Across Borders, 2018–. *Publications*: articles in The Times, The Telegraph, Family Law and Family Law Week. *Recreations*: running, tennis, cycling, archaeology and history, opera, travel, Chelsea FC. *Address*: 4 Paper Buildings, Temple, EC4Y 7EX. *T*: (020) 7427 5200, *Fax*: (020) 7353 4979. *E*: ch@4pb.com.

**HAMES, Duncan John;** Director of Policy, Transparency International UK, since 2016; *b* Herts, 16 June 1977; *m* 2011, Joanna Kate Swinson, *qv*; two *s*. *Educ*: Watford Boys' Grammar Sch.; New Coll., Oxford (BA PPE 1998). Business consultant, Deloitte Consulting, 1998–2004; Dir, Chippenham Consultants Ltd, 2005–10. Mem. Bd, 2003–09, Chm., Audit Cttee, 2008–09, SW England RDA; Mem. Bd, Culture SW, 2006–08. Mem. (Lib Dem) W Wilts DC, 2003–07. Contested (Lib Dem): Tottenham, June 2000; Watford, 2001; Westbury, 2005. MP (Lib Dem) Chippenham, 2010–15; contested (Lib Dem) same seat, 2015. PPS to Minister of State for Children and Families, 2010–11, to Sec. of State for Energy and Climate Change, 2011–12, to Dep. Prime Minister, 2012–13. Strategic Advr, Templar Executives, 2016. Member: Policy Adv. Bd, Social Market Foundn, 2010–15; Bd, Great Britain-China Centre, 2011–15. Non-exec. Dir, S London and Maudsley NHS Foundn Trust, 2016–.

**HAMES, Megan Veronica;** *see* Butler, M. V.

**HAMID, Rt Rev. David;** *see* Gibraltar in Europe, Suffragan Bishop of.

**HAMID, David;** Partner, OpCapita LLP (formerly Merchant Equity Partners), since 2006; Chairman, The Football Pools, since 2017; *b* 11 Dec. 1951; *s* of Osman and Doreen Hamid; *m* 1984, Gillian Joy; three *s* one *d*. *Educ*: Alleyne's Grammar Sch., Stevenage; Univ. of Bradford (BSc Hons Industrial Technol. and Mgt). Marketing Director: Jewellery Div., Alfred Dunhill, 1985–86; Supasnaps, 1987; Managing Director: Dixons Financial Services, 1988–90; Mastercare Ltd, 1990–95; Commercial Service Dir, Dixons Gp plc, 1995–98; Gp Man. Dir, PC World, 1998–2001; Chief Operating Officer, Dixons Gp plc, 2001–03; CEO, Halfords Gp plc, 2003–05; Partner, MEP Mayflower Hldgs, 2006–08; Chairman: Nationwide Autocentres, 2006–10; Ideal Shopping Ltd, 2011–15. Non-exec. Dir, Homeserve Membership, 2006–11; Dep. Chm., MVideo OAO (Russia), 2011–17 (Dir, 2005–17); Chm., Game Digital plc (formerly Game Retail Ltd), 2012–17. Chm., Music for Youth, 2008–15. *Recreations*: field hockey, playing in a rock band, golf. *Address*: OpCapita LLP, 2 Park Street, W1K 2HX. *Club*: Royal Automobile.

**HAMILL, Keith,** OBE 2012; FCA; Chairman, Horsforth Holdings Ltd, since 2012; *b* 7 Dec. 1952; *s* of Gerard Hamill and Edith Hamill; *m* 1975, Angela Sylvia Green; three *s*. *Educ*: Cambridge Grammar Sch. for Boys; Univ. of Nottingham (BA Politics). FCA 1989. Price Waterhouse, 1975–98 (Partner, 1987–88); Dir, Financial Control, Guinness PLC, 1988–91; Finance Director: United Distillers plc, 1991–93; Forte plc, 1993–96; W H Smith plc, 1996–2000; Chairman: W H Smith N America, 1996–2000; Collins Stewart, then Collins Stewart Tullett, later Tullett Prebon plc, 2000–13. Chairman: Alterian plc, 2000–11; Go Ltd, 2001–02; Luminar plc, 2001–06; Moss Bros Gp PLC, 2001–08; Bertram Books Ltd, 2001–07; Travelodge, 2003–10 and 2012 (Dep. Chm., 2010–12); Heath Lambert Gp Ltd, 2005–11; Fundsmith, 2010–12; Avant Homes Ltd (formerly Gladedale Ltd), 2013–14; Premier Foods, 2017–19; Deputy Chairman: Collins Stewart plc, 2006–10; Dir, Newmarket Racecourse Ltd, 2002–11; non-executive Director: Electrocomponents plc, 1999–2008; William Hill PLC, 2000–01; Tempus Gp PLC, 2000–01; TDG plc, 2001–05; Cadmus Communications Corp., 2002–07; EasyJet, 2009–17; Max Property plc, 2009–14; Samsonite, 2010–. Mem., Urgent Issues Task Force, Accounting Standards Bd, 1992–98; Chm., Financial Reporting Cttee, CBI, 1993–97. Treas., 1997–2003, Pro-Chancellor, 2003–11, Univ. of Nottingham. Dir, Greenwich and Bexley Hospice, 1999–2008. Trustee, British Internat. Sch. in Rome, 2014–. Hon. LLD Nottingham, 2012. *Recreations*: opera, horse racing, soccer, golf. *Address:* Horsforth Holdings Ltd, LDH House, Si Two, St Ives Business Park, Cambs PE27 4EE. *T:* (01480) 484250. *Clubs:* Royal Automobile; Royal Ascot Racing; Chislehurst Golf.

**HAMILTON;** *see* Baillie-Hamilton, family name of Earl of Haddington.

**HAMILTON;** *see* Cole-Hamilton.

**HAMILTON;** *see* Douglas-Hamilton.

**HAMILTON,** family name of **Duke of Abercorn,** of **Lord Belhaven,** and of **Barons Hamilton of Dalzell, Hamilton of Epsom** and **HolmPatrick.**

**HAMILTON,** 16th Duke of, *cr* 1643 (Scot.), **AND BRANDON,** 13th Duke of, *cr* 1711 (GB); **Alexander Douglas-Hamilton;** Marquess of Douglas 1633; Lord Abernethy and Jedburgh Forest 1633; Marquess of Clydesdale 1643; Earl of Angus; Earl of Arran, Lanark and Cambridge; Lord Aven and Innerdale 1643; Lord Machanshire and Polmont; Baron Dutton (GB) 1711; Premier Peer of Scotland; Hereditary Keeper of Holyrood Palace; *b* 31 March 1978; *er s* of 15th Duke of Hamilton and Sarah (*d* 1994), *d* of Sir Walter Scott, 4th Bt; *S* father, 2010; *m* 2011, Sophie Ann Rutherford; three *s. Heir: s* Marquess of Douglas and Clydesdale, *qv.*

**HAMILTON, Marquess of; James Harold Charles Hamilton;** *b* 19 Aug. 1969; *s* and heir of Duke of Abercorn, *qv*; *m* 2004, Tanya, *d* of late Douglas Nation; two *s.* A Page of Honour to the Queen, 1982–84. *Heir: s* Viscount Strabane, *qv. Address:* Barons Court, Omagh, Co. Tyrone BT78 4EZ.

**HAMILTON OF DALZELL,** 5th Baron *cr* 1886; **Gavin Goulburn Hamilton;** DL; farmer and landowner; *b* 8 Oct. 1968; *s* of 4th Baron Hamilton of Dalzell and (Ann Anastasia) Corinna (Helena) Hamilton (*née* Dixon); *S* father, 2006; *m* 1997, Harriet Louise, *yr d* of Thomas Roskill; one *s* three *d* (of whom two *d* are twins). *Educ:* Eton Coll.; Buckingham Univ. (BSc). ACA 1994. Smith & Williamson, chartered accountants, 1990–95; DHL International (UK) Ltd, 1995–2007. Director: Apley Estate, Goulburn Farms, 2007–; Apley Farm Shop, 2011–; Bridgnorth Rugby FC, 2018–. DL Shropshire, 2011. *Recreation:* shooting. *Heir: s* Hon. Francis Alexander James Goulburn Hamilton, *b* 20 Oct. 2009. *Address:* Harrington Hall, Shifnal, Shropshire TF11 9DR. *T:* (01952) 730870. *E:* gavin.hamilton@apleyestate.com. *Clubs:* Boodle's, Pratts.

**HAMILTON OF EPSOM,** Baron *cr* 2005 (Life Peer), of West Anstey in the county of Devon; **Archibald Gavin Hamilton,** Kt 1994; PC 1991; *b* 30 Dec. 1941; *yr s* of 3rd Baron Hamilton of Dalzell, GCVO, MC; *m* 1968, Anne Catharine Napier; three *d. Educ:* Eton Coll. Borough Councillor, Kensington and Chelsea, 1968–71. Contested (C) Dagenham, Feb. and Oct., 1974. MP (C) Epsom and Ewell, April 1978–2001; PPS to Sec. of State for Energy, 1979–81, to Sec. of State for Transport, 1981–82; an Asst Govt Whip, 1982–84; a Lord Comr of HM Treasury (Govt Whip), 1984–86; Parly Under-Sec. of State for Defence Procurement, MoD, 1986–87; PPS to Prime Minister, 1987–88; Minister of State, MoD, 1988–93. Member: Intelligence and Security Cttee, 1994–97; Select Cttee on Standards in Public Life, 1995; Select Cttee on Members' Interests, 1995; Jt Cttee on Nat. Security Council, 2015–. Chm., 1922 Cttee, 1997–2001 (Exec. Mem., 1995–97). Mem., NATO Parly Assembly, 2012–. Pres., European-Atlantic Gp, 2014–18. Gov., Westminster Foundn for Democracy, 1993–99. Mem. Council, Nat. Army Mus., 2013–18. Trustee, Supporting Wounded Veterans, 2017–. Mem., Garden Soc. *Address:* House of Lords, SW1A 0PW. *Clubs:* White's, Pratt's.

**HAMILTON, Rt Hon. Lord; Arthur Campbell Hamilton;** PC 2002; Lord Justice General of Scotland and Lord President of the Court of Session, 2005–12; Member of the Supplementary Panel of the Supreme Court of the United Kingdom, 2012–17; a Judge of the Court of Appeal, Botswana, since 2012; arbitrator, since 2014; a Judge of the Qatar International Court, since 2015; *b* 10 June 1942; *s* of James Whitehead Hamilton and Isobel Walker Hamilton (*née* McConnell); *m* 1970, Christine Ann Croll; one *d. Educ:* The High School of Glasgow; Glasgow Univ.; Worcester Coll., Oxford (BA; Hon. Fellow, 2003); Edinburgh Univ. (LLB). Admitted member, Faculty of Advocates, 1968; QC (Scot.) 1982; Standing Junior Counsel: to Scottish Development Dept, 1975–78; to Board of Inland Revenue (Scotland), 1978–82; Advocate Depute, 1982–85; Judge, Courts of Appeal, Jersey and Guernsey, 1988–95; Pres., Pensions Appeal Tribunals for Scotland, 1992–95; a Senator of the Coll. of Justice in Scotland, 1995–2005. Hon. Bencher, Inner Temple, 2006. *Recreations:* music, history. *Address:* 8 Heriot Row, Edinburgh EH3 6HU. *T:* (0131) 556 4663. *Club:* New (Edinburgh).

**HAMILTON (NZ), Bishop of, (RC),** since 2015; **Most Rev. Stephen Marmion Lowe;** *b* Hokitika, NZ, 3 Aug. 1962; *s* of Frank Lowe and Milly Lowe. *Educ:* Univ. of Otago (BTh); Pontifical Gregorian Univ., Rome (STL). NZ Forest Service, Hokitika and Christchurch; NZ Timberlands, Timaru. Ordained priest, 1996; Asst Priest, Mairehau, Ashburton and Greymouth; Parish Priest, Timaru N; Formation Dir, Holy Cross Seminary, Auckland, 2008–14. *Address:* PO Box 4353, Hamilton 3247, New Zealand. *E:* bishop@cdh.org.nz.

**HAMILTON, Adrian Walter;** QC 1973; commercial arbitrator and mediator, retired; a Recorder of the Crown Court, 1974–95; *b* 11 March 1923; *er s* of late W. G. M. Hamilton, banker, Fletching, Sussex and of late Mrs S. E. Hamilton; *m* 1966, Jill, *d* of S. R. Brimblecombe, Eastbourne; two *d. Educ:* Highgate Sch.; Balliol Coll., Oxford (BA 1st cl. Jurisprudence 1948; MA 1954; Jenkyns Law Prize; Paton Meml Student, 1948–49). Served with RN, 1942–46 (N Atlantic, Mediterranean, English Channel, Far East): Ord. Seaman, 1942; Sub-Lt RNVR, 1943, Lieut 1946. Cassel Scholar, Lincoln's Inn, 1949; called to Bar, Lincoln's Inn, 1949 (Bencher 1979), Middle Temple and Inner Temple; Dep. High Court Judge, 1982–95. Mem., Senate of Inns of Court and the Bar, 1976–82, Treas., 1979–82; Mem. Council, Inns of Court, 1987–91. Mem., Council of Legal Educn, 1977–87. Chairman: Appellate Cttee for Exam. Irregularities, London Univ., 1985–; Mental Health Review Tribunals, 1986–95; Lautro Disciplinary Cttees, 1991–94. Inspector, Peek Foods Ltd, 1977. *Recreations:* family, travelling, history. *Address:* 63 Abbotsbury Road, W14 8EL. *T:* (020) 7603 0185. *Club:* Garrick.

**HAMILTON, Alfred William, (Wilfred);** Deputy Secretary, Department of Enterprise, Trade and Investment, Northern Ireland, 2001–08; *b* 13 June 1948; *s* of Albert George Hamilton and Anna Hamilton (*née* Christie); *m* 1972, Sandra Magill; one *s* one *d. Educ:* Boys' Model Sch., Belfast. Dip. Admin and Mgt. Northern Ireland Civil Service: posts in mgt services, Rayner Scrutinies, NI Econ. Council and Eur. Div., Dept of Health and Social Services, 1967–91; Asst Sec., 1991; Head of Finance Div., 1991–95, Head of Finance, EU and Efficiency Div., 1995–2001, Dept of Econ. Develt. Chm., Ulster-Scots Acad. Project Steering Gp, 2010–. *Recreations:* golf, sport in general, reading. *Address:* c/o Department of Enterprise, Trade and Investment, Netherleigh, Massey Avenue, Belfast BT4 2JP.

**HAMILTON, Sir Andrew Caradoc,** 10th Bt *cr* 1646, of Silverton Hill, Lanarkshire; *b* 23 Sept. 1953; *s* of Sir Richard Hamilton, 9th Bt and Elizabeth Vidal Barton; *S* father, 2001; *m* 1984, Anthea Jane Huntingford; three *d. Educ:* Charterhouse; St Peter's Coll., Oxford (BA). *Heir: cousin* Paul Howden Hamilton [*b* 24 Dec. 1951; *m* 1980, Elizabeth Anne Harrison; two *d*].

**HAMILTON, Prof. Andrew David,** PhD; FRS 2004; President, New York University, since 2016; *b* 3 Nov. 1952; *m* 1981, Jennifer Letton; two *s* one *d. Educ:* Univ. of Exeter (BSc 1974); Univ. of British Columbia (MSc 1976); Univ. of Cambridge (PhD 1980). Asst Prof. of Chem., Princeton Univ., 1981–88; University of Pittsburgh: Associate Prof., 1988–92; Prof. of Chem., 1992–97; Hd, Dept of Chem., 1994–97; Yale University: Irénée duPont Prof. of Chem., 1997–2004; Prof. of Molecular Biophysics and Biochem., 1998–2009; Hd, Dept of Chemistry, 1999–2003; Dep. Provost for Sci. and Technol., 2003–04; Benjamin Silliman Prof. of Chemistry and Provost, 2004–09; Vice-Chancellor, Univ. of Oxford, 2009–15. Mem., EPSRC, 2011–15. *Publications:* articles in learned jls. *Address:* New York University, 70 Washington Square South, New York, NY 10012, USA.

**HAMILTON, His Honour Andrew Ninian Roberts;** a Circuit Judge, Midland Circuit, 2001–16; *b* 7 Jan. 1947; *s* of Robert Bousfield Hamilton and Margery Wensley Iowerth Hamilton (*née* Roberts); *m* 1982, Isobel Louise Goode; one *s* one *d. Educ:* Cheltenham Coll.; Birmingham Univ. (LLB). Called to the Bar, Gray's Inn, 1970; in practice, Midland and Oxford Circuit; Asst Recorder, 1993–99; a Recorder, 1999–2001. Mem. (C) Nottingham CC, 1973–91 (Chairman: Transport Cttee, 1976; Archaeology Cttee, 1987–91; Vice-Chm., Leisure Services Cttee, 1987–88; Hon. Alderman, 1991). Chairman: Nottingham Civic Soc., 1978–83 (Vice-Pres., 1983–); Nottingham Civic Soc. Sales Ltd, 1988–2001; Nottingham Park Conservation Trust, 1992–2014; Nottingham Caves Forum, 2010–; Wollaton Histl and Conservation Soc., 2011–; Dir, Nottingham and Notts United Services Club, 1994–2001. Chm., Nottingham Bar Mess, 1995–2001. External examiner, BVC, Nottingham Trent Univ., 1997–2000. Contested (C) Ilkeston, Oct. 1974. *Publications:* Nottingham's Royal Castle and Ducal Palace, 1976, 5th edn 1999; Nottingham, City of Caves, 1978, 3rd edn 2004; Historic Walks in Nottingham, 1978, 2nd edn 1985. *Recreations:* tennis, ski-ing, golf, walking, local history. *Club:* Nottingham and Notts United Services.

**HAMILTON, Angus Warnock;** a District Judge (Magistrates' Courts), since 2005; Information Technology Liaison Judge, since 2016; *b* 1 June 1957; *s* of Sir James Arnott Hamilton, KCB, MBE. *Educ:* Univ. of Leicester (LLB 1979); Univ. of Sheffield (MA Socio-Legal Studies 1980); Guildford Coll. of Law. Trainee solicitor, 1981–83; admitted solicitor, 1983; solicitor in private practice, 1983–97; solicitor/sole Principal, Hamiltons Solicitors, 1997–2005; a Dep. Dist Judge, 1998–2005; Dist Judge, E London Family Court, 2014–. Member: Gambling Appeals Tribunal, 2007–; Information Rights Tribunal, 2010–; Professional Regulation Tribunal, 2016–; Pensions Tribunal, 2016–. Mem., Equal Treatment Adv. Cttee, Judicial Studies Bd, 2008–11. Tutor, Judicial Coll., 2013–. *Publications:* (with Rosemary Jay) Data Protection Law and Practice: a guide to the Data Protection Act 1998, 1999, 2nd edn 2003; *contributions to:* Liberating Cyberspace, 1998; Staying Legal, 1999; Advising HIV+ Clients: a guide for lawyers, 1999; Advising Gay and Lesbian Clients: a guide for lawyers, 1999. *Recreations:* travel, photography, cinema, live music, weight training, scuba-diving, directing pop promo videos. *E:* angus.hamilton@mac.com. *Clubs:* Athenæum, h.

**HAMILTON, Arthur Campbell;** *see* Hamilton, Rt Hon. Lord.

**HAMILTON, Christina Mary;** *see* Slade, C. M.

**HAMILTON, Sir David,** Kt 2016; *b* 24 Oct. 1950; *s* of Agnes and David Hamilton; *m* 1969, Jean Macrae; two *d. Educ:* Dalkeith High Sch. Coalminer, 1965–84; Landscape Supervisor, Midlothian DC, 1987–89; Training Officer and Placement Officer, Craigmillar Fest. Soc., 1989–92; Chief Exec., Craigmillar Opportunities Trust, 1992–2000. Mem., Midlothian Council, 1995–2001. MP (Lab) Midlothian, 2001–15. Scottish Whip, 2011–15. Chm., Midlothian Innovation Technol. Trust, 2001–10; Director: Lothian Miners Convalescent Home, 2004–; Scottish Mining Mus., 2008–11 and 2016–. Hon. Pres., Midlothian Community Artists, 1995. *Recreations:* films, current affairs, grandchildren.

**HAMILTON, Derek Jack;** Sheriff of North Strathclyde at Greenock, since 2012; *b* Airdrie, 30 May 1961; *s* of Jack Hughes Hamilton and Janet Hamilton (*née* Shilliday); *m* 1986, Marion Ann Sutherland; one *s* two *d. Educ:* Airdrie Acad.; Univ. of Glasgow (LLB 1981; DipLP 1982). Admitted as solicitor, 1983; Partner: Bonnar & Co., Airdrie, 1986–98; Hamilton Ross, Airdrie, 1999–2009; Hon. Sheriff, 2006–12; Immigration Judge (pt-time), 2006–12; Duty Immigration Judge (pt-time), 2010–12; Convener (pt-time), 2007–12, Inhouse Convener (pt-time), 2008–12, Mental Health Tribunal for Scotland; Judge (pt-time), Social Entitlement Chamber, 2011–12. Legal Advr, GDC, 2010–12. *Recreations:* cycling, mountain biking, tennis. *Address:* Greenock Sheriff Court, Sheriff Court House, Nelson Street, Greenock PA15 1TR. *T:* (01475) 787073. *E:* sheriffdhamilton@scotcourts.gov.uk.

**HAMILTON, His Honour Donald Rankin Douglas;** a Circuit Judge, 1994–2012; *b* 15 June 1946; *s* of Allister McNicoll Hamilton and Mary Glen Hamilton (*née* Rankin); *m* 1974, (Margaret) Ruth Perrens; one *s* one *d. Educ:* Rugby Sch.; Balliol Coll., Oxford (BA). Called to the Bar, Gray's Inn, 1969 (Atkin Schol. 1970); pupillage in Birmingham, 1970–71; practised in Birmingham, 1971–94; Designated Family Judge, Birmingham, 1996–2008. Mem., Council of Mgt, CBSO, 1974–80; Dir, CBSO Soc. Ltd, 1984–99; former Trustee: City of Birmingham Orchestral Endowment Fund; CBSO Benevolent Fund. Patron, SWEET Project, Birmingham. *Recreation:* music.

**HAMILTON, Duncan Graeme;** Advocate at Scottish Bar; *b* 3 Oct. 1973; *s* of Rev. David Gentles Hamilton and Elsa Catherine Hamilton (*née* Nicolson); *m* 2003, Susan De Bruin; two *s* one *d. Educ:* Glasgow Univ. (MA 1st Cl. Hons Hist.); Edinburgh Univ. (LLB Scots Law; DipLP); Kennedy Sch. of Govt, Harvard Univ. (Kennedy Schol.). Asst Brand Manager, Proctor & Gamble, 1995; Aide and advr to Alex Salmond, MP, 1997–99. MSP (SNP) Highlands and Is, 1999–2003; Mem., Health and Community Care Cttee, 1999–2000, Enterprise and Life Long Learning Cttee, 2000–03, Justice Cttee, 2001–03, Scottish Parlt. Mem., SNP, 1994–; Asst to SNP Chief Exec., 1998–99. Bar trainee, Simpson & Marwick Solicitors, Edinburgh, 2004–05; devilling at Scottish Bar, 2005–06; called to Scottish Bar, 2006. Political advr to First Minister, Scottish Exec., later Scottish Govt, 2007–08; Standing Jun. Counsel to Scottish Govt, 2013–. Legal Mem., Mental Health Tribunal for Scotland, 2018–. Mem. Council, London Information Network on Conflict and State-building, 2003– (spokesman for Caucasus Caspian Commn, 2007–08). Columnist: Scotsman, 2003–07; Scotland on Sunday, 2009–12. *Recreations:* football, reading, friends. *Address:* c/o Faculty of Advocates, Parliament House, Edinburgh EH1 1RF.

**HAMILTON, Eben William;** QC 1981; *b* 12 June 1937; *s* of late Rev. John Edmund Hamilton, MC and Hon. Lilias Hamilton, *e d* of 1st Baron Maclay of Glasgow; *m* 1st, 1973, Catherine Harvey (marr. diss. 1977); 2nd, 1985, Themy Rusi Bilimoria, *y d* of late Brig. Rusi Bilimoria. *Educ:* Winchester; Trinity Coll., Cambridge. Nat. Service: 4/7 Royal Dragoon Guards, 1955–57; Fife and Forfar Yeomanry/Scottish Horse, TA, 1958–66.

Called to the Bar: Inner Temple, 1962, Bencher, 1985; (*ad eundem*) Lincoln's Inn, 1966; admitted (*ad hoc*): Hong Kong Bar, 1978; Singapore Bar, 1982; Cayman Bar, 2001. Dep. High Court Judge, Chancery Div., 1990–2005. Mem., Inst. of Conveyancers, 1991– (Pres., 1995–96). Jt DTI Inspector, Atlantic Computers plc, 1990–94. Trustee, Royal Scottish Corp., 2008–. FRSA 1988. *Address:* 5 Canon Lane, Cathedral Close, Chichester PO19 1PX. *Club:* Garrick.

**HAMILTON, Rt Hon. Dame Eleanor (Warwick);** *see* King, Rt Hon. Dame E. W.

**HAMILTON, Fabian;** MP (Lab) Leeds North East, since 1997; *b* 12 April 1955; *s* of late Mario Uziell-Hamilton and Her Honour Adrianne Uziell-Hamilton; *m* 1980, Rosemary Ratcliffe; one *s* two *d*. *Educ:* Brentwood Sch., Essex; Univ. of York (BA Hons). Graphic designer (own company), 1979–94; computer systems consultant, 1994–97. Leeds City Council: Mem. (Lab), 1987–97; Chm., Employment and Econ. Develt Cttee, 1994–96; Chm., Educn Cttee, 1996–98. Shadow Minister for Foreign and Commonwealth Affairs, 2016–, for Defence, 2016–17. Mem., Select Cttee on Foreign Affairs, 2001–10, on Political and Constitutional Reform, 2010–15, Internat. Develt, 2013–16. Contested (Lab) Leeds NE, 1992. Trustee, Heart Research UK (formerly Nat. Heart Res. Fund), 1999–2012. Gov., Northern Sch. of Contemporary Dance. *Recreations:* film, theatre, opera, photography, cycling. *Address:* House of Commons, SW1A 0AA. *T:* (020) 7219 3493.

**HAMILTON, Prof. George,** CVO 2017; MD; FRCS; Professor of Vascular Surgery, UCL Medical School (formerly Royal Free and University College School of Medicine), University of London, since 2003; Consultant in Vascular and General Surgery, since 1987 and Medical Director of Private Practice and Royal Free International, since 2016, Royal Free London NHS Foundation (formerly Royal Free Hampstead NHS) Trust; Consultant Vascular Surgeon, Great Ormond Street Hospital for Sick Children NHS Trust, since 1998; Serjeant Surgeon to the Queen, 2010–16 (Surgeon to the Queen, 2007–10); *b* 2 Sept. 1947; *s* of George Hamilton and Ginetta Lucaccini Hamilton; *m* 1980, Margaret Handyside; one *s* two *d*. *Educ:* St Modan's High Sch., Stirling; Univ. of Glasgow Sch. of Medicine (MB ChB 1971; MD 2002). DObstRCOG 1974; FRCS 1977; FRCSGlas *ad eundem* 2007. Charing Cross Hosp., London; Surg. Registrar, Basildon Hosp.; Royal Free Hospital, subseq. Royal Free and University College, School of Medicine: Surg. Res. Fellow, 1980; Lectr in Surgery, 1981–87; Hon. Sen. Lectr, 1987–2003; Clin. Sub-Dean, 1997–2005; Faculty (formerly Site) Tutor, Royal Free Campus, 2000–05; Divl Dir of Surgery and Associated Services, Royal Free Hampstead NHS Trust, later Royal Free London NHS Foundn Trust, 2011–18. Clin. Res. Fellow, Mass Gen. Hosp. and Harvard Sch. of Medicine, 1985–86. Surgeon to the Royal Household, 2001–07. Chm., Jt Vascular Res. Gp of GB and Ireland, 1995–98. President: Vascular Soc. of GB and Ireland, 2006–07; European Soc. for Vascular Surgery, 2012–13. Mem., British Fulbright Scholars' Assoc. *Publications:* (ed jtly) Renal Vascular Disease, 1995; contribs to learned jls of surgery and vascular surgery and disease. *Recreations:* family, good food and wine, travel, cinema, theatre, water sports, walking, ski-ing. *Address:* Vascular Surgery, Royal Free Hospital, Pond Street, NW3 2QG. *T:* (020) 7433 2952.

**HAMILTON, Sir George,** Kt 2019; QPM 2015; Chief Constable, Police Service of Northern Ireland, 2014–19; *b* Newtownards, Co. Down, 27 June 1967; *s* of Robert Hamilton and Elsie Hamilton; *m* 1989, Ruth Rainey; one *s* three *d*. *Educ:* Gransha High Sch., Bangor, Co. Down; Open Univ. (BA Politics and Econs); Univ. of Ulster (MBA Dist.). Various roles up to Detective Chief Insp., RUC, 1985–2001, to Chief Supt, Police Service of NI, 2001–07; Asst Chief Constable, Crime and Public Protection, Strathclyde Police, 2007–11; Asst Chief Constable, Criminal Justice, 2011–13, Rural Reg., 2013–14, Police Service of NI.

**HAMILTON, His Honour Iain McCormick,** CBE 2015; a Circuit Judge, 2000–14; Designated Family Judge for Greater Manchester, 2005–14; a Senior Circuit Judge, 2010–14; *b* 11 Nov. 1948; *s* of James Hamilton and Mary Isabella Hamilton; *m* 1975, Marilyn Tomlinson; one *s* two *d*. *Educ:* Heversham Grammar Sch.; Manchester Poly. (BA Hons Law). Admitted solicitor, 1974; Walls, Johnston & Co., Stockport, 1974–94; Jones Maidment Wilson, Manchester, 1994–2000; Asst Recorder, 1992–96; Recorder, 1996–2000. Pres., Stockport Law Soc., 1990–91. Chm., 1992–93 and 1996–99, Patron, 2001–, Child Concern. Hon. DH Manchester Metropolitan, 2010; Hon. LLD Bolton, 2015. *Recreations:* music, reading, cooking, watching sport, bird watching.

**HAMILTON, Ian Lethame;** Chief Executive, St George's Healthcare NHS Trust, 1999–2003; *b* 24 July 1951; *s* of Robert Hamilton and Margaret Henderson (*née* McKay). *Educ:* Larkhall Acad.; Glasgow Coll. of Technol. CIPFA 1974. Supervisory accountant, 1975–78, Asst Chief Accountant, 1978–81, Strathclyde Regl Council; Regl Finance Officer, Housing Corp., 1981–83; Dep. Dir of Finance, Wandsworth HA, 1983–88; Project Manager, King's Fund Centre for Health Services Develt, 1988–89 (on secondment); Resource Mgt Project Manager, Wandsworth HA, 1989–91; Dir of Service Develt, 1991–98, Dep. Chief Exec., 1998–99, St George's Healthcare NHS Trust. *Recreations:* gardening, reading, country walks. *Address:* 20 Artesian Road, W2 5AR.

**HAMILTON, Ian Robertson;** QC (Scot.) 1980; *b* Paisley, Scotland, 13 Sept. 1925; *s* of John Harris Hamilton and Martha Robertson; *m* 1974, Jeannette Patricia Mari Stewart, Connel, Argyll; one *s*, and one *s* two *d* by former marriage. *Educ:* John Neilson Sch., Paisley; Allan Glen's Sch., Glasgow; Glasgow and Edinburgh Univs (BL). Served RAFVR, 1943–48. Called to the Scottish Bar, 1954 and to the Albertan Bar, 1982. Advocate Depute, 1962; Dir of Civil Litigation, Republic of Zambia, 1964–66; Hon. Sheriff of Lanarks, 1967; retd from practice to work for National Trust for Scotland and later to farm in Argyll, 1969; returned to practice, 1974; Sheriff of Glasgow and Strathkelvin, May–Dec. 1984; resigned commn Dec. 1984; returned to practice. Founder, Castle Wynd Printers, Edinburgh, 1955 (published four paper-back vols of Hugh MacDiarmid's poetry, 1955–56). Founder and first Chm., The Whichway Trust, to provide adventure training for young offenders, 1988. Chief Pilot, Scottish Parachute Club, 1978–80. Student Pres., Heriot-Watt Univ., 1990–96; Rector, Aberdeen Univ., 1994–96. Hon. Research Fellow, 1997, Hon. LLD 1997, Aberdeen. Hon. Brother, Sir William Wallace Free Colliers, 1997. *Publications:* No Stone Unturned, 1952 (also New York); The Tinkers of the World, 1957 (Foyle award-winning play); The Taking of the Stone of Destiny, 1991; *autobiography:* A Touch of Treason, 1990; A Touch More Treason, 1994; contrib. various jls. *Recreation:* neophobia. *Address:* Lochnabeithe, North Connel, Oban, Argyll PA37 1QX. *T:* (01631) 710427.

**HAMILTON, Jaime Richard;** QC 2019; *b* Manchester, 21 Jan. 1971; *s* of Bryan Hamilton and Maureen Hamilton; *m* 2009, Katherine Pierpoint. *Educ:* University Coll. of Wales, Aberystwyth (LLB 1992). Called to the Bar, Gray's Inn, 1993; pupil barrister, 1 Dr Johnson's 1993–94, barrister, 9 St John Street, 1994–. *Recreations:* Captain of Gentleman Gardeners Cricket Club, author of View from the North blog, antiques. *Address:* 9 St John Street, Manchester M3 4DN. *T:* (0161) 955 9000. *E:* clerks@9sjs.com.

**HAMILTON, His Honour John;** a Circuit Judge, 1987–2006; *b* 27 Jan. 1941; *s* of late John Ian Hamilton and Mrs Margaret Walker; *m* 1965, Patricia Ann Hamilton (*née* Henman); two *s* one *d*. *Educ:* Durlston Court Prep. Sch., New Milton, Hants; Harrow (schol.); Hertford Coll., Oxford (schol.; MA Jurisp.). Called to the Bar, Gray's Inn, 1965; a Recorder, 1985. KStJ 1982. *Recreations:* golf, bridge, gardening. *Address:* Red Stack, Anstey, near Buntingford, Herts SG9 0BN. *T:* (01763) 848536.

**HAMILTON, John Robert Anderson;** QC (Scot.) 2011; Sheriff of North Strathclyde at Dumbarton, since 2017; *b* Glasgow, 14 Jan. 1969; *s* of John Anthony Hamilton, FRCSE and Edith Mary Allardice Anderson (or Hamilton); *m* 1995, Ruth Hamilton, PhD; one *s* one *d*. *Educ:* Kelvinside Acad.; Aberdeen Univ. (LLB 1990; DipLP 1991). Admitted as solicitor, 1993; in practice as solicitor, 1993–97; admitted to Faculty of Advocates, 1998; Tutor, Glasgow Law Sch., 2002–03; Advocate Depute, 2003–06; Dir, Trng and Educn, Faculty of Advocates, 2009–12. Convenor, Mental Health Tribunal Scotland, 2008–17; Judge of First-tier Tribunal (Social Entitlement Chamber), 2014–17. Member: Parole Bd for Scotland, 2014–; Scottish Legal Aid Bd, 2016–17. *Recreation:* curling. *Address:* Dumbarton Sheriff Court, Church Street, Dumbarton G82 1QR. *Clubs:* Reform Curling, Partick Curling.

**HAMILTON, Kirstie Louise, (Mrs Charles Stewart-Smith);** Director, Newsfury, since 2010; *b* 5 April 1963; *d* of Elizabeth Kate Marie Hamilton and Mark Robert Hamilton; *m* 1998, Charles Stewart-Smith; two *s*. *Educ:* Hillcrest High Sch., Hamilton, NZ. Columnist, National Business Review, NZ, 1988–89; Business Correspondent, Evening Standard, 1989–92; Business Correspondent, 1992–95, Dep. City Editor, 1995–96, Sunday Times; City Editor, The Express and Sunday Express, 1996–97; City Editor, Sunday Times, 1997–2002; Partner, Tulchan Communications, 2002–07. *Recreations:* riding, ski-ing. *Address:* 37 Stockwell Park Crescent, SW9 0DQ.

**HAMILTON, Lewis Carl David,** MBE 2009; Formula One racing driver; *b* Stevenage, 7 Jan. 1985; *s* of Anthony Hamilton. *Educ:* Cambridge Arts and Scis Sixth Form and Tutorial Coll. Enrolled on young driver prog. by McLaren Mercedes, 1997; kart racing: from age 8 until 2001; Eur. Champion, Formula A, 2000; car racing: Formula Renault UK, 2001–03, Champion (with Manor Motorsport), 2003; Formula 3 Euro Series, 2004–05, Champion (with ASM), 2005; GP2 Series, 2006, Champion (with ART Grand Prix), 2006; Formula 1, 2007–: driver for: McLaren Mercedes F1 team, 2007–12; Mercedes AMG Petronas F1 team, 2013–; Grand Prix winner: Canadian, US, Hungarian, Japanese, 2007; Australian, Monaco, British, German, Chinese, 2008; Hungarian, Singapore, 2009; Turkish, Canadian, Belgian, 2010; German, Chinese, Abu Dhabi, 2011; Canadian, Hungarian, Italian, US, 2012; Hungarian, 2013; Malaysian, Bahrain, Chinese, Spanish, British, Italian, Singapore, Japanese, Russian, US, Abu Dhabi, 2014; Australian, Chinese, Bahrain, Canadian, British, Belgian, Italian, Japanese, Russian, US, 2015; Monaco, Canadian, Austrian, British, Hungarian, German, Mexican, Brazilian, Abu Dhabi, 2016; Chinese, Spanish, Canadian, British, Belgian, Italian, Japanese, 2017; Azerbaijan, Spanish, French, German, Italian, Singapore, Russian, Japanese, Brazilian, Abu Dhabi, 2018; Bahrain, Chinese, Monaco, Canadian, French, British, Hungarian, 2019; World Champion, 2008, 2014, 2015, 2017, 2018. BBC Sports Personality of the Year, 2014. *Publications:* Lewis Hamilton: my story, 2007. *Address:* c/o Mercedes AMG Petronas Formula One Team, Operations Centre, Brackley, Northants NN13 7BD.

**HAMILTON, Sir Malcolm William Bruce S.;** *see* Stirling-Hamilton.

**HAMILTON, (Mostyn) Neil;** Member (UK Ind) Mid Wales and West, National Assembly for Wales, since 2016; legal consultant, broadcaster, writer; *b* 9 March 1949; *s* of Ronald and Norma Hamilton; *m* 1983, (Mary) Christine Holman. *Educ:* Amman Valley Grammar School; University College of Wales, Aberystwyth (BSc Econs, MSc Econs); Corpus Christi College, Cambridge (LLM). Called to the Bar, Middle Temple, 1979. MP (C) Tatton, 1983–97; contested (C) same seat, 1997. PPS to Minister of State for Transport, 1986–87; an Asst Govt Whip, 1990–92; Parly Under-Sec. of State, DTI, 1992–94. Mem., Select Cttee on Treasury and Civil Service, 1987–90; Vice-Chm., Conservative backbench Trade and Industry Cttee, 1984–90 (Sec., 1983 and 1994–97); Secretary: Cons. backbench Finance Cttee, 1987–90 and 1995–97; UK-ANZAC Parly Gp, 1984–97; Chm., All Party Anglo-Togo Parly Gp, 1988–97. Mem., Nat. Exec. Cttee, UKIP, 2011– (Dep. Chm., 2013–); Chm., UKIP Wilts, 2012–16. Contested (UK Ind) Newport W, April 2019. Chm., Sheila Childs Recruitment Ltd, 2004–15. Columnist, Sunday Express, 2007–16. Vice-Pres., Small Business Bureau, 1985–97. Vice-Pres., Cheshire Agricl Soc., 1986–. Actor: Jack and the Beanstalk, Yvonne Arnaud Th., Guildford, 2002–03; Cinderella, Lighthouse Th., Kettering, 2011; narrator, Rocky Horror Show, 30th anniversary tour, 2002–03; actor/performer, Lunch with the Hamiltons, 2006, 2007, 2008, High Jinks with the Hamiltons, 2011, Edinburgh Fest. *Publications:* UK/US Double Taxation, 1980; The European Community—a Policy for Reform, 1983; (ed) Land Development Encyclopaedia, 1981–; (jtly) No Turning Back, 1985; Great Political Eccentrics, 1999; pamphlets on state industry, schools and the NHS. *Recreations:* campaigning to restore Parliamentary sovereignty, gardening, opera, the arts, architecture and conservation, country pursuits, silence. *Address:* National Assembly for Wales, Cardiff Bay, Cardiff CF99 1NA.

**HAMILTON, Sir Nigel,** KCB 2008; DL; Head of Northern Ireland Civil Service, 2002–08; Vice Lord-Lieutenant, Belfast, since 2009; *b* 19 March 1948; *s* of James and Jean Hamilton; *m* 1974, Lorna Woods; two *s*. *Educ:* Queen's Univ., Belfast (BSc Hons); Henley Mgt Coll.; Federal Exec. Inst., Virginia; Univ. of Ulster. Joined NICS, 1970; Under Sec., Central Community Relns, Urban Regeneration, 1990–98; Permanent Secretary: Dept of Educn, 1998–2001; Dept for Regl Develt, 2001–02. Non-executive Director: Ulster Bank, 2009–17; Belfast City Airport, 2009–13. Chairman: Council, Prince's Trust, NI, 2008–17; Bryson Charitable Gp, 2008–12; New Irish Arts, 2014–. Patron, Tiny Life, 2008–. DL City of Belfast. DUniv Ulster, 2008. *Recreations:* Rugby (Pres., Ulster Referees Soc., 1996–97; Pres., Ulster Br., Irish RFU, 2010–11), golf.

**HAMILTON, Nigel John Mawdesley;** QC 1981; *b* 13 Jan. 1938; *s* of late Archibald Dearman Hamilton and Joan Worsley Hamilton (*née* Mawdesley); *m* 1963, Leone Morag Elizabeth Gordon (*d* 2006); two *s*. *Educ:* St Edward's Sch., Oxford; Queens' Coll., Cambridge. Nat. Service, 2nd Lieut, RE, Survey Dept, 1956–58. Assistant Master: St Edward's Sch., Oxford, 1962–63; King's Sch., Canterbury, 1963–65. Called to the Bar, Inner Temple, 1965, Bencher, 1989. Mem., Gen. Council of the Bar, 1989–94. Mem. (C) for Chew Valley, Avon CC, 1989–93. *Recreation:* fishing. *Address:* New Bailey Chambers, 2nd Floor, 10 Duke Street, Liverpool L1 5AS. *Club:* Flyfishers'.

**HAMILTON, Peter Bryan,** MA; Head Master of Haberdashers' Aske's School, 2002–18; *b* 28 Aug. 1956; *s* of Brian George Hamilton and Clara Hamilton (*née* Marchi); *m* 1st, 1981, Danièle Lahaye (marr. diss. 1987); one *d*; 2nd, 1993, Sylvie (*née* Vulliet); one *d*. *Educ:* King Edward VI Grammar Sch., Southampton; Christ Church, Oxford (1st Cl. Hons Modern Foreign Languages 1979; MA). Head of French, Radley Coll., 1981–89; Head of Modern Langs and Housemaster of Wren's, Westminster Sch., 1989–96; Head Master, King Edward VI Sch., Southampton, 1996–2002. Examr in French, Oxford and Cambridge Schs Exam. Bd, 1992–97. Governor: Stroud Sch., 1997–2002; Princes' Mead, 1997–2002; Durlston Court Sch., 1999–2002; Reddiford Sch., 2003; Lochinver House, 2004; Krishna Avanti Sch., 2009; Bushey Acad., 2009–14. *Recreations:* canoeing, horse-riding, hill walking, karate, sailing, ski-ing, squash, wind surfing, comparative literature, European cinema, opera, classical music, study of Arabic.

**HAMILTON, Reeta;** see Chakrabarti, R.

**HAMILTON, His Honour Richard Graham;** a Circuit Judge, 1986–97; Chancellor, Diocese of Liverpool, 1976–2002; *b* 26 Aug. 1932; *s* of late Henry Augustus Rupert Hamilton and Frances Mary Graham Hamilton; *m* 1960, Patricia Craghill Hamilton (*née* Ashburner) (*d* 2008); one *s* one *d*; partner, Mrs Sonia Abrahamson (*d* 2014). *Educ:* Charterhouse; University Coll., Oxford (MA); MA Screenwriting, Liverpool John Moores Univ., 1999. Called to the Bar, Middle Temple, 1956; a Recorder, 1974–86. Regular broadcasting work for Radio Merseyside, inc. scripts: Van Gogh in England, 1981; Voices from Babylon, 1983; A Longing for Dynamite, 1984; Dark Night, 1988 (winner of first prize for a short religious play, RADIUS); Murder Court productions (dramatised trials), Liverpool: The Maybrick Case, 1989; The Veronica Mutiny, 1990; Threatening Behaviour, 2006; writer and presenter, Ten-Minute Tales, Bay TV, 2016. *Publications:* Foul Bills and Dagger Money, 1979; All Jangle and Riot, 1986; A Good Wigging, 1988; Pistols at Dawn (short stories), 2019. *Recreations:* reading, tapestry, films. *Club:* Athenæum (Liverpool).

**HAMILTON, Dr Russell Douglas,** CBE 2010; FFPH; Director of Research and Development, Department of Health, 2004–16; *b* 6 Sept. 1955; *s* of Ronald Adrian Hamilton and June Grace Hamilton; *m* 1993, Angela Carole Shore; two *d*. *Educ:* Pimlico High Sch.; James Cook Univ. (BSc Hons 1976); Univ. of London (PhD Physiol. 1990); Brunel Univ./Henley Mgt Coll. (MBA 1993). DipM 1993; FFPH 2003. Tutor, James Cook Univ., 1976; SO in Respiratory Medicine, Flinders Med. Centre, Adelaide, 1977–79; SO, then Principal Clinical Scientist, Acad. Dept of Medicine, Charing Cross Hosp., 1980–93; Regl R&D Manager, SW RHA and NHS Exec. S and W, 1993–98; Department of Health: Regl Dir, R&D, then Hd of R&D Div. S, 1998–2003; Hd, Res. Policy and Strategy, then Dep. Dir of R&D, 2003–04. Director, National NHS R&D Programmes: in Asthma, 1998–2003; in Complex Disability, 1998–2003; in Cancer, 1998–2007. Member: Consumers in NHS Res., 1999–2004; Bd, NCRI (formerly Nat. Cancer Res. Funders Forum), 2000–16; Res. for Patient Benefits Wkg Party, 2003–04; Govt Chief Scientific Advr's Cttee, 2004–13; Bd, UK Clin. Res. Collaboration, 2004–16; Bd, Office for Strategic Coordination of Health Res., 2006–16; Bd, NIHR, 2006–16; CRUK, 2015–; Ext. Adv. Gp, NZ Health Res. Strategy, 2018–. HEFCE Panel Member: RAE 2001 Panel UoA 1; RAE 2008 Main Panel A; REF 2014 Main Panel A. Hon. DSc: Exeter, 2012; Bristol, 2017. *Publications:* contrib. res. papers esp. on respiratory physiology in health and disease; contrib. policy and strategy documents incl. Best Research for Best Health, 2006. *Recreations:* family, sailing, ski-ing, skittles, music. *Address:* 24 Queen Street, North Curry, Taunton TA3 6LE.

**HAMILTON, Simon Terence;** Member (DemU) Strangford, Northern Ireland Assembly, since 2007; *b* Newtownards, Co. Down, 17 March 1977; *s* of Frank and Muriel Hamilton; *m* 2003, Nicola Karen McAvoy; two *s*. *Educ:* Comber Primary Sch.; Regent Hse Sch., Newtownards; Queen's Univ. Belfast (BA Hons Modern Hist. and Politics 1999; BLegS Hons Law 2001). Auditor, PricewaterhouseCoopers, 2001–03; Press Officer, DUP, 2003–07. Mem. (DemU) Ards BC, 2005–10. Northern Ireland Assembly: Private Sec. to Minister of Finance and Personnel, 2011–13; Minister of Finance and Personnel, 2013–15; Minister for Health, Social Services and Public Safety, 2015–16; Minister for the Economy, 2016–17; Deputy Chairman: Cttee on Finance and Personnel, 2008–09; Cttee for the Envmt, 2011–13; Chm., Cttee for Social Develt, 2009–11. Hon. Mem., CIPFA 2015. *Recreations:* reading, walking, travelling. *Address:* 7 The Square, Comber, Co. Down BT23 5DX. *T:* (028) 9187 0900. *E:* simonhamilton@dup.org.uk.

**HAMILTON, Her Honour Susan, (Mrs Eric Kelly);** QC 1993; a Circuit Judge, 1998–2007; *m* 1977, Dr Eric Peter Kelly; two *s*. *Educ:* Hove Grammar Sch. for Girls. Called to the Bar, Middle Temple, 1975; a Recorder, 1996–98. *Publications:* The Modern Law of Highways, 1981; (contrib.) Halsbury's Laws of England, vol. 21, 4th edn, 1995, vol. 39(1), 4th edn, 1998; (contrib.) Encyclopaedia of Forms and Precedents, 5th edn, 1986. *Recreations:* sailing, gardening, tapestry, travelling. *Clubs:* Royal Southern Yacht, Bar Yacht.

**HAMILTON, Victoria Louise, (Mrs Mark Bazeley);** actress; *b* Wimbledon, 5 April 1971; *d* of Timothy Sharp and Valerie Sharp; *m* 2007, Mark Bazeley; two *s*. *Educ:* London Acad. of Music and Dramatic Art. *Theatre* appearances include RSC, NT, Peter Hall Co., West End and NY; Master Builder (Most Promising Newcomer, London Critics' Circle Awards), tour and West End, 1995; As You Like It (Best Actress, Critics' Circle Awards), Crucible, Sheffield, transf. Lyric, 2000; A Day in the Death of Joe Egg, Ambassadors, 2001, NY, 2003; Suddenly Last Summer, Albery (Best Actress, Evening Standard Awards), 2004; Albion, Almeida (Best Actress, Critics' Circle Th. Awards), 2017. *Television* includes: Victoria & Albert, 2001; To the Ends of the Earth, 2005; Lark Rise to Candleford, 2008–11; What Remains, 2013; The Game, 2014; Doctor Foster, 2015, 2017; The Crown, 2016–17; Deep State, 2018. *Films:* Before You Go, 2002; Scoop, 2007. *Address:* c/o Nicola van Gelder, Conway van Gelder Grant, Third Floor, 8–12 Broadwick Street, W1F 8HW.

**HAMILTON, Wilfred;** see Hamilton, Alfred W.

**HAMILTON, William Francis Forbes,** CA; Chairman, Macrae & Dick Ltd, 1994–2015; Vice Lord-Lieutenant, Inverness, 2002–15; *b* 19 April 1940; *s* of late Col William Hamilton, OBE, CA and of Amy Constance Hamilton (*née* Forbes); *m* 1971, Anne Davison, MB BS; one *s*. *Educ:* Inverness Royal Acad.; Edinburgh Univ. (BCom 1961). CA 1967. Macrae & Dick Ltd: Co. Sec., 1968–80; Finance Dir, 1971–80; Man. Dir, 1980–2003. Dir, Highlands & Islands Airports Ltd, 1995–2001; Chm., Menzies BMW, 1998–. Mem., Distributor Council, BL Cars, 1977–78. Member, Highland Committee: Scottish Council Develt and Ind., 1971–2007; Police Dependants' Trust, 1998–2008. Director: Highland Hospice, 1992–95; Highland Hospice Trading Co., 1995–2008. Trustee, Fresson Trust, 1991–. DL Inverness, 2000. *Recreations:* sailing, travel. *Address:* St Kilda, La Rue du Coin, Grouville, Jersey JE3 9QR. *T:* (01534) 871896. *Clubs:* Royal Highland Yacht, Royal Channel Islands Yacht.

**HAMILTON, Prof. William Trevor,** CBE 2019; MD; FRCP, FRCGP; Professor of Primary Care Diagnostics, University of Exeter, since 2010; *b* Belfast, 10 May 1958; *s* of Dr Trevor Hamilton and Esther Hamilton (*née* Rule); *m* 1984, Dr Alison Round; one *s* two *d*. *Educ:* Royal Belfast Academical Instn; Univ. of Bristol (BSc Hons Med. Microbiol. 1979; MB ChB Medicine 1982; MD by thesis 2005). MRCP 1986, FRCP 2003; MRCGP 1986, FRCGP 2002. House Officer, Frenchay Hosp. and Bristol Royal Infirmary, 1982–83; Sen. House Officer, Royal Devon and Exeter Hosp., 1983–85; Govt Med. Officer, Malawi; GP Registrar, Exeter, 1988–89; General Practitioner: Barnfield Hill Surgery, 1990–2000; Mount Pleasant Health Centre, 2005–17; Chief Medical Officer, Liverpool Victoria Friendly Soc., 2000–; Chief Medical Officer and Exec. Dir, The Exeter (friendly soc.), 2003–. Clin. Lead for NICE guideline, NG12, suspected cancer, 2012–15. *Publications:* Orthopaedics in Primary Care, 2nd edn 2005; Cancer Diagnosis in Primary Care, 2007; contrib. over 250 peer-reviewed papers to med. literature. *Recreations:* long-distance walking, tennis, sailing, bridge. *Address:* Stoke Hill Farm, Pennsylvania Road, Exeter EX4 5BW. *E:* w.hamilton@exeter.ac.uk.

**HAMILTON DALRYMPLE, Sir Hew Richard;** see Dalrymple.

**HAMILTON-RUSSELL,** family name of **Viscount Boyne**.

**HAMILTON-SMITH,** family name of **Baron Colwyn**.

**HAMLIN, Prof. Michael John,** CBE 1994; FICE, FREng; FRSE; consulting water engineer, since 1984; Principal and Vice Chancellor of the University of Dundee, 1987–94; *b* 11 May 1930; *s* of late Dr Ernest John Hamlin and Dorothy Janet Hamlin; *m* 1951, Augusta Louise, *d* of late William Thomas Tippins and Rose Louise Tippins; three *s*. *Educ:* St John's Coll., Johannesburg; Dauntsey's Sch.; Bristol Univ. (BSc); Imperial Coll. of Science and Technol., London (DIC). FIWEM (FIWES 1973); FICE 1981; FREng (FEng 1985); FRSE 1990. Asst Engineer, Lemon & Blizard, Southampton, 1951–53; Engineer: Anglo-American Corp., Johannesburg, 1954–55; Stewart, Sviridov & Oliver, Johannesburg, 1955; Partner, Rowe & Hamlin, Johannesburg, 1956–58; Univ. of Witwatersrand, 1959–60; University of Birmingham, 1961–87: Prof. of Water Engrg, 1970–87; Hd of Dept of Civil Engrg, 1980–87; Pro Vice-Chancellor, 1985–86; Vice-Principal, 1986–87. Chm., Aquatic and Atmospheric Phys. Scis Grants Cttee, NERC, 1975–79; Member: Severn Trent Water Authority, 1974–79; British National Cttee for Geodesy and Geophysics, 1979–84 (Chm., Hydrology Sub-Cttee, 1979–84); Scottish Econ. Council, 1989–93; Internat. Relns Cttee, 1992–95; Scientific Unions Cttee, 1995–99, Royal Soc. President: Internat. Commn on Water Resource Systems of the Internat. Assoc. of Hydrological Scis (IAHS), 1983–87; British Hydrological Soc., 1995–97. International Union of Geodesy and Geophysics: Mem., Council, 1992–2000; Mem., 1991–2007, Chm., 2003–07, Finance Cttee; Fellow, 2015. Chm., Scottish Centre for Children with Motor Impairment, 1991–94. Hon. Life Mem., Guild of Students, Birmingham Univ., 1980; Hon. Mem., Students' Assoc., Dundee Univ., 1994–. FRCPS (Glas) 1992; Hon. FRCGP 1993. Dist. Fellow, Internat. Med. Univ., Kuala Lumpur, 1999. Hon. LLD: St Andrews, 1989; Dundee, 1996; Hon. DEng: Birmingham, 1995; Bristol, 2000; Hon. DLitt Southern Queensland, 2003. President's Premium, IWES, 1972. OStJ 1991. *Publications:* contribs on public health engrg and water resources engrg in learned jls. *Recreations:* walking, gardening. *Address:* The Coombes, Hope Bagot, Ludlow, Shropshire SY8 3AQ.

**HAMLYN, Claire;** see Jakens, C.

**HAMLYN, Jane Sarah,** CBE 2018; Director, Frith Street Gallery, London, since 1988; Chair, Paul Hamlyn Foundation, since 2003 (Trustee, since 1987); *b* London, 17 April 1958; *d* of Baron Hamlyn, CBE and late Eileen Margaret, (Bobbie), Hamlyn; partner, 1988, James Lingwood, *qv*; one *s* two *d*. *Educ:* King Alfred Sch., London; Brighton Sch. of Art (Foundn course); City and Guilds Sch. of Art (BA 1st Cl. with Dist. Illustrative Arts); London Coll. of Printing (Postgrad. Dip. Book Prodn and Design). Asst Book Designer, John Roberts Press, 1983–85; Asst Art Editor, Folio Soc., 1985–88; freelance work with publishers, and teaching, 1987–89. Sen. Advisory Counsel, India Inst., KCL, 2012–. Hon. Dir, Royal Opera House, Covent Gdn, 2012–. *Recreations:* contemporary art, architecture and design, music and opera, India, travel. *Address:* c/o Paul Hamlyn Foundation, 5–11 Leeke Street, WC1X 9HY.

**HAMLYN, Peter John,** MD; FRCS; Hon. Consultant Neurosurgeon, University College London Hospital, since 2007; Director of Education, Institute of Sport Exercise and Health, University College Hospital, London, since 2009; *b* 10 Aug. 1957; *s* of David William Hamlyn and Paula Anne Hamlyn (*née* Bowker); *m* 1994, Geraldine Marie Frances Shepherd; two *s* (and one *s* decd). *Educ:* N Cestrian Grammar Sch.; Solihull Sixth Form Coll.; University Coll. London (BSc 1st Cl. Hons Neurosci. 1979; MB BS 1982; MD 1994 (Rogers Prize)). FRCS 1986; FInstLM (FISM 1995). Consultant Neurological and Spinal Surgeon: St Bartholomew's Hosp., 1990–2007; The Royal London Hosp., 1996–2007. Dir, Sport and Exercise Medicine, Queen Mary, Univ. of London, 2003–07. Chm., Ministerial Wkg Gp on Safety and Medicine in Sport, DCMS, 2001. Corresp. in sports medicine, Daily Telegraph, 1993–2012. Founder, 1992, and Pres., British Brain and Spine Foundn (Vice-Chm., 1997). Med. Advr, London 2012 Olympic Bid, 2004–05; Mem., London Specialist Trng Cttee in Sport and Exercise Medicine, 2005–07. Trustee, Grand Prix Trust, 2013–. *Publications:* Neurovascular Compression of the Cranial Nerves in Neurological and Systematic Disease, 1999. *Recreation:* sculpture.

**HAMM, John (Frederick),** OC 2009; MD; Chairman, Assisted Human Reproduction Canada, 2006–12; Premier of Nova Scotia, Canada, 1999–2006; *b* 8 April 1938; *m* 1964, Genesta Hartling; two *s* one *d*. *Educ:* Univ. of King's Coll., Halifax (BSc 1958); Dalhousie Med. Sch. (MD 1963). Family physician, 1963–93. MLA (PC) Pictou Centre, Nova Scotia, 1993–2006; Leader of Opposition, NS, 1995–98. Leader, PC Party of NS, 1995–2006. Mem., Provincial Med. Bd, NS, 1963–96. President: Coll. of Family Physicians, NS; Pictou Co. Med. Soc., 1971–73; Med. Soc. of NS, 1977. Pres., Aberdeen Hosp. Med. Staff, 1986–88; Chm., Aberdeen Hosp. Foundn, 1990–92. Former Warden, St George's Ch. *Recreations:* hockey, running, wood working.

**HAMMARBERG, Thomas;** international human rights adviser; Commissioner for Human Rights, Council of Europe, 2006–12; Chairman, Swedish Commission for Roma Rights, 2014–16; *b* 2 Jan. 1942; *s* of Harald and Naima Hammarberg; *m* 1997, Alfhild Petren; one *s*. *Educ:* Stockholm Sch. of Econs (BS). Foreign Editor, daily Expressen, then Swedish broadcasting, 1970–80; Secretary General: Amnesty Internat., 1980–86; Save the Children—Sweden, 1986–92; Ambassador and Special Advr to the Foreign Minister, 1994–2002; Sec. Gen., Olof Palme Internat. Center, Stockholm, 2002–06. Vice Chm., UN Cttee on the Rights of the Child, 1991–96; Special Rep. of the UN Sec. Gen. in Cambodia, 1996–2000. DJur *hc*, Stockholm, 2010; Hon. Dr PolSci Göteborg, 2013. King of Sweden Hon. Medal, 2005; Stockholm Human Rights Award, 2012; Geuzenpenning, 2014. *Publications:* books in Swedish and English on media reporting and human rights matters. *Recreation:* ski-ing. *Address:* Tistelvagen 22, 12134 Enskededalen, Sweden.

**HAMMER, James Dominic George,** CB 1983; Chairman, Certification Management Council, Zurich (formerly Eagle Star) Certification Ltd, 1996–2001; *b* 21 April 1929; *s* of E. A. G. and E. L. G. Hammer; *m* 1955, Margaret Eileen Halse; two *s* one *d*. *Educ:* Dulwich Coll.; Corpus Christi Coll., Cambridge. BA Hons Mod. Langs. Joined HM Factory Inspectorate, 1953; Chief Inspector of Factories, 1975–84; Dep. Dir Gen., HSE, 1985–89. Dir, UK SKILLS, 1990–2000. Pres., Internat. Assoc. of Labour Inspection, 1984–93; Chairman: Nat. Certification Scheme for In-Service Inspection Bodies, 1990–92; Nat. Steering Cttee, Eur. Year of Safety, Health and Hygiene at Work 1992, 1991–93; NACCB, 1992–95; Nat. Exam. Bd in Occupational Safety and Health, 1992–95. Vice Chm., Camberwell HA, 1982–91; Associate Mem., King's Healthcare, 1992–97. FIOSH 1992. *Address:* 10 Allison Grove, Dulwich, SE21 7ER. *T:* (020) 8693 2977.

**HAMMERBECK, Brig. Christopher John Anthony,** CB 1991; CBE 2007; Executive Director, British Chamber of Commerce in Hong Kong, 1994–2015; *b* 14 March 1943; *s* of Sqn Leader O. R. W. Hammerbeck and I. M. Hammerbeck; *m* 1974, Alison Mary Felice (marr. diss. 1996); one *s* two *d*. *Educ:* Mayfield Coll., Sussex. Commnd, 1965; 2nd RTR, 1965–70; Air Adjt, Parachute Sqn, RAC, 1970–72; GSO3 (Ops), HQ 20 Armoured Bde, 1972–74; psc, 1975; DAA&QMG, HQ 12 Mechanised Bde, 1976–78; Sqn Comdr, 4th RTR, 1978–80; DAAG(O), MoD, 1980–82; Directing Staff, Army Staff Coll., 1982–84; CO, 2nd RTR, 1984–87; Col, Tactical Doctrine/Op. Requirement 1 (BR) Corps, 1987–88; RCDS, 1989; Comdr, 4th Armoured Brigade, 1990–92; Dep. Comdr, British Forces Hong Kong, 1992–94. Senior Advisor: Guangzhou Foreign Trade and Investment

Bureau, 2008–; Guangzhou Regl Sub-Council, China Council for Promotion of Internat. Trade, 2008–; Vermilion Partners Ltd, 2006–15; Steve Vickers Associates Ltd, 2016–18. Mem., Gen. Cttee. European Chamber of Commerce, Hong Kong, 1996–2015 (Special Advr, 2015–17); Pres., Inst. of Export (HK), 2004–. President: Hong Kong Br., RBL, 1995–; HK Ex-Servicemen's Assoc., 1995–. Trustee, Locally Enlisted Personnel Trust, 1997–. Member: Hong Kong Inst. of Dirs, 2001–; Hong Kong Sea Cadets Council, 2004–. MCMI. Hon. Citizen, Xiamen City, China, 2006. *Recreations:* golf, ski-ing, reading, travel, hiking. *Clubs:* Army and Navy, Royal Over-Seas League; Shek O, Hong Kong (Hong Kong).

**HAMMERSLEY, (Constance) Ann**; see Cryer, C. A.

**HAMMERSLEY, Rear-Adm. Peter Gerald**, CB 1982; OBE 1965; *b* 18 May 1928; *s* of late Robert Stevens Hammersley and Norah Hammersley (*née* Kirkham); *m* 1959, Audrey Cynthia Henderson Bolton; one *s* one *d. Educ:* Denstone Coll.; RNEC Manadon; Imperial Coll., London (DIC). Served RN, 1946–82; Long Engrg Course, RNEC Manadon, 1946–50; HMS Liverpool, 1950–51; Advanced Marine Engrg Course, RNC Greenwich, 1951–53; HMS Ocean, 1953–54; joined Submarine Service, 1954; HMS Alaric, HMS Tiptoe, 1954–58; Nuclear Engrg Course, Imperial Coll., 1958–59; First Marine Engineer Officer, first RN Nuclear Submarine, HMS Dreadnought, 1960–64; DG Ships Staff, 1965–68; Base Engineer Officer, Clyde Submarine Base, 1968–70; Naval Staff, 1970–72; Asst Director, S/M Project Team, DG Ships, 1973–76; CO, HMS Defiance, 1976–78; Captain, RNEC Manadon, 1978–80; CSO (engrg) to C-in-C Fleet, 1980–82. Comdr 1964; Captain 1971; Rear-Adm. 1980; Chief Exec., British Internal Combustion Engine Manufacturers' Assoc., 1982–85; Dir, British Marine Equipment Council, 1985–92. Fellow, Woodard Schs Corp., 1992–98 (Hon. Fellow, 1998). Gov., Denstone Coll. 1986–98 (Chm., 1994–98). Founder Liveryman, Engineers' Co., 1983 (Master, 1988–89). *Recreations:* walking, gardening, golf. *Address:* Wistaria Cottage, Linersh Wood, Bramley, near Guildford GU5 0EE. *Clubs:* Army and Navy; Bramley Golf.

**HAMMERSLEY, Philip Tom**, CBE 2000 (OBE 1989); CEng; *b* 10 Feb. 1931; *s* of Tom Andrew Hammersley and Winifred Hammersley (*née* Moyns); *m* 1954, Lesley Ann Millage; two *s* one *d. Educ:* Bancroft's Sch.; Imperial Coll., Univ. of London (BSc Eng.). CEng 1965; MIMechE 1965. Tech. Officer, ICI Plastics Div., 1954–65; Clarks Ltd: Chief Engr, 1965–68; Prodn Services Manager, 1968–71; Dir, Children's Div., 1971–79; Pres., Stride-rite Footwear, Boston, Mass, 1979–81; British Shoe Corporation, Leicester: Factories Dir, 1981–87; Man. Dir, Freeman, Hardy & Willis, 1987–89; Commercial Dir, 1989–90; non-exec. Dir, BSS Gp PLC, 1991–99 (Dep. Chm., 1995; Chm., 1995–99). Vice-Chm., Leics HA, 1990–92; Chm., Leicester Royal Infirmary NHS Trust, 1992–97; Regl Chm., Trent, NHS Exec., DoH, 1997–99; Chm., Univ. Hosps of Leicester NHS Trust, 2000–06. Chm. Council, Shoe & Allied Trades Res. Assoc., 1983–86; Pres., Brit. Footwear Manufacturers Fedn, 1986–87; Chm., E Midlands Regl Council, CBI, 1988–90. Chm., Nat. Space Centre (Ops) Ltd, 2001–09; Trustee, Nat. Space Centre, 1997–2001, 2006–09. Freeman, City of London, 1983; Mem., Patten Makers' Co., 1983–. Hon. DBA De Montfort, 1999; Hon. LLD Leicester, 2008. *Recreations:* golf, theatre, music. *Address:* 3 Holywell, Hook Heath Road, Woking, Surrey GU22 0LA. *T:* (01483) 493191. *Clubs:* East India, MCC.

**HAMMERSLEY, Stephen John**, CBE 2012; Chief Executive, Pilgrims' Friend Society, since 2015; *b* Ipswich, 23 Dec. 1961; *s* of John and Janet Hammersley; *m* 1987, Susan Elizabeth; three *c. Educ:* Bramcote Hills Grammar Sch.; Durham Univ. (BSc Maths). Barclays Bank, 1983–2000; Tearfund, 2000–04; Chief Exec., UK Community Foundns (formerly Community Foundn Network), 2004–14. Chair, TLMT Trading Ltd, 2010–. *Recreation:* outdoor pursuits. *E:* sjh_123@btinternet.com.

**HAMMERTON, Alastair Rolf; His Honour Judge Alastair Hammerton;** a Circuit Judge, since 2014; *b* Sussex, 3 Nov. 1960; *s* of His Honour Rolf Eric Hammerton and Thelma Hammerton; *m* 1991, Vanessa Rumboll; one *s* two *d. Educ:* Winchester Coll.; Queens' Coll., Cambridge (BA 1982); Univ. of Virginia Sch. of Law (LLM 1984). Called to the Bar, Inner Temple, 1983, Bencher, 2004; a Recorder, 2004–14. *Recreations:* theatre, cooking, gardening. *Address:* Snaresbrook Crown Court, 75 Hollybush Hill, Snaresbrook, E11 1QW.
See also Her Honour V. L. Hammerton.

**HAMMERTON, Her Honour Veronica Lesley;** a Circuit Judge, 2005–15; *b* 1 Oct. 1954; *d* of His Honour Rolf Eric Hammerton and Thelma Hammerton; *m* 1981, David John Knight; one *s* one *d. Educ:* Cheltenham Ladies' Coll.; Girton Coll., Cambridge (BA 1976). Called to the Bar, Inner Temple, 1977; Asst Recorder, 1996–2000; a Recorder, 2000–05. Legal Mem., Mental Health Rev. Tribunal, 2003–. *Recreations:* embroidery, sailing, tennis, theatre-going.
See also A. R. Hammerton.

**HAMMETT, Ven. Barry Keith**, CB 2006; Chaplain of the Fleet, Archdeacon for the Royal Navy and Director General, Naval Chaplaincy Service, 2002–06; *b* 9 Oct. 1947; *s* of George and Irene Hammett. *Educ:* Eltham Coll.; Magdalen Coll., Oxford (BA 1971, MA 1974); St Stephen's House, Oxford; Ven. English Coll., Rome (exchange student). Ordained deacon 1974, priest 1975; Asst Curate, St Peter's, Plymouth, 1974–77; Chaplain, RN, 1977–2006; Staff Chaplain, MoD, 1986–90; Principal, Armed Forces' Chaplaincy Centre, 1996–2000. QHC 1999–2006. Hon. Canon: Portsmouth Cathedral, 2002–06; Hon. Canon Emeritus, 2006; Cathedral Chapter, Dio. in Europe (Gibraltar), 2003–06. *Recreations:* travel, historic houses, gardening, motoring, photography, genealogy. *Address:* 26 Penhurst Gardens, Chipping Norton, Oxon OX7 5ED.

**HAMMICK, Sir Jeremy (Charles)**, 6th Bt *cr* 1834, of Cavendish Square, London; landscape artist; *b* 3 Feb. 1956; *s* of Sir Stephen George Hammick, 5th Bt, OBE and Gillian Elizabeth Hammick (*née* Inchbald); *S* father, 2014; *m* 1997, Mrs Melanie Louise Stock (marr. diss. 2014); two *s. Educ:* Bournemouth Coll. of Art. *Heir: s* George Frederick Love Hammick, *b* 16 Feb. 1998.

**HAMMOND, Sir Anthony (Hilgrove)**, KCB 2000 (CB 1992); Standing Counsel to General Synod of the Church of England, 2000–13; *b* 27 July 1940; *s* of late Colonel Charles William Hilgrove Hammond and Jessie Eugenia Hammond (*née* Francis); *m* 1988, Avril Collinson. *Educ:* Malvern Coll.; Emmanuel Coll., Cambridge (BA, MA, LLM). Admitted Solicitor of Supreme Court, 1965. Articled with LCC, 1962; Solicitor, GLC, 1965–68; Home Office: Legal Assistant, 1968; Sen. Legal Assistant, 1970; Asst Legal Advr, 1974; Principal Asst Legal Advr, 1980–88; Legal Advr, 1988–92; Home Office and NI Office; Solicitor and Dep. Sec., then Dir Gen. Legal Services, DTI, 1992–97; HM Procurator Gen., Treasury Solicitor and Queen's Proctor, 1997–2000; Legal Counsel to Hakluyt & Co. Ltd, 2001–05. Mem. Bd, Inst. of Advanced Legal Studies, 1997–. Fellow, Soc. of Advanced Legal Studies, 1997. Freeman, City of London, 1991; Liveryman, Glass Sellers' Co., 1991– (Master, 2007). Hon. QC 1997. *Recreations:* bridge, music, opera, walking, birdwatching.

**HAMMOND, Christopher Mark;** Founder, CMH Contemporary Art, since 2016; *b* Glasgow, 29 May 1968; *s* of Michael Hammond and Marjorie Hammond; partner, Una Murtagh; two *d. Educ:* Wimbledon Sch. of Art. Lectr in Curating, Goldsmiths, Univ. of London, 2007–. Founder and Dir, MOT Internat. (formerly MOT), 2002–16. *Club:* Soho House.

**HAMMOND, Prof. Gerald**, PhD; FBA 1998; John Edward Taylor Professor of English Literature, University of Manchester, 1993–2006, now Emeritus; *b* 3 Nov. 1945; *s* of Frank George Hammond and Ruth Hammond (*née* Wallen); *m* 1971, Patsy Talat Naheed Khaliq; one *s* one *d. Educ:* University Coll. London (BA 1968; PhD 1974). University of Manchester: Lectr, 1971–83, Sen. Lectr, 1983–90, Reader, 1990–93, in English; Dean: Faculty of Arts, 1999–2002; Internat. and Grad. Educn, 2002–03; Faculty of Engrg and Physical Scis, 2003–04; Associate Vice Pres., Grad. Educn, 2005–06. Res. Posts Co-ordinator, British Acad., 2002–05. Distinguished Vis. Humanities Prof., Auburn Univ., Alabama, 1987; Nat. Sci. Council of Taiwan Res. Fellow, 1997–98. Chatterton Lecture, 1985, Warton Lecture, 1995, British Acad. *Publications:* (ed) The Metaphysical Poets, 1974; (ed) John Skelton: poems, 1980; The Reader and Shakespeare's Young Man Sonnets, 1981; The Making of the English Bible, 1984; (ed) Sir Walter Ralegh, 1984; (ed) Elizabethan Poetry, Lyrical and Narrative, 1984; (ed) Richard Lovelace: poems, 1987; Fleeting Things: English poets and poems 1616–1660, 1990; Horseracing: a book of words, 1992; (ed jtly) The English Bible, King James Version: the New Testament and the Apocrypha, 2012; articles in learned jls, reviews. *Recreation:* horseracing. *Address:* 29 Belfield Road, Manchester M20 6BJ. *T:* (0161) 445 2399.

**HAMMOND, His Honour James Anthony;** a Circuit Judge, 1986–2010; *b* 25 July 1936; *s* of James Hammond and Phyllis Eileen Hammond; *m* 1963, Sheila Mary Hammond, JP (*née* Stafford); three *d. Educ:* Wigan Grammar Sch.; St Catherine's Coll., Oxford (MA). Called to the Bar, Lincoln's Inn, 1959; National Service, 1959–61; a Recorder, 1980–86. Mem. (pt-time), Parole Bd, 2010–. Councillor: Up Holland UDC, 1962–66; Skelmersdale and Holland UDC, 1970–72. Chairman: NW Branch, Society of Labour Lawyers, 1975–86; W Lancs CAB, 1982–86; Pres., NW Branch, Inst. for Study and Treatment of Delinquency, 1987–98. *Recreation:* walking. *Clubs:* Wigan Hockey (Vice Pres., 1983–); Broughton Park Rugby Union Football.

**HAMMOND, (John) Martin;** Headmaster, Tonbridge School, 1990–2005; *b* 15 Nov. 1944; *s* of late Thomas Chatterton Hammond and Joan Cruse; *m* 1974, Meredith Jane Shier (*d* 2018); one *s* one *d. Educ:* Winchester Coll. (Scholar); Balliol Coll., Oxford (Domus Scholar; Hertford Scholar and (1st) de Paravicini Scholar, (2nd) Craven Scholar, 1st Cl. Hons Mods, 1963; Chancellor's Latin Prose Prize, Chancellor's Latin Verse Prize, Ireland Scholar, 1964; Gaisford Greek Prose Prize, Gaisford Greek Verse Prize (jtly), 1965; 2nd Cl. Lit. Hum. 1966). Asst Master, St Paul's Sch., 1966–71; Teacher, Anargyrios Sch., Spetsai, Greece, 1972–73; Asst Master, Harrow Sch., 1973–74; Head of Classics, 1974–80, and Master in College, 1980–84, Eton Coll.; Headmaster, City of London Sch., 1984–90. Mem., Gen. Adv. Council of BBC, 1987–91. *Publications:* Homer, The Iliad (trans.), 1987; Homer, The Odyssey (trans.), 2000; Marcus Aurelius (trans. and notes), 2006; Thucydides, The Peloponnesian War (trans.), 2009; Arrian, Alexander the Great (trans.), 2013; Josephus, The Jewish War (trans.), 2017; Procopius, The Secret History (trans.); Artemidorus, The Interpretation of Dreams (trans.). *Address:* Shepherds' Hey, Hundon Road, Barnardiston, Haverhill, Suffolk CB9 7TJ. *T:* (01440) 786441.

**HAMMOND, (Jonathan) Mark;** Member Council, General Pharmaceutical Council, since 2016; *b* 8 Aug. 1961; *s* of late Rev. Leslie Hammond and of Sherry Hammond; *m* 1993, Susan Margaret Postle; one *s. Educ:* Kingswood Sch., Bath; Magdalene Coll., Cambridge (BA Hons Hist. 1983). Department of the Environment, 1985–93: Private Sec. to Sir Gordon Manzie, 1987–89; Global Atmosphere Div., 1989–93; First Sec., Washington, 1993–97; Hd of Econ. and Envmt Policy, Surrey CC, 1997–2000; Dir, Envmt and Develt, 2000–04, Chief Exec., 2004–10, W Sussex CC; Chief Exec., Equality and Human Rights Commn, 2011–15. Lay Mem., Governing Body, NE Hants CCG, 2015–17. Vis. Prof. in Public Admin, 2011–, Sen. Fellow, Centre for Eur. Studies, 2016–18, Canterbury Christchurch Univ.; Vis. Fellow, Univ. of Bath, 2019–. Non-exec. Bd Mem., CPS, 2017–. Trustee, Council for At-Risk (formerly Assisting Refugee) Academics, 2012–. Hon. Dr Canterbury Christchurch, 2015. *Recreations:* golf, reading, crosswords. *Club:* Goodwood Golf.

**HAMMOND, Julia Jessica;** see Eccleshare, J. J.

**HAMMOND, Karen Ann;** a District Judge (Magistrates' Courts), since 2013; *b* London, 9 June 1962; *d* of Brian William Hammond and Dorothy Catherine Hammond (*née* Parker); *m* 2000; two *d. Educ:* Archbishop Tenison's Grammar Sch., Croydon; Croydon Tech. Coll. (OND 1980); Univ. of Nottingham (LLB Hons 1983); Inns of Court Sch. of Law. Called to the Bar, Middle Temple, 1985; in practice as barrister, 1985–98; Lecturer: Coll. of Law, 1998–2000; Nottingham Law Sch., 2000–05; BPP UC, 2005–13; a Dep. Dist Judge (Magistrates' Courts), 2003–13. *Recreations:* family, friends, ski-ing, film and theatre, beach-hutting. *Address:* Camberwell Green Magistrates' Court, D'Eynsford Road, SE5 7UP. *E:* djmc.karen.hammond@ejudiciary.net.

**HAMMOND, Mark;** see Hammond, Jonathan M.

**HAMMOND, Martin;** see Hammond, John M.

**HAMMOND, Mary Elaine, (Mrs P. C. Vel),** FRAM; freelance singing teacher; Sondheim Professor of Musical Theatre Vocal Studies, Royal Academy of Music (Head of Musical Theatre, 1992–2012); *b* Bristol, 16 Nov. 1940; *d* of Herbert Leslie Hammond and Winifred Elsie Hammond; *m* 1962, Peter Charles Vel; two *s. Educ:* Colston's Girls' Sch., Bristol; Royal Acad. of Music (LRAM 1961). FRAM 1998. Extensive work as a session singer encompassing wide range of music incl. opera, pop/rock, TV, film, radio and live concerts, 1962–87; singing consultant on 27 West End shows with companies incl. Cameron Mackintosh Ltd, Really Useful Gp, Bill Kenwright, NT, Donmar, Menière and RSC; coach of singers in TV, radio and pop and rock gps. Member Board: British Voice Assoc., 1993–; Actors Centre, London, 1996–2015. *Publications:* Thank You, That's All We Need for Today, 2009. *Recreation:* visiting antique fairs and car boot sales. *Address:* 164 Camden Road, NW1 9HJ. *T:* (020) 7267 3418. *E:* vox@maryhammond.co.uk.

**HAMMOND, Prof. Norman David Curle**, FBA 1998; Archaeology Correspondent, The Times, since 1967; Professor of Archaeology, Boston University, 1988–2010, now Emeritus; Associate in Maya Archaeology, Peabody Museum, Harvard University, since 1988; Senior Fellow, McDonald Institute, Cambridge University, since 2009; *b* 10 July 1944; *er s* of late William Hammond and Kathleen Jessie Hammond (*née* Howes); *m* 1972, Jean, *er d* of late A. H. Wilson and Beryl Wilson; one *s* one *d. Educ:* Varndean GS; Peterhouse, Cambridge (Trevelyan Schol.; Leaf Studentship 1964; Bartle Frere Exhibnr 1966; BA 1966; Dip. Classical Archaeol. 1967; MA 1970; PhD 1972; ScD 1987). FSA 1974 (Mem. Council, 1996–99). Centre of Latin American Studies, Cambridge: Res. Fellow, 1967–71; Leverhulme Res. Fellow, 1972–75; Res. Fellow, Fitzwilliam Coll., Cambridge, 1973–75; Sen. Lectr, Univ. of Bradford, 1975–77; Rutgers University: Vis. Prof., 1977–78; Associate Prof., 1978–84; Prof. of Archaeol., 1984–87; Distinguished Prof. of Archaeol.,

1987–88; Chm., Dept of Archaeol., Boston Univ., 2004–07 (Acting Chm., 1989–91, 2002–03). Irvine Chair of Anthropol., Calif. Acad. of Scis, 1984–85; Fellow in Pre-Columbian Studies, Dumbarton Oaks, Washington, 1988; Rockefeller Foundn Scholar, Bellagio, 1997. Visiting Professor: Univ. of California, Berkeley, 1977; Jilin Univ., Changchun, 1981; Univ. of Paris, Sorbonne, 1987; Univ. of Bonn, 1994; de Carle Dist. Prof., Univ. of Otago, NZ, 2013; Univ. of Otago, 2016; Visiting Fellow: Worcester Coll., Oxford, 1989; Peterhouse, Cambridge, 1991, 1996–97; McDonald Inst., Cambridge Univ., 1997, 2004; All Souls Coll., Oxford, 2004; Clare Hall, Cambridge, 2004. Lectures: Curl, RAI, 1985; Bushnell, Cambridge Univ., 1997; Willey, Harvard Univ., 2000; Brunswick Distinguished, MMA, 2001; Taft, Univ. of Cincinnati, 2006; Reckitt, British Acad., 2006; Holleyman, Sussex Univ., 2006; Aronui, Royal Soc. of NZ, 2011. Acad. Trustee, Archaeol. Inst. of America, 1990–93. MAE 2018. Hon. Mem., Phi Beta Kappa, 1989. Mem. editl bds, archaeol. jls, USA, UK, Mexico, 1984–; Editor, Afghan Studies, 1976–79; Consulting Editor, Liby of Congress, 1977–89; Archaeol. Consultant, Scientific American, 1979–95; Archaeol. Editor, TLS, 2009–11. Excavations and surveys: Libya and Tunisia, 1964; Afghanistan, 1966; Belize, 1970–2002 (Lubaantun, Nohmul, Cuello, La Milpa); Ecuador, 1972–84. Hon. DSc Bradford, 1999. Press Award, British Archaeol. Awards, 1994, (jtly) 1998; Soc. of Antiquaries Medal, 2001; Research Award, Shanghai Archaeol Forum, 2015. *Publications:* (ed) South Asian Archaeology, 1973; (ed) Mesoamerican Archaeology, 1974; Lubaantun: a Classic Maya realm, 1975; (ed) Social Process in Maya Prehistory, 1977; (ed with F. R. Allchin) The Archaeology of Afghanistan, 1978, 2nd edn (ed with W. Ball) 2019; (ed with G. R. Willey) Maya Archaeology and Ethnohistory, 1979; Ancient Maya Civilisation, 1982, 5th edn 1994, numerous foreign edns; (gen. editor) Archaeology Procs, 44th Congress of Americanists, 1982–84; (ed) Nohmul: excavations 1973–83, 1985; (ed) Cuello: an early Maya community in Belize, 1991; The Maya, 2000; contribs to learned and unlearned jls. *Recreations:* heraldry, genealogy, serendipity. *Address:* Wholeway, Harlton, Cambridge CB23 1ET. *T:* (01223) 262376. *Clubs:* Athenæum; Tavern (Boston).

**HAMMOND, Prof. Paul Francis**, FBA 2002; Professor of Seventeenth-Century English Literature, University of Leeds, since 1996; *b* 1953; *s* of Ronald Francis Hammond and Maureen Margaret Hammond. *Educ:* Peter Symonds' Sch., Winchester; Trinity Coll., Cambridge (BA, MA; PhD 1979; LittD 1996). Fellow, Trinity Coll., Cambridge, 1978–82; University of Leeds: Lectr in English, 1978–89; Sen. Lectr, 1989–95; Reader in Seventeenth-Century Literature, 1995–96. Vis. Fellow Commoner, Trinity Coll., Cambridge, 2007; Leverhulme Trust Res. Fellow, 2007–08. An Associate Ed., New, later Oxford, DNB, 1998–2002. *Publications:* John Oldham and the Renewal of Classical Culture, 1983; (ed) Selected Prose of Alexander Pope, 1987; John Dryden: a literary life, 1991; (ed jtly) The Poems of John Dryden, 5 vols, 1995–2005; Love Between Men in English Literature, 1996; Dryden and the Traces of Classical Rome, 1999; (ed jtly) John Dryden: Tercentenary Essays, 2000; (ed) Restoration Literature: an anthology, 2002; Figuring Sex between Men from Shakespeare to Rochester, 2002; (ed jtly) Shakespeare and Renaissance Europe, 2004; The Making of Restoration Poetry, 2006; The Strangeness of Tragedy, 2009; (ed jtly) John Milton: life, writings, reputation, 2010; (ed) Shakespeare's Sonnets: an original spelling edition, 2012; Milton and the People, 2014; Milton's Complex Words, 2017; articles on seventeenth century English and French literature in scholarly jls. *Recreations:* France and Germany. *Address:* School of English, University of Leeds, Leeds LS2 9JT. *T:* (0113) 343 4739.

**HAMMOND, Prof. Peter Jackson**, PhD; FBA 2009; Professor of Economics, University of Warwick, since 2007 (Marie Curie Professor, 2007–10); *b* Marple, Cheshire, 9 May 1945; *s* of Fred and Elsie Hammond; *m* 1979, Mrudula Patel. *Educ:* Trinity Hall, Cambridge (BA Hons Maths 1967; PhD Econs 1974). Jun. Res. Fellow, Nuffield Coll., Oxford, 1969–71; Lectr in Econs, 1971–76, Prof. of Econs, 1976–79, Univ. of Essex; Professor of Economics: Stanford Univ., Calif, 1979–2007, now Emeritus; European University Inst., 1989–91. John Simon Guggenheim Fellow, USA, 1987–88; Humboldt Res. Award, Germany, 1993–94. *Publications:* (jtly) Mathematics for Economic Analysis, 1995, 4th edn as Essential Mathematics for Economic Analysis, 2012, 5th edn 2016; (ed jtly) Handbook of Utility Theory, vol. 1, 1998, vol. 2, 2004; (jtly) Further Mathematics for Economic Analysis, 2005, 2nd edn 2008. *Recreations:* admiring, sometimes critically, those near the frontiers of human endeavour, reinforcing memories of active participation in sport, especially cricket and chess. *Address:* Department of Economics, University of Warwick, Gibbet Hill Road, Coventry CV4 7AL. *T:* (024) 7652 3052, *Fax:* (024) 7652 3032. *E:* p.j.hammond@warwick.ac.uk.

**HAMMOND, Rt Hon. Philip;** PC 2010; MP for Runnymede and Weybridge, since 1997 (C, 1997–2019; Ind, since 2019); *b* 4 Dec. 1955; *s* of Bernard Lawrence Hammond and Doris Rose Hammond; *m* 1991, Susan Carolyn, *d* of E. Williams-Walker; one *s* two *d*. *Educ:* Shenfield Sch., Brentwood; University Coll., Oxford (Open Scholar, 1st cl. PPE, MA). Various posts, Speywood Labs Ltd, 1977–81; Dir, Speywood Medical Ltd, 1981–83; established and ran medical equipment distribution co., and dir, medical equipment manufg cos, 1983–94; Partner, CMA Consultants, 1993–95; Director: Castlemead Ltd, 1984–; Castlemead Homes Ltd, 1994–2004; Consort Resources Ltd, 2000–03. Consultant, Govt of Malawi, 1995–97. Contested (C) Newham NE, June 1994. Opposition spokesman on health and social services, 1998–2001, on trade and industry, 2001–02; on local and devolved govt, 2002–05; Shadow Chief Sec. to HM Treasury, 2005 and 2007–10; Shadow Sec. of State for Work and Pensions, 2005–07; Secretary of State: for Transport, 2010–11; for Defence, 2011–14; for Foreign and Commonwealth Affairs, 2014–16; Chancellor of the Exchequer, 2016–19. Mem., Select Cttee on Envmt, Transport and the Regions, 1997–98, on Trade and Industry, 2002. Sec., Cons. Parly Health Cttee, 1997–98. *Recreations:* reading, cinema, walking. *Address:* House of Commons, SW1A 0AA. *T:* (020) 7219 4055.

**HAMMOND, Richard Mark;** television presenter and journalist, since 1990; *b* 19 Dec. 1969; *s* of Alan and Eileen Hammond; *m* 2002, Amanda, (Mindy), Etheridge; two *d*. *Educ:* Solihull Boys' Sch.; Ripon Grammar Sch.; Harrogate Coll. of Art and Technol. Presenter and producer: BBC Radio York, 1989–92; BBC Radio Stations: Leeds, Newcastle, Cleveland, Cumbria and Lancs; presenter: Men and Motors; Livetime; Top Gear, 2002–15; Brainiac: Science Abuse, 2003–06; Should I Worry About?, 2003–05; Richard Hammond's Engineering Connections, 2008–11; Richard Hammond's Invisible Worlds, 2010; Richard Hammond's Journey to the Bottom of the Ocean, 2011; Planet Earth Live, 2012; Richard Hammond's Crash Course, 2012; Richard Hammond's Miracles of Nature, 2012; Richard Hammond's Secret Service, 2013; Richard Hammond Builds a Planet, 2013; Wild Weather, 2014; Richard Hammond's Jungle Quest, 2015; The Grand Tour, 2016, 2017, 2018, 2019; columnist, Daily Mirror, 2005–. *Publications:* What Not to Drive, 2005; Richard Hammond's Car Confidential, 2006; Can You Feel the Force?, 2006; On the Edge: my story, 2007; As You Do…: adventures with Evel, Oliver and the Vice-president of Botswana, 2008; A Short History of Caravans in the UK, 2009; Or Is That Just Me?, 2009; On the Road: growing up in eight journeys - my early years, 2013. *Recreations:* motorcycling, writing, painting, photography, horse-riding, cycling, running.

**HAMMOND, His Honour Simon Tristram;** a Circuit Judge, 1993–2016; *b* 5 Jan. 1944; *s* of Philip J. Hammond and Sylvia D. (*née* Sillem); *m* 1976, Louise (*née* Weir); one *s* two *d*. *Educ:* Eastbourne Coll.; Coll. of Law. Articled to Philip J. Hammond, Leicester; admitted Solicitor, 1967; Solicitor, later Partner, Victor J. Lissack, London, 1968–76; Partner, Philip J. Hammond & Sons, Leicester, 1977–93. An Asst Recorder, 1985–90; a Recorder, 1990–93; Diversity and Community Relns Judge for Leicester, 2002–16. Asst Comr to Parly Boundary Commn for England, 1992. Member: Probation Bd, Leics and Rutland, 2003–14; Parole Bd, 2016–19. Member: Law Soc.'s Standing Cttee on Criminal Law, 1982–91; Crown Court Rules Cttee, 1988–93; Enforcement Sub-cttee, Home Office Rev. of Magistrates Court Procedure, 1989–90; Equal Treatment Adv. Cttee, Judicial Studies Bd, 2006–10. Churchwarden, 1990–. *Recreations:* horses, ski-ing, vegetable gardening, bread making, walking.

**HAMMOND, Stephen William;** MP for Wimbledon, since 2005 (C, 2005–19; Ind, since 2019); *b* 4 Feb. 1962; *s* of Bryan Norman Walter and Janice Eve Hammond; *m* 1991, Sally Patricia Brodie; one *d*. *Educ:* King Edward VI Sch., Southampton; Queen Mary Coll., London (BSc Econ Hons). Reed Stenhouse Investment Services, 1983–85; Canada Life, 1985–87; UBS Phillips & Drew, 1987–91; Dir, Kleinwort Benson Securities, 1991–98; Commerzbank, 1998–2003, Dir of Res., 1999–2001. Mem., Merton BC, 2002–06. Contested (C): Warwickshire North, 1997; Wimbledon, 2001. Shadow Minister for Transport, 2005–10; PPS to Sec. of State for Communities and Local Govt, 2010–12; Parly Under-Sec. of State, DfT, 2012–14; Minister of State, DHSC, 2018–19. Chm., All Party Parly Gp for Wholesale Financial Markets, 2010–12, for Infrastructure, 2015–, for Wholesale Financial Markets, 2015–; Mem., Treasury Select Cttee, 2015–18. Chm. Cons. Friends of India, 2010–12. *Address:* House of Commons, SW1A 0AA. *T:* (020) 7219 3401. *E:* hammonds@parliament.uk. *Clubs:* Royal Wimbledon Golf, Wimbledon Hockey, Wimbledon Civic Forum (Pres.), Wimbledon Society.

**HAMMOND BOOTH, Jonothan;** DL; Managing Director, Catapult Group, since 1994; mentor and coach, since 1994; *b* Chepstow, Gwent, 27 Aug. 1958; *s* of Alan Parry Booth and Mary Lynn Booth; *m* 1985, Beverley Close; one *s* two *d*. *Educ:* Holme Valley Grammar Sch. Trainee surveyor and auctioneer, 1977–79; European disc jockey, 1980–82; commercial radio presenter, 1983–87; BBC presenter and producer, 1987–95; television presenter, BBC and independent, 1987–94. Dir, 2003–11, Vice-Pres., 2011–, Northern Ballet. Dir, Frazier Hist. Mus., Louisville, Ky, 2011–12. Trustee, Royal Armouries, 2004–12. Gov., York St John Univ., 2013–. Freeman, Guild of Entrepreneurs, 2016–. DL W Yorks, 2018. *Publications:* Pond Life: creating the ripple effect in everything you say and do, 2006. *Recreations:* family, theatre, dance, travel, history, writing. *Address:* Catapult Group, The Old Stables, Holmfirth, W Yorks HD9 7TH. *T:* (01484) 680444. *E:* jon@thecatapultgroup.co.uk.

**HAMMOND-CHAMBERS, (Robert) Alexander;** Chairman, Ivory & Sime, 1985–91; Chairman, Dobbies Garden Centres plc, 1994–2007; *b* 20 Oct. 1942; *s* of late Robert Rupert Hammond-Chambers and Leonie Elie Noble (*née* Andrews); *m* 1968, Sarah Louisa Madeline (*née* Fanshawe); two *s* one *d*. *Educ:* Wellington College; Magdalene College, Cambridge (Hons Economics). Ivory & Sime: joined 1964; Partner, 1969; Director, 1975, upon incorporation; Dep. Chm., 1982. Chairman: Fidelity Special Values plc, 1994–2010; Hunter Property Fund Management, 2003–13; Hansa Trust, 2004– (Dir, 2002–); Sandstorm Internat. Ltd, 2008–18; Director: Internat. Biotechnology Trust plc, 2001–12; Montanaro European Smaller Companies Trust plc, 2004–18; Hampden & Co. plc, 2010–; GAMCO Asset Mgt (UK), 2015–18; Gabelli Merger Plus Trust, 2018–; Brown Advisory Funds plc, 2018–; Walter Scott & Partners Ltd, 2019–, and other cos. Chm., Assoc. of Investment Trust Cos, 2003–05 (Dep. Chm., 2002–03); Overseas Governor, Nat. Assoc. of Securities Dealers Inc., 1984–87. Chm., Edinburgh Green Belt Trust, 1991–2001. *Recreations:* cricket, photography, golf, writing, theatre. *Address:* The Old White House, 3 Liberton Tower Lane, Edinburgh EH16 6TQ. *T:* (0131) 672 1697. *Clubs:* Caledonian, Pilgrims; Hon. Co. of Edinburgh Golfers (Edinburgh).

**HAMNETT, Prof. Andrew**, DPhil; FRSC; FRSE; Principal and Vice-Chancellor, University of Strathclyde, 2001–09; *b* 12 Nov. 1947; *s* of Albert Edward Hamnett and Dorothy Grace Hamnett (*née* Stewart); *m* 1976, Suzanne Marie Parkin; three *d*. *Educ:* William Hulme's Grammar Sch., Manchester; University Coll., Oxford (Open Schol.; BA Hons Chem. 1970); St John's Coll., Oxford (Sen. Schol.; DPhil 1973); Open Univ. (BSc Maths and Stats 2015). CChem, FRSC 1991; FRSE 2002. Jun. Res. Fellow in Chemistry, Queen's Coll., Oxford, 1972–77; Deptl Res. Asst, then Lectr in Inorganic Chemistry, Oxford Univ., 1977–89; Fellow by Special Election, then Tutorial Fellow, St Catherine's Coll., Oxford, 1980–89; University of Newcastle upon Tyne: Prof. of Physical Chemistry, 1989–2000; Pro-Vice-Chancellor, 1993–2000. Killam Fellow, Univ. of BC, 1974–76. Pres., Scottish Assoc. of Marine Sci., 2010–13. Chm., Newcastle and Dist Soc. of Organists, 2013–. Sec., URC Northern Synod Trust, 2012–. DL Glasgow City, 2004–09. Hon. Fellow, Univ. of Strathclyde 2009. Hon. DSc Technical Univ. Lodz, Poland, 2005; DUniv Strathclyde, 2009; Hon. DCL Newcastle, 2010. *Publications:* (with P. A. Christensen) Techniques and Mechanism in Electrochemistry, 1994; (ed with R. G. Compton) Novel Methods of Studying the Electrode-Electrolyte Interface, 1989; (jtly) Electrochemistry, 1998, 2nd rev. edn 2007 (trans. Chinese); numerous papers and review articles on physical and inorganic chemistry. *Recreations:* music, classical languages, mathematics and statistics. *Address:* c/o University of Strathclyde, 16 Richmond Street, Glasgow G1 1XQ. *Clubs:* Rotary; Northern Counties (Newcastle upon Tyne).

**HAMNETT, Prof. Christopher Robert**, FAcSS; Professor of Geography, King's College London, 1995–2014, now Emeritus; *b* Louth, Lincs, 7 Oct. 1946; *s* of William and Mary Hamnett; *m* 1969, Barbara Pope; two *d*. *Educ:* Univ. of London ext. *Educ:* (BSc 1969); Univ. of Birmingham (Dip. Urban and Regl Studies). Open University: Res. Asst, 1970–73; Lectr, 1974–85; Sen. Lectr, 1985–95; Prof. of Geog., 1995. Banneker Prof., George Washington Univ., 1986; Vis. Prof., ANU, 1989; Sir Norman Chester Sen. Res. Fellow, Nuffield Coll., Oxford, 1993–94; Sen. Res. Fellow, Netherlands Inst. of Advanced Studies, 1992–93; Vis. Prof., Sciences-Po, Paris, 2004, 2014. Res. Dir and Mem., Nugee Cttee Inquiry, 1984–86. Westminster Housing Comr, 2005–06; Ealing Housing Comr, 2011–12. FAcSS 2007; FKC 2013; FRSA 2011. Back Award, RGS, 2012. *Publications:* (ed jtly) The Future of Cities, 1973; (ed jtly) City, Economy and Society, 1981; Cities, Housing and Profits, 1987; Winners and Losers: the housing market in Britain, 1988; (ed jtly) The Changing Social Structure, 1989; As Safe as Houses: housing wealth inheritance in Britain, 1991; (ed jtly) Housing and Housing Markets, 1991; (ed jtly) A Shrinking World, 1995; (ed) Social Geography: a reader, 1996; Shrinking the State: the political underpinnings of privatisation, 1998; Unequal City: London in the global arena, 2003; Ethnicity, Class and Aspiration: understanding London's new East End, 2011; edited books; contrib. papers to learned jls. *Recreations:* walking, ski-ing, music, art, water fights with grandchildren. *Address:* Department of Geography, King's College London, Strand, WC2R 2LS. *E:* chris.hamnett@kcl.ac.uk.

**HAMNETT, Katharine**, CBE 2011; fashion designer; *b* 16 Aug. 1947; *d* of Gp Capt. James Appleton. *Educ:* Cheltenham Ladies' Coll.; St Martin's Sch. of Art. Set up Tuttabankem (with Anne Buck), 1969–75; freelance designer in London, Paris, Milan, New York and Hong Kong, 1975–79; established Katharine Hamnett Ltd, 1979, and subseq. launched men's and women's collections, Asia, Europe, USA; transf. production to Italy, 1989, moving from manufacturing to licensing base. Vis. Prof., UAL (formerly London Inst.),

1997–. Numerous awards include British Fashion Designer of the Year, 1984. *Publications:* contribs to fashion magazines and newspapers. *Recreations:* gardening, agriculture, photography, archaeology, travel. *E:* info@katharinehamnett.com.

**HAMPDEN;** *see* Hobart-Hampden.

**HAMPDEN, 7th Viscount** *cr* 1884, of Glynde, co. Sussex; **Francis Anthony Brand;** *b* London, 17 Sept. 1970; *s* of 6th Viscount Hampden and of Cara Brand (*née* Proby); *S* father, 2008; *m* 2004, Dr Caroline Pryor, *d* of His Honour Robert Charles Pryor, *qv*; one *s* two *d. Educ:* Windlesham House Sch.; Millfield Sch.; Edinburgh Univ.; Cranfield Sch. of Mgt. *Heir:* s Hon. Lucian Anthony Brand, *b* 3 Nov. 2005. *Address:* The Estate Office, Glynde Place, Glynde, East Sussex BN8 6SX. *T:* (01273) 858224.

**HAMPEL, Rev. Canon Michael Hans Joachim;** Vice-Dean and Precentor, Durham Cathedral, since 2018; *b* Kendal, 11 Oct. 1967; *s* of Heinz and Barbara Hampel. *Educ:* King Edward VI Sch., Stratford-upon-Avon; University Coll., Durham (BA 1989); St Chad's Coll., Durham (MA 2002); Westcott House, Cambridge (CTM 1993). Ordained deacon, 1993, priest, 1994; Asst Curate, Whitworth with St Paul, Spennymoor, 1993–97; Minor Canon, Precentor and Sacrist, Durham Cathedral, 1997–2002; Sen. Tutor and Dir of Develt, St Chad's Coll., Durham, 2002–04; Res. Canon and Precentor, 2004–11, Sub-Dean, 2009–11, St Edmundsbury Cathedral; Res. Canon and Precentor, St Paul's Cathedral, 2011–18. Chaplain, 1407 (Newton Aycliffe) Sqdn, ATC, 1995–2004. Vice-Chair of Governors: King Edward VI Upper Sch., Bury St Edmunds, 2004–11; St Paul's Cathedral Sch., 2011–18; Chorister Sch., Durham Cathedral. *Publications:* contribs to books and learned jls; lyric writer for sacred anthems and songs. *Recreations:* constitutional history, art history, reading, music, theatre, cinema, food and wine, family and friends. *Address:* 7 The College, Durham DH1 3EQ. *E:* michael.hampel@durhamcathedral.co.uk.

**HAMPEL, Sir Ronald (Claus),** Kt 1995; Chairman: ICI plc, 1995–99; United Business Media (formerly United News & Media), 1999–2002; *b* 31 May 1932; *s* of Karl Victor Hugo Hampel and Rutgard Emil Klothilde Hauck; *m* 1957, Jane Bristed Hewson; three *s* one *d. Educ:* Canford Sch., Wimborne; Corpus Christi Coll., Cambridge (MA Mod. Lang. and Law; Hon. Fellow, 1996). Nat. service, 2nd Lt, 3rd RHA, 1951–52. Joined ICI, 1955; Vice-Pres., ICI US, 1973–77; Gen. Manager, Commercial, 1977–80; Chairman: ICI Paints, 1980–83; ICI Agrochemicals, 1983–85; Dir, ICI, 1985–99; Chief Operating Officer, 1991–93, Dep. Chm. and Chief Exec., 1993–95, ICI plc. Non-executive Director: Powell Duffryn, 1984–88; Commercial Union, 1988–95; BAE Systems (formerly British Aerospace), 1989–2002; ALCOA, USA, 1995–2005; Templeton Emerging Markets Investment Trust, 2003–07 (Chm., 2004–07); TI Automotive, 2007–09; Internat. Stadia Gp, 2010–16 (Chm., 2010–16); Geeknet Inc., 2011–16; Adv. Dir, Teijin, Japan, 2000–04. Dir, Amer. Chamber of Commerce, 1986–91; Chm., Cttee on Corporate Governance, 1995–98; Member: Listed Cos Adv. Cttee, Stock Exchange, 1996–99; Nomination Cttee, NY Stock Exchange, 1996–98; Adv. Cttee, Karlpreis Aachen, 1997–2001. Mem. Exec. Cttee, British North America Cttee, 1989–95. Mem., European Round Table, 1995–99. Chm. Trustees, Eden Project, 2000–07. CCMI (CBIM 1985). *Recreations:* tennis, golf, ski-ing, music. *Clubs:* MCC, All England Lawn Tennis; Royal & Ancient.

**HAMPSHER-MONK, Dame Susan Catherine;** *see* Leather, Dame S. C.

**HAMPSHIRE, Prof. Michael John,** CBE 1987; Research Professor of Electronic Information Technology, University of Salford, 1990–2004; *b* 13 Oct. 1939; *s* of Jack and Hilda May Hampshire; *m* 1962, Mavis (*née* Oakes); one *d. Educ:* Heckmondwike Grammar Sch.; Univ. of Birmingham (BSc Physics, PhD Elec. Engrg). University of Salford: Lectr, 1964; Sen. Lectr, 1972; Prof. of Solid State Electronics, 1978–85, of Electronic IT, 1985–90; Chm., Dept of Electronic and Electrical Engrg, 1981–89; Asst Man. Dir, 1989–95, Dir, 1989–98, Salford Univ. Business Services Ltd. Consultant: Ferranti, 1970–74; Volex Gp, 1977–99 (Chm., R&D Cttee, 1987–92); Thorn EMI Flow Measurement, 1980–88. Founder and Chm., Vertec (Electronics), 1982–92 (Dir, 1992–98). Commendation EPIC Award, 1982; Academic Enterprise Award, 1982; Techmart Technology Transfer Trophy, 1984. Hon. FIED 2001 (Hon. MIED 1982). *Publications:* Electron Physics and Devices, 1969; 80 pubns and patents on solid state electronics and electronic systems, vehicle multiplexing, innovation. *Recreation:* music. *Address:* 3 Brookfield, Upper Hopton, Mirfield, West Yorks WF14 8HL.

**HAMPSHIRE, Nancy Lynn Delaney, (Lady Hampshire);** *see* Cartwright, N. L. D.

**HAMPSHIRE, Susan,** CBE 2018 (OBE 1995); actress; *b* 12 May; *d* of George Kenneth Hampshire and June Hampshire; *m* 1st, 1967, Pierre Granier-Deferre (marr. diss. 1974); one *s* (one *d* decd); 2nd, 1981, Sir Eddie Kulukundis, *qv. Educ:* Hampshire Sch., Knightsbridge. *Stage:* Expresso Bongo, Saville, tour, 1959; 'that girl' in Follow That Girl, Vaudeville, 1960; Fairy Tales of New York, Comedy, 1961; Marion Dangerfield in Ginger Man, Royal Court, 1963; Past Imperfect, St Martin's and Savoy, 1964; Kate Hardcastle in She Stoops to Conquer, tour, 1966; On Approval, tour, 1966; Mary in The Sleeping Prince, St Martin's, tour, 1968; Nora in A Doll's House, Greenwich, 1972; Katharina in The Taming of the Shrew, Shaw, 1974; Peter in Peter Pan, Coliseum, 1974; Jeannette in Romeo and Jeannette, tour, 1975; Rosalind in As You Like It, Shaw, 1975; title rôle in Miss Julie, Greenwich, 1975; Elizabeth in The Circle, Haymarket, 1976; Ann Whitefield in Man and Superman, Savoy, 1978; Siri Von Essen in Tribades, Hampstead, 1978; Victorine in An Audience Called Edouard, Greenwich, 1978; Irene in The Crucifer of Blood, Haymarket, 1979; Ruth Carson in Night and Day, Phoenix, 1979; Elizabeth in The Revolt, New End, 1980; Stella Drury in House Guest, Savoy, 1981; Elvira in Blithe Spirit, Vaudeville, 1986; Marie Stopes in Married Love, Wyndham's, 1988; Countess in A Little Night Music, Piccadilly, 1989; Mrs Anna in The King and I, Sadler's Wells, 1990; Gertrude Lawrence in Noel and Gertie, Duke of York's, 1991; Felicity, Countess of Marshwood in Relative Values, Savoy, 1993; Suzanna in Suzanna Andler, Battersea, 1995; Alicia in Black Chiffon (tour), 1996; Sheila in Relatively Speaking (tour), 2000; Felicity, Countess of Marshwood in Relative Values (tour), 2002; Miss Shepherd in The Lady in the Van (tour), 2004–05; Fairy Godmother in Cinderella, Wimbledon, 2005, Woking, 2006; The Bargain (tour), 2007; Kitty in The Circle, Chichester, 2008; Mrs Bennet in Pride and Prejudice, Th. Royal, Bath (and tour), 2009; Lady Markby in An Ideal Husband, Vaudeville, 2018; *TV Serials:* Katy in What Katy Did; Andromeda (title rôle); Fleur Forsyte in The Forsyte Saga (Emmy Award for Best Actress, 1970); Becky Sharp in Vanity Fair (Emmy Award for Best Actress, 1973); Sarah Churchill, Duchess of Marlborough, in The First Churchills (Emmy Award for Best Actress, 1971); Glencora Palliser in The Pallisers; Lady Melfont in Dick Turpin; Signora Neroni in The Barchester Chronicles; Martha in Leaving, 2 series; Going to Pot, 3 series; Don't tell Father; Esme Harkness in The Grand, 2 series; Coming Home; Monarch of the Glen, 7 series; Sparkling Cyanide; The Royal; Casualty, 2010, 2013; Midsomer Murders, 2017. *Films include:* During One Night, The Three Lives of Thomasina, Night Must Fall, Wonderful Life, Paris in August, The Fighting Prince of Donegal, Monte Carlo or Bust, Rogan, David Copperfield, Living Free, A Time for Loving, Malpertuis (E. Poe Prizes du Film Fantastique, Best Actress, 1972), Neither the Sea Nor the Sand, Roses and Green Peppers, Bang, Another Mother's Son. Dir, Conservation Foundn, 1995–; Vice-Pres., Internat. Tree Foundn. Mem. Exec. Cttee, Population Concern; Pres., Dyslexia Inst.; Patron and Ambassador, Nat. Osteoporosis Soc.; Patron and Vice Pres., Juvenile Diabetes Res. Foundn. Hon. DLitt: London, 1981; City, 1984; St Andrews, 1986; Exeter, 2001; Hon. DEd Kingston, 1994; Hon. DArts Pine Manor Coll., Boston, USA, 1994. *Publications:* Susan's Story, 1981; The Maternal Instinct, 1984; Lucy Jane at the Ballet, 1989; Lucy Jane on Television, 1989; Trouble Free Gardening, 1989; Every Letter Counts, 1990; Lucy Jane and the Dancing Competition, 1991; Easy Gardening, 1991; Lucy Jane and the Russian Ballet, 1993; Rosie's First Ballet Lesson, 1996. *Recreations:* gardening, music, the study of antique furniture. *Address:* c/o Chatto & Linnit Ltd, 17 Old Park Lane, W1K 1QT.

**HAMPSON, Christopher,** CBE 1994; Chairman: RMC Group, 1996–2002; British Biotech plc, 1998–2002; *b* 6 Sept. 1931; *s* of Harold Ralph Hampson and Geraldine Mary Hampson; *m* 1954, Joan Margaret Cassils Evans; two *s* three *d. Educ:* McGill Univ. (BEng Chem. 1952). Vice-Pres., 1956–78 and Sen. Vice-Pres., 1982–84, Canadian Industries, Canada; Imperial Chemical Industries: Gen. Manager, Planning, 1978–82; Man. Dir and Chief Exec. Officer, ICI Australia, 1984–87; Exec. Dir, ICI, 1987–94; Chm., Yorkshire Electricity Gp, 1994–97. Non-executive Director: SNC-Lavalin Group, 1992–2002; TransAlta Corp., 1993–2003; BG plc, 1997–2000; Lattice Gp plc, 2000–02. Mem. Bd, 1996–99, Dep. Chm., 1999–2000, Environment Agency. *Recreations:* tennis, ski-ing. *Address:* 77 Kensington Court, W8 5DT. *Clubs:* Boodle's, Hurlingham; York (Toronto).
See also H. A. Hampson.

**HAMPSON, Christopher;** choreographer; Artistic Director, since 2012, and Chief Executive Officer, since 2015, Scottish Ballet; *b* 31 March 1973; *s* of Geoffrey and Janice Hampson. *Educ:* Royal Ballet Schs, White Lodge and Upper Sch.; Ashridge Exec. Educn, Hult Internat. Business Sch. (Exec. MBA for Creative Industries 2019). Soloist with English Nat. Ballet, 1992–99; rôles include: principal role in Square Dance; Drosselmeyer in Nutcracker; Headmistress in Graduation Ball; Dancing Master in Cinderella; also created soloist role in Symphonic Dances, and Caterpillar in Alice in Wonderland; Ballet Master, London City Ballet and Royal NZ Ballet, 1999–2000; guest teacher/coach: English Nat. Ballet; Royal Swedish Ballet; Royal NZ Ballet; Atlanta Ballet; National Th., Prague; Royal Acad. of Dance; English Nat. Ballet Sch.; Nat. Ballet of Canada; Matthew Bourne's New Adventures; Hong Kong Ballet; Genée Internat. Ballet Competition; Northern Ballet Th. Created ballets: for English National Ballet: Perpetuum Mobile, 1997; Country Garden, 1998; Concerto Grosso, 1999; Double Concerto, 2000; Nutcracker, 2002; Trapeze, 2003; for London City Ballet: Dinaresade, Canciones, 1999; for Royal New Zealand Ballet: Saltarello, 2001; Romeo and Juliet, 2002; Esquisses, 2005; Cinderella, 2007 (filmed for TVNZ, 2008); Silhouette, 2010; for National Theatre, Prague: Giselle, 2004; for Atlanta Ballet, USA: Sinfonietta Giocosa, 2005; Rite of Spring, 2011; for Royal Festival Hall: A Christmas Carol, 2000; for Royal Academy of Dance: La Vision, Caprice, 2003; for Royal Ballet: Dear Norman, 2009; for Ballet Black: Sextet, 2010; Storyville, 2012; for Scottish Ballet: Hansel and Gretel, 2013; Cinderella, 2015. Dir, Johann Strauss Gala (annually), 2005–11. Co-founder, Internat. Ballet Masterclasses, Prague, 2003. Speaker, TEDx, Glasgow; leadership talks for Inst. Good Governance; Leader, Young Leaders Rural Retreat, Dance East. Award for Best Classical Choreog., Critics' Circle, 2002; Award for Outstanding Achievement in Dance, Barclays Th., 2002. *Recreations:* music, theatre, wine, marathon running, knitting, studying for Exec. MBA with Ashridge Business School. *Address:* Scottish Ballet, Tramway, 25 Albert Drive, Glasgow G41 2PE. *E:* chris.hampson@scottishballet.co.uk.

**HAMPSON, Harold Arthur;** Managing Director, Chairman of Industries Coverage, Europe, Middle East and Africa, J P Morgan Europe, since 2016; *b* Montreal, 14 April 1965; *s* of Christopher Hampson, *qv*; *m* 1991, Rachel Mary Gibson; two *s* two *d. Educ:* St Paul's Sch., London; Trinity Coll., Cambridge (BA 1987; MA Hons; MEng). Joined J P Morgan, 1988; Equity Syndicate Manager, 1991–95; Hd, Equity Capital Mkts, 1995–99; Hd, Media Investment Banking, Europe, 2000–09; Hd of Telecom, Media, Technology, Investment Banking Europe, 2009–12; Hd of Financial Sponsor Coverage and Hd of Corporate Investment Banking, Europe, 2012–16. *Recreations:* ski-ing, running, biking, opera. *Clubs:* Buck's, Walbrook, 5 Hertford Street; Leander (Henley-on-Thames).

**HAMPSON, Dr Keith;** *b* 14 Aug. 1943; *s* of Bertie Hampson and Mary Elizabeth Noble; *m* 1st, 1975, Frances Pauline (*d* 1975), *d* of late Mathieu Donald Einhorn and of Ellen-Ruth Einhorn; 2nd, 1979, Susan, *d* of Mr and Mrs John Wilkie Cameron. *Educ:* King James I Grammar Sch., Bishop Auckland, Co. Durham; Univ. of Bristol; Harvard Univ. BA, CertEd, PhD. Personal Asst to Edward Heath, 1966 and 1970 Gen. Elections and in his House of Commons office, 1968; Lectr in American History, Edinburgh Univ., 1968–74. MP (C) Ripon, Feb. 1974–1983, Leeds North West, 1983–97; contested (C) Leeds North West, 1997. PPS to Minister for Local Govt, 1979–83, to Sec. of State for Environment, 1983, to Sec. of State for Defence, 1983–84. Member: Select Cttee on Trade and Industry, 1987–97; Public Accounts Commn, 1992–97; Vice Chairman: Cons. Parly Educn Cttee, 1975–79; Cons. Parly Defence Cttee, 1984–88 (Sec., 1984–88). Mem., Educn Adv. Cttee of UK Commn for UNESCO, 1980–84. Mem., Gen. Adv. Council, IBA, 1980–88. Vice President: WEA, 1978–97; Assoc. of Business Executives, 1979–99; Vice-Chm., Youthaid, 1979–83. UK Project Manager, DFID and FCO funds for democracy progs in Russia, 1998–2003; Sec., Internat. Adv. Bd, Moscow Sch. of Pol Studies, 2003–15; Mem., Bd of Dirs, Sch. of Civic Educn, 2016–17. Freeman, City of London, 2014. *Recreations:* DIY, music, gardening. *Club:* Carlton.

**HAMPSON, Peter,** CBE 2003; QPM 1998; Director General, National Criminal Intelligence Service, 2003–06; *b* 8 Jan. 1947; *s* of Maj. Ronald Hampson, MBE and Edith Hampson; *m* 1971, Pamela Mary Cotes; one *s* two *d. Educ:* Sandford Orleigh Sch., Newton Abbot; King's Coll. London (LLB 1982; AKC). Joined Metropolitan Police Service, 1967: Constable, 1967–71; Chief Superintendent, 1991–94; Asst Chief Constable, Surrey Police, 1994–96; Asst Inspector of Constabulary, Home Office, 1996–99; Chief Constable, W Mercia Constabulary, 1999–2003. Trustee: Community Foundn for Surrey, 2006–16 (Vice Pres., 2016–); Police Rehabilitation Trust, 2007–18. Gov., Treloar Coll., Alton, 2008–16. OStJ 1998. *Recreations:* family and friends, reading, theatre, cycling, long-distance walking, music, St John Ambulance, National Trust volunteer, Surrey Community Foundn.

**HAMPSON, Roger;** Chief Executive, London Borough of Redbridge, 2000–16; *b* Gosforth, Northumberland, 1950; *s* of William Hampson and Betty Hampson; *m* 1st, 1972, Caroline St John-Brooks (*d* 2003); one *s* one *d*; 2nd, 2008, Esther Wallington, *qv*; two *d. Educ:* Univ. of Ulster (BA Hons 1973); Univ. of Bristol (DipSocAdmin 1978). Res. Fellow, Personal Social Services Res. Unit, Univ. of Kent, 1983–86; Chief Social Services Officer, London Bor. of Bexley, 1988–94; Dir, Social Services and Housing, London Bor. of Redbridge, 1994–2000. FRSA. *Publications:* (jtly) Care in the Community: the first steps, 1988; (jtly) Directing Social Services, 1999; (with Nigel Shadbolt) The Digital Ape, 2018; articles on local govt services and others. *E:* roger.hampson@gmail.com.

**HAMPSON, Stephen Fazackerley;** Under Secretary, Scottish Executive (formerly Scottish Office), 1993–2002; *b* 27 Oct. 1945; *s* of Frank Hampson and Helen (*née* Ellis); *m* 1970, Gunilla Brunk; one *s* one *d. Educ:* University Coll., Oxford (BPhil; MA). Lectr, Aberdeen Univ., 1969–71; Economist, NEDO, 1971–75; various posts, Scottish Office, 1975–78, and at Scottish Office, then Scottish Executive, 1981–2002 (Head: Envmt Gp, 1993–2000; Enterprise and Industrial Affairs Gp, 2000–02); First Sec., FCO, New Delhi,

1978–81. Member, Board: British Trade Internat., 2000–02; Mercy Corps Scotland, 2008–10. Mem., Council, WWF Scotland, 2002–08. Hon. FCIWEM 1998. *Address*: Glenelg, Park Road, Kilmacolm PA13 4EE. *T*: (01505) 872615.

**HAMPSON, Sir Stuart**, Kt 1998; CVO 2016; DL; Chairman, The Crown Estate, 2010–16; *b* 7 Jan. 1947; *s of* Kenneth and Mary Hampson; *m* 1973, Angela McLaren; one *s* one *d*. *Educ*: Royal Masonic Sch., Bushey; St John's Coll., Oxford (BA Mod. Langs, MA, Hon. Fellow, 2001). Board of Trade, 1969–72; FCO UKMIS to UN, Geneva, 1972–74; Dept of Prices and Consumer Protection, 1974–79; Dept of Trade, 1979–82; John Lewis Partnership, 1982–2007: Dir of Research and Expansion, 1986; Dep. Chm., 1989; Chm., 1993–2007. Dep. Chm., London First, 1992–97; Chm., Centre for Tomorrow's Company, 1998–99. Chm., RSA, 1999–2001 (Treas., 1997–98; Dep. Chm., 1998–99, 2001–02). President: Royal Agricl Soc. of England, 2005–06; Employee Ownership Assoc. (formerly Job Ownership Ltd), 2005–11; Hearing Dogs for Deaf People, 2016–. High Sheriff, Bucks, 2013–14; DL Bucks, 2015. Hon. FCGI 2002. Hon. DBA: Kingston, 1998; Southampton Inst., 2001; Middlesex 2007; Hon. DSc Buckingham, 2010; Hon. LLD Warwick, 2010.

**HAMPSON, (Walter) Thomas**; singer; *b* Elkhart, Indiana, 28 June 1955; *s of* Walter Hampson and Ruthye Hampson; one *d*. *Educ*: Eastern Washington Univ. (BA Govt); Fort Wright Coll.; Music Acad. of West. Début in Hansel and Gretel, 1974; with Düsseldorf Ensemble, 1981–84; title rôle in Der Prinz von Homburg, Darmstadt, 1982; débuts: Cologne, Munich, Santa Fé, 1982–84; Metropolitan Opera, NY, Vienna Staatsoper, Covent Garden, 1986; La Scala Milan, Deutsche Oper, Berlin, 1989; Carnegie Hall, San Francisco Opera, 1990; rôles include: Marcello in La Bohème; Guglielmo in Così fan tutte; Figaro in Il Barbiere di Siviglia; Count in Le Nozze di Figaro; Ulisse in Il Ritorno d'Ulisse in Patria; Lescaut in Manon; Count in La Traviata; Vicomte de Valmont in Dangerous Liaisons (world première, 1996); Marquis de Posa in Don Carlos; Riccardo in I Puritani; Wolfram in Tannhäuser; Oreste in Iphigénie en Tauride; Amfortas in Parsifal; Mandryka in Arabella; Renato in Un Ballo in Maschera; Athanael in Thais; Iago in Otello; title rôles: Don Giovanni; Billy Budd; Hamlet; Eugene Onegin; William Tell; Werther (seldom-performed baritone version); Doktor Faust; Der Riese vom Steinfeld (world première, 2002); Macbeth; Simon Boccanegra; Wozzeck. Has performed with Wiener Philharmoniker, NY Philharmonic (Artist-in-Residence, 2009–10), LPO and Chicago Symphony orchs. Recital repertoire includes Schumann, Mahler and American Art Song. Has made numerous recordings. Founded Hampsong Foundn, 2003. Hon. RAM 1996; Hon. Mem., Wiener Konzerthaus, 2004; Mem., Amer. Acad. of Arts and Scis, 2010. Hon. Dr: San Francisco Conservatory of Music; Whitworth Coll., USA. Awards include: Gold Medal, Internat. Mahler Soc.; Lotte Lehman Medal, Music Acad. of West, 1979; Edison Prize, Netherlands, 1990 and 1992; Grand Prix du Disque, 1990, 1996, Echo Klassik, 1995, Deutsche Schallplattenpreis; Cannes Classical Award, 1994; Citation of Merit, Nat. Arts Club, 1997; Vienna Kammersänger, 1999; Austrian Medal of Honour in Arts and Scis, 2004; Edison Life Achievement Award, 2005. Commandeur de l'Ordre des Arts et des Lettres (France), 2010. *Publications*: (ed jtly) Mahler Songs: critical edition, 1993; (ed jtly) Schumann/Heine 20 Lieder und Gesänge: critical edition. *Address*: c/o Centre Stage Management, Stralauer Allee 1, 10245 Berlin, Germany.

**HAMPSTEAD, Archdeacon of**; *see* Hawkins, Ven. J. E. I.

**HAMPTON, 7th Baron** *cr* 1874; **John Humphrey Arnott Pakington**; Bt 1846; secondary school teacher; owner, Johnnie Pakington Photography, since 2010; *b* 24 Dec. 1964; *s of* 6th Baron Hampton and Jane Elizabeth Farquharson Pakington (*née* Arnott); *S* father, 2003; *m* 1996, Siena, *yr d of* Remo Caldato; one *s* one *d*. *Educ*: Exeter Coll. of Art and Design (BA Hons). Creative Dir, Band & Brown Communications, London, 1995–2010. Mem., ECB Coaches Assoc., 2010– (UK Coaching Cert. Level 2 Cricket Coach). Member: Friends of Worcester Record Office, 2001–; British Italian Soc., 2004–. *Recreations*: gardening, sport, photography. *Heir*: *s* Hon. Charles Richard Caldato Pakington, *b* 2 May 2005. *Clubs*: King's Head Members; Stoke Newington Cricket, Saracens Amateur Rugby Football.

**HAMPTON, Alison Wendy; Her Honour Judge Hampton**; a Circuit Judge, since 2002; Designated Civil Judge, Leicester and Northampton; *b* 14 March 1955; *d of* Wing Comdr Gordon Hampton, OBE, DFC and Eve Hampton; *m* 1977, Nigel Haynes. *Educ*: Abbeydale Girls' Grammar Sch., Sheffield; Leicester Univ. (LLB Hons). Called to the Bar, Gray's Inn, 1977; Circuit Jun., Midland and Oxford Circuit, 1987–88. Mem., WI, 1995–. *Recreations*: fine arts, fine food, cycling, walking, scuba diving, ski-ing, cats. *Address*: Leicester County Court, Wellington Street, Leicester LE1 6HG.

**HAMPTON, Christopher James**, CBE 1999; FRSL; playwright; *b* 26 Jan. 1946; *s of* Bernard Patrick Hampton and Dorothy Patience Hampton (*née* Herrington); *m* 1971, Laura Margaret de Holesch; two *d*. *Educ*: Lancing Coll.; New Coll., Oxford (MA; Hon. Fellow, 1997). First play: When Did You Last See My Mother?, 1964 (perf. Royal Court Theatre, 1966; transf. Comedy Theatre; prod. at Sheridan Square Playhouse, New York, 1967, Trafalgar Studios, 2011). Resident Dramatist, Royal Court Theatre, Aug. 1968–70. FRSL 1976 (Mem. Council, 1984–90). Officier, l'Ordre des Arts et des Lettres (France), 1997. *Plays*: Total Eclipse, prod. Royal Court, 1968; The Philanthropist, Royal Court and Mayfair, 1970 (Evening Standard Best Comedy Award, 1970; Plays & Players London Theatre Critics Best Play, 1970), NY, 1971, Chichester, 1985, Donmar, 2005, NY, 2009, Trafalgar Studios, 2017; Savages, Royal Court, 1973, Comedy, 1973, LA, 1974 (Plays & Players London Theatre Critics Best Play, Jt Winner, 1973; Los Angeles Drama Critics Circle Award for Distinguished Playwriting, 1974); Treats, Royal Court, 1976, Mayfair, 1976, Garrick, 2007; Able's Will, BBC TV, 1977; After Mercer, NT, 1980; The History Man (from Malcolm Bradbury) BBC TV, 1981; Total Eclipse (rev. version) Lyric, Hammersmith, 1981; The Portage to San Cristobal of A. H. (from George Steiner), Mermaid, 1982; Tales from Hollywood, LA, 1982, NT 1983 (Standard Best Comedy Award, 1983), Donmar, 2001; Les Liaisons Dangereuses (from Laclos), RSC, 1985, transf. Ambassadors, 1986, NY, 1987, 2008, 2016, Donmar, 2015 (Plays & Players London Theatre Critics Best Play, Jt Winner, 1985; Time Out Best Production Award, 1986; London Standard Best Play Award, 1986; Laurence Olivier Best Play Award, 1986; NY Drama Critics' Circle Best For. Play Award, 1987); Hotel du Lac (from Anita Brookner), BBC TV, 1986 (BAFTA Best TV Film Award, 1987); The Ginger Tree (from Oswald Wynd), BBC TV, 1989; White Chameleon, NT, 1991; Alice's Adventures Under Ground, NT, 1994; The Talking Cure, NT, 2002, Theater in der Josefstadt, Vienna, 2014; Embers (from Sándor Márai), Duke of York's, 2006; Youth Without God (from Horváth), Theater in der Josefstadt, Vienna, 2009; Appomattox, Guthrie Th., Minneapolis, 2012; The Thirteenth Tale (from Diane Setterfield), BBC TV, 2013; All About Eve (from Joe Mankiewicz), Theater in der Josefstadt, Vienna, 2018; A German Life, Bridge Th., 2019; *musicals*: Sunset Boulevard (book and lyrics with Don Black), Apollo, 1992, LA, 1993, NY, 1994, 2017, ENO, 2016 (Tony Award: Best Original Score, 1995; Best Book of a Musical, 1995), Comedy, 2008; Dracula (book and lyrics with Don Black), La Jolla, 2001, NY, 2004; Stephen Ward (book and lyrics with Don Black), Aldwych, 2013; *opera*: Waiting for the Barbarians (libretto, based on novel by J. M. Coetzee; music by Philip Glass), Erfurt, 2005, Austin, Texas, 2007; Appomattox (libretto; music by Philip Glass), San Francisco, 2007, (rev. version) Nat. Opera, Washington, 2015; The Trial (libretto based on novel by Kafka;

music by Philip Glass), ROH, 2014; *translations*: Marya, by Isaac Babel, Royal Court, 1967; Uncle Vanya, by Chekhov, Royal Court, 1970, Vaudeville, 2012; Hedda Gabler, by Ibsen, Fest. Theatre, Stratford, Ont, 1970, Almeida, Islington, 1984, rev. version, NT, 1989; A Doll's House, by Ibsen, NY, 1971, Criterion, 1973, NY, 1975, W Yorks Playhouse, 2005; Don Juan, by Molière, Bristol Old Vic, 1972; Tales from the Vienna Woods, by Horváth, NT, 1977; Don Juan Comes Back from the War, by Horváth, NT, 1978; Ghosts, by Ibsen, Actors' Co., 1978; The Wild Duck, by Ibsen, NT, 1979; The Prague Trial, by Chéreau and Mnouchkine, Paris Studio, 1980; Tartuffe, by Molière, RSC, 1983, Theatre Royal, Haymarket, 2018; Faith, Hope and Charity, by Horváth, Lyric, Hammersmith, 1989, Southwark Playhouse, 2011; Art, by Yasmina Reza, Wyndhams, 1996 (Standard Best Comedy Award and Laurence Olivier Best Comedy Award, 1997), NY (Tony Award, Best Play), 1998, Old Vic, 2016; An Enemy of the People, by Ibsen, RNT, 1997, Crucible, Sheffield, 2010, Chichester, 2016; The Unexpected Man, by Yasmina Reza, RSC, 1998, NY, 2000; Conversations After a Burial, by Yasmina Reza, Almeida, 2000; Life x 3, by Yasmina Reza, RNT, transf. Old Vic, 2000, NY 2003; Three Sisters, by Chekhov, Playhouse, 2003, Lyric Hammersmith, 2010; The Seagull, by Chekhov, Royal Court, 2007, NY, 2008; God of Carnage, by Yasmina Reza, Gielgud, 2008 (Laurence Olivier Best Comedy Award), NY (Tony Award, Best Play), 2009; Judgment Day, by Horváth, Almeida, 2009; The Father, by Florian Zeller, Ustinov Studio, Th. Royal, Bath, 2014, transf. Tricycle Th., 2015, Wyndham's, 2015, 2018, Duke of York's and NY, 2016; The Mother, by Florian Zeller, Th. Royal Bath, 2015, transf. Tricycle Th., 2016, NY, 2019; The Truth, by Florian Zeller, Menier Chocolate Factory, transf. Wyndham's, 2016; Haïm - In the Light of a Violin, by Gérald Garutti, Print Room, Coronet, 2016; The Mentor, by Daniel Kehlmann, Th. Royal, Bath, 2017, transf. Vaudeville; Christmas Eve, by Daniel Kehlmann, Th. Royal, Bath, 2017; The Lie, by Florian Zeller, Menier Chocolate Factory, 2017; The Height of the Storm, by Florian Zeller, Wyndham's, 2018, NY, 2019; The Son, by Florian Zeller, Kiln Th., 2019; *screenplays*: A Doll's House, 1973; Tales From the Vienna Woods, 1979; The Honorary Consul, 1983; The Good Father, 1986 (Prix Italia 1988); Wolf at the Door, 1986; Dangerous Liaisons, 1988 (Academy Award, and Writers Guild of America Award, for best adapted screenplay; Critics' Circle Award for best screenplay, 1989; BAFTA best screenplay award, 1990); Total Eclipse, 1995; Mary Reilly, 1996; The Quiet American, 2002; Atonement, 2007 (Hollywood Screenwriter of the Year, 2007; Richard Attenborough Screenwriter of the Year, 2008; Best Literary Adaptation, Forum Internat. Cinéma et Littérature, Monaco, 2008); Chéri, 2009; A Dangerous Method, 2012; Perfect Mothers (aka Adore), 2013; Ali and Nino, 2016; (*also directed*): Carrington, 1995 (Special Jury Prize, Cannes Fest., 1995); The Secret Agent, 1996; Imagining Argentina, 2003. *Publications*: When Did You Last See My Mother?, 1967; Total Eclipse, 1969, rev. version, 1981; The Philanthropist, 1970, 3rd edn 2005, The Philanthropist and other plays, 1991; Savages, 1974; Treats, 1976, rev. version, 2007; Able's Will, 1979; Tales from Hollywood, 1983, 2nd edn 2001; The Portage to San Cristobal of A. H. (George Steiner), 1983; Les Liaisons Dangereuses, 1985; Dangerous Liaisons: the film, 1989; The Ginger Tree, 1989; White Chameleon, 1991; (with Don Black) Sunset Boulevard, 1993; Alice's Adventures Under Ground, 1995; Carrington, 1995; Total Eclipse: the film, 1996; Plays One, 1997; The Secret Agent and Nostromo (Conrad), 1997; Collected Screenplays, 2002; The Talking Cure, 2002; Hampton on Hampton, ed Alastair Owen, 2005; Embers, 2006; Atonement: the shooting script, 2007; Appomattox, 2012; A German Life, 2019; *translations*: Isaac Babel, Marya, 1969; Chekhov, Uncle Vanya, 1971, 2nd edn 2012; Ibsen, Hedda Gabler, 1972, rev. version 1989; Ibsen, A Doll's House, 1972, 2nd edn 1989; Molière, Don Juan, 1972; Horváth, Tales from the Vienna Woods, 1977, 2nd edn 2000; Horváth, Don Juan Comes Back from the War, 1978; Ibsen, The Wild Duck, 1980; Ibsen, Ghosts, 1983; Molière, Tartuffe, 1984, 2nd edn 1991, rev. edn 2018; Horváth, Faith, Hope and Charity, 1989; Yasmina Reza, Art (Scott Moncrieff Trans. Prize, Translators' Assoc.), 1997; Ibsen, An Enemy of the People, 1997; Yasmina Reza, The Unexpected Man, 1998; Yasmina Reza, Conversations After a Burial, 2000; Yasmina Reza, Life x 3, 2000; Chekhov, Three Sisters, 2004; Yasmina Reza, Plays One, 2005; Chekhov, The Seagull, 2007; Yasmina Reza, God of Carnage, 2008; Horváth, Judgment Day, 2009; Florian Zeller, The Mother and The Father, 2015; Florian Zeller, The Truth, 2016; Daniel Kehlmann, The Mentor, 2017; Florian Zeller, The Lie, 2017; Daniel Kehlmann, Christmas Eve, 2017; Florian Zeller, The Height of the Storm, 2018; Florian Zeller, The Son, 2019. *Recreations*: travel, cinema. *Address*: 2 Kensington Park Gardens, W11 3HB. *Club*: Dramatists'.

**HAMPTON, Sir Geoffrey**; *see* Hampton, Sir L. G.

**HAMPTON, John**; a Recorder of the Crown Court, 1983–98; *b* 13 Nov. 1926; *e s of* late Thomas Victor Hampton and Alice Maud (*née* Sturgeon), Oulton Broad; *m* 1954, Laura Jessie (*d* 2017), *d of* Ronald Mylne Ford and Margaret Jessie Ford (*née* Coghill), Newcastle-under-Lyme; three *d*. *Educ*: Bradford Grammar School; University College London (LLB). Served Royal Navy, 1945–47. Called to the Bar, Inner Temple, 1952; NE Circuit; Solicitor General and Attorney General; Dep. Circuit Judge, 1975–82. Dep. Chm., Agricultural Land Tribunal, Yorks and Lancs Area, 1980–82, Yorks and Humberside Area, 1982–99; Dep. Traffic Comr, NE Traffic Area, 1988–94. *Recreations*: mountaineering, sailing. *E*: jlhampton@bigpond.com.

**HAMPTON, Prof. Kay**; Member, Scottish Human Rights Commission, 2007–15; consultant, KK Consulting, since 2011; Lead Commissioner, 2002–07, and Chairman, 2006–07, Commission for Racial Equality (Deputy Chairman, 2003–06); *b* 25 Dec. 1957; *m* Russell Hampton; two *d*. *Educ*: Univ. of Durban-Westville, SA (BA Hons 1985; MA (Sociol.) *cum laude* 1987). Res. Asst, 1978–79, Researcher, 1980–89, Inst. for Social and Econ. Res., Univ. of Durban-Westville, SA; Researcher, Strategic Planning Dept, City of Durban Municipality, 1990–93; Glasgow Caledonian University: Res. Fellow, 1994–96, Res. Dir, 1996–2000, Scottish Ethnic Minorities Res. Unit; Lectr in Sociol., 2000–06, Prof. of Communities and Race Relns, 2006–11, Sch. of Law and Social Scis. Observer, Exec. Cttee, West of Scotland Community Relns Council, 1994–98; Mem. Adv. Cttee, Scottish Poverty Information Unit, 1996–99; Member Committee: SCVO Race Equality Adv. Gp, 1996–2002; Apna Ghar (Scotland's first black-led housing assoc.), 1997–99; Board Member: Nat. Lottery Charities Bd, subseq. Community Fund, 1998–2004 (Chm. Scotland Cttee, 1998–2004); Meridian, Black and Ethnic Minority Women's Information and Resource Centre, 2000–01; Res. Advr, Black and Ethnic Minority Infrastructure in Scotland (BEMIS), 1998–99; Member: Regulatory Cttee, Law Soc. of Scotland, 2011–13; Adjudicating Panel, Gen. Teaching Council for Scotland, 2012–14; Scottish Solicitors Disciplinary Tribunal, 2013–; Public Appts Assessor, Commn for Ethical Standards in Public Life in Scotland, 2012–; Nat. Confidential Forum, Scottish Govt, 2014–16; non-executive Director: Positive Action in Housing, 1999–2002; Scottish Refugee Council, 2003; Scottish Prison Service, 2017–; Chm., Saheliya, Women's Mental Health Project, 1999–2000. Trustee, Scottish Assoc. for Mental Health, 2010–14. Mem. Editl Bd, Scottish Youth Issues Jl, 2000–04. ILTM. Mem. AUT. Patron, Ind. Academic Res. Studies Internat. Inst., 2014–. Bronze Medal for Scientific Achievement, SA Assoc. for Advancement in Scis, 1988. *Publications*: (contrib. chapter) Ageing in South Africa, 1989; articles in Scottish Youth Issues Jl, Internat. Jl of Health Promotion and Educn, SA Jl of Sociol., Jl of Scottish Anti-racist Fedn in Community Develt and Social Work, Scottish Ethnic Minorities Res. Unit occasional papers series. *Recreation*: attempting to make a difference by promoting fairness and justice!

**HAMPTON, Sir (Leslie) Geoffrey,** Kt 1998; KPMG Professor of Education Leadership, University of Wolverhampton, since 2005 (Dean of Education, 2000–06; Pro Vice Chancellor, 2006–09; Deputy Vice-Chancellor, 2009–13); *b* 2 Aug. 1952; *s* of Leslie and Irene Hampton; *m* 1975, Christine Joyce Bickley; two *s*. *Educ*: King Alfred's Coll., Winchester (Cert Ed); Southampton Univ. (BEd); Birmingham Univ. (MEd). Teacher of Technology, Pensnett Sch., Dudley, W Midlands, 1973–86 (Dep. Head, 1985–86); Dep. Head, Buckpool Sch., Dudley, 1986–93; Headteacher, Northicote Sch., Wolverhampton, 1993–99. Dir, Midlands Leadership Centre, 1999–2014; Co-Dir, Nat. ICT Res. Centre, 2001–03. Chief Advr to Minister for Sch. Standards, Black Country Challenge Prog., 2007–10. Chief Exec., Educn Central, 2013–16. Member: Nat. Adv. Gp, Basic Skills Agency, 2002–07; Bd, Black Country Partnership for Learning, 2006–; Adv. Bd, Nat. Educn Business Partnerships, 2007–08; Nat. Challenge Expert Advisers Gp, DCSF, then DFE, 2008–. Associate Dir, Specialist Schs and Academies Trust, 2005–; Leader, Educn and Skills, Black Country Consortium, 2006–. Chairman: Walsall Educn Bd, 2003–08; Wolverhampton Local Educn Partnership, 2010–. Dir, CPI (W Midlands) Ltd, Educn Consultancy, 2016–. Mem., Strategic Bd, C of E Central Educn Trust, 2015–. Hon. DEd King Alfred's Coll., Winchester, 2003. *Publications*: (contrib.) Developing Quality Systems in Education, ed G. Doherty, 1994; (jtly) Transforming Northicote, 2000; (jtly) A Guide to Teacher Professional Development, 2004. *Recreations*: DIY, cycling, gardening. *Address*: University of Wolverhampton, Executive Suite, Wulfruna Street, Wolverhampton WV1 1LY.

**HAMPTON, Sir Philip (Roy),** Kt 2007; Chairman, GlaxoSmithKline plc, 2015–19; *b* 5 Oct. 1953; *m* 1983, Amanda Lowe; two *s*. *Educ*: Lincoln Coll., Oxford (MA English 1975; Hon. Fellow 2010); INSEAD, Fontainebleau (MBA 1980). ACA 1978. Lazard Brothers, 1981–89: corporate finance rôles, 1981–86; Exec. Dir, 1987–89; Group Finance Director: British Steel, 1990–96; British Gas, then BG, 1996–2000; BT Gp, 2000–02; Gp Finance Dir, Lloyds TSB Gp plc, 2002–04; Chairman: J. Sainsbury plc, 2004–09; Royal Bank of Scotland Gp, 2009–15. Chm., UK Financial Investments Ltd, 2008–09. Non-executive Director: Belgacom, 2004–10; Anglo American plc, 2009–18. *Recreations*: history, sailing, ski-ing. *Club*: Royal Thames Yacht.

**HAMWEE,** Baroness *cr* 1991 (Life Peer), of Richmond upon Thames; **Sally Rachel Hamwee;** Member (Lib Dem), London Assembly, Greater London Authority, 2000–08 (Chairman, 2001–02, 2003–04, 2005–06 and 2007–08; Deputy Chairman, 2000–01, 2002–03, 2004–05 and 2006–07); former Consultant, Clintons, solicitors (Partner, 1984–2000); *b* 12 Jan. 1947; *d* of late Alec Hamwee and Dorothy (*née* Saunders). *Educ*: Manchester High Sch. for Girls; Girton Coll., Cambridge (MA). Admitted as solicitor, 1972. Councillor, London Borough of Richmond upon Thames, 1978–98 (Chm., Planning Cttee, 1983–94; Vice Chm., Policy and Resources Cttee, 1987–91); Chair, London Planning Adv. Cttee, 1986–94. Vice Chm., Assoc. of Liberal Democrat Councillors, 1988–99; Member: Nat. Exec., Liberal Party, 1987–88; Federal Exec., Liberal Democrats, 1989–91; Lib Dem spokesman on local govt, 1991–98, on planning and housing, 1993–98, on transport and the regions, 1997–2001, and on ODPM, subseq. DCLG, 2001–09, on Home Affairs, 2009–, H of L; Co-Chair, Lib Dem Policy Cttee on Home Affairs, Justice and Equality, 2010–; Member: Select Cttee on Econ. Affairs, 2008–10, on Adoption Legislation, 2012–13, on Inquiries Act 2005, 2013–14, on Extradition Law, 2014–15, H of L; Leader's Group on H of L Code of Conduct, 2009, on working practices of H of L, 2010–11; Secondary Legislation Scrutiny (formerly Merits of Statutory Instruments) Cttee, 2010–; Jt Cttee on Human Rights, 2015–. Member: Adv. Council, London First, 1996–98 (Dir, 1993–96); Council, Parents for Children, 1977–86; Council of Mgt, Refuge (formerly Chiswick Family Rescue), 1991–2005; Adv. Bd, Centre for Public Scrutiny; Policy and Res. Adv. Gp. Missing People, 2014–. Chm., Xfm Ltd, 1996–98. Member, Board: Arts Council London, 2006–08; Rose Th., Kingston, 2009– (Trustee, Kingston Th. Trust, 2009–). Vice-President: TCPA, 2002– (Pres., 1995–2002); Chartered Inst. of Envmtl Health; Jt Pres., London Councils, 2005–. Trustee, Safer London, 2014–. *Address*: 101A Mortlake High Street, SW14 8HQ.

**HANAN, Dame Elizabeth (Ann),** DNZM 1998; CRSNZ 2006; Deputy Mayor, Dunedin City, 1998–2004 (City Councillor, 1986–2004); *b* 21 Aug. 1937; *d* of Sir John Patrick Walsh, KBE; *m* 1966, John Murray Hanan; one *s* two *d*. *Educ*: Columba Coll.; Otago Girls' High Sch.; Otago and Canterbury Univs (BSc Univ. of NZ 1961; Dip. Recreation and Sport 1983). Secondary School Teacher, Christchurch, London and Dunedin, 1960–66, 1984–88; Supervisor and Demonstrator, Chemistry, Univ. of Otago, 1975–86; Tutor, Otago Poly., 1982–85. Member: NZ Council, 1986–88, Bd, 1989–98, Consumers' Inst. of NZ; Electrical Workers' Registration Bd, 1993–98 (Presiding Mem., 1993–97). Member: Otago Br., Fedn of Graduate Women (formerly Fedn of University Women), 1961– (Pres., 1990–92); Nat. Exec., Plunket Soc., 1972–74; Bd, Otago Mus. Trust, 1986–2001 (Chair, 1987–99); Otago Theatre Trust, 1986–2001; Friends of Otago Mus., 2013– (Patron, 2013–); Fortune Theatre (Mem., Bd of Mgt, 1995–2006; Pres., 2003–06); Discovery World, 1989–98; Mgt Cttee, Theomin Gall., 2001–07; Arrowtown Village Assoc., 2013–. Chair, Assoc. of Science and Technology Centres, 1994–96; Pres., NZ Internat. Science Fest., Dunedin, 1996–2004 (Mem. Cttee, 2004–17; Life Mem., 2010). Vice Pres., City Choir Dunedin, 2015–. Commemoration Medal, 1990, Suffrage Centennial Medal, 1993, NZ. *Publications*: Playgrounds and Play, 1981 (trans. Japanese 1993); The Clans From Newton Hall: a family history Wallace Morris, 2002; The Hanan Journey, 2009; Pioneers: Walsh family history, 2012; Elsie Hanan *née* Nimmo, 2013; The Legend of Lorenzo Resta, Macetown Miner and the Story of His House at 82 McDonnell Road, Arrowtown, 2014; The Legend of Newton Hall Fife, 2015. *Recreations*: walking, reading, computers, genealogy, theatre, travel. *Address*: 159 Highgate, Dunedin 9010, New Zealand. *T*: 027 2211739, *T*: and *Fax*: (3) 4774388. *Club*: University (Dunedin).

**HANBURY, Heather Gail;** Head Mistress, Lady Eleanor Holles School, Hampton, since 2014; *b* Belfast, 20 Sept. 1960; *d* of Douglas Adams and Jane Adams; *m* 1993, Roland Hanbury. *Educ*: Princess Gardens Sch., Belfast; Univ. of Edinburgh (MA Geog. 1983); Wolfson Coll., Cambridge (MSc Land Economy 1986); Inst. of Educn, Univ. of London (PGCE 1996). Mkt Analyst, Planning, Research and Systems plc, 1986–88; Sen. Consultant, Touche Ross Mgt Consultants, 1988–93; Hd, Corporate Fundraising, VSO, 1993–95; Teacher of Geog., Hd of Upper Sch., then Hd of Sixth Form, Blackheath High Sch., 1996–2001; Hd of Sixth Form, Haberdashers' Aske's Sch. for Girls, 2001–03; Dep. Hd, Latymer Upper Sch., 2003–08; Headmistress, Wimbledon High Sch., 2008–14. *Recreations*: bridge, cooking and entertaining, theatre, travel. *Address*: Lady Eleanor Holles School, Hanworth Road, Hampton, Middx TW12 3HF. *T*: (020) 8979 1601.

**HANBURY-TENISON, (Airling) Robin,** OBE 1981; DL; MA, FLS, FRGS; farmer; President, Survival International (Chairman, since 1969); *b* 7 May 1936; *s* of late Major Gerald Evan Farquhar Tenison, Lough Bawn, Co. Monaghan, Ireland, and Ruth, *o* surv. *c* of late John Capel Hanbury, JP, DL, Pontypool Park, Monmouthshire; *m* 1st, 1959, Marika Hopkinson (*d* 1982); one *s* one *d*; 2nd, 1983, Mrs Louella Edwards (High Sheriff of Cornwall, 2006–07), *d* of late Lt Col G. T. G. Williams, DL, and Mrs Williams, Menkee, St Mabyn, Cornwall; one *s*. *Educ*: Eton; Magdalen Coll., Oxford (MA). Made first land crossing of South America at its widest point, 1958 (Mrs Patrick Ness Award, RGS, 1961); explored Tassili N'Ajjer, Tibesti and Air mountains in Southern Sahara, 1962–66; crossed S America in a small boat from the Orinoco to Buenos Aires, 1964–65; Geographical Magazine Amazonas Expedn, by Hovercraft, 1968; Trans-African Hovercraft Expedn (Dep. Leader), 1969; visited 33 Indian tribes as guest of Brazilian Govt, 1971; Winston Churchill Memorial Fellow, 1971; British Trans Americas Expedn, 1972; explored Outer Islands of Indonesia, 1973; Eastern Sulawesi, 1974; Sabah, Brunei, Sarawak, 1976; RGS Mulu (Sarawak) Expedn (Leader), 1977–78; expedns to Ecuador, Brazil and Venezuela, 1980–81; rode across France, 1984; rode along Great Wall of China, 1986; rode through New Zealand, 1988; led mission for IUCN, Friends of the Earth and Survival Internat. to Malaysia to investigate imprisonment of envmtl protesters, 1988; rode as pilgrim to Santiago de Compostela, 1989; rode across Spain driving 300 cattle on Trans Humance, 1991; visited tribal peoples of E Siberia for Survival Internat., 1992 and 1994; rode route of proposed Pennine Bridleway, 1994; visited: tribal people of Arunachal Pradesh, NE India, 1995; Innu of Labrador, 1997; Tuareg of Ténéré desert, S Sahara, 1999, 2002, 2003; Bushmen of the Kalahari, 2005; Kimberley, Australia rock art, 2006; rode through Albania, 2007; climbed Mt Roraima, Venezuela, 2008; Maya forest res., 2009; Gran Chaco, Paraguay, 2012; return to Mulu for circuit of Mt Api, 2014. Mulu (film for C4), 1999. Chief Executive: BFSS, 1995–97; Countryside Alliance (BFSS, Countryside Business Gp and Countryside Movt), 1997–98 (Patron, 2003); organised Countryside Rally, 1997, Countryside March, 1998. Comr of Income Tax, 1965–95; Mem., SW Regl Panel, MAFF, 1993–96; Mem. of Lloyd's, 1976–95. Mem., Invest in Britain (formerly Think British) Campaign, 1987–; Trustee, Ecological Foundn, 1988–2004; President: Cornwall Wildlife Trust, 1988–95; Rain Forest Club, 2001–05; Patron: Cornwall Heritage Trust, 1994–; Countryside Alliance, 2003–. DL Cornwall, 2003. Hon. Consul of Cornwall in Kosovo, 2014. Mem. Council, RGS, 1968–70, 1971–76, 1979–82 (Vice-Pres., 1982–86); Patron's Medal, RGS, 1979; Krug Award of Excellence, 1980; Farmers Club Cup, 1998; Personality of the Year, Internat. Council for Game and Wildlife Conservation, 1998; Contribution to Countryside Award, CLA, 2000; Medal of Italian Chamber of Deputies, Pio Manzù Centre, 2000; Mungo Park Medal, RSGS, 2001. Dr *hc* Mons-Hainaut, 1992; Hon. DSc Plymouth, 2012. *Publications*: The Rough and the Smooth, 1969, 2nd edn 2005; Report of a Visit to the Indians of Brazil, 1971; A Question of Survival, 1973, 2nd edn 2005; A Pattern of Peoples, 1975, 2nd edn 2005; Mulu: the rain forest, 1980, 3rd edn 2005; Aborigines of the Amazon Rain Forest: the Yanomami, 1982; Worlds Apart (autobiog.), 1984, 3rd edn 2005; White Horses Over France, 1985, 2nd edn 2005; A Ride along the Great Wall, 1987, 2nd edn 2005; Fragile Eden: a ride through New Zealand, 1989, 2nd edn 2005; Spanish Pilgrimage: a canter to St James, 1990, 2nd edn 2005; (ed) The Oxford Book of Exploration, 1993, 3rd edn 2010; Worlds Within, 2005; (ed) The Seventy Great Journeys in History, 2006; Land of Eagles: riding through Europe's forgotten country, 2009, 2nd edn 2013; The Great Explorers, 2010; Echoes of a Vanished World: a lifetime in pictures, 2012; Beauty Freely Given, 2012; The Modern Explorers, 2013; Finding Eden: a journey into the heart of Borneo, 2017; *for children*: Jake's Escape, 1996, 2nd edn 2013; Jake's Treasure, 1998, 2nd edn 2013; Jake's Safari, 1998, 2nd edn 2013; articles in: The Times, Telegraph, Spectator, Daily Mail, Sunday Express, etc; articles and reviews in Geographical Magazine (numerous), Geographical Jl, Ecologist, Literary Review, TLS, New Scientist, Traveller, Country Life, Field, etc. *Recreations*: travelling, riding across countries. *Address*: Cabilla Manor, Bodmin, Cornwall PL30 4DW. *T*: (01208) 821224. *E*: robin@cabilla.co.uk. *W*: www.cabilla.co.uk, www.robinsbooks.co.uk. *Clubs*: Travellers, Pratt's, Geographical.

**HANBURY-TRACY,** family name of **Baron Sudeley.**

**HANCE, Very Rev. Dr Stephen John;** National Lead for Evangelism and Witness, Church of England, since 2019; *b* Kisumu, Kenya, 16 April 1966; *s* of John and Joan Hance; *m* 1990, Jacqueline Gray; two *s* one *d*. *Educ*: Portsmouth Univ. (BSc Hons 1989); Nottingham Univ. (BTh Hons 1992; MA 1993); Asbury Theol Seminary, Kentucky (DMin 2009). Ordained deacon, 1993, priest, 1994; Curate, St Jude's, Southsea, 1993–96; Team Vicar, Tollington, 1996–99; Dir of Post Ordination Trng, Kingston, 2000–05; Incumbent, Ascension, Balham Hill, 1999–2013; Canon Missioner and Dir of Mission and Evangelism, Southwark Cathedral, 2013–17; Dean of Derby, 2017–19. Mem., Gen. Synod, 2015–17. *Publications*: Going for Growth, 2003; (with J. Hance) In the Beginning, 2000; (contrib.) How to do Mission Action Planning, 2016; (contrib.) Doorways to the Sacred, 2017; (ed) Forgiveness in Practice, 2018; (contrib.) Anglican Evangelists, 2019. *Recreations*: music, theatre, travel, reading, Africa, playing rock guitar. *Address*: Church House, Great Smith Street, SW1P 3AZ.

**HANCOCK, Prof. Barry William,** OBE 2009; MD; FRCP, FRCPE, FRCR; Yorkshire Cancer Research Professor of Clinical Oncology, University of Sheffield, 1988–2009, now Emeritus; *b* 25 Jan. 1946; *s* of George Llewellyn Hancock and Sarah Hancock; *m* 1969, (Christine Diana) Helen Spray; one *s* one *d*. *Educ*: Univ. of Sheffield Med. Sch. (MB ChB 1969; MD 1977); Univ. of London (DCH 1971). FRCP 1985; FRCPE 1995; FRCR 1995. Lectr, 1974–78, Sen. Lectr, 1978–86, Reader, 1986–88, in Medicine, Univ. of Sheffield; Dir of Supraregl Gestational Trophoblastic Tumour Service (N of England and Wales), 1991–2009; Yorks Cancer Res. Dir of Cancer Res., 2000–09. Chm., Renal Clinical Studies Gp, NCRI, 2001–08. Pres., Internat. Soc. for Study of Trophoblastic Diseases, 2007–09 (Gold Medal, 2009). New Year Hons Award, Lord Mayor of Sheffield, 1999; Sheffield Community Hero Award (Health), 2002; Centenary Achievement Medal, Sheffield Univ., 2005; Excellence in Oncology Lifetime Achievement Award, Pfizer/British Oncol. Assoc., 2008; Sheffield Legends Award, Sheffield CC, 2010. *Publications*: (ed) Assessment of Tumour Response, 1982; (ed jtly) Immunological Aspects of Cancer, 1985; (ed jtly) Lymphoreticular Disease, 1985; (jtly) Lecture Notes in Clinical Oncology, 1986; (ed) Cancer Care in the Community, 1996; (ed) Cancer Care in the Hospital, 1996; (ed jtly) Gestational Trophoblastic Disease, 1997, 4th edn 2015; (ed jtly) Malignant Lymphoma, 2000; over 250 articles in med. jls. *Recreations*: railways, ornithology, philately, tennis. *Address*: (home) Treetops, 253 Dobcroft Road, Ecclesall, Sheffield S11 9LG. *T*: (0114) 235 1433; Academic Unit of Clinical Oncology, Weston Park Hospital, Whitham Road, Sheffield S10 2SJ. *E*: b.w.hancock@sheffield.ac.uk.

**HANCOCK, Brian John;** Director, PRIME Partners, since 2003; Telecommunication and Media Advisor, 2010–13, and Team Manager, 2012–13, Firstsource (formerly Conduit); *b* 8 Aug. 1950; *s* of John and Joan Hancock; *m*; one *s* one *d*. *Educ*: Poly. of Wales (BSc Chem. Engrg 1974); Aston Univ. (Post Grad. Dip. Occupnl Safety and Health, 1986); Cardiff Univ. Business Sch. (Post Grad. Cert. in Sustainable Profitable Growth and Leadership, 2007). Registered Safety Practitioner, 1994; MIOSH 1992; AMIChemE. Chemical Project Engr, Monsanto Ltd, 1974–76; Shift Prodn Supervisor, 1976–80, Asst Plant Manager, 1980–85, ReChem International Ltd; Chemical Specialist Inspector of Factories, Health and Safety Inspectorate, 1985–88; Health, Safety and Envmt Supt, BP Chemicals, 1988–92; health, safety and envmt consultant and advr, and Dir of own consultancy, 1992–2000. National Assembly for Wales: Mem., (Plaid Cymru) Islwyn, 1999–2003; contested (Plaid Cymru): Islwyn, 2003; Newport West, 2007. Governor: primary and secondary schs, 1985–2000; Ysgol Gyfun Gwynllyw, 2004– (Chm., 2011–14). Chair, Alexis Enterprises Ltd, 2003–05; Gen. Manager, Phoenix Community Transport, 2003–06; Employment Liaison Officer, Dash Trng Ltd, 2007–08; Family Job Liaison Officer, A4e, 2008–09; Volunteer, Workers' Educn Assoc., 2009–10. Mem., Risca Town Council (formerly Risca West Community Council), 2012–; Actg Clerk to Draethen, Waterloo and Rudry

Community Council, 2017 and 2018–. Chair, Plaid Cymru Cangen Ebwy Islwyn Br., 2005–. Chm., Pontywaun Boat Club. Mem., CAMRA. *Recreations:* athletics (Newport Harriers AC), Rugby, DIY. *T:* (01633) 601934. *Clubs:* Newport Harriers Athletic; Risca Rugby Football.

**HANCOCK, Christine;** Founder and Director, C3 Collaborating for Health, since 2009. *Educ:* London School of Economics (BScEcons). RGN. Formerly: Chief Nursing Officer, Bloomsbury Health Authority; General Manager, Waltham Forest Health Authority; Gen. Sec., RCN, 1989–2001; Pres., Internat. Council of Nurses, 2001–05; Eur. Dir, Oxford Health Alliance, 2006–09. Gov., De Montfort Univ., 2006–15. *Address:* C3 Collaborating for Health, CAN Mezzanine, 7–14 Great Dover Street, SE1 4YR.

**HANCOCK, Very Rev. Christopher David,** PhD; Director, Oxford House Consultancy (formerly Institute of Religion and Society in Asia, then Oxford House Research Ltd), since 2010; *b* 18 Feb. 1954; *s* of late Rev. Dr Ronald and of Vera Hancock; *m* 1975, Suzie Nichols; one *s* one *d*. *Educ:* Highgate Sch.; Queen's Coll., Oxford (BA 1975, MA 1980); Cranmer Hall, Durham (BA 1978); St John's Coll., Durham (PhD 1984). Ordained deacon 1982, priest 1983; Curate, Holy Trinity with St John, Leicester, 1982–85; Chaplain, Magdalene Coll., Cambridge, 1985–88; Lectr, Divinity Faculty, Univ. of Cambridge, 1985–88; Asst, 1988–91, Associate Prof., 1991–94, Virginia Theol Seminary, USA; Vicar, Holy Trinity, Cambridge, 1994–2002; Dean of Bradford, 2002–04; Dir, Centre for the Study of Christianity in China, KCL (formerly at Oxford), 2005–09. Chaplain (part-time), St Peter's Coll., Oxford, 2012–14; Vis. Scholar, Wolfson Coll., Oxford, 2012–14. Visiting Professor: S Asia Inst. of Advanced Christian Studies, Bangalore, 1996–; St Mary's Univ., Twickenham, 2018–. Exec. Dir, AMO Global, 2005–10. Hon. Fellow, Wycliffe Hall, Oxford, 2010–16. *Recreations:* music, sport, woodwork, walking, fishing, bird-watching, films, family. *Address:* 3 College Farm Cottages, Garford, Abingdon, Oxon OX13 5PF; 13 Westmoreland Terrace, SW1V 4AG. *Club:* Oxford and Cambridge.

**HANCOCK, Christopher Patrick;** QC 2000; a Recorder, since 2004; Deputy High Court Judge, since 2008; *b* 7 June 1960; *s* of Alan Hancock and Dr (Rosemary) Ann Turner; *m* 1985, Diane Galloway; two *s*. *Educ:* Perse Sch. for Boys, Cambridge; Trinity Coll., Cambridge (MA Hons); Harvard Law Sch. (LLM). Called to the Bar, Middle Temple, 1983, Bencher, 2011; in practice at the Bar, 1985–. Dir, Learning Partnership Trust, 2015–. Governor: Hatfield Heath Community Primary Sch., 2012–; Perse Sch., Cambridge, 2018–. *Recreations:* golf, music, watching football, family, Cub Scout leader, Group Contact and Deputy District Commissioner. *Address:* 20 Essex Street, WC2R 3AL. *T:* (020) 7583 9294.

**HANCOCK, Elisabeth Joy;** Head, Old Palace School, Croydon, 2000–04; *b* 2 Dec. 1947; *d* of Reginald Arthur Lord and Evelyn Maud Mary Lord; *m* 1970, Barry Steuart Hancock; one *d*. *Educ:* Queen's Coll., Harley Street; Nottingham Univ. (BA Hons); Univ. of Sussex (PGCE). GB East Europe Centre, 1969; Nevill Sch., Hove, 1969–72; Brighton and Hove High Sch. (GPDST), 1972–89, Dep. Hd, 1986–89; Head, Bromley High Sch. (GDST), 1989–2000. FRSA 1988. *Publications:* Teaching History, 1970. *Recreations:* theatre, opera, watching cricket. *Address:* c/o Old Palace School, Old Palace Road, Croydon CR0 1AX.

**HANCOCK, Group Captain Ethnea Mary,** RRC 1990; Director and Matron-in-Chief, Princess Mary's Royal Air Force Nursing Service, and Deputy Director, Defence Nursing Services (Organisation), 1991–94; *b* 5 April 1937; *d* of late Sydney Ludwig Hancock and Catherine Teresa Hancock (*née* O'Dea). *Educ:* Convent of the Cross, Boscombe; University Coll. Hosp., London; RGN 1958; Southlands Hosp., Shoreham; Whittington Hosp., London; RM 1960; BA Hons Open Univ. 2003. Joined PMRAFNS, 1961–65; Columbia Presbyterian Medical Center, NY, 1966–67; rejoined PMRAFNS, 1967; served RAF Hosps and Units, UK, N Africa, Cyprus, Singapore, Germany; appts include Sen. Matron, RAF Hosp., Ely, 1985–87; MoD, 1987–88; Principal Nursing Officer, PMRAFNS, 1988–91, QHNS, 1991–94. *Recreations:* home and garden, music and the arts, travelling. *Address:* Nationwide Building Society, PO Box 8888, Swindon SN3 1TS.

**HANCOCK, Frances Winifred;** *see* Done, F. W.

**HANCOCK, Prof. Gus,** PhD; Professor of Chemistry, University of Oxford, 1996–2012, now Emeritus (Head, Physical and Theoretical Chemistry Laboratory, 2005–10); Fellow, Trinity College, Oxford, since 1976; *b* Chell, 17 Nov. 1944; *s* of Reginald and Mary Hancock; *m* 1971, Rosemary Margaret Norfolk Brown; one *s* one *d*. *Educ:* Bangor Grammar Sch., Co. Down; Trinity Coll., Dublin (Louis Claude Purser Schol. and Foundn Schol.; BA Hons Natural Scis; MA); Peterhouse, Cambridge (PhD Physical Chem. 1971). Res. Asst, Univ. of Calif, San Diego, 1971–73; Wissenschaftlicher Angestellte, Univ. Bielefeld, 1973–76; Lectr in Physical Chem., Oxford Univ., 1976–96. Vis. Prof. of Chem., Stanford Univ., 1989. Hon. Dr Córdoba, Argentina, 2013. Corday Morgan Medal and Prize, 1982, Reaction Kinetics Award, 1995, Polanyi Medal, Gas Kinetics Gp, 2002, Chemical Dynamics Award, 2010, RSC; Italgas Prize for Sci. and Technol. for the Envmt, 2000. *Publications:* contrib. jls and books. *Address:* 124 Divinity Road, Oxford OX4 1LW. *T:* (01865) 275439. *E:* gus.hancock@chem.ox.ac.uk.

**HANCOCK, Heather Jane,** LVO 2013; DL; Chairman, Food Standards Agency, since 2016 (Deputy Chairman, 2015–16); Director, Amerdale Group, since 2014; *b* Colne, Lancs, 27 Aug. 1965; *d* of Colin and Pamela Margaret Wilkinson; *m* 1992, Mark Edward Hancock; two *s*. *Educ:* Colne Park High Sch.; Nelson and Colne Further Educn Coll.; St John's Coll., Cambridge (BA 1st Cl. Land Econ.; MA; Hon. Fellow). Land Agent, Carter Jonas, 1987–88; Economist, Home Office, 1988–90; Private Secretary: to Home Sec., 1990–92; to Perm. Sec., DNH, 1992–93; Hd, Millennium Commn Unit, 1993–94; Chief Exec., 1994–95, Dep. Chief Exec., 1995–96, Millennium Commn; Mgt Consultant, Deloitte and Touche, 1996–98; Chief Exec., Yorks Dales Nat. Park Authy, 1998–2000; Exec. Dir, Yorks Forward, 2000–03; Deloitte LLP: Partner, 2003–14; Mem. Bd, 2006–08; Man. Partner, Talent, Innovation and Brand, 2008–12, Talent and Brand, 2012–13, Client Experience, 2013–14; Global Man. Dir, Communications and Brand, Deloitte Touche Tohmatsu Ltd, 2011–13. Dep. Chm., London 2017 Ltd and London Championships Ltd, 2013–16. Non-exec. Chair, Wavelength Ltd, 2015–18; non-exec. Dir, Rural Solutions Ltd, 2017–. Chm., Football League Wkg Party on Structure of Football, 1997–98. Trustee: Prince's Trust, 2000–12 (Chair: Yorks and Humber Regl Council, 1999–2007; Audit Cttee, 2007–12); Internat. Business Leaders Forum, 2011–13. Chm., Rural Affairs Cttee, BBC, 2003–10. Hon. Sec., 1995–97, Pres., 2003–04 Land Soc. Founder Trustee, Yorks Dales Millennium Trust, 1996–2003; Trustee: Waterways Trust, 1998–2002; Chatsworth Settlement Trust, 2018–. Vice-Pres., Upper Wharfedale Agricl Soc., 1999–. Pres., Johnian Soc., 2012–13; Chair, Develt Cttee, St John's Coll., Cambridge, 2013–17. Gov., Giggleswick Sch., 2007–19 (Chm. of Trustees and Govs, 2013–19). DL N Yorks, 2017. *Recreation:* rural affairs and country life. *Address:* The Old Vicarage, Arncliffe, N Yorks BD23 5QD.

**HANCOCK, Herbert Jeffrey, (Herbie);** jazz pianist and composer; *b* Chicago, 12 April 1940; *s* of Wayman Edward Hancock and Winnie Hancock (*née* Griffin); *m* 1968, Gudrun Meixner; one *d*. *Educ:* Grinnell Coll., Iowa; Roosevelt Univ., Chicago; Manhattan Sch. of Music; New Sch. for Social Res. Owner and publisher, Hancock Music Co., 1962–; founder, Hancock and Joe Prodns, 1989–. Pres., Harlem Jazz Music Center Inc.; Institute Chm., Thelonious Monk Inst. of Jazz, 2004–; Creative Chair of Jazz, LA Philharmonic, 2010–; Norton Prof. of Poetry, Harvard Univ., 2014. Performances with: Chicago SO, 1952; Coleman Hawkins, Chicago, 1960; Donald Byrd, 1960–63; Miles Davis Quintet, 1963–68. Composer of music for films: Blow Up, 1966; The Spook Who Sat by the Door, 1973; Death Wish, 1974; A Soldier's Story, 1984; Jo Jo Dancer, Your Life is Calling, 1986; Action Jackson, 1988; Colors, 1988; Harlem Nights, 1989; Livin' Large, 1991; writer of score and actor in film, 'Round Midnight, 1986 (Acad. Award for best original score, 1986). Numerous awards. *Albums include:* Takin' Off, 1963; Succotash, 1964; Speak Like a Child, 1968; Fat Albert Rotunda, 1969; Mwandishi, 1971; Crossings, 1972; Sextant, 1972; Headhunters, 1973; Thrust, 1974; Man-Child, 1975; The Quintet, 1977; V. S. O. P., 1977; Sunlight, 1978; An Evening with Herbie Hancock and Chick Corea in Concert, 1979; Feets Don't Fail Me Now, 1979; Monster, 1980; Lite Me Up, 1982; Future Shock, 1983; Sound System, 1984; (with Foday Musa Suso) Village Life, 1985; (with Dexter Gordon) The Other Side of 'Round Midnight, 1987; Perfect Machine, 1988; Jamming, 1992; Cantaloupe Island, 1994; Tribute to Miles, 1994; Dis Is Da Drum, 1995; The New Standard, 1996; (with Wayne Shorter) 1 + 1, 1997; Gershwin's World, 1998; Return of the Headhunters, 1998; future 2 future, 2001; Possibilities, 2005; River: the Joni letters, 2007 (Grammy Award, 2008); The Imagine Project, 2010. *Publications:* (with Lisa Dickey) Herbie Hancock: possibilities (memoir), 2014. *Address:* Hancock Music Co., Suite 1600, 1880 Century Park East, Los Angeles, CA 90067, USA.

**HANCOCK, Janet Catherine,** LVO 2005; FRGS; HM Diplomatic Service, retired; Deputy High Commissioner, then Acting High Commissioner, Malta, 2005–09; *b* 5 Jan. 1949; *d* of Joseph Paul Knox and Alice Cecælia (*née* Ouzman); *m* 1973, Roger Arnold Hancock (marr. diss. 2006); *m* 2007, David Kemp. *Educ:* Convent of Jesus and Mary, Felixstowe and Ipswich; St Anne's Coll., Oxford (MA); Birkbeck Coll., London (MA). Entered FCO, 1971: res. analyst, 1971–94; Beirut, 1985, 1986, 1987; Hd, ME and N Africa Res. Gp, 1994–2000; Actg Dep. Head of Mission, Jerusalem, 1998; Dep. Hd of Mission, Tunis, 2000–04. FRGS 1998. Trustee, SWORDE-Teppa, Tajikistan, 2009–. Mem. Edtl Bd, Asian Affairs, 2011–. *Publications:* contrib. articles to Mediterranean Politics, Jl Royal Soc. for Asian Affairs, etc. *Recreations:* plants and birds, dalmatians, cats (Mem. Cttee, Southend and Dist. Br., Cats Protection), trying to compensate for woeful lack of classical education by studying Greek and Roman history.

**HANCOCK, Prof. Keith Jackson,** AO 1987; Vice-Chancellor, The Flinders University of South Australia, 1980–87; Senior Deputy President, Australian Industrial Relations Commission (formerly Australian Conciliation and Arbitration Commission), 1992–97 (Deputy President, 1987–92); *b* 4 Jan. 1935; *s* of late A. S. Hancock and Mrs R. D. Hancock; three *s* one *d*. *Educ:* Univ. of Melbourne (BA); Univ. of London (PhD). Tutor in Economic History, Univ. of Melbourne, 1956–57; Lectr in Economics, Univ. of Adelaide, 1959–63; Professor of Economics, 1964–87, now Emeritus, and Pro-Vice-Chancellor, 1975–79, Flinders Univ. of SA. Hon. Vis. Fellow, 1998–2018, Adjunct Prof., 2018–, Univ. of Adelaide; Professorial Fellow, Nat. Inst. of Labour Studies, 1998–2017. Chairman: Cttee of Inquiry into S Australian Racing Industry, 1972–74; Nat. Superannuation Cttee of Inquiry, 1973–77; Cttee of Review of Aust. Industrial Relns Law and Systems, 1983–85; Mem., Review Gp on Aust. Financial Instns, 1983. Chm., Energy Industry Ombudsman (SA) Ltd, 2000–09. Pres., Acad. of Social Sciences in Australia, 1981–84. FASSA 1968. Hon. Fellow, LSE, 1982. Hon. DLitt Flinders, 1987; Hon. DCom Melbourne, 2013. *Publications:* The National Income and Social Welfare, 1965; (with P. A. Samuelson and R. H. Wallace) Economics (Australian edn), 1969, 2nd edn 1975; (ed jtly) Applied Economics: readings for Australian students, 1975; Incomes Policy in Australia, 1981; (ed jtly) Japanese and Australian Labour Markets: a comparative study, 1983; (ed) Australian Society, 1989; Australian Wage Policy: infancy and adolescence, 2013; contrib. to various racing industry, superannuation, and financial and industrial law systems reports in Australia; articles in Economic Jl, Economica, Amer. Econ. Rev. and other jls. *Recreations:* bridge, sailing, music. *Address:* 6 Maturin Road, Glenelg, SA 5045, Australia. *T:* (8) 82948667. *Clubs:* Adelaide (Adelaide); Royal South Australian Yacht Squadron (Treas., 2008–12).

**HANCOCK, Rt Hon. Matthew John David, (Rt Hon. Matt);** PC 2014; MP (C) West Suffolk, since 2010; Secretary of State for Health and Social Care, since 2018; *b* Chester, 2 Oct. 1978; *s* of Michael Hancock and Shirley Hills (now Carter); *m* 2006, Martha Hoyer Millar; two *s* one *d*. *Educ:* Farndon Co. Prim. Sch.; King's Sch., Chester; W Cheshire Coll.; Exeter Coll., Oxford (BA 1st Cl. PPE 1999); Christ's Coll., Cambridge (MPhil Econ 2003). Economist, Bank of England, 2000–05; COS to George Osborne, MP, 2005–10. Parly Under-Sec. of State for Skills, 2012–13, Minister of State (Minister for Skills and Enterprise), 2013–14, BIS and DfE; Minister of State (Minister for Business, Enterprise and Energy), BIS and DECC, 2014–15; Minister for the Cabinet Office and Paymaster Gen., 2015–16; Minister of State (Minister for Digital and Culture, then Minister for Digital), DCMS, 2016–18; Sec. of State for Digital, Culture, Media and Sport, 2018. Member: Public Accounts Cttee, 2010–12; Cttee on Standards and Privileges, 2010–12. *Publications:* (with N. Zahawi) Masters of Nothing, 2011. *Recreations:* cricket, cooking, racing, walking with family, Twitter (@ MattHancock). *Address:* House of Commons, SW1A 0AA. *T:* (020) 7219 7186. *E:* matt.hancock.mp@parliament.uk. *W:* www.matt-hancock.com, www.twitter.com/MattHancock, www.facebook.com/matthancockofficial, Mobile App: Matt Hancock.

**HANCOCK, Michael Thomas,** CBE 1992; *b* 9 April 1946; *m* 1967, Jacqueline, *d* of Sidney and Gwen Elliott; one *s* one *d*. *Educ:* well. Member: Portsmouth City Council, 1971–2014 (for Fratton Ward, 1973–2014; Leader, Lib Dem Gp, 1989–97; Chm., Planning and Econ. Develt Cttee, 1991–94; Exec. Mem., Planning, Econ. Develt, Tourism and Property, 2003–14); Hampshire County Council, 1973–97 (Leader of the Opposition, 1977–81, 1989–93; Leader, Lib Dem Gp, 1989–97; Leader of Council, 1993–97). Joined SDP, 1981 (Mem., Nat. Cttee, 1984); contested Portsmouth S (SDP) 1983. MP (SDP) Portsmouth S, June 1984–1987; contested (SDP/Alliance) same seat, 1987. MP Portsmouth S, 1997–2015 (Lib Dem 1997–2014, Ind, 2014–15); contested (Ind) same seat, 2015. Lib Dem parly spokesman on defence, 1997–2001. Member: Public Admin Cttee, 1997–99; Select Cttee on Defence, 1998–2011; Panel of Chairmen, 2000–15; UK Parly Delegn to Council of Europe, 1997–2015 (Mem. Bd, Lib Dems; Chm., Youth and Support Cttee); WEU Parly Assembly (Leader, Liberal Gp); NATO Parly Assembly (Dep. Leader, Liberal Gp). Contested (Lib Dem) Wight and Hampshire South, Eur. Parly elecns, 1994. Dist Officer for Hants, IoW and CI, Mencap, 1989–97. Vice Chairman: Portsmouth Operating Co., 1992–95; Portsmouth Docks, 1992–2002. Dir, Daytime Club, BBC, 1987–90. Bd of Dirs, Drug Rehabilitation Unit, Alpha Drug Clinic, Alpha House, Droxford, 1971–. Trustee, Royal Marine Museum, 1993. Hon. Alderman, Hants, 1997. Hon. award for contrib. to Anglo-German relations, Homborn, W Germany, 1981. *Publications:* contribs to various jls. *Recreations:* people, living life to the full. *Clubs:* too many to mention.

**HANCOCK, Rt Rev. Peter;** *see* Bath and Wells, Bishop of.

**HANCOCK, Sheila,** CBE 2011 (OBE 1974); actor, director and writer; *d* of late Enrico Hancock and Ivy Woodward; *m* 1st, 1955, Alexander Ross (*d* 1971); one *d*; 2nd, 1973, John Thaw, CBE (*d* 2002); one *d*. *Educ:* Dartford County Grammar Sch.; Royal Academy of Dramatic Art. Acted in Repertory, Theatre Workshop, Stratford East, for 8 years. Associate Dir, Cambridge Theatre Co., 1980–82; Artistic Dir, RSC Regional Tour, 1983–84; acted and directed, NT, 1985–86. Dir, The Actors Centre, 1978–. Starring roles in: Rattle of a Simple Man, 1962; The Anniversary, 1966, 2005; A Delicate Balance (RSC), 1969; So What About Love?, 1969; Absurd Person Singular, 1973; Déjà Revue, 1974; The Bed Before Yesterday, 1976; Annie, 1978; Sweeney Todd, 1980; The Winter's Tale, RSC, Stratford 1981, Barbican 1982; Peter Pan, Barbican, 1982–83; The Cherry Orchard, The Duchess of Malfi, National, 1985–86; Greenland, Royal Court, 1988; Prin, Lyric, Hammersmith, 1989, Lyric, Shaftesbury Avenue, 1990; A Judgement in Stone, The Way of the World, Lyric, Hammersmith, 1992; Gypsy, W Yorkshire Playhouse, 1994 (Best Actress, Theatre Awards UK, TMA); Harry and Me, Royal Court, 1996; Lock Up Your Daughters, Chichester, 1996; Then Again…, Lyric, Hammersmith, 1997; Vassa, Albery, 1999; Under the Blue Sky, Royal Court, 2000; In Extremis, RNT, 2000; Arab-Israeli Cookbook, Gate, 2004; The Anniversary, Garrick, 2005; Cabaret, Lyric, 2006 (Olivier and Clarence Derwent Awards for best supporting role); The Birthday Party, Lyric, Hammersmith, 2008; Sister Act, Palladium, 2009; The Last of the Duchess, Hampstead Th., 2011; Barking in Essex, Wyndham's Th., 2013; Grey Gardens, Southwark Playhouse, 2016; Harold and Maude, Charing Cross Th., 2018; This is My Family, Minerva, Chichester, 2019. Has starred in several successful revues; appeared on Broadway in Entertaining Mr Sloane. Directed: The Soldier's Fortune, Lyric, Hammersmith, 1981; A Midsummer Night's Dream, RSC, 1983; The Critic, National, 1986. *Films:* The Love Child, 1987; Making Waves, 1987; Hawks, 1988; Buster, 1988; Three Men and a Little Lady, 1990; Hold Back the Night, 1999; Love and Death on Long Island, 2000; Yes, 2005; Boy in the Striped Pyjamas, 2008; Edie, 2018; The More You Ignore Me, 2018. *Television:* many successes, including The Rag Trade, Jumping the Queue, The Rivals, and several comedy series, incl. Gone to the Dogs, 1991, Gone to Seed, 1992, Brighton Belles, 1993; other appearances include: The Buccaneers, 1994; Dangerous Lady, 1994; Close Relations, 1998; Eastenders, Love or Money, The Russian Bride, 2001; Bedtime, 2001, 2002, 2003; Bait, 2002; 40 Something, 2003; Grumpy Old Women, 2003, 2004, 2005; Feather Boy, 2004; Bleak House, 2005; After Thomas, 2006; The Last Word, 2008; My Life in Verse (documentary), 2009; Suffragette City (documentary), 2010; Over the Rainbow, 2010; The Art of Water Colours (documentary), 2011; Hustle, 2012; Perspectives: the Brontes (documentary), 2013; Casualty, 2016; Delicious, 2017; Endeavour, 2017; The Dumping Ground, 2017; wrote and acted in Royal Enclosure, 1990. Chancellor, Univ. of Portsmouth, 2008–12. Awards: Variety Club, London Critics, Whitbread Trophy (for best Actress on Broadway); Carmen Silvera Award, Grand Order of Lady Ratlings, 2010; Lifetime Achievement Award, Women in Film and TV, 2011. *Publications:* Ramblings of an Actress, 1987; The Two of Us, 2004 (Author of the Year, British Book Awards, 2005); Just Me, 2008; Miss Carter's War (novel), 2014. *Recreations:* reading, music. *Address:* c/o Independent Talent Group Ltd, 40 Whitfield Street, W1T 2RH.

*See also* M. J. Byam Shaw.

**HAND, Prof. David John,** OBE 2013; PhD; FBA 2003; Professor of Statistics, Imperial College London, 1999–2011, now Emeritus Professor of Mathematics and Senior Research Investigator; Chief Scientific Advisor, Winton Capital Management, 2010–18; *b* 30 June 1950; *s* of Peter Hand and Margaret Hand; *m* 1993, Dr Shelley Channon; two *d*. *Educ:* Christ Church, Oxford (BA Maths 1972); Southampton Univ. (MSc Stats 1974; PhD Pattern Recognition 1977). CStat 1993; FIMA 2011. Statistician, Inst. of Psychiatry, 1977–88; Prof. of Statistics, Open Univ., 1988–99. Non-exec. Dir, UK Statistics Authy, 2013–. Pres., Royal Statistical Soc., 2008–09, 2010. Mem., Magic Circle, 2015–. Hon. FIA 1999. Guy Medal in Silver, Royal Statistical Soc., 2002; George Box Medal, Eur. Network for Business and Industrial Statistics, 2016. *Publications:* Discrimination and Classification, 1981; Finite Mixture Distributions, 1981; Kernel Discriminant Analysis, 1982; Artificial Intelligence and Psychiatry, 1985; Multivariate Analysis of Variance and Repeated Measures, 1987; (ed) The Statistical Consultant in Action, 1987; Analysis of Repeated Measures, 1990; (ed) Artificial Intelligence Frontiers in Statistics, 1993; (ed) AI and Computer Power: the impact on statistics, 1994; (ed) A Handbook of Small Data Sets, 1994; Elements of Statistics, 1995; Biplots, 1996; Practical Longitudinal Data Analysis, 1996; Construction and Assessment of Classification Rules, 1997; (ed) Statistics in Finance, 1998; Intelligent Data Analysis, 1999; Advances in Intelligent Data Analysis, IDA–99, 1999; Principles of Data Mining, 2001; (ed) Advances in Intelligent Data Analysis, IDA 2001, 2001; Pattern Detection and Discovery, 2002; Methods and Models in Statistics, 2004; Measurement Theory and Practice, 2004; (ed) Selected Papers of Sir David Cox, 2005; Information Generation, 2007; Statistics: a very short introduction, 2008; ROC Curves for Continuous Data, 2009; The Improbability Principle, 2014; The Wellbeing of Nations, 2014; Measurement: a very short introduction, 2016; over 300 scientific articles. *Address:* Department of Mathematics, Imperial College London, 180 Queen's Gate, SW7 2AZ. *T:* (020) 7594 2843. *E:* d.j.hand@imperial.ac.uk.

**HAND, Graham Stewart;** Global Digital Technology, FCO Services, since 2017; *b* 3 Nov. 1948; *s* of Ronald Charles Hand and Mary Fraser Hand (*née* Stewart); *m* 1973, Anne Mary Seton Campbell; one *s* one *d* (and one *s* decd). *Educ:* RMA Sandhurst; St John's Coll., Cambridge (MA 1979). Regular Army, 1969–80; FCO, 1980–2004: served UN Dept, 1980–82; Dakar, 1982–84; News Dept, FCO, 1984–87; Head of Chancery, Helsinki, 1987–90; Aid Policy Dept, ODA, 1991–92; Head of Human Rights Policy Dept, FCO, 1992–94; Dep. High Comr, Nigeria, 1994–96; RCDS, 1997; Ambassador to Bosnia and Herzegovina, 1998–2001; Chargé d'Affaires, Tajikistan, 2002; Ambassador to Algeria, 2002–04; Chief Exec., British Expertise (formerly British Consultants & Construction Bureau), 2004–13; consultant, FCO, 2014–17. *Recreations:* opera, choral singing, sailing, golf, cooking. *E:* graham.hand@talktalk.net.

**HAND, Jessica Mary;** HM Diplomatic Service; Ambassador to Angola and concurrently to São Tomé and Príncipe, since 2018; *b* 1 Sept. 1957; *d* of William Evan Pearce and Mary Elizabeth Pearce (*née* Pimm); *m* 1999, Lt Col Dr Robert Wayne Hand, US Army (retd). *Educ:* Aberdeen Univ. (MA Jt Hons, French and Internat. Relations). PA to Dir, NERC Research Vessel Base, Barry, 1976–78; sales co-ordinator for wine co., Cardiff, 1983–85; joined FCO, 1985; Second Sec., FCO, 1985–87; Dakar, Senegal, 1987–90; First Sec., UN Dept, 1990–92, African Dept (Southern), 1992–94, FCO; lang. trng, 1994–95; Ambassador to Belarus, 1996–99; Dep. Hd, Non-Proliferation Dept, FCO, 1999–2001; UK Pol Advr, Allied Forces North, 2002–04; Counsellor (Mgt), later Dir, Ops and Business Change, and Consul-Gen., Moscow, 2004–08; Dir, UK Trade & Investment, Turkey and Consul-Gen., Istanbul, 2008–12; FCO, 2012–14; Hd of Arms Export Policy, FCO, 2014–17. *Recreations:* campanology, walking, reading, cooking, music (classical, jazz and anything to dance to). *Address:* c/o Foreign and Commonwealth Office, King Charles Street, SW1A 2AH.

**HAND, His Honour John Lester;** QC 1988; a Circuit Judge, 2008–17; *b* 16 June 1947; *s* of John James and Violet Hand; *m* 1st, 1972, Helen Andrea McWatt (marr. diss.); 2nd, 1990, Lynda Ray Ferrigno; one *d*. *Educ:* Huddersfield New College; Univ. of Nottingham (LLB 1969). Called to the Bar, Gray's Inn, 1972, Bencher, 1996; Northern Circuit, 1972; Recorder, 1991–2008. Mem., Employment Appeal Tribunal, 2002–04. Judicial Mem., Parole Bd, 2018–. *Recreations:* motorcycling, windsurfing.

**HAND, Jonathan Elliott Sheerman;** QC 2019; *b* Harrogate, 25 June 1967; *s* of Malcolm and Sally Hand; *m* 1997, Lucinda Collum; one *s* one *d*. *Educ:* Oundle Sch.; Christ Church, Oxford (BA Law). Called to the Bar, Inner Temple, 1990; in practice as barrister, 1991–; Fee-paid Judge of First-tier Tribunal (Mental Health), 2019–. *Recreations:* family, farming, travel, ski-ing, Bath Rugby. *Address:* Outer Temple Chambers, 222 Strand, WC2R 1BA. *T:* (020) 7353 6381. *E:* jonathan.handqc@outertemple.com. *Club:* Army and Navy.

**HANDCOCK,** family name of **Baron Castlemaine**.

**HANDELSMAN, Harry;** Chief Executive Officer, Manhattan Loft Corporation, since 1992; *b* Munich, 17 Sept. 1949. *Educ:* York Univ., Toronto (Masters degree Econs). Member: Bd, Artangel, 2009–; Bd, South London Gall., 2016–; Develt Cttee, Southbank Centre, 2016–. Hon. FRIBA 2012. *Address:* Manhattan Loft Corporation, Edison House, 223–231 Old Marylebone Road, NW1 5QT. *T:* (020) 7535 2222.

**HANDFORD, Rt Rev. (George) Clive,** CMG 2007; Bishop in Cyprus and the Gulf, 1996–2007; President Bishop, Episcopal Church in Jerusalem and the Middle East, 2002–07; an Honorary Assistant Bishop, Diocese of Leeds (formerly West Yorkshire and the Dales), since 2014; *b* 17 April 1937; *s* of Cyril Percy Dawson Handford and Alice Ethel Handford; *m* 1962, Anne Elizabeth Jane Atherley; one *d*. *Educ:* Hatfield Coll., Durham (BA); Queen's Coll., Birmingham and Univ. of Birmingham (DipTh). Curate, Mansfield Parish Church, 1963–66; Chaplain: Baghdad, 1967; Beirut, 1967–73; Dean, St George's Cathedral, Jerusalem, 1974–78; Archdeacon in the Gulf and Chaplain in Abu Dhabi and Qatar, 1978–83; Vicar of Kneesall with Laxton, and Wellow and Rufford, 1983–84; RD of Tuxford and Norwell, 1983–84; Archdeacon of Nottingham, 1984–90; Suffragan Bishop of Warwick, 1990–96. An Hon. Asst Bishop, Dio. of Ripon and Leeds, 2007–14. ChStJ 1976. *Address:* Wayside, 1 The Terrace, Kirby Hill, Boroughbridge, York YO51 9DQ. *T:* (01423) 325406.

**HANDLEY, Ven. (Anthony) Michael;** Archdeacon of Norfolk, 1993–2002, now Emeritus; *b* 3 June 1936; *s* of Eric Harvey Handley and Janet Handley; *m* 1962, Christine May Adlington; two *s* one *d*. *Educ:* Spalding Grammar School; Selwyn Coll., Cambridge (MA Hons); Chichester Theol Coll. Asst Curate, Thorpe St Andrew, 1962–66; Anglican Priest on Fairstead Estate, 1966–72; Vicar of Hellesdon, 1972–81; RD of Norwich North, 1979–81; Archdeacon of Norwich, 1981–93. Proctor in Convocation, 1980–85; Mem., General Synod, 1990–95. Research Project, The Use of Colour, Shape, and Line Drawings as Experiential Training Resources, 1976. *Publications:* A Parish Prayer Card, 1980. *Recreations:* visiting islands, painting, bird watching. *Address:* 25 New Street, Sheringham, Norfolk NR26 8EE. *T:* (01263) 820928.

**HANDLEY, Mrs Carol Margaret;** Headmistress, Camden School for Girls, 1971–85; *b* 17 Oct. 1929; *d* of Claude Hilary Taylor and Margaret Eleanor Taylor (*née* Peebles); *m* 1952, Prof. Eric Walter Handley, CBE, FBA (*d* 2013). *Educ:* St Paul's Girls' Sch.; University Coll. London (BA; Fellow 1977). Asst Classics Mistress: North Foreland Lodge Sch., 1952; Queen's Gate Sch., 1952; Head of Classics Dept, Camden Sch. for Girls, 1956; Deputy Headmistress, Camden Sch. for Girls, 1964. Dir, Reading Classical Greek Courses, Inst. of Continuing Educn, Univ. of Cambridge, 1990–2006. Sen. Mem., Wolfson Coll., Cambridge, 1989–. Member Council: RHC, then RHBNC, 1977–95; Middx Hosp. Med. Sch., 1980–84; Mem. Governors and Council, Bedford Coll., 1981–85; Community (formerly Partnership) Gov., Comberton Village Coll., 2004– (Chm., 2006–10); Mem., Comberton Acad. Trust, 2011–17; Community Gov., Cambourne Village Coll., 2012–15. Pres., Classical Assoc., 1996–97. *Publications:* (jtly) An Independent Study Guide to Reading Greek, 1995, 2nd edn 2008; (jtly) A Greek Anthology, 2002. *Recreation:* gardening. *Address:* Colt House, 44 High Street, Little Eversden, Cambs CB23 1HE.

**HANDLEY, David Thomas,** CMG 2000; HM Diplomatic Service, retired; *b* 31 Aug. 1945; *s* of late Leslie Thomas Handley and Frances Handley (*née* Harrison); *m* 1st, 1967, Lilian Duff (marr. diss. 1977); one *s* one *d*; 2nd, 1978, Susan Elizabeth Beal; two *s* one *d* (and one *d* decd). *Educ:* Univ. of Newcastle upon Tyne (BA Jt Hons Politics and Econs). British Leyland Motor Corp., 1967–72; joined FCO, 1972: language studies, MECAS, Lebanon, 1974–76; First Sec., Budapest, 1978–81; Hd of British Interests Sect. and Chargé d'Affaires, Guatemala City, 1984–87; Counsellor: Cairo, 1990–93; FCO, 1993–2000. Hd, Gp Strategic Analysis, BAE Systems, 2000–12; Man. Dir, Veracity Worldwide, 2012–14. Co-Chair, Bd of Govs, Bedales Sch., 2005–08. *Recreations:* family, friends, fitness, fun. *Address:* The Red House, Froxfield, Hants GU23 1BB. *T:* (01730) 827039.

**HANDLEY, Ven. Michael;** *see* Handley, Ven. A. M.

**HANDLEY, Paul;** Editor, Church Times, since 1995; *b* 29 May 1958; *s* of Arnold Terence Handley and Margaret Hardy; *m* 1980, Terence MacMath; two *s* two *d*. *Educ:* Colchester Royal Grammar Sch.; Goldsmiths' Coll., Univ. of London (BA English 1980). News Editor, Church of England Newspaper, 1981–85; freelance publisher, writer, 1986–88; Reporter, Church Times, 1988–90; Press Sec. to Archbishop of Canterbury, 1990–92; freelance writer, 1992–94; News Editor, Church Times, 1994. Trustee, Sandford St Martin Trust, 2004–15. Mem. Cttee, Bloxham Faith and Literature Fest., 2012–. Founder and Judge, Church Times Green Church Awards, 2017; Judge, Church Times Green Health Awards, 2018. *Recreations:* evensong, walking. *Address:* c/o Church Times, 108–114 Golden Lane, EC1Y 0TG. *T:* (020) 7776 1060. *E:* editor@churchtimes.co.uk.

**HANDOVER, Richard Gordon,** CBE 2008; DL; Chairman, Power to Change Trust, 2014–15; *b* 13 April 1946; *s* of Gordon Handover and Hilda Handover (*née* Dyke); *m* 1972, Veronica Joan Woodhead; one *s* two *d*. *Educ:* Blundell's Sch. W H Smith, 1964–2005: various jun. managerial appts, 1964–74; sen. mgt appts, 1974–89; Man. Dir, Our Price Music, 1989–95; joined main co. bd, 1995; Man. Dir, W H Smith News, 1995–97; Gp Chief Exec., W H Smith Gp plc, subseq. W H Smith PLC, 1997–2003; Chm., 2003–05. Chm., Alexon Gp plc, 2008–11; non-executive Director: Nationwide Bldg Soc., 2000–07; Royal Mail, 2002–11. Chm., Adult Learning Inspectorate, 2002–07. Chm., Age Concern Enterprises Ltd, 1992–99; Dir, BITC, 1999–2005; Vice Chm., Kids Company, 2005–15. Chm. Govs, Dauntsey's Sch., 2005–. Chm., Wilts and Swindon Community Foundn, 2005–14. DL Wilts, 2011. *Recreations:* tennis, golf, painting.

**HANDS, Rt Hon. Gregory (William);** PC 2014; MP (C) Chelsea and Fulham, since 2010 (Hammersmith and Fulham, 2005–10); *b* 14 Nov. 1965; *s* of Edward and Mavis Hands; *m* 2005, Irina Hundt; one *s* one *d*. *Educ:* Dr Challoner's Grammar Sch.; Robinson Coll., Cambridge (BA 1989). Banker, 1989–97. Mem. (C), Hammersmith and Fulham BC, 1998–2006. An Asst Govt Whip, 2011–13; Treas. of HM Household (Dep. Chief Whip), 2013–15; Chief Sec. to the Treasury, 2015–16; Minister of State, DIT, 2016–18. *Address:* House of Commons, SW1A 0AA.

**HANDS, Guy;** Group Chairman and Chief Investment Officer, Terra Firma Capital Partners, since 2008 (Chairman and Chief Executive Officer, 2002–08); *b* 27 Aug. 1959; *s* of Christopher and Sally Hands; *m* 1984, Julia Caroline Ablethorpe; two *s* two *d*. *Educ:* Judd Sch., Tonbridge; Mansfield Coll., Oxford (BA Hons PPE, MA; Bancroft Fellow 2000). Hd of Eurobond Trading, Goldman Sachs, 1982–94 (Trading, 1986; Hd, Global Asset Structuring Gp, 1990); Founder and Man. Dir, Principal Finance Gp, Nomura Internat. plc, 1994–2001. Mem., Chancellor's Court of Benefactors, Univ. of Oxford, 2000–. Fellow, Duke of Edinburgh Award Scheme, 2001–. Philanthropic supporter of Mansfield Coll., Oxford, educnl charities for disadvantaged children, and charities in Kent and Guernsey. *Recreations:* films, wine, fine art. *Address:* Terra Firma Capital Management Ltd, Royal Chambers, St Julian's Avenue, St Peter Port, Guernsey GY1 3RE. *T:* (01481) 754660.

**HANDS, Terence David, (Terry),** CBE 2007; theatre and opera director; Director, Clwyd Theatr Cymru (formerly Theatr Clwyd), 1997–2015 (Artistic Consultant, 1996–97); *b* 9 Jan. 1941; *s* of Joseph Ronald Hands and Luise Berthe Kohler; *m* 1st, 1964, Josephine Barstow (marr. diss. 1967); 2nd, 1974, Ludmila Mikael (marr. diss. 1980); one *d*; partner, 1988–96, Julia Lintott; two *s*; 3rd, 2002, Emma (*née* Lucia). *Educ:* Woking Grammar Sch.; Birmingham Univ. (BA Hons Eng. Lang. and Lit.); RADA (Hons Dip.). Founder-Artistic Dir, Liverpool Everyman Theatre, 1964–66 (Hon. Dir, 1996); Artistic Dir, RSC Theatregoround, 1966–67; Associate Dir, 1967–77, Jt Artistic Dir, 1978–86, Chief Exec. and Artistic Dir, 1986–91, Director Emeritus, 1991–, RSC; Consultant Dir, Comédie Française, 1975–80. Vis. Prof., ATRiuM, Univ. of S Wales (formerly Univ. of Glamorgan), 2007–. Associate Mem., RADA; Hon. Fellow, Shakespeare Inst. Jt Pres., Arvon Foundn, 1990–; Hon. FRWCMD (Hon. FWCMD 2002); Hon. Fellow: NE Wales Inst. of HE, 2002; Bangor Univ., 2013. Hon. DLitt: Birmingham, 1988; Liverpool, 2006; Hon. Dr Middlesex, 1997. Chevalier des Arts et des Lettres, 1973. *Director* (for Liverpool Everyman Theatre, 1964–66): The Importance of Being Earnest; Look Back in Anger; Richard III; The Four Seasons; Fando and Lis; *Artistic Director* (for RSC Theatregoround): The Proposal, 1966; The Second Shepherds' Play, 1966; The Dumb Waiter, 1967; Under Milk Wood, 1967; *directed for RSC:* The Criminals, 1967; Pleasure and Repentance, 1967; The Latent Heterosexual, 1968; The Merry Wives of Windsor, 1968, Japan tour, 1970; Bartholomew Fair, 1969; Pericles, 1969; Women Beware Women, 1969; Richard III, 1970, 1980; Balcony, 1971, 1987; Man of Mode, 1971; The Merchant of Venice, 1971; Murder in the Cathedral, 1972; Cries from Casement, 1973; Romeo and Juliet, 1973, 1989; The Bewitched, 1974; The Actor, 1974; Henry IV, Parts 1 and 2, 1975; Henry V, 1975, USA and European Tour, 1976; Old World, 1976; Henry VI parts 1, 2 and 3 (SWET Award, Dir of the Year, Plays and Players, Best Production, 1978), Coriolanus, 1977, European tour, 1979; The Changeling, 1978; Twelfth Night, The Children of the Sun, 1979; As You Like It, Richard II, 1980; Troilus and Cressida, 1981; Arden of Faversham, Much Ado About Nothing, 1982 (European tour and Broadway, 1984), Poppy, 1982; Cyrano de Bergerac, 1983 (SWET Best Dir award), Broadway, 1984 (televised, 1984); Red Noses, 1985; Othello, 1985; The Winter's Tale, 1986; Scenes from a Marriage, 1986; Julius Caesar, 1987; Carrie (Stratford and Broadway), 1988; (with John Barton) Coriolanus, 1989; Romeo and Juliet, 1989; Singer, 1989; Love's Labours Lost, 1990; The Seagull, 1990; Tamburlaine the Great, 1992 (Evening Standard Award, London Drama Critics Award, 1993); *directed for Royal National Theatre:* The Merry Wives of Windsor, 1995; *directed for Chichester Festival Theatre:* Hadrian VII, 1995; The Visit, 1995; *directed for Birmingham Rep.:* The Importance of Being Earnest, 1995 (transf. Old Vic, 1995); *directed for Theatr Clwyd/Clwyd Theatr Cymru:* The Importance of Being Earnest, (also Birmingham and Toronto), Equus, A Christmas Carol, 1997; The Journey of Mary Kelly, The Norman Conquests, 1998; Twelfth Night, Macbeth, Under Milk Wood, 1999; Private Lives, 2000; King Lear, Bedroom Farce, The Rabbit, 2001; Rosencrantz and Guildenstern are Dead, Betrayal, Romeo and Juliet, The Four Seasons, 2002; Blithe Spirit, The Crucible, Pleasure and Repentance, 2003; One Flew Over the Cuckoo's Nest, 2004; Troilus and Cressida, Night Must Fall, 2005; A Chorus of Disapproval, Memory, 2006; Arcadia, 2007; Cherry Orchard, 2007; Macbeth, 2008; Noises Off, 2009; Mary Stuart, 2009; Pygmalion, 2009; Arden of Faversham, 2010; A Small Family Business, 2010; The Taming of the Shrew, 2011; As You Like It, 2012; Boeing Boeing, 2012; The Winslow Boy, 2013; Under Milk Wood, 2014; Hamlet, 2015; *directed for Comédie Française:* Richard III, 1972 (Meilleur Spectacle de l'Année award); Pericles, 1974; Twelfth Night, 1976 (Meilleur Spectacle de l'Année award); Le Cid, 1977; Murder in the Cathedral, 1978; *directed for Paris Opéra:* Verdi's Otello, 1976 (televised 1978); *directed for Burg Theatre, Vienna:* Troilus and Cressida, 1977; As You Like It, 1979; *directed for Royal Opera:* Parsifal, 1979; *directed for Teatro Stabile di Genova, Italy:* Women Beware Women, 1981; *directed for Schauspielhaus, Zürich:* Arden of Faversham, 1992; *directed for Recklinghausen:* Buffalo Bill, 1992; *directed for Bremen:* Simon Boccanegra, 1992; *directed for National Theatre, Oslo:* Merry Wives of Windsor, 1995; The Pretenders, 1996; The Seagull, 1998; Sag Mir Wo Die Blumen Sind, Berlin, 1993; Hamlet, Marigny Theatre, Paris, 1994; Royal Hunt of the Sun, Tokyo, 1996; *recording:* Murder in the Cathedral, 1976; *television:* Cyrano de Bergerac, 1984. *Publications:* trans. (with Barbara Wright) Genet, The Balcony, 1971; Pleasure and Repentance, 1976; (ed Sally Beauman) Henry V, 1976; Hamlet (French trans.), 1994; contribs to Theatre 72, Playback.

**HANDS, Dr Timothy Roderick;** Headmaster, Winchester College, since 2016; *b* 30 March 1956; *s* of late Rory Hands and Catherine Hands (*née* Walker); *m* 1988, Jane, *er d* of late Ian and Ann Smart; two *s*. *Educ:* Emanuel Sch., Battersea; Guildhall Sch. of Music and Drama; King's Coll. London (BA 1st Cl. English Lang. and Lit.; William Stebbing Prize, 1976, J. S. Brewer Prize, 1977, EETS and L. M. Faithfull Prizes, 1978; AKC with Credit; 1st Leathes Prizeman, 1978; Coll. Jelf Medallist; FKC 2017); St Catherine's Coll., Oxford (Sen. Schol.); Oriel Coll., Oxford (R. W. B. Burton Sen. Schol.; DPhil 1984). Stipendiary Lectr, Oriel Coll., Oxford, 1985–86; Asst Master, King's Sch., Canterbury, 1986–94 (Housemaster, Galpin's, 1990–94); Second Master, Whitgift Sch., 1994–97; Headmaster, Portsmouth Grammar Sch., 1997–2007; Master, Magdalen Coll. Sch., Oxford, 2008–16. Conductor, Schola Cantorum of Oxford, 1982–85. Mem., Editl Bd, Conf. and Common Room, 2000–13. Member: Admiralty Interview Bd, 1998–2004; Ind. State Sch. Partnership Forum, DFES, 2002–04. Mem., ISC Wkg Gp on Access to Ind. Educn, 2000–03. Mem., Ext. Adv. Bd, Oxford Univ. Faculty of English, 2006–. Headmasters' and Headmistresses' Conference: Sec., 2003–04, Chm., 2004–05, S Central Div.; Mem. Ctee, 2003–15; Mem., 2003–12, Co-Chair, 2005–12, HMC/GSA Univs Cttee; Chm., 2013–14. Bishop's Rep., Portsmouth Cathedral Council, 2001–05. Founding Chm., Portsmouth Festivities, 2000–07 (Chm., Trustees and Bd of Dirs, 2006–07; Patron, 2007–). Trustee: Portsmouth Cathedral, 1999–2005; HMS Warrior 1860, 2003–08; Schola Cantorum, Oxford, 2008–16; Oxford Preservation Trust, 2015–. Governor: Alleyn's Sch., 2005–09; St Mary's Calne, 2010–16; Bedales, 2010–17; Midhurst Rother Coll., 2016–; Cheam Sch., 2018–; Member, Council: Cheltenham Ladies' Coll., 2009; St Swithun's Sch., 2016–. *Publications:* A George Eliot Chronology, 1989; Thomas Hardy: distracted preacher, 1989; A Hardy Chronology, 1992; (contrib.) New Perspectives on Thomas Hardy, 1994; Thomas Hardy: writers in their time, 1995; (contrib.) The Achievement of Thomas Hardy, 2000; (contrib.) Oxford Reader's Companion to Hardy, 2000; Ideas to Assemble, 2006; Heads: expert advice for changing times, 2007; (contrib.) Ashgate Research Companion to Thomas Hardy, 2010; (contrib.) The Gove Legacy: education in Britain, 2015; (contrib.) Choosing an Independent School, 2016; literary and musical articles, editions and reviews. *Recreations:* classical music, sport, especially Rugby and cricket, writing. *Address:* Winchester College, College Street, Winchester SO23 9NA. *Clubs:* Athenæum, East India.

**HANDY, Charles Brian,** CBE 2000; author; *b* 25 July 1932; *s* of Archdeacon Brian Leslie Handy and Joan Kathleen Herbert Handy (*née* Scott); *m* 1962, Elizabeth Ann Hill (*d* 2018); one *s* one *d*. *Educ:* Oriel Coll., Oxford (BA 1956; MA 1966; Hon. Fellow, 1998); MIT (SM 1967). Shell Internat. Petroleum Co., 1956–65; Charter Consolidated Ltd, 1965–66; Sloan Sch. of Management, MIT (Internat. Faculty Fellow), 1967–68; London Business School, 1968–94; Prof., 1972–77; Vis. Prof., 1977–94; Fellow, 1994; Warden, St George's House, Windsor Castle, 1977–81. Chm., Royal Soc. for Encouragement of Arts, Manufactures and Commerce, 1987–89. FCGI 2000. Hon. Fellow: Inst. of Educn, London Univ., 1999; St Mary's Coll., Twickenham, 1999. Hon. DLitt: Bristol Poly., 1988; Open Univ., 1989; UEA, 1993; QUB, 1998; Middlesex, 1998; Exeter, 1999; Essex, Hull, Durham, 2000; Roehampton, 2014; Hon. LLD Dublin, 2006. Lifetime Achievement Award, Thinkers 50, 2013; Irish Presidential Dist. Service Award for Irish Overseas, 2015. *Publications:* Understanding Organizations, 1976, 4th edn 1999; Gods of Management, 1978, 2nd edn 1991; Future of Work, 1982; Understanding Schools as Organizations, 1986; Understanding Voluntary Organizations, 1988; The Age of Unreason, 1989; Inside Organizations, 1990; Waiting for the Mountain to Move, 1991; The Empty Raincoat, 1994; Beyond Certainty (essays), 1995; The Hungry Spirit, 1997; The New Alchemists, 1999; Thoughts for the Day, 1999; The Elephant and the Flea, 2001; Reinvented Lives, 2002; Myself and Other More Important Matters, 2006; The New Philanthropists, 2006; The Second Curve, 2015; 21 Letters on Life and Its Challenges, 2019. *Address:* Flat 2, 73 Putney Hill, SW15 3NT. *T:* (020) 8788 1610; Old Hall Cottages, Bressingham, Diss, Norfolk IP22 2AG. *T:* (01379) 687546. *E:* candehandy@aol.com.

**HANDYSIDE, Richard Neil;** QC 2009; *b* Cardiff, 27 Sept. 1968; *s* of Robert Handyside and Rhona Handyside (now Aldridge); *m* 1999, Philippa Betts; two *s*. *Educ:* Marlborough; Univ. of Bristol (LLB); Brasenose Coll., Oxford (BCL). Called to the Bar, Lincoln's Inn, 1993; in practice as a barrister, specialising in commercial law. *Recreations:* tennis, travel, watching Rugby. *Address:* Fountain Court, Temple, EC4Y 9DH. *T:* (020) 7583 3335, *Fax:* (020) 7353 0329.

**HANGARTNER, John Robert Wilfred;** Consultant Histopathologist, Guy's and St Thomas' Hospitals, 2002–17; *b* 5 Feb. 1955; *s* of John Hangartner and Ita Patricia (*née* Brett); *m* 1980, Jillian Mary Ansell; one *s* one *d*. *Educ:* Merchant Taylors' Sch., Northwood; Guy's Hosp. Med. Sch., Univ. of London (BSc Hons 1976; MB BS 1979); Open Univ. (MBA 1995). MRCS, LRCP 1979; MRCPath 1988, FRCPath 1997. Clin. Lectr in Histopathology, St George's Hosp. Med. Sch., 1983–88; Department of Health: SMO, 1988–91; Temp. PMO, 1991–93; PMO, 1993; Under Sec., and SPMO, 1993–97; CMO, Guardian Health Ltd, 1997–2000; Sen. Med. Advr, PPP healthcare, 1999–2000; Gp Med. Advr, Capio Healthcare (UK), 2001–03; Bd Med. Advr, CS Healthcare, 2004–13; Clin. Dir, Diagnostic and Therapeutic Services Directorate, 2004–05, Divisional Dir, Core Clinical Services Div., 2004–06, Guy's and St Thomas' NHS Foundn Trust; Clin. Dir, GSTS Pathology LLP, 2009–14. Principal Dir, Brett Cook Consulting Ltd, 2000–15. Chm., Hosp. Jun. Staff Cttee, BMA, 1984–85. FRSA 1994–2018. *Recreations:* photography, singing, sailing. *Address:* 11 Annesley Road, Blackheath, SE3 0JX. *T:* (020) 8319 3164.

**HANHAM,** family name of **Baroness Hanham**.

**HANHAM,** Baroness *cr* 1999 (Life Peer), of Kensington in the Royal Borough of Kensington and Chelsea; **Joan Brownlow Hanham,** CBE 1997; *b* 23 Sept. 1939; *d* of Alfred Spark and Mary (*née* Mitchell); *m* 1964, Dr Iain William Ferguson Hanham (*d* 2011); one *s* one *d*. *Educ:* Hillcourt Sch., Dublin. Royal Borough of Kensington and Chelsea: Mem. (C), 1970–2010; Mayor, 1983–84; Leader of Council, 1989–2000; Chairman: Town Planning Cttee, 1984–86; Social Services Cttee, 1987–89; Policy and Resources Cttee, 1989–2000. Chm., Policy Cttee, London Boroughs Assoc., 1991–95. An Opposition Whip, H of L, 2000–08; Opposition spokesman for local govt, housing, planning and the regions, 2002–07, Scotland, 2003–07, transport, 2005–07, home affairs, 2007–10; Parly Under-Sec. of State, DCLG, 2010–13. Mem., Mental Health Act Commn, 1983–90; non-exec. Mem., NW Thames RHA, 1983–94; non-exec. Dir, Chelsea and Westminster Health Care NHS Trust, 1994–2000; Chairman: St Mary's Hosp. NHS Trust, 2000–07; NHS Monitor, 2014–15. Vice-Pres., Commonwealth Inst., 1998–2000. Pres., Volunteering England, 2008–10. JP City of London Commn 1984–2009, and Inner London Family Proceedings Court, 1992–2009. Freeman: City of London, 1984; Royal Bor. of Kensington and Chelsea, 2011. *Recreations:* music, travel. *Address:* House of Lords, SW1A 0PW. *Club:* Hurlingham.

**HANHAM, Prof. Harold John;** Vice-Chancellor, University of Lancaster, 1985–95; *b* Auckland, New Zealand, 16 June 1928; *s* of John Newman Hanham and Ellie Malone; *m* 1973, Ruth Soulé Arnon, *d* of Prof. Daniel I. Arnon, Univ. of Calif, Berkeley. *Educ:* Mount Albert Grammar Sch.; Auckland UC (now Univ. of Auckland); Univ. of New Zealand (BA 1948, MA 1950); Selwyn Coll., Cambridge (PhD 1954). FRHistS 1960; FAAAS 1974. Asst Lectr to Sen. Lectr, in Govt, Univ. of Manchester, 1954–63; Prof. and Head of Dept of Politics, Univ. of Edinburgh, 1963–68; Prof. of History, 1968–73 and Fellow of Lowell House, 1970–73, Harvard Univ.; Prof. of History and Political Science, 1972–85 and Dean, Sch. of Humanities and Social Sci., 1973–84, MIT; Hon. Prof. of History, Univ. of Lancaster, 1985–. Mem., ESRC, 1986. Guggenheim Fellow, 1972–73. Hon. AM Harvard, 1968; Hon. DSc Lancaster, 1995. John H. Jenkins Prize for Bibliography, Union Coll., 1978. *Publications:* Elections and Party Management, 1969, 2nd edn 1978; The Nineteenth-Century Constitution, 1969; Scottish Nationalism, 1969; Bibliography of British History 1851–1914, 1976. *Recreations:* discovering Canada, squash. *Clubs:* Oxford and Cambridge; St Botolph (Boston).

**HANHAM, Sir William (John Edward),** 13th Bt *cr* 1667, of Wimborne, Dorsetshire; landowner, Dorset, since 2009; *b* Nairobi, Kenya, 4 Sept. 1957; *o s* of Sir Michael William Hanham, 12th Bt, DFC and Margaret Jane Hanham (*née* Thomas); *S* father, 2009; *m* 2011, Alison (Christina), *d* of John Birch and Sylvia (*née* MacNair). *Educ:* Winchester Coll.; Courtauld Inst. of Art (BA Hons History of Art). Press and PR Officer, Christie's Auctioneers, London, 1983–91; Art Dealer in Old Master Paintings, London, 1993–2009. *Recreations:* art history, gardening, bee-keeping, astronomy, sailing. *Address:* c/o Deans Court Estate Office, 2 Deans Court Lane, Wimborne, Dorset BH21 1EE. *Club:* Garrick.

**HANKES, Sir Claude,** KCVO 2006; macro-strategist and adviser; *b* 8 March 1949. *Educ:* Grey. With Manufacturers Hanover, 1968–72; Robert Fleming & Co. Ltd, 1972–77, Director 1974–77; Chm., Management Cttee, Price Waterhouse and Partners, 1983–89. Advr to Bd, (Corange) Boehringer Mannheim, 1988–94; Dep. Chm., Leutwiler and Partners Ltd, 1992–96; Chm., Shaw & Bradley Ltd, 1993–2019; Interim Chm., Roland Berger Strategy Consultants Ltd, 2003–05. Masterminded resolution to S African debt crisis, 1985–86; Chm., Adv. Cttee to Kingdom of Jordan on Strategic Economic Policy Issues, 1993–94; Advisor: to Iraq, 2003, to Iraq Governing Council, 2003–04, to Iraq on macro strategic issues, 2005–06; Trade Bank of Iraq, 2007–11. Testified to US Congress on UN Oil for Food scandal, 2004. Trustee: Windsor Leadership Trust, 1998– (Chm., 2000–07);

Hawthornden Internat. Retreat for Writers, 2008–10. Hon. Fellow and Life Mem. Council, St George's House, Windsor Castle, 2006 (Trustee and Advr, 2000–06; Lect., 2014); Hon. Mem., Coll. of St George, Windsor Castle, 2006 (Hon. Fellow and Advr 2002–06). Hon. Fellow, Corpus Christi Coll., Oxford. *Publications:* Nobel Industrier report, Stockholm, 1991. *Recreations:* gardening, art. *E:* officesirclaude@gmail.com.

**HANKES-DRIELSMA, Sir Claude Dunbar;** *see* Hankes, Sir Claude.

**HANKEY,** family name of **Baron Hankey**.

**HANKEY,** 3rd Baron *cr* 1939, of The Chart, Surrey; **Donald Robin Alers Hankey;** *b* 12 June 1938; *s* of 2nd Baron Hankey, KCMG, KCVO and Frances Bevyl Stuart-Monteth (*d* 1957); *S* father, 1996; *m* 1st, 1963, Margaretha Thorndahl (marr. diss. 1974); 2nd, 1974, Eileen Désirée (marr. diss. 1994), *yr d* of Maj.-Gen. Stuart Battye, CB; two *d*; 3rd, 1994, June, *d* of late Dr Leonard Taboroff. *Educ:* Rugby; University Coll. London (DipArch). RIBA. Founder, 1973, Chm., 1973–2006, Consultant, 2006–, Gilmore Hankey Kirke Ltd, architects, planners, engineers and conservation specialists (part of the GHK Group of cos incl. engrg, econs, sociols and mgt); founder, Gilmore Hankey Kirke SA, Paris (consultants to Commercial Union, Bovis Investissements SA, Givenchy, Mayor of Nemours). Pres., ICOMOS (UK), 2006–12 (Vice-Chm., 1997–2002; Vice Pres., 2002–06); Vice-Chm., Historic Bldgs Adv. Gp, MoD, 1999–2004. Founder and former Chm., All Party Gp on Architecture and Planning. Consultant to: World Bank; IADB in Jamaica; USAID in Jordan; EU; Yemen; Pakistan; China; World Heritage sites; specialising in conservation, design upgrading and re-use of the cultural and historic envmt, legal and admin. systems and cities mgt. FRSA; FSA; FRAI. *Recreations:* piano, the arts, cultural anthropology, tennis, skiing. *Heir:* *b* Hon. Alexander Maurice Alers Hankey, PhD [*b* 18 Aug. 1947; *m* 1970, Deborah Benson (marr. diss. 1990)]. *Address:* 8 Sunset Road, SE5 8EA.

**HANKIN, Jonas;** QC 2013; *b* 6 Aug. 1969; *s* of Roderick and Jacqueline Hankin; *m* 2006, Hannah Cartledge; two *s*. *Educ:* King's Coll. London; Inns of Court Sch. of Law. Called to the Bar, Middle Temple, 1994; in practice as a barrister, specialising in criminal law, 1994–. *Address:* No5 Chambers, Fountain Court, Steelhouse Lane, Birmingham B4 6DR. *T:* 0845 210 5555. *E:* info@no5.com.

**HANKS, Patrick Wyndham,** PhD; lexicographer, corpus linguist and onomastician; *b* 24 March 1940; *s* of Wyndham George Hanks and Elizabeth Mary (*née* Rudd); *m* 1st, 1961, Helga Gertrud Ingeborg Lietz (marr. diss. 1968); one *s* one *d*; 2nd, 1979, Julie Eyre (marr. diss. 1996); two *d*. *Educ:* Ardingly Coll., Sussex; University Coll., Oxford (BA, MA); Masaryk Univ., Brno (PhD). Editor, Dictionaries and Reference Books, Hamlyn Group, 1964–70; Man. Dir, Laurence Urdang Associates, 1970–79; Dir, Surnames Res. Project, Univ. of Essex, 1980–83; Project Manager, Cobuild, Univ. of Birmingham, 1983–87; Chief Editor, Collins English Dictionaries, 1987–90; Manager, then Chief Editor, Current English Dictionaries, OUP, 1990–2000. Adjunct Prof., Dept of Computer Sci., Brandeis Univ., 2002–06; Associate Prof., Faculty of Informatics, Masaryk Univ., Brno, 2005–08; Vis. Prof., UWE, 2007–18 (res. project, Family Names of UK, 2010–); Sen. Researcher and Vis. Prof., Inst. of Formal and Applied Linguistics, Charles Univ., Prague, 2008–10; Vis. Prof. of Computational Lexicography, 2009, Prof. in Lexicography, 2012– (res. project, Disambiguation of Verbs by Collocation), Res. Inst. for Information and Language Processing, Univ. of Wolverhampton. Vis. Scientist (corpus lexicography), AT&T Bell Labs, 1988–90; Chief Investigator, Hector project in corpus analysis, Systems Res. Center, Digital Equipment Corp., Palo Alto, CA, 1991–92. Consultant: Electronic Dictionary of the German Lang., Berlin-Brandenburg Acad. of Scis, 2003–06; Patakis Publishers, Athens, 2006–09; Inst. for the Czech Lang., Prague, 2008–09. *Publications:* (ed) Hamlyn Encyclopedic World Dictionary, 1971; (ed) Collins English Dictionary, 1979; (with J. Corbett) Business Listening Tasks, 1986; (managing editor) Collins Cobuild English Language Dictionary, 1987; (with F. Hodges) Dictionary of Surnames, 1988; (with F. Hodges) Oxford Dictionary of First Names, 1990, 2nd edn 2006; (ed jtly) New Oxford Dictionary of English, 1998; (ed) New Oxford Thesaurus of English, 2000; Dictionary of American Family Names, 2003; (ed) Lexicology: critical concepts in Linguistics, 2008; (ed with R. Giora) Metaphor and Figurative Language: critical concepts in linguistics, 2012; Lexical Analysis: norms and exploitations, 2013; (ed with R. Coates and P. McClure) Oxford Dictionary of Family Names of Britain and Ireland, 2016; articles in Computational Linguistics, Internat. Jl Corpus Linguistics, Computing and the Humanities, Internat. Jl of Lexicography, Onoma, Names, and other jls; *festschrift:* A Way with Words, 2010. *Recreations:* onomastics, philology, bridge, punting. *E:* patrick.w.hanks@gmail.com.

**HANKS, Tom;** actor and producer; *b* 9 July 1956; *s* of Amos Hanks and Janet; *m* 1st, 1978, Samantha Lewes (marr. diss. 1985); one *s* one *d*; 2nd, 1988, Rita Wilson; two *s*. *Educ:* Calif State Univ. *Films* include: Splash, Bachelor Party, 1984; The Money Pit, 1986; Dragnet, 1987; Big, Punchline, 1988; Turner and Hooch, 1989; The Bonfire of the Vanities, 1990; A League of their Own, 1992; Sleepless in Seattle, 1993; Philadelphia, 1994 (Best Actor Award, Berlin Film Fest.; Acad. Award for Best Actor); Forrest Gump (Acad. Award for Best Actor), Apollo 13, 1995; Toy Story, 1996; (also writer and dir) That Thing You Do!, 1997; Saving Private Ryan, 1998; You've Got Mail, 1999; The Green Mile, Toy Story 2, 2000; Cast Away, 2001; Road to Perdition, 2002; Catch Me If You Can, 2003; The Ladykillers, The Terminal, 2004; The Da Vinci Code, 2006; Charlie Wilson's War, 2007; Angels and Demons, 2009; Toy Story 3, 2010; (also writer and dir) Larry Crowne, 2011; Extremely Loud and Incredibly Close, 2012; Cloud Atlas, Captain Phillips, Saving Mr Banks, 2013; Bridge of Spies, 2015; A Hologram for the King, Inferno, Sully, 2016; The Post, 2018; Toy Story 4, A Beautiful Day in the Neighbourhood, 2019; *television* includes: Bosom Buddies, 1980–82; co-prod., Band of Brothers, 2001; executive producer: The Pacific, 2010; The Sixties, 2014; The Seventies, 2015; The Eighties, 2016; The Nineties, 2017; The 2000s, 2018; *theatre:* Lucky Guy, NY, 2013. Presidential Medal of Freedom (USA), 2016. *Publications:* Uncommon Type: some stories, 2017. *Address:* c/o Creative Artists Agency, 2000 Avenue of the Stars, Los Angeles, CA 90067, USA.

**HANLEY, Rt Hon. Sir Jeremy (James),** KCMG 1997; PC 1994; chartered accountant, company director, lecturer and broadcaster; *b* 17 Nov. 1945; *s* of late Jimmy Hanley and Dinah Sheridan; *m* 1973, Verna, Viscountess Villiers (*née* Stott); one *s*, one step *d*, and one *s* by previous marriage. *Educ:* Rugby. FCA 1969; FCCA 1980; FCIS 1980. Peat Marwick Mitchell & Co., 1963–66; Lectr in law, taxation and accountancy, Anderson Thomas Frankel, 1969, Dir 1969; Man. Dir, ATF (Jersey and Ireland), 1970–73; Dep. Chm., The Financial Training Co. Ltd, 1973–90; Sec., Park Place PLC, 1977–83; Chm., Fraser Green Ltd, 1986–90. Non-executive Director: ITE Gp, 1997–2009; Brass Tacks Publishing, 1997–2000; GTECH Hldgs Corp., 2001–07; Eur. Adv. Bd, Credit Lyonnais, 2000–05; NYMEX Europe, 2005–07; Willis Hldgs Inc., 2006–15; Langbar Internat., 2006–14; Blue Hackle Ltd, 2006–10; Lottomatica SpA, 2007–17; CSS Stellar plc, 2007–08; Nymex London, 2008–09; Mountfield Gp, 2008–09; Willis Ltd, 2008–17; London Asia Capital plc, 2011–14; Chairman: Internat. Trade and Investment Missions, 1997–2002; AdVal Gp plc, 1998–2003; Braingames Network plc, 2000–02; Falcon Fund Mgt Ltd, 2000–03; Onslow Suffolk Ltd, 2007–09. Sen. Consultant, Kroll Associates, 2003–04; Mem. Adv. Bd, Talal Abu-Ghazaleh Internat., 2004–05. Dir, Arab-British Chamber of Commerce, 1998–2011. Parly Advr to ICA, 1986–90. Contested (C) Lambeth Central, April 1978, 1979. MP (C) Richmond and Barnes, 1983–97; contested (C) Richmond Park, 1997. PPS to Minister of State, Privy Council Office (Minister for CS and the Arts), 1987–90, to Sec. of State for Envmt, 1990; Parly Under-Sec. of State, NI Office, 1990–93 (Minister for Health, Social Security and Agric., 1990–92, for Pol Develt, Community Relns and Educn, 1992–93); Minister of State for the Armed Forces, MoD, 1993–94; Chm. of Cons. Party and in Cabinet as Minister without Portfolio, 1994–95; Minister of State, FCO, 1995–97. Mem., H of C Select Cttee on Home Affairs, 1983–87 (Mem., Subcttee on Race Relns and Immigration, 1983–87); Jt Vice-Chm., Cons. Back-bench Trade and Industry Cttee, 1983–87. Member: British-American Parly Gp, 1983–97; Anglo-French Parly Gp, 1983–97; British-Irish Interparly Body, 1990; Life Member: CPA, 1983; IPU, 1983; Chm., Cons. Candidates Assoc., 1982–83. Member: Bow Gp, 1974–97 (Chm., Home Affairs Cttee); European Movt, 1974–97; Mensa, 1968–. Vice-Pres., British-Iranian Chamber of Commerce, 2002–06 (Chm., 2000–02). Freeman, City of London, 1989; Liveryman: Chartered Accountants' Co., 1993– (Mem., Ct of Assts, 1996–2011; Master, 2005–06); Dyers' Co., 2011–. *Recreations:* cookery, chess, cricket, languages, theatre, cinema, music. *Address:* 6 Buttsmead, Northwood, Middlesex HA6 2TL. *T:* (01923) 836861; Berry Head House, Victoria Road, Brixham, Devon TQ5 9AR. *T:* (01803) 882317. *Clubs:* Garrick, Pilgrims, Lord's Taverners, Saints & Sinners; Brixham Rotary, Brixham Cricket, Brixham Rugby.

**HANLEY, Lynsey Emma;** author; writer for The Guardian, since 2007; *b* Birmingham, 12 April 1976; *d* of Lloyd Hanley and Christine Hanley; *m* 2003, Jamie Robert Thomas O'Brien; one *s* one *d*. *Educ:* Queen Mary and Westfield Coll., London (BA Pols and Hist. 1997). Freelance journalist and reviewer, The Guardian, The Observer, New Statesman, Prospect, TLS, Daily Telegraph, 1996–. Hon. Res. Fellow, Lancaster Univ., 2009–12; Vis. Fellow, Liverpool John Moores Univ., 2013–. Hon. Res. Fellow, Lancaster Univ., 2014–. *Publications:* Estates: an intimate history, 2007, 4th edn 2017; Respectable, 2016, 2nd edn 2017. *Recreations:* walking, listening to music, friends and family, reading, cooking, concerts, sitting quietly. *Address:* c/o Caroline Dawnay, United Agents, 12–26 Lexington Street, W1F 0LE. *T:* (020) 3812 0800. *E:* sscard@unitedagents.co.uk.

**HANMER, Sir (Wyndham Richard) Guy,** 9th Bt *cr* 1774, of Hanmer, Flintshire; farmer and landowner; *b* 27 Nov. 1955; *s* of Sir John Wyndham Edward Hanmer, 8th Bt, and of Audrey Melissa, *d* of Major A. C. J. Congreve; *S* father, 2008; *m* 1986, Elizabeth Ann, *yr d* of Neil Taylor; two *s* one *d*. *Educ:* Wellington Coll. Army, Blues and Royals, 1975–81. *Recreation:* shooting. *Heir:* *s* Thomas Wyndham William Hanmer, *b* 10 May 1989. *Address:* The Stables, Bettisfield Park, Whitchurch, Shropshire SY13 2JZ. *T:* (01948) 710634.

**HANNA, Brian Petrie,** CBE 2000; *b* 15 Dec. 1941; *m* 1968, Sylvia Campbell; one *d*. *Educ:* Royal Belfast Academical Instn; Belfast Coll. of Technol.; Ulster Coll., NI Poly. (DMS). FCIEH. Belfast Corporation: Clerical Asst, City Treasurer's Dept, 1959; Health Department: Clerical Officer, 1960–61; Pupil Public Health Inspector, 1961–65; Public Health Inspector, 1965–73; Sen. Trng Advr, Food and Drink ITB, 1974–75; Principal Public Health Inspector, Eastern Gp Public Health Cttee, Castlereagh BC, 1975–77; Belfast City Council: Dep. Dir, 1978–84, Dir, 1984–92, Envmtl Health Services; Dir, Health and Envmtl Services, 1992–94; Chief Exec., 1994–2002. Royal Acad. of Engrg Vis. Prof. on Sustainable Develt, Ulster Univ., 2003–05. Member: UK Sustainable Develt Commn, 2000–04; NI Public Service Commn, 2007–10 and 2013–16; Chm., NI Local Govt Staff Commn, 2005–10 and 2013–. Non-exec. Dir, Ivy Wood Properties Ltd, 2005–15. Dep. Chm., NI Science Park, 2008–14. Pres., 2002–05, Vice-Pres., 2005–, Chartered Inst. of Envmtl Health; Vice Pres., Envmt Protection UK, 2007–11. Gov., Royal Belfast Academical Instn, 2001–; Mem. Senate, QUB, 2002–09; Chm. Bd, Envmtl Sustainability and Health Inst. (formerly Envmtl Health Sci. Inst.), Dublin Inst. of Technol., 2011–16. Chm., NI Adv. Cttee, 2004–12, Trustee, 2009–11, British Council. CCMI, until 2017 (CIMgt 2001). Hon. FRSPH 2005. Hon. DSc (Econ) QUB, 2001. *Recreations:* apart from my family, the sport of hockey (Past Pres., Irish Hockey Union).

**HANNA, Carmel;** Member (SDLP) South Belfast, Northern Ireland Assembly, 1998–2010; *b* 26 April 1946; *d* of John and Mary McAleenan; *m* 1973, Eamon Hanna; one *s* three *d*. *Educ:* Our Lady's Grammar Sch., Newry; Belfast City Hosp. (SRN); Royal Maternity Hosp. (SCM). Staff nurse in hosps in Belfast (Accident and Emergency), Guernsey, and Dublin, 1967–73; Staff Nurse, Musgrave Park Hosp., 1984–93; Social Services, South and East Belfast HSS Trust, 1993–98. Mem. (SDLP) Belfast CC, 1997–2008. Northern Ireland Assembly: Minister for Employment and Learning, 2001–02; SDLP health spokesperson; Chair, Cttee on Standards and Privileges, 2007–10; Member: Health Cttee, 1998–2010; Assembly and Exec. Review Cttee, 2007–10. Chm., All-Party Gp on Internat. Develt, 2000. *Recreations:* gardening, travel, Irish history, cooking. *Address:* 12 Bawnmore Road, Belfast BT9 6LA. *T:* (028) 9066 7577.
*See also* C. Hanna.

**HANNA, Claire;** Member (SDLP) South Belfast, Northern Ireland Assembly, since June 2015; *b* Galway, Ireland, 19 June 1980; *d* of Eamon Hanna and Carmel Hanna, *qv*; *m* 2011, Donal Lyons; three *d*. *Educ:* St Bride's Primary Sch., Belfast; Rathmore Grammar Sch.; Open Univ. (BSc Hons); Queen's Univ. Belfast (LLM). Campaigns Officer, Concern Worldwide, 2005–15. Mem. (SDLP) Belfast CC, 2011–15. *Recreations:* theatre, reading, running, listening to music, art. *Address:* Northern Ireland Assembly, Parliament Buildings, Stormont, Belfast BT4 3XX. *T:* (028) 9052 0369. *E:* claire.hanna@mla.niassembly.gov.uk; 455 Ormeau Road, Belfast BT7 3GQ. *T:* (028) 9099 6066.

**HANNA, Prof. David Colin,** PhD; FRS 1998; Professor of Physics, 1988–2007, now Emeritus, and Deputy Director, Optoelectronics Research Centre, 1989–2007, University of Southampton; *b* 10 April 1941; *s* of James Morgan Hanna and Vera Elizabeth Hanna (*née* Hopkins); *m* 1968, Sarah Veronica Jane Heigham; two *s*. *Educ:* Nottingham High Sch.; Jesus Coll., Cambridge (BA 1962); Southampton Univ. (PhD 1967). University of Southampton: Lectr, Dept of Electronics, 1967–78; Sen. Lectr, 1978–84; Reader, Dept of Physics, 1984–88. Fellow, Winchester Coll., 2001–09. Consiglio Nazionale della Ricerca Vis. Fellow, Politecnico di Milano, 1971; Alexander von Humboldt Fellow, Univ. of Munich, 1978–79. Dir-at-Large, 1996, Fellow, 1998, Optical Soc. of America. Max Born Medal and Prize, German Physical Soc., 1993; Quantum Electronics and Optics Prize, Eur. Physical Soc., 2000; Alexander von Humboldt Res. Award, Alexander von Humboldt Foundn, 2000; Charles Hard Townes Award, Optical Soc. of Amer., 2003. *Publications:* Nonlinear Optics of Free Atoms and Molecules, 1979; more than 250 papers in learned jls on lasers and nonlinear optics. *Recreations:* walking, climbing, gardening, cooking, sailing, music, theatre, travel. *Address:* Optoelectronics Research Centre, University of Southampton, Southampton SO17 1BJ. *T:* (023) 8059 2150.

**HANNAFORD, Joanne,** FBCS; Partner, Engineering, since 2014, and Head, EMEA Technology, since 2017, Goldman Sachs; *b* Rush Green, 1970; *d* of Alexander Hutchison and Georgina Hutchison; *m* 1995, Jonathan Hannaford. *Educ:* Anglia Univ. (HND Computer Sci.); Staffordshire Univ. (BSc Hons 1st Cl. Computer Sci.). FBCS 2014. Software Engr, Equities Technol., UBS, 1992–94; Lead Architect, Equities Trading, NatWest Markets, 1994–97; Goldman Sachs: Associate, 1997–98; Vice Pres., Engrg, 1998–2008; Man. Dir, Engrg, 2008–14. Mem., Adv. Bd, Govt Digital Service, 2016–.

Trustee, Founders4Schools, 2016–; Mem. Bd, WISE Campaign, 2016–. *Recreation:* tennis. *Address:* Goldman Sachs, Peterborough Court, 133 Fleet Street, EC4A 2BB. *E:* joanne.hannaford@gs.com.

**HANNAH, Prof. Leslie**, FBA 2019; Visiting Professor, London School of Economics, 2007–17, now Professor Emeritus; *b* 15 June 1947; *s* of Arthur Hannah and Marie (*née* Lancashire); *m* 1984, Nuala Barbara Zahedieh (*née* Hockton) (marr. diss. 1998), *e d* of Thomas and Deirdre Hockton; one *s*, and two step *d*. *Educ:* Manchester Grammar Sch.; St John's and Nuffield Colleges, Oxford. MA, PhD, DPhil. Research Fellow, St John's Coll., Oxford, 1969–73; Lectr in economics, Univ. of Essex, 1973–75; Lectr in recent British economic and social history, Univ. of Cambridge, and Fellow and Financial Tutor, Emmanuel Coll., Cambridge, 1976–78; London School of Economics: Dir, Business History Unit, 1978–88; Prof. of Business Hist., 1982–97; Pro-Dir, 1995–97; Acting Dir, 1996–97; Dean, City Univ. Business Sch., subseq. Sir John Cass Business Sch., City of London, 1997–2000, Vis. Prof., 2000–03; Chief Exec., Ashridge Mgt Coll., 2000–03; Prof. of Economics, Univ. of Tokyo, 2004–07, 2012–13; Dir d'Etudes Associé, Ecole des Hautes Etudes en Scis Sociales, Paris, 2007. Vis. Prof., Harvard Univ., 1984–85. Director: NRG London Reinsurance, 1986–93; London Econs Ltd, 1991–2000. *Publications:* Rise of the Corporate Economy, 1976, 2nd edn 1983; (ed) Management Strategy and Business Development, 1976; (with J. A. Kay) Concentration in Modern Industry, 1977; Electricity before Nationalisation, 1979; Engineers, Managers and Politicians, 1982; Entrepreneurs and the Social Sciences, 1983; Inventing Retirement, 1986; (with M. Ackrill) Barclays, 2001; (with K. Wada) Invisible Hand Strikes Back, 2001; contribs to jls. *Recreation:* England. *Address:* 332 Lauderdale Tower, Barbican, EC2Y 8NA. *Club:* Reform.

**HANNAH, His Honour William**; a Circuit Judge, 1988–95; *b* 31 March 1929; *s* of William Bond Hannah and Elizabeth Alexandra Hannah; *m* 1950, Alma June Marshall (*d* 2015); one *s* one *d*. *Educ:* Everton School, Notts. RAF 1947–52; Police Officer, 1952–77. Called to the Bar, Gray's Inn, 1970; in practice, NE Circuit, 1977–88; a Recorder, 1987–88; Resident Judge, Teesside, 1993–96; Dep. Chief Justice, Supreme Ct of St Helena, S Atlantic, 1996–2001. *Recreations:* golf, swimming, walking, theatre. *Address:* c/o New Court Chambers, 3 Broad Chare, Newcastle upon Tyne NE1 3DQ. *Club:* South Shields Golf.

**HANNAM, Sir John (Gordon)**, Kt 1992; *b* 2 Aug. 1929; *s* of Thomas William and Selina Hannam; *m* 1st, 1956, Wendy Macartney; two *d*; 2nd, 1983, Mrs Vanessa Wauchope (*née* Anson). *Educ:* Yeovil Grammar Sch. Studied Agriculture, 1945–46. Served in: Royal Tank Regt (commissioned), 1947–48; Somerset LI (TA), 1949–51. Studied Hotel industry, 1950–52; Managing Dir, Hotels and Restaurant Co., 1952–61; Developed Motels, 1961–70; Chm., British Motels Fedn, 1967–74, Pres. 1974–80; Mem. Council, BTA, 1968–69; Mem. Economic Research Council, 1967–85. MP (C) Exeter, 1970–97. PPS to: Minister for Industry, 1972–74; Chief Sec., Treasury, 1974. Mem., Select Cttee on Procedure, 1993–97; Secretary: Cons. Parly Trade Cttee, 1971–72; All-Party Disablement Gp, 1974–92 (Co-Chm., 1992–97); 1922 Cttee, 1987–97; Mem., Govt Adv. Cttee on Transport for Disabled, 1983–97; Chairman: Anglo-Swiss Parly Gp, 1987–97; West Country Cons. Cttee, 1973–74, 1979–81; Cons. Party Energy Cttee, 1979–92; Arts and Leisure Standing Cttee, Bow Group, 1975–84; Vice-Chairman: Arts and Heritage Cttee, 1974–79; British Cttee of Internat. Rehabilitation, 1979–92; Parly Gp on Energy Studies, 1992–97 (Hon. Mem., 1997–). Captain: Lords and Commons Tennis Club, 1975–97; Lords and Commons Ski Club, 1977–82; Cdre, House of Commons Yacht Club, 1975. Mem., Snowdon Working Party on the Disabled, 1975–76; Chm. Trustees, Snowdon Awards Scheme, 1997–2012. Vice-President: Disablement Income Gp; Alzheimer's Soc.; Council, Action Medical Research (formerly Action Research for Crippling Diseases); Disabled Motorists Gp; Disabled Drivers Assoc.; Rehabilitation UK, 2005– (Bd Mem., 1995–2005). Member: Bd, Nat. Theatre, 1979–92; Glyndebourne Festival Soc.; Council, British Youth Opera, 1989–2008 (Chm., 1997–2008; Vice-Pres., 2008–). Hon. MA Open, 1986. *Recreations:* music (opera), theatre, sailing (anything), ski-ing (fast), Cresta tobogganing (foolish), gardening; county tennis and hockey (Somerset tennis champion, 1953), croquet. *Address:* 85 Bromfelde Road, SW4 6PP. *Clubs:* All England Lawn Tennis, International Lawn Tennis, Veterans Lawn Tennis Club of GB.

**HANNAM, Timothy James**; QC 2018; a Recorder, since 2012; *b* Walsall, 26 April 1973; *s* of Roderick and Carol Hannam; *m* 2000, Susan Elizabeth Gavan; one *s* one *d*. *Educ:* Queen Mary's Grammar Sch., Walsall; Oriel Coll., Oxford (BA Juris.). Called to the Bar, Gray's Inn, 1995; in practice as barrister, specialising in crime, 1996–; Standing Counsel to Revenue and Customs Prosecutions Office, 2008–13. Gov. Repton Sch., 2014–. *Recreations:* walking, shooting, Rugby, football, reading, family. *Address:* Citadel Chambers, 190 Corporation Street, Birmingham B4 6QD. *T:* (0121) 233 8500. *E:* clerks@citadelchambers.com.

**HANNAN, Daniel John**; Member (C) South East Region, England, European Parliament, since 1999; writer and journalist; *b* 1 Sept. 1971; *s* of late Hugh R. Hannan and Lavinia M. Hannan (*née* Moffat); *m* 2000, Sara Maynard; one *s* two *d*. *Educ:* Marlborough; Oriel Coll., Oxford (MA). Leader writer, Daily Telegraph, 1996–2008. Dir, European Res. Gp, 1994–99. *Publications:* Time for a Fresh Start in Europe, 1993; Britain in a Multi-Speed Europe, 1994; The Challenge of the East, 1996; A Guide to the Amsterdam Treaty, 1997; What if we vote No?, 2004; The Case for EFTA, 2005; Direct Democracy, 2006; (with D. Carswell) The Plan: twelve months to renew Britain, 2008; The New Road to Serfdom, 2010; Why America Shouldn't Copy Europe, 2011; A Doomed Marriage: Britain and the EU, 2012; How We Invented Freedom & Why It Matters, 2013; Why Vote Leave, 2016; What Next?: how to get the best from Brexit, 2016. *Recreation:* Shakespeare. *Clubs:* Garrick, Pratt's.

**HANNAN, Menna**, see Richards, Menna.

**HANNAY**, family name of **Baron Hannay of Chiswick**.

**HANNAY OF CHISWICK**, Baron *cr* 2001 (Life Peer), of Bedford Park in the London Borough of Ealing; **David Hugh Alexander Hannay**, GCMG 1995 (KCMG 1986; CMG 1981); CH 2003; *b* 28 Sept. 1935; *s* of late Julian Hannay; *m* 1961, Gillian Rex; four *s*. *Educ:* Winchester; New Coll., Oxford (Hon. Fellow 2001). Foreign Office, 1959–60; Tehran, 1960–61; 3rd Sec., Kabul, 1961–63; 2nd Sec., FO, 1963–65; 2nd, later 1st Sec., UK Delegn to European Communities, Brussels, 1965–70; 1st Sec., UK Negotiating Team with European Communities, 1970–72; Chef de Cabinet to Sir Christopher Soames, Vice President of EEC, 1973–77; Head of Energy, Science and Space Dept, FCO, 1977–79; Head of Middle East Dept, FCO, 1979; Asst Under-Sec. of State (European Community), FCO, 1979–84; Minister, Washington, 1984–85; Ambassador and UK Permanent Rep. to Eur. Communities, Brussels, 1985–90; Ambassador and UK Perm. Rep. to UN, 1990–95; retd from Diplomatic Service, 1995. British Govt Special Rep. for Cyprus, 1996–2003; Prime Minister's Personal Envoy to Turkey, 1998; EU Presidency Special Rep. for Cyprus, 1998. Member: EU Select Cttee, H of L, 2002–06, 2008–14 (Chm., Sub-Cttee for Home Affairs, 2010–14); Intergovtl Orgns Cttee, H of L, 2007–08; Cttee on the Arctic, H of L, 2014–15; Cttee on Sexual Violence in Conflict, H of L, 2015–16; Internat. Relns Cttee, H of L, 2016–; Chm., All Party Parly Gp on UN, 2012– (Vice-Chm., 2005–11); Vice-Chm., All Party Parly Gp on EU, 2006–; Jt Convenor, All Party Parly Gp on Global Security and Non-Proliferation, 2008–; Mem. Exec., British-American Parly Gp, 2008–12; Member: Top Level Gp of Parliamentarians for Multilateral Nuclear Disarmament and Non-Proliferation, 2011–; European Leadership Network for Nuclear Disarmament and Non-Proliferation, 2013–. Mem., UN Sec.-General's High Level Panel on Threats, Challenges and Change, 2003–04. Chm., UNA of UK, 2006–11. Non-executive Director: Chime Communications, 1996–2006; Aegis, 2000–03; Mem., Ind. Adv. Panel, Tangguh, 2002–09; Mem., Bd, Salzburg Seminar, 2002–05; Mem., Adv. Bd, GPW, 2011–. Mem., Bd, Centre for European Reform, 1997–; Mem., Council of Britain in Europe, 1999–2005; Mem., Sen. European Experts Gp, 1999– (Chm., 2014–). Chm., Internat. Adv. Bd, EDHEC Business Sch., 2003–09; Mem., Internat. Adv. Bd, Judge Business Sch., Univ. of Cambridge, 2004–10. Gov., Ditchley Foundn, 2005–19 (Hon. Gov., 2019–). Mem. Court and Council, 1998–, Pro-Chancellor, 2001–06, Birmingham Univ.; Mem. Council, Univ. of Kent, 2009–15. Patron, Wyndham Place Charlemagne Trust, 2009–. Hon. DLitt Birmingham, 2003. *Publications:* Cyprus: the search for a solution, 2004; New World Disorder: the UN after the Cold War – an insider's view, 2008; Britain's Quest for a Role: a diplomatic memoir from Europe to the UN, 2012. *Recreations:* travel, gardening, photography. *Address:* 3 The Orchard, W4 1JZ. *Club:* Travellers.

**HANNAY, Prof. David Rainsford**, MD, PhD; FRCGP, FFPH; Vice Lord-Lieutenant, District of Wigtown, Dumfries and Galloway, 2009–14; *b* London, 3 Jan. 1939; *s* of Ramsay and Margaret Rainsford Hannay; *m* 1963, Janet Mary Gilliat; three *s*. *Educ:* Winchester Coll.; Trinity Coll., Cambridge (BChir 1964; MB 1965; MA; MD 1982); Univ. of Glasgow (PhD 1975). FRCGP 1988. Glasgow University: Lectr, Dept of Community Medicine, 1968–75; Sen. Lectr, Dept of Gen. Practice, 1975–84; Principal in Gen. Practice, Newton Stewart, Wigtownshire, 1984–86; Prof. of Gen. Practice, Univ. of Sheffield, 1986–96, Prof. Emeritus, 1997; Principal in Gen. Practice, Newton Stewart, 1997–2004. Dir, Primary Care Res. Network, Dumfries and Galloway, 2000–03. Non-exec. Dir, Dumfries and Galloway NHS Bd, 2010–14. FFPH 1982. *Publications:* The Symptom Iceberg: a study of community health, 1979; Lecture Notes on Medical Sociology, 1988; contrib. papers to learned jls. *Recreations:* playing bagpipes, sailing. *Address:* Cuddyfield, Carsluith, Newton Stewart, Wigtownshire DG8 7DS.

**HANNAY, Elizabeth Anne Scott**; *see* Prescott-Decie, E. A. S.

**HANNETT, John**; General Secretary, Union of Shop, Distributive and Allied Workers, 2004–18; *b* 23 June 1953; *s* of John and Mary Hannett; *m* 1979, Linda Sargeant; one *s* one *d*. *Educ:* St George's RC High Sch., Liverpool. Union of Shop, Distributive and Allied Workers: Area Organiser, 1985–90; Nat. Officer, 1990–97; Dep. Gen. Sec., 1997–2004. Member: Low Pay Commn, 2007–17; Council, ACAS, 2010–16. *Recreation:* football.

**HANNIGAN, Robert Peter**, CMG 2013; Senior Adviser, McKinsey & Co., since 2017; Executive Chairman (Europe), BlueVoyant LLC, since 2018; *b* 1965. *Educ:* Wadham Coll., Oxford (MA; Hon. Fellow 2015). Northern Ireland Office: Dep. Dir of Communications, 2000–01; Dir of Communications, 2001–04; Associate Pol Dir, 2004–05; Dir Gen., Political, 2005–07; Security Advr to Prime Minister, and Hd of Security, Intelligence and Resilience, Cabinet Office, 2007–10; Dir Gen., Defence and Intelligence, FCO, 2010–14; Dir, Govt Communications HQ, 2014–17. Mem., Defence Innovation Adv. Panel, MoD, 2017–. Trustee, Bletchley Park Trust, 2018–. Sen. Associate Fellow, RUSI, 2018; Sen. Fellow, Belfer Center, Harvard Univ., 2018–. FIET 2017. US Nat. Intelligence Distinguished Public Service Medal, 2017; Order of Sultan Qaboos (Oman), 2017. *Club:* Special Forces.

**HANNINGFIELD**, Baron *cr* 1998 (Life Peer), of Chelmsford in the co. of Essex; **Paul Edward Winston White**; DL; farmer; Member (C), 1970–2011, and Leader, 1998–99 and 2001–10, Essex County Council; *b* 16 Sept. 1940; *s* of Edward Ernest William White and Irene Joyce Gertrude White (*née* Williamson). *Educ:* King Edward VI Grammar Sch., Chelmsford (Nuffield Scholarship). Chm., 1989–92, Leader, Cons. Gp, 2001–10, Essex CC. Chairman: Council, Local Educn Authorities, 1990–92; Eastern Area, FEFC, 1992–97. Dep. Chm., LGA, 1997–2001. Mem., EU Cttee of the Regions (Vice Pres., European People's Party, 1998; Vice Pres., Transport and Information Soc. Commn, 1998–2000). Mem. Ct, Essex Univ., 1980. DL Essex, 1991. *Publications:* many contribs to local govt jls. *Recreations:* gardening, wine and food, travel, walking the dog. *Address:* Pippins Place, Helmons Lane, West Hanningfield, Chelmsford, Essex CM2 8UW. *T:* (01245) 400229.

**HANNON, Rt Rev. Brian Desmond Anthony**; Bishop of Clogher, 1986–2001; *b* 5 Oct. 1936; *s* of late Ven. Arthur Gordon Hannon and of Hilda Catherine Stewart-Moore Hannon (*née* Denny); *m* 1964, Maeve Geraldine Audley (*née* Butler); three *s*. *Educ:* Mourne Grange Prep. School, Co. Down; St Columba's Coll., Co. Dublin; Trinity Coll., Dublin (BA Hons 1959, 1st Class Divinity Testimonium 1961). Deacon 1961, priest 1962; Diocese of Derry: Curate-Assistant, All Saints, Clooney, Londonderry, 1961–64; Rector of Desertmartin, 1964–69; Rector of Christ Church, Londonderry, 1969–82; RD of Londonderry, 1977–82; Diocese of Clogher: Rector of St Macartin's Cathedral, Enniskillen, 1982–86; Canon of Cathedral Chapter, 1983; Dean of Clogher, 1985. Chm., Council for Mission in Ireland, C of I, 1987–99. Pres., CMS (Ireland), 1990–96; Chm., Irish Council of Churches, 1992–94; Co-Chm., Irish Inter-Church Meeting, 1992–94; Mem., WCC Central Cttee, 1983–92. Chm. of Western (NI) Education and Library Bd, 1985–87 and 1989–91 (Vice-Chm., 1987–89 and 1991–93). Hon. MA TCD, 1962. *Publications:* (editor/author) Christ Church, Londonderry—1830 to 1980—Milestones, Ministers, Memories, 1980. *Recreations:* walking, music, travel, sport. *Address:* Drumconnis Top, 202 Mullaghmeen Road, Ballinamallard, Co. Fermanagh, N Ireland BT94 2DZ. *T:* (028) 6638 8557. *E:* bdah@btinternet.com.

**HANNON, Richard Michael**; racehorse trainer, 1970–2013; *b* 30 May 1945; *m* 1966, Josephine Ann McCarthy; two *s* four *d* (of whom two *s* one *d* are triplets). First trainer's licence, 1970; wins include: 2000 Guineas, 1973 (Mon Fils), 1987 (Don't Forget Me), 1990 (Tirol); Irish 2000 Guineas, 1987 (Don't Forget Me), 1990 (Tirol); leading Flat trainer, 1992, 2010, 2011, 2013; trained record number of winners (182), 1993 season. *Address:* East Everleigh Stables, Marlborough, Wilts SN8 3EY.

**HANNS, Raquel**; *see* Agnello, R.

**HANRATTY, James Robert Anthony**, RD 1987; Immigration Judge (formerly Adjudicator), 1997–2014; *b* 6 Feb. 1946; *s* of late Dr J. F. Hanratty, OBE, KSG, and Irene Hanratty (*née* Belton); *m* 1975, Pamela Hoare; one *s* two *d*. *Educ:* Stonyhurst Coll.; Coll. of Law; Birmingham Coll. of Commerce. Admitted solicitor, UK 1970, Hong Kong 1982. Criminal Appeal Office, Royal Courts of Justice, 1971–74; Lawyer, LCD, H of L, 1974–81; Sen. Crown Counsel, Attorney Gen.'s Chambers, Hong Kong, 1981–85; Asst Sec., Hd, Judicial Appts Div., LCD, 1985–88; Chief Exec., Royal Courts of Justice, 1988–91; Dep. Legal Advr, then Legal Advr, to British Side of Sino-British Liaison Gp on Handover of Hong Kong to China, Hong Kong, 1991–97. Mem., Ind. Adv. Gp to advise on Windrush Affair, 2018–19. Marking Examr in Criminal Law, Law Soc., 1971–81. Pres., Council of Immigration Judges for Eng., Wales and Scotland, 2001–03. Mem. Cttee, Hong Kong Soc.,

2008–13. Joined RNR as ordinary seaman, 1971; Lieut Comdr, 1994, retd. Member: RYA, 1990–; RNSA, 2002–. Pres., Stonyhurst Assoc., 2013–14. Speaker on literary festival circuit. *Publications:* The Making of an Immigration Judge (memoir), 2016; contrib. various articles to legal jls on internat. law aspects of the Hong Kong Handover and Immigration Law. *Recreations:* sailing, tennis, watching cricket, club life, family, standing on bridges and waving at trains. *E:* jrhanratty@btinternet.com. *Clubs:* Athenæum, Hurlingham (Cttee 2000–03); Royal Yacht Squadron; RNVR Yacht (Cdre, 2002–04); Royal Hong Kong Yacht; Deauville Yacht.

HANRATTY, Judith Christine, CVO 2008; OBE 2002; Chairman, Commonwealth Education Trust, 2007–17 (Chairman, Commonwealth Institute, 2002–07); Director, Partner Re Ltd, 2005–17; *b* Wellington, NZ, 16 Aug. 1943; *d* of late John Edward Hanratty and Joyce Hanratty. *Educ:* Chilton St James Sch., NZ; St Hilda's Collegiate Sch., NZ; Victoria Univ. of Wellington, NZ (LLB; LLM; LLD). Barrister: High Court of NZ, 1966; Supreme Court of Vic, Australia, 1980; Inner Temple, 1987. Co. Sec., BP plc, 1994–2003. Non-executive Director: BP Pension Trustees, 1992–2004; London Electricity plc, 1995–97; Charles Taylor plc, 2000–12; Partnerships UK plc, 2001–05; BSI, 2002–05. Non-exec. Dir, England Golf, 2011–16. Member: Insce Brokers' Registration Council, 1993–98; Competition (formerly Monopolies and Mergers) Commn, 1997–2003; Takeover Panel, 1997–2003; Council, Lloyd's of London, 1998–2009; Gas and Electricity Mkts Authy, 2004–10. Patron, Kids' Lit Quiz, 2015–. Fellow, Lucy Cavendish Coll., Cambridge, 1998. FRSA 1994. *Recreations:* golf, croquet. *Address:* 36 Sloane Court West, SW3 4TB. *E:* judith@sloanecourtwest.com; 341 Fergusson Drive, Upper Hutt 5018, New Zealand. *Clubs:* Athenæum, Wellington, Roehampton; Royal Wimbledon Golf; Royal Wellington Golf.

HANRATTY, Mary Bridget, CBE 2003; Director of Nursing and Midwifery Education, Beeches Management Centre, Dungannon, Northern Ireland, 1997–2006; *b* 15 Nov. 1943; *d* of Edward Holland and late Rose Anne Holland; *m* 1967, (Malachy) Oliver Hanratty; two *s. Educ:* BA, MSc. RGN; RMN; RNT. Dir, Nurse Educn, 1991–97; involved in professional regulation of nurses, midwives and health visitors. Mem., 1989–2002, Vice-Pres., 1998–2002, UKCC; Mem., NMC, 2001 (Vice-Pres., 2001–05). Chair, Middletown Centre for Autism Ltd, 2016– (Vice Chair, 2013–16). *Recreations:* foreign travel, crosswords, entertaining.

HANRETTY, Gerald Francis; QC (Scot.) 2002; *b* 13 April 1958; *s* of Peter Hanretty and Margaret Hanretty (*née* Soutar); *m* 1979, Moira Walker; two *s* one *d. Educ:* St Mirin's Acad., Paisley; Univ. of Glasgow (LLB). Solicitor, 1980–89; admitted Advocate, 1990; Advocate Depute, 2001–03; Chairman (part-time): Mental Health Tribunal for Scotland, 2005–14; Police Appeals Tribunal, 2010–13. *Recreations:* family interests, reading, Formula One racing. *Address:* c/o Advocates' Library, Parliament House, Edinburgh EH1 1RF.

HÄNSCH, Dr Klaus; Member (SPD), European Parliament, 1979–2009 (President, 1994–97); *b* Sprottau, Silesia, 15 Dec. 1938; *s* of Willi Hänsch and Erna (*née* Sander); *m* 1969, Ilse Hoof. *Educ:* Univ. of Cologne (degree in Pol Sci. 1965); Univ. of Paris; Univ. of Berlin (PhD 1969). Escaped from Silesia to Schleswig-Holstein, 1945. Mil. Service, 1959–60. Res. Asst, Otto Suhr Inst., Free Univ. of Berlin, 1966–68; Ed., Dokumente, 1968–69; Advr to Rep. of FRG under Franco-German Treaty, 1969–70; Press Officer, 1970–79 and expert advr, 1977–79, to Minister for Sci. and Res., N Rhine/Westphalia; Lectr, Duisburg Univ., 1976–94 (Hon. Prof., 1994). European Parliament: Member: Foreign Affairs and Security and other cttees, 1979–94; For. Affairs, Human Rights, Common Security and Defence Policy Cttee, 1997; Vice-Chm., Party of Eur. Socialists Gp, 1997; Advr. Mem., Bundestag Cttee on EC issues, 1985–95; Chm., Delegn for relns with US, 1987–89. Member: SPD, 1964–; ÖTV (Union of Tspt and Public Service Workers). *Publications:* Kontinent der Hoffnungen: mein europäisches leben, 2010; pamphlets, contribs to books, and many articles on politics and society in France and on issues relating to unification of Europe and European security policy.

HÄNSCH, Prof. Theodor Wolfgang, PhD; Director, Division of Laserspectroscopy, Max Planck Institute for Quantum Optics, since 1986; Carl Friedrich von Siemens Professor of Physics, Ludwig Maximilians University, Munich, since 2007 (Professor of Physics, since 1986); *b* Heidelberg, 30 Oct. 1941. *Educ:* Helmholtz Gymnasium, Heidelberg; Univ. of Heidelberg (Physics Dip. 1966; PhD summa cum laude 1969). Asst Prof., Inst. of Applied Physics, Univ. of Heidelberg, 1969–70; Stanford University: NATO Postdoctoral Fellow, 1970–72; Associate Prof. of Physics, 1972–75; Prof. of Physics, 1975–86; Consulting Prof., 1988–; Exec. Dir, Max Planck Inst. for Quantum Optics, 1993–96 and 2003–04; Chm., Physics Dept, Ludwig Maximilians Univ., 2001–02. Visiting Professor: Coll. de France, 1978; Univ. of Kyoto, 1979; Univ. of Florence, 1979, 1995–; Fudan Univ., Shanghai, 1982; Ecole Normale Supérieure, Paris, 1992; Gordon Moore Dist. Schol., CIT, Pasadena, 2001. Hon. Professor: Nat. Chiang Tung Univ., HsinChu, Taiwan, 2010; Univ. System of Taiwan, 2010; Northwestern Poly. Univ., Xi'an, China, 2014. Adv. Ed., Optics Communications, 1975–; Associate Ed., Jl of Optical Soc. of America, 1981–84; Member, Editorial Board: Metrologia, 1975–83; Applied Physics B, 1983–; Springer Series in Optical Scis, 1998–; Laser Physics Rev., 2004–; Laser and Photonics Rev., 2007–; Annalen der Physik, 2011–; Internat. Jl on Atomic, Molecular, Condensate and Nano Physics, 2012–; Mem., Adv. Cttee, Physics Today, 1985–95; Mem., Bd of Editors, Physics in Perspective, 1997–2006. Fellow: APS, 1973; Optical Soc. of America, 1973; Nat. Acad. Inventors, USA, 2014. Member: Amer. Acad. Arts and Scis, 1983; Bavarian Acad. Arts and Scis, 1991; Berlin-Brandenburg Acad. Scis, 2005; German Acad. Natural Scientists, Leopoldina, 2006; Pontifical Acad. Sci., 2006; MAE 2009. Hon. Dr rer. nat. Free Univ., Berlin, 2006; Hon. Dr Bar Ilan Univ., Tel Aviv, 2008; Hon. DSc: St Andrews, 2006; Strathclyde, 2011. Awards include: Alexander von Humboldt Sen. US Scientist Award, 1977; Cyrus B. Comstock Prize, US NAS, Herbert B. Broida Prize, APS, 1983; William F. Meggers Award, Optical Soc. of America, 1985; Michelson Medal, Franklin Inst., Philadelphia, 1986; King Faisal Internat. Prize for Sci., Saudi Arabia, 1989; Einstein Medal for Laser Sci., 1995; Arthur L. Schawlow Prize for Laser Sci., APS, 1996; Arthur L. Schawlow Award and Life Mem., Laser Inst. of America, 2000; Quantum Electronics and Optics Prize, Eur. Physical Soc., 2001; Matteucci Medal, Nat. Acad. of Scis, Italy, 2002; Alfried Krupp Prize for Sci., 2002; I. I. Rabi Award, IEEE, 2005; Frederic Ives Medal, Optical Soc. of America, 2005; Otto-Hahn Prize for Chemistry and Physics, 2005; (jtly) Nobel Prize in Physics, 2005; Carl Friedrich von Siemens Prize and Chair, 2006; Ioannes Marcus Marci Medal, Czech Spectroscopic Soc., 2006; Rudolf Diesel Gold Medal, German Inst. of Interventions, 2006; Medal, Acad. of Scis of Czech Republic, 2007; James Joyce Award, UCD, 2009; Sayling Wen Excellent Lect. Award, Nat. Central Univ., Taiwan, 2010; Wilhelm Exner Medal, Wilhelm Exner Foundn, Vienna, 2012; Fitzpatrick Pioneer Award, Duke Univ., 2015. Hon. Citizen: Florence, Italy, 2006; Garching, 2006. Order of Merit: Germany, 2003 (Großes Bundesverdienstkreuz mit Stern, 2006); Bavaria, 2003 (Maximiliansorden, Constitutional Medal in Gold, 2010); Italy, 2006 (Grand Officer Cross); for Sciences and Arts (Germany), 2008. *Publications:* approx. 665 articles. *Address:* c/o Gabriele Gschwendtner (Head of Office, Manager and Personal Consultant), Faculty of Physics, Ludwig Maximilians University, Schellingstrasse 4/III, H327/H 328, 80799 Munich, Germany. *T:* (89) 21803212, (mobile) 01741 1931522, *Fax:* (89) 285192. *E:* t.w.haensch@physik.uni.muenchen.de, t.w.haensch@lmu.de.

HANSELL, Prof. David Matthew, MD; FRCP, FRCR; FRSM; Professor of Thoracic Imaging, Imperial College School of Medicine, 1998–2017, now Emeritus; Consultant Radiologist, Royal Brompton Hospital, 1989–2017 (Director, Department of Radiology, 1992–95 and 2004–14); *b* London, 3 April 1957; *s* of Peter Hansell and Jean Hansell (*née* Nicol); *m* 1981, Mary Anne Gadsden; three *d. Educ:* Framlingham Coll.; King's Coll., London and Westminster Hosp. Med. Sch. (MB BS 1981; MD 1997). MRCP 1984, FRCP 1999; FRCR 1987. FRSM 2011 (DipABRSM 2004, LRSM 2006). Registrar and Sen. Registrar in Diagnostic Radiol., Westminster Hosp., 1984–88. Vis. Asst Prof., Dept of Radiological Scis, UCLA, 1989. Academic Hd, Lung Imaging Res. Team, Nat. Heart and Lung Inst., 1994–96. Sen. Investigator, NIHR, 2013–17. Pres., Eur. Soc. of Thoracic Imaging, 2005; Pres., Fleischner Soc., 2012–13. Ed., Clinical Radiology, 2002–06; Associate Ed., Radiology (USA), 2000–03. RCR Gold Medal, 2015. *Publications:* (jtly) Imaging of Diseases of the Chest, 1990, 5th edn 2010; numerous chapters and over 350 papers on all aspects of thoracic imaging; contrib. to N Amer. and Eur. guidelines on diffuse lung diseases. *Recreations:* Baroque music, moles, trees. *Club:* Athenæum.

HANSEN, Alan David; football pundit, BBC, 1992–2014; *b* 13 June 1955; *s* of John and Anne Hansen; *m* 1980, Janette Rhymes; one *s* one *d. Educ:* Lornshill Acad. Professional footballer, Liverpool FC, 1977–91: League Champions, 1979, 1980, 1982, 1983, 1984, 1986, 1988, 1990; Capt., FA Cup winning team, 1986, 1988; winners: European Cup, 1978, 1981, 1984; League Cup, 1981, 1982, 1983, 1984. Presenter: Football's Dream Factory, BBC, 2001; Club or Country, BBC, 2003; Life After Football, BBC, 2005. Football columnist, Daily Telegraph, 2002–. *Publications:* Tall, Dark and Hansen, 1988; Matter of Opinion, 1999. *Address:* c/o Silver Fox Media, 3 Sauncey Wood, Harpenden, Herts AL5 5DP. *Clubs:* Hillside Golf; Southport and Birkdale Cricket.

HANSEN, Diana Jill; Director, Somerset House Trust, 2002–05; *b* 24 March 1948. *Educ:* Univ. of Sussex (MA 2010). HM Treasury, 1969–89; Dir, VAT Control, and a Comr, HM Customs and Excise, 1989–91; Asst Under-Sec. of State, Air, 1992, Finance, 1993, MoD (PE), Programmes, 1994, MoD; Comd Sec., HQ Land Comd, 1998–2002.

HANSEN, Prof. Jean-Pierre, DèS; FRS 2002; Professor of Theoretical Chemistry, 1997–2007, now Emeritus, and Fellow of Corpus Christi College, since 1997, University of Cambridge; *b* 10 May 1942; *s* of late Georges Hansen and Simone Flohr; *m* 1971, Martine Bechet; one *d. Educ:* Athénée Grand-Ducal de Luxembourg; Univ. de Liège (Licence en Sciences Physiques, 1964); Univ. de Paris-Sud (Orsay) (DèS 1969). CChem, FRSC 1998. Chargé de recherche, CNRS, France, 1967–73; Prof. of Physics, Univ. Pierre et Marie Curie, Paris, 1973–87; Directeur Adjoint, 1987–93, Prof. and Hd of Dept of Physics, 1987–97, Ecole Normale Supérieure, Lyons. Miller Prof., Univ. of Calif at Berkeley, 1992. Mem., Inst. Universitaire de France, 1992–97. Hon. Dr Liège, 2008. Grand Prix de l'Etat, Académie des Sciences, Paris, 1990; Prix Spécial, Soc. Française de Physique, 1998; Liquid Matter Prize, Eur. Physical Soc., 2005; Rumford Medal, Royal Soc., 2006; Grand Prix des Scis Physiques, Institut Grand-Ducal, Luxembourg, 2010; Berni J. Alder Prize, CECAM, 2013. Chevalier de l'Ordre de la Couronne de Chêne (Luxembourg), 1997. *Publications:* (jtly) Theory of Simple Liquids, 1976, 4th edn 2013; (ed jtly) Liquids, Freezing and the Glass Transition, 1991; (jtly) Basic Concepts for Simple and Complex Liquids, 2003; papers in internat. jls. *Recreations:* history of art, classical music, hill walking. *Address:* Department of Chemistry, Lensfield Road, Cambridge CB2 1EW. *T:* (01223) 336377.

HANSEN, Hon. Sir John (William), KNZM 2009 (DCNZM 2008); a Judge, High Court of New Zealand, 1995–2008; Executive Judge, South Island, 1997–2008; Senior Puisne Judge, 2005–08; *b* Fairlie, NZ, 11 May 1944; *s* of William John and Jane Hansen; *m* 1966, Ann Porter; one *s* one *d. Educ:* Wakari Prim. Sch., Dunedin; Dunedin North Intermediate Sch., Dunedin; Otago Boys' High Sch., Dunedin; Univ. of Otago (LLB 1968). Admitted solicitor, 1966, called to the Bar, 1967, Supreme Court of NZ, admitted solicitor and called to the Bar, Supreme Court of WA, 1985; Clerk, Collier & Taylor, Dunedin, 1966; Solicitor, Aspinall, Joel & Co., Dunedin, 1967; Barrister and Solicitor, John E. Farry, Dunedin, 1969; Partner, John E. Farry & Hansen, Dunedin, 1969–79; Hong Kong Judiciary, 1979–88: variously Magistrate, Coroner, Dist Court Judge, Family Court Judge, Master of the Supreme Court; High Court of New Zealand: Master, 1988; Temp. Judge, 1993–95; Ct of Appeals Judge, Solomon Is and Western Samoa, 2010–. Associate Mem., Shortland Chambers, 2010. Mem., Rulings Panel, Gas Industry Co. Ltd, 2009–; Chm., Legal Services Agency, 2009–11; Consultant, Legal Issues Centre, Otago Univ., 2010–. Chm., Dunedin (formerly Dunedin Venues) Mgt Ltd, 2010–. Foundn Pres., Otago Br., NZ Legal Assoc. Trustee: Canterbury Youth Develt Trust, 2009–; Christchurch Casino Charitable Trust, 2009–; Canterbury Cricket Trust, 2009–. Chair, Red Cross Christchurch Earthquake Commn, 2011–. Manager: Hong Kong Cricket XI to Malaysia and Singapore, 1983, to ICC Associate Mems Trophy, UK, 1986; NZ Team, Hong Kong Internat. Cricket Sixes Tournament, 2003; Member: Code of Conduct Commn, ICC, 2007–10; Bd, NZ Cricket, 2009–13. Internat. Rugby Bd Appeals Officer, 2009–; Mem., NZ RFU Appeals Council, 2009–. Capt. of Cricket, Kowloon Cricket Club, Hong Kong; Pres., Willows Cricket Club, Christchurch, 2003–. Former music reviewer, South China Morning Post, Hong Kong; book reviewer, Christchurch Press. NZ Medal, 1990. *Publications:* contribs to various legal jls. *Recreations:* Rugby, cricket, hiking, reading, book reviewing, music, poetry, law reform, cooking, wine. *Address:* Totara, Wolffs Road, RD6, Rangiora 7476, New Zealand. *T:* (3) 3125843. *E:* totaraa@xtra.co.nz. *Clubs:* MCC, London New Zealand Cricket; Valley Peace Cricket, The Willows Cricket (Christchurch, NZ).

HANSEN, Prof. Lars Peter, PhD; Professor of Statistics, since 2007, David Rockefeller Distinguished Service Professor, since 2010, and Professor of Finance, Booth Business School, since 2017, University of Chicago; *b* Urbana, Ill, 26 Oct. 1952; *s* of R. Gaurth Hansen and Anna Lou Rees Hansen; *m* 1984, Grace Tsiang; one *s. Educ:* Utah State Univ. (BS Maths and Political Sci. 1974); Univ. of Minnesota (PhD Econs 1978). Carnegie-Mellon University: Asst Prof., 1978–80; Associate Prof., 1980–81; University of Chicago: Associate Prof., 1981–84; Prof. of Econs, 1984–90; Homer J. Livingston Prof. of Econs, 1990–97; Homer J. Livingston Distinguished Service Prof. of Econs, 1997–2010. Fellow: Econometric Soc., 1985 (Pres., 2007); US Nat. Acad. of Scis, 1999; Amer. Finance Assoc., 2007; Mem., Amer. Acad. of Arts and Scis, 1993. Hon. DSc Utah, 2012. (Jtly) Nobel Prize in Econs, 2013. *Publications:* (with T. J. Sargent) Rational Expectations Econometrics, 1991; (with T. J. Sargent) Robustness, 2007; (ed with Yacine Ait-Sahalia) Handbook of Financial Econometrics, 2009; (with T. J. Sargent) Recursive Models of Dynamic Linear Economies, 2013; (with T. J. Sargent) Uncertainty Within Economic Models, 2014. *Address:* Department of Economics, University of Chicago, 1126 East 59th Street, Chicago, IL 60637, USA.

HANSENNE, Michel; Member (Christian Social Party), European Parliament, 1999–2004; *b* 23 March 1940; *s* of Henri and Charlier Georgette Hansenne; *m* 1978, Mme Gabrielle Vanlandschoot; one *s* one *d. Educ:* Liège Univ. (Dr Law 1962; degree in Econs and Finance, 1967). Research work, Univ. of Liège, 1962–72. Mem. Belgian Parliament, 1974–89; Minister: for French Culture, 1979–81; for Employment and Labour, 1981–88; for Civil Service, 1988–89; Dir-Gen., ILO, 1989–99. Mem., EPP Gp, EP, 1999–2004. *Publications:*

Emploi, les scénarios du possible, 1985; Un garde-fou pour la mondialisation: le BIT dans l'après-guerre froide, 1999; articles in national and international jls. *Address:* 28 rue des Deux Eglises, 4120 Rotheux-Rimière, Neupré, Belgium.

**HANSFORD, Peter George,** CEng, FREng, FICE; FAPM; Professor of Construction and Infrastructure Policy, University College London, 2016–18; Hon. Professor, since 2018; President, Institution of Civil Engineers, 2010–11; *b* Basingstoke, 4 March 1954; *s of* Leonard George Hansford and Avis Maud Hansford; *m* 1977, Pamela Wendy Baker; one *s* one *d*. *Educ:* Queen Mary's Sch., Basingstoke; Univ. of Nottingham (BSc Civil Engrg 1975); Cranfield Sch. of Mgt (MBA 1986). CEng 1980; FICE 1992; FAPM 2006; FREng 2013. Sen. Engr, Amey Roadstone Construction, 1975–81; Resident Engr, Maunsell Consultants Asia, 1981–85; Man. Dir, Nichols Gp, 1986–99; Exec. Dir, Infrastructure, Strategic Rail Authy, 2000–02; Partner, Gardiner & Theobald, 2003–04; Exec. Dir, Nichols Gp, 2004–12; Chief Construction Advr to UK Govt, 2012–15. Non-exec. Chm., Thomas Telford Ltd, 2008–09. Chm., Engrs Without Borders, 2012–16 (Trustee, 2010–16). Mem., Expert Witness Inst., 2009. FRSA 2004; MInstD; CCMI 2011. Hon. FICES 2014. Hon. LLD Nottingham, 2014. Sir Monty Finniston Award for Lifetime Achievement, Assoc. for Project Mgt, 2018. *Recreations:* golf, watching Rugby. *Address:* Institution of Civil Engineers, One Great George Street, Westminster, SW1P 3AA. *T:* (020) 7222 7722, *Fax:* (020) 7222 7500.

**HANSJEE, Anil;** Head of Ventures and Corporate Development, Europe, Middle East and Africa, PayPal, since 2016; *b* London, 6 Sept. 1967; *s of* Raman Hansjee and Lillian Hansjee; *m* 2008, Carina Christiansen; one *s*. *Educ:* Rygaards Internat. Sch., Copenhagen; Gammel Hellerup Gymnasium; Univ. of Edinburgh (BSc Hons Computer Sci. and Artificial Intelligence 1990); London Business Sch. (MSc Finance 1997). Consultant, Price Waterhouse, 1990–91; software engr, Swiss Bank Corp., 1992–94; Vice Pres., IT, 1994–97, Associate, 1997–2000, Chase Manhattan; Vice Pres., Bear Stearns, 2000–01; Principal, IDG Ventures, 2002–06; Dir, GP Bullhound, 2006; Hd, Corporate Develt, EMEA, Google, 2006–11; Co-founder, Google Campus London, 2011; Sen. Industrial Advr, EQT, 2011–13; Co-founder and Venture Partner, Firestartr.co, 2012–; Chief Digital Investment Officer, Modern Times Gp, 2013–15; Co-founder and Venture Partner, mojo.capital, 2015–16. Member, Board: Shazam, 2005–06; Fon, 2006–11; Sine Wave Co., 2011–13; StoryBricks, 2011–14; Culture Label, 2011–14; RollUp Media, 2011–13; Zattikka, 2012–13; Splay Sverige AB, 2013–15; Investinor, 2013–15. Advisor: Seedcamp, 2008–13; Shutl, 2013; Badoo, 2011–13; Bookingbug, 2011–14; Digital Vega, 2011–; Worldwide Computer Co., 2011–14; Creandum, 2011–13; Lepe Partners, 2011–13; MCI Funds, 2011–12; Peak Labs, 2012–14; ClusterHQ, 2012–14; Trustev, 2013–15. Mem. Bd, Policy and Public Affairs, BCS, 2010–12. FBCS 2007. Hon. Dr Computing Kingston, 2011. *Recreations:* running, football, film, art, French cuisine. *E:* anil@hansjee.net. *Club:* Chelsea Football.

**HANSON, Brian John Taylor,** CBE 1996; Joint Secretary, Panel of Reference of the Anglican Communion, 2005–08; Registrar and Legal Adviser to General Synod of Church of England, 1975–2001; Joint Principal Registrar, Provinces of Canterbury and York, 1980–2001; Registrar, Convocation of Canterbury, 1982–2001; *b* 23 Jan. 1939; *o s of* Benjamin John Hanson and Gwendoline Ada Hanson (*née* Taylor); *m* 1972, Deborah Mary Hazel, *yr d of* Lt-Col R. S. P. Dawson, OBE; two *s* three *d*. *Educ:* Hounslow Coll.; Law Society's Coll. of Law; Univ. of Wales (LLM 1994). Solicitor (admitted 1963) and ecclesiastical notary; in private practice, Wilson Houlder & Co., 1963–65; Solicitor with Church Comrs, 1965–99; Asst Legal Advr to General Synod, 1970–75; Dir of Legal Services, Archbishops' Council, 1999–2001. Reviewer, Commn for Health Improvement, 2001–04; Mem., Healthcare Commn Appeals Panel, 2005–09. Mem., Notaries Public Disciplinary Tribunal, 2001–. An Assessor to Archbp of Canterbury under the Clergy Discipline Measure, 2011–. Member: Legal Adv. Commn of General Synod, 1980–2001 (Sec., 1970–86); Gen. Council, Ecclesiastical Law Soc., 1987–2003. Chm., Chichester Dio. Bd of Patronage, 1998–2013; Vice-Pres., Chichester Diocesan Synod, 2001–15. Lay Canon, 2003–12, Lay Canon Emeritus, 2012–, Gibraltar Cathedral, Dio. in Europe. Pres., Soc. for Maintenance of the Faith, 1999–2018 (Vice Pres., 2018–). Guardian, Nat. Shrine of Our Lady of Walsingham, 1984–2015, now Guardian Emeritus; Fellow, Corp. of SS Mary and Nicholas (Woodard Schools), 1987–2015, now Hon. Fellow; Member Council: St Luke's Hosp. for the Clergy, 1985–2001 (Archbishop's Nominee, St Luke's Res. Foundn, 1998–2006); Chichester Cath., 2000–. Governor: St Michael's Sch., Burton Park, 1987–94; Pusey House, Oxford, 1993–2005 (Vice-Pres., 2005–); Quainton Hall Sch., 1994–2005. Warden of the Lower Liberty, St Andrew, Holborn, 2002–13, now Churchwarden Emeritus. Freeman, City of London, 1991; Liveryman, Co. of Glaziers and Painters of Glass, 1992–. FRSA 1996; FInstD 1998. DCL Lambeth, 2001. *Publications:* (ed) The Canons of the Church of England, 2nd edn 1975, 5th edn 1993; (ed) The Opinions of the Legal Advisory Commission, 6th edn 1985; (ed) Atkin's Court Forms, ecclesiastical vol., 1992, 2nd edn 1996; (jtly) Moore's Introduction to English Canon Law, 3rd edn 1992. *Recreations:* the family, gardening, genealogy. *Address:* Garden Cottage, Wappingthorn Farm Lane, Steyning, W Sussex BN44 3AG. *T:* (01903) 812214.

**HANSON, Sir (Charles) Rupert (Patrick),** 4th Bt *cr* 1918, of Fowey, Cornwall; Revenue Assistant, HM Inspector of Taxes, 1993–2010; *b* 25 June 1945; *s of* Sir Charles John Hanson, 3rd Bt and late Patricia Helen (*née* Brind; subseq. Mrs Miéville); *S* father, 1996; *m* 1977, Wanda Julia, *d of* Don Arturo Larrain, Santiago, Chile; one *s*. *Educ:* Eton Coll.; Polytech. of Central London. BA (CNAA) Modern Langs; Dip. in Technical and Specialised Trans. Technical, legal and commercial translator, 1977–83; TEFL (part-time), 1981–83; voluntary charity worker, 1984–85; Inland Revenue, then HMRC, 1986–2010. *Recreations:* classical music, writing poetry, tennis, walking. *Heir: s* Alexis Charles Hanson, *b* 25 March 1978.

**HANSON, Christopher John;** a Deputy District Judge (Civil), since 1998; a Judge of the Upper Tribunal (Immigration and Asylum Chamber) (formerly Senior Immigration Judge, Asylum and Immigration Tribunal), since 2009; *b* Fulford, York, 17 Sept. 1960; *m* 1985, Moira Tonkins; one *s* one *d*. *Educ:* Gravesend Co. Grammar Sch. for Boys; Poly. of Wales (BA Hons Law). Admitted as solicitor, 1987; in practice as solicitor, 1987–2002; Immigration Judge, 2002–08; Designated Immigration Judge, Asylum and Immigration Tribunal, 2008–09. *Recreations:* walking, cycling, athletics, spending time with my family. *Address:* Upper Tribunal (Immigration and Asylum Chamber), Field House, 15 Bream's Buildings, EC4A 1DZ.

**HANSON, Rt Hon. David (George);** PC 2007; MP (Lab) Delyn, since 1992; *b* 5 July 1957; *s of* late Brian George Hanson and of Glenda Doreen (*née* Jones); *m* 1986, Margaret Rose Mitchell; two *s* two *d*. *Educ:* Verdin Comprehensive, Winsford, Ches.; Hull Univ. (BA Hons, PGCE). Vice-Pres., Hull Univ. Students' Union, 1978–79. Management trainee, Co-op. Union/Plymouth Co-op. Soc., 1980–82; with Spastics Soc., 1982–89; Dir, RE-SOLV (Soc. for Prevention of Solvent Abuse), 1989–92. Councillor: Vale Royal BC, 1983–91 (Leader, Lab Gp and Council, 1989–91); Northwich Town Council, 1987–91. Contested (Lab): Eddisbury, 1983; Delyn, 1987; Cheshire W (European Parlt), 1984. PPS to Chief Sec. to HM Treasury, 1997–98; an Asst Govt Whip, 1998–99; Parly Under-Sec. of State, Wales Office, 1999–2001; PPS to the Prime Minister, 2001–05; Minister of State: NI Office, 2005–07; MoJ, 2007–09; Home Office, 2009–10; Shadow Treasury Minister, 2010–11; Shadow Minister for Police, 2011–13, for Immigration, 2013–15. Member: Speaker's Panel of Chairs, 2015–; Justice Select Cttee, 2015–; Intelligence and Security Cttee, 2016–. *Recreations:* football, family, cinema. *Address:* House of Commons, SW1A 0AA. *T:* (020) 7219 5064; (constituency office) 4 Trelawny Square, Flint, Flintshire CH6 5NN. *T:* (01352) 763159.

**HANSON, Sir Rupert;** *see* Hanson, Sir C. R. P.

**HANSON, Samantha;** *see* Bond, S.

**HANWORTH,** 3rd Viscount *cr* 1936, of Hanworth, co. Middlesex; **(David) Stephen (Geoffrey) Pollock;** Bt 1922; Baron Hanworth 1926; Professor of Econometrics and Computational Statistics, University of Leicester, since 2007; *b* 16 Feb. 1946; *er s of* 2nd Viscount Hanworth and Isolda Rosamond, *yr d of* Geoffrey Parker; *S* father, 1996; *m* 1968, Elizabeth Liberty, *e d of* Lawrence Vambe, MBE; two *d*. *Educ:* Wellington Coll.; Guildford Tech. Coll.; Sussex Univ. (BA); Univ. of Southampton (MSc); Univ. of Amsterdam (DEcon). Lectr, Dept of Economics, 1971–92, Reader in Econometrics, 1992–2007, QMC, then QMW, later QMUL. Elected Mem. (Lab), H of L, 2011. *Heir: nephew* Harold William Charles Pollock, *b* 30 April 1988.

**HAPGOOD, Mark Bernard;** QC 1994; *b* 2 April 1951; *m* 1978, Linda Fieldsend; two *d*; *m* 2008, Arzu Kebes; two *s*. *Educ:* Nottingham Univ. (LLB). Called to the Bar, Gray's Inn, 1979, Bencher, 2003. *Publications:* (ed) Paget's Law of Banking, 10th edn 1989 to 13th edn 2007; (contrib.) Halsbury's Laws of England, vol. 3 (1): Banking, reissue, 2005; Bills of Exchange, vol. 4 (1), reissue, 2002. *Recreations:* running, 16th/17th century financial documents. *Address:* Brick Court Chambers, 7–8 Essex Street, WC2R 3LD. *Club:* St Enedoc Golf.

**HAPPÉ, Prof. Francesca Gabrielle,** PhD; FBA 2014; FMedSci; Professor of Cognitive Neuroscience, since 2008, and Director and Head of Department, MRC Social, Genetic and Developmental Psychiatry Centre, since 2012, Institute of Psychiatry, Psychology and Neuroscience (formerly Institute of Psychiatry), King's College London; *b* Cambridge, 2 June 1967; *d of* Peter Bernard Happé and Gabrielle Happé (*née* Forrest); *m* Daniel Richard Gordon; two *s* one *d*. *Educ:* Burgess Hill Sch.; Corpus Christi Coll., Oxford (BA 1st Cl. Hons Exptl Psychol. 1988); University Coll. London (PhD Psychol. 1991). MRC Studentship, 1988–91. Res. Scientist, 1991–95, MRC Cognitive Develt Unit, London; Temp. Lectr in Develtl Psychol., Cambridge Univ., 1993 and 2001; Human Frontiers Sci. Prog. Fellow, Dept of Psychol. and Aphasia Res. Centre, Boston Coll., 1995–96; Sen. Scientist in Cognitive Psychol., 1996–2000, Reader in Cognitive Neurosci., 2000–08, MRC Social, Genetic and Develtl Psychiatry Centre, Inst. of Psychiatry, KCL. Co-founder, Nat. Forum for Neurosci. and Special Educn, 2012–. Pres., Internat. Soc. for Autism Res., 2013–15 (Mem. Bd, 2012–17; Fellow 2018). Member: BPsS 1989; Assoc. for Child and Adolescent Mental Health, 1990–; EPsS 1992. FMedSci 2017. Spearman Medal, BPsS, 1998; EPsS Prize, 1999; Rosalind Franklin Award, Royal Soc., 2011. *Publications:* Autism: an introduction to psychological theory, 1994 (US edn 1995; trans. Danish, 1995, Japanese, 1997, Spanish, 1998, Greek, 2003, Russian, 2006); (ed with Uta Frith) Autism and Talent, 2010; (with S. Fletcher-Watson) Autism: a new introduction to psychological theory and current debate, 2019; (ed jtly) Girls and Autism: educational, family and personal perspectives, 2019; contrib. peer-reviewed papers to learned jls. *Recreation:* making things. *Address:* Social, Genetic and Developmental Psychiatry Centre, Institute of Psychiatry, Psychology and Neuroscience (PO80), De Crespigny Park, Denmark Hill, SE5 8AF. *T:* (020) 7848 0873, *Fax:* (020) 7848 0866. *E:* francesca.happe@kcl.ac.uk.

**HAPPÉ, Rhiannon;** *see* Jones, R.

**HAQUE, Muhammed Luthful;** QC 2015; *b* Loughborough, 26 July 1973; *s of* Serajul and Dilwara Hoque; *m* 2006, Emma Louise Peacock; one *s* one *d*. *Educ:* Loughborough Grammar Sch.; Hertford Coll., Oxford (BA Hons; MA); City Univ., London (MA Law). Called to the Bar, Lincoln's Inn, 1997; in practice as barrister specialising in common and commercial law, 1997–. *Recreations:* golf, cricket, the history of typography, Sadler's Wells Dining Club. *Address:* Crown Office Chambers, 2 Crown Office Row, Temple, EC4Y 7HJ. *T:* (020) 7797 8100. *E:* haque@crownofficechambers.com.

**HARBAGE, William John Hirons;** QC 2003; a Recorder, since 2000; *b* 7 Feb. 1960; *s of* late Thomas William (John) Harbage, solicitor, and of Patricia Margaret Harbage (*née* Amis); *m* 1986, Julia Mary Herschel Dunkerley; one *s* two *d*. *Educ:* Haileybury Coll.; St John's Coll., Cambridge (BA Hons Law 1982, MA 1986). Short Service Limited Commn, 7th Duke of Edinburgh's Own Gurkha Rifles, 1979. Called to the Bar, Middle Temple, 1983; in practice as barrister, specialising in criminal law, 1983–; Asst Recorder, 1999–2000. Chm. Appeal Bd, Prescription Medicines Code of Practice Authy, 2006–. *Address:* 36 Group, 4 Field Court, Gray's Inn, WC1R 5EF. *T:* (020) 7421 8000. *E:* wharbage@36crime.co.uk. *Club:* Luffenham Heath Golf.

**HARBERD, Prof. Nicholas Paul,** PhD; FRS 2009; Sibthorpian Professor of Plant Science, University of Oxford, since 2008; Fellow, St John's College, Oxford, since 2008; *b* 15 July 1956; *s of* David and Muriel Harberd; *m* 1993, Jessica Ruth Harris; one *s* one *d*. *Educ:* Christ's Coll., Cambridge (MA; PhD 1981). Res. Project Leader, John Innes Centre, Norwich, 1990–2007. Hon. Prof., UEA, 2004–07. *Publications:* Seed to Seed, 2006; papers in learned jls incl. Nature, Science, Proc. NAS, Genes and Develt, Current Biol., Plant Cell. *Recreations:* music (playing piano, organ and Javanese gamelan music), walking. *Address:* Department of Plant Sciences, University of Oxford, South Parks Road, Oxford OX1 3RB.

**HARBERTON,** 11th Viscount *cr* 1791 (Ire.); **Henry Robert Pomeroy;** Baron Harberton 1783; Director, CHASE Africa, since 2013; *b* 23 April 1958; *s of* late Major Hon. Robert William Pomeroy and (Winifred) Anne (*née* Colegate); *S* uncle, 2004; *m* 1990, Caroline Mary, *d of* Jeremy Grindle; two *s*. *Educ:* Eton; RAC Cirencester; Univ. of Reading (MA Tropical Agricl Develt 1993). Chartered Surveyor: Portman Estate, 1981–88; P&O Properties, 1988–92; internat. develt aid in Africa and UK, 1994–; Country Dir, Rwanda and Grants Co-ordinator, Send a Cow, 2005–13. Lay Reader, C of E, 2002–. *Heir: s* Hon. Patrick Christopher Pomeroy, *b* 10 May 1995.

**HARBIDGE, Ven. Adrian Guy;** Rector, Seale, Puttenham and Wanborough, 2015–16 (Priest-in-Charge, 2010–15); *b* 10 Nov. 1948; *s of* John and Pat Harbidge; *m* 1975, Bridget West-Watson; one *s* one *d*. *Educ:* Marling Sch., Stroud; St John's Coll., Durham (BA); Cuddesdon Coll., Oxford. Purser, Mercantile Marine, 1970–73. Deacon 1975, priest 1976; Curate, Romsey Abbey, 1975–80; Vicar: St Andrew's, Bennett Road, Bournemouth, 1980–86; Chandler's Ford, 1986–99; RD of Eastleigh, 1993–99; Archdeacon of Winchester, 1999–2000; Archdeacon of Bournemouth, 2000–10, now Archdeacon Emeritus. Hon. Canon, St Peter's Cathedral, Tororo, Uganda, 2000. *Publications:* Those whom DDO hath joined together…, 1996. *Recreations:* landscape gardening, walking, cycling. *Address:* 2 Tudor Cottages, 309 Catherington Lane, Waterlooville, Hants PO8 0TE.

**HARBISON, Dame Joan (Irene)**, DBE 2004 (CBE 1992); *b* 21 Jan. 1938; *d* of Tom and Jane McAllister; *m* 1966, Jeremy Harbison (*d* 2015); one *d*. *Educ:* Victoria Coll., Belfast; QUB (BA 1960; MSc (Educnl Psychol.) 1972). Sen. Lectr, Stranmillis Coll., Belfast, 1972–97. Deputy Chm., Eastern Health and Social Services Bd, NI, 1984–89; Chair, CRE (NI), 1997–99; Chief Comr, Equality Commn for NI, 1999–2005; Mem., NI Judicial Appts Commn, 2005–09; Older People's Advocate for NI, 2008–11. Member: GDC, 1990–99; HFEA, 1990–96; Standing Adv. Commn on Human Rights, 1989–96; Regulation and Quality Improvement Authy, 2005–09; a Civil Service Comr, 2006–09. Chair, Age Concern NI. Hon. LLD Ulster, 2005. *Publications:* (with Jeremy Harbison) A Society Under Stress: children and young people in NI, 1980; (ed) Children of the Troubles, 1983; (ed) Growing Up in Northern Ireland, 1989. *Recreations:* travel, food and wine.
*See also* J. B. McAllister.

**HARBISON, Dr Samuel Alexander**, CB 1998; international health and safety consultant; HM Chief Inspector of Nuclear Installations, Health and Safety Executive, 1991–98; *b* 9 May 1941; *s* of Adam Harbison and Maude Harbison (*née* Adams); *m* 1st, 1964, Joyce Margaret Buick (marr. diss. 1991); three *d*; 2nd, 1991, Margaret Gail (*née* Vale) (*d* 2005). *Educ:* Queen's Univ., Belfast (Hons BSc); Univ. of California, Los Angeles (MSc); Univ. of London (PhD). Reactor Physicist, UKAEA, Windscale, 1962–64; Research and Teaching Asst, UCLA, 1964–66; Research at Rutherford High Energy Lab., Harwell, 1966–69; Sen. Lectr, Royal Naval Coll., Greenwich, 1969–74; Nuclear Installations Inspectorate, HSE, 1974–98. Chm., Defence Nuclear Safety Cttee, 2001–06. *Publications:* (jtly) An Introduction to Radiation Protection, 1972, 7th edn 2018; numerous sci. and tech. papers in learned jls. *Recreations:* golf, music, walking. *Address:* Winnats, Whitehill Road, Meopham, Kent DA13 0NS.

**HARBORD, Clare Mary Petre;** Corporate Affairs Director, Drax Power, since 2017; *b* London, 25 Jan. 1957; *d* of late Captain Thomas Hornsby and of Hon. Patricia Mary Hornsby (*née* Dent, now Bence); *m* 1984, Robert Harbord (marr. diss. 2005); two *s* one *d*. *Educ:* Woldingham Sch., Surrey; Southampton Univ. (BA Hons Archaeol.). Journalist, IPC Mags, 1980–85; Sen. Account Manager, Valin Pollen, 1986–88; PR Manager, Corporate Communications, Eagle Star, 1988–99; Dir, Countrywide, Porter Novelli, 1999–2003; Hd of Communications, E.ON UK, 2004–07; Dir of Communications, MoJ, 2007–11; Corporate Affairs Dir, BAA, 2011–16. FCIPR 2007. *Recreations:* archaeology, travelling, theatre, films, swimming. *Address:* Drax Power, Selby, N Yorks YO8 8PH.

**HARBORD-HAMOND**, family name of **Baron Suffield**.

**HARBORNE, Peter Gale;** HM Diplomatic Service, retired; Clerk Adviser to the European Scrutiny Committee, House of Commons, 2004–16; *b* 29 June 1945; *s* of late Leslie Herbert and Marie Mildred Edith Harborne; *m* 1976, Tessa Elizabeth Henri; two *s*. *Educ:* King Edward's Sch., Birmingham; Birmingham Univ. (BCom). Dept of Health, 1966–72; FCO, 1972–74; First Sec., Ottawa, 1974–75; First Sec., Commercial, Mexico City, 1975–78; Lloyd's Bank Internat., 1979–81; FCO, 1981–83; Head of Chancery, Helsinki, 1983–87; Dep. Head of Mission, Budapest, 1988–91; Counsellor, FCO, 1991–95; Ambassador, Slovak Republic, 1995–98; High Comr, Trinidad and Tobago, 1999–2004. *Recreations:* watching cricket, playing tennis, the arts. *Address:* Lantern House, Mollington Lane, Warmington OX17 1BS. *Club:* MCC.

**HARBOUR, Ivan William;** architect; Senior Partner, Rogers Stirk Harbour + Partners LLP, since 2011; *b* Irvine, Scotland, 3 June 1962; *s* of John Harbour and Celia Harbour (*née* Whitehead); *m* 1993, Roxanne Stacey; one *s* one *d*. *Educ:* Bartlett Sch. of Architecture and Planning, University Coll. London (BSc Hons, DipArch). Richard Rogers Partnership, later Rogers Stirk Harbour + Partners, 1985–, Sen. Dir, 1993–2011; *major projects include:* Parc Bit Masterplan, Mallorca, 1994; ECHR, Strasbourg, 1995; VR Techno Plaza, Gifu, Japan, 1995; South Bank Masterplan, London, 1996; Bordeaux Law Courts, 1999; Amano Res. Labs, Gifu, 1999; Shin-Puh-Kan Shopping Centre, Kyoto, Japan, 2001; Minami Yamashiro Sch., Kyoto Prefecture, 2003; Silvercup Studios, NY, 2003; Nippon TV HQ, Tokyo, 2004; Mossbourne Community Acad., London, 2004; Nat. Assembly for Wales, Cardiff, 2005; Berkeley Hotel, London, 2005; Antwerp Law Courts, 2006; Terminal 4, Barajas Airport, Madrid, 2006 (Stirling Prize, RIBA, 2006); E Darling Harbour Masterplan Competition, Sydney, Australia, 2006; R9 Metro Station, Kaohsiung, Taiwan, 2007; Ching Fu HQ, Kaohsiung, 2007; Maggie's Centre, London, 2008 (Stirling Prize, RIBA, 2009); Jacob K Javits Convention Centre, NY, 2008; Design for Manufacture/Oxley Woods, Milton Keynes, 2009 (Manser Medal 2008); 300 New Jersey Ave offices, Washington, 2009; Port Authy Bus Terminal, NY, 2010; Scandicci Nuovo Centro Civico, Italy, 2013; Parc 1, Seoul, 2014; 8 Chifley Sq., Sydney, 2014; Y:Cube, London, 2015; Barangaroo Masterplan, Sydney, 2015; *current projects:* 360 London, 2004–; 1201 K St, Washington, 2006–; Sporting d'Hiver, Monte Carlo, 2008–; Centre Buildings redevelt, LSE, 2013–; Internat. Quarter, London, 2014–. *Recreations:* building, cycling, drawing. *Address:* Rogers Stirk Harbour + Partners, The Leadenhall Building, 122 Leadenhall Street, EC3V 4AB. *T:* (020) 7385 1235, *Fax:* (020) 7385 8409. *E:* enquiries@rsh-p.com.

**HARBOUR, Malcolm John Charles**, CBE 2013; Director, Digital Policy Alliance, since 2002; Senior Adviser: European Policy Centre, since 2014; Teneo Cabinet DN (formerly Cabinet DN), since 2014; Associate Connected Places Catapult, since 2019; *b* 19 Feb. 1947; *s* of John and Bobby Harbour; *m* 1969, Penny Johnson; two *d*. *Educ:* Bedford Sch.; Trinity Coll., Cambridge (MA Mech Eng); Aston Univ. Business Sch. (Dip. Mgt Studies). CEng, MIMechE, 1975; FIMI 1984. Engr Apprentice, BMC Longbridge, 1967–69; Design and Develt Engr, BMC, 1969–72; Product Planning Manager, Rover-Triumph, 1972–76; Project Manager, Medium Cars, BL Cars, 1976–80; Austin-Rover: Director: Business Planning, 1980–82; Mkting, 1982–84; Sales, UK and Ireland, 1984–86; Overseas Sales, 1986–89; Founder Partner, Harbour Wade Brown, motor industry consultants, 1989–99; Founder Dir, Internat. Car Distribn Prog., 1993–2006; Project Dir, 3 Day Car Prog., 1998–99. MEP (C) W Midlands, 1999–2014. European Parliament: Cons. spokesman on internal market, 1999–2009; Member: Cttee for Legal Affairs and Internal Market, 1999–2004; Cttee for Industry, External Trade, Res. and Energy, 1999–2004; Cons. Delegn Bureau, 1999–2003; Delegn to Japan, 1999–2014; Cttee for Internal Mkt and Consumer Protection, 2004–14 (Chm., 2009–14); Cttee for Industry, Technol., Res. and Energy, 2004–09; Cttee Co-ordinator, EPP-ED Gp, 2004–09; Vice-Pres., Sci. and Technol. Panel, 2002–14; Co-Chm., Eur. Forum for the Automobile and Soc., 2000–09; Chairman: Ceramics Industry Forum, 2000–14; Cons. Technol. Forum, 2004–10; Eur. Manufg Forum, 2009–14; Rapporteur: Eur. Commn Reform, 2000; Universal Service in Electronic Communications, 2001–14; Internal Market Strategy, 2003; Motor Vehicle Type Approval, 2007; Innovative Procurement, 2008; Recreational Craft, 2011; Connected Continent, 2013. Vice Pres., Trading Standards Inst., later Chartered Trading Standards Inst., 2011–. Guardian, Birmingham Assay Office, 2007–14. Mem. Bd, Birmingham Sci. City, 2010–16. Mem. Council, Univ. of Birmingham, 2014–. Gov., Eur. Internet Foundn, 2003–14. Hon. DSc Aston, 2008. *Publications:* reports on the car industry for DTI, OECD, LGA etc. *Recreations:* choral singing, motor sport, travel, cooking. *Address:* The Cottage, Nutlands Farm, Olderrow Lane, Henley in Arden, Warwickshire B95 5NH. *T:* (01564) 637387. *E:* Harbournutlands@sky.com.

**HARCOURT;** *see* Vernon-Harcourt, family name of Baron Vernon.

**HARCOURT, Prof. Geoffrey Colin**, AC 2018 (AO 1994); PhD, LittD; FRSN, FASSA; FAcSS; Fellow and College Lecturer in Economics, Jesus College, Cambridge, 1982–98, now Emeritus Fellow (President, 1988–89 and 1990–92); Reader (*ad hominem*) in the History of Economic Theory, Cambridge University, 1990–98, now Emeritus; *b* 27 June 1931; *s* of Kenneth Kopel Harcourt and Marjorie Rahel (*née* Gans); *m* 1955, Joan Margaret Bartrop; two *s* two *d*. *Educ:* Malvern Grammar Sch.; Wesley Coll., Melbourne; Queen's Coll., Univ. of Melbourne (BCom (Hons) 1954; MCom 1956; Hon. Fellow, 1998); King's Coll., Cambridge. PhD 1960, LittD 1988, Cantab. University of Adelaide: Lectr in Econs, 1958–62; Sen. Lectr, 1963–65; Reader, 1965–67; Prof. of Econs (Personal Chair), 1967–85, Prof. Emeritus 1988; Cambridge University: Lectr in Econs and Politics, 1964–66, 1982–90; Fellow and Dir of Studies in Econs, Trinity Hall, 1964–66. Leverhulme Exchange Fellow, Keio Univ., Tokyo, 1969–70; Visiting Fellow: Clare Hall, Cambridge, 1972–73; ANU, 1997; Sugden Fellow, Queen's Coll., Univ. of Melbourne, 2002; Vis. Professorial Fellow, Univ. of NSW, 2008, 2009, 2010–16; Visiting Professor: Scarborough Coll., Univ. of Toronto, 1977, 1980; Univ. of Melbourne, 2002; Hon. Prof., Univ. of NSW, 1997, 1999, UNSW Sydney, 2016–19. Howard League for Penal Reform, SA Branch: Sec., 1959–63; Vice-Pres., 1967–74; Pres., 1974–80. Mem., Exec. Cttee, Campaign for Peace in Vietnam, 1967–75 (Chm., 1970–72). Mem., Aust. Labor Party Nat. Cttee of Enquiry, 1978–79. Pres., Econ. Soc. of Aust. and NZ, 1974–77; Mem. Council, Roy. Econ. Soc., 1990–95. Lectures: Wellington-Burnham, Tufts Univ., USA, 1975; Edward Shann Meml, Univ. of WA, 1975; Newcastle, in Pol Economy, Univ. of Newcastle, NSW, 1977; Academy, Acad. of Social Scis in Aust., 1978; G. L. Wood Meml, Univ. of Melbourne, 1982; John Curtin Meml, ANU, 1982; Special Lectr in Econs, Manchester Univ., 1983–84; Nobel Conf., Minnesota, USA, 1986; Laws, Univ. of Tennessee at Knoxville, USA, 1991; Second Donald Horne Address, Melbourne, 1992; Sir Halford Cook, Queen's Coll., Melbourne, 1995; Kingsley Martin Meml, Cambridge, 1996; Annual Colin Clark, Univ. of Qld, 1997; Bernard Haskell, Univ. of Missouri, 2006. FASSA 1971 (Exec. Cttee Mem., 1974–77; Jubilee Fellow, 2015); FAcSS (AcSS 2003); FRSN 2016. Hon. Mem., European Soc. for Hist. of Economic Thought, 2004. Distinguished Fellow: Economic Soc. of Australia, 1996; Hist. of Econs Soc., 2004; Hist. of Economic Thought Soc. of Australia, 2012. Hon. LittD De Montfort, 1997; Hon. DCom Melbourne, 2003; Hon Dr rer. pol Fribourg, 2003. (Jtly) Veblen-Commons Award, Assoc. for Evolutionary Econs, USA, 2010; Dist. Alumni Award, Univ. of Adelaide, 2015. *Publications:* (with P. H. Karmel and R. H. Wallace) Economic Activity, 1967 (trans. Italian 1969); (ed with R. H. Parker) Readings in the Concept and Measurement of Income, 1969, 2nd edn (ed with R. H. Parker and G. Whittington) 1986; (ed with L. F. Laing) Capital and Growth: Selected Readings, 1971 (trans. Spanish 1977); Some Cambridge Controversies in the Theory of Capital, 1972 (trans. Italian 1973, Polish and Spanish 1975, Japanese 1980); Theoretical Controversy and Social Significance: an evaluation of the Cambridge controversies (Edward Shann Meml Lecture), 1975; (ed) The Microeconomic Foundations of Macroeconomics, 1977; The Social Science Imperialists: selected essays (ed Prue Kerr), 1982; (ed) Keynes and his Contemporaries, 1985; (ed with Jon Cohen) International Monetary Problems and Supply-Side Economics: Essays in Honour of Lorie Tarshis, 1986; Controversies in Political Economy (selected essays, ed O. F. Hamouda), 1986; On Political Economists and Modern Political Economy (selected essays, ed C. Sardoni), 1992; Markets, Madness and a Middle Way (Second Annual Donald Horne Address), 1992; Post-Keynesian Essays in Biography: portraits of Twentieth Century political economists, 1993; (ed jtly) The Dynamics of the Wealth of Nations, Growth, Distribution and Structural Change: essays in honour of Luigi Pasinetti, 1993; (ed jtly) Income and Employment in Theory and Practice: essays in memory of Athanasios Asimakopulos, 1994; Capitalism, Socialism and Post-Keynesianism: selected essays, 1995; (ed with P. A. Riach) A 'Second Edition' of The General Theory, 2 vols, 1997 (trans. Japanese, 2004); 50 Years a Keynesian and other essays, 2001; Selected Essays on Economic Policy, 2001; (ed) L'Économie Rebelle de Joan Robinson, 2001; (ed jtly) Editing Economics: essays in honour of Mark Perlman, 2002; (with Prue Kerr) Joan Robinson: critical assessments of leading economists, 5 vols, 2002; (ed jtly) Capital Theory, 3 vols, 2005; The Structure of Post-Keynesian Economics: the core contributions of the pioneers, 2006; (with Prue Kerr) Joan Robinson, 2009; On Skidelsky's Keynes and Other Essays, 2012; The Making of a Post-Keynesian Economist, 2012; (ed with P. Kriesler) The Oxford Handbook of Post-Keynesian Economics, 2 vols, 2013; (ed with J. Pixley) Financial Crises and the Nature of Capitalist Money: mutual developments from the work of Geoffrey Ingham, 2013; (jtly) Post-Keynesian Essays from Down Under: theory and policy from an historical perspective, vol. 1, Essays on Keynes, Harrod and Kalecki, 2015, vol. 2, Essays on Policy and Applied Economics, 2016, vol. 3, Essays on Ethics, 2016, vol. 4, Essays on Theory, 2016; many articles and reviews in learned jls and chapters in edited books. *Recreations:* cricket, Australian rules football, running (not jogging), bike riding, reading, politics, gossip. *Address:* School of Economics, UNSW Sydney, Sydney, NSW 2052, Australia; 42/67 St Marks Road, Randwick, Sydney, NSW 2031, Australia. *Clubs:* Melbourne Cricket, South Australian Cricket Association.

**HARCOURT, Geoffrey David**, RDI 1978; DesRCA; freelance consultant designer, since 1962; painter in oils and watercolours, since 2005; *b* 9 Aug. 1935; *s* of William and Barbara Harcourt; *m* 1965, Jean Mary Vaughan Pryce-Jones (*d* 2009); one *s* one *d*. *Educ:* High Wycombe Sch. of Art; Royal Coll. of Art; DesRCA, Silver Medal 1960. FSIAD 1968. Designer: Latham, Tyler, Jensen, Chicago, 1960–61; Jacob Jensen, Copenhagen, 1961; Andrew Pegram Ltd, London, 1961–62; consultant, Artifort, Holland, 1962–95 (domestic and business furniture designer; many models still in prodn including RCA Silver Medal chair of 1960 by Emmemobili, Italy). Visiting Lecturer: High Wycombe Coll. of Art and Design, 1963–74; Leicester Polytechnic, 1982–93; Ext. Assessor for BA Hons degrees, Kingston Polytechnic, 1974–77, Loughborough Coll. of Art and Design, 1978–81, Belfast Polytechnic, 1977–81 and Buckinghamshire Coll. of Higher Educn, 1982–85; Ext. Examr, RCA, 1996–98. Chair design for Artifort awarded first prize for creativity, Brussels, 1978; Member: Design Awards Cttee, Design Council, 1979–80; Furniture Design Wkg Party, EDC, 1986–87; Chm., RSA Bursaries Cttee (Furniture Design Section, 1982–86, Ceramics Section, 1989–91), Woven Textiles, 1992–94, Footwear, 1996–97); approved consultant, Design Council 'Support for Design' initiative. Work exhibited: permanent collection, Stedelijk Mus., Amsterdam, 1967; Prague Mus. of Decorative Arts, 1972; Science Mus., London, 1972; Design Council, London and Glasgow, 1976 and 1981; Eye for Industry Exhibn, V&A, 1987; Nederlands Textielmuseum, 1988; Manchester Prize exhibn, City Art Gall., 1988; St George's Hall, Windsor Exhibn, Architecture Foundn, London, 1993; RCA Centennial Exhibn, 1996; RCA 175th year Exhibn, Design for Industry section, 2012. Painter in oils and watercolours; exhibited Oxfordshire Artsweek, 2011–16, Henley Royal Regatta, 2013, 2014, Henley Mgt Coll., 2015. Master, Faculty of RDI, 2003–05. Chm., Adv. Panel to Lord Lieutenant of Oxfordshire, 1998–2000. FRSA 1979. Freeman, City of London; Liveryman, Worshipful Co. of Furniture Makers, 1975–2009 (Chm., Design Awards Cttee, 1994–97). JP Thame and Henley, 1981–2000 (Chm., Youth Court Panel, 1993–95; Chm. Bench, 1996–98). *Publications:* Geoffrey Harcourt's Sketchbooks, 2 vols, 2017. *Recreations:* painting, bridge, cooking, golf. *Address:* The Old Vicarage, Benson, Oxfordshire OX10 6SF. *W:* geoffreyharcourt.com. *Clubs:* Leander (Assoc. Mem.); Goring and Streatley Golf.

**HARCOURT, Michael Franklin,** OC 2012; Associate Director, Continuing Studies Centre for Sustainability, University of British Columbia, 2009; Premier of British Columbia, 1991–96; *b* Edmonton, Alta, 6 Jan. 1943; *e s* of Frank and Stella Louise Harcourt; *m* 1971, Beckie Salo; one *s*. *Educ*: Sir Winston Churchill High Sch., Vancouver; University of British Columbia (LLB 1968). Lawyer, Vancouver, 1968–72. Alderman, 1972–80, Mayor, 1980–86, City of Vancouver. MLA (NDP) Vancouver Centre, 1986–91, Vancouver-Mt Pleasant, 1991–96; Leader of the Opposition, BC, 1987–92. Sen. Associate, Sustainable Develt Res. Inst., later Sustainable Develt Res. Initiative, UBC, 1996–2009. Director: Vancouver Port Authy, 1998–2006; Vancouver Airport Authy, 1998. Exec. Mem., Nat. Roundtable on Envmt and Economy, 1996–2005. *Publications*: (with John Lekich) Plan B: one man's journey from tragedy to triumph (autobiog.), 2004; City Making in Paradise, 2007. *Recreations*: tennis, golf, ski-ing, watching basketball and football.

**HARCOURT-SMITH, Air Chief Marshal Sir David,** GBE 1989; KCB 1984; DFC 1957; aviation consultant; Chairman, Chelworth Defence Ltd, 1991–96; Controller Aircraft, Ministry of Defence, Procurement Executive, 1986–89, retired; *b* 14 Oct. 1931; *s* of late Air Vice-Marshal G. Harcourt-Smith, CB, CBE, MVO, and of M. Harcourt-Smith; *m* 1957, Mary (*née* Entwistle) (*d* 2018); two *s* one *d*. *Educ*: Felsted Sch.; RAF College. Commnd 1952; flying appts with Nos 11, 8 and 54 Squadrons; Staff Coll., 1962; OC No 54 Squadron, 1963–65; PSO to AOC-in-C, Tech. Training Comd, 1965–67; Defence Planning Staff, 1967–68; OC No 6 Squadron, 1969–70; Central Tactics and Trials Organisation, 1970–72; OC RAF Brüggen, 1972–74; Dir of Op. Requirements, 1974–76; RCDS, 1977; Comdt, RAF Coll., Cranwell, 1978–80; Asst Chief of Air Staff (Op. Reqs), 1980–84; AOC-in-C, RAF Support Command, 1984–85. Dir, DESC, 1991–97. Gov., Downe House, 1993–96. *Recreations*: walking, golf. *Club*: Royal Air Force.

**HARDAKER, Paul James,** PhD; FRMetS, FInstP, CMet; Chief Executive, Institute of Physics, since 2012; *b* 14 Sept. 1966; *s* of late Jack Hardaker and Judith Mary Bolton (*née* James); *m* 2001, Lynwen Davies. *Educ*: Univ. of Essex (BSc 1st Cl. Hons 1988; PhD Maths 1992); Univ. of Portsmouth (Dip Mgt Studies 1998). FRMetS 1993; CMet 2001; CEnv 2005–12; FInstP 2012. Sen. Res. Fellow, Dept of Maths, Essex Univ., 1989–93; Meteorological Office, subseq. Met Office, 1993–2006; Sen. Scientist, then Hd of Internat. Business Unit, 1993–96; Weather Radar Prog. Manager and UK Hydrology Advr, 1996–99; Hd, Remote Sensing and Observations Develt, 1999–2002; Gp Hd, New Products and Services, 2002–04; Chief Govt Advr, 2004–06; Chief Exec., Royal Meteorological Soc., 2006–12. Visiting Professor: Envmtl Scis, Salford Univ., 1999–2011; Sch. of Maths, Physics and Meteorol., Univ. of Reading, 2006–. Chm., Flood Risk from Extreme Events prog., NERC, 2005–11. Non-executive Director: WeatherXChange, 2002–05; Reading PCT, 2005–07; Dep. Chm., NHS Berks West (formerly Berks West PCT), 2007–10. Interim Man. Dir, EcoConnect Ltd, 2004. Member: Bd, Soc. for the Envmt, 2006–11; Bd, Sense about Sci., 2009– (Chm., 2012–); Bd, Sci. Council, 2009–14; Adv. Council on Standards Quality, PAA\VQ-SET, 2008–12. Guest Presenter, BBC Radio Berkshire, 2008–10. Trustee, RMetS, 1996–2006. Ed., Atmospheric Sci. Letters, 1998–2006. *Publications*: contributor to: Hydrometeorology and Climatology, 1997; Weather Radar Technology for Water Resources Management, 1997; Weather Radar: principle advances and applications, 2004; Known Risk, 2005; numerous contribs to learned jls. *Recreations*: tennis, ballroom dancing, music. *Address*: Institute of Physics, 37 Caledonian Road, N1 9BU. *T*: (020) 7470 4800. *E*: paul.hardaker@iop.org.

**HARDCASTLE, Prof. Jack Donald,** CBE 1998; MChir (Cantab); FRCP, FRCS; Lead Clinician, Mid Trent Cancer Network, 1998–2005; Professor of Surgery, University of Nottingham, 1970–98, then Emeritus; *b* 3 April 1933; *s* of Albert Hardcastle and Bertha (*née* Ellison); *m* 1965, Rosemary Hay-Shunker; one *s* one *d*. *Educ*: St Bartholomew's Grammar Sch., Newbury; Emmanuel Coll., Cambridge (Senior Scholar 1954; BA, MA; Windsor Postgrad. Schol.); London Hospital (Open Scholarship 1955; MB, BChir, MChir (Distinction)). MRCP 1961; FRCS 1962; FRCP 1984. House Phys./Surg., Resident Accoucheur, London Hosp., 1959–60; Ho. Surg. to Prof. Aird, Hammersmith Postgraduate Hosp., 1961–62; London Hospital: Research Asst, 1962; Lectr in Surgery, 1963; Registrar in Surgery, 1964; Registrar in Surgery, Thoracic Unit, 1965; Sen. Registrar in Surgery, 1965; Sen. Registrar, St Mark's Hosp., London, 1968; Sen. Lectr in Surgery, London Hosp., 1968. Sir Arthur Sims Commonwealth Travelling Prof., RCS, 1985; Mayne Vis. Prof., Univ. of Brisbane, 1987. Member Council: RCS, 1987–99 (Dir, Raven Dept of Educn, 1994–99; Vice-Pres., 1995–97); Med. Protection Soc., 1995–2003 (Dir). Founder FMedSci 1998. Hon. FRCSGlas. Hunterian Orator, 1999, Gold Medal, 2000, RCS. *Publications*: Isolated Organ Perfusion (with H. D. Ritchie), 1973; various scientific papers. *Recreations*: ski-ing, walking, golf. *Address*: Field House, 32 Marlock Close, Fiskerton, Notts NG25 0UB.

**HARDCASTLE, (Jesse) Leslie,** OBE 1974; exhibition and museum consultant, since 1996; *b* 8 Dec. 1926; *s* of Francis Ernest Hardcastle and Dorothy Schofield; *m* 1968, Vivienne Mansel Richards; two *s*. *Educ*: St Joseph's College, Croydon. British Lion Film Productions, 1943–44; Royal Navy, 1944–47. British Film Inst., 1947–94; Telekinema Festival of Britain, 1951; London Film Fest. admin, 1958–91; Controller, NFT, 1968–91; Museum of the Moving Image: originator, 1981–88; Curator, 1988–94. A Governor, BFI, 2004–10. Sec., Projected Picture Trust, 1994–99; Consultant, London Film Mus., 2009– (exhibns include Charles Chaplin; Ray Harryhausen; Magnum Photographers on Set: Lights, Camera, London; Bond in Action). Co-presenter, Soho Soc. Hour, Soho Radio, 2015–. Pres., The Soho Soc.; Founder Mem., Soho Housing Assoc. *Recreations*: community work, theatre, music, cinema. *Address*: 37c Great Pulteney Street, W1F 9NT.

**HARDCASTLE, Prof. William John,** PhD; FBA 2004; FRSE; Professor of Speech Sciences and Director, Speech Science Research Centre (formerly Scottish Centre for Speech and Communication Science Research), Queen Margaret University (formerly Queen Margaret University College), Edinburgh, 2003–10, now Professor Emeritus; *b* 28 Sept. 1943; *s* of late Gilbert William Hardcastle and Gwendolen Rose Hardcastle (*née* Barber); *m* 1969, Francesca MacDonald; two *s* one *d*. *Educ*: Brisbane Grammar Sch.; Univ. of Queensland (BA 1966; MA 1967); Univ. of Edinburgh (Dip. Phonetics 1968; PhD 1971). Lectr, Inst. für Phonetik, Univ. Kiel, 1972–74; University of Reading: Lectr, Dept of Linguistic Sci., 1974–81; Reader, 1981–89; Prof. of Speech Scis, 1989–93; Queen Margaret University College, Edinburgh: Hd, Dept of Speech and Lang. Scis, 1993–99; Dean: Health Scis, 1999–2002; Res., 2002–03. Vis. Lectr, Sch. of English and Linguistics, Macquarie Univ., Sydney, 1978–79. Member: Acad. Accreditation Panel, Royal Coll. of Speech and Lang. Therapists, 1988; Res. and Commercialisation Cttee, Univs Scotland, 1996–2007; Res. Policy and Adv. Cttee, SHEFC, 1999–2004; Linguistics Panel (sub-panel Phonetics), RAE 2001, 2001; Linguistics Panel, RAE 2008, 2005–. Member Editorial Board: Speech Communication, 1982–92; Clinical Linguistics and Phonetics, 1992–; Internat. Jl Lang. and Communication Disorders, 2001–. Consultant, Lawrence Erlbaum publishers, 2000–. Pres., Internat. Clinical Phonetics and Linguistics Assoc., 1991–2001. Fellow, Inst. Acoustics, 1996–2002; FRSA 1997; FRSE 2007. Mem., Norwegian Acad. of Sci. and Letters, 2007. Hon. FRCSLT 2003. Hon. DSc Napier, 2007; Hon. DLitt Queen Margaret, 2009. *Publications*: Physiology of Speech Production, 1976; (with P. Dalton) Disorders of Fluency and their Effects on Communication, 1977, 2nd edn 1989; (ed with A. Marchal) Speech Production and Speech Modelling, 1990; (ed with J. Laver) Handbook of Phonetic Sciences, 1997, (ed with J. Laver and F. Gibbon) 2nd edn, 2010; (ed with N. Hewlett) Coarticulation: theory, data and techniques, 1999; contribs to conf. procs and vols of studies, res. papers in phonetic, linguistic and speech therapy jls. *Recreations*: walking the Scottish hills, badminton, golf, gardening. *Address*: Queen Margaret University, Musselburgh EH21 6UU. *T*: (0131) 474 0000.

**HARDEN, Peter William Mason;** Publisher, Harden's, since 1991; Managing Director, York Press, since 2011; *b* 1 June 1966; *s* of late John Harden and Susan Harden; *m* 1996, Francesca Elizabeth Freeman; three *s* one *d*. *Educ*: King's Sch., Chester; Trinity Coll., Cambridge (BA 1987). Saudi International Bank, 1987–90; publishing, mkt res. and restaurant reviewing, 1991–. FRSA. *Publications*: Harden's London Restaurants, annually, 1992–; Harden's UK Restaurants, annually, 1999–. *Recreations*: gym, running. *Address*: Harden's Ltd, Forever Beta Space, Ground Floor, 25 Holywell Row, EC2A 4XE. *T*: (020) 7839 4763. *E*: ph@hardens.com. *Club*: Hawks (Cambridge).
See also R. J. M. Harden.

**HARDEN, Richard John Mason;** independent management consultant, since 2014; Founder and Director, Viavenue Ltd (formerly A Private Room Ltd), 2016–19; *b* 26 July 1959; *s* of late John Harden and Susan Harden; *m* 2000, Jeanette Elizabeth Holland; two *d*. *Educ*: King's Sch., Chester; Christ's Coll., Cambridge (BA 1981). Called to the Bar, Middle Temple, 1982; Baring Brothers, 1983–84; Samuel Montagu, 1984–91; Publisher, Harden's, 1991–2014; publishing, mkt res., restaurant reviewing and journalism, 1991–2014. Trustee: London Soc., 2014–18; London Festival of Baroque Music, 2015–18. *Publications*: Harden's London Restaurants, annually, 1992–2015; Harden's UK Restaurants, annually, 1999–2015. *Recreation*: wandering around cities. *Address*: 30 Vincent Square, SW1P 2NW. *T*: (020) 7233 7277. *E*: rh@hardenuk.com.
See also P. W. M. Harden.

**HARDENBERGER, (Ulf) Håkan;** musician; international trumpet soloist; *b* 27 Oct. 1961; *s* of Åke and Mona Hardenberger; *m* 1986, Heidi Thomassen; two *s*. *Educ*: Paris Conservatory. Concerts as soloist with orchestras including LA Philharmonic, Chicago Symphony, Vienna Phil., London Phil., London Symphony, Philharmonia, Orch. des Bayerische Rundfunk, Accademia Nazionale di Santa Cecilia, NHK Symphony, Leipzig Gewandhaus; festivals include Lucerne, Salzburg, BBC Proms. Prof. of Trumpet, Malmö Acad. of Music; Internat. Chair in Brass Studies, RNCM, Manchester; Prince Consort Prof. of Trumpet, Royal Coll. of Music. Hon. RAM 1992. *Address*: c/o KD Schmid UK Ltd, 40 St Martin's Lane, WC2N 4ER.

**HARDIE,** family name of **Baron Hardie**.

**HARDIE, Baron** *cr* 1997 (Life Peer), of Blackford in the City of Edinburgh; **Andrew Rutherford Hardie;** PC 1997; a Senator of the College of Justice in Scotland and Lord of Session, 2000–12; *b* 8 Jan. 1946; *s* of late Andrew Rutherford Hardie and Elizabeth Currie Lowe; *m* 1971, Catherine Storrar Elgin; two *s* one *d*. *Educ*: St Mungo's Primary Sch., Alloa; St Modan's High Sch., Stirling; Edinburgh Univ. (MA, LLB Hons). Enrolled Solicitor, 1971; Mem., Faculty of Advocates, 1973; Advocate Depute, 1979–83; QC (Scot.) 1985; Lord Advocate, UK, 1997–99, Scotland, 1999–2000. Treasurer, 1989–94, Dean, 1994–97, Faculty of Advocates. Chm., Edinburgh Tram Inquiry, 2014–. Chm. of Trustees, Runciman Apse Trust, 2016–. Hon. Pres., Capability Scotland, 2012–. Hon. Bencher, Lincoln's Inn, 1998. *Address*: 4 Oswald Road, Edinburgh EH9 2HF. *T*: (0131) 667 7542.

**HARDIE, Dr Alexander,** OBE 1990; political consultant, 2012–14; *b* 5 March 1947; *s* of Alexander Merrie Hardie and Phyllis A. I. Hardie; *m* 1971, Jillian Hester Rowlands (marr. diss. 2004); one *s* two *d*. *Educ*: Aberdeen Grammar Sch.; Bristol Grammar Sch.; Univ. of Edinburgh (MA); Corpus Christi Coll., Oxford (DPhil). Jun. Research Fellow, Univ. of Bristol, 1972–73; HM Diplomatic Service, 1973–2001: FCO, 1973–77; First Secretary: Budapest, 1977–78; Bucharest, 1979–81; FCO, 1981–86; Lusaka, 1986–90; FCO, 1990–93; Counsellor, Pretoria, 1993–97; FCO, 1997–2001. Fellow and Bursar, Oriel Coll., Oxford, 2001–04. Consultant in Security Sector Reform, FCO, 2005–12; Sen. Advr, Morgan Stanley, with resp. for Africa, 2012–13. Hon. Res. Associate in Classics, Royal Holloway, London Univ., 1998–2001; Hon. Fellow in Classics, Edinburgh Univ., 2007–14, 2016–. *Publications*: Statius and the Silvae, 1983. *Recreation*: classical studies. *Address*: The Old School House, Clava, Culloden, Inverness-shire IV2 5EL. *E*: sandy304hardie@gmail.com. *Club*: Travellers.

**HARDIE, (Charles) Jeremy (Mawdesley),** CBE 1983; Research Associate, Centre for Philosophy of Natural and Social Sciences, London School of Economics, since 2000; *b* 9 June 1938; *s* of Sir Charles Hardie, CBE; *m* 1st, 1962, Susan Chamberlain (marr. diss. 1976); two *d* two *s*; 2nd, 1978, Xandra, Countess of Gowrie (marr. diss. 1994), *d* of late Col R. A. G. Bingley, CVO, DSO, OBE; one *d*; 3rd, 1994, Kirsteen Margaret Tait. *Educ*: Winchester Coll.; New Coll., Oxford (2nd Cl. Hon. Mods, 1st Cl. Lit. Hum.); Nuffield Coll., Oxford (BPhil Econs). ACA 1965, Peat, Marwick, Mitchell & Co.; Nuffield Coll., Oxford, 1966–67; Jun. Res. Fellow, Trinity Coll., Oxford, 1967–68; Fellow and Tutor in Econs, Keble Coll., Oxford, 1968–75 (Hon. Fellow, 1998). Partner, Dixon Wilson & Co., 1975–82. Chairman: Nat. Provident Instn, 1980–89 (Dir, 1972–89, Dep. Chm., 1977); Alexander Syndicate Management Ltd, 1982–95; Radio Broadland Ltd, 1983–85 (Dir, 1983–90); D. P. Mann Underwriting Agency Ltd, 1983–99; W. H. Smith Gp, 1994–99 (Dir, 1988–99; Dep. Chm., 1992–94); Touch Clarity Ltd, 2001–04; Loch Fyne Restaurants Ltd, 2002–05; Brasserie Blanc plc, 2006–11. Director: Alexanders Discount Co. Ltd, 1978–87 (Dep. Chm., 1981–84; Chm., 1984–86); John Swire & Sons Ltd, 1982–98; Amdahl (UK) Ltd, 1983–86; Mercantile House Holdings Ltd, 1984–87; Additional Underwriting Agencies (No 3) Ltd, 1985–2007; Alexanders Laing & Cruickshank Gilts Ltd, 1986–87 (Chm., 1986); Northdoor Hldgs, 1989–93; Fieldfare Internat., 2014–; Granta Publications Ltd, 2018–19; Syngrafii Inc., 2019–. Mem., Investment Cttee, Impetus Private Equity Foundn, 2013–17. Chm., Centre for Economic Policy Res., 1984–89; Treas., REconS, 1987–93; Dep. Chm., NAAFI, 1986–92 (Dir, 1981–). Member: Monopolies and Mergers Commn, 1976–83 (Dep. Chm., 1980–83); Council, Oxford Centre for Management Studies, 1978–85; Hammersmith Health Authority, 1982–83; Arts Council of GB, 1984–86; Peacock Cttee on Financing of BBC, 1985–86. Mem. Council, KCL, 1992–2004 (Dep. Chm., 1997–2004; FKC 2004). Chair: Open Foundn, 2004–09; China Dialogue, 2014–15; Flipside, 2015–17. Fellow, Centre for Social Policy, 2014–. Contested Norwich South, (SDP) 1983, (SDP/Alliance) 1987. Mem. Bd, Sainsbury Centre for Visual Arts, 2015–. Trustee: Esmée Fairbairn Foundn, 1972–2008 (Chm., 2003–07); Butler Trust, 1985–87; IPPR, 2000–09; Somerset Hse Trust, 2001–15; Internat. Hse, 2007–09; Early Intervention Foundn, 2014–17; Granta Charitable Trust, 2019–. *Publications*: (with N. Cartwright) Evidence-Based Policy: a practical guide to doing it better, 2012. *Recreations*: sailing, ski-ing, tennis, walking. *Address*: 23 Arlington Road, NW1 7ER. *T*: (020) 7387 1697.

**HARDIE, Prof. (David) Grahame,** PhD; FRS 2007; FRSE; FMedSci; Professor of Cellular Signalling, University of Dundee, since 1994; *b* 25 April 1950; *s* of Grahame McLean Hardie and Bertha Tyson Hardie; *m* 1977, Linda Margaret; four *s*. *Educ*: Downing Coll., Cambridge (BA 1971). Heriot-Watt Univ. (PhD). University of Dundee: Lectr, 1977–87; Sen. Lectr, 1987–90; Reader, 1990–94. Member: Physiol Medicine and

Infections Bd, MRC, 1997–2001; Molecular and Cell Panel, Wellcome Trust, 2001–04; Internat. Conf. Grant and Short Visits Panel, Royal Soc., 2008–10; Chairs and Prog. Grants Cttee, BHF, 2008–12; Advanced Investigator Panel, Eur. Res. Council, 2011–. FRSE 1998; FMedSci 2002. *Publications:* Biochemical Messengers, 1991; over 350 reviews, chapters and peer-reviewed scientific papers. *Recreations:* sailing, sea kayaking, cycling. *Address:* Division of Cell Signalling and Immunology, College of Life Sciences, University of Dundee, Dundee DD1 5EH. *T:* (01382) 384253. *E:* d.g.hardie@dundee.ac.uk.

**HARDIE, Brig. Donald David Graeme**, CVO 2008; TD 1968; JP; FIMMM; Lord-Lieutenant, Dunbartonshire (formerly Strathclyde Region, Districts of Dumbarton, Clydebank, Bearsden and Milngavie, Strathkelvin, Cumbernauld and Kilsyth), 1990–2007; Keeper of Dumbarton Castle, since 1996; *b* 23 Jan. 1936; *m* 1st, 1961, Rosalind Allan Ker (marr. diss. 1998); two *s*; 2nd, 1999, Sheena Roome. *Educ:* Larchfield, Blairmore and Merchiston Castle Schools. U.T.R. Management Trainee, 1956–59; F. W. Allen & Ker, 1960–61; with J. & G. Hardie & Co., 1961–2001, Dir, 1966–2001, Chm., 1990–2001; Man. Dir, 2001–05, Chm., 2005–10, Preston Stretchform Ltd (formerly Hardie Mgt Consultants, then Hardie Internat. Sales); Director: Gilbert Plastics, 1973–76; Hardie Polymers, 1976–2001; Hardie Polymers (England), 1989–2001; Ronaash, 1988–2000; Tullochan Trust Ltd (Trustee, 1996). Commissioned 41st Field Regt RA, 1955; Battery Comdr, 277 (Argyll & Sutherland Highlanders) Regt, RA TA, 1966; CO GSV OTC, 1973; TA Colonel: Lowlands, 1976; DES, 1980; Scotland, 1985; Hon. Colonel: Glasgow and Lanarks Bn, ACF, 1990–2000; 105 Air Defence Regt, RA(V), 1992–99; ACF Brig. Scotland, 1983–87; Chm., RA Council for Scotland, 1996–2001. President: Dunbartonshire SSAFA, 1992–2007; Dunbartonshire Scout Council, and Girl Guides, 1994–2007; Boys Bde, Argyll and Lennox, 1999–2007; Highland RFCA, 2005–07; Vice-Pres., Nat. Artillery Assoc., 2002–. Hon. Col Comdt, RA, 2003–07. Patron: Cornerstone, 1999–2009; Craighalbert Centre, 1999–2009. Session Clerk, Luss Parish Ch, 2015–. Chieftain, Loch Lomond Games, 1996–2009. JP Dumbarton, 1990. FIMMM (FPRI 1984). KStJ 1997. *Recreations:* fishing, curling. *Address:* East Lodge, Arden, Dunbartonshire G83 8RD. *T:* (01389) 850790. *Clubs:* Royal Scots (Edinburgh); Royal Northern and Clyde Yacht.

**HARDIE, Grahame;** *see* Hardie, D. G.

**HARDIE, Jeremy;** *see* Hardie, C. J. M.

**HARDIE, John Macdonald;** Chief Executive Officer, ITN Ltd, 2009–18; *b* Glasgow, 7 Jan. 1962; *s* of Donald and Mary Hardie; *m* 2005, Nicola Swash; two *s*. *Educ:* Glasgow Univ. (MA Hons English and Philosophy). Procter and Gamble: brand asst, 1983–86; Brand Manager, 1986–89; Associate Advertising Manager, 1989–91; Advertising Dir, 1991–94; Man. Dir, 1994–97; Mktg and Commercial Dir, ITV Ltd, 1997–2001; Walt Disney Co.: Man. Dir and Sen. Vice Pres., 2001–04; Man. Dir and Exec. Vice Pres., 2005–09; non-exec. Chm., Super RTL, 2008; CEO, Jetix NV, 2009. Chm., RTS, 2011–16. Liveryman, Marketors' Co., 2007–. *Recreations:* piano, guitar, golf, TV and cinema, writing. *Clubs:* Caledonian, Marketing Group of GB (Chm., 2012–13), Soho House, Thirty.

**HARDIE, Philip Russell**, PhD; FBA 2000; Hon. Professor of Latin Literature, Cambridge University and Senior Research Fellow, Trinity College, Cambridge, since 2006; *b* 13 July 1952; *s* of late Miles Clayton Hardie, OBE and Pauline Le Gros (*née* Clark); *m* 2012, Susan Elizabeth Griffith; one *s* (and one *s* decd). *Educ:* St Paul's Sch., London; Corpus Christi Coll., Oxford (MA; Hon. Fellow, 2016); MPhil London; PhD Cantab 1990. Editl Asst, Oxford Dictionaries, 1977–80; P. S. Allen Jun. Res. Fellow, Corpus Christi Coll., Oxford, 1980–84; Guest Faculty appt in Classical Hist., Sarah Lawrence Coll., NY, 1984–85; Cambridge University: Fellow and Coll. Lectr in Classics, Magdalene Coll., 1986–90; Fellow, 1990–2002, Emeritus Fellow, 2005, New Hall; Reader in Latin Lit., 1998–2002; Corpus Christi Prof. of Latin Lang. and Lit., and Fellow of Corpus Christi Coll., Oxford, 2002–06. Sather Prof., Univ. of Calif, Berkeley, 2016. Hon. FAHA 2014. *Publications:* Virgil's Aeneid: cosmos and imperium, 1986; The Epic Successors of Virgil, 1993; (ed) Virgil Aeneid 9, 1994; Virgil, 1998; Ovid's Poetics of Illusion, 2002; (ed) The Cambridge Companion to Ovid, 2002; (ed) The Cambridge Companion to Lucretius, 2007; Lucretian Receptions, 2009; Rumour and Renown, 2012; The Last Trojan Hero: a cultural history of Virgil's Aeneid, 2014; Ovidio Metamorfosi, vol. 5 Libri XIII–XV, 2015; Classicism and Christianity in Late Antique Latin Poetry, 2019. *Recreations:* walking, music. *Address:* Trinity College, Cambridge CB2 1TQ. *T:* (01223) 338400.

**HARDIE, Prof. Roger Clayton**, PhD; FRS 2010; Professor of Cellular Neuroscience, University of Cambridge, since 2006; *b* 1953. *Educ:* Emmanuel College, Cambridge (BA 1974); Australian Nat. Univ. (PhD 1979). Max-Planck Inst. of Biol Cybernetics, 1979–85; Dept of Zool., 1985–95, Dept of Anatomy, 1995–2006, Univ. of Cambridge. Rank Prize for Opto-electronics, 2012. *Publications:* contribs to jls incl. Nature, Science, Cell, Neuron, Current Biol. *Address:* Department of Physiology, Development and Neuroscience, University of Cambridge, Downing Street, Cambridge CB2 3EG.

**HARDIE BOYS, Rt Hon. Sir Michael**, GNZM 1996; GCMG 1996; QSO 2001; PC 1989; Governor General of New Zealand, 1996–2001; *b* Wellington, 6 Oct. 1931; *s* of Hon. Mr Justice Reginald Hardie Boys and Edith May (*née* Bennett); *m* 1957, Edith Mary Zohrab; two *s* two *d*. *Educ:* Wellington Coll.; Victoria Univ. (BA, LLB). Admitted Barrister and Solicitor, 1954; Partner, Scott Hardie Boys & Morrison, 1955–80; Chm., Legal Aid Bd, 1978–80; Judge of NZ High Court, 1980–89; Judge of the Court of Appeal, NZ, 1989–96. Pres., Wellington Dist Law Soc., 1979; Treas., NZ Law Soc., 1980. Hon. Bencher, Gray's Inn, 1994. Hon. Fellow, Wolfson Coll., Cambridge, 1995. Hon. LLD Victoria Univ. of Wellington, 1997.

**HARDING**, family name of **Baron Harding of Petherton**.

**HARDING OF PETHERTON**, 3rd Baron *cr* 1958, of Nether Compton, co. Dorset; **William Allan John Harding;** *b* 5 July 1969; *er s* of 2nd Baron Harding of Petherton and Harriet, *d* of Maj.-Gen. James Francis Hare, CB, DSO; *S* father, 2016; *m* 2000, Susannah, *o d* of Richard Ratcliff; two *s* one *d*. *Heir: s* Hon. Angus John Edward Harding, *b* 1 Sept. 2001.

**HARDING OF WINSCOMBE**, Baroness *cr* 2014 (Life Peer), of Nether Compton in the County of Dorset; **Hon. Diana Mary, (Dido) Harding;** Chair, NHS Improvement, since 2017; *b* Germany, 9 Nov. 1967; *d* of 2nd Baron Harding of Petherton; *m* 1995, John David Penrose, *qv*; two *d*. *Educ:* Univ. of Oxford (BA 1st Cl. Hons PPE); Harvard Univ. (MBA 1992). McKinsey & Co., 1988–90, 1992–95; Mktg Dir, Thomas Cook, 1995–98; Global Sourcing Dir, Kingfisher plc, 1998–99; Commercial Dir, Woolworths plc, 1999–2000; various posts, Tesco plc, 2000–08; Convenience Dir, Sainsbury plc, 2008–10; CEO, TalkTalk Telecom Gp plc, 2010–17. Non-executive Director: British Land, 2010–14; Cheltenham Racecourse; Bank of England, 2014–; UK Holocaust Meml Foundn, 2015–. Steward, Jockey Club, 2018–. *Publications:* Cool Dawn: my National Velvet, 1998. *Recreations:* horse racing, looking after my children. *Address:* House of Lords, SW1A 0PW.

**HARDING, Prof. Alan Paul**, DPhil; Chief Economic Adviser, Greater Manchester Combined Authority, since 2016; *b* 14 Sept. 1958; *s* of late Alan Harding and Ada Harding; *m* 2006, Karen Kauffman; one *s* one *d* (twins). *Educ:* Andrew Marvell Sen. High Sch., Hull; Middx Univ. (BA Humanities); LSE (MSc Econ); Nuffield Coll., Oxford (DPhil Politics). Res. Associate, Centre for Urban Studies, Univ. of Liverpool, 1988–92; Sen. Res. Fellow, 1992–94, Prof. of Urban Policy and Politics, 1994–99, European Inst. for Urban Affairs, Liverpool John Moores Univ.; Prof. of Urban and Regl Governance and Co-Dir, Centre for Sustainable Urban and Regl Futures, Univ. of Salford, 1999–2007; Prof. of Urban and Regl Governance and Dir (formerly Co-Dir), Inst. for Political and Economic Governance, Univ. of Manchester, 2007–12; Prof. of Public Policy and Dir, Heseltine Inst., Univ. of Liverpool, 2012–15. FRSA. *Publications:* European Cities Towards 2000, 1994; Regional Government in Britain: an economic solution?, 1996; Is There a 'Missing Middle' in English Governance?, 2000; Changing Cities, 2005; Bright Satanic Mills, 2007; Urban Theory, 2014; articles in Internat. Jl of Urban and Regl Res., Urban Studies, Urban Affairs Rev., British Jl of Political Sci., W European Politics, Govt and Policy, etc. *Recreations:* pre-post-modern music, travelling to see my children, enduring being a Hull City supporter, walking in North Wales. *Address:* Greater Manchester Combined Authority, Churchgate House, 56 Oxford Street, Manchester M1 6EU. *E:* Alan.Harding@greatermanchester-ca.gov.uk.

**HARDING, Andrew Howard**, FCMA; Chief Executive, Management Accounting, Association of International Certified Professional Accountants, since 2017; *b* London, 22 Oct. 1961; *s* of John and Diana Harding; *m* 1988, Candace Greig; two *s*. *Educ:* Uppingham Sch.; Univ. of Bristol (BSc(Econ) 1983); Henley Business Sch. (MBA 2002). ACA 1986; FCMA 2012; CGMA 2012. Auditor, Dearden Farrow, 1983–87; Lectr, Accountancy Tuition Centre, 1987–89; Nat. Trng Manager, Kidsons, 1989–91; Association of Chartered Certified Accountants: Trng Manager, 1991–96; Hd, Professional Standards, 1997–2000; Exec. Dir, 2000–06; Exec. Dir, 2009–11, Man. Dir, 2011–16, Chief Exec., 2016, CIMA. Chm., ATS Chemicals plc, 2014–16. *Recreations:* guitarist, cyclist, skier, scuba diver. *Address:* Association of International Certified Professional Accountants and Chartered Institute of Management Accountants, The Helicon, One South Place, EC2M 2RB. *E:* andrew.harding@aicpa-cima.com.

**HARDING, Andrew William John;** Africa Correspondent, BBC News, since 2009; *b* Epsom, 14 May 1967; *s* of John and Barbara Harding; *m* 1996, Jenny Hodgson; three *s*. *Educ:* King's Sch., Canterbury; Emmanuel Coll., Cambridge (BA Hons English Lit. 1989); City Univ. (Dip. Journalism). Moscow Corresp., Ind. Radio News and Monitor Radio, 1991–94; BBC News: Caucasus Corresp., 1994–96; Moscow Corresp., 1996–2000; E Africa Corresp., 2000–04; Asia Corresp., 2004–09. *Publications:* The Mayor of Mogadishu, 2016; These Are Not Gentle People, 2019. *Recreations:* books, boats. *Address:* c/o BBC News, 18 Bompas Road, 2193, Johannesburg, South Africa. *T:* 114822305, *Fax:* 114823400. *E:* andrew.harding@bbc.co.uk.

**HARDING, Prof. Anthony Filmer**, PhD; FBA 2001; FSA; Anniversary Professor of Archaeology, University of Exeter, 2004–15, now Emeritus; *b* 20 Nov. 1946; *s* of Edward Filmer Harding and Enid (*née* Price). *Educ:* Corpus Christi Coll., Cambridge (MA, PhD 1973). FSA 1983. Durham University: Lectr in Archaeol., 1973–88; Sen. Lectr, 1988–90; Prof. of Archaeol., 1990–2004. Guest Prof., Munich Centre for Ancient Worlds, Ludwig-Maximilians Univ., Munich, 2015–16. Pres., European Assoc. of Archaeologists, 2003–09. *Publications:* (with J. M. Coles) The Bronze Age in Europe, 1979; The Mycenaeans and Europe, 1984; Henge Monuments and Related Sites of Great Britain, 1987; Die Schwerter im ehemaligen Jugoslawien, 1995; European Societies in the Bronze Age, 2000; (with J. Ostoja-Zagórski and others) Sobiejuchy: a fortified site of the Early Iron Age in Poland, 2004; (with R. Šumberová and others) Velim: violence and death in Bronze Age Bohemia, 2007; Warriors and Weapons in Bronze Age Europe, 2007; Explorations in Salt Archaeology in the Carpathian Zone, 2013; Salt in Prehistoric Europe, 2013; (ed with H. Fokkens) The Oxford Handbook of the European Bronze Age, 2013. *Recreations:* music, gardening, walking. *Address:* Department of Archaeology, University of Exeter, North Park Road, Exeter EX4 4QE.

**HARDING, Brian John;** Director, Food and Farming Group, Department for Environment, Food and Rural Affairs, 2007–12; *b* 24 Sept. 1952; *s* of Edwin Ernest Harding and Hilda Mary Harding; *m* 1975, Pamela Bliss; one *s* one *d*. *Educ:* Queen Elizabeth's Sch., Crediton; UCL (BA Geog.). Ministry of Agriculture, Fisheries and Food, subseq. Department for Environment, Food and Rural Affairs: admin trainee, 1974–78; Private Sec. to Minister of State, 1978–80; Sec. to Zuckerman Rev. of Badgers and Bovine TB, 1980–81; Hd of Branch, Food Standards Div., 1981–84; Desk Officer (Agric.), European Secretariat, Cabinet Office, 1984–85 (on secondment); First Sec. (Agric. and Commercial), Washington, 1985–89 (on secondment); Head: Regl Mgt Div., 1990–92; Milk Div., 1992–96; Financial Policy Div., 1996–2000; Director: Policy and Corporate Strategy Unit, 2000–03; Wildlife, Countryside and Land Use, 2003–06; Sustainable Food Chain, 2006–07. *Recreations:* walking, reading, gardening, painting in water colours.

**HARDING, Daniel John;** conductor; Music Director: Swedish Radio Symphony Orchestra, since 2007; Orchestre de Paris, since 2016; *b* 31 Aug. 1975; *s* of Dr John Harding and Caroline Harding (*née* Cameron); *m* 2000, Beatrice Muthelet; one *s* one *d*. *Educ:* Chetham's Sch. of Music, Manchester; Trinity Hall, Cambridge. Assistant to Music Director: CBSO, 1993–94; Berlin Philharmonic Orch., 1995–96; Principal Conductor, Trondheim SO, 1997–2000; Music Director: die Deutsche Kammerphilharmonie, Bremen, 1999–2003; Mahler Chamber Orchestra, 2003–11, now Conductor Laureate; Principal Guest Conductor, LSO, 2006–17; Music Partner, New Japan Philharmonic, 2010–; Artistic Dir, Anima Mundi Fest., 2018–. Débuts: BBC Proms, 1996; Berlin Philharmonic Orch., 1996; Royal Opera Hse, Covent Garden, 2002. Has made numerous recordings. Chevalier, Ordre des Arts et des Lettres (France), 2002. *Recreations:* match-going Manchester United supporter, playing Championship Manager. *Address:* c/o Askonas Holt Ltd, 15 Fetter Lane, EC4A 1BW. *T:* (020) 7400 1700, *Fax:* (020) 7400 1799.

**HARDING, Prof. Dennis William**, MA, DPhil; FRSE; Abercromby Professor of Archaeology, University of Edinburgh, 1977–2007; *b* 11 April 1940; *s* of Charles Royston Harding and Marjorie Doris Harding; *m* 2006, Carole Jennifer Andrée Forbes. *Educ:* Keble Coll., Oxford (BA, MA, DPhil). Assistant Keeper, Dept of Antiquities, Ashmolean Museum, Oxford, 1965–66; Lecturer in Celtic Archaeology, 1966, Sen. Lectr, 1975–77, Univ. of Durham; University of Edinburgh: Dean, Faculty of Arts, 1983–86; Vice-Principal, 1988–91. Member: Board of Trustees, National Museum of Antiquities of Scotland, 1977–85; Ancient Monuments Board for Scotland, 1979–83; Scottish Postgrad. Studentships Awards Cttee, 1981–2001 (Chm., 1997–2001). FRSE 1986. *Publications:* The Iron Age in the Upper Thames Basin, 1972; The Iron Age in Lowland Britain, 1974, repr. 2014; (with A. J. Challis) Later Prehistory from the Trent to the Tyne, 1975; ed and contrib., Archaeology in the North: Report of the Northern Archaeological Survey, 1976; ed and contrib., Hillforts: later prehistoric earthworks in Britain and Ireland, 1976; Prehistoric Europe, 1978; (with I. M. Blake and P. J. Reynolds) An Iron Age Settlement in Dorset: excavation and reconstruction, 1993; (with T. N. Dixon) Dun Bharabhat, Cnip: an Iron Age settlement in West Lewis, 2000; (with S. M. D. Gilmour) The Iron Age

Settlement at Beirgh, Riof, Isle of Lewis, 2000; The Iron Age in Northern Britain, 2004, 2nd edn 2017; The Archaeology of Celtic Art, 2007; The Iron Age Round-house: later prehistoric building in Britain and beyond, 2009; Iron Age Hillforts in Britain and Beyond, 2012; Death and Burial in Iron Age Britain, 2015; Re-writing History: changing perceptions of the archaeological past, 2020.

**HARDING, Hazel,** CBE 2006; DL; Chairman, East Lancashire Hospitals NHS Trust, 2009–13; *b* 17 Dec. 1946; *d* of Trevlyn William Sanderson and Florence Ward Sanderson; *m* 1975, Steven Harding (marr. diss. 2002); four *d*. Member (Lab): Lancashire CC, 1985–2009 (Chm., 1997–98; Chm., Lancs Educn Authy, 1998–2001; Leader, 2001–09); Rossendale BC, 1990–94, 1995–99. Board Member: Burnley Healthcare Trust, 1997–2002; Lancs LSC, 2000–06. Local Government Association: Member: Educn Exec., 1998–2005; Children's Bd, 2005. Founder Mem., Gen. Teaching Council of England, 2000; Chm., Rochdale Local Educn Partnership, 2010–15. DL Lancs, 2009. *Recreation:* voluntary work. *Address:* 21 Hawthorne Meadows, Crawshawbooth, Rossendale, Lancs BB4 8BF. *T:* (01706) 215767.

**HARDING, Rev. James Owen Glyn;** Director and Chief Executive, National Society for the Prevention of Cruelty to Children, 1995–2000, Vice-President, since 2001; *b* 18 Oct. 1942; *s* of Walter James Harding and Elizabeth May Harding; *m* 1965, Sally Goldie; one *s* two *d*. *Educ:* Pinner Grammar Sch.; Univ. of Sussex (BA); Univ. of Exeter (Home Office Letter of Recognition in Child Care); NE Oecumenical Course. Royal Borough of Kensington and Chelsea: Child Care Officer and Sen. Child Care Officer, Children's Dept, 1968–71; Area Officer and Asst Dir, Social Services Dept, 1971–85; National Society for the Prevention of Cruelty to Children: Dir, Child Care, 1986–89; Dep. Chief Exec. and Dir of Children's Services, 1989–95. Mem., Commn of Inquiry on death of Kimberley Carlisle, 1987. Ordained deacon, 2006, priest, 2007; non-stipendiary Asst Curate, Holy Redeemer, Acomb and York Workplace Chaplaincy, 2006–12; permission to officiate and Asst Dir of Ordinands, dio. York, 2012–. Patron, Nat. Assoc. of People Abused as Children. *Publications:* (jtly) A Child in Mind, 1987; The Parentalk Guide to Being a Grandparent, 2001; contrib. to various jls on social work and children's issues. *Recreations:* writing, literature, walking, sport, the theatre. *Address:* Strathmore, 63 Station Road, Upper Poppleton, York YO26 6PZ.

**HARDING, Keith;** Member (C) Mid Scotland and Fife, Scottish Parliament, 1999–2003; *b* 21 Nov. 1938; *s* of late Cyril Dennis Harding and Ella Evelyn Harding; *m* 1974, Elizabeth Anne Fowler; one *s* one *d*. *Educ:* Chipping Norton GS; Oxford Coll. of Further Educn. Newsagent and banker. Mem. (C) Stirling DC, then Stirling Council, 1986–99 (Leader, 1993–96; Opposition Leader, 1996–99). Contested (Scottish People's Alliance) Stirling, Scottish Parly elecns, 2003.

**HARDING, Rt Rev. Malcolm Alfred Warden;** Assisting Bishop, Anglican Network in Canada, since 2009 (Bishop Suffragan, 2007–09); *b* 28 June 1936; *s* of Henry Warden Harding and Grace (*née* Walker); *m* 1962, Marylou (*née* Richards); one *s* two *d*. *Educ:* Univ. of Western Ontario (BA 1959); Huron Coll. (LTh 1962); Univ. of Manitoba (BSW 1965, MSW 1966). Ordained deacon, 1962; i/c of five rural parishes, dio. of Fredericton, 1962–63; Child Welfare Worker, Children's Aid Soc., Ont., 1963–64; Social Worker, 1966–68, Supervisor, 1968–73, Manitoba Dept of Health and Social Develt; ordained priest, 1973; Priest-in-charge, Birtle, Solsgirth, 1973–78; Rector, St George's, Brandon, 1978–92; Archdeacon of Brandon, 1986–92; Diocesan Administrator, Brandon, 1992; Bishop of Brandon, 1992–2001. Ambassador for Anglican Renewal Ministries, Canada, 2001–06. Hon. DD Huron, 1993. *Recreations:* model railroad, fishing, reading, railway enthusiast. *Address:* c/o Anglican Network in Canada, Box 1013, Burlington, ON L7R 4L8, Canada.

**HARDING, Dr Nicholas John,** OBE 2015; FRCGP, FRCP, SFFMLM; Chairman, Sandwell and West Birmingham Clinical Commissioning Group, since 2012 (Interim Chairman, 2011–12); a Founding Partner, Modality Partnership (formerly Vitality Partnership), since 2009; *b* Birmingham, 21 Dec. 1969; *s* of Dr L. K. Harding and Dr C. M. Harding; *m* 1993, Fiona Elizabeth May; three *d*. *Educ:* Univ. of Birmingham (BSc Pharmacol. 1991; MB ChB 1994). MRCGP 1998, FRCGP 2007; DRCOG 1999; PGDip (Cardiol.) 2011; FRCP 2016; SFFMLM 2017. House Officer, Queen Elizabeth and Selly Oak Hosps, Birmingham, 1994–95; SHO, City Hosp., Birmingham, 1995–99; GP Partner, Handsworth Wood Med. Centre, 1999–. Clin. Dir of Commissioning, Heart of Birmingham PCT, 2009–11; Chm., HealthWorks Local Commng Gp, 2011–. Sen. Med. Advr, NHS England, 2017–. Examiner, RCGP, 2003–16. Hon. Prof., Aston Univ., 2016–. Hon. MFPH 2014. *Address:* Handsworth Wood Medical Centre, 110–116 Church Lane, Handsworth Wood, Birmingham B20 2ES.

**HARDING, Marshal of the Royal Air Force Sir Peter (Robin),** GCB 1988 (KCB 1983; CB 1980); FRAeS; *b* 2 Dec. 1933; *s* of late Peter Harding and Elizabeth Clear; *m* 1955, Sheila Rosemary May; two *s* one *d* (and one *s* decd). *Educ:* Chingford High Sch. Joined RAF, 1952; Pilot, 12 Sqdn, 1954–57; QFI and Flt Comdr, RAF Coll., Cranwell, 1957–60; Pilot, 1 Sqdn, RAAF, 1960–62; sc 1963; Air Secretary's Dept, MoD, 1964–66; OC, 18 Sqdn, Gutersloh and Acklington, 1966–69; jssc, Latimer, 1969–70; Defence Policy Staff, MoD, 1970–71; Director, Air Staff, Briefing, MoD, 1971–74; Station Comdr, RAF Brüggen, 1974–76; ADC to the Queen, 1975; Dir of Defence Policy, MoD, 1976–78; Asst Chief of Staff (Plans and Policy), SHAPE, 1978–80; AOC No 11 Group, 1981–82; VCAS, 1982–84; VCDS, 1985; AOC-in-C, RAF Strike Comd, and C-in-C, UK Air Forces, 1985–88; Chief of Air Staff, 1988–92; Chief of the Defence Staff, 1992–94. Dep. Chm., GEC Marconi Ltd, 1995–98; Chm. and Chief Exec., Merlyn Internat. Associates, 1997–2006; Chm., Thorlock Internat. Ltd, 1999–2000. Member; Partnership Korea, 1995–99; Anglo Korean Forum, 1995–99. FRAeS 1983, Hon. CRAeS 1989; FRSA 1988 (Life Fellow 2008). Liveryman, Hon. Co. of Air Pilots (formerly GAPAN), 1989–. Member: Council, Winston Churchill Meml Trust, 1990–2008; Leonard Cheshire Conflict Recovery Centre, 1998–2005. Vice Pres., Guild of Aviation Artists, 1994–. Hon. DSc Cranfield, 1990. Comdr, Legion of Merit (USA), 1992. *Publications:* articles for professional jls, magazines and books. *Recreations:* pianoforte, bridge, birdwatching, fishing. *Clubs:* Garrick, Royal Air Force.

**HARDING, Philip Douglas;** journalist, broadcaster and international media consultant, since 2007; *b* London, 28 April 1947; *s* of Douglas Harding and Leonora Harding; *m* 1979, Margo Blythman; one *d*. *Educ:* Harrow Co. Sch. for Boys; Univ. of York (BA Hons); Wharton Business Sch. (AMP). BBC: News trainee, 1969–70; News writer, BBC Radio News, 1970–72; Producer, TV Current Affairs, 1972–81; Dep. Ed., Panorama, 1981; Dep. Ed., Nationwide, 1981–83; Ed., London Plus, 1983–84; Hd, London and SE Regl TV, 1984–85; Asst Hd, Current Affairs TV, 1985–87; Editor, Today prog., Radio 4, 1987–92; Proj. Dir, then Founding Editor, News Progs, Radio Five Live, 1993–95; Chief Political Advr, 1995–96; Controller, Editl Policy, 1996–2001; Dir, English Networks and News, World Service, 2001–07. Progs and interviews for broadcast media. Editl Trustee, Press Assoc., 2008–; Trustee: One World Media, 2007–12; CPU Media Trust, 2007–. Fellow: Radio Acad., 2000–; Soc. of Editors, 2007–. *Publications:* (contrib.) Is the BBC in Crisis?, 2014; articles in newspapers. *Recreations:* watching football, supporting QPR, walking, travelling, listening to music from across the world. *E:* phil@hardingmedia.com. *Clubs:* Frontline, h.

**HARDING, Rear Adm. Russell George,** CBE 2015 (OBE 2002); Defence Consultant, A. T. Kearney, since 2017; *b* Perth, 13 May 1960; *s* of George and Anne Harding; *m* 1983, Suzanne Pugh; two *d*. *Educ:* BRNC Dartmouth; Edinburgh Univ. (BSc Electrical Engrg 1982). Joined RN, 1978; Watchkeeper, HMS Hermione, 1983–85; flying trng, RNAS Culdrose, 1985–86; 814 Naval Air Sqn, HM Illustrious, 1987–88; 750 Naval Air Sqn as Navigation Systems Instructor, RNAS Culdrose, 1988–89; in command: HMS Brereton, 1989–91; HMS Alderney, 1991; Flight Comdr, HMS Cumberland, 1992–93; Exec. Officer and 2nd in comd, HMS Brilliant, 1993–95; Trng Way Ahead Study, MoD, 1995–96; in comd HMS Brave, 1996–98; Trng Comdr, Britannia RN Coll., Dartmouth, 1998–2000; Air Warfare Desk Officer, Directorate of Navy Resources and Plans, 2000–02, Dep. Dir, Above Water Capability area, 2003–05, MoD; Dep. to Cdre Fleet Air Arm, Navy Comd Portsmouth, 2005–06; in comd HMS Ocean, 2006–07; Hd of Air and Littoral Manoeuvre Capability, MoD, 2008–11; Dep. Comdr, Strike Force NATO, 2011–12 (Dep. Comdr, NATO Libya Operation Unified Protector, 2011); Rear Adm. Fleet Air Arm, and ACNS (Aviation and Carriers), later ACNS (Aviation, Amphibious Capability and Carriers), 2012–15. Mgt Consultant, PA Consulting Group, 2016–17. *Recreations:* running, sailing.

**HARDING, Stephen Mark;** Attorney General, Isle of Man, 2011–16; *b* Liverpool, 11 Nov. 1961; *s* of Bryan Wilfrid Harding and Beatrice Nancy Deeming (*née* Moore); *m* 1997, Frances Tracey Dean; one *s* one *d*. *Educ:* Onchan Primary Sch., IOM; King William's Coll., Castletown; Douglas High Sch.; Lancaster Univ. (BA Hons Orgn Studies). Called to the Manx Bar, 1992; NP, 1996; admitted solicitor, England, 1998; Govt Advocate, IOM, 2002–11. *Recreations:* walking, mountain biking.

**HARDINGE,** family name of **Viscount Hardinge** and **Baron Hardinge of Penshurst.**

**HARDINGE,** 8th Viscount *cr* 1846, of Lahore and King's Newton, Derbyshire; **Thomas Henry de Montarville Hardinge;** Bt 1801; *b* Carshalton, Surrey, 19 June 1993; *s* of 7th Viscount Hardinge and of Sophia Mary Hardinge (*née* Bagnell). *S* father, 2014. *Educ:* Stowe Sch.; Brunel Univ. (engrg). *Recreations:* shooting, tennis. *Heir:* *b* Hon. Jamie Alexander David Hardinge, *b* 4 Nov. 1996. *Address:* 20 Niton Street, SW6 6NJ. *Club:* East India.

**HARDINGE OF PENSHURST,** 4th Baron *cr* 1910; **Julian Alexander Hardinge;** Chairman, Mallory International, since 2002; *b* 23 Aug. 1945; *s* of 3rd Baron Hardinge of Penshurst and Janet Christine Goschen (*d* 1970), *d* of late Lt-Col Francis Cecil Campbell Balfour, CIE, CVO, CBE, MC; *S* father, 1997; *m* 1st, 1972, Anthea June West (marr. diss. 1993); two *d*; 2nd, 2001, Ulrike Adolph. *Educ:* Eton; Trinity Coll., Cambridge. A Page of Honour to HM the Queen, 1959–62. Booksellers' Association: Dir, Book Tokens Ltd, 1984–2004; Chairman: Coll. and Univ. Booksellers Gp, 1985–87; Export Booksellers Gp, 1993–95; Batch.co.uk, 2002–06 (Dir, 1998–2006); Hon. Vice Pres. Director: John Smith & Son, Booksellers, 1998–2001; ESQN Ltd, 2002–11; Hardinge Simpole Publishing, 2001–12; Baobab Ebook Services Ltd, 2013–. Chm., Mind Sports Olympiad, 1998–2002. *Heir:* *b* Hon. Hugh Francis Hardinge [*b* 9 August 1948; *m* 1st, 1970, Penelope F. Dubber; one *d*; 2nd, 1976, Christine M. Hales; one *s* one *d*]. *Address:* Upper Yewdale, 7 Links Road, Budleigh Salterton, Devon EX9 6DF.

**HARDINGE, Frances Melanie,** FRSL; children's author, since 2005; *b* Brighton, 23 Feb. 1973. *Educ:* Tunbridge Girls' Grammar Sch.; Ipswich High Sch.; Somerville Coll., Oxford (BA English Lang. and Lit.; MSt English). Tech. author and graphic designer for TAO Gp, Reading, 1997–2004. FRSL 2018. *Publications:* Fly By Night, 2005; Verdigris Deep, 2007; Gullstruck Island, 2009; Twilight Robbery, 2011; A Face Like Glass, 2012; Cuckoo Song, 2014; The Lie Tree, 2015 (Costa Book Award); A Skinful of Shadows, 2017. *Recreations:* scuba diving, role-playing games, travelling, hiking, volcano-chasing. *Address:* c/o Nancy Miles, Miles Stott Children's Literary Agency Ltd, East Hook Farm, Lower Quay Road, Hook, Haverfordwest, Pembrokeshire SA62 4LR. *E:* frances@franceshardinge.com.

**HARDMAN, Rt Rev. Christine Elizabeth;** *see* Newcastle, Bishop of.

**HARDMAN, John Nimrod,** FCA; Chairman: ASDA Group PLC (formerly ASDA-MFI), 1988–91 (Deputy Chairman, 1986–87; Director, 1984–91); Dewhurst Butchers, 1996–2006; *b* 8 Oct. 1939; *s* of late Harry John Hardman and of Florence Gladys Sybil Anne Hardman (*née* Dolby); *m* 1966, Joan McHugh (*d* 2009); one *s* one *d*. *Educ:* Quarry Bank High Sch., Liverpool; Liverpool Univ. (BComm Hons). FIGD. Duncan Watson & Short, Chartered Accts, 1962–66; RCA Corp., 1967–69; Finance Dir, Thorn Colour Tubes Ltd, 1969–75; Dir, Europe, Africa and Far East, RCA Corp. Picture Tube Div., 1976–80; Finance Director: Oriel Foods, 1981; ASDA Stores, 1981–84 (Man. Dir, 1984–89); Director: Maples Stores plc, 1995–98; Adderley Featherstone plc, 1991–2007. Director: Leeds Develt Corp., 1988–92; Yorks Electricity Bd, 1989–97. CCMI; FRSA. *Recreations:* golf, tennis, shooting, cricket. *Address:* 3 Albert Terrace, Harrogate, Yorks HG1 1HY. *Clubs:* Lord's Taverners; Liverpool Artists, Royal Liverpool Golf, Liverpool Racquets (Liverpool); Pannal Golf (Harrogate).

**HARDMAN, Richard Frederick Paynter,** CBE 1998; CGeol, FGS; consultant explorationist, since 2002; *b* 2 May 1936; *s* of late Dr Charles Ramsay Hardman and of Mary Hardman (*née* Barnsley); *m* 1st, 1960, Janet Quintrell Treloar (marr. diss.); two *s* two *d*; 2nd, 1982, Marilyn Merryweather (marr. diss.); one *d*; 3rd, 1995, Elizabeth Jane Atkinson (*d* 2008); 4th, 2009, Alice Deschampsneufs. *Educ:* Arnold Sch., Blackpool; Corpus Christi Coll., Oxford (MA). FGS 1959; CGeol 1991. Nat. Service, RN, 1954–56. Geologist with BP, in UK, Libya, Kuwait, Colombia, 1959–69; Exploration Manager with Amoco, Superior Oil and Amerada Hess, based in London and Norway, 1969–88; Exploration Dir, Amerada Hess Ltd, 1989–98; Amerada Hess International Ltd: Vice-Pres., NW Europe, 1996–98; Dir and Vice-Pres., Exploration, 1998–2001; Exploration Dir, Regal Petroleum, 2005–06. Director: DENERCO OIL A/S, 1997–2001; Atlantic Petroleum, 2003–16; Dir and Tech. Advr, FX Energy Inc., 2003–15. Mem., Programme Bd, Brit. Geol Survey, 1993–95. Mem., NERC, 1998–2003 (Chm., Sci and Innovation Strategy Bd, 2001–03); Chm., Industrial Liaison Panel, Eur. Consortium for Ocean Res. Drilling, 2010–12. Geological Society: Chm., Petroleum Gp, 1987–90; Pres., 1996–98. Chm., Petroleum Exploration Soc. of GB, 1985–86; Pres., Earth Sci. Teachers Assoc., 1993–95. Chm., Artsline, 2001–03. Chair, Friends of Southwark Cathedral, 2002–06. Petroleum Gp Silver Medal, 2002, William Smith Medal, 2003, Geol Soc.; Lifetime Achievement Award, Petroleum Gp of Geol Soc., 2014. *Publications:* (ed jtly) Tectonic Events Responsible for Britain's Oil and Gas Reserves, 1990; (ed) Exploration Britain: geological insights for the next decade, 1992; papers on chalk as an oil and gas reservoir. *Recreations:* geology, jam making, theatre, music, wide open spaces, early medieval history and art. *Address:* 42 Walcot Square, SE11 4TZ. *T:* (020) 7820 3513. *Club:* Athenæum.

**HARDMAN MOORE, John Halstead;** *see* Moore, J. H. H.

**HARDSTAFF, Veronica Mary;** community activist, Sheffield, since 2007; *b* 23 Oct. 1941; *d* of Rev. Ernest Tutt and Mary Tutt; *m* 1st, 1964 (marr. diss. 1977); one *s* one *d*; 2nd, 2007, Rev. Canon Dr Alan Roy Billings, *qv*. *Educ:* Manchester Univ. (BA Hons German);

Cologne Univ. Teacher of German and French: High Storrs Girls' GS, Sheffield, 1963–66; St Peter's Sec. Mod. Sch., Sheffield, 1969–70; Knottingley High Sch., 1977–79; Frecheville Sch., Sheffield, 1979–86; Birley Sch., Sheffield, 1986–94; supply teacher, 1999–2002. Mem. (Lab), Sheffield CC, 1971–78 and 2002–07. MEP (Lab) Lincs and Humberside S, 1994–99; contested (Lab) Yorks and Humber Reg., 1999. Vice-Chm., Jt Parly Cttee, EP-Poland, 1995–99. *Recreations:* reading, walking, classical music, playing flute, local activism! *Address:* 43 Northfield Court, Sheffield S10 1QR. *T:* (0114) 267 6549.

**HARDWICK, Very Rev. Christopher George,** PhD; Vicar, Tavistock, Gulworthy and Brent Tor, since 2015; *b* 7 Oct. 1957; *s* of Keith Hardwick and Vera Elizabeth Hardwick; *m* 1st, 1982, Linda Dorothy Hicks (marr. diss. 2010); one *s* one *d*; 2nd, 2011, Sarah Katherine Louise White. *Educ:* King Edward VI Sch., Lichfield; Ripon Coll., Cuddesdon; Open Univ. (BA 1994); Birmingham Univ. (MA 1996; PhD 2000). ACIB 1979. Ordained deacon, 1992, priest, 1993; Asst Curate, Worcester SE Team, 1992–95; Chaplain (part-time): St Richard's Hospice, Worcester, 1992–95; RNIB (New Coll.) Worcester, 1992–95; Rector: Ripple, Earls Croome with Hill Croome and Strensham, 1995–2005; Upton upon Severn and Church of the Good Shepherd, Hook Common, 2000–05; Dean of Truro, 2005–11; Priest-in-charge, Pyworthy, Pancrasweek and Bridgerule, 2011–15. RD Upton, 1997–2005; Hon. Canon, Worcester Cathedral, 2003–05. Chm., Worcester Diocesan House of Clergy, 2002–05; Proctor in Convocation, Gen. Synod, 2004–05. A Church Comr, 2007–11. *Recreations:* choral music, current affairs, reading, cooking, entertaining, sailing. *Address:* The Vicarage, 5A Plymouth Road, Tavistock, Devon PL19 8AU.

**HARDWICK, Matthew Richard;** QC 2014; *b* Haslemere, Surrey, 14 March 1969; *s* of Dr Richard Gerald Hardwick and Mrs Richard Hardwick; *m* 2002, Philippa Anne; two *s* two *d*. *Educ:* Marlborough Coll.; Trinity Coll., Cambridge (BA Classics and Law 1991); Université Libre de Bruxelles (Licence spéciale en droit européen 1993). Called to the Bar, Gray's Inn, 1994. Member: Commercial Bar Assoc.; Chancery Bar Assoc. *Recreations:* family walks and bike rides, Lakeland swims, chaotic sailing trips with family (and two dogs), chopping and stacking wood with my sons and daughters, singing (croakily). *Address:* Springhead, Marley Lane, near Haslemere, W Sussex GU27 3RE. *T:* 07788 743472. *E:* mhardwick@3vb.com.

**HARDWICK, Nicholas Lionel,** CBE 2010; Professor of Criminal Justice, Royal Holloway, University of London, since 2016; *b* 19 July 1957; *s* of Lionel and Nancy Hardwick; one *d*; *m* 1985, Susan Heaven; one *s*. *Educ:* Epsom Coll.; Hull Univ. (BA Hons English Lit. 1979). Youth Training Manager, NACRO, 1980–85; Dep. Chief Exec., Soc. Voluntary Associates, 1986; Chief Executive: Centrepoint, 1986–95; British Refugee Council, subseq. Refugee Council, 1995–2003; Shadow Chm., 2003–04, Chm., 2004–10, Ind. Police Complaints Commn; HM Chief Inspector of Prisons for England and Wales, and Chair, UK Nat. Preventive Mechanism, 2010–16; Chm., Parole Bd of England and Wales, 2016–18. Special Advr, Rough Sleeping, DoE, 1991. Chm., Housing Ombudsman Service, 2010–13. Chm., European Council for Refugees and Exiles, 1999–2003. Chm., Gtr London Radio Adv. Council, 1993–95; Mem., BBC SE Regl Adv. Cttee, 1993–95. Member: Social Security Adv. Cttee, 1994–99; Holocaust Meml Day Steering Gp, 2001–05. Bd Mem., Stonebridge HAT, 1994–97. Trustee: Youth Hostel Assoc., 2007–09; New Horizon Youth Centre, 2009– (Chair, 2016–); Prisoners Abroad, 2017–; London Housing Foundn, 2017–. Patron: Unlock, 2016–; Zahid Mubarek Trust, 2017–. FRSA 1995. Hon. Fellow, Dept of Criminology, Univ. of Leicester, 2013. Hon. Bencher, Middle Temple, 2017. Hon. DSSc Wolverhampton, 2002; Hon. DLitt Hull, 2011; Hon. DLaws Leeds Beckett, 2016. *Recreations:* walking, Spain, Queens Park Rangers FC.

**HARDWICKE, 10th Earl of,** *cr* 1754; **Joseph Philip Sebastian Yorke;** Baron Hardwicke 1733; Viscount Royston 1754; Senior Consultant, Hartwell Buck Ltd, since 2015; *b* 3 Feb. 1971; *s* of Philip Simon Prospero Rupert Lindley, Viscount Royston (*d* 1973) and Virginia Anne (*d* 1988), *d* of Geoffrey Lyon; *S* grandfather, 1974; *m* 2008, Siobhan Loftus; one *s*. *Heir:* *s* Viscount Royston, *qv*.

**HARDY;** *see* Gathorne-Hardy, family name of Earl of Cranbrook.

**HARDY, Alan;** Member (C) for Brent North, Greater London Council, 1967–86 (Chairman, Finance and Establishment Committee, 1977–81); *b* 24 March 1932; *s* of late John Robert Hardy and Emily Hardy; *m* 1972, Betty Howe (*d* 2010), *d* of late Walter and Hilda Howe. *Educ:* Hookergate Grammar Sch.; Univ. of Manchester; Inst. of Historical Res., Univ. of London (MA). Res. Asst to Sir Lewis Namier, History of Parliament Trust, 1955–56; Res. Officer and Dep. Dir, London Municipal Soc., 1956–63; Mem. British Secretariat, Council of European Municipalities, 1963–64. Member: Local Authorities' Conditions of Service Adv. Bd, 1977–81; Nat. Jt Council for Local Authorities' Services (Manual Workers), 1977–81. Mem. Bd, Harlow Develt Corp., 1968–80. Hon. Life Pres., Brent North Conservative Assoc., 1986. Contested (C) Islington SW, 1966. *Publications:* Queen Victoria Was Amused, 1976; The Kings' Mistresses, 1980. *Recreation:* admiring old things. *Address:* The Old Garden, 20 Ledger Lane, Outwood, Wakefield WF1 2PH. *T:* (01924) 823771. *Club:* Naval.

**HARDY, Amanda Jane;** QC 2015; *b* Hornchurch, Essex, 12 Dec. 1969; *d* of late V. W. M. Richards and M. V. Richards; *m* 1994, Matthew David Hardy; three *d*. *Educ:* City of London Sch. for Girls; King's Coll. London (LLB Hons; LLM Tax; AKC). Called to the Bar, Middle Temple, 1993, Bencher, 2017; in practice as barrister, specialising in revenue law. Chair, Chancery Bar Litigants in Person Scheme, 2013–17. Chancery Bar Association: Mem., Main Cttee, 2012–; Hon. Sec., 2016–18; Chair: Pro Bono Sub-cttee, 2013–17; Wellbeing and Corporate Social Responsibility Cttee, 2018–; Vice Chair, 2018–; Mem., Tech. Cttee, Soc. of Trust and Estate Planners, 2015–. Freedom, City of London, 2011; Liveryman, Tax Advisers' Co., 2014–. *Publications:* (with R. Venables) Inheritance Tax Planning, 3rd edn 1997; International Taxation of Trusts, 2004, 2014 (looseleaf); Tolley's Statutory Residence Test, 2nd edn 2017. *Recreations:* my family, reading, theatre. *Address:* 5 Stone Buildings, Lincoln's Inn, WC2A 3XT. *T:* (020) 7242 2601.

**HARDY, Andrew; His Honour Judge Hardy;** a Circuit Judge, since 2018; *b* Consett, Co. Durham, 18 Aug. 1964; *s* of Thomas Davison Hardy and Irene Hardy; *m* 1996, Erica Jane Soady; one *s* one *d*. *Educ:* Manchester Poly. (LLB Hons). Admitted solicitor, 1989; a Dep. District Judge, 2005–10; a District Judge, 2010–18. *Recreations:* cycling, football.

**HARDY, Anna Gwenllian;** *see* Somers Cocks, Hon. A. G.

**HARDY, Rev. Canon Brian Albert;** Rector, All Saints, St Andrews, 1991–96; *b* 3 July 1931; *s* of Albert Charles Hardy and Edith Maude Sarah Mabe. *Educ:* City Boys' School, Leicester; St John's Coll., Oxford (MA, DipTheol); Westcott House, Cambridge. Curate, Rugeley, Staffs, 1957–62; Chaplain, Downing Coll., Cambridge, 1962–66; Livingston (West Lothian) Ecumenical Team Ministry, 1966–74; Churches' Planning Officer for Telford, Salop, 1974–78; Chaplain, Coates Hall Theological Coll., Edinburgh, 1978–82; Rector, St Columba's by the Castle Episcopal Church, Edinburgh, 1982–91; Episcopalian Chaplain, Royal Infirmary of Edinburgh and Royal Edinburgh Hosp., 1982–86; Dean of the dio. of Edinburgh, 1986–91. Hon. Canon, Edinburgh Cathedral, 1991. *Recreation:* music, especially choral and piano. *Address:* 3/3 Starbank Road, Newhaven, Edinburgh EH5 3BN. *T:* (0131) 551 6783.

**HARDY, David Ian Brooker;** Director, Distance Education International, 2007–19; *b* 28 Sept. 1950; *s* of late Leslie Hardy and Ruth Eveline Hardy (*née* Brooker); *m* 1979, Christine Mary Wilson; two *d*. *Educ:* Bradford Grammar Sch.; Univ. of London (BSc Hons); Univ. of Leeds (Grad. Cert Ed). Chartered FCIPD. Dept of Educn, Leeds City Council, 1979–85; Department of Education and Science: Yorks and Humberside, 1985–86; Nat. Manager, Post Experience Vocational Educn, 1986–90; Asst Sec., 1990; Chief Exec., 1990–2000, Hon. Pres., 2000–01, Open Poly., then Open Learning Foundn; Chief Exec., Open Learning Internat., 2002–07. Chm., European Open Univ. Network BV, 1996–2001. Moderator, BTEC, 1982–85; Member: UGC/NAB Standing Cttee on Continuing Educn, 1986–90; Inter-Ministerial Rev. of Highly Qualified Manpower, 1989–90; CNAA, 1991–92; Bd, Eur. Assoc. Distance Teaching Univs, 1993–2001 (Pres., 1999–2001); Eur. Open and Distance Learning Liaison Cttee, 1999–2002. Vice Pres. (Europe), Internat. Council for Open and Distance Educn, 1999–2002. Advr on educn reform to govts of Kazakhstan, Kyrgyzstan, Georgia, Azerbaijan, Russian Fedn, Turkey and Romania, 2002–18; advr on univ. reform in 25 other countries. Internat. observer for election of Pres., Republic of Uzbekistan, 2016. Vis. Lectr, Immanuel Kant State Univ. of Russia, 2007–08. Hon. Mem., Central Asian Business Women's Assoc., 2007–. Mem. Council, Bradford Chamber of Commerce, 1982–86. Mem., RIIA, 2012–. MInstD 2014. *Publications:* (jtly) Onchocerciasis in Zaire, 1977; articles in learned jls on post-secondary education reform. *Recreations:* Central Asia, swimming, fell walking, travel, trackdays. *E:* d.i.b.hardy@outlook.com.

**HARDY, David Malcolm;** Chief Executive, PowerPlay Golf Holdings Limited, since 2016 (Director, since 2008); *b* 16 July 1955; *s* of Roy Hardy and late Mary Hardy; *m* 1981 (marr. diss. 1994); one *s* one *d*; *m* 1995, Marion Dorothy Brazier. *Educ:* Westcliff High Sch. ACIB; FCT. Barclays Bank, 1973–81; Barclays Merchant Bank, 1981–85; LCH.Clearnet (formerly London Clearing House), 1985–2006, Gp Chief Exec., 1987–2006; Hd, Strategic Mkt Develt, MF Global, 2007–08. Director: London Commodity Exchange (1986) Ltd, 1991–96; Internat. Petroleum Exchange of London Ltd, 1993–99; Futures and Options Assoc., 1993–2006; Inst. of Financial Markets, US, 2000–10; GCSA LLC (US), 2012– (Chm., 2013–); SBL Network Ltd, 2016–18 (Chm., 2014–16); Asterisk Network Solutions, 2018– (Chm., 2018–). Mem., Adv. Bd, Cleartrade Exchange Pte Ltd, 2011–16. Member: FSA Practitioner Panel, 2001–06. FRSA. Freeman, City of London, 1994; Liveryman, Co. of World Traders, 1993; Mem., Internat. Bankers' Co., 2005–10. Member: Futures Industry Hall of Fame, 2009; Securities Services Hall of Fame, 2009. *Recreations:* golf, photography. *E:* oak.park@mac.com. *Clubs:* Royal Automobile; West Byfleet Golf.

**HARDY, Sir David (William),** Kt 1992; Chairman, Transport Research Laboratory, 1996–2007; Chairman of Trustees, National Maritime Museum, 1995–2005 (Trustee, 1992); *b* 14 July 1930; 3rd *s* of late Brig. John H. Hardy, CBE, MC; *m* 1957, Rosemary, *d* of late Sir Godfrey F. S. Collins, KCIE, CSI, OBE; one *s* one *d*. *Educ:* Wellington Coll.; Harvard Business School (AMP). Chartered Accountant. Served 2nd RHA, 2/Lt, 1953–54. Funch Edye & Co. Inc., NY, New Orleans and Norfolk, Va, 1954–64 (Dir, 1960); Vice Pres. Finance and Admin, Imperial Tobacco, USA, 1964–70; HM Govt Co-ordinator of Industrial Advrs, 1970–72; Gp Finance Dir, Tate & Lyle Ltd, 1972–77; Dir, Ocean Transport & Trading PLC, 1977–83; Chairman: Ocean Inchcape, 1980–83; London Park Hotels, 1983–87; Globe Investment Trust, 1983–90 (Dir, 1976–90); Docklands Light Railway, 1984–87; Swan Hunter, 1986–88; MGM Assurance, 1986–2000 (Dep. Chm., 1985–86; Dir, 1985–2000); Europa Minerals, 1991–94; Bankers Trust Investment Management, 1992–94; Burmine Ltd, 1992–96; Y. J. Lovell, 1994–99; Colliers Capital UK, 2004–07; Committed Capital UK, 2004–; 100 Group Chartered Accountants, 1986–88; LDDC, 1988–92 (Dep. Chm., 1988); Deputy Chairman: LRT, 1984–87; Agricultural Mortgage Corp., 1985–92 (Dir, 1973–); Director: Sturge Holdings PLC, 1985–95; Waterford Wedgwood plc (formerly Waterford Glass), 1984–90; Paragon Group, 1985–88; Aberfoyle Holdings, 1986–91; Chelsea Harbour Ltd, 1989–90; Electra Kingsway Managers Hldgs Ltd, 1990–91; Tootal Gp, 1990–91; CIBA-GEIGY, 1991–96; Hanson, 1991–2001; J. A. Devenish, 1991–93; Stirling-Lloyd Holdings, 1992–; James Fisher & Sons, 1993–2003 (Chm., 1993–94); Milner Estates (formerly Conrad Ritblat) plc, 1996–99; Imperial Tobacco Gp, 1996–2001; Sons of Gwalia, 1996–99; Milner Consultancies, 2000–01; Fitzhardinge, 2001–04; Colliers CRE, 2004–07; Adv. Dir, HSBC Investment Banking, 1995–97. Chm., Engrg Marketing Adv. Cttee, DTI, 1989–90; Member: NEDC Cttee for Agriculture, 1970–72; Export Credit Guarantees Adv. Council, 1973–78; Industrial Develt Adv. Bd, DTI, 1992–96; Co-opted Council of Inst. of Chartered Accountants, 1974–78; Economic and Fiscal Policy Cttee, CBI, 1981–88; Council, BIM, 1974–78 (CCMI (CBIM 1975)). Mem., Develt Cttee, NACF, 1988–98; Vice Chm., St Katherine and Shadwell Trust, 2000– (Mem., 1990–); Founder Mem., Royal Albert Dock Trust, 1992–; Dir, Greenwich Millennium Trust, 1996–2001; Trustee: Mary Rose Trust, 2000–; Sir John Fisher Charitable Foundn, 2008–. Pres., Poplar, Blackwall and Dist Rowing Club, 1992–; Patron, Pitlochry Angling Club, 1994–. Gov., Chelsea Open Air Nursery Sch., 1992–2004 (Dep. Chm., 1994–2004). Hon. British Consul, Norfolk, Va, 1960–62. Member: Co. of Chartered Accountants, 1976; Co. of Shipwrights, 1990. Younger Brother, Trinity House, 1996. FCILT (FCIT 1988). Hon. LLD Greenwich, 2003. *E:* seahardy@aol.com. *Clubs:* Brooks's, Beefsteak, MCC, Flyfishers', HAC.

**HARDY, Emma Ann;** MP (Lab) Hull West and Hessle, since 2017; two *d*. Teacher, Willerby Primary Sch., 2005–15; trade union organiser, 2015–17. Mem. (Lab), Hessle Town Council, 2015–. Mem., Educn Cttee, H of C, 2017–. *Address:* House of Commons, SW1A 0AA.

**HARDY, Sir James (Gilbert),** Kt 1981; OBE 1975; Consultant, Accolade Wines Australia (formerly Hardy Wine Company, then Constellation Wines Australia), since 2003; Senior Partner, Leadership, CMLpartners Ltd Executive Search, 2011–13; *b* 20 Nov. 1932; *s* of Tom Mayfield Hardy and Eileen C. Hardy; *m* 1st, 1956, Anne Christine Jackson (marr. diss. 1991); two *s*; 2nd, 1991, Joan Margaret McInnes. *Educ:* St Peter's Coll., Adelaide, SA; S Australian Sch. of Mines; S Australian Inst. of Technol. (Dip. in Accountancy). FCPA; FAICD. National Service, 13th Field Artillery Regt, Adelaide, 1951. Elder Smith & Co. Ltd, 1951; J. C. Correll & Co., 1952; Thomas Hardy & Sons Pty Ltd, Winemakers, Adelaide, 1953–92: Shipping Clerk, Sales Rep., Sales Supervisor and Lab. Asst, 1953–62; Dir and Manager, Sydney Br., 1962–77; Regional Dir, Eastern Australia, 1977–81; Chm. of Dirs, 1981–92; Chm. of Dirs, Houghton Wines Pty Ltd, 1981–92; Dir, BRL Hardy Ltd, 1992–2002. Director: S Australian Film Corp., 1981–87; America's Cup Challenge 1983 Ltd, 1981–85; Advertiser Newspapers Ltd, 1983–88; Lorna Hodgkinson Sunshine Home Ltd, 1993–2003. Dep. Chm., Racing Rules Cttee, Yachting Fedn, 1969–81; Dir of Sailing/Captain, S Australian Challenge for the Defence of America's Cup 1984–87. Vice Pres., Internat. 12 Metre Assoc., 1986–92. Treasurer, Liquor Trade Supervisory Council of NSW, 1965–70; Fellow, Catering Inst. of Australia, 1972; Pres., Wine and Brandy Assoc. of NSW, 1980–83. NSW Chm., Aust. National Travel Assoc., 1976; Vice Pres., Royal Blind Soc. of NSW, 1980–88 (Mem. Council, 1967–91); Pres., NSW Aust. Football League and Sydney Football League, 1982–83; Pres., "One and All" Sailing Ship Assoc. of SA Inc., 1981–90; Chm., Adelaide 1998 Commonwealth Games Bid, 1990–92; Mem., Bd of Advice, Rothmans Nat. Sport Foundn, 1985–87; Trustee: Rothmans Foundn, 1987–93; Sydney Cricket and Sports Ground Trust, 1990–95; Mem., Council, Australian Nat. Maritime

Mus., 1992–97; Dir/Trustee, HM Bark Endeavour Foundn, 1996–2003. Chairman: Adv. Cttee, Life Educn Centre of SA, 1988–91; Landcare Australia Ltd Foundn, 1994–98; Adv. Cttee, Natural Heritage Trust, 1998–2009. Pres., Australia Day Regatta, Sydney, 2004–11. Member: Exec. Cttee, Neurosurgical Res. Foundn of SA, 1988–2004; Adv. Bd, John Curtin Sch. of Medical Res., ANU, Canberra, 1982–87. Dep. Grand Master, United Grand Lodge of NSW, 1977–80. Australian Yachtsman of the Year, 1981; inducted into America's Cup Hall of Fame, 1994. *Relevant publication*: Sir James Hardy: an adventurous life, by Rob Mundle, 1993. *Recreation*: yachting (skipper or helmsman in America's Cup and Admiral's Cup races). *Address*: Accolade Wines Australia, PO Box 96, Botany, NSW 1455, Australia. *T*: (2) 96665855, *Fax*: (2) 93169738. *Clubs*: Royal Ocean Racing; Australian, Tattersalls, Royal Sydney Yacht Squadron (Sydney); Cruising Yacht of Australia (NSW); Royal Perth Yacht; Royal Queensland Yacht; Fort Worth Boat (Texas, USA).

**HARDY, Joanna;** independent jewellery consultant and broadcaster; *b* London, 9 Nov. 1961; *d* of Albert Edward John Hardy and Julia Hardy; *m* 1996, Craig Emerson; one *s* one *d*. *Educ*: Littlefields Sch.; Bedales Sch.; W Surrey Sch. of Art and Design; Sir John Cass Sch. of Art and Design (Diamond Dip. 1983). FGA 1982. Rough diamond sorter/valuer, De Beers Diamond Trading Co., London, 1982–84; Asst Manager, Polished Diamond Buying Office, J C Ginder Pty Ltd, Antwerp, 1985–86; Diamond Dealer, J C Ginder Ltd, Diamond Merchants, London, 1986–89; Diamond Specialist and Antique Jewellery Valuer and Cataloguer, Phillips Fine Art Auctioneers, London, 1989–92; travelled overland through SE Asia to Australia, 1992–94; Sen. Jewellery Specialist, Dir and Auctioneer, Sotheby's, 1995–2009. Jewellery Specialist, BBC Antiques Roadshow, 2007–. FRSA 2010. Freeman, City of London, 2006; Liveryman, Goldsmiths' Co., 2013 (Mem., Ct of Assts, 2017). *Publications*: Collect Contemporary Jewellery, 2012; (with J. Self) Emerald, 2013; Ruby, 2017; contribs to jewellery mags and to newspapers. *Recreations*: music, golf, arts, travel, gardening, photography, opera, theatre. *Address*: London, SW19. *E*: joanna@joannahardy.com. *Club*: Royal Over-Seas League.

**HARDY, Prof. John,** PhD; FMedSci; FRS 2009; Professor of Neuroscience, since 2007, Chair of Molecular Biology of Neurological Disease, and Head of Department of Molecular Neuroscience, University College London. *Educ*: Univ. of Leeds (BSc 1976); Imperial Coll. London (PhD). Postdoctoral Fellow, MRC Neuropathogenesis Unit, Newcastle upon Tyne, 1979–83; Asst Prof., Swedish Brain Bank, Umeå, 1983–84; Asst Prof., 1984–89, Associate Prof., 1989–92, Dept of Biochemistry and Molecular Genetics, St Mary's Hospital Med. Sch., Imperial Coll. London; Pfeiffer Prof. of Alzheimer's Res., Univ. of S Florida, 1992–96; Consultant and Prof. of Neuroscience, Mayo Clinic, Jacksonville, Fla, 1996–2001 (Vis. Scientist, 2001–04); Sen. Investigator and Chief, Lab. of Neurogenetics, Nat. Inst. of Ageing, Bethesda, 2001–07. FMedSci 2008. Robert A. Pritzker Prize for Leadership in Parkinson's Res., 2015; Breakthrough Prize in Life Scis, 2015; Brain Prize, Lundbeck Foundn, Denmark, 2018. *Publications*: contrib. articles to jls. *Address*: UCL Institute of Neurology, Queen Square, WC1N 3BG.

**HARDY, Maj.-Gen. John Campbell,** CB 1985; LVO 1978; Administrator, Sion College, 1993–2000; *b* 13 Oct. 1933; *s* of late General Sir Campbell Hardy, KCB, CBE, DSO; *m* 1961, Jennifer Mary Kempton; one *s* one *d*. *Educ*: Sherborne Sch. Joined Royal Marines, 1952; 45 Commando, 1954; HMS Superb, 1956; Instructor, NCOs' School, Plymouth, 1957; 42 Commando, 1959; 43 Commando, 1962; Adjt, Jt Service Amphibious Warfare Centre, 1964; Company Comdr, 45 Commando, 1965; sc Bracknell, 1966; Instr, RNC Greenwich, 1967; Extra Equerry to Prince Philip, 1968–69; SO, Dept of CGRM, 1969; Rifle Company Comdr, 41 Commando, 1971; ndc Latimer, 1972; Staff of Chief of Defence Staff, 1973; Staff Officer HQ Commando Forces, 1975; CO RM Poole, 1977; COS and Asst Defence Attaché, British Defence Staff Washington, 1979; ADC to the Queen, 1981–82; Chief of Staff to Comdt Gen. RM, 1982–84; DCS (Support) to C-in-C Allied Forces N Europe, 1984–87. Col Comdt, RM, 1990–94. Dir, British Digestive Foundn, 1987–92. Gen. Comr of Taxes, 1989–2008. Gov., Dashwood Foundn, 1998–2015. *Address*: c/o National Westminster Bank plc, 31 High Street, Deal, Kent CT14 6EW. *Club*: Army and Navy.

**HARDY, John Sydney;** QC 2008; a Recorder, since 2002; *b* London, 12 Dec. 1953; *s* of Sydney and Margaret Hardy; *m* 1990, Claire McCririck; one *s* one *d*. *Educ*: Christ's Hosp.; Magdalen Coll., Oxford (BA Hons Modern Hist.). Teacher, Priory Sch., Banstead, Surrey, 1977–86. Called to the Bar, Gray's Inn, 1988, Bencher, 2014; in practice as barrister specialising in extradition and serious fraud. *Recreations*: music and opera, Rugby Union, cricket, golf, food and wine, travel. *Address*: 3 Raymond Buildings, Gray's Inn, WC1R 5BH.

**HARDY, Prof. Michael Christopher,** CMG 2010; OBE 2001; Professor of Intercultural Relations, since 2011, and Executive Director, Centre for Trust, Peace and Social Relations, since 2014, Coventry University (Director: Centre for Social Relations (formerly Institute of Community Cohesion), 2011–14; Human Security Grand Challenge Initiative, 2011–14); *b* 24 April 1949; *s* of Wilfred Alexander Hardy and Barbara Linington Hardy; *m* 1973, Dorothy Marjorie Skinner; one *s* one *d*. *Educ*: London Univ. (BSc Hons Econs ext. 1971); Univ. of London Inst. of Educn (Cert. Further and Higher Educn 1972); Brunel Univ. (MA Econs 1976). Lectr in Econs, Orpington Coll., 1973–77; Sen. Lectr in Econs, 1977–87, Hd, Sch. of Econs and Public Policy, 1986–87, Leeds Metropolitan Univ.; Hd, Sch. of Econs, 1987–95, Prof. of Internat. Business, 1990–95, Lancs Polytechnic, subseq. Univ. of Central Lancs; British Council: Dir, Private Sector Develt, 1995–97; Regl Dir for Develt Services, ME, Cairo, 1997–2001; Mem., Sen. Mgt Team and Dir, Develt Services, 2001–04; Dir, Indonesia, 2004–08; Prog. Leader, Intercultural Dialogue, 2008–11; Senior Advisor: Min. of Culture and Tourism, Govt of Azerbaijan, 2012–; UN Alliance of Civilisations, 2012–. Mem. Bd, 2014–17, Vice-Chair, 2017–18, Chair, 2019–, Internat. Leadership Assoc. Trustee, Three Faiths Forum, 2012–. Life FRSA 2012. Hon. PhD: Univ. of Mgt, Azerbaijan, 2017; Orasi Ilmiah, Univ. of Muhammadyah Jakarta, Indonesia, 2019. *Publications*: (jtly) Controversies in Applied Economics, 1987; (ed jtly) Controversy in Applied Economics, 1989; (contrib.) Management Development in Poland: building management training capacity with foreign partnerships, 1998; (ed jtly) 7th July 2007 London Bombings: a decade of reflections, 2015; Innovation: shared security and the challenges of exclusion, 2016; (ed jtly) Muslim Identity in a Turbulent Age: Islamic extremism and Western Islamophobia, 2017; Dialogue at the Edge, 2019; articles in jls incl. Municipal Jl. *Recreations*: cooking, family, gadgets, trying to keep up with my grandson William James. *Address*: Centre for Trust, Peace and Social Relations, Coventry University, Priory Street, Coventry CV1 5FB. *T*: (024) 7679 5765, *Fax*: (024) 7679 5761. *E*: mike.hardy@coventry.ac.uk.

**HARDY, Michael James Langley;** Director for Telecommunications Policy and Postal Services, Directorate-General for Information Technologies and Industries, and Telecommunications, Commission of the European Communities, 1992–93; *b* 30 Jan. 1933; *s* of James Hardy and Rosina (*née* Langley); *m* 1959, Dr Swana Metzger; one *s* two *d*. *Educ*: Beckenham Grammar Sch.; Magdalen Coll., Oxford (Exhibnr; BA 1956; MA 1959); Magdalene Coll., Cambridge (LLB 1957; LLM 1963); Exeter Sch. of Art and Design, Univ. of Plymouth (BA (Fine Art) 1996, MA 2002). Called to the Bar, Gray's Inn, 1957. Asst Lecturer, Law Faculty: Manchester Univ., 1958–59; KCL, 1959–60; Legal Officer, later Sen. Legal Officer, Legal Service, UN, 1960–73; Legal Adviser, Govt of Nepal, 1968–69 (on leave of absence from UN); Commn of the European Communities, 1973–93: Legal Adviser, Legal Service, 1973–77; Head of Div., Japan, Australia and NZ, Directorate-General for External Relations, 1978–82; Head of Commn Delegn, New York, 1982–87; Dir for Gen. Affairs, Directorate-Gen. for Telecommunications, Information Industries and Innovation, 1987–92. *Publications*: Blood Feuds and the Payment of Blood Money in the Middle East, 1963; Modern Diplomatic Law, 1968; (with T. Grumley-Grennan) Gidleigh: a Dartmoor village past and present, 2000; articles in legal and political science jls. *Recreations*: walking, talking. *Address*: Castle House, Gidleigh, Devon TQ13 8HR. *T*: (01647) 433567.

**HARDY, Rt Rev. Robert Maynard,** CBE 2001; an Hon. Assistant Bishop, Diocese of Carlisle, since 2002; *b* 5 Oct. 1936; *s* of Harold and Monica Mavie Hardy; *m* 1970, Isobel Mary, *d* of Charles and Ella Burch; two *s* one *d*. *Educ*: Queen Elizabeth Grammar School, Wakefield; Clare College, Cambridge (MA). Deacon 1962, priest 1963; Assistant Curate, All Saints and Martyrs, Langley, Manchester, 1962; Fellow and Chaplain, Selwyn College, Cambridge, 1965 (Hon. Fellow, 1986); Vicar of All Saints, Borehamwood, 1972; Priest-in-charge, Aspley Guise, 1975; Course Director, St Albans Diocese Ministerial Training Scheme, 1975; Incumbent of United Benefice of Aspley Guise with Husborne Crawley and Ridgmont, 1980; Bishop Suffragan of Maidstone, 1980–86; Bishop of Lincoln, 1986–2001; Bishop to HM Prisons, 1985–2001. Hon. DD Hull, 1992; Hon. DLitt Lincoln, 2002. *Recreations*: walking, gardening, reading. *Address*: Carleton House, Back Lane, Langwathby, Penrith, Cumbria CA10 1NB. *T*: (01768) 881210.

**HARDY, Russell;** Chairman: South Warwickshire NHS Foundation Trust, since 2015; Wye Valley NHS Trust, since 2016; *b* London, 29 Sept. 1960; *s* of Arthur Hardy and Olive Hardy (*née* Carter); *m* 2000, Kim Mitchell; one *s* one *d*. *Educ*: Fryerns Sch., Basildon; Warwick Univ. (BA Hons; MA Econs). Economist, Unilever plc, 1982–85; Sen. Manager, Deloitte Haskins & Sells, 1985–88; Kingfisher plc, 1988–92; Trading Dir, Safeway, 1992–95; Chm. and Chief Exec., Dolland & Aitchison, 1995–2005; Gp CEO, Blacks Leisure plc, 2005–07; Chairman: Hunters Moor Ltd, 2008–13; Fosse Healthcare, 2014–. Chm., Robert Jones and Agnes Hunt Orthopaedic and Dist Hosp. NHS Trust, 2009–15. Gov., Nuffield Health, 2010– (Chm., 2012–). Chm., Multiple Sclerosis Trust, 1993–2014; Trustee, UK Acquired Brain Injury Forum, 2009–16. CIMA 1985. *E*: russell.hardy2909@btinternet.com.

**HARE,** family name of **Viscount Blakenham** and **Earl of Listowel**.

**HARE, Sir David,** Kt 1998; FRSL 1985; playwright and screenwriter; *b* 5 June 1947; *s* of Clifford Theodore Rippon Hare and Agnes Cockburn Hare; *m* 1st, 1970, Margaret Matheson (marr. diss. 1980); two *s* one *d*; 2nd, 1992, Nicole Farhi, *qv*. *Educ*: Lancing Coll.; Jesus Coll., Cambridge (MA Hons; Hon. Fellow, 2001). Founded Portable Theatre, 1968; Literary Manager and Resident Dramatist, Royal Court, 1969–71; Resident Dramatist, Nottingham Playhouse, 1973; founded Joint Stock Theatre Group, 1975; US/UK Bicentennial Fellowship, 1977; founded Greenpoint Films, 1982; Associate Dir, Nat. Theatre, 1984–88, 1989–97. Chm. Jury, BFI London Film Fest., 2012. Mem., Amer. Acad. of Arts and Scis, 2012. Hon. DLit: Tel Aviv, 2001; Cambridge, 2005; UEA, 2010; Hon. DLitt GSMD, 2012. Officier, l'Ordre des Arts et des Lettres (France), 1997. *Author of plays*: Slag, Hampstead, 1970, Royal Court, then NY, 1971; The Great Exhibition, Hampstead, 1972; Knuckle (televised, 1989), Comedy, 1974; Fanshen, Joint Stock, 1975, NT 1992; The Secret Rapture, NT, 1988, NY, 1989 (dir, NY only), Lyric, 2003; Racing Demon, NT, 1990, NY, 1995; Murmuring Judges, NT, 1991; The Absence of War, NT, 1993 (televised, 1996); Skylight, NT, 1995, NY and Wyndhams, 1996, Vaudeville, 1997, Wyndhams, 2014, Broadway, 2015; Amy's View, NT, transf. Aldwych, 1997, NY 1999, Garrick, 2006; The Judas Kiss, Playhouse, then NY, 1998, Hampstead, 2012, Duke of York's, 2013, Toronto and Brooklyn Acad., 2016; Via Dolorosa, Royal Court, 1998 (also actor), NY, 1999, Duchess Th., 2002; The Breath of Life, Haymarket, 2002; The Permanent Way, Out of Joint Th. Co., NT, 2004; Stuff Happens, NT, 2004, NY 2006; The Vertical Hour, NY, 2006, Royal Court, 2008; Gethsemane, NT, 2008; Berlin/Wall, NT, Royal Court and NY, 2009 (also actor); The Power of Yes, NT, 2009; South Downs, Chichester, 2011, trans. Pinter, 2012; Behind the Beautiful Forevers, NT, 2014; The Moderate Soprano, Hampstead, 2015, trans. Duke of York's, 2018; The Red Barn, NT, 2016; I'm Not Running, NT, 2018; *author and director of plays*: Brassneck (with Howard Brenton), Nottingham Playhouse, 1973; Teeth 'n' Smiles, Royal Court, 1975, Wyndhams, 1976; Plenty, NT, 1978, NY, 1983, Albery (dir. J. Kent), 1999, NY Shakespeare Fest., 2016, Chichester, 2019; A Map of the World, Adelaide Fest., 1982, NT, 1983, NY, 1985; (with Howard Brenton) Pravda, NT, 1985; The Bay at Nice, NT, 1986, Menier Chocolate Factory, 2019; Wrecked Eggs, NT, 1986; My Zinc Bed, Royal Court, 2000; *opera libretto*: The Knife, NY Shakespeare Fest., 1987 (also directed); *TV films*: Man Above Men, 1973; Licking Hitler, 1978 (also directed); Dreams of Leaving, 1980 (also directed); Saigon—Year of the Cat, 1983; Heading Home, 1991; My Zinc Bed, 2008; Page Eight, 2011 (also directed); Turks & Caicos, 2014 (also directed); Salting the Battlefield, 2014 (also directed); BBC series: Collateral, 2018. *Directed*: The Party, NT, 1974; Weapons of Happiness, NT, 1976; Total Eclipse, Lyric, Hammersmith, 1981; King Lear, NT, 1986; The Designated Mourner, NT, 1996; Heartbreak House, Almeida, 1997; The Year of Magical Thinking, NY, 2007, NT, 2008. *Adapted*: Pirandello, The Rules of the Game, NT, 1971, Almeida, 1992; Brecht, Life of Galileo, Almeida, 1994, NT, 2006; Brecht, Mother Courage and her Children, NT, 1995; Chekhov, Ivanov, Almeida, 1997; Schnitzler (La Ronde), The Blue Room, Donmar Warehouse, 1998, NY 1999, Th. Royal, Haymarket, 2000; Chekhov, Platonov, Almeida, 2001; Lorca, The House of Bernarda Alba, NT, 2005; Gorky, Enemies, Almeida, 2006; Craig Murray, Murder in Samarkand (radio play), 2010; Young Chekhov - Ivanov, Platonov, The Seagull, Chichester, 2015, NT, 2016; Ibsen, The Master Builder, Old Vic, 2016; Uncle Vanya, Theatre Royal, Bath, 2019; Peter Gynt, after Henrik Ibsen, NT, 2019. *Films*: wrote and directed: Wetherby, 1985; Paris by Night, 1988; Strapless, 1989; (screenplay) Plenty, 1985; Damage (adapted from novel by Josephine Hart), 1992; The Secret Rapture, 1994; directed, The Designated Mourner, 1997; wrote and acted, Via Dolorosa, 2000; (screenplay) The Hours (adapted from novel by Michael Cunningham), 2002; (screenplay) The Reader (adapted from novel by Bernard Schlink), 2008; (screenplay) Wall (animation), 2017; (screenplay) Denial (adapted from book by Deborah Lipstadt), 2017; (screenplay) The White Crow, 2019. *Publications*: Slag, 1970; The Great Exhibition, 1972; Knuckle, 1974; Brassneck, 1974; Fanshen, 1976; Teeth 'n' Smiles, 1976; Plenty, 1978; Licking Hitler, 1978; Dreams of Leaving, 1980; A Map of the World, 1982; Saigon, 1983; Pravda, 1985; Wetherby, 1985; The Bay at Nice and Wrecked Eggs, 1986; The Secret Rapture, 1988; Paris By Night, 1989; Strapless, 1990; Racing Demon, 1990; Writing Lefthanded, 1991; Heading Home, 1991; Murmuring Judges, 1991; The Absence of War, 1993; Asking Around, 1993; Rules of the Game, 1994; Skylight, 1995; Mother Courage, 1995; Plays One, 1996; Plays Two, 1996; Amy's View, 1997; Ivanov, 1997; The Judas Kiss, 1998; The Blue Room, 1998; Via Dolorosa, 1998; Acting Up, 1999; My Zinc Bed, 2000; Platonov, 2001; The Hours, 2002; The Breath of Life, 2002; Collected Screenplays, 2002; The Permanent Way, 2003; Stuff Happens, 2004; The House of Bernarda Alba, 2005; Obedience, Struggle and Revolt, 2005; Enemies, 2006; The Vertical Hour, 2006; Plays Three, 2008; Gethsemane, 2008; The Reader, 2008; Berlin/Wall, 2009; The Power of Yes,

2009; Lee Miller, 2010; South Downs, 2011; Behind the Beautiful Forevers, 2014; The Blue Touch Paper (memoir), 2015; Young Chekhov—Platonov, Ivanov and The Seagull, 2015; The Moderate Soprano, 2015; Ibsen - The Master Builder, 2016; The Red Barn, 2016; I'm Not Running, 2018; Peter Gynt, 2019; Uncle Vanya, 2019.

**HARE, Ewan Nigel Christian, (Nick);** Canadian Diplomat, retired; Deputy Secretary-General (Development Co-operation) of the Commonwealth, 1993–99; *b* 11 May 1939; *m* 1985, Raina Ho; one *s* two *d*. *Educ:* Earlham Coll. (BA); Carleton Univ. (DPA). First Sec., Canadian High Commn, Accra, 1969–72; Canadian International Development Agency: Regl Dir, Asia SE, 1972–76; Regl Dir, Central and S Africa, 1976–78; Dir-Gen., Resources Br., 1978–80; Dir-Gen., UN Progs, 1980–84; Ambassador of Canada to Zaire, Rwanda, Burundi and Congo, 1984–87; Dir, Africa Trade Div., Dept of Foreign Affairs, Ottawa, 1987–88; Dir-Gen., Industrial Co-operation Prog., Canadian Internat. Develt Agency, 1988–91; Canadian High Comr to Nigeria and Ambassador to Benin, 1991–93. Internat. Electoral Observer, 2011–. Chm., Canadian Hunger Foundn—Partners in Rural Develt, 2001–08; Chair, Internat. Cttee, Canadian Comprehensive Audit Foundn, 2002–10. Board Member: Retired Hds of Mission Assoc., 2003–14; Pearson Peacekeeping Centre, 2004–10; North-South Inst., 2008–; Canadian Executive Service Orgn, 2010–16. Mem., Canadian Council for Internat. Co-operation, 2011–. *Recreations:* ski-ing, distance running, swimming, cycling. *Clubs:* Canadian Kennel; Leonberger (Ontario).

**HARE, Ivan Charles;** QC 2017; *b* Gainsborough, Lincs, 11 Nov. 1966; *s* of Norman Philip and Mary Hare; *m* 2007, Sophie Bessemer; three *d*. *Educ:* Queen Elizabeth's Grammar Sch., Gainsborough; King's Coll., London (LLB 1st Cl.); New Coll., Oxford (BCL 1st Cl.); Harvard Law Sch. (LLM); Trinity Coll., Cambridge (MA). Called to the Bar, Gray's Inn, 1991; Fellow, Trinity Coll., Cambridge, 1991–2004; in practice as barrister, Blackstone Chambers, 2004–, specialising in public law. *Publications:* (ed with C. F. Forsyth) The Golden Metwand and the Crooked Cord, 1998; (ed jtly) Constitutional Reform in the United Kingdom, 1998; (ed with J. Weinstein) Extreme Speech and Democracy, 2009; (ed and contrib.) De Smith's Judicial Review, 7th edn 2013, 8th edn 2018. *Address:* Blackstone Chambers, Temple, EC4Y 9BW. *T:* (020) 7583 1770, *Fax:* (020) 7822 7350. *E:* clerks@blackstonechambers.com.

**HARE, Margaret Flora, (Mrs David Hare);** *see* Spittle, M. F.

**HARE, Sir Nicholas (Patrick),** 7th Bt *cr* 1818, of Stow Hall, Norfolk; *b* 27 Aug. 1955; *o s* of Sir Philip Hare, 6th Bt and Anne Lisle Hare (*née* Nicholson); *S* father, 2000; *m* 1982, Caroline Keith, *d* of T. P. K. Allan; two *s*. *Educ:* Bryanston. *Heir: s* Thomas Hare, *b* 7 Aug. 1986. *Address:* Tavern House, Sopworth, Chippenham, Wilts SN14 6PR.

**HARE, Nick;** *see* Hare, E. N. C.

**HARE, Nicole, (Lady Hare);** *see* Farhi, N.

**HARE, Paul Webster,** LVO 1985; HM Diplomatic Service, retired; Project Director, Shanghai World EXPO 2010, UK Trade and Investment, 2005–08; Senior Lecturer, Frederick S Pardee School of Global Studies, Boston University, since 2015; *b* 20 July 1951; *s* of Maurice Leslie Hare and Anne Dorothy Hare (*née* Webster); *m* 1978, Lynda Carol Henderson, *d* of Ian Stuart McWalter Henderson, CBE, GM, KPM and Marie Beatrice Henderson (*née* Green); three *s* three *d*. *Educ:* Leeds Grammar Sch. (Foundn Schol.); Trinity Coll., Oxford (Open Schol., MA 1st Cl. Hons PPE 1972); Coll. of Law, London. Qualified as solicitor, with Herbert Smith & Co., London, 1973–75; TEFL, Biella and Genoa, Italy, 1976; Corporate Finance Dept, J. Henry Schroder Wagg & Co., London, 1976–78; entered HM Diplomatic Service, 1978: Private Sec. to Ambassador to EC, Brussels, 1979–80; First Sec. and Hd of Chancery, Lisbon, 1981–85; FCO, 1985–88; Consul and Dep. Dir, Investment, USA, NY, 1988–94; Dep. Hd of Mission and Counsellor (Commercial and Economic), Caracas, 1994–97; Hd, Non-Proliferation Dept, FCO, 1997–2001; Ambassador to Republic of Cuba, 2001–04; Vis. Fellow, Weatherhead Center for Internat. Relations, Harvard Univ., 2004–05. Lectr and Fellow, Center for Internat. Affairs, Boston Univ., 2009–15. Mem., Cuba Policy Gp, Brookings Instn, Washington, 2008–. Pres., Baseball Softball UK, 2000–01. Online Cuba Topics expert, New York Times, 2009–. Order of Prince Henry the Navigator (Portugal), 1985; Order of 5 May 1810, Barinas (Venezuela), 1995. *Publications:* Moncada - a Cuban Story (novel), 2010; Making Diplomacy Work: intelligent innovation for the modern world, 2015; articles for Miami Herald, Brookings Instn, Poder 360 mag., Cuban Affairs, FT, Huffington Post, The Atlantic. *Recreations:* family, music, sport. *Address:* c/o International Relations, Boston University, 152 Bay State Road, Boston, MA 02215, USA.

**HARE, Stephen;** Chief Executive Officer, Sage plc, since 2018 (Chief Financial Officer, 2014–18); *b* Withernsea, 15 April 1961; *s* of David Hare and Joyce Hare; partner, Lucinda Cowley; one *s*. *Educ:* Univ. of Liverpool (BCom Hons). Chartered Accountant 1985. GEC, then Marconi, latterly as Chief Financial Officer, 1989–2003; consultant, 2003–05; Group Chief Financial Officer: Spectris plc, 2005–06; Invensys plc, 2006–09; Operating Partner and Co Hd, Operating Support Gp, Apax Partners, 2009–14. *Recreations:* golf, travel, family. *Club:* Wentworth Golf.

**HARE, Timothy James Pitt;** Vice Lord-Lieutenant of West Yorkshire, since 2012; *b* Wetherby, 7 June 1948; *s* of Clifford Ronald Pitt Hare and Hazel Mary Hare; *m* 1977, Diana Marion Trigg; one *s* two *d* (and one *d* decd). *Educ:* Uppingham Sch. Director: James Hare Ltd, 1973–; Harecroft Estates Ltd, 1973–; Merchanting Div., Illingworth Morris, 1977–79; Sales Dir, Salts of Saltaire, 1982–83; Partner, N Deighton Farms, 1986–. High Sheriff, 2005–06, DL 2007, W Yorks. *Recreations:* country pursuits, gardening, golf, classic cars, breeding alpacas, wine, travel. *Address:* The Old Hall, The Green, North Deighton, Wetherby, N Yorks LS22 4EN. *T:* (01937) 580775. *E:* tim.hare@james-hare.com. *Club:* Sloane.

**HAREN, Sir Patrick (Hugh),** Kt 2008; PhD; FREng, FIET; Deputy Chairman, Bank of Ireland Group plc, since 2018 (non-executive Director, since 2012; Senior Independent Director, since 2017); *b* 4 Aug. 1950; *s* of James Joseph Haren and Sarah Haren; *m* 1971, Anne Elizabeth McNally; two *s*. *Educ:* Queen's Univ. Belfast (BSc 1971; PhD 1976); University Coll., Dublin (MBA 1986). FIET (FIEE 1990); FREng (FEng 1998). Power Systems Engrg, Electricity Supply Bd, Dublin, 1971–73; Engr, Superconducting Magnet Prog., CERN, Geneva, 1976–78; Electricity Supply Board, Dublin: engrg appts, 1978–84; Divl Manager, Strategic Planning, 1985–87; Regl Accountant, 1987–88; Manager, Business Ventures, 1988–89; Dir, 1989–92; Dir, Hoermann Electronics Ltd, 1990–91; Chief Exec., 1992–98, Chm., 1999–2008, NI Electricity; Chief Exec., 1998–2007, Dep. Chm., 2007–09, Chm., 2009–12, Viridian Gp Ltd. Mem. Study Cttee, Power System Operation and Control, CIGRE, 1982–86. Non-exec. Dire, Bank of Ireland (UK) plc, 2012–16. *Publications:* technical papers in power system operation and computer control. *Recreations:* ski-ing, walking, languages. *Address:* 57 Ringdufferin Road, Toye, Downpatrick BT30 9PH. *T:* (028) 4482 8584.

**HAREWOOD,** 8th Earl of, *cr* 1812; **David Henry George Lascelles;** Baron Harewood 1796; Viscount Lascelles 1812; freelance film and television producer; *b* 21 Oct. 1950; *s* of 7th Earl of Harewood, KBE, Hon. AM and Maria, (Marion), Donata (*née* Stein, later Thorpe), CBE; *S* father, 2011; *m* 1979, Margaret Rosalind Messenger; three *s* one *d*; *m* 1990, Diane Jane Howse. *Educ:* The Hall Sch.; Westminster; Bristol Univ. Productions include: *films:* Tibet - a Buddhist Trilogy, 1977; Richard III, 1995; The Wisdom of Crocodiles, 1998; *television:* Inspector Morse IV and V, 1989–90 (BAFTA Best TV Series award); Wide-Eyed & Legless, 1992; Moll Flanders, 1996; Second Sight, 1999; *stage:* Carnival Messiah, Harewood, 2007. Chairman: Harewood House Trust Ltd, 1993–; Alchemy, 2008–; Orient Foundn (Trustee, 1983–); Co-Founder, Geraldine Connor Foundn, 2012; Patron: Kala Sangam; Leeds W Indian Centre; Yorks CCC. Hon. Pres., Leeds United FC. *Heir: s* Viscount Lascelles, *qv*. *Address:* Harewood House, Harewood, Leeds, West Yorks LS17 9LG.

**HARFORD, Sir Mark (John),** 4th Bt *cr* 1934, of Falcondale, co. Cardigan; *b* 6 Aug. 1964; *er s* of Sir (John) Timothy Harford, 3rd Bt, and of Carolyn Jane Mullens; *S* father, 2010; *m* 1999, Louise Rosamond, *d* of Robert Langford, of Tadworth, Surrey; three *d*. *Heir: b* Simon Guy Harford [*b* 24 Sept. 1966; *m* 1998, Alexandra (marr. diss. 2015), *d* of Frederick Gans; two *s*].

**HARFORD, Timothy D.,** OBE 2019; Senior Columnist, Financial Times, since 2006; *b* Kent, 1973. *Educ:* Aylesbury Grammar Sch.; Oxford Univ. (MA; MPhil). Visiting Fellow, Nuffield College, Oxford, 2010–18. Hon. FSS 2017. *Publications:* The Undercover Economist, 2005; The Logic of Life, 2008; Dear Undercover Economist, 2009; Adapt, 2011; The Undercover Economist Strikes Back, 2013; Messy, 2016; Fifty Things that Make the Modern Economy, 2017.

**HARGREAVES, Adele Esther;** *see* Blakebrough, A. E.

**HARGREAVES, Andrew Raikes;** Member, Supervisory Board, Thyssen Petroleum, since 2014; *b* 15 May 1955; *s* of Col and Mrs D. W. Hargreaves; *m* 1978, Fiona Susan, *o d* of G. W. Dottridge; two *s*. *Educ:* Eton; St Edmund Hall, Oxford (MA Hons). Auctioneer and valuation expert, Christies, 1977–81; executive, Hill Samuel & Co. Ltd, 1981–83; Asst Dir, Sanwa Internat. Ltd, 1983–85; Asst Dir J. Henry Schroder Wagg & Co. Ltd, 1985–87; Consultant: Schroders plc, 1987–92; Midlands Electricity plc, 1989–97; UK Man. Dir, Daimler-Benz, subseq. DaimlerChrysler, Aerospace AG, 1997–2000; UK Chm., 2000–04, Sen. Advr and Gp Dir, Govt Affairs, 2004–12, EADS UK Ltd; Managing Director: Securisys Mgt Ltd, 2014–; Securisys Hldgs and Securisys Information Ltd, 2012–13. Contested (C) Blyth Valley, 1983. MP (C) Birmingham, Hall Green, 1987–97; contested (C) same seat, 1997. PPS to Ministers of State, FCO, 1992–97. Member: Select Cttee on Information, 1992–97; Select Cttee for Parly Comr for Admin, 1993–97; Secretary: back bench Urban and Inner Cities Cttee, 1987–91 (Chm., 1992–94); back bench Defence Cttee, 1992–94 (Vice-Chm., 1994–97). Mem., Bow Gp. Man. Partner, Gt Moreton Farm, 2011–. *Recreations:* fishing, gardening, walking, antiques, art. *Club:* Boodle's.

**HARGREAVES, David Harold,** PhD; Fellow, Wolfson College, Cambridge, 1988–2006, now Emeritus; *b* 31 Aug. 1939; *s* of Clifford and Marion Hargreaves. *Educ:* Bolton School; Christ's College, Cambridge (MA, PhD). Asst Master, Hull Grammar Sch., 1961–64; Research Associate, Dept of Sociology and Social Anthropology, Univ. of Manchester, 1964–65; Lectr, Senior Lectr then Reader, Dept of Education, Univ. of Manchester, 1965–79; Reader in Education and Fellow of Jesus College, Oxford, 1979–84; Chief Inspector, ILEA, 1984–88; University of Cambridge: Prof. of Educn, 1988–2000; Member: Gen. Bd of the Faculties, 1989–92; Local Exams Syndicate, 1990–92; Bd of Grad. Studies, 1990–92; Chairman: Council, Sch. of Humanities and Soc. Scis, 1990–92; Cttee on the Training and Develt of Univ. Teachers, 1990–92; Needs Cttee, 1991–92. Chief Executive, QCA, 2000–01. Vis. Prof., Univ. of Manchester, 2003–08. Member: Educn Res. Bd, SSRC, 1979–82; Educn Adv. Council, Royal Opera House, Covent Garden, 1985–90; Educn Adv. Council, IBA, 1988–90; ESRC, 1991–95 (Chm., Res. Centres Bd, 1992–94); Res. Cttee, Teacher Trng Agency, 1995–97; Educn Cttee, NESTA, 1999–2003; Nat. Educnl Res. Forum, 1999–2004; Jt Vice-Chm., Sec. of State for Educn and Employment's Standards Task Force, 1997–2000; Policy Advr to Sec. of State for Educn and Skills, 2001–02; Bd Mem., 1999–2000, Chm., 2002–05, British Educnl Communications and Technol. Agency. Chairman: Eastern Arts Bd, 1991–94; Internat. Adv. Council on Quality of Educn, NSW, 1993–95. Non-exec. Dir, W Suffolk Hosps NHS Trust, 1998–2000. Sen. Associate, Demos, 2003. Consultant: Lifelong Learning Foundn, 2002–04; Paul Hamlyn Foundn, 2002–07; Specialist Schs Trust, 2003–09 (Associate Dir, Develt and Res.); (on self-improving sch. systems) Nat. Coll. for Sch. Leadership, 2010–12. Trustee, Villiers Park Educnl Trust, 2004–07. Mem., Educn Cttee, LSO, 2002–05. FRSA 1984; FAcSS (Founding AcSS, 1999). Hon. FCT 2001. Hon. EdD Wolverhampton, 2002. *Publications:* Social Relations in a Secondary School, 1967; Interpersonal Relations and Education, 1972; (jtly) Deviance in Classrooms, 1975; The Challenge for the Comprehensive School, 1982; (jtly) Planning for School Development, 1990; (jtly) The Empowered School, 1991; The Mosaic of Learning, 1994; (jtly) On-the-Job Training for Surgeons, 1997; (jtly) On-the-Job Training for Physicians, 1997; Creative Professionalism, 1998; Education Epidemic, 2003; Learning for Life, 2004; A Self-improving School System, 2012; Beyond Schooling, 2019. *Recreation:* the arts.

**HARGREAVES, Prof. Ian Richard,** CBE 2012; Professor of Digital Economy, University of Wales, Cardiff, 2010–18, Professor Emeritus, 2019 (Professor of Journalism, 1998–2010); *b* 18 June 1951; *s* of Ronald and Edna Hargreaves; *m* 1st, 1972, Elizabeth Anne Crago (marr. diss. 1991); one *s* one *d*; 2nd, 1993, Adele Esther Blakebrough, *qv*; two *d*. *Educ:* Burnley Grammar Sch.; Altrincham Grammar Sch.; Queens' Coll., Cambridge (MA). Community worker, Kaleidoscope Project, 1972–73; Reporter, Keighley News, 1973–74; Journalist, Bradford Telegraph & Argus, 1974–76; Financial Times, 1976–87: Industrial Corresp.; Transport Corresp.; New York Corresp.; Social Affairs Ed.; Resources Ed.; Features Ed.; Man. Ed., 1987–88, Controller, 1988–89, Dir, 1989–90, News and Current Affairs, BBC; Dep. Editor, The Financial Times, 1990–94; Editor: Independent, 1994–96; New Statesman & Soc., then New Statesman, 1996–98; Gp Dir, Corporate and Public Affairs, BAA plc, 2003–06; Strategic Communications Dir, FCO, 2008–10. Mem. Bd, S London and Maudsley NHS Trust, 2000–03. Chm., Demos, 1997–2002. Member Board: New Statesman, 1996–2003; Greenpeace UK, 1997–2002; Presentable, 2001–03; OFCOM, 2002–08 (Sen. Partner, 2007–08); Alacrity, 2013–; Nat. Theatre of Wales, 2013–; Wales Millennium Centre, 2015–; Mem., BBC Bd, 2017–. Res. Fellow, NESTA, 2012–13; Sen. Fellow, Lisbon Council, 2013–. *Publications:* Sharper Vision: the BBC and the communications revolution, 1993; (with Ian Christie) Tomorrow's Politics: the third way and beyond, 1998; Who's Misunderstanding Whom?: science and the media, 2000; Journalism: truth or dare?, 2003; A Very Short Intro to Journalism, 2005, 2nd edn 2014; The Heart of Digital Wales: a review for the Welsh Assembly Government, 2010; Digital Opportunity: review of intellectual property and growth, 2011; A Manifesto for the UK Creative Economy, 2013; (ed) The Creative Citizen Unbound, 2016. *Recreations:* walking, tennis, football, music, poetry. *Address:* Cardiff School of Journalism, Media and Culture, 2 Central Square, Cardiff CF10 1FS. *T:* 07909 534545.

**HARGREAVES, Simon John Robert;** QC 2009; *b* Rochdale, 15 Jan. 1968; *s* of Edward Hargreaves and Christina Hargreaves; *m* 2001, Catherine Morgan; three *d*. *Educ:* Shrewsbury Sch.; Worcester Coll., Oxford (BA Juris. 1989). Called to the Bar, Inner Temple, 1991; in practice as a barrister, specialising in construction, energy and IT law,

1991–; Mem., Attorney-Gen.'s Panel of Counsel, 2003–08. *Recreations:* ski-ing, scuba diving. *Address:* Keating Chambers, 15 Essex Street, WC2R 3AA. *T:* (020) 7544 2600, *Fax:* (020) 7544 2700. *E:* shargreaves@keatingchambers.com.

**HARGREAVES, Susan Elizabeth**, OBE 2016; Chief Executive, Internet Watch Foundation, since 2011; *b* York, 1962; *d* of late Patrick John Nuttgens, CBE and of Bridget Ann Nuttgens; *m* 2006, Marcus Romer; one *s* one *d*. *Educ:* Leeds Poly. (HND Hotel Catering and Instl Mgt 1984). Gen. Manager, Red Ladder Theatre Co., 1990–95; Dep. Dir, Watermans Art Centre, 1995–96; CEO, Audiences Yorkshire, 1996–2002; Dir, Cultureworks UK, 2002–08; CEO, Soc. of Dyers and Colourists, 2008–11. Trustee, Northern Ballet Th., 2003–08. *Address:* Internet Watch Foundation, Discovery House, Chivers Way, Vision Park, Histon, Cambridge CB24 9ZR. *T:* (01223) 203030. *E:* susie@iwf.org.uk.

**HARGROVE, Dr Caroline**, FREng; CEng, FIMechE; Chief Technology Officer, Babylon Health, since 2018; *b* Montreal, Canada, 18 March 1968; *d* of Pierre Hogue and Edith Hogue (*née* Levasseur); *m* 2000, Neil Hargrove; one *s* one *d*. *Educ:* Queen's Univ., Kingston, Ont (BSc Hons 1989); Wolfson Coll., Cambridge (PhD 1994). CEng 1995; FIMechE 2016. Lectr, Univ. of Cambridge, 1994–97; Vehicle Dynamics Engr, McLaren F1 Racing, 1997–2007; Prog. Dir, 2007–12, Tech. Dir, 2012–17, Chief Technol. Officer, 2018, McLaren Applied Technologies. FREng 2017. Trustee, Nat. Saturday Clubs, 2017–. *Publications:* contribs to learned jls; patents. *Recreations:* tennis, badminton, cello, family. *Address:* Babylon Health, 60 Sloane Avenue, SW3 3DD. *E:* caroline.hargrove@babylonhealth.com.

**HARINGTON, Sir David Richard**, 15th Bt *cr* 1611, of Ridlington, Rutland; *b* 25 June 1944; *yr s* of His Honour John Charles Dundas Harington, QC, *yr s* of 12th Bt, and Lavender Cecilia Harington (*née* Denny); *S* brother, 2016; *m* 1983, Deborah (*née* Catesby); two *s*. *Educ:* Westminster; Christ Church, Oxford. *Heir: s* John Catesby Harington, *b* 7 Jan. 1984.

**HARINGTON, Michael Kenneth; His Honour Judge Harington;** a Circuit Judge, since 2000; *b* 9 Aug. 1951; *s* of late Kenneth Douglas Evelyn Herbert Harington, and Maureen Helen (*née* McCalmont); *m* 1984, Deirdre Christine Kehoe; one *s* two *d*. *Educ:* Eton Coll.; Christ Church, Oxford (MA). Called to the Bar, Inner Temple, 1974; a Recorder, 1998. *Recreations:* golf, shooting. *Address:* Gloucester County Court, Kimbrose Way, Gloucester GL1 2DE. *Club:* MCC.

**HARKER, Lisa Marie;** Director, Nuffield Family Justice Observatory, since 2019; *b* Farnborough, Kent, 3 May 1969; *d* of Dr Paul Harker and Jacqueline Harker; *m* 1999, Mark Norman; one *s* one *d*. *Educ:* Lord Digby's Sch., Sherborne; Bristol Univ. (BSc Hons Psychol.); London Sch. of Econs (MSc Social Policy and Planning). Policy Officer, Daycare Trust, 1992–95; Campaign Team Co-ordinator, Child Poverty Action Gp, 1995–97; Social Affairs Specialist, BBC News, 1997–99; UK Advocacy Co-ordinator, Save the Children UK, 1999–2000; Dep. Dir, IPPR, 2000–03; Ind. Policy Advr, 2003–07; Co-Dir, IPPR, 2007–10; Hd, Strategy Unit, then Hd, Strategy and Develt, 2011–14, Dir of Strategy, Policy and Evidence, 2014–16, NSPCC; Chief Exec., The Art Room, 2016–19. Vis. Fellow, Nuffield Coll., Oxford, 2015–. Member: London Child Poverty Commn, 2006–08; Res. Cttee, 2016–18, Strategic Adv. Network, 2019–, ESRC. Chm., Daycare Trust, 2001–06; Trustee: Aspire Oxfordshire, 2002–11; NACRO, 2006–09; KPMG Foundn, 2009–16. *Publications:* Poverty: the facts, 1996; (ed) From Welfare to Wellbeing: the future of social care, 2002; An Equal Start, 2003; Delivering on Child Poverty: what would it take?, 2006; How Safe Are Our Children?, 2013. *Recreations:* cooking for friends, playing accordion, exploring Italy by Vespa. *Address:* Nuffield Family Justice Observatory, 28 Bedford Square, WC1B 3JS. *T:* (020) 7631 0566. *E:* lharker@nuffieldfoundation.org.

**HARKNESS, Very Rev. James**, KCVO 2005; CB 1993; OBE 1978; Moderator of the General Assembly of The Church of Scotland, 1995–96; a Chaplain to the Queen in Scotland, 1996–2006 (an Extra Chaplain, 1995–96 and since 2006); Dean of the Chapel Royal in Scotland, 1996–2006; *b* 20 Oct. 1935; *s* of James and Jane Harkness; *m* 1960, Elizabeth Anne Tolmie; one *s* one *d*. *Educ:* Univ. of Edinburgh (MA). Asst Minister, North Morningside Parish Church, Edinburgh, 1959–61; joined RAChD, 1961: Chaplain: 1 KOSB, 1961–65; 1 Queen's Own Highlanders, 1965–69; Singapore, 1969–70; Dep. Warden, RAChD Centre, 1970–74; Senior Chaplain: N Ireland, 1974–75; 4th Div., 1975–78; Asst Chaplain Gen., Scotland, 1980–81; Senior Chaplain: 1st British Corps, 1981–82; BAOR, 1982–84; Dep. Chaplain Gen. to the Forces, 1985–86, Chaplain Gen., 1987–95. QHC 1982–95. Chaplain, BLESMA, 1995–2002; Nat. Chaplain, 1995–2002, Pres., 2001–06, RBL, Scotland. Chm., Bd of Dirs, Carberry, 1998–2001. Mem., Pensions Appeal Tribunals, Scotland, 1999–2005. Chm., Veterans Scotland, 2003–06. Member: Scot. Adv. Cttee, ICRF, 1995–2000; Bd, Mercy Corps, Scotland, 2001–08; Pres., Soc. of Friends, St Andrew's, Jerusalem, 1998–2005. President: ACFA, Scotland, 1996–2004; Earl Haig Fund Scotland, 2001–06; Officers' Assoc. Scotland, 2001–06. Trustee: Nat. Prayer Breakfast for Scotland, 1996–2012; Liberating Scots Trust, 1998–2001; Anglo Israel Assoc., 2001–11 (Mem., Exec. Cttee, 1995–2001); Scottish Nat. War Meml, 2003–15; Gen. Trustee, Church of Scotland, 1996–2011. Gov., Fettes Coll., 1999–2009. Patron, St Mary's Music Sch., Edinburgh, 1995–2000. FRSA 1992. DD Aberdeen, 2000. KStJ 2012 (OStJ 1988; ChStJ 1999; Dean, Order of St John, Scotland, 2005–11). *Recreation:* general pursuits. *Address:* 13 Saxe Coburg Place, Edinburgh EH3 5BR. *Clubs:* New, Royal Scots (Edinburgh).

**HARKNESS, John Diamond;** First Scottish Parliamentary Counsel to the United Kingdom, 2000–02; *b* 14 July 1944; *s* of Jack Harkness and Isabel Harkness. *Educ:* High Sch. of Glasgow; Univ. of Glasgow (MA, LLB). Legal Asst, then Sen. Legal Asst, Office of Solicitor to Sec. of State for Scotland, 1971–79; Asst, then Deputy Scottish Parliamentary Counsel, 1979–2000; Asst Legal Sec. to Lord Advocate, 1979–99. *Recreations:* reading, music, travel. *Address:* 10 The Limes, Linden Gardens, W2 4ET.

**HARLE, Prof. John Crofton**, FGS; saxophonist, composer, record producer; Professor, Guildhall School of Music and Drama, since 2018; *b* 20 Sept. 1956; *s* of Jack Harle and Joyce Harle (*née* Crofton); *m* 1st, 1985, Julia Jane Eisner (marr. diss. 2004); two *s*; 2nd, 2010, Riccarda Anne Kane. *Educ:* Newcastle Royal Grammar Sch.; Royal Military Sch. of Music, Kneller Hall (Cousins Meml Medal for Best Army Musician 1975); Royal Coll. of Music (Foundn Schol.; ARCM (Hons) 1980; Dannreuther Concerto Prize 1980); French govt scholarship for study with Daniel Deffayet, Paris Conservatoire, 1981–82. FGS (FGSM 1990). Began career as clarinettist; served as solo clarinettist, Band of Coldstream Guards; Leader of Myrha Saxophone Quartet, 1977–82; formed duo with pianist John Lenehan, 1979; actor/musician, RNT, London, 1979–85; saxophone soloist, 1980–, with major internat. orchs, incl. LSO, English Chamber Orch., LPO, Amsterdam Concertgebouw, New World Symphony; Principal Saxophone, London Sinfonietta, 1987–97; founder Mem., Michael Nyman Band, 1980; formed: Berliner Band, 1980; John Harle Band, 1988; also worked with Nash Ensemble and the Fires of London. Compositions for several ensembles, 1983–, incl. London Brass and LSO. Frequent composer and soloist on TV (incl. BBC series, Silent Witness (RTS Award for best TV theme music, 1998), BBC2 documentary, Lucien Freud—A Painted Life (RTS Best Original Music Award, 2012, Ivor Novello Award for Best Soundtrack, 2014), and History of Britain) and feature films (incl. Prick Up Your Ears (Cannes Film Fest. Award for Best Artistic Achievement in a Feature Film); regular broadcaster on BBC Radio; featured in One Man and his Sax, BBC2 TV, 1988. Has made many recordings. Major works written for him by Dominic Muldowney, Ned Rorem, Richard Rodney Bennett, Luciano Berio, Michael Nyman, Gavin Bryars, Mike Westbrook, Stanley Myers, Harrison Birtwistle, Michael Torke, John Tavener, Sally Beamish. Prof. of Saxophone, Performance and Music History, then Prof. of Saxophone, 1988–2012, Vis. Prof., 2016–18, Guildhall Sch. of Music and Drama; Vis. Prof. of Saxophone and Performance, Canterbury Christ Church Univ., 2012–16. Artistic Dir, Green Hall, Tokyo, 1986–88; Founder and Man. Dir, Harle Records, 2005–13; producer, EMI Classics, Tokyo, 2011–12; Artistic Dir and Producer, Sospiro Records, 2013–. Ed., Universal Saxophone Edn, 1983–89. Founder, Sospiro Leadership Masterclasses, 2007–; speaker and lectr on leadership and music, 2007–. Mem., Lords Taverners, 2005–; Freeman: Musicians' Co.; City of London. GLAA Young Musician, 1979, 1980. *Publications:* John Harle's Saxophone Album, 1986, reissued as John Harle's Sax Album, 1998; Rachmaninov Vocalise, 2001; The Saxophone, 2017. *Recreations:* nostalgia, New Wave British films of the 1960s, fogeydom, Viz. *Address:* The Old Malthouse, Goodnestone, Kent CT3 1PB. *T:* 07711 223313. *Club:* East India.

**HARLECH**, 7th Baron *cr* 1876; **Jasset David Cody Ormsby Gore;** *b* Oswestry, Shropshire, 1 July 1986; *o s* of 6th Baron Harlech and of Amanda, *d* of Alan Thomas Grieve, *qv*; *S* father, 2016. *Educ:* Eton Coll.; Central St Martins (BA (Hons) Graphic Design 2008). Property developer; estate management. *Heir:* none.

**HARLECH, Pamela, Lady;** journalist and producer; *b* 18 Dec. 1934; *d* of Ralph Frederick Colin and Georgia Talmey; *m* 1969, 5th Baron Harlech, KCMG, PC (*d* 1985); one *d*. *Educ:* Smith Coll., Northampton, Mass; Finch Coll. (BA). London Editor, (American) Vogue, 1964–69; Food Editor, (British) Vogue, 1971–82; freelance journalist, 1972–; prodn work for special events, 1986–87; Commissioning Editor, Thames and Hudson, Publishers, 1987–89. Chairman: Women's Playhouse Trust, 1984–94; V&A Enterprises, 1987–94; English Nat. Ballet, 1990–2000; Council, British Amer. Arts Assoc., 1990–92; Bath Shakespeare Festival, 2004–06; Trustee, V&A Mus., 1986–94; Member: Welsh Arts Council, 1981–85; Arts Council of GB, 1986–90; South Bank Bd, 1986–94; Council, Managing Bd, Crusaid, 1987–96; Council, ABSA, 1988–95 (Chm., Judging Panel for Awards, 1989–90); Bd, Th. Royal, Bath, 2001–08; Bd, Wales Millennium Centre, 2002–07. Pres., Bath Cancer Support, 1998–2016. *Publications:* Feast without Fuss, 1976; Pamela Harlech's Complete Guide to Cooking, Entertainment and Household Management, 1981; Vogue Book of Menus, 1985. *Recreations:* music, cooking, laughing.

**HARLEN, Prof. Wynne**, OBE 1991; PhD; Director, Scottish Council for Research in Education, 1990–99; *b* 12 Jan. 1937; *d* of Arthur Mitchell and Edith (*née* Radcliffe); *m* 1958, Frank Harlen (*d* 1987); one *s* one *d*. *Educ:* St Hilda's Coll., Oxford (BA 1958; MA 1961); Univ. of Bristol (PhD 1974). Asst teacher, Cheltenham Ladies' Coll., 1959–60; Lectr, St Mary's Coll. of Educn and Glos Coll. of Art, 1960–66; Research Fellow: Univ. of Bristol, 1966–73; Univ. of Reading, 1973–77; Sen. Res. Fellow, KCL, 1977–84; Sidney Jones Prof. of Science Educn, Univ. of Liverpool, 1985–90. Visiting Professor: Univ. of Liverpool, 1990–2001; Grad. Sch. of Educn, Bristol Univ., 2000–; Project Dir, Univ. of Cambridge, 2003–06. Bernard Osher Fellow, Exploratorium, San Francisco, 1995. Chair, Sci. Expert Gp, OECD Student Assessment Project, 1998–2003. President: British Educnl Res. Assoc., 1993–94; Educn Sect., BAAS, 2001–02; ASE, 2009–10. FEIS 1999. Editor, Primary Sci. Rev., 1999–2004. Purkwa Prize for contribs to sci. and educn, 2008; recognised by INNOVEC (Mexico) for contrib. to sci. educn, 2011. *Publications:* Science 5/13: a formative evaluation, 1977; Guides to Assessment: Science, 1983; New Trends in Primary Science Education, 1983; Teaching and Learning Primary Science, 1985, 2nd edn 1994; Primary Science: taking the plunge, 1985, 2nd edn 2001; The Teaching of Science, 1992, 6th edn as The Teaching of Science in Primary Schools, 2014; Enhancing Quality in Assessment, 1994; Developing Primary Science, 1997; Effective Teaching of Science: a review of research, 1999; Teaching, Learning and Assessing Science: 5–12, 2000, 4th edn 2006; Assessment of Learning, 2007; Student Assessment and Testing, 2008; Developing Teacher Assessment, 2010; Principles and Big Ideas of Science Education 2010; Assessment and Inquiry-Based Science Education: issues in policy and practice, 2013; Working with Big Ideas of Science Education, 2015; Teaching Science for Understanding, 2015; Inquiry-based Learning in Science: assessment and content implications, 2015; The Teaching of Science in Primary Schools, 2018; numerous articles in jls incl. Internat. Jl Sci. Educn, Studies in Educnl Evaluation, Cambridge Jl Educn, Curriculum Jl, Brit. Educnl Res. Jl, Res. Papers in Educn, Jl Curriculum Studies, Assessment in Educn, Studies in Sci. Educn. *Recreations:* opera, orchestral music, hill-walking, gardening, piano playing. *Address:* Haymount Coach House, Bridgend, Duns, Berwickshire TD11 3DJ.

**HARLEY, Gen. Sir Alexander (George Hamilton)**, KBE 1996 (OBE 1981); CB 1991; Master Gunner, St James's Park, 2001–08; Senior Military Adviser, Thales Defence Systems, 2003–12; *b* India, 3 May 1941; *s* of late Lt-Col William Hamilton Coughtrie Harley, 1st Punjab Regt and later Royal Indian Engineers, and Eleanor Blanche (*née* Jarvis); *m* 1967, Christina Valentine, *d* of late Edmund Noel Butler-Cole and Kathleen Mary (*née* Thompson); two *s*. *Educ:* Caterham Sch.; RMA Sandhurst. Commissioned RA 1962; 1962–73: 7 Para Regt RHA; Staff Capt. MoD; Adjutant; Canadian Staff Coll.; Mil. Asst to Chief of Jt Intelligence, MoD, 1974–75; Battery Comdr, 1975–78 (despatches); Directing Staff, Staff Coll., 1978–79; CO 19 Field Regt RA (The Highland Gunners), 1979–82; Col Defence Staff, and Operations Centre, Falklands War, MoD, 1982–84; Comdr 33 Armd Brigade, 1985–87; Chief of Ops, Northern Army Group, 1988–90; Asst Chief Jt Ops, Overseas and Gulf War, MoD, 1990–93; Administrator, Sovereign Base Areas, and Comdr British Forces Cyprus, 1993–95; DCDS Ops, and Dir Jt Ops, MoD, 1995–97. Adjt Gen., 1997–2000; ADC Gen. to the Queen, 1998–2000. Col Comdt, HAC, RHA, 1998–2003. Chm., Purple International, 2001–03. Pres., Combined Services Hockey, 1995–2000 (Hon. Vice-Pres., 2001–11); Patron: The Nordics Hockey Club, 1992–; Dan's Fund for Burns, 2003–. Hon. Vice President: Raleigh Internat., 1998–2008; Army Hockey Assoc., 2001–. Gov., King's Sch., Bruton, 2001–12; Pres., Caterham Sch., 2009–13. Visitor/Trustee, Bishop Sexey's Hosp., Bruton, 2013–. FCMI (FBIM 1982). Freeman: City of London, 2002; Wheelwrights' Co., 2002. *Clubs:* Naval and Military, Honourable Artillery Company.

**HARLEY, David Charles Mount-Stephen**, CMG 2011; *b* Hartfield, 10 Dec. 1948; *s* of Richard and Rose Harley; *m* 2008, Susanne Oberhauser; one *s* one *d*. *Educ:* Queens' Coll., Cambridge (BA 1971). EU official, 1975–2010, Dep. Sec.-Gen., EP, 2007–10; Sen. Advr, Burson-Marsteller, Brussels, 2010–11. Dir, Hartfield Consulting Ltd, 2010–. *Recreations:* theatre, literature. *E:* dcmsharley@gmail.com. *Club:* Groucho.

**HARLEY, Ian**, FCA, FCIB; Chief Executive, Abbey National plc, 1998–2002; *b* 30 April 1950; *s* of Michael Harley and Mary Harley (*née* Looker); *m* 1975, Rosalind Caroline Smith; three *s*. *Educ:* Falkirk High Sch.; Edinburgh Univ. (MA 1972). FCA 1982; FCIB 1998. Articled Clerk, Touche Ross, 1972–76; Corporate Planning Team, Morgan Crucible, 1976; joined Abbey National, 1977. Dir, Dah Sing Financial Hldgs, Hong Kong, 1998–2002; non-executive Director: Rentokil Initial plc, 1999–2007; British Energy plc,

2002–09; Remploy Ltd, 2004–10; John Menzies plc, 2009–15; Chm., Rentokil Initial Pension Trustee Ltd, 2007–15. Pres., CIB, 2001–02. Dir, Southwark Diocesan Bd of Finance, 2004–14. Chm., Ct of Govs, Whitgift Foundn, 2007–15 (Gov., 2002–). *Recreations:* reading, walking, cycling, golf. *Club:* Oriental.

**HARLEY, Ven. Michael;** Archdeacon of Winchester, 2009–15, now Archdeacon Emeritus; permission to officiate: Diocese of Winchester, since 2015; Diocese of Salisbury, since 2015; Diocese of Oxford, since 2017; *b* Ivybridge, Devon, 4 Sept. 1950; *s* of Ian Peter Harley and Joan Agnes Mabel Harley; *m* 1974, Deborah Mary Whillock; three *d*. *Educ:* Queen Elizabeth's Sch., Crediton; King's Coll., London (AKC 1973); Christ Church Coll. Canterbury (CertEd 1974); St Augustine's Coll., Canterbury; Lambeth Diploma (STh 1992); Univ. of Kent (MPhil 1995). Ordained deacon, 1975, priest, 1976; Curate, St William's, Walderslade, Chatham, 1975–78; Curate-in-charge, St Barnabas, Weeke, 1978–81; Vicar: St Mary Extra, Southampton, 1981–86; Hurstbourne Tarrant Benefice, 1986–99; Rural Dean, Andover, 1995–99; Vicar, Chandlers Ford, Winchester, 1999–2009; Master, St Cross Hosp., and Priest-in-charge, Winchester St Cross and St Faith, 2009–11. Chair, House of Clergy, 2004–09; Mem., Gen. Synod, 2005–15. Acora Link Officer, Dio. of Winchester, 1991–94; Diocesan Rural Officer, Winchester, 1994–97; Chair, Winchester Diocesan Adv. Cttee, 2017–19. Hon. Canon, Winchester Cathedral, 2007–15, now Canon Emeritus. *Recreations:* reading, music, films, theatre, cooking, history, current affairs, keeping fit, travel.

**HARLING, Christopher Charles, (Kit),** CBE 2010; FRCP, FFOM, FFPH; Consultant Occupational Physician, Derriford Hospital, Plymouth, 2006–11; Postgraduate Research Student, Institute of Sound and Vibration Research, University of Southampton, since 2016; *b* 12 Jan. 1951; *s* of Robert and Dorothy Harling; *m* 1976, Philippa Ann Capper; two *s*. *Educ:* Leeds GS; Manchester GS; Keble Coll., Oxford (MA); University Coll. Hosp. Med. Sch. (MB BS); Univ. of Plymouth (MRes Marine Biol., 2014). DAvMed 1988; FFOM 1991; FRCP 1995; FFPH (FFPHM 1999). Res. Fellow and Hon. Registrar, Inst. Envmtl and Offshore Medicine, Univ. of Aberdeen, 1979–80; Area MO, NCB, 1981–84; Consultant Occupational Physician: Sheffield HA, 1984–88; Bristol Royal Infirmary, 1988–2005; Sen. Lectr in Occupl Medicine, Univ. of Bristol, 1988–2005. Dir (part-time), NHS Plus, 2002–11. Civilian Consultant Advr in Occupational Medicine to RN, 1993–2012; Hon. Advr in Occupational Medicine to RNLI, 2005–13 (Mem., Med. and Survival Sub-cttee, 2005–13). MO, RNR, 1988–95 (PMO, HMS Flying Fox, 1994–95). Vis. Scientist, Biofouling and Ballast Water, PML Applications, Plymouth, 2015–17. Mem., Scientific Adv. Cttee, MoD, 2015–18. Hon. Sec., Specialist Trng Authy of Med. Royal Colls, 1999–2008 (Mem., 1996–98; Vice-Chm., 1998–99); Sec., 1987–90, Chm., 1990–93, Assoc. NHS Occupational Physicians; Mem. Council, 1982–84, Mem., NHS Work Gp, 1985–87, SOM; Faculty of Occupational Medicine, Royal College of Physicians: Examr, 1990–99, Dep. Chief Examr, 1993–94; Vice-Dean, 1994–96; Dean, later Pres., 1996–99; Chm., Ethics Cttee, 1999–2007. Mem., Biometrics and Forensics Gp (formerly Nat. DNA Database Ethics Gp), Home Office, 2014–19. Vice Chm., Salcombe Harbour Bd, 2006–16. Mem., RNSA, 1988–. *Publications:* papers on ethics, occupational medicine and health care workers. *Recreations:* sailing, flying, polar bears, penguins.

**HARLING, Marcus Roderick;** Partner, Construction and Engineering, Burges Salmon LLP, since 1992; *b* Plymouth, 1961; *m* 1995, Fiona; three *c*. *Educ:* University of Exeter (LLB). Admitted a solicitor, 1985. Trustee, NPG, 2018–. *Recreation:* Lake District. *E:* marcus.harling@burges-salmon.com.

**HARLOE, Prof. Michael Howard,** PhD; FAcSS; Vice-Chancellor, University of Salford, 1997–2009, now Emeritus Professor; Visiting Professor, London School of Economics, since 2009; Visiting Fellow, Kellogg College, Oxford, since 2014; *b* 11 Oct. 1943; *s* of Maurice Edward and May Cecilia Harloe; *m* 1976, Judy Rosilyn Philip; one *s* two *d*. *Educ:* Watford Boys' GS; Worcester Coll., Oxford (MA 1970); PhD Essex 1984. Res. Asst, Borough of Swindon, 1967–69; Res. Officer, LSE, 1969–72; PSO, Centre for Envmtl Studies, London, 1972–80; University of Essex: Lectr, 1980–84, Sen. Lectr, 1984–87, Reader, 1987–90, Prof., 1990–97, Dept of Sociology; Dean of Social Scis, 1988–91; Pro-Vice-Chancellor, 1992–97. FAcSS (AcSS 2000). Hon. DLitt Salford, 2010. *Publications:* (jtly) The Organisation of Housing: public and private enterprise in London, 1974; Swindon, A Town in Transition: a study in urban development and overspill policy, 1975; (ed) Captive Cities: studies in the political economy of cities and regions, 1977; (ed) New Perspectives in Urban Change and Conflict, 1981; (ed with E. Lebas) City, Class and Capital, 1981 (US edn 1982); Private Rented Housing in the United States and Europe, 1985; (jtly) Housing and Social Change in Europe and the USA, 1988; (ed and contrib.) Place, Policy and Politics, 1990; (with M. Martens) New Ideas for Housing: the experience of three countries, 1990; (ed jtly) Divided Cities: New York and London in the contemporary world, 1992; The People's Home: social rented housing in Europe and America, 1995; (ed) Sociology of Urban Communities, Vols I–III, 1996; (ed jtly) Cities After Socialism: urban and regional change and conflict in post-Socialist societies, 1996; (jtly) Working Capital: life and labour in contemporary London, 2002. *Recreations:* gardening, travel, reading, sociology, yoga. *Club:* Oxford and Cambridge.

**HARLOW, Archdeacon of;** *see* Herrick, Ven. V. A.

**HARLOW, Prof. Carol R.,** PhD; FBA 1999; Professor of Public Law, London School of Economics, University of London, 1989–2002, now Emeritus (Hon. Fellow, 2007); *b* 28 Aug. 1935; *d* of late Prof. Charles Harold Williams and Clare Williams (*née* Pollak); *m*; one *s* one *d*. *Educ:* King's Coll., London (LLB 1956; LLM 1970); LSE (PhD 1980). Lectr, Kingston Poly., 1972–76; Lectr, 1976–86, Reader, 1986–89, LSE. Jean Monnet Prof., European Univ. Inst., 1995, 1996. Bencher, Middle Temple, 2009 (Reader, 2019). Hon. QC 1996. *Publications:* Compensation and Government Torts, 1982; (jtly) Law and Administration, 1984, 3rd edn 2008; Understanding Tort Law, 1986, 3rd edn 2005; (jtly) Pressure Through Law, 1992; Accountability in the European Union, 2002; Tort Law and Beyond (Clarendon Lectures), 2004; (ed jtly) Administrative Law in a Changing State, 2009; (jtly) Process and Procedure in EU Administration, 2014; (ed jtly) Handbook of EU Administrative Law, 2016. *Recreations:* theatre, gardening, walking, painting. *Address:* Law Department, London School of Economics, Houghton Street, WC2A 2AE. *E:* c.harlow@lse.ac.uk.

**HARMAN, Rt Hon. Harriet;** PC 1997; QC 2001; MP (Lab) Camberwell and Peckham, since 1997 (Peckham, Oct. 1982–1997); *b* 30 July 1950; *d* of late John Bishop Harman, FRCS, FRCP, and Anna Charlotte Harman; *m* 1982, Jack Dromey, *qv*; two *s* one *d*. *Educ:* St Paul's Girls' Sch.; York Univ. Brent Community Law Centre, 1974–78; Legal Officer, NCCL, 1978–82. Opposition Chief Sec. to the Treasury, 1992–94; opposition front bench spokesman: on employment, 1994–95; on health, 1995–96; on social security, 1996–97; Sec. of State for Social Security, 1997–98; Solicitor-Gen., 2001–05; Minister of State, DCA, subseq. MoJ, 2005–07; Lord Privy Seal and Leader of the House of Commons, and Minister for Women and for Equality, 2007–10; Dep. Leader and Chair of Labour Party, 2007–15; Shadow Sec. of State for Internat. Develt, 2010–11, for Culture, Media and Sport, 2011–15; Shadow Dep. Prime Minister, 2011–15. Mem., NEC, Labour Party, 1993–98. *Publications:* Sex Discrimination in Schools, 1977; Justice Deserted: the subversion of the jury, 1979; The Century Gap, 1993; A Woman's Work, 2017. *Address:* House of Commons, SW1A 0AA.

**HARMAN, Sir Jeremiah (LeRoy),** Kt 1982; a Justice of the High Court, Chancery Division, 1982–98; *b* 13 April 1930; *er s* of late Rt Hon. Sir Charles Eustace Harman, PC; *m* 1960, Erica Jane (marr. diss. 1986), *e d* of late Hon. Sir Maurice Richard Bridgeman, KBE; two *s* one *d*; *m* 1987, Katharine Frances Goddard Pulay (*d* 2002), *d* of late Rt Hon. Sir Eric Sachs and *widow* of George Pulay. *Educ:* Horris Hill Sch.; Eton Coll. Served Coldstream Guards and Parachute Regt, 1948–51; Parachute Regt (TA), 1951–55. Called to the Bar, Lincoln's Inn, 1954, Bencher, 1977, Treas., 2000; QC 1968; called to Hong Kong Bar, 1978, Singapore Bar, 1980; Mem., Bar Council, 1963–67. Dir, Dunford & Elliott Ltd, 1972–79. *Recreations:* fishing, watching birds, reading, listening to music. *Address:* c/o Treasury Office, Lincoln's Inn, WC2A 3TL.

**HARMAN, Sir John (Andrew),** Kt 1997; DL; Chairman, Institute for European Environment Policy, since 2010 (Director, 2008–10); *b* 30 July 1950; *s* of John E. Harman and Patricia J. Harman (*née* Mullins); *m* 1971, Susan Elizabeth Crowther; one *s* three *d*. *Educ:* St George's Coll., Weybridge; Manchester Univ. (BSc Hons Maths); Huddersfield Coll. of Educn (Technical) (PGCE). Maths teacher, Greenhead Coll., Huddersfield, 1973–79; Head of Maths, Barnsley 6th Form Coll., 1979–90; Sen. Lectr in Maths, Barnsley Coll., 1990–97. Joined Labour Party, 1977: various posts, incl. Br. Sec., Co-ordinating Cttee Chm. and Constituency Vice-Chm.; Mem., Policy Commns on Envmt, 1995–96, and Local Govt, 1995–. Member (Lab): W Yorks CC, 1981–86 (Vice-Chm. 1982–85, Chm. 1985–86, Finance Cttee); Kirklees MDC, 1986–2000 (Leader, Council, and Labour Gp, 1986–99); Lead Comr for Intervention, Doncaster MBC, 2010–12. Dep. Chm. 1988–92, Vice-Chm. 1992–97, AMA; Local Government Association: Dep. Leader, Labour Gp, 1997–2000; Chm., Urban Commn, 1997–2000. Mem., Sec. of State's New Deal Task Force, 1997–2001; Mem., UK Delegn to Earth Summit, Rio de Janeiro, 1992. Dir, Kirklees Stadium Develt Ltd, 1993– (Chm., 1993–2016). Mem. Bd, 1995–2008, Chm., 2000–08, Envmt Agency. Director: Energy Saving Trust, 1997–2012; Aldersgate Gp, 2007–15; Nat. House Builders Council, 2009–17; Mem. Bd, Centre for Low Carbon Futures, 2010–14; Chm., One Community Foundn Ltd, 2010–19. Trustee: Nat. Coal Mining Mus., 2004–18; Forum for the Future, 2007–14; Huddersfield Choral Soc., 2014–. Contested (Lab) Colne Valley, 1987, 1992. DL W Yorks, 2012. Hon. FICE 2000; Hon. FIWM 2002; Hon. FIWEM 2002; Hon. FSE 2005. Hon. DCL Huddersfield, 2000. *Recreations:* music, reading, gardening, Huddersfield Town AFC. *Address:* 82A New North Road, Huddersfield HD1 5NE.

**HARMAN, Richard Stuart;** Chief Executive, Association of Governing Bodies of Independent Schools, since 2016; *b* 11 March 1959; *s* of late Donald George Harman and of Jean Patricia Harman (*née* Harrison); *m* 1989, Dr Karin Voth (Rev. Dr Karin Voth Harman); one *d*. *Educ:* Trinity Coll., Cambridge (BA English Lit. 1981); Exeter Univ. (PGCE). Sales Exec., Acad. Press/Harcourt Brace Internat. (Publishers), 1981–83; teacher of English and Drama, Marlborough Coll., 1984–88; Eastbourne College: Hd of English, 1988–91; Housemaster, 1991–95; Co-educn Co-ordinator, 1995–97; Registrar and Dir of Drama, 1997–2000; Headmaster: Aldenham Sch., Elstree, 2000–06; Uppingham School, 2006–16. Chm., Boarding Schs' Assoc., 2011–12; Chm., HMC, 2014–15. *Recreations:* sports, theatre, music, travel. *Address:* Association of Governing Bodies of Independent Schools, 3 Codicote Road, Welwyn, Herts AL6 9LY. *Clubs:* East India, Lansdowne.

**HARMAN, Robert Donald;** QC 1974; a Recorder of the Crown Court, 1972–97; a Judge of the Courts of Appeal of Jersey, 1986–98, and of Guernsey, 1986–99; *b* 26 Sept. 1928; *o s* of late Herbert Donald Harman, MC and Dorothy (*née* Fleming); *m* 1st, 1960, Sarah Elizabeth (*d* 1965), *o d* of late G. C. Cleverly; two *s*; 2nd, 1968, Rosamond Geraldine, 2nd *d* of late Comdr G. T. A. Scott, RN; two *d*. *Educ:* privately; St Paul's Sch.; Magdalen Coll., Oxford. Called to the Bar, Gray's Inn, 1954, Bencher, 1984; South-Eastern Circuit; a Junior Prosecuting Counsel to the Crown at Central Criminal Court, 1967–72; a Senior Treasury Counsel, 1972–74. Mem., Senate of the Inns of Court and the Bar, 1985–87. Appeal Steward, BBB of C, 1981–98. Liveryman, Goldsmiths' Co. *Address:* 2 Harcourt Buildings, Temple, EC4Y 9DA. *T:* (020) 7353 2112; The Clock House, near Sparsholt, Winchester, Hants SO21 2LX. *T:* (01962) 776461. *Clubs:* Garrick; Swinley Forest Golf.

**HARMAN, Stephen Richard;** Chairman, British Horseracing Authority, 2013–18; *b* Durham, 20 June 1956; *s* of Alec and Gill Harman; *m* 1983, Patricia Robigo; twin *s* one *d*. *Educ:* Durham Univ. (BA); Warwick Univ. (MBA). Dowty Mining, 1978–80; Shell: various UK posts, 1980–87; Dir, HK and China, 1987–93; Chief Exec., Eur. Liquefied Petroleum Gas, 1994–98; Chief Exec., Shell Marine, 1999–2002; Vice-Pres., Downstream, 2003–05; CEO, Pennzoil, 2006–10; Vice-Pres., Downstream Jt Ventures, 2010–13. Sen. Ind. Dir, UPOL, 2014–16. Chm., Ustinov Coll. Council, Durham Univ., 2013–. Trustee/Dir, Help for Heroes, 2010–; Co-Chair, Dumfries House Veterans' Charity, 2018–. *Recreations:* horseracing, golf, tennis, cricket, Rugby, historical fiction, mentoring, Cornwall, mining art. *E:* srh.harman@googlemail.com. *Clubs:* Lensbury (Teddington); Royal Cinque Ports Golf, Mullion Golf.

**HARMER, David John;** Chairman, Shaftesbury Society, 2005–07; Chief Executive, John Grooms Housing Association, 1988–2005; *b* 14 May 1940; *s* of Stanley James Arthur Harmer and Eileen Joan (*née* Callaghan); *m* 1971, Janet Arnott Dodds; one *s* one *d*; one *s* one *d* from previous *m*. *Educ:* Dulwich Coll.; Spurgeon's Coll. Surveyor, Portman Family Settled Estates, 1957–61; Ministerial Assistant, W Ham Central Mission, 1961–62; Church Pastor, Shaftesbury Soc., 1964–71; Founder, 1971, Dep. Dir, 1971–88, Shaftesbury Soc. Housing Assoc. Member: Exec., Christian Alliance Housing Assoc., 1987–90; Regl Exec., Nat. Housing Fedn, 1987–95 (Chm., 1990–93); Chm., Nat. Wheelchair Housing Assoc. Gp, 1992–95. Livability (formerly Shaftesbury Society, then Grooms-Shaftesbury): Member: Council, 1995–2010; Urban Action Cttee, 1995–99 (Chm., 1997–99); Audit Cttee, 2001–10; Pay Review Panel, 2002; Chief Exec.'s Appts Panel, 2002, 2010; Chairman: Grooms-Shaftesbury Merger Project Gp, 2006–07; Fundraising and Marketing Cttee, 2007–10; Vice Chm., Bd of Trustees, 2007–10; voluntary helper for Publicity and Fundraising; Vice Pres., 2013–. Mem., West Ham Central Mission Wkg Gp, 2000–01. Link Trustee, Nash Coll., Bromley, 2003–10 (Mem., Resources Cttee; Chm. Govs, 2005–10); Trustee, Kingsley Hall, Dagenham, 2016–. Mem., John Grooms Disability Enquiry, 2003. Mem., Inst. of Advanced Motorists, 2006–. Freeman, City of London, 2002. Diaconate Mem., Woodmansterne Baptist Ch., 2010–16. *Recreations:* housing and disability issues, Church and Christian activities, exhibition budgerigars (Sec., 2000–, Pres., 2008 and 2016, Croydon Budgerigar Soc.; Mem. Council, 2009–, Chm., 2011–16, Pres., 2018 and 2019, London and Southern Counties Budgerigar Soc.), fuchsias, family tree, Christian preaching. *Address:* Remrah, 146 Hayes Lane, Kenley, Surrey CR8 5HQ.

**HARMES, Stephen Douglas;** a District Judge (Magistrates' Courts), since 2014; *b* St Asaph, N Wales, 29 May 1959; *s* of Frank and Irene Harmes; *m* 1997, Tracey Lynne Hopkins; one *s* one *d*. *Educ:* Deeside High Sch., Queensferry, Flintshire; Univ. of Wales Inst. Sci. and Technol., Cardiff (BSc Hons Econs 1980); Inns of Court Sch. of Law. Called to the Bar, Gray's Inn, 1993; Crown Prosecutor, 1994–99; Crown Advocate, 1999–2014; First-tier Tribunal Judge (Immigration and Asylum), 2006–14. *Recreations:* tennis, Rugby. *Address:* Cardiff Magistrates' Court, Fitzalan Place, Cardiff CF24 0RZ. *T:* (029) 2046 3040. *E:* DJMC.Stephen.Harmes@ejudiciary.net. *Club:* Cardiff Castle Lawn Tennis.

**HARMSWORTH,** family name of **Viscount Rothermere** and **Baron Harmsworth**.

**HARMSWORTH, 3rd Baron** *cr* 1939, of Egham; **Thomas Harold Raymond Harmsworth**; publisher; *b* 20 July 1939; *s* of Hon. Eric Beauchamp Northcliffe Harmsworth (*d* 1988) and Hélène Marie (*d* 1962), *d* of Col Jules Raymond Dehove; *S* uncle, 1990; *m* 1971, Patricia Palmer, *d* of late M. P. Horsley; two *s* three *d*. *Educ*: Eton; Christ Church, Oxford (MA). Nat. Service, Royal Horse Guards (The Blues), 1957–59 (2nd Lieut). Stockbroker, 1962–74; DHSS, 1974–88. Pres., Dr Johnson's House Trust. *Publications*: Gastronomic Dictionary: French-English, 2003; Gastronomic Dictionary: Spanish-English, 2004; Gastronomic Dictionary: Italian-English, 2005; Gastronomic Dictionary: Portuguese-English, 2008. *Recreations*: sundry, including music. *Heir*: *s* Hon. Dominic Michael Eric Harmsworth [*b* 18 Sept. 1973; *m* 1999, Veronica Patricia, *d* of late Luis and Veronica Ausset, San Fernando, Chile; three *s* two *d* (of whom one *s* one *d* are twins)]. *Address*: The Old Rectory, Stoke Abbott, Beaminster, Dorset DT8 3JT. *T*: (01308) 868139. *Clubs*: Carlton, Brooks's.

**HARMSWORTH, Sir Hildebrand Harold**, 3rd Bt *cr* 1922; gardening writer; *b* 5 June 1931; *s* of Sir Hildebrand Alfred Beresford Harmsworth, 2nd Bt, and Elen, *d* of Nicolaj Billenstein, Randers, Denmark; *S* father, 1977, but his name does not appear on the Official Roll of the Baronetage; *m* 1960, Gillian Andrea (*d* 2005), *o d* of William John Lewis; one *s* two *d*. *Educ*: Harrow; Trinity College, Dublin. *Heir*: *s* Hildebrand Esmond Miles Harmsworth [*b* 1 Sept. 1964; *m* 1988, Ruth Denise, *d* of Dennis Miles; one *s* two *d*]. *Address*: Ewlyn Villa, 42 Leckhampton Road, Cheltenham GL53 0BB.

**HARNDEN, Prof. David Gilbert**, PhD; FRCPath; FRSE 1982; FRSB; Chairman, South Manchester University Hospitals NHS Trust, 1997–2002; *b* 22 June 1932; *s* of William Alfred Harnden and Anne McKenzie Wilson; *m* 1955, Thora Margaret Seatter; three *s*. *Educ*: George Heriot's School, Edinburgh; University of Edinburgh. BSc. Lectr, Univ. of Edinburgh, 1956–57; Sci. Mem., Radiobiology Unit, MRC, Harwell, 1957–59; Sci. Mem., Clinical and Population Cytogenetics Unit, MRC, Edinburgh, 1959–69; Prof. of Cancer Studies, Univ. of Birmingham, 1969–83; Dir, Paterson Labs, later Paterson Inst. for Cancer Res., Christie Hosp. and Holt Radium Inst., later Christie Hosp. NHS Trust, 1983–97; Hon. Prof. of Experimental Oncology, 1983–97, Prof. Emeritus, 1998–, Univ. of Manchester; Emeritus Fellow, CRC, 1997. Chairman: Educn Cttee, Cancer Res. Campaign, 1987–92; NW Regl Adv. Cttee on Oncology Services, 1991–95. Dir, Christie Hosp. (NHS) Trust, 1991–97. Trustee: New Heart/New Start, Wythenshawe Hosp. Transplant Fund, 1998–2002; Gray Lab. Cancer Res. Trust, 2000–06; Chm., Trustees, Friends of Rosie, Children's Cancer Res. Fund, 1999–2011. Hon. MRCP 1987. Chm., Editorial Bd, British Jl of Cancer, 1983–98. Mem., NRPB, 1995–99. *Publications*: papers on cancer research and human genetics in learned jls. *Recreation*: sketching people and places. *Address*: Tanglewood, Ladybrook Road, Bramhall, Stockport SK7 3NE. *T*: (0161) 485 3214. *E*: dgharnden@btinternet.com.

**HARNEY, Dr Marion**; Senior Lecturer in Conservation, since 2014 and Director, Learning and Teaching, Postgraduate Taught Programmes, since 2017, Department of Architecture and Civil Engineering, University of Bath; *b* Newcastle upon Tyne, 26 Aug. 1951; *d* of James Smith and Lavinia Christina Smith; *m* 1982, John Harney; one *s* one *d*. *Educ*: Univ. of Bristol (BA Hons English 2000); Univ. of Bath (MPhil 2005; PhD 2011). British Gas: Mgt Accountant, N Region, 1969–74; Salaries and Wages Supervisor, SW Region, 1974–84; Dir, EuroMediaCall, Bath, 1997–2001; University of Bath: Res. Officer, 2001–07; Heritage Coordinator, 2000–07; Lectr and Dir of Studies, MSc Conservation of Historic Gardens and Cultural Landscapes, 2007–14. Vis. Prof., Univ. of Westminster, 2016–. Dir, Gardens Trust, 2013– (Chair, Conservation Cttee, 2013–); Mem. Council, 2015–, Mem., Historic Envmt Adv. Gp, 2016–, Nat. Trust; Mem., ICOMOS-UK Cultural Landscapes and Historic Gardens Cttee, 2015–. Mem., Bath World Heritage Site Adv. Bd, 2007–; Chair, Bathscape Landscape Partnership Bd, 2013–17; Trustee, Hestercombe Centre for Landscape and Art, 2017–. FHEA 2014. Researcher, Pevsner Architectural Guide to Bath, 2003. *Publications*: Place-making for the Imagination: Horace Walpole and Strawberry Hill, 2013 (John Brinkerhoff Jackson Book Prize, 2015); (ed) Gardens and Landscapes in Historic Building Conservation, 2014; articles in jls incl. Architectl Rev., Studies in Hist. of Gardens and Designed Landscapes, EAAE Trans on Architectl Educn. *Recreations*: running, walking mad springer spaniel, opera, classical music, gardening, reading, watching crime dramas. *Address*: Department of Architecture and Civil Engineering, University of Bath, Bath BA2 7AY. *T*: (01225) 383977. *E*: m.harney@bath.ac.uk.

**HARNEY, Mary**; Leader, Progressive Democrats, Ireland, 1993–2006 and 2007–08; *b* March 1953; *m* 2001, Brian Geoghegan. *Educ*: Convent of Mercy, Inchicore, Dublin; Presentation Convent, Clondalkin, Co. Dublin; Trinity Coll., Dublin (BA). Contested (FF) Dublin SE, 1977. Mem. Dublin CC, 1979–91. Senator, 1977–81; TD Dublin SW, then Dublin Mid West: FF, 1981–85; Prog. Dem., 1985–2008, Ind., 2008–11; Minister: of Envmtl Protection, 1989–92; for Enterprise, Trade and Employment, 1997–2004; for Health and Children, 2004–11; Tánaiste, 1997–2006. Progressive Democrats: Co-Founder, 1985; Dep. Leader, and Spokesperson on Justice, Equality and Law Reform, 1993. Chm., Advanced Materials and Bio-Engrg Res. Centre, TCD. Chm., Pharmed Ltd; non-executive Director: Biocon Ltd, 2012–; Euro Insurances, 2012–; Ward Biotech, 2012; Diona Technol. Ltd. Chancellor, Univ. of Limerick, 2018–.

**HAROCHE, Prof. Serge**, PhD; Professor, 2001–15, now Emeritus, and Chair of Quantum Physics and Director, 2012–15, Collège de France; *b* Casablanca, Morocco, 11 Sept. 1944; *m* 1965, Claudine Zeligson; one *s* one *d*. *Educ*: Lycée Carnot, Paris; École Normale Supérieure, Paris (PhD 1971). Postdoctoral Fellow, Stanford Univ., 1972–73; Lectr, École Normale Supérieure, Paris, 1973–84; Maître du Conference, École Polytechnique, 1974–84; Prof., Paris VI Univ., 1975–2001 (Chm., Physics Dept, École Normale Supérieure, 1994–2000); Prof. (pt-time), Yale Univ., 1984–93. Vis. Prof., Harvard Univ., 1981. Mem., Inst. Universitaire de France, 1991–2000. Mem., French Acad. Scis, 1994; Foreign Mem., NAS, USA. Grand Prix Jean Ricard, French Physical Soc., 1983; Einstein Prize for Laser Sci., 1988; Humboldt Award, Humboldt Foundn, 1992; Michelson Medal, Franklin Inst., 1993; Tomassoni Award, La Sapienza Univ., Rome, 2001; Quantum Electronics Prize, Eur. Physical Soc., 2002; Townes Award, Optical Soc. of America, 2009; Gold Medal, Centre Nat. de la Recherche Scientifique, 2009; (jtly) Nobel Prize in Physics, 2012. Comdr, Légion d'Honneur (France), 2013. *Publications*: (with J.-M. Raimond) Exploring the Quantum: atoms, cavities and photons, 2006; contrib. papers to learned jls. *Address*: Département de Physique de l'École Normale Supérieure, 24 rue Lhomond, 75005 Paris, France.

**HARPER, Rt Rev. Alan Edwin Thomas**, OBE 1996; FRGS; Archbishop of Armagh, and Primate of All Ireland, 2007–12; *b* Tamworth, 20 March 1944; *m* 1967, Helen Louise McLean; one *s* three *d*. *Educ*: Leeds Univ. (BA 1965); C of I Theol Coll. Sen. Insp. of Historic Monuments, Archaeol Survey of NI, 1966–74; Asst Prin. Planning Officer, Staffs CC, 1974–75. Ordained deacon, 1978, priest, 1979; Curate Asst, Ballywillan, 1978–80; Incumbent: Moville with Greencastle, 1980–82; Christ Church, Londonderry, 1982–86; St John's, Malone, 1986–2002; Precentor, Belfast Cathedral, 1996–2002; Archdeacon of Connor, 1996–2002; Bishop of Connor, 2002–07. Preb. of St Audoen, Nat. Cathedral and Collegiate Church of St Patrick, Dublin, 1990–2001. Founder Trustee and first Chm., Ulster Historic Churches Trust, 1995–2000; Mem., 1980–95, Chm. 1988–95, Historic Monuments Council for NI. FRGS 2012. *Address*: Forth Cottage, 67 Lisnacroppin Road, Rathfriland, Newry, Co. Down BT34 5NZ. *T*: (028) 4065 1649. *E*: a.e.t.harper@gmx.com.

**HARPER, Antony Peter**, FREng, FIMechE; Industrial Strategy Challenge Director, Faraday Battery Challenge, since 2018; *b* Gateshead, 23 May 1964; *s* of Peter Harper and Brenda Harper; *m* 2002, Karen Powell; two *s*. *Educ*: Imperial Coll., London (BSc Hons Aeronautical Engrg 1986); Coventry Univ. (Post Grad. Dip. Mathematical Modelling and Computer Simulation 1994). FIMechE 2011; FREng 2016. Jaguar Cars Ltd: Hd, Computer Aided Design, 1989–97; Hd, Vehicle Packaging and Analysis, 1997–2003; on secondment as Product Devel Specialist, Ford Motor Co., 2003–05; Hd, Res. and Advanced System Develt, Jaguar Land Rover, 2005–16; Dir, Engrg Res., Jaguar Land Rover, 2016–18. Hon. Fellow, Univ. of Warwick, 2008. *Recreations*: lead guitar in a band, cycling, badminton, theatre, watching Liverpool FC. *Address*: UK Research & Innovation, Polaris House, Swindon SN2 1FL. *T*: 07827 982232. *E*: tony.harper@innovateuk.ukri.org.

**HARPER, Dr Caroline Anne**, CBE 2016 (OBE 2000); Chief Executive, Sightsavers International, since 2005; *b* 4 May 1960; *d* of Douglas and Barbara Harper. *Educ*: Bristol Univ. (BSc); Churchill Coll., Cambridge (PhD 1986). British Gas, 1985–91; Amerada Hess, 1991–2002 (Man. Dir, Amerada Hess Gas); CEO, Harper & Associates, 2002–05. Hon. DSc Bristol, 2013. *Recreations*: ski-ing, travel. *Address*: 4 Courtenay Towers, Courtenay Terrace, Hove, Sussex BN3 2WF. *E*: harper_ca@hotmail.com.

**HARPER, Air Marshal Sir Christopher (Nigel)**, KBE 2011 (CBE 2002); FRAeS; Founder and Managing Director, CH4C Global, since 2017; *b* 25 March 1957; *s* of late Denis Alan Harper and Cynthia Nancy Harper; *m* 1980, Janet Elizabeth Edwards; one *s* (and one *s* decd). *Educ*: Alleyn's Sch., Dulwich; King's Coll., London (MA Defence Studies). FRAeS 2019. Joined RAF, 1976; officer trng, RAF Henlow, 1976 (Sword of Honour); with 41 (Fighter) Sqdn, 1979–81; with Nos 31 and 14 Sqdns, 1982–85; Jaguar Qualified Weapons Instructor, 1984; Exchange tour, Canadian Air Force flying CF-18 Hornet with 421 Sqdn, 1986–89; Eurofighter Project Officer, MoD, 1989–92; RAF Staff Coll., Bracknell, 1992; MA to Minister (Armed Forces), MoD, 1992–94; OC No 41 (F) Sqdn, 1994–97; hcsc, 1997; Exec. Officer to Comdr AAFCE, 1997–99; Stn Comdr, RAF Coltishall, 1999–2001 (dispatches, Iraq, 2002); Air Cdre Typhoon, HQ 1 Gp, 2002–04; Dir, Jt Commitments, MoD, 2004–05; COS Ops, HQ Strike Comd, 2005–07; AOC No 1 Gp, 2007–09; Dep. Comdr, Jt Force Comd Brunssum, 2009–11; UK Mil. Rep. to NATO and EU, 2011–13; Dir Gen., NATO Internat. Military Staff, HQ NATO, 2013–16. Non-resident Sen. Fellow, Atlantic Council of US, 2017. Pres., RAF Flying Clubs' Assoc., 2005–; Vice Pres., RAF Charitable Trust, 2013–. Trustee, Air League, 2018–. Hon. Pres., No 1475 Sqdn ATC, 2003–; Hon. Air Cdre, No 2620 (Norfolk) Sqdn RAuxAF, 2017–. Pres., Edward Alleyn Club, 2010–11. FCMI (FIMgt 1997), CCMI 2012; CMgr 2015; MInstD 2016 (Cert. Company Direction, 2017). *Recreations*: flying, motorcycling, shooting, running, ski-ing, gastronomy, fine wine. *Clubs*: Royal Air Force (Vice Pres., 2013–17); Royal Air Squadron (Dir, 2016–); Strangers' (Norwich).

**HARPER, Prof. David Alexander Taylor**, PhD; DSc; CGeol, FGS; Professor of Palaeontology, and Principal, Van Mildert College, Durham University, since 2011; *b* 29 Sept. 1953; *s* of David and Jessie Harper; *m* 1981, Dr Maureen McCorry; two *s* one *d*. *Educ*: George Watson's Boys' Coll., Edinburgh; Walbottle Grammar Sch., Throckley; Imperial Coll. London (BSc); Queen's Univ., Belfast (PhD 1979; DSc 2005). ARSM 1975; FGS 1976; CGeol 1992; EurGeol 2004. Lectr, 1984–97, Reader, 1997–98, University Coll. Galway; Prof., Univ. of Copenhagen, 1998–2011; Res. Associate, Nat. Mus. of Scotland, 2019. Einstein Prof., Chinese Acad. of Scis, 2008; Vis. Prof., Lund Univ., 2014–; Dist. Vis. Prof., China Univ. of Geosciences, Wuhan, 2017–. Chm., Internat. Commn of Stratigraphy, 2016–. President: Internat. Palaeontol. Assoc., 2006–10; Palaeontol Assoc., 2014–16. Foreign Member: Royal Danish Acad. Scis and Letters, 2004; Royal Swedish Physiographic Soc., 2014. Hon. Fellow, Natural Hist. Mus., 2013. *Publications*: (with P. J. Brenchley) Palaeoecology: ecosystems, environments and evolution, 1998; (with Ø. Hammer) Palaeontological Data Analysis, 2006; (with M. J. Benton) Introduction to Palaeobiology and Fossil Record, 2009; contrib. peer-reviewed papers to learned jls. *Recreations*: hill walking, opera, enjoying malt whisky. *Address*: Principal's House, Van Mildert College, Durham University, Durham DH1 3LQ. *E*: david.harper@durham.ac.uk.

**HARPER, David Ross**, CBE 2002; FFPH; FRSB; Managing Director, Harper Public Health Consulting Ltd, since 2014; *b* 6 June 1955; *s* of Frank Harper and Louise Harper (*née* Mason); *m* 1978, Lorraine Chadwick; two *s* one *d*. *Educ*: Univ. of Dundee (BSc Hons Microbiol. 1977); Univ. of Birmingham (PhD Microbial Biochem. 1982). CBiol, FRSB (FIBiol 1995); FFPH 2006. Hd, Microbiol. Unit, Metropolitan Police Forensic Sci. Lab., 1981–89; Department of Health: Head: Microbiol. Pathology Services, 1989–91; Food Microbiol. Sci. Unit, 1991–94; Dangerous Pathogens, Biotechnol. and Envmtl Microbiol. Unit, 1994–2000; Envmt Br., 2000–03; Dir Gen. for Health Protection, Internat. Health and Scientific Develt, 2003–08; Chief Scientist and Hd of Profession for Scientists, 1996–2013, Dir Gen. of Health Improvement and Protection, 2008–13; Dir Gen. and Chief Scientist, Dept of Health, WHO (on secondment), 2012–13. Vis. Prof., Cranfield Univ., 2012–. Hon. Professor: Univ. of Dundee, 2007–; LSHTM, 2017–. Sen. Consulting Fellow, Chatham Hse, 2014–. Hon. FRSPH 2011. Hon. DSc Cranfield, 2010. *Publications*: articles in jls. *Recreations*: music, sport, motorcycles. *Address*: 30 Mycenae Road, SE3 7SG. *T*: 07872 492717. *E*: david@harperz.com.

**HARPER, Sir Ewan William**, Kt 2003; CBE 1997; JP; Chief Executive: United Church Schools Trust (formerly The Church Schools Company), 1990–2011; United Learning Trust, 2002–11 (Governor, 2002–11); *b* 21 June 1939; *s* of Leonard Robert Harper and Enid Harper (*née* Redman); *m* 1965, Jennifer Margaret Hoare-Scott; one *s* three *d*. *Educ*: Marlborough Coll.; Trinity Hall, Cambridge (Open Exhibnr; MA Hist.; Hon. Fellow, 2013). Man. Dir, 1972–87, Chm., 1985–87, Harper and Tunstall Ltd; Dir, Restoration of Lambeth Palace Chapel, 1987–88; Sec., Archbishops' Commn on Rural Areas, 1988–90. Mem., Hurd Commn on Office of Archbishop of Canterbury, 2000. Chm., Northants Industry Year, 1986; Vice Chm., Bd of Visitors, Wellingborough Borstal, 1970–82. Lay Mem., Chapter of Peterborough Cath., 2002–07. Member, Court: Lincoln Univ., 2011–18; Northampton Univ., 2011–. Mem., Adv. Bd, RPO, 2013–17. Governor: Benenden Sch., 1983–92 (Chm., Benenden Sch. Trust); Oundle Sch., 1992–2003; Maidwell Hall, 1993–2000; UC Northampton, 1997–2002. Trustee: Lambeth Fund, 1983–2014 (Chm., 2011–14); Maurice and Hilda Charitable Trust, 1998–; Academy Sponsors Trust, 2004–06; Oundle Music Trust, 2014–. JP Northants, 1973. Kt Comdr, Royal Order of Francis I, 2011. *Recreations*: gardening, golf, tennis, watercolours, history. *Clubs*: Athenæum, MCC.

**HARPER, Prof. Fred**, PhD; educational consultant, Central and Eastern Europe, since 1997; Dean, Seale-Hayne Faculty of Agriculture, Food and Land Use, University of Plymouth (formerly Plymouth Polytechnic), 1989–97, now Emeritus Professor of Agriculture; *b* 7 June 1947; *s* of Frederick and Queenie Elizabeth Harper; *m* 1971, Moyna Carole Hunter (marr. diss. 1996); one *d*. *Educ*: Univ. of Nottingham (BSc Hons Agric., PhD). Lecturer: Writtle Agricl Coll., Chelmsford, 1971–75; and Dir of Studies, Univ. of

Edinburgh, 1975–82; Vice-Principal and Dir of Studies, Harper Adams Agricl Coll., Shropshire, 1983–88; Principal, Seale-Hayne Coll., Devon, 1988–89. ARAgS, 1993. *Publications:* The Principles of Arable Crop Production, 1983; numerous pubns on crop physiology and production, agricl educn and overseas agriculture. *Recreations:* walking, travel, observing wildlife, watching sport. *Address:* 11 The Village, Shobrooke, Crediton, Exeter EX17 1AU. *T:* (01363) 776105.

**HARPER, Prof. John Martin,** DMus; FLSW; Director, International Centre for Sacred Music Studies, 2008–14, and Research Professor, 1998–2014, now Professor Emeritus, Bangor University; Honorary Professor of Liturgy and Music, University of Birmingham, since 2014; *b* 11 July 1947; *s* of late Geoffrey Martin and Kathleen Harper; *m* 1970, Cynthia Margaret Dean (marr. diss.); three *s*; *m* 1991, Sally Elizabeth Roper. *Educ:* King's Coll. Sch., Cambridge; Clifton Coll., Bristol; Selwyn Coll., Cambridge (Organ Scholar; MA); Birmingham Univ. (PhD 1976); MA Oxon. Dir, Edington Music Fest., 1971–78; Dir of Music, St Chad's Cathedral, Birmingham, 1972–78; Lectr in Music, Birmingham Univ., 1974–75, 1976–81; Asst Dir of Music, King Edward's Sch., Birmingham, 1975–76; Fellow, Organist, Informator Choristarum and Tutor in Music, Magdalen Coll., and Univ. Lectr in Music, Oxford, 1981–90; Prof. of Music, UC of N Wales, then Univ. of Wales, Bangor, subseq. Bangor Univ., 1991–98; Dir Gen., RSCM, 1998–2007 (Emeritus Dir, 2008). Leverhulme Fellow, 1997–98; Vis. Scholar, Sarum Coll., 2005–. Founder Dir, Centre for Advanced Welsh Music Studies, 1994–2003; Dir, Experience of Worship in Late Medieval Cathedral and Parish Church Res. Project, 2009–. Vice-Pres., Plainsong and Medieval Music Soc., 2008–. FRCO(CHM) 1972; FRSCM 2007; FLSW 2012. DMus Lambeth, 2010. Hon. FGCM 1996. Benemerenti Papal award, 1978. *Publications:* choral compositions, 1974–; (ed) Orlando Gibbons: Consort Music, 1982; The Forms and Orders of Western Liturgy, 1991; (ed) Hymns for Prayer and Praise, 1996, 2nd edn 2011–12; (ed) Music for Common Worship (7 vols), 2000–06; (contrib.) Late Medieval Liturgies Enacted, 2016; (Principal Ed.) Mass of the Blessed Virgin Mary, 2 vols, 2019; contributor to: New Grove Dictionary of Music and Musicians, 1980, 2000; Oxford DNB; articles and reviews in music jls and papers. *Address:* Bethania, 9 Llys y Tywysog, Tremeirchion, St Asaph, Denbighshire LL17 0UL.

**HARPER, (John) Michael;** Deputy Chairman, QinetiQ plc, since 2012 (non-executive Director, since 2011); *b* 2 Jan. 1945; *s* of Mark and Kathleen Harper; *m* 1st, 1968, Julia Carey (marr. diss. 1979); one *s* one *d*; 2nd, 1979, Judith Soesan; two *s* one *d*. *Educ:* King's Coll., London (BSc Eng, AKC, 1966); Imperial Coll., London (MSc 1967). Managing Director: Vickers S. Marston, 1975–80; BAJ Vickers, 1980–84; Graviner Ltd, 1984–88; Divl Man. Dir, 1988–99, Dir, 1999–2000, Williams plc; Chief Exec., Kidde plc, 2000–05. Chairman: Vitec Gp plc, 2004–12; BBA Aviation plc, 2007–14; Ricardo plc, 2009–14 (non-exec. Dir, 2003–14). Non-exec. Dir, Catlin Gp plc, 2005–10; Sen. Ind. Dir, Aerospace Technology Inst., 2014–. Chm., Fire Sector Fedn, 2018–. Trustee, Tring Park Sch., 2010–. Freeman, City of London, 2003. Liveryman: Firefighters' Co., 2004– (Master, 2012–13); Gunmakers' Co., 2014–. *Recreations:* sport generally, particularly cricket, football, Rugby; ballet, opera. *Address:* Claridges, High Street, Eggington, Beds LU7 9PQ. *Clubs:* Travellers, MCC.

**HARPER, Prof. (John) Ross,** CBE 1986; Founder, 1961, and Senior Partner, 1961–2001, Ross Harper & Murphy, Solicitors; Consultant, Harper Macleod, since 2001 (Senior Partner, 1991–2001); Professor of Law, Strathclyde University, 1986–2002, now Emeritus; *b* 20 March 1935; *s* of late Rev. Thomas Harper, BD, STM, PhD and Margaret Simpson Harper (later Clarkson); *m* 1963, Ursula Helga Renate Gathman; two *s* one *d*. *Educ:* Hutchesons' Boys' Grammar School; Glasgow Univ. (MA, LLB), Pres., Students Rep. Council, 1955. Pres., Scottish Union of Students, 1956–58; Chm., Internat. Students' Conf., 1958. Asst Solicitor, McGettigan & Co., Glasgow, 1959; founded Ross Harper & Murphy, 1961. Temp. Sheriff, 1979–89; a Parly Comr, 1997–. Pres., Law Soc. of Scotland, 1988–89 (Vice-Pres., 1987–88). Pres., Glasgow Bar Assoc., 1975–78; International Bar Association: Chm., Criminal Law Div., 1983–87; Chm., Gen. Practice Section, 1990–92 (Sec. and Treas., 1988–90); Vice-Pres., 1992–94; Pres., 1994–96. Chairman: Mining (Scotland), 1997–2007 (Jt Chm., 1993–95); Scottish Coal, 1997–2007; Alarm Protection Ltd, 2000–; Eur. Scanning Clinic Ltd, 2004–07; Admiralty Resources NL (Australia), 2005–. Chm., Finance Cttee, Greater Glasgow Health Board, 1984–87; Non-exec. Dir, Scottish Prison Service, 1993–96. Consultant, Makanyane Safari Lodge, SA, 2001–. Trustee, Nat. Galls of Scotland, 1996–99. Contested (C): Hamilton, 1970; W Renfrewshire, Feb. and Oct. 1974. Founder Chm., Soc. of Scottish Cons. Lawyers, 1982–86; Pres., Scottish Cons. & Unionist Assoc., 1989 (Hon. Sec., 1986–89). *Publications:* A Practitioner's Guide to the Criminal Courts, 1985; Glasgow Rape Case, 1985; Fingertip Criminal Law, 1986; Global Law in Practice, 1997; Beyond Reasonable Doubt (autobiog.), 2015; pamphlets on devolution, referendums, etc. *Recreations:* bridge, angling. *Address:* 3 Bungalow Court, Peppermint Grove, Perth, WA 6011, Australia. *Club:* Caledonian.

**HARPER, Joseph Charles;** QC 1992; *b* 21 March 1939; *e s* of Frederick Charles Harper and Kitty (*née* Judah); *m* 1st, 1984, Sylvia Helen Turner (marr. diss. 1994); two *s*; 2nd, 2012, Susannah Deighton. *Educ:* Charterhouse; LSE (BA, LLB, LLM). ARCM 1960. Lectr, later Hd, Dept of Law, Kingston Poly., 1965–70; called to the Bar: Gray's Inn, 1970 (Bencher, 2000); Antigua, 1985. Mem. Council, Justice, 1979–91. *Publications:* (Specialist Editor) Hill and Redman, Law of Landlord and Tenant (looseleaf), 17th edn 1982, 18th edn 1988–2013; (ed and contrib.) Halsbury's Laws of England, vol. 8(I) Compulsory Acquisition of Land, vol. 46 Town and Country Planning; (ed) Planning Encyclopedia, 2006–13. *Recreations:* music (especially playing the French horn), bibliomania. *Address:* Landmark Chambers, 180 Fleet Street, EC4A 2HG. *T:* (020) 7430 1221. *Clubs:* Garrick, Chelsea Arts.

**HARPER, Rt Hon. Mark;** PC 2015; MP (C) Forest of Dean, since 2005; *b* 26 Feb. 1970; *m* 1999, Margaret Whelan. *Educ:* Headlands Sch., Swindon; Swindon Coll.; Brasenose Coll., Oxford (BA 1991). Auditor, KPMG, 1991–95; Intel Corporation (UK) Ltd: Sen. Finance Analyst, 1995–97; Finance Manager, 1997–2000; Ops Manager, 2000–02; own accountancy practice, Forest of Dean, 2002–06. Contested (C) Forest of Dean, 2001. Shadow Minister: for Defence, 2005–07; for Disabled People, 2007–10; Parly Sec., Cabinet Office, 2010–12; Minister of State (Minister for Immigration), Home Office, 2012–14; Minister of State, DWP, 2014–15; Parly Sec. to HM Treasury (Govt Chief Whip), 2015–16. *Address:* House of Commons, SW1A 0AA.

**HARPER, Mark Eliot George;** QC 2016; *b* Nottingham, 16 May 1970; *s* of Vivian and Patricia Harper; *m* 1997, Julie Niven; two *d*. *Educ:* Arnold Hill Comprehensive Sch.; Downing Coll., Cambridge (BA Hons Law 1992; MA). Called to the Bar, Lincoln's Inn, 1993; in practice as barrister, specialising in chancery and commercial litigation, 1994–. *Recreations:* family, dog walking, weight training, pipe collecting, tattoo art, cricket, football, Rugby Union, books of Wilkie Collins, classic cinema, the making of the perfect log fire. *Address:* Kings Chambers, 36 Young Street, Manchester M3 3FT. *T:* (0161) 819 8264. *E:* mharper@kingschambers.com.

**HARPER, Michael;** see Harper, J. M.

**HARPER, Monica Celia,** CMG 2004; HM Diplomatic Service, retired; Head of International Relations, Shakespeare's Globe, 2005–06; *b* 18 Aug. 1944; *d* of late Frank Ernest Harper and Renee Alice Harper. *Educ:* Reading Univ. and Sorbonne (BA Hons); City of London Coll. (Dip. Business Studies). Entered HM Diplomatic Service, 1967; FCO, 1967–69; on secondment to internat. staff of SEATO, Bangkok, 1969–72; attached to Ecole Nat. d'Admin, Paris, 1973–74; Third Sec., BMG, Berlin, 1974–77; Second Secretary: Bonn, 1977–79; Personnel Ops Dept, FCO, 1979–82; Mexico City, 1982–84; Press and Inf. Officer, UK Delegn to NATO, 1984–88; First Sec., Western European Dept (Germany), 1989–94; Dep. Hd of Mission, Luxembourg, 1994–98; Consul Gen., Lille, 1998–2004; Counsellor, FCO, 2004. *Recreations:* music, theatre, exhibitions, travel, food. *Address:* 51 Tudor Way, Church Crookham, Hants GU52 6LX.

**HARPER, Prof. Peter Stanley,** Kt 2004; CBE 1995; DM; FRCP; University Research Professor in Human Genetics, Cardiff University, 2004–08, now Professor Emeritus; *b* 28 April 1939; *m*; two *s* three *d*. *Educ:* Exeter Coll., Oxford (BA 1961; MA, BM BS 1964; DM 1972). With Sir Cyril Clarke, Nuffield Inst. for Med. Genetics, Liverpool, 1967–69; with Dr Victor McKusick, Div. of Med. Genetics, Johns Hopkins Hosp., Baltimore, 1969–71; UWCM, Cardiff, 1971–2004, Prof. of Med. Genetics, 1981–2004. *Publications:* Myotonic Dystrophy, 1979, 3rd edn 2001; Practical Genetic Counselling, 1981, 7th edn 2010; (ed) Huntington's Disease, 1991, 3rd edn 2002; Landmarks in Medical Genetics, 2004; A Short History of Medical Genetics, 2008. *Recreations:* natural history, music. *Address:* Institute of Medical Genetics, Cardiff University, Heath Park, Cardiff CF14 4XN. *T:* (029) 2074 4057. *E:* HarperPS@cf.ac.uk.

**HARPER, His Honour Richard Saul;** a Circuit Judge, 2015–19; a Deputy High Court Judge, 2015–19; *b* 19 June 1953; *s* of Alfred and Netta Harper; *m* 1988, Amanda Louise Price; two *s* one *d*. *Educ:* Magdalen Coll., Oxford (MA). Called to the Bar, Gray's Inn, 1975; practising barrister, 1976–94; District Judge, Principal Registry of the Family Div., 1994–2015; nominated to sit in Court of Protection, 2008–19. *Publications:* Child Care Law: a basic guide for practitioners, 1991; Medical Treatment and the Law: the protection of adults and minors in the Family Division, 1999; Medical Treatment and the Law: Issues of Consent: the protection of the vulnerable: children and adults lacking capacity, 2014. *Recreations:* international affairs, reading, sport, music.

**HARPER, Robin Charles Moreton,** OBE 2018; Member (Green) Lothians, Scottish Parliament, 1999–2011; *b* 4 Aug. 1940; *s* of late Comdr C. H. A. Harper, OBE, RN and Jessicca Harper; *m* 1994, Jennifer Helen Carter (*née* Brown); one step *s*. *Educ:* Aberdeen Univ. (MA); Edinburgh Univ. (Dip. Guidance & Curriculum). Teacher: Braehead Sch., Fife, 1964–68, 1970–71; Kolanya Sch., Kenya, 1968; Amukura Sch., Kenya, 1969; teacher: English, Newbattle High Sch., 1971–72; Modern Studies, Boroughmuir High Sch., 1972–99. Rector: Edinburgh Univ., 2000–03; Aberdeen Univ., 2005–08. Co-convener, Scottish Green Party, 1999–2009. Contested (Green) Edinburgh E, 2010. Pres., EIS Local Assoc., 1989–91; Vice-Pres., Arboricultural Assoc., 2007. Trustee: Nat. Trust Scotland, 2011–17; Scottish Wildlife Trust, 2011–14 (Chair, 2014–17). Patron: Forth Children's Theatre, 1999–; Scottish Ecol Design Assoc., 2011–; Ambassador, Play Scotland, 2011–. FEIS; FRSA; FRSSA (Pres., 2009–11). Hon. FRIAS, 2008. *Publications:* Dear Mr Harper, 2011. *Recreation:* music.

**HARPER, Ross;** see Harper, J. R.

**HARPER, Rt Hon. Stephen Joseph;** PC (Can.) 2004; MP (Alliance, then C) Calgary Southwest, 2002–16; Prime Minister of Canada, 2006–15; Director, Harper and Associates Consulting Inc., since 2016; *b* 30 April 1959; *s* of late Joseph Harper and Margaret Johnstone; *m* 1993, Laureen Teskey; one *s* one *d*. *Educ:* Richview Collegiate Inst.; Univ. of Calgary. Chief Aide to Jim Hawkes, MP, 1985; Exec. Asst, then Chief Advr and Speech Writer to Deborah Grey, MP, 1989–93. Vice-Pres., 1997, Pres., 1997–2001, Nat. Citizens' Coalition. Contested (Reform) Calgary W, 1988. MP (Reform), Calgary W, 1993–97; Leader of the Opposition, 2002–04, 2004–06. Founding Mem., Reform Party, 1993; Leader, Canadian Alliance, 2002–03; Co-founder, 2003, Leader, 2004–15, Cons. Party of Canada.

**HARPER, William Ronald;** a Director, Thames Water, 1982–97; *b* 5 June 1944; *s* of William and Dorothy Harper; *m* 1969, Susan Penelope (*née* Rider); two *s* two *d*. *Educ:* Barton Peveril Grammar Sch., Eastleigh, Hants. IPFA 1965. Hampshire CC, 1960–64; Eastbourne CBC, 1964–68; Chartered Inst. of Public Finance and Accountancy, 1968–70; Greenwich London BC, 1970–74; Thames Water Authority: joined 1974; Dir of Finance, 1982; Dir of Corporate Strategy, 1984; Man. Dir, 1986; Dep. Chm., Thames Water Utilities, 1989; Thames Water PLC: Bd Mem., 1989–97; Gp Dir, Corporate Activities, 1992; Divl Dir, Products, 1994; Strategy Dir, 1996–97. Chm., Foundn for Water Res., 1989–94. Member: Council, Water Services Assoc., 1990–94; Bd of Management, Water Training, 1991–99 (Chm., 1993–99). CEN Rapporteur-Water, 1998–2013. *Address:* Sunnybank, High Street, Upton, Didcot, Oxon OX11 9JE. *T:* (01235) 851177.

**HARPIN, Richard David;** Chief Executive, HomeServe plc, since 1999 (Managing Director, Homeserve GB Ltd, 1993–99); Founder: Enterprise Trust, 2009; Growth Partner LLP, 2015; *b* Huddersfield, 10 Sept. 1964; *s* of David and Philippa Harpin; *m* 1997, Kate; two *s* one *d*. *Educ:* Royal Grammar Sch., Newcastle upon Tyne; York Univ. (BA Hons Econs). Brand Manager, Procter and Gamble, 1986–90; Harpin Ltd, 1988–; Sen. Consultant, Deloitte, 1990–91; Franchisee, Mortgage Advice Shop, Middlesbrough, 1991–92. Non-executive Chairman: Heating Components and Equipt Ltd, 1998–2004; Amsys Rapid Prototype and Tooling Ltd, 1999–2001; non-executive Director: Professional Properties Ltd, 1990–99; Baker Tilly Consulting, 1992–97; Mortgage Advice Bureau, 1997–2000. Mem., Leaders Gp, Cons. Party, 2009–. Mem., Nat. Apprenticeship Ambassadors Network, 2009–; Chm., W Midlands Apprenticeship Network, 2009–11. Enterprise Fellow, Prince's Trust, 2009–; created Scouting Entrepreneur Badge, Scout Assoc., 2010; Scouting Ambassador, 2011–. Ernst & Young Entrepreneur of the Year, 2009; PLC Awards Entrepreneur of the Year, 2011. *Recreations:* off piste and heliski-ing, swimming, private pilot's license, helicopter license. *Address:* HomeServe plc, Cable Drive, off Green Lane, Walsall WS2 7BN. *T:* (01922) 659701. *E:* richard.harpin@homeserve.com.

**HARPUM, Charles,** LLD; barrister; Fellow, Downing College, Cambridge, 1977–2001, now Emeritus; *b* 29 March 1953; *s* of Dr John Richard Harpum and Beatrice Doreen Harpum (*née* Harper). *Educ:* Queen Elizabeth Grammar Sch., Penrith; Cheltenham Grammar Sch.; Downing Coll., Cambridge (BA 1st Cl. Hons with Dist. 1975; LLB 1st Cl. Hons with Dist. 1977; Chancellor's Medal; MA 1979; LLD 2003). Called to the Bar, Lincoln's Inn, 1976, Bencher, 2001. Asst Lectr in Law, 1979–84, Lectr, 1984–98, Cambridge Univ.; a Law Comr, 1994–2001. Vis. Schol., Sch. of Law, Univ. of Va, Charlottesville, USA, 1991. Hon. QC 2018. *Publications:* (jtly) Megarry and Wade's Law of Real Property, 7th edn 2008 to 8th edn 2012; (jtly) Registered Land, 2002; (jtly) Registered Land: law and practice under the Land Registration Act 2002, 2004; numerous articles on property law in learned jls. *Recreations:* travelling, listening to classical music, drinking single island malts. *Address:* Falcon Chambers, Falcon Court, EC4Y 1AA. *T:* (020) 7353 2484.

**HARRA, James,** CB 2015; Second Permanent Secretary, HM Revenue and Customs, since 2018; *s* of James and Shirley Harra. *Educ:* Portadown Coll.; Queen's Univ. Belfast (law degree). Joined Inland Revenue as Inspector of Taxes, 1984; HM Revenue and Customs:

Dir of Corporation Tax and VAT, 2009–11; Dir of Personal Tax Customer Ops, 2011; Dir of Personal Tax Ops, 2011–12; Dir Gen., Business Tax, 2012–16; a Comr, 2012–; Dir Gen., Customer Strategy and Tax Design, 2016–17. *Address:* HM Revenue and Customs, 100 Parliament Street, SW1A 2BQ.

**HARREL, David Terence Digby;** independent consultant; Consultant, King & Wood Mallesons SJ Berwin (formerly S. J. Berwin), Solicitors, since 2007 (Partner, 1982–2007; Senior Partner, 1992–2006); *b* 23 June 1948; *s* of late Capt. H. T. Harrel, RN; *m* 1974, Julia Mary Reeves; two *s* one *d*. *Educ:* Marlborough Coll.; Bristol Univ. (LLB). William Charles Crocker: articled clerk, 1971–74; Asst Solicitor, 1974–77; Partner, 1977–79; Partner, Burton & Ramsden, 1979–81. Chairman: Kyte Gp Ltd, 2008–11; CPA Global, 2011–12; Savile Gp plc, 2011–13; Fairpoint plc, 2013–; non-executive Director: Wichford plc, 2007–11; Rathbone Brothers plc, 2007–17. Mem. Bd, ENO, 2005–16. Trustee, Clore Duffield Foundn, 1985–. *Recreations:* golf, tennis, fishing, shooting, walking, reading. *Clubs:* Swinley Forest Golf; Royal St George's Golf.

**HARRELL, Lynn Morris;** 'cellist; *b* 30 Jan. 1944; *s* of Mack Harrell, Metropolitan Opera baritone and Marjorie Harrell (*née* Fulton), violinist. *Educ:* Juilliard Sch. of Music; Curtis Inst. of Music. Principal 'Cellist, Cleveland Orch., 1963–71; Professor: College Conservatory of Music, Cincinnati, 1971–77; Juilliard Sch. of Music, 1977–86; Internat. Chair of 'Cello Studies, RAM, 1987–95; Piatigorsky Chair, Sch. of Music, USC, 1987–93; Artistic Dir, Los Angeles Philharmonic Inst., 1988–92; Principal, RAM, 1993–95; Prof. of Cello, Shepherd Sch. of Music, Rice Univ., Houston, 2002–09; Prof., Musikhochschule Lübeck, 2002–. Co-founder, 2010, and Pres., HEARTbeat (children's charity). Numerous awards and Grammys. *Recreations:* fishing, golf, chess. *Address:* c/o Columbia Artists Management Inc., 5 Columbus Circle, 1790 Broadway, New York, NY 10019–1412, USA.

**HARRHY, Eiddwen Mair;** soprano; *b* 14 April 1949; *d* of David and Emily Harrhy; *m* Greg Strange, journalist and broadcaster; one *d*. *Educ:* St Winefride's Convent, Swansea; Royal Manchester College of Music (Gold Medal Opera Prize); Paris (Miriam Licette Prize). Welsh Nat. Opera Chorus, 1970–71; Glyndebourne Festival Opera Chorus, 1971–73; début at Royal Opera House, Covent Garden, Wagner Ring Cycle, 1974; début, ENO, 1975; performances: Welsh Nat. Opera; La Scala Milan; Teatro Colon Buenos Aires; ENO; Glyndebourne; Opera North; Scottish Opera; UK and overseas orchestras; BBC promenade concerts; Australia, NZ, Hong Kong, S America, Europe, Scandinavia, USA; numerous recordings. Prof. of Vocal Studies, RCM, 2000–15; Visiting Professor: at Conservatoires in Vienna, Stockholm, Prague, Utrecht, Vilnius; Jacobs Sch. of Music, Indiana Univ., 2009; Helsinki, 2012; Nanyang Acad. of Fine Arts and Yong Siew Toh Conservatory of Music, Univ. of Singapore, 2013; Vocal Coach: Jacob's Sch. of Music, Indiana Univ., 2013–; Nat. Opera Studio, London, 2013–. Hon. DMus Swansea, 2015. FRWCMD (FWCMD 2002); FRCM 2012. FRSA 2003. *Recreations:* chamber music, skiing, golf, walking. *E:* eiddwen@crownhousemedia.com.

**HARRI, Guto;** broadcaster and communications adviser; Contributing Political Editor, GQ Magazine, since 2018; Vice President, Hanover Communications, since 2018; *b* Caerdydd, Wales, 8 July 1966; *s* of late Harri Elwyn and of Lenna Ogwen Pritchard-Jones; *m* 2000, Shireen Louise Jilla; two *s* one *d*. *Educ:* Queen's Coll., Oxford (BA); Centre for Journalism Studies, Cardiff Univ. (Dip. Journalism). Corresp., BBC Wales, 1989–96; reporter and presenter, The World at One, BBC Radio 4, 1996–99; Political corresp., BBC News, 1999–2002; Chief Political corresp., BBC News 24, 2002–04; Rome corresp., 2004–05, N America Business corresp., 2005–07, BBC News; Political corresp., Six O'Clock News, 2007–08; Sen. Policy Advr, Fleishman-Hillard, 2008; Dir of Ext. Affairs and Spokesman for Mayor of London, 2008–12; Dir of Communications, News UK (formerly News Internat.), 2012–15; Man. Dir, Ext. Communications, Liberty Global, 2016–17. Non-executive Director: Hay Literature Fest., 2016–; Hydro Industries, 2018–. Mem., S4C Authy, 2015–18. Presenter, Byd yn ei Le, S4C, 2018–. Hon. Fellow, Bangor Univ., 2008. Hon. Dr S Wales, 2018. Mem., volunteer crew, RNLI, 2013–. *Recreations:* sailing, sculling, travel, food and friends. *E:* Gutoharri@gmail.com.

**HARRIES,** family name of **Baron Harries of Pentregarth**.

**HARRIES OF PENTREGARTH,** Baron *cr* 2006 (Life Peer), of Ceinewydd in the County of Dyfed; **Rt Rev. Richard Douglas Harries;** Bishop of Oxford, 1987–2006; an Hon. Assistant Bishop, Diocese of Southwark, since 2006; Gresham Professor of Divinity, 2008–12, now Professor Emeritus; *b* 2 June 1936; *s* of late Brig. W. D. J. Harries, CBE and Mrs G. M. B. Harries; *m* 1963, Josephine Bottomley, MA, MB, BChir, DCH; one *s* one *d*. *Educ:* Wellington Coll.; RMA, Sandhurst; Selwyn Coll., Cambridge (MA 1965; Hon. Fellow, 1998); Cuddesdon Coll., Oxford. Lieut, Royal Corps of Signals, 1955–58. Curate, Hampstead Parish Church, 1963–69; Chaplain, Westfield Coll. 1966–69; Lectr, Wells Theol Coll., 1969–72; Warden of Wells, Salisbury and Wells Theol Coll., 1971–72; Vicar, All Saints, Fulham, 1972–81; Dean, King's Coll., London, 1981–87. GOE examr in Christian Ethics, 1972–76; Dir, Post Ordination Trng for Kensington Jurisdiction, 1973–79. Chm., C of E Bd for Social Responsibility, 1996–2001; Vice-Chairman: Council of Christian Action, 1979–87; Council for Arms Control, 1982–87; Member: Home Office Adv. Cttee for reform of law on sexual offences, 1981–85; ACC, 1994–2003; Bd, Christian Aid, 1994–2002; Royal Commn on H of L reform, 1999; Nuffield Council on Bioethics, 2002–07; HFEA, 2002–09. Chm., A Very Light Sleeper rev., Runnymede Commn on Antisemitism, 1994; Chm., Commn on Civil Society and Democratic Engagement, 2014–; Mem., Commn on Religion and Belief in British Public Life, 2013–16. Chairman: Southwark Ordination Course, 1982–87; Shalom; ELTSA (End Loans to Southern Africa), 1982–87; CCJ, 1992–2001; H of L Select Cttee on Stem Cell Res., 2001–02; Mem., H of L Select Cttees on Charities, 2016–17, on Citizenship and Civic Engagement, 2017–19. Pres., Johnson Soc., 1988–89. Consultant to Archbishops of Canterbury and York on Interfaith Relns, with special resp. for Jewish Christian relns, 1986–92 (Sir Sigmund Sternberg Award, 1989). Founder, Oxford Abrahamic Gp, 1992. Radio and TV work. Vis. Prof., Liverpool Hope UC, 2002; Hon. Prof. of Theol., KCL, 2006–. Lectures: Hockerill, and Drawbridge, London, 1982; Stockton, London Business Sch., 1992; Pall Mall, Inst. of Dirs, 1993; Theological, QUB, 1993; Heslington, York, 1994; Drummond, Stirling, 2007; Sarum Theol, Sarum Coll., 2009; Sir D. J. James, Cardiff, 2011; Sir D. O. Evans, Aberystwyth, 2011. FKC 1983; FRSL 1996; FLSW 2012. Hon. FMedSci 2004; Hon. FIBiol 2009. Hon. Fellow, St Anne's Coll., Oxford, 2006. Hon. DD: London, 1994; Grad. Theol Foundn, 2012; DUniv: Oxford Brookes, 2001; Open, 2006; Hon. DCL Huddersfield, 2008. President's Medal, British Acad., 2012. *Publications:* Prayers of Hope, 1975; Turning to Prayer, 1978; Prayers of Grief and Glory, 1979; Being a Christian, 1981; Should Christians Support Guerillas?, 1982; The Authority of Divine Love, 1983; Praying Round the Clock, 1983; Prayer and the Pursuit of Happiness, 1985; Morning has Broken, 1985; Christianity and War in a Nuclear Age, 1986; C. S. Lewis: the man and his God, 1987; Christ is Risen, 1988; Is There a Gospel for the Rich?, 1992; Art and the Beauty of God, 1993; The Real God, 1994; Questioning Belief, 1995; A Gallery of Reflections: the Nativity of Christ, 1995; In the Gladness of Today, 1999; God Outside the Box: why spiritual people object to Christianity, 2002; After the evil: Christianity and Judaism in the shadow of the holocaust, 2003; The Passion in Art, 2004; Praying the Eucharist, 2004; The Re-enchantment of Morality: wisdom for a troubled world, 2008; Faith in Politics?: rediscovering the Christian roots of our political values, 2010; Issues of Life and Death: Christian faith and medical intervention, 2010; The Image of Christ in Modern Art, 2013; The Beauty and the Horror: searching for God in a suffering world, 2016; Haunted by Christ: modern writers and the struggle for faith, 2018; *edited:* (jtly) Seasons of the Spirit, 1984; The One Genius; Through the Year with Austin Farrer, 1987; (jtly) Two Cheers for Secularism, 1998; (jtly) Christianity: two thousand years, 2001; (jtly) Abraham's Children: Jews, Christians and Muslims in conversation, 2006; *edited and contributed:* What Hope in an Armed World?, 1982; Reinhold Niebuhr and the Issues of Our Time, 1986; (jtly) Reinhold Niebuhr and Contemporary Politics, 2010; *contributed to:* Stewards of the Mysteries of God, 1979; Unholy Warfare, 1983; The Cross and the Bomb, 1983; Dropping the Bomb, 1985; Julian, Woman of our Time, 1985; If Christ be not raised, 1986; The Reality of God, 1986; A Necessary End, 1991; The Straits of War: Gallipoli remembered, 2000; That Second Bottle: essays on John Wilmot, Earl of Rochester, 2000; A Companion to English Renaissance Literature and Culture, 2000; Runcie: on reflection, 2002; Comparative Theology: essays for Keith Ward, 2003; Jesus in History, Thought and Culture, 2003; The Ethics of War, 2006; Britain's Next Bomb: what next?, 2006; The Price of Peace: just war in the twenty-first century, 2007; What makes us Human?, 2007; Does God Believe in Human Rights?, 2007; Intelligent Faith, 2009; British Foreign Policy and the Anglican Church, 2008; The Oxford Handbook of the Reception History of the Bible, 2011; Religion, Society and God, 2013; articles in Theology, The Times, The Observer and various other periodicals. *Recreations:* theatre, literature, walking. *Address:* House of Lords, SW1A 0PW.

**HARRIES, Dr Jennifer Margaret,** OBE 2016; Deputy Chief Medical Officer, Department of Health and Social Care, since 2019; *b* Watford, 26 Oct. 1958; *d* of Dr Peter George Higgins and late Marjorie Higgins (*née* Simpson); *m* 1986, Brian David John Harries (marr. diss. 1996); one *s* three *d*. *Educ:* Monmouth Sch. for Girls; Monmouth Sch.; Univ. of Birmingham (MB (1st) 1977; BSc Pharmacol. 1981; MB ChB 1984; PGCert Strategic Planning and Commng 2009); Cardiff Univ. (MPH 2000); Glamorgan Univ. (PGDip Health Econs 2001); Univ. of South Wales (MBA 2011). FFPH 2007. House physician, Birmingham Gen. Hosp., 1984–85; house surgeon, Sandwell Dist Gen. Hosp., 1985–86; SHO and Med. Registrar rotation, Southland Hosp., Invercargill, NZ, 1987–89; Clin. Asst, Haematol., Hereford Co. Hosp., 1995–96; Specialist Registrar (pt-time), Nat. Public Health Service Wales, 1996–2006; Dir, Public Health, Monmouthshire, 2007–09; Joint Director of Public Health: NHS Swindon and Swindon BC, 2009–11; NHS Norfolk and Waveney and Norfolk CC, 2011–13; Interim Dir, Health and Healthcare Improvement, Public Health Wales, 2013; Public Health England: Regl Dir of Public Health, S of England, 2013–17; Dep. Med. Dir, 2017–19. Hon. Res. Fellow, Univ. Hosp. of Cardiff, 2002–03; Hon. Lectr, Dept of Epidemiol., Med. Stats and Community Medicine, Univ. of Wales Coll. of Medicine, 2006–09; Vis. Prof., Univ. of Chester, 2019–. Member: Partner Bd, GMC, 2008–13; UK Jt Cttee on Vaccination and Immunisation, 2008–13; Nat. Adv. Cttee on NHS Constitution, 2011–14; NHS England Clin. Priorities Adv. Gp, 2016–19; Expert Adv. Gp for Medicinal Use of Cannabis, Home Office, 2018; Ministerial Task Force on Women's Health, DHSC, 2018–. FCMI 2010. *Publications:* articles in jls on ebola transmission and risk mitigation, infectious disease and health services mgt. *Recreations:* walking, antique button collecting, spoonerisms, Suffolk. *Address:* Department of Health and Social Care, 39 Victoria Street, SW1H 0EU. *T:* (020) 7210 4850. *E:* Jenny.Harries@dhsc.gov.uk.

**HARRIES, Prof. John Edward,** PhD; CPhys, FInstP; FRMetS; FLSW; Professor of Earth Observation, Imperial College London (formerly Imperial College of Science, Technology and Medicine), 1994–2013, Emeritus Professor of Physics and Senior Research Fellow, since 2013; on secondment as Chief Scientific Adviser to Welsh Government (formerly Welsh Assembly Government), 2010–13; *b* 26 March 1946; *s* of Brynmor and Marion Harries; *m* 1968, Sheila Margaret Basford; two *s* one *d*. *Educ:* Univ. of Birmingham (BSc Hons Physics 1967); King's Coll., London (PhD Physics 1971). Nat. Physical Lab., 1967–80; SO, later SSO, then PSO; Hd, Envmtl Standards Gp, 1976–80; Rutherford Appleton Laboratory, 1980–93; SPSO and Hd, Geophysics and Radio Div., 1980–84; DCSO, 1984; Associate Dir and Hd of Space Science Dept, 1984–93. Mem., NERC, 1995–97. President: Internat. Radiation Commn, 1992–96; RMetS, 1994–96. FLSW 2011. Fellow, Aberystwyth Univ., 2014. Hon. DSc Glamorgan, 2013. Dist. Public Service Medal, NASA, 2011; Mason Gold Medal, RMetS 2014. *Publications:* Earthwatch: the climate from space, 1991; more than 100 articles in books, jls and magazines. *Recreations:* walking, reading, music, supporting Welsh Rugby. *Address:* Spring Cottage, 129 Plymouth Road, Penarth, Vale of Glamorgan CF64 5DG. *E:* johnharries273@yahoo.com.

**HARRIES, Mark Robert;** QC 2019; *b* Newport, Gwent, 4 Oct. 1972; *s* of Robert and Ann Harries; *m* 2014, Kelly Harvey; one *d*. *Educ:* Rougemont Sch., Newport, Gwent; Queen Mary and Westfield Coll., Univ. of London (LLB Hons 1994); Inns of Court Sch. of Law (BVC 1995). Called to the Bar, Lincoln's Inn, 1995; in practice as a barrister, specialising in criminal defence. *Recreations:* Chelsea FC, wine, opera, music, tennis, family. *Address:* Carmelite Chambers, 9 Carmelite Street, EC4Y 0DR. *T:* (020) 7936 6300. *E:* mharriesqc@carmelitechambers.co.uk.

**HARRINGTON,** 12th Earl of, *cr* 1742; **Charles Henry Leicester Stanhope;** Viscount Stanhope of Mahon and Baron Stanhope of Elvaston, 1717; Baron Harrington, 1729; Viscount Petersham, 1742; *b* 20 July 1945; *s* of 11th Earl of Harrington and Eileen, *o d* of Sir John Foley Grey, 8th Bt; *S* father, 2009; *m* 1966, Virginia Alleyne Freeman Jackson, Mallow (marr. diss. 1983); one *s* one *d*; *m* 1984, Anita Countess of Suffolk and Berkshire. *Educ:* Eton. *Heir:* *s* Viscount Petersham, *qv*.
*See also* Earl of Snowdon.

**HARRINGTON, Prof. (John) Malcolm,** CBE 1992; MD; FRCP, FFOM, FFOMI, FMedSci, FFPH; Foundation Professor of Occupational Health, now Emeritus, and Director, Institute of Occupational Health, University of Birmingham, 1981–2000; *b* 6 April 1942; *s* of John Roy Harrington and Veda Naomi Harrington; *m* 1967, Madeline Mary Davies; one *d*. *Educ:* King's Coll., London (BSc, MSc); Westminster Hosp. Med. Sch. MD 1976; FFOM 1981; FRCP 1982; FFOMI 1994; MFPHM 1996, FFPH 2006. Hospital appointments, 1966–69; Lectr in Occupational Medicine, LSHTM, 1969–75; Vis. Scientist, Centers for Disease Control, Atlanta, US Public Health Service, 1975–77; Sen. Lectr in Occupational Medicine, LSHTM, 1977–80. Chm., Ind. Injuries Adv. Council, 1982–96. Ind. Review Lead, Work Capability Assessment, DWP, 2010–13. Gov., 2007–10, Lead Gov., 2009–10, Royal Devon and Exeter NHS Foundn Trust. Founder FMedSci 1998; Hon. FRSocMed 2004. *Publications:* (ed jtly) Occupational Hygiene, 1980, 3rd edn 2005; (with F. S. Gill) Occupational Health, 1983, 6th edn 2019; (ed) Recent Advances in Occupational Health, Vol. 2 1984, Vol. 3 1987; (ed jtly) Hunter's Diseases of Occupation, 10th edn 2010; papers in scientific professional jls. *Recreations:* music, gardening, cricket, reading biographies, theatre. *Address:* 1 The Cliff, Budleigh Salterton, Devon EX9 6JU. *Clubs:* Athenæum, Royal Society of Medicine.

**HARRINGTON, Dr Michael John,** CEng, FICE, FCIWEM; consultant, since 2011; Director, Michael Harrington Associates Ltd, 2011–14; *b* Neath, W Glamorgan, 6 Jan. 1953; *s* of late James Henry Harrington and of Kathleen Harrington (*née* Stitson); one *d*. *Educ*: Univ. of Wales, Cardiff (BEng 1st Cl 1976; PhD 2003); Harvard Business Sch. (AMP); Henley Management Sch. (Top Mgt Prog. 1990). CEng 1979; FICE 1996. Various construction and gen. mgt positions, 1976–95; Dir, Welsh Water, 1995–97; Managing Director: Hyder Infrastructure Services, 1997–99; Hyder Services, 1999–2001; Partner, Harrington Associates, 2001–03; Chief Information Officer and Dir, Corporate Services, Welsh Assembly Govt, 2003–11. FCIWEM (FIWEM 1996). *Recreations*: fine wine, cinema, keeping fit, theatre. *Club*: Cardiff and County.

**HARRINGTON, Patrick John;** QC 1993; a Recorder, since 1991; *b* 23 June 1949; *s* of Murtagh Joseph Harrington and Eileen Mary Harrington (*née* Kelly); *m* 1975, Susan Jane, *o c* of Captain K. W. Bradley, RN; one *s* one *d*. *Educ*: Ebbw Vale Grammar Sch.; Birmingham Coll. of Commerce (LLB Hons (London) 1972); Univ. of Wales (MA Eng. Lit. 2007). Called to the Bar, Gray's Inn, 1973, Bencher, 2001; Leader, Wales and Chester Circuit, 2000–03; Hd of Chambers, 2005–. Chm., Gwent Health Research Ethics Cttee, 1993–97. Sometime Lectr on advocacy, Univ. of Florida. Protector: Millennium Awards Trust, 2003–; Legacy Trust, 2006–14. Mem., Nat. Anti-Doping Panel, 2008–14 (Vice Pres., 2008–09). Pres., Ebbw Vale Male Choir, 2010–15. *Publications*: A Nutshell on Evidence, 1974; (with Bobby Graham) The Session Man, 2004. *Recreations*: playing and listening to music, tennis, ski-ing, classic motoring, horse racing, collecting books. *Address*: Farrar's Building, Temple, EC4Y 7BD; Broom House, Raglan, Monmouthshire NP15 2HW. *Clubs*: Cardiff and County; Ebbw Vale Rugby Football.

**HARRINGTON, Richard;** MP for Watford, since 2010 (C, 2010–19; Ind, since 2019); *b* Leeds, 4 Nov. 1957; *s* of John Harrington and Alma Harrington; *m* 1982, Jessie Benardette; two *s*. *Educ*: Leeds Grammar Sch.; Keble Coll., Oxford (MA Juris.). Graduate trainee, John Lewis Partnership, 1980–83; Co-Founder and Dir, Harvington Properties, 1983–; CEO, LSI Gp Hldgs plc, 1992–97. Non-exec. Dir, Eden Financial Ltd (formerly Eden Gp plc), 2005–. Parly Under Sec. of State, Home Office, DCLG and DFID, 2015–16, DWP, 2016–17, BEIS, 2017–19. Vice Chm., Target Seats, Cons. Party, 2012. *Recreations*: cinema, reading, taunting, citrology. *Address*: House of Commons, SW1A 0AA. *T*: (020) 7219 7180. *E*: richard.harrington.mp@parliament.uk. *Clubs*: Oriental; Oxhey Conservative; Town and Country (Watford).

**HARRIS,** family name of **Earl of Malmesbury** and of **Barons Harris, Harris of Haringey** and **Harris of Peckham**.

**HARRIS,** 8th Baron *cr* 1815, of Seringapatam and Mysore and of Belmont, Kent; **Anthony Harris;** *b* 8 March 1942; *s* of 7th Baron Harris and Laura Cecilia (*née* McCausland); *S* father, 1996; *m* 1966, Anstice (*d* 2007), *d* of Alfred Winter; two *d*. *Heir*: cousin Rear-Adm. Michael George Temple Harris, *qv*.

**HARRIS OF HARINGEY,** Baron *cr* 1998 (Life Peer), of Hornsey in the London Borough of Haringey; **(Jonathan) Toby Harris;** *b* 11 Oct. 1953; *s* of Prof. Harry Harris, FRS and of Muriel Hargest; *m* 1979, Ann Sarah Herbert; two *s* one *d*. *Educ*: Haberdashers' Aske's Sch., Elstree; Trinity Coll., Cambridge (BA Hons NatScis and Econ). Chair, Cambridge Univ. Labour Club, 1973; Pres., Cambridge Union Soc., 1974. Economics Div., Bank of England, 1975–79; Electricity Consumers' Council, 1979–86, Dep. Dir, 1983; Dir, Assoc. of CHCs for England and Wales, 1987–98. Chm., Toby Harris Associates, 1998–. Vis. Prof., London South Bank Univ., 2009–14. Non-exec. Dir, London Ambulance Service NHS Trust, 1998–2005. Chm., Nat. Trading Standards Bd, 2013–; Mem., Trading Standards Inst., 2013–. Chm., Fundraising Regulator, 2019–. Consultant Advr, KPMG, 1999–2013; Trng Advr, Infolog Ltd, 1998–2005; Sen. Associate, King's Fund, 1999–2004; Special Advr to the Bd, Transport for London, 2004–08; Mem., Public Sector Adv. Council, Anite, 2005–06. Mem., Haringey BC, 1978–2002 (Chair, Social Services Cttee, 1982–87; Leader, 1987–99). Mem. (Lab) Brent and Harrow, London Assembly, GLA, 2000–04 (Leader, Labour Gp, 2000–04); Member: Adv. Cabinet, Mayor of London, 2000–04; Metropolitan Police Authy, 2000–12 (Chm., 2000–04; rep. of Home Sec. overseeing counter-terrorism and security, 2004–12); Dep. Chair, AMA, 1991–96 (Chair, Social Services Cttee, 1986–93); Chair: Assoc. of London Authorities, 1993–95 (Dep. Chair, 1990–93; Chair, Social Services Cttee, 1984–88); Assoc. of London Govt, 1995–2000; LBTC-Training for Care, 1986–94; Local Govt Anti-Poverty Unit, 1994–97; Local Government Association: Chairman: Labour Gp, 1996–2004; Community Safety Panel, 1997–98; Mem., Exec., 1999–2003; Vice-Pres., 2005–10; Pres., London Councils, 2017–. Nat. Chair, Young Fabian Gp, 1976–77; Chair, Hornsey Labour Party, 1978, 1979, 1980; Mem., Labour Party Nat. Policy Forum, 1992–2004; Co-opted Mem., Lab. Party Local Govt Cttee, 1993–2004. Chm., Labour Peers' Gp, 2014– (Vice-Chm., 2009–12). Chm., All-Party Parly Gp on Policing, 2005–; Treas., Parly Inf. and Communications Technol. Forum (formerly Parly IT Cttee), 2005–16; Member: H of L Select Cttee Inquiry on Personal Internet Security, 2006–07; Jt Cttee on Nat. Security Strategy, 2010–14, 2017–; Chm., H of L Cttee on Olympic and Paralympic Legacy, 2013. Chair: Adv. Bd, City Security and Resilience Network, 2011–; Ind. Ref. Gp, Nat. Crime Agency, 2017–; Dep. Chair, Nat. Fuel Poverty Forum, 1981–86; Member: London Drug Policy Forum, 1990–98; Jt London Adv. Panel, 1996–97. Jt Chair: London Pride Partnership, 1995–98; London Waste Action, 1997–2000; Founding Chair, Inst. of Commissioning Professionals, 2007–08; Member: King's Fund Orgnl Audit Adv. Council, 1991–98; Exec. Cttee, RADAR, 1991–93; Nat. Nursery Exam. Bd, 1992–94; Home Office Adv. Council on Race Relations, 1992–97; Bd, London First, 1993–2002; Exec. Council, RNIB, 1993–94; Cttee of Regns of EU, 1994–2002; NHS Charter Advisor's Gp, 1997–98; London Pension Funds Authority, 1998–2000; Metropolitan Police Cttee, 1998–2000; Bd, London Develt Partnership, 1998–2000; Police Counter-Terrorism Bd, 2007–12; Police Counter-Terrorism Ministerial Adv. Gp, 2007–10; Chairman: Ind. Adv. Panel on Deaths in Custody, 2009–15; Audit Panel, Metropolitan Police, 2012; Ind. Rev. into Deaths of Young People in Prison Custody, 2014–15; Ind. Rev. into London's Preparedness to Respond to a Major Terrorist Incident, 2016. Non-exec. Dir, Cyber Security Challenge UK, 2011–. Chair: Wembley Nat. Stadium Trust, 1997–2018; Freedom Charity, 2009–15. Trustee: Evening Standard Blitz Meml Appeal, 1995–99; Help for Health Trust, 1995–97; The Learning Agency, 1996–98; Safer London Foundn, 2005–08; Bilimankwhe Arts, 2008–14. London Ambassador, CSV, 2005–12. Mem. Adv. Bd, Three Faiths Forum, 2003–08. Patron, The Larches, 2002–. Pres., Inst. of Strategic Risk Mgt, 2019–. Mem. Court, Middx Univ., 1995–. Governor: Nat. Inst. for Social Work, 1986–94; Sch. of St David and St Katherine, 1978–96; St Mary's Schs, Hornsey, 1978–96. FRSA 1993; FBCS 2011. Freeman, City of London, 1998. DUniv Middx, 1999. *Publications*: (with Nick Butler and Neil Kinnock) Why Vote Labour?, 1979; (contrib.) Economics of Prosperity, 1980; (ed with Jonathan Bradshaw) Energy and Social Policy, 1983; (contrib.) Rationing in Action, 1993; (contrib.) Whistleblowing in the Health Service: accountability, law, and professional practice, 1994. *Recreations*: reading, theatre, classical music, opera. *Address*: House of Lords, SW1A 0PW. *W*: www.lordtobyharris.org.uk, www.twitter.com/LordTobySays.

**HARRIS OF PECKHAM,** Baron *cr* 1995 (Life Peer), of Peckham in the London Borough of Southwark; **Philip Charles Harris,** Kt 1985; Chairman, Harris Ventures Ltd, since 1988; *b* 15 Sept. 1942; *s* of Charles William Harris, MC and Ruth Ellen (*née* Ward); *m* 1960, Pauline Norma Chumley (*see* Dame P. N. Harris); three *s* one *d*. *Educ*: Streatham Grammar School. Chm., 1964–88, Chief Exec., 1987–88, Harris Queensway Plc; Chm., C. W. Harris Properties Ltd, 1988–97; Chm. and Chief Exec., 1988–2012, Chm., 2012–14, Carpetright plc. Dir, Harveys Hldgs, 1986–2000; non-executive Director: Great Universal Stores, 1986–2004; Fisons Plc, 1986–94; Molyneux Estates, 1990–95; Matalan plc, 2004–06; Arsenal FC, 2005–. Mem., British Show Jumping Assoc., 1974–. Chm., Guy's and Lewisham NHS Trust, 1991–93; Vice-Chm., Lewisham Hospital NHS Trust, 1993–97; Member: Council of Governors, UMDS of Guy's and St Thomas' Hosps, 1984–98 (Hon. Fellow, 1992); Court of Patrons, RCOG, 1984–98; Chm., Generation Trust, 1984–; Dir, Outward Bound Trust, 2001–03; Lead Sponsor, Harris Fedn of S London Schools, 2007–. Dep. Chm., Cons. Party Bd of Treasurers, 1993–97. Dep. Chm., Nat. Appeal Bd, NSPCC, 1998–2007. Trustee, RA, 1998–2005. Freeman, City of London, 1992. Hon. Fellow, Oriel Coll., Oxford, 1989; FGCL 1995; Hon. FRCR 1993. Hon. DEc Richmond Coll., London, 1996; Hon. LLD South Bank, 1998. Hambro Business Man of the Year, 1983; Ernst & Young UK Entrepreneur of the Year, 2007. *Publications*: (with Ivan Fallon) Magic Carpet Ride, 2017. *Recreations*: football, cricket, show jumping, tennis. *Address*: Harris Ventures Ltd, Philip Harris House, 1A Spur Road, Orpington, Kent BR6 0PH. *E*: judy.willett@harrisventures.co.uk.

**HARRIS OF RICHMOND,** Baroness *cr* 1999 (Life Peer), of Richmond in the county of North Yorkshire; **Angela Felicity Harris;** *b* 4 Jan. 1944; *d* of late Rev. George Henry Hamilton Richards and Eva Richards; *m* 1st, 1965, Philip Martin Bowles (marr. diss. 1975); one *s*; 2nd, 1976, John Philip Roger Harris. *Educ*: Canon Slade Grammar Sch., Bolton, Lancs. Careers Advr and Employment Asst, 1974–76. Member (L, then Lib Dem): Richmond Town Council, 1978–81 and 1991–99; Richmondshire DC, 1978–89; N Yorks CC, 1981–2001. Chm., N Yorks Police Authy, 1995–2001. Dep. Chm., Assoc. of Police Authorities, 1997–2001; Chm., Adv. Cttee to the Constables' Central Cttee, 2014–15, Chm., Ind. Reference Gp, 2016, Police Fedn of England and Wales. Chm., EU Select Sub-Cttee F, H of L, 2000–04; Spokesperson, Police, 2003–10; Dep. spokesperson, NI, 2003–15; Dep. Speaker, H of L, 2008–18; a Lib Dem Whip, 2018–. Chm., Industry and Parliament Trust, 2010–14 (Dep. Chm., 2007–10); President: Nat. Assoc. of Chaplains to the Police, 2003–18; Police Treatment Centres, 2018–; Trustee: Police Rehabilitation Centre, 2004–18; Fellowship of St John UK Trust, 2015–. High Steward, Ripon Cathedral, 2011–. Companion, RAF Regt, 2008–. DL N Yorks, 1994. *Address*: House of Lords, SW1A 0PW.

**HARRIS, Prof. Adrian Llewellyn,** DPhil; FRCP; FMedSci; Cancer Research UK (formerly ICRF) Professor of Medical (formerly Clinical) Oncology, Oxford University, since 1988; Fellow of St Hugh's College, Oxford, since 1989; Consultant Medical Oncologist, Oxford University Hospitals NHS Trust, 1989–2018; *b* 10 Aug. 1950; *m* 1975, Margaret Susan Denman; one *s* one *d*. *Educ*: Univ. of Liverpool (BSc Hons Biochem. 1970; MB ChB Hons 1973); DPhil Oxon 1978. MRCP 1975, FRCP 1985. Hosp. appts, Liverpool, 1973–74; Clinical Scientist, MRC Clinical Pharmacology Unit, Radcliffe Infirmary, Oxford and Nuffield Dept of Medicine, 1975–78; Registrar in Academic Unit, Royal Free Hosp., 1978–80; Lectr and Sen. Registrar, Inst. for Cancer Res., Royal Marsden Hosp., 1980–82; Vis. Researcher, Imp. Cancer Res. Fund Mutagenesis Lab., London, 1982–83; Prof. of Clinical Oncology, Newcastle upon Tyne Univ., 1983–88. FMedSci 1998. Hon. DSc London; Hon. MD Democritus, Thrace. *Publications*: papers on growth factors in breast cancer, hypoxia and tumour angiogenesis, mechanisms by which breast cancers become resistant to treatment, hormone and drug treatment of cancer. *Recreations*: swimming, modern dance, science fiction, film, theatre. *Address*: Cancer Research UK Laboratories, Weatherall Institute of Molecular Medicine, John Radcliffe Hospital, Oxford OX3 9DS.

**HARRIS, Adrian William;** Head of Digital, Church of England, since 2016; *b* Lincoln, 21 March 1984; *s* of William Peter Harris and of Patricia Ann Harris; *m* 2014, Helen Jane Armes. *Educ*: Longsands Coll., St Neots; Canterbury Christ Church Univ. (BSc Hons Computing 2006). Hd of Digital, Conservative Party, 2011; Digital Communications Manager, 2011–13, Hd of Digital Communications, 2013–15, Tesco plc; Hd of Digital Communications, BUPA, 2015–16. Churchwarden and non-exec. Dir, St Martin-in-the-Fields, Trafalgar Square, 2016–18. *Recreations*: current affairs, swimming, walking. *Address*: Church of England, Church House, Westminster, SW1P 3AZ. *T*: 07823 883353. *E*: adrian.harris@churchofengland.org.

**HARRIS, Hon. Dame Anna Evelyn Hamilton;** *see* Pauffley, Hon. Dame A. E. H.

**HARRIS, Anthony David,** CMG 1995; LVO 1979; HM Diplomatic Service, retired; Senior Executive Officer, RFIB Middle East, Dubai, since 2006 (Deputy Chairman, RFIB Middle East Group, 2014–16); Director, RFIB Saudi Arabia Ltd, Riyadh, 2014–15 (General Manager, 2011–14); *b* 13 Oct. 1941; *s* of Reginald William Harris and Kathleen Mary Harris (*née* Daw); *m* 1st, 1970, Patricia Ann Over (marr. diss. 1988); one *s*; 2nd, 1988, Sophie Kisling (marr. diss. 2009); two *s* one *d*; 3rd, 2009, Erminia De Marco. *Educ*: Plymouth College; Exeter College, Oxford (BA 2nd cl. Hons Lit. Hum.; MA). Third Sec., Commonwealth Relations Office, 1964; Middle East Centre for Arab Studies, Lebanon, 1965; Third, later Second Sec., and Vice-Consul, Jedda, 1967; Second Sec. (Inf.), Khartoum, 1969; First Sec., FCO, 1972; First Sec., Head of Chancery and Consul, Abu Dhabi, 1975; First Sec., UK Mission to UN, Geneva, 1979; Counsellor, FCO, 1982; seconded to MoD as Regl Marketing Dir 1 (Arabian Peninsula and Pakistan), 1983; Dep. Head of Mission, Cairo, 1986; Head of Information Dept, FCO, 1990–93; Scrutiny of Security in FCO, 1993–94; Ambassador to UAE, 1994–98. Dir, Robert Fleming and Co. Ltd, 1999–2000; Advr, Technocraft Motor Corp., Iran, 2001–03; estabd Gemini Consultants, Dubai, 2001, in association with Jefferson Waterman Internat., Washington (Man. Partner, 2001–03); PR Manager, Ilyas and Mustafa Galadari Gp, Dubai, 2003–05; estabd Dubai branch, RFIB Middle East, 2006, set up RFIB Saudi Arabia Ltd, 2011. Regl Advr, Brunswick Gp, 2007–10; Middle East Consultant, M Communications, 2010–13. Mem., Adv. Bd, Consilium (Equinox Security Internat.), 2016–. Mem. Council, RSAA, 1999–2001. Dep. Chm. (Gulf Affairs), Next Century Foundn, 1999–. *Recreations*: shooting (HM the Queen's Prize, Bisley, 1964; British team to Canada, 1974), hill-walking, climbing, exploring Italy, Neolithic studies, Oriental, particularly Caucasian carpets. *Club*: Reform.

**HARRIS, Anthony Geoffrey S.;** *see* Stoughton-Harris.

**HARRIS, Anthony George,** CBE 2005 (OBE 1991); Principal, Harper Adams Agricultural College, 1977–94, retired; *b* 29 July 1929; *s* of John and Emily Kate Harris; *m* 1955, Sylvia Pyle; one *s* one *d* (and two *s* decd). *Educ*: Seale-Hayne Agricl Coll. (NDA, CDA Hons). FRSB, FRAgS. Lectr in Agric., Dorset Coll. of Agric., 1953–55; Lectr in Crop Production, Harper Adams Agricl Coll., 1955–58; Vice-Principal, Walford Coll. of Agric., 1958–66; Principal, Merrist Wood Agric. Coll., 1967–77. Chm., W Midlands Rural

Affairs Forum, 2002–05. Hon. FRASE 1999. Hon. Nuffield Schol., 2007. DUniv Open 1996. BCPC Medal, 1998. *Publications:* Crop Husbandry, 1961; Farm Machinery, 1965, 2nd edn 1974. *Recreations:* walking, reading. *Club:* Farmers.

**HARRIS, Rt Rev. Mgr Anthony John,** SCA; priest, Our Lady of the Visitation, Greenford, 1994–2004; former Assistant Priest, St Thomas More, Barking; *b* 6 May 1940; *s* of Philip John Harris and Eileen (*née* Kelly). *Educ:* St Patrick's Seminary, Thurles, Co. Tipperary (graduated in Phil. and Theol.). Ordained as Pallottine Priest, 1965; Dean of Discipline, 1965; Assistant Priest: Clerkenwell, 1965–68; Hastings, 1968–73; joined Chaplains' Br., RAF, 1973; served in UK, Germany, Cyprus and Ascension Island; Asst Principal Chaplain, 1986–92; Prin. RC Chaplain to RAF, 1992–94; VG, RAF, 1992–94. Prelate of Honour, 1992. *Recreations:* walking, swimming. *Address:* 6 Three Corners, Barnehurst, Kent DA7 6HF. *Clubs:* Royal Air Force; Essex.

**HARRIS, Prof. Anthony Leonard,** PhD; CGeol; FRSE, FGS; Professor of Geology, University of Liverpool, 1987–2001, now Emeritus; Distinguished Visiting Fellow, Cardiff University, since 2002; *b* 11 May 1935; *s* of Thomas Haydn Harris and Dora Harris (*née* Wilkinson); *m* 1959, Noreen Jones; one *s* one *d*. *Educ:* Cardiff High Sch.; University College of Wales, Aberystwyth (BSc, PhD). Geologist and Principal Geologist, British Geol Survey, 1959–71; Liverpool University: Lectr, Sen. Lectr, then Reader, 1971–87; Head, Dept of Earth Scis, 1983–94; Dean, Faculty of Science, 1994–2000. Hon. Res. Associate, 2004–10, Hon. Res. Fellow, 2010–, Nat. Mus. of Wales; Hon. Prof. in Geol., Aberystwyth Univ., 2010–. Pres., Geol Soc., 1990–92. Fellow, Geol Soc. of Amer., 1978, Sometime Captain Men's Hockey: UCW; Univ. of Wales; Edinburgh Civil Service. Major John Coke Medal, Geol Soc., 1985; C. T. Clough Meml Medal, Geol Soc. of Edinburgh, 1989; Silver Medal, Liverpool Geol Soc., 2003. *Publications:* (ed and contrib.) Caledonides of the British Isles, 1979; The Caledonian-Appalachian Orogen, 1988; papers in learned jls. *Recreations:* music, ornithology. *Address:* Department of Earth Sciences, Cardiff University, Cathays Park, Cardiff CF10 3YE; Pentwyn, St Andrews Major, Vale of Glamorgan CF64 4HD. *Clubs:* Geological Society; Rotary (Dinas Powys), Probus (Dinas Powys).

**HARRIS, Ven. Brian;** *see* Harris, Ven. R. B.

**HARRIS, Brian Nicholas,** FRICS; Consultant, CBRE (formerly Richard Ellis, then Richard Ellis St Quintin, subseq. CB Richard Ellis), Chartered Surveyors and International Property Consultants, since 1996 (Chairman of Partnership, 1984–93; Partner, 1961–96); *b* 12 Dec. 1931; *s* of Claude Harris and Dorothy (*née* Harris); *m* 1961, Rosalyn Marion Caines; two *d*. *Educ:* King Alfred's Sch., Wantage; College of Estate Management. Chartered Surveyor. Chm., City of London Br. of RICS, 1984–85; Member of Council: London Chamber of Commerce, 1985– (Dep. Chm., 1990–92; Pres., 1992–94; Bd Mem., 1989–96); ABCC, 1992–98 (Mem. Bd, 1994–98; Chm., Southern Reg., 1994–96); Australian British Chamber of Commerce (UK), 1988–2000; Mem., Aust. and NZ Trade Adv. Cttee, 1991–98. Chairman: Heathrow Airport Support Gp, 1993–99; Priority Sites Ltd, 2001–03; Educn Develt Internat. plc, 2003–05; Bann System Ltd, 2005–10; Bd Mem., London First, 1993–94. Hon. Property Advr, Order of St John, 1996–2001. Chairman: London Chamber of Commerce Educnl Trust, 2000–05; Britain Australia Soc., 2002–03. Gov., Woldingham Sch., 1986–93 (Dep. Chm., 1991–93). Mem., Court of Common Council, City of London, 1996; Sheriff, City of London, 1998–99; Mem. Ct of Assts, Co. of Glaziers and Painters of Glass, 1990– (Master, 2003); Liveryman, Co. of World Traders, 1989–. *Recreations:* flyfishing, gardening, golf. *Address:* Grants Paddock, Grants Lane, Limpsfield, Surrey RH8 0RQ. *T:* (01883) 723215. *Clubs:* Carlton, City of London, Flyfishers'; Tandridge Golf.

**HARRIS, Brian Thomas,** OBE 1983; QC 1982; *b* 14 Aug. 1932; *s* of Thomas and Eleanor Harris; *m* 1957, Janet Rosina Harris (*née* Hodgson); one *s* one *d*. *Educ:* Henry Thornton Grammar Sch.; King's Coll., Univ. of London. LLB (Hons). Called to the Bar, Gray's Inn, 1960; joined London Magistrates' Courts, 1963; Clerk to the Justices, Poole, 1967–85; Dir, Professional Conduct Dept, 1985–94, Sec., Exec. Cttee, Jt Disciplinary Scheme, 1986–94, ICAEW. Member: Juvenile Courts Committee, Magistrates' Assoc., 1973–85; NACRO Juvenile Crime Adv. Cttee, 1982–85; former member: CCETSW working party on legal trng of social workers (report, 1974); NACRO cttee on diversion (Zander report, 1975); HO/DHSS working party on operation of Children and Young Persons' Act 1969 (report, 1978); ABAFA working party on care proceedings (report, 1979). Chairman: Membership and Disciplinary Tribunal, PIA, 1994–2002; Disciplinary Tribunal, SFA, 1994–2002; Appeals Tribunal, Assoc. of Accounting Technicians, 1996–2002. Reviewer of Complaints: ICAS, 2001–10; Assoc. of Accounting Technicians, 2002–10. Pres., Justices' Clerks Soc., 1981–82. Editor: Justice of the Peace Review, 1982–85 (Legal Editor, 1973; Jt Editor, 1978–85); The Regulator and Professional Conduct Qly, 1994–98. *Publications:* Criminal Jurisdiction of Magistrates, 1969, 11th edn 1988; Warrants of Search and Entry, 1973; The Courts, the Press and the Public, 1976; The Rehabilitation of Offenders, 1976, 3rd edn 1999; New Law of Family Proceedings in Magistrates' Courts, 1979; (ed) entry on Magistrates in Halsbury's Laws of England, 4th edn 1979; (ed jtly) Clarke Hall and Morrison on Children, 1985; The Law and Practice of Disciplinary and Regulatory Proceedings, 1995, 7th edn 2013; The Tribunal Member, 1995; The Literature of the Law, 1998; Injustice, 2006; Intolerance, 2008; Passion, Poison and Power, 2010; The Calm Retreat: a short history of Olney, 2012; Tales from the Courtroom, 2013; The Surprising Mr Kipling, 2014; The Two Sided Man, 2015; Missing Books, 2016. *Recreation:* the contemplation of verse. *Address:* 24 Coneygere, Olney, Bucks MK46 4AF. *T:* (01234) 712932. *E:* brianharris2@mac.com.

**HARRIS, Carolyn;** MP (Lab) Swansea East, since 2015; *b* Swansea; *d* of Don and Pauline Marvelly; three *s*. *Educ:* Swansea Univ. Project Manager, Guiding Hands charity, 1998–2000; Wales Regl Dir, Community Logistics, 2000–03; Wales Regl Manager, children's cancer charity, 2003–05; Sen. Parly Asst and Constituency Manager, Office of Siân James, MP, 2005–15. Shadow Minister for Home Affairs, 2016–, for Women and Equalities, 2017–. Dep. Leader, Welsh Labour, 2018–. *Address:* (office) 485 Llangyfelach Road, Brynhyfryd, Swansea SA5 9EA. *T:* (01792) 462054. *E:* carolyn.harris.mp@ parliament.uk.

**HARRIS, Charles;** *see* Harris, G. C. W.

**HARRIS, Christine Elizabeth;** *see* Holt, C. E.

**HARRIS, Christopher H.;** *see* Heaton-Harris.

**HARRIS, Prof. Christopher John,** DPhil; Professor of Economics, University of Cambridge, since 1995; Fellow, King's College, Cambridge, 1995, now Emeritus; *b* 22 Sept. 1960; *s* of Colin Christopher Harris and Barbara Kay (*née* Hall); *m* 1993, Qun Li. *Educ:* Oundle Sch.; Corpus Christi Coll., Oxford (BA Maths 1981); Nuffield Coll., Oxford (MPhil Econ 1983; DPhil Econ 1984). Prize Research Fellow, Nuffield Coll., Oxford, 1983–84; Univ. Lectr in Econs, Univ. of Oxford and Fellow of Nuffield Coll., 1984–94. Vis. Prof., MIT, 1990–91; Vis. Fellow, Princeton Univ., 2000–01; British Acad. Res. Prof., 2000–03. Richard B. Fisher Mem., IAS, 2001–02. *Publications:* articles on dynamic games and theory of industrial organisation in Econometrica, Rev. of Econ. Studies, Jl of Econ. Theory, etc. *Recreations:* walking, running, swimming. *Address:* Faculty of Economics, Austin Robinson Building, Sidgwick Avenue, Cambridge CB3 9DD.

**HARRIS, Prof. Christopher John,** PhD, DSc; FIMA, FREng, FIET; Lucas Professor of Aerospace Systems Engineering, 1987–99, Professor of Computational Intelligence, 1999–2015, now Professor Emeritus, University of Southampton (Head, Department of Electronic and Computer Science, 1999–2002; Research Professor, 2003–15); *b* 23 Dec. 1945; *s* of George Harris and Hilda Harris; *m* 1965, Ruth Joy Harris; one *s* two *d*. *Educ:* Univ. of Leicester (BSc); MA Oxon; Univ. of Southampton (PhD 1972; DSc 2002). FIMA 1979; CEng 1979; FIET (FIEE 1991); FREng (FEng 1996). Lecturer: Hull Univ., 1967–72; UMIST, 1972–76; Oxford Univ., 1976–80; Fellow, St Edmund Hall, Oxford, 1976–80; Dep. Chief Scientist, MoD, 1980–84; Prof., Cranfield Inst. of Technol., 1984–86; Dir, Nat. Defence Technol. Centre in Data and Information Fusion, MoD, 2002–04. Hon. Professor: Univ. Hong Kong, 1991; Huazhong Univ., China, 1991. Achievement Medal, 1998, Faraday Medal, 2001, IEE. *Publications:* (with J. F. Miles) Stability of Linear Systems, 1980, 2nd edn 1985; (with J. M. Valenca) Stability of Input-output Dynamic Systems, 1983, 2nd edn 1987; (ed) Applications of Artificial Intelligence to $C^2$ Systems, 1988; (jtly) Intelligent Control: aspects of fuzzy logic and neural nets, 1993; (with M. Brown) Neurofuzzy Adaptive Modelling and Control, 1994; (jtly) Advanced Adaptive Control, 1995; Adaptive Neural Network Control of Robotic Manipulators, 1998; Data Based Modelling, Estimation and Control, 2002. *Recreations:* painting, scuba diving, gardening, fly fishing. *Address:* 14 Beechwood Rise, West End, Southampton, Hants SO18 3PW. *T:* (023) 8047 2363.

**HARRIS, Sir Christopher (John Ashford),** 3rd Bt *cr* 1932, of Bethnal Green, co. London; Chief Executive Officer, North Pacific Securities Ltd, since 1980; *b* Wellington, NZ, 26 Aug. 1934; *er s* of Sir Jack Wolfred Ashford Harris, 2nd Bt and Patricia, *o d* of A. P. Penman, Wahroonga, Sydney, NSW; *S* father, 2009; *m* 1957, Anna, *d* of F. H. T. de Malmanche, Auckland, NZ; one *s* two *d*. *Educ:* Wanganui Collegiate Sch., NZ. Former Mem. Bd of ten cos. *Recreations:* sailing, athletics, golf. *Heir: s* Andrew Frederick Ashford Harris [*b* 17 March 1958; *m* 1st, 1990, Terena Ann (marr. diss. 1999); one *d*; 2nd, 2004, Gabriele Schaefer]. *Address:* 21 Anne Street, Wadestown, Wellington, New Zealand. *T:* (4) 4723212. *Clubs:* Wellington, Royal Wellington Golf (Wellington, NZ).

**HARRIS, Claire Victoria;** *see* Williams, C. V.

**HARRIS, Prof. Clare Elizabeth,** PhD; FBA 2019; Professor of Visual Anthropology, since 2014, and Curator for Asian Collections, Pitt Rivers Museum, since 1998, University of Oxford; Fellow of Magdalen College, Oxford, since 2002; *b* Wallingford, 29 March 1965; *d* of Reginald Harris and Annie Harris; partner, Rupert Gill; one *s*. *Educ:* King Edward VI Upper Sch., Bury St Edmunds; Robinson Coll., Cambridge (BA Hons 1st Cl. Hist. of Art 1988); Sch. of Oriental and African Studies, Univ. of London (MA (Dist.) Art and Archaeol. 1989; PhD 1997); Univ. of Oxford (MA 1998). Res. and Teaching Asst, Univ. of London, 1992–94; Lectr, UEA, 1994–98; Lectr, Univ. of Oxford, 1998–2014; Fellow, Linacre Coll., Oxford, 1998–2001. Vis. Prof., Univ. of Leiden, 2014. *Publications:* In the Image of Tibet: Tibetan painting after 1959, 1999 (Jury Prize, Internat. Centre for Ethnohist., 2000); (with Tsering Shakya) Seeing Lhasa: British depictions of the Tibetan capital 1936–1947, 2003; (ed jtly) Ladakh: culture at the crossroads, 2005; The Museum on the Roof of the World: art, politics and the representation of Tibet, 2012 (E. Gene Smith Prize, Assoc. of Asian Studies, 2014); Photography and Tibet, 2016; articles in learned jls; chapters in edited collections; exhibn catalogues. *Recreations:* singing in gospel choir, collecting old postcards, travelling, gardening, disco dancing, visiting exhibitions, museums and historic sites. *Address:* Magdalen College, High Street, Oxford OX1 4AU. *E:* clare.harris@magd.ox.ac.uk.

**HARRIS, Colleen Lorraine,** MVO 2004; DL; Director, Colleen Harris Associates, since 2007; *b* 24 Sept. 1955; *d* of late Gladstone Meertins and Sheila Meertins; *m* 1976, Wayne Harris; two *s*. Press Officer to Prime Minister, 1987–88; various Govt PR roles, 1988–97; Hd, Media Planning for Dep. Prime Minister, 1997–98; Dep. Press Sec., 1998–2000, Press Sec., 2000–03, to Prince of Wales; Strategy and Communications Dir, CRE, 2003–06; Interim Dir of Communications, Equality and Human Rights Commn, 2007; Dir, Dignity Mgt Consultancy, 2007–09. Non-exec. Dir, Oxleas NHS Foundn Trust, 2016–17. Chm., Caribbean Bd, 2002–08. Member: CRUK, 2003–; Press Complaints Commn, 2006–09. FRSA 2006; MCIPR 2008. Member: Council, Royal Albert Hall, 2004–14; Bd, Hackney Empire, 2008–14. Trustee: YMCA Central, 2010–; Dulwich Picture Gall., 2011–18. Gov., City Lit. Inst., 2011–12. DL Gtr London, 2015; Chair, HM Gtr London Lieutenancy Ltd, 2017–. *Recreations:* music, dance, drama, radio, all forms of theatrical performance, practising the piano. *W:* www.colleenharris.co.uk. *Club:* Soho House.

**HARRIS, David Anthony;** *b* 1 Nov. 1937; *s* of late E. C. Harris and Betty Harris; *m* 1st, 1962, Diana Joan Hansford (*d* 1996); one *s* one *d*; 2nd, 1998, Mrs Alison Bunker. *Educ:* Mount Radford Sch., Exeter. Jun. Reporter, Express and Echo, Exeter, 1954–58. Nat. Service, commnd Devonshire and Dorset Regt, 1958; Staff Captain (Public Relns) GHQ, MELF, 1959. Reporter, Western Morning News, 1960–61; joined Daily Telegraph, Westminster Staff, 1961; Political Correspondent, Daily Telegraph, 1976–79; MEP (C) Cornwall and Plymouth, 1979–84. Chm., Parly Lobby Journalists, 1977–78. Mem. (C) Bromley, and Bromley, Ravensbourne, GLC, 1968–77; Chm. Thamesmead Ctee, 1971–73. Contested (C) Mitcham and Morden, Feb. 1974. MP (C) St Ives, 1983–97. PPS to Minister of State for Foreign and Commonwealth Affairs, 1987–88, to Sec. of State for Foreign and Commonwealth Affairs, 1988–89, to Dep. Prime Minister and Leader of Commons, 1989–90. Member, Select Committee: on Agriculture, 1983–87; on Broadcasting, 1988–97; on Foreign Affairs, 1991–97; on Social Security, 1991–92. Chairman: Cons. Fisheries Cttee, 1987–97; W Country Cons. MPs, 1991–92. Leading Cons. spokesman for Cornwall, 1997–2001. Chm., Seafood Cornwall, 2004–12. Mem. Council, Royal Nat. Mission to Deep Sea Fishermen, 1993–2013 (Chm., 2009–12). Churchwarden, St Piran's, Perran-ar-Worthal, 2001–05. *Recreations:* gardening, reading obituaries. *Address:* Trewedna Farm, Perranwell Station, near Truro, Cornwall TR3 7PQ.

**HARRIS, David John,** CMG 1999; PhD; Professor of Public International Law, 1981–2003, now Emeritus, and Co-Director, Human Rights Law Centre, since 1993, University of Nottingham; *b* 3 July 1938; *s* of Sidney and May Harris; *m* 1963, Sandra Jean Nelson (*d* 2015); two *s*. *Educ:* Sutton High Sch., Plymouth; KCL (LLB 1959); LSE (LLM 1961; PhD 1977). Ford Foundn Res. Fellow, Univ. of Michigan Law Sch., 1961–62; Asst Lectr, QUB, 1962–63; University of Nottingham: Asst Lectr, 1963–64; Lectr, 1964–73; Sen. Lectr in Law, 1973–81; Head, Law Dept, 1987–90. Mem., Cttee of Ind. Experts, European Social Charter, 1990–96. *Publications:* (ed) Garner's Environmental Law, 5 vols, 1973–2005; Cases and Materials on International Law, 1973, 8th edn (with S. Sivakumaran) 2015; (with S. Bailey and B. Jones) Civil Liberties: cases and materials, 1980, 5th edn 2001; The European Social Charter, 1984, 2nd edn (with J. Darcy) 2001; (with J. Shepherd) An Index to British Treaties 1969–80, 1991; (with M. O'Boyle and C. Warbrick) The Law of the European Convention on Human Rights, 1995, 4th edn (with M. O'Boyle, E. Bates and C. Buckley) 2018; (with S. Joseph) The International Covenant on Civil and Political Rights and United Kingdom Law, 1995; (with D. Gomien and L. Zwaak) Law and Practice of the European Convention on Human Rights and the European Social Charter, 1996; (with S. Livingstone) The Inter-American System of Human Rights, 1998; (with R. Burchill and A. Owers) Economic, Social and Cultural Rights: their implementation in UK law, 1999; (consultant ed.) Moeckli, Sivakumaran and Shah, International Human Rights Law, 2nd edn 2013, 3rd edn 2018. *Recreations:* travelling, walking. *Address:* School of Law, The University, Nottingham NG7 2RD. *T:* (0115) 951 5701.

**HARRIS, His Honour David Michael;** QC 1989; a Circuit Judge, 2001–12; *b* 7 Feb. 1943; *s* of Maurice and Doris Harris; *m* 1970, Emma Lucia Calma; two *s* one *d*. *Educ:* Liverpool Institute High School for Boys; Lincoln Coll., Oxford (BA 1964; MA 1967); Trinity Hall, Cambridge (PhD 1969). Asst Lectr in Law, Manchester Univ., 1967–69. Called to the Bar, Middle Temple, 1969, Bencher, 1997; Asst Recorder, 1984–88; Recorder, 1988–2001; Dep. High Ct Judge, 1993–12. *Publications:* (ed jtly) Winfield and Jolowicz on Tort, 9th edn, 1971; (ed jtly) Supplement to Bingham's Modern Cases on Negligence, 3rd edn, 1985. *Recreations:* the Arts, travel, sport.

**HARRIS, Evan;** *b* 21 Oct. 1965; *s* of Prof. Frank Harris, *qv*. *Educ:* Blue Coat Sch., Liverpool; Wadham Coll., Oxford (BA Hons Physiol.); Oxford Univ. Med. Sch. (BM BCh 1991). House Officer, John Radcliffe Hosp. and Royal Liverpool Univ. Hosp., 1991–92; Sen. House Officer (Medicine), Central Oxford Hosps, 1992–94; Hon. Registrar in Public Health, and Regl Task Force MO, Oxford Regl Postgrad. Dept of Med. Educn and Oxfordshire HA, 1994–97. Mem. Council, BMA, 1994–97 (Mem., Med. Ethics Cttee, 1999). MP (Lib Dem) Oxford W and Abingdon, 1997–2010; contested (Lib Dem) same seat, 2010. Parly Lib Dem spokesman on: NHS, 1997–99; higher educn and women's issues, 1999–2001; health, 2001–03; science, 2005–10. Chm., All Party Kidney Gp, 1999–2010; Officer, All Party Gps on Refugees, and on AIDS, 1997–2010; Member: Sci. and Technol. Select Cttee, 2003–10; Jt Select Cttee on Human Rights, 2005–10. *Publications:* contribs to med. jls. *Recreations:* chess, bridge, squash, television. *Address:* 32A North Hinksey Village, Oxford OX2 0NA. *T:* (01865) 250424. *Club:* Oxford Rotary.

**HARRIS, Prof. Frank,** CBE 1996; FMedSci; Dean, Faculty of Medicine and Biological Sciences (formerly of Medicine) and Professor of Paediatrics, University of Leicester, 1990–2000, now Professor Emeritus; Hon. Consultant Paediatrician, Leicester Royal Infirmary, 1990–2000; *b* 6 Oct. 1934; *s* of David and Miriam Harris; *m* 1963, Brenda van Embden; two *s*. *Educ:* Univ. of Cape Town (MB ChB 1957; MMed (Paed), 1963; MD 1964); CertHE Oxon 2006. FRCPE 1975; FRCP 1982; FRCPCH 1997 (Hon. FRCPCH 2000). Groote Schuur and Red Cross War Memorial Children's Hosp., Cape Town; CSIR Res. Fellow, Dept of Medicine, Univ. of Cape Town; Lectr and Sen. Lectr in Child Health, Univ. of Sheffield, 1965–74; University of Liverpool: Prof. of Child Health and Dir, Inst. of Child Health, 1974–89; Pro-Vice-Chancellor, 1981–84; Dean, Faculty of Medicine, 1985–89; Hon. Cons. Paediatrician to Royal Liverpool Children's Hosps at Myrtle Street and Alder Hey. Exec. Sec., Council of Deans of UK Med. Schs and Faculties, 1992–96. Member: Liverpool AHA and DHA, 1977–84; Mersey RHA, 1983–89; Trent RHA, 1990; Vice-Chm., Leics HA, 1993–97, 1998–2000 (non-exec. Dir, 1990–). Member: Cttee on Review of Medicines, 1981–90; Cttee on Safety of Medicines, 1990–92; Joint Planning Adv. Cttee, DoH, 1990–94; GMC, 1990–99 (Overseas Review Bd, 1992–96; Educn Cttee, 1994–99; Preliminary Proceedings Cttee, 1994–99; Registration Cttee, 1997–99; Overseas Cttee, 1997–98); NAHAT Wkg Gp on Teaching, Res. and Audit, 1992–93; Scientific Cttee, EU Alban Prog., 2003–06. Member: Exec., Univ. Hosps Assoc., 1991–98; Exec. Cttee, Assoc. of Med. Schs in Europe, 1993–99; Adv. Cttee on Med. Trng, EC, 1994–2001 (Chm., 1999–2001). Examr for RCP and Univs, UK and overseas. Founder FMedSci 1998. *Publications:* Paediatric Fluid Therapy, 1973; chapters in med. books; contribs to med. jls. *Recreations:* bridge, history. *Address:* 39 Frenchay Road, Oxford OX2 6TG.

See also E. Harris.

**HARRIS, His Honour (Geoffrey) Charles (Wesson);** QC 1989; a Circuit Judge, 1993–2017; a Senior Circuit Judge, 2014–17; *b* 17 Jan. 1945; *s* of late G. Hardy Harris and M. J. P. Harris (*née* Wesson); *m* 1970, Carol Ann Alston; two *s* one *d*. *Educ:* Repton; Univ. of Birmingham (LLB). Called to the Bar, Inner Temple, 1967, Bencher, 2009; practice on Midland and Oxford Circuit and in London, 1967–93; a Recorder, 1990–93; Designated Civil Judge: Oxford and Northampton, 1998–2001; Oxford/Thames Valley, 2001–13; Oxfordshire, Bucks, Berks, Beds and Herts, 2014–17. Member: Parole Bd, 1995–2000; Crown Court Rule Cttee, 1997–2005; Council of Circuit Judges: Mem. Cttee, 2002–11; Vice-Pres., 2009; Pres., 2010. Contested (C) Penistone, Yorks, Oct. 1974. Gov., St Clement Danes C of E Primary Sch., 1976–79. *Publications:* contrib. to Halsbury's Laws of England, 4th edn 1976, and other legal publications; magazine articles on stalking and ballooning. *Recreations:* history, architecture, deer stalking, ski-ing, mountain walking, travel. *E:* gcwharris@gmail.com. *Clubs:* Travellers, Kandahar.

See also H. J. W. Harris.

**HARRIS, Hugh Christopher Emlyn,** CBE 2009; Consultant, London First, 2011–16 (Director of Operations, 1995–99; Director, Global Network, 1999–2011); *b* 25 March 1936; *s* of Thomas Emlyn Harris, CB, CBE and Martha Anne (*née* Davies); *m* 1968, Pamela Susan Woollard; one *s* one *d*. *Educ:* The Leys Sch., Cambridge; Trinity Coll., Cambridge (BA 1959; MA). FCIPD (FIPM 1990, FIPD). Bank of England, 1959–94: Chief of Corporate Services, 1984–94; Associate Dir, 1988–94; Comr, CRE, 1995–2000 (Dep. Chm., 1996–2000). Director: BE Services Ltd, 1984–94; BE Museum Ltd, 1989–94; BE Property Holdings Ltd, 1989–94; Securities Management Trust Ltd, 1987–94; Solefield School Educational Trust Ltd, Sevenoaks, 1986–2001. Dir, London Film Commn, 1996–2000. Member: Business Leaders Team, BITC Race for Opportunity Campaign, 1994–98; Windsor Fellowship Adv. Council, 1988–94; Council, London Civic Forum, 2001–09. Vice Pres., Bankers Benevolent Fund, 1990–2011. Gov., Newham Coll. of Further Educn, 2004–14. Trustee, Learning Revolution Trust, 2014–. Chm., Broad St Ward Club, 2002–03; Liveryman, Turners' Co., 1993–. Hon. Treas., Kemsing Br., RBL, 1971–2014. FRSA. *Recreations:* tennis, watching Rugby, films, opera, ballet, bridge. *E:* hughcharris61@gmail.com.

**HARRIS, Hugh James Wesson;** Director, Ministers, Accountability and Strategy, Department of Health and Social Care, since 2018; *b* 1975; *s* of His Honour (Geoffrey) Charles (Wesson) Harris, *qv*; civil partnership 2012, Gaucho Rasmussen; one *s* one *d*. *Educ:* Magdalen Coll., Oxford (BA PPE 1997); Kennedy Sch. of Govt, Harvard Univ. (MPA 2002; Kennedy Scholar). Dep. Dir, World in 1998, Economist Pubns, 1998; Sen. Policy Advr, CBI, 1998–2000; Economist, HM Treasury, 2002–07; Asst Dir, N. M. Rothschild & Sons, 2007–09; Deputy Director: No 10 Policy Unit, 2010–13; Energy and Agric. Policy, HM Treasury, 2013–15; Dir, Media and Creative Industries, DCMS, 2015–18. *Recreations:* theatre, travel. *Address:* Department of Health and Social Care, 39 Victoria Street, SW1H 0EU.

**HARRIS, Air Cdre Irene Joyce, (Joy),** CB 1984; RRC 1976; SRN, SCM; Director, Nursing Services (RAF), and Matron-in-Chief, Princess Mary's Royal Air Force Nursing Service, 1981–84; *b* 26 Sept. 1926; *d* of late Robert John Harris and Annie Martha Harris (*née* Breed). *Educ:* Southgate County Sch.; Charing Cross Hosp.; The London Hosp.; Queen Mary's Maternity Home, Hampstead. SRN 1947, SCM 1950. Joined Princess Mary's RAF Nursing Service, 1950; gen. nursing and midwifery duties in UK, Singapore, Germany and Cyprus; Dep. Matron, 1970; Sen. Matron, 1975; Principal Matron, 1978; Dep. Dir, Nursing Services (RAF), 1981. QHNS 1981–84. *Recreations:* travel, ornithology, music, archaeology, gardening. *Address:* 51 Station Road, Haddenham, Ely, Cambs CB6 3XD. *Club:* Royal Air Force.

**HARRIS, Dr Jane;** author; *b* Belfast, 1961; *m* 1993, Tom Shankland (marr. diss. 2017). *Educ:* Univ. of Glasgow (MA 1984); Univ. of E Anglia (MA Creative Writing 1992; PhD Creative and Critical Writing 1997). Arts Council Writer in Residence, HMP Durham, 1992–94; script and novel reader for film cos and The Literary Consultancy; script ed.; teacher of creative writing, UEA; Guardian Masterclass Fiction-Writing Tutor, 2014–15; film script writer, incl. Bait, 1999, Going Down, 2000. *Publications:* The Observations, 2006; Gillespie and I, 2011; Sugar Money, 2017. *E:* janeharrisinfo@gmail.com. *W:* www.janeharris.com.

**HARRIS, Jane Rosalind;** see Rogers, J. R.

**HARRIS, Jeffery Francis,** FCA; Chairman: Essentra (formerly Filtrona), 2005–16; Cookson Group plc, 2010–12; *b* 8 April 1948; *s* of Ernest and Kathleen Veronica Harris; *m* 1976, Elizabeth Helen Hancock; two *s*. *Educ:* Rendcomb Coll., Cirencester; Southampton Univ. (BSc Hons 1970). FCA 1979. Trainee chartered accountant, 1970; with Barton Mayhew & Co., later Ernst & Young, 1980–85; UniChem, subseq. Alliance UniChem, 1985–2005: Gp Chief Accountant, 1985–86; Finance Dir, 1986–91; Dep. Chief Exec., 1991–92; Chief Exec., 1992–2001; Chm., 2001–05. Board Member: ANZAG AG (Germany), 1999–2007; Bunzl plc, 2000–09; Associated British Foods plc, 2003–07. Chm., British Assoc. of Pharmaceutical Wholesalers, 1996–98; Pres., GIRP-European Assoc. of Pharmaceutical Wholesalers, 2003–04. Chm. of Trustees, Richmond Parish Lands Charity, 2002–12. Hon. DBA Kingston Univ., 2003. *Recreations:* walking, ski-ing, cycling, gardening, opera.

**HARRIS, Jeremy Michael;** public affairs consultant and writer, since 2016; Director, Ruelle Consultancy, since 2016; Fellow of New College, Oxford, 2006–16, now Emeritus; *b* 31 Oct. 1950; *s* of late David Arnold Harris and of Beryl May Harris (*née* Howe); *m* 1st, 1983, Susan Lynn Roberts (marr. diss. 2011); one *s* one *d*; 2nd, 2014, Jennifer Butler. *Educ:* Sevenoaks Sch., Kent; Clare Coll., Cambridge (MA Hons); Nottingham Univ. (PGCE 1972). BBC News: Reporter, BBC Radio News, 1978–82; Madrid Corresp., 1982–86; Moscow Corresp., 1986–89; Foreign Affairs Corresp., 1989–90; Washington Corresp., 1990–95; Radio Presenter, BBC Current Affairs Progs incl. World Tonight, and Today, 1995–99; Archbishop of Canterbury's Sec. for Public Affairs, and Dep. Chief of Staff, Lambeth Palace, 1999–2005; Dir, Communications and Public Affairs, Univ. of Oxford, 2005–16. Mem., Editl Bd, Oxford Today, 2005–16. Mem. Bd, Oxford Playhouse, 2005–16. *Recreations:* theatre, maps, walking. *Address:* 38 Aldridge Road Villas, W11 1BW. *E:* jeremy.harris@new.ox.ac.uk, jeremy.harris@theruelleconsultancy.com.

**HARRIS, Joanne Michèle Sylvie,** MBE 2013; author; *b* 3 July 1964; *d* of Robert Ian Short and Jeannette Payen-Short; *m* 1988, Kevin Steven Harris; one *d*. *Educ:* St Catharine's Coll., Cambridge (BA Mod. and Mediaeval Langs; MA 1985; Hon. Fellow, 2012); Sheffield Univ. (PGCE 1987). Hon. DLit: Huddersfield, 2003; Sheffield, 2004. *Publications:* The Evil Seed, 1992; Sleep, Pale Sister, 1994; Chocolat, 1999; Blackberry Wine, 2000; Five Quarters of the Orange, 2001; Coastliners, 2002; (with F. Warde) The French Kitchen, 2002; Holy Fools, 2003; Jigs and Reels, 2004; Gentlemen and Players, 2005; (with F. Warde) The French Market, 2005; The Lollipop Shoes, 2007; Runemarks, 2007; Blueeyedboy, 2010; Runelight, 2011; Peaches for Monsieur le Curé, 2012; A Cat, A Hat and a Piece of String, 2012; The Gospel of Loki, 2014; The Little Book of Chocolat, 2014; Different Class, 2016; A Pocketful of Crows, 2017; The Testament of Loki, 2018; The Blue Salt Road, 2018; The Strawberry Thief, 2019. *Recreations:* mooching, lounging, strutting, strumming, priest-baiting and quiet subversion of the system. *Address:* c/o Eldon House, Sharp Lane, Almondbury, Huddersfield HD5 8XL.

**HARRIS, Very Rev. John;** Dean of Brecon, and Vicar of Brecon St Mary with Battle and Llanddew, 1993–98; *b* 12 March 1932; *s* of Richard and Ivy Harris; *m* 1956, Beryl June Roberts; two *s* one *d*. *Educ:* St David's Coll., Lampeter (BA 1955); Salisbury Theol Coll. Ordained deacon 1957, priest 1958; Curate: Pontnewynydd, 1957–60; Bassaleg, 1960–63; Vicar: Penmaen, 1963–69; St Paul, Newport, 1969–84; Maindee, 1984–93; RD of Newport, 1977–93. Canon, St Woolos Cath., 1984–93. *Recreations:* classical archæology, music, ballet, natural history. *Address:* 40 Mounton Drive, Chepstow, Monmouthshire NP16 5EH.

**HARRIS, Prof. John Buchanan,** PhD; CBiol, FRSB; Professor of Experimental Neurology, Faculty of Medical Sciences, Newcastle University, 1980–2007, now Emeritus (Director of International Postgraduate Studies, 2002–05); Head of Neurotoxicology, Chemicals Division, Health Protection Agency, Newcastle upon Tyne, 2004–07; *b* 18 Jan. 1940; *s* of John Benjamin Sargent Harris and Mary Isobel Harris; *m* 1965, Christine Margaret Holt; one *s* one *d* (and one *s* decd). *Educ:* Tiffin Sch.; Bradford Inst. of Technol.; Univ. of Bradford (PhD 1967); BPharm (London ext. 1963). MRPharmS 1964; FRSB (FIBiol 1981); CBiol 1990. Research Asst, Univ. of Bradford, 1963–67; Newcastle upon Tyne University: Sen. Res. Associate, 1967–72; Principal Res. Associate, 1972–74; Sen. Lectr, 1974–80. Wellcome Fellow, Univ. of Lund, Sweden, 1970–71; MRC/NIH Fellow, UCLA, 1977–78; Wellcome/Ramaciotti Fellow, Monash Univ., Melbourne, 1980. *Publications:* (ed) Muscular Dystrophy and Other Inherited Diseases of Skeletal Muscle in Animals, 1979; (ed jtly) Natural Toxins: animal, plant and microbial, 1986; (ed jtly) Muscle Metabolism, Vol. 4 (3) of Baillière's Endocrinology and Metabolism, 1990; (ed jtly) Medical Neurotoxicology, 1999; over 200 refereed pubns. *Address:* Institute of Neurosciences and Medical Toxicology Centre, Faculty of Medical Sciences, Newcastle University, Framlington Place, Newcastle upon Tyne NE2 4HH. *T:* (0191) 222 8046, *Fax:* (0191) 222 5772. *E:* j.b.harris@ncl.ac.uk.

**HARRIS, John Charles,** CBE 2007; solicitor; International Management and Legal Consultant, John Harris Consultancy and Associates, since 1986; *b* 25 April 1936; *s* of Sir Charles Joseph William Harris, KBE and Lady Harris (Emily (*née* Thompson)); *m* 1961, Alison Beryl Sturley; one *s* one *d*. *Educ:* Dulwich College (LCC scholarship); Clare College, Cambridge. MA, LLM. 2nd Lieut, Intelligence Corps, 1954–56. UKAEA (seconded to OECD), 1959–63; articled to Town Clerk, Poole, 1963–66; Asst Sol., then Senior Asst Sol., Poole BC, 1966–67; Asst Sol., then Principal Asst to Chief Exec. and Town Clerk, 1967–71, Dep. Town Clerk, 1972–73, County Borough of Bournemouth; County Sec., 1973–83, Chief Exec. and County Clerk, 1983–86, S Yorks CC; Dir, S Yorks Passenger Transport Exec., 1984–86; Sec. to Yorkshire and Humberside County Councils Assoc., 1984–86; Dir, S Yorks Residuary Body, 1985–86; Clerk to Lord Lieutenant of S Yorks, 1984–86; Public Sector Adviser/Associate Consultant: PA Consulting Gp, 1986–91; Daniel Bates Partnership, 1991–95; Executive Director: Solace Internat. (1992) Ltd, 1992–2000; Solace Internat. Southern Africa Pty Ltd, 1993–2001. Chair: Coal Authy, 1999–2007; Coal Forum, 2007–13. Adviser to AMA Police and Fire Cttee, 1976–86; Member: Home Office Tripartite Working Party on Police Act 1964, 1983–86; Rampton SHSA Cttee, 1989–96; Arts Council Touring Bd, 1989–92; Pontefract HA, 1990–93; Council, Local Govt

Internat. Bureau, 1993–96. Mem., Exec. Council, Solace, 1984–86; Dir, Trustee, and Mem. Bd, Homeless Internat. Ltd, 1998–2000; Dir, South Africa Housing Network Trust Ltd, 1998–2001; Jt Chm., Ivory Park/Wakefield Educn Partnership, 2002–07; Chair: Northern Counties Housing Assoc. Ltd, 1994–2000 (Mem. Bd, 1990–2009, Vice Chm., 1994, 2002–03); Northern Counties Specialised Housing Assoc. Ltd, 1994–2007; Mid Yorks Hospitals NHS Trust, 2008–09 (non-exec. Dir, 2007–08); Rossington Eco-Town Partnership, 2008–10; Little Red Bus (HDCT) Ltd, 2011–13. Chair, Guinness Northern Counties, NE Region, 2007–11; Mem. Bd, Guinness Trust Partnership, 2007–08. Director: Stray Services Ltd, 2010–; Hatfield Colliery EBT Co. Ltd, 2014–15. Chm., Soc. of County Secretaries, 1983–84; Mem., Law Society. Independent Member: W Yorks Police Authy, 1994–99; Police Cttee, AMA, 1995; MoD Police Cttee, 2003–07; MoD Police and Guarding Agency: Chm., Audit Cttee, 2004–12; Mem., Owner's Adv. Bd, 2007–12; non-exec. Mem., Mgt Bd, 2011–13. Hon. PR Officer, S Yorks and Humberside Region, Riding for Disabled Assoc., 1983–92 (Mem., Nat. Publications Cttee, 1987–90); Chair, Bd of Trustees, Art House, Wakefield, 2009–15 (Dep. Chair, 2015–18); Trustee: S Yorks Charity Inf. Service, 1977–87; Housing Assocs Charitable Trust, 1994–96; Harrogate (White Rose) Theatre Trust Ltd, 2011–18 (Chair, Friends of Harrogate Th., 2011–15); Harrogate Homeless Project, 2015– (Dep. Chair, 2016; Chair, 2016–); Scarborough Museums Trust, 2017–; Trustee and Hon. Administrator: Harrogate Royal Hall Restoration Trust, 2013–; Harrogate Internat. Partnership, 2017–18; Harrogate and District Improvement Trust, 2018–. Founder Mem./Sec., Barnsley Rockley Rotary Club, 1976–79 (Hon. Sec.); Vice-Chm. and Sec., Friends of Opera North, 1979–86; Mem., Council/Co., and Develt Cttee, Opera North, 1980–95. Convenor, Britain Stronger in Europe Volunteer Cttee, N Yorks and Harrogate, 2016. Guild of Freemen, City of London, 1967; Justice; European Movement; Actsa. Governor, Wakefield Dist Community Sch. (formerly Ackworth Moor Top, then Felkirk Community Special Sch.), 1996–2009 (Chm., 1998–2009). DL S Yorks, 1986. FRSA 1984. *Recreations:* being with family and friends, theatre and opera, foreign travel, supporting South Africa. *Address:* 7 Stray Towers, Victoria Road, Harrogate HG2 0LJ. *T:* (01423) 398847. *E:* jcharris7stray@gmail.com.

**HARRIS, John Frederick,** OBE 1986; FSA; Curator, British Architectural Library's Drawing Collection and Heinz Gallery, 1960–86; Consultant: to Collection, Canadian Centre for Architecture, 1986–88 (Member Advisory Board, 1983–88); Heinz Architectural Center, Carnegie, 1991–94; Victoria and Albert Museum Primary Galleries Project, 1996–2001; *b* 13 Aug. 1931; *s* of Frederick Harris and Maud (*née* Sellwood); *m* 1960, Eileen Spiegel, New York; one *s* one *d. Educ:* Cowley C of E School. Itinerant before 1956; Library of Royal Inst. of Architects, 1956. Mem., Mr Paul Mellon's Adv. Bd, 1966–78; Trustee, Amer. Mus. in Britain, 1974–88; Chm., Colnaghi & Co., 1982–92. President: Internat. Confedn on Architectural Museums, 1981–84 (Chm., 1979–81; Hon. Life Pres., 1984); Marylebone Soc., 1978–80; Twentieth Century Soc. (formerly Thirties Soc.), 1986– (Mem. Cttee, 1979–); Member: Council, Drawing Soc. of America, 1962–68; Council, Victorian Soc., 1974–; Nat. Council, Internat. Council of Monuments and Sites, 1976–83; Soc. of Dilettanti, 1977–; Member Committee: Soc. of Architectural Historians of GB, 1958–66; Georgian Gp, 1970–74, 1986–89; Save Britain's Heritage, 1970–; Stowe Landscape, 1980–2001 (Patron, Stowe Gardens Buildings Trust, 1986–92); Bldg Museum Proj., 1980–86; Garden History, 1980–84; Jl of Garden History, 1980–89. Member: Adv. Council, Drawings Center, NY, 1983–89; Management Cttee, Courtauld Inst. of Art, 1983–87; Somerset House Building Cttee, 1986–89; Council, Royal Archaeol. Inst., 1984–86; Adv. Cttees, Historic Bldgs and Monuments Commn, 1984–88; Ashton Meml Steering Gp, 1984–86; GLC Historic Buildings Panel, 1984–86; Ambrose Congreve Award, 1980–82; Ashmole Archive Cttee, 1985–87; Adv. Bd, Irish Architectural Archive, 1988–91; Appeal Cttee, Painshill Park Trust, 1988–89; Spencer House Restoration Cttee, 1986–95; Nat. Trust Arts Panel, 1996–; Council, Georgian Gp, 2007–; Trustee: Architecture Foundn, 1991–94; Save Europe's Heritage, 1996–; Holburne Mus., Bath, 2000–06. Andrew W. Mellon Lectr in Fine Arts, Nat. Gall., Washington, 1981; Slade Prof. of Fine Art, Univ. of Oxford, 1982–83. Exhibitions Organizer: The King's Arcadia, 1973; The Destruction of the Country House (with Marcus Binney), 1974; The Garden, 1979; Dir, British Country House Exhibn, Nat. Gall., Washington, 1982–83; many exhibns in Heinz Gall.; travelling exhibns and catalogues: Italian Architectural Drawings, 1966; Sir Christopher Wren, 1970; Designs of the British Country House, 1985. FSA 1968; FRSA 1975; Hon. FRIBA 1972; Hon. MA Oxon, 1982; Hon. Brother Art Workers' Guild, 1972. Harris Testimonial Medal, 1999. Editor, Studies in Architecture, 1976–99. *Publications:* English Decorative Ironwork, 1960; Regency Furniture Designs, 1961; (ed), The Prideaux Collection of Topographical Drawings, 1963; (jtly) Lincolnshire, 1964; (contrib.) The Making of Stamford, 1965; (jtly) Illustrated Glossary of Architecture, 1966, 2nd edn 1969; (jtly) Buckingham Palace, 1968; Georgian Country Houses, 1968; (contrib.) Concerning Architecture, 1968; Sir William Chambers, Knight of the Polar Star, 1970 (Hitchcock Medallion 1971); (ed) The Rise and Progress of the Present State of Planting, 1970; (ed jtly) The Country Seat, 1970; Catalogue of British Drawings for Architecture, Decoration, Sculpture and Landscape Gardening in American Collections, 1971; A Country House Index, 1971, 2nd edn 1979; Catalogue of the Drawings Collection RIBA: Inigo Jones and John Webb, 1972; (contrib.) Guide to Vitruvius Britannicus, 1972; (jtly) The King's Arcadia: Inigo Jones and The Stuart Court, 1973; Catalogue of the Drawings Collection RIBA: Colin Campbell, 1973; Headfort House and Robert Adam, 1973; (jtly) The Destruction of the Country House, 1974; Gardens of Delight, The Art of Thomas Robins, 1976; Gardens of Delight, The Rococo English Landscape of Thomas Robins, 1978; (jtly) Catalogue of Drawings by Inigo Jones, John Webb and Isaac de Caus in Worcester College, Oxford, 1979; A Garden Alphabet, 1979; (ed) The Garden Show, 1979; The Artist and the Country House 1979 (Sir Banister Fletcher prize, 1979), 2nd edn 1986; (contrib.) Village England, 1980; (contrib.) Lost Houses of Scotland, 1980; The English Garden 1530–1840: a contemporary view, 1981; (contrib.) John Claudius Loudon and the Early Nineteenth Century in Great Britain, Washington, 1980; (jtly) Interiors, 1981; The Palladians, 1981; Die Hauser der Lords und Gentlemen, 1982; William Talman, Maverick Architect, 1982; (contrib.) SAVE Gibraltar's Heritage, 1982; Architectural Drawings in the Cooper Hewitt Museum, New York, 1982; (contrib.) Vanishing Houses of England, 1982; (contrib.) Macmillan Encyclopedia of Architecture, 1982; (contrib.) Great Drawings from the Collection of Royal Institute of British Architects, 1983; (jtly) Britannia Illustrata Knyff & Kip, 1984; The Design of the British Country House, 1985; (jtly) Inigo Jones—Complete Architectural Drawings, 1989; (contrib.) In Honor of Paul Mellon, Collector and Benefactor, 1986; (contrib.) Canadian Centre for Architecture Building and Gardens, 1989; (contrib.) The Fashioning and Functioning of the British Country House, 1989; (jtly) Jamaica's Heritage: an untapped resource, 1991; (contrib.) Writers and their Houses, 1993; The Palladian Revival: Lord Burlington, his villa and garden at Chiswick, 1994; The Artist and the Country House, 1995; (ed jtly and contrib.) Sir William Chambers: architect to George III, 1996; (contrib.) Chambers and Adelcranz, 1997; No Voice from the Hall: early memories of a country house snooper, 1998; (contrib.) Summerson and Hitchcock, 2002; Echoing Voices: more memories of a country house snooper, 2002; (contrib.) Kinaslott, 2002; (contrib.) Description of the Idea and General-Plan for an English Park, 2004; (contrib.) L'Art anglais dans les collections de l'Institut de France, 2004; Moving Rooms: the trade in architectural salvages, 2007 (William M. B. Berger Prize, 2009); The Duke of Beaufort his House, 2007; (jtly) A Passion for Building: the amateur architect in England 1650–1850, 2007; (contrib.) John Talman: an early-eighteenth-century connoisseur, 2008; (contrib.) The Persistence of the Classical, 2008; (contrib.) Chatsworth: the attic sale, 2010; (contrib.) William Kent: designing Georgian Britain, 2013; articles in Georgian Gp Jl, Annali di Architettura, and other jls. *Recreation:* flinting.

**HARRIS, John Howard;** management consultant in children's services and education, since 2011; Director, John Harris Consulting Ltd, since 2011; *b* 27 Sept. 1956; *s* of late James Edward Harris and Mary Mildred Harris; *m* 1982, Pauline Donnelly; one *d. Educ:* St Catharine's Coll., Cambridge (BA Hons Hist. 1979); Univ. of London Inst. of Educn (PGCE (Dist.); Storey Miller Prize); Essex Inst. of Higher Educn (Dip. Professional Studies in Educn (Dist.) 1986). London Borough of Newham: teacher: Langdon Sch., 1980–82; Forest Gate Community Sch., 1982–87; Advr for Tech. and Vocational Educn Initiative, 1987–90; Essex County Council: Sen. Co. Inspector, 14–19 Curriculum, 1990–91; Principal Co. Inspector, 1991–92; Service Manager, Community Educn and Post-16 Liaison, 1992–95; Sen. Educn Officer, 1995–96; Asst Dir, Educn, 1996–99; Dir of Educn, 1999–2003, Westminster CC; Sen. Educn Exec., CAPITA Strategic Educn Services, 2003; Dir, Children, Schools and Families, Herts CC, 2003–11. Independent Chair: Doncaster Local Safeguarding Children Bd, 2014–17; Sandwell Local Safeguarding Children Bd, 2014–17; Hounslow Learning Partnership, 2014–18. Trustee: Nat. Foundn for Educnl Res., 2011–15; Change, Grow, Live, 2017–. Chm., W Herts Community Free Sch., Trust, 2013–19. *Recreations:* reading, film, travel, cycling, running (ran Paris Marathon), football (supporting Leyton Orient FC).

**HARRIS, Prof. John Morley,** DPhil; FMedSci; Lord (formerly Sir David) Alliance Professor of Bioethics, since 1997, and Director, Institute for Science, Ethics and Innovation, since 2007, University of Manchester; *b* 21 Aug. 1945; *s* of Albert Harris and Ruth Harris; *m* 1978, Sita Williams; one *s. Educ:* University of Kent at Canterbury (BA 1966); Balliol Coll., Oxford (DPhil 1976). Lectr in Philosophy, 1974–77, Sen. Lectr, 1977–79, City of Birmingham Poly.; Associate Lectr in Philosophy, Brunel Univ., 1977–79; University of Manchester: Lectr in Philosophy, 1979–84, Sen. Lectr, 1984–88, Dept of Educn; Res. Dir, Centre for Social Ethics and Policy, 1986–; Reader in Applied Philosophy, Sch. of Educn, 1988–90; Prof. of Bioethics and Applied Philosophy, 1990–97; Dir, Inst. of Medicine, Law and Bioethics, 1996–. Series Ed., Social Ethics and Policy, 1985–; Founder and a Gen. Ed., Issues in Biomedical Ethics series, 1994–. Member: Adv. Cttee on Genetic Testing, 1997–99; Human Genetics Commn, 1999–; Ethics Cttee, BMA, 1991–97 and 1999–. Chm., Values and Attitudes Wkg Party, Age Concern, 1996–99. Mem., Romanian Acad. Med. Scis, 1994–; MAE 2011. FMedSci 2001; FRSA. Hon. DLitt Kent, 2010. *Publications:* Violence and Responsibility, 1980; The Value of Life, 1985; (ed with S. Hirsch) Consent and the Incompetent Patient, 1988; (ed with A. Dyson) Experiments on Embryos, 1990; Wonderwoman and Superman: ethics and human biotechnology, 1992; (ed with A. Dyson) Ethics and Biotechnology, 1994; Clones, Genes and Immortality, 1998; (ed jtly) AIDS: ethics, justice and European policy, 1998; (ed with S. Holm) The Future of Human Reproduction, 1998; (ed jtly) A Companion to Genethics: philosophy and the genetic revolution, 2001; (ed.) Bioethics, 2001; On Cloning, 2004; Enhancing Evolution, 2007. *Recreations:* cooking, walking, driving, argument, Italy, Manchester United. *Address:* Institute for Science, Ethics and Innovation, Faculty of Life Sciences, Stopford Building, University of Manchester, Manchester M13 9PL. *T:* (0161) 275 7704.

**HARRIS, His Honour John Percival,** DSC 1945; QC 1974; a Circuit Judge, 1980–95; *b* 16 Feb. 1925; *o s* of late Thomas Percival Harris and Nora May Harris; *m* 1959, Janet Valerie Douglas; one *s* two *d. Educ:* Wells Cathedral Sch.; Pembroke Coll., Cambridge. BA 1947. Served in RN, 1943–46: Midshipman, RNVR, 1944, Sub-Lt 1945. Called to the Bar, Middle Temple, 1949, Bencher 1970. A Recorder of the Crown Court, 1972–80; Dep. Sen. Judge, Sovereign Base Areas, Cyprus, 1983–2000 (Acting Sen. Judge, 1995). *Recreations:* reading, Victorian pictures. *Address:* Tudor Court, Fairmile Park Road, Cobham, Surrey KT11 2PP. *T:* (01932) 864756.

**HARRIS, (John Robert) William,** FRCP, FRCPI; Consultant in Genito-Urinary Medicine, 1976–2011, Hon. Consultant, since 2011, Imperial College Healthcare NHS Trust (formerly St Mary's Hospital NHS Trust); *b* 25 Sept. 1943; *s* of William James Smyth Harris and Anne (*née* Glass); *m* 1st, 1968, Mary Elizabeth Keating (marr. diss. 1992; remarried 1994; she *d* 2013); one *s* one *d. Educ:* Ballymena Acad.; Queen's Univ., Belfast (MB). FRCP 1985; FRCPI 1996. Postgrad. trng, Royal Victoria Hosp., Belfast and Liverpool Sch. of Tropical Medicine, 1968–72; Consultant and Hon. Sen. Lectr, Sheffield Royal Infirmary, 1972–74; Consultant, King's Coll. Hosp., 1974–75; Med. Dir, St Mary's Hosp. NHS Trust, 1991–97. Lock Lectr, RCPSG, 1993. Internat. Health Award, 1973; Scott-Heron Medal, Royal Victoria Hosp., Belfast, 1985. *Publications:* Recent Advances in Sexually Transmitted Diseases, 1975, 4th edn 1991; papers on sexually transmitted diseases, AIDS and prostatitis. *Recreations:* walking, cinema, travel. *Address:* London Medical, 49 Marylebone High Street, W1U 5HJ. *T:* (020) 7486 4166. *Club:* Athenæum.

**HARRIS, Jonathan David,** CBE 2002 (OBE 1993); chartered surveyor; consultant; President, Royal Institution of Chartered Surveyors, 2000–01; *b* 28 Sept. 1941; *s* of Wilfred Harris and Ann Harris (*née* Godel); *m* 1964, Jeniffer Cecilia Fass; one *s* three *d. Educ:* Haberdashers' Aske's Sch. FRICS 1964. Pepper Angliss & Yarwood, Chartered Surveyors, 1959–94 (Sen. Partner, 1974–94); Director: Property Growth Assurance Co. Ltd, 1968–79; Cardinal Group, 1973–2017; Carlisle Gp, 1987–99; Cressida Gp, 1996–; Babraham Bioscience Technologies Ltd, 2002–04. Mem. Bd, Plymouth Develt Corp., 1993–96; Dep. Chm., UN Real Estate Adv. Gp, 2001–06; Chair, Total Place Asset Mgt Bd, Kent CC, 2010. Committee Member: Sackville Property Unit Trust (formerly Lazard Property Unit Trust), 1974–99; Langbourn Income Growth & Property Unit Trust, 1984–2010. Member: Real Estate Mkt (formerly Real Estate) Adv. Gp, UNECE, 1998–; Property Adv. Gp, Bank of England, 1999–2001; Professions Wkg Gp, Council for Excellence in Mgt and Leadership, 2000–02. Founder and Chairman: Harris Foundn for Life-Long Learning (formerly Continuing Professional Develt Foundn, later Educational Foundn for Life-Long Learning), 1980–; Inst. of Continuing Professional Develt, 1997–2013. Dir, Grendon Trust, 1977–98; Treas., Prison Reform Trust, 1998–2001. Trustee: Enterprise Education Trust (formerly Understanding Industry, subseq. businessdynamics), 1997–2015 (Dep. Chm., 2006–15); LPO Adv. Bd, 1996–2017 (Chm., Audit Cttee, 2016–18); Mem., Adv. Council, 2017–); Chm. of Trustees, Resource (formerly Employment Resource Centre), 2004–13; Vice Patron, Commonwealth Housing Trust, 2014–. Gov., Univ. of Westminster (formerly Poly. of Central London), 1988–99; Trustee, Manor Lodge Sch., 2002–13. Mem., Counselors of Real Estate, USA, 2005– (White Landau Meml Prize, 2009). Liveryman: Co. of Chartered Surveyors, 1977; Co. of Basketmakers, 1962. FRSA. Hon. DLitt Westminster, 1998. *Recreations:* bridge, grandchildren. *Address:* 24 Hays Mews, W1J 5PY. *T:* (020) 7495 3132.

**HARRIS, Prof. Jonathan Malcolm,** PhD; barrister; Professor of International Commercial Law, Dickson Poon Law School, King's College London, since 2011; Senior Research Fellow, Jesus College, Oxford, since 2018; *b* Portsmouth, 29 March 1972; *s* of Michael and Sylvia Harris; *m* 2008, Tricia Pickering; two *s* one *d. Educ:* Portsmouth Grammar Sch.; Jesus Coll., Oxford (BCL; MA); Univ. of Birmingham (PhD). Lectr in Law,

Univ. of Birmingham, 1995–2000; Reader in Law, Univ. of Nottingham, 2000–01; Prof. of Internat. Commercial Law, Univ. of Birmingham, 2002–11. In practice as barrister, Serle Court, 2009–. Mem., Lord Chancellor's Adv. Cttee on Private Internat. Law, 2014–. Mem., Soc. of Trust and Estate Practitioners. Hon. Mem., Assoc. of Contentious Trust and Probate Specialists. Hon. QC 2016. Co-Ed. and Co-founder, Jl Private Internat. Law, 2005–. *Publications*: The Hague Trusts Convention, 2002; (jtly) International Sale of Goods in the Conflict of Laws, 2005; (Co-Gen. Ed.) Dicey, Morris and Collins, The Conflict of Laws, 15th edn 2016. *Address*: Serle Court, 6 New Square, Lincoln's Inn, WC2A 3QS. *T*: (020) 7242 6105. *E*: JHarris@serlecourt.co.uk.

**HARRIS, Prof. Jose Ferial**, PhD; FBA 1993; Professor of Modern History, University of Oxford, 1996–2008, now Emeritus; Fellow, St Catherine's College, Oxford, 1978, now Emeritus (Vice-Master, 2003–05); *d* of Leonard Cecil Chambers and Freda Ellen Chambers (*née* Brown); *m* 1968, Prof. James William Harris, FBA (*d* 2004); one *s*. *Educ*: Dame Alice Harpur Sch., Bedford; Newnham Coll., Cambridge (MA, PhD). Res. Fellow, Nuffield Coll., Oxford, 1966–69; Lectr, 1969–74, Sen. Lectr, 1974–78, Dept of Social Sci. and Admin, LSE; Reader in Modern History, Oxford Univ., 1990–96. Vis. Res. Fellow, Princeton, 1985–86. Ford Lectr in English History, Oxford Univ., 1996–97; Leverhulme Res. Prof., Oxford Univ., 1998–2002. Vis. Res. Prof., Sch. of Advanced Studies, Univ. of London, 2006–07; Hon. Vis. Prof., Birkbeck, Univ. of London, 2007–10; Vis. Res. Fellow, Harry Ransom Center, Univ. of Texas, 2010. *Publications*: Unemployment and Politics: a study in English social policy, 1972, 2nd edn 1984; William Beveridge: a biography, 1977, 2nd edn 1997; Private Lives, Public Spirit: a social history of Britain 1870–1914, 1993, 2nd edn 1994; Ferdinand Tönnies: community and civil society, 2001; Civil Society in British History, 2003; Le Rapport Beveridge: le text fondateur de l'état providence, 2012. *Recreations*: painting, walking, river boats, family life. *Address*: 5 Belbroughton Road, Oxford OX2 6UZ.

**HARRIS, Joseph Hugh**; Vice Lord-Lieutenant of Cumbria, 1994–2007; *b* 3 June 1932; *s* of late John Frederick Harris and of Gwendolen Arden Harris; *m* 1957, Anne, *d* of Brig. Leslie Harrison McRobert, CBE. *Educ*: Aysgarth Sch.; Harrow; Royal Agricl Coll. (MRAC). Lieut, 11th Hussars, PAO. Chairman: Cumbrian Newspapers Ltd, 1987–2002; Grasmere Sports (Dir, 1977–2008). Member: Northern Regl Panel, MAFF, 1987–93; Rural Develt Commn, 1989–2000. Royal Agricultural Society: Sen. Steward, 1960–77; Dep. Pres., 1987; Trustee, 1992–2009; Hon. Dir, Royal Show, 1978–82. High Sheriff of Cumbria, 1976–77; DL 1984, JP 1971–2002, Cumbria. Chm., Penrith and Alston Bench, 1991–95. Chm. of Govs, Aysgarth Sch., 1975–78; Gov., RAC, Cirencester, 1987–90. Liveryman, Farmers' Co., 1973–. *Recreations*: shooting, country sports, conservation. *Address*: West View, Bowscar, Penrith, Cumbria CA11 9PG. *T*: and *Fax*: (01768) 885661.

**HARRIS, Air Cdre Joy**; *see* Harris, I. J.

**HARRIS, Dr Keith Murray**, CBiol, FRSB, FRES; Director, International (formerly Commonwealth) Institute of Entomology, 1985–92; *b* 26 Nov. 1932; *s* of Clifford Murray Harris and Doris (*née* Cottam); *m* 1957, Elizabeth Harrison; one *s* one *d*. *Educ*: Lewis Sch., Pengam; Univ. of Wales, Aberystwyth (BSc, DSc); Selwyn Coll., Cambridge (DipAgricSci); Imperial Coll. of Tropical Agric., Trinidad (DipTA). FRES 1960; FRSB (FIBiol 1985). Entomologist, then Sen. Entomologist, Federal Dept of Agricl Res., Nigeria, 1955–62; Sen. Res. Fellow, BM (Natural History), 1962–66; Entomologist and Sen. Scientist, RHS, Wisley, 1966–74; Principal Taxonomist, Commonwealth Inst. of Entomology, 1974–85. *Publications*: (jtly) Collins Guide to the Pests, Diseases and Disorders of Garden Plants, 1981, 4th edn (as Collins Photoguide to the Pests, Diseases and Disorders of Garden Plants), 2014; scientific research papers and articles on pests of cultivated plants, esp. pests of African cereal crops, and on taxonomy and biol. of gall midges. *Recreations*: walking, cycling, gardening, music. *Address*: 81 Linden Way, Ripley, Woking, Surrey GU23 6LP.

**HARRIS, Laura; Her Honour Judge Laura Harris**; a Circuit Judge, since 2008; *b* London, 3 July 1954; *d* of Emanuel and Patricia Harris; one *s* by Paul Krempel. *Educ*: Henrietta Barnett Sch.; Lady Margaret Hall, Oxford (BA Hons). Called to the Bar, Middle Temple, 1977, Bencher, 2019; in practice as a barrister, specialising in family law, 1977–2008; Dep. Dist Judge, Principal Registry, Family Div., 1990–2008; Recorder, 2003–08. *Recreations*: travel, theatre, visual arts, cinema, reading, walking. *Address*: Central Family Court, First Avenue House, 422-49 High Holborn, WC1V 6NP.

**HARRIS, Leonard John**; Commissioner, and Director, VAT Policy (formerly Internal Taxes), Customs and Excise, 1991–96; *b* 4 July 1941; *s* of Leonard and May Harris; *m* 1st, 1965, Jill Christine Tompkins (marr. diss.); one *s* two *d*; 2nd, 1986, Jennifer Dilys Biddiscombe (*née* Barker). *Educ*: Westminster City Sch.; St John's Coll., Cambridge. BA 1964 (Eng. Lit.), MA 1967. HM Customs and Excise: Asst Principal, 1964; Private Sec. to Chairman, 1966–68; Principal, 1969; CS Selection Bd, 1970; HM Customs and Excise, 1971; Cabinet Office, 1971–74; First Sec., UK Rep. to EEC, 1974–76, Counsellor, 1976–77; Asst Sec., HM Customs and Excise, 1977–80, Cabinet Office, 1980–83; Under Sec., 1983; Comr of Customs and Excise, 1983–87; Under Sec., MPO, 1987; Under Sec., HM Treasury, 1987–91. *Recreations*: cooking, music, naturism. *Address*: 2 Greens Row, Laundry Lane, Aston, Oxon OX18 2DG. *Club*: Oxford Naturist (Oxford).

**HARRIS, Louise Anne**; *see* Bloom, L. A. H.

**HARRIS, Mark**; Assistant Treasury Solicitor, Department for Education (formerly Education and Science), 1988–94; *b* 23 Feb. 1943; *s* of late Solomon Harris and Eva (*née* Lazarus); *m* 1972, Sharon Frances Colin; one *d*. *Educ*: Central Foundation Boys' Grammar Sch., London; London School of Economics and Political Science, London Univ. (LLB Hons). Solicitor of the Supreme Court, 1967. Entered Solicitor's Office, Dept of Employment, as Legal Asst, 1968; Sen. Legal Asst, 1973; Asst Solicitor, 1978; Legal Advr, 1987–88. Vol. mem. mgt cttee, dep. ed. and journalist, Essex Jewish News, 1996–. Vol. Mem., Mgt Cttee, and Publicity Officer, Cambridge Jewish Residents' Assoc., 2010–15. *Publications*: The Shtetl and Other Jewish Stories, 2009; The Chorister and Other Jewish Stories, 2011; The Music Makers and Other Jewish Stories, 2012; Last Days in Berlin (novel), 2016; A Virtual Reality (novel), 2018; numerous short stories, magazine and newspaper articles. *Recreations*: travel, walking, short-story and other writing, drawing, theatre, choral singing (first tenor, London Jewish Male Choir, 1988–2008, London Cantorial Singers, 2009–).

**HARRIS, Mark Philip Allen**; independent lottery/regulation adviser, since 2016; Executive Director and Member, National Lottery Committee, Gambling Commission, 2013–15; *b* 29 July 1961; *s* of Roy Allen Harris and Vivienne Harris; *m* 1993, Patricia Mary Allen; one *s* one *d*. *Educ*: Bishop's Stortford Coll.; Nottingham Univ. (LLB Hons). CPFA 1987. Audit Examr, 1983–88, Manager, 1988–91, Sen. Manager, 1991–94, District Audit; Associate Controller, Audit Commn, 1994–97; Exec. Consultant, Hammersmith Hosps NHS Trust, 1997–98; Associate Dir (Strategic Develt), Audit Commn, 1998–99; Chief Exec., Nat. Lottery Commn, 1999–2013. Mem., Alumni Council, 2005–10, Chair,

2008–10, Ashridge Business Sch. Trustee: Responsibility in Gambling Trust, 2007–09; Responsible Gambling Fund, 2009–12. *Recreations*: family, cycling, hill walking, mountaineering literature.

**HARRIS, Prof. Sir Martin (Best)**, Kt 2000; CBE 1992; DL; Chairman, Universities Superannuation Scheme Ltd, 2006–15 (Director, 1991–2015; Deputy Chairman, 2004–06); President, Clare Hall, Cambridge, 2008–13 (Hon. Fellow, 2013); *b* 28 June 1944; *s* of William Best Harris and Betty Evelyn (*née* Martin); *m* 1966, Barbara Mary (*née* Daniels); two *s*. *Educ*: Devonport High Sch. for Boys, Plymouth; Queens' Coll., Cambridge (BA, MA; Hon. Fellow, 1992); Sch. of Oriental and African Studies, London (PhD). Lecturer in French Linguistics, Univ. of Leicester, 1967; University of Salford: Sen. Lectr in French Linguistics, 1974; Prof. of Romance Ling., 1976–87; Dean of Social Sciences and Arts, 1978–81; Pro-Vice-Chancellor, 1981–87; Vice-Chancellor: Essex Univ., 1987–92; Manchester Univ., 1992–2004; Dir, Office for Fair Access, 2004–12. Chancellor, Univ. of Salford, 2004–09. Chairman: CVCP, 1997–99 (Vice-Chm., 1995–97); NW Univs Assoc., 1999–2000; Cambridge Commonwealth Trust, 2011–14; Cambridge Overseas Trust, 2011–14. Member: Internat. Cttee for Historical Linguistics, 1979–86; UGC, 1984–87; HEFCE Review of Univ. Libraries, 1992–93; Chairman: NI Sub Cttee, UFC (formerly UGC), 1985–91; Nat. Curriculum Wkg Gp for Modern Foreign Langs, 1989–90; HEFCE/CVCP Review of Postgrad. Educn, 1995–96; Clinical Standards Adv. Gp, 1996–99; DfEE Careers Review, 2000. Member: Commn for Health Improvement, 1999–2002; NW Develt Agency Bd, 2001–08 (Dep. Chm., 2002–08). Chm., Manchester: Knowledge Capital, 2004–08. Mem. Council, Philological Soc., 1979–86, 1988–92. Chm. of Govs, Centre for Inf. on Lang. Teaching, 1990–96; Vice Chm. of Governors, Parrs Wood High Sch., 1982–86; Gov., Colchester Sixth Form Coll., 1988–92; Member Governing Body: Anglia Poly., 1989–93; Plymouth Univ., 2004–09; Dep. Chm. of Govs, SOAS, Univ. of London, 2013– (Mem. Governing Body, 1990–93). Mem. High Council, Eur. Univ. Inst., 1992–96. Mem. Editorial Board: Journal Linguistics, 1982–91; Diachronica, 1983–92; French Studies, 1987–93; Jt Gen. Editor, Longman Linguistics Library, 1982–96. MAE 1991; AcSS 2001. DL Greater Manchester, 1998. Hon. Fellow: Bolton Inst., 1996; Univ. of Central Lancashire, 1999; Hon. RNCM 1996; Hon. FCP 2003; Hon. FRCSE 2005. Hon. LLD QUB, 1992; DUniv: Essex, 1993; Keele, 2006; Open, 2017; Hon. DLitt: Salford, 1995; Manchester Metropolitan, 2000; Leicester, Lincoln, 2003; Ulster, Manchester, UMIST, 2004; Exeter, 2008; Plymouth, 2009; London, 2013. *Publications*: (ed) Romance Syntax: synchronic and diachronic perspectives, 1976; The Evolution of French Syntax: a comparative approach, 1978; (ed with N. Vincent) Studies in the Romance Verb, 1982; (ed with P. Ramat) Historical Development of Auxiliaries, 1987; (ed with N. Vincent) The Romance Languages, 1988; about 35 articles in appropriate jls and collections. *Recreations*: gardening, travel, wine, music, the arts. *Address*: Director's Office, School of Oriental and African Studies, University of London, Thornhaugh Street, WC1H 0XG. *T*: (020) 7898 4014.

**HARRIS, Martin Fergus**, OBE 2010; HM Diplomatic Service; Director, Eastern Europe and Central Asia, Foreign and Commonwealth Office, since 2017; *b* Edinburgh, 17 May 1969; *s* of Rev. W. Fergus Harris and Ruth Harris; *m* 1993, Linda MacLachlan; three *d*. *Educ*: George Watson's Coll., Edinburgh; Glenalmond Coll.; Corpus Christi Coll., Cambridge (BA 1991; MA 1995; Pres., Cambridge Union, 1990); Open Univ. (MPA 2008). Joined FCO, 1991; Second Sec., UK Delegn to OSCE, 1992–96; S Asia Dept, FCO, 1997–98; First Sec., Moscow, 1999–2003; Dep. Hd of Mission, Kiev, 2003–08; Dep. Dir, Cabinet Office (on secondment), 2008–10; Ambassador to Romania, 2010–14; Minister and Dep. Hd of Mission, Moscow, 2014–17. *Recreations*: opera, church music, history. *Address*: c/o Foreign and Commonwealth Office, King Charles Street, SW1A 2AH.

**HARRIS, Mervyn Leslie Richard**; a District Judge (Magistrates' Courts) (formerly Stipendiary Magistrate), Nottinghamshire, 1991–2010; *b* 9 Aug. 1942; *s* of Albert Leslie Harris and Gladys Mary (*née* Plummer); *m* 1967, Marcia Jane Tomblin; one *s* one *d*. *Educ*: King Henry VIII Sch., Coventry; University Coll. London (LLB 1964). Admitted solicitor, 1969; Partner, Hughes & Masser, solicitors, Coventry, 1969–91. Chm. (part-time), Social Security Appeals Tribunal, 1985–91; Actg Stipendiary Magistrate, 1987–91. Clerk to local charities in Coventry and Atherstone. *Recreations*: walking, railways, railway history, watching football, Rugby and cricket.

**HARRIS, Michael David**, FRCO; Organist and Master of the Music, St Giles' Cathedral, Edinburgh, since 1996; organ recitalist, conductor and adjudicator; *b* 29 Dec. 1958; *s* of David John Harris and Muriel Harris (*née* Pearson); *m* 1987, Brigitte Johanne Hannelore Schröder; one *d*. *Educ*: King's Sch., Gloucester; Reading Sch.; St Peter's Coll., Oxford (MA); Royal Coll. of Music (ARCM); FRCO 1980. Sub Organist, Leeds Parish Church, 1982–86; Asst Dir of Music, Leeds Grammar Sch., 1982–86; Asst Organist, Canterbury Cathedral, 1986–96; Organist, King's Sch., Canterbury, 1986–96; Lectr in Music, Edinburgh Napier (formerly Napier) Univ., 1996–; Director: Scottish Chamber Choir, 1997–2010; Edinburgh Organ Acad., 1998–2010; Cantica Alba, 2010–. Organ recitals in UK, Germany, Belgium, Italy, Poland, Australia, NZ and USA. Recordings and broadcasts with choirs of Canterbury Cathedral and St Giles' Cathedral, Edinburgh. *Recreations*: railways, cooking. *Address*: St Giles' Cathedral, Edinburgh EH1 1RE.

**HARRIS, Michael Deane**; Senior Business Advisor, Fasken Martineau DuMoulin LLP, since 2013; consultant and advisor to various Canadian companies, since 2002; Premier of Ontario, 1995–2002; *b* 23 Jan. 1945; *s* of Sidney Deane Harris and Hope Gooding Harris (*née* Robinson). *Educ*: Algonquin High Sch.; North Bay Teachers' Coll. ICD.D 2005. Formerly: entrepreneur (owned and operated ventures incl. tourist resort and ski center); sch. teacher (Trustee, 1975–81, Chm., 1977–81, Nipissing Bd of Educn). MPP (PC) for Nipissing, Ontario, 1981; Parly Asst to Minister of the Envmt; Minister of Natural Resources and Minister of Energy, 1985. House Leader, 1986–89, Leader, 1990–2002, Ontario Progressive Conservative Party. Senior Business Adviser: Goodmans LLP, 2002–10; Cassels Brock & Blackwell LLP, 2010–13; Director: Canaccord Genuity Gp (formerly Capital, then Cannacord Financial Inc.), 2004–; Colliers Internat. Gp Inc. (formerly FirstService Corp.), 2006–; Element Financial Corp., 2011–15; Luminato, 2014–16; Chairman: Route1 Inc., 2009–; Magna Internat. Inc., 2011–12 (Lead Dir, 2003–11). Chm. of Trustees, Chartwell Retirement Residences (formerly Chartwell Seniors Housing Real Estate Investment Trust), 2003–; Director: Tim Horton Children's Foundn, 2002–14; New Haven Learning Centre, 2015–. Sen. Fellow, Fraser Institute, 2002. Hon. DLitt Nipissing, Ont, 2010. Freedom Medal, Nat. Citizens Coalition, Canada, 1996; E. P. Taylor Award of Merit, Jockey Club of Canada, 2000; Cam Fella Award, Standardbred Canada, 2000. *Address*: Fasken Martineau DuMoulin LLP, 333 Bay Street, Suite 2400, Bay Adelaide Centre, Box 20, Toronto, ON M5H 2T6, Canada.

**HARRIS, His Honour Sir Michael (Frank)**, Kt 2008; a Circuit Judge, 1992–2007; *b* 11 Jan. 1942; *s* of Joseph Frank Harris and Edna Harris; *m* 1969, Veronica Brend; one *s* one *d*. *Educ*: St Bartholomew's Grammar Sch., Newbury; Merton Coll., Oxford (BA). Called to the Bar, Middle Temple, 1965, Bencher, 2003; a Recorder, 1990–92. Chief Social Security Comr and Chief Child Support Comr, 2001–03; President: Social Security, Medical, Disability and Child Support Appeal Tribunals, 1998–99; The Appeals Service, 1999–2007. *Recreations*: piano playing, amateur dramatics, walking, music, theatre, travel, reading.

**HARRIS, Rear-Adm. Michael George Temple**; JP; Clerk to the Clothworkers' Co. of the City of London and Secretary to the Clothworkers' Foundation, 1992–2001; *b* 5 July 1941; *s* of late Comdr Antony John Temple Harris, OBE, RN and Doris Drake Harris; *heir-pres.* to Baron Harris, *qv*; *m* 1970, Katrina Chichester; three *d*. *Educ*: Pangbourne Coll.; RNC Dartmouth; Open Univ. (BA, Dip. Spanish 2004); Buckingham Univ. (MA 2017). FRGS 1978–2002; FNI 1988–2002. Qualified Submarines, 1963, TAS 1968; commanded HM Submarines: Osiris, 1970–72; Sovereign, 1975–77 (N Pole, 1976); 3rd Submarine Sqn, 1982–85; commanded HM Ships: Cardiff, 1980–82 (Falkland Is, 1982); Ark Royal, 1987–89; ACDS (NATO/UK), 1989–92. Exchange service with USN, 3rd Fleet Staff, 1972–75. Younger Brother of Trinity House, 1989–. Trustee, 1984–2014, Chm., 1995–2014, Belmont House, Kent; Trustee, Emmaus Hampshire, 2005–14. Mem., Ancient Soc. of Coll. Youths, 1995–. Liveryman, Clothworkers' Co., 1997– (Mem., Ct of Assistants, 2001–). Gov., Pangbourne Coll., 1997–2007. JP NW Hants, 2002–11. Churchwarden, All Hallows, Whitchurch, Hants, 2011–13. *Recreations*: fishing, bell-ringing, monumental brasses, historical and biographical research. *Address*: c/o Clothworkers' Hall, Dunster Court, Mincing Lane, EC3R 7AH. *Clubs*: Band of Brothers, Royal Navy of 1765 and 1785.

**HARRIS, Michael John**; Owner, Find Your Lightbulb Ltd, since 2009; *b* 10 March 1949; *s* of John Melton and Ivy May Harris; *m* 1971, Susan Cooper; one *s* one *d*. *Educ*: Dudley Grammar Sch.; University Coll. London (BSc Chemistry). Variety of positions in IT, incl. Head of Systems Develt for Retail Bank, Midland Bank, 1972–86; Dir, Space-Time Systems, 1986–88; Chief Executive: Firstdirect, 1988–91; Mercury Communications Ltd, 1991–95; Prudential Banking, then Egg, 1995–2000; Vice Chm., Egg plc, 2000–05; Chm., Gp Innovation, Royal Bank of Scotland, 2006–09; Co-founder and Chm., Garlik, 2006–11. *Publications*: Find Your Lightbulb: how to make millions from apparently impossible ideas, 2008. *Recreations*: tennis, walking, theatre, photography, watching Aston Villa.

**HARRIS, Rear Adm. Nicholas Henry Linton**, CB 2006; MBE 1987; Clerk to Merchant Taylors' Company, 2006–18; *b* 26 Feb. 1952; *s* of Peter N. Harris and Theodora M. F. Harris (*née* Patterson); *m* 1974, Jennifer Mary Peebles; two *d*. *Educ*: Malvern Coll.; BRNC Dartmouth. Joined RN, 1969; CO, HMS Oberon, 1985–86, HMS Sovereign, 1988–90; US Naval War Coll., 1991–92; Naval Staff, Washington, 1992–94; on staff, MoD, 1994–97; Captain, Second Submarine Sqdn, 1997–99; Dep. Flag Officer, Submarines, 1999–2000; Naval Attaché, Washington, 2000–03; FO Scotland, Northern England and NI, 2003–06. *Recreations*: cricket, golf. *Clubs*: Royal Navy of 1765 and 1785, City Naval (Chm., 2011–); RN Cricket; Broadhalfpenny Brigands Cricket (Hambledon) (Chm., 2012–); Hartley Wintney Golf.

**HARRIS, Nigel Richard**; Chief Executive, Tearfund, since 2015; *b* Bristol, 19 Feb. 1965; *s* of Richard Harris and Varna Harris; *m* 1990, Teresa Rolfe; one *s* one *d*. *Educ*: Bristol Grammar Sch.; Magdalen Coll., Oxford (BA). Investment Banker, 1988–96, Dir, 1996, Hd of Trading, London, 1997–2000, J Henry Schroder & Co.; Consultant, Tearfund, 2001; Co-Hd, Res., 2002–04, Chief Exec., 2004–08, New Philanthropy Capital; Consultant, DFID, 2008–09; COS, Save the Children UK, 2009–11; Chief Exec., Farm Africa, 2011–15. *Recreations*: time spent with family, travel, walking, ski-ing. *Address*: Tearfund, 100 Church Road, Teddington TW11 8QF. *T*: (020) 8977 9144. *E*: nigel.harris@tearfund.org.

**HARRIS, Canon Patricia Ann, (Mrs J. N. K. Harris)**; Central President, The Mothers' Union, 1989–94 (Vice-President, 1986–88); *b* 29 May 1939; *m* 1963, Rev. James Nigel Kingsley Harris, BA; one *s* one *d*. *Educ*: Trinity Coll., Carmarthen (Hon. Fellow, 1995). Teaching Dip. Teacher, 1959–63; pt-time special needs teacher, 1963–88; vol. teacher, Gloucester Prison, 1978–85. Member: Glos Dio. Synod, 1980–2001; C of E General Synod, 1985–2000 (Mem. Exec., 1991–2001, Vice Chm., 1996–2001, Chm., Trust Funds, 1996–2001, Bd of Mission); Bishops' Council, 1985–2001; Cttee, Partnership for World Mission, 1993–2000; Women's Nat. Commn, 1994–96; USPG Council, 1994–96; Cttee, Black Anglican Concerns, 1995–96; Council, 1996–, Publications Cttee, 1997–, Bible Reading Fellowship. Mothers' Union: Young Wives Leader, 1963–65; Enrolling Mem., 1967–76; Presiding Mem., 1969–74; Diocesan Social Concern Chm., 1974–80; Pres., Glos dio., 1980–85; Mem., Worldwide Council, 1995–. Hon. Lay Canon, Gloucester Cathedral, 2001–. Mem., Archbishops' Bd of Examiners, 1996–99. Paul Harris Fellow, Rotary Internat., 1995. Cross of St Augustine, 1995. *Recreations*: family, watching Rugby, cooking, craft work, gym. *Address*: 14 Shalford Close, Cirencester, Glos GL7 1WG. *T*: (01285) 885641.

**HARRIS, Rt Rev. Patrick Burnet**; an Honorary Assistant Bishop: Diocese of Europe, 1999–2017; Diocese of Gloucester, 2005–17; *b* 30 Sept. 1934; *s* of Edward James Burnet Harris and Astrid Kendall; *m* 1968, Valerie Margaret Pilbrow; two *s* one *d*. *Educ*: St Albans School; Keble Coll., Oxford (MA); Clifton Theol Coll. Asst Curate, St Ebbe's, Oxford, 1960–63; Missionary with S American Missionary Soc., 1963–73; Archdeacon of Salta, Argentina, 1969–73; Diocesan Bishop of Northern Argentina, 1973–80; Rector of Kirkheaton and Asst Bishop, Dio. Wakefield, 1981–85; Sec., Partnership for World Mission, 1986–88; Asst Bishop, Dio. Oxford, 1986–88; Bishop of Southwell, 1988–99. Asst Bp, Dio. Lincoln, 1999–2005. Mem., South Atlantic Council, 1986–2011. Chairman: Bible Reading Fellowship, 1995–98; Council, Ridley Hall, 1994–2003; Internat. Anglican Family Network, 2007–12; Pres., S Amer. Mission Soc., 1993–2010; Vice-Pres., TEAR Fund, 1994–2003. Mem., H of L, 1996–99. Hon. Fellow, Univ. of Glos, 2017. *Recreations*: ornithology, S American Indian culture, music, harvesting. *Address*: Apt B, Ireton House, Pavilion Gardens, The Park, Cheltenham, Glos GL50 2SP.

**HARRIS, Prof. Paul**; photographer and artist; Professor of Screen Media, University of Dundee, since 2014 (Dean, Duncan of Jordanstone College of Art and Design, 2014–19); *b* Birmingham, 4 June 1959; *s* of John Leonard Harris and Ethel Rose Harris; *m* 1986, Denise Hazel Bruno. *Educ*: Yardley Grammar Sch.; Birmingham Coll. of Art and Design (DA Photography 1980). Various broadcast television posts, Channel 4, BBC, ITV and freelance, 1980–92; Depute Dir, Media Centre, Dundee Inst. of Technol., 1992–94; freelance producer and lectr, 1994–96; Hd, Dept of Film and Television, Edinburgh Coll. of Art, 1996–2002; University of Abertay, Dundee: Sen. Lectr in Computer Arts and Vis. Prof., 2002–04; Prof. of Screen Media, 2004–10 (Vis. Prof. of Screen Media, 2010–); Creative Dir, Inst. of Arts, Media and Computer Games, 2009–10; Prof. of Screen Media, and Hd, Gray's Sch. of Art, Robert Gordon Univ., Aberdeen, 2010–14. Vis. Prof. of Creative Practice, Alexander Coll., Larnaca, Cyprus, 2018. Project Dir, 2001–02, Exec. Chm., 2002–07, Angus Digital Media Centre. Chairman: Growing Audiences NE, 2011–13; Regional Screen Scotland, 2014–; Member, Board: Patrick Allan-Fraser of Hospitalfield Trust, 2004–09; Scottish Screen, 2005–07 (Chm., Lottery and Investment Panel, 2005–07); Scottish Enterprise Tayside, 2007–14; Learning and Teaching Scotland, 2010–12; sound, Scotland's Fest. of New Music, 2012–16. Specialist Expert in Film and Digital Media, Communication and Journalism and Visual Arts and Design, Hong Kong Council for Accreditation of Acad. and Vocational Quals, 2014–. FRSA 2008. Chair and Ed., Creating a New North, 2012–14 (report publd 2014). *Publications*: articles in Jl of Media Practice, Internat. Jl of Educn Through Art, Jl of Audience and Reception Studies.

*Recreations*: travel, good food, fine wines, art, photography, cycling, driving, motorcycling. *Address*: Duncan of Jordanstone College of Art and Design, University of Dundee, Perth Road, Dundee DD1 4HT. *T*: (01382) 388820, *Fax*: (01382) 388305. *E*: p.harris@dundee.ac.uk.

**HARRIS, Prof. Paul Lansley**, DPhil; FBA 1998; Professor of Education, Harvard University, since 2001; *b* 14 May 1946; *s* of Joseph and Betty Harris; *m* Pascale Torracinta; three *s*. *Educ*: Chippenham Grammar Sch.; Sussex Univ. (BA Psychol.); Linacre Coll., Oxford (DPhil Psychol. 1971). Research Fellow: Center for Cognitive Studies, Harvard Univ., 1971–72; in Exptl Psychol., Oxford Univ., 1972–73; Lectr, Dept of Psychol., Lancaster Univ., 1973–76; Reader, Free Univ., Amsterdam, 1976–79; Lectr, Dept of Social Psychology, LSE, 1979–81; Oxford University: Lectr in Exptl Psychol., 1981–96; Reader, 1996–98; Prof. of Develtl Psychol., 1998–2001; Fellow, St John's Coll., 1981–2001, now Emeritus. Fellow, Center for Advanced Study in Behavioral Scis, Stanford, USA, 1992–93; John Simon Guggenheim Meml Foundn Fellow, 2005. Foreign Mem., Norwegian Acad. of Sci. and Letters, 2006–. Hon. Fellow, Cardiff Univ., 2011–. FAAAS 2015. Dr *hc*: Rennes, 2007; Lausanne, 2009. Preyer Award, European Soc. for Develtl Psychol., 2009; Cognitive Develt Soc. Book Award, 2013; Eleanor Maccoby Book Award, 2015, Mentor Award in Develtl Psychol., 2015, Amer. Psychol Assoc.; Mentor Award in Psychol., Assoc. for Psychol Sci., 2017. *Publications*: Children and Emotion, 1989; The Work of the Imagination, 2000; Trusting What You're Told: how children learn from others, 2012; articles in learned jls, incl. Child Development, Philosophical Trans. of Royal Soc., PNAS and Psychological Sci. *Recreations*: cooking, writing. *Address*: 503A Larsen Hall, Harvard Graduate School of Education, Appian Way, Cambridge, MA 02138, USA.

**HARRIS, Dame Pauline (Norma)**, DBE 2004; DL; company director; *b* 5 Jan. 1942; *d* of Bertie William Chumley and Constance Chumley (*née* Woolett); *m* 1960, Philip Charles Harris (see Baron Harris of Peckham); three *s* one *d*. *Educ*: St Helen's Sch., Streatham. Chairman: Organising Cttee, Children's Royal Variety Performance, 1985–88; Appeal Cttee, Birthright, 1988–91; Kingdom Appeal, Foetal Res. Unit, KCH, 1991–93; Co-Chm., Mencap Opera, 1993–96; Vice President: Friends of Guy's Hosp., 1991–; Mencap, 1995–; Pres., Harris HospisCare, 1997–. Dir and Mem., Special Educnl Needs Sub-cttee, Harris City Technol. Coll., Croydon, 1988–; Mem. Council, Harris Manchester Coll., Oxford, 1994–; Dir and Gov., Harris Girls' Acad., E Dulwich, 2006–; Dir, Harris Fedn of S London Schs, 2007–. Hon. Fellow: Oriel Coll., Oxford, 1994; RVC, S Mimms, 1994; Harris Manchester Coll., Oxford, 1996; Lucy Cavendish Coll., Cambridge, 1996. Trustee: Dyslexia Educn Trust, 1986–; Bacon City Technol. Coll., Bermondsey, 1990–; Mem. Cttee, Specialist Schs Trust, 2001–06; Trustee and Gov., Acad. of Peckham, 2002–. Gov., Kemnal Technol. Coll., Sidcup, 1994–. Patron: Nat. Eczema Soc., 1989–; Lewisham Children's Hosp., 1992–. Mem., British Showjumping Assoc., 1958–. DL Kent, 2005. Hon. DHL Richmond, London, 2002. *Recreations*: historic car rallying, dressage. *Address*: c/o Philip Harris House, 1A Spur Road, Orpington, Kent BR6 0PH. *T*: (01689) 886886, *Fax*: (01689) 886887. *E*: judy.willett@harrisventures.co.uk.

**HARRIS, Peter Michael**; Official Solicitor to the Supreme Court, 1993–99; *b* 13 April 1937; *m* 1963, Bridget Burke; one *s* two *d*. *Educ*: Cirencester Grammar School; Britannia Royal Naval College, Dartmouth. Cadet, RN, 1953; Lieut Comdr 1967; retired from RN 1972. Called to the Bar, Gray's Inn, 1971; Lord Chancellor's Department: Legal Asst, 1974; Circuit Administrator, Northern Circuit, 1986–93. Chm. and Trustee, Dorothy Pamela Smith Trust, 1999; Chm., Grandparents' Assoc., 2003–11. *Publications*: The Children Act 1989: a procedural handbook, 1991; The Expert Witness Pack, 1997. *Recreations*: reading, walking, gardening. *Address*: 23 Rook Wood Way, Little Kingshill, Great Missenden, Bucks HP16 0DF.

**HARRIS, Dame Philippa Jill Olivier, (Dame Pippa)**, DBE 2015; film and television producer; Co-Founder and Director, Neal Street Productions, since 2003; *b* Oxford, 27 March 1967; *d* of Dr Anthony Harris and Angela M. O. Harris (*née* Richards); *m* 1997, Richard McBrien; one *d*. *Educ*: Oxford High Sch.; Robinson Coll., Cambridge (BA Hons English 1989). Prodn asst, Jacaranda Prodns, 1989–91; Drama Ed., Carlton TV, 1993–97; BBC: Develt Exec., Films, 1997–99; Exec. Producer, Drama Serials, 1999–2001; Hd, Drama Commng, TV, 2001–03; producer/executive producer: Warriors, 1999 (BAFTA and RTS Awards); Care, 2000 (BAFTA and Prix Italia Awards); Other People's Children, 2000; The Sleeper, 2000; Love in a Cold Climate, 2001; The Cazalets, 2001; The Way We Live Now, 2001 (BAFTA and BPG Awards); The Inspector Lynley Mysteries, 2001–02; The Key, 2003; The Young Visiters, 2003; Jarhead, 2006; Starter for Ten, 2006; Stuart A Life Backwards, 2007 (Banff World TV and RTS Awards; Best TV Film, Reims Internat. TV Fest.); Things We Lost in the Fire, 2007; Revolutionary Road, 2008; Away We Go, 2009; Call the Midwife, 2012– (TRIC Best Drama Prog. of Year; TV Choice Best New Drama; Christopher Award; TV Choice Best Family Drama; Best Period Drama, Nat. TV Awards); The Hollow Crown, 2012–16 (RTS and BPG Best Single Drama Awards); Blood, 2013; Penny Dreadful, 2014–16; We Are Many, 2015; Britannia, 2017. Mem., Council, BAFTA, 2008– (Mem., Film Cttee, 2008–17; Chair, 2015–17, 2018–June 2020; Dep. Chair, 2017–18); Gov., Royal Central Sch. of Speech and Drama (formerly Central Sch. of Speech and Drama), 2010–18. Trustee: Creative Soc. (formerly New Deal of the Mind), 2009–17; Charleston Trust, 2016–. Mem., Charleston Appeal Cttee, 2013–. *Publications*: Song of Love: the letters of Rupert Brooke and Noel Olivier, 1991. *Recreations*: theatre, cinema, reading, contemporary art. *Address*: Neal Street Productions, 26–28 Neal Street, WC2H 9QQ. *T*: (020) 7240 8890. *E*: post@nealstreetproductions.com.

**HARRIS, Rebecca Elizabeth**; MP (C) Castle Point, since 2010; a Lord Commissioner of HM Treasury (Government Whip), since 2018; *b* Windsor, 22 Dec. 1967; *d* of Philip and Louise Harris; *m* Frank; one *s*. *Educ*: London Sch. of Econs and Pol Sci. (BSc). Mktg Dir, Phillimore & Co. Ltd (publishers), 1997–2007. Special Advr to Tim Yeo, MP, 2003–10. Mem. (C) Chichester DC, 1999–2003. An Asst Govt Whip, 2017–18. Mem., Select Cttee for Business, Innovation and Skills, 2010–15, for Regulatory Reform, 2012–17. *Recreation*: gardening. *Address*: House of Commons, SW1A 0AA. *T*: (020) 7219 7206. *E*: rebecca.harris.mp@parliament.uk.

**HARRIS, Ven. (Reginald) Brian**; Archdeacon of Manchester, 1980–98; a Residentiary Canon of Manchester Cathedral, 1980–98, Sub-Dean 1986–98; *b* 14 Aug. 1934; *s* of Reginald and Ruby Harris; *m* 1959, Anne Patricia Hughes; one *s* one *d*. *Educ*: Eltham College; Christ's College, Cambridge (MA); Ridley Hall, Cambridge. Curate of Wednesbury, 1959–61; Curate of Uttoxeter, 1961–64; Vicar of St Peter, Bury, 1964–70; Vicar of Walmsley, Bolton, 1970–80; RD of Walmsley, 1970–80. *Recreations*: walking, painting, music. *Address*: 9 Cote Lane, Hayfield, High Peak SK22 2HL. *T*: (01663) 746321.

**HARRIS, Rhian Sara**; Chief Executive, Lakeland Arts, since 2019; *b* 4 Dec. 1967; *m* 2001, Jonathan Hourigan; one *s* one *d*. *Educ*: Essex Univ. (BA Hons Art Hist. and Theory); City Univ. (MA Mus. and Gall. Mgt). Res. Asst, 1990–93, Sen. Picture Cataloguer, 1993–95, Wellcome Inst. for Hist. of Medicine; Curator, 1995–2001, Dir, 2001–08, Foundling Mus.; Dir, V&A Mus. of Childhood, 2008–18. Mem., Women Leaders Mus. Network, 2013–. Trustee, Jewish Mus., 2016–. *Publications*: (ed jtly and contrib.) Enlightened Self-Interest, 1997; (ed) The Foundling Museum Guidebook, 2004; (contrib.) Children, Childhood and Cultural Heritage, 2012; contrib. articles to Art Quarterly, Christies Mag., LTS Newsletter,

BBC History Online, Museums Jl, Outlook (Children England). *Recreations:* art, contemporary Welsh art, childhood studies, cinema, dance, music, travelling, pilates, gardening. *Address:* Lakeland Arts, Blackwell, The Arts & Crafts House, Bowness-on-Windermere, Cumbria LA23 3JT.

**HARRIS, Robert Dennis;** author; *b* 7 March 1957; *s* of late Dennis Harris and Audrey (*née* Hardy); *m* 1988, Gillian, *d* of Sir Derek Peter Hornby and Margaret (*née* Withers); two *s* two *d*. *Educ:* King Edward VII Sch., Melton Mowbray; Selwyn Coll., Cambridge (BA Hons English; Hon. Fellow 2013). Pres., Cambridge Union, 1978. Joined BBC TV Current Affairs Dept, 1978; Reporter, Newsnight, 1981–85, Panorama, 1985–87; Political Editor, Observer, 1987–89; Political Columnist, Sunday Times, 1989–92, 1996–97; Columnist, Daily Telegraph, 2001–02; book reviewer, Sunday Times, 2009–. Patron, Bletchley Park Trust, 2001–. Pres., Classical Assoc., 2007–08. Mem., BAFTA, 2002. FRSL 1996. Hon. DLitt Nottingham, 2012. Columnist of the Year, British Press Awards, 2003. *Publications: novels:* Fatherland, 1992 (filmed 1994); Enigma, 1995 (filmed 2001); Archangel, 1998 (televised 2005); Pompeii, 2003; Imperium, 2006; The Ghost, 2007 (filmed 2010; writer of screenplay with Roman Polanski (Eur. Film Award, César and Lumière Prizes for best adapted screenplay); Lustrum, 2009; The Fear Index, 2011; An Officer and a Spy, 2013 (Popular Fiction Book of Yr, Nat. Book Awards, 2013; Walter Scott Prize, 2014; Ian Fleming Steel Dagger Award, CWA, 2014; filmed 2019); Dictator, 2015; Conclave, 2016; The Cicero Trilogy, 2016 (adapted for stage as Imperium I and II, RSC, Stratford, 2017, transf. Gielgud, 2018); Munich, 2017; The Second Sleep, 2019; *non-fiction:* (with Jeremy Paxman) A Higher Form of Killing: the history of gas and germ warfare, 1982; Gotcha! the media, the government and the Falklands crisis, 1983; The Making of Neil Kinnock, 1984; Selling Hitler: the story of the Hitler diaries, 1986 (televised, 1991); Good and Faithful Servant: the unauthorized biography of Bernard Ingham, 1990; The Media Trilogy, 1994. *Recreations:* collecting books, walking, dove-keeping. *Address:* The Old Vicarage, Kintbury, Berks RG17 9TR. *T:* (01488) 658073. *Club:* Garrick.

**HARRIS, Robert K.;** *see* Kirby-Harris.

**HARRIS, Robert Malcolm;** HM Diplomatic Service, retired; Governor of Anguilla, 1997–2000 (Acting Governor, 1996–97); *b* 9 Feb. 1941; *m* 1984, Mary Lavinia Allmark (*née* Taggart). Joined Foreign Office, 1960, Archives Clerk, 1960–62; Istanbul, 1962–63; Cento, Ankara, 1963–65; Blantyre, 1965–69; FCO, 1969; Moscow, 1970–72; FCO, 1972–75; Second Sec., Dublin, 1975–79; Nat. Defence Coll., Latimer, 1979–80; First Sec., FCO, 1980–84; Hd of Chancery, Brunei, 1984–89; Consul, Lyon, 1989–90; First Sec., FCO, 1990–92; Chargé d'Affaires, Almaty, 1992–93; First Sec., FCO, 1993–96. *Recreations:* golf, music, gardening. *Address:* Le Bourg, 46500 Miers, France. *Club:* Golf de Montal.

**HARRIS, Robert William,** CEng, FREng, FIOA; Director, Rob Harris Design Ltd, since 2015; *b* London, 6 Dec. 1954; *s* of William Harris and Mabel Harris; *m* 1981, Susan-Jayne Ashton; one *s* one *d*. *Educ:* Warwick Univ. (BSc Hons Physics 1975); Univ. of Southampton (MSc Sound and Vibration 1977). CEng 1995; FREng 2009. Acoustic Consultant, Acoustic Technology Ltd, 1977–82; Acoustic Consultant, 1983–89, Principal, 1990–97, Arup Acoustics; Dir, Acoustics, 1998–2015, Dir, Arts and Culture UKMEA, 2009–15, Arup. Internat. auditorium acoustic designer; projects include: Glyndebourne Opera House, 1994; Bridgewater Hall, Manchester, 1996; Royal Opera House, London, 2000; City Recital Hall, Sydney, 2002; Concertgebouw, Bruges, 2002; Copenhagen Opera House, 2004; Oslo Opera House, 2008; Kings Place recital hall, London, 2008. Royal Acad. of Engrg Vis. Prof., Univ. of Southampton, 2016–19. Theatre consultant. FIOA 1990. *Publications:* numerous papers in professional jls and conf. procs on auditorium design and sound system design. *Recreations:* cycling, photography, travel, performing arts. *T:* 07534 109168. *E:* info@robharrisdesign.co.uk. *W:* www.robharrisdesign.co.uk.

**HARRIS, Robin (David Ronald),** CBE 1988; writer; *b* 22 June 1952; *s* of Ronald Desmond Harris and Isabella Jamieson Harris. *Educ:* Canford Sch.; Exeter Coll., Oxford (Stapeldon Schol., MA History, DPhil). Desk Officer, Conservative Res. Dept, 1978–81; Special Adviser: to Financial Sec. to the Treasury, 1981–83; to Home Secretary, 1983–85; Dir, Conservative Res. Dept, 1985–89; Mem., Prime Minister's Policy Unit, 1989–90; Advr to Baroness Thatcher, 1990–2003. Consultant Dir, Politeia, 2003–11. Sen. Vis. Fellow, Heritage Foundn, 2009–13. Lectr in History, Croatian Catholic Univ., 2016–17. Order of the Morning Star (Croatia), 2008. *Publications:* Valois Guyenne: a study of politics, government and society in medieval France, 1994; (ed) Margaret Thatcher: the collected speeches, 1997; Dubrovnik: a history, 2003; Beyond Friendship: the future of Anglo-American relations, 2006; Talleyrand: betrayer and saviour of France, 2007; The Conservatives: a history, 2011; Not for Turning: the life of Margaret Thatcher, 2013; Stepinac: his life and times, 2016. *Recreations:* reading, travel. *Club:* Oxford and Cambridge.

**HARRIS, Rolf;** entertainer; *b* 30 March 1930; *s* of C. G. Harris and A. M. Harris (*née* Robbins); *m* 1958, Alwen Hughes, sculptress; one *d*. *Educ:* Bassendean State Sch.; Perth Modern Sch.; Univ. of WA; Claremont Teachers' Coll. Jun. backstroke champion, Australia, 1946; teacher, Perth; paintings exhibited: RA, London, 1954, 1955; Nat. Gall., London, 2002; 80th birthday portrait of HM Queen, 2005; Clarendon Gall., Mayfair, 2011; Walker Art Gall., Liverpool, 2012; *television* includes: Rolf Harris Show, 1967–71; Rolf on Saturday-OK, 1977–79; Cartoon Time, 1984–89; Rolf's Cartoon Club, 1989–93; Animal Hospital, 1994–2004; Rolf's Amazing Animals, 1998; Rolf on Art, 2001; Rolf's Golden Jubilee, 2003; Rolf Harris' Star Portraits, 2004–07; Rolf Harris Paints His Dream, 2010; *recordings* include: Tie Me Kangaroo Down Sport, 1960; Sun Arise, 1962; Two Little Boys, 1969; Stairway to Heaven, 1993. *Publications:* Write Your Own Pop Song, 1968; Rolf Goes Bush, 1975; Picture Book of Cats, 1978; Looking at Pictures, 1978; Instant Music, 1980; Your Cartoon Time, 1986; Catalogue of Comic Verse, 1988; Every Picture Tells a Story, 1989; Win or Die: the making of a King, 1989; Your Animation Time, 1991; Personality Cats, 1992; Me and You and Poems Too, 1993; Can You Tell What it is Yet? (autobiog.), 2001; Rolf on Art, 2002; Tie Me Kangaroo Down, Sport, 2009; True Animal Tales, 2011.

**HARRIS, Rosemary Jeanne;** author; *b* 20 Feb. 1923; *yr d* of Marshal of the RAF Sir Arthur Harris, 1st Bt, GCB, OBE, AFC, LLD, and of Barbara Kyrle Money. *Educ:* privately; Thorneloe Sch., Weymouth; St Martin's, Central and Chelsea Schs of Art. Red Cross Nursing Auxiliary, London, Westminster Div., from 1941. Student, 1945–48; picture restorer, 1949; student at Courtauld Inst. (Dept of Technology), 1950; Reader, MGM, 1951–52; subseq. full-time writer. Reviewer of children's books for The Times, 1970–73. Television plays: Peronik, 1976; The Unknown Enchantment, 1981. *Publications:* The Summer-House, 1956; Voyage to Cythera, 1958; Venus with Sparrows, 1961; All My Enemies, 1967; The Nice Girl's Story, 1968; A Wicked Pack of Cards, 1969; The Double Snare, 1975; Three Candles for the Dark, 1976; *for children:* The Moon in the Cloud, 1968 (Carnegie Medal); The Shadow on the Sun, 1970; The Seal-Singing, 1971; The Child in the Bamboo Grove, 1971; The Bright and Morning Star, 1972; The King's White Elephant, 1973; The Lotus and the Grail, 1974; The Flying Ship, 1974; The Little Dog of Fo, 1976; I Want to be a Fish, 1977; A Quest for Orion, 1978; Beauty and the Beast, 1979; Greenfinger House, 1979; Tower of the Stars, 1980; The Enchanted Horse, 1981; Janni's Stork, 1982; Zed, 1982; (adapted) Heidi, by Johanna Spyri, 1983; Summers of the Wild Rose, 1987; (ed) Poetry Anthology: Love and the Merry-Go-Round, 1988; Colm of the Islands, 1989; Ticket to Freedom, 1991; The Wildcat Strike, 1995; The Haunting of Joey M'basa, 1996. *Recreations:* music, theatre, reading.

**HARRIS, Russell James;** QC 2003; *b* 10 Nov. 1961; *s* of late Donald Harris and Jean Harris (*née* Hall); *m* 1999, Nicola Richards; one *s* two *d*. *Educ:* Heolddu Comprehensive Sch., Bargoed; St John's Coll., Cambridge (MacMahon Schol., Pres. JCR, Lamour Prize, MA 1984); City Univ. (Dip Law 1985). Called to the Bar, Gray's Inn, 1986, Bencher, 2009 (Trustee, 2013); in practice as a barrister, specialising in planning and public law, 1986–; Special Advocate, 2009–. Mem. Wales Council, Prince's Trust, 2013–17. Vice Pres., London Welsh Male Voice Choir, 2017–. Series advr, The Welsh in London (BBC Wales TV), 2006. Pres., Old Chiswick Protection Soc., 2019–. *Publications:* (jtly) Environmental Law, 2001; various articles in Jl of Planning and Envmtl Law. *Recreations:* family, Wales (especially Ramsey Sound and the Farmer's Arms, St Davids). *Address:* Landmark Chambers, 180 Fleet Street, EC4A 2HG. *T:* (020) 7430 1221. *E:* russellharrisqc@ Mortonhouse.co.uk. *Clubs:* London Welsh Rugby Football (Discipline Officer, 2003–); St Davids Rugby Football (Vice-Pres., 2006–).

**HARRIS, Prof. Ruth,** DPhil; FBA 2011; Professor of Modern History, University of Oxford, since 2011; Senior Research Fellow, All Souls College, since 2016; *b* 25 Dec. 1958; *m* 1985, Dr Iain George Pears, *qv*; two *s*. *Educ:* Univ. of Pennsylvania (BA, MA); DPhil. Jun. Res. Fellow, St John's Coll., Oxford, 1983; Associate Prof., Smith Coll., Northampton, Mass; Lectr in Modern Hist., Univ. of Oxford, 1990; Fellow, New Coll., Oxford, 1990–2016. *Publications:* Murders and Madness, 1989; (ed jtly and contrib.) Clinical Diseases of the Nervous System, 1990; Lourdes: body and spirit in the secular age, 1999; The Man on Devil's Island: Alfred Dreyfus and the affair that divided France, 2010 (Wolfson History Prize, 2011; Nat. Jewish Book Award); Dreyfus: politics, emotion and the scandal of the century, 2011. *Address:* All Souls College, Oxford OX1 4AL.

**HARRIS, Sheila Lesley;** *see* Scales, S. L.

**HARRIS, Sonia Ruth; Her Honour Judge Sonia Harris;** a Circuit Judge, since 2018; *b* Coventry, 12 Sept. 1974; *d* of Philip Harris and Valerie Harris; *m* 1997, Dr Timothy Short; one *s* one *d*. *Educ:* Parkgate Infant and Jun. Sch., Coventry; Blue Coat C of E Sch., Coventry; Christ Church, Oxford (BA 1st Cl. Hons Juris. 1996); Univ. of British Columbia (LLM by res. 1997). Called to the Bar, Lincoln's Inn, 1998; pupillage, 4 New Sq., Lincoln's Inn, 1998–99; Lectr and Reader in Family Law, Univs of Durham and Birmingham, 1999–2011; Prof. of Family Law and Policy, Univ. of Birmingham, 2011–14, Hon. Prof. of Law, 2014–; a Dep. Dist Judge, 2010–14; a Dist Judge, 2014–18; a Recorder, 2016–18. Special Advr to H of L Select Cttee on Adoption, 2012. *Publications:* (with J. Miles) Family Law: text, cases and materials, 2007, 3rd edn 2015; Aboriginal Child Welfare, Self-Government and the Rights of Indigenous Children: protecting the vulnerable under international law, 2012; (ed jtly) The Futures of Legal Education and the Legal Profession, 2015. *Recreations:* hiking, ski-ing, theatre, singing. *Address:* Wolverhampton Combined Court Centre, Pipers Row, Wolverhampton WV1 3LQ. *T:* (01902) 481000. *E:* HHJ.Sonia.Harris@ejudiciary.net.

**HARRIS, Thomas, (Tom);** Director, Third Avenue Public Affairs Ltd (formerly Third Avenue Communications), since 2015; columnist, Daily Telegraph, since 2016; *b* 20 Feb. 1964; *s* of Tom Harris and Rita Harris (*née* Ralston); *m* 1998, Carolyn Moffat. *Educ:* Garnock Acad., Kilbirnie, Ayrshire; Napier Coll., Edinburgh (SHND Journalism). Trainee Reporter, E Kilbride News, 1986–88; Reporter, Paisley Daily Express, 1988–90; Press Officer: Labour Party in Scotland, 1990–92; Strathclyde Regl Council, 1993–96; Sen. Media Officer, Glasgow CC, 1996; PR Manager, E Ayrshire Council, 1996–98; Chief PR and Marketing Officer, Strathclyde PTE, 1998–2001. MP (Lab) Glasgow, Cathcart, 2001–05, Glasgow S, 2005–15; contested (Lab) same seat, 2015. Parly Under-Sec. of State, DfT, 2006–08; Shadow Minister for Envmt, Food and Rural Affairs, 2012–13. Mem., Select Cttee on Transport, 2010–12 and 2013–15, on Admin, 2010 and 2013–15. Mem., Expert Challenge Panel, ind. rev. of railway industry, 2018–19. *Publications:* Ten Years in the Death of the Labour Party, 2018. *Recreations:* tennis, astronomy, hill walking, cinema. *E:* info@thirdavenue.org.uk.

**HARRIS, Sir Thomas (George),** KBE 2002; CMG 1995; HM Diplomatic Service, retired; Chairman, European Services Forum, 2010–18; Director, International Business and Diplomatic Exchange, since 2016; *b* 6 Feb. 1945; *s* of late Kenneth James Harris and of Dorothy Harris; *m* 1967, Mei-Ling Hwang; three *s*. *Educ:* Haberdashers' Aske's School; Gonville and Caius College, Cambridge. MA. Board of Trade, 1966–69; British Embassy, Tokyo, 1969–71; Asst Private Sec. to Minister for Aerospace, 1971–72; Dept of Trade, 1972–76; Cabinet Office, 1976–78; Principal Private Sec. to Sec. of State for Trade, 1978–79; Asst Sec., Dept of Trade, 1979–83; HM Diplomatic Service: Counsellor (Commercial), British Embassy, Washington, 1983–88; Head of Chancery, Lagos, 1988–90; Dep. High Comr, Nigeria, 1990–91; Head, East African Dept, 1991–92, African Dept (Equatorial), 1992–94, FCO; Ambassador, Repub. of Korea, 1994–97; Dir-Gen., Export Promotion, DTI, 1997–99 (on secondment); Dir-Gen., Trade and Investment in the US, and Consul-Gen., NY, 1999–2004. Vice-Chm., Standard Chartered Bank Ltd, 2004–14. Special Advr, Center for Strategic and Internat. Studies, Washington, 2004–08. Chairman: Pakistan Britain Trade and Investment Forum, 2006–12; Taiwan Britain Business Council, 2007–13; Trade Policy Adv. Gp, British Bankers' Assoc., 2007–13. Member: Internat. Adv. Bd, BritishAmerican Business, 2004–14; Indonesian British Business Council, 2004–12; UK-Korea Forum for the Future, 2004–14; Philippine-British Business Council, 2004–15; Korea Britain Business Council, 2007–12; Saudi British Jt Business Council, 2005–12; Singapore British Business Council, 2005–12; Transatlantic Task Force on Trade and Investment, 2011–12. Non-executive Director: Biocompatibles plc, 2005–11; ISFL Ltd, 2007–10; Johnson Matthey plc, 2009–12; SC First Bank, Korea, 2009–14; City UK Ltd, 2010–14. Trustee: Imperial War Mus., 2005–09; Asia House, London, 2005–10; Confucius Business Inst., LSE, 2011–14; Imperial War Mus. Develt Trust, 2012–. *Publications:* (contrib.) Conflict and Consensus, 1985; (contrib.) Reforming the City: responses to the global financial crisis, 2009; contribs to Jl of Korean Hist. of Sci. Society, Thunderbird Internat. Business Rev., Asian Affairs. *Address:* 8 Oakeshott Avenue, Highgate, N6 6NS. *Club:* Oxford and Cambridge.

**HARRIS, Timothy James,** FCCT; Headteacher, Colyton Grammar School, since 2016; *b* Torquay, 2 April 1969; *s* of Reginald and Molly Mitchell; *m* 2001, Louise Thayre; one *s*. *Educ:* Bassaleg Sch.; Newcastle Univ. (BA Hons Ancient Hist. 1990); Sussex Univ. (PGCE 1992); NPQH 2014. Teacher of Hist., Easthampstead Park Sch., Bracknell, 1992–98; Hd of Hist., 1998–2007, Asst Headteacher, 2007–08, Holt Sch., Wokingham; Asst Headteacher, 2008–14, Dep. Headteacher, 2014–16, Reading Sch. Founding FCCT 2017. *Recreations:* Rugby, football, cricket. *Address:* The Meadows, Talaton, Exeter EX5 2RL. *T:* (01404) 823177, 07801 948201. *E:* ha33a@me.com. *Club:* Lansdowne.

**HARRIS, William;** *see* Harris, J. R. W.

**HARRIS, Prof. William Anthony,** PhD; FRS 2007; FMedSci; Professor of Anatomy, 1997–2018, now Emeritus, and Head, Department of Physiology, Development and Neuroscience, 2006–18, Cambridge University; Fellow, Clare College, Cambridge, since 1997; b 26 Nov. 1950; s of Louis Jacob Harris and Helen Gallendar Harris; m 1983, Christine Elizabeth Holt, qv; one s one d. Educ: Univ. of Calif, Berkeley (BA); California Inst. of Technol. (PhD 1976). Jun. Fellow, Harvard Univ., 1977–80; Faculty Mem., Univ. of Calif, San Diego, 1980–97; engaged in res. on genetic and molecular basis of neural develt. Co-founder, DanioLabs, 2002–. FMedSci 2007. Hd Coach, Cambridge Univ. Ice Hockey Club. Waddington Medal, British Soc. for Develtl Biology, 2017. *Publications*: Genetic Neurobiology, 1982; Development of the Nervous System, 2000, 3rd edn 2012. *Recreations*: ice-hockey, painting. *Address*: Clare College, Cambridge CB2 1TL.

**HARRIS, Winifred Anne Charlotte, (Lady Normington),** CBE 2007; Director, Joint International Unit, Department for Work and Pensions, Department for Business, Innovation and Skills (formerly Department for Innovation, Universities and Skills), and Department for Children, Schools and Families (formerly Department for Education and Skills), 2006–09; b 1 Jan. 1947; d of Leslie Frank Harris and Winifred Maisie Bissett Harris (née Wilson); m 1985, David John Normington (see Sir D. J. Normington). Educ: Univ. of Aberdeen (MA Hons Hist. 1969). Private Sec. to Sec. of State for Employment, 1974; First Sec. (Labour), British Embassy, Brussels, 1980–84; Area Manager (W London), MSC, 1985–86; Dir, Individual Conciliation, ACAS, 1986–88; Hd, Financial Mgt Services, 1988–91, Regl Dir, London, 1992–96, Dept for Employment; Hd, EU Div., DFEE, 1997–2003; Dep. Dir, Internat., Home Office, 2003–06. Mem., Educn Adv. Bd, Dulwich Picture Gall., 2010–15. Patron, Treloars, 2017–19 (Trustee, 2019–). Governor: Hackney Community Coll., 2010–16; New City Coll., 2016–; Mem., Bd of Govs, Univ. of Winchester, 2011– (Vice Chm., 2012–). MCIPD 1987. *Recreations*: opera, ballet, music, walking, gardening, reading, collecting antique fans.

**HARRISON;** see Graham-Harrison.

**HARRISON,** family name of **Baron Harrison**.

**HARRISON,** Baron cr 1999 (Life Peer), of Chester in the county of Cheshire; **Lyndon Henry Arthur Harrison;** b 28 Sept. 1947; s of late Charles William Harrison and Edith (née Johnson); m 1980, Hilary Anne Plank; one s one d. Educ: Oxford Sch.; Univ. of Warwick (BA Hons 1970); Univ. of Sussex (MA 1971); Univ. of Keele (MA 1978). Part time Lectr, N Staffs Polytechnic, 1973–75; Research Officer, Students' Union, UMIST, 1975–78; Union Manager, NE Wales Inst. of Higher Educn, Wrexham, 1978–89. Cheshire County Councillor, 1981–90 (Chairman: Libraries and Countryside Cttee, 1982, 1984–89; Further Educn, 1984–89; Tourism, 1985–89). Dep. Chm., NW Tourist Bd, 1987–89. MEP (Lab) Cheshire W, 1989–94, Cheshire W and Wirral, 1994–99, European Parliament: Lab spokesman on monetary union, and on ASEAN and Korea, 1994–99; Vice-President: Tourism Intergp, 1995–99; Small and Med. Size Enterprises Intergp, 1995–99. Vice Chm., ACC, 1990–97. Liaison Peer, NI Office, 2000–02; Mem., H of L Cttee on Common Foreign and Security Policy, 2000–03, on Social Policy, 2003–07, on Hybrid Instruments, 2003–, on EU, 2004–, on Equality Act 2010 and the Disabled, 2015–16, on Financial Exclusion, 2016–17; Chm., H of L Cttee on Econ. and Financial Affairs (formerly on Econ. and Financial Affairs and Internat. Trade), 2010–15. H of L Rep. on internat. trade affairs to IPU and Delegate to Parly Assembly of WTO, 2012–14. *Recreations*: chess, bridge, the arts, sport. *Address*: House of Lords, SW1A 0PW.

**HARRISON, Prof. Alan,** TD 1983 (Bar 1989, 2nd Bar 1995); PhD; FDSRCS; FDSRCSE; Professor of Dental Care of the Elderly, University of Bristol, 1987–2004, now Emeritus; b 24 July 1944; s of Lt-Col John Thomas West Harrison and Mona Evelyn (née Gee); m 1st, 1967, Pauline Lilian (née Rendell) (marr. diss. 1980); one s one d; 2nd, 1982, Margaret Ann (née Frost); two d. Educ: Rydal Sch., Colwyn Bay; Univ. of Wales (BDS, PhD). FDS RCS; FDSRCSE ad hominem; FADM. Lectr, Dental Sch. Cardiff, 1970–78; Sen. Lectr and Hon. Consultant, Univ. of Leeds, 1978–87. Vis. Asst Prof., Univ. of South Carolina, 1974–75. Mem., Inst. for Learning and Teaching in Higher Educn, 2002–. OC 390 Field Dental Team (V), 1971–73; CO 308 Evacuation Hosp. RAMC(V), 1989–94; CO 306 Field Hosp. RAMC(V), 1994–95; Hon. Col Comdt RADC, 1996–2001; Col RADC(V), 1989–2005. QHDS 1996–99. Hon. Fellow, Cardiff Univ., 2006. *Publications*: Overdentures in General Dental Practice, 1988, 3rd edn 1993; Complete Dentures: problem solving, 1999; over 160 publications in scientific jls. *Recreations*: walking, woodworking, digital photography. *E*: alan.harrison@bristol.ac.uk.

**HARRISON, Alistair;** see Harrison, W. A.

**HARRISON, Prof. Andrew,** DPhil; FRSE; FRSC; Chief Executive Officer, Diamond Light Source Ltd, since 2014; b Oxford, 3 Oct. 1959; s of Prof. Martin Harrison and Wendy Harrison; m 1988, Alison Charlotte; three d. Educ: Newcastle-under-Lyme High Sch.; St John's Coll., Oxford (BA; DPhil; Hon. Fellow 2016). Royal Soc. Univ. Res. Fellow, Univ. of Oxford, 1988–92; Lectr, then Reader, 1992–99, Prof. of Solid State Chem., 1999–2006, Univ. of Edinburgh; Associate Dir, 2006–11, Dir Gen., 2011–13, Institut Laue Langevin. Res. Fellow, McMaster Univ., 1989. Vis. Prof., Univ. of Manchester, 2014–; Hon. Prof., Univ. of Edinburgh, 2014. FRSE 2002. Hon. DSc Edinburgh, 2017. *Publications*: Fractals in Chemistry, 1995; over 100 articles in learned jls. *Recreations*: ski-ing, snowboarding, cycling on and off road, hillwalking. *Address*: Diamond Light Source Ltd, Diamond House, Harwell Science and Innovation Campus, Didcot, Oxon OX11 0DE. *T*: (01235) 778811, *Fax*: (01235) 778499. *E*: andrew.harrison@diamond.ac.uk.

**HARRISON, (Anne) Victoria, (Lady Harrison),** DPhil; Executive Secretary (Chief Executive), Wolfson Foundation, 1997–2006; d of Lawrence Greggain and Amy Isabel Greggain (née Briggs); m 1967, Brian Howard Harrison (see Sir Brian Harrison). Educ: Workington GS; Milham Ford Sch., Oxford; St Anne's Coll., Oxford (BA 1st Cl. Hons Animal Physiology 1965; Theodore Williams Schol. 1965; MA 1970; DPhil 1970). Exec. Editor, Internat. Abstracts of Biological Scis, 1971–72; MRC HQ Office, 1972–83, PSO, 1974; seconded to Science and Technology Secretariat, Cabinet Office, 1983–85, Dep. to Chief Scientific Advr, 1984–85; Head of Secretariat, MRC, 1985–89; Head of Policy Div., AFRC, 1989–94; Dir of Policy and Assessment, BBSRC, 1994–97; Consultant, DIPEx Charity, 2007–10. Mem. Bd, Inst. of Sports and Exercise Medicine, 2007–13. Trustee: Comparative Clinical Sci. Foundn, 2007–16; UCL Hosps Charity, 2007–17 (Chm., 2015–17); Hearing Dogs for Deaf People, 2011–. *Recreations*: phoning friends from the bath, armchair gardening, Yarnells Hill Book Club. *Address*: The Book House, Yarnells Hill, Oxford OX2 9BG. *Clubs*: Athenæum, Royal Society of Medicine.

**HARRISON, Air Vice-Marshal Anthony John,** CB 1997; CBE 1992 (OBE 1986); JP; Executive Vice-President and General Manager, Singapore, BAE SYSTEMS (formerly British Aerospace) plc, 1998–2005; b 9 Nov. 1943; s of Jack and Jean Harrison; m 1965, Glynn Dene Hyland-Smith; one s one d. Educ: Woodbridge Sch., Suffolk. Commnd RAF, 1963; Commanding Officer: 617 Sqdn (The Dambusters), 1982–85; RAF Bruggen, 1989–92; Dir, Jt Warfare, MoD, 1992–94; ACDS (Ops), MoD, 1994–97. Upper Freeman, GAPAN, 1985. Pres., Woodbridge RAF Assoc., 1994. FRAeS. JP Devon, 2007. *Recreations*: golf, tennis, aviation history. *Address*: Chudleigh Knighton, Devon. *Club*: Royal Air Force.

**HARRISON, Sir Brian (Howard),** Kt 2005; DPhil; FBA 2005; FRHistS; Emeritus Fellow of Corpus Christi College, Oxford, since 2004; Titular Professor of Modern History, University of Oxford, 1996–2004; b 9 July 1937; s of Howard Harrison and Mary Elizabeth (née Savill); m 1967, Anne Victoria Greggain (see A. V. Harrison). Educ: Merchant Taylors' Sch., Northwood; St John's Coll., Oxford (BA 1st Cl. Hons Mod. Hist. 1961; MA 1966; DPhil 1966; Hon. Fellow, 2010). FRHistS 1973. Nat. Service, 2nd Lieut, Malta Signal Sqdn, 1956–58. Oxford University: Sen. Schol., St Antony's Coll., 1961–64; Jun. Res. Fellow, Nuffield Coll., 1964–67; Corpus Christi College, Oxford: Fellow and Tutor in Modern Hist. and Pols, 1967–2000; Official Fellow, 2000–04; Sen. Tutor, 1984–86 and 1988–90; Vice-Pres., 1992, 1993 and 1996–98; Univ. Reader in Modern British History, 1990–2000. Editor, Oxford DNB, 2000–04. Visiting Professor: Univ. of Michigan (Ann Arbor), 1970; Harvard Univ., 1973–74; Visiting Fellow: Melbourne Univ., 1975; ANU, 1995. *Publications*: Drink and the Victorians, 1971, 2nd edn 1994; Separate Spheres: the opposition to women's suffrage in Britain, 1978; (ed with P. Hollis) Robert Lowery: Chartist and lecturer, 1979; Peaceable Kingdom: stability and change in modern Britain, 1982; (with C. Ford) A Hundred Years Ago: Britain in the 1880s in words and photographs, 1983; Prudent Revolutionaries: portraits of British feminists between the wars, 1987; (ed and contrib.) The History of the University of Oxford, Vol. 8: The Twentieth Century, 1994; (ed) Corpuscles: a history of Corpus Christi College, Oxford, 1994; The Transformation of British Politics 1860–1995, 1996; (ed jtly and contrib.) Civil Histories: essays presented to Sir Keith Thomas, 2000; New Oxford History of England series: Seeking a Role: the United Kingdom 1951–1970, 2009; Finding a Role?: the United Kingdom 1970–1990, 2010. *Recreations*: looking at architecture, cooking, listening to classical music. *Address*: The Book House, Yarnells Hill, Oxford OX2 9BG.

**HARRISON, Prof. Bryan Desmond,** CBE 1990; PhD; FRS 1987; FRSE; Professor of Plant Virology, University of Dundee, 1991–96, now Professor Emeritus; b 16 June 1931; s of John William and Norah Harrison; m 1968, Elizabeth Ann Latham-Warde; two s one d. Educ: Whitgift Sch., Croydon; Reading Univ. (BSc Hons Agric. Bot. 1952); London Univ. (PhD 1955). FRSE 1979. Postgraduate student, ARC, 1952; Scottish Hort. Res. Inst., Dundee, 1954; Rothamsted Exp. Station, 1957; Head, Virology Section, 1966, Dep. Dir, 1979, Scottish Hort. Res. Inst.; Head, Virology Dept, Scottish Crop Res. Inst., 1981–91. Visiting Professor: Japan Soc. for Promotion of Science, 1970; Organization of American States, Venezuela, 1973; Hon. Prof., Univ. of St Andrews, 1986–99; Hon. Vis. Prof., Univ. of Dundee, 1988–91; Hon. Res. Fellow (formerly Hon. Res. Prof.), James Hutton Inst. (formerly Scottish Crop Res. Inst.), 1991–; Vis. Prof., Univ. of Zhejiang, China, 2001–. Pres., Assoc. of Applied Biologists, 1980–81. Life Mem., Internat. Cttee for Taxonomy of Viruses, 1997. Hon. Member: Assoc. of Applied Biologists, 1989; Soc. for Gen. Microbiol., 1990; Phytopathological Soc. of Japan, 1992; For. Associate, US Nat. Acad. of Scis, 1998. Hon. DAgrFor Univ. of Helsinki, 1990. *Publications*: Plant Virology: the principles (with A. J. Gibbs), 1976 (trans. Russian and Chinese); research papers and reviews on plant viruses and virus diseases. *Recreations*: growing garden crops, foreign travel. *Address*: James Hutton Institute, Invergowrie, Dundee DD2 5DA. *T*: (01382) 562731, *Fax*: (01382) 562426.

**HARRISON, Bryan James;** management consultant, 2001–12; b 30 Oct. 1947; s of late James Harrison and Doris Harrison (née Burnham); m 1st, 1973 (marr. diss. 1988); two d; 2nd, 1990, Valerie Mayo; one d. Educ: Southmoor Sch., Sunderland; Exeter Univ. (BA Politics). DHSS, 1971–81; seconded to Camden and Islington AHA, 1981–82; Dist Administrator, Islington HA, 1982–84; District General Manager: Islington HA, 1984–88; Bloomsbury HA, 1988–90; Bloomsbury and Islington HA, 1990–92; Regl Gen. Manager, NE Thames RHA, 1992–94; Chief Exec., Forest Healthcare NHS Trust, 1995–99; Special Advr, Workforce and Develt, NHS Exec., 1999–2001. Non-exec. Dir, Barnet PCT, 2004–11. Trustee and Mem. Council, Marie Curie Cancer Care, 2002–08. *Recreations*: golf, reading, music, soccer, art.

**HARRISON, Rev. Cameron Elias;** international consultant on education policy; Director, Harrison Leimon Associates, since 2002; b 27 Aug. 1945; s of Elias Harrison and Herries Harrison; m 1968, Pearl Leimon; one s one d. Educ: Cumnock Acad.; Strathclyde Univ. (BSc Hons Physics); Stirling Univ. (MEd). Physics Teacher, Greenock Acad., 1968–71; Head of Physics, Graeme High Sch., 1971–79; Depute Rector, Kirkcudbright Acad., 1979–82; Rector, The Gordon Schools, 1982–91; Chief Exec., Scottish Consultative Council on the Curriculum, 1991–98. Sec.-Gen., Consortium of Instns for Develt & Res. in Educn in Europe, 1993–97; Dir, Inst. for Educnl Policy, Open Soc. Inst., Budapest, 1998–2002. Ordained, C of S, 2006; Assoc. Minister, Church of the Holy Trinity, St Andrews, 2008–. FRSA. *Publications*: Managing Change, 1989. *Recreations*: walking, singing, talking, listening, teaching, learning. *Address*: St Andrews, Fife.

**HARRISON, Prof. Carol,** DPhil; FBA 2018; Lady Margaret Professor of Divinity, University of Oxford, since 2015; Canon of Christ Church Cathedral, Oxford, since 2015; b West Hartlepool, 27 Nov. 1960; d of Keith Harrison and Margaretta Harrison; m 2010, Alexander Pokhilko; one s. Educ: Durham Wearside Sec. Sch.; Lady Margaret Hall, Oxford (BA; DPhil 1987). École Pratique des Hautes Études, Paris. Lectr, Univ. of Hull, 1987–88; Durham University: Lectr, Sen. Lectr, then Reader, 1989–2008; Prof. of Hist. and Theol. of the Latin West, 2008–15. *Publications*: Revelation and Beauty in the Thought of Saint Augustine, 1992; Augustine: Christian truth and fractured humanity, 2000; Rethinking Augustine's Early Theology: an argument for continuity, 2006; The Art of Listening in the Early Church, 2013; Reading Augustine on Music: sense, affect, voice, 2018. *Recreation*: listening. *Address*: Priory House, Christ Church, Oxford OX1 1DP. *T*: (01865) 276247. *E*: carol.harrison@theology.ox.ac.uk.

**HARRISON, Caroline Mary Alice;** QC 2013; b Haslingden, Lancs, 31 Dec. 1961; d of Peter Harrison and Patricia Harrison. Educ: Regent's Park Coll., Oxford (MA Philos. and Theol.); City Univ., London (DipLaw); King's Coll. London (MA Med. Law and Ethics). Called to the Bar, Lincoln's Inn, 1986; barrister in ind. practice, 1986–. Member: Gene Therapy Advr. Cttee, 1999–2009; Human Genetics Commn, 2004–12; Nat. Res. Ethics Expert Adv. Panel, 2010–12; Biometrics and Forensics Ethics Gp, 2018–. *Recreations*: music (especially opera and early church music), art (especially portraits), wine, fly fishing, running. *Address*: 2 Temple Gardens, EC4Y 9AY. *T*: (020) 7822 1200, *Fax*: (020) 7822 1300. *E*: CHarrisonQC@2tg.co.uk. *Club*: Royal Automobile.

**HARRISON, Catherine Jane Crozier;** see Pickstock, C. J. C.

**HARRISON, Charles Rupert;** Organist and Master of the Choristers, Chichester Cathedral, since 2014; b Nottingham, 21 March 1974; s of Richard and Valerie Harrison; m 2017, Dr Sarah Margaret Elizabeth Sanderson. Educ: Minster Sch., Southwell; Jesus Coll., Cambridge (BA 1995; MA 2000). Asst Organist, Carlisle Cathedral, 1995–99; Dir of Music, St George's Church, Belfast, 2000–03; Tutor, QUB, 2000–03; Asst Dir of Music and Sub

Organist, Lincoln Cathedral, 2003–14. *Recreations:* theatre, travel, walking, wine, flying, art. *Address:* The Royal Chantry, Cathedral Cloisters, Chichester PO19 1PX. *T:* (01243) 782595, *Fax:* (01243) 812499. *E:* organist@chichestercathedral.org.uk.

**HARRISON, Sir Colin;** *see* Harrison, Sir R. C.

**HARRISON, Rev. Fr Crispin;** *see* Harrison, Rev. Fr M. B. C.

**HARRISON, Sir David,** Kt 1997; CBE 1990; FREng; Fellow, since 1957, and Master, 1994–2000, Selwyn College, Cambridge; *b* 3 May 1930; *s* of Harold David Harrison and Lavinia Wilson; *m* 1962, Sheila Rachel Debes; one *s* one *d* (and one *s* decd). *Educ:* Bede Sch., Sunderland; Clacton County High Sch.; Selwyn Coll., Cambridge (1st Cl. Pts I and II Natural Sciences Tripos, BA 1953, PhD 1956, MA 1957, ScD 1979). CEng, FREng (FEng 1987); FRSC (FRIC 1961), FIChemE 1968. 2nd Lieut, REME, 1949. Cambridge University: Research student, Dept of Physical Chemistry, 1953–56; Univ. Asst Lectr in Chem. Engrg, 1956–61; Univ. Lectr, 1961–79; Sen. Tutor, Selwyn Coll., 1967–79; Mem., Council of the Senate, 1967–75; Mem., Univ. Council, 1995–2000; Dep. Vice-Chancellor, 1995–2000; Pro-Vice-Chancellor, 1997; Chm., Faculty Bd of Educn, 1976–78, of Engrg, 1994–2001; Vice-Chancellor: Univ. of Keele, 1979–84; Univ. of Exeter, 1984–94. Visiting Professor of Chemical Engineering: Univ. of Delaware, USA, 1967; Univ. of Sydney, 1976. Chm., Adv. Cttee on Safety in Nuclear Installations, 1993–99; Mem., Engineering Council, 1994–96. Hon. Editor, Trans Instn of Chemical Engrs, 1972–78; Member Council: Lancing Coll., 1970–82; Haileybury, 1974–84; St Edward's, Oxford, 1977–89; Bolton Girls' Sch., 1981–84; Shrewsbury Sch., 1983–2003 (Chm., 1989–2003); Taunton Sch., 1986–89; Fellow, Woodard Corporation of Schools, 1972–94; Chairman: Bd of Trustees, Homerton Coll., Cambridge, 1979–2010; UCCA, 1984–91; Voluntary Sector Consultative Council, 1984–88; Southern Univs Jt Bd, 1986–88; Church and Associated Colls Adv. Cttee, PCFC, 1988–91; CVCP, 1991–93; Bd of Management, Northcott Theatre, 1984–94; Eastern Arts Bd, 1994–98 (Mem., Arts Council of England, 1996–98); Council, RSCM, 1996–2005; Ely Cathedral Council, 2000–16 (High Bailiff, 2017–). Pres., IChemE, 1991–92 (Vice-Pres., 1989–91); Dir, Salters' Inst. of Industrial Chemistry, 1993–2015. Mem., Marshall Aid Commemoration Commn, 1982–89. FRSA 1985; FRSCM 2005; CCMI (CBIM 1990). Hon. Fellow, Homerton Coll., Cambridge, 2016. Freeman, City of London, 1998; Liveryman, Salters' Co., 1998. DUniv: Keele, 1992; York, 2008; Hon. DSc Exeter, 1995. George E. Davis Medal, IChemE, 2001. *Publications:* (with J. F. Davidson) Fluidised Particles, 1963; (also with J. F. Davidson) Fluidization, 1971, rev. edn (with J. F. Davidson and R. Clift) 1985; numerous articles in scientific and technological jls. *Recreations:* music, tennis, hill walking, good food. *Address:* 7 Gough Way, Cambridge CB3 9LN. *T:* (01223) 359315. *E:* sirdavidharrison@gmail.com. *Clubs:* Athenæum, Oxford and Cambridge; Federation House (Stoke-on-Trent).

**HARRISON, Prof. David James,** MD; FRCPath, FRCPE, FRCSE; John Reid Professor of Pathology, University of St Andrews, since 2012; Head of Specialty Pathology, NHS Lothian, since 2009; Honorary Consultant in Histopathology, Royal Infirmary of Edinburgh, since 1991; *b* Belfast, 24 March 1959. *Educ:* Campbell Coll., Belfast; Univ. of Edinburgh (BSc Hons 1980; MB ChB 1983; MD 1990). FRCPath 1998; FRCPE 2003; FRCSE 2003. University of Edinburgh: Lectr, 1986–91, Sen. Lectr, 1991–97, Reader, 1997–98, in Pathol.; Prof. of Pathol., 1998–2012; Hd, Div. of Pathol., 1998–2012; Dir, Cancer Res. Centre, 2005–08; Dir, Breakthrough Breast Cancer Res. Unit, 2007–12; Hon. Prof., Coll. of Medicine and Veterinary Medicine, 2012–; Clin. Dir, Pathol. Directorate, Lothian Univ. Hosps Div., 2001–04. Adjunct Professor: in Medicinal Chemistry, Univ. of Florida, Gainesville, 2003–; of Pathol. and Forensic Educn, Univ. of Canberra, 2004–. Chm., Med. Res. Scotland, 2009– (Mem., Scientific Adv. Bd, 2007–); Member: Biomed. and Therapeutics Res. Cttee, Chief Scientist Office, Scotland, 1998–2008 (Dep. Chm.); DoH Gene Therapy Adv. Cttee, 2000–09 (Vice-Chm., 2006–09); DoH Cttee on Carcinogenicity of Chemicals in Food, Consumer Products and the Envmt, 2000–09; Food Standards Agency/DoH Cttee on Toxicity of Chemicals in Food, Consumer Products and the Envmt, 2007–. MRC Coll. of Experts Physiological Systems and Clin. Scis Bd, 2004–; Member: CRUK Strat. Adv. Gp, 2006–; Scientific Adv. Cttee, Yorks Cancer Research, 2007–. Trustee, Melville Trust for Care and Cure of Cancer, 2008. *Publications:* (ed jtly) Muir's Textbook of Pathology, 14th edn 2008; contrib. chapters in books and jls. *Recreations:* EMMS Nazareth charity (Chm. 2002–) which operates a hospital and nursing school in the Middle East, music, hill walking. *Address:* Medical and Biological Sciences Building, University of St Andrews, North Haugh, St Andrews, Fife KY16 9TF.

**HARRISON, (Desmond) Roger (Wingate);** Chairman, Toynbee Hall, 1990–2002; Deputy Chairman, Capital Radio, 1991–2000 (Director, 1975–2000); *b* 9 April 1933; *s* of late Maj.-Gen. Desmond Harrison, CB, DSO and Kathleen Harrison (*née* Hazley); *m* 1965, Victoria Lee-Barber, MVO (*d* 2018), *d* of Rear-Adm. John Lee-Barber, CB, DSO; three *s* (and one *s* one *d* decd). *Educ:* Rugby School; Worcester College, Oxford (MA); Harvard Univ. Business Sch. Writing freelance, principally for The Times, 1951–57; joined staff of The Times, 1957–67; The Observer: joined 1967; Dir, 1970–92; Jt Managing Dir, 1977–84; Chief Exec., 1984–87. Dir, The Oak Foundn 1987–89. Chairman: Greater Manchester Cablevision, 1990–93; Sterling Publishing, 1993–96; Director: LWT and LWT (Holdings), 1976–94; Sableknight, 1981–; Trinity International Holdings, 1991–2003; Mem. Bd, Ashoka - Innovators for the Public, 2005–. Chairman: Asylum Aid, 1991–98; Royal Acad. of Dancing, 1993–2006. Governor, Sadler's Wells, 1984–95. Vice Pres., Hampshire Wildlife Trust, 2011–. *Recreations:* the arts, the environment, country pursuits, tennis. *Address:* Itchen Stoke Mill, Alresford SO24 0RA. *Clubs:* Beefsteak, Flyfishers'.

*See also* H. K. Harrison.

**HARRISON, Edward Peter Graham, (Ted),** PhD; artist, writer, cartoonist, television producer and broadcaster; *b* 14 April 1948; *s* of Rev. Peter Harrison and Joan Harrison; *m* 1968, Helen Grace Waters; one *s* one *d*. *Educ:* Grenville Coll., Bideford, Devon; University of Kent at Canterbury (BA 1968; PhD Theol. 1998); Univ. for the Creative Arts (MA Fine Art 2010). Graduate trainee, Kent Messenger, 1968–72; Reporter: Morgan-Grampian Magazines, 1972; Southern Television, 1970–73; BBC World Service, Radio 4 You and Yours, 1972–80; BBC Radio 4 Sunday, 1972–88; BBC TV Scotland Current Account, 1981–83; Presenter and Reporter, BBC Radio Scotland News and Current Affairs, 1980–85; Reporter: BBC Radio 4 World Tonight, 1981–83; BBC Radio 4 World at One and PM, 1983–87; Presenter: Radio 4 Opinions, 1986–87; Radio 4 Sunday, 1986–88 and Soundings, 1985–88; ITV series The Human Factor, 1986–92; Channel 4 series on Lambeth Conf., 1988; BBC Religious Affairs Corresp., 1988–89; presenter, Does He Take Sugar?, Radio 4, 1991–95; series ed., Ultimate Questions, ITV, 2000; dir, animation series, Wise and Wonderful, 2002; producer: Redcoats, ITV, 2003–04; Essentials of Faith, ITV, 2005; Mosque, ITV, 2005. Dir, Pilgrim Productions, Canterbury, 1992–2008; Founder, Unst Animation Studio, 2000. Contested (L) gen. elections: Bexley, 1970; Maidstone, Feb. 1974. London exhibition of caricatures, 1977; exhibition of watercolours, Oxford, Canterbury, 1981; exhibn of cartoons and paintings, Rutherford Coll., Canterbury, 2010; art installation, Innocence Betrayed, St Paul's Cathedral, 2011; Cherry Tree, artwork to honour organ donors, Guy's Hosp., 2015; public artwork, The Nightingale, St Thomas' Hosp., 2018; exhibitions: Stations of the Cross: Forces of Creation, Norwich Cathedral, 2013; North, South-East, George's Hse Gall., Folkestone, 2013; Stations of the Cross and The Twelve Apostles, St David's Cathedral, 2014; Unst Modern, Shetland, 2014; Llandaff Cathedral, 2015; Holy Wells of Wales, St David's, 2016; Sins of the World, Gloucester Cathedral, St Bride's Fleet St, London, 2017; Legends of St Padarn, Aberystwyth, Llanberis, 2017; Washington Arts Centre, 2019; In Footsteps of RS Thomas, Aberdaron, 2019. *Publications:* Modern Elizabethans, 1977; (jtly) McIndoe's Army, 1978; Marks of the Cross, 1981; Commissioner Catherine, 1983; Much Beloved Daughter, 1984; The Durham Phenomenon, 1985; Living with kidney failure, 1990; Kriss Akabusi—on track, 1991; The Elvis People, 1992; Members Only, 1994; Stigmata: a medieval mystery for a modern age, 1994; Letters to a friend I never knew, 1995; Disability: rights and wrongs, 1995; Tanni, 1996; Defender of the Faith, 1996; Diana: icon and sacrifice, 1998; Beyond Dying, 2000; Will the next Archbishop please stand up?, 2002; Diana: myth and reality, 2006; King Clone, 2010; From the Ridiculous to the Sublime, 2010; Remembrance Today, 2012; Apocalypse When?, 2012; (with R. Coles) Lives of the Improbable Saints, 2012; (with R. Coles) Legends of the Improbable Saints, 2013; Tales of Three Popes, 2014; The Death and Resurrection of Elvis Presley, 2016. *Recreation:* visiting old churches and modern art galleries.

**HARRISON, Sir Edwin Michael Harwood,** 3rd Bt *cr* 1961, of Bugbrooke; Director, Naked Coffee Ltd, since 2011; *b* London, 29 May 1981; *s* of Sir Michael James Harwood Harrison, 2nd Bt and of Rosamund Louise Harrison (*née* Clive); S father, 2019, but his name does not appear on the Official Roll of the Baronetage; *m* 2013, Magdalena Edyta Woloszyn; two *s* one *d*. *Educ:* Univ. of Western Australia (MCom Hons). Project Manager, Liberty Develt Foundn, Uganda, 2010. *Heir: s* Nile Harwood Harrison, *b* 31 Oct. 2014. *Address:* 2 Ringford Road, SW18 1RS. *T:* 07920 523290. *E:* edwin_harrison@hotmail.co.uk.

**HARRISON, George;** *see* Harrison, S. G.

**HARRISON, (George) Michael (Antony),** CBE 1980; Chief Education Officer, City of Sheffield, 1967–85; *b* 7 April 1925; *s* of George and Kathleen Harrison; *m* 1951, Pauline (*née* Roberts); two *s* one *d*. *Educ:* Manchester Grammar Sch.; Brasenose Coll., Oxford. MA (Lit. Hum.); DipEd. Military service, Lieut, 3rd Recce and Parachute Regt, 1947. Asst Master, Bedford Modern Sch., 1951–53; admin. Asst, W Riding CC, Education Dept, 1953–55; Asst Educn Officer, Cumberland CC Educn Dept, 1955–64; Dep. Educn Officer, Sheffield, 1965–67. Advr, Educn and NVQ Programmes, Dept of Employment, 1985–96. Hon. Research Fellow, Leeds Univ., 1985–89; Associate Prof., Sheffield Univ., 1991–95. Member various cttees, incl.: Taylor Cttee of Enquiry on Govt in Schools, 1975–77; UK Nat. Commn for Unesco Educn Adv. Cttee, 1977–83; Yorkshire and Humberside Econ. Planning Council, 1978–79; Technician Educn Council, 1979–83; Engineering Council, 1982–87; Board, Nat. Adv. Body on Local Authority Higher Educn, 1981–83. Pres., Soc. of Educn Officers, 1976; Vice-Pres., Standing Conf. on Schools' Science and Technology, 1980– (Chm. 1975–79). Vice-Pres., St William's Foundn, York, 1992–95. Hon. LLD Sheffield, 1988. *Recreation:* foreign travel. *Address:* 7 Eaveslea, New Road, Kirkby Lonsdale, Cumbria LA6 2AB. *T:* (015242) 73834. *E:* gmah070425@gmail.com.

**HARRISON, Prof. Henrietta Katherine,** DPhil; FBA 2014; Professor of Modern Chinese Studies, University of Oxford, since 2012; Fellow, Pembroke College, Oxford, since 2015; *b* London, 1967; *d* of (Desmond) Roger (Wingate) Harrison, *qv*. *Educ:* St Paul's Sch., Hammersmith; Newnham Coll., Cambridge (BA Classics 1989); Harvard Univ. (MA Regl Studies East Asia 1992); Univ. of Oxford (DPhil Oriental Studies 1996). Fulford Jun. Res. Fellow, St Anne's Coll., Oxford, 1996–98; Lectr in Chinese, Univ. of Leeds, 1999–2006; Prof. of Hist., Harvard Univ., 2006–12; Fellow, St Cross Coll., Oxford, 2012–15. *Publications:* China: inventing the nation, 2001; The Making of the Republican Citizen: ceremonies and symbols in China 1911–1929, 2000; The Man Awakened from Dreams: one man's life in a North China village 1857–1942, 2005; The Missionary's Curse and Other Tales from a Chinese Catholic Village, 2013. *Recreation:* needlework. *Address:* University of Oxford China Centre, Dickson Poon Building, Canterbury Road, Oxford OX2 6LU. *E:* henrietta.harrison@orinst.ox.ac.uk.

**HARRISON, John Clive,** LVO 1971; HM Diplomatic Service, retired; High Commissioner, Mauritius, 1993–97; *b* 12 July 1937; *s* of Sir Geoffrey Harrison, GCMG, KCVO; *m* 1967, Jennifer Heather Burston; one *s* two *d*. *Educ:* Winchester Coll.; Jesus Coll., Oxford. BA. Entered Foreign Office, 1960; Rangoon, 1961; Vientiane, 1964; FO, 1964; Second, later First, Sec. (Information), Addis Ababa, 1967; Ankara, 1971; seconded to Cabinet Office, 1973; First Sec., FCO, 1976; First Sec., Head of Chancery and Consul, Luxembourg, 1978; Counsellor and Head of Chancery, Lagos, 1981–84; Counsellor, attached to Protocol Dept, FCO, 1984; Hd of Consular Dept, FCO, 1985–89; Dep. High Comr, Islamabad, 1989–93. *Recreations:* gardening, tennis, golf, family holidays. *Address:* Wymering, Sheet Common, Petersfield, Hants GU31 5AT. *Clubs:* Royal Over-Seas League; Petersfield Golf.

**HARRISON, John Foster;** QC 2016; *b* Leeds, 20 Jan. 1968; *s* of Dr David Harrison and Dr Gillian Harrison; *m* 2004, Nicole Moerman; one *s* two *d*. *Educ:* Nottingham Univ. (BA Hons); Birmingham Univ. (MSocSc); Leeds Univ. (LLB Hons). Called to the Bar, Lincoln's Inn, 1994; in practice as barrister, specialising in criminal and regulatory law, 1994–. *Recreations:* cricket, social history, literature, music, long distance running. *Address:* St Pauls Chambers, Park Row House, 19–20 Park Row, Leeds LS1 5JF. *T:* (0113) 245 5866. *E:* jh@stpaulschambers.com. *Clubs:* Yorkshire County Cricket, Old Leos Cricket.

**HARRISON, John Seymour H.;** *see* Heslop-Harrison.

**HARRISON, Kate Elizabeth;** Founder Partner, Harrison Grant Solicitors, since 2004; *b* Durham, 25 Nov. 1955; *d* of Jonathan Harrison and Jean Harrison (*née* Bradbury); one *s* one *d*. *Educ:* Nottingham Girls' High Sch.; New Hall, Cambridge (BA 1978); London Sch. of Econs and Pol Sci. (LLM); DipABRSM Piano Perf. 2018. Admitted solicitor, 1981; solicitor, Lawford & Co., Gordon & James Morton, and Tooting and Balham Law Centre, 1981–85; Senior Lecturer: North East London Poly., 1985–88; Bristol Poly., 1988–92; Hd, Law, Mind (Nat. Assoc. for Mental Health), 1992–97; solicitor, Scott-Moncrief & Co., 1997–2001; Lawyer, Greenpeace, 2001–03. *Recreations:* music, film, walking, Member of London Symphony Chorus. *Address:* Harrison Grant Solicitors, 45 Beech Street, EC2Y 8AD. *T:* (020) 7826 8520. *E:* kateharrison@hglaw.co.uk.

**HARRISON, Kaye Barbara;** Headteacher, Sutton Coldfield Grammar School for Girls, 2000–10; *b* Romiley, Cheshire, 13 Sept. 1950; *d* of Henry James and Ada Patricia Morris; *m*; marr. diss. *Educ:* York Univ. (BA Maths and Educn 1971; PGCE 1972); Wolverhampton Poly. (MEd 1987). Hd of Maths, Haunton Hall, Tamworth, 1972–75; Teacher of Maths, Woodhouse Sch., Tamworth, 1975–83; Curriculum Co-ordinator and Hd of Maths, Queen Mary's High Sch., Walsall, 1983–92; Headteacher, Newport Girls' High Sch., Shropshire, 1992–2000. Member: Inland Waterways Assoc.; Shropshire Union Canal Soc.; Nat. Women's Register; U3A. *Recreations:* theatre, inland waterways, photography, walking, watercolour painting.

**HARRISON, Kristina, (Mrs J. Pattinson);** a District Judge (Magistrates' Courts), since 2005; *b* 5 June 1957; *d* of late John, (Jack), Harrison and of Sybil Mary Harrison; *m* 1985, John Pattinson; one *s* two *d*. *Educ:* Manchester Poly. (BA Hons Law, 1978). Founded

Kristina Harrison, Solicitors, Manchester, 1985, specialising in criminal law. *Recreations:* endlessly renovating old houses, all aspects of interior design, collecting handbags. *Address:* Teesside Magistrates' Court, Victoria Square, Middlesbrough TS1 2AS.

**HARRISON, Malcolm Charles William;** Group Chief Executive Officer of the Chartered Institute of Procurement and Supply, since 2018; *b* London, 7 March 1960; *s* of late William Harrison and of Audrey Harrison; *m* 1987, Belinda Clayton; one *s* three *d*. *Educ:* Oundle Sch.; Selwyn Coll., Cambridge (BA 1981; MEng 1992). Roles in production, procurement and sales, Mars, 1982–93; Purchasing Dir, Bass Brewers, 1993–96; Man. Dir, Bass Brewers Midlands, 1996–98; Ops Dir, Britvic plc, 1999–2000; Chief Procurement Officer: InBev SA, 2001–05; Nestle SA, 2006–10; Gp Dir, Plastic Packaging, Rexam plc, 2010–14; CEO, Crown Commercial Service, 2016–18. MCIPS 1993, FCIPS 2017. *Recreations:* gardening, walking, ski-ing, family. *E:* harrison.mcw@btinternet.com. *Clubs:* Leander; Hawks (Cambridge).

**HARRISON, Prof. Mark,** DPhil; FRHistS; Professor of the History of Medicine, since 2006, and Director, Wellcome Unit for the History of Medicine, since 2001, University of Oxford; Fellow, Green Templeton College, Oxford, since 2001; *b* Berkeley, Glos, 9 June 1964; *s* of Anthony Harrison and Marina Harrison (*née* Pockett). *Educ:* Katharine Lady Berkeley's Sch., Wotton-under-Edge; Univ. of Bradford (BSc 1st Cl. Hons Soc. Sci. (Hist. Maj.) 1987); Corpus Christi Coll., Oxford (DPhil Mod. Hist. 1991); Univ. of Oxford (MA 2001). Jun. Res. Fellow, Green Coll., Oxford, 1990–91; Res. Fellow, Wellcome Inst. for Hist. of Medicine, UCL, 1991–94; Lectr in Hist., 1994–97, Sen. Lectr, 1997–2000, Sheffield Hallam Univ.; University of Oxford: Sen. Res. Fellow and Actg Dir, Wellcome Unit for Hist. of Medicine, 2000–01; Reader in Hist. of Medicine, 2001–06. FRHistS 2003. *Publications:* Public Health in British India: Anglo-Indian preventive medicine, 1859–1914, 1994; (ed jtly) War, Medicine and Modernity, 1998; (ed jtly) Medicine and Modern Warfare, 1999; Climates and Constitutions: health, race, environment and British imperialism in india, 1600–1850, 1999; (ed with Peter Cain) Imperialism: critical concepts in historical studies, 3 vols, 2001; (ed with B. Pati) Health, Medicine and Empire: perspectives on colonial India, 2001; Disease and the Modern World, 1500 to the Present Day, 2004; Medicine and Victory: British military medicine in the Second World War, 2004 (Templer Medal Book Prize, Soc. of Army Histl Res., 2005); (jtly) Fractured States: smallpox, vaccination and public health policy in British India, 1800–1947, 2005; (ed with B. Pati) The Social History of Health and Medicine in Colonial India, 2009, 2011; (ed jtly) From Global Medicine to Western Medicine: the hospital beyond the West, 2009; Medicine in the Age of Commerce and Empire: Britain and its tropical colonies, 1660–1830, 2010; The Medical War: British military medicine in the First World War, 2010 (Templer Medal Book Prize, Soc. of Army Histl Res., 2011); Contagion: how commerce has spread disease, 2012; (ed with B. Pati) Society, Medicine and Politics in colonial India, 2018. *Recreations:* cycling, keeping fit, fishing, gardening, bee-keeping, natural history. *Address:* Wellcome Unit for the History of Medicine, 45–47 Banbury Road, Oxford OX2 6PE. *T:* (01865) 284629, *Fax:* (01865) 274605. *E:* mark.harrison@wuhmo.ox.ac.uk.

**HARRISON, Melissa Zoë;** novelist, columnist and critic; *b* Guildford, 5 Feb. 1975; *d* of Peter Darrell Harrison and Valerie Ann Harrison (*née* Thurley); *m* 2009, Anthony James Young. *Educ:* Howard of Effingham Comprehensive Sch.; Lincoln Coll., Oxford (BA English Lang. and Lit. 1996). Editl asst, 1996–98, jun. ed., 1998–2000, Piatkus Books; Ed. for Popular Culture, Virgin Books, 2000–01; freelance proofreader and copyeditor, 2001–06; Prodn Ed., Mixmag mag., 2006–. *Publications:* Clay, 2013; At Hawthorn Time, 2015; Rain: four walks in English weather, 2016; (ed) Spring, 2016; (ed) Summer, 2016; (ed) Autumn, 2016; (ed) Winter, 2016; All Among the Barley, 2018. *Recreations:* walking, electronic music, photography, natural history. *W:* www.melissaharrison.co.uk, www.twitter.com/m_z_harrison.

**HARRISON, Michael;** *see* Harrison, G. M. A.

**HARRISON, Dr Michael;** JP; Chairman and Medical Director, Midlands Health Consultancy Network Ltd, since 1996; *b* 1 March 1939; *s* of Frank Harrison and Ruby Wilhelmina (*née* Proctor); *m* 1962, Ann Haiser; two *d*. *Educ:* Leamington Coll.; Univ. of London (St Mary's Hosp.) (MB BS, BA). LRCP, MRCS, DPH, FFPH, MHSM, FRSPH. Hosp. med. appts, 1964–66; health MO appts, 1966–70; Birmingham RHB, 1971–74; specialist in community medicine, W Midlands RHA, 1974–76; Area MO, Sandwell AHA, 1976–83; Dist MO, 1983–88, Dist Gen. Manager, 1985–88, Sandwell HA; Sen. Clinical Lectr, Univ. of Birmingham, 1988; Regl Dir of Public Health and Regl MO, 1988–93, Exec. Dir, 1990–94, Dep. Chief Exec., 1993–94, West Midlands RHA. Cons. Advr, WHO, 1989. Pres., Assoc. for Industrial Archaeology, 1998. Pres., Droitwich Spa Saltway Rotary Club, 2001–02. FCMI. SBStJ. JP Birmingham, 1980. *Recreations:* sailing, photography, industrial archaeology. *Address:* 19 Sandles Close, Droitwich Spa, Worcs WR9 8RB. *T:* (01905) 798308.

**HARRISON, Michael;** theatre producer; Managing Director: Michael Harrison Entertainment Ltd, since 2005; Qdos Entertainment (Pantomimes) Ltd, since 2005; *b* Wallsend, Tyne and Wear, 13 Nov. 1979; *s* of Michael and Vivien Harrison; *m* 2016, Kathryn Rooney; one *s*. *Educ:* Queen Margaret Univ. Coll., Edinburgh. Productions include: The Bodyguard, Adelphi Th., 2012, Dominion Th., 2016; Gypsy, Savoy Th., 2015 (Laurence Olivier Award, 2016); Mrs Henderson Presents, Noel Coward Th., 2016; Annie, Piccadilly, Th., 2017; Young Frankenstein, Garrick Th., 2017; Dick Whittington, 2017 (Laurence Olivier Award, 2018), Snow White, 2018, Joseph and the Amazing Technicolor Dreamcoat, 2019, London Palladium; Fiddler on the Roof, Playhouse Th., 2019. Companion, Liverpool Inst. of Performing Arts, 2012. *Recreations:* theatre, family, fine dining, travel. *Address:* Qdos Entertainment, 2nd Floor, 161 Drury Lane, WC2B 5PN. *T:* (020) 7430 7909. *E:* michael@michaelharrisonentertainment.co.uk.

**HARRISON, Rev. Fr (Michael Burt) Crispin,** CR; Superior of the Community of the Resurrection, Mirfield, 1998–2003; *b* 26 April 1936. *Educ:* Univ. of Leeds (BA Phil. with Hist. 1959); Trinity Coll., Oxford (BA Theol. 1962; MA 1966); Coll. of the Resurrection, Mirfield. Ordained deacon 1963, priest 1964; Curate: St Aidan, W Hartlepool, 1963–64; All Saints, Middlesbrough, 1964–66; licensed to officiate: Dio. Wakefield, 1966–69, 1978–87 and 1998–; Dio. Christ the King, SA, 2003–06; Dio. Leeds; professed, CR, 1968; Tutor, St Peter's Coll. and Lectr, Federal Theol Seminary, S Africa, 1970–77; Tutor, Coll. of the Resurrection, 1978–84, Vice-Principal, 1984–87; Provincial and Prior, St Peter's Priory, Johannesburg, 1987–97; Canon Theologian, Dio. of Christ the King, S Africa, 1990–97. *Address:* House of the Resurrection, Mirfield, W Yorks WF14 0BN. *T:* (01924) 483337.

**HARRISON, Hon. Sir Michael (Guy Vicat),** Kt 1993; a Judge of the High Court of Justice, Queen's Bench Division, 1993–2004; *b* 28 Sept. 1939; *s* of late Hugh Francis Guy Harrison and Elizabeth Alban Harrison (*née* Jones); *m* 1966, Judith (*née* Gist); one *s* one *d*. *Educ:* Charterhouse; Trinity Hall, Cambridge (MA). Called to the Bar, Gray's Inn, 1965, Bencher, 1993; QC 1983; a Recorder, 1989–93. Dep. Chm., Parly Boundary Commn for England, 1996–2004 (Asst Comr, 1981–93). Chm., Panel for Examination of Structure Plans, Somerset, 1981, Isles of Scilly, 1982, W Sussex, 1986. Trustee, Butler Trust, 2010–. *Recreations:* tennis, sailing, fishing.

**HARRISON, Prof. Michael Jackson;** Vice-Chancellor, University of Wolverhampton, 1992–98 (Director, Wolverhampton Polytechnic (formerly The Polytechnic, Wolverhampton), 1985–92); *b* 18 Dec. 1941; *s* of Jackson Harrison and Norah (*née* Lees); *m* 1974, Marie Ghislaine Félix. *Educ:* Guildford Tech. Coll.; Univ. of Leicester (BA, MA). Lecturer in Sociology: Enfield Coll. of Technol., 1966–67; Univ. of Leeds, 1967–68; Sen. Lectr, Enfield Coll. of Technol., 1968–72; Principal Lectr, Sheffield City Polytechnic, 1972–76; Head of Dept, Hull Coll. of Higher Educn, 1976–81; Asst Dir, 1982–84, Dep. Dir, 1985, The Polytechnic, Wolverhampton. Vis. Lectr, Univ. of Oregon, 1971. Governor: Bilston Community Coll.; Thomas Telford CTC. FCMI (FBIM 1983). *Publications:* (jtly) A Sociology of Industrialisation, 1978; contribs to learned jls. *Recreations:* cinema, travelling, music. *Address:* 34 Mount Road, Penn, Wolverhampton WV4 5SW. *T:* (01902) 338807.

**HARRISON, Rt Rev. Michael Robert;** *see* Dunwich, Bishop Suffragan of.

**HARRISON, Dr Michelle;** Worldwide Chief Executive Officer, Kantar Public, since 2016 and Chief Executive Officer, Government and Public Sector Practice, since 2012, WPP; *b* Coventry, 1968; *m* 1999, Nicholas Bull; two *s* one *d*. *Educ:* Higham Lane Comprehensive Sch., Nuneaton; Univ. of Liverpool (PhD Social Sci. 1994). Res. Asst, Dept of Geog., Univ. of Liverpool, 1989–90; post-doctoral research, Univ. of Cardiff, 1994–97; Consultant to Bd Dir, Henley Centre for Forecasting, then Henley Centre, later Henley Centre Headlight Vision, 1997–2007; Chm., Inst. for Insight in the Public Services, 2006–08; CEO, TNS BMRB, 2008–15. Member: Green Fiscal Commn, 2007–10. Trustee: Involve, 2005–11; NESTA, 2012–17. *Publications:* (jtly) Consuming Interests: the social provision of foods, 2000; King Sugar: Jamaica, the Caribbean and the world sugar economy, 2001. *Recreations:* walking in Cumbria, horses. *Address:* Kantar Public, 6 More London Place, SE1 2QY. *T:* (020) 7656 5739. *E:* michelle.harrison@kantarpublic.com.

**HARRISON, Norman,** CChem, FRSC, FNI; Director of Strategic Development, Babcock International Group, 2010–14; Director, Energy at Long Crendon, since 2014; *b* 25 Jan. 1952; *s* of Robert and Elsie Harrison; *m* 1973, Jacqueline Ogden. *Educ:* John Dalton Poly. Coll., Manchester; Blackburn Tech. Coll. (DMS). CChem, 1981; MRSC 1981, FRSC 2012; FNI 2010. British Energy plc (formerly Central Electricity Generating Board, then Nuclear Electric plc): Commng Team Mem., Heysham 1 Nuclear Power Stn, 1981–85; Control Room Supervisor, Heysham 2 Nuclear Power Stn, 1985–93; Shift Manager, 1993–95, Tech. and Safety Manager, 1995–96, Hartlepool Nuclear Power Stn; Ops Manager, 1996–99, Dir, 1999–2000, Heysham 1 Nuclear Power Stn; Dir, Sizewell B Nuclear Power Stn, 2000–03; Dir, Dounreay Div., 2003–07, CEO, 2007–09, non-exec. Dir, 2016–, UKAEA. Associate, Thales UK, 2016–17. Sen. Advr to Exec., Culham Centre for Fusion Energy, 2014–16; Strategic Advr, Amec Foster Wheeler, 2014–17. Member: Nuclear Liabilities Funding Adv. Bd, 2009–15; Bd, Nuclear Industries Assoc., 2011–14; Nuclear Liabilities Fund, 2011–17. Pres., Nuclear Inst., 2011–13. Dep. Chair, Adv. Council, Radioactive Waste Mgt Ltd, 2017–. Ind. Gov., Manchester Metropolitan Univ., 2008– (Dep. Chm., 2014–). FRSA 2007. *Recreations:* travel, opera, gardening.

**HARRISON, Dame Patricia (Mary),** DNZM 2009 (DCNZM 2001); QSO 1987; Member, Otago Regional Council, 1996–2004; *b* 6 Sept. 1932; *d* of Hugh and Catherine Thomson; *m* 1957, Arthur Keith Harrison; one *s* two *d*. *Educ:* Otago Girls' High Sch.; Dunedin Teachers' Coll.; Otago Univ. (MA Hons Philosophy; James Clark Meml Prize in Philosophy 1955). Hd of Faculty, Burnside High Sch., 1973–75; Principal, Queen's High Sch., Dunedin, 1975–94. Chm., Otago Youth Wellness Trust, 1996–2008 (Trustee, 2009–). Chm., Otago Regl Access Employment Council, 1985–87. Mem. Council, Univ. of Otago, 1985–96. Board Member: YWCA, 1970–80; Southern Th. Trust, 1987–90. Volunteer, Victim Support, 2010–. Commemoration Medal (NZ), 1990; Suffrage Medal (NZ), 1993. *Publications:* Magic, Myth and Legends: a supplementary English text, 1974. *Recreations:* gardening, bridge, walking. *Address:* 31 Gladstone Road, Dalmore, Dunedin North 9010, New Zealand. *T:* (3) 4738606.

**HARRISON, Patrick Kennard,** CBE 1982; Secretary, Royal Institute of British Architects, 1968–87; *b* 8 July 1928; *e s* of late Richard Harrison and Sheila Griffin; *m* 1955, Mary Wilson, *y d* of late Captain G. C. C. Damant, CBE, RN; one *d*. *Educ:* Lord Williams's Sch., Thame; Downing Coll., Cambridge (Exhbnr in English). Wireless Fitter, RAFVR, 1947–49; Asst Principal, Dept of Health for Scotland, 1953; Private Sec. to Deptl Sec. and to Parly Secs, Scottish Office, 1958–60; Principal, Scottish Develt Dept and Regional Develt Div., Scottish Office, 1960–68. Dir, Building Mus. Project, 1990–97. Hon. Mem., Amer. Inst. of Architects, 1978. Hon. FRIAS, 1987; Hon. FRIBA, 1988. *Recreations:* gardening, travel, reading, music. *Address:* 28B Moray Place, Edinburgh EH3 6BX. *T:* (0131) 225 5342. *Clubs:* Reform; New (Edinburgh).

**HARRISON, Prof. Paul Jeffrey,** FRCPsych; Professor of Psychiatry, University of Oxford, since 2000; Fellow, Wolfson College, Oxford, since 1997; *b* 18 Oct. 1960; *s* of Walford John Harrison and Bridget Ann Harrison; *m* 1984, Sandra Hallett; three *d*. *Educ:* City of London Sch.; Balliol Coll., Oxford (BA 1982; BM BCh 1985; MA 1987); DM Oxon 1991. MRCPsych 1989, FRCPsych 2001. MRC Trng Fellow, St Mary's Hosp. Med. Sch., 1988; University of Oxford: Clinical Lectr in Psychiatry, 1991–94; Wellcome Trust Sen. Res. Fellow, 1995–97; Clinical Reader in Psychiatry, 1997–2000. Collegium Internationale Neuro-Psychopharmacologicum Schizophrenia Award, 1998; Sen. Clinical Prize, Brit. Assoc. for Psychopharmacol., 1999; A. E. Bennett Award, Soc. for Biol Psychiatry, 2004; Joel Elkes Award, Amer. Coll. of Neuropsychopharmacol., 2005; Clin. Neurosci. Award, Collegium Internat. Neuro-Psychopharmacol., 2010; Clin. Neuropsychopharmacol. Award, Eur. Coll. Neuropsychopharmacol., 2012. *Publications:* Lecture Notes on Psychiatry, 8th edn 1998 to 10th edn 2010; The Neuropathology of Schizophrenia, 2000; Shorter Oxford Textbook of Psychiatry, 5th edn 2007 to 7th edn 2017; Schizophrenia, 3rd edn 2011; articles on schizophrenia, bipolar disorder and Alzheimer's disease. *Recreations:* sport, music. *Address:* University Department of Psychiatry, Warneford Hospital, Oxford OX3 7JX. *T:* (01865) 613144.

**HARRISON, Peter;** Group Chief Executive, Schroders plc, since 2016; *b* Chester, 25 May 1966; *s* of (Stanley) George Harrison, *qv*; *m* 1994, Rachel Sarah Mabson; one *s* one *d*. *Educ:* Ruthin Sch.; King's Sch., Chester; Univ. of Bath (BSc Hons). Investment Analyst, Schroders plc, 1988–91; Portfolio Manager, Newton Investment Mgt, 1991–96; Hd, Global Equities, JP Morgan, 1996–2004; Global Chief Investment Officer, Deutsche AM, 2004–05; Chm. and Chief Exec., RWC Partners, 2006–13; Hd of Investment, Schroders plc, 2014–16. Chm., Investment Assoc., 2017–. Mem., Takeover Panel, 2017–; Mem., Internat. Business and Diplomatic Exchange. Trustee, Game and Wildlife Conservation Trust, 2012–15. Hon. DLaws Bath, 2017. *Recreations:* family, country pursuits. *Address:* Schroders plc, 31 Gresham Street, EC2V 7QA. *T:* (020) 7658 6000. *E:* peter.harrison@schroders.com.

*See also* S. *Harrison.*

**HARRISON, Prof. Peter Duncan**, PhD; Director, Institute for Advanced Studies in the Humanities (formerly Centre for the History of European Discourses), University of Queensland, since 2011; Senior Research Fellow, Ian Ramsey Centre, University of Oxford, since 2011; Australian Laureate Fellow, 2015–19; b 29 Nov. 1955; s of Duncan and Jean Harrison; m 1994, Carol Taylor; one s one d. Educ: Yeronga Infants Sch.; Bundaberg State High Sch.; Univ. of Queensland (BSc; BA Hons; PhD 1989); Yale Univ. (MA); Univ. of Oxford (MA; DLitt). Bond University: Asst Prof., 1989–93, Associate Prof., 1994–2000, of Philos.; Prof. of Hist. and Philos., 2001–06; Andreas Idreos Prof. of Sci. and Religion, and Dir, Ian Ramsey Centre, Univ. of Oxford, 2007–11; Fellow, Harris Manchester Coll., Oxford, 2007–11. Hon. Res. Consultant, Dept of Studies in Religion, Univ. of Queensland, 1990–2010. Gifford Lectr, Edinburgh, 2011; Bampton Lectr, Oxford, 2019. FAHA 1998. Centenary Medal (Australia), 2001. *Publications:* Religion and the Religions in the English Enlightenment, 1990, 2nd edn 2002; The Bible, Protestantism and the Rise of Natural Science, 1998, 2nd edn 2002; The Fall of Man and the Foundations of Science, 2007; The Cambridge Companion to Science and Religion, 2010; (ed jtly) Wrestling with Nature: from omens to science, 2011; The Territories of Science and Religion, 2015; (ed jtly) Science without God: rethinking the history of scientific naturalism, 2019. *Address:* Institute for Advanced Studies in the Humanities, Level 5 Forgan Smith Building, University of Queensland, Qld 4072, Australia.

**HARRISON, Ven. Peter Reginald Wallace**; Archdeacon of the East Riding, 1999–2006; b 22 June 1939; s of Gilbert V. W. Harrison and Mary L. W. Harrison (née Blair); m 1970, Elizabeth Mary Byzia; one s one d. Educ: Charterhouse; Selwyn Coll., Cambridge (BA Theol 1962); Ridley Hall, Cambridge. Ordained deacon 1964, priest 1965; Curate, St Luke's, Barton Hill, Bristol, 1964–69; Youth Worker and Chaplain, Greenhouse Trust, London, 1969–77; Dir, Northorpe Hall Trust, Mirfield, 1977–84; Team Rector, Drypool Team Ministry, Hull, 1984–98. *Recreations:* grandparenting, voluntary work in relationships in church and community. *Address:* 10 Priestgate, Church Street, Sutton, Hull HU7 4QR. *T:* (01482) 797110.

**HARRISON, Philippa Mary, (Mrs Anthony McConnell)**; Chairman, Investment Committee, Book Tokens Ltd, since 2009 (Director, 1996–2014; Chairman, 2011–14); b 25 Nov. 1942; d of Charles Kershaw Whitfield and Alexina Margaret Whitfield; m 1st, 1968 (marr. diss. 1976); 2nd, 2011, Anthony McConnell. Educ: Walthamstow Hall; Bristol Univ. (BA Hons); Courtauld Inst. Promotions Organiser, Associated Book Publishers, 1963–66; reader and editor, Jonathan Cape, 1967–73; Editl Dir, Hutchinson, 1974–78; Jt Editor-in-Chief, Penguin, 1979–80; Editl Dir, Michael Joseph, 1980–85; Man. Dir and Publisher, Macmillan London, 1986–88; Man. Dir, V&A Enterprises, 1990–91; Man. Dir and Publisher, Macdonald & Co., subseq. Little, Brown & Co. (UK), 1991–96; Chief Exec. and Publisher, 1996–2000, non-exec. Chm., 2000–01, Little, Brown & Co. (UK); Editl Dir, Ed Victor Literary Agency, 2002–17. Director: Royal Acad. of Arts Enterprise Bd, 1999–2014; British Mus. Co., 2002–09. Member: Bd, Book Marketing Council, 1983–88; Booker Mgt Cttee, 1987–89; Literature Panel, Arts Council, 1988–92. Mem. Council, Publishers' Assoc., 1995–2002 (Pres., 1998–99). Trustee: Eric & Salome Estorick Foundn, 1996–99; Cumbria Bldgs Preservation Trust, 2011–. CCMI (CIMgt 1987; Mem. Bd, 1999–2005); FRSA 1992. *Recreations:* walking, gardening, theatre, politics, looking at pictures, friends. *Address:* 3B Connaught House, Clifton Gardens, W9 1AL. *T:* (020) 7289 8808. *Club:* Groucho.

**HARRISON, Rachael; Her Honour Judge Rachael Harrison**; a Circuit Judge, since 2018; b Nottingham, 24 April 1971; d of Peter-Emile and Yvonne Harrison; partner, Rt Hon. Sir Peter Daniel William Coulson, qv. Educ: Chilwell Comprehensive Sch., Nottingham; Lake View Sixth Form Coll., Nottingham; Leicester Poly. (LLB Hons); Inns of Court Sch. of Law. Called to the Bar, Inner Temple, 1993; in practice as barrister, Sheffield, 1994–2018; a Recorder, 2016–18. *Recreations:* following Nottingham Panthers Ice Hockey team, reading, art, travel. *Address:* Sheffield Combined Court Centre, The Law Courts, 50 West Bar, Sheffield S3 8PH.

**HARRISON, Richard Tristan**; QC 2012; b Santiago, Chile, 13 Nov. 1968; s of Peter Alan Harrison, OBE and Maria-Luisa Harrison; m 2003, Sarah Katharine Whitten; three s one d. Educ: Cranleigh Sch.; Emmanuel Coll., Cambridge (BA Modern and Medieval Langs 1991); City Univ. (DipLaw). Called to the Bar, Inner Temple, 1993; in practice as a barrister, specialising in divorce and internat. family law, 1994–. Consultant Ed., Hersham and McFarlane Child Law and Practice, 2007–. *Recreations:* family, food, Spain. *Address:* 1 King's Bench Walk, Temple, EC4Y 7DB. *T:* (020) 7936 1500. *E:* rharrisonqc@1kbw.co.uk.

**HARRISON, Sir (Robert) Colin**, 4th Bt cr 1922; b 25 May 1938; s of Sir John Fowler Harrison, 2nd Bt, and Kathleen (d 1993), yr d of late Robert Livingston, The Gables, Eaglescliffe, Co. Durham; S brother, 1955; m 1963, Maureen, er d of late E. Leonard Chiverton, Garth Corner, Kirkbymoorside, York; one s two d. Educ: St Peter's Coll., Radley; St John's Coll., Cambridge. Commissioned with Fifth Royal Northumberland Fusiliers (National Service), 1957–59. Chm., John Harrison (Stockton) Ltd, 1963–2006. Chm., Young Master Printers Nat. Cttee, 1972–73. Heir: s John Wyndham Fowler Harrison, b 14 Dec. 1972. *Address:* Dinsdale House, 6 Uppleby, Easingwold, York YO61 3BB.

**HARRISON, Robert John; His Honour Judge Harrison**; a Circuit Judge, since 2016; a Senior Circuit Judge, since 2017; b Cardiff, 1964; s of Christopher Harrison and Daphne Harrison; m 1991, Gwenyth Ann Jones; three s. Educ: University Coll., Cardiff (LLB). Called to the Bar, Lincoln's Inn, 1988; barrister, 30 Park Place, Cardiff, 1988–2016; a Recorder, 2005–16. *Recreations:* family, cricket, hockey, Rugby, gardening. *Club:* Penarth Athletic.

**HARRISON, Roger**; see Harrison, D. R. W.

**HARRISON, Prof. Roy Michael**, OBE 2004; PhD; DSc; FRS 2017; FRSC, FRMetS; Queen Elizabeth II Birmingham Centenary Professor of Environmental Health, since 1991, and Head, Division of Environmental Health & Risk Management, since 1999, University of Birmingham; b 14 Oct. 1948; s of Wilfred Harrison and Rosa (née Cotton); m 1st, 1981, Angela Copeman (marr. diss.); one s one d; 2nd, 1989, Susan Sturt; one s. Educ: Henley Grammar Sch.; Univ. of Birmingham (BSc; PhD 1972; DSc 1988). FRMetS 1982; FRSC 1988. Res. Asst, Imperial Coll., Univ. of London, 1972–74; Lectr, Lancaster Univ., 1974–84; Reader, Univ. of Essex, 1984–91. Dist. Adjunct Prof., King Abdulaziz Univ., Jeddah, 2011–. Margary Lectr, RMetS, 1994; John Jeyes Lectr, RSC, 1995. Department of the Environment: Mem., Photochem. Oxidants Rev. Gp, 1986–97; Chairman: Quality of Urban Air Rev. Gp, 1991–97; Airborne Particles Expert Gp, 1997–99; Vice-Chm., Expert Panel on Air Quality Standards, 2003– (Mem., 1992–2002); Member: Cttee on Med. Effects of Air Pollution, 1993–2003, 2006–, Cttee on Toxicity, 2012–, DoH, then DHSC; Adv. Cttee on Hazardous Substances, 2001–06; Air Quality Expert Gp, 2002–; Mem., Sci. Adv. Council, DEFRA, 2009–12. Hon. Consulting Envmtl Toxicologist, Nat. Poisons Inf. Service, Birmingham Centre and W Midlands Poisons Unit, 1994–99. Mem., HEFCE Panel, 2001, 2008 and 2014 RAEs. Chm., Envmt Gp, RSC, 1990–91; Theme Leader for Envmt, Pollution and Human Health, NERC, 2007–12. Hon. FFOM 1998; Hon. MFPHM 1997; Hon. Mem., Chartered Inst. Envmtl Health, 2010. Hon. DSc Lancaster, 2015. Fitzroy Prize, RMetS, 2012; Envmt Prize, RSC, 2015. *Publications:* (with D. P. H. Laxen) Lead Pollution: causes and control, 1981; Pollution: causes, effects and control, 1983, 5th edn 2014; (with R. Perry) Handbook of Air Pollution Analysis, 2nd edn 1986; (jtly) Acid Rain: scientific and technical advances, 1987; (with S. Rapsomanikis) Environmental Analysis using Chromatography Interfaced with Atomic Spectroscopy, 1989; (jtly) Introductory Chemistry for the Environmental Sciences, 1991, 2nd edn (with S. J. de Mora) 1996; (with R. S. Hamilton) Highway Pollution, 1991; (jtly) Handbook for Urban Air Improvement, 1992; Understanding Our Environment: an introduction to environmental chemistry and pollution, 1992, 3rd edn 1999; (with M. Radojevic) Atmospheric Acidity: sources, consequences and abatement, 1992; (with F. E. Warner) Radioecology after Chernobyl: biogeochemical pathways of artificial radionuclides, SCOPE 50, 1993; (jtly) Urban Air Quality in the United Kingdom, 1993; (jtly) Diesel Vehicle Emissions and Urban Air Quality, 1993; (with R. E. Hester) Issues in Environmental Science and Technology, vol. 1, 1994 to vol. 48, 2019; (jtly) Airborne Particulate Matter in the United Kingdom, 1996; (with R. Van Grieken) Atmospheric Particles, 1998; (jtly) Source Apportionment of Airborne Particulate Matter in the United Kingdom, 1999; An Introduction to Pollution Science, 2006; Principles of Environmental Chemistry, 2007; many papers to learned jls. *Recreations:* mowing and other outdoor pursuits. *Address:* School of Geography, Earth and Environmental Sciences, University of Birmingham, Edgbaston, Birmingham B15 2TT. *T:* (0121) 414 3494.

**HARRISON, Sally, (Mrs R. D. Norton)**; QC 2010; b Cheshire, 4 Nov. 1968; d of (Stanley) George Harrison, qv; m 1997, Richard Damian Norton; one s one d. Educ: Howell's Sch., Denbigh (Drapers' Schol.); Reading Univ. (BSc Hons); City Univ. (CPE). Called to the Bar, Gray's Inn, 1992, Bencher, 2015; in practice as barrister, specialising in family and matrimonial law, 1992–; Hd of Chambers, St John's Bldgs, Manchester, 2013–. *Recreations:* cycling, open water swimming, reading, music. *Address:* St John's Buildings, 24A–28 St John Street, Manchester M3 4DJ. *T:* (0161) 214 1500, *Fax:* (0161) 835 3929. *E:* sally.harrisonqc@stjohnbuildings.co.uk.
See also P. Harrison.

**HARRISON, Samantha**; see Jones, S.

**HARRISON, (Stanley) George**, CBE 2003; a District Judge, Chester County Court and District Registry of High Court, 1985–2008; b 16 Aug. 1937; s of Stanley George Harrison and Elizabeth Avril Meff (née Walker); m 1st, 1963, Jennifer Lorna Harrow (d 2013); one s one d; 2nd, 2016, Davina Lesley Susan Weinronk. Educ: Wellington Coll.; Univ. of Manchester (LLB Hons). Commnd Lancs Regt (2nd Lt), 1956–58. Admitted solicitor, 1964; Partner, Wayman Hales, Chester, 1967–82; Registrar, Liverpool Co. Court, 1982–85. Mem., Lord Chancellor's Adv. Cttee on Delay in Public Law, 2002. Sec., 1985–2000, Pres., 2002, HM Assoc. of Dist Judges. Chm., Muir Housing Gp Assoc., 1986–2002. Dir, CLS Care Services, 1991–2001. *Recreations:* fishing, cricket, grass. *Address:* 4 Rathmore Drive, Oxton, Wirral CH43 2HD.
See also P. Harrison, S. Harrison.

**HARRISON, Tania**; Head of Arts, Festival Republic, including Latitude Festival and Reading and Leeds Festivals, since 2006; b Luton, 9 Aug. 1966; d of John Harrison and Barbara Patrick. Educ: Bedale Sch., N Yorks; Birmingham Univ.; Drama Centre, London; Clore Short Course. Communication Advertising Mktg Foundn (Mktg Dip.) 2003. Hd of Mktg, Mean Fiddler Music Gp, 1992–2006. Director: Hull Freedom Fest., 2013–15; Dance Umbrella, 2015–; Wrong Crowd, 2015–. Chm. Panel, Edinburgh Fosters Comedy Awards, 2011, 2013. FRSA 2013. Inspiration Award, Women of Year Awards, 2006; The Stage Award for Special Achievement in Regl Theatre, 2008; Award for Outstanding Contribn to British Art Fests, British Arts Fests Assoc., 2011; Dan Crawford Innovation Award, Empty Space Peter Brook Awards, 2014; Editors Award, Access All Areas, 2016. *Recreations:* ongoing personal development of a specialised art form known as Cultural Multi-Tasking where one learns to juggle theatre, comedy, dance, music, cabaret, poetry, live art, literature and science alongside the flamethrowing art of life. *Address:* Festival Republic, 19–25 Argyll Street, W1F 7TS. *T:* (020) 7009 3000. *E:* tharrison@festivalrepublic.com. *Club:* Groucho.

**HARRISON, Ted**; see Harrison, E. P. G.

**HARRISON, Tony**; poet; b 30 April 1937; s of Harry Ashton Harrison and Florrie (née Wilkinson-Horner). Hon. FBA 2018. *Publications:* Earthworks, 1964; Aikin Mata, 1966; Newcastle is Peru, 1969; The Loiners (Geoffrey Faber Meml Prize), 1970; The Misanthrope, 1973; Phaedra Britannica, 1975; Palladas: poems, 1975; The Passion, 1977; Bow Down, 1977; From The School of Eloquence and other poems, 1978; The Bartered Bride, 1978; Continuous, 1981; A Kumquat for John Keats, 1981; US Martial, 1981; The Oresteia, 1981; Selected Poems, 1984, expanded edn 1987; The Mysteries, 1985; Dramatic Verse 1973–85, 1985; v., 1985; The Fire-Gap, 1985; Theatre Works 1973–85, 1986; The Trackers of Oxyrhynchus, 1990; v. and other poems, 1990; A Cold Coming: Gulf War poems, 1991; The Common Chorus, 1992; The Gaze of the Gorgon (Whitbread Award for Poetry), 1992; Square Rounds, 1992; Black Daisies for the Bride, 1993; Poetry or Bust, 1993; A Maybe Day in Kazakhstan, 1994; The Shadow of Hiroshima, 1995; Permanently Bard, 1995; Plays Three: The Kaisers of Carnuntum, The Labourers of Herakles, Poetry or Bust, 1996; The Prince's Play, 1996; Prometheus, 1998 (also Dir, film, 1999); Plays One: The Mysteries, 1999; Laureate's Block and Other Poems, 2000; Plays Two: The Oresteia, The Common Chorus, The Trojan Women, 2001; Plays Four: The Misanthrope, Phaedra Britannica, The Prince's Play, 2001; Plays Five: The Trackers of Oxyrhynchus, Square Rounds, 2004; Hecuba, 2005; Under the Clock: new poems, 2005; Collected Poems, 2007; Collected Film Poetry, 2007; Fram, 2008; The Inky Digit of Defiance: selected prose 1966–2016, 2017; Polygons, 2017.

**HARRISON, Trudy Lynne**; MP (C) Copeland, since Feb. 2017; b Whitehaven, 19 April 1976; d of Alan Jeffery and Judith Jeffery; m Keith Harrison; four d. Educ: Wyndham Comp. Sch., Egremont; Univ. of Salford (FdSc). Tech. Clerk, Sellafield Ltd, 1993–98; owner and Dir, Sunny Days, 2002–06; Locality Officer, 2010–13, Regeneration Officer, 2013, Copeland BC; Proj. Manager, Wellbank proj., 2013–; Prog. Manager, Bootle2020, 2014–. Mem., Educn Cttee, H of C, 2017–. *Address:* (office) Main Street, Bootle, Millom, Cumbria LA19 5TF. *T:* (01229) 718333, (020) 7219 4002. *E:* trudy.harrison.mp@parliament.uk.

**HARRISON, Valerie, (Mrs D. M. Harrison)**; see Caton, V.

**HARRISON, Victoria**; see Harrison, A. V.

**HARRISON, (William) Alistair**, CMG 2012; CVO 1996; HM Diplomatic Service, retired; HM Marshal of the Diplomatic Corps, since 2014; b 14 Nov. 1954; s of late William Kent Harrison and Alice Rita Harrison; m 1st, 1981, Theresa Mary Morrison (marr. diss. 1991); 2nd, 1996, Sarah Judith Wood; one s two d. Educ: Newcastle Royal Grammar Sch.; University Coll., Oxford (BA 1977; MA 1980); Birkbeck Coll., London (DipEcon 1995); Open Univ. (BSc Maths 2012). Joined FCO, 1977: Third, later Second Sec., Warsaw, 1979–82; First Sec., FCO, 1982–84; Private Sec. to Parly Under-Sec., FCO, 1984–86; First Sec., UK Mission to UN, NY, 1987–92; Deputy Head: ME Dept, FCO, 1992–95; of

Mission, Warsaw, 1995–98; Foreign Policy Advr to Dir-Gen. for External Relations, EC, Brussels, 1998–2000; Hd of Chancery and Pol Counsellor, UKMIS to UN, NY, 2000–03; Hd, UN (later Internat. Orgns) Dept, FCO, 2003–05; High Comr to Zambia, 2005–08; Gov. of Anguilla, 2009–13. *Recreations:* music, bridge, ski-ing, golf. *Address:* Ambassador's Court, St James's Palace, SW1A 1BL.

**HARRISSON, Georgina Jane, (Mrs James Fern);** Deputy Secretary, Educational Services, Department of Education, New South Wales, since 2017; *b* Norwich, 17 Jan. 1978; *d* of Hugh Geoffrey and Jennifer Harrisson; *m* 2007, James Fern; two *d*. *Educ:* Univ. of Birmingham (BSc Biol Scis (Genetics) 2000). Account Manager, Prime Minister's Delivery Unit, Cabinet Office, 2002–05; Policy Advr to Premier of NSW, Australia, 2005–07 (on secondment); Hd, Performance and Delivery, DCLG, 2007–08; Actg Dir of Strategy and Performance, DCSF, 2009; Dep. Dir, Schools Directorate, DCSF, later DfE, 2009–11; Exec. Co-ordinator, Domestic Policy, Dept of Prime Minister and Cabinet, Australia, 2011–12; Exec. Dir, Strategic Initiatives, Dept of Premier and Cabinet, NSW, 2012–14; Dep. Sec., Dept of Family and Community Services, NSW, 2014–17. *Recreations:* tennis, sailing, live music.

**HARROD, Dr Tanya Olivia;** design historian; *b* 7 July 1951; *d* of Peter Kingsmill Ledger and Maria Martha Ledger (*née* Sax); *m* 1977, Henry Mark Harrod; one *s* one *d*, and two step *s*. *Educ:* St Felix Sch., Southwold; Univ. of York (BA Hist.); St Hilda's Coll., Oxford (DPhil 1978). Tutor, Open Univ., 1978–88; Architecture and Design corresp., Independent on Sunday, 1989–94; Vis. Fellow, Sch. of World Art and Museology, UEA, 1995–97; Morfudd Roberts Res. Fellow, Univ. of the Creative Arts, Farnham, 2014; Hon. Res. Fellow, V&A, 2014–19. Vis. Prof., Sch. of Humanities, RCA, 2000–10. Member, Advisory Board: Jl Design History, 1996–2009; Interpreting Ceramics, 2003– ; Burlington Magazine, 2006– . Trustee: Heritage Crafts Assoc., 2011–13; Contemporary Applied Art, 2014– . Mem., Acquisitions Cttee, Contemporary Art Soc., 2014– . Mem., Internat. Assoc. of Art Critics, 1992– . Brother, 2011, Hon. Brother, 2016, Art Workers' Guild. Jt Editor, Jl of Modern Craft, 2008– . *Publications:* (ed) Obscure Objects of Desire: reviewing the crafts in the Twentieth Century, 1997; The Crafts in Britain in the 20th Century, 1999; (contrib.) Contemporary Art and the Home, 2002; (contrib.) Out of the Ordinary: spectacular craft, 2007; (contrib.) Neocraft: modernity and the crafts, 2007; (contrib.) Craft, Space and Interior Design, 1855–2005, 2008; (ed) Ann Stokes: artists' potter, 2009; (contrib.) Contemporary British Studio Ceramics: the Grainer Collection, 2010; (contrib.) Anne Dunn, 2010; The Last Sane Man: Michael Cardew, modern pots, colonialism and the counter culture, 2012 (James Tait Black Biography Prize, 2013); The Real Thing: essays on making in the modern world, 2015; Leonard Rosoman, 2017; (ed) Craft: documents of contemporary art, 2018; contribs to Philosophical Trans Royal Soc., Burlington Mag., TLS, Spectator, Crafts, Literary Rev., Tate Etc, Frieze, Prospect. *Recreations:* swimming in seas, rivers and lakes. *Address:* 51 Campden Hill Square, W8 7JR. *T:* (020) 7727 8485.

**HARROLD, Roy Mealham;** farmer, 1947–91; *b* 13 Aug. 1928; *s* of John Frederick Harrold and Ellen Selena Harrold (*née* Mealham); *m* 1968, Barbara Mary, yr *d* of William and Florence Andrews; one *s* one *d*. *Educ:* Stoke Holy Cross Primary Sch.; Bracondale Sch., Norwich. County Chm., Norfolk Fedn of Young Farmers' Clubs, 1956–57; Mem., Nat. Council of Young Farmers, 1957–60; Mem. Council, Royal Norfolk Agric. Assoc., 1972–75, 1980–83, 1987–89; Mem., Press Council, 1976–83. Mem., UK Shareholders Assoc., 1993– . Lay Chm., Norwich East Deanery Synod, 1970–79; Member: Norwich Dio. Synod, 1970–96; Norwich Dio. Bd of Patronage, 1970–82; Norwich Dio. Bd of Finance, 1983–96; Pastoral Asst, St Peter Mancroft, Norwich, 1991–2017 (Church Warden, 1978–82, 1988–92). *Recreations:* music, opera, ballet. *Address:* Milkwood, 122 Norwich Road, Stoke Holy Cross, Norwich NR14 8QJ. *T:* (01508) 492322.

**HARROP, Andrew Jonathan Gilbert;** General Secretary, Fabian Society, since 2011; *b* Wandsworth, 27 Nov. 1976; *s* of Sir Peter John Harrop, *qv*; partner, Katie Sushila Ratna Ghose, *qv*; one *d*. *Educ:* St Paul's Sch.; Gonville and Caius Coll., Cambridge (BA Hons 1998); London Sch. of Econs and Pol Sci. (MSc 1999); London Business Sch. (MBA 2009). Res. asst to Anne Campbell, MP, 1998–99; researcher, New Policy Inst., 1999–2003; Policy Officer, 2003–06, Hd of Policy, 2006–09, Age Concern England; Dir of Policy and Public Affairs, Age UK, 2009–11. Vice Pres. and Treas., Foundn for Eur. Progressive Studies, Brussels, 2016–17. Chair of Govs, Hungerford Sch. and Children's Centre, Islington, 2017–18. Contested (Lab) NE Herts, 2005. *Recreations:* walking, cycling. *E:* andrew.harrop@fabians.org.uk.

**HARROP, Sir Peter (John),** KCB 1984 (CB 1980); Second Permanent Secretary, Department of the Environment, 1981–86; *b* 18 March 1926; *s* of late Gilbert Harrop, OBE; *m* 1975, Margaret Joan, *d* of E. U. E. Elliott-Binns, CB; two *s*. *Educ:* King Edward VII Sch., Lytham, Lancs; Peterhouse, Cambridge. MA (Hist. Tripos). Served RNVR, 1945–48 (Sub-Lt). Min. of Town and Country Planning, 1949; Min. of Housing and Local Govt, 1951; Dept of the Environment, 1970 (Chm., Yorks and Humberside Economic Planning Bd, and Regional Dir, 1971–73); Under-Sec., HM Treasury, 1973–76; Deputy Secretary: DoE, 1977–79, 1980–81; Cabinet Office, 1979–80. Chm., National Bus Co., 1988–91; non-executive Director: Nat. Home Loans Hldgs plc, 1987–92; Municipal Mutual Insurance Ltd, 1988–2001; Thames Water plc, 1989–95 (Mem., Thames Water Authority, 1986–89). Chm., UK Cttee, European Year of the Environment, 1986–88. Chairman: Richmond upon Thames Housing Trust, 1990–96; River Thames Boat Project, 2001–06 (Pres., 2006– ). Chm. of Govs, Richmond upon Thames Coll., 1993–96. Hon. Trustee, British Mus., 1987–97. *Recreation:* golf. *Address:* 19 Berwyn Road, Richmond, Surrey TW10 5BP. *Clubs:* Oxford and Cambridge, Roehampton.
*See also* A. J. G. Harrop.

**HARROW, His Honour John Michael;** a Circuit Judge, 2003–15; *b* 30 March 1946; *s* of Henry John and Edith Harrow; *m* 2000, Maria Liddle; two *s* one *d*. *Educ:* Hemsworth Grammar Sch.; Coll. of Law, Guildford. Admitted solicitor, 1969; a Recorder, 1996–2003. Chm. (pt-time), 1986–96, Dist Chm., 1996–2003, Appeals Service. Mem., Parole Bd, 2016– . *Publications:* (contrib.) Butterworth's Road Traffic Service, annually 1991–94. *Recreations:* walking, film, war history.

**HARROWBY, 8th Earl of,** *cr* 1809; **Dudley Adrian Conroy Ryder;** Baron Harrowby, 1776; Viscount Sandon, 1809; DL; chartered surveyor; *b* 18 March 1951; *s* of 7th Earl of Harrowby, TD and Jeanette Rosalthé (*née* Johnston-Saint); *S* father, 2007; *m* 1st, 1977, Sarah Nichola Hobhouse Payne (*d* 1994), *d* of Captain Anthony Payne; three *s* one *d*; 2nd, 1998, Mrs Caroline J. Coram James (*née* Marks). *Educ:* Eton; Univ. of Newcastle upon Tyne; Magdalene Coll., Cambridge (MA). FRICS 1992. Exec. Dir, Compton Street Securities Ltd, 1988–2002. Mem., Governing Council, Goldsmiths Coll., Univ. of London, 2003–09 (Mem., Finance and Resources Cttee, 2004–09). Mem., Audit Cttee, 2009–14); Governor: John Archer Sch., Wandsworth, 1986–88; Dean Close Sch., Cheltenham, 2004– . President: Staffordshire Soc., 1995–97; Stafford Historical and Civic Soc., 2008– ; Vice Pres., Glos Co. Br., CPRE, 2008– ; Mem. Cttee, Glos Br., CLA, 2011–16, 2017– . Mem., NFU, 1975– . Patron: Guild of Handicraft Trust, 1991– ; N Staffs Co. RBL, 2008–13; Oak Tree Farm Rural Project, 2014– ; Vice Patron, The Almshouse Assoc., 2018– ; Trustee, Bathtub 2 Boardroom charity, 2010– . Mem., Assoc. of Conservative Peers, 2009– . Liveryman, Co. of Goldsmiths, 1997. DL Staffs, 2017. *Recreations:* travel, fell walking, music, study of fine art and architecture. *Heir: s* Viscount Sandon, *qv*. *Address:* Sandon Estate Office, Sandon, Stafford ST18 0DA.

**HARROWER, Rt Rev. John Douglas,** OAM 2000; Bishop of Tasmania, 2000–15; Bishop assisting Primate of Anglican Church of Australia, since 2015; *b* 16 Oct. 1947; *s* of John Lawrence Harrower and Enid Dorothy Harrower; *m* 1970, Gayelene Melva Harrower; two *s*. *Educ:* Melbourne Univ. (BE 1970, BA 1973); Ridley Coll., ACT (ThL 1992); Bible Coll. of Vict., ACT (MA (Theol.) 1996, Adv. Dip. Missiol Studies 1996). CEng 1976; MIChemE 1976. Process Engr, Petroleum Refineries (Aust.) P/L, Melbourne, 1970–72; Project Officer, Tariff Bd, Melbourne, 1972–74; Director: Industry Studies Br., Industries Assistance Commn, 1975; IMPACT Project, Melbourne, 1975–78; Univ. Chaplain, Buenos Aires, 1979–81; Missionary, CMS, Argentina, 1979–88; Exec Chm., CERTEZA-ABUA, Buenos Aires, 1981–87; Gen. Sec., Argentine Univs Bible Assoc., 1981–86; ordained deacon, 1984, priest, 1986, Buenos Aires; Asst Minister, Iglesia Anglicana de San Salvador, Buenos Aires, 1984–88; Vicar: St Paul's, Glen Waverley, Vic, Aust., 1989–95; St Barnabas Anglican Ch, Glen Waverley, 1995–2000; Area Dean, Waverley-Knox, 1992–94; Archdeacon of Kew, Dio. Melbourne, 1994–2000. Dir, World Vision, Australia, 2006–16; President: SparkLit Australia (formerly SPCKA), 2004– ; Bush Church Aid Soc. of Australia, 2014– . MAICD 2007, FAICD 2009. Centenary Medal, Australia, 2003. *Publications:* in Spanish: Personal Evangelism, 1985, new edn 1996; (with Silvia Chaves) Spiritual Gifts: a body in mission, 1985, new edn 1989; 30 Days with Jeremiah, 1989, new edn 1998; in English: Cry of Hope, 2001; The God of Life, 2015; Being a Church in Mission, 2016. *Recreation:* reading. *Address:* c/o Diocese of Melbourne, The Anglican Centre, 209 Flinders Lane, Melbourne, Vic 3000, Australia. *E:* john.harrower@gmail.com.

**HARSENT, David,** FRSL, FEA; poet, novelist, dramatist, librettist; Professor of Creative Writing, University of Roehampton, since 2013; *b* 9 Dec. 1942; *s* of Albert and Mary Harsent; *m* 1989, Julia Watson; one *d*, and two *s* one *d* from former marriage. *Educ:* trifling! Hon. Res. Fellow, Royal Holloway, Univ. of London, 2005–07; Dist. Writing Fellow, 2005–08, Vis. Prof., 2009– , Sheffield Hallam Univ.; Prof. of Creative Writing, Bath Spa Univ., 2012–13. Commns from Royal Opera House and Proms; performances at S Bank Centre, Kammeroper, Vienna, Carnegie Hall, NY, Aldeburgh Fest., Wales Millennium Centre, Salzburg Fest.; *words for music:* music by Harrison Birtwistle: Gawain, opera libretto, 1991; The Woman and the Hare, song cycle, 1999; The Ring Dance of the Nazarene, song setting, 2003; The Minotaur, opera libretto, 2008; Serenade the Silkie, music by Julian Grant, 1994; When She Died, opera libretto, music by Jonathan Dove, 2002; Crime Fiction, music by Huw Watkins, 2009; The Corridor, opera libretto, music by Harrison Birtwistle, 2009; In the Locked Room, opera libretto, music by Huw Watkins, Edinburgh Internat. Fest., 2012; Songs from the Same Earth, song cycle, music by Harrison Birtwistle, Aldeburgh, 2013; The Cure, opera libretto, music by Harrison Birtwistle, Aldeburgh, 2015; The Judas Passion, music by Sally Beamish, 2017. FRSL 1999; FEA 2012; FZS 2013; FHEA 2015; Fellow, Hellenic Authors Soc., 2016. Hon. DLitt Roehampton, 2013. *Publications: fiction:* From an Inland Sea, 1985; *poetry:* Truce, 1973; After Dark, 1973; Dreams of the Dead, 1977; A Violent Country, 1979; Mister Punch, 1984; Selected Poems, 1989; Gawain: a libretto, 1991; Storybook Hero, 1992; News From the Front, 1993; The Sorrow of Sarajevo: versions of poems by Goran Simic, 1996; The Potted Priest, 1997; Sprinting from the Graveyard: versions of poems by Goran Simic, 1997; A Bird's Idea of Flight, 1998; Marriage, 2002; Legion (Forward Prize for best poetry collection), 2005; Selected Poems 1969–2005, 2007; Night, 2011 (Griffin Internat. Poetry Prize, Griffin Trust for Excellence in Poetry, 2012); Poetry: In Secret (versions of Yannis Ritsos), 2012; Fire Songs, 2014 (T. S. Eliot Prize, Poetry Book Soc.); Salt, 2017; *editor:* (with M. Susko) Savramena Britanska Poezija, 1988; Another Round at the Pillars: Festschrift for Ian Hamilton Cargo, 1999; Raising the Iron, 2004. *Recreation:* re-inventing the past for future use. *Address:* c/o United Agents, 12–26 Lexington Street, W1F 0LE.

**HARSTON, Julian John Robert Clive;** HM Diplomatic Service, retired; Assistant Secretary General, United Nations, 2007–09; Director, Harston Consulting, since 2009; *b* 20 Oct. 1942; *s* of late Col Clive Harston, ERD, and of Kathleen Harston; *m* 1st, 1966, Karen Howard Oake (*née* Longfield) (marr. diss. 2000); one *s*; 2nd, 2008, Marina Vasic (*née* Bareta); two step *d*. *Educ:* King's Sch., Canterbury; Univ. of London (BSc); Univ. of Rhodesia and Nyasaland. British Tourist Authority, 1965–70; FCO, 1970; Consul, Hanoi, 1973; 1st Secretary: Blantyre, 1975; Lisbon, 1982; Counsellor, Harare, 1984–88; FCO, 1988–91; Counsellor, UK Mission, Geneva, 1991–95; Head, Political and Civil Affairs, UN Peace Forces, Zagreb, former Yugoslavia, 1995–96; Dir, UN Liaison Office, Belgrade, Fed. Repub. of Yugoslavia, 1996; Rep. of Sec.-Gen. and Hd of Mission, UN Civilian Police Mission, Haiti, 1998–99; Dep. Special Rep. of UN Sec.-Gen. to Bosnia Herzegovina, 1999–2001; Dir, UN Dept of Peace Keeping, NY, 2001–04; Dir, UN, Belgrade, 2004–07; Hd of Mission for the Referendum in W Sahara and Special Rep. of the Sec.-Gen. in W Sahara, UN, 2007–09; Rep. of the Sec.-Gen. in Belgrade, 2009. Founder Mem., Adv. Panel to UK Defence Coll., 2013– . *Recreations:* photography, travel. *Address:* Toplicin Venac 21, Apt 21, 11000 Belgrade, Serbia. *Clubs:* East India, Special Forces.

**HART, Alan;** broadcasting consultant, since 1991; Director, Global AMG, 1995–2000; Executive Director, Eurosport Consortium, 1997–2004 (Trustee, 2004–09); *b* 17 April 1935; *s* of late Reginald Thomas Hart and Lillian Hart; *m* 1961, Celia Mary Vine; two *s* one *d*. *Educ:* Pinnerwood Primary Sch.; University College Sch., Hampstead. Reporter: Willesden Chronicle and Kilburn Times, 1952–58; Newcastle Evening Chronicle, 1958; London Evening News, 1958–59; Editorial Asst, BBC Sportsview, 1959–61; Television Sports Producer, BBC Manchester, 1962–64; Asst Editor, Sportsview, 1964–65; Editor, Sportsview, 1965–68; Editor, Grandstand, 1968–77; Head of Sport, BBC Television, 1977–81; Controller, BBC1 Television, 1981–84; Special Asst to Dir Gen., BBC, 1985; Controller, Internat. Relations, BBC, 1986–91. Dir, Eurosport, 1991–97 (Chm., 1989–91); Chm., British Eurosport, 1997–99. Advr on management of E European broadcasting services, EBU, 1991–93; Trustee, EBU sub-licence scheme, 2005–13. Chairman: Inventure Trust, 2003–07; Veterans Farm Able Foundn, 2018–19; Dir, Give Them a Sporting Chance, 2003– . Gov., S Devon Coll., 2004–13; Trustee, Friends of South Devon Coll., 2008– (Chm., 2008–16). FRTS 1983. Hon. DEd Plymouth, 2014. *Recreations:* sport, music. *Address:* Cutwellwalls, Avonwick, near South Brent, Devon TQ10 9HA.

**HART, Anelay Colton Wright;** Partner in Appleby, Hope & Matthews, 1963–95; *b* 6 March 1934; *s* of Anelay Thomas Bayston Hart and Phyllis Marian Hart; *m* 1979, Margaret Gardner (*née* Dewing) (*d* 2018). *Educ:* Stamford Sch.; King's Coll., London (LLB). Solicitor, retd. Advisory Director, World Society for the Protection of Animals, 1982–2003; RSPCA: Mem. Council, 1969–95; Hon. Treasurer, 1974–81; Chm. of Council, 1981–83, 1985–86, 1988–90; Vice-Chm. Council, 1983–84, 1986–88; Queen Victoria Silver Medal, 1984. President, Rotary Club of South Bank and Eston, 1972–73. *Recreation:* walking. *Club:* Royal Over-Seas League.

**HART, Anthony;** *see* Hart, T. A. A.

**HART, David Timothy Nelson**; QC 2003; b 18 Nov. 1958; s of late Timothy Norman Hart and Margaret Jane Hart; m Rosalind Catherine English; one s one d. Educ: Oundle Sch.; Trinity Coll., Cambridge (BA Classics and Law 1981). Called to the Bar, Middle Temple, 1982; in practice as barrister, 1983–. Mem., Area Cttee, Legal Aid Bd/Legal Services Commn, 1995–; Appeals Officer: EU Emission Trading Scheme, 2005–; Carbon Reduction Commitment, 2010–. Mem., Res. Ethics Cttee, St Thomas' Hosp., 2002–12. Publications: (contrib.) Introduction to Human Rights and the Common Law, ed English and Havers; (cons. ed. and contrib.) Burnett-Hall on Environmental Law, 2nd edn 2008 to 3rd edn 2012; numerous contribs on envmtl law issues, esp. human rights. Recreations: walking over saltmarshes, sailing, ski-ing, conversation, frequent blogger on environmental issues. Address: Lapwing House, Glebe Lane, Burnham Overy Staithe, Norfolk PE31 8JQ. E: david.hart@1cor.com. Clubs: Overy Staithe Sailing; Downhill Only (Wengen).

**HART, Most Rev. Denis James**; b Melbourne, 16 May 1941; s of Kevin James Hart and Annie Eileen (née Larkan). Educ: Xavier Coll., Kew; Corpus Christi Coll., Werribee; Corpus Christi Coll., Glen Waverley. Ordained priest, 1967; Chaplain, Repatriation Hosp., Heidelberg, 1967–68; Asst Priest, N Balwyn, 1968; Asst Priest and Master of Ceremonies, St Patrick's Cathedral, Melbourne, 1969–74; Prefect of Ceremonies, Archdio. Melbourne, 1970–96; Advocate and Notary, Regional Matrimonial Tribunal, 1975–85; Exec. Sec., Nat. Liturgical Commn, Aust. Catholic Bps' Conf., 1975–90; Parish Priest, St Joseph's, W Brunswick, 1987–96; Vicar Gen. and Moderator of the Curia, 1996–2001; Aux. Bp, Archdio. Melbourne, 1997–2001; Titular Bp of Vagada, 1997–2001. Member: Congregation for Eastern Churches, 2014–; Pontifical Council for Culture, 2014–; Congregation for Divine Worship and Disciple of the Sacraments, 2016–. Australian Catholic Bishops' Conference: Member: Commn for Liturgy, 2000–12; Permanent Cttee, 2002–18; Chm., Cttee for Finance and Admin., 2002–12; Vice Pres., 2009–12; Pres., 2012–18; Vice Pres., Internat. Commn for English in the Liturgy, 2008–16. Recreations: walking, music, reading.

**HART, Edwina**, MBE 1998; Member (Lab) Gower, National Assembly for Wales, 1999–2016; Minister for Economy, Science and Transport (formerly for Business, Enterprise, Technology and Science, and for Transport), 2013–16; b 26 April 1957; d of late Eric G. Thomas and Hannah J. Thomas; m 1986, Robert B. Hart; one d. Member: Employment Appeal Tribunal, 1992–99; Broadcasting Council for Wales, 1995–99; Adv. Cttee Wales, EOC, 1998–99. Nat. Pres., BIFU, 1992–94; Chair, Wales TUC, 1997–98. National Assembly for Wales: Sec. for Finance, 1999–2000; Minister for Finance, Local Govt and Communities, 2000–03, for Social Justice and Regeneration, 2003–07, for Health and Social Services, 2007–11. Chm., Equal Opportunity Cttee, 2000–02; Mem., SW Wales Regl Cttee, 1999–2007. Non-executive Director: Chwarae Teg, 1994–99; Wales Millennium Centre, 1997–99. Trustee, GFG Foundn, 2018–. Mem., Council, 1998–99, Ct of Govs, 2000–11, Univ. of Wales, Swansea. Pres., Gower Fest., 2017. CStJ 2013. Recreations: reading, music, cookery.

**HART, Dr (Everard) Peter**, CChem, FRSC; Rector, Sunderland Polytechnic, 1981–90; b 16 Sept. 1925; s of Robert Daniel Hart and Margaret Stokes; m Enid Mary Scott; three s one d. Educ: Wyggeston Grammar Sch., Leicester; Loughborough Coll.; London Univ. (BSc, PhD). Asst Lectr, Lectr and Sen. Lectr, Nottingham and Dist Technical Coll., 1951–57; Sunderland Technical College, later Sunderland Polytechnic: Head of Dept of Chemistry and Biology, 1958–69; Vice-Principal, 1963–69; Dep. Rector, 1969–80. Member: Cttee for Sci. and Technol., CNAA, 1974–77; Gen. Council, Northern Arts, 1982–90. Royal Institute of Chemistry: Mem. Council, 1963–65, 1970–73; Vice-Pres., 1973–75. FRSA 1985. Hon. DCL Sunderland, 1994. Recreations: music, opera, theatre, travel. Address: Redesdale, North End, Durham City DH1 4NE. T: (0191) 384 8305.

**HART, Sir Graham (Allan)**, KCB 1996 (CB 1987); PhD; Permanent Secretary, Department of Health, 1992–97; b 13 March 1940; s of Frederick and Winifred Hart; m 1964, Margaret Aline Powell; two s. Educ: Brentwood Sch.; Pembroke Coll., Oxford (Hon. Fellow 1997); Univ. of Essex (MA 2008; PhD 2015). Assistant Principal, 1962, Principal, 1967, Ministry of Health; Asst Registrar, General Medical Council, 1969–71; Principal Private Sec. to Secretary of State for Social Services, 1972–74; Asst Sec., 1974, Under Sec., 1979, DHSS; Under Sec., Central Policy Review Staff, 1982–83; Dep. Sec., DHSS, then DoH, 1984–89; Sec., Home and Health Dept, Scottish Office, 1990–92. Chairman: King's Fund, 1998–2004; Citizens Advice (formerly NACAB), 1999–2004 (Chm., Governance Rev. Gp, 1998–99); Pharmacy Practice Res. Trust, 1999–2005; Appts Cttee, GDC, 2002–08; NI Hospice Review Team, 2003; Mem., Audit Commn, 1999–2004. Dir, NHBC, 2004–12. Trustee, British Lung Foundn, 2006–12; Treas., Hist. of Parlt Trust, 2011–. Publications: The Cambridgeshire Committee for Scandalous Ministers 1644–45, 2017. Address: 1 Priory Lodge, Priory Park, SE3 9UY. T: (020) 8297 6537.

**HART, Prof. Graham John**, PhD; FMedSci; Professor of Sexual Health and HIV Research, since 2006, and Dean, Faculty of Population Health Sciences, since 2011, University College London; b Middlesbrough, 7 June 1957; s of late Trevor Hart and Doris Hart; civil partnership 2016, m 2016, Christopher James Thow. Educ: Whinney Banks Secondary Modern Sch.; Univ. of Leicester (BA 1st Cl. Hons 1978); Univ. of Kent (PhD 1982). Lectr in Med. Sociol., Middx Hosp. Med. Sch., 1986–93; Sen. Lectr, UCL, 1993–94; Associate Dir, MRC Social and Public Health Scis Unit, Univ. of Glasgow, 1994–2005. Publications: (Co-Ed.) Social Aspects of AIDS book series, 1989–99; (Gen. Ed.) Health, Risk and Society book series, 1994–2002; contrib. papers to BMJ, AIDS, Jl AIDS, Archives Internal Medicine, AIDS Care, Sexually Transmitted Infections, Social Sci. and Medicine, Jl Adolescence. Recreations: novels, theatre, art, gardens, dogs, walking, running, gym. Address: School of Life and Medical Sciences, University College London, Gower Street, WC1E 6BT. T: (020) 7679 6814. E: g.hart@ucl.ac.uk.

**HART, Guy William Pulbrook**, OBE 1985; HM Diplomatic Service, retired; b 24 Dec. 1931; s of late Ernest Guy Hart and Muriel Hart (née Walkington); m 1954, Elizabeth Marjorie (née Bennett) (d 2013); one s one d (and one d decd). Educ: Cranleigh School. Commissioned, Intelligence Corps, 1951–60. British Cellophane Ltd, 1960–62; CRO, 1962; Consular Officer, Kuala Lumpur, 1963–67; Hungarian Language Course, 1967; Second Sec. (Inf.), Budapest, 1968–71; News Dept, FCO, 1971–74; Second Sec. (Econ.), later First Sec. (Inf.), British Mil. Govt, Berlin, 1974–78; First Sec. (Comm.), Port of Spain, 1978–82, Budapest, 1982–85; Asst Head, Inf. Dept, FCO, 1986; Ambassador to the Mongolian People's Republic, 1987–89; High Comr to Seychelles, 1989–91; Head of British delegn, EC monitor mission, Zagreb, 1993–94; Mem., UN Observer mission, SA election; CSCE observer, election in former Yugoslav republic of Macedonia, 1994. Publications: White Month's Return: Mongolia comes of age, 1993. Recreations: Alpine sports, shooting, painting. Address: 1 Marsh Mill, Wargrave Road, Henley on Thames, Oxon RG9 3JD.

**HART, Dr James Maurice**, CBE 2007; QPM 1999; Commissioner, City of London Police, 2002–06; law enforcement and security consultant; b 10 Sept. 1947; s of late Lewis Hart and Beatrice Withington; m 1993, Julie Anne Russell; two s. Educ: Wayneflete Sch., Esher; Kingston Coll.; City Univ. (BSc Hons Systems and Mgt; PhD 1995). Joined Surrey Police, 1966; transf. to Metropolitan Police, as Chief Inspector, 1983; posts at Heathrow Airport, New Scotland Yard and Notting Hill; Chief Superintendent, 1989; Divl Comdr, Wandsworth, 1990–94; Hd, Diplomatic Protection Br., 1994; Asst Chief Constable, Surrey Police, 1994–98: Head: Support Services, 1994–95; Territorial Policing, 1995–96; Specialist Ops, 1997–98; City of London Police: Asst Comr, 1998–2002; Dep. to Comr and Operational Hd, 1998–99; Head, Support Services, 2000–01. Association of Chief Police Officers: Chm., Firearms Licensing Cttee, 1999–2002; Chm., Econ. Crime Cttee, 2002–06. CCMI 2006 (FIMgt 1998). Hon. DSc City, 2004. Publications: (jtly) Neighbourhood Policing: theoretical basis for community sector policing, 1981. Recreations: ski-ing, creating home and garden, walking, cooking and eating.

**HART, Matthew Jason**; dancer, choreographer, singer and actor; b 13 July 1972; s of Colin Dennis Hart and Susan Jean Hart (now Rose). Educ: Arts Educational Sch., London; Royal Ballet Sch., London. Dancer: London Fest. Ballet, 1984–87; Royal Ballet soloist, 1991–96; Rambert Dance Co., 1996–2000; George Piper Dances, 2001–03; freelance, 2003–; choreographer: Nat. Youth Dance, 1990; Royal Ballet, 1991–2000; Royal Ballet Sch., 1992–98, 2010, 2012; Birmingham Royal Ballet, 1993; London City Ballet, 1995–96; English Nat. Ballet, 1996; Dance Umbrella, 1996; English Nat. Ballet Sch., 1999, 2012; Ballet Deutsche Oper am Rhein, 2000; Hong Kong Ballet, 2001; London Studio Centre, 2002, 2007, 2011; George Piper Dances, 2002; K Ballet Co., Tokyo, 2003; Millennium Dance, 2000, 2005, 2006, 2013; Central Sch. of Ballet, 2009, 2012; London Children's Ballet, 2010; Sarasota Ballet, Fla, 2011, 2012, 2013, 2015; ENB2, 2012; New English Ballet Th., 2015. Created rôles as: (for Royal Opera House 2): Toad, in Wind in the Willows, 2002; The Devil, in The Soldier's Tale, 2004, 2005, 2009; Oswald Moving, in Ashworks, 2005; Pinocchio (title rôle), 2005; The King of the Mountains, in The Thief of Baghdad, 2008; (for Arc Dance Co.) The Prince, in The Anatomy of a Storyteller, 2004; (for Royal Opera House 2) Tom Rakewell, in Pleasure's Progress, 2010; other appearances include: On Your Toes (musical), 2004; Mrs Henderson Presents (film), 2005; Riot at the Rite (film for BBC2), 2006; Babes in Arms (musical), Chichester Fest. Th., 2007; Viva La Diva, 2007; A Midsummer Night's Dream, 2008, Romeo and Juliet, 2008, Regent's Park; Margot (film for BBC2), 2009; dance appearances include: Betrothal in a Monastery (opera), Glyndebourne, 2006; The Prince in Matthew Bourne's Swan Lake, 2006. Dance coach and critic, Strictly Dance Fever, BBC, 2006. Address: 12c Theed Street, SE1 8ST.

**HART, Michael**, CBE 1990; MA; Education Consultant, European Commission, 1990–93; b 1 May 1928; yr s of late Dr F. C. Hardt; m 1956, Lida Dabney Adams, PhD (Wisconsin Univ.). Educ: Collège Français, Berlin; Landerziehungsheim Schondorf; Keble Coll., Oxford (Exhib.; 1st Cl. Hons History, 1951). Administrative Asst, UNRRA, 1945–47; Asst Master and Head of History, Sherborne Sch., 1951–56; Head of History, 1956–61, and Housemaster of School House, 1961–67, Shrewsbury Sch.; Headmaster of Mill Hill Sch., 1967–74; HM Inspector of Schs, DES, 1974–76; Headmaster, European Sch., Mol, Belgium, 1976–80; Headmaster, European Sch., Luxembourg, 1980–89; Dir, European Classes, Alden Biesen, Belgium, 1989–92. FRSA. Commandeur de l'Ordre de Mérite (Luxembourg), 1989. Publications: The EEC and Secondary Education in the UK, 1974; The European Dimension in Primary and Secondary Education, 1992; contrib. to Reader's Digest World Atlas and Atlas of British Isles. Recreations: dogs, history, music, bridge. Address: 13 St Luke's Court, Hyde Lane, Marlborough, Wilts SN8 1YU.

**HART, Prof. Michael**, CBE 1993; FRS 1982; FInstP; Professor of Physics, University of Manchester, 1984–93, now Emeritus; Chairman, National Synchrotron Light Source, Brookhaven National Laboratory, 1995–2000; b 4 Nov. 1938; s of Reuben Harold Victor Hart and Phyllis Mary (née White); m 1963, Susan Margaret (née Powell); three d. Educ: Cotham Grammar Sch., Bristol; Bristol Univ. (BSc, PhD, DSc). FInstP 1971. Research Associate: Dept of Materials Science and Engrg, Cornell Univ., 1963–65; Dept of Physics, Bristol Univ., 1965–67; Lectr in Physics, 1967–72, Reader in Physics, 1972–76, Bristol Univ.; Sen. Resident Res. Associate of Nat. Research Council, NASA Electronics Research Center, Boston, Mass, 1969–70; Special Advisor, Central Policy Review Staff, Cabinet Office, 1975–77; Wheatstone Prof. of Physics and Head of Physics Dept, KCL, 1976–84; Science Programme Co-ordinator (part-time, on secondment), Daresbury Lab., SERC, 1985–88. Prof. of Applied Physics, De Montfort Univ., 1993–98; Hon. Prof. in Engrg, Warwick Univ., 1993–98; Vis. Prof. in Physics, Bristol Univ., 2000–05. Amer. Crystallographic Assoc.'s Bertram Eugene Warren Award for Diffraction Physics (jtly with Dr U. Bonse), 1970; Charles Vernon Boys Prize of Inst. of Physics, 1971. Publications: numerous contribs to learned jls on x-ray optics, defects in crystals and synchrotron radiation. Recreations: tennis, cookery, flying kites. Address: 2 Challoner Court, Merchants Landing, Bristol BS1 4RG. T: (0117) 921 5291. E: michael_hart@blueyonder.co.uk.

**HART, Michael**, FCII; non-executive Chairman, Furness Building Society, 2005–09 (Director, 2000–09); b 28 Sept. 1937; s of William and Kathleen Hart; m (separated); two s two d. FCII 1971. Man. Dir, 1987–94, Chm., 1994–95, Provincial Insurance plc; Chief Exec., Sun Life and Provincial (Hldgs) plc, 1995–97, retired. Non-exec. Chm., Flemings European Fledgeling Investment Trust plc, 1998–2006; Director: Inter American Insurance Ltd, 1998–2001; Active Languages Ltd, 1999–2008; Time Group Ltd, 2001–04; PremierLine Ltd, 2003–06; Home & Legacy Holdings Ltd, 2003–06. Mem. Council, Lancaster Univ., 1998–2006. Chm. Trustees, Brewery Arts Centre, 1997–2011. Recreations: walking, wine. Address: 17 Whinlatter Drive, Kendal LA9 7HE. T: (01539) 736586.

**HART, Miranda Katherine**; actress, comedienne and writer; b Torquay, 14 Dec. 1972; d of Captain David Hart Dyke, qv. Educ: Downe House Sch., Berks; Univ. of West of England (BA Hons Politics); Acad. of Live and Recorded Arts. PA/Office Manager, Macmillan Cancer Support, 1998–2001; PA, Comic Relief, 2001–03; actress in television series: Vicar of Dibley, 2004; Absolutely Fabulous, 2004; Smack the Pony, 2004; Nighty Night, 2005; Hyperdrive, 2006–07; Not Going Out, 2006–09; Angelo's, 2007; Monday, Monday, 2009; Miranda (also writer), 2009–14; Call the Midwife, 2012–15; actress in film, Spy, 2015; actress in musical, Annie, Piccadilly Th., 2017. Stand-up show, My, What I Call Live, Show, UK tour, 2014. Hon. Trustee, Comic Relief, 2010–; Patron: Spear, 2011–; Theatres Trust, 2018–; Ambassador, Prince's Countryside Fund, 2019–. Publications: Is it Just Me?, 2012; Best of Miranda, 2014; Peggy & Me, 2016; Miranda's Daily Dose of Such Fun!, 2017; The Girl with the Lost Smile, 2017. Recreations: theatre, musicals, TV and film, animals, tennis, touch tennis, nature, travel, free swimming, swimming. Address: c/o Troika Talent, 180 Great Portland Street, W1W 5QZ.

**HART, Prof. Oliver Simon D'Arcy**, PhD; Professor of Economics, since 1993, and Andrew E. Furer Professor, since 1997, Harvard University; b 9 Oct. 1948; s of late Philip Montagu D'Arcy Hart, CBE and Ruth Hart; m 1974, Rita Goldberg (who retains maiden name); two s. Educ: University Coll. Sch.; King's Coll., Cambridge (BA 1969); Univ. of Warwick (MA 1972); Princeton Univ. (PhD 1974). Lectr in Econs, Univ. of Essex, 1974–75; Asst Lectr in Econs, subseq. Lectr, Univ. of Cambridge, 1975–81; Fellow of Churchill Coll., Cambridge, 1975–81; Prof. of Economics, LSE, 1982–85; Prog. Dir, Centre for Economic Policy Res., 1983–84; Prof. of Economics, MIT, 1985–93. Centennial Vis. Prof., LSE, 1997–. Sec.-Treas., Amer. Law and Econs Assoc., 2004–05 (Pres., 2006–07); Vice-Pres., AEA, 2006–07. Fellow: Econometric Soc., 1979 (Mem. Council, 1983–89, 1994–99); Amer. Acad. of Arts and Scis, 1988; Eur. Corporate Governance Inst., 2002; Amer. Finance Assoc., 2016. Corresp. FBA 2000. MNAS 2016. Hon. Fellow, Churchill Coll., Cambridge, 2018. Editor, Review of Economic Studies,

1979–83. Dr *hc* Free Univ. of Brussels, 1992; Univ. of Basel, 1994; Univ. of Paris-Dauphine, 2009; Copenhagen Business Sch., 2009; Hon. DSc (Econ) London Business Sch., 2011; Hon. LLD Warwick 2012; Hon. PhD Bologna, 2018. (Jtly) Nobel Prize for Economics, 2016. *Publications:* Firms, Contracts, and Financial Structure, 1995; articles in Jl of Pol Economy, Qly Jl of Econs, Amer. Econ. Rev., Econometrica. *Recreations:* playing the piano, swimming. *Address:* Department of Economics, Harvard University, Cambridge, MA 02138, USA.

**HART, Peter;** *see* Hart, E. P.

**HART, Roger Dudley,** CMG 1998; HM Diplomatic Service, retired; Ambassador to Peru, 1999–2003; *b* 29 Dec. 1943; *s* of Alfred John Hart and Emma Jane Hart; *m* 1968, Maria de Los Angeles (Angela) de Santiago Jimenez; two *s*. *Educ:* St Olave's Grammar Sch., London; Univ. of Birmingham (BA 1965). Entered FO 1965; served British Mil. Govt W Berlin, Bahrain and FCO; First Sec. (Aid), Nairobi, 1975–78; First Sec. (Commercial), Lisbon, 1978–83; FCO, 1983–85; RCDS 1985; BNSC, 1986; Consul-Gen., Rio de Janeiro, 1986–90; Dep. Hd of Mission, Mexico City, 1990–93; Head of Nationality, Treaty and Claims Dept, FCO, 1993–95; Ambassador to Angola, and (non-resident) to São Tomé and Príncipe, 1995–98. Citizen, 1989, Pedro Ernesto Medal, 1990, Rio de Janeiro. *Recreations:* travel, classical music, old silver. *Address:* 7 Rosscourt Mansions, 4 Palace Street, SW1E 5HZ. *Club:* Canning.

**HART, Samuel Kinsford;** Co-founder and Director, Hart Bros Restaurants Ltd, since 2003; *b* London, 29 Sept. 1974; *s* of Tim and Stefa Hart; *m* 2002, Robin; three *c*. *Educ:* Eton; Univ. of Manchester (BA Econs). Pres., Los Hermanos Duende SA de CV, Mexico, 1996. Mem., Gran Orden de Caballeros del Vino. *Publications:* (jtly) Modern Spanish Cooking, 2006; (jtly) Barrafina: a Spanish cookbook, 2011. *Recreations:* lunch, wine, cycling, gardening, music and dancing. *Address:* Quo Vadis, 26–29 Dean Street, W1D 3LL. *T:* (020) 7437 9585. *E:* sam@hartsgroup.co.uk. *Clubs:* Quo Vadis, Groucho; Velo (Rocacorba, Spain).

**HART, Simon Anthony;** MP (C) Carmarthen West and Pembrokeshire South, since 2010; Parliamentary Secretary, Cabinet Office, since 2019; *b* 15 Aug. 1963; *s* of Anthony Hart and Judith Hart (*née* Christie); *m* 1998, Abigail Kate Holland; one *s* one *d*. *Educ:* Radley Coll., Oxon; RAC Cirencester (Rural Estate Mgt). MRICS (ARICS 1985–99). Llewellyn Humphreys, Chartered Surveyors, 1988–98; Balfour, Burd & Benson, Chartered Surveyors, 1998–99; Regl Public Relns Officer, 1999, Dir of Campaign for Hunting, 1999–2003, Chief Exec., 2003–10, Chm., 2015–, Countryside Alliance. Prime Minister's Trade Envoy to Panama, Costa Rica and Dominican Republic, 2017–. Member: Pol and Constitutional Select Cttee, 2010–12; Welsh Affairs Select Cttee, 2012–15; Envmt, Food and Rural Affairs Select Cttee, 2015–17; Digital, Culture, Media and Sport Select Cttee, 2017–; Cttee on Standards in Public Life, 2017–. Exec. Mem., 1922 Cttee, 2015–17. Mem., OSCE Parly Assembly, 2016–17. Chm., United and Cecil Club, 2015–18. Master and Huntsman, S Pembrokeshire Hunt, 1988–99. Trustee, Sundorne Estate, 1995–2015. *Recreations:* all aspects of country sports, cricket. *Address:* House of Commons, SW1A 0AA. *Club:* Cresselly Cricket.

**HART, Prof. Stephen Malcolm,** PhD; Professor of Latin American Film, Literature and Culture, since 2002, and Leverhulme Trust Senior Research Fellow, 2015–17, University College London; *b* London, 25 Aug. 1959; *s* of Bryan Hart and Barbara Hart; *m* 1978, Danielle Elizabeth Degaute; one *s* three *d*. *Educ:* Downing Coll., Cambridge (BA 1980; PhD 1985). Lectr, Westfield Coll., London, 1984–91; Associate Prof., Univ. of Kentucky, 1991–98; Sen. Lectr, 1998–2000, Reader, 2000–02, UCL. Gen. Ed., Tamesis, 1999–. Corresp. Mem., Peruvian Acad. of Language, 2013. Order of Merit (Peru), 2004; Order of Merit (Nat. Univ. of Trujillo, Peru), 2014. *Publications:* Gabriel García Márquez, 2010; César Vallejo: a literary biography, 2013; Latin American Cinema, 2015. *Recreations:* jogging, cinema, theatre, art. *Address:* Department of Spanish, Portuguese and Latin American Studies, School of European Languages, Culture and Society, 305 Foster Court, University College London, Gower Street, WC1E 6BT. *T:* (020) 7679 3036. *E:* stephen.malcolm.hart@ucl.ac.uk.

**HART, Prof. Susan Jane Ritchie,** PhD; FRSE; Dean, Durham University Business School, since 2016; *b* Edinburgh, 18 July 1960; *d* of Thomas Hart and Jean Sutherland McDonald Forbes Hart; one *s* one *d*. *Educ:* Bearsden Acad.; Strathclyde Univ. (BA Hons 1982; PhD 1987); Mktg Res. Soc., Strathclyde (Dip. 1985). Lectr, Dept of Mktg, Strathclyde Univ., 1987–92; Professor of Marketing: Heriot-Watt Univ., 1993–95; Stirling Univ., 1995–98; Strathclyde University: Prof. of Mktg, 1998–2016; Hd, Dept of Mktg, 2002–04; Exec. Dean, Internationalisation, 2011–15; Associate Dep. Principal, 2015–16; Vice Dean, 2005–08, Dean, 2008–15, Strathclyde Business School. Ed., Jl Mktg Mgt, 2000–. FRSE 2009; Fellow, Leadership Trust Foundn, 2010. Mem. Bd, Assoc. to Advance Collegiate Schs of Business, 2011–. *Publications:* Marketing Changes, 2003; New Product Development, 1996; Product Strategy and Management, 2007. *Recreations:* cycling, ski-ing. *Address:* Durham University Business School, Mill Hill Lane, Durham DH1 3LB.

**HART, (Thomas) Anthony (Alfred),** MA; Headmaster, Cranleigh School, 1984–97; *b* 4 March 1940; *er s* of Rev. Arthur Reginald Hart and Florence Ivy Hart; *m* 1971, Daintre Margaret Withiel (*née* Thomas); one *s* one *d*. *Educ:* City of Bath Sch.; New Coll., Oxford (2nd Cl. Hons PPE; MA); Pres., Oxford Union, 1963. Served with VSO, Mzuzu Secondary Sch., Nyasaland, 1959–60. Asst Principal and Principal, Min. of Transport, 1964–69; seconded to Govt of Malaŵi as Transport Adviser, 1969–70; Principal, DoE and CSD, 1970–73; Head, Voluntary Services Unit, Home Office, 1973–75; Asst Sec., CSD and HM Treasury, 1975–84. *Recreation:* enjoying Cyprus. *Address:* PO Box 59340, Pissouri, 4607, Cyprus. *T:* (25) 222802. *E:* daintrecyprus@cytanet.com.cy.

**HART, Prof. Vaughan Anthony,** PhD; Professor of Architecture, since 2005, and Director, Centre for Advanced Studies in Architecture, 1994–2001 and 2010–14, University of Bath; *b* Belfast, 23 Oct. 1960; *s* of Ronald Hart and Mary Hart (*née* Glass); *m* 1999, Charlotte Courtman-Davies; one *s*. *Educ:* Univ. of Bath (BSc 1983; BArch 1985); Trinity Hall, Cambridge (MPhil 1987; PhD 1991). University of Bath: Res. Officer, 1991–93; Lectr in Architecture, 1993–95; Sen. Lectr, 1995–97; Reader in Architectural Hist., 1997–2005; Hd, Dept of Architecture and Civil Engrg, 2008–10; Member: Senate, 2010–11; Court, 2011–. Vis. Prof. of Architecture, Univ. of Kent, 2010–. Sen. Fellow, Paul Mellon Centre for Studies in British Art, London, 2005; Vis. Fellow, St John's Coll., Oxford, 2005; Sen. Vis. Fellow, Centre for Advanced Study in Visual Arts, Nat. Gall. of Art, Washington, 2009. Mem., Adv. Bd, Helsinki Collegium for Advanced Studies, Univ. Helsinki, 2012–18. Exhibitions curated: Paper Palaces, Fitzwilliam Mus., Cambridge, 1997; Palladio's Rome, British Sch. at Rome, 2008; Virtual Reality, Sorbonne, Paris, 2009. Work displayed in Royal Acad. Summer Exhibns, 1986 (winner, student prize), 1993, 1995. Trustee, Holburne Mus., Bath, 2011–16; Trustee and Mem. Council, Oriental Ceramics Soc., 2014–19 (Asst Hon. Sec., 2017–19). *Publications:* Art and Magic in the Court of the Stuarts, 1994, 2nd edn 2014; (trans. jtly) Sebastiano Serlio on Architecture, vol. 1, 1996, vol. 2, 2001, 2nd edn (2 vols) 2005 (Chinese edn 2014); St Paul's Cathedral: Christopher Wren, 1995, 2nd edn 1999; Paper Palaces: the rise of the Renaissance architectural treatise, 1998; Nicholas Hawksmoor: rebuilding ancient wonders, 2002, 2nd edn 2007 (Best Book on British Art Prize, Amer. Coll. Art Assoc., 2005); (trans. jtly) Palladio's Rome, 2006, 2nd edn 2009 (Japanese edn 2011); Sir John Vanbrugh: storyteller in stone, 2008; Inigo Jones: the architect of kings, 2011; Sansovino's Venice, 2017. *Recreations:* swimming, collecting Chinese porcelain, playing chess with Christopher, supporting Fulham FC. *Address:* c/o Department of Architecture and Civil Engineering, University of Bath, Bath BA2 7AY. *T:* (01225) 386361, *Fax:* (01225) 386691. *E:* v.hart@bath.ac.uk.

**HART-DAVIS, Dr Adam John;** freelance writer, since 1994; *b* 4 July 1943; *yr s* of Sir Rupert Hart-Davis; *m* 1st, 1965, Adrienne Alpin (marr. diss. 1995); two *s*; 2nd, 2010, Susan Blackmore. *Educ:* Eton; Merton Coll., Oxford (BA 1st Cl. Hons Chemistry 1966; Hon. Fellow 2006); York Univ. (DPhil 1968). Post-doctoral Research: Univ. of Alberta, Edmonton, 1969–71; Univ. of Oxford, 1971; College Science Editor, Clarendon Press (OUP), 1971–77; Researcher, 1977–83, Producer, 1983–94, Yorkshire Television. Presenter: TV series: Local Heroes, 1992–2000; Hart-Davis on History, 1998, 1999; Secret City, 2000; What the Romans Did for Us, 2000; What the Victorians Did for Us, 2001; Science Shack, 2001, 2003; Adam Hart-Davis says Come to Your Senses, 2001; Tomorrow's World, 2002; What the Tudors Did for Us, 2002; What the Stuarts Did for Us, 2002; Industrial Nation, 2003; What the Ancients Did for Us, 2005; How London Was Built, 2005, 2006, 2007; The Cosmos: a beginner's guide, 2007; Just Another Day, 2007; How Britain Was Built, 2008; radio series: Inventors Imperfect, 1999–2003; High Resolution, 2001; Elements of Surprise, 2001; Engineering Solutions, 2004, 2006, 2007; Eureka Years, 2004, 2005, 2007, 2008. Mem., ASME, 2014–15. Pres., Tavistock Fest. of Music and Arts, 2013–16. Member: Newcomen Soc.; Assoc. of Polelathe Turners; Patron: Wrexham Science Fest., 1998; Cycle West, 2000; Brede Steam Engine Soc., 2002; Theatre Odyssey, 2002; The Garden Sci. Trust, 2003; Museum of Sci. and Industry, Manchester, 2003; ACT, 2003; Ideas 21; Assoc. of Lighthouse Keepers, 2003; Bognor Birdman, 2004; Holgate Windmill Preservation Soc., 2004; Crank It Up, 2004; Transplant Links Community, 2008; Engineering Explained, 2008; Life Pres., Ellenroad Trust, 2004. Hon. Member: British Toilet Assoc.; Associates of Discovery Museum, 2003; S Hams Soc., 2009; Hon. MRI 2005. Comp ILE 2005. Hon. Fellow: Soc. of Dyers and Colourists, 2005; British Sci. Assoc., 2010; Hon. FRSC 2007; Hon. FRPS 2007. DUniv: York, 2000; Brunel, 2007; Open, 2009; Hon DTech: Loughborough, 2001; UWE, 2005; Hon. DSc: Sheffield, Bradford, 2001; Birmingham, 2002; Bristol, Sheffield Hallam, Leicester, 2003; QUB, 2004; Hon. DCL Northumbria, 2002; Hon. DLitt Bath, 2004. Gerald Frewer Meml Trophy, Instn of Engrg Designers, 1999; first medal for public promotion of engrg, Royal Acad. of Engrg, 2002; Sir Henry Royce Meml Medal, IIE, 2003; Judges' Award for Educnl TV, RTS, 2003; ASME Ralph Coats Roe Medal, 2014. *Publications:* Don't Just Sit There!, 1980; (with Hilary Lawson) Where There's Life…, 1982; Scientific Eye, 1986; Mathematical Eye, 1989; World's Weirdest "True" Ghost Stories, 1991; (with Susan Blackmore) Test Your Psychic Powers, 1995; Thunder, Flush and Thomas Crapper, 1997; Science Tricks, 1997; (with Paul Bader) The Local Heroes Book of British Ingenuity, 1997; (with Paul Bader) More Local Heroes, 1998; Amazing Math Puzzles, 1998; Eurekaaargh!, 1999; (with Paul Bader) The Local Heroes Book of DIY Science, 2000; Chain Reactions, 2000; What the Victorians Did for Us, 2001; (with Emily Trosciankco) Henry Winstanley and the Eddystone Lighthouse, 2002; What the Tudors and Stuarts Did for Us, 2002; Talking Science, 2004; What the Past Did for Us, 2004; Why Does a Ball Bounce?, 2005; (with Emily Trosciankco) Taking the Piss, 2006; Just Another Day, 2006; (with Paul Bader) The Cosmos: a beginner's guide, 2007; (ed) History: the definitive visual guide, 2007; String: unravel the secrets of a little ball of twine, 2009; (ed) Science: the definitive visual guide, 2009; The Book of Time, 2011; (ed) Engineers, 2012; Inventions, 2012; The Science Book, 2014; Pavlov's Dog, 2015; Schrodinger's Cat, 2015; Very Heath Robinson, 2017. *Recreations:* green woodwork, drinking wine, chess, growing vegetables, drawing, watercolour painting, U3A ukulele band, choir, folk group, cycling, lip-reading.
*See also* P. D. Hart-Davis.

**HART-DAVIS, (Peter) Duff;** author and journalist; *b* 3 June 1936; *er s* of Sir Rupert Hart-Davis; *m* 1961, Phyllida Barstow; one *s* one *d*. *Educ:* Eton; Worcester Coll., Oxford (BA 1960). Nat. Service, Coldstream Guards, 1955–57. Joined Sunday Telegraph, 1961; Editor, News Background page, 1966–70; feature writer, 1971–75; Literary Editor, 1975–76; Asst Editor, 1976–78. Country Columnist, Independent, 1986–2001. *Publications:* Ascension: the story of a South Atlantic island, 1972, 2nd edn 2016; Peter Fleming, 1974; Monarchs of the Glen, 1978; Hitler's Games, 1986; (ed) The Letters and Journals of Sir Alan Lascelles: Vol. 1, End of an Era, 1986; Vol. 2, In Royal Service, 1989; Armada, 1988; Country Matters, 1989; The House the Berrys Built, 1990; Wildings: the secret garden of Eileen Soper, 1991; Further Country Matters, 1992; When the Country Went to Town, 1997; Raoul Millais, 1998; Fauna Britannica, 2002; Audubon's Elephant, 2003; (ed) Pavilions of Splendour, 2004; Honorary Tiger, 2005; (ed) King's Counsellor, 2006; Philip de László: his life and art, 2010; The War that Never Was: the true story of the men who fought Britain's most secret battle, 2011; Among the Deer, 2011; Man of War, 2012; Our Land at War, 2015; *fiction:* The Megacull, 1968; The Gold of St Matthew, 1970; Spider in the Morning, 1972; The Heights of Rimring, 1980; Level Five, 1982; Fire Falcon, 1983; The Man-eater of Jassapur, 1985; Horses of War, 1991. *Recreations:* opera, wine, cutting and splitting firewood, deer. *Address:* Owlpen Farm, Uley, Glos GL11 5BZ. *T:* (01453) 860239.
*See also* A. J. Hart-Davis.

**HART DYKE, Captain David,** CBE 1990; LVO 1980; RN; Clerk to Worshipful Company of Skinners, 1990–2003; *b* 3 Oct. 1938; *s* of late Comdr Rev. Eric Hart Dyke and Mary Hart Dyke; *m* 1967, Diana Margaret, *d* of Sir William Luce, GBE, KCMG; two *d*. *Educ:* St Lawrence College, Ramsgate; BRNC Dartmouth. RN 1958; served Far East and Middle East; navigation specialist; Exec. Officer, HMS Hampshire, 1974–76; Staff, RN Staff Coll., 1976–78; Comdr, HM Yacht Britannia, 1978–80; Captain HMS Coventry; action in Falklands, 1982; ACOS to C-in-C Fleet, 1982–84; Asst Naval Attaché, Washington, 1985–87; Dir, Naval Recruiting, 1987–89. ADC to the Queen, 1988–89. *Publications:* Four Weeks in May: the loss of HMS Coventry - a captain's story, 2007. *Recreations:* water-colouring, garden design, military history, tennis. *Address:* Hambledon House, Hambledon, Hants PO7 4RU. *T:* (023) 9263 2380.
*See also* M. K. Hart.

**HART DYKE, Sir David (William),** 10th Bt *cr* 1677, of Horeham, Sussex; educator; *b* 5 Jan. 1955; *s* of Sir Derek William Hart Dyke, 9th Bt and Dorothy Moses; *S* father, 1987. *Educ:* Ryerson Polytechnical Institute (BA). Educator, Scientists in School, 2012–; educational staff, Green Venture, 2016–. Member, Board of Directors: Ontario Envmt Network, 2009–; Earth Day Hamilton-Burlington, 2010– (Coordinator, 2016–). Contested (Green Party) Hamilton E-Stoney Creek, 2008, 2011. *Recreations:* portage camping, ice hockey, reading. *Heir: cousin* Thomas Guy Hart Dyke, *b* 1976. *Address:* 28 King Street West, Apt 14B, Stoney Creek, ON L8G 1H4, Canada.

**HART DYKE, Miranda Katherine;** *see* Hart, M. K.

**HART-LEVERTON, Colin Allen;** QC 1979; a Recorder of the Crown Court, 1979–2001; *b* 10 May 1936; *s* of Monty Hart-Leverton and Betty (*née* Simmonds); one *s*; *m* 1990, Kathi Jo, *d* of Hal and Jan Davidson. *Educ:* Stowe; self-taught thereafter. Mem., Inst. of Taxation, 1957 (youngest to have ever qualified); called to the Bar, Middle Temple, 1957 (youngest to have ever qual.). Contested (L): Bristol West, 1959 (youngest cand.); Walthamstow West, 1964. Prosecuting Counsel, Central Criminal Court, 1974–79; Dep. Circuit Judge, 1975; Attorney-at-Law, Turks and Caicos Islands, Caribbean, 1976. Occasional television and radio broadcasts. Professional pianist with various well-known jazz bands. *Recreations:* table-tennis, jazz. *Address:* 1MCB, Third Floor, 15 New Bridge Street, EC4V 6AU. *T:* (020) 7452 8900.

**HARTE, (Catherine) Miriam;** DL; Chairman, Tees, Esk and Wear Valley NHS Foundation Trust, since 2019; *b* 3 Aug. 1960; *d* of Joseph and Mary Harte, Waterford, Eire. *Educ:* Trinity Coll., Dublin (BA Law 1981). Chartered Accountant, 1985; FCA 1995. Trainee, Arthur Andersen & Co., 1981–86; Finance Manager, UK and Europe/US, Procter & Gamble, 1986–97; Director: Bede's World, 1998–2001; Beamish, North of England Open Air Mus., 2001–07; owner and Dir, culture, heritage, fundraising and project mgt consultancy, 2007; Interim Manager, Hancock Project, Gt North Mus., 2008–09. Business Advr, Creative United, 2015–. Board Member: MLA NE (formerly NE MLAC), 2001–07; NE Tourism Adv. Bd, 2004–07. Dir, Audiences NE, 2004–12. Non-executive Director: Sunderland City Hosps Trust, 2007–16; Northumberland Tyne and Wear Mental Health Foundn, 2017–19. Mem. Bd, Thirteen Housing Gp (formerly Tees Valley Housing) Ltd, 2015–. DL Co. Durham, 2007. *Recreations:* walking, cooking, theatre, travelling. *Address:* Thorn Cottage, 125 Kells Lane, Low Fell NE9 5XY. *T:* (0191) 487 9258. *E:* miriamharte@gmail.com.

**HARTE, Julia Kathleen;** *see* McKenzie, J. K.

**HARTE, Miriam;** *see* Harte, C. M.

**HARTER, Dr Andrew Charles,** CBE 2017; DL; FREng, FIET; FBCS; Founder and Chief Executive Officer, RealVNC Ltd, since 2002; Fellow, St Edmund's College, Cambridge, since 2002; Chairman, Cambridge Network, since 2014; *b* Yorks, 5 April 1961; *s* of late Roy Harter and Jean Dorothy Harter (*née* Brook); *m* 2004, Lily Bacon; two *s. Educ:* Queen Elizabeth Grammar Sch., Wakefield; Fitzwilliam Coll., Cambridge (BA 1983); Corpus Christi Coll., Cambridge (PhD 1990). CEng 2002; FIET 2002; FREng 2011. Principal Res. Engr, Olivetti and Oracle Res. Lab., 1990–99; Dir of Res. and Engrg, AT&T Labs Res., 1999–2002. Vis. Fellow, Univ. of Cambridge Computer Lab., 2002–. Trustee: RAEng, 2013–; Britten Sinfonia, 2013–; Centre for Computing Hist., 2013–; IET, 2014– (Vice-Pres., 2019–). FLCM 1979; FBCS 2007. FRSA 2014. High Sheriff, 2018–19, DL, 2019, Cambs. Turing Lect., IET, 2018. Hon. DSc Anglia Ruskin, 2015. Silver Medal, 2010, MacRobert Award, 2013, RAEng; Faraday Medal, IET, 2016. *Publications:* Three-dimensional Integrated Circuit Layout, 1991, 2nd edn 2009; patents and papers on computer systems. *Recreations:* golf, ski-ing, Rugby, flying, music, opera, theatre, badgers. *Address:* 15 Tenison Avenue, Cambridge CB1 2DX. *T:* 07734 251812. *E:* ach3@cam.ac.uk. *Club:* Athenæum.

**HARTER, Caryl, (Mrs David Harter);** *see* Churchill, C.

**HARTILL, Edward Theodore,** OBE 2004; FRICS; Business Development Advisor, Corderoy, international chartered quantity surveyors and cost consultants, 2008–09; City Surveyor, City of London Corporation (formerly Corporation of London), 1985–2008; *b* 23 Jan. 1943; *s* of late Clement Augustus Hartill and Florence Margarita Hartill; *m* 1975, Gillian Ruth Todd; two *s*, and two *s* from previous marr. *Educ:* Priory Sch. for Boys, Shrewsbury; Coll. of Estate Management, London Univ. BSc (Estate Management); FRICS 1978. Joined Messrs Burd and Evans, Land Agents, Shrewsbury, 1963; Estates Dept, Legal and Gen. Assce Soc., 1964–73; Property Investment Dept, Guardian Royal Exchange Assce Gp, 1973–85 (Hd Office Manager, 1980–85). Vis. Lectr in Law of Town Planning and Compulsory Purchase, Hammersmith and W London Coll. of Advanced Business Studies, 1968–78. Royal Institution of Chartered Surveyors: Member: Gen. Practice Divl Council, 1989–97 (Pres., 1992–93); Governing Council, 1990–2004; Hon. Treas., 2000–04. Mem., Assoc. of Chief Estates Surveyors and Property Managers in Local Govt (formerly Local Authority Valuers Assoc.), 1985–2007 (Mem., Nat. Council, 1988–2007; Pres., 1996–97; Hon. Mem., 2007); Mem., Govt Study Team on Professional Liability, 1988–89; Mem. Steering Gp, 1992–99, and Chm., Property Services Sub-Gp, 1992–99, Construction Industry Standing Conf.; Founder Mem. and Chm., Property Services NTO, 1999–2004; Vice-Chm., Asset Skills, 2004–07 (Chm., 2003). University of London: Member: Council, 2004–08; Bd of Trustees, 2008–15; Estates Cttee, 2004–08, 2017– (Dep. Chm., 2006–08, 2017–); Investments Cttee, 2008–15 (Dep. Chm., 2009–15); Estates Sub-Gp, 2014–16 (Acting Chm., 2014–15); Chm., Senate House Project Bd, 2006–12; Dep. Chm., Univ. Marine Biol Station, 2009–13 (Mem., Bd of Trustees, 2008–13); Chm., Safety Cttee, 2009–15. Gov. and Trustee, Coram (formerly Coram Family), 2006–14 (Vice Chm., 2007–08; Chm., 2008–14; Hon. Vice Pres., 2014). Hon. Mem., Investment Property Forum, 1995–2008. Hon. Associate, Czech Chamber of Appraisers, 1992. Mem., British Schs Exploring Soc. Life Fellow, RSA (FRSA 1993). Liveryman, Chartered Surveyors' Co., 1985– (Mem., Court of Assistants, 1991–2009; Master, 2003–04). *Recreations:* hill walking, travel, cars, watching GT racing. *Address:* 215 Sheen Lane, East Sheen, SW14 8LE. *T:* (020) 8878 4494.
*See also* R. J. Hartill.

**HARTILL, Rosemary Jane;** broadcaster and facilitator; *b* 11 Aug. 1949; *d* of late Clement Augustus Hartill and Florence Margarita Ford. *Educ:* Wellington Girls' High Sch., Salop; Bristol Univ. (BA (Hons) English). Editor: Tom Stacey (Publishing) Ltd, 1970–73; David and Charles Ltd, 1973–75; Sen. Non-fiction Editor, Hamish Hamilton Children's Books Ltd, 1975–76; freelance journalist and broadcaster, 1976–82; freelance book and ballet reviewer, TES, 1976–80; Religious Affairs Reporter, 1979–82, Religious Affairs Corresp., 1982–88, BBC; Reporter: BBC Everyman Prog., 1987; ITV Human Factor series, 1989–92; Presenter: BBC Woman's Hour (NE edns), 1989–90; Meridian Books (BBC World Service), and numerous other progs. Founder, Rosemary Hartill & Associates, 1996; Co-Founder, Voyager TV Ltd, 1997; non-executive Director: Shared Interest, 1996–2005; Ethical Investment Res. Service, 1997–2001. Board Member: Nat. Probation Service, Northumbria, 2001–07; (non-exec.) Northumberland Tyne and Wear Strategic HA, 2002–05; Courts Bd, Northumbria, 2004–07; Youth Justice Bd for England and Wales, 2004–08. Facilitator: Alternatives to Violence Project, Britain, 1996– (Trustee, 1997–2000); Barter Books book gps, Alnwick, 2003–; Mem. mgt gp, Newcastle Conflict Resolution Network, 2005–13. Mem., Soc. of Friends (Mem., Former Yugoslavia Project Mgt Gp, 2000–02); Mem., Central Cttee, Quaker Communications, 2010–12; Mem., Parly Engagement Working Gp, Scotland, 2017–); Trustee, The Friend, 2004–10. FRSA 2001. Hon. DLitt: Hull, 1995; Bristol, 2000. Sandford St Martin Trust personal award for outstanding contrib. to religious broadcasting, 1994, and other awards. *Publications:* (ed) Emily Brontë: poems, 1973; Wild Animals, 1978; In Perspective, 1988; Writers Revealed, 1989; Were You There?, 1995; (ed) Florence Nightingale, 1996. *Recreations:* being in Northumberland, wildlife, theatre, music, film, books, exploring modern art and architecture. *Address:* 101b/17 St Stephen Street, Edinburgh EH3 5AB.
*See also* E. T. Hartill.

**HARTING, Henry Maria Robert Egmont M.;** *see* Mayr-Harting.

**HARTINGTON, Marquess of;** courtesy title of heir of Duke of Devonshire, not used by current heir.

**HARTLAND, Michael;** *see* James, M. L.

**HARTLAND-SWANN, Julian Dana Nimmo,** CMG 1992; HM Diplomatic Service, retired; Thai-Europe business consultant, since 1997; *b* 18 Feb. 1936; *s* of late Prof. J. J. Hartland-Swann and of Mrs Kenlis Hartland-Swann (*née* Taylour); *m* 1st, 1960, Ann Deirdre Green (*d* 2000); one *s* one *d*; 2nd, 2004, Julie Katherine Ryan. *Educ:* Stowe; Lincoln Coll., Oxford (History). HM Forces, 1955–57. Entered HM Diplomatic Service, 1960; 3rd Sec., Brit. Embassy, Bangkok, 1961–65; 2nd, later 1st Sec., FO, 1965–68; 1st Sec., Berlin, 1968–71; 1st Sec. and Head of Chancery, Vienna, 1971–74; FCO, 1975–77; Counsellor, 1977; Ambassador to Mongolian People's Republic, 1977–79; Counsellor and Dep. Head of Mission, Brussels, 1979–83; Head of SE Asian Dept, FCO, 1983–85; Consul Gen., Frankfurt, 1986–90; Ambassador to Burma (Myanmar), 1990–95; Exec. Dir, Eur. Business Inf. Centre, Delegn of the EC to Thailand, 1995–97. *Recreations:* French food, sailing, restoring ruins. *Address:* Résidence Hof Ten Berg, Clos Hof Ten Berg 30, 1200 Brussels, Belgium.

**HARTLEY, Prof. Brian Selby,** PhD; FRS 1971; Professor of Biochemistry, Imperial College, University of London, 1974–91, now Emeritus; Director, 1982–91, Senior Research Fellow, 1991–94, Centre for Biotechnology; *b* 16 April 1926; *s* of Norman and Hilda Hartley; *m* 1949, Kathleen Maude Vaughan; three *s* one *d. Educ:* Queens' Coll., Cambridge (BA 1947, MA 1952); Univ. of Leeds (PhD 1952). ICI Fellow, Univ. of Cambridge, 1952; Helen Hay Whitney Fellow, Univ. of Washington, Seattle, USA, 1958; Fellow and Lectr in Biochemistry, Trinity Coll., Cambridge, 1964; Scientific Staff, MRC Laboratory of Molecular Biology, 1961–74. Founder and Mem. Sci. Bd, Biogen, 1978; Chairman: Agrol Ltd, 1993–2000; BioConversion Technologies Ltd, 2006–09; Biocaldol Ltd, 2009–10 (Sen. Scientific Advr, 2010–12); Chm. and Res. Dir, E3 Biotechnology Ltd, 2012–. Mem. Council: EMBO (European Centre for Molecular Biology), 1978–84; Royal Soc., 1982–84. Hon. Mem., Amer. Soc. of Biological Chemists, 1977. British Drug Houses Medal for Analytical Biochemistry, 1969. *Publications:* over 150 papers and articles in scientific jls and books. *Recreations:* gardening, genealogy. *Address:* Grove Cottage, 21 Smith Street, Elsworth, Cambridge CB23 4HY.

**HARTLEY, Caroline Mary;** *see* Rookes, C. M.

**HARTLEY, David Fielding,** PhD; CEng; FBCS, CITP; Fellow, Clare College, Cambridge, since 1986 (Steward, 2002–05); Director, University Computing Service, University of Cambridge, 1970–94; *b* 14 Sept. 1937; *s* of late Robert M. Hartley and Sheila E. Hartley, LRAM; *m* 1960, Joanna Mary (*d* 1998), *d* of late Stanley and Constance Bolton; one *s* two *d. Educ:* Rydal Sch.; Clare Coll., Cambridge (MA, PhD 1963). FBCS 1968; CEng 1990; CITP 2004. University of Cambridge: Sen. Asst in Research, Mathematical Lab., 1964–65; Asst Dir of Research, 1966–67; Univ. Lectr, 1967–70; Jun. Research Fellow, Churchill Coll., Cambridge, 1964–67; Fellow, Darwin Coll., Cambridge, 1969–86; Chief Exec., UK Educn and Res. Networking Assoc., 1994–97; Exec. Dir, Cambridge Crystallographic Data Centre, 1997–2002. Museum Dir, Nat. Mus. of Computing, 2012–13. British Computer Society: Mem. Council, 1970–73, 1977–80, 1985–90, 1998–2002; Vice Pres. (Technical), 1985–87, (External Relns), 1987–90; Dep. Pres., 1998–99; Pres., 1999–2000. Mem., Computer Conservation Soc., 2007– (Chm., 2007–11; Hon. Treas., 2014–18). Chm., Inter-University Cttee on Computing, 1972–74; Mem., Computer Bd for Univs and Research Councils, 1979–83. Mem. Council of Management, Numerical Algorithms Gp Ltd, 1979–2006 (Chm., 1986–97); adviser to Prime Minister, Information Technology Adv. Panel, 1981–86; DTI Hon. Adviser in Information Technology (on sabbatical leave), 1983; Mem. various Govt, Res. Council and Industry cttees and consultancies. Mem., BBC Science Consultative Gp, 1984–87. Hon. Mem., Univ. of Cambridge Computer Lab., 2011–. Dir, CADCentre Ltd, 1983–94. Sec., Clare Alumni Assoc., 2003–18. Governor, Rydal Sch., 1982–88. Medal of Merits, Nicholas Copernicus Univ., Poland, 1984. Mem., Editl Bd, Computer Jl, 2010–12. *Publications:* papers in scientific jls on operating systems, programming languages, computing service management. *Address:* Clare College, Cambridge CB2 1TN.

**HARTLEY, Prof. Frank Robinson;** DL; CChem, FRSC; Vice-Chancellor, Cranfield University (formerly Cranfield Institute of Technology), 1989–2006; *b* 29 Jan. 1942; *s* of Sir Frank Hartley, CBE; *m* 1st, 1964, Valerie Peel (*d* 2005); three *d*; 2nd, 2009, Charmaine Harvey. *Educ:* King's College Sch., Wimbledon (Sambrooke Schol.; Fellow, 2003); Magdalen Coll., Oxford (Demy; BA, MA, DPhil, DSc). FRAeS 1996. Post-doctoral Fellow, Commonwealth Scientific and Industrial Research Organisation, Div. of Protein Chemistry, Melbourne, Aust., 1966–69; Imperial Chemical Industries Research Fellow and Tutor in Physical Chemistry, University Coll. London, 1969–70; Lectr in Inorganic Chemistry, Univ. of Southampton, 1970–75; Professor of Chemistry and Head of Dept of Chemistry and Metallurgy, 1975–82, Acting Dean, 1982–84, Principal and Dean, 1984–89, RMCS, Shrivenham. Chm., Cranfield IT Inst., 1989–90 (Dir, 1986–89); Man. Dir, CIT (Holdings) Ltd, 1993–2006 (Dir, 1989–93); Chm., CIM Inst., 1990–2006; Dir, Cranfield Ventures Ltd, 1990–2006 (Man. Dir, 2000–06); non-executive Director: T & N, 1989–98; Eastern Regl Adv. Bd, National Westminster Bank, 1990–92; Kalon, 1994–99; Kenwood, 1995–99; Hunting-BRAE Ltd, 1999–2006; Bedfordshire TEC, 1994–96. Sen. Travelling Fellow, ACU, 1986. Special Advr to Prime Minister on defence systems, 1988–91; Special Advr to H of L Select Cttee on Sci. and Technol., 1994–95; Mem., Parly Scientific Cttee, 1986– (Mem. Council and Gen. Purposes Cttee, 1992–98; Vice-Pres., 1995–98). Member: Internat. Adv. Bd, Kanagawa Acad. of Sci. and Technol., Japan, 1989–98; Bd, Internat. Foundn for Artificial Intelligence, 1990–98. Vice Pres., Cranfield Trust, 1989–; Chm., Lorch Foundn, 1995–2006; Dir, Shuttleworth Trust, 1994–97. Member: Council, IoD, 2000–; Eastern Regl Bd, CBI, 2000–06. Chairman: Sen. Council for Devon, Teignmouth Br., 2008–13; Teignmouth and Dawlish Ramblers, 2010–16. Gov., Welbeck Coll., 1984–89; Mem. Council, Bath Univ., 1982–89. DL Beds, 2005. Mem., Oxford Union. FRSA 1988. Editor-in-Chief, Brassey's New Battlefield Weapons Systems and Technology series, 1988–. *Publications:* The Chemistry of Platinum and Palladium (Applied Science), 1973; Elements of Organometallic Chemistry (Chemical Soc.), 1974, Japanese edn 1981, Chinese edn 1989; (with C. Burgess and R. M. Alcock) Solution Equilibria, 1980, Russian edn 1983; (with S. Patai) The Chemistry of the Metal—Carbon Bond, vol. 1 1983, vol. 2 1984, vol. 3 1985, vol. 4 1987, vol. 5 1989; Supported Metal Complexes, 1985, Russian edn 1987; The Chemistry of Organophosphorus Compounds, vol. 1, 1990, vol. 2, 1992, vol. 3, 1994, vol. 4, 1996; Chemistry of the Platinum Group Metals, 1991; papers in inorganic, coordination and organometallic chemistry in major English, Amer. and Aust. chemical jls. *Recreations:* gardening, swimming, rambling, reading. *Club:* Shrivenham.

**HARTLEY, Rt Rev. Helen-Ann Macleod;** *see* Ripon, Area Bishop of.

**HARTLEY, Janice Lindsay,** CB 2017; Implementation and Delivery Director, Universal Credit Programme, Department for Work and Pensions, 2012–19; *b* Paisley, 10 March 1964; *d* of Albert Edward and Janet Connie; *m* 1998, Peter Hartley; one *s* one *d. Educ:* Linwood High Sch.; Leeds Metropolitan Univ. (BA Hons Business and Mgt). Various roles,

DHSS, 1982–97; Modernising Services Team, DSS, 1997–2000; Department for Work and Pensions: Digital Office Infrastructure Project, 2000–04; Hd, IT Service Delivery, 2004–10; IT Service Delivery Dir, 2010–12. *Recreations:* reading, cycling.

**HARTLEY, John Robert;** education consultant, since 2016; *b* 4 Oct. 1955; *s* of Peter and Josephine Hartley; *m* 1982, Susanna Newton; two *s* one *d. Educ:* Oundle Sch.; St Catharine's Coll., Cambridge (BA 1977, PGCE). Physics teacher, Aylesbury GS, 1978–83; Sen. Physicist, Hazelwick Sch., Crawley, 1983–87; Hd of Sci., St Joseph's RC Comprehensive Sch., Swindon, 1988–90; Dep. Headteacher, Moulsham High Sch., Chelmsford, 1991–97; Headteacher, Notley High Sch., Braintree, 1997–2003; Headteacher, Saffron Walden County High Sch., 2004–15; Chief Exec., Saffron Acad. Trust, 2012–15. Nat. Leader of Educn, 2011–15. *Recreations:* fell-walking, cycling, local and social history. *Address:* John Hartley Education Consultants, c/o 16 Wentworth Road, Oxford OX2 7TQ. *E:* johnandsuehartley@gmail.com.

**HARTLEY, Julian Matthew Frederick;** Chief Executive, Leeds Teaching Hospitals NHS Trust, since 2013; *b* Keighley, W Yorks, 24 Feb. 1967; *s* of Max and Rosalind Hartley; *m* 1997, Karina Wood; one *s* one *d. Educ:* Bingley Grammar Sch.; Durham Univ. (BA Hons; MBA); King's Coll., Cambridge (PGCE). Chief Executive: Tameside and Glossop PCT, 2002–05; Blackpool Teaching Hosps, 2005–09; University Hosp. of S Manchester, 2009–12; Man. Dir, NHS Improving Quality, 2012–13. *Publications:* Leadership in the NHS: connecting for the future NHS Confederation, 2005; Placing Ladders, 2008. *Recreations:* tennis, theatre, Manchester United. *Address:* Leeds Teaching Hospitals NHS Trust, St James' Hospital, Beckett Street, Leeds LS9 7TF. *E:* julian.hartley@leedsth.nhs.uk.

**HARTLEY, Prof. Keith;** Professor of Economics, 1987–2008, now Emeritus, and Director, Centre for Defence Economics, 1990–2008, University of York; *b* 14 July 1940; *s* of Walter and Ivy Hartley; *m* 1966, Winifred Kealy; one *s* two *d. Educ:* Univ. of Hull (BSc Econs; PhD 1974). Dir, Inst. for Res. in Social Scis, Univ. of York, 1982–94. NATO Res. Fellow, 1977–79 and 1986–87; QinetiQ Vis. Fellow, 2009. *Publications:* Political Economy of NATO, 1999; (with J. Brauer) Economics of Regional Security, 2000; (with T. Sandler) Economics of Defense, 2001; (with T. Sandler) Economics of Conflict, 2003; (with T. Sandler) Handbook of Defense Economics, vol. 2, 2007; (with C. Tisdell) Microeconomic Policy, 2008; Economics of Defence Policy, 2011; (with D. Braddon) Handbook of the Economics of Conflict, 2011; The Political Economy of Aerospace Industries, 2014; The Economics of Arms, 2017. *Recreations:* walking, angling, football, reading, military history. *Address:* Economics Department, University of York, York YO10 5DD. *T:* (01904) 433753. *E:* kh2@york.ac.uk.

**HARTLEY, Richard Anthony;** QC 2008; a Recorder, since 2002; *b* Crewe, 7 Nov. 1962; *s* of Dr Tony Hartley and Renée Hartley; *m* 1987, Clare Meeke; two *s* two *d. Educ:* Haslington Co. Primary Sch.; Sandbach Sch.; Liverpool Univ. (LLB Hons 1984). Called to the Bar, Middle Temple, 1985; in practice as barrister, Manchester, specialising in personal injury, sports law and clinical negligence cases, 1985–. *Recreations:* football (Manchester City), squash, snowboarding, cycling, classic cars and motorbikes, hill walking, a pint with friends. *Address:* Cobden House Chambers, 19 Quay Street, Manchester M3 3HN. *T:* (0161) 833 6000.

**HARTLEY, Richard Leslie Clifford;** QC 1976; *b* 31 May 1932; *s* of late Arthur Clifford Hartley, CBE and Nina Hartley. *Educ:* Marlborough Coll.; Sidney Sussex Coll., Cambridge (MA). Called to the Bar, Gray's Inn, 1956, Bencher, 1986. Former Chairman: Appeal Bd, Jockey Club; Appeal Bd, HRA. *Recreations:* golf, tennis, horse racing. *Address:* 15 Chesham Street, SW1X 8ND. *T:* (020) 7235 2420. *Clubs:* Garrick, MCC; Woking Golf; Rye Golf; St Enodoc Golf; New Zealand Golf (Weybridge).

**HARTLEY, Prof. Susan Elaine, (Mrs D. I. Grimley),** OBE 2019; DPhil; Director, York Environmental Sustainability Institute, University of York, since 2010; *b* Dover, 17 July 1962; *d* of Prof. John Roger Hartley and Lita Mary Hartley; *m* 1986, David Ian Grimley. *Educ:* Roundhay Sch., Leeds; St Hugh's Coll., Oxford (BA Biochem. 1984); Univ. of York (DPhil Ecol. 1987). Post-doctoral researcher, Univ. of York, 1987–89; Post-doctoral researcher, 1990–96, PSO, 1996–2000, Centre for Ecol. and Hydrol., Banchory; University of Sussex: Reader in Ecol., 2001–03; Prof. of Ecol., 2004–10; Dir of Res., Sch. of Life Scis, 2009–10. Pres., British Ecol Soc., 2015–17. Trustee, Royal Botanic Gdns, Kew, 2016–; Member, Board: Natural England, 2018–; Castle Howard Arboretum Trust, 2018–. Mem., Methodist Ch. *Publications:* (ed jtly) Biotic Interactions in the Tropics, 2005; (ed jtly) The Ecology of Plant Secondary Metabolites: from genes to ecosystems, 2012; contribs to learned jls. *Recreations:* travel, photography, walking, gardening, modern art. *Address:* York Environmental Sustainability Institute, Environment Building, Wentworth Way, University of York, York YO10 5NG. *T:* (direct) (01904) 328640, (office) (01904) 328866. *E:* sue.hartley@york.ac.uk.

**HARTMANN, Dr Peter,** Hon. KBE 1992; Ambassador of Germany to France, 1998–2001; *b* 9 Oct. 1935; *m* Baroness Lonny von Blomberg-Hartmann (*d* 2008). *Educ:* Frankfurt; Rome (LPH); Cologne; Fribourg Univ. (DPhil). Foreign Service, 1965; Washington, 1966; Karachi, 1968; EC Brussels, 1971; Buenos Aires, 1978; Head, Foreign Relations Office, CDU, 1981–84; Federal Chancellery: Head, European Policy, 1984–87; Asst Under-Sec., Foreign, Security and Develt Policy, 1987–90; Dep. Under-Sec., Foreign Security Policy, and Advr to Federal Chancellor, 1991–93; Ambassador to UK, 1993–95; Under Sec. of State, Foreign Min., Germany, 1995–98. *Address:* 14163 Berlin, Beuckestrasse 6, Germany.

**HARTMANN, Tessa,** CBE 2016; Managing Director, Hartmann Media Ltd (formerly TFF Marketing Ltd), since 1995; *b* Stirlingshire; *d* of John Fortune-Fraser and late Tessa Fortune-Fraser; *m* 1996, Alexander Hartmann; two *s* two *d. Educ:* High Sch. of Glasgow; Aiglow Coll., Switzerland; Univ. of Stirling (BA Business). Graduate intern, Kennedy Foundn, Washington, DC, 1992; Account Manager, FKB Carlson, London, 1993–95; Man. Dir, Hartmann House Jersey, 2015–. Founder, Scottish Fashion Awards, 2006; Jersey Style Awards, 2017. Political commentator; columnist, Sunday Times Scotland, 2013–14; Fashion Editor at Large, The Herald, 2011–14. MCIM 1997. DUniv Glasgow Caledonian, 2012. *Recreation:* support and nurture of fashion design and textile manufacture.

**HARTNETT, David Anthony,** CB 2003; a Commissioner, 2000–12, and Permanent Secretary for Tax, 2008–12, HM Revenue and Customs (a Deputy Chairman, 2003–05; Director-General, 2005–08; Acting Chairman and Permanent Secretary, 2007–08); *b* 25 Feb. 1951; *s* of late George Peter Hartnett and Mary Christine Hartnett (*née* O'Donoghue); *m* 1977, Aileen Patricia Mary O'Dempsey; two *s* one *d. Educ:* Hampton Sch.; Birmingham Univ. (BA Hons Latin). Inland Revenue, 1976–2005: Inspector of Taxes, 1976–86; Investigation Manager, 1986–91; Dir, Financial Intermediaries and Claims Office, 1991–96; Asst Dir, Personal Tax Div., 1996–98; Dir, Savings and Investment and Capital and Valuation Divs, 1998–99; Dir, Capital and Savings Div., 1999–2000. Vice-Chm., OECD Forum on Tax Admin., 2009–12. Advr, Hldgs Bd, HSBC, 2013–; non-exec. Dir, HSBC Turkey, 2016–18. Gov., St Mary's Univ., 2014–. *Recreation:* Marcus Tullius Cicero.

**HARTNOLL, Mary Charmian,** CBE 1990; Director of Social Work, Glasgow City Council, 1996–98; *b* 31 May 1939; *d* of Rev. Sydney W. Hartnoll and Margaret Hartnoll. *Educ:* Colston's Girls' Grammar Sch., Bristol; Bedford Coll., Univ. of London (BA Hons); Univ. of Liverpool (HO Cert. in Child Care). Child Care Officer, Dorset CC, 1961–63; various posts, County Borough of Reading, 1963–74; Asst Dir, Berks CC, 1974–75; Divl Officer, Reading, 1975–77; Dir of Social Work: Grampian Regl Council, 1978–93; Strathclyde Regl Council, 1993–96. Chm., E Park, Glasgow, 2000–01; Convener, Scottish Commn for Regulation of Care, 2001–06. Hon. LLD Robert Gordon Univ., 1993. *Recreations:* natural history, walking, music, theatre going. *Address:* 36 Norfolk Road, Aberdeen AB10 6JR.

**HARTOP, Barry;** Chief Executive, Telenor Business Solutions (formerly Nextra (UK) Ltd), 2001–03; *b* 15 Aug. 1942; *s* of Philip William Hartop and Constance Winifred (*née* Drew); *m* 1966, Sandra Swan; one *s* one *d. Educ:* Durham Univ. (BSc Hons Chem. Engrg). Prodn and technical mgt, Lever Bros Ltd, 1965–72; Unilever PLC: Chm., Cost Reduction and R&D, 1972–80; Man. Dir, European Business Centre, 1980–83; Chm. and Man. Dir, Lever Industrial Ltd, 1983–89; Man. Dir, Gestetner Hldgs, 1989–92; Chief Executive: WDA, 1994–96; Millennium Exhibn, 1996; Man. Dir, Norsk Data, 1997–2001. Chairman: Hammicks Bookshops Ltd, 1994–98; Locum Gp Ltd, 1997–2002; Reed Health Gp plc, 2003–06. Chief Consultant, Business Relns (Defence) 2e2 Ltd, 2003–13. Governor: Royal Grammar Sch., Guildford, 1991–2015 (Chm., RGS Foundn, 2004–11); Hoe Valley Sch., Woking, 2016–18. Mem., Guildford Vision Gp, 2016–. *Recreations:* keep fit, gardening, travel. *Address:* 9 Castle Street, Farnham, Surrey GU9 7HR. *T:* (01252) 209037. *Club:* County (Guildford).

**HARTRIDGE, David Charles,** CMG 2001; Senior Trade Advisor, White & Case LLP (formerly Senior Director, White & Case International Trade), Geneva, since 2002; *b* 22 April 1939; *s* of Sidney George Hartridge and Mabel Kate (*née* Hunt); *m* 1965, Dorothy Ann Ling (marr. diss. 1997; remarried 2014); two *d. Educ:* Windsor Grammar Sch.; Oriel Coll., Oxford (MA). BoT, 1961–71; First Sec., UK Mission, Geneva, 1971–75; Asst Sec., DTI, 1977–79; Counsellor, UK Repn to EEC, Brussels, 1979–80; Chef de Cabinet, GATT, 1980–85; Dir, GATT and WTO, 1985–2001, Dir, Services Div., 1993–2001, Dir-in-Charge, May–Sept. 1999; Special Advr to DG, WTO, 2001–02. *Recreations:* bird watching, music, history. *Address:* Hollow Stones, Nailsworth Hill, Nailsworth, Stroud, Glos GL6 0AW. *T:* (01453) 836884.

**HARTWELL, Sir (Francis) Anthony (Charles Peter),** 6th Bt *cr* 1805, of Dale Hall, Essex; marine consultant; Director, International Diamond Drilling, West Africa, since 1999; survey and inspection assignments, oil, gas and shipping services, Lagos, Nigeria, since 2000; Marine Superintendent/Consultant, Peacegate Oil and Gas Ltd, Lagos, Nigeria, since 2008; *b* 1 June 1940; *o s* of Sir Brodrick William Charles Elwin Hartwell, 5th Bt and of his 1st wife, Marie Josephine Hartwell, *d* of S. P. Mullins; *S* father, 1993; *m* 1968, Barbara Phyllis Rae (marr. diss. 1989), *d* of H. Rae Green; one *s. Educ:* Thames Nautical Coll., HMS Worcester. Cadet, RNR. Master's Foreign Going (Cl. 1) Cert. MNI, MRIN. Captain (Master Mariner), 1972. Sea Service Navigating Officer, Asst Nautical Inspector, then Cargo Supt (Overseas Containers Ltd) London, P&O Group, 1958–71; Chief Officer/Master, North Sea ops, Ocean Inchcape Ltd, 1972–73; P&O Cadet Trng Officer, 1973–75; overseas port management, Nigeria, Papua New Guinea and Saudi Arabia, 1975–87; Branch Manager, Lloyds Agency, Dammam, Saudi Arabia, 1987–89; marine surveyor and nautical consultant, Saudi Arabia, The Maldives, Nigeria, Cyprus, 1989–93; Man. Dir, Universal UKI Ltd, Nigeria, 1999. *Recreations:* ocean sailing, scuba diving, photography. *Heir: s* Timothy Peter Michael Charles Hartwell [*b* 8 July 1970; *m* 2002, Diana Katherine, *d* of Ronald McKelvie Sinclair, Edinburgh; one *s*]. *Clubs:* Cachalots-Southampton Master Mariners'; Old Worcester's Association.

**HARTWELL, Prof. Leland Harrison,** PhD; Virginia G. Piper Professor of Personalized Medicine and Chief Scientist, Center for Sustainable Health, Biodesign Institute, Arizona State University, since 2010; *b* Los Angeles, 30 Oct. 1939; *s* of Marjorie Hartwell (*née* Taylor); *m* Theresa Naujack. *Educ:* CIT (BS 1961); MIT (PhD 1964). Fellow, Salk Inst., 1964–65; Asst Prof., 1965–67, Associate Prof., 1967–68, Univ. of Calif, Irvine; Associate Prof., 1968–73, Prof. of Genome Scis, 1973–2010, now Emeritus, Univ. of Washington, Seattle; Pres. and Dir, Fred Hutchinson Cancer Res. Center, Seattle, 1997–2010, now Dir Emeritus. Res. Prof., American Cancer Soc., 1990–. (Jtly) Nobel Prize for Physiol. or Medicine, 2001. *Publications:* articles in learned jls. *Address:* Center for Sustainable Health, Biodesign Institute, Arizona State University, PO Box 875001, Tempe, AZ 85287–5001, USA.

**HARTY, Bernard Peter,** CBE 1998; Chairman, Imerys (UK) Pension Fund (formerly English China Clay Pension Fund), 2000–08; *b* 1 May 1943; *s* of William Harty and Eileen Nora (*née* Canavan); *m* 1965, Glenys Elaine Simpson; one *d. Educ:* St Richards Coll., Droitwich; Ullathorne Grammar Sch., Coventry. CPFA 1966. Accountant, Coventry CBC, 1961–69; Forward Budget Planning Officer, Derbyshire CC, 1969–72; Chief Accountant, Bradford CBC, 1972–74; Chief Finance Officer, Bradford MDC, 1973–76; County Treasurer, Oxfordshire CC, 1976–83; Chamberlain, 1983–99, and Town Clerk, 1996–99, City of London Corp.; Man. Dir, Barbican Centre, 1994–95. Chm., London Pension Fund Authy, 1999–2001. Dir, Dexia Public Finance Bank, 1994–2000; Chairman: London Processing Centre Pension Fund, 2001–03; Alstom Pension Trust, 2004–05. Mem. Nat. Cttee, Information Technol. Year 1982 (IT82); Chm., IT82 Local Govt Cttee, 1982. Chm., Foundn for IT in Local Govt, 1988–91. Chm., Treasury Management Panel, 1991–94; Superannuation Investments Panel, 1994–95; CIPFA; Member: Local Govt Sub Gp, Financial Law Panel, 1993–95; HM Treasury Cttee on Local Authy Borrowing, 1994–95. Chm., Charlton Kings Parish Council, Cheltenham, 2008–10. Freeman, City of London, 1983; Liveryman, Worshipful Co. of Tallow Chandlers, 1984; Founder Mem., Co. of Information Technologists (Hon. Liveryman, 1997). Hon. DPhil London Guildhall Univ., 1997. Commander, Nat. Order of Merit (France), 1996. *Publications:* papers in professional jls. *Recreations:* theatre, music, National Trust, sport. *E:* bernardharty@aol.com.

**HARVERSON, Patrick Richard,** LVO 2013; Managing Partner, Milltown Partners LLP, since 2013; *b* 8 Nov. 1962; *s* of late John and Quinn Harverson. *Educ:* London Sch. of Econs (BSc (Econ) Internat. Relns). Financial Times, 1988–2000: stockmarket reporter; economics writer; NY Correspondent; Sports Correspondent; Dir of Communications, Manchester United FC, 2000–04; Communications Sec. to the Prince of Wales, 2004–13, and to the Duchess of Cornwall, 2005–13. *Recreation:* football.

**HARVEY,** family name of **Baron Harvey of Tasburgh**.

**HARVEY OF TASBURGH,** 3rd Baron *cr* 1954, of Tasburgh, Norfolk; **Charles John Giuseppe Harvey;** Bt 1868; *b* 4 Feb. 1951; *s* of late Hon. John Wynn Harvey (*d* 1989) (*yr s* of 1st Baron Harvey of Tasburgh) and of Elena Maria-Teresa, *yr d* of late Giambattista, Marchese Curtopassi; *S* uncle, 2010; *m* 1979, Margaret, *d* of Cecil Walter Brown; one *s* three *d. Educ:* Eton; Trinity Coll., Oxford. *Heir: s* Hon. John Charles Giuseppe Harvey, *b* 11 May 1993.

**HARVEY, Alan James, (Tim)**, RDI 1991; production designer, film and television; *b* 14 Oct. 1936; *s* of Ernest Harvey and Ida Harvey; *m* 1958, Sheila Todd; one *s* one *d*. *Educ*: Hampton Grammar Sch.; Manchester Univ. (BA Hons Architecture). Designer: BBC TV N Region, 1960–64; Telefis Eireann, 1964–66; BBC Scotland, 1966–69; BBC London, 1969–88; freelance film designer, 1988–; *films* include: Henry V, 1989; Much Ado About Nothing, 1993; Mary Shelley's Frankenstein, 1994; Othello, 1995; Hamlet, 1996; The Magic Flute, 2006; Sleuth, 2007. US Emmy Award, 1974, 1976; BAFTA Design Awards, 1976, 1985, 1987; Design Award, RTS, 1982. *Recreations*: football, Italian language and culture, family. *Address*: 2 Cambridge Court, Clevedon Road, Twickenham, Middx TW1 2HT.

**HARVEY, Prof. Andrew Charles**, FBA 1999; Professor of Econometrics, University of Cambridge, 1996–2014, now Emeritus; Fellow, Corpus Christi College, Cambridge, since 1996; *b* 10 Sept. 1947; *s* of Richard Arthur Harvey and Margaret Frances Harvey (*née* Clark); *m* 1969, Lavinia Mary Young; one *s* one *d*. *Educ*: Leeds Modern Sch.; Univ. of York (BA); LSE (MSc). Economist and statistician, Central Bureau of Stats, Nairobi, 1969–71; Lectr, Univ. of Kent at Canterbury, 1971–77; Vis. Prof., Univ. of British Columbia, 1977–78; London School of Economics: Sen. Lectr, 1978–81; Reader, 1981–84; Prof. of Econometrics, 1984–96. Fellow, Econometric Soc., 1990. *Publications*: The Econometric Analysis of Time Series, 1981, 2nd edn 1990; Time Series Models, 1981, 2nd edn 1993; Forecasting, Structural Time Series Models and the Kalman Filter, 1989; Dynamic Models for Volatility and Heavy Tails, 2013. *Recreations*: football, opera, hill-walking. *Address*: Faculty of Economics, Sidgwick Avenue, Cambridge CB3 9DD.

**HARVEY, Anthony Peter**; Chairman, The Broad Oak Consultancy, 1991–2016; *b* 21 May 1940; *s* of late Frederick William Henry Harvey and Fanny Evelyn Harvey (*née* Dixon); *m* 1963, Margaret Hayward; three *s* one *d*. *Educ*: Hertford Grammar Sch. MCLIP. Dept of Oriental Printed Books, British Museum, 1958–60; British Museum (Natural History): Dept of Palaeontology, 1960–75; Librarian, 1963–75; Head, Dept of Library Services, 1981–88; Co-ordinator of Planning and Development, 1985–88; Head of Marketing and Develt, 1988–91. Director: Natural History Mus. Develt Trust, 1990–91; BM (Natural Hist.) Internat. Foundn, 1990–91. Chm., Heathfield Partnership, 1997–99; Director: Welshpool Partnership, 2002–06; Welshpool Projects, 2007–10. Chm., Geology Inf. Gp, 1975–78, Liby Cttee, 1981–84, Geol Soc.; Chm., N Powys DFAS, 2005–08 and 2012– (Prog. Sec., 2000–03; Vice Chm., 2002–05; Trustee, 2005–08); Member: Printing Hist. Soc., 1965–; Garden Hist. Soc., 1988–; Soc. for Hist. of Natural Hist., 1963– (Treas., 1964–2004; Hon. Mem., 2004–). Trustee: Britain Australia Bicentennial Trust, 1988–; Montgomery Co. Regeneration Assoc., 2002–16; Oriel Davies Gall., 2003–10 (Chm., 2005–10); Montgomeryshire Wildlife Trust, 2004–08 (Sec., 2006); Trustee and Dir, Gwasg Gregynog (Gregynog Press), 2006– (Hon. Treas., 2007–16). Councillor, Welshpool Town Council, 2004–12 (Chm., Finance and Gen. Purposes Cttee, 2007–10, Vice Chm., 2010–11). Mem., Governing Body, Ch in Wales, 2010–12. Freeman, City of London, 1985; Liveryman, Co. of Marketors, 1991–2014. *Publications*: (ed) Secrets of the Earth, 1967; (ed) Directory of Scientific Directories, 1969, 4th edn 1986; Prehistoric Man, 1972; Guide to World Science, vol. 1, 1974; (ed) Encyclopedia of Prehistoric Life, 1979; European Sources of Scientific and Technical Information, 1981, 7th edn 1986; numerous contribs to learned jls, ref. works and periodicals. *Recreations*: garden history and design, transport history, bibliography. *Address*: Oak Cottage, 23 High Street, Welshpool, Powys SY21 7JP. *T*: (01938) 559087.

**HARVEY, Barbara Fitzgerald**, CBE 1997; FSA 1964; FBA 1982; Fellow of Somerville College, Oxford, 1956–93, now Emeritus Fellow; Reader (*ad hominem*) in Medieval History, Oxford University, 1990–93; *b* 21 Jan. 1928; *d* of Richard Henry Harvey and Anne Fitzgerald (*née* Julian). *Educ*: Teignmouth Grammar Sch.; Bishop Blackall Sch., Exeter; Somerville Coll., Oxford (Schol.). First Cl. Final Honour Sch. of Modern History, Oxford, 1949; Bryce Student, Oxford Univ., 1950–51; BLitt Oxon 1953. Assistant, Dept of Scottish History, Edinburgh Univ., 1951–52; Asst Lectr, subseq. Lectr, Queen Mary Coll., London Univ., 1952–55; Tutor, Somerville Coll., Oxford, 1955–93; Vice-Principal, 1976–79, 1981–83. Assessor, Oxford Univ., 1968–69. Ford's Lectr, Oxford, 1989. Mem., Royal Commn on Historical MSS, 1991–97. Pres., Henry Bradshaw Soc., 1997–2007. Hon. Vice-Pres., RHistS, 2003–. Gen. Editor, Oxford Medieval Texts, 1987–99. *Publications*: Documents Illustrating the Rule of Walter de Wenlok, Abbot of Westminster 1283–1307, 1965; Westminster Abbey and its Estates in the Middle Ages, 1977; (ed with L. C. Hector) The Westminster Chronicle 1381–94, 1982; Living and Dying in England 1100–1540: the monastic experience, (jtly, Wolfson Foundn History Prize), 1993; (ed) The Twelfth and Thirteenth Centuries: short Oxford history of the British Isles, 2001; The Obedientiaries of Westminster Abbey and their Financial Records *c* 1275 to 1540, 2002; contribs to Economic History Rev., Trans Royal Historical Soc., Bulletin of Inst. of Historical Research, etc. *Address*: 6 Ritchie Court, 380 Banbury Road, Oxford OX2 7PW. *T*: (01865) 554766.

**HARVEY, Caroline**; *see* Trollope, Joanna.

**HARVEY, Prof. Charles Richard Musgrave**, (3rd Bt *cr* 1933, but does not use the title); retired economic consultant; *b* 7 April 1937; *s* of Sir Richard Musgrave Harvey, 2nd Bt, and Frances Estelle (*d* 1986), *er d* of late Lindsay Crompton Lawford, Montreal; *S* father, 1978; *m* 1967, Celia Vivien, *d* of late George Henry Hodson; one *s* one *d*. *Educ*: Marlborough; Pembroke Coll., Cambridge (BA 1960, MA 1964). Fellow, Institute of Development Studies, Sussex, 1972–2002; Sen. Res. Fellow, Botswana Institute for Development Policy Analysis, Gaborone, 1996–2001. *Heir*: *s* Paul Richard Harvey [*b* 2 June 1971; *m* 2004, Prudence Ruth Daniels; one *s* one *d*].
See also T. C. Harvey.

**HARVEY, Christopher John, (Kit), H.**; *see* Hesketh Harvey.

**HARVEY, (Christopher) Paul (Duncan)**, CMG 2004; HM Diplomatic Service, retired; *b* 21 July 1956; *s* of late Prof. William John Harvey and of Margaret Anne Harvey; *m* 1989, Anasaini Kamakorewa; one *s* one *d*. *Educ*: Royal Belfast Academical Instn; University Coll., Oxford (MA); Downing Coll., Cambridge. Tutor in Geog., Cambridge Centre for 6th Form Studies, 1982–85; joined FCO, 1986: 2nd Sec., Suva, 1988–90; 1st Sec., Brussels, 1990–94; FCO, 1995–98; UK Rep. to Sierra Leone Peace Talks, Lomé, 1999; UK Special Rep. for Peace in Sierra Leone, 1999–2000; Deputy High Comr, Kenya, 2000–03; on secondment to Coalition Provisional Authy, Iraq, 2003–04; liaison officer, Operation Bracknell, 2005; Internat. Security Directorate, FCO, 2005–08. *Recreations*: books, organic gardening.

**HARVEY, Prof. David William**, PhD; Distinguished Professor of Anthropology, since 2001 and Director, Center for Place, Culture and Politics, 2008–13, Graduate Center, City University of New York; *b* 31 Oct. 1935; *s* of Frederick and Doris Harvey. *Educ*: St John's Coll., Cambridge (BA (Hons), MA, PhD). Lectr, Univ. of Bristol, 1961–69; Prof. of Geography, Johns Hopkins Univ., 1969–86; Oxford University: Halford Mackinder Prof. of Geography, 1987–93; Fellow, St Peter's Coll., 1987–93; Supernumerary Res. Fellow, St John's Coll., 2001–; Prof. of Geography, Johns Hopkins Univ., 1993–2001. Guggenheim Meml Fellow, 1976–77. Corresp. FBA 1998. Dr (*hc*): Buenos Aires, 1997; Roskilde, 1997; Uppsala, 2000. Outstanding Contributor Award, Assoc. of Amer. Geographers, 1980; Gill Meml Award, RGS, 1982; Anders Retzius Gold Medal, Swedish Soc. for Anthropology and Geography, 1989; Patron's Medal, RGS, 1995; Vautrin Lud Internat. Prize in Geography, 1995. *Publications*: Explanation in Geography, 1969, 4th edn 1978; Social Justice and the City, 1973, 3rd edn 1989; The Limits to Capital, 1982, 2nd edn 1984; The Urbanisation of Capital, 1985; Consciousness and the Urban Experience, 1985; The Urban Experience, 1989; The Condition of Postmodernity, 1989; Justice, Nature and the Geography of Difference, 1996; Spaces of Hope, 2000; Spaces of Capital, 2001; Paris, Capital of Modernity, 2003; The New Imperialism, 2003; A Brief History of Neoliberalism, 2005; Spaces of Global Capitalism, 2006; The Enigma of Capital and the Crises of Capitalism, 2010; Rebel Cities: from right to the city to the urban revolution, 2012; Seventeen Contradictions and the End of Capitalism, 2014. *Address*: PhD Program in Anthropology, Graduate Center, City University of New York, 365 Fifth Avenue, New York, NY 10016, USA.

**HARVEY, Dame DeAnne Shirley**; *see* Julius, Dame D. S.

**HARVEY, Diane Catherine**; *see* Redgrave, D. C.

**HARVEY, Rt Rev. Donald Frederick**; Bishop of Eastern Newfoundland and Labrador, 1993–2004; Episcopal Vicar, Anglican Network in Canada, since 2014 (Moderator, 2004–14); *b* St John's, Newfoundland, 13 Sept. 1939; *s* of Robert Joseph and Elsie May Harvey (*née* Vaters); *m* 1964, Gertrude, *d* of George and Jessie Hiscock. *Educ*: St Michael's Sch., 1956; Memorial Univ. (BA 1985; MA 1987); Queen's Theol Coll. (MDiv 1986). Sch. teacher, 1956–57; ordained deacon, 1963, priest, 1964; served in parishes: Portugal Cove, 1963–64, 1973–76; Twillingate, 1965; King's Cove, 1965–68; Happy Valley, Labrador, 1968–73; St Michael & All Angels, St John's, 1976–83; Anglican Chaplain, Meml Univ. of Newfoundland, 1984–87; Rector, and Dean, Cathedral of St John the Baptist, St John's, 1989–92. Rural Dean of Labrador, 1968–73; Dean, Anglican Church in N America, 2010–14. Lectr in Pastoral Theol., Queen's Coll., 1984–94; Sessional Lectr, English, Meml Univ. of Newfoundland, 1985–89. Hon. DD: Huron Coll., 1996; Nashotah Hse, 2009. *Address*: 501–7 Tiffany Lane, St John's, NL A1A 4B7, Canada.

**HARVEY, Dr Felicity Ann Hope, (Mrs G. D. Royce)**, CBE 2008; Director General for Public and International Health, Department of Health, 2012–16; *b* London, 6 June 1956; *d* of Charles Harvey and Audrey Harvey (*née* Haslett, later Livingston Booth); *m* 1986, George David Royce; two *s*. *Educ*: Richmond Co. Sch. for Girls, Surrey; St Bartholomew's Med. Coll., London (MB BS 1980); London Hosp. Med. Coll., London Univ. (Postgrad. Dip. Clin. Microbiol. 1983); Henley Mgt Coll. (MBA 1997). MRCPath; FFPH 2003. Hse surgeon, Essex Co. Hosp., Colchester, and hse physician, St Bartholomew's Hosp., London, 1980–81; Lectr, Dept of Med. Microbiol., Royal London Hosp. Med. Coll., 1981–83; Lectr and Hon. Sen. Registrar in Med. Microbiol., King's Coll. Sch. of Medicine and Dentistry, 1983–90; Department of Health: SMO, 1990–94; Private Sec. to CMO, 1994–96; Hd, Quality Mgt, NHS Exec., 1997–2000; Dir, Prison Health, HM Prison Service and DoH, 2000–02; Dir and Hd, Medicines Pharmacy and Industry, DoH, 2003–09; HM Treasury: Director: Prime Minister's Delivery Unit, 2009–10; Performance and Reform Unit, 2011–12; Prime Minister's Implementation Unit, Cabinet Office, 2012. Vis. Prof., Inst. of Global Health Innovation, Imperial Coll. London, 2016–. Non-exec. Dir, Guy's and St Thomas' NHS Foundn Trust, 2016–; Ind. non-exec. Dir, Mediclinic Internat. plc, 2017–. Member: UN Taskforce on Global Health Crises, 2016–17; Ind. Oversight and Adv. Cttee, WHO Health Emergencies Prog., 2016– (Chair). Trustee, Royal Trinity Hospice, London, 2016–. Mem., BMA, 1980. Hon. FRCP 2017. *Recreations*: Scottish country dancing, singing, acting, family pursuits. *E*: felicity.harvey@hotmail.com. *Club*: Reform.

**HARVEY, Dr Helen Lesley**; Headmistress, St Swithun's School, 1995–2010; *b* 7 April 1950; *d* of George Frederick Cox and Olive Cox; *m* 1975, Dr H. Hale Harvey (marr. diss. 1999); one *s* one *d*. *Educ*: Lordswood Sch., Birmingham; Bedford Coll., Univ. of London (BSc); Chester Beatty Cancer Res. Inst., Surrey (PhD). Asst Mistress, Greylands Coll., IoW, 1975–76; Asst Mistress, 1976–89, Dep. Headmistress, 1989–90, Headmistress, 1990–94, Upper Chine Sch., Shanklin, IoW. *Recreations*: sailing, walking.

**HARVEY, Jack**; *see* Rankin, I. J.

**HARVEY, Prof. Jake Burns**, RSA 1989 (ARSA 1977); Professor of Sculpture, Edinburgh College of Art, 2001–11, now Emeritus (Head, School of Sculpture, 1998); *b* 3 June 1948; *s* of George and Nan Harvey; *m* 1971, Penelope F. Proctor; one *s* two *d*. *Educ*: Edinburgh Coll. of Art (DA). *Recreation*: fishing. *Address*: Maxton Cross, Maxton, Melrose, Roxburghshire TD6 0RL. *T*: and *Fax*: (01835) 822650.

**HARVEY, John Barton**; author; *b* London, 21 Dec. 1938; *s* of Thomas Harvey and Helen Harvey (*née* White); partner, Sarah Boiling; one *d*; one *s* one *d* by a previous marriage. *Educ*: St Aloysius Coll., London; Goldsmiths' Coll., Univ. of London (Cert. Teacher Trng); Hatfield Poly. (BA English); Univ. of Nottingham (MA American Studies); Birkbeck Coll., Univ. of London (CertHE Hist. of Art). Teacher of English and drama: Heanor-Aldercar Secondary Sch., 1964–68; Harrow Way Community Sch., 1968–72; Stevenage Girls' Sch., 1972–75. Adaptations for radio: The End of the Affair by Graham Greene, 1998 (Sony Radio Drama Silver Award, 1999); The Heart of the Matter by Graham Greene, 2001; The Frederica Quartet by A. S. Byatt, 2002; (with Shelley Silas) The Raj Quartet by Paul Scott, 2005; The Inspector Chen Mysteries, 2015–18; adaptations for television: Anna of the Five Towns by Arnold Bennett, 1985; The Old Wives' Tale (as Sophia and Constance) by Arnold Bennett, 1988; The Secret House of Death by Ruth Rendell, 1996; dramatisation for stage: Darkness, Darkness, Nottingham Playhouse, 2016. Pres., Bromley House Liby, Nottingham, 2016–. Member: Crime Writers' Assoc., 1990; Mystery Writers of America, 1990; Private Eye Writers of America, 2000; Soc. of Authors, 2008. Hon. DLitt: Nottingham, 2009; Herts, 2013. Cartier Diamond Dagger for Sustained Excellence in Crime Writing, 2007, Short Story Dagger, 2014, CWA. *Publications*: *fiction*: Lonely Hearts, 1989 (adapted for TV, 1992); Rough Treatment, 1990 (adapted for TV, 1993); Cutting Edge, 1991; Off Minor, 1992; Wasted Years, 1993; Cold Light, 1994 (Grand Prix du Roman Noir Etranger du Cognac, 2000); Living Proof, 1995; Easy Meat, 1996; Still Water, 1997; Last Rites, 1998 (Sherlock Award for Best British Detective, 1999); Now's the Time, 1999; In a True Light, 2001; Flesh & Blood, 2004 (Silver Dagger for Fiction, CWA); Ash & Bone, 2005 (Prix du Polar Européen, 2007); Darkness & Light, 2006; Gone to Ground, 2007; Cold in Hand, 2008; Nick's Blues, 2008; Minor Key, 2009; Far Cry, 2009; A Darker Shade of Blue, 2010; Good Bait, 2012; Darkness, Darkness, 2014; Going Down Slow, 2017; Body & Soul, 2018; *editor*: Blue Lightning, 1998; Men from Boys, 2003; *poetry*: Ghosts of a Chance, 1992; Bluer than This, 1998; Out of Silence, 2014; Aslant, 2019. *Recreations*: reading, walking, listening to music, looking at art, going to the cinema, watching Notts County and Spurs, being forever in search of a perfect flat white. *E*: john@mellotone.co.uk. *Clubs*: Detection; Notts County FC Supporters (Hon. Life Mem.).

**HARVEY, Jonathan Paul**; writer and playwright, since 1987; *b* Liverpool, 13 June 1968; *s* of Brian Harvey and Maureen Harvey; partner, Paul Hunt. *Educ*: Blue Coat Sch., Liverpool; Univ. of Hull (BSc Hons Psychol. and Educn). Special needs teacher, Abbey

Wood Sch., London, 1990–93. *Plays for theatre include:* The Cherry Blossom Tree, Liverpool Playhouse, 1987; Mohair, Royal Court Th. Upstairs, 1988; Wildfire, Royal Court Th. Upstairs, 1992; Beautiful Thing, Bush, 1993 (John Whiting Award, 1994); Babies, Royal Court (George Devine Award, Evening Standard Award for Most Promising Playwright), 1994; Boom Bang-a-Bang, Bush, 1995; Rupert Street Lonely Hearts Club, Donmar Warehouse (Best New Play, Manchester Evening News Awards), 1995; Swan Song, Hampstead, 1997; Hushabye Mountain, Hampstead, 1998; Guiding Star, NT, 1999; Out in The Open, Hampstead, 2001; Closer to Heaven, Arts, 2001; Canary, Liverpool Playhouse, 2008; Corrie!, Lowry, and tour, 2010; Dusty, Th. Royal, Bath, 2018; Musik, Assembly Rooms, Edinburgh, 2019; *television* includes: Gimme, Gimme, Gimme, 1999–2000; At Home with the Braithwaites, 2003; The Catherine Tate Show, 2006; Lilies, 2007; Beautiful People, 2008–09; Rev, 2010; Shameless, 2012; Great Night Out, 2013; Coronation Street, 2014–16; Tracey Ullman's Show, 2016; *film* includes Beautiful Thing, 1996; *radio* includes: Take That, Lennon and Sid (play), 1994; What Does the K Stand For?, 2014–17. *Publications:* All She Wants, 2012; The Confusion of Karen Carpenter, 2013; The Girl Who Just Appeared, 2014; The Secrets We Keep, 2015; The History of Us, 2016. *Address:* c/o Independent Talent Management, 40 Whitfield Street, W1T 2RH.

**HARVEY, Kenneth George,** CBE 2011; Chairman, Pennon Group (formerly South West Water) plc, 1997–2015; *b* 22 July 1940; *s* of George Harvey and Nellie Harvey (*née* Gilmore); *m* 1st, 1963, Wendy Youldon (*d* 1982); one *s* one *d*; 2nd, 1990, Anne Model. *Educ:* Urmston Grammar Sch., Manchester; City Univ. (BSc, 1st Cl. Hons Elec. Eng). Student Apprentice, Westinghouse, 1958–63; Southern and London Electricity Boards, 1963–81; London Electricity Board: Engineering Dir, 1981–84; Dep. Chm., 1984–89; Chm. and Chief Exec., NORWEB plc (formerly North Western Electricity Bd), 1989–95. Chairman: Greater Manchester Buses South Ltd, 1993–95; Intercare Gp plc, 1996–2004; Comax plc, 1997–99; Beaufort Group plc, 1998–2004; non-executive Director: Lattice Gp, 2000–02; Nat. Grid plc (formerly Nat. Grid Transco), 2002 (Sen. Ind. Dir, 2006). Pres., Electricity Assoc., 1992–93. Chm., Royal Exchange Theatre Co., Manchester, 1994–98. *Recreations:* sport, gardening, DIY, theatre.

**HARVEY, Michael Llewellyn Tucker;** QC 1982; a Recorder, 1986–2016; a Deputy High Court Judge, 1995–2016; *b* 22 May 1943; *s* of late Rev. Victor Llewellyn Tucker Harvey and Pauline Harvey (*née* Wybrow); *m* 1972, Denise Madeleine Neary; one *s* one *d*. *Educ:* St John's Sch., Leatherhead; Christ's Coll., Cambridge (BA Hons Law, LLB, MA). Called to the Bar, Gray's Inn, 1966 (Uthwatt Schol. 1965, James Mould Schol. 1966; Bencher, 1991). *Publications:* joint contributor of title 'Damages' in Halsbury's Laws of England, 4th edn 1975. *Recreations:* shooting, golf. *Address:* 2 Crown Office Row, Temple, EC4Y 7HJ. *T:* (020) 7797 8100. *Clubs:* Athenæum; Hawks (Cambridge); Burhill Golf.

**HARVEY, Rt Rev. Murray Alexander;** *see* Grafton, NSW, Bishop of.

**HARVEY, Sir Nicholas (Barton),** Kt 2012; strategic management and communications consultant, since 2015; Chairman, Lawthority Ltd, since 2016; Chief Executive Officer, Liberal Democrats, since 2017; *b* 3 Aug. 1961; *s* of Frederick Barton Harvey and Christine Diana Rosalind (*née* Gildea); *m* 2003, Kate Fox; one *s* one *d*. *Educ:* Queen's Coll., Taunton; Middlesex Poly. (BA Hons). Communications and Marketing Consultant: Profile Public Relns, 1984–86; Dewe Rogerson Ltd, 1986–91; Westminster Consortium, 1991–92. MP (Lib Dem) N Devon, 1992–2015; contested (Lib Dem) same seat, 2015, 2017. Lib Dem spokesman: on transport, 1992–94; on trade and industry, 1994–97; on regions, 1997–99; on health, 1999–2001; on culture, media and sport, 2001–03; on defence, 2006–10; Minister of State (Minister for the Armed Forces), MoD, 2010–12. Chair, Lib Dem Campaigns and Communications, 1994–99. Mem., Parly Assembly, Council of Europe, 2005–07. Associate, Global Partners Governance, 2013–; Chm., Joseph Rowntree Reform Trust, 2015–18. *Recreations:* travelling, walking, playing piano, soccer enthusiast.

**HARVEY, Paul;** *see* Harvey, C. P. D.

**HARVEY, Prof. Paul Dean Adshead,** FBA 2003; FSA, FRHistS; Professor Emeritus, University of Durham, since 1985; *b* 7 May 1930; *s* of John Dean Monroe Harvey and Gwendolen Mabel Darlington (*née* Adshead); *m* 1968, Yvonne Crossman (*d* 2014). *Educ:* Bishop Feild Coll., St John's, Newfoundland; Warwick Sch.; St John's Coll., Oxford (BA 1953; MA; DPhil 1960); FRHistS 1961, FSA 1963. Asst Archivist, Warwick County Record Office, 1954–56; Asst Keeper, Dept of Manuscripts, British Museum, 1957–66; Lectr, 1966–70, Sen. Lectr, 1970–78, Dept of History, Univ. of Southampton; Prof. of Mediaeval Hist., Univ. of Durham, 1978–85. Mem., Adv. Council on Public Records, 1984–89. Vice-President: Surtees Soc., 1978–; British Records Assoc., 2005– (Chm., 1995–2000); Dugdale Soc., 2007–. Hon. Fellow, Portsmouth Polytechnic, 1987. Jt Gen. Editor, Southampton Records Series, 1966–78; Gen. Editor, Portsmouth Record Series, 1969–2002. *Publications:* (with H. Thorpe) The printed maps of Warwickshire 1576–1900, 1959; A medieval Oxfordshire village: Cuxham 1240–1400, 1965; (ed with W. Albert) Portsmouth and Sheet Turnpike Commissioners' minute book 1711–1754, 1973; (ed) Manorial records of Cuxham, Oxfordshire, circa 1200–1359, 1976; The history of topographical maps: symbols, pictures and surveys, 1980; (ed) The peasant land market in medieval England, 1984; Manorial records, 1984; (ed with R. A. Skelton) Local maps and plans from medieval England, 1986; Medieval maps, 1991; Maps in Tudor England, 1993; (with A. McGuinness) A guide to British medieval seals, 1996; Editing historical records, 2001; Manors and Maps in Rural England: from the tenth century to the seventeenth, 2010; Medieval Maps of the Holy Land, 2012; contribs to: The Victoria History of the County of Oxford, vol. 10, 1972; History of Cartography, vol. 1, 1987; Agrarian History of England and Wales, vol. 3, 1991; articles in learned jls and periodicals. *Recreation:* British topography and topographical writings. *Address:* Lyndhurst, Farnley Hey Road, Durham DH1 4EA. *T:* (0191) 386 9396. *Club:* Athenæum.

**HARVEY, Prof. Paul H.,** CBE 2008; DPhil, DSc; FRS 1992; Professor in Zoology, University of Oxford, 1996–2014, now Emeritus; Fellow of Jesus College, Oxford, 1996–2014, now Emeritus; *b* 19 Jan. 1947; *s* of Edward Walter Harvey and Eileen Joan (*née* Pagett); *m*; two *s*. *Educ:* Queen Elizabeth's Grammar Sch., Hartlebury; Univ. of York (BA 1st Cl. Hons, DPhil); Univ. of Oxford (MA, DSc). Lectr in Biology, Univ. of Wales, Swansea, 1971–73; University of Sussex: Lectr in Biology, 1973–84; Reader, 1984–85; University of Oxford: Lectr in Zoology, 1985–89; Reader, 1989–96; Hd, Dept of Zoology, 1998–2011; Fellow, Merton Coll., Oxford, 1985–96. Vis. Lectr in Biology, Harvard Univ., 1978–79; Visiting Professor: Harvard Univ., 1980; Univ. of Washington, Seattle, 1982; Princeton Univ., 1984–85; Imperial Coll. London, 1995–. Sec., Zoological Soc. of London, 2000–11. MAE 2007. Scientific Medal, Zool Soc., 1986; J. Murray Luck Award, Nat. Acad. of Scis, USA, 1997; Frink Medal, Zool Soc., 2011. *Publications:* The Comparative Method in Evolutionary Biology, 1991; edited books; scientific papers. *Recreations:* walking, cooking. *Address:* 72 Old High Street, Headington, Oxford OX3 9HW. *T:* 07850 412883.

**HARVEY, Peter Kent;** DL; Chairman, Poole Hospital NHS Foundation Trust, 2001–10; Pro-Chancellor, Bournemouth University, 2011–17; *b* 1 Feb. 1946; *s* of late John Alan Harvey and Joan Harvey; *m* 1976, Wendy Anne Wills; one *d*. *Educ:* Bishop Wordsworth's Sch., Salisbury; Liverpool Univ. (LLB Hons). Articled Clerk, 1968–71, Asst Solicitor, 1971, IoW CC; Asst Solicitor, Bournemouth BC, 1971–73; Dorset County Council: Sen. Asst Solicitor, 1973; Actg Asst Clerk, 1973–74; Dep. County Solicitor, 1974–85; County Solicitor and Dep. Chief Exec., 1985–91; Chief Exec., and Clerk to the Dorset Lieutenancy, 1991–99. Clerk to Dorset Fire Authy, 1991–99, to Dorset Police Authy, 1991–2006. Director: Dorset TEC, 1991–99; Dorset Business Link, 1997–99; Chairman: Dorset Strategic Bd of Young Enterprise, 1996–99; Poole Bay Primary Care Trust, 2000; Chair, Conduct and Competency Panels, NMC, 2012–16. Trustee: Dorset Health Trust, 2000–08 (Chm., 2000–06); Caxton Foundn, 2011–13. Trustee and Sec., Police Partnership Trust, 1997–2005. Hon. DEd Bournemouth, 2018. DL Dorset, 1999. *Recreations:* golf, sailing, gardening. *Address:* White Cottage, Dogdean, Wimborne, Dorset BH21 4HA.

**HARVEY, Richard John,** FIA; Chairman, PZ Cussons, 2010–16; *b* 11 July 1950; *s* of Lester Harvey and Jean Rose Harvey; *m* 1971, Karen Vowles; one *s* two *d*. *Educ:* Univ. of Manchester (BSc Hons Maths). FIA 1975. Personal Pensions Manager, Phoenix Assurance, 1983–85; Mkting Manager, Sun Alliance, 1985–87; Gen. Manager, Sun Alliance Life (NZ), 1987–92; Chief Exec., Norwich Union Hldgs (NZ), 1992–93; Norwich Union: Gen. Manager (Finance), 1993–94; Actuary, 1994; Gp Finance Dir, 1995–97; Dep. Gp Chief Exec., 1997; Gp Chief Exec., 1998–2000; Dep. Gp Chief Exec., 2000–01, Gp Chief Exec., 2001–07, CGNU, later Aviva plc. Chm., ABI, 2003–05. Advocate, 2007–08, Patron, 2008, Concern Universal. *Recreations:* theatre, ski-ing, squash.

**HARVEY, Robert Lambart;** author, journalist and historian; *b* 21 Aug. 1953; *s* of Hon. John and Elena Harvey; *m* 1981, Jane Roper (*d* 2018); one *s*. *Educ:* Eton; Christ Church, Oxford (BA 1974, MA 1978). Staff Correspondent, The Economist, 1974–81, Asst Editor, 1981–83; Columnist and Leader Writer, Daily Telegraph, 1987–91; global syndicated columnist, 2016–. MP (C) SW Clwyd, 1983–87. Mem., House of Commons Select Cttee on Foreign Affairs, 1984–87. Mem., Wilton Park Council, 1984–88; For. Sec.'s Rep., Adv. Bd for Woodrow Wilson Chair of Internat. Politics, 1985–92. Pres., Montgomery Cons. Assoc., 2005–08 and 2017–. *Publications:* Portugal: birth of a democracy, 1978; Fire Down Below: a study of Latin America, 1988; (ed) Blueprint 2000, 1989; The Undefeated: a study of modern Japan, 1994; The Return of the Strong: the drift to global disorder, 1995; Clive: the life and death of a British Emperor, 1998; Liberators: Latin America's struggle for independence 1810–1830, 2000; Cochrane: the life and exploits of a fighting captain, 2000; A Few Bloody Noses: the American War of Independence, 2001; The Fall of Apartheid, 2002; Comrades: the rise and fall of world Communism, 2003; Global Disorder, 2003; The War of Wars: the epic struggle between Britain and France 1789–1815, 2007; (ed) The World Crisis, 2007; The Mavericks: the military commanders who changed the course of history, 2008; Simon Bolivar, 2011. *Recreations:* the arts, films, music, swimming, walking. *Clubs:* Brooks's, Lansdowne.

**HARVEY, Sheila Elizabeth;** *see* Healy, S. E.

**HARVEY, Stephen Frank;** QC 2006; *b* 2 Nov. 1951; *s* of Frank George Harvey and Muriel Irene Harvey (*née* Stancombe); *m* 1973, Felicity Anne Murphy (marr. diss. 2000); one *s* two *d*. *Educ:* University Coll. London (LLB Hons); Inns of Court Sch. of Law. ACIArb. Mech. engrg industry, 1968–70; NHS, 1970–72; legal dept, local authy, 1972–76; financial services, 1976–78; called to the Bar, Gray's Inn, 1979; Asst Prosecutor, Essex CC, 1979–82; in private practice as a barrister, 1982–; Hd of Chambers, 1 Gray's Inn Square, 2013–16. *Recreations:* sailing, fishing. *Address:* 3 Paper Buildings, Temple, EC4Y 7EU.

**HARVEY, Tamara Catherine;** Artistic Director, Theatr Clwyd, since 2015; *b* Mochudi, Botswana, 5 Nov. 1977; *d* of Prof. Charles Richard Musgrave Harvey, *qv*; *m* 2012, William Jared Zeuss; one *s* one *d*. *Educ:* Univ. of Bristol (BA Hons Eng. Lit. 2000). Freelance theatre dir, 2000–15. Trustee: Peggy Ramsay Foundn, 2008–; Nat. Student Drama Fest., 2014–; Gladstone's Liby, 2019–. *Recreation:* watching cricket. *Address:* c/o Casarotto Ramsay & Associates Ltd, 3rd Floor, 7 Savoy Court, Strand, WC2R 0EX. *T:* (020) 7287 4450. *E:* mel@casarotto.co.uk.

**HARVEY, Tim;** *see* Harvey, A. J.

**HARVEY, William Graeme;** naturalist; *b* 15 Jan. 1947; *s* of late Jack Harvey and Grace (*née* Wilson); *m* 1st, 1970, Pamela Garnham (marr. diss. 1989); one *s* two *d*; 2nd, 1999, Pauline Maria Hayes (CBE 2013). *Educ:* Simon Langton Grammar Sch., Canterbury; University Coll., Oxford (BA Geography; MA). British Council, 1969–2000: Tanzania, 1970–73; Indonesia, 1974–76; Personnel, 1976–80; Madras, 1980–83; Educnl Contracts, 1983–86; Rep., Bangladesh, 1986–90; Gen. Manager, Tech. Co-operation Trng, 1990–92; Regl Dir, Eastern and Central Africa, and Dir, Kenya, 1993–98; Dir, Internat. Partnerships, 1998–2000. MBOU. Mem., Records Cttee, Sussex Ornithol Soc., 2011–19. Mem., Editl Bd, Indian Birds, 2007–. *Publications:* Birds in Bangladesh, 1990; A Photographic Guide to the Birds of India, 2002; Tails of Dilli (children's stories), 2004; Atlas of the Birds of Delhi and Haryana, 2006; contrib. UK, African and Asian ornithol and conservation jls and books. *Recreations:* bird watching, conservation, gardening, poetry, 20th century pop music, Coronation Street. *Address:* Pound Farm, Blackham, near Tunbridge Wells, E Sussex TN3 9TY. *E:* billharvey08@gmail.com. *Club:* Madras (Chennai) (Life Mem.).

**HARVIE, Amanda;** Managing Director, The Harvie Consultancy, since 2009; *b* Glasgow, 5 Jan. 1965; *d* of James Harvie and Dawn Harvie; *m* 2015, Gavin Wallace Hewitt, *qv*. *Educ:* Craigholme Sch., Glasgow; Royal Holloway and Bedford New Coll., Univ. of London (BA Hons). MCIPR 1992. Arts mktg consultant, 1986–88; PR consultant, 1988–95; Regl Manager, Prince's Scottish Youth Business Trust, 1995–99; Chief Executive: Aberdeen and Grampian Chamber of Commerce, 1999–2003; Scottish Financial Enterprise, 2003–07; sabbatical, 2007–08; independent business consultant, 2008–09. Non-exec. Dir, horsescotland, 2012–14. Member: Financial Services Strategy Gp, then Financial Services Implementation Gp, Scottish Govt, 2003–07; Financial Services Sector Adv. Bd, UK Trade and Investment, 2006–07; Shadow Chancellor's Financial Services Implementation Adv. Gp, 2009–10. Contested (C) Aberdeen S, 2010. Member: Scottish Conservatives Commn, 2010; Scottish Exec., Scottish Conservative and Unionist Party, 2011–12. Mem., Guild of Public Relns Practitioners, 2006–15. Trustee, Reform Scotland, 2008–10. FRSA 2013. Burgess, City of Aberdeen, 2002. *Recreations:* equestrian sports, the countryside, art, literature, music, travel. *T:* 07710 786807. *E:* amanda@theharvieconsultancy.com.

**HARVIE, Prof. Christopher,** PhD; Member (SNP) Scotland Mid and Fife, Scottish Parliament, 2007–11; *b* 21 Sept. 1944; *s* of George Harvie and late Isobel Harvie (*née* Russell); *m* 1980, Virginia Roundell (*d* 2005); one *d*. *Educ:* Kelso High Sch.; Royal High Sch., Edinburgh; Univ. of Edinburgh (MA 1st Cl. Hons Hist. 1966; PhD 1972). Lectr, then Sen. Lectr in Hist., Open Univ., 1969–80; Prof. of British and Irish Studies, Eberhard-Karls Univ., Tübingen, 1980–2007, now Emeritus. Hon. Professor: of Politics, Univ. of Wales, Aberystwyth, 1996; of Hist., Strathclyde Univ., 1999–2009. Global Horizons Guest Lectr, Nat. Geographic Soc., 2015. Has made broadcasts and TV films. Bundesverdienstkreuz (Germany), 2012. *Publications:* The Lights of Liberalism, 1976; Scotland and Nationalism, 1977, 4th edn 2004; Scotland since 1914, 1981, 4th edn 2016; The Centre of Things: British political fiction, 1991; Cultural Weapons, 1992; The Rise of Regional Europe, 1993; Fool's Gold: the story of North Sea oil, 1993; Travelling Scot, 1999; The Oxford Short History of Scotland, 2002, 2nd edn 2014; Scotland's Transport, 2002; Mending

Scotland, 2004; Floating Commonwealth: the Atlantic world, 2008; Broonland: the last days of Gordon Brown, 2010; Scotland the Brief, 2011; 1814 Year of Waverley, 2013; Dalriada: a novel of the Clyde at war, 2015; Iron Road: the survival and success of the railway, a world account, 2019; Who are we neutral against?: a sequel to Dalriada, 2019; articles in learned jls, Scotsman, Guardian, etc; *festschrift*: View from Zollernblick, 2013. *Recreations:* walking, painting, music, travel by train and ship. *Address:* West Avenel, 50 High Cross Avenue, Melrose TD6 9SU; Llwyn Gog, 4 Pwllhobi Terrace, Llanbadarn, Aberystwyth SY23 3SN; Bert-Brecht-Bau, Wilhelmstraße 50, Tübingen, Germany.

**HARVIE, Sir John (Smith), (Sir Jack),** Kt 1997; CBE 1992; Senior Partner, J. S. Harvie & Co., since 1993; *b* 9 Aug. 1936; *s* of Alexander Wood Harvie and Margaret Isabella Smith Harvie; *m* 1958, Elizabeth Maxwell; one *s* two *d. Educ:* Ibrox Secondary Sch., Glasgow. Served HLI, 1954–57; Founder, J. S. Harvie & Co., 1959; Chairman: Central Building Contractors (CBC) Ltd, 1971–; City Link Developments (Glasgow) Ltd, 1984–. *Recreations:* travel, reading. *Address:* Auchencraig, Mugdock, Milngavie, Glasgow G62 8EJ.

**HARVIE, Jonathan Alexander;** QC 1992; *b* 21 March 1950; *s* of late Anthony Bedford Harvie and of Winifred Jean Harvie (*née* Treliving); *m* 1981, Antonia Mary Lea, *d* of late Rev. His Honour Christopher Gerald Lea, MC; two *s* one *d. Educ:* King's Sch., Canterbury; Brasenose Coll., Oxford (BA Jurisprudence). Called to the Bar: Middle Temple, 1973 (Bencher, 2003); Bahamas, 2004. An Asst Recorder, 1994–2000; a Recorder, 2000–02. Life Mem., Internat. Soc. of Dendrologists. *Recreations:* gardening, racing, golf, music. *Address:* Blackstone Chambers, Blackstone House, Temple, EC4Y 9BW. *T:* (020) 7583 1770. *Clubs:* White's, Pratt's; Swinley Forest Golf; Vincent's (Oxford).

**HARVIE, Patrick;** Member (Green) Glasgow, Scottish Parliament, since 2003; *b* 18 March 1973; *s* of Dave and Rose Harvie. *Educ:* Dumbarton Acad.; Manchester Metropolitan Univ. Youth Worker, then Develt Worker, PHACE West, subseq. PHACE Scotland, 1997–2003. *Recreations:* computing, reading, cinema, food and drink. *Address:* Scottish Parliament, Edinburgh EH99 1SP. *T:* (0131) 348 6363. *E:* patrick.harvie.msp@parliament.scot.

**HARVIE-WATT, Sir James,** 2nd Bt *cr* 1945, of Bathgate, Co. Lothian; FCA; company director; *b* 25 Aug. 1940; *s* of Sir George Harvie-Watt, 1st Bt, QC, TD and Bettie, *o d* of Paymaster-Capt. Archibald Taylor, OBE, RN; *S* father, 1989; *m* 1966, Roseline, *d* of late Baron Louis de Chollet, Fribourg, Switzerland, and Frances Tate, Royal Oak, Maryland, USA; one *s* one *d. Educ:* Eton; Christ Church, Oxford (MA). FCA 1975 (ACA 1965). Lieut London Scottish (TA), 1959–67. With Coopers & Lybrand, 1962–70; Executive, British Electric Traction Co. Ltd, and Director of subsid. companies, 1970–78; Man. Dir, Wembley Stadium Ltd, 1973–78; Chairman: Cannons Sports & Leisure Ltd, 1990–93; A H Ball Gp, then Langley & Johnson, then Medi@Invest, 1995–2002; Oliver & Saunders Gp, 1997–2011. Director: Lake & Elliot Industries Ltd, 1988–93; Penna Consulting plc, 1995–2013; US Smaller Companies Investment Trust PLC, 1998–2000; Wellington Mgt Portfolios (Ire.), 2000–02, and other cos. Mem. Executive Cttee, London Tourist Board, 1977–80; Member: Sports Council, 1980–88 (Vice-Chm., 1985–88; Mem. Sports Council enquiries into: Financing of Athletics in UK, 1983; Karate, 1986); Indoor Tennis Initiative Bd, 1986–89. Chm., Crystal Palace Nat. Sports Centre, 1984–88; Dir, National Centres Bd, 1987–88. Member Management Cttee: Nat. Coaching Foundn, 1984–88; Holme Pierrepont Nat. Water Sports Centre, 1985–88; Mem., Stella Artois Tournament Cttee, 1990–94; International Tennis Hall of Fame: Dir, 1996–2005 and 2006–14; Mem., Exec. Cttee, 1997–2005 and 2006–14 (Chm., 2001–05); Chm., Internat. Council, 2006–11. Mem. Council, NPFA, 1985–90. FRSA 1978. OStJ 1964, and Mem. London Council of the Order, 1975–84. *Recreations:* shooting, tennis, golf, photography, walking. *Heir: s* Mark Louis Harvie-Watt [*b* 19 Aug. 1969; *m* 1996, Miranda, *d* of Martin Thompson; two *s* one *d*]. *Address:* 18 St Mary Abbots Terrace, W14 8NX. *T:* (office) (020) 7602 7353. *E:* harviewattjames@gmail.com. *Clubs:* White's, Pratt's, All England Lawn Tennis and Croquet, Queen's (Vice-Chm., 1987–90; Chm., 1990–93; Dir, 1987–2006); Swinley Forest Golf.

**HARWERTH, Noël,** JD; Chairman, UK Export Finance, since 2017; *b* 16 Dec. 1947; *d* of Ben and Ira Vida Harwerth; *m* 1976, Seth Melhado. *Educ:* Univ. of Texas (BS); Univ. of Texas Sch. of Law (JD). Chief Tax Officer: Kennecott Copper Co., 1978–82; Dun & Bradstreet, NY, 1982–88; Citigroup, NY, 1988–98; Chief Operating Officer, Citibank Internat. plc, London, 1998–2003. Partnership Dir, London Underground, 2003–08; Dep. Chm., 2013, then Chm., Sumitomo Mitsui Bank Europe; Chm., GE Capital Bank Ltd, 2011; non-executive Director: RSA (formerly Royal & SunAlliance) plc, 2004–13; Corus Gp, 2005–07; Logica Gp, 2007–12; Impellam Gp, 2008–11; Alent, 2012–15; Standard Life, 2012–17; London Metal Exchange, 2012–; Sirius Minerals, 2015–; CHAPS Co., 2016–. Dir, Dominion Diamond Corp. (formerly Harry Winston Diamond Corp.), 2008–. Non-executive Member: Horserace Totalisator Bd, 2006–11; Bd, British Horseracing Authy, 2014–. Fulbright Comr. *Recreations:* golf, horse-racing, shooting, opera. *Clubs:* University, Cosmopolitan (New York); Wentworth Golf; Millbrook Golf (New York); Saratoga Golf and Polo.

**HARWOOD, John Warwick;** Vice Lord-Lieutenant of Oxfordshire, 2009–19; *b* 10 Dec. 1946; *s* of late Dennis G. and Mrs W. G. Harwood; *m* 1967, Diana, *d* of late Harford Thomas; one *s* one *d. Educ:* Univ. of Kent at Canterbury (BA Hons); Univ. of London (MA). Admin. Officer, GLC, 1968–73; Private Sec. to Leader of ILEA, 1973–77; Head of Chief Exec.'s Office, London Bor. of Hammersmith and Fulham, 1977–79; Asst Chief Exec., London Bor. of Hammersmith and Fulham, 1979–82; Chief Exec., London Bor. of Lewisham, 1982–89; Hon. Clerk, S London Consortium, 1983–89; Chief Exec., Oxfordshire CC, 1989–2000; Clerk, Lieutenancy for Oxfordshire, 1989–2001; Chief Exec., Learning and Skills Council, 2000–03; Interim Chief Exec., Cumbria CC, 2004; Chm., CfBT Educn Trust (formerly CFBT), 2004–12. Sen. Associate Fellow, Warwick Business Sch., Univ. of Warwick, 2004–07. Chief Exec., Food Standards Agency, 2006–08. Director: N Oxfordshire Business Venture Ltd, 1989–98; Thames Business Advice Centre Ltd, 1989–99; Heart of England TEC, 1990–2001 (Chm., 2000–01); South East Regional Investment Ltd, 1998–2000. Member: Commn on Future of Voluntary Sector, 1995–96; Business Link Accreditation Adv. Bd, 1996–2000; Care Quality Commn, 2010–14. Chair, Local Authorities Race Relations Information Exchange, 1990–2000; Mem. Exec. Cttee, TCPA, 1981–89. Chm., Parrott & Lee Foundn, 1998–; Pres., Oxon CPRE, 2013–; Trustee: Oxfordshire Community Foundn, 1996–2004; Oxfordshire Victoria County History Trust Appeal, 1997–; Northmoor Trust, 2003–10 (Chm., 2005–10); Oxfordshire Youth (formerly Assoc. for Young People), 2011–18; Cogges Heritage Trust, 2011–; Marriott Trust, 2013–; Young Dementia UK Homes, 2013–. Mem. Ct, Oxford Brookes Univ., 1999–2010. DL Oxfordshire, 2001. Hon. MA Kent, 1995. *Publications:* (contrib.) The Renaissance of Local Government, 1995; (contrib.) Understanding British Institutions, 1998. *Recreations:* walking, cooking, gardening. *Address:* West End House, Wootton, Oxon OX20 1DL. *E:* jharwood.cqc@gmail.com. *Club:* Reform.

**HARWOOD, Air Vice-Marshal Michael John,** CB 2012; CBE 2004 (MBE 1995); QCVS 1991; Director: Matrix Blue Ltd, since 2012; Military Mutual, since 2014; *b* Buenos Aires, 29 Oct. 1958; *s* of (John) Alan (Douglas) Harwood and Mavis Verna Harwood; *m* 1981, Cheryl Kay South; two *d. Educ:* Merchant Taylors' Sch., Northwood; King's Coll. London (MA Defence Studies 1996). No 4 Adv. Flying Trng Sch. and Standards Sqn, RAF Valley, 1980–83; No 63 Sqn, RAF Chivenor, 1983–84; No IV (Army Cooperation) Sqn, RAF Gütersloh, 1985–87; Strike Attack Operational Evaluation Unit, Central Trials and Tactics Orgn, Boscombe Down, 1987–92; OC Night, then Sqn Exec. Officer, No 1 (Fighter) Sqn (Harriers), RAF Wittering, 1992–95; Directorate of Public Relns, MoD, London, 1995–96; COS's Outer Office, PJHQ (UK), Northwood, 1996–98; OC No 20 Sqn (Harrier Operational Conversion Unit), RAF Wittering, 1998–2000; Comdr British Forces Operation Bolton, Saudi Arabia, 2000; Station Comdr and Harrier Force Comdr, RAF Cottesmore, 2001–03; ACOS (Operational Trng), RAF Strike Command, 2003–05; Dir HCSC and Asst Comdt (Air), Shrivenham, 2005–07; UK Air Component Comdr and AOC 83 Expeditionary Air Gp, Qatar, 2008; Hd, British Defence Staff US, and Defence Attaché, Washington, DC, 2008–12; British Rep. to UN Mil. Staff Cttee, 2011. Air Experience Flight pilot, RAF Air Cadet Orgn, 2014–. Hon. Prof., Sch. of Politics and Internat. Relns, Univ. of Nottingham, 2014–. *Recreations:* family, bookshops, walking and talking. *E:* mjh.matrix@gmail.com. *Club:* Royal Air Force.

**HARWOOD, Richard John,** OBE 2014; QC 2013; *b* Sutton-in-Ashfield, 30 Aug. 1970; *s* of John and Frances Harwood; *m* 2005, Grainne O'Rourke; one *s* one *d* and one step *s. Educ:* Nottingham High Sch.; Jesus Coll., Cambridge (BA 1991; LLM 1992); Inns of Court Sch. of Law. Called to the Bar: Middle Temple, 1993; NI, 2016; in practice as barrister, 1993–; Mem., Bar Liby, Belfast, 2016–. Dep. Chm., Adv. Panel on Standards for Planning Inspectorate, 2007–10. Mem. (C) Merton LBC, 1998–2006. Contested (C) Bolsover, 1997. Case Ed., Jl Planning and Envmt Law, 2000–. *Publications:* Planning Enforcement, 1996, 2nd edn 2013; Historic Environment Law, 2012; Planning Permission, 2016; (jtly) Planning Policy, 2018. *Recreations:* astronomy, art, history, watching my children play football. *Address:* 39 Essex Chambers, 81 Chancery Lane, WC2A 1DD. *T:* (020) 7832 1111. *E:* clerks@39essex.com.

**HARWOOD, Sir Ronald,** Kt 2010; CBE 1999; FRSL; writer; *b* 9 Nov. 1934; *s* of late Isaac Horwitz and Isobel Pepper; *m* 1959, Natasha Riehle (*d* 2013); one *s* two *d. Educ:* Sea Point Boys' High Sch., Cape Town; RADA. FRSL 1974. Actor, 1953–60. Artistic Dir, Cheltenham Festival of Literature, 1975; Presenter: Kaleidoscope, BBC, 1973; Read All About It, BBC TV, 1978–79. Visitor in Theatre, Balliol Coll., Oxford, 1986. TV plays include: The Barber of Stamford Hill, 1960; (with Casper Wrede) Private Potter, 1961; The Guests, 1972; Breakthrough at Reykjavik, 1987; Countdown to War, 1989; adapted several of Roald Dahl's Tales of the Unexpected for TV, 1979–80; TV series, All the World's a Stage, 1984; screenplays include: A High Wind in Jamaica, 1965; One Day in the Life of Ivan Denisovich, 1971; Evita Perón, 1981; The Dresser, 1983; Mandela, 1987; The Browning Version, 1994; Cry, The Beloved Country, 1995; Taking Sides, 2002; The Pianist, 2002 (Academy Award, 2003); Being Julia, 2004; The Diving Bell and the Butterfly, 2007 (BAFTA Award, 2008; Humanitas Prize, 2008; Prix Jacques Prévert Du Scénario, 2008); Love in the Time of Cholera, 2007; Quartet, 2012. Directed: The Odd Couple, 1989; Poison Pen, 1993; Royal Exchange, Manchester; Another Time, Steppenwolf Theatre, Chicago, 1991. Chairman: Writers Guild of GB, 1969; Council, RSL, 2001–04 (Mem., 1998–2001); Yvonne Arnaud Th., 2009–13; Member: Lit. Panel, Arts Council of GB, 1973–78; Cttee, Royal Literary Fund, 1995–2005 (Pres., 2005–); Cttee, English PEN, 1987–93 (Pres., 1989–93); Pres., Internat. PEN, 1993–97. Gov., Central Sch. of Speech and Drama, 1993–98. Trustee, Booker Foundn, 2002. Hon. DLitt: Keele, 2002; Aberdeen, 2013; Dr *hc* Nat. Acad. for Theatre and Film Arts, Sofia, 2007; Hon. Fellow: Central Sch. of Speech and Drama, 2007; Univ. of Chichester, 2009. Stefan Mitrov Ljubiša Prize, Budra Festival, Montenegro, for services to European literature and human rights, 2000; Nat. Jewish Th. Lifetime Achievement Award, 2014. Chevalier, Nat. Order of Arts and Letters (France), 1996. *Publications:* novels: All the Same Shadows, 1961; The Guilt Merchants, 1963; The Girl in Melanie Klein, 1969; Articles of Faith, 1973; The Genoa Ferry, 1976; Cesar and Augusta, 1978; Home, 1993 (Jewish Qly prize for fiction, 1994); *short stories:* One. Interior. Day.—adventures in the film trade, 1978; (co-ed) New Stories 3, 1978; *biography:* Sir Donald Wolfit, CBE—his life and work in the unfashionable theatre, 1971; (ed) The Ages of Gielgud, 1984; (ed) Dear Alec: Guinness at seventy-five, 1989; *essays:* (ed) A Night at the Theatre, 1983; (ed) The Faber Book of Theatre, 1993; *plays:* Country Matters, 1969; The Ordeal of Gilbert Pinfold (from Evelyn Waugh), 1977; A Family, 1978; The Dresser, 1980 (New Standard Drama Award; Drama Critics Award); After the Lions, 1982; Tramway Road, 1984; The Deliberate Death of a Polish Priest, 1985; Interpreters, 1985; J. J. Farr, 1987; Ivanov (from Chekhov), 1989; Another Time, 1989; Reflected Glory, 1992; Poison Pen, 1993; The Collected Plays of Ronald Harwood, 1993; Ronald Harwood: Plays 2, 1995; Taking Sides, 1995; The Handyman, 1996; Goodbye Kiss, 1997; Equally Divided, 1998; Quartet, 1999 (screenplay, 2012); Mahler's Conversion, 2001; An English Tragedy, 2008; Collaboration, 2008; Heavenly Ivy, 2010; *screenplays:* The Pianist, and Taking Sides, 2002; *musical libretto:* The Good Companions, 1974; *historical:* All the World's a Stage, 1983. *Recreation:* watching cricket. *Address:* c/o Judy Daish Associates, 2 St Charles Place, W10 6EG. *T:* (020) 8964 8811. *Clubs:* Garrick, MCC.

**HASAN, Wajid Shamsul;** High Commissioner for Pakistan in the United Kingdom, 1994–97 and 2008–13; *b* 5 Jan. 1941; *s* of late Syed Shamsul Hasan and Ameer Begum; *m* Zarina Wajid Hasan; one *s. Educ:* Karachi Univ. (LLB 1964); Master in Internat. Relations 1962. Freelance journalist, 1960; joined Jang Group of Newspapers, 1962; Editor, The News (English lang. daily), 1969; Founding Editor, MAG (English Weekly), 1981. Chm., Nat. Press Trust, 1989–90. Press Adviser, 1991–94, Adviser, 1997–2007, to Hon. Benazir Bhutto. TV commentator on S Asia and Middle East. *Publications:* contrib. articles to all major newspapers of Pakistan. *Recreation:* reading. *Clubs:* Royal Over-Seas League, Travellers.

**HASELGROVE, Prof. Colin Cliff,** PhD; FBA 2009; FSA; Professor of Archaeology, since 2005 and Head, School of Archaeology and Ancient History, 2006–12, University of Leicester; *b* London, 1951; *s* of Dennis Haselgrove and Evelyn Haselgrove; *m* 1998, Pamela Lowther. *Educ:* Westminster Sch.; Univ. of Sussex (BSc Hons Biochem.); Trinity Coll., Cambridge (BA Hons Archaeol. and Anthropol. 1974; PhD Archaeol. 1987). FSA 1989. Department of Archaeology, University of Durham: Lectr, 1977–89; Sen. Lectr, 1989–93; Reader, 1993–95; Prof., 1995–2004. Visiting Professor: Ecole Normale Supérieure, Paris, 1997; JW Goethe Univ., Frankfurt, 2003. Mem., Unité Mixte Recherche 8546 CNRS, 1999–; Corresp. Mem., German Archaeol Inst., 2005–. *Publications:* Iron Age Coinage in South-East England, 1987; Reconstructing Iron Age Societies, 1997; Iron Age Coinage and Ritual Practice, 2005; Les mutations de la fin de l'age du fer, 2006; The Earlier Iron Age in Britain and the Near Continent, 2007; The Later Iron Age in Britain and Beyond, 2007; The Traprain Environs Project, 2009; The Later Prehistory of North-West Europe, 2015; Cartimandua's Capital?: The Late Iron Age Royal Site at Stanwick, North Yorkshire, 2016. *Recreations:* gardening novice, French food, wine and markets, reading. *Address:* School of Archaeology and Ancient History, University of Leicester, University Road, Leicester LE1 7RH. *T:* (0116) 252 2611, *Fax:* (0116) 252 5005. *E:* cch7@le.ac.uk.

**HASELHURST,** family name of **Baron Haselhurst**.

**HASELHURST,** Baron *cr* 2018 (Life Peer), of Saffron Walden in the County of Essex; **Alan Gordon Barraclough Haselhurst,** Kt 1995; PC 1999; *b* 23 June 1937; *s* of late John Haselhurst and Alyse (*née* Barraclough); *m* 1977, Angela (*née* Bailey); two *s* one *d. Educ:* King Edward VI Sch., Birmingham; Cheltenham Coll.; Oriel Coll., Oxford. Pres., Oxford Univ. Conservative Assoc., 1958; Sec., Treas. and Librarian, Oxford Union Soc., 1959–60; Nat. Chm., Young Conservatives, 1966–68. MP (C) Middleton and Prestwich, 1970–Feb. 1974, Saffron Walden, July 1977–2017. PPS to Sec. of State for Educn, 1979–82. Chairman: of Ways and Means and a Dep. Speaker, H of C, 1997–2010; Admin Cttee, 2010–15; Member: Financial Services Cttee, 1997–2017; Audit Cttee, 2010–15; Liaison Cttee, 2010–15; Ecclesiastical Cttee, 2010–15. Mem., H of C Select Cttee on European Legislation, 1982–97, on Catering, 1991–97, on Transport, 1992–97; Chm., All Party Parly Cricket Gp, 2010–17 (Hon. Sec. 1993–2010; Pres., 2018–). Member: Home Affairs Sub-cttee, European Cttee, H of L, 2018–; Parly and Pol Sub-cttee, Honours Cttee, 2019–. Chm., Rights of Way Review Cttee, 1983–93. Commonwealth Parliamentary Association: Chm., UK Br., 2010–15; Chm., Exec. Cttee, 2011–14. Chairman: Manchester Youth and Community Service, 1974–77; Commonwealth Youth Exchange Council, 1978–81; Chm. Trustees, Community Development (formerly Projects) Foundn, 1986–97. *Publications:* Occasionally Cricket, 1999; Eventually Cricket, 2001; Incidentally Cricket, 2003; Accidentally Cricket, 2009; Unusually Cricket, 2010; Fatally Cricket, 2013; Politically Cricket, 2016. *Recreations:* gardening, theatre, music, watching cricket. *Clubs:* MCC; Essex CC (Mem., Exec. Cttee, 1996–2008); Yorkshire CC; Middlesex CC.

**HASELOCK, Rev. Canon Jeremy Matthew,** FSA; Residentiary Canon and Precentor, 1998–2017, Vice Dean, 2004–17, Norwich Cathedral; Chaplain to the Queen, since 2013; *b* 20 Sept. 1951; *s* of late Kenneth Pool Haselock and Pamela Haselock (*née* Bolus). *Educ:* Univ. of York (BA Hons History 1973); Univ. of York Centre for Mediaeval Studies (BPhil 1974); St Stephen's House, Oxford (BA Theol. 1982, MA 1985). Deacon 1983, priest 1984; Asst Curate, St Gabriel, Pimlico, 1983–86; Asst Priest, St John, Lafayette Sq., Washington, 1985; Asst Curate, St James, Paddington, 1986–88; Domestic Chaplain to Bp of Chichester, 1988–91; Vicar of Boxgrove, 1991–98; Chichester Dio. Liturgical Advr, 1991–98; Preb. of Fittleworth and Canon of Chichester Cathedral, 1994–2000. Proctor in Convocation and Mem., Gen. Synod, 1995–2010. Chm., Norwich Dio. Liturgical Cttee, 1998–2006; Member: C of E Liturgical Commn, 1996–2006; C of E Liturgical Publishing Gp, 2001–03; Chichester DAC for Care of Churches, 1991–98; Norwich DAC for Care of Churches, 1998–2017; Pubns Cttee, 1988–93, Archaeol Working Party, 1997–99, Council for Care of Churches; Cathedrals Fabric Commn for England, 2003–11; Bishoprics and Cathedrals Cttee, Church Comrs, 2006–13; Council, Guild of Church Musicians, 2001 (Sub-Warden, 2005–11; Warden, 2011–17). Vis. Prof. in Liturgics, 2010–11, Adj. Prof. in Liturgics, 2013–, Nashotah House. Chm. of Govs, Boxgrove Sch., 1991–98; Gov., Norwich Sch., 1998–2017. Chaplain Gen., 2001–04, Chancellor, 2005–08, Bailiff, 2008–11, now Bailiff Emeritus, Order of St Lazarus of Jerusalem (Dep. Ecclesiastical Grand Prior, 2011–13); EGCLJ 2009. FSA 2007. Hon. FGCM 2008. Hon. DMus Nashotah Hse, 2013. *Publications:* (with Roger Greenacre) The Sacrament of Easter, 1989, 3rd edn 1995; (with P. Hurst) Norfolk Rood Screens, 2012; chapters in works on history, art and architecture of English cathedrals; articles, reviews and papers on liturgical and artistic matters. *Recreations:* foreign travel, collecting Oriental porcelain, music and theatre, especially opera, reading, church crawling, conversation, cooking and entertaining, wine. *Address:* 3 The Terrace, Old Ford Road, E2 9PH. *T:* (020) 8980 6087. *Club:* Athenæum.

**HASKARD, Prof. Dorian Oliver,** DM; FRCP, FMedSci; Professor of Cardiovascular Medicine, since 1995, Head of Vascular Sciences, National Heart and Lung Institute, 2004–17, and Head of Immunology and Inflammation, Department of Medicine, 2010–17, Imperial College London (formerly Royal Postgraduate Medical School, then Imperial College School of Medicine) at Hammersmith Hospital (British Heart Foundation Sir John McMichael Professor of Cardiovascular Medicine, 1995–2016); *b* 8 July 1951; *s* of Oliver Patrick Miller Haskard and Anna Caroline (*née* Worthington); *m* 1980, Kathleen Ann Keitzman; three *s. Educ:* Eton Coll.; St Edmund Hall, Oxford (MA; DM 1989); Middlesex Hosp. Med. Sch. FRCP 1994. Res. Fellow, Southwestern Med. Sch., Dallas, 1984–86; Wellcome Trust Sen. Res. Fellow in Clinical Sci., UMDS, Guy's Hosp., 1987–90; Royal Postgraduate Medical School, Hammersmith Hospital: Sen. Lectr in Rheumatology, 1990–94; Reader, 1994. FMedSci 2001. *Publications:* papers on the immune system in vascular disease. *Recreation:* gardening. *Address:* National Heart and Lung Institute, Imperial College London, Hammersmith Hospital, Du Cane Road, W12 0NN. *T:* (020) 8383 3064.

**HASKEL,** family name of **Baron Haskel**.

**HASKEL,** Baron *cr* 1993 (Life Peer), of Higher Broughton in the Metropolitan County of Greater Manchester; **Simon Haskel;** *b* Kaunas, Lithuania, 9 Oct. 1934; *s* of late Isaac and Julia Haskel; *m* 1962, Carole Lewis, New York, USA; one *s* one *d. Educ:* Salford Coll. of Advanced Technol. (BSc Textile Technol.). ATI. Nat. Service commn, RA, 1959. Joined Perrotts Ltd, 1961; Chm., Perrotts Gp and associated cos, 1973–97. An opposition whip, H of L, 1994–97; an opposition spokesman on trade and industry, 1995–97; a Lord in Waiting (Govt Whip), 1997–98; front bench spokesman on trade and industry, on treasury, and on social security, 1997–98. Mem., Select Cttee on Sci. and Technol., 1995–97, 1999–2003, 2007–10; Dep. Chm. of Cttees, H of L, 2002–; Dep. Speaker, H of L, 2002–. Labour Party: Sec., 1972 Industry Gp, 1976–81; Sec., 1981–90, Chm., 1990–96, Finance and Industry Gp. Chm., Thames Concerts Soc., 1982–90; Pres., Inst. of Jewish Policy Res. (formerly Inst. of Jewish Affairs), 1998–2015. Chm. Trustees, The Smith Inst., 1999–2009. Hon. President: Envmtl Industries Commn, 2000–14; Technitex Faraday, 2002–12; Materials UK, 2006–16. Patron: Soc. of Ops Engrs, 2000–04; Chronic Disease Res. Foundn, 2000–05. FRSA 1979. DUniv Bolton, 2007. *Recreations:* music, cycling. *Address:* House of Lords, SW1A 0PW. *T:* (020) 7219 4076.

*See also* J. E. Haskel.

**HASKEL, Prof. Jonathan Edward,** CBE 2018; PhD; Professor of Economics, Imperial College Business School, since 2008; Member, Monetary Policy Committee, Bank of England, since 2018; *b* London, 13 Aug. 1963; *s* of Baron Haskel, *qv;* *m* 1997, Sue Alexander; two *d. Educ:* King's Coll. Sch., Wimbledon; Univ. of Bristol (BSc Econs 1984); London Sch. of Econs and Pol Sci. (MSc Econs 1985; PhD Econs 1990). Temp. Lectr, Univ. of Bristol, 1987–88; Res. Officer, Centre for Business Strategy, London Business Sch., 1988–90; Lectr, 1990–97, Reader, 1997–98, Prof., 1998–2008, Hd of Econs Dept, 2003–08, QMW, later QMUL. Res. Fellow, Labour Econs Prog., Centre for Econ. Policy Res., 1999–; Res. Associate, IZA, Bonn, 2001–. Visiting Professor: Stern Sch. of Business, NY Univ., 1997; Tuck Sch. of Business, Dartmouth Coll., 2012–; Vis. Res. Schol., ANU, 1995. Non-exec. Dir, UK Statistics Authy, 2016–. Member: Reporting Panel, Competition Commn, 2001–09; Competition Decisions Cttee, FCA, 2015–; Enforcement and Competition Decisions Cttee, Payment System Regulator, 2015–. Mem. Council, REconS, 2012–16. Mem., Editl Bd, Economica, 1998–2016. *Publications:* (with S. Westlake) Capitalism Without Capital: the rise of the intangible economy, 2017; contribs to learned jls incl. Amer. Econ. Rev., Econ. Jl, Jl Econ. Perspectives, Rev. Econs and Stats, Canadian Jl Econs, Internat. Jl Industrial Orgn, Jl Industrial Econs, Rev. Income and Wealth, Oxford Bull. Econs and Stats, Economica, Oxford Econ. Papers, Eur. Econ. Rev., Scandinavian Jl Econs. *Recreations:* running, cycling. *Address:* Imperial College Business School, Tanaka Building, Room 296, South Kensington Campus, SW7 2AZ. *T:* (020) 7594 8563, *Fax:* (020) 7594 5915. *E:* j.haskel@imperial.ac.uk.

**HASKINS,** family name of **Baron Haskins**.

**HASKINS,** Baron *cr* 1998 (Life Peer), of Skidby in the co. of the East Riding of Yorkshire; **Christopher Robin Haskins;** Chairman: Northern Foods, 1986–2002; Express Dairies plc, 1998–2002; *b* 30 May 1937; *s* of Robin and Margaret Haskins; *m* 1959, Gilda Horsley; three *s* two *d. Educ:* Trinity Coll., Dublin (BA Mod). Ford Motor Co., Dagenham, 1960–62; Northern Foods, formerly Northern Dairies, 1962–2002. Chm., Better Regulation Task Force, 1997–2002; Member: New Deal Task Force, 1997–2001; Efficiency and Reform Bd, Cabinet Office, 2010–. Mem. Bd, Yorks and Humber Regl Develt Agency, 1998–2008; Chm., Humber LEP, 2011–. Member: Culliton Irish Industrial Policy Review Gp, 1991–92; Commn for Social Justice, 1992–94; UK Round Table on Sustainable Develt, 1995–98; Hampel Cttee on Corporate Governance, 1996–97. Member: H of L Europe Sub-Cttee D, 2003–06, Sub-Cttee A, 2007–12; Select Cttee on Small and Med. Sized Enterprises Exports, 2012–13; H of L EU Financial Affairs Sub-Cttee, 2015–17; Chm., European Movement, 2004–06. Trustee: Runnymede Trust, 1989–98; Demos, 1993–2000; Civil Liberties Trust, 1997–99; Legal Assistance Trust, 1998–2004; Lawes Agricl Trust, 1999–2016. Pro-Chancellor, Open Univ., 2005–14. Hon. LLD: Hull, 1999; Dublin, 2000; Nottingham, Huddersfield, 2003; DU: Leeds Metropolitan, 1998; Essex, 2000; Hon. DSc: Cranfield, 2000; Lincoln, 2003; Bradford, 2005. *Recreations:* writing, only-in-emergency harvest tractor-driver, cricket, Hull City FC. *Address:* Quarryside Farm, Main Street, Skidby, near Cottingham, East Yorks HU16 5TG. *T:* (01482) 842692.

**HASLAM, Andrew Peter;** QC 2018; a Recorder, since 2008; *b* Sheffield, 9 March 1968; *s* of Peter Haslam and Anne Haslam (*née* Spink, now Harbige); *m* 2003, Tracey Samantha Hunt; two *s* one *d. Educ:* Ashville Coll., Harrogate; Univ. of Leicester (LLB Hons). Called to the Bar, Gray's Inn, 1991; in practice as barrister, Leeds, specialising in criminal law, 1991–. *Recreations:* music, squash, family, Leeds United Football Club. *Address:* St Pauls Chambers, 3rd Floor, Park Row House, 19–20 Park Row, Leeds LS1 5JF. *T:* (0113) 245 5866. *E:* aph@stpaulschambers.com.

**HASLAM, Christopher Peter de Landre;** HM Diplomatic Service, retired; Ambassador (non-resident) to Marshall Islands, Micronesia and Palau, 1999–2003; Deputy High Commissioner to Fiji Islands, Tuvalu, Kiribati and Nauru, 1999–2003; *b* 22 March 1943; *s* of late Jack Harold Haslam and Molly Patricia Haslam; *m* 1969, Lana Whitley; two *s. Educ:* Ashley Co. Secondary, Hants. Admiralty, 1960–66; joined HM Diplomatic Service, 1966: Jakarta, 1969–72; Attaché, Sofia, 1972–74; FCO, 1974–78; Canberra, 1978–82; Second Sec. (Commercial), Lagos, 1982–86; FCO, 1986–89; First Sec. (Commercial), Copenhagen, 1989–93; FCO Inspectorate, 1993–96; First Sec. (Commercial and Econ.), Colombo, 1996–99. *Recreations:* reading, lobbying MP and local authorities on current issues.

**HASLAM, Sir David (Antony),** Kt 2018; CBE 2004; Chair, National Institute for Health and Care Excellence, since 2013; Professor of General Practice, University of Nicosia, since 2014; *b* 4 July 1949; *s* of Norman and Mary Haslam; *m* 1974, Barbara Flannery; one *s* one *d. Educ:* Monkton Combe Sch.; Birmingham Univ. (MB ChB 1972). DObstRCOG 1974; MRCGP (Dist.) 1976, FRCGP 1989; DFFP 1998; FFPH 2003; FRCP 2004. GP, Ramsey Health Centre, Huntingdon, 1976–2011. Nat. Clin. Advr, Healthcare Commn, 2005–09; Nat. Professional Advr, Care Quality Commn, 2009–13. Vis. Prof. in Primary Health Care, De Montfort Univ., Leicester, 2000–. Chm. of Council, 2001–04, Pres., 2006–09, RCGP. Mem., Postgrad. Medical Educn and Trng Bd, 2003–10; Co-Chm., Modernising Med. Careers Prog. Bd, 2007–09; Chm., NHS Evidence Adv. Cttee, 2008–13; Member: Nat. Quality Bd for NHS, 2009–; NHS Future Forum, 2011–12. Chair, Adv. Bd, Kaleidoscope Health & Care, 2016–; Mem., Bd of Dirs, State Health Services Orgn, Cyprus, 2018–. Pres., BMA, 2011–12. FAcadMed 2010. DUniv Birmingham, 2014; Hon. ScD UEA, 2016. *Publications:* Sleepless Children, 1984 (also US, Dutch, German, Spanish, Finnish, Swedish, Indonesian, Hebrew, Hungarian, Chinese and Bulgarian edns); Eat It Up, 1986 (also Dutch and Hungarian edns); Travelling With Children, 1987 (also Dutch edn); Parent Stress, 1989 (also Dutch, Finnish and Polish edns); The Expectant Father, 1990, 2nd edn 1998; Bulimia: a guide for sufferers and their families, 1994 (also US and Czech edns); Food Fights, 1995 (also US, German and Chinese edns); Coping with a Termination, 1996; Your Child's Symptoms Explained, 1997 (also Czech, Polish, Romanian and Greek edns); Stress Free Parenting, 1998 (also Bulgarian and Russian edns); A–Z Guide to Children's Health, 1999; (ed) The Guide to Your Child's Symptoms, 1999; (ed) Not Another Guide to Stress in General Practice, 2000; contrib. numerous articles and papers to med. jls. *Recreations:* music, photography, travel; ran London Marathon, 2006. *Address:* Purbeck House, Martinstown, Dorchester, Dorset DT2 9LB. *T:* (01305) 889125. *E:* david@haslam.org.

**HASLAM, (Gordon) Edward;** Partner and Head of Mining, Strategia Worldwide, since 2018; *b* 17 April 1944; *s* of Eric and Marjorie Haslam; *m* 1972, Caroline Rosemary Harrington; three *s. Educ:* King Edward VII Grammar Sch., Sheffield. Man. Dir, Western Platinum Ltd, SA, 1997–99; CEO, Lonmin plc, 1999–2004. Chm., Talvivaara Mining Co. plc, 2007–12; non-exec. Dir, 2011–, Sen. Ind. Dir and Dep. Chm., 2015–, Centamin plc. Pres., Internat. Platinum Assoc., 1990. FInstD 1995; CCMI 2002. *Publications:* Platinum Group Metals and the Quality of Life, 1989. *Recreations:* aviation (holds Private Pilot's Licence), sailing (qualified Yachtmaster), fly fishing.

**HASLAM, Rev. Gregory Paul;** Minister, Westminster Chapel, 2002–16; *b* Liverpool, 13 June 1953; *s* of late Wilfred Haslam and Jean Elizabeth Haslam (*née* Stackhouse); *m* 1975, Ruth Carson Munro; three *s. Educ:* Bootle Grammar Sch., Liverpool; Newton-le-Willows Grammar Sch., Merseyside; Bede Coll., Durham Univ. (BA 1975); Padgate Coll. (PGCE 1976); London Theol Seminary. Religious Educn Teacher, Hindley High Sch., Wigan, 1976–78; Minister, Winchester Family Church, Hants, 1980–2002. *Publications:* Chosen for Good, 1986; Could You Fall Away?, 1988; Elisha - a sign and a wonder, 1995; Preach the Word!, 2006; Let My People Grow, 2006; A Radical Encounter with God, 2007; Moving in the Prophetic, 2009; The Man Who Wrestled With God, 2009; Should Christians Embrace Evolution?, 2010; The Jonah Complex, 2012; Proclaiming Christmas, 2012; If I Had Only One Sermon to Preach, 2013; articles in Evangelicals Now, New Frontiers, Christianity, Cover to Cover Every Day, Closer to God, Daily Bread. *Recreations:* reading, cinema, cycling, motor cycling, walking, apologetics.

**HASLAM, Rev. John Gordon;** non-stipendiary Church of England priest; a Chaplain to the Queen, 1989–2002; *b* 15 July 1932; *s* of Ernest Henry Haslam and Constance Mabel (*née* Moore); *m* 1st, 1957, Margaret Anne Couse (*d* 1985); two *s* one *d*; 2nd, 1987, Marian Kidson Clarke. *Educ:* King Edward's Sch., Birmingham; Birmingham Univ. (LLB); Queen's Coll., Birmingham. National Service, RA, 1956–58 (2nd Lieut). Solicitor's Articled Clerk, Johnson & Co., Birmingham, 1953–56; Asst Solicitor, 1958–62, Partner, 1962–75, Pinsent & Co., Solicitors, Birmingham; a Chm. of Industrial Tribunals, 1976–92, Regl Chm., 1992–96, part-time Chm., 1996–2001. Ordained deacon and priest, Birmingham dio., 1977; Hon. Curate: St Michael's, Bartley Green, Birmingham, 1977–79; St Mary's, Moseley, Birmingham, 1980–96; Hon. Hosp. Chaplain, 1980–88; temp. service as priest in many Birmingham parishes, 1983–96; licensed to officiate, Hereford dio., 1996–. *Recreations:* gardening, steam railways, fell walking. *Address:* 16 Mill Street, Ludlow, Salop SY8 1BE. *T:* (01584) 876663.

**HASLAM, Jonathan,** CBE 1997; FRGS; Managing Director, Haslamedia Ltd, since 2005; *b* 2 Oct. 1952; *s* of Arthur and Irene Florence; *m* 1981, Dawn Rachel Saunders; two *s*. *Educ:* Cowbridge Grammar Sch., Glam; Plymouth Poly. (BSc Hons Geog. 1975); Croydon Coll. of Art and Technol. (HNC Business Studies). MCIPR 1997. FRGS 2010. Mgt Trainee, National Westminster Bank, 1975–79; Information Officer: COI, 1979–82; Dept of Industry, 1982–84; Sen. Inf. Officer, Home Office, 1984–86; Chief Press Officer, then Dep. Hd of Inf., Dept of Employment, 1986–89; Dep. Dir of Inf., Home Office, 1989–91; Dep. Press Sec. to Prime Minister, 1991–95; Head of Inf. and Press Sec. to Minister, Min. of Agriculture, 1995–96; Chief Press Sec. to Prime Minister, 1996–97; Dir of Communications, DFEE, 1997; Dir of Corporate Affairs, London Metal Exchange, 1997–2003; Gp Dir of Communications, Jarvis plc, 2003–05; Chm., The Spokesman, 2003–06. Dir, MIP Communications Ltd, 2008–. Sen. Advr, Smith Square Partners LLP, 2010–. Chm., Friends of Dulwich Coll., 2007–10 (Dep. Chm., 2006–07); Gov., Bishop Challoner Sch., 2007–14 (Trustee, 2014–16). *Recreations:* long walks, photography, travel, reading, golf, music, running for fitness.

**HASLAM, Prof. Jonathan George,** FBA 2009; Professor of the History of International Relations, University of Cambridge, 2004–15, now Emeritus; Fellow, Corpus Christi College, Cambridge, since 1993; George F. Kennan Professor, School of Historical Studies, Institute for Advanced Study, Princeton, since 2015; *b* Copthorne, Sussex, 15 Jan. 1951; *s* of Edgar Alfred Haslam and Marjorie May Haslam; *m* 2006, Karina Urbach; one *s*. *Educ:* London Sch. of Econs (BSc (Econ.) 1972); Trinity Coll., Cambridge (MLitt 1978). Lectr, Univ. of Birmingham, 1975–84; Associate Prof., Johns Hopkins Univ., 1984–86; Visiting Associate Professor: Stanford Univ., 1986–87; Univ. of Calif, Berkeley, 1987–88; University of Cambridge: Sen. Res. Fellow, King's Coll., 1988–92; Asst Dir of Studies, 1991–2000; Reader, 2000–04. Visiting Professor: Stanford Univ., 1994 and 2005; Yale Univ., 1996; Harvard Univ., 2001. Member: Inst. for Advanced Study, Princeton, 1998; Soc. of Scholars, Johns Hopkins Univ., 2010–. *Publications:* Soviet Foreign Policy, 1930–33: the impact of the Depression, 1983; The Soviet Union and the Struggle for Collective Security in Europe, 1933–39, 1984; The Soviet Union and the Politics of Nuclear Weapons in Europe, 1969–87, 1990; The Soviet Union and the Threat from the East, 1933–41, 1992; The Vices of Integrity: E. H. Carr, 1892–1982, 1999; No Virtue Like Necessity: realist thought in international relations since Machiavelli, 2002; The Nixon Administration and the Death of Allende's Chile: a case of assisted suicide, 2005; Russia's Cold War: from the October Revolution to the Fall of the Wall, 2011; Near and Distant Neighbors: a new history of Soviet intelligence, 2015. *Recreations:* foreign languages, music, study of the martial arts, gardening. *Address:* Institute for Advanced Study, Einstein Drive, Princeton, NJ 08540, USA. *Club:* Athenæum.

**HASLAM, Mark Stanley Culloden;** Partner, BCL Solicitors LLP (formerly BCL Burton Copeland), since 1998; *b* Nairobi, 16 June 1957; *s* of Nigel Haslam and Daphne Haslam; *m* 1996, Helen Fiona Copsey; three step *s*. *Educ:* Wellington Coll.; Pembroke Coll., Cambridge (BA Law 1978). Admitted solicitor, 1981; Partner: Claude Hornby & Cox, 1985–95; Magrath & Co., 1995–98. Pres., London Criminal Courts Solicitors' Assoc., 2001. *Recreations:* Rugby, cricket, horseracing, theatre. *Address:* Brook Place, 23 Brook Farm Road, Cobham, Surrey KT11 3AX. *T:* (01932) 864735, (office) (020) 7430 2277, 07976 294270, *Fax:* (office) (020) 7430 1101. *E:* mhaslam@bcl.com. *Clubs:* Brook Cricket, Sandown Park racecourse, Esher Rugby.

**HASLAM, Michael Trevor,** TD 1991; MD; retired consultant psychiatrist and medical director; *b* 7 Feb. 1934; *s* of Gerald Haslam and Edna Beatrice Haslam (*née* Oldfield); *m* 1959, Shirley Dunstan Jefferies; one *s* two *d*. *Educ:* Sedbergh Sch.; St John's Coll., Cambridge (MA 1960, MD 1971); St Bartholomew's Hosp.; Univ. of Leeds (MA (Theol) 2003). FRCP(Glas.) 1979; FRCPsych 1980. Captain, RAMC, 1960–62; hosp. posts, York, 1962–64, Newcastle upon Tyne, 1964–67; Consultant Psychiatrist: Doncaster, 1967–70; York, 1970–89; Medical Director: Harrogate Clinic, 1989–91; SW Durham Mental Health NHS Trust, 1993–96; S Durham Health Care NHS Trust, 1996–98. Hon. Sec., 1986–92, Chm., 1992–2003, Hon. Sec. and Treas., 2006–15, Soc. of Clinical Psychiatrists; former Cttee Chm., RCP. Freeman: City of London, 1973; City of Glasgow, 2011; Liveryman, Soc. of Apothecaries, 1973. *Publications:* Psychiatric Illness in Adolescence, 1975; Sexual Disorders, 1978 (trans. Spanish 1980); Psychosexual Disorders, 1979; Psychiatry Made Simple, 1982, 2nd edn 1990 (trans. Polish 1997); Transvestism, 1993; (ed) Psychiatry in the New Millennium, 2003; Clifton Hospital: an era, 1997; Close to the Wind, 2006; Shrink in the Clink, 2008; Alzheimer, 2009; A History of the Society of Clinical Psychiatrists, 2014; Reggie Raindrop, 2017; Sedbergh Revisited, 2017; articles in learned jls. *Recreations:* writing, music, fives, squash, croquet, travel. *Address:* Chapel Garth, Crayke, York YO61 4TE. *T:* (01347) 823042.

**HASLAM, Miranda Jayne;** *see* Moore, Miranda J.

**HASLAM, Nicholas Ponsonby;** Chief Executive Officer, Nicky Haslam Studio, since 2016; *b* Gt Missenden, Bucks, 27 Sept. 1939; *s* of William Heywood Haslam and Diamond Louise Constance, (Diana), Haslam (*née* Ponsonby). *Educ:* Eton. Asst Art Dir, American Vogue, Condé Nast, USA, 1962–64; Art Dir, Show Mag., NY, 1964–66; owner, Arabian horse ranch, Phoenix, Arizona, 1965–70; worked in film business, LA, 1970–72; Founder, and Dir, Nicholas Haslam, later CEO, NH Design, 1972–2016. Launched singing career initially at Bellamy's restaurant, 2009, followed by engagements at Savoy Hotel, Annabel's, St James's Th. and private venues; released CD Midnight Matinee, 2013. Internat. Interior Designer of the Year, Andrew Martin Awards, 2016. *Publications:* Sheer Opulence, 2002, 2nd edn 2010; Redeeming Features (autobiog.), 2009; Folly de Grandeur, 2013; A Designer's Life, 2014. *Recreations:* history, biography, painting. *Address:* Flat 1, 165 Cromwell Road, SW5 0SQ. *E:* nickyhaslam@email.com. *Club:* Travellers.

**HASLAM, Richard Michael,** FSA; writer on architecture; adviser; painter; *b* 27 Sept. 1944; *s* of Cecil Henry Cobden Haslam and Sylvia Lois Haslam (*née* Assheton); *m* 1980, Charlotte Sophia Dorrien Smith (*d* 1997); two *s* one *d*. *Educ:* Eton Coll. (Oppidan Schol.); New Coll., Oxford (BA 1966, MA 1967); Courtauld Inst. of Art (MA 1969). FSA 1987. Res. Asst to Sir Nikolaus Pevsner, 1969–71; Statistician, 1971–72, and Mem., Lloyd's. Curator, Clough Williams-Ellis exhibn, Heinz Gall., RIBA, 1997. National Trust: Member: Architectl Panel, 1978–2015; Cttee for Wales, 1980–88; Properties Cttee, 1985–2005; Council, 2005–11; Member: Historic Buildings Council for Wales, 1980–98; Royal Commn on Ancient and Historical Monuments of Wales, 1986–98; Stowe Adv. Panel, 1989–; Prize Jury, Premio Dedalo Minosse for commng a building, 1998– (Chm., 2008–11). Trustee, Venice in Peril Fund, 1992– (Hon. Sec., 2011–). Brother, Art Workers' Guild, 2011–. *Publications:* The Buildings of Wales: Powys, 1979, 2nd edn (jtly) 2013; From Decay to Splendour: the repair of church treasures, 1985; Clough Williams-Ellis's Drawings, 1996; (jtly) The Buildings of Wales: Gwynedd, 2009; articles on English, Welsh and Italian subjects in Country Life, Garden History, Arte Lombarda, Perspectives on Architecture and other jls. *Recreations:* walking, Italy, family life. *Address:* Bramley Grange, Bramley, Tadley, Hants RG26 5DJ; Parc, Llanfrothen, Gwynedd LL48 6SP.

**HASLETT, Prof. Christopher,** CBE 2017 (OBE 2004); FRCP, FRCPE, FMedSci; FRSE; Sir John Crofton Professor of Respiratory Medicine (formerly Professor of Respiratory Medicine) and Director, Rayne Laboratories, since 1990 and Director, Queen's Medical Research Institute, since 2005, University of Edinburgh; Hon. Consultant Physician, Lothian Acute Hospitals Trust, since 1990; *b* 2 April 1953; *s* of James and Elizabeth Haslett; *m* 1973, Jean Margaret Hale; one *s* one *d*. *Educ:* Wirral Grammar Sch.; Univ. of Edinburgh Med. Sch. (BSc 1st Cl. Hons Pathology 1974; MB ChB Hons 1974; Ettles Schol.; Leslie Gold Medal for most distinguished grad. 1977). MRCP 1979, FRCP 1991; FRCPE 1988. Jun. med. posts, Edinburgh, 1977–79; Rotating Med. Registrar, Ealing Hosp. and Hammersmith Hosp., 1980–82; MRC Travelling Fellow, Nat. Jewish Hosp., Denver, 1982–85; MRC Sen. Clin. Fellow and Sen. Lectr, Dept of Medicine, RPMS, Hammersmith Hosp., 1986–90; University of Edinburgh: Associate Dean (Res.), 1996–2001; Head, Div. of Clin. Sci. and Community Health, 1998–2001; Dir, MRC/Univ. of Edinburgh Centre for Inflammation Res., Queen's Med. Res. Inst., 2002–09. Vice-Chairman: Res. Cttee, Nat. Asthma Campaign, 1990–94; MRC Molecular and Cellular Medicine Bd, 1994–98; Mem., MRC Systems A Grants Cttee, 1990–92; Chairman: Lung Injury Section, European Respiratory Soc., 1994–98 (Sec., 1991–94); MRC ROPA Infection and Immunity Panel, 1995, 1996. Medal and Prize for Sci., Saltire Soc., 1996; Gilston Lecture and Medal, Intensive Care Soc., 1998; Sir James Black Medal, RSE, 2014; numerous lectures in UK and abroad. FMedSci 1998. *Publications:* (Sen. Ed.) Davidson's Textbook of Medicine, 17th edn 1995, 18th edn 1999; (ed jtly) ARDS—Acute Respiratory Distress Syndrome in Adults, 1997; numerous articles in learned jls concerning inflammatory cell biology and inflammatory lung disease. *Recreations:* Rugby Union (spectating only, these days), contemporary fiction, cooking, eating and drinking (not necessarily in that order), collecting fine wines. *Address:* Queen's Medical Research Institute, 47 Little France Crescent, Edinburgh EH16 4TJ. *T:* (0131) 242 6561. *E:* C.Haslett@ed.ac.uk.

**HASSALL, Craig Steven;** Chief Executive, Royal Albert Hall, since 2017; *b* Australia, 2 Dec. 1964; *s* of Frank Hassall and Brenda Hassall (*née* Zell, now Millan). *Educ:* Univ. of Sydney (BEc). Corporate Inf. Manager, 1987–90, Planning Manager, 1990–92, Opera Australia; Man. Dir, Bell Shakespeare Co., 1993–94; Mktg Dir, Opera Australia, 1995–97; Hd, Cultural Olympiad, Sydney 2000 Olympic Games, 1997–2001; Dep. Gen. Manager, Sydney Theatre Co., 2002–05; Man. Dir, English National Ballet, 2005–12; Chief Operating Officer, Raymond Gubbay Ltd, 2012–13; Chief Exec., Opera Australia, 2013–17. Artistic Advr, London 2012 Olympic Games, 2010–12. *Recreations:* theatre, music, heritage. *Address:* Royal Albert Hall, Kensington Gore, SW7 2AP.

**HASSALL, Eric Ronald,** CBE 1999; FIMMM, FRICS; Deputy Chairman, Coal Authority, 1997–2000; Chairman, British Geological Survey Board, 1994–2001; *b* 16 Nov. 1930; *s* of George Arthur Hassall and Margaret Hassall; *m* 1953, Joan Wilson; two *s* three *d*. *Educ:* Leigh Grammar Sch.; Wigan Mining Coll.; Coll. of Estates Management, Manchester Business Sch. CEng. National Coal Bd, 1947–72; Wardell Armstrong: Partner, 1972–81; Sen. Partner, 1981–91; Chairman, 1991–94. Crown Mineral Agent, 1988–92. Mem., NERC, 1993–98. Dep. Pro-Chancellor, Keele Univ., 2003–08. Pres., IMinE, 1997–99. Hon. DSc Staffordshire, 1995; DUniv Keele, 2009. *Publications:* contribs on mining technology. *Recreations:* golf, sport, reading, engineering, science, painting, family, local history. *Address:* 32 Repton Drive, Newcastle under Lyme, Staffs ST5 3JF. *T:* (01782) 619835. *E:* erhjh@hotmail.co.uk. *Clubs:* Newcastle under Lyme Golf; Little Aston Golf.

**HASSALL, Tom Grafton,** OBE 1999; FSA; archaeologist; Fellow, St Cross College, Oxford, since 1974; *b* 3 Dec. 1943; *s* of late William Owen Hassall and Averil Grafton Beaves; *m* 1967, Angela Rosaleen Goldsmith; three *s*. *Educ:* Dragon Sch., Oxford; Lord Williams's Grammar Sch., Thame; Corpus Christi Coll., Oxford (BA History). FSA 1971. Asst local ed., Victoria County History of Oxford, 1966–67; Director: Oxford Archaeological Excavation Cttee, 1967–73; Oxfordshire Archaeological Unit, 1973–85; Associate Staff Tutor, Oxford Univ. Dept for External Studies, 1978–85; Sec. and Chief Exec., RCHME, 1986–99; archaeological consultant, 1999–; Res. Associate, Inst. of Archaeol., Oxford, 1999–2005. Vis. Fellow, Kellogg Coll., Oxford, 1999–2007. Trustee, Oxford Preservation Trust, 1973–; Chairman: Standing Conf. of Archaeol Unit Managers, 1980–83; British Archaeological Awards, 1983–88; Victoria History of Oxfordshire Trust, 1997–2003; Kelmscott Mgt Cttee, 2000–05; Adv. Cttee on Historic Wreck Sites, 2002–11; Historic Wrecks Panel, English Heritage, 2011–17; President: Council for British Archaeology, 1983–86; Oxfordshire Architectural and Historical Soc., 1984–92; ICOMOS, UK, 1997–2003 (Chm., World Heritage Cttee, 2002–07); Mem., Ancient Monuments Adv. Cttee, Historic Buildings and Monuments Commn, 1984–93. Guest Lectr, Swan Hellenic Cruises, 1981–99. Crew mem., Athenian Trireme, 1987. Hon. MCIfA (Hon. MIFA 1999). *Publications:* Oxford: the city beneath your feet, 1972; specialist articles on archaeology. *Recreation:* boating. *Address:* 80 Rewley Road, Oxford OX1 2RQ. *Club:* Athenæum.

**HASSAN, Dame Anna (Patricia Lucy),** DBE 2006; education consultant, advisor, coach and mentor to head teachers and school leaders, since 2004; Headteacher, 1993–2008, Executive Headteacher, 2008–09, Millfields Community School, Hackney; Executive Headteacher, Daubeney Primary School, Hackney, 2008–09; *b* 16 March 1946; *d* of late Angelo Fusco and Rosa Fusco (*née* Forte), Banbridge, Co. Down; *m* 1971, Nevzat Hassan; one *s*. *Educ:* St Patrick's Primary Sch., Banbridge; Santa Giovanna Antia, Sora, Italy; Assumption Convent, Ballynahinch, Co. Down; Coloma Teacher Trng Coll. (Teaching Cert.); NE London Poly. (BEd); London Univ. Inst. of Educn (NPQH). St Joseph's Primary Sch., Rotherhithe, 1969–78; restaurateur, 1973–79; teacher: St Mary's Primary Sch., Banbridge, 1976–79; Baden Powell Sch., Hackney, 1980–85; Headteacher, Grasmere Primary Sch., Hackney, 1987–93. Tutor, NPQH course, London Univ. Inst. of Educn, 2001–. London Challenge Advr, Aspiring Head Teachers' Wave Prog., Nat. Coll. for Leadership of Schs and Children's Services, 2010–13. Advr to educators in NI, Italy, China, India and Emirates. Hon. Fellow, Gloucestershire Univ., 2005. Member: London Diocesan Bd for Schs, 2012–; Nida Trust, 2012–. Chair, Outstanding for All, Haringey Educn Commn, 2012–13; Mem. Bd, Standing Adv. Council for Religious Educn, Hackney, 2004–14. Governor: Hackney Community Coll., 2003–14; Leys Primary Sch., Barking and Dagenham, 2014–. Chm. Bd, Oak Community Acads Trust, 2014–. *Publications:* (contrib.) Improving Schools, Improve Communities, 2003; contrib. educnl jls and pubns. *Recreations:* trained classical singer, going to opera and theatre, enjoys listening to most types of music, reads historical novels and mystery/detective stories, enjoys all types of puzzles.

**HASSAN, Mamoun Hamid;** producer, director and writer; Dean (formerly Director) of Editing, International Film and Television School, Cuba, 1997–2002, now Visiting Lecturer; *b* Jedda, 12 Dec. 1937; *s* of late Dr Hamid Hassan and of Fatma Hassan (*née* Sadat); *m* 1966, Moya Jacqueline Gillespie, MA Oxon; two *s*. Formerly script writer, editor and director; Head of Production Board, British Film Inst., 1971–74; Head of Films Branch, UNRWA, Lebanon, 1974–76; First Hd of Directing, Nat. Film and Television Sch., 1976–78; Bd Mem., 1978–84, Man. Dir, 1979–84, Nat. Film Finance Corp.; Hd of Editing, Nat. Film and Television Sch., 1993–97 (Gov., 1983–92). Member: Cinematograph Films Council, 1977–78; Scottish Film Production Fund, 1983–87; Consultant, Aust. Film Council, 1984; Advr, European Script Fund, 1989–90; Sen. Consultant for UNESCO,

Harare, Zimbabwe, 1991–93. Visiting Lecturer: UCLA; California Inst. of the Arts; Eur. Film Coll., Denmark; Satyajit Ray Inst. of Film & Television, Calcutta. Films produced include: No Surrender, 1985; co-writer and co-prod., Machuca, 2004; writer, co-prod. and supervising ed., La Buena Vida, 2008; Editing Consultant, My Brother the Devil, 2012; Creative Consultant, Araña, 2019. Producer and presenter, Movie Masterclass, C4 series, 1988, 2nd series, 1990. *Publications:* articles in THES. *Address:* 9 South Hill Park Gardens, Hampstead, NW3 2TD.

**HASSELL, Julia Elizabeth;** see Simpson, J. E.

**HASSELL, Prof. Michael Patrick,** CBE 2002; FRS 1987; Professor of Insect Ecology, 1979–2007, Honorary Principal Research Fellow, since 2007, Imperial College London; *b* 2 Aug. 1942; *s* of Albert Marmaduke Hassell and Gertrude Hassell (*née* Loeser); *m* 1st, 1966, Glynis Mary Everett (marr. diss. 1981); two *s*; 2nd, 1982, Victoria Anne Taylor; one *s* one *d*. *Educ:* Whitgift School; Clare College, Cambridge (BA 1964, MA); Oriel College, Oxford (DPhil 1967; DSc Oxford 1980. NERC Research Fellow, Hope Dept of Entomology, Oxford, 1968–70; Imperial College London: Lectr, 1970–75, Reader, 1975–79, Dept of Zoology and Applied Entomology; Dep. Head, 1984–92, Head, 1993–2001, Dept of Biology; Dir, Silwood Park, 1988–2004; Principal, 2001–04, Dean, 2004–07, Faculty of Life Scis. Vis. Lectr, Univ. of California, Berkeley, 1967–63; Storer Life Sciences Lectr, Univ. of California, Davis, 1985. Non-exec. Dir, Ealing, Hammersmith and Hounslow HA, 1996–98. Mem., NERC, 1991–94. Trustee, Natural Hist. Mus., 1999–2008; Chm., Nat. Biodiversity Network Trust, 2012–. President: British Ecological Soc., 1998–2000; Royal Entomological Soc., 2016–17. MAE 1998. Scientific Medal, Zoological Soc., 1981; Gold Medal, 1994, Award, 2010, British Ecol Soc.; Wheldon Prize, Oxford Univ., 1995. *Publications:* Insect Population Ecology (with G. C. Varley and G. R. Gradwell), 1973; The Dynamics of Competition and Predation, 1975; The Dynamics of Arthropod Predator-Prey Systems, 1978; The Spatial and Temporal Dynamics of Host-Parasitoid Interactions, 2000; research papers and review articles on dynamics of animal populations, esp. insects. *Recreations:* natural history, hill walking. *Address:* Barnside, Buckland Brewer, Bideford, Devon EX39 5NF.

**HASSELL, Hon. William Ralph Boucher,** AM 2000; JP; Proprietor, Hassell Advisory Services, consultants and advisers on community issues and campaigns, 1992–94, and since 1997; *b* 6 June 1943; *s* of John Boucher Hassell and Dorothy Leslie Hassell (*née* Wright); *m* 1974, Susan Vicki Long; one *s* two *d*. *Educ:* Western Australian govt schs; Hale Sch., Perth; Univ. of Western Australia (LLB); Univ. of Reading, UK (MA; Rotary Foundn Graduate Fellow, 1967–68). Barrister and Solicitor; Partner in law firm, Lohrmann, Tindal and Guthrie, WA, 1968–80. MP (L) Cottesloe, WA, 1977–90; Minister for Police and Traffic, 1980–83, for Community Welfare, 1980–82, for Employment and Trng, 1982–83; Leader of the Opposition, 1984–86. Agent Gen. for WA, London, 1994–97; Official Rep., Britain and Europe, Govt of WA, 1997. Dir, Govt Employees Superannuation Bd, WA, 2000–03. Dir, Antares Energy Ltd, 2004–09. Member: Commonwealth Superannuation Complaints Tribunal, 2003–08; Innovation Australia (formerly Commonwealth Industry R&D Bd), 2005–09 (Mem., Engrg and Manufg Cttee, 2000–06; Chm., Automotive Cttee, 2005–09; Chm., Innovation Grants Cttee, 2008–09); Quality Review Cttee, Inst. of Chartered Accountants in Australia, 2008–16. Chm., Liberal Party of Western Australia Pty Ltd, 2006–11. Member: Appeal Cttee, Archbp's Appeal for Anglicare, 1987–94 and 1997– (Chm., 1991–94); Bd, Multiple Sclerosis Soc. of WA (Vice-Pres.), 1990–94 and 1997–; Adv. Bd, Constitutional Centre of WA, 1997–2014 (Chm., 2011–14); Nat. Bd, Multiple Sclerosis Australia, 2013–17. Councillor, 2011–, Dep. Mayor, 2013–, City of Nedlands, WA. Pres., W Australian-German Business Assoc., 2010–14, 2015–16. Hon. Consul for Germany, WA, 1998–2010. JP WA, 1994–. Chm., Order of Australia Assoc., WA Br., 2015–18. Centenary Medal, Australia, 2003; Cross, Order of Merit (Germany), 2009. *Publications:* Parliamentary newsletter, 1987–90; various articles. *Recreations:* bridge, tennis, reading. *Address:* 20 Loneragan Street, Nedlands, WA 6009, Australia. *T:* (8) 93809991. *E:* wrbhassell@gmail.com. *Clubs:* Weld (Perth); Dalkeith Tennis.

**HASTE, Norman David,** OBE 1997; FREng; FICE; consultant in project management in energy sector, since 2013; *b* 4 Nov. 1944; *s* of Jack Haste and Edith Eleanor Haste (*née* Jarvis); *m* 1968, Judith Ann Graham; two *d*. *Educ:* Royal Coll. of Advanced Technol., Salford. FICE 1984; FREng (FEng 1996); FCIHT (FIHT 1996). Contracts Manager, McConnell Dowell SE Asia (Singapore), 1981–84; John Laing Construction Ltd: Dir, Special Projects, 1984–85; Project Director: Main Civil Engrg Works, Sizewell B Power Station, 1985–90; Second Severn Crossing, 1990–95; Terminal 5, Heathrow Airport, 1996–2002; Chief Exec., Cross London Rail Links, 2002–05; Ops Dir, High-Point Rendel, 2005–06; Chief Operating Officer, Laing O'Rourke Middle E and S Asia, 2006–09; Laing O'Rourke: Advr on Nuclear New Build, 2009–11; Exec. Dir, Nuclear New Build, 2011–12. Chm., Severn River Crossing PLC, 2000–06. Dir, Transnet, South Africa, 2006–10. Non-exec. Dir, C. Spencer Ltd (Hull), 2013–16, Advr, Spencer Gp, 2016; Adv. role on ITER project, Fusion for Energy, 2015–18. Pres., Smeatonian Soc. of Civil Engrs, 2019. Trustee, RAEng, 2015–18. Hon. DEng West of England, 1997; Hon. DSc: Salford, 1998; Hull, 2013. *Recreations:* golf, music, theatre.

**HASTIE, Prof. Nicholas Dixon,** CBE 2006; PhD; FMedSci; FRS 2002; FRSE; Member, Scientific Staff, Medical Research Council Human Genetics Unit, Edinburgh, since 1982 (Director, 1994–2015); Director of Academic Development, Medical Research Council Institute of Genetics and Molecular Medicine, Edinburgh, since 2016 (inaugural Director, 2007–16); *b* 29 March 1947; *s* of Duncan Sidney Hastie and Eleanor Stella Hastie; *m* 1975, Alison Clayton Todd; one *s* one *d*. *Educ:* Colwyn Bay Grammar Sch.; Univ. of Liverpool (BSc 1969); King's Coll., Cambridge (PhD 1973). FRSE 1993. Res. Fellow, Edinburgh Univ., 1973–75; Cancer Res. Scientist and Associate Res. Prof., Roswell Park Meml Inst., Buffalo, USA, 1975–82. Hon. Prof., Univ. of Edinburgh, 1993; Internat. Res. Schol., Howard Hughes Med. Inst., 1992–97. Eur. Ed., Genes & Develt, 1991–97. Mem., EMBO, 1990. Member: Scientific Adv. Bd, Inst. of Molecular Pathol., Vienna, 1993–2000; Molecular and Cellular Medicine Bd, 1996–2000, Strategy Develt Gp, 1996–99, MRC; Scientific Adv. Cttee, Lister Inst., 1997; Internat. Scientific Adv. Bd, Develtl Genetics Prog., Sheffield, 2000; Cancer Res. UK Scientific Exec. Bd, 2002; Chairman, Scientific Advisory Board: Wellcome Trust Centre for Human Genetics, Oxford, 2000–; Wellcome Trust, Sanger Inst., 2004–10; Chm., Adv. Bd, Cambridge Inst. of Medical Res., 2000. Numerous distinguished lectures. Charter Fellow, Molecular Medicine Soc., 1996; FMedSci 1998. Gov., Beatson Cancer Res. Inst., 1999. Hon. DSc: Edinburgh, 2005; Dundee, 2014; Hon. DM Sheffield, 2014. Genetics Soc. Medal, 2008. *Publications:* contrib. numerous papers to various internat. jls incl. Nature, Cell and Science. *Recreations:* reading, gardening, cooking, travelling, walking, gym. *Address:* MRC Institute of Genetics and Molecular Medicine, University of Edinburgh, Crewe Road, Edinburgh EH4 2XU. *T:* (0131) 467 8401.

**HASTIE, Sir Robert (Cameron),** KCVO 2008; CBE 1983; RD 1968 (Bar 1978); JP; Chairman, Bernard Hastie & Co. Ltd, UK and Australia, 1973–2008; Lord-Lieutenant, West Glamorgan, 1995–2008 (Vice Lord-Lieutenant, 1991–95); *b* Swansea, 24 May 1933; *s* of B. H. C. Hastie and M. H. Hastie; *m* 1961, Mary Griffiths; two *s* one *d*. *Educ:* Bromsgrove Sch. Joined RN, National Service, 1951; Midshipman 1953; qual. RNR Ocean comd, 1963; progressive ranks to Captain RNR, 1974, in comd HMS Cambria, 1974–77; Aide-de-Camp to the Queen, 1977; Commodore RNR 1979–82. Pres., Swansea Unit Sea Cadet Corps, 1982–96. Chairman: Mumbles Lifeboat Station Cttee, 1987–95; Milford Haven Port Authy, 1994–2000. Mem., W Wales Cttee, CBI, 1982–96; Vice Pres., RNLI, 1999– (Mem. Council, 1991–2006; Trustee and Dep. Treas., 1999–2004). President: Glam W Area Scout Council, 1995–2008 (Chm., 1989–96); RFCA Wales, 2005–08. DL West Glamorgan, 1974; JP Swansea, 1989; High Sheriff of W Glamorgan County, 1977–78. KStJ 2006 (CStJ 1996). *Recreations:* farming, sailing, shooting. *Address:* Upper Hareslade Farm, Bishopston, Swansea SA3 3BU. *T:* (01792) 232957. *Clubs:* Naval; Royal Naval Sailing Association (Portsmouth); Bristol Channel Yacht (Swansea); Royal Sydney Yacht Squadron (Sydney, Aust.).

**HASTIE, Robert David;** Artistic Director, Sheffield Theatres, since 2016; *b* Scarborough, 27 July 1977; *s* of David and Janet Hastie. *Educ:* Scarborough Coll.; Peterhouse, Cambridge (MA); Royal Acad. of Dramatic Art (BA). Actor with NT, RSC, Chichester Fest. Th., Sheffield Ths and Lamb Players; Associate Dir, Donmar Warehouse, 2014–19. Plays directed include: My Night With Reg, Donmar Warehouse, 2014; Breaking the Code, Manchester Royal Exchange, 2016; Julius Caesar, Sheffield Crucible, 2017; Macbeth, Globe, 2018; Standing at the Sky's Edge, Sheffield Crucible, 2019. *Address:* Sheffield Theatres Trust, 55 Norfolk Street, Sheffield S1 1DA. *T:* (0114) 249 5999.

**HASTIE-SMITH, Richard Maybury,** CB 1984; FIPD 1986; Chairman: Incorporated Froebel Educational Institute, 1993–2003; Templeton Estates Ltd, 1994–2003; *b* 13 Oct. 1931; *s* of Engr-Comdr D. Hastie-Smith and H. I. Hastie-Smith; *m* 1956, Bridget Noel Cox; one *s* two *d*. *Educ:* Cranleigh Sch. (Schol.); Magdalene Coll., Cambridge (Schol.; MA). HM Forces, commnd Queen's Royal Regt, 1950–51. Entered Administrative Class, Home CS, War Office, 1955; Private Sec. to Permanent Under-Sec., 1957; Asst Private Sec. to Sec. of State, 1958; Principal, 1960; Asst Private Sec. to Sec. of State for Defence, 1965; Private Sec. to Minister of Defence (Equipment), 1968; Asst Sec., 1969; RCDS, 1974; Under-Sec., MoD, 1975, Cabinet Office, 1979–81; Dep. Under-Sec. of State, MoD, 1981–91. Mem., Civil Service Appeal Bd, 1992–99; Non-Service Mem., Home Office Assessment Consultancy Unit for police, prison and fire services, 1992–2003. Chm. Council, Cranleigh and Bramley Schs, 1993–99; Mem. Council, Surrey Univ. Roehampton (formerly Roehampton Inst.), 1993–2003. Chm., 1983–94, Vice-Pres., 1994–, Magdalene Coll. Assoc. *Address:* 18 York Avenue, East Sheen, SW14 7LG. *T:* (020) 8876 4597.

See also Rev. T. M. Hastie-Smith.

**HASTIE-SMITH, Rev. Timothy Maybury;** Team Vicar, Bibury with Winson, and Barnsley, Gloucestershire, since 2014; National Director, Scripture Union, 2010–19; *b* London, 8 March 1962; *s* of Richard Maybury Hastie-Smith, *qv*; *m* 1987, Joanne Elizabeth, *e d* of David Ide and late Marion Ide; one *s* two *d*. *Educ:* Cranleigh Sch. (St Nicholas Scholar); Magdalene Coll., Cambridge (BA 1984); Wycliffe Hall, Oxford (Cert. Theol. 1988). Lay Chaplain, Felsted Sch., 1984–85; ordained deacon, 1988, priest, 1989; Asst Curate, St Ebbe's with Holy Trinity and St Peter-le-Bailey, Oxford, 1988–91; Sen. Chaplain and Admissions Tutor, Stowe Sch., 1991–98; Headmaster, Dean Close Sch., Cheltenham, 1998–2008; Vicar of Kempsford, Glos, 2009–14. Prin. Consultant, Perrett Laver, 2009–10. Dir, Knockout Ltd, 1987–90. Chairman: TISCA, 2001–07; HMC West, 2007–08; HMC, 2008. Trustee: Havelock Trust, 2009–14; David Ross Educnl Trust, 2010–14. Governor: St Hugh's Sch., Woodhall Spa, 1995–2001; Orwell Park Sch., 1997–2003; Aldro Sch., 1997–2011; Hatherop Castle Sch., 1998–2011; Blue Coat Sch., Birmingham, 1999–2006; Beachborough Sch., 2000–07; Swanbourne House Sch., 2000–14; Winterfold House, 2004–08; Bibury C of E Primary Sch., 2015–. Fellow, Univ. of Gloucestershire, 1998. Freeman, Haberdashers' Co., 2012–. *Recreations:* theatre, reading, psephology, cinema, chicken husbandry, Gloucester RUFC, travel, Tottenham Hotspur, an extremely energetic Labrador. *Address:* The Vicarage, Bibury, Cirencester, Glos GL7 5NT. *T:* (01285) 740301. *E:* tim.hastie-smith@hotmail.com. *Clubs:* Coningsby, East India, National, Carlton.

**HASTILOW, Nigel Graham;** journalist and writer; *b* 22 Feb. 1956; *s* of late Michael Alexander Hastilow; *m* 1980, Fiona Mary Findlay. *Educ:* Mill Hill Sch.; Birmingham Univ. (BA Eng. Lang. and Lit.). Reporter: Solihull News, 1978–80; Evening Mail, Birmingham, 1980–85; Mktg Manager, Birmingham Post & Mail Ltd, 1985–87; Birmingham Post: Political Editor, 1987–90; Asst Editor, 1990–91; Dep. Editor, 1991–92; Exec. Editor, 1992–93; Editor, 1993–99; W Midlands Dir, Inst. of Dirs, 2000–01; W Midlands Regl Dir, 2001–11, Dir of Enterprise, 2011–18, Inst. of Chartered Accts; Editl Dir, Heart Media Gp, 2003–05. Contested (C), Birmingham, Edgbaston, 2001. *Publications:* The Last of England, 2004; Tomorrow's England, 2008; The Smoking Gun, 2011; Murder on the Brussels Express, 2014; The Trials of Eldred Pottinger, 2019. *Recreations:* usual sporting and cultural interests, air guitar. *Address:* Corner Cottage, Manor Road, Wickhamford, Worcs WR11 7SA.

**HASTINGS;** see Abney-Hastings, family name of Earl of Loudoun.

**HASTINGS,** family name of **Baron Hastings of Scarisbrick**.

**HASTINGS,** 23rd Baron *cr* 1290; **Delaval Thomas Harold Astley;** Bt 1660; *b* 25 April 1960; *er s* of 22nd Baron Hastings and Catherine Rosaline Ratcliffe (*née* Hinton); *S* father, 2007; *m* 1987, Veronica, *er d* of Richard Smart; one *s* two *d*. *Educ:* Radley; Durham Univ. *Heir: s* Hon. Jacob Astley, *b* 5 Sept. 1991.

**HASTINGS OF SCARISBRICK,** Baron *cr* 2005 (Life Peer), of Scarisbrick in the County of Lancashire; **Michael John Hastings,** CBE 2002; Global Head of Corporate Citizenship and Diversity, KPMG, since 2006; *b* 29 Jan. 1958; *s* of Petain and Olive Hastings; *m* 1990, Jane; one *s* two *d*. *Educ:* Scarisbrick Hall Sch., Lancs; London Bible Coll. (BA (Hons)); Westminster Coll., Oxford (PGCE). Teacher (Hd of Religious Studies), 1981–85; Govt Policy Consultant, 1985–90; presenter and reporter: TV AM and GMTV, 1990–94; BBC SE, 1994–95; Hd of Public Affairs, 1996–2003, Hd of Corporate Social Responsibility, 2003–06, BBC; Hd of Corporate Social Responsibility, KPMG, 2006. Non-exec. Dir, British Telecom (Community Support Cttee), 2004– (Mem., Responsible Business Bd). Comr, CRE, 1993–2001. Vice Pres., UNICEF UK. Chm., Millennium Promise UK. Trustee: Crime Concern, 1988–2008 (Chm., 1995–2008); Vodafone Gp Foundn, 2008–. Patron: Springboard for Children, 2005– (Chm., 1992–98); ZANE, 2005–. Chancellor, Regent's Univ. London, 2017–. *Recreations:* cycling, country walking, cinema, friends. *Address:* House of Lords, SW1A 0PW.

**HASTINGS, Archdeacon of;** see Dowler, Ven. R. E. M.

**HASTINGS, Alfred James,** CB 1999; Clerk of the Journals, House of Commons, 1991–2001; *b* 10 Feb. 1938; *s* of William Hastings and Letitia (*née* Loveridge); *m* 1972, Susan Edge; three *s*. *Educ:* Leamington College; New College, Oxford (MA). A Clerk of the House of Commons, 1960–2001: Registrar of Members' Interests, 1987–91; Clerk of the Cttee of Privileges, and subseq. of the Cttee on Standards and Privileges, 1991–97; Commons Clerk, Jt Cttee on Parly Privilege, 1997–99. *Recreations:* music, high fidelity sound reproduction. *Address:* 26 Feilden Grove, Headington, Oxford OX3 0DU.

**HASTINGS, Alison Jane;** media consultant, since 2002; Specialist Partner, Alder Media, since 2015; *b* 14 Aug. 1965; *d* of Len and Jackie Hastings; one *d*; *m* 2007, Dr David Fleming, *qv*; one *d*, and two step *s* one step *d. Educ:* Folkestone Girls' Grammar Sch.; Canterbury Coll.; Harlow Coll. (Nat. Council for Trng in Journalism). Hd, Editl Staff Develt, Thomson Regl newspapers, 1994–95; Dep. Ed., 1995–96, Ed., 1996–2002, Newcastle Evening Chronicle. Member: Press Complaints Commn, 1998–2002; Gambling Commn, 2015–. Non-executive Director: Clatterbridge Cancer Centre, 2012–; Archant, 2016–; Mobatility Operations plc, 2018–. Member: Adv. Bd, Pagefield Communications, 2015–; Expert Adv. Bd, Sharing Economy, 2016–. Mem. Council, Durham Univ., 2015–. Trustee, BBC Trust, 2006–14; Mem., Press Assoc. Trust, 2016–. Vice Pres., British Bd of Film Classification, 2008–18. *Recreations:* time with family, travelling, reading, watching films. *E:* alisonhastingsmedia@aol.com.

**HASTINGS, Sir Max (Macdonald),** Kt 2002; FRSL; author and journalist; *b* 28 Dec. 1945; *s* of late Macdonald Hastings and Anne Scott James, author and journalist; *m* 1st, 1972, Patricia Mary Edmondson (marr. diss. 1994); one *s* one *d* (and one *s* decd); 2nd, 1999, Mrs Penny Grade. *Educ:* Charterhouse (Scholar); University Coll., Oxford (Exhibnr). Researcher, BBC TV Great War series, 1963–64; Reporter, Evening Standard, 1965–67; Fellow, US World Press Inst., 1967–68; Roving Correspondent, Evening Standard, 1968–70; Reporter, BBC TV Current Affairs, 1970–73; Editor, Evening Standard Londoner's Diary, 1976–77; Columnist, Daily Express, 1981–83; columnist, Sunday Times, 1985–86; Editor, The Daily Telegraph, 1986–95; Dir, 1989–95, Editor-in-Chief, 1990–95, The Daily Telegraph plc; Editor, The Evening Standard, 1996–2002; contributor, Daily Mail, 2002–18; Contrib. Ed., Financial Times, 2009–13; contributor, The Times, 2018–; Reviewer: Sunday Times, 2002–; NY Review of Books, 2002–. As War Correspondent, covered Middle East, Indochina, Angola, India-Pakistan, Cyprus, Rhodesia and S Atlantic. Mem., Press Complaints Commn, 1991–92. Churchill Fellow, Westminster Coll., Fulton, Mo, 2011. TV documentaries: Ping-Pong in Peking, 1971; The War about Peace, 1983; Alarums and Exercursions, 1984; Cold Comfort Farm, 1985; The War in Korea (series), 1988; We Are All Green Now, 1990; Spies, in series Cold War, CNN, 1998; Hitler's Germany, 2000; The Falklands: reluctant heroes, 2002; Winston's War, 2003; The Falklands Legacy, 2012; The Necessary War, 2014. President: CPRE, 2002–07; Sir Walter Scott Soc. of Edinburgh, 2012–13. Trustee: Nat. Portrait Gall., 1995–2004; Game Conservancy, 2014–18 (Vice Pres., 1992). Patron, Labrador Rescue Trust, 2017–. Liddell-Hart Lecture, KCL, 1994; Mountbatten Lecture, Edinburgh Univ., 2004; Leonard Stein Lectures, Oxford Univ., 2009. FRHistS 1988; FRSL 1996. Hon FKC, 2004. Hon. DLitt: Leicester, 1992; Nottingham, 2005. Journalist of the Year, British Press Awards, 1982 (cited 1973 and 1980); What The Papers Say, Granada TV: Reporter of the Year, 1982; Editor of the Year, 1988; Duke of Westminster Medal for military literature, RUSI, 2008; Literary Award for Lifetime Achievement, Chicago Pritzker Library, 2012; Friuladria Prize, Gorizia Internat. Hist. Fest., 2014. *Publications:* America 1968: the fire this time, 1968; Ulster 1969: the struggle for civil rights in Northern Ireland, 1970; Montrose: the King's champion, 1977; Yoni: the hero of Entebbe, 1979; Bomber Command, 1979 (Somerset Maugham Award for Non-Fiction, 1980); (with Len Deighton) The Battle of Britain, 1980; Das Reich, 1981; (with Simon Jenkins) The Battle for The Falklands, 1983 (Yorkshire Post Book of the Year Award); Overlord: D-Day and the battle for Normandy, 1984 (Yorkshire Post Book of the Year Award); Victory in Europe, 1985; (ed) Oxford Book of Military Anecdotes, 1985; The Korean War, 1987; Outside Days, 1989; Scattered Shots, 1999; Going to the Wars, 2000; Editor, 2002; Armageddon, 2004; Warriors, 2005; Country Fair, 2005; Nemesis, 2007; Finest Years, 2009; Did You Really Shoot the Television?: a family fable, 2010; All Hell Let Loose, 2011 (RUSI Duke of Westminster Medal for Military Literature, 2012); Catastrophe: Europe goes to war 1914, 2013; The Secret War, 2015; Vietnam: an epic tragedy 1945–1975, 2018; Chastise: the Dambusters' story 1943, 2019. *Recreations:* shooting, fishing. *Address:* c/o The Wylie Agency, 17 Bedford Square, WC1B 3JA. *Club:* Brooks's.

**HASTINGS, Dr Michael Harvey,** FRS 2010; FMedSci; Research Scientist and Group Leader in Circadian Neurobiology, since 2001, and Head, Division of Neurobiology, since 2016, Medical Research Council Laboratory of Molecular Biology; *b* Sheffield, 10 June 1956; *s* of Harvey Hastings and Susan Hastings (née Binks); *m* 1986, Angela Charlotte Roberts; one *s* two *d. Educ:* Abbeydale Boys' Grammar Sch., Sheffield; Univ. of Liverpool (BSc Marine Biol. 1977; PhD Marine Biol. 1980); Univ. of Manchester (PGCE 1981). University of Cambridge: post-doctoral res. asst, Dept of Anatomy, 1981–84; Demonstrator in Anatomy, 1984–88; Lectr in Anatomy, 1988–98; Reader in Neurosci., 1998–2001; Fellow and Coll. Lectr, Queens' Coll., Cambridge, 1987–90. FMedSci 2008. *Publications:* contrib. res. papers, reviews and commentaries. *Recreations:* birdwatching, African safaris, reading, family holidays. *Address:* MRC Laboratory of Molecular Biology, MRC Centre, Francis Crick Avenue, Cambridge CB2 0QH. *T:* (01223) 267045. *E:* mha@mrc-lmb.cam.ac.uk.

**HASTINGS, Lady Selina (Shirley);** writer; *b* 5 March 1945; *d* of 16th Earl of Huntingdon and Countess of Huntingdon, (Margaret Lane). *Educ:* St Paul's Girls' Sch.; St Hugh's Coll., Oxford (MA). Daily Telegraph, 1968–82; Literary Ed., Harper's & Queen, 1987–95. *Publications:* Nancy Mitford: a biography, 1985; Evelyn Waugh, 1994; Rosamond Lehmann, 2002; The Secret Lives of Somerset Maugham, 2009; The Red Earl: the extraordinary life of the 16th Earl of Huntingdon, 2014. *Address:* c/o Rogers, Coleridge & White, 20 Powis Mews, W11 1JN. *T:* (020) 7221 3717.

**HASTINGS BASS,** family name of **Earl of Huntingdon**.

**HATCH, Prof. David John,** FRCA; Professional Standards Advisor, Royal College of Anaesthetists, 2001–09; Professor of Paediatric Anaesthesia (first chair), University of London, 1991–2002, now Emeritus; *b* 11 April 1937; *s* of James Frederick Hatch and Marguerite Fanny (née Forge); *m* 1960, Rita Goulter; two *s* two *d. Educ:* Caterham Sch.; University Coll. London (MB BS 1961). MRCS, LRCP 1960; FRCA 1965. Fellow in Anesthesiology, Mayo Clinic, USA, 1968–69; Consultant in Anaesthesia and Respiratory Measurement, Gt Ormond St Children's Hosp., 1969–91. Pres., Assoc. Paediatric Anaesthetists, 1993–95; Vice-Pres., RCAnaes, 1991–93; Member: Med. Soc. of London, 1990–2002; GMC, 1994–2003 (Chm., Cttee on Professional Performance, 1999–2004; Chm., Assessment Gp, 2003–). Hewitt Lectr, RCAnaes, 1999. Hon. FRCPCH 2010. John Snow Medal, 2001, Foundn Award, 2015, Assoc. of Anaesthetists of GB and Ire.; Gold Medal, RCAnaes, 2003. *Publications:* (with E. Sumner) Neonatal Anaesthesia and Intensive Care, 1981, 3rd edn 1995; Paediatric Anaesthesia, 1989, 2nd edn 1999; contribs on paediatric anaesthesia, intensive care and professional self-regulation. *Recreations:* sailing, badminton, magic (Member: Christian Magicians UK, 2007– (Sec., 2011–15); Magic Circle, 2009– (Welfare Officer, 2012–); Associate Mem., Inner Magic Circle, 2015).

**HATCH, Lionel;** independent artist, designer and writer, since 2018; *b* 20 Aug. 1949; *s* of Douglas Hatch and Clarice Hatch (née Aldred); *m* Vivien Smith (marr. diss. 1984); one *s*; 2nd, 2016, Stella Nesbitt. *Educ:* Bolton Coll. of Art and Design. Jun. Art Dir, Royds, 1970–71; Art Director: Rileys, 1971–72; Cogent Elliott, 1972–73; Stowe Bowden, 1973–75; McDonalds, 1975–77; Yeoward Taylor Bonner, 1977–79; Creative Gp Hd, J Walter Thompson, 1979–80; graphic design consultant, 1980–86; Co-founder and Creative Dir, The Chase, 1986–2017. Conducted Graphic Design Student Workshops, Staffordshire Univ., 2010. Projects, drawings and design effectiveness studies exhibited internationally; exhibitions include: Twelve International Lettering Artists, 1983; New York Type Directors Club, 1984; Pitcairn Galleries; Manchester Art Gall.; Octagon Th.; Bolton Art Gall.; work held in private collections. Best in Show, The Roses Awards, 1987, 2009; Grand Global Award, NY Advertising Fest., 1994; DBA Design Effectiveness Award, 2003; Best in Show, 2010, Gold Award, 2012, Fresh Awards; Bronze Award, Cannes Advertising Fest., 2010; Writing for Design, Book D&AD Awards, 2011. *Publications:* The Chase by The Chase: how a design consultancy thinks it thinks, 1993; Fifty Designers' Current Favourite Typefaces, 2010; The Wood that Doesn't Look Like an Elephant, 2017; When Shrimps Learn to Whistle: a novel; artworks, design projects and design effectiveness studies in books, jls and other pubns. *Recreations:* keeping a curious mind, beachcomber, gardener. *E:* line.thepod@yahoo.co.uk.

**HATCH, Dr Marshall Davidson,** AM 1981; FRS 1980; FAA 1975; Chief Research Scientist, 1970–97, Hon. Research Fellow, 1997–2006, Division of Plant Industry, CSIRO, Canberra; *b* 24 Dec. 1932; *s* of Lloyd Davidson Hatch and Alice Endesby Hatch (née Dalziel); *m* 1st (marr. diss.), 1963, Lyndall P. Clarke. *Educ:* Newington Coll., Sydney; Univ. of Sydney (BSc, PhD). FAA 1975. Res. Scientist, Div. of Food Res., CSIRO, 1955–59; Post Doctoral Res. Fellow, Univ. of Calif., Davis, 1959–61; Res. Scientist, Colonial Sugar Refining Co. Ltd, Brisbane, 1961–66 and 1968–69 (Reader in Plant Biochemistry, Univ. of Queensland, Brisbane, 1967). Foreign Associate, Nat. Acad. of Sciences, USA, 1990. Rank Prize, Rank Foundn, UK, 1981; Internat. Prize for Biology, Japan Soc. for Promotion of Science, 1991. *Publications:* 164 papers, reviews and chaps in scientific jls and text books in field of photosynthesis and other areas of plant biochemistry. *Recreations:* ski-ing, cycling, reading. *Address:* PO Box 480, Jamison, ACT 2614, Australia. *T:* (2) 62515159.

**HATCH, Steven Thomas;** Vice-President, Northern Europe, Facebook, since 2016; *b* Romsey, 27 March 1970; *s* of Thomas Albert Hatch and Winifred Margaret Hatch; *m* 2000, Sophie Webster; one *s* one *d*. Media Planner, DDB, 1992–96; Sen. Planner, PHD, 1997–98; Bd Strategist, Y&R, 1998–99; Mediaedge:cia, then MEC: Hd of Strategy, 1999–2008; Man. Dir, 2008–11; CEO, 2011–14; Regl Dir, UK, Facebook, 2014–16. Non-exec. Dir, Reach plc (formerly Trinity Mirror plc), 2015–. Chm., Technol. Gp, CBI, 2016–. *Recreations:* yoga, cooking, running, sailing. *Address:* Facebook, 1 Rathbone Square, Fitzrovia, W1T 1FB. *E:* sth@fb.com.

**HATCHER, Prof. (Melvyn) John,** PhD, LittD; FAcSS; Professor of Economic and Social History, University of Cambridge, since 1995 (Chairman, Faculty of History, 2005–08); Fellow, Corpus Christi College, Cambridge, since 1976 (Vice-Master, 2000–06); *b* 7 Jan. 1942; *s* of John Edward Hatcher and Lilian Florence Hatcher (née Lepper); *m* 1967, Janice Miriam Ranson; two *d. Educ:* Owen's GS, Islington; London School of Economics, London Univ. (BSc(Econ), PhD); MA, LittD 1994, Cantab. Salesman, Reckitt and Coleman Ltd, 1960–63; Res. Fellow, Inst. of Historical Research, London, 1966–67; Lectr, 1967–74, Sen. Lectr, 1974–75, in History, Univ. of Kent; Vis. Prof., Univ. of Colorado at Boulder, USA, 1975–76; Lectr in History, 1976–86, Reader in Economic and Social History, 1986–95, Univ. of Cambridge. Vice-Chm., ESRC Econ. Affairs Cttee, 1979–84. Fellow, Huntington Liby, Calif, USA, 1986; Sen. Vis. Fellow, Stanford Univ. Humanities Center, 2008–09. FAcSS (AcSS 2001). Editor, Economic History Review, 1996–2001. *Publications:* Rural Society and Economy in the Duchy of Cornwall 1300–1500, 1970; English Tin Production and Trade before 1550, 1973; A History of British Pewter, 1974; Plague, Population and the English Economy 1348–1530, 1977; (jtly) Medieval England: rural society and economic change 1086–1348, 1978; (contrib.) The Agrarian History of England and Wales, vol. II 1042–1350, 1988; The History of the British Coal Industry: before 1700, 1993; (jtly) Medieval England: towns, commerce and crafts 1086–1348, 1995; (jtly) Modelling the Middle Ages, 2001; The Black Death: an intimate history, 2008; (jtly) Seven Centuries of Unreal Wages, 2019; articles in learned jls. *Recreations:* jazz, football. *Address:* Corpus Christi College, Cambridge CB2 1RH. *T:* (01223) 338000. *E:* mjh1001@cam.ac.uk.

**HATFIELD, Richard Paul,** CB 2012; CBE 1991; Director-General, International, Strategy (formerly Networks) and Environment Group, Department for Transport, 2009–12; *b* 8 Feb. 1953; *m* 1982, Penelope Charlotte Bratton. *Educ:* Whitgift Sch., Croydon; University Coll., Oxford (MA). Admin. trainee, MoD, 1974; Private Secretary to: Under Sec. of State (Army), 1978–80; Cabinet Sec., 1982–85; Ministry of Defence: Asst Private Sec. to Defence Sec., 1986; Head: Defence Lands, 1986–88; Overseas Div., 1988–91; Programme and Policy Div., 1991–93; Dir Gen., Mgt and Orgn, 1993–96; Dep. Under Sec. of State (Policy), subseq. Policy Dir, 1996–2001; Personnel Dir, 2001–08; Dir Gen., Safety, Service Delivery and Logistics, DfT, 2008–09. Non-exec. Trustee, Charity for Civil Servants (formerly Civil Service Benevolent Fund), 2007–13. Member: Finance and Develt Cttee, Nat. Mus. of RN, 2012–16; Bd, HMS Trincomalee, 2014–; Chm., Nat. Mus. of RN (Operations), 2016–.

**HATFIELD, Sally Anne, (Mrs Nicholas Simpson);** QC 2013; a Recorder, since 2004; Assistant Coroner (formerly Assistant Deputy Coroner), Manchester, Central, since 2010; *b* Portsmouth, 3 May 1964; *d* of Michael and Anne Hatfield; *m* 1992, Nicholas Simpson; one *s* two *d. Educ:* Portsmouth High Sch.; Lincoln Coll. Oxford (BA 1st Cl. Hons Juris. 1986); Inns of Court Sch. of Law. Called to the Bar, Inner Temple, 1988; in practice as barrister, Doughty St Chambers, London, 1989– and Byrom St Chambers, Manchester, 2008–. Gov., Kingsway Sch., Stockport, 2006–. *Publications:* (jtly) Butterworth's Guide to the Mental Capacity Act 2005, 2007; (contrib. ed.) Butterworths Personal Injury Litigation Service. *Recreations:* cooking, birdwatching, school governing, the arts, fair trade, family and friends. *Address:* Byrom Street Chambers, 12 Byrom Street, Manchester M3 4PP. *T:* (0161) 829 2100. *E:* sally.hatfield@byromstreet.com.

**HATFULL, Martin Alan;** Director, Martin Hatfull Ltd, since 2017; Senior Adviser, Kreab Worldwide, since 2017; *b* 7 June 1957; *s* of late Alan Frederick Hatfull; *m* 1980, Phyllis Julia Mary Morshead; two *s. Educ:* Dulwich Coll.; Worcester Coll., Oxford (BA Lit.Hum. 1980). Joined Foreign and Commonwealth Office, 1980; Second, later First, Sec., Tokyo, 1982–86; EU Dept (External), FCO, 1987–88; Private Sec. to Parly Under Sec. of State, FCO, 1988–91; First Sec., UK Rep. to EU, Brussels, 1991–95; Dep. Head, EU Dept (External), FCO, 1995–96; Head, Commonwealth Co-ordination Dept, FCO, 1996–98; Counsellor (Economic and Commercial), Rome, 1998–2002; Minister, Tokyo, 2003–08; Ambassador to Indonesia, 2008–11; Internat. Trade Advr to Diageo plc (on secondment from FCO), 2011–12; Dir, EU Balance of Competences, FCO, 2012–13; Dir, Govt Relns, 2013–14, Internat. Public Affairs, 2014–16, Diageo plc. Vice-Chm., UK-ASEAN Business Council, 2015–19 (Mem. Bd, 2013–19); Mem. Bd, UK-India Business Council, 2014–18. Chm., Anglo-Indonesian Soc., 2018–; Dep. Chm., Japan Soc., 2018–. Trustee, City & Guilds London Art Sch., 2018–.

**HATHERTON,** 8th Baron cr 1835; **Edward Charles Littleton;** agronomist; b 24 May 1950; s of Mervyn Cecil Littleton (d 1970) (g s of 3rd Baron) and Margaret Ann (d 2000), d of Frank Sheehy; S cousin, 1985; m 1974, Hilda Maria, d of Rodolfo Robert; one s two d. Heir: s Hon. Thomas Edward Littleton, b 7 March 1977. Address: PO Box 1341-2150, Moravia, Costa Rica.

**HATLEY, Tim;** set and costume designer for theatre and film, since 1989; b Lincoln, 28 Feb. 1967; s of Edward Hatley and Margaret Hatley; partner, Rasshied Din. Educ: Bearwood Coll., Berks; Central St Martins Sch. of Art and Design, London (BA 1st Cl. Hons 1989). Theatre productions include: National Theatre: Out of a house walked a man (with Complicite), 1995; Stanley, 1996; The Caucasian Chalk Circle, 1997; Flight, 1997; Darker Face of the Earth, 1998; Sleep with Me, 1998; Hamlet, 2000; Humble Boy, 2001; The Talking Cure, 2002; Vincent in Brixton, 2003; Henry V, 2003; Present Laughter, 2007; Rafta Rafta, 2007; Welcome to Thebes, 2010; Timon of Athens, 2012; A Small Family Business, 2014; Great Britain, 2014; 3 Winters, 2015; other productions: Chatsky, Almeida, 1994; The Three Lives of Lucie Cabrol, Complicite, West End, 1995; Suddenly Last Summer, Comedy, 1999; Private Lives, Albery, transf. NY, 2001 (Tony Award for Best Set Design, 2002); Spamalot, NY, 2004; Shrek the Musical, NY, 2008 (Tony Award for Best Costume Design, 2009); Mrs Klein, Almeida, 2009; My Fair Lady, Châtelet, Paris, 2010; Betty Blue Eyes, Novello, 2012; The Bodyguard, Adelphi, UK tour, Cologne, 2012; Quatermaine's Terms, Wyndham's, 2013; Ghosts, Almeida, transf. NY, 2014; The Pajama Game, Chichester, transf. West End, 2014; Singing in the Rain, Châtelet, Paris, 2015; Mr Foote's Other Leg, Hampstead, transf. Th. Royal, Haymarket, 2015; Temple, Donmar, 2015; Carmen, Royal Ballet, 2015; Little Eyolf, Almeida, 2015; Dreamgirls, Savoy, 2016; The Stepmother, Chichester, 2017; The Slaves of Solitude, Hampstead, 2017; In Praise of Love, Ustinov Th., Bath, 2018; Don Quixote, ROH, 2019. Films: Stage Beauty, 2003; Closer, 2004; Notes on a Scandal, 2006. Exhibitions: Vivienne Westwood - a London Fashion, Mus. of London, 1999; Diaghilev and the Ballet Russes, V&A, 2010. Olivier Award for best set design: for Stanley, 1997; for Humble Boy and Private Lives, 2002. Address: c/o Judy Daish Associates Ltd, 2 St Charles Place, W10 6EG. T: (020) 8964 8811. E: judy@judydaish.com.

**HATT, Paul William David;** Secretary, Royal Hospital Chelsea, 2007-16; b 21 Nov. 1949; s of late William Oliver Hatt and Henrietta Hatt (née McGregor); m 1975, Cecilia Anne Freeman; two s two d. Educ: Sir Joseph Williamson's Sch., Rochester; Lincoln Coll., Oxford (Schol., BA Hons English Lang. and Lit., PGCE, MA); Nat. Defence Coll. Joined Ministry of Defence, 1973: Principal, 1980-85; on secondment to FCO, as First Sec., UK Delegn to NATO, Brussels, 1985-89; Asst Sec., 1990; Head, Defence Lands, 1990-92; Dir, Proliferation and Arms Control Secretariat, 1992-97; Head, Resources and Programmes (Army), 1997-98; Asst Under Sec., 1998; Comd Sec., RAF Logistics Comd, 1998-2000; Fellow, Center for Internat. Affairs, Harvard Univ., 2000-01; Comd Sec. to Second Sea Lord and C-in-C Naval Home Comd, and Asst Under-Sec. of State (Naval Personnel), MoD, 2001-06; Project Dir, Royal Naval Museum, 2006. Recreations: sedentary pursuits, including family, literature and music. E: hatt_paul@hotmail.com.

**HATTER, Maria Lisa;** see Williams, M. L.

**HATTER, Sir Maurice,** Kt 1999; Chairman, IMO Precision Controls Ltd, 1970; b 6 March 1929; s of Ralph and Sarah Hatter; m 1999, Irene Noach. Royal Signals, 1949. Formed an electronics manufacturer sold to Thorn, 1968. Pres., World ORT, 2004-08, Pres. Emeritus, 2008. Founded Hatter Inst. of Cardiology, at UCH, 1990. Hon. Life Pres., Charlton Athletic FC, 2000. Hon. Fellow, UCL, 1995. Hon. PhD Haifa, Israel, 1996. Recreations: tennis, boating, underwater archaeology.

**HATTERSLEY,** Baron cr 1997 (Life Peer), of Sparkbrook in the co. of West Midlands; **Roy Sydney George Hattersley;** PC 1975; Deputy Leader of the Labour Party, 1983-92; b 28 Dec. 1932; s of Frederick Roy Hattersley, Sheffield; m 1956, Molly Hattersley, qv (marr. diss. 2013); m 2013, Maggie Pearlstine. Educ: Sheffield City Grammar Sch.; Univ. of Hull (BSc (Econ)). Journalist and Health Service Executive, 1956-64; Mem. Sheffield City Council, 1957-65 (Chm. Housing Cttee and Public Works Cttee). MP (Lab) Birmingham, Sparkbrook, 1964-97. PPS to Minister of Pensions and National Insurance, 1964-67; Jt Parly Sec., DEP (formerly Min. of Labour), 1967-69; Minister of Defence for Administration, 1969-70; Labour Party spokesman: on Defence, 1972; on Educn and Sci., 1972-74; Minister of State, FCO, 1974-76; Sec. of State for Prices and Consumer Protection, 1976-79; principal opposition spokesman on environment, 1979-80, on home affairs, 1980-83, on Treasury and economic affairs, 1983-87, on home affairs, 1987-92. Mem., H of L, 1997-2017. Visiting Fellow: Inst. of Politics, Univ. of Harvard, 1971, 1972; Nuffield Coll., Oxford, 1984-. Dir, Campaign for a European Political Community, 1966-67. Columnist: Punch; The Guardian; The Listener, 1970-2009; Columnist of the Year, Granada, 1982. FRSL 2010. Hon. DSc Sheffield Hallam; Hon. DCL: Hull; West Midlands. Publications: Nelson, 1974; Goodbye to Yorkshire (essays), 1976; Politics Apart, 1982; Press Gang, 1983; A Yorkshire Boyhood, 1983; Choose Freedom: the future for Democratic Socialism, 1987; Economic Priorities for a Labour Government, 1987; Who Goes Home? 1995; 50 Years On, 1997; Blood & Fire, 1999; A Brand from the Burning: the life of John Wesley, 2002; The Edwardians, 2004; Campbell-Bannerman, 2007; Borrowed Time: the story of Britain between the wars, 2007; In Search of England, 2009; David Lloyd George: the great outsider, 2010; The Devonshires: the story of a family and a nation, 2013; The Catholics, 2017; novels: The Maker's Mark, 1990; In That Quiet Earth, 1991; Skylark Song, 1994; Between Ourselves, 1994; Buster's Diaries, 1998; Buster's Secret Diaries, 2007. Clubs: Reform, Garrick.

**HATTERSLEY, Prof. Andrew Tym,** CBE 2017; DM; FRS 2010; FRCP, FMedSci; Professor of Molecular Medicine, University of Exeter Medical School (formerly Peninsula Medical School); Consultant Physician, Royal Devon and Exeter NHS Foundation Trust, since 1995. Educ: Emmanuel Coll., Cambridge (BA 1981); Univ. of Oxford (BM BCh 1984; DM 1990). MRCP 1987; FRCP 1999. Registrar in Medicine, Hammersmith Hosp.; MRC Res. Fellow, Diabetes Res. Lab., Radcliffe Infirmary, Oxford; Lectr in Medicine, Queen Elizabeth Hospital, Birmingham. Lectures include: Don Steiner, Univ. of Chicago, 2006; Victor Horsley, BMA, 2007; Dorothy Hodgkin Prize, Diabetes UK, 2007; William Osler Prize, Assoc. of Physicians, 2007; Charlotte Branchaud, McGill Children's Hosp., 2007; Sir Stanley Davidson, RCP, 2008; Falch, Univ. of Bergen, 2010; Gordon Cumming Meml, MRC; Carter, Brit. Genetics Soc., 2013; Croonian, RCP, 2014; Kroc, Univ. of Chicago, 2014; Claes Hellerstrom, Univ. of Brussels, 2014; Tizard, Perinatal Medicine Soc., 2014; Albert Renold, EASD, 2015. FMedSci 2004. Novartis Award in Diabetes, 2003; Moxon Trust Medal, RCP, 2011; Innovation in Pediatric Diabetes Care Prize, Internat. Soc. of Paediatric and Adolescent Diabetes, 2012; Naomi Berrie Award, Univ. of Columbia, 2014; Rolf Luft Award, Karolinska Inst., 2015; Clin. Endocrinol. Trust Award, Europ. Endocrine Soc.; GlaxoSmithKline Prize, Royal Soc., 2016; EASD-NovoNordisk Prize for Excellence, 2016. Publications: over 550 contribs to jls incl. Science, Nature Genetics, New England jl Medicine, Lancet. Address: University of Exeter Medical School, Barrack Road, Exeter EX2 5DW.

**HATTERSLEY, Edith Mary, (Molly); Molly, Lady Hattersley;** educational consultant, 1990; Visiting Fellow, Institute of Education, University of London (Management Development Centre), 1990-97; b 5 Feb. 1931; d of Michael and Sally Loughran; m 1956, Roy Sydney George Hattersley (see Baron Hattersley) (marr. diss. 2013). Educ: Consett Grammar Sch.; University College of Hull. BA Hons English (London), CertEd (Hull). Assistant Mistress at schools in Surrey and Yorkshire, 1953-61; Sen. Mistress, Myers Grove Sch., Sheffield, 1961-64; Dep. Headmistress, Kidbrooke Sch., SE3, 1965-69; Headmistress, Hurlingham Sch., SW6, 1969-74; Headmistress, Creighton Sch., N10, 1974-82; Asst Educn Officer, then Dep. Dir of Educn, ILEA, 1983-90. Advr on educnl matters to Trustees of BM, 1978-86. Chairman of Cttee, Assoc. of Head Mistresses, 1975-77; Pres., Secondary Heads Assoc., 1980-81; Chm., Soc. of Educn Consultants, 1994-96. Mem. Ct of Governors, LSE, 1970-99. FRSA 1982-2010. Recreation: reading.

**HATTON;** see Finch Hatton, family name of Earl of Winchilsea.

**HATTON, Alison Lee;** see Booth, A. L.

**HATTON, Andrew John; His Honour Judge Andrew Hatton;** a Circuit Judge, since 2012; Director of Training for Courts and Joint Dean of Faculty, Judicial College, since 2016; b Bolton, 15 Sept. 1964; s of Thomas William and Margery Hatton; m 1990, Caroline Sarah Ann Headley; one s one d. Educ: Bolton Sch.; Leeds Poly. (LLB Hons 1986); Inns of Court Sch. of Law; Liverpool John Moores Univ. (LLM 2015). Called to the Bar, Gray's Inn, 1987; in practice as barrister, 1987-2012; a Dep. Dist Judge (Magistrates' Courts), 2005-12; a Recorder, 2009-12; Internat. Criminal Judge, EU Mission in Kosovo, 2011-12; UN apptd Judge of Residual Special Ct for Sierra Leone, 2013-. Mem., Honourable Soc. of Gray's Inn, 1986. Recreations: ski-ing, golf, theatre. Address: Judicial College, 9th Floor, Thomas More Building, Royal Courts of Justice, Strand, WC2A 2LL.

**HATTON, Prof. Angela Dawn,** PhD; FRSB; Director, Science and Technology, National Oceanography Centre, since 2016; b Knutsford, 1969; d of John Hatton and Irene Hatton; m 2000, Stephen Teape; one s one d. Educ: Liverpool Poly. (BSc Hons Applied Biol. 1991); Univ. of East Anglia (PhD Marine Biogeochem. 1995). Postdoctoral Res. Associate, UEA, 1995-97; Scottish Association for Marine Science: NERC Res. Fellow, 1997-2003; Lectr, 2003-06; Sen. Lectr, 2006-12; Prof., 2012-14; Leader, Dynamic Ocean Theme, 2012-14; Associate Dir for Res., 2014-16. Chm., Sci. Bd (formerly Sci. and Innovation Strategy Bd), NERC, 2015-. FRSB (FSB 2011). Address: National Oceanography Centre, European Way, Southampton SO14 3ZH. E: angela.hatton@noc.ac.uk.

**HATTON, His Honour David William,** QC 1996; a Circuit Judge, 2012-19; b 29 May 1953; s of Thomas William Hatton and Margery Hatton; m 1994, Janet Elizabeth Bossons; one s one d. Educ: Bolton Sch.; Univ. of Bristol (LLB Hons). Called to the Bar, Gray's Inn, 1976, Bencher, 2005. Recorder, 1994-2012. Recreations: reading, music, walking, football. Club: Bolton Wanderers Football.

**HATTON, James Andrew;** a District Judge (Magistrates' Courts), since 2018; b Birkenhead, Wirral, 20 Feb. 1980; s of Michael Hatton and Elizabeth Hatton; m 2005, Rachel Lyth; two s. Educ: Bebington High Sch.; Leeds Metropolitan Univ. (LLB Hons Law). Admitted solicitor, 2004; a Dep. District Judge (Magistrates' Courts), 2012-18. Recreations: golf, football, travel. Address: Manchester Magistrates' Court, Crown Square, Manchester M60 1PR.

**HAUGH, Leslie John;** independent consultant, since 2002; Principal Finance Officer, Home Office, 2000-02; b 20 Aug. 1947; s of John Lamont Haugh and Robina Speed Haugh (née Stenhouse); one s one d. Educ: Buckhaven High Sch. ACMA 1980; FCCA 1998. HM Treasury, 1964; MPBW, 1965-67; BoT, then DTI, 1967-76; Dept of Employment, 1976-84; Dep. Accountant and Comptroller Gen., HM Customs and Excise, 1984-92; Accounting Advr, Home Office, 1992-98; seconded to Systems Union, 1998-2000. Recreations: golf (badly), bridge (badly), saying no. Club: Crail Golfing Society.

**HAUGHEY,** family name of **Baron Haughey**.

**HAUGHEY,** Baron cr 2013 (Life Peer), of Hutchesontown in the City of Glasgow; **William Haughey,** Kt 2012; OBE 2003; Joint Owner and Executive Chairman, City Facilities Management Holdings (formerly City Refrigeration Holdings (UK)) Ltd, since 1985; b Glasgow, 2 July 1956; s of Thomas Haughey and Margaret Haughey (née Morton); m 1978, Susan Moore (CBE 2016); one s. Educ: Holyrood Sen. Secondary Sch., Glasgow; Springburn Coll., Glasgow. Engrg supervisor, Turner Refrigeration Ltd, 1973-83; Hd of Engrg, UTS Carrier (USA), UAE, 1983-85. Former Chm., Scottish Enterprise Glasgow. Former non-exec. Dir, Celtic FC. Est. City Charitable Trust, 2010. Hon. DTech Glasgow Caledonian, 2005. Loving Cup, 2001, St Mungo Prize, 2007, City of Glasgow. Address: City Facilities Management Holdings Ltd, Caledonia House, 2 Lawmoor Street, Glasgow G5 0US.

**HAUGHEY, Hon. Caroline Philippa, (Mrs Mark Braid);** OBE 2019; QC 2018; b Newry, Co. Down, 14 Dec. 1975; d of Baron Ballyedmond, OBE and Mary Gordon Haughey; m 2004, Mark Braid; four d. Educ: Wycombe Abbey Sch.; Trinity Coll., Dublin (LLB); Inns of Court Sch. of Law. Called to the Bar, Middle Temple, 1999; in practice as a barrister, 1999-, Furnival Chambers, 2000-. Mem., Disciplinary Panel, Bar Standards Bd, 2011-17. Author, Modern Slavery Act 2015 Rev., 2016; Mem., Prime Minister's Modern Slavery Task Force, 2016-; Jt legal expert advr, Ind. Review of the Modern Slavery Act 2015, 2018-19. Trustee: Kalisher Trust, 2013-; Concord Prison Charity, 2016-. Member: Provost's Council, TCD, 2017-; Human Trafficking Adv. Council, McCain Foundn, 2017-. Recreations: cooking, reading, supporting husband in cricket. Address: Furnival Chambers, Furnival Street, EC4A 1JQ. T: (020) 7405 3232. E: clerks@furnivallaw.co.uk.

**HAUGHEY, Denis;** Member (SDLP) Ulster Mid, Northern Ireland Assembly, 1998-2003; b 3 Oct. 1944; s of Henry Haughey and Elizabeth Falls; m 1970, Maureen McCarron; one s two d. Educ: St Patrick's Coll., Armagh; Queen's Univ., Belfast (BA Hons Modern History and Pol Sci.). Mem., Northern Ireland Assembly, 1982-86; Minister, Office of First and Dep. First Ministers, NI Assembly, 1999-2000, 2001-02. Mem., Cttee of the Regions, EU, 1994-2002. Social Democratic and Labour Party: Founder Mem., 1970; Vice-Chair, 1971-73; Chair, 1973-78; Internat. Sec., 1978-2001. Recreations: reading (history, biography), music, travel. Address: 66 Fairhill Road, Cookstown, Co. Tyrone BT80 8DE. T: (028) 8676 3349.

**HAUSER, Andrew;** Executive Director, Markets, Bank of England, since 2018; b Norwich, 24 Jan. 1970; s of David Paul Hauser and Margaret Julia Hauser; m 2002, Demelza Mary; two s. Educ: St John's Coll., Oxford (BA 1st Cl. PPE); London Sch. of Econs and Pol Sci. (MSc Econs (Dist.); Ely Devons Prize). Bank of England: analytical and mgt roles, 1992-2001; Private Sec. to Dep. Gov., Financial Stability, 2001-03; Sen. Advr to Rachel Lomax, 2003; Hd, Internat. Economic Analysis, 2004; UK Exec. Dir (Alternate), IMF, Washington (on secondment), 2004-06; Hd, Bank of England Inflation Report, 2006-09; Private Sec. to Gov., 2009-12; Hd, Sterling Mkts, 2012-14; Hd, Fair and Effective Mkts Rev., Jt Bank of England/HM Treasury/FCA, 2014-15; Exec. Dir, Banking, Payment and

Financial Resilience, 2015–18. Non-exec. Dir and Chm., Audit and Risk Cttee, NHS Litigation Authy, 2013–17. *Recreations:* music, architecture, Rugby. *Address:* Bank of England, Threadneedle Street, EC2R 8AH. *E:* andrew.hauser@bankofengland.co.uk.

HAUSER, Dr Hermann Maria, Hon. KBE 2015 (Hon. CBE 2002); FRS 2012; Founder Director, Amadeus Capital Partners Ltd, since 1997; Director, Globespan-Virata Inc. (formerly ATM Ltd, later Virata), 2001–03 (Chairman, 1992–2001); *b* 23 Oct. 1948; *s* of Hermann Hauser and Gerti Pizl; *m* 1982, Pamela Raspe; one *s* one *d*. *Educ:* Vienna Univ. (MA Physics); Cavendish Lab., Univ. of Cambridge (PhD Physics 1977). Co-founder, Acorn (BBC) Computers, 1978 (500,000 BBC micro computers sold by 1984); Founder, IQ (Bio) Ltd, 1982; Vice-Pres. Research, Olivetti, Italy, 1986–88; Dir, Harlequin Ltd, 1986–99; Founder, IXI Ltd, 1987; formation of ARM Ltd (jt venture between Acorn and Apple), 1987; Founder and Chm., Active Book Co., 1988; Co-Chm., CTO of EO Inc., 1991; Founder: Vocalis Ltd, 1992; Electronic Share Information Ltd, 1993; Advanced Rendering Technology Ltd, 1995; Founder/Chairman: SynGenix Ltd, 1993; Advanced Displays Ltd, 1993–94; Advanced Telecommunications Modules Ltd, 1993; UK Online Ltd, 1994; Entertainment Online Ltd, 1995. Hon. DSc Bath, 1990; Hon. DSc Loughborough, 1998. *Recreations:* tennis, squash, ski-ing, swimming, piano. *Address:* (office) Suite 1, 2nd Floor, 2 Quayside, Cambridge CB5 8AB. *T:* (01223) 707000.

HAUSER, Wolfhart Gunnar; Chairman, FirstGroup plc, 2015–19; *b* 5 Dec. 1949; *s* of Josef Hauser and Eva Bargenda; *m* 1981, Dr Susanne Sandhagen; two *s*. *Educ:* Ludwig Maximilians Univ., Munich (MD 1978). Chief Executive Officer: TÜV Product Service GmbH, 1988–97; TÜV Süd AG, 1998–2002; Bd Dir, 2002–15, Chief Exec., 2005–15, Intertek Gp plc. *Recreations:* ski-ing, tennis, golf. *Club:* Rotary (Munich).

HÄUSSER, Prof. Michael Andreas, PhD; FMedSci; FRS 2015; Professor of Neuroscience, since 2001, and Wellcome Trust Principal Research Fellow, since 2011, Wolfson Institute for Biomedical Research, University College London. *Educ:* Univ. of Oxford (PhD 1992). Postdoctoral Research: Max Planck Inst. for Medical Res., Heidelberg, 1992–95; École Normale Supérieure, Paris, 1995–97; University College London: Wellcome Trust Career Develt Res. Fellow, 1997–2001; Wellcome Trust Sen. Res. Fellow, 2001–11. FMedSci 2012. *Publications:* articles in scientific jls. *Address:* Wolfson Institute for Biomedical Research, Cruciform Building, University College London, Gower Street, WC1E 6BT.

HAVARD, Dai; *b* 7 Feb. 1950; *m* 1986, Julia Watts (marr. diss.). *Educ:* Univ. of Warwick (MA). Union studies tutor, 1971–75; researcher, 1975–79; Educn Officer, 1975–82; Official, MSF, 1989–2001. MP (Lab) Merthyr Tydfil and Rhymney, 2001–15.

HAVELOCK-ALLAN, Hon. Dame Alison Lee Caroline, (Lady Havelock-Allan); *see* Foster, Hon. Dame A. L. C.

HAVELOCK-ALLAN, His Honour Sir (Anthony) Mark (David), 5th Bt *cr* 1858, of Lucknow; QC 1993; commercial arbitrator; a Senior Circuit Judge, Bristol Mercantile Court, 2001–17; a Deputy High Court Judge, Commercial Court and Admiralty Court, 2002–17; Principal Judge, Bristol Technology and Construction Court, 2005–17; *b* 4 April 1951; *s* of Sir Anthony James Allan Havelock-Allan, 4th Bt and Valerie Babette Louise Hobson, actress (who *m* 2nd, J. D. Profumo, CBE; she *d* 1998); *S* father, 2003; *m* 1st, 1976, Lucy Clare (marr. diss. 1984), *y d* of late Alexander Mitchell-Innes; 2nd, 1986, Alison Lee Caroline Foster (*see* Hon. Dame A. L. C. Foster); one *s* two *d*. *Educ:* Eton; Durham Univ. (BA Hons Law 1972); Trinity Coll., Cambridge (LLB 1974; Dip. in Internat. Law, 1976). Called to the Bar, Inner Temple, 1974, Bencher, 1995; Asst Recorder, 1993–96; a Recorder, 1997–2001. Mem., Market Supervision and Review Cttee, Lloyd's of London, 2019–. Pres., British Assoc. for Cemeteries in S Asia, 2016–. FCIArb 1991. *Recreations:* salmon fishing and foreign travel (preferably combined). *Heir:* *s* Henry Caspar Francis Havelock-Allan, *b* 6 Oct. 1994. *Address:* c/o 20 Essex Street Chambers, 20 Essex Street, WC2R 3AL. *T:* (020) 7842 1200. *Clubs:* Garrick, Royal Automobile.

HAVENHAND, Martin Stephen; Chairman, Rotherham NHS Foundation Trust, since 2014; *b* 14 Oct. 1950; *s* of Mark Havenhand and Jessie Brough; *m*; two *s* one *d*. *Educ:* Sheffield Business Sch.; Centre for Managing Change, London (MSc Managing Change). Asst Chief Officer (Recreation, Culture and Health), S Yorks MCC, 1980–85; Dir of Leisure Services, then of Envmt, Trafford MBC, 1985–93; Chief Executive: Bassetlaw DC, 1993–99; Yorkshire Forward, 1999–2006. Chairman: Advance Gp Hldgs, 2006–13; Nat. Metals Technol. Centre, 2006–13. Exec. Chm., Yorkshire 2012, 2006–10. Non-exec. Dir, Yorks Water, 2008–17. Hon. Dr Bradford Business Sch. *Recreations:* sport, lifelong learning. *Address:* Rotherham NHS Foundation Trust, Rotherham Hospital, Moorgate Road, Rotherham, S Yorks S60 2UD.

HAVERGAL, Giles Pollock, CBE 2002 (OBE 1987); director and actor; Director, Citizens' Theatre Glasgow, 1969–2003; *b* 9 June 1938; *s* of Henry McLeod Havergal and Margaret Graham Hyacinth Havergal (*née* Chitty). *Educ:* Harrow Sch.; Christ Church, Oxford (MA). Trainee Dir, Oldham Repertory, 1963; Director: Her Majesty's Theatre, Barrow-in-Furness, 1964; Palace Theatre, Watford, 1965–69. FRSAMD 1988; FRSE 1994. Hon. DLitt: Glasgow, 1987; Strathclyde, 1996. DDra RSAMD, 1997. St Mungo Prize, City of Glasgow, 1995. *Address:* c/o Alan Brodie Representation Ltd, Paddock Suite, The Courtyard, 55 Charterhouse Street, EC1M 6HA. *T:* (020) 7253 6226.

HAVERS, Hon. Nigel (Allan); actor; *b* 6 Nov. 1951; *yr s* of Baron Havers, PC, and of Carol Elizabeth (who *m* 1993, Charles Frederick Hughesdon, AFC); *m* 1st, 1974, Carolyn Cox (marr. diss. 1989; she *d* 2011); one *d*; 2nd, 1989, Polly Bloomfield (*d* 2004); 3rd, 2007, Georgiana Bronfman. *Educ:* Arts Educational Sch. Researcher, Jimmy Young Programme, BBC Radio 2. *Television* includes: The Glittering Prizes; Nicholas Nickleby; A Horseman Riding By; Upstairs Downstairs; Don't Wait Up, 1983–90; Strangers and Brothers, 1984; The Charmer, 1987; Proof, 1987; A Perfect Hero, 1991; Sleepers, The Good Guys, 1992; The Heart Surgeon, 1997; Dangerfield, 1998 and 1999; The Gentleman Thief, 2001; Manchild, 2002, 2003; Coronation Street, 2009–13; Downton Abbey, 2011; Murder on the Blackpool Express, 2017; *films* include: Chariots of Fire, 1981; A Passage to India, 1985; The Whistle Blower; Empire of the Sun, 1988; *theatre* includes: The Importance of Being Earnest, NT, 1982, Harold Pinter Th., 2014; Art, 2001; See You Next Tuesday, Albery, 2003; Rebecca, nat. tour, 2004–05; Single Spies, nat. tour, 2008; *radio* includes, Mrs Dale's Diary. *Publications:* Playing with Fire (autobiog.), 2006. *Address:* 28 Bramham Gardens, SW5 0HE. *Club:* Garrick.

*See also* Hon. P. N. Havers.

HAVERS, Hon. Philip Nigel; QC 1995; *b* 16 June 1950; *s* of Baron Havers, PC and of Carol Elizabeth (*née* Lay) (who *m* 1993, Charles Frederick Hughesdon, AFC); *m* 1976, Patricia Frances Searle; one *s* one *d*. *Educ:* Eton Coll.; Corpus Christi Coll., Cambridge. Called to the Bar, Inner Temple, 1974, Bencher, 2001. A Recorder, 1990–2000; a Dep. High Ct Judge, 2002–. *Recreations:* tennis, music, wine, gardening, travel. *Address:* 1 Crown Office Row, Temple, EC4Y 7HH. *T:* (020) 7797 7500. *Club:* Garrick.

*See also* Hon. N. A. Havers.

HAVERY, His Honour Richard Orbell; QC 1980; a Judge of the Technology and Construction Court of the High Court, 1998–2007; *b* 7 Feb. 1934; *s* of late Joseph Horton Havery and Constance Eleanor (*née* Orbell). *Educ:* St Paul's; Magdalen Coll., Oxford (MA 1961); Imperial Coll. London (MSc 2010). Called to the Bar, Middle Temple, 1962, Bencher, 1989 (Autumn Reader, 2017); an Asst Recorder, 1982–86; a Recorder, 1986–93; a Circuit Judge and Official Referee, 1993–98. Pres., Madrigal Soc., 2009–11. *Publications:* (with D. A. McI. Kemp and M. S. Kemp) The Quantum of Damages: personal injury claims, 3rd edn, 1967; (Gen. Ed.) History of the Middle Temple, 2011. *Recreations:* music, croquet, steam locomotives. *Clubs:* Athenæum, Garrick, Hurlingham; Leander (Henley-on-Thames).

HAVILLAND; *see* de Havilland.

HAVLICEK, Sasha; Founder and Chief Executive Officer, Institute for Strategic Dialogue, since 2006; *b* London, 30 May 1975; *d* of Milan Havlicek and Marina Mahler. *Educ:* St Paul's Girls' Sch., London; London Sch. of Econs and Political Sci. and King's Coll. London (BA European Studies); London Sch. of Econs and Political Sci. (MSc Political Theory). Sen. Dir, EastWest Inst., 1999–2006. Expert Advr, UK Counter-Extremism Commn, 2019. *E:* sh@isdglobal.org.

HAWARD, Birkin Anthony Christopher, RIBA; Consultant, van Heyningen and Haward Architects, since 2010 (Joint Principal, 1982–2010); *b* 28 Sept. 1939; *s* of Birkin Haward and Muriel Haward (*née* Wright); *m* 1st, 1963, Rose Hargreaves Heap (marr. diss. 1975; she *d* 1993); one *s* one *d*; 2nd, 1977, Joanna van Heyningen, *qv*; one *s* one *d*. *Educ:* Northgate Grammar Sch., Ipswich; Architectural Assoc. RIBA 1969. Dir, Foster Associates, 1969–83; formed van Heyningen and Haward Architects, 1982. Studio teacher: Cambridge Univ. Sch. of Architecture, 1969–75; Bartlett Sch. of Architecture, 1976–81; RCA, 1981–84. Vis. critic, Univ. of Pennsylvania, 1976, and most UK architectural schs. Award-winning buildings include: Haward House, London, 1976; Newnham Coll. Rare Books Liby, Cambridge, 1981; 2nd Haward House, London, 1986; Clovelly Visitor Centre, 1989; Wilson Court, Cambridge, 1994; Jacqueline du Pré Music Bldg, Oxford, 1995; King Alfred's Sch., London, 1997; Gateway to the White Cliffs (NT), Dover, 1999; West Ham Station, Jubilee Line Extension, 1999; Nat. Centre for Early Music, York, 2000; Polhill Inf. Centre, Bedford, 2000; Khoan and Michael Sullivan Chinese Painting Gall., Ashmolean Mus., Oxford, 2001; Sutton Hoo Visitor Centre (NT), 2002; Music Res. Centre, Univ. of York, 2004; Trinity Centre, Ipswich, 2005; Kaleidoscope, Lewisham, 2006; RSPB Centre, Rainham Marshes, 2007; Stelios Ioannou Centre for Classical and Byzantine Studies, Oxford, 2008; Performing Arts Centre, Latymer Upper Sch., London, 2008; Lerner Ct, Clare Coll., Cambridge, 2009. Ext. Examr, 1984–87, Mem., Steering Cttee, 1991–96, RIBA. Member: Architectural Panel, NT, 1995–; Council, AA, 2000–03; Fabric Adv. Cttee, St Paul's Cathedral, 2003–. Assessor, Heritage Lottery Fund, 1996–99; Architectural Advr, Arts Council Lottery Panel, 1996–2001. Trustee, William Morris Gall., 2003–. Exhibitions: Kent Design, Maidstone, 2000; University Challenge: buildings for higher educn, Building Centre, 2001; New Connections, Municipal Arts Soc. of NY, 2001; Winning Designs, Bristol Arch. Centre, RIBA, London and Cube Gall., Manchester, 2002; Diverse City, RIBA, London, 2003; Celebration of Architectural Competitions, Cube Gall., Manchester, 2003, RIAS, Edinburgh, 2004; one man exhibition: Beardsmore Gall., 2012, 2014, 2016, 2018; Salthouse Ch, 2019. *Publications:* contribs to major newspaper and architectural jls. *Recreations:* drawing, painting, theatre, church-crawling, 19th and 20th century stained glass, gardening. *Address:* c/o van Heyningen and Haward Architects, 1a Harmood Street, NW1 8DN. *T:* (020) 3362 4488.

HAWARD, Joanna; *see* van Heyningen, J.

HAWARD, John Anthony William; farmer, since 2008; consultant, since 1999; *b* 8 Feb. 1958; *s* of Anthony Ivor Haward and Joan Haward; partner, Janie Wilson; one *d*. *Educ:* City of London Sch. Joined: DoE, 1977; Spastics Soc., 1987; Mgt Advr and Hd of Chief Exec.'s Office, Berks CC, 1988; Dir of Corporate Strategy, Southwark Council, 1994; Advr, UN Mission to Kosovo, 1999; Chm., Local Govt Modernisation Team, DETR, subseq. ODPM, 2000–03; Dir of Local Govt Practice SE, ODPM, then DCLG, 2004–07. Expert Adviser: to Govt of Kosovo, 2011–14; to Govt of Macedonia, 2014–15. Proprietor, Le Puget, 2008–. *Publications:* Impact of Advanced Information Systems, 1984; Devolved Management, 1989; Project Management, 1991. *Recreations:* walking, reading, history, cooking, wine. *Address:* 40bis rue de l'Olivette, 09500 Mirepoix, France. *E:* john@lepuget.com.

HAWARDEN, 9th Viscount *cr* 1793 (Ire.); Robert Connan Wyndham Leslie Maude; Bt 1705; Baron de Montalt 1785; *b* 23 May 1961; *s* of 8th Viscount and Susannah Caroline Hyde, *d* of late Maj. Charles Phillips Gardner; *S* father, 1991; *m* 1995, Judith Anne, *y d* of late John Bates; one *s* two *d*. *Educ:* St Edmund's Sch., Canterbury; RAC Cirencester. *Heir:* *s* Hon. Varian John Connan Eustace Maude, *b* 1 Sept. 1997. *Address:* Great Bossington Farm House, Bossington, Adisham, near Canterbury, Kent CT3 3LN.

HAWES, Ven. Arthur John; Archdeacon of Lincoln, 1995–2008, now Archdeacon Emeritus; Canon and Prebendary of Lincoln Cathedral, 1995–2008, now Canon Emeritus; Associate Priest, Barnham Broom and Upper Yare, Norwich, since 2017; *b* 31 Aug. 1943; *s* of late John and Sylvia Hawes; *m* 1969, Melanie Harris; one *s* one *d*. *Educ:* City of Oxford High Sch. for Boys; Chichester Theol Coll.; Richmond Fellowship (Cert. in Human Relns, 1968); Univ. of Birmingham (Dip. in Pastoral Studies, 1972; Dip. in Liturgy and Architecture, 1975); Univ. of E Anglia (BA Hons 1986). Ordained deacon 1968, priest 1969; Asst Curate, St John the Baptist, Kidderminster, 1968–72; Priest-in-charge, St Richard's, Droitwich, 1972–76; Rector: Alderford with Attlebridge and Swannington, 1976–92; St Faith's, Gaywood, King's Lynn, 1992–95. Chaplain, Hellesdon and David Rice Hosps, Yare Clinic, 1976–92; Rural Dean of Sparham, 1981–91; Hon. Canon of Norwich Cathedral, 1988–95. Mem., General Synod, 2000–08 (Mem., Mission and Public Affairs Council, 2000–09; Chm., Mental Health Adv. Cttee, 1995–2009). Chm., Norwich Diocesan Bd for Social Responsibility, 1990–95. Mental Health Act Comr, 1986–94. Pres., Lincs Rural Housing Assoc., 1998–2007; Chm., East Midlands Develt Centre, 2003–05; non-exec. Dir, Lincolnshire Partnership Trust, 2002–06; Mental Health Act Advr to Lincolnshire Partnership Foundn Trust, 2006–08; Training Consultant, Lincolnshire Partnership Trust, 2008–12. Vice Pres., British Assoc. for Study of Spirituality, 2010–16. Chaplaincy Co-ordinator for Saga Cruises, 2009–. Co-Chair, Nat. Spirituality and Mental Health Forum, 2009–11. Vis. Fellow, Staffordshire Univ., 2010–13. Patron, MIND, 1995–2008; Ambassador, Norfolk Mind, 2018–. Langton Award for Community Service, Lambeth Palace, 2016. *Publications:* (ed jtly) The Ann French Memorial Lectures, 1996; (contrib.) Jewels for the Journey, 2007; (contrib.) Spirituality and Mental Health, 2011; (contrib.) Spirituality and End of Life Care, 2013; (ed) Crossing the River: the contribution of spirituality to humanity and its future, 2014; (contrib.) Ageing, Don't Panic, 2017; High Days and Holy Days, 2019; contribs to theol jls. *Recreations:* golf, medieval art and architecture, theatre, music, grandchildren, garden. *Address:* Sunnyside Farmhouse, 29 Market Street, Shipdham, Thetford, Norfolk IP25 7LY. *T:* (01362) 822441, *T:* 07803 249834. *E:* arthur.hawes@yahoo.co.uk.

**HAWES, Very Rev. Joseph Patricius;** Dean of St Edmundsbury, since 2018; *b* 21 March 1965; *s* of Charles Hawes and late Barbara Hawes; civil partnership, Rev. Christopher Eyden. *Educ:* St Chad's Coll., Durham (BA 1987); King's College London (MA 2012); St Stephen's House, Oxford. Ordained deacon, 1991, priest, 1992; Curate, Clapham Team Ministry, 1991–96; Priest-in-charge, St Michael and All Angels, Barnes, 1996–97; Team Vicar, Barnes Team Ministry, 1997–2003; Vicar, All Saints, Fulham, 2003–18. Hon. Canon, Gaborone, Botswana, 2011–. *Recreations:* cooking, scuba diving, hiking, gardening, theatre and opera. *Address:* The Deanery, The Great Churchyard, Bury St Edmunds IP33 1RS.

**HAWES, Patrick Thomas,** FRCO, FLCM; composer and conductor, since 1989; *b* Grimsby, 5 Dec. 1958; *s* of John William Alfred Hawes and Catherine Agnes Hawes; civil partnership 2011, Andrew Berry. *Educ:* De Aston Sch., Market Rasen; Durham Univ. (MA 1981). FRCO 1984. Asst Dir, Music, Pangbourne Coll., 1981–90; Composer in Residence: Charterhouse, 1990–97; Classic FM, 2006–08. *Compositions:* Quanta Qualia, 2004; Bluebird Variations, 2004; O Lord Our Governor, 2005; Towards the Light, 2006; When Israel Was a Child, 2007; Song of Songs, 2008; Lazarus Requiem, 2008; Highgrove Suite, 2010; Angel, 2014; Revelation, 2017; The Great War Symphony, 2018. *Recreations:* horse racing, theatre, ballet, opera, running, cooking. *W:* www.patrickhawes.com.

**HAWKE,** family name of **Baron Hawke**.

**HAWKE,** 12th Baron *cr* 1776, of Towton; **William Martin Theodore Hawke;** *b* 23 June 1995; *s* of 11th Baron Hawke and of Bronwen, *d* of William James, MRCVS; *S* father, 2009. *Educ:* Stowe; Royal Agricultural Univ. (BSc Hons Real Estate Mgt).

**HAWKER, Ven. Alan Fort;** Archdeacon of Malmesbury, 1999–2010, now Archdeacon Emeritus; *b* 23 March 1944; *s* of Albert Hawker and Florence Lilian Hawker (*née* Fort); *m* 1968, Jeanette Dorothy Law; one *s* three *d*. *Educ:* Buckhurst Hill County High Sch.; Hull Univ. (BA Hons Soc. Studies 1965); Clifton Theol Coll. (DipTh 1968). PACTA 1973. Asst Curate, St Leonard and St Mary, Bootle, 1968–71; Asst Curate (with charge), St Paul, Fazakerley, 1971–73; Vicar, St Paul, Goose Green, 1973–81; Team Rector, St Mary, Southgate (Crawley), 1981–98; Canon and Prebendary, Chichester Cathedral, 1991–98; Proctor in Convocation, 1990–2010; RD of E Grinstead, 1993–98; Archdeacon of Swindon, 1998–99. Chm., Gen. Synod Working Party on Clergy Discipline and Reform of Ecclesiastical Courts, 1994–2001; Member: Gen. Synod Standing Cttee, 1995–98; Gen. Synod Business Cttee, 2000–10; C of E Clergy Discipline Commn, 2003–10. CEDR Accredited Mediator. Vice Chair, Council, Glos Univ., 2002–08. *Publications:* Under Authority, 1996. *Recreations:* walking, railways, theatre, reading, music. *Address:* 21 Paddocks Close, Wolston, Warwicks CV8 3GW. *T:* (024) 7654 4021. *E:* alanandjen68@gmail.com.

**HAWKER, Prof. Craig Jon,** PhD; FRS 2010; FRSC; Professor of Materials, Chemistry and Biochemistry, and Director of Materials Research Laboratory, since 2004, Ruth and Alan J. Heeger Chair in Interdisciplinary Science, since 2010, Director, Dow Materials Institute, since 2011, and Clarke Professor and Director, California Nanosystems Institute, since 2013, University of California, Santa Barbara; *b* Toowoomba, Australia, 11 Jan. 1964. *Educ:* Univ. of Queensland (BSc 1st Cl. Hons 1984); Wolfson Coll., Cambridge (Ribbands Schol.; PhD 1988). FRSC 2013. Post-doctoral Res. Associate, Cornell Univ., 1988–90; Queen Elizabeth II Res. Fellow, Univ. of Queensland, 1990–93; Mem., res. staff, IBM Almaden Res. Center, 1993–2004. Hon. Prof. of Chemistry, Univ. of Queensland, 2001–; Prof., King Fahd Univ. of Petroleum and Minerals, Saudi Arabia, 2011–. Consultant to: Hitachi Data Systems, 2002–05; Mitsubishi Chem. Co., 2004–; Eastman Kodak, 2005–06; Ciba Speciality Chemicals, 2005–06; BASF, 2006–08; Allergan, 2006–; Promerus, 2006. Member, Scientific Advisory Board: NSEC, Univ. of Wisconsin, Madison, 2003–; Australian Inst. Bioengrg and Nanotechnol., 2004–; MIT Inst. for Soldier Nanotechnologies, 2004–; Molecular Foundry, Lawrence Berkeley Nat. Lab., 2005–; Materials Res. Lab., Univ. of Illinois, 2006–. Mem., RACI. *Publications:* contribs to jls incl. Jl Amer. Chem. Soc., Adv. Materials, Jl Polymer Sci., Polymer Chem., Chem. Sci., Macromolecules. *Address:* Department of Chemistry and Biochemistry, University of California, Santa Barbara, Santa Barbara, CA 93106–9510, USA.

**HAWKER, David Gordon;** international education consultant; *b* 11 Feb. 1954; *s* of Gordon Hawker and Peggy Hawker (*née* Lewis); *m* 1987, Judy Tongue; one *s* one *d*. *Educ:* Whitgift Sch., Croydon; Northampton Grammar Sch.; Wadham Coll., Oxford (BA Hons French and German; PGCE). Teacher, 1976–85; Exams Officer, Oxford Schs Exams Bd, 1985–86; Exams Sec., Inst. of Linguists, 1986–89; Schs Advr, Calderdale MBC, 1989–92; Sen. Professional Officer, Sch. Exams and Assessment Council, 1992–93; Asst Chief Exec., SCAA, 1994–97; Hd, Curriculum and Assessment, QCA, 1997–99; Dir of Educn, 1999–2002, Dir of Children's Services, 2002–07, Brighton & Hove City Council; Dep. Chief Exec., Westminster City Council, 2007–08; Dir Gen. for Children, Educn, Lifelong Learning and Skills, Welsh Assembly Govt, 2008–10; Dir Gen., Arms Length Body Reform Prog., DfE, 2010–11. Hon. Prof., Durham Univ., 2012–18. Chm., Assoc. of Dirs of Educn and Children's Services, 2004–07 (Chm., Standards, Performance and Inspection Cttee, 2007–08). Consultant to OECD, World Bank and British Council on educnl evaluation and assessment, 2000–18; Mem., Gen. Educn Sub-Bd, Open Soc. Inst., 2007–13. Prof., College of Teachers, 2007–16; Vis. Res. Fellow, Univ. of Sussex, 2011–14; Vis. Professorial Fellow, Inst. of Educn, London, 2012–16. Trustee: 4Children, 2006–08; Educnl Develt Trust (formerly CfBT Educnl Trust), 2011–19; CfBT Schs Trust, 2013–19; Educators Internat., 2013–. *Publications:* Core Skills Framework for Modern Languages, 1990; Review of Assessment and Testing, 1995; A Higher Vision for LEAs, 2001; Methodological Recommendations for a Quality Monitoring Framework for the Russian Education System, 2002; (contrib.) Contemporary Issues in the Early Years, 5th edn 2009; (contrib.) Parents, Personalities and Power: Welsh medium schools in South East Wales, 2013; Baseline Assessment in an International Context, 2014; (contrib.) Handbook of International Development and Education, 2015; (jtly) Checking the Possibility of Equating a Mathematics Assessment between Russia, Scotland and England for Children Starting School, 2018. *Recreations:* music, travel. *Address:* Withypool, Lye Head, Bewdley, Worcs DY12 2UP. *T:* 07970 909891. *E:* davidandjudyhawker@gmail.com.

**HAWKER, Hon. David Peter Maxwell,** AO 2012; MP (L) Wannon, Vic, 1983–2010; Speaker, House of Representatives, 2004–08; *b* Adelaide, 1 May 1949; *s* of David Hawker and Pamela Gavin Hawker (*née* Anderson); *m* 1973, Penelope Ann Ahern; three *s* one *d*. *Educ:* Geelong Grammar Sch.; Univ. of Melbourne (BEng). Man. Dir, Newlands Pty Ltd (agricl business), 1973–. Shadow Minister for Land Transport, 1990–93; Opposition Whip, 1994–96; Mem., Speaker's panel, 1998–2004. House of Representatives Standing Committees: Dep. Chm., Industry, Sci. and Technol., 1989–90; Chairman: Finance, Admin and Public Admin, 1996–98; Econs, Finance and Public Affairs, 1998–2004; Dep. Chm., Jt Standing Cttee on Foreign Affairs, Defence and Trade, 2008–10 (Chm., Defence Sub-cttee, 1999–2001); Mem., Jt Select Cttee on Republic Referendum, 1999, on Intelligence Services, 2001–. Chm., Govt Members Wool Cttee, 1996–2004. Chm., Liberal Party Fed. Rural Cttee, 1987–90. Dir, Abbeyfield Australia Ltd, 2011–. Chairman: Heart Morass Cttee of Govs, 2011–; Motorcycle Expert Adv. Panel, Govt of Vic (formerly Motorcycle Adv. Gp, VicRoads), 2011–; Victorian Shooting Sports Facilities Prog., 2014–15; Mem., Victorian Hunting Adv. Cttee, 2013–14. Patron, Field and Game Australia, 2008–. Life Gov., Brauer Coll. Alumni Assoc., 2007–. *Publications:* Who Reaps the Benefits?: a chronicle of the wheat debate, 1989; (jtly) The Heart of Liberalism, 1994; Striking a Balance: the lack of adequate and comparable services for regional Australia, 1996. *Recreations:* shooting, golf, cycling. *Address:* PO Box 1089, Barwon Heads, Vic 3227, Australia. *Clubs:* Melbourne; Royal Melbourne Golf.

**HAWKER, Graham Alfred,** CBE 1999; Chief Executive, Hyder (formerly Welsh Water) plc, 1991–2000 (Director of Finance, 1989–91); *b* 12 May 1947; *s* of Alfred Hawker and Sarah Rebecca (*née* Bowen); *m* 1967, Sandra Ann Evans; one *s* one *d*. *Educ:* Bedwellty Grammar Sch. CIPFA 1969; FCCA 1981. Trainee Acct, Caerphilly DC, 1964–66; Abercarn District Council: Acct, 1966–67; Chief Acct, 1967–68; Dep. Treas., 1968–70; Chief Auditor, Taf Fechan Water Bd, 1970–74; Welsh Water Authority: Audit Manager, 1974–78; Div. Finance Manager, 1978–84; Chief Acct, 1984–86; Dir, Planning and Develt, 1986–87; Dir, Finance, 1987–91. A Dir, Bank of England, 1998–2000. Chairman: Dŵr Cymru Ltd, 1993–2000; Hyder Consulting (formerly Acer), 1993–2000; Swalec, 1996–2000. Dep. Chm., 1998–2000, Chief Exec., 2000–04, Welsh Develt Agency. Chairman: BITC (Wales), 1994–2000; New Deal Task Force Adv. Cttee (Wales), 1997–98; Member: CBI Council for Wales, 1994–97; New Deal Adv. Cttee (UK), 1997–98; Prince of Wales' Review Cttee on Queen's Awards, 1999. Prince of Wales Ambassador's Award for Corporate Social Responsibility, 1999. CCMI. DL Gwent, 1998–2017. Hon. Fellow, Univ. of Wales, Cardiff, 1999. Hon. Dr Glamorgan, 1996. *Recreations:* family, walking, wine. *Address:* St Teilo House, Llantilio Pertholey, Abergavenny NP7 6NY.

**HAWKER, Stephen,** CB 2005; FIET; FICPEM; Senior Civil Servant, Ministry of Defence, retired 2006; company director; *b* 1948; *s* of Derek Hawker and Pamela Hawker (*née* Holland); *m* 1989; one *s* one *d*. *Educ:* Worksop Coll.; Pembroke Coll., Oxford (MA 1970); Univ. of Nottingham (PGCE 1971). FIET (FIEE 2004); FICPEM 2009. Hd of Dept, King James's Coll. of Henley, 1971–78; MoD, 1978–2006; on secondment: to NI Office, 1981–83 and 1998–2000; to Cabinet Office, 1989–92. Nat. Security Adv, Defence Strategy and Solutions, 2006–08. Man. Dir, SHD Consulting Ltd, 2006–16. Cityforum Sen. Associate, 2014–. Chm., Critical-Link Ltd, 2014–. Non-exec. Dir, FCO Services, 2009–19. Mem. Adv. Bd, BAE Systems Applied Intelligence (formerly Detica, then BAE Systems Detica), 2007–14; Member: Adv. Council on Nat. Records and Archives, 2011–17; Security Vetting Appeals Panel, 2015–. Vis. Prof., Cranfield Univ., 2006–12; Dist. Fellow, Reading Univ., 2019. Member, Audit Committee: EPSRC, 2013–18; Manchester Metropolitan Univ., 2019–.

**HAWKES, Prof. David John,** PhD; FREng; CPhys, FInstP; FIPEM; FMedSci; Professor of Computational Imaging Science, and Director, Centre of Medical Image Computing, University College London, since 2005; *b* 16 Jan. 1953; *s* of Roy and Joyce Hawkes; *m* 1978, Elizabeth Anne Nicholson; two *d*. *Educ:* Christ Church, Oxford (BA 2nd cl. Hons Natural Scis (Physics)); Univ. of Birmingham (MSc Radiobiol.); Univ. of Surrey (PhD 1982). FIPEM 1993; CPhys, FInstP 1997. Principal Physicist and Hd, Imaging and Med. Physics, St George's Hosp., London, 1984–88; Sen. Lectr, 1988–93, Reader in Radiol Scis, 1993–98, Guy's Hosp.; Prof. of Computational Imaging Sci., 1998–2004, and Chm., Div. of Imaging Scis, Sch. of Medicine, 2002–04, KCL. Dir, Interdisciplinary Res. Collaboration in Med. Images and Signals, 2003–07. Sen. Investigator, NIHR, 2010. Hon. Consultant Physicist, Guy's and St Thomas' NHS Trust, 1989–. FREng 2003; FBIR 2007; Fellow, Soc. of Med. Image Computing and Computer Assisted Interventions, 2009; FMedSci 2011. Business Fellow, London Technol. Network, 2003. William Roentgen Hon. Lect., Eur. Congress of Radiol., Vienna, 2006; Crookshank Lect. and Medal, RCR, 2008. *Publications:* (ed with A. Colchester) Information Processing in Medical Imaging, 1991; (ed jtly) Medical Image Registration, 2000; over 270 peer reviewed papers on med. imaging. *Recreations:* sailing, ski-ing, windsurfing, hill-climbing, trekking, mountain biking, musician. *Address:* Centre of Medical Image Computing, Department of Medical Physics, University College London, Gower Street, WC1E 6BT.

**HAWKES, Sir (John) Garry,** Kt 2009; CBE 1999; company director; Chief Executive, Gardner Merchant, 1978–98; Director, Trusthouse Forte, 1983–93; *b* 26 Aug. 1939; *s* of John and Joyce Hawkes; *m* 1963, Peggy Lee (*d* 2019); one *d*. *Educ:* Rowlinson Sch., Sheffield; Huddersfield Coll. of Technology. Joined Gardner Merchant, 1963; Regl Dir, 1972–76; European Man. Dir, 1976; Man. Dir, Gardner Merchant Ltd, 1977–95. Directeur Général, Sodexo SA, 1995–98; Chm., Cheese Cellar Co., 2000–07; Vice-Chm., Accord plc, 2005–07 (Dir, 2000–07); Dir, Investors in People, 2000–06; non-exec. Dir, Internat. Skills Standards Orgn. Chairman: Nat. Council, NTO, 1997–2001; British Trng Internat., 1997–2001; ARAMARK UK, 2000–04; Edexcel, 2000–05; Basic Skills Agency, 2002–07; Guidance Accreditation Bd, 2002–05; Vice Chm., London Qualifications, 2003–05. Pres., Hospitality Action, 1996–2004. Trustee, Edge Foundn, 2014– (Chm., 2004–09; Pres., 2009–14). FIH (FHCIMA 1982). Hon. Fellow: Huddersfield Univ., 1996; Oxford Brookes Univ., 1997. *Recreations:* theatre, modern design, travel. *Address:* Coalpit, Rookery Way, Haywards Heath, W Sussex RH16 4RE.

**HAWKES, Nigel John Mytton,** CBE 1999; journalist; *b* 1 Sept. 1943; *s* of late R. W. Hawkes, MBE and K. M. Hawkes; *m* 1971, Jo Beresford; two *s* one *d*. *Educ:* Sedbergh Sch.; St Catherine's Coll., Oxford (MA). Mem., editl staff, Nature, 1966–69; Sci. Editor, Science Jl, 1969–70; Associate Editor, Telegraph Mag., 1970–72; The Observer: Sci. Corresp., 1972–81; Foreign News Editor, 1981–83; Diplomatic Corresp., 1983–87; Diplomatic Editor, 1987–90; The Times: Science Editor, 1990–2000; Health Editor, 2000–08. Columnist, BMJ, 2007–16. Dir, Straight Statistics, 2008–11; Mem., Adv. Bd, Ultrasis plc, 2008–14. Gov., British Nutrition Foundn, 1999–2006 (British Nutrition Foundn Award, 1992). Chm., Friends of Woodchurch Windmill, 2002–06. Health Journalist Award, MJA, 2007; Freelance Journalist Award, MJA, 2011. *Publications:* The Computer Revolution, 1971; Early Scientific Instruments, 1978; (ed and contrib.) Tearing Down the Curtain, 1989; Structures, 1991; Man on the Move, 1992; numerous science and technology titles for children and teenagers. *Recreations:* walking, opera. *Address:* Well House, Front Road, Woodchurch, Kent TN26 3QE. *T:* (01233) 860518.

**HAWKES, Richard Charles;** Chief Executive Officer, British Asian Trust, since 2015; *b* Wolverhampton, 1 Dec. 1964; *s* of Geoffrey Lawrence Hawkes and Vivienne Wendy Hawkes; *m* 1996, Emily Catto; one *s* two *d*. *Educ:* Wolverhampton Grammar Sch.; Univ. of Manchester (BA Econs 1987). Pres., Univ. of Manchester Students' Union, 1988; Nat. Sec., NUS, 1989–90; Consultant, UN, 1990–92; Internat. Dir, Austrian NUS, 1992–94; Chief Exec., Sense International, 1994–2006; Internat. Dir, VSO, 2006–09; Chief Exec., Scope, 2010–15. Chairman: Bond, 2004–08; Motivation Charitable Trust, 2016–; Member: Progs Bd, Sightsavers, 2007–; IDS BBC Charity Appeals Adv. Cttee, 2009–14; Trustee: iPartner India, 2006–15 (Chm., 2009–15); Skills—Third Sector, 2009–14; Voluntary Organisations Disability Gp, 2011–15. *Recreations:* family, sport, politics. *Address:* 49 Jerome Drive, St Albans AL3 4LT. *T:* (01727) 750246. *E:* Richard.Hawkes@britishasiantrust.org.

**HAWKESBURY, Viscount; Luke Marmaduke Peter Savile Foljambe;** Director, Savills PLC, since 2012; *b* 25 March 1972; *s* and heir of 5th Earl of Liverpool, *qv*; *m* 2013, Katharine, *d* of Jeffrey and Sandra Davis; two *d*. *Educ:* Ampleforth; Roehampton Inst. With

Property Vision Ltd, 1999–2001; with Savills PLC (formerly FPDSavills Ltd), 2001–; Associate Dir, 2009–12. *Recreations:* golf, shooting, fishing. *Clubs:* Quo Vadis, 5 Hertford Street, Pratt's.

**HAWKESWORTH, Prof. Christopher John,** DPhil; FRS 2002; FRSE; Wardlaw Professor of Earth Sciences, and Deputy Principal and Vice-Principal (Research), University of St Andrews, 2009–14, now Professor Emeritus; Senior Research Fellow, University of Bristol, since 2014; *b* 18 Dec. 1947; *s* of Desmond and Ann Hawkesworth; *m* 1972, Elizabeth Celia Williams; one *d. Educ:* Trinity Coll., Dublin (BA Hons); St Edmund Hall, Oxford (DPhil). NERC Res. Fellow, Univ. of Leeds, 1975–78; Open University: Lectr, 1978–83; Sen. Lectr, 1983–88; Prof., 1988–2000; Prof. of Earth Scis, Bristol Univ., 2000–09. Internat. Sec., Geochemical Soc., 1995–97; Member: NERC Earth Scis and Technology Bd, 1996–99; Res. and Knowledge Exchange Cttee, SFC, 2011–15. Pres., European Assoc. for Geochemistry, 1997–98; Sci. Sec., Geol Soc. of London, 1999–2002; Vice-Pres., European Union of Geosciences, 2001–03. Fellow: American Geophysical Union, 2000; Geochemical Soc., 2001; FRSE 2012. Hon. DSc Copenhagen, 2000. Maj. John Coke Medal, Geol. Soc. of London, 1996; Schlumberger Medal, Mineralog. Soc., 2002; Wolfson Merit Award, Royal Soc., 2008; Wollaston Medal, Geol Soc. of London, 2012; Robert Bunsen Medal, Eur. Geoscis Union, 2014. *Publications:* (ed jtly) The Early Earth: physical, chemical and biological development, 2002; edited jointly: Continental Basalts and Mantle Xenoliths, 1983; Mantle Metasomatism, 1987; Understanding the Earth, II, 1992; Chemical Geology, festschrift for A. W. Hofmann, 1997; 320 scientific papers. *Recreations:* hill walking, sports, photography, reading predominantly non-fiction, gardening. *Address:* Woodbine Cottage, Kirtlington, Oxon OX5 3HA. *T:* (01869) 350304. *E:* c.j.hawkesworth@bristol.ac.uk.

**HAWKESWORTH, Gareth;** *see* Hawkesworth, W. G.

**HAWKESWORTH, His Honour (Thomas) Simon (Ashwell);** QC 1982; a Circuit Judge, 1999–2011; *b* 15 Nov. 1943; *s* of late Charles Peter Elmhirst Hawkesworth and Felicity Hawkesworth; *m* 1st, 1970, Jennifer Lewis (marr. diss. 1989); two *s*; 2nd, 1990, Dr May Bamber, MD, MRCP; twin *s. Educ:* Rugby Sch.; The Queen's Coll., Oxford (MA). Called to the Bar, Gray's Inn, 1967, Bencher 1990; a Recorder, 1982–99. Mem., Mental Health Tribunal, 2009–13.

See also W. G. Hawkesworth.

**HAWKESWORTH, His Honour (Walter) Gareth;** a Circuit Judge, 1999–2018; *b* 29 Dec. 1949; *s* of late Charles Peter Elmhirst Hawkesworth and of Felicity Hawkesworth (*née* Ashwell); *m* 1982, Barbara Joyce Tapper; one *s* one *d,* and one step *d. Educ:* Rugby Sch.; Magdalene Coll., Cambridge (Schol.; BA 2nd Cl. Hons Law, MA); Council of Legal Educn. Called to the Bar, Gray's Inn, 1972; joined Fenners Chambers, Cambridge, 1974; a Recorder, 1995–99; Resident Judge, Cambridge Crown Court, 2007–15; Hon. Recorder, City of Cambridge, 2013–15. *Recreations:* gardening, theatre, travel.

See also T. S. A. Hawkesworth.

**HAWKEY, Rev. Dr James Douglas Thomas;** Canon Theologian of Westminster Abbey, since 2019; Chaplain to the Queen, since 2017; *b* Brighton, 23 Aug. 1979; *s* of Anthony Douglas Hawkey and Susan Jennifer Hawkey (*née* Berntsen); *m* 2012, Carol Ripley. *Educ:* Girton Coll., Cambridge (BA 1st Cl. Theol. and Religious Studies 2001; Montefiore Prize; Gibson Greek Testament Prize; Sir Arthur Arnold Schol.); Selwyn Coll., Cambridge (MPhil 2002; PhD 2007; Gosden Schol.). Ordained deacon, 2007, priest, 2008; Curate, St Mary's Portsea, Portsmouth, 2007–10; Westminster Abbey: Minor Canon, 2010–15; Precentor, 2013–15; Fellow, 2015–, Dean and Dir of Studies in Theol., 2015–18, Clare Coll., Cambridge; Asst Diocesan Dir of Ordinands, Dio. of Ely, 2016–18. Member: Council, USPG, 2013–17; Malines Conversations Gp, 2013–; Internat. Reformed/ Anglican Dialogue, 2015–; Chm., UK Develt Cttee, Anglican Centre in Rome, 2014–. Trustee, Cambridge Inst. on Religion and Internat. Studies, 2017– (Mem., Council of Reference, 2015–17). Advr, Center for Empathy in Internat. Affairs, 2018–. Chaplain to High Sheriff of Cambs, 2017–18; Chaplain to Drapers' Co., 2016–17. Lyttelton Lectr, Eton Coll., 2018; Vis. Lectr, Dept of Theol. and Religious Studies, KCL, 2019–. Gov., City of Portsmouth Girls' Sch., 2007–10 (Chm., Personnel Cttee); Mem., Council, Queen's Coll., London, 2008–13. *Publications:* (contrib.) Church Times Book of 100 Best Prayers, 2006; (contrib. and ed jtly) God's Song and Music's Meaning, 2018; Walking Together on the Way: learning to be the Church - local, regional, universal. An Anglican Commentary, 2018; articles in learned jls incl. Ecclesiology, Theology, One in Christ, Ecumenical Rev. *Recreations:* international affairs, arts, cooking, British countryside, Italy. *Address:* The Chapter Office, Dean's Yard, Westminster, SW1P 3PA. *E:* jamiehawkey@gmail.com.

**HAWKEY, Prof. Peter Michael,** MD, DSc, PhD; FRCPath; Professor of Clinical and Public Health Bacteriology, Medical School, University of Birmingham, since 2001; Honorary Consultant, Queen Elizabeth Hospital, Birmingham, since 2017; *b* London, 21 Feb. 1951; *s* of Reginald Hawkey and Joan Hawkey; *m* 2006, Susan Fiona Cole; two *d* and one step *s* two step *d. Educ:* Univ. of East Anglia (BSc Hons Plant and Gen. Microbiol. 1972); King's Coll. Hosp., Univ. of London (MB BS 1978); Univ. of Bristol (MD 1983); Univ. of Leeds (DSc 2002); Univ. of Birmingham (PhD 2017). FRCPath 1984. Lectr and Hon. Sen. Registrar, Univ. of Bristol, 1979–85; University of Leeds: Lectr, 1985–88; Sen. Lectr, 1988–90; Reader, 1990–93; Prof. of Med. Microbiol., 1993–2001; Hon. Consultant, 1985–2001; Hon. Consultant, Heart of England Hosp., 2001–17; W Midlands Regl Microbiologist, then W Midlands Lead Public Health Microbiologist, HPA, later PHE, 2005–17. Chairman: DoH Cttee on controlling Clostridium difficile infection, 2007–14; Scientific Cttee, Nat. External Quality Assessment Service, 2010–. Garrod Medal, British Soc. for Antimicrobial Chemotherapy, 2017. *Publications:* (ed with D. Lewis) Medical Bacteriology: a practical approach, 1989, 2nd edn 2004; (ed with S. H. Gillespie) Medical Parasitology: a practical approach, 1995; (ed jtly) Principles and Practice of Clinical Bacteriology, 1997, 2nd edn 2006; over 250 articles on antibiotic resistance and hospital infection. *Recreations:* motor racing, restoring old sporting cars, gardening, ski-ing, horse riding, breeding Burmese cats. *Address:* Institute of Microbiology and Infection, University of Birmingham B15 2TT. *T:* (0121) 414 3113. *E:* p.m.hawkey@bham.ac.uk. *Club:* Farmers.

**HAWKHEAD, Sir Anthony Gerard, (Sir Tony),** Kt 2011; CBE 2003; Vice Chair, NHS Birmingham and Solihull Clinical Commissioning Group, since 2018; *b* 7 Oct. 1957; *s* of late Harry and Mary Hawkhead; *m* 1981, Marion Small; one *d* (one *s* decd). *Educ:* Whitefriars Sch., Cheltenham. Various policy and finance jobs, MoD, 1978–87; Inner Cities Unit, DTI, 1987; Leader, Govt's N Peckham Task Force, 1988–89; Hd, Business and Econ. Develt, LDDC, 1989–91; Chief Executive: E London Partnership, 1991–96; Groundwork UK, 1996–2014; Action for Children, 2014–18. Member: Supervisory Bd, DEFRA, 2011–15; UK Nat. Adv. Bd on Social Investment, 2016–18. Chm., W Warks Develt Trust, 2011–14. FRSA. Hon. FCIWEM 2005; Hon. Fellow, Inst. of Employability Professionals, 2013. *Recreations:* tennis, cricket, racquetball, music, wine, France. *Clubs:* Mandarins Cricket; W Warks Sports; Warwickshire CC.

**HAWKINS, Very Rev. Alun John;** Dean of Bangor, 2004–11; *b* 28 May 1944; *m* 1971, Ann Deborah Williams, HMI; two *s. Educ:* King's Coll. London (BA, AKC 1966); Univ. of Wales, Bangor (BD 1981); St Deiniol's, Hawarden. Lecturer: in English and Drama, St Mary's Coll. of Educn, Bangor, 1969–77; in Educn, UCNW, Bangor, 1977–79; Chief Examiner, Drama and Th. Arts, Associated Examg Bd, 1971–76. Ordained deacon, 1981, priest, 1982; Curate, Dwygyfylchi, 1981–84; Rector, Llanberis, 1984–89; Tutor, Diocesan NSM Course, 1985–90, Dir of Ordinands, 1986–90, Dio. Bangor; Vicar, Knighton and Norton, 1989–93; Canon Residentiary and Missioner, Bangor Cathedral, and Vicar in Bangor Rectorial Benefice, 1993–2000; Archdeacon of Bangor, 2000–04. Chaplain, Knighton Hosp., 1989–93. Chm., Governing Body, Church in Wales, 2007–11. Archbishop's Commissary, 2004. *Address:* Carreg Wen, 9 Cil y Graig, Llanfairpwll, Anglesey LL61 5NZ. *T:* (01248) 717403.

**HAWKINS, Prof. Anthony Donald,** CBE 2000; PhD; FRSE; Managing Director, Loughine Ltd, since 2002; Director, Aquatic Noise Trust, since 2011; *b* 25 March 1942; *s* of Kenneth St David Hawkins and Marjorie Lillian Hawkins; *m* 1966, Susan Mary Fulker; one *s. Educ:* Poole Grammar Sch.; Bristol Univ. (BSc 1st Cl. Hons Zoology, 1963; PhD 1968). Dept of Agriculture and Fisheries for Scotland: Scientific Officer, Marine Lab., Aberdeen, 1965, Chief Scientific Officer, 1987; Dir of Fisheries Res., Scottish Office Agriculture and Fisheries Dept, subseq. Dir of Fisheries Res. Services, Scottish Exec., 1987–2002; Hon. Res. Prof., 1987–, Prof. of Marine Resource Mgt, 2002–06, Univ. of Aberdeen; Chm., N Sea Commn Fisheries Partnership, 2002–05. Consultant to FAO, Peru, 1975; Hon. Lectr, Univ. of St Andrews, 1983. Rapporteur, North Sea Regl Adv. Council, 2004–. FRSE 1988. A. B. Wood Medal and Prize, Inst. of Acoustics, 1978. *Publications:* (ed and contrib.) Sound Reception in Fish, 1976; (ed and contrib.) Aquarium Systems, 1981; pubns on marine science, fish physiology, salmon biology, and impact of underwater noise on fishes and invertebrates. *Recreations:* angling, whippet breeding. *Address:* Kincraig, Blairs, Aberdeen AB12 5YT. *T:* (01224) 868984. *E:* a.hawkins@btconnect.com.

**HAWKINS, Catherine Eileen,** CBE 1992; debt consultant; *b* 16 Jan. 1939; *d* of Stanley Richard Hawkins and Mary-Kate Hawkins. *Educ:* La Retraite High Sch., Clifton. SRN, CMB (Pt 1), HVCert, DN London, Queen's Inst. of Nursing Cert, IRCert, DipIT. General nursing, student, 1956–59; Staff Nursing, Charing Cross Hosp., SRN, 1960–61; Pt 1 midwifery, St Thomas' Hosp., 1961; Health Visitor Student, LCC, RCN, 1961–62; LCC Health Visitor, 1962–63; Bristol CC HV, 1963–64; Project Leader, Bahrain Public Health Service, 1964–66; Field Work Teacher, HV, 1966–68; Health Centre Administrator, 1968–71; Administrator, Res. Div., Health Educn Council, 1971–72; Sen. Nursing Officer, Community Services, 1972–74; Area Nurse Service Capital Planning, Avon AHA, 1974–79; Dist Nursing Officer, Bristol and Weston DHA, 1979–82; Chief Nursing Officer, Southmead DHA, 1982–84; Regional Nursing Officer, 1984, Regl Gen. Manager, 1984–93, SW RHA. Non-exec. Dir, N Bristol NHS Trust, 1999–2003. WHO Consultant in Health Service Mgt, Middle East Br., 1999–2006. *Address:* Dun An Octa, Haggard, Ramsgrange, Co. Wexford, Y34 P268, Eire.

**HAWKINS, Christopher James;** Deputy Chairman, Black Country Development Corporation, 1992–98; non-executive chairman of a number of cos, 1988–99; *b* 26 Nov. 1937; *s* of Alec Desmond Hawkins and Christina Barbara; *m* Susan Ann Hawkins; two *d. Educ:* Bristol Grammar Sch.; Bristol Univ. BA (Hons) Economics. Joined Courtaulds Ltd, Head Office Economics Dept, 1959; seconded to UK aid financed industrial and economic survey of Northern Nigeria, 1960; similar mission to Tunisia to work on 5 year plan, 1961; Research Div. Economist, Courtaulds Ltd, 1961–66, Building Develt Manager, 1965–66; Lectr in Economics, 1966, Sen. Lectr, 1973–83, Univ. of Southampton. MP (C) High Peak, 1983–92. *Publications:* Capital Investment Appraisal, 1971; Theory of the Firm, 1973; The British Economy: what will our children think?, 1982; Britain's Economic Future: an immediate programme for revival, 1983; articles in Jl of Industrial Economics, Amer. Economic Review. *Recreations:* reading, music, sailing.

**HAWKINS, Rt Rev. David John Leader;** Area Bishop of Barking, 2002–14; *b* 30 March 1949; *s* of John Mitchell and Monica Mary Hawkins; *m* 1973, Carole Gladwin; three *d. Educ:* Kingsmead Sch.; Wrekin Coll.; London Coll. of Divinity (ALCD 1973); St John's Coll., Nottingham; Nottingham Univ. (BTh, LTh 1973). Teacher, Mbiruri Secondary Sch., Embu, Kenya, 1968–69. Ordained deacon, 1973, priest, 1974; Curate, St Andrew's, Bebington, 1973–76; Founding Warden, Bida Bible Trng Centre, Northern Nigeria, 1976–82; Vicar, St John's, Bida, and Acting Archdeacon, Bida Archdeaconry, 1979–82; Priest i/c, St Matthew's with St Luke's, Oxford, 1983–86; Vicar, 1986–99, Team Rector, 1999–2002, St George's, Leeds. Diocese of Chelmsford: Hd Bishop for Mission and Parish Develt, 2004–14; Hd Bishop for Youth, 2005–14; Archbp's Advr for Black Majority Churches, 2006–14; Lead Bishop: Global Christian Forum, 2005–; for 2012 Olympic and Paralympic Games, 2006–13. Canon Emeritus, Kaduna, Nigeria, 1982. Chaplain, Yorks CCC, 1986–2002. Dir, Ashlar House, 1986–2001; Exec. Trustee, St George's Crypt, 1986–2002; Chair, Leeds Faith in Schs, 1993–2002; Pres., Global Day of Prayer, London, 2012– (Chm., 2007–12). Patron: Commn for Mission; Haven Hse, Woodford, 2012–. Life Pres., Bardsey Bird and Field Observatory, 2008. *Recreations:* painting, music, bird watching, mountain walking, sailing, running, poetry.

**HAWKINS, James Bruce,** MA; Vice Chancellor and Global Head of School Heads, Whittle School & Studios, since 2018; *b* Sussex, 10 Dec. 1965; *s* of Dr Philip John Clare Hawkins and José Phyllis Hawkins (*née* Thorneloe); *m* 1999, Zoë Antonia Neeves; one *d. Educ:* King Edward VI Sch., Camp Hill, Birmingham; Brasenose Coll., Oxford (MA Maths; PGCE). Asst Master, Radley Coll., 1988–92; Hd of Maths, Forest Sch., 1992–97; Dep. Hd, Chigwell Sch., 1997–2002; Head Master, Norwich Sch., 2002–11; Head Master, Harrow Sch., 2011–18. Vice-Pres., Internat. Boys' Sch. Coalition, 2014–18. Trustee: Compassion UK, 2002–11; Norman's Foundn, 2003–11; Harrow Mission, 2016–18; West London Zone, 2016–18. Governor: Old Sch., Henstead, 2003–11; The Open Acad., Norwich, 2008–11; City Acad., Norwich, 2009–11; Orley Farm Sch., 2011–18; Aysgarth Sch., 2011–18; Wellesley House, 2011–18; Francis Holland Schs Trust, 2016–18. *Recreations:* music, films, cafés, theatre. *Clubs:* Conduit, Sloane.

**HAWKINS, Dr John,** OBE 2001; Programme (formerly Project) Manager, Knowledge and Learning Centres, British Council, 2001–04; *b* 13 Oct. 1944; *s* of Maurice and Anna Hawkins; *m* 1968, Pamela June Donnelly; one *s* one *d. Educ:* Reading Univ. (BSc Physical Properties of Materials; PhD); Univ. of East Anglia (MA Develt Studies, 1994). Joined British Council, 1971; served Lahore, Islamabad, Bogotá, and Buenos Aires; Budget Department: Management Accountant, 1980–85; Dir, 1985–91; Manager, HQ Relocation Project, 1991–92; Head, Accommodation Services, 1992–93; Regl Dir, W Africa, 1994–97; Dir, Africa and S Asia, 1997–2000; Acting Dir of Finance, 2000; Special Projects, 2000–01. Voluntary work for Kings Church, Wokingham, 2004–; Trustee: DISCET UK, 2004–; Mustard Tree Foundn, Reading, 2015–. JP Reading, 2006–14. *Recreations:* walking, carpentry. *Address:* 50 Gipsy Lane, Earley, Reading RG6 7HD.

**HAWKINS, Prof. John Alan,** PhD; Professor of English and Applied Linguistics, University of Cambridge, 2004–11, now Emeritus; Distinguished Professor, University of California, Davis (Professor of Linguistics, 2007). *Educ:* Trinity Hall, Cambridge (BA 1970; PhD 1975). Lectr, Univ. of Essex, 1973–77; Univ. of Southern Calif, 1977–2004, Prof. of

Linguistics, 1987–2004; Max Planck Inst. for Psycholinguistics, Nijmegen, 1982–85. *Publications*: Definiteness and Indefiniteness, 1978; Word Order Universals, 1983; A Comparative Typology of English and German, 1986; A Performance Theory of Order and Constituency, 1994; Efficiency and Complexity in Grammars, 2004; (with Luna Filipovic) Criterial Features in L2 English, 2012; Cross-linguistic Variation and Efficiency, 2014. *Address*: Department of Linguistics, University of California, Davis, 270 Kerr Hall, One Shields Avenue, CA 95616, USA.

HAWKINS, Prof. John David, FBA 1993; Professor of Ancient Anatolian Languages, School of Oriental and African Studies, University of London, 1993–2005, now Emeritus; *b* 11 Sept. 1940; *s* of John and Audrey Hawkins. *Educ*: Bradfield Coll.; University Coll., Oxford (BA 1962; MA 1965); Inst. of Archaeol., Univ. of London (Postgrad. Dip. 1964). School of Oriental and African Studies, University of London: Res. Fellow, 1964–67; Lectr, then Sen. Lectr, 1967–93. *Publications*: The Hieroglyphic Inscription of the Sacred Pool Complex at Boğazköy-Hattusa, 1995; Corpus of Hieroglyphic Luwian Inscriptions, vol. I, parts 1–3, 2000. *Recreations*: gardening, political cartoons, caricature. *Address*: c/o School of Oriental and African Studies, University of London, Thornhaugh Street, WC1H 0XG. *T*: (020) 7734 5409.

HAWKINS, Ven. John Edward Inskipp; Archdeacon of Hampstead, since 2015; *b* 6 June 1963; *s* of Jeremy and Elizabeth Hawkins; *m* 1st, 1986, Emma Woodhead (*d* 1990); 2nd, 1999, Desiree Shakes; two step *d*. *Educ*: King's Coll. London (BD 1985); Queen's Coll., Birmingham. Ordained deacon, 1988, priest, 1989; Curate, Holy Trinity, Birchfield, 1988–92; Curate, 1992–93, Team Vicar, 1993–99, All Saints, Poplar; Vicar, St John, W Hendon, 1999–2015; Area Dean, W Barnet, 2004–09; Priest-in-charge, St Matthias, Colindale, 2007–15; Preb., St Paul's Cathedral, 2013–.

HAWKINS, John Mark; HM Diplomatic Service, retired; Ambassador to Qatar, 2008–12; *b* 30 April 1960; *s* of John Clement Hawkins and Diana Margaret Hawkins (*née* Townsend); *m* 1991, Rosemarie Anne Kleynhans; two *s*. *Educ*: Bedford Sch.; New Coll., Oxford (MA Modern Hist.). Mgt trainee, J. Sainsbury plc, 1981–82; joined HM Diplomatic Service, 1982; FCO, 1982–84; Third, later Second, Sec. (Chancery), Pretoria/Cape Town, 1984–88; FCO, 1989–93; First Sec. (Commercial), New Delhi, 1993–96; Internat. Dir, Invest in Britain Bureau, 1997–99; Counsellor and Dir, Trade and Investment Promotion for Spain, Madrid, 2000–04; Consul Gen., Dubai, 2004–08; Fellow, Sheikh Nasser bin Muhammed Al Sabah Prog., Durham Univ., 2012; special unpaid leave, HM Diplomatic Service, 2012–15. Mem., Adv. Bd, Delancey Real Estate Mgt, 2013–; Sen. Advr, ME, Jockey Club and Ascot Racecourse, 2015–. *Recreations*: travel, family, sport, especially horseracing. *Clubs*: Royal Over-Seas League; Mandarins Cricket.

HAWKINS, Neil Grant; Principal, Concord College, 2005–Sept. 2020; Global Principal, Concord International, from Sept. 2020; *b* Aldershot, 5 Nov. 1965; *s* of Philip and Mary Hawkins; *m* 1989, Vanessa Pond; one *s*. *Educ*: Brentwood Sch.; Robinson Coll., Cambridge (BA Hist. 1988; PGCE). Teacher of History: Norwich Sch., 1989–92; Cranleigh Sch., 1992–94; Head of History: Cranleigh Sch., 1994–98; Sevenoaks Sch., 1998–2000; Dir of Studies, Leys Sch., 2000–05. Mem., Soc. of Heads, 2005–. *Recreations*: running, philosophy, reading, chatting, watching sport. *Address*: Concord College, Acton Burnell, Shrewsbury, Shropshire SY5 7PF. *T*: (01694) 731631. *E*: theprincipal@concordcollegeuk.com. *Club*: Rotary (Shrewsbury) (Hon. Mem.).

HAWKINS, Nicholas John; corporate barrister and company director; Partner, Gunnercooke LLP, since 2016; *b* 27 March 1957; *s* of late Arthur Ernest Hawkins, PhD, FInstP, CPhys and of Patricia Jean Hawkins, BSc, BA (*née* Papworth); *m* 1st, 1979, Angela Margaret Turner, MA Oxon, CPFA (marr. diss. 2000); two *s* one *d*; 2nd, 2001, Jenny Cassar; one step *s* one step *d*. *Educ*: Bedford Modern Sch.; Lincoln Coll., Oxford (MA); Inns of Court Sch. of Law. ACIArb. Called to the Bar, Middle Temple, 1979 (Harmsworth Sen. Scholar). Practised from chambers in Birmingham and Northampton, 1979–86; worked in construction and recruitment, 1986–87; Company Legal Advr, Access, 1987–89; Gp Legal Advr, Lloyds Abbey Life plc, 1989–92; Corporate Lawyer, AMJ internat. law firm, Sultanate of Oman, 2005–06; Barrister: Harris Hagan, Solicitors, 2006–07; Gambling Governance, 2006–07; Advr, Plus Mkts, 2006–07; Consultant Hd of Gambling Law, Halliwells LLP, Solicitors, 2007; Legal Dir, 2007–11, Co. Sec., 2008–11, Danoptra Hldgs Ltd, later Danoptra Ltd; Hd of Legislation, Sport and Gambling Law, Spring Law Solicitors, 2011–12; Chief Exec., Acoustic Sensing Technology (UK) Ltd, 2012–14; practised from chambers in Leeds and London, 2015–16. Mem., Bar Council, 1988–95; Chm., Bar Assoc. for Commerce, Finance and Industry, 1994–95. Contested (C) Huddersfield, 1987. MP (C) Blackpool S, 1992–97, Surrey Heath, 1997–2005. PPS to Ministers of State, MoD, 1995–96, to Sec. of State for Nat. Heritage, 1996–97; opposition frontbench spokesman: on legal affairs, 1999–2001, 2002–03; on home affairs, 2000–03; on internat. develt, 2001–02. Member: Transport Select Cttee, 1993–95; Home Affairs Select Cttee, 1998–99; DCMS Select Cttee, 2004–05; Sec., Cons. backbench Educn Cttee, 1993–95; Vice Chairman: Cons. backbench Culture, Media and Sport (formerly Nat. Heritage) Cttee, 1997–2005; Cons. backbench Home Affairs Cttee, 1997–2005; Chm., Cons. backbench Sports Cttee, 1994–2005; Vice-Chairman: All-Party Sports Cttee, 1997–2005; All-Party Gp on Insurance and Financial Services, 1995–2005. Chm., W Lancs Support Gp, Marie Curie Cancer Care, 1992–96. *Publications*: booklets and articles on Conservative policy, transport hist., sport, legal and employment matters, and on gambling and sports law. *Recreations*: cricket, music, theatre, transport history, Rugby, soccer, swimming. *Address*: Gunnercooke LLP, 1 Aire Street, Leeds, W Yorks LS1 4PR. *Clubs*: MCC; Lord's Taverners.

HAWKINS, Nicholas Simon; barrister; owner, Nick Hawkins Initiatives, since 2017; Director, The Hawkins Consultancy, since 2019; *b* Southsea, 9 April 1959; *s* of Jim and Jill Hawkins; *m* 1984, Sue Davey; one *s* one *d*. *Educ*: King's Sch., Grantham; Lincoln Coll., Oxford (BA PPE 1981; MA 1985); Inns of Court Sch. of Law. Royal Navy: Gen. and Professional Naval Trng, 1977–82; Lieutenant: Supply Officer, Naval Party 2200, 1982–83; Captain's Sec., HMS Antrim, 1983–84; Manpower Systems Analyst, HMS Centurion, 1984–87; Supply Officer, HMS Sheffield, 1987–89; Lieutenant Commander: legal trng, 1989–92; called to the Bar, Inner Temple, 1991; in practice as a barrister, Normanton Chambers, 2018–; Staff Legal Adviser: to FO Scotland and NI, 1992–94; to FO Portsmouth, 1994–96; Comdr, Naval Prosecuting Authy, 1996–99; Chief Crown Prosecutor: CPS Wilts, 1999–2003; CPS Hants and IoW, 2003–11; CPS Wessex, 2011–13; CPS Direct, 2013–14; Chief Operating Officer, Ind. Police Complaints Commn, 2014–15; Chief Exec., Legal Ombudsman, 2015–17. Vis. Prof., Univ. of Portsmouth, 2014–. *Publications*: (contrib.) The Routledge International Handbook on Hate Crime, 2014. *Recreations*: cricket, football, keep fit, walking, travel, musical theatre, family. *Address*: Langley Road, Claverdon, Warwickshire CV35 8PU. *T*: 07584 419084. *E*: nickshawkins@icloud.com.

HAWKINS, Prof. Philip Nigel, PhD; FRCP, FRCPath; FMedSci; Professor of Medicine, and Head, Centre for Amyloidosis and Acute Phase Proteins, University College London, since 1999; Head, NHS National Amyloidosis Centre, Royal Free Hospital, London, since 1999; *b* London, 1959; *s* of Dr Warren Hawkins and Dr Margaret Hawkins (*née* Segar); *m* Dr Libi Deller; one *s*. *Educ*: Haberdashers' Aske's Sch., Elstree; Univ. of London (MB BS Hons 1982; PhD 1990). FRCP 1994; FRCPath 2004. Trng posts at St George's Hosp. Med. Sch., 1982–84 and RPMS, Hammersmith Hosp., 1984–89; Sen. Lectr in Medicine, 1990–94, Reader, 1994–99, RPMS, Hammersmith Hosp. MRC Trng Fellow, 1987–89. Goulstonian Lectr, 1995. Mem., Assoc. Physicians of GB and Ireland, 1993. FMedSci 2004. Wellcome Trust Univ. Award, 1997. *Publications*: contrib. papers on amyloidosis and inherited inflammatory disorders to learned jls. *Recreations*: thinking outside the box, sailing, windsurfing, walking on the beach, vehicle technology. *Address*: National Amyloidosis Centre, UCL Medical School, Royal Free Hospital, Rowland Hill Street, NW3 2PF. *T*: (020) 7433 2815. *E*: p.hawkins@ucl.ac.uk. *Club*: Hayling Island Sailing.

HAWKINS, Dr Phillip Thomas, FRS 2013; Group Leader in Signalling, Babraham Institute, Cambridge, since 2003. *Educ*: Univ. of Bristol (BSc 1st Cl. Biochem. 1980; PhD Biochem. 1983). Postdoctoral Fellow, S. K. & F. Research Ltd, Welwyn, 1985–87; Postdoctoral Fellow, 1987–88, Lister Fellow, 1988–90, Molecular Neurobiol. Unit, MRC Centre, Cambridge; Babraham Institute, Cambridge: Lister Fellow, AFRC Inst. of Animal Physiol. and Genetics Res., 1990–93; BBSRC Sen. Res. Fellow, 1993–98; BBSRC Advanced Fellow, 1998–2003. *Publications*: contribs to learned jls incl. Nature, Cell, Science. *Address*: Babraham Institute, Babraham Research Campus, Cambridge CB22 3AT.

HAWKINS, Sir Richard Caesar, 9th Bt *cr* 1778, of Kelston, Somerset; *b* 29 Dec. 1958; *yr s* of Sir Humphry Hawkins, 7th Bt and of Anita, *d* of C. H. Funkey; *S* brother, 1999; *m* 1992, Ernestine Ehrensperger; one *s*. *Educ*: Hilton Coll., Natal; Witwatersrand Univ. Chartered Accountant (SA). Manager, 7 casinos and hotels, Sun International, SA, 2001–. Gov., Pridwin Prep. Sch., 2002–. *Heir*: *s* Jonathan Caesar Hawkins, *b* 23 June 1992. *Address*: PO Box 410838, Craighall Park, Johannesburg 2024, South Africa.

HAWKINS, His Honour Richard Graeme; QC 1984; a Circuit Judge, 1989–2012; *b* 23 Feb. 1941; *s* of late Denis William Hawkins and Norah Mary (*née* Beckingsale); *m* 1969, Anne Elizabeth, *d* of late Dr and Mrs Glyn Edwards, The Boltons, Bournemouth; one *s* one *d*. *Educ*: Hendon County Sch.; University College London (LLB Hons 1962). Called to the Bar, Gray's Inn, 1963, Bencher, 2003. A Recorder, 1985–89. Mem., Hon. Soc. of Gray's Inn, 1959–. Liveryman, Curriers' Co., 1995–. *Recreations*: sailing, University of the Third Age. *Club*: Garrick.

HAWKINS, Rt Rev. Richard Stephen; Suffragan Bishop of Crediton, 1996–2004; an Honorary Assistant Bishop, Diocese of Exeter, since 2005; *b* 2 April 1939; *s* of late Ven. Canon John Stanley Hawkins and Elsie Hawkins (*née* Briggs); *m* 1966, Valerie Ann Herneman; one *s* one *d* (and one *s* one *d* decd). *Educ*: Exeter School; Exeter Coll., Oxford; St Stephen's House, Oxford. MA (Oxon); BPhil (Exeter Univ.); CQSW. Asst Curate, St Thomas, Exeter, 1963–66; Team Vicar of Clyst St Mary, Clyst Valley Team Ministry, 1966–78; Bishop's Officer for Ministry and Joint Director, Exeter-Truro Ministry Training Scheme, 1978–81; Team Vicar, Central Exeter Team Ministry, 1978–81; Diocesan Director of Ordinands, Exeter, 1979–81; Priest-in-charge, Whitestone with Oldridge, 1981–87; Archdeacon of Totnes, 1981–88; Suffragan Bishop of Plymouth, 1988–96; Chapter Canon, Exeter Cathedral, 2006–09. *Address*: 3 Westbrook Close, Whipton, Exeter EX4 8BS. *T*: (01392) 462622.

HAWKINS, Prof. Robert Edward, PhD; FRCP; Cancer Research UK Professor, and Director of Medical Oncology, Christie Hospital NHS Trust, Manchester, and University of Manchester, since 1998; Chief Executive Officer, Cellular Therapeutics Ltd, since 2015 (Director, since 2010); *b* 10 Nov. 1955; *s* of George Edward Russell Hawkins and Rosemary Anne Hawkins; *m* 1989, Gek Kee Lim; one *s*. *Educ*: Trinity Coll., Cambridge (BA (Maths) 1977); UCL (MB BS 1984); MRC Lab. of Molecular Biol., Cambridge (PhD 1994). MRCP 1988, FRCP 1999. MRC Trng Fellow, 1989–92, CRC Sen. Res. Fellow, 1992–96, MRC Lab. of Molecular Biol., Cambridge; Prof. of Oncology, Univ. of Bristol, 1996–98; Hon. Consultant, Christie Hosp. NHS Trust, Manchester, 1998–. Co-ordinator: EU Framework Prog. 6: ATTACK (Adoptive engineered T-cell Targeting to Activate Cancer Killing) Project, 2006–11; EU Framework Prog. 7: ATTRACT (Advanced Teaching and Training for Adoptive Cell Therapy), 2010–13; ATTACK clinical trial network, 2013–; NIHR/Efficacy and Mechanisms Evaluation Prog./MRC METILDA trial in metastatic melanoma, 2013–. Member: MRC Molecular and Cellular Medicine Bd, 2012–; World Immunotherapy Council, 2012–. Pres., Soc. for Cellular Therapy of Cancer, 2012–. Clinical Ed., British Jl of Cancer, 1996–2003. *Publications*: over 160 papers on cancer res. with emphasis on renal cancer, antibody technology, gene and immunotherapy. *Recreation*: golf. *Address*: Medical Oncology, Christie Hospital and University of Manchester, Wilmslow Road, Manchester M20 4BX. *T*: (0161) 446 3208, *Fax*: (0161) 446 3269. *E*: robert.hawkins@ics.manchester.ac.uk.

HAWKINS, Sally Cecilia; actress; *b* Lewisham, London, 27 April 1976; *d* of Colin Hawkins and Jacqui Hawkins. *Educ*: James Allen Girls' Sch.; RADA. *Theatre* includes: As You Like It, Buckingham Palace Gala; Romeo and Juliet, The Cherry Orchard, Th. Royal, York, 1999; Much Ado About Nothing, A Midsummer Night's Dream, Regents Park, 2000; Country Music, Royal Court, 2004; House of Bernarda Alba, RNT, 2005; The Winterling, Royal Court, 2006; Mrs Warren's Profession, NY, 2010; Constellations, Royal Court, transf. Duke of York's, 2012; *films* include: All Or Nothing, 2002; Layer Cake, 2004; Vera Drake, 2005; Waz, 2007; Cassandra's Dream, Happy-Go-Lucky (Best Actress, LA Film Critics, NY Film Critics, Boston Film Critics, Silver Bear Award, 2008, Amer. Nat. Soc. of Film Critics, 2009; Breakthrough Award, Hollywood Film Fest., 2008; Peter Sellers award for Comedy, Evening Standard Film Awards, Golden Globe for Best Actress in a Comedy or Musical, 2009), 2008; An Education, Desert Flower, 2009; Happy Ever Afters, It's a Wonderful Afterlife, Made in Dagenham, 2010; Never Let Me Go, Submarine, Love Birds, Jane Eyre, 2011; Great Expectations, 2012; Blue Jasmine, 2013 (Best Supporting Actress, Empire Award, 2014); The Phone Call (short), 2013; The Double, 2014; Godzilla, 2014; Paddington, 2014; X + Y, 2015; Paddington 2 (British Actress, London Film Critics' Circle Award, 2017), Maudie, 2017 (Audience Choice Award, Vancouver Film Fest., 2017); The Shape of Water, 2018 (Best Actress, Boston Film Critics, Dallas-Fort Worth Film Critics, Dorian Award, Houston Film Critics, London Film Critics, National Soc. of Film Critics, Online Film Critics, 2017); Godzilla: King of the Monsters, 2019; Eternal Beauty, 2019; *television* includes: Tipping the Velvet, 2002; The Young Visiters, 2003; Byron, 2003; Promoted to Glory, 2003; Little Britain, 2003–05; Bunk Bed Boys, 2004; Fingersmith, 2005; 20,000 Streets Under the Sky, 2005; Shiny Shiny Bright New Hole in My Heart, 2006; Man to Man with Dean Learner, 2006; Persuasion, 2007 (Best Performance by an Actress, TV Film, Golden Nymph Award, 2007; Best Actress, RTS, 2008); Little Crackers, 2011; Room on the Broom, 2012; How and Why, 2014; The Hollow Crown: Henry VI Parts 1 and 2, 2016. Film Actress of the Year, Glamour Awards, 2014; British or Irish Actress of the Year, London Film Critics' Circle Award, 2018. *Recreations*: painting, writing, cycling, walking, meditating, playing with young nieces and nephews. *Address*: c/o Conway van Gelder Grant Ltd, 8–12 Broadwick Street, W1F 8HW. *T*: (020) 7287 0077. *E*: elaine@conwayvg.com.

HAWKINS, Prof. Stephen John, PhD, DSc; CBiol, FRSB, FMBA; Professor of Natural Sciences, Southampton University, 2010–17, now Emeritus (Dean, Faculty of Natural and Environmental Sciences, 2010–15); Lankester Fellow, Marine Biological Association of the UK, Plymouth, since 2016; *b* 12 Jan. 1956; *s* of Kenneth and Marjorie Hawkins; *m* 1997,

Dr Elspeth Jack. *Educ:* Univ. of Liverpool (BSc Marine Biology 1976; PhD 1980; DSc 2008). MIBiol 1980, FRSB (FIBiol 2009). NERC Post-doctoral Fellow, Marine Biological Assoc., Plymouth, 1979–80; Lectr in Zoology, Univ. of Manchester, 1980–87; Lectr, 1987–90, Sen. Lectr, 1990–95, in Marine Biology, Univ. of Liverpool; University of Southampton: Dir, Centre for Envmtl Scis, 1995–99; Hd, Biodiversity and Ecology Div., 1996–99; Prof. of Envmtl Biology, 1995–2006 (pt-time, 1999–2006); Dir and Sec., Marine Biol Assoc. of UK, 1999–2007 (Vice-Pres., 2010–); Prof. of Marine Biol., Univ. of Plymouth, 2006–07; Prof. of Natural Scis, and Head, Coll. of Natural Scis, 2007–10, Actg Pro-Vice Chancellor, Res. and Enterprise, 2010, Bangor Univ. Partnership for the Observation of Global Oceans Vis. Prof., Argentina, 2010; Vis. Prof., Nat. Univ. of Singapore Soc., 2016–17; Erskine Fellow, Univ. of Canterbury, NZ, 2017. Chairman: Bioadapt Panel, 2011–13, Living Earth Panel, 2014–15, Agence Nat. de la Recherche, France; Biodiversa Panel, 2015–16. Vice-Pres., European Marine Res. Stations Network, 2000–07. Mem., Sci. Adv. Council, DEFRA, 2009–11; Chm., Welsh Govt Technical Adv. Gp on Marine Conservation Zones, 2009–11. Mem., Adv. Bd, Biodiversity Res. Centre Academia Sinica, Taiwan, 2010–. Trustee: Nat. Biodiversity Network, 2000–04; Nat. Marine Aquarium, Plymouth, 2000–04; Freshwater Biol Assoc., 2014–17. FHEA 2003; FMBA 2016. *Publications:* (with H. D. Jones) Marine Field Course Guide: Rocky Shores, 1992; (with D. Raffaelli) Intertidal Ecology, 1996, 2nd edn 1999; over 300 peer-reviewed papers and book chapters. *Recreations:* cricket, ski-ing, fishing, sailing, occasional fieldwork, watching Rugby. *Address:* Ocean and Earth Science, National Oceanography Centre Southampton, Waterfront Campus, European Way, Southampton SO14 3ZH; Marine Biological Association of the UK, The Laboratory, Citadel Hill, Plymouth PL1 2PB. *Clubs:* Braunton Cricket (Vice-Pres., 1995–2007); Barnstaple Rugby Football.

**HAWKSWORTH, Prof. David Leslie,** CBE 1996; DSc; CBiol, FRSB, FLS; mycologist, systematist, and environmental and forensic biologist; Scientific Associate, Natural History Museum, London, since 2006; Honorary Research Associate, Royal Botanic Gardens, Kew, since 2014; *b* Sheffield, 5 June 1946; *e s* of late Leslie Hawksworth and Freda Mary (*née* Dolamore); *m* 1st, 1968, Madeleine Una Ford (marr. diss. 1998); one *s* one *d*; 2nd, 1999 (marr. diss. 2008); 3rd, 2009, Patricia E. J. Wiltshire. *Educ:* Herbert Strutt Grammar Sch., Belper; Univ. of Leicester (BSc 1967; PhD 1970; DSc 1980). FLS 1969; FRSB (FIBiol 1982); CBiol 1986. Mycologist, Commonwealth Mycological Inst., Kew, 1969–81; sci. asst to Exec. Dir, CAB, 1981–83; Dir, Internat. Mycol Inst., CAB Internat., 1983–97. Visiting Professor: Univ. of Riyadh, 1978; Univ. of Reading, 1984–98; Univ. of Assiut, 1985; Univ. of Kent, 1990–; Royal Holloway, Univ. of London, 1992–; Univ. Complutense, Madrid, 2000–01; Birkbeck, Univ. of London, 2012–17; Univ. of Southampton, 2015–; Jilin Agricultural Univ., 2016–; Res. Prof., Universidad Complutense de Madrid, 2001–16; Prof. of Biology, 2007–09, Prof. of Ecology, 2013–14, Univ. of Gloucestershire. Mem. Council, English Nature, 1996–99. President: British Lichen Soc., 1986–87 (Hon. Mem., 1997); Eur. Congress of Mycologists, 1989; Br. Mycol Soc., 1990 (Centenary Fellow, 1996); Internat. Mycol Assoc., 1990–94 (Sec.-Gen., 1977–90; Hon. Pres., 1994–); Internat. Union of Biol Sci., 1994–97; Professional Mem., Chartered Soc. of Forensic Scis (formerly Forensic Sci. Soc.), 2011. Vice-Pres., Linnean Soc., 1985–88; Treasurer and Editor-in-Chief, Systematics Assoc., 1972–86; Treas., Internat. Congress of Systematic and Evolutionary Biol., 1989–96; Chairman: Internat. Commn on Taxonomy of Fungi, 1982–2002; Ruislip-Northwood Woods Adv. Working Party, 1979–82; Internat. Cttee on Bionomenclature, 1994–2012; Chief Rapp., CAB Internat. Review Confs, 1985, 1990, 1993, 1996. Dir, MycoNova, 1998–2003. FRSA 1997. Hon. Member: Soc. Lichenologica Italiana, 1989; Ukrainian Botanical Soc., 1992; Mycol Soc. of America, 1994; Assoc. Latinoamericana de Micología, 1996; Japanese Soc. for Lichenology, 2002. Editor: The Lichenologist, 1970–90; Systema Ascomycetum, 1986–98; Mycosystema, 1987–2008; Sen. (formerly Exec.) Editor, Mycological Research, 2000–08; Editor-in-Chief: Biodiversity and Conservation, 2006–; IMA Fungus, 2010–. Mem., Mole Valley DC, 2016– (Cabinet Mem., 2018–19). FD *hc* Umeå, 1996. First Bicent. Medal, Linnean Soc., 1978; Acharius Medal, Internat. Assoc. for Lichenology, 2002; Josef Adolf von Arx Award, KNAW-CBS Fungal Biodiversity Centre, Utrecht, 2011; Ainsworth Medal, 2014, Fellow Medal, 2018, Internat. Mycol Assoc.; Founders' Award, Eur. Congress of Mycologists, 2015. *Publications:* (jtly) Dictionary of the Fungi, 6th edn 1971 to 8th edn 1995; (ed jtly) Air Pollution and Lichens, 1973; Mycologist's Handbook, 1974; (ed) The Changing Flora and Fauna of Britain, 1974; (jtly) Lichens as Pollution Monitors, 1976; (ed jtly) Lichenology: progress and problems, 1976; (jtly) Lichenology in the British Isles 1568–1975, 1977; (jtly) Key Works to the Fauna and Flora of the British Isles and Northwestern Europe, 4th edn 1978, 5th edn 1988; (ed) Advancing Agricultural Production in Africa, 1984; (jtly) The Lichen-Forming Fungi, 1984; (jtly) The British Ascomycotina, 1985; (ed jtly) Coevolution and Systematics, 1986; (ed jtly) Coevolution of Fungi with Plants and Animals, 1988; (ed jtly) Living Resources for Biotechnology, 1988; (ed) Prospects in Systematics, 1988; (jtly) International Mycological Directory, 1990; (ed) Frontiers in Mycology, 1991; (ed) Improving the Stability of Names, 1991; (ed) The Biodiversity of Microorganisms and Invertebrates: their role in sustainable agriculture, 1991; (jtly) Lichen Flora of Great Britain and Ireland, 1992; (jtly) Biodiversity and Biosystematic Priorities: microorganisms and invertebrates, 1993; (jtly) IMI: retrospect and prospect, 1993; (ed) Identification and Characterization of Pest Organisms, 1994; Glossary of Terms Used in Bionomenclature, 1994; (ed) Ascomycete Systematics: problems and perspectives in the nineties, 1994; (jtly) The Biodiversity of Microorganisms and the Role of Microbial Resource Centres, 1994; (ed jtly) Microbial Diversity and Ecosystem Function, 1995; (ed jtly) Biodiversity Information: needs and options, 1997; (ed) The Changing Wildlife of Great Britain and Ireland, 2001; (ed jtly) International Code of Botanical Nomenclature (Vienna Code), 2006; (ed jtly) Arthropod Diversity and Conservation, 2006; (ed jtly) Forest Diversity and Management, 2006; (ed jtly) Human Exploitation and Biodiversity, 2006; (ed jtly) Marine, Freshwater and Wetlands Biodiversity Conservation, 2006; (ed jtly) Vertebrate Conservation and Biodiversity, 2007; Plant Conservation and Biodiversity, 2007; Biodiversity and Conservation in Europe, 2008; (ed jtly) Plantation Forests and Biodiversity: oxymoron or opportunity, 2009; (ed jtly) Protist Diversity and Geographical Distribution, 2009; (ed) Management and Conservation of Biodiversity, 2010; (ed) Methods and Practice in Biodiversity and Conservation, 2010; Terms used in Bionomenclature: the naming of organisms (and plant communities), 2010; (ed jtly) International Code of Nomenclature for algae, fungi and plants, 2012, 2018; numerous papers on biodiversity, biol nomenclature, fungi (including lichens), forensic mycology. *Recreations:* bibliography, Huxley family, natural history, second-hand books. *Address:* Milford House, 10 The Mead, Ashtead, Surrey KT21 2LZ. *E:* d.hawksworth@nhm.ac.uk, d.hawksworth@kew.org, councillor.hawksworth@molevalley.gov.uk.

**HAWLEY, Prof. Christine Elizabeth,** CBE 2008; RIBA; Professor of Architectural Studies, 1993–2016, now Emeritus Professor of Architectural Design, and Dean and Head of The Bartlett, Faculty of the Built Environment, 1999–2009, University College London; *b* 3 Aug. 1949; *d* of John and Margaret Hawley; *m* 1973, Clyde; two *s* one *d*. *Educ:* City of London Sch. for Girls; Architectural Assoc. (AADipl 1975). ARCUK 1985. Lectr, AA, 1978–86; Hd, Sch. of Architecture, Univ. of East London, 1986–93. Visiting Professor: Univ. of Lund, Sweden, 2008; Chinese Univ. of Hong Kong, 2009, 2011; Hong Kong Univ., 2016; Chisholm Fellowship, Univ. of Western Australia, 2012; One Siew May Prof., NUS, 2019. Recent built work includes: social housing for Internat. Bauausstellung, Berlin, 1989; Kantine, Städel Acad., Frankfurt, 1992; exhibn pavilions, Osaka and Nagoya Expo, 1993; social housing for Gifu, Japan; mus. for Roman remains at Camuntum, Lower Austria, 1997. Advr, CABE, 2001–04. Curator, Bi-City Biennale of Urbanism\Architecture, Hong Kong, 2015–16. FRSA. Annie Spink Award, RIBA, 2016. *Publications:* articles in a number of prof. jls inc. GA, Architecture and Urbanism and Architects' Jl. *Recreations:* swimming, reading, film, art. *Address:* 10 Lyndhurst Square, SE15 5AR.

**HAWLEY, Sir James (Appleton),** KCVO 2010; TD 1969; Lord-Lieutenant of Staffordshire, 1993–2012; *b* 28 March 1937; *s* of late John J. Hawley and Mary Hawley, JP; *m* 1961, Susan, *d* of Alan Stott, JP, DL; one *s* two *d*. *Educ:* Uppingham; St Edmund Hall, Oxford (MA Jurisp.). Called to the Bar, Middle Temple, 1961. Nat. Service, 2nd Lieut South Staffs Regt, Cyprus; Lieut to Major, Staffs Yeomanry Regt (QORR). Chairman: John James Hawley (Speciality Works) Ltd, 1961–98; J. W. Wilkinson & Co., 1970–98; Dir, Stafford Railway Building Soc., 1985–2003. Pres., Made-Up Textiles Assoc., 1984–85; Chm., Camping Trade Assoc., 1977–78. President: Staffs and Birmingham Agricl Soc., 2004–05; Walsall Soc. for the Blind, 2001– (Chm., 1977–92); Lichfield Fest., 2006–14; RFCA W Midlands, 1998–2004; Trustee, Armed Forces Meml, 2003–16; Patron, Staffs Wildlife Trust, 2014–17; formerly Patron, President or Trustee of many other organisations in Staffs. Freeman: City of London, 1986; Newcastle-under-Lyme, 2011; Co. of Staffs, 2012. Liveryman, Saddlers' Co., 1986–. JP Staffs 1969; High Sheriff, Staffs, 1976–77; DL Staffs 1978. DUniv: Staffordshire, 2003; Keele, 2009. KStJ 1993. *Recreations:* family, Staffordshire, outdoor pursuits. *Address:* The Hollies, Stafford Road, Eccleshall, Stafford ST21 6JP. *Clubs:* Oxford and Cambridge; Walsall.

**HAWLEY, Ven. John Andrew;** Archdeacon of Blackburn, 2002–15; permission to officiate, Dioceses of Sheffield, York and Leeds, since 2016; Acting Archdeacon of Doncaster, since 2019; *b* 27 April 1950; *s* of Willie and Constance May Hawley. *Educ:* Stannington County Jun. Sch.; Ecclesfield Grammar Sch.; King's Coll., London (BD, AKC 1971); Wycliffe Hall, Oxford. Ordained deacon, 1974, priest, 1975; Asst Curate, Holy Trinity, Hull, 1974–77; Sen. Curate, Bradford Cathedral, 1977–80; Vicar, All Saints, Woodlands, Doncaster, 1980–91; Team Rector, Dewsbury, 1991–2002; Actg Archdeacon of Lancaster, 2010–11; Acting Vicar of Goole, 2016–19. Proctor in Convocation, 1996–2002; Bishop's Adviser on Urban Priority Areas, 2002–15; on Hosp. and Hospice Chaplaincy, 2013–15; Archbishop of York's Assessor for Clergy Discipline Measure, 2015–; Bp of Sheffield's Enquirer for C4 Faculties, 2016–. Chm., Wakefield Diocesan House of Clergy, 2000–02. Hon. Canon, Wakefield Cathedral, 1998. Member: Nat. Archdeacons' Forum, 2010–15; Pastoral Measure Rev. Gp, C of E, 2000–03; House for Duty Wkg Gp, C of E, 2010–12. Chm., Belonging to Blackburn with Darwen Campaign, 2003–04. *Recreations:* cricket, golf, fell walking, quiet holidays in Scotland, studying St Paulinus of York. *Address:* 35 Woodland Avenue, Goole, E Yorks DN14 6QT. *T:* (01405) 762678, 07544 952645.

**HAWLEY, Dr Robert,** CBE 1997; FREng, FIET, FIMechE, FInstP; FRSE; Chairman: Engineering Council, 1999–2002; Particle Physics and Astronomy Research Council, 1998–2001; *b* 23 July 1936; *s* of William and Eva Hawley; *m* 1st, Valerie (*née* Clarke) (marr. diss. 2002); one *s* one *d*; *m* 2nd, 2002, Pamela Elizabeth (*née* Neesham). *Educ:* Wallasey Grammar Sch.; Wallasey Technical Coll.; Birkenhead Technical Coll.; Durham Univ. (BSc 1959; PhD 1963); Newcastle upon Tyne Univ. (DSc 1976). FIET (FIEE 1970); FREng (FEng 1979); FIMechE 1987; FInstP 1971. FRSE 1997. Student apprentice, BICC, Prescot, 1952–55; C. A. Parsons & Co. Ltd: Head of Res. Team, 1961–64; Chief Elec. Engr, 1970–74; Dir of Prodn and Engrg, 1974–76; Man. Dir, NEI Parsons Ltd, 1976–84; NEI plc: Man. Dir, Power Engrg Gp, 1984–89; Man. Dir, 1989–92; Chm., NEI ABB Gas Turbines Ltd, 1990–92; Chief Executive: Nuclear Electric plc, 1992–96; British Energy plc, 1995–97. Mem. Bd, Rolls-Royce plc, 1989–92. Non-executive Chairman: Rotork plc, 1997–98; INBIS Group plc, 1997–2000; ERAtech Ltd, 1997–2000; Taylor Woodrow plc, 1999–2003; Rocktron, 2001–05; Berkeley Resources Ltd, 2006–; Lister Petter Investment Hldgs Ltd, 2006–; Carron Acquisition Co. Ltd, 2006–09; non-executive Director: W. S. Atkins Ltd, 1994–97; Tricorder Technology, 1997–2001; Colt Telecom Gp, 1998–2010; Rutland Trust, 2001–07; Consultant, ABB Ltd, 1993–97; Advr, SEMA Gp, 1995–97; Adv. Dir, HSBC Investment Bank, 1998–2004. Member: NE Indust. Develt Bd, DTI, 1989–92; Bd, Northern Develt Co., 1989–92; Industrial Develt Adv. Bd, DTI, 1994–2000; Pres., Partnership Korea, DTI, 1995–2002. Chairman: Hawley Cttee on Corporate Governance Information Management, 1993–98; Hawley Gp on Engrg Profession, DTI and Engrg Council, 1999–2001. Mem., Annual Review Sub-group, and Chm., Energy Wkg Pty, 1986–87, ACARD; Member: DFEE Women's Issues Wkg Gp, 1996–97; Mgt and Leadership in the Professions, DFEE, 2000–. Institution of Electrical Engineers: Vice Pres., 1991–95; Dep. Pres., 1995–96; Pres., 1996–97. Member Council: Fellowship of Engrg, 1981–84; Foundn for Sci. and Technol., 1999–2001 (Dep. Chm., 2002–); Royal Instn, 2000–; Mem., Nat. Centre for Univs and Business (formerly Council for Industry and Higher Educn), 2000–. Pres., Energy Industries Club, 1989–91. Mem., Boat and Shoreworks Cttee, RNLI, 1992–95. Trustee, Daphne Jackson Trust, 2000–. Chm., 2002–07, Pres., 2007–, Anglo-Korean Soc. Lectures include: C. A. Parsons Meml, IEE and Royal Soc., 1977; Hunter Meml, IEE, 1990; Blackadder, NEC Inst., 1992; Wilson Campbell Meml, Univ. of Newcastle upon Tyne, 1994; Bowden, UMIST, 1994; J. G. Collier Meml, Univ. of Brunel, 1997; Higginson, 1998, Temple Chevallier, 2001, Durham; Armstrong, 2001, Newcastle upon Tyne; Royce, IIE, 2001; Mountbatten, IEE, 2002; Bridge, Engineers' Co., 2002; Blumein, IEE, 2005. Member: Court, Univ. of Newcastle upon Tyne, 1979–; Bd of Advrs, Elec. Engrg, Univ. of London, 1982–86; Court, Loughborough Univ., 2003–; Chm., Council, Univ. of Durham, 1997–2002; Vice-Chancellor, World Nuclear Univ., 2006–. Freeman, City of London, 1985; Master, Engrs' Co., 2005–06. Mem., Nat. Acad. of Engrg of Korea, 2001. FRSE 1997; FCGI 2003. Hon. FINucE 1994; Hon. FIEE 2003. Hon. Fellow, Liverpool John Moores Univ., 2002. Hon. DSc: Durham, 1996; City, 1998; Cranfield, 2002; Hon. DEng: South Bank, 1997; West of England, 1997; Newcastle upon Tyne, 2002; UMIST, 2002; Hon. DTech: Staffordshire 2000; Abertay Dundee, 2001; Robert Gordon, Aberdeen, 2002. DUniv Surrey, 2002. Waverley Gold Medal, RSA, 1960; Achievement Medal, for outstanding contribs to power engrg, IEE, 1989. Premio Vicente Lecuna Medal, Venezuela, 1997; Order of Diplomatic Service Gwanghwa Medal, Korea, 1999. *Publications:* (with A. Maitland) Vacuum as an Insulator, 1967; (with A. A. Zaky): Dielectric Solids, 1970; Conduction and Breakdown in Mineral Oil, 1973; Fundamentals of Electromagnetic Field Theory, 1974; technical papers on electrical breakdown in vacuum, liquids and solids, electrical machine design and power generation. *Recreations:* gardening, writing, philately. *Address:* Summerfield, Rendcomb, near Cirencester, Glos GL7 7HB. *T:* (01285) 831610, *Fax:* (01285) 831801. *Club:* Athenæum.

**HAWORTH, Baron** *cr* 2004 (Life Peer), of Fisherfield in Ross and Cromarty; **Alan Robert Haworth;** Secretary, Parliamentary Labour Party, 1992–2004; *b* 26 April 1948; *s* of late John Haworth and Hilma Haworth (*née* Westhead); *m* 1st, 1973, Gill Cole; 2nd, 1991, Maggie Rae. *Educ:* Barking Regl Coll. of Technol. (BScSoc London Univ. ext.). Cttee

Officer, 1975–85, Sen. Cttee Officer, 1985–92, Parly Labour Party. *Publications:* (ed jtly) Men Who Made Labour, 2006. *Recreations:* hill walking, mountaineering. *Address:* House of Lords, SW1A 0PW.

HAWORTH, Sir Christopher, 4th Bt *cr* 1911, of Dunham Massey, Co. Chester; *b* 6 Nov. 1951; *s* of Sir Philip Haworth, 3rd Bt and Joan Helen Haworth (*née* Clark); *S* father, 2019; *m* 1994, Susan Rachel, *d* of David Ives and widow of Jonathan Dent; one *s* one *d*, and two step *s*. *Heir: s* Oliver Jonathan Christopher Haworth, *b* 20 Oct. 1996.

HAWORTH, Glennis; *see* Haworth, S. G.

HAWORTH, Graham Thomas, RIBA; Director, Haworth Tompkins Architects, since 1991; *b* 15 Jan. 1960; *m* 2008, Lottie Cole; one *d*, and two *s* one *d* from a previous relationship. *Educ:* Univ. of Nottingham (BArch); Jesus Coll., Cambridge (DipArch). RIBA 1989. Architect: Skidmore Owings Merrill, 1986–87; Bennetts Associates, 1988–90. Projects include: Royal Court Th., 2000; Coin Street Housing, 2001; Hayward Gall. extension, 2003; Young Vic Th., London Liby, 2005; Liverpool 1, 2007; Royal Coll. of Art, 2008. *Recreations:* contemporary arts, theatre, walking, fishing, painting. *Address:* Haworth Tompkins, 33 Greenwood Place, NW5 1LB. *E:* graham.haworth@haworthtompkins.com.

HAWORTH, John Leigh W.; *see* Walker-Haworth.

HAWORTH, (John) Martin, PhD; Headmaster, Wallington County Grammar School, 1990–2010; *b* 22 Jan. 1949; *s* of Reginald and Hilda Haworth; *m* 1973, Brenda Dawe; two *d*. *Educ:* London Bible Coll. (BD 1972); Univ. of Birmingham (MA 1973; PhD 1982); Univ. of Warwick (MEd 1984). RE teacher, Plymstock Sch., 1973–77; Hd, RE and Hd, 6th Form, Coundon Court Sch., 1977–84; Dep. Hd, Wisewood Sch., 1985–90. FRSA. *Recreations:* karate (1st Dan), running, church, theatre, concerts, opera. *E:* JMartinHaworth@gmail.com.

HAWORTH, His Honour Jonathan Mayo; a Circuit Judge, 1996–2016; *b* 5 Oct. 1948; *s* of George Henry Haworth and Elsa Sophia Haworth; *m* 1973, Brigitte Ilse Müller; one *s* one *d*. *Educ:* King Edward VII Grammar Sch., Sheffield; King's Coll., London (LLB Hons). Called to the Bar, Middle Temple, 1971; practised from Fenners Chambers, Cambridge, 1973–96. *Recreations:* reading, computers, music, cricket.

HAWORTH, Martin; *see* Haworth, J. M.

HAWORTH, Peter Aynge; Master of the Senior (formerly Supreme) Court Costs Office, since 2006; *b* 27 March 1951; *s* of Arthur Haworth and Mary Haworth (*née* Aynge); *m* 1975, Margaret Elaine Knowles; three *d*. *Educ:* Towneley High Sch., Burnley; Univ. of Liverpool (LLB 1972). Admitted as solicitor, 1975; Partner, Southerns Solicitors, 1978–2003; a Dep. District Judge, Northern Circuit, 1992–; Solicitor Advocate, 1998; Dep. Master and Costs Judge, 2002–06. Mem., Civil Procedure Rule Cttee, 1996–99; Solicitor Mem. and Chm., Solicitors' Disciplinary Tribunal, 1999–2006. A Lieut Bailiff of Guernsey, 2003–. *Recreations:* yachting, ski-ing, hot air ballooning, fell walking, theatre. *Address:* Senior Court Costs Office, Thomas More Building, Royal Courts of Justice, Strand, WC2A 2LL. *Clubs:* Royal London Yacht; Royal Ocean Racing; City Livery Yacht.

HAWORTH, Russell Adam; Chief Executive Officer, Nominet, since 2015; *b* Warrington, Cheshire, 20 Sept. 1971; *s* of John Haworth and Marilyn Haworth (*née* Adams); *m* 2006, Elizabeth Anne Turenne; two *s*. *Educ:* St Wilfred's Primary Sch.; Bridgewater High Sch.; Leicester De Montfort Univ. (BSc 1st Cl. Hons Mech. Engrg); Kellogg Sch. of Mgt, Northwestern Univ. (MBA). Strategy Consultant, PA Consulting, 1995–98; Manager, Corporate Finance Advisory, Deloitte, 1998–2000; Dir, Corporate Finance, 2000–01, Vice Pres., Hd of Americas for Corporate Develt, 2001–08, Reuters; Sen. Vice Pres., Hd of Strategy and Business Develt, 2008–10, Man. Dir, ME and N Africa, 2010–14, Thomson Reuters. Member: Bd, TechUK, 2017–; Adv. Bd, CyLon, 2018–. Chair, Digital Leaders, 2018–. Mem., Adv. Bd, Innovation Council, CBI, 2018–. Mem., Young Presidents Orgn, 2008–. FBCS 2019. CIM Award, 1996; Tech. CEO of Year, CEO Monthly Mag., 2018. *Recreations:* tennis, golf, swimming, cycling.

HAWORTH, Prof. (Sheila) Glennis, (Mrs L. F. H. Busk), CBE 2007; MD; FRCP, FRCPath; FRCPCH; FMedSci; Professor of Developmental Cardiology, Institute of Child Health, 1991–2009, and British Heart Foundation Professor of Developmental Cardiology, 1991–2004, University College London, now Professor Emeritus; Founder, 2001, and Lead Clinician, 2001–09, UK Pulmonary Hypertension Service for Children; *b* 31 May 1939; *d* of Richard and Elizabeth Haworth; *m* 1st, 1970, Prof. T. J. McElwain (*d* 1990); 2nd, 1993, Maj.-Gen. Leslie Francis Harry Busk, *qv*. *Educ:* Royal Free Hosp. Sch. of Medicine, Univ. of London (MB BS 1964; MD 1976). FRCP 1981; FRCPath 1991; FRCPCH 1997. Fellow in Fetal Physiol. and Neonatol., Columbia Univ., NY, 1967–69; Med. Registrar, RPMS, 1970; Registrar, then Sen. Lectr, Royal Brompton Hosp., London, 1971–76; Hon. Consultant in Paediatric Cardiol., Hosp. for Sick Children, Great Ormond St, 1976–2009; Institute of Child Health: Sen. Lectr, 1976–82; Sub-Dean, 1982–85; Reader, 1982–88; Prof. of Paediatric Cardiol., 1989–90. Pres., Pulmonary Vascular Res. Inst., 2014–16. Involved with practice of medicine overseas for over 30 years, incl. improvement of pulmonary hypertension care. FACC 1986; FMedSci 1999. *Publications:* clinical and basic science papers on the develt of the pulmonary circulation, the pathogenesis and treatment of pulmonary hypertension in childhood and paediatric cardiology. *Recreations:* playing the piano, opera, travel. *Address:* Bushwood, Witheridge Hill Bottom, Highmoor, Henley-on-Thames, Oxon RG9 5PE. *T:* (01491) 641223. *E:* s.haworth@ich.ucl.ac.uk.

HAWTHORN, Ven. Christopher John; Archdeacon of Cleveland, 1991–2001, now Archdeacon Emeritus; *b* 29 April 1936; *s* of late Rev. John Christopher Hawthorn and Susan Mary Hawthorn; *m* 1964, Elizabeth Margaret Lowe; three *s* one *d*. *Educ:* Marlborough Coll.; Queens' Coll., Cambridge (MA Hons); Ripon Hall, Oxford. Deacon 1962, priest 1963; Asst Curate, Sutton-in-Holderness, 1962–66; Vicar: St Nicholas, Hull, 1966–72; Christ Church, Coatham, 1972–79; St Martin's-on-the-Hill, Scarborough, 1979–91; RD Scarborough, 1982–91. Proctor in Convocation, 1987–90; Canon of York, 1987–2001, now Canon Emeritus. *Recreations:* gardening, fell walking, sport. *Address:* 11 Holly Tree Lane, Haxby, York YO32 3YJ. *T:* (01904) 591008.

HAWTHORNE, Prof. John P., PhD; FBA 2013; Professor of Philosophy, University of Southern California, since 2015 (part-time, 2013–15). *Educ:* Univ. of Manchester (BA 1985); Syracuse Univ. (PhD 1991); MA Oxon. Former positions at Univ. of NSW, ANU, Arizona State Univ. and Syracuse Univ.; Waynflete Prof. of Metaphysical Philosophy, Univ. of Oxford, 2006–15; Fellow, Magdalen Coll., Oxford, until 2015. Visiting Professor: Rutgers Univ.; Princeton Univ., 2009–13. *Publications:* Knowledge and Lotteries, 2004; Metaphysical Essays, 2006; (with Herman Cappelen) Relativism and Monadic Truth, 2009; (with David Manley) The Reference Book, 2012. *Address:* School of Philosophy, University of Southern California, Mudd Hall of Philosophy, 3709 Trousdale Parkway, Los Angeles, CA 90089-0451, USA.

HAWTIN, Brian Richard, CB 1997; Deputy Director General, Technical Secretariat, Organisation for the Prohibition of Chemical Weapons, 2003–06; *b* 31 May 1946; *s* of late Dick Hawtin and Jean (*née* Middleton); *m* 1969, Anthea Fry; two *d*. *Educ:* Portsmouth Grammar Sch.; Christ Church, Oxford (MA). Ministry of Defence, 1967–2002: Asst Private Sec. to Permt Under Sec. of State, 1970; seconded to FCO as First Sec., UK Delegn to NATO, Brussels, 1978–80; Asst Sec., 1981; RCDS 1987; Private Sec. to Sec. of State for Defence, 1987–89; Asst Under Sec. of State (material/naval), 1989–92, (Progs), 1992–94, (Home and Overseas), 1994–96, (Policy), 1997–99; Fellow, Center for Internat. Affairs, Harvard Univ., 1996–97; Dir Gen., Internat. Security Policy, 1999–2002; Chm., MoD Grievance Appeal Panel, 2007–14. *Recreations:* walking, antiques, grandchildren, travel.

HAWTIN, Rt Rev. David Christopher; Bishop Suffragan of Repton, 1999–2006; an Honorary Assistant Bishop, Diocese of Sheffield, since 2007; *b* 7 June 1943; *m* 1968, Elizabeth Ann (*née* Uden) (*d* 2010); one *s* two *d*; *m* 2019, Linda Blenkinship. *Educ:* King Edward VII Sch., Lytham St Annes; Keble Coll., Oxford (BA 1965; MA 1970); William Temple Coll., Rugby; Cuddesdon Coll., Oxford. Ordained deacon, 1967, priest 1968; Curate: St Thomas, Pennywell, Sunderland, 1967–71; St Peter's, Stockton, 1971–74; Priest in charge, St Andrew's, Leam Lane, Gateshead, 1974–79; Rector, Washington (incl. LEP), 1979–88; Diocesan Ecumenical Officer, Durham, 1988–92; Archdeacon of Newark, 1992–99. Gen. Synod Rep. for E Midlands Ministry Trng Course, 1997–99. Member: Gen. Synod, 1983–99 (Mem., Bd for Mission and Unity, 1986–91); BCC, 1987–90; Churches Together in England, 1990–2006 (Enabling Gp, 1991–99; Dep. Moderator, CTE Forum, 1995–99); Council of Churches for Britain and Ireland, 1990–2006; Chairman: Diocesan Bd of Educn, Southwell, 1993–99; E Midlands Consortium for Educn and Trng for Ministry, 1996–2001; Derby Diocesan Council for Mission and Unity, 1999–2001; Derby Diocesan Pastoral Cttee, 1999–2006; E Midlands Ministry Trng Course, 2002–06. Churches Project Co-ordinator, Nat. Garden Fest., Gateshead, 1988–91. Local Unity Advr, Durham Ecumenical Relations Gp, 1991–92; Consultant: Council for Christian Unity, 1991–96; Methodist/Anglican Panel for Unity in Mission, 2009–15; Member: CCU Local Unity Panel, 1999–2009 (Chm., 2003–06); Churches Together in England Gp for Local Unity, 2001–06. Member: N Notts and N Derbys Coalfield Alliance Bd, 1999–2003; Derbys Partnership, 2001. *Address:* 29 Arran Way, Rothwell, Leeds LS26 0WB.

HAWTIN, Michael Victor; Secretary, TALK, 2012–17 (Chairman, 2009–12); *b* 7 Sept. 1942; *s* of Guy and Constance Hawtin; *m* 1966, Judith Mary Eeley; one *s* one *d*. *Educ:* Bournemouth Sch.; St John's Coll., Cambridge (MA); Univ. of Calif, Berkeley (MA). Asst Principal, 1964–69, Principal, 1969–77, HM Treasury; seconded to Barclays Bank, 1969–71; Asst Sec., HM Treasury, 1977–83, Under Sec. (Principal Finance Officer), PSA, 1983–86; Under Sec., HM Treasury, 1986–88; Dir, Resource Management Gp and Principal Establishment and Finance Officer, ECGD, 1988–92; Dir, Underwriting Gp, ECGD, 1992–95; consultancy work for EU and IMF, 1996–2001. Chm., Relate W Surrey, 2000–09. *Recreations:* music, travel.

HAWTON, Prof. Keith Edward, DSc, DM; FRCPsych, FMedSci; Consultant Psychiatrist, Oxford Health NHS Foundation Trust (formerly Oxfordshire Mental Healthcare Unit, then Oxfordshire Mental Healthcare NHS Trust, later Oxfordshire and Buckinghamshire Mental Health NHS Foundation Trust), since 1984; Professor of Psychiatry, since 1996, and Director, Centre for Suicide Research, since 1998, University of Oxford; *b* 23 Dec. 1942; *s* of Leslie William Hawton and Eliza Hawton; *m* 1978, Joan Kirk; two *d*. *Educ:* Balliol Coll., and Med. Sch., Oxford (MB 2001; BChir 1969; DM 1980; DSc 2001); St John's Coll., Cambridge (MA 1970). FRCPsych 1990. Trng in psychiatry, 1970–73; Res. Psychiatrist, Clin. Lectr and Clin. Tutor in Psychiatry, Dept of Psychiatry, Oxford Univ., 1974–84. Boerhaave Vis. Prof., Leiden Univ., 1990–91. Sen. Investigator, Nat. Inst. for Health Res., 2009–16. FMedSci 2013. Stengel Res. Award, Internat. Assoc. for Suicide Prevention, 1995; Dublin Award, Amer. Assoc. Suicidology, 2001; Res. Award, American Foundn for Suicide Prevention, 2002; Morselli Medal, Internat. Assoc. Suicide Res., 2013. *Publications:* Attempted Suicide: a practical guide, 1982, 2nd edn 1987; Sex Therapy: a practical guide, 1985; Cognitive Behaviour Therapy for Psychiatric Problems, 1989; Suicide and Stress in Farmers, 1998; The International Handbook of Suicide and Attempted Suicide, 2000; Prevention and Treatment of Suicidal Behaviour: from science to practice, 2005; By Their Own Young Hand: deliberate self-harm and suicidal ideas in adolescents, 2006; Suicide, 2013. *Recreations:* fishing, cricket, wines, golf. *Address:* Centre for Suicide Research, University Department of Psychiatry, Warneford Hospital, Oxford OX3 7JX.

HAY, family name of Marquis of Tweeddale, Earls of Erroll and Kinnoull, and of Baron Hay of Ballyore.

HAY, Lord; Harry Thomas William Hay; property manager; *b* 8 Aug. 1984; *s* and heir of Earl of Erroll, *qv*; *m* 2017, Clementine Camilla Curtis, *e d* of Prof. Simon Travis. *Educ:* Stowe Sch.; Northumbria Univ. *Recreations:* country pursuits, ski-ing, horse racing. *Club:* Puffin's.

HAY OF BALLYORE, Baron *cr* 2014 (Life Peer), of Ballyore in the City of Londonderry; William Alexander Hay; Member for Foyle, 1998–2014 (DemU, 1998–2007, when elected Speaker), and Speaker, 2007–14, Northern Ireland Assembly; *b* 16 April 1950; *m* (marr. diss.); three *s* two *d*. *Educ:* Newbuildings Primary Sch.; Faughen Valley High Sch. Mem. (DemU), Derry CC, 1981–2010. Contested (DemU) Foyle, 2001, 2005. *Address:* House of Lords, SW1A 0PW.

HAY, Alasdair George, CBE 2017; QFSM 2011; Chief Officer, Scottish Fire and Rescue Service, 2012–19; *b* Edinburgh, 24 Dec. 1961; *s* of Alistair and Zandra Hay; *m* 1983, Caroline Lees; three *s*. *Educ:* Gracemount High Sch., Edinburgh; Univ. of Abertay, Dundee (MBA); Dundee Coll. (Post Grad. Dip. HR Mgt). MIFireE 1994. Fire officer, Essex Co. Fire and Rescue Service, 1983–92; Sen. Instructor, Scottish Fire Service Trng Sch., 1992–94; Tayside Fire and Rescue: Station Officer, 1994–95; Temp. Asst Divl Officer, 1995–97; Temp. Divl Officer III, Dep. Comdr Tech. Services, 1997; Asst Divl Officer, 1997–99; Divl Officer III, Dep. Divl Comdr Ops, 1999–2002; Divl Officer I, Comdr Tech. Services, 2002–04; Area Mgr B, Hd of Personnel, 2004–07; Asst Chief Fire Officer, 2007–08; Dep. Chief Fire Officer, 2008–11; Chief Fire Officer, 2012; Advr, Scottish Fire and Rescue Service Adv. Unit, 2011–12. Has undertaken courses on Exec. Mentoring, Safety for Sen. Execs and Task Orientated Negotiation. Co-opted Trustee, Chief Fire Officers Assoc., 2012–17; Mem., Nat. Fire Chiefs Council, 2018 (Co-opted Trustee, 2017–18). *Recreations:* family, playing tennis, watching Rugby and football, reading, history.

HAY, Dame Barbara (Logan), DCMG 2008 (CMG 1998); LVO 2008; MBE 1991; HM Diplomatic Service, retired; Consul-General, Los Angeles, 2009–13; *b* 20 Jan. 1953; *d* of late Alfred Hay and Isabella Hay (*née* Burgon). *Educ:* Boroughmuir Sen. Secondary Sch., Edinburgh. Joined Diplomatic Service, 1971; Russian language training, 1974–75; served Moscow and Johannesburg, 1975–80; Asst Private Sec. to Perm. Under-Sec. and Head of Diplomatic Service, 1981–83; FCO and Montreal, 1983–88; First Sec. (Inf.), Moscow, 1988–91; Consul-Gen., St Petersburg, 1991–92; Jt Assistance Unit (Central Europe), FCO, 1992–94; Ambassador, Republic of Uzbekistan and (non-res.), Republic of Tajikistan,

1995–99; Counsellor, FCO, 1999–2000; Consul-Gen., St Petersburg, 2000–04; Consul-Gen., and Dir of Trade and Investment Promotion, Istanbul, 2004–09. Co-Chair, Uzbek-British Trade and Industry Council, 2015–. Trustee, Cure Parkinson's Trust, 2015–. *Recreations:* theatre, travel, music, keeping in touch with friends.

**HAY, Charles John,** MVO 1996; HM Diplomatic Service; High Commissioner to Malaysia, since 2019; *b* Aberdeen, 22 Sept. 1965; *s* of John Hay and Avril Hay; *m* 2001, Pascale Sutherland; two *d*. *Educ:* Univ. of Southampton (BA Hons 1987); Open Univ. (MBA 1999). Commnd Gordon Highlanders, 1988; Platoon Comdr, 1988–91; ADC to D Comd British Forces, Cyprus, 1992; joined FCO, 1993; Second Sec. (Political), Prague, 1994–97; First Secretary: FCO, 1998–99; Econ. and Finance, UK Perm. Repn to EU, Brussels, 1999–2003; Hd, G8 Presidency Team, 2004–05; Counsellor (Political) and Dep. Hd of Mission, Madrid, 2006–09; Asst Dir, HR, FCO, 2009–11; Dir, Consular Services, FCO, 2011–14; Ambassador to Republic of Korea, 2015–18. Mem., Royal Co. of Archers (Queen's Bodyguard for Scotland), 2016. FRSA. Hon. DBA Korean Nat. Univ. of Transportation, Chungju, 2015. Hon. Citizen: Chungju, 2015; Jung-gu, 2016; Seoul, 2018. *Recreations:* P. G. Wodehouse, crime fiction, walking, sending gloating tasteless postcards to friends when travelling, trying to keep up my languages, golf, archery. *Address:* c/o Foreign and Commonwealth Office, King Charles Street, SW1A 2AH. *E:* charles.hay@fco.gov.uk.

**HAY, Rt Rev. Mgr George Adam;** Canon, Plymouth Cathedral Chapter, 1994, now Emeritus; *b* 14 Nov. 1930; *s* of late Sir William Rupert Hay, KCMG, KCIE, CSI, and late Sybil Ethel, *d* of Sir Stewart Abram. *Educ:* Ampleforth College, York; New Coll., Oxford (BA Hons, MA); Venerable English Coll., Rome (STL). National Service as Midshipman RNVR, 1949–50; student, Oxford, 1950–53; Venerable English Coll., Rome, 1953–60. Ordained priest at Rome, 1959; Curate, Sacred Heart Church, Exeter, and part-time RC Chaplain to students at Exeter Univ., 1960; Chaplain to students at Exeter Univ. and Priest-in-charge, Crediton, 1966–78; Rector, Venerable English Coll., Rome, 1978–84; Parish Priest: St John the Baptist, Dartmouth, 1984; Sacred Heart and St Teresa, Paignton, 1984–91; St Boniface, Okehampton and Holy Family, Chagford, 1991–97; Our Lady and St Denis, St Marychurch, Torquay, 1997–2003; Church of the Holy Spirit, Bovey Tracey, 2003–09. *Recreations:* fly fishing, mountain walking. *Address:* 30 The Roundway, Kingskerswell TQ12 5BW.

**HAY, Lady (Helen) Olga;** *see* Maitland, Lady H. O.

**HAY, Sir John (Erroll Audley),** 11th Bt *cr* 1663 (NS) of Park, Wigtownshire; *b* 3 Dec. 1935; *o s* of Sir Arthur Thomas Erroll Hay, 10th Bt, ISO, ARIBA and his 1st wife, Hertha Hedwig Paula Louise (*d* 1994), *d* of Ludwig Stölzle, Nagelberg, Austria; *S* father, 1993. *Educ:* Gordonstoun; St Andrews Univ. (MA). *Heir:* none.

**HAY, Sir Malcolm John Robert D.;** *see* Dalrymple-Hay.

**HAY, Peter,** CBE 2012; Director, Peter Hay Consultancy Ltd, since 2017; Chair, Turning Point, since 2018; *b* 17 July 1962; *s* of Martin and Ann Hay; *m* 1989, Carmel Corrigan; one *s* two *d* (and one *s* decd). *Educ:* UC, Swansea (BA Hons 1983); Univ. of Exeter (BPhil 1985); Open Univ. (MBA 1995). CQSW 1985. Humberside County Council: Social worker, 1985–88; Team Ldr Assessment, Grimsby, 1988–89; Prin. Practitioner, Scunthorpe, 1989–92; Area Manager, Grimsby, 1992–96; North East Lincolnshire Council: Asst Dir, Child Care, 1996–97; Acting Dir of Social Services, 1997–98, Dir, 1998–2002; Dir of Community Care, 2002–03; Strategic Dir, Social Care and Health, then Adults and Communities, subseq. People Directorate, Birmingham CC, 2003–17. Pres., ADASS, 2011–12 (Vice Pres., 2010–11). Chm., Res. in Practice for Adults, 2011–15; Ind. Chair, Oxford Dio. Safeguarding Panel, 2018–. Trustee/Board Member: Community Integrated Care, 2012–18; SCIE, 2013–; Hanover Housing, 2017–; Goodgym, 2017–. Hon. Dr Birmingham City, 2019. Chair, Social Worker of the Year Awards, 2017–. *Recreations:* family life, gardening, a good book, a whole range of music, watching sport - preferably a winning Worcester Warriors Rugby team. *E:* peter_hay@btinternet.com. *W:* www.peterhay.online.

**HAY, Rev. Richard,** CMG 1992; Vicar, St Paul's, Addlestone, 1999–2007; Rural Dean of Runnymede, 2002–07; *b* 4 May 1942; *s* of Prof. Denys Hay, FBA, FRSE and Sarah Gwyneth Morley; *m* 1969, Miriam Marguerite Alvin England; two *s*. *Educ:* George Watson's Coll., Edinburgh; Edinburgh Univ.; Balliol Coll., Oxford (BA Hons, Mod. Hist.); Cranmer Hall, Durham. Assistant Principal, HM Treasury, 1963–68; Secretary, West Midlands Economic Planning Council, 1966–67; Private Sec. to Financial Sec., Treasury, 1967–68; Principal, Treasury, 1968–73; European Commission: Member, Cabinet of Sir Christopher (later Lord) Soames, Vice-Pres., 1973–75; Dep. Chef de Cabinet, 1975–77; Chef de Cabinet to Mr Christopher (now Lord) Tugendhat, Member, 1977–79; Dir, Economic Structures and Community Interventions, Directorate-Gen. for Economic and Financial Affairs, 1979–81; Dep. Dir-Gen., 1981–86, Dir-Gen., 1986–91, Directorate-General for Personnel and Admin, EC; Special Advr, EC, 1991. Consultant, Sharing of Ministries Abroad, 1992–94. Ordained deacon, 1996, priest, 1997; Curate, St Clement and All Saints, Hastings, 1996–99. Hon. Asst Minister, St Paul's, Woking, 2008–. Chairman: AIACE-UK, 2009– (Dep. Chm., 2009); AIACE-Internat., 2011–15. Trustee, Walsingham, 2008–13 (Chm. of Trustees, 2010–13). *Address:* 15 Fox Close, Pyrford, Surrey GU22 8LP.

**HAY, Robert Colquhoun,** CBE 1988; WS; Sheriff Principal of North Strathclyde, 1989–98; *b* 1933; *s* of late J. B. Hay, dental surgeon, Stirling and Mrs J. Y. Hay; *m* 1958, Olive Black; two *s* two *d*. *Educ:* Univ. of Edinburgh (MA, LLB). Legal practice, 1957–63, 1968–76; Depute Procurator Fiscal, Edinburgh, 1963–68; Temp. Sheriff, 1984–89; Chm., 1976–81, Pres., 1981–89, Industrial Tribunals for Scotland. Mem., Sheriff Court Rules Council, 1989–95 (Chm., 1993–95). Comr, Northern Lighthouse Bd, 1989–98 (Vice-Chm., 1991–92; Chm., 1992–93). Hon. Sheriff, Dumbarton, 1999. Comr for Clan Hay, 1995–2002. *Publications:* contrib. Laws of Scotland: Stair Memorial Encyclopaedia, 1988.

**HAY, Robin William Patrick Hamilton;** a Recorder, 1985–2005; barrister; *b* 1 Nov. 1939; *s* of William R. Hay and Dora Hay; *m* 1969, Lady Olga Maitland, *qv*; two *s* one *d*. *Educ:* Eltham; Selwyn Coll., Cambridge (MA, LLB). Called to the Bar, Inner Temple, 1964. Legal Advisor: Disciplinary Panel, Inst. and Faculty of Actuaries, 2006–; Statutory Cttees, RPSGB, later Gen. Pharmaceutical Council, 2006–16. Legal Mem., Res. Ethics Cttee, Nat. Hosp. for Neurology and Neurosurgery, 2001–12; Chm., Appeal Panel, Postgrad. Med. Educn and Trng Bd, 2005–09; Legal Assessor: GMC, 2002–; NMC, 2007–; GCC, 2009–; GDC, 2010–16; HCPC, 2012–. Lay Panellist, ACCA, 2010–. Chm., Nat. (formerly Young) Musicians Symphony Orchestra, 1990–2001. *Recreations:* church tasting, gastronomy, choral singing. *Address:* Lamb Chambers, Lamb Building, Temple, EC4Y 7AS. *Club:* Garrick.

**HAY, Prof. Roderick James,** DM; FRCP, FRCPath, FMedSci; Chairman, International Foundation for Dermatology, 2002–16, now Special Adviser; Professor of Dermatology, Queen's University Belfast, 2004–07, now Emeritus; Professor of Cutaneous Infection, King's College London, 2009–17, now Emeritus; Consultant Dermatologist, London Bridge Hospital, since 2017; *b* 13 April 1947; *s* of Kenneth Stuart Hay and Margery Geidt (*née* Winterbotham); *m* 1973, Delyth Price; two *d*. *Educ:* Wellington Coll.; Merton Coll.,

Oxford (BA 1968; BM BCh 1971; MA 1979; DM 1980); Guy's Hosp. Med. Sch. MRCP 1974, FRCP 1981; MRCPath 1981, FRCPath 1992. House physician and surgeon, SHO and Dermatol. Registrar, Guy's Hosp., 1971–75; London School of Hygiene and Tropical Medicine: Wellcome Res. Fellow, 1975–77; Lectr, 1977–79; Sen. Lectr, 1979–83; Reader in Clinical Mycology, 1983–89; Hon. Cons. Dermatologist, 1979–2002, Dean, 1993–2000, St John's Inst. of Dermatol.; Mary Dunhill Prof. of Cutaneous Medicine, London Univ., 1990–2002; Clinical Dir, Dermatology, Guy's and St Thomas' NHS Trust, 1996–2000; Dean for Ext. Affairs, GKT, 1998–2002; Queen's University Belfast: Dean, Fac. of Medicine and Health Scis, 2002–05; Hd, Sch. of Medicine and Dentistry (formerly Sch. of Medicine), 2002–07; Consultant Dermatologist, King's Coll. Hosp. NHS Trust, 2008–16. Inaugural René Touraine Lectr, Eur. Acad. Dermatol., 2012; Gerald Levene Oration, RSocMed, 2014; Joseph Plenk Lect., 2015. Non-exec. Dir, Eastern Health and Social Services Bd, 2002–10. Chm. and Trustee, Grants and Res. Cttee, Dunhill Med. Trust, 2015–17; Chair, Technical Adv. Cttee, and Trustee, LEPRA, 2017–. FMedSci 2000. Clarence Livingood Award, Amer. Acad. of Dermatology, 2008; Sir Archibald Grey Medal, British Assoc. of Dermatologists, 2011; Medal of Achievement in Global Dermatology, Internat. League of Dermatological Socs, 2019. *Publications:* A Clinician's Guide to Fungal Disease, 1981; Medical Mycology, 1996; contribs to med. and scientific jls on immunology and treatment of fungal infections and epidemiology of skin disease. *Recreations:* gardening, music. *Address:* Hunters Moon, Plum Lane, Shipton under Wychwood, Oxon OX7 6DZ; International Foundation for Dermatology, Willan House, 4 Fitzroy Square, W1T 5HQ. *T:* (020) 7388 6515.

**HAY, Sir Ronald Frederick Hamilton,** 12th Bt *cr* 1703, of Alderston; *b* 1941; *s* of Sir Ronald Nelson Hay, 11th Bt and Rita, *d* of John Munyard; *S* father, 1988, but his name does not appear on the Official Roll of the Baronetage; *m* 1978, Kathleen, *d* of John Thake; two *s* one *d*. *Heir: s* Alexander James Hay, *b* 1979.

**HAY, Prof. Ronald Thomas,** PhD; FRS 2010; FRSE; Professor of Molecular Biology, College of Life Sciences, University of Dundee, since 2005; *b* Dundee. *Educ:* Heriot-Watt Univ. (BSc Biochem. 1975); MRC Virol. Unit, Glasgow (PhD 1979). Damon Runyon-Walter Winchell Cancer Fund Postdoctoral Fellow, Harvard Med. Sch., 1979–82; Staff Scientist, MRC Virol. Unit, Glasgow, 1982–85; University of St Andrews: Lectr, then Reader, later Prof. of Molecular Biol., 1985–2005; Dep. Dir, Centre for Biomolecular Scis. Mem., EMBO, 2009. FRSE 1996; FMedSci 2005. *Publications:* contribs to jls incl. Nat. Cell Biol., EMBO Jl, Nat. Structural Molecular Biol., Molecular Cell, Nature, Genes and Develt, Cancer Res., Oncogene, Jl Hepatol., Trends Cell Biol. *Address:* College of Life Sciences, University of Dundee, Dundee DD1 5EH.

**HAY, Prof. Simon Iain,** DPhil, DSc; FRCPE; FMedSci; Professor of Health Metrics Sciences, University of Washington, since 2015; *b* Rinteln, Germany, 15 Jan. 1971; *s* of Robert Hay and Julia Hay (*née* Harmsworth, now Perry); *m* 2002, Sarah Tomlin; one *s* one *d*. *Educ:* Univ. of Bristol (BSc Hons 1992); Univ. of Oxford (DPhil 1996; DSc 2014). FRCPE 2014. University of Oxford: Postgrad. Res. Asst, 1993–96; Postdoctoral Res. Officer, 1996–99; Sen. Res. Fellow, 1999–2008; Reader of Infectious Disease Epidemiol., 2008–12; Prof. of Epidemiology, 2012; Res. Fellow, St John's Coll., Oxford, 2012–17; Sen. Res. Fellow, Wellcome Trust, 2006–17. Pres., RSTM&H, 2013–15. FMedSci 2015. Scientific Medal, ZSL, 2008; Back Award, RGS, 2012; Bailey K. Ashford Medal, Amer. Soc. of Tropical Medicine and Hygiene, 2013; Chalmers Meml Medal, RSTM&H, 2015. *Publications:* over 400 articles in learned jls. *Recreations:* gardening, music, reading, travel, natural history. *Address:* Institute for Health Metrics and Evaluation, Department of Health Metrics Sciences, University of Washington, 2301 Fifth Avenue, Suite 600, Seattle, WA 98121, USA. *T:* (206) 8972878. *E:* sihay@uw.edu.

**HAY, Stephen James,** FCA; Deputy Chief Executive Officer, Regulation, NHS Improvement, 2016–19; *b* Cuckfield, 22 March 1965; *s* of Brian and Joy Hay; *m* 1999, Nathalie; two *s*. *Educ:* Ardingly Coll.; Univ. of Lancaster (BSc Mgt Scis). FCA 1991. With KPMG, 1988–2003; Man. Dir and Mem. Bd, Monitor, 2004–16. Non-exec. Dir, and Chm., Audit and Risk Cttee, DCLG, 2009–15.

**HAY-CAMPBELL, (Thomas) Ian,** LVO 1994; HM Diplomatic Service, retired; Deputy Head of Mission, Oslo, 2001–05; *b* 19 May 1945; *s* of Thomas Neil Hay-Campbell and Anthea Joan Hay-Campbell (*née* Carey); *m* 1970, Margaret Lorraine (*née* Hoadley); four *s*. *Educ:* Wanganui Collegiate Sch., NZ; Victoria Univ. of Wellington (BA Hons History). Radio Journalist, NZBC, Wellington, 1969–72; Radio Producer, subseq. Editor, BBC World Service, 1972–84; joined FCO, 1984; First Sec., FCO, 1984–87; Dep. Head of Mission, Kinshasa, 1987–90; FCO, 1990–94; Head of Press and Public Affairs Section, Moscow, 1994–97; Dep. High Comr, Harare, 1998–2001. *Recreations:* modern history, family history research, reading, trams. *Address:* Flat 1, Glenthorne, 4 West Road, Guildford, Surrey GU1 2AT. *T:* (01483) 572646.

**HAY DAVISON, Ian Frederic;** *see* Davison.

**HAY-PLUMB, Paula Maria;** Finance Director, Rosling King LLP, 2011–18; *b* 18 March 1960; *d* of Henry Sephton Green and Eileen Green (*née* Millburn); *m* 1984, Martin Hay-Plumb; one *s* one *d*. *Educ:* Univ. of Exeter (BSc Hons 1980). ACA 1983; MCT 1989. Qualified as chartered accountant with Peat, Marwick, Mitchell; Marks and Spencer plc, 1984–88; Olympia & York Canary Wharf Ltd, 1989–93; Finance Dir, 1994–96, Man. Dir (Ops), 1996–99, Chief Exec., 1999–2002, English Partnerships; Corporate Finance and Gp Reporting Dir, Marks and Spencer plc, 2003–05. Chairman: DETR Coalfields Task Force, 1997–98 (reported 1998); Nat. Australia Gp Common Investment Fund Trustee Ltd, 2007–10; non-executive Director: Skipton Building Soc., 2006–10; Forensic Science Service Ltd, 2006–12; Nat. Audit Office, 2010–14; Hyde Housing Assoc., 2012–; Aberforth Smaller Companies Trust plc, 2014–; Oxford Univ. Hosps NHS Foundn Trust, 2017–. A Crown Estate Comr, 2015–. Trustee: Coalfields Regeneration Trust, 1999–2008, Calthorpe Estates, 2017–. *Recreations:* music, theatre.

**HAYASHI, Keiichi;** Justice of the Supreme Court of Japan, since 2017; *b* 8 Feb. 1951. *Educ:* Kyoto Univ. (BA Law); Stanford Univ. (MA Political Scis). Joined Min. of Foreign Affairs, Japan, 1974; Director: 2nd SE Asia Div., 1991–93; Treaties Div., 1993–96; Counsellor, London, 1996–99; Deputy Director-General: N American Affairs Bureau, 1999–2000; Treaties Bureau, 2000–02; Dir-Gen., Internat. Legal Affairs Bureau, 2002–05; Ambassador to Ireland, 2005–08; Dep. Vice-Minister for Foreign Affairs, 2008; Asst Cabinet Sec., 2008–10; Ambassador from Japan to the Court of St James's, 2011–16. *Publications:* If You Know about Ireland, You Will Better Understand Japan, 2009.

**HAYCOCKS, Myra Anne;** *see* Kinghorn, M. A.

**HAYDAY, Anthony Victor;** HM Diplomatic Service, retired; Ambassador to Madagascar, 1987–90; *b* 1 June 1930; *s* of Charles Leslie Victor Hayday and Catherine (*née* McCarthy); *m* 1966, Anne Heather Moffat (*d* 1995); one *s* one *d*. *Educ:* Beckenham and Penge Grammar School. Royal Air Force, 1949–50; HM Foreign (later Diplomatic) Service, 1950; Brazzaville, 1953; British Information Services, New York, 1955; FO, 1958; Vice Consul, Houston, 1961; 2nd Secretary, Algiers, 1962; FO (later FCO), 1966; 1st Secretary, New Delhi, 1969; Head of Chancery, Freetown, 1973; on secondment to Commonwealth

Secretariat, 1976–80; Dep. High Comr, Calcutta, 1981–85; Consul-Gen., Cleveland, 1985–87. *Recreations:* birdwatching, athletics. *Address:* Meadow Cottage, Swillbrook, Malmesbury, Wilts SN16 9GA. *Clubs:* Blackheath Harriers; Bengal (Calcutta).

**HAYDEN, Hon. Sir Anthony Paul,** Kt 2013; **Hon. Mr Justice Hayden;** a Judge of the High Court, Family Division, since 2013; Vice President, Court of Protection, since 2018; *b* 24 June 1961. Called to the Bar, Middle Temple, 1987; a Recorder, 2000–13; QC 2002. *Address:* Royal Courts of Justice, Strand, WC2A 2LL.

**HAYDEN, Ven. David Frank;** Archdeacon of Norfolk, 2002–12; *b* 25 Jan. 1947; *s* of Donald and Margaret Hayden; *m* 1st, 1968, Ruby Cowles (*d* 2015); two *d*; 2nd, 2016, Elisabeth Thorpe. *Educ:* Tyndale Hall, Bristol (DipTh 1969, BD 1971); London Univ. Ordained deacon, 1971, priest, 1972; Curate: St Matthew's, Silverhill, 1971; Galleywood Common, 1975; Rector, Redgrave cum Botesdale with Rickinghall, 1979–84; RD, Hartismere, 1981–84; Vicar, Cromer, 1984–2002; Hosp. Chaplain (pt-time), 1984–2000; RD, Repps, 1995–2002. Hon. Canon, Norwich Cathedral, 1996–2002. *Recreations:* boating, walking. *Address:* Church Farm House, Church Lane, Oulton Broad, Lowestoft, Suffolk NR32 3JN.

**HAYDEN, Prof. Jacqueline, (Mrs. E. M. Dunbar),** CBE 2013; Dean, Postgraduate Medical Studies, Health Education North West and Universities of Manchester, Lancashire and Liverpool, 1997–2016; *b* Croydon, 4 Dec. 1950; *d* of late Robert Leslie James Hayden and Dorothy Blanche Hayden; *m* 1976, Edward Milne Dunbar; two *s*. *Educ:* Croydon High Sch. GPDST; St George's Hosp. Med. Sch., Univ. of London (MB BS 1974; DSc (Med) 2013). MRCP 1976, FRCP 1996; DCH 1977; MRCGP 1979, FRCGP 1987; DRCOG 1979; FRCPE 2012. Preregistration House Officer: St James' Hosp., Balham, 1974–75; Ashford Hosp., Middx, 1975; Postregistration Hse Officer, Medicine Oxford, 1975–76; Gen. Practice Trng Scheme, Oxford, 1976–79; Principal, Unsworth Medical Centre, Bury, 1979–2010. Regl Advr in Gen. Practice, North West RHA and Univ. of Manchester, 1991–96. Associate, GMC, 2005–. Non-exec. Dir, Plymouth Hosps NHS Trust, 2016–; Mem. Cttee, Med. Practitioner Tribunal Service, 2016–. FAcadMed 2011; Founding Sen. Fellow, FMLM, 2016. Hon. FRCPsych, 2018. Hon. DSc: St George's London, 2013; Lancaster, 2017; Edge Hill, 2018. *Publications:* (jtly) A Guide for New Principals, 1996; *contributor:* The Medical Annual, 1987; The Practice Receptionist, 1989; The Child Surveillance Handbook, 1990, 2nd edn 1994; Change and Teamwork in Primary Care, 1993; Professional Development in General Practice, 1996; The Very Stuff of General Practice, 1999; Medical Management, 2012; over 30 jl articles and editorials. *Address:* 12 Mercers Road, Heywood, Lancs OL10 2NP. *T:* (01706) 625470; 2 Cliff Terrace, Devonport Hill, Kingsand, Cornwall PL10 1NJ. *T:* 07976 247104. *E:* jackyhayden@aol.com, jacky.hayden@btinternet.com.

**HAYDEN, Hon. William George,** AC 1989; cattle farmer, Brisbane Valley; Governor-General of Australia, 1989–96; *b* Brisbane, 23 Jan. 1933; *s* of G. Hayden, Oakland, Calif, USA; *m* 1960, Dallas, *d* of W. Broadfoot; one *s* two *d* (and one *d* decd). *Educ:* Brisbane State High Sch.; Univ. of Qld (BEcon). Public Service, Qld, 1950–52; Police Constable, Qld Police Force, 1953–61. MHR (Lab) for Oxley, Qld, 1961–88. Parly Spokesman on Health and Welfare, 1969–72; Minister for Social Security, Australian Govt, 1972–75; Federal Treasurer, June–Nov. 1975; Leader of Australian Labor Party and the Opposition, 1977–83; spokesman on defence, 1976–77 and on economic management, 1976–83; Minister for Foreign Affairs, 1983–87, and for Trade, 1987–88. Adjunct Prof. of Humanities, Qld Univ. of Technol., Brisbane, 1996. Chm., Editl Cttee, Quadrant Jl, 1998–2004. Res. Vis. Fellow, Jane Franklin Hall, Univ. of Tasmania, 2000. Patron: (Qld Br.) Australian Inst. Internat. Affairs; (Qld Br.) Australian Fabian Soc.; Member: Gen. Sir John Monash Foundn; Assoc. of Former Mems of Parlt of Australia. Hon. FRACP 1995. Hon. Dr: Griffith Univ., 1990; Univ. of Central Qld, 1992; Hon. LLD Univ. of Qld, 1990; Hon. DLitt Univ. of S Qld, 1997. Australian Humanist of the Year, 1996. Kt, Order of St John in Australia, 1989. Gwandhwa Medal, Order of Diplomatic Merit, Korea. Commander, Order of Three Stars (Latvia). *Publications:* Hayden: an autobiography, 1996. *Address:* PO Box 7829, Waterfront Place, Brisbane, Qld 4001, Australia.

**HAYDER, Mo;** writer of crime fiction; *b* UK, 2 Jan. 1962; one *d*. *Educ:* American Univ., Washington (MA Film Making 1991); Bath Spa Univ. (MA Creative Writing 2000). *Publications:* Birdman, 2000; The Treatment, 2001; Tokyo, 2003; Pig Island, 2005; Ritual, 2008; Skin, 2009; Gone, 2010; Hanging Hill, 2011; Poppet, 2013; Wolf, 2014. *Address:* c/o Gregory & Company, David Higham, 7–12 Noel Street, W1F 8GQ. *T:* (020) 7434 5900.

**HAYDON, Alec Guy;** QC 2019; *b* Kent, 10 Dec. 1969; *s* of Patrick Guy Haydon and Christine Mary Haydon; *m* 2012, Sabina Rakcheyeva; two *s*. *Educ:* Sir Joseph Williamson's Mathematical Sch., Rochester; St John's Coll., Cambridge (BA 1st Cl. Law 1992); Harvard Law Sch. (LLM). Called to the Bar, Gray's Inn, 1993; in practice as a barrister, specialising in commercial litigation, Brick Court Chambers, 1995–. *Recreations:* running, cycling, motor racing. *Address:* 47 Lee Road, Blackheath, SE3 9RT; Brick Court Chambers, 7–8 Essex Street, WC2R 3LD. *T:* (020) 7379 3558. *E:* alec.haydon@brickcourt.co.uk. *Club:* Royal Automobile.

**HAYDON, Christopher;** *see* Wilkinson, C.

**HAYES, Sir Brian,** Kt 1998; CBE 1992; QPM 1985; security consultant, since 1998; Deputy Commissioner of Metropolitan Police, 1995–98; *b* 25 Jan. 1940; 2nd *s* of James and Jessie Hayes; *m* 1960, Priscilla Rose Bishop; one *s* three *d*. *Educ:* Plaistow County Grammar Sch.; Sheffield Univ. (BA Hons 1st Cl. Mod. Langs). Metropolitan Police, 1959–77; seconded Northern Ireland, 1971–72; Police Adviser, Mexico, 1975 and 1976, Colombia, 1977 and 1993; British Police representative, EEC, 1976–77; Asst Chief Constable, Surrey Constabulary, 1977–81; Dep. Chief Constable, Wiltshire Constabulary, 1981–82; Chief Constable, Surrey Constabulary, 1982–91; Inspector of Constabulary for SE England, 1991–95. Vice-Pres., ACPO, 1990–91. Chm., Police Athletic Assoc., 1989–91 (Nat. Sec., 1984–88); Pres., Union Sportive des Polices d'Europe, 1990–92. Special Advr on Security to FA, 1997–2002; Security Consultant, TRI-MEX Internat. Ltd, 1999–2002. Freeman, City of London, 1998. OStJ 1987. Police Long Service and Good Conduct Medal, 1981; Cruz al Mérito Policial (Spain), 1998. *Recreations:* karate, rowing, cycling, swimming, golf.

**HAYES, Sir Brian (David),** GCB 1988 (KCB 1980; CB 1976); Permanent Secretary, Department of Trade and Industry, 1985–89, retired (Joint Permanent Secretary, 1983–85); *b* 5 May 1929; *s* of late Charles and Flora Hayes, Bramerton, Norfolk; *m* 1958, Audrey Jenkins (*d* 2014); one *s* one *d*. *Educ:* Norwich Sch.; Corpus Christi Coll., Cambridge. BA (Hist.) 1952, PhD (Cambridge) 1956. RASC, 1947–49. Joined Min. of Agriculture, Fisheries and Food, 1956; Asst Private Sec. to the Minister, 1958; Asst Sec., 1967; Under-Sec., Milk and Poultry Gp, 1970–73; Dep. Sec., 1973–78; Permanent Sec., 1979–83. Director: Guardian Royal Exchange, 1989–99; Tate & Lyle, 1989–98; Adv. Dir, Unilever plc, 1990–99. Chm., CBI Educn Foundn, 1991–96. Dir, SANE, 1990–2007. Lloyd's Members' Ombudsman, 1994–2007. *Recreations:* reading, television, opera.

**HAYES, Christine;** *see* Farnish, C.

**HAYES, Christine Isobel, (Kirsty);** HM Diplomatic Service; Ambassador to Portugal, 2014–18; *b* Aberdeen, 2 Feb. 1977; *d* of Robert Colin and Rowena Antoinette Paton; *m* 2002, Peter Richard Hayes, *qv*; one *s* one *d*. *Educ:* Dame Alice Harpur Sch.; Inst. of Archaeol., University Coll. London (BA Hons Archaeol.); Sch. of Oriental and African Studies, Univ. of London (MA Internat. Studies and Diplomacy); Kingston Business Sch. (MA HR Strategy). Inst. of Archaeol., 1998–99; entered FCO, 1999; Dept of Envmt Policy, FCO, 1999–2000; Vice-Consul (Pol and Econ.), Hong Kong, 2000–01; Private Sec. to Ambassador, Washington, 2001–05; EU Dept, FCO, 2005–07; Human Resources Dept, FCO, 2007–08; Consultant, UNDP Regl Centre, Colombo, Sri Lanka, 2009–10; Head: Corporate Communications, FCO, 2010; Internat. Orgns Dept, 2011–13. *Recreations:* eventing, show jumping, yoga, scuba diving, swimming. *Address:* Foreign and Commonwealth Office, King Charles Street, SW1A 2AH. *E:* Kirsty.hayes@fco.gov.uk. *Club:* Farmers.

**HAYES, Helen Elizabeth;** MP (Lab) Dulwich and West Norwood, since 2015; *b* 8 Aug. 1974. *Educ:* Balliol Coll., Oxford (BA Hons PPE); London Sch. of Econs and Pol Sci. (MSc Social Policy and Admin). Jt Man. Dir, Town Centres Ltd, subseq. Urban Practitioners, 1998–2012; Partner, Allies and Morrison, 2011–15. Mem. (Lab) Southwark LBC, 2010–16. Mem., Communities and Local Govt Select Cttee, 2015–. *Address:* House of Commons, SW1A 0AA.

**HAYES, Jeremy Joseph James;** barrister; freelance journalist and broadcaster; *b* 20 April 1953; *s* of Peter and Daye Hayes; *m* 1979, Alison Gail Mansfield; one *s* one *d*. *Educ:* Oratory Sch.; LLB London. Called to the Bar, Middle Temple, 1977; leading counsel in high profile criminal trials. Formerly Political Ed., Punch mag.; freelance columnist and restaurant reviewer, London Paper, 2006–; paper reviewer, Stephen Nolan Show, BBC Radio 5 Live, 2013–. MP (C) Harlow, 1983–97; contested (C) same seat, 1997. PPS to Minister of State, NI Office, 1992–94, DoE, 1994–97. Member, Select Committee: on Social Services, 1987–90; on Health, 1990–91; on National Heritage, 1996–97; formerly: Member: All Party Parly Gp on Human Rights; All Party Parly Gp on Race Relations; Vice Chm., All Party AIDS Cttee; Chm., All Party ASH Gp. Promoter: Parents' Aid (No 2) Bill; Sexual Offences Bill; Sponsor: Video Recordings Act; Protection of Children against Tobacco Act; Freedom of Information (Medical Records) Act. Mem., Amnesty Internat. Fellow: Industry and Parliament Trust; All Party Armed Forces Trust. Hon. Dir, State Legislative Leaders Foundn, USA. Vice Pres., Wendens Ambo Cricket Club. Freeman, City of London. Lord of the Manor, High Easter, 2002–. *Publications:* An Unexpected MP, 2014. *Recreations:* proud father of Francesca (teacher in Cambridge) and Lawrence (paramedic in Leatherhead), proud grandfather of twins Sam and Will, dining at the Savile, propping up the bar at El Vino, Fleet Street. *Address:* Goldsmith Chambers, Goldsmith Building, Temple, EC4Y 7BL. *W:* jerryhayes.co.uk, www.twitter.com/jerryhayes1. *Clubs:* Savile; Essex.

**HAYES, John Allan;** QC 2013; **His Honour Judge Hayes;** a Circuit Judge, since 2018; a Deputy High Court Judge, since 2018; *b* Sheffield, 17 May 1968; *s* of Mike and Mary Hayes; *m* 1994; Dr Sarah; three *s* one *d*. *Educ:* Tapton Sch., Sheffield; Pembroke Coll., Oxford (BA 1st Cl. Hons Juris. 1990). Tutor and researcher, Free Univ., Berlin, 1990–91; called to the Bar, Lincoln's Inn, 1992; in practice as barrister, 1992–2018; a Recorder, 2016–18. *Publications:* contribs to Family Law Jl. *Recreations:* fell running, orienteering, outdoor swimming. *Address:* Leeds Combined Court Centre, 1 Oxford Row, Leeds LS1 3BG.

**HAYES, Rt Hon. Sir John (Henry),** Kt 2018; CBE 2016; PC 2013; MP (C) South Holland and The Deepings, since 1997; *b* 23 June 1958; *s* of late Henry John Hayes and Lily Hayes; *m* 1997, Susan Jane Hopewell; two *s*. *Educ:* Colfe's Grammar Sch., London; Univ. of Nottingham (BA Hons, PGCE). Joined The Data Base Ltd, 1983, Dir, 1986–99. Mem., Nottinghamshire CC, 1985–98. Contested (C) Derbyshire NE, 1987, 1992. Shadow Schools Minister, 2000–01; Opposition Pairing Whip, 2001–02; Shadow Agriculture and Fisheries Minister, 2002–03; Shadow Housing and Planning Minister, 2003–05; Shadow Transport Minister, 2005; Shadow Minister: for Vocational Educn and Skills, 2005–07; for Lifelong Learning, Further and Higher Educn, 2007–10; Minister of State: for Further Educn Skills and Lifelong Learning, BIS and DFE, 2010–12; for Energy, DECC, 2012–13; (Minister without Portfolio), Cabinet Office, 2013–14; DfT, 2014–15; Home Office, 2015–16; DfT, 2016–18; Sen. Parly Advr to the Prime Minister, 2013–15. Member, Select Committee: Agriculture, 1997–99; Educn and Employment, 1998–99; Administration, 2001–02; Mem., Cttee of Selection, 2001–02. A Vice-Chm., Cons. Party, 1999–2000. Adjunct Associate Prof., Richmond, The American Internat. Univ. in London, 2002–10. Fellow: Chartered Instn for Further Educn, 2017; City & Guilds, 2017. *Recreations:* the arts (particularly English painting, poetry and prose), good food and wine, many sports (including darts and boxing), gardening, making jam, antiques, architecture, aesthetics. *Address:* House of Commons, SW1A 0AA. *T:* (020) 7219 1389. *Clubs:* Carlton; Spalding, Spalding Gentlemen's Soc. (Lincs).

**HAYES, John William,** CBE 1995; Chairman, Law Society Pension Scheme, 2002–13 (Director, Law Society Pensions Archive and Communications Forum, since 2013); *b* 10 Feb. 1945; *s* of late Dick Hayes and Bridget Isobel Hayes; *m* 1970, Jennifer Hayes (*née* Harvey); two *s* one *d*. *Educ:* Nottingham High Sch.; Morecambe Grammar Sch.; Victoria Univ. of Manchester (LLB). Solicitor. Articled Thomas Foord, 1966–69; Worthing Borough Council, 1966–69; Nottingham County Borough Council, 1969–71; Somerset CC, 1971–74; Asst, Dep. Clerk and Dep. Chief Exec., Notts CC, 1974–80; Clerk and Chief Exec., Warwicks CC, 1980–86; Sec.-Gen., Law Soc., 1987–96; Chm., OPRA, 1996–2001. Chm., Local Govt Gp, Law Soc., 1981–82; Sec., Warwicks Probation Cttee, 1983–86; Clerk to Warwicks Magistrates' Courts' Cttee, 1983–86; Clerk to Lord Lieut of Warwicks, 1980–86. Chm., Ind. Inquiry into River Vessel Safety, 1992. Chairman: Disciplinary Appeals Cttee, CIPFA, 2001–10; Actuarial Profession Disciplinary Bd, 2004–09. Chm., Coventry Dio. Church Urban Fund, 1989–91; Member: Bishop of Coventry's Board of Social Responsibility, 1981–86; Inner Cities' Task Force, 1985–86. Mem., Ind. Remuneration Panel, 2001–04, Ind. Mem., Standards Cttee, 2001– (Chm., 2006–09), W Sussex CC; Mem., Ind. Remuneration Panel, IoW Council, 2015–. Legal Assessor, British Council of Osteopathy, 1998–2003. Mem. Council, Warwick Univ., 1980–90; Gov., Univ. of Chichester (formerly UC Chichester), 2001–07. Gov., Kingsley School, 1986–92; Foundn Gov., All Saints C of E Primary Sch., Freshwater IoW, 2013–17 (Chm., 2014–17); Gov., South Bersted Primary Sch., 2018–. Trustee, St Andrew's (Norton) Trust, 2016–19. Hon. LLD De Montfort, 1996. *Recreations:* cricket, music, idleness.

**HAYES, Kirsty Isobel;** *see* Hayes, C. I.

**HAYES, Patricia Jane,** CB 2019; Director General, Roads, Devolution and Motoring, Department for Transport, since 2016; *b* 9 June 1966; *d* of William and Emily Rennie; *m* 1992, Andrew Hayes; three *s*. *Educ:* Armagh Girls' High Sch.; Pembroke Coll., Oxford (BA PPE 1987, MA). Various posts, Dept of Transport and DETR, 1987–96; First Sec., Transport, British Embassy, Washington, 1996–99; Sec., Sustainable Develt Commn, 2000–02; Department for Transport: Hd, Charging and Local Transport Div., 2002–04; Hd, NW East Midlands Div., 2004–06; Hd, Talent Mgt and People Develt, 2006–07; Dir,

Road and Vehicle Safety and Standards, 2007–11; Dir of Roads, 2011–13; Dir, Motoring, Freight and London, 2013; Dir, Aviation, 2013–16. *Address:* Department for Transport, Great Minster House, 33 Horseferry Road, SW1P 4DR. *T:* (020) 7944 5212.

**HAYES, Dr Peter Richard;** HM Diplomatic Service; International Strategy Adviser, Information Commissioner's Office (on secondment), since 2018; *b* 11 April 1963; *s* of late Jasper Terence Hayes and of Greta Louvain Hayes; *m* 2002, Christine, (Kirsty), Isobel Paton (*see* C. I. Hayes); one *s* one *d*. *Educ:* County Sch., Ashford, Surrey; Univ. of Surrey (BSc Physics); King's Coll. London (PhD 1989). Post-doctoral res. associate, KCL, 1989–90; SSO, NPL, 1990–93; Team Leader, Mgt and Technology Services, DTI, 1993–94; Head of Competition Issues, Cabinet Office, 1994–96; Asst Dir, Internat., OST, 1997–98; Dep. Hd, Envmt, Sci. and Energy, FCO, 1998–2000; Dir, Nuclear Decommng, DTI, 2000–01; Counsellor, then Consul Gen., Washington, 2001–05; Principal Private Sec. to Sec. of State for Foreign and Commonwealth Affairs, 2005–07; High Comr, Sri Lanka and non-resident to Maldives, 2008–10; Hd of Public Affairs, London Stock Exchange Gp (on secondment), 2011–12; Hd, Counter Proliferation, FCO, 2012; Dir, Overseas Territories, FCO, 2012–16; Commissioner: of the British Antarctic Territory, 2012–16; of the British Indian Ocean Territory, 2012–16. *Publications:* contrib. to acad. physics pubns and jls. *Recreation:* family. *Address:* Foreign and Commonwealth Office, King Charles Street, SW1A 2AH. *Club:* Farmers.

**HAYES, Dr William;** President, St John's College, University of Oxford, 1987–2001 (Hon. Fellow, 2001); Senior Research Fellow, Clarendon Laboratory, Oxford University, since 1987; Pro-Vice-Chancellor, University of Oxford, 1990–2001; *b* 12 Nov. 1930; *s* of Robert Hayes and Eileen Tobin; *m* 1962, Joan Ferriss (*d* 1996); two *s* one *d*. *Educ:* University Coll., Dublin (MSc, PhD); Oxford Univ. (MA, DPhil). FInstP 1960. St John's College, Oxford: 1851 Overseas Schol., 1955–57; Official Fellow and Tutor, 1960–87; Principal Bursar, 1977–87; University Lectr, 1962–85, Prof., 1985–87, Oxford Univ.; Dir and Head of Clarendon Lab., Oxford, 1985–87. Oxford University: Mem., Gen. Bd of the Faculties, 1985–88; Mem., Hebdomadal Council, 1989–2000; Chm., Curators of Univ. Chest, 1992–2000; Delegate, OUP, 1991–2001. Temporary research appointments at: Argonne Nat. Lab., 1957–58; Purdue Univ., 1963–64; RCA Labs, Princeton, 1968; Univ. of Illinois, 1971; Bell Labs, 1974. Mem., Physics Cttee, SERC, 1982–85. Sen. Foreign Fellow, American Nat. Sci. Foundn, 1963–64; Fellow, American Physical Soc., 1990. Hon. MRIA 1998. Hon. DSc: NUI, 1988; Purdue Univ., 1996. *Publications:* (ed) Crystals with the Fluorite Structure, 1974; (with R. Loudon) Scattering of Light by Crystals, 1978; (with A. M. Stoneham) Defects and Defect Processes in non-metallic Solids, 1985; contribs to Procs of Royal Soc., Jl of Physics, Physical Rev., etc. *Recreations:* walking, reading, listening to music. *Address:* St John's College, Oxford OX1 3JP. *T:* (01865) 277300.

**HAYES, William;** General Secretary, Communication Workers Union, 2001–15; *b* 8 June 1953; *s* of William and Margaret Hayes; *m* 1995, Dian Lee; one *s* one *d*. *Educ:* St Swithin's Secondary Modern; Univ. of Liverpool (Dip. Trade Union Studies). Fitter-welder, 1968–71; factory worker, 1971–73; unemployed, 1973–74; joined Post Office, 1974, Postman; Lay Official, Union of Post Office Workers, subseq. UCW, then CWU, 1992; Nat. Official, CWU, 1992–2001. Member: Stop the War Coalition, 2016–; Labour Party Conference Arrangement Cttee, 2017–. *Recreations:* films, music, books, Liverpool FC.

**HAYFORD;** *see* Casely-Hayford.

**HAYHOE, Thomas Edward George;** Chairman, West London NHS Trust (formerly West London Mental Health NHS Trust), since 2015; *b* Wickham, Hants, 3 March 1956; *s* of Capt. George Hayhoe, RN and Carenza Hayhoe (*née* Lee); *m* 1st, 1978, Helen Kendal (marr. diss. 1998); one *d*; 2nd, 1999, Natalie Jobling. *Educ:* Corpus Christi Coll., Cambridge (BA Hons Hist. 1977); Graduate Sch. of Business, Stanford Univ. (MBA 1980). Pres., Cambridge Students Union, 1977–78; Harkness Fellow, 1978–80. Mgt consultant, McKinsey & Co., 1980–85; Gp Planning and Develt Manager, 1985–88, Gen. Manager, Stationery and Cards, 1988–92, WH Smith plc; mgt consultant and entrepreneur, Brackenbury Gp, subseq. The Chambers, 1992–2010. Chm., Gamestation Ltd, 2000–02. Dir and Dep. Chm., Ealing, Hammersmith and Hounslow HA, 1985–2000; Chm., W London Pathol. Consortium, 2000–04. Chairman: Building Better Health W London Ltd, 2005–10; W Middlesex Univ. Hosp. NHS Trust, 2010–15; Dir, Medihome Ltd, 2005–09. Chm., Fitness to Practise Panel, Nursing and Midwifery Council, 2012–. Trustee, Versus Arthritis (formerly Arthritis Res. UK), 2012–. Contested (SDP) Wycombe, 1987. Cdre, Ranelagh Sailing Club, 1991–92. *Recreations:* sailing, cycling, singing, opera, ballet. *Address:* 21 Tabor Road, W6 0BN. *E:* tom@hayhoe.net. *Club:* Royal Ocean Racing (Rear Cdre, 2007–08; Vice Cdre, 2008–10).

**HAYMAN,** family name of **Baroness Hayman**.

**HAYMAN,** Baroness *cr* 1995 (Life Peer), of Dartmouth Park in the London Borough of Camden; **Helene Valerie Hayman,** GBE 2012; PC 2001; Lord Speaker, House of Lords, 2006–11; *b* 26 March 1949; *d* of late Maurice Middleweek and Maude Middleweek; *m* 1974, Martin Hayman; four *s*. *Educ:* Wolverhampton Girls' High Sch.; Newnham Coll., Cambridge (MA; Hon. Fellow 2008). Pres., Cambridge Union, 1969. Worked with Shelter, Nat. Campaign for the Homeless, 1969; Camden Council Social Services Dept, 1971; Dep. Dir, Nat. Council for One Parent Families, 1974. Vice-Chairman: Bloomsbury HA, 1988–90 (Mem., 1985–90); Bloomsbury and Islington HA, 1991–92 (Mem., 1990–91); Chm., Whittington Hosp. NHS Trust, 1992–97. Contested (Lab) Wolverhampton SW, Feb. 1974; MP (Lab) Welwyn and Hatfield, Oct. 1974–1979. Parliamentary Under-Secretary of State: DETR, 1997–98; DoH, 1998–99; Minister of State, MAFF, 1999–2001. Member: Select Cttee on the Assisted Dying for the Terminally Ill Bill, 2004–05; Constitution Cttee, 2005–06. Chairman: Cancer Res. UK, 2001–05; Human Tissue Authy, 2005–06; Cambridge Univ. Health Partners, 2014–17. Member: Human Fertilisation and Embryology Authy, 2005–06; GMC, 2013–18. Member: RCOG Ethics Cttee, 1982–96; UCL/UCH Cttee on Ethics of Clinical Investigation, 1987–96 (Vice-Chm., 1990–96); Council, UCL, 1992–97; Review Cttee, Anti-Terrorism, Crime and Security Act, 2002–03; Bd, Roadsafe, 2002–06; Chm., Ethics and Governance Council, UK Biobank, 2015–18. Jt Pres., Hansard Soc., 2010–11. Hon. Joint President: UK Br., CPA, 2006–11; IPU, 2006–11. Trustee: Royal Botanical Gardens, Kew, 2002–06; Tropical Health and Educn Trust, 2005–06; Sabin Vaccine Inst., 2011–15; Malaria Consortium, 2013–16; Disasters Emergency Cttee, 2014–; Chair, Malaria No More UK, 2019–. Hon. Dr: Middx; N London; Brunel, 2012; Birmingham, 2014; Hon. DSc Herts, 1999; Hon. LLD Wolverhampton, 2007. *Address:* House of Lords, SW1A 0PW. *T:* (020) 7219 5083.

**HAYMAN, Andrew Christopher,** CBE 2006; QPM 2004; security commentator, analyst and strategic adviser, since 2008; Assistant Commissioner, Special Operations, in charge of counter terrorism, royalty and diplomatic protection and security of London, 2005–08; *b* 31 July 1959; *s* of Geoffrey and Valerie Hayman; *m* 1993, Jane Nicola Corbett; two *d*. *Educ:* Exeter Univ. (MA); Fitzwilliam Coll., Cambridge (Postgrad. Dip. in Applied Criminology). Joined Essex Police, 1978; Chief Inspector, Ops, 1993–95; Divl Comdr, Supt and Chief Supt, 1995–98; Metropolitan Police: Comdr, i/c Drugs and Crime, 1998–2001; Dep. Asst Comr, Anti Corruption, and Dep. to Dep. Comr, 2001–02; Chief Constable, Norfolk Constabulary, 2002–05. Security commentator, ITV, NBC and The Times, 2008–11. Mem., Adv. Council on Misuse of Drugs, 2001–06; Chm., Drugs Cttee, 2001–06, Terrorism Cttee, 2006–08, Security Advr, 2008–, ACPO. Broadcaster, Policing Britain, BBC Radio 4, 2009. Ext. Examr, Cambridge Univ., 2001–08. Anglia Ruskin (formerly Anglia Polytechnic) University: Gov., 2000–11 (Chm., Appeals Cttee, 2010–11); Vis. Fellow, 2011–. Chm. of Govs, St Mary's Kelvedon Primary Sch., 2009–. *Publications:* (with M. Gilmore) The Terrorist Hunters, 2009. *Recreations:* gardening, theatre, reading, keeping fit.

**HAYMAN, (Anne) Carolyn,** OBE 2003; independent innovator; Chair, Preventable Surprises, 2015–17; *b* 23 April 1951; *d* of Walter Kurt Hayman, *qv* and late Margaret Riley Crann; *m* 1980, Peter John Bury (marr. diss. 2012); two *d*. *Educ:* Putney High Sch. for Girls; Newnham Coll., Cambridge (BA Classics and Philosophy); Sch. of Oriental and African Studies (MSc Econ). Admin. Trainee, ODM, 1975–78; Advr, Central Policy Review Staff, 1978–80; Senior Consultant, Office Automation: EOSYS, 1980–82; Coopers & Lybrand, 1982–83; Jt Man. Dir, Korda & Co., 1983–95; Exec. Dir, Rutherford Ventures, 1995–96; Chief Exec., Foyer Fedn, 1996–2004; Co-founder and Chief Exec., Peace Direct, 2004–14. Co. Sec., Sri Lanka Campaign for Peace and Justice, 2010–15; Dir, Network for Social Change, 2015–. Chairman: Cambridge Animation Systems, 1990–96; Atraverda, 1992–97. Dir, Technology & Law, 1982–85. Member: Commonwealth Develt Corp., 1994–99; Working Gp on 14–19 Reform, 2003–04. Member: Council, Pitcom, 1981–83; Council for Industry and Higher Educn, 1992–97; Board, Industrial Res. and Tech. Unit, 1995–97; Quaker UN Cttee, 2006–11. Trustee: Solar Aid, 2008–11; Global Greengrants Fund UK, 2016–; Britain Yearly Meeting (Quakers), 2019–. Editor, Work and Society, 1984–86. *Recreations:* music, swimming, cycling, applying agroecological techniques to my vegetable patch. *Address:* 36A Lawford Road, NW5 2LN. *T:* (020) 7916 2689.

**HAYMAN, George Edward;** QC 2018; *b* St Albans, 25 Aug. 1975; *s* of Andy Hayman and Ruth Hayman; *m* 2009, Amy Long; two *s* one *d*. *Educ:* Heathfield High Sch., Cheshire; Downing Coll., Cambridge (BA 1997). Called to the Bar, Middle Temple, 1998; in practice as barrister, specialising in commercial chancery. *Recreations:* family, cooking, piano. *Address:* Maitland Chambers, 7 Stone Buildings, Lincoln's Inn, WC2A 3SZ. *T:* (020) 7406 1200. *E:* ghayman@maitlandchambers.com. *Clubs:* Athenæum, Soho House.

**HAYMAN, His Honour John David Woodburn;** a Circuit Judge, 1976–92; *b* 24 Aug. 1918; *m* Jane (*née* Davison) (*d* 2015); two *s* four *d*. *Educ:* King Edward VII Sch., Johannesburg; St John's Coll., Cambridge (MA, LLM). Served with S African Forces, 1940–42 (discharged on medical grounds). Called to the Bar, Middle Temple, 1945. Sometime Lecturer in Law: University Coll. of Wales, Aberystwyth; Leeds Univ.; Cambridge Univ.

**HAYMAN, Susan Mary;** MP (Lab) Workington, since 2015; *b* Upper Buckleybury, 28 July 1962; *d* of John Bentley and Rita Bentley; *m* 1997, Ross Hayman; one *s* one *d*, and one step *s* one step *d*. *Educ:* St Bartholomew's Comp. Sch., Newbury; Anglia Ruskin Univ. (BA Hons Eng. Lit.). Bookseller, Heffers Bookshop, 1984–86; proof-reader and copy editor, Goodfellow and Egan, 1986–88; self-employed proof-reader and copy editor, 1988–97; Asst to Tess Kingham, MP, 1997–2001, to Michael Foster, MP, 2001–05; Communications Consultant, Copper Consultancy, 2005–14; self-employed communications consultant, 2014–15. Mem. (Lab) Cumbria CC, 2013–15. Shadow Sec. of State for Envmt, Food and Rural Affairs, 2017–. *Recreations:* music, theatre, gardening, walking the dog, fell walking. *Address:* House of Commons, SW1A 0AA. *T:* (020) 7219 4554. *E:* sue.hayman.mp@parliament.uk.

**HAYMAN, Prof. Walter Kurt,** MA; ScD (Cambridge); FRS 1956; FIC; Professor of Pure Mathematics, University of York, 1985–93, now Emeritus; Senior Research Fellow, Imperial College, London, since 1995; *b* 6 Jan. 1926; *s* of late Franz Samuel Haymann and Ruth Therese (*née* Hensel); *m* 1st, 1947, Margaret Riley Crann, MA Cantab (*d* 1994), *d* of Thomas Crann, New Earswick, York; three *d*; 2nd, 1995, Dr Waficka Katifi (*d* 2001); 3rd, 2007, Marie Jennings, MBE (*d* 2015). *Educ:* Gordonstoun Sch.; St John's Coll., Cambridge. Lecturer at King's Coll., Newcastle upon Tyne, 1947, and Fellow of St John's Coll., Cambridge, 1947–50; Lecturer, 1947, and Reader, 1953–56, Exeter; Prof. of Pure Maths, 1956–85, and Dean of RCS, 1978–81, Imperial Coll., London (FIC 1989). Visiting Lecturer at Brown Univ., USA, 1949–50, at Stanford Univ., USA (summer) 1950 and 1955, and to the American Mathematical Soc., 1961. Co-founder with Mrs Hayman of British Mathematical Olympiad; Vice-Pres., London Mathematical Soc., 1982–84. Foreign Member: Finnish Acad. of Science and Letters; Accademia Nazionale dei Lincei, Rome; Corresp. Mem., Bavarian Acad. of Science. Hon. DSc: Exeter, 1981; Birmingham, 1985; NUI, 1997; Hon. Dr rer. nat. Giessen, 1992; Hon. DPhil Uppsala, 1992. 1st Smiths Prize, 1948, shared Adams Prize, 1949, Cambridge Univ.; Jun. Berwick Prize, 1955, Sen. Berwick Prize, 1964, de Morgan Medal, 1995, London Mathematical Soc. *Publications:* Multivalent Functions (Cambridge, 1958, 2nd edn 1994) Meromorphic Functions (Oxford, 1964); Research Problems in Function Theory (London, 1967, 2nd edn with Eleanor Lingham, 2019); Subharmonic Functions, vol. I, 1976, vol. II, 1989; papers in various mathematical journals. *Recreations:* music, travel, television. *Address:* Department of Mathematics, Imperial College London, SW7 2AZ; 104 Cranford Lane, Harlington, Middx UB3 5HB.

*See also* A. C. Hayman.

**HAYMAN-JOYCE, Lt-Gen. Sir Robert (John),** KCB 1996; CBE 1989 (OBE 1979); DL; Chairman, Raytheon Systems Ltd, 2000–12; *b* 16 Oct. 1940; *s* of late Major T. F. Hayman-Joyce and B. C. Bruford; *m* 1968, Diana Livingstone-Bussell; two *s*. *Educ:* Radley Coll.; Magdalene Coll., Cambridge (MA). Commnd 11th Hussars (PAO), 1963; CO Royal Hussars (PWO), 1980–82; Comdr RAC, 1 (BR) Corps, 1983–85; Dir, UK Tank Programme, 1988; Dir Gen., Fighting Vehicles and Engr Equipment, later Land Fighting Systems, MoD (PE), 1989–92; Dir, RAC, 1992–94; Military Sec., MoD, 1994–95; MGO, 1995–98, and Dep. Chief of Defence Procurement (Ops), 1996–98. Non-exec. Dir, Alvis plc, 1999–2004. Col Comdt RAC, 1995–99; Hon. Col, Royal Yeomanry, 2002–10. Chairman: Trustees, Tank Mus., 1995–2002; Monmouthshire Hunt, 1998–2002; London Internat. Horse Show, 2010–16 (Vice Pres., 2016–). Patron: Retired Officers Assoc., 2000–09; Soc. for Welfare of Horses and Ponies, 2003–09; Firing Line (Mus. of the Welsh Soldier), 2011–; Arts Alive, 2011–. DL Gwent, 1997. Hon. DSc Cranfield, 1998. *Recreations:* ski-ing, horses, birdwatching. *Address:* Ty Isha, Mamhilad, Pontypool, Monmouthshire NP4 0JE. *Clubs:* Cavalry and Guards; Leander (Henley-on-Thames); Monmouthshire Hunt (Chm., 2009–).

**HAYMES, Rev. Dr Brian;** Minister, Bloomsbury Central Baptist Church, 2000–05; *b* 8 Dec. 1940; *s* of Reginald and Ella Haymes; *m* 1965, Jennifer Christine Frankland; two *d*. *Educ:* King's Coll. Sch., Wimbledon; Univ. of Bristol (BA 1965); Univ. of Exeter (MA 1973; PhD 1976). Baptist Minister: St George, Bristol, 1965–69; South Street, Exeter, 1969–77; Mansfield Road, Nottingham, 1977–81; Tutor, 1981–85, Principal, 1985–94, Northern Baptist Coll., Manchester; Principal, Bristol Baptist Coll., 1994–2000. Lecturer (part-time) in Christian Ethics: Univ. of Manchester, 1983–93; Univ. of Bristol, 1996–2000. Pres., Baptist Union of GB, 1993–94. *Publications:* The Concept of the Knowledge of God, 1986; (jtly) On Being the Church, 2008; (jtly) The Communion of

Saints, 2014; (jtly) God after Christendom?, 2015. *Recreations:* reading, watching cricket and Rugby. *Address:* 1 Colville Grove, Timperley, Altrincham, Cheshire WA15 6NA. *T:* (0161) 374 0813.

**HAYNES, Alison Wendy;** *see* Hampton, A. W.

**HAYNES, Dana Rebecca;** *see* Arnold, D. R.

**HAYNES, Ernest Anthony, (Tony),** CIGEM; Regional Chairman, British Gas plc, East Midlands, 1983–87; *b* 8 May 1922; *s* of Joseph Ernest Haynes and Ethel Rose (*née* Toomer); *m* 1946, Sheila Theresa (*née* Blane); two *s* two *d*. *Educ:* King Edward VI Grammar Sch., Totnes, S Devon. Joined Devonshire Regt, 1940; RMC Sandhurst, 1941; commnd Hampshire Regt, 1941; served in N Africa, Italy and NW Europe; Captain, 1945. Govt rehabilitation course for ex-officers, 1947–48; joined Torquay and Paignton Gas Co., 1949; appts with: West Midlands and Northern Gas Boards; Gas Council; Eastern; Dep. Chm., North Eastern, 1977–78; Dep. Chm., North Thames Gas, 1979–82. Vice-Pres., Internat. Colloquium about Gas Marketing, 1983–84. Silver Medal, IGasE, for paper, Energy Conservation—a marketing opportunity. *Recreations:* golf, flyfishing.

**HAYNES, Lawrence John;** Chairman, Magnox Ltd, since 2019; *b* 6 Dec. 1952; *s* of Donald H. Haynes and Irene E. Haynes (*née* Langford); *m* 1978, Carol Anne Nelson; one *d*, and two step *d*. *Educ:* Heriot-Watt Univ. (BA Hons Business Law 1983). FCIHT (FIHT 1995); FCILT (FCIT 1996). RAF technician, 1969–78; Head of Contracts, British Aerospace (Space Systems), 1983–89; Legal Dir, 1989–90, Man. Dir, 1990–91, Microtel Communications; Man. Dir, British Aerospace Communications, 1991–92; Project Dir, British Aerospace, 1992–94; Chief Exec., Highways Agency, 1994–99; Partner and Hd of Ops, Eur. BPO, PricewaterhouseCoopers, 1999–2000; Chief Executive: 186k Ltd, 2000–02; Govt Services Gp, British Nuclear Fuels plc, 2003–04; British Nuclear Gp, 2004–07; Dir, BNFL plc, 2005–07; Chief Exec., White Young Green Plc, 2007–09; Pres. of Nuclear, 2009–13, Pres. of Marine and Nuclear, 2013–14, Pres., Land and Sea Div., 2014–16, Rolls-Royce plc; Chm., Rolls-Royce Power Systems, 2014–16. Non-executive Director: Network Rail Ltd, 2010–14; Louis Berger Inc., 2017–18. Chm., RAF Benevolent Fund, 2014–. FRSA 1994. Hon. DEng Heriot-Watt, 2010. *Recreations:* sailing, ski-ing.

**HAYNES, Prof. Peter Howard,** FRS 2019; PhD; Professor of Applied Mathematics, University of Cambridge, since 2001 (Head, Department of Applied Mathematics and Theoretical Physics, 2005–15); Fellow, Queens' College, Cambridge, since 1986; *b* 23 July 1958; *s* of late Bernard Archibald Haynes and of Stella Iris Haynes (*née* Whitehead); *m* 1989, Kathleen Mary Crease; two *s*. *Educ:* Royal Grammar Sch., Guildford; Queens' Coll., Cambridge (BA 1979, MA 1983, PhD 1984). Res. Associate, Dept of Atmospheric Scis, Univ. of Washington, 1984–85; University of Cambridge: Royal Soc. Meteorol Office Res. Fellow, 1986–90; Asst Dir of Res., 1991; Lectr, 1991–99, Reader in Atmospheric Sci., 1999–2001. Mem., Atmospheric Scis Peer Review Cttee, NERC, 1997–2001. Mem. and Chm. Steering Cttee, Prog. on Transport in Atmosphere and Ocean, ESF, 1996–2000; Mem., Scientific Steering Cttee, Stratospheric Processes and Climate Project, World Climate Res. Prog., 2005–10. Chaire d'attractivité, Univ. Fédérale Toulouse Midi-Pyrénées, 2015–. MAE 1998. *Publications:* contribs to Jl Fluid Mechanics, Jl Atmospheric Scis, Jl Geophysical Res., Qly Jl Royal Meteorol Soc., Jl Physical Oceanography, Physics of Fluids, and others. *Recreations:* orienteering, running, reading, family. *Address:* Department of Applied Mathematics and Theoretical Physics, Centre for Mathematical Sciences, Wilberforce Road, Cambridge CB3 0WA. *T:* (01223) 337862, *Fax:* (01223) 765900. *E:* phh@damtp.cam.ac.uk.

**HAYNES, Timothy Hugh Penzer;** Headmaster, Tonbridge School, 2005–18; *b* 2 April 1955; *s* of Barry and Felicia Haynes. *Educ:* Shrewsbury Sch.; Univ. of Reading (BA Hist.); Pembroke Coll., Cambridge (PGCE). Assistant Master: Hampton Sch., 1980–82; St Paul's Sch., London, 1982–95 (Surmaster, 1992–95); Headmaster, Monmouth Sch., 1995–2005. *Address:* North Parade House, 12 Hereford Road, Monmouth NP25 3PB.

**HAYS, Irene;** *see* Lucas, I.

**HAYTER, 4th Baron** *cr* 1927, of Chislehurst, Kent; **George William Michael Chubb;** Bt 1900; *b* 9 Oct. 1943; *s* of 3rd Baron Hayter, KCVO, CBE and Elizabeth Anne Chubb (*née* Rumbold); *S* father, 2003; *m* 1983, Waltraud, *yr d* of J. Flackl, Sydney; one *s*. *Educ:* Marlborough; Nottingham Univ. (BSc). Managing Director: Chubb Malaysia, 1972–79; Chubb Australia, 1979–82; Dir, Business Develt for Physical Security, Chubb Security plc, 1982–89; Managing Director: Uniqey Ltd, 1989–90; William Chubb Associates, 1991–2005; Dir, UELS Ltd, 1996–. Liveryman, Weavers' Co. (Mem., Ct of Assts; Upper Bailiff, 1999–2000). *Heir: s* Hon. Thomas Frederik Flackl Chubb, *b* 23 July 1986.

**HAYTER OF KENTISH TOWN,** Baroness *cr* 2010 (Life Peer), of Kentish Town in the London Borough of Camden; **Dianne Hayter;** *b* 7 Sept. 1949; *d* of late Alec Hayter and late Nancy Hayter; *m* 1994, Prof. (Anthony) David Caplin. *Educ:* Trevelyan Coll., Durham Univ. (BA Hons Sociology and Social Admin); Univ. of London (PhD 2004). Research Assistant: General and Municipal Workers Union, 1970–72; European Trade Union Confedn (ETUC), Brussels, 1973; Research Officer, Trade Union Adv. Cttee to OECD (TUAC-OECD), Paris, 1973–74; Fabian Society: Asst Gen. Sec., 1974–76; Gen. Sec., 1976–82; Mem. Exec. Cttee, 1986–95; Chm., 1992–93; Journalist, A Week in Politics, Channel Four, 1982–84; Dir, Alcohol Concern, 1984–90; Chief Exec., European PLP, 1990–96; Dir of Corporate Affairs, Wellcome Trust, 1996–99; Chief Exec., Pelican Centre, 1999–2001. Res. Student, QMW, 2001–04. Member: Royal Commn on Criminal Procedure, 1978–80; Bd, Nat. Patient Safety Agency, 2001–04; Dr Foster Ethics Cttee, 2001–10; Financial Services Consumer Panel, 2001–05 (Vice Chm., 2003–05); Bd, NCC, 2001–08; Determinations Panel, Pensions Regulator, 2005–10; Insolvency Practices Council, 2006–10; Bd for Actuarial Standards, Financial Reporting Council, 2006–11; Surveyors Ombudsman Service Bd, 2007–08; NEST Corporation, 2010; Chair: Consumer Panel, Bar Standards Bd, 2006–09; Property Standards Bd, 2008–10; Legal Services Consumer Panel, 2009–11. Shadow Minister for Women and Equalities, 2015–17. Vis. Prof., Univ. of Westminster, 2011–. An Opposition Whip, H of L, 2011–15; Shadow Minister for Cabinet Office, 2012–17, for Consumer Affairs, BIS, then BEIS, 2012–19, for Brexit, 2016–19; Shadow Dep. Leader of H of L, 2017–. Chair, Camden Alcoholics Support Assoc., 1996–2003, Mem., 2003–12. Member: Exec. Cttee, London Labour Party, 1977–83; Nat. Constitution Cttee Labour Party, 1987–98; Labour Party NEC, 1998–2010 (Vice-Chm., 2006–07; Chm., 2007–08); Chm., Holborn & St Pancras Labour Party, 1990–93. Member: Labour Party; Soc. of Labour Lawyers; GMB; Jewish Labour Movt; Co-op. Party; Labour Arab Gp; Socialist Educn Assoc. JP Inner London, 1976–90. *Publications:* The Labour Party: crisis and prospects (Fabian Soc.), 1977; (contrib.) Labour in the Eighties, 1980; (contrib.) Prime Minister Portillo and Other Things that Never Happened, 2003; Fightback: Labour's Traditional Right in the 80s, 2005; (ed jtly) Men Who Made Labour, 2006; (contrib.) From the Workhouse to Welfare, 2009; (contrib.) The Prime Ministers Who Never Were, 2011. *Recreations:* reading, politics. *Address:* House of Lords, SW1A 0PW. *E:* hayterd@parliament.uk. *W:* www.twitter.com/HayteratLords.

**HAYTER, Sir Paul (David Grenville),** KCB 2007; LVO 1992; Clerk of the Parliaments, House of Lords, 2003–07; *b* 4 Nov. 1942; *s* of late Rev. Canon Michael George Hayter and Katherine Patricia Hayter (*née* Schofield); *m* 1973, Hon. Deborah Gervaise, *d* of Baron Maude of Stratford-upon-Avon, TD, PC; two *s* one *d*. *Educ:* Eton (King's Scholar); Christ Church, Oxford (MA). Clerk, Parlt Office, House of Lords, 1964; seconded as Private Sec. to Leader of House and Chief Whip, House of Lords, 1974–77; Clerk of Cttees, 1977; Principal Clerk of Cttees, 1985–90; Prin. Finance Officer, 1991–94; Reading Clerk, 1991–97; Principal Clerk of Public Bills, subseq. Clerk of Legislation, 1994–2003; Clerk Asst, 1997–2003. Sec., Assoc. of Lord-Lieutenants, 1977–91. Chm., CPRE Northants, 2007–17. *Recreations:* music, gardening, botanising, local history, archery, painting. *Address:* Walnut House, Charlton, Banbury OX17 3DR.

**HAYTHORNTHWAITE, Richard Neil;** Chairman: MasterCard Inc., since 2006; Arc International, since 2015; QIO Technologies, since 2015; Advisory Partner, Moelis & Company, since 2018; *b* 17 Dec. 1956; *s* of Christopher Scott Haythornthwaite and Angela Mary Haythornthwaite (*née* Painter); *m* 1979, Janeen Marie Dennis; one *s* one *d*. *Educ:* Colston's Sch., Bristol; Queen's Coll., Oxford (MA Geol.); Massachusetts Inst. of Technol. (SM Mgt). With BP, 1978–95, Pres., BP Venezuela, 1993–95; Commercial Dir, Premier Oil, 1995–97; Blue Circle Industries: Chief Exec., Heavy Bldgs Materials, Europe and Asia, 1997–99; Gp CEO, 1999–2001; Chief Exec., Invensys plc, 2001–05; Man. Dir, 2006–08, Sen. Adviser, 2008–14, Star Capital Partners Ltd. Non-executive Director: Cookson Gp plc, 1999–2003; ICI plc, 2001–08; Lafarge SA, 2001–03; Chairman: Network Rail, 2009–12; Centrica, 2014–19. Chief Operating Officer, 2008–12, Chm. of Operating Businesses, 2013–15, Advr, 2016–17, PSI UK. Chair: Better Regulation Commn, 2006–08; Risk and Regulation Adv. Council, 2008–09. Chairman: Centre for Creative Communities, 1996–2006; Almeida Theatre, 2001–08; South Bank Centre, 2008–15; Web Foundn, 2013–16; Creative Industries Fedn, 2017–. Trustee: NMSI, 2002–07; British Council, 2003–08. *Recreations:* cycling, travel, arts. *Clubs:* Royal Automobile, 67 Pall Mall, 5 Hertford Street.

**HAYTON, Dr David John;** Legal Consultant, Lennox Paton, Nassau, Bahamas, since 2019; *b* 13 July 1944; *s* of Arthur Hayton and Beatrice (*née* Thompson); *m* 1979, Linda Patricia Rae; one *s*. *Educ:* Newcastle Royal GS; Univ. of Newcastle upon Tyne (LLB 1st Cl. Hons 1966; LLD 1980); MA 1973, LLD 2006, Cantab. Called to the Bar, Inner Temple, 1968, and Lincoln's Inn *aeg* (Bencher, 2004). Lectr, Sheffield Univ., 1966–69; private practice, Lincoln's Inn, 1970–2005; Lectr, QMC, London, 1970–73; Lectr, Univ. of Cambridge and Fellow of Jesus Coll., 1973–87; Prof. of Law, 1987–2005, Dean, Law Faculty, 1988–90, KCL; FKC 2005; Chm., London Univ. Bd of Studies in Law, 1992–95. Vis. Lectr, Inns of Court Sch. of Law, 1971–84, Hon. Reader, 1984–96. An Asst Recorder, 1984–92; a Recorder, 1992–2000; Actg Justice, Supreme Ct, Bahamas, 2000, 2001; Justice of the Caribbean Ct of Justice, 2005–19. Dep. Chm., Trust Law Cttee, 1994–2005; Mem., Law Panel, 2001 RAE, HEFCE. Chm., Council, Pension Trustees Forum, 1992–95. Hon. Sec., SPTL, 1996–2001. Head of UK Delegns to The Hague Confs on Private Internat. Law, 1984, 1988. *Publications:* Registered Land, 1973, 3rd edn 1981; Hayton & Tiley: Capital Transfer Tax, 1975, 2nd edn 1978; Hayton & Marshall: Cases & Commentary on Trusts, 6th edn 1975 to 12th edn 2005; Underhill & Hayton: Law of Trusts and Trustees, 13th edn 1979 to 19th edn 2016; Law of Trusts, 1989, 4th edn 2003; Hayton Report on Financial Services and Trust Law, 1990; (ed) European Succession Laws, 1991, 3rd edn 2002; (ed) Principles of European Trust Law, 1999; (ed) Modern International Developments in Trust Law, 1999; (ed) Extending the Boundaries of Trust and Similar Ring-fenced Funds, 2002; (ed) Towards an EU Directive on Protected Funds, 2009; (ed) The International Trust, 3rd edn 2011; (contrib.) Halsbury's Laws of England, vol. 98, Trusts and Powers, 5th edn 2013; contribs to chapters in books on trusts, tax and estate planning; articles in learned jls. *Recreations:* health club, watching Rugby and cricket, reading novels, wine tasting. *Address:* Lennox Paton, 3 Bayside Executive Park, West Bay Street and Blake Road, N–4875, Nassau, Bahamas. *T:* 5025000. *Clubs:* Athenæum, MCC, Queen's Park Cricket (Trinidad), Tranquility Tennis (Trinidad).

**HAYTON, Michael Pearson;** QC 2013; a Recorder, since 2012; Leader, Northern Circuit, since 2017; *b* Preston, Lancs, 3 Nov. 1970; *s* of Michael Derek Hayton and Dylis Barbara Hayton; *m* 2004 (marr. diss. 2015); one *s*. *Educ:* Queen Elizabeth's Grammar Sch., Blackburn; St Anne's Coll., Oxford (MA Juris.). Called to the Bar, Lincoln's Inn, 1993; in practice as barrister, specialising in regulatory crime and crime, 1993–. *Recreations:* Rugby Union, golf, olive oil production. *Address:* 2 Hare Court, Temple, EC4Y 7BH; Deans Court Chambers, 24 St John Street, Manchester M3 4DF. *T:* (0161) 214 6000, *Fax:* (0161) 214 6001. *E:* hayton@deanscourt.co.uk. *Clubs:* Vincent's (Oxford); Royal Birkdale Golf.

**HAYTON, Philip John;** Newscaster, BBC TV News, 1985–2005; *b* 2 Nov. 1947; *s* of Austin and Jennie Hayton; *m* 1972, Thelma Gant; one *s* one *d*. *Educ:* at various schs in USA and UK. Pirate radio disc jockey, 1967; joined BBC, 1968; reporter: Radio Leeds, 1968–71; and newscaster, TV Leeds, 1971–74; TV News: reporter, 1974–80; Foreign Corresp., 1980–83; reporter and newscaster, 1983–2005, Six O'clock and Nine O'clock News, World News and News 24. Full-time stockmarket investor, 2005–. *Recreations:* theatre, walking, investment, foreign travel. *E:* pjhayton1@gmail.com.

**HAYWARD, Baron** *cr* 2015 (Life Peer), of Cumnor in the County of Oxfordshire; **Robert Antony Hayward,** OBE 1991; Chief Executive, British Beer and Pub Association (formerly Brewers and Licensed Retailers), 1999–2009; *b* 11 March 1949; *s* of late Ralph and of Mary Hayward. *Educ:* Abingdon Sch.; Maidenhead Grammar Sch.; University Coll. of Rhodesia; BSc Econ Hons London (external). Personnel Officer, Esso Petroleum, 1971–75; Personnel Manager: Coca Cola Bottlers (S & N) Ltd, 1975–79; GEC Large Machines, 1979–82; Dir Gen., British Soft Drinks Assoc., 1993–99. MP (C) Kingswood, 1983–92; contested (C): Kingswood, 1992, Christchurch, July 1993. PPS to Minister for Corporate and Consumer Affairs, 1985–87, to Minister for Industry, 1986–87, to Sec. of State for Transport, 1987–89. Mem., Commons Select Cttee on Energy, 1983–85. Advr to Chm., Cons. Party, 2009–10; Chm., Govt Review of Equality Legislation, 2013. Adviser: Terrence Higgins Trust, 2012–14; Dignity in Dying, 2012– (Treas., 2014–). Chm., Trade Assoc. Forum, CBI, 2007–08. Dir, Stonewall Gp, 1997–2003. Trustee: Central YMCA, 2011– (Dep. Chm., 2014–); YMCA Training, 2014–. Founder Mem., 1996–99, Pres., 1999–2003, King's Cross Steelers RFC. *Recreations:* Rugby, psephology. *Address:* 11 Grosvenor Park, SE5 0NQ; House of Lords, SW1A 0PW.

**HAYWARD, Alexander;** engineering and transport historian, and museum consultant, since 2018; Director of Collections, Research and Learning, Queensland Museum Network, 2015–18; *b* 26 Nov. 1960; *s* of Peter and Nikki Hayward; *m* 1990, Rosy Nicholson; one *s* one *d*. *Educ:* Univ. of Sydney (BA 1982, MA 1986); Univ. of Leicester (MSc 1989). LTCL 1982; AMA 1993, FMA 2010. Curator, Science Mus., London, 1990–98; Suffolk County Council: Mus Officer, 1998–2001; Hd of Heritage, 2001–05; Keeper of Sci. and Technol., Nat. Museums of Scotland, 2005–15. Expert Advr, Heritage Lottery Fund, 2000–04; Scottish Rep., UK Science, Technology and Industry Subject Specialist Network, 2005–15; Founding Chm., Scottish Technology and Industry Collections Knowledge Network, 2006–11 (Mem. Cttee, 2012–15); Founding Mem., Dounreay Heritage Adv. Panel, 2010–15; Member: BT Connected Earth Consulting Gp,

2006–07; Cttee, Museums Galleries Scotland (formerly Scottish Museums Council) Collections Recognition (formerly Significance) Scheme, 2006–13; Council, Royal Scottish Soc. of Arts, 2009–15 (Vice Pres., 2010–13); Council, Newcomen Soc., 2013–15; Cttee, Engrg Heritage Qld, 2016–18; Exec. Cttee, Asia Pacific Network of Sci. and Technol. Centres, 2017–18. FRSSA 2007. *Publications:* The Traction Engine in Scotland, 2011. *Recreations:* enjoying the history of technology, music of G. F. Handel and British dance bands of 1920s. *Address:* Tettenhall House, Hinstock, Market Drayton, Shropshire TF9 2TJ.

**HAYWARD, Anthony Bryan,** PhD; FRSE; Chairman, Glencore (formerly Glencore, then Glencore Xstrata), since 2014 (Senior Independent Director, 2011–13; interim Chairman, 2013–14); Partner, St James's Asset Management, since 2017; Founder and Chairman, Genel Energy plc, 2015–17 (Chief Executive Officer, 2011–15); *b* Slough, 21 May 1957; *s* of Bryan and Mary Hayward; *m* 1985, Maureen Fulton (marr. diss. 2013); one *s* one *d*; *m* 2015, Lina Ramirez; one *s*. *Educ:* Univ. of Aston in Birmingham (BSc); Univ. of Edinburgh (PhD Geol 1982). Joined BP, 1982; BP Exploration, 1982–99: various tech. and commercial posts, London, Aberdeen, France, China and Glasgow; Exploration Manager, Colombia; Pres., Venezuela, 1995–97; Gp Vice Pres. and Mem. Upstream Exec. Cttee, 1997–2000; Gp Treas., 2000–02; Exec. Dir and Chief Exec., Exploration and Prodn, 2003–07; Gp Chief Exec., BP plc, 2007–10. Partner and Mem. Adv. Bd, AEA Capital, 2007–; founder, Vallares plc, 2011. Mem. Bd, TNK-BP, 2003–08, 2010–11. Member: UK Business Council, 2008–10; US Business Council, 2008–13; World Econ. Forum Community of Chairmen, 2014–. Chm., Develt Bd, Aston Univ., 2013–; Mem., Chm.'s Adv. Bd, British Mus., 2013–. *Recreations:* sailing, ski-ing, cycling, watching sport, art.

**HAYWARD, Francesca Natasha;** Principal Dancer, Royal Ballet, since 2016; *b* Kenya, 4 July 1992. *Educ:* Royal Ballet Sch. Joined Royal Ballet, 2011; repertoire includes: Juliet, Manon, Clara and the Sugar Plum Fairy in The Nutcracker, Perdita in The Winter's Tale, The Girl in The Invitation, Princess Stephanie in Mayerling, Principal Woman in Rhapsody, Lise in La Fille Mal Gardée, Princess Aurora in The Sleeping Beauty, and Alice in Alice's Adventures in Wonderland. Awards include: Lynne Seymour Award for Expressive Dance, 2009; Young British Dancer of Year, 2010; Royal Ballet Sch.; Silver and Audience Choice Award, Adeline Genée, Royal Acad. of Dance, 2010; Emerging Artist Award, Nat. Dance Awards, 2014; hClub 100 Rising Star Award, Hospital Club, 2015. *Recreations:* violin, travelling, history. *Address:* Royal Opera House, Bow Street, Covent Garden, WC2E 9DD. *E:* Francesca.Hayward@roh.org.uk.

**HAYWARD, Prof. Geoffrey Francis;** Professor of Education and Head, Faculty of Education, University of Cambridge, since 2014; *b* Wendover, Bucks, 1955; *s* of Harry Robin Hayward and Patricia Vivien Hayward (*née* Turner); partner, Jill Johnson; two *s*. *Educ:* Lord Williams Sch., Thame; New Coll., Oxford (BA Zool.; DPhil 1983). Postdoctoral Res. Fellow, Univ. of Liverpool, 1980–81; Lecturer: Wakefield Dist Coll., 1982–87; Liverpool Inst. of Higher Educn, 1987–89; Lectr, 1989–2008, Reader in Educn, 2008–10, Univ. of Oxford; Prof. of Educn, Univ. of Leeds, 2011–14. *Publications:* Applied Genetics, 1992; Applied Ecology, 1992; Getting to Grips with GNVQs: a handbook for teachers, 1995; Higher Education in Crisis: the corporate eclipse of the university, 2001; Balancing the Skills Equation: key issues for policy and practice, 2004; Education for All, 2008; Improving Learning by Widening Participation in Higher Education, 2009; contribs to jls and chapters in books. *Recreations:* gardening, fishing, walking. *Address:* Faculty of Education, University of Cambridge, 184 Hills Road, Cambridge CB2 8PQ. *T:* (01223) 767713. *E:* gfh22@cam.ac.uk.

**HAYWARD, Gerald William;** HM Diplomatic Service, retired; *b* 18 Nov. 1927; *s* of late Frederick William Hayward and Annie Louise (*née* Glasscock); *m* 1956, Patricia Rhonwen (*née* Foster Hall); one *s* three *d*. *Educ:* Tottenham Grammar School; London and Hong Kong Univs. HM Forces, 1946–57. Joined HM Foreign (subseq. HM Diplomatic) Service, 1957; served Bangkok, Hong Kong, Copenhagen, Kuala Lumpur; FCO, 1980–82; (part-time), Cabinet Office, 1984–92. *Address:* Fosters, 9 Ashley Road, Sevenoaks, Kent TN13 3AW. *T:* (01732) 451227.

**HAYWARD, Guy Alexander;** Global Chief Executive Officer, Forsman & Bodenfors (formerly KBS), since 2015; *b* London, 18 Feb. 1964; *s* of I. A. C. Hayward and S. E. A. Hayward; three *d*; *m* 2012, Astrid Boesze; one *d*. *Educ:* St Edward's Sch., Oxford; Christ Church, Oxford (BA Hons Modern Langs). Joined J Walter Thompson Co., later JWT Gp as grad. trainee, 1987; Account Director: JWT Barcelona, then London, 1990–92; WCRS, London, 1992–94; Wieden + Kennedy, Amsterdam, 1994–97; Founding Partner, 180, Amsterdam, 1998–2009; CEO, JWT UK Gp, 2009–11; Global Business Develt Dir, BETC Worldwide, 2011–14. *Address:* 252 West 76th Street, New York, NY 10023, USA. *E:* guy.hayward@rocketmail.com. *Clubs:* Every House; Vincent's (Oxford).

**HAYWARD, His Honour Richard Michael;** a Circuit Judge, 1996–2016; *b* 12 July 1946; *s* of George Michael Hayward and Esmé Mary Florence Hayward (*née* Howard); *m* 1969, Laura Louise Buchan; two *s* one *d*. *Educ:* Highgate Sch.; Inns of Court Sch. of Law. Called to the Bar, Middle Temple, 1969; in practice at the Bar, 1970–96; Asst Recorder, 1990–94; Recorder, 1994–96. *Recreations:* golf, painting, horses, gardening. *Clubs:* Boodle's; Rye Golf; Royal & Ancient Golf (St Andrews).

**HAYWARD SMITH, His Honour Rodger;** QC 1988; a Circuit Judge, 2002–13; *b* 25 Feb. 1943; *s* of late Frederick Ernest Smith and Heather Hayward (*née* Rodgers); *m* 1975, Gillian Sheila (*née* Johnson); one *s* one *d*. *Educ:* Brentwood Sch.; St Edmund Hall, Oxford (MA). Called to the Bar, Gray's Inn, 1967; a Recorder, 1986–2002 (Asst Recorder, 1981–86); a Deputy High Ct Judge, 1990–2002. A Legal Assessor, GMC, 2000–02. *Publications:* (ed jtly and contrib.) Jackson's Matrimonial Finance and Taxation, 5th edn 1992 to 7th edn 2002. *Recreations:* amateur dramatics (Chm., Barnes Community Players, 2017–19), walking. *Address:* 1 King's Bench Walk, Temple, EC4Y 7DB.

**HAYWOOD, Dr Elizabeth Zaidée, (Lady Hain);** Partner, Haywood Hain LLP, since 2008; *b* Paisley, 11 Nov. 1955; *d* of Lt Comdr Douglas Inglefield Haywood and Zaidée Maud Elsie Haywood (*née* Honywood); *m* 2003, Peter Gerald Hain (*see* Baron Hain). *Educ:* Univ. of Wales, Cardiff (BSc Econ) 1st Cl. 1986); University Coll., Swansea (PhD 1989). Palmer Publications, NY, 1975–78; Eur. Parlt, 1978–82; Eur. Affairs Manager, Welsh Develt Agency, 1989–94; Dir, Wales, CBI, 1994–2000; Communications Dir, Assoc. of Train Operating Cos, 2000–01; Man. Dir, KMC Internat., 2001–08. Non-executive Director: SP Energy Networks, 2015–18; Hendre Gp, 2015– (Vice Chm., 2016–); Natural Resources Wales, 2016–. Trustee and Mem. Bd, Leonard Cheshire Disability, 2015–. *Recreations:* gardening, travel, writing a novel. *Address:* Haywood Hain LLP, 368 Anchor House, Smugglers Way, SW18 1EL. *E:* elizabeth@haywoodhain.com.

**HAYWOOD, (June) Sandra T.;** *see* Tyler-Haywood.

**HAYWOOD, Nigel Robert,** CVO 2006; HM Diplomatic Service, retired; Governor of the Falkland Islands and Commissioner for South Georgia and the South Sandwich Islands, 2010–14; *b* 17 March 1955; *yr s* of Leslie and Peggy Haywood; *m* 1979, (Mary) Louise Smith; three *s*. *Educ:* Truro Sch.; New Coll., Oxford (MA English, MPhil Comparative Philology); RMA Sandhurst; Bournemouth Univ. (MSc Biodiversity Conservation). MCIL (MIL 1988). Lt, RAEC, 1977–80. Joined HM Diplomatic Service, 1983: Second, later First Sec., Budapest, 1985–89; FCO, 1989–92; Dep. Consul-Gen., Johannesburg, 1992–96; Counsellor and Dep. Head, UK Delegn to OSCE, Vienna, 1996–2000; Asst Dir (Personnel), FCO, 2000–03; Ambassador to Estonia, 2003–07; Consul-Gen., Basra, 2008–09. Director: Angling Trust, 2014–; UK Overseas Territories Conservation Forum, 2014–; Falkland Islands Trust, 2015–. Member: Philological Soc., 1981–; Golden Scale Club, 1982– (Hon. Pres., 2002–); British Ecol Soc., 2010–; Cttee, Piddle, Frome and W Dorset Fisheries Assoc., 2014–; Royal Entomological Soc., 2016–; Linnean Soc., 2017–. Chm., SW Veterans Athletics Club, 2016–. Research student in conservation biol., Bournemouth Univ., 2015–. Bard of Cornish Gorsedd, 1976. *Publications:* (contrib.) The One That Got Away, 1991; occasional articles and reviews in angling press. *Recreations:* fishing (especially saltwater fly fishing), marathon running, butterfly and moth conservation, archery, recorders, renaissance lute, bassoon. *Address:* 6 Tom's Mead, Corfe Castle, Dorset BH20 5HH. *Clubs:* Oxford and Cambridge, Flyfishers'; Purbeck Runners.

**HAZAREESINGH, Dr Sudhir Kumar,** FBA 2006; Lecturer in Politics, University of Oxford, since 1990; Fellow and Tutor in Politics, Balliol College, Oxford, since 1990; *b* 18 Oct. 1961; *s* of late Kissoonsingh Hazareesingh and of Thara Hazareesingh; partner, Dr Karma Nabulsi, Fellow of St Edmund Hall, Oxford. *Educ:* Balliol Coll., Oxford (BA 1st Cl. Hons Politics and Phil. 1984; MPhil Internat. Relns 1986); DPhil Politics Oxon 1990. University of Oxford: Open Prize Res. Fellow, Nuffield Coll., 1987–90; Lectr in Politics, Exeter Coll., 1989–90; Sen. Tutor, Balliol Coll., 1997–2001. Prof. Invité, Inst. des Etudes Politiques, Paris, 2006; British Acad. Res. Reader, 2001–03; Acad. Visitor, Dept of Pol Sci., Princeton Univ., 2002; Dir d'Etudes Invité, Ecole des Hautes Etudes en Scis Sociales, Paris, 2003; Vis. Fellow, Remarque Inst., NY Univ., 2004; Enseignant, Ecole Doctorale, Institut d'Etudes Politiques, Paris, 2009–10. Maître de Conférences, Ecole Pratique des Hautes Etudes, Paris (Section 4), 2000. Chevalier, Ordre des Palmes Académiques (France), 2003; Grand Prix du Mémorial and Medal of Honour, Ajaccio (France), 2006; Prix d'Histoire du Sénat (France), 2011; Grand Prix du Livre d'Idées (France), 2015. *Publications:* Intellectuals and the French Communist Party: disillusion and decline, 1991; Political Traditions in Modern France, 1994; From Subject to Citizen: the Second Empire and the emergence of modern French democracy, 1998; (with V. Wright) Francs-Maçons sous le Second Empire: le Grand Orient de France à la veille de la Troisième République, 2001; Intellectual Founders of the Republic: five studies in Nineteenth-Century French political thought, 2001; (ed and contrib.) The Jacobin Legacy in Modern France, 2002; The Saint-Napoleon: celebrations of sovereignty in 19th century France, 2004 (trans. French 2007); The Legend of Napoleon, 2004 (trans. French 2006); (with E. Anceau and V. Wright) Les Préfets de Gambetta, 2007; Le Mythe Gaullien, 2010; In the Shadow of the General, 2012; How The French Think, 2015 (trans. French 2015). *Recreations:* swimming, cinema, reading, listening to music. *Address:* Balliol College, Oxford OX1 3BJ. *T:* (01865) 277758, *Fax:* (01865) 277803. *E:* sudhir.hazareesingh@balliol.ox.ac.uk.

**HAZEL, George McLean,** OBE 2005; PhD; CEng; Independent Consultant, George Hazel Consultancy, since 2012; *b* 27 Jan. 1949; *s* of George McLean Hazel and Agnes Steven Hazel (*née* Willins); *m* 1974, Fiona Isabella Gault; one *s* two *d*. *Educ:* Heriot-Watt Univ. (BSc Civil Engrg; MSc Transportation); Cranfield Inst. of Technol. (PhD 1986). CEng 1975, MICE 1975. Transportation engr, Lothian Regl Council and Edinburgh CC, 1971–79; Prof. and Hd of Civil Engrg, Napier Univ., 1979–89; Dir, Oscar Faber Ltd (transport consultancy), 1989–93; Dir of Transportation, 1993–96, of City Develt, 1996–2000, Edinburgh CC; Dir, later Chm., McLean Hazel Ltd, later MRC McLean Hazel Ltd, 2000–11. Vis. Prof., Robert Gordon Univ., 2000–09. Pres., Instn of Highways and Transportation, 2003–04. FIHT 1976; FILT 1978. *Publications:* (with Roger Parry) Making Cities Work, 2004. *Recreations:* ski-ing, gardening, restoring vintage cars. *Address:* 332 Lanark Road, Edinburgh EH14 2LH. *T:* (office) 07974 235209, (home) (0131) 441 7787. *E:* george@georgehazel.com.

**HAZELL, Malcolm John,** CVO 1988; AM 2009; consultant to government and business, since 2008; Official Secretary to the Governor-General of Australia, 2003–08; Secretary, Order of Australia, 2003–08; an Extra Equerry to the Queen, since 2010; *b* 17 Dec. 1948; *s* of Neville John and Joan Nell Hazell; *m* 1976, Rhondda Leonie Seels; two *s*. *Educ:* C of E Grammar Sch., Brisbane; Univ. of Qld (BA Hons); Templeton Coll., Oxford; Graduate, Australian Inst. of Co. Dirs, 2009. Admin. Trainee, Public Service Bd, 1972; Exec. Officer to Comr, Nat. Capital Develt Commn, 1973–74; Private Sec., then Sen. Private Sec., to Prime Minister, Aust., 1975–79, 1980–81; Sen. Private Sec. to Minister for Aviation and Minister Assisting Prime Minister, 1982–83; various sen. mgt positions, Dept of Prime Minister and Cabinet, Canberra, 1982–85; Commonwealth Dir, Bicentennial Royal Visits to Aust., 1986–89; Asst Sec. and Hd, Internat. Div., Office of Security and Intelligence Coordination, 1989–94; Hd, S Pacific Forum Task Force, 1994; Asst Sec. and Hd, Cabinet Secretariat, Dept of Prime Minister and Cabinet, 1994–98; Sen. Advr to Prime Minister, 1998–2003. Secretary: Official Estabts Trust, 1985–87, 1995–96; Australian Bravery Decorations Council, 2003–08. Chm., ACT Block Grant Authy, 2009. Dir, Constitution Educn Fund Australia, 2012–18. Hon. Sec., Royal Australian Inst. of Public Admin, 1973–75. Member: Australian Inst. Company Dirs, 2007– (Fellow 2009); Ind. Communications Cttee, Australian Govt, 2015–. Mem., ACT Selection Cttee, Winston Churchill Memorial Trust, 2009–18. Mem., Commonwealth Day Celebration Cttee, ACT, 2010–16. Vice Pres., Canberra Grammar Sch. Foundn, 1993–96; Dir, Canberra Grammar Sch., 1994–2006 (Vice Chm., 2005–06). Dir, Southern Highlands Internat. Piano Comp., 2010–16. Foundn Chm., Anglican Dio. Canberra and Goulburn, Diocesan Schs Council, 1998–2002. Hon. Lay Canon, St Saviour's Cathedral, Goulburn, 2002. FAICD 2009. KStJ 2008 (CStJ 2004). Tenth Anniversary of Independence Medal (PNG), 1987. *Recreations:* music, cricket, family. *Address:* 46 Gledden Street, Chifley, ACT 2606, Australia. *T:* (2) 62822274. *E:* mjhazell48@gmail.com. *Club:* Commonwealth (Canberra).

**HAZELL, Peter Frank;** Chairman, Axa PPP, since 2017; *b* 4 Aug. 1948; *s* of Frank Henry Hazell and Kathleen Hazell; *m* 1972, Maureen Pamela Church; one *s* one *d*. *Educ:* Hertford Coll., Oxford (MA PPE 1969; BPhil Econs 1971). Partner: Deloitte Haskins & Sells, 1980–90; Coopers & Lybrand, 1990–98; UK Managing Partner, PricewaterhouseCoopers, 1998–2000. Chm., Argent Gp plc, 2001–16; non-executive Director: UK Coal, 2003–11; Smith & Williamson, 2004–16; Brit Insce, 2004–12; Axa UK, 2013–; Axa Ireland, 2014–; Canopius Managing Agents, 2014–. Member: Competition Commn, 2002–10; NERC, 2004–11. Mem. Court, Univ. of Greenwich, 2010–. *Recreations:* cricket, Rugby, opera, ballet, theatre, hill walking. *Address:* Axa UK plc, 5 Old Broad Street, EC2N 1AD. *T:* (020) 7920 5260. *Club:* MCC.

**HAZELL, Prof. Robert John Davidge,** CBE 2006; Professor of Government and the Constitution, University College London, since 1998 (Founder and Director, Constitution Unit, 1995–2015); *b* 30 April 1948; *s* of Peter Hazell and Elizabeth Complin Fowler; *m* 1981, Alison Sophia Mordaunt Richards; two *s*. *Educ:* Eton (King's Schol.); Wadham Coll., Oxford (Minor Schol.; MA Hons). Called to the Bar, Middle Temple, 1973, Bencher, 2012; Barrister, 1973–75; Lay Magistrate, Highbury Corner, 1978–96. Home Office, 1975–89, working in Immigration Dept, Policy Planning Unit, Gaming Bd, Race Relns, Broadcasting, Police and Prison Depts; CS travelling fellowship to investigate freedom of inf. in Australia, Canada, NZ, 1986–87; Dir, Nuffield Foundn, 1989–95. Sen. Fellow, Inst.

for Govt, 2010–. Vice-Chm., Assoc. of Charitable Foundns, 1992–95. Mem. Council, Hansard Soc., 1997–2015 (Vice-Chm., Commn on Scrutiny Role of Parlt, 1999–2001). Vice-Chm., Ind. Commn on Proportional Repn, 2002–03. Trustee, Citizenship Foundn, 1991–2000; Mem. Council, Justice, 1995–. FAcSS (AcSS 2011). FRSA 1991. Haldane Medal, RIPA, 1978. *Publications:* Conspiracy and Civil Liberties, 1974; (ed) The Bar on Trial, 1978; An Assembly for Wales, 1996; (ed) Constitutional Futures, 1999; (ed) The State and the Nations, 2000; (ed) The State of the Nations 2003, 2003; (ed) Devolution, Law Making and the Constitution, 2005; (ed) The English Question, 2006; (ed) Constitutional Futures Revisited, 2008; Hung Parliaments: the challenges for Westminster and Whitehall, 2009; Does Freedom of Information Work?: the impact of FOI on central government in the UK, 2010; The Conservative-Lib Dem Agenda for Constitutional Reform, 2010; The Politics of Coalition: how the Conservative-Liberal Democrat coalition works, 2012; Special Advisers: who they are, what they do and why they matter, 2014; The Politics of Judicial Independence in the UK's Changing Constitution, 2015; articles in legal and govt jls. *Recreations:* bird-watching, badgers, opera, canoeing, sailing. *Address:* 94 Constantine Road, NW3 2LS. *T:* (020) 7267 4881; (office) The Constitution Unit, School of Public Policy, University College London, 29 Tavistock Square, WC1H 9QU. *T:* (020) 7679 9349, *Fax:* (020) 7679 4978. *E:* r.hazell@ucl.ac.uk.

HAZLERIGG, family name of **Baron Hazlerigg**.

HAZLERIGG, 3rd Baron *cr* 1945, of Noseley; **Arthur Grey Hazlerigg**; Bt 1622; *b* 5 May 1951; *s* of 2nd Baron Hazlerigg, MC, TD and Patricia, *d* of John Pullar; *S* father, 2002; *m* 1999, Shan (*née* McIndoe); one *s* three *d* (incl. twin *d*) by previous marriage. *Heir:* s Hon. Arthur William Grey Hazlerigg [*b* 13 May 1987; *m* 2017, Kate Braithwaite]. *Address:* Noseley Hall, Billesdon, Leics LE7 9EH. *T:* (0116) 259 6487, *Fax:* (0116) 259 6989. *E:* arthur@noseleyhall.co.uk. *Clubs:* MCC; Leicester Tigers Rugby Football.

HAZLEWOOD, Charles Matthew Egerton; conductor; *b* 14 Nov. 1966; *s* of Rev. Canon Ian Hazlewood and Helen Hazlewood; *m* 1993, Henrietta Lang; three *s* one *d*. *Educ:* Christ's Hosp.; Keble Coll., Oxford (Organ Schol.; BA Hons). ARCO 1985. Founder and Music Dir, Excellent Device! (formerly Eos), 1991–2009; Music Director: Broomhill Opera, 1993–2001; Wiltons Music Hall, 1999–2003; and Co-founder, Dimpho di Kopane, Cape Town, 2000–08 (composer and Music Dir, The Mysteries, Beggar's Opera, The Snow Queen); and Founder, Army of Generals (formerly Harmonieband), 2002–; Principal Guest Conductor, BBC Concert Orch., 2005–09; Founder, Charles Hazlewood's All Star Collective, 2008–; Founder Artistic Director: Orch. in a Field, 2009–; The British Paraorchestra, 2011–; Founder, Soweto Messiah Project, Johannesburg, 2012–. Débuts: Carnegie Hall, 2003; BBC Proms, 2006; Royal Concertgebouw Orch., 2009; Orch. of the Age of Enlightenment, 2009; Malmo SO, 2009; Gothenburg SO, 2010; Philharmonia, 2010; Copenhagen Philharmonic, 2015; Swedish Radio SO, 2015; Metropol Orkest, 2015; Hague Residentie Orkest, 2017; Danish Radio SO, 2017; CBSO, 2017. Author, conductor and presenter of television films: Vivaldi Unmasked, 2001; The Genius of Mozart, 2003; Beethoven, 2005; Stripping Pop, 2005; Tchaikovsky, 2007; How Pop Songs Work, 2008; The Birth of British Music, 2009; Come Clog Dancing, 2010; Come Bell Ringing, 2011; Scrapheap Orchestra, 2011; My Beatles Black Album, 2017; Tones, Drones and Arpeggios: The Magic of Minimalism, 2018; music dir and conductor of film, U-Carmen E-Khayelitsha, 2005 (Golden Bear for best film, Berlin Film Fest.); conductor and presenter, BBC radio programmes: Discovering Music; The Charles Hazlewood Show. Composer: Dead Dog in a Suitcase (new version of The Beggar's Opera for Kneehigh Th.), 2014, transf. UK and world tour; The Tin Drum (opera, for Kneehigh Th.), 2017, UK tour; Ubu Karaoke (musical, for Kneehigh Th.), 2018. First Prize, Conducting Comp., EBU, 1995; Sony Radio Academy Award, 2005, 2006, 2008. *Recreations:* cooking, film. *Address:* c/o Intermusica, 9 Kingsway, WC2B 6XF. *T:* (020) 7608 9900. *E:* info@charleshazlewood.com, skhan@intermusica.co.uk. *W:* www.charleshazlewood.com.

HAZZARD, Chris; MP (SF) South Down, since 2017; *b* Drumaness, Co. Down, 20 Aug. 1984; *m* Lisa. *Educ:* Our Lady and St Patrick's Coll., Knock; Queen's Univ. Belfast. Press officer, SF. Mem. (SF) S Down, NI Assembly, 2012–17. Minister for Infrastructure, NI, 2016–17. Mem., Educn Cttee, 2012–16, Public Accounts Cttee, 2013–14, NI Assembly. *Address:* c/o Sinn Féin, 55 Falls Road, Belfast BT12 4PD.

HEAD, family name of **Viscount Head**.

HEAD, 2nd Viscount *cr* 1960, of Throope; **Richard Antony Head**; *b* 27 Feb. 1937; *s* of 1st Viscount Head, GCMG, CBE, MC, PC, and Dorothea, Viscountess Head (*d* 1987), *d* of 9th Earl of Shaftesbury, KP, GCVO, CBE, PC; *S* father, 1983; *m* 1974, Alicia Brigid, *er d* of Julian Salmond; two *s* one *d*. *Educ:* Eton; RMA Sandhurst. The Life Guards, 1957–66 (Captain), retd. Trainer of racehorses, 1968–83. *Recreation:* golf. *Heir:* s Hon. Henry Julian Head, *b* 30 March 1980. *Address:* Throope Manor, Bishopstone, Salisbury, Wilts SP5 4BA. *T:* (01722) 718318.

HEAD, (John) Philip (Trevelyan); His Honour Judge Head; a Circuit Judge, since 2004; *b* 6 July 1953; *s* of Walter Raleigh Trevelyan Head and Rosemary Constance Beatrice Head (*née* Borwick); *m* 1983, Erica Lesley Cox; two *c*. *Educ:* Marlborough Coll.; Merton Coll., Oxford (MA); Univ. of Virginia (LLM). Fulbright Schol., 1974–75. Called to the Bar, Middle Temple, 1976; Asst Recorder, 1996–2000, Recorder, 2000–04. Mem., Parole Bd for Eng. and Wales, 2006–09; Judicial Mem., Restricted Patients Panel, 2011–12. Oxford Univ. Hockey Blue, 1974. *Recreations:* travel, books. *Address:* Leicester Crown Court, 90 Wellington Street, Leicester LE1 6HG. *Clubs:* Savile, Sette of Odd Volumes.

HEAD, Michael Edward, CVO 1991; UK Member, European Commission on Racism and Intolerance (Council of Europe), 1996–2013 (Chairman, 2001–05); *b* 17 March 1936; *s* of Alexander Edward Head and Wilhelmina Head; *m* 1963, Wendy Elizabeth, *d* of R. J. Davies; two *s* two *d*. *Educ:* Leeds, Kingston, and Woking Grammar Schools; University College London (BA; Pollard Prize for History); Univ. of Michigan (MA). 2nd Lieut, Royal Artillery (Nat. Service), 1958–60. Home Office, 1960; Private Sec. to Parly Under Secs of State, 1964–66; Sec., Deptl Cttee on Liquor Licensing (Erroll), 1971–72; Asst Sec., 1974–84: Probation and After Care Dept; Community Programmes and Equal Opportunities Dept; Criminal Dept; Asst Under Sec. of State, General Dept, 1984, Criminal Justice and Constitutional Dept (Registrar of the Baronetage), 1986, Broadcasting Dept, 1991, Equal Opportunities and Gen. Dept, 1991 (Head of Dept, 1991–96). Dir, Rehab UK, 1996–2005. Member: Surrey Probation Cttee, 1997–2001; Surrey Probation Bd, 2001–07. Vice Chm., Woking Community Leisure Ltd, 1996–98. Mem. Cttee, Arts Soc. Mayford (formerly Mayford Decorative and Fine Arts Soc.), 2013–19 (Vice Chair, 2016–19). *Recreations:* theatre, reading. *Address:* Rustlings, Castle Road, Horsell, Woking, Surrey GU21 4ET. *T:* and *Fax:* (01483) 772929. *E:* mhead90120@btinternet.com. *Clubs:* 1900; County (Guildford); Rotary (Woking Dist).

HEAD, Sir Patrick (Michael Charles), Kt 2015; RDI 1993; FREng; Director of Engineering, Williams Grand Prix Engineering Ltd, 2004–11; *b* June 1946. *Educ:* University Coll. London (degree Mech. Engrg 1970). Joined Lola, chassis manufacturer, 1970; Williams Grand Prix Engineering Ltd: Co-Founder and designer, 1977; Tech. Dir, 1986–2004. Dir, Williams Hybrid Power Ltd, 2008–14.

HEAD, Peter Richard, CBE 2011 (OBE 1998); FREng, FICE, FIStructE; Founder, 2011, and Chief Executive Officer, since 2014, Ecological Sequestration Trust (Chairman, 2011–14); Founder and Chairman, Resilience Brokers Ltd, since 2017; *b* 27 Feb. 1947; *s* of Robert Cyril Head and Vera Alice (*née* Kent); *m* 1970, Susan Florence East; one *s* one *d*. *Educ:* Tiffin Boys' Sch., Kingston-upon-Thames; Imperial Coll., London (BSc 1st Cl. Hons Eng 1969). FREng (FEng 1996); FICE 1995; FIStructE 1995; FCIHT (FIHT 1995). Freeman Fox & Partners, 1969–80: team leader for design of: Avonmouth Bridge, M5, 1971–74; Myton Swing Bridge, Hull, 1974–75 (Dep. Resident Engr, construction of Myton Bridge, 1977–80); Section Engr, construction of Friarton Bridge, Perth, 1975–77; G. Maunsell & Partners subseq. Maunsell, later part of AECOM Gp, then FaberMaunsell, 1980–2004: designer of bridges over docks on Dockland Light Rly, London, 1981–84; Project Director: Second Severn Crossing, 1984–96; design and construction, Kap Shui Mun Bridge, Hong Kong, 1994–96; Dir responsible for studies and choice of bridge for third crossing of Forth Estuary, 1993–2004; Man. Dir, 1995–97; Chief Exec., Europe, 1997–2002; Corporate Develt Dir, 2002–04; Dir for supervision of construction, Rion Antirion Bridge, Greece, 1997–2004; Dir and Leader of Global Planning, 2004–11, Consultant, 2011–12, Arup; Proj. Dir, Dongtan Eco-city, Shanghai, 2005–08; Maunsell Structural Plastics Ltd, 1984–97: Dir and designer, Aberfeldy Bridge, 1992 and Bonds Mill Bridge, Stonehouse, Glos, 1994; inventor, Advanced Composite Construction System and Spaces bridge concept. Chm., London First Sustainability Unit, 2000; Comr, GLA Sustainable Develt Commn, 2002–09; Chm., Steel Construction Inst., 2003–06 (Dep. Chm., 1999–2003); Vice-Pres., Construction Industry Res. Assoc., 1999–2004; Member: 2012 Olympics Construction Task Force, 2005–10; TG09 Sustainable Develt Solutions Network Urban Sustainable Develt Goal, 2011–15; Chm., South Bd, Groundwork Trust, 2018– (Dir, London Bd, 2008–18); UNISDR FRAF FIST Wkg Gp, 2018–; Chm., Trust Bd, Inst. for Sustainability, 2009–15; Sci. Advr, Planetary Health Commn, 2014–15. Mem., Adv. Bd, 2019 Global Assessment Report, UN Office for Disaster Risk Reduction, 2018–. Visiting Professor: Univ. of Surrey, 2000–05; Univ. of Bristol, 2008–; Univ. of Westminster, 2011–14; Hood Fellow, Univ. of Auckland, 2010–11. Innovation Champion, Thames Gateway, 2008–10. Internat. Brunel Lecture Series, ICE, 2008–09. FCGI 2001; FRSA 2008. Hon. DEng Bristol, 2008. Premier Gold Award/PRW Award for Excellence in Design, 1993; Silver Medal, Royal Acad. Engrg, 1995; Laureate Award of Merit Internat. Assoc. of Bridge and Structural Engrg, 1998; Telford Prize, ICE, 2006; Frank Whittle Medal, RAEng, 2008; Lorenzo H. Zambrano Lifetime Achievement Award, CEMEX, 2016. *Publications:* numerous papers in learned jls and conf. proc. covering sustainability, major bridge projects and pioneering work in advanced composite materials, sustainable cities and low carbon urban develt. *Recreations:* hill-walking, gardening, painting, grandchildren. *Address:* Ecological Sequestration Trust, 10 Queen Street Place, EC4R 1BE. *E:* peter.head@ecosequestrust.org; Parkside, 11 Manor Way, Beckenham, Kent BR3 3LH. *T:* 07917 231655.

HEAD, Philip; see Head, J. P. T.

HEAD, Philip John, FRICS; programme and project management consultant, since 2012; *b* 24 Nov. 1951; *s* of Dennis George Head and Marjorie Head; *m* 1974, Barbara Fox; two *s*. *Educ:* Surbiton Grammar Sch.; Herefordshire Tech. Coll.; Univ. of Reading (BSc Hons Estate Management). FRICS 1985. Estates Surveyor, 1973–77, Sen. Commercial Surveyor, 1977–78, Milton Keynes Develt Corp.; Welsh Development Agency, 1978–93: Develt and Funding Manager, 1981–83; Dep. Commercial Dir, 1983–84; Commercial Dir, 1984–87; Exec. Dir, Property and Regional Services, 1987–91; Chief Exec., 1991–93; Hd of Property Services, 1994–98, Asst Dir, 1998–2001, FEFCE; Asst Dir, 2001–02, Dir, Infrastructure and Property Services, 2002–10, LSC; Dir of Capital, Skills Funding Agency, 2010–12. Gov., Gloucestershire Coll., 2014–. *Recreations:* member of Rotary Club of Cardiff West (Hon. Sec.), gardening, family. *E:* philipjhead@btinternet.com.

HEAD, Sir Richard (Douglas Somerville), 6th Bt *cr* 1838, of Rochester, Kent; Assistant Gardener, RHS Garden, Wisley, 1979–2009; *b* 16 Jan. 1951; *s* of Major Sir Francis Head, 5th Bt, and of Susan, Lady Head (*née* Ramsay); *S* father, 2005; *m* 1991, Edwina Mansell (marr. diss. 1999). *Educ:* Eton; Bristol Poly. (BA Fine Arts 1974); London Univ. Inst. of Educn (PGCE 1975); RA Schs (David Murray Landscape Studentship). Artist in pen and ink, gouache, oil paint, drypoint. Mixed exhibitions: Michael Parkin Fine Arts, 1988; Christie's 20th Century Old Etonian Artists, 1990; Sally Hunter Fine Arts, 1997; Russell Gallery Mixed Christmas Show, 2007, 2008, 2009; solo exhibition, The First Gallery, Southampton, 2005. *Recreations:* music, painting, drawing, garden volunteer at Clandon Park. *Heir:* cousin Patrick John Somerville Head [*b* 4 Oct. 1943; *m* 1st, 1971, Karen Carla Schaufele (marr. diss. 1986); two *d*; 2nd, 1995, Joan Fay Crawford]. *Address:* 6 Viscount Gardens, Byfleet, Surrey KT14 6HE.

HEAD, Sandra Anne; see Phinbow, S. A.

HEADFORT, 7th Marquis of, *cr* 1800; **Thomas Michael Ronald Christopher Taylour**; Bt 1704; Baron Headfort, 1760; Viscount Headfort, 1762; Earl of Bective, 1766; Baron Kenlis (UK), 1831; *b* 10 Feb. 1959; *o s* of 6th Marquis of Headfort and of Hon. Elizabeth Nall-Cain, *d* of 2nd Baron Brocket; *S* father, 2005; *m* 1987, Susan Jane (*d* 2008), *er d* of late C. A. Vandervell and of Mrs Vandervell; two *s* two *d*. *Educ:* Harrow; RAC Cirencester. Estate agent with John D. Wood & Co., London, 1981–87; property consultant, 1995–2003, Dir, 2003–11, Bective Davidson, later Bective Leslie Marsh Ltd, London; Dir, Central London Estate Agents Ltd; Sen. Consultant, Sotheby's Internat. Realty, 2011–12. Mem., Irish Peers Assoc. *Heir:* s Earl of Bective, *qv*. *Address:* Swinbrook Manor Farm, Swinbrook, near Burford, Oxon OX18 4DY. *Club:* Turf.

HEAL, Anne Elizabeth; Chair: Customer Challenge Group, Thames Water, since 2015; Volunteering Matters, since 2015; *b* Bangor, N Wales, 7 Oct. 1962; *d* of John and Elizabeth Heal; *m* 1986, Stuart Fowler; one *s* three *d*. *Educ:* Perse Sch. for Girls, Cambridge; Somerville Coll., Oxford (MA PPE); London Business Sch. (Sloan Fellow; MSc Mgt). Employee Relns, Ford Motor Co., 1983–85; reporter, Citycall, 1985; Associate Dir, Charles Barker, 1986–88; BT: Dir, Strategic Planning and Hd, Chm.'s and CEO's offices, 1988–2001; Gp Dir, Regulatory Affairs, 2002–05; Managing Director: Strategy, Openreach, 2006–15; BT Volunteering, 2013–15. Board Member: Women in Technol. and Telecoms, 2005–12; Ofqual, 2012–18; Director: Office of Rail and Road, 2016–; London Design and Engrg UTC, 2018–; Member: Bank of England Enforcement Decision Making Cttee, 2018–; Regulatory Decisions Cttee, FCA, 2019–. Non-exec. Dir, ELEXON, 2017–. Lay Advr, RCPath, 2016–17; Lay Mem., GDC, 2017–. Gov., Unicorn Sch., Kew, 2008–16 (Co-Chm., 2014–16). Trustee: NCVO, 2015–; Ballet Boyz, 2015–; Mem., Governance and Nominations Cttee, Diabetes UK, 2018– (Chair, 2019–). FRSA. *Recreations:* opera, ballet, sport, running, vegetable gardening and slug management. *Address:* Volunteering Matters, The Levy Centre, 18–24 Lower Clapton Road, E5 0PD. *T:* (020) 3780 5872. *E:* anneheal01@gmail.com.

**HEAL, Prof. (Barbara) Jane**, PhD; FBA 1997; Professor of Philosophy, University of Cambridge, 1999–2012, now Emeritus; Fellow, St John's College, Cambridge, since 1986 (President, 1999–2003); *b* 21 Oct. 1946; *d* of William Calvert Kneale and Martha Kneale (*née* Hurst); *m* 1968, John Gauntlett Benedict Heal (marr. diss. 1987); one *s* one *d*. *Educ:* Oxford High Sch. for Girls; New Hall, Cambridge (BA 1968; PhD 1973). Sarah Smithson Res. Fellow, Newnham Coll., Cambridge, 1971–74; Harkness Fellow, Commonwealth Fund of NY, and Vis. Fellow, Princeton Univ. and Univ. of Calif at Berkeley, 1974–76; Lectr in Philosophy, Univ. of Newcastle upon Tyne, 1976–86; Univ. Asst Lectr, 1986–91, Lectr, 1991–96, Reader, 1996–99, in Philosophy, Univ. of Cambridge. *Publications:* Fact and Meaning, 1989; Mind, Reason and Imagination, 2003; articles in Mind, Philosophical Qly, etc. *Recreations:* reading, walking. *Address:* St John's College, Cambridge CB2 1TP. *T:* (01223) 338668.

**HEAL, Dr Felicity Margaret,** FBA 2015; Lecturer in History, University of Oxford, 1980–2011, now Emeritus; Fellow, Jesus College, Oxford, 1980–2011, now Emeritus; *b* Hemel Hempstead, 24 Sept. 1945; *d* of John and Winifred Chandler; *m* 1988, Dr Clive Holmes; two step *s*; one *d* by a previous marriage. *Educ:* Lewes Girls' Grammar Sch., Sussex; Newnham Coll., Cambridge (BA Hist. 1967; PhD Hist. 1970). Res. Fellow, Newnham Coll., Cambridge, 1970–73; Staff Tutor, Open Univ., 1976–78; Lectr in Hist., Sussex Univ., 1977–79; University of Oxford: Chair, Faculty of Hist., 1999–2001; Dep. Hd, Humanities Div., 2009–11. Vis. Fellow, Univs of Yale and Stanford, 1975–76. Consultant Ed., Oxford DNB, 1995–. *Publications:* Of Prelates and Princes: a study of the economic and social position of the Tudor Episcopate, 1980; Hospitality in Early Modern England, 1990; (with C. Holmes) The Gentry in England and Wales 1500–1700, 1994; Reformation in Britain and Ireland, 2003; The Power of Gifts: gift-exchange in early modern England, 2014. *Recreations:* music, especially of the Baroque, travel, gardening. *Address:* Jesus College, Turl Street, Oxford OX1 3DW. *T:* (01865) 510068. *E:* felicity.heal@jesus.ox.ac.uk.

**HEAL, Jane;** *see* Heal, B. J.

**HEAL, Oliver Standerwick,** PhD; furniture restorer, since 2004; *b* 18 April 1949; *s* of late Anthony Standerwick Heal; *m* 1990, Annik Coatalen; one *s*. *Educ:* Leighton Park Sch., Reading; Bucks Chiltern UC (BA Hons (Furniture Conservation and Restoration) 2004); Brunel Univ. (PhD 2009). Joined Heal's, 1970; Dir, Heal & Son Ltd, 1974–83, Chm., 1977–83; Chm., Heal & Son Holdings PLC, 1981–83 (Dir, 1975–83); Dir, Staples & Co. Ltd, 1981–84; Chm., Heal Textil GmbH, 1984–90; VRP multi-carte, France, 1990–91; Commercial Dir, Faïenceries de Quimper, France, 1992–94; sales agent, furnishing fabrics, France, 1994–2000. Liveryman, Furniture Makers' Co., 1978–. *Publications:* Sir Ambrose Heal and the Heal Cabinet Factory 1897–1939, 2014; article in Jl of Furniture History Soc. *Recreation:* vintage cars. *Club:* Vintage Sports Car (Chipping Norton).

**HEAL, Sharon;** Director, Museums Association, since 2014; *b* Leeds, 27 Oct. 1967; *d* of John Heal and Josephine Heal; *m* 1996, Alexander Shanks; one *d*. *Educ:* Roundhay High Sch., Leeds; London Coll. of Printing. Editor, Museums Jl, 2005–10; Hd, Pubns and Events, Mus Assoc., 2010–14. *Publications:* (contrib.) Museums and Public Value, 2013. *Recreations:* horse riding, book club. *Address:* Museums Association, 42 Clerkenwell Close, EC1R 0AZ. *T:* (020) 7566 7800. *E:* sharon@museumsassociation.org.

**HEAL, Sylvia Lloyd;** JP; *b* 20 July 1942; *d* of late John Lloyd Fox and Ruby Fox; *m* 1965, Keith Heal; one *s* one *d*. *Educ:* Elfed Secondary Modern School, Buckley, N Wales; Coleg Harlech; University College Swansea (BSc Econ 1968). Social worker, health service and Dept of Employment, 1968–70 and 1980–90; Nat. Officer, Carers Nat. Assoc., 1992–97. MP (Lab) Mid Staffordshire, March 1990–1992; contested (Lab) Mid Staffordshire, 1992; MP (Lab) Halesowen and Rowley Regis, 1997–2010. PPS to Sec. of State for Defence, 1997–2000; First Dep. Chm. of Ways and Means and a Dep. Speaker, H of C, 2000–10. Mem., Select Cttee on Educn, Sci. and Arts, 1990–92; opposition spokesperson on health and women's issues, 1991–92. Mem. Council, ASA, 1992–97; Mem., Exec. Council, SSAFA, 1990–91. Hon. Fellow, Univ. of Wales, 2003. JP Surrey, 1973. *Recreations:* walking, theatre, listening to male voice choirs, gardening. *Address:* Meadlake, 15 Vicarage Avenue, Egham, Surrey TW20 8NW.

**HEALD, Bill;** *see* Heald, R. J.

**HEALD, Rt Hon. Sir Oliver,** Kt 2014; PC 2016; QC 2012; MP (C) North East Hertfordshire, since 1997 (North Hertfordshire, 1992–97); *b* 15 Dec. 1954; *s* of late John Anthony Heald and Joyce Heald; *m* 1979, Christine Whittle; one *s* two *d*. *Educ:* Reading Sch.; Pembroke Coll., Cambridge. Called to the Bar, Middle Temple, 1977, Bencher, 2013; practice in E Anglia and London, 1977–95 and 1997–2001. Contested (C) Southwark and Bermondsey, 1987. PPS to Minister of Agric., Fisheries and Food, 1994–95; Parly Under-Sec. of State, DSS, 1995–97; an Opposition Whip, 1997–2000; Opposition spokesman: on home affairs, 2000–01; on health, 2001–02; on work and pensions, 2002–03; Shadow Leader, H of C, 2003–05; Shadow Sec. of State for Constitutional Affairs, and Shadow Chancellor of Duchy of Lancaster, 2005–07; Solicitor General, 2012–14; Minister of State, MoJ, 2016–17. Private Member's Bill—Animal Welfare (Service Animals) Act, 2019. Member: Employment Select Cttee, 1992–94; Admin Select Cttee, 1998–2000; Select Cttee on Modernisation of H of C, 2003–05; Select Cttee on Work and Pensions, 2007–12; Cttee on Standards in Public Life, 2008–12; Cttee of Selection, 2009–10; Cttee on Standards and Privileges, 2010–12; Ecclesiastical Cttee, 2010–12; Governance Select Cttee, 2014–15; Ind. High-Level Commn on Sexual Misconduct, Accountability and Culture Change (Oxfam), 2018–. Vice-Chm., Rules Cttee, Council of Europe, 2012. Chm. of Exec., Soc. of Conservative Lawyers, 2007–12. *Recreations:* sports, family, sailing. *Address:* House of Commons, SW1A 0AA.

**HEALD, Prof. Richard John, (Bill),** CBE 2012 (OBE 1998); FRCS, FRCSE; Surgical Director, Pelican Cancer Foundation, Basingstoke, since 2000; *b* 11 May 1936; *o s* of late Jack and Muriel Heald, St Albans; *m* 1969, Denise (*née* Boncey); three *d*. *Educ:* Gonville and Caius Coll., Cambridge (BA 1st Cl. Hons 1957 (Coll. Prize); MA 1960; MB 1960, MChir 1965); Guy's Hosp., London. FRCSE 1964; FRCS 1965. Consultant Surgeon: N Hants Hosp., Basingstoke, 1973–; specialist in colorectal cancer surgery and internat. teacher of surgical technique. Personal Chair, Univ. of Southampton, 1998–. B. V. Petrovsky Hon. Prof., Nat. Res. Centre of Surgery, Russia, 2011. Sir Peter Freyer Meml Lect., NUI, 2011. Mem. Council, RCS, 1989–2001 (Vice-Pres., 1996–98); Pres., Sections of Coloproctol. and of Surgery, RSocMed; Pres., Internat. Colon and Rectal Club—Surgical Dir, TIC, Shanghai, 2005; Colostomy Assoc., 2008. Israel Soc. of Colon and Rectal Surgery, 2007. Hon. Member: Swiss Surgical Soc., 2000; Polish Soc. of Surgical Oncol., 2008 (Gold Medal, 2008). Hon. FRSocMed 2001; Hon. Fellow: Assoc. of Coloproctol. of GB and Ireland, 2001; German Surgical Soc., 2004; Austrian Surgical Soc., 2004; Assoc. Française de Chirurgie, 2005; Amer. Soc. of Colon and Rectal Surgeons, 2012; Surgical Soc. of Rome, 2012; Hon. FACS 2013; Hon. FRCSI 2014. Hon. Dr Linkoping, Sweden, 1997. Gold Medal in Surgery, Assoc. of Surgery of Netherlands, 2001; Centenary Medal, French Cancer Soc., 2005; Herczel Award (Bronze Placket), Hungarian Coloproctology Assoc., 2011. *Publications:* contrib. papers on rectal cancer surgery, particularly total mesorectal excision for rectal cancer to jls incl. Jl RSocMed, Lancet. *Recreation:* sailing. *Address:* Pelican Cancer Foundation, The Ark, Dinwoodie Drive, Basingstoke, Hants RG24 9NN. *T:* (01256) 314848. *Club:* Royal Southampton Yacht.
*See also* T. H. Henman.

**HEALE, Simon John Newton;** Chief Executive, London Metal Exchange, 2001–06; *b* 27 April 1953; *s* of James Newton Heale and Ruth Elizabeth Heale; *m* 1982, Catriona Jean, *d* of Lt-Gen. Sir Robin Macdonald Carnegie, KCB, OBE; one *s* two *d*. *Educ:* Winchester Coll.; Oriel Coll., Oxford (BA 1975). Chartered Accountant, 1978. Finance Dir, Swire Japan, 1982–85; Pres., Oceanroutes Inc., 1985–88; Gen. Manager Cargo, Cathay Pacific, 1988–90; Chief Operating Officer, Dragonair, 1990–94; Dep. Man. Dir, Cathay Pacific Airways, 1994–97; Jardine Fleming: Gp Finance Dir, 1997–99; Chief Operating Officer, 1999–2001. Non-executive Director: LCH.Clearnet Gp Ltd, 2003–06; Morgan Advanced Materials (formerly Morgan Crucible Co.) plc, 2005–14; KAZ Minerals (formerly Kazakhmys) plc, 2007–18 (Chm., 2013–17); Marex Spectron (formerly Marex Financial), 2007–18 (Chm., 2016–18); Panmure Gordon & Co. plc, 2007–11 (Interim Chm., 2009–11); PZ Cussons, 2008–13; Coats plc, 2011–14 (Sen. Ind. Dir, 2013–14); Chairman: GMS, 2014–19; Energean Oil and Gas plc, 2017–. Chief Exec., China Now Fest., 2007–08. Treas. and Trustee, Macmillan Cancer Support, 2010–16. *Recreations:* travel, reading, walking, labradors and Jack Russells.

**HEALEY, Sir Charles Edward C.;** *see* Chadwyck-Healey.

**HEALEY, Rt Hon. John;** PC 2008; MP (Lab) Wentworth and Dearne, since 2010 (Wentworth, 1997–2010); *b* 13 Feb. 1960; *s* of Aidan Healey, OBE and Jean Healey; *m* 1993, Jackie Bate; one *s*. *Educ:* Christ's Coll., Cambridge (schol., BA 1982). Charity campaigner, 1984–90; Campaigns Manager, Issue Communications, 1990–92; Head of Communications, MSF, 1992–94; Campaigns Dir, TUC, 1994–97. PPS to Chancellor of the Exchequer, 1999–2001; Parly Under-Sec. of State, DFES, 2001–02; Econ. Sec., 2002–05, Financial Sec., 2005–07, HM Treasury; Minister of State (Minister for Local Govt), 2007–09, (Minister for Housing), 2009–10, DCLG; Shadow Minister for Housing, 2010; Shadow Sec. of State for Health, 2010–11; Shadow Minister for Housing and Planning, 2015–16; Shadow Sec. of State for Housing, 2016–. Contested (Lab) Ryedale, 1992. *Address:* House of Commons, SW1A 0AA. *E:* john.healey.mp@parliament.uk.

**HEALEY, Prof. John Francis,** PhD; FBA 2011; Professor of Semitic Studies, University of Manchester, 1997–2013, now Emeritus; *b* Leeds, 10 Feb. 1948; *s* of George Healey and Frances Healey; *m* 1972, Elizabeth Anne Warman; one *s* one *d*. *Educ:* St Michael's Coll., Leeds; University Coll., Dublin, NUI (BA, MA Semitic Langs and Greek); Sch. of Oriental and African Studies, Univ. of London (PhD 1977). Lectr in Semitic Langs, University Coll., Cardiff, 1974–80; Lectr in Hebrew and Semitic Philol., Univ. of Durham, 1981–89; University of Manchester: Lectr, 1989–92; Sen. Lectr, 1992–95; Reader, 1995–97. *Publications:* Leshono Suryoyo: first studies in Syriac, 1980, 2nd edn 2005; The Early Alphabet, 1990; The Nabataean Tomb Inscriptions of Mada'in Salih, 1993; (with H. J. W. Drijvers) The Old Syriac Inscriptions of Edessa and Osrhoene, 1999; The Religion of the Nabataeans: a conspectus, 2001; (with G. R. Smith) A Brief Introduction to the Arabic Alphabet, 2009; Aramaic Inscriptions and Documents of the Roman Period, 2009; Law and Religion between Petra and Edessa: studies in Aramaic epigraphy on the Roman frontier, 2011; approx. 120 learned articles and contribs to edited works. *Recreations:* travel in the Middle East where possible, The Guardian, The Tablet. *Address:* School of Arts, Languages and Cultures, Faculty of Humanities, University of Manchester, Oxford Road, Manchester M13 9PL. *T:* (0161) 434 4956. *E:* john.healey@manchester.ac.uk.

**HEALEY, Prof. Patsy,** OBE 1999; PhD; FBA 2009; Professor, School of Architecture, Planning and Landscape, University of Newcastle upon Tyne, 1988–2002, now Emeritus; *b* Loughborough, Leics, 1 Jan. 1940; *d* of late Cecil Terence Ingold, CMG and Leonora Mary Ingold (*née* Kemp); *m* 1st, 1961, Ian Nevill Healey (*d* 1972); 2nd, 1977, David Reiach Hunter (*d* 1979). *Educ:* Walthamstow Hall, Sevenoaks; University Coll., London (BA Geog.); Regent St Poly. (DipTP); London Sch. of Econs (PhD Urban and Regl Planning). MRTPI 1973. Teacher, Llwyn-y-bryn Grammar Sch. for Girls, then Eltham Green Comp. Sch., 1962–65; Planning Officer, Lewisham LBC, then GLC, 1965–69; Res. Fellow, 1969–72; Kingston Poly., 1972–74; Principal Lectr and Dean of Faculty, Oxford Poly., 1974–87. Chair, Glendale Gateway Trust, 2012–15. Member: ESRC cttees; Joseph Rowntree Housing and Neighbourhood Res. Cttee; RTPI cttees; HEFCE; RAE Panel 2001. Mem. Bd, Tyne and Wear Develt Corp., 1990–98. FAcSS (AcSS 1999). Hon. DLaw Newcastle, 2015. Gold Medal, RTPI, 2007. *Publications:* (ed jtly) Planning Theory: prospects for the 1980s, 1982; Local Plans in British Land Use Planning, 1983; (ed jtly) Land Policy: problems and alternatives, 1985; (jtly) The Political Economy of Land: urban development in an oil economy, 1985; (jtly) Land Use Planning and the Mediation of Urban Change, 1988; (ed jtly) Rebuilding the City: property-led urban regeneration, 1992; (ed jtly) Managing Cities: the new urban context, 1995; (jtly) Negotiating Development, 1995; (ed jtly) Making Strategic Spatial Plans: innovation in Europe, 1997; Collaborative Planning: shaping places in fragmented societies, 1997, 2nd edn 2006; (jtly) Planning, Governance and Spacial Strategy in Britain, 2000; (ed jtly) The Governance of Place, 2001; (ed jtly) Urban Governance, Institutional Capacity and Social Milieux, 2002; Urban Complexity and Spatial Strategies: towards a relational planning for our times, 2007; (ed jtly) Critical Readings in Planning Theory (3 vols), 2008; Making Better Places: the planning project in the twenty-first century, 2010; (ed jtly) Crossing Borders: international exchange and planning practices, 2010; contrib. papers to learned jls. *Recreations:* gardening, walking, history and archaeology, literature. *Address:* School of Architecture, Planning and Landscape, Newcastle upon Tyne University, Newcastle upon Tyne NE1 7RU. *E:* Patsy.Healey@newcastle.ac.uk.
*See also* T. Ingold.

**HEALY OF PRIMROSE HILL,** Baroness *cr* 2010 (Life Peer), of Primrose Hill in the London Borough of Camden; **Anna Mary Healy;** *b* London, 10 May 1955; *d* of late Martin Michael Healy and Kathleen Elizabeth Healy; *m* 1992, Jon Cruddas, *qv*; one *s*. *Educ:* St Aloysius Convent Grammar Sch., London; Royal Holloway Coll., London Univ. (BA Hons Modern Hist., Econ. Hist. and Politics 1976); Birkbeck Coll., London (MSc (Econ) Politics 1982); City Univ. (Postgrad. Dip. Periodical Journalism 1982). Labour Party: PA to Hd of Internat. Dept, 1978–81; PA to Dir of Communications, 1981–82; journalist on various pubns incl. Internat. Broadcasting, 1982–85; Campaigns Press Officer, 1985–88; Parly Press Sec., H of C, 1988–96; Press Officer to Leader of Opposition, 1996–97; Special Adviser: to Sec. of State for NI, 1997–98; to Sec. of State, Cabinet Office, 1998–99; to Minister for Transport, 2000–01; to Minister for Cabinet Office, 2001–03; Hd, Office of Jon Cruddas, MP, 2003–07; Special Advr to Leader of H of C, 2007–10; COS to Leader of the Opposition, H of C, May–Sept. 2010. *Recreations:* music, film, literature. *Address:* House of Lords, SW1A 0PW. *T:* (020) 7219 8912, 07946 524824. *E:* healyab@parliament.uk.

**HEALY, Alexandra;** QC 2011; *b* 18 Nov. 1968; *d* of Alexander Patrick Healy, III and Janet Mary Healy; *m* 1999, Ken Millett; one *s* one *d*. *Educ:* Ward Freman Sch., Buntingford; Trinity Hall, Cambridge (BA 1991). Called to the Bar, Gray's Inn, 1992, Bencher, 2015; in practice as barrister, specialising in criminal fraud. Sec., Criminal Bar Assoc., 2007–08;

Mem., Bar Council Remuneration Cttee, 2008– (Co-Chair, 2012–). Dir, Bar Mutual Indemnity Fund, 2010–. *Recreations:* family, walking, singing (while walking). *Address:* Foundry Chambers, Quality House, 5–9 Quality Court, Chancery Lane, WC2A 1HP.

**HEALY, Maurice Eugene**, OBE 2001; Director, National Consumer Council, 1987–91; *b* 27 Nov. 1933; *s* of late Thomas Healy and Emily Healy (*née* O'Mahoney); *m* 1958, Jose Barbara Speller Dewdney; two *d* (and one *d* decd). *Educ:* Downside School; Peterhouse, Cambridge (BA Classics). Nat. service, Royal Artillery, 1954–56. BoT, 1956–60; Consumers' Assoc., working on Which?, 1960–76; Head of Editl Dept and Editor of Which?, 1973–76; Nat. Consumer Council, 1977–91. Chairman, Consumer Policy Committee: BSI, 1993–98; ISO, 1996–98; Member: Council, Bureau Européen des Unions de Consommateurs, 1977–91; Council, Insurance Ombudsman Bureau, 1991–2001 (Chm., 1996–2001); Code of Banking Practice Review Cttee, 1991–99; Ind. Management Cttee, Optical Consumer Complaints Service, 1992–99; Bd, Jazz Services Ltd, 1992–2001; Consumer Panel, PIA, 1993–98; Council, Funeral Ombudsman Service, 2001–03; Assessor to Auld Cttee on reform of shop hours, 1984. Chm., Patients' Assoc., 1991–93. Trustee, European Res. Inst. for Consumer Affairs, 1990–2007. Chm. of Governors, Highgate Wood School, 1983–86. Chm., Friends of Queens Wood, 2000–08. Bereavement counsellor: Cruse, 2006–11; N London Hospice, 2012–14. FRSA. Hon. Mem., Inst. of Consumer Affairs. *Publications:* contribs to Which? and Nat. Consumer Council and other jls and conf. papers. *Recreations:* jazz, Irish music, Shona sculpture. *Address:* 15 Onslow Gardens, Muswell Hill, N10 3JT. *T:* (020) 8883 8955.

**HEALY, Sheila Elizabeth**; Member, Arts Council England, and Chair, South West Regional Arts Council, 2010–17; *b* 20 Oct. 1954; *m* 2007, Richard Harvey; one *s*, and one step *s* one step *d*. *Educ:* Trinity Coll., Dublin (BA Hons, MA Econs and Social Studies). Residential Social Worker, Brent LBC, 1978–80; Community Worker, Pensioners' Link, 1980–83; Policy Officer, GLC, 1983–85; Hd, Urban Prog., and Hd, Policy and Performance, Wolverhampton MBC, 1985–90; Asst City Sec., Quality and Business Services, Nottingham CC, 1990–92; Chief Exec., City Challenge and Dir of Envmt, Walsall MBC, 1992–97; Corporate Dir, Envmt and Econ., 1997–2000, Community Governance, 2000–03, Bor. of Telford & Wrekin; Regl Associate, W Midlands, IDeA, 2003–04; Regl Dir, Local Govt, ODPM, 2004–06; Chief Exec., Cornwall CC, 2006–08; Interim Chief Exec., Shropshire CC, 2008–09; Dir, H & H Horizons, 2009–16. Dir and Vice-Chm., Ikon Gall., Birmingham, 2000–04. Chair: Audiences Central, W Midlands, 2000–06; Audience Agency, 2014–18. Member: Bd, Situations Internat. Public Art Producers; Tate St Ives Adv. Council, 2006–; Leading Museums Gp, 2009–13; Bd, Kneehigh Th. Co., 2011–16; Catalyst Fund Panel, HEFCE, 2014–18. *Recreations:* walking, theatre, reading, cinema, travel, contemporary and modern art. *Address:* Aisling House, New Street, Marnhull, Dorset DT10 1NP. *E:* sheila@porthkea.myzen.co.uk.

**HEALY, Siobán Mary**; QC 2010; *b* Leamington Spa, 6 Aug. 1965; *d* of Dr Peter Healy and Dr Mary Healy (*née* Daly). *Educ:* Trinity Sch., Leamington Spa; Brasenose Coll., Oxford (BA Hons Juris.); Northwestern Univ., Chicago (LLM). Admitted solicitor, 1990; called to the Bar, Inner Temple, 1993; in practice as barrister and arbitrator, specialising in commercial law, particularly internat. arbitration, insurance and reinsurance, shipping, internat. trade, sport and professional negligence. *Recreations:* ski-ing, ski touring/mountaineering, trail running and hiking in the Alps and S American volcanoes. *Address:* 5 King's Bench Walk, Temple, EC4Y 7DS. *T:* (020) 7910 8300, *Fax:* (020) 7910 8400.

**HEALY, Tim T.**; *see* Traverse-Healy.

**HEALY-PRATT, James Simon**; Partner, Stewarts Law LLP, since 2006; HM Assistant Coroner: for East Sussex, since 2016; for West Sussex, since 2019; *b* Westminster, 1 March 1968; *m* 1994, Paula Healy; two *s*. *Educ:* Downside Sch., Som; Durham Univ. (BA Hons Law 1990); Inns of Court Sch. of Law; University Coll. London (LLM Air and Space Law 1994). Called to the Bar: Gray's Inn, 1991; NY, 1997; in practice as barrister, 1991–92; Sen. Legal Advr, Global Aerospace, 1992–2000; Gp Gen. Counsel, Amlin plc, 2000–06; admitted as solicitor, 2006. Lectr in Air Law (pt-time), Cranfield Univ., 2012–; Course Dir, Judicial Coll., 2019–. Mem., Coroners' Soc. (Hon. Treas., 2017–). *Publications:* (Contributing Ed.) Margo on Aviation Insurance, 3rd edn 2001; contrib. articles to Jl Air and Space, Jl Personal Injury Law. *Recreations:* helicopters, motorcycles, West of Ireland, Newcastle United FC. *Address:* Stewarts Law LLP, 5 New Street Square, EC4A 3BF. *T:* (020) 7822 8000. *E:* jhp@stewartslaw.com.

**HEANEY, Albert Lawrence**; Director, Social Services and Integration, Welsh Government, since 2013; *b* Co. Armagh, NI, 1964; *s* of Laurence and Elizabeth Heaney; *m* Heather; one *s*. *Educ:* Portadown Coll. Grammar Sch.; Univ. of Glamorgan (BA Hons Sociol. with Professional Studies; MBA; Cert. in Using Systemic Family Therapy). CQSW 1988; CMS 1995; DMS 1996. Sen. Residential Social Worker, 1988–89; Social Worker, Mid Glamorgan CC, 1989–91; Social Work Therapist, Brynfynnon, 1991–94; Team Manager, Merthyr Tydfil CB, 1994–99; Service Mgr, 1999–2001, Area Manager, S and W Wales, 2001–05, NSPCC; Asst Dir, Social Services, 2005–08, Corporate Dir, Social Services, 2008–13, Caerphilly CBC. Chm., Dance Sport Wales, 2011–13. Pres., Assoc. of Dirs of Social Services Wales, 2012. *Recreations:* dance sport, reading. *Address:* Welsh Government, Cathays Park, Cardiff CF10 3NQ. *T:* (029) 2082 3219. *E:* Albert.Heaney@wales.gsi.gov.uk.

**HEAP, Sir Brian**; *see* Heap, Sir R. B.

**HEAP, Sir Peter (William)**, KCMG 1995 (CMG 1987); HM Diplomatic Service, retired; *b* 13 April 1935; *s* of Roger and Dora Heap; *m* 1st, Helen Wilmerding; two *s* two *d*; 2nd, Dorrit Breitenstein; 3rd, 1986, Ann Johnson; one step *s* one step *d*. *Educ:* Bishop Road Secondary Modern Sch., Bristol; Bristol Cathedral Sch.; Merton Coll., Oxford. 2nd Lt Glos Regt and RWAFF, 1954–56. Joined Diplomatic Service, 1959; Third Sec., Dublin, 1960; Second Sec., Ottawa, 1960; First Sec., Colombo, 1963–66; seconded to MoD, 1966–68; FO, 1968–71; Dep. Dir-Gen., British Information Services, New York, 1971–76; Counsellor, Caracas, 1976–80; Head of Energy, Science and Space Dept, FCO, 1980–83; High Comr to the Bahamas, 1983–86; Minister and Dep. High Comr, Lagos, 1986–89; British Trade Comr, Hong Kong, and Consul-Gen., Macau, 1989–92; Ambassador to Brazil, 1992–95. Advr to Bd, HSBC Investment Bank, 1995–98; Mem., Adv. Bd, Tetra Strategy, 2010–14; Consultant: Amerada Hess plc, 1996–2006; BOC Gp, 1997–2001; Adv. Bd, CFS Partners, 2001–10; Internat. Business Consultant, Nabas Legal, 2010–14; Dep. Chm., RCM Gp, 2001–05; non-exec. Dir, D. S. Wolf Internat., 1998–99; non-executive Chairman: Regal Petroleum plc, 2005–06; Moorgate Capital, 2010–. Chairman: Brazilian Chamber of Commerce in GB, 1996–2010, now Chm. Emeritus; Britain Brazil Business Forum, 1998–2003; Labour Finance and Industry Gp, 2003–09; Trustees, Commonwealth Countries League, 2015–. Mem., Internat. Cttee, CBI, 1997–2002. Member, Council: Anglo Brazil Soc., 1999–; Friends of the Bahamas, 2000–; Chm., Friends of Sri Lanka Assoc., 2011–. Chm., Maria Nobrega Charitable Trust (UK), 2003–10. Gov., Greycoat Hosp. Sch., 2001–12. Freeman, City of London, 2001. *Address:* (home) 6 Carlisle Mansions, Carlisle Place, SW1P 1HX.

**HEAP, Sir (Robert) Brian**, Kt 2001; CBE 1994; FRS 1989; FRSC; FRSB; Master, St Edmund's College, Cambridge, 1996–2004 (Hon. Fellow, since 2004); Research Associate, Centre for Development Studies, University of Cambridge, 2012–17, Distinguished Fellow, since 2017; *b* 27 Feb. 1935; *s* of late Bertram Heap and Eva Mary Heap (*née* Melling); *m* 1961, Marion Patricia Grant; two *s* one *d*. *Educ:* New Mills Grammar Sch.; Univ. of Nottingham (BSc, PhD); King's Coll., Cambridge (MA, ScD). FRSB (FIBiol 1973). FRSC 1987. Univ. Demonstrator, Cambridge, 1960; Lalor Res. Fellow, ARC Babraham, Cambridge, 1963; Staff Mem., AFRC Babraham, 1964–95: Hd, Dept of Physiology, 1976; Hd, Cambridge Res. Station, 1986; Dir, Inst. of Animal Physiol. and Genetics Res., Cambridge and Edinburgh, 1989–93; Dir of Science, AFRC, 1991–94; Dir, AFRC, subseq. BBSRC Babraham Inst., 1993–94. Vis. Prof., Univ. of Nairobi, 1974; Vis. Res. Fellow, Murdoch Univ., 1976; Special Prof., 1988–2010, Hon. Prof., 2011–16, Univ. of Nottingham; Vis. Prof., Univ. of Guelph, 1990; Vis. Sen. Fellow, Sch. of Clin. Medicine, Univ. of Cambridge, 1994–2001; Res. Associate, Faraday Inst., St Edmund's Coll. Cambridge, 2006–. Mem., Scientific Adv. Bd, Merck, Sharp and Dohme, 1990–98; Consultant: R. W. Johnson Pharmaceutical Res. Inst., NJ, 1993–98; Ligand Pharmaceuticals, La Jolla, San Diego, 1994–97; Principal Scientific Advr, ZyGEM, NZ, 2005–10; Chief Scientific Advr, Cambridge Malaysian Commonwealth Studies Centre, 2014–. UK Rep. NATO Sci. Cttee, Brussels, 1998–2005. Member: Exec. Council, ESF, 1994–97; Council, Royal Soc., 1994–2001 (Foreign Sec. and Vice-Pres., 1996–2001); Nuffield Council on Bioethics, 1997–2001; Bd, Eur. Advanced Translational Res. Infrastructure in Medicine, 2008–11; Bd, African Technol. Policy Studies Network Bd, 2008–13; Chair: Governing Council, Cambridge Theological Fedn, 2006–10; Cambridge Genetics Knowledge Park, 2002–07; Public Health Genomics, Cambridge, 2008–12; Vice-Chm., 2004–10, Pres., 2010–13, European Acads Sci. Adv. Council. Specialist Advr, Select Cttee on sci. and engrg at heart of govt policy, 2009. Member Committee: Soc. for Study of Fertility, 1967–72; Jls of Reproduction and Fertility Ltd; Bibliography of Reproduction, 1967–70; Soc. and Jl of Endocrinology, 1980–84; Placenta; Oxford Reviews of Reproductive Biology, 1981–94; Exec. Editor, Philosophical Trans of Royal Soc., 2004–07. Consultant: WHO, Geneva, 1975–82; China, 1981–85. Chairman: Ciba Foundn Symposium, 1978; Harden Conf., 1984. President: Inst. of Biol., 1996–98; Internat. Soc. Sci. and Religion, 2006–08. Judge: Templeton Prize, 2001–04; Kilby Awards, 2002. Member, Advisory Board: John Templeton Foundn, 2004–06, 2008–11; Faraday Inst. of Sci. and Religion, 2006–; Trustee: Cambridge Overseas Trust, 2002–08; European Trust, 2002–08; Commonwealth Trust, 2003–08; Sino-British Fellowship Trust, 2004–16; Sense about Science, 2004–10; Cambridge Malaysian Educn and Develt Trust, 2010–13; Cambridge China Develt Trust, 2010–; Mahathir Sci. Award Foundn, 2012–17; Chm. Trustees, Academia Europaea, 2003–10. Lectures: Hammond, Soc. for Study of Fertility, 1986; Linacre, Oxford Univ., 1993; Annual, RASE, 1995; Robinson Meml, Univ. of Nottingham, 1997; Rutherford Meml, South Africa, 1999. Fellow, World Acad. of Art and Sci., 2009. FRAgS 1995. Hon. FRASE 1995; Hon. FZS 2007; Hon. Foreign Fellow, Korean Acad. of Sci. and Technol., 1998. Hon. Fellow, Green Templeton (formerly Green) Coll., Oxford, 1997. Hon. DSc: Nottingham, 1994; York, 2001; St Andrews, 2007. Research Medallist, RASE, 1976; Inventor's Award, AFRC, 1980; Marshall Medal, Soc. for Study of Reproduction, 2000. *Publications:* sci. papers on reproductive biology, endocrinology, biotechnology, sustainability, science advice and policy, energy and development, in various biol and med. jls. *Recreations:* music, hiking, kite flying. *Address:* St Edmund's College, Cambridge CB3 0BN.

**HEAPHY, Clive Andrew**; Chief Finance Officer (formerly Corporate Director, Finance and Governance), Birmingham City Council, since 2018; *b* Burton upon Trent, 16 June 1961; *s* of Daniel Joseph Heaphy and Amelda Heaphy; *m* 1985, Deborah Ann Jones; one *s* one *d*. *Educ:* Portsmouth Poly. (BSc Hons Engrg Geology and Geotechnics 1982). CIPFA 1986. Trainee Accountant, Westminster CC, 1982–83; various roles, Coventry CC, 1983–91; Finance Manager (Housing), Milton Keynes BC, 1991–94; Man. Consultant, Chapman Hendy Associates, 1994–97; Dir, Resources, S Oxon Housing Assoc., 1997–2000; Director of Finance: English Churches Housing Gp, 2000–03; Sport England, 2003–06; FCO Services, 2006–08; Dir, Finance and Corp. Resources, Central Beds Council, 2008–10; interim Dir, Finance, OFSTED, 2010; Dir, Finance and Corp. Services, London Borough of Brent, 2010–13; Dir, i-Max Solutions Ltd, 2013–15; Dir of Finance Ops, 2013–17, Finance Dir, 2017, High Speed Two Ltd; interim Chief Financial Officer, London Bor. of Haringey, 2017–18. MInstD. Trustee, Inst. of Cancer Res., 2012–. *Recreations:* golf, current affairs, cycling, walking, photography. *Address:* Birmingham City Council, Council House, Victoria Square, Birmingham B1 1BB. *T:* (0121) 303 3758. *E:* clive.heaphy@birmingham.gov.uk.

**HEAPPEY, James Stephen**; MP (C) Wells, since 2015; *b* Nuneaton, 30 Jan. 1981; *s* of Stephen and Anita Heappey; *m* 2009, Kate; one *s* one *d*. *Educ:* Queen Elizabeth's Hosp., Bristol; Univ. of Birmingham (BA Hons Pol Sci.); RMA, Sandhurst. Commnd Army, 2004; Platoon Comdr, 1st Bn, Royal Glos, Berks and Wilts Regt, 2004–06; ADC to GOC, NI, 2006–07; The Rifles: Regtl Signals Officer, 4th Bn, 2007–09; Adjt, 2nd Bn, 2009–11; Exec. Officer, Army Gen. Staff, 2011–12. Parly Asst to Rt Hon. Dr Liam Fox, MP, 2012–13; consultant project manager, 2013–14. PPS to Sec. of State for Transport, 2017–. *Recreations:* cooking, cricket, golf, Rugby, tennis, family. *Address:* House of Commons, SW1A 0AA. *T:* (020) 7219 4289; 5 Cathedral View Offices, Wookey Hole Road, Wells, Som BA5 2BT. *T:* (01749) 343255. *E:* james.heappey.mp@parliament.uk.

**HEAPS, Jeremy David P.**; *see* Pickett-Heaps.

**HEAPS, John Edward**; Chief Executive, Britannia Building Society, 1993–99; *b* 24 Feb. 1939; *m* 1985, Shirley (*née* Jones); two *d*; one *s* one *d* from previous marr. *Educ:* Calday Grange Grammar Sch., W Kirby; Oldershaw Grammar Sch., Wallasey; Univ. of Liverpool. FCIB (FCBSI 1992). Colne Building Society: Sec., 1972; Chief Exec., 1972–80; Chief Exec. and Dir, 1980–83; Britannia Building Society: Dep. Gen. Manager, 1983–87; Gen. Manager, 1987–91; Inf. Systems Dir, 1991; Dep. Man. Dir, 1991–93. Chm., BSA, 1998–99 (Mem. Council, 1994; Dep. Chm., 1996–98); Dir, Bldg Socs Trust, 1997–99. Non-exec. Dir, Police Mutual Assurance Soc., 2001–08. Dir, Staffs TEC, 1996–99. Trustee, Keele Develt Trust, 1996–2001. Mem. Court, Univ. of Keele, 1994–2008. MCMI. *Recreation:* family pursuits. *Address:* Jardene, School Lane, Little Neston, Cheshire CH64 4DQ.

**HEAPS, John Robert**; Chairman, Yorkshire Building Society, since 2015; Partner, Eversheds LLP, 1985–2015 (Head of Litigation, 1999–2008; Chairman, 2010–14); *b* Ilkley, W Yorks, 8 July 1953; *s* of Dennis Heaps and Madeleine Heaps (*née* Coburn); *m* 1981, Vivienne Anne Smith; two *s*. *Educ:* St Thomas Aquinas Grammar Sch., Leeds; Ratcliffe Coll., Leics; Univ. of Liverpool (LLB 1975). Admitted solicitor, 1978; solicitor, Freshfields, 1978–84. Mem., Business and Oversight Bd, Law Society, 2013–. International Bar Association: Mem. Council, Legal Practice Div., 2006–08; Co. Chm., World Orgns Cttee, 2009–12. Mem. Bd, CPR Inst., 2012–16. Member, Board: Garden Bridge Trust, 2013–; CityUK, 2017–. *Publications:* (contrib.) Privilege and Confidentiality: an international handbook, 2006, 2nd edn 2012. *Recreations:* golf, fishing, family, cricket, opera, theatre. *Address:* Yorkshire Building Society, Broadgate, The Headrow, Leeds LS1 8EQ. *T:* (01274) 472262. *Clubs:* Pannal Golf, Alwoodley Golf.

**HEARD, Prof. Edith,** PhD; FRS 2013; Director General, European Molecular Biology Laboratory, since 2019; Professor of Epigenetics and Cellular Memory, Collège de France, since 2012; b 5 March 1965. *Educ:* Francis Holland Girls' Sch., London; Emmanuel Coll., Cambridge (BA 1st Cl. Natural Scis 1986); Imperial Cancer Res. Fund, London (PhD Biochem. 1990). Postdoctoral Fellow, 1990–93, Sen. Res. Scientist, 1993–2000, Pasteur Institute, Paris; Vis. Scientist, Cold Spring Harbor Lab., 2000–01; Curie Institute, Paris: Jun. Gp Leader, 2001–06; Sen. Gp Leader, Mammalian Develt Epigenetics team, 2006–08; Co-Dir, Genetics and Develtl Biol. Unit, 2008–10; Dir, Genetics and Develtl Biol. Unit, 2010–18. Mem., EMBO, 2005. Otto Mangold Prize, German Soc. for Develtl Biol., 2007; Silver Medal, Centre Nat. de la recherche scientifique, 2008; Jean Hamburger Prize, Ville de Paris, 2009; Grand Prix de la Fondation pour la Recherche Médicale, 2011; Prix de la Fondation Allianz, Inst. de France, 2013. *Publications:* contribs to learned jls incl. Science, Nature, Genes and Develt, Cancer Res., Proc. NAS, Cell Develt, Cell Stem Cell, Molecular Cell, Develtl Cell. *Address:* European Molecular Biology Laboratory, Meyerhofstrasse 1, 69117 Heidelberg, Germany.

**HEARN, Barry Maurice William,** FCA; Chairman: World Snooker Ltd, since 2010; Matchroom Sport (formerly Matchroom) Ltd, since 1982; b 19 June 1948; s of George Sydney and Barbara Winifred Hearn; m 1970, Susan Clark; one s one d. *Educ:* Buckhurst Hill Grammar School. Owner and Chm., Leyton Orient FC, 1995–2014. Chm., Professional Darts Corp., 2001–. *Publications:* The Business, 1990. *Recreations:* football, fishing, poker, golf. *Address:* Matchroom Sport Ltd, Mascalls, Mascalls Lane, Brentwood, Essex CM14 5LJ. *T:* (01277) 359900.
See also E. J. Hearn.

**HEARN, David Anthony;** General Secretary, Broadcasting Entertainment Cinematograph Theatre Union, 1991–93 (General Secretary, 1987–90, Joint General Secretary, 1984–87, Broadcasting and Entertainment Trades Alliance); Chairman, Litho and Digital Impressions Ltd, since 1997; b 4 March 1929; s of James Wilfrid Laurier Hearn and Clara (née Barlow); m 1952, Anne Beveridge; two s. *Educ:* Trinity Coll., Oxford (MA). Asst to Gen. Sec., Assoc. of Broadcasting Staff, 1955; subseq. Asst Gen. Sec., then Dep. Gen. Sec.; Gen. Sec., Assoc. of Broadcasting and Allied Staffs, 1972–84. Dir, Nat. Campaign for the Arts Ltd, 1986–93. Chm., Film and Electronic Media Cttee, Fedn of Entertainment Unions, 1991–93; Mem., British Screen Adv. Council, 1987; President: Internat. Fedn of Audio Visual Unions, 1991–93 (Gen. Sec., W European Sect., 1984–91); Eur. Cttee of Trade Unions in Arts, Mass Media and Entertainment, 1992–93. Sen. Res. Fellow, Nuffield Coll., Oxford, 1970–71. *Address:* 4 Stocks Tree Close, Yarnton, Kidlington, Oxon OX5 1LU. *T:* (01865) 374613.

**HEARN, Donald Peter;** Bursar and Fellow of Clare College, Cambridge, 2001–13, now Emeritus Fellow; b 2 Nov. 1947; s of late Peter James Hearn and Anita Margaret Hearn; m 1973, Rachel Mary Arnold; two d. *Educ:* Clifton College; Selwyn College, Cambridge (MA). FCA. Ernst & Whinney, 1969–79; Group Financial Controller, Saga Holidays, 1979–83; Chief Financial Officer, Lee Valley Water Co., 1983–86; Finance Dir, 1986–2001, Sec., 1989–2001, RHS; Gen. Comr for Taxes, 1990–2008. Mem., F and GP Cttee, RPMS, Univ. of London, 1991–97; Imperial College: Chm., Audit Cttee, 1996–2005; Mem. Court, 1998–2005; Chm., House Cttee, 1998–2001; Gov., 2001–05; Member: Selwyn Coll. Assoc. Cttee, 1997–2001; Cambridge Univ. Audit Cttee, 2002–07; Trustee, Cambridge Univ. Staff Pension Scheme, 2002– (Chm., Investments Cttee, 2002–). Director: Fitzwilliam Museum Enterprise, 2003–; Cambridge Colleges Funding plc, 2014–. Trustee: Chelsea Physic Gdn, 2002–16 (Treas., 2003–16); Cambridge Univ. Botanic Gdn, 2003–; Chm., Cambridge Univ. Farm, 2008–. Treasurer: Cambridge Past, Present and Future, 2013–16; Isaac Newton Trust, 2016–; Interim Bursar: Jesus Coll., Cambridge, 2016–17; Newnham Coll., Cambridge, 2018–19. Governor, Woldingham Sch., 1990–93. Hon. FRHS. *Recreation:* gardening. *Address:* Clare College, Trinity Lane, Cambridge CB2 1TL.

**HEARN, Edward John;** Managing Director, Matchroom Sport Ltd (Director, since 2004); b Epping, 8 June 1979; s of Barry Maurice William Hearn, qv; m 2010, Chloe Rouse; two d. Commercial Dir, Euro Pro Tour Ltd, 2001; Director: Professional Darts Corp. Ltd, 2009–; World Snooker Hldg Ltd, 2010–; World Snooker Ltd, 2010–; World Series of Darts Ltd, 2015–; Matchroom Boxing Ltd, 2016–; Matchroom Boxing USA Ltd, 2018–. *Address:* Matchroom Sport Ltd, Mascalls, Mascalls Lane, Brentwood, Essex CM14 5LJ. *T:* (01277) 359900. *E:* info@matchroom.com.

**HEARN, Rt Rev. George Arthur;** Bishop of Rockhampton, 1981–96; Vicar of Canterbury, diocese of Melbourne, 1996–2001; b 17 Nov. 1935; s of Albert Frederick and Edith Maxham Hearn; m 1957, Adele Taylor (d 2006); two s one d. *Educ:* Northcote High School; University High School; La Trobe Univ., Melbourne. BA, ThL 1965, DipRE, ThSchol, Aust. Coll. of Theology; MACE. Deacon 1964, priest 1965, Diocese of Gippsland; Curate of Traralgon, 1964–66; Vicar of Omeo, 1966–69; Rector of Wonthaggi, 1969–73; Rector of Kyabram, dio. Bendigo, 1973–77; Field Officer, Dept of Christian Education, Diocese of Melbourne, 1977–79; Dir, Gen. Bd of Religious Education, 1978–81. *Recreations:* gardening, reading, golf, music. *Address:* 2 Arthur Street, Doncaster, Vic 3108, Australia.

**HEARN, Prof. John Patrick,** PhD; Professor of Physiology, University of Sydney Medical School, since 2004; Executive Director, Worldwide Universities Network, since 2009; Chairman, Australia Africa Universities Network, since 2010; b Limbdi, India, 24 Feb. 1943; s of late Lt-Col Hugh Patrick Hearn, Barrister, and Cynthia Ellen (née Nicholson); m 1967, Margaret Ruth Patricia McNair; four s one d. *Educ:* Crusaders' Sch., Headley, Hants; St Mary's Sch., Nairobi, Kenya; University Coll., Dublin (BSc, MSc); ANU, Canberra (PhD). Lectr in Zool., 1967–69, and Dean of Science, 1968–69, Strathmore Coll., Nairobi; Res. Scholar, ANU, 1969–72; scientist, MRC Reproductive Biology Unit, Edinburgh, 1972–79; Consultant Scientist, WHO Special Prog. of Res. in Human Reproduction, Geneva, 1978–79; Zoological Society of London: Dir, Wellcome Labs of Comparative Physiology, 1979–80; Dir of Science and Dir, Inst. of Zool., 1980–87; Dep. Sec., AFRC, 1987–90; Dir, MRC/AFRC Comparative Physiology Res. Gp, 1983–89; Dir, Wisconsin Regl Primate Res. Center and Prof. in Physiol., Med. Sch., Univ. of Wisconsin-Madison, 1989–96; Consultant Scientist, WHO Res. Prog. in Family and Reproductive Health, Geneva, 1996–98; Australian National University: Dir, Res. Sch. of Biol Scis, 1998–2001; Dep. Vice-Chancellor (Res.), 2001–04; Dep. Vice-Chancellor (Academic and Internat.), then Vice Pres. (Internat.), Univ. of Sydney, 2004–13. Exec. Chm., Hearn International Pty Ltd, 2013–. Rapporteur and Chm., WHO Asia Pacific Regl Panel in Reproductive Health, 1999–2005; Member: Futures Gp on Bioecon. 2020, OECD, 2008–10; Expert Gp on Internationalisation in Higher Educn, OECD, 2011–13; Innovation, Higher Educn and Res. in Develt Gp, OECD, 2011–15; Educn Adv. Gp, British Council, 2014–. Chm., Australian Biotechnol. Adv. Council, 2001–04; Member: Bd, Australian Nuclear Sci. and Technol. Orgn, 2008–12; Adv. Gp on Australia-Africa Relns, Dept of For. Affairs and Trade, Australia, 2015–. Mem. Bd, Sports Knowledge Australia, 2004–10; Chm., Sydney Confucius Inst., 2008–13. Vis. Prof. in Biology (formerly in Zoology), UCL, 1979–93; Vis. Prof., New England Primate Res. Center, Harvard Univ. Med. Sch., 1989–91; Hon. Res. Fellow, CSIRO Wildlife and Ecology, 1997–99. Pres., Internat. Primatological Soc., 1984–88; Chm., Soc. for Reproductive Biology, 2000–04. Hon. DSc UCD, 2015. Scientific Medal, Zool Soc. London, 1983; Osman Hill Medal, Primate Soc. of GB, 1986; Australian Centenary Medal, 2001. *Publications:* (ed with H. Rothe and H. Wolters) The Biology and Behaviour of Marmosets, 1978; (ed) Immunological Aspects of Reproduction and Fertility Control, 1980; (ed) Reproduction in New World Primates, 1982; (ed) Advances in Animal Conservation, 1985; (ed) Reproduction and Disease in Captive and Wild Animals, 1988; (ed) Conservation of Primate Species studied in Biomedical Research, 1994; 220 papers on develtl, reproductive and stem cell physiol. in scientific jls; 10 papers on reform of univ. higher educn and res. *Recreations:* running, swimming (Mem., Bronte Surf and Life Saving Club). *Address:* 207A Old Teachers College A22, University of Sydney, NSW 2006, Australia. *T:* (4) 23783287, *Fax:* (2) 93514462. *E:* john.hearn@sydney.edu.au. *Club:* Athenæum.

**HEARN, Sarah Penelope;** see Chambers, S. P.

**HEARNDEN, Dr Arthur George,** OBE 1990; General Secretary, Independent Schools Joint Council, 1985–97; b 15 Dec. 1931; s of Hugh and Violet Hearnden; m 1962, Josephine McNeill; one s two d. *Educ:* Methodist Coll., Belfast; Christ's Coll., Cambridge (MA); Wadham Coll., Oxford (DPhil). Teacher, Friends' Sch., Lisburn, 1952–55; NI short service commn, Royal Signals, 1955–57; Capt., CCF, 1957–65; teacher, various schs, incl. Aldenham (1959–67), and in exchange posts, Lycée d'Aix-les-Bains and Bunsengymnasium, Heidelberg, 1957–68; Res. Officer, Oxford Univ., 1969–71; Lectr in Comparative Education, Inst. of Education, Univ. of London, 1972–74; Secretary: Standing Conf. on Univ. Entrance, 1975–84; Overseas Res. Students Awards Scheme, 1982–84. Chairman: Internat. Cttee, Soc. for Res. in Higher Educn, 1977–81; Internat. Baccalaureate Feasibility Study, 1979–80. Member: DES Adv. Cttee on AS level, 1985–91; Hanover Univ./VW Commn on German Univ. Hist., 1985–91; Sch. Exams and Assessment Council, 1988–91; Funding Agency for Schs, 1994–98 (Chm. of Finance, 1997–98); Press Complaints Commn, 1999–2005. Educnl Advr, Royal Ballet Sch., 2001–03. Pres., Ind. Schs Assoc., 1997–2002; Hon. Vice Pres., Council of British Internat. Schs (formerly Indep. Schs in EC), 1997–2010; Chm., HSBC Bursary Fund, 1998–2002; Trustee: Hall Sch. Charitable Trust, 1988–2009 (Chm, 1997–2009); Youth for Britain-Worldwide Volunteering, 1993–2000 (Chm., 1995–2000); Millwood Educn Trust, 2002–11 (Chm., 2007–11). Governor: Wychwood Sch., 1983–90; Abbotsholme, 1985–92; Oxford High Sch., 1985–92; Abingdon Sch., 1988–99; Dunottar Sch., 1990–92; Newton Prep. Sch., 1992–2014; Alpha Plus Schs, 2010–15. Sec., Hethe PCC, 1998–2007, 2009–12; Mem., Hethe Parish Council, 2003–05. *Publications:* Paths to University, 1973; Bildungspolitik in der BRD und DDR, 1973 (trans. Education in the Two Germanies, 1974); Education, Culture and Politics in West Germany, 1974; Methods of Establishing Equivalences, 1976; (ed and contrib.) The British in Germany, 1978; (ed) From School to University, 1980; Red Robert, a Life of Sir Robert Birley, 1984; A Flying Start: the story of The Manor, 2007; reports and articles in learned jls. *Recreations:* family, theatre. *Address:* Eversleigh, Middle Street, Islip, Oxon OX5 2SF. *T:* (01865) 848039. *Club:* Athenæum.

**HEARNE, Sir Graham (James),** Kt 1998; CBE 1990; Chairman: Catlin Group Ltd, 2003–12; Enterprise Oil plc, 1991–2002 (Chief Executive, 1984–91); b 23 Nov. 1937; s of Frank Hearne and Emily (née Shakespeare); m 1961, Carol Jean (née Brown); one s two d (and one d decd). *Educ:* George Dixon Grammar Sch., Birmingham. Admitted solicitor, 1959: Pinsent & Co., Solicitors, 1959–63; Fried, Frank, Harris, Shriver & Jacobson, Attorneys, NYC, 1963–66; Herbert Smith & Co., Solicitors, 1966–67; IRC, 1967–68; N. M. Rothschild & Sons Ltd, 1968–77; Finance Dir, Courtaulds Ltd, 1977–81; Chief Exec., Tricentrol, 1981–83; Gp Man. Dir, Carless, Capel and Leonard, 1983–84. Non-executive Director: N. M. Rothschild & Sons Ltd, 1970–2010; Northern Foods, Ltd, 1976–82; BPB Industries, 1982–91; Reckitt & Colman, 1990–97; Courtaulds, 1991–98; Wellcome, 1991–95; The Wellcome Foundn, 1991–95; Gallaher Gp plc, 1997–2007 (Dep. Chm., 1997–2007); BTR plc, 1998–99; Invensys (formerly BTR Siebe) plc, 1999–2003; Braemar Shipping Services (formerly Seascope Shipping Hldgs plc, then Seascope Gp plc), 1999–2015 (Chm., 2002–15); Wellstream Hldgs plc (formerly Wellstream Internat. Ltd), 2003–11; Stratic Energy Corp., 2005–10 (Chm., 2005–10); Bumi plc (formerly Vallar plc), 2010–13; Genel Energy plc (formerly Vallares), 2011–16. Chairman: Caradon, then Novar, plc, 1999–2005; Rowan Cos plc (formerly Inc.), 2004–17; part-time Member: British National Oil Corp., 1975–78; Dover Harbour Bd, 1976–78. Chm., Brindex (Assoc. of British Indep. Oil Exploration Cos), 1986–88. Trustee: Philharmonia Orch. Trust, 1982–2008; Chichester Fest. Theatre Trust, 1988–98; Hayward Foundn, 1992–2002. High Sheriff, Greater London, 1995. *Address:* 5 Crescent Place, SW3 2EA. *Clubs:* Reform, Brooks's, MCC.

**HEARTY, Michael John;** Board Member and Chairman, Audit Committee, Blackpool Teaching Hospitals NHS Foundation Trust, since 2016; Independent Advisor: Public Health England, since 2016; Betsi Cadwaladr University Health Board, since 2018; b Blackpool; s of Patrick Brian and Joan Hearty; m 1990, Janet; one d. *Educ:* Holy Family Prim. Sch.; St Thomas of Canterbury Sec. Mod. Sch.; Victoria Univ. of Manchester (BA Hons Econs 1983); Liverpool John Moores Univ. (CPFA 1994). Department of Health and Social Security, subseq. Department of Social Security, later Benefits Agency, then Department for Work and Pensions: Clerical grades, 1975–77; Exec. Officer, 1984–90; Higher Exec. Officer (Trainee Accountant), 1990–94; Sen. Exec. Officer (Accountant), 1994–99; Prin. Accountant, 1999–2002; Head: Accounting Gp, 2002–04; Finance, Planning and Performance, 2004–05; Business Mgt Div., 2005–06; Dep. Dir, Gp Finance Directorate, 2005–06; Dep. Dir, Financial Accounting, 2006–07, Dir of Finance, 2007–10, DCSF, later DFE; Dir Gen., Strategic Planning, Finance and Performance, subseq. Finance and Corporate Services, Welsh Assembly Govt, later Welsh Govt, 2010–15. Non-executive Director: Audit Cttee, DoH, 2007–14; Treasury Solicitors' Dept, 2008–10; HM Revenue and Customs, 2018–. Member, Board: CIPFA, 2012–15 (Fellow, 2016); Lancs and S Cumbria Integrated Care System, 2017–; Associate Mem., Hywel Dda Univ. Health Bd, 2018–. Chm. of Govs, Carr Head Prim. Sch., Poulton-le-Fylde, 2006–10. *Recreations:* shareholder and season ticket holder of Everton FC (with daughter, Rachael), travel, playing guitar.

**HEASLIP, Rear-Adm. Richard George,** CB 1987; Flag Officer Submarines, and NATO Commander Submarine Forces Eastern Atlantic, 1984–87; b 30 April 1932; s of Eric Arthur Heaslip and Vera Margaret (née Bailey); m 1959, Lorna Jean Grayston, Halifax, NS, Canada; three s one d (incl. twin s and d). *Educ:* Royal Naval Coll., Dartmouth. CO HMS Sea Devil, 1961–62; Exec. Officer, HMS Dreadnought (1st British nuclear submarine), 1965–66; CO HMS Conqueror (nuclear submarine), 1971–72; CO Second Submarine Sqdn, 1975–77; Staff, SACLANT, 1980–82; Staff, CDS, 1982–84; Dep. Asst COS (Ops), Staff of SACEUR, 1984. ADC 1984–85. Dir-Gen., ESU, 1987–90. Member: European Atlantic Gp Cttee, 1988–89; Bureau, Standing Conf. of Atlantic Orgns, 1988–89. Chm., RN Football Assoc., 1976–84; President: London Submarine Old Comrades Assoc., 1987–2007; Conqueror Assoc., 2003–. Mem., Ferndown Town Council, 2006–08. Vice-Pres., Dorset CPRE, 2015– (Vice-Chm., 2010–14; Chm., 2014–15). Chm., W Parley Parish Council, 2011–13. *Publications:* End to End, 2007. *Recreations:* walking (Land's End to John O'Groats, 2002); music, gardening. *Address:* 2 Longfield Drive, West Parley, Dorset BH22 8TY. *E:* rgheaslip@hotmail.com.

**HEATH, Allister Georges Freund**; Editor, The Sunday Telegraph, since 2017; *b* Mulhouse, France, 1977; *s* of Alexander and Sylviane Heath; *m* 2002, Neda; two *d. Educ*: Coll. Emile Zola, Kingersheim, France; Lycée Lambert, Mulhouse; London Sch. of Econs and Pol Sci. (BSc Econs 1998); Hertford Coll., Oxford (MPhil Econs 2000). Ed., European Jl and Hd of Res., Eur. Foundn, 2000–02; Associate Ed., 2006–08, Contributing Ed. 2008–11, Spectator; Econs Corresp., 2002, Econs Ed. and Leader Writer, 2002–05, Dep. Ed., 2005–06, Ed., 2007–08, The Business; Ed., City A. M., 2008–14; Dep. Dir of Content and Dep. Ed., The Telegraph, 2014–17. Columnist, Daily Telegraph, 2012–. Wincott Vis. Prof. of Business Journalism, Univ. of Buckingham, 2005–07. Chm., 2020 Tax Commn, 2011–12 (author, The Single Income Tax: Final Report of the 2020 Tax Commn, 2012). *Publications*: Flat Tax: towards a British model, 2006; (with D. B. Smith) At a Price: the true cost of public spending, 2006. *Recreation*: family. *Address*: The Telegraph, 111 Buckingham Palace Road, SW1W 0DT. *E*: allister_heath@yahoo.co.uk.

**HEATH, Angela**; *see* Heath, L. A.

**HEATH, Prof. Anthony Francis**, CBE 2013; PhD; FBA 1992; Professor of Sociology, University of Oxford, 1999–2010, now Emeritus; Director, Centre for Social Investigation, Nuffield College, Oxford, since 2014 (Official Fellow, 1987–99, Fellow, 1999–2010, now Emeritus); Professor of Sociology, University of Manchester, since 2010; *b* 15 Dec. 1942; *s* of Ronald John Heath and Cicely Florence (*née* Roberts); *m* 1983, Dr Mary-Jane Pearce, MRCGP, FRCPsych; two *s* one *d. Educ*: Merchant Taylors', Crosby; Trinity Coll., Cambridge (BA 1st cl. Classics pt I, 1st cl. Econs pt II; PhD 1971). Asst Principal, HM Treasury, 1965–66; Fellow of Churchill Coll., 1967–70, Asst Lectr, Faculty of Econs, 1968–70, Cambridge Univ.; Univ. Lectr and Fellow of Jesus Coll., Oxford, 1970–86. Dir, 1983, 1987, 1992 and 1997 British Election Studies, Co-Dir, Centre for Res. into Elections and Social Trends, 1994–2010, ESRC. *Publications*: Rational Choice and Social Change, 1976; (jtly) Origins and Destinations, 1980; Social Mobility, 1981; (jtly) How Britain Votes, 1985; (jtly) Understanding Political Change, 1991; (jtly) Labour's Last Chance, 1994; (jtly) The Rise of New Labour, 2001; (jtly) Unequal Chances: ethnic minorities in Western labour markets, 2007; (jtly) The Political Integration of Ethnic Minorities in Britain, 2013; (jtly) Unequal Attainments: ethnic educational inequalities in ten western countries, 2014; contribs to Jl of Royal Stat. Soc., Amer. Jl of Sociol., Ethnic and Racial Studies, Eur. Sociol Rev., Eur. Jl of Sociol., Eur. Jl of Pol Res., Sociology, British Jl of Pol Sci., British Jl of Sociol., Electoral Studies, Acta Sociologica, Oxford Rev. of Educn. *Recreations*: piano playing, cross-country running. *Address*: 72 Lonsdale Road, Oxford OX2 7EP. *T*: (01865) 553512. *Clubs*: Achilles; Hawks (Cambridge).

**HEATH, Rt Hon. David (William St John)**, CBE 1989; PC 2015; Chairman, Western Region, Consumer Council for Water, since 2015; *b* 16 March 1954; *s* of Eric Heath and Pamela Heath; *m* 1987, Caroline Netherton; one *s* one *d. Educ*: Millfield Sch.; St John's Coll., Oxford (MA Physiological Scis); City Univ. FADO 1979. In practice as optician, 1979–86. Somerset County Council: Councillor (Lib Dem), 1985–97; Leader, 1985–89; Chm., Educn Cttee, 1996–97. Vice Chm., Assoc. of County Councils, 1993–97. Chm., Avon & Somerset Police Authy, 1993–96; Vice Chm., Cttee of Local Police Authorities, 1993–97. Mem., Audit Commn, 1995–97. Contested (Lib Dem) Somerton and Frome, 1992. MP (Lib Dem) Somerton and Frome, 1997–2015. Lib Dem spokesman on European affairs, 1997–98, on foreign affairs, 1999–2001, on work, family and pensions, 2001–03, on home and legal affairs, 2003–05; on constitutional affairs, and shadow to Leader of the House, 2005–07 and 2009–10; shadow to Sec. of State for Justice and Lord Chancellor, 2007–09; Parly Sec. (Dep. Leader), Office of the Leader of the H of C, 2010–12; Minister of State, DEFRA, 2012–13. Leader, Liberal Gp, OSCE Parly Assembly, 2009–10. Mem., Academic Council, Wilton Park, 2007–10. Lay Mem. Bd, Solicitors Regulation Authy, 2015–. Mem., Witham Friary Friendly Soc., 1984–. FRSA 1995. *Recreations*: cricket, Rugby football, pig breeding until recently. *Address*: The Yard, Witham Friary, near Frome, Somerset BA11 5HF. *T*: (01749) 850458.

**HEATH, (Lettyce) Angela**; non-executive Director, The North West London Hospitals (formerly Northwick Park and St Mark's) NHS Trust, 1996–2002; *b* 27 May 1944; *d* of late Frank Buchanan Ryde and Emily Rose Ryde (*née* Davies); *m* 1985, Roger Heath (marr. diss. 2015). *Educ*: Birmingham Univ. (BA 1966; MA 1968); Birkbeck Coll., London (MSc 1999). Department of the Environment, 1971–96: Admin. Trainee, 1971; Private Sec. to Minister of Housing, 1979; Asst Sec., 1983; Central Policy Planning Unit, 1983–85; Local Govt Div., 1985–87; Personnel Management, 1987–90; Housing Corp. Finance, 1990–91; Under-Sec., 1992; Regl Dir for London, 1992–94; Dir, Regeneration Progs, Govt Office for London, 1994–95; Dir, Local Govt, 1995–96. Vis. Sen. Fellow, Sch. of Public Policy, Univ. of Birmingham, 1997–99. JP Middlesex, 1997–2003. FRSA 1995. *Address*: 22A The Dale, Wirksworth, Derbyshire DE4 4EJ.

**HEATH, Michael John**, MBE 2001; freelance cartoonist, since 1956; Cartoons Editor, The Spectator, since 1989; *b* 13 Oct. 1935; *s* of George Heath and Alice (Queenie) Stewert Morrison Bremner; *m* 1st, 1959, Hanne Sternkopf (marr. diss. 1992); two *d*; 2nd, 2003, Martha Swift (marr. diss. 2012); two *d*; partner, Hilary Penn. *Educ*: no education to speak of (Devon, Hampstead and Brighton); Brighton Art Coll. Trained as animator, Rank Screen Services, 1955; started placing cartoons in Melody Maker, 1955; contributed to: Lilliput; Tatler; John Bull; Man about Town; Men Only; Honey; Punch, 1958–89; Spectator, 1958–; Private Eye, 1964–2016 (strips include The Gays, The Regulars, Great Bores of Today, Baby); Sunday Times, 1967–; London Standard, 1976–86, 1995–96; Mail on Sunday, 1985–; The Independent, 1986–97 (Political Cartoonist, 1991–96), 2003–; London Daily News, 1987. Pocket Cartoonist of the Year, Cartoonists Club of GB, 1977; Glen Grant Cartoonist of the Year, 1978; What the Papers Say Cartoonist of the Year, 1982; Pont Award for drawing the British Character, 2001; Lifetime Achievement Award, Cartoon Fedn of GB, 2010. *Publications*: Private Eye Cartoon Library, 1973, 2nd edn 1975; The Punch Cartoons of Michael Heath, 1976; Book of Bores, No 1, 1976, No 2, Star Bores, 1979, No 3, Bores Three, 1983; Love All, 1982; Best of Heath (foreword by Malcolm Muggeridge), 1984; Welcome to America, 1985; Heath's Nineties, 1997; The Battle for Britain, 2017. *Recreations*: listening to Charlie Parker and Thelonious Monk, walking, learning to paint, my dachshund Charlie Barker.

**HEATH, His Honour Michael John**; a Circuit Judge, 1995–2017; Resident Judge, Lincoln Combined Court Centre, 2000–10; *b* Grimsby, 12 June 1948; *s* of late Norman Heath and Dorothy Heath; *m* 1972, Heather, *d* of late Christopher Croft and of Mrs D. Croft, Hetton-le-Hole; two *s. Educ*: Barcroft County Sch., Wintringham; Grammar Sch., Grimsby; Leeds Univ. (Lindsey Sen. Scholar 1966; LLB). FCIArb. Asst Solicitor, R. A. C. Symes and Co., Scunthorpe, 1975, Partner, 1977; Dep. Dist Judge, 1987–95; a Recorder, 1993–95; Solicitor Advocate (All Courts), 1994; Ethnic Minorities Liaison Judge, Lincolnshire, 1995–2008; Resident Judge, Grimsby Crown Court, 1999–2001; Magistrates' Liaison Judge, 2004–10. Chm., Humberside Area Criminal Justice Strategy Cttee, 2000–03; Member: Courts Bd, Lincolnshire, 2004–06; Lincolnshire Probation Bd, 2004–06. Hon. Recorder, City of Lincoln, 2001–10. *Recreations*: soccer, cricket, foreign languages.

**HEATH, Maj.-Gen. Michael Stuart**, CB 1994; CBE 1991; CEng, FIET; Director of Corporate Strategy, NXT plc, 2000–01; *b* 7 Sept. 1940; *s* of late Bernard Stuart Heath and of Blanche Dorothy Ellen Heath (*née* Fairey); *m* 1965, Frances Wood; one *s* one *d. Educ*: St Albans Sch.; Welbeck Coll.; Royal Military Coll. of Science (BSc Eng Upper 2nd cl. Hons London). Commissioned REME, 1961; served Malaya, BAOR, Edinburgh, to 1971; RMCS and Staff Coll., 1972–73; Armour Sch., Bovington, 1974–75; Comd 7 Field Workshop, BAOR, 1976–77; Nat. Defence Coll., 1978; Berlin Field Force, 1978–80; Comd Maint., HQ 2 Armd Div., BAOR, 1981–82; MoD, 1982–85; RCDS, 1986; Dir, Support Planning (Army), MoD, 1987–89; Comd Maint., HQ BAOR, 1990–91; Dir Gen., Electrical and Mechanical Engrg, subseq. Equipment Support (Army), MoD, 1991–93; Team Leader, Army Costs Study Team, 1994. Dir Gen., Engrg Council, 1995–98. Chm., 20/20 Speech Ltd, 1999–2000. *Recreations*: walking, music, photography, web design. *Address*: c/o Barclays Bank, 167 High Street, Bromley, Kent BR1 1NL.

**HEATH-BROWN, Prof. David Rodney, (Roger),** PhD; FRS 1993; Professor of Pure Mathematics, University of Oxford, 1999–2016; Fellow of Worcester College, Oxford, 1999–2016, now Emeritus Fellow; *b* 12 Oct. 1952; *s* of Basil Heath-Brown and Phyllis Joan (*née* Watson); *m* 1992, Ann Louise Sharpley; two *d. Educ*: Welwyn Garden City Grammar Sch.; Trinity Coll., Cambridge (BA, MA, PhD). Jun. Res. Fellow, Trinity Coll., Cambridge, 1977–79; Oxford University: Fellow and Tutor in Pure Maths, Magdalen Coll., 1979–98, Emeritus Fellow, 1999; Reader in Pure Maths, 1990–98. Corresp. Mem., Akad. der Wissenschaften, Göttingen, 1999. Jun. Berwick Prize, 1981, Sen. Berwick Prize, 1996, Pólya Prize, 2009, London Math. Soc. *Publications*: numerous mathematical papers in learned jls. *Recreations*: field botany, bridge, gardening. *Address*: Mathematical Institute, Radcliffe Observatory Quarter, Woodstock Road, Oxford OX2 6GG. *T*: (01865) 273535.

**HEATHCOAT-AMORY, Rt Hon. David (Philip)**; PC 1996; FCA; *b* 21 March 1949; *s* of late Roderick and Sonia Heathcoat-Amory; *m* 1978, Linda Adams; one *s* one *d* (and one *s* decd). *Educ*: Eton Coll.; Oxford Univ. (MA PPE). Qual. as Chartered Accountant with Price Waterhouse & Co., 1974; FCA 1980. Worked in industry, becoming Asst Finance Dir of British Technology Gp, until 1983 when resigned to fight Gen. Election. MP (C) Wells, 1983–2010; contested (C) same seat, 2010. PPS to the Financial Sec. to the Treasury, 1985–87, to the Home Secretary, 1987–88; an Asst Govt Whip, 1988–89; a Lord Comr of HM Treasury, 1989; Parly Under Sec. of State, DoE, 1989–90, Dept of Energy, 1990–92; Dep. Govt Chief Whip and Treasurer, HM Household, 1992–93; Minister of State, FCO, 1993–94; HM Paymaster General, 1994–96; Shadow Chief Sec. to HM Treasury, 1997–2000. Chm., London and Devonshire Trust Ltd, 2005–. Trustee, Nat. Heritage Meml Fund, 2014–17. *Recreations*: fishing, shooting, music, growing trees. *Address*: 12 Lower Addison Gardens, W14 8BQ. *T*: (020) 7603 3083. *Clubs*: Beefsteak, White's.

**HEATHCOAT AMORY, Sir Ian**, 6th Bt *cr* 1874; DL; *b* 3 Feb. 1942; *s* of Sir William Heathcoat Amory, 5th Bt, DSO, and Margaret Isabel Dorothy Evelyn (*d* 1997), *yr d* of Sir Arthur Havelock James Doyle, 4th Bt; *S* father, 1982; *m* 1972, Frances Louise, *d* of J. F. B. Pomeroy; four *s. Educ*: Eton. Chairman: Lowman Manufacturing Co. Ltd, 1976–; DevonAir Radio Ltd, 1983–90; Dir, Watts Blake Bearne & Co. PLC, 1984–88. Mem., Devon CC, 1973–85. JP Devon, 1980–93; DL Devon, 1981. *Heir: s* William Francis Heathcoat Amory [*b* 19 July 1975; *m* 2011, Tatiana Rose Sloane; three *s* one *d*]. *Address*: Calverleigh Court, Tiverton, Devon EX16 8BB.

**HEATHCOTE, Dr (Frederic) Roger**, CBE 2005; Chief Executive, Employment Tribunals Service, 2000–04; *b* 19 March 1944; *s* of late Frederic William Trevor Heathcote and Kathleen Annie Heathcote; *m* 1st, 1970, Geraldine Nixon (marr. diss. 1986); 2nd, 1986, Mary Campbell Syme Dickson; one *s* one step *d. Educ*: Bromsgrove Sch.; Birmingham Univ. (BSc (Hons) Physics, PhD). Res. Associate, Birmingham Univ., 1969–70; joined CS as Asst Principal, Min. of Technology (later DTI), 1970; Private Secretary to: Secretary (Industrial Develt), 1973; Permanent Under Sec. of State, Dept of Energy, 1974; Department of Energy: Principal, 1974; Asst Sec., 1978; Dir of Resource Management (Grade 4), 1988; Under Sec., Coal Div., 1989–91; Prin. Estabt and Finance Officer, 1991–92; Hd of Services Mgt Div., DTI, 1992–96; Dir, Export Control and Non-Proliferation, DTI, 1996–2000; UK Gov., IAEA, and UK Rep., Exec. Council of Orgn for the Prohibition of Chemical Weapons, 1996–2000. Non-exec. Dir, Trafalgar House Property Ltd, 1988–94. Gov., British Coll. of Osteopathic Medicine, 2004– (Chm., 2006–). *Recreations*: reading, gardening, lapidary, painting. *Address*: 8B The Crescent, Surbiton, Surrey KT6 4BN.

**HEATHCOTE, Sir Mark Simon Robert**, 10th Bt *cr* 1733, of London; OBE 1988; *b* 1 March 1941; *o s* of Brig. Sir Gilbert Simon Heathcote, 9th Bt, CBE and Patricia Margaret Heathcote (*née* Leslie); *S* father, 2014; *m* 1975, Susan Mary, *d* of Lt-Col George Ashley; two *s. Educ*: Eton; Magdalene Coll., Cambridge (BA 1963; MA 1981). P & O Orient Lines, 1963–70; Counsellor, FO, 1971–94; BP plc, 1994–2000; FCO, 2000–05. *Heir: s* Alastair Robert Heathcote [*b* 18 Aug. 1977; one *d* by Camilla Harvey].

**HEATHCOTE, Roger**; *see* Heathcote, F. R.

**HEATHCOTE, Sir Timothy Gilbert**, 12th Bt *cr* 1733, of Hursley, Hampshire; *b* 25 May 1957; *er s* of Sir Michael Heathcote, 11th Bt and Victoria (*née* Wilford); *S* father, 2007. Is in remainder to Earldom of Macclesfield. *Heir: b* George Benjamin Heathcote [*b* 2 Feb. 1965; *m* 1999, Dr Kate Rogers; two *s* one *d*].

**HEATHCOTE-DRUMMOND-WILLOUGHBY**, family name of **Baroness Willoughby de Eresby**.

**HEATHER, Christopher Mark**; QC 2017; *b* Norwich, 1971; *s* of Julian and Sandra Heather; *m* 2009, Angela Neillis; one *d. Educ*: Hewett Sch., Norwich; Girton Coll., Cambridge (BA 1994). Called to the Bar, Middle Temple, 1995; in practice as barrister, 1998–. *Recreations*: festivals, running, making bread, wine, violin, opera, Lego. *Address*: Tanfield Chambers, 2–5 Warwick Court, WC1R 5DJ. *T*: (020) 7421 5300. *E*: cheather@tanfieldchambers.co.uk.

**HEATHERWICK, Thomas Alexander**, CBE 2013; RA 2013; RDI 2004; Founder and Principal, Heatherwick (formerly Thomas Heatherwick) Studio, since 1994; *b* 17 Feb. 1970. *Educ*: Manchester Metropolitan Univ. (BA Hons Three Dimensional Design 1992); Royal Coll. of Art (MA Furniture 1994). Founded Heatherwick Studio to combine architecture, urban planning and product design; notable projects include: UK Pavilion, Shanghai Expo 2010, 2010 (Lubetkin Prize, RIBA, 2010); new Routemaster bus, London, 2010; London 2012 Olympic Flame Cauldron, 2012; Bombay Sapphire Distillery, Hants, 2014 (Civic Trust Award, 2017); Nanyang Learning Hub, Singapore, 2015; Zeitz Mus. of Contemporary Art Africa, Cape Town, 2017 (RIBA Internat. Prize, 2018); (with Fosters & Partners) Bund Finance Centre, Shanghai, 2017; Coal Drops Yard, London, 2016–18 (NLA Award, 2016); Vessel, NY, 2017–19. FRSA 2004; Sen. FRCA 2012; FRIBA 2007; Hon. FGCL, 2016. DUniv: Sheffield Hallam, 2005; Brighton, 2008; Hon. Dr: Manchester Metropolitan, 2007; UAL, 2013; Cardiff, 2016; Hon. LLD Dundee, 2007. *Address*: Heatherwick Studio, 356–364 Gray's Inn Road, WC1X 8BH. *T*: (020) 7833 8800. *E*: studio@heatherwick.com.

**HEATHFIELD, Ven. Simon David**; Archdeacon of Aston, since 2014; *b* 1967; *m* Rachel; two *c. Educ*: Birmingham Univ. (BMus 1988); Fitzwilliam Coll., Cambridge (BTh 1999); Ridley Hall, Cambridge. RAF Officer; Insurance Manager; Auxiliary Nurse; Church and

Community Youth Worker, N Kent and Oxford; ordained deacon, 1999, priest, 2000; Curate, Church of the Good Shepherd, Heswall, 1999–2002; Vocation and Ministry Advr, Church Pastoral Aid Soc., 2002–05; Team Rector, Walthamstow, 2006–14; Area Dean, Waltham Forest, 2012–14. *Address:* 175 Harborne Lane, Selly Oak, Birmingham B29 6SS.

**HEATHWAITE, Prof. (Ann) Louise, (Mrs A. G. Mackie),** CBE 2018; PhD; FRSB; FRSE; Professor of Land and Water Systems Science, Lancaster Environment Centre, since 2004 and Cross-Faculty Associate Dean for Research, since 2018, Lancaster University; *b* Huddersfield, 1961; *d* of Ron Heathwaite and Eileen Heathwaite (*née* Throup); *m* 1994, Alistair G. Mackie. *Educ:* Boston Spa Comprehensive Sch.; Univ. of E Anglia (BSc 1st Cl. Hons Envmtl Sci. 1982); Univ. of Bristol (PhD 1987). Res. Officer, MAFF and Scientific Officer, Soil Survey of England and Wales, 1982–83; NERC Postdoctoral Res. Asst, Dept of Geography, Oxford Univ., 1987–88; Envmtl Hydrologist, Higher Scientific Officer, Chief Scientist's Directorate, NCC, 1988–89; Department of Geography, University of Sheffield: Lectr, 1989–95; Sen. Lectr, 1996–97; Prof., 1998–2004. Theme Leader, Sustainable Use of Natural Resources, NERC, 2008–12 (Mem. Council, 2013–17, 2018–). Chief Scientific Advr, Rural Affairs and Envmt, subseq. Rural Affairs, Food, and the Envmt, Scottish Govt, 2012–17. Member: Sci. Adv. Council, DEFRA, 2011–17; Steering Bd, UK Collaborative on Develt Sci., 2012–17; Adv. Cttee, CEH, 2016–18; UKRI Industrial Strategy Challenge Fund Transforming Food Prodn Adv. Bd, 2018–; Royal Soc. Global Envmt Res. Cttee, 2019–. Pres., Freshwater Biol Assoc., 2017–. FRSB (FSB 2010) FRSE 2015. *Publications:* (ed jtly) Nitrate: processes, patterns and management, 1993; (with K. Göttlich) Mires: process, exploitation and conservation, 1993; (ed with J. M. R. Hughes) The Hydrology and Hydrochemistry of British Wetlands, 1995; The Impact of Land Use Change on Nutrient Loads from Diffuse Sources, 1999; (jtly) Wetland Ecology and Eco-Hydrology, 2004; (ed jtly) Nutrient Mobility within River Basins: a European perspective, 2005; (ed jtly) Dynamics and Biogeochemistry of River Corridors and Wetlands, 2005; over 160 pubns in internat. peer-reviewed jls. *Recreations:* fell running, sheepdogs. *Address:* Lancaster Environment Centre, Lancaster University, Lancaster LA1 4YQ. *T:* (01524) 510225. *E:* louise.heathwaite@lancs.ac.uk.

**HEATLEY, Brian Antony;** Secretary, Green House (green think tank), 2011–14; *b* 20 April 1947; *s* of Thomas Russell Heatley and Margaret Ross (*née* Deacon); *m*; one *d*. *Educ:* Sheen Grammar Sch.; St John's Coll., Cambridge (BA); Balliol Coll., Oxford; Warwick Univ. (MPhil). Volunteer teacher, Ethiopia, 1969–71; Department of Trade and Industry, 1974–89: appts include Financial Services, Consumer Protection and Radio Communications; Head, Small Firms and Enterprise Br., 1989–90, Head, Resource Planning Br., 1990–93, Dept of Employment; Head of Adults and Trng Strategy, Dept of Employment, then DFEE, 1993–96. Student teacher, Sheffield Univ., 1996–97; Maths teacher, Graveney Sch., Tooting, 1997–2001. Policy Co-ordinator and Mem., Nat. Exec., 2004–09, Mem., Policy Cttee, 2009–10, Green Party; co-author, Green Party Gen. Election Manifesto, 2010, 2015. *Recreations:* walking, history, photography, food. *Address:* Lorton Barn, Lorton Lane, Weymouth, Dorset DT3 5QH.

**HEATON, Clive William;** QC 2006; **His Honour Judge Heaton;** a Circuit Judge, since 2011; Designated Family Judge for Humberside and North Lincolnshire, since 2016; *b* 20 July 1957; *s* of William and Dilys Heaton; *m* 1980, Susan Margaret Taylor (*d* 2007); two *s*; *m* 2012, Angela Catherine Finnerty, *qv*. *Educ:* Huddersfield New Coll.; Keble Coll., Oxford (MA); Chester Coll. of Law. Admitted solicitor, 1982; called to the Bar, Gray's Inn, 1992; in practice, specialising in family and child care law; Recorder, 2003–11; Dep. High Ct Judge, Family Div., 2009–; authorised to sit in Admin. Ct, 2012–18. Mem., Standards Cttee, Bar Standards Bd, 2008–11; Chm., Leeds Family Law Bar Assoc., 2011. Course Dir, Judicial Coll., 2016–19. *Publications:* (with Heather Swindells) Adoption: the modern procedure, 2006; (with L. McCallum and R. Joghi) The Forced Marriage Act, 2009. *Address:* Leeds Combined Court Centre, 1 Oxford Row, Leeds LS1 3BG.

**HEATON, Frances Anne;** Chairman: Lazards London Directors' Pension Scheme, 2006–15 (Director, 2002–15); Schroder Pension Trustee Ltd, 2008–14; *b* 11 Aug. 1944; *d* of John Ferris Whidborne and Marjorie Annie (*née* Maltby); *m* 1969, Martin Heaton; two *s*. *Educ:* Queen Anne's, Caversham; Trinity Coll., Dublin (BA, LLB). Called to the Bar, Inner Temple, 1967. Dept of Econ. Affairs, 1967–70; HM Treasury, 1970–80; seconded to S. G. Warburg & Co. Ltd, 1977–79; Lazard Brothers & Co. Ltd, 1980–2001, Dir, 1987–2001; seconded as Dir Gen., Panel on Takeovers and Mergers, 1992–94. Director: W. S. Atkins, 1990–2003 (Dep. Chm., 1996–2003); Bank of England, 1993–2001; Elementis plc (formerly Harrisons & Crosfield), 1994–99; Commercial Union, 1994–98; BUPA, 1998–2001; Legal & General Gp plc, 2001–10; AWG plc, 2002–07; Jupiter Primadona Growth Trust, 2005–14; BMT Gp, 2007–14. Mem., Cttee on Standards in Public Life, 1997–2003. *Recreations:* riding, gardening, bridge.

**HEATON, John;** *see* Heaton, W. J.

**HEATON, Dr Rebecca Jane;** Head, Sustainability and Policy, Drax Group, since 2015; Member, Committee on Climate Change, since 2017; *b* Bristol, 31 March 1971; *d* of Arthur Daniel Heaton and Beryl Marjorie Heaton (*née* Sampson); *m* 2004, Piers Nesbitt; one *s*. *Educ:* University Coll. of North Wales, Bangor (BSc 1st Cl. Hons Forestry 1993); Cardiff Univ. (PhD 2000). FICFor 2011. Post-doctoral scientist, Cardiff Univ., 1999–2001; Project Manager, Bronzeoak Ltd, 2001–02; Sen. Consultant, ADAS, 2002–06; Sustainability Manager, BP, 2006–09; Strategic Issues Specialist, Shell, 2009–15. *Recreations:* vegetable growing, bee keeping, hill walking, mountain marathons. *Club:* Farmers.

**HEATON, Sir Richard (Nicholas),** KCB 2019 (CB 2011); Permanent Secretary, Ministry of Justice, since 2015; Clerk of the Crown in Chancery, since 2015; *b* 5 Oct. 1965; *s* of late David Heaton, OBE. *Educ:* Rugby Sch.; Worcester Coll., Oxford (BA 1987). Called to the Bar, Inner Temple, 1988, Bencher, 2013. Home Office, 1991–96; Legal Secretariat to the Law Officers, 1996–98; Home Office, 1998–2000; Cabinet Office, 2000–01; Lord Chancellor's Dept, subseq. DCA, 2001–06, Legal Advr, 2004–06; Dir-Gen., Legal Gp, DWP, and Solicitor to DWP and DoH, 2007–09; Dir-Gen., Strategy, Information and Pensions, DWP, 2009–12; First Parliamentary Counsel, 2012–15; Permanent Sec., Cabinet Office, 2012–15. Chm. of Trustees, United St Saviour's Charity, 2014–. *Recreations:* India, pictures. *Address:* Ministry of Justice, 102 Petty France, SW1H 9AJ.

**HEATON, (William) John;** consultant to the betting industry, since 2004; Chief Executive, Betting & Gaming Consultancy Ltd, since 2004; *b* 12 Jan. 1954; *s* of Ronald and Hilda Heaton; one *s* two *d*; *m* 2011, Karen Macdonald. *Educ:* Wigan Grammar Sch.; Sheffield Univ. (LLB). Admitted Solicitor, 1975. Principal Solicitor, Manchester CC, 1976–83; Horserace Totalisator Board: Co. Sec. and Solicitor, 1983–96; Chief Exec., 1997–2004. Chm., Scotbet Ltd, 2011–. Mem. Council, Assoc. of British Bookmakers, 2015–. *Recreations:* Rugby, golf. *Address:* 3 Vicarage Drive, SW14 8RX. *E:* john@heaton.co.uk. *Clubs:* Richmond Rugby (Pres., 2015–18; Chm., 2015–); Royal Mid Surrey Golf.

**HEATON, Sir Yvo (Robert) Henniker-,** 4th Bt *cr* 1912; *b* 24 April 1954; *s* of Sir (John Victor) Peregrine Henniker-Heaton, 3rd Bt, and of Margaret Patricia, *d* of late Lieut Percy Wright, Canadian Mounted Rifles; *S* father, 1971; *m* 1978, Freda, *d* of B. Jones; one *s* one *d*. Mem., North West Leics DC, 1987–95. Chm., Kegworth Cons. Assoc., 1988–94. Gov., Ashby Willesley Sch., 1996–2000. *Publications:* Corporate Computer Insurance, 1990. *Heir:* s Alastair (John) Henniker-Heaton, *b* 4 May 1990.

**HEATON-HARRIS, Christopher;** MP (C) Daventry, since 2010; Minister of State, Department for Transport, since 2019; *b* 28 Nov. 1967; *s* of David Barry Heaton-Harris and Ann Geraldine Heaton-Harris; *m* 1990, Jayne Yvonne Carlow; two *d*. *Educ:* Tiffin Grammar Sch. for Boys, Kingston upon Thames. Dir, What 4 Ltd, 1995–2003. Contested (C) Leicester South, 1997, July 2004. MEP (C) East Midlands, 1999–2009. An Asst Govt Whip, 2016–17; Vice Chamberlain of HM Household (Govt Whip), 2017–18; Comptroller of HM Household (Govt Whip), 2018; Parly Under-Sec. of State, DExEU, 2018–19. Pres., EU Sports Platform, 2009–10. *Recreation:* grade 5 soccer referee. *Address:* (office) 78 St George's Avenue, Northampton NN2 6JF; House of Commons, SW1A 0AA.

**HEATON-JONES, Peter;** MP (C) North Devon, since 2015; *b* Kingston upon Thames, 2 Aug. 1963; *s* of Richard Howard Heaton-Jones and Eileen Heaton-Jones (*née* Lewis). *Educ:* Esher Grammar Sch.; Southlands Coll. (BA Hons Sociol. and Geog. Univ. of London); London Coll. of Printing (CNAA Dip. Journalism). Sen. Broadcast Journalist, BBC, 1986–97; Hd, Mktg, ABC, Australia, 1998–2000; freelance broadcaster and media consultant, 2000–06; Press Sec., NSW Parlt, 2007–08; Agent, Cons. Party, 2008–10; Sen. Parly Asst, 2010–15. Mem. (C) Swindon BC, 2010–14. PPS, DWP, 2016–17, to Sec. of State for Work and Pensions, 2017–18, to Lord Chancellor, and Sec. of State for Justice, 2018–. Mem., Envmtl Audit Select Cttee, 2015–17. *Address:* House of Commons, SW1A 0AA. *E:* peter.heatonjones.mp@parliament.uk.

**HEAVEN, Derick R.;** Chief Executive Officer, Sugar Industry Authority, Jamaica, 2002–15; Chairman, Jamaica Cane Products Sales, 2015–16; *b* 19 Dec. 1940; *m* 1966, Thyra Reid; two *s* one *d*. *Educ:* Cornwall Coll.; Jamaica Sch. of Agriculture. Mem., St Catherine Parish Council, 1974–76; MP for South St Catherine, 1976–80; Parly Sec., Min. of Foreign Affairs, then Minister of Trade and Commerce, 1980; involved in farming and business interests, 1980–89; Consul-General, New York, 1989–92; Ambassador to Japan and (non-resident) to People's Republic of China and Republic of Korea, 1992–94; High Comr for Jamaica in London, 1994–99, and Ambassador (non-resident) to Scandinavia, Spain and Portugal; CEO, Sugar Co. of Jamaica Ltd, 1999–2002. Chm., Commonwealth Fund for Tech. Co-operation, 1996–99. *Recreations:* reading, travelling, sports.

**HEBBLETHWAITE, Rev. Dr Brian Leslie;** University Lecturer in Divinity, Cambridge, 1977–99, and Life Fellow of Queens' College, since 1994; *b* 3 Jan. 1939; *s* of Alderman Cyril Hebblethwaite and Sarah Anne Hebblethwaite; *m* 1991, Emma Sian (marr. diss. 2003), *d* of late John Ivor Disley, CBE; one *d*. *Educ:* Clifton Coll.; Magdalen Coll., Oxford (BA LitHum 1961; MA 1967); Magdalene Coll., Cambridge (BA Theol 1963; MA 1968; BD 1984; DD 2006); Westcott House, Cambridge; Univ. of Heidelberg. Curate, All Saints', Elton, Bury, 1965–68; Cambridge University: Bye-Fellow and Chaplain, 1968, Fellow and Dean of Chapel, 1969–94, Queens' Coll.; Univ. Asst Lectr in Divinity, 1973–77; Sen. Proctor, 1998–99; Examng Chaplain to Bishop of Manchester, 1977–98; Canon Theologian, Leicester Cathedral, 1982–2001. Pres., Soc. for Study of Theology, 1989–91. Lectures: Teape, Delhi, Calcutta and Bangalore, 1983–84; (jtly) Gifford, Glasgow, 2001; Hensley Henson, Oxford, 2002. Editor for Ethics, Theologische Realenzyklopädie, 1980–2007. *Publications:* Evil, Suffering and Religion, 1976, rev. edn 2000; The Problems of Theology, 1980; (ed jtly) Christianity and Other Religions, 1980, rev. edn 2001; The Adequacy of Christian Ethics, 1981; (ed jtly) The Philosophical Frontiers of Christian Theology, 1982; The Christian Hope, 1984, rev. edn 2010; Preaching Through the Christian Year 10, 1985; The Incarnation, 1987; The Ocean of Truth, 1988; (ed jtly) Divine Action, 1990; The Essence of Christianity, 1996; Ethics and Religion in a Pluralistic Age, 1997; Philosophical Theology and Christian Doctrine, 2004; In Defence of Christianity, 2005; (ed jtly) The Human Person in God's World, 2006; The Philosophical Theology of Austin Farrer, 2007; *festschrift:* Truth, Religious Dialogue and Dynamic Orthodoxy, ed by J. J. Lipner, 2005. *Recreations:* watching cricket, architecture, books. *Address:* The Old Barn, 32 High Street, Stretham, Ely, Cambs CB6 3JQ. *T:* (01353) 648279. *Club:* Athenæum.

**HEBDITCH, Maxwell Graham,** CBE 1994; Director, Museum of London, 1977–97; *b* 22 Aug. 1937; *s* of late Harold Hebditch, motor engr, Yeovil, and Lily (*née* Bartle); *m* 1963, Felicity Davies; two *s* one *d*. *Educ:* Yeovil Sch.; Magdalene Coll., Cambridge (MA). FSA, FMA. Nat. Service Commn, RAF, 1956–58. Field Archaeologist, Leicester Museums, 1961–64; Asst Curator in Archaeology, later Curator in Agricultural and Social History, City Museum, Bristol, 1965–71; Dir, Guildhall Mus., London, 1971–74; Dep. Dir, Mus. of London, 1974–77. Hon. Curator, Lyme Regis Mus., 2000–08 (Trustee, 2008–14). Chm., Mus. Trng Inst., subseq. Cultural Heritage NTO, 1997–2004 (Bd Mem., 1990–). Co-Dir, Mus. Leadership Prog., UEA, 1994–2000. Mem., EC Cttee of Cultural Consultants, 1990–92. Chm., UK Nat. Cttee, ICOM, 1981–87; Pres., Museums Assoc., 1990–92 (Vice-Pres., 1988–90); Chm., Taunton Cultural Consortium, 2004–13. Trustee: Mus. in Docklands, 1997–2005; Lyme Regis Mus., 2008–15; Weymouth Mus. Trust, 2011–14; Dorset County Mus., 2014–. Hon. DLitt City, 1992. *Publications:* contribs to archaeological and museological jls and books. *Recreations:* museums and monuments. *Address:* 4 St John Way, Dorchester, Dorset DT1 2FG.

**HEBER-PERCY, Sir Algernon (Eustace Hugh),** KCVO 2014; Lord-Lieutenant for Shropshire, 1996–2019 (Vice Lord-Lieutenant, 1990–96); *b* 2 Jan. 1944; *s* of Brig. A. G. W. Heber-Percy, DSO and Daphne Wilma Kenyon (*née* Parker Bowles); *m* 1966, Hon. Margaret Jane Lever, *y d* of 3rd Viscount Leverhulme, KG, TD; one *s* three *d*. *Educ:* Harrow; Mons OTC. Lieut Grenadier Guards, 1962–66. Farmer and landowner. Chm., Mercia Regional Cttee, Nat. Trust, 1990–99; Trustee, Nat. Gardens Scheme, 1990–2005. Pres., Shropshire and Mid Wales Hospice, 1988–; Chm., Walker Trust Cttee, 1990– (Mem., 1990–). Hon. Colonel: 5th Bn, Shropshire and Herefordshire LI (Vol.), 1998–99; W Midlands Regt, 1999–2005. Gov., Shrewsbury Sch., 2004–14. DL Shropshire, 1986; High Sheriff of Shropshire, 1987. Hon. DLitt: Chester, 2017; Harper Adams, 2018. *Recreations:* gardening, country sports. *Address:* Hodnet Hall, Hodnet, Market Drayton, Shropshire TF9 3NN. *T:* (01630) 685202. *Club:* Cavalry and Guards.

**HECHT, Kimberlee;** *see* Colin, K.

**HECHT, Samuel,** RDI 2008; Co-founder and Partner, Industrial Facility UK, since 2002; *b* London, 7 Aug. 1969; *s* of Jack and Maureen Hecht; *m* 2001, Kimberlee Colin, *qv*; two *s*. *Educ:* Mill Hill Sch., London; Central St Martin's, London (BA Hons Industrial Design with dist.); Royal Coll. of Art (MA Industrial Design). IDEO: industrial designer, San Francisco, 1994–96; Sen. Designer, Tokyo, 1996–99; Hd of Design, London, 1999–2002; Creative Dir, Muji Europe, 2004–07. Creative Advisor; Muji Japan, 2002–; Herman Miller Inc., 2008–. Sen. Tutor, RCA, 2007–10. Vis. Prof., Karlsruhe HFG, Germany, 2011–13. FRSA 2012. *Publications:* (jtly) Things That Go Unseen, 2002; (jtly) Product as Landscape, 2004; (contrib.) Phaidon Design Classics, 2007; (jtly) Usefulness in Small Things, 2011; (jtly) Industrial Facility, 2018. *Address:* Industrial Facility, Clerks Well House, 20 Britton Street, EC1M 5UA. *E:* mail@industrialfacility.co.uk.

**HECKMAN, Prof. James Joseph,** PhD; Henry Schultz Distinguished Service Professor, University of Chicago, since 1994 (Henry Schultz Professor, 1985–94); *b* 19 April 1944; *s* of John Jacob Heckman and Bernice Irene Medley Heckman; *m* 1st, 1964, Sally Lentz (marr. diss. 1971); 2nd, 1979, Lynne Pettler; one *s* one *d. Educ:* Colorado Coll. (BA Math 1965); Princeton (MA Econ 1968; PhD Econ 1971). Instructor-Associate Prof., Columbia Univ., 1970–74; Associate Prof., 1973–77, Prof. of Econs, 1977–, Univ. of Chicago; Yale Univ. (on leave), 1988–90. Guggenheim Fellow, 1977–78; Fellow, Center for Advanced Study in Behavioral Sci., 1977–78. Member: Amer. Acad., 1985–; NAS, 1992–; Resident Mem., Amer. Philosophical Soc., 2008–; Fellow: Econometric Soc., 1980; American Statistical Assoc., 2001; Soc. of Labor Economics, 2004; Amer. Assoc. for the Advancement of Science, 2009; Nat. Acad. of Educn, USA, 2010. Hon. MA Yale, 1989; Hon. PhD Colorado Coll., 2001; Hon. LLD: Chile, 2002; Univ. Autónoma del Estado de México, 2003; Montreal, Bard Coll., 2004; Hon. Dr Catholic Univ. of Chile, 2009; Hon. DSc (Econ) UCL, 2013; Hon. DSocSc Lignan, China, 2014. John Bates Clark Medal, American Econ. Soc., 1983; Nobel Prize for Economics, 2000; Jacob Mincer Award for Lifetime Achievement, Soc. of Labor Economics, 2005; Ulysses Medal, UC Dublin, 2006. President's Gold Medal (Italy), 2008; Frisch Medal, Econometric Soc., 2014. *Publications:* Longitudinal Analysis of Labor Market Data, 1985; Inequality in America: what role for human capital policies?, 2003; (with E. Leamer) Handbook of Econometrics, vol. 5 2001, vol. 6A 2007 and vol. 6B 2007; (ed jtly) Global Perspectives on the Rule of Law, 2009; Giving Kids a Fair Chance, 2012; (ed jtly) The Myth of Achievement Tests: the GED and the role of character in American life, 2014; other books and over 200 articles. *Recreations:* hiking, bicycling, reading, music. *Address:* Department of Economics, University of Chicago, 1126 E 59th Street, Chicago, IL 60637, USA.

**HECTOR, Alistair Gordon;** Headmaster, George Heriot's School, Edinburgh, 1998–2013; *b* 5 Oct. 1955; *s* of Gordon Matthews Hector, CMG, CBE; *m* 1980, Rosemary Ann Craig; two *s* one *d. Educ:* Edinburgh Acad.; Univ. of St Andrews (MA); Univ. of Erlangen, Germany. Lektor in English, Univ. of Erlangen, 1978–80; Head of German, Merchiston Castle Sch., Edinburgh, 1980–85; Head of Dept, German, 1986–89, Modern Langs, 1989–95, King Edward's Sch., Bath; Dep. Headmaster, Warwick Sch., 1995–97. *Recreations:* sport, walking, music, travel, family.

**HEDEGAARD, Connie,** Silver Cross, Order of Dannebrog, 2005; Chair, KR Foundation, since 2015; *b* Copenhagen, 15 Sept. 1960; *d* of Knud Hedegaard Koksbang and Elinor Hedegaard Koksbang; *m* 1992, Jacob Andersen; two *s. Educ:* Univ. of Copenhagen (MA Lit. and Hist.). Journalist, Hd of Radio News and columnist, Danish TV, 1990–2004. MP, Denmark, 1984–90 and 2005–09; Minister: for Envmt, 2004–07, and for Nordic Cooperation, 2005–07; for Climate and Energy, 2007–09; for UN Climate Change Conf., Copenhagen, 2009. Mem., EC, 2010–14. Mem. Bd, Danfoss, 2016–. *Publications:* The 20th Century: the 100 most influential people in Denmark (with C. Hagen Pedersen), 1999; Da Klimaet blev Hot, 2008. *Address:* KR Foundation, c/o Klub #8, Linnésgade 25, 1361 Copenhagen, Denmark.

**HEDGER, John Clive,** CB 1998; Chairman, Berkshire Healthcare NHS Foundation Trust, 2009–16; *b* 17 Dec. 1942; *s* of late Leslie John Keith Hedger and Iris Hedger (*née* Friedlos); *m* 1966, Jean Ann Felstead; two *s* one *d. Educ:* Quirister Sch., Winchester; Victoria Coll., Jersey; Univ. of Sussex (BA 1965; MA 1966). Dept of Educn and Science, 1966; Asst Private Sec., 1970; Sec., Cttee of Enquiry on Educn of Handicapped, 1974–76; Under Sec., DES, 1988–92; Dep. Sec., Dept for Educn, 1992–95; Dir of Ops, DFEE, 1995–2000. Chm., Sector Skills Council for Lifelong Learning, later Lifelong Learning UK, 2005–07; Trustee, Rathbone (formerly Rathbone Training), 2000–09; Trustee and non-exec. Dir, Nat. Foundn for Educnl Research, 2004–12. Mem. Council, Radley Coll., 1998–2007; Gov., Mary Hare Sch., 2006–14; Trustee, Langley Acad. Trust, 2012–. *Recreations:* walking, gardening, grandchildren, cycling in Dorset. *Address:* Hillrise Barn, Fairfield Road, Shroton, Blandford Forum, Dorset DT11 8QA. *T:* (01258) 863762.

**HEDGES, Very Rev. Jane Barbara;** Dean of Norwich, since 2014; *b* 6 April 1955; *d* of John William Henry Taylor and Elizabeth Taylor; *m* 1982, Christopher Hedges; two *s. Educ:* Durham Univ. (BA Hons). Ordained deaconess, 1980, deacon 1987, priest 1994; Deaconess, Holy Trinity with St Columba, Fareham, 1980–83; Team Vicar, Southampton City Centre Team, 1983–88; Stewardship Advr, Portsmouth Dio., 1988–93; Residentiary Canon, Portsmouth Cathedral, 1993–2001; Team Rector, Honiton Team Ministry, 2001–06; Canon Steward, 2006–14, and Archdeacon, 2006–09, 2011–14, Westminster Abbey. Hon. LLD Portsmouth, 2006. *Recreations:* walking, listening to classical music, animal welfare, sporting events with sons, touring abroad/pilgrimages. *Address:* The Deanery, The Close, Norwich NR1 4EG. *T:* (01603) 280300. *E:* dean@cathedral.org.uk.

**HEDGES, (Jonathan) Mark;** Editor, Country Life, since 2006; *b* 24 Feb. 1964; *s* of John and Mary Hedges; two *s* one *d. Educ:* Radley Coll., Abingdon; Univ. of Durham (BSc Geol. 1985). Tattersalls, Newmarket, 1985–88; Ed., Shooting Times, 1998–2000; Publisher, The Field, Shooting Times, Sporting Gun and Anglers' Mail, 2000–02; Ed., Horse & Hound, 2002–03, 2004; Editor-in-Chief, Country and Leisure Media, IPC, 2002–06. *Publications:* Dog, 2000. *Recreations:* shooting, fly fishing, leaning on a fork, the countryside. *Address:* Country Life, Pinehurst 2, Pinehurst Road, Farnborough Business Park GU14 7BF. *T:* (01252) 555060. *E:* mark.hedges@ti-media.com. *Club:* Athenæum.

**HEDGES, Matthew James;** HM Diplomatic Service; Ambassador to Paraguay, since 2017; *b* Merthyr Tydfil, 23 April 1973; *s* of David and Mary Hedges. *Educ:* St Anne's Coll., Oxford (BA Modern Langs 1996); Princeton Univ. (MPA 2016). Grad. trainee, Macmillan Publishers, 1996–99; entered FCO, 1999; Desk Officer, Security Policy Dept, FCO, 1999–2000; Advr, UK Mission to UN, NY, 2000; FCO, 2001; Second Sec. (Political), Rabat, 2002–05; Team Leader, EU Directorate, FCO, 2005–06; on secondment to H of C as Sen. Clerk, Internat. Develt Select Cttee, 2006–08; Head: Governor's Office, Turks and Caicos Is, 2008; Political Section, Tokyo, 2009–12; Dep. Hd of Mission, Rangoon, 2012–15. *Recreations:* theatre, reading, opera, art, travel. *Address:* c/o Foreign and Commonwealth Office, King Charles Street, SW1A 2AH. *E:* matthew.hedges@fco.gov.uk.

**HEDGES, Michael Irving Ian,** CBE 2005; QPM 1995; Chief Constable, South Yorkshire Police, 1998–2004; *b* 27 Jan. 1948; *s* of Arthur and Helen Hedges; *m* 1968, Beryl Janet Smith; one *s. Educ:* Holyrood Sch., Chard, Som.; King's College, London (LLB). Constable, Somerset and Bath Police, 1967–72; transf. to Metropolitan Police, 1972–87; Chief Superintendent, Thames Valley Police, 1987–88; Asst Chief Constable, Avon and Somerset Police, 1988–93; Dep. Chief Constable, South Yorkshire Police, 1993–98. RHS Medal for Gallantry, 1968. *Recreations:* swimming, reading, golf, fly fishing, gardening; an active Rotarian.

**HEDGES, Michael John;** Member (Lab) Swansea East, National Assembly for Wales, since 2011; *b* Swansea, 8 July 1956; *s* of William John Hedges and Rosemary June Hedges; *m* 1996, Anne Rachel Hopkins; two *d. Educ:* Swansea Univ. (BSc Hons Materials Sci. and Technol.); Cardiff Univ. (PGCE). Researcher, BSC, 1978–81; Researcher and Lectr in Computing, 1981–83; Lectr in Computing, Coleg Morgannwg, 1983–2011. Mem. (Lab), Swansea Council, 1989– (Leader, 1997–2001). Chair, Climate Change, Envmt and Rural Affairs Cttee, 2017–. *Recreations:* football, cricket, Rugby. *Address:* 4 Glyncollen Drive, Ynysforgan, Swansea SA6 6RR. *T:* (01792) 791774. *E:* mike.hedges@assembly.wales. *Clubs:* Morriston Working Men's; Ynystawe Cricket and Football, Morriston Rugby, Morriston Golf, Glais Rugby.

**HEDLEY, Air Vice-Marshal Bruce Haakon,** MBE 2000; Director Joint Warfare, Joint Forces Command, since 2016; *b* Reading, 28 Feb. 1967; *s* of Brian Hedley and Signy Hedley; *m* 1987, Stella Jane Betts; two *s. Educ:* Maiden Earley Comp. Sch.; King's Coll. London (MA Defence Studies). Joined RAF 1985; OC 3 (Fighter) Sqdn, 2002–05; Dep. Principal Staff Officer to Chief of Defence Staff, 2007–09; Station Comdr, RAF Valley, 2009–11; Force Effects Coordinator and Dir of Communications, II Marine Expeditionary Force, 2011–12; Comdt Air Warfare Centre, 2012–15; HCSC 2016. Pres., RAF Badminton Assoc., 2012–; Chm., RAF Bobsleigh, Luge and Skeleton Assoc., 2013–. *Recreation:* keen runner. *Address:* Director Joint Warfare, Joint Forces Command, Northwood Headquarters, Sandy Lane, Northwood, Middx HA6 3HP. *T:* (01923) 955024. *E:* JFC-DJW@mod.uk. *Club:* Royal Air Force.

**HEDLEY, Rev. Charles John Wykeham,** PhD; Rector, St James's, Piccadilly, 1999–2009; English language teacher, Beijing and Chengdu, 2009–12; *b* 26 June 1947; *s* of Harry and Elisabeth Hedley. *Educ:* Christ's Hospital, Horsham; Royal Holloway Coll., Univ. of London (BSc; PhD 1973); Fitzwilliam Coll., Cambridge (MA); Westcott House, Cambridge. Deacon 1976, priest 1977; Asst Curate, St Anne's, Chingford, 1976–79; Curate, St Martin-in-the-Fields, 1979–86; Chaplain, Christ's Coll., Cambridge, 1986–90; Team Rector of Gleadless, Sheffield, 1990–99. *Recreations:* walking, classical music. *E:* charleshuk@outlook.com.

**HEDLEY, Sir Mark,** Kt 2002; DL; a Judge of the High Court, Family Division, 2002–13; *b* 23 Aug. 1946; *s* of late Peter and Eve Hedley; *m* 1973, Erica Britton; three *s* one *d. Educ:* Framlingham College; Univ. of Liverpool (LLB Hons). Called to the Bar, Gray's Inn, 1969, Bencher, 2002; VSO, Sudan, 1969–70; practice at Liverpool Bar, 1971–92; Head of Chambers, 1983–92; a Recorder, 1988–92; a Circuit Judge, 1992–2001. Vis. Prof., Liverpool Hope Univ., 2013–. Chancellor, Dio. Liverpool, 2002–18. Reader in C of E, 1975–. Hon. LLD Liverpool, 2003; Hon. Fellow, Liverpool John Moores Univ., 2005. DL Merseyside, 2015. *Recreations:* cricket, railways. *Address:* 55 Everton Road, Liverpool L6 2EH.

**HEDLEY, Richard Philip; His Honour Judge Hedley;** a Circuit Judge, since 2018; Designated Civil Judge for Leicester and Northampton, since 2019. *Educ:* Univ. of Leicester (LLB); Univ. of Cambridge (Dip. Notarial Practice). Called to the Bar, Middle Temple, 1983; a Recorder, 2002–18; a District Judge, 2012–18. *Publications:* (Asst Ed.) Byles on Bills of Exchange, 26th edn 1988; (with William Hedley) Hedley on Bills of Exchange and Bankers' Documentary Credits, 4th edn 2001. *Recreations:* music, cricket, golf, rowing. *Address:* County Court at Leicester, 90 Wellington Street, Leicester LE1 6HG. *T:* (0116) 222 5700.

**HEDWORTH, (Alan) Toby;** QC 1996; a Recorder, since 1995; *b* 23 April 1952; *s* of late John William Swaddle Hedworth and Margaret Ena Hedworth (*née* Dodds); *m* 1987, Kathleen Mary (*née* Luke); two *d. Educ:* King's Sch., Tynemouth; Royal Grammar Sch., Newcastle upon Tyne; St Catharine's Coll., Cambridge (MA). Called to the Bar, Inner Temple, 1975, NI 2012; Head, Trinity Chambers, Newcastle upon Tyne, 1999–. Vice Chm., Northumberland and Newcastle Soc., 1997–. *Recreations:* Newcastle United, the English Lake District, motoring, the built environment. *Address:* The Custom House, Quayside, Newcastle upon Tyne NE1 3DE. *T:* (0191) 232 1927. *Club:* Northern Counties (Newcastle upon Tyne).

**HEEGER, Prof. Alan Jay,** PhD; Presidential Chair, since 2003, and Professor of Physics, since 1982, and Professor of Materials, since 1987, University of California, Santa Barbara; *b* 22 Jan. 1936; *s* of Peter Jacob Heeger and Alice Minkin Heeger; *m* 1957, Ruth Chudacroft; two *s. Educ:* Univ. of Nebraska (BS 1957); Univ. of Calif, Berkeley (PhD 1961). University of Pennsylvania: Prof. of Physics, 1962–82; Director: Lab. for Res. on Structure of Matter, 1974–80; Inst. for Polymers and Organic Solids, 1983–99. Founder, 1990, Chm., 1990–99, Uniax Corp. Member: NAS; NAE. Holds numerous hon. degrees. Buckley Prize, APS, 1983; Balzan Foundn Prize, 1995; Nobel Prize in Chem., 2000. *Recreations:* ski-ing, walking. *Address:* Department of Physics, University of California at Santa Barbara, Santa Barbara, CA 93106, USA. *T:* (805) 8933184, *Fax:* (805) 8934755. *E:* ajhe@physics.ucsb.edu.

**HEELEY, Michelle Louise, (Mrs Ashley Bayliss);** QC 2017; *b* Birmingham, 18 Jan. 1978; *d* of Ronald Heeley and Geraldine Heeley; *m* 2009, Ashley Bayliss; two *s. Educ:* King Edward VI Handsworth Sch.; Nottingham Trent Univ. (LLB Hons Europe 2000); Nottingham Law Sch. (BVC 2001). Called to the Bar, Gray's Inn, 2001; in practice as a barrister, specialising in crime and regulatory law, No 5 Chambers, Birmingham, 2001–; a Recorder, 2012–. *Recreations:* drumming, reading, juggling, acting, supporter of Aston Villa FC. *Address:* No 5 Chambers, Fountain Court, Steelhouse Lane, Birmingham B4 6DR. *T:* (0121) 606 0500. *E:* mlh@no5.com.

**HEFFER, Simon James,** PhD; columnist, Daily Telegraph and Sunday Telegraph, since 2015; *b* 18 July 1960; *er s* of late James Heffer and Joyce Mary Heffer (*née* Clements); *m* 1987, Diana Caroline, *d* of Sqdn Ldr P. A. Clee; two *s. Educ:* King Edward VI Sch., Chelmsford; Corpus Christi Coll., Cambridge (BA 1982; MA 1986; PhD 2009). Medical journalist, 1983–86; Leader Writer and Parly Sketch Writer, Daily Telegraph, 1986–91; Dep. Ed. and Political Corresp., Spectator, 1991–94; Dep. Ed., Daily Telegraph, 1994–95; columnist, Daily Mail, 1993–94 and 1995–2005; Associate Ed. and columnist, Daily Telegraph, 2005–11; columnist, Daily Mail, 2011–15. Member, Board: Britten Sinfonia, 2005–09; Elgar Foundn and Birthplace Trust, 2009–16; New Queen's Hall Orchestra, 2013–. Fellow Commoner, Corpus Christi Coll., Cambridge, 2010; Professorial Res. Fellow in Mod. Hist., Humanities Res. Inst., Univ. of Buckingham, 2018–. Sen. Advr, Sanctuary Counsel, 2019–. FRHistS 2017. *Publications:* Moral Desperado: a life of Thomas Carlyle, 1995; Power and Place: the political consequences of King Edward VII, 1998; Like the Roman: the life of Enoch Powell, 1998; Nor Shall My Sword: the reinvention of England, 1999; Vaughan Williams, 2000; Great British Speeches, 2007; Strictly English, 2010; A Short History of Power, 2011; High Minds: the Victorians and the birth of modern Britain, 2013; Simply English, 2014; The Age of Decadence: Britain 1880–1914, 2017; Staring at God: Britain in the Great War, 2019. *Recreations:* cricket, music, bibliophily, my family. *Address:* The Daily Telegraph, 111 Buckingham Palace Road, SW1W 0DT. *Clubs:* Beefsteak, Garrick, MCC, Pratt's.

**HEFFERNAN, Margaret Anne Windham;** author; *b* Corpus Christi, Texas, 15 June 1955; *d* of Jack Edward Windham and Sally Anne Windham; *m* 1st, 1983, Michael Francis Heffernan (*d* 1985); 2nd, 1991, Lindsay Boyd Nicholson; one *s* one *d. Educ:* Girton Coll., Cambridge (BA 1977). Producer, BBC TV, 1983–91; Man. Dir, IPPA, 1991–93; Consultant, Boston, MA, 1993; Chief Executive Officer: InfoMation Corp., 1996–97; ZineZone Corp., 1997–99; iCast Corp., 1999–2002. Non-executive Director: Bath Consultancy Gp, 2009–11; RADA Enterprises, 2014–; Merryck and Co., 2015–. Vis. Prof.,

Simmons Coll., Boston, 2004–08. Mem., Adv. Bd, Sch. of Mgt, 2008–, Vis. Lectr, 2009–, Univ. of Bath. Mem. Council, RADA, 2003–14. Trustee: Bath Festivals, 2010–15; London Liby, 2013–15; Centre for Effective Dispute Resolution, 2018–. *Plays:* Eve Blinked, 2006; Power Play, 2009; Wilful Blindness, 2009; Mrs Updike, 2011. Hon. DBA Bath, 2011. *Publications:* The Naked Truth: a working woman's manifesto, 2004; How She Does It, 2007; Women on Top, 2008; Wilful Blindness, 2011, rev. edn 2019; A Bigger Prize: why competition isn't everything and how we do better, 2014; Beyond Measure: the big impact of small change, 2015; More than a Dream: feminist utopias, 2016. *Recreations:* singing, earwigging, mowing, arguing, turnarounds. *E:* margaret@mheffernan.com.

**HEFFERNAN, Prof. Michael John,** PhD; FBA 2015; Professor of Historical Geography, University of Nottingham, since 1999; *b* Worcs, 7 June 1959; *s* of Patrick and Kathleen Heffernan; *m* 2013, Berta Turnbull; one *s*. *Educ:* Queen Elizabeth I Grammar Sch., Hartlebury; Univ. of Wales, Swansea (BSc 1980); St John's Coll., Cambridge (PhD 1987). Loughborough University: Lectr in Histl Geog., 1985–90; Sen. Lectr, 1990–95; Reader, 1995–99. Vis. Prof., UCLA, 1999–2000; Alexander Von Humboldt Res. Fellow, Univ. of Heidelberg, 1999–2000. Ed., Jl Histl Geog., 1996–2005. FRHistS 2010. Marion I. Newbigin Award, RSGS, 2001. *Publications:* The Meaning of Europe, 1998. *Recreations:* skiing, canoeing, walking in the Pyrenees. *Address:* School of Geography, University of Nottingham, Sir Clive Granger Building, University Park, Nottingham NR7 2RD. *E:* mike.heffernan@nottingham.ac.uk. *Club:* Geographical.

**HEGARTY, Frances;** see Fyfield, F.

**HEGARTY, Dr John,** FInstP; Provost of Trinity College Dublin, 2001–11; Director, Innovation Advisory Partners, since 2012; *b* Mayo, 17 April 1948; *s* of John and Delia Hegarty; *m* 1975, Neasa Ní Chinnéide; two *s*. *Educ:* National Univ. of Ireland, Maynooth (BSc 1969; Higher DipEd 1971); National Univ. of Ireland, Galway (PhD 1976); Trinity Coll. Dublin (DSc 2001). FInstP 1986. Res. Associate, Univ. of Wisconsin-Madison, 1977–80; Res. Scientist, Bell Labs, Murray Hill, NJ, 1980–86; Prof. of Laser Physics, TCD, 1986–2001. Founder and Dir, Optronics Ireland, 1989–2000. Coordinator, Eur. Consortium on Microcavities, 1993–2000. Member: Bd, Nat. Res. Support Fund, Ireland, 1995–98; Higher Educn Authy, Ireland, 1998–2001; Tech. Adv. Panel on Information and Communications Technol., Sci. Foundn Ireland, 2000–01. Chm., Deans and Vice Presidents for Res. under CHIU, 2000. Fellow, TCD. MRIA. Hon. LLD QUB, 2008; Hon. DSc UCD, 2013. *Publications:* contribs to jls incl. Physical Rev., Optical and Quantum Electronics, IEEE Jl Quantum Electronics, Applied Physics Letters, Jl Luminescence, Jl Crystal Growth, Optics Letters, Electronics Letters. *Recreations:* reader of all forms of literature from biography to novels which enrich the soul and ease me to sleep at night, sailing and a love of the power and unpredictability of the sea, cycling for leisure, especially around W Kerry. *Address:* Provost's Office, Trinity College, Dublin 2, Ireland. *T:* (1) 8961558, *Fax:* (1) 8962303.

**HEGARTY, Sir John (Kevin),** Kt 2007; Founding Director, Bartle Bogle Hegarty Ltd, since 1982 (Worldwide Creative Director, 1982–2012, and Group Chairman, 1991–2012); *b* 20 May 1944; *s* of Matthew and Anne Hegarty; *m* (separated); one *s* one *d*. *Educ:* Challoner Grammar Sch.; Hornsey Sch. of Art; London Coll. of Printing. Junior Art Dir, Benton & Bowles, 1965–66; Art Director: John Collings and Partners, 1966–67; Cramer Saatchi, 1967–70; Saatchi & Saatchi: Founding Shareholder, 1970; Dep. Creative Dir, 1971–73; Founding Partner and Creative Dir, TBWA, London, 1973–82. Hon. Prof., London Inst., 1998. FRSA 1992. Wine maker, Domaine de Chamans. *Publications:* Hegarty on Advertising: turning intelligence into magic, 2011; Hegarty on Creativity: there are no rules, 2014. *Recreations:* tennis, ski-ing. *Address:* (office) 60 Kingly Street, W1B 5DS. *Clubs:* Groucho; Century.

**HEGARTY, Kevin John;** QC 2010; a Recorder, since 2003; *b* London, 9 Jan. 1960; *s* of John Hegarty and Josephine Hegarty; *m* 1984, Alison Day; one *s* two *d*. *Educ:* St Michael's Sch., Stevenage; Univ. of Newcastle upon Tyne (LLB Hons); Salford Univ. (MA). Called to the Bar, Middle Temple, 1982; in practice as a barrister, Manchester, then Birmingham, specialising in crime and regulatory law, 1990–; Hd, St Philips Chambers, 2011–14. *Recreations:* squash, classical guitar, gardening. *Address:* St Philips Chambers, 55 Temple Row, Birmingham B2 5LS. *Clubs:* Sloane; Stratford upon Avon Squash.

**HEGARTY, Most Rev. Séamus;** Bishop of Derry, (RC), 1994–2011; *b* 26 Jan. 1940; *s* of James Hegarty and Mary O'Donnell. *Educ:* Kilcar National School; St Eunan's Coll., Letterkenny; St Patrick's Coll., Maynooth; University Coll., Dublin. Priest, 1966; postgrad. studies, University Coll., Dublin, 1966–67; Dean of Studies 1967–71, President 1971–82, Holy Cross College, Falcarragh; Bishop of Raphoe, 1982–94. *Publications:* contribs to works on school administration and student assessment. *Recreations:* bridge, angling.

**HEGARTY, Seamus,** PhD; researcher and academic; Director, National Foundation for Educational Research, 1994–2005; *b* 19 Oct. 1945; *s* of James Hegarty and Mary Hegarty; *m* 1972, Carol Halls; two *s* one *d*. *Educ:* St Colman's Coll., Fermoy; University Coll., Dublin (BSc, HDipEd); Univ. of London Inst. of Educn (PhD 1975). Mgt trng, 1969–70; teaching, 1970–75; research, 1975–94. Visiting Professor: Reading Univ., 1996; Inst. of Educn, Univ. of London, 1996–98; Univ. of Aberystwyth (formerly Univ. of Wales, Aberystwyth), 2004–08; Univ. of Warwick, 2005–; Manchester Metropolitan Univ., 2005–09; QUB, 2005–09; Marie Curie Res. Fellow, TCD, 2011–12. Pres., Consortium of Instns for Develt and Res. in Educn in Europe, 2000–02; Chairman: Internat. Assoc. for the Evaluation of Educnl Achievement, 2005–12; Learning Standards Gp, Learning Metrics Task Force, 2012–13; Mem., Nat. Council for Special Educn, 2007–12. FAcSS 2015. Hon. Dr: Free Univ. of Brussels, 1997; Oxford Brookes, 2001; London, 2006; DUniv York, 1999. MInstD 1994. Ed., Educnl Res., 1983–2005; Founder Ed., European Jl Special Needs Educn, 1986–. *Publications:* Able to Learn?: the pursuit of culture-fair assessment, 1978; Educating Pupils with Special Needs in the Ordinary School, 1981; Integration in Action, 1982; Recent Curriculum Development in Special Education, 1982; The Making of a Profession, 1983; Training for Management in Schools, 1983; Research and Evaluation Methods in Special Education, 1985; Meeting Special Needs in Ordinary Schools, 1987, 2nd edn 1993; Developing Expertise: INSET for special educational needs, 1988; Review of the Present Situation of Special Education, 1988; Boosting Educational Achievement, 1989; Educating Children and Young People with Disabilities: principles and the review of practice, 1993; New Perspectives in Special Education: a six-country study of integration, 1994; Review of the Present Situation in Special Needs Education, 1995; The Role of Research in Mature Education Systems, 1997; (with M. Alur) Education and Children with Special Needs: from segregation to inclusion, 2002. *Recreations:* contemporary fiction, music, board games, golf, walking. *Club:* West Middlesex Golf.

**HEGARTY, His Honour Thomas Brendan;** QC 1992; a Circuit Judge, 1996–2013; *b* 6 June 1943; *s* of Thomas Hegarty and Louise (*née* Conlan); *m* 1972, Irene Letitia Hall; one *s* one *d*. *Educ:* St Joseph's Coll., Dumfries; St John's Coll., Cambridge (BA 1964; LLB 1965; MA 1970). Called to the Bar, Middle Temple, 1970; a Recorder, 1988–96. *Club:* Manchester Tennis and Racquet.

**HEGDE, Mridul,** CB 2013; non-executive Director and Chair, Risk Committee, HSBC UK Bank plc, since 2018; *b* Mangalore, India, 24 March 1967; *d* of Taranath Hegde and Kasturi Hegde (*née* Bhat); *m* 1st, 1994, Brian Brivati (marr. diss.); one *s* one *d*; 2nd, 2009, Philip J. Tansley; one *d*. *Educ:* Ravenspark Acad.; Balliol Coll., Oxford (BA PPE); Birkbeck Coll., Univ. of London (MSc Econs). AEU, 1988–89; HM Treasury, 1990–94, Speechwriter to the Chancellor, 1992–94; Policy Advr, Policy and Planning Directorate, BBC, 1996–97; DCMS, 1997–2002; HM Treasury: Team Leader, Public Services, 2002–04; Director: Public Spending, 2004–08; Financial Stability, 2008–12; Exec. Dir, Strategy, Financial Reporting Council, 2012–14. Non-exec. Dir, UK Municipal Bonds Agency, 2015–19.

**HEGDE, Dr Ramanujan Shankar,** FRS 2016; Programme Leader, MRC Laboratory of Molecular Biology, since 2011; *b* Kumta, India, 1 April 1970; *s* of Shankar Timmaya Hegde and Chandrakala Shankar Hegde; *m* 2000, Maryann Helen Kivlen. *Educ:* Univ. of Chicago (BA Hons); Univ. of California, San Francisco (MD; PhD 1998). Nat. Cancer Inst. Scholar, USA, 1999–2001; Investigator, 2001–08, Sen. Investigator, 2008–11, NIH. *Publications:* primary res. articles in Nature, Science, Cell and other jls. *Recreation:* science. *Address:* MRC Laboratory of Molecular Biology, Francis Crick Avenue, Cambridge CB2 0QH. *E:* rhegde@mrc-lmb.cam.ac.uk.

**HEGGESSEY, Lorraine Sylvia;** public/motivational speaker and media consultant, since 2010; Chief Executive Officer, Royal Foundation of the Duke and Duchess of Cambridge (formerly of the Duke and Duchess of Cambridge and Prince Harry, then the Duke and Duchess of Sussex), 2017–19; *b* 16 Nov. 1956; *d* of Sam and Doris Heggessey; *m* 1985, Ronald de Jong, musician and composer; two *d*. *Educ:* Durham Univ. (BA Hons English Lang. and Lit.). BBC: News Trainee and Sub Editor, 1979–83; Producer: Panorama, 1983–86; This Week, 1986–91; Editor, Biteback, 1991–92; Series Producer, The Underworld, 1992–94; Exec. Producer, BBC Science (QED, Animal Hospital, The Human Body, Minders), 1994–97; Head of Children's Programmes, 1997–99; Dep. Chief Exec., BBC Productions, 1999–2000; Controller, BBC1, 2000–05; Chief Exec., talkbackThames, 2005–10; Exec. Chair, Boom Pictures, 2012–14. Ind. Ext. Advr, Channel 4 Growth Fund, 2015–. Chm., Grierson Trust, 2014–. *Recreations:* ski-ing, yoga, open water swimming, hiking, having fun with my family and friends, theatre, cinema.

**HEGGS, Renée Fanny Madeleine, (Miguette);** a Social Security Commissioner, 1981–2002; a Child Support Commissioner, 1993–2002; *b* 29 Nov. 1929; *d* of Emilio and Graziella Calderan; *m* 1953, Geoffrey Ellis Heggs (*d* 2017); two *s* one *d*. *Educ:* Notting Hill and Ealing High Sch., GPDST; LLB (London) 1952. Legal Researcher, Wiggin and Dana, Conn, USA, 1953–54; admitted Solicitor, 1955; practising Solicitor, 1955–81. Chm., Nat. Inscce Local Tribunal, 1976–81; pt-time Chm. of Industrial Tribunals, 1978–81; Pres., Appeal Tribunal under London Building Acts, 1979–81; Legal Mem., 1985–2000, Dep. Regl Chm., 1995–2000, Mental Health Review Tribunal. Mem., UK Assoc. of Women Judges, 2004–. Liveryman, City of London Solicitors' Co., 2005–. *Recreations:* music, travelling. *Address:* 12 Audley Road, Ealing, W5 3ET. *T:* (020) 8997 0305. *Club:* Royal Over-Seas League.

**HEGINBOTHAM, Prof. Christopher John,** OBE 2009; PhD; healthcare consultant; Chief Executive, Institute of Social Commissioning, 2011–13; Director, Values Based Commissioning Ltd, 2011–18; *b* 25 March 1948; *s* of late Joseph William Heginbotham and Marjorie Heginbotham; *m* 1st, 1988, Barbara Joyce, *d* of Charles and Lois-Ella Gill, Cincinnati, Ohio (marr. diss. 2008); two *d*; 2nd, 2011, Christine Sconce, *d* of Roland and Mary Sanderson, Preston, Lancs. *Educ:* Univ. of Birmingham (BSc Hons 1969); Univ. of Essex (MSc 1972); MA Wales 1989; MPhil Cambridge 2001; Univ. of Lancaster (PhD 2017); Univ. of York (MA 2018). Area Manager, Circle Thirty Three Housing Trust, 1977–80; Assistant Borough Housing Officer, London Borough of Haringey, 1980–82; Nat. Dir, MIND (Nat. Assoc. for Mental Health), 1982–88; Fellow in Health Services Management, King's Fund Coll., London, 1989–93; Chief Executive: Riverside Mental Health NHS Trust, 1993–96; E and N Herts HA, 1996–2000; Chm. and Chief Exec., Eastern Region Specialised Commissioning Gp, 2000–01; Chief Exec., S Warwicks Gen. Hosps NHS Trust, 2001–03; Chief Exec., Mental Health Act Commn, 2003–08; University of Central Lancashire: Prof. of Mental Health Policy and Mgt, 2005–11, now Emeritus; Co-Dir, Inst. for Philosophy, Diversity and Mental Health, 2006–10; Dep. Hd, 2008–10, Actg Hd, 2010, Internat. Sch. for Communities, Rights and Inclusion. Member: Hampstead DHA, 1981–87; Waltham Forest DHA, 1989–92 (Vice-Chm., 1991–92); Chm., Redbridge and Waltham Forest FHSA, 1992–93; non-exec. Dir, Lancs Care NHS Foundn Trust, 2008–. Member: Nat. Adv. Council on Employment of Disabled People, 1983–90; Bd, World Fedn for Mental Health, 1985–89 (rep., UN Commn on Human Rights, 1985–91); Bd, Internat. Acad. of Law and Mental Health, 1987–89; Bd, Global Health Equity Foundn, Geneva, 2011–. Vis. Res. Fellow, Univ. of Glasgow Inst. of Law and Ethics in Medicine, 1987–91; Vis. Sen. Fellow, Health Services Mgt Centre, Univ. of Birmingham, 1994–2001; Hon. Prof., Inst. of Clin. Educn, Med. Sch., Univ. of Warwick, 2005–; Vis. Prof., Univ. of Cumbria, 2012–15. FRSPH 2014; FRSA 2015. *Publications:* Housing Projects for Mentally Handicapped People, 1981; Promoting Residential Services for Mentally Handicapped People, 1982; Webs and Mazes: approaches to community care, 1984; The Rights of Mentally Ill People, 1987; Return to Community, 1990; (with T. Campbell) Mental Illness: prejudice, discrimination and the law, 1990; (with C. Ham) Purchasing Dilemmas, 1992; Philosophy, Psychiatry and Psychopathy, 2000; Values-based Commissioning of Health and Social Care, 2012; (with K. Newbigging) Commissioning Health and Wellbeing, 2013; (ed with K. Newbigging) Public Health, 2016. *Recreations:* medieval history, art history, writing (medieval history and medieval art history), walking, cycling, travel. *Address:* Bankfield House, Whitebeck Lane, Priest Hutton, Carnforth, Lancs LA6 1JL.

**HEGLEY, John Richard;** freelance poet and performer; *b* 1 Oct. 1953; *s* of René Robert Hegley and Joan Hegley; one *d*. *Educ:* Univ. of Bradford (BSc Hons Social Scis (European Lit./Hist. of Ideas)). Actor/musician: Inter-action Prof. Dogg's Troup, 1978; Soapbox Children's Th., 1979; John Peel Radio sessions, 1983–84; presenter, Word of Mouth, TV poetry series, 1990; BBC on-line Poet-in-Residence, 1998; played Vernon Hines in Pyjama Game, 1999; Hearing with Hegley, BBC Radio series, 1997–99; performed, 21st Edinburgh Fest., 2004; Keats House Poet-in-Residence, 2012. Hon. LLD Luton 2000. *Publications:* Glad to Wear Glasses, 1990; Can I Come Down Now, Dad?, 1992; Five Sugars, Please, 1993; Love Cuts, 1995; The Family Pack, 1997; Beyond Our Kennel, 1998; Dog, 2000; My Dog is a Carrot, 2002; The Sound of Paint Drying, 2003; Uncut Confetti, 2006; Stanley's Stick, 2012; Peace, Love and Potatoes, 2012; I am a Poetato, 2013; New and Selected Potatoes, 2013. *Address:* Troika, 180 Great Portland Street, W1W 5QZ.

**HEHIR, Christopher Joseph; His Honour Judge Hehir;** a Circuit Judge, since 2015; *b* Glasgow, 15 Nov. 1966; *s* of Joseph Hehir and Monica Hehir (*née* Miller); *m* 2008, Katherine Punch; one *s* two *d*. *Educ:* St Aloysius Coll., Glasgow; Charters Comprehensive Sch., Ascot; Merton Coll., Oxford (BA Juris 1988). Called to the Bar, Inner Temple, 1990; in practice as barrister, specialising in criminal law, 1990–2015; a Recorder, 2009–15.

*Publications:* (contrib.) EU Law in Criminal Practice, 2013. *Recreations:* family, wasting time online, fretting about the fortunes of Celtic FC. *Address:* Southwark Crown Court, 1 English Grounds, SE1 2HU.

HEIDEN, Paul; Senior Independent Director, London Stock Exchange Group plc, since 2014 (non-executive Director, since 2010); *b* 3 Feb. 1957; *s* of Ronald Joseph and Hilda Primrose Heiden; *m* 1979, Susan; one *s* one *d*. *Educ:* Stratford Grammar Sch.; Imperial Coll., London (BSc 1st cl. Hons Biol.). ARCS; ACA. Accountant, Peat Marwick Mitchell, 1979–84; Financial Controller: Mercury Communications, 1984–88; Hanson plc, 1988–92; Rolls-Royce: Finance Dir, Aerospace, 1992–97; Bd Dir, 1997–2002; Man. Dir, Industrial Businesses, 1997–99; Finance Dir, 1999–2002; Chief Exec., FKI plc, 2003–08; Chairman: Talaris Ltd, 2008–12; Intelligent Energy plc, 2012–17. Non-executive Director: Bunzl, 1999–2005; Filtrona, 2005–06; United Utilities plc, 2006–13; Meggitt plc, 2010–; Chm., A-Gas (Orb) Ltd, 2015–17. *Recreations:* golf, ski-ing, spectator sports. *Clubs:* Nottingham Golf (Hollinwell); Ratcliffe on Trent Golf; Loch Lomond Golf.

HEIGL, Peter Richard; HM Diplomatic Service, retired; Resident Deputy High Commissioner, Republic of Kiribati, 2004–06; *b* 21 Feb. 1943; *s* of late Joseph William Heigl and Violet Heigl (*née* Gatti); *m* 1965, Sally Lupton; three *s* one *d*. *Educ:* Worthing Technical High Sch. Min. of Power, 1963–66; Min. of Technology, 1966–70; DTI, 1970–74; FCO, 1974; served: Kuala Lumpur, 1974–78; Accra, 1978–81; FCO, 1981–84; 1st Sec., Riyadh, 1984–86; Consul (Commercial), Jedda, 1986–89; FCO, 1989–91; Dep. Head of Mission, Khartoum, 1991–93; Chargé, Phnom Penh, 1994; Dep. Head of Mission, Kathmandu, 1994–99; High Comr to the Bahamas, 1999–2003. *Recreations:* family, travel, swimming, reading, local history. *Address:* c/o Foreign and Commonwealth Office, King Charles Street, SW1A 2AH.

HEILBRON, Hilary Nora Burstein; QC 1987; *b* 2 Jan. 1949; *d* of Dr Nathaniel Burstein and Dame Rose Heilbron, DBE. *Educ:* Huyton College; Lady Margaret Hall, Oxford (MA). Called to the Bar, Gray's Inn, 1971; Bencher, 1995. DTI Inspector into Blue Arrow plc, 1989–91. Chairman: London Common Law and Commercial Bar Assoc., 1992–93; Jt Gen. Council of Bar and Law Soc. indep. working party into civil justice, 1993. Dir, The City Disputes Panel Ltd, 1994–2007 (Chm., 2006–07). Vice-Chm., Marshall Aid Commemoration Commn, 1998–2002; Member: Adv. Council, Centre for Dispute Resolution, 1996–2002; Civil Justice Council, 1998–2002; Bar Assoc. of NSW; Court, London Court of Internat. Arbitration, 2016–. *Publications:* A Practical Guide to International Arbitration in London, 2008; Rose Heilbron, Legal Pioneer of the 20th Century: inspiring advocate who became England's first woman judge, 2012. *Recreations:* travel, gardening. *Address:* Brick Court Chambers, 7–8 Essex Street, WC2R 3LD. *T:* (020) 7379 3550.

HEIM, Paul Emil, CMG 1988; Chairman, Taxation Disciplinary Board (formerly Tribunal), 2000–04 (Vice Chairman, Appeal Committee, 2004–08); *b* 23 May 1932; *s* of George Heim and Hedy Heim (*née* Herz); *m* 1962, Elizabeth, *er d* of late Lt-Col G. M. Allen, MBE; one *s* two *d*. *Educ:* Prince of Wales School, Nairobi; King's Coll., Univ. of Durham (LLB). Called to the Bar, Lincoln's Inn, 1955, Bencher, 1986. Dep. Registrar, Supreme Court of Kenya, then Sen. Dep. Registrar, Magistrate and Acting Registrar, and Hd, Judicial Dept (HMOCS), 1954–65, Reserve Police Officer, 1955–57; admitted Advocate, Supreme Court, 1959; Administrator, European Court of Human Rights, Strasbourg, 1965, European Commn of Human Rights, Strasbourg, 1966; Principal Administrator, Political Directorate, Council of Europe, 1967, Dep. Head, Private Office, 1969; Head of Div., then Dir, European Parlt, 1973–81; Registrar, European Court of Justice, 1982–88; Pres., Heads of Admin of EC Instns, 1986–88; Special Advr, European Court of Justice, 1988–89; a Chairman: Financial Services Tribunal, 1988–2002; Value Added Tax Tribunal, 1989–2003; Pres., FIMBRA Appeal Tribunals, 1990–2001; a Dep. Chm., PIA Appeal Tribunal, 1994–2002. Chm., European Law Gp, Lincoln's Inn, 1988–2008. Vis. Prof., Leicester Univ., 1988–2000; Hon. Res. Fellow, Univ. of Exeter, 1988–98. Chm., George Heim Meml Trust, 1998–; Dep. Chm., 1999–2009, Chm., 2009–14, Luxembourg Soc.; Chm., Langport Area Develt Trust (formerly Langport Forum), 2007–09 (Dep. Chm., 2001–06). Treas., Somerset Anne Frank Awards, 2013–16. Grand Officer, Order of Merit (Luxembourg), 1998. *Address:* Wearne Wyche, Langport, Somerset TA10 9AA.

HEIN, Prof. Jotun John; Professor of Bioinformatics, University of Oxford, and Fellow of University College, Oxford, since 2001; *b* Denmark, 19 July 1956; *s* of Piet Hein and Gerd Erikson; two *d*. *Educ:* Aarhus Univ. (Licentiate in Sci. 1990). Asst Prof., 1990–94, Associate Prof., 1994–2001, Aarhus Univ. *Recreations:* reading, golf, tennis, badminton. *Address:* Department of Statistics, University of Oxford, 24–29 St Giles', Oxford OX1 3LB. *T:* (01865) 272860.

HEINE, Prof. Volker, FRS 1974; Professor of Theoretical Physics, University of Cambridge, 1976–97; Fellow of Clare College, Cambridge, since 1960; *b* 19 Sept. 1930; *m* 1955, M. Daphne Hines; one *s* two *d*. *Educ:* Otago Univ. (MSc, DipHons); Cambridge Univ. (PhD). FInstP. Demonstrator, Cambridge Univ., 1958–63, Lectr 1963–70; Reader in Theoretical Physics, 1970–76. Vis. Prof., Univ. of Chicago, 1965–66; Vis. Scientist, Bell Labs, USA, 1970–71. For. Mem., Max-Planck Inst., Stuttgart, 1980–. Fellow, Amer. Phys. Soc., 1987. Maxwell Medal, Inst. of Physics, 1972; Royal Medal, Royal Soc., 1993; Paul Dirac Medal, Inst. of Physics, 1993; Max Born Medal, Inst. of Physics and German Physical Soc., 2001. *Publications:* Group Theory in Quantum Mechanics, 1960; (jtly) Solid State Physics Vol. 24, 1970, Vol. 35, 1980; articles in Proc. Royal Soc., Jl Physics, Physical Review, etc. *Address:* Cavendish Laboratory, 19 J. J. Thomson Avenue, Cambridge CB3 0HE.

HEINEY, Paul; freelance writer and broadcaster; *b* 20 April 1949; *s* of Norbert Wisniewski and Evelyn Mardlin; name changed to Heiney by Deed Poll, 1971; *m* 1980, Elizabeth Mary Purves, *qv*; one *d* (one *s* decd). *Educ:* Parson Cross Primary Sch., Sheffield; High Storrs Grammar Sch. for Boys. Stagehand, Birmingham Rep. Th., 1968; electrician, Mermaid Th., 1969; BBC: asst film recordist, 1969–71; Radio Humberside, 1971–74; television presenter, programmes include: That's Life!, 1978–82; In at the Deep End, 1982–85; Travel Show, 1984–87; Food and Drink, 1991; Watchdog, 2001–09; Trading Places, ITV, 1988–2000; Victorian Farming Year, ITV, 2002–05; Countrywise and Countrywise Kitchen, ITV, 2009–; BBC Radio, includes: reporter: Newsbeat, Radio 1, 1974–76; Today, Radio 4, 1976–78; Radio 2 (occasionally), 1984–96; End of the Line, Radio 4, 1993–94; A Year in Harness, Radio 4, 1996; Home Truths, 2005. Patron, Wolverstone Project, 2006–. Younger Brother, Trinity House, 2019–. Hon. DCL East Anglia, 2006. *Publications:* The Sailing Weekend Book, 1984 (Best Book of the Sea, King George's Fund for Sailors); The English and their Horses, 1987; In at the Deep End, 1989; Farming Times, 1993; Second Crop, 1994; George Soper's Horses, 1997; Ham and Pigs, 1998; Domino's Effect (novel), 1999; Golden Apples (novel), 1999; The Nuts and Bolts of Life, 2003; The Traditional Farming Year, 2004; Can Cows Walk Upstairs?, 2005; Maritime Britain, 2005; Do Cats Have Belly Buttons?, 2007; Farm Fatale, 2012; Can Crocodiles Cry, 2015; One Wild Song: a voyage in a lost son's wake, 2015. *Recreations:* sailing, ploughing with Suffolk Punches. *Address:* c/o Jo Gurnett, 7 Old Park Lane, W1K 1QR. *T:* (020) 7440 1850. *E:* pheiney@me.com. *Clubs:* Royal Cruising (Cdre, 2019–), Ocean Cruising; Suffolk Horse Society.

HEIS, Richard; Chief Restructuring Officer, Steinhoff International Holdings, since 2018; *b* Manchester, 26 May 1962; *s* of Jan and Valerie Ann Heis; *m* 1993, Elizabeth Anne Hill; two *s* one *d*. *Educ:* Stockport Grammar Sch.; Birmingham Univ. (LLB). Joined KPMG, 1983; auditor, London and Hong Kong, 1983–89; Restructuring and Insolvency Manager, London, 1989–97; Restructuring and Insolvency Partner, 1997–2017. Chair, Tech. Cttee, R3, 2007–10. Mem., Banking Liaison Panel, HM Treasury, 2009–17. Dir, Insol Internat., 2011–18. Liquidator: Barings Bank, 2001–05; New Millennium Experience Co., 2001–02; Supervisor, Marconi plc scheme, 2003; Administrator: Connaught plc, 2010–17; MF Global UK, 2011–; Alpari (UK), 2015–17. *Recreations:* golf, cycling, tennis, bridge, Cornwall. *Address:* Steinhoff International Holdings NV, 5th Floor Festival House, Jessop Avenue, Cheltenham GL50 3SH. *E:* richard.heis@steinhoff.co.uk. *Clubs:* Wilderness Golf, St Enodoc Golf.

HEISBOURG, François; Special Adviser, Fondation pour la Recherche Stratégique, Paris, since 2005 (Director, 2001–05); Senior Adviser (Europe), International Institute of Strategic Studies, since 2019 (Chairman, 2001–19); *b* 24 June 1949; *s* of late Georges Heisbourg and of Hélène Heisbourg (*née* Pinet); *m* 1989, Elyette, *d* of Georges Levy; two *s*. *Educ:* Landon School, Bethesda, Maryland; Collège Stanislas, Paris; Inst. d'Etudes Politiques, Paris; Ecole Nationale d'Administration, Paris. French Foreign Ministry: Asst to Head of Economics Dept, 1978; Mem., Policy Planning Staff, 1979; 1st Sec., French Mission to UN, NY, 1979–81; Diplomatic Adviser to Minister of Defence, 1981–84. Vice-Pres., Thomson SA, Paris, 1984–87; Dir, IISS, 1987–92; Sen. Vice-Pres., Matra Défense-Espace, Paris, 1992–98; Hd, French Interministerial gp on study of internat. relations and strategic affairs, 1999–2000; Prof., Inst. d'Etudes Politiques, Paris, 1999–2001. Chm., Geneva Centre for Security Policy, 1998–2018. Member: Presidential White Paper Commn on Defence and Nat. Security, 2007–08, 2012–13; Internat. Commn on Nuclear Non-proliferation and Disarmament, 2008–10. Numerous foreign orders. *Publications:* Emiliano Zapata et la Révolution mexicaine, 1978; (with P. Boniface) La Puce, les Hommes et la Bombe, 1986; (contrib.) The Conventional Defence of Europe, 1986; (contrib.) Conventional Arms Control and East-West Security, 1989; (ed) The Changing Strategic Landscape, 1989; (ed) The Strategic Implications of Change in the Soviet Union, 1990; (contrib.) The Shape of the New Europe, 1992; (contrib.) Western Europe and the Gulf War, 1992; Les Volontaires de l'An 2000, 1995; Warfare, 1997; European Defence: making it work, 2000; Hyperterrorisme: la nouvelle guerre, 2001; La Fin de l'Occident? L'Amérique, l'Europe et le Moyen-Orient, 2005; (with J. L. Marret) Le Terrorisme en France Aujourd'hui, 2006; L'Épaisseur du Monde, 2007; Iran: le choix des armes?, 2007; Après Al Qaida, 2009; Vainqueurs et Vaincus, 2010; (ed) Les armes nucléaires ont-elles un avenir?, 2011; Espionnage et renseignement: le vrai dossier, 2012; La Fin du Rêve Européen, 2013; Secrètes Histoires, 2015; Comment perdre la guerre contre le terrorisme, 2016; Cet étrange nazi qui a sauvé mon père, 2019; contribs to internat. jls. *Recreations:* hiking, old atlas collecting. *E:* f.heisbourg@frstrategie.org. *Club:* Travellers (Paris).

HEISER, Sir Terence Michael, (Sir Terry), GCB 1992 (KCB 1987; CB 1984); Permanent Secretary, Department of the Environment, 1985–92; *b* 24 May 1932; *s* of David and Daisy Heiser; *m* 1957, Kathleen Mary Waddle; one *s* one *d*. *Educ:* Grafton Road Primary Sch., Dagenham; London Evacuee Sch., Sunninghill, Berks; Windsor County Boys' Sch., Berks; Birkbeck Coll., Univ. of London; BA (Hons English). Served in RAF, 1950–52; joined Civil Service 1949, served with Colonial Office, Min. of Works, Min. of Housing and Local Govt; Principal Private Sec. to Sec. of State for the Environment, 1975–76; Under Secretary: Housing Directorate, 1976–79; Local Govt Finance Directorate, 1979–81; Dep. Sec., DoE, 1981–85. Non-exec. Director: Abbey National plc, 1992–2001; Sainsbury plc, 1992–2000; Wessex Water plc, 1993–98. Mem. Bd, PIA, 1994–2000; Mem., Senior Salaries Review Bd, Office of Manpower Econs, 1998–2003. Chm., Gen. Advice Council, BBC, 1992–96. Mem., Adv. Panel on Spoliation, DCMS, 2000–18. Mem., Exec. Cttee, 1993–2002, Southern Region Cttee, 2003–04, Nat. Trust; Mem., V&A Theatre Mus. Cttee, 2004–06 (Trustee, V&A Mus., 1993–2003); Trustee, Prince of Wales Phoenix Trust, 1996–2001. Governor, Birkbeck Coll., London, 1990–2002; Mem. Council, Sussex Univ., 1999–2008. Freeman, City of London, 1990. Hon. Fellow, Birkbeck Coll., London, 1988. Hon. DLitt Bradford, 1988. *Recreations:* reading, walking, talking. *Club:* Garrick.

HELAISSI, Sheikh Abdulrahman Al-, Hon. GCVO; retired; Saudi Arabian Ambassador to the Court of St James's, 1966–76; *b* 24 July 1922. *Educ:* Universities of Cairo and London. Secretary to Embassy, London, 1947–54; Under-Sec., Min. of Agriculture, 1954–57; Head of Delegn to FAO, 1955–61; Ambassador to Sudan, 1957–60; Representative to UN, and to various confs concerned with health and agriculture; Delegate to Conf. of Non-aligned Nations, Belgrade, 1961; Ambassador: Italy and Austria, 1961–66; UK and Denmark (concurrently), 1966–76. Versed in Islamic Religious Law. *Publications:* The Rehabilitation of the Bedouins, 1959. *Address:* PO Box No 8062, Riyadh-11482, Saudi Arabia.

HELE, Desmond George K.; *see* King-Hele.

HELFGOTT, Sir Ben, Kt 2018; MBE 2000; *b* Pabianice, Poland, 22 Nov. 1929; *s* of late Moishe Helfgott and Sarah Helfgott; *m* 1966, Arza; three *s*. Holocaust concentration camp survivor. Weightlifting: gold medal, lightweight class, World Maccabiah Games, 1950, 1953, 1957; British Champion, 11 stone, 1954, lightweight, 1955, 1956, 1958; bronze medal, Commonwealth Games, Cardiff, 1958; Captain, British weightlifting team, Olympic Games, Melbourne, 1956, Rome, 1960; Member, British weightlifting team: World Championship, Vienna, 1954, Munich, 1955, Stockholm, 1958, Warsaw, 1959; World Fest. of Youth, Warsaw, 1955, Moscow, 1957. Company dir, 1965–80. Chairman: '45 Aid Soc. Holocaust Survivors, 1963–2016 (Pres., 2016–); Polin - Inst. of Polish Jewish Studies, 1994–; Member, Executive: Central British Fund, 1965–84 (Jt Treas., 1976–84); Weiner Liby, 1978–2014; Dep., Bd of Deputies of British Jews, 1982– (Chm., Yad Vashem Cttee, 1985–2005); Trustee: Bd of Mgt, Holocaust Educn Trust, 1988–2018 (Patron, 2018–); Holocaust Meml Day Trust, 2005–11 (Treas., 2005–08; Pres., 2012–); Founding Patron and Mem., Adv. Gp, Perm. Holocaust Exhibn, Imperial War Mus., 1995–; Mem. Exec. of Negotiating and Allocations Cttees, 1995–, Mem. Leadership Council, 2014–, Conf. on Jewish Material Claims Against Germany; Member: Exec., World Confedn of Holocaust Survivor Orgns, 1998–; Internat. Holocaust Remembrance Alliance (formerly Task Force for Internat. Cooperation on Holocaust Educn, Remembrance and Res.), 1998–; Prime Minister's Holocaust Commn, 2013–; Pres., Yad Vashem UK Foundn, 2005–; Mem. Assembly of Founders, Foundn for Preservation of Jewish Heritage in Poland, 2009–. Freeman, City of London, 2015. Hon. Fellow, Univ. of Cumbria, 2014. DUniv Southampton, 2006; Hon. DLit Inst. of Educn, London, 2012. Lifetime Achievement Award, Jewish News, 2012; UK Points of Life Award, 2014; Lifetime Dedication Award, Holocaust Educn Trust, 2018. Comdr's Cross, Order of Merit (Poland), 2005 (Knight's Cross, 1994). *E:* benhelfgott@gmail.com.

**HELIĆ, Baroness** *cr* 2014 (Life Peer), of Millbank in the City of Westminster; **Arminka Helić;** Chief of Staff, 2006–15 and Senior Special Adviser, 2010–15 to Rt Hon. William Hague, MP; *b* Bosnia-Herzegovina; adopted British nationality, 2002. Expert on foreign, defence and security policy. Freelance consultant, BBC and ITV, 1993–94; Internat. Affairs and Defence Advr, H of C, 1997–98; Advr to Shadow Sec. of State for Foreign Affairs and for Defence, 1998–2000; Risk Analyst, MMC Ventures Ltd, 2001–02; Sen. Special Advr to Shadow Sec. of State for Foreign Affairs, 2002–05. Architect of Preventing Sexual Violence Initiative, 2012–; Member: Adv. Bd on Preventing Sexual Violence Initiative, FCO, 2015–; Adv. Bd, Centre for Women, Peace and Security, LSE, 2015–; Bd, Trust Fund for Victims, Internat. Criminal Ct, 2015–. Mem., Internat. Relns Cttee, H of L, 2016–. *Address:* House of Lords, SW1A 0PW.

**HELLARD, Rebecca Jane;** Director of Finance and Resources, Liverpool City Council, 2012–18; *b* 11 July 1966; *d* of Hugh Somerled Matheson Macdonald and Sarah Jane Macdonald (*née* Tuffs); one *s* one *d*. *Educ:* Cambridge Coll. of Arts and Technol. (BA Hons Econs). ACCA 1995. Philips Financial Services, 1991–94; Manager, PricewaterhouseCoopers, 1994–97; Breckland Council: Finance and Performance Manager, 1997–99; Finance Dir, 1999–2002; Dep. Chief Exec., 2002–04; Chief Exec., 2004–06; Strategic Dir Corporate Services, Bradford CC, 2007–12. *Recreations:* sports - gym, running, swimming.

**HELLAWELL, Keith,** QPM 1990; writer and broadcaster; Expert Adviser to Home Secretary on international drugs issues, 2001–02; Director, Huddersfield Rugby League Club, since 2002; *b* 18 May 1942; *s* of Douglas Hellawell and Ada Alice Hellawell (*née* Battye); *m* 1963, Brenda Hey; one *s* two *d*. *Educ:* Kirkburton Sec. Mod. Sch.; Dewsbury Tech. Coll.; Barnsley Coll. of Mining; Inst. of Criminol., Cambridge Univ.; London Univ. (LLB 1972); Cranfield Inst. of Tech. (MSc 1982); Police Staff Coll. Huddersfield Borough Police, 1962; seconded to Home Office, 1975–78, incl. service in NI; Asst Chief Constable, W Yorks Police, 1983; Dep. Chief Constable, Humberside Police, 1985; Chief Constable: Cleveland Police, 1990; W Yorks Police, 1993–98; UK Anti-Drugs Co-ordinator, 1998–2001. Advr, Crimestoppers Trust, 1994–. Chairman: Catapult Presentation plc, 2001; Sterience Ltd; Howells Associates; Goldshield Gp plc, 2006–09; Sports Direct, 2009–18; Smart Witness Ltd, 2016–; non-executive Director: Evans of Leeds plc, 1998–99; Universal Vehicles Gp plc, 2001; Dalkia plc, 2002–06; Mortice Ltd, 2010–. Member: Adv. Council on Misuse of Drugs, 1994–98; Bd, Northern Counties Housing Assoc. Ltd, 1996–98; St John's Council, W Yorks, 1983–85 and 1993–; Council, NSPCC (Trustee, 1993–2000; Chm., Services to Children's Cttee, 1996–); Trustee, Children in Crisis. Mem., Editl Bd, Forensic Medicine Jl, 1996–. Hon. LLD Bradford, 1998; Hon. DSSc Leeds, 1998; Hon. DCL Huddersfield, 1998. OStJ 1996. *Publications:* The Outsider (autobiog.), 2002. *Recreations:* design, gardening, reading, sport.

**HELLER, Angela Mary;** *see* Flowers, A. M.

**HELLER, Lucy Lauris;** Chief Executive Officer, ARK, since 2012 (Managing Director, ARK Schools, since 2004); *b* London, 8 Feb. 1959; *d* of late Lukas Heller and Caroline Carter; *m* 1990, Sir Charles (Abraham Grierson) Elton, Bt, *qv* (marr. diss. 2007); one *s* one *d*; partner, Sir Adrian (Frederick Melhuish) Smith, *qv*. *Educ:* Hampstead Comp. Sch.; Lady Margaret Hall, Oxford (BA Hons PPE). Banker, Bankers Trust, 1981–87; Man. Dir, Capital Mkts Gp, Manufacturers Hanover, 1987–90; Gp Treas., Booker, 1990–95; Exec. Chm., Verso, 1995–98; Gen. Manager, The Observer, Guardian Media Gp, 1998–99; Jt Man. Dir, TSL Education, 2000–03. Member, Board: Standard Life Foundn, 2017–; Educn Endowment Fund, 2018–. Mem., Marshall Aid Commn, 2002–09. Mem. Bd, Bush Th., 1989–2005. *Publications:* Euro Commercial Paper, 1988. *Address:* ARK, 65 Kingsway, WC2B 6TD. *T:* (020) 3116 0710. *E:* lucy.heller@arkonline.org.

**HELLER, Sir Michael Aron,** Kt 2013; FCA; Chairman: London & Associated Properties plc, since 1977 (Director, since 1971); Bisichi Mining plc, since 1981 (Director, since 1972); *b* London, 15 July 1936; *s* of Simon and Nettie Heller; *m* 1965, Morven Livingstone; two *s* one *d*. *Educ:* Harrogate Grammar Sch.; St Catharine's Coll., Cambridge (BA 1958; MA 1963; Fellow Commoner). ACA 1961, FCA 1971. Exec. Dir, Kenyon Son & Craven Ltd, 1961–68; Exec. Dir, 1968–70, non-exec. Dir, 1971–91, United Biscuit (Hldgs) plc; non-exec. Dir, 1965–2018, non-exec. Chm., 1977–2018, Electronic Data Processing plc. Dep. Chm., Centre for Policy Studies, 1993–. Hon. Fellow, UCL, 2007. Hon. Dr: Technion, Haifa, 2010; Sheffield Hallam, 2010. *Recreations:* walking, collecting modern British and French post-Impressionist paintings, opera, ballet. *Address:* 24 Bruton Place, W1J 6NE. *T:* (020) 7415 5000. *E:* M.Heller@lap.co.uk. *Club:* Royal Automobile.

**HELLINGA, Dr Lotte,** FBA 1990; Secretary, Consortium of European Research Libraries, 1994–2002; a Deputy Keeper, British Library, 1985–95 (Acting Director, Humanities and Social Sciences, 1990–91); *b* 9 Sept. 1932; *d* of Arie Querido and Catharina Geertruida Querido (*née* Nagtegaal); *m* Wytze Hellinga (*d* 1985); one *s*. *Educ:* Univ. of Amsterdam. Lectr, then Sen. Lectr, Univ. of Amsterdam, 1967–76; Asst Keeper, British Liby, 1976–85. Vice Pres., Bibliographical Soc., 1996–2010. Correspondent, Royal Netherlands Acad. of Scis, 1989–. Gutenberg Preis, Mainz, 1989; Gold Medal, Bibliographical Soc., 2009; Bernard Breslauer Prize, Internat. League of Antiquarian Booksellers, 2010. *Publications:* The Fifteenth Century Printing Types of the Low Countries, 1966; Caxton in Focus, 1982 (trans. Japanese 1991); (ed jtly) The Cambridge History of the Book in Britain, vol. III, 1999; Impresores, editores, correctores y cajistas Siglo XV, 2006 (trans. Italian, as Fare un libro nel Quattrocento, 2015); Catalogue of Books printed in the XVth century now in the British Library, vol. XI (England), 2007; Printing in England in the Fifteenth Century, 2009; William Caxton and Early Printing in England, 2010 (trans. Japanese 2013); Texts in Transit: manuscripts to proof and print in the fifteenth century, 2014; Incunabula in Transit: people and trade, 2018; numerous articles in learned jls. *Address:* 40A Canonbury Square, N1 2AW. *T:* (020) 7359 2083.

**HELLIWELL, Prof. John Richard,** DPhil, DSc; FInstP, FRSC, FRSB; Professor of Structural Chemistry, University of Manchester, 1989–2012, now Emeritus; *b* 19 Sept. 1953; *s* of Henry Smith Helliwell and Amy (*née* Southam); *m* 1978, Madeleine Berry; one *s* one *d* (and one *s* decd). *Educ:* Ossett Sch.; Univ. of York (BSc 1st cl. Hons Physics 1974; DSc 1996); Balliol Coll., Univ. of Oxford (DPhil Molecular Biophysics 1978). CPhys, FInstP 1986; CChem, FRSC 1995; CBiol, FRSB (FIBiol 1998). MRC Res. Asst and Jun. Res. Fellow, Linacre Coll., Oxford, 1978; Lectr in Biophysics, Keele Univ., jtly with SERC Daresbury Lab., 1979–83; SSO, then PSO, SERC Daresbury Lab., 1983–85; Lectr in Physics, York Univ., 1985–88; part-time with SERC, subseq. CCLRC, then STFC, Daresbury Lab., 1985–93, 2001–06, Hon. Scientist, 2007–; CCLRC Dir of Synchrotron Radiation Sci., Daresbury Lab., 2002. Vis. Res. Scholar, Cornell Univ., 1994; Visiting Professor: Univ. of Chicago, 1994; of Crystallography, Birkbeck Coll., London Univ., 2002–. Leader, UK Delegn, World Congress of Biophysics, New Delhi, 1999; Internat. Union of Crystallography Rep. to Internat. Council of Scientific and Tech. Inf., 2005–14, and to Cttee on Data for Sci. and Technol., 2012–; Chm. and Mem., Sci. Adv. Cttee, Spanish Nat. Synchrotron 'ALBA', 2010–14; Chairman: ALBA Beamtime Panel, 2011–14; Eur. Spallation Neutron Source Neutron Macromolecular Crystallography Sci. and Tech. Adv. Panel, 2013–. Mem., Open Res. Data Task Force, 2017–. Conference Lectures: Yugoslav-Italian Crystallographic Assoc., 1989; Soc. of Crystallographers of Australia, 1994 (1987 Fellow (Hon.), 1994); British Crystallographic Assoc., 1995; 2nd Internat. Conf. on Life Science, Japan, 1996; Dame Kathleen Lonsdale Meml, British Crystallographic Assoc., 2011; other Lectures: Ilyas Haneef Meml, Univ. of Leeds, 1993; Herzenberg Symposium, Yale Univ., 1995; Chem. Dept Dedication, Univ. of Toledo, 1998; K. Banerjee Meml, and Silver Medal, Indian Assoc. for Cultivation of Sci., Calcutta, 2000; 150th Anniv. W. L. Bragg, Univ. of Manchester, 2001; Weizmann Inst., Israel, 2002; Royal Instn, 2004; US Nat. Liby of Medicine, Bethesda, 2006. Transactions Symposium Orgnr, Amer. Crystallographic Assoc., 1999; Chm. of Prog. Cttee, British Crystallographic Assoc. Annual Conf. 2015. Mem., Gen. Assembly, Univ. of Manchester, 2004– (Mem. Court, UMIST, 1996–2004). Pres., Eur. Crystallographic Assoc., 2006–09; Fellow, Amer. Crystallographic Assoc., 2015. Corresp. Mem., Royal Acad. of Scis and Arts of Barcelona, 2015; Hon. Member: Nat. Inst. of Chem., Slovenia, 1997–; British Biophysical Soc., 2016; British Crystallographic Assoc., 2019. Jt Main Ed., Jl Synchrotron Radiation, 1994–99; Editor-in-Chief, Internat. Union of Crystallography's Jls, 1996–2005; Co-Editor: Jl Applied Crystallography, 1995–2014; Crystallography Reviews, 2006–. Patterson Award, Amer. Crystallographic Assoc., 2014; Max Perutz Prize, Eur. Crystallographic Assoc., 2015. *Publications:* Macromolecular Crystallography with Synchrotron Radiation, 1992; (ed jtly) Time-resolved Macromolecular Crystallography, 1992; (ed jtly) Synchrotron Radiation in the Biosciences, 1994; (ed jtly) Time-resolved Diffraction, 1997; (jtly) Macromolecular Crystallization and Crystal Perfection, 2010; Perspectives in Crystallography, 2015; Skills for a Scientific Life, 2016; The Whys of a Scientific Life, 2018; original res. papers and reviews in scientific jls. *Recreations:* family, cycling (Mem., Cycle Touring Club). *Address:* c/o School of Chemistry, University of Manchester, Oxford Road, Manchester M13 9PL. *E:* john.helliwell@manchester.ac.uk.

**HELLYER, Bartle Grimston, (Bart);** Vice Lord-Lieutenant of Rutland, since 2018; *b* Bishop Burton, 30 Oct. 1950; *s* of Andrew Hellyer and Diana Hellyer; *m* 1996, Rebecca Hemsley (*d* 2004). *Educ:* Uppingham Sch.; Univ. of Exeter (LLB 1973). Admitted solicitor, 1976; articled clerk, then Asst Solicitor, Allen & Overy, 1974–76; Asst Solicitor, Roythorne & Co., 1977–78; self-employed as solicitor/legal expert witness for severe personal injury claims, 1979–2010. Founding Mem., Spinal Injuries Assoc., 1974– (Bd Mem. and Legal Advr, 1974–79; Chm., 2005–08). Trustee: Friends of Launde Abbey, 2013–; Peterborough Cathedral Develt Trust, 2014–. Mem., High Sheriffs' Assoc. Freeman, City of London, 2013; Liveryman, Framework Knitters' Co., 2013. High Sheriff, 2012, DL, 2014, Rutland. *Recreations:* thoroughbred horse breeding and racing (Member, Thoroughbred Breeders' Association), concerts, theatre, cricket, countryside preservation. *Address:* Rowells Lodge, Ridlington, Oakham LE15 9AH. *T:* (01572) 820260, 07850 934610, *Fax:* (01572) 820270. *E:* bgh@globalnet.co.uk. *Club:* Army and Navy.

**HELLYER, Hon. Paul Theodore;** PC (Canada) 1957; FRSA 1973; Syndicated Columnist, Toronto Sun, 1974–84; *b* Waterford, Ont, Canada, 6 Aug. 1923; *s* of A. S. Hellyer and Lulla M. Anderson; *m* 1st, 1945, Ellen Jean (*d* 2004), *d* of Henry Ralph, Toronto, Ont; two *s* one *d*; 2nd, 2005, Sandra Dorothy Bussiere. *Educ:* Waterford High Sch., Ont; Curtiss-Wright Techn. Inst. of Aeronautics, Glendale, Calif; University of Toronto (BA). Fleet Aircraft Mfg Co., Fort Erie, Ont. Wartime service, RCAF and Cdn Army. Propr Mari-Jane Fashions, Toronto, 1945–56; Treas., Curran Hall Ltd, Toronto, 1950 (Pres., 1951–62). Elected to House of Commons, 1949; re-elected, 1953; Parly Asst to Hon. Ralph Campney, Minister of Nat. Defence, 1956; Associate Minister of Nat. Defence, 1957; defeated in gen. elections of June 1957 and March 1958; re-elected to House of Commons in by-election Dec. 1958 and again re-elected June 1962, April 1963, Nov. 1965, June 1968, and Oct. 1972; defeated gen. election July 1974; Minister of National Defence, 1963–67; Minister of Transport, 1967–69, and Minister i/c Housing, 1968–69; resigned 1969 on question of principle relating to housing. Chm., Federal Task Force on Housing and Urban Develt, 1968. Served as a Parly Rep. to NATO under both L and C administrations. Joined Parly Press Gallery, Oct. 1974. Distinguished visitor, York Univ., 1969–70. Founder and Leader, Action Canada party, 1971; joined Progressive Cons. Party, 1972; Candidate for leadership of Progressive Cons. Party, Feb. 1976; re-joined Liberal Party, Nov. 1982, resigned Dec. 1996; Leader, Canadian Action Party, 1997–2004. Exec. Dir, The Canada Uni Assoc., 1991–92. *Publications:* Agenda: a Plan for Action, 1971; Exit Inflation, 1981; Jobs for All—Capitalism on Trial, 1984; Canada at the Crossroads, 1990; Damn the Torpedoes, 1990; Funny Money: a common sense alternative to mainline economics, 1994; Surviving the Global Financial Crisis: the economics of hope for Generation X, 1996; Arundel Lodge: a little bit of old Muskoka, 1996; The Evil Empire: globalization's darker side, 1997; Stop: think, 1999; Goodbye Canada, 2001; One Big Party: to keep Canada independent, 2003; Light at the End of the Tunnel: a survival plan for the human species, 2010; A Miracle in Waiting: economics that make sense, 2010; The Money Mafia: a world in crisis, 2014; Hope Restored: an autobiography, 2018. *Recreations:* philately, music. *Address:* Suite 506, 65 Harbour Square, Toronto, ON M5J 2L4, Canada. *Club:* National.

**HELM, James Ernest;** Director of Communications, Metropolitan Police Service, since 2018; *b* Guisborough, N Yorks, 3 Sept. 1968; *s* of Ernest Helm and Marion Helm; *m* 2000, Charlotte Coleman-Smith (*d* 2018); three *s*. *Educ:* Stokesley Sch., N Yorks; Trinity Hall, Cambridge (BA Social and Pol Sci. 1991; MA). Voluntary teacher, South Africa, 1992; reporter, Newcastle Evening Chronicle, 1992–94; BBC News: correspondent, producer, presenter, 1994–2007; Dublin Corresp., 2002–07; PR consultant, Blue Rubicon, and freelance writer, 2007–09; Client Dir, COI, 2009–10; Dir of Communications, DFID, 2010–16; Partner, Portland Communications, 2016–18. Mem., Stokesley Agricl Soc. *Recreations:* family time, playing and watching sport esp. Middlesbrough FC, walking. *W:* www.twitter.com/jameshelm1.

**HELM, Marie Theresa C.;** *see* Conte-Helm.

**HELME, Nicola Margaret;** *see* Padfield, N. M.

**HELME, Philippa Ann;** Principal Clerk, Table Office, House of Commons, since 2014; *b* Binfield, Berks, 27 Aug. 1960; *d* of late Wing Comdr James Michael Helme, DFC, AFC and Diana Wentworth Helme (*née* Howitt); *m* 1988, Robin Stephen Galliver; two *s* three *d*. *Educ:* Sherborne Sch. for Girls; St Anne's Coll., Oxford (BA 1981). House of Commons, 1983–: Sec. to Chm. of Ways and Means, 1992–95; Clerk: Welsh Affairs Cttee, 1995–2000; Sci. and Technol. Cttee, 2000–02; on secondment as Parly Advr, Cabinet Office, 2002–05; Clerk, Defence Cttee, 2005–07; Hd, Office of the Chief Exec., 2008–10; Deputy Hd, Cttee Office, 2010–14. Trustee, Industry and Parliament Trust, 2017–. *Address:* House of Commons, SW1A 0AA. *T:* (020) 7219 3312. *E:* helmep@parliament.uk.
*See also* N. M. Padfield.

**HELMER, Roger;** Member for East Midlands, European Parliament, 1999–2017 (C, 1999–2012, UK Ind, 2012–17); *b* 25 Jan. 1944; *s* of Charles Henry Helmer and Nellie Ethel Helmer; *m* 1st, 1967, Veronica Logan (marr. diss. 1984); one *s* one *d*; 2nd, 1987, Sara Thomas (*née* Winterbottom). *Educ:* King Edward VI Sch., Southampton; Churchill Coll., Cambridge (BA, MA). Various mkting and gen. mgt posts with major multinationals, Procter & Gamble, Readers' Digest, and Guinness Plc, UK and overseas, especially E and SE Asia, 1965–98. Hon. Chm., Freedom Assoc., 2007–10. *Recreation:* walking the dog.

**HELTAY, Laszlo Istvan;** Founder and Music Director, Academy of St Martin in the Fields Chorus, 1975–99; *b* Budapest, 5 Jan. 1930; *s* of Laszlo Heltay and Gizella Somogy; *m* 1964, Hilary Nicholson. *Educ:* Franz Liszt Acad. of Music, Budapest (MA); Merton Coll., Oxford (MLitt; Hon. Fellow, 1997). Associate Conductor, NZBC Symphony Orchestra and Dir, NZ Opera Co., 1964–67; Conductor, Phoenix Opera Co., 1970–73; Founder and Music Dir, Brighton Fest. Chorus, 1968–95; Dir of Music, Royal Choral Soc., 1985–95; Music Dir, Chorus of Radio Televisión Española SA, Madrid, 1997–2002. Has conducted major orchestras including: Philharmonia, Royal Philharmonic, London Philharmonic, Dresden Philharmonic, Dallas Symphony, Budapest Philharmonic; also radio orchestras and choirs. Choral music for film, Amadeus, 1984. Has made recordings. Hon. DMus Sussex, 1995. Internat. Kodaly Medal, 1982. *Recreations:* chess, reading, dog-walking.

**HELY-HUTCHINSON,** family name of **Earl of Donoughmore.**

**HELY HUTCHINSON, Hon. Timothy Mark,** CBE 2019; Group Chief Executive, Hachette UK (formerly Chief Executive, Hachette Livre UK), 2004–17; *b* 26 Oct. 1953; *s* of Earl of Donoughmore, *qv* and late Sheila (*née* Parsons). *Educ:* Eton Coll. (Oppidan Schol.); Magdalen Coll., Oxford (William Doncaster Schol.; MA Mod. Langs and Phil.). Various appts, Macmillan Publishers, 1975–82; Managing Director: Macdonald & Co. (Publishers) Ltd, 1982–86; Headline Book Publishing PLC, 1986–93; Chief Exec., Hodder Headline Ltd, 1993–2004. Director: WH Smith plc, 1999–2004; Inflexion plc, 2000–03; Chm., WH Smith News, 2001–04. Dir, Publishers Assoc., 1998–2004. Venturer of the Year Award, Brit. Venture Capital Assoc., 1990. Chevalier de la Legion d'Honneur (France). *Recreations:* opera, horse-racing, bridge. *Address:* Scatterford, Newland, Glos GL16 8NG. *Club:* Athenæum.

**HEMANS, Simon Nicholas Peter,** CMG 1992; CVO 1983; HM Diplomatic Service, retired; Partner, Cranmore Co., 1997–2001; *b* 19 Sept. 1940; *s* of late Brig. Peter Rupert Hemans, CBE, and Margaret Estelle Hemans (*née* Melsome); *m* 1970, Ursula Martha Naef; three *s* one *d*. *Educ:* Sherborne; London School of Economics (BScEcon). Joined Foreign Office, 1964; British Embassy, Moscow, 1966–68; FO, 1968–69; Dep. Commissioner, Anguilla, March–Oct. 1969; FO, 1969–71; UK Mission to UN, New York, 1971–75; British Embassy, Budapest, 1975–79; FO, 1979–81; Dep. High Comr, Nairobi, 1981–84; Head of Chancery, Moscow, 1985–87; Head of Soviet Dept, FCO, 1987–90; Asst Under-Sec. of State (Africa), FCO, 1990–92; Ambassador, Ukraine, 1992–95; High Comr to Kenya, 1995–97. *Publications:* trans., Savchuk, The Streets of Kiev, 1996. *Recreation:* travel. *Address:* 73 Cranmore Lane, Aldershot, Hants GU11 3AP.

**HEMERY, David Peter,** CBE 2003 (MBE 1969); DL; Founder and President, 21st Century Legacy, since 2007; *b* 18 July 1944; *s* of Peter Ronald Bentley Hemery and Eileen Beatrice Price; *m* 1981, Vivian Mary Bruford; two *s*. *Educ:* Boston Univ. (BSc Internat. Business 1968; DEd Social Psychology 1984); St Catherine's Coll., Oxford (CertEd 1970); Harvard Univ. (MEd 1972). Commonwealth Games: Gold Medal, 110m Hurdles, 1966, 1970; Captain, England Team, 1970; Olympic Games: Gold Medal, 400m Hurdles, 1968 (World Record); Bronze Medal, 400m Hurdles, 1972; Silver Medal, 4×400m, 1972. Teacher, Coach and Housemaster, Millfield Sch., 1970–71 and 1972–73; Dir, Sobell Sports Centre, 1973–75; Teacher and Coach, Boston Univ., 1976–83; coaching course for Nat. Coaching Foundn, 1983–85; mgt trng. Mem., Nat. Cttee, 1999–, and Exec., 2001–15 (Vice Chm., 2004–15; Life Vice Pres., 2015), BOA; Pres., UK Athletics, 1998–2002; Chm., Confedn of British Sport, 2006–08. Dir, Developing Potential Ltd, 1997–2010; Dep. Chm., Performance Consultants Internat. Ltd, 2006–11. Pres., Marlborough Jr AC, 2003–. Coach and Advr, sch. to internat. level; wrote prog. for schs, Be the Best You Can Be!, secondary version, 2008, primary version, 2011. Patron, British Assoc. of Sport and Exercise Medicine, 2009–. DL Wilts, 2016. Eur. Olympic Laurel Award, Eur. Olympic Cttee, 2011. *Publications:* Another Hurdle (autobiog.), 1975; The Pursuit of Sporting Excellence, 1986, 2nd edn as Sporting Excellence: what makes a champion, 1991; Athletics in Action, 1987; Winning without Drugs, 1989; How to Help Children Find the Champion Within Themselves, 2005. *Recreations:* family, sport, cycling, walking, gardening, human potential, spiritual understanding. *Address:* White Acre, Fyfield, Marlborough, Wilts SN8 1PX. *T:* (01672) 861676, 07866 459336.

**HEMINGFORD, 3rd Baron** *cr* 1943, of Watford; **Dennis Nicholas Herbert;** Deputy Chief Executive, Westminster Press, 1992–95 (Editorial Director, 1974–92); *b* 25 July 1934; *s* of 2nd Baron Hemingford and Elizabeth McClare (*d* 1979), *d* of Col J. M. Clark, Haltwhistle, Northumberland; *S* father, 1982; known professionally as Nicholas Herbert; *m* 1958, Jennifer Mary Toresen Bailey (OBE 1997), DL (*d* 2018), *d* of F. W. Bailey, Harrogate; one *s* three *d*. *Educ:* Oundle Sch.; Clare Coll., Cambridge (MA). Reuters Ltd, 1956–61; The Times: Asst Washington Corresp., 1961–65; Middle East Corresp., 1965–68; Dep. Features Editor, 1968–70; Editor, Cambridge Evening News, 1970–74. Vice-Pres., Guild of British Newspaper Editors, 1979, Pres., 1980–81. Mem. Bd, Assoc. of British Editors (Hon. Sec., 1985–95), 1985–95. Member: Council, Europa Nostra, 1999–2005; Culture Cttee, UK Commn, UNESCO, 2000–04; Council, Friends of British Library, 2005–11 and 2012–18; Council, U3A, Cambridge, 2010–12; Chm., East Anglia Regl Cttee, Nat. Trust, 1990–2000. Pres., Huntingdonshire Family History Soc., 1985–2019. Trustee: Bell Educnl Trust, 1985–90; Ely Cathedral Restoration Trust, 1993–2014. (Jtly) Self Publisher of Year Award, 2010. *Publications:* Successive Journeys: a family in four continents, 2008 (First Prize, non-fiction, Self Publishing Awards, David St John Thomas Charitable Trust and Writing Mag., 2010). *Heir: s* Hon. Christopher Dennis Charles Herbert [*b* 4 July 1973; *m* 2009, Chey Louise Fabing, *o d* of Mrs Anne Fabing; one *s* one *d*]. *Address:* The Coach House, 4 Common Lane, Hemingford Abbots, Huntingdon PE28 9AN. *T:* (01480) 466234.

*See also Lady Goodhart, H. T. Moggridge.*

**HEMINGWAY, Prof. Janet,** CBE 2012; PhD; FRS 2011; FMedSci; Professor of Insect Molecular Biology and Director, Liverpool School of Tropical Medicine, University of Liverpool, since 2001; *b* 13 June 1957; *d* of Brian Hemingway and Mollie Hemingway; one *d*. *Educ:* Sheffield Univ. (BSc 1st cl. Genetics); LSHTM, London Univ. (PhD); Hon. Fellow 2017). Lectr, Univ. of California, Riverside, 1981–82; MRC Res. Fellow, 1982–84, Royal Soc. Jun. Res. Fellow and Sen. Lectr, 1984–94, LSHTM; Prof. of Molecular Entomology, Cardiff Univ., 1994–2001. CEO, Gates Foundn Innovative Vector Control Consortium, 2005–14; Sen. Tech. Advr on Neglected Tropical Diseases to Bill and Melinda Gates Foundn, 2015–. Foreign Mem., NAS, USA, 2009. FMedSci 2006. Hon. FRCP 2008. Hon. DSc: Sheffield, 2009; Warwick, 2014; Chester, 2016. Sci. and Technol. Award, Welsh Woman of the Year, 2000; Public service, BT Merseyside Woman of the Year 2003. *Publications:* over 280 articles in scientific jls. *Recreations:* breaking and riding Arabian horses, squash, tennis, ski-ing, reading. *Address:* Liverpool School of Tropical Medicine, Pembroke Place, Liverpool L3 5QA. *E:* janet.hemingway@lstmed.ac.uk.

**HEMINGWAY, Wayne Andrew,** MBE 2006; Co-Founder and Partner, HemingwayDesign, since 1999; Co-Founder, Vintage Festival, since 2009; *b* 19 Jan. 1961; *s* of Billy Two Rivers and Maureen Hemingway; *m* 1982, Gerardine Astin (MBE 2006); two *s* two *d*. *Educ:* University Coll. London (BSc Hons Geog. and Town Planning); Surrey Univ. (MA Fashion). Co-Founder (with Gerardine Hemingway), Red or Dead, 1982, sold, 1999 (Designer of the Year, 1996, 1997, 1998). Mem., Trustee Bd, Design Council CABE, 2010–. Vis. Prof. of Urban Studies, Northumberland Univ., 2004–. Hon. DA Wolverhampton, 2005. *Publications:* Just Above the Mantelpiece, 1998; Mass Market Classics - The Home, 2000. *Recreations:* running, general sport, my kids. *Address:* HemingwayDesign, 15 Wembley Park Drive, Wembley HA9 8HD. *T:* and *Fax:* (020) 8903 1074. *E:* info@hemingwaydesign.co.uk.

**HEMINSLEY, Stephen John;** Director of Finance, Planning and Performance, Employment and Wellbeing Groups, Department for Work and Pensions, 2009–10; *b* 19 Dec. 1951; *s* of John and Joyce Margaret Heminsley; *m* 1980, Yvonne Lesley Stephenson; one *s* one *d*. *Educ:* Joseph Leckie Sch., Walsall. CIPFA 1986. Department of Health and Social Security, later Department of Social Security: Office Supervisor, 1972–77; Internal Auditor, 1977–88; Project Manager, DSS Financial Systems Strategy, 1988–90; Director of: Finance (Contributions Agency), 1990–95; Business Planning (CSA), 1995–97; Strategy and Planning (Benefits Agency), 1997–2000; Pensions, subseq. Children and Pensioners, 2000–01; Dir, Nat. Services, 2001–04, Acting Dir Gen., Service Delivery, 2004, Bd of Inland Revenue; Dir, Orgnl Design, subseq. Orgnl Develt, 2004–07, Dir, Finance Transformation, 2007–08, HMRC; Dir, Corporate Services, then Dir of Finance and Corporate Services, Healthcare Commn, later Care Quality Commn, 2008–09. Mem., Central Govt Panel, CIPFA, 1997–2016. Trustee: Newbrough Town Hall, 2012–14; Dementia Care, Newcastle, 2014–17; Chm., Fourstones Community Ventures Ltd, 2016–. Mem., Warden Parish Council, Northumberland, 2013– (Chm., 2017–). Gov., Newbrough Primary Sch., 2017–. FCPFA 2018. *Recreations:* walking, Rugby Union, family, guitarist. *E:* steveheminsley@gmail.com. *Club:* Handsworth Rugby Union Football.

**HEMM, Amanda Jane;** *see* Roocroft, A. J.

**HEMMING, John Alexander Melvin;** *b* 16 March 1960; *s* of Melvin John and Doreen Hemming; *m* 1981, Christine Margaret (*née* Richards); one *s* two *d*; one *s* one *d* by Emily Rohaise Cox. *Educ:* King Edward's Sch., Birmingham; Magdalen Coll., Oxford (MA Physics 1981). Founded: John Hemming & Co., subseq. JHC plc, 1983; MarketNet, 1994; Music Mercia International, 1997. Mem., Birmingham CC, 1990–2008 (Dep. Leader, 2004–05; Leader, 1998–2005, Chm., 2005–15, Lib Dem Gp). Contested: (L) Birmingham Hall Green, 1983; (L/All) Birmingham Small Heath, 1987; (Lib Dem) Birmingham Yardley, 1992, 1997, 2001. MP (Lib Dem) Birmingham Yardley, 2005–15; contested (Lib Dem) same seat, 2015, 2017. Chm., Birmingham Lib Dem City Exec. Cttee, 2009–. *Recreation:* jazz piano in John Hemming and The Jazz Lobbyists.

**HEMMING, John Henry,** CMG 1994; DLitt; FRGS, FSA, FRSL; Chairman, Hemming Group Ltd (Managing Director of Municipal Publications Ltd), 2011–15 (Director, since 1962; Deputy Chairman, 1967–76; Joint Chairman, 1976–2011); Director and Secretary, Royal Geographical Society, 1975–96; *b* 5 Jan. 1935; *s* of late Henry Harold Hemming, OBE, MC, and Alice Louisa Weaver, OBE; *m* 1979, Sukie, *d* of late M. J. Babington Smith, CBE; one *s* one *d*. *Educ:* Eton Coll.; McGill Univ.; Magdalen Coll., Oxford (Hon. Fellow, 2004); DLitt Oxon 1981. FSA 1998. Chairman: Brintex Ltd, 1979− (Man. Dir, 1963–70, Dep. Chm. 1976–78); Newman Books, 1979–. Member, Iriri River Expedition, Brazil, 1961; Leader, Maracá Rainforest Project, Brazil, 1987–88; Co-Chm., Jordan Badia R&D Prog., 1992–2004. Member Bd, British Council, 1993–2002; Member Council: Anglo-Brazilian Soc., 1963–2006; Pro Natura Internat., 1991–2007; Hakluyt Soc., 1996–2016. Corresp. Mem., Academia Nacional de la Historia, Venezuela. Dep. Chm., Lepra, 1998–2011; Founding Trustee, Survival International, 1969–2003; Trustee: Gilchrist Educnl Trust, 1988–; Anglo-Peruvian Soc., 1996– (Chm. Trustees, 1996–2007); Rainforest Foundn, 1997–; John Ellerman Foundn, 1998–2010; Global Diversity Foundn, 1999–; Cusichaca Trust, 1999–; Earthwatch Trust, 2004–16; Chairman: British Empire and Commonwealth Mus. Trust, 1990–99; Rainforest Club, 1997–2002; Greencard Trust, 1997–2009 (Mem. Council, 1989–2009); Amazon Charitable Trust, 2008–; Patron: Earth Love Fund, 1996–; Wilderness Trust, 2003–. FRGS 1962; FRSL 2013. Hon. DLitt Warwick, 1989; DUniv Stirling, 1991. Mungo Park Medal, RSGS, 1988; Founder's Medal, RGS, 1990; Washburn Medal, Boston Mus. of Sci., 1990; Citation of Merit, Explorers' Club, NY, 1997; Special Award, Instituto Nacional de Cultura, Peru, 1997; President's Medal, British Acad., 2018. Grand Cross, Orden al Mérito (Peru), 2007 (Officer, 1986); Gran Oficial, Orden El Sol del Peru, 2010; Comendador, Order of Cruzeiro do Sul (Brazil), 1998. *Publications:* The Conquest of the Incas, 1970 (Robert Pitman Literary Prize, 1970, Christopher Award, NY, 1971), rev. edn 1993 (US rev. edn 2012); (jt) Tribes of the Amazon Basin in Brazil, 1972; Red Gold: The Conquest of the Brazilian Indians, 1978; The Search for El Dorado, 1978; Machu Picchu, 1981; Monuments of the Incas, 1982, 3rd rev. edn 2010; The New Incas, 1983; (ed) Change in the Amazon Basin (2 vols), 1985; Amazon Frontier: the defeat of the Brazilian Indians, 1987; Maracá, 1988; Roraima: Brazil's northernmost frontier, 1990; Maracá Rainforest Island, 1993; (ed) The Rainforest Edge, 1994; The Golden Age of Discovery, 1998; Die If You Must, 2003; Tree of Rivers: the story of the Amazon, 2008; Naturalists in Paradise: Wallace, Bates and Spruce in the Amazon, 2015; People of the Rainforest: the Villas Boas brothers, explorers and humanitarians of the Amazon, 2019. *Recreations:* writing, travel. *Address:* 10 Edwardes Square, W8 6HE. *T:* (020) 7602 6697. *E:* j.hemming@hgluk.com. *Clubs:* Boodle's, Beefsteak (Chm., 2002–04), Geographical.

*See also L. A. Service.*

**HEMMING, Lindy;** costume designer for theatre, since 1970 and cinema, since 1983; *b* Haverfordwest, Wales, 21 Aug. 1948; *d* of Alan Hemming and Jean Hemming (*née* Alexander); one *s* one *d*; partner, Robert A. Starrett, cartoonist. *Educ:* Llandovery Coll., Carmarthenshire; Robert Jones and Agnes Hunt Orthopaedic Hosp.; Royal Acad. of Dramatic Art. Costume designer: *theatre:* Hampstead Th. Club; Open Space Th.; NT/RSC (Barbican and Stratford upon Avon); West End theatres; *films* include: My Beautiful Launderette, 1985; Life is Sweet, 1990; Naked, 1993; Four Weddings and a Funeral, 1994; Funny Bones, 1995; GoldenEye, 1995; Tomorrow Never Dies, 1997; The World is Not Enough, 1999; Topsy Turvy, 1999 (Acad. Award, 2000); Tomb Raiders 1, 2001; Die Another Day, 2002; Tomb Raiders 2, 2003; Batman Begins, 2005; Casino Royale, 2006; Dark Knight, 2008 (Designers' Guild Award, 2009); Clash of the Titans, 2010; The Dark Knight Rises, 2012; Paddington, 2014; Wonder Woman, 2014 (Designers' Guild Award, 2016); Paddington 2, 2017; Wonder Woman II, 2018. Guest Curator, Designing Bond, 50th Anniversary, Barbican, 2012. Member: British Film Designers' Guild; BAFTA; Acad. of Motion Pictures, USA. Woman of Year, Media Craft Awards, 1996; Siân Phillips Award, BAFTA Cymru, 2018. *Publications:* contrib. articles and features to newspapers and mags. *Recreations:* eating good food, people watching, travelling, caring for some very needy olive trees in Italy. *Address:* 105 Willoughby House, Barbican, EC2Y 8BL; Casa Lorenzino, Fertigliana no 12, 54010 Bigliolo, Aulla, Italy. *T:* 7860493995. *E:* LindyHmm@aol.com.

**HEMMING, Martin John,** CB 2003; Director General Legal Services and Legal Adviser, Ministry of Defence, 1998–2009; *b* 29 May 1949; *s* of late Albert Reuben Hemming and Constance Rosaline Hemming; *m* 1976, Kathleen Siân Davies; one *s* one *d*. *Educ:* Tudor Grange Grammar Sch., Solihull; Fitzwilliam Coll., Cambridge (BA 1971; MA 1976); London School of Economics and Political Science (LLM 1973). Called to the Bar, Gray's Inn, 1972, Bencher, 2006; practising barrister, 1974–82; Sen. Legal Asst, Treasury

Solicitor's Dept, 1982–85; Legal Advr (Grade 6), MoD, 1985–88; Asst Treasury Solicitor, 1988–98. Dep. Legal Advr, FCO, 2009–13. Associate Fellow, RUSI, 2013. *E*: martin.hemming@gmail.com. *Club*: Oxford and Cambridge.

**HEMMINGS, Dr Brian Arthur**, PhD; FRS 2009; Senior Scientist, Friedrich Miescher Institute for Biomedical Research, Basel, 1990–2014 (Group Leader, 1983–89), now Emeritus. *Educ*: Univ. of Nottingham (BSc 1972); Univ. of East Anglia (PhD 1975). Res. Fellow, Biochemisches Institut der Universität, Freiburg, 1975–77; Fogarty Vis. Fellow, NIH, Bethesda, 1977–80; MRC Res. Fellow, Med. Scis Inst., Univ. of Dundee, 1980–82; FMI Res. Associate, Rockefeller Univ., NY, 1982–83. Vis. Prof., Faculty of Medicine, Katholieke Universiteit, Leuven, 2000. Member: Scientific Cttee, Swiss Cancer League, 2001–12; Royal Soc. Subcttee (SC6) for Cell Regulation and Signal Transduction, 2011–14. *Publications*: contrib. articles in jls.

**HEMPHILL**, 6th Baron *cr* 1906, of Rathkenny and Cashel; **Charles Andrew Martyn Martyn-Hemphill**; Director, Waverton Investment Management (formerly J. O. Hambro Investment Management), since 2011; *b* Dublin, 8 Oct. 1954; *s* of 5th Baron Hemphill and (Olivia) Anne, *d* of late Major Robert Francis Ruttledge, MC, *S* father, 2012; *m* 1985, Sarah Jane Frances Lumley; two *s* three *d*. *Educ*: Downside Sch.; St Benet's Hall, Oxford (BA History; MA). With Deutsche Asset Mgt (formerly Morgan Grenfell Asset Mgt), 1979–2005; Spencer Hse Capital Mgt, 2006–11. Chm. of Governors, St Mary's Sch., Ascot. Trustee: Dulverton Trust; UCL Hosp. Charitable Trust. *Recreations*: ski-ing, golf. *Heir*: *s* Hon. Richard Patrick Lumley Martyn-Hemphill, *b* 17 May 1990. *Address*: 66 Manville Road, SW17 8JL; Dunkelin, Kiltulla, Athenry, Co. Galway, Ireland. *Clubs*: White's, Hurlingham; New Zealand.

**HEMPLEMAN-ADAMS, Sir David (Kim)**, KCVO 2017 (LVO 2007); OBE 1998 (MBE 1994); DL; company director; explorer and mountaineer; *b* 10 Oct. 1956; *m* Claire (marr. diss. 2017); three *d*. *Educ*: Writhlington Comp. Sch.; Manchester Univ.; Bristol Poly. (post-grad. Business Studies). Ascents: Mt McKinley, Alaska Range, 1980; Kilimanjaro, Tanzania, 1981; Mt Everest, Himalayas, 1993; Vinson Massif, Antarctica, 1994; Aconcagua, Andes, 1994; Mt Carstensz, Indonesia, 1995. Arctic/Antarctic expeditions: first solo unsupported expedition to magnetic North Pole, 1984; leader of first unsupported gp expedition to geomagnetic North Pole, 1992; first Briton to walk solo and unsupported to South Pole, 1996; first person to climb highest peaks of all seven continents and trek to magnetic and geographic North and South Poles, 1998; first person to walk solo and unaided by new route to geomagnetic North Pole, 2003; has reached the Poles 14 times. Hot-air balloon flights: first to cross Andes, 1998; first to cross North-West Passage, 1999; first to fly solo to North Pole, 2000; first to fly solo across Arctic Ocean, 2000; first to cross Atlantic in open wicker-basket, 2003. Led first British yacht to sail around North Pole in one season, NE/NW Passage, 2016. Director: Hempleman Investments; Global Resins; Ultimate Adventures. Founder, Mitchemp Trust. Trustee, Duke of Edinburgh Award, 2006–. DL, 2004, High Sheriff, 2016–17, Wilts. Member: RGS; RSGS; Hon. Co. of Air Pilots (formerly GAPAN); Royal Soc. Hon. DSc Leicester, 1998. 42 FAI Aviation world records; Fifty awards. Polar Medal and Clasp, 2013. KStJ 2016 (CStJ 2011). *Publications*: Race Against Time: North Geomagnetic Pole expedition, 1993; Toughing it Out, 1996; Walking on Thin Ice, 1998; At the Mercy of the Winds, 2000; (jtly) At the Heart of the Great Alone, 2009; No Such Thing as Failure, 2015; Open Water, Breaking Ice, 2017. *Clubs*: Alpine, Travellers; Explorers (New York).

**HEMPSALL, Dr David Stuart**, MA; Headmaster, Queen Elizabeth's Grammar School, Blackburn, 1995–2007; *b* 4 Jan. 1947; *s* of Harold and Freda Hempsall; *m* 1st, 1969, Patricia Land (*d* 2004); one *s* one *d*; 2nd, 2006, Diane Ewart-Jones. *Educ*: Manchester GS; Sidney Sussex Coll., Cambridge (MA); Univ. of Kent (PhD). Assistant Master: Sir William Nottidge Sch., Whitstable, 1971–72; Rugby Sch., 1973–85 (Head of History, 1977–85); Headmaster, Scarborough Coll., 1985–95. Hon. Treas., HMC, 2002–07. Chm. of Govs, The King's Sch., Chester, 2009–12. Trustee, Peel Foundn, 1995–. Hon. Sec., Limey Valley Residents' Assoc., 2009–. FRSA. Sec., Christ Ch Walshaw PCC, 2010–. *Publications*: articles in hist. and educnl learned jls. *Recreations*: do-it-yourself, hill-walking, music, sport, reading. *Address*: c/o Queen Elizabeth's Grammar School, West Park Road, Blackburn BB2 6DF. *T*: (01254) 686300.

**HEMSLEY, Oliver Alexander**; Executive Director, Numis Corporation plc, 2016–17 (Chief Executive Officer, 2000–16); *b* Oakham, Rutland, 27 Sept. 1962; *s* of Archie and Valerie Hemsley; *m* 1995, Charlotte Baddeley; two *s* one *d*. *Educ*: Stamford Sch., Lincs. Marine Underwriter, Alston Brockbank Underwriting Ltd, 1981–89; Chief Executive Officer: Hemsley & Co. Securities Ltd, 1990–92; Raphael Zorn Hemsley Ltd, 1992–2000. Mem., Adv. Bd, Palamon Capital Partners, 2017–. *Recreations*: hunting, kitchen gardening, flora and fauna, reading. *Clubs*: Garrick, City of London.

**HEMSLEY, Stephen Glen**, FCA; non-executive Chairman, Domino's Pizza Group (formerly Domino's Pizza UK and Ireland) plc, since 2010 (Executive Chairman, 2008–10); Chairman, Franchise Brands plc (formerly Franchise Brands Worldwide Ltd), since 2008; *b* Bromley, 3 Aug. 1957. *Educ*: Bromley Grammar Sch. for Boys; Univ. of Kent at Canterbury (BA Hons). FCA 1982. Stoy Hayward & Co., Chartered Accountants, 1978–83; Corp. Finance Manager, Sarasin Internat. Securities, 1983–84; Investment Controller, 1984–88, Sen. Investment Controller, 1988–89, Investment Dir, 1989–92, 3i plc; Domino's Pizza plc: Chief Financial Officer, 1998–2000; CEO, 2000–07. *Recreations*: sailing, ski-ing, shooting. *Address*: Domino's Pizza Group plc, 1 Thornbury, West Ashland, Milton Keynes MK6 4BB. *T*: (01908) 580604. *E*: stephenhemsley@hotmail.com. *Club*: Royal Thames Yacht.

**HENDERSON**, family name of **Baron Faringdon**.

**HENDERSON, Anne Frances**; *see* Milton, Rt Hon. A. F.

**HENDERSON, Barry**; *see* Henderson, J. S. B.

**HENDERSON, Bernard Vere**, CBE 1987; Chairman: Anglian Water, 1981–94; British Waterways Board, 1994–99; *b* 8 July 1928; *s* of late Percy Cecil and Ruth Elizabeth Henderson; *m* 1952, Valerie Jane Cairns (*d* 2019); two *s* one *d*. *Educ*: Ampleforth Coll.; Harvard Business Sch. Served Army, RE, 1946–49. P. C. Henderson Group, 1949–80 (Man. Dir, 1958–80). Chm., Water Services Assoc., 1990–91. Chm., Australia and NZ Trade Adv. Cttee, 1994–95. Pres., Pipeline Industry Guild, 1992–94. *Recreations*: countryside, cruising. *Address*: Lessudden Bank, St Boswells, Melrose TD6 0DU.

**HENDERSON, Charles Edward**, CB 1992; FIA; Chairman: Total Holding UK (formerly Total Oil Holdings, then TotalFinaElf Holding UK), 1998–2005; Total Exploration and Production UK (formerly Total Oil Marine, then TotalFinaElf Exploration UK), 1998–2005; *b* 19 Sept. 1939; *s* of late David Henderson and of Giorgiana Leggatt Henderson; *m* 1966, Rachel Hilary Hall, *d* of late Dr Stephen Hall, FRCP and Dr Mary Hall; one *d* one *s*. *Educ*: Charterhouse; Pembroke Coll., Cambridge (MA). FIA 1965. Actuarial Trainee, subseq. Asst Investment Sec., Equity & Law Life Assurance Soc., 1960–70; ECGD, 1971–73; DTI, 1973–74; Dept of Energy, 1974–88: Asst Sec., 1975; Under Sec., 1982; Atomic Energy Div., 1982; Oil Div., 1985; Prin. Estabt and Finance Officer, 1986–88; Head, Office of Arts and Libraries, 1989–92; Dep. Sec., DTI, 1992–96. Mem., Competition (formerly Monopolies and Mergers) Commn, 1998–2007. Dir, Aluminium Corp. Ltd, 1981–84. Sen. Associate, Cambridge Energy Res. Associates, 1998–2002. President: Soc. for Underwater Technology, 1999–2001; Inst. of Petroleum, 2000–02. *Recreations*: making and listening to music, mountaineering, golf. *Address*: 17 Sydney House, Woodstock Road, W4 1DP. *T*: (020) 8994 1345.

*See also* Julian Hall.

**HENDERSON, Douglas John**; Partner, Harley Street Hearing, since 2006; Director: Ossian Services Ltd, since 2009; North West Hearing, since 2014; *b* 9 June 1949; *s* of John and Joy Henderson; *m* 1st, 1974, Janet Margaret Graham (marr. diss.); one *s*; 2nd, 2002, Geraldine Daly; one *d*. *Educ*: Waid Academy, Anstruther, Fife; Central Coll., Glasgow; Univ. of Strathclyde. Apprentice, Rolls Royce, 1966–68; Clerk, British Rail, 1969; Research Officer, GMWU, 1973–75; Regional Organiser, GMWU, then GMB, 1975–87. Mem. Exec., Scottish Council, Labour Party, 1979–87 (Chm., 1984–85). MP (Lab) Newcastle upon Tyne N, 1987–2010. Opposition spokesman on trade and industry, 1988–92, on local govt, 1992–94, on public service, 1994–95, on home affairs, 1995–97; Minister of State: (Europe), FCO, 1997–98; (Minister for the Armed Forces), MoD, 1998–99. Sec., All Party Athletes Gp, 2002–10; Chairman: Northern Gp of Lab MPs, 2000–01; GMB Parly Gp, 2002–10 (Sec., 1987–97); Mem. UK Delegn to Council of Europe and WEU, 2005–10; Chm., Defence Cttee, Eur. Security and Defence Assembly, 2009–10. Chm., Falkirk FC, 2015– (Dir, 2013–). *Recreations*: athletics, mountaineering. *Clubs*: Elswick Harriers, Lemington Labour, Newburn Memorial, Dinnington, Union Jack (Newcastle).

**HENDERSON, Fergus**, MBE 2005; Chef and Co-Owner, St John Restaurant, London, since 1994 (Michelin Star, 2009); *b* 31 July 1963; *s* of Brian and Elizabeth Henderson; *m* 1993, Margot Clayton; one *s* two *d*. *Educ*: King Alfred's Sch.; Architectural Assoc. RIBA pt 2. Chef, French House Dining Room, 1992–94. *Publications*: Nose to Tail Eating: a kind of British cooking, 1999, 4th edn 2004; (jtly) Beyond Nose to Tail, 2007; Complete Nose to Tail, 2012; The Book of St John, 2019. *Recreation*: cooking. *Address*: St John Restaurant, 26 St John Street, EC1M 4AY. *T*: (020) 7553 9842. *E*: sarah@stjohnrestaurant.com. *Club*: Groucho.

**HENDERSON, Prof. Gavin Douglas**, CBE 2004; Principal, Royal Central School of Speech and Drama (formerly Central School of Speech and Drama), University of London, since 2007; *b* 3 Feb. 1948; *s* of Magnus Reg Henderson and Sybil (*née* Horton); *m* 1st, 1973, Jane Williams (marr. diss. 1977); 2nd, 1983, Carole Becker (marr. diss. 1992); two *s*; 3rd, 1992, Mary Jane Walsh. *Educ*: Brighton Coll.; Brighton Coll. of Art; Kingston Art Coll.; University Coll. London; Slade Sch. of Fine Art. Solo trumpet, St Bartholomew's Church, Brighton, 1963–2014; Leader and Dir, Henderson Brass Consort, 1968–75; Principal Trumpet, Worthing Municipal and Concert Orchs, 1969–70; Dep. Front of House and Publicity Manager, Victoria Theatre, Stoke-on-Trent, 1970–71; Founder and Dir, Crawley Fest., 1971–73; Artistic Director: York Fest. Mystery Plays, 1972–76; Portsmouth Fest., 1974–76; Chief Exec., New Philharmonia and Philharmonia Orchs, 1975–78; Dir, S Hill Park Arts Centre and Founder, Wilde Theatre, Bracknell, 1979–84; Artistic Director: Brighton Internat. Fest., 1983–94; Dartington Internat. Summer Sch., 1985–2010; Court in the Act, Royal Acad. of Arts, 1993; Mem., Adv. Bd, London Contemporary Dance Trust, 1986–87; Pres. and Artistic Advr, Bournemouth Fest., 1996–98 (Artistic Dir, 1994–96); Principal, Trinity Coll. of Music, 1994–2005; Principal and Chief Exec., Trinity Laban, 2005–06. Chairman: Clarion Concert Agency, 1972–75; Palindrome Prodns Ltd, 1994–2003; World Circuit Arts, 1995–2004; Nat. Foundn for Youth Music (formerly Youth Music Trust), 1998–2007. Writer and presenter, A View of …, BBC TV Series, 1983. Member: Music Panel and Opera Cttee, 1973–75, Regl Cttee, 1981–84, Arts Council of GB; Arts Council of England, 1994–98 (Chm., Music Panel, 1994–2003); Arts Cttee, RSA, 1991–94; Chairman: British Arts Fests Assoc., 1994–2002 (Dep. Chm., 1987–94); Brighton Youth Orch. Trust, 1998–2005; Regency Soc., 1999–2006; Antony Dale Secret Garden Trust, 2010–; Brighton Hippodrome CIC, 2015–; Member: Exec. Cttee, SE Arts Assoc., 1982–89 (Chm., Festival Panel, 1986–89); Exec. Bd, European Fests Assoc., 1988–94 (Vice Pres., 1994–2003, Pres., 2003–05); Southern Arts Bd, 1990–93; Arts Initiative in Mgt Cttee, Gulbenkian Foundn, 1982–83. Trustee: Electro-Acoustic Music Soc., 1984–90; Brighton Early Music Fest., 2005–; Theatres Trust, 2014–. Judge: Prudential Awards, 1992; Audi Young Musician of the Year, 1993; Barclays New Stages, 1994; British Gas Working for Cities, 1995; Olivier Awards, 2001–02; Chm., Royal Over-Seas League Music Competition, 2007–. External Examiner: UEA, 2008–13; Middlesex Univ., 2014–. Pres., Nat. Piers Soc., 1986–. One-man exhibitions: Gall. 185, Brighton, 1968; Mulberry Gall., Lancaster, 1969. Mem. Bd, Trinity Coll., London, 1994–2008; Governor: Brighton Univ. (formerly Poly.), 1987–95; Chetham's Sch., Manchester, 1994–2011; Feoffee, Chetham's Hosp., 2007–14. Pres., ISM, 2010–11. Mem., Royal Soc. of Musicians, 1996–. Lecture-performances: Piers of the Realm, 1968–; Picasso, Diaghilev and the Commedia dell'Arte, 2002–; Conductors Unbecoming, 2015–. Liveryman, Musicians' Co., 1995. Freeman, City of London, 1995. Hon. Fellow: Univ. of Sussex, 1991; Univ. of Brighton, 1993; Laban, 2000; Hon. FTCL 1998; Hon. FRCM 2002; Hon. FRNCM 2003; Hon. FRBC (Hon. FBC 2010); Hon. CTL 2007. Hon. MA Sussex, 1992. Europe Award, E Sussex CC, 1992; Sir Charles Groves Award, 2005; BACS Gold Award, 2007. *Publications*: Picasso and the Theatre, 1982; articles for Resurgence, Classical Music, Tempo, Musical Times, Stage, and Listener. *Recreations*: seaside pierage, Savile snooker, cooking seafood, vintage motor-racing. *Address*: Royal Central School of Speech and Drama, University of London, Eton Avenue, NW3 3HY. *Clubs*: Beefsteak, Garrick, Savile (Hon. Life Mem.), Royal Over-Seas League (Hon. Mem.), Academy, Acts and Actors.

**HENDERSON, Prof. George David Smith**, FSA; Professor of Medieval Art, Cambridge, 1986–96, then Emeritus; Fellow of Downing College, Cambridge, 1974–94; *b* 7 May 1931; *yr s* of late Very Rev. Prof. George David Henderson, DLitt, DTh, DD and Jenny Holmes McCulloch Henderson (*née* Smith); *m* 1957, Isabel Bisset Murray, OBE, Hon. FSAScot; one *s* one *d*. *Educ*: Aberdeen Grammar Sch.; Univ. of Aberdeen (MA 1953); Courtauld Inst., Univ. of London (BA 1956); Trinity Coll., Cambridge (MA, PhD 1961). Research Fellow, Barber Inst. of Art, Univ. of Birmingham, 1959–60; Graham Robertson Research Fellow, Downing Coll., Cambridge, 1960–63; University of Manchester: Asst Lectr in History of Art, 1962–64; Lectr, 1964–66; University of Edinburgh: Lectr in Fine Arts, 1966–71; Reader in Fine Arts, 1971–73; University of Cambridge: Lectr in History of Art, 1974–79; Head of Dept, 1974–88; Reader in Medieval Art, 1979–86; a Syndic, Fitzwilliam Museum, 1974–88. Mem., Ely Cathedral Fabric Adv. Cttee, 1990–98. *Publications*: Gothic, 1967; Chartres, 1968; Early Medieval, 1972, repr. 1993; (ed with Giles Robertson) Studies in Memory of David Talbot Rice, 1975; Bede and the Visual Arts (Jarrow Lect.), 1980; Losses and Lacunae in Early Insular Art (Garmonsway Lect.), 1982; Studies in English Bible Illustration, 1985; From Durrow to Kells, 1987; (contrib.) The Eadwine Psalter, 1992; (contrib.) Emulation and Innovation in Carolingian Culture, 1993; Vision and Image in Early Christian England, 1999; (with Isabel Henderson) The Art of the Picts: sculpture and metalwork in early medieval Scotland, 2004 (a Historians of British Art Book Prize, 2006); articles in UK and Amer. jls and papers in procs of internat. confs;

*Festschrift:* New Offerings, Ancient Treasures: studies in medieval art for George Henderson, ed. P. Binski and W. Noel, 2001. *Recreations:* listening to Wagner, porphyrology, looking for agates. *Address:* The Old Manse, Nigg by Tain, Ross and Cromarty IV19 1QR.

**HENDERSON, Prof. Gideon Mark,** PhD; FRS 2013; Professor of Earth Sciences, University of Oxford, since 2006; Fellow of University College, Oxford, since 1999; Chief Scientific Adviser, Department for Environment, Food and Rural Affairs, since 2019; *b* Glasgow, 29 July 1968; *s* of Prof. Paul Henderson, *qv*; *m* 2000, Catherine Mary Wheatley; two *s*. *Educ:* Altwood Comp., Maidenhead; Hertford Coll., Oxford (BA Earth Scis 1989); St John's Coll., Cambridge (PhD Geochem. 1994). Post-doctoral Fellow, 1994–96, Associate Res. Scientist, 1996–99, Lamont-Doherty Earth Observatory, Columbia Univ.; Lectr, 1999–2006, Hd, Dept of Earth Scis, 2013–17, Univ. of Oxford. Mem., NERC, 2018–. *Publications:* The Cambridge Handbook of Earth Science Data (with P. Henderson), 2009; articles in scientific jls. *Address:* Department of Earth Sciences, University of Oxford, South Parks Road, Oxford OX1 3AN. *T:* (01865) 272000. *E:* gideonh@earth.ox.ac.uk.

**HENDERSON, Giles Ian,** CBE 1992; Master, Pembroke College, Oxford, 2001–13, now Honorary Fellow; *b* 20 April 1942; *s* of late Charles David Henderson and Joan K. Firmin; *m* 1971, Lynne Fyfield; two *s* one *d*. *Educ:* Michaelhouse, Natal; Univ. of Witwatersrand (BA); Magdalen Coll., Oxford (Sen. Mackinnon Scholar; MA, BCL). Fulbright Award, 1966–67. Associate in Law, Univ. of California at Berkeley, 1966–67; joined Slaughter and May, 1968; admitted Solicitor, 1970; Partner, Slaughter and May, 1975, Sen. Partner, 1993–2001. Member: Hampel Cttee on Corporate Governance, 1995–98; Financial Reporting Council, 1998–2001; Takeover Appeal Bd, 2016–; Chm., Law Gp, UK-China Forum, 1997–2000. Non-executive Director: Land Securities plc, 2000–02; Standard Life Assurance Co., 2001–03. Chairman: Nuffield Med. Trust, 2003–15; Conf. of Oxford Colls, 2007–09; Dir, Cumberland Lodge, 2007–08. Mem. Council, Univ. of Oxford, 2007–13. Trustee, Tanaka UK Japan Educnl Foundn, 2014–. *Recreations:* tennis, walking, watching Rugby, opera and ballet.

See also M. G. F. Henderson.

**HENDERSON, Gordon;** MP (C) Sittingbourne and Sheppey, since 2010; *b* Gillingham, Kent, 27 Jan. 1948; *s* of William John Butler Henderson and Pauline Henderson (*née* Pullen); *m* 1993, Louise Claire Crowder; one *s* two *d*. *Educ:* Fort Luton Secondary Sch. for Boys. Woolworths, 1964–79; restaurateur, 1979–83; Agent, Cons. Party, 1983–85; GEC Marconi, 1985–93; Unwins Wine Gp, 1993–2003; Beams UK Ltd, 2003–08; mgt consultant, 2008–10. Mem. (C) Kent CC, 1989–93. Contested (C): Luton S, 2001; Sittingbourne and Sheppey, 2005. *Recreations:* reading, writing. *Address:* House of Commons, SW1A 0AA. *T:* (020) 7219 7144; (office) Top Floor, Unit 10, Periwinkle Court, Church Street, Milton Regis, Sittingbourne, Kent ME10 2JZ. *E:* gordon.henderson.mp@parliament.uk.

**HENDERSON, Prof. Graham,** CBE 2011; DL; Vice-Chancellor and Chief Executive, Teesside University, 2003–15; *b* 23 Aug. 1952; *s* of Thomas and Elizabeth Henderson; *m* 1987, Joan Younger; two *s* one *d*. *Educ:* Heaton Grammar Sch.; Lanchester Poly. (BSc Hons); City Univ. (MSc with Dist.); Nene Coll. (FE Teachers' Cert.). Trainee Accountant, 1970–71, Trainee Operational Res. Scientist, 1973–74, NCB; Lectr, Sch. of Maths, Mgt and Business Studies, Nene Coll., Northampton, 1975–79; Lectr, then Sen. Lectr, then Prin. Lectr, Sch. of Business Analysis, Newcastle Poly., 1979–89; Asst Dir, Newcastle Poly., later Newcastle Business Sch., Univ. of Northumbria, 1989–97; Dir, Sunderland Business Sch., Univ. of Sunderland, 1997–99; Dep. Vice-Chancellor, Univ. of Teesside, 1999–2003. Member: CBI Regl Council, 2003–09, 2012–15; Bd, Univs for the NE, 2003–15 (Chm., 2005–09); Bd, NE Chamber of Commerce, 2005–10 (Mem. Council, 2009–15); Nat. Exec., Million+ (formerly Campaign for Mainstream Univs), 2005–10; Bd, Universities UK, 2010–15 (Member: Business and Ind. Policy Network (formerly Employability Business and Ind. Policy Cttee), 2008–15; Student Quality and Participation Policy Network (formerly Student Experience Policy Cttee), 2008–15); Chairman: Regl Council, NE Higher Skills Network, 2006–09; Regl Sci., Technol., Engrg and Maths NE Bd, 2009–11; Membership Adv. Gp, Leadership Foundn for Higher Educn, 2010–15; Redcar and Cleveland Foundn for Jobs, 2014–18. Member, Corporation Board: Hartlepool Coll., 1999–2004; Laurence Jackson Sch., 1999–2003; Darlington Coll. of Technology, 1999–2006; Member Board: Univ. Alliance, 2011–15; Birmingham City Univ., 2013–; York St John Univ., 2015–. Vice-Chm., Transparent Approach to Costing Develt and Implementation Gp, HEFCE, 2013–18. Director: Middlesbrough Town Centre Co., 2003–06; Durham and Tees Valley LSC, 2005–07; NE Regl LSC, 2007–10; Mem. Bd, Tees Valley Unlimited, 2006–15. Pres., 2013–17, Hon. Sec., 2015–17, Chm., 2017–18, Guisborough RU FC. Trustee: Capt. Cook Birthplace Trust, 2003–17 (Chm., 2015–17); Trincomalee Trust, 2003–07; Member: Areté Learning Trust, 2015–; Teesside Learning Trust, 2017–; Our Children First Multi Acad. Trust, 2017–; Patron: Middlesbrough Older Persons' Forum, 2011–; Community Campus, 2013–; Theatre Hullabaloo, 2015–. CCMI 2010. Hon. Fellow, Nat. Centre for Entrepreneurship in Educn, 2015. DL N Yorks 2012. *Recreations:* Rugby Union and football (spectator), walking, ballroom dancing, golf.

**HENDERSON, Guy;** Chief Executive Officer, Ascot Racecourse, since 2015; *b* Cape Town, SA, 9 Jan. 1958; *s* of William Herriot Henderson and Rosalind Campbell Henderson; *m* 1988, Sophie Jane Wingfield Digby; two *s* two *d*. *Educ:* St Peter's Coll., Radley; Downing Coll., Cambridge (BA 1979; MA). Admitted as solicitor, England and Wales, 1982, Hong Kong, 1993; Allen & Overy, 1980–2012, Partner, 1990–2012; Consultant Mediator, Maurice Turnor Gardner LLP, 2012–13. Chm., Cobham plc Pension Fund, 2008–09. Member, Board: The Horse Trust, 2005–12 (Chm., 2007–12); Wincanton Racecourse, 2010–15 (Chm., 2012–14); Trustee, Injured Jockeys Fund, 2016–. *Recreations:* sailing, ski-ing, nature conservation. *Address:* Ascot Racecourse, High Street, Ascot, Berks SL5 7JX. *T:* (01344) 878501. *E:* guy.henderson@ascot.co.uk. *Clubs:* Farmers; Hong Kong, Shek O Country; Royal Ascot Racing (Chm., 2016–).

**HENDERSON, Harry;** DL; Chairman, Witan Investment Trust plc, since 2003 (Director, since 1988); *b* London, 25 April 1952; *s* of J. R. Henderson and K. S. Beckwith-Smith; *m* 1977, Sarah M. C. Lowther; one *s* one *d*. *Educ:* Eton Coll. Commnd 9th/12th Royal Lancers (Prince of Wales's), 1971. Partner, Cazenove & Co., 1982–2002. DL Berks 2008. *Recreations:* ski-ing, shooting. *Address:* West Woodhay House, Newbury, Berks RG20 0BS. *T:* (01488) 668233, 07710 253491. *E:* harry@woodhay.com. *Club:* Whites.

**HENDERSON, Rear Adm. Iain Robert,** CB 2001; CBE 1991; DL; Registrar and Secretary, Order of the Bath, since 2006 (Gentleman Usher of the Scarlet Rod, 2002–06); Vice Lord-Lieutenant for Hampshire, since 2018; *b* 1 April 1948; *s* of John and Christina Henderson; *m* 1976, Rosalind Margaret Arkell; two *s* two *d*. *Educ:* Epsom Coll. BRNC 1965; qualified as: rotary wing pilot, 1971; fixed wing pilot, 1974; Exec. Officer, HMS Plymouth, 1980–82; CO, HMS Ariadne, 1984–85, HMS Charybdis, 1985; Trng Comdr, BRNC, 1986–87; Directorate of Naval Officer Appointments (Seaman) (Air), 1988–90; CO, HMS London, 1990–91; AD Warfare Directorate of Naval Plans, 1991–93; CO, RNAS Yeovilton, 1993–96; Comdr, Naval Base, Portsmouth, 1996–98; FONA, 1998–2000; AOC No 3 Gp and FOMA, 2000–01. ADC to the Queen, 1996–98. Chief Exec., Sue Ryder Care, 2001–07. Freeman, City of London, 1992; Liveryman, Co. of Upholders, 1996–; Mem., Ct of Assts, Guild of Freemen, City of London, 1997–2003. DL Hants, 2006. *Recreation:* equestrian and country pursuits.

**HENDERSON, Ian Francis;** QC 2016; *b* London, 23 Feb. 1967; *s* of George Henderson and late Theresa Henderson; *m* 1990, Natalie Maria Wilkins; two *s* one *d*. *Educ:* City of London Poly. (LLB Hons Business Law 1989). Called to the Bar, Inner Temple, 1990; in practice as barrister specialising in criminal law, 8 King's Bench Walk, 1990–2000, Farringdon Chambers, 2000–. *Recreations:* spending time with family and friends, playing sport and in particular football, eclectic music taste ranging from 1980s new romantic to jazz, eating, spending time in Norfolk. *Address:* Farringdon Chambers, 180 Bermondsey Street, SE1 3TQ. *T:* (020) 7089 5700. *E:* ianhenderson@farringdon-law.co.uk.

**HENDERSON, Ian James,** CBE 2001; FRICS; farmer, since 2007; Chairman, Circle Property plc, since 2016; *b* 18 July 1943; *s* of Robert and Sheila Henderson; *m* 1972, Sheila Sturrock; one *s* one *d*. *Educ:* Wellington Coll.; Coll. of Estate Mgt, London Sch. of Econs and Pol Sci. (BSc Estate Mgt). FRICS 1978. Joined Land Securities, 1971; Chief Exec., Land Securities Gp PLC, 1997–2004. Chm., New West End Co. Ltd, 2000–08; Vice-Chm., London Regl Bd, Royal & Sun Alliance, 1998–; Mem., President's Cttee, London First, 2002–13. Chm., London Mayoral Commn into W End Central Retail Area Planning and Develt Policy, 2006–07. Non-executive Chairman: Treveria plc (formerly Dawnay Day Treveria), 2005–09; Ishaan Real Estate PLC, 2006–13; Evans Mgt Ltd, 2008–12; Dep. Chm., Capital & Counties Properties plc, 2010–16; non-exec. Dir, Capital Shopping Centres Gp plc, 2010–12 (non-exec. Dir, Liberty Internat. PLC, 2005–10); consultant, Quintain Estates and Development plc, 2005–08. Chm., St Martin-in-the-Fields Develt Trust, 2005–11; Vice Chm., Bd of Mgt, Central and Cecil Housing Trust, 1992–2007 (Vice Pres., 2007–). Pres., British Property Fedn, 2002–03. Comr, Commonwealth War Graves Commn, 2002–10. Trustee, Natural Hist. Mus., 2005–13 (Chm., Estates Adv. Bd, 2013–16; Property Cttee, 2016–18); Council Mem., Royal Albert Hall, 2005–16; Chm. Govs, Dolphin Square Charitable Foundn, 2005–16. Pres., Lighthouse Club, 2005–08; Vice Pres., Cambridge Land Soc., 2005–; Pres., Edenbridge and Oxted Agricultural Show, 2015–16. *Clubs:* Brooks's, Naval and Military.

**HENDERSON, Ivan John;** public affairs consultant, Ivan Henderson Consultancy, since 2008; Member (Lab), Essex County Council, since 2013 (Labour Group Leader); *b* 7 June 1958; *s* of Margaret Bloice and step *s* of late Michael Bloice; *m* 1992, Jo'anne Atkinson; two *s*; one *s* one *d* from a previous marriage. *Educ:* Sir Anthony Deane Comprehensive Sch., Harwich. British Rail, Sealink, 1975–97: dock operative; Union Orgnr, Docks, and Exec. Officer, RMT, 1991–94. Member (Lab): Harwich Town Council, 1986–97 and 2011–; Tendring DC, 1995–97 and 2011– (Labour Gp Leader). MP (Lab) Harwich, 1997–2005; contested (Lab) same seat, 2005; contested (Lab) Clacton, 2010. PPS to Minister of State: Home Office, 2001–02; ODPM, 2002–03; PPS to Sec. of State, DWP, 2003–04; PPS to Paymaster-General, HM Treasury, 2004–05. Member: All Party Cancer Gp; All Party Maritime Gp; All Party Town Centre Mgt Gp; All Party Gp against Drug Abuse; All Party China Gp; All Party India Gp; All Party Gp on Animal Welfare; All Party Gp on Child Abduction; Labour Parly TU Gp; Seaside Gp, Labour MPs; Chm., All Party Parly Sea Cadets Gp, 2004–05; Vice Chm., All Party Parly Gp Ports and Shipping, 2001–05. Parly Spokesman for Clacton, 2006. Member: Bd, Harwich Haven Authy, 2007–13; Essex Fire Authy, 2014–17. Mem., Essex Wildlife Trust, 2001–. *Recreation:* football (coach for Little Oakley Memorial FC). *Address:* Harwich, Essex. *T:* 07889 367822. *E:* ivanhenderson4labour@yahoo.co.uk. *Club:* Harwich and Dovercourt Cricket (Vice Pres., 1997).

**HENDERSON, James Brodie;** Chief Executive, Bell Pottinger, 2013–17; *b* São Paulo, Brazil, 30 Dec. 1964; *s* of Ian and Veronica Henderson; *m* 1991, Alexandra Fisher (marr. diss. 2017); one *s* three *d*. *Educ:* Haileybury; Buckingham Univ. (LLB). Partner, College Hill PR, 1989–2004; Founder, 2004, Man. Dir, 2004–10, Pelham PR; Man. Dir, Pelham Bell Pottinger, 2010–12. Trustee, Children In Crisis, 2013–16. *Recreations:* theatre, travel, running, family. *T:* 07774 444163.

**HENDERSON, James Frowyke;** a District Judge (Magistrates' Courts), 2004–18; *b* 17 Dec. 1954; *s* of James Murray Henderson and Myrtle Elizabeth Jean Henderson; *m* 1989, Jane Elisabeth; one *s*. *Educ:* King's Sch., Tynemouth; Univ. of Newcastle upon Tyne (LLB); Univ. of Northumbria (LLM 2006; Sutherland Prize, 2006); Univ. of Cambridge (Postgrad. Dip. Applied Criminol. 2011; MSt 2012; Inst. of Criminol. Annual Prize, 2012). Called to the Bar, Middle Temple, 1984; Tutorial Studentship, 1980–83, Lectr in Laws, 1984–86, KCL; barrister in criminal practice, 1986–2004; Actg Stipendiary Magistrate, 1999–2000; Dep. Dist Judge (Magistrates' Courts), 2000–04. Occasional Lectr, British Acad. of Forensic Sci., 1980–83; Lectr (pt-time), PCL, 1983–84. FRSA 2008. *Publications:* contrib. numerous academic articles on criminal law and evidence to King's Coll. Law Jl, Criminal Bar Assoc. Newsletter, 4 Brick Court Chambers Law Review. *Recreations:* playing mandolin and guitar and various sized recorders, 4th Dan Black Belt in Goshin-Do (a modern Ju-Jitsu style), member of Scotch Malt Whisky Soc. *Club:* Oxford and Cambridge.

**HENDERSON, (James Stewart) Barry;** management consultant; *b* 29 April 1936; *s* of James Henderson, CBE and Jane Stewart Henderson (*née* McLaren); *m* 1961, Janet Helen Sprot Todd; two *s*. *Educ:* Lathallan Sch.; Stowe Sch. Nat. Service, Scots Guards, 1954–56; electronics and computer industries, 1957–65; Scottish Conservative Central Office, 1966–70; computer industry, 1971–74; management consultant, 1975–86; paper industry, 1987–90; Dir, British Paper and Board Industry Fedn, 1990–92; Partner, Henderson Consulting, 1993–. Contested (C): E Edinburgh, 1966; E Dunbartonshire, 1970; Fife NE, 1987. MP (C): East Dunbartonshire, Feb.–Sept. 1974; E Fife, 1979–83; Fife NE, 1983–87. PPS to Economic Sec. to HM Treasury, 1984–87. Member: Select Cttee on Scottish Affairs, 1979–87; H of C Chairmen's Panel, 1981–83; Chm., Scottish Cons. Back Bench Cttee, 1983–84; Vice-Chm., PITCOM, 1986–87. Mem., ODPM Right to Manage review, 2001–04. Area Bd Mem., CityWest Homes, 2003–05. Comr, Strathclyde Tram Public Inquiry, 1996. Trustee, St Andrews Links Trust, 1979–87. Comr, Gen. Assembly of Church of Scotland, 1986. Sec., 1997–2000, Vice-Chm., 2000–02, Pimlico Village Housing Co-op; Chm., Westminster Soc., 2004–08; Sec., Fedn of Bath Residents' Assocs, 2014–18. *Publications:* pamphlets on Scottish, European and environmental issues. *Address:* 3 Royal View, Victoria Bridge Road, Bath BA2 3GG.

**HENDERSON, Jane Elisabeth,** CB 2004; counsellor in private practice; Vice-Chair, Yeovil District Hospital Foundation Trust, since 2016 (non-executive Director, since 2013); *b* 2 May 1952; *m* 1979, Clive Abbott; one *s* one *d*. *Educ:* Tunbridge Wells Grammar Sch.; Somerville Coll., Oxford (BA 1973; BPhil 1975; MA); Birkbeck Coll., Univ. of London (MSc 1983); Bath Centre for Counselling and Psychotherapy (Dip. Humanistic and Integrative Counselling 2016). Joined NI Office, 1975, Pvte Sec. to Perm. Sec., 1977–79; HM Treasury, 1979–81; CSSB, 1984–85; Industrial Econs Div., HM Treasury, 1985–86; Dept of Employment, 1986–88; SW Regl Dir, Employment Service, 1988–92; Trng, Enterprise and Educn Directorate, Dept of Employment, 1992–94; Dir of Finance and Funding, HEFCE, 1994–96; Dir of Resources, Rural Develt Commn, 1996–97; Regl Dir, Govt Office for the SW, 1998–2005; Strategic Advr on Sustainable Communities, IDeA,

2005–06; Chief Exec., SW of England Regl Develt Agency, 2006–12. Chm., Bd of Govs, Bath Spa Univ., 2013–16 (Mem. Bd, 2011–16; Chm., 2012–13). Trustee, Dementia UK, 2011–13. Hon. LLD Exeter, 2005; Hon. DBus Plymouth, 2010.

**HENDERSON, Very Rev. Janet;** freelance writer; Spiritual and Pastoral Care Manager, St Michael's Hospice, Harrogate, 2013–15 (Trustee, 2008–13); *b* 12 May 1957; *d* of John Wilson Henderson and Megan (née Williams); *m* 1996, David Michael Challoner. *Educ:* Addenbrooke's Sch. of Nursing, Cambridge (RGN 1982); Durham Univ. (BA Hons 1988). Staff Nurse, Cambridge AHA, 1982–85; ordained deacon, 1988, priest, 1994; Asst Curate, St Peter and St Paul, Wisbech, 1988–90; Parish Deacon, Bestwood Team Ministry, Nottingham, 1990–93; Lectr, St John's Coll., Nottingham, 1993–97; Associate Priest NSM, St Michael and All Angels, Bramcote, Nottingham, 1994–97; Lectr, Cambridge Theol Fedn, and Tutor, Ridley Hall Theol Coll., 1997–2001; Dean, Women's Ministry, Dio. of Southwell, 2001–07; Priest-in-Charge, St Patrick's, Nuthall, 2001–07; Residentiary Canon, Ripon Cath., 2007–11; Archdeacon of Richmond, 2007–13; Residentiary Canon, and Diocesan Advr on Non-stip. Ministry, Dio. of Ripon and Leeds, 2011–13; Dean of Llandaff, 2013. Dir, 2008–13, part-time Tutor, 2014–15, St John's Coll., Durham Univ. *Publications:* (ed jtly) Pastoral Prayers, 1996; articles in British Jl of Theological Educn, Anvil. *Recreations:* playing the double bass and piano, walking.

**HENDERSON, Maj. Gen. John McNiven Ross,** CB 2014; Chief Executive, Staffordshire County Council, since 2015. *Educ:* Heriot-Watt Univ. (BSc Mech. Engrg 1984); Cranfield Univ. (MSc Defence Technol. 1995). Joined REME, 1982; Electrical Mech. Engr, 15th/19th Hussars, 1988–90; Co. Comdr 1 Bn REME, 1998–2000; Mil. Asst, SACEUR, 2000–02; CO 2 Bn REME, 2002–04; Comdr, Provincial Reconstruction Team, Afghanistan, 2004; HCSC 2005; DCS 1st Armoured Div., 2005–06; Comdr 102 Logistic Bde, 2006–08; Logistics Dir, British Army, 2008–11; rcds 2011; GOC British Forces Germany, 2012–15. *Address:* Staffordshire County Council, County Buildings, Martin Street, Stafford ST16 2LH.

**HENDERSON, Rt Rev. Julian Tudor;** see Blackburn, Bishop of.

**HENDERSON, Rt Hon. Sir Launcelot (Dinadan James),** Kt 2007; PC 2017; **Rt Hon. Lord Justice Henderson;** a Lord Justice of Appeal, since 2016; *b* 20 Nov. 1951; *er s* of Baron Henderson of Brompton, KCB; *m* 1989, Elaine Elizabeth Webb (marr. diss. 2016); two *s* one *d. Educ:* Westminster Sch.; Balliol Coll., Oxford (MA). Fellow of All Souls Coll., Oxford, 1974–81, 1982–89 and 2008–. Called to the Bar, Lincoln's Inn, 1977, Bencher, 2004; practised as Barrister (Chancery), 1978–2006; Standing Junior Counsel: to Inland Revenue (Chancery), 1987–91; to Inland Revenue, 1991–95; QC 1995; a Dep. High Ct Judge, Chancery Div., 2001–07; a Judge of the High Ct, Chancery Div., 2007–16. Trustee, Samuel Courtauld Trust, 2005–13; Chm., Trust Law Cttee, 2016–. *Recreations:* botany, art, music, books. *Address:* Royal Courts of Justice, Strand, WC2A 2LL.

See also Rt Rev. R. C. A. Henderson.

**HENDERSON, Lisa Margaret, (Mrs Blair Davidson);** QC (Scot.) 2016; *b* Aberdeen, 21 Sept. 1969; *d* of William Henderson and Alison Henderson; *m* 1998, Blair Davidson. *Educ:* Albyn Sch. for Girls, Aberdeen; Univ. of Aberdeen (LLB 1990; DipLP 1991). MCIArb 2017, FCIArb 2019. Admitted solicitor, 1994; John G. Gray & Co., Edinburgh, Solicitors, 1991–94; admitted to Faculty of Advocates, 1995; called to the Bar, Middle Temple, 2019. Lead Tutor, 2012–17, Tutor, 2017–, Personal Injury Elective, Dip. in Legal Practice, Edinburgh Univ. Law Sch. (author, Personal Injury Elective, 2011–17). Hon. Sen. Lectr, Glasgow Univ. Sch. of Medicine, 2012–18; Vis. Lectr, Pavia Univ., 2014–15. Fellow, British Amer. Project, 2004 (Vice Chair, British Amer. Project UK). *Address:* Advocates Library, Parliament House, Edinburgh EH1 1RF. *T:* (clerks) (0131) 226 5071. *E:* lisa.henderson@advocates.org.uk.

**HENDERSON, Mark;** lighting designer, since 1981; *b* 26 Sept. 1957; *s* of Gordon Henderson and Margaret Henderson (née Moakes); two *s. Educ:* Sherwood Hall Tech. Grammar Sch., Mansfield. Chief electrician for Kent Opera, English Music Th., London Contemporary Dance, Sadler's Wells and Opera North, 1978–; lighting designs for: *theatre:* numerous West End productions including: Grease, Follies, Carmen Jones, Rowan Atkinson in Revue, Home, Design for Living; Neville's Island, 1994; Passion, 1996; West Side Story, 1998; Spend, Spend, Spend, 1999; The Real Thing, 2000 (also NY); Sunset Boulevard, 2001; Our House, Chitty Chitty Bang Bang, 2002; A Few Good Men, 2005; The Sound of Music, 2006; Enron, 2009; The Bodyguard, Sweeney Todd, 2012 (What's On Stage Award for Lighting Design, 2013); Funny Girl, Gypsy (Best Lighting Design, Olivier Awards, 2016), 2015; Lady Day at Emerson's Bar, Don Juan in Soho, 2017; RNT productions include: Cat on a Hot Tin Roof (also NY), 1988; Hamlet (also NY), 1989; Les Parents Terribles, 1994; The Oedipus Plays, 1996; Amy's View, Copenhagen, Antony and Cleopatra, 1998; Battle Royal, 1999; All My Sons, 2001; Mourning Becomes Electra, 2003; The History Boys, 2004 (also NY; Tony Award for Lighting Design (Play), 2006); The Alchemist, 2006; The Habit of Art, Burnt by the Sun, (Best Lighting Design, Olivier Awards, 2010), 2009; Emperor and Galilean, One Man Two Guvnors, 2011; Coriolanus, 2014 (What's On Stage Award for Lighting Design, 2015); The Hard Problem, 2015; RSC productions include: Macbeth, Kiss Me Kate, The Lion, the Witch and the Wardrobe; Imperium, 2017; Almeida Theatre productions include: Phèdre, The Ice Man Cometh, 1998; Vassa, Plenty, 1999; Richard II, Coriolanus, 2000; Lulu, 2001; Old Vic productions include: Girl from the North Country, 2017; Fanny and Alexander, 2018; Broadway productions include: The Judas Kiss, Democracy, Racing Demon, Indiscretions, Les Liaisons Dangereuses; *opera* productions include: The Flying Dutchman (Royal Opera); Anna Karenina, The Silver Tassie, 2000, ENO; Othello, Glyndebourne, 2001; Tosca, ROH, 2006; Don Carlo, ROH, 2017; *dance* productions include: Agora, Shadows in the Sun (London Contemp. Dance Th.); Quicksilver (Rambert Dance Co.); Tales of Beatrix Potter, The Judas Tree, Daphnis and Chloë, Sleeping Beauty (Royal Ballet); The Nutcracker, 1999; Giselle, 2016 (English Nat. Ballet); *films* include: The Tall Guy, 1988; Under Milk Wood, 1992; televised opening of Millennium Centre, Cardiff (BAFTA Cymru, 2005). Olivier Awards: Lighting Designer of the Year, 1992; Best Lighting Designer, 1995, 2000, 2002. *Address:* c/o PBJ Management, 22 Rathbone Street, W1T 1LG.

**HENDERSON, Mark;** Chief Executive, Home Group Ltd, since 2008; *b* 12 Oct. 1962; *s* of Ralph and Mary Henderson; *m* 1987, Lindsey Robertson; one *s* one *d. Educ:* Univ. of Dundee (BSc Hons). Planning Technician: Dunfermline DC, 1979–87; Dundee DC, 1987–91; Strategic Policy Manager, Clackmannanshire, 1994–96; Partnership Funding Officer, Angus Council, 1996–97; Asst Dir (Regeneration), N Lincs Council, 1997–2000; Dir of Ops, One Northeast, 2000–03; Chief Exec., Northumberland CC, 2003–08. Mem., Dundee DC, 1992–96. *Recreations:* classic motorcycle racer, supporter of Dunfermline Athletic FC and Newcastle United FC. *Address:* Home Group Ltd, 2 Gosforth Park Way, Gosforth Business Park, Newcastle-upon-Tyne NE12 8ET.

**HENDERSON, Mark Giles Fyfield;** Director of Communications, Wellcome Trust, since 2016 (Head of Communications, 2012–16); *b* Lambeth, 22 Aug. 1974; *s* of Giles Ian Henderson, *qv; m* 2009, Niki Vivien; one *s* one *d. Educ:* Winchester Coll.; Balliol Coll., Oxford (BA 1st Cl. Hons Modern Hist. 1996). The Times, 1996–2011: sci. corresp., 2000–06; Sci. Ed., 2006–11. Award for Statistical Excellence in Journalism, Royal Statistical Soc.; Med. Journalists' Assoc. awards; Eur. Best Cancer Reporter, Eur. Sch. of Oncol. *Publications:* 50 Genetics Ideas You Really Need to Know, 2009; The Geek Manifesto: why science matters, 2012. *Recreations:* ski-ing, popular science, cricket, football, Twitter. *Address:* Wellcome Trust, 215 Euston Road, NW1 2BE. *T:* (020) 7611 8540. *E:* m.henderson@wellcome.ac.uk. *Club:* Queens Park Rangers Football.

**HENDERSON, Michael John Glidden,** FCA; Chairman, Advisory Board, Quexco Inc. (USA), since 2005 (Executive Vice-Chairman, 2002–05); *b* 19 Aug. 1938; *s* of William Glidden Henderson and Aileen Judith Henderson (née Molloy); *m* 1965, Stephanie Maria Dyer; four *s. Educ:* St Benedict's Sch., Ealing. FCA 1971. Took articles with William Dyson Jones & Co., 1956; qual. as chartered accountant, 1961; Whinney Smith & Whinney & Co., 1963; Goodlass Wall & Lead Industries, later Cookson Group plc, 1965; Cookson Group: Dir, 1975; Man. Dir, 1979; Chief Exec., 1984–90; Chm. and Chief Exec., 1990–91; Exec. Dir, Ronar Services Ltd, 1991–2006. Chairman: Henderson Crossthwaite, subseq. Investec Henderson Crossthwaite, Hldgs Ltd, 1995–2000; Cyril Sweett Ltd, then Cyril Sweett Gp plc, subseq. Sweett Gp plc, 2010–14 (non-exec. Dir, 1998–2014); Dir, Tioxide Gp, 1987–90; non-executive Director: Guinness Mahon Holdings, 1988–2000; Three Counties Financial Mgt Services Ltd, 1991–2009; ECO-BAT Technologies, 1999–2002. Mem., Innovation Adv. Bd, DTI, 1988–93. Trustee, Natural History Mus. Develt Trust, 1990–2000. Member: Council, St Augustine's Soc., 2007–15; Investment Cttee, Handicapped Children's Pilgrimage Trust, 2013–18. Mem., Catholic Union, 2008– (Mem. Council, 2012–; Chm., Membership and Commns Cttee, 2013–17; Exec. Cttee, 2016–). Chm., Exec. Cttee and Trustee, Catholic Union Charitable Trust Ltd, 2013–. FRSA 1989. Governor: St George's Coll., Weybridge, 1990–2011 (Dep. Chm., 2002–11; Chm., F and GP Cttee, 1991–2011); Cranmore Sch., W Horsley, 1992– (Chm., 2012–; Dep. Chm., 1998–2012; Chm., F and GP Cttee, 1992–2012); St Teresa's Convent, Effingham, 2002–14 (Chm., F and GP Cttee, 2003–11; Vice Chm., 2011–14). Mem., Effingham and Fetcham Pastoral Council, 2012–15. KC*HS 2016 (KHS 2005; KCHS 2010) (Mem. Council and Treas., S Section, 2007–15). *Recreations:* tennis, golf, watching all sports, reading, music, visiting and being involved with family including 16 grandchildren, gardening in woodland. *Address:* 34 Frenchlands Gate, Ockham Road South, East Horsley, Surrey KT24 6BF. *T:* (01483) 283844. *E:* mike.henderson3@btopenworld.com. *Clubs:* MCC, Queen's; Wisley Golf (Dir, 2002–07; Dep. Chm., 2004–07); Horsley Sports (Chm., 1982–87); Sussex Cricket; Surrey Cricket; Thurlestone Golf; Salcombe Yacht; Kingsbridge Tennis.

**HENDERSON, Nicholas John,** LVO 2018; National Hunt racehorse trainer, since 1978; *b* 10 Dec. 1950; *s* of late John Ronald Henderson, CVO, OBE; *m* 1st, 1978, Diana Amanda Thorne (marr. diss. 2006); three *d*; 2nd, 2018, Sophie Jean Waddilove. *Educ:* Eton. Amateur rider, 1970–78 (rode 75 winners, incl. Imperial Cup, Sandown and Liverpool Foxhunters); Asst Trainer to Fred Winter, 1973–78. Trained over 2,300 winners, incl. See You Then (Champion Hurdle, 1985, 1986, 1987), Brown Windsor (Whitbread Gold Cup, 1989), Remittance Man (Champion Chase, 1992), Punjabi (Champion Hurdle, 2009), Binocular (Champion Hurdle, 2010); Long Run (Cheltenham Gold Cup, 2011); Finian's Rainbow (Champion Chase, 2012); Sprinter Sacre (Champion Chase, 2013, 2016); Bobs Worth (Cheltenham Gold Cup, 2013); Buveur D'Air (Champion Hurdle, 2017, 2018); Altior (Champion Chase, 2018, 2019). Leading Nat. Hunt trainer, 1986–87, 1987–88, 2012–13; Champion Nat. Hunt trainer, 2016–17, 2017–18; Piper Heidsieck Trainer of the Year, 1986, 1987, 1988. *Address:* Seven Barrows, Lambourn, Hungerford, Berks RG17 8UH.

**HENDERSON, Prof. Paul,** CBE 2003; DPhil; Director of Science, Natural History Museum, 1995–2003; *b* 7 Nov. 1940; *s* of Thomas William Henderson and Dorothy Violet (née Marriner); *m* 1966, Elizabeth Kathryn Ankerson; one *s* one *d. Educ:* King's Coll. Sch., Wimbledon; Univ. of London (BSc 1963); Univ. of Oxford (DPhil 1966). FGS 1990; CGeol 1990; FLS 1997. Asst Lectr in Chemistry, Glasgow Univ., 1967–68; Lectr in Geochem., Chelsea Coll., Univ. of London, 1968–76; British Museum (Natural History), subseq. Natural History Museum: PSO, 1977, Grade 6, 1984, Dep. Keeper, 1987, Keeper, 1989–95, Deputy Director, Associate Dir, Earth Scis, 1992–95. Visiting Professor: Univ. of Bern, Switzerland, 1989; UCL, 1990–98 (Hon. Prof., 1999–). Pres., Mineralogical Soc., 1989–91 (Mem. Council, 1974–76 and 1986–89); Vice-Pres., Geol Soc., 2002–08; Member Council: Eur. Assoc. for Geochem., 1986–94; Internat. Mineralog. Assoc., 1989–94; Vice-Pres., Linnean Soc. of London, 2018–. Member: Sci. Adv. Bd, 1994–99, Expert Commn, 2001–02, Museum für Naturkunde, Berlin; Sci. Adv. Cttee, 2000–01, Conseil Scientifique, 2002–06, Muséum Nat. d'Histoire Naturelle, Paris. Trustee, Horniman Mus. and Public Park Trust, 2004–12. Fourmarier Medal, Belgian Geol Soc., 1989. *Publications:* Inorganic Geochemistry, 1982; (ed) Rare Earth Element Geochemistry, 1984; (with G. M. Henderson) Cambridge Handbook of Earth Science Data, 2009; James Sowerby: the enlightenment's natural historian, 2015 (Excellence in Biography Award, Council on Botanical and Horticl Libraries, USA, 2016; Inspirational Book of the Year, Garden Media Guild, 2016); contribs to jls on geochem. and mineral chem. *Recreations:* music, mineralogy, history, Paris, wine. *Address:* Department of Earth Sciences, University College London, Gower Street, WC1E 6BT. *E:* p.henderson@ucl.ac.uk.

See also G. M. Henderson.

**HENDERSON, Air Vice-Marshal Peter William,** CB 2000; MBE 1982; CEng, FRAeS; Director General, Equipment Support (Air), and Member, Air Force Board, 1999–2000; *b* 5 Nov. 1945. *Educ:* King's Sch., Macclesfield; RAF Tech. Coll., Henlow; RAF Coll. Cranwell (BSc Hons 1969). Inspectorate of Flight Safety, 1975; RAF Germany, 1978; RAF Staff Coll., 1982; RAF Abingdon, 1982–84; Dept of Air Mem. for Supply and Orgn, 1984–87; Mem., Ordnance Bd, 1987–90; Stn Comdr, Abingdon, 1990–92; Logistic Comd Project Sponsor, HQ RAF Support Comd, 1992–95; Dir 1995–97, Dir Gen., 1997–99, RAF Support Mgt; Mem., Air Force Bd and Defence Logistics Mgt Bd, 1999–2000, retd. *Recreations:* gardening, motoring, offshore sailing. *Club:* Royal Air Force.

**HENDERSON, Dr Richard,** CH 2018; FRS 1983; Member of the Scientific Staff, Medical Research Council Laboratory of Molecular Biology, Cambridge, since 1973 (Director, 1996–2006); Fellow of Darwin College, Cambridge, 1981–2012, now Emeritus Fellow; *b* 19 July 1945; *s* of late John and Grace Henderson; *m* 1st, 1969, Penelope FitzGerald (marr. diss. 1988); one *s* one *d* (and one *d* decd); 2nd, 1995, Jade Li. *Educ:* Hawick High Sch.; Boroughmuir Secondary Sch.; Edinburgh Univ. (BSc); Corpus Christi Coll., Cambridge (Hon. Fellow, 2003); PhD Cantab 1970. Helen Hay Whitney Fellow, Yale Univ., 1970–73. Mem., MRC, 2008–14. Founder FMedSci 1998. Foreign Associate, Acad. of Sci., USA, 1998. Hon. DSc Edinburgh, 2008. William Bate Hardy Prize, Cambridge Phil Soc., 1978; Ernst Ruska Prize for Electron Microscopy, Ernst Ruska Foundn, 1981; Lewis S. Rosenstiel Award, Brandeis Univ., 1991; Louis Jeantet Award, Jeantet Foundn, Geneva, 1993; Gregori Aminoff Prize, Royal Swedish Acad. of Scis, 1999; Alexander Hollaender Award, US NAS, 2016; Copley Medal, Royal Soc., 2016; (jtly) Nobel Prize in Chemistry, 2017. *Publications:* research pubns and reviews in scientific jls. *Recreations:* kayaking, wine-tasting, hillwalking. *Address:* MRC Laboratory of Molecular Biology, Francis Crick Avenue, Cambridge CB2 0QH. *T:* (01223) 267000.

**HENDERSON, Rt Rev. Richard Crosbie Aitken,** DPhil; Team Vicar, Heart of Eden Team Ministry, 2011–12; an Honorary Assistant Bishop, Diocese of Carlisle, 2011–14; *b* 27 March 1957; *s* of Baron Henderson of Brompton, KBE; *m* 1985, Anita Julia Whiting; one *s* two *d*. *Educ*: Westminster Sch.; Magdalen Coll., Oxford (MA, DPhil 1984); St John's Coll., Nottingham (DipTh Univ. of Nottingham 1984; Dip Pastoral Studies 1986). Ordained deacon, 1986, priest, 1987; Curate, Chinnor with Emmington and Sydenham, Dio. Oxford, 1986–89; Diocese of Cork, Cloyne and Ross: Incumbent, Abbeystrewry Union, 1989–95; Ross Union, 1995–98; Canon, Cork and Ross Cathedrals, 1993–95; Prebendary of Cork, 1995–98; Dean of Ross, 1995–98; Bishop of Tuam, Killala and Achonry, 1998–2011. *Publications*: The Jealousy of Jonah, 2006. *Recreations*: woodwork, metalwork, horticulture.
*See also* Rt Hon. Sir L. D. J. Henderson.

**HENDERSON, Richard Mitchell,** CB 2007; WS; Solicitor to the Scottish Executive, and Head of the Government Legal Service for Scotland, 1999–2007; President, Law Society of Scotland, 2007–09 (Vice-President, May–Aug. 2007); *b* 17 April 1947; *s* of Thomas Alex Henderson and Hester Susan England Henderson (*née* Mitchell); *m* 1970, Frances Lesley Eadie; one *s* one *d*. *Educ*: Cellardyke Primary Sch., Anstruther; Strathallan Sch.; Univ. of Edinburgh (LlB Hons 1969). Admitted Solicitor, 1971; WS 2006; Solicitor to the Sec. of State for Scotland, 1998. Chm., Scottish Cttee, Admin. Justice and Tribunals Council, 2009–13. *Recreations*: golf (occasional and erratic), walking, being in the fresh air.

**HENDERSON, Sir Richard (Yates),** KCVO 2006; TD 1966; JP; Lord-Lieutenant of Ayrshire and Arran, 1991–2006; *b* 7 July 1931; *s* of late John Wishart Henderson and Dorothy (*née* Yates); *m* 1957, Frances Elizabeth Chrystal; two *s* one *d* (and one *s* decd). *Educ*: Rugby; Hertford Coll., Oxford (BA); Glasgow Univ. (LLB). Served Royal Scots Greys, 1950–52; Ayrshire Yeomanry TA, 1953–69. Partner, Mitchells Roberton, Solicitors, Glasgow, 1958–90; Trustee, TSB, Glasgow, 1966–74; Dir, West of Scotland TSB, 1974–83. Hon. Sheriff, S Strathclyde, Dumfries and Galloway at Ayr, 1997. Ensign, Royal Company of Archers, Queen's Body Guard for Scotland, 2004–. Hon. Col, Ayrshire Yeo. Sqn, Scottish Yeo., 1992–97; Pres., Lowlands TAVRA, 1996–2000. DL Ayrshire, 1970–90. *Recreations*: shooting, tennis, golf. *Address*: Blairston, by Ayr KA7 4EF. *T*: (01292) 441601. *Club*: Western (Glasgow).

**HENDERSON, Roger Anthony,** QC 1980; a Recorder of the Crown Court, 1983–2012; a Deputy High Court Judge, 1987–2012; *b* 21 April 1943; *s* of late Dr Peter Wallace Henderson, MC and Dr Stella Dolores Henderson; *m* 1968, Catherine Margaret Williams (*d* 2013); three *d* (and one *d* decd). *Educ*: Radley Coll.; St Catharine's Coll., Cambridge (Scholar; 1st Cl. Hons degree in Law, MA; Adderley Prize for Law, 1964). Inner Temple: Duke of Edinburgh Award, 1962; Major Scholarship, 1964; called to the Bar, 1964; Bencher, 1985. Counsel to King's Cross Inquiry, 1988. Mem., Bar Council, 1988–91; Chm., Public Affairs Cttee of Bar, 1989–90. Chm., Civil Service Arbitration Tribunal, 1994–; Member: Exec. Council, British Acad. of Forensic Sciences, 1977–90 (Pres., 1986–87); Council of Legal Educn, 1983–90. Chm., Assoc. of Regulatory and Disciplinary Lawyers, 2003–09; Vice Pres., Health and Safety Lawyers' Assoc., 2005–. Gov., London Hosp. Med. Coll., 1989–96 (Chm., Council, 1993–96); Chm., Special Cttee, St Peter's Hosps, 1989–92; Mem. Council, QMW, 1993–2005; Mem. Council, Southampton Univ., 2009–12; Chm., Med. Coll. of St Bartholomew's Hosp. Trust, 2012–18. FRSA 1994. Hon. Fellow, QMC, London, 2006. *Recreations*: fly-fishing, gardening, shooting. *Address*: Holbury Mill, Lockerley, Romsey, Hants SO51 0JR. *T*: (01794) 340583; 7A Berkeley Gardens, W8 4AP. *Clubs*: Boodle's; New Zealand Golf.

**HENDERSON, Victor Joseph,** CMG 2000; HM Diplomatic Service, retired; Senior Consultant, MEC International Ltd, since 2001; *b* 10 Jan. 1941; *s* of Frederick Ilwyn Henderson and Mary Elizabeth Henderson; *m* 1966, Heather Winifred Steed; one *s* one *d*. *Educ*: Rhondda Co. Grammar Sch. for Boys; King's Coll., London (BA Hons Spanish 1961). Joined HM Diplomatic Service, 1966: MECAS, Lebanon, 1967–69; Third Sec. (Commercial), Jedda, 1969–72; Second Sec. (Commercial), Bahrain, 1972–75; FCO, 1975–78; Second, later First Sec., Caracas, 1978–82; Consul, Jerusalem, 1982–87; FCO, 1987–90; First Sec. (Political, later Commercial), Helsinki, 1990–94; Dep. Head, Jt Export Promotion Directorate, FCO/DTI, 1995–97; Ambassador to the Yemen, 1997–2001. Analyst (pt-time), BBC Monitoring Services, 2006–. Chm., British Yemeni Soc., 2006–08. *Recreations*: watching cricket, reading, listening to music (especially jazz). *Address*: c/o MEC International Ltd, Granville House, 132-135 Sloane Street, SW1X 9AX.

**HENDERSON-SELLERS, Prof. Ann,** PhD, DSc; Professor, Department of Environment and Geography (formerly Physical Geography), Macquarie University, 2008–12, now Emerita; *b* 7 March 1952; *d* of Thomas William Futtit and Ruth Forester Fielding; *m* 1974, Prof. Brian Henderson-Sellers. *Educ*: Sheffield Girls' High Sch.; Pate's, Cheltenham; Univ. of Bristol (BSc Hons Maths); Univ. of Leicester (PhD 1976, DSc 1999). University of Liverpool: Lectr, 1977–82; Sen. Lectr, 1982–86; Reader, 1986–88; Personal Chair in Physical Geography, 1988; Prof. of Physical Geog., and Dir, Climatic Impacts Centre, Macquarie Univ., 1988–96; Dep. Vice-Chancellor, R&D, RMIT, 1996–98; Dir, Envmt, Australian Nuclear Sci. and Technol. Orgn, 1998–2005; Dir, World Climate Res. Prog., WMO, 2006–07. Vis. Lectr, Univ. of Witwatersrand, S Africa, 1979; Vis. Res. Fellow, NASA Goddard Inst. for Space Studies, 1981–82; Vis. Prof., Univ. of Louvain-la-Neuve, Belgium, 1983; Vis. Scientist, Nat. Center for Atmospheric Res., USA, 1985–2003. Hon. DSc Bristol, 2011. *Publications*: (jtly) Atmospheric Pollution, 4th edn 1981; The Origin and Evolution of Planetary Atmospheres, 1983; Satellite Sensing of a Cloudy Atmosphere, 1984; (jtly) Contemporary Climatology, 1986, 2nd edn 1999; (jtly) The Climate Modelling Primer, 1987, 4th edn 2013; (jtly) The Greenhouse Effect: living in a warmer Australia, 1989; (ed jtly) Vegetation and Climate Interactions in Semi-Arid Regions, 1991; (ed jtly) Climate Change Atlas, 1995; (ed) Future Climates of the World: a modelling perspective, 1995, 2nd edn as Future of the World's Climate, 2012; (ed jtly) Climate Change: developing Southern Hemisphere perspectives, 1996; (ed jtly) Assessing Climate Change, 1997; (jtly) The Great North Walk Companion, 2009; 453 articles in tech. jls. *Recreation*: collecting Winnie the Pooh books in different languages.

**HENDERSON-STEWART, Sir David (James),** 2nd Bt *cr* 1957; *b* 3 July 1941; *s* of Sir James Henderson-Stewart, 1st Bt, MP, and of Anna Margaret (*née* Greenwell); *S* father, 1961; *m* 1972, Anne, *d* of Count Serge de Pahlen; three *s* one *d*. *Educ*: Eton Coll.; Trinity Coll., Oxford. *Heir*: *s* David Henderson-Stewart [*b* 2 Feb. 1973; *m* 1997, Xenia Yagello; two *s* two *d* (of whom one *s* one *d* are twins)]. *Address*: 90 Oxford Gardens, W10 5UW. *T*: (020) 8964 4356.

**HENDON, David Anthony,** CBE 2006; FREng, FIET; Director, Information Economy and Life Sciences, Department for Business, Innovation and Skills, 2010–11; Director, Hendon Communications Strategy Ltd, since 2011; Senior Vice President, Rivada Networks, since 2017; *b* 19 Oct. 1949; *s* of Anthony Leonard Hendon and Constance Audrey Hendon (*née* Clayton); *m* 1976, Gillian Anne Iles; one *s* two *d*. *Educ*: Royal Grammar Sch., Guildford; Southampton Univ. (BSc Eng 1972). FIET (FIEE 2000); CEng 1978; FREng 2002. MoD, 1973–84 (Principal, 1981–84); Asst Dir (Engrg), Home Office, 1984–88; Dep. Dir, 1988–92, Dir, 1992–98, Technol., Policy, Communications and Inf. Industries Directorate, DTI; Chief Exec., Radiocommunications Agency, 1998–2002; Hd of Communications and Inf. Industries Directorate, DTI, 2002–03; Dir, Business Relns, then Inf. Economy, DTI, later BERR, subseq. BIS, 2003–10. Chm. Bd, Eur. Telecommunications Standards Inst., 1995–99. Chm., Radio Spectrum Internat. Consulting Ltd, 1998–2002. Sen. Advr, Ofcom, 2011–17. Chair: 4G/TV Co-existence Oversight Bd, DCMS, 2013–18; Strategic Adv. Bd, 5G Innovation Centre, Univ. of Surrey, 2013–. Non-executive Director: Multiple Access Communications Ltd, 2012–; Continuum Bridge Ltd, 2013–19. Member: PPARC, 2002–06; EPSRC, 2006–09. Vis. Prof., Univ. of Surrey, 2013–. Trustee, Radio Communications Foundn, 2003– (Vice-Chm., 2009–). Spastics Society, later Scope: Mem. Council, 1987–96; Vice-Chm., 1991–93; Chm., Audit Cttee, 1993–98; Hon. Life Mem., 1996. Chm., White Lodge Centre, Chertsey, 1980–85. Gov., Guildford Co. Sch., 1994–98. *Recreations*: grandchildren, food and wine, Maine Coon cats. *Address*: 2 Ellis Avenue, Onslow Village, Guildford GU2 7SR. *T*: (01483) 823108.

**HENDRICK, Sir Mark (Phillip),** Kt 2018; CEng; MP (Lab and Co-op) Preston, since Nov. 2000; *b* 2 Nov. 1958; *s* of Brian Francis Hendrick and Jennifer (*née* Chapman); *m* 2008, Yannan Yu. *Educ*: Liverpool Poly. (BSc Hons Electrical and Electronic Engrg); Univ. of Manchester (MSc Computer Sci.; Cert Ed). CEng 1987. Trainee Technician, Signal and Telecommunications, BR, 1975–78; Student Engr, 1979–81; RSRE Malvern, MoD, 1979; Special Systems Unit, STC plc, 1980; AEG Telefunken, Seligenstadt, Germany, 1981; Design Engr, Daresbury Lab., SERC, 1982–84 and 1985–88; Lectr, Stockport Coll., 1989–94. MEP (Lab and Co-op) Lancashire Central, 1994–99; contested (Lab) NW Reg., 1999. PPS to Sec. of State, DEFRA, 2003–06, FCO, 2006–07, to Minister of Justice, 2007–08. Member: Internat. Develt Select Cttee, 2008–10; Foreign Affairs Select Cttee, 2012–17; Internat. Trade Select Cttee, 2018–; Chm., All Party Parly China Gp, 2010–12. *Recreations*: football supporter (Manchester City and Preston North End), travel, chess, German and French. *Address*: c/o House of Commons, SW1A 0AA; (constituency office) PTMC, Marsh Lane, Preston PR1 8UQ. *T*: (01772) 883575. *Clubs*: Parkfield Labour; Lonsdale (Preston).

**HENDRICKS, Barbara;** American soprano; *b* 20 Nov. 1948; *d* of Rev. M. L. Hendricks and Della Hendricks; *m*; one *s* one *d*. *Educ*: Univ. of Nebraska (BS Chem. and Math. 1969); Juilliard Sch. of Music, NY (Schol.; BM); studied under Jennie Tourel. Début, l'Incoronazione di Poppea, San Francisco Opera, 1976; has appeared with opera cos of Berlin, Boston, Florence, Glyndebourne, Hamburg, La Scala, Milan, LA, Royal Opera, Covent Garden, etc; concert performances with major orchestras; numerous recordings. Launched own record label, Arte Verum, 2005. Goodwill Ambassador, UN High Commn for Refugees, 1987. Hon. Dr Juilliard, NY, 2000. Prince of Asturias Prize, 2000. Commandeur des Arts et des Lettres (France), 1986; Chevalier de la Légion d'Honneur (France), 1993; St George's Cross (Catalonia, Spain), 2006.

**HENDRICKS, Rt Rev. Paul Joseph;** an Auxiliary Bishop, Diocese of Southwark, (RC), since 2006; *b* 18 March 1956; *s* of Gerald Hendricks and Grace Hendricks (*née* Deacon). *Educ*: Holy Innocents Primary St., Orpington; St Mary's Grammar Sch., Sidcup; Corpus Christi Coll., Oxford (BA Physics 1977, MA); Gregorian Univ., Rome (PhL 1985). Ordained deacon, 1983, priest, 1984; Asst Priest, St Boniface Church, Tooting, 1985–89; Lectr in Philosophy, St John's Seminary, Wonersh, 1989–99; Parish Priest, Our Lady of Sorrows, Peckham, 1999–2006. *Recreations*: reading, walking, cats, music. *Address*: 95 Carshalton Road, Sutton SM1 4LL. *T*: (020) 8643 8007. *E*: bishop.hendricks@gmail.com.

**HENDRIE, Dr Gerald Mills;** musicologist, composer, harpsichordist and organist; Professor of Music, The Open University, 1969–90; *b* 28 Oct. 1935; *s* of James Harold Hendrie and Florence Mary MacPherson; *m* 1st, 1962, Dinah Florence Barsham, BMus, PhD (*d* 1985); two *s*; 2nd, 1986, Dr Lynette Anne Maddern, MB, BS. *Educ*: Framlingham Coll., Suffolk; Royal Coll. of Music; Selwyn Coll., Cambridge (MA, MusB, PhD). FRCO, ARCM. Director of Music, Homerton Coll., Cambridge, 1962–63; Lectr in Music, Univ. of Manchester, 1963–67; Prof. and Chm., Dept of Music, Univ. of Victoria, BC, Canada, 1967–69; Reader in Music, subseq. Prof., The Open Univ., 1969–90; Dir of Studies in Music, St John's Coll., Cambridge, 1981–84, Supervisor, 1977–84. Vis. Fellow in Music, Univ. of WA, 1985. *Publications*: Musica Britannica XX, Orlando Gibbons: Keyboard Music, 1962, 3rd rev. edn 2010; G. F. Handel: Anthems für Cannons, 3 vols, 1985, 1987, 1991; Anthems für the Chapel Royal, 1992; Utrecht Te Deum and Jubilate, 1998; Gilbert and Sullivan: Iolanthe (critical edn in full score), 3 vols, 2018, vocal score 2019; articles for Die Musik in Geschichte und Gegenwart; musical compositions include: Five Bagatelles for piano, 1980; Four Excursions for piano, 1983; Three Pieces for flute and piano, 1985; Specula Petro for organ, 1988; Quintet for Brass, 1988; Choral: Hommage à César Franck for organ, 1990; Le Tombeau de Marcel Dupré (for organ): Toccata and Fugue, 1991; Prelude and Fugue, 1991; Prelude and Fugue on the name BACH, 1992; Two Sketches on the name BACH, 1993; Sonata No 1, In Praise of St Asaph, for organ, 1994; Four Consolations (after Boethius) for unaccompanied choir, 1996; Requiem, for soprano, chorus, organ, 1997; Sonata No 2, In Praise of Reconciliation, for organ, 1998, for piano, 1998; Premier Livre d'Orgue, 1999; Deuxième Livre d'Orgue, 2000; Missa Aquitaniae, for soprano, chorus, organ, 2003; Sounats Campanetos/Ring out, Sing out, Noël Gascon, for SATB accompanied, 2005; Sonata No 3, Sonate en Trio, for organ, 2006; A Handful of Rags for piano, 2013; Another Handful of Rags for piano, 2014; Twelve New Rags for piano, 2018; Pastoral and Fughetta, for organ, 2018–19; much church music. *Recreations*: walking, gardening. *Address*: Au Village, 32190 Caillavet, France. *T*: 562644104.

**HENDRIE, Robert Andrew Michie;** HM Diplomatic Service, retired; Ambassador to Uruguay, 1994–98; *b* 4 May 1938; *s* of John Hendrie, Edinburgh and Effie Campbell (*née* Mackay); *m* 1964, Consuelo Liaño Solórzano; two *d*. *Educ*: Bradford Grammar Sch.; Trinity Hall, Cambridge (BA, MA). Joined HM Diplomatic Service, 1961; MECAS, Beirut, 1961–62; Political Residency, Bahrain, 1962–65; Tehran, 1965–69; Tripoli, 1968–69; Latin America Dept, FCO, 1969–73; Lima, 1973–75; Buenos Aires, 1975–80; Asst Hd, Central Africa Dept, ME Dept and Inf. Dept, FCO, 1980–86; Consul-General: Lille, 1986–90; Dubai, UAE, 1990–94. Mem., S Atlantic Council, 2001–; Vice Pres., British Uruguayan Soc., 2012–17. Mem., RSAA, 2003–. MCIL (MIL 1987). Freeman, City of London, 2012. *Recreations*: reading, walking, watching Rugby, languages. *Address*: c/o Foreign and Commonwealth Office, King Charles Street, SW1A 2AH. *Clubs*: Canning, Roehampton.

**HENDRON, Joseph Gerard;** Member (SDLP) Belfast West, Northern Ireland Assembly, 1998–2003; *b* 12 Nov. 1932; *m* 1974, Sally (*née* Lennon); three *s* one *d*. *Educ*: St Malachy's Coll.; Queen's Univ., Belfast (MB 1957). FRCGP 1987. GP, W Belfast. Mem. (SDLP) Belfast CC, 1981–93. MP (SDLP) Belfast W, 1992–97; contested (SDLP) same seat, 1983, 1987, 1997. Chm., Health, Social Services and Public Safety Cttee, NI Assembly. Mem., Parades Commn, 2006–10.

**HENDRY, Andrew Egan Henderson, (Drew);** MP (SNP) Inverness, Nairn, Badenoch and Strathspey, since 2015; *b* 31 May 1964; *m* Jackie; four *c*. Shop worker, latterly Dir, multinat. appliance manufr; Founder and Chm., Teclan Ltd, 1999–2016. Mem. (SNP), Highland Council, 2007–15 (Leader, SNP Gp, 2011–15; Leader of Council, 2012–15). SNP Gp Leader, H of C, 2015–17; SNP spokesperson on Business, Energy and Industrial

Strategy, 2017–. Mem., Business, Energy and Industrial Strategy Select Cttee, 2017–. Vice Pres., Conf. of Maritime Peripheral Regions, 2012. *Address:* House of Commons, SW1A 0AA. *T:* (020) 7219 6118.

**HENDRY, Rt Hon. Charles**, CBE 2019; PC 2015; *b* 6 May 1959; *s* of late Charles William Righton Hendry and Margaret Anne Hendry; *m* 1995, Mrs Sallie A. Moores; two *s*, and one step *s* one step *d*. *Educ:* Rugby Sch.; Univ. of Edinburgh (BCom Hons 1981). Account Dir, Ogilvy and Mather PR, 1983–86; Burson-Marsteller: Associate Dir (PR), 1986–88; Sen. Counsellor, Public Affairs, 1990–92. Non-executive Chairman: Agenda Gp Ltd, 2001–05 (Dir and Chief Exec., 1999–2001); IncrediBull Ideas Ltd, 2003–04. Special Adviser to: Rt Hon. John Moore, 1988; Rt Hon. Anthony Newton, 1988–89; Chief of Staff to Leader of Cons. Party, 1997; Hd of Business Liaison, Cons. Party, 1997–99. Vice-Chm., Battersea Cons. Assoc., 1981–83. Contested (C): Clackmannan, 1983; Mansfield, 1987; MP (C) High Peak, 1992–97; contested (C) same seat, 1997; MP (C) Wealden, 2001–15. PPS to Sec. of State for Educn and Employment, 1995; a Vice Chm., Cons. Party, 1995–97; an Opposition Whip, 2001–02; Shadow Minister: for youth affairs, 2002–05; for industry and enterprise, 2005; for energy, science and technology, 2005–07; for Energy, Industry and Postal Affairs, 2007–08; for Energy, 2008–10; Minister of State, DECC, 2010–12; Prime Minister's Trade Envoy to Azerbaijan, Kazakhstan and Turkmenistan, 2012–15; Comr, UK Pavilion, Expo 2017, Kazakhstan. Dep. Chm., Cons. Party, 2003–05. Member, Select Committee: on Procedure, 1992–94; on NI Affairs, 1994–97; on Culture, Media and Sport, 2003–04; on Energy and Climate Change, 2009–10. Secretary: Conservative Back bench Social Services Cttee, 1992–94; Cons. Back bench Home Improvement Sub-Cttee, 1993–94; Cons. Back bench Urban Affairs Cttee, 1994; Jt Chm., All-Party Parly Gp on Homelessness, 1992–96; Vice Chm., All Party Parly Internet Gp, 2005–08; Chm., British-Swiss Parly Gp, 2007–10. Sec., E Midlands Area Cons. MPs, 1992–97. Chm., Forewind Ltd, 2013–15; Vice-Chm., Atlantic Petroleum, 2017–; non-exec. Dir, Independent Oil & Gas, 2017–; Dir, London Power Corp., 2017–. Led Hendry Ind. Rev. of Tidal Lagoons, 2016–17 (Report, 2017). Vis. Prof., Univ. of Edinburgh, 2012–. President: British Youth Council, 1992–97; Nat. Energy Action, 2013–15; BIEE, 2014–; Russo-British Chamber of Commerce, 2011–; British Chamber of Commerce, Kazakhstan, 2015–; Trustee: Drive for Youth, 1989–99; Friends of NACAB, 1992–95; Big Issue Foundn, 1995–97 (Patron, 1997–2010); British Youth Parlt, 2003–10; Patron, Nuclear Inst., 2016–. Hon. Fellow, Energy Inst., 2013. *Recreations:* family, opera, ski-ing.

**HENDRY, Sir David (Forbes),** Kt 2009; PhD; FBA 1987; FRSE; FAcSS; Professor of Economics, 1982–2018, and Director, Economic Modelling, Institute for New Economic Thinking (formerly Institute for Economic Modelling) at Oxford Martin School, 2010–18, University of Oxford; Fellow, since 1982, and Senior Research Fellow, since 2018, Nuffield College, Oxford; *b* 6 March 1944; *s* of Robert Ernest Hendry and Catherine Helen (*née* Mackenzie); *m* 1966, Evelyn Rosemary (*née* Vass); one *d*. *Educ:* Aberdeen Univ. (MA 1st Cl. Hons); LSE (MSc Distinction, PhD). Fellow, Econometric Soc., 1975; FRSE 2002. London School of Economics: Lectr, 1969; Reader, 1973; Prof. of Econometrics, 1977–82; Leverhulme Personal Res. Prof. of Econs, Univ. of Oxford, 1995–2000. Vis. Professor: Yale Univ., 1975; Univ. of Calif, Berkeley, 1976; Catholic Univ. of Louvain, 1980; Univ. of Calif, San Diego, 1981, 1989–90; Vis. Research Prof., Duke Univ., 1987–91. Chm., Res. Assessment Panel in Econs, HEFC, 1996. Pres., Royal Economic Soc., 1992–95 (Hon. Vice Pres., 1995–). Fellow, Jl of Econometrics, 1997. Founding Fellow, Internat. Assoc. for Applied Econometrics, 2017. Hon. Fellow, Internat. Inst. of Forecasters, 2001. Hon. Foreign Member: Amer. Economic Assoc., 1991; Amer. Acad. of Arts and Scis, 1994; Hon. Mem., Argentine Assoc. of Political Econ., 2010. Hon. LLD: Aberdeen, 1987; St Andrews, 2002; Hon. DSc Nottingham, 1998; Hon. DPhil: Norwegian Univ. of Sci. and Technol., 2001; Lund, 2006; Hon. Dr Oec: St Gallen, 2001; Aarhus, 2013; Dr *hc* Carlos III, 2009. FAcSS (AcSS 2012). Guy Medal in Bronze, Royal Statistical Soc., 1986; Thomson Reuters Citation Laureate, 2013; Lifetime Achievement Award, ESRC, 2014. Editor: Rev. of Econ. Studies, 1971–75; Econ. Jl, 1976–80; Oxford Bulletin of Economics and Statistics, 1983. *Publications:* (ed with K. F. Wallis) Econometrics and Quantitative Economics, 1984; PC-GIVE, 1989; (with A. J. Neale and N. R. Ericsson) PC-NAIVE, 1991; Econometrics: alchemy or science?, 1993, 2nd edn 2000; (jtly) Cointegration, Error Correction and the Econometric Analysis of Non-stationary Data, 1993; Dynamic Econometrics, 1995; (ed with M. S. Morgan) The Foundations of Econometric Analysis, 1995; (with J. A. Doornik) Empirical Econometric Modelling, 1996; (with J. A. Doornik) An Interface to Empirical Modelling, 1996; (with J. A. Doornik) Modelling Dynamic Systems using PcFiml, 1997; (with M. P. Clements) Forecasting Economic Time Series, 1998; (with M. P. Clements) Forecasting Non-Stationary Economic Time Series, 1999; (ed with N. R. Ericsson) Understanding Economic Forecasts, 2001; (with H. M. Krolzig) Automatic Econometric Model Selection, 2001; (with J. A. Doornik) Econometric Modelling Using PcGive (3 vols), 2001; (with J. A. Doornik) Interactive Monte Carlo Experimentation in Econometrics Using PcNaive, 2001; (ed with M. P. Clements) Companion to Economic Forecasting, 2002; (with B. Nielson) Econometric Modelling: a likelihood approach, 2007; (ed with M. P. Clements) Oxford Handbook of Economic Forecasting, 2011; (with J. A. Doornik) Empirical Model Discovery and Theory Evaluation, 2014; Introductory Macro-econometrics: a new approach, 2015; (with J. L. Castle and M. P. Clements) Forecasting: an essential introduction, 2019; (with J. L. Castle) Modelling our Changing World, 2019; papers in econometrics, statistics and economics jls. *Recreation:* golf. *Address:* Nuffield College, Oxford OX1 1NF; 26 Northmoor Road, Oxford OX2 6UR. *T:* (01865) 515588.

**HENDRY, Drew;** *see* Hendry, A. E. H.

**HENDRY, Ian Duncan,** CMG 1996; HM Diplomatic Service, retired; Constitutional Adviser, Overseas Territories Directorate (formerly Overseas Territories Department), Foreign and Commonwealth Office, since 2005; *b* 2 April 1948; *s* of Duncan William Hendry and Edna Beatrice Hendry (*née* Woodley); *m* 1st, 1973, Elizabeth Anne Southall (marr. diss.); one *s* one *d*; 2nd, 1991, Sally Annabel Hill. *Educ:* Uppingham Sch.; King's Coll., London (LLB, LLM). Called to the Bar, Gray's Inn, 1971; Asst Legal Advr, FCO, 1971–82 and 1985–86; Legal Advr, BMG, Berlin, 1982–85; Legal Counsellor: FCO, 1986–91; UK Perm. Representation to EC, 1991–95; FCO, 1995–99; Dep. Legal Advr, FCO, 1999–2005. *Publications:* (with M. C. Wood) The Legal Status of Berlin, 1986; (jtly) The External Relations of the European Communities, 1996; (with S. Dickson) British Overseas Territories Law, 2011, 2nd edn 2018; articles in Internat. and Comparative Law Qly and German Yearbook of Internat. Law. *Recreations:* travel, gardening, swimming, percussion, the exotic. *Address:* Woodlands Cottage, Sturmer, Haverhill, Suffolk CB9 7UW.

**HENDRY, Jamie Lovat;** theatre and film producer, since 2006; *b* London, 24 July 1985; *s* of John Hendry and Dee Hendry; *m* 2015, Annaliese Briggs; one *s* one *d*. *Educ:* St Paul's Sch., London; Univ. of Warwick (BSc Hons Computer Sci.). Major West End productions include: Legally Blonde the Musical, 2009; La Cage aux Folles, 2008; Soho Cinders, 2012; Let it Be, 2012; Neville's Island, 2014; Impossible, 2015; The Wind in the Willows (musical), 2017. Films include The Wind in the Willows, 2018. Mem., SOLT, 2009–. *Recreations:* squash, tennis, motor racing, theatre. *Address:* c/o Jamie Hendry Productions, 13 Regent Street, SW1Y 4LR. *T:* (020) 7183 5630. *E:* jamie@jamiehendryproductions.com. *Clubs:* Ivy, Soho House.

**HENDRY, Prof. Martin Anthony,** MBE 2015; PhD; FRSE, FInstP; Professor of Gravitational Astrophysics and Cosmology, since 2011, and Head, School of Physics and Astronomy, since 2012, University of Glasgow; *b* Glasgow, 13 Nov. 1967; *s* of William Hendry and Anne Hendry; *m* 2001, Ruth Wilkinson; one *d*. *Educ:* Univ. of Glasgow (BSc Hons 1st Cl. Maths and Astronomy 1988; PhD Cosmology 1992). Res. Fellow, Univ. of Sussex, 1992–96; University of Glasgow: Res. Associate, 1996–98; Lectr in Astronomy, 1998–2003; Sen. Lectr in Phys and Astronomy, 2003–11. Science in Society Fellow, STFC, 2010–12. FRSE 2011; FInstP 2012. *Publications:* over 250 scientific articles in astrophysics and cosmology. *Recreations:* classical music and choral singing, walking, hill climbing, cinema going, watching sports. *Address:* School of Physics and Astronomy, University of Glasgow, Glasgow G12 8QQ. *T:* (0141) 330 5685, *Fax:* (0141) 330 5299. *E:* martin.hendry@glasgow.ac.uk.

**HENDRY, Stephen Gordon,** MBE 1993; professional snooker player, 1986–2012; *b* 13 Jan. 1969; *s* of Gordon John Hendry and Irene Agnes (*née* Anthony); *m* 1995, Amanda Elizabeth Theresa Tart; two *s*. *Educ:* Inverkeithing High Sch. Embassy World Champion, 1990, 1992, 1993, 1994, 1995, 1996, 1999 (record number of wins); Benson & Hedges Masters Champion, 1989, 1990, 1991, 1992, 1993, 1996; UK Professional Champion, 1989, 1990, 1994, 1995, 1996; World Doubles Champion, 1987. *Publications:* Remember My Name, 1989. *Recreations:* golf, music, cars. *Club:* Lord's Taverners (Scotland).

**HENDY, Christopher Rupert,** FREng, CEng, FICE, Eur Ing; Technical Director for Transportation (formerly for Highways and Transportation), Atkins Consultants UK, since 2012; *b* Cambridge, 31 July 1970; *s* of Philip Robert Hendy and Anne Hendy; *m* 1994, Wendy Joan Edwin; two *s*. *Educ:* Winchester Coll.; Selwyn Coll., Cambridge (BA Engrg 1992; MA 1995). CEng 1998; FREng 2013; FICE 2006. W S Atkins plc: Engr, 1992–2001; Gp Engr, 2001–06; Chief Engr, 2006–07; Tech. Dir for Bridge Engrg, 2007–12; Chair, Bridge Engrg, 2009–. Chairman: UK Steel Bridge Gp, Steel Construction Inst., 2006–; UK Bridge Cttee, BSI, 2013–; fib UK, 2014–. Eur Ing 1998. Silver Medal, RAEng, 2012; Gold Medal, ICE, 2016. *Publications:* Designers' Guide to EN 1994-2, Steel and Concrete Composite Bridges, 2006; Designers' Guide to EN 1992-2, Concrete Bridges, 2007; Designers' Guide to EN 1993-2, Steel Bridges, 2007; contrib. papers to ICE Jls. *Recreations:* family, golf, tennis, cricket, walking, watching Rugby, juggling. *Address:* Atkins, Woodcote Grove, Ashley Road, Epsom KT18 5BW. *T:* (01372) 756307. *E:* chris.hendy@atkinsglobal.com.

**HENDY, John Giles;** QC 1987; *b* 11 April 1948; *s* of late Jack Hendy and Hon. Mary Hendy; *m*; three *d*. *Educ:* Ealing Technical Coll. (LLB London Univ. ext.); Queen's Univ., Belfast (DipLL, LLM). Called to the Bar, Gray's Inn, 1972; Bencher, 1995. Dir, Newham Rights Centre, 1973–76; Lectr, Middlesex Polytechnic, 1976–77; Barrister, 1977–. Vis. Prof., Sch. of Law, KCL, 1999–2008; Hon. Prof., Faculty of Law, UCL, 2014–. Chairman: Inst. of Employment Rights, 1989–; Employment Law Bar Assoc., 2003–05. Pres., Internat. Centre for Trade Union Rights, 2011–; Vice-Pres., Campaign for Trade Union Freedom, 2014–. *Publications:* (jtly) Personal Injury Practice, 2nd edn 1993, 3rd edn 1999; Redgrave's Health and Safety, 2nd edn 1994, 3rd edn 1998; (jtly) Munkman on Employer's Liability, 12th edn 1995 to 15th edn 2009; (jtly) A Manifesto for Labour Law, 2016; (contrib.) Bullen & Leake & Jacobs Precedents of Pleading, 18th edn, 2016; (jtly) Rolling Out the Manifesto for Labour Law, 2018; contrib. articles on labour law to jls incl. Industrial Law Jl, Eur. Human Rights Law Rev. *Address:* Old Square Chambers, 10–11 Bedford Row, WC1R 4BU. *T:* (020) 7269 0300, *Fax:* (020) 7405 1387.

*See also* Sir P. G. Hendy.

*[Created a Baron (Life Peer), 2019 but title not gazetted at time of going to press.]*

**HENDY, Sir Peter (Gerard),** Kt 2013; CBE 2006; Chair, Network Rail, since 2015; *b* 19 March 1953; *s* of late Jack Hendy and Hon. Mary Hendy; *m* 1999, Sue Pendle; one *s* one *d*. *Educ:* Latymer Upper Sch.; Univ. of Leeds (BA Econs and Geog.). London Transport, 1975–89, Dist Ops Manager, 1986–89; Man. Dir, Centre W London Buses Ltd, 1989–98; Divl Dir, First Gp, 1997–98; Dir, New World First Bus, Hong Kong, 1998–99; Dep. Dir, UK Bus for First Gp plc, 1998–2001; Man. Dir, Surface Transport, 2001–06, Comr, 2006–15, Transport for London. Chair: Commn for Integrated Transport, 2005–10 (Mem., 2004–05); London Legacy Develt Corp., 2017–. Member: Industrial Tribunals, 1993–98; Council, Confedn of Passenger Transport, 1994–2000. President: CILT, 2011–12 (Vice-Pres., 2008–); UITP, 2013–15. Trustee, Sci. Mus. Gp, 2019–. FCILT (FCIT 1985); FIHT 2005; FICE 2015. Hon. DSc City, 2010; Hon. DEng Bath, 2013; Hon. LLD Leeds, 2015; Hon. DLitt QMUL, 2018. *Recreations:* bus driving, cycling, travel, reading, my family. *Address:* Network Rail, Walker Suite, General Offices, Waterloo Station, SE1 8SW. *Clubs:* Groucho; Widcombe Social.

*See also* J. G. Hendy.

**HENEAGE, James Arthur;** Managing Director, Ottakar's plc, 1988–2006; *b* 31 Oct. 1957; *s* of Simon and Elizabeth Heneage; *m* 1987, Charlotte Shott; two *s* two *d*. *Educ:* Worth Abbey. Commnd Grenadier Guards, 1977–82. Advertising Executive: D'Arcy Macmanus Masius, 1982–84; Ogilvy & Mather, 1984–87; founded Ottakar's, 1987. Chm., Cheltenham Lit. Fest., 2006–. Dir, Prince's Rainforest Project, 2007–09. *Publications:* The Walls of Byzantium, 2013; Towers of Samarcand, 2014; The Lion of Mistra, 2015; A World on Fire, 2018. *Recreations:* history, cartooning, playing piano in a band, Tintin. *Address:* Buddens House, Bowerchalke, Salisbury, Wilts SP5 5BN.

**HENES, John Derek;** Head, UK Delegation to UK/French Channel Tunnel Intergovernmental Commission, 1997–2006; *b* 8 June 1937; *s* of Frederick William Kingaby Henes and Joan Elizabeth Henes (*née* Colbourne); *m* 1981, Virginia Elizabeth Evans (*d* 2011); one *s* one *d*. *Educ:* Christ's Hospital; Gonville and Caius College, Cambridge (MA). Ministry of Aviation, 1963; Dept of Trade, 1971; Private Sec. to Christopher Chataway, 1973–74, to Lord Beswick, 1974–75; Asst Sec., 1975; Dept of Transport, 1983–96; Under Sec., 1989. *Recreations:* reading, music. *Address:* 1e Cambridge Road, Twickenham, Middx TW1 2HN.

**HENFREY, Claire;** *see* Dove, C.

**HENIG,** family name of **Baroness Henig.**

**HENIG,** Baroness *cr* 2004 (Life Peer), of Lancaster in the County of Lancashire; **Ruth Beatrice Henig,** CBE 2000; DL; PhD; Deputy Speaker, House of Lords, since 2015; *b* 10 Nov. 1943; *d* of Kurt and Elfriede Munzer; *m* 1st, 1966, Stanley Henig, *qv* (marr. diss. 1993); two *s*; 2nd, 1994, Jack Johnstone (*d* 2013). *Educ:* Wyggeston Girls' Grammar Sch., Leicester; Bedford Coll., London (BA Hons 1st cl. (Hist.) 1965) Lancaster Univ. (PhD 1978). Lancaster University: Lectr, then Sen. Lectr, in Hist., 1968–2002; Hd, Hist. Dept, 1995–97; Dean, Arts and Humanities, 1997–2000. Mem. (Lab) Lancaster E, 1981–2005, Chm., 1999–2000, Lancs CC. Chairman: Lancs Police Authy, 1995–2005; Security Industry Authy, 2007–13. Mem., EU External Affairs Sub Cttee, 2012–15, EU Cttee, 2014–15, H of L. Non-exec. Chair, Securigroup, 2016–. Parly Patron: Be Your Best Foundn/Rock Challenge UK, 2006–18; Seashell Trust, 2007–. Chm., Assoc. Police Authorities, 1997–2005. Chairman: Adult Coll., Lancaster, 1981–91; Bd, Duke's Playhouse Theatre, Lancaster, 1987–95; Bd, Storey Creative Industries Centre, Lancaster, 2007–11. JP

Lancaster, 1984–2004 (Mem., Lancs Adv. Cttee for Appt of Justices, 2000–04); DL Lancs, 2002. *Publications*: The League of Nations, 1973; Versailles and After, 1984, 2nd edn 1995; Origins of the Second World War, 1985; Origins of the First World War, 1989, 3rd edn 2002; (with Chris Culpin) Europe 1870–1945, 1997; The Weimar Republic, 1998; (with Simon Henig) Women and Political Power, 2000; A History of the League of Nations, 2010. *Recreations*: bridge, fell-walking, real ale, wine appreciation, gardening, travel. *Address*: House of Lords, SW1A 0PW. *E*: ruthhenig@gmail.com.

**HENIG, Prof. Stanley**; Professor of European Politics, 1982–97 and Head of Department of European Studies, 1990–97, University of Central Lancashire (formerly Preston, then Lancashire, Polytechnic); Deputy Pro-Chancellor, University of Lancaster, 2006–11; *b* 7 July 1939; *s* of Sir Mark Henig and Grace (*née* Cohen); *m* 1st, 1966, Ruth Beatrice Munzer (*see* Baroness Henig) (marr. diss. 1993); two *s*; 2nd, 2002, Christine Carole Swann. *Educ*: Wyggeston Grammar Sch.; Corpus Christi Coll., Oxford. BA 1st Cl. Hons, 1961; MA 1965 Oxon. Teaching Asst, Dept of Politics, Univ. of Minnesota, 1961; Research Student, Nuffield Coll., 1962; Lecturer in Politics, Lancaster Univ., 1964–66; MP Lancaster, 1966–70; Lectr in Politics, Warwick Univ., 1970–71; Lectr, Civil Service Coll., 1972–75; Preston, subseq. Lancashire, Polytechnic: Head of Div. of Social Admin, later Sch. of Social Studies, 1976–85; Dean, Faculty of Social Studies, 1985–90. Sen. Res. Fellow, Federal Trust, 2001–. Mem., Lancaster CC, 1981–99 (Leader, 1991–99); Dep. Ldr, Lab. Gp, ADC, 1995–97; Sec., Lab. Gp, LGA, 1997–99. Governor, British Inst. of Recorded Sound, 1975–80. Sec., later Man. Dir, Historic Masters Ltd, 1983–2011; Sec., Historic Singers Trust, 1985–2011. Mem. Cttee, Internat. Ernest Bloch Soc., 2011– (Ed., Newsletter, 2011–). Chm., Court, RNCM, 1986–89. Dep. Chm., James Madison Charitable Trust, 2015–. Asst Editor, Jl of Common Market Studies, 1964–72, Editor, 1973–76. *Publications*: (ed) European Political Parties, 1969; External Relations of the European Community, 1971; (ed) Political Parties in the European Community, 1979; Power and Decision in Europe, 1980; Uniting of Europe, 1997; (jtly) Enrico Caruso—Recollections and Retrospective, 1999; (ed) The Kosovo Crisis, 2001; (ed) Modernizing Britain: central, devolved, federal, 2002; Modernising British Government: constitutional challenges and federal solutions, 2006; Federalism and the British, 2008; (contrib.) The First Lives of Alfredo Catalani, 2011; (contrib.) Ernest Bloch Studies, 2016; articles and reviews on opera and opera singers in numerous jls. *Recreation*: collector of old gramophone records and operatic memorabilia. *Address*: 10 Yealand Drive, Lancaster LA1 4EW. *T*: (01524) 69624.

**HENLEY**, 8th Baron *cr* 1799 (Ire.); **Oliver Michael Robert Eden**; PC 2013; Baron Northington (UK) 1885; *b* 22 Nov. 1953; *er s* of 7th Baron Henley and of Nancy Mary, *d* of Stanley Walton, Gilsland, Cumbria; *S* father, 1977; *m* 1984, Caroline Patricia, *d* of A. G. Sharp, Mackney, Oxon; three *s* one *d*. *Educ*: Clifton; Durham Univ. (BA 1975). Called to the Bar, Middle Temple, 1977. A Lord in Waiting (Govt Whip), 1989; Parliamentary Under-Secretary of State: DSS, 1989–93; Dept of Employment, 1993–94; MoD, 1994–95; Minister of State, DFEE, 1995–97; Opposition spokesman on home affairs, 1997–98, on legal affairs, 2005–10; Opposition Chief Whip, H of L, 1998–2001; Parly Under-Sec. of State, DEFRA, 2010–11; Minister of State, Home Office, 2011–12; Parly Under-Sec. of State, DWP, 2016–17; a Lord in Waiting (Govt Whip), 2016–17; Parly Under-Sec. of State, BEIS, 2017–19. Elected Mem., H of L, 1999. Mem., Cumbria CC, 1986–89. Chm., Penrith and the Border Conservative Assoc., 1987–89. Pres., Cumbria Assoc. of Local Councils, 1981–89. Pres., Cumbria Trust for Nature Conservation, 1988–89. *Heir*: *s* Hon. John Michael Oliver Eden, *b* 30 June 1988. *Address*: Scaleby Castle, Carlisle, Cumbria CA6 4LN. *Clubs*: Brooks's; Pratt's; Northern Counties.

**HENLEY, Darren Richard**, OBE 2013; Chief Executive, Arts Council England, since 2015; *b* 16 Feb. 1973. *Educ*: Univ. of Hull (BA Hons Politics 1994); Univ. of South Wales (MSc Mgt 2017); Univ. of Buckingham (MA Hist. of Art 2018); Middlesex Univ. (DProf 2019). Freelance radio journalist for stations incl. Invicta, LBC, IRN, Classic FM and BBC GLR, 1989–94; Sen. Broadcast Journalist, ITN Radio, 1994–95; Classic FM: Prog. Editor, Classic Newsnight, 1995–96; News Manager, 1996–99; News and Prog. Manager, 1999–2000; Man. Editor, 2000–04; Station Manager, 2004–06; Man. Dir, 2006–15; Managing Director: theJazz, 2006–08; Xfm, 2008; Choice FM, 2008; Launch Dir, Global Television, 2012. Dir, Independent Radio News Ltd, 2008–12. Member: Broadcast Journalism Trng Council, 2000–03; SE Regl Arts Council, 2002–04; Adv. Council, 2005–07, Business Develt Cttee, 2007–11, Philharmonia Orch.; DFE (formerly DCSF)/DCMS Music Prog. Bd, 2007–10; Media Bd, Prince's Foundn for Children and the Arts, 2007–12; Steering Gp, In Harmony, 2009–11; Creative and Cultural Industries Task Force, 2009; Adv. Bd, City Music Foundn, 2012–15; Cultural Adv. Gp, Birmingham City Univ., 2012–15; Creative Industries Council, BEIS/DCMS, 2015–; UK Council, Creative Industries Fedn, 2015–; Mem. and Chm., In Tune Nat. Year of Music Legacy Gp (formerly Steering Gp, Nat. Year of Music), 2009–10; Bd Dir, Canterbury Fest. and Th. Trust, 2001–15 (Vice Chm., 2007–09; Vice Pres., 2009–15); Chairman: Music Manifesto Partnership and Advocacy Gp, 2007–10; Henley Review of Funding and Delivery of Music Educn, DfE/DCMS, 2010–11 (report publd 2011); Henley Review of Cultural Educn, DfE/DCMS, 2011 (report publd 2012); Communities in Tune Adv. Gp, DCLG, 2012–15; Mayor of London's Music Educn Adv. Gp, 2013–15; Co-Chm., Cultural Educn Bd, 2013–15; Member: Monitoring Bd, Nat. Plan for Music Educn, DfE/DCMS, 2012–13; Scottish Govt Instrumental Music Gp, 2013. Comr, Univ. of Warwick Commn on Future of Cultural Value, 2013–15. Trustee: Future Talent, 2006–10; Associated Bd, Royal Schs of Music, 2013–15; Global Charities, 2013–15. Patron, Mayor of London's Fund for Young Musicians, 2011–15. Companion, Liverpool Inst. for Performing Arts, 2016. Fellow: Radio Acad., 2011; London Coll. of Music, 2012. FRSA 1998. Hon. Fellow: Canterbury Christ Church Univ., 2010; Trinity Laban Conservatoire of Music and Dance, 2011; Liverpool John Moores Univ., 2015; GSMD, 2015; Arts Univ. Bournemouth, 2017; Honorary Member: RNCM, 2012; ISM, 2013; RCM, 2015. CCMI 2010. Hon. DLitt: Hull, 2014; York St John, 2019; DUniv: Birmingham City, 2014; Buckinghamshire New, 2014; Univ. of the Arts, London, 2018; Hon. MA, Univ. for Creative Arts, 2016; Hon. DArts, Sunderland, 2019. Gold Medal, Arts and Culture, 2000, Gold Medal, Best Music Prog., 2007, NY Internat. Radio Fest.; Chm.'s Award, 2007, Programmer of the Yr, 2009, Gold Award, 2012, Arqiva Commercial Radio Awards; Gold Award, Music Programming, Sony Radio Acad. Awards, 2009; Making Music Sir Charles Groves Prize, 2012; President's Medal, British Acad., 2015. *Publications*: The Story of Classical Music, 2004; (with Aled Jones) Aled: the autobiography, 2005; Famous Composers, 2005; G4: the official book, 2005; (with John Suchet) The Classic FM Friendly Guide to Beethoven, 2006; The Classic FM Friendly Guide to Music, 2006; More Famous Composers, 2007; (with Hayley Westenra) Hayley Westenra: in her own voice, 2007; The Classic FM Friendly Music Quiz Book, 2007; The Incredible Story of Classical Music, 2008; (with V. McKernan) The Original Liverpool Sound: the Royal Liverpool Philharmonic story, 2009; (with S. Jackson and T. Lihoreau) The Classic FM Hall of Fame, 2011; (with S. Jackson) Everything you Ever Wanted to Know about Classical Music... but were too afraid to ask, 2012; (with S. Jackson) 50 Moments that Rocked the Classical Music World, 2014; (with S. Jackson and T. Lihoreau) The Big Book of Classical Music, 2014; (with T. Lihoreau and D. Ross) Charting the Classics, 2014; (with J. Sorrell and P. Roberts) The Virtuous Circle: why creative and cultural education count, 2014; The Classic FM Handy Guide to the Orchestra, 2015; The Classic FM Handy Guide to Everything You Ever Wanted To Know About Classical Music, 2015; The Arts Dividend: why investment in culture pays, 2016; Creativity: why it matters, 2018; (with D. Easlea) Decca: the supreme record company, 2019; *with* T. Lihoreau: The Classic FM Pocket Book of Music, 2003; The Classic FM Book of Quotes, 2004; The Classic FM Book of Trivia, 2004; The Classic FM Friendly Guide to Mozart, 2005; Classic Ephemera, 2005; The Classic FM Friendly Guide to Elgar, 2007; Classic FM 101 Questions & Answers About Classical Music, 2008; Classic Ephemera: a musical miscellany, 2009; The A to Z of Classic FM Music, 2010; The Classic FM Quiz Book, 2012. *Recreations*: arts and culture, train travel. *Address*: Arts Council England, 21 Bloomsbury Street, WC1B 3HF. *T*: 0845 300 6200. *E*: chief.executive@artscouncil.org.uk. *Club*: Gillingham Football.

**HENMAN, Timothy Henry**, OBE 2004; professional tennis player, 1993–2007; *b* 6 Sept. 1974; *s* of Anthony and Jane Henman; *m* 1999, Lucy, *d* of Prof. Richard John, (Bill), Heald, *qv*; three *d*. *Educ*: Reed's Sch., Cobham. Mem., British Davis Cup Team, 1995–2004, 2007. Winner: Nat. Championships, 1995, 1996, 1997, (doubles) 1999; Silver Medal (doubles), Olympic Games, 1996; Sydney Internat. Tournament, 1997; President's Cup, Tashkent, 1997, 1998; Swiss Indoor Championships, (doubles) 1997, 1998, 2001; Monte Carlo Open, (doubles) 1999, 2004; CA Trophy, Vienna, 2000; Samsung Open, Brighton, 2000; Copenhagen Open, 2001; Australian Hardcourt Championships, 2002; Legg Mason Classic, Washington, 2003; BNP Paribas Masters, Paris, 2003. Mem. Bd, AELTC, 2011– (Chm., Tennis sub-cttee, 2015–). Most Improved Player of the Year Award, ATP, 1996. *Address*: c/o IMG, Building 6, Chiswick Park, 566 Chiswick High Road, W4 5HR.

**HENNESSY**, family name of **Barons Hennessy of Nympsfield** and **Windlesham**.

**HENNESSY OF NYMPSFIELD**, Baron *cr* 2010 (Life Peer), of Nympsfield in the County of Gloucestershire; **Peter John Hennessy**, FBA 2003; FRHistS; FAcSS; Attlee Professor of Contemporary British History, since 2001, and Patron, Mile End Institute, since 2015, Queen Mary University of London; *b* 28 March 1947; *s* of William Gerald and Edith Hennessy; *m* 1969, Enid Mary Candler; two *d*. *Educ*: Marling Sch., Stroud; St John's Coll., Cambridge (BA 1969; Hon. Fellow, 2010), PhD Cantab 1990; LittD Cantab 2009; LSE (Hon. Fellow, 2000); Harvard, 1971–72 (Kennedy Meml Scholar). FRHistS 1993. Reporter, THES, 1972–74, The Times, 1974–76; Lobby corresp., Financial Times, 1976; Whitehall corresp., The Times, 1976–82; journalist, The Economist, 1982; home leader writer and columnist, The Times, 1982–84; columnist: New Statesman, 1986–87; The Independent, 1987–91; Director, 1989–93; The Tablet, 2003–11; Prof. of Contemporary History, QMW, Univ. of London, 1992–2000; Chm., Kennedy Meml Trust, 1995–2000. Co-Founder and Co-Dir, 1986–89, Mem. Bd, 1989–98, Inst. of Contemporary British Hist. (Hon. Fellow, 1995). Vis. Prof. of Govt, Strathclyde Univ., 1989–2004; Gresham Prof. of Rhetoric, 1994–97; Vis. Lectr, Dept of Politics, Univ. of Strathclyde, 1983–84 (Hon. Res. Fellow, 1985–89); Visiting Fellow: Policy Studies Inst., 1986–91 (Sen. Fellow, 1984–85); Council Mem., 1991–97); Univ. Depts of Politics, Reading 1988–94, Nottingham 1989–95; RIPA, 1989–92; Hon. Res. Fellow, Dept of Politics and Sociology, Birkbeck Coll., London, 1990–91; Vis. Scholar, Centre for Australian Public Sector Management, Griffith Univ., Brisbane, 1991; Associate, Cold War Studies Prog., LSE, 2010–. Member: Steering Gp, Sharman Review of Audit and Accountability for Central Govt, 2000–01; Cabinet Office Adv. Gp on Security and Intelligence Records, 2004–10; Joint H of C—H of L Cttee on H of L Reform Bill, 2011–12; Chief of Defence Staff's Strategic Adv. Panel, 2011–; BASIC Trident Commn, 2011–14; Sen. Advisory Gp, RCDS, 2013–; FCO Diplomatic Excellence External Panel, 2013–; No 10 History Steering Gp, 2014–; H of L Select Cttee on Sci. and Technol., 2014–17; RUSI Ind. Surveillance Review, 2014–15; H of L Constitution Cttee, 2019–. Vice-President: Politics Assoc., 1985–90; RHistS, 1990–2000; Pres., Johnian Soc., 1995. Trustee: Attlee Foundn, 1985–98 (Patron, 1998–); Geffrye Mus., 2002–04; Orwell Meml Trust, 2002–04. Patron: Bletchley Park Trust, 2011–16; Mile End Gp, 2011–13. Mem. Bd, Inst. of Histl Res., 1992–97; Member: Council, Gresham Coll., 1996–97 (Fellow, 1997); Council of Reference, Westminster Abbey Inst., 2013–; Gov., 2001–, Mem., Council of Mgt, 2011–, Ditchley Foundn. Member: Advisory Board: Global Strategy Forum, 2015–; Cambridge Security Initiative, 2015–; Council, Foundn for Sci. and Technol., 2017–. Fellow, Goodenough Coll., 2018–. Dir, The Tablet, 2003–11. FRSA 1992. FAcSS (Founding AcSS 1999). Presenter: Under Fire, TV, 1985–87; Radio 4 Analysis programme, 1986–92; writer and presenter, What Has Become of Us, TV, 1994; numerous other radio and TV productions. Curator, Secret State exhibn, Nat. Archives, 2004. Hon. Vis. Prof., Strategy and Security Inst., Univ. of Exeter, 2012–; Hon. Prof., QUB, 2013–. Hon. Fellow, St Benet's Hall, Oxford, 2008. Hon. DLitt: Univ. of W England, 1995; Univ. of Westminster, 1996; Kingston, 1998; Strathclyde, 2005; Reading, 2011; Glos, 2012; DUniv Open, 2009. Hon. Bencher, Middle Temple, 2012. Hon. Capt., RNR, 2017–. Times Higher Educn Lifetime Achievement Award, 2008; Norton Medlicott Medal, Historical Assoc., 2010; Diamond Jubilee Award for Pol Studies Communication, Pol Studies Assoc., 2010; Minerva Medal, Royal Philosophical Soc. of Glasgow, 2017–18. *Publications*: (with Keith Jeffery) States of Emergency, 1983; (with Michael Cockerell and David Walker) Sources Close to the Prime Minister, 1984; What the Papers Never Said, 1985; Cabinet, 1986; (ed with Anthony Seldon) Ruling Performance, 1987; Whitehall, 1989, rev. edn 2001; Never Again: Britain, 1945–51, 1992 (Duff Cooper Prize, 1993; NCR Book Award for Non-Fiction, 1993); The Hidden Wiring: unearthing the British Constitution, 1995; Muddling Through: power, politics and the quality of government in postwar Britain, 1996; The Prime Minister: the office and its holders since 1945, 2000; The Secret State, 2002, 2nd edn 2010; Having It So Good: Britain in the fifties (Orwell Prize for Political Writing), 2006; (ed) The New Protective State: government, intelligence and terrorism, 2007; Cabinets and the Bomb, 2007; Distilling the Frenzy: writing the history of one's own times, 2012; Establishment and Meritocracy, 2014; The Kingdom to Come: thoughts on the union before and after the Scottish referendum, 2015; (with James Jinks) The Silent Deep: the Royal Navy submarine service since 1945, 2015 (Duke of Westminster Medal for Military History, 2015; Mountbatten Maritime Prize for Military Literature, 2016); (with Robert Shepherd) Reflections: conversations with politicians, vol. 1 2016, vol. 2 2019; Winds of Change: Britain in the early sixties, 2019. *Recreations*: reading, listening to music, searching for the British Constitution. *Address*: House of Lords, SW1A 0PW. *T*: (020) 7219 3000. *Clubs*: Savile, Grillions, Naval.

**HENNESSY, Sir James (Patrick Ivan)**, KBE 1982 (OBE 1968; MBE 1959); CMG 1975; HM Diplomatic Service, retired; *b* 26 Sept. 1923; *s* of late Richard George Hennessy, DSO, MC; *m* 1947, Patricia (*d* 2015), *o d* of late Wing Comdr F. H. Unwin, OBE; five *d* (one *s* decd). *Educ*: Bedford Sch.; King's Coll., Newcastle; Sidney Sussex Coll., Cambridge; LSE. Served RA, 1942–44; seconded IA, 1944–46, Adjt and Battery Comdr, 6th Indian Field Regt. Apptd to HM Overseas Service, Basutoland, District Officer, 1948; Judicial Comr, 1953; Dist Comr, 1954–56; Jt Sec., Constitutional Commn, 1957–59; Supervisor of Elections, 1959; Sec. to Exec. Council, 1960; seconded to Office of High Comr, Cape Town/Pretoria, 1961–63; Perm. Sec. for local govt, 1964; MLC, 1965; Sec. for External Affairs, Defence and Internal Security, 1967; Prime Minister's Office, 1968. Retired, later apptd to HM Diplomatic Service; FO, 1968–70; Chargé d'Affaires, Montevideo, 1971–72; High Comr to Uganda and Ambassador (non-resident), Rwanda, 1973–76; Consul-Gen.,

Cape Town, 1977–80; Governor and C-in-C, Belize, 1980–81; HM Chief Inspector of Prisons for England and Wales, 1982–87. Mem., Parole Bd, 1988–91. Trustee, Butler Trust, 1988–98. *Address*: c/o 2 Seeliger Road, Kommetjie 7975, Cape Town, South Africa.

**HENNESSY, Brig. Mary Brigid Teresa, (Rita),** CBE 1988 (MBE 1967); RRC 1982; Matron-in-Chief, Queen Alexandra's Royal Army Nursing Corps, 1985–89 and Director of Defence Nursing Service, 1986–89; *b* 27 Jan. 1933; *d* of late Bartholomew and Nora Agnes Hennessy. *Educ*: Convent of Mercy, Ennis, Co. Clare; Whittington Hosp., Highgate, London; Victoria Maternity Hosp., Barnet. SRN; SCM. Joined QARANC, 1959; service in Britain, Singapore, Malaya, Germany; various hosp. appts, 1959–74; seconded to office of Chargé d'affaires, Peking, 1965–67; Dep. Matron, Hongkong, 1976; Lt-Col 1979; Col 1982; Brig., Matron-in-Chief and Dir of Army Nursing Services, 1985. QHNS 1985–89. *Recreations*: music, theatre, gardening.

**HENNESSY, Patrick James;** Mayoral Director, Communications, Greater London Authority, since 2016; *b* 10 July 1963; *s* of late Thomas Michael Hennessy and of Elizabeth Anne Hennessy; *m* (marr. diss.); one *s* one *d*; partner, Marcela Benedetti. *Educ*: Colet Court Sch.; Eton Coll.; Lady Margaret Hall, Oxford (BA Hons 1985). Reporter: Express and Echo, Exeter, 1985–88; The Sun, 1988–92; Political Corresp., Daily Express, 1992–96; Dep. Political Ed., Evening Standard, 1996–2004; Political Ed., Sunday Telegraph, 2004–13; Dep. Dir of Communications, Labour Party, 2013–15. Judge, Spectator Parliamentarian of Year Awards, 2006–13. *Recreations*: football, music, reading. *Address*: Greater London Authority, City Hall, Queen's Walk, SE1 2AA. *Club*: Chelsea Football.

**HENNESSY, Richard Patrick,** FCA; Chief Financial Officer, The Really Useful Group Ltd, 2004–06; *b* 16 Nov. 1953; *s* of Graham Harold Hennessy and Dolores Hennessy (*née* Ellul); *m* 1979, Angela Carthew; one *s* one *d*. *Educ*: Newcastle Univ. (BA Hons Econs and Accounting). FCA 1979. Manager, Peat Marwick Mitchell, London, 1976–80; Sen. Manager, Peat Marwick Mitchell & Co., Hong Kong, 1980–82; Gp Financial Accountant, Hongkong & Shanghai Banking Corp. Ltd, 1982–84; Financial Controller, Saudi British Bank, 1984–88; Sen. Gp Financial Accountant, Hongkong & Shanghai Banking Corp. Ltd, 1988–92; Gp Chief Accountant, HSBC Holdings plc, 1992–95; Chief Financial Officer, Midland, subseq. HSBC, Bank plc, 1996–2003. Mem. Banking Sub-Cttee, ICAEW, 1993–2003. Events Chm., Arts and Crafts Movement in Surrey, 2012–16. Mem., Soc. of London Theatre, 2004–06. Trustee, Iwokrama Internat. Centre for Rain Forest Conservation and Develt, 2006–12. *Recreations*: family, motor sport, music, walking, swimming, painting and stained glass. *Address*: Oak Meadows, 65 Park Road, Woking, Surrey GU22 7BZ.

**HENNIKER,** 9th Baron *cr* 1800 (Ire.); **Mark Ian Philip Chandos Henniker-Major;** Bt 1765; Baron Hartismere (UK) 1866; *b* 29 Sept. 1947; *s* of 8th Baron Henniker and Margaret Osla (*née* Benning); *S* father, 2004; *m* 1st, 1973, Lesley Antoinette Masterton-Smith (*née* Foskett) (marr. diss. 1996); one *s* three *d* (and one *s* decd); 2nd, 1996, Bente Toft (*née* Petersen) (marr. diss. 2015); one *s*. *Educ*: Eton; Trinity Coll., Cambridge (MA); LLM (London); London Inst. of World Affairs (Dip.). FCIArb; AMRAeS. Solicitor (retired/non-practising). *Heir*: *s* Hon. Edward George Major Henniker-Major, *b* 22 April 1985. *Address*: 217 Bull Road, Thornham Parva, Eye, Suffolk IP23 8ES. *T*: (01379) 783854. *E*: mhenniker_anglab@btinternet.com.

**HENNIKER, Sir Adrian Chandos,** 9th Bt *cr* 1813, of Newton Hall, Essex; *b* 18 Oct. 1946; *s* of Brig. Sir Mark Chandos Auberon Henniker, 8th Bt, CBE, DSO, MC and Kathleen Denys (*d* 1998), *d* of John Anderson; *S* father, 1991, but his name does not appear on the Official Roll of the Baronetage; *m* 1971, Ann (*d* 2019), *d* of Stuart Britton; twin *d*. *Educ*: Marlborough. *Heir*: none. *Address*: The Coach House, Llwyndu, Abergavenny, Gwent NP7 7HG.

**HENNIKER HEATON, Sir Yvo Robert;** *see* Heaton.

**HENNIKER-MAJOR,** family name of **Baron Henniker.**

**HENNING, (William) Brian;** Chairman, Sport Northern Ireland, 2012–16; Director: UK Sport, 2012–16; Beulah Business Solutions, since 2012; *b* City of Armagh, 14 July 1954; *s* of William John Henning and Jane Elizabeth Henning; *m* 2006, Yvonne Anna Palnoch (*née* Magowan); two *s* one *d*. *Educ*: Newry Grammar Sch.; Univ. of Ulster. Sen. Quantity Surveyor, Bruce Shaw Partnership, 1978–84; Sen. Surveyor, Farrans Construction, 1984–86; Man. Dir, Cresta Building Services (NI) Ltd, 1988–92; Property and Develt Dir, Crestacare plc, 1992–98; Chief Executive: Cusp Gp, 1998–2007; Lotus Gp, 2008–12. Chm., Lisburn City Centre Mgt, 2002–06. Vice Chm., NI Council for Integrated Educn, 1991; Chair, NI Regl Bd, RICS, 2018–. Mem., Cinemagic (Ireland) Ltd, 2007–. Trustee, Age NI, 2013–14. *Recreations*: active interest in all sports esp. athletics, Rugby Union (Manager, Ulster Rugby Under 18, 2005–06), soccer, golf, ski-ing, resistance training and yoga, landscape management, family and friends. *Address*: Beulah, 33 Newry Road, Banbridge BT32 3HP. *T*: (028) 4062 8214.

**HENRIQUES, Hon. Sir Richard (Henry Quixano),** Kt 2000; a Judge of the High Court of Justice, Queen's Bench Division, 2000–13; Presiding Judge, North Eastern Circuit, 2001–04; *b* 27 Oct. 1943; *s* of late Cecil Quixano Henriques and Doreen Mary Henriques; *m* Joan Hilary, (Toni), (*née* Senior); one *s* and one step *s*. *Educ*: Bradfield Coll., Berks; Worcester Coll., Oxford (BA). Called to the Bar, Inner Temple, 1967; Bencher, 1994. A Recorder, 1983–2000; QC 1986; Mem., Northern Circuit (Leader, 1995–98). Member: Gen. Council of the Bar, 1993–98; Criminal Justice Liaison Cttee, 1993–95; Northern Circuit Exec. Cttee, 1993–98. Conducted Ind. Rev. into Operation Midland, 2016. Council Mem., Rossall Sch., 1985–95. Patron, Blackpool Boys and Girls Club, 2017–. *Recreations*: bridge, golf, the Turf. *Address*: c/o Royal Courts of Justice, Strand, WC2A 2LL. *Clubs*: Royal Lytham and St Anne's Golf, Fleetwood Golf.

**HENRY, Claire Louise,** MBE 2013; independent consultant, Claire Henry Associates, since 2019; Director, Improvement and Transformation, Hospice UK, 2017–19 (Chief Executive: National Council for Palliative Care, 2014–17; Dying Matters Coalition, 2014–17); *b* Leicester, 29 April 1965; *d* of Victor Henry and Burnice Henry; *m* 2005, Lionel Cunnington. *Educ*: Casterton Community Coll.; Rutland Sixth Form Coll.; Bournemouth Univ. (BSc Hons). RGN; Royal Marsden Hosp. (Postgrad. Dip. Cancer Care). Staff Nurse, 1987–92, Sen. Staff Nurse, 1992–93, Boston, Lincs; Macmillan nurse, 1993–2000; Proj. Manager, Cancer Services Collaborative Improvement Partnership, 2000–01; Nat. Associate Dir, 2001–04, Nat. Prog. Dir, 2005–13. End of Life Care Prog., NHS; Hd, Progs for Long-term Conditions and End of Life Care, NHS Improving Quality, 2013–14. *Publications*: (contrib.) Nursing in Primary Care: a handbook for students, 2001; (contrib.) Advance Care Planning in End of Life Care, 2011; (jtly) Pathways Through Care at the End of Life, 2013. *Recreations*: walking, history, season ticket holder at Leicester Tigers Rugby. *E*: clh.associatesrutland@gmail.com.

**HENRY, Colin Glen;** Chief Executive, Silverwells Consultants Ltd, since 2016; Senior Advisor, McKinsey & Company, since 2017; *b* Aberdeen, 18 Jan. 1965; *s* of Fulton Henry and Joan Henry; partner, 2005, Ian Macdonald. *Educ*: Uddington Grammar Sch. Merchandiser, Marks and Spencer plc, 1984–97; Man. Dir, Coats Viyella plc, 1997–2000;

Sen. Vice Pres., Polo Ralph Lauren Inc., 2000–03; Sen. Vice Pres., Umbro plc, 2003–09; Chief Product Officer, Esprit GmbH, 2010–12; Chief Exec., Jaeger Ltd, 2013–15. Hon. Prof., Glasgow Caledonian Univ., 2014–. Hon. FRCA 2008. *Recreations*: oenophilia, St Emilion, Wolfie the Jack Russell. *T*: 07796 957123. *E*: cgh1000@mac.com. *Clubs*: Soho House, 67 Pall Mall.

**HENRY, Prof. (Diana) Kristin, (Mrs G. G. Blakey),** FRCP, FRCPath; Professor of Pathology, Imperial College School of Medicine (formerly Charing Cross and Westminster Medical School), London University, 1987–98, now Emeritus Professor, Imperial College London; *d* of late Colin Neil Thorburn Henry and of Vera (*née* Christensen); *m* 1st, 1960, Charles Michael Yates (marr. diss.); 2nd, 1967, George Gavin Blakey (*d* 2013); one *s* one *d*. *Educ*: Malvern Girls' Coll.; St Thomas's Hosp. Med. Sch. (MB BS). FRCP 1982; FRCPath 1977. Junior appts at Chelsea Hosp. for Women and Brompton Hosp., 1960–64; Res. Registrar, Bd of Governors, Hosp. of Diseases of the Chest, 1964–66; MRC Fellow in Immunology, Middx Hosp., 1966–69; Lectr, RPMS, 1969–74; Reader, 1974–82, Prof. of Histopathology, 1982–84, Westminster Med. Sch., London Univ.; Prof. of Histopathology, Charing Cross & Westminster Med. Sch., 1984–87. Mem., Editl Bd, Histopathology, 1975–2003; Founding Ed., Current Diagnostic Pathology, 1993–; Asst Ed., Internat. Jl of Surgical Pathology, 1999–. British Council Lectr and Foundn Lectr to Coll. of Pathologists, Sri Lanka, 1987. Member: Thymic Tumour Panel, MRC, 1974–79; Pathology Panel, Brit. Nat. Lymphoma Investigation, MRC, 1975–87 (Expert Pathologist representing BNLI in Nat. Cancer Inst. (USA) study of lymphomas, 1976–81 (report pub. 1982)). Mem., Kettering Prize Award Cttee, Gen. Motors Cancer Res. Foundn, 1981–82. Co-founder, British Lymphoma Pathology Gp, 1974–; founder Mem., Eur. Bone Marrow Pathology Gp, 1992–; Mem., Melanoma Study Gp, 1989–. Treas., 1981–94, Pres., 1994–96, Cunningham Gold Medal, President's Medal, British Div., Internat. Acad. of Pathology; Pres., Internat. Acad. of Pathology, 2010–12 (Vice-Pres. for Europe, 1998–2008; Chm., Educn Cttee, 2000–11; Gold Medal, 2012); Founder, Arab British Sch. of Pathology, 2001. *Publications*: Systematic Pathology, vol. 7: 3rd edn, The Thymus, Lymph Nodes, Spleen and Lymphatics (ed with W. St C. Symmers and contrib.), 1992; (with G. Farrer-Brown) A Colour Atlas of Thymus and Lymph Node Pathology with Ultrastructure, 1981; (contrib.) The Human Thymus in Disease, 1981; (contrib.) Ultrastructure of the Small Intestine, 1982; (contrib.) Bone Marrow Transplantation in Mucopolysaccharidoses, 1984; numerous contribs to learned jls in field of haematopathology (incl. Lymphoma Study Gp pubns), malignant melanoma and oncology. *Recreations*: painting, driving, animal welfare. *Address*: Imperial College London at Charing Cross Hospital, Fulham Palace Road, W6 8RF. *T*: (020) 8846 7133. *Club*: Sloane.

**HENRY, Edward Joseph Aloysius,** QC 2018; *b* London, 26 Nov. 1961; *s* of Richard Aloysius Francis Xavier Henry and Philomena Marguerita Henry; *m* 1st, 1992, Miranda Mary (marr. diss. 2014), *d* of Kenneth and Mary Bromage; three *s*; 2nd, 2014, Marketa Josephine, *d* of Jindrich and Zdenka Slavikova; one *d*. *Educ*: Worth Sch.; Jesus Coll., Cambridge (BA Hons Hist.; Titular Exhibnr); City Univ. (DipLaw). Called to the Bar, Lincoln's Inn, 1988; in practice as a barrister, specialising in criminal and regulatory offence, QEB Hollis Whiteman (formerly Chambers of Daniel Hollis, QC), 1989–. Trustee: Release, 2010–19; Fine Cell Work, 2011– (Dep. Chm., 2014–). *Recreations*: singing, theatre, parenting my infant daughter, buying the occasional bolt of cloth, medico-legal history. *Address*: QEB Hollis Whiteman, 1–2 Laurence Pountney Hill, EC4R 0EU. *T*: (020) 7933 8855. *E*: barristers@qebhw.co.uk. *Club*: Garrick.

**HENRY, Hugh;** Member (Lab) Renfrewshire South, Scottish Parliament, 2011–16 (Paisley South, 1999–2011); *b* 12 Feb. 1952; *s* of Joseph and Mary Henry; *m* Jacqueline (*née* Muldoon); one *s* two *d*. *Educ*: Glasgow Univ. (BAcc). Worked in accountancy, teaching and social work. Member (Lab): Renfrew DC, 1985–96; Renfrewshire Council, 1995–99 (Leader, 1995–99). Scottish Executive: Dep. Minister for Health and Community Care, 2001–02, for Social Justice, 2002–03, for Justice, 2003–07; Minister for Educn and Young People, 2007; Convenor, European Cttee, Scottish Parlt, 1999–2016. Mem., Cttee of the Regions, EU.

**HENRY, John Philip;** Chairman, Cheltenham Civic Society, 2001–09; Vice-Chairman, Gloucestershire Hospitals NHS Trust, 2002–10 (non-executive Director, 2002–10); *b* 8 Oct. 1946; *s* of late L. Henry, MD, FRCS and P. M. Henry, MB, ChB; *m* 1992, Gillian Mary Richardson; one *s* one *d*. *Educ*: Cheltenham Coll.; Queen's Coll., Oxford (MA). Psychologist, Road Research Lab., 1968; Admin Trainee, DoE, 1972; Principal, 1976; Private Sec., Minister for Housing and Construction, 1981–83; Asst Sec., 1983–89; Regl Dir, Yorks and Humberside Regl Office, Depts of the Envmt and Transport, 1990–94; Prin. Finance Officer, Property Hldgs, DoE, 1994–95; Hd of Agencies Gp, OPS, Cabinet Office, 1995–96. Non-exec. Dir, E Glos NHS Trust, 2000–02. Chm., Holst Birthplace Trust, 1999–2001. Chm. Govs, St James' Primary Sch., Cheltenham, 2001–14; Governor: Arthur Dye Primary Sch., Cheltenham, 2009–19; Pate's Grammar Sch., Cheltenham, 2010–18. *Recreations*: arts, architecture, literature. *Address*: 19 Montpellier Terrace, Cheltenham, Glos GL50 1UX.

**HENRY, Rt Hon. Sir John (Steele),** KNZM 2009 (DCNZM 2001); PC 1996; Judge, Court of Appeal, New Zealand, 1995–2000; *b* 3 July 1932; *s* of Hon. Sir Trevor Ernest Henry and Audrey Kate (*née* Sheriff); *m* 1957, Jennefer Lynne Stevenson; one *s* two *d*. *Educ*: King's Coll., Auckland; Auckland Univ. (LLB 1955). QC (NZ) 1980; High Court Judge, 1984–95; Acting Judge, Supreme Court, NZ, 2002–07. Commemoration Medal (NZ), 1990. *Recreations*: fishing, tramping, golf. *Address*: 310 Riddell Road, Glendowie, Auckland 1071, New Zealand. *T*: (9) 5758526. *Club*: Northern (Auckland).

**HENRY, Keith Nicholas,** FREng; Chairman: Regal Petroleum plc, 2008–17; Greenko Group plc, 2013–16 (non-executive Director, 2012–16); *b* 3 March 1945; *s* of Kenneth G. Henry and Barbara Henry; *m* 1974, Susan Mary Horsburgh; two *d*. *Educ*: Bedford Sch.; London Univ. (BSc Hons Civil Engrg (ext.) 1967); Birmingham Univ. (MSc Foundn Engrg 1969). With Internat. Mgt and Engrg Gp Ltd, 1969–71; Project Engr, then Manager, Brown & Root, 1971–77; Engrg Manager, Brown & Root Far East, 1977–80; Brown & Root (UK) Ltd: Engrg Manager, 1980–84; Commercial Dir, 1984–85; Technical Dir and Chief Engr, 1985–88; Managing Director: Brown & Root Vickers Ltd, 1987–89; Brown & Root Marine, 1989; Chief Executive: Brown & Root Ltd, 1990–95; Nat. Power plc, 1995–99; Gp Exec. Vice-Pres. and Chief Exec., Engrg and Construction, Kvaerner E&C PLC, 2000–03; Dep. Chm., Petroleum-Geo Services ASA, 2003–06; Chairman: Burren Energy plc, 2006–08 (Dir, 2005–08); Petrojarl ASA, 2006; Helius Energy plc, 2009–11; Mediterranean Oil & Gas plc, 2012–14. Non-executive Director: Enterprise Oil, 1995–2002; Emerald Energy plc, 2004–09; South East Water Ltd, 2005–07; High Point-Rendel Ltd, 2006–; First Calgary Petroleums Ltd, 2008; Sterling Energy plc, 2009–16; KSK Power Ventur plc, 2014–18. FREng (FEng 1988). *Recreation*: shooting. *E*: keithhenry@btinternet.com. *Club*: Royal Automobile.

**HENRY, Dr Kenneth Ross,** AC 2007; Secretary to the Treasury, Department of the Treasury, Australia, 2001–11; Special Adviser to the Prime Minister of Australia, 2011–12; *b* 27 Nov. 1957; *s* of John Desmond Henry and Heather Audrey McKay; *m* 1979, Naomi Jayne Smith; one *s* one *d*. *Educ*: Chatham High Sch., Taree; Univ. of New South Wales (BCom Hons); Univ. of Canterbury, NZ (PhD Econs). Res. Officer, Australian Bureau of

Stats, 1979–80; Asst Lectr, 1980–81, Lectr, 1982–84, Univ. of Canterbury, NZ; Department of the Treasury, Australia: Sen. Finance Officer, 1984–85, Chief Finance Officer, 1985–86, Taxation Policy Div.; Private Sec., Office of Treas., 1986–89; Sen. Advr to Treas., 1989–91; Principal Advr, 1991–92; Minister (Econ. and Financial Affairs), Australian Delegn to OECD, Paris, 1992–93; First Asst Sec., Taxation Policy Div., 1994–97; Chair, Taxation Taskforce, 1997–98; Exec. Dir, Econ. Gp, 1998–2001. Non-executive Director: Nat. Australia Bank, 2011–19 (Chm., 2015–19); Australian Securities Exchange, 2013–. Exec. Chm., Australian Nat. Inst. of Public Policy, ANU, 2012–14. Mem., Econ. Soc. of Australia, 1999. *Recreations:* care of native fauna, reading, music. *Club:* Commonwealth (Canberra).

**HENRY, Kristin;** *see* Henry, D. K.

**HENRY, Sir Lenworth George, (Sir Lenny),** Kt 2015; CBE 1999; stand-up comedian, since 1975; actor; *b* 29 Aug. 1958; *s* of late Winston Henry and Winifred Henry; *m* 1984, Dawn R. French (marr. diss. 2010); one adopted *d*. *Educ:* Blue Coat Secondary Mod. Sch.; W. R. Tewson Sch.; Preston Coll.; Open Univ. (BA); Royal Holloway, Univ. of London (MA; PhD 2018). Trustee, Comic Relief, 1987–. Chancellor, Birmingham City Univ., 2016–. Won New Faces Talent Show, 1975; stand-up show, Have You Seen This Man, tour, 2001–02; So Much Things To Say, Wyndhams, 2003; Where You From?, tour, 2007; Cradle to Rave, tour, 2011; *TV appearances* include: Fosters, 1976–77; Tiswas, 1978–81; 3 of a Kind, 1981–84; The Lenny Henry Show, 1984, 1985, 1987, 1988, 1995, 2004; Lenny Henry Tonight, 1986; Xmas Specials, 1987, 1988, 1994, 1995; Chef, 1992, 1994, 1996; Lenny's Big Amazon Adventure, 1997; Lenny Goes to Town, 1998; Hope and Glory, 1999, 2000; Lenny's Big Atlantic Adventure, 2000; Lenny Henry in Pieces, 2002, 2003; This Is My Life, 2003; Lenny's Britain, Lenny Henry: So Much Things to Say, 2007; The Syndicate, Danny and the Human Zoo, 2015; Broadchurch, 2017; The Long Song, 2018; *radio drama series:* Bad Faith, 2008, 2010, 2011; *films:* Coast to Coast, 1984; Work Experience, 1989; Alive and Kicking, 1990; True Identity, 1990; *theatre:* Othello, W Yorks Playhouse, transf. Rose Th., Kingston, then Trafalgar Studios, 2009; The Comedy of Errors, NT, 2011; Fences, Th. Royal, Bath, transf. Duchess Th., 2013 (Best Actor, Critics' Circle Th. Awards, 2014); Rudy's Rare Records, Birmingham Rep., 2014; Educating Rita, Chichester Festival Th., 2015; The Resistible Rise of Arturo Ui, Donmar Warehouse, 2017; King Hedley II, Th. Royal Stratford E, 2019. Lifetime Achievement Award, British Comedy Awards, 2003; Alan Clarke Award for Outstanding Contribution to TV, BAFTA, 2016. *Publications:* Quest for the Big Woof; Charlie and the Big Chill, 1995; (jtly) Charlie, Queen of the Desert, 1996; Who Am I, Again? (memoir), 2019. *Recreations:* huge fan of R'n'B, hiphop, funk, avid reader, tennis, comics, enjoying my family. *Address:* c/o PBJ Management Ltd, 22 Rathbone Street, W1T 1LG. *T:* (020) 7287 1112. *Clubs:* Groucho, Soho House.

**HENRY, Patricia;** *see* Robertson, P.

**HENRY, Sir Patrick (Denis),** 3rd Bt *cr* 1923, of Cahore, co. Londonderry; businessman; *b* 20 Dec. 1957; *s* of Denis Valentine Henry (*d* 1983), *yr s* of 1st Bt, and Elizabeth Henry (*née* Walker); *S* uncle, 1997, but his name does not appear on the Official Roll of the Baronetage; *m* 1997, Georgina Ravenscroft (marr. diss.). *Educ:* Corpus Christi Coll., Oxford (BA (Hons) Modern History 1978). *Club:* Blackburn Rovers.

**HENRY, Peter Clifford; His Honour Judge Henry;** a Circuit Judge, since 2009; *b* Johannesburg, 28 Oct. 1954; *s* of Ian Clifford Henry and Pamela Joan Henry; *m* 1980, Elisabeth Stephens; one *s* one *d*. *Educ:* Uppingham Sch.; Exeter Univ. (LLB Hons). Called to the Bar, Inner Temple, 1977; in practice as barrister, specialising in criminal law; a Recorder, 2001–09; Legal Assessor to GMC, 2007–09. *Recreations:* motorsport, flying, painting, cycling, cricket. *Address:* Courts of Justice, London Road, Southampton, Hants SO15 2XQ. *T:* (023) 8021 3200, *Fax:* (023) 8021 3234. *Clubs:* Vintage Sports Car; Linkenholt Cricket.

**HENRY, Simon Peter;** Chief Financial Officer and Executive Director, Royal Dutch Shell plc, 2009–17; *b* Eckington, Derbyshire, 13 July 1961; *s* of Peter Garland Henry and Marina Henry (*née* Moore); *m* 1986, Jonquil Ruth Porter; two *s* one *d*. *Educ:* King Ecgbert Comprehensive Sch., Sheffield; Churchill Coll., Cambridge (BA 1st Cl. Hons Maths 1982; MA 1986). CIMA 1989, FCMA 2009. Joined Shell, 1982: engr, Stanlow Refinery, 1982; various manufg, internal audit and finance appts, Shell UK Ltd, 1982–92; Finance Manager of Mktg, Egypt, 1992–94; Controller, Upstream business, Egypt, 1994–96; Oil Products Finance Advr, Asia Pacific, 1996–98; Finance Dir, Mekong Cluster, 1998–99; Gen. Manager, Finance, SE Asian Retail business, 1999–2001; Hd, Investor Relns, 2000–04; Chief Financial Officer, Exploration and Prodn, 2004–09. Non-executive Director: Lloyds Banking Gp, 2014–; Rio Tinto, 2017–. Member: Cttee, 100 Gp of UK Finance Directors, 2010–17; Adv. Cttee, Centre for Eur. Reform, 2011–. Chair, Eur. Round Table Chief Financial Officer Taskforce, 2012–17. *Recreations:* sport, still playing football at 57, travel, family.

**HENRY, Wendy Ann;** Foster Dog Co-ordinator, Mayhew Animal Home, 2009; *d* of Bernard and Elsa Henry; *m* 1980, Tim Miles; one *d*. *Educ:* Queen Mary School, Lytham. Reporter, Daily Mail, Manchester, 1975–76, News of the World, 1976–79; Features Editor, Woman Magazine, 1979–81; Asst Editor, The Sun, 1981–85; Editor: Sunday Magazine, 1985–86; The News of the World, 1986–88; Dep. Editor, The Sun, 1988; Editor, The People, 1988–89; Ed.-in-Chief, The Globe, Florida, 1990–93; Man. Ed., current affairs TV Prog., 1993–95; Ed., weekend section, Daily News, NY, 1995–97; Ed.-in-Chief, Successful Slimming, and Editl Dir, New Publications, Globe Communications, USA, 1997–99; Ed., Real Homes mag., 1999–2001; Launch Ed., Parkhill Publishing, 2001–09. Foster Dog Co-ordinator, Battersea Dogs' and Cats' Home, 2003–08. Mem., Women in Journalism. *Recreations:* husband, dogs, sleeping.

**HENSCHEL, Ruth Mary;** *see* Ashton, R. M.

**HENSHALL, Dr Christopher Harry;** independent consultant in health, research and innovation policy, since 2010; *b* 16 Feb. 1954; *s* of late Henry James Henshall and Edna Geraldine Henshall (*née* Watkins). *Educ:* Barnard Castle Sch., Co. Durham; Gonville and Caius Coll., Cambridge (BA Natural Sciences 1975; PhD 1983). Univ. of Nottingham (MA in Child Development 1976). Lectr in Psychol., Univ. of Warwick, 1981–84; Res. Fellow, Univ. of Southampton, 1984–85; Prog. Dir, Health Promotion Res. Trust, 1985–88; Sec., Health Services Res. Cttee, MRC, 1988–91; Research and Development Division, Department of Health: Sen. Principal, 1991; Asst Sec., 1993; Dep. Dir, R&D, 1996–2001; Dir, Sci. and Engrg Base Gp, OST, DTI, 2001–04. Hon. Prof., Dept of Public Health and Policy, LSHTM, 2001–05; Pro Vice-Chancellor for Ext. Relns, Univ. of York, 2005–10; Associate Prof., Health Economics Res. Gp, Brunel Univ. London, 2010–15. Mem., Internat. Adv. Gp, Initiative to Improve Health in Asia, NUS, 2010–15. Health Technology Assessment International: Pres., 2003–05; Chm., Policy Forum, 2004–07 and 2010–16. Chm., Asia Policy Forum, 2013–16. Mem. Bd, Alberta Res. and Innovation Authy, 2009–14; Bd Dir, Alberta Innovates Health Solutions, 2014–16. Hon. Fellow, Centre for Health Econs, Univ. of York, 2010–13; Vis. Fellow, Office of Health Econs, 2017–. *Recreations:* hill walking (Munroist number 3053), opera, music, wine. *Address:* 13 St Mary's Grove, N1 2NT. *T:* 07769 931610. *E:* consulting@chrishenshall.co.uk.

**HENSHALL, Very Rev. Nicholas James;** Dean of Chelmsford, since 2014; *b* Mossley, Lancs, 6 April 1962; *s* of late Rt Rev. Michael Henshall; *m* 1991, Christine Margaret Goodacre; one *s* two *d*. *Educ:* Manchester Grammar Sch.; British Sch. of Archaeology, Athens; Wadham Coll., Oxford (BA 1985; MA 1988); Ripon Coll., Cuddesdon. Ordained deacon, 1988, priest, 1989; Curate, St Mary's, Blyth, Northumberland, 1988–92; Vicar, St Margaret's, Scotswood, Newcastle, 1992–2002; Canon Precentor, Derby Cathedral, 2002–08; Vicar, Christ Church, Harrogate, 2008–14; Acting Archdeacon of Richmond, 2013–14. *Publications:* regular articles in The Tablet. *Recreations:* walking, cooking. *Address:* Chelmsford Cathedral, 53 New Street, Chelmsford CM1 1TY. *T:* (01245) 294492. *E:* dean@chelmsfordcathedral.org.uk.

**HENSHALL, Valentine Ruth, (Ruthie);** actress, singer and dancer; *b* 7 March 1967; *d* of David Henshall and Gloria Diana Mary Henshall; *m* 2004, Timothy Michael Howar (marr. diss. 2011); two *d*. *Educ:* Bullers Wood Grammar Sch. for Girls; Laine Theatre Arts, Epsom. *Theatre:* Chorus Line (tour), 1986; West End début, Cats, New London Th., 1987–88; Miss Saigon, Th. Royal, Drury Lane, 1990, NY 2000; Children of Eden, Prince Edward Th., 1991; The Sisterhood, Henry VIII, Valentine's Day, Chichester Fest., 1992; Fantine in Les Miserables, Palace Th., 1993–94, 10th anniv. concert, Royal Albert Hall, 1995; She Loves Me, Savoy, 1994 (Best Actress in a Musical, Laurence Olivier Awards, 1995); Crazy for You, Prince Edward Th., 1995; Oliver!, Palladium Th., 1996; Divorce Me, Darling, Chichester Fest., 1997; Chicago, Adelphi, 1998, NY, 1999, Cambridge Th., 2010, (21st anniv. revival) Phoenix Th., 2018; Ziegfeld Follies of 1936, NY, 1999; Vagina Monologues, NY, 1999, Arts Th., London, 2002; Putting it Together, NY, 1999; Peggy Sue Got Married, Shaftesbury, 2001; Woman in White, Palace Th., 2005; The Other Woman, NY, 2006; Stair Way to Paradise, NY, 2007; Marguerite, Th. Royal Haymarket, 2008; Blithe Spirit, Th. Royal Bath, transf. Apollo, 2011; An Intimate Evening with Ruthie Henshall (tour), 2013; Billy Elliot, Victoria Palace, 2014; Follies, Royal Albert Hall, 2015. *Television:* a Judge, Dancing on Ice, 2008–09; The Case, 2011; Curb Your Enthusiasm, HBO, 2011; *film:* A Christmas Carol, 2004; *album:* I've Loved These Days, 2013. Many cast recordings. *Recreations:* I'm a mother of two small children—recreation, what's that? *Address:* 7 Pond Cottages, Manningtree Road, Stutton, Ipswich, Suffolk IP9 2TG. *T:* (01473) 328159. *W:* www.ruthiehenshall.com. *Club:* Soho House.

**HENSHAW, Andrew Raywood;** QC 2013; a Deputy High Court Judge, since 2017; *b* Towcester, Northants, 22 April 1962; *s* of Raywood and Patricia Henshaw; *m* 1998, Claire O'Connor; two *s* one *d*. *Educ:* Sponne Sch., Towcester; Downing Coll., Cambridge (BA Hons 1983). Admitted solicitor, 1986; Solicitor, Linklaters & Paines, 1986–2000; called to the Bar, Inner Temple, 2000; in practice as barrister, specialising in commercial, public and EU law, 2000–. *Recreations:* music, bridge, ski-ing. *Address:* Brick Court Chambers, 7–8 Essex Street, WC2R 3LD. *T:* (020) 7379 3550. *E:* andrew.henshaw@brickcourt.co.uk.

**HENSHAW, Sir David (George),** Kt 2004; Chief Executive, Liverpool City Council, 1999–2006; Chairman, Sir David Henshaw Partnership Ltd, since 2010; Interim Chairman, Natural Resources Wales, since 2018; *b* 7 March 1949; *s* of George Ronald Henshaw and Ethel Irene Henshaw; *m* 1st 1978, Rosemary St C. Herbert (marr. diss. 2000); two *s*; 2nd, 2000, Alison Joy Jones. *Educ:* Sheffield Poly. (BA Public Admin 1973); Univ. of Birmingham (MScSoc 1975). Corporate Planning Officer, S Yorks MCC, 1974–84; Prin. Asst County Clerk, then Asst Chief Exec., Essex CC, 1984–89; Chief Exec., Knowsley MBC, 1989–99. Clerk to Merseyside Police Authy, 1989–2000. Dir and Dep. Chm., Mersey Partnership, 1993–2006; Mem. Bd, Improvement and Devel Agency for Local Govt, 2001–03. Non-executive Director: Albany Investment Trust plc, 2004–12; Hedra plc, 2006–08. Dep. Chm., Nat. Task Force on Crime Reduction, 2000–02; non-exec. Dir, Home Office Correctional Services Bd, 2002–05; Hd, Redesign of CSA, 2006–07; Member: Independent Rev. of Higher Educn Pay and Conditions, 1999; Strategy Gp, Civil Service Mgt Bd, 2002–03; Bd, Council for Museums, Libraries and Archives, 2004–06; Public Services Productivity Panel, HM Treasury, 2005–07. Chairman: NW Strategic Health Authy, 2006–11; Bd, NESTA Public Services Innovation Lab., 2008–12; Manchester Acad. of Health Scis, 2009–12; Our Life North West, 2009–11; Alder Hey Children's NHS Foundn Trust, 2011–19; Nat. Mus Liverpool, 2017–; Liverpool World Heritage Task Force, 2017–; Wirral Univ. Hosp. NHS Foundn Trust, 2019– (Interim Chm., 2018–19); Interim Chairman: Morecambe Bay Univ. Hosps Foundn Trust, 2012–13; Dorset Healthcare Univ. NHS Foundn Trust, 2013–14; St George's Univ. Hosps NHS Foundn Trust, 2016–17. Advr, Prime Minister's Delivery Unit, 2001–04; Public Service Reform Advr, States of Jersey Govt, 2014–18. Jt Chm., SOLACE Enterprises, 1998–2005; Pres., SOLACE, 2000–01. Trustee: North West Heritage Trust, 2008–14; NESTA, 2010–12; Alder Hey Charitable Trust, 2011–18; N Wales Bldg Preservation Trust, 2017–. Chm., Faenol Festival Trust, 2007–10. Gov., Liverpool John Moores Univ., 2009–12 (Hon. Fellow, 2004). Fellow, Liverpool Univ., 1998; Vis. Fellow, Royal Inst. of Technol., Melbourne, Aust., 1997–2002. FRSA 2005. DUniv Sheffield Hallam, 2006. *Recreations:* golf, opera, walking, tennis, active member morris tours. *Clubs:* Royal Automobile; Royal Liverpool Golf; Royal St Davids Golf (Harlech).

**HENSHAW, Prof. Denis Lee,** PhD; Professor of Physics, University of Bristol, 1995–2011, now Emeritus Professor of Human Radiation Effects; Scientific Director, Children with Cancer UK, since 2011; *b* 4 May 1946; *s* of late Frederick Henshaw and Evelyne May (*née* Fox); *m* 1994, Wassana. *Educ:* Westfield Coll., Univ. of London (BSc 1969); Univ. of Nottingham (PhD 1974). Teacher, Mundella GS, 1969–70; University of Bristol: Res. Associate, 1973–82; Res. Fellow, 1982–90; Sen. Res. Fellow, 1990–95. Dir, Track Analysis Systems Ltd, Bristol, 1984–. Trustee, Children with Leukaemia, 2004–11. Fellow, Collegium Ramazzini, 2017–. Associate Ed., Internat. Jl Radiation Biol., 1995–2016. *Publications:* over 260 scientific pubns. *Recreation:* Italian language and culture. *Address:* Atmospheric Chemistry Group, School of Chemistry, University of Bristol, Cantocks Close, Bristol BS8 1TS.

**HENSHAW, Frank Charles,** CBE 1993; DL; FRICS; General Manager, Milton Keynes Development Corporation, 1980–92; *b* 28 Aug. 1930; *s* of Frank and Edith Annie Henshaw; *m* 1966, Patricia Jane McDonald; one *s* one *d*. *Educ:* Towcester Grammar Sch.; Coll. of Estate Management. FRICS 1959. Nat. service, RAF, 1948–50. Quantity Surveyor: Northants CC, 1947–53; Coventry City Council, 1953–63; Prin. Quantity Surveyor, Midlands Housing Consortium, 1963–65; Chief Quantity Surveyor: Runcorn Develt Corp., 1965–70; Sheffield City Council, 1970–71; Milton Keynes Development Corporation: Chief Quantity Surveyor, 1971–74; Exec. Dir, 1974–78; Dep. Gen. Manager, 1978–80. Chm., Milton Keynes Housing Assoc., 1985–88; Dep. Chm., Central Milton Keynes Shopping Mgt Co., 1978–89. Pres., Milton Keynes and N Bucks TEC, 1992–95 (Dir, 1990–92). DL Bucks, 1995. Hon. Fellow, De Montfort Univ., 1993. DUniv Open, 1994. OON 1989. *Recreations:* golf, travel. *Club:* Woburn Golf and Country.

**HENSHER, Dr Philip Michael,** FRSL; novelist; *b* 20 Feb. 1965; *s* of R. J. Hensher and M. Hensher. *Educ:* Tapton Sch., Sheffield; Lady Margaret Hall, Oxford (BA); Jesus Coll., Cambridge (PhD 1992). Clerk, H of C, 1990–96. Chief Book Reviewer, Spectator, 1994–;

Art Critic, Mail on Sunday, 1996–; columnist, The Independent. Associate Prof. of English, Univ. of Exeter, 2005–12; Prof. of Creative Writing, Univ. of Bath Spa, 2013–. Mem., Booker Prize Jury, 2001. FRSL 1998 (Mem. Council, 2000–05). *Publications*: Other Lulus, 1994; Kitchen Venom, 1996 (Somerset Maugham Award); Pleasured, 1998; The Bedroom of the Mister's Wife (short stories), 1999; The Mulberry Empire, 2002; The Fit, 2004; The Northern Clemency, 2008; King of the Badgers, 2011; Scenes from Early Life, 2012; The Missing Ink (essays), 2012; The Emperor Waltz, 2014; (ed) The Penguin Book of the British Short Story (2 vols), 2015; Tales of Persuasion (short stories), 2016; The Friendly Ones, 2018; (ed) The Penguin Book of the Contemporary British Short Story, 2018. *Recreation*: ceramics. *Address*: 83A Tennyson Street, SW8 3TH.

**HENSMAN, Claire Theresa**; Lord-Lieutenant of Cumbria, since 2013; *b* 5 July 1948; *d* of Dr Peter Wallace Henderson and Dr Stella Dolores Henderson; *m* 1973, Peter Richard Wavell Hensman; one *s* two *d*. *Educ*: Sherborne Sch. for Girls; London Sch. of Econs and Pol Sci. (BA Laws). Investment Exec., Hill Samuel, 1970–73; Investment Analyst, M&G Investment Mgt, 1973–76; Pension Fund Advr, NM Rothschild, 1976–78; Gen. Comr of Income Tax, 1987–2000. Non-executive Director: Westmorland Hosp. NHS Trust, 1992–98; Univ. of Cumbria, 2010–19. Mem. Council, High Sheriffs' Assoc., 2007–13. Mem. Council, Lancaster Univ., 1993–2006 (Dep. Pro-Chancellor, 2001–06; Hon. Fellow, 2007). High Sheriff, Cumbria, 2007–08. Trustee: Frieda Scott Ch Trust, 2004–13; Lake District Calvert Trust, 2013–; Chair, Lakeland Arts Support Trust, 2011–; Patron, Bendrigg Trust, 2013–. President: Cumbria Alcohol and Drug Adv. Service, 2009–; Cumbria Community Foundn, 2013–; Young Cumbria, 2013–; Cumbria Scouts, 2013–; SSAFA (Cumbria), 2013–; Vice-Pres., NW of Eng. and IoM RFCA, 2013–. Gov., Sedbergh Sch., 2013–. *Recreations*: gardening, music, ski-ing. *Address*: Hill Top, Crosthwaite, Kendal, Cumbria LA8 8JB. *E*: c.hensman@hilltop.uk.com. *Club*: Down Hill Only.

**HENSON, Christine Ruth**; QC 2015; **Her Honour Judge Henson**; a Circuit Judge, since 2015. *Educ*: Univ. of Warwick (BA 1992). Called to the Bar, Middle Temple, 1994; a Recorder, 2013–15.

**HENSON, Judith Rosalind**; *see* Mackrell, J. R.

**HENSON, Marguerite Ann, (Mrs Nicky Henson);** *see* Porter, M. A.

**HENSON, Nicholas Victor Leslie, (Nicky)**; actor; *b* 12 May 1945; *s* of Leslie Henson and Billie Collins; *m* 1st, 1968, Una Stubbs (marr. diss.); two *s*; 2nd, 1986, Marguerite Porter, *qv*; one *s*. *Educ*: St Bede's, Eastbourne; Charterhouse. Formerly popular song writer; Founder Mem., Young Vic; first stage appearance, 1962; London stage: All Square, Vaudeville, 1963; Camelot, Drury Lane, 1964; Passion Flower Hotel, Prince of Wales, 1965; Canterbury Tales, Phoenix, 1968; Ride Across Lake Constance, Mayfair, 1973; Hamlet, Greenwich, 1973; Midsummer Night's Dream, Regent's Park, 1973; Cinderella, Casino, 1973; Mardi Gras, Prince of Wales, 1976; Rookery Nook, Her Majesty's, 1980; Noises Off, Savoy, 1982; The Relapse, Lyric, 1983; Sufficient Carbohydrate, Albery, 1984; Journey's End, Whitehall, 1986; The Three Sisters, Royal Court, 1990; Matador, Queen's, 1991; Reflected Glory, Vaudeville, 1992; An Ideal Husband, Globe, 1993, NY, 1996, Australia, 1997; Rage, Bush, 1994; Enter the Guardsman, Donmar, 1997; Alarms and Excursions, Gielgud, 1998; Passion Play, Comedy, 2000; Frame 312, Donmar, 2002; Jumpers, Piccadilly, 2003, NY, 2004; *Young Vic*: Scapino, Waiting for Godot, She Stoops to Conquer, Taming of the Shrew, Measure for Measure, Soldier's Tale, Oedipus, Romeo and Juliet, The Maids, Look Back in Anger, Rosencrantz and Guildenstern are Dead, Charley's Aunt; *National Theatre*: Cherry Orchard, Macbeth, The Woman, The Double Dealer, A Fair Quarrel, Browning Version, Provok'd Wife, Elephant Man, Mandragola; *Royal Shakespeare Co.*: Man and Superman, Merry Wives of Windsor, As You Like It, Twelfth Night; *television series*: Life of Balzac, 1976; Seagull Island, 1981; Happy Apple, 1983; Thin Air, 1988; The Green Man, 1990; The Healer, 1994; Preston Front, 1994; Shine on Harvey Moon, 1994; Blue Dove, 2002; Downton Abbey, 2009–13; 30 films, incl. Vera Drake, 2004, Syriana, 2005, Blitz, 2010; Truth or Dare, 2011; Tommy's Honour, 2016. Dir, Bang Bang, Mercury Th., Colchester, 2017. *Recreation*: music. *Address*: c/o Meg Poole, 191 Kingston Road, Teddington TW11 9JN. *W*: www.nickyhenson.me.uk.

**HENTON, (Margaret) Patricia (Stuart)**, MBE 2017; FRSE, FCIWEM, FCIWM, CGeol, FGS; Director of Environment and Business (formerly Environment Protection), Environment Agency, 2005–10; *b* 30 Oct. 1949; *d* of Robert Stuart Sanderson and Lois Lindsay Sanderson; *m* 1971, Richard George Henton; one *s* one *d*. *Educ*: George Watson's Coll., Edinburgh; Univ. of Manchester (BSc Hons Geol./Geog. 1970). FGS 1974; FCIWEM 1979; FCIWM 2006 (MInstWM 1981); CGeol 1990. Geologist, Associated Portland Cement Manufacturers, 1970–71; Hydrogeologist, Clyde River Purification Bd, 1972–75; Geologist, NCB Opencast Exec., 1975; Inspector, 1975–79, Hydrologist, 1979–83, Forth River Purification Bd; Associate, 1983–85, Sen. Associate, 1985–90, Dir, Scotland and NI, 1990–95, Aspinwall & Co. Ltd; Dir, Envmtl Strategy, 1995–2000, Chief Exec., 2000–02, SEPA. Dir, Scotland and NI Forum for Envmtl Res., 1996–2002; non-exec. Dir, Coal Authy, 2010–17. Chm., Ind. Regulatory Challenge Panel, HSE, 2012–. Member: Sec. of State for Scotland's Adv. Gp on Sustainable Develt, 1993–98; Regulatory Agencies Strategy Bd, DEFRA, 2003–05 (Chm., 2004–05). Chm., Adv. Panel, Forestry Commn, 2003–05; Mem. Council, NERC, 1999–2001; Additional Mem., Water Panel, Competition Commn, 1998–2000. Member: Adv. Cttee for Scotland, 2000–08, Council, 2003–09, Scottish Cttee, 2018–, RSPB; Bd, British Geol Survey, 2009–11; Council, Geol Soc. of London, 2011–18; Bd, UK Carbon Capture and Storage Res. Centre, 2012–16; Adv. Bd, Internat. Centre for Mathematical Scis, 2018–; Trustee: Royal Botanic Garden, Edinburgh, 2010–18; British Trust for Ornithology, 2010–14; Inst. for Eur. Envmtl Policy, 2011–. Pres., CIWEM, 1995–96. Mem., Audit Cttee, Heriot-Watt Univ., 2003–05. FRSE 2002. *Recreations*: travel, bird watching, the Silk Road, hill-walking, gardens. *Address*: 4 Jeffrey Avenue, Edinburgh EH4 3RW.

**HENWOOD, John Philip**, MBE 1998; Chairman: Byerley Ltd, since 2000; G4S Secure Solutions (Jersey) Ltd, since 2010; *b* 27 Aug. 1945; *s* of late Snowdon William Henwood and Amy Doris Henwood (*née* Stickley); *m* 1970, Sheila Patricia Renault (marr. diss. 1994). *Educ*: St Lawrence Sch.; Victoria Coll., Jersey. Joined Channel Television Ltd, later Channel Television Group, then ComProp Ltd, 1962: ops trainee, 1962–64; cameraman, 1964–65; Hd of Studio, 1965–66; Dep. Ops Manager, 1966–70; Producer/Dir (setting up commercial prodn unit), 1970–77; Hd, News and Features, 1977–83; Programme Controller, 1983–86; Dir of Progs, 1986–87; Chief Exec. and Man. Dir, 1987–2000; Dir, 1986–2004. Chairman: Jersey Telecom Gp Ltd, 2002–09; Jersey Tourism Bd, 2013–17; Visit Jersey Ltd, 2014–17; Director: ITV Network, 1987–99; Jersey Finance, 2001–09 (Vice-Chm.); Kleinwort Benson Channel Islands Hldgs, 2003–12; Kleinwort Benson Bank, 2007–12; Flying Brands Ltd, 2007–12; Bailiwick Investments Ltd, 2008–; LFH Internat., 2009–. Chm., Producers' Industrial Relns Service Ltd, 1997–2000. Mem., States of Jersey Review Panel of Machinery of Govt, 1999–2001. Sen. Steward, CI Racing and Hunt Club, 1998 and 2009; Pres., Jersey Race Club, 1998–2001; Mem., Horserace Writers and Photographers Assoc.; racing correspondent: TV Times Channel Is region, 1970s; Jersey Evening Post, 2001– (columnist, 2016–). President, Jersey Branch: CIM, 1999–2018; IoD, 2005–08 (Chm., 2001–02; Lifetime Achievement Award, 2016). Trustee: ITV Retirement Benefits Scheme, 1997–2000; Durrell Wildlife Conservation Trust, 2006–12; St John Youth and Community Trust, 2009–19; Lloyds Bank Foundn, 2016–. Friend, RA. *Recreations*: the turf – horse racing and the thoroughbred, writing (incl. regular current affairs newspaper column), current affairs, ski-ing, international travel.

**HENWOOD, Stephen Hugh**, CBE 2013; TD 1985; FRGS; Chairman: Nuclear Decommissioning Authority, 2008–17; Aerospace Technology Institute, since 2014; Lake District National Park Partnership, since 2018; *b* Newcastle upon Tyne, 11 June 1953; *s* of Hugh Henwood and Cicely Henwood (*née* Gordin); *m* 1981, Gill Rennie; one *s* two *d*. *Educ*: Leeds Grammar Sch.; Liverpool Univ. (BA Hons Econs); Harvard Business Sch. (Advanced Mgt Prog.). Tate & Lyle plc: financial and operational roles, 1977–85; Strategic Planner and Asst to UK Man. Dir, 1985–87; Man. Dir, Tate & Lyle Distribution Services, 1987–89; Divl Dir, Finance and Planning, Tate & Lyle Sugars, 1989–92; BAE Systems plc: Finance Dir, Mil. Aircraft Div., 1992–96; Man. Dir, Royal Ordnance, 1996–99; Gp Financial Controller, 1999–2000; Gp Man. Dir, Progs, 2000–02; Internat. Partnerships, 2002–06; Chm., NP Aerospace, 2006–07. Hon. Treas. and Mem. Council, RGS, 2008–14 (FRGS 2008; Hon. Fellow 2014). FCMA 1989; FRAeS 2000–10. Trustee, Army Mus Ogilby Trust, 2002–18. Regtl Col, London Scottish, 2000–07; Dep. Hon. Col, London Regt, 2000–07. Chm. Bd, Univ. of Cumbria, 2010–14. *Recreations*: walking, bird-watching. *Address*: Keen Ground, Hawkshead, Ambleside, Cumbria LA22 0NW. *E*: stephen.henwood@mesuri.com. *Club*: Army and Navy.

**HEPBURN, James Douglas**; Member (SNP) Cumbernauld and Kilsyth, Scottish Parliament, since 2011 (Scotland Central, 2007–11); Minister for Business, Fair Work and Skills, since 2018; *b* 21 May 1979; *s* of Iain Hepburn and Mary (*née* Irvine, now Hunter); *m* 2006, Julie Shackleton; one *s* one *d*. *Educ*: Univ. of Glasgow (MA 2002). Sen. Vice-Pres., Students' Rep. Council, 1999–2000. Front of house asst, Citizens' Th., Glasgow, 2001–02; temp. data processor, Scottish Power, 2002; Res. Asst to Alex Neil, MSP, 2002–07. Minister for Sport, Health Improvement and Mental Health, 2014–16, for Employability and Training, 2016–18, Scottish Parlt. *Recreations*: football, reading, writing, cinema. *Address*: Scottish Parliament, Holyrood, Edinburgh EH99 1SP. *T*: (0131) 348 6574, *Fax*: (0131) 348 6979.

**HEPBURN, Sir John Alastair Trant Kidd B.**; *see* Buchan-Hepburn.

**HEPBURN, Stephen;** MP (Lab) Jarrow, since 1997; *b* 6 Dec. 1959; *s* of Peter and Margaret Hepburn. *Educ*: Springfield Comprehensive Sch., Jarrow; Newcastle Univ. Former Res. Asst to Donald Dixon, MP. Mem. (Lab) S Tyneside MBC, 1985–97 (Chair: Finance Cttee, 1989–90; Tyne & Wear Pensions, 1989–97; Dep. Leader, 1990–97). Member: Defence Select Cttee, 2000–01; NI Affairs Select Cttee, 2004–; Scottish Affairs Select Cttee, 2015–17; Secretary: All Party Football Gp; All Party Football Team. *Recreation*: sports. *Address*: House of Commons, SW1A 0AA. *T*: (constituency office) (0191) 420 0648. *Clubs*: Neon (Jarrow); Iona (Hebburn).

**HEPBURNE SCOTT**, family name of **Lord Polwarth**.

**HEPHER, Michael Leslie**; Chief Executive, 1996–98, and Chairman, 1997–98, Charterhouse plc; *b* 17 Jan. 1944; *s* of Leslie and Edna Hepher; *m* 1st, 1971, Janice Morton (marr. diss. 2004); one *s* two *d*; 2nd, 2006, Raissa Chtcherbakova. *Educ*: Kingston Grammar School. FIA; Associate, Soc. of Actuaries; FLIA. Provident Life Assoc., UK, 1961–67; Commercial Life Assurance, Canada, 1967–70; Maritime Life Assurance Co., Canada, 1970–79; Chm. and Man. Dir, Abbey Life Group, UK, subseq. Lloyds Abbey Life, 1980–91; Gp Man. Dir, BT, 1991–95. Non-executive Chairman: HambroFraserSmith, 1999–2000; Telecity plc, 2000–05; Lane Clark and Peacock LLP, 2003–05; non-executive Director: Kingfisher, 1997–2010; Canada Life Assurance Co., 1999–; Catlin Gp Ltd, 2003–10; Great-West Life, 2006–; Chartis UK, 2010–12. *Recreations*: reading, golf. *Address*: (office) 35 Piccadilly, W1J 0DW.

**HEPPELL, John;** *b* 3 Nov. 1948; *m* 1974, Eileen Golding; two *s* one *d*. *Educ*: Rutherford Grammar Sch.; SE Northumberland Technical Coll.; Ashington Technical Coll. Fitter: NCB, 1964–70; various cos, 1970–75; diesel fitter, 1975–78, workshop supervisor, 1978–89, British Rail. Mem. (Lab) Nottinghamshire CC, 1981–93. MP (Lab) Nottingham E, 1992–2010. PPS to Leader of House of Lords, 1997–98; PPS to Dep. Prime Minister and Sec. of State for Envmt, Transport and the Regions, 1998–2001; a Lord Comr of HM Treasury (Govt Whip), 2001–05; Vice-Chamberlain of HM Household, 2005–07; an Asst Govt Whip, 2009–10. Member: Cttee of Selection, 1997–2007; Children, Schs and Families Select Cttee, 2007–09.

**HEPPELL, Prof. Stephen John**; Felipe Segovia Professor of Learning Innovation, Universidad Camilo José Cela, Madrid, since 2014; Professor of New Media Environments, Bournemouth University, since 2007; Emeritus Professor, Anglia Ruskin University (formerly Anglia Polytechnic University), since 2004; *b* Chalfont St Peter, 10 Aug. 1950; *s* of Donald Albert William Heppell and Brenda Mary Heppell; *m* 1974, Carole Lynda Chapman; one *s* two *d*. *Educ*: Chenies Co. Primary Sch.; Dr Challoner's Grammar Sch., Amersham; Univ. of Reading (BA Hons Econs); Univ. of East London (PGCE); South Bank Univ. (MSc). Secondary sch. teacher, E London, Essex and S London, 1974–83; Essex Inst. of Higher Educn, then Anglia Higher Education College, later Anglia Polytechnic, subseq. Anglia Polytechnic University: Lectr, 1983–87; Dir, Learning Technology Res. Centre, later Ultralab, 1985–2004; Prof., 1987–2004. CEO, Learning Possibilities Plus, 2009–. Vis. Prof., Universidad Camilo José Cela, Madrid, 2011–14. Trustee: Creative Skillset, 2008–14; BAFTA, 2011– (Mem. Council, 2009–); Mem., Adv. Bd, Educurious, 2011–. *Publications*: Help your Child with Computers at Home, 1994; papers and jls on technol. in learning, design of learning envmts and educnl policy. *Recreations*: a lifetime of competitive sailing from club to world championship level, currently (with Carole) owns and races a 1907 Oyster Smack 'My Alice' and a 1933 Brightlingsea One Design 'Aina', very fond of fish and chips, and silicon chips. *Address*: Heppell.net Ltd, 41 Belmont Close, Wickford, Essex SS12 0HR. *T*: 07929 621295, *Fax*: (01268) 475435. *W*: www.heppell.net, www.twitter.com/stephenheppell. *Clubs*: Brightlingsea Sailing; Colne Yacht.

**HEPPELL, (Thomas) Strachan**, CB 1986; Deputy Secretary, Department of Health (formerly Department of Health and Social Security), 1983–95; Chairman, Management Board, European Medicines Evaluation Agency, 1994–2000; *b* 15 Aug. 1935; *s* of late Leslie Thomas Davidson Heppell and Doris Abbey Heppell (*née* Potts); *m* 1963, Felicity Ann Rice; two *s*. *Educ*: Acklam Hall Grammar Sch., Middlesbrough; The Queen's Coll., Oxford. National Assistance Board, Ministry of Social Security/DHSS: Asst Principal, 1958; Principal, 1963–73 (seconded to Cabinet Office, 1967–69); Asst Director of Social Welfare, Hong Kong, 1971–73; Asst Sec., DHSS, 1973–78 (Social Security Adviser, Hong Kong Govt, 1977); Under Sec., DHSS, 1979–83. Chm., Family Fund Trust, 1997–2003; Mem., Broadcasting Standards Commn, 1996–2003; Expert Mem., Fairness Cttee, OFCOM, 2003–04; Mem., Adv. Bd, Institut des Sciences de la Santé, 2004–06; Chair: Audit Adv. Cttee, EMEA, 2004–12; Eur. Inst. for Health, 2006–10. Vis. Fellow, LSE, 1997–2000. *Publications*: contribs on health, social welfare and regulatory affairs. *Recreations*: gardening, travelling.

**HEPPLE, Tyson Julian,** CB 2017; Director General, Immigration Enforcement, Home Office, since 2018; *b* Weston-super-Mare, 29 March 1968; *s* of George and Denise Hepple; *m* 2004, Anne Davies; two *d*. *Educ:* St Brendan's Coll., Bristol; Univ. of Reading (BA Hons Politics and Internat. Relns 1989). Home Office: various roles, incl. criminal and policing policy and ministerial private offices, 1990–2006; Reform Dir, 2006–09; Dir, Policing Policy and Ops, 2009–11; Dir, Civil Liberties and Public Protection, 2011–12; Dir, Internat. Criminality and Extradition, 2012–14; Interim Dir Gen., HM Passport Office, 2014–15; Dir, Asylum Ops, 2015–16; Dir, Immigration and Protection, 2017–18. Gov., Heber Primary Sch., London. *Recreations:* Reading Football Club, Somerset County Cricket Club, rock band, Marillion. *Address:* Home Office, 2 Marsham Street, SW1P 4DF. *E:* tyson.hepple@homeoffice.gsi.gov.uk.

**HEPPLEWHITE, Rosalind Mary Joy, (Ros);** Chair, Leicestershire and Rutland Probation Board, 2001–04; *b* 20 Dec. 1952; *d* of Anne and Anthony Phillips; *m* 1971, Julian Hepplewhite; one *s* one *d*. *Educ:* University College London (BA Hons). Asst House Governor, 1980–83, and Hosp. Sec., 1983–84, Bethlem Royal and Maudsley Hosps; Unit Administrator (Mental Health), Hammersmith and Fulham HA, 1984–85; Unit Gen. Manager (Mental Health and Mental Handicap), 1985–88, Dir, Corporate Develt, 1988–89, Brighton HA; Nat. Dir, MIND (Nat. Assoc. of Mental Health), 1989–91; Chief Exec., CSA, 1992–94; Chief Exec. and Registrar, GDC, 1996–2000. Mem., Council on Tribunals, 2002–05. JP Leicester, 2002–05. Chair, Trustees, Salisbury Women's Refuge, 2019–. *Recreation:* home and family.

**HEPWORTH, Noel Peers,** OBE 1980; international public financial management consultant, since 2008; *b* 22 Dec. 1934; *m* 1963, Jean Margaret Aldcroft; one *s* three *d*. *Educ:* Crewe County Grammar Sch.; London Univ. CPFA (IPFA 1958); DPA 1963. Nat. Service, RAF, 1953–55. NW Gas Bd, 1951–58; Asst City Treasurer, Manchester, 1965–72; Dir of Finance, Croydon, 1972–80; Dir, CIPFA, 1980–96. Chairman: Inst. of Public Finance Ltd, 1996–2002; CIPFA Internat., 2002–08. Financial Advr to London Boroughs Assoc. and AMA, 1972–80; Mem., London Treasurers' Adv. Body, 1972–80; Member: Dept of Envmt Property Adv. Group, 1980–88; Audit Commn, 1983–91; Adv. Bd, Treasury Solicitor Agency, 1996–99. Pres., Internat. Consortium on Governmental Financial Management, 1987–92; Proj. Dir, Eur. Fedn of Accountants single Eur. currency project, 1996–2001. Chm., FEE Public Sector Cttee, 1988–2003. Chm., Croydon Almshouse and Relief in Need Charities, 1996–2017. FRSA 1985. Freeman, City of London, 1991. Hon. DSc (Econ) Hull; Hon. LLD Brighton; Hon. DSc City. Mem., Editl Adv. Bd, Public Money and Mgt. *Publications:* Finance of Local Government, 1970, 7th edn 1984, Japanese edn 1983; Housing Rents, Costs and Subsidies, 1978, 2nd edn 1981; contribs to technical and financial jls, local govt press and nat. and internat. press. *Recreations:* gardening, walking.

**HERALD, John Pearson;** Sheriff of North Strathclyde, 1992–2012; *b* 12 July 1946; *s* of Andrew James Herald and Martha Wilson or Herald; *m* 1969, Catriona McDougall Anderson; one *d*. *Educ:* Hillhead High Sch., Glasgow; Univ. of Glasgow (LLB). Partner, Carlton Gilruth, Dundee, 1971–91; Dir, William Halley & Sons, Dundee, 1988–91. Depute Town Clerk, Newport-on-Tay, 1970–75; Temp. Sheriff, 1984–91; Chm., Industrial Tribunals, 1984–91. Sec., Angus Legal Aid Cttee, 1979–87; Mem., Legal Aid Central Cttee, 1981–87; Chm., Dundee CAB, 1972–79 and 1982–91. *Recreations:* reading, soccer.

**HERBECQ, Sir John (Edward),** KCB 1977; a Church Commissioner, 1982–96; *b* 29 May 1922; *s* of late Joseph Edward and Rosina Elizabeth Herbecq; *m* 1947, Pamela Filby (*d* 2009); one *d*. *Educ:* High Sch. for Boys, Chichester. Clerical Officer, Colonial Office, 1939; Asst Principal, Treasury, 1950; Private Sec. to Chm., UK Atomic Energy Authority, 1960–62; Asst Sec., Treasury, 1964; Asst Sec., 1968, Under Sec., 1970, Dep. Sec., 1973, Second Permanent Sec., 1975–81, CSD. Dep. Chm., Review Body for Nursing Staff, Midwives, Health Visitors and Professions Allied to Medicine, 1986–91 (Mem., 1983–91); Chm., Malaŵi Civil Service Review Commn, 1984–85. Member: C of E Pensions Bd, 1985–89; Chichester Diocesan Bd of Finance, 1983–97 (Chm., 1989–97). *Recreations:* was Scottish country dancing (ISTD Supreme Award with Hons), now walking, watching cricket, reading. *Address:* 2 The Stables, Mill Lane, Prestbury, Cheltenham, Glos GL52 3NE. *T:* (01242) 571291.

**HERBERG, Javan William;** QC 2011; *b* London, 22 Nov. 1965; *s* of Dr Lewis Jacob Herberg and Mary Herberg; partner, Dr Jessica Boyd; five *s* one *d*. *Educ:* University College Sch.; University Coll. London (LLB); Merton Coll., Oxford (BCL). Called to the Bar, Lincoln's Inn, 1992; in practice as a barrister, specialising in commercial law, financial services, public law and human rights, Blackstone Chambers, 1992–. Chair, Constitutional and Administrative Law Bar Assoc., 2012–14. Gov., Richard Cobden Primary Sch., 2016–. *Publications:* (contrib.) Human Rights Law and Practice, 1999, (ed jtly) 3rd edn 2009. *Recreations:* chamber music, opera, playing 2nd violin, fell walking. *Address:* Blackstone Chambers, Blackstone House, Temple, EC4Y 9BW. *E:* javanherberg@blackstonechambers.com.

**HERBERT,** family name of **Earls of Carnarvon, Pembroke,** and **Powis,** and **Baron Hemingford.**

**HERBERT,** 19th Baron *cr* 1461; **David John Seyfried Herbert;** Director, David Seyfried Ltd; *b* 3 March 1952; *s* of late John Beeton Seyfried and Lady Cathleen Blanche Lily Eliot, *d* of 6th Earl of St Germans and *gd* of 9th Duke of Beaufort; Herbert Barony, in abeyance since death of 10th Duke of Beaufort, 1984, called out of abeyance in his favour, 2002; *co-heir* to Barony of Botetourt 1305; assumed additional surname of Herbert by Royal Licence, 2002; *m* 1975, Jane, *d* of Dr Ian Francis Bishop; one *s* one *d*. *Educ:* Harrow. *Heir: s* Dr the Hon. Oliver Richard Seyfried Herbert, MB BS, FRCA, FFPMRCA [*b* 17 June 1976; *m* 2003, Sarah, (Sally), *d* of Ian Fergusson, FRCS; one *s* two *d*]. *Address:* David Seyfried Ltd, Design Centre, Chelsea Harbour, SW10 0XE.

**HERBERT, Lord; Reginald Michael Henry Herbert;** *b* 21 Oct. 2012; *s* and *heir* of Earl of Pembroke and Montgomery, *qv*.

**HERBERT, Dr Andrew James,** OBE 2010; FBCS; FREng; Distinguished Engineer, 2005–11, and Chairman, 2010–11, Microsoft Research, Cambridge; Fellow, Wolfson College, Cambridge, 2001–11, now Emeritus Fellow; Project Manager (part-time), EDSAC Replica Project, National Museum of Computing, Bletchley Park, since 2011; *b* 30 March 1954; *s* of Edward James Herbert and Catherine Beatrice Herbert (*née* Blaxley); *m* 1st, 1976, Jane Elizabeth Cherry (*d* 2015); two *s* one *d*; 2nd, 2018, Dr Jasmin Fisher, FRSB. *Educ:* Gillingham Grammar Sch.; Univ. of Leeds (BSc Hons 1st cl. (Computational Sci.) 1975); St John's Coll., Cambridge (PhD (Computer Sci.) 1978). Asst Lectr, 1978–83, Lectr 1983–85, Computer Lab., Cambridge Univ.; Technical Dir, APM Ltd, Cambridge, 1985–98; Chief Architect, ANSA Project, 1985–98; Chief Tech. Officer, Digitivity Inc., 1996–98; Dir, Advanced Technol., Citrix Systems Inc., 1998–2000; Asst Dir, 2001–03, Man. Dir, 2003–10, Microsoft Research, Cambridge. Mem., EPSRC, 2006–11. Vis. Prof., UCL. Trustee, Nat. Mus. of Computing, 2016– (Chm., Trustees, 2017–). FBCS 2005; FREng 2007. *Publications:* (with R. M. Needham) The Cambridge Distributed Computing System, 1982; (ed with K. Spärk Jones) Computer Systems: theory, technology and applications, 2004. *Recreations:* restoring and flying vintage aircraft (private pilot's licence and IMC rating), computer and software conservation. *Address:* 27 Millington Road, Cambridge CB3 9HW.

**HERBERT, Brian Douglas;** Director of Performance Review, East Anglian Regional Health Authority, 1989–91; *b* 29 May 1930; *s* of Stanley and Kathleen Herbert; *m* 1st, 1952, Linda (marr. diss.); two *s* one *d*; 2nd, 1973, Lila; one *d*. *Educ:* Ipswich School. IPFA. Local Govt Finance, 1946–63; Health Service: Asst Treasurer, NW Metropolitan RHB, 1963; Group Treasurer, SW Middlesex HMC, 1967; Area Treasurer, Ealing, Hammersmith and Hounslow AHA(T), 1973; Regional Treasurer, 1981, Dir of Finance and Administration, 1985, E Anglian RHA. *Address:* 3 Dane Drive, Cambridge CB3 9LP. *T:* (01223) 574305.

**HERBERT, Rt Rev. Christopher William;** Bishop of St Albans, 1995–2009; an Honorary Assistant Bishop: Diocese of Guildford, since 2009; Diocese of Winchester, since 2010; Diocese of Chichester, 2013–14; Diocese of Salisbury, and Archbishop's Delegate, 2011; *b* 7 Jan. 1944; *s* of Walter Meredith Herbert (who *m* 1950, Dorothy Margaret Curnock) and late Hilda Lucy (*née* Dibbin); *m* 1968, Janet Elizabeth Turner; two *s*. *Educ:* Monmouth School; St David's Coll., Lampeter (BA); Univ. of Bristol (PGCE); Wells Theol Coll.; Univ. of Leicester (MPhil 2002; PhD 2008). Asst Curate, Tupsley, Hereford, 1967–71; Asst Master, Bishop's Sch., Hereford, 1967–71; Adv. in Religious Educn, 1971–76, Dir of Educn, 1976–81, Dio. of Hereford; Vicar, St Thomas on the Bourne, Farnham, Surrey, 1981–90; Archdeacon of Dorking, 1990–95. Dir, Post-ordination Training, Dio. of Guildford, 1984–90; Hon. Canon of Guildford, 1984–95. Mem., Fabric Adv. Cttee, Canterbury Cathedral, 2016–. Lectr, NADFAS, 2009–. Dir and Trustee, Abbeyfield Soc., 2009–15; Trustee, Abbeyfield Res. Foundn, 2015–18. Vis. Prof. of Christian Ethics, Univ. of Surrey, 2016–. Hon. DLitt Hertfordshire, 2003; Hon. DArts, Bedfordshire, 2008. Hon. Citizen, Fano, Italy, 2008. Royal Patron's Award, Abbeyfield Soc., 2018. *Publications:* The New Creation, 1971; A Place to Dream, 1976; St Paul's: A Place to Dream, 1981; The Edge of Wonder, 1981; Listening to Children, 1983; On the Road, 1984; Be Thou My Vision, 1985; This Most Amazing Day, 1986; The Question of Jesus, 1987; Alive to God, 1987; Ways into Prayer, 1987; Help in your Bereavement, 1988; Prayers for Children, 1993; Pocket Prayers, 1993; The Prayer Garden, 1994; Words of Comfort, 1994; Pocket Prayers for Children, 1999; Pocket Words of Comfort, 2004; Seeing and Believing, 2008; Pocket Prayers for Commuters, 2009; Health, 2012; Foreshadowing the Reformation: art and religion in the 15th century Burgundian Netherlands, 2016. *Recreations:* walking, cycling, reading, gardening, writing unpublished novels. *Address:* 1 Beacon Close, Boundstone, Farnham, Surrey GU10 4PA. *T:* (01252) 795600. *W:* www.threeabbeys.me.uk.

**HERBERT, David Richard;** QC 2013; a Recorder, since 2009; *b* Leicester, 1 March 1968; *s* of Richard and Dorothy Herbert; *m* 1997, Rebecca (*see* R. M. Herbert); one *s* one *d*. *Educ:* Rugby Sch.; Southampton Univ. (BA Hons Hist. 1990); City Univ. (CPE 1991). Called to the Bar, Gray's Inn, 1992. *Recreations:* ski-ing, Rugby, cycling, medieval and ancient history, eating chocolate, family. *Address:* 36 Group, 4 Field Court, Gray's Inn, WC1R 5EF. *T:* (020) 7421 8000.

**HERBERT, Jeffrey William,** FREng, FIMechE; EurIng; engineer and industrialist; *b* 21 July 1942; *s* of Alexander William John Herbert and Amy (*née* Whitwell); *m* 1965, Sheila Heane; one *s* two *d*. *Educ:* Loughborough Univ. (DLC, BEng Mech. and Prodn Engrg). MIET (MIEE 1968); FIMechE 1992; CEng, FREng (FEng 1993). Managing Director: Rover-Triumph Cars Ltd, 1976–81; GEC Diesels Ltd, 1981–85; Exec. Dir, Industry, Charter Consolidated PLC, 1985–89; Chief Exec., 1990–96, Chm., 1996–2001, Charter plc. Chairman: Cape plc, 1995–96; Anderson Gp plc, 1987–95; Esab AB, 1994–2001; British South Africa Co., 1996–2001; Howden Gp plc, 1997–2001; Howden Africa Hldgs Ltd, 1997–2001; Claverham Ltd, 1998–2000; Concentric Gp, 1999–2004; Deputy Chairman: Vickers plc, 1997–2000 (non-exec. Dir, 1991–2000); House of Fraser plc, 2001–06; non-executive Director: M & G Investment Trust, 1992–2002; F. T. Everard & Sons, 2002–07; Veolia Water East Ltd (formerly Tendring Hundred Water Services Ltd), 2003– (Chm., 2005–); Affinity Water Ltd, 2012–16. Mem. Council, 1995–2003, Hon. Treas., 1997–2003, Royal Acad. of Engrg. Trustee, Thrombosis Res. Inst., 2004–. Chm., Finance Cttee, Dedham Parish Council, 2018–. CCMI; FRSA 1993. Freeman, City of London, 1993; Liveryman, Wheelwrights' Co., 1993. Hon. DTech Loughborough, 1999; Hon. BSc Loughborough, 2011. *Recreations:* shooting, walking, wine, veteran and classic cars, living in Portugal. *Address:* Baytrees, Long Road West, Dedham, Colchester, Essex CO7 6EL.

**HERBERT, Mark Jeremy;** QC 1995; Commissioner, Royal Court of Jersey, since 2013; Editor, Private Client Business, since 2017; *b* 12 Nov. 1948; *yr s* of late Kenneth Falkner Herbert and Kathleen Ellis Herbert; *m* 1977, Shiranikha Pullenayegum. *Educ:* Lancing Coll.; King's Coll., London (BA). Called to the Bar, Lincoln's Inn, 1974, Bencher, 2004; in practice at Chancery Bar, 1975–; a Dep. High Ct Judge, 2004–15. *Publications:* (contrib.) Whiteman on Capital Gains Tax, 4th edn 1988; Drafting and Variation of Wills, 1989; (contrib.) Arbitration of Trust Disputes, 2016. *Recreations:* bell-ringing, theatre, travel, Italy. *Address:* Pump Court Tax Chambers, 16 Bedford Row, WC1R 4EF. *T:* (020) 7414 8080.

**HERBERT, Nicholas;** *see* Hemingford, 3rd Baron.

**HERBERT, Rt Hon. Nicholas Le Quesne, (Rt Hon. Nick),** CBE 2016; PC 2010; MP (C) Arundel and South Downs, since 2005; *b* 7 April 1963; civil partnership 2008, Jason Eades. *Educ:* Haileybury; Magdalene Coll., Cambridge (BA Hons 1985). British Field Sports Soc., 1990–96, latterly Dir of Political Affairs; Chief Exec., Business for Sterling, 1998–2000; Dir, Reform, 2002–05. Contested (C) Berwick-upon-Tweed, 1997. Shadow Sec. of State for Justice, 2007–09, for Envmt, Food and Rural Affairs, 2009–10; Minister of State, MoJ and Home Office, 2010–12. *Address:* House of Commons, SW1A 0AA.

**HERBERT, Rebecca Mary; Her Honour Judge Herbert;** a Circuit Judge, since 2019; *b* Ashby de la Zouch, 20 June 1970; *d* of Michael and Susan Collins; *m* 1997, David Richard Herbert, *qv*; one *s* one *d*. *Educ:* Twycross House Sch., Leics; Manchester Univ. (LLB). Called to the Bar, Gray's Inn, 1993; a Recorder, 2016–19. Chair, Police Appeals Tribunal, 2016. *Recreations:* dogs, horses, chickens, baking interesting cakes. *Address:* Luton Crown Court, 7 George Street, Luton LU1 2AA.

**HERBERT, Prof. Robert Louis,** PhD; Alumnae Foundation Professor of Art, 1990–96, Andrew W. Mellon Professor of Humanities, 1996–97, now Emeritus, Mount Holyoke College, Mass; *b* 21 April 1929; *s* of John Newman Herbert and Rosalia Harr Herbert; *m* 1953, Eugenia Randall Warren; one *s* two *d*. *Educ:* Wesleyan Univ., Middletown, Conn (BA 1951); Yale Univ. (MA 1954, PhD 1957). Fulbright Scholar, Paris, 1951–52; Faculty, Yale Univ., 1956–90: Associate Prof., 1963; Prof., 1966; Departmental Chm., 1965–68; Robert Lehman Prof. of Hist. of Art, 1974–90. Guggenheim Fellow, 1971–72; Slade Prof. of Fine Art, Oxford, 1978. Organizer of exhibitions: Barbizon Revisited, Boston Museum of Fine Arts and others, 1962–63; Neo-Impressionism, Solomon R. Guggenheim Mus., 1968; J. F. Millet, Musées Nationaux, Paris, and Arts Council, London, 1975–76; Léger's Le Grand Déjeuner, Minneapolis Inst. of Arts and Detroit Inst. of Arts, 1980; Seurat,

Musées Nationaux, Paris and Metropolitan Mus., NY, 1991; Peasants and 'Primitivism': French prints from Millet to Gauguin, Mount Holyoke Coll., RI Sch. of Design, and Univ. of Chicago, 1995–96; Seurat and the Making of La Grande Jatte, Art Inst. of Chicago, 2004. Fellow, Amer. Acad. of Arts and Sciences, 1978; Mem., Amer. Philosophical Soc., 1993. Chevalier, 1976, Officier, 1990, Ordre des Arts et des Lettres. *Publications*: Barbizon Revisited, 1962–63; Seurat's Drawings, 1963; The Art Criticism of John Ruskin, 1964; Modern Artists on Art, 1964, rev. edn 2000; Neo-Impressionism, 1968; David, Voltaire, 'Brutus' and the French Revolution, 1972; J. F. Millet, 1975; (ed jtly) Société Anonyme and Dreier Bequest at Yale University: a catalogue raisonné, 1984; Impressionism: art, leisure and Parisian society, 1988; Monet on the Normandy Coast, 1994; Nature's Workshop: Renoir's writings on the decorative arts, 2000; Seurat: Drawings and Paintings, 2001; From Millet to Léger, 2002; Seurat and the Making of "La Grande Jatte", 2004; A Woman of Amherst, 2008; articles in learned jls.

**HERBERT, Robin Arthur Elidyr,** CBE 1994; DL; JP; President Emeritus, Royal Horticultural Society, since 1994; Chairman, Leopold Joseph Holdings PLC, 1978–2004; *b* 5 March 1934; *s* of late Sir John Arthur Herbert, GCIE and Lady Mary Herbert; *m* 1st, 1960, Margaret Griswold Lewis (marr. diss. 1988); two *s* two *d*; 2nd, 1988, Philippa Harriet King. *Educ*: Eton; Christ Church, Oxford (MA); Harvard Business School (MBA). MRICS. 2nd Lieut Royal Horse Guards, 1953–54; Captain Royal Monmouthshire R.E, 1962–68. Chairman: Union Discount Co. of London, later Union PLC, 1990–96 (Director, 1989–96); Lands Improvement Holdings PLC; Foreign & Colonial Income Growth Investment Trust, 1994–2004; Director: Nat. Westminster Bank, 1972–92; Agricl Mortgage Corp., 1985–93; Marks & Spencer, 1986–91; Consolidated Gold Fields, 1986–89 (Dep. Chm., 1988–89); F&C Smaller Companies Investment Trust, 1985–2001; Federated Aggregates, 1991–95; SWOAC Holdings, 1990–98. Financial Advisor: Water Superannuation Fund, 1986–89; Nat. Rivers Authy, 1989–96. Mem. Council, BBA, 1992–98. Dep. Chm., Countryside Commn, 1971–80; Member: Council, National Trust, 1969–87 (Mem., Exec. Cttee, 1969–84); Chm. Cttee for Wales, 1969–84); Nat. Water Council, 1980–83; Welsh Develt Agency, 1980–86; Darwin Initiative Adv. Cttee, 1993–99; Royal Parks Agency Adv. Gp, 1993–2000. Chm., Global Heritage Fund UK, 2011–. Royal Horticultural Society: Mem. Council, 1971–74 and 1979–94; Pres. and Chm. Council, 1984–94. Pres., Welsh Historic Gardens Trust, 2011–13; Trustee: Royal Botanic Gardens, Kew, 1987–97 (Chm., 1991–97); Nat. Botanic Gdn of Wales, 1994–2007; Botanic Gdns Conservation Internat., 1991–2012. Chm., Flowers & Plants Assoc., 1998–2006. DL 1968, JP 1964, High Sheriff 1972, Monmouthshire. *Recreations*: dendrology, walking. *Address*: Neuadd, Llanbedr, Crickhowell, Powys NP8 1SP. *T*: (01873) 812164. *Clubs*: Brooks's, Pratt's, Beefsteak.

**HERBISON, Nancy Maureen;** *see* Argenta, N. M.

**HERDAN, Bernard Laurence,** CB 2007; *b* 23 Nov. 1947; *s* of late Dr Gustav Herdan and Estelle Muriel Innes Herdan (*née* Jackson); *m* 1971, Janet Elizabeth Hughes; one *d* (and one *d* decd). *Educ*: Bristol Grammar Sch.; Churchill Coll., Cambridge (BA Hons 1969, MA); Bath Univ. (DMS 1972). Systems Designer, BAe, 1969–73; Prog. Manager, ESA, 1973–84; Managing Consultant, BIS Mackintosh, 1984–85; Man. Dir, Defence Technology Enterprises, 1985–89; Commercial Dir, Meteorological Office, 1990–95; Chief Executive: Driving Standards Agency, 1995–99; UK Passport Agency and Criminal Records Bureau, subseq. Passport and Records Agency, then UK Passport Service, 1999–2006; Exec. Dir for Service Planning and Delivery, Identity and Passport Service, 2006–08; interim Chief Exec., SIA, 2008–09; Chief Exec., Nat. Fraud Authy, 2009–11. Advr to Comr, City of London Police, 2011–13. Non-executive Director: MoD, 2012–13; Legal Ombudsman, 2015–19; non-exec. Bd Mem., Disclosure and Barring Service, 2012–16. Chair, Fitness to Practise Panels, GMC, 2014– (Mem., 2012–13); Mem., Fitness to Practise Panels, NMC, 2019–. Mem., Barristers Disciplinary Tribunal Panels, Bar Standards Bd, 2013–15. Associate, Univ. of Birmingham Business Sch., 2009. Dep. Chm., Bedford Hosp. NHS Trust, 2004–09. Trustee: Victim Support, 2010–15; Bedford CAB, 2010–12; Corporate Alliance Against Domestic Violence, 2011–14; Fostering Network, 2012–14; Alzheimer's Soc., 2013–. MInstD 1986. Hon. DBA Bedfordshire, 2008. Editor-in-Chief, Space Communication and Broadcasting, 1982–86. *Publications*: papers in professional jls. *Recreations*: horse riding, foreign travel, theatre, the arts. *Address*: Lowstead, Highford Lane, Hexham, Northumberland NE46 2DP. *T*: 07881 500877.

**HEREFORD, 19th Viscount** *cr* 1550; **Charles Robin de Bohun Devereux;** Bt 1611; Premier Viscount of England; *b* 11 Aug. 1975; *s* of 18th Viscount Hereford and Susan Mary, *oc* of Major Maurice Godley; *S* father, 2004; *m* 2010, Louisa Jane, *y d* of William Knight, Holland Park; one *s* one *d*. *Educ*: Stowe; UEA (BA Hons Hist. of Art and Architecture). Bonhams Auctioneers: Valuer, 1998–; Departmental Dir, 2007–; UK Dir, 2010–; Dir of Private Clients, 2017–. *Heir*: *s* Hon. Henry Walter de Bohun Devereux, *b* 11 Feb. 2015. *Address*: 98 Elms Crescent, SW4 8QT. *Club*: White's.
*See also* Hon. E. M. de B. Devereux.

**HEREFORD, Bishop of;** *no new appointment at time of going to press.*

**HEREFORD, Dean of;** *see* Tavinor, Very Rev. M. E.

**HEREFORD, Archdeacon of;** *see* Chedzey, Ven. D. C.

**HERFT, Most Rev. Roger Adrian,** AM 2012; Archbishop of Perth and Metropolitan of the Province of Western Australia, 2005–17; *b* 11 July 1948; *s* of Richard Clarence and Esmie Marie Herft; *m* 1976, Cheryl Oranee Jayasekera; two *s*. *Educ*: Royal College, Colombo; Theological Coll. of Lanka. BTh, BD (Serampore). Employed at Carson Cumberbatch & Co. Ltd, 1966–69; theol coll., 1969–73; deacon 1972, priest 1973; Assistant Curate: Holy Emmanuel Church, Moratuwa, 1972; St Luke's Church, Borella, with chaplaincy to Colombo Prison, 1973; Vicar: Holy Emmanuel, Moratuwa, 1976; SS Mary and John Nugegoda, 1979; Parish Consultant, Diocese of Waikato, NZ, 1983; Bishop of Waikato, 1986–93; Bishop of Newcastle, NSW, 1993–2005. Chaplain, Lambeth Conf. of Bishops, 1998; Archbishop of Canterbury's rep. on L'Arche Internat. Church Leaders' Commn, 1998–2013; Anglican Co-Chair, Internat. Anglican-Orthodox Theol Dialogue Commn, 2008. Sub-Prelate, WA Commandery, Order of St John of Jerusalem, Australia, 2005. *Publications*: (co-ed) Encounter with Reality, 1971; Christ's Battlers, 1997. *Recreations*: reading, avid follower of cricket.

**HERISSONE, Prof. Rebecca Louise,** PhD; FBA 2019; Professor of Musicology, since 2014, and Director of Research, Department of Music, since 2015, University of Manchester; *b* Reading, 12 June 1971; *d* of Derek Heape and Gillian Heape (*née* Carter, later Neill); *m* 1998, Dr Peter Herissone-Kelly; one *s* one *d*. *Educ*: Churchill Coll., Cambridge (BA 1st Cl. Hons Music 1992; MA Music 1996); King's Coll. London (MMus Histl Musicol. (Dist.) 1993); Emmanuel Coll., Cambridge (PhD Music 1996). Res. Fellow, Emmanuel Coll., Cambridge, 1995–96 and 1997–99; Temp. Lectr in Music, Univ. of Cambridge, 1996–97; Lectr in Music, Lancaster Univ., 1999–2005; University of Manchester: Lectr in Musicol., 2006–07; Sen. Lectr in Musicol., 2007–13; Hd of Music, 2011–14; Hd, Div. of Art Hist., Drama and Music, 2017–18. Ed., Music & Letters, 2007–19. *Publications*: Music Theory in Seventeenth-Century England, 2000; To Fill, Forbear and Adorne: the organ accompaniment of restoration music (monograph), 2006; (ed) The Ashgate Research Companion to Henry Purcell, 2012; Musical Creativity in Restoration England, 2013 (Biennial Diana McVeagh Prize, N Amer. British Music Studies Assoc., 2014); (ed with A. Howard) Concepts of Creativity in Seventeenth-Century England, 2017; contrib. articles to Jl Amer. Musicol Soc., Music & Letters, Jl Royal Musical Assoc., Musical Qly. *Address*: Martin Harris Centre for Music and Drama, University of Manchester, Coupland Street, Manchester M13 9PL. *T*: (0161) 275 4980. *E*: rebecca.herissone@manchester.ac.uk.

**HERMAN, David Joseph;** Consultant on Eastern Europe, General Motors Corporation, 2002; Vice President, Russia and the Commonwealth of Independent States, General Motors, 1998–2002; Chairman, Sollers OJSC, 2007–15; *b* 14 Jan. 1946; *m* Isabel Roehrenbach; two *d*. *Educ*: New York Univ. (BA Govt Affairs 1967); LSE; Harvard Univ. Grad. Sch. (JD 1971). Attorney, Legal Staff, General Motors, NY, 1973; Manager, Sales Develt (USSR), GM Internat. Ops, 1976; Special Asst to Man. Dir, GM España, 1979–82; Managing Director: GM Chile, Santiago, 1982; GM Colombia, 1984–86; GM Continental, Antwerp, 1986–88; Exec. Dir, Eur. Parts & Accessories, GM Europe, 1988–89; Pres. and Chief Exec. Officer, SAAB Automobile, 1989–92; Chm. and Man. Dir, Adam Opel AG, 1992–98. Vice Pres., Gen. Motors Corp., 1992–2002. Dir, Golden Telecom, 2002–. *Recreations*: golf, opera, bridge.

**HERMANN, Alexander Henry Baxter;** HM Diplomatic Service, retired; *b* 28 Dec. 1917; *m* Rita Rosalind Fernandes. Joined Foreign Service, 1939; served 1942–55; Peking, Ahwaz, Chengtu, Chungking, Shanghai, Quito, Panama, Tamsui; Foreign Office, 1956; Commercial Counsellor and Consul-General, Rangoon, 1957–61; HM Consul-General at Marseilles, also to Monaco, 1961–65; Diplomatic Service Inspector, 1965–66; Counsellor, Hong Kong Affairs, Washington, 1967–70, 1974–77; Consul-General, Osaka, 1971–73. *Address*: 32 Old Place, Aldwick, Sussex PO21 3AX.

**HERMER, Richard Simon;** QC 2009; *b* Cardiff, 1968; *m*; two *d*. *Educ*: Cardiff High Sch.; Manchester Univ. (BA Hons). Called to the Bar, Middle Temple, 1993. *Address*: Matrix Chambers, Griffin Building, Gray's Inn, WC1R 5LN. *E*: richardhermer@matrixlaw.co.uk.

**HERMITAGE, Peter Andrew,** QPM 1996; management consultant on security, government and police matters, since 2000; *b* 26 Sept. 1948; *s* of late Thomas Henry Hermitage and Freda Helen Hermitage; *m* 1971, Brenda Howard; one *s* one *d*. *Educ*: Chatham House GS, Ramsgate. Joined Kent Constabulary, 1968: numerous operational, investigative and organisational roles, incl. Dir, Jun. Comd Course, Police Staff Coll., Bramshill, 1986–87; Asst Chief Constable, Kent, 1990–94; Asst Inspector of Constabulary, Home Office, 1994–96; Dir, Nat. Police Training (with rank of Chief Constable), 1996–99. Mem. Bd, Security Industry Authy, 2003–06 (Acting Chm., 2003–04; Chm., 2004–06). Dir, Office of Ind. Adjudicator, 2010–. Non-exec. Dir, Perpetuity Res. and Consultancy Internat., 2006–10. Chairman: E Kent Hosps NHS Trust, 2000–03; Trustees, Michael Yoakley's Charity, 2015–. Ed., Police Jl, 1997–99. Vice-Pres., Police Mutual Asscce Soc., 1997–99. Gov., Canterbury Christ Church Univ. (formerly UC), 1999– (Vice Chm., 2003–; Dep. Pro-Chancellor, 2005–09; Pro-Chancellor, 2009–13; Hon. Fellow, 2014). MRSPH (MRSH 1992); FCIPD (FIPD 1997); MInstD 1999. FRSA 2010. *Recreations*: Rugby, fly fishing, painting water colours, family, Rotary. *Address*: 4 Ealham Close, Canterbury, Kent CT4 7BW.

**HERMON, Peter Michael Robert;** Head of Information Systems, CL-Alexanders Laing and Cruickshank Holdings Ltd, 1989–90; *b* 13 Nov. 1928; British; *m* 1954, Norma Stuart Brealey; two *s* two *d*; *m* 2017, Patricia Florence Cheek. *Educ*: Nottingham High Sch.; St John's Coll., Oxford (1st cl. hons Maths; Univ. Maths Prize, 1953); Merton Coll., Oxford. Leo Computers Ltd, 1955–59; Manager, Management and Computer Divs, Dunlop Co., 1959–65; Information Handling Div, BOAC, 1965–68; Management Services Dir, BOAC, and Mem. Bd of Management, 1968–72; Mem. of Board, BOAC, 1972; British Airways: Gp Management Services Dir, 1972–78; Board Mem., 1978–83; Management Services Dir, 1978–82; Man. Dir, European Services Div., 1982–83. Man. Dir, Tandem Computers Ltd, 1983–84; Dir, Tandem UK, 1983–85; Head of Systems and Communications, Lloyd's of London, 1984–86; Information Systems Dir, Harris Queensway, 1986–88. Mem. Bd of Dirs, Internat. Aeradio Ltd, 1966–83, Chm., 1982–83; Chm., Internat. Aeradio (Caribbean) Ltd, 1967–83; Mem. Bd, SITA, 1972–83, Chm., 1981–83. *Publications*: Hill Walking in Wales, 1991; (jtly) User-Driven Innovation: the world's first business computer, 1996; Lifting the Veil: a plain language guide to the Bible, 2006. *Recreations*: hill walking, music, cats. *Address*: White Flints, Quentin Way, Wentworth, Virginia Water, Surrey GU25 4PS.

**HERMON, Sylvia, (Lady Hermon);** MP for North Down, since 2001 (UU, 2001–10; Ind, since 2010); *b* 11 Aug. 1955; *d* of Robert and Mary Paisley; *m* 1988, Sir John (Charles) Hermon, OBE, QPM (*d* 2008); two *s*. *Educ*: UCW, Aberystwyth (LLB 1st Cl. Hons); Coll. of Law, Chester. Lectr in Law, QUB, 1978–88; PR Consultant, 1993–96. *Publications*: A Guide to EEC Law in Northern Ireland, 1986. *Recreations*: swimming, ornithology. *Address*: House of Commons, SW1A 0AA.

**HERMON-TAYLOR, Prof. John,** FRCS; Professor of Surgery, St George's Hospital Medical School, 1976–2002, now Professor Emeritus; Professor Affiliate (formerly Visiting Professor), Division of Nutritional Sciences (formerly Diabetes and Nutritional Sciences), Faculty of Life Sciences and Medicine (formerly School of Medicine), King's College London, since 2008; *b* 16 Oct. 1936; *s* of late Hermon Taylor, FRCS; *m* 1971, Eleanor Ann Pheteplace, of Davenport, Iowa; one *s* one *d*. *Educ*: Harrow Sch. (Shepherd-Churchill Open Major Entrance Schol.); St John's Coll., Cambridge (travelling schol., 1955; BA 1957, MB BChir 1960, MChir 1968); London Hosp. Med. Coll. (Open Entrance Schol., 1957, prizes in Med., Path., and Obst.). FRCS 1963 (Hallett Prize, 1962). Training in surgery, 1962–68; MRC Travelling Fellow to Mayo Clinic, USA, 1968–69 (Vis. Prof., 1980, 1985); Senior Lectr, 1970, Reader in Surgery, 1971–76, London Hosp. Med. Coll. Pearce-Gould Vis. Prof., Middlesex Hosp., 1982; Vis. Prof., Pakistan Inst. of Med. Scis, Islamabad, 1989. Hon. Consultant in Gen. Surgery to RN, 1989–2002. Mem. Council, Assoc. of Surgeons of GB and Ireland, 1981–84; Dir, James IV Assoc. of Surgeons, 1983–86. Member: Council, Action Research, 1988–97; Scientific Cttee, British Digestive Foundn, 1991–95; Medical Adv. Cttee, British Liver Trust, 1995–96; Health Services Res. and Clin. Epidemiol. Adv. Cttee, Wellcome Trust, 1996–2001 (Mem., Clinical Panel, 1985–88); wkg gp on Crohn's disease and paratuberculosis, Scientific Cttee on Animal Health and Animal Welfare, EC, 1998–2000. Director: BioScience Internat. Inc., 1987–2013; HAV Vaccines Ltd, 2009–. Mem., numerous professional bodies, UK and overseas. Innovator of the Year award, Times Newspaper/Barclays Bank, 1988. *Publications*: scientific papers on purification and biochem. of enteropeptidase, diseases of pancreas, peptide chem., enzyme activation in gastric disorders, on causation and specific treatment of Crohn's disease, mycobacterial genetics, epidemiology of breast cancer, biol res. on common solid tumours, a new virally vectored T-cell vaccine against Mycobacterium avium subspecies paratuberculosis to treat Crohn's disease. *Recreations*: fishing, sailing, shooting, growing soft fruit and vegetables. *Address*: Division of Nutritional Sciences, Faculty of Life Sciences and Medicine, Franklin-Wilkins Building, King's College London, Stamford Street, SE1 9NH. *T*: (020) 7848 4511. *E*: j.hermon@kcl.ac.uk.

**HERN, Jane Carolyn;** Registrar, Royal College of Veterinary Surgeons, 1997–2011; *b* 22 Sept. 1954; *d* of George Kenneth Hern and Elizabeth Ellen Hern (*née* Byford). *Educ:* Girton Coll., Cambridge (BA Hons Law 1976; MA). Articles with Lovell, White & King, 1977–79; admitted as solicitor, 1979; LCD, 1979–87, Law Commn, 1981–86; Law Soc., 1987–96: Asst Sec.-Gen., 1992–95; Dir, Management and Planning Directorate, 1995–96; Actg Sec.-Gen., 1996. Chairman: UK Inter-Professional Gp, 2005–15; Skills for Justice Appeals Cttee, 2005–18; Audit Cttee, Gen. Osteopathic Council, 2010–15. Mem. Bd, QAA, 2010–16 (Chm., Audit Cttee, 2015–16). *Recreations:* eating, drinking, reading crime thrillers, visiting places of historic interest.

**HERNANDEZ, David Anthony; His Honour Judge Hernandez;** a Circuit Judge, since 2004; *b* 15 Sept. 1953; *s* of Andrew and Daphne Hernandez; *m* 1987, Lesley Newton, *qv*; one *s* one *d*. *Educ:* Bury Grammar Sch.; St Catherine's Coll., Oxford (MA Jurisprudence). Called to the Bar: Lincoln's Inn, 1976; Trinidad and Tobago, 1981; barrister, practising family law, 1976–2004; Jt Head, Young Street Chambers, Manchester, 2001–04. Asst Recorder, 1996–2000, Recorder, 2000–04. Chm., Rent Assessment Cttee (Northern Panel), 1984–2004. *Recreations:* Tai Chi, listening to jazz, travel. *Address:* Manchester Crown Court, Courts of Justice, Crown Square, Manchester M3 3FL. *T:* (0161) 954 1800.

**HERON, Mark Nicholas B.;** *see* Bryant-Heron.

**HERON, Raymond,** CBE 1984; retired; Deputy Director, Propellants, Explosives and Rocket Motor Establishment, Ministry of Defence (Procurement Executive), 1977–84; *b* 10 April 1924; *s* of Lewis and Doris Heron; *m* 1948, Elizabeth MacGathan (*d* 2006); one *s* one *d*. *Educ:* Heath Grammar Sch., Halifax; Queen's Coll., Oxford (BA Physics). Shell Refining and Marketing Co., 1944–47; RN, Instructor Branch, 1947–52; Rocket Propulsion Estabt, Min. of Supply (later Min. of Technology), 1952–67; Cabinet Office, 1967; Asst Dir, Min. of Technology, 1967–73; Dep. Dir, Explosives Research and Development Estabt, MoD, 1973; Special Asst to Sec. (Procurement Exec.), MoD, 1973–74; Head of Rocket Motor Exec. and Dep. Dir/2, Rocket Propulsion Estabt, MoD (PE), 1974–76. *Publications:* articles in scientific and technical jls. *Recreations:* music, hill walking, golf. *Address:* 9 Grange Gardens, Wendover, Aylesbury, Bucks HP22 6HB. *T:* (01296) 622921. *Club:* Ashridge Golf.

**HERON-MAXWELL, Sir Nigel (Mellor),** 10th Bt *cr* 1683; *b* 30 Jan. 1944; *s* of Sir Patrick Ivor Heron-Maxwell, 9th Bt and D. Geraldine E., *yr d* of late Claud Paget Mellor; *S* father, 1982; *m* 1972, Mary Elizabeth Angela (*d* 2010), *o d* of late W. Ewing, Co. Donegal; one *s* one *d*. *Educ:* Milton Abbey. Volunteer Watchkeeper, Charlestown Lookout, Nat. Coastwatch Instn, 2012–16. *Heir: s* David Mellor Heron-Maxwell [*b* 22 May 1975; *m* 2012, Emma Louise Ranger; one *s* one *d*].

**HERRICK, Ven. Vanessa Anne;** Archdeacon of Harlow, since 2017; *b* London, 27 March 1958; *d* of Robert Renaut and Dorothy Joan Renaut (*née* Tuckey); *m* 1980, David William Herrick; two *s*. *Educ:* Grey Coat Hospital, Westminster; Trinity Coll. of Music (LTCL 1975); Univ. of York (BA Hons Music 1980); St John's Coll., Nottingham (CTh 1981); Ridley Hall, Cambridge (CTh; MA Pastoral Theology 1996). Freelance music teacher, 1980–84; Regl Co-ordinator (E Anglia), Foundn for Study of Infant Deaths, 1990–94. Ordained deacon, 1996, priest, 1997; Asst Curate, Cathedral Parish of St James, Bury St Edmunds, 1996–99; Chaplain and Fellow, Fitzwilliam Coll., Cambridge and Tutor in Pastoral Theology, Ridley Hall, Cambridge, 1999–2002; Diocese of Ely: Dir of Ministry and Dir of Ordinands, 2003–11; Dean of Women's Ministry, 2007–11; Rector: Wimborne Minster, 2012–17; Northern Villages, 2015–17. Canon, Ely Cathedral, 2003–11; Canon and Preb., Salisbury Cathedral, 2014–17. *Publications:* Jesus Wept: reflections on vulnerability in leadership, 1998; Face Value: God in the place of encounter, 2002; Take Up Your Cross: daily readings for Lent, 2005. *Recreations:* long-distance walking, singing, theatre, cinema, contemporary arts, knitting, novice golfer. *Address:* Glebe House, Church Lane, Sheering, Bishop's Stortford CM22 7NR. *T:* (01279) 734524. *E:* a.harlow@chelmsford.anglican.org.

**HERRIDGE, Michael Eric James;** HM Diplomatic Service, retired; Deputy High Commissioner to South India, 1999–2003; *b* 23 Sept. 1946; *s* of late Robert James Herridge and Mary Herridge (*née* Beckitt); *m* 1968, Margaret Elizabeth Bramble; one *d*. *Educ:* Ashley Sch., Hampshire; Bournemouth Coll. Joined HM Diplomatic Service, 1966; Prague, 1969–72; Nairobi, 1972–75; FCO, 1975–79; Second Sec., Lagos, 1979–82; Second, then First, Sec., UKMIS NY, 1982–86; FCO, 1986–90; First Sec., Madrid, 1990–95; FCO, 1995–99. *Recreations:* genealogy, gardening, photography. *Address:* Cheddar, Somerset.

**HERRIES OF TERREGLES, Lady,** (16th in line, of the Lordship *cr* 1490); **Theresa Jane Kerr, (Marchioness of Lothian);** *b* Sutton, Surrey, 24 Jan. 1945; *yr d* of 16th Duke of Norfolk, KG, PC, GCVO, GBE, TD, and Lavinia Mary, Duchess of Norfolk, LG, CBE; *S* sister, 2017; *m* 1975, Michael Andrew Foster Jude Kerr (*see* 13th Marquess of Lothian); two *d* (and one *d* decd). *Educ:* Convent in Arundel; Convent of Sacred Heart, Woldingham, Surrey. Charity worker; pilgrimage helper and organiser, Handicapped Children's Pilgrimage Trust, 1965–74; Mem. Cttee, Malcolm Sergeant Cancer Fund for Children (Scotland), 1975–90. *Recreations:* tennis (Sussex County Champion, 1969; Sussex County Team, 1968–74), riding, swimming, ski-ing. *Heir: d* Lady Clare Kerr [*b* 25 Jan. 1979; *m* 2010, Nicholas Richard Hurd (*see* Rt Hon. N. R. Hurd); one *s* one *d*]. *Address:* Monteviot, Jedburgh TD8 6UH. *Club:* All England Tennis.

**HERRIN, Jeremy Reid;** Artistic Director, Headlong, since 2013; *b* New York, 19 Jan. 1970; *s* of John Edward Herrin and Heather Yeoman Herrin; partner, Deborah Bruce; one *s* one *d*. *Educ:* Oundle Sch.; Royal Scottish Acad. of Music and Drama (BA Dramatic Studies). Asst Dir, Royal Court, 1994–96; Staff Dir, NT, 1996–99; Associate Dir, Live Th., Newcastle upon Tyne, 2000–08; Dep. Artistic Dir, Royal Court Th., 2009–12. Co-Dir, Stage Dirs UK, 2015–. Director: theatre productions: Marble, Abbey, Dublin, 2009; Much Ado About Nothing, 2011, The Tempest, 2013, Globe; Death and the Maiden, Harold Pinter, 2011; South Downs, Chichester, 2011, transf. Harold Pinter, 2012; Children's Children, Almeida, 2012; This House, NT, 2012, Chichester, 2016; Absent Friends, Harold Pinter, 2012; Uncle Vanya, Chichester, 2012; Another Country, Chichester, 2013, transf. Trafalgar Studios, 2014; Wolf Hall and Bring Up the Bodies, RSC (Evening Standard Award for Best Dir), transf. Aldwych, 2014, NY, 2015; The Moderate Soprano, Hampstead, 2015; Noises Off, NY, 2016, Lyric Hammersmith, 2019; The Plough and the Stars, NT, 2016; Junkyard, Bristol Old Vic, 2017; Common, NT, 2017; Labour of Love, Noël Coward Th., 2017; All My Sons, Old Vic, 2019; for Royal Court: The Face, transf. Duke of York's, The Vertical Hour, 2007; Tusk Tusk, The Priory, 2009; Kin, 2010; The Heretic, Haunted Child, 2011; Hero, 2012; No Quarter, 2013; for Headlong: People, Places and Things, NT, 2015, transf. Wyndhams, 2016; The Absence of War, Rose Th., Kingston and Crucible, Sheffield, 2015; The Nether, Royal Court, transf. Duke of York's, 2015; radio productions: The Vertical Hour, 2008; Flare Path, 2011; South Downs, 2012. *Recreations:* music, film, family. *Address:* Headlong, 17 Risborough Street, SE1 0HG. *E:* info@headlong.co.uk.

**HERRINGTON, Dr Richard Jeremy,** FGS; Head, Earth Sciences Department, Natural History Museum, since 2013; *b* Basingstoke, 17 June 1959; *s* of John Herrington and Barbara Herrington; *m* 1982, Denise Elaine Browne; two *s*. *Educ:* Vyne Sch., Basingstoke; Queen Mary's 6th Form Coll., Basingstoke; Royal Sch. of Mines, Imperial Coll. London (BSc Hons Mining Geol.; PhD 1991; DIC 1991). FGS 1991. Geologist, Cominco Ltd, 1980–87; Natural History Museum: Sen. Res. Fellow, 1991–95; Researcher, 1995–2009; Individual Merit Researcher, 2009–. Visiting Professor: Royal Sch. of Mines, Imperial Coll. London; Camborne Sch. of Mines, Univ. of Exeter. Fellow, Soc. of Economic Geologists, 1992. *Publications:* Gold (jtly), 1999; over 85 papers in internat. jls incl. Nature, Geol., Earth and Planetary Sci. Letters, Nature Geosci., Earth Sci. Reviews, Economic Geol., Mineralium Deposita. *Recreations:* walking, sailing, gardening. *Address:* Natural History Museum, Cromwell Road, SW7 5BD. *T:* (020) 7942 5528. *E:* r.herrington@nhm.ac.uk.

**HERRMANN, Georgina,** OBE 2001; DPhil; FBA 1999; Reader in the Archaeology of Western Asia, University College London, 1993–2002, Visiting Hon. Research Professor, 2002–Sept. 2020, Emeritus Reader, from Sept. 2020; *b* 20 Oct. 1937; *d* of John Walker Thompson and Gladys Elaine Thompson; *m* 1965, Prof. Luke John Herrmann (*d* 2016); two *s*. *Educ:* Inst. of Archaeology, Univ. of London (post-grad. dip. 1963); St Hugh's Coll., Oxford (DPhil 1966). FSA 1968. Sec., Foreign Office, 1956–61; J. R. MacIver Jun. Res. Fellow, Oxford, 1966–68; Calouste Gulbenkian Fellow, Cambridge, 1974–76; Regents' Prof., Univ. of Calif at Berkeley, 1986; Leverhulme Res. Fellow, 1989–91; part-time Lecturer: Inst. of Archaeology, London Univ., 1985–91; in Mesopotamian Archaeology, UCL, 1991–93. Dir, excavations at Merv, Turkmenistan, 1992–2001. Hon. Foreign Mem., Amer. Inst. of Archaeology, 1997. Editor, Iran (jl of British Inst. of Persian Studies), 1966–81. Laureate, Rolex Award for Enterprise, 1996. *Publications:* Ivories from Nimrud, III (with M. Mallowan), 1974, IV, 1986, V, 1992, VI (with S. Laidlaw), 2009, VII (with S. Laidlaw), 2013; The Iranian Revival, 1977; Iranische Denkmaler (recording Sasanian rock reliefs), 8–11, 1977–83, and 13, 1989; (ed) Furniture of Western Asia, Ancient and Traditional, 1996; Monuments of Merv I, 1999; (ed jtly) After Alexander: Central Asia before Islam, 2007; Ancient Ivory: masterpieces of the Assyrian empire, 2017. *Recreations:* planting trees, labradors, walking. *Address:* The Old Vicarage, Penrhos, Raglan, Usk, Mon NP15 2LE. *T:* (01600) 780524. *Club:* Athenæum.

**HERROD, His Honour Donald;** QC 1972; a Circuit Judge, 1978–95; *b* 7 Aug. 1930; *o s* of Wilfred and Phyllis Herrod, Doncaster; *m* 1959, Kathleen Elaine Merrington, MB, ChB; two *d*. *Educ:* grammar schs, Doncaster and Leeds. Called to the Bar, 1956. A Recorder of the Crown Court, 1972–78. Member: Parole Bd, 1978–81; Judicial Studies Bd, 1982–86. *Recreation:* golf.

**HERRON, Michael;** Director, Information Management, 2008–10, and Chief Information Officer, 2010, Department for Transport; *b* 7 Jan. 1954; *s* of John Herron and Eileen Herron (*née* Mann); *m* 1989, Tessa Garland; two *s*. *Educ:* West End London Polytech. (BA Hons). Mgt trainee, Aérospatiale, 1978; Sales Manager, MM Electronics, 1979–80; Gen. Manager, York Mill Ltd, 1981–86; DTI, 1986–95; Cabinet Office, 1995–2004; Dir, Business Delivery Services, DfT, 2004–08. *Recreations:* cooking, wine, motor-cycling, rock 'n roll music, ski-ing. *Address:* 9 Ropemakers Fields, E14 8BX. *Club:* Royal Automobile.

**HERSCHBACH, Prof. Dudley Robert;** Baird Professor of Science, Harvard University, 1976–2003, now Baird Professor Emeritus; Professor of Physics, Texas A&M University, since 2005; *b* 18 June 1932; *s* of Robert D. Herschbach and Dorothy E. Herschbach; *m* 1964, Georgene L. Botyos; two *d*. *Educ:* Campbell High School; Stanford Univ. (BS Math 1954, MS Chem. 1955); Harvard Univ. (AM Physics 1956, PhD Chem. Phys 1958). Junior Fellow, Soc. of Fellows, Harvard, 1957–59; Asst Prof., 1959–61, Associate Prof., 1961–63, Univ. of California, Berkeley; Prof. of Chemistry, Harvard Univ., 1963–76. Hon. DSc: Toronto, 1977; Dartmouth Coll., 1992; Charles Univ., Prague, 1993; Wheaton Coll., 1995; Franklin & Marshall Coll., 1998; Harvard, 2011; Edinburgh, 2016. (Jtly) Nobel Prize for Chemistry, 1986; US Nat. Medal of Sci., 1991; Heyrovský Medal, Czech Acad. of Scis, 1992; Walker Prize, Boston Mus. of Sci., 1994; Gold Medal, Amer. Inst. of Chemists, 2011. *Publications:* over 400 research papers, chiefly on quantum mechanics, chemical kinetics, reaction dynamics, molecular spectroscopy, collision theory, in Jl of Chemical Physics, Jl of Phys. Chemistry, Molecular Physics, Phys. Review. *Recreations:* tennis, biking, hiking, kayaking, poetry. *T:* (617) 6949850, (office) (617) 4953218.

**HERSEY, David Kenneth;** lighting designer; founder Chairman, DH Design Ltd, since 1972; *b* 30 Nov. 1939; *s* of Ella Morgan Decker and C. Kenneth Hersey; *m* Demetra Marastis; one *s* two *d*. *Educ:* Oberlin Coll., Ohio. Left NY for London, 1968; lighting designer for theatre, opera and ballet cos, incl. Royal Opera House, ENO, Glyndebourne, Ballet Rambert, London Contemporary Dance, Scottish Ballet; lighting consultant to Nat. Theatre, 1974–84; many productions for RSC. Chm., Assoc. of Lighting Designers, 1984–86. *Designs include:* Evita, 1978 (Tony award, 1980); Nicholas Nickleby, 1980; Cats, 1981 (Tony and Drama Desk awards, 1983); Song and Dance, 1982; Guys and Dolls, 1982; Starlight Express, 1984; Les Misérables, 1985 (Tony award, 1987); Porgy and Bess, 1986; Chess, 1986; Miss Saigon, 1989 (Drama Desk award, 1991); Oliver, 1995; Martin Guerre, Jesus Christ Superstar, 1996; My Fair Lady, 2001; South Pacific, The Coast of Utopia, Anything Goes, 2002; Love's Labours Lost, 2003; The Dark, 2004; Porgy and Bess, 2006; Equus, 2007, Broadway, 2008; Measure for Measure, 2010; Showboat, 2016; Fiddler on the Roof (Knight of Illumination Award for best lighting for a musical), 2017. Hon. Dr Middx, 2002. Olivier Award for best lighting designer, 1995. *Recreation:* sailing (Millennium Odyssey Round the World Yacht Rally, 1998–2000). *Address:* DH Design Ltd, 64 New Cavendish Street, W1G 8TB.

**HERSHKO, Avram,** PhD, MD; Distinguished Professor, Department of Biochemistry, Technion - Israel Institute of Technology, since 1998 (Associate Professor, 1972–80; Professor, 1980); *b* 31 Dec. 1937; *s* of Moshe Hershko and Shoshana Hershko; *m* 1963, Judith Leibowitz; three *s*. *Educ:* Hebrew Univ., Jerusalem (MD 1965; PhD 1969). Physician, Israel Defence Forces, 1965–67. Post-doctoral Fellow, Univ. of San Francisco, 1969–72. Mem., Israel Acad. of Scis, 2000; Foreign Associate, NAS, 2003. Israel Prize for Biochemistry, 1994; Gairdner Award, Gairdner Foundn, 1999; Lasker Prize for Basic Medical Res., 2000; Wolf Foundn Prize in Medicine, 2001; Louisa Gross Horwitz Award, 2001; (jtly) Nobel Prize in Chemistry, 2004. *Publications:* articles in learned jls. *Address:* Department of Biochemistry, Ruth and Bruce Rappaport Faculty of Medicine, Technion - Israel Institute of Technology, PO Box 9649, Haifa 31096, Israel.

**HERSOV, Gregory Adam;** freelance theatre director, since 1976; Artistic Director, Royal Exchange Theatre, Manchester, 1987–2014; *b* 4 May 1956; *s* of late Dr Lionel Hersov and of Zoe (*née* Menell). *Educ:* Bryanston; Mansfield Coll., Oxford (MA). Regl dirs trainee, Thames TV, Redgrave Th., Farnham, 1976–78; Royal Exchange Theatre: asst dir, 1980–83; Associate Dir, 1983–85; Associate Artistic Dir, 1985–87; productions include: One Flew Over the Cuckoo's Nest, 1982; Death of a Salesman, 1985; A Doll's House, 1987; The Alchemist, 1987; All My Sons, 1988; The Voysey Inheritance, 1989; The Crucible, 1990; Blues for Mr Charlie, 1992; Romeo and Juliet, 1992; Venice Preserv'd, 1994; Animal Crackers, Royal Exchange Th. Internat. Fest. and Lyric, 1995–99; King Lear, 1999; Uncle Vanya, 2001; The Seagull, 2003; Harvey, 2005; Cyrano de Bergerac, 2006;

The Tempest, 2007; Antigone, 2008; Palace of the End, 2009; Pygmalion, 2010; As You Like It, 2011; A Doll's House, 2013; Look Back in Anger, RNT, 1999. Chm., Talawa Theatre Co., 2012–. *Address*: London. *E*: greg.hersov@icloud.com.

**HERTFORD, 9th Marquess of,** *cr* 1793; **Henry Jocelyn Seymour;** Baron Conway of Ragley 1703; Baron Conway of Killultagh 1712; Earl of Hertford, Viscount Beauchamp 1750; Earl of Yarmouth 1793; DL; *b* 6 July 1958; *s* of 8th Marquess of Hertford and of Comtesse Louise de Caraman Chimay; *S* father, 1997; *m* 1990, Beatriz, *d* of Jorge Karam; two *s* two *d*. DL Warwicks, 2012. High Steward, Stratford upon Avon, 2016. ARAgS 2015. *Heir*: *s* Earl of Yarmouth, *qv*. *Club*: Sloane.

**HERTFORD, Bishop Suffragan of,** since 2015; **Rt Rev. Noel Michael Roy Beasley;** *b* 1968; *m* Lizzie; one *s* one *d*. *Educ*: Imperial Coll. London (BSc 1991); Oriel Coll., Oxford (DPhil 1995); Cranmer Hall, Durham; St John's Coll., Durham (BA 1998). Ordained deacon, 1999; priest, 2000; Curate, St Nicholas, Newport, with Longford, Chetwynd and Forton, Dio. of Lichfield, 1999–2003; Chaplain, 2003–07, Tutor in Mission and Vice Principal, 2007–10, Westcott House, Cambridge; Dep. Dir, 2003–08, Dir, 2008–10, Partnership for Child Develt, Dept of Infectious Disease Epidemiology, Imperial Coll. London; Dir of Mission, Dio. of Oxford, 2010–15. Hon. Canon, Christ Church, Oxford, 2014–15. *Address*: Bishopswood, 3 Stobarts Close, Knebworth SG3 6ND.

**HERTFORD, Archdeacon of;** *see* Mackenzie, Ven. J.

**HERTRICH, Rainer;** Co-Chief Executive Officer, European Aeronautic Defence and Space Company, 2000–05; *b* 6 Dec. 1949. *Educ*: apprenticeship and business training, Siemens AG; Technical Univ. of Berlin; Univ. of Nuremberg (Bachelor of Commerce). Messerschmitt-Bölkow-Blohm GmbH: Information Processing Supervisor, Controlling Dept, Mil. Aircraft Div., 1977; Hd, Controlling Dept, 1978, CFO, 1983, Service Div. (Ottobrunn); Hd, Controlling and Finance Dept, Dynamics Div., 1984; CFO and Mem. Div. Mgt, Marine and Special Products Div., 1987; DaimlerBenz Aerospace, subseq. DaimlerChrysler Aerospace AG: Hd of Divl Controlling, Central Controlling Section, Deutsche Aerospace AG, 1990; Sen. Vice Pres., Corporate Controlling, 1991; Hd, Aeroengines business unit, 1996; Mem., Exec. Cttee, 1996; Pres. and CEO, 2000; President and CEO, Motoren und Turbinen Union München GmbH, 1996.

**HERTZ, Prof. Noreena Tamar,** PhD; writer, academic, broadcaster, campaigner, corporate and political adviser; Economics Editor, ITV News, 2016–17; Visiting Professor, University College London, since 2014; Director, Global Reach International, since 2001; *b* London, 24 Sept. 1967; *d* of Jonathan Hertz and Leah Hertz (*née* Treiser); *m* 2012, Daniel Cohen, *qv*. *Educ*: N London Collegiate Sch.; Westminster Sch.; University Coll. London (BA Philos. and Econs 1987; Hon. Fellow, 2010); Wharton Sch., Univ. of Pennsylvania (MBA Finance and Mktg 1991); King's Coll., Cambridge (PhD Mgt and Econs 1996). Hd, Strategy and Res., Centre for ME Competitive Strategy, 1996–97; Judge Business School, University of Cambridge: Lectr in Internat. Business and Sen. Res. Fellow, Econs Strategy Gp, 1997–2001; Sen. Associate, 2001–07; Associate Dir, Centre for Internat. Business and Mgt, 2003–13; Fellow, 2009–15; Miliband Fellow, Dept of Govt, LSE, 2002–03; Prof. of Global Political Econ., Dept of Econs, Utrecht Univ., 2005–06; Fellow, Centre for Global Governance, LSE, 2007–09; Prof. of Globalisation, Sustainability and Mgt, Duisenberg Sch. of Finance and Erasmus Univ., 2009–13. Vis. Prof., Rotterdam Sch. of Mgt, Erasmus Univ., 2008–09. Consultant: to clients operating in Russia, incl. IFC, Russian Govt, Municipality of Yaroslavl, St Petersburg Stock Exchange, Credit Suisse First Boston, KPMG, Access Industries, 1991–2000; to multinat. corps, 2000–; to Govts, incl. Norwegian, Tanzanian, Dutch, Israeli, Palestinian and Jordanian; to Africa Commn, Dutch Central Bank; to NGOs, incl. Project (RED), Make Poverty History Coalition, Jubilee Debt Campaign. Member: Bd, Global Strategy Gp, Rights and Humanity, 2004–07; Econs and Politics Adv. Bd, Citigroup, 2007–09; Adv. Bd, Edelman, 2009–12; Bd, Warner Music Gp, 2014–. Presenter and creator of television programmes: The End of Politics, 2002; Noreena's Agenda, 2005; The Million Pound Footballers Giveaway, 2007; Host, MegaHertz: London Calling, Sirius XM Radio, 2017–. Trustee, IPPR, 2011–. *Publications*: Russian Business Relationships in the Wake of Reform, 1997; The Silent Takeover: global capitalism and the death of democracy, 2001; IOU: the debt threat and why we must defuse it, 2004; Eyes Wide Open: how to make smart decisions in a confusing world, 2013; contribs to acad. jls on business ethics, sustainability, business-govt-society nexus, globalisation, consumer power, risk mgt, equality and women's rights; contribs to newspapers incl. The Times, Guardian, Washington Post, FT, Daily Beast, Handelsblatt, La Repubblica, Der Spiegel, Die Welt, S China Morning Post, Wall Street Jl. *Recreations*: acting, contemporary art, feminist literature, current affairs, contemporary dance, ballet, giraffes. *Address*: University College London, 2 Taviton Street, WC1H 0BT. *T*: (020) 7679 8580, *Fax*: (020) 7679 8552. *E*: nh@noreena.com.

**HERTZBERGER, Herman;** Kt, Order of Orange-Nassau (Netherlands) 1991; Companion, Order of Dutch Lion (Netherlands) 1999; architect; owner of architectural practice, AHH (formerly Architectuurstudio HH), 1958–2015, Advisor, since 2015; *b* Amsterdam, 6 July 1932; *s* of Herman Hertzberger and Margareta Johanna Alberta Hertzberger (*née* Prins); *m* 1958, Johanna van Seters (*d* 2019); one *s* two *d*. *Educ*: Technical Univ., Delft (Bouwkundig ingenieur). Jt Ed., Forum (Dutch mag.), 1959–63; teacher, Acad. of Architecture, Amsterdam, 1965–69; Professor: Technical Univ., Delft, 1970–99; Univ. of Geneva, 1986–93; teacher, Berlage Inst., Amsterdam, 1999–2000; guest teacher, Acad. of Architecture, Amsterdam, 2000–09. Visiting Professor: American and Canadian univs, 1966–81, 1987, 1993, 1996; Univ. of Geneva, 1982–86. Chm., Berlage Inst., Amsterdam, 1990–95. Hon. FRIBA 1991; Hon. FRIAS 1996; Hon. FAIA 2004. Hon. Member: Acad. Royale de Belgique, 1975; Bund Deutscher Architekten, 1983; Akademie der Künste Berlin, 1993; Academie delle Arti del Disegno, Florence, 1995; Acad. d'Architecture de France, 1997; Royal Inst. Dutch Architects, 2002. Projects include: *schools*: Delft Montessori, 1966; Amsterdam Montessori and Willemspark, Amsterdam, 1983; De Evemaar, Amsterdam, 1986; Polygoon, Almere, 1992; Anne Franksch., Papendrecht, 1994; De Koperwiek, Venlo, 1997; Montessori Coll. Oost, Amsterdam, 2000; Stedelijk Dalton Lyceum, Dordrecht, 2008; Municipal Grammar, Leiden, 2009; Istituto Comprensivo Raffaello, Rome, 2012; De Bron, Amersfoort, 2012; *residential developments*: Kassel, Germany, 1982; Het Gein, Amersfoort-Schothorst, 1989; Papendrecht, 1996; Düren, Germany, 1996; Paradijssel, Capelle aan den IJssel, 2000; Ypenburg, 2005; *other projects*: urban renewal, Haarlemmer Houttuinen, Amsterdam, 1982; office buildings, Min. of Social Welfare and Employment, 1990, Benelux Trademarks Office, 1993, The Hague; Public Liby and Centre for Art and Music, Breda, 1993; urban design/masterplan for Stralauer Halbinsel, Berlin, 1998; exhibn design, Fresh Facts, Dutch Pavilion, Venice 8th Internat. Architecture Biennale, 2002 (Leone d'Oro Award for Best Foreign Pavilion); office complex with studios and housing, Mediapark, Cologne, 2004; theatre and congress centre, Apeldoorn, 2004; office bldg, HQ Waternet, Amsterdam, 2005; Faculty of Sci., Univ. of Amsterdam, 2009; NHL Univ., Leeuwarden, 2010; Faculty of Sci., Univ. of Utrecht, 2011. Dr *hc* Geneva, 2011. Awards include: Berliner Architekturpreis, 1989; Premio Europa Architettura Fondazione Tetraktis Award, 1991; Premios Vitruvio Trayectoria Internacional, 1998; Oeuvre Award for Architecture, Netherlands Foundn for Visual Arts, Design and Architecture, 2004; Gold Medal, RIBA, 2012; Medal in Architecture, Thomas Jefferson Foundn, 2015. *Publications*: Lessons for Students in Architecture, 1991, 6th edn 2009 (Japanese edn 1995, German edn 1995, Dutch, Italian, Portuguese and Chinese edns 1996, Persian edn 1998, Greek edn 2002, Korean and French edns 2010); Herman Hertzberger: projects, 1995; Chassé Theater, 1995; Space and the Architect: lessons in architecture 2, 2000, 2nd edn 2008 (Dutch edn 1999; Chinese edn 1999, 2nd edn 2000); Articulations, 2002; Shelter for Culture: Herman Hertzberger and Apeldoorn, 2004; The Theatres of Herman Hertzberger, 2005; Waternet Double Tower, 2006; Space and Learning: lessons in architecture 3, 2008 (Dutch edn 2008); The Schools of Herman Hertzberger, 2009; NHL University, 2011; Architecture and Structuralism, 2015; contribs to jls incl. Forum, World Architecture, Harvard Educnl Rev., RIBA Jl, Building Ideas, Summarios, Spazio e Società, L'Architecture d'Aujourd'hui, Techniques & Architecture, Archithese, Berlage Cahiers, AIT; *relevant publications*: Hertzberger's Amsterdam, ed by Maarten Kloos, 2007; Herman Hertzberger, by Robert McCarter, 2015. *Address*: AHH, Gerard Doustraat 220, 1073 XB Amsterdam, The Netherlands. *T*: 206765888. *E*: office@ahh.nl.

**HERTZELL, David John;** a Law Commissioner, 2007–14; Consultant, BLM, since 2015; *b* London, 26 Nov. 1955; *s* of Clifford and Barbara Hertzell; *m* 1984, Anne Tootill; one *s* two *d*. *Educ*: George Abbot Sch., Guildford; Brasenose Coll., Oxford (BA Mod. Hist.); Guildford Coll. of Law. Davies Arnold Cooper Solicitors: trainee, 1981; admitted solicitor, 1983; Partner, 1989–2007; Man. Partner, 1992–96, 2000–06. *Recreations*: squash, cycling, sailing (anything).

**HERVEY,** family name of **Marquess of Bristol**.

**HERVEY, Sir Roger Blaise Ramsay,** KCVO 1991; CMG 1980; HM Diplomatic Service; Ambassador to Mexico, 1992–94; *b* 3 Oct. 1934. HM Forces, 1953–55. Joined Diplomatic Service, 1958; Bonn, 1958; FO, 1961; Prague, 1963; First Sec., FO, 1965; Office of Political Advr, Singapore, 1968; FCO, 1970; First Sec. and Head of Chancery, Bogotá, 1974; Counsellor, FCO, 1976; Counsellor, The Hague, 1979; Minister, Madrid, 1982; Asst Under Sec. of State (Protocol) and Vice Marshal of Diplomatic Corps, 1986. *Address*: c/o Foreign and Commonwealth Office, SW1A 2AH.

**HERVEY-BATHURST, Sir Frederick (William John),** 8th Bt *cr* 1818, of Lainston, Hants; *b* London, 18 Sept. 1965; *s* of Sir Frederick John Charles Gordon Hervey-Bathurst, 7th Bt and of Caroline Hervey-Bathurst, *d* of Sir William Randle Starkey, 2nd Bt; *S* father, 2011; *m* 1991, Annabel Peta Warburg; one *s* one *d*. *Educ*: Harrow Sch.; Univ. of Buckingham (BA Hons). Chartered Financial Planner. Director: Chestergate Financial Planning Ltd, 1996–2011; Clarendon Financial Planning Ltd, 2011–. Chm., Head and Neck Cancer Foundn, 2015–. *Recreations*: fly fishing, reading, walking, carpentry, bonfires, deer park. *Heir*: *s* Frederick Benjamin Guy Hervey-Bathurst, *b* 9 March 1998. *Address*: Somborne Park, Stockbridge, Hants SO20 6QT. *T*: 07899 845610, (office) (01794) 388594. *E*: fhb@clarendonfp.co.uk.

**HERZ, Robert Henry,** FCA; Chairman, Financial Accounting Standards Board, 2002–10; *b* New York City, 18 June 1953; *s* of James and Susan Herz; *m* 1978, Louise; one *s* one *d*. *Educ*: Univ. of Manchester (BA (Econ) 1st Cl. Hons 1974). FCA 1977; CPA 1979 (Gold Medal); CGMA. Partner, Coopers & Lybrand, 1985–98; Partner and Mem., US and Global Bds, PricewaterhouseCoopers, 1998–2002. Mem., Internat. Accounting Standards Bd, 2001–02. Director: Fannie Mae, 2011–; Morgan Stanley, 2012–; Sen. Advr, WebFilings, 2011–. Chairman: Transnat. Auditors Cttee, 2000–02; SEC Resolutions Cttee, AICPA; Mem., Internat. Central Mkts Cttee, NY Stock Exchange. Mem., Adv. Bd, Manchester Business Sch., 2008–; Exec.-in-Residence, Columbia Business Sch., 2010–. Pres., Coopers & Lybrand Foundn, later PricewaterhouseCoopers Foundn, 1994–2002. Trustee and Chair, Finance Cttee, Kessler Foundn, 2003–. Hon. LLD Manchester, 2017. Elijah Watt Sells Award, AICPA, 1979. *Publications*: (jtly) Foreign Currency Translation, 1982; (jtly) The Coopers & Lybrand SEC Manual, 1993; (jtly) The Value Reporting Revolution, 2000; Accounting Changes: chronicles of convergence, crisis and complexity in financial reporting, 2013. *Recreations*: travel, golf, softball, volleyball.

**HESELTINE,** family name of **Baron Heseltine**.

**HESELTINE,** Baron *cr* 2001 (Life Peer), of Thenford in the County of Northamptonshire; **Michael Ray Dibdin Heseltine,** CH 1997; PC 1979; Chairman, Haymarket Group, since 1999 (Director, since 1997); *b* 21 March 1933; *s* of late Col R. D. Heseltine, Swansea, Glamorgan; *m* 1962, Anne Harding Williams (*see* Lady Heseltine); one *s* two *d*. *Educ*: Shrewsbury Sch.; Pembroke Coll., Oxford (BA PPE; Hon. Fellow 1986). Pres. Oxford Union, 1954. National Service (commissioned), Welsh Guards, 1959. Director of Bow Publications, 1961–65; Chm., Haymarket Press, 1966–70. Contested (C): Gower, 1959; Coventry North, 1964. MP (C): Tavistock, 1966–74; Henley, 1974–2001. Vice-Chm., Cons. Parly Transport Cttee, 1968; Opposition Spokesman on Transport, 1969; Parly Sec., Min. of Transport, June–Oct. 1970; Parly Under-Sec. of State, DoE, 1970–72; Minister for Aerospace and Shipping, DTI, 1972–74; Opposition Spokesman on: Industry, 1974–76; Environment, 1976–79; Sec. of State for the Environment, 1979–83 and 1990–92, for Defence, 1983–86; Pres., BoT, 1992–95; First Sec. of State and Dep. Prime Minister, 1995–97. Pres., Assoc. of Conservative Clubs, 1978; Vice-Pres., 1978, Pres., 1982–84, Nat. Young Conservatives; Pres., Conservative Gp for Europe, 2001. Advr to govt on local growth, until 2017; Chm., Ind. Adv. Panel, Regl Growth Fund, 2010–17; author of report, No Stone Unturned in Pursuit of Growth, 2012; Mem., Nat. Infrastructure Commn, 2015–17; Chm., Thames Estuary 2050 Growth Commn, 2016–17; Co-Chm., Estate Regeneration Adv. Panel, 2016–17. Mem. Council, Zoological Soc. of London, 1987–90; Vice-Pres., RHS, 2009–. Patron, Nat. Centre for Competitiveness, Univ. of Luton, 2001. Freeman: City of Liverpool, 2012; City of London, 2012. Hon. Fellow: Leeds Polytechnic, 1988; Univ. of Wales, Swansea, 2001. Hon. FCIM 1998 (Pres., 2006–08); Hon. Fellow: Marketing Soc., 2011; Liverpool John Moores Univ., 2013; Univ. of Northampton, 2013. Hon. LLD Liverpool, 1990; Hon. Dr Univ. of S Wales, 2013; hon. degree, Aston Univ., 2013. *Publications*: Reviving the Inner Cities, 1983; Where There's a Will, 1987; The Challenge of Europe, 1989; Life in the Jungle (memoirs), 2000; (with Anne Heseltine) Thenford: the creation of an English garden, 2016. *Address*: c/o House of Lords, SW1A 0PW. *Clubs*: Brooks's, Carlton, Pratt's, White's, Beefsteak.
*See also* R. W. D. Heseltine.

**HESELTINE, Lady;** Anne Edna Harding Heseltine; a Trustee, National Gallery, 2008–16; *b* London, 23 Oct. 1934; *d* of William and Edna Williams; *m* 1962, Michael Ray Dibdin Heseltine (*see* Baron Heseltine); one *s* two *d*. *Educ*: Bedford Coll., Univ. of London (BA Hons 1956). Career in publishing and art dealing at Victor Gollancz Ltd, Crane Kalman Gall. and Bury St Gall. Mem., Bd of Visitors, Ashmolean Mus., Oxford, 1987–2006, Fellow, 2006; Chm. Adv. Bd, Oxford Univ. Mus. of Natural History, 2009–12; Distinguished Friend, Univ. of Oxford, 1999; Trustee: Imperial War Mus., 1990–97; V & A Mus., 1997–2002; Burlington Mag., 2003–; The Sixteen (choir and orch.), 2017–; former Mem. Council, Attingham Foundn; Mem. Adv. Bd, Arts Centre, Univ. of Warwick, 2016–. Hon. Fellow, Royal Holloway, Univ. of London, 2011. *Publications*: (with Michael

Heseltine) Thenford: the creation of an English garden, 2016. *Recreations:* travelling, art history, collecting, gardens, fox and stag hunting. *Address:* Thenford House, near Banbury, Oxon OX17 2BX.
*See also* R. W. D. Heseltine.

**HESELTINE, Rupert William Dibdin;** Executive Chairman, Haymarket Media Group, since 2009; *b* London, 9 July 1967; *s of* Baron Heseltine, *qv* and Lady Heseltine, *qv*; *m* 2000, Sarah Caroline Fitch; two *s* one *d. Educ:* Harrow; Oxford Poly. With Peter Isaacson Pubns, Australia, 1989; Maxwell Business Communications; joined Haymarket Gp, 1994; consumer mags div., Car Hi-Fi; Wine & Spirit Internat., Wilmington plc; Haymarket Group: Advertising Dir, PR Week; Associate Publisher, Gramophone; Publisher, What Hi-Fi? Sound & Vision; Dir, Haymarket Gp Ltd, 2001–; Deputy Chairman: Haymarket Exhibns, 2004–05; Haymarket Media Gp, 2005–09. *Address:* Haymarket Media Group, Bridge House, 69 London Road, Twickenham TW1 3SP. *T:* (020) 8267 5000.

**HESELTINE, Rt Hon. Sir William (Frederick Payne),** GCB 1990 (KCB 1986; CB 1978); GCVO 1988 (KCVO 1982; CVO 1969; MVO 1961); AC 1988; QSO 1990; PC 1986; Deputy Chairman, P & O Australia Ltd, 1998–2001 (Director, 1990–2001); *b* E Fremantle, W Australia, 17 July 1930; *s of* late H. W. Heseltine; *m* 1st, Ann Elizabeth (*d* 1957), *d of* late L. F. Turner, Melbourne; 2nd, Audrey Margaret (*d* 2013), *d of* late S. Nolan, Sydney; one *s* one *d*; 3rd, 2016, Diana, *d of* late Dr W. A. D. Loftus, Bega, NSW. *Educ:* Christ Church Grammar Sch., Claremont, WA; University of Western Australia (1st class hons, History). Prime Minister's dept, Canberra, 1951–62; Private Secretary to Prime Minister, 1955–59; Asst Information Officer to The Queen, 1960–61; Acting Official Secretary to Governor-General of Australia, 1962; Asst Federal Director of Liberal Party of Australia, 1962–64; attached to Household of Princess Marina for visit to Australia, 1964; attached to Melbourne Age, 1964; Asst Press Secretary to the Queen, 1965–67, Press Secretary, 1968–72; Assistant Private Secretary to the Queen, 1972–77, Dep. Private Secretary, 1977–86, Private Sec., and Keeper of the Queen's Archives, 1986–90. Chm., NZI Insurance Australia Ltd, 1992–98 (Dep. Chm., 1991–92); Director: West Coast Telecasters Ltd, 1991–96; NZI Insurance NZ, 1996–98. Pres., Royal Western Australian Histl Soc., 1998–2001. Senator, Murdoch Univ., 2000–06. *Address:* 3/57 Prince Albert Street, Mosman, NSW 2088, Australia. *Club:* Weld (Perth).

**HESFORD, Stephen;** author, since 2015; *b* 27 May 1957; *s of* late Bernard Hesford and of Nellie Hesford; *m* 1984, Elizabeth Anne Henshall; two *s. Educ:* Univ. of Bradford (BScSoc Econs/Politics 1978); Poly. of Central London (Post-grad. Dip. in Law 1980). Called to the Bar, Gray's Inn, 1981. Contested (Lab) S Suffolk, 1992. MP (Lab) Wirral W, 1997–2010. PPS to Leader of H of L, 2005–07, to Solicitor Gen. and to Minister of State, MoJ, 2007–09. Mem., Health Select Cttee, 1999–2001. Founder: and Sec., All-Party Parly Gp on Primary Care and Public Health, 1998–2010; and Vice-Chm., All-Party Parly Gp on Autism. Mem. Bd, Mind, 1998–2001. Trustee, Alcohol Concern, 2012–14. Vis. Lectr in Politics, Univ. of Chester, 2010–15. Mem. Bd and Gov., Edge Hill Univ., 2013–15. FRSPH (FRIPHH 1998); Fellow, Soc. of Public Health; FRSA 2006. *Recreations:* watching football, reading. *Club:* Lancashire County Cricket (Life Mem.).

**HESKETH, 3rd Baron** *cr* 1935, of Hesketh; **Thomas Alexander Fermor-Hesketh,** KBE 1997; PC 1991; Bt 1761; Executive Chairman: Towcester Racecourse, since 1995; British Mediterranean Airways, 1994–2007; *b* 28 Oct. 1950; *s of* 2nd Baron and Christian Mary, OBE 1984, *o d of* Sir John McEwen, 1st Bt of Marchmont, DL, JP; *S* father, 1955; *m* 1977, Hon. Claire, *e d of* 3rd Baron Manton; one *s* two *d. Educ:* Ampleforth. A Lord in Waiting (Govt Whip), 1986–89; Parly Under-Sec. of State, DoE, 1989–90; Minister of State, DTI, 1990–91; Capt. of Gentlemen-at-Arms (Govt Chief Whip in H of L), 1991–93. Chm., Cons. Party Foundn, 2003–10; Treas., Cons. Party, 2003–05. Non-executive Deputy Chairman: Babcock Internat., 1993–2010; Freestream Aircraft Ltd, 2009–; ind. Dir, Air Astana JSC, 2007–; non-exec. Dir, BAE Systems, 1993–2005. President: British Racing Drivers' Club, 1994–99; Remote Sensing and Photogrammetry Soc., 1995–2002. Hon. FSE; Hon. FIET 1982. Heir: *s* Hon. Frederick Hatton Fermor-Hesketh, *b* 13 Oct. 1988. *Address:* c/o Towcester Racecourse, London Road, Towcester, Northants NN12 6LB. *Clubs:* White's, Turf, Pratt's.
*See also* J. Goodwin.

**HESKETH, Very Rev. Dr Philip John;** DL; Dean of Rochester, since 2016 (Acting Dean, 2010, 2011–12 and 2014–16); *b* Southport, 15 Nov. 1964; *s of* Ronald Hesketh and Jacqline Hesketh; *m* 1989, Dr Sugina Kamalagharan; one *s* three *d. Educ:* St Ninians, Isle of Man; King's Coll. London (BD 1986; AKC 1986; PhD 1994); Ripon Coll., Cuddesdon (Dip. HR 1988; DipMin 1994). Community Worker, Vauxhall Mission, 1986–91; ordained deacon, 1994, priest, 1995; Curate, Holy Cross, Bearsted with St Mary's, Thurnham, Kent, 1994–98; Vicar, St Stephen's, Chatham, Medway, 1998–2005; Canon Pastor, Rochester Cathedral, 2005–16. Ext. Tutor, SE Inst. of Theol Educn, 1996–2004. DL Kent, 2019. *Recreations:* walking, keeping rare breed pigs, music. *Address:* The Deanery, The Precinct, Rochester, Kent ME1 1SR. *E:* Dean@rochestercathedral.org.

**HESKETH, Ven. Ronald David,** CB 2004; Chaplain-in-Chief and Archdeacon, Royal Air Force, 2001–06; *b* 16 June 1947; *s of* William Ronald Hesketh and Mary Hagar Hesketh; *m* 1971, Vera Ruth Taylor; one *s* one *d. Educ:* King David Sch., Liverpool; Bede Coll., Univ. of Durham (BA Hons 1968); Ridley Hall, Cambridge; St Michael's Coll., Llandaff (DPS 1971); Dip in Reformation Studies, Open Univ., 1977. Ordained deacon, 1971, priest, 1972; Curate, Southport, 1971–73; Asst Chaplain, Mersey Mission to Seamen, 1973–75; RAF Chaplain, 1975–98; Command Chaplain, 1998–2001; Canon, Lincoln Cathedral, 2001–06; Vocations Officer, Worcester Dio., 2006–11; Force Chaplain, West Mercia Police, 2009–. Chaplain and Almoner, St John Fellowship, Priory of England and the Islands, OStJ, 2018–; Almoner, Hon. Co. of Glos, 2018–. Mem., Gen. Synod of C of E, 2001–05. QHC 2001–06. Mem. Council, RAF Benevolent Fund, 2001–04; Chm., Naval, Military and Air Force Bible Soc., 2006–14. Vice Pres., Friends of St Clement Danes, 2001–. FRGS 2002; FCMI 2006. *Recreations:* theatre, travel, philately, antiquarian books. *Address:* Whistledown, Twyning Green, Twyning GL20 6DQ. *T:* (01684) 299773. *E:* ron@hesketh.org.uk. *Club:* Royal Air Force.

**HESKETH HARVEY, Christopher John, (Kit);** writer, broadcaster and cabaret performer; *b* Zomba, Nyasaland, 30 April 1957; *s of* Noel Harvey and Susan Mary Harvey (*née* Ford); *m* 1986, Catherine, (Kate), Rabett; one *s* one *d. Educ:* Cathedral Choir Sch., Canterbury; Tonbridge Sch.; Clare Coll., Cambridge (BA English Lit. 1978); St Catherine's Coll., Oxford (Postgrad. Th. Studies). Staff producer, Music and Arts, BBC TV, 1980–85; *lyricist and star.* (at Vaudeville Th.): Kit and the Widow: Lavishly Mounted, 1991; January Sale, 1994; Salad Days, 1996; Meat on the Bone, 1998; Tom Foolery; starred with Joan Rivers, Haymarket Th. and London Palladium, 2002 and 2006; Cowardly Custard (UK tour), 2011; Abanazar in Aladdin, Guildford, 2012; *plays:* Five O'clock Angel, Hampstead Th., 1998; The Caribbean Tempest, Barbados, 2000; *screenwriter:* Maurice, 1986; Birkin, 1994; Hans Christian Andersen, 2000; *opera translations* include: Bartered Bride, Royal Opera, 2001; Il Turco in Italia, 2002, La Belle Hélène, 2006, ENO; Bluebeard, 2007; Véronique, 2009; The Merry Widow, Grand, Leeds, 2010; The Magic Flute, Scottish Opera, 2012; *librettist:* (with James McConnel) Orlando, Barbican, 1988 (Vivian Ellis Award); (with James McConnel) Killing Rasputin, Bridewell, 1998; The Life and Death of Alexander Litvinenko, Grange Park Opera, 2020; *television* includes: co-writer, Vicar of Dibley, 1994; Lavishly Mounted; Mounting the Hustings; *radio* includes: Cocktails; panellist, Just a Minute, 1996–. *Recreations:* mushrooming, surfing, playing the piano execrably. *Address:* Park House, Stoke Ferry, King's Lynn, Norfolk PE33 9SF; c/o PBJ Management, 22 Rathbone Street, W1T 1LG. *T:* (020) 7287 1112. *Clubs:* Garrick, Saints and Sinners.

**HESKETT, Rt Rev. Ralph;** see Hallam, Bishop of, (RC).

**HESLAM, (Mary) Noelle, (Mrs David Heslam);** see Walsh, M. N.

**HESLOP, David Thomas,** OBE 1987; CIGEM; Regional Chairman, British Gas plc Southern, 1988–94; *b* Sept. 1932; *s of* late John Heslop and Frances Mary (*née* Brooks); *m* 1952, Barbara Mary Seddon; one *s* one *d. Educ:* Henley Management Coll. (GMC 1974); Harvard Business Sch. (AMP 1981). CIGEM (CompIGasE 1990). Commercial Sales Officer, Scottish Gas, 1960; Marketing Develt Man., West Midlands Gas, 1965; Sales Man., South Eastern Gas, 1972; Dir of Sales, North Western Gas, 1976; HQ Dir of Sales, British Gas, 1982. Pres., Internat. Gas Marketing Colloquium, 1986–89. FCIM 1977; CCMI (CBIM 1990). *Recreation:* church activities. *Address:* Prestolee, Rhinefield Road, Brockenhurst, Hants SO42 7SR.

**HESLOP, Martin Sydney;** QC 1995; a Recorder of the Crown Court, since 1993; *b* 6 Aug. 1948; *s of* late Sydney Heslop and of Patricia (*née* Day); *m* 1994, Aurea Jane (*née* Boyle). *Educ:* St George's Coll., Weybridge; Bristol Univ. LLB Hons 1971. Called to the Bar, Lincoln's Inn, 1972; Jun. Treasury Counsel, 1987; First Jun. Treasury Counsel, 1992–93; Sen. Treasury Counsel, 1993–95. An Asst Recorder, 1989–93. *Recreations:* sailing, travel, photography, fine wine and food. *Address:* 2 Hare Court, Temple, EC4Y 7BH. *T:* (020) 7353 5324. *Clubs:* Royal London Yacht, Bar Yacht; Exe Sailing.

**HESLOP, Neil,** OBE 2002; Chief Executive, Leonard Cheshire Disability, since 2016; *b* Newcastle upon Tyne, 14 Nov. 1964; *s of* Jack Heslop and Carol Heslop; *m* 1994, Nicola Jane Cottell; two *d. Educ:* Clark's Coll.; Guildford Grammar Sch.; RNIB New Coll., Worcester; Univ. of Newcastle (LLB Hons); Cranfield Sch. of Mgt (MBA); Chartered Inst. of Mktg (DipM). Nortel Networks: graduate trainee, 1989; Acquisition Proj. Manager, 1989–91; Strategic Planning Manager, 1992–94; Founder and Dir, China Medica Ltd, 1994–96; Cellnet, then BT Cellnet, later $O_2$: Mktg Ops Manager, 1996–98; Strategic Prog. Manager, 1998–99; Hd of Strategy, 2000–01; Gen. Manager Retail and Online Ops, $O_2$ UK, 2001–04; CEO, Cincinnati Bell Wireless Inc., 2004–06; Chief Operating Officer, i-wireless LLC, 2006–08; Man. Dir, Kontroll Freax Ltd, 2009–11; interim Chief Operating Officer, JJB Sports, 2011–12; interim CEO, KFX Technology, 2012–13; Man. Dir, RNIB Solutions, RNIB, 2013–16. Co-founder and Trustee, Blind in Business, 1992–. Non-exec. Dir, CTIA, 2004–05. *Recreations:* walking, cycling, supporting Newcastle United Football Club, supporting Harlequins Rugby Union. *Address:* Leonard Cheshire Disability, 66 South Lambeth Road, Vauxhall, SW8 1RL. *T:* (020) 3242 0200. *E:* neil.heslop@leonardcheshire.org.

**HESLOP, Sean Martin,** MA; Executive Principal, Folkestone Academy and Marlowe Academy, 2013–15 (Principal, Folkestone Academy, 2009–13); *b* 31 Oct. 1967; *s of* late Roy Heslop and of Eileen Heslop; *m* 2005, Céline Gagnon. *Educ:* Queens' Coll., Cambridge (BA 1989); King's Coll., London (PGCE); Inst. of Educn, Univ. of London (MA Dist.). Teacher of English, Queen Elizabeth's Sch., Barnet, 1994–97; Hd of English, St Olave's Sch., Orpington, 1997–2000; Dep. Headteacher, Ravens Wood Sch., Bromley, 2000–04; Headmaster, Tiffin Sch., Kingston, 2004–09. Res. Associate, Nat. Coll. of Sch. Leadership, 2003. Consultant, Thinking & Learning Schs Alliance, 2002–04. FRSA 2007. *Publications:* contrib. articles on social capital, knowledge capital and change process to educn mgt jls. *Recreations:* walking, reading, bird-watching.

**HESLOP-HARRISON, Prof. John Seymour, (Pat),** PhD; Professor of Molecular Cytogenetics and Cell Biology, University of Leicester, since 2000; *b* Belfast, NI, 14 March 1959; *s of* Prof. John Heslop-Harrison, FRS and Yolande Heslop-Harrison; *m* 1995, Trude Schwarzacher; two *s. Educ:* Univ. of Massachusetts; University Coll. of Wales, Aberystwyth (BSc 1980); Peterhouse, Cambridge (PhD 1983). Stone Res. Fellow, Peterhouse, Cambridge, 1982–85; Scientific Officer: Plant Breeding Inst., Cambridge, 1985–90; John Innes Centre, Norwich, 1990–2000. Principal Investigator, South China Botanical Garden, Chinese Acad. of Scis, 2019–. Associate Ed., Chromosome Res., 1994–2012, now Emeritus Ed.; Chief Ed., Annals of Botany, 2008–. Member: Cttee, Global Musa Genomics Consortium, 2001–; Sub-panel, UK REF 2014. Vice-Pres., 2007–09, Pres., 2009–11, Soc. for Exptl Biol.; Mem. Bd, 2004–, Second Vice Pres., 2015–, Eur. Cytogeneticists Assoc. Reviewer and assessor for grants, res. progs/site visits. *Publications:* contribs to acad. jls. *Recreations:* enjoying the natural and built environment, walking, photography, technology and art. *Address:* Department of Genetics and Genome Biology, University of Leicester, Leicester LE1 7RH. *T:* (0116) 252 3397. *E:* phh@molcyt.com.

**HESS, Edward John Watkin; His Honour Judge Hess;** a Circuit Judge, since 2015; a Deputy High Court Judge, since 2016; Designated Family Judge for Wiltshire, since 2018; Deputy National Lead Judge, Financial Remedies Court, since 2018; *b* Rochdale, 29 Oct. 1962; *s of* John and Valerie Hess; *m* 1988, Elizabeth Bannan; two *s* one *d. Educ:* Rugby Sch.; Peterhouse, Cambridge (BA 1984; MA). Called to the Bar, Middle Temple, 1985; barrister, Harcourt Chambers, 1985–2010 (Treas., 1998–2010); Dep. Dist Judge, Co. Courts, 2002–04; Principal Registry of Family Div., 2004–10; a Recorder, 2009–15; Dist Judge (Principal Registry of the Family Div., sitting at Central Family Ct), 2010–15. Mem. Council (C), RBKC, 1988–98 (Mayor, 1997–98); Chm., Housing and Social Services Cttee, 1993–96). Contested (C) Wigan, 1992. Chm., Cambridge Univ. Cons. Assoc., 1984; Treas., Cambridge Union, 1983–84; Chm., Coningsby Club, 1992. Chm., Holton Players, 2012–. *Publications:* (jtly) Pensions on Divorce: a practitioner's handbook, 2008, 3rd edn 2018; (ed) The Collected Works of Kit Arnold, 2011; (jtly) Dictionary of Financial Remedies (annually), 2014–; Wheatley Manor, Its Owners and Occupants: 956–2015, 2015; Standard Family Orders Handbook, vol. 1 and vol. 2, 2018. *Recreations:* lawn tennis, Real tennis, cricket, amateur dramatics. *Address:* Swindon Combined Court, The Law Courts, Islington Street, Swindon SN1 2HG. *Clubs:* Travellers, MCC.

**HESS, Nigel John;** composer for television, film, theatre and concert hall; *b* 22 July 1953; *s of* John and Sheila Hess; *m* 1996, Lisa Claire Telford; one *d. Educ:* Weston-super-Mare Grammar Sch. for Boys; St Catharine's Coll., Cambridge (MA; Hon. Fellow 2016). Composed scores for: *theatre,* including: Troilus and Cressida, Julius Caesar, Much Ado About Nothing and Cyrano de Bergerac (NY Drama Desk Award, 1985), Comedy of Errors, Hamlet, Love's Labour's Lost, Love's Labour's Won, Othello, The Winter's Tale, The Swan Down Gloves, A Christmas Carol, Twelfth Night (all for Royal Shakespeare Company); The Merry Wives of Windsor, Romeo and Juliet, Henry VIII, The Knight of the Burning Pestle, Nell Gwynn (all for Shakespeare's Globe); The Secret of Sherlock Holmes; *television,* including: A Woman of Substance; Deceptions; Anna of the Five Towns; All Passion Spent; Vanity Fair; Campion; Testament (Novello Award for Best TV Theme, 1988); Summer's Lease (TRIC Award for Best TV Theme, 1989); The London Embassy; The One Game; Titmuss Regained; Maigret; Growing Pains; Classic Adventure;

Dangerfield; Just William; Wycliffe; Hetty Wainthropp Investigates (Novello Award for Best TV Theme, 1997); Badger; Ballykissangel; New Tricks; Stick with Me Kid; *films*, including: An Ideal Husband, 1999; Ladies in Lavender, 2004; *concert music* includes: Thames Journey; East Coast Pictures, 1985; The Way of Light, 1985; Global Variations, 1990; Stephenson's Rocket, 1991; The Winds of Power, 1993; Scramble!, 1994; To the Stars!, 1996; The TV Detectives, 1998; Monck's March, 2002; New London Pictures, 2003; The Food of Love, 2005; Piano Concerto (commnd by Prince of Wales), 2007; Shakespeare Pictures, 2008; A Christmas Overture, 2007; Jubilate Deo, 2010; March Barnes Wallis, 2013; Chansons de Normandie, 2014; A Celebration Overture, 2015; *ballet*, The Old Man of Lochnagar, 2007; devised Admission: One Shilling—the story of Dame Myra Hess and her wartime concerts, for Nat. Gall., 2009. Has made numerous recordings. Arranged and directed music for the Queen's private 90th birthday celebrations, Windsor Castle, 2016 and for the Prince of Wales's 70th birthday celebrations, Buckingham Palace, 2018. *Address*: c/o Bucks Music Ltd, Roundhouse, 212 Regents Park Road Entrance, NW1 8AW. *T*: (020) 7221 4275, *Fax*: (020) 7229 6893. *E*: nigel@myramusic.co.uk.

**HESSAYON, Dr David Gerald,** OBE 2007; gardening author; Chairman: Expert Publications Ltd, since 1988; Hessayon Books, since 1993; *b* 13 Feb. 1928; *s* of Jack and Lena Hessayon; *m* 1951, Joan Parker Gray (*d* 2001); two *d*. *Educ*: Salford Grammar Sch.; Leeds Univ. (BSc 1950); Manchester Univ. (PhD 1954). CBiol; FRSB (FIBiol 1971); FCIHort (FIHort 1986). Res. Fellow, UC of Gold Coast, 1953. Pan Britannica Industries Ltd: Technical Man., 1955–60; Tech. Dir, 1960–64; Man. Dir, 1964–91; Chm., 1972–93; Chm., Turbair Ltd, 1972–93. Chm., British Agrochemicals Assoc., 1980–81. Patron, Essex Gardens Trust, 1996–. FCMI (FBIM 1972). Hon. DSc: CNAA, 1990; Hertfordshire, 1994; Leeds, 2008. Lifetime Achievement Trophy, Nat. British Book Awards, 1992; Veitch Gold Meml Medal, RHS, 1992; Lifetime Achievement Award, Garden Writers' Guild, 2005; Outstanding Achievement Award, Romantic Novelists' Assoc., 2014. *Publications*: Be Your Own Gardening Expert, 1959, rev. edn 1977; Be Your Own House Plant Expert, 1960; Potato Growers Handbook, 1961; Silage Makers Handbook, 1961; Be Your Own Lawn Expert, 1962, rev. edn 1979; Be Your Own Rose Expert, 1964, rev. edn 1977; (with J. P. Hessayon) The Garden Book of Europe, 1973; Vegetable Plotter, 1976; Be Your Own House Plant Spotter, 1977; Be Your Own Vegetable Doctor, 1978; Be Your Own Garden Doctor, 1978; The House Plant Expert, 1980, rev. edn 1991; The Rose Expert, 1981, rev. edn 1996; The Lawn Expert, 1982, rev. edn 1997; The Cereal Disease Expert, 1982; The Tree and Shrub Expert, 1983; The Armchair Book of the Garden, 1983; The Flower Expert, 1984, rev. edn 1999; The Vegetable Expert, 1985; The Indoor Plant Spotter, 1985; The Garden Expert, 1986; The Gold Plated House Plant Expert, 1987; The Home Expert, 1987; Vegetable Jotter, 1989; Rose Jotter, 1989; House Plant Jotter, 1989; The Fruit Expert, 1990; Be Your Own Greenhouse Expert, 1990; The Bio Friendly Gardening Guide, 1990; The Bedding Plant Expert, 1991, rev. edn 1996; The Garden DIY Expert, 1992; The Rock and Water Garden Expert, 1993; The Flowering Shrub Expert, 1994; The Greenhouse Expert, 1994; The Flower Arranging Expert, 1994; The Container Expert, 1995; The Bulb Expert, 1995; The Easy-care Gardening Expert, 1995; The Vegetable & Herb Expert, 1997, rev. edn as The New Vegetable & Herb Expert, 2014; The Evergreen Expert, 1998; The Pocket Flower Expert, 2001; The Pocket Tree & Shrub Expert, 2001; The Pocket Garden Troubles Expert, 2001; The Pocket House Plant Expert, 2002; The Pocket Vegetable Expert, 2002; The Garden Revival Expert, 2004; The House Plant Expert Book 2, 2005; The Pest & Weed Expert, 2007; The Orchid Expert, 2008; The Bedside Book of the Garden, 2008; The Green Garden Expert, 2009; The Expert Vegetable Notebook, 2009; The Best of Experts, 2010; The Complete Garden Expert, 2012; The Indoor Plant & Flower Expert, 2013. *Recreations*: American folk music, The Times crossword. *Address*: Sloe House, Halstead, Essex CO9 1PA.

**HESSELL TILTMAN, Sir John,** KCVO 2003 (LVO 1997); Director of Property Services, HM Household, 1996–2003 (Deputy Director, 1991–96); *b* 27 Aug. 1942; *s* of Henry Hessell Tiltman and Rita Florence Hessell Tiltman; *m* 1969, Monique Yvonne Françoise Louge; one *s* one *d*. *Educ*: Brighton Coll.; Brighton Coll. of Art (DipArch 1965). ARIBA 1968. Project Architect, GLC, 1965–68; Property Services Agency, Department of the Environment, 1969–90: Project Architect, 1969–76; Project Manager: PO and BT works, 1976–82; RN works, 1982–85; Chief Architect, work in RN Trng Estabts, 1985–88; Hd of Royal Palaces Gp, 1988–90; Project Dir, reconstruction of fire-damaged areas of Windsor Castle, 1993–97; Dir, Time and Space Project, Nat. Maritime Mus., Greenwich, 2004–06; Mem., Parly Estate Bd, 2006–09. *Recreations*: overseas travel, bridge, French, classical concerts and opera. *Address*: 18 rue Sainte Anne, 31000 Toulouse, France.

**HESTER, Prof. Ronald Ernest,** DSc, PhD; CChem, FRSC; Professor of Chemistry, University of York, 1983–2001, now Emeritus; *b* 8 March 1936; *s* of Ernest and Rhoda Hester; *m* 1958, Bridget Ann Maddin; two *s* one *d*. *Educ*: Royal Grammar Sch., High Wycombe; London Univ. (BSc; DSc 1979); Cornell Univ. (PhD 1962). CChem 1975; FRSC 1971. Res. Fellow, Cambridge Univ., 1962–63; Asst Prof., Cornell Univ., 1963–65; University of York: Lectr, 1965–71; Sen. Lectr, 1971–76; Reader, 1976–83. Science and Engineering Research Council: Chm., Chemistry Cttee, 1988–90; Mem., Science Bd, 1988–90; Mem., Council, 1990–94. Chm., Envmt Group, RSC, 1982–85. European Editor, BioSpectroscopy, 1994–2003; Mem., Editorial Bd, Biopolymers, 2004–06. *Publications*: (jtly) Inorganic Chemistry, 1965; (ed with R. J. H. Clark) Advances in Infrared and Raman Spectroscopy, 12 vols, 1975–85; (ed with R. J. H. Clark) Advances in Spectroscopy, 14 vols, 1986–98; (ed with R. M. Harrison) Issues in Environmental Science and Technology, 45 vols, 1994–2018; 350 research papers. *Recreations*: tennis, golf, ski-ing, travel. *Address*: Department of Chemistry, University of York, York YO10 5DD. *T*: (01904) 432557.
See also S. A. M. Hester.

**HESTER, Stephen Alan Michael;** Chief Executive, RSA Insurance Group, since 2014; *b* 14 Dec. 1960; one *s* one *d*. *Educ*: Lady Margaret Hall, Oxford (BA PPE). Credit Suisse First Boston, 1982–2001: various posts, including: Co-Hd, European Investment Banking, 1993–96; Mem. Exec. Bd, 1996–2001; Chief Financial Officer, 1996–2000; Hd, Fixed Income Div., 2000–01; Abbey National plc: Finance Dir, 2002; Chief Operating Officer, 2003–04; Chief Executive: British Land Co. plc, 2004–08; Royal Bank of Scotland Group plc, 2008–13. Non-exec. Dep. Chm., Northern Rock, 2008; Sen. Ind. Dir, Centrica plc, 2016–. *Recreations*: ski-ing, country sports, horticulture.

**HETHERINGTON, Prof. Alistair MacCulloch,** PhD; Melville Wills Professor of Botany, University of Bristol, since 2006; *b* Glasgow, 3 Feb. 1957; *s* of James Kilmurry Hetherington and Jessie Flora Hetherington (*née* McCulloch); *m* 1984, Nichola Jane Conolly; two *s* one *d*. *Educ*: Atholl Prep. Sch., Milngavie; Aberdour Primary Sch., Aberdour; Woodmill High Sch., Dunfermline; Univ. of St Andrews (BSc; PhD 1983). Res. Fellow, Univ. of Edinburgh, 1982–84; University of Lancaster: Lectr, 1984–91; Sen. Lectr, 1991–94; Prof., 1994–2006. Vis. Prof., UCD, 2004–; Hon. Prof., Tianjin Agricl Univ., China, 2009–; Christensen Vis. Fellow, St Catherine's Coll., Oxford, 2001–02; Vis. Fellow, Magdalen Coll., Oxford, 2013. Mem., Scientific Adv. Council, DEFRA, 2009–11. Chair, Integrative and Systems Biol. Strategy Cttee, BBSRC, 2010–14; Mem. Governing Council, Marine Biol Assoc. of UK, 2011–14. Trustee, New Phytologist Trust, 2006–; Dir (Trustee), Nat. Gdn of Wales, 2008–10. Ed. in Chief, New Phytologist, 2012–. *Publications*: (ed jtly) Post-translational Modifications in Plants, 1993; (ed with C. Grierson) Practical Systems Biology, 2007; contribs to scientific jls. *Recreation*: hill walking. *Address*: Life Sciences Building, University of Bristol, 24 Tyndall Avenue, Bristol BS8 1TQ. *T*: (0117) 394 1188. *E*: Alistair.Hetherington@bristol.ac.uk.

**HETHERINGTON, Roger Rooke; His Honour Judge Hetherington;** a Circuit Judge, since 2003; *b* 2 April 1951; *s* of Dr Stephen Hetherington and Jeanette Hetherington; *m* 1976, Charlotte Elizabeth Bourne; one *s* two *d*. *Educ*: Sherborne Sch.; Trinity Coll., Cambridge (BA Hons). Called to the Bar, Middle Temple, 1973; in practice as barrister, 1973–2003; Asst Recorder, Western Circuit, 1997–2000; Recorder, 2000–03; Resident Judge, Portsmouth and Newport (I of W) Crown Courts, 2011–19. Hon. Recorder, City of Portsmouth, 2011–. *Recreations*: golf, racing. *Address*: Portsmouth Combined Court Centre, Courts of Justice, Winston Churchill Avenue, Portsmouth PO1 2EB. *Clubs*: Royal Naval (Portsmouth); Huntercombe Golf.

**HETHERINGTON, Dr Stephen Francis,** MBE 2017; Chairman, HQ Theatres Trust, 2013–17 (Chairman, HQ Theatres, 2007–13); *b* 20 May 1949; *s* of Jack Hetherington and Constance Alice, (Billie), Hetherington (*née* Harper); three *d*. *Educ*: Northern Sch. of Music; Royal Acad. of Music; Warwick Univ. (MA); Birmingham Univ. (PhD 2014). Trumpeter, with symphony orchs, 1969–75. Formed Hetherington Seelig (with J. Seelig), 1981; Dir, Hetherington Seelig Theatres Ltd, 1981–2007: co. presented opera, ballet, theatre and music worldwide; consultant to govts and cultural instns; formed business plans for Lowry Project (Nat. Landmark Millennium Project for the Arts), 1995, Chief Exec., 1996–2001; led Birmingham CC's bid to become European Capital of Culture 2008; Chm., Southend's bid for city status as part of Queen's Jubilee celebrations, 2011–12. Founder and Trustee, OHMI Trust, 2011–. FRSA 2018. Hon. Fellow, Exeter Univ., 2013. *Recreations*: sailing, flying. *E*: stephen@hetherington.biz.

**HEW, Becky;** *see* Francis, B.

**HEWES, Robin Anthony Charles;** Chief Executive, New Millennium Experience Co., 2001 (Finance Director, 2000–01); *b* 15 April 1945; *s* of late Leslie Augustus Hewes and Lily Violet Hewes (*née* Norfolk); *m* 1967, Christine Diane Stonebridge; one *s* two *d*. *Educ*: Colchester Royal Grammar School; Bristol Univ. (LLB Hons 1966). Inspector of Taxes, 1966; Department of Industry, 1974; Cabinet Office (Management and Personnel Office), 1985–87; Dir, Enterprise and Deregulation Unit, DTI, 1987–88; Lloyd's of London: Head, later Dir, Regulatory Services, 1988–94 (nominated Member, Council of Lloyd's and Lloyd's Regulatory Bd, 1993–94); Dir, Finance and Mem., Lloyd's Mkt Bd, 1994–2000. Non-exec. Dir, Comforto-Vickers (formerly Vickers Business Equipment Div.), 1984–88. Hereditary Freeman, Bor. of Colchester, 1967. Lloyd's Silver Medal, 1996; Queen's Diamond Jubilee Medal, 2012. *Address*: 38 Plovers Mead, Wyatts Green, Brentwood, Essex CM15 0PS. *T*: (01277) 822891.

**HEWETSON, Ven. Christopher;** Archdeacon of Chester, 1994–2002, now Archdeacon Emeritus; *b* 1 June 1937; *s* of Edward and Mary Hewetson; *m* 1963, Alison Mary Croft; four *d*. *Educ*: Shrewsbury Sch.; Trinity Coll., Oxford (MA); Chichester Theol Coll. Assistant Master: Dragon Sch., Oxford, 1960–64 and 1966–67; The Craig, Windermere, 1964–66. Ordained deacon, 1969, priest, 1970; Assistant Curate: SS Peter and Paul, Leckhampton, 1969–71; All Saints, Wokingham, 1971–73; Vicar, St Peter's, Didcot, 1973–82; Rector, All Saints, Ascot Heath, 1982–90; Chaplain, St George's Sch., Ascot, 1985–88; RD, Bracknell, 1986–90; Priest i/c, Holy Trinity, Headington Quarry, 1990–94; Hon. Canon, Christ Church, Oxford, 1992–94; RD, Cowley, 1994. Mem., Chester Cath. Chapter, 2001–02. Bishop's Advr for Spirituality, dio. Exeter, 2003–07. *Address*: 70 East Street, South Molton, Devon EX36 3DQ.

**HEWETSON, Sir Christopher (Raynor),** Kt 1984; TD 1967; DL; Partner, Lace Mawer (formerly Laces), Solicitors, Liverpool, 1961–95; President, Law Society, 1983–84; *b* 26 Dec. 1929; *s* of Harry Raynor Hewetson and Emma Hewetson; *m* 1962, Alison May Downie, *d* of late Prof. A. W. Downie, FRCP, FRS; two *s* one *d*. *Educ*: Sedbergh Sch.; Peterhouse, Cambridge (MA). National Service, 2nd Lieut 4th RHA, 1951–53; Territorial Service, 1953–68: Lt-Col commanding 359 Medium Regt, RA, TA, 1965–68. Qualified as solicitor, 1956. Mem. Council, Law Society, 1966–87; Vice-Pres., 1982–83; President, Liverpool Law Society, 1976. Gov., Coll. of Law, 1969–94 (Chm., 1977–82). Hon. Col, 33 Signal Regt (V), 1992–94. DL Merseyside, 1986, High Sheriff, Merseyside, 1998. *Recreations*: golf, walking, music. *Address*: 24c Westcliffe Road, Birkdale, Southport, Merseyside PR8 2BU. *T*: (01704) 567179. *Clubs*: Army and Navy; Athenæum (Pres., 1997–98) (Liverpool); Royal Birkdale Golf (Capt., 1993–94) (Southport).

**HEWETT, Prof. Paul Charles,** PhD; Professor of Observational Cosmology and Astrophysics, University of Cambridge, since 2007; Fellow of Corpus Christi College, Cambridge, since 1984; *b* London, 4 Dec. 1956; *s* of Henry Charles John Hewett and Iris Joyce Hewett. *Educ*: St Dunstan's Coll., Catford, London; Univ. of Edinburgh (BSc Astrophys 1979; PhD Astrophys 1983); Corpus Christi Coll., Cambridge (MA 1993). Institute of Astronomy, University of Cambridge: SERC Fellow, 1982–84; Res. Fellow, 1984–87; Royal Soc. Univ. Res. Fellow, 1987–90; Sen. Asst in Res., 1990–92; Asst Dir of Res., 1992–2000; John Couch Adams Astronomer, 1995–2000; Reader in Observational Astrophys, 2000–07; Dep. Dir, 2008–11; Dir, 2012–13. *Publications*: over 250 articles on cosmology and astrophys in learned jls. *Recreations*: reading, wine (Wine Steward, Corpus Christi College, Cambridge, 2000–). *Address*: Corpus Christi College, Cambridge CB2 1RH. *T*: (01223) 338000, *Fax*: (01223) 338061. *E*: phewett@ast.cam.ac.uk.

**HEWETT, Sir Richard Mark John,** 7th Bt *cr* 1813, of Nether Seale, Leicestershire; computer programmer; freelance website developer, since 2012; *b* 15 Nov. 1958; *er s* of Sir Peter John Smithson Hewett, 6th Bt, MM and of Jennifer Ann Cooper Hewett (*née* Jones); *S* father, 2001; *m* 2019, Alexandra Pia Beatrix Erika Pleuger (*née* Heinrich). *Educ*: Bradfield Coll.; Jesus Coll., Cambridge (BA Nat. Scis 1980). Career in geophysical software develt; Seismograph Service Ltd, 1980–91; Schlumberger Geco-Prakla, 1991–2000; WesternGeco, 2000–09. *Recreations*: folk music, SF, choral singing, folk harp, astronomy, amateur radio. *Heir*: *b* David Patrick John Hewett [*b* 24 June 1968; *m* 1997, Kate Elizabeth Ormand; two *s* one *d*]. *Address*: Dursley, Glos.

**HEWISH, Prof. Antony,** MA, PhD; FRS 1968; FInstP; Professor of Radio Astronomy, University of Cambridge, 1971–89, now Emeritus (Reader, 1969–71); Fellow of Churchill College, since 1961; *b* 11 May 1924; *s* of late Ernest William Hewish and Frances Grace Lanyon Pinch; *m* 1950, Marjorie Elizabeth Catherine Richards; one *s* (one *d* decd). *Educ*: King's Coll., Taunton; Gonville and Caius Coll., Cambridge (BA 1948, MA 1950, PhD 1952; Hamilton Prize, Isaac Newton Student, 1952; Hon. Fellow, 1976). FInstP 1998. RAE Farnborough, 1943–46; Research Fellow, Gonville and Caius Coll., 1952–54; Asst Dir of Research, 1954–62; Fellow, Gonville and Caius Coll., 1955–61; Lectr in Physics, Univ. of Cambridge, 1962–69. Dir, Mullard Radio Astrophysics Observatory, Cambridge, 1982–87. Visiting Prof. in Astronomy, Yale, 1963; Prof. of the Royal Instn, 1977; Vikram Sarabhai Prof., Physical Res. Lab., Ahmedabad, India, 1988. Lectures: Karl Schwarzschild, Bonn, 1971; Lindsay Meml, Maryland, 1972; Larmor, Cambridge, 1973; Harland, Exeter, 1974; Kelvin, IEE, 1975; Halley, Oxford, 1979; Selby, Cardiff, 1983; Krishnan Meml, New

Delhi, 1989; Gold, Cornell, 1992; Saha Meml, Calcutta, 1993; Birla Meml, Hyderabad, 1993; Waynick Meml, Penn State, 2000. Fellow, Science Mus., London, 2009. MAE 1993. Foreign Mem., Belgian Royal Acad., 1990; Foreign Hon. Mem., Amer. Acad. of Arts and Sciences; Foreign Fellow, Indian Nat. Sci. Acad., 1982; Hon. Fellow: Instn of Electronics and Telecommunication Engrs, India, 1985; Tata Inst. of Fundamental Sci., Bombay, 1996. Hon. DSc: Leicester, 1976; Exeter, 1977; Manchester, 1989; Santa Maria, Brazil, 1989; Univ. Teknologi Malaysia, 1997; Hon. ScD Cambridge, 1996. Eddington Medal, Royal Astronomical Soc., 1969; Charles Vernon Boys Prize, Inst. of Physics and Physical Soc., 1970; Dellinger Gold Medal, Internat. Union of Radio Science, 1972; Michelson Medal, Franklin Inst., 1973; Hopkins Prize, Cambridge Phil Soc., 1973; Holweck Medal and Prize, Soc. Française de Physique, 1974; Nobel Prize for Physics (jtly), 1974; Hughes Medal, Royal Soc., 1977; Vainu Bappu Prize, Indian Nat. Sci. Acad., 1996. Hon. Citizen, Kwangju, S Korea, 1995. *Publications:* Papers in Proc. Royal Society, Phys. Soc., Mon. Not. Royal Astr. Soc., etc. *Recreations:* music, gardening, cliff-walking. *Address:* Margaret House, Church End, Barley, Royston SG8 8JS. *T:* (01763) 847927. *E:* ah120@mrao.cam.ac.uk.

HEWISON, Erica Jane; *see* Bolton, Erica J.

HEWISON, Prof. Robert Alwyn Petrie, DLitt; cultural historian; Theatre Critic, Sunday Times, 1981–2016; Professor of Cultural Policy and Leadership Studies, City University, 2006–12; *b* 2 June 1943; *s* of Robert John Petrie Hewison and Nancy Courtenay (*née* Henderson); *m* 1st, 1981, Jackie Staples (marr. diss. 1986); one *d*; 2nd, 1986, Erica Jane Bolton, *qv*; two *d*. *Educ:* Bedford Sch.; Ravensbourne Coll. of Art and Design; Brasenose Coll., Oxford (BA 1965; MA 1970; MLitt 1972; DLitt 1989). Grad. trainee, Southern Television, 1966; independent writer and critic, 1967–. Guest Curator: J. B. Speed Art Mus., Louisville, Ky, 1978; Museo Correr, Venice, 1983; Ashmolean Mus., Oxford, 1996; Tate Gall., London, 2000. Vis. Prof., De Montfort Univ., 1993–95; Prof. in Literary and Cultural Studies, 1995–2000, pt-time Prof., Dept of English, 2001, Hon. Prof., Ruskin Liby and Res. Centre, 2002, Univ. of Lancaster; Slade Prof. of Fine Art, Oxford Univ., 1999–2000; Adjunct Prof., Grad. Sch. of Architecture, Planning and Preservation, Columbia Univ. NY, 2017–19. Associate Prod., film, Effie Gray, 2014. Mem., Writers' Guild of GB, 1968–. Associate, Demos think-tank, 2003–. *Publications:* John Ruskin: the argument of the eye, 1976; Under Siege: literary life in London 1939–45, 1977, rev. edn 1988; Ruskin and Venice, 1978; Irreverence, Scurrility, Profanity, Vilification and Licentious Abuse: Monty Python, the case against, 1981, 2nd edn 1990; (ed) New Approaches to Ruskin: 13 essays, 1981; In Anger: culture in the Cold War 1945–60, 1981, rev. edn 1988; (ed) The Ruskin Art Collection at Oxford: the rudimentary series, 1984; Footlights!: a hundred years of Cambridge comedy, 1986; The Heritage Industry: Britain in a climate of decline, 1987; Too Much: art and society in the Sixties 1960–75, 1988; Future Tense: a new art for the Nineties, 1990; Culture and Consensus: England, art and politics since 1940, 1995, rev. edn 1997; Ruskin and Oxford: the art of education, 1996; (ed) Ruskin's Artists: studies in the Victorian visual economy, 2000; (jtly) Ruskin, Turner and the Pre-Raphaelites, 2000; Ruskin's Venice, 2000; (with John Holden) Experience and Experiment: the UK branch of the Gulbenkian Foundation 1956–2006, 2006; John Ruskin, 2007; Ruskin on Venice: 'The Paradise of Cities', 2009; John Byrne: art and life, 2011; (with John Holden) The Cultural Leadership Handbook, 2011; (with Chris Orr) Chris Orr: the making of things, 2013; Cultural Capital: the rise and fall of creative Britain, 2014; Ruskin and his Contemporaries, 2018; (ed) Giotto and his works in Padua, 2018. *Recreation:* gardening. *Address:* 120 The Vale, Acton Park, W3 7JT.

HEWITT, family name of Viscount Lifford.

HEWITT, (Alison) Claire; Head Mistress, Manchester High School for Girls, since 2009; *b* Barnsley, 1964; *d* of Jack Thickett and Una Thickett; *m* 1987, Richard Hewitt. *Educ:* Wakefield Girls' High Sch.; Sheffield Univ. (BSc Chem. 1985; PGCE 1986; NPQH 2004). Chemistry teacher, Harrogate Ladies' Coll., 1986–91; Hd of Chemistry, Fulneck Sch., 1991–94; Hd of Chemistry, then Dir of Studies, later Dep. Hd, Sheffield High Sch., 1994–2005; Headteacher, King Edward VI Grammar Sch., Louth, 2005–08. *Recreations:* walking, cycling, puzzles, listening to a wide range of classical and contemporary music. *Address:* Manchester High School for Girls, Grangethorpe Road, Manchester M14 6HS. *T:* (0161) 224 0447, *Fax:* (0161) 224 6192. *E:* admin@mhsg.manchester.sch.uk.

HEWITT, Angela Mary, CC 2015 (OC 2000); OBE 2006; FRSC 2006; concert pianist; Artistic Director, Trasimeno Music Festival, since 2005; *b* 26 July 1958; *d* of Godfrey Hewitt and Marion Hewitt (*née* Hogg). *Educ:* Royal Conservatory of Music, Toronto (ARCT 1972); Univ. of Ottawa (BMus 1977). First recital at age 9; American début, Kennedy Center, Washington, 1976; Wigmore Hall début, 1985; Proms début, 1990; recitals and concerto appearances throughout N America, Europe, Far East, Australia, NZ, Mexico, etc; numerous radio and TV broadcasts, UK and overseas; has made numerous recordings, incl. all the major keyboard works of J. S. Bach. Winner of competitions, in N America and Europe, incl. First Prize, Toronto Internat. Bach Piano Comp., 1985. Hon. Fellow, Peterhouse, Cambridge, 2014. Hon. DMus Ottawa, 1995; Hon. LLD: Queen's, Kingston, 2002; Toronto, 2009; DUniv Open, 2006. Juno Award, Canada, for Best Instrumental Recording of Year, 1999, 2001, 2004; Governor Gen.'s Award for Performing Arts, Canada, 2002; Listeners' Award, BBC Radio 3, 2003; Artist of the Year, Gramophone Awards, 2006; Instrumentalist of the Year, MIDEM, Cannes, 2010; Governor Gen.'s Lifetime Achievement Award for Classical Music, Canada, 2018. *Recreations:* travelling, cooking wheat-free meals, seeing friends, going to the theatre. *Address:* c/o HarrisonParrott, The Ark, 201 Talgarth Road, W6 8BJ. *E:* info@harrisonparrott.co.uk.

HEWITT, Prof. (Brian) George, PhD; FBA 1997; Professor of Caucasian Languages, School of Oriental and African Studies, London University, 1996–2015, now Emeritus; *b* 11 Nov. 1949; *s* of late Thomas Douglas Hewitt and Joan (*née* Cousins); *m* 1976, Zaira Kiazimovna Khiba; two *d*. *Educ:* Doncaster Grammar Sch. for Boys; St John's Coll., Cambridge (BA 1972; Dip. in Linguistics 1973; MA 1976; PhD 1982). Open Henry Arthur Thomas Schol. in Classics, 1969–72; John Stewart of Rannoch Univ. Schol. and Coll. Graves Prize, 1971; Warr Classical Student, 1972–73; British Council Exchange Postgrad. Student, Tbilisi, Georgia, 1975–76, 1979–80; Marjory Wardrop Scholar for Georgian Studies, 1978–81. Lectr in Linguistics, Hull Univ., 1981–88; Lectr in Linguistics and Caucasian Langs, 1988–92, Reader in Caucasian Langs, 1992–96, SOAS. Member, Editorial Board: Revue des Etudes Géorgiennes et Caucasiennes, 1985–; Central Asian Survey, 1993–2015. Mem. Council, Philological Soc., 1985–90; First Pres., Societas Caucasologica Europaea, 1986–88 and 1988–90. Hon. Rep. for Republic of Abkhazia in UK, 1993–. Hon. Member: Internat. Cherkess Acad. of Scis, 1997–; Abkhazian Acad. of Scis, 1997; Writers' Union of Abkhazia, 2003–. Mem. Bd of Managers, Marjory Wardrop Fund, Oxford, 1983–. Honour and Glory of Abkhazia Medal, 2004; Medal for Services, Foreign Min. of Abkhazia, 2013; Medal for Collaborative Work, Min. of Defence, Abkhazia, 2015. *Publications:* Lingua Descriptive Studies 2: Abkhaz, 1979; Typology of Subordination in Georgian and Abkhaz, 1987; (ed and contrib.) Indigenous Languages of the Caucasus 2: North West Caucasus, 1989; (ed and contrib.) Caucasian Perspectives, 1992; (ed and contrib. jtly) Subject, Voice and Ergativity: selected essays, 1995; Georgian: a learner's grammar, 1995, 2nd edn 2005; Georgian: a structural reference grammar, 1995; A Georgian Reader, 1996; (with Zaira Khiba) Abkhaz Newspaper Reader (with supplements), 1998; (ed and contrib.) The Abkhazians: a handbook, 1998; The Languages of the Caucasus: scope for study and survival (inaugural lecture), 1998; Introduction to the Study of the Languages of the Caucasus, 2004; Abkhazian Folktales, 2005; (with Zurab Dzhopua) Pages from Abkhazian Folklore, 2008; Abkhaz: a comprehensive self-tutor, 2010; Discordant Neighbours: a reassessment of the Georgian-Abkhazian and Georgian-South Ossetian conflicts, 2013; articles on Caucasian langs and politics in encycs, Central Asian Survey, Bedi Kartlisa, Revue des Etudes Géorgiennes et Caucasiennes and online, incl. www.opendemocracy.net. *Recreation:* classical music. *Address:* c/o Department of Near and Middle East, School of Oriental and African Studies, Thornhaugh Street, Russell Square, WC1H 0XG. *E:* gh2@soas.ac.uk.

HEWITT, Prof. (Charles) Nicholas, PhD; CSci; CChem; FRSC; Distinguished Professor of Atmospheric Chemistry, Lancaster University, since 2016 (Professor of Atmospheric Chemistry, 1993–2016); *b* 23 Sept. 1953; *s* of Peter Hewitt and Amanda Hewitt (*née* Rodwell); *m*; one *s* one *d*. *Educ:* Queen Elizabeth's Grammar Sch. for Boys, Barnet; Lancaster Univ. (BA 1976; PhD 1985). CChem 1985. Lancaster University: New-Blood Lectr, 1985–91; Sen. Lectr, 1991–93; Hd, Dept of Envmtl Scis, 1996–99. Vis. Fellow and Fulbright Schol., Univ. of Colo, Boulder, 1988–89; Vis. Scientist, Nat. Center for Atmospheric Res., Boulder, Colo, 1994–95, 2010. Member: Photochemical Oxidant Rev. Gp, DoE, 1991–99; Scientific Steering Cttee, Eurotrac-2 (a Eureka project), 1996–2002. Chm., Envmtl Chemistry Gp, RSC, 1996–98. Wolfson Res. Merit Award, Royal Soc., 2010. *Publications:* Instrumental Analysis of Pollutants, 1991; Methods of Environmental Data Analysis, 1992; (with W. T. Sturges) Global Atmospheric Chemical Change, 1993; (with G. Davison) Air Pollution in the United Kingdom, 1997; Reactive Hydrocarbons in the Atmosphere, 1999; (with A. Jackson) Handbook of Atmospheric Science, 2003; (with A. Jackson) Atmospheric Science for Environmental Scientists, 2009; numerous articles in learned jls. *Recreation:* being outdoors. *Address:* Lancaster Environment Centre, Lancaster University, Lancaster LA1 4YQ. *T:* (01524) 593931.

HEWITT, Claire; *see* Hewitt, A. C.

HEWITT, Sir (Cyrus) Lenox (Simson), Kt 1971; OBE 1963; company chairman and director; *b* 7 May 1917; *s* of Cyrus Lenox Hewitt and Ella Louise Hewitt; *m* 1942, Alison Hope (*née* Tillyard) (*d* 2011); one *s* two *d* (and one *d* decd). *Educ:* Scotch Coll., Melbourne; Melbourne Univ. (BCom). FCPA, FCIS, LCA. Broken Hill Proprietary Co. Ltd, 1933–46; Asst Sec., Commonwealth Prices Br., Canberra, 1939–46; Economist, Dept of Post War Reconstruction, 1946–49; Official Sec. and Actg Dep. High Comr, London, 1950–53; Commonwealth Treasury: Asst Sec., 1953–55; 1st Asst Sec., 1955–62; Dep. Sec., 1962–66; Chm., Australian Univs Commn, 1967; Secretary to: Prime Minister's Dept, 1968–71; Dept of the Environment, Aborigines and the Arts, 1971–72; Dept of Minerals and Energy, 1972–75. Lectr, Econs and Cost Accountancy, Canberra UC, 1940–49, 1954. Acting Chairman: Pipeline Authority, 1973–75; Petroleum and Minerals Authority, 1974–75; Chairman: Qantas Airways Ltd, 1975–80 (Dir, 1973–80); Qantas Wentworth Hldgs Ltd, 1975–80; QH Tours Ltd, 1975–80 (Dir, 1974–80); Petroleum and Minerals Co. of Aust. Pty Ltd, 1975; Austmark Internat. Ltd, 1983–88; Northern Mining Corp. NL, 1984–85; State Rail Authority of NSW, 1985–88; Director: East/Aust. Pipeline Corp. Ltd, 1974–75; Mary Kathleen Uranium Ltd, 1975–80; Aust. Industry Develt Corp., 1975; Santos Ltd, 1981–82; Pontello Constructions Ltd, 1980–82; Aberfoyle Ltd, 1981–89; Endeavour Resources Ltd, 1982–86; Ansett Transport Industries Ltd, 1982–88; Short Brothers (Australia) Ltd, 1981–91; Airship Industries PLC, 1984–88; Qintex Australia Ltd, 1985–90; British Midland Airways (Australia) Pty Ltd, 1985; Universal Telecasters Securities Ltd, 1986–90; Mirage Management Ltd, 1986–91; Qintex Ltd, 1987–90; Qintex America Ltd, 1987–90; Fortis Pacific Aviation Ltd, 1987–2001; Fortis Aviation Group Ltd, 1988–2001. Dep. Chm., Aust. Atomic Energy Commn, 1972–77; Chairman: Exec. Cttee, IATA, 1976–77 (Mem., 1975–80); Orient Airlines Assoc., 1977; Mem., Judicial Commn of NSW, 1986–89. Tony Jannus Award, 1989. Centenary Medal (Australia), 2001. *Clubs:* Brooks's; Melbourne (Melbourne); Union, University and Schools (Sydney).
*See also* Rt Hon. P. H. Hewitt.

HEWITT, Prof. David Sword, PhD; FRSE; Regius Professor of English Literature, University of Aberdeen, 2007–08, now Professor Emeritus; *b* 22 April 1942; *s* of Rev. George Hewitt and Elisabeth Hewitt; *m* 1967, Angela Williams; one *s* one *d*. *Educ:* Melrose Grammar Sch.; George Watson's Coll.; Univ. of Edinburgh (MA 1964); Univ. of Aberdeen (PhD 1969). University of Aberdeen: Asst Lectr, Lectr, Sen. Lectr, then Reader in English, 1964–94; Prof. of Scottish Literature, 1994–2007. Treas., Assoc. of Scottish Literary Studies, 1972–96. Elder, 1969–, Session Clerk, 2001–13, Cathedral Church of St Machar, Old Aberdeen. FRSE 1990; FEA 1996. Pres., Edinburgh Sir Walter Scott Club, 1988–89. Ed.-in-Chief, Edinburgh Edition of the Waverley Novels, 1987–2012; Man. Ed., Clarendon Dickens, 2014–. *Publications:* (ed) Scott on Himself, 1981; editions of Scott novels: The Antiquary, 1995; (jtly) Redgauntlet, 1997; (jtly) The Heart of Midlothian, 2004; Rob Roy, 2007; contrib. Oxford DNB. *Recreations:* listening to classical music and opera, visiting churches and art galleries, literature and drama. *Address:* 21 Ferryhill Place, Aberdeen AB11 7SE. *T:* (01224) 580834. *E:* david.hewitt@abdn.ac.uk.

HEWITT, Francis Anthony; Chairman, Northern Ireland Transport Holding Company, since 2015 (non-executive director, since 2011); *b* 1 July 1943; *s* of Joseph and Mary Hewitt; *m* 1st, 1968, Carol Burch; two *d*; 2nd, 2003, Wendy Austin. *Educ:* Queen's Univ., Belfast (BScEcon). FCIM. NI Min. of Agriculture, 1961–63; HM Customs and Excise, 1963–72; NI Min. of Commerce Rep. in W Germany, 1973–78; NI Dept of Commerce, 1978–82; HM Consulate-Gen., LA, 1982–84; Industrial Development Board for Northern Ireland: Exec. Dir, Marketing, 1984–88; Dep. Chief Exec., 1988–96; Chief Exec., NI Growth Challenge, 1996–2000; Dep. Perm. Sec., NI Dept of Culture, Arts and Leisure, 2000–02; Chief Exec., NI Chamber of Commerce, 2002–08; Mem., NI Legal Services Commn, 2003–06. Non-exec. Dir, Invest Northern Ireland, 2008–. Mem. Bd and NI Chair, Big Lottery Fund, 2009–16. Chm., NI Science Park, 2008–14. Member Board: Ilex Urban Regeneration Co., 2010–13; Strategic Investment Bd for NI, 2010–16. Trustee, Grand Opera Hse, Belfast, 2007–09. Hon. Consul, Federal Republic of Germany, 2002–14. Cross of Order of Merit (Germany), 2011. *Recreations:* music, walking, gun dogs, classic cars.

HEWITT, Gavin Wallace, CMG 1995; Ambassador to Belgium, 2001–03; Chief Executive, Scotch Whisky Association, 2003–13; non-executive Chairman, Findr Ltd, since 2015; *b* 19 Oct. 1944; *s* of George Burrill and Elisabeth Murray Hewitt; *m* 1st, 1973, Heather Mary Clayton (marr. diss. 2009); two *s* two *d*; 2nd, 2015, Amanda Harvie, *qv*. *Educ:* George Watson's Coll., Edinburgh; Edinburgh Univ. (MA). Min. of Transport, 1967–70; on secondment from MoT as Third, later Second, Sec. to UK Delegn, EEC, Brussels, 1970–72; FCO, 1972–73; First Sec., British High Commn, Canberra, 1973–78; FCO, 1978–81; First Sec. and Head of Chancery, HM Embassy, Belgrade, 1981–84; Mem., Jt FCO/BBC Review Gp, BBC External Services, 1984; Counsellor on loan to Home Civil Service, 1984–87; Counsellor, Head of Chancery and Dep. Perm. Rep., UK Mission to UN, Geneva, 1987–91; Head, SE Asia Dept, FCO, 1992–94; Ambassador: to Croatia, 1994–97; to Finland, 1997–2000. Non-executive Director: Bladnoch Distillery Ltd, 2015–17; Artisanal Spirits Co. (formerly Scotch Malt Whisky (Hldgs) Ltd), 2015–. Consultant to Fasmar Ltd, 2018–. Member: Exec., Scottish Council Develt and Industry,

2004–14; CBI Trade Assoc. Council, 2004–13; Exec. Gp, Scotland Food and Drink, 2008–13; Food and Drink Leadership Forum, 2008–10; Internat. Adv. Bd, Asia Scotland Inst., 2013–17. Pres., spiritsEUROPE (formerly Eur. Spirits Orgn), 2011–13. Member: Bd of Geneva English Sch., 1989–91 (Vice-Chm., 1990–91); Gen. Convocation, Heriot-Watt Univ., 2005–11; Patron, British Sch. of Brussels, 2001–03. Chm., Friends of Abbotsford Cttee, 2019–. Keeper of the Quaich, 2009. Liveryman, Distillers' Co., 2014–. *Recreations:* music, tinkering, walking.

**HEWITT, George;** see Hewitt, B. G.

**HEWITT, Guy Arlington Kenneth;** Consulting Specialist, Development Solutions Inc., since 2018; High Commissioner for Barbados in the United Kingdom, 2014–18; *b* London, 1967; *s* of Radcliffe and Elaine Hewitt; *m* 1995, Michelle Kirton; one *s* one *d. Educ:* Univ. of W Indies (BSc Hons Sociol. and Pol Sci.; MSc Develt Studies); Univ. of Kent (Postgrad. DipTh). Prog. Coordinator, Caribbean Policy Develt Centre, 1993–95; Advr, Commonwealth Secretariat, 1995–2003; Dir, Caribbean Exams Council, 2003–10; Caribbean Manager, City & Guilds Inst., 2010–14. Chm. Bd, Queen Elizabeth Hosp., 2009–11. Dep. Chm., Barbados Vocational Trng Bd, 2010–14. Ordained Minister of Religion, 2004. *Publications:* Gender Budgets Make Cents, 2001; Gender Budgets Make More Cents, 2002; Engendering Budgets, 2003; Father a Nation: Barbados and the legacy of Emile Barrow, 2016. *Recreations:* gardening, scuba diving, volunteering. *Clubs:* Rotary, Kent.

**HEWITT, John Andrew;** Corporate Director Resources, Durham County Council, since 2016; *b* Co. Durham, 3 Oct. 1971; *s* of Frank and Mary Hewitt; *m* 1997, Shirley Vaulks; one *s* one *d. Educ:* Ferryhill Comprehensive Sch.; Sunderland Univ. (BA 1st Cl. Hons Business and Mgt); Teesside Univ. (MBA). CIPFA 1993. Accountant, Sedgefield BC, 1988–2001; Hd of Finance, Durham Police, 2001–04; Dep. Chief Exec., Co. Durham Fire Service, 2004–14; Corporate Dir Business and Resources, S Tyneside Council, 2014–16. *Recreations:* football, tennis, golf. *Address:* Durham County Council, County Hall, Durham DH1 5UL. *Club:* Bishop Auckland Golf.

**HEWITT, Sir Lenox;** see Hewitt, Sir C. L. S.

**HEWITT, Martin James,** QPM 2014; Chair, National Police Chiefs' Council, since 2019; *b* London, 23 March 1966; *s* of Graham and Maureen Hewitt; *m* 2007, Louise Philpott; two *s* two *d. Educ:* Salesian Coll., Battersea; Royal Mil. Acad. Sandhurst; Univ. of Leicester (Postgrad. Dip. Criminal Justice Studies 2000). Commnd RA, 1987; served RA, 1987–93. Police Officer, Kent Police, 1993–2005; Metropolitan Police Service: Detective Chief Superintendent, 2005–09; Comdr, Organised Crime, 2009–12; Dep. Asst Comr, 2012–14; Asst Comr, 2014–19. Associate Fellow, RUSI, 2012–. Vice Chair, Nat. Police Chiefs' Council, 2015–19. Chm., Metropolitan Police Amateur Boxing Club, 2011–. *Recreations:* trying to keep ahead of four kids, two dogs and a tortoise, reading military history, keeping fit, cinema, watching and talking about Rugby and American football. *Address:* National Police Chiefs' Council, 10 Victoria Street, SW1H 0NN. *T:* (020) 3276 3793. *E:* martin.hewitt@npcc.pnn.police.uk.

**HEWITT, Michael Earling;** central banking and financial markets consultant; *b* 28 March 1936; *s* of late Herbert Erland Hewitt and Dorothy Amelia Hewitt; *m* 1st, 1961, Elizabeth Mary Hughes Batchelor (marr. diss. 2000); one *s* one *d;* 2nd, 2004, Galina Andreevna Utkina (marr. diss. 2008); 3rd, 2012, Olga Dolgova (marr. diss. 2018). *Educ:* Christ's Hospital; Merton College, Oxford (Chancellor's Prize for Latin Prose, 1958; MA (Modern Hist.)); BSc Econ London. Bank of England, 1961–94: Economic Adviser, Govt of Bermuda, 1970–74; Financial Forecaster, 1976–78; Adviser, Financial Instns, 1981–83; Head of Financial Supervision, Gen. Div., 1984–87; Head of Finance and Industry Area, 1987–88; Senior Advr, Finance and Industry, 1988–90; Dir of Central Banking Studies, 1990–94; Project Manager (IMF), EC Technical Assistance for CIS Trng Prog. for Central Bank of Russian Fedn, 1994–99, and Nat. Bank of Ukraine, 1997–98; Resident Advr, Egyptian Capital Mkt Authy, 2000–02; Expert: Banking Sector Reform Project, Macedonia, 2003–04; Accounting Reform Project, Nat. Bank of Romania, 2006; Strengthening Financial Sector of Ukraine Project, 2008–10; Evaluation of banking sector support prog., Syria, 2011; Advr to Gov., Nat. Bank of Macedonia, 2004–05. Chm., OECD Gp of Experts on Systemic Risks in Securities Markets, 1988–90. *Recreations:* chess, wine, travel. *Address:* Villiers Lodge, 5A Villiers Road, Southsea, Hants PO5 2HG.

**HEWITT, Nicholas;** see Hewitt, C. N.

**HEWITT, Sir Nicholas Charles Joseph,** 3rd Bt *cr* 1921; *b* 12 Nov. 1947; *s* of Sir Joseph Hewitt, 2nd Bt and Marguerite, *yr d* of Charles Burgess; *S* father, 1973; *m* 1969, Pamela Margaret, *o d* of Geoffrey J. M. Hunt, TD; two *s* one *d. Heir: s* Charles Edward James Hewitt [*b* 15 Nov. 1970; *m* 2002, Alison, *d* of Peter Brown, Hobart, Tas; one *s*]. *Address:* Colswayn House, Huttons Ambo, Yorks YO60 7HJ. *T:* (01653) 696557.

**HEWITT, Rt Hon. Patricia Hope;** PC 2001; Chair: UK India Business Council, 2009–17; Advisory Board, Oxford India Centre, since 2018; Norfolk and Waveney Sustainability and Transformation Partnership, since 2017; *b* 2 Dec. 1948; *d* of Sir (Cyrus) Lenox (Simson) Hewitt, *qv*, and late Alison Hope Hewitt; *m* 1981, William Jack Birtles, *qv*; one *s* one *d. Educ:* C of E Girls' Grammar Sch., Canberra; Australian Nat. Univ.; Newnham Coll., Cambridge (MA. MA Oxon; AMusA (piano). Public Relations Officer, Age Concern (Nat. Old People's Welfare Council), 1971–73; Women's Rights Officer, Nat. Council for Civil Liberties, 1973–74, Gen. Secretary 1974–83; Press and Broadcasting Sec., 1983–88, Policy Co-ordinator, 1988–89, to Leader of Opposition; Sen. Res. Fellow, 1989, Dep. Dir, 1989–94, Inst. for Public Policy Res.; Head, then Dir, of Research, Andersen Consulting, 1994–97. Non-executive Director: BT Gp plc, 2008–14 (Sen. Ind. Dir, 2009–14); Eurotunnel, 2010–; Bupa, 2013–14; Mem., Adv. Cttee, Barclays Asia Pacific, 2009–12; Mem., Global Adv. Bd, Sutherland Global Services, 2012–; Sen. Advr, FTI Consulting, 2015–. Associate, Newnham Coll., Cambridge, 1984–97 (Hon. Associate, 2013–); Vis. Fellow, Nuffield Coll., Oxford, 1992–2001. Dep. Chair, Commn on Social Justice, 1993–95; Vice-Chairman: Healthcare 2000, 1995–96; British Council, 1997–98. Contested (Lab) Leicester E, 1983. MP (Lab) Leicester W, 1997–2010. Economic Sec., HM Treasury, 1998–99; Minister of State, DTI, 1999–2001; Sec. of State for Trade and Industry, and Minister for Women, 2001–05; Sec. of State for Health, 2005–07. Mem., Select Cttee on Social Security, 1997–98. Member: Asia Task Force, 2009–14; UK India Round Table, 2009–16. Chair, Katha Children's Trust, 2011–16. FRSA 1992. *Publications:* Your Rights (Age Concern), 1973; Rights for Women (NCCL), 1975; Civil Liberties, the NCCL Guide (co-ed 3rd edn), 1977; The Privacy Report (NCCL), 1977; Your Rights at Work (NCCL), 1978, 2nd edn 1981; The Abuse of Power, 1981; (jtly) Your Second Baby, 1990; About Time: the revolution in work and family life, 1993. *Recreations:* reading, theatre, music, gardening. *Address:* FTI Consulting LLP, Public Affairs Division, 200 Aldersgate Street, EC1A 4HD. *T:* (020) 3727 1224. *E:* patricia.hewitt@fticonsulting.com.

**HEWITT, Penelope Ann,** CBE 2003; Senior District Judge (Chief Magistrate), Bow Street Magistrates' Court, 2000–03; *b* 4 May 1932; *d* of late William Mottershead, JP, MB ChB and Eileen Mottershead; *m* 1954, Peter Nisbet Hewitt (*d* 2018); one *s* two *d. Educ:* Howell's Sch., Denbigh; BA Open Univ., 1975. Called to the Bar, Gray's Inn, 1978, Bencher, 2001; in practice, Liverpool, 1978–90; Mem., Northern Circuit; District Judge (Magistrates' Courts) (formerly Stipendiary Magistrate), Leeds, 1990–2000. Lay Chm., Bolton Deanery Synod, 1984–90. Member: British Acad. of Forensic Scis, 1979–2005; Magisterial Cttee, Judicial Studies Bd, 1993–98. JP Bolton, 1968–90. *Recreations:* music, reading, opera, embroidery.

**HEWITT, Peter John,** CBE 2008; executive coach and consultant, since 2016; Chief Executive, Guy's and St Thomas' Charity, 2009–16; *b* 17 Nov. 1951; *m* 1st, 1977, Joan Coventry (marr. diss. 1999); three *d;* 2nd, 2013, Dr Judith Bell. *Educ:* Barnard Castle Sch.; Leeds Univ. (BA, MA). Inter-action, Kentish Town, 1976; Arts Officer, N Tyneside MBC, 1977–82; Northern Arts, 1982–97 (Chief Exec., 1992–97); Corporate Affairs Dir, Tees HA, 1997–98; Chief Exec., Arts Council of England, later Arts Council England, 1998–2008. FKC 2014; FRSA. *Recreations:* arts, walking, cycling. *Address:* 15 Murray Road, Berkhamsted HP4 1JD.

**HEWITT, Sarah Louise;** see Singleton, S. L.

**HEWITT, Sheila Iffat;** JP; Regional Chairman, Eastern and Southern Areas, Legal Services Commission (formerly Legal Aid Board), 1998–2004; *b* Pakistan, 6 Oct. 1952; *m* 1973, Anthony Hewitt; two *s. Educ:* London Sch. of Econs and Pol Sci. (BSc Econ). ACIB 1975. Member: London Rent Assessment Panel, 1985–2002; Immigration Appeals Tribunal, 1992–; Appeal Tribunal Competition Commn, 2000–10; Ind. Assessor, OCPA, 2000–13. Mem., Radio Authority, 1998–2003. Non-exec. Bd Mem., Mid Surrey HA, 1992–95; Chm., Surrey Heartlands NHS Trust, 1995–98. Member: GMC, 2001–11; Fitness to Practise Panel, NMC, 2008–16. JP Surrey, 1987. *Recreations:* mountain trekking, tennis. *Address:* Calderwood, Wilmerhatch Lane, Epsom, Surrey KT18 7EH. *T:* (01372) 273730. *Club:* Royal Automobile.

**HEWITT-DYER, Christine Helen,** CB 2019; Director of People, National Church Institutions, Church of England, since 2019; *b* Southsea, 22 June 1961; *d* of John Setchell and Margaret Setchell; *m* 2013, Stuart Dyer; three *s* by a former marriage. *Educ:* Queen Anne Grammar Sch., York; Queen Elizabeth's Grammar Sch., Mansfield; Univ. of Leeds (BSc 1st Chem. Scis 1982). FCIPD 2012. Scientist, Lab. of Govt Chemist, 1982–86; sci. and econ. policy posts, DTI, 1986–96; cross govt sci. policy, OST, 1996–99; Dep. Dir, HR Strategy and Policy, DTI, 2000–05; Dir, Strategy, ACAS, 2005–08; Dep. Dir, Innovation Infrastructure, DIUS, subseq. BERR, 2008–11; Dep. Dir, HR Strategy, Talent and Learning, BIS, 2011–13; HR Dir, DSTL, MoD, 2013–15; Dir, People, Capability and Change, DCLG, then MHCLG, 2015–19. Trustee, HCT Gp, 2012–. *Recreations:* tennis, walking, Christian Aid. *E:* christine.hewittdyer@churchofengland.org.

**HEWLETT, Rev. David Jonathon Peter,** PhD; Principal, Queen's Foundation for Ecumenical Theological Education, since 2003; *b* 8 Feb. 1957; *s* of Vincent and late Daphne Hewlett; *m* 1978, Penelope Skilton; three *s* one *d. Educ:* Durham Univ. (BA 1st cl. Hons 1979; PhD 1984). Ordained deacon, 1983, priest, 1984; Asst Curate, St James, New Barnet, 1983–86; Lectr in Systematic Theol., C of I Theol Coll., Dublin, and TCD, 1986–90; Jt Dir, SW Ministry Trng Course, and Priest i/c, Feock, Dio. of Truro, 1990–95; Principal, SW Ministry Trng Course, 1995–2003. Hon. Fellow, Dept of Theol., Exeter Univ., 1995–2003. Canon Emeritus, Truro Cathedral, 2003; Hon. Canon. Birmingham Cathedral, 2014–. *Recreation:* music. *Address:* Queen's Foundation for Ecumenical Theological Education, Somerset Road, Edgbaston, Birmingham B15 2QH. *T:* (0121) 454 1527, *Fax:* (0121) 454 8171. *E:* d.hewlett@queens.ac.uk.

**HEWLETT-DAVIES, Mrs Janet Mary;** journalist; public affairs consultant; *b* 13 May 1938; *d* of Frederick Charles and Margaret Ellen Hewlett; *m* 1964, Barry Davies (*d* 2016). *Educ:* King Edward VI High School for Girls, Birmingham. Journalist, West Midlands 1956–59; BBC, 1959–65; Films Division, Central Office of Information, 1966–67; Press Officer: Prime Minister's Office, 1967–72; HM Customs and Excise, 1972–73; Principal Information Officer, Dept of Trade and Industry, 1973–74; Dep. Chief Press Secretary to Prime Minister, 1974–76; Head of Information, Dept of Transport, 1976–79; Director of Information: DoE, 1979–82; DHSS, 1982–86; Dir of Public Affairs, Pergamon, BPCC and Mirror Gp of Cos, 1986–87. Vice-Chm., WHO Working Gp on Information and Health, 1983. *Recreations:* Shakespeare's Globe, Brighton, acting. *Address:* 44 Sussex Square, Brighton BN2 1GE. *T:* (01273) 693792. *Club:* Reform.

**HEWSON, (Charles) Andrew (Dale);** Chairman, Johnson & Alcock Ltd, authors' agents, 2003, now Chairman Emeritus; *b* Tyrringham, N Bucks, 30 Dec. 1942; *s* of George Dale Hewson and Irene Hewson (*née* Richardson); *m* 1st, 1969, Margaret Cumming Watson (*d* 2002); one *d;* 2nd, 2012, Carmela Margery Bromhead; one step *s. Educ:* Bury Lawn Kindergarten, Newport Pagnell; St Stephen's Prep. Sch., Dundrum, Co. Dublin; Angusfield House Prep. Sch., Edinburgh; Trinity Coll., Glenalmond; Univ. of St Andrews (MA Hons). Front of House and Box Office Manager, Newcastle Playhouse, 1967–68; Agent, 1969–77, Man. Dir/Sole Proprietor, 1977–2003, John Johnson Ltd (merged with Michael Alcock Mgt, 2003). Trustee, Fenton Arts Trust, 2005–12. *Recreations:* early morning swimming, hill walking in good boots, gardening in challenging French terrain, the arts, food for free, my grandchildren. *Address:* 62 Thornhill Road, N1 1JU. *T:* (020) 7607 2108; Roquedur le Haut, Sumène, 30440 Gard, France. *T:* (4) 67825911. *E:* andrew@johnsonandalcock.co.uk. *Clubs:* Garrick, Groucho.

**HEWSON, John Robert,** AM 2001; PhD; investment banker and company director; *b* 28 Oct. 1946; *s* of Donald Hewson and late Eileen Isabella Hewson (*née* Tippett); *m* 1st, Margaret; two *s* one *d;* 2nd, 1988, Carolyn Judith Somerville; one *d;* 3rd, 2007, Jessica Wilson. *Educ:* Univ. of Sydney (BEc Hons); Univ. of Saskatchewan (MA 1969); Johns Hopkins Univ. (MA, PhD 1971). Economist, IMF, 1971–74; Res. Economist, Reserve Bank of Australia, 1976; Economic Advr to Fed. Treas., 1976–82; University of New South Wales: Prof. of Econs, 1978–87; Head, Sch. of Econs, 1983–86; Dir, Japanese Econs Management Studies Centre, 1984–87. Dir, Macquarie Bank, 1985–87. MP (L) Wentworth, NSW, 1987–95; Shadow Minister for Finance, 1988–89; Shadow Treas., 1989–90; Leader of the Opposition, Australian Parlt, 1990–94; Shadow Minister for Industry, Commerce, Infrastructure and Customs, 1994–95. Prof. of Mgt and Dean, Macquarie Grad. Sch. of Mgt, 2002–04. Chairman: John Hewson Gp Pty Ltd, 1995–2015; Gold and Resources Develt Ltd, 1996–98 (Dir, 2000–04); Australian Bus Manufacturing Co., 1999; Universal Bus Co. Pty Ltd, 2000–; Global Renewables Ltd, 2000–04; Belle Property Pty Ltd, 2000–03; Strategic Capital Mgt Pty Ltd, 2000–04; X Capital Health, 2004–; Pisces Gp, 2008; General Security Australia Insurance Brokers Pty Ltd; Vice-Chm., Qingdao Pacific Coach Co., 2001–; Mem., Adv. Council, ABN AMRO Australia Ltd, 1998–2004 (Chm., 1996–98). Chm., RepuTex Rating Cttee, 2003–04. Chairman: Leadership Foundn Pty, 1998–2003; Investment Adv. Cttee, Australian Olympic Foundn, 2001; Foundn for New England Reg Art Mus., 2001–03; Adv. Cttee, Dunmore Lang Coll. Foundn, 2002–03; Business Leaders Forum on Sustainable Develt, 2003–09; Member, Advisory Group: Gp Training Australia, 2003–; Australia Worldwide, Solutions for a Sustainable Future, 2003–. Chairman: Osteoporosis Australia Council, 1997–; Arthritis Res. Taskforce Ltd, 2003–; KidsXpress; Director: Exec. Bd, Asia-Aust. Inst., 1999–; Positive Ageing Foundn, 1999–2003; Pres., Arthritis Foundn of Australia, 1997–2002. Chm., Freehand Gp, 2004–. Columnist, Australian Financial Review, 1998–. *Publications:*

Liquidity Creation and Distribution in the Eurocurrency Market, 1975; (jtly) The Eurocurrency Markets and their Implications, 1975; Offshore Banking in Australia, 1981. *Recreations:* jazz, sport, cars, theatre, motor sports. *Clubs:* Australian; Australian Golf, Royal Sydney Golf.

**HEWSON, Paul David, (Bono),** Hon. KBE 2007; singer and songwriter; *b* 10 May 1960; *s* of late Robert Hewson and of Iris Hewson; *m* 1982, Alison Stewart; two *s* two *d*. *Educ:* Mount Temple Sch., Dublin. Co-founder and lead singer, U2, 1978–; nat. and internat. tours. *Albums include:* Boy, 1980; October, 1981; War, 1983; Under a Blood Red Sky, 1983; The Unforgettable Fire, 1984; Wide Awake in America, 1985; The Joshua Tree, 1987; Rattle and Hum, 1988; Achtung Baby, 1991; The Fly, 1991; Zooropa, 1993; Pop, 1997; All That You Can't Leave Behind, 2000; How to Dismantle an Atomic Bomb, 2004; No Line on the Horizon, 2009; Songs of Innocence, 2014; Songs of Experience, 2017. 22 Grammy Awards, 1987, 1988, 1992, 1993, 1994, 2000, 2001, 2004, 2005. Director: Elevation Partners, 2004–15; Fender Musical Instruments Corpn, 2014–; co-founder, The Rise Fund, 2016. Co-founder and Director: Debt, AIDS, Trade, Africa, 2002–; ONE Campaign to Make Poverty History (USA), 2004–; Make Poverty History (UK), 2005–. *Publications:* On the Move, 2007.

**HEWSTONE, Prof. Miles Ronald Cole,** DPhil, DSc; FBA 2002; Professor of Social Psychology and Director, Centre for the Study of Intergroup Conflict, since 2001, and Professor of Social Psychology and Public Policy, Blavatnik School of Government, since 2016, University of Oxford; Fellow, New College, Oxford, since 2001; Global Innovation Chair for Social Conflict and Cohesion, University of Newcastle, Australia, since 2017; *b* 4 Aug. 1956; *s* of Ronald Keith and late Audrey Cole Hewstone; *m* 1986, Claudia Maria Hammer; one *s* one *d*. *Educ:* Univ. of Bristol (BSc 1st Cl. Hons Psychol. 1978); Trinity Coll., Oxford (DPhil 1981); Univ. of Tübingen, Germany (Habilitation); Univ. of Oxford (DSc 2007). University of Bristol: Lectr in Psychol., 1985–88; Reader in Social Psychol., 1988–91; Prof. of Social Psychol. (Personal Chair), 1991–92; Ordinarius Prof. of Social Psychol., Univ. of Mannheim, 1992–94; Prof. of Psychol., UWCC, 1994–2001. Mem., Social Integration Commn, 2014–. Invited Fellow, Center for Advanced Study in Behavioral Scis, Stanford, Calif, 1987–88 and 1999–2000. Hon. FBPsS 2003 (FBPsS 1986). Spearman Medal, 1987, Presidents' Award, 2001, BPsS; Kurt Lewin Award for Dist. Res. Achievement, Eur. Assoc. for Exptl Social Psychol., 2005; Kurt Lewin Award, Soc. for Psychol Study of Social Issues, 2012; Codol Medal, Eur. Assoc. of Social Psychol., 2014; Godon Allport Intergp Relns Prize, Soc. for Psychol Study of Social Issues, 2015. *Publications:* Understanding Attitudes to the European Community: a social psychological study in four member states, 1986; (ed jtly) Contact and Conflict in Intergroup Encounters, 1986; Causal Attribution: from cognitive processes to collective beliefs, 1989; (ed with A. Manstead) The Blackwell Encyclopedia of Social Psychology, 1995; (ed jtly) Psychology, 2005; (ed jtly) Introduction to Social Psychology, 4th edn 2008 to 6th edn 2015; (ed jtly) The Sage Handbook of Prejudice, Stereotyping and Discrimination, 2010; (ed with R. Martin) Minority Influence and Innovation: antecedents, processes and consequences, 2010; (ed with G. Hodson) Advances in Intergroup Contact, 2013. *Address:* New College, Oxford OX1 3BN. *E:* miles.hewstone@psy.ox.ac.uk.

**HEXHAM AND NEWCASTLE, Bishop of, (RC),** since 2019; **Rt Rev. Robert John Byrne,** CO; *b* 22 Sept. 1956; *s* of Sidney and Monica Byrne (née Rigby). *Educ:* St Bede's Coll., Manchester; King's Coll. London (BD; AKC); Pontifical Univ. of St Thomas Aquinas, Rome. Entered Birmingham Oratory, 1980; Chaplain, St Philip's Coll., Edgbaston, 1984–88; ordained priest, 1985; Parish Priest, St Aloysius, Oxford, 1990–99; Founder, 1990, Provost, 1993–2011, Oxford Oratory; Nat. Ecumenical Officer and Sec., Dept of Dialogue and Unity, Bishops' Conf. of Eng. and Wales, 2012–14 (Mem., Dept of Dialogue and Unity, 2014, and Dept of Christian Life and Worship, 2016); Aux. Bishop of Birmingham and Titular Bishop of Cuncacestre, 2014–19. Sec., Perm. Deputation, Internat. Fedn of the Congregations of the Oratory, 2000–11. Chair, EWARC, 2019. Trustee and Gov., Oratory Sch., 1996–2019. Prison Chaplain, 1988–2013. Mem., Clockmakers' Co., 2008–. *Recreations:* history, opera, travel. *Address:* Bishop's House, 800 West Road, Newcastle upon Tyne NE5 2BJ. *T:* (0191) 228 0003. *E:* bishop.robert@rcdhn.org.uk. *Club:* Travellers.

**HEY, Prof. Anthony John Grenville,** CBE 2005; DPhil, CEng, FREng, FIET, FBCS, FInstP; Senior Data Science Fellow, eScience Institute, University of Washington, since 2014; Chief Data Scientist, UK Science and Technology Facilities Council, since 2015; *b* 17 Aug. 1946; *s* of late Colin Grenville Hey and Phyllis Gwendolen Rhodes; *m* 1969, Jessie Margaret Nancy; two *s* one *d*. *Educ:* King Edward's Sch., Birmingham; Worcester Coll., Oxford (Open Schol., 1964; BA Physics 1967); St John's Coll., Oxford; DPhil Oxon, 1970. CEng; FREng 2001; FInstP 2005. University of Southampton: Lectr in Physics, 1974–86; Prof. of Computation, Sch. of Electronics and Computer Sci., 1986–2005; Dir, UK e-Science Core Prog., EPSRC, 2001–05 (on secondment); Microsoft Corporation: Vice-Pres. for Tech. Computing, 2005–07; Corporate Vice-Pres. for Ext. Res., 2007–11; Vice-Pres. for Res. Connections, 2011–14. Sabbaticals at CIT, MIT and IBM Research. Mem., Advanced Scientific Computing Adv. Cttee, Office of Sci., US Dept of Energy, 2010–. Member: Bd, Washington State Life Scis Discovery Fund, 2006–13; Bd, CodePlex Foundn, 2010–; Council, Res. Data Alliance, 2013–. Mem., PPARC, 2006–07. Vis. Prof., Univ. of Southampton, 2006–. Co-Chm., UK E-infrastructure Leadership Council, 2012–. FAAAS 2010; FACM 2017; Hon. Fellow, Cardiff Univ., 2005. Hon. DCL Newcastle, 2008; Hon. DSc: Drexel, USA, 2013; Swansea, 2014; Southampton, 2017. *Publications:* (with Ian Aitchison) Gauge Theories in Particle Physics, 1982, 4th edn 2013; (with Patrick Walters) The New Quantum Universe, 1987, 2nd edn 2003; (with Robin Allen) The Feynman Lectures on Computation, 1996; (with Patrick Walters) Einstein's Mirror, 1997; (ed) Fenyman and Computation, 1998; (co-ed) The Fourth Paradigm: data-intensive scientific discovery, 2009; (with Gyuri Pápay) The Computing Universe: a journey through a revolution, 2014. *Recreations:* reading, writing, hill-walking, long-term supporter of Southampton FC. *Address:* Science and Technology Facilities Council, Rutherford Appleton Laboratory, Harwell Campus, Didcot OX11 0QX. *E:* tony.hey@stfc.ac.uk.

**HEY, Prof. John Denis;** Professor of Economics and Statistics, University of York, 1984–2016 (part-time, 1997–2010), now Professor Emeritus; *b* 26 Sept. 1944; *s* of George Brian Hey and Elizabeth Hamilton Hey (née Burns); *m* 1968, Margaret Robertson Bissett (marr. diss. 1998); one *s* two *d*. *Educ:* Manchester Grammar Sch.; Cambridge Univ. (MA); Edinburgh Univ. (MSc). Econometrician, Hoare & Co., 1968–69; Lectr in Economics, Univ. of Durham, 1969–73, Univ. of St Andrews, 1974–75; Lectr in Social and Economic Statistics, Univ. of York, 1975–81, Sen. Lectr, 1981–84; Professore Ordinario: Univ. of Bari, 1998–2006; Luiss Guido Carli, Italy, 2006–10. Co-Dir, Centre for Experimental Economics, Univ. of York, 1986–. Economic Consultant, Wise Speke & Co., 1972–87. Editor: Bulletin of Economic Research, 1984–87; Economic Journal, 1986–96. *Publications:* Statistics in Economics, 1974; Uncertainty in Microeconomics, 1979; Britain in Context, 1979; Economics in Disequilibrium, 1981; Data in Doubt, 1983; (ed jtly) Surveys in the Economics of Uncertainty, 1987; (ed) Current Issues in Microeconomics, 1989; (ed jtly) A Century of Economics, 1990; Experiments in Economics, 1991; (ed) The Future of Economics, 1992; (ed jtly) Recent Developments in Experimental Economics, 1993; (ed) The Economics of Uncertainty, 1997; Intermediate Microeconomics, 2003; Microeconomia, 2007; articles in academic economics jls. *Recreations:* gym, opera. *Address:* Department of Economics and Related Studies, University of York, Heslington, York YO10 5DD. *T:* (01904) 433786.

**HEYCOCK, Prof. Caroline Bridget,** PhD; FBA 2019; Professor of Syntax, University of Edinburgh, since 2007; *b* Folkestone, 22 Nov. 1960; *d* of Edward Alfred Heycock and Bridget Heycock (née Halsey); *m* 2004, Robert Sandler. *Educ:* St Columba's Sch., Kilmacolm, Renfrewshire; King's Coll., Cambridge (Open Schol.; BA 1st Cl. Modern Langs 1983); Univ. of Pennsylvania (PhD Linguistics 1991). Teacher of English: Shimizugaoka High Sch., Japan, 1983–84; Ritsumeikan Univ., Japan, 1984–85; Assistant Professor of Linguistics: Oakland Univ., USA, 1991–92; Yale Univ., 1992–94; Lectr in Linguistics, Univ. of Edinburgh, 1994–99; Asst Prof. of Linguistics, Univ. of Delaware, 1997–98; Reader in Linguistics, Univ. of Edinburgh, 1999–2007. *Publications:* Layers of Predication, 1994; (ed jtly) Language Acquisition: knowledge representation and processing, 1999; (ed jtly) Current Issues in Germanic Syntax, 2012; (ed jtly) Syntactic Variation in Insular Scandinavian, 2017. *Recreations:* mountain walking, running, drawing, printmaking, beachcombing, (re)learning languages, crosswords. *Address:* School of Philosophy, Psychology and Language Sciences, University of Edinburgh, 3 Charles Street, Edinburgh EH8 9AD. *T:* (0131) 651 1999. *E:* caroline.heycock@ed.ac.uk.

**HEYES, Prof. Cecilia Mary,** PhD, DSc; FBA 2010; Senior Research Fellow in Theoretical Life Sciences, All Souls College, Oxford, since 2008; Professor of Psychology, University of Oxford, since 2009; *b* Ashford, Kent, 6 March 1960; *d* of James Joseph Heyes and Helen Mary Heyes (née Henneker); partner, Martin Eimer, *qv*. *Educ:* Highworth Grammar Sch., Ashford; University Coll. London (BSc 1981; PhD 1984); Univ. of Oxford (DSc 2016). Harkness Fellow, Evolutionary Epistemology, Lehigh Univ., Univ. of Chicago and Tufts Univ., 1984–86; Res. Fellow, Psychol., Trinity Hall, Cambridge, 1986–89; Department of Psychology, University College London: Lectr, 1988–93; Sen. Lectr, 1993–96; Reader, 1996–2000; Prof., 2000–08. *Publications:* (ed jtly) Social Learning and the Roots of Culture, 1996; (ed jtly) Evolution of Cognition, 2001; (ed jtly) Selection Theory and Social Construction, 2001; Cognitive Gadgets: the cultural evolution of thinking (monograph), 2018; contrib. papers to peer-reviewed jls of exptl psychol. and cognitive neurosci. *Recreation:* nice cup of tea and a sit down. *Address:* All Souls College, Oxford OX1 4AL. *T:* (01865) 279394. *E:* cecilia.heyes@all-souls.ox.ac.uk.

**HEYES, David Alan;** *b* 2 April 1946; *s* of Harold and Lilian Heyes; *m* 1968, Judith Egerton Gallagher; one *s* one *d*. *Educ:* Open Univ. (BA). Local govt manager, Manchester, 1962–86; trade union organiser, 1986–87; local govt manager, Oldham, 1987–90; self employed, computer graphics business, 1990–95; manager, CAB, Manchester, 1995–2001. MP (Lab) Ashton under Lyne, 2001–15.

**HEYGATE, Sir Richard John Gage,** 6th Bt *cr* 1831, of Southend, Essex; Chairman, Anglo Cathay Enterprises, since 2012; Managing Partner, UK office, Oneida Associés, since 2008; International Consultant, China Railway Group, since 2015; *b* 30 Jan. 1940; *s* of Sir John Edward Nourse Heygate, 4th Bt and his 2nd wife, Gwyneth Eliot (*d* 1994), 2nd *d* of J. E. H. Lloyd; *S* brother, 1991; *m* 1st, 1968, Carol Rosemary (marr. diss. 1972), *d* of Comdr Richard Michell; 2nd, 1974, Jong Ja (marr. diss. 1988), *d* of In Suk, Seoul; one *d*; 3rd, 1988, Susan Fiona, *d* of late Robert Buckley; two *s*. *Educ:* Repton; Balliol Coll., Oxford. IBM (UK) Ltd, 1967–70; McKinsey & Company Inc., 1970–77; Director: Olaf Foods, 1977–85; Index Gp, 1985–87; Principal, McKinsey and Co. Inc., 1987–98; CEO, Sophron Partners Ltd, 1998–2005. Director: Isis Technology, 1999–2000; Propero Ltd, 2000–03; Web Connectivity, 2008–11; Chairman: Storks Nest Wine, 2003–04; Mouse Smart Software, 2004–06; Welford Technology Partners, 2005–10; Red Unida, subseq. Icareertech Ltd, 2010–14. Internat. Agent, China Railway Engrg No 3 Gp, 2015–; Mem. Adv. Bd, Fortone Gp, China, 2015–16; Chairman, Advisory Board: Beyond Laboratory, 2018–; Treleaven Capital, 2018–. Dir, 88 Initiative, 2015–. Mem., Finance Cttee, Cancer Res., 1992–98. *Publications:* (with Michael Daunt) Endangered Species, 2008; (with Philip Carr-Gomm) The Book of English Magic, 2009. *Heir:* s Frederick Carysfort Gage Heygate, *b* 28 June 1988. *Address:* 34 Abercrombie Street, SW11 2JD.

**HEYHOE, David Charles Ross,** CB 1998; Director, Greenwich Hospital, 1998–2002; *b* 29 June 1938; *s* of late Cecil Ross Heyhoe and Clara Beatrice (née Woodard Knight); *m* 1972, Pauline Susan (née Morgan); one *s* one *d*. *Educ:* Beckenham and Penge Grammar Sch.; Worcester Coll., Oxford (Schol.; MA Lit.Hum.). Served HM Forces, 1957–59. Asst Principal, War Office, 1963; Asst Private Sec. to Minister (Army), 1966; Principal, MoD, 1967; Asst Sec., 1975; Res. Associate, Inst. for Strategic Studies, 1975–76; Private Sec. to Leader of H of C, 1981–84; Asst Under Sec. of State, MoD, 1986–97. Mem., Royal Patriotic Fund Corp., 1998–2002. Dir, Pollen Estate Trustee Co. Ltd, 2002–07. *Recreations:* books, sport. *Address:* 49 Westmoreland Road, Barnes, SW13 9RZ. *Clubs:* Roehampton, Rosslyn Park FC.

**HEYHOE, Rosemary;** Director, Human Resources Operations, Department of Trade and Industry, 2003–05; *b* 17 Sept. 1946; *d* of Herbert Arthur Mears and Mabel Mears (née Foster); *m* 1978, Richard John Heyhoe; two *d*. *Educ:* Wallington County Sch. for Girls. Bd of Trade, 1965–70; NEDO, 1970–73; DTI, 1973–74; Metrication Bd, 1974–75; Private Sec., Parly Under-Sec. of State, Dept of Prices and Consumer Protection, 1975–77; Personnel, DTI, 1977–82; privatisation team, Nat. Maritime Inst., 1982; internal consultancy, 1982–92; office of Principal Establishment and Finance Officer, DTI, 1992–97; Dir of Resources and Services, OFT, 1997–2001; Dir resp. for Civil Emergency Planning, DTI, 2001–03. *Recreations:* family, opera, travel. *Address:* 50 Tachbrook Street, Pimlico, SW1V 2NA.

**HEYLIN, Angela Christine Mary, (Mrs M. Minzly),** LVO 2008; OBE 1997; *b* 17 Sept. 1943; *d* of Bernard Heylin and Ruth Victoria Heylin; *m* 1971, Maurice Minzly; one *s*. *Educ:* Apsley Grammar Sch.; Watford Coll. Charles Barker plc: Chief Exec., 1989–92; Chm., 1992–97; UK Pres., BSMG Worldwide, 1997–2000. Non-executive Director: Provident Financial, 1997–2003; Mothercare plc, 1997–2004; Austin Reed Gp plc, 2001–06. Mem. Adv. Bd, Mercer Delta Consulting, 2004–06. Prime Minister's Adv. Panel, Citizen's Charter, 1993–97. Trustee, Historic Royal Palaces, 1998–2007. Chm., Public Relations Consultants' Assoc., 1990–92. Chm., House of St Barnabas, 2001–04. *Publications:* Putting it Across, 1991. *Recreations:* theatre, gardening, music. *Address:* 7 Ormonde Court, 10–14 Belsize Grove, NW3 4UP. *T:* (020) 7813 3488, 07767 491508. *E:* angela@heylin.com.

**HEYMAN, Prof. Jacques,** MA, PhD; FICE; FSA; FREng; Professor of Engineering, 1971–92, and Head of Department of Engineering, 1983–92, University of Cambridge, now Emeritus Professor; Fellow of Peterhouse, 1949–51, and 1955–92, now Emeritus Fellow; *b* 8 March 1925; *m* 1958, Eva Orlans (*d* 1982); three *d*. *Educ:* Whitgift Sch.; Peterhouse, Cambridge. Senior Bursar, Peterhouse, 1962–64; University Demonstrator, Engineering Dept, Cambridge Univ., 1951, University Lectr, 1954, Reader, 1968. Vis. Professor: Brown Univ., USA, 1957–58; Harvard Univ., 1966. Consultant Engineer: Ely Cathedral, 1972–2005; St Albans Cathedral, 1978–2000; Lichfield Cathedral, 1986–91; Worcester Cathedral, 1986–90; Gloucester Cathedral, 1989–90. Member: Architectural Adv. Panel, Westminster Abbey, 1973–98; Cathedrals Fabric Commn (formerly Cathedrals Adv. Commn) for England, 1981–2001; Council, ICE, 1960–63 and 1975–78; Smeatonian

Soc. of Civil Engrs, 1982– (Pres., 2004); Fabric Adv. Cttee, Ely Cathedral, 2005–15. Hon. FRIBA 1998. Hon. DSc Sussex, 1975; Dr *hc* Univ. Politécnica de Madrid, 2008. James Watt Medal, 1973. Cross of St Augustine, 2005. *Publications*: The Steel Skeleton, vol. 2 (with Lord Baker, M. R. Horne), 1956; Plastic Design of Portal Frames, 1957; Beams and Framed Structures, 1964, 2nd edn 1974 (trans. Spanish 2002); Plastic Design of Frames, vol. 1, 1969 (paperback 1980), vol. 2, 1971; Coulomb's Memoir on Statics, 1972, reprinted 1997 (trans. Italian 1999); Equilibrium of Shell Structures, 1977; Elements of Stress Analysis, 1982; The Masonry Arch, 1982; Estructuras de Fábrica (collection of papers on masonry construction, trans. Spanish), 1995, republished as vol. 1, 2015, further papers, vol. 2, 2015; The Stone Skeleton, 1995 (trans. Spanish 1999, Italian 2014); Elements of the Theory of Structures, 1996; Arches, Vaults and Buttresses (collected papers 1966–95), 1996; Structural Analysis, a Historical Approach, 1998 (trans. Spanish 2004); The Science of Structural Engineering, 1999 (trans. Spanish 2001); Basic Structural Theory, 2008 (trans. Spanish 2011); Geometry and Mechanics of Historical Structures (collected papers 1993–2014), 2016; articles on plastic design, masonry construction and general structural theory. *Address*: 3 Banhams Close, Cambridge CB4 1HX. *T*: (01223) 357360.

HEYMANN, Amanda; *see* Rowlatt, A.

HEYN, Andrew Richard, OBE 2014; HM Diplomatic Service; Consul General, Hong Kong and (non-resident) Macao, since 2016; *b* Prinsted, W Sussex, 14 Jan. 1962; *s* of Lt Comdr Denis Heyn and Una Heyn; *m* 1988, Jane Carmel Mulvenna; one *d*. *Educ*: Dr Challoner's Grammar Sch., Amersham; Univ. of Manchester (BA Hons Politics). DTI, 1985–88; entered FCO, 1989; Second Sec., Caracas, 1991–94; Hd, Amsterdam Intergovtl Conf. Unit, FCO, 1994–96; First Sec., Lisbon, 1996–2000; Asst Dir, HR Dept, FCO, 2000–05; Counsellor, Dep. Hd of Mission and Dir, Trade and Investment, Dublin, 2005–09; Ambassador to Burma, 2009–13; Hd, Commercial and Econ. Diplomacy Dept, FCO, 2013–14; Dir, Leadership, Governance and Diversity Strategy, CS Gp, Cabinet Office, 2014–16. *Recreations*: tennis, football, cinema, karaoke, suffering in support of Leeds United. *Address*: c/o Foreign and Commonwealth Office, King Charles Street, SW1A 2AH. *Club*: Donnybrook Tennis (Dublin).

HEYTESBURY, 7th Baron *cr* 1828; **James William Holmes à Court**; Bt 1795; *b* 30 July 1967; *s* of 6th Baron Heytesbury and of Alison Jean (*née* Balfour); *S* father, 2004; *m* 1995, Polly Jane Kendrick (*d* 2014). *Educ*: Bryanston; Southampton Univ. (BSc Hons). *Heir*: cousin Peter Michael Hamilton Holmes à Court [*b* 1968; *m* 1995, Divonne Jarecki; two s (twins) two *d* (twins)].

HEYWOOD, Dr Ann, FRICS, FCIOB; higher education consultant, since 2013; Principal, College of Estate Management, Reading, 2007–13; *b* 9 March 1955; *d* of Philip Tassell and Mary (*née* Wicks). *Educ*: Maidstone Grammar Sch. for Girls; Bedford Coll., Univ. of London (BSc 1975); Coll. of Estate Mgt; PhD Salford Univ. 2003. FRICS 1987; FCIOB 2012. MAFF, 1975–81; Rural Planning Services, 1981–86; Founder and Man. Partner, CPM, 1986–99; owner, Principal Purpose, sustainability consultancy, 2003–08. Specialist Advr to H of C Select Cttee, 1987–88. Chair, Presidential Commn for Sustainability, RICS, 2005–07. Mem., Exec. Bd, Construction Industry Council, 2009–12. Hon. Fellow: HK Inst. of Surveyors, 2013; University Coll. of Estate Mgt, 2017. Green Surveyor of the Year, RICS, 1998–99. *Recreations*: walking, cinema, travel, stone carving.

HEYWOOD, Barry; *see* Heywood, R. B.

HEYWOOD, Mark Adrian; QC 2010; a Recorder, since 2007; *b* 28 June 1962; *s* of Philip Gerard Heywood and Jennifer Jane Heywood; *m* 1990, Frances Jane Reid; two *s* one *d*. *Educ*: Taunton Sch.; Gonville and Caius Coll., Cambridge (BA Hons Law 1984); Inns of Court Sch. of Law. Called to the Bar, Gray's Inn, 1985, Bencher, 2014; Jun. Treasury Counsel, 2001–08; Sen. Treasury Counsel, 2008–; First Sen. Treasury Counsel, CCC, 2015–18. *Recreations*: sailing, motorcycling, mountains, classic tractors, agricultural machines and rural crafts. *Address*: 5 King's Bench Walk, Temple, EC4Y 7DN. *T*: (020) 7353 5638, *Fax*: (020) 7353 6166.

HEYWOOD, Matthew David, RIBA; Director, Matthew Heywood Ltd, since 2003; *b* 26 Dec. 1970; *s* of late David Main Heywood and of Patricia Ann Heywood, *qv*; *m* 2002, Sarah Elizabeth Casemore; one *s*. *Educ*: Dundee Univ. (BSc Architecture, BArch Hons). RIBA 1996. Architect: T. P. Bennett Partnership, 1994–96; Future Systems, 1996–2003 (Associate Dir, 2001–03). *Recreations*: member of Ascension Church, Balham Hill, London. *Address*: Matthew Heywood Ltd, 23 Berber Road, SW11 6RZ. *T*: (020) 7352 7583. *E*: email@matthewheywood.com.

HEYWOOD, Patricia Ann, (Mrs Michael Brown), OBE 2007; World Wide President, Mothers' Union, 2001–06; *b* 8 Feb. 1943; *d* of George and Joan Robinson; *m* 1st, 1965, David Main Heywood (*d* 1999); two *s*; 2nd, 2012, Michael Brown. *Educ*: Kendal High Sch.; Whitelands Coll., London. Teacher, 1964–68 and 1975–81. Joined Mothers' Union, 1973; Diocesan Pres., St Andrew's, Dunkeld and Dunblane, and Mem., Central Executive, 1992–95; Provincial Pres. for Scotland and Mem., Trustee Bd, 1995–2000. *Recreations*: reading, gardening, walking, crafts. *Address*: 6 Hillside Road, Ashtead, Surrey KT21 1RX. *See also* M. D. *Heywood*.

HEYWOOD, Sir Peter, 6th Bt *cr* 1838, of Claremont, Lancashire; company director, retired; *b* 10 Dec. 1947; *s* of Sir Oliver Kerr Heywood, 5th Bt and of Denise Wymondham, 2nd *d* of late Jocelyn William Godefroi; *S* father, 1992; *m* 1970, Jacqueline Anne, *d* of Sir Robert Frederick Hunt, CBE; two *d*. *Educ*: Bryanston Sch.; Keble Coll., Oxford (BA Hons). Founder and Chair of Trustees, Genesis Trust, 1995–. *Heir*: twin *b* Michael Heywood [*b* 10 Dec. 1947; *m* 1972, Caroline Awdry Greig; one *s* one *d*].

HEYWOOD, His Honour Peter Leslie; a Circuit Judge, 2008–19; *b* Bangor, N Wales, 23 Sept. 1949; *s* of Rev. Geoffrey Thomas Heywood and Irene Heywood (*née* Williams); *m* 1975, Ann Davina Morris; one *s* one *d*. *Educ*: John Bright's Grammar Sch., Llandudno; University Coll. of Wales, Aberystwyth (LLB 1977). Justices' Clerk, N Wilts, 1981–88; called to the Bar, Gray's Inn, 1988; barrister in private practice, specialising in crime, 1988–2008. Liaison Judge to Dyfed Magistrates, 2008–13, to Wales Probation Trust, 2013–14. Dir, Bala Lake Railway Co., 2016–. *Recreations*: flyfishing (Mem., Cross Hands and Dist. Angling Assoc.), Rugby, mountain biking.

HEYWOOD, Dr (Ronald) Barry; Director, British Antarctic Survey, 1994–97; *b* 28 Sept. 1937; *s* of Ronald Heywood and Edith Henrietta Heywood (*née* Bradbury); *m* 1965, Josephine Despina Panagopoulos; two *d*. *Educ*: Ashby Grammar Sch., Leics; Birmingham Univ. (BSc 1959; MSc 1961); Queen Mary Coll., London Univ. (PhD 1970). MRSB (MIBiol 1967). British Antarctic Survey: Biologist, 1961–68; Hd, Freshwater Res., 1968–83; Chief Scientist, Offshore Biol Prog., 1978–86; Hd, Marine Life Scis Div., 1986–87; Dep. Dir, 1988–94. UK Delegate: IOC Regl Cttee for Southern Ocean, 1987–97; SCAR, 1995–97 (Mem., Wkg Gp on Human Biol and Medicine, 1995–97); Council of Managers of Nat. Antarctic Progs, 1994–97. Chairman: Eur. Bd for Polar Sci., 1995–97; Jt Exec., Eur. Bds for Marine and Polar Sci., 1995–97; Mem., British Nat. Cttee Antarctic Res., 1994–97. Pres., British Antarctic Survey Club, 2009–. Hon. Associate, RHC, 1981. Polar Medal, 1967 and Clasp, 1986. *Publications*: University Research in Antarctica, 1993; papers on freshwater and marine physics and biol. *Recreations*: walking, music, U3A Lectr on Western Classical Music. *Address*: Magdalene House, Glapthorn Road, Oundle, Peterborough PE8 4JA. *Club*: Antarctic.

HEYWOOD, Suzanne Elizabeth, (Lady Heywood of Whitehall); Managing Director, Exor Group, since 2016; *b* Southampton, 25 Feb. 1969; *d* of Gordon Cook and late Mary Cook (*née* Brindley); *m* 1997, Jeremy John Heywood (Baron Heywood of Whitehall, GCB, CVO) (*d* 2018); two *s* one *d* (of whom one *s* one *d* are twins). *Educ*: on schooner Wavewalker sailing around world, recreating Capt. Cook's third voyage, 1976–86; Somerville Coll., Oxford (BA Zool. 1990); King's Coll., Cambridge (PhD 1993). HM Treasury: fast stream trainee, 1993–95; Private Sec. to Financial Sec., 1995–96; Grade 7, 1996–97; McKinsey & Company, Inc.: Consultant, 1997–2007; Partner, 2007–13; Dir (Sen. Partner), and Global Hd, Organisation Design Service Line, 2013–15. Non-executive Director: Economist Gp, 2015– (Audit Cttee, 2016–; Remuneration Cttee, 2018–); CNH Industrial, 2016– (Chm., 2018–); Dir, Chanel, 2018–. Adjunct Lectr, Sch. of Econs and Mgt, Tsinghua Univ., 2014–15. Trustee, Royal Opera House, 2013– (Chm., Finance and Ops Cttee, 2014–; Dep. Chm., 2016–); Member: Govg Body, RAM, 2014–16 (Mem., Audit Cttee, 2014–16); Council, RA, 2015–16; Trustee, RA Trust, 2014–. Trustee, New Entrepreneurs Foundn, 2013–14. *Publications*: (jtly) Reorg, 2016; articles in Wall Street Jl, McKinsey Qly and Eur. Business Rev. on range of organisational topics. *Recreations*: family, adventure travel, opera, ballet, wide range of music, art, writing.

HEYWOOD, Prof. Vernon Hilton; Emeritus Professor, University of Reading, since 1988; *b* 24 Dec. 1927; *s* of Vernon William and Marjorie Elizabeth Heywood; *m* 1st, 1952, María de la Concepción Salcedo Manrique; four *s*; 2nd, 1980, Christine Anne Brighton. *Educ*: George Heriot's Sch., Edinburgh; Edinburgh Univ. (BSc, DSc); Pembroke Coll., Cambridge (PhD). Lecturer 1955–60, Sen. Lectr 1960–63, Reader 1963–64, Professor 1964–68, Dept of Botany, Univ. of Liverpool; University of Reading: Prof. of Botany and Hd of Dept of Botany, 1968–88; Dean, Faculty of Science, 1978–81. Dir, 1987–92, Consultant Dir, 1993, Botanic Gardens Conservation Internat.; Chief Scientist (Plant Conservation), IUCN, 1988–92; Exec. Editor, Global Biodiversity Assessment, UNEP, 1993–98. Hon. Professor: Botanical Inst., Nanjing, 1989–; Univ. Juan Agustín Maza, Mendoza, Argentina, 1997–; Hon. Fellow, Royal Botanic Garden, Edinburgh, 1995–. Storer Lectr, Univ. of California, Davis, 1990; Regents' Lectr, Univ. of Calif, Riverside, 1998. Chm., European Plants Specialist Gp, Species Survival Commn of IUCN, 1984–87; Pres. Emeritus, Internat. Council on Medicinal and Aromatic Plants, 2003– (Pres., 1994–2003); Member of Board: Genetic Resources Communications Systems Inc., 1990–94; Yves Rocher Foundn, 1991–; Conservatoire Botanique National, Porquerolles, 1991–, Bailleul, 1993–, Nancy, 1996–. Pres., Internat. Assoc. of Botanic Gdns, 2012–17; Trustee: Royal Botanic Gardens, Kew, 1983–87; IUCN, UK, 1993–2005. Corresponding Mem., Botanical Soc. of Amer., 1987–. Hon. FLS 1999. Councillor of Honour, Consejo Superior de Investigaciones Científicas, Spain, 1970. Linnean Medal, Linnean Soc. of London, 1987; Hutchinson Medal, Chicago Horticl Soc., 1989; Royal Botanic Gdn Edinburgh Medal, 2002. Order of the Silver Dog, 1989, Insignia de Oro, 2003 (Gran Canaria). *Publications*: Principles of Angiosperm Taxonomy (with P. H. Davis), 1963, 2nd edn 1963; (ed jtly) Flora Europaea: vol. 1 1964 (2nd edn 1993), vol. 2 1968, vol. 3 1972, vol. 4 1976, vol. 5 1980; Plant Taxonomy, 1967, 2nd edn 1976; Flowering Plants of the World, 1978, 2nd edn 1985; (jtly) Our Green and Living World, 1984; Las Plantas con Flores, 1985; (jtly) Botanic Gardens and the World Conservation Strategy, 1987; The Botanic Gardens Conservation Strategy, 1989; (jtly) International Directory of Botanic Gardens V, 1990; (jtly) Conservation of Medicinal Plants, 1991; (jtly) Conservation Techniques in Botanic Gardens, 1991; (jtly) Tropical Botanic Gardens: their role in conservation and development, 1991; (jtly) Proceedings of the International Symposium on Botanical Gardens, 1991; (jtly) Conservation des ressources végétales, 1991; (jtly) Centres of Plant Diversity: a guide and strategy for their conservation: vol. 1 1994, vol. 2 1995, vol. 3 1996; (ed) Global Biodiversity Assessment, 1995; Les Plantes à Fleurs, 1996; (jtly) Conservation of the Wild Relatives of Cultivated Plants Native to Europe, 1997; Use and Potential of Wild Plants in Farm Households, 1998; (jtly) In situ Conservation: a critical review of good practices, 2006; (ed jtly) Do Conservation Targets Help?, 2006; (jtly) Flowering Plant Families of the World, 2007; (jtly) Flowering Plants: a concise pictorial guide, 2011; (with D. Hunter) Crop Wild Relatives: a manual of *in situ* conservation, 2011; (jtly) European Code of Conduct for Botanic Gardens on Invasive Alien Species, 2013; over 500 papers in sci. jls. *Recreations*: cooking, travel, music, writing. *Address*: White Mead, 22 Wiltshire Road, Wokingham RG40 1TP. *T*: (0118) 978 0185.

HEYWOOD, Victoria Mary Taylor, (Lady Jones), CBE 2012; Chairman, Royal Society of Arts, 2012–18; *b* 25 June 1956; *d* of late Kenneth Heywood Taylor and of Gillian Dorothea Taylor (*née* Black); *m* 1st, 1988, Christopher Wright (marr. diss. 1994); one *s*; 2nd, 2004, Sir Clive William Jones, *qv*. *Educ*: Truro High Sch.; Fortismere Sch.; Central Sch. of Speech and Drama (Dip. Drama). Stage manager, 1977–84; Gen. Manager, London Bubble Th. Co., 1986–89; Exec. Dir, Contact Th., Manchester, 1989–93; Gen. Manager, London Internat. Fest. of Th., 1994; Executive Director: English Stage Co. (Royal Court Th.), 1994–2001; Royal Shakespeare Company, 2003–12. Vice-Chairman: Lyric Th., Hammersmith, 1999–2004; Young Vic Th., 2002–06; Mem Bd, Nat. Th., 2018–. Member: Soc. of London Theatres, 1999–; Council, C&G, 2012–; Chairman: Warwick Commn into Future of Cultural Value, 2013–15; 14/18 Now, 2013–. Trustee, Shakespeare Birthplace Trust, 2004–12. Lay Mem., Warwick Univ., 2008–13. Chm., Mountview Acad. of Arts, 2013–. FRSA 2005. Hon. DLitt Birmingham, 2009; Hon. DArts Ohio, 2012. *Recreation*: writing.
*See also* Baron Taylor of Goss Moor.

HEYWORTH, Michael Paul, MBE 2007; PhD; Director, Council for British Archaeology, since 2004; *b* 30 July 1961; *s* of Allan Keith Heyworth and Jean Barbara Heyworth (*née* Kersey); *m* 1st, 1995, Dr Catherine Jane Mortimer (marr. diss. 2014); one *s* one *d*; 2nd, 2016, Louise Ennis. *Educ*: Univ. of Sheffield (BA Hons Prehist. and Archaeol. 1982); Univ. of Bradford (MA Scientific Methods in Archaeol. 1983; PhD 1991); OU Business Sch. (Professional Cert. in Mgt 2003). MCIfA (MIFA 2004); FSA 2001. Res. Asst, 1983–86, Postgrad. res. student, 1986–87, Univ. of Bradford; SO, 1987–89, Higher SO, 1989–90, Ancient Monuments Lab., English Heritage; Council for British Archaeology: Sen. Bibliographer, British and Irish Archaeol Bibliography, 1990–92; Inf. Officer, 1992–94; Dep. Dir and Inf. Officer, 1994–2002; Dep. Dir, 2002–04. Institute of Field Archaeologists: Mem. Council, 1985–88; Hon. Treas., 1986–88; Ed., Technical Papers, 1989–94. Co-Dir, Internet Archaeology, electronic jl, 1995–; Vice Chm., Archaeology Data Service, 1998–; Chairman: Archaeology Trng Forum, 2005–11; British Archaeol Awards, 2009–13; Adv. Bd, Nat. Heritage Protection Plan, 2011–14; Adv. Gp, Portable Antiquities Scheme, 2015–; Heritage 2020, 2015–; Acomb and Westfield Neighbourhood Forum, 2018–. Sec., All Party Parly Archaeology Gp, 2007–. Vice Pres., Eur. Forum of Heritage Assocs, 1993–98. Mem., Yorks and Humber Regl Cttee, Heritage Lottery Fund, 2009–15. Trustee: York Archaeol Trust, 1996–2007; Yorks Philosophical Soc., 2003–06; Heritage Alliance (formerly Heritage Link), 2005–11. MCMI 2003–16. FRSA 2014–17. *Publications*: (jtly) The Hamwic Glass, 1998; compiled and edited: British Archaeological Bibliography (with I. Holroyd), 1990, 1991, 1992; Archaeology in Britain, 1992; British

Archaeological Yearbook 1995–96; various papers, articles and reports; over 40 Ancient Monuments Lab. tech. reports on wide variety of technol material. *Recreations:* football, current affairs, local issues. *Address:* Council for British Archaeology, Beatrice de Cardi House, 66 Bootham, York YO30 7BZ. *T:* (01904) 671417, *Fax:* (01904) 671384. *E:* mikeheyworth@archaeologyuk.org.

**HIBBARD, Prof. Bryan Montague,** MD, PhD; FRCOG; Professor of Obstetrics and Gynaecology, University of Wales College of Medicine (formerly Welsh National School of Medicine), 1973–91, now Emeritus Professor; *b* 24 April 1926; *s* of Montague Reginald and Muriel Irene Hibbard; *m* 1955, Elizabeth Donald Grassie (*d* 2019). *Educ:* Queen Elizabeth's Sch., Barnet; St Bartholomew's Hosp. Med. Coll., London (MD); PhD (Liverpool). MRCS 1950; FRCOG 1965. Formerly: Sen. Lectr, Liverpool Univ.; Consultant Obstetrician and Gynaecologist, Liverpool RHB, and Univ. Hosp. of Wales. Chairman, Joint Standing Committee: Obstetric Anaesthesia, RCOG/RCAnaes, 1988–91; RCOG/RCM, 1988–91; Member: Cttee on Safety of Medicines, 1979–83; Maternity Services Adv. Cttee, 1981–85; Council, RCOG, 1982–88, 1989–92; S Glam HA, 1983–88; Medicines Commn, 1986–89. President: Welsh Obst. and Gynaecol Soc., 1985–86; History of Medicine Soc. of Wales, 1995–96. Hon. Curator of Museum, RCOG, 1986–2000 (Hon. Librarian, 1992–94). Mem. Editl Bd, Confidential Enquiries into Maternal Deaths, 1985–96 (Chm., Clinical Sub-Group, 1990–96). Pres., Contemp. Art Soc. for Wales, 2008–18. Hon. FRANZCOG 1997. *Publications:* Principles of Obstetrics, 1988; The Obstetric Forceps, 1988; The Obstetrician's Armamentarium, 2000; numerous contribs to world medical literature. *Recreations:* collecting 18th century drinking glasses, fell walking, coarse gardening. *Address:* The Clock House, Cathedral Close, Llandaff, Cardiff CF5 2ED. *T:* (029) 2056 6636.

**HIBBERT;** see Holland-Hibbert, family name of Viscount Knutsford.

**HIBBERT, Rev. Barrie Edward;** Associate Minister, Flinders Street Baptist Church, Adelaide, 2000–03; *b* 9 June 1935; *s* of Joseph and Eva Hibbert, Gisborne, NZ; *m* 1st, 1957, Ellen Judith Eade (*d* 2010); one *s* two *d*; 2nd, 2013, Gillian Mary Arnold Collins. *Educ:* Victoria Univ. of Wellington, NZ (BA); Melbourne Coll. of Divinity, Vic, Australia (LTh); NZ Baptist Theol Coll. Minister: Baptist churches in Gore, Tawa and Dunedin, NZ, 1962–79; Flinders St Baptist Church, Adelaide, SA, 1979–87; Bloomsbury Central Baptist Church, London, 1987–99. *Address:* 53/32 Ayre Street, South Plympton, SA 5038, Australia. *T:* (8) 82978558.

**HICHENS, Antony Peverell,** RD 1969; Chairman, D. S. Smith (formerly David S. Smith (Holdings)) plc, 1999–2006; *b* 10 Sept. 1936; *s* of late Lt-Comdr R. P. Hichens, DSO (and Bar), DSC (and 2 Bars), RNVR, and Catherine Gilbert Enys; *m* 1963, Sczerina Neomi Hobday, DL; one *d*. *Educ:* Stowe; Magdalen Coll., Oxford (MA Law); Univ. of Pennsylvania, Wharton Sch. (MBA). Midshipman, RNVR, 1954–56. Called to Bar, Inner Temple, 1960. Rio Tinto-Zinc Corp., 1960–72; Financial Dir, Redland, 1972–81; Man. Dir and Chief Financial Officer, Consolidated Gold Fields, 1981–89; Chairman: Y. J. Lovell (Holdings), 1990–94; Caradon, 1990–98; Lasmo plc, 2000–01 (Dep. Chm., 1992–2000); Dep. Chm., Candover Investments plc, 1989–2005 (non-exec. Dir, 1989–2010). Mem. (non-exec.), British Coal Corp., 1992–97. Mem., Takeover Panel, 2001–10. Waynflete Fellow, Magdalen Coll., Oxford, 1997–. *Publications:* Gunboat Command: the life of Lieutenant Commander Robert Hichens DSO\* DSC\*\* RNVR, 2007. *Recreations:* travel, wine, shooting. *Address:* Slape Manor, Netherbury, near Bridport, Dorset DT6 5LH. *T:* (01308) 488232. *Clubs:* Brooks's, Naval.

**HICKEY, Alexander Frederick;** QC 2016; *b* Hereford, 1 Aug. 1972; *s* of Peter Anthony Hickey and Juliet Fredericka Hickey (now Mrs Forrest); *m* 2000, Rebecca Jane Parkyns; one *s* one *d*. *Educ:* Hereford Cathedral Sch. (Hd Chorister, 1986); Christ Church, Oxford (Choral Schol., Christ Church Cathedral Choir; MA Juris. 1994). Called to the Bar, Lincoln's Inn, 1995; in practice as barrister, specialising in commercial and internat. law, mainly in construction, engrg and energy disputes, 1995–. Judicial Asst to Court of Appeal (Civil Div.), 1997; Mem. Cttee, Technol. and Construction Bar. Mem., All Saints, W Dulwich PCC. Tenor: St Bartholomew the Great choir, 1995–2004; Tonus Peregrinus; freelance professional tenor. Mem., Contessa 32 Class Assoc. *Recreations:* singing, sailing, cycling, reading history. *Address:* 4 Pump Court, Temple, EC4Y 7AN. *T:* (020) 7842 5555. *E:* ahickey@4pumpcourt.com; 20 Fawnbrake Avenue, Herne Hill, SE24 0BY. *T:* (020) 7738 5801. *E:* afhickey@icloud.com.

**HICKEY, Most Rev. Barry James,** OAM 1982; Archbishop of Perth (Australia), (RC), 1991–2012, now Emeritus; *b* 16 April 1936; *s* of G. Hickey. *Educ:* Christian Brothers Coll., WA; St Charles Seminary, WA; Propaganda Fide Coll., Rome; Univ. of WA. Dir, Centrecare, Perth (Catholic Family Welfare), 1972–82; Episcopal Vicar for Social Welfare, 1982–84; Parish Priest of Highgate, WA, 1983–84; Bishop of Geraldton, WA, 1984–91. Mem., Bd of Inst. of Family Studies, Melbourne, 1980–83; Chairman: Nat. Liturgical Commn, 1995–2000; Bishops' Cttee for the Media, 2000–06; Bishops' Cttee for Evangelisation and Mission, 2000–03; Bishops' Commn for Aborigines and Torres Strait Islanders, 2006–11. Mem., Australian Citizenship Council, 1998–2000. Centenary Award (Federation Medal), Australia, 2003. *Recreations:* tennis, walking. *Address:* Gibney House, 50 Vincent Street, Mt Lawley, WA 6050, Australia.

**HICKEY, Christopher John,** CMG 2009; Director, British Council Schools, 2013–16; *b* 8 Nov. 1951; *s* of late William Joseph Hickey and Evelyn Mary Hickey; *m* 1984, Pauline Donovan; one *s* one *d*. *Educ:* Monmouth Sch.; Univ. of Sheffield (BA French and Spanish); Univ. of Leeds (PGCE); University Coll. London (MPhil French Lit.); London Business Sch. (Sen. Exec. Prog.). Dip. TEFL (RSA). English Teacher, Univ. of Rennes and Franco-American Inst., 1975–78; joined British Council, 1978: English teaching asst, 1978–80; Asst English Lang. Officer, Morocco, 1981–83; Regl Lang. Advr, London, 1983–86; First Sec. (Educn), British Embassy, Abidjan, 1986–90; English Lang. Officer, Barcelona, 1990–93; Hd, Educnl Enterprises, Madrid, 1993–95; Dep. Dir, 1996–99, Dir, 1999–2000, Educnl Enterprises, London; Director and Cultural Counsellor, British Embassy: Greece, 2000–03; Spain, 2003–09; France, 2009–13. Chm. Bd, British Council Sch., Madrid, 2003–09; Member, Board: British Hispanic Foundn, Madrid, 2003–09; Coll. Franco-Britannique, Paris, 2009–13. *Recreations:* literature, languages, the arts, walking, restaurants. *Address:* c/o British Council, 10 Spring Gardens, SW1A 2BN. *E:* chrishickey100@gmail.com.

**HICKEY, Simon Roger Greenwood; His Honour Judge Hickey;** a Circuit Judge, since 2012; *b* Alton, Hants, 1 Dec. 1961; *s* of Bill and Bunty Hickey; *m* 1991, Alison Black; two *s* one *d*. *Educ:* Pocklington Sch., E Yorks; Leicester Univ. (LLB Hons). Called to the Bar, Gray's Inn, 1985 (Holt Schol., 1985; Harold Langrish Prize (Best Constitnl Essay), 1985); in practice as barrister, 1985–2009; a Recorder (Crime), 2002–12; a Recorder (Civil), 2004–12; a Dep. Dist Judge (Crime), 2006–09; a District Judge (Magistrates' Courts), 2009–12. *Recreations:* cycling, reading, cooking. *Address:* Newcastle-upon-Tyne Crown Court, The Quayside, Newcastle upon Tyne NE1 3LA. *Club:* Royal Air Force.

**HICKEY, Dr Stephen Harald Frederick;** Lay Member and Vice-Chair, Wandsworth Clinical Commissioning Group, since 2013; *b* 10 July 1949; *s* of late Rev. Dr James Peter Hickinbotham and Ingeborg Hickinbotham; name changed by Deed Poll to Hickey, 1976; *m* 1976, Dr Janet Elizabeth Hunter; three *s*. *Educ:* St Lawrence Coll., Ramsgate; Corpus Christi Coll., Oxford (BA, MA); St Antony's Coll., Oxford (DPhil). Joined DHSS, 1974; Asst Private Sec. to Sec. of State, 1978–79 and 1984–85; Asst Sec., DHSS, later DSS, 1985–94; seconded to Rank Xerox (UK), 1989–90; Chief Exec., Civil Service Coll., 1994–98; Prin. Finance Officer, 1998–2002, Dir, Corporate Services, 2000–02, Dir, Corporate Develt Gp, 2002–03, DSS, then DWP; Acting Chief Exec., Highways Agency, 2003; Director General: Driver, Vehicle, Operator Gp, DfT, 2003–07; Safety, Service Delivery and Logistics Gp, DfT, 2007–08. Chair, Community Transport Assoc. (UK), 2010–16. Mem., Ind. Transport Commn, 2011–. Non-exec. Dir, Wandsworth NHS PCT, 2009–13 (Vice Chair, 2011–13). Trustee: St George's Hosp. Charity, 2008–16 (Chair, 2012–16); Disabled Living Foundn, 2009–14. Ind. Mem., Governance, Risk and Audit Cttee, Bar Standards Bd, 2019–. *Publications:* Workers in Imperial Germany: the miners of the Ruhr, 1985; The Great Little College: corpuscles on Corpus Christi College, Oxford, 1945–2017, 2017. *Recreations:* music, tennis, walking, history.

**HICKFORD, Michael Francis;** Hospital Chaplain, NHS Highland, 2011–13 (Hospital and Community Healthcare Chaplain, 2004–10); Rector, St Ninian's, Invergordon, 2012–13; *b* 7 Oct. 1953; *s* of Frank Hickford and Cherryl Wendy Rosalind (*née* Mitchell). *Educ:* Gravesend Grammar Sch.; Edinburgh Theological Coll. Chaplain, St John's Cathedral, Oban, 1986–89; Rector, St Mungo, Alexandria, Dunbartonshire, 1989–95; Priest i/c, St James the Great, Dingwall with St Anne, Strathpeffer, 1995–2003; Dean of Moray, Ross and Caithness, 1998–2003; Provost and Rector, 2003–04, Hon. Canon, 2007, Chapter Canon, 2012, St Andrew's Cathedral, Inverness; Interim Priest, St Andrew's, Tain with St Ninian's, Invergordon, 2011–12. *Recreations:* music, cookery, ornithology, railways.

**HICKINBOTTOM, Rt Hon. Sir Gary (Robert),** Kt 2009; PC 2017; FCIArb; **Rt Hon. Lord Justice Hickinbottom;** a Lord Justice of Appeal, since 2017; *b* 22 Dec. 1955; *s* of Samuel Geoffrey Hickinbottom and Jean Irene Hickinbottom (*née* Greaney); *m* 1st, 1982 (marr. diss. 2001); two *s* two *d*; 2nd, 2004, Georgina Caroline Hamilton. *Educ:* Queen Mary's Grammar Sch., Walsall; University Coll., Oxford (MA); DipICArb, 1997. FCIArb 1995. Lectr, Poly. of Central London, 1980–81; admitted Solicitor, 1981; Solicitor Advocate (all Courts), 1997; Partner, McKenna & Co., subseq. Cameron McKenna, 1986–2000; Lectr, University Coll., Oxford, 1987–89; Registered Mediator, 1991; Parking Adjudicator, Parking Appeals Service and Nat. Parking Adjudication Service, 1994–2000; Asst Recorder, 1994–98; Recorder, 1998–2000; Circuit Judge, 2000–09; Dep. High Ct Judge, 2001–09; a Judge of the High Ct, QBD, 2009–17; Chief Social Security Comr and Child Support Comr, 2003–09; Chief Pensions Appeal Comr, 2005–09; Designated Civil Judge: for S and W Wales, 2005–07; for Wales, 2007–08; Dep. Sen. Pres. of Tribunals, 2008–09; Pres., Administrative Appeals Chamber, Upper Tribunal, 2008–09; Judge, Supreme Ct, Falklands Is, 2006–; Liaison Judge for Northern and N Eastern Circuits, 2012–13, for Midland, Wales and Western Circuits, 2013–16, QBD; Sen. Liaison Judge for Diversity, 2012–16. Asst Comr, Boundary Commn of England, 2000. Member: Gen. Council of Bar and Law Soc. Jt Wkg Party on Civil Courts, 1992–93; Law Soc. Wkg Party on Gp Actions, 1994–2000; Judicial Technol. Bd, 2004–05, 2010–13. Bencher, Middle Temple, 2009. Pres., Solicitors Assoc. of Higher Court Advocates, 2009–. Knight Principal, Imperial Soc. of Kts Bachelor, 2019– (Mem., 2009–; Mem. Council, 2017–). Freeman of the City of London, 2010; Liveryman: Arbitrators' Co., 2010– (Ct Asst, 2011–; Master, 2018–19); Bakers' Co., 2012–. *Publications:* various articles on law and legal procedure. *Recreations:* choral singing, opera, ballet, sport. *Address:* Royal Courts of Justice, Strand, WC2A 2LL. *Clubs:* Reform; London Welsh.

**HICKMAN, Claire Josephine;** see Moreland, C. J.

**HICKMAN, Dr Clive,** FREng; Chief Executive, Manufacturing Technology Centre Ltd, since 2010; *b* Coseley, 19 Nov. 1954; *s* of Jack Hickman and Marjorie Hickman; *m* 1979, Judith Elcock; one *s* one *d*. *Educ:* Wolverhampton Poly. (BSc (1st)); Aston Univ. (PhD 1984); Loughborough Univ. (MBA). CEng 1989; FIMechE 1992. Dir, Motor Industry Res. Assoc., 1988–96; Man. Dir, Ricardo UK Ltd, 1997–2005; Chief Exec., Tata Motors Eur. Tech. Centre plc and Hd, Engrg, Tata Motors Ltd, 2005–10. Chm., Midlands Engine Innovation Gp, 2016–; Mem. Bd, Women's Business Council, 2016–. Vice Pres. and Trustee, IMechE, 2012–. FREng 2015. Hon. DSc Cranfield, 2011; Hon. DTech Loughborough, 2013; Hon. DEng Birmingham, 2015. *Publications:* (ed jtly) Vehicle Systems Integration: the way ahead, 2000.

**HICKMAN, Sir (Richard) Glenn,** 4th Bt *cr* 1903; *b* 12 April 1949; *o s* of Sir Alfred Howard Whitby Hickman, 3rd Bt, and Margaret Doris (*d* 1996), *o d* of Leonard Kempson; *S* father, 1979; *m* 1981, Heather Mary Elizabeth, *er d* of late Dr James Moffett, Swindon, and Jan for Gwendoline Moffett; two *s* one *d*. *Educ:* Eton. *Heir:* *s* Charles Patrick Alfred Hickman [*b* 5 May 1983; *m* 2014, Alicia Lorraine Newson; two *s*]. *Address:* Manor Farm House, Liddington, Wilts SN4 0HD. *Club:* Turf.

**HICKMAN, Richard Michael,** CBE 2002; Chief Inquiry Reporter, Scottish Executive (formerly Scottish Office), 1997–2002; *b* 30 April 1942; *m* 1st, 1964, Lorna Dixon (marr. diss. 1992); two *s*; 2nd, 1993, Sandie Jane Randall; one step *s* one step *d*. *Educ:* Kingswood Sch., Bath; LSE (BA Hons Geog.); Regent St Polytechnic (DipTP); Univ. of British Columbia (MA Community and Regional Planning). MRTPI 1966. Planning Depts of LCC, 1963–65, of GLC, 1965–67; Scottish Develt Dept, 1969–78; Scottish Office Inquiry Reporters' Unit, 1979–2002. *Recreations:* walking, sailing, travel.

**HICKMAN, Dr Thomas Richard;** QC 2019; Reader in Public Law, University College London, since 2012; *b* England, 1977; *s* of Richard and Sally Hickman; *m* 2012, Maria Isabel Pereira Garcia; one *s* one *d*. *Educ:* Marlborough Sch., St Albans; Selwyn Coll., Cambridge (MA; PhD 2003); Univ. of Toronto (LLM Hons). Called to the Bar, Lincoln's Inn, 2003. *Publications:* (jtly) Human Rights: judicial protection in the United Kingdom, 2008; Public Law After the Human Rights Act, 2010. *Recreations:* family, marriage, Netflix. *Address:* Blackstone Chambers, Blackstone House, Temple, EC4Y 9BW. *E:* th@blackstonechambers.com.

**HICKMET, Richard Saladin;** barrister-at-law; *b* 1 Dec. 1947; *s* of late Ferid Hickmet and Elizabeth Hickmet; *m* 1973, Susan (*née* Ludwig); three *d*. *Educ:* Millfield Sch.; Sorbonne; Hull Univ. (BA). Called to the Bar, Inner Temple, 1974. Mem., Wandsworth Borough Council, 1978–83 (Chm., Leisure and Amenities Cttee, 1980–83; privatised street cleansing, refuse collection, parks maintenance). Contested (C): Glanford and Scunthorpe, 1987; Eastbourne, Oct. 1990. MP (C) Glanford and Scunthorpe, 1983–87; High Sheriff, Somerset, 2017–18. *Recreations:* squash, hunting. *Address:* The Chantry, Rhode, North Petherton, Somerset TA5 2AD. *T:* (01278) 663388, *Fax:* (01278) 663981. *E:* law@richardhickmet.co.uk.

**HICKS;** see Joynson-Hicks.

**HICKS, Dr Brendan Hamilton,** FRCP; Regional Postgraduate Dean Director, NHS Kent, Surrey and Sussex (formerly South East Region), 1996–2004; *b* 22 Feb. 1942; *s* of Bryan Hamilton Hicks and Winifrede (*née* O'Leary); *m* 1966, Jackie Ann Box; one *s* one *d*. *Educ:* St Brendan's Coll., Bristol; Guy's Hosp. Med. Sch., Univ. of London (BSc 1962; MB BS 1965; MD 1976). FRCP 1982. Jun. med. posts, Guy's Hosp., RPMS and

Brompton Hosp., 1965–67; Governors' Res. Schol. and Lectr in Medicine, Guy's Hosp. Med. Sch., 1967–72; NIH Internat. Fellow (US Public Health Service/MRC), Univ. of Michigan, Ann Arbor, 1972–73; Sen. Lectr in Medicine, Undergrad. Tutor and Hon. Consultant Physician, Guy's Hosp. and Med. Sch., 1974–80; Sen. Lectr in Medicine, UMDS of Guy's and St Thomas' Hosps, and Consultant Physician to Guy's and St Thomas' and Lewisham Hosps, 1981–95; Postgrad. Dean and Trust Dir, Postgrad. Med. and Dental Educn, Guy's and St Thomas' Hosp., 1985–95. Hon. Prof., Univ. of Brighton, 2002–. Mem. Cttee, Friends of Greenwich Park, 2007– (Chm., 2009–11). Hon. DSc Brighton, 2005. *Publications*: contrib. chapter in: A Short Textbook of Medicine, ed jtly, biennially, 1978–92; Principles of Clinical Medicine, ed Rees and Williams, 1995; contrib. papers in Metabolism, Diabetic Medicine, Clin. Endocrinol., etc. *Recreations*: drawing, glass-blowing, stained glass. *Address*: 60 Greenwich Park Street, SE10 9LT. *T*: (020) 8858 7363. *E*: brendan.hicks@btinternet.com.

**HICKS, Dr Colin Peter,** CB 2007; CChem, FRSC; Director General, British National Space Centre, 1999–2006; *b* 1 May 1946; *s* of George Stephen Frederick Hicks and Irene Maud (*née* Hargrave); *m* 1967, Elizabeth Joan Payne; two *d*. *Educ*: Rutlish Grammar Sch., Merton; Univ. of Bristol (BSc, PhD). Lectr in Chemistry, Univ. of W Indies, Jamaica, 1970–73; ICI Res. Fellow, Univ. of Exeter, 1973–75; DTI, 1975–2006; NPL, 1975–80; Laboratory of Govt Chemist, 1984–87; Sec., Ind. Develt Adv. Bd, 1988–90; Hd, Res. and Technol. Policy Div., 1990–94; Hd of Envmt and Energy Technologies Div., 1994–96; Dir, Envmt, 1996–99. Mem., NERC, 2002–06. Pres., Eurisy, 2006–15. Mem. Council, 2006–13, Trustee Bd, 2009–13, BUGB. *Address*: 41 Teddington Park, Teddington TW11 8DB.

**HICKS, His Honour John Charles;** QC 1980; a Judge of the Technology and Construction Court of the High Court (formerly the Official Referees' Courts), 1993–2000; a Circuit Judge, 1988–2000; *b* 4 March 1928; *s* of late Charles Hicks and late Marjorie Jane Hicks; *m* 1957, Elizabeth Mary, *o d* of late Rev. J. B. Jennings; (one *s* one *d* decd). *Educ*: King Edward VI Grammar Schs, Chelmsford and Totnes; London Univ. LLM 1954. Served RA (National Service), 1946–48. Admitted solicitor, 1952; called to the Bar, Middle Temple, 1966; a Recorder, 1978–88. Legal Dept, Thomas Tilling Ltd, 1953–54; Partner in Messrs Burchells, solicitors, 1955–65; Methodist Missionary Soc., Caribbean, 1965–66. Jl Sec., Methodist Conf., 1989–97. *Publications*: (contrib. precedents) George on the Sale of Flats, 1957, 4th edn 1978; (contrib. precedents) Precedents for the Conveyancer, 2004; (ed jtly) The Constitution and Discipline of the Methodist Church in the Caribbean and the Americas, 1967, with annual supplements to 1987; (ed) The Constitutional Practice and Discipline of the Methodist Church, 6th edn 1974, 7th edn 1988, with annual supplements, 1974–97; An Absolute Wreck: the loss of the Thomas W Lawson, 2015; articles in Mod. Law Rev., Cambridge Law Jl, Law & Justice, Conveyancer, and Epworth Rev. *Recreations*: singing, organ practice, theatre, opera, the Methodist Constitution. *Address*: Flat 3, 17 Montagu Square, W1H 2LE. *T*: (020) 7935 6008. *E*: john.hicks@montagusquare.net.

**HICKS, Maureen Patricia;** tourism consultant and freelance tour director, since 2004, now specialising in worldwide railway tours; *b* 23 Feb. 1948; *d* of Ron and Nora Cutler; *m* 1973, Keith Hicks; one *s* one *d*. *Educ*: Ashley Secondary School; Brockenhurst Grammar School; Furzedown College of Education. Teacher's Cert. Secondary Teacher, Drama and English, 1969–70; Marks & Spencer Management, 1970–74; Asst Area Educn Officer, 1974–76; Dir, Motor Museum, 1976–82; Project Dir, Stratford-upon-Avon Visitor Mgt Nat. Pilot Project, 1992–96; Dir of Fundraising and Marketing, Myton Hamlet Hospice, Warwick, 1997–2001; Stratford Upon Avon Town Centre Project Manager, 2000–04. Mem., Stratford DC, 1979–84. MP (C) Wolverhampton North East, 1987–92; contested (C) Wolverhampton NE, 1992. PPS to Minister of State and Parly Under-Sec. of State, FCO, 1991–92; Sec., H of C Tourism Cttee, 1987–92. Non-executive Director: David Clarke Associates, 1992–96; S Warwicks Combined Care (formerly Mental Health Services) NHS Trust, 1994–2002. Trustee: Kingsley Sch., Leamington Spa, 2001– (Chm., 2019–); Earl Mountbatten Hospice, IoW, 2009–16 (Vice Chm., 2012–16; Chair, Finance, Audit and Resources, 2013–16). Hon. Fellow, Wolverhampton Univ., 1992. *Recreations*: USA, travel, theatre, golf, bridge.

**HICKS, Sir Robert,** Kt 1996; Chairman: Resound Health Ltd, 2004–15; Marjon University Tenancies Ltd, since 2012; *b* 18 Jan. 1938; *s* of W. H. Hicks; *m* 1st, 1962, Maria Elizabeth Ann Gwyther (marr. diss. 1988); two *d*; 2nd, 1991, Mrs Glenys Foote. *Educ*: Queen Elizabeth Grammar Sch., Crediton; University Coll., London; Univ. of Exeter. Taught at St Austell Grammar Sch., 1961–64; Lecturer in Regional Geography, Weston-super-Mare Technical Coll., 1964–70. MP (C): Bodmin, 1970–Feb. 1974, Oct. 1974–1983; Cornwall SE, 1983–97. An Asst Govt Whip, 1973–74; Member: Select Cttee of House of Commons, European Legislation, 1973, 1976–97; Speaker's Panel, 1992–97; Vice-Chm., Cons. Parly European Affairs Cttee, 1979–81; Chairman: Cons. Parly Agric. Cttee, 1979–81 (Vice-Chm., 1972–73 (Chm., Horticultural Sub-Cttee), and 1974–79); Westcountry Gp of Cons. MPs, 1976–77; UK Gp, Parly Assoc. for Euro-Arab Co-operation, 1982–97; Vice-Chm., Cons. Party ME Council, 1992–97 (Treasurer, 1980–92); Parly Adviser to British Hotels, Restaurants and Caterers Assoc., 1974–97, to Milk Marketing Bd, 1985–97. Chairman: Westcountry Enterprises, 1997–2003; Midas Consortium, 2003–05. Pres., Plymouth Albion RFC, 1991–96. Chm., Silvanus Trust, 1999–2010. Trustee, Peninsula Med. Sch. Foundn, 1997–2002. Chm., Bd of Govs, Plymouth Coll., 2004–09. *Recreations*: cricket, gardening, golf. *Address*: Burndoo, Luckett, Callington, Cornwall PL17 8NH. *Clubs*: Farmers', MCC.

**HICKS, Robin Edgcumbe;** freelance local journalist; Member, Management Board, Royal Smithfield Show, 1998–2004; *b* 6 Dec. 1942; *s* of late Ronald Eric Edgcumbe Hicks and Fredrica Hicks; *m* 1970, Sue (*née* Dalton); one *s* one *d*. *Educ*: Bancroft's Sch.; Seale Hayne Coll. (NDA; Dip. Farm Management); Univ. of Reading (DipAgric Extension). ARAgS 1995. Farm worker, 1961–63; Agricl Advr, MAFF, 1967–69; Producer/Presenter, BBC Farming Today, 1969–71; Churchill Fellow, 1973; various production posts, radio and television, 1971–77; Hd of Marketing and Develt, RASE, 1977–79; Hd of Network Radio, BBC South and West, 1979–88; Chief Exec., RASE, 1989–91; Dir, Royal Smithfield Show, 1992–98; Dir, P&O Events Ltd, 1992–98; Chief Exec., Consortium of Rural TECs, 1998–99; Dir, Expocentric.com, 1999–2001. Editor: Blablablah, 2006–09; www.heraultwhatson.info, 2009–14; Reporter: French News, 2004–08; The Connexion, 2009–13; TheFrenchPaper, 2009–14. Consultant, Landscape '99; PR Consultant, Beziers Airport, 2007–14. Mem., Bristol and Weston HA, 1986–88; Vice-Chm., Radio Acad., 1986–88; Trustee: St George's Music Trust, 1981–88; Head Injury Recovery Trust, 1986–94; Rural Housing Trust, 1990–92; Avon Valley Railway Heritage Trust, 2015–16 (Chm., 2015–16); Trustee and Farm Advr, Lawrence Weston Community Farm, 2016–. Member: Exec. Cttee, SW Arts, 1981–85; SW Concerts Bd, 1981–88. Hon. Life Mem., Royal Smithfield Club, 2005–. Freeman, City of London, 1977; Liveryman, Drapers' Co., 1981. Confrère, Petit Pâté de Pézenas, 2012. Volunteer and grassland advr, Riding for Disabled Assoc. Avon Riding Centre, 2016–. *Recreations*: family and friends, being back in England and exploring, playing the farmer at community farm and at Riding for Disabled Association. *Address*: 232 The Crescent, Hannover Quay, Bristol BS1 5JR. *Clubs*: Farmers'; Midi Cricket (Pres., 2005–06; Hon. Life Pres., 2006); Probus (Bristol) (Chm., 2016–17).

**HICKS, Sophia Margaret Rawle;** Founder and Chief Executive Officer, Sophie Hicks Agency, since 2014; *b* London, 19 Feb. 1965; *d* of Timothy and Penelope Hicks. *Educ*: Francis Holland Sch.; St Mary's Coll., Twickenham (BA Hons French Lit. 1988). Ed Victor Ltd: Literary Agent, 1989–92; Dir, 1992–99; Man. Dir, 1999–2014. *Recreations*: reading, theatre, walking, bird watching, running. *Address*: Sophie Hicks Agency, 60 Grays Inn Road, WC1X 8AQ. *E*: sophie@sophiehicksagency.com. *Club*: Groucho.

**HICKS, Thomas;** *see* Steele, Tommy.

**HICKS, William David Antony;** QC 1995; *b* 11 June 1951; *s* of Maj.-Gen. William Michael Ellis Hicks, CB, OBE; *m* 1982, Jennifer Caroline Ross; one *s* two *d*. *Educ*: Eton Coll.; Magdalene Coll., Cambridge (MA Econs). Called to the Bar, Inner Temple, 1975. Chm., Salmon and Trout Conservation, 2018–. Trustee, Community Wholecare Centres, 2019. Freeman, Fishmongers' Co., 2012. *Recreations*: fishing, Real tennis, painting, walking, bee keeping. *Address*: Landmark Chambers, 180 Fleet Street, EC4A 2HG. *Clubs*: Flyfishers', MCC.

**HICKS BEACH,** family name of **Earl St Aldwyn**.

**HICKSON, Prof. Ian David,** PhD; FRS 2010; Professor of Molecular Aging, since 2010, and Director, Centre for Chromosome Stability, since 2015, University of Copenhagen; *b* Blackpool, 19 Aug. 1957; *s* of Leslie Hickson and Margaret Hickson; *m* 1st, 1978, Julie Hickson (marr. diss. 2007); one *s* one *d* (and one *d* decd); 2nd, 2009, Dr Ying Liu. *Educ*: Arnold Sch., Blackpool; Univ. of Newcastle upon Tyne (BSc; PhD 1982). Lectr, Univ. of Newcastle upon Tyne, 1983–88; Sen. Scientist, 1989–95, Principal Scientist, 1995–99, ICRF; Prof. of Molecular Oncology, Univ. of Oxford, 1999–2010; Dep. Dir, CRUK Oxford Cancer Centre, 1999–2010. FMedSci 2010. *Publications*: over 200 articles in learned scientific jls. *Recreations*: swimming, cinema, food and drink, family. *Address*: Centre for Chromosome Stability, Department of Cellular and Molecular Medicine, Panum Institute, Building 22.1.21, University of Copenhagen, 2200 Copenhagen N, Denmark.

**HICKSON, Peter Charles Fletcher;** Chairman, Orbis Charitable Trust, since 2015 (Trustee, since 2008); *b* Cambridge, 30 May 1945; *s* of Geoffrey and Jane Hickson; *m* 1972, Rosemary Dawson; three *s* one *d*. *Educ*: Uppingham Sch.; Fitzwilliam Coll., Cambridge (BA 1967; MA). Chief Accountant, Doulton Glass Industries Ltd, 1970–78; Finance Director: Wimpey Asphalt Ltd, 1978–80; Tarmac Buildings Products Ltd, 1980–84; Dep. Chief Exec., United Scientific Hldgs plc, 1985–89; Man. Dir, Tern plc, 1989–91; Finance Dir, MAI plc, 1991–96; Gp Finance Dir, Powergen plc, 1996–2002; Chairman: Anglian Water, 2003–09; Communisis plc, 2007–17; Chemring Gp plc, 2010–16. Non-executive Director: Meridian Broadcasting Ltd, 1991–96; Anglia TV plc, 1994–96; RAC plc, 1994–2002; Marconi Corp. plc, 2004–07; Scottish Power plc, 2006–07; London & Continental Railways Ltd, 2007–11; Kazakhmys plc, 2009–11; Harworth Gp (formerly UK Coal, then Coalfield Resources) plc, 2011–16. Trustee, Sonoro Music, 2016–. Chm. Govs, St John's Sch., Leatherhead, 2003–14. *Recreations*: music, golf, cricket. *Address*: Orbis Charitable Trust, 10 Lower Thames Street, EC3R 6AF. *T*: (020) 7608 7260. *E*: pcfhickson@yahoo.co.uk. *Clubs*: Oxford and Cambridge, MCC, City of London; Wimbledon; Royal Wimbledon Golf, Wimbledon Park Golf; Real de Golf Las Brisas (Marbella).

**HIDDLESTON, Adam Wallace; His Honour Judge Hiddleston;** a Circuit Judge, since 2015; a Judge of the First-Tier Tribunal, Health, Education and Social Care Chamber (Mental Health), since 2014; *b* Ndola, Zambia, 1 April 1965; *s* of late George Hiddleston and Dr Patricia Hiddleston (*née* Wallace); *m* 2010, Sophie Olivia Eggar; one *s* one *d*. *Educ*: Loretto Sch.; Univ. of Newcastle upon Tyne (LLB Hons). Pegasus Schol., NZ, 1993. Called to the Bar: Inner Temple, 1990, Bencher, 2013; Eastern Caribbean Supreme Court, BVI, 2011; in practice as barrister, 1990–2015; a Recorder, 2012–15. Legal Assessor: GMC, 2007–15; GDC, 2010–15; NMC, 2012–15; HCPC, 2012–15. Member: Gen. Council of Bar, 2008–15 (Mem., Professional Conduct Cttee, 2009–15); Cttee, Council of HM Circuit Judges, 2016–. Chm., Disciplinary Cttee, CIPFA, 2014–15; Mem. Exec., Bar Human Rights Cttee, 2010–12. Wine Treas., 2002–06, Circuit Jun., 2006–08, Western Circuit. *Recreations*: family, Munro bagging, ski-ing, Scotland (mountains, glens, lochs and drams). *Address*: Croydon Crown Court, The Law Courts, Altyre Road, Croydon, Surrey CR9 5AB. *Club*: Athenæum.

**HIDER, David James;** Director, Internal Communications Project, British Gas, 1994–95; *b* 5 Nov. 1934; *s* of Edward James Hider and Marguerite Noel Hider (*née* James); *m* 1963, Margaret Gilbert Macdonald Watson; two *s* one *d*. *Educ*: Roan Sch., Greenwich; King Edward VII Nautical Coll., Poplar. Master Mariner; DMS; CIGEM. Merchant Navy, 1952–67 (to Chief Officer); South Eastern Gas: Commercial Asst, 1967; Conversion Unit Manager, 1969; Area Service Manager, Sussex, 1973; Regl Service Manager, 1976; Dir of Marketing, 1981; British Gas: Dir of Service, 1983; Dir of Domestic Marketing, 1990; Regl Chm., British Gas S Western, 1990–94. Mem., SW IDB, 1997–99; Vice Chm., Bristol Regeneration Partnership, 2000–03; Chm., Bristol Partnership Regeneration Progs Mgt Gp (formerly Bristol Regeneration Partnership), 2003–04. Chm., Avon Youth Assoc., 1996–2015. Chm. and Man. Dir, St Peter's Hospice Enterprises, 2000–10; Trustee, CLIC, 2000–04. Gov., UWE, 1993–2004. *Publications*: contribs to Jl IGasE. *Recreations*: swimming, walking, cooking.

**HIDER, Prof. Robert Charles,** PhD; CChem, FRSC; Professor of Medicinal Chemistry, King's College, London, since 1987; *b* 14 Aug. 1943; *s* of Charles Thomas Hider and Josephine Mary (*née* Breitbach); *m* 1967, Shirley Christine Nickels; one *s* one *d*. *Educ*: King's Coll., London (BSc Chem. and Physics 1964; PhD Chem. 1967; FKC 1997). Wellcome Res. Fellow, St Thomas' Hosp., 1967–70; Lectr, then Reader, Dept of Chem., Essex Univ., 1970–87; King's College, London: Head, Sch. of Life, Basic Med. and Health Scis, then of Health & Life Scis, 1994–2000; Head, Dept of Pharmacy, 2000–03; Head, Sch. of Biomed. Scis, subseq. Sch. of Biomed. and Health Scis, 2002–07. Associated with develt of medicines for thalassaemia, anaemia, and renal failure. Visiting Professor: Dept of Biochem., Univ. of Calif, Berkeley, 1977 and 1980; Coll. of Pharmaceutical Scis, Zhejiang Univ., 2009–; Chiang Mai Univ., 2012–. Paul Ehrlich Lectr, BioIron, 2013. Hon. MRPharmS, 1995. Hanbury Meml Medal, 2014; Thousand Talents Award, China, 2014. Member, Editorial Board: Toxicon, 1986–98; Biometals, 1990–; Analytical Biochem., 2017–. *Publications*: contrib. articles on pharmaceutically active peptides and metal chelating agents to pharmaceutical, biochem. and chem. jls. *Recreations*: arachnology, natural history, Australian philately. *Address*: 257 Point Clear Road, St Osyth, Essex CO16 8JL. *T*: (01255) 821335.

**HIELSCHER, Sir Leo (Arthur),** AC 2004; Kt 1987; Foundation Chairman, Queensland Treasury Corporation, since 2010 (Chairman, 1988–2010); *b* 1 Oct. 1926; *s* of Leslie Charles Hielscher and Elizabeth Jane Petersen; *m* 1948, Mary Ellen Pelgrave (*d* 2017); one *s* one *d* (and one *s* decd). *Educ*: Brisbane State High Sch.; Univ. of Queensland (BComm, AAUQ). FCPA; FAIM. Queensland Public Service, 1942; RAAF, 1945–47; Asst Under Sec. (Budget), Qld Treasury, 1964–69, Dep. Under Treasurer, 1969–74; Under Treas. of Qld (CS Hd of Treasury Dept of Qld Govt), 1974–88. Eisenhower Exchange Fellow, 1973. *Publications*: Sir Leo Hielscher: Queensland made, 2014. *Recreations*: fishing, boating, theatre. *Address*: 3301/15 Cansdale Street, Yeronga, Brisbane, Qld 4104, Australia. *T*: (home) (7) 38926296, *T*: (business) (7) 38424611. *E*: slahielscher@bigpond.com. *Clubs*: Brisbane, Tattersalls (Brisbane).

**HIGGINS**, family name of **Baron Higgins**.

**HIGGINS**, Baron *cr* 1997 (Life Peer), of Worthing, in the co. of West Sussex; **Terence Langley Higgins**, KBE 1993; PC 1979; DL; *b* 18 Jan. 1928; *s* of late Reginald and Rose Higgins, Dulwich; *m* 1961, Dame Rosalyn Higgins, *qv*; one *s* one *d*. *Educ*: Alleyn's Sch., Dulwich; Gonville and Caius Coll., Cambridge (BA (Hons) 1958; MA 1963; Pres., Cambridge Union Soc., 1958). Brit. Olympic Team (athletics) 1948, 1952. NZ Shipping Co., 1948–55; Lectr in Economic Principles, Dept of Economics, Yale Univ., 1958–59; Economist with Unilever, 1959–64. Dir, 1980–92, Consultant, 1992–2003, Lex Service Group (Chm., Lex Pension Fund Trustees, 1994–2002); Dir, First Choice Holidays (formerly Owners Abroad) plc, 1992–97. MP (C) Worthing, 1964–97. Opposition Spokesman on Treasury and Economic Affairs, 1966–70; Minister of State, Treasury, 1970–72; Financial Sec. to Treasury, 1972–74; Opposition Spokesman: on Treasury and Econ. Affairs, 1974; for Trade, 1974–76; Principal Opposition Spokesman, H of L, on social security, 1997–2001, on work and pensions, 2001–06. Chairman: Select Cttee on Procedure, 1980–83; Select Cttee on Treasury and CS, 1983–97 (Mem., 1980–97); House of Commons Liaison Cttee, 1984–97; Sec., Cons. Parly Finance Cttee, 1965–66; Chm., Cons. Parly Cttee on Sport, 1979–81, on Transport, 1979–91; Member: Public Accounts Commn, 1984–97 (Chm., 1996–97); Exec. Cttee, 1922 Cttee, 1980–97. Mem., H of L, 1997–2019. Member: H of L Select Cttee on Speakership of H of L, 2005, on Personal Service Companies, 2014; Jt Cttee on the Conventions of Parlt, 2006. Mem., Claims Resolution Tribunal for Dormant Accounts in Switzerland, 1998–2002. Member: Council, RIIA, 1979–85; Council, IAM, 1979–98. Governor: NIESR, 1989–; Dulwich Coll. 1980–95; Alleyn's Sch., 1995–99. Special Fellow, PSI, 1986 (Mem. Council, 1989–95); Trustee, Industry and Parlt Trust, 1985–91; Hon. Mem., Keynes College, Univ. of Kent, 1976–. DL W Sussex, 1989. *Address*: House of Lords, SW1A 0PW. *Clubs*: Reform, Yale; Hawks (Cambridge); Koninklijke Haagsche Golf.

*See also* D. J. Campbell.

**HIGGINS, Andrew James**, PhD; MRCVS; FRSB; Editor-in-Chief, The Veterinary Journal (formerly British Veterinary Journal), 1991–2015, Honorary Editor-in-Chief, since 2016 (Deputy Editor, 1990–91); *b* 7 Dec. 1948; *s* of late Edward James Higgins and Gabrielle Joy Higgins, *d* of late Sir John Kelland; *m* 1981, Nicola, *d* of late Peter Eliot and of Jenifer Eliot; one *s* three *d*. *Educ*: St Michael's Coll., Leeds; Royal Veterinary Coll., Univ. of London (BVetMed 1973; PhD 1985); Centre for Tropical Med., Univ. of Edinburgh (MSc 1977). FRSB (FIBiol 1993). Commnd RAVC 1973. Vet. Officer to Sultan of Oman, 1975–76; Vet. Advr, ME and N Africa, Wellcome Foundn, 1977–82; Scientific Dir and Chief Exec., Animal Health Trust, 1988–99. Cons., FAO, 1981–86. Mem., Lord Chancellor's Adv. Sub-cttee for W Suffolk, 1999–2008. Member: Conservation and Welfare Cttee, 1987–96, Ethics Cttee, 1994–2014, Welfare Cttee, 1998–2013, Zool Soc. of London; Vet. Res. Club, 1989–; Vet. Panel, BEF, 1993–2009 (Chm., 2004–09); Govt Adv. Cttee on Quarantine, 1997–98; Greyhound Board of Great Britain: Mem., Impartiality (formerly UK Accreditation Service) Cttee, 2009–19, Disciplinary Cttee, 2009–; Chairman: Ind. Anti-doping and Medication Control Review, 2009–10; Doping and Medication Adv. Panel, 2010–12; Ind. Doping and Medication Advr, 2012–14. Trustee: Soc. for Protection of Animals Abroad, 1985–98 (Vice-Chm., 1986–89); Dogs Trust (formerly Nat. Canine Defence League), 1999–2009; RCVS Trust, 2001–06; Animals in War Meml Fund, 2001–08; Kennel Club Charitable Trust, 2016–; Scientific Adviser: World Horse Welfare (formerly Internat. League for the Protection of Horses), 2006– (Trustee and Mem. Council, 1999–2006); Phang Nga Elephant Park, 2015–; Chairman: Retired Greyhound Trust, 2008–15; Southern Thailand Elephant Foundn, 2018–; Pres., Anglo-Italian Soc. for the Protection of Animals. Hon. Advr, UK Jockey Club, 1988–89; Fédération Equestre Internationale: Hon. Scientific Advr, 1990–2010; Chm., Medication Adv. Gp, 2005–08; Mem., Vet. Cttee, 2006–10. Man. Consultant, Compton Fundraising Consultants Ltd, 2000–15; Chm., Strata Technology Ltd, 2002–11. Hon. Mem., Kennel Club, 2015–. Scientific Fellow, Zool Soc. of London. Univ. of London Laurel, 1971; Ciba-Geigy Prize for Res. in Animal Health, 1985; Equine Veterinary Jl Open Award and medal, 1986; Centenary Prize, Central Vet. Soc., 1986; George Fleming Prize, British Vet. Jl, 1987; President's Award, Vet. Mktg Assoc., 1997. *Publications*: (contrib.) An Anatomy of Veterinary Europe, 1972; (ed and contrib.) The Camel in Health and Disease, 1986; (ed) The Equine Manual, 1995, 2nd edn 2005; With the SAS and Other Animals, 2011, 2nd edn 2016; papers in sci. and gen. pubns and communications to learned socs. *Recreations*: countryside, opera, writing, the Asian elephant. *Club*: Royal Society of Medicine.

**HIGGINS, Bernard Franklin**, FRSE; Chair, National Galleries of Scotland, since 2017; Strategic Adviser, Scottish National Investment Bank, since 2018; *b* Paisley, 12 Dec. 1960; *s* of James Love Higgins and Mary Muir Mulheron; *m* 2017, Sharon Christine Ward; two step *d*, and two *s* four *d* from previous marriages. *Educ*: Holyrood Secondary Sch.; Univ. of Glasgow (BSc Hons Maths 1983). FFA 1986; FCIB 2004. Actuarial Student, then Gen. Manager Sales, 1995–97, Standard Life; Chief Executive: Retail Banking, RBS Gp, 1997–2006; Retail, HBOS, 2006–07; Tesco Bank, 2008–18. Chm., Kyckr Ltd, 2018–; non-executive Director: Buccleuch, 2012–; Glasgow Life, 2017–; Arabian Centres, 2018–. Trustee: Edinburgh Internat. Cultural Summit, 2014–; Burrell Renaissance, 2017–. Vis. Prof., Strathclyde Univ., 2017–; Hon. Prof., Edinburgh Business Sch., 2017–. FRSE 2018. *Recreations*: reading, poetry, art, football, travel, Italy. *Address*: 7 Doune Terrace, Edinburgh EH3 6DY. *Clubs*: Groucho, Two Brydges, Soho House, Ivy, Academy, 5 Hertford Street; New (Edinburgh).

**HIGGINS, Charlotte Elizabeth**, FSA; Chief Culture Writer (formerly Chief Arts Writer), The Guardian, since 2008; *b* Stoke-on-Trent, 6 Sept. 1972; *d* of Peter and Pamela Higgins. *Educ*: Newcastle-under-Lyme Sch.; Balliol Coll., Oxford (MA 1994). Asst Ed., Histl Collections, 1994–95; Sub-ed., Vogue, 1995–96; Chief Sub-ed., World of Interiors, 1996–97; The Guardian: Dep. Ed., Space mag., 1997–99; Classical Music Ed., 2000–04; Arts Corresp., 2004–08. Associate Fellow, Centre for Study of Greek and Roman Antiquity, Corpus Christi Coll., Oxford, 2012–. FSA 2017. Hon. DA Staffordshire, 2016. *Publications*: Latin Love Lessons, 2007; It's All Greek to Me, 2008; Under Another Sky, 2013; This New Noise, 2015; Red Thread, 2018. *Recreation*: chamber music. *Address*: The Guardian, Kings Place, 90 York Way, N1 9GU. *E*: charlotte.higgins@theguardian.com.

**HIGGINS, Prof. Christopher Francis**, PhD; FRSE, FMedSci; Vice-Chancellor and Warden, 2007–14, and Pro-Chancellor, 2014–15, Durham University, Emeritus Professor, 2015; *b* 24 June 1955; *s* of Prof. Philip John Higgins and Betty Ann Higgins (*née* Edmonds); *m* 1st, 1978, Elizabeth Mary Joy (marr. diss. 1994); two *d*; 2nd, 1994, Suzanne Wilson Higgins (marr. diss. 2001); three *d*. *Educ*: Univ. of Durham (BSc 1st Cl. Hons Botany 1976; PhD 1979). FRSE 1989. NATO-SERC postdoctoral Fellow, Univ. of California, Berkeley, 1979–81; University of Dundee: Lectr, 1981–87; Reader and Prof. of Molecular Genetics, 1987–89; Lister Inst. Res. Fellow, 1983–89; Oxford University: Principal Scientist, ICRF, and Dep. Dir, ICRF Labs, Inst. of Molecular Medicine, 1989–93; Fellow, Keble Coll., 1989–93; Nuffield Prof. of Clin. Biochemistry, and Fellow, Hertford Coll., 1993–97; Dir, MRC Clinical Scis Centre, and Prof. and Hd of Div. of Clinical Scis, Imperial Coll. London, 1998–2007. Howard Hughes Internat. Res. Scholar; Fellow, EMBO, 1988. Mem., BBSRC, 1997–2000; Mem., Governing Council, John Innes Centre, 1994–2000; Mem. Exec. Council, AMRC, 2003–07. Chairman: Spongiform Encephalopathy Adv. Cttee, 2004–11; Scientific Adv. Bd, Microscience; Mem., Nat. Expert Panel on New and Emerging Infections; Scientific Advr, Select Cttee on Stem Cells, H of L, 2001–02; Mem., Human Genetics Commn, 2005–08. Charity Trustee: Future Harvest, 2001–05; 2 Higher Ground, 2001–04; Kennedy Inst. for Rheumatology, 2004–07; Suffolk Acads Trust, 2015–; Britten-Pears Foundn, 2017–. Gov., W Suffolk Coll., 2015–. Founding Editor and Editor-in-Chief, Molecular Microbiology, 1987–2003. Mem. Bd, One NorthEast RDA, 2008–12. Chm. Trustees, Nat. Youth Choir, 2010–. DL Co. Durham, 2008–15. Founder FMedSci 1998 (Mem., Council, 2000–03); FRSA. Hugh Bean Prize for Violin, 1970, Exhibr, 1970–73, RCM; Fleming Medal, Soc. for Gen. Microbiol., 1987; CIBA Medal and Prize, Biochemical Soc., 1995. *Publications*: numerous research papers in learned jls. *Recreations*: five daughters, medieval farm house, classical music and opera. *E*: chris.higgins@durham.ac.uk, chrishigginsxx@yahoo.com.

**HIGGINS, Clare Frances Elizabeth**; actress; *d* of James Stephen Higgins and Paula Cecilia (*née* Murphy). *Educ*: St Philomena's Convent Sch., Derbys; Ecclesbourne Sch., Derbys; LAMDA. *Theatre includes*: A View from the Bridge, Harrogate; The White Devil, Oxford Playhouse; Beethoven's Tenth, Vaudeville; Jenkin's Ear, Royal Court; Ride Down Mount Morgan, Wyndhams; A Letter of Resignation, Comedy, 1997; Heartbreak House, 2000, The Secret Rapture, 2001, Chichester; Royal Exchange, Manchester: Measure for Measure; Rollo; Blood Black and Gold; The Deep Man; Greenwich: Time and the Conways; The Rivals; A Streetcar Named Desire; Royal Shakespeare Company: A Midsummer Night's Dream, 1989; Hamlet, 1989; Antony and Cleopatra, 1992; Royal National Theatre: The Futurists, 1986; The Secret Rapture, 1988; Richard III, 1990; King Lear, 1990; Napoli Milionaria, 1991; The Absence of War, 1993 (televised, 1996); The Children's Hour, 1994 (Critics' Circle Award, 1995); Sweet Bird of Youth, 1995 (Olivier Award, Critics' Circle Award, Time Out Award, 1995); The Walls, 2001; Vincent in Brixton, 2002 (Olivier Award, Evening Standard Award, Critics' Circle Award, 2003); Major Barbara, 2008; A Slight Ache, 2008; Oedipus, 2008; All's Well That Ends Well, 2009; Hamlet, 2010; The Seagull, Present Laughter, W Yorks Playhouse, 1998; Who's Afraid of Virginia Woolf, Bristol Old Vic, 2002, Th. Royal, Bath, 2014; Hecuba, 2004 (Olivier Award, 2005), Phaedra, 2006, Donmar Warehouse; Death of a Salesman, The Night of the Iguana, Lyric, 2005; The Fever, Royal Court, 2009; Mrs Klein, Almeida, 2009; Other Desert Cities, Old Vic, 2014; Clarion, Arcola, 2015. *Television includes*: Pride and Prejudice; Unity; Byron; The Concubine; Mitch; The Citadel; Cover Her Face; Foreign Body; Beautiful Lies; After the War; Downtown Lagos; Circle of Deceit; Man of the Month, The Syndicate; Parade's End; Downton Abbey; Homefront, Eastenders, Dr Who, The Worst Witch. *Films include*: 1919; Hellraiser; Hellbound; The Fruit Machine; Bad Behaviour, 1993; Let it Come Down, 1995; Easter House, 1995; Small Faces, 1996; House of Mirth, 1999; The Libertine, 2004; The Golden Compass, 2007. *Address*: c/o Conway van Gelder Grant Ltd, 8–12 Broadwick Street, W1F 8HW.

**HIGGINS, Daniel John P.**; *see* Pearce-Higgins.

**HIGGINS, His Honour David Edward Alexander**; a Circuit Judge, 2003–15; a Deputy High Court Judge, 2007; *b* 15 Dec. 1945; *s* of Edward and Rena Higgins; *m* 1971, Rosalind Jane Reading; two *d*. *Educ*: St Peter's Sch., York; Newcastle Univ. (LLB). Partner, Herbert Smith (Solicitors), 1976–2003; a Recorder of the Crown Court, 2000–03. *Recreations*: opera, equine sports, Italy. *Address*: c/o Circuit Secretariat, Rose Court, 2 Southwark Bridge, SE1 9HS.

**HIGGINS, Jack**; *see* Patterson, Harry.

**HIGGINS, Prof. James**, PhD; FBA 1999; Professor of Latin American Literature, University of Liverpool, 1988–2004, now Emeritus; *b* 28 May 1939; *s* of Peter and Annie Higgins; *m* 1962, Kirstine Anne Atwell; one *s* (and one *s* decd). *Educ*: Our Lady's High Sch., Motherwell; Univ. of Glasgow (MA); Univ. of Lyons (LèsL); PhD Liverpool 1968. Department of Hispanic Studies, Liverpool University: Asst Lectr, 1964–67; Lectr, 1967–73; Sen. Lectr, 1973–83; Reader, 1983–88; Head of Dept, 1988–97. Visiting Professor: Univ. of Pittsburgh, 1968; Univ. of Waterloo, Ont, 1974; Univ. of West Indies, Trinidad, 1979; Univ. of Wisconsin-Madison, 1990; Hon. Professor: Univ. of San Marcos, Lima, 1984; Univ. of Stirling, 2006–12. Corresp. Fellow, Peruvian Acad., 2002. Comdr, Order of Merit (Peru), 1988. *Publications*: Visión del hombre y de la vida en las últimas obras poéticas de César Vallejo, 1970; César Vallejo: an anthology of his poetry, 1970; The Poet in Peru, 1982; A History of Peruvian Literature, 1987; César Vallejo: a selection of his poetry (with trans), 1987; César Vallejo en su poesía, 1990; Cambio social y constantes humanas: la narrativa corta de J. R. Ribeyro, 1991; Hitos de la poesía peruana, 1993; Myths of the Emergent: social mobility in contemporary Peruvian fiction, 1994; The Literary Representation of Peru, 2002; Lima: a cultural and literary history, 2005; Historia de la literatura peruana, 2006; John Barbour's The Bruce: a free translation in verse, 2013; numerous articles. *Recreations*: reading, gardening, walking, football, whisky, Scottish literature. *Address*: Flat 6, Carlton House, 15 Snowdon Place, Stirling FK8 2NR. *T*: (01786) 470641.

**HIGGINS, Prof. Dame Joan (Margaret)**, DBE 2007; PhD; Professor of Health Policy, 1992–2004, now Emerita, and Director, Manchester Centre for Healthcare Management, 1998–2004, University of Manchester; *b* 15 June 1948; *d* of Kenneth and Kate Higgins; *m* 1983, John P. Martin (*d* 1997); two step *s* (and one step *s* decd). *Educ*: Rutherford Coll. of Advanced Technol. (BA Hons (Sociol.), London Univ. (ext.), 1969); Univ. of York (Dip. Soc. Admin 1971); Univ. of Southampton (PhD 1979). Res. Asst, then Lectr, Portsmouth Poly., 1971–74; University of Southampton: Lectr, 1974–86, Sen. Lectr, 1986–89, in Social Policy; Prof. of Social Policy, 1989–92. Chm., Christie Hosp. NHS Trust, Manchester, 2002–07. Chairman: Manchester FHSA, 1992–96; Manchester HA, 1996–99; Patient Information Adv. Gp, 2001–08; NHS Litigation Authy, 2007–13; Regl Chm., NHS Exec. NW, 1999–2001; Interim Chm., Nat. Treatment Agency for Substance Misuse, 2001; non-executive Director: Southampton and SW Hampshire HA, 1981–90; Wessex Regl HA, 1990–92. Member: Care Record Develt Bd, 2004–07 (Chm., Ethics Adv. Gp, 2004–07); Nat. Information Governance Bd, 2007–09; Ind. Mem., H of L Appts Commn, 2008–13; Chm., Queen's Counsel Selection Panel, 2009–12 (Mem., 2005–09). Pres., European Health Mgt Assoc., 2001–03. Hon. FRCOG 2012. *Publications*: The Poverty Business: Britain and America, 1978; States of Welfare: comparative analysis in social policy, 1981; (jtly) Government and Urban Poverty, 1983; The Business of Medicine: private health care in Britain, 1988. *Recreations*: travel, gardening, walking, reading, cooking, wine, theatre, modern art, printmaking, book arts. *Address*: Flat 402, 6 Naoroji Street, WC1X 0GD.

**HIGGINS, John Andrew**; Assistant Auditor General, National Audit Office, 1989–99; *b* 19 Feb. 1940; *s* of George Henry and Mildred Maud Higgins, of Hendon; *m* 1965, Susan Jennifer Mathis; one *s*. *Educ*: Hendon County Sch.; Hastings Grammar Sch. ARCO. Exchequer and Audit Department: Asst Auditor, 1958; Auditor, 1968; Sen. Auditor, 1971; Chief Auditor, 1977; Dep. Dir, 1981; Office of Auditor Gen. of Canada, 1983–84; Dir, Nat. Audit Office, 1984.

Treas., Crawley and Horsham Dist Organists' Assoc., 1994–2006; Trustee and Treas., Crawley Open House, 1999–. Mem., Crawley Horticultural Soc. *Recreations:* classical organ playing, golf, bridge (Mem., Crawley Horticultural Society Bridge section), gardening, supporting Crystal Palace and Crawley Town. *Address:* Zaria, 65 Milton Mount Avenue, Pound Hill, Crawley, Sussex RH10 3DP. *T:* (01293) 417075.

**HIGGINS, John Patrick,** MBE 2008; professional snooker player; *b* Motherwell, 18 May 1975; *s* of late John and Josephine Higgins; *m* 2000, Denise Whitton; two *s* one *d*. *Educ:* St Aidan's Primary Sch.; St Aidan's High Sch. Turned professional, 1992; won first tournament, 1994; wins include: Grand Prix, 1994, 1999, 2005, 2008; British Open, 1995, 1998, 2001, 2004; Internat. Open, 1995, 1996; UK Championship, 1998, 2000, 2010; Masters, 1999, 2006; World Snooker Championship, 1998, 2007, 2009, 2011; Welsh Open, 2000, 2010, 2011, 2015; Shanghai Masters, 2012; Bulgarian Open, 2013; Internat. Championship, 2015; Australian Open, 2015; China Championship, 2016. *Address:* 76 Royal Gardens, Bothwell, Glasgow G71 8SY. *T:* (01698) 852995. *E:* john.higgins30@hotmail.co.uk.

**HIGGINS, John Stuart,** CBE 2005; Director General, DigitalEurope, 2011–17; Chairman, Global Digital Foundation, since 2017; *b* 26 June 1954; *s* of Robert Brian Higgins and Josephine Mary Higgins; *m* 1977, Ailsa Elizabeth Ann Gibson; three *d*. *Educ:* Cardinal Langley Sch., Middleton; Univ. of East Anglia (BSc Hons Maths and Phys); CDipAF. Systems Analyst, then Project Manager, London Brick Co., 1976–81; Business Manager, Triad Computing Systems, 1982–85; Director: Wilkins Computer Systems, 1986–90; Softwright Systems, then SSA, 1991–96; CEO, Res Rocket Surfer, CA, 1997–98; Director General: Computing Services and Software Assoc., 1998–2002; Intellect, 2002–12. Sen. Advr, Burson Marstellar, 2017–. Chairman: GRID Computing Task Force, Information Age Partnership, 2004; IP Forum Business Opportunities Gp, 2005; CBI Trade Assoc. Council, 2009–11; Vice Chm., UK Security and Resilience Industry Suppliers' Community, 2008–11; Member, Board: Eur. Internet Forum, 2015–17; Pro Europa, 2015–. Vice-Pres., Eur. Information, Communications and Consumer Electronics Technology Industry Assoc., 2006–08; Pres., Eur. Commn Strategic Policy Forum on Digital Entrepreneurship, 2014–16. Mem., UK Space Leadership Council, 2012–16. University of Warwick: Lay Mem. Council, 2003–15; Chm., Audit Cttee, 2010–15; Chm., Eur. Adv. Bd. FRSA. Editor's Award for outstanding contrib. to UK IT, Computing Awards for Excellence, 2008. *Recreations:* tennis, the outdoors, music, theatre. *E:* john.higgins@globaldigitalfoundation.org.

**HIGGINS, Dame Julia (Stretton),** DBE 2001 (CBE 1996); DPhil; FRS 1995; FREng; Senior Research Investigator, Imperial College London, since 2007 (Professor of Polymer Science, 1989–2007); President, Institute of Physics, 2017–19; *b* 1 July 1942; *d* of late George Stretton Downes, CBE and Sheilah D. M. Downes (née Gavigan). *Educ:* Somerville Coll., Oxford (MA, DPhil 1968; Hon. Fellow, 1996). CChem 1991, FRSC 1991; CEng 1994, FREng 1999; FIM 1994; FCGI 1994; FInstP 1996; FIChemE 1997. Physics teacher, Mexborough Grammar Sch., 1966–68; Dept of Chemistry, Univ. of Manchester, 1968–72; Res. Fellow, Centre de Recherche sur les Macromolecules, Strasbourg, 1972–73; physicist, Inst Laue-Langevin, Grenoble, 1973–76; Imperial College, London: Dept of Chem. Engrg, 1976–; Dean, City and Guilds Coll., 1993–97; Dir, Graduate Sch. of Engrg and Physical Scis, 2002–06; Principal, Faculty of Engrg, 2006–07. Vis. Academic, Institut für Makromolekulare Chemie, Freiburg, 1988. Trustee, Nat. Gall., 2001–10. Chm., EPSRC, 2003–07 (Mem., 1994–2000); Science and Engineering Research Council: Member: Neutron Beam Res. Cttee, 1979–83 and 1988–91; Polymers and Composites Cttee, 1989–94 (Chm., 1991–94); Materials Commn, 1991–94; Facilities Commn, 1993–94; Member: CCLRC, 1995–2000; Sci. and Engrg Cttee, British Council, 1993–98; Council for Sci. and Technol., 1998–2004; Chm., Adv. Cttee for Maths Educn, 2008–12. Foreign Sec. and Vice Pres., Royal Soc., 2001–06; President: IChemE, 2002–03; BAAS, 2003–04; Vice-Pres. and Mem. Council, RAEng, 2008–. Foreign Associate, Nat. Acad. Engrg, USA, 1999. Hon. DSc: Nottingham, 1999; QUB, Leicester, 2002; Oxon, Sheffield, 2003; Kent, Exeter, Leeds, Sheffield Hallam, 2004; Bath, 2005; Keele, 2006; Birmingham, 2007; Manchester, Liverpool, 2008; Loughborough, 2009; Melbourne, 2011; Cardiff, 2011; UCL, 2012; Kingston, 2015; Hon. DEng Heriot-Watt, 2000. *Publications:* (with H. Benoît) Polymers and Neutron Scattering, 1994; contrib. articles on polymer science to learned jls. *Address:* Department of Chemical Engineering, Imperial College London, SW7 2AZ. *T:* (020) 7594 5565.

*See also* G. P. S. Downes.

**HIGGINS, Rt Hon. Sir Malachy (Joseph),** Kt 1993; PC 2007; a Lord Justice of Appeal, Supreme Court of Judicature, Northern Ireland, 2007–14; *b* 30 Oct. 1944; *er s* of late James and May Higgins; *m* 1980, Dorothy Ann, *d* of Dr Leslie Grech, Malta; three *d*. *Educ:* St MacNissi's Coll., Garron Tower; Queen's Univ., Belfast (LLB); Middle Temple (BL). Called to NI Bar, 1969 (Bencher, 1993), to Irish Bar, 1978; QC (NI), 1985; County Court Judge, 1988–93; Recorder of Londonderry, 1990–93; County Court Judge for Co. Armagh, 1993; Judge of the High Court of Justice, NI, 1993–2007 (Family Div., 1996–2001); Sen. Judge, QBD, 2004–07. Chairman: Criminal Justice Issues Gp, 2008–; Judicial Studies Bd for NI, 2009–. Judge in Residence, 1999–2001, Chm. Bd of Visitors, 2005–, QUB. Chm., Children Order Adv. Cttee, 1996–2001. *Recreations:* gardening, golf, sailing, walking. *Address:* Ashdene, Comber, Co. Down BT23 5SP. *Clubs:* Royal Ulster Yacht, Royal Belfast Golf.

**HIGGINS, Michael D(aniel);** President of Ireland, since 2011; *b* Limerick, 18 April 1941; *m* 1974, Sabina Coyne; three *s* one *d*. *Educ:* University Coll., Galway; Univ. of Manchester; Univ. of Indiana (MA Sociol.; Dist. Alumni Service Award 2014). Vis. Prof., Univ. of Southern Illinois; Lectr in Political Sci. and Sociol., UC, Galway. Mem. (Lab), Galway CC, 1974–93 (Mayor, 1982–83 and 1991–92). Member: Seanad, 1973–77 and 1983–87; Dáil (TD) (Lab) Galway W, 1981–82 and 1987–2011; Minister for Arts, Culture and Gaeltacht, 1993–97. Hon. Adjunct Prof., Irish Centre for Human Rights, NUI. Patron, Inst. of Irish Studies, Univ. of Liverpool, 2019–. MRIA 2012. Hon. FRCPI 2014; Hon. FRCSI 2016; Hon. Fellow: Inst. of Engrs of Ireland, 2016; Coll. of Anaesthesiologists of Ireland, 2018. Hon. Life Member: Irish Writers' Union, 2012; Law Soc., 2014. Hon. Fellow: TCD, 2012; Galway Mayo Inst. of Technol., 2013. Hon. LLD: NUI, 2012; TCD, 2013; Liverpool, 2015; Edinburgh, 2016; WA, 2017; Melbourne, 2017; Hon. Dr: Middlesex, 2013; Vytautas Magnus, Kaunas, 2018; Hon. DHL Indiana, 2014; Hon. Dr English Lang., Lit. and Phil., Athens, 2018. Seán McBride Peace Prize, Internat. Peace Bureau, Helsinki, 1991; Sorbonne Medal, Paris, 2013; Gold Medal, Histl Soc., TCD, 2013; Lifetime Achievement Award, UCD, 2013; Fr Aengus Finucane Award, Concern Worldwide, 2014; Trinity Praeses Elit Award Dublin Univ. Law Soc., 2014; Lifetime Achievement Award, Gerard Manley Hopkins Soc., Ireland, 2014; St Vincent de Paul Social Justice Award, 2015; T K Whitaker Award for Outstanding Contribn to Public Life, Inst. Banking, Ireland, 2016. Freedom: Cork City, 2014; Limerick City and Co., 2014; Key of City of Lisbon, 2015. Orden Nacional Jose Matias Delgado (El Salvador), 2013; OM, 5 Nov. 1811 (El Salvador), 2013; Dip. of Honour (Chile), 2016; Gran Collar, Orden del Sol (Peru), 2017. *Publications:* (jtly) Causes for Concern: Irish politics, culture and society, 2007; Renewing the Republic, 2011; When Ideas Matter: speeches for an ethical republic; *poetry:* The Betrayal, 1990; (with M. Mulcahy) The Season of Fire, 1993; An Arid Season, 2004; New and Selected Poems, 2011. *Address:* Áras an Uachtaráin, Phoenix Park, Dublin 8, Ireland. *T:* (01) 6171000.

**HIGGINS, Very Rev. Michael John,** OBE 2003; Dean of Ely, 1991–2003, now Emeritus; *b* 31 Dec. 1935; *s* of Claud John and Elsie Higgins; *m* 1976, Bevyl Margaret Stringer; one *d*. *Educ:* Whitchurch Grammar Sch., Cardiff; Univ. of Birmingham (LLB 1957); Gonville and Caius Coll., Cambridge (LLB 1959, PhD 1962); Harvard Univ.; Ridley Hall, Cambridge. Lectr in English Law, Univ. of Birmingham, 1961–63. Ordained, 1965; Curate, Ormskirk Parish Church, dio. of Liverpool, 1965–68; Selection Sec., ACCM, 1968–74; Vicar, Frome and Priest-in-charge of Woodlands, dio. of Bath and Wells, 1974–80; Rector of Preston, and Leader of Preston Town Centre Team Ministry, dio. of Blackburn, 1980–91. *Publications:* The Vicar's House, 1988. *Recreations:* music, walking, travel. *Address:* Twin Cottage, Great Dunham, Norfolk PE32 2LR.

**HIGGINS, Peter Raymond,** RDI 2009; interior designer; Creative Director, Land Design Studio, since 1992; *b* London, 26 March 1948; *s* of late Donald Higgins and of Anneliese Higgins; *m* 2006, Shirley Walker; one *s*. *Educ:* Architectural Assoc. Sch. of Architecture (5th Yr Prize 1975). RIBA 1988. Design Dept, BBC TV, 1977–85; Associate Dir, Imagination Ltd, 1985–88; freelance designer, 1988–92; Land Design Studio, 1992–: conceptual masterplanning and exhibition design includes: River & Rowing Mus., Henley, 1998; Nat. Waterfront Mus., Swansea, 2005; UK Pavilion, Expo 2005, Japan, 2005; Golden Age of Couture, V&A, 2007; Pompeii and Herculaneum, BM, 2013. External Examiner: Leeds Metropolitan Univ., 2000–04; Kingston Univ., 2005–09; Manchester Metropolitan Univ., 2009–14; Univ. of Brighton, 2014–; Vis. Prof., Central St Martins Coll. of Art and Design, 2003–; Vis. Lectr, RCA, 2016–18. *Publications:* (contrib.) Takeover, 2001; (contrib.) Reshaping Museum Space, 2005; (contrib.) The International Handbook of Museum Studies, 2015. *Recreation:* football. *Address:* Land Design Studio, 5 Spring Grove Road, Richmond TW10 6EH. *T:* (020) 8332 6699. *E:* peter@landdesignstudio.co.uk.

**HIGGINS, Phillip John;** Corporate Director (formerly Corporate Manager), Cardiff County Council, 1999–2006; *b* 9 May 1946; *s* of Eugene Oswald Higgins and Dorothy Mary Higgins; *m* 1969, Anne Elizabeth Watkin; one *s* two *d*. *Educ:* Stand Grammar Sch., Manchester; Coll. of Commerce, Manchester. IMTA 1972. Accountant, Halifax CBC, 1972–74; Sen. Accountant, West Yorks CC, 1974–76; Gp Accountant, 1976–80, Principal Asst, loans and investments, 1980–82, Principal Asst, technical, 1982–85, Gtr Manchester Council; Asst Co. Treas., S Glamorgan CC, 1985–88; Dir of Finance, Cardiff Bay Develt Corp., 1988–99. Treas., S Wales Magistrates' Courts Cttee, 1999–2006. *Recreations:* reading political history, the countryside. *Address:* Wisteria Cottage, Llantrithyd, Cowbridge, Vale of Glamorgan CF71 7UB. *T:* (01446) 781676.

**HIGGINS, Roisin Anne;** QC (Scot.) 2015; *b* Bellshill, 13 May 1972; *d* of Colin Kirk Higgins and Anne Marie Higgins; *m* 2018, Duncan James Batchelor; two *s*. *Educ:* Fernhill Sch., Rutherglen; St Aloysius' Coll., Glasgow; Univ. of Glasgow (LLB Hons; DipLP). Solicitor, 1995–99; an Advocate, 2000–15. Mem. Cttee, The Intellectual Property Lawyers' Orgn, 2011–. *Publications:* (jtly) Confidentiality: counselling, psychotherapy and the law in Scotland, 2001. *Recreations:* reading, family time, visiting the Hebrides. *Address:* Advocates Library, Parliament House, Parliament Square, Edinburgh EH1 1RF. *T:* (0131) 226 2881, *Fax:* (0131) 225 3642. *E:* roisin.higgins@axiomadvocates.com.

**HIGGINS, Dame Rosalyn,** GBE 2019 (DBE 1995); JSD; FBA 1995; QC 1986; a Judge, 1995–2009, and President, 2006–09, International Court of Justice; *b* 2 June 1937; *d* of Lewis Cohen and Fay Inberg; *m* 1961, Terence Langley Higgins (*see* Baron Higgins); one *s* one *d*. *Educ:* Burlington Grammar Sch., London; Girton Coll., Cambridge (Scholar; BA 1958, 1st Cl. Law Qualifying 1, 1st Cl. Triposs Pt II; 1st Cl. LLB 1959); Yale Law Sch., (JSD 1962). UK Intern, Office of Legal Affairs, UN, 1958; Commonwealth Fund Fellow, 1959; Vis. Fellow, Brookings Instn, Washington, DC, 1960; Jun. Fellow in Internat. Studies, LSE, 1961–63; Staff Specialist in Internat. Law, RIIA, 1963–74; Vis. Fellow, LSE, 1974–78; Professor of International Law: Univ. of Kent at Canterbury, 1978–81; LSE, London Univ., 1981–95. Gen. course, Hague Acad. of Internat. Law, 1991. Visiting Professor of International Law: Stanford Univ., 1975; Yale Univ., 1977. Bencher, Inner Temple, 1989. Mem., UN Cttee on Human Rights, 1984–95. Hague Lectures on Internat. Law, 1982. Internat. Legal Advr, Chilcot Inquiry, 2009–16. Pres., British Inst. of Internat. and Comparative Law, 2011–16; Vice Pres., Amer. Soc. of Internat. Law, 1972–74 (Certif. of Merit, 1971, 1995). Membre de l'Institut de Droit International, 1993 (Associé, 1987). Hon. doctorates include: Dr *hc* Univ. of Paris XI, 1980; Hon. LLD: LSE, 1995; Cambridge, 1996; Hon. DCL Oxford, 2002. Manley Hudson Medal, 1998; Balzan Prize, Internat. Balzan Foundn, 2007. Membre de l'Ordre des Palmes Académiques (France), 1988. *Publications:* The Development of International Law through the Political Organs of the United Nations, 1963; Conflict of Interests: international law in a divided world, 1965; The Administration of the United Kingdom Foreign Policy through the United Nations, 1966; (ed with James Fawcett) Law in Movement—essays in memory of John McMahon, 1974; UN Peacekeeping: documents and commentary: Vol. I, Middle East, 1969; Vol. II, Asia, 1971; Vol. III, Africa, 1980; Vol. IV, Europe, 1981; Problems and Process, 1994; Themes and Theories: selected essays, speeches and writings in international law, 2009; Oppenheim's International Law: the United Nations (2 vols), 2017; articles for law jls and jls of internat. relations. *Recreations:* golf, cooking, eating.

*See also* D. J. Campbell.

**HIGGINSON, Prof. Irene Julie,** OBE 2008; PhD; FRCP, FFPHM, FMedSci; Professor of Palliative Care and Policy, since 1996, Director, Cicely Saunders Institute, since 2010, and Vice Dean (Research), Florence Nightingale Faculty of Nursing, Midwifery and Palliative Care, King's College London; Scientific Director, Cicely Saunders International, since 2002; Honorary Consultant in Palliative Medicine: King's College London, since 1996; Guy's and St Thomas' Hospitals, since 2002; Lewisham Hospital, since 2004; *b* Lowton, Lancs, 25 Oct. 1958; *d* of William Leslie Higginson and Kathleen Lucille Higginson (née Rogers). *Educ:* Culcheth High Sch.; Univ. of Nottingham (BMedSci Hons 1980; BM BS 1982); Univ. of London (PhD 1992). MFPHM 1995, FFPHM 1997; FRCP 2005. Sen. Lectr, LSHTM, 1995–96, Dir, R&D and Consultant, Kensington, Chelsea and Westminster HA, 1995–96; Dir, Res., Educn and Quality, St Christopher's Hospice, London, 1996–2001; Dean, Grad. Studies, Guy's, King's and St Thomas' Sch. of Medicine, London, 2002–05. NIHR Sen. Investigator, 2009–. FMedSci 2013. *Publications:* (ed with J. Hanratty) Palliative Care in Terminal Illness, 1994; (ed with E. Bruera) Cachexia: anorexia in cancer patients, 1996; (ed with J. M. Addington-Hall) Palliative Care for Non-Cancer Patients, 2001; (ed jtly) Research Methods in Palliative Care, 2007; (ed jtly) Textbook of Palliative Medicine, 2009, 2nd edn 2014; over 600 papers in jls incl. Lancet, BMJ, Jl of AMA, PLOS Medicine, BMC Medicine, Palliative Medicine, Jl of Pain Symptom Mgt. *Address:* Cicely Saunders Institute of Palliative Care, Policy and Rehabilitation, King's College London, Bessemer Road, SE5 9PJ. *T:* (020) 7848 5516, *Fax:* (020) 7848 5517. *E:* irene.higginson@kcl.ac.uk. *Club:* Athenæum.

**HIGGINSON, Lucy Amanda;** equestrian writer and media consultant, since 2015; Founder and Owner, Lucy Higginson Ltd, since 2015; *b* 13 March 1970; *d* of late Keith Higginson and of Judith Britain; *m* 1999, Dr Alexis Warnes; one *s* one *d*. *Educ:* Manchester

High Sch. for Girls; Univ. of Durham (BA Hons). Dep. Ed., The Field, 1996–2002; Dep. Ed., 2002, Ed., 2002–14, Horse & Hound. Member: Selection Panel, British Horse Soc. Hall of Fame, 2005–; Adv. Panel, London Riding Club, 2015–. *Recreations:* riding across country, spaniel walking, fraternising with rowers (sometimes even in a boat), open water swimming. *Address:* Villiers House, Common Lane, Eton College, Windsor, Berks SL4 6EG. *E:* lucy@lucyhigginson.co.uk.

**HIGGS, Air Vice-Marshal Barry,** CBE 1981; Assistant Chief of Defence Staff (Overseas), 1985–87; *b* 22 Aug. 1934; *s* of late Percy Harold Higgs and of Ethel Eliza Higgs; *m* 1957, Sylvia May Wilks; two *s. Educ:* Finchley County Secondary Grammar Sch. Served with Nos 207, 115, 138, 49 and 51 Sqdns, 1955–70; sc 1968; Forward Policy (RAF), 1971–73; ndc 1974; Comd No 39 (PR) Sqdn, 1975–77; Asst Dir Defence Policy, 1978–79; Comd RAF Finningley, 1979–81; RCDS 1982; Dep. Dir of Intelligence, 1983–85. Dir Gen., Fertiliser Manufacturers Assoc., 1987–98. ARAgS 1998. Francis New Meml Medal, Internat. Fertiliser Soc., 1999. *Recreations:* boating, the outdoors, theatre. *Address:* 6 Renaissance Mews, Grove Road, Lymington SO41 3AH. *T:* 07899 891918. *Club:* Royal Air Force.

**HIGGS, Prof. Douglas Roland,** DSc; FRCP, FRCPath; FRS 2005; Professor of Haematology, since 1996, Director, MRC Molecular Haematology Unit, since 2001, and Director, MRC Weatherall Institute of Molecular Medicine, since 2012, University of Oxford; *b* 13 Jan. 1951. *Educ:* Alleyn's Sch.; King's Coll. London; King's Coll. Hosp. Med. Sch. (MB BS 1974); DSc London 1990. FRCP 1993; FRCPath 1994. SHO, 1975, Registrar in Haematol., 1976, King's Coll. Hosp., London; University of Oxford: MRC Trng Fellow, Nuffield Dept of Clinical Medicine, 1977–80; Scientific Officer (Clinical), MRC Molecular Haematol. Unit, 1980–2001; Hon. Consultant in Haematol., John Radcliffe Hosp., Oxford, 1985–. FMedSci 2001. *Address:* MRC Molecular Haematology Unit, MRC Weatherall Institute of Molecular Medicine, John Radcliffe Hospital, Headington, Oxford OX3 9DS.

**HIGGS, Jonathan Alexander Cameron;** QC 2011; a Recorder, since 2016; *b* Chelmsford, 23 Sept. 1963; *s* of Brian James Higgs, QC and of Jean Cameron Higgs (*née* DuMerton); *m* Caroline Sarah Darley Knight; two *s* two *d. Educ:* Downside; Chelmer Inst. of Higher Educn (BA Hons Law). Called to the Bar, Middle Temple, 1987. *Recreations:* tennis, watching birds. *Address:* 5 King's Bench Walk, EC4Y 7DN. *T:* (020) 7353 5638.

**HIGGS, Prof. Peter Ware,** CH 2013; PhD; FRS 1983; FRSE; Professor of Theoretical Physics, University of Edinburgh, 1980–96, now Emeritus; *b* 29 May 1929; *s* of Thomas Ware Higgs and Gertrude Maud (*née* Coghill); *m* 1963, Jo Ann (*d* 2008), *d* of Jo C. and Meryl Williamson, Urbana, Ill; two *s. Educ:* Cotham Grammar Sch., Bristol; King's Coll., Univ. of London (BSc, MSc; PhD 1954). FRSE 1974. Royal Commn for Exhibn of 1851 Sen. Student, KCL, 1953–54 and Univ. of Edinburgh, 1954–55; Sen. Res. Fellow, Univ. of Edinburgh, 1955–56; ICI Res. Fellow, UCL, 1956–57 and Imperial Coll., 1957–58; Lectr in Maths, UCL, 1958–60; Lectr in Mathematical Physics, 1960–70, and Reader in Math. Physics, 1970–80, Univ. of Edinburgh. FKC 1998. Hon. Fellow, Swansea Univ., 2008. Hon. FInstP 1998. Hon. DSc: Bristol, 1997; Edinburgh, 1998; Glasgow, 2002; KCL, 2009; UCL, 2010; Cambridge, 2012; Heriot-Watt, 2012; Durham, 2013; Manchester, 2013; St Andrews, 2014; Libre de Bruxelles, 2014; QUB, 2015; TCD, 2016. (Jtly) Hughes Medal, Royal Soc., 1981; (jtly) Rutherford Medal, 1984, Paul Dirac Medal, 1997, Inst. of Physics; James Scott Prize, 1993, Royal Medal, 2000, RSE; (jtly) High Energy Particle Physics Prize, Eur. Physical Soc., 1997; (jtly) Wolf Prize in Physics, 2004; Oskar Klein Medal, Swedish Royal Acad. of Scis, 2009; (jtly) Sakurai Prize, APS, 2010; Edinburgh Award, 2011; Nonino Prize, 2013; (jtly) Edinburgh Medal, 2013; (jtly) Nobel Prize in Physics, 2013; (jtly) Prince of Asturias Award, Fundación Príncipe de Asturias, 2013; Copley Medal, Royal Soc., 2015; Medal, Royal Commn for Exhibn of 1851, 2017; Carla Fendi Foundn Prize, 2018. *Publications:* papers on molecular vibrations and spectra, classical and quantum field theories, and on spontaneous breaking of gauge symmetries in theories of elementary particles. *Recreations:* walking, swimming, listening to music. *Address:* 2 Darnaway Street, Edinburgh EH3 6BG. *T:* (0131) 225 7060.

**HIGHAM, Catherine Mary;** *see* Ennis, C. M.

**HIGHAM, Prof. Charles Franklin Wandesforde,** ONZM 2016; PhD, ScD; FRSNZ; FRAS; FSA; FBA; Research Professor, University of Otago, New Zealand, since 2005 (Professor of Anthropology, 1968–2003; James Cook Fellow, 2003–05); *b* 19 Oct. 1939; *s* of Ernest Harry Hamilton Higham and Eileen Florence Emily Higham (*née* Woodhead); *m* 1964, Pauline Askew; two *s* two *d. Educ:* Raynes Park Co. Grammar Sch.; St Catharine's Coll., Cambridge (Rugby blue, 1961–62; BA, MA; PhD 1966; ScD 1991; Hon. Fellow, 2008). FSA 1984; FRAS 1986. Lectr in Prehist., Univ. of Otago, 1967–68. Vis. Prof., Univ. of London, 1978; Benians Fellow, St John's Coll., Cambridge, 1991–92; Vis. Scholar, St Catharine's Coll., Cambridge, 2003–08. Mortimer Wheeler Lectr, 1983, Reckitt Lectr, 2002, British Acad.; Golson Lectr, ANU, 2010; Keble Lectr, Oxford, 2010; McDonald Lectr, Univ. of Cambridge, 2011. FRSNZ 1992; Corresp. FBA 2000; Fellow, NZ Acad. of Humanities, 2009. Grahame Clark Medal, British Acad., 2012; Mason Durie Medal, Royal Soc. of NZ, 2014. Mem. editl bds various learned jls. *Publications:* The Archaeology of Mainland Southeast Asia, 1989; (with R. Bannanurag) The Excavation of Khok Phanom Di: Vol. I, The Excavation, Chronology and Human Burials, 1990; (ed with R. Bannanurag) The Excavation of Khok Phanom Di: Vol. II, The Biological Remains Part I, 1991; The Bronze Age of Southeast Asia, 1996; The Civilisation of Angkor, 2001; Early Cultures of Mainland Southeast Asia, 2002; The Encyclopaedia of Ancient Asian Civilizations, 2004; The Excavation of Khok Phanom Di: Vol. VII, Summary and Conclusions, 2004; (ed with A. Kijngan) The Origins of the Civilization of Angkor: Vol. II, The Excavation of Noen U-Loke and Non Muong Kao, 2007, Vol. III, The Excavation of Ban Non Wat: introduction, 2009, Vol. IV, The Neolithic Occupation, 2011, Vol. V, The Bronze Age, 2012, Vol. VI, The Iron Age: summary and conclusions, 2012; Early Thailand: from Prehistory to Sukhothai, 2012; The Origins of the Civilization of Angkor, 2013; Early Mainland Southeast Asia: from first humans to Angkor, 2014; edited with R. Thosarat: Khok Phanom Di: Vol. III: The Material Culture Part I, 1993; Khok Phanom Di: prehistoric adaptation to the world's richest habitat, 1994; The Excavation of Khok Phanom Di: Vol. IV, The Biological Remains, Part II, 1996; The Excavation of Nong Nor, a Prehistoric Site in Central Thailand, 1998; Prehistoric Thailand: from first settlement to Sukhothai, 1998; The Excavation of Khok Phanom Di: Vol. V, The People, 1999; The Excavation of Khok Phanom Di: Vol. VI, The Pottery, 2004; The Origins of the Civilization of Angkor: Vol. I, The Excavation of Ban Lum Khao, 2005. *Recreation:* classical guitar. *Address:* Department of Anthropology and Archaeology, PO Box 56, Dunedin, New Zealand. *T:* (3) 4798750; 1 Newbury Street, Company Bay, Dunedin, New Zealand. *T:* (3) 4761056. *Club:* Hawks (Cambridge).

**HIGHAM, Geoffrey Arthur;** Chairman, Rugby Group PLC, 1986–96 (Director, 1979–96); Director and Trustee, Building Centre Group, 1982–2001 (Chairman, 1984–88); *b* 17 April 1927; *s* of Arthur Higham and Elsie Higham (*née* Vickerman); *m* 1st, 1951, Audrey Hill (*d* 2006); one *s* one *d*; 2nd, 2007, Jenny Voice (*née* Cummins). *Educ:* King William's Coll., IOM; St Catharine's Coll., Cambridge (MA MechScis). Served RE, 1945–48. Metal Box Co., 1950–64; Montague Burton, 1964–65; Cape Industries, 1965–85: Man. Dir, 1971–80; Chm., 1980–85; Industrial Dir, Charter Consolidated, 1980–87; Director: Pirelli Gen., 1987–2006; Pirelli UK, 1997–2006; Travers Morgan, 1988–91; Try Gp, 1989–99; Vale Housing Assoc., 1998–2008; Sovereign Housing Assoc., 2007–10. Chm., BIM Foundn, 1981–83; Vice Chm., Council, BIM, 1984–88; Mem. Council, CBI, 1994–96; Mem. Council, 1978–88, Chm., 1980–82, UK S Africa Trade Assoc. Trustee, Mansfield Coll., Oxford, 1988–95. CCMI (CBIM 1975); FRSA 1989. *Recreations:* music, cricket, gardening. *Address:* 32 East St Helen Street, Abingdon, Oxfordshire OX14 5EB. *Clubs:* Army and Navy, Middlesex CC.
*See also* N. G. Higham.

**HIGHAM, Prof. Jennifer Mary,** MD; FRCP, FRCOG; Principal, St George's, University of London, since 2016; *b* Warrington, Cheshire, 5 July 1961; *d* of late Stanley Higham and of Margaret Higham (*née* Baldwin); *m* 1992, Ed Naylor; one *s* two *d. Educ:* Thorpe Grammar Sch.; University Coll. London (MB BS 1985; MD 1993). MRCOG 1992, FRCOG 2005; FRCP 2018. Sen. Registrar, St Mary's Hosp., 1995–96; Consultant Gynaecologist, Imperial Coll. Healthcare Trust, 1997–2015; Hd, Undergrad. Medicine, 2006–09, Vice Dean, Institutional Affairs, and Dir of Educn (formerly Dep. Principal), Faculty of Medicine, 2010–15, Imperial Coll. London. Sen. Vice Dean, Lee Kong Chian Sch. of Medicine, Singapore, 2013–15. Non-executive Director: W Middx Univ. Hosp. NHS Trust, 2009–15; St George's Univ. Hosps NHS Foundn Trust, 2016–. Medical Schools Council: Mem., 2010–14, Chm., 2014–16, Educn Sub-cttee; Mem., Assessment Board, 2014–; Chm., 2016–; Member: Bd, Health Educn NW London, 2013–15; Jt Bd, Brighton and Sussex Med. Sch., 2013–16; Bd, UCEA Clinical Staff Adv. Gp, 2013–16; Pres., and Chm., Strategy Bd, Health Scis Acad., 2014–15. Governor: Chelsea and Westminster Hosp., 2011–15; Kingston Univ., 2015–. Trustee: Imperial Coll. Trust, 2009–15; St Mary's Develt Trust, 2014–15. Calman Lect., Acad. of Med. Educators, 2017. FHEA 2002; FFSRH (FFFP 2005). Hon. FAcadMed, 2017. Hon. DMed Brighton and Sussex Med. Sch., 2018. Mentor of Year, Women of Future Awards, 2011; Pres. and Rector's Award for Outstanding Contribn to Teaching Excellence, Imperial Coll. London, 2013; Imperial Coll. Medal, 2014; Nanyang Educn Gold Award, 2015. *Publications:* contrib. res. papers on abnormal uterine bleeding, gynaecol., educn, use of simulation in educn and trng. *Recreations:* art, food, ski-ing. *Address:* Principal's Office, St George's, University of London, Cranmer Terrace, SW17 0RE. *E:* jhigham@sgul.ac.uk.

**HIGHAM, John Arthur,** QC 1992; Partner, 2004–15, Consultant, 2016–17, White & Case; *b* 11 Aug. 1952; *s* of late Frank Greenhouse Higham and of Muriel (*née* King); *m* 1st, 1982, Francesca Mary Antonietta Ronan (decd); one *s* two *d*; 2nd, 1988, Catherine Mary Ennis, *qv*; two *s* one *d. Educ:* Shrewsbury Sch.; Churchill Coll., Cambridge (scholar, MA, LLM). Called to the Bar, Lincoln's Inn, 1976; an Asst Recorder, Midland and Oxford Circuit, 1998–2000; Recorder, 2000–10; admitted solicitor and authorised as solicitor advocate, 1999; Consultant, 1999–2000, Partner, 2000–04, Stephenson Harwood. *Publications:* (ed jtly) Loose on Liquidators, 2nd edn 1981; (ed jtly) The Law and Practice of Corporate Administration, 1994, 2nd edn as Corporate Administrations and Rescue Procedures, 2005. *Recreations:* music, cricket, gardening. *T:* 07377 671597. *E:* johnhigham125@gmail.com.

**HIGHAM, Commander Michael Bernard Shepley,** CVO 1999; RN; Grand Secretary, United Grand Lodge of England, 1980–98; Secretary, Grand Charity, 1981–98; *b* 7 June 1936; *s* of late Anthony Richard Charles Higham, TD, FRCS and Mary Higham (*née* Shepley); *m* 1st, 1970, Caroline Verena Wells (marr. diss. 1996); one *s* one *d*; 2nd, 1997, Andrea Svedberg, *d* of late Elias Svedberg and Astrid Svedberg. *Educ:* Epsom Coll. Joined RN, 1954; served: HM Ships Triumph (twice), Eagle, Cavendish and Chichester; in offices of: C-in-C Portsmouth and C-in-C Plymouth; Flag Officers Plymouth, Scotland and NI; Adm. Comdg Reserves; on staff of C-in-C Fleet; retd RN, 1977. Called to the Bar, Middle Temple, 1968. Grand Secretary's Office, 1977–98, Dep. Grand Sec., 1978–80; Past Jun. Grand Warden, 1986–2005; Past Sen. Grand Warden, 2006. Mem., RNSA. Mem., Nankersey Male Choir. *Publications:* Freemasonry from Craft to tolerance, 1985. *Recreation:* sailing. *Address:* Oyster Shell, Restronguet Passage, Mylor, Falmouth, Cornwall TR11 5ST. *Club:* Royal Cornwall Yacht (Falmouth).

**HIGHAM, Nicholas Geoffrey, (Nick);** journalist and broadcaster; *b* 1 June 1954; *s* of Geoffrey Arthur Higham, *qv*; *m* 1981, Deborah Starling; one *s* one *d. Educ:* Bradfield Coll., Berks; St Catharine's Coll., Cambridge (BA Hons English 1975). Freelance journalist, 1978–88; correspondent, BBC News, 1988–2018 (media, 1988–91; arts and media, 1991–2003; BBC News 24, 2003–08); presenter, Meet the Author, 2009–16. Columnist, Marketing Week, 1990–2006. *Recreations:* theatre, armchair history. *T:* 07850 929588. *E:* highamnews@gmail.com.

**HIGHAM, Prof. Nicholas John,** PhD; FRS 2007; Richardson Professor of Applied Mathematics, since 1998, and Royal Society Research Professor, since 2018, University of Manchester; *b* Salford, 25 Dec. 1961; *s* of Kenneth Frederick Higham and Doris Higham (*née* Wilson); *m* 1998, Françoise Marie Louise Tisseur; two *s. Educ:* Univ. of Manchester (BSc Hons Maths 1982; MSc Numerical Analysis and Computing 1983; PhD Numerical Analysis 1985). University of Manchester: Lectr, 1985–89; Sen. Lectr, 1989–92; Reader, 1992–96; Prof. of Applied Maths, 1996–98. Vis. Asst Prof. of Computer Sci., Cornell Univ., 1988–89; Nuffield Foundn Sci. Res. Fellow, 1991–92; Royal Soc. Leverhulme Trust Sen. Res. Fellow, 1999–2000; Royal Soc. Wolfson Res. Fellow, Royal Soc., 2003–08. MAE 2016. Fellow, SIAM, 2009 (Pres., 2017–18). Alston S. Householder Award VI, 1987; Leslie Fox Prize, IMA, 1988; Jun. Whitehead Prize, 1999, Fröhlich Prize, 2008, LMS. *Publications:* Handbook of Writing for the Mathematical Sciences, 1993, 2nd edn 1998; Accuracy and Stability of Numerical Algorithms, 1996, 2nd edn 2002; (with D. J. Higham) MATLAB Guide, 2000, 3rd edn 2017; Functions of Matrices: theory and computation, 2008; (ed) Princeton Companion to Applied Mathematics, 2015; contrib. numerous scientific papers. *Recreations:* photography, playing keyboards, gardening. *Address:* School of Mathematics, University of Manchester, Manchester M13 9PL. *T:* (0161) 275 5822, *Fax:* (0161) 275 5819.

**HIGHFIELD, Ashley Gilroy Mark,** CEng; Chief Executive, Johnston Press plc, 2011–18; *b* 3 Oct. 1965; *s* of Roy Highfield and Sheila Highfield; one *d. Educ:* Elizabeth Coll., Guernsey; Royal Grammar Sch., High Wycombe; City Univ., London (BSc (Hons) Business Computing Systems). MBCS. Mgt Consultant, Coopers and Lybrand, 1988–94; Hd of IT and New Media, NBC Europe, 1994–95; Man. Dir, Flextech Interactive, Flextech Television, 1996–2000; Dir, Future (formerly New) Media and Technol., BBC, 2000–08; Chief Exec., Project Kangaroo, 2008; Man. Dir and Vice Pres., Consumer and Online, Microsoft UK, 2009–11. Non-executive Director, 1999–2000: Xrefer.com Ltd; Multimap.com Ltd; Improveline.com Ltd; WayAheadGroup (ticketing) Ltd; non-exec. Dir, William Hill plc, 2008–17; Chm., Oyster Yachts, 2018–. Gov., BFI, 2008–15. FRSA; FRTS. *Recreations:* motor racing, reading, architecture, music, film. *Clubs:* Soho House, Ivy.

**HIGHFIELD, Dr Roger Ronald,** FRSB; Science Director, Science Museum Group, since 2019; *b* Griffithstown, Wales, July 1958; *s* of Ronald and Dorothea Highfield; *m* 1992, Julia Brookes; one *s* one *d. Educ:* Chase Side Primary Sch., Enfield; Christ's Hosp., Horsham; Pembroke Coll., Oxford (Domus Schol.; MA Chem. 1980); DPhil Oxon 1983. FRSB (FIBiol 2004). Clin. reporter, Pulse mag. for GPs, 1983–84; news ed., Nuclear Engrg Internat., 1984–86; Technol. Corresp., 1986, Technol. Ed., 1987–88, Sci. Ed., 1988–2008,

Columnist, 2009–15, Daily Telegraph; Ed., New Scientist, 2008–11; Dir, External Affairs, Nat. Mus. of Sci. and Industry, subseq. Sci. Mus. Gp, 2011–19. Visiting Sabbatical Fellow: Queen Elizabeth Hse, Oxford Univ., 1989; Balliol Coll., Oxford, 1994; Visiting Professor of Public Engagement: Dunn Sch., Univ. of Oxford, 2018–; Dept of Chem., UCL. Mem., UKRI-MRC, 2018–. Former contributor to Economist, Guardian, New Scientist, Sunday Times, Observer; sci. ed., Esquire, 1996–98; contrib. High Life, Spectator, Condé Nast Traveller and Science, Wired UK, Newsweek. Contrib. BBC radio, incl. Scope, Acid Test, Sci. Now, Leading Edge and Museum of Curiosity, Infinite Monkey Cage. Member: Communications and Public Engagement Cttee, RAEng; Health Protection and Society Adv. Gp, HPA; Bioscis Futures Forum; Sci. and Media Expert Gp, BIS; Adv. Cttee, Sci. Mus.; Sci. Policy Adv. Gp, Royal Soc., 2013–16; Editl Adv. Gp, Mosaic, 2014–; Longitude Prize Cttee, 2014–; Editl Bd, Chemistry World, RSC, 2015–. Judge: BBC Samuel Johnson Prize for Non-Fiction, 2010; British Press Awards, 2013, 2014, 2015, 2016, 2017; Scientific Breakthrough Award, Wired, 2016; Royal Soc. Insight Investment Sci. Book Prize, 2016; Eur. Inventor Award, 2017–. Curator, TEDxLondon, 2016; Guest Curator, Wired Live, 2017, 2018. Hon. Fellow, BAAS. Science Writers' Award, Assoc. of British Sci. Writers, 1987, 1995, 1997, 1998; Specialist Writer of the Year, British Press Awards, 1988; Medical Journalism Award for consumer news, 1998; Tony Thistlethwaite Award, MJA, 2007; Wilkins-Bernal-Medawar Medal, Royal Soc., 2012. *Publications:* The Arrow of Time: the quest to solve time's greatest mystery, 1990; The Private Lives of Albert Einstein, 1993; Frontiers of Complexity: the search for order in a chaotic world, 1995; Can Reindeer Fly?: the science of Christmas, 1998; The Science of Harry Potter: how magic really works, 2002; After Dolly: the uses and misuses of human cloning, 2006; (ed) A Life Decoded, by Craig Venter, 2007; Supercooperators: the mathematics of evolution, altruism and human behaviour (or, why we need each other to succeed), 2011; (ed) Life at the Speed of Light, by Craig Venter, 2013; The Dance of Life: symmetry, cells and how we became human, 2019. *Recreations:* Twitter (@RogerHighfield), cooking, drinking, dining. *Address:* Science Museum, Exhibition Road, SW7 2DD. *W:* www.rogerhighfield.com.

**HIGHT, David William,** PhD; FRS 2016; FREng, FICE; Senior Consultant, Geotechnical Consulting Group, since 2008 (Founding Director, 1983–2008); *b* Maidenhead, 17 Aug. 1943; *s* of John Hight and Florence Hight; *m* 1st, 1966, Susan Morgan (*d* 2003); one *s* one *d*; 2nd, 2009, Deborah Jane Vaughan (*d* 2017). *Educ:* Maidenhead Grammar Sch.; Imperial Coll. of Sci., Technol. and Medicine, London (DIC 1965; MSc 1971; PhD 1983). Civil Engr, Scott Wilson Kirkpatrick and Partners, 1965–73; Res. Asst, 1973–78, Lectr, 1978–83, Imperial Coll. London. Visiting Professor: MIT, 1983; Imperial Coll. London, 1993–2012; Dist. Vis. Prof., NUS, Singapore, 2000. FICE 1997; FREng 2001. *Publications:* Characterisation and Engineering Properties of Natural Soils, vols 1 and 2, 2003, vols 3 and 4, 2007; Engineering in the Lambeth Group, 2004. *Recreations:* theatre, sport, music, horticulture. *Address:* Windrush, East Williamston, Tenby, Dyfed SA70 8RU. *T:* (01834) 814070. *E:* d.w.hight75@gmail.com.

**HIGHTON, David Peter;** Chair, Maidstone and Tunbridge Wells NHS Trust, since 2017; *b* 22 May 1954; *s* of Allan Peter Highton and May Comrie Highton (née Doughty); *m* 2005, Wendy Ann Attree; one *d*. *Educ:* Borden Grammar Sch., Sittingbourne; Univ. of Bristol (BSc Hons Econs 1975). ACA 1978, FCA 1989. Chartered Accountant, Turquands Barton Mayhew, 1975–79; Financial Accountant, Tunnel Avebe Starches Ltd, 1979–81; Financial Controller: R. P. Martin plc, 1981–83; Grand Metropolitan Brewing, 1983–87; Regl Finance Dir, Prudential Property Services, 1987–90; Dir of Finance and Chief Exec., Ealing HA, 1990–92; Dir of Finance, Riverside Hosps, 1992–94; Chief Executive: Chelsea and Westminster Hosp., 1994–2000; Oxford Radcliffe Hosps NHS Trust, 2000–03; Managing Director: Hyperium Consulting, 2003–11; Clinicenta Ltd (formerly Patient Choice Partners), 2003–10; Exec. Dir, Corporate Develt, Hamad Med. Corp., Qatar, 2011–17; Ministerial Advr on Private Sector Involvement and Public Private Partnership to Minister of Public Health, Qatar, 2016–17. Non-exec. Chm., Sussex Health Care Audiology, 2011–18; non-exec. Director: Healthwork UK, 2000–05 (Chm., 2001–05); Skills for Health, 2007–11 (Chm., 2002–03); Clearview Healthcare, Delhi, 2010–14; Chair, Demelza Hospices, 2018–. Health Advr, Servita Ltd, 2018–. Trustee, NHS Confedn, 2009–10. *Publications:* contribs to health mgt jls. *Recreations:* Rugby, books, films, good food. *Address:* Maidstone and Tunbridge Wells NHS Trust, c/o Maidstone Hospital, Hermitage Lane, Maidstone, Kent ME16 9QQ. *Clubs:* Sittingbourne Rugby (Pres., 2000–09; Vice-Pres., 2009–), Imperial Medicals Rugby (Vice Pres.).

**HIGNELL, Alastair James,** CBE 2009; Rugby Union football player and cricketer, retired; Rugby commentator, BBC Radio Live, 1996–2008; *b* Cambridge, 4 Sept. 1955; *s* of Anthony and Patricia Hignell; *m* 1980, Jeannie Hobart; two *s*. *Educ:* Denstone Coll.; Fitzwilliam Coll., Cambridge (BA 1978; PGCE). Player: Glos CCC, 1974–83; England Rugby, 1975–79. Teacher of History: Bristol Cathedral Sch., 1978–83; Sherborne Sch., 1983–85; commentator: BBC Radio, 1985–89; ITV West, 1989–96. Patron, MS-UK, 2002–11; Trustee, Leonard Cheshire Disability, 2012–. Hon. MA Bristol, 2004. Helen Rollason Award, BBC Sports Awards, 2008. *Publications:* Higgy: matches, microphones and MS, 2011. *Recreations:* family, sport, theatre, history, travel, art, singing. *E:* alastairhignell@btconnect.com. *W:* www.alastairhignell.com. *Clubs:* Hawks; England Rugby Internationals, Cambridge University Rugby Union Football; Gloucestershire CC, Rugby Union Writers, Lord's Taverners.

**HII, Sir Yii Ann,** KBE 2012 (Hon. KBE 2007); Group Chairman, Investwell Group of Companies, since 1993 (Chief Executive Officer, 1993); *b* Sarawak, Malaysia, 30 Jan. 1960; *s* of Hii Ka Kai and Sia Kiu Leng; *m* 1986, Dr Soo Hian Beh; two *s* four *d*. *Educ:* Deakin Univ., Australia (BSc Hons Civil Engrg 1983). Founder, Investwell Gp of Cos, 1993. *Address:* (office) 101 Cecil Street, #20–06, Tong Eng Building, Singapore 069533. *T:* 63241955, *Fax:* 63241966. *E:* mcompany@singnet.com.sg.

**HILAIRE, Dr Ernest;** Member (Lab) Castries South, House of Assembly, St Lucia, since 2016; Chairman, Citizenship by Investment Programme, 2015. *Educ:* Univ. of West Indies (BSc 1st Cl. Hons Political Sci. and Sociol. (Double Major) 1993); Darwin Coll., Cambridge (MPhil Internat. Relns 1996); London Sch. of Econs and Pol Sci. (PhD Internat. Relns 2005); McKinsey Faculty (Mini MBA 2007); Univ. of Notre Dame (Exec. Cert. Negotiations and Conflict Mgt 2009). CEO, Cricket World Cup, St Lucia Inc., 2005–07; Associate, McKinsey and Co., 2007–08; Tournament Dir, ICC WT20 WI 2010, 2008–09; CEO, WI Cricket Bd, 2009–12; High Comr for St Lucia in UK, 2012–15. Chm., Citizenship by Investment Prog., 2015. Chair: Sports St Lucia Inc.; Nat. Skills Develt Centre.

**HILARY, John Jephson;** Head of Trade Policy, Labour Party, 2017–18; *b* London, 11 Aug. 1964; *s* of David and Phoebe Hilary; *m* 1995, Janet Wood. *Educ:* Corpus Christi Coll., Cambridge (BA Hons Classics 1986); Sch. of Oriental and African Studies, Univ. of London (MA Chinese Politics 1992). Campaigns Officer, Amnesty Internat., 1989–91; Sub-Ed., BBC World Service, 1993–94; Ed., VSO, 1994–97; freelance trade policy consultant, 1997–2001; Trade Policy Advr, Save the Children, 2001–03; Dir of Campaigns and Policy, 2004–08, Exec. Dir, 2008–16, War on Want. Hon. Prof., Sch. of Politics and Internat. Relns, Univ. of Nottingham, 2013–. *Publications:* The Poverty of Capitalism, 2013; (ed) Free Trade and Transnational Labour, 2014. *Recreations:* cricket, birdwatching, classical music, modern art.

**HILBORN, Rev. Dr David Henry Kyte;** Principal, Moorlands College, since 2019; *b* 4 Jan. 1964; *s* of Edwin Henry and Constance May Hilborn; *m* 1988, Mia Alison Kyte (*see* Rev. M. A. K. Hilborn); one *s* one *d*. *Educ:* Langley Park Sch. for Boys; Nottingham Univ. (BA English; PhD Theol. and English); Mansfield Coll., Oxford (MA Theol.). Ordinand, Mansfield Coll., Oxford, 1985–89; Minister, Keyworth URC, 1989–92; research and teaching, Nottingham Univ., 1992–94; Minister: City Temple URC, 1994–99 (Jt Minister, 1997–99); Queen's Park URC, 2000–02; Theol Advr, then Head of Theology, Evangelical Alliance (UK), 1997–2006; ordained deacon and priest, C of E, 2002; Curate, St Mary's, Acton, 2002–06; Dir of Studies, 2006, Dir, N Thames Ministerial Trng Course, and Asst Dean, 2007–12, St Mellitus Coll.; Principal, St John's Coll., Nottingham, 2012–18. SFHEA 2018. *Publications:* Picking Up the Pieces: can Evangelicals adapt to contemporary culture?, 1997; (ed) Faith, Hope and Homosexuality, 1998; (ed) The Nature of Hell, 2000; (jtly) One Body in Christ: the history and significance of the Evangelical Alliance, 2001; (ed) 'Toronto' in Perspective, 2001; (ed) God and the Generations, 2002; (contrib.) Evangelicalism and the Orthodox Church, 2002; (contrib.) Faith, Health and Prosperity, 2003; (ed) Movement for Change: evangelicals and social transformation, 2004; (ed) The Atonement Debate, 2008; articles in theological books and jls. *Recreations:* cricket, poetry, classic rock and pop. *Address:* Moorlands College, Sopley, Christchurch, Dorset BH23 7AT. *T:* (01425) 460714.

**HILBORN, Rev. Mia Alison Kyte;** Hospitaller, Head of Spiritual Health Care and Chaplaincy Team Leader, Guy's and St Thomas' Hospital NHS Foundation Trust (formerly NHS Trust), since 2001; *b* 7 March 1963; *d* of late Harry Stephen Broadbelt and Jean Margaret Broadbelt; *m* 1988, Rev. David Henry Kyte Hilborn, *qv*; one *s* one *d*. *Educ:* City Univ. (BSc (Hons) Econs and Psychol.); Mansfield Coll., Oxford (MA Theol.); Univ. of London (MA Psychol. of Religion). Ordination, URC, 1989; Minister, Friary URC, West Bridgford, Nottingham, 1989–94; City Temple URC, 1994–2000, Jt Minister, 1997–99; Free Church Chaplain, St Bart's Hosp., and Children's Chaplain, Bart's and The London NHS Trust, 1997–2001; Associate Minister, Queen's Park URC, 2000–02; ordained deacon, and priest, C of E, 2002; Hon. Asst Curate, N Lambeth Parish, 2002–09; Permission to Officiate, Stepney Area, London Dio., 2009–12; Asst Priest, St Paul's and St Mark's, Old Ford, 2009–12; Hon. Asst Priest, St Anne and All Saints, S Lambeth, 2017–. Franciscan tertiary, 2010. Senior Brigade Chaplain (formerly Hd of Chaplaincy), London Fire Brigade, 2005–; Hd of Chaplaincy, London Fire and Emergency Planning Authy, 2005–18; Chaplain and Trustee, Firefighters Meml Trust, 2015– (Sub-chaplain, 2013–15); Chair, Chaplaincy Leadership Forum and Exec., 2013–16. Governor: Evelina Hosp. Sch., 2005–14 (Chair, 2013–14); Guy's and St Thomas' NHS Foundn Trust, 2010–13. Trustee, Cecily Northcote Trust, 2015–17. *Recreations:* reading, theatres, studying theology, bioethics. *Address:* The Chaplaincy, St Thomas' Hospital, Westminster Bridge Road, SE1 7EH.

**HILBORNE, Stephanie Vera,** OBE 2010; Chief Executive, Women in Sport, since 2019; *b* 3 March 1968; *d* of Derek Vance Hilborne and Mary Elizabeth Hilborne (née Drewett); one *s* one *d*. *Educ:* Lady Eleanor Holles Sch.; Bristol Univ. (BSc 1st Cl. Hons Biol.); University Coll. London (MSc Conservation 1993). Principal Officer, Wildlife and Countryside Link, 1994–97; Asst CEO, 1998–2000, CEO, 2000–04, Notts Wildlife Trust; Chief Exec., The Wildlife Trusts, 2004–19. FRSA 1996. Hon. DSc Bristol, 2015. *Recreations:* walking/rambling, swimming, badminton. *Address:* Women in Sport, House of Sport, 4th Floor, 190 Great Dover Street, SE1 4YB.

**HILDEBRAND, Peter;** Regional Employment Judge, London South, 2008–19; an Employment Judge, 2019; *b* Lurgan, Co. Armagh, 28 June 1954; *s* of William Robert Perry Hildebrand and Olive Hildebrand; *m* 1980, Ann Purdon; one *s* two *d*. *Educ:* Campbell Coll., Belfast; Pembroke Coll., Cambridge (BA 1975). Admitted solicitor, 1978; Sacker and Partners, 1976–81, 1982–86; Stephenson Harwood, 1981–82; Burd Pearse, Exeter, 1986–97; Fee Paid Chm., Exeter, 1993–97, Salaried Chm., Leeds, 1997–2008, Employment Tribunal. *Recreations:* various. *Address:* Regional Office of Employment Tribunal, Victory House, 30–34 Kingsway, WC2B 6EX. *Club:* Reform.

**HILDER, Carolyn Hayley Jane; Her Honour Judge Hilder;** a Circuit Judge, since 2017; Senior Judge, Court of Protection, since 2017; *b* Shipston-on-Stour, 8 July 1969; *d* of Duncan Hilder and Denise Hilder; *m* 1997, Stuart Jarvis; two *d*. *Educ:* Oswestry Sch.; Trinity Hall, Cambridge (BA 1990); Queen Mary and Westfield Coll., Univ. of London (PhD 2010). Called to the Bar, Lincoln's Inn, 1991; a District Judge, 2010–17. *Address:* Court of Protection, First Avenue House, PO Box 70185, High Holborn, WC1A 9JA.

**HILDITCH, David William;** Member (DemU) Antrim East, Northern Ireland Assembly, since 1998; *b* 23 July 1963; two *s*. *Educ:* Carrickfergus Grammar Sch. Carrickfergus Borough Council: Mem. (DemU), 1991–2013; Dep. Mayor, 1994–96; Mayor, 1997–98. *Address:* East Antrim Democratic Unionist Party, 2 Joymount, Carrickfergus, Co. Antrim BT38 7DN. *T:* (028) 9332 9980.

**HILDRETH, (Henry) Jan (Hamilton Crossley);** independent consultant; Chairman: South West London and St George's Mental Health (formerly Pathfinder) NHS Trust, 1994–2004; High Performance Sports Ltd, 1995–2011; *b* 1 Dec. 1932; *s* of Maj.-Gen. Sir (Harold) John (Crossley) Hildreth, KBE, and late Mrs Joan Elise Hallett (née Hamilton); *m* 1958, Wendy Moira Marjorie, *d* of late Arthur Harold Clough, CMG, OBE and Marjorie Violet Clough; two *s* one *d*. *Educ:* Wellington Coll.; The Queen's Coll., Oxford (Hon. Mods (Nat. Sci.), BA PPE 1956, MA). National Service in RA, BAOR, 1952–53; 44 Parachute Bde (TA), 1953–58. Baltic Exchange, 1956; Royal Dutch Shell Group, 1957: served Philippines (marketing) and London (finance); Kleinwort, Benson Ltd, 1963; NEDO, 1965; Member of Economic Development Cttees for the Clothing, the Hosiery and Knitwear, and the Wool Textile industries; Mem., London Transport Bd, subseq. LTE, 1968–72: main responsibilities Finance, Marketing, Corp. Plan, Data Processing, and Estates; Asst Chief Exec., John Laing & Son Ltd, 1972–74; Dir-Gen., Inst. of Directors, 1975–78. Director: Minster Trust Ltd, 1979–94; Monument Oil and Gas plc, 1984–88; non-exec. dir of several cos, 1983–96; Chairman: Carroll Securities Ltd, 1986–91; Sea Catch PLC, 1987–94; Scallop Kings PLC, 1987–97. Member: Cttee, GBA, 1978–86 and 1997–2000; Council, ISIS, 1979–82; Exec. Cttee, Industrial Soc., 1973–84 (Hon. Life Mem., 1984); Council, British Exec. Service Overseas, 1975–91; Council, SCOPE (formerly Spastic Soc.), 1980–83, 1985 (Chm. Audit Cttee, 1990–92; Hon. Treas., 1992–97); Review Body for Nursing and Midwifery Staff and Professions Allied to Medicine, 1989–95; Council, St George's Hosp. Med. Sch., 1995–2002; Dir, Contact A Family, 1980–89. Constituency Chm., 1986–89, Pres., 1989–92, Wimbledon Cons. Assoc. Governor: Wellington Coll., 1974–2003; Eagle House Sch., 1986–2003. FCILT. FRSA. *Recreations:* cross-country, mountain and road running (London Marathon, 1981–2005), photography, water mills, and others. *Address:* 50 Ridgway Place, Wimbledon, SW19 4SW. *Clubs:* Athenæum; Vincent's (Oxford); Thames Hare and Hounds.

**HILDRETH, Paul Adrian;** UK and international advisor on cities, regions and local economies, since 2005; *b* London, 4 Feb. 1952; *s* of Cyril Leyland and Joan Hildreth; *m* 1987, Victoria Anne Gauld; two *s*. *Educ:* Nobel Grammar Sch., Stevenage; Aberystwyth Univ. (BScEcon Econs 1974; MScEcon 1977); Birmingham Univ. (MSc Public Service Mgt 2006). Greater London Council: Asst Trng Officer, 1976–78; Trng Officer, 1978–79; Career Develt Officer, 1979–81; London Transport Finance, 1981; Policy Asst to Chm., Industry and Employment Cttee, 1981–83; Actg Hd, Inner City Policy, 1983–85; Chief Asst (Housing and Social Services), City of Westminster, 1985–88; London Borough of Croydon: Asst Bor. Sec., 1988–92; Hd, Econ. Prog., 1992–98; Hd, Econ. and Strategic Develt, 1998–2003; on secondment as Policy Advr, ODPM, 2003–05. Vis. Policy Fellow, Centre for Sustainable Urban Futures, Univ. of Salford, 2005–16. Non-exec. Dir, Cambridge Econometrics, 2008–. Associate, Centre for London, 2013–. Member: Expert Panel on Cities and Regl Policy, DCLG, 2005–09; Panel for Architecture, Built Envmt and Planning, REF 2014, 2011–14; Bd, Regl Studies Assoc., 2012–19 (Chm., Policy Cttee, 2015–19). Expert assignments, Council of Europe, 2008–. Enabler, CABE, 2009–12. MCIPD 1981; Mem., Instn of Econ. Develt, 1999. Fellow, Regl Studies Assoc., 2014–. *Publications:* contrib. papers to peer-reviewed jls on sub.-nat. econ. policy, cities and governance. *Recreations:* mountain hiking, ski-ing, tennis, member of St Mary's Church, Reigate. *Address:* 1 Belmont Road, Reigate, Surrey RH2 7ED. *T:* (01737) 223252. *E:* pahildreth@yahoo.com.

**HILDYARD, Marianna Catherine Thoroton, (Lady Falconer of Thoroton);** QC 2002; **Her Honour Judge Hildyard;** a Circuit Judge, since 2012; *b* 24 Nov. 1955; *d* of Sir David Hildyard, KCMG, DFC and Millicent Hildyard, *d* of Sir Edward Baron; *m* 1985, Charles Leslie Falconer (*see* Baron Falconer of Thoroton); three *s* one *d*. *Educ:* Council of Legal Educn. Called to the Bar, Inner Temple, 1977, Bencher, 2009. Asst Recorder, 1999; Recorder, 1999–2012; a Dep. High Court Judge, 2009–12. Mem. Bd, Bar Services Bd. Chm., Deborah Hutton Campaign; Ambassador, Nat. Aids Trust. *Recreations:* gardening, my children. *Address:* Luton County Court, 2nd Floor, Cresta House, Alma Street, Luton, Beds LU1 2PU.

*See also* Hon. Sir R. H. T. Hildyard.

**HILDYARD, Hon. Sir Robert Henry Thoroton,** Kt 2011; **Hon. Mr Justice Hildyard;** DL; a Judge of the High Court of Justice, Chancery Division, since 2011; *b* 10 Oct. 1952; *s* of Sir David (Henry Thoroton) Hildyard, KCMG, DFC and Millicent Hildyard, *d* of Sir Edward Baron; *m* 1980, Isabella Jane Rennie (marr. diss. 2010); two *d* (and one *d* decd); *m* 2012, Lucy Gibson; one *d*. *Educ:* Eton Coll.; Christ Church, Oxford (BA Hons Hist.). Called to the Bar, Inner Temple, 1977; Bencher, Lincoln's Inn, 2005. Jun. Counsel to Crown (Chancery), 1992–94; QC 1994; a Deputy High Court Judge, 2002–11; Attorney Gen., Duchy of Lancaster, 2006–11. Mem., Financial Reporting Review Panel, 2002–08. Mem., Adv. Council, Attingham Trust, 2011–. DL Notts 2014. *Address:* Royal Courts of Justice, 7 Rolls Building, Fetter Lane, EC4A 1NL. *Club:* Garrick.

*See also* M. C. T. Hildyard.

**HILHORST, Rosemary,** OBE 2003; Director, Pakistan, British Council, since 2016; *b* 10 April 1954; *d* of late Raymond Bowditch and of June Ebdon; *m* 1981, Francis Hilhorst; one *s* one *d*. *Educ:* UCL (BSc Hons (Physics) 1975); Chelsea Coll. Centre for Sci. Educn, London (PGCE (Integrated Sci.) 1976); London Business Sch. (Sen. Exec. Prog. 2003). Sci. teacher and hd of sci. depts, Sussex, Dorset, Italy and Tanzania, 1976–85; British Council, 1985–: Asst Dir, Sudan, 1986–89; mgt posts, HQ, London, 1989–91, and 1994–97; Director: Slovakia, 1991–94; Tanzania, 1997–2000; Central and E Europe, 2000–01; Connecting Futures, 2002–03; Director: Portugal, 2003–08; Russia, 2008–11; Regional Dir, EU, 2011–15; Dir, Shakespeare Lives, 2015–16. Member: Exec. Cttee, Tanzania Br., Britain-Tanzania Assoc., 1997–2000; Selection Cttee, Tanzania Bd, 1997–2000, Portuguese Bd, 2003–08, United World Colls; Governing Body, British Assoc. for Central and Eastern Europe, 2000–02. *Recreations:* gardening, running, family.

**HILL;** *see* Clegg-Hill, family name of Viscount Hill.

**HILL;** *see* Erskine-Hill.

**HILL,** family name of **Marquess of Downshire** and **Baron Hill of Oareford**.

**HILL, 9th Viscount** *cr* 1842; **Peter David Raymond Charles Clegg-Hill;** Bt 1727; Baron Hill 1814; *b* 17 Oct. 1945; *s* of Major Hon. Frederick Raymond Clegg-Hill, 2nd *s* of 6th Viscount and Alice Dorothy (*née* Chapman); *S* cousin, 2003; *m* 1973, Sharon Ruth Deane, NZ (marr. diss. 2000; she changed her name to Savanna Dawson; they re-married 2002); one *s* five *d* (and one *s* decd, Paul Andrew Raymond Clegg-Hill, *b* 1979, *d* 2003). *Heir: s* Hon. Michael Charles David Clegg-Hill [*b* 29 Feb. 1988; *m* 2010, Stephanie Riley; two *d*]. *E:* Moyadrift@yahoo.co.uk.

**HILL OF OAREFORD,** Baron *cr* 2010 (Life Peer), of Oareford in the County of Somerset; **Jonathan Hopkin Hill,** CBE 1995; PC 2013; Independent National Director, Times Newspapers, since 2017; Senior Adviser: Freshfields Bruckhaus Deringer, since 2017; UBS, since 2018; Deloitte, since 2018; Institution of Civil Engineers, since 2018; Aviva, since 2018; Member, European Commission, 2014–16; *b* 24 July 1960; *s* of Rowland Louis Hill and Paddy Marguerite (*née* Henwood); *m* 1988, Alexandra Jane Nettelfield; one *s* two *d*. *Educ:* Highgate Sch.; Trinity Coll., Cambridge (MA). RIT & Northern, 1983; Hamish Hamilton, 1984–85; Conservative Research Dept, 1985–86; Special Advr to Rt Hon. Kenneth Clarke at Dept of Employment, DTI and DoH, 1986–89; Lowe Bell Communications, 1989–91; No 10 Policy Unit, 1991–92; Political Sec. to Prime Minister, 1992–94; Sen. Consultant, Bell Pottinger Consultants, 1994–98; Founding Dir, Quiller Consultants, 1998–2010; Parly Under-Sec. of State for Educn, 2010–13; Leader of the H of L and Chancellor of the Duchy of Lancaster, 2013–14. Chm., Ditchley Foundn, 2017–; Mem. Bd, Centre for Policy Studies, 2017–; Trustee: Nat. Literacy Trust, 1995–2009; Teach First, 2017–; Mem. Adv. Bd, Reform, 2004–10. Governor: Highgate Sch., 1995–2010; Hanford Sch., 2004–10. *Publications:* (with Baroness Hogg) Too Close to Call, 1995. *Recreations:* reading, gardening, walking on Exmoor. *Address:* House of Lords, SW1A 0PW.

**HILL, Prof. Adrian Vivian Sinton,** DPhil, DM; FRCP; FMedSci; Director, The Jenner Institute, since 2005, and Professor of Human Genetics, since 1996, University of Oxford; Fellow, Magdalen College, Oxford, since 2004; *b* 9 Oct. 1958; *s* of late Fergus Hill and of Helen (*née* O'Donovan); *m* 1994, Sunetra Gupta, *qv*; two *d*. *Educ:* Belvedere Coll., Dublin; Trinity Coll., Dublin (Foundn Scholar; Hon. Fellow, 2008); Magdalen Coll. and Lincoln Coll., Oxford (BA 1979; BM BCh 1982; MA 1982; DPhil 1986; DM 1993). FRCP 1999. University of Oxford: Research Fellow: Exeter Coll., 1983–86, 1994–99; St John's Coll., 1988–90; Balliol Coll., 1990–93; Wellcome Trust Principal Res. Fellow, Wellcome Trust Centre for Human Genetics, 1995–2010; Chm., Centre for Clinical Vaccinology and Tropical Medicine, 2005–. Hon. Consultant Physician, Oxford Radcliffe Hosps, 1993–. FMedSci 1999. *Publications:* research papers on human genetics, vaccines and infectious diseases, esp. malaria. *Recreations:* music, travel. *Address:* The Jenner Institute, Roosevelt Drive, Oxford OX3 7DQ. *T:* (01865) 617610. *E:* adrian.hill@ndm.ox.ac.uk.

**HILL, Alastair Malcolm,** OBE 2000; QC 1982; *b* 12 May 1936; *s* of Prof. Sir Ian George Wilson Hill, CBE, LLD, FRCP, FRSE and Lady (Audrey) Hill; *m* 1969, Elizabeth Maria Innes; one *s* one *d*. *Educ:* Trinity Coll., Glenalmond; Keble Coll., Oxford (Stevenson-Chatterton Schol.; BA Hons Jurisp. 1959). Nat. Service, RHA, 1954–56. Called to the Bar, Gray's Inn, 1961; South Eastern Circuit; a Recorder, 1982. Former Trustee, Disability Law Service. *Recreations:* collecting prints and watercolours, opera, fly-fishing.

**HILL, Allen;** *see* Hill, H. A. O.

**HILL, Andrea;** Chief Executive, Suffolk County Council, 2008–11; *b* 12 Feb. 1964; *d* of Michael and Sheila Large; *m* 1984, Phil Hill (marr. diss. 2012); three *s*. *Educ:* N London Poly. (BA 1st Cl. Hons Modern Studies); Univ. of Birmingham (MBA Public Sector). Thurrock Borough Council: Policy Performance Rev. Officer, 1985–87; Principal Asst, 1987–90; Hd of Strategy Planning, 1990–94; Asst Chief Exec., Cambridge CC, 1994–99; Dir of Policy and Community, 1999–2000, Dep. Chief Exec., 2000–01, N Herts DC; Chief Executive: Colchester BC, 2001–04; Bedfordshire CC, 2004–08. Dir, Customer Service Direct, 2008–11. Mem. Bd, Living East, Regl Cultural Consortium for E of England, 2002–07. Non-exec. Dir, Univ. Campus Suffolk, 2008–11. Dir, DanceEast, 2010–11. Trustee, Ipswich Town Charitable (formerly Community) Trust, 2008–11. *Recreations:* marathon running, ski-ing, sailing, windsurfing.

**HILL, Prof. (Anthony) Edward,** OBE 2010; PhD; Executive Director, National Oceanography Centre, since 2010 (Director, 2005–10); Professor of Oceanography, University of Southampton, since 2007; *b* 30 Dec. 1959; *s* of Antony Sidney Hill and Philomena Hill (*née* Ward); *m* 1989, Jacqueline Patricia Caukwell; two *s*. *Educ:* Bishop Wulstan RC High Sch., Rugby; Univ. of Sheffield (BSc (Applied Maths) 1st class 1981); UCNW, Bangor (MSc 1983; PhD (Physical Oceanography) 1987). Lectr in Oceanography, 1986–95, Sen. Lectr, 1995–99, UCNW, Bangor, subseq. Univ. of Wales, Bangor; Dir, Proudman Oceanographic Lab., NERC, 1999–2005. Hon. Vis. Prof., Univ. of Liverpool, 1999–2004; Hon. Prof., Univ. of Southampton, 2005–07. Interim Dir, British Antarctic Survey, 2012. Chm. Bd, Nat. Centre for Ocean Forecasting, 2005–07; Chm., Governing Bd, Nat. Partnership for Ocean Prediction, 2017–; Hd, UK Delegn to Intergovtl Oceanographic Commn of UNESCO, 2017–. Member: Exec. Bd, NERC, 2001–16 (Mem., Sci. and Innovation Strategy Bd, 2008–11); Steering Cttee, Global Climate Observing System, 2007–10; Council, Marine Biology Assoc., 2008–10; Exec. Cttee, Partnership for Observation of Global Ocean, 2014–16; Adv. Gp, Future of the Sea Foresight Project, Govt Office of Sci., 2016–17; Greenwich Forum, 2016–18; Scientific Advisory Board: Helmholtz Centre for Ocean Res. (GEOMAR), Germany, 2009–17; Inst. of Oceanology of Chinese Acad. of Scis., 2015–. FIMarEST, CMarSci 2016. Hon. Fellow, Bangor Univ., 2014. Hon. DSc Sheffield, 2011. *Publications:* numerous res. contribns on oceanography of continental shelf seas to acad. jls. *Recreations:* oil painting, visiting historical monuments, walking, crazy adventures with sons Oliver and Patrick, including ascent of the Old Man of Hoy (Aug. 2016), Old Man of Stoer (2017) and Am Buachaille (2018). *Address:* National Oceanography Centre, Empress Dock, European Way, Southampton SO14 3ZH.

**HILL, Antony James de Villiers;** consultant; Headmaster, St Mark's School, Southborough, Mass, 1994–2006; *b* 1 Aug. 1940; *s* of James Kenneth Hill and Hon. Yvonne Aletta Hill, *d* of 2nd Baron de Villiers; *m* 1974, Gunilla Els-Charlotte Emilie (Elsa) Nilsson; one *d*. *Educ:* Sydney Grammar School; Sydney Univ. (BA Hons); Boston Univ. (MEd). Law Clerk, 1962–64; Antarctic Expedition, 1964–65; Master, Canberra Grammar Sch., 1965–66; Instructor, Himalayan Mountaineering Inst., Darjeeling, 1967–68; Master, Sydney C of E Grammar Sch., 1967–72, 1977; Mem. Faculty: Phillips Acad., Andover, Mass, 1972–74; Boston Univ., 1974–76; Senior Master, King's Sch., Parramatta, 1977–81; Headmaster: Christ Church Grammar Sch., WA, 1982–87; Melbourne C of E Grammar Sch., later Melbourne Grammar Sch., 1988–94; Dir, Wesley College Inst. for Educnl Innovation, Melbourne, 2006–07. *Recreations:* running, climbing, sailing, theatre, music, reading. *Address:* 22 Dartmouth Street, Boston, MA 02116, USA. *T:* (617) 8696935. *Clubs:* Weld (Perth, WA); Savage (Melbourne).

**HILL, Charles;** *see* Hill, R. C.

**HILL, Charles Edward;** Head, Departmental Security Unit, Department for International Development, since 2016; *b* 31 March 1963; *s* of Anthony and Jennifer Hill; *m* 1996, Suzanne Victoria Stock; one *s* one *d*. *Educ:* Royal Holloway Coll., Univ. of London (BA Hist.). Joined HM Diplomatic Service, 1990; Third Sec. (Chancery), Doha, 1993–96; Dep. Hd of Mission, Almaty, 1997–2000; Parly Clerk, FCO, 2000–02; Hd, Central Asia and S Caucasus Section, FCO, 2002–04; Dep. Hd of Mission, Muscat, 2004–08, Oslo, 2009–13; Hd, Policy and Trng, Security Dept, FCO, 2013–16. *Recreations:* travel, tennis, backgammon, CFC. *Address:* Department for International Development, 22 Whitehall, SW1A 2EG.

**HILL, Christopher Frederick;** Chief Executive, Hargreaves Lansdown plc, since 2017 (Chief Financial Officer, 2017); *b* Reading, 5 June 1971; *s* of Gordon and Sally Hill; *m* 1998, Vanessa; three *c*. *Educ:* Cheltenham Coll.; Keble Coll., Oxford (MA Modern Hist.). ACA. Accountant: Arthur Andersen, 1993–2000; Gen. Electric Co., 2000–03; Finance Dir, VWR, 2005–07; Gp Financial Controller, 2007–09, Chief Financial Officer, 2009–11, Travelex; Chief Financial Officer, IG Gp plc, 2011–16. AMCT. *Recreations:* sailing, ski-ing, cycling, cricket, golf, tennis. *Address:* Hargreaves Lansdown, One College Square, Anchor Road, Bristol BS1 5HL. *T:* (0117) 980 9541. *E:* christopher.hill@hl.co.uk. *Clubs:* MCC; Royal Dart Yacht.

**HILL, Rt Rev. Christopher John,** KCVO 2014; Bishop of Guildford, 2004–13; Clerk of the Closet to the Queen, 2005–14; *b* 10 Oct. 1945; *s* of Leonard and Frances V. Hill; *m* 1976, Hilary Ann Whitehouse; three *s* one *d*. *Educ:* Sebright Sch., Worcs; King's Coll., London (BD Hons; Relton Prize for Theology, 1967; MTh 1968; AKC 1967). Deacon 1969, priest 1970. Asst Curate, Dio. of Lichfield: St Michael's, Tividale, 1969–73; St Nicholas, Codsall, 1973–74; Asst Chaplain to Archbp of Canterbury for Foreign Relations, 1974–81; Archbp's Sec. for Ecumenical Affairs, 1982–89; Hon. Canon of Canterbury Cathedral, 1982–89; Chaplain to the Queen, 1987–96; Canon Residentiary, 1989–96, Precentor, 1990–96, St Paul's Cathedral; Bishop Suffragan of Stafford, 1996–2004. Honorary Assistant Bishop: Dio. of Gloucester, 2014–; Dio. of Canterbury, 2014–; Dio. of London, 2014–18; Dio. of Ely, 2015–. Anglican Secretary: Anglican-RC Internat. Commn (I), 1974–81, Internat. Commn (II), 1983–90 (Mem., 1990–91); Anglican-Lutheran Eur. Commn, 1981–82; Consultant: C of E—German Churches Commn, 1987–90; C of E—Nordic-Baltic Churches Commn, 1989–92; Co-Chairman: C of E—French Lutheran and Reformed Conversations, 1994–98; Meissen Theol Conf., 1998–2010; Chm., C of E Council for Christian Unity, 2008–12 (Mem., 1989–96); Vice-Chm., Faith and Order Adv. Gp, 1998–2007 (Mem., 1996–2008). Member: Legal Adv. Commn, Gen. Synod of C of E, 1991–2013; House of Bishops, Gen. Synod of C of E, 1999–2013 (Chm., Women Bishops' Gp, 2005–06; Mem., Theol Gp, 2006–10; Mem., Faith and Order Commn, 2010–13); Wkg Pty on Women in the Episcopate, 2001–04 (Vice-Chm., 2003–04); Wkg Party on Bishops' Legal Costs, Fees Adv. Commn, 2003; Liturgical Commn, 2003–06; Discipline Commn, 2004–13; Anglican-RC Internat. Commn III, 2011–18 (Consultant,

2019–); Wkg Gp on Ordinariate, 2011–13. Pres., Conf. of Eur. Churches, 2013–18 (Vice-Pres. 2009–13); Chm., Severn Forum, 2017–. Entered H of L 2010. Mem. Council, KCL, 2009–15. Guestmaster, Nikaean Club, 1982–89. Co-Chm., London Soc. of Jews and Christians, 1991–96; Vice-Chm., 1993–2002, Chm., 2002–15, Pres., 2019–, Ecclesiastical Law Soc. Pres., Gloucester Assoc. of Parish and Town Councils, 2015–. DD Lambeth 2014; DUniv Surrey, 2015. *Publications:* (ed jtly) Anglicans and Roman Catholics: the search for unity, 1995; (ed jtly) Documents in the Debate: papers on Anglican orders, 1997; miscellaneous ecumenical, ecclesiological and legal articles. *Recreations:* Radio 3, walking, detective stories, Italian food, GWR, unaffordable wine. *Address:* Hillview, West End, Ruardean, Glos GL17 9TP. *Clubs:* Athenæum, Sette of Odd Volumes, Nobody's Friends.

**HILL, Prof. Christopher John,** DPhil; FBA 2007; Sir Patrick Sheehy Professor of International Relations, University of Cambridge, 2004–16, now Emeritus Professor of International Relations; Fellow, Sidney Sussex College, Cambridge, since 2004; Wilson E. Schmidt Distinguished Professor of International Relations, School of Advanced International Studies Europe, Johns Hopkins University, Bologna, since 2017; *b* 20 Nov. 1948; *s* of Peter Alan Hill and Sylvia Dawn Hill; *m* 1970, Maria McKay; one *s* one *d*. *Educ:* Merton Coll., Oxford (BA 1st Cl. Hons Modern History 1970); Nuffield Coll., Oxford (DPhil 1979). London School of Economics and Political Science: Noel Buxton Student in Internat. Relns, 1973–74; Lectr, 1974–90, Sen. Lectr, 1990–91, in Internat. Relns; Montague Burton Prof. of Internat. Relns, 1991–2004; Convenor, Dept of Internat. Relns, 1994–97; Vice Chm., Academic Bd, 1999–2002; University of Cambridge: Dir, Centre of Internat. Studies, 2004–09; Jt Hd, 2009–10, Hd, 2012–14, Dept of Politics and Internat. Studies. Vis. Prof., Dartmouth Coll., NH, 1985; Visiting Fellow: RIIA, 1980–81; Woodrow Wilson International Centre for Scholars, Washington, 1984; European University Inst., Florence, 1992–93, 1998; UCSD, 2003; Univ. of Siena, 2003; Robert Schumann Centre of Advanced Studies, European University Inst., Fiesole, 2015; Academic Visitor, St Antony's Coll., Oxford, 2009; Vis. Researcher, Centre des Études Européennes, Paris, 2015. Hon. PhD Peloponnese, 2015. Ufficiale dell'Ordine della Stella d'Italia, 2017. *Publications:* (ed) National Foreign Policies and European Political Co-operation, 1983; Cabinet Decisions in Foreign Policy, 1991; (ed jtly) Two Worlds of International Relations, 1994; (ed) The Actors in Europe's Foreign Policy, 1996; (ed jtly) European Foreign Policy: key documents, 2000; The Changing Politics of Foreign Policy, 2003, 2nd edn as Foreign Policy in the Twenty-First Century, 2016; (ed jtly) International Relations and the European Union, 2005, 3rd edn 2017; (ed jtly) National and European Foreign Policies, 2011; The National Interest in Question: foreign policy in multicultural societies, 2013; (jtly) The Art of Attraction: soft power and the UK's role in the world, 2014; The Future of British Foreign Policy: security and diplomacy in a world after Brexit, 2019; many articles in learned jls and contribs to books. *Recreations:* Wolverhampton Wanderers FC, the visual arts. *Address:* Sidney Sussex College, Cambridge CB2 3HU. *E:* cjh68@cam.ac.uk.

**HILL, Ven. Colin,** PhD; Archdeacon of West Cumberland, 2004–08; *b* 4 Sept. 1942; *s* of William Albert Hill and Annie Hill; *m* 1965, Kathleen Chadbourne; three *d*. *Educ:* Leicester Univ. (BSc (Maths) 1964); Ripon Hall, Oxford; Open Univ. (PhD (Sociol. of Religion) 1988). Ordained deacon, 1966, priest, 1967; Assistant Curate: Ch of the Martyrs, Dio. Leicester, 1966–69; St Crispin's Ch, Braunstone, 1969–71; Lectr, Ecumenical Inst., Teesside, 1971–72; Vicar, St Thomas and St James, Worsbrough, 1972–78; Chs' Develt Officer for Mission and Ministry for Telford, Dios Lichfield and Hereford, 1978–96; Canon Res., and Canon Treas., Carlisle Cathedral, and Diocesan Sec., Carlisle, 1996–2004; Vice Dean, Carlisle Cathedral, 2004. Rural Dean: Telford, Dio. Lichfield, 1980–96; Telford Severn Gorge, Dio. Hereford, 1980–96; Preb., Hereford Cathedral, 1983–96. *Publications:* (contrib.) A Workbook in Popular Religion, 1986; (contrib.) A Deanery Workbook, 1988; What's Good for the Organisation: appraisal schemes, 1991; (contrib.) Religious Movements in a Neo-Weberian Perspective, 1992; Loosing the Apron Strings: devolution to deaneries, 1996; Appointing the Rural Dean, 2004; Deans and Deaneries: lessons from Norway, 2006. *Recreations:* social housing, Scandinavian travel, cultivation of bonsai. *Address:* Telford House, 1A Briery Bank, Arnside, Cumbria LA5 0HW.

**HILL, Rev. Canon Colin Arnold Clifford,** OBE 1996; Vicar of Croydon and Chaplain to Archbishop Whitgift Foundation, 1973–94; Chaplain to the Queen, 1990–99; *b* 13 Feb. 1929; *s* of William and May Hill; *m* 1st, 1957, Shirley (*d* 1961); one *s*; 2nd, 1971, Irene Chamberlain; one step *s*. *Educ:* Reading Sch.; Bristol Univ.; Ripon Hall Theol Coll., Oxford; Univ. of Wales, Bangor (MPhil 2003). Ordained deacon, Sheffield Cathedral, 1957, priest, 1958; Rotherham Parish Church; Vicar of Brightside, 1960; Rector of Easthampstead, Bracknell, 1964; Chaplain, RAF Staff Coll., Bracknell, 1968. Hon. Canon, Canterbury, 1975, Canon Emeritus, 1984; Hon. Canon, Southwark, 1984, Canon Emeritus, 1994. Proctor in Convocation and General Synod, Dio. Oxford, 1970–73, Dios of Canterbury and Southwark, 1980–84. Religious Advr, London Borough of Croydon, 1973–94; Chairman: Church Tenements Trust, 1973–94; Croydon Industrial Mission, 1975–94. Chm., Croydon Crime Prevention Initiative, 1989–94; Vice Chm., Croydon Police Consultative Cttee, 1985–94. Founder, Bracknell Samaritans, 1968; Founder Chm., Croydon Youth Counselling Agency, 1974–94. *Recreation:* grandson. *Address:* Silver Birches, 70 Preston Crowmarsh, Wallingford, Oxon OX10 6SL. *T:* 07837 249949. *E:* colinatsb@clara.co.uk.

**HILL, Damon Graham Devereux,** OBE 1997; motor racing driver, retired; analyst and commentator, Sky Sports F1, since 2012; *b* 17 Sept. 1960; *s* of late Graham Hill, OBE and Bette Hill; *m* 1988, Georgie Hill; two *s* two *d*. *Educ:* Haberdashers' Aske's Sch. Began motorcycle racing, 1979; Formula 3, 1986; Formula 3000, 1988; Formula 1, 1992–99: Brabham team, 1992; with Williams Team, 1991–96: test driver, 1991; driver, 1993–96; Grand Prix wins: 3 in 1993, 6 in 1994, 4 in 1995, 8 in 1996 (Argentina, Australia, Brazil, Canada, France, Germany, Japan, San Marino), 1 in 1998; Drivers' World Championship, 1996; with Arrows team, 1997; with Jordan team, 1998–99. Chairman: P1 Internat. Ltd, 2001; Damon Hill BMW, Warwick, 2001. Numerous awards incl. BBC Sports Personality of the Year, 1994 and 1996. *Publications:* Grand Prix Year, 1994; Championship Year, 1996; Watching the Wheels, 2016. *Club:* British Racing Drivers' (Pres., 2006–11).

**HILL, David Arnold,** CBE 2015; DPhil; Chairman and Owner, Environment Bank Ltd, since 2007; Owner and Director, Environmental Markets Exchange, since 2010; *b* Derby, 18 April 1958; *s* of Arnold Hill and Phyllis Joan Hill; *m* 1989, Dr Kathleen Raw; one *s* two *d*. *Educ:* Noel Baker Sch., Derby; Univ. of Loughborough (BSc Hons 1st Cl. 1979); Wolfson Coll., Oxford (DPhil 1982). Ecologist, Game Conservancy, 1982–86; Sen. Ecologist, RSPB, 1986–89; Dir of Develt, British Trust for Ornithology, 1989–92; Owner and Chief Exec., Ecoscope Applied Ecologists, 1992–2002, subseq. merged with RPS Gp plc, Chief Scientific Advr, 2002–06; Chief Exec., David Hill Ecology and Envmt, 2007–. Non-exec. Dir, Jt Nature Conservation Cttee, 2006–16. Dep. Chm., Natural England, 2011–16 (non-exec. Dir, 2006–; Chairman: Developer Industry Gp, 2011–16; Innovation Gp, 2013–16); Chairman: Northern Upland Chain Local Nature Partnership, 2012–; Plantlife, 2015–; Dir, NatureSpace Partnership Ltd, 2018–. Mem., Ecosystem Markets Taskforce, 2011–13; Comr, RSA Food, Farming and Countryside Commn, 2018–. Vis. Prof. in Ecol., Oxford Brookes Univ., 2006–. Mem., Bd of Trustees, Esmée Fairbairn Foundn, 2017–. *Publications:* The Pheasant, 1986; The Avocet, 1989; Bird Census Techniques, 1992, 2nd edn 2000; Managing Habitats for Conservation, 1996; The Handbook of Biodiversity Methods, 2005. *Recreations:* wildlife photography, bird watching, walking, mountain biking, travelling to remote places, fly fishing, my family. *E:* dhill@davidhillecology.com.

**HILL, David Christopher,** CBE 2018; Executive Director, Children, Schools and Families, Surrey County Council, since 2018; *b* London, 30 March 1959; *s* of Stanley and Joyce Hill; *m* 1988, Joanne Susan Thorogood; two *d*. *Educ:* Brittons Sch., Rainham, Essex; Brunel Univ. (MSc; CQSW 1983). Social Worker, London Bor. of Greenwich, 1983–87; Area Dir, Family Welfare Assoc., 1987–89; Gen. Manager, City of Westminster, 1989–96; Head of Children's Services: Havering LBC, 1996–2000; Tower Hamlets LBC, 2000–05; Director of Children's Services: Merton LBC, 2005–08; Croydon LBC, 2008–10; Exec. Dir, Schools, Children and Families, 2010–13, Exec. Dir, Schs, Children, Families and Adult Services, 2013–18, Essex CC. Pres., Assoc. of Dirs of Children's Services, 2016–17 (Vice Pres., 2015–16). Member: Social Work Reform Bd, 2010–; Bd, Coll. of Social Work, 2010–. Trustee, Who Cares Trust, 2010–. *Recreations:* music - choral, brass, piano, theatre performance, all sports. *Address:* Surrey County Hall, Penrhyn Road, Kingston upon Thames KT1 2TW. *T:* 0345 600 9009. *E:* davechill5@sky.com.

**HILL, David Graeme;** Director, Environmental Quality, Department for Environment, Food and Rural Affairs, since 2018; *b* Newcastle upon Tyne, 4 Nov. 1975; *s* of Graeme Hill and Eileen Hill; *m* 2005, Sophie Watson; two *s*. *Educ:* Ponteland High Sch., Northumberland; Corpus Christi Coll., Oxford (BA Hons PPE). Civil Service: fast stream, 1998–2002; Private Secretary: to Minister for Housing and Planning, 2000; to the Dep. Prime Minister, 2000–01; to Sec. of State for Transport, Local Govt and Regions, 2001–02; Propriety and Ethics Team, Cabinet Office, 2003–04; Dep. Dir, Strategy and Performance, 2005–07, Housing Supply, 2007–08, DCLG; Dep. Dir, Internat. Climate Change, DECC, 2009–11; Principal Private Sec. to Sec. of State for Communities and Local Govt, 2011–13; Dir, Strategy and Private Office, 2013–15, Communications, 2014–15, DCLG (Bd Mem., 2013–15); Dir of Apprenticeships, BIS and DFE, later DFE, 2015–17; Dir, Strategic Commng and Policy, Essex CC, 2017–18. Trust Mem., Cromwell Acad., Cambs, 2015–16. *Recreations:* gardening, golf, cricket, football (Newcastle United). *Address:* Department for Environment, Food and Rural Affairs, 2 Marsham Street, SW1P 4DF. *E:* david.hill@defra.gov.uk.

**HILL, David Neil,** MBE 2019; MA, FRCO, FRSCM; Musical Director, Bach Choir, since 1998; Principal Conductor, Yale University Schola Cantorum, since 2013; Professor of Choral Conducting, Yale University, since 2013; *b* 13 May 1957; *s* of James Brian Greatrex Hill and Jean Hill; *m* 1st, 1979, Hilary Llystyn Jones (marr. diss.); one *s* one *d*; 2nd, 1994, Alice Mary Wills; one *s* one *d*. *Educ:* Chetham's School of Music, Manchester; St John's College, Cambridge (organ student; toured Aust. 1977, USA and Canada, 1978, Japan, 1979; MA). FGCM 2003; FRSCM 2008. Sub-Organist, Durham Cathedral, 1980–82; Organist and Master of Music: Westminster Cathedral, 1982–88; Winchester Cathedral, 1988–2002; Organist and Dir of Music, St John's Coll., Cambridge, 2003–07. Conductor: Alexandra Choir, 1979–87; Waynflete Singers, Winchester, 1988–2002; Associate Chorus Master, 1987–98, Artistic Dir, 1992–98, Philharmonia Chorus; Principal Conductor, Southern Sinfonia, 2003–; Principal Conductor, Leeds Philharmonic, 2005–; Chief Conductor, BBC Singers, 2007–17; Associate Guest Conductor, Bournemouth SO, 2009–. Dir, Southern Cathedrals' Fest., triennially 1990–2002. Vis. Prof. of Choral Conducting, RAM, 1986–. Mem. Council, RCO, 1984–; President: Cathedral Organists' Assoc., 2006–07; IAO, 2007–09. Recordings with choirs and orchs incl. Westminster Cathedral Choir (Gramophone award, 1985); concerts and tours abroad, including tours to Australia, USA and Philippines. Hon. RAM 2010. Hon. DMus Southampton, 2003. *Recreations:* drawing, reading, wine, cars. *Address:* c/o Ralph Blackbourn, Rayfield Allied, Studio 26 China Works, 100 Black Prince Road, SE1 7SJ. *Club:* Athenæum.

**HILL, David Rowland;** Director, Bell Pottinger Group, 2007–13; *b* 1 Feb. 1948; *s* of Rowland Foster Hill and Rita Maud Hill; *m* 1974, Janet Gibson (marr. diss. 1992); one *s* one *d*. *Educ:* King Edward VI Sch., Birmingham; Brasenose Coll., Oxford Univ. (BA PPE). Unigate Ltd, 1970–72; Asst to Rt Hon. Roy Hattersley, MP, 1972–76; Political Advr, Dept of Prices and Consumer Protection, 1976–79; Head of Staff: Rt Hon. Roy Hattersley, 1979–83; Dep. Leader of Labour Party's Office, 1983–91; Dir of Campaigns and Communications, Lab Party, 1991–93; Chief Spokesperson for Labour Party, 1993–98; Dir, Bell Pottinger Good Relations, subseq. Good Relations, 1998–2003; Man. Dir, Keith McDowall Associates, subseq. Good Relations Political Communications, 2000–03; Dir of Communications, Prime Minister's Office, 2003–07. *Recreations:* cinema, watching sport, foreign travel.

**HILL, Dawn Elysea,** CBE 2018; Chairman, Black Cultural Archives, since 2012; *b* Jamaica, 25 Sept. 1939; *d* of Leslie and Ruby Franklin; *m* 1974, Dr Martin M. J. D. Hill (*d* 2015); one *s* one *d*. *Educ:* Camperdown High Sch., Jamaica; Leicester Coll. of Arts and Technol.; Leicester Gen. Hosp. (SRN 1960); London Sch. of Econs and Pol Sci. (Dip. Social Admin; Dip. Personnel Mgt 1974). NHS nursing appts incl. Sen. Theatre Sister and Superintendent, Neuro-Surgical Theatres, Whittington Hosp., 1960–71; Sen. Personnel Officer, Hackney Hosps, 1975–82; Principal Officer, Personnel and Industrial Relns, Southwark Social Services, 1982–89; Hd, Personnel and Payroll, Lambeth Bor. of Southwark, 1989–92; Management Consultant: Dawn Hill & Associates, Consultancy, 1993–95; Focus Consultancy Ltd, 1995–2003; DJB Consultancy, 2002–09. Chm., Mgt Bd, Blackliners HIV and AIDS and Sexual Health Services, 1991–2002; Mem. Bd, African and Caribbean Family Mediation Service, 1996–2002. Panel Mem., Lambeth Educn Appeals, Admissions, Exclusions and Employee Dismissals, 2007–. Mem., Lambeth Liby Commn, 2011–12. Founder, 1972, and formerly Mgt Advr, Rainbow Community Nursery, Hackney. Chm. Govs, Norwood Girls' Sch., Lambeth, 1992–2000; Governor: Evelina Children's Hosp. Sch., St Thomas' Hosp., 2001– (Chm. Govs, 2001–11); Guy's and St Thomas' Hosp. NHS Foundn Trust, 2009–15 (non-exec. Dir, 1999–2007). Trustee and Vice Chm., Black Cultural Archives, 1998–2001; Trustee, Mary Seacole Meml Statue Appeal, 2011–16; Pres., Mary Seacole Trust, 2017–. Mem., Friends of Georgian Soc. of Jamaica (UK). *Recreations:* ballet, music, fashion, art, paintings, football, tennis. *Address:* 111 Helix Road, SW2 2JR. *T:* (020) 8473 9256, 07947 371639.

**HILL, Edward;** see Hill, A. E.

**HILL, Rev. Mgr Edward Peter;** Parish Priest, St Andrew's Church, Tenterden, 2003–14; *b* 8 Aug. 1943; *s* of Leslie John Hill and Constance Irene Hill. *Educ:* Holy Family RC Primary Sch., Morden; John Fisher Independent Sch., Purley; St Joseph's Jun. Seminary, Mark Cross, Sussex; St John's Seminary, Wonersh. Ordained priest, 1968; Assistant Priest: St Saviour, Lewisham, 1968–72; St Thomas of Canterbury, Wandsworth, 1972–78; St Peter, Woolwich, 1978–82; served as RAF Chaplain, 1982–2000: Cranwell, Wildenrath, Brampton, Brize Norton, Rheindahlen; Asst Principal Chaplain, Support Command, Brampton, and Personnel and Trng Comd, Innsworth; Prin. RC Chaplain and Dir, Chaplaincy Services 2, RAF, 1997–2000; held rank of Gp Captain; QHC 1997–2000; Officiating Chaplain (RC), RAF Brize Norton, 2000–03. Prelate of Honour to the Pope, 1997. *Recreation:* most sports (interest in, only now, as spectator and studier). *Club:* Royal Air Force.

**HILL, (Eleanor Mary) Henrietta**; QC 2015; *b* Leeds, 30 Sept. 1973; *d* of Roger Hill and Carol Hill (*née* Wright, now Lawson); *m* 2012, Richard Kenyon; two *s*. *Educ*: Gateways Sch., Leeds; Emmanuel Coll., Cambridge (BA Hons Law 1994; MA); Harvard Univ. (Herchel Smith Fellow 1995–96). Called to the Bar, Inner Temple, 1997; in practice as a barrister, Cloisters Chambers, 1997–2000, Doughty St Chambers, 2000–; Asst Coroner, Inner S London, 2013–; Dep. Queen's Bench Master, 2015–. Pegasus Fellow, Center for Constitutional Rights, NY, 2002. *Publications*: Blackstone's Guide to the Race Relations (Amendment) Act 2000, 2001; (with Richard Kenyon) Promoting Equality and Diversity: a practitioner's guide, 2007; (contrib.) Halsbury's Laws, Vol. 88A, Rights and Freedoms, 2013. *Recreations*: family life, local history, travel. *Address*: Doughty Street Chambers, 54 Doughty Street, WC1N 2LS. *T*: (020) 7404 1313, *Fax*: (020) 7404 2283. *E*: h.hill@doughtystreet.co.uk.

**HILL, Emma Rhian**, CBE 2012; Creative Director and Co-Owner, Hill and Friends, since 2015; *b* Kingston-upon-Thames, 5 Aug. 1969; *d* of Keith Hill and Valerie Christine Hill (*née* Edwards). *Educ*: Wimbledon Sch. of Art (Art Foundn Dip. (Dist.) 1989); Ravensbourne Sch. of Design (BA Hons Fashion 1992). Designer, Accessories: Burberry, 1992–94; Liz Claiborne, 1994–97; Senior Designer, Accessories: Calvin Klein, 1998–2000; Marc Jacobs, 2000–02; Vice Pres., Accessories, Gap Inc., 2002–05; Consultant Designer: Chloe, 2006–07; Halston, 2007–08; Creative Dir, Mulberry, 2008–13. Hon. Fellow, UAL, 2014. *Club*: Soho House.

**HILL, Felicity**; *see* Green, F.

**HILL, Lt Gen. Giles Patrick**, CBE 2014; Deputy Commander, Resolute Support Mission, Afghanistan, 2019–20; *b* Leeds, 6 Jan. 1967; *s* of Donald and Patricia Hill; *m* 1995, Chantal Larocque; one *s*. *Educ*: Lawnswood Sch., Leeds; Cranfield Univ. (MA Mil. Sci. and Technol. 2001). Joined Army, 1989; CO, 1st Bn, Parachute Regt, 1996–98; HCSC 2011; Comdr, 16 Air Assault Bde, 2011–13; Dep. Commanding Gen., US 82nd Airborne Div., 2013–15; GOC 1st (UK) Div., 2015–16; ACDS (Defence Engagement), 2017–19.

**HILL, Graham Chadwick**, FRSC; Headmaster, Dr Challoner's Grammar School, Amersham, 1993–2001, Trustee, 2001–10; *b* 11 Jan. 1942; *s* of Harold Hill and Harriet (*née* Chadwick); *m* 1st, 1964, Elizabeth Wadsworth (*d* 2013); two *d* (and one *d* decd); 2nd, 2015, Katherine Anderson. *Educ*: Bacup and Rawtenstall Grammar Sch.; Trinity Coll., Cambridge (BA, MA, PGCE Dist, AdvDipEd). FRSC 1985. Asst Science Master, Marlborough Coll., 1965–70; Sen. Chemistry Master, 1970–75, Sen. Science Master, 1975–78, Bristol Grammar Sch.; Dep. Headmaster, Dr Challoner's Grammar Sch., 1978–86, 1989–93; Sen. Fellow, Univ. of York, 1986–87. Chm., 1987–89, Trustee, 1991–93 and 2001–06, ASE. FRSA 1993. Guinness Award for Sci. Teachers, 1968; Bronze Medallion, RSC, 1986. *Publications*: Chemistry in Context, 1978, 7th edn 2017; Chemistry in Context Laboratory Manual and Study Guide, 1982, 6th edn 2011; Chemistry Counts, 1986, 3rd edn 2003; Letts Revise Science, 1990; Science Scene (booklets, books and teachers' guides), 1990–92; Materials, 1992; Science for GCSE, 1998, 2nd edn 2001; Foundation Science for GCSE, 2001; Synoptic Skills in A level Chemistry, 2003; AQA GCSE Science, 2006; AQA GCSE Additional Science, 2007; co-author and editor: AQA GCSE Chemistry, 2007; AQA GCSE Physics, 2007; AQA GCSE Biology, 2007; OCR Chemistry for AS, 2008; Edexcel Chemistry for AS, 2008; OCR Chemistry for A2, 2009; Edexcel Chemistry for A2, 2009; Edexcel International GCSE Chemistry, 2013, 2nd edn 2017; Edexcel A Level Chemistry 1, 2015; Edexcel A Level Chemistry 2, 2015; contribs to learned jls. *Recreations*: walking, gardening, theatre, wildlife, travel.

**HILL, Harry Douglas**; Co-Founder, and Deputy Chairman, 2014–18, Learning Technologies Group plc (formerly In-Deed Online plc) (Chairman, 2010); Deputy Chairman, Hunters Property plc, since 2016 (Executive Director, 2013–15; Interim Chief Executive, 2015–16); *b* Yorks, 4 April 1948; *s* of Jack and Kathleen Hill; *m* 1986, Mandy Elizabeth Glenys; five *s*. *Educ*: Barnsley Grammar Sch.; Coll. of Estate Mgt. Chartered surveyor. Chief Exec., 1988–2007, Chm., 2007–09, Countrywide plc. Non-exec. Dir, Rightmove plc, 2003–08; Director: Jupiter Second Split plc, 2004–14; Milton Homes plc, 2008–09. *Recreations*: fishing, bird watching, cycling, National Hunt racing, restaurant in Portugal (owner).

**HILL, Henrietta**; *see* Hill, E. M. H.

**HILL, Hilary M.**; *see* Murray Hill.

**HILL, Prof. (Hugh) Allen (Oliver)**, FRS 1990; CChem, FRSC; Professor of Bioinorganic Chemistry, Oxford, 1992–2004, now Emeritus; Fellow and Praelector, 1965–2004, Hon. Fellow, 2007, The Queen's College, Oxford; *b* 23 May 1937; *s* of Hugh Rankin Stewart Hill and Elizabeth Hill (*née* Burns); *m* 1967, Boglárka Anna Pinter; two *s* one *d*. *Educ*: Royal Belfast Academical Institution; QUB (BSc 1959; PhD 1962); Wadham Coll., Oxford (MA 1964; DSc 1986; Hon. Fellow, 2002). Oxford University: Weir Jun. Fellow, UC, 1964–65; Deptl Demonstrator, 1965–67, Lectr, 1967–90, in Inorganic Chemistry; Reader in Bioinorganic Chemistry, 1990–92; Sen. Proctor, 1976–77. Vis. appts, Harvard, Univ. of Sydney, Univ. of California, 1970–82; Vis. Prof., Harvard Med. Sch., 1996–2002; Pacific Coast Lects, 1981; Robinson Lectr, RSC, 1994. Chm., Davy Faraday Cttee, 1996–98; Mem. Council, Royal Instn, 1995–98. Hon. DSc QUB, 1996. Interdisciplinary Award, RSC, 1987; Chemistry and Electrochemistry of Transition Metals Award, RSC, 1990; Mullard Award, Royal Soc., 1993; Breyer Medal, RACI, 1994; Royal Medal, Royal Soc., 2010. *Publications*: Physical Methods in Advanced Inorganic Chemistry (with P. Day), 1968; papers in professional jls. *Recreations*: gardening, music. *Address*: The Queen's College, Oxford OX1 4AW. *T*: (01865) 279120. *E*: allen.hill@queens.ox.ac.uk.

**HILL, Sir James Frederick**, 4th Bt *cr* 1917; OBE 2000; DL; *b* 5 Dec. 1943; *s* of Sir James Hill, 3rd Bt and Marjory, *d* of late Frank Croft; *S* father, 1976; *m* 1966, Sandra Elizabeth, *o d* of J. C. Ingram; one *s* three *d*. Dir, Yorkshire Bldg Soc., 1972–96. Chairman: British Wool Fedn, 1987–90; Sir James Hill (Wool) Ltd, 1991–. Chm., Specialist Schs and Acads Trust, 2007–09. DL West Yorks, 1994. DUniv Bradford, 1997. *Heir*: *s* James Laurence Ingram Hill [*b* 22 Sept. 1973; *m* 2003, Kate Elizabeth, *d* of T. Horsfield, Silkstone, Yorks; one *s* two *d*]. *Address*: Roseville, Moor Lane, Menston, Ilkley, West Yorks LS29 6AP. *T*: (01943) 874624. *Clubs*: Royal Automobile; Bradford (Yorks); St Enodoc Golf.

**HILL, James Michael**; QC 2006; a Recorder, since 2002; *b* 5 Oct. 1960; *s* of late Michael Hill and Doreen Hill; *m* 1986, Carolyne Dent; two *d*. *Educ*: Durham Johnston Sch.; Manchester Univ. (LLB Hons 1982). Called to the Bar, Inner Temple, 1984; N Eastern Circuit; in practice, specialising in criminal law and regulatory law; Hd, Fountain Chambers, 2010–. Former Gov., Red House Sch., Norton-on-Tees. Former Mem., Durham Town and Gown Soc. *Recreations*: playing golf, watching hockey, supporting Newcastle United. *Address*: Fountain Chambers, Cleveland Business Centre, 1 Watson Street, Middlesbrough TS1 2RQ. *T*: (01642) 804040, *Fax*: (01642) 804060. *E*: amallett@fountainchambers.co.uk; St John's Buildings, 24a–28 St John Street, Manchester M3 4DJ. *T*: (0161) 214 1500; Henderson Chambers, 2 Harcourt Buildings, Temple, EC4Y 9DB. *T*: (020) 7583 9020. *Clubs*: Durham County; Wynyard Golf; Whitley Bay and Tynemouth Hockey.

**HILL, Jane**; presenter, BBC TV News, since 1997; *b* Eastbourne, E Sussex, 10 June 1969; *d* of David and Margaret Hill; civil partnership 2013, Sara Shepherd. *Educ*: Micklefield Sch., E Sussex; Queen Mary Coll., London Univ. (BA Hons Politics 1991). Voluntary and freelance rôles with BBC local radio, 1986–91; asst and researcher to Senate Democrats, Washington, DC, 1991; researcher, Radio 5 Live, 1994–95; trainee, BBC Regl News Trainee Scheme, 1995–96; regl TV journalist, 1995–97; presenter: BBC TV News, incl. One O'Clock, Six O'Clock and Ten O'Clock News and BBC News Channel, 1997–; Saturday PM, BBC Radio 4, 2017–. Mem., Adv. Bd, British-American Project, 2016–. Active with charities in field of diversity and inclusion, and Parkinson's disease. Mem., BAFTA, 2018–. Hon. Fellow QMUL, 2017. *Recreations*: the arts, particularly theatre and cinema, food, dog walking, the gym, The Archers. *Club*: Soho House.

**HILL, Jeremy**; *see* Hill, P. J. O.

**HILL, Dame Jessica E.**; *see* Ennis-Hill.

**HILL, John**; *b* 28 April 1922; *s* of William Hallett Hill and Emily Hill (*née* Massey); *m* 1952, Hilda Mary Barratt (*d* 2007); (one *s* decd). *Educ*: Merchant Taylors' Sch., Crosby; Liverpool Univ. (BCom); Inst. of Public Finance and Accountancy, 1954. City Treasurer of Liverpool, 1974–82. Mem., Merseyside Residuary Body, 1985–88. Hon. Sen. Res. Fellow, Inst. of Local Govt Studies, Birmingham Univ., 1982–93. *Recreation*: music. *Address*: 325 Northway, Lydiate, Merseyside L31 0BW. *T*: (0151) 526 3699.

**HILL, Sir John Alfred Rowley**, 11th Bt *cr* 1779, of Brook Hall, Londonderry; *b* 29 Feb. 1940; *s* of Sir George Alfred Rowley Hill, 9th Bt and his 2nd wife, Jessie Anne (*née* Roberts; *d* 1995); *S* half-brother, 1992; *m* 1966, Diana Anne Walker (marr. diss. 1981); one adopted *s* one adopted *d*. *Heir*: kinsman Allan Claude Hill [*b* 10 Feb. 1936; *m* 1970, Rachel St Just (marr. diss. 1978); one *s* one *d*]. *Address*: 5 Wherry Close, March, Cambs PE15 9BX.

**HILL, John Cameron**, TD 1959; FRICS; Member, Lands Tribunal, 1987–99; *b* 8 April 1927; *s* of Raymond Cameron Hill and Margaret (*née* Chadwick); *m* 1954, Jane Edna Austin; one *s* one *d*. *Educ*: Bishop Vesey's Grammar Sch., Sutton Coldfield; Trinity Coll., Oxford; College of Estate Management, London Univ. (BSc EstMan). Hillier Parker May & Rowden, 1953–88, Partner, 1962–88. Served TA (Major), 1949–73; Metropolitan Special Constabulary (Comdt), 1973–86. Liveryman, Farriers' Co. *Publications*: (jtly) Valuations: principles into practice, 1980, 4th edn 1993; (jtly) Handbook of Rent Review, 1981, rev. edns to 1988. *Recreations*: shooting, DIY. *Address*: Hastoe House, Hastoe, Tring, Herts HP23 6LS. *T*: (01442) 822084. *Club*: Honourable Artillery Company.

**HILL, John Lawrence**; Chairman, Britannia Building Society, 1990–94; Chief Executive, Loss Prevention Council, 1986–96; *b* 21 July 1934; *s* of late Sidney Hill and Hilda Wardle Hill; *m* 1960, Elizabeth Godfrey; one *s* three *d*. *Educ*: Abbotsholme Sch.; Sidney Sussex Coll., Cambridge (MA). National Service, Royal Corps of Signals, 1953–55. Royal Dutch Shell Group, 1959–67; PA Consulting Group, 1967–86; Director: Britannia Building Soc., 1984–94; Britannia Life, 1989–94. Director: Loss Prevention Certification Bd, 1986–96; Nat. Approval Council for Security Systems, 1990–96. Governor, Inst. of Risk Management, 1987–93. *Recreations*: golf, bridge, music, greyhound rescue. *Address*: 23 Harvey Road, Guildford, Surrey GU1 3LU. *T*: (01483) 566413. *Clubs*: Hawks (Cambridge); Royal & Ancient Golf, Worplesdon Golf.

**HILL, Prof. Jonathan Michael**, PhD; RIBA; Professor of Architecture and Visual Theory, since 2005, and Director, MPhil/PhD Architectural Design, since 2000, Bartlett School of Architecture, University College London; *b* Maidstone, 1958; *s* of George Wharton Hill and Margaret Mary Hill. *Educ*: King's Coll., Taunton; Wellington Sch.; Architectural Assoc. Sch. of Architecture (AA Dip (Hons) 1983; RIBA Pt 3 1985); Bartlett Sch. of Architecture, University Coll. London (MSc Hist. of Mod. Architecture 1990; PhD Architecture (Architectural Design) 2000). ARB (ARCUK 1985); RIBA 1994. Bartlett School of Architecture, University College London: Lectr, 1989–99, Sen. Lectr, 1999–2005, in Architecture; Head, 2004–05; Dir of Design, 2011–12. Fellow, Akademie Schloss Solitude, Stuttgart, 1998–99; Vis. Sen. Fellow, Dept of Architecture, National Univ. of Singapore, 2004. FRSA 1995. Jt Ed., Design Research in Architecture, book series, 2010–. *Publications*: The Illegal Architect, 1998; (ed) Occupying Architecture: between the architect and the user, 1998; (ed) Architecture—the Subject is Matter, 2001; Actions of Architecture: architects and creative users, 2003; Immaterial Architecture, 2006; Drawing Research, 2006; (ed jtly) Critical Architecture, 2007; Weather Architecture, 2012; A Landscape of Architecture, History and Fiction, 2016; The Architecture of Ruins, 2019. *Recreations*: walking, gardens. *Address*: Bartlett School of Architecture, University College London, 22 Gordon Street, WC1H 0QB. *T*: (020) 3108 9672. *E*: jonathan.hill@ucl.ac.uk.

**HILL, Dame Judith (Eileen)**, DBE 2012 (CBE 2001); DL; FRCN; Chief Executive, Northern Ireland Hospice, 2005–14. Sen. Nurse and Tutor, Countess Mountbatten House, Southampton; Chief Nursing Officer, Dept of Health, Social Services and Public Safety, NI, 1995–2005. Chair, NI Palliative Care Services Rev. (Report, Partnerships in Caring, 2000). Vis. Prof., Sch. of Nursing, Univ. of Ulster. Chair, Mgt Cttee and Policy and Practice Cttee, All Ireland Inst. of Hospice and Palliative Care, 2011–16. DL Belfast, 2013. FRCN 2009. Hon. DSc Ulster, 2011. Outstanding Achievement Award, RCN, NI, 2008; Paul Harris Fellow Award, Rotary Club Belfast, 2013.

**HILL, Rt Hon. Keith**; *see* Hill, Rt Hon. T. K.

**HILL, Leslie Francis**; Chairman: HartHill Partnership Ltd, 2004–08; British Music Rights Ltd, 2005–07; ITV, 1994–2002 (Director, 1987–2002); Director, Carlton Communications PLC, 1994–2004; *b* 2 Sept. 1936; *s* of late Elizabeth May and Francis Alfred Hill; *m* 1972, Christine Susan (*née* Bush); two *s*. *Educ*: Cotham Grammar School. FCA. Qualified as Chartered Accountant; with Ware, Ward (now Ernst & Young), 1952–62, Peat, Marwick, Mitchell, 1962–65; IPC Group, 1965–70, finally Finance Director, Music for Pleasure, continuing as such with EMI Group to 1971; EMI Group: Exec. Dir, Rest of World Div., 1972–73; Man. Dir, EMI NZ, 1973–74; Asst Dir, Group Music, 1975–76; Managing Director: EMI Records UK, 1976–78; EMI Music, Europe, 1979–80; Jt Man. Dir, HAT Group plc, 1980–86; Dir, ITN, 1987–95; Man. Dir, 1987–91, Chm. and Chief Exec., 1991–95, Central Independent Television. *Recreations*: listening to music, reading, fitness, watching cricket.

**HILL, Prof. Leslie James**, PhD; FBA 2003; Professor of French Studies, University of Warwick, 1998–2014, now Emeritus. *Educ*: Gonville and Caius Coll., Cambridge (BA (Mod. Langs) 1972; MA 1976; PhD (French) 1976). University of Cambridge: Res. Fellow in French, Selwyn Coll., 1974–76; Lectr in French and Dir of Studies in Mod. Langs, Clare Coll., 1976–79; University of Warwick: Lectr in French Studies, 1979–93; Sen. Lectr, 1993–96; Reader, 1996–98. *Publications*: Beckett's Fiction: in different words, 1990; Marguerite Duras: apocalyptic desires, 1993; Blanchot: extreme contemporary, 1997; Bataille, Klossowski, Blanchot: writing at the limit, 2001; The Cambridge Introduction to Jacques Derrida, 2007; Radical Indecision: Barthes, Blanchot, Derrida, and the future of criticism, 2010; Maurice Blanchot and Fragmentary Writing: a change of epoch, 2012;

Nancy Blanchot: a serious controversy, 2018. *Recreations:* photography, organic vegetable gardening. *Address:* Department of French Studies, School of Modern Languages and Cultures, University of Warwick, Coventry CV4 7AL. *E:* leslie.hill@warwick.ac.uk.

**HILL, Mark;** *see* Hill, N. M.

**HILL, Mark Roger;** antiques and collectables expert, author and publisher, since 2002; *b* Guildford, 2 Feb. 1975; *s* of Roger and Angela Hill; partner, Philip Reicherstorfer. *Educ:* Royal Grammar Sch., Guildford; Reading Univ. (BA Hons Hist. of Art and Architecture). Jun. cataloguer, Bonhams, 1996–98; Specialist, Sotheby's, 1998–2000; Channel Manager, 2000, Dir, Auction Hse Services and Live Auctions, 2001–02, icollector.com; Consultant and author: Price Guide Co. (UK) Ltd and Dorling Kindersley, 2002–08; Miller's, 2008–; author and publisher, Mark Hill Publishing Ltd, 2006–; Accredited Lectr, Arts Soc., 2015–. Co-presenter, BBC TV: Cracking Antiques, 2010; Antiques Uncovered, 2012; Collectaholics, 2014, 2015; specialist, Antiques Roadshow, 2007–; antiques columnist, Daily Mail, 2012–. Patron, King's Lynn Arts Centre, 2011–15. Freeman: City of London, 2013; Arts Scholars' Co. (formerly Co. of Art Scholars, Dealers and Collectors), 2009–. *Publications:* Fat Lava: West German ceramics of the 1960s and 70s, 2006, 4th edn 2016; Michael Harris: Mdina glass and Isle of Wight studio glass, 2006; Frank Thrower and Dartington Glass, 2007; Hi Sklo Lo Sklo: post war Czech glass design from masterpiece to mass-produced, 2008; Caithness Glass: loch, heather and peat, 2011; Alla Moda: Italian ceramics of 1950s–70s, 2012; (Gen. Ed.) Berànek & Skrdlovice: legends of Czech glass, 2014; The Horrors of War by Pierre-Georges Jeanniot, 2014; Sklo: Czech glass design from the 1950s–70s, 2017. *Recreations:* growing bonsai, art, reading, collecting, drinking wine. *E:* books@markhillpublishing.com. *Club:* Groucho.

**HILL, Martin Henry Paul;** HM Diplomatic Service, retired; property management; *b* 17 May 1961; *s* of John and Jacqueline Hill; *m* 1985, Kim Cherie Lydyard; three *d*. *Educ:* Pembroke Coll., Cambridge (BA Langs and Econs, MA). Food Standards Div., MAFF, 1983–84; Parly Clerk to Lord Privy Seal, 1985–86; Ministry of Agriculture, Fisheries and Food: Financial Mgt Team, 1986; EC Div., 1987; Sugar, Oils and Fats Div., 1988; Principal Private Sec. to Food Safety Minister, 1989–90; Trade Policy and Tropical Foods Div., 1990–92; First Sec., Agric., Fisheries and Food, Bonn, 1993–96; joined HM Diplomatic Service, 1996; SE Asian Dept, FCO, 1996–98; Dep. High Comr, Colombo, 1998–2001; Commercial Counsellor, Bangkok, 2002–05; Counsellor (Econ., Sci. and Innovation), Ottawa, 2006–09; Dep. High Comr, Ottawa, 2009–11; Dep. Hd of Mission, Bogota, 2011; Hd, Counter Proliferation Dept, FCO, 2011–12; Hd, Strategy and Network Dept, Consular Directorate, FCO, 2012–13. *Recreations:* squash, travel, reading, diving, music.

**HILL, Martyn Geoffrey;** tenor singer; *b* 14 Sept. 1944; *s* of Norman S. L. Hill and Gwendoline A. M. Hill (*née* Andrews); three *s* one *d*; *m* 2004, Julie Ann Moffat. *Educ:* Sir Joseph Williamson's Mathematical School, Rochester, Kent; King's College, Cambridge; Royal College of Music (ARCM); vocal studies with Audrey Langford. Prof. of Vocal Studies, Trinity Coll. of Music, 1997–2011. Concert, oratorio, recital and operatic appearances throughout the world with major orchestras, conductors and choirs; numerous radio, TV and gramophone recordings. Hon. DMus Leicester, 2009. *Address:* c/o Owen White Management, 139 Brookwood Road, SW18 5BD.

**HILL, Matthew;** Chief Operating Officer, Travelopia, since 2018; *b* London, 1970; *m* 2002, Jacqui; two *d*. *Educ:* Univ. of Warwick (BSc Hons Econs). Joined Unilever, 1993; mktg roles, then Global Vice Pres., Mktg, 2003–10, Unilever; Chief Mktg Officer, H. J. Heinz, 2010–11; Chief Commercial Officer and Man. Dir, H. J. Heinz UK and Ireland, 2011–13; Pres. and CEO, Europe, H. J. Heinz, subseq. Kraft Heinz Co., 2013–16. *Recreations:* running, golf.

**HILL, Max Benjamin Rowland;** QC 2008; a Recorder, since 2004; Director of Public Prosecutions, since 2018; *b* Hatfield, 10 Jan. 1964; *s* of Thomas Rowland Hill and Shirley Ann Hill; *m* 1993, Heather Faith Coombs; two *d*. *Educ:* Royal Grammar Sch., Newcastle-upon-Tyne; St Peter's Coll., Oxford (Scholar; BA Hons Juris. 1986). Called to the Bar, Middle Temple, 1987, Bencher, 2012; in practice as barrister specialising in crime; Hd of Chambers, 18 Red Lion Ct, 2012–18; Leader, SE Circuit, 2014–16. Ind. Reviewer of Terrorism Legislation, 2017–18. Chairman: Bd of Trustees, Scene and Heard, 2005–11; Criminal Bar Association, 2011–12 (Vice Chm., 2010–11); Kalisher Scholarship Trust, 2014–18 (Trustee). Co-founder, High Stakes Persuasion, 2014–18. Academic Advr, Curriculum for Cohesion, 2014–17; Steering Gp, Understanding Conversion to Islam in Prison, 2018. Patron, Scene and Heard, 2011–. FRSA. *Publications:* (contributing ed.) Practitioner's Guide to Terrorist Trials, 2007; (contrib.) Investigating Terrorism, 2015. *Recreations:* theatre, tennis, travel, indoor rowing. *Address:* Crown Prosecution Service, 102 Petty France, SW1H 9EA. *T:* (020) 3357 1898. *E:* cpsprivateoffice@cps.gov.uk.

**HILL, Rt Rev. Michael Arthur;** Bishop of Bristol, 2003–17; an Honorary Assistant Bishop, Diocese of Bath and Wells, since 2018; *b* 17 April 1949; *s* of Arthur and Hilda Hill; *m* 1972, Anthea Jean Hill (*née* Longridge); one *s* four *d*. *Educ:* N Cheshire Coll. of FE (Dip. in Business Studies); Brasted Place Coll.; Ridley Hall, Cambridge (GOE); Fitzwilliam Coll., Cambridge (Postgrad. Cert. in Theology). Junior Exec. in printing industry, 1968–72. Mem., Scargill House Community, 1972–73; ordained deacon, 1977, priest, 1978; Curate: St Mary Magdalene, Addiscombe, Croydon, 1977–80; St Paul, Slough, 1980–83; Priest in charge, 1983–90, Rector, 1990–92, St Leonard, Chesham Bois; RD, Amersham, 1990–92; Archdeacon of Berkshire, 1992–98; Area Bishop of Buckingham, 1998–2003. Entered H of L, 2009. *Publications:* Reaching the Unchurched, 1992; Lifelines, 1997. *Recreations:* playing guitar, listening to music, cricket, soccer, Rugby League and Union, reading.

**HILL, Michael Robert;** MP (Lab) Hartlepool, since 2017; *b* Heywood, Lancs, 12 May 1963; *s* of late Robert Hill and of Pauline Hill; *m* Glynis; two *s*. *Educ:* Lancaster Univ. (BA Drama and Dramatics and Theatre Arts). Worked in theatre, in educn, then at Rochdale Bor. Liby; Shop Steward, then Deptl Convenor for Libraries; Asst Br. Sec., Rochdale NALGO; Br. Sec., Rochdale UNISON, until 2000; Regl Organiser, Northern Reg., 2000–17, Regl Political Officer, 2012–17, UNISON. Labour Party: Sec., Heywood and Middleton constituency; Trade Union Liaison Officer, Northern Reg., 2012–17; Vice Chair, Labour North, 2016–17. Mem., Petitions Cttee, H of C, 2017–. Contested (Lab) Richmond (Yorks), 2015. *Address:* House of Commons, SW1A 0AA.

**HILL, Michael Thomas;** HM Diplomatic Service, retired; Administrator, Ascension Island, 2005–08; *b* 2 Jan. 1945; *s* of late Roland Hill and Anne Hill (*née* McIlwraith); *m* 1977, Elizabeth Louise, *d* of Derrick Charles Carden, CMG; three *s* one *d*. *Educ:* Bathgate Acad. Joined Foreign Office, 1963; served UKMIS NY, Vientiane, Kaduna, Sana'a; Dep. Hd of Mission, Ulan Bator, 1978–81; Consul, Port of Spain, 1981–85; FCO, 1985–88; Asst to Dep. Governor, Gibraltar, 1988–93; First Sec. and Hd of Aid Sect., Nairobi, 1993–96; FCO, 1996–2000; High Comr, Vanuatu, 2000–05. *Recreations:* golf, gardening, walking. *Address:* 14 Romsey Road, Winchester SO23 8TP.

**HILL, Michael William;** Director, Science Reference Library, British Library, 1973–86; *b* 1928; *o s* of late Geoffrey William Hill, Ross on Wye and Torquay; *m* 1st, 1957, Elma Jack Forrest (*d* 1967); one *s* one *d*; 2nd, 1969, Barbara Joy Youngman. *Educ:* King Henry VIII Sch., Coventry; Nottingham High Sch.; Lincoln Coll., Oxford (MA, MSc). MRIC 1953; CChem; FCLIP (FIInfSc 1982). Research Chemist, Laporte Chemicals Ltd, 1953–56; Morgan Crucible Group: Laboratory Head, 1956; Asst Process Control Manager, 1958; Group Technical Editor, 1963; Asst Keeper, British Museum, 1964; Dep. Librarian, Patent Office Library, 1965; Keeper, and Dir, Nat. Ref. Library of Science and Invention, BM, 1968–73; British Library: Mem., Organising Cttee, 1970–73; Associate Dir, Sci. Technology and Industry, 1986–88. Various consultancies in Europe, Asia and developing countries, 1974–92. Pres., Fédn Internat. de Documentation et Information, 1985–90. Member: Exec. Cttee, Nat. Central Library, 1971–74; EEC/CIDST Working Parties on Patent documentation, 1973–80, and on Information for Industry, 1976–80; Board, UK Chemical Inf. Service, 1974–77; Adv. Cttee for Scottish Science Reference Library, 1983–87; Chairman: Circle of State Librarians, 1977–79; Council, Aslib, 1979–81; Vice Pres., IATUL, 1976–81; Founder, Western European Round Table on Information and Documentation, subseq. European Council of Information Assocs, 1980. Series Editor (with I. McIlwaine), Guides to Information Sources. *Publications:* Patent Documentation (with Wittmann and Schiffels), 1979; Michael Hill on Science, Technology and Information (ed by P. Ward), 1988; National Information Policies and Strategies, 1994; The Impact of Information on Society, 1998, 2nd edn 2005; papers on librarianship, documentation and information science in jls and conf. proceedings. *Address:* 137 Burdon Lane, Cheam, Surrey SM2 7DB. *T:* (020) 8642 2418. *Club:* Oxford and Cambridge.

**HILL, (Nicholas) Mark;** QC 2009; *b* Birmingham, 7 Aug. 1965; *s* of David Hill and Stanlene Hill. *Educ:* Tudor Grange Comp. Sch., Solihull; Solihull Sixth Form Coll.; King's Coll., London (LLB Hons 1986; AKC 1986); Univ. of Wales (LLM Canon Law 1994). Called to the Bar, Middle Temple, 1987; Mem. *ad eundem*, Inner Temple, 2008, Bencher, 2011; in practice as a barrister, 3 Pump Court, 1988–2011, Francis Taylor Building, 2012–. Recorder, 2005–; Dep. Judge of Upper Tribunal (Asylum and Immigration), 2015–. Mem., Legal Aid Commn, 1995–2000, Legal Adv. Commn, 2001–, General Synod of C of E. Deputy Chancellor: dio. of Winchester, 1994–2006; dio. of York, 2007–; dio. of Blackburn, 2010–; Chancellor: dio. of Chichester, 1999–; dio. of Gibraltar in Europe, 2004–; dio. of Leeds (formerly W Yorks and the Dales), 2015–. Founder Mem., Anglican-RC Colloquium of Canon Lawyers, 1999–; Mem., Standing Cttee, Ecclesiastical Judges Assoc., 2008–; Convener, Interfaith Legal Advrs Network, 2008–; Co-Chm., Belief in Mediation and Arbitration, 2012–15. Member: Eur. Consortium for Ch and State Research, 2004– (Pres., 2012); Internat. Consortium for Law and Religion Studies, 2007–. Fellow, 1999–, Hon. Prof. of Law, 2006–, Centre for Law and Religion, Cardiff Univ.; Sen. Visitor, Emmanuel Coll., Cambridge, 2007; Ecumenical Fellow in Canon Law, Ven. English Coll., Rome, 2013–; Extraordinary Prof., Univ. of Pretoria, 2014–; Vis. Prof., Dickson Poon Sch. of Law, KCL, 2015–. Fellow, Internat. Acad. for Freedom of Religion and Belief, 2004–. Ed., Ecclesiastical Law Jl, 2002–; Member: Internat. Adv. Bd, Revista General de Derecho Canónico y Derecho Eclesiástico del Estado, 2004–; Editl Adv. Bd, Oxford Jl for Law and Religion, 2011–. *Publications:* Ecclesiastical Law, 1995, 3rd edn 2007; (ed jtly) English Canon Law, 1998; (ed) Faithful Discipleship: clergy discipline in Anglican and Roman Catholic canon law, 2001; (ed) Religious Liberty and Human Rights, 2002; (ed jtly) Jowitt's Dictionary of English Law, 2010; (ed jtly) Butterworths Costs Service, 2010; Religion and Law in the United Kingdom, 2011, 2nd edn 2014; Religion and Discrimination Law in the European Union, 2012; (ed jtly) Magna Carta, Religion and the Rule of Law, 2015; (ed jtly) Great Christian Jurists in English History, 2017; regular contrib. to legal periodicals on law and religion. *Recreations:* exotic travel, domestic theatre. *Address:* Francis Taylor Building, Temple, EC4Y 7BJ. *T:* (020) 7353 8415. *E:* mark.hill@ftb.eu.com. *Clubs:* Athenæum; Nikæan.

**HILL, Rt Rev. Peter;** *see* Barking, Area Bishop of.

**HILL, Prof. Peter David,** FRCP, FRCPsych, FRCPCH; Emeritus Professor, University of London, since 1998; Consultant Child and Adolescent Psychiatrist, in private practice, since 2003; *b* Eastbourne, 16 March 1945; *s* of Derryck and Phyllis Hill; *m* 1972, Christine Seed; two *s* one *d*. *Educ:* Leighton Park Sch., Reading; Selwyn Coll., Cambridge (BA 1966; MB BChir 1969); St Bartholomew's Hosp. Med. Sch. FRCP 1994; FRCPsych 1987; FRCPCH 1997. Hosp. posts, St Bartholomew's Hosp., London, 1969–72; Registrar and Sen. Registrar, Maudsley Hosp., 1972–79; Sen. Lectr, 1979, then Prof. of Child Mental Health, 1979–98, St George's Hosp. Med. Sch., Univ. of London; Consultant, St George's Hosp., 1979–98; Hon. Consultant, St Thomas' Hosp., 1981–89; Consultant Psychiatrist, 1998–2003, Hon. Consultant, 2003–10, Gt Ormond St Hosp. Vis. Prof., St George's, Univ. of London, 1999–. Advr, Select Cttee on Health, 1995–97. Med. Advr to British Army, 1995–2007; Consultant Advr, Huntercombe Manor Hosp., Maidenhead, 1998–2014; Specialist Advr, Health Adv. Service, 1999–2003. Chm., Faculty of Child and Adolescent Psychiatry, RCPsych, 1993–97. Pres., Union Européenne de Médecins Spécialistes (Child and Adolescent Psychiatry), 2002–06. *Publications:* (jtly) Essentials of Postgraduate Psychiatry, 1979, 3rd edn 1997; (jtly) A Manual of Practical Psychiatry, 1986; Adolescent Psychiatry, 1989; (jtly) The Child Surveillance Handbook, 1990, 2nd edn 1994; (jtly) The Child with a Disability, 1996; (jtly) Child Mental Health in Primary Care, 2001; (jtly) A Perfect Start, 2007; (jtly) A Handbook for the Assessment of Children's Behaviours, 2012; contrib. papers and chapters on child and adolescent psychiatry, psychopharmacol. and child mental health services. *Recreations:* jazz trumpet, contemplation, rural wildlife. *Address:* 35 Great James Street, WC1N 3HB. *T:* (020) 7486 2332. *E:* ali@127harley.com. *Club:* Royal Society of Medicine.

**HILL, (Peter) Jeremy (Oldham),** CMG 2019; HM Diplomatic Service; Legal Counsellor, Foreign and Commonwealth Office, since 2017; *b* 17 April 1954; *m* 1981, Katharine Hearn; one *s* one *d*. Joined FCO as Asst Legal Advr, 1982; First Sec. (Legal Advr), Bonn, 1987–90; on loan as Legal Counsellor, Law Officers' Dept, 1991–95; Legal Counsellor, UK Rep., Brussels, 1995–98; Hd, Southern European Dept, FCO, 1999–2001; Ambassador to: Lithuania, 2001–03; Bulgaria, 2004–07; Asst Dir, CPDS, 2008–13, 2015–17; Dep. Hd, OSCE Mission, Odessa, Ukraine, 2014.

**HILL, Peter Whitehead;** Editor, Daily Express, 2003–11; *b* 6 April 1945; *s* of Becket and Edith Hill; *m* 1st, 1984, Vera Marshall (marr. diss. 1998); one *d*; 2nd, 2004, Marjorie Francis; one *s*. *Educ:* Hulme Grammar Sch., Oldham; Manchester Univ. Reporter, Colne Valley Guardian, 1961–62; sub-editor: Huddersfield Examr, 1962–63; Manchester Evening News, 1963–65; leader writer, Oldham Evening Chronicle, 1965–67; sub-ed., Daily Telegraph, 1967–74; sub-ed., Daily Mirror, 1974–78; Chief Sub-Ed., Sunday People, 1970–80; Chief Sub-Ed., Night Ed., Associate Ed., and Dep. Ed., 1978–98, Ed., 1998–2003, Daily Star. Mem., Press Complaints Commn, 2003–08. Columnist, Daily Express, 2011–18. *Recreations:* bridge, tennis, ski-ing, upholstery. *Address:* c/o Daily Express, 10 Lower Thames Street, EC3R 6EN. *Clubs:* Reform, Andrew Robson Bridge.

**HILL, (Robert) Charles;** QC (NI) 1974; Member, Standing Advisory Commission on Human Rights under Northern Ireland Constitution Act 1973, 1991–96 (Chairman, 1992–95); *b* 22 March 1936; *s* of Benjamin Morrison Hill and Mary A. Hill (*née* Roche); *m* 1961, Kathleen Allen (*d* 2010); three *s* one *d*. *Educ:* St Malachy's Coll., Belfast; Queen's Univ. Belfast (LLB); Trinity Coll., Dublin (MA). Called to the Bar: Inn of Court, NI, 1959, Bencher, 1988; Gray's Inn, 1971; King's Inns, Dublin, 1986; Sen. Counsel, Ireland, 1987. Official Referee under Finance Acts, 1976; Dep. County Court Judge, 1979–80. Chairman:

Statutory Body, Pharmaceutical Soc. of NI, 1977–92; Poison Bd of NI, 1982–92. *Recreations:* history of art, forestry, shooting. *Address:* The Bar Library, Royal Courts of Justice, Chichester Street, Belfast BT1 3JQ. *T:* (028) 9024 1523. *Club:* Kildare Street and University (Dublin).

**HILL, Sir Robert (Charles Finch)**, KBE 1991; FREng; part-time lecturer, University of Bath, since 1995; President, Institute of Marine Engineers, 1995–96; *b* 1 May 1937; *s* of late Frances Margaret Hill (*née* Lumsden) and Ronald Finch Hill; *m* 1971, Deborah Mary (*née* Windle); one *s* one *d*. *Educ:* Nautical Coll., Pangbourne; RNEC Manadon; RNC Greenwich. BSc(Eng); CEng, FREng (FEng 1992). HMS Thermopylae, 1964–65; HMS Repulse, 1967–71; MoD (PE), 1971–74; RNEC Manadon, 1975–77; HMS Cleopatra, 1977–78; Nuclear Power Manager, Chatham, 1979–80; MoD (PE), 1980–84; RCDS 1985; HMS Raleigh in Comd, 1986–87; CSO (Engrg) to C-in-C Fleet, 1987–89; Chief Abovewater Systems Exec., 1989–91; Dep. Controller of the Navy (Vice-Adm.), 1989–93; Chief Naval Engr Officer, 1989–93; Dir Gen. Submarines, 1991–93; retd. Independent Director: British Energy plc, 1999–2003; SEA (Group) Ltd, 1999–2007. Trustee, Bath Theatre Trust, 2003–. Mem. Council, Univ. of Bath, 2000–06. Hon. FIMarEST 2002. Hon. DTech Plymouth, 1995; Hon. DEng Bath, 2005. *Recreations:* rhythm guitar, theatre, sailing. *Club:* Royal Over-Seas League.

**HILL, Hon. Robert Murray**, AC 2012; Adjunct Professor of Sustainability, United States Studies Centre, University of Sydney, since 2009; Chairman, CRC for Low Carbon Living, since 2012; *b* 25 Sept. 1946; *s* of C. M. Hill; *m* 1969, Diana Jacka; two *s* two *d*. *Educ:* Scotch Coll., Mitcham, SA; Univ. of Adelaide (LLB 1968; BA 1982); Univ. of London (LLM 1970). In practice as barrister and solicitor, SA, 1970–. Senator (L) S Australia, 1981–2006; Fed. Shadow Minister for Foreign Affairs, 1989–93, for Defence, 1993, for Public Admin, 1993–94, for Educn, Sci. and Technol., 1994–96; Leader of the Opposition in Senate, 1993–96; Leader of the Govt in Senate, 1996–2006; Minister for the Envmt, 1996–98, for the Envmt and Heritage, 1998–2001, for Defence, 2001–06; Perm. Rep. of Australia to the UN, 2006–09. Liberal Party of Australia: Campaign Ctee., 1975–77; Chm., Constitutional Cttee, 1977–81; Vice-Pres., 1977–79, Pres., 1985–87, SA Div.; Mem., Fed. Exec., 1985–87 and 1990–2006. Chm., Australian Carbon Trust, 2009. Chancellor, Univ. of Adelaide, 2010–14.

**HILL, Rev. Roger Anthony John;** Bishop's Missioner, Diocese of Manchester, 2007–11; Chaplain to the Queen, 2001–15; *b* 23 March 1945; *s* of Arthur and Gladys Hill; *m* 1972, Joanna Reading; three *s*. *Educ:* Univ. of Liverpool (BA 1967); Linacre Coll., Oxford (BA 1969; MA); Ripon Hall, Oxford. Ordained deacon, 1970, priest, 1971; Curate: St Peter, St Helier, Southwark, 1970–74; Dawley Parva, 1974–76; Team Vicar, 1976–81, Rector, 1981–88, Central Telford; Rector: Newark, 1988–2002; St Ann, Manchester, 2002–07. RD Newark, 1990–95; Area Dean, Hulme, 2005–07. Hon. Canon: Southwell Minster, 1998–2002; Manchester Cathedral, 2002–11, now Canon Emeritus. *Recreations:* walking, travel. *Address:* 4 Four Stalls End, Littleborough, Lancs OL15 8SB. *T:* (01706) 374719.

**HILL, Roger Jonathan;** Director of Community and Partnership, Sodexo Justice Services, since 2011; *b* Epsom, Surrey, 9 July 1955; *s* of John and Mary Hill; *m* 1993, Elizabeth Durrans; one *d*. *Educ:* Nork Park Sch., Banstead, Surrey; Newcastle upon Tyne Poly. (CQSW); Sunderland Univ. Business Sch. (MBA). Probation Officer, 1978–95; Asst Chief Probation Officer, Durham, 1995–2001; Chief Probation Officer: Lincs, 2001–04; London, 2004–05; Dir, Nat. Probation Service, 2005–09; Dir of Offender Mgt (SE England), Nat. Offender Mgt Service, MoJ, 2009–11. *Recreations:* contemporary music, guitar, listening and playing, photography, building renovation and DIY, walking. *Address:* Sodexo Justice Services, One Southampton Row, WC1B 5HA. *T:* (01203) 1164340, 07767 238595. *E:* roger.hill@sodexo.com.

**HILL, Shaun Donovan;** consultant and writer; chef and restaurateur; *b* 11 April 1947; *s* of George Herbert Hill and Molly Hill; *m* 1966, Anja Toivonen; one *s* two *d*. *Educ:* London Oratory; St Marylebone Grammar Sch. Cook: Carrier's Restaurant, Islington, 1967–71; Gay Hussar, 1971–73; Intercontinental Hotel, London, 1973–75; Head Chef: Montcalm Hotel, London, 1976–77; Capital Hotel, London, 1978; Lygon Arms, Broadway, Worcs, 1979–81; Gidleigh Park, Chagford, 1985–94; Head Chef, Merchant House, Ludlow, 1994–2005; Head Chef and Owner, The Walnut Tree, Abergavenny, 2007–. *Publications:* Gidleigh Park Cookery Book, 1990; Shaun Hill's Cookery Book, 1994; (with John Wilkins) Archestratus: the life of luxury, 1994; Shaun Hill's Cooking at the Merchant House, 2000; How To Cook Better, 2004; (with J. Wilkins) Food in Ancient Cultures, 2005; (jtly) Cook, 2005; (jtly) The Cook's Book, 2005; Salt is Essential, 2016. *Recreations:* wine, travel. *Address:* 24 Droitwich Road, Worcester WR3 7LH. *E:* shaun@thewalnuttreeinn.com.

**HILL, Ven. Simon James;** Archdeacon of Taunton, since 2016; Warden of Readers, Diocese of Bath and Wells, since 2016; *b* 1964. *Educ:* Univ. of Sheffield (BA 1985); Univ. of Exeter (PGCE 1988); Univ. of Bristol (MA 2009); Ripon Coll., Cuddesdon. Ordained deacon, 1995, priest, 1996; Curate: St James, Manston, 1995–98; Team Vicar, St Peter and St Paul, Dorchester, 1998–2003; Dir, Berinsfield Prog., Ripon Coll., Cuddesdon, 1998–2003; Rector, St Andrew, Backwell, N Somerset, 2003–10; Dir of Clergy Develt, Dio. of Bath and Wells, 2010–16; Preb., Wells Cathedral, 2014–16. *Address:* c/o Diocese of Bath and Wells, The Old Deanery, St Andrew's Street, Wells, Som BA5 2UG.

**HILL, Stephen Guy,** OBE 2017; Executive Chairman (formerly Chairman and Chief Executive), D'Aval Ltd (formerly Harbour Group), since 2006; *b* 19 July 1960; *s* of Michael Lawrence Hill and Joan Florence Hill (*née* Luce). *Educ:* King Edward VII Sch., Lytham; St John's Coll., Cambridge (Wright Prize 1980; Whitehead Scholar; MA 1st Cl. Hons Law 1982); Harvard Business Sch. (PMD 1991). Consultant, Boston Consulting Gp, 1982–85; Exec. Asst to Chm., Guinness plc, 1985–87; Pearson plc, 1987–2002: Dir of Strategy, 1987–92; Managing Director: Watford Observer Newspapers, 1992–93; Oxford & County Newspapers Ltd, 1993–95; Chief Executive: Westminster Press Ltd, 1995–96; Financial Times Newspaper, 1996–98; Financial Times Gp Ltd, 1998–2002; Mem., Mgt Bd, 1998–2002; Chm., Interactive Data Corp. (formerly Data Broadcasting Inc.), 1998–2002; Chief Exec., Sporting Exchange Ltd (Betfair), 2003–05. Non-executive Director: Royal & Sun Alliance Gp plc, 2000–04; Psion plc, 2003–06; Channel 4, 2005–11; IG Gp plc, 2011–; Applerigg Ltd, 2013–; AZTEC Ltd, 2014–16; Chm., 2Degrees.com, 2010–13. Mem. Bd Ofcom, 2014–15. Mem. Adv. Bd, Judge Business Sch., Cambridge Univ., 2007–16 (Mem., Circle of Patrons, 2017–). Mem. Council, Whitechapel Art Gall., 2000–03. Trustee, Action on Hearing Loss (formerly RNID), 2008–17 (Hon. Treas., 2008–12; Dep. Chm., 2012–13; Chm., 2013–17; Hon. Vice Pres., 2017–); Chm., Alzheimer's Soc., 2016–. *Recreations:* triathlon, gardening, travel, classic cars. *Club:* Royal Automobile.

**HILL, Prof. Stephen Roderick,** PhD; Professor of Management, University of London, 2001–11, Professor Emeritus, 2012; Principal, Royal Holloway, University of London, 2002–09; *b* 15 March 1946; *s* of Alan Hill, CBE and Enid Hill (*née* Malin); *m* 1st, 1970, Jane Severn (marr. diss. 1993); one *s* one *d*; 2nd, 1996, Siobhan Rosser. *Educ:* University College Sch.; Balliol Coll., Oxford (BA Modern Hist.); London Sch. of Econs (MSc Sociol.; PhD 1973). Lectr in Sociol., Bedford Coll., London, 1968–70; London School of Economics: Lectr in Industrial Relns, 1971–74; Lectr, 1974–82, Reader, 1982–91, in Sociol.; Prof. of Sociol., 1991–2001; Pro-Dir, 1996–2001; Prof. of Mgt, 2001–02; Actg Dir, 2001; Dep. Dir, 2001–02; Mem. Ct, 1991–2001; Mem. Council, 1996–2002; Pres., LSE Foundn Inc., 2000–02. Ed., British Jl Sociol., 1995–2002. Member: Corporate Social Responsibility Steering Gp, DTI, 2003–04; Scholarly Commns Gp, JISC, 2004–10. Mem. Bd, Surrey Bridges, 2002–08; Dir, Higher Educn SE, 2003–10; Chair, Southern Univs Mgt Services, 2003–07. Member, Court: City Univ., 2001–06; Henley Mgt Coll., 2005–08; Mem. Council, St George's, Univ. of London, 2004–09; Trustee, Univ. of London, 2008–09. Trustee, Citizens Advice Richmond (formerly Richmond CAB Service, then Richmond CAB), 2010– (Vice-Chair Trustees, 2012–16; Chair Trustees, 2016–). Fellow, Wellington Coll., 2009–16. *Publications:* The Dockers, 1976; Competition and Control at Work, 1981; with N. Abercrombie and B. S. Turner: The Dominant Ideology Thesis, 1980; The Penguin Dictionary of Sociology, 1984, 5th edn 2006; Sovereign Individuals of Capitalism, 1986; (ed) Dominant Ideologies, 1990; (with M. White, C. Mills and D. Smeaton) Managing to Change?, 2004; (with P. McGovern, C. Mills and M. White) Market, Class, and Employment, 2007. *Recreations:* fell-walking, dinghy sailing. *E:* stephen.hill@rhul.ac.uk.

**HILL, Stephen Russell,** CB 2004; OBE 1982; Managing Director, Steve Hill Consultancy Ltd, since 2004; Chief Executive, Defence Aviation Repair Agency, 1999–2003; *b* 27 March 1942; *s* of late Henry Rowland Hill and Kathleen Bertha Hill; *m* 1964, Muriel Chisholm; one *s* one *d*. *Educ:* St Philip's Grammar Sch., Birmingham; Hendon CAT; BA Open Univ. 1980; Dip. Accounting and Finance 1988. CEng 1975; FIMechE 1985; FRAeS 1986. Marine Engr, BP Tanker Co., 1958–65; Civil Engrg projects, BP Refinery, Grangemouth, 1965–66; RAF, 1966–91: appts incl. Chief Engr, RAF Coningsby, 1981–84; Air Cdre, Dir of Support Mgt, 1989–91; Business Develt, BAe, 1991–95; Projects and Technical Dir, Serco Defence, 1995–96; Chief Exec., Naval Aircraft Repair Orgn, 1996–99. FCMI (FIMgt 1987). *Recreation:* hill walking.

**HILL, Dr Stuart John;** Vice Chair, Dudley and Walsall Mental Health Partnership NHS Trust, 2013–14 (non-executive Director, 2010–14); *b* 23 March 1950; *s* of late Maurice William Hill and of Dorothy Alice Hill (*née* Raynor); *m* 1st, 1972 (marr. diss. 1991); one *s* one *d*; 2nd, 1994, Frances Irene Susan Entwistle (*d* 2017); one step *s*. *Educ:* Ecclesbourne GS, Duffield, Derbys; Peterhouse, Cambridge (schol.; BA Hons 1st cl. Engrg; Baker Prize; PhD Metallurgy and Materials Sci. 1977). BR Research Dept, 1975–77; GKN Technology Ltd, 1977–89; Business Devell Exec., GKN Automotive Div., 1989–90; Develt Dir, GKN Powder Metallurgy Div., 1990–91; Dir, Tech. Strategy, BRB, 1991–93; Man. Dir, BR Production Services, 1993–96; Chief Land Registrar and Chief Exec., HM Land Registry, 1996–99; Chief Exec., Housebuilders Fedn, 1999–2000; Managing Director: AEA Technology Envmt, 2000–05; AEA Technology Rail, 2005–06; Delta Rail Gp Ltd, 2006; Founding Dir, later Consultant, Kynnersley Mgt Services, 2007–11. Chair, Standards Cttee, W Midlands Police Authy, 2010–12. Lay Member: Solicitors Disciplinary Tribunal, 2009–; Professional Conduct Cttee, Nat. Register of Public Service Interpreters, 2012–16; Member: Disciplinary Cttee, CIMA, 2011–16 (Vice Chair, 2013–16); Jt Regulatory Cttee, Fixed Charge Receivership Scheme, RICS/Insolvency Practitioners Assoc., 2013–16; FRC Disciplinary Tribunals, 2013–; RCVS Preliminary Investigation Cttee, 2015–18. FRSA 1996. *Publications:* (trans.) F. Schmelz *et al*, Universal Joints and Driveshafts, 1992, 2nd edn 2005; ed and contrib. books and learned jls on driveline components and engrg mgt. *Recreations:* volunteer at Wightwick Manor (NT), family history research.

**HILL, Sunetra;** see Gupta, S.

**HILL, Susan Elizabeth, (Lady Wells),** CBE 2012; novelist and playwright; *b* 5 Feb. 1942; *d* of late R. H. and Doris Hill; *m* 1975, Stanley William Wells (*see* Sir S. W. Wells); two *d* (and one *d* decd). *Educ:* grammar schs in Scarborough and Coventry; King's Coll., Univ. of London (BA Hons English 1963; Fellow, 1978). FRSL 1972. Literary critic, various jls, 1963–; numerous plays for BBC, 1970–; Presenter, Bookshelf, Radio 4, 1986–87. Founder and Publisher, Long Barn Books, 1996; Founder Publisher and Ed., Books and Company, qly mag., 1997–2000. Patron, Prince of Wales Hospice, Pontefract, 2000–. Chm., Chipping Campden Cricket Club, 1999–2010. *Publications:* The Enclosure, 1961; Do me a Favour, 1963; Gentleman and Ladies, 1969; A Change for the Better, 1969; I'm the King of the Castle, 1970; The Albatross, 1971; Strange Meeting, 1971; The Bird of Night, 1972; A Bit of Singing and Dancing, 1973; In the Springtime of the Year, 1974; The Cold Country and Other Plays for Radio, 1975; (ed) The Distracted Preacher and other stories by Thomas Hardy, 1979; The Magic Apple Tree, 1982; The Woman in Black: a ghost story, 1983 (adapted for stage, 1989); (ed) Ghost Stories, 1983; (ed) People, an anthology, 1983; Through the Kitchen Window, 1984; Through the Garden Gate, 1986; The Lighting of the Lamps, 1987; Lanterns Across the Snow, 1987; Shakespeare Country, 1987; The Spirit of the Cotswolds, 1988; Family (autobiog.), 1989; Air and Angels, 1991; The Mist in the Mirror: a ghost story, 1992; Mrs de Winter, 1993; (ed) Contemporary Women's Short Stories, 1995; (with Rory Stuart) Reflections from a Garden, 1995; Listening to the Orchestra (short stories), 1996; (ed) The Second Penguin Book of Women's Short Stories, 1997; The Service of Clouds, 1998; The Boy Who Taught the Bee-keeper to Read and Other Stories, 2003; The Various Haunts of Men, 2004; The Pure in Heart, 2005; The Risk of Darkness, 2006; The Man in the Picture (novella), 2007; The Vows of Silence, 2008; The Beacon, 2008; Howard's End is on the Landing: a year of reading from home, 2009; The Shadows in the Street, 2010; The Small Hand, 2010; A Kind Man, 2010; The Betrayal of Trust, 2011; Dolly, 2012; A Question of Identity, 2012; The Black Sheep, 2013; Printer's Devil Court, 2014; The Soul of Discretion, 2014; The Travelling Bag and Other Ghostly Stories, 2016; From the Heart, 2017; Jacob's Room is Full of Books, 2017; The Comforts of Home, 2018; The Benefit of Hindsight, 2019; *for children:* One Night at a Time, 1984; Mother's Magic, 1986; Can it be True?, 1988; Susie's Shoes, 1989; Stories from Codling Village, 1990; I've Forgotten Edward, 1990; I Won't Go There Again, 1990; (ed) The Walker Book of Ghost Stories, 1990; Pirate Poll, 1991; The Glass Angels, 1991; Beware, Beware!, 1993; King of King's, 1993; The Battle for Gullywith, 2008; *play:* The Ramshackle Company, 1981. *Address:* Glaven Farm, Little Thornage, Holt, Norfolk NR25 7JE. *E:* mail@susan-hill.com.

**HILL, Dame Susan Lesley,** DBE 2018 (OBE 2005); PhD; FRSB; Chief Scientific Officer, Department of Health, since 2002; *b* Swindon, 14 April 1955; *d* of late Albert Leslie George Hill and Edna Mary Hill (*née* Bennett); civil partnership 2006, Dawn Alison Chaplin. *Educ:* Ashton Keynes Primary Sch.; Hreod Burna High Sch., Swindon; Coventry Univ. (MPhil 1986); Birmingham Univ. (PhD 1988). FRSB (FIBiol 2001). Hd, Respiratory Lab., Princess Margaret's Hosp., Swindon, 1976–80; Sen. Res. Asst, Dept of Medicine, Univ. of Birmingham, 1980–83; Chief Respiratory Physiologist, Gen. Hosp., Birmingham, 1983–88; Sen., then Prin. Clinical Scientist, S Birmingham HA, 1988–94; Res. Fellow, 1988–94, Sen. Res. Fellow, 1994–2002, Univ. of Birmingham; Consultant Clin. Scientist and Hd, Lung Resource Centre, 1994–2002, Clin. Governance Lead and Clin. Dir, Respiratory Medicine, 2000–03, University Hosp. Birmingham NHS Trust. Chm., W Midlands Regl Cttee, 1995–2002, Associate Dir, 2000–02, Healthcare Scientists. Department of Health: Nat. Dir for Audiology/Physiol Diagnostics, 2005–; SRO UK Modernising Scientific Careers prog., 2008–; Science and Society Lead, 2008–; Jt Nat. Clin. Dir for Respiratory Disease and Home Oxygen Services, 2009–. Hon. Prof. of Respiratory Medicine, Univ. of Birmingham, 2002–. Mem., Exec. Bd, Conf. of Clin. Scientists Orgns,

1995–2001. Chair: UK Healthcare Sci. Nat. Occupational Standards project, 1995–2002; Nat. Physiol Measurement Bd, 2006–; Home Oxygen Services Bd, 2009–; Co-Chair: Healthcare Sci. Prog. Bd, Med. Educn England, 2009–; Respiratory Prog. Bd, 2009–; Member: Sci. in Health Gp, Sci. Council, 2002–; Med. Technologies Adv. Cttee, NICE, 2008–; Ministerial Med. Technol. Strategic Gp, 2009–; Adv. Bd, Sci. for All, 2009–; Exec. Bd, Life Scis Industry, 2010–; Bd, Technician Council, 2010–. Mem., wkg party on Audiol Medicine, RCP, 2003–04. Vice-Pres., British Lung Foundn, 2008– (Member: Exec. Cttee, 1992–98; Breathe Easy Cttee, 1993–2000; Mem. and Chm., Midlands Cttee, 1996–2004). Member, Executive Board: British Thoracic Soc., 1992–2002; Assoc. Clin. Scientists, 2000–02; Sec., Fedn for Healthcare Sci., 2001–02. Gov., De Montfort Univ., 2009–. Cofounder and Dir, Chronic Obstructive Pulmonary Disease biannual internat. conf. series, 1997– (co-ed., conf. proc.); European Respiratory Journals: Mem., Bd of Dirs, 1998–2001; Ed., Buyers Guide, 1998–2001. Hon. MRCP 2002, Hon. FRCP 2010. Hon. DSc: Keele, 2007; De Montfort, 2008; Aston, 2009; Wolverhampton, 2009. *Publications*: Issues in Infection: the interaction between lung defences and bacteria: time for reappraisal, 1996; Practical Handbook of Respiratory Function Testing, 1999; contrib. papers and editl reviews to scientific jls on lung inflammation, infection and pathophysiol., Chronic obstructive pulmonary disease, bronchiectasis and asthma and on quality of service delivery. *Recreations*: cooking, fine dining, house renovation, reading, walking. *Address*: NHS England, 6th Floor, Zone B, Skipton House, 80 London Road, SE1 6LH. *E*: sue.l.hill@nhs.net.

**HILL, Rt Hon. (Trevor) Keith**; PC 2003; Chair, Lambeth Living, 2009–15; *b* 28 July 1943; *s* of late George Ernest Hill and Ena Ida (*née* Dakin); *m* 1972, Lesley Ann Sheppard. *Educ*: Corpus Christi Coll., Oxford (BA, MA); UCW, Aberystwyth (DipEd). Res. Asst in Politics, Univ. of Leicester, 1966–68; Belgian Govt Scholar, Brussels, 1968–69; Lectr in Politics, Univ. of Strathclyde, 1969–73; Res. Officer, Labour Party Internat. Dept, 1974–76; Political Liaison Officer, NUR, subseq. Nat. Union of Rail, Maritime and Tspt Workers, 1976–92. MP (Lab) Streatham, 1992–2010. An Asst Govt Whip, 1998–99; Parly Under-Sec. of State, DETR, 1999–2001; Treasurer of HM Household (Dep. Chief Whip), 2001–03; Minister of State (Minister for Housing and Planning), ODPM, 2003–05; PPS to Prime Minister, 2005–07. Chairman: Regulatory Panel, Assoc. of Residential Managing Agents, 2013–16; London Bor. of Hammersmith and Fulham Residents' Commn on Council Housing, 2015–16. *Publications*: (contrib.) European Political Parties, 1969; (contrib.) Electoral Behaviour, 1974. *Recreations*: walks, books, films, music. *Address*: 110 Wavertree Road, Streatham Hill, SW2 3ST. *T*: (020) 8674 0434.

**HILL, Vernon William, II**; Founder and Chairman, Metro Bank UK, 2010–19; *b* San Francisco, 18 Aug. 1945; *s* of Vernon W. Hill; *m* 1973, Shirley; four *c*. *Educ*: Wharton Sch., Univ. of Pennsylvania (BS Finance). Founder and Chm., Commerce Bancorp, 1973–2007. *Publications*: Fans not Customers, 2012. *Recreation*: golf.

**HILL, Prof. William George**, OBE 2004; FRS 1985; FRSE 1979; Professor of Animal Genetics, University of Edinburgh, 1983–2002, now Emeritus; *b* 7 Aug. 1940; *s* of late William Hill and Margaret Paterson Hill (*née* Hamilton); *m* 1971, Christine Rosemary Austin; one *s* two *d*. *Educ*: St Albans School; Wye Coll., Univ. of London (BSc 1961); Univ. of California, Davis (MS 1963); Iowa State Univ.; Univ. of Edinburgh (PhD 1965; DSc 1976). University of Edinburgh: Asst Lectr, 1965–67, Lectr, 1967–74, Reader, 1974–83, in Genetics; Hd, Dept of Genetics, 1989–90; Hd, Inst. of Cell, Animal and Population Biol., 1990–93; Hd, Div. of Biol Scis, 1993–98; Dean and Provost, Faculty of Sci. and Engrg, 1999–2002. Visiting Professor/Research Associate: Univ. of Minnesota, 1966; Iowa State Univ., 1967–78; N Carolina State Univ., 1979, 1985, 1992–2005. Consultant Geneticist: Cotswold Pig Develt Co., 1965–99; British Friesian Cattle Soc., 1978–88; Holstein Friesian Soc., 1988–98. Chm., Org Cttee, 4th World Congress, 1990, Pres., 5th World Congress, Genetics Applied to Livestock Prodn; Chm., Org Cttee, 4th Internat. Conf. Quantitative Genetics, 2012; Pres., British Soc. Animal Sci., 1999–2000 (Vice-Pres., 1997–99); Vice-Pres., Genetics Soc., 2004–08. Chm., Nat. Consultative Cttee, Animal Genetic Resources, 2001–02; Member: Scientific Study Group, Meat and Livestock Commn, 1969–72; Cattle Res. Consultative Cttee, 1985–86; AFRC Animals Res. Grant Bd, 1986–92; Dir's Adv. Gp, AFRC Animal Breeding Res. Orgn, 1983–86; Tech. Cttee, 1992–99 (Chm., 1995–97), Develt Cttee, 1992–98, Animal Data Centre; Inst. Animal Physiology and Genetics Res., 1986–93; Bd Govs, Roslin Inst., 1994–2002; Council, Royal Soc., 1993–94; Commonwealth Scholarship Commn, 1998–2004 (Dep.-Chm., 2002–04). Mem. 1996, Chm. 2001, RAE Biol Sci. Panel. Editor: Animal Prodn, 1971–78; Genetics, 1993–94; Livestock Prodn Sci., 1994–95; Genetics Res. (formerly Genetical Res.), 1996–2012; Proceedings of Royal Soc. B, 2005–08. Hon. DSc N Carolina State, 2003; Dr *hc* Edinburgh, 2005. *Publications*: (ed) Benchmark Papers in Quantitative Genetics, 1984; (ed) Evolution and Animal Breeding, 1989; numerous papers on quantitative and population genetics, biometrics and animal breeding, in sci. jls. *Recreations*: farming, bridge. *Address*: 31/7 Salisbury Road, Edinburgh EH16 5AA. *T*: (0131) 667 3680. *Club*: Farmers.

**HILL-NORTON, Vice Adm. Hon. Sir Nicholas (John)**, KCB 1991; *b* 13 July 1939; *s* of Admiral of the Fleet Baron Hill-Norton, GCB; *m* 1966, Ann Jennifer, *d* of Vice-Adm. D. H. Mason, CB, CVO; two *s* one *d*. *Educ*: Marlborough Coll.; BRNC, Dartmouth; US Naval War Coll., Newport, RI. Royal Navy, 1957–95; commanded: HMS Antelope, 1974–76; Fishery Protection Sqdn, 1978–80; HMS Southampton, 1980–81; HMS Invincible, 1983–85; Flag Officer, Gibraltar, 1987–90; Flag Officer Surface Flotilla and Comdr, Anti-Submarine Warfare Striking Force Atlantic, 1990–92; Dep. Chief of Defence Staff, 1992–95. Defence Adviser: GEC-Marconi, 1995–99; BAE SYSTEMS, 1999–2000; Director: Matra Marconi Space, 1996–99; Marconi N America, 1997–2000; Lear Astronics (USA), 1996–99. Mem., UK Adv. Bd, Tenix Pty (Australia), 2003–07. Chm., British Greyhound Racing Bd, 2000–02. Vice Pres., RUSI, 1999–2003; Chm., King George's Fund for Sailors, 2003–07. *Recreations*: travel, cooking, country sports, golf, woodland management. *Club*: Royal Navy of 1765 and 1785.

**HILL-TOUT, Paul Edward**; Director, Forestry Commission, 2003–10; a Forestry Commissioner, 2004–10; *b* 24 Aug. 1957; *s* of Walter Tony Hill-Tout and Evelyn Mary Hill-Tout; *m* 1982, Lin; one *s* five *d*. *Educ*: King's Coll. London (BA Geog.); Christ Church, Oxford (MSc Forestry and Land Mgt). Joined Forestry Commn, 1980; has held various appts across the orgn and GB. *Recreations*: owns and manages a woodland in Devon, hiking, camping, travel, all eras of history.

**HILL-TREVOR**, family name of **Baron Trevor**.

**HILL-WOOD, Sir Samuel Thomas**, 4th Bt *cr* 1921, of Moorfield, Glossop, co. Derby; senior account manager, software; *b* 24 Aug. 1971; *er s* of Sir David Basil Hill-Wood, 3rd Bt and of Jennifer Anne, *d* of Peter McKenzie-Strang; *S* father, 2002; *m* 2014, Emma Jane Dixon; one *s* one *d* (twins). *Educ*: Wellington Coll.; Kingston Univ. (BA Hons, MA). *Recreations*: golf, fishing, cricket, football, shooting. *Heir*: *s* George David Hill-Wood, *b* 1 Aug. 2018. *Address*: Dacre Farm, Sandpit Lane, Farley Hill, Reading, Berkshire RG7 1XJ.

**HILLCOAT, Polly**; *see* Borland, P.

**HILLEL, Mira B.**; *see* Bar-Hillel.

**HILLEN, John Malcolm; His Honour Judge Hillen**; a Circuit Judge, since 2005; Resident Judge, Blackfriars Crown Court, since 2014; *b* 13 May 1952; *s* of late Clarence Albert Hillen and of Winifred Hillen (*née* Bristow); *m* 1985, Monica Lilian Marie Curtice; one *s* one *d*. *Educ*: King Edward VI Grammar Sch., Aston (Hales Scholar); Lincoln Coll., Oxford (Open Exhibn; MA Modern Hist.); Coll. of Law. Called to the Bar, Middle Temple, 1976, Bencher, 2018; in practice as barrister, specialising in criminal law, 1978–2005; Asst Recorder, 1997–2000; Recorder, 2000–05. Chair, Central London (Crime) Leadership Gp, 2016–. Trustee and Mem. Cttee, Barristers' Benevolent Assoc., 1996–. *Recreations*: fair-weather gardening, hibernation. *Address*: c/o Blackfriars Crown Court, 1–15 Pocock Street, SE1 0BJ. *T*: (020) 7922 5800.

**HILLENBRAND, Prof. Carole**, CBE 2018 (OBE 2009); PhD; FBA 2007; FRSE; FRAS; FRHistS; Professor of Islamic History, University of Edinburgh, 2000–08, now Emerita; Professor of Islamic History, University of St Andrews, since 2013; *b* Southery, Norfolk, 3 May 1943; *e d* of William Thomas Jordan and Lilian Margaret Jordan (*née* Lister); *m* 1968, Robert Hillenbrand, *qv*; two *d*. *Educ*: Perse Girls' Sch., Cambridge; Girton Coll., Cambridge (BA 1965); Somerville Coll., Oxford (BA 1972; Hon. Fellow 2009); Univ. of Edinburgh (PhD 1979). University of Edinburgh: Lectr in Arabic, 1979–90; Reader in Arabic, 1990–2000; Hd, Dept of Islamic and Middle Eastern Studies, 1997–2002 and 2006–08. Visiting Professor: Dartmouth Coll., 1994, 2005; Univ. of Groningen, Netherlands, 2002; Sen. Res. Fellow, Univ. of St Louis, 2011, 2013, 2015, 2017. Vice-Pres., British Soc. for Middle Eastern Studies, 2003–09. Corresp. Fellow, Medieval Acad. of America, 2012–. FRSE 2000. King Faisal Internat. Prize in Islamic Studies, 2005; British Soc. for Islamic and Middle Eastern Studies Award, 2015; British Acad./Naef Al-Rodhan Prize for Transcultural Understanding, 2016; (jtly) Medal, RAS, 2019. *Publications*: (ed jtly) Qajar Iran: political, social and cultural change, 1800–1925, 1984; The Waning of the Umayyad Caliphate, 1989; A Muslim Principality in Crusader Times: the early Artuqid State, 1990; The Crusades, Islamic Perspectives, 1999 (trans. Russian, Indonesian, Turkish); (ed) The Sultan's Turret, 1999; Turkish Myth and Muslim Symbol: the Battle of Manzikert, 2007 (trans. Turkish); Introduction to Islam: beliefs and practices in historical perspective, 2015 (trans. Japanese, Czech, Hungarian, Italian, Korean, Chinese); contribs to books and articles in jls. *Recreations*: travel, cinema. *Address*: Islamic and Middle Eastern Studies, University of Edinburgh, 19 George Square, Edinburgh EH8 9LD; Department of Medieval History, University of St Andrews, 71 South Street, St Andrews KY16 9BA.

**HILLENBRAND, Prof. Robert**, DPhil; FBA 2008; FRSE; Honorary Professorial Fellow and Professor Emeritus, Islamic and Middle Eastern Studies, University of Edinburgh, since 2007; Professor of Islamic Art, University of St Andrews, since 2013; *b* Damgarten, Germany, 2 Aug. 1941; *s* of Fritz Hillenbrand and Margaret Hillenbrand (*née* Meinck); *m* 1968, Carole Jordan (*see* C. Hillenbrand); two *d*. *Educ*: Trinity Coll., Cambridge (BA 1963); Trinity Coll., Oxford (DPhil 1974). Department of Fine Art, Univ. of Edinburgh, 1971–2007, Prof. of Islamic Art, 1989–2007. Slade Prof. of Art, Univ. of Cambridge, 2008; Visiting Professor: Princeton Univ.; UCLA; Bamberg Univ.; Dartmouth Coll.; Groningen Univ.; American Univ. in Cairo. Hon. Prof., Univ. of St Andrews, 2011–12. Kevorkian Lectures, New York Univ., 1993. Dir, Centre for the Advanced Study of the Arab World, 2006–07; Vice-Pres., British Inst. of Persian Studies, 1993–2011. Hon. Mem., Deutsche Morgenländische Gesellschaft, 2013. Alice Hitchcock Medallion, Soc. of Architectural Historians of GB, 1996; Iris Foundn Scholar's Award for Outstanding Contribn to the Decorative Arts, New York, 2008; Lifetime Award, Assoc. of Iranian Studies, 2018; Medal, RAS, 2019. FRSE 1991. *Publications*: (jtly) Islamic Architecture in North Africa, 1976; (ed) Proceedings of the 10th Congress of the Union Européenne des Arabisants et Islamisants, 1982; (ed) The Islamic Book, 1984; Islamic Architecture: form, function and meaning, 1994 (trans. Persian, 1998, 2000); (ed) The Art of the Saljuqs in Iran and Anatolia, 1994; The 'Amiriya in Rada': the history and restoration of a sixteenth-century Madrasa in the Yemen, 1997; (ed jtly) The Art and Archaeology of Ancient Persia: new light on the Parthian and Sasanian empires, 1998; Islamic Art and Architecture, 1999 (trans. German and Turkish, 2005; Persian and Danish, 2008); (ed jtly) Ottoman Jerusalem: the living city, 1517–1917, 2000; (ed) Persian Painting from the Mongols to the Qajars, 2001; The Architecture of Ottoman Jerusalem: an introduction, 2002; Studies in Medieval Islamic Art and Architecture, vol. 1, 2001, vol. 2, 2006; (ed) Shahnama: text and image in the Persian Book of Kings, 2004 (Book of the Year Prize, Islamic Republic of Iran, 2006); (ed) Image and Meaning in Islamic Art, 2005; (ed) Ayyubid Jerusalem: the Holy City in context, 1187–1250, 2009; The Sheikh Zayed Grand Mosque, 2010; Studies in the Islamic Arts of the Book, 2012; The Sheikh Zayed Grand Mosque: a landmark of modern Islamic architecture, 2012; (ed jtly) Ferdowsi, the Mongols and the History of Iran, 2013; 170 book chapters and articles in jls. *Recreations*: travel, cinema, hill-walking. *Address*: Islamic and Middle Eastern Studies, University of Edinburgh, 19 George Square, Edinburgh EH8 9LD.

**HILLHOUSE, Prof. Edward William**, PhD; FRCP; Chief of Scientific, Academic and Faculty Affairs, Hamad Medical Corporation, Doha, Qatar, 2013 (Senior Policy Advisor, then Chief Policy Advisor and Chief of Medical, Academic and Research Affairs, 2011–13); Professor of Medicine, Weill Cornell Medical College, New York, 2012; Professor of Medicine, and Dean, Faculty of Medicine and Health, University of Leeds, 2002–11, now Emeritus Professor; *b* 16 March 1950; *s* of William and Joan Hillhouse; *m* 1993, Nicola Judith; three *s* three *d*. *Educ*: All Saints Sch., Wimbledon; Rutlish Sch., Merton; St Thomas's Hosp. Med. Sch., Univ. of London (BSc 1st Cl. Hons 1972; PhD 1975; MB BS 1981). FRCP 1995. Res. Fellow, Tufts Univ., Boston, 1986–87; Lectr in Medicine, King's Coll. Hosp., London, 1988–90; Sen. Lectr in Metabolic Medicine, Univ. of Newcastle, 1990–93; Sen. Lectr in Medicine, Univ. of Bristol, 1993–95; Prof. of Medicine, and Dir of Molecular Res. Inst., Univ. of Warwick, 1995–2002. Non-exec. Dir, Leeds Teaching Hosps NHS Trust, 2003. Dir, Internat. Assoc. of Academic Health Centers, 2010–; Consultant, Assoc. of Academic Health Centers, Washington DC, 2011–. Associate, Shift Health, Toronto, 2018–. *Publications*: over 150 articles in learned jls. *Recreations*: yoga, tennis, watching Leeds United FC, reading, history, fine wine. *Address*: Hamad Medical Corporation, PO Box 3050, Doha, Qatar. *E*: ehillhouse@hmc.org.qa.

**HILLHOUSE, Sir (Robert) Russell**, KCB 1991; FRSE; Permanent Under-Secretary of State, Scottish Office, 1988–98; *b* 23 April 1938; *s* of Robert Hillhouse and Jean Russell; *m* 1966, Alison Janet Fraser (*d* 2015); two *d*. *Educ*: Hutchesons' Grammar Sch., Glasgow; Glasgow Univ. (MA). FRSE 1995: Scottish Education Dept, 1962; HM Treasury, 1971; Asst Secretary, Scottish Office, 1974; Scottish Home and Health Dept, 1977; Under Sec. (Principal Finance Officer), Scottish Office, 1980; Under Sec., 1985–87, Sec., 1987–88, Scottish Educn Dept. Director: Bank of Scotland, 1998–2001; Scottish Provident Instn, 1999–2001. Chairman: Hebrides Ensemble, 1999–2003; Upper Deeside Access Trust, 1998–2003; Edinburgh Competitive Fest. Assoc., 2010–14. Gov., RSAMD, 2000–08. DUniv Glasgow, 1999; Hon. LLD Aberdeen, 1999; Hon. DLitt Napier, 1999. FRSA 1992. *Recreations*: making music, enjoying the countryside. *Address*: 12 Russell Place, Edinburgh EH5 3HH. *T*: (0131) 476 0503. *Club*: New (Edinburgh).

**HILLIARD, Jonathan Adam**; QC 2016; *b* Southampton, 21 July 1980; *s* of Dr Brian Hilliard and Dr Margaret Hilliard; *m* 2016, Anna Littler. *Educ*: King Edward VI Sch., Southampton; Sidney Sussex Coll., Cambridge (MA Hons Law); Gonville and Caius Coll., Cambridge (LLM). Called to the Bar, Lincoln's Inn, 2003; in practice as barrister, specialising in chancery and commercial law, 2003–. Gov., Swiss Cottage Sch. Develt and Res. Centre, 2015– (Vice Chm., 2016–). *Publications:* (with Dr J. O'Sullivan) The Law of Contract, 2004 to 7th edn 2016. *Recreations:* music, sport, literature, travel. *Address:* Wilberforce Chambers, 8 New Square, Lincoln's Inn, WC2A 3QP. *T:* (020) 7306 0102, *Fax:* (020) 7306 0095. *E:* jhilliard@wilberforce.co.uk.

**HILLIARD, Lexa;** *see* Hilliard, P. A.

**HILLIARD, Nicholas Richard Maybury;** QC 2008; **His Honour Judge Hilliard;** a Senior Circuit Judge, since 2012; Recorder of London, since 2015; *b* 1 May 1959; *s* of His Honour Judge Christopher Richard Hilliard and Anne Margaret Hilliard; *m* 2011, Jane Dorothy Garioni. *Educ:* Bradfield Coll.; Lincoln Coll., Oxford (MA). Called to the Bar, Middle Temple, 1981, Bencher, 2003; Recorder, 2001–12; Leader, SE Circuit, 2011–12. Standing Counsel to DTI, 1993–95; Jun. Treasury Counsel, 1995–2000; Sen. Treasury Counsel, Central Criminal Court, 2001–08; Resident Judge, Woolwich Crown Court, 2012–13; Common Serjeant, City of London, 2013–15; Asst Coroner, W Sussex, 2014–. Hon. Recorder, Greenwich, 2013. Vice-Chm., 2004–05, Chm., 2005–06, Criminal Bar Assoc. Mem., Common Council, City of London, 1994–96, 2005–09. Mem., Commn of Lieutenancy, City of London, 2014–. Trustee: Ben Kinsella Trust, 2010–12 (Patron, 2015–); Crisis, 2011–16; Finding Rhythms, 2014–17. Vice Pres., Sheriffs' and Recorders' Fund, 2015–. Gov., City of London Acad., Islington, 2014–17. Patron, Prison Advice and Care Trust, 2018–. Liveryman: Feltmakers' Co. (Mem., Ct of Assts, 2005–; Master, 2017–18); Vintners' Co., 2019; Hon. Liveryman: Cutlers' Co., 2014; Curriers' Co., 2015; Security Professionals' Co., 2016; Needlemakers' Co., 2017. Mem., Pilgrims. Contrib. Ed., Archbold, Criminal Pleading, Evidence and Practice, 1994–; Ed., Criminal Appeal Reports, 1994–2000. *Address:* Central Criminal Court, Old Bailey, EC4M 7EH. *Clubs:* Garrick, Beefsteak, MCC; Woking Golf.

**HILLIARD, Piers Alexandra, (Lexa);** QC 2009; *b* London, 23 Feb. 1956; *d* of Joanne Hilliard; *m* 2003, Stephen Sands. *Educ:* London Sch. of Econs and Pol Sci. (LLB Hons); King's Coll., London (Postgrad. Dip. EC Law). Lectr in Law, Durham Univ., 1984–87; called to the Bar, Middle Temple, 1987; in practice as a barrister, 1990–. *Publications:* (contrib.) Directors: duties, liabilities and remedies, 2009. *Recreations:* walking, sailing. *Address:* Wilberforce Chambers, 8 New Square, Lincoln's Inn, WC2A 3QP. *Club:* British Classic Yacht.

**HILLIER, Andrew Charles;** QC 2002; *b* 4 May 1949; *s* of late William Hillier and Rosemary (*née* Dutton); *m* 1971, Dr Geraldine Morris; one *s* one *d*. *Educ:* St Louis Sch.; Beaumont Coll.; Trinity Coll., Dublin (BA Hons); Bristol Univ. (PhD 2016). Called to the Bar, Gray's Inn, 1972, Bencher, 2009; in practice as a barrister, 1972–2012. Trustee, Advocate (formerly Bar Pro Bono Unit), 2014–. Volunteer Advr, SW London Law Centres, 2015–. Res. Associate, Bristol Univ., 2017–. *Publications:* Tolley's Employment Act, 1982. *Recreations:* gardening in France, Britain in China in the 19th century.

**HILLIER, Bevis;** author, art historian, journalist; *b* 28 March 1940; *s* of late Jack Ronald Hillier and Mary Louise Hillier (*née* Palmer). *Educ:* Reigate Grammar Sch.; Magdalen Coll., Oxford (demy). Gladstone Memorial Prize, 1961. Editorial staff, The Times, 1963–68 (trainee, Home News Reporter, Sale Room Correspondent); Editor, British Museum Society Bulletin, 1968–70; Guest Curator, Minneapolis Inst. of Arts, USA, 1971; Editor, The Connoisseur, 1973–76; Antiques Correspondent, 1970–84, Dep. Literary Editor, 1980–82, The Times; Editor, The Times Saturday Review, 1982; Features Editor, 1982–83, Exec. Editor, 1983–84, Telegraph Sunday Magazine; Columnist and Associate Editor, Los Angeles Times, 1984–88; Editor, Sotheby's Preview, 1990–93. Co-founder and first Chm., Thirties Soc. (now Twentieth Century Soc.), 1979; Pres., Betjeman Soc., 2006– (Vice-Pres., 1988–2006). FRSA 1967; FRSL 1997. Hon. DLitt Winchester, 2009. Commendatore, Order of Merit (Italy), 1976. *Publications:* Master Potters of the Industrial Revolution: The Turners of Lane End, 1965; Pottery and Porcelain 1700–1914, 1968; Art Deco of the 1920s and 1930s, 1968; Posters, 1969; Cartoons and Caricatures, 1970; The World of Art Deco, 1971; 100 Years of Posters, 1972; Travel Posters, 1973; Victorian Studio Photographs, 1974; (jtly) Façade, 1974; Austerity/Binge, 1975; Punorama, 1975; Dead Funny, 1975; (ed with Mary Banham) A Tonic to the Nation: The Festival of Britain 1951, 1976; The New Antiques, 1977; Fougasse, 1978; Ealing Film Posters, 1981; Bevis Hillier's Pocket Guide to Antiques, 1981; Greetings from Christmas Past, 1982; The Style of the Century 1900–1980, 1983; John Betjeman: a life in pictures, 1984; Mickey Mouse Memorabilia, 1986; Young Betjeman, 1988; Early English Porcelain, 1992; (jtly) Art Deco Style, 1997; John Betjeman: new fame, new love, 2002; Betjeman: the bonus of laughter, 2004; The Wit and Wisdom of G. K. Chesterton, 2010; The Virgin's Baby: the battle of the Ampthill succession, 2013; Going for a Song: an anthology of poems about antiques, 2014; contributor to books, and periodicals incl. The Spectator, The Connoisseur, Apollo, Trans English Ceramic Circle, Proc. Wedgwood Soc., etc. *Recreations:* piano, collecting. *Address:* Flat 23, Hospital of St Cross, St Cross Road, Winchester, Hants SO23 9SD. *T:* (01962) 855294. *Club:* Garrick.

**HILLIER, Gillian Frances,** OBE 2017; Director of Careers and Further Education, Department for Education, since 2017; *b* Wakefield, 15 Nov. 1970; *d* of Anthony Langford and Angela Langford (*née* Wright, later Charlton); *m* 2004, Stephen Martin Hillier, *qv*; one *s* one *d* (twins). *Educ:* Harrogate Grammar Sch.; Nottingham Univ. (BA Politics); Birkbeck Coll., Univ. of London (MSc Political Admin). Exec. Officer, Lord Chancellor's Dept, 1991–94; Professional Officer, Teacher Training Agency, 1995–2000; Dep. Dir, Greenwich Educn Action Zone, 2000–02; Sch. Workforce Team Leader, DfES, 2002–03; Policy Advr to Prime Minister, 2003–05; Change Prog. Mgr, Local Transformation, DfES, 2005–06; Dep. Dir, Workforce Develt Div., DCSF, 2008–09; Department for Education: Deputy Director: Qualifications Systems Div., 2010–12; Young People, 2012–13; Free Schs Capital, 2014–16; Sch. Improvement, 2016–17. *Recreation:* listening to my children singing in Sheffield Cathedral Choir and the National Youth Girls/Boys Choirs. *Address:* Department for Education, 2 St Paul's Place, Sheffield S1 2JF. *T:* (0114) 274 2431. *E:* gillian.hillier@education.gov.uk.

**HILLIER, Malcolm Dudley;** designer and author; *b* 1 Aug. 1936. *Educ:* St Paul's School; Guildhall School of Music (LGSM). Advertising career, Colman Prentis and Varley; later Dir of Television, S. H. Benson, 1958–74; started garden design co. (with Colin Hilton), and opened flower shop, specialising in dried flowers, 1974; formed design partnership, 1992; writer since 1985. *Publications:* Complete Book of Dried Flowers, 1986; Malcolm Hillier's Guide to Arranging Dried Flowers, 1987; Flowers, 1988; Container Gardening, 1991; Roses, 1991; Pot Pourri, 1991; Malcolm Hillier's Christmas, 1992; Little Scented Library, 1992; Garlands, 1994; Container Gardening throughout the Year, 1995; Good Food Fast, 1995; Malcolm Hillier's Colour Garden, 1995; Entertaining, 1997; Cat's Christmas, 1998; Flowers, 2000; Rites of Passage, 2013. *Recreations:* photography, poetry writing, pottery.

**HILLIER, Meg;** MP (Lab and Co-op) Hackney South and Shoreditch, since 2005; *b* 14 Feb. 1969; *m* 1997; one *s* two *d*. *Educ:* St Hilda's Coll., Oxford (BA Hons PPE); City Univ. (Dip. Newspaper Journalism). Reporter, S Yorks Times, 1991; Petty Officer, P & O European Ferries, 1992; PR Officer, Newlon Housing Gp, 1993; reporter, 1994–95, features editor,

1995–98, Housing Today; freelance, 1998–2000. Mem. (Lab) Islington BC, 1994–2002 (Chair, Neighbourhood Services Cttee, 1995–97); Mayor, Islington, 1998–99. Mem. (Lab) NE, London Assembly, GLA, 2000–04. Mem. Bd, Transport for London, 2004–05. PPS to Sec. of State for Communities and Local Govt, 2006–07; Parly Under-Sec. of State, Home Office, 2007–10; Shadow Sec. of State for Energy and Climate Change, 2010–11. Mem., Public Accounts Select Cttee, 2011– (Chm., 2015–). Trustee, War Memls Trust, 2001–. *Recreations:* local history, cycling. *Address:* House of Commons, SW1A 0AA.

**HILLIER, Paul Douglas,** OBE 2006; conductor and singer; *b* 9 Feb. 1949; *s* of Douglas and Felicity Hillier; *m* 1st, 1977, Lena-Liis Kiesel (marr. diss. 2002); two *d*; 2nd, 2004, Else Torp; two *d*. *Educ:* Guildhall School of Music and Drama, London (AGSM). Vicar-Choral, St Paul's Cathedral, 1974–76; Musical Dir, Hilliard Ensemble, 1973–90; Prof. of Music, Univ. of Calif., Davis, 1990–96; Prof. of Music and Dir, Early Music Inst., Indiana Univ., Bloomington, 1996–2003. Artistic Dir and Principal Conductor, Estonian Philharmonic Chamber Choir, 2001–07; Chief Conductor and Artistic Dir, Ars Nova, Copenhagen, 2003–; Conductor: Western Wind Chamber Choir, 1985–89; Klemetti Inst. Chamber Choir, Finland, 1989–93; Dir, Theatre of Voices, 1989–; Artistic Director: Nat. Chamber Choir of Ireland, 2008–; Coro Casa da Musica, Porto, 2009–. Hon. Prof., Univ. of Copenhagen, 2003–07. Gen. Editor, Fazer Editions of Early Music, Helsinki, 1992–99. Edison Prize (Holland), 1989; Estonian Cultural Prize, 2004; Grammy Awards for Best Choral Perf., 2007, for Best Small Ensemble Perf., 2010. White Star of Estonia, 2007; Knight, Order of Dannebrog (Denmark), 2013. *Publications:* 300 Years of English Partsongs, 1983; Romantic English Partsongs, 1986; The Catch Book, 1987; The Music of Arvo Pärt, 1997; (ed) Steve Reich, Writings on Music, 2002; On Pärt, 2005. *Recreations:* reading, walking.

**HILLIER, Dr Richard John;** independent scholar (late antiquity); Headmaster, Yehudi Menuhin School, 2010–17; *b* Winchester, 27 April 1961; *s* of David and Shirley Hillier; *m* 1984, Elaine Hall; two *s*. *Educ:* King's Sch., Peterborough; St John's Coll., Cambridge (BA 1982; MA 1986); Univ. of Durham (PGCE 1983; PhD 1990). Classics teacher: St Leonard's Sch., St Andrews, 1986–87; Durham Sch., 1987–91; Course Tutor, Open Univ., 1989–91; Repton School: Hd of Classics, 1991–98; Housemaster and classics teacher, 1997–2006; Headmaster, Oratory Prep. Sch., 2006–10. Vis. Fellow, St John's Coll., Durham, 2018–. *Publications:* Arator on the Acts of the Apostles: a Baptismal commentary, 1993; contrib. articles to Jl Theol Studies, Studia Patristica, Anglo-Saxon England. *Recreations:* academic research (late antiquity); music and theatre, travel (Mediterranean), spending time in Northumberland and Scottish Borders, gardening, family and dog. *Address:* 8 Crossgate Moor Gardens, Durham DH1 4HS. *E:* richardjhillier@gmail.com.

**HILLIER, Stephen Martin;** Director, Althemis Ltd, 2013–17; Chief Executive, Training and Development Agency for Schools, 2011–12; *b* 30 May 1957; *s* of Alfred Harley and Mabel Hillier; *m* 2004, Gillian Frances Langford (*see* G. F. Hillier); one *s* one *d* (twins). *Educ:* City of London Polytech. (BA Hons); Birkbeck Coll., Univ. of London (MSc). Exec. Officer, Schs Council, 1978–81; Department of Education and Science: Exec. Officer, Curriculum Br., 1981–82; HEO, student loans policy, 1982–85; Private Sec. to Minister of State, 1985–87; Sen. Exec. Officer, Teachers' Br., 1987–88; Teamleader, Grant-Maintained Schs, DfEE, 1988–93; Dep. Chief Exec., Teacher Trng Agency, 1994–99; Department for Education and Skills, then Department for Innovation, Universities and Skills, later Department for Business, Innovation and Skills: Divl Manager, Post-16 Educn and Trng, 1999–2001; Dep. Dir, Sch. Workforce Unit, 2001–03; Dir, Sch. Workforce Gp, 2004–06; Dir, Skills Gp, 2006–09; Regl Dir, Govt Office for E Midlands, 2010–11. Trustee: NFER, 2011–13; Mercia Learning Trust, 2013–17. Chair of Govs, Valley Park Primary Sch., Sheffield, 2015–18; Community Gov., King Ecgbert Acad., Sheffield, 2013–17. Hd Steward, Sheffield Cathedral, 2018–. *Recreation:* enjoying life in the Peak District and Yorkshire with our young twins Amélie and Seth. *Address:* 77 Crescent Road, Sheffield S7 1HN. *T:* 07711 847278. *E:* ginger1511@icloud.com.

**HILLIER, William Edward,** CEng, FIET; Visiting Industrial Fellow, Engineering Department, Cambridge University, 1996–98 and 1999–2018; *b* 11 April 1936; *s* of William Edward and Ivy Hillier; *m* 1958, Barbara Mary Thorpe (*d* 2017); one *s* one *d*. *Educ:* Acton Grammar School; Open Univ. (BA). FIET (FIEE 1990). Missile Electronics Engineer, De Havilland Propellers, 1958–60; Semiconductor Test Equipment Design and Production Manager, 1960–64, Semiconductor Production Manager, 1965–70, Texas Instruments; Computer Aided Engineering Services Manager, up to Tech. Dir, CAD, Racal Redac, 1970–85 (Dep. Man. Dir, 1982–85); Dir, Application of Computers and Manufg Engrg Directorate, 1985–94, and Hd of IT, 1991–94, SERC; Corporate Industrial Marketing, EPSRC, 1994–96. Chairman: Computing and Control Div., IEE, 1993–94; Indust. Adv. Bd, Sch. of Manufg and Mech. Engrg, Birmingham Univ., 1997–2000. Dir, Heritage Rly Assoc., 2000–. FCMI. *Publications:* articles in professional papers. *Recreation:* railway preservation. *Address:* 19 Simon de Montfort Drive, Evesham, Worcs WR11 4NR. *T:* (01386) 443449.

**HILLING, Julie Ann;** *b* Oxford; *d* of Arthur Hilling and Penelope Hilling (*née* Whiting). *Educ:* Cedars Sch., Leighton Buzzard; Nottingham Univ. (BSc Chem.); Manchester Poly. (Dip. Youth and Community Work). Community worker: St Ann's Tenants' and Residents' Assoc., 1977–80; Sneinton Hermitage Community Assoc., 1980–81; youth worker: St Helen's BC, 1982–86; Wigan Council, 1986–2004; Learning Organiser, NASUWT, 2004–06; Sen. Regl Organiser, TSSA, 2006–10. MP (Lab) Bolton W, 2010–15; contested (Lab) same seat, 2015, 2017. PPS to Shadow Minister for Women and Equalities, 2010–12; an Opposition Whip, 2012–15. Member: Transport Select Cttee, 2010–12; Standards and Privileges Cttee, 2011–12; Chair, All Party Parly Gp on Rail of the North, 2010–15; Co-Chair, All Party Parly Gp on Youth Affairs, 2010–15.

**HILLMAN, David,** RDI 1997; FCSD; FRCA; Director, Studio David Hillman, since 2007; *b* 12 Feb. 1943; *s* of late Leslie Hillman and Marjorie Joan Hillman (*née* Nash); *m* 1st, 1963, Eileen Margaret Griffin (marr. diss. 1968); one *s* one *d*; 2nd, 1983, Jennie Diana Burns; two *s*. *Educ:* Aristotle Central Sch.; London Sch. of Printing and Graphic Art (NDD Graphic Design 1962). AGI 1977; FCSD 1979; Sen. FRCA 2004. Design Asst, Sunday Times mag., 1962–65; Art Editor, London Life, 1965–66; Designer/Editor, Design for Living section, Sunday Times mag., 1966–68; Art Dir and Dep. Editor, Nova, 1968–75; freelance practice, 1975–78; Dir, Pentagram Design, 1978–2007. Exhibn, Hillman in Print, The Hub, Sleaford, 2009, James Hockey & Foyer Galls, Univ. for Creative Arts, Farnham, 2010. Mem., Alliance Graphique Internat., 1977– (UK Pres., 1996–2000; Internat. Pres., 2000–03). *Publications:* (ed jtly) Ideas on Design, 1986; Puzzlegrams, 1989; Pentagames, 1992; (ed jtly) Nova, 1993; (ed jtly) The Compendium, 1993; (jtly) Puzzlegrams Too, 1994; (ed jtly) Pentagram, Book 5, 1999; (jtly) Century Makers, 1999; (jtly) Terence Donovan, The Photographs, 2000; (ed jtly) Pentagram Profile, 2004; (ed with Diana Donovan) Terence Donovan Fashion, 2012; (ed with Diana Donovan) Terence Donovan Portraits, 2016. *Recreations:* ski-ing, modern jazz. *Address:* Glebe Wood House, Bodmin Street, Holsworthy, Devon EX22 6BH. *T:* (01409) 255563.

**HILLMAN, Prof. John Richard,** PhD; FRSE; FLS, FRSB, FCIHort; Scientific Adviser, Arab Academy of Sciences, since 2002; Hon. Research Fellow, James Hutton Institute, since 2011 (Director and Chief Executive, Scottish Crop Research Institute, 1986–2005);

b 21 July 1944; s of late Robert Hillman and Emily Irene Hillman (née Barrett); m 1967, Sandra Kathleen Palmer; two s. Educ: Chislehurst and Sidcup Grammar Sch. for Boys; University Coll. of Wales, Aberystwyth (BSc 1965; PhD 1968). FRSE, FRSB (FIBiol 1985); FLS 1982; FCIHort (FIHort 1997). Univ. of Nottingham: Asst Lectr in Physiology and Environmental Studies, 1968; Lectr, 1969; Univ. of Glasgow: Lectr in Botany, 1971; Sen. Lectr, 1977; Reader, 1980; Prof. of Botany, 1982. Visiting Professor: Univ. of Dundee, 1986–; Univ. of Strathclyde, 1986–; Univ. of Edinburgh, 1988–; Univ. of Glasgow, 1991–; Adjunct Prof., Petra Univ., Jordan, 2015–. Bawden Lectr, Brighton, 1993. Chm., Agric., Hort. and Forestry Sector Panel, UK Technology Foresight Prog., 1995–97 (Chm., Agric. Nat. Resources and Envmt Sector Panel, 1994–95); Founder and Dep. Chm., Mylnefield Research Services Ltd, 1993–2005; Founder, Mylnefield Trust. Pres., Agriculture & Food Sect., British Sci. Assoc. (formerly BAAS), 2000–. Member: Bd, BioIndustry Assoc., 1998–2005 (Chm., Industrial Biotechnol. Cttee, 1998–2004); Court, Univ. of Abertay Dundee, 1998–2005; Res. and Knowledge Transfer Cttee, SHEFC (later SFC), 2003–07; Commercial Farmers Gp, 2006–. Mem., Exec. Council, Scotia Agriculture Club, 2003– (Vice-Pres., 2005–07; Pres., 2007–09). Chm., Angus Cons. and Unionist Party, 2007–10. FCMI (FBIM 1987); FRSA 1997; FRAgS 2004. Hon. DSc: Strathclyde, 1994; Abertay Dundee, 1996. British Potato Industry Award, 1999; Internat. Potato Industry Award, 2000; Dr Hardie Award, Virus-Tested Stem Cutting Assoc., 2001; Scottish Horticl Medal, Royal Caledonian Horticultural Soc., 2003. Publications: (ed) Isolation of Plant Growth Substances, 1978; (ed with A. Crozier) The Biosynthesis and Metabolism of Plant Hormones, 1984; (ed with C. T. Brett) Biochemistry of Plant Cell Walls, 1985; (ed with A. Badran and E. Baydoun): Universities in Arab Countries: an urgent need for change, 2018; Major Challenges Facing Higher Education in the Arab World: quality assurance and relevance, 2019; papers on plant physiol., biotechnol., food security and future of agriculture in learned jls. Recreations: horology, economics, antique woodworking and plumbing tools. Address: c/o James Hutton Institute, Invergowrie, Dundee DD2 5DA. T: (01382) 562731. Club: Farmers.

HILLS, Andrew Worth; Director, BBC Monitoring, 1996–2003; b 1 Sept. 1949; s of late Roland Frederick Hills and Margaret Eunice (née Johnson); m 1st, 1974, Frances Mary Ralston (marr. diss. 1992); three s; 2nd, 1992, Mary Sandra Caraffi. Educ: Abingdon Sch.; Corpus Christi Coll., Cambridge (BA 1971; MA 1975). United Kingdom Atomic Energy Authority, 1971–96: Gen. Sec., AEE Winfrith, 1981–84; Principal Finance and Programmes Officer, 1984–86; Authority Personnel Officer, 1986–89; Exec. Dir, Finance and Personnel, 1989–91; Mem., UKAEA, 1991–94; Managing Director: Sites and Personnel, 1991–92; Corporate Services, 1992–94; Services Div., 1994–95; Dir, Special Projects, 1995–96. Recreations: church-crawling, music, reading. Address: Craven Lodge, Speen Lane, Newbury RG14 1RJ.

HILLS, Barrington William; racehorse trainer, 1969–2011 and 2014–15; b 2 April 1937; s of William George Hills and Phyllis (née Biddle); m 1st, 1959, Maureen (marr. diss. 1977), d of late Patrick Newson; two s (twins) (and one s decd); 2nd, 1977, Penelope Elizabeth May, d of John Richard Woodhouse; two s. Educ: Robston Hall, Gloucester; St Mary's Convent, Newmarket; Mr Whittaker's, Worcester. National Service, King's Troop, RHA. Major race winners include: Prix de l'Arc de Triomphe, 1973 (Rheingold); 1,000 Guineas, 1978 (Enstone Spark), 2009 (Ghanaati); 2,000 Guineas, 1979 (Tap on Wood), 2004 (Haafhd); Irish Derby, 1987 (Sir Harry Lewis); Irish 1,000 Guineas, 1993 (Nicer), 1999 (Hula Angel); St Leger, 1994 (Moonax); Irish Oaks, 1994 (Bolas); Prix Royal-Oak, 1994 (Moonax). George Ennor Trophy, Horserace Writers and Photographers Assoc., 2009. Recreations: hunting, shooting, golf. Address: c/o Wetherdown House, Lambourn, Hungerford, Berks RG17 8UB. T: (01488) 71548. Club: Turf.

HILLS, Col David Henry, MBE 1986; Under Treasurer, 1997–2012, Hon. Bencher, 2012, Honourable Society of Lincoln's Inn; b 23 May 1946; s of Air Vice-Marshal (Eric) Donald Hills, CB, CBE and Pamela Mary, d of Col A. P. Sandeman; m 1970, Josephine Anne, d of Wing Comdr J. W. Abbott; two s one d. Educ: Mount St Mary's Coll.; RMA Sandhurst. Commnd 2nd Lt Royal Highland Fusiliers, 1967; regimental service, Scotland, Singapore, NI, 1967–77; Staff HQ 8 Bde, Londonderry, 1977–79; Staff Coll., Camberley, 1980; regimental service, Germany, 1981–83; MoD, 1983–85; loan service, Zimbabwe, 1985; DCOS HQ 1 Infantry Bde, 1987–88; Comd 1st Bn Royal Highland Fusiliers, 1988–90; Staff, RMA Sandhurst, 1990–93; Dep. COS Rear Support HQ ARRC, Germany and Croatia, 1993–96; DACOS G4 Ops and Plans HQ Land, 1996–97. Sec., Council of the Inns of Ct, 2007–09; Jt Rep., Council of the Inns of Ct to the Bar Standards Bd, 2008–09. Recreations: tennis, golf, ski-ing, bridge. Address: 15 Church Street, Whitchurch, Hants RG28 7AD.

HILLS, Jacqueline Sukie; see Binns, J. S.

HILLS, Sir John (Robert), Kt 2013; CBE 1999; FBA 2002; FAcSS; Richard Titmuss Professor of Social Policy, since 2015, and Chair, Centre for Analysis of Social Exclusion, since 2016 (Director, 1997–2016), London School of Economics (Professor of Social Policy, since 1997); b 29 July 1954; s of Derrick Walter Hills and Valerie Jean Hills (née Gribble); m 1989, Anne Elizabeth Power. Educ: Nottingham High Sch.; Abingdon Sch.; St John's Coll., Cambridge (BA 1976, MA); Birmingham Univ. (MSocSc 1980). Min. of Finance, Botswana, 1976–78; DoE, 1979–80; Treasury Cttee, H of C, 1980–82; Inst. for Fiscal Studies, 1982–84; Commn of Inquiry into Taxation, Zimbabwe, 1984–86; Welfare State Prog., LSE, 1986–97. Mem., Pensions Commn, 2003–06; Chair, Nat. Equality Panel, 2008–10. Ind. Review of Fuel Poverty for DECC, 2011–12 (report publd 2012). FAcSS (AcSS 2009). Publications: (ed) The State of Welfare: the welfare state in Britain since 1974, 1990, 2nd edn (jtly), 1998; Unravelling Housing Finance: subsidies, benefits and taxation, 1991; The Future of Welfare, 1993, 2nd edn 1997; (ed jtly) The Dynamic of Welfare, 1995; (ed) New Inequalities: the changing distribution of income and wealth in the UK, 1996; (jtly) Paying for Health, Education and Housing, 2000; (ed jtly) Understanding Social Exclusion, 2002; Inequality and the State, 2004; (ed jtly) A More Equal Society?, 2005; Ends and Means: the future roles of social housing in England, 2007; (ed jtly) Towards a More Equal Society, 2009; (jtly) An Anatomy of Economic Inequality, 2010; (jtly) Wealth in the UK: distribution, accumulation and policy, 2013; Good Times, Bad Times: the welfare myth of them and us, 2014, rev. edn 2017; (jtly) Social Policy in a Cold Climate, 2016; (ed jtly) Decent Incomes for All, 2019. Recreation: fell walking. Address: Centre for Analysis of Social Exclusion, London School of Economics, Houghton Street, WC2A 2AE.

HILLS, Philip, CMG 2003; Chief Executive, Project and Export Finance, HSBC, 1990–2004; b 10 Feb. 1946; s of Frank and Lilian Elizabeth Patricia Hills; m 1969, Margaret Elizabeth Susan Harris; four d. Educ: Colfe's Grammar Sch., London. N. M. Rothschild & Sons Ltd, 1963–76 (Manager, Export Finance, 1969–76); Dir, Export Finance, Grindlay Brandts Ltd, 1976–81; HSBC Gp, 1981–2004. Director: Anthony Gibbs & Sons Ltd, 1981–88; Samuel Montagu & Co. Ltd, 1988–90. Chm., Export and Shipbuilding Policy Cttee, BBA, 1990–2001. Recreations: sport, travel, cookery. Address: HSBC Bank plc, 8 Canada Square, E14 5HQ.

HILLS, Dr Philip David; Headmaster, Oxford High School GDST, since 2017; b Colchester, May 1974; s of David John Hills and Linda Phyllis Hills (née Buck); m 1997, Prof. Alison Elizabeth Scott; one s two d. Educ: Colchester Royal Grammar Sch.; Trinity Coll., Cambridge (BA 1995; MPhil 1996; PhD Classics 2000). Res. Fellow, Jesus Coll., Cambridge, 1999–2001; Lectr, Faculty of Classics, Cambridge Univ., 2000–01; Asst Master, Eton Coll., 2001–05; Head of Classics: Bristol GS, 2005–07; St Paul's Sch., 2007–10; Dep. Hd, Hampton Sch., 2010–17. Foundn Gov., SS Philip and James C of E (Voluntary Aided), 2015–. Publications: Horace, 2005; contrib. educn-related articles to jls incl. TES. Recreations: football, theatre, politics. Address: Oxford High School GDST, Belbroughton Road, Oxford OX2 6XA. T: (01865) 559888. E: oxfordhigh@oxf.gdst.net. Club: Lansdowne.

HILLS, Prof. Richard Edwin, FRS 2014; Professor of Radio Astronomy, 1990–2012, and Deputy Head, Department of Physics, 1999–2003, University of Cambridge, Emeritus Professor of Radio Astronomy, 2012; Fellow of St Edmund's College, Cambridge, since 1993; b 30 Sept. 1945; s of Ronald Hills and Betty Dorothy Hills (née Davies); m 1973, Beverly Bevis; two s. Educ: Bedford Sch.; Queens' Coll., Cambridge (BA Physics); Univ. of California, Berkeley (PhD Astronomy). Research Scientist, Max Planck Inst. for Radio Astronomy, Bonn, 1972–74; Research Associate, 1974–84, Asst Dir of Research, 1984–90, Cavendish Lab., Cambridge; Project Scientist, James Clerk Maxwell Telescope, 1975–87. Project Scientist, Atacama Large Millimetre Array, Chile, 2007–12. FRAS. Jackson-Gwilt Medal, RAS, 1989; MacRobert Award, Fellowship of Engineers, 1990. Publications: contribs to professional jls. Recreations: travel, DIY, music. Address: c/o Cavendish Laboratory, J. J. Thomson Avenue, Cambridge CB3 0HE. T: (01223) 337369.

HILLS, Sarah Tien Mee; see Lee, S. T. M.

HILLSBOROUGH, Earl of; Edmund Robin Arthur Hill; b 21 May 1996; s and heir of Marquess of Downshire, qv. Educ: Eton; Univ. of Edinburgh.

HILLSON, Dr Rowan Mary, MBE 2006; FRCP; Consultant Physician, Diabetes and Endocrinology, General Internal Medicine, Hillingdon Hospital, 1989–2012, Hon. Consultant Physician, 2012–13; National Clinical Director for Diabetes, Department of Health, 2008–13; b London, 10 May 1951; d of Rodney and Kathleen Hillson. Educ: Edgbaston High Sch., Birmingham; Univ. of Birmingham (MB ChB 1974; MD 1983). MRCP 1976, FRCP 1994. Hon. Sen. Registrar, 1980–84, Sen. Registrar, 1984–89, Diabetes and Endocrinol., Gen. Internal Medicine, Radcliffe Infirmary and John Radcliffe Hosp., Oxford; diabetes and endocrinol., and gen. internal medicine roles, London Deanery, 1997–2008; Hon. Sen. Lectr, 1999–2012, and Clin. Tutor, 1998–2012, Imperial Coll. Med. Sch. Mem., Appraisal Cttee, 2005–08, Vice Chm., Vascular Topic Selection Panel, 2008–11, NICE. British Diabetic Association, later Diabetes UK: pioneered and supervised Outward Bound courses for people with diabetes, 1981–96; Member: Educn Cttee, 1989–91; Med. and Scientific Cttee, 1990–92; Chm., Sports and Exercise Wkg Party, 1991–93; Council of Healthcare Professionals, 2013–. Royal College of Physicians: Regl Advr, NW London, 2001–04 (CPD Advr, 2004–08); Mem. Council, 2007–10, 2013–16; Trustee, 2013–16. Mem. Cttee, Assoc. British Clin. Diabetologists, 2006–08. Mem., Council of Healthcare Professionals, 2013–19. Trustee, Diabetes Care Trust (ABCD) Ltd, 2013–. Hon. DSc Brunel, 2011. Publications: Diabetes: a beyond basics guide, 1987, rev. edn 1992, 2nd edn 1996; Diabetes: a young persons guide, 1988; Diabetes Beyond Forty, 1988, 2nd edn as Late Onset Diabetes, 1996; Diabetes: a new guide, 1992, 2nd edn as Diabetes: the complete guide, 1996, 3rd edn 2002 (Spanish edn 2005); Thyroid Disorders, 1991, 3rd edn 2002; Practical Diabetes Care, 1996, 2nd edn 2002 (Polish edn 1997, Russian edn 2000); Diabetes Care: a practical manual, 2008, 2nd edn 2015; contrib. articles to learned jls on diabetes and other med. topics. Recreations: observing the natural world, enjoying ballet, theatre and classical music, very amateur photography.

HILSENRATH, Rebecca Jane; Chief Executive Officer, Equality and Human Rights Commission, since 2015 (Chief Legal Officer, 2014–15); b Twickenham, 23 Feb. 1965; d of David Martin Loewe and Susan Flora Loewe; m 1992, Michael Hilsenrath; four s. Educ: Putney High Sch.; Newnham Coll., Cambridge (Exhibnr; BA Hons Law 1987); Coll. of Law. Trainee and asst solicitor, Linklaters, 1988–93; Legal Advisor: DfES, 2001–04; Attorney Gen.'s Office, 2004–08; CEO, LawWorks (Solicitors Pro Bono Gp), 2008–14. Member: Governance Expert Gp, Educn and Employers Taskforce, 2009–11; Wkg Gp on Access to Justice for Litigants in Person, Civil Justice Council, 2011–. Non Lay Mem., Office for Legal Complaints, 2017–. Mem., Mgt Cttee, Bar Pro Bono Unit, 2008–17. Trustee: Mary Ward Legal Centre, 2007–12; Nat. Pro Bono Centre, 2010–17. Chair, Assoc. of Chief Execs, 2019–. Governor: Hertsmere Jewish Primary Sch., 1998–2009 (Chair of Govs, 2001–09); (and Trustee) Yavneh Coll., Borehamwood, 2000–10. Hon. LLD BPP, 2017; Hon. Dr Hertfordshire, 2019. Publications: (as Jane Diamond): A Place Called F, 2011; Visiting Sins, 2013. Recreations: spending time in our family home in Llanegryn, mid-Wales, making myself heard above my four sons, writing novels. Address: 31 Deacons Hill Road, Elstree, Herts WD6 3HY. T: 07884 226444. E: rebecca@hilsenrath.com.

HILSON, Malcolm Geoffrey, OBE 2001; HM Diplomatic Service, retired; High Commissioner, Vanuatu, 1997–2000; b 28 Sept. 1942; s of Geoffrey Norman and Mildred Alice Hilson; m 1965, Marian Joan Freeman; two s. Educ: Bedford Modern School. Entered Foreign Office, 1961; served Jakarta, Singapore, Bombay, Kuala Lumpur and FCO; First Sec., Kaduna, 1982–86; FCO, 1986–90; New Delhi, 1990–93; FCO, 1993–97. Recreations: gardening, bowls, golf, bell ringing. Address: Chestnuts, Long Lane, Southrepps, Norfolk NR11 8NL.

HILSUM, Prof. Cyril, CBE 1990; PhD; FRS 1979; FREng; Visiting Professor of Physics, University College London, since 1988; b 17 May 1925; s of Benjamin and Ada Hilsum; m 1947, Betty Cooper (d 1987); one d (and one d decd). Educ: Raine's Sch., London; University Coll., London (BSc, PhD). FREng (FEng 1978); FIEEE 1984. Joined Royal Naval Scientific Service, 1945; Admiralty Res. Lab., 1947–50, and Services Electronics Res. Lab., 1950–64, working first on infra-red res., then on semiconductors; Royal Signals and Radar Estab., 1964–83, working first on compound semiconductors, later on flat panel electronic displays; CSO, 1974–83; Chief Scientist, Gen. Electric Co. Res. Labs, 1983–85; Dir of Res., GEC plc, 1985–93. Mem., SERC, 1984–88. Pres., Inst. of Physics, 1988–90; Hon. FInstP 2001 (FInstP 1960). Foreign Associate, US National Acad. of Engrg, 1983. Hon. DEng: Sheffield, 1992; Nottingham Trent, 1997. Max Born Medal and Prize, 1987, Glazebrook Medal and Prize, 1997, Inst. of Physics; Faraday Medal, IEE, 1988; Braun Prize, Soc. for Inf. Display, 1998; Royal Medal, Royal Soc., 2007. Publications: Semiconducting III-V Compounds, 1961; over 100 scientific and technical papers. Recreation: ballroom dancing. Address: 12 Eastglade, Pinner, Middx HA5 3AN. T: (020) 8866 8323.
See also L. Hilsum.

HILSUM, Lindsey; International Editor, Channel 4 News, since 2004; b 3 Aug. 1958; d of Prof. Cyril Hilsum, qv and late Betty Hilsum. Educ: City of Worcester Grammar Sch. for Girls; Exeter Univ. (BA Hons Spanish and French). Freelance journalist in Latin America, 1980–82; Information Officer, UNICEF, Nairobi, 1982–86; stringer, BBC and Guardian, Nairobi, 1986–89; producer, BBC World Service, 1989–93; freelance journalist, 1993–96; Channel 4 News: diplomatic corresp., 1996–2004; Beijing corresp., 2006–08. Specialist Journalist of the Year, 2003, Journalist of the Year, 2005, RTS; Amnesty Award, 2004; James Cameron Award, James Cameron Meml Trust, 2005; Charles Wheeler Award, British Journalism Rev., 2011; One World Journalist of Year, 2011; Special Internat.

Award, Political Studies Assoc., 2011; Mungo Park Medal, RSGS, 2014; Patron's Medal, RGS, 2017. *Publications:* Sandstorm: Libya in the time of revolution, 2012; In Extremis: the life of war correspondent Marie Colvin, 2018; contribs to Granta, NY Rev. of Books, Sunday Times, Guardian, Observer, etc. *Recreations:* horse riding, duck watching. *Address:* Channel 4 News, ITN, 200 Gray's Inn Road, WC1X 8XZ. *T:* (020) 7430 4606, *Fax:* (020) 7430 4608. *E:* lindsey.hilsum@itn.co.uk.

**HILTON OF EGGARDON**, Baroness *cr* 1991 (Life Peer), of Eggardon in the County of Dorset; **Jennifer Hilton**, QPM 1989; *b* 12 Jan. 1936; *d* of John Robert Hilton, CMG and Margaret Frances Hilton. *Educ:* Bedales Sch.; Manchester Univ. (BA Hons Psychology 1970; MA (Research) 1971); London Univ. (Dip. Criminology 1977; Dip. History of Art 1982). Joined Metropolitan Police, 1956; Univ. Scholarship, 1967; Police Staff Coll. (Directing Staff), 1973–74; Met. Police Management Services Dept, 1975–76; Supt then Chief Supt, Heathrow Airport, Battersea, Chiswick, 1977–83; New Scotland Yard (Traffic, Courts, Obscene Publications, Planning, Neighbourhood Policing), 1983–87; Comdr, 1984; Head of Training, Metropolitan Police, 1988–90. House of Lords: Opposition Whip, 1991–95; opposition spokesperson on the envmt, 1991–97: Member: EC Sub-Cttee on Envmt, 1991–95 (Chm., 1995–98); Science and Technol. Cttee, 1993–95, 2004–07, 2010–15; EC Sub-Cttee on Defence and Foreign Affairs, 2000–03; Foreign Relns Cttee, 2016–; Chm., Adv. Panel on Works of Art, 1998–2003. Mem., OSCE Election Monitoring Panel, 1998–. *Publications:* The Gentle Arm of the Law, 1967, 2nd edn 1973; (with Sonya Hunt) Individual Development and Social Experience, 1975, 2nd edn 1981; articles in Police Jl, Police Review, etc. *Recreations:* gardening, history, art, travel. *Address:* House of Lords, SW1A 0PW.

**HILTON, (Alan) John Howard;** QC 1990; a Recorder, 1986–2004; *b* 21 Aug. 1942; *s* of Alan Howard Hilton and Barbara Mary Campbell Hilton; *m* 1st, 1968, Jasmina Laila Hamzavi; 2nd, 1978, Nicola Mary Bayley, *qv*; one *s*. *Educ:* Haileybury and Imperial Service Coll.; Manchester Univ. (LLB Hons). Called to the Bar, Middle Temple, 1964. *Recreations:* opera, cooking, magic, 19th century paintings of ladies, enjoying adjournments. *Clubs:* Garrick, Les Six.

**HILTON, Prof. (Andrew John) Boyd,** DPhil; FBA 2007; Professor of Modern British History, University of Cambridge, 2007; Fellow of Trinity College, Cambridge, since 1974; *b* 19 Jan. 1944; *s* of Kenneth Boyd Hilton and Irene Beryl Hilton; *m* 1971, Mary à Beckett; one *s* two *d*. *Educ:* William Hulme's Grammar Sch.; Manchester; New Coll., Oxford (BA 1966; DPhil 1972). Res. Lectr, Christ Church, Oxford, 1969–74; Lectr, 1988–97, Reader, 1997–2007, Faculty of History, Univ. of Cambridge; Trinity College, Cambridge: Tutor, 1978–88, 1990–91, 1994–96; Sen. Tutor, 1985–88; Dean, 1991–93; Steward, 2000. James Ford Special Lectr, Univ. of Oxford, 1995. FRHistS 1986. *Publications:* Corn, Cash, Commerce: the economic policies of the Tory governments 1815–1830, 1969; The Age of Atonement: the influence of evangelicalism on social and economic thought, 1988; A Mad, Bad, and Dangerous People? England 1783–1846: the new Oxford history of England, 2006; (contrib.) St John's College, Cambridge: a history, 2011. *Recreations:* too few to mention. *Address:* 1 Carlyle Road, Cambridge CB4 3DN; Trinity College, Cambridge CB2 1TQ. *T:* (01223) 338425. *E:* ajbh1@cam.ac.uk.

**HILTON, Anthony Victor;** Financial Editor, Evening Standard, since 2002 (City Editor, 1984–89 and 1996–2002; Managing Director, 1989–95); Business and Economics columnist, Independent, Evening Standard, since 2012; *b* 26 Aug. 1946; *s* of Raymond Walwork Hilton and Miriam Eileen Norah Hilton (*née* Kydd); *m* 1st, 1969, Patricia Moore; one *s*; 2nd, 1989, Cynthia June Miles; two *s* one *d*. *Educ:* Univ. of Aberdeen (MA Hons Econs 1968). Financial columnist: Guardian, 1968; Observer, 1969; Daily Mail, 1971; Sunday Express, 1972; Editor, Accountancy Age, 1974–79; NY corresp., Sunday Times, 1979–82; City Editor, The Times, 1982–83; Dir, Associated Newspapers, 1989–95. Dir, London Forum, 1993–94; Mem. Council, London First, 1996–98 (Dir, 1993–96). Mem. Cttee, St John's Ambulance Charity Appeal, 1992–94. Vice Pres., Children's Film Unit, 1993–96. Vis. Prof., London Met. Univ., 2011–13. Hon. Dr Aberdeen, 2010. *Publications:* How to communicate financial information to employees, 1979; City within a state: a portrait of the City of London, 1987. *Recreations:* canal cruising, cycling, bonfires. *Address:* Priory Hall, Hadleigh, Suffolk IP7 5AZ. *T:* (01473) 823185. *Clubs:* Reform, Lansdowne.

**HILTON, Boyd;** *see* Hilton, A. J. B.

**HILTON, Brian James George,** CB 1992; non-executive director of public companies; Deputy Secretary, Department of Trade and Industry, 1994–99; *b* 21 April 1940; *s* of late Percival William Hilton and Gladys Hilton (*née* Haylett); *m* 1965, Mary Margaret Kirkpatrick (separated); one *s* two *d*. *Educ:* St Marylebone Grammar Sch., London. Export Credits Guarantee Dept, 1958–68; Board of Trade, 1968–71; Foreign and Commonwealth Office, 1971–74: First Secretary to UK Delegn to OECD, Paris; Asst Sec., Dept of Industry, 1976–84; RCDS 1981; Hd, Financial Services Div., DTI, 1984–87; Hd, Central Unit (Under Sec.), DTI, 1987–89; Dep. Sec., MAFF, 1989–91; Dir, Citizen's Charter Unit, Cabinet Office, 1991–94. Complaints Ombudsman, LIFFE, 2007–10. Chm., Channel Mgt Agency, Lloyd's, 2014–; non-exec. Dir, SCOR Insurance Ltd, 2009–. Foundation Governor, Hampden Gurney Primary Sch., London W1, 1976–; Gov., RAU (formerly RAC), Cirencester, 1990–91, 2005–13 (Chm., 2011–13). MRAC 2004. *Recreations:* cricket, Rugby, music, opera, gardening, fly fishing. *Address:* 1 Lake View, Shoyswell Manor, Sheepstreet Lane, Etchingham, E Sussex TN19 7AZ.

**HILTON, Cara Laura;** Policy and Public Affairs Manager, Civil Engineering Contractors Association Scotland, since 2016; *b* Falkirk, 1975; *d* of Ian Peattie and Catherine Peattie, *qv*; *m* 2006, Simon Hilton; two *s* one *d*. *Educ:* Grangemouth High Sch.; Open Univ. (Dip. Child Develt 2008); Univ. of Strathclyde (BA Politics 1997); Univ. of Leicester (MA Eur. Law (Dist.) 2004). Asst Statistical Officer, NHS Exec., 1997–98; Educn Planning Asst, City of York Council, 1998–99; res. asst, USDAW, 1999–2007; researcher, Karen Whitefield, MSP, 2007–11; Parly Asst, Thomas Docherty, MP, 2012–13. Mem. (Lab) Fife Council, 2012–15. Mem. (Lab) Dunfermline, Scottish Parlt, Oct. 2013–2016; contested (Lab) same seat, 2016. Contested (Lab) Dunfermline and Fife W, 2017. *Recreations:* spending time with family and friends, cooking.

**HILTON, John Howard;** *see* Hilton, A. J. H.

**HILTON, Jonathan James Robert,** CEng, FIMechE; Managing Director, Celeratis Ltd, since 2015; *b* Eastbourne, 14 April 1964; *s* of John and Anne Hilton; *m* 2000, Judy Oliver; one *s* (and one *s* decd). *Educ:* Hatfield Poly. (BSc Hons Mech. Engrg 1986). CEng 1990; FIMechE 2002. Undergrad. apprentice, 1982–87, engine designer, 1987–89, Rolls Royce; Mech. engr, Graesby Dynamics Ltd, 1989–91; engine designer, 1991–94, Chief Engr, 1995–97, Cosworth; Chief Engr, TWR F1 Engines, 1998–2002; Tech. Dir, Engine Div., Renault F1 Team, 2003–06; Co-founder and Man. Dir, Flybrid Automotive Ltd, 2007–13; Commercial Dir, 2014–15, non-exec. Dep. Chm., 2015–17, Torotrak PLC. Trustee, IMechE, 2011– (Vice Pres., 2013–16; Pres., 2016–17). *Publications:* named inventor on over 40 published patents. *Recreations:* family, sailing, surfing, motorsport. *Address:* Celeratis Ltd, Magog House, Chase Park Road, Yarkley Hastings, Northampton NN7 1HF. *T:* (01604) 696878. *E:* JHilton@celeratis.com.

**HILTON, Matthew James;** Chief Executive Officer, seAp Advocacy, since 2018; *b* 25 Jan. 1967; *s* of Ronald and Mary Hilton; *m* 1995, Elizabeth Sarah Jones; two *s* one *d*. *Educ:* St John Fisher High Sch., Wigan; Univ. of Sheffield (BA 1988, MA 1989); Imperial Coll., London (MBA 2000). English teacher, Prague, 1990–92; joined DTI, 1992; Private Sec. to Sec. of State and Minister for Energy and Industry, 1994–97; Dir, Business Support Rev., 2001–03; Principal Private Sec. to Sec. of State, 2003–05; Dir of Strategy and Communications, then Dir of Communications, DTI, subseq. BERR, 2005–07; Dir, Employment Relations, BERR, subseq. BIS, 2007–11; Dir of Higher Educn Student Support, 2011–12, Dir of Higher Educn, 2012–14, BIS; Dep. Vice Chancellor (Ops) and Univ. Sec., Kingston Univ., 2014–17. Trustee, Nat. Deaf Children's Soc., 2006–15 (Chm., 2011–15); Gov., BRIT Sch., 2018–. *Club:* Gentlemen of Lewes Cricket.

**HILTON, Nicola Mary;** *see* Bayley, N. M.

**HILTON, Rachel;** *see* Whetstone, R. M. J.

**HILTON, Ronald;** Chief Executive, Staffordshire County Council, 2007–10; Managing Partner, Ron Hilton Consultancy Ltd, 2010–13; *b* Washington, Co. Durham, 16 Feb. 1946; *s* of James and Muriel Hilton; *m* 1968, Frances Biggs; two *s*. *Educ:* Washington Grammar Sch.; Teesside Poly. (BSc Hons). Dir, Worcester CC, 1980–85; Dep. Chief Exec., Dir of Envmt and Econ. Develt, and Dir, Stockport Direct Services, Stockport CC, 1985–2002; Corporate Dir of Develt, 2002–05, Dep. Chief Exec., 2005–07, Staffs CC. Clerk to Lord Lieutenancy of Staffs, 2007–10; Sec., Adv. Cttee, Staffs Magistrates. Chm., W Midlands Assembly Regl Adv. Gp, 2003–07. Dir, Stockport Business Link, 1998–2001. Mem., NW Business Adv. Service, 1998–2002. Econ. Develt Advr to LGA, 1997–2002. Non-exec. Dir, South Staffs and Shropshire NHS Founds Trust, 2010–16 (Vice Chm. and Sen. Ind. Dir, 2012–16). Mem. Adv. Bd, Senn Delaney, 2010–14. Mem., Regeneration and Res. Cttee, Co. Surveyors' Soc., 2003–07. Trustee, Salford Univ. Campus, 1995–2002; Gov., Staffordshire Univ., 2007–10. FRSA 2008. *Recreation:* golf. *Club:* Bramall Park Golf.

**HILTON, Prof. Sean Robert,** MD; FRCGP; Professor of General Practice and Primary Care, St George's (formerly St George's Hospital Medical School), University of London, 1993–2012, now Emeritus (Director, International Relations, 2011–12); Professor of Medical Education, University of Nicosia, since 2012; *b* 31 Oct. 1949; *s* of Harold and Doris Hilton; *m* 1994, Lesley Wood; two *s* one *d*. *Educ:* Weymouth Grammar Sch.; St George's Hosp. Med. Sch., London (MB BS 1974; MD 1991). FRCGP 1990. NHS GP Principal, Kingston-upon-Thames, 1979–2009; St George's Hospital Medical School, University of London, subseq. St George's, University of London: Sen. Lectr in Gen. Practice, 1987–93; Dean of Undergrad. Medicine, 1997–2002; Vice-Principal, 2003–07; Dep. Principal, 2008–11; non-exec. Dir, St George's Healthcare Trust, 2003–11. Gov., Anglo-European Coll. of Chiropractic, 2003–12 (Chm., 2006–12); Mem. Council, Acad. of Medical Educators, 2007– (Pres., 2011–14). Chm., DIPEx Charity, Oxford, 2016–; Trustee, Princess Alice Hospice, Esher, 2012–. FHEA 1999; FAcadMed 2009, Hon. FAcadMed 2019. MRSocMed. Hon. Fellow, St George's, Univ. of London, 2017. Hon. DSc: Kingston, 2012; Nicosia, 2018. *Publications:* (with M. Levy) Asthma in Practice, 1987, 4th edn 1999; (jtly) Asthma at Your Fingertips, 1993, 3rd edn 2006; more than 100 peer reviewed papers and book chapters on gen. practice, primary care and med. educn. *Recreations:* music (especially Schubert and songs of Jackson Browne), gardening and trees, football, cricket, WW1. *Address:* St George's, University of London, Cranmer Terrace, SW17 0RE. *T:* (020) 8286 2857. *E:* shilton.shx@gmail.com. *Club:* MCC.

**HIMSWORTH, Emma Katherine, (Mrs N. P. Buller);** QC 2012; *b* London, 17 Feb. 1968; *d* of Prof. Richard Lawrence Himsworth, *qv*; *m* 2000, Nigel Pearson Buller; two *s*, and one step *d*. *Educ:* South Hampstead High Sch.; Univ. of Edinburgh (BSc Biol Scis (Hons Biochem.)); City Univ. (DipLaw). Called to the Bar, Gray's Inn, 1993, Bencher, 2018; in practice, One Essex Court, 1995–, specialising in intellectual property law and related aspects of commercial and competition law; appointed to hear trade mark appeals, 2013–. Liveryman, Goldsmiths' Co., 2004. *Address:* One Essex Court, Temple, EC4Y 9AR. *T:* (020) 7583 2000, *Fax:* (020) 7583 0118. *E:* ehimsworth@oeclaw.co.uk.

**HIMSWORTH, Prof. Richard Lawrence,** MD; FRCP; Professor of Health Research and Development, 1993–2002, and Director, Institute of Public Health, 1999–2002, Cambridge University; Fellow, Girton College, Cambridge, since 1995; *b* 14 June 1937; *s* of Sir Harold Himsworth, KCB, FRS; *m* 1966, Sara Margaret Tattersall; two *s* one *d*. *Educ:* Westminster Sch.; Trinity Coll., Cambridge (MB BChir 1961, MD 1971); University Coll. Hosp. Med. Sch.; University Coll. London (MA in History of Medicine 2005). FRCP 1977; FRCPE 1988; FRCPGlas 1990; FFPH (FFPHM 2002). Lectr in Medicine, UCH Med. Sch., 1967–71; MRC Travelling Fellow, New York, 1969–70; MRC Scientific Staff, Clinical Res. Centre, 1971–85: Asst Dir, 1978–82; Head, Endocrinology Res. Gp, 1979–85; Consultant Physician, Northwick Park Hosp., 1972–85; Regius Prof. of Medicine, Univ. of Aberdeen, and Hon. Consultant Physician, Aberdeen Royal Infirmary, 1985–93. Hon. Prof., UEA, 1994. Associate Dir, R&D, Anglia and Oxford RHA, 1994–98; Dir, R&D, Eastern (formerly Anglia and Oxford) Region, NHS Exec., DoH, 1998–2002. Member: NW Thames RHA, 1982–85; Scottish Nat. Med. Adv. Cttee, 1990–92; Gen. Council, King Edward's Hosp. Fund for London, 1980– (Mem. London Commns, 1990–92, 1995–97). Mem. Ct, Imperial Coll., London, 2002–09. Liveryman, 1976–, Mem. Ct of Assts, 1995–, Prime Warden, 2007–08, Goldsmiths' Co. Hon. DSc Anglia Poly., 2000. *Publications:* scientific and medical papers. *Address:* Park House, 39 High Street, Balsham, Cambridge CB21 4DJ. *T:* (01223) 893975.
See also E. K. Himsworth.

**HINCE, Dr Trevor Anthony;** Director and Secretary, Lister Institute for Preventive Medicine, 2004–15, Member, since 2016; *b* 17 Aug. 1949; *s* of late Gerald Arthur Hince and Beryl Doris Hince (*née* Franklin); *m* 1st, 1972, Carol Jean Tarabella (marr. diss. 1996); 2nd, 1996, Sarah Elizabeth Verrall. *Educ:* Forest Grammar Sch., Winnersh; University Coll. London (BSc Hons 1971); Middlesex Hosp. Med. Sch. (PhD 1976); Brunel Univ./Henley Mgt Coll. (MSc 1988). Middlesex Hospital Medical School: Research Asst, 1971–76; Temp. Lectr in Pathology, 1976–79; Cancer Research Campaign: Asst Scientific Sec., 1980–86; Scientific Sec., 1986–89; Dep. Dir, Scientific Dept, 1989–96; Scientific Dir, 1996–2002; Dep. Dir Gen., 1998–2002; Dir, Res. Mgt and Planning, CRUK, 2002–04. Member: Inst. of Cancer Res., 2004–; CRUK, 2015–. Trustee, Gibb Res. Fellowship Fund, 2004–15. *Publications:* papers in scientific jls. *Recreations:* walking, gardening, music, wildlife conservation. *Address:* Sharlands Corner, Blackboys, Uckfield, East Sussex TN22 6HN.

**HINCH, Prof. Edward John,** PhD; FRS 1997; Professor of Fluid Mechanics, University of Cambridge, 1998–2014; Fellow of Trinity College, Cambridge, since 1971; *b* 4 March 1947; *s* of Joseph Edward Hinch and Mary Grace Hinch (*née* Chandler); *m* 1969, Christine Bridges; one *s* one *d*. *Educ:* Edmonton County Grammar Sch.; Trinity Coll., Cambridge (BA 1968; PhD 1973). Asst Lectr, 1972–75, Lectr, 1975–94, Reader, 1994–98, Univ. of Cambridge. Fellow, APS, 2003; MAE 2011; For. Associate, NAE, 2012. Hon Dr Inst Nat. Poly. de Toulouse, 2010. Fluid Mechanics Prize, Euro Mech, 2010; Fluid Dynamics Prize,

APS, 2010. Chevalier de l'ordre national du Mérite (France), 1997. *Publications:* Perturbation Methods, 1991; papers on fluid mechanics and its applications in scientific jls. *Address:* Trinity College, Cambridge CB2 1TQ. *T:* (01223) 338427.

**HINCHCLIFFE, Peter Robert Mossom,** CMG 1988; CVO 1979; HM Diplomatic Service, retired; Ambassador to Jordan, 1993–97; *b* 9 April 1937; *s* of Herbert Peter and Jeannie Hinchcliffe; *m* 1965, Archbold Harriet Siddall; three *d*. *Educ:* Elm Park, Killylea, Co. Armagh, Prep. Sch.; Radley Coll.; Trinity Coll., Dublin (BA (Hons), MA). Military service, short service commission, W Yorks Regt, 1955–57; TCD, Dublin Univ., 1957–61; HMOCS: West Aden Protectorate, South Arabian Fedn, 1961–67; Admin. Asst, Birmingham Univ., 1968–69; FCO: 1st Sec., Near Eastern Dept, 1969–70; 1st Sec., UK Mission to UN, 1971–74; 1st Sec. and Head of Chancery, Kuwait, 1974–76; Asst Head of Science and Technology and Central and Southern African Depts, FCO, 1976–78; Dep. High Comr, Dar es Salaam, 1978–81; Consul-Gen., Dubai, 1981–85; Hd of Information Dept, FCO, 1985–87; Ambassador to Kuwait, 1987–90; High Comr to Zambia, 1990–93. Chm., Hutton and Paxton Community Council, 2001–05. Hon. Fellow, Edin. Univ. 1997–2008; Sen. Res. Fellow, QUB, 1997–2000; Hon. Adjunct Fellow, Curtin Univ., WA, 2002. *Publications:* Time to Kill Sparrows (poetry anthology), 1999; (with B. Milton-Edwards): Jordan: a Hashemite Legacy, 2001, 2nd edn 2008; Conflicts in the Middle East since 1945, 2001, 3rd edn 2007; Without Glory in Arabia: the British retreat from Aden, 2006. *Recreations:* golf, tennis, writing poetry. *Address:* The Old Bakery, Willis Wynd, Duns, Berwickshire TD11 3AD. *Clubs:* East India, Devonshire, Sports and Public Schools; Duns Golf; Royal Co. Down Golf (Newcastle, Co. Down).

**HINCHINGBROOKE, Viscount; Luke Timothy Charles Montagu;** *b* 5 Dec. 1969; *er s* and *heir* of Earl of Sandwich, *qv*; *m* 2004, Julie, *d* of Thomas L. Fisher, Chicago; two *s*. *Educ:* Westminster Sch.; Columbia Univ., NY. Director: Kinexus Ltd, 1996–97; Wide Multimedia, 1997–2001; Chief Executive Officer: Wide Learning, 1997–2001; Met Film Sch., 2003–09 (non-exec. Dir, 2003–17). Trustee: Dalai Lama Centre for Compassion, 2015–; Inner Compass Initiative, 2016–. *Heir: s* Hon. William James Hayman Montagu, *b* 2 Nov. 2004. *Address:* c/o Mapperton House, Beaminster, Dorset DT8 3NR.

**HINCHLIFFE, David Martin;** consultant on health and social care policy; *b* 14 Oct. 1948; *s* of late Robert Victor Hinchliffe and Muriel Hinchliffe; *m* 1982, Julia (*née* North); one *s* one *d*. *Educ:* Lawefield Lane Primary Sch., Wakefield; Cathedral C of E Secondary Modern Sch., Wakefield; Leeds Polytechnic (Cert. in Social Work); Bradford Univ. (MA Social Work and Community Work); Huddersfield Polytechnic (Cert Ed); Leeds Univ. (MA Local and Regl Hist.). Social Work with Leeds Social Services, 1968–79; Social Work Tutor, Kirklees Metropolitan Borough Council, 1980–87. MP (Lab) Wakefield, 1987–2005. An opposition front bench spokesman on personal social services and community care, 1992–95. Chairman: Health Select Cttee, 1997–2005; Select Cttee on Adoption and Children Bill, 2001 and 2002. Chm., Nat. Coal Mining Mus. for England, 2013–16. Hon. Mem., Nat. Council, NSPCC. *Publications:* Rugby's Class War, 2000; (ed) A Westminster XIII: Parliamentarians and Rugby League, 2002; (jtly) Rugby's Berlin Wall, 2005; They Walked On Water: the story of Wembley, 1968, 2013. *Recreations:* Rugby League - supporter of Wakefield Trinity RLFC, genealogy, local history. *Club:* Wakefield Labour.

**HINCHLIFFE, Thomas Richard;** QC 2016; *b* Harrogate, 19 Sept. 1972; *s* of Stephen Hinchliffe and Sandra Hinchliffe; *m* 2002, Lucy Deborah Buttress; one *s* one *d*. *Educ:* Eton Coll.; Brasenose Coll., Oxford (MA Chem.). Called to the Bar, Middle Temple, 1997; in practice as a barrister specialising in intellectual property law, 3 New Square, 1998–. *Publications:* Terrell on the Law of Patents, (contrib.) 15th edn 2000, 16th edn 2006, (ed) 18th edn 2016. *Recreations:* cycling, running, triathlon, family. *Address:* 3 New Square, Lincoln's Inn, WC2A 3RS. *T:* (020) 7405 1111, *Fax:* (020) 7405 7800. *Club:* Welwyn Wheelers Cycling.

**HINCKS, Tim;** Co-Chief Executive Officer, Expectation, since 2016; *b* Windsor, 18 Aug. 1967; *s* of David Hincks and Geraldine Hincks; *m* 2000, Pippa Healy; two *s* one *d*. *Educ:* Weald Comp. Sch., Billingshurst; Bristol Univ. (BSocSc Econs and Politics). Hair gel factory, Billingshurst, 1989–90; Policy Researcher, Nat. Consumer Council, 1990; TV Researcher, Food and Drink prog., BBC Westminster and Newsnight, BBC, 1990–99; Endemol UK: Chief Creative Officer, 1999–2007; CEO, 2007–12; Chm., 2012–16; Pres., Endemol Gp, 2012–14, Endemol Shine Gp, 2014–16. Mem., Exec. Cttee, Edinburgh Internat. Television Fest., 2006– (Exec. Chm., 2007–10). *Recreations:* my kids, Arsenal FC, member of popular rock and beat combo No Expectations.

**HIND, Andrew Fleming,** CB 2011; FCA; Visiting Professor of Charity Governance and Finance, Cass Business School, City, University of London (formerly City University London), since 2011; Chair, Fundraising Standards Board, 2015–16; *b* 29 Sept. 1955; *s* of Andrew Hind and Mary Hind; *m* 1985, Christina; three *s*. *Educ:* Portsmouth Grammar Sch.; Southampton Univ. (BSc). FCA 1979. Ernst & Young, 1976–80; Pannell Kerr Forster, Kenya, 1980–83; Divl Financial Controller, Balfour Beatty Ltd, 1983–86; Dir of Finance, 1986–89, Dep. Chief Exec., 1989–91, ActionAid; Dir of Finance and Corporate Services, Barnardo's, 1992–95; Dir of Finance and Business Develt, 1995–2002, Chief Operating Officer, 2002–04, BBC World Service; Chief Exec., Charity Commn, 2004–10; Editor, Charity Finance Mag., 2011–15. Charity Finance Directors' Group: Co-founder, 1988; Mem., Exec. Cttee, 1988–94; Chm., 1992–94. Member: Commn on Effectiveness and the Voluntary Sector, NCVO, 1990; Charity Awards Judges Panel, 2001–04, 2011–18 (Chm., 2003–04, 2011–18); Audit Cttee, Commonwealth Secretariat, 2004–06; Commn on the Future of Volunteering, 2006–08; Professional Standards Authy for Health and Social Care (formerly Council for Healthcare Regulatory Excellence), 2009–16 (Chm., Audit Cttee, 2009–16); Information Commn, 2010–15. Chm., Public Sector Adv. Bd, ICAEW, 2007–10. Trustee: Internat. Fundraising Gp, 1992–95; VSO, 1995–98; UNICEF UK, 1995–2002 (Treas., 1996–2002); Baring Foundn, 2010–; Trustee and Treas., Diana, Princess of Wales Meml Fund, 1999–2004. *Publications:* (ed jtly) Charity Managers and Charity Trustees - Meeting the Challenges of the 1990s, 1993; (ed) The Charity Finance Handbook, 1994; The Governance and Management of Charities, 1995. *Recreations:* golf, tennis, travel, collecting old books on Africa. *Address:* 11 Byng Road, High Barnet, Herts EN5 4NW. *T:* 07703 109063. *E:* andrew@andrewhind.co.uk.

**HIND, Rt Rev. Dr John William;** Bishop of Chichester, 2001–12; an Honorary Assistant Bishop, Diocese of Portsmouth, since 2012; *b* 19 June 1945; *s* of late Harold Hind and Joan Mary Hind; *m* 1966, Janet Helen McLintock; three *s*. *Educ:* Watford Grammar Sch.; Leeds Univ. (BA 1966). Asst Master, Leeds Modern Sch., 1966–69; Asst Lectr, King Alfred's Coll., Winchester, 1969–70; Cuddesdon Theol Coll.; Deacon 1972, Priest 1973; Asst Curate, St John's, Catford, 1972–76; Vicar, Christ Church, Forest Hill, 1976–82 and Priest-in-Charge, St Paul's, Forest Hill, 1981–82; Principal, Chichester Theol Coll., 1982–91; Area Bishop of Horsham, 1991–93; Bishop of Gibraltar in Europe, 1993–2001. Canon Residentiary and Bursalis Preb., Chichester Cathedral, 1982–90. Mem., H of L, 2008–12. Chm., Faith and Order Commn (formerly Faith and Order Adv. Gp), C of E, 1991–2012; Mem., Faith and Order Commn, WCC, 1999–2014 (Vice-Moderator, 2006–14). DD Lambeth, 2009. *Recreations:* cooking, languages.

**HIND, Kenneth Harvard,** CBE 1995; barrister; *b* 15 Sept. 1949; *s* of George Edward and Brenda Hind; one *s* one *d*; *m* 2008, Sue Hall, JP; one step *d*. *Educ:* Woodhouse Grove Sch., Bradford; Leeds Univ. (LLB 1971); Inns of Court Sch. of Law. Pres., Leeds Univ. Union, 1971–72. Called to the Bar, Gray's Inn, 1973; practised North Eastern circuit, 1973–83. MP (C) West Lancashire, 1983–92; contested (C): W Lancashire, 1992; Selby, 1997. PPS to Minister of State: for Defence Procurement, 1986–87; for Employment, 1987–89; for Northern Ireland, 1989–90; PPS to Sec. of State for Northern Ireland, 1990–92. Officer, 1995–97, Chm., 1997–2002, Conservative Candidates Assoc. Member: Soc. of Conservative Lawyers, 1983–; Justice, Internat. Commn of Jurists, 1983–. Mem. (C), Ribble Valley BC, 2005–. Sen. Vice Chm., Ribble Valley Conservative Assoc., 2009– (Chm., 2006–09); Mem., Conservative Nat. Convention. Hon. Vice-Pres., Central and West Lancs Chamber of Industry and Commerce, 1983–92. *Recreations:* music, sailing Enterprise, cricket. *Address:* Newton Chambers, The Beeches, Waddington Road, Clitheroe, Lancs BB7 2HN.

**HINDLEY, Julia Carolyn;** *see* Newton, J. C.

**HINDLEY, Michael John;** Director, Michael Hindley and Associates, since 1999; Member (Lab), Lancashire County Council, 2001–05; *b* 11 April 1947; *s* of John and Edna Hindley; *m* 1980, Ewa Agnieszka (*née* Leszczyc-Grabianka); one *d*. *Educ:* Clitheroe Royal Grammar School; London University (BA Hons); Lancaster University (MA); Free University of West Berlin; Univ. of Glamorgan (Postgrad. Dip. Internat. Law). Labour Councillor, Hyndburn District Council, 1979–84 (Leader, 1981–84); contested (Lab) Blackpool North, 1983. MEP (Lab) Lancashire E, 1984–94, Lancashire S, 1994–99. Mem., Exec. Bd, War on Want, 1998–2009. Special Advr, Centre for Socio-Eco-Nomic Develt, Geneva, 2014–. Associate Prof., Georgetown Univ., Washington, 1993–2008. Expert Advr on Trade Issues, Eur. Econ. and Social Cttee, 2009–. *Recreations:* walking, reading, music, travel. *Address:* 27 Commercial Road, Great Harwood, Lancs BB6 7HX. *T:* (01254) 887017. *Club:* Reform.

**HINDLEY, Stephen Lewis,** CBE 2006; DL; FICE, FCIOB, FRICS; Executive Chairman, Midas Group Ltd, since 2002; *b* 11 March 1949; *s* of Arthur Stanley Hindley and Ann Hindley; *m* 1973, Moira Ann Williamson; two *d*. *Educ:* St Philip's Grammar Sch., Birmingham; Salford Univ. (BSc). FICE 1997; FCIOB 2001; FRICS 2013. Civil engr, Trafalgar House Gp, 1970–76; Project Manager, John Mowlem plc, 1976–89; Man. Dir, E. Thomas (subsid. co. of John Mowlem), 1989–98; Chief Exec., 1998–2001, Chm. and CEO, 2001–05, Midas Gp Ltd. Chairman: Construction Council, CBI, 2011–15; Heart of the SW LEP, 2014–; Devon Community Foundn, 2014–. Trustee, Children's Hospice SW, 2012–. DL Devon, 2009. *Recreations:* running, hill-walking, sailing, golf, classic cars, motor sport. *Address:* Midas Group, Midas House, Pynes Hill, Exeter EX2 5WS. *T:* (01392) 356200, *Fax:* (0870) 8553814. *E:* shindley@midasgroup.co.uk. *Club:* Royal Automobile.

**HINDLIP,** 6th Baron *cr* 1886; **Charles Henry Allsopp;** Bt 1880; *b* 5 Aug. 1940; *e s* of 5th Baron Hindlip and Cecily Valentine Jane, *o d* of Lt-Col Malcolm Borwick, DSO; *S* father, 1993; *m* 1968, Fiona Victoria Jean Atherley (*d* 2014), *d* of late Hon. William Johnston McGowan, 2nd *s* of 1st Baron McGowan, KBE; one *s* three *d*. *Educ:* Eton. Coldstream Guards, 1959–62; joined Christie's, 1962; Gen. Manager, Christie's New York, 1965–70; Christie, Manson & Woods: Dir, 1970; Dep. Chm., 1985; Chm., 1986–96; Chm., Christie's Internat., 1996–2002; Dep. Chm., Agnew's, 2003–04. Trustee, Chatham Historic Dockyard, 1989–2000. Chevalier de la Légion d'Honneur (France), 1998. *Publications:* An Auctioneer's Lot: triumphs and disasters at Christie's, 2016. *Recreations:* painting, shooting, ski-ing. *Heir: s* Hon. Henry William Allsopp [*b* 8 June 1973; *m* 2012, Hon. Naomi Gummer, *e d* of Baron Chadlington, *qv*]. *Address:* Lydden House, King's Stag, Dorset DT10 2AU. *Clubs:* White's, Pratt's, Beefsteak; Corviglia Ski.

**HINDMARCH, Anya,** CBE 2017 (MBE 2009); Founder and Chairman, since 1987, and Chief Creative Officer, since 2011, Anya Hindmarch; *b* Burnham, 7 May 1968; *d* of Michael and Susan Hindmarch; *m* 1996, Hugh James Seymour; four *s* one *d*. *Educ:* New Hall Sch. Business Ambassador, DIT (formerly UKTI), 2010–18; Mem., Adv. Bd for Mayor of London, 2013–. Mem. Exec. Bd, British Fashion Council, 2010–. Trustee: RA, 2008–; Design Mus., 2009–; Mothers for Children, 2009–. Gov., Univ. of the Arts, 2010–15. Hon. DArts Anglia Ruskin, 2011; DUniv Essex, 2017. *Recreations:* art, architecture, graphic design, photography. *Address:* Anya Hindmarch Ltd, The Stable Block, Plough Brewery, 516 Wandsworth Road, SW8 3JX. *T:* (020) 7501 0177, *Fax:* (020) 7501 0170. *Club:* Chelsea Arts.

**HINDMARSH, Irene,** JP, MA; Principal, St Aidan's College, University of Durham, 1970–88; Pro-Vice-Chancellor, University of Durham, 1982–85; *b* 22 Oct. 1923; *d* of Albert Hindmarsh and Elizabeth (*née* White). *Educ:* Heaton High Sch.; Lady Margaret Hall, Oxford (MA Hons French); King's Coll., Univ. of Durham (PGCE). Taught at St Paul's Girls' Sch., London, 1947–49, Rutherford High Sch., Newcastle upon Tyne, 1949–59; Interchange Teacher, Lycée de Jeunes Filles, Dax, Landes, France, 1954–55; Lectr in Educn and French, King's Coll., Durham, 1959–64; Headmistress, Birkenhead High Sch., GPDST, 1964–70. Vis. Prof., New York State Univ., Syracuse, Cornell, Harvard, 1962; Delegate of Internat. Fedn of Univ. Women to UNO, NY, to Commns on Human Rights and Status of Women, 1962; Vis. Professor: Fu-Dan Univ., Shanghai, 1979, and again, 1980; SW China Teachers' Univ., Beibei, Sichuan, and Fu-Dan Univ., Shanghai, 1986. Delegate/Translator to internat. confs of FIPESO, 1963–70; Chairman: Internat. Cttee of Headmistresses' Assoc., 1966–70; Internat. Panel of Joint Four, 1967–70. Mem. of Council, Chillingham Wild Cattle Assoc., 1988–98. Editor, Internat. Bull. of AHM, 1966–70. JP Birkenhead 1966, Durham 1974. FRSA 1989. *Publications:* various articles on educnl topics in AGM papers of Assoc. of Head Mistresses; contribs to prelim. papers of FIPESO meetings; seminar papers to symposia on lit. topics, Sèvres, under auspices of Council of Europe; contrib. re St Aidan's to Durham History from the Air. *Recreations:* travel, music, theatre, films, art, architecture. *Address:* 8 Dickens Wynd, Merryoaks, Elvet Moor, Durham DH1 3QR.

**HINDS, Rt Hon. Damian (Patrick George);** PC 2018; MP (C) East Hampshire, since 2010; *b* London, 27 Nov. 1969; *s* of Francis Hinds and Bridget Hinds; *m* 2007, Jacqui Morel; one *s* two *d*. *Educ:* Sir Ambrose Grammar Sch., Altrincham; Trinity Coll., Oxford (BA PPE 1992). Res. analyst, Mercer Mgt Consulting, 1992–95; Holiday Inn: Pricing Manager, 1995–96, Mktg Manager, 1996–99, Holiday Inn Europe; Vice Pres., e-Commerce, 2000–01, Vice Pres., Commercial, 2001–03, Holiday Inn and Intercontinental, EMEA; Strategy Dir, Greene King plc, 2005–07; freelance advr to hotel trade, 2003–05 and 2007–10. An Asst Govt Whip, 2014–15; Exchequer Sec., HM Treasury, 2015–16; Minister of State (Minister for Employment), DWP, 2016–18; Sec. of State for Educn, 2018–19. *Recreation:* music. *Address:* House of Commons, SW1A 0AA. *T:* (020) 7219 7057. *E:* damian.hinds.mp@parliament.uk.

**HINDS, Prof. Edward Allen,** DPhil; FRS 2004; Professor of Physics, Imperial College London, since 2002; *b* 8 Sept. 1949; *s* of Lawrence and Ruth Hinds; *m* 1972, Ann Carter; one *s* three *d*. *Educ:* Jesus Coll., Oxford (BA 1971; DPhil 1974). Professor of Physics: Yale Univ., 1977–95; Univ. of Sussex, 1995–2002. Alfred P. Sloan Fellow, 1981–85; Alexander von Humboldt Res. Award, 1998–2003; EPSRC Sen. Res. Fellow, 1999–2004; Royal Soc.

Res. Prof., 2006–. *Publications:* articles in academic physics jls. *Recreations:* music, physics. *Address:* 213 The Blackett Laboratory, Imperial College London, Prince Consort Road, SW7 2BW. *E:* ed.hinds@imperial.ac.uk.

**HINDS, Lesley Adelaide;** Member (Lab) City of Edinburgh Council, 1996–2017 (Lord Lieutenant and Lord Provost, City of Edinburgh, 2003–07); *b* Dundee, 3 Aug. 1956; *d* of late Kenneth Nicol and of Ena Nicol; *m* 1977, Martin Hinds; one *s* two *d*. *Educ:* Kirkton High Sch., Dundee; Dundee Coll. of Educn. Primary sch. teacher, Deans Primary, W Lothian, 1977–80. Mem. (Lab), Edinburgh DC, 1984–96 (Leader, 1993–96). Chair, Health Scotland, 2001–07. Director: N Edinburgh Area Renewal; N Edinburgh Arts; Pilton Partnership. Formerly Chm., Edinburgh Internat. Conf. Centre; Chair: Edinburgh Fest. Soc., 2003–07; Edinburgh Mil. Tattoo Ltd, 2003–07. Contested (Lab): Edinburgh Western, Scottish Parlt, 2011; Edinburgh Northern and Leith, Scottish Parlt, 2016. Convener, Transport and Envmt Cttee, Edinburgh CC, 2012–17. *Recreations:* theatre, dance, swimming, travel. *T:* (0131) 539 4499. *E:* hinds@blueyonder.co.uk.

**HINDUJA, Gopichand Parmanand;** President, Hinduja Group of Companies, since 1962; *b* 29 Feb. 1940; *s* of Parmanand Deepchand Hinduja and Jamuna Parmanand Hinduja; *m* 1963, Sunita Gurnani; two *s* one *d*. *Educ:* Jai Hind Coll., Bombay, India. Joined family business, 1958; Head, Hinduja Gp's ops in Iran, 1958–78; resident in UK, 1982–; jtly (with brother) initiated diversification and expansion of Hinduja Gp. Pres., Hinduja Foundn, 1962–. Member: Adv. Council, Hinduja Cambridge Trust, 1991–; Duke of Edinburgh's Award Fellowship, 1987–. Patron: Balaji Temple, UK; Swaminarayan Hindu Mission, London. Chm., Gurnanak Trust, Teheran. MInstD. Hon. LLD Westminster, 1996; Hon. DEc Richmond Coll., 1997. *Recreations:* Indian music, travel, sailing, yoga. *Address:* Hinduja Group of Companies, c/o Sangam Ltd, New Zealand House, 80 Haymarket, SW1Y 4TE. *T:* (020) 7839 4661. *Clubs:* Royal Automobile, Annabel's.
*See also* S. P. Hinduja.

**HINDUJA, Srichand Parmanand;** Chairman, Hinduja Group of Companies, since 1962; *b* 28 Nov. 1935; *s* of Hinduja Parmanand Deepchand Hinduja and Jamuna Parmanand Bajaj; *m* 1963, Madhu Srichand Menda; two *d*. *Educ:* National Coll., Bombay, India; Davar Coll. of Commerce, Mumbai. Joined family business; jtly (with brother) initiated diversification and expansion of Hinduja Gp. Chm., Hinduja Foundn, 1962–. Global Co-ordinator, IndusInd, 1962; Pres., IndusInd Internat. Fedn, 1996. Member, Advisory Council: Dharam Indic Res. Centres, Columbia, USA and Cambridge, UK; Hinduja Cambridge Trust, 1991–; Judge Inst. of Mgt, Cambridge, 1997. Mem., Duke of Edinburgh's Award Fellowship. Patron, Centre of India/US Educn, USA. Mem. Corp., Massachusetts Gen. Hosp. Hon. LLD Westminster, 1996; Hon. DEc Richmond Coll., 1997. *Publications:* Indic Research and Contemporary Crisis, 1995; The Essence of Vedic Marriage for Success and Happiness, 1996. *Recreations:* sports in general, but particularly tennis, volleyball and cricket, Indian classical music. *Address:* Hinduja Group of Companies, c/o Sangam Ltd, New Zealand House, 80 Haymarket, SW1Y 4TE. *T:* (020) 7839 4661. *Clubs:* Royal Over-Seas League, Les Ambassadeurs.
*See also* G. P. Hinduja.

**HINE, Dame Deirdre (Joan),** DBE 1997; FRCP, FFPH; President: Royal Medical Benevolent Fund, 2008–12; Age Cymru, 2011–17; British Medical Association, 2005–06; Royal Society of Medicine, 2000–02 (Chairman, Press Board, 2004–08); *b* 16 Sept. 1937; *d* of late David Alban Curran and Noreen Mary Curran (*née* Cliffe); *m* 1963, Raymond Hine (*d* 2018); two *s*. *Educ:* Heathfield House, Cardiff; Charlton Park, Cheltenham; Welsh Nat. Sch. of Medicine (MB BCh). DPH 1964; FFPH (FFPHM 1978); FRCP 1993. Asst MO, Glamorgan CC, 1963–74; Specialist in Community Medicine, S Glam HA, 1974–82; Sen. Lectr in Geriatric Medicine, Univ. of Wales Coll. of Medicine, 1982–84; Dep. Chief MO, Welsh Office, 1984–87; Dir, Welsh Breast Cancer Screening Service, 1987–90; CMO, Welsh Office, 1990–97. Member: Audit Commn, 1998–99; H of L Appt Commn, 2000–05; Chm., Commn for Health Improvement, 1999–2004. Non-exec. Dir, Dŵr Cymru, 2001–10. Vice President: Marie Curie Cancer Care, 1998–; British Lung Foundn, 2005–. Chairman: No Smoking Day, 1998–2001; BUPA Foundn, 2004–11. Chm., C. difficile Public Inquiry, NI, 2009–11. *Publications:* papers on health promotion, health care of elderly, breast cancer screening, epidemiol. of old age in jls and text books; Calman-Hine report on cancer services. *Recreations:* travel, theatre, reading, canal cruising.
*See also* P. D. Curran.

**HINE, Rt Rev. John Franklin Meldon;** Auxiliary Bishop in Southwark, (RC), and Titular Bishop of Beverly, 2001–13, now Emeritus; Parish Priest, St Andrew's Church, Tenterden, since 2013; *b* 26 July 1938; *s* of Lt Comdr Jack F. W. Hine, RN and Moira E. Hine. *Educ:* Stonyhurst; Mayfield Coll.; Ven. English Coll., Rome; Pontifical Gregorian Univ., Rome (PhL 1958; STB 1961). Assistant Priest: Worcester Park, S London, 1963–70; Maidstone, 1970–73; Chatham, 1973–78; Parish Priest, Bearsted and Harrietsham, and Sec., subseq. Chm., Diocesan Schs' Commn for Kent, 1978–86; VG and Chancellor, Southwark Diocese, 1986–2001. Prelate of Honour, 1986. *Recreations:* golf, walking. *Address:* The Presbytery, 47 Ashford Road, Tenterden, Kent TN30 6LL.

**HINE, Vice Adm. Nicholas William,** CB 2018; Second Sea Lord and Deputy Chief of the Naval Staff, since 2019; *b* Carlisle, 4 Feb. 1966; *s* of late Rod Hine and of Margaret Hine (*née* Byers); *m* 1996, Zoe Thompson; one *d*. *Educ:* John Taylor High Sch., Staffs; City Univ., London (BSc Mgt and Systems 1989); King's Coll. London (MA Defence Studies 1999). Joined RN, 1984; Commanding Officer: HMS Blackwater, 1995–97; HMS Talent, 1999–2000; Hd, Admiralty Pilots, 2008; Naval Advr to Iraqi Govt, 2009; rcds 2009; CO, HMS Westminster, 2011–12; Defence Policy Advr, HM Treasury, 2012–15; ACNS (Policy), 2015–19. MInstD 2015; FRSA. *Address:* Navy Command HQ, Leach Building, Whale Island, Portsmouth PO2 8BY.

**HINE, Air Chief Marshal Sir Patrick (Bardon),** GCB 1989 (KCB 1983); GBE 1991; Air Officer Commanding-in-Chief, RAF Strike Command and Commander-in-Chief, United Kingdom Air Forces, 1988–91; Joint Commander, British Forces, Gulf War, 1990–91; Military Adviser to British Aerospace plc, 1992–99; *b* 14 July 1932; parents decd; *m* 1956, Jill Adèle (*née* Gardner); three *s*. *Educ:* Peter Symonds Sch., Winchester. Served: No 1 Sqn, 1952–54; CFS Staff Instructor and Mem., Pelicans aerobatic team, 1956–57; No 111 Sqn and Mem., Black Arrows aerobatic team, 1957–59; No 93 Sqn, 1959–60; commanded: No 92 Sqn, 1962–64; No 17 Sqn, 1970–71; RAF Wildenrath, 1974–75; Dir, Public Relations (RAF), 1975–77; RCDS 1978; SASO, HQ RAF, Germany, 1979; ACAS (Policy), 1979–83; C-in-C RAF Germany and Comdr, Second Allied Tactical Air Force, 1983–85; VCDS, 1985–87; Air Mem. for Supply and Orgn, 1987–88. Air ADC to the Queen, 1989–91. King of Arms, Order of the British Empire, 1997–2011. CCMI; FRAeS. Winner, Carris Trophy, Hants, IoW and Channel Islands Golf Championship, and Brabazon Trophy, 1949; English Schoolboy Golf Internat., 1948–49; Inter-Services Golf, 1952–57. QCVSA 1960. *Recreations:* golf, caravanning, photography, travelling, cruising. *Clubs:* Royal Air Force; Colonels (Founder Mem.); Royal & Ancient Golf (St Andrews) (Captain, 2010–11), Brokenhurst Manor Golf (Pres., 2012–), Seniors.

**HINES, James Philip;** QC 2015; *b* London, 13 May 1960; *s* of late Robert Henry Hines and of Shelagh Mary Hines; *m* 1993, Siân Spier; three *s* two *d*. *Educ:* St Benedict's Sch., Ealing; Ealing Coll., London (LLB). Called to the Bar, Gray's Inn, 1982, Bencher, 2019. *Recreations:* gardening, travel. *Address:* 3 Raymond Buildings, Gray's Inn, WC1R 5BH. *T:* (020) 7400 6400. *E:* james.hines@3rblaw.com.

**HINES, Richard Peter Treadwell D.;** *see* Davenport-Hines.

**HINGLEY, Robert Charles Anthony;** non-executive Chairman, Law Debenture Corporation, since 2018 (Director, since 2017); *b* 11 May 1960; *s* of Anthony Hingley and Ruth Hingley; *m* 1993, Arabella Ballard; one *s* one *d*. *Educ:* Rugby Sch.; Corpus Christi Coll., Cambridge (BA Hons 1981). Admitted Solicitor, 1984; Articled Clerk/Solicitor, Coward Chance, 1982–85; J. Henry Schroder & Co. Ltd, 1985–2000: Dir of Investment Banking, 1994; Hd of German Investment Banking, 1995–96; Hd of Financial Instns Gp, 1997–2000; Citigroup Investment Bank: Man. Dir and Global Co-Hd of Financial Instns Gp, 2000–03; Hd of German Investment Banking, 2001–03; Vice-Chm., Lexicon Partners, 2005–10; Chief Financial Officer, Save the Children, 2007; Dir-Gen., Panel on Takeovers and Mergers, 2007–10; Man. Dir, 2010–12, Sen. Advr, 2012–15, Lazard & Co. Ltd; Dir of Investment Affairs, ABI, 2012–14; Partner, Ondra Partners LLP, 2015–17. Dir, Waterstones Hldgs, 2012–16; Chairman: Phoenix Spree Deutschland Ltd, 2015–; Euroclear UK and Ireland Ltd, 2018–. Consultant: Strutt & Parker LLP, 2014–17; BNP Real Estate Ltd, 2017–19. Trustee: Arvon Foundn, 2006–15; Save the Children, 2007–15; Park Th., 2015–. Governor: Rugby Sch., 2007–; Chelsea Acad., 2008–16. *Recreations:* golf, cricket, reading, dog-walking. *E:* roberthingley@aol.com. *Clubs:* MCC, Queen's.

**HINKLEY, Prof. David Victor,** PhD; Professor of Statistics, University of California at Santa Barbara, since 1995; *b* 10 Sept. 1944; *s* of Eric Samson Hinkley and Edna Gertrude (*née* Alger); *m*; one *s* one *d*. *Educ:* Birmingham Univ. (BSc 1965); Imperial Coll., London (PhD 1969). MA Oxon 1990. Asst Lectr in Maths, Imperial Coll., London, 1967–69; Asst Prof. in Stats, Stanford Univ., 1969–71; Lectr in Maths, Imperial Coll., 1971–73; Associate Prof. and Prof. in Stats, Univ. of Minnesota, 1973–80; Prof. in Maths, Univ. of Texas, 1980–91; Prof. of Statistical Sci., and Fellow of St Anne's Coll., Oxford Univ., 1989–95. Editor: Annals of Statistics, 1980–82; Biometrika, 1991–92. *Publications:* Theoretical Statistics, 1973; Problems and Solutions in Theoretical Statistics, 1977; Statistical Theory and Modelling, 1990; Bootstrap Methods and Their Application, 1997; articles in statistical and scientific jls. *Recreations:* photography, botanical observation. *Address:* Department of Statistics and Applied Probability, University of California at Santa Barbara, CA 93106-3110, USA. *T:* (805) 8932129.

**HINKLEY, Sarah Ann, (Sally),** CBE 1995; Director, Performance and Change Management Group, Cabinet Office, 1999–2002; *b* 28 March 1950; *d* of Eric David Booth and Mary Booth; *m* 1st, 1980, Nigel Dorling (marr. diss. 1988); one *s*; 2nd, 1998, Alan Hinkley; one step *d*. *Educ:* Kendal High Sch.; Callington Grammar Sch.; Girton Coll., Cambridge (BA 1972; MA). Joined Dept of the Environment, 1974: Private Sec. to Permanent Sec., 1980–81; Principal, 1981–86; Asst Sec., 1987; Hd, Central Policy Planning Unit, 1987–88; Dir of Finance and Resources, Historic Royal Palaces, 1989–92; Department of National Heritage, later of Culture, Media and Sport, 1992–99: Hd, Nat. Lottery Div. and Dir of Finance, 1992–94; Hd, Broadcasting Policy Div., 1994–95; Under Sec., 1995; Hd, Libraries, Galls and Museums Gp, 1995–98; Hd, Educn, Trng, Arts and Sports Gp, 1998–99; Exec. Dir, Professional Standards, ICAEW, 2003–05. FRSA 1998. *Recreations:* singing alto with Teddington Choral Society, novel and poetry writing, supporting and enjoying my family, tending the garden.

**HINKS, Frank Peter;** QC 2000; writer and illustrator of children's stories; *b* 8 July 1950; *s* of Henry John Hinks and Patricia May Hinks (*née* Adams); *m* 1982, Susan Mary, *d* of Col J. A. Haire; three *s*. *Educ:* Bromley Grammar Sch.; St Catherine's Coll., Oxford (schol.; BA 1st Cl. Hons 1971; BCL 1st Cl. Hons 1972; MA). Called to the Bar, Lincoln's Inn, 1973, Bencher, 2008; in practice at the Bar, 1974–. Churchwarden, St Peter and St Paul, Shoreham, 1995–2005, 2010–. Liveryman, Innholders' Co. *Publications:* include: The Vicar's Chickens, 1992; The Land of Lost Hair, 1992; Creatures of the Forest, 1993; The Crystal Key, 1995; Ramion (collected stories), 2003 (trans. Korean, 2006); The Dim Daft Dwarves, 2004; The Bands of Evil, 2004; The Magic Magpie, 2004; The Cruel Count, 2004; Realm of Ramion (collected stories), 2004; The Seven Stones of Iliana, 2005; The Black Marchesa, 2005; Gary and the Frog Prince, 2005; The Embodiment of Evil, 2005; Swords of Ramion (collected stories), 2005; The Kingdom of the Deep, 2009; The Blizzard Wizard, 2010; The Body Collector, 2012; Boris and the Dumb Skulls, 2014; Seas of Ramion (collected stories), 2015; Rock of Ramion (collected stories), 2017; The Dream Thief, 2018; Frankie and the Dancing Furies, 2018; The Gift of Evil, 2019. *Recreations:* collecting jugs, gardening. *Address:* 6 New Square, Lincoln's Inn, WC2A 3QS.

**HINSLIFF, Gabrielle Seal;** journalist and author; columnist and feature writer, The Guardian, since 2014; *b* Chelmsford, 4 July 1971; *d* of Geoffrey Hinsliff and Judith Elizabeth Hinsliff; *m* 2006, James Clark; one *s*. *Educ:* Queens' Coll., Cambridge (BA Hons Eng. 1993); Centre for Journalism Studies, Univ. of Cardiff (Dip. Journalism 1994). Reporter, Grimsby Evening Telegraph, 1994–96; Daily Mail: News Reporter, then Health Reporter, 1996–97; Political Reporter, then Political Correspondent, 1997–2000; Chief Political Correspondent, 2000–04, Political Ed., 2004–09, The Observer; columnist, The Times, 2013–14; Political Ed.-at-Large, Grazia, 2012–15; Political Ed., The Pool, 2015–19. Member: Family Friendly Working Hours Taskforce, DWP, 2010–11; Resolution Foundn Commn on Living Standards, 2011–12. Trustee, 4Children, 2009–12. *Publications:* Half a Wife: the working family's guide to getting a life back, 2012. *Recreations:* my family, travel, gossip, dancing. *W:* www.twitter.com/gabyhinsliff.

**HINTON, Prof. Geoffrey Everest,** CC 2018; FRS 1998; FRSCan; PhD; Professor of Computer Science, 2001–14, University Professor, 2006–14, University of Toronto, now Distinguished Emeritus Professor; Vice President and Engineering Fellow, Google, since 2013; *b* 6 Dec. 1947; *s* of Prof. Howard Everest Hinton, FRS and late Margaret Rose Hinton; *m* 1997, Jacqueline Ford; one *s* one *d*. *Educ:* King's Coll., Cambridge (BA Exptl Psychology 1970); Univ. of Edinburgh (PhD Artificial Intelligence 1978). Fellow: Sussex Univ., 1976–78; UCSD, 1978–80; Faculty Mem., Computer Sci. Dept, Carnegie-Mellon Univ., 1982–87; Fellow, Canadian Inst. for Advanced Res. and Prof. of Computer Science and Psychology, Univ. of Toronto, 1987–98; Dir, Gatsby Computational Neurosci. Unit, UCL, 1998–2001. Pres., Cognitive Science Soc., 1992–93. Fellow, Amer. Assoc. for Artificial Intelligence, 1991; FRSCan 1996. Hon. Fellow, Amer. Acad. of Arts and Scis, 2003; Dist. Fellow, Canadian Inst. for Advanced Res., 2014. Hon. DSc: Edinburgh, 2001; Sussex, 2011. Award for contribs to IT, IT Assoc. of Canada/NSERC, 1992; NSERC Herzberg Medal, 2010; Killam Prize in Engrg, Canada Council for Arts, 2012; IEEE/RSE James Clerk Maxwell Medal, 2016; (jtly) A. M. Turing Award, Assoc. for Computing Machinery, 2019. *Publications:* (ed jtly) Parallel Models of Human Associative Memory, 1989; Connectionist Symbol Processing, 1992; (ed jtly) Unsupervised Learning: foundations of neural computation, 1999; numerous papers and articles in learned jls. *Address:* Department of Computer Science, University of Toronto, 6 King's College Road, Toronto, ON M5S 3G4, Canada. *T:* (416) 978 7564, *Fax:* (416) 978 1455.

**HINTON, Leslie Frank;** writer and journalist; Chief Executive Officer, Dow Jones & Company, 2007–11; publisher, Wall Street Journal, 2008–11; *b* 19 Feb. 1944; *s* of late Frank Arthur Hinton and Lilian Amy Hinton (*née* Bruce); *m* 1st, 1968, Mary Christine Weadick (marr. diss. 2009); four *s* one *d*; 2nd, 2009, Katharine Margaret Raymond. *Educ:* British Army schs in Germany, Libya, Egypt, Ethiopia and Singapore. Reporter, Adelaide News, SA, 1960–65; desk editor, British United Press, London, 1965–66; reporter, The Sun, 1966–69; writer editor, Adelaide News, 1969–70; reporter, The Sun, 1971–76; US corresp., News Internat., NYC, 1976–78; news editor, 1978–80, Managing Editor, 1980–82, The Star, NYC; Associate Editor, Boston Herald, 1982–85; Editor-in-Chief, Star Mag., 1985–87; Exec. Vice Pres., 1987–90, Pres., 1990–91, Murdoch Magazines, NYC; Pres. and Chief Exec. Officer, News America Publishing Inc., NYC, 1991–93; Chm. and Chief Exec. Officer, Fox Television Stations Inc. and Fox News Inc., LA, 1993–95; Exec. Chm., News International Ltd, 1995–2007. Director: British Sky Broadcasting plc, 1999–2003; Johnston Press plc, 2005–07. Chairman: Code of Practice Cttee, Press Complaints Commn, 1998–2007; Council, CPU, 1999–2007; Director: Press Standards Bd of Finance, 2003–07; Press Assoc., 1996–2007; Associated Press, 2011. Member Board of Trustees: Amer. Sch. in London, 1999–2007; Graduate Sch. of Journalism, City Univ. of New York, 2008–11. Mem., Bd of Advrs, Dept of Ophthalmol., Columbia Univ., 2010–. *Publications:* The Bootle Boy: an untidy life in news (memoir), 2018.

**HINTZ, B. Jürgen;** Group Chief Executive, Novar plc (formerly Caradon plc), 1998–2006; *b* 3 May 1942; *s* of Karl-Heinz Hintz and Elsbeth Parr; *m* 2nd, 1996, Kirsty MacMaster; one *s* one *d*, and one step *d*. *Educ:* Univ. of N Carolina State (BSc). Physicist, 1964–75; Procter & Gamble Inc.: various positions, 1976–89; Dir, 1989–91; Chief Exec., CarnaudMetalBox, 1991–95. Non-executive Director: Apple Computers Inc., 1994–97; Inchcape plc, 1994–98. Chm., Supervisory Bd, Head NV, then Head BV (Mem., 2003–). *Recreations:* ski-ing, tennis.

**HINTZE, Prof. Almut,** Dr phil, Dr hab.; FBA 2015; Zartoshty Brothers Professor of Zoroastrianism, School of Oriental and African Studies, University of London, since 2010; *b* Flinsbach, Germany, 7 June 1957; *d* of Gerhard Hintze and Valborg Hintze (*née* Schimrigk); *m* 1996, Eugenio Federico Biagini; one *s*. *Educ:* Univ. of Heidelberg (BA Classics 1984); Univ. of Oxford (MPhil Gen. Linguistics and Comparative Philol. 1986); Univ. of Erlangen (Dr phil Indo-Iranian Studies 1990); Free Univ. of Berlin (Dr hab. Indo-Eur. Studies 1997). Heisenberg Jun. Res. Prof., Univ. of Cambridge, 1997–2000; Res. Fellow, Clare Hall, Cambridge, 1997–2001; Zartoshty Lectr, 2001–05, Sen. Lectr, 2005–08, Reader, 2008–10, SOAS, Univ. of London. *Publications:* Der Zamyād-Yašt, 1994; Lohn im Indo-Iranischen, 2000; A Zoroastrian Liturgy, 2007; (with F. M. Kotwal) The Khorda Avesta and Yašt Codexei, 2008; Change and Continuity in the Zoroastrian Tradition, 2013. *Recreations:* music (playing the flute and piano), swimming, cycling. *Address:* Department of Religions and Philosophies, SOAS, University of London, Thornhaugh Street, Russell Square, WC1H 0XG. *T:* (020) 7898 4598, *Fax:* (020) 7898 4699. *E:* ah69@soas.ac.uk.

**HINTZE, Sir Michael,** Kt 2013; AM 2013; Executive Chairman, CQS, since 2019 (Founder, Chief Executive and Senior Investment Officer, 1999–2019); *b* Harbin, China, 27 July 1953; *s* of Michael Hintze and Veronica Hintze (*née* Lange, later Yakubovsky); *m* Dorothy; four *c*. *Educ:* Univ. of Sydney (BSc Physics and Pure Maths; BEng Electrical Engrg); Univ. of NSW (MSc Acoustics); Harvard Business Sch. (MBA). Electrical Design Engr, Civil and Civic Pty Ltd, Australia, 1976; served Australian Army, Royal Australian Electrical and Mech. Engrs (Captain), 1979–80; with Salomon Bros, NY, 1982–84; Goldman Sachs, London, 1984–96, rôles incl. Exec. Dir and Hd of UK Trading; Man. Dir and Eur. Hd of Convertibles, then Man. Dir, Leveraged Funds Gp, Credit Suisse First Boston, London, 1996–99. Estabd Hintze Family Charitable Foundn, 2005. Advr to Finance and Audit Cttee, Prince's Council, Duchy of Cornwall, 2014–; Mem., Bd of Superintendence, Vatican Bank, 2014–. Trustee: IEA; Nat. Gall., 2008–16; NPG, 2017–. Patron, Prince's Trust Australia; Sen. Vice-Patron, Royal Navy and Royal Marines Charity, 2013–. Special Friend of Aircraft Carrier HMS Queen Elizabeth. Hon. DBus NSW. GCSG 2008 (KCSG 2005). (Jtly) Prince of Wales Award for Arts Philanthropy, 2009. *Address:* CQS Investment Management Ltd, 4th Floor, One Strand, WC2N 5HR.

**HIPKIN, John;** Member (Ind), since 2008, and Leader, Independent Group, since 2013, Cambridge City Council (Member (Lib Dem), 1992–2007); Member (Ind) and Leader, Independent Group, Cambridgeshire County Council, 2013–17; *b* 9 April 1935; *s* of Jack Hipkin and Elsie Hipkin; *m* 1963, Bronwyn Vaughan Dewey (marr. diss. 1985); four *s* one *d*; one *d*; *m* 2004, Marie-Louise Holland; one *d*. *Educ:* Surbiton Grammar Sch. for Boys; LSE (BScEcon). Asst Teacher, 1957–65; Research Officer: King's Coll., Cambridge, 1965–68; Univ. of East Anglia, 1968–71; Sec., Schools Council Working Party on Whole Curriculum, 1973–74; Dir, Adv. Centre for Educn, 1974–77; Hd of English, Meridian Sch., Royston, Herts, 1977–95. Mayor of Cambridge, 2005–06. Chm., Planning Cttee, Cambridge CC, 2016–18. *Publications:* (jtly) New Wine in Old Bottles, 1967; The Massacre of Peterloo (a play), 1968, 2nd edn 1974; (ed jtly) Education for the Seventies, 1970. *Recreations:* theatre, foreign travel, history, medieval music. *Address:* 15 Oxford Road, Cambridge CB4 3PH. *T:* (01223) 564126.

**HIPKINS, Michael Francis,** PhD; Director, Financial Support for Learners, Department for Business, Innovation and Skills (formerly Director, Student Finance, Department for Education and Skills, then Department for Innovation, Universities and Skills), 2004–11; *b* 12 March 1951; *s* of Leonard Sidney Hipkins and Stella Frances Irving Graham; *m* 1977, Barbara Wilson; one *s* (and one *s* decd). *Educ:* Imperial Coll., London (BSc 1972; PhD 1976). MInstP 1987. EMBO Long-term Fellow, CNRS, France, 1976; Lectr, Univ. of Glasgow, 1976–86; Principal, 1988, Grade 5, 1990, DES, subseq. DFE, DFEE then DFES. Member, Council: Univ. of Bath, 2011–17; Bucks New Univ., 2011– (Dep. Chair, 2014–16; Chair, 2016–).

**HIRD, Christopher Clarke;** Founder and Managing Director, Dartmouth Films, since 2008; *b* Northallerton; *s* of George Kenneth Hird and Muriel Hird (*née* Clarke); partner, Anna Haworth; one *s* two *d*. *Educ:* Pocklington Sch., York; St Edmund Hall, Oxford (BA PPE). Investment analyst, Simon & Coates, stockbrokers, 1969–73; journalist: Investors Guardian, 1973–74; The Economist, 1974–76; Daily Mail, 1976–78; Dep. Editor, New Statesman, 1978–80; Editor, Insight, Sunday Times, 1980–82; Reporter, Diverse Reports, Channel Four Television, 1982–86; Founder and Jt Man. Dir, FulcrumTV, 1986–2007; Jt Founder, Fulcrum Res., 1986–2007. Man. Editor, 2013–14, non-exec. Dir, 2015–, Bureau of Investigative Journalism. Non-executive Director: City Limits, 1981–85; New Statesman, 1985–88; Pensions and Investment Res. Consultants, 1986–88. Non-exec. Dir, 1998–2001, Chair, 2001–05, Sheffield Internat. Documentary Fest.; Founding Chair, docsociety (formerly British Documentary Film Foundn), 2005–10; non-executive Director: Index on Censorship, 2004–10 (Patron, 2010–); Bridge Documentary Foundn, 2017–; Trustee: Wincott Foundn, 2004–; Grierson Trust, 2008–14 (Patron, 2014–); Centre for Investigative Journalism, 2012–16; One World Media, 2013–; Crispin Aubrey Legacy Fund, 2013–; Theatre Royal, Stratford East, 2018–; Picture People, 2019–; Patron, London Film Sch., 2014–. Mem., BAFTA, 2014–. *Publications:* Your Employer's Profits, 1975; (contrib.) Demystifying Social Statistics, 1979; Challenging the Figures, 1983; (with Richard Belfield) The Index of Nominees and Their Beneficial Owners, 1987; (jtly) Murdoch: the decline of an empire, 1991; (jtly) Murdoch: the great escape, 1994. *Recreations:* work, socialising with family and friends. *Address:* Dartmouth Films, West Wing, Somerset House, WC2R 1LA. *T:* (020) 7845 5855. *E:* christo@dartmouthfilms.com. *Club:* h.

**HIRSCH, Andrew Mark;** Chief Executive Officer, John Brown Media, since 2001; *b* London, 22 March 1959; *s* of Walter Hirsch and Doris Hirsch; *m* 1990, Jane O'Rourke; two *s*. *Educ:* Beal Grammar Sch. for Boys. Family furniture business, 1977–86; sales exec., Sydney, 1986–88; Publishing Dir, Pearl & Dean, 1988–92; John Brown Media, 1992–: set up NY office, 2000; led mgt buyout, 2004. *Recreations:* tennis, football, movies, travel, spending time with family. *Address:* John Brown Media, 8 Baldwin Street, EC1V 9NU. *T:* (020) 7565 3000. *E:* andrew.hirsch@johnbrownmedia.com.

**HIRSCH, Prof. Sir Peter (Bernhard),** Kt 1975; MA, PhD; FRS 1963; Isaac Wolfson Professor of Metallurgy in the University of Oxford, 1966–92, Emeritus, 1992; Fellow, St Edmund Hall, Oxford, 1966–92, now Emeritus; *b* 16 Jan. 1925; *s* of Ismar Hirsch and Regina Meyerson; *m* 1959, Mabel Anne Kellar (*née* Stephens) (*d* 2016), *widow* of James Noel Kellar; one step *s* one step *d*. *Educ:* Sloane Sch., Chelsea; St Catharine's Coll., Cambridge (Hon. Fellow, 1982). BA 1946; MA 1950; PhD 1951. Reader in Physics in Univ. of Cambridge, 1964–66; Fellow, Christ's Coll., Cambridge, 1960–66, Hon. Fellow, 1978. Has been engaged on researches with electron microscope on imperfections in crystalline structure of metals and on relation between structural defects and mechanical properties. Chairman: Metallurgy and Materials Cttee (and Mem., Eng. Bd), SRC, 1970–73; UKAEA, 1982–84 (pt-time mem., 1982–94); Technical Adv. Gp on Structl Integrity, 1993–2002; Member: Elec. Supply Res. Council, 1969–82; Council for Scientific Policy, 1970–72; Tech. Adv. Cttee, Advent, 1982–89; Tech. Adv. Bd, Monsanto Electronic Materials, 1985–88; Chm., Materials, Processes Adv. Bd, Rolls-Royce, 1996–2000. Chm., Isis Innovation Ltd, 1988–96; Director: Cogent Ltd, 1985–89; Rolls-Royce Associates, 1994–97; Oxford Med. Imaging Analysis, OMIA, 2000–01. FIC 1988. Hon. Fellow: RMS, 1977; Japan Soc. of Electron Microscopy, 1979; Japan Inst. of Metals, 1989; Inst. of Materials, 2002. Associate Mem., Royal Acad. of Sci., Letters and Fine Arts, Belgium, 1995; Hon. Member: French Electron Microscopy Soc.; Spanish Electron Microscopy Soc., 1974; Materials Res. Soc., India, 1990; Chinese Electron Microscopy Soc., 1992; For. Hon. Mem., Amer. Acad. of Arts and Scis, 2005; For. Associate, US NAE, 2001; For. Mem., Russian Acad. of Scis, 2006. Hon. DSc: Newcastle, 1979; City, 1979; Northwestern, 1982; Hon. ScD East Anglia, 1983; Hon. DEng: Liverpool, 1991; Birmingham, 1993. Rosenhain Medal, Inst. of Metals, 1961; C. V. Boys Prize, Inst. of Physics and Physical Sci., 1962; Clamer Medal, Franklin Inst., 1970; Wihuri Internat. Prize, Helsinki, 1971; Royal Soc. Hughes Medal, 1973; Metals Soc. Platinum Medal, 1976; Royal Medal, Royal Soc., 1977; A. A. Griffith Medal, Inst. of Materials, 1979; Arthur Von Hippel Award, Materials Res. Soc., 1983; (jtly) Wolf Prize in Physics, Wolf Foundn, 1983–84; Dist. Scientist Award, Electron Microscopy Soc. of America, 1986; Holweck Prize, Inst. of Physics and French Physical Soc., 1988; Gold Medal, Japan Inst. of Metals, 1989; Acta Metallurgica Gold Medal, 1997; Heyn Medal, German Soc. for Materials Sci., 2002; Lomonosov Gold Medal, Russian Acad. of Scis, 2005. *Publications:* Electron Microscopy of Thin Crystals (with others), 1965; (ed) The Physics of Metals, vol. 2, Defects, 1975; (ed jtly) Progress in Materials Science, vol. 36, 1992; (ed) Topics in Electron Diffraction and Microscopy of Materials, 1999; (ed jtly) Fracture, Plastic Flow, and Structural Integrity, 2000; Methods for the Assessment of the Structural Integrity of Components and Structures, 2003; numerous contribs to learned jls. *Recreation:* walking. *Address:* 104A Lonsdale Road, Oxford OX2 7ET.

**HIRSCH, Prof. Steven Richard,** MD; FRCP; FRCPsych; expert witness in psychiatry and private practitioner, Wimbledon, until 2018; Professor of Psychiatry, Imperial College School of Medicine (formerly Charing Cross and Westminster Medical School), 1975–2002, now Emeritus; *m* 1st, 1964, Maureen; two *d*; 2nd, 2004, Teresa (*d* 2008); one *s* one *d*; 3rd, 2011, Dr Olga Goldina. *Educ:* Amherst Coll., Mass (BA Hons); Johns Hopkins Univ. (MD); London Univ. (MPhil). Res. worker, MRC Social Psychiatry, 1971–73; Hon. Sen. Registrar, Maudsley Hosp., 1971–73; Lectr in Psychiatry, Inst. of Psychiatry, Univ. of London, 1972–73; Sen. Lectr and Hon. Cons., Depts of Psychiatry, Westminster Hosp. and Queen Mary's Hosp., 1973–75. Dir, Teaching Governance, W London Mental Health NHS Trust, 2002; Vis. Consultant, Priory Hosp., 2002–15. *Publications:* (ed with M. Shepherd) Themes and Variations in European Psychiatry: an anthology, 1974; (with J. Leff) Abnormalities in parents of schizophrenics: review of the literature and an investigation of communication defects and deviances, (monograph) 1975; (ed with R. Farmer) The Suicide Syndrome, 1980; (ed with P. B. Bradley) The Psychopharmacology and Treatment of Schizophrenia, 1986; Psychiatric Beds and Resources: factors influencing bed use and service planning (report of a working party, RCPsych), 1988; (ed with J. Harris) Consent and the Incompetent Patient: ethics, law and medicine, 1988; (ed with D. Weinberger) Schizophrenia, 1995, 2nd edn 2003; chapters in books and abstracts; numerous contribs to scientific pubns. *Address:* Department of Psychiatry, Division of Neuroscience, Imperial College, Hammersmith Hospital, Du Cane Road, W12 0HS. *T:* 07968 065464, (home) (020) 8946 8554.

**HIRST, Christopher;** Global Chief Executive Officer, Havas, since 2019 (Chairman and Chief Executive Officer, UK and Europe, 2015–19); *b* Cannock, W Midlands, 4 April 1971; *s* of Richard and Patricia Hirst; *m* 2000, Ann Jenkins; two *s*. *Educ:* Haydon Bridge Co. High Sch.; Brasenose Coll., Oxford (MEng Engrg Sci.); Harvard Business Sch. (AMP). Account Dir, Bartle Bogle Hegarty, 1996–99; Client Services Dir, Fallon, 1999–2003; Man. Dir, 2003–09, CEO, 2009–15, Grey London. Member: Council, IPA, 2012–; Council, Creative Industries Fedn, 2015–; Council, EMEA Facebook, 2018–. Trustee, MOBO, 2016–. *Publications:* No Bullsh*t Leadership, 2019. *Recreations:* eating, drinking, reading, writing, tennis. *T:* 07881 907712. *E:* chrishirst6@gmail.com. *Clubs:* Soho House, Groucho.

**HIRST, Damien;** artist; *b* Bristol, 7 June 1965; *s* of Mary Brennan; three *s* by Maia Norman. *Educ:* Goldsmiths' Coll., Univ. of London (BA Fine Art 1989). Solo exhibitions include: ICA, 1991; Emmanuel Perrotin, Paris, 1991; Cohen Gall., NY, 1992; Regen Projects, LA, 1993; Galerie Jablonka, Cologne, 1993; Milwaukee Art Mus., 1994; Dallas Mus., 1994; Kukje Gall., Seoul, 1995; White Cube Gall., 1995, 2003, 2007, 2014, 2019; Max Gandolph-Bibliothek, Salzburg, 1996; Gagosian Gall., NY, 1996, 2018, Hong Kong, 2017, LA, 2018; Bruno Bischofberger, Zurich, 1997; Astrup Fearnley, Oslo, 1997; Southampton City Art Gall., 1998; Tate Gall., 1999; Wallace Collection, 2009; Paul Stolper Gall., 2014; Punta della Dogana and Palazzo Grassi, Venice, 2017; Houghton Hall, 2018; retrospective exhibn, Saatchi Gall., 2003; Gagosian Gall., London, 2006; Serpentine Gall., 2006; (retrospective) Tate Modern, 2012; The Complete Spot Paintings 1986–2011, Gagosian Galls, 2012; (retrospective) New Art Gall., Walsall, 2015; Schizophrenogenesis, Paul Stolper Gall., London, 2014; Treasures from the Wreck of the Unbelievable, Venice, 2017. Gp exhibitions in UK, Europe, USA and Australia. Co-founder and owner, Pharmacy, Notting Hill, 1998–2003 (contemp. restaurant design award, Carlton London Restaurant Awards, 1999); founder, Number 11, The Quay, Ilfracombe, 2004. Turner Prize, 1995. *Publications:* I Want to Spend the Rest of My Life Everywhere, With Everyone, One to One, Always,

Forever, Now, 1997; Theories, Models, Methods, Approaches, Assumptions, Results and Findings, 2000; (illus.) Meaningless Static, by Paul Fryer, 2000; (with Gordon Burn) On the Way to Work, 2001; From the Cradle to the Grave: selected drawings, 2004. *Address:* c/o White Cube Gallery, 144–152 Bermondsey Street, SE1 3TQ.

**HIRST, Joanne Elizabeth;** a District Judge (Magistrates' Courts), since 2018; *b* Hyde, Cheshire, 25 Feb. 1966; *d* of Malcolm Harrison and Margaret Harrison (*née* Cawkwell); *m* 1989, Carl Philip Hirst; two *d*. *Educ:* Fairfield High Sch. for Girls, Manchester; Nottingham Trent Univ. (LLB Hons 1996); Manchester Metropolitan Univ. (DipLP (Dist.) 1997). Admitted as solicitor, 1997; solicitor, 1997–2002, Legal Team Manager, 2002–06, Manchester Courts Service; Judicial Develt Manager, HM Courts Service, 2006–12; a Dep. Dist Judge (Magistrates' Courts), 2009–18; Consultant Judicial Expert, MoJ, 2012–14. Mem., Fitness to Practise Cttee, Health Care Regulation, 2014–18. Law Soc. Prize, 1997; Justices Clerks' Soc. Prize, 1998. *Recreations:* travel, reading, fine dining. *Address:* Doncaster Magistrates' Court, College Road, Doncaster, S Yorks DN1 3HS.

**HIRST, John Raymond,** CBE 2014; FCA; Chief Executive, Met Office, 2007–14; *b* Nicosia, Cyprus, 9 Aug. 1952; *m* Anne; one *s* one *d*. *Educ:* Leeds Univ. (BA). FCA; ACT. ICI plc, 1979–97: CEO, ICI Autocolor, 1990–95; Gp Treas., 1995–96; CEO, ICI Perf. Chemicals, 1996–97; Gp CEO, Premier Farnell plc, 1998–2005. Chairman: Asbis, 2006–09; British Standards Instn, 2019–; non-executive Director: Hammerson plc, 2003–14 (Chm., Audit Cttee); Marsh UK Ltd, 2014–; Ultra Electronics plc, 2015– (Chm., Audit Cttee, 2015–); Anglian Water Services, 2015– (Chm., Audit Cttee, 2015–). UK Permanent Rep., WMO, 2007–14 (Chm., Audit Cttee, 2010–14). Dir, Epilepsy Research UK, 2006–. Trustee, SUDEP Action (formerly Epilepsy Bereaved), 2008– (Chm.). CCMI. Hon. DSc Exeter, 2013.

**HIRST, Prof. Judy,** DPhil; FRS 2018; Professor of Biological Chemistry, since 2018, and Interim Director, MRC Mitochondrial Biology Unit, since 2019, University of Cambridge; Fellow, since 2011 and Dean, since 2017, Corpus Christi College, Cambridge; *b* Huddersfield, 8 March 1972; *d* of Rodney Graham Hirst and Mary Hirst (*née* Carter); partner, Peter Alan Connor. *Educ:* King James' Sch., Huddersfield; Greenhead Coll., Huddersfield; St John's Coll., Oxford (BA 1994; MA 1997); Lincoln Coll., Oxford (DPhil 1997). Wellcome Trust Prize Internat. Res. Fellow, Scripps Res. Inst., La Jolla, Calif, 1998–99; Principal Investigator, MRC Mitochondrial Biol. Unit, Univ. of Cambridge, 1999–. *Recreations:* classical music, cycling, hiking and mountain climbing, travel. *Address:* MRC Mitochondrial Biology Unit, University of Cambridge, Cambridge Biomedical Campus, Hills Road, Cambridge CB2 0XY. *E:* jh@mrc-mbu.cam.ac.uk.

**HIRST, Larry,** CBE 2007; Chairman, IBM Europe, Middle East and Africa, 2008–10; *b* 4 Nov. 1951; *s* of late Harold Hirst and Joan Hirst; *m* 1978, Ellen Alison; one *s* one *d*. *Educ:* Univ. of Hull (BSc Hons Maths 1973). Kodak, 1973–77; IBM Corp., 1977–2010: Dir Ops, E Europe, Russia, 1989–90; Exec. Asst to Chm., 1992–93; Vice Pres., Financial Services, EMEA, 1994–2001; Chief Exec., UK, Ireland and SA, 2001–08; Chm., IBM Netherlands, 2003–10. Non-executive Director: MITIE Gp plc, 2010–18 (Sen. Ind. Dir, 2015–18); ARM Hldgs plc, 2011–16 (Chm., Remuneration Cttee, 2012–16); Mem., Internat. Adv. Bd, BA, 2012–16. Chm., e-skills UK Sector Skills Council for IT and Telecoms, 2001–10; Exec. Chm., Information Age Partnership, 2001–03; Chairman: Transition to Teaching Council, 2007–10; UKTI Technol. Bd, 2008–13; Mem., President's Cttee, 2001–08, Internat. Adv. Bd, 2008–10, CBI. Comr, UK Commn for Employment and Skills, 2007–10; UK Business Ambassador, 2009–12. Adjunct Prof., 2011–, Chm., Data Sci. Inst., 2014–, Imperial Coll. London (Chm., Digital Cities Exchange Bd, 2011–14); Mem. Adv. Bd, Res. Inst. in Sci. of Cyber Security, 2012–. Member: S African President's Internat. Adv. Bd, 2006–10; Bd, IMD Business Sch., Lausanne, 2008–10; Internat. Advr, Monetise Gp, 2011–15; Ambassador: Everywoman, 2000–; Black British Business, 2014–. *Recreations:* golf, woodland maintenance hopefully not at the same time, reading biographies, gadgets, technology futures. *E:* larryhirst@hirst-works.com.

**HIRST, Sir Michael (William),** Kt 1992; LLB, CA; company director; business consultant; Founder, Michael Hirst Associates; Chairman: Pagoda Public Relations Ltd, 2000–19; Millstream Associates Ltd, 2000–16; *b* 2 Jan. 1946; *s* of late John Melville Hirst and Christina Binning Torrance or Hirst; *m* 1972, Naomi Ferguson Wilson; one *s* two *d*. *Educ:* Glasgow Acad., Glasgow; Univ. of Glasgow (LLB). CA 1970. Exchange Student, Univ. of Iceland, 1967; Partner, Peat, Marwick Mitchell & Co., 1978–83; Consultant, Peat Marwick UK, 1983–92. Pres., Glasgow Univ. Conservative Club, 1967; National Vice-Chm., Scottish Young Conservatives, 1971–73; Chm., Scottish Conservative Candidates Assoc., 1978–81; Vice-Chairman: Pty Organisation Cttee, 1985; Conservative Party in Scotland, 1987–89; Pres., 1989–92, Chm., 1993–97, Scottish Cons. & Unionist Party. Contested (C): Central Dunbartonshire, Feb. and Oct. 1974; E Dunbartonshire, 1979; Strathkelvin and Bearsden, 1987 and 1992. MP (C) Strathkelvin and Bearsden, 1983–87. PPS to Parly Under-Secs of State, DoE, 1985–87. Mem., Select Cttee on Scottish Affairs, 1983–87. Director: Children's Hospice Assoc., Scotland, 1993–2005; Erskine Hosp. Ltd (formerly Princess Louise Scottish Hosp.), 1980–2011 (Mem., Exec. Bd, 1997–2011). Co-Chm., Global Network of Parly Champions for Diabetes, 2015–. Mem., Bd of Trustees, Diabetes UK (formerly British Diabetic Assoc.), 1988–2006 (Hon. Sec., 1993–98; Vice Chm., 1998–2001; Chm., 2001–06); Pres., Internat. Diabetes Fedn, 2012–15 (Vice-Pres., 2006–09; Pres.-Elect, 2009–12); Chm., Park Sch. Educnl Trust, 1988–2009; Mem. Court, Glasgow Caledonian Univ., 1993–98 (Chm., Audit Cttee, 1993–98). Mem. Council, Imperial Soc. of Kts Bachelor, 2002– (Chm. Scottish Div., 2002–); Registrar, 2017–). Chm., Friends of Kippen Kirk Trust, 2004–. FRSA 1993; MCIPR (MIPR 2003). Hon. FRCPE 2012. Hon. DLitt Glasgow Caledonian, 2004. *Recreations:* golf, walking, ski-ing. *Address:* Glentirran, Kippen, Stirlingshire FK8 3DY. *T:* (01786) 870283. *Clubs:* Carlton; The Western (Glasgow).

**HIRST, Neil Alexander Carr;** Senior Policy Fellow, Grantham Institute for Climate Change, Imperial College London, since 2009; *b* 16 May 1946; *s* of Theodore James Hirst and Valerie Adamson Hirst; *m* 1984, Caroline Rokeby Collins; two *d*. *Educ:* Canford Sch.; Lincoln Coll., Oxford (BA 1st Cl. Hons PPE); Cornell Univ., USA (Telluride Schol., MBA). Jun. reporter, Eastbourne Gazette and Herald Chronicle, 1964–65; entered Civil Service, 1970: Asst Principal, Min. of Technol., 1970–73; Asst Private Sec. to Ministers for Industry and Energy and Sec. of State for Trade, 1973–75; Principal, Oil and Gas Div., then Atomic Energy Div., Dept of Energy, 1975–80; on secondment to Private Finance Dept, Goldman Sachs, NY, 1981; returned to Dept of Energy for public flotation of Britoil, 1982; Asst Sec., Atomic Energy Div., 1983–85; Counsellor (Energy), Washington DC, 1985–88; Oil and Gas Div., Dept of Energy, 1988–92; Department of Trade and Industry: coal privatisation legislation, 1992–94; Labs Unit (privatisation of Nat. Engrg Lab. and Nat. Chemical Lab.), 1995; Under Sec. and Hd, Atomic Energy Div., 1995; Dir, Nuclear Industries, 1996–98; Dep. Dir Gen., Energy, 1998–2002; Hd, Energy Mkts Unit, 2002–04; Dir, Office of Energy Technol. and R&D, 2004–08, Dir, Global Dialogue, 2008–09, Internat. Energy Agency. Mem., UKAEA, 1996–98; Chm., Nuclear Safety Wkg Gp of the G8 Summit nations, 1998. Mem., Dorset Natural Hist. and Archaeol Soc., 2000. *Publications:* The Energy Conundrum: climate change, global prosperity, and the tough decisions we have to make, 2018. *Recreations:* gardening, music, theatre, walking. *Address:* 3 Stockwell Park Road, SW9 0AP. *T:* (020) 7735 9615. *Club:* Oxford and Cambridge.

**HIRST, Prof. Paul Heywood;** Professor of Education, University of Cambridge, 1971–88, now Emeritus, and Fellow of Wolfson College (formerly University College), Cambridge, 1971, now Emeritus; *b* 10 Nov. 1927; *s* of late Herbert and Winifred Hirst, Birkby, Huddersfield. *Educ:* Huddersfield Coll.; Trinity Coll., Cambridge (BA 1948, MA 1952); Cert. Educn Cantab, 1952; DipEd London, 1955; MA Oxon (by incorporation), Christ Church, Oxford, 1955. Asst Master, William Hulme's Grammar Sch., Manchester, 1948–50; Maths Master, Eastbourne Coll., 1950–55; Lectr and Tutor, Univ. of Oxford Dept of Educn, 1955–59; Lectr in Philosophy of Educn, Univ. of London Inst. of Educn, 1959–65; Prof. of Educn, King's Coll., Univ. of London, 1965–71. Visiting Professor: Univ. of British Columbia, 1964, 1967; Univ. of Malawi, 1969; Univ. of Puerto Rico, 1984; Univ. of Sydney, 1989; Univ. of Alberta, 1989; Inst. of Educn, Univ. of London, 1991–96. De Carle Lectr, Univ. of Otago, 1976; Fink Lectr, Univ. of Melbourne, 1976. Vice-Pres., Philosophy of Educn Soc. of GB; Member: UGC Educn Sub-Cttee, 1971–80; Educn Cttee, 1972–82, Academic Policy Cttee, 1981–87, Chm., Research Cttee, 1988–92, CNAA; Swann Cttee of Inquiry into Educn of Children from Ethnic Minorities, 1981–85. Chm., Univs Council for Educn of Teachers, 1985–88. Member Court: Univ. of Derby, 1996; Univ. of Glos, 2006. Hon. Mem., Royal Norwegian Soc. of Scis and Letters, 1996. Hon. DEd CNAA, 1992; Hon. DPhil Cheltenham and Gloucester Coll. of Higher Educn, 2000; Hon. DLitt Huddersfield, 2002. *Publications:* (with R. S. Peters) The Logic of Education, 1970; (ed with R. F. Dearden and R. S. Peters) Education and the Development of Reason, 1971; Knowledge and the Curriculum, 1974; Moral Education in a Secular Society, 1974; (ed) Educational Theory and its Foundation Disciplines, 1984; (with V. J. Furlong) Initial Teacher Training and the Role of the School, 1988; (ed with P. A. White) Philosophy of Education: major themes in the analytic tradition, 1998; papers in: Philosophical Analysis and Education (ed R. D. Archambault), 1965; The Study of Education (ed J. W. Tibble), 1966; The Concept of Education (ed R. S. Peters), 1966; Religious Education in a Pluralistic Society (ed M. C. Felderhof), 1985; Education, Values and Mind (ed D. E. Cooper), 1986; Partnership in Initial Teacher Training (ed M. Booth *et al*), 1990; Beyond Liberal Education (ed R. Barrow and P. White), 1993; The Aims of Education (ed R. Marples), 1999; Education in Morality (ed J. M. Halstead and T. H. McLaughlin), 1999; Leaders in Philosophy of Education (ed L. J. Waks), 2008; Religious Upbringing and the Costs of Freedom (ed P. Caws and S. Jones), 2010. *Recreation:* music, especially opera. *Address:* Flat 3, 6 Royal Crescent, Brighton BN2 1AL. *T:* (01273) 684118. *Club:* Athenæum.

**HIRST, Simon David; His Honour Judge Hirst;** a Circuit Judge, since 2015; *b* Oldham, 26 Oct. 1970; *s* of David Roy Hirst and Catherine Christine Hirst; *m* 1999, Jo Kiddle; one *d*. *Educ:* Hulme Grammar Sch., Oldham; Hull Univ. (LLB). Inns of Court Sch. of Law. Called to the Bar, Lincoln, 1993; a Recorder, 2009–15. *Recreations:* football, running, cycling. *Address:* Lincoln Crown Court, The Castle, Castle Hill, Lincoln LN1 3GA. *T:* (01522) 525222.

**HISCOCK, Prof. Simon John,** DPhil; Professor of Botany and Director, Botanic Garden and Harcourt Arboretum, University of Oxford, since 2015; *b* Winterbourne, Newbury, 11 June 1963; *s* of Peter Hiscock and June Hiscock; partner, 1992, Dr Suzanne O'Shea. *Educ:* Park House Sch., Newbury; St Bartholomew's Sch., Newbury; Worcester Coll., Oxford (BA Botany 1985; PGCE 1989; DPhil 1993). Sch. Master, St Bartholomew's Sch., Newbury, 1987–89; Post-doctoral Res. Asst, Univ. of Oxford, 1993–97; BBSRC David Phillips Res. Fellow, Univ. of Oxford, 1997–2000, Univ. of Bristol, 2000–02; University of Bristol: Lectr in Plant Scis, 2002–04; Dir, Botanic Garden, 2003–15 (Hon. Dir, 2015–16); Reader in Plant Scis, 2004–07; Prof. of Botany, 2007–15 (Hon. Prof. of Botany, 2015–). Mem., Peer Rev. Coll., NERC, 2004–; Core Mem., NERC Rev. Panel E, 2013–. Linnean Society of London: Fellow, 1991; Mem. Council, 2013–; Vice-Pres., 2014; Scientific Sec. (Botany), 2014–. Erskine Fellow, Univ. of Canterbury, Christchurch, 2007. Trustee, New Phytologist Trust, 2017–. Editor: Annals of Botany, 2008–17; AoB Plants, 2011–17; Editor in Chief, Plants, People, Planet. *Publications:* (with Christopher Thorogood) A Field Guide to the Wild Flowers of the Algarve, 2014. *Recreations:* botanical illustration, cricket, natural history, real ale (CAMRA Member), Mediterranean Europe travel. *Address:* University of Oxford Botanic Garden, Rose Lane, Oxford OX1 4AZ. *T:* (01865) 610302. *E:* simon.hiscock@obg.ox.ac.uk; Minnibrook Cottage, Winterbourne, Newbury, Berks RG20 8BA.

**HISCOCK, Stephen John;** HM Diplomatic Service, retired; High Commissioner to Guyana, and (non resident) Ambassador to Suriname, 2002–06; *b* 16 June 1946; *s* of Lionel Percy Hiscock and Dorothy Mabel Hiscock (*née* Wright); *m* 1st, 1967, Gillian Denise Roe; two *s*; 2nd, 1983, Dee Mary Forster; two *s* one *d*. *Educ:* Devonport High Sch. for Boys, Plymouth. With Inland Revenue, 1963–65; entered Foreign Office, 1965; FCO, 1965–68; Kuala Lumpur, 1968–72; Lusaka, 1972–76; FCO, 1976–78; Second Sec., Islamabad, 1978–82; First Secretary: Seoul, 1982–86; FCO, 1986–88; Dep. High Comr, Georgetown, 1988–93; FCO, 1993–96; Consul-Gen., Brisbane, 1997–2001; Commercial Counsellor (temp.), Bangkok, 2001–02; Dep. Hd of Mission (temp.), Kabul, March–April 2002. Mem., OAS Election Observation Mission to Guyana, 2006. Sensitivity Reviewer, FCO, 2008–. Dir, Commonwealth Boxing Council Ltd, 2008. Ind. Mem., Kent Police Authy, 2008–12. Gov., Bethany Sch., Goudhurst, 2008–12. *Recreations:* social tennis, walking. *Address:* The Reading Room, 5 School Lane, Greens Norton, Northants NN12 8BU. *Club:* Towcestrians.

**HISCOX, Robert Ralph Scrymgeour;** Chairman, Hiscox Ltd (formerly Hiscox plc), 1996–2013, Honorary President, 2013–17; *b* 4 Jan. 1943; *s* of late Ralph Hiscox, CBE and Louisa Jeanie Hiscox; *m* 1st, 1966, Lucy Mills (marr. diss. 1978; she *d* 1996); two *s*; 2nd, 1985, Lady Julia Elizabeth Meade, 3rd *d* of Earl of Clanwilliam; three *s*. *Educ:* Rugby Sch.; Corpus Christi Coll., Cambridge (MA). ACII. Member of Lloyd's, 1967–98 (Dep. Chm., 1993–95; Dep. Chm., First Market Bd, 1993–95); Chairman: Lloyd's Underwriting Agents' Assoc., 1991; Lloyd's Corporate Capital Assoc., 1998–99; Lloyd's Market Assoc., 1999–2000. Director: Roberts & Hiscox, 1973–98; Hiscox Hldgs Ltd, 1987–99; R. K. Harrison Hldgs Ltd, 1990–99; Hiscox Syndicates Ltd, 1991–2013; Hiscox Insce Co., 1996–2013. Non-exec. Dir, Grainger (formerly Grainger Trust) plc, 2002–12. Mem., Mus. and Galls Commn, 1996–2000. Dir, Public Catalogue Foundn, 2004–12. Treasurer and Trustee: Campaign for Museums, 1998–2004; 24 Hour Mus., 2000–01; Treas., Friends of the Tate Gallery, 1990–93; Trustee: Wilts Bobby Van Trust, 1998– (Chm., 2002–); Kenneth Armitage Foundn, 2005– (Chm., 2011–); Paolozzi Foundn, 2009– (Chm., 2011–); Chairman: Swindon Mus. and Art Gall. Trust, 2015–18; Image Cinemas Ltd, 2019–. Founder and Patron, Sculpture in the City, 2011–17; Patron: Friends of Erlestoke Prison, 2012–; Marlborough Brandt Gp, 2015–18 (Trustee, 2012–15). High Sheriff, 2011, DL 2013, Wilts. Lloyds Gold Medal, 2013. *Recreations:* family life, country life, the arts, changing things. *Address:* Rainscombe Park, Oare, Marlborough, Wilts SN8 4HZ. *E:* roberthiscox@gmail.com. *Clubs:* Queen's, Shikar, White's.

**HISLOP, David Seymour;** QC 2010; *b* Dunedin, NZ, 17 July 1955; *s* of Alfred George Hislop and Eileen Mary Hislop; *m* 1986, Donna Joyce Bradley; one *s* one *d*. *Educ:* Whangarei Boys High Sch.; Auckland Univ. (LLB). Commercial Litigation Solicitor and Counsel, Nicholson Gribbin Solicitors, 1979–84; Litigation Partner, Thorne Dallas & Partners, 1984–88; called to the Bar, Gray's Inn, 1989; specialist defence barrister in field of serious organised crime and fraud. *Publications:* (contrib.) A Practitioner's Guide to the Law and Regulation of Financial Crime, 2011; contribs to New Law Jl, Archbold News, Butterworth's Human Rights Commentaries. *Recreations:* food, fine wine, Rugby, family. *E:* davidhislopqc@aol.com, d.hislop@doughtystreet.co.uk.

**HISLOP, Ian David;** Editor, Private Eye, since 1986; writer and broadcaster; *b* 13 July 1960; *s* of late David Atholl Hislop and Helen Hislop; *m* 1988, Victoria Hamson (*see* V. Hislop); one *s* one *d. Educ:* Ardingly College; Magdalen College, Oxford (BA Hons Eng. Lang. and Lit.; Underhill Exhibn; Violet Vaughan Morgan Scholarship). Joined Private Eye, 1981, Dep. Editor, 1985–86. Columnist, The Listener, 1985–89; Television critic, The Spectator, 1994–96; Columnist, Sunday Telegraph, 1996–2003. *Radio:* broadcaster: Newsquiz, 1985–90; 4th Column, 1992–96; Lent Talk, 1994; Words on Words, 1999; The Hislop Vote, 2000; A Revolution in 5 Acts, 2001; The Real Patron Saints, 2002; A Brief History of Tax, 2003; The Choir Invisible, 2003; There'll be Blue Birds over the White Cliffs of Dover, 2004; Are We Offensive Enough?, 2004; Looking for Middle England, 2006; Lord Kitchener's Image, 2007; We Three Kings, 2008; The Six Faces of Henry VIII, 2009; (contrib.) A History of The World in 100 Objects, 2010; The Verse that Stings, 2014; I, Object!, 2018; radio scripts (with Nick Newman): Gush, 1994; Greed All About It, 2010; What Went Wrong with the Olympics, 2010; The News at Bedtime, 2011; Trial by Laughter, 2016, adapted for stage, Watermill, Newbury, 2018, and nat. tour; *television:* performer, Have I Got News For You, 1990–; documentary presenter: Canterbury Tales, 1996; School Rules, 1997; Pennies from Bevan, 1998; Great Railway Journeys East to West, 1999; Who Do You Think You Are?, 2004; Not Forgotten, 2005; Not Forgotten: shot at dawn, 2007; Scouting for Boys, 2007; Not Forgotten: the men who wouldn't fight, 2008; Ian Hislop Goes Off the Rails, 2008; Marlow on Hogarth, 2008; Ian Hislop's Changing of the Bard, 2009; Not Forgotten: soldiers of Empire, 2009; Ian Hislop's Age of the Do-Gooders, 2010; When Bankers Were Good, 2011; Stiff Upper Lip: An Emotional History of Britain, 2012; Ian Hislop's Olden Days, 2014; Ian Hislop's Victorian Benefits, 2016; Ian Hislop on the First Great Immigration Row, 2017; television scripts (with Nick Newman): Spitting Image, 1984–89; The Stone Age, 1989; Briefcase Encounter, 1990; The Harry Enfield Programme, 1990–92; Harry Enfield and Chums, 1994–98; Mangez Merveillac, 1994; Dead on Time, 1995; Gobble, 1996; Sermon from St Albions, 1998; Songs and Praise from St Albions, 1999; Confessions of a Murderer, 1999; My Dad's the Prime Minister, 2003, 2004; (screenplay) A Bunch of Amateurs, 2008; (screenplay) The Wipers Times, 2013 (Best Single Drama, BPG, 2014), adapted for stage, 2016, performed Arts, 2017, 2018. Curator, I Object: Ian Hislop's Search for Dissent, British Mus., 2018. Editors' Ed., 1991, Ed. of the Year, 1998, British Soc. of Mag. Editors; Award for political satire, Channel 4 Political Awards, 2004; Political Comedy Award, Channel 4, 2006; Voice of the Listener and Viewer Award for Excellence in Broadcasting, 2009; Diamond Jubilee Award for Best Political Satire, Political Studies Assoc., 2010; Liberty Human Rights Long Walk Award, 2011; Mark Boxer Award for Outstanding Edit Contrib. to Mags, 2017. *Publications:* various Private Eye collections and Private Eye Annual, 1985–; contribs to newspapers and magazines on books, current affairs, arts and entertainment, 2003–. *Address:* c/o Private Eye, 6 Carlisle Street, W1D 3BN. *T:* (020) 7437 4017.

**HISLOP, Victoria;** writer; *b* Bromley, 8 June 1959; *d* of John and Mary Hamson; *m* 1988, Ian David Hislop, *qv;* one *s* one *d. Educ:* Tonbridge Grammar Sch. for Girls; St Hilda's Coll., Oxford (BA Hons English). PA to Sales Dir, Sidgwick & Jackson, 1982–84; Account Dir, Good Relations, 1985–88; Account Dir, Wolff Olins, 1988–90; freelance journalist, nat. newspapers and mags incl. Daily Telegraph, Sunday Telegraph, Sunday Times, Woman & Home, Good Housekeeping, Condé Nast Traveller, 1990–. Ambassador: for tourism, Greek Tourist Orgn, 2012–; Lepra Health in Action, 2013–. Hon. LittD Sheffield, 2018. *Publications:* The Island, 2005 (British Book Award for Newcomer of Year, 2007); The Return, 2008; The Thread, 2011; The Last Dance, 2012; (ed) The Story: love, loss and the lives of women, 2013; The Sunrise, 2014; Cartes Postales from Greece, 2016; Those Who Are Loved, 2019. *Recreations:* music, tennis, Greek language and culture. *Address:* c/o Peter Strauss, Rogers Coleridge & White, 20 Powis Mews, W11 1JN. *T:* (020) 7221 3717. *E:* victoria@victoriahislop.com.

**HITCHCOCK, Patricia Ann, (Mrs P. S. Brooke-Ball);** QC 2011; a Recorder, since 2018; *b* Epsom, Surrey, 3 Feb. 1956; *d* of Eldred Arnold Hitchcock and Muriel, (Emma), Hitchcock (*née* Bilsland); *m* 1987, Peter Stuart Brooke-Ball; one *s* one *d. Educ:* Westminster Sch.; Brasenose Coll., Oxford (BA Hons Eng. Lang. and Lit. 1978); City Univ., London (DipLaw 1987). Publishing trainee, Rainbird Publishing Gp, 1978–79; Asst Ed., Albany Books, 1979; Paperback Buyer, Brentano's Univ. Bookstore, LA, 1980–81; freelance proofreader, Graphic Typesetting Service, LA, 1981–82; Prodn Ed., Sage Publications, LA, 1982; Senior Editor: Robert Nicholson Publications, 1982–84 (Mother, NUJ Chapel); Quill Publications, 1984–85; freelance contributor and ed., 1985–86; called to the Bar, Inner Temple, 1988; joined Cloisters Chambers, Temple, started as common law barrister specialising in criminal defence, now specialising in catastrophic clin. negligence, personal injury, mental health, inquests and medical law; CEDR accredited mediator, 2003. *Publications:* (contrib.) Butterworths Personal Injury Litigation Service, 2003–; (contrib.) Lewis & Buchan: Clinical Negligence, a practical guide, Pt edn 2012, 8th edn 2018; contrib. articles in Solicitors Jl, AVMA Medical, Legal Jl etc. *Recreations:* friends and family, food and wine, ballet, theatre, travel, yoga. *Address:* Cloisters, 1 Pump Court, Temple, EC4Y 7AA. *T:* (020) 7827 4000. *E:* phi@cloisters.com.

**HITCHENS, Rear Adm. Gilbert Archibald Ford,** CB 1988; Director General Ship Refitting, Ministry of Defence, 1985–87, retired; *b* 11 April 1932; *m* 1961, Patricia Hamilton; one *s* one *d.* BA Hons. Joined Royal Navy, 1950; Commander, 1968; Guided Weapons Staff Officer, Min. of Technology, 1968–70; Exec. Officer, RNEC, 1970–72; Senior Officer while building and Weapon Engineer Officer, HMS Sheffield, 1973–75; MoD (Navy), 1975–77; Naval Attaché, Tokyo and Seoul, 1977–79; Asst Dir, Manpower Requirements, MoD (Navy), 1979–80; Dir, Officers' Appts (Eng.), 1980–82; Captain, HMS Defiance, 1982–84; ADC to the Queen, 1984; CSO Engrg to C-in-C Fleet, 1984–85. Mem., Plymouth DHA, 1989–90. Admiralty Gov., Royal Naval Benevolent Trust, 1989–96. Competitor, Commonwealth Winter Games, 1958. Chairman: RN Ski and Mountaineering Club, 1984–86; Govs, Devonport High Sch. for Boys, 1993–97. Liveryman, Ironmongers' Co., 1994. *Recreations:* any activity in the high hills.
See also Sir T. M. Hitchens.

**HITCHENS, Peter Jonathan;** journalist and author; *b* 28 Oct. 1951; *s* of late Comdr Eric Ernest Hitchens and of Yvonne Jean Hitchens (*née* Hickman); *m* 1983, Eve Ross; two *s* one *d. Educ:* Leys Sch., Cambridge; Oxford Coll. of Further Educn; Univ. of York (BA 1973). Journalist: Socialist Worker, 1972; Swindon Evening Advertiser, 1973–76; Coventry Evening Telegraph, 1976; Daily Express, 1977–2001: sometime industrial reporter, Labour Corresp., Dep. Pol Ed., Diplomatic Corresp., Moscow Corresp., Washington Corresp., Asst Ed.; resigned 2001; reporter and columnist, Mail on Sunday, 2001–. Orwell Prize for Journalism, 2010. *Publications:* The Abolition of Britain, 1999; (contrib.) The Rape of the Constitution, 2000; Monday Morning Blues, 2000; The Abolition of Liberty, 2004; The Broken Compass, 2009; The Rage against God, 2010; The War We Never Fought, 2012; Short Breaks in Mordor, 2014; The Phoney Victory, 2018. *Recreations:* long train journeys, second-hand bookshops. *Address:* Mail on Sunday, 2 Derry Street, W8 5TS. *T:* (020) 3615 3258. *E:* peter.hitchens@mailonsunday.co.uk.

**HITCHENS, Sir Timothy Mark, (Sir Tim),** KCVO 2018 (LVO 1997); CMG 2012; HM Diplomatic Service, retired; President, Wolfson College, Oxford, since 2018; *b* 7 May 1962; *s* of Rear Adm. Gilbert Archibald Ford Hitchens, *qv; m* 1985, Sara Kubra; one *s* one *d. Educ:* Dulwich Coll.; Christ's Coll., Cambridge (BA). Foreign and Commonwealth Office, 1983–2017; Tokyo, 1985–89; Private Sec. to Minister of State, FCO, 1991–94; Speechwriter to Foreign Sec., 1994–95; First Sec., Islamabad, 1995–97; Asst Pvte Sec. to the Queen, 1998–2002; Hd, Africa Dept (Equatorial), FCO, 2003–05; Minister, Paris, 2005–08; Dir, Eur. Pol Affairs, FCO, 2008–10; Africa Dir, FCO, 2010–12; Ambassador to Japan, 2012–16; Dir Gen. Economic, FCO, and Mem., FCO Bd, 2017. Chief Exec., Commonwealth Summit 2018, 2017–18. *Recreations:* walking, gardening, Kendo. *Address:* Wolfson College, Linton Road, Oxford OX2 6UD.

**HITCHIN, Prof. Nigel James,** DPhil; FRS 1991; Savilian Professor of Geometry, University of Oxford, 1997–2016; Fellow of New College, Oxford, 1997–2016, now Emeritus Fellow; *b* 2 Aug. 1946; *s* of Eric Wilfred Hitchin and Bessie (*née* Blood); *m* 1973, Nedda Vejarano Bernal; one *s* one *d. Educ:* Ecclesbourne Sch., Duffield; Jesus Coll., Oxford (BA 1968; Hon. Fellow, 1998); Wolfson Coll., Oxford (MA, DPhil 1972). Res. Asst, Inst. for Advanced Study, Princeton, 1971–73; Instructor, Courant Inst., New York Univ., 1973–74; SRC Res. Asst, 1974–77, SRC Advanced Res. Fellow, 1977–79, Oxford Univ.; Fellow and Tutor in Maths, St Catherine's Coll., Oxford, 1979–90 (Hon. Fellow, 2014); Prof. of Maths, Univ. of Warwick, 1990–94; Rouse Ball Prof. of Maths, Univ. of Cambridge, 1994–97; Fellow of Gonville and Caius Coll., Cambridge, 1994–97 (Hon. Fellow, 2008). Vis. Prof., SUNY, Stony Brook, 1983. Hon. DSc: Bath, 2003; Warwick, 2014. London Mathematical Society: Pres., 1994–96; Jun. Whitehead Prize, 1981; Sen. Berwick Prize, 1990; Polya Prize, LMS, 2002; Sylvester Medal, Royal Soc., 2000; Shaw Prize in Math. Scis, 2016. *Publications:* Monopoles, Minimal Surfaces and Algebraic Curves, 1987; (with M. F. Atiyah) The Geometry and Dynamics of Magnetic Monopoles, 1988; (with G. B. Segal and R. S. Ward) Integrable Systems: twistors, loop groups and Riemann surfaces, 1999; articles in learned jls. *Address:* Hampden Manor, 81 Mill Street, Kidlington OX5 2EB.

**HITCHING, His Honour Alan Norman;** a Circuit Judge, 1987–2006; Resident Judge, Blackfriars Crown Court, 1998–2006; *b* 5 Jan. 1941; *s* of late Norman Henry Samuel Hitching and Grace Ellen Hitching; *m* 1st, 1967, Hilda Muriel (*née* King) (*d* 2000); one *d* two *s;* 2nd, 2003, Susan Mary (*née* Banfield), *widow* of Michael Henry Cotton. *Educ:* Forest Sch., Snaresbrook; Christ Church, Oxford (BA 1962; Radcliffe Exhibnr and Dixon Scholar, 1962; BCL 1963; MA). Harmsworth Entrance Scholar, Middle Temple, 1960; Astbury Scholar and Safford Prize, Middle Temple, 1964; called to the Bar, Middle Temple, 1964, Bencher, 2005; Standing Counsel, Inland Revenue, SE Circuit, 1974–87; Dep. Circuit Judge, 1981–85, 2006–09; a Recorder, 1985–87. Cropwood Fellow, Inst. of Criminology, Cambridge, 1990. Vice-Pres., John Grooms Assoc. for the Disabled, 1991–2007 (Chm., 1981–89; Vice-Chm., 1978–81 and 1989–91). Licensed Reader, dio. of Chelmsford, 1987–2001; ordained deacon, 2001, priest, 2002; NSM, High Ongar, Chelmsford, 2001–05; permission to officiate, Chelmsford dio., 2005–; Chaplain, Metropolitan Police, 2010–15. Trustee, Tower Hamlets Mission, 2009–. *Recreations:* people, pottery, poetry, preaching. *Address:* c/o Middle Temple, Treasury Office, Middle Temple Lane, EC4Y 9AT.

**HITCHINGS, (Christian Nicholas) Henry,** FRSL; freelance writer; Theatre Critic, London Evening Standard, since 2009; consultant editor, Oxford English Dictionary, since 2015; *b* Guildford, 11 Dec. 1974; *s* of Paul Barrington Knowles Hitchings and Mary Nichola Hitchings (*née* Adams). *Educ:* Eton Coll.; Christ Church, Oxford (BA 1996); University Coll. London (PhD 2002). FRSL 2015. Chair, Drama Section, Critics' Circle, 2018–. Pres., Johnson Soc., Lichfield, 2018. *Publications:* Dr Johnson's Dictionary, 2005; The Secret Life of Words, 2008 (John Llewellyn Rhys Prize, Booktrust, 2008; Somerset Maugham Award, Soc. of Authors, 2009); Who's Afraid of Jane Austen?, 2009; The Language Wars, 2011; Sorry! The English and their Manners, 2013; (ed) Browse: the world in bookshops, 2016; The World in Thirty-Eight Chapters or Dr Johnson's Guide to Life, 2018. *Recreations:* walking, wine, local history. *Address:* c/o Rogers, Coleridge & White Ltd, 20 Powis Mews, W11 1JN. *Club:* Blacks.

**HITCHINGS, Prof. Roger Alan,** FRCS; FRCOphth; Ophthalmic Surgeon, 1978–2008, Consultant, 1981–2008 and Director, Research and Development, 2000–08, Moorfields Eye Hospital, now Honorary Consultant Ophthalmologist; Professor of Glaucoma and Allied Studies, Institute of Ophthalmology, University College London, 1999–2008, now Emeritus; *b* 30 May 1942; *s* of Alan and Mary Hitchings; *m* 1966, Virmati Talwar; two *d. Educ:* Steyning Grammar Sch.; Royal Free Hosp. (MB BS). FRCS 1971; FRCOphth 1988. Resident Surgical Officer, Moorfields Eye Hosp., 1969–73; Res. Fellow, Wills Eye Hosp., 1973–75; Sen. Lectr, Univ. of London, 1975–79; Consultant Ophthalmic Surgeon, KCH, 1979–81. Vis. Prof., Nat. Univ. Hosp. Singapore, 2010–13. President: Eur. Glaucoma Soc., 2000–08; World Glaucoma Assoc., 2001–03 (Member: Bd of Govs, 2003–15; Council, 2016–); Mem., German Ophthalmological Soc., 2006. Chm., Eur. Glaucoma Soc. Foundn, 2008–. Lectures: Duke Elder, 1997, Bowman, 2008, Royal Coll. Ophthalmologists; Shaffer, Amer. Acad. Ophthalmologists, 2000; Spaeth Commemorative, Amer. Glaucoma Soc., 2001; Ida Mann, Oxford Univ., 2002; Goldmann, Glaucoma Res. Soc., 2006; Bartisch, Univ. of Dresden, 2009. Internat. Scholar Award, American Glaucoma Soc., 2014. *Publications:* Atlas of Clinical Ophthalmology, 1984, 3rd edn 2005; The Refractory Glaucomas, 1995; Glaucoma: a practical guide, 2000; Glaucoma (2 vols), 2009, 2nd edn 2014; over 250 peer-reviewed papers on glaucoma and allied subjects. *Recreations:* Rotary, Probus, history, gardening, travel.

**HITCHINGS, Sandra Caroline;** *see* Dinneen, S. C.

**HITCHMOUGH, Andrew John;** QC 2013; *b* Warrington, 18 Sept. 1968; *s* of Joseph Neil Hitchmough and Enid Hitchmough; *m* 2003, Sarah Baker. *Educ:* Abraham Guest High Sch., Wigan; Winstanley Coll., Wigan; Southampton Univ. (LLB 1st Cl. Hons). Called to the Bar, Inner Temple, 1991; in practice as barrister, specialising in tax, 1991–. *Recreations:* boating, diving, shooting, fly fishing, ski-ing. *Address:* Pump Court Tax Chambers, 16 Bedford Row, WC1R 4EF. *T:* (020) 7414 8080, *Fax:* (020) 7414 8099. *E:* ahitchmough@pumptax.com.

**HIVES,** family name of **Baron Hives**.

**HIVES,** 3rd Baron *cr* 1950, of Duffield, co. Derby; **Matthew Peter Hives;** engineer; Director, DWN Investments Ltd, since 2013; *b* 25 May 1971; *s* of Hon. Peter Anthony Hives (*d* 1974) and Dinah (*née* Wilson-North); *S* uncle, 1997; *m* 2017, Dr Davina Meredith, *y d* of David Meredith and Sandra Meredith (*née* Burke), County Offaly, Ireland. *Educ:* Haileybury; Newcastle Univ. (BEng); Aberdeen Univ. (MSc). MIMechE. Formerly with

**HIX, Hilary Anne**; see Ross, H. A.

**HIX, Mark**, MBE 2017; restaurateur, chef and food writer; Owner: Hix Oyster & Chop House, London, since 2008; Hix Oyster and Fish House, Dorset, since 2008; Hix Restaurant, London, since 2009; Hix Restaurant and Champagne Bar, since 2010; The Tramshed, since 2012; Hixter, since 2013; Hixter Bankside, since 2014; Director of Food, Browns Hotel, London, since 2008; *b* 10 Dec. 1962; *s* of Ernest and Gill Hix; *m* Suzie Hix (marr. diss.); three *d*. *Educ*: Colfox Sch.; Weymouth Coll. Commis Chef, Grosvenor Hse Hotel, 1981–83; Commis Chef, later Chef de Partie, Dorchester, 1983–84; Sous Chef, then Hd Chef, Mr Pontacs/Candlewick Room, 1985–90 (Michelin Red M award); Hd Chef, Le Caprice; Exec. Hd Chef, 1990–2008, Chef Dir, 1992–2008, Caprice Hldgs Ltd, overseeing Le Caprice and The Ivy (Michelin Red M award); Chef Director: J. Sheekey, Covent Gdn, 1998–2008; Daphne's, 2000–08; Bam-Bou, 2000–08; Pasha, 2000–08. Recipe column: Independent on Saturday mag. (Glenfiddich Award, Best Newspaper Cookery Writer, 2003); Country Life. Best Cookery Writer, Guild of Food Writers, 2005; Chef of the Year, GQ Mag., 2008; Restaurateur of the Year, Tatler, 2009; Chef of the Year, Catey Awards, 2010. *Publications*: The Ivy: the restaurant and its recipes, 1997; (with A. A. Gill) Le Caprice: the book, 1999; Eat Up, 2000; British, 2003, 2nd edn 2005; Fish Etc, 2004; (with M. Gluck) The Simple Art of Food and Wine, 2005; British Regional Food: in search of the best British food today, 2006; British Seasonal Food, 2008; Hix Oyster and Chop House, 2010; Mark Hix on Baking, 2012. *Recreations*: fishing, foraging, shooting, golf, art collecting. *E*: mhix@hixfoodetc.co.uk. *Clubs*: Groucho, Soho House, Royal Automobile; Stoke Park Golf.

**HOAD, Pamela Joan**; see Gordon, P. J.

**HOAR, Rev. Ronald William Cecil**; Chairman, Manchester and Stockport Methodist District, 1979–95; President of the Methodist Conference, 1991–92; *b* 31 Oct. 1931; *s* of Cecil Herbert William and Lilian Augusta Hoar; *m* 1956, Peggy Jean (née Stubbington); three *s* two *d*. *Educ*: Shedfield Church of England Primary Sch., Hants; Price's Sch., Fareham, Hants; Richmond Coll., Univ. of London (BD). Methodist Minister: Wells, Somerset, 1955–58; Bermondsey, London, 1958–62; Westminster and Chelsea, 1962–67; Bristol Mission, 1967–76; Great Yarmouth and Gorleston, 1976–79. *Publications*: Methodism in Chelsea to 1963, 1963; A Good Ideal: a history of the Bristol Methodist Mission, 1973; Advertising the Gospel, 1991. *Recreations*: DIY, watching sport, oil painting, gardening. *Address*: 73 Summerset Village, 180 Ruapehu Drive, Fitzherbert, Palmerston North 4110, New Zealand.

**HOARE, Alexander Simon**; private banker; Managing Partner, C. Hoare & Co., since 2009 (Chief Executive, 2001–09); *b* 1 April 1962; *s* of Christopher E. B. Hoare and late Sylvia M. Hoare; *m* 2012, Claudia, *d* of David and Suzanne Martin; one *s*. *Educ*: Winchester Coll.; Univ. of Edinburgh (BComm Hons). ACIB 1990. Consultant Analyst, PA Consulting Gp, 1985–87; joined C. Hoare & Co., 1987–. Non-exec. Dir, Jupiter Green Investment Trust Plc, 2006–09. *Address*: C. Hoare & Co., 37 Fleet Street, EC4P 4DQ. *Club*: St Mawes Billiards and Social.

**HOARE, Sir Antony**; see Hoare, Sir C. A. R.

**HOARE, Rev. Brian Richard**; Methodist Minister, 1971–2000; Methodist Evangelism Secretary, 1996–2000; President of the Methodist Conference, 1995–96; *b* 9 Dec. 1935; *s* of William Charles Hoare and Kathleen Nora Hoare (née Thwaites); *m* 1962, Joyce Eleanor Davidson; one *s* one *d*. *Educ*: Southwell Minster Grammar Sch., Notts; Westminster Coll., London (Teacher's Cert.); Richmond Coll., Univ. of London (BD 1971). Ops Clerk, RAF, 1954–56. Teacher, Col Frank Seely Secondary Sch., Calverton, Notts, 1959–62; Travelling Sec., subsequently Nat. Sec., Colls of Educn Christian Union, Inter-Varsity Fellowship, London, 1962–68. Chaplain Hunmanby Hall Sch., Filey, 1971–74; Minister, Hull Methodist Mission, 1974–77; New Testament Tutor, Cliff Coll., Sheffield, 1977–86; Superintendent Minister, Longton Central Hall, Stoke-on-Trent, 1986–88; Divl Sec. 1988–89, Dep. Gen. Sec. 1989–95, Home Mission Div. Member: World Methodist Council, Nairobi, 1986, Singapore, 1991, Rio de Janeiro, 1996, Brighton, 2001; World Methodist Exec. Cttee, Bulgaria, 1992, Estonia, 1994. Chairman: Epworth Old Rectory, 2000–08; Pratt Green Trust, 2007–15. *Publications*: (ed) Methods of Mission, 1979; Evangelism in New Testament Practice and Methodist Tradition, 1984; Hymns and Songs for Worship, 1985; Celebrate and Sing, 1991; 20 Things to do in a Decade of Evangelism, 1991; By the Way: six studies in incidental evangelism, 1995; New Creation: a full length musical presentation, 1995; Singing Faith, 1998; (ed) Leisure and Mission, 2000; (jtly) More than a Methodist, 2003; Cover to Cover: studies in Revelation, 2006; hymns and songs (words and music) published in a variety of books. *Recreations*: music, literature, travel. *Address*: 5 Flaxdale Close, Knaresborough, N Yorks HG5 0NZ.

**HOARE, Sir (Charles) Antony (Richard), (Tony)**, Kt 2000; FRS 1982; FREng; Principal Researcher, 1999–2015, Consultant, 2015–17, and Visitor, since 2017, Microsoft Research Ltd, Cambridge; Honorary Member, Cambridge University Computing Laboratory, since 2007; *b* 11 Jan. 1934; *s* of late Henry S. M. Hoare and Marjorie F. Hoare; *m* 1962, Jill Pym; one *s* one *d* (and one *s* decd). *Educ*: King's Sch., Canterbury; Merton Coll., Oxford (MA, Cert. Stats; Hon. Fellow, 2003); Moscow State Univ. Computer Div., Elliott Brothers, London, Ltd, 1960–68: successively Programmer, Chief Engr, Tech. Man., Chief Scientist; National Computer Centre, 1968; Prof. of Computer Science, QUB, 1968–77; Oxford University: Fellow, Wolfson Coll., 1977–99; Prof. of Computation, then James Martin Prof. of Inf. Engrg, 1977–99. Lee Kuan Yew Distinguished Visitor, Singapore, 1992; Einstein Prof., Chinese Acad. of Sci., 2006. Dist. FBCS 1978; MAE 1989; FREng 2005. For. Mem., Accademia Nazionale dei Lincei, 1988; Corresp. Mem., Bavarian Acad. of Scis, 1997; Foreign Associate: US NAE, 2006; US NAS, 2017. Fellow, Computer Hist. Mus., Mountain View, Calif, 2011. Hon. Fellow: Kellogg Coll., Oxford, 1999; Darwin Coll., Cambridge, 2001. Hon. DSc: Southern California, 1979; Warwick, 1985; Pennsylvania, 1986; Belfast, 1987; York, 1989; Essex 1991; Bath, 1993; Oxford Brookes, 2000; QMC, 2005; Heriot-Watt, 2007; Athens Univ. of Econs and Business, 2007; Warsaw, 2012; Madrid, 2013; St Petersburg (Inf. Technologies, Mechanics and Optics), 2013. A. M. Turing Award, Assoc. Comp. Mach., 1980; Harry Goode Meml Award, Amer. Fedn of Inf. Processing Socs, 1981; Faraday Medal, IEE, 1985; Computer Pioneer Award, 1991, John von Neumann Medal, 2011, IEEE; Kyoto Prize, Inamori Foundn, 2000; F. L. Bauer Prize, Technical Univ. Munich, 2007; Distinguished Achievement Award, Special Interest Gp on Programming Langs, ACM, 2012; 20 Year ICFEM Most Influential Person Award, 2018. *Publications*: Structured Programming (with O.-J. Dahl and E. W. Dijkstra), 1972; Communicating Sequential Processes, 1985; (with C. B. Jones) Essays in Computing Science, 1988; (with He Jifeng) Unifying Theories of Programming, 1998; articles in Computer Jl, Commun. ACM, and Acta Informatica; *festschrift*: A Classical Mind, 1994; Reflections on the Work of C. A. R. Hoare, 2010. *Recreations*: walking, reading, listening to music.

**HOARE, Sir Charles James**, 9th Bt *cr* 1784, of Annabella, Cork; International Secretary, Christian Action Research and Education, 1998; *b* 15 March 1971; *s* of Sir Timothy Edward Charles Hoare, 8th Bt, OBE and of Felicity Anne (née Boddington); *S* father, 2008; *m* 2000, Hon. Eleanor Filumena Flower, *o d* of Viscount Ashbrook, *qv*; one *s* two *d*. *Educ*: Pimlico Sch.; Durham Univ. (BA); London Sch. of Econs (MSc). Mem., Mgt Bd, Centre on Religion and Global Affairs. OStJ. *Heir*: *s* Edward Harry William Hoare, *b* 13 Feb. 2006.

**HOARE, Christopher Henry St John, (Toby)**; Executive Chairman, since 2005, and Chief Executive Officer, Europe, since 2006, J. Walter Thomson Group; Chairman, Geometry Global, since 2013; *b* 2 Feb. 1960; *s* of J. Michael Hoare and Ann St J. Hoare; *m* 1986, Hon. Sarah Jane Dixon-Smith; two *s* one *d*. *Educ*: Harrow. Distillers Co. Ltd, 1979–80; Express Newspapers, 1980–84; Centaur Communications, 1984–85; Dorland Advertising, 1985–87; Young & Rubicam, 1987–99; Gp Chief Exec., Bates UK Ltd, 1999–2002; Chm., Bates Gp Europe, 2002–04; CEO, Team HSBC, WPP Gp, 2004–05. Chm.; Mus. of Brands, London, 2018–. Governor, Harrow Sch., 2002–17. Freeman, City of London, 1987; Liveryman, Co. of Distillers, 1982. *Recreations*: shooting, golf, theatre, football. *Address*: 17 Stanley Crescent, W11 2NA. *T*: (020) 7221 5159; The Old Rectory, Bradfield St George, Bury St Edmunds, Suffolk IP30 0DH. *Clubs*: Garrick; Royal Newmarket & Worlington Golf, Swinley Forest Golf.

**HOARE, David Alexander**; Chairman, Teenage Cancer Trust, since 2010; Founder and Chair, KAN Ventures, since 2014; *b* Dublin, 31 Jan. 1950; *s* of John Hoare and Daphne Hoare; *m* 1975, Janet Mary, Jammy, Shorter; two *s* one *d*. *Educ*: Marlborough Coll.; Univ. of Birmingham (BSc Chem. Engrg 1972); Stanford Business Sch. (MBA 1977; Harkness Fellow). Fawley Refinery, Esso Petroleum, 1972–75; Partner, Boston and London, Bain & Co., 1977–87; Co-Founder and Dir, Talisman Mgt Ltd, 1987–2015; Chief Exec., Cope Allman Packaging plc, 1987–92; Duncton plc, later Moneybarn Ltd: Co-Founder, 1992; Chm., 1992–2009; Dir, 2009–14; Chief Exec., Investors in Educn Ltd, 1992–93; Chief Operating Officer, 1992–93, non-exec. Dir, 1996–2004, Paragon Gp of Cos plc; Chief Executive: Laura Ashley plc, 1997–98; Thorn UK Ltd, 1998–99; Founder Dir, South West Sussex Radio Ltd, 1998–2005; Chairman: Virgin Express Hldgs plc, 1999–2005; Target Worldwide Express Ltd, 2002–06; Fairline Boats Hldgs Ltd, 2005–07; Sparck Hldgs BV, 2005–08; V Ships Gp, 2007–11; DX Gp plc, 2010–14. Advr, Eden McCallum, 2002–14. Dir, Inst. for Turnaround, 2013–14. Chair, Office for Standards in Educn, 2014–16; Trustee, Academies Enterprise Trust, 2014. *Recreations*: tennis, ski-ing, cycling, golf, sailing, family. *Address*: 40 Chepstow Place, W2 4TA. *E*: davidhoare2000@btinternet.com. *Clubs*: Queen's; Campden Hill Lawn Tennis.

**HOARE, Sir David (John)**, 9th Bt *cr* 1786, of Barn Elms, Surrey; Managing Partner, C. Hoare & Co., Bankers, 2006–18 (Chairman, 2001–06); *b* 8 Oct. 1935; *s* of Sir Peter William Hoare, 7th Bt, and Laura Ray Hoare, *o d* of Sir John Esplen, 1st Bt, KBE; *S* brother, 2004; *m* 1st, 1965, Mary Vanessa Cardew (marr. diss. 1978); one *s*; 2nd, 1984, Virginia Victoria Graham Labes. *Educ*: Eton. Commnd Nat. Service, 1954–56. Joined Hoare's Bank, 1959: Man. Partner, 1964–88; Dep. Chm., 1988–2001. Dir, Mitre Court Property Holding Co., 1964. Chm., Internat. Atlantic Salmon Club, 1995–2015. Trustee, West Country Rivers Trust, 1996. *Recreations*: fishing, golf, shooting, ski-ing, forestry. *Heir*: *s* Simon Merrik Hoare [*b* 11 Oct. 1967; *m* 1st, 1999, Aurélie, *d* of Jean-François Catoire (marr. diss. 2009); two *s*; 2nd, 2011, Sandra, *d* of Alain Sortais; two *s*]. *Address*: Luscombe Castle, Dawlish, Devon EX7 0PU; C. Hoare & Co., 37 Fleet Street, EC4P 4DQ. *Clubs*: White's; Royal St George's Golf, Swinley Forest Golf.

**HOARE, Henry Cadogan**; Senior Partner, C. Hoare & Co., Bankers, until 2018 (Chairman, 1988–2001); *b* 23 Nov. 1931; *s* of late Henry Peregrine Rennie Hoare and of Lady Beatrix Fanshawe, *d* of 6th Earl Cadogan, CBE; *m* 1st, 1959, Pamela Bunbury (marr. diss. 1970); two *s* one *d*; 2nd, 1977, Caromy Maxwell Macdonald. *Educ*: Eton; Trinity Coll., Cambridge (MA). Career in banking. *Address*: c/o C. Hoare & Co., 37 Fleet Street, EC4P 4DQ.

**HOARE, Michelle S., (Brie)**; see Stevens-Hoare.

**HOARE, Rt Rev. Dr Rupert William Noel**; Dean of Liverpool, 2000–07, now Dean Emeritus; an Honorary Assistant Bishop, Diocese of Manchester, since 2008; *b* 3 March 1940; *s* of Julian Hoare and Edith Hoare (née Temple); *m* 1965, Gesine (née Pflüger); three *s* one *d*. *Educ*: Rugby School; Trinity Coll., Oxford (BA 1961, MA 1967); Kirchliche Hochschule, Berlin; Westcott House and Fitzwilliam House, Cambridge (BA 1964); Birmingham Univ. (PhD 1973). Deacon 1964, priest 1965, Dio. Manchester; Curate of St Mary, Oldham, 1964–67; Lecturer, Queen's Theological Coll., Birmingham, 1968–72; Canon Theologian of Coventry Cathedral, 1970–75; Rector, Parish of the Resurrection, Manchester, 1972–78; Residentiary Canon, Birmingham Cathedral, 1978–81; Principal, Westcott House, Cambridge, 1981–93; Bishop Suffragan of Dudley, 1993–99. *Publications*: (trans. jtly) Bultmann's St John, 1971; (contrib.) Queen's Sermons, 1973, Queen's Essays, 1980; The Trial of Faith, 1988; articles in Theology. *Recreations*: hill walking, gardening, listening to music. *Address*: 14 Shaw Hall Bank Road, Greenfield, Saddleworth, Oldham OL3 7LD.

**HOARE, Simon James**; MP (C) North Dorset, since 2015; *b* Cardiff, 28 June 1969; *s* of Colin and Maria Hoare; *m* 2000, Kate, *y d* of William Lund, FRCS; three *d*. *Educ*: Bishop Hannon High Sch., Cardiff; Greyfriars, Oxford (BA Hons Modern Hist.). Business and public affairs consultant to land owners, farmers, public sector and property develt cos; family business in oil sector; Man. Dir, Community Connect Ltd, 2002–15. Member (C): W Oxfordshire DC, 2004–15 (Cabinet Mem., Resources, 2007–15); Oxfordshire CC, 2013–15. PPS to Minister of State for Agric., Fisheries and Food, 2016–17, to Home Office, 2017–. Chm., NI Affairs Select Cttee, 2019–. *Recreations*: gardening, collecting, horse racing, family. *Address*: House of Commons, SW1A 0AA. *T*: (020) 7219 5697. *E*: simon.hoare.mp@parliament.uk. *Clubs*: Garrick, Royal Over-Seas League; Blandford Constitutional; Newport Boat (Pembrokeshire).

**HOARE, Toby**; see Hoare, C. H. St J.

**HOBAN, Mark Gerard**; chartered accountant; Chairman, Flood Re, since 2015; *b* 31 March 1964; *s* of Tom Hoban and Maureen Hoban (née Orchard); *m* 1994, Fiona Jane Barrett. *Educ*: London Sch. of Econs (BSc Econs 1985). ACA 1989. With Coopers & Lybrand, then PricewaterhouseCoopers, 1985–2001, Sen. Manager, 1992–2001. Contested (C) South Shields, 1997. MP (C) Fareham, 2001–15. An Opposition Whip, 2002–03; Shadow Minister for Educn, 2003–05; Shadow Financial Sec., HM Treasury, 2005–10; Shadow Minister for Wearside, 2007–10; Financial Sec., HM Treasury, 2010–12; Minister of State, DWP, 2012–13. Mem., Select Cttee on Sci. and Technology, 2001–03. Non-executive Director: London Stock Exchange, 2015–; CityUK, 2016–; Borsa Italiana SpA, 2017–; Senior Adviser: IHS Markit (formerly Markit) Gp Ltd, 2014–; PwC, 2015–. Vis. Prof., St Mary's Univ., 2016–. Hon. Vice-Pres., Soc. of Maritime Industries, 2003–10. Freeman, City of London, 2003; Liveryman, Fruiterers' Co., 2003. *Recreations*: cooking, entertaining, reading, travel. *Address*: 20 The Vale, Locks Heath, Southampton SO31 6NL.

**HOBART, David Anthony,** CB 2004; Chief Executive, City of London Law Society, since 2011; Gentleman Usher to the Queen, since 2007; *b* 24 Dec. 1951; *m* 1977, Mandy Wilson; one *s* one *d*. *Educ:* Magdalene Coll., Cambridge (MPhil); LLB Open Univ. rcds; jsdc; psc. Various planning and financial programming posts in MoD; promoted to Air Vice-Marshal, 2001; ACDS (Policy), 2001–04; Chief Exec., Bar Council, 2004–11. *Recreations:* golf, ski-ing. *Address:* City of London Law Society, 4 College Hill, EC4R 2RB. *Clubs:* Royal Air Force; Wildernesse (Kent), Royal Cinque Ports Golf (Deal).

**HOBART, Sir John Vere,** 4th Bt *cr* 1914, of Langdown, Co. Southampton; *b* 9 April 1945; *s* of Lt-Comdr Sir Robert Hampden Hobart, 3rd Bt, RN and Sylvia (*d* 1965), *d* of Harry Argo; *heir-pres.* to Earl of Buckinghamshire, *qv*; *S* father, 1988; *m* 1980, Kate, *o d* of late George Henry Iddles; two *s*. *Educ:* Royal Agricl Coll., Cirencester. Mem. (C) Isle of Wight Council, 2009–. *Heir: s* George Hampden Hobart, *b* 10 June 1982.

**HOBART-HAMPDEN,** family name of **Earl of Buckinghamshire**.

**HOBBS, Prof. Angela Hunter,** PhD; Professor of the Public Understanding of Philosophy, University of Sheffield, since 2012; *b* Rudgwick, Sussex, 12 June 1961; *d* of Anthony Hobbs and Rosemary Hobbs (*née* Davies); one *d*. *Educ:* Coll. of Richard Collyer, Horsham, Sussex; New Hall, Cambridge (BA Classics 1983; MA 1986; PhD Classics 1991). W. H. D. Rouse Fellow in Classics, Christ's Coll., Cambridge, 1989–92; Warwick University: Lectr in Philosophy, 1992–2001; Associate Prof. in Philosophy, 2001–09; Sen. Fellow in the Public Understanding of Philosophy, 2009–12. Member: Exec. Cttee, British Philosophical Assoc., 2013–; Exec. Cttee and Trustee, Forum for European Philosophy, 2015–; Adv. Cttee, Speakers' Corner Trust, 2015–. Chair, Arts and Ideas Trust, 2011–16; Patron, Philosophy in Educn Project, 2015–; Hon. Patron, Philosophy Foundn, 2011–. World Economic Forum, Davos: Speaker, 2016; Council on Values, Ethics and Innovation, 2018–19. Associate Fellow, Crick Centre, 2014–. Judge, Man Booker Internat., 2019. Contributor to radio progs, incl. In Our Time and Desert Island Discs, and TV progs, newspapers, audio books and websites. FRSA 2010. *Publications:* (contrib.) Concise Oxford Dictionary of Politics, 1996, 3rd edn 2008; (contrib.) Routledge Encyclopedia of Philosophy, 1998; Plato and the Hero, 2000; (contrib.) Plato's Symposium: issues in interpretation and reception, 2006; (contrib.) Maieusis: essays in ancient philosophy in honour of Myles Burnyeat, 2007; (contrib.) In Our Time, 2009; (contrib.) Oxford Encyclopedia of Ancient Greece and Rome, 2010; (contrib.) Philosophy Bites Back, 2012; (contrib.) The Philosophy Shop, 2012; (contrib.) Continuum Companion to Plato, 2012; (contrib.) Religion and Atheism: beyond the divide, 2016; (contrib.) Rereading Ancient Philosophy: old chestnuts and sacred cows, 2017; (contrib.) In Our Time: celebrating 20 years of essential conversation, 2018; Plato's Republic: a Ladybird expert book, 2019; contribs to Philosophy, Psychiatry and Psychol., Philosophical Inquiry, Common Knowledge; contribs to special issues of Jl Philosophy in Schs and Classical Receptions Jl. *Recreations:* theatre, music, reading, walking, travelling, canoeing, swimming, cricket. *Address:* Department of Philosophy, University of Sheffield, 45 Victoria Street, Sheffield S3 7QB. *T:* (0114) 222 0594, (0114) 222 0571. *E:* a.hobbs@sheffield.ac.uk. *W:* www.angiehobbs.com, www.twitter.com/drangiehobbs.

**HOBBS, Christina;** *see* Dodwell, C.

**HOBBS, Prof. (Frederick David) Richard,** CBE 2019; FRCGP, FRCP; FMedSci; FESC; Nuffield Professor of Primary Care, and Head, Nuffield Department of Primary Care Health Sciences, University of Oxford, since 2011; Fellow, Harris Manchester College, Oxford, since 2011; *b* 2 Nov. 1953; *s* of Frederick Derek Hobbs and Nancy Elizabeth (*née* Wilde); *m* 1st, 1977, Jane Marilyn Porter (marr. diss. 2005); one *s* one *d*; 2nd, 2014, Lesley Martine Roberts. *Educ:* King Edward VI Camp Hill Sch., Birmingham; Bristol Univ. (MB, ChB 1977). MRCGP 1981, FRCGP 1990; FRCP 2000. House officer posts, Bath Royal United Hosp., 1977–78; Sen. house officer posts, Selly Oak Hosp., Birmingham, 1978–80; GP trainee, Univ. Health Centre, Birmingham, 1980–81; Principal in general practice, Bellevue Med. Centre, Birmingham, 1981– (part-time, 1992–); Birmingham University: part-time Sen. Lectr in General Practice, 1985–92; Prof. and Hd, Dept of Primary Care Clinical Scis (formerly Primary Care and Gen. Practice), 1992–2011; Asst Dean, Sch. of Medicine, 1993–96; Hd, Div. of Primary Care, Public and Occupational Health, 1998–2001; Associate Dean, Sch. of Medicine, 2002–09; Hd, Sch. of Health and Pop. Scis, 2009–11. Nat. Dir, NIHR English Sch. for Primary Care Res., 2009–; Dir, NIHR Collaboration for Leadership in Applied Health Res. and Care Oxford, 2013–. FMedSci 2002; FESC 2002. *Publications:* 12 books; 30 book chapters; over 450 peer-reviewed articles. *Recreations:* gardening, travel, interests in music (passive), wine and good food. *Address:* Nuffield Department of Primary Care Health Sciences, University of Oxford, Radcliffe Primary Care Building, Radcliffe Observatory Quarter, Walton Street, Oxford OX2 6GG.

**HOBBS, Jennifer Lynn,** MBE 1992; Principal, St Mary's College, Durham University, 1999–2007; *b* 5 March 1944; *d* of Henry Edwin Hobbs and Jean Hobbs (*née* Kennedy). *Educ:* St Paul's Girls' Sch., London; Newnham Coll., Cambridge (BA (Hons) Geog 1966; MA 1970). VSO teacher, Malacca Girls' High Sch., Malaysia, 1966–68; Geography Editor, Overseas Educ. Dept, Macmillan Education, 1968–73; British Council, 1973–94: various posts in UK; Nepal, 1979–83; Yugoslavia/Croatia, 1988–92; on secondment, Univ. of Durham, 1992–94; University of Durham, 1994–2007: Dir, Internat. Office, 1994–2004; Associate Dean for Student Support Services, 2004–05. Mem., Durham Cathedral Council, 2001–07. FRSA 2003. Governor: Durham Sch., 1998–2005; Durham High Sch. for Girls, 2007–10; Pilgrims' Sch., Winchester, 2009–16 (Vice-Chm., 2014–15). Chm., 2010–12, Mem., 2013, Portsmouth and Winchester Diocesan Bd of Educn. Trustee and Dir, Winchester Action on Climate Change Ltd, 2018–. *Recreations:* classical music, choral singing, sport, walking, birdwatching, gardening, environmental sustainability issues.

**HOBBS, Dr Jeremy Alexander;** HM Diplomatic Service; Head, Americas Research Group, Foreign and Commonwealth Office, since 2017; *b* Dunfermline, 8 Feb. 1961; *s* of late Brian Hobbs and of Patricia Hobbs (*née* Bullman); *m* 1983, Ana Maria Erendira Granados; one *s* one *d*. *Educ:* Monterey Prep. Sch., Wynberg, SA; Arthur Mellows Village Coll., Glinton, Peterborough; Portsmouth Poly. (BA Latin American Studies); Univ. of Essex (MA Latin American Govt and Politics; PhD Govt 1991). Entered FCO, 1991; Sen. Res. Officer, FCO, 1991–95; Second Sec. (Pol/Tech. Cooperation), Bogota, 1995–99; Principal Res. Officer, FCO, 1999–2003; First Sec. (Pol), Mexico City, 2003–06; Sen. Principal Res. Officer, FCO, 2006–13; Chargé d'Affaires, Quito, 2012; Ambassador to Paraguay, 2013–17. *Recreations:* swimming, rowing, reading, listening to music, cooking. *Address:* 18 Groves Close, Colchester, Essex CO4 5BP. *E:* jeremy.hobbs@fco.gov.uk.

**HOBBS, Prof. Kenneth Edward Frederick,** ChM, FRCS; Professor of Surgery, Royal Free Hospital School of Medicine, University of London, and Consultant Surgeon, Royal Free Hampstead NHS Trust (formerly Royal Free Hospital), 1973–98, then Emeritus Professor; Chairman, Joint Board of Surgery, University College London Medical School and Royal Free Hospital School of Medicine, 1993–98; Dean, University of London Faculty of Medicine, 1994–98; *b* 28 Dec. 1936; *s* of late Thomas Edward Ernest Hobbs and Gladys May Hobbs (*née* Neave). *Educ:* West Suffolk County Grammar Sch., Bury St Edmunds; Guy's Hosp. Med. Sch., Univ. of London (MB BS 1960). ChM Bristol 1970; FRCS 1964. Lectr in Surgery, Univ. of Bristol, 1966–70; Surgical Res. Fellow, Harvard Univ., 1968–69; Sen. Lectr in Surgery, Univ. of Bristol, 1970–73; University of London: Vice-Dean, Faculty of Medicine, 1986–90; Mem. Senate, then Council, 1985–98; Chm., Acad. Adv. Bd in Medicine, 1986–90; Dep. Chm., Acad. Council Standing Sub-Cttee in Medicine, 1986–90. Mem., Systems Bd, MRC, 1982–86; Chm., Grants Cttee A, MRC, 1984–86; Member: Med. Sub-Cttee, UGC, 1986–89; Med. Cttee, UFC, 1991–92; GMC, 1996–2001 (Dep. Chm., Professional Conduct Cttee, 1999–2001; Professional Mem., Fitness to Practise Cttee, 2002–06; Mem., Fitness to Practise Panels, 2009–); Mason Med. Res. Foundn, 1988–98 (Chm., 1993–98). Vis. Prof., Univs in China, Ethiopia, S Africa, Europe, USA, West Indies. Secretary: Patey Soc., 1979–82; 1942 Club, 1985–88; Trustee and Bd Mem., Stanley Thomas Johnson Foundn, Berne, 1976–2004 (Chm., 1997–2004). Gov., Norfolk and Norwich Univ. Hosp. Foundn Trust, 2008–. Hon. Fellow, Chinese Univ. of Hong Kong, 2002. Hon. FCSSL 1995. Internat. Master Surgeon, Internat. Coll. of Surgeons, 1994. FRSocMed 1973. *Publications:* chapters on aspects of liver surgery in textbooks; contribs to professional jls. *Recreations:* gourmet cooking and dining, the countryside. *Address:* Apartment 10, Westlegate Tower, 14–18 Westlegate, Norwich NR1 3LJ. *T:* (01603) 613529. *Club:* Royal Society of Medicine.

**HOBBS, Maj.-Gen. Sir Michael (Frederick),** KCVO 1998; CBE 1982 (OBE 1979; MBE 1975); Governor, Military Knights of Windsor, 2000–12; *b* 28 Feb. 1937; *s* of late Brig. Godfrey Pennington Hobbs and Elizabeth Constance Mary Hobbs; *m* 1967, Tessa Mary Churchill; one *s* two *d*. *Educ:* Eton College. Served Grenadier Guards, 1956–80; Directing Staff, Staff Coll., 1974–77; MoD, 1980–82; Commander 39 Inf. Bde, 1982–84; Dir of PR (Army), 1984–85; Commander, 4th Armoured Div., 1985–87; retired. Director: Duke of Edinburgh's Award, 1988–98; Outward Bound Trust, 1995–2006.

**HOBBS, Peter Thomas Goddard;** HM first non-police Inspector of Constabulary, 1993–98; *b* 19 March 1938; *s* of late Reginald Stanley Hobbs, BEM, Gloucester and of Phyllis Gwendoline (*née* Goddard); *m* 1964, Victoria Christabel, *d* of late Rev. Alan Matheson, Clifton Campville, Staffs; one *d*. *Educ:* Crypt Sch., Glos; Exeter Coll., Oxford (Waugh Scholar; MA). Nat. Service, 2nd Lt, RASC, 1957–59; Capt., RCT, TA, 1959–68. With ICI Ltd, 1962–79 (Jt Personnel Manager, Mond Div.); Gp Personnel Dir, Wellcome Foundn and Wellcome PLC, 1979–92. Chemical Industries Association: Dep. Chm., Pharmaceuticals and Fine Chemical Jt Industrial Council, 1979–89; Chairman: Trng Cttee, 1985–89; Employment Affairs Bd, 1989–91; Mem. Council, 1989–92; Chm., Chem. Industry Educn Centre, Univ. of York, 1992–94. Dir, Employment Conditions Abroad Ltd, 1984–91 and 1993. Confederation of British Industry: Member: Task Force on Vocational Educn and Trng, 1989–90; Educn and Trng Cttee, 1990–94; Business in the Community: Member, Target Team: for Industrial/Educn Partnerships, 1988–90; for Priority Hiring, 1988–91; Founder Chm., Employers' Forum on Disability, 1986–93; Mem., Nat. Adv. Council on Employment for People with Disabilities, 1991–93; Trustee, Learning from Experience Trust, 1988– (Chm., 1992–93 and 1998–2008). Member: Council, Contemporary Applied Arts, 1990–92; Industry Adv. Gp, Nat. Curriculum Council, 1990–92; Personnel Standards Lead Body, 1992–94; Council, EDEXCEL (formerly BTEC), 1995–98. Non-exec. Dir, Forensic Sci. Service, 1996–2006. Director: and Dep. Chm., Roffey Park Inst., 1989–93; Centre for Enterprise, London Business Sch., 1989–92; Mem. Adv. Council, Mgt Centre Europe, Brussels, 1989–97. Gov., Kent Coll., Canterbury, 2013–. Trustee, Canterbury Archaeol Trust, 2013–; Dir, Industrial Buildings Preservation Trust, 2016–. CCIPD 1988 (Internat. Vice Pres., 1987–89, 1990–91); FInstD 1989 (Mem., Employment Cttee, 1989–93); FRSA 1992. Dr hc Internat. Mgt Centres, 2000. *Recreations:* history, archaeology, opera, turning the soil. *Address:* 105 Blenheim Crescent, W11 2EQ. *T:* (020) 7727 3054. *Club:* Oxford and Cambridge.

**HOBBS, Philip John;** racehorse trainer, since 1985; *b* 26 July 1955; *s* of Tony and Barbara Hobbs; *m* 1982, Sarah Louise Hill; three *d*. *Educ:* King's Coll., Taunton; Univ. of Reading (BSc). Rode 160 winners as a jockey; has trained over 2000 winners, 1985–. *Recreations:* ski-ing, shooting. *Address:* Sandhill Racing Stables, Bilbrook, Minehead, Somerset TA24 6HA. *T:* (01984) 640366, *Fax:* (01984) 641124. *E:* pjhobbs@pjhobbs.com. *Club:* Sportsman.

**HOBBS, Richard;** *see* Hobbs, F. D. R.

**HOBBS, Prof. Roger Edwin,** PhD, DSc; FICE; Director, Tension Technology International, since 1986; Professor of Engineering Structures, Imperial College of Science, Technology and Medicine, London, 1990–2003, now Emeritus; *b* 24 Feb. 1943; *s* of Edwin Daniel Hobbs and Phyllis Eileen (*née* Chapman); *m* 1st, 1965, Barbara Ann Dalton (*d* 1987); one *s* two *d*; 2nd, 1989, Dorinda Elizabeth Mitchell. *Educ:* Imperial Coll., London (PhD 1966; DSc Eng 1996). FICE 1995; FCGI 1996. Imperial College, London: Res. Asst, 1966–70; Lectr in Civil Engrg, 1970–83; Sen. Lectr, 1983–86; Reader in Structural Engrg, 1986–90; Hd, Dept of Civil Engrg, 1994–97. *Publications:* technical papers on steel structures, wire and high strength fibre ropes, offshore pipelines. *Recreations:* walking, France, preferably in combination. *Address:* Department of Civil and Environmental Engineering, Imperial College London, SW7 2AZ.

**HOBBY, Russell Keith;** Chief Executive, Teach First, since 2017; *b* Abingdon, 22 Jan. 1972. *Educ:* Corpus Christi Coll., Oxford (BA 1st Cl. Hons PPE 1993). Damascus Tech Ltd, 1993–95; Second Sight Ltd, 1995–98; joined Hay Gp, 1998, Associate Dir, 1999–2010; Gen. Sec., Nat. Assoc. of Head Teachers, 2010–17. *Publications:* The School Recruitment Handbook, 2004.

**HOBCRAFT, Kathleen Elizabeth;** *see* Kiernan, K. E.

**HOBDAY, Peter James;** journalist and broadcaster; *s* of Arthur John Hobday and Dorothy Ann Hobday (*née* Lewis); *m* 1st, 1959, Tamara Batcharnikoff (*d* 1984); one *s* one *d*; 2nd, 1996, Victoria Fenwick. *Educ:* St Chad's Coll., Wolverhampton; Wolverhampton Univ. Wolverhampton Express and Star, 1960; Business magazine, 1960–61; The Director, 1961–74; joined BBC, 1970: World Service, 1970–74; Financial World Tonight, 1974–82, Moneybox, 1977–80, Radio 4; Money Programme, 1979–80, Newsnight, 1980–82, BBC TV; Today programme, Radio 4, 1982–96; Masterworks, Radio 3, 1996–2000. Hon. Dr de Montfort, 1996; Hon. DLitt Wolverhampton, 2008. *Publications:* Man the Industrialist, 1970; Saudi Arabia Today, 1974; In the Valley of the Fireflies, 1995; Managing the Message, 2000; The Girl in Rose: Haydn's last love, 2004. *Recreation:* growing olives in Italy. *Address:* 67 Highlever Road, W10 6PR. *Club:* Athenæum.

**HOBHOUSE, Anna Catrina, (Kate);** Chairman, Fortnum & Mason plc, since 2008; *b* Sydney, 30 July 1962; *d* of late Garfield Howard Weston and Mary Ruth Weston (*née* Kippenberger); *m* 1988, William Arthur Hobhouse; four *s* one *d*. *Educ:* Francis Holland Sch.; Univ. of Bristol (BA Ancient Mediterranean Studies). Mem., Bd of Dirs, Fortnum & Mason plc, 1998–. Trustee, Garfield Weston Foundn, 2000–. *Address:* Fortnum & Mason plc, 181 Piccadilly, W1A 1ER. *T:* (020) 7973 5610. *E:* helen.smith@fortnumandmason.co.uk.

*See also* G. G. Weston, G. H. Weston.

**HOBHOUSE, Sir Charles (John Spinney),** 7th Bt *cr* 1812, of Broughton-Gifford, Bradford-on-Avon and of Monkton Farleigh, Wiltshire; *b* 27 Oct. 1962; *s* of Sir Charles Chisholm Hobhouse, 6th Bt, TD and of Elspeth Jean, *yr d* of late Thomas George Spinney; *S* father, 1991; *m* 1993, Katrina (marr. diss. 1997), *d* of Maj.-Gen. Sir Denzil Macarthur-

Onslow, CBE, DSO; *m* 2009, Annette Welshman; two *s*. *Recreations:* sport, travel. *Heir:* s Benjamin Charles Spinney Hobhouse, *b* 26 Oct. 2009. *Address:* Monkton Farleigh Manor, Bradford-on-Avon, Wilts BA15 2QE.

**HOBHOUSE, Kate;** *see* Hobhouse, A. C.

**HOBHOUSE, Penelope, (Mrs John Malins),** MBE 2014; VMH; gardener, garden writer and garden consultant, since 1976; *b* 20 Nov. 1929; *d* of late Captain J. J. L.-C. Chichester-Clark, DSO and Bar, MP and Marion Chichester-Clark (later Mrs C. E. Brackenbury); *m* 1st, 1952, Paul Hobhouse (marr. diss. 1982; he *d* 1994); two *s* one *d*; 2nd, 1983, Prof. John Malins (*d* 1992). *Educ:* Girton Coll., Cambridge (BA Hons Econs, 1951; MA). National Trust tenant of Tintinhull House garden, 1980–93. Hon. DLitt: Birmingham, 1998; Essex (Writtle Coll.), 1998. VMH 1996. *Publications:* The Country Gardener, 1976, revd edn 1989; The Smaller Garden, 1981; Gertrude Jekyll on Gardening, 1983; Colour in your Garden, 1985; The National Trust: A Book of Gardening, 1986; Private Gardens of England, 1986; Garden Style, 1988; Painted Gardens, 1988; Borders, 1989; The Gardens of Europe, 1990; Flower Gardens, 1991; Plants in Garden History, 1992; Penelope Hobhouse on Gardening, 1994; Penelope Hobhouse's Garden Designs, 1997; Penelope Hobhouse's Natural Planting, 1997; A Gardener's Journal, 1997; Gardens of Italy, 1998; The Story of Gardening, 2002; The Gardens of Persia, 2003; In Search of Paradise, 2006. *Recreations:* reading Trollope and Henry James, Italy. *Address:* Dairy Barn, Pitcombe, Bruton, Som BA10 0PF.

**HOBHOUSE, Wera Benedicta;** MP (Lib Dem) Bath, since 2017; *b* Hanover, Germany, Feb. 1960; *m* 1990, William Hobhouse; two *s* two *d*. Radio journalist; professional artist; teacher of modern langs. Mem., Rochdale MBC, 2004–14 (C, 2004–05, Lib Dem 2005–14). Mem., Cttee on Exiting the EU, H of C, 2017–. Contested (Lib Dem): Heywood and Middleton, 2010; NE Somerset, 2015. *Address:* House of Commons, SW1A 0AA.

**HOBLEY, Anthony Robert;** Chief Executive, Carbon Tracker Initiative, since 2014; *b* Purley, 24 Nov. 1966; *s* of Brian and Linda Hobley; *m* 2001, Geraldine Marie Ismail (marr. diss. 2010); *m* Lisa Walker. *Educ:* St Leonards C of E Middle Sch., Chelsham; Warlingham Comprehensive Sch.; Plymouth Univ. (BSc 1st Cl. Hons Chem. with Physics 1988); Darwin Coll., Cambridge; De Montfort Univ. (CPE Law 1991); University Coll. London (LLM Envmtl Law). Trainee solicitor, Ince & Co., 1992–94; admitted as solicitor, 1994; Solicitor, Envmt Law Dept, Nabarro Nathanson, 1994–96; Sen. Solicitor, Envmt Law Team, CMS Cameron McKenna, 1996–2001; Sen. Solicitor, Global Climate Change Team, Baker & McKenzie, 2001–05; Chm., Carbon Mkts Assoc. (formerly London Climate Change Services), 2003–08; Global Hd, Climate Change and Carbon Finance, Norton Rose Gp, 2007–14; Partner, Norton Rose LLP, 2007–14. Mem., Police Liaison Cttee, Caterham Police, Surrey Constabulary, 1984–85. Sec., Climate Change Wkg Gp, UK Envmt Law Assoc., 1998–99; Chair, Legal Sub-gp, UK Emissions Trading Gp, 1999–2000. Member: Bd, Verified Carbon Standards Assoc., 2007–; Bd and Dir, Carbon Mkts & Investors Assoc., 2008–. Founder and Mem., Steering Cttee, Business for a Clean Economy (Australia), 2009–11. *Recreations:* running, ski-ing, some sailing, reading. *Address:* Carbon Tracker Initiative, 2nd Floor, 40 Bermondsey Street, SE1 3UD. *E:* ahobley@carbontracker.org.

**HOBLEY, Brian,** FSA; historical and archaeological researcher and writer; Chief Urban Archaeologist, City of London, 1973–89; Director, Hobley Archaeological Consultancy Services Ltd, 1989–92; *b* 25 June 1930; *s* of William Hobley and Harriet (*née* Hobson); *m* (marr. diss. 1992); one *s* one *d*. *Educ:* Univ. of Leicester (BA Hons 1965); Univ. of Oxford (MSt 1994). FSA 1969; AMA 1970. Field Officer, Coventry Corp., 1965; Keeper, Dept Field Archaeology, Coventry Museum, 1970. Lectr, Birmingham Univ. Extra-mural Dept, 1965–74. Chm. Standing Cttee, Arch. Unit Managers, 1986–89; Jt Sec., British Archaeologists and Developers Liaison Gp, 1986–89. MCMI (MBIM 1978); MCIfA (MIFA 1982). *Publications:* (ed jtly) Waterfront Archaeology in Britain and Northern Europe, 1981; Roman Urban Defences in the West, 1983; Roman Urban Topography in Britain and the Western Empire, 1985; Roman and Saxon London: a reappraisal, 1986; British Archaeologists and Developers Code of Practice, 1986; The Rebirth of Towns in the West AD 700–1050, 1988; The Circle of God: an archaeological and historical search for the Sacred: a study in continuity, 2015; reports in learned jls incl. Proc. 7th, 8th, 9th and 12th Internat. Congresses of Roman Frontier Studies, Tel Aviv, Univ. Israel and Bucharest Univ., Rumania on excavations and reconstructions at The Lunt Roman fort, Baginton near Coventry. *Recreations:* classical music, chess. *Address:* 46 Healey Court, Coten End, Warwick CV34 4XP.

**HOBLEY, Christopher Mathias James;** Director, Market Access and Budget, Department for Exiting the European Union, since 2017; *b* Roehampton, 27 June 1976; *s* of John Hobley and Uta Hobley von Tschurtschenthaler; *m* 2008, Rahila Mian; two *d*. *Educ:* Marlborough Coll.; Univ. of Edinburgh (MA Hons Hist.); London Sch. of Econs and Political Sci. (MSc Eur. Studies). DTI, 2001–08; First Sec., Soc. and Employment, UK Perm. Repn to the EU, 2008–12; Dep. Dir (actg), Energy Efficiency, DECC, 2013; Deputy Director: Corporate Governance and Co. Law Reform, BERR, 2013–15; Steel, BIS, 2015–16; Market Access and Budget, DExEU, 2016–17. *Publications:* (ed jtly) A Students Guide to European Integration: by students for students, 2004. *Recreations:* family - proud father of Alia and Inaya, happy husband to Rahila, running, hiking, ski-ing, live music, plenty of travelling. *Address:* Department for Exiting the European Union, 9 Downing Street, SW1A 2AL. *T:* 07808 847124. *E:* chris.hobley@dexeu.gov.uk.

**HOBMAN, Anthony Hugh Burton;** Member, Electoral Commission, 2010–17; Senior Advisor, Lincoln Pensions (formerly Lincoln International Pensions Advisory) Ltd, since 2013; *b* 5 July 1955; *s* of late David Burton Hobman, CBE and of Erica Agatha Hobman (*née* Irwin); *m* 1st, 1978, Catherine Fenton (marr. diss. 1994); one *s* two *d*; 2nd, 2001, Victoria Richards (*née* Maynard); one *d* and two step *s*. *Educ:* De La Salle Coll.; Cardinal Newman Sch., Hove; N Staffs Polytech. (BA Hons (Modern Studies) 1976). Barclays Bank plc: Graduate Mgt Trainee, 1976–81; various roles in Marketing, Project, Change and Service Mgt, 1982–95; Proshare (UK) Ltd: Hd, Private Investor Services, 1996–99; Chief Exec., 1999–2000; Chief Executive: Money Channel plc, 2000–01; Occupational Pensions Regulatory Authy, 2002–05; The Pensions Regulator, 2005–10; Consumer Financial Educn Body, subseq. Money Advice Service, 2010–12. Member: Consultative Cttee, Co. Law Review, DTI, 1999–2000; Adv. Gp, Employer Task Force on Pensions, DWP, 2003–04; Man. Bd, Cttee of Eur. Insce and Occupational Pensions Supervisors, 2009–10 (Chair, Occupational Pensions Cttee, 2007–09); Simple Financial Products Steering Gp, 2012. Gov., Pensions Policy Inst., 2005–. Trustee, David Hobman Charitable Trust, 1987–96. *Recreations:* ski-ing, theatre, opera, wine, watching Time Team. *Address:* 20 Wilbury Gardens, Hove, E Sussex BN3 6HY. *T:* (01273) 727183. *E:* tonyhobman@gmail.com. *Club:* Reform.

**HOBOLT, Prof. Sara Binzer,** PhD; FBA 2017; Sutherland Professor of European Institutions, London School of Economics and Political Science, since 2012; *b* Copenhagen, 28 Dec. 1977; *d* of Carsten Hobolt and Naja Binzer; *m* 2009, Dominik Mattmann; three *s*. *Educ:* Goldsmiths Coll., Univ. of London (BA 1st Cl. Hons Politics and Public Policy 2001); St John's Coll., Cambridge (MPhil Political Sci. 2002; PhD Political Sci. 2006). Postdoctoral Fellow, Nuffield Coll., Oxford, 2005–06; Fellow in Politics, Lincoln Coll., Oxford, 2006–11; Lectr in Comparative European Politics, Univ. of Oxford, 2006–11; Associate Mem., Nuffield Coll., Oxford, 2009–. Hon. Prof. in Political Sci., Univ. of Southern Denmark, 2009–. *Publications:* Europe in Question: referendums on European integration, 2009; (with J. Tilley) Blaming Europe?, 2014; (ed with O. Cramme) Democratic Politics in a European Union Under Stress, 2014. *Recreation:* family. *Address:* Department of Government, London School of Economics and Political Science, Houghton Street, WC2A 2AE. *E:* s.b.hobolt@lse.ac.uk.

**HOBSBAWM BAMPING, Julia Nathalie,** OBE 2015; Founder, Chief Executive and Director, Editorial Intelligence Ltd, since 2003; Chief Executive, Julia Hobsbawm Consulting Ltd, since 2005; *b* 15 Aug. 1964; *d* of Prof. Eric John Ernest Hobsbawm, CH, FBA and Marlene (*née* Schwarz); *m* 2004, Alaric Bamping; two *s* one *d*, and one step *s* one step *d*. *Educ:* Camden Sch. for Girls; Poly. of Central London. Asst, Martin Dunitz Med. Publrs, 1982; Publicity Officer, Penguin Books, 1983; Head of Publicity, Virago Press, 1985–87; Researcher: Books by my Bedside, Thames TV, 1987–89; Wogan, BBC, 1989–90; Forward Planning Editor, John Gau Productions, 1990–91; Fundraising Consultant, 1000 Club and High Value Donors, Labour Party, 1991–92; founded Julia Hobsbawm Associates, 1992, then, Hobsbawm Macaulay Communications, 1993 (Chair, 1993–2001); Chief Exec., HMC-Hobsbawm Media + Marketing Communications Ltd, 2001–05. Strategic Counsel to Edelman, 2009–12. Vis. Prof., London College, 2003–; Hon. Visiting Professor in Networking: Cass Business Sch., 2011–18; Univ. Campus Suffolk, then Univ. of Suffolk, 2012–; Hon. Vis. Prof. in Workplace Social Health, Cass Business Sch., 2018–. Member: Commng Panel, ESRC Culture of Consumption Res. Panel, 2002–07; Public Value Adv. Panel, Arts Council, 2006–07; President's Panel, CIPR, 2007–08; Global Agenda Council on Informed Societies, World Econ. Forum, 2010–14; FCO Diplomatic Excellence Panel, 2014–. Founder, Names Not Numbers, ideas conf., 2009–. Vice Pres., Hay Fest. of Lit., 2001–18. Mem., Nat. Develt Cttee, Treehouse, 2007–13. Trustee: Facial Surgery Res. Foundn, 2000–08 (Patron, 2008–); In-Kind Direct, 2003–07; Jewish Community Centre for London, 2004–05; Jewish Mus., London, 2017–18. FRSA 2003. Presenter, The Human and Machine Podcast, 2018–. Media Woman of the Year, First Women Awards, 2012. *Publications:* (with Robert Gray) The Cosmopolitan Guide to Working in PR and Advertising, 1996; (ed) Where the Truth Lies: trust and morality in PR and journalism, 2006, 2nd edn as Where the Truth Lies: trust and morality in the business of PR, journalism and communication, 2010; (with John Lloyd) The Power of the Commentariat: how much do commentators influence politics and public opinion?, 2008; The See-Saw: 100 ideas for work life balance, 2009; Fully Connected: working and networking in 2020, 2014; Fully Connected: surviving and thriving in an age of overload, 2017; Fully Connected: social health in an age of overload, 2018; The APPlied Human at Work: the world of the worker in the digital era, 2019. *Recreations:* conversation, reading, walking, thinking. *W:* www.juliahobsbawm.com. *Clubs:* Arts, Groucho, Ivy, Soho House.

**HOBSON, John;** Director, Construction Industry, Department of Trade and Industry, 2001–02; *b* 30 March 1946; *s* of late John Leslie Hobson and Beatrice Edith Hobson; *m* 1970, Jeanne Gerrish (marr. diss. 1996); one *s* one *d*. *Educ:* Northampton Grammar Sch.; Manchester Grammar Sch.; King's Coll., Cambridge (MA Mathematics). Joined Min. of Transport, 1967; Asst Private Sec. to Sec. of State for the Environment, 1970–72; Private Sec. to Head of CS, 1974–78; Assistant Secretary: Dept of Transport, 1979–80; DoE, 1980–86; Under-Sec., subseq. Dir, DoE, subseq. DETR, 1986–2001 (Dir of Construction, 1997–2001). Trustee, Sustainability First, 2003–14. JP Warwicks, 2002–16.

**HOBSON, John Graham;** QC 2000; a Recorder, since 2000; *s* of late John Herbert Hobson and Lilian May Hobson (*née* Mott); *m* 1976, Shirley June Palmer; one *s* one *d*. *Educ:* Monkton Combe Sch.; St John's Coll., Cambridge (LLM). Admitted Solicitor, 1968; Director: W Stepney Neighbourhood Law Centre, 1973–75; Southwark Law Project, 1975–80; called to the Bar, Inner Temple, 1980; Supplementary Panel of Counsel to Treasury, 1992–2000; Standing Counsel to Rent Assessment Panel, 1997–2000; Asst Recorder, 1999–2000. Special Advr, NI Affairs Cttee for Enquiry into Planning System in NI, H of C, 1995–96. Hon. Standing Counsel, CPRE, 2002–. *Recreations:* playing the 'cello, rowing, fishing, watching football. *Address:* Landmark Chambers, 180 Fleet Street, EC4A 2HG. *Clubs:* Travellers, London Rowing.

**HOBSON, Prof. John Montagu,** PhD; FBA 2015; Professor of Politics and International Relations, University of Sheffield, since 2005; *b* Montreal, 27 Dec. 1962; *s* of Timothy John Hobson and Nora Hobson; partner, Cecelia Thomas; one *s* two *d*. *Educ:* Hatfield Poly. (BA); London Sch. of Econs and Political Sci. (MSc; PhD 1991). Lectr in Internat. Relns, La Trobe Univ., Melbourne, 1992–97; Sen. Lectr in Internat. Relns, Univ. of Sydney, 1997–2004; Reader in Internat. Relns, Univ. of Sheffield, 2004–05. *Publications:* (with Linda Weiss) States and Economic Development, 1995; The Wealth of States, 1997; The State and International Relations, 2000; (ed with Stephen Hobden) Historical Sociology of International Relations, 2002; The Eastern Origins of Western Civilisation, 2004; (ed with Leonard Seabrooke) Everyday Politics of the World Economy, 2007; (ed with Colin Tyler) Selected Writings of John A. Hobson, 1932–1938: the struggle for the international mind, 2011; The Eurocentric Conception of World Politics: Western international theory, 1760–2010, 2012. *Recreations:* piano, bass, music writing. *Address:* Department of Politics, University of Sheffield, Elmfield, Northumberland Road, Sheffield S10 2TU. *T:* (0114) 222 1669, *Fax:* (0114) 222 1717. *E:* J.M.Hobson@sheffield.ac.uk.

**HOBSON, Prof. Marian Elizabeth,** CBE 2002; FBA 1999; Professor of French, Queen Mary (formerly Queen Mary and Westfield College), University of London, 1992–2005, now Professorial Research Fellow; *b* 10 Nov. 1941; *d* of Baron Hobson and Doris Mary Hobson; *m* 1968, Michel Jeanneret, Corresp. FBA; one *s*. *Educ:* Newnham Coll., Cambridge. Asst Lectr in French, Univ. of Warwick, 1966–71; Maître-assistante, Univ. of Geneva, 1974–76; Fellow of Trinity Coll., Cambridge (first woman Fellow), 1977–92; Univ. Lectr, Univ. of Cambridge, 1985–92. Visiting Professor: Univ. of Calif, 1990; Johns Hopkins Univ., 1995, 2005; Univ. de Paris, 1997; Harvard Univ., 2007; Eugene Freehling Vis. Prof., Univ. of Michigan, 2006; Occasional Lecturer: Ren Min Univ., Beijing, 1999, 2004; Normal Sch. of Eastern China, Shanghai, 2011; Visitor, Inst. of Advanced Study in Eur. Culture, Jiao-Tong Univ., Shanghai, 2014. Chevalier des palmes académiques (France), 1997. *Publications:* The Object of Art, 1982; Jacques Derrida: opening lines, 1998; (ed with Simon Harvey) Diderot's Lettre sur les aveugles, Lettre sur les sourds et muets, 2000; Diderot and Rousseau: networks of enlightenment, 2011; (ed) Diderot's Le Neveu de Rameau, 2013, 2nd edn 2015. *Address:* 21 Church Lane, Trumpington, Cambridge CB2 9LA.

**HOBSON, Paul;** Director, Modern Art Oxford, since 2013; *b* Wath-upon-Dearne, 18 July 1970; *s* of Alan and Carol Hobson; civil partnership, Stephen Webb. *Educ:* Brasenose Coll., Oxford (MA Modern Hist. 1991); City Univ., London (MA Arts Mgt and Policy 1995); Middlesex Univ. (MA Aesthetics and Contemp. Visual Theory 2003). Researcher, Hayward Gall., S Bank Centre, 1993–94; Develt Manager, ENO, 1994–97; Hd, Royal Acad. Trust, RA, 1997–2000; Hd, Strategy and Develt, Serpentine Gall., 2001; Dir, Private

Arts Foundn, 2002–07; Interim Dir, Showroom Gall., 2007; Dir, Contemporary Art Soc., 2007–13. FRSA. *Publications:* Life is More Important than Art, 2008. *Recreations:* culture, swimming, water polo, contemporary art and dance. *Address:* Modern Art Oxford, 30 Pembroke Street, Oxford OX1 1BP. *T:* (01865) 722733.

**HOCHGREB, Prof. Simone,** PhD; FRAeS; Professor of Engineering, University of Cambridge, since 2002; *b* 24 July 1962; *d* of Osmar Hochgreb and Nilce F. Hochgreb; *m* 1998, Stephen Vandermark; one *d*. *Educ:* Univ. of São Paulo (BSME 1985); Princeton Univ. (PhD 1991). FRAeS 2011. Asst Prof., MIT, 1991–99; Principal Investigator, Sandia Nat. Labs, Calif, 1999–2000; Man. Engr, Exponent, 2000–02. Vis. Prof., Instituto Tecnológico de Aeronáutica, S J Campos, Brazil, 2014–17. Fellow, Combustion Inst. *Publications:* contrib. transactions on combustion and flame. *Address:* Department of Engineering, University of Cambridge, Trumpington Street, Cambridge CB2 1PZ. *E:* sh372@cam.ac.uk.

**HOCHHAUSER, Andrew Romain;** QC 1997; FCIArb; a Recorder, since 2004; a Deputy High Court Judge, since 2013; *b* 16 March 1955; *s* of late Jerome Romain, MD, FRCSE and Ruth Hochhauser. *Educ:* Highgate Sch.; Univ. of Bristol (LLB Hons); London Sch. of Econs (LLM Hons); Courtauld Inst. of Art (MA Hons). FCIArb 1995. Called to the Bar, Middle Temple, 1977 (Harmsworth Scholar), Bencher, 2000 (Dep. Treas. elect, 2019). Part-time Mem., Law Faculty, LSE, 1979–86. Hon. Counsel, Westminster Abbey, 2004–; Vice-Chm., Inns of Ct Coll. of Advocacy, 2016–. Chairman: Dance Umbrella, 2007–14; Paintings in Hosps, 2018– (Vice-Chm., 2013–17). Trustee: V&A Mus., 2011–19; Propeller Theatre Co., 2012–15; Shelter from the Storm, 2014–18; Ensemble Plus Ultra, 2016–; Nat. Aids Trust, 2017–. Governor: Central Sch. of Ballet, 2015–16; Univ. of the Arts London, 2016–; Chm., Ethics Cttee, Courtauld Inst. of Art, 2019. FRSA 2013. *Recreations:* collecting paintings, swimming with sharks, contemporary dance. *Address:* Essex Court Chambers, 24 Lincoln's Inn Fields, WC2A 3EG. *T:* (020) 7813 8000. *Club:* Garrick.

**HOCKÉ, Jean-Pierre;** international consultant; United Nations High Commissioner for Refugees, 1986–89; *b* 31 March 1938; *s* of Charles and Marie Rose Hocké; *m* 1961, Michèle Marie Weber; two *s*. *Educ:* Univ. of Lausanne (grad. Econ. and Business Admin). With commercial firms in Switzerland and Nigeria, 1961–67; joined Internat. Cttee of Red Cross, 1968: Hd of Operations Dept, 1973; Mem., Directorate, 1981. Mem., Jean Monnet Foundn, Lausanne, 1984–2015; Chm., Bd, InterAssist, Bern, 1990–2004; Mem., Bd of Dirs, Africa Humanitarian Action, Addis Abeba, 1994–. Chm., Property Commn refugees and displaced, Bosnia, 1996–2004. Jury Mem., Prix européen de L'essai Charles Veillon, 2000–. Mem., Bd of Dirs, Lemania Gp of Schs, 2007–. Hon. Dr Lausanne, 1987. *Address:* 7 rue de l'Eglise, 1299 Crans-près-Céligny, Switzerland. *T:* (22) 7768404, 793553855. *E:* jphocke@bluewin.ch.

**HOCKENHULL, Lt Gen. James Richard,** OBE 2003; Chief of Defence Intelligence, since 2018; *b* Havant, Hants, 27 July 1964; *s* of William and Jean Hockenhull; *m* 1990, Karen Elizabeth Harrison; two *d*. *Educ:* Royal Hosp. Sch.; Univ. of York (BA Hons Politics); Cranfield Univ. (MA Mil. Studies). Commnd RA and Internat. Corps, 1982; Operational deployments incl. NI, Iraq and Afghanistan; CO Jt Support Gp, NI, 2001–03; Chief G5 (Planning), HQ ARRC, 2007–08; Head: Information Superiority Army HQ, 2009–11; Mil. Strategic Planning, MoD, 2011–13; Dir, Adv. Gp, Kabul, Afghanistan, MoD, 2013–14; Dir, Cyber Intelligence and Inf. Integration, 2015–18. Vis. Fellow, Pembroke Coll., Cambridge. Pres., Army Equitation Assoc. Hon. Col Comdt, Intelligence Corps, 2014–. QCVS 2000; US Bronze Star, 2006; Officer, Legion of Merit (USA), 2017. *Recreations:* recreational ski-ing, agricultural cricket, competitive tennis. *E:* jhockenhull3@gmail.com. *Club:* Philippics Cricket.

**HOCKLEY, (Charles) Dair F.;** *see* Farrar-Hockley.

**HOCKLEY, Rear Adm. Christopher John,** CBE 2014; DL; Chief Executive Officer, MacRobert Trust, since 2014; *b* Orpington, Kent, 24 Aug. 1959; *s* of late Peter William Hockley and of Valerie Joan Hockley; *m* 2005, Kate Elizabeth Henderson; one *s* one *d*, and three step *s*. *Educ:* Dulwich Coll.; Royal Naval Engrg Coll. (BSc Hons; MSc). CMarEng 1988; CEng 1988; FIMarEST 2010. Joined RN, 1977; MEO, HMS Edinburgh, HMS Invincible, 1997–99; Dep. Team Leader, Future Aircraft Carrier Proj., 1999–2002; Mil. Asst to Chief of Defence Procurement, 2002–05; Through Life Support Dir, Defence Logistics Orgn, 2005–07; Naval Base Comdr, HM Naval Base Clyde, and ADC to the Queen, 2007–11; FO Scotland, Northern England and NI, FO Regl Forces and FO Reserves, 2011–14. FCMI 2011. DL Aberdeenshire, 2018. *Recreations:* boating, walking, watching Rugby.

**HOCKMAN, Stephen Alexander;** QC 1990; *b* 4 Jan. 1947; *s* of Nathaniel and Trude Hockman; *m* 1998, Elizabeth St Hill Davies. *Educ:* Eltham Coll.; Jesus Coll., Cambridge (MA). Called to the Bar, Middle Temple, 1970, Bencher, 1996 (Treas., 2015). Leader, SE Circuit, 2000–03. Mem., Apostrophe Chambers, 2011–. Chm., Bar Council, 2006 (Vice-Chm., 2005). *Recreations:* philosophy, politics, the arts. *Address:* 6 Pump Court, Temple, EC4Y 7AR. *T:* (020) 7797 8400.

**HOCKNEY, Damian;** Member, London Assembly, Greater London Authority, 2004–08 (UK Ind, 2004–05; Veritas, 2005; One London, 2005–08). Career in publishing. Vice-Chm., UKIP, 2001–03; Dep. Leader, Veritas, Jan.–July 2005; Leader, One London Party, 2005. Former Mem., Metropolitan Police Authy. Contested (Veritas) Broxtowe, 2005.

**HOCKNEY, David,** OM 2012; CH 1997; RA 1991 (ARA 1985); artist; *b* Bradford, 9 July 1937; *s* of late Kenneth and Laura Hockney. *Educ:* Bradford Grammar Sch.; Bradford Sch. of Art; Royal Coll. of Art. Lecturer: Maidstone Coll. of Art, 1962; Univ. of Iowa, 1964; Univ. of Colorado, 1965; Univ. of California, Los Angeles, 1966, Berkeley, 1967. One-man shows: Kasmin Ltd, London, 1963, 1965, 1966, 1968, 1969, 1970, 1972; Alan Gallery, New York, 1964–67; Museum of Modern Art, NY, 1964–68; Stedelijk Museum, Amsterdam, 1966; Whitworth Gallery, Manchester, 1969; Louvre, Paris, 1974; Galerie Claude Bernard, Paris, 1975 and 1985; Nicholas Wilder, LA, 1976; Galerie Neundorf, Hamburg, 1977; Warehouse Gall., 1979; Knoedler Gall., 1979, 1981, 1982, 1983, 1984, 1986 and 1988; André Emmerich Gall., 1979, 1980, annually 1982–95; Tate, 1986, 1988; Hayward Gall., 1983 and 1985; L. A. Louver, LA, 1986, 1989, 1995, 1998, 2005, 2007, 2009, 2018; Annely Juda, 1997, 2003, 2005, 2006, 2009, 2014, 2015, 2016, 2017; Nat. Portrait Gall., 2003; Royal Acad. of Arts, 1995, 1999, 2002, 2004, 2005, 2007, 2012, 2016; Arts Club of Chicago, 2008; Kunsthalle Würth, Schwäbisch Hall, 2009; PaceWildenstein, NY, 2009; Royal W of England Acad., Bristol, 2010; Guggenheim Mus., Bilbao, Metropolitan Mus. of Art, NY, Getty Centre, LA, Centre Georges Pompidou, Paris, Tate Britain, 2017; PACE Gall., NY, 2018; LA Co. Mus. of Art, 2018; touring show of drawings and prints: Munich, Madrid, Lisbon, Teheran, 1977; USA and Canada, 1978; Tate, 1980; Saltaire, Yorks, New York and LA, 1994; drawing retrospective, Hamburg, London, LA, 1996; Retrospective Exhibitions: Whitechapel Art Gall., 1970; LA County Mus. of Art, Metropolitan Mus. of Art, Tate Gall., 1988–89; Manchester City Art Galls, 1996; Centre Georges Pompidou, Paris, 1999; Bonn Mus., 1999; Mus. of Fine Arts, Boston, LA County Mus. of Art, Nat. Portrait Gall., 2006–07; Nottingham Contemporary, 2009–10; Dulwich Picture Gall., 2014; Early Drawings, Offer Waterman, London, 2015. Exhibitions of photographs: Hayward Gall., 1983; Nat. Mus. of Photography, Film and Television, 1991. 1st Prize, John Moores Exhibn, Liverpool, 1967. Designer: The Rake's Progress, Glyndebourne, 1975, La Scala, 1979; The Magic Flute, Glyndebourne, 1978; L'Enfant et les sortilèges and Nightingale, Double Bill, and Varii Capricci, Covent Garden, 1983; Tristan und Isolde, LA, 1987; Turandot, Chicago, San Francisco, 1990; Die Frau ohne Schatten, Covent Garden, 1992, LA, 1993; designing costumes and sets for Parade and Stravinsky triple bills, Metropolitan Opera House, NY, 1981. Films: A Bigger Splash, 1975; A Day on the Grand Canal with the Emperor of China or surface is illusion but so is depth, 1988; television: Secret Knowledge, 2001; Hockney on Photography, 2011. Hon. DLitt Oxford, 1995; Hon. DFA Yale, 2005. Shakespeare Prize, Hamburg Foundn, 1983; First Prize, Internat. Center of Photography, NY, 1985; Silver Progress Medal, RPS, 1988; Praemium Imperiale, Japan Art Assoc., 1989; Fifth Annual Gov's Award for Visual Arts in California, 1994. *Publications:* (ed and illustrated) 14 Poems of C. P. Cavafy, 1967; (illustrated) Six Fairy Tales of the Brothers Grimm, 1969; 72 Drawings by David Hockney, 1971; David Hockney by David Hockney (autobiog.), 1976; The Blue Guitar, 1977; David Hockney: Travels with Pen, Pencil and Ink: selected prints and drawings 1962–77, 1978; Paper Pools, 1980; (with Stephen Spender) China Diary, 1982; Hockney Paints the Stage, 1983; David Hockney: Cameraworks, 1984 (Kodak Photography Book Award); David Hockney: A Retrospective, 1988; Hockney on Photography (conversations with Paul Joyce), 1988; Hockney's Alphabet, 1991 (ed Stephen Spender); That's the Way I See It (autobiog.), 1993; Hockney on Art: photography, painting and perspective, 1999; Secret Knowledge: rediscovering the lost techniques of the old masters, 2001, 2006; Hockney's Portraits and People, 2003; Hockney's Pictures, 2004; David Hockney Portraits, 2006; (with Martin Gayford) A History of Pictures: from the cave to the computer screen, 2016; (with Martin Gayford) A History of Pictures for Children, 2018. *Address:* c/o 7508 Santa Monica Boulevard, Los Angeles, CA 90046, USA.

**HODDER, Elizabeth;** Commissioner, Equal Opportunities Commission, 1996–2002 (Deputy Chairwoman, 1996–2000); Chairman, Lifespan Healthcare NHS Trust, 2000–02 (non-executive Director, since 1993); *b* 5 Sept. 1942; *er d* of John Scruton and Beryl Haynes, High Wycombe; *m* 1st, 1962, Barry Quirke (marr. diss. 1970); two *d*, 2nd, 1971, Prof. Bramwell Hodder (*d* 2006); three step *s* two step *d*. *Educ:* High Wycombe High Sch.; Queen Mary Coll., Univ. of London. Member: Nat. Consumer Council, 1981–87; Building Societies Ombudsman Council, 1987–; Code of Banking Practice Review Cttee, 1992–2002; Comr and Chm., Consumers' Cttee, Meat and Livestock Commn, 1992–98. Founder and Hon. Pres., Nat. Stepfamily Assoc., 1985–; several positions in local and national organs. *Publications:* The Step-parents' Handbook, 1985; Stepfamilies Talking, 1989; The Book of Old Tarts, 2001. *Recreations:* Italy, cooking, painting, hill-walking. *Address:* 4 Ascham Road, Cambridge CB4 2BD. *T:* (01223) 301086.

**HODDER, Prof. Ian Richard,** CMG 2019; PhD; FBA 1996; Dunlevie Family Professor, School of Humanities and Sciences, Stanford University, since 2002; *b* 23 Nov. 1948; *s* of late Prof. Bramwell William Hodder and Noreen Victoria Hodder; *m* 1st, 1975, Françoise Marguerite Hivernel; two *s*; 2nd, 1987, Christine Ann Hastorf; two *s*. *Educ:* Inst. of Archaeology, London (BA 1971); Peterhouse, Cambridge (PhD 1975). Lectr, Dept of Archaeology, University of Leeds, 1974–77; University of Cambridge: Univ. Asst, then Univ. Lectr, Dept of Archaeology, 1977–90; Reader in Prehistory, 1990–96; Dir, Cambridge Archaeol. Unit, 1990–2000; Fellow of Darwin Coll., 1990–2000; Prof. of Archaeology, 1996–2000; Prof., Dept of Cultural and Social Anthropology, 1999–2001, Co-Dir, Archaeol. Centre, 1999–2002, Stanford Univ. Adjunct Asst Prof. of Anthropology, SUNY, 1984–89; Visiting Professor: Dept of Anthropology, Univ. of Minnesota (and Adjunct Prof.), 1986–93; Van Giffen Inst. for Pre- and Proto-history, Amsterdam, 1980; Univ. of Paris I, Sorbonne, 1985; Fellow: Centre for Advanced Study in Behavioural Scis, Calif, 1987; McDonald Inst., Univ. of Cambridge, 2001–02; Guggenheim Fellow, 2005–06; Hon. Prof., Inst. of Archaeol., UCL. Hon. DSc Bristol, 2009; Hon. Dr Leiden, 2010. *Publications:* Spatial Analysis in Archaeology (with C. Orton), 1976; Symbols in Action, 1982; The Present Past, 1982; Reading the Past, 1986; The Domestication of Europe, 1990; Theory and Practice in Archaeology, 1992; The Archaeological Process, 1999; Archaeology Beyond Dialogue, 2004; The Leopard's Tale, 2006; Entangled: an archaeology of the relationships between humans and things, 2012; Where Are We Heading? The Evolution of Humans and Things, 2018. *Recreations:* music (playing violin and piano), tennis, golf, sailing, travel. *Address:* Department of Anthropology, Stanford University, Stanford, CA 94305–2034, USA.

**HODDINOTT, Rear-Adm. Anthony Paul,** CB 1994; OBE 1979; Chairman, International Legal Assistance Consortium, 2002–11; *b* 28 Jan. 1942; *s* of late Comdr Peter Hoddinott, RN and Marjorie Hoddinott (*née* Kent); *m* 1965, Ellen Ruby, High, Burton; one *s* two *d*. *Educ:* St Michael's, Otford; Bloxham; BRNC Dartmouth. Served HM Ships Chawton, Trump, Dreadnought, Repulse, Porpoise; in Comd, HMS Andrew, 1973–75; Staff of Comdr Third Fleet, USN, 1975–76; in Comd, HMS Revenge, 1976–79; Comdr, Submarine Tactics and Weapons Gp, 1979–81; in Comd, HMS Glasgow, 1981–83 (South Atlantic, 1982); Asst Dir, Naval Warfare, 1983–85; NATO Defence Coll., Rome, 1985; Dep. UK Mil. Rep. to NATO, Brussels, 1986–88; COS (Submarines), 1988–90; Naval Attaché and Comdr, British Naval Staff, Washington, 1990–94, retd. Exec. Dir, Internat. Bar Assoc., 1995–2000. Dir, Warship Preservation Trust, 1995–2006; Trustee, RN Submarine Mus., 1999–08 (Chm., Soc. of Friends, 1999–2014). Liveryman, Fan Makers' Co., 1998– (Mem., Ct of Assistants, 2007–; Master, 2016–17; Chm., Charity Cttee, 2017–). Dir, Bentley Drivers Club, 2013–16 (Chm., Mid-West Reg., 2013–16). *Recreations:* theatre, classic Bentley cars, family, travel. *Address:* 45 Oaklands Road, Petersfield, Hants GU32 2EY.

**HODDLE, Glenn;** Director, Glenn Hoddle Academy, Montecastillo, Spain, 2008–11; First-Team Coach, Queens Park Rangers Football Club, 2014–15; *b* 27 Oct. 1957; *s* of late Derek Hoddle and of Teressa (*née* Roberts); *m* 1979, Christine Anne Stirling (marr. diss. 1999); one *s* two *d*; *m* 2000, Vanessa Shean (marr. diss.). *Educ:* Burnt Mill Sch., Harlow. Professional football player: Tottenham Hotspur, 1976–86 (won FA Cup, 1981, 1982, UEFA Cup, 1984); AS Monaco, 1986–91 (won French Championship, 1988); Player/Manager: Swindon Town, 1991–93; Chelsea, 1993–96; Coach, England Football Team, 1996–99; Manager: Southampton, 2000–01; Tottenham Hotspur, 2001–03; Wolverhampton Wanderers, 2004–06. 53 England caps, 1980–88; represented England in World Cup, Spain, 1982, Mexico, 1986. Regular pundit, Sky TV. *Publications:* Spurred to Success (autobiog.), 1998; (with David Davies) Glenn Hoddle: the World Cup 1998 Story, 1998.

**HODGE, Rt Hon. Lord; Patrick Stewart Hodge;** PC 2013; a Justice of the Supreme Court of the United Kingdom, since 2013; *b* 19 May 1953; *s* of George Mackenzie Hodge and Helen Russell Hodge; *m* 1983, Penelope Jane Wigin; two *s* one *d*. *Educ:* Croftinloan Sch.; Trinity Coll., Glenalmond; Corpus Christi Coll., Cambridge (Scholar, BA; Hon. Fellow, 2014); Edinburgh Univ. (LLB). Scottish Office, 1975–78; admitted Faculty of Advocates, 1983; Standing Junior Counsel: to Dept of Energy, 1989–91; to Inland Revenue in Scotland, 1991–96; QC (Scot.) 1996; a Judge of Courts of Appeal of Jersey and Guernsey, 2000–05; Procurator to Gen. Assembly of Church of Scotland, 2000–05; a Senator of the College of Justice in Scotland, 2005–13. Comr (pt time), Scottish Law Commn,

1997–2003. Bencher, Middle Temple, 2011. Hon. Prof., Stellenbosch Univ., SA, 2014–; Vis. Prof., E China Univ. of Pol Sci. and Law, 2018–. Trustee, David Hume Inst., 2008–13. Gov., Merchiston Castle Sch., Edinburgh, 1998–2012. Hon. LLD Glasgow, 2014. *Publications*: Scotland and the Union, 1994; various legal articles. *Recreations*: opera, ski-ing. *Address*: Supreme Court, Parliament Square, SW1P 3BD. *Club*: Bruntsfield Links Golfing Society.

**HODGE, Sir Andrew (Rowland)**, 3rd Bt *cr* 1921, of Chipstead, Kent; *b* 4 Dec. 1968; *o s* of Sir John Rowland Hodge, 2nd Bt, MBE and of his 4th wife, Vivien Jill, *d* of A. S. Knightley; *S* father, 1995, but his name does not appear on the Official Roll of the Baronetage; *m* 2008, Dr Joyce Inma; one *s*. *Educ*: Stella Maris Coll., Malta; Benjamin Britten High Sch., Suffolk. Estate agent, 1986–91 and 1993–94. *Recreations*: tennis, ski-ing. *Heir*: *s* Aston Rowland Hodge, *b* 10 Sept. 2008.

**HODGE, David Ralph**; QC 1997; **His Honour Judge Hodge**; a Circuit Judge, since 2005; Specialist Chancery Judge, Northern Circuit, since 2005; *b* Prestatyn, 13 July 1956; *er s* of Ralph Noel Hodge, CBE and late Jean Margaret Hodge; *m* 2003, Jane Woosey. *Educ*: St Margaret's, Liverpool; University Coll., Oxford (BA Jurisprudence 1977; BCL 1978). Called to the Bar, Inner Temple, 1979; admitted to Lincoln's Inn, 1980 (Bencher, 2000); in practice at Chancery Bar, 1980–2005; an Asst Recorder, 1998–2000; a Recorder, 2000–05; a Dep. High Ct Judge, 2004–05; nominated Judge: of Ct of Protection (pt-time), 2007–; of Upper Tribunal (Tax and Chancery Chamber) (pt-time), 2013–; of Upper Tribunal (Lands Chamber) (pt-time), 2014–. Member: Council of Circuit Judges, 2007– (Chm., Civil Sub-Cttee, 2017–); Incorporated Council of Law Reporting, 2010–. Chm., Bar Representation Cttee, 1997–98, Jt Chm., Students' Activities Exec. Cttee, 2008–14, Lincoln's Inn. Tutor Judge, Judicial Coll. Specialist Jurisdictions Course, 2010–; Jt Course Dir, Specialist Civil Jurisdictions Course, 2018–. Dep. Chancellor, Dio. of Blackburn, 2016–; Chancellor, Dio. of Oxford, 2019–. Mem., Gen. Synod Legal Adv. Commn, 2016–. *Publications*: contrib. chapter on Chancery Matters to The Law and Practice of Compromise, 4th edn, 1996 to 8th edn 2015; Rectification: the modern law and practice governing claims for rectification for mistake, 2010, 2nd edn 2015; (ed) Atkin's Court Forms titles: on Compromise & Settlements, 2013; on Declaratory Judgements, 2014; on Injunctions, 2014; on Interim Remedies, 2014. *Recreations*: wife, theatre, advocacy training, Shelley. *Address*: c/o Manchester Civil Justice Centre, 1 Bridge Street West, Manchester M60 9DJ. *Clubs*: Garrick; Athenæum (Liverpool).

**HODGE, Douglas**; actor and director; *b* Plymouth, 25 Feb. 1960; *s* of Harry and Christine Hodge; partner, Tessa Peake-Jones; one *s* one *d*. *Educ*: Gillingham Grammar Sch.; Howard Sch., Kent; Royal Acad. of Dramatic Art; Nat. Youth Theatre. Actor: *films* include: Salome's Last Dance, 1988; Diamond Skulls, 1989; The Trial, 1993; Saigon Baby, 1995; Hollow Reed, 1996; Vanity Fair, 2004; Scenes of a Sexual Nature, 2006; The Descent 2, 2009; Robin Hood, 2010; Tulip Fever, 2017; *television* includes: Capital City, 1989–90; Anglo Saxon Attitudes, 1992; Middlemarch, 1994; The Way We Live Now, 2001; Redcap, 2003–04; Mansfield Park, 2007; One Night, 2012; Bert and Dickie, 2012; Secret State, 2012; The Town, 2012; Penny Dreadful, 2015; Falling Water, The Night Manager, 2016; Decline and Fall, 2017; Unforgotten, 2017; *theatre* includes: Moonlight, No Mans Land, 1993, Coriolanus, 1994; Almeida and Comedy; The Collection, The Lover, Donmar Warehouse, 1998; The Caretaker, Comedy, 2000; Three Sisters, Playhouse, 2003; Dumb Show, Royal Court, 2004; Guys and Dolls, Piccadilly, 2005; Titus Andronicus, Shakespeare's Globe, 2006; La Cage aux Folles, Playhouse, 2008 (Best Actor in a Musical: Olivier Awards, 2009; Tony Awards, 2010); Inadmissible Evidence, Donmar Warehouse, 2011; Torch Song Trilogy, Menier, 2012; Charlie and the Chocolate Factory, Th. Royal, 2013; National Theatre: King Lear, 1986; Pericles, Blinded by the Sun, 1994; Betrayal, 1998; A Matter of Life and Death, 2007; Fire and Air, Classic Stage Co., NY, 2018. Director: *film*: Victoria Station, 2003; *theatre*: The Dumb Waiter, Oxford Playhouse, 2004; See How They Run, Duchess, 2006; Absurdia, Donmar, 2008; Last Easter, Birmingham Rep., 2008; Dimetos, Donmar Warehouse, 2009; Cyrano de Bergerac, NY, 2012; writer and director: Pacha Mama's Blessing, Almeida, 1989. Singer and songwriter; albums: Cowley Road Songs, 2005; Nightbus, 2019. Associate Dir, Donmar Th., 2007–09. Mem. Council, NYT, 1986–2006. *Recreations*: dive master, black belt karate. *Address*: c/o Lindy King, United Agents, 12–26 Lexington Street, W1F 0LE. *Club*: Soho House.

**HODGE, Sir James (William)**, KCVO 1996; CMG 1996; HM Diplomatic Service, retired; Chairman, Society of Pension Professionals (formerly Consultants), 2007–19; *b* 24 Dec. 1943; *s* of late William Hodge and Catherine Hodge (*née* Carden); *m* 1970, Frances Margaret, *d* of late Michael Coyne and of Teresa Coyne (*née* Walsh); three *d*. *Educ*: Holy Cross Academy, Edinburgh; Univ. of Edinburgh (MA (Hons) English Lang. and Lit.). Commonwealth Office, 1966; Third Secretary, Tokyo, 1967; Second Secretary (Information), Tokyo, 1970; FCO, 1972; First Sec. (Development, later Chancery), Lagos, 1975; FCO, 1978; First Sec. (Economic), 1981, Counsellor (Commercial), 1982, Tokyo; Counsellor: Copenhagen, 1986; FCO, 1990; RCDS, 1994; Minister, British Embassy, Peking, 1995–96; Ambassador to Thailand and (non-resident) to Lao People's Democratic Republic, 1996–2000; Consul-General, Hong Kong and (non-resident) Macao, 2000–03. MCIL 1990. FRSA 2009. Hon. DLitt Ulster, 2003; Hon. LLD Liverpool, 2004. Kt Grand Cross (1st cl.), Order of the White Elephant (Thailand), 1996. *Recreations*: books, music. *Clubs*: Oriental, MCC; Royal Scots (Edinburgh); Foreign Correspondents' (Hong Kong); Jockey (Macau).

**HODGE, John Dennis**; President, J. D. Hodge & Co., International Management and Aerospace Consultants, 1987–2003; *b* 10 Feb. 1929; *s* of John Charles Henry Hodge and Emily M. Corbett Hodge; *m* 1952, Audrey Cox; two *s* two *d*. *Educ*: Northampton Engineering Coll., University of London (now City Univ.). Vickers-Armstrong Ltd, Weybridge, England (Aerodynamics Dept), 1950–52; Head, Air Loads Section, Avro Aircraft Ltd, Toronto, Canada, 1952–59; Tech. Asst to Chief, Ops Div., Space Task Group, NASA, Langley Field, Va, USA, 1959; Chief, Flight Control Br., Space Task Group, NASA, 1961; Asst Chief of Flight Control, 1962, Chief, Flight Control Div., Flight Ops Directorate, NASA, MSC, 1963–68; Manager, Advanced Missions Program, NASA, Manned Spacecraft Centre, 1968–70; Dir, Transport Systems Concepts, Transport Systems Center, 1970; Vice-Pres., R&D, The Ontario Transportation Develt Corp., 1974–76; Department of Transportation, Washington, 1976–82; Chief, R&D Plans and Programs Analysis Div., 1976–77; Actg Dir, Office of Policy, Plans and Admin, 1977–79; Associate Administrator, for Policy, Plans and Program Management, Res. and Special programs Admin, 1979–82; Dir, Space Station Task Force, NASA, Washington, 1982–84; Dep. Associate Administrator for Space Station, NASA, Washington, 1984–85, Actg Associate Administrator, 1985–86. FAIAA 1991. Hon. ScD City Univ., London, Eng., 1966. NASA Medal for Exceptional Service, 1967 and 1969; Dept of Transportation Meritorious Achievement Award, 1974; Special Achievement Award, 1979; Presidential Rank Award of Meritorious Executive, NASA, 1985. *Publications*: contribs to NASA publications and various aerospace jls. *Recreations*: reading, golf. *Address*: 1951 Sagewood Lane #224, Reston, VA 20191–5412, USA.

**HODGE, Rt Hon. Dame Margaret (Eve)**, DBE 2015 (MBE 1978); PC 2003; MP (Lab) Barking, since June 1994; *b* 8 Sept. 1944; *d* of late Hans and Lisbeth Oppenheimer; *m* 1st, 1968, Andrew Watson (marr. diss. 1978); one *s* one *d*; 2nd, 1978, Henry Egar Garfield Hodge (later Hon. Sir Henry Hodge, OBE) (*d* 2009); two *d*. *Educ*: Bromley High Sch.; Oxford High Sch.; LSE (BSc Econ 1966). Teaching and internat. market research, 1966–73. London Borough of Islington: Councillor, 1973–94; Chair of Housing, 1975–79; Dep. Leader, 1981; Leader, 1982–92. Chair: Assoc. of London Authorities, 1984–92; London Res. Centre, 1985–92; Vice-Chair, AMA, 1991–92. Member: HO Adv. Cttee on Race Relations, 1988–92; Local Govt Commn, 1993–94; Board, Central and Inner London North TEC, 1990–92; Labour Party Local Govt Cttee, 1983–92. Parly Under-Sec. of State, DfEE, 1998–2001; Minister of State, DFES, 2001–05; Minister of State: (Minister for Employment and Welfare Reform (formerly for Work), DWP, 2005–06; DTI, 2006–07; DCMS, 2007–08 and 2009–10. Chair: Educn Select Cttee, H of C, 1997–98; Public Accounts Select Cttee, 2010–15; London Gp of Labour MPs, 1996–98; All Party Parly Gp on Responsible Taxation, 2015–; former mem., govt and local govt bodies. Sen. Consultant, Price Waterhouse, 1992–94. Director: London First, 1992; (non-exec.) UCH and Middlesex Hosp., 1992–94; Mem. Bd, Westminster Foundn for Democracy, 2015–; Trustee and Mem. Bd, Social Market Foundn, 2018–; Co-Chair, Govern Up, 2015–. Chair: Circle 33 Housing Trust, 1993–96; Fabian Soc., 1997–98; Th. Royal Stratford East, 2016–. Gov., LSE, 1990–99; Mem. Council, Univ. of London, 1994–98; Chair, Council, Royal Holloway, Univ. of London, 2018–. Vis. Prof., Public Policy Unit, KCL, 2015–; Vis. Fellow, Blavatnik Sch. of Govt, Univ. of Oxford, 2016–18. Mem., Editl Bd, Political Qly, 2016–. Hon. Fellow, Polytechnic of North London. Hon. DCL City, 1993; DUniv South Wales, 2014. Freeman, City of London, 2013. *Publications*: Quality, Equality and Democracy, 1991; Beyond the Town Hall, 1994; Elected Mayors and Democracy, 1997; Called To Account, 2016 (Best Non-fiction Book, Parliamentary Awards, 2016); contribs to numerous jls and newspapers. *Recreations*: family, opera, piano, travel, cooking. *Address*: c/o House of Commons, SW1A 0AA.

**HODGE, Michael**, MBE 1975; HM Diplomatic Service, retired; *b* 12 June 1944; *s* of late Howard Jack Hodge and Iris Amy Hodge (*née* Treasure); *m* 1966, Wilhelmina Marjorie Glover; one *s* one *d*. *Educ*: Cotham Grammar Sch., Bristol. With Prison Commn, 1961–62; joined HM Diplomatic Service, 1962: FO, 1962–65; Third Sec., Belgrade, 1965–67; Commercial Officer, Paris, 1968–70; Third, later Second, Sec., Bahrain Residency, 1970–72; Second Secretary: (Information), Kaduna, 1972–73; (Commercial), Kampala, 1973–74; FCO, 1974–78; First Sec. (Econ.), Copenhagen, 1978–82; FCO, 1983–87; on loan to ICI Agrochemicals, 1987–89; First Sec. (Commercial), Paris, 1989–92; Head, Services Planning and Resources Dept, FCO, 1992–96; Consul Gen., Chicago, 1996–99. Chm., Battle Meml Hall, 2001–05. Pres., Rotary Club of Battle, 2004–05, 2010–11, 2015–16. Chm., Treasure Hse Educnl Support, 2012–16. Paul Harris Fellow, 2005. Kt, First Class, Order of Dannebrog (Denmark), 1978. *Recreations*: music, organising events, travel, steam railways. *Club*: Royal Over-Seas League.

**HODGE, Michael John Davy V.**; *see* Vere-Hodge.

**HODGE, Patricia**, OBE 2017; actress; *b* 29 Sept. 1946; *d* of Eric and Marion Hodge; *m* 1976, Peter Owen (*d* 2016); two *s*. *Educ*: Wintringham Girls' Grammar Sch., Grimsby; St Helen's Sch., Northwood, Middx; Maria Grey Coll., Twickenham; London Acad. of Music and Dramatic Art. Theatre début, No-one Was Saved, Traverse, Edinburgh, 1971; *West End theatre* includes: Popkiss, Globe, 1972; Two Gentlemen of Verona (musical), 1973; Pippin, Her Majesty's, 1973; Hair, Queen's, 1974; The Mitford Girls, Globe, 1981 (transf. from Chichester); Benefactors, Vaudeville, 1984; Noël and Gertie, Comedy, 1989–90; Shades, Albery, 1992; Separate Tables, Albery, 1993; The Prime of Miss Jean Brodie, Strand, 1994; A Day in the Death of Joe Egg, Trafalgar Studios, 2019; National Theatre: A Little Night Music, 1995; Money (Best Supporting Actress, Laurence Olivier Awards, 2000); Summerfolk, 1999; Noises Off, 2000; His Dark Materials, 2003; The Country Wife, Th. Royal, 2007; Calendar Girls, Noel Coward, 2009; *other appearances* include: The Beggar's Opera, Nottingham Playhouse, 1975; Pal Joey, and Look Back In Anger, Oxford Playhouse, 1976; Then and Now, Hampstead, 1979; As You Like It, Chichester Fest., 1983; Lady in the Dark, Edinburgh Fest., 1988; Heartbreak House, Almeida, 1997; The Clean House, Crucible Th., Sheffield, 2006, and nat. tour, 2008; Calendar Girls, UK tour, 2008; The Breath of Life, Lyceum, Sheffield, 2011; Dandy Dick, nat. tour, 2012; Relative Values, Th. Royal, Bath, 2013, transf. Harold Pinter Th., 2014; Travels With My Aunt, Chichester Fest., 2016; Copenhagen, Chichester Fest., 2018; *television plays and films* include: The Girls of Slender Means, 1975; The Naked Civil Servant, 1975; Hay Fever, 1984; The Death of the Heart, 1985; Hotel du Lac, 1986; Heat of the Day, 1988; The Shell Seekers, 1989; The Secret Life of Ian Fleming, 1989; The Moonstone, 1997; The Falklands Play, 2002; Marple: The Sittaford Mystery, 2006; Maxwell, 2007; *television series and serials* include: Rumpole of the Bailey, 7 series, 1978–90; Edward and Mrs Simpson, 1978; Holding the Fort, 3 series, 1979–82; The Other 'Arf, 1979–80, 1981; Nanny, 1980; Jemima Shore Investigates, 1982; The Life and Loves of a She-Devil, 1986; Rich Tea and Sympathy, 1991; The Cloning of Joanna May, 1992; The Legacy of Reginald Perrin, 1996; Sweet Medicine, 2003; Miranda, 3 series, 2009–14; Downton Abbey, 2015; A Very English Scandal, 2018; Four Weddings and a Funeral, 2019; *films* include: Betrayal, 1983; The Leading Man, 1996; Jilting Joe, 1997; Before You Go, 2002; Surviving Christmas with the Relatives, 2018. Hon. DLitt: Hull, 1996; Brunel, 2001; Leicester, 2003. Female Performer of the Year, Spoken Word Awards, 2003. *Address*: c/o Paul Lyon-Maris, Independent Talent Group Ltd, 40 Whitfield Street, W1T 2RH. *T*: (020) 7636 6565.

**HODGE, Patrick Stewart**; *see* Hodge, Rt Hon. Lord.

**HODGE-DALLAWAY, Simeilia**; Founder, Artistic Director and Chief Executive Officer, Artistic Directors of the Future, since 2014; *b* London, 3 Feb. 1983; *d* of Steve Dallaway and Charmaine Miller; partner, Reginald Edmund McKamie, Jr. *Educ*: Univ. of Roehampton (BA Drama and Th. Studies 2004). Administrator and Producer, Kali Th. Co., 2004–06; trained as theatre director, Young Vic and NT, 2006–08; Project Manager, Black Play Archive, RNT, 2008–10; teacher in secondary schs, E London and Essex; Project Asst, Open Stage initiative, Theatre Royal Stratford East, 2012–13; Co-Founder, Exec. Dir and Creative Producer, Black Lives, Black Words Internat. Project, 2014–16; Founder, Artistic Dir and CEO, Beyond the Canon Ltd, 2016–. Trustee, Dirs Guild of GB, 2017–19. *Publications*: (ed) The Oberon Book of Monologues for Black Actors: classical and contemporary speeches from Black British plays, Vol. 1, 2013; (ed) Audition Speeches for Black, South Asian and Middle Eastern Actors, 2016; (ed) Artistic Directors of the Future Talks Brexit, 2018. *Recreations*: theatre, art exhibitions, travelling, family, dance, cinema, reading. *Address*: Flat 44, Sapphire Court, 15 Warton Road, E15 2GF. *T*: 07984 642547. *E*: sim@adofthefuture.com.

**HODGES, Prof. John Russell**, MD; FRCP, FMedSci; Professor of Cognitive Neurology, University of Sydney, since 2016; *b* 7 Jan. 1952; *s* of Edward and Gwen Hodges; *m* 1952, Dr Carol Ann Gregory; two *s* one *d*. *Educ*: Kingsbridge Sch.; Royal London Hosp. Med. Sch. (MB BS Hons 1975, MD 1988). MRCP 1977, FRCP 1993. Lectr in Medicine, Southampton Univ., 1980–82; Registrar in Neurology, Radcliffe Infirmary, Oxford,

1982–85; MRC Res. Fellow, 1985–86; Lectr in Clinical Neurol., Radcliffe Infirmary, Oxford, 1986–90; MRC Travelling Fellow, UCSD, 1988–89; Lectr, Univ. of Cambridge, 1990–97; MRC Prof. of Behavioural Neurol., Univ. of Cambridge, 1997–2007; Principal Res. Fellow and Federation Fellow, Nat. Health and Med. Res. Council, Australia, 2007–16; Prof. of Cognitive Neurol., Univ. of NSW, then UNSW Australia, 2007–16. Dir, Alzheimer's Res. Trust Centre, Cambridge, 1998. Chm., British Neuropsychiatric Assoc., 1982–2001; Pres., Res. Gp on Aphasia, World Fedn of Neurol., 1998–. FMedSci 2002. *Publications:* Transient Amnesia, 1991; Cognitive Assessment for Clinicians, 1994; Memory Disorders in Psychiatric Practice, 2000; Early Onset Dementia: a multidisciplinary approach, 2001; contrib. numerous scientific papers to learned jls. *Recreations:* playing the saxophone, cinema, literature, fishing. *Address:* Brain and Mind Centre, University of Sydney, NSW 2006, Australia.

**HODGES, John William,** CMG 2003; CEng, FICE; development infrastructure consultant, 2003–19; *b* 14 Nov. 1942; *s* of John Henry Hodges and Lilian Elizabeth Hodges; *m* 1962, Barbara Park; two *s* (and one *s* decd). *Educ:* Shoreditch Comprehensive Sch.; Brixton Sch. of Building; Westminster Coll. CEng 1968; FICE 1983. Exec. Engr, Govt of Zambia, 1965–68; Engr, UK Transport Res. Labs, 1969–73; Overseas Development Administration: Engrg Advr, 1974–84; Sen. Engrg Advr, 1985–86; Head: Pacific, 1987–89; Contracts, 1990–93; Chief Engrg Advr, 1994–2002. *Recreation:* restoration and rallying of classic cars.

**HODGES, Lew;** not for profit consultant; *b* 29 Feb. 1956. *Educ:* University Coll. London (BA (Hons) Classics); MBA London Business Sch., 1990. Chartered Accountant 1981. Subsidy Officer, then Asst Dir of Finance, Arts Council, 1981–87; Head of Finance, CNAA, 1987–89; Finance Dir, Arts Council of GB, subseq. of England, 1989–96; Dir, Corporate Services, Sports Council, 1996–97; Hd of Finance, RNT, 1997–2000; Dir of Finance and Mgt Resources, London Arts, 2000–01; Dir of Finance and Planning, Arts & Business, 2001–05; Chief Operating Officer (formerly Dir of Finance and Resources), Leadership Foundn, 2006–16; Chief Operating Officer, ACEVO, 2016–17. Mem., Inner London Probation Cttee, 1996–2001. Board Member: LAMDA, 2002–07; English Touring Th., 2002–11; Greenwich Fest., 2002–06; Artsadmin, 2002–13; Space, 2007–13; Nat. Youth Jazz Coll., 2009–; Wac Arts, 2014–; Protein, 2014–; Guildhall Sch. Trust, 2018–.

**HODGES, Nicholas Rudy;** Chief Executive Officer, London International Group plc, 1993–99; *b* 26 Aug. 1939; *s* of Edward William Hodges and Gwendoline Winifred Hayward (*née* Golding); *m* 1st, 1959, Valerie Joyce Dyke (marr. diss. 1988; now Hedges); one *s* two *d*; 2nd, 1988, Christine Winifred Mary Dodd. *Educ:* Colchester Royal Grammar Sch. Salesman and Mktg, Nestlé Ltd, 1961–63; Kimberley Clark Ltd: Salesman, 1963–65; Product and Mktg Manager, 1965–67; Area Manager, 1967–69; Regl Manager, 1969–72; Regl Manager, Golden Wonder Ltd, 1972–74; Sales Dir, Johnson & Johnson Consumer, 1974–80; Man. Dir, Sangers, 1980–82; London International Group: Sales/Mktg Dir, 1982–88; World Wide Mkt Dir, Hosp. Products, 1988–90; European Man. Dir, 1990–93. Sen. non-exec. Dir and Dep. Chm., Taylor-Nelson Sofres, 1998–2002. Liveryman: Glovers' Co., 1986–2013; Co. of World Traders, 1989–2017 (Mem. Court, 1999–2003). MCIM (MInstM 1972). *Recreations:* good food and wine, golf, fishing, horse racing. *Address:* PO Box 307, Applecross, WA 6953, Australia. *Clubs:* Royal Dornoch Golf, Burnham Beeches Golf.

**HODGES, Paula;** QC 2014; Partner, Herbert Smith Freehills (formerly Herbert Smith) LLP, since 1996; *b* Swansea, 20 Feb. 1965; *d* of Colin and Ann Hodges; *m* 2010, John Balsdon; three *c*. *Educ:* Olchfa Comprehensive Sch., Swansea; Girton Coll., Cambridge (BA Law 1986). Admitted solicitor, 1989; trainee solicitor, 1987–89, Asst Solicitor, 1989–96, Herbert Smith LLP. Pres., London Ct of Internat. Arbitration, 2019–. *Publications:* (contrib.) Liquefied Natural Gas: the law and business, 2006, 2nd edn 2012; (contrib.) Arbitration in England, 2013. *Recreations:* family, Chelsea Football Club, music, pilates, travel, French burgundy. *Address:* Herbert Smith Freehills LLP, Exchange House, Primrose Street, EC2A 2EG. *T:* (020) 7374 8000, *Fax:* (020) 7374 0888. *E:* paula.hodges@hsf.com.

**HODGES, Prof. Richard Andrew,** OBE 1995; PhD; FSA 1984; President, American University of Rome, since 2012; *b* 29 Sept. 1952; *s* of Roy Clarence Hodges and Joan (*née* Hartnell); *m* 1st, 1976, Deborah Peters (marr. diss. 1998); one *s* one *d*; 2nd, 2008, Kim Bowes; one *s*. *Educ:* City of Bath Boys' Sch.; Univ. of Southampton (BA, PhD). Sheffield University: Lectr in Prehistory and Archaeology, 1976–86; Sen. Lectr, 1986–93; Prof., 1993–95; Prof. of Visual Arts and Dir, Inst. of World Archaeology, Sch. of World Arts and Museology, UEA, 1995. Leverhulme Res. Fellow, 1980, Dir, 1988–95 (on secondment), British Sch. at Rome; Director: Prince of Wales's Inst. of Architecture, 1996–98; Univ. of Pennsylvania Mus., Philadelphia, 2007–12. Special Advr to Minister of Culture, Albania, 1999; Mem. Bd, Packard Humanities Inst., 2003– (Advr to proj., Albania, 2000–06). Visiting Professor: in Medieval Studies, SUNY-Birmingham, 1983; in Medieval Archaeology, Siena Univ., 1984–87; in Archaeology, Copenhagen Univ., 1987–88; Sheffield Univ., 2006–09; Charles Eliot Norton Lectr, Amer. Inst. of Archaeology, 2005; Dalrymple Lectr, Univ. of Glasgow, 2009. Director: Roystone Grange landscape project, Derbyshire, 1978–88; San Vincenzo excavations, S Italy, 1980–98; co-director: Sheffield-Siena archaeological project, Montarrenti, Tuscany, 1982–87; Butrint excavations, Albania, 1994–2012; San Pietro d'Asso excavations, Tuscany, 2010. Scientific Dir, Butrint Foundn, 1995–2012; Principal Investigator, Colline Metalifere project, Tuscany, for Eur. Res. Council and Siena Univ., 2015–. Pres., LoveItaly!, 2015–. *Publications:* Walks in the Cotswolds, 1976; The Hamwih Pottery, 1981; (with G. Barker) Archaeology and Italian Society, 1981; Dark Age Economics, 1982, 2nd edn 1989; (with P. Davey) Ceramics and trade, 1983; (with D. Whitehouse) Mohammed, Charlemagne and the origins of Europe, 1983; (with John Mitchell) San Vincenzo al Volturno, 1985; Primitive and Peasant Markets, 1988; (with B. Hobley) Rebirth of the town in the West, 1988; The Anglo-Saxon Achievement, 1989; Wall to Wall History, 1991 (British Archaeological Book of the Year, 1992); (with K. Smith) Recent Developments in the Archaeology of the Peak District, 1991; (ed) San Vincenzo 1, 1993; (ed) San Vincenzo 2, 1995; (with J. Mitchell) La Basilica di Iosue a San Vincenzo al Volturno, 1995; Light in the Dark Ages, 1997; (with W. Bowden) The Sixth Century, 1998; Towns and Trade in the Age of Charlemagne, 2000; Visions of Rome: Thomas Ashby, archaeologist, 2000; (with R. Francovich) Villa to Village, 2003; (with W. Bowden and K. Lake) Byzantine Butrint, 2004; Goodbye to the Vikings?, 2006; (with L. Bejko) Eternal Butrint, 2006; New Directions in Albanian Archaeology, 2006; (with K. Bowes and K. Francis) Between Text and Territory, 2006; (with I. Hansen) Roman Butrint, 2006; The Rise and Fall of Byzantine Butrint, 2008; (with W. Bowden) Butrint 3: excavations at the Triconch Palace, 2011; (with S. Leppard and J. Mitchell) San Vincenzo Maggiore and its Workshops, 2011; Dark Age Economics: a new audit, 2012; (jtly) Butrint 4: the archaeology and histories of an Ionian town, 2012; (with S. Gelichi) From One Sea to Another, 2012; (with S. Gelichi) New Directions in Early Medieval European Archaeology, 2015; The Archaeology of Mediterranean Placemaking, 2016; Travels with an Archaeologist, 2017; (with G. Bianchi) Origins of a New Economic Union (7th–12th centuries). *Recreations:* hill walking, music, watching cricket. *Address:* American University of Rome, Via Pietro Roselli 4, 00153 Rome, Italy.

**HODGES, Dr Wilfrid Augustine,** FBA 2009; Professor of Mathematics, 1987–2006, Professorial Fellow, 2006–08, Queen Mary, University of London (formerly Queen Mary College, then Queen Mary and Westfield College); *b* Reading, 27 May 1941; *s* of Herbert Arthur Hodges and Vera Joan Hodges (*née* Willis); *m* 1965, Helen Marcia Hurst Ward; one *s* two *d*. *Educ:* King's Sch., Canterbury; New Coll., Oxford (BA 1965; DPhil 1970). Actg Asst Prof. of Philosophy, UCLA, 1967–68; University of London: Bedford College, 1968–84, Queen Mary College, then Queen Mary and Westfield College, later Queen Mary, 1984–2008: Lectr, in Philosophy and Maths, 1968–74, in Maths, 1974–81; Reader in Mathematical Logic, 1981–87. Vis. Associate Prof. of Maths, Univ. of Colo at Boulder, 1979–80. President: British Logic Colloquium, 1990–95; Eur. Assoc. for Logic, Lang. and Information, 1995–96; Internat. Union of Hist. and Philosophy of Sci., 2010–11 (Pres., Div. of Logic, Methodology and Philosophy of Sci., 2008–11). *Publications:* Logic, 1977, 2nd edn 2001; Building Models by Games, 1985; Model Theory, 1993; A Shorter Model Theory, 1997; (with I. Chiswell) Mathematical Logic, 2007; contrib. articles to mathematical and logical jls. *Recreations:* piano, Dartmoor. *Address:* Herons Brook, Sticklepath, Okehampton, Devon EX20 2PY. *T:* (01837) 840154. *E:* wilfrid.hodges@btinternet.com.

**HODGKIN, Prof. Jonathan Alan,** PhD; FRS 1990; Professor of Genetics, Oxford University, 2000–16, now Emeritus; Fellow of Keble College, Oxford, 2000–16, now Emeritus; *b* 24 Aug. 1949; *s* of Sir Alan Hodgkin, OM, KBE, FRS and of Marion Hodgkin, *d* of late F. P. Rous; *m* 2005, Patricia Etsuko Kuwabara. *Educ:* Bryanston Sch., Dorset; Merton Coll., Oxford (BA; Hon. Fellow, 2001); Darwin Coll., Cambridge (PhD). SRC Res. Fellowship, 1974–76; Staff Scientist, MRC Lab. of Molecular Biology, 1977–2000; Associate Hd, Dept of Biochem., Univ. of Oxford, 2005–17. Vis. Prof., Univ. of Wisconsin, 1990. Mem., EMBO, 1989. *Publications:* contribs to scientific jls. *Recreations:* archaeology, cooking, cinema. *Address:* 82a Lonsdale Road, Oxford OX2 7ER. *T:* (01865) 552340.

**HODGKIN, Mark William Backhouse;** Director, Bury Street Capital Ltd, since 2005; *b* 26 Jan. 1949; *s* of David Kenneth and Brigit Louise Hodgkin; *m* 1978, Madeleine Alison Newton; three *d*. *Educ:* Australian National Univ. (BEc). A. Fifer Ltd, 1972–74; Laurence Prust & Co., 1974–76; Man. Dir, Rivkin & Co. (Overseas), 1976–92; Vice Pres., Bankers Trust, 1992–93; Man. Dir, West Merchant Bank (WestLB Gp), 1993–98; Chief Exec., Panmure Gordon, subseq. WestLB Panmure, Ltd, 1996–2000; CEO, Compass Capital Ltd, 2001–03; Chief Operating Officer, Cross Asset Mgt Ltd, 2003–05. Dir, Hawkesbury Capital Mgt Pte Ltd, 2005–11. *Recreations:* sailing, theatre, opera.

**HODGKINS, Christopher Ian;** jazz trumpet player, band leader, composer, music business educator and broadcaster; Owner, Bell CDs, since 2004; *b* Westcliff-on-Sea, 16 Aug. 1950; *s* of William and Lucy Hodgkins; *m* 1996, Mary Patterson; one *s*. *Educ:* Ealing Coll. of Further Educn (HND Business and Finance 1985); London Mgt Centre, Poly. of Central London (MBA 1990). DipM 1991; FCIM 2005. Professional musician, 1968–; Dir, Welsh Jazz Fest., 1974–81; Administrator, Welsh Jazz Soc., 1978–81; Dir, Jazz Services Ltd, 1985–2014. Chm., Nat. Jazz Archive, 2005–14. Secretariat, All Pty Parly Jazz Appreciation Gp, 2006–. Member: Concert Artistes Assoc., London; Cullercoats Crescent Club and Inst. *Recreations:* jazz, music, reading, walking, writing, book collecting, trumpet playing. *Address:* 41 Bedford Road, West Ealing, W13 0SP. *T:* (020) 8840 4643. *E:* chris.hodgkins3@googlemail.com.

**HODGKINSON, Sir Michael Stewart,** Kt 2003; Chairman, Keolis UK Ltd, since 2011; *b* 7 April 1944; *s* of Stewart Gordon Hodgkinson and Ruth Phyllis Hodgkinson; *m* 1988, Elspeth Holman; one *s* two *d*. *Educ:* Nottingham Univ. (BA Hons Industrial Econs). ACMA 1969. Finance: Ford of Europe, 1965–69; British Leyland, 1969–75; Finance and Admin. Dir, Leyland Cars Engrg, 1975–78; Man. Dir, Land Rover Ltd, 1978–83; Gp Dir, Watney Mann & Truman Brewers, 1983–85; Dep. Chief Exec., Express Dairies, 1985–89; Chief Exec., Grand Metropolitan Foods, Europe, 1989–92; Gp Airports Dir, 1992–99, Chief Exec., 1999–2003, BAA plc. Chairman: Post Office, 2003–07; First Choice plc, 2004–07; Dep. Chm., TUI Travel plc, 2007–; non-executive Director: Royal Mail, 2003–07; Dublin Airport Authy plc, 2004–11; Crossrail Ltd, 2009–12. Mem. Bd, Transport for London, 2000–12. *Recreations:* golf, theatre, travel.

**HODGKINSON, Neil Robert;** Editor-in-Chief, Reach plc (formerly Trinity Mirror) North East, Humber and Lincoln, since 2018 (Editor-in-Chief, Humber and Lincoln, Trinity Mirror plc, 2016–18); Editor, Hull Daily Mail, since 2011; *b* 28 May 1960; *s* of Robert Hodgkinson and Faith Hodgkinson; *m* 1st, 1984, Jacqueline Dawn Proctor; 2nd, 1993, Christine Elizabeth Talbot; 3rd, 2006, Emma Louise Schofield; one *s*. *Educ:* Baines Grammar Sch., Poulton-le-Fylde; Central Lancashire Poly. (Dip. Journalism). Trainee journalist to Dep. News Editor, W Lancs Evening Gazette, 1979–87; News Editor, then Dep. Editor, Lancs Evening Post, 1987–92; Dep. Ed., Yorkshire Evening Post, 1992–96; Editor, Lancs Evening Post, 1996–99; Editor and Dir, Yorkshire Evening Post, 1999–2006; Editl Dir, Cumbrian Newspapers Ltd, 2006–11. *Recreation:* Rugby Union youth coach. *Address:* Hull Daily Mail, Blundells Corner, Beverley Road, Hull HU3 1XS. *T:* (01482) 315250.

**HODGSON,** family name of **Baroness Hodgson of Abinger** and **Baron Hodgson of Astley Abbotts**.

**HODGSON OF ABINGER,** Baroness *cr* 2013 (Life Peer), of Abinger in the County of Surrey; **Fiona Ferelith Hodgson,** CBE 2012; *d* of Keith Storr Allom and Jean Ferelith Maxwell Robertson; *m* 1982, Robin Granville Hodgson (*see* Baron Hodgson of Astley Abbotts); three *s* one *d* (and one twin *s* decd). *Educ:* Queen Anne's Sch., Caversham; Guildford High Sch. Res. Exec., Reader's Digest Assoc. Ltd, 1980–83; Director: Johnson Bros & Co. Ltd, 1989–; Johnson Bros Design, 1991–2006. Non-exec. Dir, Barnet DHA, 1992–94. Mem. Bd, Cons. Party, 2009–12; Pres., Nat. Cons. Convention, 2013 (Vice Pres., 2009–11); Hon. Vice Pres., Cons. Women's Orgn (Dep. Chm., 2002–05; Chm., 2005–08; Pres., 2008–11); Chm., Cons. Party Conf., 2011. Cons. Party Whip, 2014–17. Co-Chm., All-Party Parly Gp on Women, Peace and Security, 2014–. Mem., Armed Forces Parly Scheme, 2014–. Member: Farm Animal Welfare Council, 1989–97; Gen. Council and Appeals Cttee, Wellbeing, 1993–2006; Adv. Cttee on Animal Foodstuffs, Food Standards Agency, 2001–04; Council of Internat. Social Services UK, 2003–04; Indep. Health Forum, 2003–04; Indep. Sector Working Gp on licensing and revalidation of private doctors, 2006–09; Indep. Sector Assessment and Adv. Cttee, Indep. Doctors Fedn, 2010–14; Women's Justice Taskforce, Prison Reform Trust, 2010–15; Steering Bd, Foreign Sec.'s Initiative on Preventing Sexual Violence, 2012–; Select Cttee on Sexual Violence, 2015–16; Select Cttee on the Rural Economy, 2017–18. Chairman: Adv. Bd, Gender Action for Peace Security, 2009–; Governance Bd, Indep. Sector Complaints and Adjudication Service, 2012–. Member: European Union of Women, 2006–18; UN Women UK, 2009–16; Cons. Human Rights Commn, 2009–; Assoc. of Oxfam, 2009–15. Trustee, Chalker Foundn, 2010–. Patron: Afghan Connection, 2011–; Cons. Friends of Internat. Develt, 2012–. Student, RCDS, 2017–18. FRGS 2011. *Recreations:* travel, riding, walking, reading, cookery. *Address:* House of Lords, SW1A 0PW. *T:* (020) 7219 3000.

**HODGSON OF ASTLEY ABBOTTS,** Baron *cr* 2000 (Life Peer), of Nash in the co. of Shropshire; **Robin Granville Hodgson,** CBE 1992; Chairman, Johnson Bros & Co. Ltd, Walsall, since 1989 (Director, since 1970); *b* 25 April 1942; *s* of late Henry Edward and Natalie Beatrice Hodgson; *m* 1982, Fiona Ferelith Allom (*see* Baroness Hodgson of Abinger); three *s* one *d* (and one twin *s* decd). *Educ:* Shrewsbury Sch.; Oxford Univ. (BA Hons 1964); Wharton Sch. of Finance, Univ. of Pennsylvania (MBA 1969). Investment Banker, New York and Montreal, 1964–67; Industry in Birmingham, England, 1969–72; Gp Chief Exec., 1979–95, Chm., 1995–2002, Granville plc, then Granville Baird Ltd; Chairman: Rostrum Gp Ltd, 2000–07; Nova Capital Mgt Ltd, 2002–; Carbo plc, 2002–05; RFIB Group Ltd, 2007–15; Tenet Gp Ltd, 2007–12; EIS Optics Ltd (formerly Telescope Holdco), 2009–11; Cash Management Systems Ltd, 2014–; CMS Payments Intelligence Ltd, 2014–; Director: Community Hospitals plc, 1982–83 and 1995–2001; Domnick Hunter Gp, 1992–2002; Staffordshire Building Soc., 1995–2005; Marston's (formerly Wolverhampton and Dudley Breweries) plc, 2002–14. Mem., W Midlands Industrial Develt Bd, 1989–97. Contested (C) Walsall North, Feb. and Oct. 1974; MP (C) Walsall North, Nov. 1976–1979. Opposition spokesman on trade and industry, H of L, 2002–06. Official Reviewer: Charities Act, 2006, 2012; Pt 2, Transparency of Lobbying, Non Party Campaigning and Trade Union Administration Act 2014, 2015–. Chm., Unshackling Good Neighbours Task Force, Cabinet Office, 2011. Chm., Birmingham Bow Gp, 1972–73; National Union of Conservative Associations: Mem. Exec. Cttee, 1988–98; Vice Pres., 1995–96; Chm., 1996–98; Chm., W Midlands Area, 1991–94. Dep. Chm., Cons. Party, 1998–2000; Chairman: Nat. Cons. Convention, 1998–2000; Trustees, Cons. Party Pension Fund, 2000–06. Member: Council for the Securities Industry, 1980–85; Securities and Investments Board, 1985–89; Dir, SFA, 1991–2001; Chm., Nat. Assoc. of Security Dealers and Investment Managers, 1979–85. Chm., Armed Forces Charities Adv. Cttee, 2009–. Pres., NCVO, 2009–12. Trustee and Hon. Fellow, St Peter's Coll., Oxford; Associate, St George's House, Windsor. Liveryman, Goldsmiths' Co., 1983. *Publications:* Britain's Home Defence Gamble, 1978; Britain's Demographic Challenge, 2017. *Recreations:* squash, fishing, theatre. *Address:* House of Lords, SW1A 0PW.

**HODGSON, (Adam) Robin;** DL; Chief Executive, Hampshire County Council, 1985–95; *b* 20 March 1937; *s* of Thomas Edward Highton Hodgson, CB; *m* 1962, Elizabeth Maureen Linda Bovenizer; one *s* two *d*. *Educ:* William Ellis Sch., London; Worcester Coll., Oxford (MA 1969); BSc Open Univ. 1997. Admitted Solicitor, 1964. Asst Solicitor, LCC and GLC, 1964–66; Sen. Asst Solicitor, Oxfordshire CC, 1966–71; Asst Clerk, Northamptonshire CC, 1972–74; Dep. County Sec., E Sussex CC, 1974–77; Dep. Chief Exec. and Clerk, Essex CC, 1977–85. Chm., Winchester Diocesan Bd of Finance, 1996–2006. Mem. Council, Univ. of Southampton, 1996–2002; Governor, Univ. of Portsmouth, 1996–2003. Mem. Gen. Chiropractic Council, 1996–2004. DL Hampshire, 1996. *Recreations:* music, drama, geology. *Address:* Tara, Dean Lane, Winchester, Hampshire SO22 5RA. *T:* (01962) 862119.

**HODGSON, Christine Mary,** FCA; Chairman, since 1997, and Group Head of Corporate Social Responsibility, Capgemini UK plc; Group Executive Committee, Capgemini SA; *b* Preston, 17 Nov. 1964; *d* of Anthony Frederick and Audrey Pickles; *m* 1999, Howard Osmond Paul Hodgson, *qv*; one *s*. *Educ:* Elmslie Girls' Sch., Blackpool; Loughborough Univ. (BSc 1st Cl. Hons Accounting and Financial Mgt). ACA 1990. With Coopers & Lybrand, 1985–94; Ronson plc, 1994–97. Chm., Careers & Enterprise Co., 2015–. Non-executive Director: Ladbrokes Coral Gp (formerly Ladbrokes) plc, 2012–17; Standard Chartered Bank, 2013–. Board Member: BITC; Professional Services Business Council. Member: Audit Cttee, Queen Elizabeth Diamond Jubilee Trust; Business Adv. Gp, DFE; Internat. Trade Council, CBI; Prime Minister's Financial and Professional Services' Business Council. *Address:* Capgemini UK plc, 40 Holborn Viaduct, EC1N 2PB.

**HODGSON, George Wilson;** HM Diplomatic Service; Ambassador to Senegal, and concurrently to Cape Verde and Guinea Bissau, 2015–19; *b* London, 17 Oct. 1980; *s* of Clive Alexander Hodgson and Dr Elizabeth Ann Hodgson; *m* 2010, Constance Maljette; two *s* one *d*. *Educ:* City of London Sch.; Pembroke Coll., Oxford (BA 1st Cl. Hons PPE); Woodrow Wilson Sch., Princeton Univ. (MPA 2008). Joined FCO, 2002; Desk Officer, EU Directorate, FCO, 2002–03; Second Secretary: Kabul, 2004; UK Representation to EU, 2005–06; First Sec., Islamabad, 2008–10; Political Counsellor, Kabul, 2010–11; Sen. Advr to Special Rep. for Afghanistan and Pakistan, State Dept, Washington (on secondment), 2011–12; Head: Parly and Communications Dept, FCO, 2012–14; Ebola Taskforce, 2014–15. *Recreations:* hiking, tennis, squash, cricket. *Address:* c/o Foreign and Commonwealth Office, King Charles Street, SW1A 0AA. *E:* george.hodgson@fco.gov.uk.

**HODGSON, Guy Andrew Keith;** District Judge (Magistrates' Courts) (formerly Stipendiary Magistrate), Bradford, 1993–2009; *b* 19 March 1946; *s* of Herbert and Kathleen Hodgson; *m* 1968, Kay Bampton; three *s*. *Educ:* Pocklington Sch.; Nottingham Poly. (LLB London Ext.). Articled to M. M. Rossfield, Solicitor, York; Legal Asst, Thames Valley Police, 1970–71; Asst Prosecutor, Suffolk Police, 1971–72; Asst Solicitor, Gotelee & Goldsmith, Ipswich, 1972–74; Partner, Close Thornton, Darlington, 1974–93. *Recreations:* travel, reading, painting, hobby farming, vintage tractors, family interests, canal narrow boats.

**HODGSON, Howard Osmond Paul;** author, scriptwriter and lyricist; Chairman and Chief Executive Officer, Memoria Ltd, since 2002; *b* 22 Feb. 1950; *s* of late Osmond Paul Charles Hodgson and of Sheila Mary (*née* Ward; now Mrs Baker); *m* 1st, 1972, Marianne Denise Yvonne (marr. diss. 1998), *d* of Samuel Katibien, Aix-en-Provence, France; two *s* one *d* (and one *s* decd); 2nd, 1999, Christine Mary Pickles (*see* C. M. Hodgson); one *s*. *Educ:* Aiglon Coll., Villars, Switzerland. DipFD 1970; MBIFD; Affiliated MRSPH (MRSH 1970). Asst Man., Hodgson & Sons Ltd, 1969–71; life assce exec., 1971–75; acquired: Hodgson & Sons Ltd, 1975 (floated USM, 1986); Ingalls from House of Fraser, 1987; launched Dignity in Destiny Ltd, 1989; merger with Pompes Funèbres Générales, France, Kenyon Securities and Hodgson Hldgs plc to form PFG Hodgson Kenyon Internat. plc, 1989; launched: Bereavement Support Service, 1990; PHKI Nat. Training Sch., 1990; retd, 1991, to pursue career in broadcasting and writing. Chief Executive: Halkin Hldgs, 1993; Hoskins Brewery plc, 1993; Ronson plc, 1995–97 (acquired Ronson plc and LGW plc, 1994, Home Shopping Marketing Ltd and associated cos, the business of DCK Marketing Ltd and Smiths Packaging Ltd, 1995; Group renamed Ronson plc, 1995; resigned, 1997); CEO, Colibri Internat., 1998–2001. Founder: Low Cost Funeral Ltd, 2016; Qualitas Alliance, 2017. Presenter, How Euro Are You, BBC2, 1991–92; panellist, Board Game, Radio 4, 1992–2001. Hon. Vice Pres., Royal Soc. of St George, 1989. USM Entrepreneur of the Year, 1987. *Publications:* How to Become Dead Rich, 1992; Six Feet Under, 2000 (film script, 2001); Exhumed Innocent?, 2002; Charles: the man who will be king, 2007 (US edn as The King and Di, 2009). *Recreations:* cricket, yachting, ski-ing, English/British Royal history, Aston Villa FC. *Address:* St Julian's, Malta. *E:* hhodgson@memoria.org.uk.

**HODGSON, Prof. Humphrey Julian Francis,** DM; FRCP, FMedSci; Dame Sheila Sherlock Professor of Medicine, UCL Medical School (formerly Royal Free and University College Medical School), University College London, 1999–2011; Visiting Professor, University of Namibia, Windhoek, since 2011; *b* 5 April 1945; *s* of late Harold Robinson Hodgson and Celia Frances Hodgson (*née* Hodgson); *m* 1971, Shirley Victoria Penrose; one *s* one *d*. *Educ:* Westminster Sch.; Christ Church, Oxford (BA, BSc); St Thomas's Hosp. Med. Sch. (BM BCh, DM). FRCP 1983. Trng posts at St Thomas' and Royal Free Hosps, 1970–76; Radcliffe Travelling Fellow, University Coll., Oxford, at Massachusetts Gen. Hosp., Boston, 1977; Consultant Physician, Hammersmith Hosp., 1977–99; Royal Postgraduate Medical School, London: Sen. Lectr in Medicine, 1978–89; Reader, 1989–91; Prof. of Gastroenterology, 1991–95; Vice Dean, 1986–97; Prof. of Medicine, RPMS, then ICSM, 1995–99; Jt Med. Dir, Hammersmith Hosps NHS Trust, 1994–97; Vice Dean, Royal Free Campus, Royal Free and University Coll. Med. Sch., later UCL Med. Sch., 2001–09. Chairman: Scientific Co-ordinating Cttee, Arthritis Res. Campaign (formerly Arthritis and Rheumatism Council for Res.), 1996–2003; Trustees, Polymyalgia Rheumatica Giant Cell Arteritis UK, 2018–. Pres., British Assoc. for Study of the Liver, 2003–05; Acad. Registrar, 1992–97, Sen. Censor and Vice-Pres., 2008–11, Ed., Clinical Medicine, 2011–17, RCP. FMedSci 2002. *Publications:* Textbook of Gastroenterology, 1984; Gastroenterology: clinical science and practice, 1994; (with S. Shorvon) Physicians and War, 2016; multiple articles on clinical and laboratory aspects of gastrointestinal and liver disease and on develt of bioartificial live support systems. *Recreations:* walking, reading, academic travel. *Address:* UCL Institute for Liver and Digestive Health, Royal Free Hospital Campus, University College Medical School, Upper Third Floor, Rowland Hill Street, Hampstead, NW3 2PF. *T:* (020) 7433 2850; 40 Onslow Gardens, N10 3JU. *T:* (020) 8883 8297.

**HODGSON, Ian Geoffrey;** magazine editor, author, writer and horticultural consultant; Editor-at-Large, Garden News and Garden Answers magazines, since 2013; Editor-in-Chief, RHS Media, 2006–11 and Editor, The Garden, 1993–2011, Royal Horticultural Society; *b* Mirfield, W Yorks, 2 May 1958; *s* of Geoffrey Walter Hodgson and Mary Hodgson; *m* 1993, Judith Lesley Allen; one *s*. *Educ:* Royal Botanic Gardens, Kew (Dip. Horticulture); Univ. of Sheffield (BSc Landscape Design and Plant Sci.; Dip. Landscape Arch.; MA Landscape Design). Tech. writer, Garden News, 1986–87; Tech. Ed., Practical Gardening Magazine, 1987–89; Ed., The Gardener, 1989–93. Trustee, Plant Heritage, 2011–17. *Publications:* Growing Bromeliads, 1990; RHS Container Gardening, 2013; Great Garden Design, 2015; New Wild Garden, 2016. *Recreations:* music (especially classical and contemporary big band jazz); collecting old gardening books and gardening ephemera (especially history of plant hunting), garden and planting design, foreign travel (especially for natural history).

**HODGSON, Keith Stephen,** OBE 1997; Director, Management Support Unit, Board of Inland Revenue, 1998–2001; *b* 29 Oct. 1946; *s* of Leonard Arthur and Florence Hodgson; *m* 1969, Jean Moran. *Educ:* Wolverhampton Municipal Grammar Sch. Min. of Transport, 1965–68; Board of Inland Revenue, 1968–2001; Private Sec. to Chm. of Bd, CS Pay Res. Unit, 1978–81; Dep. Controller of Stamps, 1982–90; Dir, Stamp Office, 1990–98. FRSA 1998. *Publications:* (contrib.) Managing Change in the New Public Sector, 1994; (contrib.) Creating a Good Impression: three hundred years of the Stamp Office and Stamp Duties, 1994. *Recreations:* Freemasonry, golf, wine, Rugby. *Address:* Tenterden, Kent. *Club:* Tenterden Golf (Captain, 2011; Pres., 2017–).

**HODGSON, Dame Patricia (Anne), (Dame Patricia Donaldson),** DBE 2004 (CBE 1995); Member of Board, Centre for Data Ethics and Innovation, since 2018; Member, UK Artificial Intelligence Council, since 2019; *b* 19 Jan. 1947; *d* of Harold Hodgson and Pat Smith; *m* 1979, George Donaldson; one *s*. *Educ:* Brentwood High Sch.; Newnham Coll., Cambridge (MA; Associate Fellow, 1994–97; Hon. Fellow, 2013); LRAM (Drama) 1968. Conservative Res. Dept, Desk Officer for public sector industries, 1968–70; freelance journalism and broadcasting in UK and USA during seventies; Chm., Bow Gp, 1975–76; Editor, Crossbow, 1976–80. BBC: joined as educn producer for Open Univ. (part of founding team pioneering distance learning techniques), 1970; most of prodn career in educn, specialising in history and philosophy, with spells in current affairs on Today and Tonight; Secretariat, 1982–83, Dep. Sec., 1983–85, The Sec., 1985–87; Hd of Policy & Planning, 1987–92; Dir of Policy & Planning, 1993–2000; Dir of Public Policy, 2000; Chief Exec., ITC, 2000–04. Principal, Newnham Coll., Cambridge, 2006–12 (Vis. Bye Fellow, 2004). Chm., Higher Educn Regulation Rev. Gp, 2004–06; Mem., HEFCE, 2005–11; Chm., School Teachers' Rev. Body, 2012–14. Non-executive Director: GCAP Media plc, 2004–06; Competition Commn, 2004–11 (Mem., Monopolies and Mergers, subseq. Competition, Commn, 1993–97); Member: Statistics Commn, 2000–05; Cttee on Standards in Public Life, 2004–08; BBC Trust, 2007–11; Ind. Commn on Freedom of Information, 2015–16; Bd, Ofcom, 2011–17 (Dep. Chair, 2012–14; Chair, 2014–17). Dir, BARB, 1987–98. Mem., (C) Haringey BC, 1974–77. Mem., London Arts Bd, 1991–96. Trustee, PYBT, 1992–95. Gov., Wellcome Trust, 2004–08; Mem. Adv. Bd, Judge Inst., Cambridge, 1996–2002. DU Essex, 2001; Hon. DSc City, 2002. *Television series* include: English Urban History, 1978; Conflict in Modern Europe, 1980; Rome in the Age of Augustus, 1981. *Publications:* (ed) Paying for Broadcasting, 1992; (ed) Public Purposes in Broadcasting, 1999; (ed) Culture and Communications, 2003; articles in various newspapers and jls. *Recreation:* quietness. *Club:* Oxford and Cambridge.

**HODGSON, Randolph Arthur,** OBE 2006; owner, Neal's Yard Dairy, since 1979; *b* 29 Sept. 1956; *s* of Arthur Ralph and Monica Olive Hodgson; *m* 1982, Anita Leroy (*d* 2015); two *s* one *d*; *m* 2016, Jemima Cordle; one *s*. *Educ:* Downside Sch.; King's Coll., London (BSc Hons). Chm., Specialist Cheesemakers Assoc., 1990–94 and 2000–11. *Recreations:* cheese-making, farming.

**HODGSON, Robin;** *see* Hodgson, A. R.

**HODGSON, Sharon;** MP (Lab) Washington and Sunderland West, since 2010 (Gateshead East and Washington West, 2005–10); *b* 1 April 1966; *d* of Joan Cohen (*née* Wilson); *m* 1990, Alan Hodgson; one *s* one *d*. *Educ:* Heathfield Sen. High Sch., Gateshead; Newcastle Coll. Payroll/account clerk, Tyneside Safety Glass, 1982–88; Northern Rock Bldg Soc., Gosforth, 1988–92; Payroll administrator, Burgess Microswitch, 1992–94; Administrator, Total Learning Challenge, 1998–99; Lab. Party Orgnr, 1999–2002; Labour Link Co-ordinator, UNISON, 2002–05. PPS to Minister of State, Home Office, 2006–07, to Minister of State, MoD, 2007–08, to Minister of State, DoH, 2008–09; an Asst Govt Whip, 2009–10; Opposition Whip, 2010; Shadow Minister: for Children and Families, 2010–13, 2015–16; for Women and Equalities, 2013–15; for Public Health, 2016–. Mem., Children, Schs and Families Select Cttee, 2007–10. *Address:* (office) Units 1–1a, Vermont House, Concord, Washington, Tyne and Wear NE37 2SQ; House of Commons, SW1A 0AA. *W:* www.sharonhodgson.org.

**HODGSON, Ven. Thomas Richard Burnham;** Archdeacon of West Cumberland, 1979–91, now Archdeacon Emeritus; *b* 17 Aug. 1926; *s* of Richard Shillito Hodgson and Marion Thomasina Bertram Marshall; *m* 1952, Margaret Esther (*d* 2007), *o d* of Evan and Caroline Margaret Makinson; one *s* one *d*. *Educ:* Heversham Grammar School; London Coll. of Divinity, Univ. of London. BD, ALCD. Deacon 1952, priest 1953, dio. Carlisle; Curate of Crosthwaite, Keswick, 1952–55; Curate of Stanwix, Carlisle, 1955–59; Vicar of St Nicholas', Whitehaven, 1959–65; Rector of Aikton, 1965–67; Vicar of Raughtonhead with Gaitsgill, 1967–73, and Domestic Chaplain to Bishop of Carlisle, 1967–73, Hon. Chaplain, 1973–79; Hon. Canon of Carlisle, 1973–91; Vicar of: Grange-over-Sands, 1973–79; Mosser, 1979–83. Mem., General Synod of C of E, 1983–90. Director of

Ordination Candidates, 1970–74; RD of Windermere, 1976–79; Surrogate, 1962–91. *Publications:* Saying the Services, 1989; Speaking in Church, 2004. *Address:* 41 Waverley Court, Waverley Gardens, Carlisle CA3 9JN. *T:* (01228) 528809.

HODGSON, Rear Adm. Timothy Charles, MBE 1999; Director Submarine Capability, since 2016; *b* Gloucester, 4 May 1963; *s* of Michael Hodgson and Nancy Hodgson; *m* 1990, Jane Lee Williams. *Educ:* Monmouth Sch.; Marling Sch., Stroud; Trinity Hall, Cambridge (BA Engrg 1986); Defence Sch. of Langs (Russian Interpreter 1994); King's Coll. London (MA Defence Studies 2000); Saïd Business Sch., Oxford (MPLA 2015). CEng 1990; FIMechE 2011. Joined RN, 1982; HMS Revenge, 1988–91; Asst Naval Attaché, Moscow, 1994–97; HMS Trenchant, 1997–99; Directorate of Equipt Capability (Underwater Battlespace), 2000–03; Team Leader, Nuclear Propulsion Capability Study, 2003–04; Principal Inspector Reactor Plant, Defence Nuclear Safety Regulator, 2004–06; CSO Engrg (Submarines), 2007–10; Chief Engr (Marine Engrg), Future Submarines, 2010–12; Hd, In Service Support Team, Defence Equipment and Support, 2012–15; Hd, Nuclear Capabilities, MoD, 2015–16. *Recreations:* cycling, walking. *Address:* DG Nuclear, Ministry of Defence, Main Building, Whitehall, SW1A 2HB.

HODIVALA-DILKE, Prof. Kairbaan Michael, PhD; FMedSci; Professor of Angiogenesis, since 2009, and Deputy Director, since 2012, Barts Cancer Institute, Barts and the London School of Medicine and Dentistry, Queen Mary University of London; *b* London, 6 Oct. 1966; *d* of Jimmy and Soonu Hodivala; *m* 1994, Michael Charles Dilke; one *s* one *d*. *Educ:* Green Sch. for Girls, Isleworth; Univ. of Southampton (BSc); University Coll. London/Imperial Cancer Res. Fund (PhD 1994). Tech. Asst, Jodrell Labs, Kew Gdns (pt-time), 1984–86; Wellcome Trust Malaria Res. Team, Imperial Coll. London, 1988; Postdoctoral Fellow, MIT, Boston, 1994–99; Laboratory Head and Senior Lecturer: Guy's and St Thomas' Hosp., 1999–2004; Barts Cancer Inst., QMUL, 2005–09. Mem., EMBO. FMedSci 2015. Hooke Medal, British Soc. for Cell Biol., 2015. *Recreations:* cooking and eating with friends and family, falling asleep in front of the TV, travelling, drawing. *Address:* Barts Cancer Institute, Barts and the London School of Medicine and Dentistry, Queen Mary University of London, Charterhouse Square, EC1M 6BQ. *T:* (020) 7882 8576. *E:* k.hodivala-dilke@qmul.ac.uk.

HODKINSON, Gregory Scott; Chairman, Arup Group, 2014–19; *b* Newcastle, Australia, 10 June 1955; *s* of Barrie and Deirdre Hodkinson; *m* 1989, Siobhán O'Connor; two *s* three *d*. *Educ:* N Sydney Boys' High Sch.; Univ. of New South Wales; Macquarie Univ. (BA). Joined Arup, 1972: work in Australia and UK, 1972–88; Founding Principal, NY Office, 1988–2004; Chm., Americas Reg., 2004–11; Chm., Eur. Business, 2011–14. Non-exec. Dir, BritishAmerican Business, 2005–. Trustee, Water Aid, 2007–14. FRSA. *Recreation:* sailing. *Clubs:* Brook (New York); Shelter Island Yacht.

HODKINSON, Prof. Henry Malcolm, DM; FRCP; Barlow Professor of Geriatric Medicine, University College London, 1985–91, now Emeritus; medical expert witness, since 1990; barrister; *b* 28 April 1931; *s* of Charles and Olive Hodkinson; *m* 1st (marr. diss.); four *d*; 2nd, 1986, Judith Marie Bryant, *qv*. *Educ:* Manchester Grammar Sch.; Brasenose Coll., Oxford (MA; DM 1975); Middlesex Hospital; Westminster Univ. (Dip. in Law, 2000). FRCP 1974. Consultant Physician in Geriatrics to: Enfield and Tottenham Gps of Hosps, 1962–70; Northwick Park Hosp., 1970–78 (also Mem., Scientific Staff of Clin. Res. Centre); Sen. Lectr in Geriatric Medicine, 1978–79, Prof. of Geriatric Medicine, 1979–84, RPMS. Called to the Bar, Middle Temple, 2001; in practice as a barrister, 2001–08. Vice Pres., Research into Ageing, 1996–2016 (Governor, 1983–96). *Publications:* An Outline of Geriatrics, 1975, 2nd edn 1981 (trans. Spanish, Dutch, German, Italian and Japanese); Common Symptoms of Disease in the Elderly, 1976, 2nd edn 1980 (trans. Turkish); Biochemical Diagnosis of the Elderly, 1977; (ed) Clinical Biochemistry of the Elderly, 1984; (with J. M. Hodkinson) Sherratt? A Natural Family of Staffordshire Figures, 1991; approx. 100 papers in learned jls, 1961–. *Recreation:* English glass and ceramics. *Address:* 8 Chiswick Square, Burlington Lane, Chiswick, W4 2QG. *T:* (020) 8747 0239.

HODKINSON, James Clifford; Chairman, Furniture Village, since 2002; non-executive Director of various companies; *b* 21 April 1944; *s* of John and Lily Hodkinson; *m* 1969, Janet Lee; one *d*. *Educ:* Salesian Coll., Farnborough. Trainee Manager, F. W. Woolworth Ltd, London, 1962–71; Manager, B & Q, Bournemouth, 1972–74; Sales Manager, B & Q (Retail) Ltd, 1974–76; Man. Dir, B & Q (Southern) Ltd, 1976–79; Dir, 1976–79, Ops Dir, 1979–84, Ops and Personnel Dir, 1984–86, B & Q (Retail) Ltd; Man. Dir, 1986–89, Chief Exec., 1989–92, B & Q plc; Internat. Develt Dir, Kingfisher plc, 1992–94; Chm. and Chief Exec., B & Q plc, 1994–98; Chief Exec., New Look Retailers Ltd, 1998–2000. *Recreation:* shooting.

HODKINSON, Judith Marie, (Mrs H. M. Hodkinson); *see* Bryant, Judith M.

HODSON, Alan Charles; Chairman, Charity Bank, since 2019; *b* Bowers Gifford, 13 April 1962; *s* of John and Audrey Hodson; *m* 1986, Christiane Hyde; one *s* one *d* (and one *d* decd). *Educ:* Culford Sch.; St Peter's Coll., Oxford (MA). With Rowe & Pitman, later S. G. Warburg, then SBC, subseq. UBS, 1984–2005 (Global Hd of Equities, UBS, 2000–04); Chm., Great Ormond St Hosp. Children's Charity, 2007–15. Director: JP Morgan Elect Ltd, 2012– (Chm., 2018–); Harbourvest Global Private Equity, 2013–; Woodford Patient Capital, 2016–19. *Recreations:* golf, tennis. *Clubs:* Royal and Ancient Golf, Royal St George's Golf, Worplesdon Golf, Royal Wimbledon Golf.

HODSON, Beverley Cliffe, OBE 2003; non-executive Director, Randstad (formerly Vedior NV), 2006–15; *b* 14 June 1951; *d* of Clifford Vernon Hodson and Frances Jeanne Hodson; *m* Peter John Cottingham (marr. diss. 2015); one *s* and three step *d*. *Educ:* Blackheath High Sch.; Newnham Coll., Cambridge (BA 1st cl. hons; Exhibnr; Cambridge Tennis Blue (Ladies Captain)). Boots, 1978–96; Sears, 1996–97; Man. Dir, UK Retail, WH Smith Gp, 1997–2004. Non-executive Director: GWR Trent FM Radio, 1990–97; M&G Gp plc, 1998–99; Legal & General, 2000–07; Robert Wiseman Dairies plc, 2005–10; Iforce Ltd, 2005–11; First Milk, 2005–11; NFU Mutual, 2008–12. Member, Council: Univ. of Gloucester, 2008– (Chm., then Mem., F and GP Cttee, 2008–17); Cheltenham Coll., 2004–13. Hon. Associate, Newnham Coll., Cambridge, 2012–. Dir, Clifton Court, Putsborough, Devon, 2015–. *Recreations:* ski-ing, tennis, reading, theatre, opera, wine, food.

HODSON, His Honour Christopher Robert; a Circuit Judge, 1993–2011; Resident Judge, Warwick and Coventry Crown Courts, 2007–11; *b* 3 Nov. 1946; *s* of James and Elizabeth Hodson; *m* 1970, Jean Patricia Anne Dayer; one *s* one *d*. *Educ:* King's Sch., Worcester. Called to the Bar, Lincoln's Inn, 1970; practised, Birmingham, 1971–93; a Recorder, 1988–93. Hon. Recorder, City of Coventry, 2007–11. *Address:* c/o Crown Court Office, Warwickshire Justice Centre, Newbold Terrace, Leamington Spa CV32 4EL.

HODSON, Prof. Daniel Houghton, FCT; Chairman, Berry Palmer and Lyle Holdings plc, 2008–19 (Director, 2000–19); *b* 11 March 1944; *s* of late Henry Vincent Hodson and Margaret Elizabeth (*née* Honey); *m* 1979, Diana Mary Ryde; two *d*. *Educ:* Eton; Merton Coll., Oxford (MA Hons PPE). FCT 1979. Chase Manhattan Bank, 1965–73; joined Edward Bates & Sons Ltd, 1973, Dir 1974–76; Unigate plc: Gp Treas., 1976–81; Gp Finance Dir, 1981–87; Pres., Unigate Inc., 1986–87; Chief Exec., 1987–88, Chm. 1988,

Davidson Pearce Gp plc; Dep. Chief Exec., Nationwide Building Soc., 1989–92; Chief Exec., LIFFE, 1993–98. Director: The Post Office, 1984–95; Ransomes plc, 1993–98; Independent Insurance Gp plc, 1995–2003; London Clearing House, 1996–98; Rolfe and Nolan plc, 1999–2003; Norland Managed (formerly Reliance Environmental) Services Ltd, 1999–2006; NASDAQ OMX NLX, 2013–17; Convergex Ltd, 2015–17; Vote Leave, 2015–; Chairman: Medialink Internat., 1999–2003; Insulation and Machining Services Ltd, 2001–07; Henderson Value Trust (formerly SVM Global Fund) plc, 2004–14. Chairman: European Cttee, Options and Futures Exchanges, 1996–98; Exec. Cttee, Financial Services Negotiation Forum, 2016–17. Association of Corporate Treasurers: Chm., 1985–86; Pres., 1992–93. Gresham Prof. of Commerce, 1999–2002; Prof. Emeritus, Gresham Coll. Chm., Design and Artists Copyright Soc., 1999–2005. Chm., Lokahi Foundn, 2005–14; Exec. Chm., People's Pledge, 2012–13; Hon. Treas., Business for Britain, 2013–17. Dep. Chm., Classical Opera Co., 1997–2005; Trustee: Hanover Band, 2012–14; Chichester Cathedral Restoration and Develt Trust, 2012–. Governor: Yehudi Menuhin Sch., 1984–2005; Peter Symonds Coll., Winchester, 2000–02; St Paul's Girls' Sch., 2006–17; Collyers Coll., 2011–15; Sutton's Hosp. in Charterhouse, 2012–; Chm., Bd of Govs, Univ. of Winchester (formerly King Alfred's Coll., Winchester, then University Coll., Winchester), 2001–06; Mem. Council, Gresham Coll., 2006– (Vice Chm., 2012–). Founding Editor, Corporate Finance and Treasury Management, 1984–. Master, Mercers' Co., 2008–09. Hon. DBA Winchester, 2009. *Recreations:* music, travel, photography, reading. *Address:* Chepynge House, 22 Maltravers Street, Arundel BN18 9BU. *T:* (01903) 883234. *Club:* Brooks's.

HODSON, His Honour David; *see* Hodson, His Honour T. D. T.

HODSON, Prof. Howard Peter, PhD; FREng, FRAeS; FASME; Professor of Aerothermal Technology, 2000–13, and Director, Whittle Laboratory, 2005, Department of Engineering, University of Cambridge; Fellow, Girton College, Cambridge, since 1984; *b* 18 Feb. 1957; *s* of Edward Hodson and late Kathleen Janette Hodson; *m* 1978, Dr Jane Brooks. *Educ:* Churchill Coll., Cambridge (BA Engrg 1978, MA 1982; PhD 1983). CEng 1999, FREng 2005; FRAeS 1999. Engr, Perkins Engine Co. Ltd, 1978–79; Res. Asst, Whittle Lab., Cambridge, 1982–85; Department of Engineering, University of Cambridge: Sen. Asst in Res., 1985–89; Lectr, 1989–98; Reader in Thermofluid Engrg, 1998–2000; Girton College, Cambridge: Lectr, 1985–; Dir of Studies, 1985–2000; Actg Bursar, 1994. Dir and Sec., Cambridge Turbomachinery Consultants Ltd, 1983–2005. FASME 2002. *Publications:* contrib. papers to jls of ASME, AIAA and IMechE. *Recreations:* gardening, classic vehicle restoration.

HODSON, John; Chief Executive, Singer & Friedlander Group, 1993–2004 (Director, 1987–2004; Chairman, 1999–2003); *b* 19 May 1946; *s* of Arthur and Olga Hodson; *m* 1971, Christina McLeod; one *s* two *d*. *Educ:* Worcester Coll., Oxford (PPE). Joined Singer & Friedlander, 1969: Asst Dir, 1974–83; Dir, 1983–2004; Head of Investment Dept, 1985–90. Chairman: UBC Media PLC; SEC Investment Trust; Cenkos Securities; non-executive Director: Prestbury Gp plc; Domino's Pizza UK & Ireland plc. *Recreations:* tennis, family.

HODSON, Sir Michael (Robin Adderley), 6th Bt *cr* 1789; Captain, Scots Guards, retired; *b* 5 March 1932; *s* of Major Sir Edmond Adair Hodson, 5th Bt, DSO, and Anne Elizabeth Adderley (*d* 1984), *yr d* of Lt-Col Hartopp Francis Charles Adderley Cradock, Hill House, Sherborne St John; *S* father, 1972; *m* 1st, 1963, Katrin Alexa (marr. diss. 1978), *d* of late Erwin Bernstiel, Dinas Powis, Glamorgan; three *d*; 2nd, 1978, Catherine, *d* of late John Henry Seymour, Wimpole St, W1. *Educ:* Eton. *Heir: b* Patrick Richard Hodson [*b* 27 Nov. 1934; *m* 1961, June, *o d* of H. M. Shepherd-Cross; three *s*]. *Address:* Kilgeddin House, Llanfair Kilgeddin, Monmouthshire NP7 9BB.

HODSON, Simon James; Partner, DAC Beachcroft LLP; *b* London, 9 May 1956; *s* of Gordon Hodson and Anne Hodson; *m* 1982, Gail Lees; one *s* one *d*. *Educ:* Marlborough House Sch., Kent; Lancing Coll.; Queen Mary Coll., Univ. of London (LLB); Coll. of Law, Lancaster Gate. Admitted as solicitor, 1981; Solicitor, Clifford Turner, 1981–84; solicitor, 1984, Partner, 1985–, Sen. Partner, 2005–15, Beachcrofts, then Beachcroft Stanleys, later Beachcroft LLP, subseq. DAC Beachcroft LLP. Non-executive Director: Fresca Gp Ltd, 2009–; CH & Co. Catering Gp (Hldgs) Ltd, 2015–; Brand Foundn, 2015–; First Equity Ltd, 2017–; 4Most ESOT Ltd, 2018–. Gov., Marlborough Hse Sch., Kent, 2002–. *Recreations:* theatre, ski-ing, fishing, anything outdoors. *Address:* DAC Beachcroft LLP, The Walbrook Building, 25 Walbrook, EC4N 8AF. *T:* (020) 7242 1011, *Fax:* (020) 7831 6630. *E:* shodson@dacbeachcroft.com. *Club:* City Law.

HODSON, His Honour (Thomas) David (Tattersall); an Assistant Surveillance Commissioner, 2013–15; *b* 24 Sept. 1942; *s* of late Thomas Norman Hodson and Elsie Nuttall Hodson; *m* 1969, Patricia Ann Vint; two *s* one *d*. *Educ:* Sedbergh Sch.; Manchester Univ. (LLB). Leader Writer, Yorkshire Post, 1964–65; called to the Bar, Inner Temple 1966, Bencher, 2001; in practice on Northern Circuit, 1967–87; Junior, 1969; a Recorder, 1983–87; a Circuit Judge, 1987–2010; a Sen. Circuit Judge and Hon. Recorder of Newcastle upon Tyne, 1997–2010. Mem., Parole Bd, 1996–97; pt-time judicial Mem., Parole Bd, 2010–14; Chm., Northumbria Area Criminal Justice Strategy Cttee, 2001–03. Pres., S Lancs Br., Magistrates' Assoc., 1994–96. Mem. Court, Univ. of Newcastle upon Tyne, 2000–09. Chancellor, Dio. of Newcastle, 2009–13 (Dep. Chancellor, 2003–09). Hon. Mem., N Eastern Circuit, 2007. Hon. LLD Sunderland, 2002. *Publications:* One Week in August: the Kaiser at Lowther Castle, August 1895, 1995. *Recreations:* music, family history. *Address:* c/o Ministry of Justice, North Eastern Region, 17th Floor, West Riding House, Albion Street, Leeds LS1 5AA.

HOERNER, John Lee; consultant to Tesco Stores plc, 2008–16; Chief Executive, Central European Clothing, Tesco, 2005–08; *b* Lincoln, Nebraska, 23 Sept. 1939; *s* of Robert Lee Hoerner and Lulu Alice (*née* Stone); *m* 1st 1959, Susan Kay Morgan (marr. diss. 1971); one *s* one *d*; 2nd, 1973, Anna Lea Thomas. *Educ:* Lincoln High Sch.; Univ. of Nebraska (BS Business Admin 1961). Senior buying and merchandising positions, Hovland Swanson, Lincoln, Neb, 1959–68; Gen. Merchandise Manager, Ladies Div., Woolf Bros, Kansas City, Mo, 1968–72; Womenswear Merchandise Manager, Hahne & Co., NJ, Associated Dry Goods Corp., 1972–73; real est. develt and venture capital, McLean, Va, 1973–74; Associated Dry Goods Corporation: Gen. Merchandise Manager, 1974–76; Sen. Vice Pres. and Dir of Stores, 1976–79; Sen. Vice Pres. and Gen. Merchandise Manager, 1979–81; Pres. and CEO, H. & S. Pogue Co., Cincinnati, Ohio, 1981–82; Pres. and CEO, 1982–85, Chm. and CEO, 1985–86, L. S. Ayres & Co., Indianapolis, Ind., Associated Dry Goods Corp., later May Dept Stores Co.; Burton Group, subseq. Arcadia Group, 1987–2000: Chairman: Debenhams, 1987–92; Harvey Nichols, 1988–91; Gp Chief Exec., 1992–2000; Chief Exec., Clothing, 2001–04; Clothing and Internat. Sourcing, 2004–08, Tesco. Chm., British Fashion Council, 1997–2000. Non-exec. Dir, BAA, 1998–2004. Mem., Council of Trustees, Battersea Dogs' and Cats' Home (formerly Dogs' Home, Battersea), 1991–2006 (Vice-Chm., 1995–2002; Chm., 2002–06). Lifetime Achievement Award, Univ. of Nebraska, 2008. *Publications:* Ayres Adages, 1983; The Director's Handbook, 1991; Recipes for Retailers, 2014; How to Sell, 2015. *Recreations:* riding, flying, dogs. *Address:* Hawling Lodge, Hawling, Cheltenham, Glos GL54 5SY. *T:* (01451) 850223. *Clubs:* Groucho; Royal Air Squadron.

**HOEY, Catharine Letitia**; MP (Lab) Vauxhall, since June 1989; *b* 21 June 1946; *d* of Thomas Henry and Letitia Jane Hoey. *Educ*: Lylehill Primary Sch.; Belfast Royal Acad.; Ulster Coll. of Physical Educn (Dip. in PE); City of London Coll. (BSc Econs). Lectr, Southwark Coll., 1972–76; Sen. Lectr, Kingsway Coll., 1976–85; Educnl Advr, London Football Clubs, 1985–89. PPS to Minister of State (Minister for Welfare Reform), DSS, 1997–98; Parliamentary Under-Secretary of State: Home Office, 1998–99; DCMS (Minister for Sport), 1999–2001. Mayor of London's Comr for Sport, 2009–17. Chairman: Countryside Alliance, 2005–14; London Sport, 2014–17. Hon. Vice Pres., British Wheelchair Basketball. *Address*: House of Commons, SW1A 0AA. *T*: (020) 7219 3000. *Club*: Surrey CC (Hon. Vice Pres.).

**HOFFBRAND, Prof. (Allan) Victor**, DM, DSc; FRCP, FRCPath, FMedSci; Professor of Haematology and Honorary Consultant, Royal Free Hospital School of Medicine, 1974–96, now Emeritus Professor of Haematology, University College London (formerly Royal Free and University College Medical School); *b* 14 Oct. 1935; *s* of late Philip Hoffbrand and Minnie (*née* Freedman); *m* 1963, Irene Jill Mellows; two *s* one *d*. *Educ*: Bradford Grammar Sch.; Queen's Coll., Oxford (BA 1956; MA 1960; BM BCh 1959; DM 1972); Royal London Hospital; DSc London 1987. FRCP 1976; FRCPath 1980. Jun. hosp. posts, Royal London Hosp., 1960–62; Res. and Registrar posts, RPMS, 1962–65; MRC Fellow, New England Med. Centre, Boston, 1967–68; Sen. Lectr, RPMS, 1968–74. Fellow Commoner, Queen's Coll., Oxford, 2012–13. Member: Amer. Soc. Hematology; Brit. Soc. Haematology; Eur. Haematology Assoc. (Mem. Council, 1994–99). FMedSci 2000; Hon. FRCPE 1986. Hon. DSc: QMUL, 2012; UCL 2019. Sultan Bin Khalifa Grand Internat. Thalassaemia Award, 2018; Wallace H. Coulter Lifetime Achievement Award, Amer. Soc. Hematology, 2018; President's Medal, RCP, 2018. *Publications*: (ed with S. M. Lewis) Postgraduate Haematology, 1972, 7th edn 2016; (ed) Recent Advances in Haematology, 1977, 8th edn 1996; (with J. E. Pettit) Hoffbrand's Essential Haematology, 1980, 7th edn (with P. A. H. Moss) 2016; (with J. E. Pettit) Blood Diseases Illustrated, 1987, 5th edn, as Color Atlas of Clinical Hematology, 2019; (with A. B. Mehta) Haematology at a Glance, 2000, 4th edn 2014; papers on megaloblastic anaemia, iron chelation, leukaemia and related disorders. *Recreations*: music, antiques, gardening, bridge. *Address*: 12 Wedderburn Road, NW3 5QG.

**HOFFMAN, Dustin Lee**; actor; *b* 8 Aug. 1937; *s* of Harry Hoffman and Lillian Hoffman; *m* 1st, 1969, Anne Byrne (marr. diss. 1980); two *d*; 2nd, 1980, Lisa Gottsegen; two *s* two *d*. *Educ*: Santa Monica City Coll.; Pasadena Playhouse. Stage début in Sarah Lawrence Coll. prodn, Yes is For a Very Young Man; Broadway début, A Cook for Mr General, 1961; appeared in: Harry, and Noon and Night, Amer. Place Theatre, NY, 1964–65; Journey of the Fifth Horse, and Star Wagon, 1965; Fragments, Berkshire Theatre Festival, Stockbridge, Mass, 1966; Eh?, 1966–67; Jimmy Shine, Broadway, 1968–69; Death of a Salesman, Broadway, 1984; London début, Merchant of Venice, Phoenix, 1989. Dir, All Over Town, Broadway, 1974. Films: The Graduate, 1967; Midnight Cowboy, John and Mary, 1969; Little Big Man, Who Is Harry Kellerman and Why Is He Saying Those Terrible Things About Me?, 1971; Straw Dogs, Alfredo, Alfredo, 1972; Papillon, 1973; Lenny, 1974; All The President's Men, 1975; Marathon Man, 1976; Straight Time, 1978; Agatha, Kramer vs Kramer (Acad. Award), 1979; Tootsie, 1983; Death of a Salesman, 1985 (Emmy Award); Ishtar, 1987; Rain Man, 1989 (Academy Award; Golden Globe Award); Family Business, 1990; Billy Bathgate, 1991; Hook, 1992; Accidental Hero, 1993; Outbreak, 1995; American Buffalo, Sleepers, 1996; Mad City, Wag the Dog, 1997; Sphere, 1998; Moonlight Mile, Confidence, 2003; Runaway Jury, Finding Neverland, I Heart Huckabees, 2004; Meet the Fockers, 2005; Stranger than Fiction, Perfume, 2006; Mr Magorium's Wonder Emporium, 2007; Last Chance Harvey, 2009; Little Fockers, 2010; Barney's Version, 2011; Chef, 2014; The Choir, The Cobbler, The Program, 2015; The Meyerowitz Stories, 2017. Director, Quartet, 2012. Record: Death of a Salesman. Obie Award as best off-Broadway actor, 1965–66, for Journey of the Fifth Horse; Drama Desk, Theatre World, and Vernon Rice Awards for Eh?, 1966; Oscar Award nominee for The Graduate, Midnight Cowboy, and Lenny; Kennedy Center Honors, 2012. *Address*: 11661 San Vicente Boulevard, Suite 222, Los Angeles, CA 90049–5110, USA.

**HOFFMAN, Gary Andrew**; Chairman: Hastings Insurance Group, since 2018 (Chief Executive, 2012–18); Coventry Building Society, since 2018; *b* 21 Oct. 1960; *m* 2003. *Educ*: Queens' Coll., Cambridge. With Barclays Bank plc, 1982–2008: Man. Dir, Telephone Banking, 1995–98; Chief Exec., UK Retail Banking, 1998; Man. Dir, Customer Service and Delivery, 1999–2001; Chief Exec., 2001–05, Chm., 2005–06, Barclaycard; Exec. Dir, 2004–08; Chm., UK Banking, 2005–06; Gp Vice Chm., 2006–08; Chief Exec., Northern Rock, 2008–09; Co-Chief Exec., Northern Rock plc and Northern Rock (Asset Mgt) plc, 2010; Chief Exec., NBNK Investments plc, 2011–12. *Recreations*: running, watching Coventry City FC.

**HOFFMAN, Mark Nicholas Hamilton, (Nick)**; Partner, McKinsey & Company, since 2006; *b* London, 14 Dec. 1969; *s* of Mark Hoffman and Mary Josephine Pyles Hoffman; *m* 2014, Amanda Cupples. *Educ*: Eton Coll.; Harvard Univ. (AB summa cum laude 1993; MBA 2000). Business Analyst, McKinsey & Co., 1994–96; Special Asst to Dir, State Hermitage Mus., St Petersburg, 1997–99; Associate, McKinsey & Co., 2001–06. Trustee: Gilbert Trust for the Arts, 2006– (Chm., 2006–10); V&A Mus., 2016–. *Recreations*: arts, sculling, ski-ing. *Address*: 51 Artesian Road, W2 5DB. *T*: 07768 003834. *E*: mnhhoffman@gmail.com. *Club*: Leander.

**HOFFMAN, Thomas Dieter Dirk**, MBE 2018; Chairman, Stour Festival Company Ltd, since 2014 (Member, Board of Directors, since 2008); *b* Cambridge, 9 Aug. 1945; *s* of late Dirk Hoffman and Marie-Luise Leyser; *m* 1971, Verena Mary Fairs (*d* 2018); one *s*. *Educ*: St John's College Sch., Cambridge; The Leys Sch., Cambridge; Univ. of Exeter (LLB); INSEAD (Adv. Mgt Prog. for Bankers 1990). ACA 1971, FCA 1981. Spicer & Pegler, Cambridge, 1963–65, 1969–70; Arthur Andersen, London, 1970–72; Corp. Finance Dept, William & Glyn's Bank, London, 1972–76; Investment Banking Div., Hill Samuel & Co., London, 1976–78; Dir, Capital Markets Div., Lloyds Bank International, London, 1978–84; Dep. Man. Dir, Fuji International Finance, London, 1984–89; Hd, Corp. Banking in UK, ABN Bank, 1989–91; Gen. Manager, UK and Ireland, Banco Espirito Santo, 1991–2003; non-exec. Dir, Espirito Santo plc, 2003–05; Sen. Advr, Banif Financial Gp, Portugal, 2004–12. Chm., Portuguese Chamber of Commerce and Industry, 1998–2001 (Hon. Vice Pres., 2003–). City of London Corporation: Mem., Ct of Common Council, 2002–; Member: Planning and Transportation Cttee, 2002–13; Community Services Cttee, 2002–04; Mkts Cttee, 2002–17; Port Health and Envmtl Services Cttee, 2004–19; Culture, Heritage and Libraries Cttee, 2005–; Livery Cttee, 2005–11; Gresham Cttee, 2005– (Chm., 2011–14); Finance Cttee, 2006–19; Investment Cttee, 2006–; Financial Investment Bd, 2011–; Chief Commoner, 2019–20; Dep. Gov., Hon. The Irish Soc., 2009–10 (Mem. Court, 2002–11). Member, Board of Governors: City of London Sch. for Girls, 2002– (Chm., 2003–06); City of London Sch. for Boys, 2003–06; City of London Freemen's Sch., 2003–06. Member: Council, Univ. of Exeter, 2003–06 (Mem. Audit Cttee, 1998–2005; Chm., 2003–05); Bd of Govs, Birkbeck Coll., Univ. of London, 2003–11 (Fellow, 2012–); Council of Govs, King's College Hosp., London, 2004–11; Council, Gresham Coll., 2009– (Vice Chm., 2013–14); Trustee/Almoner, Christ's Hosp. Foundn, 2006–10 (Chm., Finance Cttee, 2006–08); Mem., Council of Govs, Guy's and St Thomas' NHS Foundn Trust, 2012–18. Member, Advisory Board: London Fest. Orch., 1996–2008 (Chm., 2004–08); Sixteen Choir and Orch., 2001–08 (Chm., 2004–08); Trustee: Maryport Heritage Trust, Cumbria, 1989–96; Portuguese Arts Trust, 1992–2002; Clergy Support Trust (formerly Corp. of Sons and Friends of the Clergy), 1996–; City of London Fest., 2003–15; Mitchell City of London Trust, 2018–; Age UK (London), 2018–; Member, Board of Governors: GSMD, 2002–12 (Chm., 2009–12); Mus. of London, 2008–19; Barbican Centre, 2009–. Hon. Treas., Guildhall Histl Assoc., 2008–. Trustee, Guildhall Sch. Trust, 2007–12. Fellow, Royal Commonwealth Soc., 1964. FRSA; Mem., Royal Soc. for Asian Affairs. Liveryman, Tylers' and Bricklayers' Co., 1979– (Master, 2006–07). *Publications*: articles on rowing, accounting and taxation in the EU, internat. finance, histories of guilds outside London. *Recreations*: listening to music, drinking fine wine, eating crab, collecting and reading histories of medieval guilds, collection of 1800 books on rowing from 34 countries donated to Leander Club in 2012. *Address*: 72 Gainsford Street, Tower Bridge Square, SE1 2NB; The Retreat, Barrack Square, Winchelsea, E Sussex TN36 4EG. *Clubs*: City Livery; Leander.

**HOFFMANN**, family name of **Baron Hoffmann**.

**HOFFMANN, Baron** *cr* 1995 (Life Peer), of Chedworth in the County of Gloucestershire; **Leonard Hubert Hoffmann**, Kt 1985; PC 1992; a Lord of Appeal in Ordinary, 1995–2009; international commercial arbitrator, since 2009; *b* 8 May 1934; *s* of B. W. and G. Hoffmann; *m* 1957, Gillian Lorna Sterner; two *d*. *Educ*: South African College Sch., Cape Town; Univ. of Cape Town (BA); The Queen's Coll., Oxford (Rhodes Scholar; MA, BCL, Vinerian Law Scholar). Hon. Fellow, 1992). Advocate of Supreme Court of S Africa, 1958–60. Called to the Bar, Gray's Inn, 1964, Bencher, 1984; QC 1977; a Judge, Courts of Appeal of Jersey and Guernsey, 1980–85; a Judge of the High Court of Justice, Chancery Div., 1985–92; a Lord Justice of Appeal, 1992–95. Non-permanent Judge, HK Court of Final Appeal, 1998–. Stowell Civil Law Fellow, University Coll., Oxford, 1961–73 (Hon. Fellow, 1995); Vis. Prof., Faculty of Law, Oxford Univ., 2009–; Hon. Prof. of Intellectual Property Law, QMUL, 2009–. Member: Royal Commn on Gambling, 1976–78; Council of Legal Educn, 1983–92 (Chm., 1989–92); Chm., Financial Markets Law Cttee, 2009–13. Pres., British-German Jurists Assoc., 1991–2009. Dir, ENO, 1985–90, 1991–94. Chm., Arts Council Adv. Cttee on London Orchs, 1993. Pres., Heath and Hampstead Soc., 2004–. Hon. Fellow, Chartered Inst. of Taxation, 2006. Hon. DCL: City, 1992; UWE, 1995; Gloucestershire, 2003. GBS 2014. *Publications*: The South African Law of Evidence, 1963. *Address*: Brick Court Chambers, 7–8 Essex Street, WC2R 3LD.

**HOFFMANN, Prof. Jules Alphonse**, PhD; Professor of Integrative Biology, Institute for Advanced Study, University of Strasbourg; Director, Research Unit 9022, 1978–2005, and Director, Institute of Molecular and Cellular Biology, 1993–2005, Centre national de la recherche scientifique, now Distinguished Class Research Director; *b* Echternach, Luxembourg, 2 Aug. 1941; *m* Daniele; two *c*. *Educ*: Univ. of Strasbourg (PhD Biol. 1969). Lab. Asst, Fac. of Scis, Univ. of Strasbourg, 1962; Centre national de la recherche scientifique: Res. Trng Asst, 1963; Res. Asst, 1964–68; Res. Associate, 1969–73; post-doctoral trng, Philipps Univ., Marburg an der Lahn, 1973–74; Res. Dir, CNRS, 1974–2009. Member: French Académie des Sciences, 1992 (Pres., 2007–08); German Acad. of Scis Leopoldina, 1987; EMBO, 1995; MAE 1993; Foreign Associate: Amer. Acad. of Arts and Scis, 2003; Russian Acad. of Scis, 2009; NAS, USA, 2008. (Jtly) Robert Koch Prize, 2004; (jtly) Balzan Prize, 2007; Keio Prize for Med. Scis, 2010; (jtly) Nobel Prize for Physiology or Medicine, 2011; Canada Gairdner Award, 2011; (jtly) Shaw Prize, 2011; Gold Medal, CNRS, 2011. *Publications*: Progress in Ecdysone Research, 1980; (ed jtly) Biosynthesis, Metabolism and Modes of Action of Invertebrate Hormones, 1985; (ed with R. A. B. Ezekowitz) Innate Immunity, 2002; articles in jls. *Address*: UPR 9022 du CNRS, Institut de Biologie, Moléculaire et Cellulaire, 15 rue René Descartes, 67084 Strasbourg Cedex, France.

**HOFFMANN, Prof. Roald**; Frank H. T. Rhodes Professor of Humane Letters, Cornell University, 1996–2009, now Emeritus; *b* 18 July 1937; *s* of Hillel Safran and Clara (*née* Rosen, who *m* 2nd, Paul Hoffmann); *m* 1960, Eva Börjesson; one *s* one *d*. *Educ*: Columbia Univ. (BA); Harvard Univ. (MA, PhD). Junior Fellow, Society of Fellows, Harvard Univ., 1962–65; Associate Professor, to Professor, 1965–74, John A. Newman Prof. of Physical Science, 1974–96, Cornell Univ. Member: Nat. Acad. of Sciences; Amer. Acad. of Arts and Sciences. Foreign Member: Royal Soc., 1984; Indian Nat. Acad. of Sciences; Royal Swedish Acad. of Sciences; USSR Acad. of Sciences; Finnish Acad. of Sciences. Hon. DTech Royal Inst. of Technology, Stockholm, 1977; Hon. DSc: Yale, 1980; Hartford, 1982; Columbia, 1982; City Univ. of NY, 1983; Puerto Rico, 1983; La Plata, 1984; Uruguay, 1984; State Univ. of NY at Binghamtom, 1985; Colgate, 1985; Rennes, 1986; Ben Gurion, 1989; Lehigh Univ., 1989; Carleton Coll., 1989; Maryland, 1990; Athens 1991; Thessaloniki, 1991; Bar Ilan, 1991; St Petersburg, 1991; Barcelona, 1992; Ohio State, 1993. Nobel Prize for Chemistry, 1981. *Publications*: (with R. B. Woodward) The Conservation of Orbital Symmetry, 1970; Solids and Surfaces, 1988; (with V. Torrence) Chemistry Imagined, 1993; The Same and Not the Same, 1995; (with S. Leibowitz Schmidt) Old Wine, New Flasks, 1997; (ed jtly) Beyond the Finite, 2010; Roald Hoffmann on the Philosophy, Art and Science of Chemistry, 2011; *fiction*: The Metamict State (poetry), 1987; Gaps and Verges (poetry), 1990; Memory Effects (poetry), 1999; (with Carl Djerassi) Oxygen (drama), 2000; Soliton (poetry), 2002; Catalista (poetry), 2002; Roald Hoffmann Izbrannie Stichotvorenia (poetry), 2010 (bilingual, Russian/English edn); Something That Belongs to You (drama), 2015; many scientific articles. *Address*: Department of Chemistry and Chemical Biology, Cornell University, Ithaca, NY 14853–1301, USA.

**HOFFORD, Leo**; QC (Scot.) 2008; *b* Singapore, 12 March 1958; *s* of Donald Hartley Hofford and Moira Macgregor (*née* Cartner); *m* 1993, Jackie Paterson; one *s* two *d*. *Educ*: Glenalmond; Edinburgh Univ. (BA, LLB, DipLP). Admitted as solicitor, 1985; called to the Scottish Bar, 1990. *Publications*: (contrib.) Parliament House Portraits. *Recreations*: writing, reading, tennis, all winter sports, piano. *Address*: 14 Chester Street, Edinburgh EH3 7RA. *T*: 07739 639086. *E*: hoffordleo@hotmail.com.

**HOFMEYR, Stephen Murray**; QC 2000; a Recorder, since 2005; a Deputy High Court Judge, since 2008; *b* 10 Feb. 1956; *s* of late Jan Murray Hofmeyr and of Stella Mary Hofmeyr (*née* Mills); *m* 1980, Audrey Frances Cannan; two *s* one *d*. *Educ*: Diocesan Coll., Rondebosch; Univ. of Cape Town (BCom, LLB); University Coll., Oxford (MA Juris.). Advocate, Supreme Court of S Africa; called to the Bar, Gray's Inn, 1982; Attorney and Conveyancer, Supreme Court of S Africa, 1984–85; in practice at the Bar, 1987–; Barrister, Eastern Caribbean Supreme Ct, 2005, and Supreme Ct of the Bahamas, 2012. *Publications*: (ed jtly) Carver on Charterparties, 2017. *Recreations*: walking, ski-ing, tennis, golf. *Address*: Acre Holt, One Tree Hill Road, Guildford GU4 8PJ. *T*: (01483) 834733; 7 King's Bench Walk, Temple, EC4Y 7DS. *Clubs*: Vincent's (Oxford); Guildford Golf.

**HOGAN, Prof. Brigid Linda Mary**, PhD; FRS 2001; Professor of Cell Biology, Duke University Medical Center, since 2018 (George Barth Geller Professor and Chair, Department of Cell Biology, 2002–18); *b* 28 Aug. 1943; *d* of Edmond Hogan and Joyce Hogan (*née* Willcox). *Educ*: Wycombe High Sch. for Girls; Newnham Coll., Cambridge (MA, PhD 1968). Postdoctoral Fellowship, MIT, 1968–70; Lectr, Univ. of Sussex,

1970–74; ICRF, London, 1974–84; NIMR, London, 1985–88; Prof. of Cell Biol., Vanderbilt Univ. Med. Sch., 1988–2002; Investigator, Howard Hughes Med. Inst., 1993–2002. Fellow, Amer. Acad. of Arts and Scis, 2001. Member: Nat. Acad. of Medicine (formerly Inst. of Medicine), 1996; Nat. Acad. of Sciences, USA, 2005. *Address:* Department of Cell Biology, Duke University Medical Center, Box 3709, Durham, NC 27710, USA.

**HOGAN, Sir Patrick,** KNZM 1999; CBE 1991; Proprietor, Cambridge Stud, 1975–2018; *b* 20 Oct. 1939; *s* of Thomas Hogan and Sarah Margaret Small; *m* 1961, Justine Alice Heath; two *d. Educ:* Goodwood Sch., Cambridge, NZ; St Peter's Convent Sch., Cambridge; Marist Brothers, Hamilton. Partner, with brother, Fencourt Thoroughbred Stud, 1965–75; estabd Cambridge Stud in partnership with wife, 1975; first to apply modern methods of promotion of progeny for sale with huge benefits to the industry as a whole. Pres., NZ Thoroughbred Breeders Assoc., 1993–96; Dir, NZ Thoroughbred Mktg Bd, 1997–99. Patron: Cambridge Chamber of Commerce, 1990–; Equine Res. Foundn, 1992. Life Mem., Cambridge Jockey Club Inc. (formerly Pres.). Hon. MSc Sport and Exercise Sci. Waikato Inst. of Technol., 2002; Hon. Dr Waikato, 2013. BMW Award for Outstanding Contribn to Racing Excellence in NZ, 1991. *Recreations:* tennis, Rugby, racing. *Clubs:* Cambridge, Hautapu Rugby Football (Cambridge); Waikato Racing (Hamilton); Auckland Racing.

**HOGAN-HOWE,** family name of **Baron Hogan-Howe**.

**HOGAN-HOWE,** Baron *cr* 2017 (Life Peer), of Sheffield in the County of South Yorkshire; **Bernard Hogan-Howe,** Kt 2013; QPM 2003; Commissioner, Metropolitan Police, 2011–17; *b* 25 Oct. 1957; *s* of Bernard Howe and Cecilia Hogan-Howe; *m* Marion White (MVO 2011). *Educ:* Hinde House Comprehensive Sch.; Merton Coll., Oxford (MA Juris.; Hon. Fellow 2013); Sheffield Univ. (MBA). Joined S Yorks Police, 1979; Dist Comdr, Doncaster W Area, 1996–97; Merseyside Police: Asst Chief Constable and Hd, Community Affairs, 1997–99; Hd, Area Ops, 1999–2001; Asst Comr, Metropolitan Police, 2001–04; Chief Constable of Merseyside, 2004–09; HM Inspector of Constabulary, 2009–11. Mem., Cabinet, ACPO, 2001–04. Mem., Financial System Vulnerabilities Cttee, HSBC, 2017–; Advr, Powerscourt, 2018–. Hon. Fellow, Liverpool John Moores Univ., 2010. Hon. LLD: Sheffield Hallam, 2012; Sheffield, 2013. *Recreations:* horse riding, playing football, supporting Sheffield Wednesday FC, opera.

**HOGARTH, Adrian John;** Parliamentary Counsel, since 2002; *b* 7 July 1960; *s* of late Prof. Cyril Alfred Hogarth and Dr Audrey Hogarth, JP, DL; *m* 1996, Archana (*née* Singh); one *s* one *d. Educ:* Magdalene Coll., Cambridge (BA Archaeol. and Anthropol. Law 1981; LLM 1982; MA). Called to the Bar, Inner Temple, 1983; Coll. Supervisor, Magdalene Coll., Cambridge, 1983–85; Asst Parly Counsel, 1985–89; Sen. Asst Parly Counsel, 1989–92; Principal Asst Parly Counsel, 1992–94, seconded to Law Commn; Dep. Parly Counsel, 1994–2002; Sen. Parly Counsel, Law Commn, 2011–15 (on secondment). Mem. Council, Commonwealth Assoc. of Legislative Counsel, 2015–. FRSA. *Recreations:* cricket, tennis, travel, reeling. *Address:* Office of the Parliamentary Counsel, 1 Horse Guards Road, SW1A 2HQ. *Clubs:* Lansdowne; Cypos? Cricket.

**HOGARTH, Andrew Allan;** QC 2003; *b* 21 July 1951; *s* of late William Allan Hogarth and Margaret Hogarth; *m* 1975, Elinor Mary Williams; four *s. Educ:* Harrow Sch.; Trinity Coll., Cambridge (MA 1973). Called to the Bar, Lincoln's Inn, 1975; in practice as barrister, specialising in employment law, 1975–. Head of Chambers, 2005–15. *Address:* 12 King's Bench Walk, Temple, EC4Y 7EL. *T:* (020) 7583 0811. *E:* hogarth@12kbw.co.uk.

**HOGBIN, Ann Denise,** CBE 2008; multi sport operations consultant, since 2012; Founder, ADH Sport Ltd, 2012–14; *b* Dover, 20 Dec. 1953; *d* of Gordon and Josephine Hogbin. *Educ:* Dover Grammar Sch. for Girls; Canterbury Tech. Coll. (Adv. Secretarial Course). Proj. Manager, British Olympic Assoc., 1973–94; Chief Exec., Commonwealth Games England, 1991–2011. Member: Team England HQ staff at Commonwealth Games, 1974, 1978, 1986, 1990; Fedn staff, Commonwealth Games, 1982; Team GB HQ staff at Olympics Games, Montreal, 1976, Seoul, 1988, Barcelona, 1992, and at Winter Olympics, Innsbruck, 1976, Sarajevo, 1984, Albertville, 1992; Gen. Team Manager, Commonwealth Games, Victoria, 1994; Chef de Mission: Team England, Commonwealth Games, Kuala Lumpur, 1998, Manchester, 2002, Melbourne, 2006; Team England, Commonwealth Youth Games, Edinburgh, 2000, Bendigo, 2004, Pune, 2008; Gen. Team England Manager, Commonwealth Games, Delhi, 2010; Dep. Chef de Mission, Operations, ParalympicsGB, 2012. *Recreations:* cycling, dining, cooking, travel.

**HOGBIN, Walter,** CBE 1990; FREng, FICE; Consultant, Taylor Woodrow, 1997–99; Chairman, Taylor Woodrow International Ltd, 1983–96; *b* 21 Dec. 1937; *s* of Walter Clifford John Hogbin and Mary Hogbin; *m* 1968, Geraldine Anne-Marie Castley; two *s. Educ:* Kent Coll., Canterbury; Queens' Coll., Cambridge (MA). Joined Taylor Woodrow, 1961; Taylor Woodrow International Ltd: Divl Dir, 1975–77; Dir, 1977–79; Man. Dir, 1979–85; Dir, 1984–96, Jt Man. Dir, 1988–92, Taylor Woodrow plc; Chm., Taylor Woodrow Construction Supervisory Bd, 1991–93. Vice-Pres., Eur. Construction Industry Fedn, 1992–94; Member: Adv. Council, ECGD, 1983–88; Overseas Projects Bd, 1986–91; Export Gp for Construction Ind., 1980–97 (Chm., 1988–90); Eur. Internat. Contractors Fedn, 1988–97 (Pres., 1994–97). Col, Engr and Logistic (formerly Transport) Staff Corps, RE, 1986–2000. FREng (FEng 1994). FRSA. Telford Gold Medal, ICE, 1979. *Recreations:* golf, gardening. *Address:* Codrington Court, Wapley Road, Chipping Sodbury, S Glos BS37 6RY. *Club:* Athenæum.

**HOGG,** family name of **Viscount Hailsham** and of **Baroness Hogg**.

**HOGG,** Baroness *cr* 1995 (Life Peer), of Kettlethorpe, in the county of Lincolnshire; **Sarah Elizabeth Mary Hogg, (Viscountess Hailsham);** Chairman, Frontier Economics, 1999–2013; Lead Independent Director, HM Treasury, 2011–17; *b* 14 May 1946; *d* of Baron Boyd-Carpenter, PC; *m* 1968, Rt Hon. Douglas Martin Hogg (*see* Viscount Hailsham); one *s* one *d. Educ:* St Mary's Convent, Ascot; Lady Margaret Hall, Oxford University (1st Cl. Hons PPE; Hon. Fellow, 1994). Staff writer, Economist, 1967, Literary Editor, 1970, Economics Editor, 1977; Economics Editor, Sunday Times, 1981; Presenter, Channel 4 News, 1982–83; Econs Editor, and Dep. Exec. Editor, Finance and Industry, The Times, 1984–86; Asst Editor, and Business and City Editor, The Independent, 1986–89; Econs Editor, Daily Telegraph and Sunday Telegraph, 1989–90; Hd, Prime Minister's Policy Unit, 1990–95; Dir, 1995–97, Chm., 1997–99, London Economics. Director: London Broadcasting Co., 1982–90; Royal Nat. Theatre, 1988–91. A Gov., BBC, 2000–04. Non-executive Director: Foreign and Colonial Smaller Cos Investment Trust, 1995–2002 (Chm., 1997–2002); Nat. Provident Instn, 1996–99; GKN, 1996–2006 (Dep. Chm., 2003–06); The Energy Group, 1996–98; 3i Group plc, 1997–2010 (Dep. Chm., 2000–02; Chm., 2002–10); Scottish Eastern Investment Trust, 1998–99; Martin Currie Portfolio Investment Trust, 1999–2002; P&O, 1999–2000; P&O Princess, 2000–03; Carnival Corp., 2003–08; Carnival plc, 2003–08; BG Group, 2005–16; Cadbury plc, 2008–10; John Lewis Partnership, 2011–18; Financial Conduct Authy, 2016–; Sen. Ind. Dir, Royal Mail Gp, 2019–; Nat. Dir, Times Newspapers Ltd, 2015–. Member: Internat. Adv. Bd, Nat. Westminster Bank, 1995–98; Adv. Bd, Bankinter, 1995–98. Chairman: Financial Reporting Council, 2010–14 (Mem., 2004–14; Dep. Chm., 2007–10); Hogg Tendering Adv. Cttee for LIBOR, 2012–14. Mem., Takeover Panel, 2011–19. Member: House of Lords Select Cttee on Sci. and Technol., 1996–99; H of L Monetary Policy and Econs Cttee, 2000–03. Member: REconS, 1996–2000; Council, IFS, 1998–2005; Cemmap, 2002–04. Governor: Centre for Economic Policy Research, 1985–92; IDS, 1987; Univ. of Lincoln, 2002–05; London Business Sch., 2004–10; Fellow, Eton Coll., 1996–2008. Trustee: St Mary's Sch., Ascot, 1994–; Trusthouse Foundn, 2003–15; Cicely Saunders Internat., 2009–11; Queen Elizabeth Diamond Jubilee Trust, 2012–; Historic Lincoln Trust, 2013–; NIESR, 2014–15. Hon. MA Open Univ., 1987; Hon. DLitt Loughborough, 1992; Hon. LLD Lincoln, 2001; Hon. DPhil: City, 2002; Cranfield, 2006. Wincott Foundation Financial Journalist of the Year, 1985; Sunday Times Non-Executive Directors Lifetime Achievement Award, 2017. *Publications:* (with Jonathan Hill) Too Close to Call, 1995; Katherine's House, 2019. *Address:* House of Lords, SW1A 0PW.
*See also* Hon. Sir T. P. J. Boyd-Carpenter, Hon. C. M. Hogg.

**HOGG, Hon. Charlotte Mary;** Chief Executive Officer, Visa Europe, and Executive Vice-President, Visa, since 2017; *b* London, 26 Aug. 1970; *d* of Viscount Hailsham, *qv*, and Baroness Hogg, *qv*; *m* 1999, Stephen Kenneth Sacks; two *c. Educ:* St Mary's Sch., Ascot; Hertford Coll., Oxford (BA); Harvard Univ. (Kennedy Schol.). Principal, McKinsey & Co., 1994–2001; Man. Dir, Morgan Stanley, 2001–07; Discover Financial Services, 2007–08; Man. Dir, UK and Ireland, Experian, 2008–11; Hd, Retail and Intermediaries, Santander UK, 2011–13; Chief Operating Officer, 2013–17, Dep. Gov. for Markets and Banking, 2017, Bank of England. Non-exec. Dir, BBC Worldwide, 2010. Mem., Finance Cttee, OUP, 2006–. Gov., Nottingham Trent Univ., 2010. Trustee, First Story, 2008– (Chm., 2008–12). *Recreation:* eventing. *Address:* The Cottage, Kettlethorpe Hall, Kettlethorpe, Lincs LN1 2LD.

**HOGG, Sir Christopher (Anthony),** Kt 1985; Chairman: Financial Reporting Council, 2006–10; Reuters Group (formerly Reuters Holdings) PLC, 1985–2004 (Director, 1984–2004); GlaxoSmithKline, 2002–04 (Director, SmithKline Beecham, subseq. GlaxoSmithKline, 1993–2004); *b* 2 Aug. 1936; *s* of late Anthony Wentworth Hogg and Monica Mary (*née* Gladwell); *m* 1st, 1961, Anne Patricia (*née* Cathie) (marr. diss. 1997); two *d*; 2nd, 1997, Miriam Stoppard, *qv. Educ:* Marlborough Coll.; Trinity Coll., Oxford (MA; Hon. Fellow 1982); Harvard Univ. (MBA). National Service, Parachute Regt, 1955–57. Harkness Fellow, 1960–62; IMEDE, Lausanne, 1962–63; Hill, Samuel Ltd, 1963–66; IRC, 1966–68; Courtaulds plc, 1968–96: Chief Exec., 1979–91; Chm., 1980–96; Chm., Courtaulds Textiles, 1990–95; Dep. Chm., 1995–96, Chm., 1996–2002, Allied Domecq. Dir, Air Liquide SA, 2000–05. Advr, Corporate Governance Cttee, Financial Reporting Council/Stock Exchange (Cadbury Cttee), 1992. Member: Indust. Develt Adv. Bd, 1976–81; Cttee of Award for Harkness Fellowships, 1980–86; Internat. Council, J. P. Morgan, 1988–2003; Court, Bank of England, 1992–96. Chm. Bd, RNT, 1995–2004. Trustee, Ford Foundn, 1987–99. For. Hon. Mem., Amer. Acad. of Arts and Scis, 1991. Hon. FCSD 1987; Hon. Fellow, London Business Sch., 1992; Hon. FCGI 1992; Hon. FCA 2013. Hon. DSc: Cranfield Inst. of Technol., 1986; Aston, 1988. BIM Gold Medal, 1986; Centenary Medal, Soc. of Chemical Industry, 1989; Hambro Businessman of the Year, 1993. *Publications:* Masers and Lasers, 1963. *Recreations:* grandchildren, friends, golf.
*See also* C. M. Hogg, Hon. H. Legge.

**HOGG, Cressida Mary, (Mrs Henry Legge),** CBE 2014; Chairman, Land Securities Ltd, since 2018 (non-executive Director, since 2014); *b* London, 27 July 1969; *d* of Sir Christopher Anthony Hogg, *qv*; *m* 1995, Hon. Henry Legge, *qv*; three *d. Educ:* St Paul's Girls' Sch.; St John's Coll., Oxford (BA PPE). JP Morgan, London, 1990–93; 3i Group plc, 1995–2014: Managing Partner, Infrastructure, 3i Infrastructure plc, 2009–14; Global Hd of Infrastructure, Canada Pension Plan Investment Bd, 2014–18. Non-executive Director: Troy Asset Mgt, 2018–; London Stock Exchange Gp, 2019–. Mem., Infrastructure Adv. Council, 2010–13. *Recreations:* music, reading, equestrian sports, walking. *Address:* Land Securities Ltd, 100 Victoria Street, SW1E 5JL.

**HOGG, David Alan,** CB 1997; Director-General and General Counsel and Solicitor, HM Revenue and Customs, 2005–09; *b* 8 Oct. 1946; *s* of Donald Kenneth Hogg and Alwyn Lilian Hogg (*née* Chinchen); *m* 1st, 1969, Geraldine Patricia Smith (marr. diss. 1979); one *s* one *d*; 2nd, 1981, Pauline Pamela Papworth; two *s. Educ:* Brighton Coll.; Coll. of Law. Admitted solicitor, 1969; in private practice, 1969–78; Treasury Solicitor's Department: Sen. Legal Asst, 1978–85; Asst Treasury Solicitor, 1985–89; Dept of Energy, 1989–90; Treasury Solicitor's Department: Principal Asst Solicitor and Hd, Litigation Div., 1990–93; Dep. Treasury Solicitor, 1993–97; Solicitor and Legal Adviser: DETR, 1997–2001; DTLR, 2001–02; ODPM and Dept for Transport, 2002–03; ODPM, 2003–04; Actg Solicitor, HM Customs and Excise, 2004–05. Vice Pres., Valuation Tribunal for England, 2009–10. *Recreations:* inland waterways, theatre, reading, watching sport. *E:* mrdahogg@gmail.com.

**HOGG, Prof. Dorothy,** MBE 2001; Professor, 2004–07, and Head, Jewellery and Silversmithing Department, 1985–2007, Edinburgh College of Art, now Professor Emeritus; craft artist in residence, Victoria and Albert Museum, 2008; *b* 19 May 1945; *d* of William Hogg and Alice Hogg (*née* Murdoch); *m* 1973, Lachlan MacColl; one *s. Educ:* Glasgow Sch. of Art (Dip of Art); Royal Coll. of Art (Master of Design, Silver Medal for work of special distn); Moray House Coll. of Educn, Edinburgh (CertEd). Freelance designer, 1970–; Lecturer: Glasgow Sch. of Art, 1972–73; Duncan of Jordanstone Coll. of Art, 1974–85; Lectr, 1985–98, Reader, 1998–2004, Edinburgh Coll. of Art. External examr, UK instns. Chm. Contemp. Cttee, and Trustee, Scottish Goldsmiths Trust, 2000–05; Purchase Advr, 1997–2001, and Selected Index Advr, 2000–03, Crafts Council, London; Specialist Advr, Scottish Arts Council, 2003–05. Trustee, Crafts Council, 2008–. Solo retrospective exhibn, Scottish Gall., Edinburgh, 1994, 2014; many group exhibns, UK, Germany, Italy, Japan and USA, 1967–. Work in public and private collections incl. Royal Mus. of Scotland, Crafts Council, Goldsmiths' Co., Aberdeen Art Gall. and Mus., Koch Ring Collection, V&A, and Mus. of Arts and Design, NY; awarded first craft residency, V&A, 2008. Co-curator: A Sense of Jewellery, Goldsmiths' Centre, 2015; 50 Secrets of Magic Craftsmanship, Elements Fest., Edinburgh, 2017; Modernist Jewellery, Mus. of Scotland, 2018. Freeman, City of London, 1998; Mem., Incorporation of Goldsmiths, City of Edinburgh, 1992; Freeman, Co. of Goldsmiths, London, 1997. FRSA 2007. Hon. FRCA 2006. Lifetime Achievement Medal, Goldsmiths' Craft and Design Council, 2010. *Recreations:* drawing, gardening, architectural heritage concerns. *Address:* c/o The Scottish Gallery, 16 Dundas Street, Edinburgh EH3 6HZ. *T:* (0131) 558 1200, *Fax:* (0131) 558 3900. *E:* dorothy_hogg@hotmail.com.

**HOGG, Gilbert Charles;** author, since 2000; *b* 11 Feb. 1933; *s* of Charles and Ivy Ellen Hogg; *m* 1st, Jeanne Whiteside; one *s* one *d* (marr. diss. 1973); 2nd, 1979, Angela Christina Wallace (*d* 2016); 3rd, 2017, Maureen Lundy. *Educ:* Victoria University Coll., Wellington, NZ (LLB 1956). Called to the New Zealand Bar and admitted Solicitor, 1957; admitted Solicitor, GB, 1971. Served RNZAC (TF), 1955–62 (Lieut). Partner, Phillips, Shayle-George and Co., Solicitors, Wellington, 1960–66; Sen. Crown Counsel, Hong Kong, 1966–70; Editor, Business Law Summary, 1970–79; Divl Legal Adviser, BSC, 1974–79; British Gas Corporation, subseq. British Gas: Dir of Legal Services, 1979–84; Sec., 1984–90; Dir, Regulatory Ops, 1990–95; solicitor and regulatory consultant, 1995–2000.

Mem., Competition Commn (formerly Monopolies and Mergers Commn), 1998–2003. Mem., Professional Ethics Cttee, 1994–97, and Council, Energy Section, 1993–98, Internat. Bar Assoc. Chairman: Phoenix House, 1996–2004; Charterhouse-in-Southwark, 1999–2004; Trustee, IBA Educn Trust, 1995–98. *Publications:* Teaching Yourself Tranquillity, 2005; The Happy Humanist, 2011; *novels:* A Smell of Fraud, 1974; The Predators, 2002; Caring for Cathy, 2008; Blue Lantern, 2009; Present Tense, 2010; The Cruel Peak, 2012; Codename Wolf, 2013; Don't Cry for the Brave, 2014; The Unforgiving Shore, 2015; Rendezvous with Death, 2016; Night Shelter, 2017; Bill Batley's Notebook, 2019. *Address:* 73 Ellerby Street, SW6 6EU. *T:* (020) 7736 8903. *E:* gilhogg@hotmail.com. *W:* www.gilhogg.co.uk.

**HOGG, Jill Alison;** *see* Douglas, J. A.

**HOGG, Hon. Dame Mary (Claire), (Hon. Dame Mary Koops),** DBE 1995; a Judge of the High Court of Justice, Family Division, 1995–2016; *b* 15 Jan. 1947; *d* of Rt Hon. Baron Hailsham of St Marylebone, PC, KG, CH, FRS; *m* 1987, Eric Koops (LVO 1997); one *s* one *d. Educ:* St Paul's Girls' Sch. Called to the Bar, Lincoln's Inn, 1968 (Bencher, 1995), NI, 1993; QC 1989; Asst Recorder, 1986–90; Recorder, 1990–95. Mem. Council, Children's Soc., 1990–95; Trustee, Harrison Homes, 1983–2009. Gov., Univ. of Westminster, 1992– (Poly. of Central London, 1983–92). FRSA 1991. Freeman, City of London, 1981. Hon. LLD Westminster, 1995.
*See also* Viscount Hailsham.

**HOGG, Sir Michael Edward L.;** *see* Lindsay-Hogg.

**HOGG, Sir Piers Michael James,** 9th Bt *cr* 1846, of Upper Grosvenor Street, Middlesex; *b* 25 April 1957; *e s* of Sir Michael Hogg, 8th Bt and of Elizabeth Anne Thérèse, *e d* of Sir Terence Falkiner, 8th Bt; *S* father, 2001; *m* 1982, Vivien (marr. diss. 1996), *y d* of Dr Philip Holman; one *s* one *d*; *m* 2016, Hazel, *d* of Harry Hewett. *Educ:* St Paul's Sch. *Heir: s* James Edward Hogg, *b* 11 Sept. 1985.

**HOGG, Rear-Adm. Robin Ivor Trower,** CB 1988; FNI; Managing Director, Robstar Productions Ltd, since 1998; *b* 25 Sept. 1932; *s* of Dudley and Nancy Hogg; *m* 1st, 1958, Susan Bridget Beryl Grantham; two *s* two *d*; 2nd, 1970, Angela Sarah Patricia Kirwan. *Educ:* The New Beacon, Sevenoaks; Bedford School. Directorate of Naval Plans, 1974–76; RCDS 1977; Captain RN Presentation Team, 1978–79; Captain First Frigate Sqdn, 1980–82; Director Naval Operational Requirements, 1982–84; Flag Officer, First Flotilla, 1984–86; COS to C-in-C Fleet, 1986–87, retd. CEO, Colebrand Ltd, 1988–97; Managing Director: Raidfleet Ltd, 1988–2000; Shinbond Ltd, 1998–2000. Chm., 2011–13, Pres., 2013–, CPRE for Devon (Chm., Plymouth and South Hams, 2007–). FCMI; FRSA. *Recreation:* private life. *Address:* c/o Barclays Bank, Blenheim Gate, 22/24 Upper Marlborough Road, St Albans AL1 3AL. *T:* (01752) 872366.

**HOGGARD, Robin Richard;** Head, Risk and Compliance Unit, London School of Economics and Political Science, since 2017; *b* 26 Nov. 1956; *s* of George Lawrence Hoggard and Frances Mary Christine Hoggard (*née* Stephenson); *m* 1988, Tonoko Komuro; one *s*. *Educ:* Cheadle Hulme Sch.; Univ. of Newcastle upon Tyne (BA Hons Politics 1979); SOAS, Univ. of London (MSc 1982). HM Diplomatic Service, 1982–2007: FCO, 1982; Tokyo, 1984–89; FCO, 1989–91; DTI, 1991–93; UK Deleg. to NATO, 1994–98; Counsellor (Mgt) and Consul Gen., Tokyo, 1998–2003; Counsellor, FCO, 2003–04; Hd of Res. Analysts, FCO, 2004–07; Dir of Govt Relns (formerly of Ext. Relns), 2007–16, Dir of Governance, Legal and Policy Div., 2016–17, LSE. *Address:* London School of Economics and Political Science, Houghton Street, WC2A 2AE.

**HOGGER, Henry George,** CMG 2004; FRGS; HM Diplomatic Service, retired; Senior Consultant, MEC International Ltd, since 2005; *b* 9 Nov. 1948; *s* of late Rear-Adm. Henry Charles Hogger, CB, DSC and Ethel Mary Hogger; *m* 1972, Fiona Jane McNabb; two *s* two *d. Educ:* Winchester Coll.; Trinity Hall, Cambridge (MA Hons). FRGS 2010. Joined FCO 1969; MECAS, Lebanon, 1971–72; served Aden, Caracas, Kuwait; FCO, 1978–82; Head of Chancery, Abu Dhabi, 1982–86; FCO, 1986–89; Counsellor and Dep. Head of Mission, Amman, 1989–92; High Comr, Namibia, 1992–96; Head, Latin America, later Latin America and Caribbean Dept, FCO, 1996–2000; Ambassador to Syria, 2000–03; Governorate Co-ordinator for Basra, Coalition Provisional Authy, Iraq, 2003–04 (on secondment). Chm., Council for British Research in the Levant, 2008–13. Co-Chair, Damask Rose Trust, 2008–19. Mem., Inst. of Advanced Motorists. *Recreations:* golf, sailing, music, travel. *Address:* Shop Farm House, Briantspuddle, Dorchester, Dorset DT2 7HY.

**HOGGETT, Anthony John Christopher,** PhD; QC 1986; a Recorder, 1988–2006; *b* 20 Aug. 1940; *s* of late Christopher Hoggett and Annie Marie Hoggett; *m* 1968, Brenda Marjorie Hale (*see* Baroness Hale of Richmond) (marr. diss. 1992); one *d*. *Educ:* Leeds Grammar Sch.; Hymers Coll., Hull; Clare Coll., Cambridge (MA, LLB); PhD Manchester. Asst Juridique, Inst. of Comparative Law, Paris, 1962–63; Lectr in Law, Univ. of Manchester, 1963–69; called to Bar, Gray's Inn, 1969, Head of Chambers, 1985–96; Asst Recorder, 1982. Res. Fellow, Univ. of Michigan, 1965–66. Mem., Civil Service Final Selection Bd for Planning Inspectors, 1987–91. Dir, Eur. Youth Parlt Internat., 1993–2003. Mem. Adv. Council, Rural Bldgs Preservation Trust, 1994–2002 (Trustee, 2000–02). Mem. Editl Bd, Envmtl Law Reports, 1992–2006. *Publications:* articles in Criminal Law Rev., Mod. Law Rev. and others. *Recreation:* music. *Address:* Kings Chambers, 36 Young Street, Manchester M3 3FT.

**HOHN, Sir Christopher,** KCMG 2014; philanthropist; Co-founder and Trustee, Children's Investment Fund Foundation, since 2002; Founder and Managing Partner, Children's Investment Fund, since 2003; *b* Addlestone, Surrey, 1967; *m* 1995, Jamie Cooper (marr. diss. 2014); four *c* (incl. triplets). *Educ:* Southampton Univ. (BA 1st Cl. Hons Accounting and Business Econs 1988); Harvard Business Sch. (MBA 1993; Baker Schol.). With Apax Partners, private equity gp, 1994–96; hedge fund manager, Perry Capital, USA, 1996–2003 (Hd, London ops, 1998–2003). *Address:* c/o Children's Investment Fund Foundation, 7 Clifford Street, W1S 2FT.

**HØJ, Prof. Peter Bordier,** PhD; Vice Chancellor and President, University of Queensland, since 2012; *b* Hundested, Denmark, 29 April 1957; *s* of John and Bodil Høj; *m* 1983, Dr Robyn Van Heeswijk (*d* 2003); one *s* one *d*; partner, Prof. Mandy Thomas. *Educ:* Univ. of Copenhagen (MSc; PhD 1987). FTSE 2004. Foundn Prof. of Viticultural Sci., Univ. of Adelaide, 1995–97; Man. Dir, Wine Res. Inst., 1997–2004; CEO, Australian Res. Council, 2004–07; Vice Chancellor and Pres., Univ. of S Australia, 2007–12. Director: Provisor Pty Ltd, 2002–04; CRC Viticulture, 2002–04. Co-Dep. Chair, Strengthened Export Controls Steering Gp, Dept of Defence, Australia, 2012–16. Member: Cttee, Nat. Res. Infrastructure, 2009–11; Australian Qualifications Framework Council, 2011–13; Australian Res. Cttee, 2012–14; Adv. Bd, edX Univ., 2014–17; Adv. Bd, Med. Res. Future Fund, Res. Australia, 2016–. Chair, Go8, 2017–; Member, Board: Educn Australia, 2008–10; Open Univs Australia, 2008–09; Univs Australia, 2009–13 (Dep. Chair and Lead Vice Chancellor of Res., 2011–13); CSIRO, 2011–14; Mem. Council, Hanban, 2017–. Mem. Council, Australian Inst. Marine Scientists, 2005–07. DUniv. Copenhagen, 2008; S Australia, 2014. *Publications:* contrib. scientific pubns. *Recreations:* soccer, biking, classical music, bush walking, wine show judging. *Address:* c/o University of Queensland, Brisbane, Qld 4072, Australia.

**HOLBOROW, Jonathan;** Editor, Mail on Sunday, 1992–98; Member, Editorial Integrity Board, Express Newspapers, 2000–02; *b* 12 Oct. 1943; *s* of late Prof. Eric John Holborow and of Cicely Mary (*née* Foister); *m* 1st, 1965, Susan Ridings (*d* 1993); one *s* one *d*; 2nd, 1994, Vivien Ferguson. *Educ:* Charterhouse. Reporter, Maidenhead Advertiser, 1961–65; Lincs Echo, 1965–66; Lincoln Chronicle, 1966–67; Daily Mail, Manchester, 1967–69; Scottish News Editor, Daily Mail, Glasgow, 1969–70; Daily Mail, Manchester: Northern Picture Editor, 1970–72; Northern News Editor, 1972–74; Daily Mail, London: Dep. News Editor, 1974–75; News Editor, 1975–80; Editor, Cambrian News, Aberystwyth, 1980–82; Asst Editor, then Associate Editor, Mail on Sunday, 1982–86; Dep. Editor, Today, 1986–87; Daily Mail: Asst Editor, then Associate Editor, 1987–88; Dep. Editor, 1988–92; Dir, Associated Newspapers Ltd, 1992–98. Chm., Folkestone and Hythe Cons. Assoc., 2004–09; Mem., Area Mgt Exec., Kent Conservatives, 2009–12 (Dep. Chm., 2010–12). *Recreation:* golf.

**HOLBOROW, Prof. Leslie Charles,** MA; QSO 2009; Vice-Chancellor, Victoria University of Wellington, 1985–98, now Emeritus Professor; *b* 28 Jan. 1941; *s* of George and Ivah Vivienne Holborow; *m* 1965, Patricia Lynette Walsh (*d* 2012); one *s* two *d*; partner, 2013, Elizabeth Mcleay. *Educ:* Henderson High Sch.; Auckland Grammar Sch.; Univ. of Auckland (MA 1st Cl. Hons Philosophy); Oxford Univ. (BPhil). Jun. Lectr, Auckland Univ., 1963; Commonwealth schol. at Merton Coll., Oxford, 1963–65; Lectr, then Sen. Lectr, Univ. of Dundee (until 1967 Queen's Coll., Univ. of St Andrews), 1965–74, Mem. Court, 1972–74; University of Queensland, Brisbane: Prof. of Philosophy, 1974–85; Pres., Academic Bd, 1980–81; Pro-Vice-Chancellor (Humanities), 1983–85. Sen. Fellow, Centre for Strategic Studies, Victoria Univ. of Wellington, 2003–14. Pres., Qld Br., Aust. Inst. of Internat. Affairs, 1984–85; Nat. Pres., 1987–90, Hon. Vice Pres., 1991–, Mem., Standing Cttee, 2002–, Nat. Inst. of Internat. Affairs; Member: NZ Cttee for Pacific Economic Co-operation, 1986–97; Bd, Inst. of Policy Studies, 1986–98; Bd, NZ Inst. of Econ. Res., 1986–91; Bd, Victoria Univ. Foundn, 1990–98; NZ Cttee for Security Co-operation in Asia Pacific, 1994–. Chair: NZ Vice-Chancellors' Cttee, 1990, 1996; Cttee on Univ. Academic Progs, 1993–95; Bd, NZ Univs Acad. Audit Unit, 2003–08; Member: Council, ACU, 1990–91, 1996; Educn Sub-Commn, UNESCO Commn for NZ, 1997–2000. Member: Musica Viva Nat. Bd, 1984–85; Bd of Management, Music Fedn of NZ, 1987–90; Bd, NZ Sch. of Dance, 2010–16; Bd, Mahara Gall., 2015– (Chair, 2016–). Trustee: NZ String Quartet, 1988–2011; Lilburn Residence Trust, 2005–15; Chm., NZ String Quartet Foundn, 1999–. Hon. LLD Victoria Univ. of Wellington, 1998. *Publications:* articles on NZ foreign policy, opera reviews, contrib. philosophical and legal jls. *Recreations:* tramping, golf, listening to music. *Address:* 16 Ames Street, Paekakariki, Wellington 5034, New Zealand. *Clubs:* Wellington, Victoria University Staff (Wellington).

**HOLBOURN, Oliver Gerald;** Head of Strategy, Economics and Corporate Development, Royal Bank of Scotland Group, since 2018; *b* Hammersmith, 23 Sept. 1977; *s* of Gilbert and Gillian Holbourn; *m* 2006, Charlotte; two *s* one *d. Educ:* Tonbridge Sch.; Pembroke Coll., Oxford (BA Hons Jurisprudence). Bank of America Merrill Lynch, 2000–13: various posts incl. Hd, Equity Syndicate, and Hd, UK Origination for Equity Capital Mkts; UK Financial Investments Ltd: Hd, Capital Mkts, 2013–14; Hd, Mkt Investments, 2014–16; Chief Exec., 2016–18. *Recreation:* tennis. *Club:* Queen's.

**HOLBROOK, Rt Rev. John Edward;** *see* Brixworth, Bishop Suffragan of.

**HOLBROOK, Peter,** CBE 2015; Chief Executive, Social Enterprise UK, since 2010; *b* Tooting, London, 12 March 1971; *s* of Keith Holbrook and Pamela Holbrook (now O'Brien). *Educ:* Tamworth Manor High Sch.; Univ. of Central Lancashire (BSc Hons Envmtl Mgt). Res. and Media Officer, Greenpeace UK, 1993–94; London Shops Manager, Oxfam GB, 1994–98; Retail and Mktg Manager, Focus on Blindness, 1998–2001; Founding Chief Exec., Sunlight Develt Trust, 2001–10. Chair, Social Enterprise World Forum, 2012–. Member: Mutuals Taskforce, Cabinet Office, 2010–; Employee Engagement Taskforce, BIS, then BEIS, 2010–; EU Social Business Expert Gp, 2012–. Trustee, Big Society Trust, 2010–. Mem., House of St Barnabas, 2013–. *Recreations:* theatre, film, festivals, literature, social entrepreneurship. *Address:* Social Enterprise UK, Third Floor, Fire Station, 139 Tooley Street, SE1 2HZ. *T:* (020) 3589 4950, *Fax:* (020) 7403 7184.

**HOLCROFT, Sir Charles (Anthony Culcheth),** 4th Bt *cr* 1921, of Eaton Mascott, Berrington, co. Salop; *b* Ludlow, Shropshire, 22 Oct. 1959; *e s* of Sir Peter George Culcheth Holcroft, 3rd Bt and of Rosemary Rachel (*née* Deas, now Firbank); *S* father, 2009; *m* 1986, Mrs Elizabeth Carter, *y d* of late John Raper, Powys; one *s* one *d*, and one step *s*. *Educ:* Royal Agricultural Coll., Cirencester; Univ. of Manchester Inst. of Sci. and Technol. (BSc Hons Computing Sci. 1999). *Recreations:* the countryside, tennis, fencing. *Heir: s* Toby David Culcheth Holcroft, *b* 5 Feb. 1990. *Address:* AP de Correos 225, 07210 Algaida, Mallorca, Spain. *E:* cholcroft@gmail.com; Wrentnall House, Wrentnall, Pulverbatch, Shrewsbury, Shropshire SY5 6HA. *T:* 07450 209834.

**HOLCROFT, Christopher Mark,** FRGS; Principal, Holcroft Services, since 2017; *b* Burnley, Lancs, 8 March 1966; *s* of Raymond and Anne Holcroft; *m* 1998, Jane Anne Senton; one *s* two *d. Educ:* Burnley Grammar Sch.; London Sch. of Econs and Pol Sci. (BSc Hons Geog.). CGeog (GIS) 2011. Cartographer, LSE, 1988–90; freelance cartographer, The Independent, 1989–90; Geographic Information Systems Specialist, Informatix (Japan), 1990–95; Corporate Sales, Autodesk, 1996–98; Corporate Mktg Manager, Cadcorp, 1998–2004; Sen. Product Manager, Ordnance Survey, 2004–05; Business Develt Manager (Asia Pacific), Cadcorp, 2005–07; Chief Executive: AGI, 2007–12; RMetS, 2012–13; Dir of Strategic Business Develt, Ordnance Survey Internat., 2013–15; Principal Consultant, Informed Solutions Ltd, 2015–16. Aircraft Refueller, Aircraft Restoration Co., 2017–. Member: UK Geographic Inf. Panel, DCLG, 2007–08; UK Location Council, DEFRA, 2009–12; Ordnance Survey Derived Data Adv. Gp, 2011–13; Geographic Inf. Customer Gp, BIS, then BEIS, 2012–17; Readers Panel for the Queen's Anniv. Prizes for Higher and Further Educn, Royal Anniversary Trust, 2012–. Charity Volunteer, Wood Green Animal Charity, 2016–. Columnist and editl contributor, GIS Professional, 2004–18. FRGS 1993. Past Chair's Award, AGI, 2011, 2012. *Recreations:* family, bass guitar, singing, classical piano, weather observations, aviation, history. *Address:* Aircraft Restoration Company, Building 425, Duxford Airfield, Duxford, Cambs CB22 4QR. *T:* 07879 697626. *E:* chris.holcroft@gmail.com.

**HOLCROFT, Lt Col Patrick Roy,** LVO 2013; OBE 1986; Lord-Lieutenant of Worcestershire, since 2012; *b* Birmingham, 17 March 1948; *e s* of Oliver and Gabrielle Holcroft (*née* Perry); *m* 1982, Annie Kathleen Roberts; three *s. Educ:* Downside Sch.; RMA Sandhurst; Nottingham Univ. (BA Hons 1972). Commnd 2nd Bn, Grenadier Guards, 1969; Instructor, RMA Sandhurst, 1975–77; psc 1980; The Captain, 1st Bn, Queen's Co., 1981–82; SO2 (MO1), MoD (A), 1982–84; MA to Adjt Gen. (Lt Col), MoD (A), 1984–87. Robert Fleming & Co.: investment analyst, 1988–90; Dir, Fleming Investment mgt, 1990–92; CEO, Robert Fleming Insce Brokers, 1992–2001; led mgt buy-out, 2001, co.

renamed RFIB Gp; CEO, RFIB Gp, 2001–09; non-exec. Dir, 2009–13. Non-executive Director: Griffin Insce Assoc., 2002–13; Thomas Miller Hldgs, 2010–16. Trustee: Grenadier Guards, 1992– ; Hedley Foundn, 1995– ; Lloyds Patriotic Fund, 2004–13; Nuffield Trust for Forces of the Crown, 2011–19. CStJ 2017. *Recreations:* country sports, cricket, golf, theatre, cooking. *Address:* c/o Lieutenancy Office, County Hall, Spetchley Road, Worcester, Worcs WR5 2NP. *Clubs:* Cavalry and Guards, Pratt's.

**HOLDAWAY, Prof. Richard,** CBE 2013; PhD; FREng; Director, Space Science and Technology, Science and Technology Facilities Council (formerly Council for the Central Laboratory of the Research Councils), 1998–2015; *b* 22 Feb. 1949; *s* of Maurice Holdaway and Margaret Holdaway; two *s*. *Educ:* Univ. of Southampton (BSc Aeronautics/Astronautics Engrg 1970; PhD Astrodynamics 1974). Design Engr, Harrier, Hawker Siddeley Aviation, 1970; Proj. Engr, Appleton Lab., 1974–80; Project Engr, then Div. Head (Space), Rutherford Appleton Lab., 1980–98. Visiting Professor: Univ. of Southampton, 1995– ; Univ. of Kent, 1996– ; Beijing Univ. of Aeronautics and Astronautics, 2006–. FAIAA 1996; FREng 2001. *Publications:* 80 jtly edited books and articles on space technology. *Recreations:* sport (squash, soccer, hockey), season ticket holder and fanatical supporter of Portsmouth Football Club.

**HOLDEN, Amanda Juliet;** musician, writer; *b* 19 Jan. 1948; *d* of Sir Brian Warren and Dame Josephine Barnes, DBE; *m* 1971, Anthony Ivan Holden, *qv* (marr. diss. 1988); three *s*. *Educ:* Benenden Sch.; Lady Margaret Hall, Oxford (MA); Guildhall Sch. of Music and Drama (Piano Accompanying Schol.; LGSM); American Univ., Washington (Hall of Nations Schol.; MA); ARCM; LRAM. Music staff: St Michael's Comprehensive, Watford, 1970–72; Watford Sch. of Music, 1971–75; Guildhall Sch., 1973–87; Founder, Music Therapy Dept, Charing Cross Hosp., London, 1973–75. Mem., Opera Adv. Bd, Royal Opera House, 1998; Advr, Opera Genesis Prog., ROH2, 2006–09. Has translated *c* 60 opera libretti, 1985–, including: The Coronation of Poppea (Monteverdi), Les Boréades, Castor and Pollux (Rameau), Orfeo ed Euridice/Orphée, Armide (Gluck), Agrippina, Alcina, Ariodante, Partenope, Rodelinda (Handel), La finta giardiniera, Il re pastore, Idomeneo, Die Entführung, The Marriage of Figaro, Don Giovanni, The Magic Flute, La clemenza di Tito, The Barber of Seville, La Cenerentola, L'elisir d'amore, Maria Stuarda, Lucia di Lammermoor, Beatrice and Benedict, The Bartered Bride, Lohengrin, Rigoletto, A Masked Ball, Aida, Falstaff, Faust, The Pearl Fishers, The Fair Maid of Perth, Carmen, Werther, La bohème, Tosca, Madam Butterfly, Il Trittico, Pagliacci (Leoncavallo), Francesca da Rimini (Rachmaninov), Volo di notte (Dallapiccola), Experimentum Mundi (Battistelli), Caligula (Glanert); Passion (Dusapin); The Snow Queen (Abrahamsen); *cartoon film script:* Rhinegold, 1995; *play translation,* Amphitryon (Kleist); *adaptations for concert hall:* The Epic of Gilgamesh (Martinů); Der Freischütz; *libretti:* The Selfish Giant (after Wilde); The Silver Tassie (after O'Casey) (Outstanding Achievement in Opera (jtly), Laurence Olivier Awards, 2001); Family Matters (after Beaumarchais), The Piano Tuner (after Daniel Mason); Bliss (after Peter Carey). *Publications:* The Magic Flute (arr. for children), 1990; (contrib.) The Mozart Compendium, 1990; (trans.) Lohengrin, 1993; (ed) The Viking Opera Guide, 1993; (ed) The Penguin Opera Guide, 1995, 2nd edn 1997; (ed) The New Penguin Opera Guide, 2001; (ed) The Penguin Concise Guide to Opera, 2005; (ed) The Opera Guide, 2015, 2nd edn 2017. *Recreations:* birdwatching, gardening, swimming, chamber music. *W:* www.amandaholden.org.uk.

**HOLDEN, Anthony Ivan;** writer; *b* 22 May 1947; *s* of late John Holden and Margaret Lois Holden (*née* Sharpe); *m* 1st, 1971, Amanda Juliet Warren (*see* A. J. Holden) (marr. diss. 1988); three *s*; 2nd, 1990, Cynthia Blake, *d* of Mrs George Blake, Brookline, Mass. *Educ:* Tre-Arddur House Sch., Anglesey; Oundle Sch.; Merton Coll., Oxford (MA Hons Eng. Lang. and Lit.; Editor, Isis). Trainee reporter, Thomson Regional Newspapers, Evening Echo, Hemel Hempstead, 1970–73; home and foreign corresp., Sunday Times, 1973–77; columnist (Atticus), Sunday Times, 1977–79; Washington corresp. and US Editor, Observer, 1979–81; Features Editor and Asst Editor, The Times, 1981–82; freelance journalist and author, 1982–85 and 1986–; Exec. Editor, Today, 1985–86; music critic, The Observer, 2002–08. Fellow, Center for Scholars and Writers, NY Public Liby, 1999–2000. Broadcaster, radio and TV; TV documentaries include: The Man Who Would Be King, 1982; Charles at Forty, 1988; Anthony Holden on Poker, 1992; Who Killed Tchaikovsky, 1993. Member, Board of Governors: South Bank Centre, 2002–08; Shakespeare North Trust, 2006–. Pres., Internat. Fedn of Poker, 2009–13. Young Journalist of 1972; commended for work in NI, News Reporter of the Year, British Press Awards, 1976; Columnist of the Year, British Press Awards, 1977. Opera translations: Don Giovanni, 1986; La Bohème, 1986; The Barber of Seville, 1987. *Publications:* (trans. and ed) Aeschylus' Agamemnon, 1969; (contrib.) The Greek Anthology, 1973; (trans. and ed) Greek Pastoral Poetry, 1974; The St Albans Poisoner, 1974, 2nd edn 1996; Charles, Prince of Wales, 1979; Their Royal Highnesses, 1981; Of Presidents, Prime Ministers and Princes, 1984; The Queen Mother, 1985, 3rd edn 1995; (trans.) Mozart's Don Giovanni, 1987; Olivier, 1988; Charles, 1988; Big Deal, 1990, 3rd edn 2002; (ed) The Last Paragraph, 1990; A Princely Marriage, 1991; The Oscars, 1993; The Tarnished Crown, 1993; (contrib.) Power and the Throne, 1994; Tchaikovsky, 1995; Diana: her life and legacy, 1997; Charles: a biography, 1998; William Shakespeare: his life and work, 1999; (ed jtly) The Mind Has Mountains, 1999; (ed jtly) There are Kermodians, 1999; The Drama of Love, Life and Death in Shakespeare, 2000; Shakespeare: an illustrated biography, 2002; The Wit in the Dungeon: the life of Leigh Hunt, 2005; All In, 2005; The Man Who Wrote Mozart, 2006; Bigger Deal, 2007; Holden on Hold'em, 2008; (ed jtly) Poems that Make Grown Men Cry, 2014; (ed jtly) Poems that Make Grown Women Cry, 2016; (ed jtly) He Played for His Wife and other stories, 2017. *Recreations:* poker, Arsenal FC, Lancashire CC. *Address:* c/o Rogers Coleridge White, 20 Powis Mews, W11 1JN. *T:* (020) 7221 3717.

**HOLDEN, Prof. David William,** PhD; FRS 2004; FMedSci; Regius Professor of Infectious Diseases, Imperial College London, since 2017 (Professor of Molecular Microbiology, 1997; Director, MRC Centre for Molecular Bacteriology and Infection, 2012–19); *b* 3 Nov. 1955; *s* of John and Bronwen Holden; *m* 2000, Belinda Sinclair. *Educ:* George Watson's Coll., Edinburgh; Univ. of Durham (BSc Hons (Botany) 1977); UCL (PhD 1982). Research Fellow: Agriculture Canada, 1982–84; Univ. of Wisconsin, 1985–88; NIMR, London, 1988–90; Royal Postgraduate Medical School, London: Lectr, 1990–93; Sen. Lectr, 1993–95; Prof., 1995–97. Scientific Founder and Consultant, Microscience Ltd, 1997–2005. FMedSci 2002. *Publications:* over 140 articles in learned jls; several patents. *Recreations:* cycling, reading, climbing. *Address:* Section of Microbiology, MRC Centre for Molecular Bacteriology and Infection, Imperial College London, Armstrong Road, SW7 2AZ. *T:* (020) 7594 3073, *Fax:* (020) 7594 3095. *E:* d.holden@imperial.ac.uk.

**HOLDEN, His Honour Derek;** a Circuit Judge, 1984–2000; a Chairman, Asylum and Immigration Tribunal (formerly Immigration Appeal Tribunal), 2000–11; *b* 7 July 1935; *s* of Frederic Holden and Audrey Holden (*née* Hayes); *m* 1961, Dorien Elizabeth Holden (*née* Bell); two *s*. *Educ:* Cromwell House; Staines Grammar Sch. Served Army; Lieut East Surrey Regt, 1953–56. Qualified as Solicitor, 1966; Derek Holden & Co., Staines, Egham, Camberley, Feltham, Basingstoke and Ashford, 1966–84; Consultant, Batt Holden & Co., 1966–84; Principal, Dorien Property Co., 1974–84; Partner, Black Lake Securities, 1978–84. A Recorder, 1980–84; President: Social Security Appeal Tribunals and Medical Appeal Tribunals, Vaccine Damage Tribunals, and Disability Appeals Tribunal, 1990–92; Child Support Tribunal, 1993; Chm., Tribunals Cttee, Judicial Studies Bd, 1991–93; Mem., Criminal Injuries Compensation Appeal Panel, 2000–08; Chm., Ind. Appeals Body, ICSTIS, 2001–11. Mem., Royal Yachting Assoc., 1975– (Dept of Trade Offshore Yachtmaster Instr with Ocean Cert.; Advanced Open Water Diving Cert., 2000); Principal, Chandor Sch. of Sailing, Lymington, 1978–85. *Recreations:* sailing, snow-boarding, photography, music, scuba-diving. *Address:* 2 Aspen Court, St Ann's Park, Virginia Water, Surrey GU25 4TD. *Clubs:* Western (Glasgow); Leander, Remenham (Henley); Burway Rowing (Laleham); Eton Excelsior Rowing (Windsor); Staines Boat; Port Solent Yacht.

**HOLDEN, Sir John David,** 4th Bt *cr* 1919; *b* 16 Dec. 1967; *s* of David George Holden (*d* 1971) (*e s* of 3rd Bt), and of Nancy, *d* of H. W. D. Marwood, Foulrice, Whenby, Brandsby, Yorks; *S* grandfather, 1976; *m* 1987, Suzanne Cummings; three *d*. Heir: *uncle* Brian Peter John Holden [*b* 12 April 1944; *m* 1984, Bernadette Anne Lopez, *d* of George Gerard O'Malley].

**HOLDEN, John Stewart;** Lay Member and Vice Chair, Bath and North East Somerset Clinical Commissioning Group, 2013–19; *b* 23 July 1945; *s* of William Stewart Holden and Jenny Holden (*née* Brelsford); *m* 1st, 1970, Pamela (marr. diss. 1984); 2nd, 1984, Margaret Newport. *Educ:* Merchant Taylors'; Emmanuel Coll., Cambridge (BA Hons Natural Scis/Law 1967; MA). British Petroleum and subsidiaries, 1964–93: Manager, Gas (Western Hemisphere), 1981–84; Area Oil Co-ordinator and Dir, BP (Schweiz) AG, 1984–87; Dir, Alexander Duckham & Co., 1991–93; Manager, European Lubricants & Bitumen, 1991–93; Develt Dir, Electricity Pool, 1994–96; Chief Exec., Companies House and Registrar of Cos for England and Wales, 1996–2002; Registrar of Political Parties, 1998–2000; Board Member: UK Passport Service, 2002–07; Criminal Records Bureau, 2002–06. Mem., Home Office Review of Criminal Records Bureau, 2002. Mem., Audit Cttee, Ind. Police Complaints Commn, 2005–09. Board Member and Audit Chair: Wiltshire PCT, 2006–13; NHS Bath and NE Somerset, 2012–13. *Publications:* The Watlington Branch, 1974; The Manchester and Milford Railway, 1979, 2nd edn 2007. *Recreations:* flying, Italian opera, history, industrial archaeology.

**HOLDEN, Sir Michael (Peter),** 8th Bt *cr* 1893, of Oakworth House, Keighley, Yorkshire; freelance railway management consultant; Managing Director, Coledale Consulting, since 2006; *b* Altrincham, Cheshire, 19 June 1956; *s* of Sir Paul Holden, 7th Bt and Vivien Mary Holden (*née* Oldham); *S* father, 2016; *m* 1990, Irene Yvonne Salmon; three *d*. *Educ:* Leys Sch., Cambridge; Portsmouth Poly. (BA Business Studies 1978). British Rail: Asst Station Manager, Richmond, 1978–79; Station Manager, Twickenham, 1979–81; Asst Station Manager, Clapham Junction, 1981–84; Duty Station Manager, King's Cross, 1984; Area Customer Services Manager, Slough, 1985–86; Area Relief Manager, King's Cross, 1986; Area Manager, NE Essex, 1986–88, Watford, 1988–91; Ops Manager, SW Div., Network SE, 1991–94; Prodn Manager, Railtrack SW, 1994–96; Zone Dir, Railtrack E Anglia, 1996–98; Regl Dir, Southern Railtrack, 1999–2003; Man. Dir, South Eastern Trains, 2003–06; CEO, Directly Operated Railways, 2011–15. Mem., British Transport Police Authy, 2004–13. Trustee, Railway Children Charity, 2008–18; Dir, Railway Children Africa, 2016– ; President: Railway Study Assoc., 2014–15; Retired Railway Officers' Soc., 2019–20; Woking District Rotary, 2019–20; Surrey Swimming, 2019–20. Tech. Officer, Woking Swimming Club, 2008– ; Treas., Pinewood Gymnastics Club Ltd, 2011–13. FIRO 2000. *Recreations:* trekking, swimming, travel. Heir: none. *Address:* Coledale, Cedar Road, Woking, Surrey GU22 0JH. *T:* (01482) 723993. *E:* holdmch@aol.com.

**HOLDEN, Patrick Brian,** MA, PhD; FCIS; Chairman: Ainsfield PLC, since 1991; Holden Homes (Southern) Ltd, since 1984; *b* 16 June 1937; *s* of Reginald John and Winifred Isabel Holden; *m* 1972, Jennifer Ruth (*née* Meddings), MB, BS (marr. diss. 2001). *Educ:* Allhallows Sch. (Major Schol.); St Catharine's Coll., Cambridge (BA Hons Law 1960, MA 1963); Univ. of Central Lancs (PhD). FCIS 1965. Served Royal Hampshire Regt, 1955–57 (regular commn), seconded 1 Ghana Regt, RWAFF. Fine Fare Group: Sec., 1960–69; Legal and Property Dir, 1965–69; Pye of Cambridge Gp, 1969–74; Dir, Pye Telecom. Ltd, 1972–74; Sec., then Dir, Oriel Foods Gp, 1975–81; Gp Sec., Fisons plc, 1981–83; Dir, Legal Affairs, Nabisco, 1983–85. Non-exec. Dir, Mortimer Growth II plc, 1997–2007. Sec., New Town Assoc., 1974–75. Lloyd's Name, 1984– . Trustee, Cartoon Mus., 2012– . *Publications:* Map of Tewin and its Rights of Way, 1991; A–Z of Dog Training and Behaviour, 1999 (trans. Chinese 2001); The Old School House: a Dickensian school, 2000; Agility: a step by step guide, 2001 (trans. German 2002); (jtly) Lively Limericks—Ribald Rhymes, 2015. *Recreations:* dogs, bridge, walking, cartoons, limericks, travel. *Address:* The Old School House, Lower Green, Tewin, Herts AL6 0LD. *T:* (01438) 717573. *Club:* Naval and Military.

**HOLDEN, Patrick Hyla,** CBE 2005; Director, Sustainable Food Trust, since 2010; International Ambassador, Soil Association, since 2010 (Director, 1995–2010); *b* 9 Sept. 1950; *s* of Dr Hyla Montgomery Holden and Joan Elizabeth Holden; *m* 1st, 1977, Louise Richards (marr. diss.); two *s* two *d*; 2nd, 2002, Rebecca Mary Hiscock; four *s*. *Educ:* Dulwich Hamlet Primary Sch.; Alleyn's Sch., Dulwich; Mount Grace Comp. Sch., Potters Bar; Emerson Coll., Sussex (biodynamic agric. course). Farmer, 240-acre mixed organic dairy farm, W Wales, 1973– (pt-time, 1988–); Dir, British Organic Farmers, 1988–92. Mem., UK Register of Organic Food Standards Bd, 1987–97. Patron: Soil Assoc. Land Trust, 2010– ; Bio-Dynamic Agricl Assoc., 2011– ; Living Earth Land Trust, 2011–. Ashoka Fellow, 2016. *Recreations:* Hebridean Islands, all year swimming, tennis, hill walking, Bach. *Address:* 38 Richmond Street, Totterdown, Bristol BS3 4TQ. *T:* (0117) 987 1467. *E:* patrickholden@me.com. *Club:* Farmers.

**HOLDEN, Robert David,** CBE 2009; independent consultant for long-term complex projects, since 2011; Chairman, UK Submarine Delivery Agency, since 2016; *b* Manchester, 6 April 1956; *s* of Robert Holden and Gladys Holden; *m* 1993, Jill Benson; one *s* one *d*. *Educ:* Lancaster Univ. (BA Financial Control and Econs 1977). ACA 1980. With Arthur Young; joined Vickers Shipbuilding and Engineering Ltd, 1983, Finance Dir, 1994; Finance Dir, GEC Marine, 1995; London & Continental Railways Ltd: Finance Dir, 1996–99; CEO, 1999–2009; CEO, Crossrail Ltd, 2009–11. Dir, Cammell Laird Shipbuilders, 1990–96. Chairman: Eurostar (UK) Ltd, 1998–2010; High Speed 1 Ltd, 2011–18; London City Airport, 2018– ; non-executive Director: Eurostar Gp Ltd, 1999–2010; Viridor Ltd, 2012–16; Nuclear Decommissioning Authy, 2015– ; Electricity North West, 2016– ; NNB Generation Co. (SZC) Ltd, 2016–. Mem., Exec. Cttee, Railway Industry Pension Scheme, 2008–14. Mem. Council, UCL, 2005–12. Hon. FICE 2010.

**HOLDEN, Susan Anne;** Chief Executive Officer, Chilterns Area of Outstanding Natural Beauty, since 2015; *b* Morden, 13 May 1966; *d* of John Holden and Sheila Holden. *Educ:* Newnham Coll., Cambridge (BA Geog. 1987; MA); Henley Sch. of Mgt (Dip. Mgt). Various roles, Shell Internat. and Shell UK, 1988–93; National Trust: Property Manager, 1996–99; Area Manager, 1999–2002; Business Admin Dir, 2002–05; Chief Exec., Woodland Trust, 2005–14; Exec. Dir, Earthwatch Inst. (Europe, ME and India), 2014–15. Welsh Govt Appointee, Brecon Beacons Nat. Park Authy, 2018–. FRSA. Trustee: Geographical Assoc., 2017– ; Sea Changers, 2017–. *Address:* Chilterns Area of Outstanding Natural Beauty, The Lodge, 90 Station Road, Chinnor OX39 4HA. *E:* sueholden@chilternsaonb.org.

**HOLDER, Eric H., Jr**; Attorney General of the United States of America, 2009–15; Partner, Covington & Burling, Washington, DC, 2001–09 and since 2015; *b* New York City, 21 Jan. 1951; *s of* Eric Holder and Miriam R. Holder; *m* Sharon Malone; three *c*. *Educ*: Stuyvesant High Sch., NYC; Columbia Univ. (BA American Hist. 1973); Columbia Law Sch. (JD 1976). Called to the Bar, NY, 1977; Public Integrity Section, Dept of Justice, 1976–88; Associate Judge, Superior Court, DC, 1988–93; US Attorney, DC, Dept of Justice, 1993–97; Dep. Attorney Gen., 1997–2001; Actg Attorney Gen., 2001. Mem., Ad Hoc Adv. Gp, US Sentencing Commn. Member Board: Columbia Univ.; Nat. Center for Victims of Crime; Meyer Foundn; Save the Children Foundn. Hon. Bencher, Middle Temple, 2012.

**HOLDER, Sir (John) Henry**, 4th Bt *cr* 1898, of Pitmaston, Moseley, Worcs; Production Director and Head Brewer, Elgood & Sons Ltd, North Brink Brewery, Wisbech, 1975–93, retired; *b* 12 March 1928; *s of* Sir John Eric Duncan Holder, 3rd Bt and Evelyn Josephine (*d* 1994), *er d of* late William Blain; *S* father, 1986; *m* 1st, 1960, Catharine Harrison (*d* 1994), *yr d of* late Leonard Baker; twin *s* one *d*; 2nd, 1996, Josephine Mary (*d* 2013), *d of* late A. Elliott and *widow of* G. Rivett. *Educ*: Eton Coll.; Birmingham Univ. (Dip. Malting and Brewing); Dip. in Safety Management, British Safety Council. Mem., Inst. of Brewing and Distilling (Diploma Mem., Inst. of Brewing). National Service, RAC; commnd 5th Royal Tank Regt, 1947. Shift Brewer, Mitchells & Butlers Ltd, 1951–53; Brewer, Reffels Bexley Brewery Ltd, 1953–56; Asst Manager, Unique Slide Rule Co., 1956–62; Brewer, Rhymney Brewery Co. Ltd, 1962–75. *Heir: er* twin *s* Nigel John Charles Holder, *b* 6 May 1962. *Address*: Thornhill House, Great Longstone, Derbyshire DE45 1TB.

**HOLDER, Most Rev. Dr John Walder Dunlop**, CBE 2011; Archbishop of the West Indies, 2009–18; Bishop of Barbados, 2000–18; *b* Barbados, 1948; *m* 1988, Betty Lucas-Holder; one *s*. *Educ*: Modern High Sch., Barbados; Codrington Coll. (DTh); Univ. of West Indies (BA Theol.); Univ. of the South (STM); Univ. of London (PhD); Cert. in HIV/AIDS Educn and Counselling. Ordained deacon, 1974, priest, 1975; Curate, St George Cathedral, St Vincent, 1975–77; Lectr in Old Testament, Codrington Coll., Barbados, 1977–2000. Member: Adv. Gp, Anglican Observer at UN, 2003–06, 2010–; Metropolitan Council of Cuba, 2010–; Alternate Deleg., Standing Cttee and Finance Cttee, Anglican Communion, 2011–; Church in the Province of the West Indies: Chm., Provincial Social Justice and Human Rights Commn, 2003–; Chm., Provincial Commn on Doctrine, 2009–; Chair, Provincial Synod, 2009–. Chairman: Joe Forte Trust, 2000–; Aubrey Collymore Scholarship Cttee, 2000–; Barbados Christian Council, 2007–11; Member: Privy Council, Barbados, 2001–; Adv. Cttee, Chronic Disease Task Res. Centre, Barbados, 2010–. Chm., Codrington Coll. Trust, 2011– (Mem., Bd of Mgt, 2003–). *Publications*: A Layman's Guide to the Bible, Part 1: an examination of the Bible in its Socio-Political, Historical and Literary Context, Part 2: outlines of the books in the Bible, 1989; Religion and Theology: a journey into the experiential, 1990; The Issue of Race: a search for a biblical perspective, 1993; The Intertestamental Period, 1994; The Ten Commandments, 1995; Is This the Word of the Lord?: in search of biblical theology and hermeneutics, 2000; (contrib.) The Anglican Communion and Homosexuality, 2008; (contrib.) The Africana Bible, 2010. *Recreations*: walking, swimming, reading, listening to music.

**HOLDERNESS, Sir Martin (William)**, 4th Bt *cr* 1920, of Tadworth, Surrey; Financial Planner, Succession Group, independent financial advisers, since 2014; *b* 24 May 1957; *s of* Sir Richard William Holderness, 3rd Bt and of Pamela Mary Dawsett (*née* Chapman); *S* father, 1998; *m* 1st (marr. diss. 2013); one *s* one *d*; 2nd, 2014, Amanda Jane (*née* Hayes). *Educ*: Bradfield Coll., Berkshire; Portsmouth Poly. (BA Accountancy 1979). CA 1983; MSFA 1995. Articled KMG Thomson McLintock, 1978–83; financial adviser, 1984–; Man. Dir, MH Financial Mgt Ltd, 2002–14. *Recreations*: theatre, films, football, family life. *Heir: s* Matthew William Thornton Holderness, *b* 23 May 1990. *Club*: Two Brydges.

**HOLDERNESS-RODDAM, Jane Mary Elizabeth**, CBE 2004; LVO 1999; Chairman, Riding for the Disabled Association, 2000–10, now Hon. Life Vice-President; *b* 7 Jan. 1948; *d of* Jack and Anne Bullen; *m* 1974, Timothy David Holderness-Roddam, *qv*. *Educ*: Westwing Sch., Thornbury, Glos. SRN, Middlesex Hosp., London, 1970. Owner, W Kington Stud Farm. Olympic Team Gold Medallist, Equestrian 3 day Event, 1968. President: Fortune Centre of Riding Therapy, 1969–; British Equestrian Trade Assoc., 2004–; British Eventing, 2004– (Chm., 1999–2004). Chairman: Nat. Riding Fest., 1999–2010; Council, British Equestrian Fedn, 2010–; Pres., Caspian Horse Soc., 2007–; Trustee: World Horse Welfare, 2007–13; Brooke, 2013–; Patron, Side Saddle Assoc., 2008–. Dir, Nat. Equine Database, 2009–13. Hon. Freeman, Co. of Loriners, 2001; Yeoman, Co. of Saddlers, 2005. Hon. Dr UWE, 2004. Queen's Award for Equestrianism, British Horse Soc., 2009. *Publications*: equestrian books include: Competitive Riding, 1988; Complete Book of Eventing, 1988; Showing, 1989; Show Jumping, 1990; Fitness for Horse and Rider, 1993; Practical Cross Country, 1994; The Life of Horses, 1999; Horse Riding in a Weekend, 2004; contrib. to equestrian magazines. *Recreations*: travel, antique collecting. *Address*: Church Farm, West Kington, Chippenham, Wilts SN14 7JE. *T*: (01249) 782050, *Fax*: (01249) 782940. *E*: jhroddam@aol.com.

**HOLDERNESS-RODDAM, Timothy David**; Director, Abercrombie & Kent Ltd, 1972–2015; *b* 23 Nov. 1942; *s of* David and Susan Holderness-Roddam; *m* 1974, Jane Mary Elizabeth Bullen (*see* J. M. E. Holderness-Roddam). *Educ*: Radley Coll. Served 14th/20th King's Hussars, 1960–65; ADC to GOC, Malta and Libya, 1962–65. Partner, West Kington Farms, 1988–. Man. Dir, UM Gp, 1993–2000; Dep. Chm., Countrywide Farmers plc, 2004–13. Chairman: Horse Trials Support Gp, 1974–2010; Blenheim Palace Internat. Horse Trials, 2016–. Director: British Eventing Ltd, 2010–17; British Equestrian Fedn, 2017–. Trustee, Friends of Conservation, 1976–. *Recreations*: travel, shooting, country pursuits. *Address*: Church Farm, West Kington, Chippenham, Wilts SN14 7JE. *T*: (01249) 782050, *Fax*: (01249) 782940. *E*: TimRoddam@westkingtonfarms.co.uk. *Club*: Cavalry and Guards.

**HOLDGATE, Sir Martin (Wyatt)**, Kt 1994; CB 1979; PhD; FRSB; President: Zoological Society of London, 1994–2004; Freshwater Biological Association, 2002–10; *b* 14 Jan. 1931; *s of* late Francis Wyatt Holdgate, MA, JP, and Lois Marjorie (*née* Bebbington); *m* 1963, Elizabeth Mary (*née* Dickason), *widow of* Dr H. H. Weil; two *s*. *Educ*: Arnold Sch., Blackpool; Queens' Coll., Cambridge (BA 1952; MA 1956; PhD 1955). FRSB (FIBiol 1967). Jt Leader and Senior Scientist, Gough Is Scientific Survey, 1955–56; Lecturer in Zoology: Manchester Univ., 1956–57; Durham Colleges, 1957–60; Leader, Royal Society Expedition to Southern Chile, 1958–59; Asst Director of Research, Scott Polar Research Institute, Cambridge, 1960–63; Senior Biologist, British Antarctic Survey, 1963–66; Dep. Dir (Research), The Nature Conservancy, 1966–70; Director: Central Unit on Environmental Pollution, DoE, 1970–74; Inst. of Terrestrial Ecology, NERC, 1974–76; Dep. Sec., 1976, Dir-Gen. of Res., 1976–79, Chief Scientist, 1979–85, Depts of the Environment and of Transport; Dep. Sec., Environment Protection and Chief Envmt Scientist, DoE, and Chief Scientific Advr, Dept of Transport, 1985–88; Dir Gen., IUCN, 1988–94. Hon. Professorial Fellow, UC Cardiff, 1976–83. Member: NERC, 1976–87; SERC (formerly SRC), 1976–87; ABRC, 1976–88; Bd, World Resources Inst., Washington, 1985–94; China Council for Internat. Co-operation on Envmt and Develt, Beijing, 1992–94; Chairman: Review of Scientific Civil Service, 1980; Renewable Energy Adv. Gp, 1992; Energy Adv. Panel, 1993–96; Internat. Inst. for Envmt and Develt, 1994–99; Co-Chm., Intergovtl Panel on Forests, UN Commn on Sustainable Develt, 1995–97; Mem., Royal Commn on Envmtl Pollution, 1994–2002; Trustee: Nat. Heritage Meml Fund and Heritage Lottery Fund, 1995–98; Cumbria Wildlife Trust, 2004–15. Chm., British Schools Exploring Society, 1967–78; Vice-Pres., Young Explorer's Trust, 1981–90 (Chm., 1972, 1979–81). President: Governing Council, UN Environment Prog., 1983–84; Global 500 Forum, 1992–97; Chm., Commonwealth Expert Gp on Climate Change, 1988–89. Chm., Governing Council, Arnold Sch., 1997–2004. Pres., Friends of the Lake District, 2014–18, now Pres. Emeritus. Hon. Mem., IUCN, 2000. Hon. FZS 2005. Hon. Fellow: RHBNC, 1997; Univ. of Cumbria, 2015. Hon. DSc: Durham, 1991; Sussex, 1993; Lancaster, 1995; QMUL, 2006. Bruce Medal, RSE, 1964; UNEP Silver Medal, 1983; UNEP Global 500, 1988; Patron's Medal, RGS, 1992; Livingstone Medal, RSGS, 1993. Comdr, Order of the Golden Ark (Netherlands), 1991. *Publications*: A History of Appleby, 1956, rewritten as The Story of Appleby in Westmorland, 2006; Mountains in the Sea, The Story of the Gough Island Expedition, 1958; (ed jtly) Antarctic Biology, 1964; (ed) Antarctic Ecology, 1970; (with N. M. Wace) Man and Nature in the Tristan da Cunha Islands, 1976; A Perspective of Environmental Pollution, 1979; (ed jtly) The World Environment 1972–82, 1982; (ed jtly) The World Environment 1972–92, 1992; From Care to Action: making a sustainable world, 1996; The Green Web: a union for world conservation, 1999; Penguins and Mandarins: memories of natural and un-natural history, 2003; Arnold: the story of a Blackpool school, 2009; numerous papers and articles on Antarctica, environment and conservation. *Address*: Fell Beck, Hartley, Kirkby Stephen, Cumbria CA17 4JH. *Club*: Athenæum.

**HOLDHAM, Susan Pauline, (Mrs Charles Llewellyn)**; a District Judge (Magistrates' Courts), since 2014; *b* Stoke-on-Trent, 11 Oct. 1960; *d of* late James Stanley Holdham and Betty Holdham; *m* 1992, Charles Llewellyn; one *s*. *Educ*: Blythe Bridge High Sch.; Univ. of Bristol (LLB Hons 1982); Inns of Court Sch. of Law. Called to the Bar, Gray's Inn, 1983, Middle Temple *ad eundem*; in practice as barrister: SE Circuit, 1983–99; Criminal Appeal Office, 1999–2014; a Dep. Dist Judge (Magistrates' Courts), 2006–14. *Publications*: (with A. Beldam) The Court of Appeal Criminal Division: a practitioner's guide, 2012, 2nd edn 2018. *Recreations*: medieval history, sighthounds, theatre, cocktails, opera. *Address*: c/o Westminster Magistrates' Court, 181 Marylebone Road, NW1 5BR.

**HOLDING, John Francis**; HM Diplomatic Service, retired; business adviser and director, and active Rotarian in New Zealand, since 1996; *b* 12 Aug. 1936; *s of* late Francis George Holding, CA, Inland Revenue, and Gwendoline Elizabeth Holding (*née* Jenkins); *m* 1st, 1970, Pamela Margaret Straker-Nesbit (marr. diss. 1984); two *d*; 2nd, 1993, Susan Ann Clark (marr. diss. 1999). *Educ*: Colwyn Bay Grammar Sch.; LSE (externally). Mil. service, 1955–57; Min. of Housing and Local Govt, 1957; CRO (later FCO), 1964; served Karachi, Islamabad and Kinshasa; First Sec., 1973; Canberra, 1973–78; The Gambia, 1978–80; Grenada and Barbados, 1984–87; Dep. High Comr, Dhaka, 1987–90; Consul-General, Auckland, and Dir UK Trade Promotion in NZ, 1990–96. *Recreations*: tennis, walking, photography, pianoforte. *Address*: 3A Walton Street, Remuera, Auckland 1050, New Zealand.

**HOLDING, Malcolm Alexander**; HM Diplomatic Service, retired; Consul-General, Naples, 1986–90; *b* 11 May 1932; *s of* Adam Anderson Holding and Mary Lillian (*née* Golding); *m* 1955, Pamela Eve Hampshire; two *d*. *Educ*: King Henry VIII Sch., Coventry. Foreign Office, 1949–51; HM Forces, 1951–53; FO, 1953–55; Middle East Centre for Arab Studies, 1956–57; Third Secretary (Commercial), Tunis, 1957–60; Second Sec. (Commercial), Khartoum, 1960–64; Second, later First Sec. (Commercial), Cairo, 1964–68; Consul, Bari, 1969; FCO, 1970–73; First Sec., British Dep. High Commission, Madras, 1973–75; FCO, 1976–78; Canadian National Defence Coll., Kingston, Ontario, 1978–79; Counsellor (Commercial), Rome, 1979–81; Consul-Gen., Edmonton, 1981–85. Commendatore, Order of Merit of the Republic of Italy, 1980. *Address*: 18 Strand Court, The Strand, Topsham, Exeter EX3 0AZ.

**HOLDING, Dr Peter**; Executive Head, Beechview Academy, since 2017; Chief Executive Officer, Marlow Education Trust, since 2016; *b* Leigh-on-Sea, 5 April 1954; *s of* John and Joan Holding; *m* 2007, Sarah Woodman. *Educ*: Brockway High Sch., USA; Univ. of Pennsylvania (BA); Open Univ. (MA Ed.); Shakespeare Inst. (MA); Univ. of Michigan (PhD 1988); Westminster Coll., Oxford (PGCE). Asst Lectr in English and Film Studies, Univ. of Michigan, 1978–82; Head: of Drama, Forest Sch., London, 1982–87; of English, Rugby Sch., 1988–94; Dep. Hd, Lawrence Sheriff Sch., Rugby, 1994–97; Headmaster, Sir William Borlase's GS, Marlow, 1997–2018. Chm., Bucks Assoc. of Secondary Heads, 2003–12; Mem. Bd, Bucks Acad. for Sch. Leadership, 2004–10; Nat. Leader of Educn, 2012–; Trustee: Nat. Assoc. for Able Children in Educn, 1997–2011; La Retraite Sch., 2012–16; Chair of Trustees, Bucks Learning Trust, 2013–16. Gov., Parlaunt Park Primary Acad., Slough, 2016–18. *Publications*: Romeo and Juliet: text and performance, 1989. *Recreations*: theatre, opera, travel, cooking. *Address*: Beechview Academy, Guinions Road, High Wycombe.

**HOLDRIDGE, Ven. Bernard Lee**; Archdeacon of Doncaster, 1994–2001; *b* 24 July 1935; *s of* Geoffrey and Lucy Medlow Holdridge. *Educ*: Grammar Sch., Thorne; Lichfield Theol Coll. Ordained deacon, 1967, priest, 1968; Curate, Swinton, S Yorks, 1967–71; Vicar, St Jude, Hexthorpe, Doncaster, 1971–81; Rector, St Mary, Rawmarsh with Parkgate, 1981–88; RD of Rotherham, 1986–88; Vicar, Priory Church of St Mary and St Cuthbert, Worksop, with St Giles, Carburton and St Mary the Virgin, Clumber Park, dio. of Southwell, 1988–94; permission to officiate, dio. of Guildford, 2006–16. Dignitary in Convocation, 1999–2001. Chairman: DAC for Care of Churches and Churchyards, Southwell, 1990–94; ACS, 1998–2003. Guardian, Shrine of Our Lady of Walsingham, 1996–. *Recreations*: foreign travel, reading, theatre, a glass of wine with friends. *Address*: Flat 35, Denehyrst Court, York Road, Guildford, Surrey GU1 4EA. *T*: (01483) 570791.

**HOLDSWORTH, Ven. Dr John Ivor**; Executive Archdeacon for the Diocese of Cyprus and the Gulf, 2010–19; Chaplain, St Helena's Church, Larnaca, 2010–19; *b* 10 Feb. 1949; *s of* Harold Holdsworth and Edith Mary Holdsworth; *m* 1971, Susan Annette Thomas; one *s* one *d*. *Educ*: Leeds Grammar Sch.; University Coll. of Wales, Aberystwyth (BA); University Coll., Cardiff (BD, MTh); St David's University Coll., Lampeter (PhD 1992). Ordained deacon 1973, priest 1974; Curate, St Paul's, Newport, 1973–77; Vicar: Abercrave and Callwen, 1977–86; Gorseinon, 1986–97; Principal and Warden, St Michael's Theol Coll., Llandaff, 1997–2003; Archdeacon of St Davids, Vicar of Steynton, and Canon of St Davids Cathedral, 2003–10. Presenter, HTV Wales Religious Affairs, 1988–98. Vis. Prof., Glyndwr Univ., 2012–18. *Publications*: Communication and the Gospel, 2003; Dwelling in a Strange Land, 2003; SCM Study Guide to the Old Testament, 2005; Getting Started with the Bible, 2007; Lies, Sex and Politicians: communicating the Old Testament in contemporary culture, 2010; Conversations with the New Testament, 2014; Conversations with the Old Testament, 2016; Everyday Conversations with Matthew, 2019. *Recreations*: walking, armchair supporter of Leeds United and Yorkshire County Cricket Club, broadcasting.

**HOLDSWORTH, Very Rev. Kelvin;** Provost, St Mary's Episcopal Cathedral, Glasgow, since 2006; *b* 22 Oct. 1966; *s* of John Stuart Holdsworth and Joyce Holdsworth (*née* Kew). *Educ:* Manchester Poly. (BSc Hons Computing Sci. and Maths 1989); Univ. of St Andrews (BD Hons Practical Theol. and Christian Ethics 1992); Univ. of Edinburgh (MTh Ministry 1996). Lay Worker, St Benet's Ecumenical Chaplaincy, QMW, 1992–95; ordained deacon, 1997, priest, 1998; Precentor, St Ninian's Cathedral, Perth, 1997–2000; Rector, St Saviour's Ch, Bridge of Allan, 2000–06. Contested (Lib Dem) Stirling, 2005. Dir, Newscan Pubns, 2006–09; Mem. Editl Bd, 2005–09, Ed., 2010–14, Inspires (mag. of Scottish Episcopal Ch). Hon. FR.CPSGlas 2018. *Recreations:* politics, blogging, bookbinding, opera criticism, sinking other people's yachts. *Address:* St Mary's Episcopal Cathedral, 300 Great Western Road, Glasgow G4 9JB. *T:* (0141) 339 6691. *E:* provost@thecathedral.org.uk. *Club:* Arlington Baths (Glasgow).

**HOLDSWORTH HUNT, Christopher;** Founder Director and Managing Director, KBC Peel, Hunt Ltd (formerly Peel, Hunt plc), 1989–2004; Chairman, Melchior Japan Investment Trust plc, 2006–10; *b* 2 Aug. 1942; *s* of late Peter Holdsworth Hunt and Monica (*née* Neville); *m* 1st, 1969, Charlotte Folin (marr. diss. 1974); 2nd, 1976, Joanne Lesley Starr Minoprio (*née* Reynolds); two *s. Educ:* Summer Fields, St Leonards; Eton Coll.; Tours Univ. Commnd Coldstream Guards, 1961–64. Joined Murton & Adams, Stockjobbers, 1964; firm acquired by Pinchin Denny, 1969; Partner, Pinchin Denny, 1971; firm acquired by Morgan Grenfell, 1986; Dir, Morgan Grenfell Securities, 1987–88. Non-exec. Dir, Octopus IHT AIM VCT plc, 2008–10. *Recreations:* opera, ballet, theatre, golf, tennis, walking. *Address:* 1 Hillsleigh Road, W8 7LE. *T:* (020) 7229 9903. *Clubs:* White's, City of London, Pratt's; Sunningdale Golf; Swinley Forest Golf.

**HOLE, Christopher Charles Maximilian, (Max),** CBE 2015; Chairman and Chief Executive Officer, Universal Music Group International, 2013–15; *b* London, 26 May 1951; *s* of Frederick and Barbara Mary Hole; *m* 1999, Jan Ravens; three *s*, and two step *s. Educ:* Haileybury; Univ. of Kent. Founder: Gemini Artists, 1972–74; Criminal Records, 1976–81; Dir, A&R, 1982–87, Man. Dir, UK, 1987–90, WEA; Man. Dir, East West Records, 1990–98; Universal Music Group International: Sen. Vice Pres., Mktg and A&R, 1998–2005; Pres., Asia Pacific, 2005–10; Chief Operating Officer, 2010–13. Non-exec. Chm., Metropolis, 2016–. Mem. Bd, ENO, 2012–15. Trustee, EMI Music Sound Foundn, 2013–15. *Recreations:* cricket, music, spending time at his houses in Cornwall and Corfu. *Clubs:* MCC, Groucho.

**HOLE, Christopher James B.;** *see* Bradley-Hole.

**HOLE, Very Rev. Derek Norman;** Provost of Leicester, 1992–99, now Emeritus; *b* Plymouth, 5 Dec. 1933; *s* of Frank Edwin Hole and Ella Evelyn Hole (*née* Thomas). *Educ:* Public Central Sch., Plymouth; Lincoln Theological College. Nat. service, RAF, 1952–54. Asst Librarian, Codrington Liby, Oxford, 1954–56. Ordained deacon, 1960, priest, 1961; Asst Curate, St Mary Magdalen, Knighton, Leicester, 1960–62; Domestic Chaplain to Archbishop of Cape Town, 1962–64; Asst Curate, St Nicholas, Kenilworth, 1964–67; Rector, St Mary the Virgin, Burton Latimer, 1967–73; Vicar, St James the Greater, Leicester, 1973–92; Chaplain to the Queen, 1985–92. Hon. Canon, Leicester Cathedral, 1983–92. Rural Dean, Christianity South, Leicester, 1983–92; Chm., House of Clergy, 1986–94; Vice-Pres., Diocesan Synod, 1986–94; Member: Bishop's Council, 1986–99; Assoc. of English Cathedrals, 1992–99; Cathedral Music Wkg Party, 1993–99. Chaplain to: Lord Mayor of Leicester, 1976–77, 1994–95, 1996–97; High Sheriffs of Leics, 1980–85, 1987–88, 1995–96, 1999–2000, 2001–02, 2007–08, 2013–14; Leicester High Sch., 1983–93; Haymarket Theatre, Leicester, 1980–83, 1993–95; Leicester Br., RAFA, 1978–92; Master of Merchant Taylors' Co., 1995–96; Leicester Guild of Freemen, 1996–99; Royal Soc. of St George, 2000–06; Mayor of Oadby and Wigston BC, 2005–06; Leics br., Royal Soc. of St George, 2006–10; Leics br., British Korean Veterans Assoc., 2006–. Commissary to Bishop of Wellington, NZ, 1998–2012. Priest Associate, Actors' Church Union, 1995– (Mem., 1980–95); Vice-Pres., English Clergy Assoc., 1993–. Chm. Leicester Diocesan Redundant Churches Uses Cttee, 1985–99. Dir and Trustee, Leicester Charity Orgn Soc., 2001–05 (Mem., 1983–2001); Trustee: Leicester Church Charities, 1983–2015; Leics Historic Churches Preservation Trust, 1989–2014; Bernard Fawcett Meml Trust, 1993–99; North Meml Homes, 1999–2012; President: Leicester Rotary Club, 1987–88; Friends, Ch of St Mary the Virgin, Burton Latimer, 2000–; Leics Probus Club, 2010–11; Leics Book Soc., 2011–12; Vice-President: Leics County Scout Council, 1992–99; Leics Guild of the Disabled, 1992–99; Leicester Cathedral Old Choristers' Assoc., 1999–; Chm., Friends, Ch of St James the Greater, Leicester, 2012–. Patron, Victoria County History of Leics Trust, 2008–; Mem., Victorian Soc., 1986–2011; Hon. Life Mem., Leics Br., BRCS, 1995; Mem., Bd of Mgt, Britain-Australia Soc., 2001–05 (Chm., Leics Br., 2000–08; Treas., 2008–11). Governor: Alderman Newton's Sch., Leicester, 1976–82; Leicester High Sch., 1992–2004; Alderman Newton Foundn, 1992–2007; Leicester GS, 1992–99 (Trustee, 1999–2006; Patron, 2006–); St John's C of E Sch., Leicester, 1997–2000. Mem. (Ind.), Burton Latimer UDC, 1971–73. Sen. Fellow, De Montfort Univ., 1998–; Mem. of Ct, Univ. of Leicester, 2011–. Freeman, City of London, 2003; Liveryman, Framework Knitters' Co., 2003– (Chaplain to Master, 2004–). Hon. DLitt De Montfort, 1999; Hon. LLD Leicester, 2005. Paul Harris Award, Rotary Club, 2012; High Sheriff of Leics's Award, 2014. *Publications:* (contrib.) Century to Millennium: St James the Greater, Leicester 1899–1999, compiled by Dr A. McWhirr, 1999. *Recreations:* bridge, music, walking, reading biographies and Victorian history. *Address:* 25 Southernhay Close, Leicester LE2 3TW. *T:* (0116) 270 9988, 07799 892615. *E:* dnhole@btinternet.com.

**HOLE, Max;** *see* Hole, C. C. M.

**HOLES, Prof. Clive Douglas,** FBA 2002; Khalid Bin Abdullah Al-Saud Professor for the Study of the Contemporary Arab World, University of Oxford, 1997–2014; Fellow, Magdalen College, Oxford, 1997–2014, now Emeritus; *b* 29 Sept. 1948; *s* of Douglas John Holes and Kathryn Mary (*née* Grafton); *m* 1st, 1980, Gillian Diane Pountain (marr. diss.); two *s*; 2nd, 2004, Deidre Margaret Thorn. *Educ:* High Arcal Grammar Sch., Dudley, Worcs; Trinity Hall, Cambridge (BA Hons 1969; MA 1973); Univ. of Birmingham (MA 1972); Wolfson Coll., Cambridge (PhD 1981). UNA volunteer teacher, Bahrain, 1969–71; British Council Officer, Kuwait, Algeria, Iraq, Thailand and London, 1971–76 and 1979–83; Lectr in Arabic and Applied Linguistics, Univ. of Salford, 1983–85; Dir, Lang. Centre, Sultan Qaboos Univ., Oman, 1985–87; University of Cambridge: Lectr in Islamic Studies, 1987–96; Reader in Arabic, 1996; Fellow, Trinity Hall, 1989–96. Pres., Council for British Res. in the Levant, 2018–. Fellow: British Soc. for Middle Eastern Studies, 1989; Anglo-Oman Soc., 1990; Bahrain-British Soc., 1991. Mem., Philological Soc., 1984–. *Publications:* Colloquial Arabic of the Gulf and Saudi Arabia, 1984, 2nd edn 2010; Language Variation and Change in a Modernising Arab State, 1987; Gulf Arabic, 1990; Breakthrough Arabic, 1992; (ed) Perspectives on Arabic Linguistics, Vol. 5, 1993; Modern Arabic: structures, functions and varieties, 1995, 2nd edn 2004; Dialect, Culture and Society in Eastern Arabia, Vol. I, 2001, Vol. II, 2005, Vol. III, 2016; Poetry and Politics in Contemporary Bedouin Society, 2009; The Nabati Poetry of the United Arab Emirates, 2011; (ed) Arabic Historical Dialectology, 2018; articles in professional jls concerned with Arabic language, culture, society and literature. *Recreations:* keeping fit, watching Wolverhampton Wanderers FC, visiting the Middle East, volunteering. *Address:* The Barn House, 36 Beckbury, Shifnal, Shropshire TF11 9DG.

**HOLFORD, Prof. John Aldred Kam,** PhD; FR.HistS; Robert Peers Professor of Adult Education, University of Nottingham, since 2007; *b* Bromley, Kent, 18 April 1953; *s* of Trafford Holford, solicitor, and Norah Holford (*née* Kam), artist and teacher; *m* 1980, Hilary Rankin; two *d. Educ:* Bryanston Sch., Dorset; Merton Coll., Oxford (BA PPE 1974); Univ. of Edinburgh (PhD Sociol. 1984); Univ. of Surrey (MSc Educnl Studies 1988). FRAS 1998; FR.HistS 2002. Tutor Organiser for Trade Union Studies and North Kent, WEA, 1979–88; University of Hong Kong: Staff Tutor, later Sen. Staff Tutor, in Social Scis, Dept of Extramural Studies, 1988–92; Sen. Lectr in Social Scis, Sch. of Professional and Continuing Educn, 1992–95; University of Surrey: Sen. Lectr, 1996–2000; Prof., 2000–07; Hd, Educnl Studies, 2003–04; Founding Hd, Politics, 2004–05; Hd, Law and Politics, 2005–07; Dir, Centre for Res. into Higher, Adult and Vocational Educn, Univ. of Nottingham, 2010–14. Ed., Internat. Jl Lifelong Educn, 2005– (Reviews Ed., 1998–2004). Hon. Prof., Univ. of Hong Kong, 2001–. Co-ordinator: EU res. projects on lifelong learning and citizenship, 1999–; (jtly) Eur. Soc. for Res. in Educn of Adults, Policy Studies Network, 2009–. Member: TUC SE Educn Adv. Cttee, 1979–88; Cttee and Council, Univs' Assoc. for Lifelong Learning, 2008–16 (Chm., Research Cttee, 2009–14); Adv. Bd, Centre for Nepal Studies (UK), 2008–; Pres., Internat. Soc. for Comparative Adult Educn, 2017–; Jt Sec., Centenary Commn on Adult Educn, 2019. Mem. Senate, 1997–2003 and 2006–07, Mem. Council, 1999–2003, Chm., Acad. Assembly, 1999–2003, Univ. of Surrey. Hon. Advr, Hong Kong Telephone Co. Staff Assoc., 1989–95. Governor: George Abbot Sch., Guildford, 1996–2007 (Chm., Curriculum Cttee, 2003–07); W Notts Coll., Mansfield, 2010–19 (Chm., Standards Cttee, 2015–19). Trustee, People Can (formerly Novas Scarman Gp), 2010–13. *Publications:* (jtly) Unemployment, 1982; Reshaping Labour, 1988; Union Education in Britain, 1993; (jtly) The Hong Kong Adult Education Handbook, 1995; (jtly) Towards a Learning City, 1997; (ed jtly) International Perspectives on Lifelong Learning, 1998; (jtly) The Theory and Practice of Learning, 1998, 2nd edn 2003; (jtly) Quality in Adult Continuing Education: Hong Kong perspectives, 1999; Planning to Learn, 1999; (jtly) Lifelong Learning and Citizenship in Europe, 2003; (jtly) Patterns of Lifelong Learning: policy and practice in an expanding Europe, 2008; (ed jtly) Citizenship, Learning and Education, 2009; (ed jtly) Lifelong Learning in Europe: national patterns and challenges, 2013; (ed jtly) Adult Education Policy and the European Union, 2014; (ed jtly) Adult and Lifelong Education: global, national and local perspectives, 2016; (ed jtly) The Palgrave International Handbook of Adult and Lifelong Education and Learning, 2018; (ed jtly) The Learning Adult, 2018; contrib. chapters in books and articles to learned jls; occasional journalism. *Recreations:* collecting and reading books, beekeeping, working for democracy and socialism. *Address:* c/o School of Education, University of Nottingham, Nottingham NG8 1BB. *T:* (0115) 951 4486. *E:* john.holford@nottingham.ac.uk.

**HOLFORD, Prof. Karen Margaret,** CBE 2018; PhD; FREng; Deputy Vice-Chancellor, Cardiff University, since 2017; *b* Huntley, Glos, 1962; *d* of Eric Lionel Holford and Joan Holford (*née* Bradley); *m* 1996, Mark David Voss; one *s* one *d. Educ:* Huntley Primary Sch., Glos; Newent Comprehensive Sch., Glos; Univ. of Wales Inst. of Sci. and Technol. (BEng Hons 1984); University Coll., Cardiff (PhD 1987). Undergrad. apprentice, Rolls Royce (Aero) Ltd, 1980–84; Sen. Engr, AB Electronic Products, 1987–90; University of Wales College, Cardiff, then University of Wales, Cardiff, later Cardiff University: Lectr, then Sen. Lectr in Mechanical Engrg, 1990–2006; Prof. of Mechanical Engrg, 2006–10; Dir, Sch. of Engrg, 2010–12; Pro Vice-Chancellor, and Hd of Coll. of Physical Scis and Engrg, 2012–17. Mem., STFC, 2017–. FR.Eng 2015. *Recreations:* sport including football, tennis and motor sport. *Address:* Cardiff University, Main Building, Park Place, Cardiff CF10 3AT. *E:* DeputyVC@cardiff.ac.uk.

**HOLFORD-STREVENS, Bonnie Jean;** *see* Blackburn, B. J.

**HOLGATE, Andrew James Headley;** Literary Editor, Sunday Times, since 2008 (Deputy Literary Editor, 1999–2008); *b* Reigate, 31 Dec. 1958; *s* of Headley Holgate and Evelyn Holgate (*née* Owen); *m* 1986, Gün Akyuz; one *s* one *d. Educ:* Christ's Hosp., W Sussex; Durham Univ. (BA Hons Hist. 1981). Bookseller, then Mktg Manager, Hatchard's, 1983–88; Mktg Officer, Chatto & Windus, 1988–89; Mktg Manager, Hatchard's, 1989–90; Ed., W Mag., WH Smith, 1990–99. *Publications:* (ed jtly) The Cost of Letters, 1998; (ed jtly) The Test of Time, 1999. *Recreations:* reading, art, theatre, walking, gardening, sport, failing to learn Italian. *Address:* c/o News UK, 1 London Bridge Street, SE1 9GF.

**HOLGATE, Hon. Sir David (John),** Kt 2014; **Hon. Mr Justice Holgate;** a Judge of the High Court, Queen's Bench Division, since 2014; President, Upper Tribunal (Lands Chamber), 2016–19; Liaison Judge for the Planning Court, since 2017; *b* 3 Aug. 1956; *s* of late John Charles Holgate and of Catherine Philbin Holgate (*née* Rooney); civil partnership 2006, Alexander Nicholas Constantine. *Educ:* Davenant Foundation Grammar Sch., Loughton; Exeter Coll., Oxford (BA Hons 1977). Called to the Bar, Middle Temple, 1978, Bencher, 2004; admitted to Hong Kong Bar, 2001; QC 1997; Recorder, 2002–14; Dep. High Court Judge, 2008–14. Mem., Supplementary Panel, Jun. Counsel to the Crown (Common Law), 1986–97; Standing Jun. Counsel to the Inland Revenue in rating and valuation matters, 1990–97. *Recreations:* music, particularly opera, travel, reading. *Address:* Royal Courts of Justice, Strand, WC2A 2LL. *Club:* Travellers.

**HOLGATE, Nicholas Ian;** Town Clerk, Royal Borough of Kensington and Chelsea, 2011–17; *b* 26 March 1962; *s* of late John Holgate and of Josephine Holgate (*née* Neve); *m* 2005, Natalie Cronin. *Educ:* Hall Grove Sch., Bagshot; Charterhouse; Trinity Coll., Cambridge (BA 1984). ACMA. HM Treasury, 1984–2004: Private Secretary to Chief Sec. to the Treasury, 1991–92; to Sec. of State for Nat. Heritage, 1992–93; Govt Res. Fellow, 1993–94; Team Leader: Strategy, Finance and Purchasing, 1995–98; Educn and Trng, 1998–2001; Dir, Welfare Reform, Budget and Public Finances Directorate, 2001–04; Chief Operating Officer, then Dir Gen., Corporate Strategy and Services, DCMS, 2004–08; Exec. Dir, Finance, Inf. Systems and Property, Royal Bor. of Kensington and Chelsea, 2008–11. *Recreations:* food, film, games.

**HOLGATE, Prof. Stephen Townley,** CBE 2011; MD, DSc; FRCP, FRCPE, FRCPath, FMedSci, FIBMS, FRSB; Medical Research Council Clinical Professor of Immunopharmacology, University of Southampton, and Hon. Consultant Physician, School of Medicine, Southampton University Hospital Trust (formerly Southampton General Hospital), since 1987; *b* 2 May 1947; *s* of William Townley Holgate and Margaret Helen (*née* Lancaster); *m* 1972, Elizabeth Karen Malkinson; three *s* one *d. Educ:* London Univ. (BSc 1968; MB BS 1971; MD 1979); DSc Soton 1991. FRCP 1984; FRCPE 1995; FRCPath 1999; CBiol, FRSB (FIBiol 1999); FIBMS 2009. House Physician and Surgeon, Charing Cross Hosp., 1971–72; Sen. Hse Physician, Nat. Hosp. for Nervous Diseases and Brompton Hosp., 1972–74; Registrar in Medicine, Salisbury and Southampton Gen. Hosps, 1974–76; Lectr in Medicine, 1976–80, Sen. Lectr, 1980–86, Reader and Prof. (personal Chair), 1986–87, Univ. of Southampton. MRC/Wellcome Trust Res. Fellow, Harvard Univ., 1978–80. Mem., Royal Commn on Envtml Pollution, 2002–08; Chairman: Population and Systems Medicine Bd, MRC, 2007–12; MRC Translational Res. Gp, 2014– (Mem., 2012–); REF 2014 Main Panel A. Member: Med. Sci Cttee, Sci. Europe,

2012–; Horizon 2020 Scientific Panel for Health, EC, 2014–; NERC, 2018–. Trustee, Cancer Res. UK, 2014–. MAE 2013 (Chair, Clinical Medicine and Vet. Sci. Section, 2015–). Founder FMedSci, 1998; FAAAAS; FERS. FRSA 1997. Hon. CSci 2009. Hon. MD: Ferrara, Italy, 1997; Jagiellonian, Poland, 1999; Naples Federico II, 2012; Hon. DSc Exeter, 2015. Rhône Poulenc Rorer World Health Award, 1995; (jtly) King Faisal Internat. Prize in Medicine, 1999; Paul Ehrlich Award, Eur. Acad. of Allergy, Asthma and Clin. Immunol., 2008; Sci. Achievement Award, Amer. Thoracic Soc., 2012; William Frankland Award, BSACI, 2012; J. Allyn Taylor Internat. Prize in Medicine, Robarts Res. Inst., Canada, 2016. *Publications:* (ed jtly) Asthma and Rhinitis: implications for diagnosis and treatment, 1995, 2nd edn 2000; (jtly) Health Effects of Air Pollutants, 1999; (ed jtly) Allergy, 1999, 4th edn 2012; Difficult Asthma, 1999; (ed jtly) Middleton's Allergy: principles and practice, 2 vols, 6th edn 2004 to 9th edn 2019; 1016 peer-reviewed articles. *Recreations:* gardening, walking, theatre. *Address:* Clinical and Experimental Sciences, Level F South Pathology and Laboratory Block, Southampton General Hospital, Southampton SO16 6YD.

**HOLL-ALLEN, Jonathan Guy;** QC 2018; *b* Poole, Dorset, 7 April 1966; *s* of Robert Holl-Allen and Barbara Shakespeare (*née* Holl); *m* 1996, Julie Freemantle; two *d. Educ:* St Edward's Sch., Oxford; Corpus Christi Coll., Cambridge (BA 1988; LLM 1989; MA 1992). Called to the Bar, Inner Temple, 1990; in practice as a barrister, specialising in medical and regulatory law, and public service pensions. *Recreations:* theatre, the classics, cryptic crosswords, Stoke City FC. *Address:* Serjeants' Inn Chambers, 85 Fleet Street, EC4Y 1AE. *T:* (020) 7427 5000. *E:* jholl-allenqc@serjeantsinn.com.

**HOLLAND, Sir Anthony;** *see* Holland, Sir J. A.

**HOLLAND, Charlotte Kate;** a District Judge (Magistrates' Courts), since 2018; *d* of Peter Holland and Sandra Holland. Called to the Bar, Lincoln's Inn, 1996; in practice as a barrister, Old Colony House Chambers, Manchester, 1996–2001, Lincoln House Chambers, Manchester, 2001–18. *Recreations:* gardening, cycling. *Address:* Leeds Magistrates' Court, Westgate, Leeds LS1 3BY.

**HOLLAND, Hon. Sir Christopher (John),** Kt 1992; a Judge of the High Court of Justice, Queen's Bench Division, 1992–2007; a Judge of the Employment Appeal Tribunal, 1994–2007; *b* 1 June 1937; *er s* of late Frank and Winifred Mary Holland; *m* 1967, Jill Iona Holland; one *s* one *d. Educ:* Leeds Grammar Sch.; Emmanuel Coll., Cambridge (MA, LLB). National Service (acting Lance-Corp.), 3rd Royal Tank Regt, 1956–58. Called to the Bar, Inner Temple, 1963, Bencher, 1985; commenced practice on North Eastern Circuit (Presiding Judge, 1993–97); QC 1978; a Recorder, 1992. Mem., Criminal Injuries Compensation Bd, 1992. Mem., Oxford Univ. Appeal Court, 2009–15. Vice Chm., Cttee of Inquiry into Outbreak of Legionnaires' Disease at Stafford, 1985; Chm., Azelle Rodney Inquiry, 2010–13. Chm., Lower Washburn Parish Council, 1975–91. *Address:* c/o Royal Courts of Justice, Strand, WC2A 2LL.

**HOLLAND, David Moore;** QC 2011; a Recorder, since 2016; a Deputy High Court Judge, since 2018; *b* Belfast, 22 Nov. 1961; *s* of John Holland and Olive Holland; two *s* one *d*; *m* 2013, Sarah Morley. *Educ:* Campbell Coll., Belfast; Pembroke Coll., Cambridge (BA Hons Law 1984; MA); Univ. of Toronto (LLM; Commonwealth Scholar). Called to the Bar, Inner Temple, 1986; in practice as a barrister, specialising in property law and costs, 1988–; Dep. Adjudicator to HM Land Registry, 2009–13; Judge of First-tier Tribunal (Property Chamber) (pt-time), 2013–. *Recreations:* watching cricket and football, food and wine. *Address:* Landmark Chambers, 180 Fleet Street, EC4A 2HG. *E:* clerks@landmarkchambers.co.uk. *Clubs:* MCC, Century; Lancashire County Cricket, Surrey County Cricket, Arsenal Football, Spirochaetes Hockey.

**HOLLAND, Rt Rev. Edward;** an Hon. Assistant Bishop, Diocese of London, and Hon. Assistant Bishop, Diocese in Europe, since 2002; *b* 28 June 1936; *s* of Reginald Dick Holland and Olive Holland (*née* Yeoman). *Educ:* New College School; Dauntsey's School; King's College London (AKC). National Service, Worcestershire Regt, 1955–57; worked for Importers, 1957–61; KCL, 1961–65. Deacon 1965, priest 1966, Rochester; Curate, Holy Trinity, Dartford, 1965–69; Curate, John Keble, Mill Hill, 1969–72; Precentor, Gibraltar Cathedral, and Missioner for Seamen, 1972–74; Chaplain at Naples, Italy, 1974–79; Vicar of S Mark's, Bromley, 1979–86; Suffragan Bishop of Gibraltar in Europe, 1986–95; Area Bishop of Colchester, 1995–2001. Mem., Churches Conservation Trust, 1998–2011; Chm., Friends of Anglican Centre in Rome, 2002–15. *Recreations:* travel, being entertained and entertaining. *Address:* 37 Parfrey Street, Hammersmith, W6 9EW. *T:* (020) 8746 3636.

**HOLLAND, James;** historian, writer and broadcaster; *b* Salisbury, 27 June 1970; *s* of Martin and Jans Holland; *m* 1995, Rachel Thwaites; one *s* one *d. Educ:* Chafyn Grove Prep. Sch., Salisbury; King's Sch., Bruton, Som; Univ. of Durham (BA Hons Hist. 1992). Publicity Manager, Penguin Books UK, 1997–2001. Contributions to television programmes include: Victory in Europe, 2005; Battle of Britain: the real story, 2010; Dambusters: the race to smash the German dams, 2012; The Battle for Malta, 2013; Cold War, Hot Jets, 2013; Normandy '44: the battle beyond D-Day, 2014; television series: Nazi Megastructures, 2014–17; Hunting Nazi Treasure, 2017. Co-Founder, Chm. and Prog. Dir, Chalke Valley Hist. Fest., 2011–. Trustee, Barnes Wallis Meml Trust, 2012–. *Publications: non-fiction*: Fortress Malta: an island under siege, 2003; Together We Stand: North Africa - turning the tide in the West 1942–43, 2005; Heroes: the greatest generation and the Second World War, 2007; Italy's Sorrow: a year of war 1944–45, 2008; The Battle of Britain, 2010; Dam Busters: race to smash the dams 1943, 2012; The Authors' XI: a season of English cricket from Hackney to Hambledon, 2013; (ed) An Englishman at War: the wartime diaries of Stanley Christopherson, 2014; The War in the West: a new history, vol. 1: Germany ascendent 1939–41, 2015, vol. 2: the allies strike back 1941–43, 2017; Burma '44: the battle that turned the war in the East, 2016; RAF100: the official story, 2018; Big Week, 2018; Normandy '44: D-Day and the battle for France, 2019; Ladybird Expert series: Battle of Britain, 2017; The Battle of the Atlantic, 2018; Blitzkrieg, 2018; *fiction*: The Burning Blue, 2004; A Pair of Silver Wings, 2006; The Odin Mission, 2008; Darkest Hour, 2009; Blood of Honour, 2010; Hellfire, 2011; Duty Calls: Dunkirk, 2011; Duty Calls: Battle of Britain, 2012; Devil's Pact, 2013. *Recreations:* cricket, walking. *Address:* Maud's Cottage, Broad Chalke, Salisbury, Wilts SP5 5QH. *T:* (01722) 781111. *E:* james@jholland.co.uk. *Club:* Royal Air Force.
*See also* T. Holland.

**HOLLAND, Sir (John) Anthony,** Kt 2003; Chairman: Northern Ireland Parades Commission, 2000–05; Standards Board for England, 2001–08; Joint Insolvency Monitoring Unit, 2001–05; Complaints Commissioner, Financial Services Authority, 2004–14; *b* 9 Nov. 1938; *s* of John and Dorothy Rita Holland; *m* 1963, Kathleen Margaret Anderson; three *s. Educ:* Ratcliffe Coll., Leics; Nottingham Univ. (LLB 1959); Financial Planning Cert., Chartered Insce Inst., 1997; Univ. of the West of England (MPhil 1998); Heythrop Coll., Univ. of London (MA with Dist. 2016). Admitted Solicitor of Supreme Court, 1962; notary public. Joined Foot & Bowden, 1964, Partner, 1964–90, Sen. Partner, 1990–97; Principal Ombudsman, PIA, 1997–2000. Chairman: Social Security Appeals Tribunal, 1974–97; South Western Regl Adv. Council, BBC, 1984–87; a Chm., SFA, 1993–2001; Access Dispute (formerly Access Dispute Resolution) Cttee, 2002–10; Dep. Chm., Regulatory Decisions Cttee, 2002–04; Mem., Investigatory Powers Tribunal, 2009–14; Member: Council, Law Soc., 1976–95 (Vice-Pres., 1989–90; Pres., 1990–91; Chm., Young Solicitors Gp, 1972); Marre Cttee on future of the Legal Profession, 1986–88; Council, Justice, 1991–2003 (Chm., Exec. Bd, 1996–99); Mem. Council, Howard League for Penal Reform, 1992–2002; Hon. Mem., SPTL, 1992. Mem. Bd, Pension Protection Fund, 2007–13; Lay Mem., Speaker's Cttee for Ind. Parly Standards Authy, 2011–14. President: Plymouth Law Soc., 1986–87; Cornwall Law Soc., 1988–89. Mem., Plymouth Diocesan Finance Cttee, 1986–94. Chm., Plymouth Chamber of Commerce and Industry, 1994–96. Governor: Plymouth Coll., 1976–93; Coll. of Law, 1991–97. Hon. Mem., Canadian Bar Assoc., 1990. Liveryman, Tallow Chandlers' Co. Hon. LLD Plymouth, 2014. *Publications:* (jtly) Principles of Registered Land Conveyancing, 1966; (jtly) Landlord and Tenant, 1968; (Jt Adv. Ed.) Mines and Quarries Section, Butterworth's Encyclopædia of Forms and Precedents, 1989; (Gen. Ed.) Cordery on Solicitors, 9th edn, 1995–2004. *Recreations:* opera, literature, the cinema. *Address:* 262 Lauderdale Tower, Barbican, EC2Y 8BY. *T:* (020) 7638 5044. *Clubs:* Athenæum; Clifton (Bristol); Royal Western Yacht (Plymouth).

**HOLLAND, John Lewis;** Managing Director, Herts & Essex Newspapers, 1990–2000; *b* 23 May 1937; *s* of George James Holland and Esther Holland; *m* 1958, Maureen Ann Adams; one *s* one *d. Educ:* Nottingham Technical Grammar Sch. Trainee Reporter, Nottingham Evening News, subseq. Jun. Reporter, Mansfield Br. Office, 1953–55; Sports Reporter, Mansfield Reporter Co., 1955–56; Sports Reporter, subseq. Sports Editor, Aldershot News Group, 1956–59; News Editor, West Bridgford & Clifton Standard, Nottingham, 1959–61; Chief Sports Sub Editor, Bristol Evening Post, and Editor, Sports Green 'Un (sports edn), 1961–64; Editor, West Bridgford & Clifton Standard, Nottingham, and Partner, Botting & Turner Sports Agency, Nottingham, 1964–66; Birmingham Evening Mail: Dep. Sports Editor, 1966–71; Editor, Special Projects Unit (Colour Prodn Dept), 1971–75; Editor, 1975–79, and Gen. Man., 1979–81, Sandwell Evening Mail; Marketing/Promotions Gen. Man., Birmingham Post & Mail, 1981–82; Editor, The Birmingham Post, 1982–86. Director: Birmingham Post & Mail Circulation and Promotions, 1986–88; Birmingham Post & Mail Publications and Promotions, 1988–90; Birmingham Convention and Visitor Bureau, 1982–90. President: Chartered Inst. of Marketing, 1989–90; Chiltern Newspaper Proprietors Assoc., 1995–99 (Vice-Pres., 1994–95). Member: Hertford Business Club, 1994–2000; Soc. of Cambs Area Golf Captains, 1999–2007. *Recreations:* journalism, golf, keeping horses, gardening, keep fit. *Address:* Carob Lodge, Marathounda, PO Box 60151, Paphos 8101, Cyprus. *Clubs:* Press (Birmingham); Heydon Grange Golf (Captain, 1998–99) (Royston); Tsada Golf (Captain, 2003–04), Secret Valley Golf, Elea Golf (Cyprus).

**HOLLAND, Rt Rev. Dr Jonathan Charles;** Principal, St Francis Theological College, Southern Queensland, since 2016; Executive Director, Ministry Education Commission, Diocese of Brisbane; *b* Perth, 26 Sept. 1956; *s* of late Rt Rev. Alfred Charles Holland; *m* 1980, Kerry Anne Minchin; two *s* one *d. Educ:* Univ. of Western Australia (BA Hons 1978); Queen's Coll., Oxford (BA Hons 1982); Univ. of Queensland (MA 1999; PhD 2007). Ordained deacon, 1982, priest, 1983; Rector: Church of the Ascension, Midland, 1989–93; Christ Church, St Lucia, Qld, 1993–2006. Archbishop's Examining Chaplain, 1995–2006; Canon, St John's Cathedral, 2004–06; an Asst Bishop, Dio. of Brisbane, Qld, 2006–16. *Publications:* Eyes Delight: six paintings and their theological meaning, 1999; Jesus Unbound: the story of Jesus of Nazareth, 2008; Anglicans, Trams and Paw Paws: the story of the Diocese of Brisbane 1945–1980, 2013; The Destiny and Passion of Philip Nigel Warrington Strong, 2019. *Recreations:* reading, poetry, gardening. *Address:* 201 Pfingst Road, Wavell Heights, Qld 4012, Australia. *T:* (7) 35147401. *E:* jholland@anglicanchurchsq.org.au. *Club:* Australian (Sydney).

**HOLLAND, Julian Miles, (Jools),** OBE 2003; DL; pianist and broadcaster; *b* 24 Jan. 1958; *s* of Derek Holland and June Rose Holland (*née* Lane); one *s* one *d* by Mary Leahy; *m* 2005, Christabel Durham; one *d. Educ:* Invicta Sherington Sch.; Shooters Hill Sch. Keyboard player with Squeeze, 1974–80; band leader, Rhythm & Blues Orch., 1993–; regular tours in UK. Architect: Helicon Mountain, Greenwich; gatehouse, Witton Castle. *Television:* presenter: The Tube, 1981–86; Juke Box Jury, 1989; Sunday Night, 1990; The Happening, 1990; Later with Jools Holland, 1993–; presenter and writer, Jools' History of the Piano, 2002; actor and writer, The Groovy Fellers, 1988; writer and producer: Walking to New Orleans, 1985; Mr Roadrunner, 1991; Beat Route, 1998; Jools Meets the Saint, 1999; *radio:* presenter, The Jools Holland Show; *films:* musical director, Spiceworld the Movie, 1997; writer of film score, Milk, 1999. *Solo albums:* A World Of His Own, 1990; Full Complement, 1991; The A-Z Geographer's Guide To The Piano, 1993; Solo Piano, 1995; Sex & Jazz & Rock & Roll, 1996; Lift The Lid, 1997; Sunset Over London, 1999; Hop The Wag, 2000; Small World Big Band, 2001; More Friends, 2002; Friends 3, 2003; Swinging The Blues, Dancing The Ska, 2005; Moving Out To The Country, 2006; The Informer, 2008; Rockinghorse, 2010; The Golden Age of Song, 2012; jt album, Tom Jones and Jools Holland, 2004; (with Ruby Turner) Jools and Ruby, 2015; (with Marc Almond) A Lovely Life to Live, 2018. DL Kent, 2006. *Publications:* Beat Route, 1998; (with Dora Loewenstein) Rolling Stones: a life on the road, 1998; Barefaced Lies & Boogie-Woogie Boasts: the autobiography, 2007. *Address:* One Fifteen, 1 Globe House, Middle Lane Mews, N8 8PN.

**HOLLAND, Katharine Jane;** QC 2010. *Educ:* Hertford Coll., Oxford (BCL; MA). FCIA 2010; DipICArb 2010. Called to the Bar, Middle Temple, 1989. *Address:* Landmark Chambers, 180 Fleet Street, EC4A 2HG. *T:* (020) 7430 1221, *Fax:* (020) 7421 6060.

**HOLLAND, Kevin John William C.;** *see* Crossley-Holland.

**HOLLAND, Neil Ridgway;** HM Diplomatic Service; Director of Protocol and Vice-Marshal of the Diplomatic Corps, since 2017; *b* Peterborough, 7 Aug. 1971; *s* of Keith Graham Holland and Angela Mary Holland; *m* 2000, Sarah Holmes; one *s* three *d. Educ:* Univ. of Southampton (BA Mod. Hist. and Politics). Security Policy Dept, FCO, 2003–04; First Secretary: Berlin, 2005–08; Washington, 2008–13; Dep. Hd of Mission, Dublin, 2013–17. *Recreations:* walking, cinema, reading, golf, cricket, music. *Address:* Foreign and Commonwealth Office, King Charles Street, SW1A 2AH. *T:* (020) 7008 0989.

**HOLLAND, Norman James Abbott;** Group Standards Manager, Philips UK, 1983–90; President, British National Electrotechnical Committee, 1993–99; *b* 16 Dec. 1927; *s* of James George Holland and May Stuart Holland; *m* 1951, Barbara Florence Byatt; one *s* one *d. Educ:* Sir Walter St John's Grammar Sch.; Regent Street Polytechnic. UK Delegate: IEC Council, 1987–92 (Delegn Leader, 1993–99; Mem. Bd, 1998–99); CENELEC Gen. Assembly, 1987–92 (Delegn Leader, 1993–99); Chm., Electrotechnical Sector Bd, 1993–99, Mem., Standards Bd, 1993–99, BSI. Member: IEC Finance Cttee, 1985–91; Engrg Council, 1985–91; Bd, Electronic Engrg Assoc., 1985–92 (Chm., Standards Policy Gp); NACCB, 1987–92. *Recreation:* golf. *Address:* 12 Pine Road, Chandler's Ford, Hants SO53 1LP.

**HOLLAND, Prof. Peter William Harold**, PhD, DSc; FRS 2003; Linacre Professor of Zoology, University of Oxford, since 2002 (Head, Department of Zoology, 2011–16); Fellow, Merton College, Oxford, since 2002; b 17 Aug. 1963; s of late William Harold Bolton and of Christine (née Bartrop) and step s of Franklin Holland; m 1996, Amanda Susan Horsfall; two s. Educ: Marple Hall Sch.; Queen's Coll., Oxford (MA); NIMR, London (PhD 1987); DSc Reading 2002. University of Oxford: Demonstrator, Dept of Zool., 1987–91; Browne Res. Fellow, Queen's Coll., 1988–91; Royal Soc. Univ. Res. Fellow, 1991–94; Prof. of Zool., Univ. of Reading, 1994–2002. Member: Cttee, British Soc. Develtl Biol., 1990–95; Genes Develtl Biol. Cttee, BBSRC, 1997–99; Council, Marine Biol. Assoc., 1998–2001, 2003– (Gov., 2003–); Funding Panel, NSF, 2002–03; Comparative Genomics Wkg Gp, NIH, 2004–06; Individual Merit Promotion Panel, BBSRC, 2004–10. Hon. Res. Fellow, Natural History Mus., 2005–; Invitation Fellow, Japan Soc. for Promotion of Sci., 2016; Yen Kwo-Yung Lectr, Chinese Univ. of Hong Kong, 2017; Vis. Prof., Univ. of Barcelona, 2019. FLS 2002; FMBA 2014. Scientific Medal, Zool. Soc. of London, 1996; De Snoo van 't Hoogerhuijs Medal, 1999; Genetics Soc. Medal, 2004; Blaise Pascal Medal, European Acad. of Scis, 2005; Kowalevsky Medal, St Petersburg Soc. of Naturalists, 2006; Linnean Medal for Zoology, Linnean Soc., 2012; Frink Medal, Zool Soc. of London, 2016. Publications: (ed with C. Stern) Essential Developmental Biology, 1993; (ed jtly) The Evolution of Developmental Mechanisms, 1994; Swifter than the Arrow: Wilfred Bartrop, football and war, 2009; The Animal Kingdom, 2011; res. papers in scientific jls. Recreations: the natural world, Lepidoptera, sporting history, fishing. Address: Merton College, Oxford OX1 4JD.

**HOLLAND, Richard**; District Judge (Magistrates' Courts) (formerly Stipendiary Magistrate), Leicestershire, 1999–2011; b 23 Jan. 1951; s of late Clifford Holland and Mary Holland (née Gledhill, later Smithies); m 2001, Ann, d of Charles and Mavis Mortimer, Wakefield. Educ: Colne Valley High Sch., W Yorks; Queen Mary Coll., Univ. of London (BA Hons 1971). Admitted Solicitor 1974. Articled Clerk, Magistrates' Courts Service, WR of Yorks, 1972–74; Sen. Court Clerk, 1974–75, Dep. Justices' Clerk, 1975–79, Oldham; Justices' Clerk, Rochdale, 1979–89; Justices' Clerk, and Clerk to the Magistrates' Courts Cttee, Wakefield Metropolitan Dist, 1990–97; Justices' Clerk and Chief Exec., Leeds City, 1997–99. Recreations: birdwatching, canal boating, the sport of Kings, feigning indolence.

**HOLLAND, Stuart (Kingsley)**; political economist; Chief Executive, Alter-Europe, 1998–2003; Director, Associate Research in Economy and Society Ltd, 1993–98; b 25 March 1940; s of late Frederick Holland and May Holland, London; m 1976, Jenny Lennard; two c. Educ: state primary schs; Christ's Hosp.; Univ. of Missouri (Exchange Scholar); Balliol Coll., Oxford (Domus Scholar; 1st Cl. Hons Mod. History); St Antony's Coll., Oxford (Sen. Scholar; DPhil Econs). Econ. Asst, Cabinet Office, 1966–67; Personal Asst to Prime Minister, 1967–68; Res. Fellow, Centre for Contemp. European Studies, Univ. of Sussex, 1968–71, Assoc. Fellow and Lectr, 1971–79. Vis. Scholar, Brookings Instn, Washington, DC, 1970. Adviser to Commons Expenditure Cttee, 1971–72; Special Adviser to Minister of Overseas Develt, 1974–75. MP (Lab) Vauxhall, 1979–89; Opposition frontbench spokesman on overseas develt and co-operation, 1983–87, on treasury and economic affairs, 1987–89; Prof. of Econs, Eur. Univ. Inst., Florence, 1989–93. Res. Specialist, RIIA, 1972–74; Associate, Inst. of Develt Studies, 1974–89 (Gov., 1983–91). Consultant: Econ. and Social Affairs Cttee, Council of Europe, 1973; Open Univ., 1973. Rapporteur, Trades Union Adv. Cttee, OECD, 1977. Chm., Public Enterprise Gp, 1973–75. European Community Commission: Mem., Expert Cttee on Inflation, 1975–76; Consultant to Directorate Gen. XVI, 1989; Dir, Proj. on Econ. and Social Cohesion, 1991–93; Adviser: to Merger Task Force, DG IV, 1991–93; to Region of Tuscany, 1992–96. Member: Council, Inst. for Workers' Control, 1974–; UN Univ. Working Party on Socio-Cultural Factors in Develt, Tokyo, 1977. Vis. Prof., Faculty of Econs, Univ. of Coimbra, 2003–; Sen. Scholar, Inst. for Social and Eur. Studies, Köszeg, Hungary, 2014–15; Sen. Res. Fellow, Inst. for Advanced Studies, Köszeg, Hungary, 2016–18. Lubbock Lectr, Oxford Univ., 1975; Tom Mann Meml Lectr, Australia, 1977. Mem., Labour Party, 1962–; Mem. sub-cttees (inc. Finance and Econ. Policy, Indust. Policy, Sector), Nat. Exec. Cttee, Labour Party, 1972–89; Executive Member: Labour Coordinating Cttee, 1978–81; European Nuclear Disarmament Campaign, 1980–83; Mem., Economic Cttee, Socialist International, 1984–. Hon. MRTPI 1980. Dr hc Roskilde Univ., Denmark, 1992. Publications: (jtly) Sovereignty and Multinational Corporations, 1971; (ed) The State as Entrepreneur, 1972; Strategy for Socialism, 1975; The Socialist Challenge, 1975; The Regional Problem, 1976; Capital versus the Regions, 1976; (ed) Beyond Capitalist Planning, 1978; Uncommon Market, 1980; (ed) Out of Crisis, 1983; (with Donald Anderson) Kissinger's Kingdom, 1984; (with James Firebrace) Never Kneel Down, 1984; The Market Economy, 1987; The Global Economy, 1987; The European Imperative: economic and social cohesion in the 1990s, 1993; Towards a New Bretton Woods: alternatives for the global economy, 1994; (with Ken Coates) Full Employment for Europe, 1995; Europe in Question: constitution, cohesion and enlargement, 2004; Europe in Question: and what to do about it, 2014; Beyond Austerity: democratic alternatives for Europe, 2016; contrib. symposia; articles in specialist jls and national and internat. press. Recreation: singing in the bath. E: sholland@fe.uc.pt.

**HOLLAND, Thomas**, FRSL; historian, translator and novelist; b Oxford, 5 Jan. 1968; s of Martin and Jans Holland; m 1993, Sadie Lowry; two d. Educ: Chafyn Grove Prep. Sch.; Canford Sch.; Queens' Coll., Cambridge (BA 1989). FEA 2008. Chairman: Soc. of Authors, 2009–11; PLR Adv. Cttee, 2016–. Presenter: Making History, BBC Radio 4, 2011–; Islam: the Untold Story, Channel 4, 2012; ISIS: the Origins of Violence, Channel 4, 2017. Pres., Stonehenge Alliance. FRSL 2016. Publications: The Vampyre, 1995; Supping with Panthers, 1996; Deliver us from Evil, 1997; The Sleeper in the Sands, 1998; The Bonehunter, 2001; Rubicon, 2003; Persian Fire, 2005; Millennium, 2008; In the Shadow of the Sword, 2012; (trans.) Herodotus, The Histories, 2013; Dynasty: the rise and fall of the House of Caesar, 2015; Athelstan: the making of England, 2016; Æthelflæd: England's forgotten founder, 2019; Dominion: the making of the Western mind, 2019. Recreations: elite international cricketer (hitter of a six and bowler of the Prince of Udaipur), walking ancient roads, dinosaurs, hedgehogs. Address: c/o PEW Literary Agency Ltd, 46 Lexington Street, W1F 0LP.

See also J. Holland.

**HOLLAND-HIBBERT**, family name of **Viscount Knutsford**.

**HOLLAND-KAYE, (William) John**, FRICS; Chief Executive, Heathrow Airport Holdings Ltd, since 2014. Educ: Peterhouse, Cambridge (BA 1986; MA 1991); INSEAD, France (MBA). Man. Dir, Nat. Sales Div., Bass Brewers, 1999–2002; appts with Taylor Woodrow, incl. Ops Dir, Taylor Woodrow Develts and Commercial Dir, Taylor Woodrow Inc., 2002–07; Divl Chm., Taylor Wimpey plc, 2007–09; Commercial Dir, BAA, 2009–12; Develt Dir, Heathrow, 2012–14. Recreations: cooking, books, swimming, hill walking. Address: Heathrow Airport Ltd, The Compass Centre, Nelson Road, Hounslow, Middx TW6 2GW.

**HOLLAND-MARTIN, Robert George, (Robin)**; Director, Henderson (formerly Henderson Administration Group) plc, 1983–98; b 6 July 1939; y s of late Cyril Holland-Martin and Rosa, d of Sir Gerald Chadwyck-Healey, 2nd Bt, CBE; m 1976, Dominique, 2nd d of Maurice Fromaget; two d. Educ: Eton. Cazenove & Co., 1960–74 (partner, 1968–74); Finance Director, Paterson Products Ltd, 1976–86; Consultant: Newmarket Venture Capital plc (formerly Newmarket Co.), 1982–94; Investindustrial Gp of Cos, 1997–2014. Non-executive Director: Dorling Kindersley Hldgs plc, 1992–2000; Fine Art Soc. plc, 1995–2018 (Chm., 2016–18); Service Point Solutions (formerly Grupo Picking Pack) SA (Spain), 1998–2006; Grapes Direct Ltd, 2000–06. Hon. Dep. Treasurer, Cons. and Unionist Party, 1979–82. Mem., Trustee Bd (formerly Council), Metropolitan Hospital-Sunday Fund, 1964–2002 (Chm., 1977–2002); Mem. Council, Homoeopathic Trust, 1970–90 (Vice Chm., 1975–90). Victoria & Albert Museum: Mem. Adv. Council, 1972–83; Mem. Cttee, Associates of V&A, 1976–85 (Chm., 1981–85); Dep. Chm., Trustees, 1983–85. Mem., Visiting Cttee for Royal Coll. of Art, 1982–93 (Chm., 1984–93). Trustee: Blackie Foundn Trust, 1971–96 (Chm., 1987–96; Pres., 1998–2018); King's Med. Res. Trust, 2000–17; C&G of London Art Sch., 2001–19 (Chm., 2002–19). Mem., Court of Assts, Fishmongers' Co., 1999– (Prime Warden, 2010–11). Address: 94 Old Church Street, SW3 6EP. T: (020) 7352 7871. Club: White's.

**HOLLANDE, François Gérard Georges**, Hon. GCB 2014; President of France, 2012–17; b Rouen, 12 Aug. 1954; s of Georges Hollande and Nicole Hollande (née Tribert); two s two d by Marie-Ségolène Royal; former partner, Valérie Trierweiler. Educ: Lycée Pasteur, Neuilly; Faculté de Droit, Paris (Licencié en Droit); Ecole des hautes études commerciales, Paris (Dip.); Inst. d'études politiques, Paris; Ecole Nat. d'Admin. Auditor, 1980–84, Clerk, 1984, Court of Auditors; Lectr, 1982–88, Prof. of Econs, 1988–91, Inst. d'études politiques. Special Advr to Pres. of France, 1981; Chief of Staff to Sec. of State, 1983–84. Member: Ussel CC, 1983–89; Limousin Regl Council, 1992 and 1998–2001 (Vice-Pres., 1998–2001); Tulle CC, 1995–2001 (Mayor, 2001–08); Mem. (Soc.) Corrèze, Nat. Assembly, 1988–93 and 1997–2012; MEP, 1999; Pres., Gen. Council of Corrèze, 2008–12. Joined Socialist Party, 1979, Nat. Sec., 1994–97, First Sec., 1997–2008; Vice Pres., Socialist Internat., 1999. Pres., Fondation La France S'Engage, 2017–. Publications: (jtly) l'Heure de choix, 1991; Devoirs de vérité, 2006; Changer de destin, 2012.

**HOLLANDER, Prof. Anthony Peter**, PhD; Pro-Vice-Chancellor for Research and Impact, University of Liverpool, since 2017; b London, 4 Feb. 1964; s of Otto Hollander and Miriam Hollander; m 1st, 1990, Catriona Lamont (marr. diss. 2013); two s one d; 2nd, 2015, Dr Anna Salerno. Educ: Christ's Coll. Finchley; Univ. of Bath (BSc 1987; 1st Cl. Hons Pharmacol.); Univ. of Bristol (PhD Pathol. 1990). Postdoctoral Scientist, McGill Univ., Montreal, 1990–93; Lectr, 1993–99, Reader, 1999–2000, Univ. of Sheffield; Prof. of Rheumatol. and Tissue Engrg, 2000–14, Hd, Sch. of Cellular and Molecular Medicine, 2009–14, Univ. of Bristol; Prof. of Stem Cell Biol. and Hd, Inst. of Integrative Biol., 2014–17, Associate Pro-Vice-Chancellor (Enterprise), 2016–17, Univ. of Liverpool. CSO, Azellon Cell Therapeutics, 2009– (Dir, 2009–). Pres., Internat. Cartilage Repair Soc., 2012–13. Publications: over 100 articles in learned jls. Recreations: cooking, opera, theatre, reading, walking, ski-ing. Address: Office of the Pro-Vice-Chancellors, University of Liverpool, The Foundation Building, 765 Brownlow Hill, Liverpool L69 7ZX. T: (0151) 794 2220. E: A.Hollander@liv.ac.uk.

**HOLLANDER, Charles Simon**; QC 1999; a Recorder, since 2000; a Deputy High Court Judge; b 1 Dec. 1955; s of Paul and Eileen Hollander; m 1986, Heather Pilley; two s two d. Educ: University College Sch.; King's Coll., Cambridge (BA 1977; MA 1981). Called to the Bar, Gray's Inn, 1978, Bencher, 2008; in practice at the Bar, 1978–. Mem., Bar Standards Bd, 2006– (Chm., Standards Cttee, 2006–). CEDR accredited mediator. Publications: Documentary Evidence, 1985, 10th edn 2009; Conflicts of Interest and Chinese Walls, 2000, 3rd edn 2008; (ed jtly) Phipson on Evidence, 15th edn 2000, 16th edn 2005. Recreations: tennis, food, wine. Address: Brick Court Chambers, 7/8 Essex Street, WC2R 3LD. T: (020) 7379 3550.

**HOLLANDS, Maj.-Gen. Graham Spencer**; b 14 Feb. 1942; s of Ernest Darrell Hollands and Gwendoline Isobel Hollands (née Matheson); m 1968, Lesley Clair Billam; one s one d. Educ: King Edward VI Sch., Bath; RMA Sandhurst; RMCS; Staff Coll., Camberley. Commissioned RA, 1963; served BAOR and UK; MoD, 1980–81; CO 25 Field Regt RA, 1981–84; CO 3rd Regt RHA, 1984–85; COS Artillery Div., HQ 1 (BR) Corps, 1985–86; Comdr, British Trng Teams, Nigeria, 1986–87; CRA 2nd Inf. Div., 1987–89; DCOS, HQ BAOR, 1989–92; Comdr Artillery, 1st British Corps, 1992–94. Chief Exec., W Kent Coll., 1994. Recreations: golf, ski-ing, country pursuits.

**HOLLENDEN**, 4th Baron cr 1912, of Leigh, Kent; **Ian Hampden Hope-Morley**; part-owner and Trustee, The Hampden Estate; b 23 Oct. 1946; e s of 3rd Baron Hollenden and Sonja (née Sundt); S father, 1999; m 1st, 1972, Beatrice (née d'Anchald) (marr. diss. 1985); one s one d; 2nd, 1988, Caroline (née Ash); two s. Educ: Maidwell Hall; Eton Coll. Shipbroker: Asmarine SA, Paris, 1969–72; Eggar Forrester, London, 1972–77; Mktg Mgr, British Shipbuilders, 1977–79; Shipbroker, Galbraith Wrightson, 1979–86; Proprietor, The Hampden Wine Company, Thame, 1988–98. Recreations: shooting, ski-ing. Heir: s Hon. Edward Hope-Morley, b 9 April 1981. Address: The Estate Office, Great Hampden, Great Missenden, Bucks HP16 9RE. Club: Brooks's.

**HOLLERN, Catherine Molloy**; MP (Lab) Blackburn, since 2015; b Dumbarton, 12 April 1955; two d; partner, John. Work study manager, Newman's Footwear; Contracts Manager, Blackburn Coll. Mem. (Lab), Blackburn with Darwen Council, until 2015 (Leader Lab Gp, 2004–15; Leader of Council, 2004–07 and 2010–15). Shadow Minister for Defence, 2016, for Communities and Local Govt, 2016–17. Address: House of Commons, SW1A 0AA.

**HOLLICK**, family name of **Baron Hollick**.

**HOLLICK**, Baron cr 1991 (Life Peer), of Notting Hill in the Royal Borough of Kensington and Chelsea; **Clive Richard Hollick**; Director, Honeywell Inc., since 2003; b 20 May 1945; s of late Leslie George Hollick and Olive Mary (née Scruton); m 1977, Susan Mary Woodford (see Lady Hollick); three d. Educ: Taunton's Sch., Southampton; Univ. of Nottingham (BA Hons). Joined Hambros Bank Ltd, 1968, Dir, 1973–96; Chairman: Shepperton Studios Ltd, 1976–84; Garban Ltd (USA), 1983–97; Founder and Chm., Meridian Broadcasting Ltd, 1992–96; Chief Executive: Mills & Allen Internat., subseq. MAI PLC, 1974–96; United News & Media, subseq. United Business Media plc, 1996–2005; Man. Dir, 2005–06, Partner, 2006–09, Sen. Advr, 2009–10, Kohlberg Kravis Roberts; Partner, then Sen. Advr, G. P. Bullhound, 2010–18; Director: Logica plc, 1987–91; Avenir Havas Media SA, 1989–92; Satellite Information Systems Ltd, 1990–94; British Aerospace, 1992–97; Anglia Television, 1994–97; TRW Inc., 2000–02; Diageo plc, 2001–11 (Sen. Dir, 2004–11); Nielsen Inc., 2007–09; Pro Sieben Sat1 (formerly Pro Sieben Media) AG, 2007–14; BMG Music Rights Mgt, 2009–14; Chm., WePredict Ltd, 2013–15; Member, Advisory Board: Jefferies Inc., 2011–17; Ambassador Th. Gp, 2011–16; Market Share Inc., 2013–17. Special Advr to Pres. of BoT and Sec. of State for Trade and Industry, 1997–98; Prime Minister's Trade and Investment Envoy to Kenya and Tanzania, 2014–. Chm., South Bank Centre, 2002–08. Dir, Bureau of Investigative Journalism, 2018–. Member: Nat. Bus Co. Ltd, 1984–91; Adv. Cttee, Dept of Applied Econs, Univ. of

Cambridge, 1989–97; Financial Law Panel, 1993–97; Commn on Public Policy and British Business, 1995–97; H of L Select Cttee on Econ. Affairs, 2010– (Chm., 2014–17); H of L Artificial Intelligence Cttee, 2017–18; H of L Intergenerational Fairness Cttee, 2018–19. Mem. Adv. Bd, Royal Soc., 2010–. Chm., Galleon Trust, 1992–97. Founding Trustee, IPPR, 1988–. Gov., LSE, 1997–2003. Hon. LLD Nottingham, 1993. *Recreations:* reading, theatre, music, cinema, golf, countryside.

HOLLICK, Lady; Susan Mary Woodford-Hollick, OBE 2011; Founder and Director, Little Garden Day Nursery (formerly Bringing Up Baby Ltd), since 1989; *b* 16 May 1945; *d* of late Ulric Cross, DSO, DFC, ORTT and Joan Woodford; *m* 1977, Clive Richard Hollick (*see* Baron Hollick); three *d*. *Educ:* La Retraite Convent High Sch., London; Univ. of Sussex (BA Hons). Producer/Dir, World in Action, Granada TV, 1969–81; Founding Commissioning Ed. for multicultural progs, Channel 4 TV, 1980–84. Chm., Index on Censorship, 1993–2000. Member: Arts Council England (formerly Arts Council of England), 2002–09 (Chair, London Regl Council (formerly London Arts Bd), 2000–09); Adv. Bd, Tate Modern, 2000–09; Chair: Tate Members' Council, 1999–2005; Leaders Quest Foundn, 2011–14; Stuart Hall Foundn, 2015–; Director: AMREF UK, 2007–11; AMREF Internat. Bd, 2008–15; Free Word, 2009–15. Trustee: Hollick Family Charitable Trust, 1997–; Theatre de Complicite, 2009–; Reprieve, 2014–; Music for My Mind, 2015–. Mem., BAFTA. FRSA. *Publications:* The Good Nursery Guide, 1992. *Recreations:* the arts, television, cinema, tennis, golf. *Club:* Queenwood Golf (Ottershaw, Surrey).

HOLLIDAY, Rev. Canon Peter Leslie; Group Chief Executive, St Giles Hospice, 2000–15; a Chaplain to the Queen, 2015–18; Member of the Chapter, and Chair, Finance Committee, Lichfield Cathedral, since 2019; *b* Sutton Coldfield, 3 July 1948; *s* of John Kenneth Holliday and Marjorie Doris Holliday; *m* 1969, Ruth Mary Page; one *s* two *d*. *Educ:* Bishop Vesey's Grammar Sch.; Birmingham Univ. (BCom 1970; MA 1992); Queen's Theol Coll., Birmingham. FCA 1979. Articled clerk, Peat, Marwick, Mitchell & Co., 1970–73; Dir, Chart Tutors Ltd, 1974–81; ordained deacon, 1983, priest, 1984; Curate, Burton on Trent, 1983–87; Priest-in-charge, Longdon, and Subchanter, Lichfield Cathedral, 1987–93; Vicar, Stratford upon Avon, 1993–2000; Chancellor's Vicar, 2002–13, Canon Custos, 2013–18, now Canon Emeritus, Lichfield Cathedral. Chm., Chart Foulks Lynch plc, 1981–88; Dir, Cowan De Groot plc, 1985–87. Chief Exec., Mary Stevens Hospice, 2011–13; Chair, ehospice, 2017–; Deputy Chair: Hospice UK, 2007–15 (Chair, Adv. Council, 2007–15); Lichfield Cathedral Sch., 2008–18. Trustee, Bury Hospice, 2016–19. Dir, Stratford Music Festival, 1997–2019. Contested (C) Warley E, Oct. 1974. *Recreations:* classical music, family and friends, gardening, travel. *Address:* 60 Needlers End Lane, Coventry CV7 7AB. *Club:* Burton (Burton on Trent; Chaplain, 2006–).

HOLLIDAY, Steven John, FREng; Chief Executive, National Grid, 2007–16; *b* Exeter, 26 Oct. 1956; *s* of Michael and Jean Holliday; *m* 1996, Kate Patterson; three *d*. *Educ:* Univ. of Nottingham (BSc Mining Engrg 1978). Esso/Exxon, 1978–97: Ops Manager, Fawley Refinery, Esso UK, 1988–92; Supply and Transportation Divl Dir, Esso UK, 1992–94; Regl Vice-Pres. Gas, Exxon Co. Internat., 1994–97; Bd Dir, British Borneo Oil and Gas, 1997–2000; National Grid: Bd Dir responsible for Transmission, 2001–03; Gp Dir responsible for UK Gas Distribution and Business Services, 2003–07. Non-exec. Dir, Marks & Spencer, 2004–14. Lead non-exec. Dir, DEFRA, 2016–17; Chm., Youth Full-Time Social Action Review, 2017–18. Vice Chm., BITC, 2014–; Vice Chm., Careers and Enterprise Co. (formerly Enterprise for Educn) Ltd, 2015–. Chm., Crisis, 2012–. Pres., Energy Inst., 2019–. FREng 2010. *Recreations:* sports, Rugby, ski-ing, arts.

HOLLIGER, Heinz; oboist, composer and conductor; *b* Langenthal, Switzerland, 21 May 1939; *m* Ursula Holliger, harpist. *Educ:* Berne Conservatoire; Paris; Basle; studied with Cassagnaud, Lefèbure, Veress, Pierlot and Boulez. Played with Basle Orch., 1959–63; Prof. of oboe, Freiburg Music Acad., 1965–2003. Has appeared as soloist and conductor at all major European music festivals, and with Chamber Orch. of Europe, English Chamber Orch., etc; has directed all major Swiss orchs, Cleveland Orch., Philharmonia, Vienna Philharmonic, Vienna SO, CBSO, Berlin Philharmonic, Concertgebouw, etc. Has inspired compositions by Berio, Penderecki, Stockhausen, Henze, Martin and others. *Compositions include:* Der magische Tänzer, Trio, Dona nobis pacem, Pneuma, Psalm, Cardiophonie, Kreis, Siebengesang, H for wind quintet, string quartet Atembogen, Scardanelli-Cycle, Gesänge der Frühe, (S)irato for orch., Violin Concerto, Partita, Puneigä. Has won many international prizes, including: Geneva Competition first prize, 1959; Munich Competition first prize, 1961; Sonning Prize; Frankfurt Music Prize; Ernst von Siemens Prize. *Address:* Konzertgesellschaft, Peter Merian-Strasse 28/Postfach, 4002 Basel, Switzerland.

HOLLINGBERY, Sir George, KCMG 2019; MP (C) Meon Valley, since 2010; *b* 12 Oct. 1963; *m* 1991, Janette Marie White; one *s* two *d*. *Educ:* Radley Coll.; Lady Margaret Hall, Oxford (BA Human Scis 1985); Wharton Sch., Univ. of Pennsylvania (MBA 1991). Stockbroker, Robert Fleming Securities, 1985–89; non-exec. Dir and shareholder, Lister Bestcare Ltd, 1991–95; Dir and Founder, Pet Depot Ltd, 1994–99; Chm. and Founder, Companion Care Vet. Gp, 1998–2001; property investment business, 2005–. Mem. (C) Winchester CC, 1999–2010. Contested (C) Winchester, 2005. PPS to Secretary of State for Home Dept, 2012–15; a Lord Comr of HM Treasury (Govt Whip), 2015–16; PPS to the Prime Minister, 2016–18; Minister of State, DIT, 2018–19. Mem., Communities and Local Govt Select Cttee, 2010–15. Mem. Exec., 1922 Cttee, 2012–. *Address:* House of Commons, SW1A 0AA.

HOLLINGHURST, Alan James, FRSL; writer; *b* 26 May 1954; *s* of James Kenneth Hollinghurst and Elizabeth Lilian Hollinghurst (*née* Keevil). *Educ:* Canford Sch.; Magdalen Coll., Oxford (BA 1975; MLitt 1979; Hon. Fellow 2013). On staff, TLS, 1982–95. Vis. Prof., Univ. of Houston, 1998; Old Dominion Fellow, Princeton Univ., 2004. FRSL 1995. Hon. DLit UCL, 2012. *Publications:* The Swimming-Pool Library, 1988 (Somerset Maugham Award, E. M. Forster Award, AAAL); The Folding Star, 1994 (James Tait Black Meml Prize); The Spell, 1998; The Line of Beauty (Man Booker Prize), 2004; The Stranger's Child, 2011; The Sparsholt Affair, 2017; *translations:* Racine, Bajazet, 1991; Racine, Berenice and Bajazet, 2012. *Recreations:* looking at buildings and pictures, listening to music. *Address:* 15 Tanza Road, NW3 2UA. *Club:* Cranium.

HOLLINGHURST, Rt Rev. Anne Elizabeth; *see* Aston, Bishop Suffragan of.

HOLLINGHURST, Edmund, FREng, FICE, FIStructE; FCIHT; Director and Partner, 1986, then Senior Partner, Gifford & Partners; *b* 27 June 1944; *s* of Rev. Dr George Frederick Hollinghurst and Rachel Hollinghurst (*née* Cooper); *m* 1986, Glenys Helen Davis; three *d*. *Educ:* Dragon Sch., Oxford; Kingswood Sch., Bath; Sidney Sussex Coll., Cambridge (MA). CEng 1971; FCIHT (FIHT 1985); FICE 1995; FIStructE 1995; FREng (FEng 1997). Trainee, Ove Arup & Partners, 1962–63; Engineer: Ninham Shand, Cape Town, SA, 1965–66; Ove Arup & Partners, London, Africa and Middle East, 1967–70; Kier Ltd, UK and overseas, 1970–73; Gifford & Partners, 1973–86, seconded as staff consultant, Asian Develt Bank, 1978. Mem., Royal Fine Art Commn, 1996–99. Vis. Prof., Univ. of Southampton. Major designs include: Bray Viaduct, Devon; Kwai Chung, Hong Kong; Dee Crossing, Wales; Second Severn Crossing; Camel Estuary Bridge, Cornwall; Kingston Bridge, Glasgow; River Tyne Millennium Bridge. Fédération Internationale de la Précontrainte Design Award, for Bray Viaduct, 1994. *Publications:* contrib. to ICE and IStructE texts. *Recreation:* sailing.

HOLLINGSWORTH, Michael Charles; Chairman, Venture Television Ltd (trading as Venture Artists, Venture Broadcasting, and Venture Correspondents), 2007 (Chief Executive, 1993–2007); *b* 22 Feb. 1946; *s* of Albert George Hollingsworth and Gwendoline Marjorie Hollingsworth; *m* 1st, 1968, Patricia Margaret Jefferson Winn (marr. diss. 1987); one *d*; 2nd, 1989, Anne Margaret Diamond (marr. diss. 1999); four *s* (and one *s* decd). *Educ:* Carlisle Grammar Sch.; Ruskin Coll., Oxford. Programme Editor, Anglia Television, 1964–67; Producer, BBC Local Radio, 1967–74; Northern Editor, Today, Radio Four, 1974–75; Editor, News and Current Affairs: Southern Television Ltd, 1975–79; ATV Network/Central, 1979–82; Sen. Producer, Current Affairs, BBC TV, 1982–84; Dir of Programmes, TV-am Ltd, 1984–86; Man. Dir, Music Box Ltd, 1986–89. Agent and consultant to television and radio cos, and to charities. FRSA. *Recreation:* DIY (house renovation).

HOLLINGSWORTH, Timothy Philip, OBE 2017; Chief Executive Officer, Sport England, since 2018; *b* Farnborough, Kent, 10 April 1967; *s* of Michael and Marjorie Hollingsworth; *m* 2000, Emma Houston; two *s*. *Educ:* Lancing Coll., Sussex; Sevenoaks Sch., Kent; Univ. of Exeter (BA Hons English and Drama; MA Drama 1990). Press Officer, 1993–95, Hd of Communications, 1995–2000, CBI; Hd, Corporate and Internal Communications, Granada plc, 2000–01; Dir, HBL Media, 2001–04; Dir, Policy and Communications, 2004–10, Chief Operating Officer, 2010–11, UK Sport; CEO, British Paralympic Assoc., 2011–18. Mem. Bd, Youth Sport Trust, 2011–18; Trustee: Nat. Paralympic Heritage Trust, 2015–18; Football Foundn, 2018–. Hon. LLD: Exeter, 2014; Bath, 2014. *Recreations:* theatre, current affairs, guitar, family, sport, Fulham FC. *Address:* Sport England, 21 Bloomsbury Street, WC1B 3HF.

HOLLINGTON, Robin Frank; QC 1999; a Recorder, since 2004; a Deputy High Court Judge, Chancery Division, since 2013; *b* 30 June 1955; *s* of late Reginald Barrie Hollington and Eleanor Gwendoline Hollington (*née* Paxton); *m* 1988, Jane Elizabeth Cadogan Gritten; one *s*. *Educ:* Haileybury; University Coll., Oxford (MA); Univ. of Pennsylvania (LLM). Called to the Bar, Lincoln's Inn, 1979, Bencher, 2007; Hd, New Square Chambers, 2010–14. *Publications:* Minority Shareholders' Rights, 1990, 8th edn as Shareholders' Rights, 2016. *Recreations:* lawn tennis, golf. *Address:* New Square Chambers, 12 New Square, Lincoln's Inn, WC2A 3SW. *T:* (020) 7419 8000. *Clubs:* Royal Automobile, MCC; Walton Heath Golf.

HOLLINGWORTH, Rt Rev. Hon. Dr Peter John, AC 2001 (AO 1988); OBE 1976; Governor General of the Commonwealth of Australia, 2001–03; *b* 10 April 1935; *m* 1960, Kathleen Ann Turner; three *d*. *Educ:* Murrumbeena and Lloyd Street State Schools; Scotch Coll., Melbourne; Trinity Coll., Univ. of Melbourne (BA 1958; MA 1981); Australian Coll. of Theol. (ThL 1959); Univ. of Melbourne (Dip. Social Studies, 1970). Commercial Cadet, Broken Hill Pty, 1952–53. Ordained, 1961; Priest in charge, St Mary's, N Melbourne, 1960–64; Brotherhood of St Laurence: Chaplain and Dir of Youth Work, 1964–68; Assoc. Dir, 1969–79; Exec. Dir, 1980–90; Canon, St Paul's Cathedral, Melbourne, 1980–85; Bishop in the Inner City, dio. of Melbourne, 1985–90; Archbishop of Brisbane and Metropolitan, Province of Queensland, 1990–2001. Chairman: Social Responsibilities Commn, Gen. Synod, Anglican Church of Aust., 1992–98; Nat. Council for the Centenary of Fedn, 2000. Mem., Australian Assoc. of Social Workers, 1970–78. Paul Harris Fellow, Rotary Internat., 1989; FAIM 1997; Hon. Fellow: Trinity Coll., Melbourne, 1998; St John's Coll., Brisbane, 2006. Hon. LLD: Monash, 1986; Melbourne, 1990; DUniv: Griffith, 1993; Qld Univ. of Technol., 1994; Univ. of Central Qld, 1995; DLitt Univ. of Southern Qld, 1999; DLitt Lambeth 2001. KStJ 2001; Nat. ChLJ 1998–2001; GCLJ 1998. Australian of the Year, 1991; Albert Nelson Marquis Lifetime Achievement Award, 2019. *Publications:* Australians in Poverty, 1979; The Powerless Poor, 1972; The Poor: victims of affluence, 1975; Kingdom Come!, 1991; Public Thoughts of an Archbishop, 1996. *Recreations:* writing, reading, swimming, music, the arts, philanthropy, welfare. *Address:* PO Box 18081, Collins Street East, Melbourne, Vic 8003, Australia.

HOLLINGWORTH, Robert Matthew; Founder and Director, I Fagiolini, since 1986; Reader in Music, University of York, since 2012; *b* Epsom, Surrey, 19 May 1966; *s* of Anthony and Juliana Hollingworth; *m* 1996, Catherine Pierron; two *d*. *Educ:* Hereford Cathedral Sch.; New Coll., Oxford (BA Hons Music 1988); Guildhall Sch. of Music and Drama. Course Director: Dartington Summer Schs, 1994–; Lacock Courses, 1996–. Freelance conductor, BBC Singers, Netherlands Chamber Choir, 2002–. *Recreations:* cricket, scandi-noir, family, garden, Monty Python and Goon Show. *Address:* Music Department, University of York, Heslington, York YO10 5DD. *E:* robert@roberthollingworth.com.

HOLLINRAKE, Kevin Paul; MP (C) Thirsk and Malton, since 2015; *b* Easingwold, 28 Sept. 1963; *m* Nikky; four *c*. *Educ:* Easingwold Sch.; Sheffield Poly. Prudential Property Services: Branch Manager, Haxby, then Burnley, Lancs, 1985–87; Area Manager, 1987–91; Jt Founder, 1992, Man. Dir, 1992–2015, Chm., 2015–, Hunters Property Gp; Co-owner, Vizzihome, 2008–13; Chm., Shoptility.com, 2013–. PPS to Leader of H of C and Lord Pres. of Council, 2016–17, to Sec. of State for Envmt, Food and Rural Affairs, 2017–. Mem., Communities and Local Govt Cttee, 2015–. *Address:* House of Commons, SW1A 0AA.

HOLLINS, family name of Baroness Hollins.

HOLLINS, Baroness *cr* 2010 (Life Peer), of Wimbledon in the London Borough of Merton and of Grenoside in the County of South Yorkshire; Sheila Clare Hollins, FRCPsych; FRCPCH; Professor of Psychiatry of Disability, St George's, University of London (formerly St George's Hospital Medical School), 1990–2011, now Emeritus; *b* 22 June 1946; *d* of late Captain Adrian Morgan Kelly, Bristol, and of Monica Dallas Kelly (*née* Edwards); *m* 1969, Martin Prior Hollins, *s* of late Harry Pryor Hollins; one *s* three *d*. *Educ:* Notre Dame High Sch., Sheffield; St Thomas' Hosp. Med. Sch., London (MB BS). MRCPsych 1978, FRCPsych 1988; FRCPCH. Sen. Registrar in Child Psychiatry, Earls Court Child Guidance Unit and Westminster Children's Hosp., 1979–81; Sen. Lectr in Psychiatry of Learning Disability, 1981–90, Hd, Div. of Mental Health, 2003–05, St George's Hosp. Med. Sch.; Winston Churchill Fellow, 1993; Hon. Consultant: Wandsworth Community Health Trust and Richmond, Twickenham and Roehampton Healthcare Trust, 1981–99; SW London Community Trust, 1999–2002; SW London and St George's Mental Health Trust, 2002–11. On secondment to Policy Div., DoH, as pt-time Policy Advr on learning disability, 1993–94 and 2001–03; Member: Minister's Adv. Gp on Learning Disability, 1999–2001; Learning Disability Task Force, 2001–04; Expert Panel, Ind. Enquiry into Access to Healthcare for People with Learning Disabilities, 2007–08; Prime Minister's Standing Commn on Carers, 2007–09; Chairman: NHS Wkg Party on Breast and Cervical Screening in Learning Disability, 1999–2000; External Adv. Gp, Nat. Confidential Inquiry into Suicides and Homicides, 2007–11; Dep. Chm., Nat. Specialist Commissioning Adv. Gp, 2006–08; Chair, Ext. Ref. Gp on Workforce for Learning Disability Services, Health Educn England, 2015–. Hon. Prof., Dept of Theol. and

Religion, Univ. of Durham, 2012–. Royal College of Psychiatrists: Vice-Pres., 2003–04; Pres., 2005–08; Chm., Exec. Cttee, Psychiatry of Learning Disability Faculty, 1994–98; Mem., Ct of Electors, 1999–2005; Mem., Bd of Internat. Affairs, 2001–05. Pres., 2012–13, Chm., Bd of Sci., 2013–, BMA. Mem., Acad. of Med. Royal Colls, 2005–08. Mem., Community Care and Disability Sub-cttee, Joseph Rowntree Foundn, 1989–93. Exec. Chm., Books Beyond Words Community Interest Co., 2010–. Mem., Pontifical Commn for the Protection of Minors, 2014–17. FRSocMed. Hon. FRCP 2007. Mem., Lay Community of St Benedict. Hon. DD London, 2013; Hon. MD Sheffield, 2014; Hon. LLD Bath, 2014; Hon. DS Worcester, 2014; Hon. DLitt Durham, 2016. *Publications:* (ed with M. Craft) Mental Handicap: a multi-disciplinary approach, 1985; (with M. Grimes) Going Somewhere: pastoral care for people with mental handicap, 1988; (with J. Curran) Understanding Depression in People with Learning Disabilities, 1996; (with L. Sireling) Understanding Grief, 1999; editor and joint author 57 titles in Books Beyond Words series, including: Hug Me, Touch Me, 1994 (Best Author, Read Easy Awards Book Trust and Joseph Rowntree Foundn); (with J. Bernal) Getting on with Epilepsy, 1999; Looking After My Breasts, 2000; (jtly) George Gets Smart, 2001; with L. Sireling: When Dad Died, 1990, 3rd edn 2004; When Mum Died, 1990, 3rd edn 2004; with V. Sinason: Jenny Speaks Out, 1992; Bob Tells All, 1992; Mugged, 2002; Supporting Victims, 2007; (jtly) You're in Prison, 2013; (with Hugh Grant and Nigel Hollins) The Drama Group, 2015; with Patricia Scotland and Noelle Blackman: When Dad Hurt Mum, 2014; Finding a Safe Place from Abuse, 2015; contrib. numerous peer-reviewed papers on mental health and learning disability. *Recreations:* family, walking, music. *Address:* House of Lords, SW1A 0PW. *T:* (020) 7219 0520. *E:* hollinss@parliament.uk.
*See also* J. M. Kelly.

**HOLLINS, Peter Thomas;** Chair: CLIC Sargent, since 2014; University Hospital Southampton NHS Foundation Trust, since 2016; *b* 22 Oct. 1947; *m* 1973, Linda Pitchford; two *d*. *Educ:* Hertford Coll., Oxford (2nd Cl. Hons Chem.). British Oxygen, 1970–73; ICI UK, 1973–89; ICI Holland, 1989–92; EVC Brussels, 1992–98; Chief Exec., British Energy, 1998–2001. Dir Gen., then Chief Exec., British Heart Foundn, 2003–13. Holds various non-exec. directorships. *Recreations:* fluent in Dutch, German and French, classical music, travelling, Rugby, hill-walking. *Address:* c/o CLIC Sargent, No1 Farriers Yard Assembly London, 77–85 Fulham Palace Road, W6 8JA.

**HOLLIS, Rt Rev. Crispian;** *see* Hollis, Rt Rev. R. F. C.

**HOLLIS, Geoffrey Alan;** Director, Drew Associates, 1997–2009; *b* 25 Nov. 1943; *s* of late William John Hollis and of Elsie Jean Hollis (*née* Baker); *m* 1967, Ann Josephine Prentice; two *s*. *Educ:* Hastings Grammar Sch.; Hertford Coll., Oxford (MA); Polytechnic of Central London (Dip. Management Studies). International Computers, 1966; International Publishing Corp., 1967; Gulf Oil, 1969; MAFF, 1974–96; seconded to FCO, First Sec., 1977–80, UK Perm. Rep., EC, Brussels; Under Sec. and Hd of Meat, later Livestock Gp, 1991–96. Non-executive Director: Lucas Ingredients (Dalgety plc), 1991–95; E and N Herts HA, 1998–2001; Mem., Welwyn Hatfield PCT, 2001–06. Chm., Welwyn & Hatfield CAB, 2006–12. Admitted to Co. of Clockmakers, 1997. Clocks Advr, St Albans Dio. *Recreations:* chess, golf, horology. *Address:* 12 Lodge Drive, Hatfield, Herts AL9 5HN.

**HOLLIS, His Honour Keith Martin John;** a Circuit Judge, 2000–13; mediator and legal consultant, since 2013; *b* 9 June 1951; *s* of Eric and Joan Hollis; *m* 1979, Mariana Roberts; one *s* one *d*. *Educ:* Whitgift Sch., Croydon. Admitted Solicitor, 1975; Partner, Davies Brown & Co., solicitors, 1976–82; Sole Principal, then Sen. Partner, Hollis Wood & Co., Solicitors, 1982–92; Dist Judge, 1992–2000; Associate Mem., 1 Crown Office Row Chambers, 2014–. Accredited Mediator 2013. Dir of Studies, Commonwealth Magistrates' and Judges' Assoc., 1999–2010; Mem., Working Pty on Latimer House Guidelines on Parly Supremacy and Judicial Independence in the Commonwealth, 2000. Chm., New Sussex Opera, 2011–13; Trustee, Sussex Community Foundn, 2015– (Chm., 2016–). *Recreations:* singing, bassoon playing, listening to music, hill-walking, cooking. *Address:* Crown Office Row, 119 Church Street, Brighton BN1 1UD.

**HOLLIS, Kim;** QC 2002; Director of Public Prosecutions, British Virgin Islands, since 2016; *b* 19 Sept. 1957; *d* of Gurbaksh Singh Salariya and Jean Taylor; *m* 1987, Andrew Charles Hollis; two *s*. *Educ:* Cheltenham Ladies' Coll.; QMC, Univ. of London (LLB Hons). Called to the Bar, Gray's Inn, 1979, Bencher, 2008. Vice Chm., 2005–11, Chm., 2011–14, Race and Religion Cttee, then Diversity Cttee, later Equality and Diversity Cttee, Bar Council; Hd, Equality and Diversity Cttee, Criminal Bar Assoc., 2004–. Chair: Minority Lawyers Conf., 2009; Bar Conf., 2010 (Vice Chair, 2009); N London Bar Mess, 2011–14. Mem., FCO Diplomatic Excellence Panel, 2013–; Diversity Advr to FCO, 2014–. Chair, Assoc. of Women Barristers, 2009–10; Vice Pres., British Assoc. of Counselling and Psychotherapy, 2014–. (Jtly) Most Successful Lawyers' Award, Soc. of Asian Lawyers, 2005; Lifetime Achievement Award, Soc. of Asian Lawyers, 2015. *Recreations:* opera, theatre, ski-ing. *Address:* 6 Essenden Road, St Leonards on Sea, E Sussex TN34 0NW. *T:* (284) 4689656. *E:* Kimhollis2@msn.com, KHollis@gov.vg. *Clubs:* National Liberal, Royal Over-Seas League.

**HOLLIS, Posy;** *see* Simmonds, P.

**HOLLIS, Richard Graham;** designer and writer; *b* 4 Dec. 1934; *s* of late George Harry Hollis and Mary Dorothy Hollis (*née* Doughty); *m* 1974, Posy Simmonds, *qv*; one *s* (and one *s* decd) from a previous marr. *Educ:* Aldenham Sch.; Chelsea Sch. of Art; Wimbledon Coll. of Art; Central Sch. of Arts and Crafts. RDI 2005. Nat. Service, 2nd Lieut, RASC. Lecturer: London Sch. of Printing and Graphic Arts, 1959–61; Chelsea Sch. of Art, 1961–63; staff designer, Galeries Lafayette, Paris, 1963–64; Hd, Dept of Graphic Design, W of England Coll. of Art, Bristol, 1964–66; Art Ed., New Society weekly, 1966–68; Sen. Lectr, Central Sch. of Art and Design, 1967–69 and 1976–78. Consultant Designer: Sadler's Wells Th., 1959–61; Finmar Ltd, 1962–64; Modern Poetry in Translation, 1964–2003; Whitechapel Art Gall., 1969–72 and 1976–85; Art Ed. and designer, Pluto Press, 1972–76. Solo travelling exhibn, Libby Sellers Gall., 2012, Centre Pompidou, Paris, Univ. of Art and Design, Lausanne, Artists' Space, NY, 2013. *Publications:* Graphic Design: a concise history, 1994, rev. and expanded edn 2001; (with Lutz Becker) Avant-Garde Graphics 1918–1934, 2005; Swiss Graphic Design: the origins and growth of an international style 1920–1965, 2006; About Graphic Design, 2012; Henry van de Velde: the artist as designer, 2019. *Address:* 22 Lloyd Square, WC1X 9AJ.

**HOLLIS, Rt Rev. (Roger Francis) Crispian;** Bishop of Portsmouth, (RC), 1988–2012, now Emeritus; *b* 17 Nov. 1936; *s* of Christopher and Madeleine Hollis. *Educ:* Stonyhurst College; Balliol Coll., Oxford (MA); Venerable English College, Rome (STL). National Service as 2nd Lt, Somerset Light Infantry, 1954–56. Ordained priest, 1965; Assistant in Amesbury, 1966–67; RC Chaplain, Oxford Univ., 1967–77; RC Assistant to Head of Religious Broadcasting, BBC, 1977–81; Administrator, Clifton Cathedral, Bristol, 1981–87; Auxiliary Bishop of Birmingham (Bishop in Oxfordshire), 1987–88. Chm., Dept of Mission and Unity, 2001–05, Chm., Dept for Internat. Affairs, 2005–09, Catholic Bishops' Conf. of England and Wales. *Recreations:* occasional golf, walking, cricket watching. *Address:* Stable House, Fairview, Mells, Somerset BA11 3PP.

**HOLLOBONE, Philip Thomas;** MP (C) Kettering, since 2005; *b* 7 Nov. 1964. *Educ:* Dulwich Coll.; Lady Margaret Hall, Oxford (MA 1987). Industry res. analyst, 1987–2003. Served TA, 1984–93. Member (C): Bromley BC, 1990–94; Kettering BC, 2003–. Contested (C): Lewisham E, 1997; Kettering, 2001. *Address:* House of Commons, SW1A 0AA.

**HOLLOWAY, Adam James Harold;** MP (C) Gravesham, since 2005; *b* 1965; *s* of Rev. Roger Holloway, OBE and Anne (*née* Alsop). *Educ:* Cranleigh Sch.; Magdalene Coll., Cambridge (BA Social and Pol Sci. 1987); RMA Sandhurst; Imperial Coll. of Sci. and Technol. (MBA). Travelled with the Afghan Resistance, 1982; classroom asst, Pace Coll., Soweto, S Africa, 1985. Grenadier Guards, 1987–92 (Captain); service in Gulf War, 1991. Presenter, 1992–94: World in Action (undercover, living homeless in London for 3 months, as homeless psychiatric patient for 2 months, as Muslim refugee in Serb territory, Bosnia, living homeless in NYC for 2 weeks); Disguises (undercover reports from UK and Balkans as psychiatric patient/refugee); Sen. Reporter, ITN, 1994–97: Bosnia reporter, Sarajevo siege, 1994; News at Ten Special Reports; Reporter, Tonight with Trevor MacDonald (undercover as asylum seeker in Calais), 2001; Iraq War (Northern front) reports for ITN and Sky News, 2003. PPS to Minister of State, FCO, 2011–12. Member: Defence Select Cttee, 2006–10 and 2012–14; Public Admin Select Cttee, 2014–15; Foreign Affairs Select Cttee, 2015–17; Chairman: 1922 Home Affairs Cttee, 2017–; All Pty Drone Gp, 2018–. Dep. Chm., Cons. Middle East Council, 2010–17. Chm., Council for Arab-British Understanding, 2009–14. Trustee: Christian Aid, 1997–2001; MapAction, 2004–10. *Publications:* In Blood Stepp'd in Too Far?: towards a realistic policy for Afghanistan, 2009. *Recreation:* being with my family and godchildren. *Address:* House of Commons, SW1A 0AA. *T:* (020) 7219 3000. *E:* hollowaya@parliament.uk, ajhholloway@gmail.com. *Clubs:* Pratt's; Gravesend and Perry Street Conservative; Nutley Social.

**HOLLOWAY, His Honour Frederick Reginald Bryn;** a Circuit Judge, 1992–2012; *b* 9 Jan. 1947; *s* of William Herbert Holloway and Audrey (*née* Hull-Brown); *m* 1974, Barbara Bradley; two *s*. *Educ:* Mill Mead, Shrewsbury; Wrekin Coll., Wellington, Salop; Coll. of Law. Entered chambers in Liverpool, 1972; Asst Recorder, 1984–89; Recorder, 1989–92. *Recreations:* gardening, Shrewsbury Town FC, cricket, tennis.

**HOLLOWAY, James Essex,** CBE 2012; Director (formerly Keeper), Scottish National Portrait Gallery, 1997–2012; *b* 24 Nov. 1948; *s* of Roland David Holloway and Nancy Briant Holloway (*née* Evans). *Educ:* Marlborough Coll.; Courtauld Inst. of Art, London Univ. (BA Hons). Res. Asst, Nat. Gall. of Scotland, 1972–80; Asst Keeper, Nat. Mus. of Wales, 1980–83; Dep. Keeper, Scottish Nat. Portrait Gall., 1983–97. Chm., Abbotsford Trust, 2016–. *Publications:* The Discovery of Scotland, 1978; James Tassie, 1986; Jacob More, 1987; William Aikman, 1988; Patrons and Painters: art in Scotland 1650–1760, 1989; The Norie Family, 1994. *Recreations:* motorbikes, India, French horn. *Address:* 20 India Street, Edinburgh EH3 6HB. *Clubs:* New, Puffin's (Edinburgh).

**HOLLOWAY, Michael John,** OBE 2009; HM Diplomatic Service, retired; Special Representative of Secretary of State for Foreign Affairs, since 2015; *b* Minster-in-Kent, 14 Jan. 1957; *s* of Robert Lawrence Holloway and Jean Olive Dormedy. *Educ:* St Edmund's Sch., Canterbury; Univ. for Creative Arts, Canterbury. Joined FCO, 1976; Finance Dept, FCO, 1976–77; Vice Consul, Dubai, 1978; Asst Mgt Officer/Accountant, Bucharest, 1979–81; African/Middle East Floater, 1981–82; Asst Reviewer, FCO, 1984–87; Vice Consul, Barcelona, 1988–90; Parly Desk Officer, Europe Dept, FCO, 1990–92; Know How Fund Manager, Czech and Slovak Republics, 1992–93, FCO/ODA; Hd, Press and Public Diplomacy, Mexico City, 1994–97; Hd of Trade and Consul, Rio de Janeiro, 1998–2002; Dir, Immigration, Dhaka, 2002–03; Dep. Hd, Resource Mgt Unit, Europe Directorate, FCO, 2003–05; Consul-Gen., Spain and Dir of Consular Services, 2005–10; Ambassador to Panama, 2011–13. Non-exec. Bd Mem., King's Gp, 2013–; Mem. and Trustee, King's Gp Academies, 2016–. Member (C): Dover DC, 2015– (Cabinet Mem. for Community Services and Safety, and Tourism, 2017–); Sandwich Town Council, 2015–. *Recreations:* dogs, painting, gardening, walking.

**HOLLOWAY, Neil John;** Senior Vice President, Business Development, Skytap Inc., since 2017; *b* 14 May 1960; *s* of Jenny Holley; *m*; one *s* one *d*. *Educ:* Univ. of Bath (BSc 1982); Jesus Coll., Cambridge (MPhil 1984). Man. Dir, Migent UK, 1988–90; Microsoft UK, 1990–2003; Dir, 1994–96; Dep. Gen. Manager, 1996–98; Man. Dir, 1998–2003; Vice-Pres., 2000–05 and Vice-Pres., Sales, Marketing and Services, 2003–05, Pres., 2005–07, Microsoft Europe, ME and Africa; Vice Pres., Business Strategy, Microsoft Internat., 2007–12; Corporate Vice Pres., Sales and Ops, Microsoft Business Solutions, 2012; Vice Pres., US Dynamics, Microsoft, 2016–17. Hon. DSc Bath, 2008. *Recreations:* golf, swimming.

**HOLLOWAY, Reginald Eric,** CMG 1984; HM Diplomatic Service, retired; *b* 22 June 1932; *s* of late Ernest and Beatrice Holloway; *m* 1958, Anne Penelope, *d* of late Walter Robert and Doris Llian Pawley; one *d*. *Educ:* St Luke's, Brighton. Apprentice reporter, 1947–53; served RAF, 1953–55; journalist in Britain and E Africa, 1955–61; Press Officer, Tanganyika Govt, 1961–63; Dir, British Inf. Service, Guyana, 1964–67; Inf. Dept, FCO, 1967–69 (Anguilla, 1969); 2nd, later 1st Sec., Chancery in Malta, 1970–72; E African Dept, FCO, 1972–74; Consul and Head of Chancery, Kathmandu, 1974–77 (Chargé d'Affaires *ai*, 1975 and 1976); Asst Head, S Asian Dept, FCO, 1977–79; Counsellor, 1979; Inspector, 1979–81; Consul-Gen., Toronto, 1981–85; Sen. British Trade Comr, Hong Kong, 1985–89, and Consul-Gen. (non-resident), Macao, 1986–89; Consul-Gen., Los Angeles, 1989–92. Business consultant, 1992–97; tree farmer, 1998–2001. Chm., Canadian Urban Inst., 1993–98. *Publications:* The Evolution and Demise of the Larger Format Press Camera, 2008. *Recreations:* gardening, old press cameras. *Address:* 6811 Carmella Place, Niagara Falls, ON L2J 4J4, Canada.

**HOLLOWAY, Richard Arthur;** Managing Director, Thames, 2011–17; *b* Watford, 16 March 1949; *s* of Gordon Roy Holloway and Iris Harriet Holloway; *m* (marr. diss.). *Educ:* Watford Grammar Sch. Producer, 1982, Controller of Entertainment, 1992–98, Central Television; Hd of Entertainment, 1998–2010, Dir of Entertainment, 2010–11, Pearson Television, then Thames Television, later talkbackThames; executive producer: Pop Idol, 2001–03; X Factor, 2004–17; Britain's Got Talent, 2007–17. FRTS 2009. Lifetime Achievement Award, RTS, 2009. *Recreations:* golf, gardening, all things Italian. *Clubs:* Ivy, Soho House.

**HOLLOWAY, Rt Rev. Richard Frederick;** Bishop of Edinburgh, 1986–2000 and Primus of the Episcopal Church in Scotland, 1992–2000; Chairman: Scottish Arts Council, 2005–10; Sistema Scotland, 2007–18; Joint Board, Scottish Arts Council and Scottish Screen, 2007–10; *b* 26 Nov. 1933; *s* of Arthur and Mary Holloway; *m* 1963, Jean Elizabeth Kennedy, New York; one *s* two *d*. *Educ:* Kelham Theol Coll.; Edinburgh Theol Coll.; Union Theol Seminary, New York (STM); BD (London). FRSE 1995. Curate, St Ninian's, Glasgow, 1959–63; Priest-in-charge, St Margaret and St Mungo's, Glasgow, 1963–68; Rector, Old St Paul's, Edinburgh, 1968–80; Rector, Church of the Advent, Boston, Mass, USA, 1980–84; Vicar, St Mary Magdalen's, Oxford, 1984–86. Gresham Prof. of Divinity, 1997–2001. Member: Human Fertilisation and Embryo Authority, 1991–97; Broadcasting Standards Commn, 2001–03; Chm., Edinburgh Voluntary Orgns Council,

1991–95. FRSE 1995. DUniv: Strathclyde, 1994; Open, 2005; Hon. DLitt: Napier, 2000; St Andrews, 2017; Hon. DD: Aberdeen, 1995; Glasgow, 2001; Hon. LLD Dundee, 2009; DUniv Stirling, 2010; Hon. Dr Drama Royal Conservatoire of Scotland, 2012. *Publications:* Let God Arise, 1972; New Vision of Glory, 1974; A New Heaven, 1978; Beyond Belief, 1982; Signs of Glory, 1983; The Killing, 1984, 2nd edn as Behold Your King, 1995; (ed) The Anglican Tradition, 1984; Paradoxes of Christian Faith and Life, 1984; The Sidelong Glance, 1985; The Way of the Cross, 1986; Seven to Flee, Seven to Follow, 1987; Crossfire: faith and doubt in an age of certainty, 1988; Another Country, Another King, 1991; Who Needs Feminism?, 1991; Anger, Sex, Doubt and Death, 1992; The Stranger in the Wings, 1994; (jtly) Churches and How to Survive Them, 1994; Limping Towards the Sunrise, 1995; Dancing on the Edge, 1997; Godless Morality, 1999; Doubts and Loves: what is left of Christianity, 2001; On Forgiveness, 2002; Looking in the Distance, 2004; How to Read the Bible, 2006; Between the Monster and the Saint: reflections on the human condition, 2008; Leaving Alexandria: a memoir of faith and doubt, 2012; A Little History of Religion, 2016; Waiting for the Last Bus, 2018. *Recreations:* long-distance walking, reading, cinema, music. *Address:* 6 Blantyre Terrace, Edinburgh EH10 5AE.

**HOLLOWAY, Prof. Robin Greville**, PhD, MusD; composer; Fellow of Gonville and Caius College, Cambridge, since 1969, and Professor of Musical Composition, University of Cambridge, 2001–11, now Emeritus; *b* 19 Oct. 1943; *s* of Robert Charles Holloway and Pamela Mary Jacob. *Educ:* St Paul's Cathedral Choir Sch.; King's Coll. Sch., Wimbledon; King's Coll., Cambridge (MA 1968; PhD 1972; MusD 1976); New Coll., Oxford. Lectr in Music, 1975–99, Reader in Music, 1999–2001, Cambridge Univ. *Compositions* include: Garden Music, 1962; First Concerto for Orchestra, 1966–69; Scenes from Schumann, 1969–70; Evening with Angels, 1972; Domination of Black, 1973–74; Sea Surface full of Clouds, 1974–75; Clarissa, 1976 (premièred ENO, 1990); Romanza, 1976; The Rivers of Hell, 1977; Second Concerto for Orchestra, 1978–79; Serenade in C, 1979; Aria, 1980; Peer Gynt, 1980–97; Brand, 1981; Women in War, 1982; Second Idyll, 1983; Seascape and Harvest, 1984; Viola Concerto, 1984; Serenade in E flat, 1984; Ballad for harp and orch., 1985; Inquietus, 1986; Double Concerto for clarinet and saxophone, 1988; The Spacious Firmament, 1989; Violin Concerto, 1990; Boys and Girls Come Out to Play, 1992; Gilded Goldbergs, 1992–98; Missa Caiensis, 1993–2001; Third Concerto for Orchestra, 1994; Canterbury Concerto for clarinet and orch., 1997; Scenes from Antwerp, 1998; Double Bass Concerto, 1998; Symphony, 1999; Spring Music, 2002; String Quartet no 1, 2003; String Quartet no 2, 2004; Fourth Concerto for Orchestra, 2006; Five Temperaments, 2008; Fifth Concerto for Orchestra, 2009; Reliquary, 2010; String Quartet no 4, trio for oboe, violin and piano, 2011; C'est l'extase, after Debussy, for soprano and orchestra, 2012; Europa and the Bull, for tuba and orchestra, 2014; Winter Music for ensemble, 2015; String Quartet no 5, 2016; For Ever Singing As They Shine, for organ and orchestra, 2017; Piano Trio, 2018; Phacton's Journey: Son of the Sun, for trumpet and orchestra. *Publications:* Wagner and Debussy, 1978; On Music: essays and diversions 1963–2003, 2003; Essays and Diversions II, 2008; numerous articles and reviews. *Recreation:* playing on two pianos. *Address:* Gonville and Caius College, Cambridge CB2 1TA. *T:* (01223) 335424.

**HOLLOWS, Dame Sharon**, DBE 2001; Principal, Charter Academy, Portsmouth, 2009–16; consultant on management and leadership, since 2004; *b* 14 Dec. 1958; *d* of Jack and Margaret Hollows; one *s* one *d*. *Educ:* Haslingden Grammar Sch.; W London Inst. of Higher Educn; Greenwich Univ. (MA Ed). Teacher, 1979–93: Furness Jun. Sch. and Manor Special Sch., Brent; St James' Jun. Sch. and Manor Primary Sch., Newham; Head Teacher, Calverton Primary Sch., Newham, 1994–2002; Adv. Head Teacher, Plumcroft Primary Sch., Greenwich, 2002–04; Dir, Sharon Hollows Consultancy Ltd, 2004–12. Mem., Standards Task Force, 2000–02. *Recreations:* horse riding, motor cycling, eating.

**HOLM, Sir Ian**, Kt 1998; CBE 1989; actor, since 1954; *b* 12 Sept. 1931; *s* of Dr James Harvey Cuthbert and Jean Wilson Cuthbert; *m* 1st, 1955, Lynn Mary Shaw (marr. diss. 1965); two *d*; and one *s* one *d*; 2nd, 1982, Sophie Baker (marr. diss. 1986); one *s*; 3rd, 1991, Penelope Alice Wilton (*see* Dame P. A. Wilton) (marr. diss. 2002); one step *d*; 4th, 2003, Sophie de Stempel. *Educ:* Chigwell Grammar Sch., Essex. Trained RADA, 1950–53 (interrupted by Nat. Service); joined Shakespeare Memorial Theatre, 1954, left after 1955; Worthing Rep., 1956; tour, Olivier's Titus Andronicus, 1957; re-joined Stratford, 1958: roles include: Puck; Ariel; Gremio; Lorenzo; Prince Hal; Henry V; Duke of Gloucester; Richard III; The Fool in Lear; Lennie in The Homecoming (also on Broadway, 1966) (Evening Standard Actor of the Year, 1965); left RSC, 1967; Moonlight, Almeida, 1993 (Evening Standard Actor of the Year, Critics Circle Award); King Lear, RNT, 1997 (Olivier award for Best Actor, 1998); The Homecoming, Comedy, 2001. Major film appearances include: Young Winston, The Fixer, Oh! What a Lovely War, The Bofors Gun, Alien, All Quiet on the Western Front, Chariots of Fire (Best Supporting Actor: Cannes, 1981; BAFTA, 1982); Return of the Soldier; Greystoke; Brazil; Laughterhouse; Dance With a Stranger; Wetherby; Dreamchild; Another Woman; Hamlet; Kafka; Naked Lunch; Blue Ice; Mary Shelley's Frankenstein, 1994; The Madness of King George, Big Night, Night Falls on Manhattan, 1995; Lochness, 1996; A Life Less Ordinary, The Sweet Hereafter, The Fifth Element, 1997; Simon Magus, eXistenZ, The Match, Joe Gould's Secret, 1998; Esther Kahn, Beautiful Joe, 1999; Bless the Child, Fellowship of the Ring, 2001; From Hell, 2002; Return of the King, 2003; The Emperor's New Clothes, Garden State, Strangers with Candy, 2004; Chromophobia, Beyond Friendship, The Treatment, Lord of War, 2005; The Hobbit: An Unexpected Journey, 2012; The Hobbit: The Battle of the Five Armies, 2014. TV series include: J. M. Barrie in trilogy The Lost Boys (RTS Best Actor Award, 1979); We, the Accused, 1980; The Bell, 1981; Game, Set and Match, 1988; other TV appearances include: Lech Walesa in Strike, 1981; Goebbels in Inside the Third Reich, 1982; Mr and Mrs Edgehill, 1985; The Browning Version, 1986; Uncle Vanya, 1990; The Last Romantics, 1991; The Borrowers, 1992; The Deep Blue Sea, 1994; Landscape, 1995; King Lear, 1997; Alice Through the Looking Glass, 1998. *Publications:* (with Steven Jacobi) Acting My Life (autobiog.), 2004. *Recreations:* tennis, walking, general outdoor activities. *Address:* c/o Markham, Froggatt & Irwin, 4 Windmill Street, W1T 2HZ.

**HOLM, Niels**; Official Secretary to Governor-General of New Zealand, 2010–14; *b* Rotherham, NZ, 12 Jan. 1955; *s* of Helge Holm and Janet Holm; *m* 1975, Suzette Parks. *Educ:* Canterbury Univ., Christchurch (MA Hons 1975; Dip. Teaching 1976). Teacher, Dannevirke High Sch., 1977–78; joined Dept of Trade and Industry, NZ, 1979; Private Sec. to Minister of For. Affairs and Overseas Trade, 1982–84, to Minister for Overseas Trade, 1984–85; Japanese lang. trng, 1985–87; Trade Comr, Tokyo, 1987; joined Min. of For. Affairs and Trade, 1988; First Sec., 1988–90; N Asia Div., 1990–92; Dep. Hd of Mission, Manila, 1992–95; Econ. First Sec., Tokyo, 1995–99; Internat. Security and Arms Control Div., 1999; Dep. Dir, Asia-Pacific Econ. Cooperation Div., 1999–2001; Ambassador to Iran and High Comr to Pakistan, 2001–04, and concurrently first Ambassador to Afghanistan, 2003–04; Regl Dep. Dir, Pacific Div., 2005–07; High Comr to PNG, 2007–10. *Recreations:* reading, ski-ing, travel.

**HOLMAN, Hon. Sir (Edward) James**, Kt 1995; **Hon. Mr Justice Holman**; a Judge of the High Court of Justice, Family Division, since 1995; *b* 21 Aug. 1947; *o s* of late Dr Edward Theodore Holman and Mary Megan Holman, MBE (*née* Morris), formerly of Ringwood, Hants, and Manaccan, Cornwall; *m* 1979, Fiona Elisabeth, *er d* of late Dr Ronald Cathcart Roxburgh, FRCP; two *s* one *d*. *Educ:* Dauntsey's; Exeter College, Oxford (BA Jurisp., MA). Called to the Bar, Middle Temple, 1971, Bencher, 1995; QC 1991; Western Circuit; in practice, 1971–95; Standing Counsel to HM Treasury (Queen's Proctor), 1980–91; a Recorder, 1993–95; Family Div. Liaison Judge, Western Circuit, 1995–2002. A Legal Assessor, UK Central Council for Nursing, Midwifery and Health Visiting, 1983–95. Member: Family Proceedings Rules Cttee, 1991–95; Supreme Court Procedure Cttee, 1992–95; ex-officio Mem., Bar Council, 1992–95. Chm., Family Law Bar Assoc., 1992–95 (Sec., 1988–92). Mem., Council, RYA, 1980–83, 1984–87, 1988–91. *Recreations:* sailing, ski-ing, music. *Address:* Royal Courts of Justice, Strand, WC2A 2LL. *Clubs:* Royal Ocean Racing (Mem. Cttee, 1984–87); Royal Yacht Squadron, Ocean Cruising.

**HOLMAN, Sir John (Stranger)**, Kt 2010; Salters Professor of Chemical Education, University of York, 2000–04, Emeritus Professor of Chemistry, 2010; Senior Adviser, Gatsby Foundation, since 2011; *b* Bath, 16 Sept. 1946; *s* of Leslie Holman and Elizabeth Holman; *m* 1969, Wendy North; two *s* one *d*. *Educ:* Royal Grammar Sch., Guildford; Gonville and Caius Coll., Cambridge (BA Hons 1967). CChem 1985; FRSC 1985. Chemistry teacher: Radley Coll., 1967–71; Bristol Grammar Sch., 1972–76; Hd of Sci., Watford Grammar Sch., 1976–84; educnl consultant, author and pt-time teacher, 1984–94; Headmaster, Watford Grammar Sch. for Boys, 1994–2000. Dir, Nat. Sci. Learning Centre, 2004–10; Nat. Dir, Sci., Technol., Engrg and Maths prog., 2006–10. Chm., Teacher Develt Trust, 2014–. Pres., RSC, 2016–18. Trustee, Natural History Mus., 2011–. Lord Lewis Award, RSC, 2014; Kavli Educn Medal, Royal Soc., 2014. *Publications:* (with G. Hill) Chemistry in Context, 1978, 7th edn 2017; (jtly) Chemistry[3], 2009, 3rd edn 2017; Good Career Guidance, 2015; author/ed. of 15 other text books; contrib. articles to numerous educnl jls. *Recreations:* spending time with my large family, growing, cooking and eating food, walking, cycling, reading novels, biography and poetry. *Address:* Chemistry Department, University of York, York YO10 5DD. *E:* john.holman@york.ac.uk.

**HOLMAN, Rev. Michael Mark**, SJ; Principal, Heythrop College, University of London, 2012–16; *b* 4 Nov. 1954; *s* of Michael and Sonja Holman. *Educ:* Wimbledon Coll.; Heythrop Coll., Univ. of London (BA); Weston Jesuit Sch. of Theol. (MDiv); Fordham Univ., NY (MSc). Entered Society of Jesus, 1974; ordained priest, 1988; Dep. Headmaster, Mt St Mary's Coll., 1992–94; Headmaster, Wimbledon Coll., 1995–2004; Provincial Superior (British Province), 2005–11. FRSA. *Recreations:* classical music, hill walking, Ignatian spirituality.

**HOLMAN, His Honour Richard Christopher**; a Senior Circuit Judge, 2002–11 (a Circuit Judge, 1994–2011); Designated Civil Judge, 1998–2011; *b* 16 June 1946; *s* of Frank Harold Holman and Joan (*née* Attrill); *m* 1st, 1969, Susan Whittaker, MBE, DL (*d* 2007); two *s*; 2nd, 2009, Kathleen Hendry. *Educ:* Watford Grammar Sch. for Boys; Eton Coll.; Gonville and Caius Coll., Cambridge (MA 1968). Admitted as solicitor, 1971; Partner, Foysters, later Davies Wallis Foyster, 1973–94, Man. Partner, 1988–89; Dep. Dist Registrar of High Court and Dep. Registrar of County Court, 1982–88; Asst Recorder, 1988–92; a Recorder, 1992–94. Member: NW Legal Aid Area Cttee, 1980–94; Civil Procedure Rule Cttee, 1997–2002. Mem. Council, Manchester Law Soc., 1983–90. Gov., Pownall Hall Sch., Wilmslow, 1990–98 (Chm., 1993–98). Trustee, Crossroads Care Cheshire East, 2008–11. *Recreations:* golf, gardening, theatre, music. *Club:* Wilmslow Golf (Captain, 1999; Pres., 2019).

**HOLMES OF RICHMOND**, Baron *cr* 2013 (Life Peer), of Richmond in the London Borough of Richmond upon Thames; **Christopher Holmes**, MBE 1993; Director of Paralympic Integration, London Organising Committee of the 2012 Olympic Games and Paralympic Games, 2009–13; *b* Peterborough, 15 Oct. 1971; *s* of Michael John Holmes and Margaret Mary Holmes. *Educ:* Harry Cheshire High Sch., Kidderminster; King's Coll., Cambridge (BA 1994; MA 1998). Paralympic swimmer; winner of Paralympic Gold Medals: 6 at Barcelona Games, 1992; 3 at Atlanta Games, 1996. Public speaker, 1992–. Admitted Solicitor, 2004; with Ashurst, 2002–07. Non-executive Director: Disability Rights Commn, 2002–07; UK Sport, 2005–13; Equality and Human Rights Commn, 2013–17; Channel 4, 2016– (Dep. Chair, 2018–); Mem., Pensions Client Bd, 2009–10. Chm., EdTech Leadership Gp, 2019–. Member: Digital Skills Cttee, H of L, 2014–15; Social Mobility Cttee, H of L, 2015–16; Financial Exclusion Select Cttee, H of L, 2016–17; AI Cttee, H of L, 2017–18; Intergenerational Fairness and Provision Select Cttee, H of L, 2018–19. Diversity Advr to Civil Service, 2015–. Patron: Youth Sport Trust, 1995–; British Paralympic Assoc., 2004–; Help for Heroes, 2008–. Ambassador, Queen Elizabeth Diamond Jubilee Trust, 2013–. Chancellor, BPP Univ., 2017– (Dep. Chancellor, 2015–17). Hon. LLD: Bath, 2012; BPP Law Sch., 2014. *Publications:* contrib. articles to Daily Telegraph, Observer, Spectator and European. *Recreations:* ski-ing, reading, wine. *Address:* Kew, Surrey. *T:* 07961 358136. *E:* cholmes128@btinternet.com. *Club:* Hawks' (Cambridge).

**HOLMES, Prof. Andrew Bruce**, AC 2017 (AM 2004); FRS 2000; FAA; FTSE; CSIRO Fellow, CSIRO Materials Science and Engineering, 2008–14, now Emeritus; University Laureate Professor, University of Melbourne, 2009–14, now Emeritus; Emeritus Professor and Distinguished Research Fellow, Imperial College London, since 2009; *b* 5 Sept. 1943; *s* of late Bruce Morell Holmes and Frances Henty Graham Holmes; *m* 1971, Jennifer Lesley; three *s*. *Educ:* Scotch Coll., Melbourne; Univ. of Melbourne (BSc, MSc); University Coll. London (PhD 1971; Hon. Fellow, 2012); ScD Cantab 1997; DSc Oxon 2011. Royal Soc. European Postdoctoral Fellow, ETH Zürich, 1971–72; University of Cambridge: Demonstrator, 1972–77; Lectr, 1977–94; Dir, Melville Lab. for Polymer Synthesis, 1994–2004; Reader in Organic and Polymer Chemistry, 1995–98; Prof. of Organic and Polymer Chemistry, 1998–2004; Fellow, Clare Coll., Cambridge, 1973–; Dir, Cambridge Quantum Fund, 1995–2004; Mem., CUP Syndicate, 2000–04; ARC Fedn and VESKI Fellow, and Prof. of Chem., Univ. of Melbourne/CSIRO Molecular and Health Technologies, 2004–09; Prof. of Chem., Imperial Coll., London, 2004–09. Member: Internat. Sci. Adv. Bd, A*Star Inst. of Materials Res. and Engrg, Singapore, 2008–11; External Rev. Panel, Internat. Council for Sci., 2013–14; Internat. Sci. Adv. Bd, CREATE, Nat. Res. Foundn, Singapore, 2017–; Internat. Sci. Adv. Bd, Internat. Workshop on Advanced Materials, Ras Al Khaimah, UAE, 2017–; Main Panel B REF, 2018–. Principal Ed., Jl Materials Res., 1994–99; Chm., Editl Bd, Chemical Communications, 2000–03; Member: Bd of Editors, Organic Syntheses, Inc., 1996–2001; Publishing Bd, RSC, 2003–06; Publishing Adv. Cttee, CSIRO, 2006–14; Editl Bd, New Jl of Chemistry, 2000–03; International Advisory Board: Macromolecular Chem. and Physics, 1999–2006; Jl Mater. Chem., 1996–2006; Chemical Communications, 2004–12; Chem. World, 2004–18; Aust. Jl of Chem., 2004–18; Bulletin, Chemical Soc. of Japan, 2004–; Beilstein Jl Organic Chem., 2005–18; Angewandte Chemie, 2006–13; Associate Ed., Organic Letters, 2006–18. Mem. Bd, Veski, 2011–14. Vis. Fellow, La Trobe Univ., 1977; Visiting Professor: Univ. of Calif, Berkeley, 1984; Univ. of Calif, Irvine, 1991; Royal Soc. Leverhulme Sen. Res. Fellow, 1993–94; Wilsmore Fellow, Univ. of Melbourne, 2002–03; Hans Kupczyk Foundn Guest Prof., Univ. of Ulm, Germany, 2009; Newton Abraham Vis. Prof. and Fellow, Lincoln Coll., Univ. of Oxford, 2011–12. Fellow: Materials Res. Soc., 2013; Amer. Assoc. for the Advancement of Sci., 2017; Hon. Fellow, Chemical Res. Soc. of India, 2013. Lectures: W. G. Dauben, Univ. of Calif, Berkeley, 1999–2000; Aggarwal, Cornell Univ., 2002; Tilden, RSC, 2003; Merck-Karl

Pfister, MIT, 2005; W. Heinlen Hall, Bowling Green State Univ., Ohio, 2006; Merck Res., RSC, 2008; Merck, Univ. of Cambridge, 2009; Robert Robinson, Oxford, 2010; Ta-shue Chou, Academia Sinica Taiwan, 2010; H. Dudley Wright Colloquium, Univ. of Geneva, 2012; Chemical Record, Chemical Soc., Japan, 2013; Nozoe, Internat. Symposium on Novel Aromatic Compounds, Taipei, 2013; C. N. R. Rao, Chem. Res. Soc. India, 2014; McRae, Queens Univ., Ont, 2014. President: Australian Council of Learned Academies, 2016; Australian Acad. of Sci., 2014–18 (Mem. Council, 2007–18). FAA 2006; FTSE 2006; FRACI 2014; Fellow, Nat. Acad. of Inventors, 2016. Hon. FRSC, 2013. Dr *hc* Hasselt, 2010. Alfred Bader Award, 1994, Materials Chem. Award, 1995, John B. Goodenough Award, 2011, RSC; Descartes Prize, EU, 2003; Macro Gp Medal UK for Outstanding Achievement, 2003; Royal Medal, Royal Soc., 2011; Glenn Award, Energy and Fuels Div., American Chem. Soc., 2015. *Publications:* contribs to various learned chem., physics and materials sci. jls on subject of synthesis and properties of polymeric and organic semiconductor materials and of natural products. *Recreations:* musical appreciation, walking. *Address:* Bio21 Institute, University of Melbourne, 30 Flemington Road, Vic 3010, Australia. *T:* (3) 83442344, *Fax:* (3) 83442384. *E:* aholmes@unimelb.edu.au.

**HOLMES, Andrew Christopher; His Honour Judge Holmes;** a Circuit Judge, since 2019; *b* Carlisle, 6 Dec. 1977; *s* of late Nigel Holmes and of Rev. Susan Holmes; *m* 2010, Luciana Ricart; one *s* one *d*. *Educ:* Austin Friars Sch., Carlisle; Univ. of Leeds (LLB Hons 1999 (Hughes Prize)). Called to the Bar, Lincoln's Inn, 2000 (Wolfson Schol.; Kennedy Schol.; Student of Year); in practice as barrister: Broad Chare Chambers, Newcastle upon Tyne, 2000–10; 42 Bedford Row, 2010–16; Dep. Dist Judge, 2010–16; Dist Judge, 2016–19. Mem., North-Eastern Circuit, 2002– (Jun., 2010). Dir, Internat. Law Students' Assoc., 2014–. *Recreations:* cricket, history, music. *Address:* Wood Green Crown Court, Lordship Lane, N22 5LF. *Clubs:* National Liberal; Surrey County Cricket.

**HOLMES, Andrew Mayhew;** Chairman, Highland Perthshire Ltd, since 2010; *b* Haltwhistle, Northumberland, 20 June 1947; *s* of Walter Holmes and Nancy Holmes; *m* 1970, Catherine Roth; three *s* one *d*. *Educ:* Millom Sch.; Harrogate Grammar Sch.; Leeds Univ. (BSc Civil Engrg); Newcastle Univ. (MSc Civil Engrg). MICE 1973. Various engrg posts, 1968–94; Dep. Dir, Transportation, Lothian Region, 1994–96; Dep. Dir, Develt, Edinburgh, 1996–98; Dir, City Develt, Edinburgh CC, 1998–2008. Mem., Mobility and Access Cttee for Scotland, 2008–. Trustee, Nat. Mus of Scotland, 2009–; Mem. Bd, Historic Envmt Scotland, 2015–. *Publications:* articles in engrg and transport jls. *Recreations:* mountaineering, gardening, travelling in Italy. *Address:* Strathtummel, Lower Oakfield, Pitlochry PH16 5DS. *E:* a.m.holmes@btinternet.com. *Club:* Italian Alpine.

**HOLMES, David,** CB 1985; Director, Corporate Resources, British Airways plc, 1996–99; Chairman, British Airways Regional, 1998–99; *b* 6 March 1935; *s* of late George A. Holmes and Annie Holmes; *m* 1963, Ann Chillingworth; one *s* two *d*. *Educ:* Doncaster Grammar Sch.; Christ Church, Oxford (MA); Birkbeck Coll., Univ. of London (BA). Asst Principal, Min. of Transport and Civil Aviation, 1957; Private Sec. to Jt Parly Sec., 1961–63; HM Treasury, 1965–68; Principal Private Sec. to Minister of Transport, 1968–70; Asst Sec., 1970, Under Sec., 1976, Dep. Sec., 1982–91, Dept of Transport; Dir, Govt and Industry Affairs, British Airways, 1991–95. Trustee, RAC Foundn, 2003–11 (Chm., 2003–09). *Recreations:* history, archaeology, music. *Address:* Dormer Lodge, 31 Little Park Gardens, Enfield, Middx EN2 6PQ. *Club:* Oxford and Cambridge.

**HOLMES, David Charles,** CBE 2014; Chief Executive, Family Action, since 2013; *b* Wallasey, 29 Dec. 1967; *s* of Denis and Rene Holmes; *m* 1992, Tracey Angela Chippendale; one *s*. *Educ:* London Sch. of Econs and Pol Sci. (LLB Hons 1989); Univ. of Bristol (LLM 1990). Admitted as solicitor, 1993; Solicitor: Clifford Chance, 1991–94; Mayer Brown, 1994–95; Department of Health: Dep. Hd, Emergency Care, 1995–96; Head: Legal Services, Medicines Control Agency (on secondment), 1996–97; Hosp. Policy, 1997–99; Children's Safeguarding Unit, 1999–2002; Dep. Dir, Adoption and Children's Trusts, 2002–03; Deputy Director: Looked After Children and Adoption, DFES, 2003–05; Children's Services, London Bor. of Haringey, 2005–06; Chief Exec., British Assoc. for Adoption and Fostering, 2006–13. Chair: End Child Poverty Coalition, 2013–15; Connaught Gp, 2013–15. Trustee, Children England, 2011– (Vice Chair, 2012–14; Chair, 2014–); Chair, Naomi Hse, 2013–. FRSA 2016. Chief Exec. of the Year, HR Distinction Awards, 2016. *Recreations:* enjoying family time, music, Spanish language, literature and culture, sport. *Address:* Family Action, 24 Angel Gate, City Road, EC1V 2PT, *T:* (020) 7241 7601. *E:* david.holmes@family-action.org.uk.

**HOLMES, David Robert,** Registrar, University of Oxford, and Professorial Fellow, St John's College, Oxford, 1998–2006; *b* 2 May 1948; *s* of late Leslie Howard Holmes and Joyce Mary Holmes (*née* Stone); *m* 1st, 1974, Lesley Ann Crone (marr diss. 1989); one *s* one *d*; 2nd, 1989, Susan, *d* of William John and Edna Bayley. *Educ:* Preston GS; Merton Coll., Oxford (MA; Hon. Fellow, 2000; Chancellor's Prize for Latin Prose, Oxford Univ., 1968). University of Warwick: Admin. Asst, 1970–74; Asst Registrar, 1974–78; seconded as Asst Registrar, Univ. of Sheffield, 1975–76; Sen. Asst Registrar, 1978–82; University of Liverpool: Acad. Sec., 1982–86; Dep. Registrar and Acad. Sec., 1987–88; Registrar and Sec., Univ. of Birmingham, 1988–98. Chairman: Oxford Mutual Ltd, 2006–; Stipends and Allowances Cttee, Merton Coll., Oxford, 2008–; Member: Council, Univ. of Warwick, 2006–09; Academic Council, BPP Univ. (formerly Coll. of Professional Studies), 2007–18 (Chm., 2014–18, 2019–); non-exec. Bd Mem., 2017–18). Trustee: Ind. Schs Governing Body, Foundn for Schs of Edward VI in Birmingham, 2006–14 (Chm., 2008–14); James Martin 21st Century Foundn, 2006–09; Arthur Thomson Trust, 2008–. Hon. DCL Oxon, 2006. *Publications:* (contrib.) Beyond the Limelight, 1986; Perspectives, Policy and Practice in Higher Education, 1998; The State of UK Higher Education, 2001. *Recreations:* reading the classics, squash, cricket, golf, tennis, music, gardening. *Address:* 2 Windsor Court, Prince of Wales Mansions, 1 York Place, Harrogate, N Yorks HG1 1JB. *T:* (01423) 550078. *Clubs:* Pannal Golf; Harrogate Squash and Fitness.

See also Sir J. E. Holmes.

**HOLMES, Eamonn,** OBE 2018; broadcast journalist; presenter, This Morning, ITV, since 2006; *b* 3 Dec. 1959; *s* of Leonard Holmes and Josephine Holmes; three *s* one *d*. *Educ:* St Malachy's Coll., Belfast. Reporter, Ulster TV, 1980–86; presenter of TV programmes including: Good Evening Ulster, Ulster TV, 1982–86; Open Air, 1986–91, Holiday, 1989–92, Jet Set, 2001–07, BBC; GMTV, 1993–2005; Anchor, Sunrise, Sky News, 2005–16; presenter, Eamonn Holmes Show, BBC Radio Five Live, 2004–09. Mem. Adv. Panel, DCMS Free-to-Air Events Listing Rev., 2009. Mem. Bd, Manchester United Charitable Foundn, 2007–. DUniv: Staffs, 2004; QUB, 2006. *Publications:* Eamonn Holmes: this is my life (autobiog.), 2006. *Recreation:* watching Manchester United. *E:* info@eamonn.tv.

**HOLMES, George Dennis,** CB 1979; FRSE; Director-General and Deputy Chairman, Forestry Commission, 1977–86, retired; *b* 9 Nov. 1926; *s* of James Henry Holmes and Florence Holmes (*née* Jones); *m* 1953, Sheila Rosemary Woodger; three *d*. *Educ:* John Bright's Sch., Llandudno; Univ. of Wales (BSc (Hons)); FRSE 1982; FICFor. Post-grad. Research, Univ. of Wales, 1947; appointed Forestry Commission, 1948; Asst Silviculturist, Research Div., 1948; Asst Conservator, N Wales, 1962; Dir of Research, 1968; Comr for Harvesting and Marketing, 1973. Mem., Scottish Legal Aid Bd, 1989–94. Hon. Prof., Univ. of Aberdeen, 1984–2000. Pres., Capability Scotland, 2003–13. Hon. DSc Wales, 1985. *Publications:* contribs to Forestry Commission pubns and to Brit. and Internat. forestry jls. *Recreations:* golf, fishing. *Address:* Flat 7, Westwood House, 2 Tudor Court, Liphook, Hants GU30 7GJ. *T:* (01428) 288774.

**HOLMES, Janice Elizabeth;** *see* Ward, J. E.

**HOLMES, Sir John (Eaton),** GCVO 2004 (CVO 1998); KBE 1999; CMG 1997; Chairman, Electoral Commission, since 2017; *b* 29 April 1951; *s* of late Leslie Howard Holmes and Joyce Mary (*née* Stone); *m* 1976, Margaret Penelope Morris; three *d*. *Educ:* Preston Grammar Sch.; Balliol Coll., Oxford (BA 1st Cl. Hons Lit. Hum., MA). HM Diplomatic Service, 1973–2007: FCO, 1973–76; 3rd Sec., then 2nd Sec., Moscow, 1976–78; Near East and N Africa Dept, FCO, 1978–82; Asst Private Sec. to Foreign Sec., 1982–84; 1st Sec. (Economic), Paris, 1984–87; Asst Hd of Soviet Dept, FCO, 1987–89; seconded to Thomas de la Rue & Co., 1989–91; Counsellor, Econ. and Commercial, New Delhi, 1991–95; Head of European Union Dept (External), FCO, 1995; on secondment as Private Sec. (Foreign Affairs), 1996–99 and Principal Private Sec., 1997–99, to the Prime Minister; Ambassador to Portugal, 1999–2001; Ambassador to France, 2001–07; Under-Sec. Gen. for Humanitarian Affairs, UN, 2007–10. Chm., Adv. Bd, CargoLogicAir, 2016–19. Dir, Ditchley Foundn, 2010–16. Chm. Bd, Internat. Rescue Cttee UK, 2012–. Member: Council, Radley Coll., 2010–; Exec. Cttee, Pilgrims, 2011–17. *Publications:* The Politics of Humanity, 2013. *Recreations:* sport (tennis, cricket, golf), music, reading. *Address:* Electoral Commission, 3 Bunhill Row, EC1Y 8YZ.

See also D. R. Holmes.

**HOLMES, Dr John Ernest Raymond;** Director, Quality and Performance, United Kingdom Atomic Energy Authority, 1989–90; *b* Birmingham, 13 Aug. 1925; *s* of late Dr John K. Holmes and of Ellen R. Holmes; *m* 1949, Patricia Clitheroe; one *s* one *d*. *Educ:* King Edward's School, Birmingham; University of Birmingham (BSc, PhD). Asst Lectr in Physics, Manchester Univ., 1949–52; Research Scientist, AERE Harwell, 1952–59; Atomic Energy Establishment, Winfrith: Research Scientist, 1959–66; Chief Physicist, 1966–73; Dep. Dir, 1973–86; Dir, 1986–89. *Publications:* technical papers on nuclear power. *Address:* Flat 1, St Antony's School House, Westbury, Sherborne, Dorset DT9 3QF. *T:* (01935) 817335.

**HOLMES, Jonathan Roy;** Managing Director, Jon Holmes Media Ltd, since 2006; *b* 26 June 1950; *s* of Roy Coulson Holmes and Margery Eleanor Heathcote Holmes (*née* Adams); *m* 1981, Margaret Helen Shipman; one *s* two *d*. *Educ:* Oundle Sch., Northants; Leeds Univ. (BA Hons (Political Studies) 1971). Reporter, Leicester Mercury, 1971–72; Dir, Pointon York Gp, 1972–80; Founder and Man. Dir, Park Associates Ltd, 1981–98; Partner, Benson McGarvey & Co., 1983–2001; Chm. and CEO, SFX Sports Gp, 1998–2006. Non-executive Director: Sportech plc, 2007–10; Brand Meets Brand Ltd, 2011–17. Chairman: Leicester City FC, 2003; Cultivate East Midlands, 2006–11. Co-Founder and Chm., Mick Fitzgerald Racing Club, 2012–. Hon. MBA De Montfort, 2005. *Recreations:* theatre, sport, esp. football, cricket and National Hunt racing, causing trouble. *Address:* Westhorpe Lodge, Westhorpe, Southwell, Notts NG25 0ND. *T:* 07802 461706. *E:* jon@jonholmesmedia.com. *Clubs:* Garrick, Groucho, MCC.

**HOLMES, Dame Kelly,** DBE 2005 (MBE 1998); National Schools Sports Champion, 2006–08; Director, Double Gold Enterprises, since 1996; *b* 19 April 1970; *d* of Michael Norris and of late Pamela Thomson. *Educ:* Hugh Christie Sch., Tonbridge. Nursing Asst for mentally handicapped, 1987; served Army, 1988–97. International athlete, 1993–2005: winner: Commonwealth Games: Gold, 1994 and 2002, Silver, 1998, 1500m; European Championships: Silver, 1500m, 1994; Bronze, 800m, 2002; World Championships: Silver, 1500m, Bronze, 800m, 1995; Silver, 800m, 2003; Olympic Games: Bronze, 800m, 2000; Gold, 1500m and 800m, 2004; Silver, World Indoor Championships, 2003; 1500m, 1st World Athletics Final, 2004. Founder and Chair, Dame Kelly Holmes Legacy Trust, 2008–. Pres., Commonwealth Games England. Performance of Year Award, IAAF, 2004; BBC Sports Personality of Year, 2004; European Athlete of Year, 2004; World Female Athlete of Year, 2004. *Publications:* (with R. Lewis) My Olympic Ten Days, 2004; (with F. Blake) Black, White and Gold: my autobiography, 2005; (with G. Walden) Katy and the Shooting Star, 2008; Running Life: mindset, fitness and nutrition for positive wellbeing, 2018.

**HOLMES, Prof. Kenneth Charles,** PhD; FRS 1981; Director of the Department of Biophysics, Max-Planck-Institute for Medical Research, Heidelberg, 1968–2003; Professor of Biophysics, Heidelberg University, 1972–99, now Emeritus; *b* 19 Nov. 1934; *m* 1957, Mary Scruby; one *s* three *d*. *Educ:* St John's Coll., Cambridge (MA 1959); London Univ. (PhD 1959). Res. Associate, Children's Hosp., Boston, USA, 1960–61; Mem., Scientific Staff, MRC Lab. of Molecular Biology, Cambridge, 1962–68. Mem., EMBO; Scientific mem., Max Planck Gesellschaft, 1972–; Mem., Heidelberg Acad. of Scis, 1991. Corresp. Mem., Soc. Royale des Scis, Liège. *Publications:* (with D. Blow) The Use of X-ray Diffraction in the Study of Protein and Nucleic Acid Structure, 1965; papers on virus structure, molecular mechanism of muscular contraction and the structure of actin. Aaron Klug - a long way from Durban: a biography, 2017. *Recreations:* rowing, singing. *Address:* Emeritus Group Biophysics, Max-Planck-Institute for Medical Research, Jahnstrasse 29, 69120 Heidelberg, Germany. *T:* (6221) 486270.

**HOLMES, Maj. Gen. Matthew John,** CBE 2019; DSO 2007; Commandant General, and Commander, UK Amphibious Forces, Royal Marines, since 2019; *b* Chalfont St Giles, 29 June 1967; *s* of Christopher Holmes and Linda Holmes; *m* 2002, Lea Margaret Brocklebank; one *s* one *d*. *Educ:* Desborough Sch.; St Austell Coll.; Univ. of Exeter (BA (Hons) Econs); King's Coll. London (MA Defence Studies). Joined Royal Marines, 1988; CO 42 Cdo RM, 2006–08; MA VCDS and Second Perm. Under Sec., 2010–12; COS, Standing Jt Force HQ, 2016–18; Dep. Advr to Minister of Interior Affairs, Afghanistan, 2018–19. Mem., Windsor Leadership Trust, 2007–. *Recreations:* water sports, ski-ing, shooting. *Address:* c/o Royal Marines, Whale Island, Portsmouth PO2 8ER. *E:* matt.holmes556@mod.gov.uk. *Club:* Naval and Military.

**HOLMES, Maurice Colston,** OBE 1985; Director, Safety, British Railways Board, 1989–92; *b* 15 Feb. 1935; *s* of Charles Edward Holmes and Ellen Catherine Mary Holmes (*née* Colston); *m* 1985, Margaret Joan Wiscombe. *Educ:* Presentation Coll., Reading. British Rail: Divl Man., Liverpool Street, 1976–79; Chief Operating Man., 1979–80, Dep. Gen. Man., 1980–82, Southern Region; Dir of Operations, BRB, 1982–88. Dir and Trustee, Railway Pension Trustee Co. Ltd, 1994–96. Pres., British Transport Pension Fedn, 1993–. Col, RE, Engrg and Logistic Staff Corps (TA), 1990–2001. *Recreations:* travel, transport, gardens. *Address:* 9 High Tree Drive, Earley, Reading, Berks RG6 1EU. *T:* (0118) 966 8887.

**HOLMES, Michael Harry;** Chairman, fountains plc, 2007–09; *b* 10 March 1945; *s* of Harry Albert Holmes and Doris Rachel (*née* Linihan); *m* 1968, Ellen van Caspel; three *s*. *Educ:* Alleyn's Sch., Dulwich; Gonville and Caius Coll., Cambridge (MA). Costain Civil Engineering Ltd, 1966–70; Ready Mixed Concrete Ltd, 1970–73; Pioneer Concrete Ltd, 1973–77; Rentokil Group plc, 1977–95: Regl Man. Dir, UK Property Services, 1988–91;

Regl Man. Dir, N America, Caribbean and E Africa, 1992–95; self-employed, 1995–97; Chief Executive: Chesterton Internat. plc, 1997–2001; Orbis plc, 2002–08. *Recreations:* fishing, sailing, old cars, motorcycles, theatre. *Address:* Beechcroft, Hophurst Hill, Crawley Down, W Sussex RH10 4LW. *T:* (01342) 716101. *Club:* Oriental.

**HOLMES, Michael John;** Member (Ind) South West Region, England, European Parliament, 1999–2002 (UK Ind, 1999–2000, subseq. non-aligned); retired; *b* 6 June 1938; adopted *s* of Albert and Elsie Holmes; *m* 1974, Carolyn Allen Jee; two *s* one *d*. *Educ:* Sevenoaks Sch. SSC, Royal Warwicks Regt, 1958–60. Sales and Mkting Exec., Sunday Times, Evening Standard, and Observer, 1962–69; Owner Publisher, Independent Gp of Free Newspapers, 1970–87; voluntary and charity work, 1987–99. European Parliament: Voting Member: Fisheries Cttee; Budgetary Control Cttee. Leader, UK Independence Party, 1998–2000. *Recreations:* travel, reading, politics. *Address:* Highfield House, North Street, Charminster, Dorchester, Dorset DT2 9QS. *T:* (01305) 268599.

**HOLMES, Prof. Patrick,** PhD; Professor of Hydraulics, Imperial College of Science, Technology and Medicine, 1983–2003; Dean, City and Guilds College, 1988–91; *b* 23 Feb. 1939; *s* of Norman Holmes and Irene (née Shelbourne); *m* 1963, Olive (née Towning); one *s* one *d*. *Educ:* University Coll. of Swansea, Univ. of Wales (BSc 1960, PhD 1963). CEng, MICE. Res. Engr, Harbour and Deep Ocean Engrg, US Navy Civil Engrg Lab., Port Hueneme, Calif, 1963–65; Lectr, Dept of Civil Engrg, Univ. of Liverpool, 1966–72, Sen. Lectr, 1972–74, Prof. of Maritime Civil Engrg, 1974–83. Vis. Prof., Univ. of the WI, Trinidad, 2001. Chm., Environment Cttee, SERC, 1981–85. Pres., Conf. of European Schs of Advanced Engrg Educn and Res., 1993–95. Hon. Mem., C&G, 1992 (FCGI 1999). *Publications:* (ed) Handbook of Hydraulic Engineering (English edn), by Lencastre, 1987; articles on ocean and coastal engineering, wave motion, wave loading, coastal erosion and accretion, and harbour and breakwater design, in Proc. ICE and Proc. Amer. Soc. of Civil Engrs. *Recreations:* golf, yachting, walking, choral music. *Address:* Cliff Hanger, 2A Claybush Road, Ashwell, Baldock, Herts SG7 5RA. *T:* (01462) 742979.

**HOLMES, Paul Robert;** Chairman, Executive Officers, Chesterfield Liberal Democrats; *b* 16 Jan. 1957; *s* of Frank and Dorothy Holmes; *m* 1978, Raelene Palmer; three *c*. *Educ:* York Univ. (BA Hons Hist); Sheffield Univ. (PGCE). Teacher, Chesterfield Boys' High Sch., 1979–84; Hd of History, Buxton Coll., 1984–90; Hd of Sixth Form, Buxton Community Sch., 1990–2001. Mem., Chesterfield BC, 1987–95, 1999–2002. MP (Lib Dem) Chesterfield, 2001–10; contested (Lib Dem) same seat, 2010. Lib Dem spokesman on disability, 2001–05, and on work and pensions, 2002–05, on housing, 2007, on home affairs and justice, 2008–10; Shadow Minister for Arts and Heritage, 2006–07. Member: Educn and Skills Select Cttee, 2001–07; Children, Schs and Families Cttee, 2008–10. Chm., Lib Dem Parly Party, 2005–07. *Recreations:* reading, walking, history.

**HOLMES, Prof. Peter Henry,** OBE 2007; PhD; FRCVS; FRSE; Professor of Veterinary Physiology, University of Glasgow, 1982–2008, now Emeritus; *b* Cottingham, E Yorks, 6 June 1942; *s* of Frank Holmes and Edna Holmes (née Wiles); *m* 1965, Ruth Helen Mack; two *d*. *Educ:* Beverley Grammar Sch.; Univ. of Glasgow (BVMS 1966; PhD 1969). MRCVS 1966. University of Glasgow: Asst Lectr, 1966–69, Lectr, 1969–76, Sen. Lectr, 1976–80, Reader, 1980–82, in Vet. Physiol.; Hd, Dept of Vet. Physiol., 1978–97; Vice-Principal for Res., 1997–2004; Territorial Vice-Principal for Faculties of Vet. Medicine, Medicine and Biomed. and Life Scis, 1997–2005; Mem., Sen. Mgt Cttee, 1997–2005; Chm., Univ. Res. Planning and Strategy Cttee, 1997–2004. Jt Chm., Univs of Glasgow and Strathclyde Synergy Partnership, 1997–2004. Chairman: Livestock Res. Strategy Cttee, Natural Resources Dept, ODA, 1992–97; (Founding) Internat. Steering Cttee, Prog. against African Trypanosomiasis, UN, 1997–2002; Strategic Sci. Adv. Panel, Scottish Exec. Envmt and Rural Affairs Dept, 2005–08; Strategic and Tech. Adv. Gp for Neglected Tropical Diseases, WHO, 2013–15 (Mem., 2010–13); Member: SFC (formerly SHEFC), 2003–10 (Chm., Res. Policy Adv. Cttee, 2003–05; Chm., Res. and Knowledge Transfer Cttee, 2005–10); DTI Res. Council Econ. Impact Wkg Gp (Warry Cttee), 2006. Mem. Council, Treas. and Pres., Assoc. of Vet. Teachers and Res. Workers, 1985–92; Mem., Vet. Policy Gp, BVA, 1993–97; Mem. Council, Treas. and Chm., UFAW, 1991–98. Chm., Res. Awards Cttee, 2005–08, Fellowship Sec., 2008–11, RSE. FRSE 1999. Hon. FRCVS 2007. Hon. DUniv Strathclyde, 2004; Hon. DSc Hull, 2013. Comdr, Ordre des Palmes Académiques (France), 2009. *Publications:* (ed jtly) The Trypanosomiases, 2003; numerous research papers and reviews on the pathophysiology and control of parasite infections in domestic animals and man. *Recreations:* cycling, gardening, golf, painting. *Address:* 2 Barclay Drive, Helensburgh G84 9RD. *T:* (01436) 674165. *E:* peter.holmes@glasgow.ac.uk.

**HOLMES, Peter Rodney;** HM Diplomatic Service, retired; *b* 29 July 1938; *m* Anne Cecilia Tarrant; one *s* three *d*. Diplomatic Service: served Strasbourg, Belgrade, Paris, Cento, Ankara; Stockholm, 1974; Consul, Douala, 1978; Dep. Head of Mission, Bahrain, 1983; Commercial Counsellor, Santiago, 1987; Ambassador to Honduras, 1995–98. *Address:* 15 Cavalier Way, Alton, Hampshire GU34 1QX.

**HOLMES, Peter Sloan;** development consultant, since 2010; Chief Executive: Sheridan Group, 2004–10 (Director, 2000–10); Sheridan Millennium Ltd, 2000–07; *b* 8 Dec. 1942; *s* of George H. G. and Anne S. Holmes; *m* 1966, Patricia McMahon; two *s*. *Educ:* Rossall Sch.; Magdalen Coll., Oxford (BA English Lang. and Lit.). Teacher, Eastbourne Coll., 1965–68; Head of English, Grosvenor High Sch., Belfast, 1968–71; Lectr, then Sen. Lectr, Stranmillis Coll. of Educn, Belfast, 1971–75; Department of Education for Northern Ireland: Inspector, 1975–83 (Sen. Inspector, 1980; Staff Inspector, 1982); Asst Sec., 1983–87; Under Sec., 1987; Dep. Sec., 1996–2000. Chairman: Arts & Business NI, 2000–06; Bytes Project, 2009–13. Mem. Court, Univ. of Stirling, 2011–16. *Recreations:* singing, cycling, gliding. *Address:* 15a Ochlochy Park, Dunblane, Perthshire FK15 0DU. *T:* (01786) 824525, 07801 989938.

**HOLMES, Richard Gordon Heath,** OBE 1992; FBA 1997; FRSL; writer, biographer and lecturer; Professor of Biographical Studies, School of English and American Studies, University of East Anglia, 2001–07; *b* 5 Nov. 1945; *s* of late Dennis Patrick Holmes and Pamela Mavis Holmes (née Gordon); partner, Rose Tremain, *qv*. *Educ:* Downside Sch.; Churchill Coll., Cambridge (BA; Hon. Fellow, 2011). FRSL 1975. Reviewer and historical features writer for The Times, 1967–92. Mem. Cttee, Royal Literary Fund, 1990–. Vis. Fellow, Trinity Coll., Cambridge, 2000, 2002. Lectures: Ernest Jones Meml, British Inst. of Psycho-Analysis, 1990; John Keats Meml, RCS, 1995; Johan Huizinga Meml, Univ. of Leiden, 1997; Seymour Biography, ANU, 2008; Wordsworth, Univ. of London, 2011; Dibner, Smithsonian Inst., Washington, 2012; Gesellschaft für englische Romantik, Ludwig Maximilian Univ., Munich, 2013; Byron, Univ. of Nottingham, 2014; Leon Levy Biography, NY, 2014; James Bryce Meml, Univ. of Oxford, 2017. Hon. DLitt: UEA, 2000; E London, 2015; Kingston, 2008. US Biographers Internat. Orgn Award, 2018. *Publications:* Thomas Chatterton: the case re-opened, 1970; One for Sorrow (poems), 1970; Shelley: the pursuit, 1974 (Somerset Maugham Award, 1977); Gautier: my fantoms (trans.), 1976, enlarged edn 2008; Inside the Tower (radio drama documentary), 1977; (ed) Shelley on Love, 1980; Coleridge, 1982; (with Peter Jay) Nerval: the chimeras, 1985; Footsteps: adventures of a romantic biographer, 1985; (ed) Mary Wollstonecraft and William Godwin, 1987; (ed with Robert Hampson) Kipling: something of myself, 1987; De Feministe en de Filosoof, 1988; Coleridge: vol. 1, Early Visions (Whitbread Book of the Year Prize), 1989, vol. 2, Darker Reflections (Duff Cooper Memorial Prize), 1998; To the Tempest Given (radio drama documentary), 1992; Dr Johnson & Mr Savage, 1993 (James Tait Black Meml Prize, 1994); The Nightwalking (radio drama documentary), 1995 (Sony Award); (ed) Coleridge: selected poems, 1996; Insights: the Romantic poets and their circle, 1997, enlarged edn 2005; Clouded Hills (radio documentary), 1999; Runaway Lives (radio documentary), 2000; Sidetracks: explorations of a romantic biographer, 2000; Romantics and Revolutionaries: Regency portraits, 2002; The Frankenstein Project (radio documentary), 2002; (ed) Classic Biographies (series), 2004; A Cloud in a Paper Bag (radio documentary), 2007; The Age of Wonder, 2008 (Royal Soc. Book Prize 2009; US Nat. Book Critics Circle Award for Non Fiction, 2010; US NAS Communication Award, 2010); Anaesthesia (radio drama), 2009; Thomas Lawrence Portraits, 2010; Falling Upwards: how we took to the air, 2013; This Long Pursuit: reflections of a romantic biographer, 2016. *Recreations:* sailing, Norfolk hill-walking, French gardening, hot-air ballooning, stargazing. *Address:* c/o HarperCollins, 1 London Bridge Street, SE1 9GF.

**HOLMES, Robin Edmond Kendall;** Head of Judicial Appointments, Lord Chancellor's Department, 1992–98; *b* 14 July 1938; *s* of Roy Frederick George and Kaye Holmes; *m* 1964, Karin Kutter (*d* 2016); two *s*. *Educ:* Wolverhampton Grammar Sch.; Clare Coll., Cambridge (BA); Birmingham Univ. (LLM). Articles, Wolverhampton CBC, 1961–64; admitted solicitor, 1964; Min. of Housing and Local Govt, subseq. DoE, 1965–73 and 1976–82; Colonial Secretariat, Hong Kong, 1973–75; Lord Chancellor's Dept, 1982–98; Grade 3, 1983–98; Circuit Administrator, Midland and Oxford Circuit, 1986–92. *Recreation:* travelling.

**HOLMES, Roger;** Managing Director, Change Capital Partners, since 2005; *b* 21 Jan. 1960. Strategy Consultant, then Principal, McKinsey & Co.; Kingfisher: Finance Dir, B & Q, 1994–97; Man. Dir, Woolworths, 1997–99; Chief Exec., electrical retailing div., 1999–2000; Marks and Spencer plc: Head, UK retailing business, 2001–02; Exec. Dir, 2001–04; Chief Exec., 2002–04. *E:* rholmes@changecapitalpartners.com.

**HOLMES, Roger de Lacy,** CB 2002; Chief Executive, St John Ambulance, 2002–07; *b* 15 Jan. 1948; *s* of Stephen and Muriel Holmes; *m* 1st, 1970, Jennifer Anne Heal (marr. diss. 2005); one *s* one *d*; 2nd, 2005, Rosalind Joy Halstead. *Educ:* Huddersfield New Coll.; Balliol Coll., Oxford (BA). DTI, 1969–74; Dept of Prices and Consumer Protection, 1974–77; Dept of Industry, 1977–79; Asst to Chm., British Leyland, 1980–82; Company Sec., Mercury Communications, 1982–83; Jt Sec. and Dir, Corporate Affairs, ICL, 1984; Exec. Dir, Dunlop Holdings, 1984–85; Euroroute, 1985–86; Chloride Group: Man. Dir, Power Electronics, 1986–88; Corporate Affairs Dir, 1989–92; Dep. Master and Comptroller, Royal Mint, 1993–2001. Non-executive Director: Cygnet Health Care, 1993–2000; Yorks Ambulance Service NHS Trust, 2006–12. Mem. Council, Univ. of London, 2003–08. CStJ 2007 (OStJ 2004). *Recreations:* golf, bridge.

**HOLMES, Timothy Charles;** Executive Director, UK-Korea Forum for the Future, 2010–14; *b* 26 April 1951; *s* of late Ronald William Holmes and Barbara Jean (née Mickleburgh); *m* 1973, Anna-Carin Magnusson; one *s* one *d*. *Educ:* Bec Sch.; Selwyn Coll., Cambridge (MA); Univ. of Aix-Marseille. Joined FCO, 1974; Second, later First, Sec., Tokyo, 1976–80; seconded to Invest in Britain Bureau, Dept of Industry, 1981–83; FCO, 1983–86; First Sec., Islamabad, 1986–90; FCO, 1990–94; Dep. Head of Mission and Commercial and Econ. Counsellor, Seoul, 1994–97; Dep. Hd of Mission, 1997–2002, Consul-Gen., 2000–02, The Hague; Dir, Asia Pacific, Internat. Gp, Trade Partners UK, then UK Trade & Investment, 2002–04; Consul Gen., Sydney and Dir Gen., Trade and Investment, 2004–08; Dep. CEO and Dir, Corporate Prog., Asia House, 2009–11. Gen. Sec., Workability Internat., 2011–12. Exec. Dir, Pakistan-Britain Trade and Investment Forum, 2009–12. FLS 2012. *Publications:* The Wild Flowers of Islamabad, 1990. *Recreations:* botany, ornithology, reading.

**HOLMES, Prof. William Neil;** Professor of Physiology, University of California, since 1964; *b* 2 June 1927; *s* of William Holmes and Minnie Holmes (née Lloyd); *m* 1955, Betty M. Brown, Boston, Mass; two *s* two *d*. *Educ:* Adams Grammar Sch., Newport, Salop; Liverpool Univ. (BSc, MSc, PhD, DSc); Harvard Univ., Cambridge, Mass. National Service, 2nd Bn RWF, 1946–48. Visiting Scholar in Biology, Harvard Univ., 1953–55; Post-grad. Research Schol., Liverpool Univ., 1955–56; ICI Fellow, Glasgow Univ., 1956–57; Asst Prof. of Zoology, 1957–63, Associate Prof. of Zoology, 1963–64, Univ. of British Columbia, Canada; John Simon Guggenheim Foundn Fellow, 1961–62; Visiting Professor of Zoology: Univ. of Hull, 1970; Univ. of Hong Kong, 1973, 1982–83 and 1987. Scientific Fellow, Zoological Soc. of London, 1967; External examiner: for undergraduate degrees, Univ. of Hong Kong, 1976–79, 1985–88; for higher degrees, Univs of Hong Kong and Hull, 1976–; Consultant to: Amer. Petroleum Inst., Washington, DC (environmental conservation), 1972–74; US Nat. Sci. Foundn (Regulatory Biology Prog.), 1980–83; US Bureau of Land Management (petroleum toxicity in seabirds), 1982–. Mem. Editorial Bd, American Journal of Physiology, 1967–70. Member: Endocrine Soc., US, 1957–; Soc. for Endocrinology, UK, 1955–; Amer. Physiological Soc., 1960–; Zoological Soc. of London, 1964–. *Publications:* numerous articles and reviews in Endocrinology, Jl of Endocrinology, Gen. and Comp. Endocrinology, Cell and Tissue Res., Archives of Environmental Contamination and Toxicology, Environmental Res., Jl of Experimental Biology. *Recreations:* travel, old maps and prints, carpentry and building. *Address:* 117 East Junipero Street, Santa Barbara, CA 93105, USA. *T:* (805) 6827256. *Club:* Tennis (Santa Barbara).

**HOLMES à COURT,** family name of **Baron Heytesbury**.

**HOLMES à COURT, Janet Lee,** AC 2007 (AO 1995); Chairman: Heytesbury Pty Ltd, Australia, 1991–2009; John Holland Group, 1991–2012 (Chairman, Advisory Board, 2013–14); *b* 29 Nov. 1943; *m* 1966, (Michael) Robert (Hamilton) Holmes à Court (*d* 1990); three *s* one *d*. *Educ:* Perth Modern Sch.; Univ. of Western Australia (BSc Chemistry; DipEd). Former Chemistry Teacher, Perth. Member Board: Reserve Bank of Australia, 1992–97; Rio Tinto Community Investment (formerly WA Future) Fund, 2006–15. Bd Mem., Aust. Res. Council, 2003–05; Board Director: Vision 2020 Aust., 2004–13; Aust. Inst. of Architects Foundn, 2016–; Bd Advr, State Bldgs Adv. Bd, 2016–. Comr, Tourism WA, 2002–07. Chairman: Australian Children's TV Foundn, 1986–; Black Swan Theatre Co., Perth, 1991–2005; WA Symphony Orch., 1998–; Member: Bd, Australian Urban Design Res. Centre, WA, 2005– (Chm., 2005–14); Bd, Australian Nat. Acad. of Music, 2009–; Bd, Australian Major Performing Arts Gp, 2010–18; Chamber of Arts and Culture WA, 2010–; Internat. Adv. Bd, NY Philharmonic, 2015–18; Bd of Advrs, Centenary Trust for Women, 2015–. Gov., Sony Foundn Australia, 1999–2009. Hon. FAIB 1998; Hon. FAHA 2011. DUniv: Qld, 1994; Murdoch, 1997; S Australia, 2017; Hon. DLitt WA, 1997; Hon. DBus: Ballarat, 2007; Charles Sturt, 2008; Hon. DArts Edith Cowan, 2011. Veuve Clicquot Business Woman of the Year, 1996; John Shaw Medal, Roads Australia, 2014. *Address:* PO Box 7255, Cloisters Square, WA 6850, Australia.

**HolmPATRICK,** 4th Baron *cr* 1897; **Hans James David Hamilton;** *b* 15 March 1955; *s* of 3rd Baron Holmpatrick and Anne Loys Roche (*d* 1998), *o d* of Commander J. E. P. Brass, RN (retd); *S* father, 1991; *m* 1984, Mrs Gill du Feu, *e d* of K. J. Harding; one *s* and one step *s*. *Heir: b* Hon. Ion Henry James Hamilton, *b* 12 June 1956.

**HOLROYD, Andrew;** *see* Holroyd, W. A. M.

**HOLROYD, Charles William, (Bill),** CBE 2012; DL; Founder and Chairman, OnSide Youth Zones, since 2008; *b* Ravenglass, Cumbria, 7 Feb. 1953; *s* of Clarence Vernon Holroyd and Dorcas Elizabeth Holroyd; *m* 1996, Julie Rae Eastwood; two *s* two *d*. *Educ:* Keswick Sch.; Blackpool Coll. (HND Hotel and Catering Admin). Gen. Manager, THF Supplies, 1976–81; CEO, Holroyd Meek Ltd, 1981–95. Chairman: Millies Cookies, 1995–2004; Positive Solutions, 2000–05; TD4, 2005–15; non-exec. Dir, AO.com (formerly DRL Ltd), 2003–15. Chairman: Young Presidents' Orgn, 1996; World Presidents' Orgn, 2009. DL 2008, High Sheriff 2015, Cheshire. *Publications:* What Could Possibly Go Wrong, 2011. *Recreations:* old cars, trekking, rallying, cycling, motorcycling, building restoration. *Address:* Abbots Moss Hall, Tarporley Road, Oakmere, Northwich, Cheshire CW8 2ES. *T:* 07930 418339, (01606) 301499. *E:* bill@abbotsmoss.com.

**HOLROYD, Dame Margaret;** *see* Drabble, Dame M.

**HOLROYD, Sir Michael (de Courcy Fraser),** Kt 2007; CBE 1989; CLit 2004; author; *b* London, 27 Aug. 1935; *s* of Basil Holroyd and Ulla (*née* Hall); *m* 1982, Margaret Drabble (*see* Dame Margaret Drabble). *Educ:* Eton Coll.; Maidenhead Public Library. Vis. Fellow, Pennsylvania State Univ., 1979. Chm., Soc. of Authors, 1973–74; Chm., Nat. Book League, 1976–78; Pres., English PEN, 1985–88. Chm., Strachey Trust, 1990–95. Member: BBC Archives Adv. Cttee, 1976–79; Arts Council of England (formerly of GB), 1992–95 (Vice-Chm., 1982–83, Chm., 1992–95, Literature Panel); Chm., Public Lending Right Adv. Cttee, 1997–2000. Vice-Pres., Royal Literary Fund, 1997–. Pres., Stephen Spender Trust, 1998–. Nat. Gov., Shaw Fest. Theatre, Ontario, 1993–2014. FRSL 1968 (Mem. Council, 1977–87; Chm. Council, 1998–2001; Vice Pres., 2001–03; Pres., 2003–10; Pres. Emeritus, 2010); FRSA. Saxton Meml Fellowship, 1964; Bollingen Fellowship, 1966; Winston Churchill Fellowship, 1971. Hon. DLitt: Ulster, 1992; Sheffield, 1993; Warwick, 1993; East Anglia, 1994; LSE, 1998; Sussex, 2009. Heywood Hill Prize, 2001; David Cohen British Lit. Prize, 2005; Golden Award, PEN, 2006. *Publications:* Hugh Kingsmill: a critical biography, 1964; Lytton Strachey, 2 vols, 1967, 1968 (Yorkshire Post Prize, 1968), rev. edn 1994 (Prix du Meilleur Livre Etranger, 1995); A Dog's Life: a novel, 1969, rev. edn 2014; (ed) The Best of Hugh Kingsmill, 1970; (ed) Lytton Strachey By Himself, 1971; Unreceived Opinions, 1973; Augustus John, 2 vols, 1974, 1975, rev. edn 1996; (with M. Easton) The Art of Augustus John, 1974; (ed) The Genius of Shaw, 1979; (ed with Paul Levy) The Shorter Strachey, 1980; (ed with Robert Skidelsky) William Gerhardie's God's Fifth Column, 1981; (ed) Essays by Divers Hands, vol. XLII, 1982; Bernard Shaw: Vol. I, The Search for Love 1856–1898, 1988 (Irish Life Arts Award, 1988); Vol. II, The Pursuit of Power 1898–1918, 1989; Vol. III, The Lure of Fantasy 1918–1950, 1991; Vol. IV, The Last Laugh 1950–1991, 1992; Vol. V, The Shaw Companion, 1992; abridged edn, 1997; Basil Street Blues, 1999; Works on Paper: the craft of biography and autobiography, 2002; Mosaic: portraits in fragments, 2004; A Strange Eventful History, 2008 (James Tait Black Meml Prize, Sheridan Morley Prize, 2009); A Book of Secrets, 2010; On Wheels, 2012; (ed with Rebecca John) The Good Bohemian: the letters of Ida John, 2017; Ancestors in the Attic, 2 vols, 2017; Facts and Fiction: a book of storytelling, 2018; various radio and television scripts. *Recreations:* listening to stories, watching people dance, avoiding tame animals, being polite, music, siestas. *Address:* c/o AP Watt at United Agents, 12–26 Lexington Street, W1F 0LE.

**HOLROYD, Robert Anthony;** Headmaster, Repton School, 2003–14; *b* 9 Dec. 1962; *s* of Anthony Holroyd and Jean Elizabeth Holroyd; *m* 1988, Penelope Claire Riddell; two *d*. *Educ:* Birkenhead Sch.; Christ Church, Oxford (Schol. 1981; BA 1st cl. Hons (Mod. Langs) 1985; MA 1988; PGCE 1989). Asst Master, Oakham Sch., 1985–86; Colegio Anglo Colombiano, Bogota, 1986–88; Hd of Dept and Housemaster, Radley Coll., 1989–2003. *Recreations:* the hills and the classics.

**HOLROYD, (William) Andrew (Myers),** CBE 2009 (OBE 2003); Chair and Compliance Officer, Jackson Lees Group (formerly Jackson Canter) Ltd, since 2016 (Chief Executive Officer, 2014–17); President, Law Society, 2007–08; *b* 13 April 1948; *s* of Bill Holroyd and Joan Holroyd; *m* 1975, Caroline Skerry; two *d*. *Educ:* Univ. of Nottingham (BA Law 1969). Admitted solicitor, 1974; Partner, Jackson & Canter, Liverpool, 1977–2014. Lay Canon, Liverpool Cathedral, 2009–. Gov., Liverpool John Moores Univ., 2009–18 (Hon. Fellow, 2008). Trustee, Liverpool Community Spirit, 2011. Hon. DLaws Nottingham, 2009. *Recreations:* music, golf. *Address:* c/o Jackson Lees Group Ltd, 3rd Floor, Walker House, Exchange Flags, Liverpool L2 3YL. *Club:* Woolton Golf (Liverpool).

**HOLROYD, William Arthur Hepworth,** FHSM; Chief Executive, North Durham Health Authority, 1992–93; *b* 15 Sept. 1938; *s* of late Rev. Harry Holroyd and Annie Dodgshun Holroyd; *m* 1967, Hilary Gower; three *s*. *Educ:* Kingswood Sch., Bath; Trinity Hall, Cambridge (MA History); Manchester Univ. (DSA). Hospital Secretary: Crewe Memorial Hosp., 1963–65; Wycombe General Hosp., 1965–67; secondment to Dept of Health, 1967–69; Dep. Gp Sec., Blackpool and Fylde HMC, 1969–72; Regional Manpower Officer, Leeds RHB, 1972–74; District Administrator, York Health Dist, 1974–82; Regional Administrator, Yorkshire RHA, 1982–85; Dist Gen. Man., Durham HA, 1985–92. Non-exec. Dir, York Waterworks, plc, 1996–99. Member: National Staff Cttee for Admin. and Clerical Staff in NHS, 1973–82; General Nursing Council for England and Wales, 1978–83; English Nat. Board for Nursing, Midwifery and Health Visiting, 1980–87; NHS Trng Authority, 1988–91. Director, Methodist Chapel Aid Ltd, 1978–2011 (Chm., 2000–11). Mem. Ind. Monitoring Bd (formerly Bd of Visitors), HM Prison Full Sutton, 1995–2008. *Publications:* (ed) Hospital Traffic and Supply Problems, 1968; Reassuring 18th Century Protestants: the librettist's intended message for Handel's Messiah, 2018. *Recreations:* walking, music, visiting the Shetland Isles, research into Handel's Messiah libretto.

**HOLROYDE, Geoffrey Vernon;** Director, Coventry (formerly Coventry Lanchester) Polytechnic, 1975–87; *b* 18 Sept. 1928; *s* of late Harold Vincent Holroyde and Kathleen Olive (*née* Glover); *m* 1960, Elizabeth Mary, *d* of Rev. E. O. Connell; two *s* two *d*. *Educ:* Wrekin Coll.; Birmingham Univ. (BSc); Birmingham Conservatoire (BMus 1995); ARCO. Royal Navy, 1949–54 and 1956–61; School-master, Welbeck Coll., 1954–56; English Electric, becoming Principal of Staff Coll., Dunchurch, 1961–70; British Leyland, Head Office Training Staff, 1970–71; Head, Sidney Stringer Sch. and Community Coll., Coventry, 1971–75; Higher Educn Adviser to Training Commn, 1987–88; Dir, GEC Management Coll., Dunchurch, 1989–92. Chairman: Industrial Links Adv. Gp to Cttee of Dirs of Polytechnics, 1980–87; National Forum for the Performing Arts in Higher Educn, 1987–91; Develt Training Steering Gp, 1983–88; Mem., W Midlands RHA, 1985–89 (Chm., Non Clinical Res. Cttee; Vice-Chm., AIDS Task Force); Mem., RSA Educn Industry Forum, 1986–90. Dir of Music, St Mary's Church, Warwick, 1962–72; Dir, Coventry Cathedral Chapter House Choir, 1982–95; Asst Dir, Warwickshire County Youth Chorale, 1999–2006. Mem., Exec. Cttee, British Fedn of Young Choirs, 1993–95. Member: Council, Upper Avon Navigation Trust, 1994–2001; Steering Cttee, Assoc. of Inland Navigation Authorities, 1997–2003. Governor, 1978–91, Trustee, 1979–91, Chm., Governing Body, 1984–89, Brathay Hall Trust; Chm. Trustees, St Mary's Hall, Warwick, 1984–90; Governor: Mid Warwicks Coll. of Further Educn, 1976–87; Kings School, Worcester, 1983–88; Coten End Co. Jun. Sch., Warwick, 2006–15. Hon. Dir of Music, 2006–14, Organist Emeritus, 2015, Holy Trinity, Gosport. Hon. Life Mem., RSCM, 1970; Hon. Life Fellow, Birmingham Conservatoire, UCE, 2002. *Publications:* Managing People, 1968; Delegations, 1968; Communications, 1969; Organs of St Mary's Church, Warwick, 1969; 900 years of Music in St Mary's Warwick, 2010; History of the Handel Organ, Gosport, 2017. *Recreations:* music (organ and choir), canals, sailing, outdoor pursuits. *Address:* 38 Coten End, Warwick CV34 4NP. *T:* (01926) 492329.

**HOLROYDE, Rt Hon. Sir Timothy Victor, (Sir Tim),** Kt 2009; PC 2017; **Rt Hon. Lord Justice Holroyde;** a Lord Justice of Appeal, since 2017; *b* 18 Aug. 1955; *s* of Frank Holroyde and Doreen Holroyde; *m* 1980, Miranda Elisabeth Stone; two *d*. *Educ:* Bristol Grammar Sch.; Wadham Coll., Oxford (BA Hons Juris.). Called to the Bar, Middle Temple, 1977, Bencher, 2005; in practice on Northern Circuit, 1978–2008; QC 1996; Recorder, 1997–2008; a Judge of the High Court of Justice, QBD, 2009–17; a Presiding Judge of the Northern Circuit, 2012–15. Mem., Sentencing Council, 2015–18 (Chm., 2018–). *Recreation:* tennis. *Address:* Royal Courts of Justice, Strand, WC2A 2LL.

**HOLST, Dame Alison (Margaret),** DNZM 2011; CBE 1987; QSM 1983; food writer, 1966–2014; *b* Dunedin, NZ, 1 Feb. 1938; *d* of Arthur Hollier Payne and Margaret Ardagh Ursula Payne (*née* Dickie); *m* 1961, Dr Peter Eugene Holst; one *s* one *d*. *Educ:* Opoho Prim. Sch., Dunedin; Dunedin North Intermediate Sch.; Otago Girls High Sch., Dunedin; Univ. of Otago (BHSc 1960). Lectr, Sch. of Home Sci., Univ. of Otago, 1961–65. Television and radio presenter. Hon. DSc Otago, 1997. *Publications:* Here's How, 1966; Meals with the family, 1967; Food Without Fuss, 1972; (ed) The New Zealand Radio and Television Cookbook, 1974; More Food Without Fuss, 1974; Simply Delicious, 1975; Lamb for all Seasons, 1976; What's Cooking?, 1978; Kitchen Diary, 1–12, 1978–89; Alison Holst's Food Processor Book, 1980; Alison Holst's Microwave Book, 1982; Let's Cook, 1982; Alison Holst Cooks, 1984; Dollars and Sense, 1984; Let's Cook Some More, 1984; Cooking Class 1, 1986, 2, 1987, 3, 1988; Family Cookbook, 1987; Lambtastic, 1987; New Zealand Recipe Notes, 1987; Microwave Menus 1, 1988, 2, 1989; Complete Cooking Class, 1989; Meals Without Meat, 1990; Recipes to Remember, 1990; Barbecue Cooking, 1991; Best of Alison Holst, 1991; Best of Home Cooking, 1991; Cooking the New Zealand Way, 1991; Food for Healthy Appetites, 1991; Kitchen Diary Collection, 1991; New Kitchen Diary, 1–3, 1991–93; New Microwave Cookbook, 1991; Mini Money Meals, 1992; Family Favourites, 1993; Everyday Cookery, 1993; Breakfasts and Brunches, 1994; Marvellous Muffins, 1994; Alison's Kitchen, 1995; Cooking for Christmas, 1995; Food for Young Families, 1995; Best Potato Recipes, 1995; Good Food, 1995; Chocolate Temptations, 1996; Sausage Book, 1996; Soup Book, 1997; Ultimate Collection, 2000; Alison's Pantry, 2003; Cool Food for Warmer Days, 2006; Fast and Fun Family Food, 2009; (with Barbara Larson) Home-Grown Cook, 2011; with Simon Holst: Bread Book, 1997; More Marvellous Muffins, 1997; Best Baking, 1998; Best Mince Recipes, 1998; Very Easy Vegetarian, 1998; School Lunches and After School Snacks, 1999; Sensational Salads, 1999; Really Easy Chicken Recipes, 2000; Baby Food and Beyond, 2000; Healthy and Delicious Muffins, 2000; More for Less Cookbook, 2001; Quick and Easy Twenty Minute Meals, 2001; 100 Favourite Muffins and Slices, 2003; 100 Favourite Cakes and Biscuits, 2004; 100 Favourite Twenty Minute Dishes, 2004; 100 Great Ways to use Slow Cookers, 2006; Food to Go, 2006; New Zealand Diabetes Cookbook, 2006; Year-Round Ways to use Slow Cookers, 2007; Popular Potatoes, 2008; Kiwi Favourites, 2008; Marvellous Mince and Sensational Sausages, 2009; New Zealand Barbecue Book, 2009; New Zealand Bread Book, 2010; My Own Kiwi Favourites, 2010; Delicious Slow Cooker Recipes, 2011. *Recreations:* walking, reading, cooking, gardening. *Address:* PO Box 482, Orewa 0946, New Zealand.

**HOLT, Alexis Fayrer B.;** *see* Brett-Holt.

**HOLT, Dr Andrew Anthony,** CBE 2004; Head, Information Services Division, Department of Health, 1990–2005; *b* 4 Jan. 1944; *s* of Josef Holzmann and Livia Holzmann; *m* 1969, Janet Margery; three *s*. *Educ:* Latymer Upper Sch.; University Coll. London (BSc Maths 1965; PhD 1969). ICI Paints Div., 1968–70; entered Civil Service, 1970: Principal, Treasury, 1974–78; Head, Operational Research: Inland Revenue, 1978–87; DHSS, 1987–90. Tutor, Open Univ., 1972–; Nat. Subject Advr for Maths and Stats, Univ. of the Third Age, 2012–16. *Publications:* History of Teddington, 2005; contrib. to jls and OR Society papers.

**HOLT, Catherine;** *see* Johnstone, C.

**HOLT, Prof. Christine Elizabeth, (Mrs W. A. Harris),** PhD; FRS 2009; FMedSci; FRSB; Professor of Developmental Neuroscience, University of Cambridge, 2003–19, now Emeritus; Fellow, Gonville and Caius College, Cambridge, since 1997; *b* 28 Aug. 1954; *d* of (Robert) Clifford Holt and Elizabeth, (Betty), Gertrude Ann Holt (*née* Buist); *m* 1983, Prof. William Anthony Harris, *qv*; one *s* one *d*. *Educ:* St Elizabeth's Sch., Stocksfield; Harrogate Coll.; St Clare's, Oxford; Sussex Univ. (BSc Hons Biol Scis); King's Coll., London (PhD Zool. 1982). FRSB (FSB 2011). Postdoctoral Fellow, UCSD, 1982 and 1984–89 (Alexander von Humboldt Fellow, 1986–87; McKnight Scholar, 1986–89); Jun. Res. Fellow, Worcester Coll., Oxford, 1983–84; Asst Prof.-in-Residence, 1989–92, Asst Prof. 1992–96, Associate Prof., 1996–97, UCSD (Pew Scholar in Biomed. Scis, 1991–96); Lectr, 1997–99, Reader in Develtl Neurobiol., 1999–2003, Cambridge Univ. Mem., EMBO, 2005–. FMedSci 2007. Remedios Caro Almela Prize in Develtl Neurobiol., Instituto de Neurociencias, Universidad Miguel Hernández-csic, Alicante, 2011; Ferrier Medal, Royal Soc., 2016; Champalimaud Vision Award, Champalimaud Foundn, 2016. *Publications:* contrib. papers to sci. jls. *Recreations:* music, fell walking, art, wildlife. *Address:* Department of Physiology, Development and Neuroscience, Anatomy Building, University of Cambridge, Downing Street, Cambridge CB2 3DY. *T:* (01223) 333750. *E:* ceh33@cam.ac.uk.
*See also* R. C. S. Holt.

**HOLT, Prof. David, (Tim),** CB 2000; PhD; FSS; President, Royal Statistical Society, 2005–07 (Vice-President, 2003–04); Chair, UK Data Forum, 2012–17; *b* 29 Oct. 1943; *s* of late Ernest Frederick Holt and Catherine Rose (*née* Finn); *m* 1966, Jill Blake; one *s* one *d*. *Educ:* Coopers' Company's Sch.; Exeter Univ. (BSc Maths 1966; PhD Mathematical Stats 1969). FSS 1973. Res. Fellow, Univ. of Exeter, 1969–70; Survey Statistician, Statistics Canada, 1970–73 (Consultant, 1974–75); University of Southampton: Lectr in Social Stats, 1973–80; Leverhulme Prof. of Social Stats, 1980–2005; Dean, Social Sci. Faculty, 1981–83; Dep. Vice Chancellor, 1990–95; Dir, CSO, 1995–96; Hd, Govt Statistical Service, 1995–2000; Dir, ONS, and Registrar Gen. for England and Wales, 1996–2000. Consultant: NZ Dept of Stats, 1981; OPCS, 1983, 1987, 1991; ESRC, 1990; Australian Bureau of Stats, 1990; EU, 2001–02; UN, 2001–02; IMF, 2002; Scientific Advr to Chief Scientist, DHSS, 1983–88. Vis. Fellow, Nuffield Coll., Oxford, 1995–2003. Associate Editor: Jl Royal Statistical Soc. B, 1983–88; Survey Methodology, 1988–2002; Editor: Jl Royal Statistical Soc. A: Stats and Society, 1991–94; Jl Official Stats, 2001–. Vice-President: Internat. Assoc. of Survey Statisticians, 1989–91 (Scientific Sec., 1985–87); UN Statistical Commn, 1997–99; Mem., Internat. Statistical Inst., 1985 (Vice-Pres., 1999–2001); Fellow, Amer. Statistical Assoc., 1990; Founding Academician, Acad. of Social Scis, 1999. Trustee, Newitt Trust, 1990–. Hon. DSc (SocSci) Southampton, 1999. *Publications:* (jtly) Analysis of Complex Surveys, 1989; papers in academic jls. *Recreations:* golf, travelling, bridge.

**HOLT, Dame Denise Mary,** DCMG 2009 (CMG 2002); HM Diplomatic Service, retired; Ambassador to Spain, 2007–09; *b* 1 Oct. 1949; *d* of William Dennis and Mary Joanna Mills; *m* 1987, David Holt; one *s*. *Educ*: New Hall Sch., Chelmsford; Bristol Univ. Res. Analyst, FCO, 1970–84; First Sec., Dublin, 1984–87; Head of Section, FCO, 1988–90; First Sec., Brasilia, 1991–93; Dep. Hd, Eastern Dept, FCO, 1993–94; Asst Dir, Personnel, 1996–98; Dep. Hd of Mission, Dublin, 1998–99; Dir, Personnel, FCO, 1999–2002; Ambassador to Mexico, 2002–05; Dir for Migration and Overseas Territories, FCO, 2005–07. Non-executive Director: HSBC Bank plc, 2011–18; HSBC Bank UK plc, 2018–; Scottish Power Renewable Energy Ltd, 2011–12; Scottish Power Energy Network Hldgs, 2012–14; M&S Bank, 2013– (Chm., 2013–); Iberdrola SA, 2014–; non-exec. Dir and Gov., Nuffield Health, 2013–. Member: Bd, Ofqual, 2010–13; NHS Pay Review Bd, 2010–14; Ind. Chm., Nominations Cttee, Alzheimer's Soc., 2011–17. Member: Mgt Council, Canada Blanch Centre for Contemp. Spanish Studies, LSE, 2010– (Chair, 2019–); Internat. Adv. Panel, Univ. of Birmingham, 2012–13; Chm., Inst. of Latin American Studies (formerly for Study of the Americas), Sch. of Advanced Studies, Univ. of London, 2012–15; Chair, Council, Univ. of Sussex, 2019–; Member: Adv. Council, Wilton Park, 2012–15; Council, Bristol Univ., 2014–16. Trustee, FCO Liby, 2012–. Chm. Trustees, Anglo-Spanish Soc., 2010–13. Hon. DLaws Bristol, 2012. *Recreations*: theatre, reading, needlework. *E*: ddpholt@aol.com.

**HOLT, Prof. Douglas Brewster,** PhD; Founder and President, Cultural Strategy Group, since 2010. *Educ*: Stanford Univ. (AB); Univ. of Chicago (MBA); Northwestern Univ. (PhD). Brand manager: Clorox Co.; Dole Packaged Foods; Assistant Professor: Penn State Univ., 1992–97; Univ. of Illinois, 1997–2000; Associate Prof., Harvard Business Sch., 2000–04; L'Oréal Prof. of Marketing, Univ. of Oxford, 2004–10; Fellow, Worcester Coll., Oxford, 2004–10. Founding Partner, Amalgamated, advertising agency, 2004–09. *Publications*: (ed jtly) The Consumer Society Reader, 2000; How Brands Become Icons: the principles of cultural branding, 2004; Cultural Strategy: using innovative ideologies to build breakthrough brands, 2010; articles in learned jls. *Address*: Cultural Strategy Group, 2945 Juilliard Street, Boulder, CO 80305, USA.

**HOLT, Elaine Karen,** FCILT; *b* Oxford, 5 June 1966; *d* of Michael and June Brown; *m* 1995, Stephen Holt. *Educ*: Stroud Girls' High Sch. British Airways: Reservations Agent, 1985–87; Sales Agent, 1987–89; Project Exec., 1989–90; Support Exec., 1990–92; British Airways (Galileo): Nat. Acct Manager, 1992–96; Manager, Nat. Accts, 1996–97; Hd of Sales, 1997–98; Managing Director: FirstInfo, 2000; TotalJourney, 2001; Commercial Services Dir, First Great Western, 2001–03; Regl Dir, First South & Wales, 2003–04; Dir, First Rail, 2004–06; Man. Dir, First Capital Connect, 2006–09; Chm. and Chief Exec., Directly Operated Railways, 2009–11; Chm., East Coast, 2009–11; Bd Dir, Rail Franchise Procurement Team, National Express, 2012; Rail Franchise Director, RATP Dev UK, 2014–. Non-executive Director: Highways England (formerly Highways Agency), 2013– (Chair: Safety Cttee, 2015–18; Remuneration Cttee, 2018–); Corserv Ltd, 2016– (Chm., Remuneration Cttee, 2016–); Cormac Ltd, 2017–. Guest Vice Pres. Guest Experience, Carnival Cruises UK, 2014–16. Mem. Bd, Rail Delivery Gp, Assoc. of Train Operating Cos, 2011–12. Ind. Shareholder Advisor, Bristol City Council, 2016–. FCILT 2010; Fellow, Inst. of Professional Sales. *Recreations*: running, keep fit, yoga, painting and drawing. *Address*: 1 Hockley Mill, Church Lane, Twyford, Winchester SO21 1NT. *E*: ekholt@icloud.com.

**HOLT, Jason Bruno Acker,** CBE 2015; Chief Executive Officer, Holts Group of Companies, since 1998; *b* London, 17 Nov. 1969; *s* of Robert Acker Holt and Dorothy Olivia Holt; *m* 1996, Shona Glover; three *d*. *Educ*: Highgate Sch.; Univ. of Leeds (BA Hons Geog.); Univ. of Westminster (DipLaw). Trainee solicitor, Paisner & Co., 1994–96; admitted solicitor, 1996; solicitor, Eversheds, 1996–98; trainee gemmologist, 1998–2000, Dir and Gemmologist, 2000–, Holts Gems. Founding Director: Holts Acad., 1998–2016; Holition, 2006–. Writer of report, Making apprenticeships more accessible to small and medium-sized enterprises (Holt Rev.), 2012; Chairman: Apprenticeship Stakeholder Bd, 2015–17; Apprenticeship Ambassador Network, 2018. Vice-Chm., British Jewellers' Assoc., 2014. Fellow, Gemmological Assoc. FCGI 2018. Liveryman, Goldsmiths' Co., 2014–. *Recreations*: sailing, cycling, family, magic, failing not to be an embarrassment to my kids. *E*: jbaholt@btinternet.com.

**HOLT, His Honour John Frederick;** a Circuit Judge, 1998–2015; *b* 7 Oct. 1947; *s* of Edward Basil Holt and Monica Holt; *m* 1970, Stephanie Ann Watson; three *s*. *Educ*: Ampleforth; Bristol Univ. (LLB). Called to the Bar, Lincoln's Inn, 1970; barrister, E Anglian Chambers, 1970–98 (Head of Chambers, 1993–98); Asst Recorder, 1989–92; a Recorder, 1992–98. ECB cricket coach. *Recreations*: village cricket, classic motor cars. *Clubs*: Strangers (Norwich); MG Car, Octagon Car, Jaguar Drivers; Twinstead Cricket.

**HOLT, John Michael,** MD, FRCP; Consultant Physician, John Radcliffe Hospital (formerly Radcliffe Infirmary), Oxford, 1974–2000, now Emeritus; Fellow, 1968–2000, now Emeritus, and Vice Principal, 1999–2000, Linacre College, Oxford; *b* 8 March 1935; *s* of late Frank Holt, BSc and of Constance Holt; *m* 1959, Sheila Margaret Morton (*d* 2017); one *s* three *d*. *Educ*: St Peter's Sch., York; Univ. of St Andrews. MA Oxon; MD St Andrews; MSc Queen's Univ. Ont. Registrar and Lectr, Nuffield Dept of Medicine, Radcliffe Infirmary, Oxford, 1964–66, Cons. Physician 1968; Chm., Medical Staff, Oxford Hosps, 1982–84. University of Oxford: Med. Tutor, 1967–73; Dir of Clinical Studies, 1971–76; Mem., Gen. Bd of Faculties, 1987–91; Chm., Clinical Medicine Bd, 1992–94. Civilian Advr in Medicine, RAF, 1994–2000. Formerly Examiner in Medicine: Univ. of Oxford; Hong Kong; London; Glasgow; Dublin; RCP. Censor, RCP, 1995–97. Member: Assoc. of Physicians; Soc. of Apothecaries; Cttee on Safety of Medicines, 1979–86; Oxford RHA, 1984–88. Pres., Oxford Medical Alumni, 2003–07. Editor, Qly Jl of Medicine, 1975–92. *Publications*: papers on disorders of blood and various med. topics in BMJ, Lancet, etc. *Recreation*: sailing. *Address*: Old Whitehill, Tackley, Oxon OX5 3AB. *T*: (01869) 331241. *Club*: Oxford and Cambridge.

**HOLT, Karen Jane, (Mrs Paul Smith); Her Honour Judge Karen Holt;** a Circuit Judge, since 2014; *b* Woking, 13 May 1964; *d* of Michael Holt and Christine Holt; *m* 1993, Paul Smith; one *s* one *d* (and one *s* decd). *Educ*: Univ. of Leeds (LLB). Called to the Bar, Lincoln's Inn, 1987; barrister, 1987–2014; a Recorder, 2009–14. *Recreations*: travel, family, school governor (secondary). *Address*: Isleworth Crown Court, 36 Ridgeway Road, Isleworth TW7 5LP. *T*: (020) 8380 4500.

**HOLT, Her Honour Mary;** a Circuit Judge, 1977–95; *d* of Henry James Holt, solicitor, and of Sarah Holt (*née* Chapman); unmarried. *Educ*: Park Sch., Preston; Girton Coll., Cambridge (MA, LLB, 1st cl. Hons). Called to the Bar, Gray's Inn, 1949 (Atkin Scholar). Practised on Northern circuit. Former Vice-Chm., Preston North Conservative Assoc.; Member: Nat. Exec. Council, 1969–72; Woman's Nat. Advisory Cttee, 1969–70; representative, Central Council, 1969–71. MP (C) Preston N, 1970–Feb. 1974. Contested (C) Preston N, Feb. and Oct. 1974. Dep. Pres., Lancs Br., BRCS, 1976–95. Freedom of Cities of Dallas and Denton, Texas, 1987. Badge of Honour, BRCS, 1989. *Publications*: 2nd edn, Benas and Essenhigh's Precedents of Pleadings, 1956. *Recreation*: walking. *Club*: Royal Over-Seas League.

**HOLT, Oliver Charles Thomas;** Chief Sports Writer, Mail on Sunday, since 2015; *b* 22 May 1966; *s* of Thomas and Eileen Holt; *m* 1995, Sarah Llewellyn-Jones; one *s* two *d*. *Educ*: King's Sch., Macclesfield; Christ Church, Oxford (BA Hons Modern Hist.). Reporter, Daily Post & Echo, Liverpool, 1990–93; The Times: Motor Racing Corresp., 1993–97; Football Corresp., 1997–2000; Chief Sports Corresp., 2000–02; Chief Sports Writer, The Mirror, 2002–15. Sports Writer of the Year, British Press Gazette, 2005, 2006; Sports Columnist of the Year, Sports Journalists' Assoc., 2012. *Publications*: The Bridge, 1998; If You're Second, You're Nothing: Ferguson and Shankly, 2006; End of the Rainbow: England's quest for glory in South Africa, 2010; Miracle at Medinah, 2012. *Recreations*: Marlon Brando, Bob Dylan, Stockport County. *Address*: c/o Mail on Sunday, Northcliffe House, 2 Derry Street, W8 5TS.

**HOLT, (Robert Charles) Stephen; His Honour Judge Stephen Holt;** a Circuit Judge, since 2009; *b* Wylam, Northumberland, 30 July 1952; *s* of (Robert) Clifford Holt and Elizabeth Gertrude Ann Holt (*née* Buist); civil partnership 2005, Jonathon Charles Hill. *Educ*: Gordonstoun Sch.; Newcastle Univ. (BSc Hons). Called to the Bar, Gray's Inn, 1978; a Recorder, 2005–09. Mem., Parole Bd, 2010–. Hon. Recorder of Norwich, 2013–. *Recreations*: walking, sailing, gardening, reading. *E*: sholt100@gmail.com. *Clubs*: Royal Automobile; Norfolk.
See also C. E. Holt.

**HOLT, Stuart;** Headmaster, Clitheroe Royal Grammar School, 1991–2004; *b* 12 Sept. 1943; *s* of Alan and Irene Holt; *m* 1968, Valerie Hollows; one *s* one *d*. *Educ*: Leeds Univ. (BSc Upper 2nd Cl. Hons Zool., MPhil); Univ. of Lancaster (MA Educn). Biol. Master, Adwick Sch., Doncaster, 1968–71; Hd of Biol., King's Sch., Pontefract, 1971–73; Hd of Sci., Whitley High Sch., Wigan, 1973–78; Dep. Hd Curriculum, Wright Robinson High Sch., Manchester, 1978–84; Headmaster, Failsworth Sch., Oldham, 1984–91. Mem., Rotary Internat. *Recreations*: Rossendale Male Voice Choir, theatre, photography, Italy, fell-walking, cabinet making. *Address*: c/o Clitheroe Royal Grammar School, York Street, Clitheroe, Lancs BB7 2DJ.

**HOLT, Thelma Mary Bernadette,** CBE 1994; Managing Director, Thelma Holt Ltd, since 1990; Associate Producer, Royal Shakespeare Company, since 2004; *b* 4 Jan. 1932; *d* of David Holt and Ellen Finagh (*née* Doyle); *m* 1st, 1956, Patrick Graucob (marr. diss. 1968; remarried 2011); 2nd, 1969, David Pressman (marr. diss. 1970). *Educ*: St Ann's Sch., Lytham; RADA. Actress, 1953; Founder, Open Space Theatre (with Charles Marowitz), 1968; Dir, Round House Theatre, 1977; Exec. Producer, Theatre of Comedy, 1983; Head of Touring and Commercial Exploitation, Royal Nat. Theatre, 1985 (Laurence Olivier/Observer Award for Outstanding Achievement, 1987); Exec. Producer, Peter Hall Co., 1989; formed Thelma Holt Ltd, 1990, productions include: The Three Sisters, 1990; Tango at the End of Winter, 1991; Electra, Hamlet, Les Atrides, La Baruffe Chiozotte, Six Characters in Search of an Author, The Tempest, 1992; Much Ado About Nothing, 1993; Peer Gynt, The Clandestine Marriage, 1994; The Seagull, A Midsummer Night's Dream, Antony and Cleopatra, The Glass Menagerie, 1995; Observe the Sons of Ulster Marching Towards the Somme, A Doll's House, 1996; The Maids, Les Fausses Confidences, Oh Les Beaux Jours, Shintoku-Maru, 1997; The Relapse, 1998; Macbeth, King Lear, 1999; Miss Julie, 2000; Semi-Monde, 2001; Via Dolorosa, The Tempest, 2002; Pericles, Ghosts, Hamlet, The Taming of the Shrew, 2003; We Happy Few, Hamlet, 2004; Man and Boy, Primo (NT, NY), Twelfth Night, 2005; The Crucible, Hay Fever, Breakfast with Mugabe, Titus Andronicus, The Canterbury Tales, 2006; Coriolanus, Kean, The Giant, 2007; Measure for Measure, Twelfth Night, The English Samurai, 2009; Ghosts, Bedroom Farce, Musashi, 2010; Ruby Wax Losing It, 2011; Cymbeline, Volcano, All That Fall, 2012; Anjin, 2013; Forbidden Broadway, 2014; for Royal Shakespeare Company: The Jacobeans, 2003; The Taming of the Shrew/The Tamer Tamed, All's Well that Ends Well, Othello, 2004; A Midsummer Night's Dream, 2005; Written on the Heart, 2012; Anjin - The Shogun and the English Samurai, 2013; Hamlet and Kafka on the Shore, 2015; Ninagawa Macbeth, 2017; Imperium, 2018; Don Quixote, 2018. Member: Arts Council, 1993–98 (Chm., Drama Adv. Panel, 1994–98); Council, RADA, 1985–2011. Director: Stage One (formerly Theatre Investment Fund) Ltd, 1982–; Citizens Theatre, Glasgow, 1989– (Vice-Pres., 1997–); Almeida Th., 2001–09; Chm., Yvonne Arnaud Th., 2002–05; Trustee, Rose Th., 2009–. Cameron Mackintosh Vis. Prof. of Contemporary Theatre, Oxford Univ., 1998; Fellow, St Catherine's Coll., Oxford, 1998–2003, then Emeritus. Patron, OUDS, 2001. Companion, Liverpool Inst. for Performing Arts, 2002; Dist. Friend of Oxford Univ., 2006. DUniv Middlesex, 1994; Hon. MA Open, 1988; Hon. DLitt UEA, 2003; Hon DA Plymouth, 2010. Special Award for Individual Achievement, TMA Awards, 2006. Order of the Rising Sun, Gold Rays with Rosette (Japan), 2004. *Recreation*: bargain hunting at antique fairs. *Address*: Noël Coward Theatre, 85 St Martin's Lane, WC2N 4AU. *T*: (020) 7812 7455. *E*: thelma@dircon.co.uk.

**HOLT, Tim;** *see* Holt, David.

**HOLTAM, Rt Rev. Nicholas Roderick;** *see* Salisbury, Bishop of.

**HOLTBY, Christopher Bruce,** OBE 2000; HM Diplomatic Service; Consul General, Melbourne, since 2016; *m* Polly Jane; one *s* two *d*. Entered CS, 1992; Desk Officer, NATO and Eur. Policy Dept, 1992–93, Navy Resources and Progs Dept, 1993–94, MoD; Second Sec., UK Delegn to NATO and WEU, Brussels, 1994–98; Hd, Policy and Ops Section, Balkans Dept, 1998–99, Hd, Kosovo Rev. Team, 1999–2000, MoD; Hd, Kosovo Section, FCO, 2000–02; UK Liaison Officer and Policy Advr on Asia and Pacific to EU High Rep., EU Council Secretariat, Brussels, 2002–07; Dep. Hd, Security Policy Dept, FCO, 2007–11; Ambassador to Estonia, 2012–16. *Address*: c/o Foreign and Commonwealth Office, King Charles Street, SW1A 2AH.

**HOLTEN, Kasper;** freelance stage director, since 2017; Chief Executive Officer, Royal Danish Theatre, since 2018; *b* Copenhagen, 29 March 1973; *s* of Henning Holten and Bodil Nyboe Andersen; partner, Signe Fabricius; two *d*. *Educ*: Univ. of Copenhagen. Asst dir to leading stage dirs, 1992–; début as stage dir, Musikteatret Undergrunden Odense, 1993; Dramaturg, Aalborg Teater, 1996–2000; Artistic Dir, Aarhus Sommeropera, 1996–99; Director of Opera: Royal Danish Th., 2000–11; ROH, 2011–17. Stage productions include: Ring, Copenhagen, 2003–06; Le Nozze di Figaro, Theater an der Wien, 2007; Die Frau Ohne Schatten, Copenhagen, 2011; Lohengrin, Deutsche Oper Berlin, 2012; Eugene Onegin, ROH, 2013; Don Giovanni, ROH, L'Ormindo, Sam Wanamaker Playhouse, Idomeneo, Wiener Staatsoper, 2014; Król Roger, ROH, 2015; Carmen, Bregenz Festival, Austria, 2017. Dir of prodns of opera, drama, musical and operetta in Denmark, Sweden, Norway, Finland, Iceland, Latvia, Russia, France, Germany, Italy, Austria, UK, USA, Japan, Australia and China; dir, film, Juan, 2010. Mem., Arts Council Denmark (Music), 1995–99. Knight, Order of the Dannebrog (Denmark), 2003; Ingenio et Arti Medal (Denmark), 2011. *T*: (Denmark) 31577273. *E*: kasper@holten.com.

**HOLTHAM, Gerald Hubert,** FLSW; Hodge Professor of Regional Economy, Cardiff Metropolitan University, since 2016; Managing Partner, Cadwyn Capital LLP, since 2005; Adviser to Finance Minister, Welsh Assembly Government, 2012–14; *b* Aberdare, 28 June 1944; *s* of late Denis Arthur Holtham and Dilys Maud Holtham (*née* Bull); *m* 1st, 1969, Patricia Mary Blythin (marr. diss. 1976); one *d*; 2nd, 1979, Edith Hodgkinson; one *s* one *d*.

*Educ:* King Edward's Sch., Birmingham; Jesus Coll., Oxford (BA 1st Cl. PPE); Nuffield Coll., Oxford (MPhil Econ). ODI, 1973–75; Economist, OECD, Paris, 1975–82; Head, Gen. Econ. Div., Dept of Econs, OECD, 1982–85; Vis. Fellow, Brookings Inst., Washington, 1985–87; Chief Internat. Economist, Shearson Lehman, 1988–91; Econs Fellow, Magdalen Coll., Oxford, 1991–92; Chief Economist, Lehman Brothers, Europe, 1992–94; Dir, IPPR, 1994–98; Dir, Global Strategy, Norwich Union Investment Mgt, 1998–2000; Chief Investment Officer, Morley Fund Mgt, 2000–04. Chm., Ind. Commn on Financing, Welsh Assembly Govt, 2008–10. Vis. Prof., Univ. of Strathclyde, 1990–93; Hon. Prof., then Vis. Prof., Cardiff Univ. Business Sch., 2004–13; Affiliated Prof., London Business Sch., 1992–99. FLSW 2015. Hon. Fellow, Swansea Univ., 2011. *Publications:* (with Roger Busby) Main Line Kill (novel), 1967; (with Arthur Hazlewood) Aid and Inequality in Kenya, 1975; (jtly) Empirical Macroeconomics for Interdependent Economies, 1988; (with Ralph Bryant and Peter Hooper) External Deficits and the Dollar, 1988; articles on economics in learned jls. *Recreations:* gardening, windsurfing, listening to jazz. *Address:* 13 Lansdowne Gardens, SW8 2EQ. *T:* (020) 7622 8673.

**HOLWELL, Peter,** FCA; Principal, University of London, 1985–97; *b* 28 March 1936; *s* of Frank Holwell and Helen (*née* Howe); *m* 1959, Jean Patricia Ashman; one *s* one *d*. *Educ:* Palmers Endowed Sch., Grays, Essex; Hendon Grammar Sch.; London Sch. of Econs and Pol Science (BSc Econ). FCA 1972; MBCS 1974; FRSocMed 1991. Articled Clerk, 1958–61, Management Consultant, 1961–64, Arthur Andersen and Co.; University of London: Head of Computing, Sch. Exams Bd, 1964–67; Head of University Computing and O & M Unit, 1967–77; Sec. for Accounting and Admin. Computing, 1977–82; Clerk of the Court, 1982–85; Dir, School Exams Council, 1988–94; Mem., Univ. of London Exams and Assessments Council, 1991–96. Chm., UCCA Computing Gp, 1977–82. Chm., City and E London FHSA, 1994–96; Mem., Quality Cttee, NHS Canterbury and Coastal CCG, 2013–16. Director: Zoo Operations Ltd, 1988–92; London E Anglian Gp Ltd, 1990–93; non-exec. Mem., NE Thames RHA, 1990–94. Consultant: POW Sch. of Architecture and the Bldg Arts, 1998–99; Chatham Historic Dockyard Trust, 1999–2001. FZS, 1988–2001 (Treas., 1991–92). Chm., St Mark's Res. Foundn and Educnl Trust, 1995–2000; Trustee: Samuel Courtauld (formerly Home House) Trust, 1985–97; Leeds Castle Foundn, 2001–03. Mem. Council, Sch. of Pharmacy, Univ. of London, 1996–2001; Vice-Chm., Wye Coll., 1996–2000. *Recreations:* military history, music, travel. *Address:* Hookers Green, Bishopsbourne, Canterbury, Kent CT4 5JB.

**HOM, Ken,** Hon. OBE 2009; BBC TV presenter; author; *b* 3 May 1949; *s* of late Thomas Hom and Ying Fong Hom. *Educ:* Univ. of Calif, Berkeley. Public television producer, 1974–75; cookery teacher, 1975–78; Cookery prof., Calif. Culinary Acad., San Francisco, 1978–82; Presenter: BBC TV series: Ken Hom's Chinese Cookery, 1984; Hot Chefs, 1991; Ken Hom's Hot Wok, 1996; Ken Hom Travels with a Hot Wok, 1998; Foolproof Chinese Cookery, 2000; The Noodle Road (series), Korean Broadcasting Service, 2009; Exploring China: A Culinary Adventure, 2012. Consultant Chef, Maison Chin, Bandara Hotel, Bangkok, 2008–13; Exec. Consultant Chef, MEE restaurant (Michelin Star, 2015), Copacabana Palace Hotel, Rio de Janeiro, 2014–. Hon. Chm., Inst. for Advancement of Sci. and Art of Chinese Cuisine, NY, 1993–. Founding Patron, Oxford Gastronomica, 2007. Ambassador: Action Against Hunger, 2008–; Prostate Cancer UK; GREAT Britain Campaign. Hon. Dr Oxford Brookes, 2007. *Publications:* Ken Hom's Encyclopaedia of Chinese Cookery Techniques, 1984 (US edn as Chinese Technique, 1981); Ken Hom's Chinese Cookery, 1984, anniversary edn, 2009; Ken Hom's Vegetable and Pasta Book, 1987; Ken Hom's East Meets West Cuisine, 1987; Fragrant Harbour Taste, 1988; Asian Vegetarian Feast, 1988; Ken Hom's Quick and Easy Chinese Cookery, 1988; The Taste of China, 1989; The Cooking of China, 1992; Ken Hom's Chinese Kitchen, 1993; Ken Hom's Hot Wok, 1996; Ken Hom's Asian Ingredients and Posters, 1997; Ken Hom Travels with a Hot Wok, 1997; Easy Family Dishes: a memoir with recipes, 1998 (Andre Simon Award, 1999; US edn as Easy Family Recipes from a Chinese-American Childhood, 1998); Ken Hom Cooks Thai, 1999; Foolproof Chinese Cookery, 2000; Quick Wok, 2001; Foolproof Thai Cookery, 2002; Foolproof Asian Cookery, 2003; 100 Top Stir Fries, 2004; Simple Chinese Cookery, 2005; Simple Thai Cookery, 2006; Simple Asian Cookery, 2007; (with Wynnie Chan) The Ken Hom Nutri Wok Kit Recipe Book, 2008; Complete Chinese Cookbook, 2011; Classic Chinese Recipes, 2011; My Kitchen Table: 100 quick stir-fry recipes, 2011; My Kitchen Table: easy Chinese suppers, 2012; Asian, 2012; (with Ching-He Huang) Exploring China: a culinary adventure: 100 recipes from our journey, 2012; (with Pierre-Jean Pébeyre) Truffle, 2014; My Stir-fried Life, 2016. *Recreations:* Bordeaux vintage wine, bicycling, reading, swimming.

**HOMA, Peter Michael,** CBE 2000; healthcare consultant; Chair, NHS Leadership Academy, since 2017; *b* 3 Jan. 1957; *s* of late Karol Anthony Homa and Anne Kathleen Homa (*née* Dixon); *m* 2006, Deborah Hallas; one *s* one *d* from previous marriage. *Educ:* Ernest Bevin Sch., London; Univ. of Sussex (BA Hons Econs 1979); Univ. of Hull (MBA 1993); Henley Management Coll. and Brunel Univ. (DBA 1998). Comp IHM 2003 (MHSM 1985, FHSM 1999). Self-employed, 1979–81; nat. admin. trainee, SW Thames RHA, 1981–82; Operational Services Adminr, St George's Hosp., London, 1983–84; Dep. Unit Adminr, Bristol Children's and Maternity Hosps, 1984–86; Dep. Unit Gen. Manager, Acute Services, Bromsgrove and Redditch HA, 1986–89; Leicester Royal Infirmary: Associate Gen. Manager, 1989–90; Unit. Gen. Manager, 1990–93; Chief Exec., Leicester Royal Infirmary NHS Trust, 1993–98; Hd, Nat. Patients' Access Team, NHS Exec., 1998–99; Chief Executive: Commn for Health Improvement, 1999–2003; St George's Healthcare NHS Trust, 2003–06. Visiting Professor: LSE, 2000–03; Univ. of Lincoln, 2006–09; Univ. of Surrey, 2006–09; Univ. of Nottingham, 2008–11; Nottingham Business Sch., 2017–. Chm., NHS Leadership Acad., 2017–; Mem., Adv. Bd, Nottingham Business Sch., 2017–. Pres., IHSM, 1998–99 (Vice-Chm., 1996–97; Chm., 1997–98). Trustee, Point of Care Foundn, 2017–. Hon. DLaws Nottingham, 2017. *Recreations:* running, cycling, reading, writing, picture framing. *Address:* The Stable Yard, Poultney Lane, Kimcote, Leics LE17 5RX. *E:* peter.homa@btinternet.com.

**HOMAN, Maj.-Gen. John Vincent,** CB 1980; CEng, FIMechE; Facilities Manager, Matra Marconi Space (formerly Marconi Space Systems), Portsmouth, 1982–92; *b* 30 June 1927; *s* of Charles Frederic William Burton Homan and Dorothy Maud Homan; *m* 1953, Ann Bartlett (*d* 2018); one *s* one *d* (and one *d* decd). *Educ:* Haileybury; RMA Sandhurst; RMCS Shrivenham. BSc (Eng). Commnd, REME, 1948; Lt-Col 1967; Comdr REME 2nd Div., 1968–70; Col 1970; MoD 1970–72; CO 27 Comd Workshop REME, 1972–74; Brig. 1974; Dep. Dir, Electrical and Mechanical Engineering, 1st British Corps, 1974–76; Dir of Equipment Management, MoD, 1976–77; Dir Gen., Electrical and Mechanical Engrg, MoD, 1978–79; Maj.-Gen. 1978; Sen. Army Mem., RCDS, 1980–82. Col Comdt, REME, 1982–88. *Address:* Roedean, 25 The Avenue, Andover, Hants SP10 3EW. *T:* (01264) 351196.

**HOMDEN, Dr Carol Ann,** CBE 2013; Chief Executive, Thomas Coram Foundation for Children (Coram) (formerly Coram Family), since 2007; *b* 9 April 1960; *d* of Dick Homden and Beryl Homden (*née* Kinnersley, now Rabbage); *m* Steve Caplin; two *s*. *Educ:* Shrewsbury High Sch.; Univ. of East Anglia (BA Hons English Lit.; PhD 1986). Publicity Asst, Poly. of N London, 1985–86; Polytechnic of Central London, subsequently University of Westminster: PR Officer, 1986–87; Dir, Corporate Communications, 1987–97; Dir, Mktg and Develt, 1997–99; Dir, Mktg and Public Affairs, BM, 1999–2003; Commercial Dir, Prince's Trust, 2003–07. Chair: Avenues Trust, 2005–11; Nat. Autistic Soc., 2012–. Member: Youth Justice Board, 2015–17; Assoc. for Child and Adolescent Mental Health, 2016–. *Publications:* The Plays of David Hare, 1986. *Recreations:* cottage in Suffolk, visiting museums. *Address:* Coram, 41 Brunswick Square, WC1N 1AZ. *T:* (020) 7520 0305. *E:* carol@coram.org.uk.

**HOME;** *see* Douglas Home, and Douglas-Home, family name of Baroness Dacre and Earl of Home.

**HOME, 15th Earl of,** *cr* 1605; **David Alexander Cospatrick Douglas-Home,** KT 2013; CVO 1997; CBE 1991; Baron Home 1473; Baron Dunglass 1605; Baron Douglas (UK) 1875; Chairman: Coutts & Co., 1999–2013; Coutts & Co. Ltd (formerly Coutts Bank von Ernst, then RBS Coutts Bank Ltd), 2004–17 (Director, 1999, Chairman, 2000, Coutts (Switzerland); Chairman, Bank von Ernst (Switzerland), 2003); *b* 20 Nov. 1943; *o s* of Baron Home of the Hirsel (Life Peer), KT, PC (who disclaimed his hereditary peerages for life, 1963) and Elizabeth Hester (*d* 1990), *d* of Very Rev. C. A. Alington, DD; *S* father, 1995; *m* 1972, Jane Margaret, *yr d* of late Col J. Williams-Wynne, CBE, DSO; one *s* two *d*. *Educ:* Eton College; Christ Church, Oxford (BA 1966). Director: Morgan Grenfell & Co. Ltd, 1974–99; Morgan Grenfell Egyptian Finance Co. Ltd, 1975–77; Morgan Grenfell (Scotland), then Deutsche Morgan Grenfell (Scotland) Ltd, 1978–99 (Chm., 1986–99); Morgan Grenfell (Asia) Ltd, 1978–82 (Dep. Chm., 1979–82); Arab Bank Investment Co., 1979–87; Agricultural Mortgage Corp., 1979–93; Arab-British Chamber of Commerce, 1975–84; Tandem Group (formerly EFG plc), 1981–96 (Chm., 1993–96); Credit for Exports, 1984–94; Deutsche Morgan Grenfell (Hong Kong), 1989–99; Deutsche Morgan Grenfell Asia Pacific Holdings Pte Ltd, 1989–99; Morgan Grenfell Thai Co., 1990–96; K & N Kenanga Bhd, 1995–99; Kenanga DMG Futures Sdn Bhd, 1995–99; Deutsche Morgan Grenfell Group plc, 1996–99 (Chm., Jan.–March, 1999); Wheatsheaf Investments Ltd (formerly Deva Gp), 1999–2010; Deva Gp Ltd (formerly Deva Hldgs), 1999–2010; Dubai Financial Services Authy, 2005–11; Chairman: Morgan Grenfell Export Services, 1984–99; Morgan Grenfell Internat. Ltd, 1987–99; Cegelec Controls Ltd, 1991–94; K & N Kenanga Holdings Bhd, 1993–99; Grosvenor Estate Hldgs, 1993–99; Grosvenor Gp Ltd, 2007–10 (Dep. Chm., 2005–07); MAN Ltd, 2000–09; Trustee, Grosvenor Estate, 1993–2010. Chm., Committee for Middle East Trade, 1986–92 (Mem., 1973–75). Governor: Ditchley Foundn, 1977–2011; Commonwealth Inst., 1988–98. Trustee, RASE, 1999–2004 (Hon. Trustee, 2004–). Pres., Old Etonian Assoc., 2002–03. Elected Mem., H of L, 1999. *Recreation:* outdoor sports. *Heir: s* Lord Dunglass, *qv*. *Address:* 43 Chelsea Towers, Chelsea Manor Street, SW3 5PN. *T:* (020) 3730 1690; The Hirsel, Coldstream, Berwickshire TD12 4LP. *T:* (01890) 882345. *Club:* Turf.
*See also* Viscount Lifford.

**HOME, Anna Margaret,** OBE 1993; Chair, Children's Media Foundation, since 2012; *b* 13 Jan. 1938; *d* of James Douglas Home and Janet Mary (*née* Wheeler). *Educ:* Convent of Our Lady, St Leonard's-on-Sea, Sussex; St Anne's Coll., Oxford (MA (Hons) Mod. Hist.). BBC Radio Studio Man., 1960–64; Res. Asst, Dir, Producer, Children's TV, 1966–70; Exec. Producer, BBC Children's Drama Unit, 1970–81: responsible for series such as Lizzie Dripping, Bagthorpe Saga, Moon Stallion; started Grange Hill, 1977; Controller of Programmes SE, later Dep. Dir of Programmes, TVS (one of the original franchise gp), 1981–86; Hd of Children's Programmes, BBC TV, 1986–98; Chief Exec., Children's Film and Television Foundn, 1998–2012. Chair: Cinemagic, 1999–2005; Eurokidnet, 2002–06; Children's Television Trust Internat., 2005–11; Kidnet, 2006–12; Save Kids TV, 2006–12; Board Member: Screen South, 2002–; Unicorn Th. for Children, 2004–11; Mem. Adv. Bd, Ability Media, 2009–13. Chm., 2nd World Summit on TV for Children, London, 1998. Chairman: Showcommotion Children's Media Fest., 2005–09; Children's Media Conf., 2010–. Trustee, Prince of Wales Arts and Kids Foundn, 2005–14. FRTS 1987. Pye Award for distinguished services to children's television, 1984; Eleanor Farjeon Award for services to children's literature, 1989; Judges Award, RTS, 1993; Lifetime Achievement Award, Women in Film and TV, 1996; BAFTA Special Award for Lifetime Achievement in Children's Programmes, 1997. *Publications:* Into the Box of Delights: a history of children's television, 1993. *Recreations:* theatre, literature, travel, gardening. *Address:* 3 Liberia Road, N5 1JP.

**HOME, Sir William (Dundas),** 14th Bt *cr* 1671 (NS), of Blackadder, Co. Berwick; consultant tree surgeon and horticulturalist; *b* 19 Feb. 1968; *s* of late John Home, *er s* of 13th Bt, and of Nancy Helen, *d* of H. G. Elliott, Perth, WA (she *m* 1993, Rt Hon. Sir John Grey Gorton, GCMG, AC, CH); *S* grandfather, 1992; *m* 1995, Dominique Meryl, *d* of Sydney Fischer, OBE; one *s* one *d*. *Educ:* Cranbrook Sch., Sydney, NSW. Member: Bd, Internat. Soc. of Arboriculture, 1991 (Founding Mem., Australian Chapter, 1997); Aust. Inst. of Horticulture, 1992; Nat. Arborists' Assoc. of Aust., 1999. *Recreations:* golf, scuba diving, fishing, tennis. *Heir: s* Thomas John Home, *b* 24 Nov. 1996. *Address:* 53 York Road, Queen's Park, NSW 2022, Australia. *Club:* Royal Sydney Golf (Sydney).

**HOME ROBERTSON, John David;** Member (Lab) East Lothian, Scottish Parliament, 1999–2007; *b* 5 Dec. 1948; *s* of late Lt-Col J. W. Home Robertson and Mrs H. M. Home Robertson; *m* 1977, Catherine Jean Brewster; two *s*. *Educ:* Ampleforth Coll.; West of Scotland Coll. of Agriculture. Farmer. Mem., Berwicks DC, 1975–78; Mem., Borders Health Bd, 1976–78. Chm., Eastern Borders CAB, 1977. MP (Lab) Berwick and E Lothian, Oct. 1978–83, E Lothian 1983–2001. Opposition Scottish Whip, 1983–84; opposition spokesman on agric., 1984–87, 1988–90, on Scotland, 1987–88; PPS to Minister of Agriculture, Fisheries and Food, 1997–98; PPS to Minister for Cabinet Office, 1998–99; Member: Select Cttee on Scottish affairs, 1980–83; Select Cttee on Defence, 1990–97; British-Irish Parly Body, 1993–99. Chm., Scottish Gp of Lab MPs, 1983. Dep. Minister for Rural Affairs, Scottish Exec., 1999–2000. Convener, Holyrood Progress Gp, 2000–05. Mem., Press Complaints Commn, 2008–11. Founder, Paxton Trust, 1989 (Man. Trustee, 2009–11); Mem., Mgt Cttee, Edinburgh Direct Aid, 2005–09; Trustee, Friends of Union Chain Bridge, 2015–. Pres., Berwickshire Naturalists Club, 2015.

**HOMER, Dame Linda Margaret, (Dame Lin),** DCB 2016 (CB 2008); a Commissioner, Chief Executive Officer and Permanent Secretary for Tax, HM Revenue and Customs, 2012–16; *b* 4 March 1957; *d* of John and Jean Risebrow; *m* 1979, Ian James Homer; three *d*. *Educ:* University Coll. London (LLB). Admitted solicitor, 1980; Lawyer, Reading BC, 1979–82; Solicitor, then Asst Chief Exec., 1982–94, Dir, Corporate Services, 1994–97, Herts CC; Chief Executive: Suffolk CC, 1998–2002; Birmingham CC, 2002–05; Dir Gen., Immigration and Nationality, then Chief Exec., Border and Immigration Agency, later UK Border Agency, Home Office, 2005–11; Permanent Sec., DfT, 2011–12. Public Interest Mem., ICAS, 2017–; Mem. Bd, Harwich Haven Authy, 2019–. Mem. Council, Birmingham Univ., 2016–. Trustee and Mem. Bd, Centre for Ageing Better, 2016–; Gov., Nuffield Health, 2019–. DUniv Birmingham, 2010. *Recreations:* ski-ing, alpine walking, gardening.

**HOMMEN, Johannes Henricus Maria, (Jan);** Chief Executive Officer: ING Group, 2009–13 (Member, 2005–09, Chairman, 2008–09, Supervisory Board); KPMG Nederland, 2014–15; *b* 29 April 1943; *s* of Joseph Hommen and Johanna van Herpen; *m* 1969, Gertrudis, (Tucke), van Enschot; two *s* two *d*. *Educ:* St Jans Lyceum, Gymnasium B, Den

Bosch; Univ. of Tilburg (Business 1970). Controller, Lips Aluminium, 1970–74; Financial Dir, Alcoa Nederland, 1974–78; Alcoa, USA: Asst Treas., 1978–86, Vice Pres. Treas., 1986–91; Exec. Vice Pres. and Chief Financial Officer, 1991–97; Philips Electronics: Chief Financial Officer, Netherlands, 1997–2005; Vice Chm., 2002–05; Chm., Reed Elsevier, 2005–09. Chairman, Supervisory Board: Academic Hosp., Maastricht, 2001–09; TNT, 2005–09; Tias Nimbas Business Sch., Univ. of Tilburg, 2005–09 (Chm., Bd of Trustees, 2013–); Brabantse Ontwikkelings Maatschappij, 2013–17; United World Coll. Nederland, 2016–; Member, Supervisory Board: Ahold Delhaize (formerly Ahold), 2003–07, 2013– (Chm., Bd of Trustees, 2013–17; Vice Chm., 2016–); Campina, until 2009; Operating Partner, Advent Internat. Inc., 2016–. Commander, Orde van Oranje Nassau (Netherlands), 2013. *Recreations:* golf, tennis, swimming, reading, music, chess. *Address:* Hondsbergselaan 14, 5062 JS Oisterwijk, Netherlands.

**HONDERICH, Prof. Edgar Dawn Ross, (Ted),** PhD; Grote Professor of the Philosophy of Mind and Logic, University College London, 1988–98, now Emeritus; Chairman, Royal Institute of Philosophy, 2006–11; *b* 30 Jan. 1933; *s* of John William Honderich and Rae Laura Armstrong, Baden, Canada; *m* 1st, 1964, Pauline Ann Marina Goodwin (marr. diss. 1972), *d* of Paul Fawcett Goodwin and Lena Payne, Kildare; one *s* one *d*; 2nd, 1989, Jane Elizabeth O'Grady (marr. diss. 1998), *d* of Major Robert O'Grady and Hon. Joan Ramsbotham, Bath; 3rd, 2003, Ingrid Coggin Purkiss, *d* of Maurice Edward Henry Coggin and Eleonora Illeris, Cambridge. *Educ:* Kitchener Sch., Kitchener, Canada; Lawrence Park Sch., Toronto; University Coll., Univ. of Toronto (BA 1959); University Coll. London (PhD 1968). Literary Editor, Toronto Star, 1957–59; Lectr in Phil., Univ. of Sussex, 1962–64; Lectr in Phil., 1964–73, Reader in Phil., 1973–83, Prof. of Phil., 1983–88, and Head of Dept of Philosophy, 1988–93, UCL; Chm., Bd of Phil Studies, Univ. of London, 1986–89. Vis. Prof., Yale Univ., and CUNY, 1970. Editor: Internat. Library of Philosophy and Scientific Method, 1966–98; Penguin philosophy books, 1967–98; The Arguments of the Philosophers, 1968–98; The Problems of Philosophy: their past and present, 1984–98; radio, television, journalism. *Publications:* Punishment: the supposed justifications, 1969, 5th edn as Punishment: the supposed justifications reconsidered, 2005; (ed) Essays on Freedom of Action, 1973; (ed) Social Ends and Political Means, 1976; (ed with Myles Burnyeat) Philosophy As It Is, 1979; Violence for Equality: inquiries in political philosophy (incorporating Three Essays on Political Violence, 1976), 1980, 3rd edn as Terrorism for Humanity: inquiries in political philosophy, 2003; (ed) Philosophy Through Its Past, 1984; (ed) Morality and Objectivity, 1985; A Theory of Determinism: the mind, neuroscience, and life-hopes, 1988, 2nd edn, as The Consequences of Determinism, 1990; Mind and Brain, 1990; Conservatism, 1990, revd edn as Conservatism: Burke, Nozick, Bush, Blair?, 2005; How Free Are You? The Determinism Problem, 1993, 2nd edn 2002 (trans. German, Japanese, Chinese, Swedish, Italian, Polish, Romanian, French, Spanish); (ed) The Oxford Companion to Philosophy, 1995, new edn 2005; Philosopher: a kind of life, 2000; After the Terror, 2002, 2nd edn 2003; Political Means and Social Ends: collected papers, 2003; On Consciousness: collected papers, 2004; On Determinism and Freedom: collected papers, 2005; Humanity, Terrorism, Terrorist War (USA edn as Right and Wrong, and Palestine, 9/11, Iraq, 7/7...), 2006; Radical Externalism: Honderich's Theory of Consciousness discussed, ed Anthony Freeman, 2006; Actual Consciousness, 2014; (ed) Philosophers of Our Times: Royal Institute of Philosophy annual lectures, 2014; Mind: your consciousness is what? where?, 2017; *relevant publication:* Ted Honderich on Consciousness, Determinism, and Humanity, ed. Prof. D. Caruso, 2018; phil articles in Amer. Phil Qly, Analysis, Inquiry, Jl of Theoretical Biol., Mind, Phil., Pol Studies, Proc. Aristotelian Soc., Jl of Consciousness Studies, Jl of Ethics, Rechtsphilosophische Hefte, etc. *Recreations:* uxorious daily walk in Highgate or Queen's Wood, wine, inexpensive restaurants. *Address:* 66 Muswell Hill Road, N10 3JR. *T:* (020) 8350 4936. *E:* t.honderich@ucl.ac.uk. *Club:* Garrick.

**HONE, David;** landscape and portrait painter; President, Royal Hibernian Academy of Arts, 1978–83; *b* 14 Dec. 1928; *s* of Joseph Hone and Vera Hone (*née* Brewster); *m* 1962, Rosemary D'Arcy; two *s* one *d*. *Educ:* Baymount School; St Columba's College; University College, Dublin. Studied art at National College of Art, Dublin, and later in Italy. Hon. RA, HRSA (ex-officio). *Recreations:* walking dogs, photography. *Address:* 4 Ailesbury Gardens, Sydney Parade, Dublin 4, Ireland. *T:* (1) 2692809.

**HONE, Michael Stuart,** OBE 1993 (MBE 1978); JP; HM Diplomatic Service, retired; Ambassador and Consul-General, Iceland, 1993–96; *b* 19 May 1936; *s* of William John Hone and Marguerite (*née* Howe); *m* 1st, 1957; three *s*; 2nd, 1983, Dr Elizabeth Ann Balmer; one *s* one *d*. *Educ:* Westham Secondary Sch. Entered RN 1951; joined CRO, 1961; served Kingston, Nairobi, Lisbon, Bridgetown; FCO 1972; served Beirut, Baghdad, Canberra; Resident British Rep., St Vincent and Grenadines; Chief Secretary and Acting Gov., St Helena, 1990. JP Hasting and Rother, 2001. *Recreations:* family, garden. *Address:* Hillcroft, Station Road, Crowhurst, Battle, E Sussex TN33 9DB. *T:* (01424) 830444.

**HONE, His Honour Richard Michael,** QC 1997; a Senior Circuit Judge at the Central Criminal Court, 2005–17; *b* 15 Feb. 1947; *s* of Maj. Gen. Sir Ralph Hone, KCMG, KBE, MC, TD, QC and Sybil Mary Hone (*née* Collins); *m* 1st, Sarah Nicholl-Carne (marr. diss.); two *s*; 2nd, Diana Pavel; two *s*. *Educ:* St Paul's Sch. (Schol.); University Coll., Oxford (MA). Called to the Bar, Middle Temple, 1970 (Bencher, 1994; Cocks' Referee, 1988–94); an Asst Recorder, 1987–91; a Recorder, 1991–2004. Mem., Bar Professional Conduct Cttee, 1993–97; Chm., Jt Regulations Cttee, Inns of Court and Bar, 1995–2000; Legal Mem., Mental Health Review Tribunals, 2000–. Freeman, City of London, 2004; Liveryman, Ironmongers' Co., 2008– (Mem. Ct, 2017–). President: Freemasons' Grand Charity, 2012–16; Masonic Charitable Foundn, 2016–. KStJ 2000 (Asst Dir of Ceremonies, 1996). *Recreations:* wine, travel, fine art. *Address:* 7 Caroline Place Mews, W2 4AQ. *E:* richardhone@btopenworld.com. *Clubs:* Boodle's, Garrick, Pratt's, Beefsteak.

**HONEY, Elizabeth;** *see* Filkin, E. J.

**HONEY, Michael John;** Chief Executive, London Ambulance Service, 1996–2000; *b* 28 Nov. 1941; *s* of Denis Honey and Mary Honey (*née* Henderson); *m* 1967, Katharine Mary Harrison; four *d*; *m* 1996, Elizabeth Filkin, *qv*. *Educ:* Clifton College; Regent Street Polytechnic (DipArch); Columbia Univ. MArch (Urban Design); MSc (City Planning). City Planner, Boston Redevelopment Authority, 1968–70; Corporate Planning Manager, Bor. of Greenwich, 1970–74; Head, Exec. Office, Bor. of Croydon, 1974–80; Chief Executive: Bor. of Richmond upon Thames, 1980–88; LDDC, 1988–90; Gloucestershire CC, 1990–96. *Recreation:* sailing.

**HONEY, Air Vice-Marshal Robert John,** CB 1991; CBE 1987; Air Secretary, 1989–94; *b* 3 Dec. 1936; *s* of F. G. Honey; *m* 1956, Diana Chalmers; one *s* one *d*. *Educ:* Ashford Grammar Sch. Joined RAF as pilot, 1954; served: Germany, 1956–59; Singapore, 1961–64; Canada, 1968–69; India, 1982; UK intervening years; Dep. Commander RAF Germany, 1987–89. Dir, RAF Sports Bd, 1994–2001. Mountaineering expedns to Mulkila, India, 1979, Masherbrum, Pakistan, 1981, Greenland, 1998. *Recreations:* climbing, mountaineering, ski-ing, watercolour painting, croquet.

**HONEY, Sophie Margaret,** MBE 2005; HM Diplomatic Service; Ambassador to Slovenia, since 2015; *b* 18 Nov. 1972; partner, Peter Savizon; one *s* one *d*. *Educ:* Pembroke Coll., Oxford (BA Phys and Philos.); Birkbeck, Univ. of London (MSc Econs). Consultant, Logica plc, 1996–99; joined FCO, 1999; Desk Officer, G8 Team, 1999–2000; Sec. to Cabinet Cttees on Econs and Sci., Cabinet Office, 2000–01; First Sec. (Political and Press), Harare, 2001–04; Hd, Common Foreign and Security Policy Team, Europe Directorate, 2004–05, Private Sec. to Minister for Europe, 2005–07, Dep. Hd, Counter Terrorism Dept, 2007–09, FCO; Hd, Political and Econ. Team, Mexico City, 2009–10; Hd, Near East Gp, FCO, 2010–14; Single Mkt and Financial Services, HM Treasury, 2014–15. *Recreations:* hanging out with my kids, cooking, rollerblading. *Address:* c/o Foreign and Commonwealth Office, King Charles Street, SW1A 2AH.

**HONEYBALL, Mary;** writer and commentator; Member (Lab) London Region, European Parliament, Jan. 2000–2019; *b* 12 Nov. 1952; *d* of Stanley James Honeyball and Betty Gath Honeyball (*née* Tandy); *m* 2019, His Honour Inigo Geoffrey Bing, *qv*. *Educ:* Pate's Grammar Sch. for Girls, Cheltenham; Somerville Coll., Oxford (MA). Admin. Officer, GLC, 1975–77; Negotiations Officer, Soc. of Civil and Public Servants, 1977–83; Political Organiser, RACS, 1983–85; Gen. Sec., Newham Voluntary Agencies Council, 1986–90; Chief Exec., Gingerbread Lone Parents' Charity, 1992–94; Gen. Sec., Assoc. of Chief Officers of Probation, 1994–98; Chief Exec., Nat. Childbirth Trust, 1999–2000. Mem. (Lab) Barnet LBC, 1978–86. FRSA. Governor: Grahame Park Comprehensive Sch., London NW, 1978–84; Sir Francis Drake Primary Sch., SE8, 1986–90; Deptford Green Comprehensive Sch., SE8, 1986–90. *Recreations:* modern fiction, art. *E:* maryhoneyball@gmail.com. *Club:* Reform.

**HONEYBORNE, James Christopher;** Creative Director, Freeborne Media Ltd, since 2019; *b* Bristol, 7 Aug. 1970; *s* of Christopher Honeyborne and Veronica Honeyborne; *m* 2016, Renée Godfrey; two *s* one *d*. *Educ:* Ampleforth Coll.; Univ. of Newcastle upon Tyne (1st Cl. BSc Hons Biol. of Plants and Animals 1992). BBC Natural Hist. Unit, 1993–2019: Producer and Dir, 1999–2007; Series Producer, 2008–13; Exec. Producer, 2013–19; major productions include: Wildlife on One, 2001–04; Meerkats the Movie, 2007; Africa, 2013; Big Blue Live, 2015; Blue Planet II, 2017. *Publications:* (jtly) Blue Planet II, 2017. *Recreations:* freediver, photographer, forager, beachcomber. *Address:* Freeborne Media Ltd, Hartwell House, 55–61 Victoria Street, Bristol BS1 6AD. *E:* james@freebornemedia.com.

**HONOUR, Simon John Langdale B.;** *see* Buck-Honour.

**HONYWOOD, Sir Filmer (Courtenay William),** 11th Bt *cr* 1660; FRICS; Regional Surveyor and Valuer, South Eastern Region, Central Electricity Generating Board, 1978–88; *b* 20 May 1930; *s* of Col Sir William Wynne Honywood, 10th Bt, MC, and Maud Naylor (*d* 1953), *d* of William Hodgson Wilson, Hexgreave Park, Southwell, Notts; *S* father, 1982; *m* 1956, Elizabeth Margaret Mary Cynthia (*d* 1996), *d* of Sir Alastair George Lionel Joseph Miller of Glenlee, 6th Bt; two *s* two *d*. *Educ:* Downside; RMA Sandhurst; Royal Agricultural College, Cirencester (MRAC Diploma). Served 3rd Carabiniers (Prince of Wales' Dragoon Guards). Farmed, 1954–64 (Suffolk Co. Dairy Herd Prodn Awards, 1955 and 1956); joined Agricl Land Service, MAFF, Maidstone, 1964; Asst Land Comr, 1966; Surveyor, Cockermouth, Cumbria, 1973–74; Senior Lands Officer, South Eastern Region, CEGB, 1974–78; pt time Sen. Valuer, Inland Revenue Valuation Service, Folkestone, 1989–90. Consultant on agricultural compensation/restoration, UK Nirex Ltd, 1988–90; Land Agency consultant, Nuclear Electric plc, 1993–94. Examiner in Agriculture: Incorporated Soc. of Estates & Wayleaves Officers, 1989–95; Soc. of Surveying Technicians, 1996–97. *Heir:* *s* Rupert Anthony Honywood, *b* 2 March 1957. *Address:* Greenway Forstal Farmhouse, Hollingbourne, Maidstone, Kent ME17 1QA. *T:* (01622) 880418.

**HOOD,** family name of **Viscounts Bridport** and **Hood**.

**HOOD,** 8th Viscount *cr* 1796, of Whitley, co. Warwick; **Henry Lyttelton Alexander Hood;** Bt 1778; Baron (Ire.) 1782, GB 1795; Partner, Hunters, Solicitors, since 1991; a Lord in Waiting to the Queen, since 2008; *b* 16 March 1958; *e s* of 7th Viscount Hood and Diana Maud Hood, CVO (*née* Lyttelton); *S* father, 1999; *m* 1991, Flora, *yr d* of Comdr M. B. Casement, OBE, RN; three *s* two *d* (of whom one *s* one *d* are twins). *Educ:* Edinburgh Univ. (MA 1981). Qualified as solicitor, 1987. *Heir:* *s* Hon. Archibald, (Archie), Lyttelton Samuel Hood, *b* 16 May 1993.

**HOOD, Prof. Christopher Cropper,** CBE 2011; DLitt; FBA 1996; FAcSS; Gladstone Professor of Government, Oxford University, 2001–14, now Emeritus; Fellow of All Souls College, Oxford, 2001–14, now Emeritus; *b* 5 March 1947; *s* of David White Hood and Margaret Cropper; *m* 1979, Gillian Thackway White; two *d*. *Educ:* Univ. of York (BA 1968; DLitt 1987); Univ. of Glasgow (BLitt 1971). Lectr in Politics, Glasgow Univ., 1972–77 and 1979–86; Res. Fellow, Univ. of York, 1977–79; Prof. of Govt and Public Administration, Univ. of Sydney, 1986–89; Prof. of Public Admin and Public Policy, LSE, 1989–2000. Chair, Politics and Internat. Relations Section, British Acad., 2002–05. Chm., Wkg Party on Personalised Medicine, Nuffield Council on Bioethics, 2008–10. Vis. Res. Fellow, Zentrum für interdisziplinäre Forschung, Univ. of Bielefeld, 1982 and 1989; Sen. Teaching Fellow, Nat. Univ. of Singapore, 1984–85; Fellow, US Nat. Acad. of Public Administration, 2010–; Professorial Fellow, ESRC, 2011–14. FAcSS (AcSS 2001). Hon. Dr Erasmus, Rotterdam, 2017. *Publications:* Limits of Administration, 1976; (ed jtly) Big Government in Hard Times, 1981; (with A. Dunsire) Bureaumetrics, 1981; The Tools of Government, 1983; Administrative Analysis, 1986; (ed jtly) Delivering Public Services in Western Europe, 1988; (with A. Dunsire) Cutback Management in Public Bureaucracies, 1989; (with M. W. Jackson) Administrative Argument, 1991; Explaining Economic Policy Reversals, 1994; (ed jtly) Rewards at the Top, 1994; The Art of the State, 1998; (with C. Scott *et al*) Regulation inside Government, 1999; (jtly) Telecommunications Regulation, 1999; (with Henry Rothstein and Robert Baldwin) The Government of Risk: understanding risk regulation regimes, 2001; (ed jtly) Rewards at the Top: Asian and Pacific Rim states, 2003; (ed jtly) Controlling Modern Government, 2004; (with Martin Lodge) Politics of Public Service Bargains, 2006; (ed with David Heald) Transparency: the key to better governance?, 2006; (with H. Margetts) The Tools of Government in the Digital Age, 2007; The Blame Game, 2011; (ed jtly) Forging a Discipline, 2014; (ed jtly) When the Party's Over: the politics of fiscal squeeze in perspective, 2014; (with R. Dixon) A Government that Worked Better and Cost Less?, 2015; (with R. Himaz) A Century of Fiscal Squeeze Politics: 100 years of austerity, politics and bureaucracy in Britain, 2017. *Address:* All Souls College, Oxford OX1 4AL. *T:* (01865) 279379. *W:* www.christopherhood.net.

**HOOD, Very Rev. (Elizabeth) Lorna,** OBE 2017; Minister, Renfrew North, 1979–2016; Chaplain to the Queen in Scotland, since 2008; Moderator of the General Assembly of the Church of Scotland, 2013–14; *b* Irvine, 21 April 1953; *d* of James Mitchell and Elizabeth Mitchell (*née* Sharpe); *m* 1979, Peter Hood; one *s* one *d*. *Educ:* Glasgow University (MA 1974; BD Hons 1977). Ordained Minister, C of S, 1978; Moderator, Paisley Presbytery, 1995–96; Nominations Convenor, Church of Scotland, Renfrew North, 1996–99; Vice-Convenor: Bd of Ministry, 2005–06; Assembly Arrangements Cttee, 2010–13. Mem., Bd of Studies, Inst. of Counselling, Glasgow, 2000–16. Gen. Trustee, C of S, 2001–18; Trustee: Hope Trust, 2010–; C of S Trust, 2015–; Chair: Scottish Bd, Remembering Srebrenica UK, 2015–; YouthLink Scotland, 2016–. Hon. DD Glasgow, 2014. Point of Light Award, 2015. *Recreations:* golf, reading, travel. *Address:* 4 Thornly Park Drive, Paisley PA2 7RR.

**HOOD, Sir John (Antony),** KNZM 2014; PhD; President and Chief Executive, Robertson Foundation, since 2010; Chair, Rhodes Trust, since 2011. *Educ:* Westlake Boys' High Sch., Auckland; Univ. of Auckland (BE; PhD 1976); Worcester Coll., Oxford (Rhodes Schol. 1976; MPhil 1978). With Fletcher Hldgs, subseq. Fletcher Challenge, Ltd, 1979–97: Head, Fletcher Challenge Paper, Fletcher Challenge Building, then Fletcher Construction Co.; Vice-Chancellor: Univ. of Auckland, 1999–2004; Univ. of Oxford, 2004–09. Formerly: Chm., Tonkin and Taylor Ltd; Director: ASB Bank Ltd; Fonterra Co-operative Gp Ltd; BG Gp plc, 2007–; Study Gp Pty Ltd, 2011–; Matakina Ltd; WPP plc, 2014–; Chairman: Urenco, 2012–; BMT Gp, 2015–. Gov., NZ Sports Foundn. Hon. Dr Beida, 2005; Hon. LLD: Auckland, 2004; UBC, 2006; Hon. PhD (Business Admin) Korea, 2008. Sir Peter Blake Medal, 2009.

**HOOD, Sir John Joseph Harold,** 3rd Bt *cr* 1922, of Wimbledon, Co. Surrey; *b* 27 Aug. 1952; *e s* of Sir Harold Joseph Hood, 2nd Bt and Hon. Ferelith Rosemary Florence Kenworthy, *o d* of 10th Baron Strabolgi; *S* father 2005, but his name does not appear on the Official Roll of the Baronetage.

**HOOD, Very Rev. Lorna;** *see* Hood, Very Rev. E. L.

**HOOD, (Martin) Sinclair (Frankland),** FSA; FBA 1983; archaeologist; *b* 31 Jan. 1917; *s* of late Lt-Comdr Martin Hood, RN, and late Mrs Martin Hood, New York; *m* 1957, Rachel Simmons (*d* 2016); one *s* two *d*. *Educ:* Harrow; Magdalen Coll., Oxford. FSA 1953. British Sch. at Athens: student, 1947–48 and 1951–53; Asst Dir, 1949–51; Dir, 1954–62; Vice-Pres., 1996–. Student, British Inst. Archaeology, Ankara, 1949–48. Geddes-Harrower Vis. Prof. of Greek Art and Archaeology, Univ. of Aberdeen, 1968. Took part in excavations at: Dorchester, Oxon, 1937; Compton, Berks, 1946–47; Southwark, 1946; Smyrna, 1948–49; Atchana, 1949–50; Sakca-Gozu, 1950; Mycenae, 1950–52; Knossos, 1950–51, 1953–55, 1957–61, 1973 and 1987; Jericho, 1952; Chios, 1952–55. Hon. Dr, Univ. of Athens, 2000. *Publications:* The Home of the Heroes: The Aegean before the Greeks, 1967; The Minoans, 1971; The Arts in Prehistoric Greece, 1978; various excavation reports and articles. *Address:* The Old Vicarage, Great Milton, Oxford OX44 7PB. *T:* (01844) 279202. *Club:* Athenæum.

**HOOD, Nicholas;** *see* Hood, W. N.

**HOOD, Peter Charles Freeman G.;** *see* Gregory-Hood.

**HOOD, Prof. Roger Grahame,** CBE 1995; DCL; FBA 1992; Professor of Criminology, 1996–2003, and Director of the Centre for Criminological Research, 1973–2003, University of Oxford; Fellow of All Souls College, Oxford, 1973–2003, now Emeritus; *b* 12 June 1936; 2nd *s* of Ronald and Phyllis Hood; *m* 1963, Barbara Blaine Young (marr. diss. 1985); one *d*; *m* 1985, Nancy Stebbing (*née* Lynah) (*d* 2019). *Educ:* King Edward's Sch., Five Ways, Birmingham; LSE (BSc Sociology); Downing Coll., Cambridge (PhD); DCL Oxon 1999. Research Officer, LSE, 1961–63; Lectr in Social Admin, Univ. of Durham, 1963–67; Asst Dir of Research, Inst. of Criminology, Univ. of Cambridge, 1967–73; Fellow of Clare Hall, Cambridge, 1969–73; Reader in Criminology, Oxford Univ., 1973–96; Sub-Warden, All Souls Coll., Oxford, 1994–96. Vis. Prof., Univ. of Virginia Sch. of Law, 1980–90, and 2005–11; Dist. Vis. Prof., Univ. of Hong Kong, 2003–04; Adjunct Prof., City Univ., Hong Kong, 2008–11. Expert Consultant, UN, on death penalty, 1988, 1995–96, 2000 and 2005. Member: Parole Bd, 1972–73; SSRC Cttee on Social Sciences and the Law, 1975–79; Judicial Studies Bd, 1979–85; Parole System Review, 1987–88; Foreign Secretary's Death Penalty Expert Gp (formerly Panel), 1998–2015. Pres., British Soc. of Criminology, 1986–89. Hon. QC 2000. Hon. LLD: Birmingham, 2008; Edinburgh Napier, 2011. Sellin-Glueck Award, Amer. Soc. of Criminology, 1986; Cesare Beccaria Medal, Internat. Soc. of Social Defence and for a Humane Criminal Policy, 2011; Eur. Criminology Award, Eur. Soc. of Criminology, 2012. *Publications:* Sentencing in Magistrates' Courts, 1962; Borstal Re-assessed, 1965; (with Richard Sparks) Key Issues in Criminology, 1970; Sentencing the Motoring Offender, 1972; (ed) Crime, Criminology and Public Policy: Essays in Honour of Sir Leon Radzinowicz, 1974; (with Sir Leon Radzinowicz) Criminology and the Administration of Criminal Justice: a bibliography, 1976; (with Sir Leon Radzinowicz) A History of English Criminal Law, vol. 5, The Emergence of Penal Policy, 1986; The Death Penalty: a world-wide perspective, 1989, 5th edn (with Carolyn Hoyle) 2015; Race and Sentencing, 1992; (with Stephen Shute) The Parole System at Work, 2000; (with Martina Fielzer) Differences or Discrimination?, 2004; (with Stephen Shute and Florence Seemungal) A Fair Hearing?: ethnic minorities in the Criminal Court, 2005; (with Florence Seemungal) A Rare and Arbitrary Fate, 2006; (jtly) A Penalty without Legitimacy, 2009; (jtly) Public Opinion on the Mandatory Death Penalty in Trinidad, 2011; Enhancing EU Action on the Death Penalty in Asia, 2012; The Death Penalty in Malaysia, 2013; (ed with Surya Deva) Confronting Capital Punishment in Asia: human rights, politics and public opinion, 2013; contribs to ed vols on the death penalty. *Address:* 36 The Stream Edge, Fisher Row, Oxford OX1 1HT. *T:* (01865) 243140, 07528 116429. *E:* roger.hood@all-souls.ox.ac.uk.

**HOOD, Sinclair;** *see* Hood, M. S. F.

**HOOD, Susan Elizabeth A.;** *see* Acland-Hood.

**HOOD, (William) Nicholas,** CVO 2012; CBE 1991; Chairman: Wessex Water Authority, 1987–89; Wessex Water plc, 1989–99; *b* 3 Dec. 1935; *s* of Sir Tom Hood, KBE, CB, TD and of Joan, *d* of Richmond P. Hellyar; *m* 1st, 1963, Angela Robinson (marr. diss. 1990); one *s* one *d*; 2nd, 1994, Ann E. H. Reynolds (marr. diss. 2003); 3rd, 2007, Patricia Lang. *Educ:* Clifton Coll. FIWEM 1992. Served DCLI, 1955–57. NEM General Insce Assoc. Ltd and Credit Insce Assoc. Ltd, 1958–64; G. B. Britton UK Ltd, eventually Sales and Marketing Dir, 1964–70; UBM Gp Plc, eventually Dir of Central Reg., 1970–84; Man. Dir, UBM Overseas Ltd, 1972–82; Dir, HAT Gp Ltd, 1984–86. Director: Bremhill Industries Plc, 1987–93; Winterthur Life UK (formerly Provident Life Assoc.) Ltd, 1988–2007 (Chm., 2002–07); Western Adv. Bd, Nat. Westminster Bank, 1990–92; CU Environmental Trust Plc, 1992–98; APV plc, 1994–97; QHIT plc, 1998–2003; Brewin Dolphin plc, 2000–12 (Dep. Chm., 2005–12); Dep. Chm., Azurix, 1998–99; Chairman: MHIT plc, 1998–2003; Frogmat Ltd, 2001–09; Mem., Strategic Adv. Bd, First Gp, 2005–. Dep. Chm., BITC, 1999–2007. Mem., DTI/DoE Adv. Cttee on Business and the Envmt, 1991–93. Chm., Water Aid Council, 1990–95; Chm., Water Services Assoc., 1995; Pres., IWSA, 1997–99 (Vice-Pres., 1993–97); Life Vice-Pres., Internat. Water Assoc., 2001; Hon. Life Vice-Pres., Amer. Waterworks Assoc., 1996; Member: Water Trng Council, 1987–99; Foundn for Water Res., 1989–99; Sustainability South West, 2000–02. Director: Harbourside Centre, 1996–99; Harbourside Foundn, 1998–2001; Clifton College Services Ltd, 2000–14; Royal United Hosp., Bath, 2012–17. Chairman: Bristol 2000, 1995–98; At-Bristol, 1998–2001 (Life Pres., 2002). Mem., Prince of Wales Council for Duchy of Cornwall, 1993–2011. Chm. Trustees, Penny Brohn Cancer Centre (formerly Bristol Cancer Help Centre), 2000–07; Trustee, West Country Rivers, 2000–16; Chm., Walk the Walk, 2006–13. Dir, West of England Philharmonic Orch., 2003–07. Gov., Merchants' Acad., 2010–17. Master, Soc. of Merchant Venturers, 2007–08. CCMI (CBIM 1990). Hon. MBA UWE, 2002. *Recreations:* fishing, painting. *Address:* One Queen's Parade, Bath BA1 2NJ. *T:* (01225) 334423. *Clubs:* Army and Navy, Boodle's, MCC.

**HOODLESS, Donald Bentley,** OBE 2005; Chairman, Northern Ireland Housing Executive, 2012–16; *b* 14 Oct. 1942; *s* of Ernest William Hoodless and Rosina Mary Hoodless; *m* 1965, Elisabeth Marian Anne Frost Plummer (*see* Dame E. M. A. F. Hoodless); two *s*. *Educ:* Univ. of Durham (BA Hons Econs 1964); Central London Poly. (Dip. Public Admin London Univ. 1968). FCIH 1997. Dir, Circle 33 Housing Trust, 1975–86; Chief Executive: Notting Hill Housing Trust, 1986–93; Circle 33 Housing Trust, 1993–2005. Chm., Skills for Care, 2005–08; Member Board: Housing Corp., 2005–08; Tenant Services Authy, 2008–12. Chm., Royal Nat. Orthopaedic Hosp., 2002–10. Mem. (Lab), Islington LBC, 1968–82 (Leader, 1982). *Recreations:* golf, Arsenal Football Club, reading. *Address:* 10 Eclipse Building, 26 Laycock Street, N1 1AH. *T:* and *Fax:* (020) 7359 0231. *E:* donald@hoodless.org. *Club:* Highgate Golf.

**HOODLESS, Dame Elisabeth (Anne Marian Frost),** DBE 2004 (CBE 1992); Executive Director, Community Service Volunteers, 1986–2011; *b* 11 Feb. 1941; *d* of late Raymond Evelyn Plummer, TD and Maureen Grace Plummer (*née* Frost); *m* 1965, Donald Bentley Hoodless, *qv*; two *s*. *Educ:* Redland High Sch., Bristol; Univ. of Durham (BA (Social Studies) 1962); LSE (DASS, CQSW 1963). Asst Dir, 1963–75, Dep. Dir, 1975–86, CSV. Churchill Fellow, consultant to US Govt VISTA (Volunteers in Service to America) prog., 1966; Commonwealth Youth Fellow, consultant to Govt of Jamaica, Nat. Youth Service prog., 1974. Mem. (Lab) London Borough of Islington, 1964–68. Dep. Chm., Speaker's Commn on Citizenship, 1987–90; Member: Personal Social Services Council, 1973–80; DoH Wkg Gp on Volunteering in the NHS, 1994–96; Sec. of State's Adv. Gp on Citizenship Educn, 1997–98. Member: IBM Community Adv. Bd, 1988–91; Bd, Innovations in Civic Participation, USA, 2001–11 (Vice-Chm., 2006–11); Bd, Attend (formerly Nat. Assoc. of Hosp. and Community Friends), 2002–06 (Vice Pres., 2006–). Pres., Volonteurope (European Network of Volunteer Agencies), 1988–2011; Chairman: Nat. Network of Volunteer Involving Agencies, 2004–11; Internat. Assoc. for Nat. Youth Service, 2007–11. Trustee, UK Disasters Emergency Appeal, 2010–12. Freeman, City of London, 1992. JP Inner London Youth Courts, 1969–2011 (Chm.). Chm. Govs, Barnsbury Sch. for Girls, 1971–89; Governor: Reeves Foundn, 1981–2003; Redland High Sch., 2011–16. DUniv Sheffield Hallam, 2004. *Publications:* Getting Money from Central Government, 1981; Managing Innovation, 1997; (contrib.) Any Volunteers for a Good Society, 2002; Citoyenneté active: intégrer la théorie à la pratique par le volontariat, 2002; Senior Volunteers: solutions waiting to happen, 2003. *Recreations:* grandchildren, growing orchids, ballet, shopping. *Address:* 10 The Eclipse Building, 26 Laycock Street, N1 1AH. *T:* (020) 7359 0231. *E:* donald@hoodless.org.

**HOOK, Prof. Andrew Dunnet,** PhD; FBA 2002; FRSE; Bradley Professor of English Literature, University of Glasgow, 1979–98, now Professor Emeritus; *b* 21 Dec. 1932; *s* of Wilfred Thomas Hook and Jessie Hook (*née* Dunnet); *m* 1966, Judith Ann Hibberd (*d* 1984); one *s* (and one *s* one *d* decd). *Educ:* Univ. of Edinburgh (MA 1st Cl. Hons 1954); Princeton Univ. (PhD 1960). Asst Lectr in English Lit., 1961–63, Lectr in American Lit., 1963–71, Univ. of Edinburgh; Sen. Lectr in English, Univ. of Aberdeen, 1971–79. Vis. Fellow, Dept of English, Princeton Univ., 1999–2000; Gillespie Vis. Prof., Coll. of Wooster, Ohio, 2001–02; Visiting Professor: Dartmouth Coll., 2003, 2006, 2007; Univ. of St Thomas, St Paul, Minnesota, 2005. FRSE 2000. *Publications:* (ed) Scott: Waverley, 1972; (ed with J. Hook) Charlotte Bronte: Shirley, 1974; (ed) John Dos Passos: Twentieth Century Views, 1974; Scotland and America: a study of cultural relations 1750–1835, 1975, 2nd edn 2008; American Literature in Context 1865–1900, 1983, 2nd edn 2016; (ed) History of Scottish Literature 1660–1800, 1987; Scott Fitzgerald, 1992; (ed with R. Sher) The Glasgow Enlightenment, 1995; From Goosecreek to Gandercleugh: studies in Scottish-American literary and cultural history, 1999; (ed with D. Mackenzie) Scott: The Fair Maid of Perth, 1999; F. Scott Fitzgerald: a literary life, 2002; (ed with C. Elliott) Francis Jeffrey's American Journal: New York to Washington 1813, 2011; (ed) Eliza Oddy: A Mississippi Diary from St Paul, Minnesota to Alton, Illinois, October 1894 to May 1895, 2013. *Recreations:* golf, watching sport on TV. *Address:* 5 Rosslyn Terrace, Glasgow G12 9NB. *T:* (0141) 334 0113. *E:* nassau@palio2.vianw.co.uk.

**HOOK, David Morgan Alfred,** FREng; Partner, 1963–93, Managing Director, 1984–88, Deputy Chairman, 1989–90, G. Maunsell & Partners; *b* 16 April 1931; *m* 1957, Winifred (*née* Brown); two *s* one *d*. *Educ:* Bancroft's School; Queens' College, Cambridge (MA). FICE, FIStructE; FREng (FEng 1985). Holland & Hannen and Cubitts, 1954–58; Nuclear Civil Constructors, 1958–62; G. Maunsell & Partners (Consulting Engineers), 1962–93. Liveryman, Engineers' Co., 1985. *Publications:* papers in Jl of IStructE. *Recreations:* golf, bowls, bridge. *Club:* Oxford and Cambridge.

**HOOK, Neil Kenneth,** MVO 1983; HM Diplomatic Service, retired; Consul-General, Osaka, 2001–05; UK Commissioner-General, Expo 2005; *b* 24 April 1945; *s* of George Edward Hook and Winifred Lucy Hook (*née* Werrell); *m* 1973, Pauline Ann Hamilton; one *s* one *d*. *Educ:* Varndean Grammar Sch., Brighton; Sheffield Univ. (Dip. Management Studies). Joined Diplomatic Service, 1968; served FCO, Moscow, Tokyo; Dhaka, 1980–83; S Africa Dept, FCO, 1984; S Asia Dept, FCO, 1985–86; Tokyo, 1987–92; N America Dept, FCO, 1993–95; Ambassador to Turkmenistan, 1995–98; FCO, 1998–99; High Comr, Swaziland, 1999–2001. *Recreations:* ballads, bridge, Hash House Harriers, photography, walking.

**HOOKEM, Michael;** Member (UK Ind) Yorkshire and the Humber Region, European Parliament, 2014–19; *b* Hull, 9 Oct. 1953. Served RAF, 1970–74; Commando Engr, RE, 1980–89; Property Manager, Residential Property Gp Ltd, 2011–13. Dep. Leader, UKIP, 2018–19. Dep. Whip, 2016–17, Co-ordinator, Cttee on Fisheries, 2016–18, Hd, UK Delegn, 2018, Europe of Freedom and Direct Democracy Gp, European Parlt. Chm., Yorks and N Lincs Regl Cttee, UKIP, 2012–14. Contested (UK Ind): Kingston upon Hull E, 2010; Wentworth and Dearne, 2015; Great Grimsby, 2017; Yorks and the Humber Reg., EP, 2019.

**HOOKER, Prof. Morna Dorothy,** DD; Lady Margaret's Professor of Divinity, University of Cambridge, 1976–98; Fellow of Robinson College, Cambridge, since 1976; *b* 19 May 1931; *d* of Percy Francis Hooker, FIA, and Lily (*née* Riley); *m* 1978, Rev. Dr W. David Stacey, MA (*d* 1993); one step *s* two step *d*. *Educ:* Univ. of Bristol (research schol.; MA 1956); Univ. of Manchester (research studentship; PhD 1966); MA Oxford 1970 and Cambridge 1976; DD Cambridge 1993. Research Fellow, Univ. of Durham, 1959–61; Lectr in New Testament Studies, King's Coll., London, 1961–70; Lectr in Theology, Oxford, and Fellow, Linacre Coll., 1970–76 (Hon. Fellow, 1980); Lectr in Theology, Keble Coll., 1972–76. Visiting Fellow, Clare Hall, Cambridge, 1974; Visiting Professor: McGill Univ., 1968; Duke Univ., 1987 and 1989; York St John Univ., 2007–12. FKC 1979. Lectures: T. W. Manson meml, 1977; A. S. Peake meml, 1978; Henton Davies, 1979; Ethel M. Wood, 1984; James A. Gray, Duke Univ., 1984; W. A. Sanderson, Melbourne, 1986; Didsbury, Manchester, 1988; Brennan, Louisville, 1989; St Paul's, 1989; Perkins, Texas, 1990; Shaffer, Yale, 1995; John Albert Hall, Victoria, BC, 1996; Smyth, Columbia Decatur,

1996; Chuen King, Hong Kong, 2001; Lund, Chicago, 2003; Newell, Anderson Univ., 2006; C. K. Barrett, Durham, 2010; Hugh Price Hughes, Hinde Street Methodist Church, London, 2010; Fernley-Hartley, 2011; Manchester Wesley Res. Centre, 2014. Pres., SNTS, 1988–89. Jt Editor, Jl of Theological Studies, 1985–2005. Hon. Fellow, Westminster Coll., Oxford, 1996. Hon. DLitt Bristol, 1994; Hon. DD Edinburgh, 1997. Burkitt Medal for Biblical Studies, British Acad., 2004. *Publications:* Jesus and the Servant, 1959; The Son of Man in Mark, 1967; (ed jtly) What about the New Testament?, 1975; Pauline Pieces, 1979; Studying the New Testament, 1979; (ed jtly) Paul and Paulinism, 1982; The Message of Mark, 1983; Continuity and Discontinuity, 1986; From Adam to Christ, 1990; A Commentary on the Gospel according to St Mark, 1991; Not Ashamed of the Gospel, 1994; The Signs of a Prophet, 1997; Beginnings, 1997; Paul: a short introduction, 2003; Endings, 2003; (ed) Not in Word Alone, 2003; Paul: a beginner's guide, 2008; The Drama of Mark, 2010; (with Frances Young) Holiness and Mission, 2010; contribs to jls incl. New Testament Studies, Jl of Theological Studies, Theology, Epworth Review, Novum Testamentum, Scottish Jl Theol., Jl for Study of New Testament, Expository Times, Bulletin of John Rylands Liby. *Recreations:* Molinology, walking, music. *Address:* Robinson College, Grange Road, Cambridge CB3 9AN.

**HOOKS, Air Vice-Marshal Robert Keith**, CBE 1979; CEng, FRAeS; RAF retired; *b* 7 Aug. 1929; *s* of late Robert George Hooks and Phyllis Hooks; *m* 1954, Kathleen (*née* Cooper); one *s* one *d*. *Educ*: Acklam Hall Sch.; Constantine Coll., Middlesbrough; BSc(Eng) London. Commnd RAF, 1951; served at RAF stations West Malling, Fassberg, Sylt, 1952–55; RAF Technical Coll., Henlow, 1956; Fairey Aviation Co., 1957–58; Air Ministry, 1958–60; Skybolt Trials Unit, Eglin, Florida, 1961–63; Bomber Command Armament Sch., Wittering, 1963–65; OC Engrg Wing, RAF Coll., Cranwell, 1967–69; HQ Far East Air Force, 1969–71; Supt of Armament A&AEE, 1971–74; Director Ground Training, 1974–76; Director Air Armament, 1976–80; Vice-Pres. (Air), Ordnance Board, 1980; Dir Gen. Aircraft 2, MoD (Procurement Exec.), 1981–84; Divl Dir (European Business), Westland Helicopters, 1984–85; Projects Dir, Helicopter Div., Westland plc, 1985–87. Dep. Man. Dir, E H Industries Ltd, 1987–94. *Address:* 34 Thames Crescent, Maidenhead, Berks SL6 8EY. *Club:* Royal Air Force.

**HOOLE, John George Aldick**; independent curator and researcher; Arts and Culture Worker, Oxford Brookes University, 2003–08; *b* 3 Feb. 1951; *s* of John Aldick Hoole and Pamela Betty Coleman; *m* 1975, Lindsey G. Rushworth; one *s* one *d*. *Educ*: Univ. of East Anglia (BA Hons History of Art). Asst Keeper of Art, Southampton Art Gall., 1974–78; Asst Dir, Museum of Modern Art, Oxford, 1978–82; Curator, Barbican Art Gall., 1982–98; Dir, Barbican Art Galls, 1998–2001. Chair, Chiltern Sculpture Trust, 2003–08. *Publications:* (with Margaret Simons) James Dickson Innes, 1887–1914, 2013. *Recreation:* horticulture. *Address:* 54 Western Road, Oxford OX1 4LG. *T:* (01865) 245268.

**HOOLEY, John Rouse**; DL; Chief Executive, West Sussex County Council, 1975–90; Clerk to the Lieutenancy of West Sussex, 1976–90; *b* 25 June 1927; *s* of Harry and Elsie Hooley; *m* 1953, Gloria Patricia Swanston; three *s* one *d*. *Educ*: William Hulme's Sch., Manchester; Lincoln Coll., Oxford; Manchester Univ. LLB London. Admitted Solicitor (Hons), 1952. Served Lancashire Fusiliers, 1946–48. Asst Solicitor, Chester, Carlisle and Shropshire, 1952–65; Asst Clerk, Cornwall, 1965–67; Dep. Clerk and Dep. Clerk of the Peace, W Sussex, 1967–74; County Sec., W Sussex, 1974–75. Member: Chichester HA, 1990–95 (Chm., 1993–95); W Sussex HA, 1995–96. Chm., Downland Housing Gp, 1990–2003. DL W Sussex, 1991. *Recreations:* reading, music. *Address:* Wellington Grange, Broyle Road, Chichester PO19 6ED.

**HOON, Rt Hon. Geoffrey (William)**; PC 1999; Chairman, OffGrid, since 2018 (non-executive Director, since 2016); Director, CyDefence, since 2017; *b* 6 Dec. 1953; *s* of Ernest and June Hoon; *m* 1981, Elaine Ann Dumelow; one *s* two *d*. *Educ*: Nottingham High Sch.; Jesus College, Cambridge (MA). Called to the Bar, Gray's Inn, 1978. Labourer at furniture factory, 1972–73; Lectr in Law, Leeds Univ., 1976–82. Vis. Prof. of Law, Univ. of Louisville, 1979–80. In practice at Nottingham, 1982–85. MP (Lab) Ashfield, 1992–2010. An Opposition Whip, 1994–95; opposition spokesman on IT, 1995–97; Parly Sec., 1997–98, Minister of State, 1998–99, Lord Chancellor's Dept; Minister of State, FCO, 1999; Sec. of State for Defence, 1999–2005; Lord Privy Seal and Leader of H of C, 2005–06; Minister of State for Europe, FCO, 2006–07; Parly Sec. to HM Treasury (Govt Chief Whip), 2007–08; Sec. of State for Transport, 2008–09. European Parliament: Mem. (Lab) Derbyshire, 1984–94; Mem., Legal Affairs Cttee, 1984–94; President: Standing Delegn to China, 1987–89; Standing Delegn to US, 1989–92. Man. Dir, Internat. Business, AgustaWestland, 2011–17. Chm. and Trustee, Twycross Zoo, 2017–; Chm., Twyford Zool Soc., 2018–. Chm., Friends of Music, 1992–94; Vice-Chm. and Gov., Westminster Foundn, 1994–97. *Recreations:* football, running, cinema, music, cycling.

**HOOPER**, family name of **Baroness Hooper**.

**HOOPER, Baroness** *cr* 1985 (Life Peer), of Liverpool and of St James's in the City of Westminster; **Gloria Dorothy Hooper**, CMG 2002; *b* 25 May 1939; *d* of late Frances and Frederick Hooper. *Educ*: University of Southampton (BA Hons Law); Universidad Central, Quito, Ecuador (Lic. de Derecho Internacional). Admitted to Law Society, Solicitor, 1973; Partner, Taylor and Humbert, subseq. Taylor Garrett, 1974–84. MEP (C) Liverpool, 1979–84; contested (C) Merseyside West, European Parly elecn, 1984. Baroness in Waiting, 1985–87; Parly Under Sec. of State, DES, 1987–88, Dept of Energy, 1988–89, DoH, 1989–92; Dep. Speaker, H of L, 1993–2018. Member: Parly Delegns to Council of Europe and WEU, 1992–97, 2002–08; EU Select Cttee, Sub Cttee B, Internal Market (formerly Sub Cttee on Finance, Econs and Internat. Trade, later Econ. and Financial Affairs), 2009–; Chm., All-Party Parly Gp for Latin America, 2009–15, on Dance, 2017–; Vice Chm., All Party Parly Gp for Japan, 2011–; Vice Chm., British Gp, IPU, 2017– (Mem., Exec. Cttee, 2010–). Chm., Adv. Cttee, UCL Inst. of Americas, 2012–. Pres., Canning House, 1997–2002. Chm., Dance Teachers' Benevolent Fund, 2009–15. FRGS 1982; Fellow, Industry and Parlt Trust, 1983; FRSA 1986. Hon. DLaws Southampton, 2009. Order of Francisco de Miranda (Venezuela); Order of Boyaca Gran Cruz (Colombia); Order of Merit (Ecuador); Order of Bernardo O'Higgens (Chile); Dame, Order of St Gregory the Great (Holy See). *Publications:* Cases on Company Law, 1967; Law of International Trade, 1968. *Recreations:* theatre, walking. *Address:* House of Lords, Westminster, SW1A 0PW. *T:* (020) 7219 3000.

**HOOPER, Rt Hon. Sir Anthony**, Kt 1995; PC 2004; a Lord Justice of Appeal, 2004–12; *b* 16 Sept. 1937; *s* of late Edwin Morris Hooper and Greta Lillian Chissim; *m* 1st, Margrethe Frances (*née* Hansen) (marr. diss. 1986); one *s* one *d*; 2nd, Heather Christine (*née* Randall) (*d* 2005); 3rd, Fiona Mary (*née* Baigrie). *Educ*: Sherborne; Trinity Hall, Cambridge (Scholar; MA, LLB). Hon. Fellow, 2009). 2nd Lieut, 7th RTR, 1956–57. Called to the Bar, Inner Temple, 1965, Bencher, 1993; admitted to Law Society of British Columbia, 1969; QC 1987; a Recorder, 1986–95; a Judge of the High Ct of Justice, QBD, 1995–2004; Presiding Judge, NE Circuit, 1997–2000. Associate Mem., Matrix Chambers, 2013–. Asst Lectr and Lectr, Univ. of Newcastle upon Tyne, 1962–65; Asst and Associate Prof., Faculty of Law, Univ. of British Columbia, 1965–68; Prof. Associé, Univ. de Laval, 1969–70; Prof., Osgoode Hall Law Sch., York Univ., 1971–73. Visiting Professor: Univ. de Montréal, 1972, 1973; Osgoode Hall, 1984; Judicial Fellow and Hon. Prof., UCL, 2012–. Mem., Criminal Procedure Rules Cttee, 2004–12. Chm., Public Concern at Work Whistleblowing Commn, 2013. Pres., British Acad. of Forensic Scis, 2001–03. Chm. Govs, Inns of Court Sch. of Law, 1996–99; Chm., Expert Witness Inst., 2013–17. Gen. Ed., Blackstone's Criminal Practice, 2008–14. *Publications:* (ed) Harris's Criminal Law, 21st edn 1968; articles in legal jls.
*See also* R. Hooper.

**HOOPER, David John**; QC 2010; *b* London, 14 Oct. 1946; *s* of John and Rachel Hooper; *m* 1976, Nicole; one *s*. *Educ*: Highfield Coll., Chertsey; Univ. of Kent; Jesus Coll., Cambridge. Called to the Bar, Middle Temple, 1971; in practice at the Bar, specialising in internat. criminal law. *Recreations:* beer sampling, walking, reading. *Address:* (chambers) 25 Bedford Row, WC1R 4HD. *T:* (020) 7067 1500. *E:* davidhooper@btopenworld.com.

**HOOPER, Lt Gen. Ivan**, CB 2017; Chief Executive Officer, Information Systems and Services, since 2018; *b* Fareham, Hants, 25 Nov. 1963; *s* of Douglas Owen and Roma Rosemary Hooper; *m* 1992, Helen Windybank; two *s*. *Educ*: Saltash Sch.; University Coll. of Wales, Aberystwyth (BSc Econs); Cranfield Univ. (MA). Commnd Army, 1986; on Directing Staff, RMA Sandhurst, 1992–93; in command: 216 (Parachute) Signals Sqdn; 21 (Air Support) Signal Regt, Iraq; JSCSC, 2004–06; Comdr, 1st (UK) Signal Bde, HQ ARRC, 2008–10; Hd, Delivery Team, Battlefield Communications Information Systems, 2010–14; Dir Ops, Inf. Systems and Services, MoD, 2014–17. *Recreations:* mountaineering (Pres., Army Mountaineering Assoc., 2010–), sailing, Cornish Pilot Gig rowing. *Clubs:* Alpine; Royal Signals Yacht (Cdre).

**HOOPER, Rt Rev. Michael Wrenford**; Bishop Suffragan of Ludlow and Archdeacon of Ludlow, 2002–09; Honorary Assistant Bishop, Diocese of Worcester, since 2010; *b* 2 May 1941; *m* 1968, Rosemary Anne Edwards; two *s* two *d*. *Educ*: Crypt Sch., Gloucester; St David's Coll., Lampeter; St Stephen's House, Oxford. Ordained deacon, 1965, priest, 1966; Asst Curate, St Mary Magdalene, Bridgnorth, Shropshire, dio. of Hereford, 1965–70; Vicar of Minsterley and Rector of Habberley, 1970–81; Rural Dean of Pontesbury, 1976–81; Rector and Rural Dean of Leominster, 1981–97; Archdeacon of Hereford, 1997–2002; Prebendary of Hereford Cathedral, 1981–2002. *Recreations:* walking, cycling, dogs, reading, music. *Address:* 6 Avon Drive, Eckington, Pershore WR10 3BU. *T:* (01386) 751589. *E:* bishopmichael@btinternet.com.

**HOOPER, Ven. Paul Denis Gregory**; Archdeacon of Leeds, 2012–16, now Archdeacon Emeritus; *b* Winchester, 24 April 1952; *s* of Robert and Mary Hooper; *m* 1983, Judith Innes Rollison; three *s*. *Educ*: Eastbourne Coll.; Manchester Univ. (BA Town and Country Planning 1975); Wycliffe Hall, Oxford (BA Theology 1980; MA 1985). Sen. Planning Officer, Plymouth City Council, 1975–78; ordained deacon, 1981, priest, 1982; Curate, St George's, Leeds, 1981–84; Youth Officer, 1984–87, Communications Officer, 1987–96, Dio. of Ripon; Chaplain to Bishop of Ripon, 1987–95; Vicar, St Mark's, Harrogate, 1995–2009; Dir of Clergy Develt, Dio. of Ripon and Leeds, 2009–12. Gov., St Aidan's C of E High Sch., Harrogate, 1997–2012. *Publications:* Being Young in an Old Church, 1986. *Recreations:* sailing, hill-walking, music, motor caravanning, civic design, modern literature. *Address:* 9 Fulwith Gate, Harrogate, N Yorks HG2 8HS. *T:* (01423) 550485. *E:* ven.paul.hooper@outlook.com.

**HOOPER, Richard**, CBE 2005; Managing Partner, Hooper Communications, since 1988; *b* 19 Sept. 1939; *s* of late Edwin Morris Hooper and Greta Lillian (*née* Goode); *m* 1964, Meredith Jean Rooney; two *s* one *d*. *Educ*: Sherborne Sch.; Worcester Coll., Oxford (BA German and Russian, 1963; MA). National Service, 2nd Lieut 7th RTR, BAOR, 1958–59. Gen. trainee, BBC, 1963; Radio Producer, BBC Further Educn, 1964–66; Harkness Fellow, USA, 1967–68; Sen. Radio and TV Producer, BBC Open Univ. Prodns, 1969–72; Dir, National Develt Prog. in Computer Assisted Learning, 1973–77; Man. Dir, Mills & Allen Communications, 1978–79; Dir, Prestel, Post Office Telecommunications, 1980–81; Chief Exec., Value Added Systems and Services, BT, 1982–86; Man. Dir, Super Channel, 1986–88. Chm., Radio Authy, 2000–03; Dep. Chm., OFCOM, 2002–05; Chairman: Ind. Review of Postal Services Sector, 2008– (report updated 2010); Broadband Stakeholder Gp, 2010–; Digital Copyright Exchange Feasibility Study, 2011–. Non-exec. Chm., IMS Gp plc, 1997–2002; Chairman: Informa (formerly T & F Informa) plc, 2005–07 (Sen. non-exec. Dir, 1999–2005); Copyright Hub Ltd, 2013–16; non-executive Director: MAI, 1993–96; United News & Media, 1996–97; LLP Gp plc, 1997–98; Informed Sources Internat., 1997–99; Superscape plc, 2000–02; UK eUniversities Worldwide, 2002–04; hibu (formerly Yell Gp) plc, 2006–14 (Sen. Ind. Dir, 2009–); Sen. Ind. Dir, VocaLink Hldgs Ltd, 2008–17; Principal Mentor, Bird & Co. Boardroom and Exec. Mentoring, 2009–. Special Staff Consultant to President Lyndon Johnson's Commn on Instructional Technology, 1968. *Publications:* (ed) Colour in Britain, 1965; (ed) The Curriculum, Context, Design and Development, 1971; Unnatural Monopolies, 1991; contrib. to books and jls. *Recreations:* the family, theatre, golf. *Clubs:* Garrick; Vincent's (Oxford).
*See also* Rt Hon. Sir A. Hooper, T. G. Hooper.

**HOOPER, Susannah Jemima**; *see* Storey, S. J.

**HOOPER, Thomas George**; film director; *b* London, 5 Oct. 1972; *s* of Richard Hooper, *qv*. *Educ*: Highgate Sch.; Westminster Sch.; University Coll., Oxford (BA Hons English Lit.). Director: *films*: Painted Faces (short film), 1992; Red Dust, 2004; The Damned United, 2009; The King's Speech, 2010 (Acad. Award for Best Dir, BAFTA Award (jtly) for Outstanding British Film, Directors Guild of America Award for Outstanding Directing, 2011); Les Misérables, 2012; The Danish Girl, 2015; Cats, 2019; *television*: Quayside, 1996; Byker Grove, 1997; Eastenders, 1997–98; Cold Feet, 1999; Love in a Cold Climate, 2001; Daniel Deronda, 2002; Prime Suspect 6: The Last Witness, 2003; Elizabeth I, 2005 (Emmy Award for Best Dir of a Miniseries, 2006); Longford, 2006; John Adams, 2008; His Dark Materials, 2019. Non-exec. Dir, Channel 4, 2017–. Member: Bd, Directors UK, 2006–07; London Coordinating Cttee, Directors Guild of America, 2010–. Gov., BFI, 2011–18. *Address:* c/o Independent Talent Group, 40 Whitfield Street, W1T 2RH.

**HOOPER, His Honour Toby Julien Anderson**; QC 2000; a Circuit Judge, 2007–16; *b* 14 Dec. 1950; *o s* of Lt Col Denys Anderson Hooper and late Paula Hooper (*née* Glascoe); *m* 1981, Anna, *d* of late Dr Brian Locke, FRCR and of Rachel Locke; one *s* two *d*. *Educ*: Durham Univ. (BA Hons 1972). Called to the Bar, Inner Temple, 1973, Bencher, 2000; in practice at the Bar, 1974–2007; Asst Recorder, 1998–2000; a Recorder, 2000–07. Mem., Parole Bd, 2010–13. Bar Council: Additional Mem., Remuneration Cttee, 1998–2003 (Vice-Chm. (Civil), 2000–03); Mem. (as SE Circuit Rep.), 2000–03; Chm., Pupillage Bd, 2001–03; Mem., General Management Cttee, 2003–05; Mem. (co-opted), Costs Sub-Cttee, Civil Justice Council, 2002–04; Mem., Incorporated Council of Law Reporting, 2004–07. Hon. Sec., Incorp. Inns of Court Mission (Gainsford Youth Club, Covent Garden), 1979–90. Gov., Worcester Sixth Form Coll., 2016–. Trustee, Heart of Mercia Multi-Acad. Trust, 2019–. Hon. Fellow, Univ. of Worcester, 2017. Hon. Freeman, City of Hereford, 2016. *Publications:* (ed) Inner Temple Advocacy Handbook, 1998, 7th edn 2004; (Gen. Ed.) Bar Council Taxation and Retirement Benefits Handbook, 3rd edn 2000, 4th edn 2002; (contrib.) Financial Crime and Corporate Misconduct, 2019. *Recreations:* choral singing, walking.

**HOOTON, His Honour Patrick Jonathan;** a Circuit Judge, 1994–2010; *b* 30 June 1941; *s* of late John Charles Hooton, CMG, MBE, QC (Bermuda) and of Patricia Jessica Hooton (*née* Manning); *m* 1st, 1970, Anne Josephine Wells; one *s*; 2nd, 1980, Jocelyn Margaret East; one *s* one *d*. *Educ:* Downside Sch., Somerset; Trinity Coll., Cambridge. Commonwealth Develt Corp., 1964–68; Van Moppes & Co., 1969–71; called to the Bar, Gray's Inn, 1973; practised on Western Circuit, 1973–94. Mem., Club Taurino, 1994–. *Recreations:* field sports, sailing, ski-ing, Southampton FC and Hampshire CC. *Clubs:* Lawyers' Fishing; Hampshire CC.

**HOPCROFT, George William;** HM Diplomatic Service, retired; consultant on international relations; *b* London, 30 Sept. 1927; *s* of late Frederick Hopcroft and Dorothy Gertrude (*née* Bourne); *m* 1951, Audrey Joan Rodd; three *s* one *d*. *Educ:* Chiswick County Sch. for Boys (sch. 'MP' July 1945); London Univ. (BCom); Brasenose Coll., Oxford; INSEAD, Fontainebleau; Univ. of Miami. Auditor with Wm R. Warner, 1946; entered Export Credits Guarantee Dept, 1946; Asst Trade Comr, Madras, 1953–57; Sen. Credit Underwriter, ECGD, 1957–64; on secondment to HM Treasury, 1964; joined FO, 1965; First Sec. (Commercial), Amman, 1965–69; First Sec. (Econ.), Bonn, 1969–71; First Sec. (Comm.), Kuala Lumpur, 1971–75; FCO, 1975–78; Counsellor (Comm. and Econ.), Bangkok, 1978–81; FCO 1981; Lloyds of London antibiosis underwriter, 1982–92. Founder Mem., Export and Overseas Trade Adv. Panel (EOTAP), 1982–; operational expert in for. affairs, attached to Govt of Belize, 1982–83. Mem., FCO Assoc. *Recreations:* leisure and circumnavigation (Pilot's A Licence, 1956), German and French literature, song, film, sport (Civil Service ½ mile champion, 1947; Venables Bowl for coxless pairs, Amateur Rowing Assoc. of E, Colombo, 1957; double-marathon in 6 hours, 1959 & 1960; Kow Yai sen. marathon, 1979; British Masters Athletic Fedn M80 400m and 800m champion, 2008 and 2009, M85 400m and 800m champion, 2013), serendipity. *Clubs:* Civil Service, Royal Over-Seas League; British (Bangkok).

**HOPE,** family name of **Marquess of Linlithgow,** and of **Barons Glendevon, Hope of Craighead** and **Rankeillour.**

**HOPE OF CRAIGHEAD,** Baron *cr* 1995 (Life Peer), of Banff in the District of Perth and Kinross; **James Arthur David Hope,** KT 2009; PC 1989; FRSE; Deputy President of the Supreme Court of the United Kingdom, 2009–13; Convenor, Cross Bench Peers, House of Lords, 2015–19; *b* 27 June 1938; *s* of late Arthur Henry Cecil Hope, OBE, WS, Edinburgh and Muriel Ann Neilson Hope (*née* Collie); *m* 1966, Katharine Mary Kerr, *d* of W. Mark Kerr, WS, Edinburgh; twin *s* one *d*. *Educ:* Edinburgh Acad.; Rugby Sch.; St John's Coll., Cambridge (Open Schol. 1956, BA 1962, MA 1978; Hon. Fellow, 1995); Edinburgh Univ. (LLB 1965). FRSE 2003. National Service, Seaforth Highlanders, 1957–59 (Lieutenant 1959). Admitted Faculty of Advocates, 1965; Standing Junior Counsel in Scotland to Board of Inland Revenue, 1974–78; Advocate-Depute, 1978–82; QC (Scotland) 1978; Dean, Faculty of Advocates, 1986–89; Lord Justice-Gen. of Scotland and Lord Pres. of Court of Session, 1989–96; a Lord of Appeal in Ordinary, 1996–2009; Second Sen. Law Lord, 2009; Chief Justice, Abu Dhabi Global Mkts Courts, 2015–. Chm., Med. Appeal Tribunal, 1985–86; Legal Chm., Pensions Appeal Tribunal, 1985–86. Mem., Scottish Cttee on Law of Arbitration, 1986–89. HM Lord High Comr to Gen. Assembly of C of S, 2015–16. Mem. Bd of Trustees, Nat. Liby of Scotland, 1989–96. Chm. Bd, Inst. of Advanced Legal Studies, 2000–13. President: Stair Soc., 1993–2013; Internat. Criminal Law Assoc., 2000–13; Commonwealth Magistrates' and Judges' Assoc., 2003–06 (Hon. Life Vice-Pres., 2009). Chm., Sub-Cttee E (Law and Instns), H of L Select Cttee on EU, 1998–2001. Hon. Professor of Law: Aberdeen, 1994–; Strathclyde, 2013– (Chancellor, 1998–2013; Fellow, 2000). Chm., Botanic Cottage Trust, 2009–12. Fellow, Soc. of Writers to the Signet, 2011. Hon. Member: Canadian Bar Assoc., 1987; Soc. of Legal Scholars (formerly SPTL), 1991; Hon. Fellow, Amer. Coll. of Trial Lawyers, 2000. Hon. Bencher: Gray's Inn, 1989; Inn of Court of NI, 1995. Hon. LLD: Aberdeen, 1991; Strathclyde, 1993; Edinburgh, 1995; Glasgow, 2013; BPP, 2014; Abertay, 2014; DUniv Strathclyde, 2013. David Kelbie Award, Inst. Contemporary Scotland, 2007. *Publications:* (ed jtly) Gloag & Henderson's Introduction to the Law of Scotland, 7th edn 1968, asst editor, 8th edn 1980 and 9th edn 1987, (contrib.) 11th edn 2001; (ed jtly) Armour on Valuation for Rating, 4th edn 1971, 5th edn 1985; (with A. G. M. Duncan) The Rent (Scotland) Act 1984, 1986; Lord Hope's Diaries, vols I, II and III, 2018, vols IV and V, 2019; (contrib.) Stair Memorial Encyclopaedia of Scots Law; (contrib.) Court of Session Practice. *Recreations:* walking, ornithology, music. *Address:* 34 India Street, Edinburgh EH3 6HB. *T:* (0131) 225 8245; House of Lords, SW1A 0PW. *Club:* New (Edinburgh).

**HOPE OF THORNES,** Baron *cr* 2005 (Life Peer), of Thornes in the County of West Yorkshire; **Rt Rev. and Rt Hon. David Michael Hope,** KCVO 1995; PC 1991; DPhil; Vicar, St Margaret's, Ilkley, 2005–06; Archbishop of York, 1995–2005; *b* 14 April 1940. *Educ:* Nottingham Univ. (BA Hons Theol); Linacre Coll., Oxford (DPhil; Hon. Fellow, 1993). Curate of St John, Tuebrook, Liverpool, 1965–70; Chaplain, Church of Resurrection, Bucharest, 1967–68; Vicar, St Andrew, Warrington, 1970–74; Principal, St Stephen's House, Oxford, 1974–82; Warden, Community of St Mary the Virgin, Wantage, 1980–87; Vicar of All Saints', Margaret Street, 1982–85; Bishop of Wakefield, 1985–91; Bishop of London, 1991–95. Mem., H of L, 2005–15. Prelate, Order of British Empire, 1991–95; Dean of the Chapels Royal, 1991–95. Hon. DD: Nottingham, 1999; Hull, 2005. *Publications:* The Leonine Sacramentary, 1971; Living the Gospel, 1993; Signs of Hope, 2001; (with Hugh Little) Better to Travel Hopefully, 2007. *Address:* 35 Hammerton Drive, Hellifield, Skipton, N Yorks BD23 4LZ.

**HOPE, Sir Alexander (Archibald Douglas),** 19th Bt *cr* 1628 (NS), of Craighall; OBE 2011; Managing Director, DNEG (formerly Double Negative VFX Ltd), since 1998; *b* London, 16 March 1969; *s* of Sir John Carl Alexander Hope, 18th Bt and of Merle Pringle, *d* of late Robert Douglas; *S* father, 2007; *m* 2002, Emmeline Grace, *d* of Simon H. Barrow; two *s*. *Educ:* Eton; Univ. of Bristol (BSocSc). *Heir: s* William John Hope, *b* 7 March 2004. *E:* alex@dneg.com. *Club:* Soho House.

**HOPE, His Honour Antony Derwin;** a Circuit Judge, 2002–14; *b* 22 Aug. 1944; *s* of John and Lorna Hope; *m* 1979, Heidi Saure; one *s* one *d*. *Educ:* Leighton Park Sch., Reading; Coll. of Estate Mgt (BSc Estate Mgt); Coll. of Law. Called to the Bar, Middle Temple, 1970; in practice as barrister, London and Winchester, 1971–2002; Judge: Bolton Crown Court, 2002–04; Portsmouth Crown Court, 2004–06; Resident Judge, Southampton Crown Court, 2006–14. UK Delegate to Internat. Assoc. of Judges, 2006–11. Hon. Recorder of Southampton, 2008–. *Publications:* The 1990–91 Planning Acts, 1993; Charles Dickens: from Portsmouth to Pickwick, 2012; Charles Dickens: my life story (3 vols), 2018. *Recreations:* cricket, walking, studying history, foreign travel, classic cars, membership of Dickens Fellowship.

**HOPE, Prof. Charles Archibald,** DPhil; Director, and Professor of the History of the Classical Tradition, Warburg Institute, University of London, 2002–10, now Emeritus Professor; *b* 11 April 1945; 2nd *s* of Sir Archibald Philip Hope, 17th Bt, OBE, DFC, AE and of Ruth, *y d* of Carl Davis; *m* 1st, 1977, Jennifer Katharine Hadley (marr. diss.); one *s*; 2nd, 2003, Donatella Sparti; one *d*. *Educ:* Eton; Balliol Coll., Oxford (BA 1967; DPhil 1975); Courtauld Inst., London (MA 1968); MA Cantab 1972. Res. Lectr, Christ Church, Oxford, 1968–72; Jun. Res. Fellow, King's Coll., Cambridge, 1972–76; Warburg Institute: Lectr in Renaissance Studies, 1976–92; Sen. Lectr, 1972–2002; Dep. Dir, 1999–2002. Slade Prof. of Fine Art, Oxford Univ., 1985–86. *Publications:* Masterpieces of Renaissance Painting, 1979; Titian, 1980; (ed) Autobiography of Benvenuto Cellini, 1984; contrib. learned jls. *Address:* Warburg Institute, Woburn Square, WC1H 0AB.

**HOPE, Christopher David Tully,** FRSL; writer; *b* 26 Feb. 1944; *s* of Dennis Tully and Kathleen Mary Hope (*née* McKenna); *m* 1967, Eleanor Klein (marr. diss. 1994); two *s*. *Educ:* Christian Brothers College, Pretoria; Univ. of Natal (BA Hons 1970); Univ. of Witwatersrand (MA 1973). FRSL 1990. Founder and Dir, Franschhoek Literary Fest., S Africa, 2007–10. Writer of libretto, A Distant Drum (play for music), Carnegie Hall, 2014. Co-founder, Fynarts Fest., Hermanus, SA, 2013–. Pringle Prize, English Acad. of Southern Africa, 1972; Cholmondeley Award, Soc. of Authors, 1974; Arts Council Bursary, 1982; Travelex, Travel Writers' Award, 1997. *Publications:* Cape Drives, 1974; A Separate Development, 1981 (David Higham Prize for Fiction); In the Country of the Black Pig, 1981; Private Parts and Other Tales, 1982 (rev. edn as Learning to Fly and Other Tales, 1990) (Internat. PEN Silver Pen Award); Kruger's Alp, 1984 (Whitbread Prize for Fiction); Englishmen, 1985; The Hottentot Room, 1986; Black Swan, 1987; White Boy Running, 1988 (CNA Award, S Africa); My Chocolate Redeemer, 1989; Moscow! Moscow!, 1990; Serenity House, 1992; The Love Songs of Nathan J. Swirsky, 1993; Darkest England, 1996; (ed jtly) New Writing, 1996; Me, the Moon and Elvis Presley, 1997; Signs of the Heart: love and death in Languedoc, 1999; Heaven Forbid, 2002; Brothers Under the Skin: travels in tyranny, 2003; My Mother's Lovers, 2006; The Garden of Bad Dreams, 2008; Shooting Angels, 2011; Jimfish, 2015; The Café de Move-on Blues, 2018; contribs to BBC, newspapers, jls. *Recreation:* getting lost. *Address:* c/o Rogers, Coleridge & White, 20 Powis Mews, W11 1JN.

**HOPE, Derwin;** see Hope, A. D.

**HOPE, Marcus Laurence Hulbert,** OBE 1998; HM Diplomatic Service, retired; Consul-General, Montreal, 1998–2002; *b* 2 Feb. 1942; *s* of late Laurence Frank Hope, OBE; *m* 1980, Uta Maria Luise Müller-Unverfehrt; one *s*. *Educ:* City of London Sch.; Sydney C of E Grammar Sch.; Univ. of Sydney (BA); Univ. of London (BA Hons); Open Univ. (Dip. Physical Sci. 2006). Joined HM Diplomatic Service, 1965; Third Sec., CRO, 1965; MECAS, 1966; Second Sec., Tripoli, 1968; FCO, 1970; First Sec., 1972; Head of Chancery, Dubai, 1974; First Sec. (Commercial), Bonn, 1976; FCO, 1980; NATO Defence Coll., Rome, 1984; Counsellor, Beirut, 1984–85; Counsellor and Head of Chancery, Berne, 1985–89; Dep. Head of Mission and Counsellor (Commercial and Aid), Jakarta, 1989–92; Hd, Western Europe Dept, FCO, 1992–95; Ambassador to Zaire, also (non-resident) to the Congo, 1996–98. Trustee, Congo Church Assoc., 2002–16. FRAS 2004. JP Wandsworth, 2003–12. *Recreations:* classical guitar, astronomy, scuba diving. *Address:* 29 Narbonne Avenue, SW4 9JR.

**HOPE, Philip Ian;** Partner, Hope Consulting and Training, since 2017 (Director, 2015); *b* 19 April 1955; *s* of A. G. Hope and Grace Hope; *m* 1980, Allison, *d* of John and Margaret Butt; one *s* one *d*. *Educ:* Wandsworth Comp. Sch.; St Luke's Coll., Exeter Univ. (BEd). Teacher, Kettering Sch. for Boys; Youth Policy Advr, NCVO; Hd, Young Volunteer Resources Unit, Nat. Youth Bureau; Mgt and Community Work Consultant, Framework, 1985–96; Dir, Framework in Print publishing co-operative. Member (Lab and Co-op): Kettering BC, 1983–87; Northants CC, 1993–97. Contested (Lab and Co-op) Kettering, 1992. MP (Lab and Co-op) Corby, 1997–2010; contested (Lab and Co-op) same seat, 2010. PPS to Minister of State for Housing and Planning, 1999–2001, to Dep. Prime Minister, 2001–03; Parliamentary Under-Secretary of State: ODPM, 2003–05; DfES, then Dept for Children, Schools and Families, 2005–07; a Parly Sec. and Minister for the Third Sector, Cabinet Office, 2007–08; Minister for the E Midlands, 2008–10; Minister of State, DoH, 2008–10. Member: Public Accounts Select Cttee, 1997–98; NI Grand Cttee, 1997–2005; Cttee of Selection, 1999–2005; Chairman: All-Party Parly Gp for charities and voluntary orgns, 1997–2001; All-Party Lighting Gp, 2001–05. Vice Chm., PLP Social Security Deptl Cttee, 1997–2001; Mem., Leadership Campaign Team with responsibility for educn, 1997–99. Dir, Improving Care Ltd, 2010–15. Adjunct Prof. for Ageing and Health, Global Health Inst., Imperial Coll. London, 2010–. *Publications:* Making Best Use of Consultants, 1993; (jtly) Performance Appraisal, 1995; various curriculum and training packs for schs and youthworkers and information booklets for young people. *Recreations:* tennis, juggling, computing, gardening.

**HOPE, Prof. Ronald Anthony, (Tony),** PhD; FRCP, FRCPsych; Professor of Medical Ethics, University of Oxford, 2000–12; Fellow, St Cross College, Oxford, 1990–2012, now Emeritus; *b* 16 March 1951; *s* of Ronald Sidney Hope and Marion Nuttall Hope (*née* Whittaker); *m* 1981, Sally Louise Hirsh; two *d*. *Educ:* Dulwich Coll.; New Coll., Oxford (Bosanquet Open Schol. in Medicine; MA, PhD 1978; BM BCh 1980). FRCPsych 1997; FRCP 2011. W. H. Rhodes Travel Schol., 1969; doctoral res. in neurobiol. at NIMR, 1973–76; preclinical trng, Middx Hosp., 1976–77; clinical trng, Univ. of Oxford, 1977–80; House surgeon, Royal United Hosp., Bath, 1980–81; House physician, John Radcliffe Hosp., Oxford, 1981; SHO-Registrar rotation in Psychiatry, Oxford, 1981–85; Wellcome Trust Trng Fellow in Psychiatry, Oxford hosps, 1985–87; University of Oxford: Clin. Lectr in Psychiatry, 1987–90; Leader, Oxford Practice Skills Project, 1990–95; Lectr in Practice Skills, 1995–2000; Reader in Medicine, 1996–2000; Dir, Ethox (Oxford Centre for Ethics and Communication in Health Care Practice), 1999–2005; Hon. Consultant Psychiatrist, Warneford Hosp. Oxford, 1990–2012. Chairman: Wellcome Trust Strategy Cttee on Med. Humanities, 2005–08; Wkg Party on Ethics and Dementia, Nuffield Council on Bioethics, 2007–09. Res. Prize and Medal, RCPsych, 1989. *Publications:* Oxford Handbook of Clinical Medicine, 1985 (trans. 9 langs), 4th edn 1998; Essential Practice in Patient-Centred Care, 1995; Manage Your Mind, 1995 (trans. 5 langs), 3rd edn 2018; Medical Ethics and Law: the core curriculum, 2003, 2nd edn 2008; Medical Ethics: a very short introduction, 2004, 2nd edn 2018; Empirical Ethics in Psychiatry, 2008; contrib. numerous papers and chapters, mainly in fields of Alzheimer's Disease and med. ethics. *Recreations:* family, literature, wine, writing. *Address:* St Cross College, Oxford OX1 3LZ.

**HOPE-DUNBAR, Sir David,** 8th Bt *cr* 1664; *b* 13 July 1941; *o s* of Sir Basil Douglas Hope-Dunbar, 7th Bt, and of his 2nd wife, Edith Maude Maclaren (*d* 1989), *d* of late Malcolm Cross; *S* father, 1961; *m* 1971, Kathleen, *yr d* of late J. T. Kenrick; one *s* two *d*. *Educ:* Eton; Royal Agricultural College, Cirencester. MRICS (ARICS 1966). Founder, Dunbar & Co., now Allied Dunbar PLC. *Recreations:* fishing, shooting. *Heir: s* Charles Hope-Dunbar, *b* 11 March 1975. *Address:* Banks Farm, Kirkcudbright DG6 4XF. *T:* (01557) 330424.

**HOPE HAILEY, Prof. Veronica,** PhD; Professor of Management Studies (formerly of Strategy and Human Resources), since 2012, Dean, School of Management, since 2013, and Vice President, since 2017, University of Bath; *b* Nottingham, 30 Nov. 1956; *d* of Morrison Gilbert Hope and Pauline Hope; *m* 1st, 1979, Charles Philip Edwards (marr. diss. 1994); three *d*; 2nd, 1995, John Martin Hailey, *qv*; two *d*. *Educ:* Univ. of York (BA Hons 1978); Aston Univ. (MSc 1986); Univ. of Manchester (PhD 1993). Res. Fellow, Judge Inst., Univ. of Cambridge, 1993–96; Professor of Human Resource Mgt, Cranfield Sch. of Mgt, Cranfield Univ., 1996–2004; of Strategy, Univ. of Bath, 2004–06; Associate Dean and Prof. of Human Resource Mgt, Cass Business Sch., City Univ., 2006–12. Mem. Council, Chartered Assoc. of University Business Schs, 2016–. Trustee, Help for Heroes, 2014–

(Chair, Nominations Cttee, 2016–). MCIPD 1986. *Publications:* (with J. Balogun) Exploring Strategic Change, 1999, 4th edn 2015; Strategic Human Resource Management, 1999; contribs to internat. jls. *Recreations:* family, dog walking, cooking, pilates, church. *Address:* University of Bath, Claverton Down, Bath BA2 7AY. *T:* (01225) 388388. *E:* v.hope.hailey@bath.ac.uk.

**HOPE JOHNSTONE,** family name of **Earl of Annandale and Hartfell**.

**HOPE-MORLEY,** family name of **Baron Hollenden**.

**HOPES, Rt Rev. Alan Stephen;** *see* East Anglia, Bishop of, (RC).

**HOPETOUN, Earl of; Andrew Victor Arthur Charles Hope;** DL; *b* 22 May 1969; *s* and *heir* of Marquess of Linlithgow, *qv*; *m* 1993, Skye, *e d* of Major Bristow Bovill; twin *s* two *d*. *Educ:* Eton; Exeter Coll., Oxford. A Page of Honour to the Queen Mother, 1985–87. Mem., Royal Co. of Archers, 2002–. DL W Lothian, 2018. *Heir: s* Viscount Aithrie, *qv*. *Address:* Hopetoun House, South Queensferry, West Lothian EH30 9SL.

**HOPEWELL, Peter David F.;** *see* Fraser-Hopewell.

**HOPGOOD, Richard Simon;** Director, Henry Smith Charity, 2002–12; *b* 7 Oct. 1952; *s* of Ronald and Daphne Hopgood; *m* 1988, Elizabeth Wakefield; one *d*. *Educ:* Christ's Hosp.; Wadham Coll., Oxford (BA). On staff of Church Comrs, 1977–98 (Dep. Sec., Policy and Planning, 1994–98); Dir of Policy and Dep. Sec.-Gen., Archbishops' Council, 1999–2002. Trustee: Escaping Victimhood, 2013–18; Inst. for Voluntary Action Res., 2013–. *Recreations:* reading, photography, writing.

**HOPKIN, Sir Deian (Rhys),** Kt 2009; PhD; FRHistS; Vice-Chancellor and Chief Executive, London South Bank University (formerly South Bank University), 2001–09, now Professor Emeritus; President, National Library of Wales, 2011–15; *b* 1 March 1944; *s* of late Islwyn Hopkin and Charlotte Hopkin (nee Rees); *m* 1st, 1966, Orian Jones (marr. diss. 1989); two *d*; 2nd, 1989, Lynne Hurley; two *s*. *Educ:* Llandovery Coll.; University Coll. of Wales, Aberystwyth (BA 1965; PhD 1981). FRHistS 1984. Lectr, 1967–84, Sen. Lectr, 1984–91, Hd of Dept, 1989–91, Dept of History, UCW Aberystwyth; Staff Tutor, Open Univ., 1974–76; Dean, Human Scis, 1992–96, Vice-Provost, 1996–2001, City of London Poly., then London Guildhall Univ. Chm., Cityside Regeneration Ltd, 1997–2002. Member: Council, Nat. Liby of Wales, 1975–88; Gen. Adv. Council, BBC, 1988–95; Exec., UK Arts and Humanities Service, 1996–2002; Skills for Health UK, 2004–08; Bd, Foundn Degree Forward, 2007–11; Learning and Skills Council, 2007–09; Council for Industry and Higher Educn, 2007–09; Public Interest Gen. Council, 2007–13; Educn Honours Cttee, Cabinet Office, 2010–16; Higher Educn Commn, 2012–. Expert Advr, First Minister of Wales, 2012–. Chairman: Univs UK Skills Task Gp, 2006–09; Local Economy Policy Unit, 2010–. Member: London Eur. Progs Cttee, 2000–05; Bd, Central London Partnership, 2001–06; One London Ltd, 2002–05; South Bank Employers Gp, 2005–07; Vice Chm., London Higher, 2006–08. Member: Hackney Community Coll. Corp., 2000–02; Lambeth Coll. Corp., 2002–05; Council, City and Guilds Inst. of London, 2009–; Council, Essex Univ., 2011–15. Freeman: City of London, 2003; Co. (formerly Guild) of Educators, 2004 (Liveryman, 2015; Trustee, 2017). FCGI 2010 (Hon. Mem., 2008). Chairman: UNIAID Foundn, 2004–09; 2014–18 Wales Remembers/Cymru'n Cofio 1914–18, 2012–; Patron: Bishopsgate Inst., 2008–11; Hillcroft Coll., 2009–16; Southwark Theatres and Educn Partnership, 2008–12; Futureversity (formerly Summer Univ.), 2008–13; Cerebra, 2009–15; Trustee: Bishopsgate Foundn, 1999–2003; Aldgate and Allhallows Foundn, 2004–06; Council for Academics-at-Risk (formerly Vice-Chm., Council for Assisting Refugee Academics), 2005–; Campaign for Learning, 2009–; Inst. of Historical Res. Trust, 2009–14; North-West Univ., S Africa, 2009–15. Chm. Emeritus, Univ. Centre, Jersey, 2011–15; Prof. Emeritus, Univ. of E London, 2010; Hon. Prof., Univ. of Essex, 2015–. FRSA 1997. Hon. FCIBSE 2008. Hon. Fellow: Univ. of Wales, Aberystwyth, 2003; Univ. of Wales, Trinity St Davids, 2012. Hon. DLitt: Glamorgan, 2008; London, 2017; Hon. LLD McGill, 2010; DUniv Open, 2012. *Publications:* (ed jtly) History and Computing, 1987; (ed jtly) Class, Community and the Labour Movement: Wales and Canada 1850–1930, 1989; (ed jtly) The Labour Party in Wales 1900–2000, 2000; Universities in the Modern Economy, 2002; contrib. articles to Internat. Rev. Social Hist., Llafur, etc. *Recreations:* music (especially jazz), writing, broadcasting. *Address:* 43 Beadon Road, Bromley, Kent BR2 9AS. *T:* (020) 8289 7912. *Club:* Athenæum.

**HOPKIN, Prof. Julian Meurglyn,** CBE 2011; MD; FRCP, FRCPE, FMedSci; FLSW; Professor of Experimental Medicine, since 2012 (Professor of Experimental Medicine, then Professor of Medicine, 1999–2010; Professor Emeritus, 2010), Chairman, Advisory Board, College of Medicine, since 2012, and Rector, Medicine and Health, since 2019, Swansea University (formerly University of Wales, Swansea) (Head, School of Medicine, 2001–08; Rector, 2008–10); Honorary Consultant Physician, Swansea Bay (formerly Abertawe Bro Morgannwg) University Health Board (formerly Swansea Hospitals), 1999–2010 and since 2012; *b* 30 Aug. 1948; *s* of Meurglyn Hopkin and Mair Hopkin (*née* Watkins); *m* 1st, 1973, Janina Macczak (*d* 2009); two *s* one *d*; 2nd, 2011, Amanda Louise Moorhouse. *Educ:* Maesydderwen Sch., Ystradgynlais; Univ. of Wales (MB BCh; MD 1981); Univ. of Edinburgh (MSc 1978); MA Oxon 1992. FRCP 1988; FRCPE 2000. Med. House Officer and Registrar, Univ. Hosps of Wales, Oxford and Edinburgh, 1972–77; MRC Advanced Student and Clinical Scientist, MRC, Edinburgh, 1977–79; Lectr in Medicine, Univ. of Birmingham, 1979–84; Clinical Sen. Lectr and Consultant Physician, Oxford, 1984–98; Fellow, Brasenose Coll., Oxford, 1992–98. Visiting Professor: Univ. of Osaka, 1994; Tor Vergata Univ., Rome, 2001; Univ. of Kyoto, 2002. Dir, Allerna Therapeutics, 2007–11; non-exec. Dir, Abertawe Bro Morgannwg Univ. NHS Trust, 2008–09; Ind. Mem. (Univ.), Swansea Bay Univ. Health Bd, 2019–. Chm., Trustees, St David's Med. Foundn, 2008–. FMedSci 2005; FLSW 2011. Hon. Fellow, Swansea Univ., 2011. (Jtly) Daiwa-Adrian Prize in Medicine, Daiwa Anglo-Japanese Foundn, 2001. Hon. Druid, Bardic Circle of Isle of Britain, 2008. *Publications:* Pneumocystis Carinii, 1991; (contrib.) Oxford Textbook of Medicine, 2nd edn 1987 to 5th edn 2010; contribs on clinical medicine, human genetic variation, allergy and infection and lung diseases to Lancet, BMJ, Nature and Science. *Recreations:* the outdoors, ski-ing and trudging. *Address:* Hafod, Llanrhidian, Gwyr SA3 1EH. *T:* (01792) 390033. *E:* j.m.hopkin@swan.ac.uk.

**HOPKIN, Sir Royston (Oliver),** KCMG 2005 (CMG 1995); Chairman and Managing Director, Spice Island Beach Resort (formerly Spice Island Inn), since 1987; Owner, Blue Horizons Cottage Hotel, 1978–2015; Tourism Ambassador at Large, Grenada, since 2013; *b* 10 Jan. 1945; *s* of late Curtis Hopkin and Audrey Hopkin; *m* 1st, 1975, Floreen Hope (decd); one *s* one *d*; 2nd, 1983, Betty Grell-Hull; one *d*. *Educ:* Grenada Boys' Secondary Sch. British Amer. Insce Co., 1963–65; joined family business, Ross Point Inn, 1965, Manager, 1969–78. Member: Grenada Tourist Bd, 1965–83; Grenada Bd of Tourism, 1998–2001; Pres., Grenada Hotel Assoc., 1969–89; Caribbean Hotel Association: Dir, 1970–; Pres., 1994–96; Chm., 1996–98; Chm., Memship Policy Cttee, 2000–06; Caribbean Tourism Organization: Dir, 1990–98; Exec. Cttee, 1994–98. Chm., Caribbean Alliance (formerly Action) for Sustainable Tourism, 2002– (Vice-Chm., 1996–2002). Mem. Bd of Trustees, Queen Elizabeth Home, Grenada, 1996– (Dep. Chm., 2006–); Trustee, Duke of Edinburgh's Award of Grenada, 2004–10. Numerous awards incl. Caribbean Hotelier of the Year, 1991; Special Service Award, Grenada Bd of Tourism, 2006; Lifetime Achievement Award: Caribbean Hotel and Tourism Assoc., 2011; Caribbean Tourism Orgn, 2012; 40th Anniv. Independence Award, Most Outstanding Hotelier, 2014. *Recreations:* reading, tennis, travelling. *Address:* Mace Point Villa, True Blue, Box 6, St George's, Grenada, West Indies. *T:* (home) 4444584, (business) 4444258. *E:* roystonhopkin@spicebeachresort.com.

**HOPKINS, Adrian Mark;** QC 2003; *b* 16 May 1961; *s* of Thomas and Brenda Hopkins; *m* 2010, Tanno Udema. *Educ:* Warwick Sch.; St Peter's Coll., Oxford (Exhibnr; BA Hons Juris. 1983). Called to the Bar, Lincoln's Inn, 1984; in practice, specialising in healthcare law, clinical negligence and professional disciplinary hearings. Member: Supplementary Panel, Counsel to Treasury (Common Law), 1995–99; Attorney Gen.'s London B Panel for Crown's Civil Litigation, 1999–2002; Mem., Bar's and Council of the Inns of Court's Disciplinary Tribunals, 2005–12. Contributing Ed., Medical Law Reports, 1999–. *Address:* Serjeants' Inn Chambers, 85 Fleet Street, EC4Y 1AE. *T:* (020) 7427 5000.

**HOPKINS, Sir Anthony;** *see* Hopkins, Sir P. A.

**HOPKINS, Anthony Strother,** CBE 1996; BSc(Econ); FCA; Civil Service Commissioner for Northern Ireland, 2009–12; *b* 17 July 1940; *s* of Strother Smith Hopkins, OBE, and Alice Roberta Hopkins; *m* 1965, Dorothy Moira (*née* McDonough); one *s* two *d*. *Educ:* Campbell Coll., Belfast; Queen's University of Belfast (BScEcon). Manager, Thomson McLintock & Co., Chartered Accountants, London, 1966–70; Principal, Dept of Commerce, N Ireland, 1970–74; Northern Ireland Development Agency, 1975–82, Chief Executive, 1979–82; Under Secretary, 1982–88, Second Perm. Sec., 1988–92, Dept of Economic Development for N Ireland; Dep. Chief Exec., 1982–88, Chief Exec., 1988–92, Industrial Develt Bd for NI; Sen. Partner, Deloitte & Touche (formerly Touche Ross & Co.), NI, Chartered Accountants, 1992–2001; Dep. Chm., 1995–96, Chm., 1997–2007, Laganside Corp. Chairman: MMB for NI, 1995–2003; NI Higher Educn Council, 2002–09. Dep. Chm., Probation Bd for NI, 1997–98. Member: NI Tourist Bd, 1992–98; Council, NI Chamber of Commerce and Industry, 1992–95; NI Skills Task Force, 1999–2003. Mem., Bd of Advrs, Crescent Capital (formerly Hambro NI Ventures), 1995–2007 (Mem., Investment Cttee, 2003–); Dir, QUBIS Ltd, 2005–2007. Chm., Kestrel Superyachts Ltd, 2007–14. Vis. Prof., Univ. of Ulster, 1992–. Mem. Adv. Bd, Ulster Business Sch., 1992–99. Member, Appeal Committee: Relate, 1994–97; Mencap (NI), 1997–2005; Mem., Management Cttee, Ulster Garden Villages Ltd Charitable Trust, 2003– (Chm., 2006–). Hon. Treas., Prince's Trust NI Appeal, 1995–97. CCMI (CBIM 1990; Chm. NI Regl Bd, 1992–97). DUniv Ulster, 2010. *Recreations:* golf, sailing. *Clubs:* Royal Belfast Golf, Royal Ulster Yacht (Co. Down).

**HOPKINS, Prof. Antony Gerald,** PhD; FBA 1996; Smuts Professor of Commonwealth History, University of Cambridge, 1994–2002, now Emeritus; Fellow, Pembroke College, Cambridge, 1994–2002, now Emeritus; Walter Prescott Webb Professor of History, University of Texas at Austin, 2002–13; *b* 21 Feb. 1938; *s* of George Henry Hopkins and Queenie Ethel (*née* Knight); *m* 1964, Wendy Beech; two *s*. *Educ:* St Paul's Sch.; QMC, Univ. of London (BA); SOAS (PhD). Asst Lectr, Lectr, then Reader, 1964–77, Prof. of Economic History, 1977–88, Univ. of Birmingham; Prof. of Internat. History, Grad. Inst. of Internat. Studies, Univ. of Geneva, 1988–94. DUniv Stirling, 1996; Hon. DLitt Birmingham, 2013. Forkosch Prize, Amer. Historical Assoc., 1995. *Publications:* An Economic History of West Africa, 1973, revd 1988; (with P. J. Cain) British Imperialism: innovation and expansion 1688–1914, 1993, (with P. J. Cain) British Imperialism: crisis and deconstruction 1914–90, 1993, joint 2nd edn as British Imperialism 1688–2000, 2001, 3rd edn 2016; (ed) Globalization in World History, 2002; (ed) Global History: interactions between the universal and the local, 2006; American Empire: a global history, 2018; articles in learned jls. *Recreation:* worrying. *Address:* Pembroke College, Cambridge CB2 1RF.

**HOPKINS, Prof. Colin Russell,** PhD; Professor of Molecular Cell Biology, 2000–06, Senior Research Investigator, 2006–10, Imperial College of Science, Technology and Medicine; *b* 4 June 1939; *s* of Bleddyn Hopkins and Vivienne Russell (*née* Jenkins); *m* 1964, Hilary Floyd; one *s* one *d*. *Educ:* UC, Swansea, Univ. of Wales (BSc; PhD 1964). University of Liverpool: Asst Lectr, Dept of Physiol., Med. Sch., 1964–66; Lectr, Dept of Histology, 1966–70; Sen. Lectr, Dept of Histology and Cell Biol. (Medical), 1971–75; Fulbright Fellow, Dept of Cell Biol., 1970, Fulbright Travelling Schol. and Vis. Associate Prof., 1971–72, Rockefeller Univ., NY; Prof. and Head, Dept of Medical Cell Biol., Univ. of Liverpool, 1975–86; Rank Prof. of Physiological Biochem., ICSTM, 1986–91; Dir, MRC Lab. for Molecular Cell Biol., UCL, 1991–2000. *Publications:* Cell Structure and Function, 1964; numerous scientific papers. *Recreations:* natural history, music.

**HOPKINS, David Rex Eugène;** Director of Quality Assurance/Administration, Ministry of Defence, 1983–90; *b* 29 June 1930; *s* of late Frank Hopkins and Vera (*née* Wimhurst); *m* 1st, 1955, Brenda Joyce Phillips (*d* 2005); two *s* one *d* (and one *d* decd); 2nd, 2006, Gwyneth Vick (*née* Rees) (*d* 2019). *Educ:* Worthing High Sch.; Christ Church, Oxford (MA 1950: Dip. in Econs and Pol Science, 1951). National Service Commn, RA, 1952; service in Korea. Asst Principal, WO, 1953; Principal, WO, 1957, MoD 1964; Asst Sec., 1967; Home Office, 1969–70; RCDS, 1971; Defence Equipment Secretariat, 1972; Dir, Headquarters Security, 1975; Financial Counsellor, UK Delegn to NATO, 1981–83. *Recreations:* church life, travel, fell-walking, military history. *Address:* The Limes, Crosby Garrett, Kirkby Stephen, Cumbria CA17 4PW. *T:* (01768) 371997.

**HOPKINS, Prof. David William;** PhD; Professor and Dean of the Central Faculty, Scotland's Rural College, since 2018; *b* London, 12 March 1963; *s* of Robert David Hopkins and Frances Margaret Hopkins; two *s* one *d*. *Educ:* Manchester Poly. (HND Biol. 1983; BSc Biol. 1985); Univ. of Newcastle (PhD Soil Sci. 1988). Postdoctoral Res. Scientist, Univ. of Newcastle, 1988–90; Lectr, then Sen. Lectr, Biol Scis, Univ. of Dundee, 1990–99; Prof. of Envmtl Sci. and Hd of Sch., Univ. of Stirling, 1999–2006; Dir of Sci., Scottish Crop Res. Inst., Dundee, 2006–11; Prof. of Envmtl Biol. and Hd, Sch. of Life Scis, Heriot-Watt Univ., 2011–14; Prof. of Soil Sci. and Dean of Agriculture, Food and Envmt, RAU, 2014–18. Adjunct Prof. of Antarctic Studies, Univ. of Canterbury, Christchurch, 2006–. Res. Fellow, RSE, 2002. *Publications:* over 100 res. articles. *Address:* Scotland's Rural College, Peter Wilson Building, West Mains Road, Edinburgh EH9 3JG.

**HOPKINS, Prof. David William Richard,** PhD; Professor of Educational Leadership, University of Bolton, since 2016; *b* 30 Jan. 1949; *s* of David Clifford Hopkins and Thelma Hopkins; *m* 1985, Marloes de Groot (marr. diss. 2013); two *s* one *d*; partner, 2014, Trish Franey. *Educ:* Univ. of Reading (BA Hons Politics 1970); UCNW, Bangor (PGCE 1971); Univ. of Sheffield (MEd 1976); Simon Fraser Univ., BC (PhD 1980). Outward Bound instructor, 1969–72; teacher, Minsthorpe High Sch. and Community Coll., 1973–75; mountain guide and grad. student, 1976–80; Lectr, Simon Fraser Univ., BC, 1980–82; Sen. Lectr, W Glam Inst. for Higher Educn, 1983–85; Tutor, Inst. of Educn, Univ. of Cambridge, 1985–96; Prof., Hd of Sch. and Dean of Educn, Univ. of Nottingham, 1996–2002; now Emeritus; Dir, Standards and Effectiveness Unit, DfES, 2002–05; HSBC Prof. of Internat. Leadership, Inst. of Educn, Univ. of London, 2005–09, now Emeritus. Hon. Prof., Univ. of Hull, 2002; Professorial Fellow, Univ. of Melbourne, 2005; Visiting Professor: Univ. of Edinburgh, 2007–; Catholic Univ. of Santiago, 2007–; Chinese Univ.

of HK, 2007–; Univ. of Wales, 2008–; Univ. of Cumbria, 2013–. Dir of Educn, Bright Tribe Trust, 2012–15. Chm., Leicester City Partnership Bd, 1999–2002. Chm., Professional Standards Cttee, British Mountain Guides, 1997–2002. Mem., All Souls Gp, 2003. Trustee: Outward Bound, 2008–12; Adventure Learning Schs Charity, 2013– (Exec. Dir, 2010–13). Freeman, Guild of Educators, 2005. IFMGA 1978; FRSA 2002. Hon. DEd Nottingham Trent, 2014. *Publications:* over 40 books including: A Teacher's Guide to Classroom Research, 1985, 5th edn 2014; Evaluation for School Development, 1989; (jtly) The Empowered School, 1991; (jtly) Personal Growth through Adventure, 1993; (jtly) School Improvement in an Era of Change, 1994; Improving the Quality of Education for All, 1996, 2nd edn 2002; (jtly) Models of Learning, 1997, 2nd edn 2002; (ed jtly) The International Handbook of Educational Change, 4 vols, 1998, 2nd edn 2010; (jtly) Improving Schools: performance and potential, 1999; School Improvement for Real, 2001; Every School a Great School, 2007; (jtly) System Leadership in Practice, 2009; (ed jtly) Powerful Learning, 2011; Exploding the Myths of School Reform, 2013; contrib. numerous articles on educn. *Recreations:* mountaineering, ski-ing, modern literature, current affairs, friends and family. *Address:* 6 Calver Mill, Calver, Hope Valley, Derbys S32 3YU; L'Aiguillette, 35 Chemin des Grands Bois, 74400 Argentière-Mt Blanc, France. *W:* www.profdavidhopkins.com. *Clubs:* Alpine, Frontline; Climbers'.

**HOPKINS, Emma Kate,** OBE 2014; HM Diplomatic Service; Ambassador to Bulgaria, since 2015; *b* Bolton; *m* 2006, Steven Hopkins; two *d. Educ:* Fitzwilliam Coll., Cambridge (BA Hons Law 1994). Called to the Bar, Middle Temple, 1995; in practice as a barrister, 1996–2001; Home Office: Sen. Adv. Lawyer, Legal Advr's Branch, 2001–06; Hd, Organised Immigration Crime, Organised and Financial Crime Unit, 2006–08; Sen. Legal Advr, UK Border Agency, 2009; Hd, EU/Internat. Team, Legal Advr's Branch, Home Office, 2009–12; Hd, Preventing Sexual Violence Initiative, FCO, 2012–15. *Address:* c/o Foreign and Commonwealth Office, King Charles Street, SW1A 2AH.

**HOPKINS, Jameson, (Jamie);** Chief Executive Officer, Workspace Group plc, 2012–19 (non-executive Director, 2010–12); *b* Bournemouth, 11 Oct. 1968; one *s* one *d. Educ:* BSc Hons Estate Mgt. Dir, Investment Dept, Savills plc, 1990–98; Investment Dir, Delancey Estates, 1998–2002; CEO, Napeley Ltd, 2002–08 (non-exec. Dir, 2008–10); Dir, Chester Properties, 2009–12.

**HOPKINS, John Humphrey David;** Golf Correspondent, The Times, 1993–2010; *b* 26 March 1945; *s* of late Leslie Charles Hopkins and Mary Eileen Hopkins (*née* Ellis); *m* 1970, Suzanne Ernestine Kommenda (marr. diss. 1998); one *s* one *d*; *m* 2006, Ysobel Jane Jones (marr. diss. 2019). *Educ:* Llandaff Cathedral Sch., Cardiff (Choral Schol.); Wrekin Coll., Telford, Salop. Sunday Times: Rugby Corresp., 1976–80; Golf Corresp., 1980–91; golf and Rugby writer, Financial Times, 1991–93. *Publications:* Life with the Lions, 1977; The British Lions, 1980; Nick Faldo in Perspective, 1985; Golf: the four Majors, 1988; Golfer's Companion, 1990; Golf in Wales: the Centenary 1895–1995, 1995; Fore! The Best of John Hopkins on Golf, 2013. *Recreations:* squash, golf, Rugby, theatre, reading. *Address:* West House, St Hilary, Cowbridge CF71 7DP. *Clubs:* Royal Automobile, MCC; Jesters; Cardiff and County (Cardiff); Royal and Ancient (St Andrews), Royal Porthcawl Golf.

**HOPKINS, Julian;** *see* Hopkins, R. J.

**HOPKINS, Kathryn;** *see* Stone, K.

**HOPKINS, Kelvin Peter;** MP (Lab) Luton North, since 1997; *b* 22 Aug. 1941; *s* of late Prof. Harold Horace Hopkins, FRS and Joan Avery Frost; *m* 1965, Patricia Mabel Langley; one *s* one *d. Educ:* Nottingham Univ. (BA Hons Politics, Economics, Maths with Stats). Economic Dept, TUC, 1969–70 and 1973–77; Lectr, St Albans Coll. of Further Educn, 1971–73; Policy and Res. Officer, NALGO, then UNISON, 1977–94. Shadow Sec. of State for Culture, Media and Sport, 2016. Member: Public Administration Select Cttee, 2002–10 and 2011–15; Transport Select Cttee, 2010–11; Eur. Scrutiny Cttee, 2007–16; Public Admin and Constitnl Affairs Cttee, 2015–; Chm., All Party Parly Gp on Alcohol Misuse, 1998–2001, for Social Sci. and Policy, 2010; Co-Chm., All Party Parly Gp for Further Educn and Lifelong Learning, 2005; Secretary: All Party Parly Gp for Jazz Appreciation, 1997–2001; All Party Parly Gp on Conflict Issues, 2007–10. Founder Mem., Old Testament Prophets, 1997–. Columnist, Socialist Campaign Gp News, 1998–2008. Gov., Luton Sixth Form Coll., 1993–. Hon. Fellow: Univ. of Luton, 1993; Univ. of Bedfordshire, 2010. *Publications:* NALGO papers. *Recreations:* music, wine, collecting antique glassware. *Address:* House of Commons, Westminster, SW1A 0AA. *T:* (020) 7219 6670; (home) (01582) 722913; 3 Union Street, Luton LU1 3AN. *T:* (01582) 488208.

**HOPKINS, Kristan Frederick;** Special Adviser to Secretary of State for Northern Ireland, since 2018; *b* 8 June 1963; one *d. Educ:* Leeds Univ. (BA). Served Army, Duke of Wellington's Regt. Lectr (pt-time) in media theory, communications and digital media. Chairman: Bradford Vision; Yorks and Humber Regl Housing Bd. Mem. (C) Bradford MDC, 1998–2010 (Leader, 2006–10). Contested (C): Leeds W, 2001; Halifax, 2005. MP (C) Keighley, 2010–17; contested (C) same seat, 2017. Parly Under-Sec. of State, DCLG, 2013–15; Vice Chamberlain of HM Household (Govt Whip), 2015–16; Parly Under-Sec. of State, NI Office, 2016–17.

**HOPKINS, Melanie Claire;** HM Diplomatic Service; High Commissioner to Fiji, (non-resident) High Commissioner to Kiribati and Tuvalu, (non-resident) Ambassador to the Republic of the Marshall Islands and the Federated States of Micronesia, and Head, South Pacific Network, since 2016; *b* Hereford, 9 Aug. 1973; *d* of Robert Hopkins and Susan Hopkins; partner, Alessandro Truppia; two *d. Educ:* Univ. of Nottingham (Mod. Langs and Mgt); City Univ. (Political Communications). Private sector, 1997–2002; joined FCO, 2003; desk officer, FCO, 2002–04; on secondment to Spanish Min. of Foreign Affairs, 2004; Hd, Political Section and Press and Public Affairs, Havana, 2004–07; Second Sec., UK Mission to the UN, Geneva, 2008–11; Hd, Common Security and Defence Policy, Eur. Directorate, FCO, 2012; Hd, Australasia and Pacific, Asia Pacific Dept, FCO, 2012–14; Dep. Hd, Security Policy Dept, FCO, 2014–16; (non-resident) High Comr to Tonga, 2016–19. *Recreations:* theatre, arts. *Address:* British High Commission, 47 Gladstone Road, Suva, Fiji. *T:* 3229120. *E:* melanie.hopkins@fco.gov.uk.

**HOPKINS, Sir Michael (John),** Kt 1995; CBE 1989; RA 1992; RIBA; RWA; Founding Partner, Hopkins Architects (formerly Michael Hopkins & Partners), since 1976; *b* 7 May 1935; *s* of late Gerald and Barbara Hopkins; *m* 1962, Patricia Ann Wainwright (*see* P. A. Hopkins); one *s* two *d. Educ:* Sherborne Sch.; Architectural Assoc. (AA Dip. 1964). RIBA 1966; RWA 1989. Worked in offices of Sir Basil Spence, Leonard Manasseh and Tom Hancock; partnership with Norman Foster, 1969–75 and with Patricia Hopkins, 1976–; *projects include:* own house and studio, Hampstead, 1976 (RIBA Award, 1977; Civic Trust Award, 1979); brewery bldg for Greene King, 1979 (RIBA Award, 1980); Patera Bldg System, 1984; Res. Centre for Schlumberger, Cambridge, 1984 (RIBA and Civic Trust Awards, 1988); infants sch., Hampshire, 1986 (RIBA and Civic Trust Awards, 1988); Mound (formerly Bicentenary) Stand, Lord's Cricket Ground, 1987 (RIBA, Civic Trust Awards, 1988); R&D Centre, Solid State Logic, 1988 (RIBA Award, 1989; Civic Trust Award, 1990); London office and country workshop for David Mellor, 1989 and 1991 (RIBA Award, 1989; Civic Trust Award, 1990; RIBA Award, 1993); redevelt of Bracken House, St Paul's, for Ohbayashi Corp., 1992 (RIBA Award, 1992; Civic Trust Award, 1994); offices at New Square, Bedfont Lakes, 1992; Glyndebourne Opera House, 1994 (RIBA Award, 1994; Civic Trust Award, 1995); Inland Revenue Centre, Nottingham, 1995 (Civic Trust Award, 1997); Queen's Bldg, Emmanuel Coll., Cambridge, 1995 (RIBA Award, 1996); Lady Sarah Cohen House, 1996; Saga Gp HQ, 1999; Jubilee Campus, Nottingham Univ., 1999 (RIBA and BCI Awards); Dynamic Earth, Edinburgh, 1999 (Civic Trust and RIBA Awards); Westminster Underground Station, 1999 (BCI Award, 2000, Civic Trust Award 2002); Portcullis House, Westminster, 2000 (Civic Trust and RIBA Awards); Wildscreen @ Bristol, 2000 (Civic Trust Award); Pilkington Labs, Sherborne Sch., 2000; Housing, Charterhouse, 2000; Parade Ground, Goodwood Racecourse, 2001 (Civic Trust Award 2003); The Forum, Norwich, 2001; Manchester Art Gall., 2002; Haberdashers' Hall, 2002; Nat. Coll. of Sch. Leadership, Nottingham Univ. (RIBA Award), 2002; GEK HQ, Athens, 2003 (RIBA Award, 2004); Norwich Cathedral Refectory, 2004 (RIBA and Civic Trust Award, 2005) and Hostry, 2009 (RIBA Award, 2010); Inn The Park, London, 2004 (Civic Trust Award, 2006); Wellcome Trust HQ, London, 2004 (RIBA Award, 2005); Evelina Children's Hosp., London, 2005 (RIBA and Civic Trust Award, 2006); Utopia, Broughton Hall Pavilion, Yorkshire, 2005 (RIBA Award, 2006, Civic Trust Award, 2007); Alnwick Garden Pavilion, Northumberland, 2006; Shin-Marunouchi Towers, Japan, 2007; LTA's Nat. Tennis Centre, Roehampton, 2007; Dubai Gate Village, 2007; Northern Arizona Univ., 2007 (RIBA Award, 2009); Bryanston Sch. Sci. Bldg, 2007; Faculty of Envmtl Studies, Yale Univ., 2008 (RIBA Award, 2010); North and South Colls, Rice Univ., 2010; Velodrome, Olympic Park, 2011; Chepauk Stadium, Chennai, 2011; Long House, Cockthorpe, Norfolk, 2011; MCA Pune Internat. Cricket Centre, 2012; Macmillan Cancer Centre, UCH, London, 2012. Pres., Architectural Assoc., 1997–99 (Vice Pres., 1987–93); Trustee, British Mus., 1993–2004. Hon. FAIA 1996; Hon. FRIAS 1996. Hon. Mem., Bund Architekten, 1996. Dr *hc* RCA 1994; Hon. DLitt Nottingham, 1995; Hon. DTech London Guildhall, 1996. RIBA Royal Gold Medal (with Patricia Hopkins), 1994. *Recreations:* Blackheath, sailing, Caturegio. *Address:* 49A Downshire Hill, NW3 1NX. *T:* (020) 7435 1109; (office) 27 Broadley Terrace, NW1 6LG. *T:* (020) 7724 1751.

**HOPKINS, Prof. Nicholas Peter;** Professor of Law, University of Reading, since 2013; a Law Commissioner, since 2015; *b* Portsmouth, 5 Jan. 1971; *s* of Derek Charles Hopkins and Patricia Josephine Hopkins. *Educ:* St Edmund's Sch., Portsmouth; Queen Mary Coll., Univ. of London (LLB Hons). Res. Asst, Law Commn, 1992–93; Lectr in Law, Durham Univ., 1993–98; University of Southampton: Lectr, 1998–2002; Sen. Lectr, 2002–09; Reader, 2009–11; Prof. of Law, 2011–13. *Publications:* The Informal Acquisition of Rights in Land, 2000; Land Law: text, cases and materials, 2009, 3rd edn 2015; (ed) Modern Studies in Property Law, 2013; Land Law: core text, 2017; contribs to Law Qly Rev., Modern Law Rev., Legal Studies, Conveyancer and Property Lawyer, Housing Theory and Society. *Recreations:* cooking, piano, dogs. *Address:* Law Commission, 1st Floor Tower, 52 Queen Anne's Gate, SW1H 9AG. *T:* (020) 3334 5304. *E:* nicholas.hopkins@lawcommission.gsi.gov.uk.

**HOPKINS, Patricia Ann, (Lady Hopkins);** Partner, Hopkins Architects (formerly Michael Hopkins & Partners), since 1976; *b* 7 April 1942; *d* of Denys Wainwright, MB, Dsc, FRCS and Dr Shelagh Wainwright, MB, ChB; *m* 1962, Michael John Hopkins (*see* Sir Michael Hopkins); one *s* two *d. Educ:* Wycombe Abbey Sch.; Architectural Assoc. (AA Dip. 1968). Own practice, 1968–76; in partnership with Michael Hopkins, 1976–. Buildings include: own house and studio, Hampstead, 1976 (RIBA Award, 1977; Civic Trust Award, 1979); Hopkins office, Marylebone, London, 1985; Fleet Velmead Infants Sch., Hants, 1986 (RIBA Award, Civic Trust Award, 1988); Masterplan, 1988, Raphael Cartoon Gall., 1993, V&A Mus.; Glyndebourne Opera House, 1994 (RIBA Award, Royal Fine Art Commn Award, 1994; Civic Trust Award, FT Award, 1995); Queen's Bldg, Emmanuel Coll., Cambridge, 1995 (RIBA Award, Royal Fine Art Commn Award, 1996); Jewish Care residential home for the elderly, 1996; Preachers Court, Charterhouse, 2000; Wildscreen @ Bristol, 2000 (Civic Trust, DTLR Urban Design Awards); Haberdashers' Hall, 2002 (Wood Award, 2003); Manchester Art Gall., 2002 (RIBA Award, Civic Trust Award, 2003); Villas at Emirates Hills, Dubai, 2003; West Wing, Ickworth House, 2006; Alnwick Garden Pavilion, 2006; Long House, Cockthorpe, Norfolk, 2011. Member: Nat. Lottery Bd, Arts Council England (formerly Arts Council of England), 1994–2000; Foundn Campaign Bd, 1994–2000, Council, 2014–, AA. Trustee, Nat. Gall., 1998–2005. Gov., Queen's Coll., Harley St, 1997–2015. Hon. FRIAS 1996; Hon. FAIA 1997. Hon. DTech London Guildhall, 1996. *Recreations:* family, friends, Blackheath, Caturegio. *Address:* 49A Downshire Hill, NW3 1NX. *T:* (020) 7435 1109; (office) 27 Broadley Terrace, NW1 6LG. *T:* (020) 7724 1751.

**HOPKINS, Paul Andrew;** QC 2009; a Recorder, since 2006; *b* Maesteg, Wales, 1 Feb. 1966; *s* of late Clifford Hopkins and Marjorie Hopkins (*née* Forrester); *m* 1994, Lisa Danielle Richards; one *s. Educ:* Maesteg Comprehensive Sch.; Univ. of Birmingham (LLB Hons 1987; NFU Mutual Assce Prize for Commercial Law); Inns of Court Sch. of Law. Called to the Bar, Gray's Inn, 1989 (Pres., Gray's Inn Student Barristers, 1988–89), Bencher, 2013; Mem. Wales and Chester Circuit (Leader, 2017–); in practice as barrister specialising in family law, 1989–; Hd, Family Law Dept, 2001–12, Dep. Hd, 2011–12, Hd, 2012–, of Chambers, 9 Park Place, Cardiff. Door Tenant: 4 Paper Bldgs, Temple, 2011–; Linenhall Chambers, Chester, 2017–. Approved Counsel, 2009–12, Queen's Counsel, 2017–, Panel of Advocates to Welsh Assembly Govt, later Welsh Govt, 2009–12. Dir, Family Contact, Cardiff, 1999–2014. Ext. Examr, Bar Professional Trng Course, Cardiff Law Sch., 2010–13. Member: Family Law Bar Assoc., 1993–; Assoc. of London Welsh Lawyers, 2012–. Mem., Children in Wales, 2012–. Mem., Gorsedd of the Bards, 2018–. *Recreations:* travel, gardening, sport, choral music (Member: Nat. Eisteddfod of Wales Choir, 2012; Cor Tabernacl (Tabernacle Chapel) Cardiff Choral Soc. Choir, 2013–15; Cor Meibion Taf Cardiff (Taf Male Voice Choir), 2013–17). *Address:* (chambers) 9 Park Place, Cardiff CF10 3DP. *T:* (029) 2038 2731, *Fax:* (029) 2022 2542. *E:* clerks@9parkplace.co.uk. *Club:* Cameo (Cardiff).

**HOPKINS, Sir (Philip) Anthony,** Kt 1993; CBE 1987; actor since 1961; *b* Port Talbot, S Wales, 31 Dec. 1937; *s* of late Richard and of Muriel Hopkins; *m* 1st, 1968, Petronella (marr. diss. 1972); one *d*; 2nd, 1973, Jennifer (marr. diss. 2002), *d* of Ronald Lynton; 3rd, 2003, Stella Arroyave. *Educ:* Cowbridge, S Wales; RADA; Cardiff Coll. of Drama. London début as Metellus Cimber in Julius Caesar, Royal Court, 1964; National Theatre: Juno and the Paycock, A Flea in Her Ear, 1966; The Dance of Death, The Three Sisters, As You Like It (all male cast), 1967; The Architect and the Emperor of Assyria, A Woman Killed with Kindness, Coriolanus, 1971; Macbeth, 1972; Pravda, 1985 (Laurence Olivier/Observer Award for outstanding achievements, 1985; (jtly) Best Actor, British Theatre Assoc. and Drama Magazine Awards, 1985; Royal Variety Club Stage Actor Award, 1985); King Lear, 1986; Antony and Cleopatra, 1987. Other stage appearances include: The Taming of the Shrew, Chichester, 1972; Equus, USA, 1974–75, 1977 (Best Actor Award, NY Drama Desk, Amer. Authors and Celebrities Forum Award, Outer Critics Circle Award, 1975; LA Drama Critics' Award, 1977); The Tempest, LA, 1979; Old Times, New York, 1984; The Lonely Road, Old Vic, 1985; M. Butterfly, Shaftesbury, 1989; Director: Dylan Thomas: return journey, Lyric, Hammersmith, 1992; August, Theatr Clwyd, 1994. *Films:* The Lion in Winter, 1968; The Looking Glass War, 1969; Hamlet, 1969; When Eight Bells Toll, 1971; Young Winston, 1972; A Doll's House, 1973; The Girl from Petrovka, 1974; All Creatures Great and Small, 1974; Juggernaut, 1974; Audrey Rose, 1977; A Bridge Too Far, 1977; International Velvet, 1978; Magic, 1978; The Elephant Man, A Change of Seasons, 1980; The Bounty (Variety Club Film Actor Award), 1984; The Good Father, 1986; 84 Charing Cross Road (Best Actor Award, Moscow Film Fest.), 1986; The Dawning, 1988; A Chorus of Disapproval, 1989; Desperate Hours, 1991; The Silence of the Lambs, 1991 (Acad., BAFTA and NY Film Critics Circle, Awards for Best Actor, 1992); Freejack, Howard's End, Chaplin, 1992; Bram Stoker's Dracula, The Trial, The Innocent, The Remains of the Day, 1993 (BAFTA Best Actor Award); Shadowlands, 1994; The Road to Wellville, Legends of the Fall, 1995; Nixon, 1996; August (also dir), 1996; Surviving Picasso, 1996; Amistad, 1998; The Edge, 1998; The Mask of Zorro, 1998; Meet Joe Black, 1999; Instinct, 1999; Titus, 2000; Hannibal, 2001; Hearts in Atlantis, 2002; Bad Company, 2002; Red Dragon, 2002; The Human Stain, 2004; Alexander, 2005; Proof, 2006; The World's Fastest Indian, 2006; Bobby, 2006; All the King's Men, 2006; Fracture, 2007; Beowulf, 2007; The Wolfman, 2010; You Will Meet a Tall Dark Stranger, 2011; Thor, 2011; The Rite, 2011; 360, 2012; Hitchcock, 2013; Thor: The Dark World, 2013; Noah, 2014; Kidnapping Freddy Heineken, 2015; Misconduct, 2016; Transformers: The Last Knight, 2017; Thor: Ragnarok, 2017. *American television films:* QB VII, 1973; Dark Victory, 1975; Bruno Hauptmann in The Lindbergh Kidnapping Case (Emmy Award), 1976; The Voyage of the Mayflower, 1979; The Bunker (Emmy Award, 1981), The Acts of Peter and Paul, 1980; The Hunchback of Notre Dame, 1981; The Arch of Triumph, 1984; Hollywood Wives, 1984; Guilty Conscience, 1984; The Tenth Man, 1988; To Be the Best, 1991; Westworld (TV series), 2016, 2018; *BBC television:* Pierre Bezukhov in serial, War and Peace (SFTA Best TV Actor award), 1972; Kean, 1978; Othello, 1981; Little Eyolf, 1982; Guy Burgess in Blunt (film), 1987; Donald Campbell in Across the Lake, 1988; Heartland, 1989; Gwyn Thomas: A Few Selected Exits, 1993; The Dresser, 2015; King Lear, 2018; Ind. TV performances incl. A Married Man (series), 1983. Fellow, BAFTA, 2008. Hon. Fellow, St David's Coll., Lampeter, 1992. Hon. DLitt Wales, 1988. Commandeur, Ordre des Arts et des Lettres (France), 1996. *Recreations:* reading, walking, piano.

HOPKINS, Philippa Mary, (Mrs Edward Howells); QC 2018; *b* Cambridge, 11 June 1971; *d* of late John and of Charity Hopkins; *m* 1996, Edward Howells; three *s. Educ:* Perse Sch. for Girls, Cambridge; Merton Coll., Oxford (BA Juris. 1992; BCL 1993; Eldon Law Schol. 1994). Called to the Bar, Middle Temple, 1994. *Publications:* (jtly) Colman, Lyon & Hopkins, Practice and Procedure of the Commercial Court, 5th edn 2000, 6th edn 2008; (ed and contrib.) Arnould's Law of Marine Insurance and Average, 17th edn 2008, 19th edn 2018. *Recreations:* reading, walking, countryside, theatre, family life, church. *Address:* Essex Court Chambers, 24 Lincoln's Inn Fields, WC2A 3EG. *T:* (020) 7813 8000, *Fax:* (020) 7813 8080. *E:* clerksroom@essexcourt.net.

HOPKINS, (Richard) Julian; Development Director, 2006–10, and part-time Development Adviser, 2010–11, St Albans Cathedral; *b* 12 Oct. 1940; *s* of late Richard Robert Hopkins, CBE and Grace Hilda (*née* Hatfield); *m*; two *s* one *d*; *m* 3rd, 2005, Stella Louise (*née* Marino). *Educ:* Bedford School. Asst Manager, London Palladium, 1963; Central Services Manager, BBC, 1965; joined RSPCA as Accounts Manager, 1972, appointed Admin. and Finance Officer, 1976; Exec. Dir, 1978–82; Gen. Manager, Charity Christmas Card Council, 1982–83; Admin. and Devlt Dir, War on Want, 1984–88; Dir, CARE Britain, 1988–94; Dir, ORBIS USA, ORBIS Internat., NY, 1994–95; Exec. Vice Pres., American SPCA, NY, 1995–2000; Develt Dir, IUCN, Washington, DC, 2000–05. Dir, and Mem. Exec. Cttee, World Soc. for Protection of Animals, 1980–82; Mem., Farm Animal Welfare Council, 1980–83. FCMI. *Publications:* novels: Conducting Terror, 2007; In The Thick Of It, 2010. *Recreations:* genealogy, opera, orchestral music, writing, 6 grandchildren. *E:* julianhop2010@gmail.com.

HOPKINS, Robert John, PhD; author and environmentalist; Catalyst and Outreach Manager, Transition Network, since 2007; *b* Chiswick, London, 24 June 1968; *s* of late John Murray Hopkins and of Heather Mary Elmhirst (*née* King); *m* 2007, Emma Louise Schofield; four *s. Educ:* Univ. of West of England (BSc 1st Cl. Hons Envmtl Quality and Resource Mgt 1996); Univ. of Plymouth (MSc Soc. Res. 2007; PhD 2010). Teacher and course co-ordinator, Practical Sustainability course, Kinsale Further Educn Coll., Co. Cork, Ire., 2000–05. Vis. Fellow, Univ. of Plymouth, 2012–; Ashoka Fellow, 2008. Hon. DSc UWE, 2013. *Publications:* The Transition Handbook: from oil dependency to local resilience, 2007; The Transition Companion: making your community more resilient in uncertain times, 2011; The Power of Just Doing Stuff: how local action can change the world, 2013. *Recreations:* gardening, swimming, time with my children. *Address:* Transition Network, 43 Fore Street, Totnes, Devon TQ9 5HN. *T:* (01803) 865669. *E:* robhopkins@transitionnetwork.org.

HOPKINS, Russell, OBE 1989; FDSRCS; Consultant Oral and Maxillo-Facial Surgeon, Cardiff Royal Infirmary, 1968–95; Director of Medical Audit, South Glamorgan Health Authority, 1991–95; *b* 30 April 1932; *s* of Charles Albert Hopkins and Frances Doris Hopkins; *m* 1970, Jill Margaret Pexton; two *s* one *d. Educ:* Barnard Castle Sch.; King's Coll., Durham Univ. (BDS 1956); Royal Free Hosp., London Univ. LRCP, MRCS 1964; FDSRCS 1961. Gen. dental practice, 1956–58; SHO, Oral Surgery, Nottingham Gen. Hosp., 1958–59; Registrar, Oral Surgery, St Peter's Hosp., Chertsey, 1959–61; Sen. Registrar, Royal Victoria Infirmary, Newcastle upon Tyne, 1965–68; Consultant, 1968–95, Gen. Manager, 1985–91, Univ. Hosp. of Wales, Cardiff. Member: Central Cttee, Hosp. Med. Services, 1975–88; Jt Consultant Cttee, London, 1980–93 (Chm., Welsh Sub-Cttee, 1986–93); Chairman: Med. Bd, S Glamorgan, 1980–82; Welsh Council, BMA, 1991–94 (Chm., Welsh Consultant and Specialist Cttee, 1989–93); BMA Gen. Managers' Gp, 1988–90; Glan-Y-Môr NHS Trust, 1995–99; Brô Morgannwg NHS Trust, 1999–2005 (Lead Chair, 2002–04). Pres., BAOMS, 1992–93; Mem., Eur. Assoc. of Max.-Fac. Surgery, 1980–95; Fellow, BMA, 1998–2016. Ext. Examr, Univ. of Hong Kong, 1990–93. *Publications:* Pre-Prosthetic Oral Surgery, 1986; A Journey Through a Life, 2014; chapters in numerous medical works. *Recreations:* grass cutting, photography, reading, having joints replaced! *Address:* 179 Cyncoed Road, Cardiff CF23 6AH. *T:* (home) (029) 2075 2319.

HOPKINS, Sidney Arthur; Managing Director, Guardian Royal Exchange plc, 1990–94; *b* 15 April 1932; *m* 1955, Joan Marion Smith; one *d. Educ:* Battersea Grammar Sch. ACII. Joined Royal Exchange Assce, 1948, Man., Organisation and Methods, 1966; Guardian Royal Exchange Assurance Ltd: Chief Claims Man. (UK), 1974; Man., Home Motor, 1976; Asst Gen. Man. (Life), 1979; Guardian Royal Exchange Assurance plc: Asst Gen. Man. (Field Operations), 1983; Gen. Man. (UK), 1985; Guardian Royal Exchange (UK) Ltd: Man. Dir, 1987; Guardian Royal Exchange plc: Dir, 1986; Dep. Chief Exec., 1989. Dir, Residuary MMB, 1994–2002. Freeman, City of London; Liveryman, Company of Insurers. *Recreations:* sports, films. *Address:* Woodlands, 8 Littleworth Lane, Esher, Surrey KT10 9PF.

HOPKINSON, family name of **Baron Colyton**.

HOPKINSON, Ven. Barnabas John; Archdeacon of Wilts, 1998–2004; *b* 11 May 1939; *s* of late Prebendary Stephan Hopkinson and Mrs Anne Hopkinson; *m* 1968, Esmé Faith (*née* Gibbons); three *d. Educ:* Emanuel School; Trinity Coll., Cambridge (MA); Lincoln Theological Coll. Curate: All Saints and Martyrs, Langley, Manchester, 1965–67; Great St Mary's, Cambridge, 1967–70; Chaplain, Charterhouse School, 1970–75; Team Vicar of Preshute, Wilts, 1975–81; RD of Marlborough, 1977–81; Rector of Wimborne Minster, Dorset, 1981–86; RD of Wimborne, 1985–86; Archdeacon of Sarum, 1986–98; Priest-in-charge, Stratford-sub-Castle, 1987–98. Canon of Salisbury Cathedral, 1983–2004, now Emeritus. *Recreations:* gardening, amateur dramatics. *Address:* Tanners Cottage, Frog Street, Bampton, Devon EX16 9NT.

HOPKINSON, Prof. Brian Ridley, FRCS; Professor of Vascular Surgery, University of Nottingham, 1996–2003, now Emeritus; Consultant General Surgeon, Queen's Medical Centre, Nottingham, 1973–2003; *b* 26 Feb. 1938; *s* of Edward Alban Ernest Hopkinson and May Olive Hopkinson (*née* Redding); *m* 1962, Margaret Ruth Bull; three *s* one *d. Educ:* Birmingham Univ. (MB ChB 1961; ChM 1972). FRCS 1964. Hse Surgeon, 1961–62, Resident Surgical Officer, 1964–65, Hallam Hosp., W Bromwich; Registrar, Cardiac Surgery, Queen Elizabeth Hosp., Birmingham, 1965–66; Buswell Res. Fellow, Buffalo, NY, 1966–67; Sen. Surgical Registrar, Birmingham Gen. Hosp. and Wolverhampton Royal Infirmary, 1967–69; Lectr in Surgery, Univ. of Birmingham, 1969–73; Consultant Gen. Surgeon specialising in vascular surgery, Queen's Med. Centre, Nottingham, 1973–96. Hon. Prof., Chinese Med. Univ., Shenyang, China, 1999. Various BMA posts including: Sec. and Chm., Nottingham Div., 1975–83; Chm., Trent Regl Council, 1992–95; Chm., Regl Consultant and Specialist Cttee, 1987–92; Chm., Annual Reps' Meeting, 1998–2001; Vice Pres., 2002–. Hon. Life Fellow, British Assoc. of Clinical Anatomists, 2017. Licensed Lay Reader, C of E, St Jude's, Mapperley. Lifetime Achievement Award: Vascular Soc. of GB and Ireland, 2012; Indian Vascular Soc., 2014. *Publications:* Endovascular Surgery for Aortic Aneurysms, 1997; Operative Atlas of Endovascular Aneurysm Surgery, 1999; contrib. Lancet. *Recreations:* swimming, motor caravanning, coal fired steamboats. *Address:* Lincolnsfield, 18 Victoria Crescent, Private Road, Sherwood, Nottingham NG5 4DA. *T:* (0115) 960 4167.

HOPKINSON, Bryan; Strategy Co-ordinator, United Nations Mission in Kosovo, 2006–08; Political Consultant, Skorgg International, 2000–14; *b* 24 Nov. 1956; *s* of Brian Hopkinson and Florance Hopkinson (*née* Richardson), Huddersfield; *m* 1987, Stephanie Burd (*née* Perkins). *Educ:* King James's Grammar Sch., Huddersfield; King's Coll., Cambridge (BA, MA). Joined FCO, 1980; Kampala, 1981–84; songwriter and musician, 1985–87; rejoined FCO, 1987; Lisbon, 1989–93; FCO, 1993–95; Ambassador to Bosnia-Herzegovina, 1995–96; Hon. Dir, British Council, Sarajevo, 1995–96; International Crisis Group: Director: Bosnia Proj., Sarajevo, Jan.–July 1999; Kosovo Proj., Pristina, July–Dec. 1999; Montenegro Proj., Podgorica, Jan.–June 2000; Political Dir, OSCE Mission in Kosovo, 2002–04. Dir, Skraffstat, 2014–18. *Publications:* Corizel and Ulia (novel), 2016; numerous Balkans reports. *Recreations:* walking, music, board and computer games. *Address:* Apt 206, 1535 The Melting Point, Commercial Street, Huddersfield, W Yorks HD1 3DN. *T:* (01484) 469804.

HOPKINSON, Prof. David Albert, MD; Professor of Human Biochemical Genetics, University College London, 1993–2000, now Emeritus; Director, Medical Research Council Human Biochemical Genetics Unit, 1976–2000; *b* 26 June 1935; *s* of George Albert and Lily Hopkinson; *m* 1st, 1959, Josephine Manze; two *s* one *d*; 2nd, 1980, Yvonne Edwards. *Educ:* Chesterfield Grammar Sch.; St Catharine's Coll., Cambridge; Royal London Hosp. Med. Coll. (MA, MD); Open Univ. (BSc Hons 1st Cl. Geol. 2008). FGS 2009. Royal London Hospital: House Surgeon and House Physician, 1959–60; Jun. Lectr, Biochem., 1960; Resident Pathologist, 1961; Scientific Staff, MRC Human Biochemical Genetics Unit, 1962–2000. Volunteer Advr and Social Policy Coordinator, Chiltern CAB, 2002–. Hon. Life Mem., Internat. Forensic Haemogenetics Soc., 1992. *Publications:* Handbook of Enzyme Electrophoresis in Human Genetics, 1976. *Recreations:* vegetable gardening, hill and mountain walking, furniture restoration, watching Rugby. *Address:* Swan Cottage, 42 Church Street, Great Missenden, Bucks HP16 0AZ.

HOPKINSON, David Hugh Laing, CBE 1986; RD 1965; DL; Deputy Chairman and Chief Executive, M&G Group PLC, 1979–87; Chairman, Harrisons and Crosfield, 1988–91 (Deputy Chairman, 1987–88, Director, 1986–91); Deputy Chairman, ECC Group (formerly English China Clays), 1986–91 (Director, since 1975); *b* 14 Aug. 1926; *s* of late Cecil Hopkinson and Leila Hopkinson; *m* 1951, Prudence Margaret Holmes, OBE, JP, DL; two *s* two *d. Educ:* Wellington Coll.; Merton Coll., Oxford (BA 1949). RNVR and RNR, 1944–65. A Clerk of the House of Commons, 1948–59; Robert Fleming, 1959–62; M&G Investment Management, 1963–87 (Chm., 1975–87); Director: Lloyds Bank Southern Regional Board, 1977–88; BR (Southern) Bd, 1978–87 (Chm., 1983–87); Wolverhampton and Dudley Breweries, 1987–96; Mem., Adv. Gp of Governor of Bank of England, 1984. Mem., Housing Corp., 1986–88. Director: English Chamber Orchestra and Music Soc., 1970–89; Charities Investment Managers, 1970–2014; Merchants Trust, 1976–99; RTZ Pension Trustees, 1993–99; SE Arts Board, 1994–97. Member: General Synod of C of E, 1970–90; Central Bd of Finance, 1970–90; a Church Comr, 1973–82, 1984–94; Mem., Chichester Dio. Bd of Finance, 1970–2001 (Chm., 1977–88); Chm., Chichester Cathedral Finance Cttee, 2000–05. Chm., Church Army Bd, 1987–98. Trustee: Nat. Assoc. of Almshouses; Chichester Cathedral Development Trust; Pallant House Gall., Chichester, 1992–2002 (Chm. of Trustees); Royal Pavilion, Brighton; RAM Foundn; Edward James Foundn, 1990–2002 (Chm.). Governor: Sherborne Sch., 1970–96 (Vice-Chm., Bd, 1987–96); Wellington Coll., 1978–96. DL 1986, High Sheriff, 1987–88, W Sussex. Hon. Fellow: St Anne's Coll., Oxford, 1984–2017; Chichester Univ., 2007–. Dist. Friend, Univ. of Oxford, 2007. *Recreations:* travelling, walking, opera. *Address:* St John's Priory, Poling, Arundel, W Sussex BN18 9PS. *T:* (01903) 882393. *Club:* Brooks's.

HOPKINSON, George William; Deputy Director and Director of Studies, Royal Institute of International Affairs, 1999–2000; retired writer and speaker on international relations; *b* 13 Sept. 1943; *s* of William Hartley Hopkinson and Mary (*née* Ashmore); *m* 1st, 1973, Mary Agnes Coverdale (marr. diss. 1997); one *s*; 2nd, 2010, Virginia Frances Dewhurst. *Educ:* Tupton Hall Grammar Sch.; Pembroke Coll., Cambridge (BA 1965; MA 1969). Inland Revenue, 1965–73; CSD, 1973–81; HM Treasury, 1981–86; Ministry of Defence, 1986–97: Hd, Defence Arms Control Unit, 1988–91; Vis. Fellow, Global Security Programme, Cambridge Univ., 1991–92 (on secondment); Hd, Defence Lands Service, 1992–93; Asst Under-Sec. of State (Policy) 1993–97; Royal Institute of International Affairs: Hd of Internat. Security Prog., 1997–99. Associate Fellow: RUSI, 1997–2008; RIIA, 2000–03; Sen. Vis. Fellow, WEU Inst., Paris, 2001. *Publications:* The Making of British Defence Policy, 2000; The Atlantic Crises, Britain, Europe and Parting from the United States, 2017; The New Geopolitics of Terror: demons and dragons, 2017; contribs to books on security policy, international affairs and arms control; occasional papers. *Recreations:* reading, walking. *Address:* Gloucester House, The Southend, Ledbury, Herefordshire HR8 2HD. *Club:* Oxford and Cambridge.

**HOPKINSON, Giles,** CB 1990; Under-Secretary, Departments of the Environment and Transport, 1976–90, retired; *b* 20 Nov. 1931; *s* of late Arthur John Hopkinson, CIE, ICS, and Eleanor (*née* Richardson); *m* 1956, Eleanor Jean Riddell; three *d. Educ:* Marlborough Coll.; Leeds Univ. (BSc). E. & J. Richardson Ltd, 1956–57; Forestal Land, Timber and Rly Co. Ltd, 1957–58; DSIR: Scientific Officer, 1958–61; Sen. Scientific Officer, 1961–64; Private Sec. to Perm. Sec., 1963–64; Principal, MoT, 1964–71; Asst Sec., DoE, 1971; Under-Secretary: DoE (Personnel Mgt and Trng), 1976; Dept of Transport (Ports and Freight Directorate), 1979; Dir, London Region, PSA, DoE, 1983–90. *Recreations:* enjoying music, paintings, furniture, limited travel within Britain, current affairs, writing (memoir). *Address:* 12 Barn Hill, Stamford, Lincs PE9 2AE.

**HOPKINSON, Simon Charles;** restaurateur, chef, writer; *b* 5 June 1954; *s* of late Bruce and Dorothie Hopkinson. *Educ:* St John's Coll. Sch., Cambridge (chorister); Trent Coll., Derbyshire. Normandie Hotel, Birtle, 1972; Hat and Feather Restaurant, Knutsford, 1973; St Non's Hotel, St David's, 1973–74; Druidstone Hotel, Broadhaven, 1974–75; chef and proprietor: Shed Restaurant, Dinas, 1975–77; Hoppy's Restaurant, 1977–78; Egon Ronay Inspector, 1978–80; private chef, London, 1980–83; Hilaire Restaurant, Kensington, 1983–87; co-proprietor, Bibendum, 1987–2016 (head chef, 1987–95). Presenter, TV series: The Good Cook, 2011; Simon Hopkinson Cooks, 2013. Cookery writer for The Independent and Food Illustrated. Glenfiddich Awards, 1995, 1997, 1998, 2000. *Publications:* (with Lindsey Bareham) Roast Chicken and Other Stories, 1994 (André Simon Meml Award (jtly), 1994); (contrib.) The Conran Cook Book, 1997; (with Lindsey Bareham) The Prawn Cocktail Years, 1997; Gammon & Spinach, 1998; Roast Chicken and Other Stories: Second Helpings, 2001; Week In Week Out, 2007; The Vegetarian Option, 2009; The Good Cook, 2011; Simon Hopkinson Cooks, 2013 (John Avery Award, André Simon Meml Fund, 2013). *Recreations:* poker, wine. *Address:* c/o David Higham Associates, 7th Floor, Waverley House, 7–12 Noel Street, W1F 8GQ.

**HOPKIRK, Jennifer;** DL; Vice Lord-Lieutenant for Buckinghamshire, 2006–11; *b* 4 Dec. 1941; *d* of Bertie and Lilian Manser; *m* 1967, Paddy Hopkirk; two *s* one *d. Educ:* Clifton High Sch., Bristol; St Godric's, Hampstead. Commercial TV film prodn, 1960–69. Various posts with Central London Cttee, RNLI, 1977–2004; Mem., Bucks Br., NSPCC, 1985– (Chm., 2006–09; Pres., 2009– ); Co-Vice Chm., London Cttee, British Paraplegic Sports Soc., 1986–94. Patron, Chilterns MS Centre, 2006–12. High Sheriff Bucks, 2005–06, DL Bucks, 2006. *Recreations:* reading, gardening, tennis, bridge, Lucas Terriers, 6 grandchildren. *Address:* Penn, Buckinghamshire. *Club:* Queen's.

**HOPKIRK, Joyce, (Mrs W. J. Lear);** writer; *b* 2 March; *d* of Walter Nicholson and Veronica (*née* Keelan); *m* 1st, 1962, Peter Hopkirk (marr. diss. 1966; he *d* 2014); one *d*; 2nd, 1974, William James Lear; one *s. Educ:* Middle Street Secondary Sch., Newcastle upon Tyne. Reporter, Gateshead Post, 1955; Founder Editor, Majorcan News, 1959; Reporter, Daily Sketch, 1960; Royal Reporter, Daily Express, 1961; Ed., Fashion Magazine, 1967; Women's Ed., Sun, 1967; Launch Ed., Cosmopolitan, 1971–72 (launched 1972); Asst Ed., Daily Mirror, 1973–78; Women's Ed., Sunday Times, 1982; Editl Dir, Elle, 1984; Asst Ed., Sunday Mirror, 1985; Ed.-in-Chief, She Magazine, 1986–89; Dir, Editors' Unlimited, 1990–92; Founder Ed., Chic Magazine 1994. Mem., Competition Commn, 1999–2004. Co-Chm., PPA Awards, 1998. Editor of the Year, 1972; Women's Magazines Editor of the Year, 1988. FRSA 1990. *Publications:* Successful Slimming, 1976; Successful Slimming Cookbook, 1978; (jtly) Splash!, 1995; (jtly) Best of Enemies, 1996; (jtly) Double Trouble, 1997; Unfinished Business, 1998; Relative Strangers, 1999; The Affair, 2000. *Recreations:* conversation, sleeping, gardening, boating.

**HOPLEY, Damian Paul;** Founder and Group Chief Executive Officer, Rugby Players' Association, since 1998; *b* London, 12 April 1970; *s* of Leo and Margaret Hopley. *Educ:* St Benedict's Sch., Ealing; Harrow Sch.; Univ. of St Andrews (MTh); Hughes Hall, Cambridge (PGCE). Cambridge Univ. Rugby Blue, 1992; player: London Wasps RFC, 1990–97; England Rugby Sevens, 1993–97 (winning team, Rugby World Cup Sevens, 1993; Captain, 1996); England Nat. Team, 1995 (3 Caps). *Recreations:* golf, yoga, cycling, piano, wellbeing, wine. *Address:* Rugby Players' Association, Regal House, 70 London Road, Twickenham TW1 3QS. *T:* (020) 3053 6677. *E:* dhopley@therpa.co.uk. *Clubs:* Soho House; Hawks (Cambridge).

**HOPMEIER, Michael Andrew Philip; His Honour Judge Hopmeier;** a Circuit Judge, since 2009; *b* Oldham, 25 Oct. 1950; *s* of Lucian Hopmeier and Yolanda Hopmeier. *Educ:* Dulwich Coll.; Wadham Coll., Oxford (MA); University Coll. London (LLM). Called to the Bar, Middle Temple, 1974, Bencher, 2014; Asst Recorder, 1990–94; Recorder, 1994–2009. Hon. Vis. Prof., City Univ., London, 2014– ; Hon. Prof., Univ. of WI, Jamaica, 2016–. *Publications:* (ed) Millington and Sutherland Williams on the Proceeds of Crime, 4th edn, 2013. *Recreations:* sailing, ski-ing, travel, music. *Address:* Southwark Crown Court, 1 English Grounds, (off Battlebridge Lane), Southwark, SE1 2HU. *Clubs:* Bar Yacht; Weirwood Sailing, Emsworth Sailing.

**HOPPEN, Prof. (Karl) Theodore,** PhD; FBA 2001; FRHistS; Professor of History, University of Hull, 1996–2003; *b* 27 Nov. 1941; *s* of Paul Ernst Theodore Hoppen and Edith Margaretha Hoppen (*née* Van Brussel); *m* 1st, 1970, Alison Mary Buchan (*d* 2002); one *s* two *d*; 2nd, 2007, Anne Patricia Drakeford. *Educ:* Glenstal Abbey Sch., Co. Limerick; University Coll., Dublin (BA 1961; MA 1964); Trinity Coll., Cambridge (PhD 1967). University of Hull: Asst Lectr, 1966–68; Lectr, 1968–74; Sen. Lectr, 1974–86; Reader, 1986–96. Benjamin Duke Fellow, Nat. Humanities Center, NC, 1985–86; Vis. Fellow, Sidney Sussex Coll., Cambridge, 1988; Res. Reader in Humanities, British Acad., 1994–96. FRHistS 1978. Hon. MRIA 2010. Mem. Editl Bd, Dictionary of Irish Biography, 2003–13 (9 vols publd 2009). *Publications:* The Common Scientist in the Seventeenth Century, 1970, 2nd edn 2008; (ed) Papers of the Dublin Philosophical Society 1683–1709, 1982, 2nd edn 2008; Elections, Politics and Society in Ireland 1832–1885, 1984; Ireland since 1800: conflict and conformity, 1989, 2nd edn 1999; The Mid-Victorian Generation 1846–1886, vol. in New Oxford History of England, 1998; (ed with Mary E. Daly) Gladstone: Ireland and beyond, 2011; Governing Hibernia: British politicians and Ireland 1800–1921, 2016 (Irish Histl Res. Prize, 2017); contrib. numerous articles to learned jls. *Recreations:* idleness, bel canto operas. *Address:* 1 Greyfriars Crescent, Beverley HU17 8LR. *T:* (01482) 861343. *E:* K.T.Hoppen@hull.ac.uk. *Club:* Oxford and Cambridge.

**HOPPER, Prof. Andrew,** CBE 2007; PhD; FRS 2006; FREng, FIET; Professor of Computer Technology and Head of Department, Computer Laboratory, University of Cambridge, since 2004; *b* Warsaw, Poland, 9 May 1953; *s* of William John Hopper and Maria Barbara Wyrzykowska; *m* 1988, Prof. Alison Gail Smith; one *s* one *d. Educ:* Quintin Kynaston Sch., London; University Coll. of Swansea (BSc); Trinity Hall, Cambridge (PhD 1978; Hon. Fellow, 2011). FREng (FEng 1996); FIET (FIEE 1993). University of Cambridge: Res. Asst, 1977–79; Asst Lectr, 1979–83; Lectr, 1983–92; Reader in Computer Technol., 1992–97; Prof. of Communications, Dept of Engrg, 1997–2004; Fellow, 1981–2011, Dir of Studies in Computer Sci., 1981–93, Corpus Christi Coll., Cambridge. Res. Dir, Acorn Computers Ltd, Cambridge, 1979–84; Man. Dir, Olivetti Oracle Res. Lab., Cambridge, subseq. AT&T Labs Cambridge, 1986–2002; Director: Qudos Ltd, Cambridge, 1985–89; Virata Corp. (formerly Advanced Telecommunications Modules Ltd), 1993–2001; Acorn Computer Gp plc, Cambridge, 1996–98; Adaptive Broadband Ltd, 1998–2001; Telemedia Systems Ltd, Cambridge, 2000–03 (Chm., 1995–2003); Real VNC Ltd, 2002– (Chm., 2002–); Solarflare Inc. (formerly Level 5 Networks Ltd), 2002–08; Ubisense (formerly Ubiquitous Systems) Ltd, 2003–15 (Chm., 2006–15); Chairman: Cambridge Broadband Ltd, 2000–05; Adventiq Ltd, Cambridge, 2005–09; Vice-Pres., Res., Ing. C. Olivetti & C., SpA, Italy, 1993–98. Pres., IET, 2012–13 (Dep. Pres., 2010–12); Treas. and Vice Pres., Royal Soc., 2017–. Clifford Paterson Lecture, Royal Soc., 1999. Hon. Fellow: Univ. of Wales, Swansea, 2005; Corpus Christi Coll., Cambridge, 2013. Hon. DSc (Eng) QUB, 2010. Silver Medal, Royal Acad. of Engrg, 2003; Sigmobile, outstanding contribn award, 2004, Test of Time Award, 2016, ACM (USA); Mountbatten Medal, IEE, 2004; MacRobert Award, RAEng, 2013; Bakerian Medal and Lect., Royal Soc., 2017. *Publications:* (jtly) Local Area Network Design, 1986. *Recreations:* ski-ing (Univ. of Cambridge half-blue), flying, farming. *Address:* Computer Laboratory, William Gates Building, J. J. Thomson Avenue, Cambridge CB3 0FD.

**HOPPER, Prof. Stephen Donald,** AC 2012; PhD; FLS; Winthrop Professor of Biodiversity, University of Western Australia, 2012–20; *b* 18 June 1951; *s* of Donald Arthur Hopper and Patricia Love Hopper; *m* 1975, Christine Rigden; two *s* one *d. Educ:* Univ. of Western Australia (BSc 1st Cl. Hons 1973; PhD 1978). Pt-time music teacher (guitar and mandolin), Zenith Music, Claremont, WA, 1970–75; botany lab. demonstrator, Univ. of WA, 1973–77; contractual botanist, Western Australian Herbarium, Dept of Agriculture, 1977; Res. Officer (flora conservation), Dept of Fisheries and Wildlife, 1977–85; Sen. Res. Scientist, flora conservation, 1985–88, Sen. Principal Res. Scientist and Officer i/c, 1988–92, Dept of Conservation and Land Mgt, Western Australian Wildlife Res. Centre; Dir, Kings Park and Botanic Garden, Perth, WA, 1992–99; CEO, Botanic Gdns and Park Authy (which manages Kings Park and Botanic Gdn and Bold Park), 1999–2004; Foundn Prof. of Plant Conservation Biol., Univ. of WA, 2004–06; Dir, Royal Botanic Gardens, Kew, 2006–12. Co-presenter, TV prog., The West, 2003. Corresp. Mem., Botanical Soc. of America, 2007. FLS 2007; FTSE 2011–17. Hon. DSc: Western Australia, 2010; Sussex, 2012. *Publications:* (jtly) Western Australia's Endangered Flora, 1990; (jtly) Leaf and Branch, 1990; (jtly) The Banksia Atlas, 1991; Kangaroo Paws and Catspaws, 1993; (ed jtly) Gondwanan Heritage, 1996; (with P. Nikulinsky) Life on the Rocks, 1999, 2nd edn 2008; (with P. Nikulinsky) Soul of the Desert, 2005; (jtly) Orchids of Western Australia, 2008; (jtly) Nyoongar Boodja Koomba Bardip Kooratan (Nyoongar land – long story short): a history of ancient Nyoongar land and people, 2018; jl articles, reports and peer-reviewed scientific papers. *Recreations:* music, walking, photography, travelling. *Address:* Centre of Excellence in Natural Resource Management, University of Western Australia, Proudlove Parade, Albany, WA 6330, Australia.

**HOPPER, William Joseph;** author; merchant banker, retired; *b* 9 Aug. 1929; *s* of I. Vance Hopper and Jennie Josephine Hopper; one *d* by a former marriage. *Educ:* Langside Elementary Sch., Glasgow; Queen's Park Secondary Sch., Glasgow; Glasgow Univ. (MA 1st Cl. Hons (Mod. Langs) 1953). Educn Officer, RAF, 1953–55. Financial Analyst, W. R. Grace & Co., NY, 1956–59; London Office Manager, H. Hentz & Co., Members, NY Stock Exchange, 1960–66; Gen. Manager, S. G. Warburg & Co. Ltd, 1966–69; Director: Hill Samuel & Co. Ltd, 1969–74; Morgan Grenfell & Co. Ltd, 1974–79 (Adviser, 1979–86) (bond issue for EIB selected as Deal of the Year by Institutional Investor, 1976); Wharf Resources Ltd, Calgary, 1984–87; Manchester Ship Canal Co., 1985–87; Chairman: Robust Mouldings, 1986–90; GCP (Australia) Ltd, 2010–12; Exec. Chm., Shire Trust, 1986–91; Advr, Yamaichi Internat. (Europe), 1986–88. Exec. Chm., WJ Hopper & Co. Ltd, investment bankers and placement agents, 1996–2009. MEP (C), Greater Manchester West, 1979–84. Co-founder (1969) and first Chm., Inst. for Fiscal Studies, London (Mem., Exec. Cttee, 1969–2015; Mem. Council, 2015); Treasurer, Action Resource Centre, 1985–94; Trustee: Nat. Hosp. for Nervous Diseases Develt Fund, 1986–90; Hampstead, Wells and Campden Trust, 1989–2000. Chm. Cttee of Management, Rosslyn Hill Unitarian Chapel, 1995–98 and 2004–10. Mem., London Dist and SE Provincial Assembly of Unitarian and Free Christian Churches, 2000–04. Governor, Colville Primary Sch., Notting Hill Gate, 1978–80. Vis. Fellow and Exec. in Residence, Manchester Business Sch., 2009–12. Author in Residence, Edinburgh Bookfest, 2009; Writer in Residence, Drucker Inst., Claremont, Calif, 2010. *Publications:* A Turntable for Capital, 1969; (with Kenneth Hopper) The Puritan Gift: triumph, collapse and revival of an American dream, 2007 (trans. Mandarin, 2013). *Recreations:* singing in church choir, watching old films, chatting to friends. *Address:* 9a Flask Walk, NW3 1HJ. *T:* (020) 7435 6414. *Club:* Garrick.

**HOPPIT, Prof. Julian,** PhD; FBA 2012; FRHistS; Astor Professor of British History, University College London, since 2006; *b* Knutsford, Cheshire, 14 Aug. 1957; *s* of Geoffrey and May Hoppit; *m* 1984, Karin Horowitz. *Educ:* Watford Boys Grammar Sch.; Selwyn Coll., Cambridge (BA 1979; PhD 1984). FRHistS 1988. Res. Fellow, Pembroke Coll., Cambridge, 1982–83; Coll. Fellow, Magdalene Coll., Cambridge, 1983–86; Lectr, then Reader, 1987–2001, Prof., 2001–06, Dept of Hist., UCL. Ed., Histl Jl, 2009–12. Treas., RHistS, 2001–05. *Publications:* Risk and Failure in English Business, 1700–1800, 1987; Failed Legislation, 1660–1800, 1997; A Land of Liberty?: England, 1689–1727, 2000; Britain's Political Economies: parliament and economic life, 1660–1800, 2017; contrib. articles to Past and Present, Econ. Hist. Rev., Histl Jl. *Recreations:* golf, gardening, cooking. *Address:* Department of History, University College London, Gower Street, WC1E 6BT. *T:* (020) 7679 3603. *E:* j.hoppit@ucl.ac.uk.

**HOPSON, Christopher Ian;** Chief Executive, NHS Providers (formerly Foundation Trust Network), since 2012; *b* 9 April 1963; *s* of David Joseph Hopson and Susan Hopson (*née* Buckingham); *m* 1994, Charlotte Gascoigne; two *s. Educ:* Marlborough Coll.; St Andrew's Sch., Del, USA (ESU Scholarship); Univ. of Sussex (BA Hons Pols 1985); Cranfield Sch. of Mgt (MBA 1992). Social Democratic Party: constituency agent, 1985–87; Researcher to Rosie Barnes, MP, 1987–88; Dir, Elections and Campaigns, 1988–89; Chief Exec. (Nat. Sec.), 1989; consultant, corporate communications strategy, 1989–91; Pol Advr to Sec. of State, Dept of Nat. Heritage, 1992; Granada Media Group: Corp. Affairs Dir, 1993–99; Bd Dir, 1996–99; Man. Dir, Result e-learning business, 1999–2002; Consultant, DfES, 2002–04; HM Revenue and Customs: Dir, Communications and Mktg, 2005–07; Dir, Change and Capability, 2007; Bd Dir, 2006–08; Dir, Customer Contact, 2008–12. Member: Standards Policy and Strategy Cttee, BSI, 2015–; NHS Assembly, 2019–. Mem. Council, RTS, 1993–97. Trustee, Foyer Fedn, 1999–2010 (Chm. of Trustees, 2004–10). *Recreations:* family, reading, theatre, cinema, football (West Ham), good food and wine (not necessarily in that order). *Address:* NHS Providers, One Birdcage Walk, SW1H 9JJ. *T:* (020) 7304 6805. *E:* chris.hopson@nhsproviders.org.

**HOPTON, Nicholas Dunster;** HM Diplomatic Service; Director, EU External and Security, Foreign and Commonwealth Office, since 2019; *b* Manchester, 8 Oct. 1965; *s* of David Samuel Hopton, MD, FRCS and Janet Sealy Hopton (*née* Dunster), MBE, DL; *m* 1993, Alejandra Echenique; three *s* two *d. Educ:* St Peter's Sch., York; Magdalene Coll., Cambridge (BA 1989); La Sapienza Univ., Rome. Entered FCO, 1989; European Communities Dept, FCO, 1990–91; Second Sec. (Pol/Inf.), Rabat (and Nouakchott), 1991–95; News Dept, FCO, 1995–97; EU Dept (Ext.), FCO, 1997–98; Private Sec. to Minister for Europe, FCO, 1998–2000; First Sec., Rome, 2000–03; Counsellor (EU/Econ.), Paris, 2003–07; Nat. Security Strategy Team, Cabinet Office, 2007–08; No 10 Policy Unit, 2008; Hd, Internat. Orgns Dept, FCO, 2008–11; Ambassador to Yemen,

2012–13; Ambassador to Qatar, 2013–15; Chargé d'Affaires, Tehran, 2015–16; Ambassador to Iran, 2016–18. Vis. Academic, St Antony's Coll., Oxford, 2013–14. *Publications:* In Pieces, 1999 (Spanish edn, 2004). *Recreations:* squash, sailing, hill walking, music, gardening. *Address:* c/o Foreign and Commonwealth Office, King Charles Street, SW1A 2AH. *E:* Nicholas.Hopton@fco.gov.uk. *Clubs:* Royal Automobile; Hawks (Cambridge).

**HOPWOOD, Sir David (Alan),** Kt 1994; FRS 1979; John Innes Professor of Genetics, University of East Anglia, Norwich, 1968–98, now Emeritus Professor of Genetics; Head of the Genetics Department, John Innes Centre, 1968–98, now Emeritus Fellow; *b* 19 Aug. 1933; *s* of Herbert Hopwood and Dora Hopwood (*née* Grant); *m* 1962, Joyce Lilian Bloom; two *s* one *d*. *Educ:* Purbrook Park County High Sch., Hants; Lymm Grammar Sch., Cheshire; St John's Coll., Cambridge (MA, PhD; Hon. Fellow, 2007). DSc (Glasgow). Whytehead Major Scholar, St John's Coll., Cambridge, 1951–54; John Stothert Bye-Fellow, Magdalene Coll., Cambridge, 1956–58 (Hon. Fellow, 1991); Res. Fellow, St John's Coll., 1958–61; Univ. Demonstrator, Univ. of Cambridge, 1957–61; Lectr in Genetics, Univ. of Glasgow, 1961–68. Pres., Genetical Soc. of GB, 1985–87. Foreign Fellow, Indian Nat. Science Acad., 1987. Hon. Professor: Chinese Acad. of Med. Scis, 1987; Insts of Microbiology and Plant Physiology, Chinese Acad. of Scis, 1987; Huazhong Agricl Univ., Wuhan, China, 1989; Jiao Tong Univ., Shanghai, 2004; Guangxi Univ., Nanning, China, 2004. Hon. FIBiol 2001. Hon. Fellow: UMIST, 1990; Magdalene Coll., Cambridge, 1992. Hon. Member: Spanish Microbiol. Soc., 1985; Hungarian Acad. of Scis, 1990; Soc. for Gen. Microbiol., 1990 (Pres., 2000–03); Kitasato Inst., Tokyo, 1997. Hon. DSc: Eidgenössische Technische Hochschule, Zürich, 1989; UEA, 1998; Athens, 2012. Mendel Medal, Czech Acad. of Scis, 1995; Stuart Mudd Prize, Internat. Union of Microbiol Socs, 2002; Ernst Chain Prize, Imperial Coll. London, 2003; André Lwoff Prize, Fedn of Eur. Microbiol Socs, 2003; Prize Medal, Soc. for Gen. Microbiol., 2011. *Publications:* Streptomyces in Nature and Medicine, 2007; numerous articles and chapters in scientific jls and books. *Recreations:* cooking, gardening, natural history. *Address:* John Innes Centre, Colney Lane, Norwich NR4 7UH. *T:* (01603) 450000, *Fax:* (01603) 450778.

**HORAM, Baron** *cr* 2013 (Life Peer), of Grimsargh in the County of Lancashire; **John Rhodes Horam;** Member, Electoral Commission, 2012–18; *b* 7 March 1939; *s* of Sydney Horam, Preston; *m* 1987, Judith Jackson. *Educ:* Silcoates Sch., Wakefield; St Catharine's Coll., Cambridge (BA 1960; Fellow Commoner, 2010). Marketing Executive, Rowntree & Co., 1960–62; leader and feature writer: Financial Times, 1962–65; The Economist, 1965–68; Man. Dir, Commodities Research Unit Ltd, 1968–70 and 1983–92; Dep. Chm., 1992–95, non-exec. Dir, 1997–, CRU Internat. Ltd. MP Gateshead West, 1970–83 (Lab, 1970–81, SDP, 1981–83); MP (C) Orpington, 1992–2010. Parly Under-Sec. of State, Dept of Transport, 1976–79; Labour spokesman on econ. affairs, 1979–81; Parly spokesman on econ. affairs, SDP, 1981–83; Parly Sec., OPSS, 1995; Parly Under-Sec. of State, DoH, 1995–97. Chm., Envmtl Audit Select Cttee, 1997–2003; Member: Foreign Affairs Select Cttee, 2005–10; EU Cttee, H of L, 2015–. Mem. Exec., 1922 Cttee, 2004–07. Chm., St Catharine's Soc., Cambridge, 2005–13 (Pres., 2014–15). *Address:* 6 Bovingdon Road, SW6 2AP.

**HORBURY, Rev. Prof. William,** PhD, DD; FBA 1997; Professor of Jewish and Early Christian Studies, University of Cambridge, 1998–2009; Fellow of Corpus Christi College, Cambridge, since 1978; *b* 6 June 1942; *m* 1966, Katharine Mary, *d* of late Rt Rev. D. R. Feaver; two *d*. *Educ:* Charterhouse; Oriel Coll., Oxford (MA 1967); Clare Coll., Cambridge (MA 1968; PhD 1971); Westcott House, Cambridge; DD Cantab 2000. Res. Fellow, Clare Coll., Cambridge, 1968–72; ordained deacon, 1969, priest, 1970; Vicar, Great Gransden, and Rector, Little Gransden, 1972–78; Cambridge University: Dean of Chapel, Corpus Christi Coll., 1978–85; Univ. Lectr in Divinity, 1984–96; Reader, 1996–98; Dir, Jewish Inscriptions Project, Divinity Faculty, 1989–95. Leverhulme Emeritus Fellow, 2010–11. T. W. Manson Meml Lect., 2009. NSM, St Botolph, Cambridge, 1990–2015. Pres., British Assoc. for Jewish Studies, 1996. Hon. DD Aberdeen, 2009; Hon. DTheol Münster, 2014. *Publications:* (ed jtly) Suffering and Martyrdom in the New Testament, 1981; (ed jtly) Essays in Honour of Ernst Bammel, 1983; (ed) *Templum Amicitiae:* essays on the Second Temple, 1991; (jtly) Jewish Inscriptions of Graeco-Roman Egypt, 1992; (jtly) The Jewish-Christian Controversy, 1996; Jews and Christians in Contact and Controversy, 1998; Jewish Messianism and the Cult of Christ, 1998; (ed) Hebrew Study from Ezra to Ben-Yehuda, 1999; (ed jtly) The Cambridge History of Judaism, vol. iii, The Early Roman Period, 1999; Christianity in Ancient Jewish Tradition, 1999; Messianism among Jews and Christians: twelve Biblical and historical studies, 2003, 2nd edn 2016; Herodian Judaism and New Testament Study, 2006; Jewish War under Trajan and Hadrian, 2014; articles in Vetus Testamentum, Jl of Theol Studies, New Testament Studies, Palestine Exploration Qly, Jewish Studies Qly, and other jls. *Recreations:* railways, cats. *Address:* Corpus Christi College, Cambridge CB2 1RH; 5 Grange Road, Cambridge CB3 9AS. *T:* (01223) 363529.

See also W. A. Feaver.

**HORDER, Prof. Jeremy Christian Nicholas,** DPhil; FBA 2014; Professor of Criminal Law, London School of Economics and Political Science, since 2013; *b* 25 Feb. 1962; *s* of John and Sylvia Horder; one *d*. *Educ:* Felsted Sch.; Univ. of Hull (LLB Law 1984); Keble Coll., Oxford (BCL, MA; DPhil 1990). Oxford University: Jun. Res. Fellow, Jesus Coll., 1987–89; Tutorial Fellow, Worcester Coll., 1989–2005; Reader in Criminal Law, 2001–06; Prof. of Criminal Law, 2006–10; Edmund Davies Prof. of Criminal Law, KCL, 2010–13. A Law Comr for England and Wales, 2005–10. Hon. Bencher, Middle Temple, 2012. Hon. LLD Hull, 2012. *Publications:* Provocation and Responsibility, 1992; Excusing Crime, 2004; Homicide and the Politics of Law Reform, 2012; Criminal Misconduct in Office: law and politics, 2018. *Recreations:* supporting Arsenal Football Club, reading crime fiction, swimming, running. *Address:* Department of Law, London School of Economics and Political Science, Houghton Street, WC2A 2AE. *T:* (020) 7955 7246. *E:* j.horder@lse.ac.uk.

**HORDERN, His Honour (Alfred) Christopher (Willoughby);** QC 1979; a Circuit Judge, 1983–2003; *m;* one *s* two *d*. *Educ:* Oxford Univ. (MA). Called to the Bar, Middle Temple, 1961; a Recorder of the Crown Court, 1974–83. *Recreations:* ski-ing, sailing, gardening of course.

**HORDERN, Rt Hon. Sir Peter (Maudslay),** Kt 1985; PC 1993; DL; Chairman, Fina (formerly Petrofina (UK)), 1987–98 (Director, 1973–98); *b* 18 April 1929; British; *s* of C. H. Hordern, MBE; *m* 1964, Susan Chataway; one *s* one *d* (and one *s* decd). *Educ:* Geelong Grammar Sch., Australia; Christ Church, Oxford, 1949–52 (MA). Mem. of Stock Exchange, London, 1957–74. Chm., Foreign & Colonial Smaller Cos (formerly Foreign & Colonial Alliance Investment), 1986–97 (Dir, 1976–99); Dir, TR Technology, 1975–98. MP (C) Horsham, 1964–74 and 1983–97, Horsham and Crawley, 1974–83. Chm., Cons. Parly Finance Cttee, 1970–72; Member: Exec., 1922 Cttee, 1968–97 (Jt Sec., 1988–97); Public Accts Cttee, 1970–97; Public Accounts Commn, 1984–97 (Chm., 1988–97). Mem. Bd, British Liby, 1996–99. DL West Sussex, 1988. *Recreations:* golf, reading and travel.

**HORE, Julia Mary;** see Yeomans, J. M.

**HORE-RUTHVEN,** family name of **Earl of Gowrie.**

**HORE RUTHVEN, Hon. Malise Walter Maitland Knox;** see Ruthven, Hon. M. W. M. K. H.

**HORGAN, Sharon;** actor, writer, director and producer; Creative Director, Merman, since 2014; *b* Hackney, London, 13 July 1970; *d* of John Horgan and Ursula Campbell; *m* 2004, Jeremy Rainbird; two *d*. *Educ:* Sacred Heart Convent Sch., Drogheda; Brunel Univ. (English and Amer. Studies). *Television:* co-creator and writer: Pulling (also actor), 2006–09; Dead Boss (also actor), 2012; Catastrophe (also actor), 2015–17, 2019 (BAFTA for Writer - Comedy (jtly), 2016); Motherland, 2016, 2017; The Circuit, 2016; creator, writer and exec. prod., Divorce, 2016–18; actor: Free Agents, 2009; The Increasingly Poor Decisions of Todd Margaret, 2009–16; The Borrowers, 2011; Psychobitches, 2012–14; Bad Sugar, 2012; Man Up (film), 2015; Game Night (film), 2018; Women on the Verge (also co-creator), 2018; This Way Up (also exec. prod.), 2019. *Recreations:* cycling, running, sketching, comics. *Clubs:* Soho House, Union, Groucho.

**HORLEY, Sandra,** CBE 2011 (OBE 1999); Chief Executive, Refuge, since 1983; *b* Sarnia, Canada, 11 Jan. 1952; *m* 1983, Julian Nieman; one *d*. *Educ:* McGill Univ. (BA Dist. Sociol. 1977). Homelessness Officer, Shrewsbury and Atcham BC, 1978–79; Dir, Haven Project (for homeless and abused women), 1979–82; Housing Advr, London Bor. of Lambeth, 1982–83. Mem. Bd, Stonham Housing Assoc., 1996–99. Hon. Fellow, London Southbank Univ., 2006. Voluntary Sector Achiever of Year and Outstanding Achiever of Year, Dods and Scottish Widows Women in Public Life Awards, 2008. *Publications:* Love and Pain, 1990; The Charm Syndrome, 1991, new edn as Power and Control, 2003. *Address:* Refuge, 4th Floor, International House, 1 St Katharine's Way, E1W 1UN. *T:* (020) 7395 7700.

**HORLICK, Vice-Adm. Sir Edwin John, (Sir Ted),** KBE 1981; FREng, FIMechE, MIMarEST; part-time consultant; *b* 28 Sept. 1925; *m* Jean Margaret (*née* Covington) (*d* 1991); four *s*. *Educ:* Bedford Modern Sch. Joined RN, 1943; Sqdn Eng. Officer, 2nd Frigate Sqdn, 1960–63; Ship Dept, MoD, 1963–66; First Asst to Chief Engineer, HM Dockyard, Singapore, 1966–68; Asst Dir Submarines, 1969–72; SOWC 1973; Fleet Marine Engineering Officer, Staff of C-in-C Fleet, 1973–75; RCDS 1976; Dir Project Team Submarine/Polaris, 1977–79; Dir Gen. Ships, 1979–83; Chief Naval Engineer Officer, 1981–83. FREng (FEng 1983). *Recreations:* golf, Rugby administration, DIY.

**HORLICK, Sir James Cunliffe William,** 6th Bt *cr* 1914, of Cowley Manor, Gloucester; *b* 19 Nov. 1956; *o s* of Sir John James Macdonald Horlick, 5th Bt and June, *d* of Douglas Cory-Wright, CBE; *S* father, 1995; *m* 1st, 1985, Fiona Rosalie (marr. diss. 1998), *e d* of Andrew McLaren; three *s;* 2nd, 1999, Mrs Gina Hudson. *Educ:* Eton. *Heir: s* Alexander Horlick, *b* 8 April 1987.

**HORLICK, Nicola Karina Christina, (Mrs M. F. D. Baker);** Chief Executive Officer: Bramdean Asset Management, since 2004; Money&Co., since 2013; *b* Nottingham, 28 Dec. 1960; *d* of Michael Robert Dudley Gayford and Suzanna Christina Victoria Gayford (*née* Czyzewska); *m* 1st, 1984, Timothy Piers Horlick (marr. diss. 2005); two *s* three *d* (and one *d* decd); 2nd, 2006, Martin Francis Damian Baker. *Educ:* Cheltenham Ladies' Coll.; Birkenhead High Sch., GDST; Phillips Exeter Acad., USA (ESU Schol.); Balliol Coll., Oxford (BA Juris.). S. G. Warburg, 1983–91, Dir, 1989–91; Managing Director: Morgan Grenfell Investment Mgt, 1991–97; SG Asset Mgt (UK), 1997–2003. Chm., Rockpool Investments LLP, 2011–15; Founder and Chm., Glentham Capital, 2013–. *Publications:* Can You Have It All?, 1997, 3rd edn 1999. *Recreations:* theatre, listening to music, ski-ing. *Address:* Money&Co., Kings House, 174 Hammersmith Road, W6 7JP. *T:* (020) 3143 4000. *E:* chani@moneyandco.com.

**HORLICK, Sir Ted;** see Horlick, Sir Edwin John.

**HORLOCK, Timothy John;** QC 1997; a Recorder, since 2000; *b* 4 Jan. 1958; *s* of Sir John Harold Horlock, FRS; *m;* four *s*. *Educ:* Manchester Grammar Sch.; St John's Coll., Cambridge (MA). Called to the Bar, Middle Temple, 1981 (Bencher, 2007); Asst Recorder, 1997–2000. *Recreations:* football, tennis, cricket. *Address:* Deans Court Chambers, 24 St John Street, Manchester M3 4DF.

**HORN, Bernard Philip;** Chairman: Social Finance Ltd, 2008–16; Econiq (Ireland), since 2007; *b* 22 April 1946; *s* of late Robert Horn and Margaret Mary Horn; *m* 1988, Clare Margaret Gilbert; one *s* two *d*, and two *s* one *d* by previous marriage. *Educ:* Catholic Coll., Preston; John Dalton Faculty of Technol., Manchester (DMS); Harvard Business Sch. With National Westminster Bank, 1965–2000: Sen. Internat. Exec., Corp. Financial Services, 1986–88; Chief of Staff, 1989–90; Gen. Manager, Gp Strategy and Communications, 1990–91; Chief Exec., Internat. Businesses, 1991–96; Dir, 1999–2000; Exec. Dir, Gp Ops, 1996–2000. Chairman: Netik Hldgs Ltd, 2002–10; Eontec Ltd, 2003–04; E-Box, 2004–15; Sen. Advr, InvestCloud Inc., 2015– (non-exec. Dir, 2013–15); non-exec. Dir, InvestCloud Inc. (USA), 2018–. Mem., Commn on Unclaimed Assets, 2005–07. Chm., Magic Bus (UK) (Indian charity), 2007–18; Vice Pres., Enham Trust, 2015– (Trustee, 2007–14). Samaritan, 2017–. Freeman, City of London, 2001; Mem., Co. of Information Technologists, 2001–14. *Recreations:* music, theatre. *E:* bph@bernardhorn.com. *Clubs:* Royal Automobile, Hurlingham.

**HORN, Helen Margaret,** MBE 1994; freelance consultant, since 2015; Head of Operations, Waterloo Foundation, since 2019; *b* 27 April 1961; *d* of Kenneth and Mary Horn. *Educ:* Dover Grammar Sch. for Girls; Thanet Tech. Coll.; Heidelberg Univ. HM Diplomatic Service, 1981–2007: former diplomatic postings: Warsaw; Zurich; Dhaka; Dubai; Kinshasa; Vienna; Johannesburg; Ambassador to Guinea, 2003–04; Consul-Gen., Brisbane, 2004–05; Pretoria, 2006–07; Hd, SE Asia Maritime Team, FCO, 2007; Dir, Qld Br., ESU, 2007–09; Humanitarian Programme Manager Africa, Christian Aid, 2009–11; Dir, Humanitarian Partnership Agreement, Australia, 2011–13; CEO, Womankind Worldwide, 2013–15; Gen. Manager, 2015–18, Chief Operating Officer, 2018–19, Res. Inst. for Care of Older People. Trustee: People in Aid, 2014–15; Ethiopiaid, 2015–. *Recreations:* African wildlife, outdoor pursuits, swimming, Pilates, theatre.

**HORN-SMITH, Sir Julian (Michael),** Kt 2004; Senior Adviser: UBS, since 2007; CVC, since 2009; Alix Partners Ltd, since 2017; non-executive Director, Lloyds Banking Group (formerly Lloyds TSB Group) plc, 2006–12; *b* 14 Dec. 1948. *Educ:* London Univ. (BSc Econ); Bath Univ. (MSc). Vodafone, then Vodafone AirTouch, subseq. reverted to Vodafone Gp plc, 1984–2006: Dir, 1996–2006; Chief Exec., Internat., 1999; Chief Operating Officer, 2001–04; Dep. Chief Exec., 2005–06. Dep. Chm. and Sen. Ind. Dir, Asia Resource Minerals plc (formerly Bumi plc), 2011–14; non-executive Director: Smiths Gp plc, 2000–06; Digicel Gp (Caribbean and Pacific), 2006–13; Digicel Gp Ltd, 2006–; De La Rue plc, 2009–13; Acer Gp, 2011–13; Veon Ltd, 2016–; Chairman: Sage Gp, 2006–07; eBuilder AB, 2016–. Chm., Altimo Adv. Bd (Alfa Telecoms), 2006–11; Co-Chair, Turkish British Tatlidil, 2010–. Pro Chancellor, Bath Univ., 2010–18. DLaws Bath, 2007. *Address:* 23 Prince's Gate Mews, SW7 2PS. *Clubs:* Army and Navy; Royal Ascot Racing.

**HORNBLOWER, Prof. Simon,** DPhil; FBA 2004; Senior Research Fellow in Classical Studies, All Souls College, Oxford, 2010–16; *b* 29 May 1949; *s* of George Alexander Hornblower and Edith Faith Hornblower; *m* 1st, 1975, Jane Custance (marr. diss. 1989); 2nd, 2010, Esther Eidinow. *Educ:* Eton Coll. (Schol.); Jesus Coll., Cambridge (Schol.; 1st cl. (Classical Tripos Pt I) 1969); Balliol Coll., Oxford (BA 1st cl. (Lit.Hum.) 1971); DPhil Oxon 1978. Prize Fellow, All Souls Coll., Oxford, 1971–77; Lectr in Ancient Hist., Univ. of Oxford, and Tutorial Fellow, Oriel Coll., Oxford, 1978–97; University College London: Sen. Lectr, Dept of Greek and Latin and of Hist., 1997–98; Prof. of Classics and Ancient Hist., 1998–2010; Grote Prof. of Ancient Hist., 2006–10. Mem., Inst. for Advanced Study, Sch. of Historical Studies, Princeton, NJ, 1994–95. *Publications:* Mausolus, 1982; The Greek World 479–323 BC, 1983, 4th edn 2011; Thucydides, 1987; Commentary on Thucydides, 3 vols, 1991, 1996 and 2008; (ed) Greek Historiography, 1994; (ed jtly) Cambridge Ancient History, vol. 6, 1994; (ed jtly) Ritual, Finance, Politics, 1994; (ed jtly) Oxford Classical Dictionary, 3rd edn 1996, 4th edn 2012; (ed jtly) Greek Personal Names: their value as evidence, 2000; Thucydides and Pindar, 2004; (ed jtly) Pindar's Poetry, Patrons and Festivals, 2007; Thucydidean Themes, 2011; (ed) Herodotus, Histories Book V, 2013; Lykophron, Alexandra, Text, Translation and Commentary, 2015; (ed jtly) Herodotus, Histories Book VI, 2017; Lykophron's Alexandra, Rome, and the Hellenistic World, 2018; (ed jtly) The Returning Hero: Nostoi and Traditions of Mediterranean Settlement, 2018. *Address:* 34A Arlington Square, N1 7DP.

**HORNBY, Andrew Hedley;** Chief Executive, The Restaurant Group, since 2019; *b* 21 Jan. 1967; *s* of James and Clare Hornby; *m* Catherine. *Educ:* Univ. of Oxford; Harvard Business Sch. (MBA). Boston Consulting Gp; Blue Circle; ASDA, 1996–99: Dir of Corp. Develt; Retail Man. Dir; Man. Dir, George; Halifax, subseq. HBOS plc: Chief Exec., Halifax Retail, 1999–2001; Chief Exec., Retail Div., 2001–05; Chief Operating Officer, 2005–06; Chief Exec., HBOS plc, 2006–09; Gp Chief Exec., Alliance Boots, 2009–11; Chief Exec., Coral, 2011–16; Chief Operating Officer, Ladbrokes Coral Gp, 2016–18; Jt Chief Operating Officer, GVC Hldgs, 2018–19.

**HORNBY, Jonathan Peter;** Founding Partner, CHI & Partners (formerly Clemmow Hornby Inge Ltd), advertising agency, 2001; Chief Executive, The&Partnership, since 2013; *b* Leamington Spa, 29 March 1967; *s* of Sir Derek Peter Hornby and Sonia Margaret Hornby (*née* Beesley); two *s* one *d*; *m* 2003, Clare Griffiths; two *d. Educ:* Marlborough Coll.; Univ. of Edinburgh (MA Hons). Joined Ogilvy & Mather, 1990, Account Dir, 1993–94; Brand Account Dir, 1995–96, Client Services Dir, 1996–98, Collett Dickenson Pearce & Partners; Jt Man. Dir, TBWA GGT Simons Palmer, 1998–2001. Trustee, Sentebale, 2011– (Chm., 2018–). *Recreations:* sailing, eventing, tennis. *Address:* The&Partnership, Charlotte Building, 17 Gresse Street, 6 Evelyn Yard (off Rathbone Place), W1T 1QL. *Clubs:* Soho House, George, Thirty, Marketing Group of Great Britain, 5 Hertford Street, Annabel's; Campden Hill Lawn Tennis; Charlton Hunt.

**HORNBY, His Honour Keith Anthony Delgado;** a Circuit Judge, 1995–2015; *b* 18 Feb. 1947; *s* of late James Lawrence Hornby and Naomi Ruth Hornby (*née* Delgado); *m* 1970, Judith Constance Fairbairn (*d* 2010); two *s* one *d. Educ:* Oratory Sch.; Trinity Coll., Dublin (BA Hons Legal Sci.). Lectr in Commercial Law, PCL, 1969–70; called to the Bar, Gray's Inn, 1970; practised on SE Circuit, 1970–95; Asst Recorder, 1988–92; Recorder, 1992–95; a Circuit Judge: Bow County Court, 1995–2012 (Lead Judge, 2007–12); Central London County Court, 2013–14; Mayors and City of London Court, 2014–15. Mem., Equal Treatment Adv. Cttee, Judicial Studies Bd, 2006–10. Gov., Oratory Sch., 2007–. *Recreations:* art, theatre, cricket, squash, golf. *Clubs:* Hurlingham; Refreshers Cricket (Pres., 2011–), Old Oratorian Cricket (Pres., 2011–).

**HORNBY, Richard;** Director of Finance and Estates, Home Office, since 2016; *b* Bradford, 10 Dec. 1969; *s* of Michael Hornby and Caroline Hornby; *m* 2004, Zoë Phillips; two *s. Educ:* Univ. of Kent (BA Theol.). CIPFA 1997. Hd, Financial Services, Liberata plc, 2000–03; Hd of Finance, City of Westminster, 2003; Divl Dir, Housing, Regeneration and Envmt, Lambeth Council, 2003–09; Treas., Sussex Police Authy, 2009–12; County Treas., W Sussex CC, 2009–14; Chief Finance Officer, Coastal W Sussex CCG, 2014–16. Chm., W Sussex Finance Officers Assoc., 2010. Former Hon. Sec., Soc. of County Treasurers (Hon. Auditor, 2010). Gov., Univ. of Chichester, 2010–12. *Recreations:* classical music, collecting art. *Address:* Home Office, 2 Marsham Street, SW1P 4DF. *T:* (020) 7035 1605. *E:* richard.hornby@homeoffice.gov.uk.

**HORNE, Sir (Alan) Gray (Antony),** 3rd Bt *cr* 1929; *b* 11 July 1948; *s* of Antony Edgar Alan Horne (*d* 1954) (*o s* of 2nd Bt), and of Valentine Antonia, *d* of Valentine Dudensing; *S* grandfather, 1984; *m* 1980, Cecile Rose, *d* of Jacques Desplanche. *Heir:* none. *Address:* Château du Basty, 24210 Thenon, Dordogne, France.

**HORNE, Alexander James;** advisor to multiple sports and leisure clients, since 2015; Co-founder and non-executive Chairman, NotLost, since 2016; *b* Cambridge, 13 July 1972; *s* of Martin and Phyll Horne; *m* 2005, Lisa Quail; two *d. Educ:* Manchester Univ. (BSc Maths 1993). ACA 1997. Trainee, Coopers & Lybrand, Manchester, 1993–96; Business Recovery Services Manager, Manchester, 1996–98; Financial Restructuring Sen. Manager, Bangkok, 1999–2000; Business Restructuring/Turnaround Sen. Manager, London, 2000–03; Finance Dir, FA, 2003–06; Man. Dir, Wembley Stadium, 2006–08; Chief Operating Officer, FA, 2008–10; Gen. Sec., Football Assoc., 2010–15; UK Chm., FanZone Ltd, 2015–17. Chm., NSPCC Sports Bd, 2013–.

**HORNE, David Oliver,** FCA; Chairman and Chief Executive, Lloyds Merchant Bank, 1987–92; *b* 7 March 1932; *s* of Herbert Oliver Horne, MBE and Edith Marion Horne (*née* Sellers); *m* 1959, Joyce Heather (*née* Kynoch); two *s* two *d. Educ:* Fettes College, Edinburgh. Director: S. G. Warburg & Co., 1966–70; Williams & Glyn's Bank, 1970–78; Lloyds Bank International, 1978–85; Managing Dir, Lloyds Merchant Bank, 1985–87. Dep. Chm., Serif, 1993–97; Director: Waterman Partnership Hldgs, 1992–2003; Black Arrow Gp, 1993–. *Recreation:* golf. *Address:* Four Winds, 5 The Gardens, Esher, Surrey KT10 8QF. *T:* (01372) 463510.

**HORNE, Sir Gray;** see Horne, Sir A. G. A.

**HORNE, Marilyn (Bernice);** mezzo-soprano; Director, Voice Program, Music Academy of the West, Santa Barbara; *b* 16 Jan. 1934; *m* 1960, Henry Lewis (marr. diss.); one *d. Educ:* Univ. of Southern California. US opera début, 1954; sings at Covent Garden, La Scala, Metropolitan Opera and other major venues; rôles include Adalgisa, Amneris, Carmen, Eboli, Isabella, Mignon, Orlando, Rosina, Tancredi, concerts and recitals. *Publications:* (with J. Scovell): Marilyn Horne - My Life (autobiog.), 1983; Marilyn Horne: the song continues, 2004. *Address:* c/o Colombia Artists Management, 5 Columbus Circle, 1790 Broadway, 6th Floor, New York, NY 10019–1412, USA.

**HORNE, Michael Andrew;** QC 2016; *b* Newcastle-upon-Tyne, 24 Nov. 1969; *s* of Dr Michael Horne and Eileen Horne; *m* 1996, Karen Scriven; one *s* two *d. Educ:* Royal Grammar Sch., Newcastle-upon-Tyne; Trinity Hall, Cambridge (BA Law 1991; MA 1995); Inns of Court Sch. of Law. Called to the Bar, Gray's Inn, 1992; in practice as barrister, specialising in healthcare law, clinical negligence, and court of protection and healthcare regulatory proceedings, 1992–. *Publications:* (Contributing Ed.) Med. Law Reports. *Recreations:* scuba diving, walking with my dogs, Newcastle United, photography. *Address:* Serjeants' Inn Chambers, 85 Fleet Street, EC4Y 1AE. *T:* (020) 7427 5000. *E:* mhorneQC@serjeantsinn.com.

**HORNE, Robert Drake;** Adviser on Education, Pakistan, 2017–18; *b* 23 April 1945; *s* of late Harold Metcalfe Horne and Dorothy Katharine Horne; *m* 1972, Jennifer Mary (*née* Gill); three *d. Educ:* Mill Hill Sch.; Oriel Coll., Oxford (MA Classics). Asst Master, Eton Coll., Windsor, 1967–68; DES, later DFE, then DFEE, 1968–97; seconded to Cabinet Office, 1979–80; Under Sec., 1988–97; Dir of Finance and Planning, Employment Service, 1995–97; First Asst Sec., Dept of Educn (formerly Employment and Educn), Trng and Youth Affairs, Canberra, 1998–2001. Budget Planning Advr, Dept of Educn, PNG, 2004–06; Financial Advr, Targeted Budget Support Prog., Vietnam, 2007–08; Economic Advr, Higher Educn Sector Develt Prog., Vietnam, 2009–11; Sen. Researcher, Finance for Tech. Educn, PNG, 2012–14; Advr on Higher Educn, Laos, 2015–16. *Recreations:* voluntary activities with fellow retirees, reading and reminiscence. *Address:* 53 Gulfview Road, Blackwood, SA 5051, Australia.

**HORNER, Christian,** OBE 2013; Team Principal, Aston Martin Red Bull (formerly Red Bull) Racing, Formula One, since 2005; *b* Leamington Spa, 16 Nov. 1973; *m* 2015, Geri Halliwell; one *s. Educ:* Warwick Sch. for Boys. Won Formula Renault scholarship, 1991; racing driver: with Manor Motorsport, race winner and highest placed rookie, British Formula Renault, 1992; F3000, 1996; Internat. F3000, 1997, driver and entrant in own racing team, Arden Internat.; retired from competitive driving to run Arden Internat., 1998; entered Arden Internat. in F3000 and Euro F3000 Championships. *Recreations:* tennis, ski-ing, water ski-ing. *Address:* Aston Martin Red Bull Racing, Bradbourne Drive, Tilbrook, Milton Keynes MK7 8BJ. *T:* (01908) 279702, *Fax:* (01908) 279703.

**HORNER, Dr Susan Margaret,** MBE 2013; education and arts consultant, since 2010; *b* Kingston-upon-Thames, 15 July 1948; *d* of William and Marjorie Galyer; *m* 1974, Peter Horner. *Educ:* Birmingham Univ. (BA Hons); Hughes Hall, Cambridge (PGCE); Leeds Univ. (PhD 1990). Teacher of English, Sheffield: Rowlinson Sch., 1971–73; Abbeydale Grange Sch., 1974–79; High Green Sch., 1980–84; Educn Advr, Sheffield, 1984–92; English Officer, Nat. Curriculum Council, 1992–94, SCAA, 1994–98; Sen. Manager, 1998–2008, Dir of Curriculum, 2009–10, QCA. Advr to Govts of Oman and Rwanda on curriculum and assessment, 2012–. Adviser: Clore Duffield Foundn, 2011–; RSC, 2012–; Grimm & Co., 2016–; Rothschild Foundn, 2018–. Chair, RSA Acads Trust, 2012–18; Trustee: First Story, 2011–; Min. of Stories, 2013–; IVE (formerly CapeUK), 2013–. Gov., Coventry Univ., 2018–. Author, Magic Dust that Lasts, report on writers in schs, Arts Council England, 2010. *Publications:* contrib. nat. curriculum and assessment advice and specifications. *Recreations:* literature, theatre, travel, birdwatching. *Address:* 14 Whirlow Park Road, Sheffield S11 9NP. *T:* (0114) 236 3465. *E:* sue@suehorner.com. *W:* www.suehorner.com.

**HORNER, Hon. Sir (Thomas) Mark,** Kt 2013; **Hon. Mr Justice Horner;** a Judge of the High Court of Justice, Northern Ireland, since 2012; President, Lands Tribunal, Northern Ireland, since 2015; *b* Belfast, 3 July 1956; *s* of Dr Thomas Horner and Mabel Horner; *m* 1981, Karin van der Ree; two *s* one *d. Educ:* Campbell Coll., Belfast; St Catharine's Coll., Cambridge (BA 1978); Inst. of Professional Legal Studies, Queen's Univ. Belfast (Professional Cert.). Called to the Bar, NI, 1979; QC (NI), 1996. Chm., Judges' Council, NI, 2015–. *Recreations:* reading, golf, watching Rugby. *Address:* Royal Courts of Justice, Chichester Street, Belfast BT1 3JF.

**HORNSBY, Timothy Richard,** CBE 2008; MA; Chair, International Tree Foundation, since 2014; *b* 22 Sept. 1940; *s* of late Harker William Hornsby and Agnes Nora French; *m* 1971, Dr Charmian Rosemary Newton; one *s* one *d. Educ:* Bradfield Coll.; Christ Church, Oxford Univ. (MA 1st Cl. Hons Modern History). Harkness Fellow, USA, at Harvard, Columbia, Henry E. Huntington Research Inst., 1961–63; Asst Prof., Birmingham Southern Coll., Alabama, 1963–64; Research Lectr, Christ Church, Oxford, 1964–65; Asst Principal, Min. of Public Building and Works, 1965–67; Private Sec. to Controller General, 1968–69; HM Treasury, 1971–73; Prin., then Asst Sec., DoE, 1975; Dir, Ancient Monuments and Historic Buildings, 1983–88, and Dir of Rural Affairs, 1984–88, DoE; Dir Gen., Nature Conservancy Council, 1988–91; Dir, Construction Policy Directorate, DoE, 1991; Chief Executive: Royal Bor. of Kingston upon Thames, 1991–95; Nat. Lottery Charities Bd, 1995–2001. A Comr, Nat. Lottery Commn, 2001–08 (Chm., 2004–05); Ind. Mem., Consumer Council for Water, 2005–14; Mem. Bd, Audience Agency, 2014–. Chair, Harkness Fellows Assoc., 2002–. Chm. Trustees, Horniman Mus. and Gardens, 2004–14; Trustee: Charles Darwin Trust, 2002–10; Internat. Inst. for Envmt and Develt, 2005–11; Royal Botanical Gardens, Kew, 2007–14; Castle Howard Arboretum, 2008–19; Field Lane, 2014–; British Architectural Trust Bd, 2014–; HOST, 2015–; King's Coll. Hosp. Charity, 2016–. Gov., Legacy Trust, 2007–14; Comr, Marshall Aid Commemoration Commn, 2011–16. FRSA. *Recreations:* conservation, talking, opera. *Address:* c/o International Tree Foundation, Unit 1 King's Meadow, Osney Mead, Oxford OX2 0DP. *E:* thornsby99@gmail.com. *Club:* Athenæum.

**HOROWITZ, Anthony,** OBE 2014; FRSL; children's writer; *b* 5 April 1955; *s* of late Mark and Celia Joyce Horowitz; *m* 1988, Jill Green; two *s. Educ:* Rugby Sch.; Univ. of York (BA). Screenwriter: *film:* Stormbreaker, 2006; *television* includes: Robin of Sherwood; Poirot; Midsomer Murders; Murder in Mind; Crime Traveller; (with J. Green) Foyle's War (series), 2002–15 (Lew Grade People's Award, 2003); Collision (series), 2009; Injustice (series), 2011; New Blood (series), 2016; writer of play, Dinner with Saddam, 2015. FRSL 2018. *Publications:* Devil's Doorbell, 1983; Night of the Scorpion, 1985; Groosham Grange, 1989; Myths and Legends, 1991; Granny, 1995; Falcon's Malteser, 1995; The Switch, 1997; Public Enemy No 2, 1997; The Devil and His Boy, 1999; Horowitz Horror, 1999; Unholy Grail, 1999; More Horowitz Horror, 2000; Mindgame (play), 2000; Stormbreaker, 2000; Point Blanc, 2001; Skeleton Key, 2002 (Red House Children's Book Award, 2003); Eagle Strike, 2003; Scorpia, 2004; The Killing Joke (adult novel), 2004; Ark Angel, 2005; Raven's Gate, 2005; Evil Star, 2006; Nightrise, 2007; Snakehead, 2007; Crocodile Tears, 2009; More Bloody Horowitz, 2010; Scorpia Rising, 2011; The House of Silk, 2011; Oblivion, 2012; Russian Roulette, 2013; Moriarty, 2014; Trigger Mortis, 2015; Magpie Murders, 2016; The Word is Murder, 2017; Forever and a Day, 2018. *Recreations:* scuba-diving, cinema, walking in Suffolk. *Address:* c/o United Agents, 12–26 Lexington Street, W1F 0LE. *T:* (020) 3214 0800.

**HOROWITZ, His Honour Michael;** QC 1990; a Circuit Judge, 2004–13; *b* 18 Oct. 1943; *s* of late David and Irene Horowitz; *m*; one *d* (one *s* decd). *Educ:* St Marylebone Grammar School; Pembroke College, Cambridge (BA 1966; LLB 1967). Pres., Cambridge Union Soc., 1967; English-Speaking Union Debating Tour of USA, 1967. Called to the Bar, Lincoln's Inn, 1968, Bencher, 1997; Asst Recorder, 1987; a Recorder, 1991–2004. Senate of Inns of Court and Bar, 1982–85; Mem., Professional Conduct Cttee, Bar Council, 1997–2000. Dir, Bar Mutual Indemnity Fund, 1999–2004. *Publications:* (contrib.) Rayden on Divorce, 17th edn 1997, 18th edn 2005; Essential Family Practice, 2002. *Recreations:* reading history, listening.

**HOROWITZ, Prof. Myer,** OC 1990; Adjunct Professor of Education, University of Victoria, since 1998; Professor Emeritus of Education, since 1990, President Emeritus, since 1999, University of Alberta; *b* 27 Dec. 1932; *s* of Philip Horowitz and Fanny Cotler; *m* 1956, Barbara, *d* of Samuel Rosen and Grace Midvidy, Montreal; two *d. Educ:* High Sch., Montreal; Sch. for Teachers, Macdonald Coll.; Sir George Williams Univ. (BA); Univ. of

Alberta (MEd); Stanford Univ. (EdD 1965). Teacher, Schs in Montreal, Sch. Bd, Greater Montreal, 1952–60. McGill University: Lectr in Educn, 1960–63; Asst Prof., 1963–65; Associate Prof., 1965–67; Asst to Dir, 1964–65; Prof. of Educn, 1967–69 and Asst Dean, 1965–69; University of Alberta: Prof. and Chm., Dept Elem. Educn, 1969–72; Dean, Faculty of Educn, 1972–75; Vice-Pres. (Academic), 1975–79; Pres., 1979–89. Hon. Dr: McGill, 1979; Concordia, 1982; Athabasca, 1989; British Columbia, 1990; Alberta, 1990; Victoria, 2000; Brock, 2000; Calgary, 2005; Royal Roads, 2012. Diamond Jubilee Medal, 2012. *Address*: A459 MacLaurin Building, University of Victoria, PO Box 3010 STN CSC, Victoria, BC V8W 3N4, Canada.

**HORRELL, Roger William**, CMG 1988; OBE 1974; HM Diplomatic Service, retired; *b* 9 July 1935; *s* of William John Horrell and Dorice Enid (*née* Young); *m* 1970, Patricia Mildred Eileen Smith (*née* Binns) (marr. diss. 1975); one *s* one *d*. *Educ*: Shebbear College; Exeter College, Oxford (MA). Served in Devonshire Regt, 1953–55; HM Colonial Service, Kenya, 1959–64; joined Foreign Office, 1964; Economic Officer, Dubai, 1965–67; FCO, 1967–70; First Sec., Kampala, 1970–73; FCO, 1973–76; First Sec., Lusaka, 1976–80; Counsellor, FCO, 1980–93. *Recreations*: watching cricket and Rugby Union – now mostly on TV; playing bridge. *Address*: 51 Oatlands Drive, Weybridge, Surrey KT13 9LU. *Club*: Reform.

**HORRIDGE, Prof. (George) Adrian**, FRS 1969; FAA 1971; Professor, Research School of Biological Sciences, Australian National University, 1969–92, now Emeritus Professor; *b* Sheffield, England, 12 Dec. 1927; *s* of George William Horridge and Olive Stray; *m* 1954, Audrey Anne Lightburne; one *s* four *d*. *Educ*: King Edward VII Sch., Sheffield; St John's Coll., Cambridge (BA 1949; PhD 1954; ScD 1968). Fellow, St John's Coll., Cambridge, 1953–56; on staff, St Andrews Univ., 1956–69; Dir, Gatty Marine Laboratory, St Andrews, 1960–69. Vis. Fellow, Churchill Coll., Cambridge, 1993–94. *Publications*: Structure and Function of the Nervous Systems of Invertebrates (with T. H. Bullock), 1965; Interneurons, 1968; (ed) The Compound Eye and Vision of Insects, 1975; Monographs of the Maritime Museum at Greenwich nos 38, 39, 40, 54, 1979–82; The Prahu: traditional sailing boat of Indonesia, 1982 (Oxford in Asia), translated as Perahu Layar Nusantara, 2015; Sailing Craft of Indonesia, 1985 (Oxford in Asia); Outrigger Canoes of Bali & Madura, Indonesia, 1986; (contrib.) The Austronesians, 1995; What Does the Honeybee See?, 2009; The Discovery of a Visual System: the honeybee, 2019; contribs 260 scientific papers to jls, etc, on behaviour and nervous systems of lower animals, and vision of the honeybee. *Recreations*: optics, mathematics, cultivating *Vanessa itea*, marine biology, sailing, language, arts, boat construction in Indonesia, rose gardening. *Address*: 76 Mueller Street, Yarralumla, ACT 2600, Australia. *W*: www.Adrian-Horridge.org.

**HORROBIN, James**, FWCB; artist blacksmith, since 1966; *b* 22 March 1946; *s* of Harry Horrobin and Betty Mary Horrobin; *m* 1st, 1966, Shirley Fitzgerald (marr. diss. 1983); one *s* one *d*; 2nd, 2007, Gabrielle Ridler. *Educ*: apprenticeship with his father on Exmoor, 1961–66; Hereford Tech. Coll. Set up own workshop, W Somerset, 1969; Lectr, Haystack Sch. of Craft, Maine, and Nat. Ornamental Metal Mus., Memphis, 1984–85. Chm., British Artist Blacksmith Assoc., 1983. Featured artist, Crafts Council exhibn, 1990. Commissions include: gates for Metalwork Gall., V&A Mus., 1981; portcullis and railings, Richmond Terrace, Whitehall, 1986; staircase, Chelsea residence of Charles Saatchi, 1989; screens, gate, address plates and emblem, 66 Cheapside, London, 1991; screens, railings and figure of Koko, Savoy Th., London, 1993; dossal rail, plaques and choir stalls, Church of Heavenly Rest, NY, 1997; lanterns, portico of St Paul's Chapel, Broadway, NY, 1998; gates, summer garden, Antony House, Cornwall, 1999; cloister railings, St John of Lattingtown, NY, 2003; Churchill Meml Screen, St Paul's Cathedral, London, 2003–04; screen, Torre Abbey, Devon, 2008; restoration of garden gates and new entrance gates, Bradfield Hall, Devon, 2010–11. FWCB 1996 (Silver Medal, 1996, Tonypandy Award, 2006, Co. of Blacksmiths). *Recreations*: painting, art history, architecture, reading, swimming, surfing, travel. *Address*: Furze View, Timberscombe, Minehead, Somerset TA24 7TY. *T*: (01643) 841402. *E*: jh@doverhay.co.uk. *W*: www.doverhay.co.uk.

**HORROCKS, Prof. Geoffrey Charles**, PhD; Fellow, St John's College, Cambridge, since 1983; Professor of Comparative Philology, University of Cambridge, 1997–2016, now Emeritus; *b* 3 Feb. 1951; *s* of Roland Horrocks and Marjorie Horrocks (*née* Atkinson); *m* 1973, Gillian Elizabeth Tasker; two *d*. *Educ*: Manchester Grammar Sch.; Downing Coll., Cambridge (BA 1972; PhD 1978). Employee Relns Manager, Mobil North Sea Ltd, 1972–73; Res. Fellow, Downing Coll., Cambridge, 1976–77; Lectr in Linguistics, SOAS, 1977–83; Lectr in Classics, Univ. of Cambridge, 1983–97. Hon. Dr Nat. and Capodistrian, Athens, 2012. *Publications*: Space and Time in Homer, 1981; Generative Grammar, 1987; Greek: a history of the language and its speakers, 1997, 2nd edn 2010; (with J. Clackson) The Blackwell History of Latin Language, 2007; Cambridge Grammar of Medieval and Early Modern Greek: vol. 4, syntax, 2019; contrib. numerous articles in jls of general, theoretical and historical linguistics, and Classics. *Recreations*: travel, guitar, football, gardening, gossip, talking to the members of my family (in no particular order). *Address*: St John's College, Cambridge CB2 1TP. *T*: (01223) 338600.

**HORROCKS, Prof. Ian Robert**, PhD; FRS 2011; Professor of Computer Science, University of Oxford, since 2007; Fellow of Oriel College, Oxford, since 2007; *b* Liverpool, 11 March 1958; *s* of William Joseph Horrocks and Barbara Francis Horrocks; *m* 1981, Maureen Mary Healy. *Educ*: Univ. of Manchester (BSc Hons Computer Sci. 1981; MSc 1995; PhD 1997). Res. Associate, Dept of Computer Sci., Univ. of Manchester, 1981–83; Tech. Dir, Scientex Ltd, 1983–94; Department of Computer Science, University of Manchester: Res. Associate, 1998–99; Lectr, 1999–2002; Sen. Lectr, then Reader, 2002–03; Prof., 2003–07. Vis. Scientist, Istituto per la Ricerca Scientifica e Tecnologica, Trento, 1997–98. Chief Scientist, Cerebra Inc., Carlsbad, Calif, 2001–06. *Publications*: contrib. numerous articles to computer sci. jls and confs. *Recreations*: mountain biking, ski-ing, reading, cinema, music. *Address*: Department of Computer Science, Wolfson Building, Parks Road, Oxford OX1 3QD. *T*: (01865) 273939, *Fax*: (01865) 521093. *E*: ian.horrocks@cs.ox.ac.uk.

**HORROCKS, Jane**; actress; *b* 18 Jan. 1964; *d* of John and Barbara Horrocks; partner, Nick Vivian; one *s* one *d*. *Educ*: Fearns Co. Secondary Sch., Rossendale, Lancs; RADA (Dip.). *Films*: The Dressmaker, 1989; The Witches, 1990; Life is Sweet, 1991 (Best Supporting Actress, LA Critics Award, 1992); Little Voice, 1998; Chicken Run, 2000; The Corpse Bride, 2006; Sunshine on Leith, 2013; Absolutely Fabulous: the movie, 2016; Swimming with Men, 2018; *plays*: Road, Royal Court, 1987; The Rise and Fall of Little Voice, RNT and Aldwych, 1992–93; Cabaret, Donmar Warehouse, 1993–94; Sweet Panic, Duke of York's, 2003; Absurd Person Singular, Garrick, 2007; The Good Soul of Szechuan, Young Vic, 2008; Aunt Dan and Lemon, Royal Court, 2009; (musical) Annie Get Your Gun, Young Vic, 2009; East is East, Trafalgar Studios, 2014; If You Kiss Me, Kiss Me, Young Vic, 2016; King Lear, Old Vic, 2016; Instructions for Correct Assembly, Royal Court, 2018; Pinter Five, Harold Pinter Th., 2018; *television*: Road, 1987; Storyteller, 1988; Bad Girl, 1992; Suffer the Little Children, 1994 (Best Actress Award, RTS, 1995); Absolutely Fabulous, 1992–94, 2001–04, 2011; Mirrorball, 2000; The Street, 2006, 2007; The Amazing Mrs Pritchard, 2006; Gracie, 2009; The Road to Coronation Street, 2010; This is Jinsy, 2011; Trollied, 2011–13; True Love, 2011; The Cruise, 2014; Inside No. 9, 2015. *Address*: c/o United Agents, 12–26 Lexington Street, W1F 0LE.

**HORROCKS, Paul John**; DL; Director, Essential Communications, since 2010; Partner, Gordon Burns Partnership, since 2011; Editor, Manchester Evening News, 1997–2009; *b* 19 Dec. 1953; *s* of Joe and Eunice Horrocks; *m* 1976, Linda Jean Walton; two *s* one *d*, and one step *d*. *Educ*: Bolton Sch. Reporter, Daily Mail, 1974; Manchester Evening News: gen. reporter, 1975–80; crime corresp., 1980–87; news editor, 1987–91; Asst Editor, 1991–95; Dep. Editor, 1995–97. Dir, Soc. of Editors, 2001–10 (Pres., 2007); Member: PCC, 2002–06; Defence Press and Broadcasting Adv. Cttee, 2007–09; Appts Panel, IPSO, 2014–. Chm., Bury NHS PCT, 2010–13; non. exec. Dir, NHS Greater Manchester, 2010–13; Member: Appeals Bd, Royal Manchester Children's Hosp., 2007–; Ethics Panel, Gtr Manchester Police Crime Comr, 2014–. Communications Adviser: NHS Gtr Manchester Service Transformation, 2011–; Univ. of Bolton, 2012–. Vice-Pres., Community Foundn for Greater Manchester, 2000–08; Mem., Organising Council, Commonwealth Games, Manchester 2002, 1998–2002. Mem., Bd of Govs, Univ. of Bolton, 2010–. Chm., Regl Press Awards, UK Soc. of Editors, 2013–. Trustee: Tatton Park Trust, 2008–; Fusilier Mus., Bury, 2016–. Patron, Francis House Children's Hospice, 1999–. DL Greater Manchester, 2011. *Recreation*: hill walking.

**HORROCKS, Peter John Gibson**, CBE 2015; Vice-Chancellor, Open University, 2015–18; *b* 8 Oct. 1959; *s* of James Nigel Gibson Horrocks and Ellen Elizabeth Gibson Horrocks; *m* 1987, Katharine Rosemary Rogers; two *s* one *d*. *Educ*: King's Coll. Sch., Wimbledon; Christ's Coll., Cambridge (BA). BBC: Dep. Ed., Panorama, 1988–90; Editor: Election '92; Public Eye, 1992–94; Here and Now, 1994; Newsnight, 1994–97; Election '97; Panorama, 1997–2000; Hd of Current Affairs, 2000–05; Hd of TV News, 2005–07; Hd of Multimedia Newsroom, 2007–09; Director: BBC World Service, 2009–15; BBC Global News, 2010–15. Chm., SE Midlands LEP, 2019–.

**HORSBRUGH-PORTER, Sir (Andrew) Alexander (Marshall)**, 5th Bt *cr* 1902, of Merrion Square, City and Co. of Dublin; Counsel, Ogier, since 2017; *b* 19 Jan. 1971; *s* of Sir John Horsbrugh-Porter, 4th Bt and of Lavinia Rose (*née* Turton); *S* father, 2013; *m* 2005, Jennie, *d* of Keith Downing; one *s* one *d*. *Educ*: Winchester Coll.; Univ. of Birmingham (BSc Politics and Econ. Hist.). Qualified Solicitor, 1998, Insolvency Practitioner, 2007. Solicitor: Davies Arnold Cooper, 1996–2000; Ince & Co., 2000–03; Attorney, Ritch & Conolly, Cayman Islands, 2004–11; Sen. Associate, Mourant Ozannes, Guernsey, 2011–15; Advocate, Royal Court of Guernsey, 2014–; Dir, David Rubin & Partners (CI) Ltd, 2015–16. *Publications*: (contrib.) Personal Insolvency: a practical guide, 2013; contribs INSOL Jl. *Recreations*: cricket, tennis, golf, history, reading. *Heir*: *s* William John Ernest Horsbrugh-Porter, *b* 25 Sept. 2006. *Address*: Flat 5, St Martins Court, St Martins, Guernsey GY4 6LL. *T*: (01481) 263006. *E*: alex.horsbrugh-porter@ogier.com. *Club*: MCC.

**HORSBURGH, John Millar Stewart**; QC (Scot.) 1980; Sheriff of Lothian and Borders at Edinburgh, 1990–2011; *b* 15 May 1938; *s* of late Alexander Horsburgh and Helen Margaret Watson Millar or Horsburgh; *m* 1966, Johann Catriona Gardner, MB, ChB, DObst RCOG; one *s* one *d*. *Educ*: Hutchesons' Boys' Grammar Sch., Glasgow; Univ. of Glasgow (MA Hons, LLB). Admitted to Scots Bar, 1965; Advocate-Depute, 1987–89. Part-time Mem., Lands Tribunal for Scotland, 1985–87. *Address*: 8 Laverockbank Road, Edinburgh EH5 3DG. *T*: (0131) 552 5328.

**HORSFALL, Sir Edward (John Wright)**, 4th Bt *cr* 1909, of Hayfield, Glusburn, co. York; *b* 17 Dec. 1940; *s* of Sir John Horsfall, 3rd Bt, MC, TD and Cassandra Nora Bernadine Horsfall (*née* Wright); *S* father, 2005; *m* 1965, Rosemary King; three *s*. *Educ*: Uppingham. Dir, Hayfield Textiles Ltd, 1961–78. Mem. (C) Cotswold DC, 2003–15 (Cabinet Mem., 2004–10). *Recreations*: theatre, travel, the arts, music. *Heir*: *e s* David Edward Horsfall [*b* 3 Sept. 1966; *m* 1996, Maria Gloria Sandoval; one *d*]. *Address*: York House, 4 The Mead, Cirencester, Glos GL7 2BB. *T*: (01285) 652012.

**HORSHAM, Bishop Suffragan of**; no new appointment at time of going to press.

**HORSHAM, Archdeacon of**; *see* Windsor, Ven. J. F.

**HORSHAM, Lisa**; *see* Cameron, L.

**HORSLEY, Very Rev. Canon Dr Alan Avery Allen**; Provost of St Andrew's Cathedral, Inverness, 1998–; Canon Emeritus, Peterborough Cathedral, since 1986; *b* 13 May 1936; *s* of Reginald James and Edith Irene Horsley; *m* 1966, Mary Joy Marshall, MA; two *d*. *Educ*: St Chad's Coll., Durham (BA 1958); Birmingham Univ.; Pacific Western Univ., Calif (MA 1984; PhD 1985); Queen's Coll., Birmingham. Ordained deacon 1960, priest 1961, Peterborough; Assistant Curate: Daventry, 1960–63; St Giles, Reading, 1963–64; St Paul's, Wokingham, 1964–66; Vicar of Yeadon, dio. Bradford, 1966–71; Rector of Heyford and Stowe Nine Churches, dio. Peterborough, 1971–78; RD of Daventry, 1976–78; Vicar of Oakham with Hambleton and Egleton (and Braunston and Brooke from 1980), 1978–86; Non-Residentiary Canon of Peterborough Cathedral, 1979–86; Chaplain: Catmose Vale Hosp., 1978–86; Rutland Memorial Hosp., 1978–86; Vicar of Lanteglos-by-Fowey, dio. Truro, 1986–88; Daventry ATC, 2005; Northants Burma Star Assoc., 2008–91; Priest in Charge: St Mary in the Fields, Culloden, 1988–91; St Paul, Strathnairn, 1988–91; Vicar, Mill End and Heronsgate with West Hyde, 1991–2001; acting RD, Rickmansworth, 1998–2000, RD, 2000–01. Permission to officiate: dio. Truro, 1998–2005; dio. Peterborough, 2003–. Hon. Assistant Priest: All Saints', Northampton, 2003–10 (Choirs' Chaplain, 2005–10); Holy Sepulchre, Northampton, 2010–14. *Publications*: (with Mary J. Horsley) A Lent Course, 1967, 3rd edn 2007; Lent with St Luke, 1978, 3rd edn 1997; Action at Lanteglos and Polruan, 1987, 2nd edn 2016; The Parish Church at Mill End, Rickmansworth, Hertfordshire: Pt I, 1999, 2nd edn 2000; Pt II, 2000; Forty-One Men: a biblical course for Lent, 2008; (with Lee Dunleavy) Kalendar for All Saints Church with St Katherine and St Peter in Northampton, 2008, 2nd edn 2009; Kalendar for St Crispin's Group, Northampton, 2011; contribs to Rutland Record Soc. Jl. *Recreations*: music, piano and organ, cultivation of flowers, historical research. *Address*: 22 Vyner Close, Thorpe Astley, Leicester LE3 3EJ. *T*: (0116) 289 2695, 07503 321553. *E*: canonalanahorsley@gmail.com.

**HORSLEY, (Christine) Ruth**; *see* Mercer, C. R.

**HORSLEY, Nicola Jane**; *see* Spence, N. J.

**HORSLEY, Stephen Daril**; Director of Operations, Clinicard Ltd, since 2014; *b* 23 June 1947; *s* of Donald Vincent Horsley and Marie Margaret Horsley; *m* 1974, Vivienne Marjorie Lee; one *s* two *d*. *Educ*: Guy's Hosp.; Manchester Business Sch. (MBSc 1985); Manchester Univ. (MA Health Ethics and Law 2004). FRCP 1988 (MRCP 1976); FFPH. Gen. Hosp. Medicine, Truro, 1971–75; Community Medicine, Yorks RHA, 1975–79; District Community Physician, E Cumbria HA, 1979–82; District MO, S Cumbria HA, 1982–85; Specialist in Community Medicine, Oxford RHA, 1985–86; Regl MO, N Western RHA, 1986–94; Consultant in Public Health, Morecambe Bay HA, 1994–2000; Locum Consultant in Public Health: St Helens and Knowsley DHA, 2000–02; St Helens PCT,

April 2002; Director of Public Health: Northants Heartlands PCT, 2002–06; Northants Teaching PCT, 2007–13 (Acting Dir, 2006–07); Interim Director of Public Health: Plymouth CC, 2013–14; Sheffield CC, 2015–16. Vis. Prof. of Public Health, Leicester Univ., 1997–. *Publications:* contribs to BMJ, Community Medicine. *Recreations:* wind surfing, walking.

**HORSMAN, Malcolm;** *b* 28 June 1933. *Educ:* Open Univ. (BSc 2006); King's Coll. London (MA 2007); Birkbeck, Univ. of London (MRes 2008). Commnd Sherwood Foresters, Nat. Service, 1952. Director, Slater Walker Securities Ltd, 1967–70; Chm., Ralli International Ltd, 1969–73; Director: The Bowater Corporation Ltd, 1972–77; Tozer Kemsley & Millbourn (Holdings) Ltd, 1975–82. Member: Study Group on Local Authority Management Structures, 1971–72; South East Economic Planning Council, 1972–74; Royal Commission on the Press, 1974–77; Institute of Contemporary Arts Ltd, 1975–78; Council, Templeton Coll. (formerly Oxford Centre for Management Studies), 1973–84; Chm., British Centre, Internat. Theatre Inst., 1982–84 (Mem. Exec. Council, 1980–87). Visiting Fellow, Cranfield Univ. (formerly Cranfield Institute of Technology)/The School of Management, 1977–97. Vis. Lectr, Univ. of Transkei, 1977. Chm., Nat. Youth Theatre, 1982–90 (Dep. Chm. 1971–82); Director: Hackney New Variety Ltd (Hackney Empire Trust), 1995–97; Gate Theatre, 1997–2000; Member: Court, RCA, 1977–80; Editorial Bd, DRAMA, 1978–81; Royal Court Develt Cttee, 1995–98; Council, Birthright, 1974–85; Council, Anti-Slavery Internat., 1998–2000. Chairman: Alice Hoffman Homes, later Hoffman De Visme Foundn, 1992–98; Open School Trust, 1998–2000. *Club:* Harlequins Rugby Football.

**HORSMAN, Michael John;** Special Professor, Nottingham University Business School, 2003–06; Independent Member, House of Commons Senior Pay Panel, 2003–16; *b* 3 March 1949; *s* of late Graham Joseph Vivian Horsman and Ruth (*née* Guest); *m* 1977, Dr Anne Margaret Marley; three *s*. *Educ:* Dollar Acad.; Glasgow Univ. (MA Hist. and Politics, 1st cl. Hons, 1971); Balliol Coll., Oxford (Snell Exhibnr, Brackenbury Scholar). Entered Civil Service, 1974; Private Sec. to Chm., MSC, 1978–79; Dept of Employment, 1979–84, on secondment to Unilever, 1981–82; Dir, PER, 1984–85; Hd, Finance Policy, and Resource Controller, MSC, 1985–87; Hd, Ops Br., Employment Service, 1987–89; Regl Dir, London and SE, Employment Service, 1989–92; Dir, Office of Manpower Economics, 1992–2003. *Recreations:* historical research, literature, cycling.

**HORT, Sir Andrew (Edwin Fenton),** 9th Bt *cr* 1767, of Castle Strange, Middlesex; *b* 15 Nov. 1954; *e s* of Sir James Fenton Hort, 8th Bt and Joan, *d* of Edward Peat; *S* father, 1995; *m* 1986, Mary, *d* of Jack Whibley; one *s* one *d*. *Heir: s* James John Fenton Hort, *b* 26 Nov. 1989. *Address:* Welle House, East Prawle, Kingsbridge, Devon TQ7 2BU.

**HORTA-OSÓRIO, António Mota de Sousa;** Group Chief Executive, Lloyds Banking Group, since 2011; *b* Lisbon, 28 Jan. 1964. *Educ:* Colégio de São João de Brito, Lisbon; Universidade Católica Portuguesa (Licenciatura Mgt and Business Admin doctoral degree 1987); INSEAD (MBA 1991; Henry Ford II Prize); Harvard Business Sch. (AMP 2003). Asst Prof. in Finance and Econometrics, Universidade Católica Portuguesa, 1985–90 (Guest Prof., MBA Prog. in Financial Strategic Planning, 1992–96); Vice Pres. and Hd, Capital Mkts, Citibank Portugal, 1987–90; Corporate Finance, Goldman Sachs Internat., NY and London, 1991–93; Banco Santander SA, 1993–2010: CEO, Banco Santander de Negócios Portugal, 1993–2000; CEO, Banco Santander Brasil, 1997–2000; CEO, 2000–06, Chm., 2006–10, Banco Santander Totta; Exec. Vice Pres., and Mem., Mgt Cttee, 2000–10; CEO, Santander UK plc, 2006–10. Non-executive Director: Abbey National plc, 2004–06; Bank of England, 2009–11; Champalimaud Foundn, 2011–; Sociedade Francisco Manuel dos Santos BV, 2011–; Exor, 2015–. Guest Prof., Portuguese Banking Trng Inst., 1985–90. Member, Governing Body: Universidade Católica Portuguesa, 2007–10; London Business Sch., 2010–15; Member, Advisory Council: Saïd Business Sch., Univ. of Oxford, 2008–12; Judge Business Sch., Univ. of Cambridge, 2009–11; CityUK, 2010–12. Chm., Wallace Collection, 2015–. Freeman, City of London, 2018. Hon. Dr: Edinburgh, 2011; Bath, 2012; Warwick, 2015. Foreign Policy Assoc. Medal, 2019. Order of Merit Grã-Cruz (Portugal), 2014; Comdr, Order of Civil Merit (Spain), 1998; Order of Southern Cross (Brazil), 1998; Encomienda de Numero, Orden de Isabel la Católica (Spain), 2009. *Recreations:* tennis, scuba diving, ski-ing. *Address:* Lloyds Banking Group plc, 25 Gresham Street, EC2V 7HN. *Clubs:* Queen's; Clube VII (Lisbon).

**HORTON,** family name of **Baroness Bowles of Berkhamsted**.

**HORTON, Claire Ellen;** Chief Executive, Battersea Dogs & Cats Home, since 2010; *b* Skipton, Yorks, 20 May 1962; *d* of Michael and Mildred Weir; *m* 1985, Paul Horton; one *s*. *Educ:* Dudley Girls High Sch.; Univ. of Warwick Business Sch. (MBA 2007). Special Constable, W Midlands Police Constabulary, 1980–87; Area Manager, NSPCC, 1988–93; Regl Dir, Cats Protection League, 1994–99; Dir, Brewed Infusion Ltd, 1999–2002; Chief Exec., Univ. of Warwick Students' Union, 2002–08; Chief Operating Officer, Variety Club of GB, 2008–10. Non-executive Director: Membership Solutions Ltd, 2005–15; Animal Health and Welfare Bd for England, DEFRA, 2014–; Chm., Assoc. of Dogs and Cats Homes, 2015–. Ind. Chair and Panel Mem., Appeals Service, Worcester CC, 2004–08. FRSA 2012; FInstD 2012. Hon. LLD Roehampton, 2015. *Publications:* (jtly) Universities and their Unions, 2006. *Recreations:* enjoying poverty through horse ownership, writing, reading, eating, but *not* cooking. *Address:* Battersea Dogs & Cats Home, 4 Battersea Park Road, SW8 4AA. *T:* (020) 7627 9207. *E:* c.horton@battersea.org.uk.

**HORTON, Geoffrey Robert;** Economic Consultant, Horton 4 Consulting, since 1998; *b* 23 July 1951; *s* of late Leonard Horton and Joan Horton; *m* 1991, Dianne Alexandra Craker; two *d*. *Educ:* Bristol Grammar Sch.; Exeter Coll., Oxford (MA); University Coll. London (MSc Econ). Economic asst, HM Treasury, 1974–76; Lectr in Econs, University Coll. of Swansea, 1976–78; Economic Advr, HM Treasury, 1978–85; Chief Economist, DRI (Europe) Ltd, 1985–88; Sen. Economic Advr, Dept of Energy, 1988–90; Sen. Consultant, Nat. Economic Research Associates, 1990–92; Dir, Regulation and Business Affairs, Office of Electricity Regulation, 1990–95; Dir Gen., Electricity Supply for NI, 1992–95; Dir of Consumer Affairs, OFT, 1995–98. Member: Panel of Experts for Reform of the Water Service in NI, 2003–06; Energy and Climate Security Panel, BERR, later DECC, 2007–10. Award for Gallantry, Royal Humane Soc., 2005. *Publications:* articles and research papers on economics. *Recreations:* reading, cooking, sailing. *Address:* 84 Berglen Court, 7 Branch Road, E14 7JX. *T:* (020) 7001 1677. *E:* Geoff@Horton4.co.uk.

**HORTON, Mark Anthony; His Honour Judge Horton;** a Circuit Judge, since 2008; *b* Crediton, Devon, 30 Sept. 1953; *s* of Robert Anthony Horton, DFC and Helene Renee Horton; *m* 1986, Madeleine Curry (marr. diss.); two *s*. *Educ:* Blundell's Sch., Tiverton; Birmingham Univ. (LLB Hons). Called to the Bar, Middle Temple, 1976; in practice as barrister specialising in crime and personal injury; Hd, Criminal Dept, St John's Chambers, Bristol, 1995–2008; Recorder, 2000–08. *Recreations:* tennis, football, Rugby, languages, French, German, Spanish, Russian. *Address:* Bristol Crown Court, The Law Courts, Small Street, Bristol BS1 1DA.

**HORTON, Matthew Bethell;** QC 1989; *b* 23 Sept. 1946; *s* of Albert Leslie Horton, BSc, FRICS and Gladys Rose Ellen Harding; *m* 1972, Liliane Boleslawski (marr. diss. 1984); one *s* one *d*. *Educ:* Sevenoaks School; Trinity Hall, Cambridge (Open Exhibn, Hist.; Squire Law Scholar; 1st Cl. Hons Law 1967; MA 1967; LLM 1968); Astbury Scholar, Middle Temple, 1968. Called to the Bar, Middle Temple, 1969. Western Circuit; Mem., Parly Bar Mess, 1977. Member: Cttee, Jt Planning Law Conf., 1983–97; European Environmental Law Cttee, Internat. Bar Assoc.; Admin. Law Cttee of Justice. *Recreations:* ski-ing, windsurfing, tennis. *Address:* 39 Essex Chambers, 81 Chancery Lane, WC2A 1DD. *Club:* Tramp.

**HORTON, Prof. Peter,** DPhil, DSc; FRS 2010; Professor of Biochemistry, 1990–2008, now Emeritus, and Chief Research Advisor, Grantham Centre for Sustainable Futures, since 2014, University of Sheffield. *Educ:* Univ. of York (BA 1st Cl. Hons Biol.; DPhil; DSc); Dip. Teaching and Learning in Higher Educn. FHEA. Postdoctoral trng, Purdue Univ.; University of Sheffield: Lectr, then Reader, Dept of Molecular Biol. and Biotechnol., 1978–90; Chm., Robert Hill Inst., 1989–2003; Res. Advr, Project Sunshine, 2011–14. Ext. Advr to Internat. Rice Res. Inst. *Publications:* contribs to jls incl. Nature, Jl Exptl Botany, Jl Biol Chem. *Address:* Department of Molecular Biology and Biotechnology, University of Sheffield, Firth Court, Western Bank, Sheffield S10 2TN.

**HORTON, Dr Richard Charles,** FRCP; Editor, since 1995, and Publishing and Editorial Director, since 2001, The Lancet; *b* 29 Dec. 1961; *s* of Ole Bjarne Kverneland and Barbara Gwendoline Beddow, and adopted *s* of Charles Kenneth Horton and Clarice Audrey Ward; *m* 1998, Ingrid Johanna Wolfe; one *d*. *Educ:* Bristol GS; Univ. of Birmingham (BSc 1st, MB ChB Hons). FRCP 1997. Sen. House Officer, Queen Elizabeth Hosp., Birmingham, 1987–88; Clin. Res. Fellow, Royal Free Hosp., London, 1988–90; Asst Editor, 1990–93, N American Editor (New York), 1993–95, The Lancet. Med. Columnist, The Observer, 1996–98. Visiting Professor: Cleveland Clinic, USA, 1997, 2007; Duke Univ., USA, 2000; Yale Univ., 2000; Arthur Thomson Vis. Prof., Univ. of Birmingham, 2000; Arnold Johnson Vis. Prof., McMaster Univ., Canada, 2000; Mayo Clinic, USA, 2002; Potiker Prof., Cleveland Clinic, USA, 2002; Hon. Professor: LSHTM, 2000–; UCL, 2005–; Univ. of Oslo, 2013–. Writer and Presenter, The Citadel (TV), 1998. Member: Exec. Cttee, UK Medical Journalists Assoc., 1991–93, 1995–97; Internat. Cttee of Medical Jl Editors, 1995–; Evaluation Gp, Acheson Ind. Inquiry into Inequalities in Health, 1998; RCP Wkg Party on Defining and Maintaining Professional Values in Medicine, 2004–05; Co-Chair, WHO Scientific Adv. Gp on Internat. Clinical Trials Registration, 2006–; Chair, RCP Wkg Party on Physicians and the Pharmaceutical Industry, 2007–08. Sen. Associate, Nuffield Trust, 2008–; Member: Council, Acad. of Med. Scis, 2010–13; Council, Univ. of Birmingham, 2010–14; Ind. Adv. Gp, WHO AFRO, 2015–. President: World Assoc. of Med. Editors, 1995–96; US Council of Science Editors, 2005–06; Foundn Council, Global Forum for Health Res., 2003–06. Patron, Medsin, 2006–; Chair, Health Metrics Network, 2010–12; Co-Chair, Ind. Expert Advr Gp on women's and children's health, 2012–15 (annual reports, 2012, 2013, 2014). Fellow, Amer. Acad. for Advancement of Sci., 1997; Founder FMedSci 1998. Hon. FRCPCH, 2013. Foreign Associate, US Inst. of Medicine, 2012. Hon. MD: Umeå, 2007; Birmingham, 2008; Gothenburg, 2014. Med. Pubn of the Year, Med. Journalists' Assoc., 2004; Edinburgh Medal, 2007; Dean's Medal, John's Hopkins Sch. of Med., 2009. *Publications:* Second Opinion: doctors, diseases and decisions in modern medicine, 2003; Doctors in Society, 2005; Innovating for Health, 2009; books and articles on cardiovascular pharmacol., gastroenterol., global health and journalology; reviews and essays in New York Review of Books, London Review of Books, TLS. *Recreation:* horizontal reflection. *Address:* The Lancet, 125 London Wall, EC2Y 5AS. *T:* (020) 7424 4929.

**HORTON, Roger Graham;** non-executive Chairman, Centre for Agriculture and Biosciences International, since 2018; *b* 11 June 1957; *s* of late Bertram Horton and of Joan Horton; *m* 1986, Deborah; two *d*. Sales and mktg roles with Internat. Thomson, 1977–87; Editl Dir, McGraw-Hill, Europe, 1987–94; Man. Dir, 1994–2003, CEO, 2003–17, Taylor & Francis Gp. *Publications:* business and industry related articles. *Recreations:* Reading FC home games fanatic, rock 'n' roll bass player, occasional barn dance caller, golf. *Address:* c/o Centre for Agriculture and Biosciences International, Noseworthy Way, Wallingford OX10 8DE. *T:* (01491) 832111.

**HORTON, Dame Rosemary Anne, (Dame Rosie),** DNZM 2011; QSO 2004; QSM 1993; *b* Christchurch, NZ; *d* of Ellis George Moon and Olga Reama Moon (*née* Raphael); *m* 1st, Donald Ronald Keith Smith (marr. diss.); one *d*; 2nd, Henry Michael Horton. Patron: Starship Foundn (Vice-Chm., 1991–2014); NZ Breast Cancer Foundn (Founder Trustee and Chm., 1995–2005; Chm., Bequest Cttee; former Chair, Friends of Starship); Rautakauri Music Therapy Trust; World Child Cancer; Yellow Belle for NZ Women's Refuge; Abbeyfield NZ; Ambassador for: Macular Degeneration; Centre for Brain Res., Univ. of Auckland; former Chair: Aotea Women's Cttee; Aotea Performing Arts Trust; former Vice Chair, Laura Fergusson Trust (former Chm., Laura Fergusson Women's Cttee); Edge Bd of Mgt. Trustee, Athlae Lyon Starship Res. Trust; Former Trustee: Arts Regl Service Trust; Parks and Wilderness Trust; SPCA; Dame Malvina Major Trust; Women's Refuge Foundn; Bethany Adv. Bd; Salvation Army; Prince of Wales Trust; Santa Parade Trust; NZ/UK Link Foundn. Henry A. Rosso Award for Ethical Fundraising, Fundraising Inst. NZ, 2000; Mayors Living Legend Award, Auckland, 2007; Catherine Variety Sheridan Award, 2008; Distinguished Citizen Award, Auckland City, 2010; EY ASB Entrepreneur of the Year, 2013. Commemoration Medal, 1990. *Recreations:* bridge, collecting Aboriginal art, travel, ballet, opera, theatre. *Address:* 179 Victoria Avenue, Remuera, Auckland, New Zealand. *T:* 274986586. *E:* rosiehorton@ihug.co.nz.

**HORVITZ, Prof. (Howard) Robert,** PhD; Professor of Biology, Massachusetts Institute of Technology, since 1986; *b* 8 May 1947; *s* of late Oscar Horvitz and Mary Horvitz; *m* 1993, Martha Constantine Paton; one *d*. *Educ:* Massachusetts Inst. of Technol. (BS Maths 1968; BS Econs 1968); Harvard Univ. (AM Biol. 1972; PhD Biol. 1974). Asst Prof. of Biol., 1978–81, Associate Prof. of Biol., 1981–86, MIT; Investigator, Howard Hughes Med. Inst., 1988–. Foreign Mem., Royal Soc., 2009. (Jtly) Nobel Prize in Physiol. or Medicine, 2002. *Address:* Department of Biology, Massachusetts Institute of Technology, 77 Massachusetts Avenue, Cambridge, MA 02139, USA.

**HORWELL, Richard Eric;** QC 2006; a Recorder, since 2004; *b* 14 Nov. 1953; *s* of John and Edna Horwell; *m* 2002, Lindsay; one *s*. *Educ:* Ewell Castle Sch.; Council of Legal Educn. Called to the Bar, Gray's Inn, 1976, Bencher, 2009; Jun. Treasury Counsel, 1991–96; Sen. Treasury Counsel, 1996–2002; First Sen. Treasury Counsel, 2002–06. *Recreations:* motor sport, travel, photography, film, dogs. *Address:* 3 Raymond Buildings, Gray's Inn, WC1R 5BH.

**HORWICH, Prof. Alan,** PhD; FRCR, FMedSci; Professor of Radiotherapy, 1986, and Dean, 1992–97 and 2005–13, Institute of Cancer Research and Royal Marsden Hospital; *b* 1 June 1948; *s* of William and Audrey Horwich; *m* 1981, Pauline Amanda Barnes; two *s* one *d*. *Educ:* William Hulme's Grammar Sch., Manchester; University College Hosp. Med. Sch. (MB BS 1971; PhD 1981). MRCP 1974, FRCP 1994; FRCR 1981. Postgrad. medicine, London, 1971–74; Fellowship in Oncology, Harvard, 1975; res. on ribonucleic acid tumour viruses, ICRF, 1976–79; radiation oncology, Royal Marsden Hosp. and Inst. of Cancer Res., 1979–; Dir, Clinical R&D, Royal Marsden Hosp., 1994–2005; Hd,

Clinical Labs, Inst. of Cancer Res., 1995–2011. Chm., MRC Testicular Tumour Working Party, 1988–94. Civilian Consultant to RN, 1989–2013. Warden, RCR, 1998–2002. FMedSci 2003. *Publications:* Testicular Cancer: investigation and management, 1991, 2nd edn 1996; Combined Radiotherapy and Chemotherapy in Clinical Oncology, 1992; Oncology: a multidisciplinary text book, 1995; Systemic Treatment of Prostate Cancer, 2010; numerous articles in med. jls on urological cancers and lymphomas. *Address:* Royal Marsden Hospital, Downs Road, Sutton, Surrey SM2 5PT. *T:* (020) 8661 3274.
*See also* P. G. *Horwich.*

**HORWICH, Prof. Paul Gordon**, PhD; Professor of Philosophy, New York University, since 2005; *b* 7 Feb. 1947; *s* of William Horwich and Audrey (*née* Rigby). *Educ:* Brasenose Coll., Oxford (BA Physics); Yale Univ. (MA Physics & Phil.); Cornell Univ. (MA, PhD Phil. 1975). Massachusetts Institute of Technology: Asst Prof. in Philosophy, 1973–80; Associate Prof., 1980–87; Prof. of Philosophy, 1987–95; Prof. of Philosophy, UCL, 1994–2000; Kornblith Prof. of Philosophy, Grad. Center, CUNY, 2000–05. *Publications:* Probability and Evidence, 1982; Asymmetries in Time, 1987; Truth, 1992, 2nd edn 1998; Meaning, 1998; From a Deflationary Point of View, 2004; Reflections on Meaning, 2005; Truth - Meaning - Reality, 2010; Wittgenstein's Metaphilosophy, 2012. *Recreations:* opera, ski-ing, summers in Tuscany. *Address:* Department of Philosophy, New York University, 5 Washington Place, New York, NY 10003, USA. *Club:* Black's.
*See also* A. *Horwich.*

**HORWITZ, Prof. Frank Martin**, PhD; Professor of Global Human Resource Management - Emerging Markets, Cranfield School of Management, Cranfield University, 2014–18; *b* Bloemfontein, S Africa; *m* 1976, Dianne; one *s* two *d*. *Educ:* Grey Coll.; Univ. of Witwatersrand (BA (SocSci); PhD 1985). Higher Dip. Personnel Mgt; Masters in Personnel Mgt. Sen. Lectr, Wits Business Sch., Univ. of Witwatersrand, 1982–83; Graduate School of Business, University of Cape Town, 1981–2009: Dir, MBA Course, 1986–91; Dir of Res., 1993–2001; Acad. Dir, 2002–03; Dir, 2004–09; Prof. of Internat. HR Mgt, and Dir, Cranfield Sch. of Mgt, Cranfield Univ., 2009–13. Visiting Professor: Haskayne Sch. of Business, Univ. of Calgary, 1992–93; Nanyang Business Sch., Singapore, 2001–02; Rotterdam Sch. of Mgt, Erasmus Univ., 2003–05. Mem. Bd of cos; Consultant in organisational change and human capital strategies for cos in Canada, Namibia, SA and UK. *Publications:* (jtly) Managing Resourceful People, 1991; (jtly) On the Edge: how South African companies cope with change, 1992; (jtly) Employment Equity and Affirmative Action: an international comparison, 2003; (jtly) Managing Human Resources in Africa, 2004; (ed with P. Budhwar) Handbook of Human Resource Management in Emerging Markets, 2016; contrib. articles to learned jls incl. Human Resources Mgt Jl, Internat. Jl Cross-Cultural Mgt, Jl Internat. Compensation and Benefits, Business in the Contemporary World, Internat. Jl Human Resource Mgt, Internat. Jl Manpower. *Recreations:* cycling, good wine, playing guitar. *Address:* Cranfield School of Management, Cranfield University, Cranfield, Bedford MK43 0AL.

**HORWOOD, Dr Joseph William**, FSS, CStat; FIMA; CMath, CSci; Chief Scientist, 1994–2010, non-executive Director, 2010–12, Centre for Environment, Fisheries and Aquaculture Science; Chief Fisheries Science Adviser, Department for Environment, Food and Rural Affairs, 1994–2010; *b* Birmingham, 1948; *s* of Jennifer Horwood. *Educ:* King Edward VI Sch., Stratford upon Avon; Univ. of London (BSc ext.); Univ. of E Anglia (ScD 1992). FSS 1970; CStat 1993; FIMA 1992; CMath 1992; CSci 2005. Marine and Fisheries Scientist, CEFAS, 1970–2010, now Emeritus Fellow. Member: Scientific Cttee, Internat. Whaling Commn, 1976–89; Scientific, Tech. and Econ. Cttee on Fisheries, EU, 1990–92; UK Marine Sci. Co-ordination Cttee, 2008–10; Marine Protected Areas Sub-Cttee, JNCC, 2009–19 (Chair, 2017–18). Chm., Sci. Adv. Cttee, CEFAS, 2006–12. International Council for Exploration of the Sea: Mem. Adv. Cttee on Fisheries Mgt, 1990–93; Vice Pres., 2000–03; Pres., 2006–09. Mem. Bd, Marine Biol Assoc., 1998–2001. Natural England: non-exec. Dir, 2009–18; Mem., Audit and Risk Cttee, 2010–11; Mem., Sci. Adv. Cttee, 2010–18; Mem., Jt Nature Conservancy Council, 2014–18; Dir, JNCC Support Co., 2014–18. *Publications:* The Sei Whale: population biology, ecology and management, 1987; Population Biology and Exploitation of the Minke Whale, 1989; contrib. scientific pubns. *Recreation:* being outside. *Address:* CEFAS Laboratory, Pakefield Road, Lowestoft NR33 0HT. *T:* (01502) 524563. *E:* jwh.jwh@btinternet.com. *Clubs:* Southwold Golf; Rookery Park Golf.

**HORWOOD, Martin Charles**; Member (Lib Dem) South West Region, European Parliament, since 2019; *b* 12 Oct. 1962; *s* of Don Horwood, ISO and Nina Horwood; *m* 1995, Dr Shona Arora; one *s* one *d*. *Educ:* Queen's Coll., Oxford (BA 1984). Account Exec., Ted Bates Advertising, 1985–86; Dir of Develt, British Humanist Assoc., 1986–88; Creative Co-ordinator, Help the Aged, 1988–90; Donor Marketing Manager, Oxfam, 1990–95; Dir of Communications and Fundraising, Oxfam (India), 1995–96; Dir of Fundraising, Alzheimer's Soc., 1996–2001; Sen. Consultant, 2001–03, Hd of Consultancy, 2003–05, Target Direct Marketing; Dir of Engagement and Impact, Development Initiatives Ltd, 2015–16. MP (Lib Dem) Cheltenham, 2005–15; contested (Lib Dem) same seat, 2015, 2017. Lib Dem spokesman on envmt, 2006–10. Member: Select Cttee on Communities and Local Govt (formerly ODPM), 2005–07; Envmtl Audit Select Cttee, 2007–10; Sec., All-Party Gp for corporate responsibility, 2005; Chm., All-Party Gp for tribal peoples, 2007–15; Chairman: Lib Dem Transport Cttee, 2010–11; Lib Dem Internat. Affairs Cttee, 2011–15. *Recreations:* cycling, drawing, astronomy. *Address:* European Parliament, 60 Rue Wiertz, 1047 Brussels, Belgium.

**HORWOOD-SMART, Rosamund, (Mrs R. O. Bernays)**; QC 1996; a Recorder, since 1995; *b* 21 Sept. 1951; *d* of late John Horwood-Smart and Sylvia Horwood-Smart; *m* 1st, 1983, Richard Blackford (marr. diss. 1994); one *s* one *d*; 2nd, 1996, Richard O. Bernays. *Educ:* Felixstowe Coll.; Cambridgeshire High Sch. for Girls; Inns of Court Sch. of Law. Called to the Bar, Inner Temple, 1974, Bencher, 1998. Trustee: Nat. Music Day, 1992–98; Prisoners of Conscience Appeal Fund, 1990–2001 (Chm., then Patron); Toyota Trevelyanshi Trust, 1990–2007; Temple Music Foundn, 2006–; Handel House, 2008–16; Longborough Fest. Opera, 2014–; Grange Fest., 2016–. Patron, New English Ballet Theatre, 2011–. Vice Pres., Internat. Students House, 2007– (Gov., 1978–2007; Chm., 2001–07). *Recreations:* music, gardening, theatre.

**HOSIE, Stewart**; MP (SNP) Dundee East, since 2005; *b* 3 Jan. 1963; *m* 1997, Shona Robison, *qv*; one *d*. *Educ:* Carnoustie High Sch.; Dundee Coll. of Technol. Gp Inf. Systems Manager, MIH, 1988–93; systems analyst, 1993–96; Year 2000/EMU Project Manager, Stakis/Hilton, 1996–2000. Nat. Sec., 1999–2003, Dep. Leader, 2014–16, SNP. Contested (SNP): Kirkcaldy, 1992, 1997; Kirkcaldy, Scottish Parlt, 1999. *Address:* (office) 8 Old Glamis Road, Dundee DD3 8HP; House of Commons, SW1A 0AA.

**HOSKER, Edmund Nigel Ronald**, CBE 2017; Director, International Energy and EU, Department for Business, Energy and Industrial Strategy (formerly Director, International Energy, EU and Energy Security, later Energy Resilience, Department of Energy and Climate Change), 2011–17; *b* 25 April 1958; *s* of Ronald Reece Hosker and Hilda Gertrude Hosker (*née* Harrington); *m* 1983, Elizabeth Miranda Thornely; three *d*. *Educ:* Slough Grammar Sch.; St Catharine's Coll., Cambridge (BA Hons English 1979). Joined Department of Trade and Industry, 1979: Private Sec. to Minister for Industry and subseq. to Sec. of State for Trade and Industry, 1983–84; Principal, 1984; on secondment to British Embassy, Washington, 1990–94; Asst Sec., 1994; transf. to Cabinet Office, 1995–97; Dir of Finance, DTI, 1997–2000; Dir, Finance and Resource Mgt, DTI, 2000–02; on secondment to Scottish Power, 2003; Dir, Europe and World Trade, DTI, subseq. BERR, 2003–08 (Acting Dir Gen. for Markets, 2005); Dir, Energy Markets Unit, BERR, 2008; Acting Dir Gen. for Corporate Services, then Corporate Support and Shared Services, later Corporate and Professional Services, subseq. Acting Chief Operating Officer, DECC, 2008–11. Mem., Admin. Bd, EU Agency for Cooperation of Energy Regulators, 2016–. Chair, Governing Bd, Internat. Energy Agency, 2013–17. FEI 2017.

**HOSKER, Sir Gerald (Albery)**, KCB 1995 (CB 1987); HM Procurator General, Treasury Solicitor and Queen's Proctor, 1992–95; *b* 28 July 1933; *s* of Leslie Reece Hosker and Constance Alice Rose Hosker (*née* Hubbard); *m* 1956, Rachel Victoria Beatrice Middleton; one *s* one *d*. *Educ:* Berkhamsted Sch., Berkhamsted, Herts; Law Soc. Coll. of Law. Admitted Solicitor, 1956; Corporate Secretary 1964; Associate of the Faculty of Secretaries and Administrators 1964. Articled to Derrick Bridges & Co., 1951–56; with Clifford-Turner & Co., 1957–59; entered Treasury Solicitor's Dept as Legal Asst, 1960; Sen. Legal Asst, 1966; Asst Solicitor, 1973; Under Sec. (Legal), 1982; Dep. Treasury Solicitor, 1984–87; Solicitor to the DTI, 1987–92. Conducted enquiry into: Customs and Excise aspects of Simon de Danser case, 1999; C. W. Cheney Pension Fund for DSS, 2001; Public Inquiry Comr, Falkland Is, 1999–2000. Dir, RAFM Investments Ltd, 2003–09. Mem. Bd, Inst. of Advanced Legal Studies, Univ. of London, 1992–95; Governor, Lyonsdown Sch., New Barnet, 1996–2006 and 2009–12. Trustee, RAF Mus., 1998–2009; Mem., Governing Bodies Forum, Mus Assoc., 2005–09. FRSA 1964–2014. Hon. QC 1991. *Recreations:* the study of biblical prophecy, walking. *Address:* (office) c/o Treasury Solicitor, 102 Petty France, SW1H 9AJ. *Club:* Royal Over-Seas League.

**HOSKING, Barbara Nancy**, CBE 1999 (OBE 1985); Deputy Chairman, Westcountry Television, 1997–99 (non-executive Director, 1992–99); *b* 4 Nov. 1926; *d* of late William Henry Hosking and Ada Kathleen Hosking (*née* Murrish); civil partnership, 2017, Margaret Sheila Hyde, *qv*. *Educ:* West Cornwall School for Girls, Penzance; Hillcroft College, Surbiton; and by my friends. Secretary to Town Clerk, Council of Isles of Scilly, and local corresp. for BBC and Western Morning News, 1945–47; Editl Asst, The Circle, Odeon and Gaumont cinemas, 1947–50; Asst to Inf. Officer, Labour Party, 1952–55; Asst to Gen. Manager, Uruwira Minerals Ltd, Tanzania, 1955–57; Asst to Gen. Sec., Labour Party, 1958–65; Press and Inf. Officer posts, Civil Service, 1965–77; Controller of Inf. Services, IBA, 1977–86; Political Consultant, Yorkshire TV, 1987–92. Mem. (Lab), Islington BC, 1962–64. Non-exec. Dir, Camden and Islington Community Health Services NHS Trust, 1992–93. Pres., Media Soc., 1987–88; Jt Vice-Chm., NCVO, 1987–92. Mem. Council, Family Policy Studies Centre, 1994–97. Trustee: Charities Aid Foundn, 1987–92; 300 Gp, 1988–91; Nat. Literacy Trust, 1993–99. Associate, Women's Advertising Club of London, 1994–. Patron, Clean-Break Theatre Co., 1992–. Hon. Vice Pres., London Cornish Assoc., 1992; Bard, Gorsedd Kernow. Occasional radio broadcaster. FRTS 1988; FRSA (Mem. Council, 1992–96). DUniv Ulster, 1996. Special citation, Internat. Women's Forum, NY, 1983, Boston, 1996. *Publications:* Exceeding My Brief: memoirs of a disobedient civil servant, 2017; contribs to Punch, New Scientist, Spectator. *Recreations:* opera, lieder, watching politics. *Club:* Reform (Trustee, 2018–).

**HOSKING, Prof. Geoffrey Alan**, OBE 2015; FBA 1993; FRHistS; Professor of Russian History, 1984–2007, now Emeritus, and Leverhulme Personal Research Professor, 1999–2004, University College London; *b* 28 April 1942; *s* of Stuart William Steggall Hosking and Jean Ross Hosking; *m* 1970, Anne Lloyd Hirst; two *d*. *Educ:* Maidstone Grammar Sch.; King's Coll., Cambridge (MA, PhD); St Antony's Coll., Oxford. FRHistS 1998. Asst Lectr in Government, 1966–68, Lectr in Government, 1968–71, Univ. of Essex; Vis. Lectr in Political Science, Univ. of Wisconsin, Madison, 1971–72; Lectr in History, Univ. of Essex, 1972–76; Sen. Research Fellow, Russian Inst., Columbia Univ., New York, 1976; Sen. Lectr and Reader in Russian History, Univ. of Essex, 1976–84; Dep. Dir, SSEES, London Univ., 1996–98. Vis. Prof., Slavisches Inst., Univ. of Cologne, 1980–81; Mem., IAS, Princeton, 2006–07. BBC Reith Lectr, 1988 (The Rediscovery of Politics: authority, culture and community in the USSR). Member: Council, Writers and Scholars Educnl Trust, 1985–2007; Overseas Policy Cttee, 1994–2000, Internat. Engagement Cttee, 2010–14, British Acad.; Council, RHistS, 2002–06; Jury, Booker Prize for Russian Fiction, 1993. Member: Internat. Academic Council, Mus. of Contemporary History (formerly Mus. of the Revolution), Moscow, 1994–; Admin. Bd, Moscow Sch. of Pol Studies, 1992–2000; Exec. Cttee, Britain-Russia Centre, 1994–2000. Trustee, J. S. Mill Inst., 1992–96; Governor, Camden Sch. for Girls, 1989–94. Member: Editl Bd, Jl of Contemporary History, 1988–99; Editl Cttee, Nations and Nationalism, 1994–2012; Editl Bd, Nationalities Papers, 1997–2005; Editl Bd, Reviews in History, 1999–2004; Editl Bd, Ab Imperio, 2002–17; Editl Bd, Otechestvennaia Istoriia, 2007–12. Hon. Dr Russian Acad. Scis, 2000. *Publications:* The Russian Constitutional Experiment: Government and Duma 1907–14, 1973; Beyond Socialist Realism: Soviet fiction since Ivan Denisovich, 1980; A History of the Soviet Union, 1985, 3rd edn 1992 (Los Angeles Times Hist. Book Prize, 1986) (trans. Russian 1994); The Awakening of the Soviet Union, 1990, 2nd edn 1991; (with J. Aves and P. J. S. Duncan) The Road to Post-Communism: independent political movements in the Soviet Union 1985–91, 1992; Russia: people and Empire 1552–1917, 1997 (trans. Russian, 2000); (ed with George Schöpflin) Myths and Nationhood, 1997; (ed with Robert Service) Russian Nationalism Past and Present, 1998; (ed with Robert Service) Reinterpreting Russia, 1999; Russia and the Russians: a history, 2001 (history prize, Ind. Publisher Book Awards, USA, 2002), 2nd edn 2012; Rulers and Victims: the Russians in the Soviet Union, 2006 (Alec Nove Book Prize, 2008); Trust: money, markets and society, 2010; Russian History: a very short introduction, 2012; Trust: a history, 2014 (trans. Russian, 2016). *Recreations:* music, chess, walking. *Address:* School of Slavonic and East European Studies, University College London, Gower Street, WC1E 6BT; Flat 15, Julian Court, 150 Camden Road, NW1 9HU. *T:* (020) 7267 5543. *E:* geoffreyhosking@mac.com.

**HOSKING, John Everard**, CBE 1990; JP; DL; Chairman, Agra Europe (London) Ltd, 1989–94 (Director and Chief Executive, 1974–89); Vice-President, Magistrates' Association, since 1990 (Chairman of Council, 1987–90); *b* 23 Oct. 1929; *s* of J. Everard Hosking, OBE and E. Margaret (*née* Shaxson); *m* 1953, Joan Cecily Whitaker, BSc (*d* 2017); two *s*. *Educ:* Marlborough Coll.; Wye Coll., London Univ. (BScA 1953). NDA 1954. Farming and forestry in Kent, 1953–69; Man. Dir, Eastes and Loud Ltd, 1965–69; Director: Newgrain-Kent, 1969–74; Ashford Corn Exchange Co., 1965–69; Agroup Ltd, 1987–94; Bureau Européen de Recherches SA, 1987–90; European Intelligence Ltd, 1987–94. Tax Comr, 1980–2004. Chairman: Centre for European Agricultural Studies Assoc., 1977–83; European Agricultural Outlook Conference, 1981–95; Kent Magistrates' Courts Cttee, 1984–88; Member: Kent Police Authority, 1970–74; Lord Chancellor's Adv. Ctte on the Appointment of Magistrates, 1977–89; Central Council, Magistrates' Courts Cttees, 1980–83; Bar Council Professional Conduct Cttee, 1983–86; Senate of Inns of Court and the Bar Disciplinary Tribunal, 1983–86; Council, Commonwealth Magistrates' and Judges' Assoc., 1989–92; Lord Chief Justice's Working Party on Mode of Trial, 1989; Lord Chancellor's Adv. Cttee on Legal Educn and Conduct, 1991–94. Pres., Kent Magistrates'

Assoc., 2001–12, now Life Vice-Pres. (Chm., 1973–78). Pres., Wye Coll. Agricola Club, 1995–2004. Vice-Patron, Ashford Community Arts Trust, 2001–11. Governor: Ashford Sch., 1976–2006 (Chm., 1994–2001); Wye Coll., Univ. of London, 1995–2000; Mem. Governing Council, Church Schs Co., 1999–2001. Patron, Ashford Sch. Foundn, 2016–. Ed., Common Agricl Policy Monitor, 1994–2011. JP Kent, 1962 (Chm., Ashford Bench, 1975–85); DL Kent, 1992. British Univs Ploughing Champion, 1952. *Publications:* (ed) Rural Response to the Resource Crisis in Europe, 1981; The Agricultural Industry of West Germany, 1990. *Recreations:* the arts, the countryside. *Address:* Pett House, Charing, Kent. *Club:* Farmers.

**HOSKINS, Sir Brian (John),** Kt 2007; CBE 1998; PhD; FRS 1988; Chair, Grantham Institute for Climate Change, Imperial College London, since 2014 (Director, 2008–14); Professor of Meteorology, University of Reading, since 1981; *b* 17 May 1945; *s* of George Frederick Hoskins and Kathleen Matilda Louise Hoskins; *m* 1968, Jacqueline Holmes; two *d. Educ:* Bristol Grammar Sch.; Trinity Hall, Cambridge (BA 1966; MA, PhD 1970; Hon. Fellow 2011). FRMetS 1970 (Hon. FRMets 2001); Fellow, Amer. Meteorol Soc., 1985 (Hon. Mem., 2014); FAAAS 2012; FEI 2012. Post-doctoral Fellow, Nat. Center for Atmospheric Res., Boulder, Colo, 1970–71; Vis. Scientist, GFD Program, Univ. of Princeton, 1972–73; Univ. of Reading: Post-doctoral Fellow, 1971–72, Gp Leader, 1973–, Atmospheric Modelling Gp; Reader in Atmospheric Modelling, 1976–81; Head, Dept of Meteorol., 1990–96. Royal Soc. Res. Prof., 2001–10. Special Advr to Sec. of State for Transport, 1990. Meteorological Office: Chm., SAC, 1995–2013; non-exec. Dir, 2000–13. Member: NERC, 1988–94; Jt Scientific Cttee, World Climate Res. Prog., 1995–2004 (Vice Chm., 2000–04); Royal Commn on Envmtl Pollution, 1998–2005; Intergovtl Panel on Climate Change, 2005–07; UK Govt Climate Change Cttee, 2008–18; Mem. Council, 2000–01, Chair, Global Envmtl Res. Cttee, 1999–2006, Royal Soc. Pres., IAMAS, 1991–95. Mem., Academia Europaea, 1989; Corresp. Academician, Real Acad. de Ciencias y Artes de Barcelona, 1994; Foreign Associate, US NAS, 2002; Foreign Mem., Chinese Acad. of Scis, 2002; FAAAS 2012. Hon. Fellow, Geol Soc. of India, 2015. Lectures: Starr Meml, MIT, 1989; Bernard Haurwitz Meml, Amer. Meteorol Soc., 1995; Welsh, Univ. of Toronto, 2006; 12th IMO Lectr, 2011; Bjerknes, Amer. Geophysical Union, 2014. Hon. Mem., Amer. Meteorol Soc., 2014. Hon. FCGI 2011. Hon. DSc: Bristol, 2008; UEA, 2009. Royal Meteorological Society: Pres., 1998–2000; Symons Meml Lecture, 1982; L. F. Richardson Prize, 1972; Buchan Prize, 1976; Symons Medal, 2006; Charles Chree Silver Medal, Inst. of Physics, 1987; Carl-Gustaf Rossby Res. Medal, Amer. Meteorol Soc., 1988; Vilhelm Bjerknes Prize, Eur. Geophys. Soc., 1997; Buys Ballot Medal, Royal Netherlands Acad., 2014; Gold Medal, Internat. Union of Geodesy and Geophysics, 2015. *Publications:* (ed with R. P. Pearce) Large-scale Dynamical Processes in the Atmosphere, 1983; (with Dr I. N. James) Dynamics of the Midlatitude Atmosphere, 2014; 180 papers in meteorol jls. *Recreations:* music, sport, gardening. *Address:* Anchor House, Green Lane, Pangbourne, Berks RG8 7BG. *T:* (0118) 984 1308.

**HOSKINS, Paul Trevor;** Director of Music, Purcell School, since 2018; *b* Benghazi, Libya, 15 Oct. 1966; *s* of Trevor Hoskins and Jenny Hoskins (*née* Lloyd); *m* 1992, Clare Holmes; one *s* two *d. Educ:* Christ's Hosp. Sch., Horsham; Gonville and Caius Coll., Cambridge (BA Hons 1989); Royal Coll. of Music. Conductor, Cambridge New Music Players, 1992; Music Dir, Rambert (formerly Rambert Dance Co.), 1996–2018; as freelance conductor, débuts with: English Nat. Ballet, 1993; Opera Factory, 1994; BBC Nat. Orch. of Wales, 1998; Royal Ballet, 2001; New York City Ballet, 2001; San Francisco Ballet, 2001; Royal Swedish Ballet, 2008; Swedish Radio Symphony Orch., 2010; Scottish Ballet, 2011; South African Nat. Dance Trust, 2015; Nat. Ballet of Canada, 2016. Gov., Childs Hill Sch., 2006–19. *Recreations:* family, home, sport, crosswords, cinema. *Address:* Purcell School, Aldenham Road, Bushey, Herts WD23 2TS. *E:* p.hoskins@purcell-school.org.

**HOSKYNS, Sir Robin Chevallier,** 18th Bt *cr* 1676, of Harewood, Herefordshire; *b* 5 July 1989; *o s* of Sir (Edwyn) Wren Hoskyns, 17th Bt, FRCPCH and of Jane Hoskyns (*née* Sellers); *S* father, 2015. *Heir: uncle* John Chandos Hoskyns [*b* 4 April 1961; two *d* by Jennifer Biondi].

**HOSSAIN, Ajmalul;** QC 1998; *b* 18 Oct. 1950; *s* of late Asrarul Hossain, barrister and Senior Advocate, Supreme Court of Bangladesh, and Rabia Hossain; *m* 1970, Nasreen Ahmed; two *s. Educ:* King's Coll., London (LLB Hons 1976; LLM 1977). FCIArb 1994. Called to the Bar, Lincoln's Inn, 1976 (Buchanan Prize), Bencher, 2012; SE Circuit; in practice at the Bar, Bangladesh, 1977–, England, 1978–; Supreme Court of Bangladesh: enrolled in High Court Div., 1977, Appellate Div., 1986; Senior Advocate, 1998. Pt-time Chm., Southampton Reg., Employment (formerly Industrial) Tribunals, 1995–2005. Member: Internat. Court of Arbitration, 2006–09, Commn on Arbitration, 2009–, Internat. Chamber of Commerce, Paris; Code of Conduct Commn, Internat. Cricket Council, 2006–15; Ethics Cttee, Fédération Internationale de l'Automobile, Paris, 2013–. Member: Supreme Court Bar Assoc., Bangladesh, 1986; Chancery Bar Assoc., 2002. Fellow, Soc. for Advanced Legal Studies, 2000. *Recreations:* travelling, bridge. *Address:* Selborne Chambers, 10 Essex Street, WC2R 3AA. *T:* (020) 7420 9500, *Fax:* (020) 7420 9555. *E:* ajmalul.hossain@selbornechambers.co.uk; A. Hossain & Associates, 3B Outer Circular Road, Maghbazar, Dhaka 1217, Bangladesh. *T:* (2) 8311492, *Fax:* (2) 9344356.

**HOSSAIN, (Syed Mohammad) Sa'ad (Ansarul);** QC 2013; *b* Belfast, 11 Aug. 1971; *s* of Quamer and Mary Hossain; *m* 2000, Anna Thomas; two *s* one *d. Educ:* Methodist Coll., Belfast; Gonville and Caius Coll., Cambridge (BSc Hons Natural Scis 1992). Called to the Bar, Gray's Inn, 1995, Bencher, 2017; in practice as barrister, specialising in commercial law, 1996–. *Recreations:* running, surfing, tennis, trekking. *Address:* One Essex Court, Temple, EC4Y 9AR. *T:* (020) 7583 2000, *Fax:* (020) 7583 0118. *E:* shossain@oeclaw.co.uk.

**HOTHAM,** family name of **Baron Hotham**.

**HOTHAM, 8th Baron** *cr* 1797; **Henry Durand Hotham;** DL; Bt 1621; *b* 3 May 1940; *s* of 7th Baron Hotham, CBE, and Lady Letitia Sibell Winifred Cecil (*d* 1992), *er d* of 5th Marquess of Exeter, KG; *S* father, 1967; *m* 1972, Alexandra Stirling Home, *d* of late Maj. Andrew S. H. Drummond Moray; two *s* one *d. Educ:* Eton; Cirencester Agricultural Coll. Late Lieut, Grenadier Guards; ADC to Governor of Tasmania, 1963–66. DL Humberside, 1981. *Heir: s* Hon. William Beaumont Hotham [*b* 13 Oct. 1972; *m* 2005, Katrina Heyward; one *s* two *d*]. *Address:* The Dower House, Mere Lane, South Dalton, Beverley, E Yorks HU17 7PL.

**HOTHFIELD, 6th Baron** *cr* 1881; **Anthony Charles Sackville Tufton;** DL; Bt 1851; *b* 21 Oct. 1939; *s* of 5th Baron Hothfield, TD and Evelyn Margarette (*d* 1989), *e d* of late Eustace Charles Mordaunt; *S* father, 1991; *m* 1975, Lucinda Marjorie, *d* of Captain Timothy John Gurney; one *s* one *d. Educ:* Eton; Magdalene Coll., Cambridge (MA). MICE. DL Cumbria, 2004. *Recreations:* Real tennis, lawn tennis, bridge, shooting. *Heir: s* Hon. William Sackville Tufton, MD [*b* 14 Nov. 1977; *m* 2006, Elizabeth, *o d* of Robin Burgess; two *s* one *d*]. *Address:* Drybeck Hall, Appleby, Cumbria CA16 6TF. *Clubs:* Hawks (Cambridge); Jesters; almost every Real tennis club.

**HOTOPF, Prof. Matthew Hugo,** CBE 2018; PhD; FRCPsych; FMedSci; Professor of General Hospital Psychiatry, since 2004 and Vice Dean of Research, since 2017, Institute of Psychiatry, Psychology and Neuroscience, King's College London; *b* London, 3 Aug. 1965; *s* of late Prof. (William Hugh) Norman Hotopf and Jill E. Hotopf; *m* 1999, Emma Staples; two *s* one *d. Educ:* University Coll. London (BSc Psychol. 1986); St Bartholomew's Hosp. Med. Sch. (MB BS 1989); London Sch. of Hygiene and Tropical Medicine (MSc Epidemiol. 1996); Inst. of Psychiatry (PhD Psychiatric Epidemiol. 1999). MRCPsych 1994, FRCPsych 2016. MRC Clin. Trng Fellow, Inst. of Psychiatry, 1995–98; Sen. Lectr in Psychiatry, Guy's, King's and St Thomas' Sch. of Medicine, 1999–2002; Reader in Psychol Medicine, Inst. of Psychiatry, 2002–04. Consultant Liaison Psychiatrist, S London and Maudsley NHS Foundn Trust, 1998– (non-exec. Dir, 2016–17). NIHR Sen. Investigator, 2007. FMedSci 2017. *Publications:* (jtly) Chronic Fatigue and its Syndromes, 1998; (ed jtly) Practical Psychiatric Epidemiology, 2003; articles in med. and psychiatric jls incl. on impact of mil. service on mental health, impact of mental disorders on mortality and physical health, and mental capacity.

**HOTSPUR;** *see* McGrath, J. A.

**HOTTEN, Christopher Peter;** QC 1994; a Recorder, 1990–2017; *b* 7 July 1949; *s* of Alan John Hotten and Ida Lydia Hotten; *m* 1973, Lone Elisabeth Nielsen; one *s* two *d. Educ:* Hornchurch Grammar Sch.; Leicester Univ. (LLB). Called to the Bar, Inner Temple, 1972. Trustee and volunteer, Gordon Russell Design Mus., Broadway. *Recreations:* golf, going to the gym, history of art.

**HOTUNG, Sir Joseph (Edward),** Kt 1993; Chairman, Ho Hung Hing Estates Ltd, 1962–2011; *b* 25 May 1930; *s* of Edward Sai-kim Hotung and Maud Alice (*née* Newman); *m* 1957, Mary Catherine McGinley (marr. diss. 1969); two *s* two *d. Educ:* St Francis Xavier Coll., Shanghai; St Louis Coll., Tientsin; Catholic Univ. of America (BA); Univ. of London (LLB ext.). With Marine Midland Bank, 1957–60. Director: HSBC Hldgs plc, 1991–98; Hongkong & Shanghai Banking Corp. Ltd, 1991–96; Hongkong Electric Hldgs Ltd, 1984–97; China & Eastern Investment Co. Ltd, 1989–98. Member: Judicial Services Commn, Hong Kong, 1990–97; Inland Revenue Bd of Review, Hong Kong, 1989–95. University of Hong Kong: Mem. Council, 1984–96; Chm. and Trustee, Staff Terminal Benefits Scheme, 1987–96; Mem. Council, Business Sch., 1990–96; Chm., Arts Develt Council, Hong Kong, 1994–96; Dir, E Asian Hist. of Sci. Foundn, 1991–2001; Member: Governing Body, SOAS, 1997–2005; St George's Hosp. Med. Sch., London Univ., 2001–07. Trustee: British Mus., 1994–2004, now Trustee Emeritus; Asia Soc., NY, 1991–97; MMA, NY, 2000–05, now Trustee Emeritus. Hon. Mem., Freer Gall. of Art and Sackler Gall., Washington, 1990. Honorary Fellow: Hong Kong Univ., 1995; SOAS, 2009. Hon. DLitt Hong Kong, 1997; Hon. DSc Econs London, 2003. NACF Award, 1993. *Recreation:* Oriental art. *Address:* 1203 Prince's Building, 10 Chater Road, Central, Hong Kong. *T:* 25229929. *Clubs:* Reform, Beefsteak; Hong Kong (Hong Kong); Century Assoc. (New York).

**HOUGH, Sir James,** Kt 2018; OBE 2013; PhD; FRS 2003; FRSE; CPhys, FInstP; FRAS; Kelvin Professor of Natural Philosophy, 2009–11, now Emeritus (Professor of Experimental Physics, 1986–2009), Associate Director, Institute for Gravitational Research, since 2009 (Director, 2000–09), and Research Professor in Natural Philosophy, since 2010, University of Glasgow; *b* 6 Aug. 1945; *s* of Frederick and Lillias Hough; *m* 1972, Anne Park McNab (*d* 2000); one *s* one *d. Educ:* Univ. of Glasgow (BSc 1st Cl. Hons Natural Philosophy 1967; PhD 1971). FInstP 1993; CPhys 2002. University of Glasgow: Res. Fellow, 1970–72; Lectr in Natural Philosophy, 1972–83; Sen. Lectr, 1983–86. Chief Exec., Scottish Univs Physics Alliance, 2011–15. Vis. Fellow, JILA, Univ. of Colorado, 1983; PPARC Sen. Fellow, 1997–2000. RSE Gunning Victoria Prize Lectr, 2008. Member: PPARC, 2005–07; Scottish Science Advrs Council, 2010–15; Council, Inst. of Physics, 2011–15. FRAS 1983; FRSE 1991; FAPS 2001; FRSA 2012. Max Planck Res. Prize, 1991; Duddell Medal and Prize, Inst. of Physics, 2004; Royal Medal, RSE, 2016; Gold Medal, RAS, 2018. *Publications:* contribs to learned jls and to books and conf. reports. *Recreations:* sports cars, photography. *Address:* Institute for Gravitational Research, School of Physics and Astronomy, University of Glasgow, Glasgow G12 8QQ. *T:* (0141) 330 4706, *Fax:* (0141) 330 6833. *E:* james.hough@glasgow.ac.uk.

**HOUGH, Prof. James Harley,** PhD; CPhys, FInstP; FRAS; Professor of Astrophysics, University of Hertfordshire (formerly Hatfield Polytechnic), 1989–2015, now Emeritus (Director of Astronomy Research, 2003–10); *b* 2 July 1943; *s* of John Harley Hough and Sarah Ann (*née* Lomax); *m* 1966, Monica Jane Dent; one *s* one *d. Educ:* Prince Henry's GS, Otley, Yorks; Univ. of Leeds (BSc 1st Cl. Hons; PhD 1967). FRAS 1997; FInstP 1998. Res. Fellow, Univ. of Calgary, 1967–71; SERC Res. Fellow, Univ. of Durham, 1971–72; Hatfield Polytechnic, subseq. Univ. of Hertfordshire: Lectr, 1972–83; Reader in Astronomy, 1983–89; Hd of Physical Scis, 1987–98; Dean of Natural Scis, 1998–2003. Particle Physics and Astronomy Research Council: Mem. Council 1997–2000; Chm., Educn and Trng Panel, 1998–2001; Mem. or Chm., numerous SERC/PPARC Cttees and Bds, 1980–. Daiwa-Adrian Prize for UK-Japan scientific collaborations, 1998; Herschel Medal, RAS, 2010. *Publications:* PPARC reports on future of UK Ground-Based Astronomy; numerous scientific papers in learned jls, mostly on active galaxies, star formation, interstellar dust, astrobiology and astronomical polarimetry. *Address:* Centre for Astrophysics Research, University of Hertfordshire, Hatfield AL10 9AB. *T:* 07443 046193.

**HOUGH, Jonathan Anthony;** QC 2014; barrister; *b* Colchester, 3 June 1973; *s* of Kenneth and Ellen Josephine Hough; *m* 2005, Caroline Elizabeth Brennan; one *d. Educ:* Bradford Grammar Sch.; St Hugh's Coll., Oxford (BA 1st Cl; MA); City Univ. (DipLaw). Called to the Bar, Middle Temple, 1997; in practice as barrister, specialising in commercial, public and administrative law, 1997–. *Publications:* (ed) Jackson & Powell on Professional Liability, 7th edn 2012, 8th edn 2017. *Recreations:* family and friends, reading, theatre, riding. *Address:* 4 New Square, Lincoln's Inn, WC2A 3RJ. *T:* (020) 7822 2000, *Fax:* (020) 7822 2001. *E:* j.hough@4newsquare.com. *Club:* Garrick.

**HOUGH, Julia Marie, (Judy);** *see* Taylor, Judy.

**HOUGH, Robert Eric,** CBE 2015; DL; Chairman, Northwest Regional Development Agency, 2009–12 (Board Member, 2007–12); *b* 18 July 1945; *s* of Gordon Hough and Joyce Hough (*née* Davies); *m* 1975, Pauline Elizabeth Arch; two *s. Educ:* William Hulme's Grammar Sch., Manchester; Univ. of Bristol (LLB 1967). Admitted solicitor, 1970; NP, 1982–92; Partner, Slater Heelis, solicitors, Manchester, 1974–89; Peel Holdings: Dir, 1986–; Exec. Dep. Chm., 1989–2002; non-exec. Dep. Chm., 2002–09; Manchester Ship Canal Company: non-exec. Chm., 1987–89; Exec. Chm., 1989–2002; Chairman: Liverpool Airport Ltd, 1997–2009, 2014–; Doncaster Sheffield Airport, 1999–2009, 2012–; Durham Tees Valley Airport, 2003–09, 2012–19. Non-executive Chairman: New East Manchester Ltd, 2002–10; Cheshire Building Soc., 2006–08 (non-exec. Dir, 2002–08); Turley Associates Ltd, 2008–14 (non-exec. Dir, 2003–14); non-executive Director: Brammer plc, 1993–2003 (non-exec. Dep. Chm., 1998–2003); PJ Kennedy Investments Ltd, 1997–2011; Alfred McAlpine plc, 2003–08; Styles & Wood Gp plc, 2006–18; Provident Financial plc, 2007–13. Mem., 2000–04, Mem. Exec. Bd, 2006–07, NW Regl Assembly; Member: NW Regl Leaders Bd, 2013–16; Transport for the North Partnership

Bd, 2015–16. Pres., Manchester Chamber of Commerce, 1994–95; Chm., Organising Cttee, 1995–99, Vice-Pres., 1999–2002, Manchester Commonwealth Games 2002; Mem., NW Business Leadership Team, 1997–2009, 2016– (Chm., 2000–03); Chm., Liverpool City Reg. LEP, 2012–16. Member: Learning and Skills Council, 2009–10; Adv. Council, Tate Liverpool, 2013–16. Gov., Univ. of Manchester, 2005–15 (Dep. Chm. Govs, 2012–15); Regent, Liverpool Hope Univ., 2015. Mem., Law Soc. DL 1997, High Sheriff 2004, Gtr Manchester. Hon. Fellow, Liverpool John Moores Univ., 2016. Hon. DBA Manchester Metropolitan, 1996; Hon. DLitt Salford, 1996. Medal of Honour, Univ. of Manchester, 2016. *Recreations:* golf, gardening, walking. *Address:* Peel Airports Ltd, Peel Dome, intu Trafford Centre, Trafford City, Manchester M17 8PL. *T:* (0161) 629 8202, *Fax:* (0161) 629 8333. *E:* rhough@peel.co.uk. *Club:* Hale Golf.

**HOUGH, Stephen,** CBE 2014; concert pianist; composer; writer; *b* 22 Nov. 1961. *Educ:* Chetham's Sch. Music, Manchester; Royal Northern Coll. of Music (Fellow, 1993); Juilliard Sch. Numerous recitals and concerto appearances with LSO, LPO, RPO, Philharmonia, Chicago SO, Philadelphia Orchestra, Cleveland Orchestra, NY Philharmonic, LA Philharmonic, San Francisco SO, Boston SO, Pittsburgh SO, Orchestre Nat. de France, Deutsches Symphonie Orchester, Berlin Philharmonic, Russian Nat. Orchestra; festival performances incl.: Ravinia, Mostly Mozart, Waldbühne, Hollywood Bowl, Blossom, Proms, Le Grange de Meslay, La Roque d'Antheron, Edinburgh, Sapporo, Salzburg, Tanglewood. *Recordings:* Hummel Piano Concertos and Sonatas; 3 Liszt Recitals; 3 Piano Albums; Schumann Recital; Brahms Piano Concertos Nos 1 and 2; Complete Britten Piano Music; Schubert Sonatas; Mendelssohn Piano Concertos; (with Robert Mann) Complete Beethoven and Brahms Violin Sonatas; Chopin Ballades and Scherzos; Scharwenka Piano Concerto No 4, and Sauer Piano Concerto No 1 (Gramophone Record of the Year, 1996); (with Steven Isserlis) Cello Sonatas of Grieg, Rachmaninoff, Franck and Rubinstein; Piano Concertos of Lowell Liebermann; Brahms Sonata; (with Michael Collins and Steven Isserlis) Clarinet Trios; Complete Piano and Orchestra Music of Saint-Saëns (Gramophone CD of the Year, 2003; Gold Disc Award, Gramophone Mag., 2008); Complete Rachmaninoff Piano Concertos; English Piano Album; piano music of York Bowen, Franck and Mompou; Mozart Album; Beethoven and Mozart Piano and Wind Quartets; Spanish Album; Stephen Hough in recital; music of Corigliano Tsontakis, Copland and Weber; Complete music for piano and orchestra by Tchaikovsky; Chopin: Late Masterpieces; Chopin Complete Waltzes (Diapason d'Or de l'Année, 2011); Broken Branches (compositions by Stephen Hough); Liszt and Grieg Piano Concertos; French Album; Brahms Piano Concertos (with Salzburg Mozarteum Orch.); In The Night (recital disc); Dream Album. Internat. Chair of Piano Studies, RNCM, 2003– (Dayas Gold Medal, 1981); Scriabin and Janáček recital; Dvorak and Schumann piano concertos (with CBSO and Andris Nelsons). Vis. Prof. of Piano, RAM, 2002– (Hon. RAM 2002). Hon. Bencher, Middle Temple, 2017. Hon. Mem., Royal Philharmonic Soc., 2018. MacArthur Fellowship, MacArthur Foundn, 2001–. Writer of cultural blog for Daily Telegraph website, 2008–. Hon. DMus Liverpool, 2011. Internat. Terence Judd Award, 1982; Naumburg Internat. Piano Competition, 1983; Jean Gimbel Lane Prize in Piano Perf., Northwestern Univ., 2009; Royal Philharmonic Soc. Instrumentalist Award, 2010. *Compositions:* Suite R-B and other enigmas, 2003; Three Marian Hymns for children's choir and organ, 2005; On Falla, 2005; Advent Calendar, 2005; Threnody (In Memoriam C. G. H.), 2006; 3 Songs From War, 2006; Mass of Innocence and Experience, 2006; The Loneliest Wilderness: elegy for cello and orch., 2006; Missa Mirabilis, 2007 (orchestral version, 2011); Londinium Magnificat and Nunc Dimittis, 2007; Three Grave Songs, 2007; Herbstlieder, 2008; Un Piccolo Sonatina, 2008; Was mit den Tränen geschieht: trio for piccolo, contrabassoon and piano, 2008; Requiem Æternum: after Victoria, 2009; Other Love Songs for SATB and piano duet, 2010; Sonata for piano (broken branches), 2010; Piano Sonata no 2 (notturno luminoso), 2012; December: a choral album, 2012; Sonata for cello and piano (les adieux), 2013; Dappled Things: a cycle of six songs for baritone and piano, 2014; Piano Sonata III (Trinitas), 2015; Just As I Am, anthem for SATB and organ, 2015; The Mad Tea Party for violin and piano, 2015; Tributes, 2015; Sonata for Viola and Piano, 2015; Paradise, for piccolo and piano, 2016; Piano Sonata no 4 (Vida Breve), 2016; Ding Dong Merrily for choir and organ, 2017; Hallowed for SATB unaccompanied, 2017; Partita for piano, 2019; Sonatina for organ, 2019. *Publications:* (contrib.) The Way We Are Now, 2006; The Bible as Prayer, 2007; (contrib.) Elgar: an anniversary portrait, 2007; (contrib.) Britten's Century: celebrating 100 years of Britten, 2013; vols of transcriptions incl. Rodgers and Hammerstein, 1999, Franck, Choral No 3, 2000; The Final Retreat (novel), 2018; Rough Ideas (misc. writings), 2019. *Recreations:* writing, reading, painting. *Address:* HarrisonParrott Ltd, The Ark, 201 Talgarth Road, W6 8BJ. *W:* www.stephenhough.com.

**HOUGHAM, John William,** CBE 1996; Commissioner and Deputy Chairman, Disability Rights Commission, 2000–07; *b* 18 Jan. 1937; *s* of late William George Hougham and Emily Jane (*née* Smith); *m* 1961, Peggy Edith Grove (*d* 2006); one *d* (one *s* decd). *Educ:* Sir Roger Manwood's Sch., Sandwich; Leeds Univ. (BA Hons). National Service: commnd 2nd Lieut RA, 1955–57. British Home Stores, 1960–63; Ford Motor Company Ltd, 1963–93: Director: Industrial Relns, Ford España SA, 1976–80; Industrial Relns, Mfg, Ford of Europe Inc., 1982–86; Personnel, and Exec. Bd Mem., Ford UK, 1986–93. Mem. Bd, Personnel Mgt Services Ltd, 1989–93. Chm., ACAS, 1993–2000; Member: Review Body on Doctors' and Dentists' Remuneration, 1992–93; Adv. Bd of CS Occupational Health Service, 1992–96; Employment Appeal Tribunal, 1992–93 and 2000–07; Bluewater Chaplaincy Team, 2013–. Member: Engrg ITB, 1987–90; IPM Nat. Cttee for Equal Opportunities, 1987–92; CBI Employment Policy Cttee, 1987–93; Council, CRAC, 1988–2000; Bd, Trng and Employment Agency for NI, 1990–93; Council, Engrg Trng Authy, 1990–93; Chairman: Employment Occupational Standards Council, 1994–97; Employment NTO, 1997–2002, subseq. ENTO, 2002–04; Adv. Cttee, ESRC Future of Work Prog., 1998–2005. Vis. Prof., Univ. (formerly Poly.) of E London, 1991–2000; Vis. Fellow, City Univ., 1991–2000. Pres., Manpower Soc., 1997–2001; Mem. Adv. Council, Involvement & Participation Assoc., 1997–2000 (Vice-Pres., 1994–97, Hon. Vice-Pres., 1997–); Chm. Disciplinary Cttee, British Health Trades Assoc., 2000–. Governor: St George's C of E Sch., Gravesend, 1990–2008; Gravesend GS for Boys, 1990–2003. Trustee: Ellenor Lions Hospices (formerly Ellenor Foundn), 2004–13; Kent Workplace Mission, 2014–. St John Ambulance: Comdr, Kent, 2007–12; Mem., County Priory Gp, 2013–; Pres., Northfleet, 2014–18; County Vice-Pres., 2016–18. Reader, dio. of Rochester, 1998–. Trustee and Vice-Chm., Kent Workplace Mission, 2015–. CCIPD (CIPM 1986); CCMI (CIMgt 1986); FRSA 1998. Freeman, City of London, 1995. Liveryman, Wheelwrights' Co., 2009. Member, Editorial Advisory Board: Human Resource Mgt Jl, 1991–2000; People Mgt Mag., 1993–2003. Hon. LLD Leeds, 1997; Hon. DBA De Montfort, 1997. CStJ 2015 (SBStJ 2009). *Publications:* (contrib.) Legal Intervention in Industrial Relations (ed William McCarthy), 1992. *Recreations:* collecting books on Kent, watching cricket and Rugby football, family history. *Address:* 12 Old Road East, Gravesend, Kent DA12 1NQ. *T:* (01474) 352138.

**HOUGHTON,** family name of **Baron Houghton of Richmond**.

**HOUGHTON OF RICHMOND,** Baron *cr* 2017 (Life Peer), of Richmond in the County of North Yorkshire; **John Nicholas Reynolds Houghton,** GCB 2011 (KCB 2008); CBE 2000 (OBE 1992); DL; Constable, HM Tower of London, since 2016; *b* 18 Oct. 1954; *s* of Frank and Margaret Houghton; *m* 1982, Margaret Glover; one *s* one *d*. *Educ:* Woodhouse Grove Sch., Bradford; RMA, Sandhurst; St Peter's Coll., Oxford (MA). Commissioned, Green Howards, 1974; psct 1985–86; CO, 1 Green Howards, 1991–94; hcsc 1997; Comdr, 39th Inf. Bde (NI), 1997–99; DMO, MoD, 1999–2002; COS HQ ARRC, 2002–04; ACDS (Ops), MoD, 2004–05; Dep. Comdg Gen., Multinational Force, Iraq, 2005–06; Chief of Jt Ops, MoD, 2006–09; Vice Chief of Defence Staff, 2009–13. Col, Yorks Regt, 2006–11; Col Comdt, Intelligence Corps, 2008–14; Chief of Defence Staff, 2013–16; ADC Gen. to the Queen, 2009–16. Trustee: Historic Royal Palaces, 2016–; Royal Armouries, 2016–; RUSI, 2017–. Officer, Legion of Merit (USA), 2006; DL Gtr London, 2018. *Recreations:* golf, shooting, history, family, watching sport, travel. *Address:* HM Tower of London, EC3N 4AB.

**HOUGHTON, Brian Thomas,** CB 1991; Director, International Division (formerly International Tax Policy Division), Inland Revenue, 1987–91; *b* 22 Aug. 1931; *s* of Bernard Charles Houghton and Sadie Houghton; *m* 1953, Joyce Beryl (*née* Williams); three *s* one *d*. *Educ:* City Boys' Sch., Leicester; Christ's Coll., Cambridge (Scholar; BA 1st cl. (Mod. Langs); MA 1957). Inland Revenue, 1957; Private Sec. to Chief Sec., HM Treasury, 1966–68; Assistant Secretary: Inland Revenue, 1968–75; HM Treasury, 1975–77; Under Sec., 1977, Principal Finance Officer and Dir of Manpower, Inland Revenue, 1977–83; Policy Div. Dir, Inland Revenue, 1983–87. Consultant, OECD, 1991–93. Vis. Professorial Fellow, QMW, 1992–97. *Recreation:* sailing. *Address:* 19 Rookes Lane, Lymington, Hants SO41 8FP. *T:* (01590) 670375.

**HOUGHTON, Sir John (Theodore),** Kt 1991; CBE 1983; FRS 1972; Chief Executive (formerly Director General) of the Meteorological Office, 1983–91; Chairman, Royal Commission on Environmental Pollution, 1992–98 (Member, 1991–98); *b* 30 Dec. 1931; *s* of Sidney M. Houghton, schoolmaster, and Miriam Houghton; *m* 1st, 1962, Margaret Edith Houghton (*née* Broughton) (*d* 1986), MB, BS, DPH; one *s* one *d*; 2nd, 1988, Sheila Houghton (*née* Thompson). *Educ:* Rhyl Grammar Sch.; Jesus Coll., Oxford (Scholar). BA hons Physics 1951, MA, DPhil 1955. Research Fellow, RAE Farnborough, 1954–57; Lectr in Atmospheric Physics, Oxford Univ., 1958–62; Reader, 1962–76; Professor, 1976–83; Fellow, Jesus Coll., Oxford, 1960–83, Hon. Fellow 1983; on secondment as Dir (Appleton), 1979–83, and Dep. Dir, 1981–83, Rutherford Appleton Laboratory, SERC, Hon. Scientist, 1992–. Member: Astronomy, Space and Radio Bd, SERC (formerly SRC), 1970–73 and 1976–81; Exec. Cttee, WMO, 1983–91 (Vice-Pres., 1987–91); Astronomy and Planetary Sci. Bd, SERC, 1987–93; Meteorological Cttee, 1975–80; Jt Organising Cttee, Global Atmospheric Res. Programme, 1976–79; Exec. Management Bd, British Nat. Space Centre, 1986–91; UK Govt Panel on Sustainable Develt, 1994–2000; Chairman: Jt Scientific Cttee, World Climate Research Programme, 1981–84; Earth Observation Adv. Cttee, ESA, 1982–93; Scientific Assessment, Intergovtl Panel for Climate Change, 1988–2002; Jt Scientific and Tech. Cttee, Global Climate Observing System, 1992–95; John Ray Initiative, 1997–2006 (Pres., 2006–). Pres., RMetS, 1976–78 (Hon. Mem.). Trustee, Shell Foundn, 2000–10. MAE 1988; Fellow, Optical Soc. of America; FInstP. Lectures: Cherwell-Simon Meml, 1983–84; Halley, 1992; Templeton, 1992; Oxford Univ.; Bakerian, Royal Soc., 1991. Hon. Mem., Amer. Met. Soc.; Hon. FRIBA 2001. Hon. Fellow: Univ. of Wales, Lampeter, 1994; Univ. of Wales, Bangor, 2003; Univ. of Wales, Aberystwyth, 2006; Glyndwr Univ., 2015. Hon. DSc: Wales, 1991; UEA, 1993; Leeds, 1995; Heriot-Watt, 1996; Greenwich, 1997; Glamorgan, 1998; Reading, 1999; Birmingham, 2000; Gloucestershire, 2001; Hull, 2002; Oxford, 2006; DUniv Stirling, 1992; Hon. DLaws Dalhousie, 2010. Buchan Prize, RMetS, 1966; Charles Chree medal and prize, Inst. of Physics, 1979; (with F. W. Taylor, C. D. Rodgers and G. D. Peskett) Rank Prize for opto-electronics, 1989; Symons Meml Medal, RMetS, 1991; Glazebrook Medal and Prize, Inst. of Phys, 1990; Global 500 Award, UN Envmt Programme, 1994; Gold Medal, RAS, 1995; Internat. Meteorological Orgn Prize, 1998; Japan Prize, Foundn of Sci. and Technol., Japan, 2006; Champion for Wales, Welsh Assembly, 2008; Albert Einstein Sci. Award, World Cultural Council, 2009. *Publications:* (with S. D. Smith) Infra-Red Physics, 1966; The Physics of Atmospheres, 1977, 3rd edn 2002; (with F. W. Taylor and C. D. Rodgers) Remote Sounding of Atmospheres, 1984; Does God play dice?, 1988; Global Warming: the complete briefing, 1994, 5th edn 2015; The Search for God: can science help?, 1995; In The Eye of the Storm, 2013 (autobiog.); papers in learned jls on atmospheric radiation, spectroscopy, remote sounding from satellites and climate change. *Recreations:* walking, sailing. *Address:* c/o Hadley Centre, Meteorological Office, Fitzroy Road, Exeter EX1 3PB.

**HOUGHTON, Peter;** Consultant, Lansdowne House Consulting, since 2011; *b* 7 Dec. 1957; *s* of late Peter Houghton and of Verde Cicely Houghton. *Educ:* Barnsley Grammar Sch.; Keble Coll., Oxford (BA Classics); Aberdeen Univ. (Cert Health Econs 1988). NHS nat. admin trainee, 1981–83; Dep. Administrator, Royal Nat. Orthopaedic Hosp., London, 1983–85; Gen. Manager, Mental Health and Learning Disability Services, Cambridge, 1985–91; Chief Exec., Hinchingbrooke Healthcare NHS Trust, Huntingdon, 1991–93; Actg Dir of Planning, E Anglian RHA, 1993–94; Director: Strategic Develt, Anglia and Oxford Reg., NHS Exec., 1994–99; Eastern Reg., NHS Exec., DoH, 1999–2002; Chief Exec., Norfolk, Suffolk and Cambs Strategic HA, 2002–05; Dir, NHS Nat. Leadership Network, DoH, 2005–06; Chief Exec., SW London and St George's Mental Health NHS Trust, 2006–09; Dir of Innovation, SE Coast SHA, 2009–11. Mem., Inst. Health Mgt, 1984. *Recreations:* classical music and opera, travel, gardening, cycling.

**HOUGHTON, Sir Stephen (Geoffrey),** Kt 2013; CBE 2004; Leader, Barnsley Metropolitan Borough Council, since 1996 (Member (Lab), since 1988); *b* Barnsley, 27 April 1958; *s* of William and Ivy Houghton; *m* 1985, Karen Eastwood; one *s* one *d*. *Educ:* Barnsley Coll. (NHC Electrical and Electronic Engrg); Univ. of Birmingham (MSc Local Governance). British Coal: apprentice electrician, 1974–78; electrician, 1978–85; Electrical Inspector, 1985–93; Manager, Bargaining for Skills Prog., Barnsley & Doncaster TEC, 1993–96. Mem., Audit Commn, 2005–11. Mem. Bd, 1999–2005, Dep. Chm., 2003–05, Yorkshire Forward RDA. Houghton Rev. into rôle of local authorities in tackling worklessness, 2008 (report published, 2009). Mem., Doncaster and Wirral Councils Improvement Bd, 2010–. Non-executive Director: Barnsley Hosp. Foundn Trust, 2012–; Municipal Bonds Agency, 2015–. Chm., Special Interest Gp of Municipal Authorities, 1998–; Local Govt Improvement Peer, 2008–. *Publications:* contribs to jls and discussion documents and pamphlets of Local Govt Information Unit, Solace Foundn, LGA, Centre for Econ. and Social Inclusion and Progress. *Recreations:* cricket, football, walking, running. *Address:* 7 Paddock Grove, Cudworth, Barnsley S72 8GF. *T:* (01226) 717348, 07968 130102. *E:* cllrstephenhoughton@barnsley.gov.uk.

**HOULDEN, Rev. Prof. (James) Leslie;** Professor of Theology, King's College, London, 1987–94, now Emeritus; *b* 1 March 1929; *s* of late James and Lily Alice Houlden. *Educ:* Altrincham Grammar Sch.; Queen's Coll., Oxford. Asst Curate, St Mary's, Hunslet, Leeds, 1955–58; Chaplain, Chichester Theological Coll., 1958–60; Chaplain Fellow, Trinity Coll., Oxford, 1960–70; Principal, Cuddesdon Theol Coll., later Ripon Coll., Cuddesdon, 1970–77; King's College, London: Lectr, 1977; Sen. Lectr in New Testament Studies,

1985; Dean, Faculty of Theology and Religious Studies, 1986–88; Head, Dept of Biblical Studies, 1988–89; Actg Dean, 1993–94; FKC 1994. Hon. Canon of Christ Church Oxford, 1976–77. Member: Liturgical Commn, 1969–76; Doctrine Commn of C of E, 1969–76; Gen. Synod of C of E, 1980–90. Editor, Theology, 1983–91. DD Lambeth, 2005. *Publications:* Paul's Letters from Prison, 1970; (ed) A Celebration of Faith, 1970; Ethics and the New Testament, 1973; The Johannine Epistles, 1974; The Pastoral Epistles, 1976; Patterns of Faith, 1977; Explorations in Theology 3, 1978; What Did the First Christians Believe?, 1982; Connections, 1986; Backward into Light, 1987; (ed jtly) The World's Religions, 1988; History, Story and Belief, 1988; (ed jtly) Dictionary of Biblical Interpretation, 1990; Truth Untold, 1991; (ed) Austin Farrer: the essential sermons, 1991; Bible and Belief, 1991; Jesus: a question of identity, 1992; (ed jtly) Austin Farrer, Words for Life, 1993; (ed) The Interpretation of the Bible in the Church, 1995; (ed jtly) Companion Encyclopedia of Theology, 1995; The Public Face of the Gospel, 1997; (ed jtly) The Common Worship Lectionary: a scripture commentary, Year A, 2001, Year B, 2002, Year C, 2003; The Strange Story of the Gospels, 2002; (ed) Jesus in History, Thought and Culture: an encyclopedia, 2003, reissued as Jesus: the complete guide, 2005; (jtly) Services for Weekdays, 2006; (with J. Woodward) Praying the Lectionary, 2007; (ed jtly) Decoding Early Christianity, 2007; *contributed to:* The Myth of God Incarnate, 1977; Incarnation and Myth, 1979; Alternative Approaches to New Testament Study, 1985; The Reality of God, 1986; A New Dictionary of Christian Ethics, 1986; The Trial of Faith, 1988; God's Truth, 1988; Embracing the Chaos, 1990; Tradition and Unity, 1991; Using the Bible Today, 1991; Fundamentalism and Tolerance, 1991; Anchor Bible Dictionary, 1992; The Resurrection of Jesus Christ, 1993; Crossing the Boundaries, 1994; Divine Revelation, 1997; New Soundings, 1997; Theological Liberalism, 2000; The Oxford Bible Commentary, 2001; reviews and articles in learned jls. *Address:* 23 The Court, Temple Balsall, Knowle, Solihull B93 0AN.

**HOULDER, Bruce Fiddes**, CB 2014; QC 1994; DL; a Recorder, since 1991; Director of Service Prosecutions (Armed Forces), 2008–13; *b* 27 Sept. 1947; *s* of late Charles Alexander Houlder and Jessie Houlder (*née* Fiddes); *m* 1974, Stella Catherine Mattinson; two *d*. *Educ:* Felsted Sch., Dunmow. Called to the Bar, Gray's Inn, 1969, Bencher, 2001. Bar Council: Mem., 1995–97, 1998–2000, 2003–05; Vice Chm., Professional Standards Cttee, 1996–98; Chairman: Public Affairs Cttee, 1999–2000 (Vice Chm., 1996–98); Equal Opportunities Cttee, 2003; Bar Quality Adv. Panel, 2007–08; Vice-Chm., Bar IT Panel, 2004–08; Judicial Studies Board: Mem., Criminal Cttee, 2003–06; Mem., Working Pty on Criminal Justice Reforms; Chm., Criminal Bar Assoc. of England and Wales, 2001–02 (Vice Chm., 2000–01); Member: Criminal Law Adv. Cttee, Law Commn, 2007–; Service Justice Bd, 2009–13; Sheffield Hallam Univ. Law and Criminology Adv. Cttee, 2012–. Tutor, Judicial Coll., 2010–. Dir, Barco Ltd, 2003–08. DL Greater London, 2009; Rep. Lieut for London Bor. of Hillingdon, 2014–. DUniv Sheffield Hallam, 2015. *Recreations:* watercolour painting, opera, cycling, theatre, music. *E:* bhqc@aol.com. *Club:* Garrick.

**HOULDING, Rev. Preb. David Nigel Christopher;** Vicar, St Stephen's with All Hallows, Hampstead, since 1985; *b* Fawkham, Kent, 25 July 1953; *s* of Reginald Houlding and Vera Houlding (*née* Bellini). *Educ:* King's Sch., Canterbury; King's Coll., London (AKC 1976); St Augustine's Coll., Canterbury. Lay Chaplain, Christian Medical Coll., Vellore, S India, 1976–77; ordained deacon, 1977, priest, 1978; Curate, All Saints, Hillingdon, 1977–81; Asst Priest, St Alban the Martyr, Holborn, 1981–85; Area Dean, N Camden, 2001–03; Preb., Consumpta per Mare, St Paul's Cathedral, 2004–. Chair: House of Clergy, Dio. of London, 2000; C of E Appts Cttee, 2004; Mem., Archbishops' Council, 2003. Pres., Church Union, 2012–. Trustee, Additional Curates Soc., 1996–; Master Gen., Soc. of the Holy Cross, 1997–. Gov., St Stephen's House, Oxford, 2001–. Hon. DD Nashotah House, Wisconsin, 2005. *Publications:* Consecrated Women? Reception and Communion, 2004; In this sign, Conquer, 2006; Who is this Man: Christ in the renewal of the Church, 2006. *Recreations:* capital cities of Europe, France, house restoration, dining. *Address:* All Hallows House, 52 Courthorpe Road, Hampstead, NW3 2LD. *T:* (020) 7267 7833, 07710 403294. *E:* fr.houlding@lineone.net. *Club:* National Liberal.

**HOULDSWORTH, Sir Richard (Thomas Reginald)**, 5th Bt *cr* 1887, of Reddish and Coodham; Farm Manager, since 1988; *b* 2 Aug. 1947; *s* of Sir Reginald Douglas Henry Houldsworth, 4th Bt, OBE, TD and Margaret May (*d* 1995), *d* of late Cecil Emilius Laurie; *S* father, 1989; *m* 1st, 1970, Jane Elizabeth (marr. diss. 1982), *o d* of Alistair Orr; two *s*; 2nd, 1992, Ann Catherine Tremayne; one *s*. *Educ:* Bredon School, Tewkesbury, Glos; Blanerne School, Denholm, Roxburghshire. *Recreations:* shooting, fishing, tennis, squash, horse racing. *Heir:* s Simon Richard Henry Houldsworth [*b* 6 Oct. 1971; *m* 2003, Rosamond Louise Frayling-Kelly]. *Address:* April Cottage, Naunton, Cheltenham, Glos GL54 3AA.

**HOULIHAN, Michael Patrick;** Director General, Japan House London, since 2016; *b* 27 Sept. 1948; *s* of Michael Houlihan and Kathleen (*née* Small); *m* 1969, Jane Hibbert; one *s* one *d*. *Educ:* St Francis Xavier's Coll., Liverpool; Univ. of Bristol (BA Hons Hist.). Imperial War Museum: Research Asst, 1971–75, Dep. Keeper, 1975–76, Dept of Exhibits; Keeper, Dept of Permanent Exhibns, 1976–84; Dep. Dir, 1984–94, Dir, 1994–98, Horniman Mus. and Gardens; Dir, subseq. Chief Exec., Nat. Museums and Galls of NI, 1998–2003; Dir Gen., Amgueddfa Cymru—Nat. Museum Wales (formerly Nat. Museums and Galls of Wales), 2003–10; Chief Exec., Mus. of NZ Te Papa Tongarewa, 2010–14; Special Advr on Mil. Heritage, Min. of Culture and Heritage, NZ, 2014. Chairman: Collections Trust (formerly MDA), 2003–09; ICOM UK, 2008–10; Dep. Chm., ICOM NZ, 2012. Member: British Commn for Military Hist., 1982–; NI Cttee, British Council, 1998; Bd, NI Mus Council, 1998. Vis. Prof., Ulster Univ., 1999. Trustee: Nat. Self-Portrait Collection of Ireland, 1998–2003; Nat. Coal Mining Mus., 2004–10. Mem. Council, Goldsmiths Coll., Univ. of London, 1997–98. *Publications:* Trench Warfare 1914–18, 1974; (with B. Yale) No Man's Land, 1984. *Recreations:* military history, cycling, Romanesque architecture, battlefields.

**HOULSBY, Prof. Guy Tinmouth**, DSc; FREng; Professor of Civil Engineering, University of Oxford, since 1991 (Head, Department of Engineering Science, 2009–14); Fellow of Brasenose College, Oxford, since 1991; *b* 28 March 1954; *s* of late Lt Col Thomas Tinmouth Houlsby, TD and Vivienne May Houlsby (*née* Ford); *m* 1985, Jenny Lucy Damaris Nedderman; two *s*. *Educ:* Trinity College, Glenalmond; St John's College, Cambridge (MA, PhD); DSc Oxon 2003. CEng 1983, FREng 1999; FICE 1997. Engineer, Binnie and Partners, 1975–76; Babtie Shaw and Morton, 1976–77; Research Student, Cambridge, 1977–80; Oxford University: Jun. Res. Fellow, Balliol Coll., 1980–83; Lectr in Engineering, 1983–91; Fellow, Keble College, 1983–91. Rankine Lect., British Geotech. Soc., 2014. *Publications:* (with A. M. Puzrin) Principles of Hyperplasticity, 2006; contribs to learned jls on soil mechanics and tidal energy. *Recreations:* ornithology, woodwork, gardening. *Address:* 25 Purcell Road, Marston, Oxford OX3 0HB. *T:* (01865) 722128; Barhill, Borgue, Dumfries and Galloway DG6 4UE. *T:* (01557) 870949.

**HOULSTON, Prof. Richard Somerset**, MD, PhD, DSc; FRS 2017; FMedSci; FRCP, FRCPE; FRCPath; FRSB; Group Leader, since 1993, and Professor of Molecular and Population Genetics, since 2007, Institute of Cancer Research, London; Hon. Consultant in Medical Genetics, Royal Marsden Hospitals NHS Trust, since 1993; *b* Reading, 10 July 1956; *s* of William Richard Houlston and Edith Marion Houlston. *Educ:* Park House Secondary Modern Sch., Newbury; St Bartholomew's Sch., Newbury; Charing Cross Hosp. Med. Sch., Univ. of London (BSc 1978; MB BS (Dist.) Pathol. 1981); Inst. of Psychiatry, King's Coll. London (MSc 1985); Univ. of London (MD 1992; PhD 1993); Imperial Coll., London (DSc 2013). MRCPath 1988, FRCPath 1997; MRCP 1993, FRCP 1998; FRCPE 1998; FRSB (FSB 2011). Hse Officer, Surgery, Walsgrave Hosp., Coventry, 1981; Hse Officer, Medicine, Charing Cross Hosp., 1982; SHO, 1982–83, Registrar, 1983–84, Pathol., Kingston Hosp.; Fellow, Wellcome Trust. Inst. Psychiatry, KCL, 1984–85; Lectr, KCL, 1985–88, ICRF, London, 1988–92; Specialist Registrar, Southampton Univ., 1992–93. FMedSci 2010. *Publications:* contrib. over 600 peer-reviewed articles, primarily focused on cancer genetics. *Recreations:* cycling, outdoor swimming, bridge. *Address:* Institute of Cancer Research, Sutton, Surrey SM2 5NG. *T:* (020) 8722 4175, *Fax:* (020) 8722 4359. *E:* richard.houlston@icr.ac.uk. *W:* www.twitter.com/HoulstonLab_ICR.

**HOULT, Helen Isabel;** *see* Cleland, H. I.

**HOURIGAN, Rhian Sara;** *see* Harris, R. S.

**HOUSDEN, Sir Peter (James)**, KCB 2010; Permanent Secretary, Scottish Government, 2010–15; *b* 7 Dec. 1950. Teacher, Madeley Court Sch., Telford, 1975–79; Professional Asst, Humberside LEA, 1979–82; Asst Dir of Educn, Notts LEA, 1982–86; Sen. Educn Officer, Lancs LEA, 1986–88; Dep. Chief Educn Officer, Notts LEA, 1988–91; Dir of Educn, 1991–94, Chief Exec., 1994–2001, Notts CC; Dir Gen., Schs, DfES, 2001–05; Permanent Sec., ODPM, then DCLG, 2005–10. Mem., Chartermark Panel, 1997–2001. Advr, LGA, 1997–2001. Chm., Nottingham Drug Action Team, 1994–2000; Mem., Adv. Council on Misuse of Drugs, 1998–2003; Mem., Ind. Adv. Gp, Windrush Inquiry, 2019–. Associate Fellow, Warwick Univ. Business Sch., 1996–2002; Hon. Prof., Univ. of Nottingham, 2017–. Mem., Adv. Gp, Welsh Centre for Public Policy, 2018–. Trustee: Work Foundn, 2007–11; RNLI, 2014–. Mem. Ct, Univ. of Greenwich, 2008–10. DUniv Nottingham Trent, 2014.

**HOUSE, James Michael;** QC 2015; *b* Oxford, 3 May 1970; *s* of Peter House and Judith House; *m* 1997, Kirsten Esther; one *s* one *d*. *Educ:* Chew Valley Comp. Sch.; Lancaster Univ. (BA Hons Politics and Internat. Relns); Univ. of Central England (CPE). Called to the Bar, Inner Temple, 1995; in practice as barrister specialising in criminal law. *Recreations:* my family, cycling, sailing, golf, triathlon. *Address:* 7 Bedford Row, WC1R 4BS. *T:* (020) 7242 3555. *E:* jhouse@7br.co.uk.

**HOUSE, Prof. Margaret A.**, OBE 2018; PhD; Vice-Chancellor and Chief Executive Officer, Leeds Trinity University, since 2013. *Educ:* Gumley House Grammar Sch., Isleworth; Plymouth Poly. (BSc Hons Geog. 1978); Middlesex Univ. (PhD Water Quality Indices 1981). Middlesex University, 1986–2012: Dean: Sch. of Social Scis, 2000–02; Health and Social Scis, 2002–05; Dep. Vice Chancellor Academic, 2005–12. Chair: Audit Cttee, 2013–, Small and Specialist Instns Network Gp, 2014–, Yorkshire Universities; Higher Educn Access Rewarding Transforming, 2014–. *Address:* Office of the Vice-Chancellor, Leeds Trinity University, Brownberrie Lane, Horsforth, Leeds LS18 5HD.

**HOUSE, Roger Keith;** a District Judge (Magistrates' Courts) (formerly Metropolitan Stipendiary Magistrate), 1995–2013; Chairman, Youth Court, 1995–2013; *b* 24 Jan. 1944; *s* of Donald Stuart House and Kathleen Mary House; *m* 1971, Elizabeth Anne Hall; two *s*. *Educ:* Wychwood Prep. Sch.; Sherborne. Admitted Solicitor, 1972; Asst Solicitor with various firms, 1972–76; sole practitioner, 1976–95. *Recreations:* singing, reading, walking the countryside, shooting, surfing.

**HOUSE, Sir (William) Stephen**, Kt 2013; QPM 2004; Deputy Commissioner, Metropolitan Police Service, since 2018; *b* 19 Oct. 1957; *s* of William Cullingford House and Alice Reid House; *m* 1987, Caroline Jose; one *s* two *d*. *Educ:* Kelvinside Acad., Glasgow; University College Sch., Hampstead; Aberdeen Univ. (MA Hons Hist./Eng. Lit.); Brunel Univ. (MBA). Joined Sussex Police, 1981; Supt, W Yorks Police, 1994–98; Asst Chief Constable, Staffs Police, 1998–2001; Dep. Asst Comr, 2001–05, Asst Comr, 2005–07, Metropolitan Police Service; Chief Constable: Strathclyde Police, 2007–12; Police Scotland, 2012–15; Asst Comr, Metropolitan Police Service, 2018. *Recreations:* reading (science fiction and history), running, hill walking.

**HOUSLAY, Prof. Miles Douglas**, PhD; FRSE; FMedSci; FRSB; Professor of Pharmacological Innovation (part-time), King's College London, since 2011; Chief Executive, BioGryffe Consulting Ltd, since 2011; Chief Scientific Officer, Mironid Ltd, since 2014 (Director, 2014–16); *b* 25 June 1950; *s* of Edwin Houslay and Georgina Houslay; *m* 1972, Rhian Gee; two *s* one *d*. *Educ:* UC Cardiff (BSc Hons Biochem. 1971); King's Coll., Cambridge (PhD Biochem. 1974). ICI Res. Fellow, Dept Pharmacol., Univ. of Cambridge, 1974; Res. Fellow, Queens' Coll., Cambridge, 1975; Lectr in Biochem., 1976–82, Reader, 1982–84, UMIST; University of Glasgow: Gardiner Prof. of Biochemistry, 1984–2011, now Emeritus; Chair, Neurosci. and Molecular Pharmacol., 2008–11; Co-Dir, Inst. of Neurosci. and Psychol., 2010–11; Prof. of Pharmacol. (pt-time), Univ. of Strathclyde, 2011–15. Ed.-in-Chief, Cellular Signalling, 1987–2014. Chairman: Cell Bd Grant Panel, MRC, 1990–93; Project Grant Panel, Wellcome Trust, 1996–2000, BHF, 1997–99; former Member: Grant Panels for MRC, AFRC, SHHD, Brit. Diabetic Assoc. and Health Res. Bd (Eire); RAE panels, HEFC, 1992, 1996. Selby Fellow, Aust. Acad. Scis, 1984. Minshull Meml Lectr, Univ. of Edinburgh, 1990. Trustee, BHF, 1997. Consultant and mem. scientific adv. bds at various pharmaceutical cos in UK, Europe and USA, including: Celgene Corp., 2002–05; Fission Pharmaceuticals, 2007–12; Chm., Scientific Adv. Bd, BioTheryX Corp., 2011–14. FRSE 1986; FMedSci 1998; FRSB 2016. Colworth Medal, Biochem. Soc., 1984; Most Cited Scientist in Scotland, Edinburgh Sci. Fest. Award, 1992; Joshua Lederburg Soc. Award, Celgene Corp., 2012. *Publications:* Dynamics of Biological Membranes, 1982; (contrib.) Molecular Aspects of Cellular Regulation, 1985; (ed jtly) Molecular Mechanism of Desensitization to Signal Molecules, 1987; (ed jtly) Activation and Desensitization of Transducing Pathways, 1990; G-proteins as mediators of signal transduction, 1990; Cyclic Nucleotide-phosphodiesterases, 1990; Phosphodiesterases in Health and Disease, 2006; Phosphodiesterases as Therapeutic Targets, 2011; over 490 contribs on cell signalling systems to learned jls. *Recreations:* walking (hill, coastal and desert), reading, electric mountain bike riding, photography, reading, driving, cooking, music. *E:* miles.houslay@kcl.ac.uk.

**HOUSSEMAYNE du BOULAY, Sir Roger (William)**, KCVO 1982 (CVO 1972); CMG 1975; HM Diplomatic Service, retired; Vice Marshal of the Diplomatic Corps, 1975–82; *b* 30 March 1922; *s* of Charles John Houssemayne du Boulay, Captain, RN, and Mary Alice Veronica, *née* Morgan; *m* 1957, Elizabeth (*d* 2014), *d* of late Brig. Home, late RM, and Molly, Lady Pile; one *d*, and two step *s*. *Educ:* Winchester; Oxford. Served RAFVR, 1941–46 (Pilot). HM Colonial Service, Nigeria, 1949–58; HM Foreign, later Diplomatic, Service, 1959; FO, 1959; Washington, 1960–64; FCO 1964–67; Manila, 1967–71; Alternate Director, Asian Development Bank, Manila, 1967–69, and Director, 1969–71; Counsellor and Head of Chancery, Paris, 1971–73; Resident Comr, New Hebrides, 1973–75. Adviser: Solomon Is Govt, 1986; Swaziland Govt, 1992. *Recreation:* painting. *Address:* Anstey Cottage, Swallowfield Park, Reading, Berks RG7 1TG.

**HOUSTON, Anne Catherine**, OBE 2015; Independent Chair, North Ayrshire Child Protection Committee, since 2014; *b* 28 Aug. 1954; *d* of Robert and Marta Houston. *Educ:* Glasgow Coll. of Technol. (HNC Applied Physics and Electronics 1975); Jordanhill Coll. of Further Educn (CQSW, Dip SW, 1980); OU Business Sch. (mgt of non-profit enterprises 1992); Social Enterprise Acad., Edinburgh (ILM Cert. in Leadership and Mgt 2009). Various sen. mgt posts in soc. work related fields; Counselling Manager, 1990–94, Dir, 1994–2006, ChildLine Scotland; Dep. Chief Exec., ChildLine UK, 2003–06, Dir, ChildLine UK within NSPCC, 2006; Chief Exec., CHILDREN 1ST, 2004–14. Mem., Partnership Drugs Initiative, Lloyds TSB Foundn for Scotland, 2001–12. Chm., Child Protection Cttees Scotland, 2015–; Vice Chair, Nat. Strategic Gp, Scotland, Stop It Now!, 2007–14. Member: Stop and Search Adv. Gp, Scottish Govt, 2015–; Child Sexual Exploitation Ministerial Gp, 2015–16; Human Trafficking and Exploitation Oversight Gp, 2016–; Nat. Child Protection Leadership Gp, 2017–. Trustee, Cattanach Trust, 2007–17 (Vice Chm., 2011–17); Chm., Postcode Culture Trust, 2012–14. Mem. Counselling Team, consultant on Human Relns and Counselling Course, and student tutor, Scottish Inst. of Human Relns, 1989–94; Member: Adv. Cttee on Prison Mgt, Scottish Prison Service, 1994–2000; Cross Party Parly Gp for Children, 2003–06; Bd, Coalition of Care and Support Providers Scotland (formerly Community Care Providers Scotland), 2009–14; Scottish Govt Early Years Task Force, 2011–14; Bd, Care Inspectorate, 2014–; Putting the Baby in the Bathwater Coalition, 2014–; Vice Chairman: Scottish Alliance on Children's Rights, 1999–2005 (Founder Mem.); Scottish Pre-school Play Assoc., 2000–06; Antibullying Network Adv. Cttee, 2001–06; Chm., Justice for Children Alliance, 2007–14. Treas., Assoc. of Chief Officers of Scottish Voluntary Orgns, 2000–04. Mem., Annie Dow Heroism Award panel, 2014–. FRSA. DUniv West of Scotland, 2015. *Publications:* Beyond the Limit: children living with parental alcohol misuse, 1998; Young People Helping Young People: international telephone helpline guidelines, 2000. *Recreations:* reading, music, gardening, food and wine. *E:* anne@achouston.plus.com.

**HOUSTON, (Robert) Graham;** Chairman, Scottish Qualifications Authority, 2009–17; *b* Glasgow, 7 Oct. 1948; *s* of David Houston and Catherine Houston; *m* 1976, Jenifer Hastie; one *d* (and one *s* decd). *Educ:* Penilee Secondary Sch., Glasgow. Regl Dir, Ellerman Travel and Leisure Ltd, 1976–86; Dir, Scotland, Industrial Soc., 1986–2003; exec. business coach, 1990–. Mem. Bd, UK Skills, 1996–2010; Vice Chm., BBC Scotland Broadcasting Council, 2002–07. Mem. (SNP), Stirling Council, 2007– (Leader, 2008–12). Mem. Bd, Scottish Police Authy, 2012–18. Vice-Pres., COSLA, 2017–. Contested (SNP) Glasgow Craigton, Feb. and Oct. 1974. *Recreations:* golf, tai chi, reading, gardening. *Address:* Stirling Council, Old View Forth, Stirling FK8 2ET.

**HOUSTON, Stewart,** CBE 2007; FRAgS; Managing Director, Microware Pig Systems, since 1989; *b* Hebburn, Co. Durham, 24 Oct. 1946; *s* of Alfred and Jean Houston; *m* 1970, Janet Margaret Pugh; two *s*. *Educ:* Jarrow Grammar Sch. Full-time farmer until 1989. Non-executive Director: Agric. and Horticulture Develt Bd, 2008–15; Animal Health Welfare Bd, DEFRA, 2011–; Scottish Agricl Colls, 2012–14. Chairman: Nat. Pig Assoc., 2003–13; British Pig Exec., 2004–15. Mem. Bd, Food Standards Agency, 2016–. FRAgS 2010. Liveryman: Farmers' Co., 2007–; Butchers' Co., 2012–. *Recreations:* fly fishing, Sunderland Football Club. *Address:* Wayside, Thornborough, Bedale, N Yorks DL8 2RQ. *T:* (01677) 470656. *E:* stewart@mpsagri.co.uk. *Clubs:* Farmers (Chm., 2013); Tanfield Fishing.

**HOUSTOUN-BOSWALL, Sir (Thomas) Alford,** 8th Bt *cr* 1836; founder and Chairman, The Harrodian School, since 1993; international economics and business consultant; *b* 23 May 1947; *s* of Sir Thomas Houstoun-Boswall, 7th Bt, and Margaret Jean, *d* of George Bullen-Smith; *S* father, 1982; *m* 1st, 1971, Eliana Michele (marr. diss. 1996), *d* of Dr John Pearse, New York; one *s* one *d*; 2nd, 2007, Malgosia, *d* of Grzegorz Stepnik. *Educ:* Lindisfarne College. Partner, Rosedale-Engel, Houstoun-Boswall Partnership, Bermuda; Director, Stair & Co., New York (specialising in fine 18th century English furniture and works of art); Pres., Houstoun-Boswall Inc. (Fine Arts), New York. Lecturer, New York Univ. and Metropolitan Museum of Art, New York. *Heir:* *s* Alexander Alford Houstoun-Boswall, *b* 16 Sept. 1972. *Address:* The Harrodian School, Lonsdale Road, SW13 9QN; 18 rue Basse, 06410 Biot, France; 11 East 73rd Street, New York, NY 10021, USA.

**HOVELL-THURLOW-CUMMING-BRUCE,** family name of **Baron Thurlow**.

**HOVEN, Helmert Frans van den;** Knight, Order of Netherlands Lion, 1978; Commander, Order of Orange Nassau, 1988; Hon. KBE 1980. Chairman, Unilever NV, 1975–84; Vice-Chairman, Unilever Ltd, 1975–84; *b* 25 April 1923; *m* 1st, 1950, Dorothy Ida Bevan (marr. diss. 1981); one *s*; 2nd, 1981, Cornelia Maria van As. *Educ:* Grammar and Trade schs in The Netherlands. Joined Unilever NV, Rotterdam, 1938; transf. to Unilever Ltd, London, 1948, then to Turkey, 1951, becoming Chm. of Unilever's business there, 1958; Chm., Unilever's Dutch margarine business, Van den Bergh en Jurgens BV, 1962; sen. marketing post, product gp, Margarine, Edible Fats and Oils, 1966; Mem. Bds of Unilever, and responsible for product gp, Sundry Foods and Drinks, 1970; Dir, Fidelity Investments, 1984–2012; non-exec. Dir, Hunter Douglas NV, 1984–2016; formerly: Mem. Supervisory Bd of Shell; Chm. Supervisory Bds of ABN/Amro Bank and various other cos; Mem., Eur. Adv. Bd, AT & T and Rockwell. Pres., ICC, Paris, 1984–86. Mem. Council, North Western (Kellogg) Business Sch., 1984–2006. *Recreations:* rowing, walking.

**HOW, Timothy Francis;** Chairman: Woburn Enterprises Ltd, since 2011; Roys (Wroxham) Ltd, since 2014; *b* 29 Dec. 1950; *s* of Mervyn Henry How and Margaret Helen How; *m* 1975, Elizabeth Mary Howard; four *d*. *Educ:* Churchill Coll., Cambridge (MA); London Business Sch. (MSc Business Studies). Gen. Manager, Polaroid (UK) Ltd, 1979–83; Man. Dir, Bejam Gp PLC, 1983–89; Chief Exec., Majestic Wine PLC, 1989–2008. Non-executive Director: Henderson Gp plc, 2008–17; Rayner & Keeler Ltd, 2008–13 (Chm., 2009–13); Dixons Carphone (formerly DSG Internat., later Dixons Retail) plc, 2009–17; Chairman: Framlington AIM VCT plc, later Downing Income 4 VCT plc, 2004–13; Enotria Wine Gp Ltd, 2012–14. Chm., Wine and Spirit Trade Assoc., 2009–11. Dir, Norfolk and Norwich Univ. Hosps Foundn Trust, 2013–. Dir, Moller Centre, Churchill Coll., Cambridge, 2015–. Gov., Peabody Trust, 2008–14. *Recreations:* sailing, golf. *Address:* Norvista, Main Road, Brancaster Staithe, Norfolk PE31 8BY. *Clubs:* Sloane; Oxford and Cambridge Sailing, Brancaster Staithe Sailing.

**HOWAR, Valentine Ruth;** *see* Henshall, V. R.

**HOWARD;** *see* Fitzalan-Howard.

**HOWARD,** family name of **Earls of Carlisle, Effingham,** and **Suffolk,** and of **Barons Howard of Lympne, Howard of Penrith, Howard of Rising** and **Strathcona**.

**HOWARD DE WALDEN,** Baroness (10th in line), *cr* 1597; **Mary Hazel Caridwen Czernin;** *b* 12 Aug. 1935; *e d* of 9th Baron Howard de Walden and 5th Baron Seaford (*d* 1999) and Countess Irene Harrach; *S* to Howard de Walden Barony of father, called out of abeyance in her favour, 2004; *m* 1957, Count Joseph Czernin (*d* 2015); one *s* five *d*. *Heir:* *s* Hon. Peter John Joseph Czernin, *qv*.

**HOWARD OF EFFINGHAM, Lord;** Edward Mowbray Nicholas Howard; *b* 11 May 1971; *s* and *heir* of Earl of Effingham, *qv*, and *s* of Anne M. Howard (who *m* 1978, Prof. Peter Gonville Stein, FBA); *m* 2002, Tatiana Tafur; one *s* one *d* (twins). *Heir:* *s* Hon. Frederick Henry Charles Howard, *b* 19 March 2007.

**HOWARD OF LYMPNE,** Baron *cr* 2010 (Life Peer), of Lympne in the County of Kent; **Michael Howard,** CH 2011; PC 1990; QC 1982; *b* 7 July 1941; *s* of late Bernard and Hilda Howard; *m* 1975, Sandra Clare, *d* of Wing-Comdr Saville Paul; one *s* one *d*, and one step *s*. *Educ:* Llanelli Grammar School; Peterhouse, Cambridge. MA, LLB; President of the Union, 1962. Major Scholar, Inner Temple, 1962; called to the Bar, Inner Temple, 1964, Bencher, 1992. Junior Counsel to the Crown (Common Law), 1980–82; a Recorder, 1986. Contested (C) Liverpool, Edge Hill, 1966 and 1970; Chm., Bow Group, 1970–71. MP (C) Folkestone and Hythe, 1983–2010. PPS to Solicitor-General, 1984–85; Parly Under-Sec. of State, DTI, 1985–87; Minister of State, DoE, 1987–90; Secretary of State for: Employment, 1990–92; the Environment, 1992–93; the Home Dept, 1993–97; Shadow Foreign Sec., 1997–99; Shadow Chancellor, 2001–03; Leader of the Conservative Party and Leader of the Opposition, 2003–05. Member: H of L Appts Commn, 2010–17; Commn on Freedom of Information, 2015–16. Jt Sec., Cons. Legal Cttee, 1983–84; Jt Vice-Chm., Cons. Employment Cttee, 1983–84; Vice-Chm., Soc. of Cons. Lawyers, 1985. Pres., Atlantic Partnership; Chairman: Entrée Gold Inc., 2013–18 (Dir, 2007–18); Soma Oil and Gas Ltd, 2013–18; Sen. Ind. Dir, Watchstone Gp Ltd (formerly Quindell), 2015–. Chm., Hospice UK (formerly Help the Hospices), 2010–18. *Recreations:* watching football (Swansea, Liverpool) and baseball (New York Mets). *Address:* House of Lords, SW1A 0PW. *Clubs:* Carlton, Pratt's, Coningsby (Chm., 1972–73).

**HOWARD OF PENRITH,** 3rd Baron *cr* 1930, of Gowbarrow, co. Cumberland; **Philip Esme Howard;** Chief Investment Officer, Beazley Group, 2013–15; *b* 1 May 1945; *e s* of 2nd Baron Howard of Penrith and Anne (*née* Hotham, *widow* of Anthony Bazley); *S* father, 1999; *m* 1969, Sarah Sophia Walker; two *s* two *d*. *Educ:* Ampleforth Coll.; Christ Church, Oxford. Journalist, Scotsman, then Daily Mail, 1967–71; Dir, Deltec Trading Co. Ltd, 1972–77; Partner, Phillips and Drew, 1977–84; Man. Dir, Lehman Brothers, 1984–97; Chm., Tarchon (formerly Esperia) Capital Mgt Ltd, 1999–2013. Non-exec. Dir, Schroders plc, 2008–18. Chm., London Youth Support Trust, 2000–. *Heir:* *s* Hon. Thomas Philip Howard, *b* 8 June 1974. *Address:* 45 Erpingham Road, SW15 1BQ. *T:* (020) 8789 7604. *Clubs:* Turf, Portland.

**HOWARD OF RISING,** Baron *cr* 2004 (Life Peer), of Castle Rising in the County of Norfolk; **Greville Patrick Charles Howard;** Chairman, Wicksteed Leisure Ltd, 1984–2003, and since 2013; *b* 22 April 1941; *s* of Col Henry and Patience Howard; *m* 1981, Mary Cortlandt (*née* Culverwell); two *s* one *d*. *Educ:* Eton. Private Sec. to Rt Hon. Enoch Powell, MBE, PC, 1968–70. Chm., Fortress Holdings plc, 1995–2004. Dir, Keep Trust, 1980–89. Chm., Nat. Playing Fields Assoc., 2004–13. Mem. (C) King's Lynn and W Norfolk DC, 2003–. *Address:* Castle Rising, Norfolk. *Club:* White's.

**HOWARD, Charles Anthony Frederick;** QC 1999; *b* 7 March 1951; *s* of late Hon. John Algernon Frederick Charles Howard and Naida Howard (later Mrs Geoffrey Royal); *m* 1st, 1978, Geraldine Dorman (marr. diss.); one *s* one *d*; 2nd, 1999, Rosie Boycott (*see* Baroness Boycott); one step *d*. *Educ:* Sherborne Sch.; St John's Coll., Cambridge (Open Hist. Schol.; BA 1972; MA 1976; McMahon Student). Called to the Bar, Inner Temple, 1975. Mem., Family Law Bar Assoc. *Recreations:* walking with my labradors, theatre, history. *Address:* 1 King's Bench Walk, Temple, EC4Y 7DB. *T:* (020) 7936 1500. *Clubs:* Groucho; Somerset CC.

*See also* Earl of Effingham.

**HOWARD, Sir David (Howarth Seymour),** 3rd Bt *cr* 1955, of Great Rissington, co. Gloucester; Chairman, Charles Stanley Group PLC (formerly Charles Stanley & Co.), Stockbrokers, since 1999 (Managing Partner/Managing Director, 1971–2014); Lord Mayor of London, 2000–01; *b* 29 Dec. 1945; *s* of Sir Edward Howard, 2nd Bt, GBE; *S* father, 2001; *m* 1968, Valerie Picton Crosse, *o d* of Derek W. Crosse; two *s* two *d*. *Educ:* Radley Coll.; Worcester Coll., Oxford (MA Hons). Director: Personal Investment Mgt and Financial Advrs Assoc. (formerly Assoc. of Pvte Client Investment Managers and Stockbrokers, then Wealth Mgt Assoc.), 2001–; CISI (formerly Securities Inst., then Securities and Investment Inst., 2002–14 (Chm., Exam. Bd, 2003–14; Hon. FCSI); Financial Services Skills Council, 2004–07. Mem., Sutton BC, 1974–78; Common Councilman, City of London, 1972–86, Alderman, 1986–2015, Sheriff, 1997–98. Master, Gardeners' Co., 1990–91. Chm., London Gardens Soc., 1996–. Pres., Chartered Mgt Inst., 2008–10 (Pres., City Br., 2002–12). Pro-Chancellor and Chm. Council, City Univ., 2003–08. President: City of London Lectrs Assoc., 2010–; Guildhall Histl Assoc., 2015–. KStJ 2000. Grand Cordon (1st class), Order of Independence (Jordan), 2001. *Recreation:* gardening. *Heir:* *s* Robert Picton Seymour Howard, *b* 28 Jan. 1971. *Clubs:* City Livery, United Wards, Lime Street and Cornhill Ward.

**HOWARD, Prof. David Martin,** PhD; FREng; Professor of Electronic Engineering, and Founding Head, Department of Electronic Engineering, Royal Holloway, University of London, since 2016; *b* Chatham, Kent, 13 April 1956; *s* of Jack Bruère Howard and Phyllis Joan Howard; *m* 2001, Clare Wake; one *s* one *d*. *Educ:* Throwley House Sch.; King's Sch., Rochester; University Coll. London (BScEng Electrical and Electronic Engrg 1978; PhD 1984). FIOA 1991; CEng 1993; FIET 1996; FREng 2016. Lectr in Experimental Phonetics, UCL, 1979–90; University of York: Lectr, 1990–93, Sen. Lectr, 1993–96, in Music Technol.; Prof. of Music Technol., 1996–2016; Hd, Dept of Electronics, 1996–2000 and 2012–16. *Publications:* (with J. A. S. Angus) Acoustics and Psychoacoustics, 1996, 5th edn 2017 (trans. Chinese); (with D. T. Murphy) Voice Science, Acoustics and Recording, 2007; Choral Singing and Healthy Voice Production, 2015. *Recreations:* sailing dinghies and yachts (RYA Day Skipper), ski-ing, organist, choir director, choir singer, keyboard instruments. *Address:* Department of Electronic Engineering, Founder's Building, Royal Holloway, University of London, Egham, Surrey TW20 0EX.

**HOWARD, Prof. Deborah Janet,** PhD; FSA, FSAScot; FRSE; FBA 2010; Professor of Architectural History, University of Cambridge, 2001–13, now Emerita (Head, Department of History of Art, 2002–06 and 2007–09; Director of Research, 2014–17); Fellow of St John's College, Cambridge, since 1992; *b* 26 Feb. 1946; *d* of Thomas Were Howard, OBE and Isobel Howard (*née* Brewer); *m* 1975, Prof. Malcolm Sim Longair, *qv*; one *s* one *d*. *Educ:* Loughton High Sch. for Girls; Newnham Coll., Cambridge (BA 1st Cl. Hons Architecture and Fine Arts 1968; MA 1972); Courtauld Inst. of Art, Univ. of London (MA 1969; PhD 1973). FSA 1984; FSAScot 1991; FRSE 2004. Leverhulme Fellow in History of Art, Clare Hall, Cambridge, 1972–73; Lectr in History of Art, UCL, 1973–76; pt-time Lectr, 1982–90, Sen. Lectr, 1990–91, Reader, 1991, Dept of Architecture, Univ. of Edinburgh; pt-time Lectr, Courtauld Inst. of Art, Univ. of London, 1991–92; Cambridge University: Librarian, Faculty of Architecture and History of Art, 1992–96; Reader in Architectl History, 1996–2001; Principal Investigator, ERC Synergy Grant, Domestic Devotions, 2013–17. Kennedy Prof. of Renaissance Studies, Smith Coll., Mass, 2006; Vis. Prof., Harvard (Villa i Tatti), 2007; Robert Johnson-La Palme Vis. Prof., Princeton Univ., 2009; McGeorge Fellow, Univ. of Melbourne, 2012; Daphne Mayo Vis. Scholar, Univ. of Qld, 2012; Leverhulme Emeritus Fellow, 2017–19. Member: Royal Fine Art Commn for

Scotland, 1987–95; Royal Commn on Ancient and Historical Monuments of Scotland, 1990–99; Scientific Cttee, Centro di Studi di Architettura Andrea Palladio, Vicenza, Italy, 2011–; Scientific Adv. Bd, Max Planck Insts—Bibliotheca Hertziana, Rome, and Kunsthistorisches Institut, Florence, 2008–14; Comitato Scientifico, Centro di Studi di Architettura 'Andrea Palladio', Vicenza, 2011–; Chm., Soc. of Architectl Historians of GB, 1997–2000. Trustee: British Archtl Liby Trust, 2001–10; British Archtl Trust Bd (formerly RIBA Trust), 2010–16; Venice in Peril, 2015–. Co-curated exhibn, Madonnas and Miracles, Fitzwilliam Mus., 2017. Hon. FRIAS 1995. Hon. LittD UCD, 2014. *Publications*: (jtly) The Art of Claude Lorrain, 1969; Jacopo Sansovino: architecture and patronage in Renaissance Venice, 1975, 2nd edn 1987; The Architectural History of Venice, 1980, 2nd edn 1987, rev. and enlarged edn 2002; (ed and jtly) The Architecture of the Scottish Renaissance, 1990; (ed) William Adam, 1990; (ed) Scottish Architects Abroad, 1991; Scottish Architecture from the Reformation to the Restoration 1560–1660, 1995; (ed) Architecture in Italy 1500–1600 by Wolfgang Lotz, 2nd edn, 1995; (jtly) La Scuola Grande della Misericordia di Venezia, 1999; Venice & the East: the impact of the Islamic world on Venetian architecture, 2000; (ed with L. Moretti) Architettura e musica nella Venezia del Rinascimento, 2006; (with L. Moretti) Sound and Space in Renaissance Venice: architecture, music, acoustics, 2009; Venice Disputed: Marc'Antonio Barbaro and Venetian architecture 1550–1600, 2011; (ed with L. Moretti) The Music Room in Early Modern France and Italy: sound, space and object, 2012; (ed jtly) Architecture and Pilgrimage: Southern Europe and beyond, 1000–1500, 2013; (ed with H. McBurney) The Image of Venice: Fialetti's View and Sir Henry Wotton, 2014; (ed with C. Corsato) Santa Maria Gloriosa dei Frari: immagini di devozione, spazi della fede/Devotional Spaces, Images of Piety, 2015; (ed jtly) Madonnas and Miracles: the holy home in Renaissance Italy, 2017; (with A. Brundin and M. Laven) The Sacred Home in Renaissance Italy, 2018; (ed jtly) La Chiesa di San Giacomo dall'Orio, Venezia, 2018; numerous articles and book reviews in learned jls. *Recreations*: mountain walking (completed Scottish Munros, 2011), music, photography, gardening. *Address*: St John's College, Cambridge CB2 1TP. *T*: (01223) 339360.

**HOWARD, Air Vice Marshal Graham John,** CB 2014; Assistant Chief of Defence Staff (Logistic Operations), 2011–14; Director, Estates and Facilities Management, Loughborough University, since 2019; *b* Spalding, Lincs, 29 Aug. 1960; *s* of Albert John Howard and Josephine Ann Howard (*née* Mason); *m* 1st, 1985, Penelope Ann Tiffany Richmond (marr. diss. 2004); two *d*; 2nd, 2006, Jacqueline Samantha (*née* Wilson); one step *d*. *Educ*: Gleed Boys' Sch.; Spalding Grammar Sch.; King's Coll., London (MA Defence Studies 1998). FCILT 2008. Commnd RAF, 1979; jun. logistics roles, 1980–95; acsc 1996; SO 1 Logistic Ops HQ Strike Comd, 1997–98; OC, Tactical Supply Wing, 1998–2000; PJHQ, 2000–04; CO, RAF Stafford, 2004–06; HCSC 2006; Strategic Delivery Unit, British Embassy, Kabul, 2006; Comdr, Jt Force Logistics HQ, PJHQ, 2007–08; Hd, Defence Logistics Policy, 2008–10; Hd, Defence Support Chain Ops and Movements, 2010–11. Reserve Officer, RAF, 2015–. Dir, Mgt Consulting, Corporate Ops, KPMG LLP, 2015–19. President: Movement Control Assoc., 2008–; Tactical Supply Wing and Servicing Commando Assoc., 2012–. *Recreations*: family, keeping fit, travel, renovating a listed property.

**HOWARD, Prof. Ian George,** RSA 1998; Principal, Edinburgh College of Art, 2001–11; Emeritus Professor, University of Edinburgh, since 2011; *b* 7 Nov. 1952; *s* of Harold Geoffrey Howard and Violet Howard (*née* Kelly); *m* 1977, Ruth D'Arcy; two *d*. *Educ*: Aberdeen Grammar Sch.; Univ. of Edinburgh; Edinburgh Coll. of Art. MA Hons Fine Art 1975; Postgrad. Dip. 1976. Lectr in Painting, Gray's Sch. of Art, Aberdeen, 1977–86; Head of Painting, Duncan of Jordanstone Coll. of Art, Dundee, 1986–95; Prof. of Fine Art (personal chair), Dundee Univ., 1995–2001; Mem., Faculty of Fine Art, British Sch. at Rome, 1996–2002; Dean, Duncan of Jordanstone Coll. of Art and Design, 1999–2001; Prof., Heriot-Watt Univ., 2001–11. Dir, Dundee Contemporary Arts Ltd, 1997–2004. Treas., Royal Scottish Acad., 2008–13. Numerous exhibns internationally; work in collections, including: Arts Council England; Contemporary Art Soc.; Edinburgh City Art Centre; Hunterian Art Gall., Glasgow; Fleming Collection, London; Royal Scottish Acad., V&A Mus.; Royal Collection Trust. Trustee, Nat. Galls of Scotland, 2010–14. Hon. Vice-Principal, Univ. of Edinburgh, 2009–11. Dr hc Edinburgh, 2007. *Publications*: Heretical Diagrams, 1995; Emblemata, 1998; Uncertain Histories, 2000. *Recreations*: travel, cooking, wild mushrooms. *Address*: Royal Scottish Academy, The Mound, Edinburgh EH2 2EL. *W*: http://ianhoward-art.net.

**HOWARD, Prof. (James) Kenneth,** OBE 2010; RA 1991 (ARA 1983); painter; Professor of Perspective, Royal Academy of Arts, 2001–11; *b* 26 Dec. 1932; *s* of Frank and Elizabeth Howard; *m* 1st, Ann Howard (*née* Popham), dress designer (marr. diss. 1974); 2nd, 1990, Christa Gaa (*née* Köhler), RWS (*d* 1992); 3rd, 2000, Dora Bertolutti. *Educ*: Kilburn Grammar School; Hornsey School of Art; Royal College of Art (ARCA). NEAC 1962 (Pres., 1998–2003); ROI 1966 (Hon. ROI 1988; Hon. Fellow 2007); RWA 1981; RWS 1983. British Council scholarship to Florence, 1958–59; taught various London Art Schools, 1959–73; Official Artist for Imperial War Museum in N Ireland, 1973, 1978; painted for the British Army in N Ireland, Germany, Cyprus, Hong Kong, Brunei, Nepal, Belize, Norway, Lebanon, Canada, Oman, 1973–; one man exhibitions: Plymouth Art Centre, 1955; John Whibley Gallery, 1966, 1968; New Grafton Gallery, 1971–2000; Jersey, 1978, 1980, 1983; Hong Kong, 1979; Nicosia, 1982; Delhi, 1983; Lowndes Lodge Gall., 1987, 1989, 1990, 1991; Sinfield Gall., 1991, 1993, 1995; Bankside Gall., 1996; Everard Reid Gall., Johannesburg, 1998; Richard Green Gall., 2002, 2003, 2004, 2005, 2006, 2009, 2011, 2013, 2015, 2016, 2017; RA Friends Room, 2009; Belle Shenkman Room, RA, 2016; Portland Gall., 2018, 2019. Works purchased by Plymouth Art Gall., Imperial War Mus., Guildhall Art Gall., Ulster Mus., Nat. Army Mus., Hove Mus., Sheffield Art Gall., Southend Mus.; commissions for UN, BAOR, Drapers' Co., Stock Exchange, States of Jersey, Banque Paribas, Royal Hosp. Chelsea. Freeman: City of London, 2007; Painter-Stainers' Co., 2007 (Liveryman, 2007–). Hon. RBA 1989; RBSA 1991; Hon. SGA 2008. First Prize: Hunting Group Award, 1982; Sparkasse Karlsruhe, 1985. Gen. Editor, Art Class series, 1988. *Publications*: contribs to: The War Artists, 1983; 60th Vol. of The Old Water-Colour Societies' Club, 1985; Painting Interiors, 1989; Art of Landscape and Seascape, 1989; Visions of Venice, 1990; Venice: the artist's vision, 1990; 20th Century Painters and Sculptors, 1991; Oils Masterclass, 1996; (jtly) Ken Howard: a personal view—Inspired by Light, 1998; Dictionary of Artists in Britain since 1945, 1998; Britain's Paintings, 2003; St Ives 1975–2005: art colony in transition, 2007; Light and Dark, 2011; Ken Howard's Switzerland: in the footsteps of Turner, 2013; *relevant publication*: The Paintings of Ken Howard, by Michael Spender, 1992. *Recreations*: cinema, opera. *Address*: 8 South Bolton Gardens, SW5 0DH. *T*: (020) 7373 2912; (studio) St Clements Studio, Mousehole, Cornwall TR19 6TR. *T*: (01736) 731596; (studio) Ramo e Corte del Paludo, 6262 Cannaregio, Venice, Italy. *T*: 0415202277. *Clubs*: Arts, Chelsea Arts.

**HOWARD, Hon. John (Winston),** OM 2012; AC 2008; Prime Minister of Australia, 1996–2007; *b* 26 July 1939; *s* of Lyall F. Howard and Mona Howard; *m* 1971, Alison Janette Parker; two *s* one *d*. *Educ*: Canterbury Boys' High Sch.; Sydney Univ. Solicitor of NSW Supreme Court, 1962. MP (L) for Bennelong, NSW, 1974–2007. Minister for Business and Consumer Affairs, Australia, 1975; Minister assisting Prime Minister, May 1977; Minister for Special Trade Negotiations, July 1977; Federal Treasurer, 1977–83; Dep. Leader of the Opposition, 1983–85; Leader, Parly Liberal Party, 1985–89 and 1995–2007; Leader of the Opposition, Australia, 1985–89, 1995–96. Chm., Manpower and Labour Market Reform Gp, 1990–93. Chm., Internat. Dem. Union, 2002–. Hon. LLD Notre Dame. Centenary Medal, Australia, 2003; Gold Olympic Order, IOC, 2003; US Presidential Medal of Freedom, 2009. *Publications*: Lazarus Rising, 2010; The Menzies Era, 2014. *Recreations*: cricket, films, reading, golf. *Address*: GPO Box 36, Sydney, NSW 2001, Australia. *Club*: Australian (Sydney).

**HOWARD, Prof. Jonathan Charles,** DPhil; FRS 1995; Professor of Genetics, Institute for Genetics, University of Cologne, 1994–2011, now Emeritus; Director, Instituto Gulbenkian de Ciência, Oeiras, Portugal, 2012; Max-Planck Fellow, Max-Planck Institute of Plant Breeding, Cologne, 2013; *b* 24 June 1943; *s* of John Eldred Howard and Marghanita (*née* Laski); *m* 1990, Maria Leptin; two *s*. *Educ*: Westminster Sch.; Magdalen Coll., Oxford (BA Zool. 1964; DPhil Medicine 1969). Mem., Scientific Staff, MRC, at Cellular Immunology Res. Unit, Sir William Dunn Sch. of Pathology, Univ. of Oxford, 1968–73; Weir Jun. Res. Fellow, University Coll., Oxford, 1970–73; Babraham Institute, Cambridge: Mem. Staff, Dept of Immunology, 1974–94; Head of Dept, 1985–94; Res. Fellow, Clare Hall, Cambridge, 1975–78; sabbaticals at: Depts of Pathology and Cell Biol., Stanford Univ., 1983, 1987; Div. of Biol., CIT, 1983; EMBL, 1992. Mem., EMBO, 1993; MAE 2008. *Publications*: Darwin, 1982; papers in learned jls on immunology and evolution. *Recreations*: fishing, piano. *Address*: Institut für Genetik, Universität zu Köln, Zülpicher Strasse 47, 50674 Köln, Germany. *T*: (221) 4704864; Heinestrasse 19, 50931 Köln, Germany. *T*: (221) 4200320.

**HOWARD, Prof. Judith Ann Kathleen,** CBE 1996; FRS 2002; Professor of Chemistry, University of Durham, since 1991; *b* 21 Oct. 1945; *d* of James and Kathleen Duckworth. *Educ*: Univ. of Bristol (BSc Hons 1966; DSc 1986); Somerville Coll., Oxford (DPhil 1971). CChem, FRSC 1991; EurChem 1996; CPhys, FInstP 1996. Sen. Res. Fellow, 1987–91, Reader, 1991, Univ. of Bristol; Sen. Fellow, Royal Soc. Leverhulme Trust, 1996–97; Sir Derman Christopherson Fellow, Univ. of Durham, 1997–98; EPSRC Sen. Res. Fellow, 1998–2003. DUniv Open, 1998; Hon. DSc: Bristol, 2004; Bath, 2005; E Anglia, 2015. *Publications*: (contrib.) Encyclopedia of Inorganic Chemistry, 1994; Crystallographic Instrumentation, 1998; Implications of Molecular and Materials Structure for New Technologies, 1999; over 1500 jl articles. *Recreations*: music, reading, hiking, art, swimming. *Address*: Department of Chemistry, University of Durham, Durham DH1 3LE. *T*: (0191) 334 2047, *Fax*: (0191) 334 2051. *E*: j.a.k.howard@durham.ac.uk.

**HOWARD, Kenneth;** *see* Howard, J. K.

**HOWARD, Sir Laurence,** KCVO 2017; OBE 2004; PhD; Lord-Lieutenant of Rutland, 2003–18; *b* 29 March 1943; *s* of Henry Lovering Howard and Beryl Cicely Howard; *m* 1966, Christine Mary Kinver; one *s* one *d*. *Educ*: Strode's Sch.; Nottingham Univ. (BSc 1967); Leicester Univ. (PhD Neurophysiol. 1971). Wolfson Fellow, 1970–73; Leicester University: Lectr, 1974, Sen. Lectr, 1988–90, in Physiology; Sub-Dean, Med. Sch., 1990–2003; Associate Lectr in Physiology, 2003–06. Chairman: Bd of Visitors, HM Prison Stocken, 1988–91; Leicester Magistrates' Courts Cttee, 1997–2002; Central Council, Magistrates' Courts Cttees, 2002–03; Pres., Leics and Rutland Magistrates' Assoc., 2004–18; Mem., Unified Courts Admin Bd, 2002–04. Chm. Council, Peterborough Cathedral, 2015–. President: Leics and Rutland Headway, 2005–; Leics and Rutland Community Foundn, 2010–; Rutland Sinfonia, 2012–; Rutland Agricl Soc., 2019–20. Patron, Leicester Charity Link, 2010–. Freeman, City of London, 1966; Hon. Freeman, Oakham, 2018. JP Rutland, 1979 (Chm. Bench, 1988–94). Hon. Fellow, UC Northampton, 2001. Hon. Air Cdre, 504 (Notts) Sqdn, 2008–18. Hon. LLD Leicester, 2013. *Publications*: articles on physiology in scientific jls. *Recreations*: travel, horse riding, music. *Address*: Daventry House, Main Street, Whissendine, Rutland LE15 7ET. *T*: (01664) 474662. *E*: laurence@whiss64.plus.com.

**HOWARD, Margaret;** freelance broadcaster, writer and concert presenter, since 1969; presenter, with Classic FM, 1992–99; *b* 29 March 1938; *d* of John Bernard Howard and Ellen Corwena Roberts. *Educ*: St Mary's Convent, Rhyl, N Wales; St Teresa's Convent, Sunbury; Guildhall Sch. of Music and Drama; Indiana Univ., Bloomington, USA; Open Univ. (BA Hons Hum. 2013). LGSM; LRAM 1960. Joined BBC, 1955; Clerk Messenger, 1955–58; Studio Manager, 1958–65; Presentation Asst, BBC TV, 1963–65 (on attachment); British govt tech. asst, Nigerian Broadcasting Corp., 1965–66 (on secondment); BBC World Service Announcer, 1967–69; Teaching Asst, Dept of Radio and TV, Indiana Univ., 1969–70; Reporter: The World This Weekend, BBC Radio 4, 1970–74; Edition, BBC TV, 1971; Tomorrow's World, BBC TV, 1972; Editor and Presenter: Pick of the Week, BBC Radio 4, 1974–91; Classic Reports, Classic FM, 1992–94; Howard's Week, Classic FM, 1994–97; Presenter: It's Your World, BBC World Service, 1981–86; Masterclass, 1994–99, Music and the Mind, concert series with Medici Quartet, 1995, Classic FM; concerts: Haydn's Seven Last Words from the Cross, Medici Quartet, 2001, 2002; Viva Verdi, Opera Nazionale Italiana, UK tour, 2001; Interviewer/Presenter, Strictly Instrumental, occasional BBC series, 1980–85; consultant and recording artist, Classical Communications Ltd, 2003–10. Radio critic, The Tablet, Sunday Express; columnist, The Universe; record columnist, Chic magazine. Female UK Radio Personality of the Year, Sony Awards, 1984; Sony Radio Awards Roll of Honour, 1988; Voice of the Listener Award for excellence, 1991; Radio Personality of the Year, TRIC Awards, 1996; inducted into Radio Acad. Hall of Fame, 2013. *Publications*: Margaret Howard's Pick of the Week, 1984; Court Jesting, 1986. *Recreations*: swimming, tasting wine, dog walking, Nordic walking. *Address*: 1 Burnes Vale, Rottingdean, Brighton, E Sussex BN2 7DW. *T*: (01273) 306343. *Club*: Rottingdean (Brighton).

**HOWARD, Martin Lloyd,** CB 2007; Chief of Assessments Staff, Cabinet Office (on loan from GCHQ), 2014–16; consultant on national security issues, since 2016; *b* 1 Oct. 1954; *s* of late Leonard Lloyd Howard and of Joan Mary Howard; *m* 1993, Caroline Jane Delves. *Educ*: Gravesend Grammar Sch. Joined MoD, 1975; apptd Sen. CS, 1993; Dir, Central and Eastern Europe, MoD, 1993–94; Private Sec. to Sec. of State for NI (on loan), 1994–96; Dep. Chief, Assessments Staff, Cabinet Office (on loan), 1996–98; Ministry of Defence: Hd, Overseas Secretariat, 1998–99; Dir of News, 1999–2001; Dir Gen., Corporate Communications, 2001–03; Dep. Chief of Defence Intelligence, 2003–04; Dir Gen., Operational Policy, 2004–07; Asst Sec. Gen. (Ops), NATO, 2007–11; Dir, Cyber Policy Support, later Cyber Policy and Internat. Relns, GCHQ, 2011–14. Vis. Sen. Fellow, LSE, 2016–17. *Recreations*: classical and contemporary guitar, sailing, reading, music. *Address*: c/o HR Department, GCHQ, Hubble Road, Cheltenham, Glos GL51 0EX.

**HOWARD, Prof. Maurice,** OBE 2016; PhD; Professor of Art History, University of Sussex, 2001–16, now Emeritus; *b* Isleworth, London, 16 June 1948; *s* of Henry George Howard and Elsie May Howard (*née* Minter). *Educ*: Walpole and Langley Grammar Schs; Christ's Coll., Cambridge (BA Hons 1970); Courtauld Inst. of Art (MA 1972); Univ. of London (PhD 1985). Lecturer in Art History: Pennsylvania State Univ., 1972–73; Univ. of St Andrews, 1974–76; University of Sussex: Lectr in Art Hist., 1976–96; Reader, 1996–2001. Hon. Res. Fellow, V&A Mus., 2001–06, 2008–11. Chm., 1991–94, Pres., 2013–17, Soc. of Architectural Historians of GB; Pres., Soc. of Antiquaries of London,

2010–14 (Dir, 2007–10). *Publications*: The Early Tudor Country House: architecture and politics 1490–1550, 1987; The Tudor Image, 1995; (jtly) Ornament: a social history since 1450, 1996; (jtly) The Vyne: a Tudor house revealed, 2003; The Building of Elizabethan and Jacobean England, 2007; (ed jtly) Painting in Britain 1500–1630: production, influences and patronage, 2015 (Exemplary Multi-authored Book, Historians of British Art, 2016). *Recreations*: opera, tennis. *Address*: Arts Building, University of Sussex, Falmer, Brighton BN1 9QN. *T*: (01273) 606755. *E*: M.Howard@sussex.ac.uk.

**HOWARD, Sir Michael (Eliot)**, OM 2005; CH 2002; Kt 1986; CBE 1977; MC 1943; DLitt; FBA 1970; FRHistS; Emeritus Professor of Modern History, University of Oxford, since 1989; *b* 29 Nov. 1922; *y s* of late Geoffrey Eliot Howard, Ashmore, near Salisbury, and of Edith Julia Emma, *o d* of Otto Edinger; civil partnership 2006, Mark Anthony James. *Educ*: Wellington; Christ Church, Oxford (BA 1946, MA 1948; Hon. Student, 1990). Served War, Coldstream Guards, 1942–45. Asst Lecturer in History, University of London, King's Coll., 1947; Lecturer, 1950; Lecturer, then Reader, in War Studies, 1953–63; Prof. of War Studies, 1963–68; University of Oxford: Fellow of All Souls Coll., 1968–80 (Hon. Fellow, 2014); Chichele Prof. of History of War, 1977–80; Regius Prof. of Modern History and Fellow of Oriel Coll., 1980–89 (Hon. Fellow, 1990); Robert A. Lovett Prof. of Military and Naval Hist., Yale Univ., 1989–93. Vis. Prof. of European History, Stanford Univ., 1967; Kluge Vis. Prof., Library of Congress, 2003. Ford's Lectr in English History, Oxford, 1971; Radcliffe Lectr, Univ. of Warwick, 1975; Trevelyan Lectr, Cambridge, 1977; Leverhulme Lectr, 1996; Lee Kuan Yew Distinguished Visitor, Nat. Univ. of Singapore, 1996. FKC. Pres. and co-Founder, Internat. Institute for Strategic Studies; Vice-Pres., Council on Christian Approaches to Defence and Disarmament; Pres., Army Records Soc. Hon. Gov., Ditchley Foundn, 2011–. Gov., Wellington Coll., 1979–90. For. Hon. Mem., Amer. Acad. of Arts and Scis, 1983. Hon. LittD Leeds, 1979; Hon. DLit London, 1988; Hon. DHumLit Lehigh Univ., Pa, USA, 1990. Chesney Meml Gold Medal, RUSI, 1973; NATO Atlantic Award, 1989. *Publications*: The Coldstream Guards, 1920–46 (with John Sparrow), 1951; Disengagement in Europe, 1958; Wellingtonian Studies, 1959; The Franco-Prussian War, 1961 (Duff Cooper Memorial Prize, 1962); The Theory and Practice of War, 1965; The Mediterranean Strategy in the Second World War, 1967; Studies in War and Peace, 1970; Grand Strategy, vol. IV (in UK History of 2nd World War, Military series), 1971 (Wolfson Foundn History Award, 1972); The Continental Commitment, 1972; War in European History, 1976; (with P. Paret) Clausewitz On War, 1977; War and the Liberal Conscience, 1978; (ed) Restraints on War, 1979; The Causes of Wars, 1983; Clausewitz, 1983; Strategic Deception in World War II, 1990; The Lessons of History, 1991; (ed with W. R. Louis) The Oxford History of the Twentieth Century, 1998; The Invention of Peace, 2000 (Pol Book Prize, Friedrich Ebert Stiftung); The First World War, 2002; Captain Professor: a life in war and peace (autobiog.), 2006; Liberation or Catastrophe?: reflections on the history of the 20th century, 2007. *Address*: The Old Farm, Eastbury, Hungerford, Berks RG17 7JN. *Clubs*: Athenæum, Garrick, Pratt's, Reform.

**HOWARD, Michael Newman**; QC 1986; arbitrator; a Recorder of the Crown Court, since 1993; *b* 10 June 1947; *s* of late Henry Ian Howard and Tilly Celia Howard. *Educ*: Clifton College; Magdalen College, Oxford (MA, BCL). Lecturer in Law, LSE, 1970–74; called to the Bar, Gray's Inn, 1971, Bencher, 1995; in practice at Bar, 1971–; Asst Recorder, 1989–93; Leader of Admiralty Bar, 1999–. Visiting Professor: Law, Univ. of Essex, 1987–92; Maritime Law, UCL, 1996–99; Maritime Law, Tulane Univ., 2011–. Mem. of Panel, Lloyd's Salvage Arbitrators, 1987–2009. *Publications*: Phipson on Evidence, ed jtly, 12th edn 1976 to 14th edn 1990, Gen. Ed., 15th edn 2000; (jtly) Foreign Currency: claims, judgements and damages, 2016; *contributions to*: Frustration and Force Majeure, 1991, 2nd edn 1995; Consensus ad Idem: essays for Guenter Treitel, 1996; Halsbury's Laws of England, 4th edn (Damages), 2005; Butterworth's Commercial Court and Arbitration Pleadings, 2005; Palmer on Bailment, 3rd edn, 2009; articles and reviews in legal periodicals. *Recreations*: books, music, sport. *Address*: Quadrant Chambers, Quadrant House, 10 Fleet Street, EC4Y 1AU. *T*: (020) 7583 4444, *Fax*: (020) 7583 4455. *E*: michael.howard@quadrantchambers.com. *Clubs*: Royal Automobile, Oxford and Cambridge, Garrick.

**HOWARD, Nicola**; QC 2019; a Recorder, since 2016; *b* Folkestone, 18 Dec. 1971; *d* of Brian Howard and Betty Stabbs; *m* 2006, Brian Lloyd St Louis, *qv*; one *s* one *d*. *Educ*: Dover Grammar Sch. for Girls; Univ. of Hull (BSc Hons 1993); Westminster Univ. (DipLaw 1994). Called to the Bar, Middle Temple, 1995; in practice as a barrister, specialising in criminal law (financial and corporate crime), 1995–. *Recreations*: family, food, films, theatre. *Address*: 25 Bedford Row, WC1R 4HD. *T*: (020) 7067 1500. *E*: clerks@25bedfordrow.com.

**HOWARD, Philip Ewen**; Co-owner, Elystan Street, since 2016; *b* Johannesburg, SA, 5 June 1966; *s* of Francis and Lynne Howard; *m* 1990, Jennifer Collier; one *s* one *d*. *Educ*: Bradfield Coll.; Univ. of Kent at Canterbury (BSc Microbiol. 1987). Commis Chef, Roux Restaurants, 1987–88; Chef de Partie: Harveys, 1988–89; Bibendum, 1989–90; Head Chef and Co-owner, The Square, W1, 1991–2016; Co-owner: The Ledbury, 2005–; Kitchen W8, 2009–; Sonny's Kitchen, 2012–; Union, France, 2017–; Perilla, 2017–; Lorne, 2017–; Gezellig, 2019–. 2 Michelin Stars, 1994, 1998; 4 AA Rosettes, 2012; AA Restaurant of Year, 2007. Catey Award for Restaurateur of Year, 2011; Restaurateurs Chefs Chef of Year, AA, 2013; London Restaurant Festival Chef of Year, 2017. *Publications*: The Square: The Cook Book, vol. 1: savoury, 2012; The Square: The Cook Book, vol. 2: sweet, 2013. *Recreations*: ski-ing, running, travelling. *Address*: Elystan Street, 43 Elystan Street, SW3 3NT.

**HOWARD, Rebecca Mary**; *see* Sabben-Clare, R. M.

**HOWARD, Stephen Lee**, LVO 2015; Chief Executive, Business in the Community, 2008–16 (Managing Director, 2005–08); *b* 25 March 1953; *s* of Richard and Marilyn Howard; *m* 1976, Holly Grothe; three *s*. *Educ*: Michigan State Univ. (BA 1975); Univ. of Michigan Law Sch. (JD *cum laude* 1978). In practice as lawyer, Providence, RI, 1978–85; Cookson America Inc.: General Counsel, 1985–86; Vice-Pres., Corporate Develt and General Counsel, 1986–91; Cookson Group plc: Chief Exec., Gp Develt, 1991–92; Dir and Chief Exec., Engineered Prods Div. and Gp Corporate Develt, 1992–94; Chief Exec., Ceramic and Engineered Prods Div. and Gp Corporate Develt, 1994–97; Gp Jt Man. Dir, 1995–97; Gp Chief Exec., 1997–2004; Chief Exec., Novar plc, 2004–05. Non-executive Director: SEGRO plc (formerly Slough Estates plc), 2001–10; Balfour Beatty plc; In Kind Direct, 2008–16. Mem., Adv. Bd, Veolia. Chairman: Power to Change, 2016–; Thames Reach, 2016–; Anthemis Inst., 2017–. Dep. Chm., Habitat, Humanity GB. Gov., St George's Coll. *Recreations*: tennis, basketball. *Club*: Royal Automobile.

**HOWARD, Victoria**; *see* Barnsley, V.

**HOWARD-JOHNSTON, Angela Maureen**; *see* Huth, A. M.

**HOWARD-LAWSON, Sir John (Philip)**, 6th Bt *cr* 1841, of Brough Hall, Yorkshire; *b* 6 June 1934; *s* of Sir William Howard Lawson, 5th Bt and Joan Eleanor (*d* 1989), *d* of late Arthur Cowie Stamer, CBE; assumed by Royal Licence surname and arms of Howard, 1962, of Howard-Lawson, 1992; *S* father, 1990; *m* 1960, Jean Veronica (*née* Marsh) (*d* 2001); two *s* one *d*. *Educ*: Ampleforth. *Heir*: *s* Philip William Howard [*b* 28 June 1961; *m* 1st, 1988, Cara Margaret Browne (marr. diss. 1992); 2nd, 1993, Isabel Anne Oldridge de la Hey; one *d*]. *Address*: Wood House, Otters Holt, Culgaith, Penrith, Cumbria CA10 1SG. *T*: (01768) 88315.

**HOWARTH**, family name of **Baron Howarth of Newport**.

**HOWARTH OF BRECKLAND**, Baroness *cr* 2001 (Life Peer), of Parson Cross in the County of South Yorkshire; **Valerie Georgina Howarth**, OBE 1999; founding Chief Executive, ChildLine, 1987–2001; *b* 5 Sept. 1940. *Educ*: Abbeydale Girls' Grammar Sch.; Univ. of Leicester. MBASW; Associate Mem., ADASS. Caseworker, Family Welfare Assoc., 1963–68; London Borough of Lambeth: Sen. Child Care Worker and Trng Officer, 1968–70; Area Co-ordinator, 1972–76; Chief Co-ordinator of Social Work, 1972–76; Asst Dir of Personal Services, 1976–82; Dir of Social Services, London Borough of Brent, 1982–86. Board Member: Food Standards Agency, 2000–07; Nat. Care Standards Commn, 2001–04; Children and Family Courts Adv. and Support Services, 2004–12 (Chm., 2008–12). Founder Member: King's Cross Homelessness Project (first Chm.), 1986–87; London Homelessness Forum, 1986–87; Home Office Steering Gp on Child Witnesses, 1991–97; Telephone Helplines Assoc. (first Chm.); NCH Commn considering Children as Abusers, 1991–92. Dir and Mem. Cttee, ICSTIS, 1988–2000; Mem., NSPCC Professional Adv. Panel, 1993–94; UK Rep., Euro Forum for Child Welfare, 1994–97. Member: Sub cttee G on EU, H of L, 2005–10 (Chm., 2007–10); EU Select Cttee, H of L, 2007–10; Sub cttee D on Agric. and Fisheries, H of L, 2010–. Trustee, Livability (formerly John Grooms Assoc. for Disabled People, later Grooms-Shaftesbury), 1987– (Chair, 2007–10); Pres., 2005–14; Sen. Vice-Pres., 2014–); Trustee: Lucy Faithfull Foundn, 1992– (Vice Chm.); NCVCCO, 1990–95 (Vice Chm.); Stop It Now, 1992–2009 (Chm.); Nat. Children's Bureau, 1993–94; Michael Sieff Foundn, 1994–2004; Little Hearts Matter, 2002– (Patron, 2002–); Children's Internat. Helplines Assoc., 2003–07 (Chm. Trustees, 2003–07; Pres., 2007–); Patron, TRACKS, 2011–. DUniv Open, 2007. *Recreations*: gardening, reading, walking, people, church activities. *Address*: House of Lords, SW1A 0PW. *E*: howarthv@parliament.uk.

**HOWARTH OF NEWPORT**, Baron *cr* 2005 (Life Peer), of Newport in the county of Gwent; **Alan Thomas Howarth**, CBE 1982; PC 2000; *b* 11 June 1944; *e s* of late T. E. B. Howarth, MC, TD and Margaret Howarth; *m* 1967, Gillian Martha (marr. diss. 1996), *d* of Mr and Mrs Arthur Chance, Dublin; two *s* two *d*; partner, 2001, Baroness Hollis of Heigham, PC (*d* 2018). *Educ*: Rugby Sch. (scholar); King's Coll., Cambridge (major scholar in History; BA 1965). Sen. Res. Asst to Field-Marshal Montgomery on A History of Warfare, 1965–67; Asst Master, Westminster Sch., 1968–74; Private Sec. to Chm. of Conservative Party, 1975–79; Dir, Cons. Res. Dept, 1979–81; Vice-Chm., Conservative Party, 1980–81. MP: Stratford on Avon, 1983–97, (C) 1983–95, (Lab) 1995–97; (Lab) Newport E, 1997–2005. PPS to Dr Rhodes Boyson, MP, 1985–87; an Asst Govt Whip, 1987–88; Lord Comr of HM Treasury, 1988–89; Parliamentary Under-Secretary of State: DES, 1989–92 (Schools Minister, 1989–90; Minister for Higher Educn and Sci., 1990–92); DFEE, 1997–98 (Employment Minister and Minister for Disabled People); DCMS, 1998–2001 (Minister for the Arts). Secretary: Cons. Arts and Heritage Cttee, 1984–85; PLP Social Security Cttee, 1996–97; Member: Nat. Heritage Select Cttee, 1992–94; Social Security Select Cttee, 1995–97; Intelligence and Security Cttee, 2001–05; Ad Hoc Cttee on Internat. Orgns, 2008–09; Chm., All Party Parly Gp on Charities and Vol. Sector, 1992–97; Treas., 1993–97, Vice-Pres., 2002–, All Party Arts and Heritage Gp; Co-Chairman: All Party Parly Gp on Architecture and Planning, 2005–11; All Party Parly Gp on Arts, Health and Wellbeing, 2014–; Hon. Treas. and Vice-Chm., All Party Parly Gp for Drug Policy Reform, 2013–18. Chm., Friends, Huntington's Disease Assoc., 1988–97; Mem. Adv. Council, Nat. Listening Library, 1992–97; Vice-Pres., British Dyslexia Assoc., 1994–97; Chm., UK Literary Heritage Wkg Gp, 2006–12; Mem. Bd, Norwich Heritage and Econ. Regeneration Trust, 2006–16. Mem. Bd, Poetry Archive, 2006–13. Mem. Court: Univ. of Warwick, 1987–97; Univ. of Birmingham, 1992–97. Mem. Bd, Inst. of Historical Res., 1992–97. Gov., Royal Shakespeare Theatre, 1984–97; Chm., Trustees and Govs, Royal Pavilion Museums Foundn (formerly Friends of Royal Pavilion Art Gall. and Mus), Brighton and Hove, 2006–11. Patron, Norfolk Community Law Service, 2019. FSA 2007. Hon. Dr Canterbury Christ Church, 2019. *Publications*: (jtly) Monty at Close Quarters, 1985; jt author of various CPC pamphlets. *Recreations*: books, the arts, walking. *Address*: House of Lords, SW1A 0PW.

**HOWARTH, Prof. David Ross**; Professor of Law and Public Policy, University of Cambridge, since 2015; Fellow, Clare College, Cambridge, since 1987; *b* 10 Nov. 1958; *s* of George Albert Howarth and Jean Howarth (*née* Rowbotham); *m* 1985, Edna Helen Murphy; two *s*. *Educ*: Queen Mary's Grammar Sch., Walsall; Clare Coll., Cambridge (BA 1981); Yale Univ. (MA 1982; LLM 1983; MPhil 1985). University of Cambridge: William Senior Res. Fellow in Comparative Law, 1985–87; Lectr, 1987, Clare Coll.; Asst Lectr, 1987–92, Lectr, 1992–2005, Reader in Private Law, 2005–15, Dir, Graduate Prog., 2011–12, Dept of Land Economy; Dir, MPhil in Public Policy, Dept of Politics and Internat. Studies, 2012–16; Associate Fellow, Cambridge Centre for Sci. and Policy, 2010–. Mem. (Lib Dem), Cambridge CC, 1987–2004 (Leader, 2000–03; Hon. Councillor, 2010). MP (Lib Dem) Cambridge, 2005–10. Lib Dem Shadow to Energy Minister, 2005–07; Solicitor-Gen., 2007, Sec. State for Justice, 2008–10. Member: Envmtl Audit Select Cttee, 2005–07; Constitnl Affairs, later Justice, Select Cttee, 2005–08. Member: Electoral Commn, 2010–18; Council of Advrs, Rand Europe, 2012– (non-exec. Dir, 2015–); Founding Mem., Cambridge Cttee for Public Policy, 2012–15; Co-Chair, Univ. of Cambridge Strategic Res. Initiative in Public Policy, 2013–. Hon. Bencher, Middle Temple, 2018. *Publications*: Textbook on Tort, 1995; (jtly) Tort: cases and materials, 2000, 7th edn 2015; (jtly) The Law of Tort, 2001, 3rd edn 2015; (jtly) Reinventing the State, 2007; Law as Engineering: thinking about what lawyers do, 2013; numerous articles in learned jls and edited books. *Address*: Clare College, Cambridge CB2 1TL. *T*: (01223) 333200.

**HOWARTH, Elgar**; freelance musician; *b* 4 Nov. 1935; *s* of Oliver and Emma Howarth; *m* 1958, Mary Bridget Neary; one *s* two *d*. *Educ*: Manchester Univ. (MusB); Royal Manchester Coll. of Music (ARMCM 1956; FRMCM 1970). Royal Opera House, Covent Garden (Orchestra), 1958–63; Royal Philharmonic Orchestra, 1963–69; Mem., London Sinfonietta, 1968–71; Mem., Philip Jones Brass Ensemble, 1965–76; freelance conductor, 1970–; Principal Guest Conductor, Opera North, 1985–88; Musical Advisor, Grimethorpe Colliery Brass Band, 1972–2007. Hon. RAM 1989; FRNCM 1994; FRWCMD (FWCMD 1997); FRCM 1999. Hon. Fellow, UC Salford, 1992. DUniv: Birmingham, 1993; York, 1999; Hon. DMus Keele, 1995; DLitt: Salford, 2003; Huddersfield, 2009. Olivier Award for Outstanding Achievement in Opera (for Die Soldaten, and The Prince of Hamburg, ENO), 1997. *Publications*: various compositions mostly for brass instruments.

**HOWARTH, Rt Hon. Sir George (Edward)**, Kt 2019; PC 2005; MP (Lab) Knowsley, since 2010 (Knowsley North, Nov. 1986–1997; Knowsley North and Sefton East, 1997–2010); *b* 29 June 1949; *m* 1977, Julie Rodgers; two *s* (one *d* decd). *Educ*: Liverpool Polytechnic. Formerly: engineer; teacher; Chief Exec., Wales TUC's Co-operative Centre, 1984–86. Former Mem., Huyton UDC; Mem., Knowsley BC, 1975–86 (Dep. Leader,

1982). Parliamentary Under-Secretary of State: Home Office, 1997–99; NI Office, 1999–2001. Mem., Intelligence and Security Cttee, 2005–16. *Address:* House of Commons, SW1A 0AA.

HOWARTH, Sir (James) Gerald (Douglas), Kt 2012; Chairman, Addveritas Ltd, since 2017; *b* 12 Sept. 1947; *s* of late James and Mary Howarth, Hurley, Berks; *m* 1973, Elizabeth Jane, *d* of late Michael and Muriel Squibb, Crowborough, Sussex; two *s* one *d*. *Educ:* Haileybury and ISC Jun. Sch.; Bloxham Sch.; Southampton Univ. (BA Hons). Commnd RAFVR, 1968. Gen. Sec., Soc. for Individual Freedom, 1969–71; entered internat. banking, 1971; Bank of America Internat., 1971–77; European Arab Bank, 1977–81 (Manager, 1979–81); Syndication Manager, Standard Chartered Bank, 1981–83; Dir, Richard Unwin Internat., 1983–87; Jt Man. Dir, Taskforce Communications, 1993–96. Dir, Freedom Under Law, 1973–77; estabd Dicey Trust, 1976. Mem., Hounslow BC, 1982–83. MP (C): Cannock and Burntwood, 1983–92; Aldershot, 1997–2017. Parliamentary Private Secretary: to Parly Under-Sec. of State for Energy, 1987–90; to Minister for Housing and Planning, 1990–91; to Rt Hon. Margaret Thatcher, MP, 1991–92; Shadow Defence Minister, 2002–10; Parly Under-Sec. of State, MoD, 2010–12. Member: Select Cttee on Sound Broadcasting, 1987–92; Home Affairs Select Cttee, 1997–2001; Defence Select Cttee, 2001–03. Chairman: Lords and Commons Family and Child Protection Gp, 1999–2005; All Party RAF Gp, 2005; All Party Parly Gp on Ukraine, 2015–17; All Party Parly Gp on Egypt, 2015–17; Vice-Chairman: Parly Aerospace Gp, 1997; All-Party Photography Gp, 2004–15; Jt Sec., Cons. Parly Aviation Cttee, 1983–87; Vice-Chm., Cons. Parly Envmt, Transport and the Regions Cttee, 1997–99; Jt Vice-Chm., Cons. Parly Home Affairs Cttee, 2000–02. Mem. Exec., 1922 Cttee, 1999–2002; Chm., 92 Gp, 2001–07, 2013–17. Chm., Conservative Way Forward, 2013–17 (Pres., 2017–). President: British Air Display Assoc. (formerly Air Display Assoc. Europe), 2002–; Historic Aircraft Assoc., 2019–; Mem. Council, Air League. Trustee: Vulcan to the Sky Trust, 2006–; British Forces Foundn, 2008–. Jt Patron, Aerobility (formerly British Disabled Flying Assoc.), 2009–. CRAeS 2004. Liveryman, Hon. Co. of Air Pilots (formerly GAPAN), 2011. Britannia Airways Parly Pilot of the Year, 1988. Contributor to No Turning Back Gp pubns. *Recreations:* flying (private pilot's licence, 1965), photography, normal family pursuits. *T:* 07850 638023. *Club:* Royal Air Force.
*See also* J. R. Cartlidge.

HOWARTH, John; Member (Lab) South East Region, European Parliament, since 2017; *b* Newcastle upon Tyne, 31 Oct. 1958; *s* of John Howarth and Freda Howarth (*née* Robinson); one *s* one *d*; *m* 2012, Jane Coney; one step *d*. *Educ:* Highfield Comp. Sch., Felling on Tyne; Univ. of Essex (BA Hons Econs; MA Hist. and Theory of 20th Century Art 1982). Pol Organiser, Labour Party, 1983–88; Dir of Mktg, ICS Gp, 1988–94; Founder and Dir, Public Impact Communications, 1994–2017; Consultant, Instinctif Partners, 2014–17. Member (Lab): Berks CC, 1993–98; Reading BC, 2001–07. Mem., SE England Assembly, 2002–07. *Recreations:* unnecessarily loud guitar, music, food and cooking, writing, photography, football and golf, talking a lot. *Address:* European Parliament, Rue Wiertz 60, 1047 Brussels, Belgium. *E:* john.howarth@ep.europa.eu. *W:* www.johnhowarthmep.uk. *Club:* Newcastle United Football.

HOWARTH, Judith; soprano; *b* 11 Sept. 1962; *m* 1986, Gordon Wilson. *Educ:* Royal Scottish Acad. of Music and Drama. Rôles include: *Royal Opera:* 1985–86: Oscar, in Un Ballo in Maschera (also in Florida); Elvira, in L'Italiana in Algeri; Iris, in Semele; 1989–: Adele, in Die Fledermaus; Ännchen, in Der Freischutz; Gilda, in Rigoletto; Liu, in Turandot; Marguerite de Valois, in Les Huguenots; Marzelline, in Fidelio; Morgana, in Alcina; Musetta, in La Bohème; Norina, in Don Pasquale; *Opera North:* 1992–: Cressida, in Troilus and Cressida; Norina; Susanna, in Le Nozze di Figaro; *English National Opera:* Madame Mao, in Nixon in China; Fiorilla, in Il Turko in Italia; Leila, in Les Pêcheurs des Perles; Butterfly, in Madame Butterfly; *Minnesota Opera:* Maria, in Maria Stuarda; Butterfly, in Madame Butterfly; Marguerite, in Faust; Violetta, in La Traviata; début at Deutsche Oper and at Vienna Staatsoper as Ellen Orford, in Peter Grimes; other rôles and productions include: Violetta, in La Traviata, Glyndebourne Touring Opera; Anne Trulove, in The Rake's Progress, Brussels; Marie, in La Fille du Régiment, Geneva; Hasse's Solimano and Cavalli's La Didone, Berlin; Countess Olga Sukarev, in Fedora, Washington; Soprano Heroines, in Les Contes d'Hoffmann, Nedda, in I Pagliacci, Florida; Aithra, in Die Ägyptische Helena, Santa Fe; Ellen Orford, in Peter Grimes, Toulouse, Santiago de Chile, Oviedo, Iceland; Pamina, in Die Zauberflöte, Strasbourg; title rôle in Maria Stuarda, Butterfly in Madame Butterfly, WNO; Katerina, in The Greek Passion, Palermo, Graz. Many concerts and festival appearances, incl. Salzburg, Aix-en-Provence, Edinburgh, Tanglewood.

HOWARTH, Paul John Arton; Managing Director, National Nuclear Laboratory, since 2009; *b* Manchester, 6 Aug. 1970; *s* of Dr Graham Arton and Edith May Howarth; *m* 1995, Victoria Dawn Cooper; three *s*. *Educ:* Knutsford High Sch.; Univ. of Birmingham (BSc Hons Phys and Astrophys; PhD Nuclear Phys 1995); Univ. of Salford (MSc Business Admin). British Nuclear Fuels plc, 1995–2006: Consultant Physicist, BNFL Instruments, 1995–96; Royal Soc. Fellowship, Kyushu Technol. Transfer Centre, then Japan Atomic Energy Res. Inst., 1997–98; Res. and Technol. Commercial Manager, 1998–2000; Special Asst to Dir of Technol. and Ops, 2000–01; Hd of Technol. for Nuclear Generation, Berkeley Labs, 2001–02; Prog. Dir for Advanced Reactor Res., then Hd, Gp Science and Skills Strategy, 2002–06; Executive Director: Dalton Nuclear Inst., Univ. of Manchester, 2007–09; Battelle Energy UK, 2011–. Vis. Prof., Univ. of Manchester, 2009–. Non-exec. Dir, NPL, 2015–; Chm., Centre of Nuclear Excellence, 2015–. Mem. Bd, Assoc. of Independent Res. and Technol. Orgns, 2014–. FREng 2014. *Recreations:* cycling, hockey, fell walking, squash. *Address:* Whirlwind, 1 Hermitage Lane, Goostrey, Cheshire CW4 8HB. *E:* paul.ja.howarth@nnl.co.uk.

HOWARTH, Peter Andreas; Managing Director, Show Media Ltd, since 2002; *b* 12 Sept. 1964; three *s*; partner, Emma Tucker. *Educ:* Gonville and Caius Coll., Cambridge (BA English 1986). Projects Manager, Paul Smith Ltd, 1986–88; Head of Menswear, Nicole Farhi, 1988–91; Style Ed., 1991–93, Style Dir, 1993–95, GQ; Editor: Arena, 1995–96; Esquire, 1996–2002. *Publications:* (ed) Fatherhood, 1997.

HOWARTH, Robert Lever; Member (Lab), Bolton County Borough, then Metropolitan Borough, Council, 1972–2004 (Leader, Labour Group, 1975–2004) Leader of the Council, 1980–2004); *b* 31 July 1927; *s* of James Howarth and Bessie (*née* Pearson); *m* 1952, Josephine Mary Doyle; one *s* one *d*. *Educ:* Bolton County Grammar Sch.; Bolton Technical Coll. Draughtsman with Hawker Siddeley Dynamics. MP (Lab) Bolton East, 1964–70. Lectr in Liberal Studies, Leigh Technical Coll., 1970–76; Senior Lectr in General Studies, Wigan Coll. of Technology, 1977–87 Dep. Chm., 1986–87, Chm., 1987–88 and 2002–03, Manchester Airport. Mem. (Lab), Bolton BC, 1958–60, 1963–66; Freeman, 2001, Hon. Alderman, 2004, Bolton MBC. *Recreations:* gardening, reading, walking, films.

HOWARTH, Stephen Frederick; HM Diplomatic Service, retired; UK Permanent Representative to Council of Europe, Strasbourg (with personal rank of Ambassador), 2003–07; *b* 25 Feb. 1947; *s* of Alan Howarth and Alice Howarth (*née* Wilkinson); *m* 1966, Jennifer Mary Chrissop; one *s* two *d*. *Educ:* Switzerland; Rossall Sch.; Norwich Sch. Joined HM Diplomatic Service, 1966; FCO, 1966–71; Vice Consul, Rabat, 1971–74; Second Sec., Washington, 1975–80; Second, later First, Sec., Near East and N Africa Dept, FCO, 1980–82; seconded to Ecole Nationale d'Admin, Paris, 1982–83; Asst Head, Trade Relations and Export Dept, FCO, 1983–84; Dep. Head of Mission, Dakar, 1984–88; Asst Head of Cultural Relations Dept, FCO, 1989–90; Counsellor and Dep. Head, Perm. Under Sec.'s Dept, FCO, 1990–92; Head of Consular Dept, later Div., 1993–97; Minister, Paris, 1997–2002. *Publications:* contribs to jl of Institut Internat. de l'Admin Public, ENA Mensuel, Paris. *Recreations:* books, buildings, landscape, gardens. *Address:* Le Matha, Caplong, Ste Foy-la-Grande, 33220, France.

HOWARTH, Rt Rev. Toby Matthew; *see* Bradford, Area Bishop of.

HOWATCH, Susan; writer; *b* 14 July 1940; *d* of George Stanford Sturt and Ann Sturt; *m* 1964, Joseph Howatch (separated 1975); one *d*. *Educ:* Sutton High Sch. GPDST; King's Coll. London (LLB 1961; FKC 1999). Established Starbridge Lectureship in Theology and Natural Science, Cambridge University, 1992. Hon. LittD Hope Coll., Mich, 2012. *Publications:* The Dark Shore, 1965; The Waiting Sands, 1966; Call in the Night, 1967; The Shrouded Walls, 1968; April's Grave, 1969; The Devil on Lammas Night, 1970; Penmarric, 1971; Cashelmara, 1974; The Rich are Different, 1977; Sins of the Fathers, 1980; The Wheel of Fortune, 1984; *Starbridge novels:* Glittering Images, 1987; Glamorous Powers, 1988; Ultimate Prizes, 1989; Scandalous Risks, 1991; Mystical Paths, 1992; Absolute Truths, 1994; *St Benet's trilogy:* A Question of Integrity, 1997, renamed as The Wonder Worker; The High Flyer, 1999; The Heartbreaker, 2003. *Recreation:* reading theology. *Address:* c/o Aitken Alexander Associates Ltd, 291 Gray's Inn Road, WC1X 8EB. *T:* (020) 7373 8672.

HOWATSON, William, FRAgS; freelance rural affairs journalist; Member (Lib Dem), Aberdeenshire Council, since 1999; Provost of Aberdeenshire, 2007–12 and since 2017; *b* 22 Jan. 1953; *s* of William Smith Howatson and Bessie Howatson; *m* 1985, Hazel Symington Paton; two *d*. *Educ:* Lockerbie Acad.; Univ. of Edinburgh (MA Hons 1975). Reporter: Scottish Farmer newspaper, 1979–83; Dumfries and Galloway Standard, 1983–84; Agricl Ed. and Leader Writer, 1984–96, columnist, 1996–2005, The Press and Journal, Aberdeen; columnist, The Courier, Dundee, 2012–16. Chm., Guild of Agricl Journalists, 1995. Member: Scottish Water and Sewerage Customers Council, 1995–99; Health Educn Bd for Scotland, 1996–2003, subseq. NHS Health Scotland, 2003–05 (Vice Chm., 2003–05); E Areas Bd, Scottish Natural Heritage, 1997–2003 (Vice Chm., 1999–2003); Bd, SEPA, 1999–2005 (Chm. E Regl Bd, 2003–05); Rail Passenger Cttee for Scotland, 2001–03; Scottish Agricl Wages Bd, 2008–18. Non-exec. Dir, Angus NHS Trust, 1998–99; Chairman: Aberdeen City Community Health Partnership, 2008–12; NHS Grampian, 2011–14 (non-exec. Mem., 2007–11). Mem. Bd of Mgt, Angus Coll., 1996–2009; Gov., Macaulay Land Use Res. Inst., 1998–2003. Assessor to Court, Univ. of Aberdeen, 2010–12. FRAgS 2003. JP S Aberdeenshire, 1999–2007. Netherthorpe Award, Guild of Agricl Journalists, 1984. *Publications:* (contrib.) Farm Servants and Labour in Lowland Scotland 1770–1914, 1984. *Recreations:* gardening, hill-walking, cooking, reading Scottish history. *Address:* Stone of Morphie, Hillside, Montrose, Angus DD10 0AA. *T:* (01674) 830746. *E:* billhowatson@btinternet.com.

HOWDEN, Alan Percival; Director, Picturedrome Media Ltd, 2001; non-executive Director, UK Film and Television Production Co. Ltd, 2001–15; *b* 28 Aug. 1936; *s* of C. P. Howden and Marian Grindell; *m* 1981, Judith South; one *d*. *Educ:* Sale Grammar Sch.; UMIST (BSc Tech Mech. Engrg). Joined BBC, 1964: Programme Exec., 1964–70; Sen. Programme Exec., 1970–77; Hd of Purchased Programmes, 1977–83; Gen. Manager, Programme Acquisition, 1983–91; Controller, Prog. Acquisition, 1991–99; Advr, Prog. Acquisition, BBC TV, 1999–2000. Mem. Bd, BBC Enterprises, 1989–94. British Film Institute: Gov., 1994–2001; Chm., Film Educn Rev. Cttee for DCMS, 1998–99; British Federation of Film Societies: Vice-Chm., 1965–80; Chm., 1980–82; Vice Pres., 1982. MInstD 1994. *Recreations:* theatre, early music, English countryside.

HOWDEN, Robert Ellis, OBE 2016; President, British Cycling Federation, since 2013 (Director, 1998–2000 and 2001–17; Chairman, 2013–17); *b* Barnsley, 11 June 1955; *s* of Leonard and Elizabeth Howden; *m* 1975, Ceri; one *d*. *Educ:* Wombwell High Sch.; Thornes House Sch., Wakefield; Wakefield Coll. Managing Director: Grass Concrete Ltd, 1981–; Chantry Contractors Ltd, 1981–. FRSA 2007. *Recreations:* cycling, painting, history. *Address:* c/o Duncan House, 142 Thornes Lane, Thornes, Wakefield, W Yorks WF2 7RE. *T:* (01924) 379443, *Fax:* (01924) 290289. *E:* bobhowden@grasscrete.com. *Club:* Wakefield Cycling.

HOWDLE, Prof. Peter David, MD; FRCP; Professor of Clinical Medicine, University of Leeds, 2006–09, now Emeritus; Consultant Physician, St James's University Hospital, Leeds, 1987–2009; *b* 16 June 1948; *s* of George Henry Howdle and Mary Jane Howdle (*née* Baugh); *m* 1972, Susan Ruth Lowery. *Educ:* King's Sch., Pontefract; Univ. of Leeds Med. Sch. (BSc 1969; MB ChB 1972; MD 1985). FRCP 1992. Jun. med. appts, St James's Univ. Hosp., Leeds, 1972–82; University of Leeds: Lectr in Medicine, 1982–87, Sen. Lectr, 1987–96; Prof. of Clinical Educn, 1996–2006; Hd, Acad. Unit of Gen. Surgery, Medicine and Anaesthesia, Univ. of Leeds Med. Sch., 1999–2005; Hd, Section of Medicine, Surgery and Anaesthesia, Leeds Inst. of Molecular Medicine, 2005–09. Vis. Lectr (Fulbright Schol.), Harvard Univ., 1984–85. Coeliac UK: Med. Advr, 1995–2011; Gov. and Trustee, 2006–11; Chm., Health Adv. Council, 2006–11; Chm., Guidelines Develt Gps, NICE, 2008–12; Med. Vice-Chair, Adv. Cttee on Clinical Excellence Awards Yorks and Humber Sub-cttee, 2009–15. Vice-Pres., Methodist Conf., 2002–03; Co-Chm., Jt Implementation Commn for the Anglican-Methodist Covenant, 2003–14; Chairman: Wesley Study Centre Cttee, St John's Coll., Durham Univ., 2009–14; Strategy and Resources Cttee, Methodist Council, 2012–19. Lambeth Cross for Ecumenism, 2017. *Publications:* Comprehensive Clinical Hepatology, 2000; Your Guide to Coeliac Disease, 2007; contrib. over 100 articles mainly on coeliac disease and mucosal immunity. *Recreations:* classical music, modern literature, Methodist history and liturgy. *E:* p.d.howdle@leeds.ac.uk.

HOWE; *see* Hogan-Howe.

HOWE, family name of **Baroness Howe of Idlicote**.

HOWE, 7th Earl *cr* 1821; **Frederick Richard Penn Curzon**; PC 2013; Baron Howe, 1788; Baron Curzon, 1794; Viscount Curzon, 1802; farmer; Deputy Leader, House of Lords, since 2015; Chairman, London and Provincial Antique Dealers' Association, 1999–2010, Honorary President, since 2010; *b* 29 Jan. 1951; *s* of Chambré George William Penn Curzon (*d* 1976) (*g s* of 3rd Earl) and Enid Jane Victoria Curzon (*née* Fergusson) (*d* 1997); *S* cousin, 1984; *m* 1983, Elizabeth Helen Stuart, DL; one *s* three *d*. *Educ:* Rugby School; Christ Church, Oxford (MA Hons Lit. Hum.; Chancellor's Prize for Latin Verse, 1973). AIB. Entered Barclays Bank Ltd, 1973; Manager, 1982; Sen. Manager, 1984–87. Director: Adam & Co., 1987–90; Provident Life Assoc. Ltd, 1988–91. A Lord in Waiting (Govt Whip), 1991–92; front bench spokesman, H of L, on employment and transport, 1991, on environment and defence, 1992; Parly Sec., MAFF, 1992–95; Parly Under-Sec. of State, MoD, 1995–97; opposition front bench spokesman on health, H of L, 1997–2010; Parly Under-Sec. of State, DoH, 2010–15; Minister of State, MoD, 2015–19; elected Mem., H of L, 1999. Governor: King William IV Naval Foundation, 1984–; Trident Trust,

1985–2008; Trustee, Milton's Cottage, 1985–2012 (Chm., 2006–11); Member: Council, RNLI, 1997–2014 (Pres., Chilterns Br., 1985–); Council of Mgt, Restoration of Appearance and Function Trust, 2000–10 (Chm., 2008–10); President: S Bucks Assoc. for the Disabled, 1984–; Nat. Soc. for Epilepsy, 1986–2010 (Vice-Pres., 1984–86); Penn Country Br., CPRE, 1986–92; Abbeyfield Beaconsfield Soc., 1991–2013. Patron: Demand, 2000–10; Chiltern Soc., 2001–. Hon. FRCP 2008. *Recreations:* spending time with family, music. *Heir: s* Viscount Curzon, *qv. Address:* c/o House of Lords, SW1A 0PW.

**HOWE OF IDLICOTE,** Baroness *cr* 2001 (Life Peer), of Shipston-on-Stour in the County of Warwickshire; **Elspeth Rosamund Morton Howe,** CBE 1999; JP; Chairman: Broadcasting Standards Commission, 1997–99 (Chairman, Broadcasting Standards Council, 1993–97); BOC Foundation for the Environment and Community, 1990–2003; *b* 8 Feb. 1932; *d* of late Philip Morton Shand and Sybil Mary (*née* Sissons); *m* 1953, Richard Edward Geoffrey Howe (Baron Howe of Aberavon, CH, PC, QC) (*d* 2015); one *s* two *d. Educ:* Bath High Sch.; Wycombe Abbey; London Sch. of Econs and Pol Science (BSc 1985; Hon. Fellow, 2001). Vice-Chm., Conservative London Area Women's Adv. Cttee, 1966–67, also Pres. of the Cttee's Contact Gp, 1973–77; Mem., Conservative Women's Nat. Adv. Cttee, 1966–71. Member: Lord Chancellor's Adv. Cttee on appointment of Magistrates for Inner London Area, 1965–75; Lord Chancellor's Adv. Cttee on Legal Aid, 1971–75; Parole Board, 1972–75. Dep. Chm., Equal Opportunities Commn, 1975–79. Co-opted Mem., ILEA, 1967–70; Member: Briggs Cttee on Nursing Profession, 1970–72; Justice Cttee on English Judiciary, 1992. Chairman: Hansard Soc. Commn on Women at the Top, 1990–91; The Quality of Care, Local Govt Management Bd Inquiry and Report, 1991–92; Archbishop's Commn on Cathedrals, 1992–94. Director: Kingfisher (formerly Woolworth Holdings) PLC, 1986–2000; United Biscuits (Holdings) PLC, 1988–94; Legal & General Group, 1989–97; Chm., Opportunity 2000 Target Team, Business in the Community, 1990–99. President: Peckham Settlement, 1976–; Women's Gas Fedn, 1979–93; Fedn of Personnel Services, subseq. of Recruitment and Employment Services, 1980–94; UNICEF UK, 1993–2002; Member Council: NACRO, 1974–93; PSI, 1983–92; St George's House, Windsor, 1989–93; Vice-Pres., Pre-Sch. Playgroups Assoc., 1979–83. Trustee, Westminster Foundn for Democracy, 1992–96. Has served as chm. or mem. of several sch. governing bodies in Tower Hamlets; Governor: Cumberlow Lodge Remand Home, 1967–70; Wycombe Abbey, 1968–90; Froebel Educn Inst., 1968–75; LSE, 1985–2006; Mem. Bd of Governors, James Allen's Girls' Sch., 1988–93; Mem. Council, Open Univ., 1996–2003 (Vice-Chm. Council, 2001–03). JP Inner London Juvenile Court Panel, 1964–92 (Chm. of Court, 1970–90). Hon. LLD: London, 1990; Aberdeen, 1993; Liverpool, 1994; DUniv: Open, 1993; South Bank, 1996; Hon. DLitt: Bradford, 1990; Sunderland, 1995. *Publications:* Under Five (a report on pre-school education), 1966. *Address:* House of Lords, SW1A 0PW.

**HOWE, Hon. Brian Leslie,** AO 2008 (AM 2001); *b* 28 Jan. 1936; *s* of John P. Howe and Lillian M. Howe; *m* 1962, Renate Morris; one *s* two *d. Educ:* Melbourne High Sch.; Melbourne Univ. (BA, DipCrim); McCormick Theol Seminary, Chicago (MA). Ordained Minister of Methodist Church, 1963; parishes at Eltham, Morwell and Fitzroy, 1960–69; Dir, Centre for Urban Research and Action, Fitzroy, and Lectr in Sociology, Swinburne Inst. of Technology, 1970–77. Professorial Associate, Centre for Public Policy, Univ. of Melbourne, 1996–; Woodrow Wilson School of Public and International Affairs, Princeton University: Res. Fellow, Centre of Domestic and Comparative Policy Studies, 1997; Frederick H. Schultz Class of 1951 Prof., 1998. MP (ALP) Batman, Vic, 1977–96; Minister: for Defence Support, 1983–84; for Social Security, 1984–89; for Community Services and Health, 1990–91; for Health, Housing and Community Services, 1991–93; for Housing, Local Govt and Community (then Human) Services, 1993–94; for Housing and Regional Develt, 1994–96; Minister assisting the Prime Minister for Social Justice, 1988–93, for Commonwealth-State Relations, 1991–93; Dep. Prime Minister of Australia, 1991–95. Life Mem., ALP, 2005. Bd Mem., 2003–08, Fellow, 2011, Australia & NZ Sch. of Govt. Life Mem., Victorian Council of Social Service, 2007. Patron, Royal Melbourne Philharmonic Orch., 1998–. Charter Mem. and Mem. Bd, Brotherhood of St Laurence, 1998– (Life Mem., 2005). Hon. Fellow, Queen's Coll., Univ. of Melbourne, 2000. Hon. FPIA (Hon. FRAPI 1995). STD *hc* Melbourne Coll. of Divinity, 2009; Hon. DLitt Melbourne, 2014; Hon. Dr Social Work Sydney, 2015. *Publications:* Weighing up Australian Values, 2007; numerous papers, contribs to books, jls and conf. procs. *Recreations:* golf, reading, films, Australian Rules football. *Address:* PO Box 459, North Carlton, Vic 3054, Australia.

**HOWE, Prof. Christine Joyce,** PhD; Professor of Education, University of Cambridge, 2006–17, now Professor Emerita; Fellow, Lucy Cavendish College, Cambridge, 2007–17; *b* Birmingham, 21 Nov. 1948; *d* of Walter Virgil Howe and Joyce Winifred Howe (*née* Barmby); *m* 1979, William John Robertson; one *s* one *d. Educ:* Univ. of Sussex (BA 1st Cl. Hons); Univ. of Cambridge (PhD 1975). Lectr, Sussex Univ., 1974–76; Strathclyde University: Lectr, 1976–90; Sen. Lectr, 1990–95; Reader, 1995–98; Prof. of Psychol., 1998–2006. Mem., ESRC, 2004–08. Chm., Develtl Section, BPsS, 2006–08. FAcSS (AcSS 2008). *Publications:* Learning Language in a Conversational Context, 1983; Language Learning: a special case for developmental psychology, 1993, re-issued 2018; Group and Interactive Learning, 1994; Gender and Classroom Interaction, 1997; Conceptual Structure in Childhood and Adolescence: the case of everyday physics, 1998, re-issued 2016; Peer Groups and Children's Development, 2010; Educational Dialogues: understanding and promoting productive interactions, 2010; approx. 300 published articles and chapters. *Recreations:* bridge, tennis, hill-walking, music, theatre.

**HOWE, Prof. Christopher Barry,** MBE 1997; PhD; FBA 2001; Professor, Chinese Business Management, School of Oriental and African Studies, University of London, 2001–03, now Emeritus (Research Professor, 2003–06); Research Professor, School of East Asian Studies, University of Sheffield, 2006–08 (Hon. Professor, since 2009); *b* 3 Nov. 1937; *s* of Charles Roderick Howe and Patricia (*née* Creeden); *m* 1967, Patricia Anne Giles; one *s* one *d. Educ:* William Ellis Sch., London; St Catharine's Coll., Cambridge (MA); PhD London. Economic Secretariat, FBI, 1961–63; Sch. of Oriental and African Studies, London Univ., 1963–2006: Head, Contemp. China Inst., 1972–78; Prof. of Economics with ref. to Asia, 1979–2001. Member: Hong Kong Univ. and Polytechnic Grants Cttee, 1974–93; UGC, 1979–84; ESRC Res. Develt Gp, 1987–88; Hong Kong Res. Grants Council, 1994–99; HEFCE Wkg Party on Chinese Studies, 1998; China Panel, British Acad., 2002–. Foreign Advr to Haut Conseil de l'évaluation de la recherche et de l'enseignement supérieur, Paris (formerly l'Agence d'évaluation de la recherche et de l'enseignement supérieur), 2010–. Fellow, 48 Gp Club, 2003. *Publications:* Employment and Economic Growth in Urban China 1949–57, 1971; Industrial Relations and Rapid Industrialisation, 1972; Wage Patterns and Wage Policy in Modern China 1919–1972, 1973; China's Economy: a basic guide, 1978; (ed) Studying China, 1979; (ed) Shanghai: revolution and development, 1980; (ed) The Readjustment in the Chinese Economy, 1984; (with Kenneth R. Walker) The Foundations of the Chinese Planned Economy, 1989; (ed) China and Japan: history, trends and prospects, 1990; The Origins of Japanese Trade Supremacy, 1996; (ed with C. H. Feinstein) Chinese Technology Transfer in the 1990s, 1997; (with R. A. Ash and Y. Y. Kueh) China's Economic Reform, 2003; (with T.

Kambara) China and the Global Energy Crisis, 2007; China's Struggle for Science and Innovation, 2019. *Recreations:* music, walking, cycling, swimming. *Address:* 12 Highgate Avenue, N6 5RX. *T:* (020) 8340 8104.

**HOWE, Prof. Daniel Walker,** FRHistS; Rhodes Professor of American History, 1992–2002; Fellow of St Catherine's College, Oxford, 1992–2002, now Fellow Emeritus; *b* 10 Jan. 1937; *s* of Maurice Langdon Howe and Lucie Walker Howe; *m* 1961, Sandra Shumway; two *s* one *d. Educ:* Harvard (BA); Magdalen Coll., Oxford (MA); Univ. of California at Berkeley (PhD). Lieut, US Army, 1959–60. Yale University: Instructor, 1966–68; Asst Prof., 1968–73; University of California at Los Angeles: Associate Prof., 1973–77; Prof., 1977–92; Chm., History Dept, 1983–87. Harmsworth Vis. Prof., Oxford, 1989–90. Fellow: Charles Warren Center, Harvard, 1970–71; Nat. Endowment for Humanities, 1975–76; Guggenheim Foundn, 1984–85; Res. Fellow, Huntington Library, 1991–92, 2002–03. FRHistS 2002. Hon. DHum Weber State Univ., 2014. Amer. Historian Laureate, 2008; Pulitzer Prize in History, 2008. *Publications:* The Unitarian Conscience, 1970, 2nd edn 1988; Victorian America, 1976; The Political Culture of the American Whigs, 1980; Making the American Self, 1997; What Hath God Wrought, 2007; articles in learned jls. *Recreations:* music, grandchildren. *Address:* St Catherine's College, Oxford OX1 3UJ. *T:* (01865) 271700; 3814 Cody Road, Sherman Oaks, CA 91403, USA.

**HOWE, Darren Francis;** QC 2015; a Recorder, since 2012; a Deputy High Court Judge, since 2016; *b* Cuckfield, Sussex, 3 April 1969; *s* of Peter John Howe and Carmel Howe; *m* 2006, Antonio Delgado. *Educ:* Chailey Comprehensive Sch.; Haywards Heath Sixth Form Coll.; Univ. of Hull (LLB Hons); Inns of Court Sch. of Law. Called to the Bar, Gray's Inn, 1992; in practice as barrister, Brighton, 1993–2006, London, 2006–; a Dep. District Judge, 2010–13. *Publications:* (contrib.) DIY Divorce and Separation: the expert guide to representing yourself, 2014. *Recreations:* running, off-road cycling, travel, cinema, music. *Address:* 1GC Family Law, 10–11 Lincoln's Inn Fields, WC2A 3BP. *T:* (020) 7797 7900. *E:* clerks@1gc.com. *Club:* h.

**HOWE, Prof. Denis;** Professor of Aircraft Design, 1973–92, College of Aeronautics, Cranfield Institute of Technology, now Professor Emeritus, Cranfield University; *b* 3 Sept. 1927; *s* of Alfred and Alice Howe; *m* 1st, 1954, Audrey Marion Wilkinson; two *s* three *d*; 2nd, 1981, Catherine Bolton. *Educ:* Watford Grammar Sch.; MIT (SM); College of Aeronautics (PhD). CEng, FIMechE, FRAeS. Project Engineer, Fairey Aviation Co., 1945–54; College of Aeronautics, Cranfield Institute of Technology: Lectr, Sen. Lectr and Reader, 1954–73; Head of College, 1986–90; Dean of Engineering, 1988–91. *Publications:* Aircraft Conceptual Design Synthesis, 2000; Aircraft Loading and Structural Layout, 2004; contribs to learned jls. *Recreations:* gardening, church administration. *Address:* 78 Albert Road, Gourock PA19 1NL. *T:* (01475) 633468.

**HOWE, Derek Andrew,** CBE 1991; former public affairs and political consultant and company director; *b* 31 Aug. 1934; *o s* of late Harold and Elsie Howe; *m* 1st, 1958, Barbara (*née* Estill); two *d*; 2nd, 1975, Sheila (*née* Digger), MBE (*d* 1990); one *s*; 3rd, 1996, Penny (*née* James) (*d* 2012). *Educ:* City of Leeds Sch.; Cockburn High Sch., Leeds. Journalist, Yorkshire Evening News, 1951–61; Conservative Central Office, 1962–70; Parliamentary Liaison Officer, 1970–73; Special Adviser, 1973–75; Press Officer, Leader of HM Opposition, 1975–79; special adviser to: Paymaster Gen., 1979–81; Chancellor of Duchy of Lancaster, 1981; Political Secretary, 10 Downing Street, 1981–83 and Special Adviser to Leader of the House of Commons, 1982–83. Chm., Churchill Clinic, 1996–99 (Dep. Chm., 1995–96). Trustee, London Youth Trust, 1985–2005 (Chm. Trustees, 1988–2004). Freeman of the City of London. *Recreations:* gardening, reading, antiques, philately, Freemasonry. *Address:* The Vines, Kimpton, near Andover, Hampshire SP11 8NU; 47 Old Market Street, Usk NP15 1AL.

**HOWE, Eric James,** CBE 1990; Data Protection Registrar, 1984–94; *b* 4 Oct. 1931; *s* of Albert Henry Howe and Florence Beatrice (*née* Hale); *m* 1967, Patricia Enid (*née* Schollick); two *d. Educ:* Stretford Grammar Sch.; Univ. of Liverpool (BA Econs 1954). FIDPM 1990; FBCS 1972. NCB, 1954–59; British Cotton Industry Res. Assoc., 1959–61; English Electric Computer Co., 1961–66; National Computing Centre, 1966–84: Dep. Dir, 1975–84; Mem. Bd of Dirs, 1976–84. Chairman: National Computer Users Forum, 1977–84; Focus Cttee for Private Sector Users, DoI, 1982–84; Member: User Panel, NEDO, 1983–84; Council, British Computer Soc., 1971–74 and 1980–83; NW Regional Council, CBI, 1977–83. Chm. Bd, N Wales Housing Assoc., 2003–05 (Bd Mem., 1997–2006). Rep. UK, Confedn of Eur. Computer Users Assocs, 1980–83. *Recreations:* gardening, golf.

**HOWE, Geoffrey Michael Thomas;** Chairman: Jardine Lloyd Thompson Group plc, since 2006 (Director, 2002–04, Joint Deputy Chairman, 2004–06); Nationwide Building Society, 2007–15 (Director, 2005–15); *b* 3 Sept. 1949; *s* of Michael Edward Howe and Susan Dorothy Howe (*née* Allan); *m* 1995, Karen Mary Webber (*née* Ford); two *d. Educ:* Manchester Grammar Sch.; St John's Coll., Cambridge (MA). Solicitor. Stephenson Harwood, 1971–75; joined Clifford Chance, 1975; Partner, Corporate Dept, 1980; Man. Partner, 1989–97; Gen. Counsel and Dir, Robert Fleming Hldgs Ltd, 1998–2000; Chm., Railtrack Gp plc, 2002. Director: Gateway Electronic Components Ltd, 2000–; Investec plc, 2003–10; Close Brothers Gp, 2011–. *Recreations:* opera, wine, antiques, paintings.

**HOWE, Ven. George Alexander;** Chief of Staff and Chaplain to Bishop of Carlisle, and Diocesan Director of Ordinands, Diocese of Carlisle, 2011–15; Archdeacon of Westmorland and Furness, 2000–11, now Archdeacon Emeritus; *b* 22 Jan. 1952; *s* of late Eugene Howe and Olivia Lydia Caroline Howe (*née* Denroche); *m* 1980, Jane Corbould; one *s* one *d. Educ:* Liverpool Inst. High Sch.; Univ. of Durham (BA 1973); Westcott House, Cambridge. Ordained deacon, 1975, priest, 1976; Curate: St Cuthbert, Peterlee, 1975–79; St Mary, Norton, Stockton-on-Tees, 1979–81; Vicar, Utd Benefice of Hart with Elwick Hall, 1981–85; Rector, St Edmund, Sedgefield, 1985–91; Rural Dean of Sedgefield, 1988–91; Vicar, Holy Trinity, Kendal, 1991–2000; Rural Dean of Kendal, 1994–99. Hon. Canon, Carlisle Cathedral, 1994–. Diocesan Ecumenical Officer (formerly Bishop's Advr for Ecumenical Affairs), dio. of Carlisle, 2001–11. Chm., Church and Community Fund, 2007–13. *Recreations:* listening to The Archers, walking the dog, good food and wine, cartology. *Address:* 29 Forge Bank, Bosbury, Ledbury, Herefordshire HR8 1QU.

**HOWE, Jeremy Peter;** Editor, The Archers, BBC Radio 4, since 2018; *b* London, 16 Nov. 1956; *s* of Robert and Marjorie Howe; *m* 1st, 1981, Elizabeth Milicevic (*d* 1992); two *d*; 2nd, 1998, Jennifer Howarth. *Educ:* Dulwich Coll.; St Edmund Hall, Oxford (BA Hons English). Associate Dir, York Th. Royal, Colchester Mercury, then freelance dir, Royal Court, Lyric Belfast, Nottingham Playhouse, 1981–86; Drama Producer, BBC NI, 1986–89; Asst Commng Ed., Film 4/Channel 4, 1989–91; Ed., Drama, BBC Radio 3, 1991–94; Exec. Producer, Television, Bristol, BBC, 1994–2006; Commng Ed., Drama, 2006–16, Drama and Fiction, 2016–18, BBC Radio 4. *Publications:* Mummydaddy, 2012. *Recreations:* my family, writing, travelling Europe, being in the desert. *Address:* c/o The Archers, BBC Birmingham, The Mailbox, Royal Mail Street, Birmingham B1 1RF. *E:* jeremy.howe@bbc.co.uk.

**HOWE, John Francis**, CB 1996; OBE 1974; Chairman, Citylink Telecommunications Ltd, since 2004; *b* 29 Jan. 1944; *s* of late Frank and Marjorie Howe; *m* 1981, Angela Ephrosini (*née* Nicolaides); one *d* one step *d*. *Educ*: Shrewsbury Sch.; Balliol Coll., Oxford (Scholar; MA). Pirelli General Cable Works, 1964; joined MoD as Asst Principal, 1967; Principal, 1972; Civil Adviser to GOC NI, 1972–73; Private Sec. to Perm. Under-Sec. of State, 1975–78; Asst Sec., 1979; seconded to FCO as Defence Counsellor, UK Delegn to NATO, 1981–84; Head, Arms Control Unit, MoD, 1985–86; Private Sec. to Sec. of State for Defence, 1986–87; Asst Under-Sec. of State (Personnel and Logistics), 1988–91; Dep. Under-Sec. of State (Civilian Management), 1992–96; Dep. Chief of Defence Procurement (Support), 1996–2000; on secondment to Thomson CSF Racal, subseq. Thales, plc, 2000–02, Sen. Defence Advr, 2001–02. Vice Chm., 2002–09, non-exec. Mem., Adv. Bd, 2009–, Thales UK plc. Chm., Security and Resilience Industry Suppliers' Community, 2009–11; Pres., EuroDefense UK, 2010–. Chm., Frederick Bonnart-Braunthal Scholarship Trust, 2014–16 (Trustee, 2002–16); Trustee: MapAction, 2010–15; RUSI, 2011–17. *Recreations*: travel, garden labour, paintings, charity work. *Club*: Athenæum.

**HOWE, Martin**, CB 1995; PhD; self-employed consultant on competition policy, 1998–2010; Director, Competition Policy Division, Office of Fair Trading, 1984–96; *b* 9 Dec. 1936; *s* of late Leslie Wistow Howe and Dorothy Vernon Howe (*née* Taylor Farrell); *m* 1959, Anne Cicely Lawrenson; three *s*. *Educ*: Leeds Univ. (BCom (Accountancy)); Sheffield Univ. (PhD). Asst Lectr, Lectr, Sen. Lectr, in Economics, Univ. of Sheffield, 1959–73; Senior Economic Adviser: Monopolies Commn, 1973–77; Office of Fair Trading, 1977–80; Asst Secretary, OFT and DTI, 1980–84. Consultant, UNCTAD, 1996–98. Special Prof., Univ. of Nottingham Business Sch., 1994–2003. Associate, Europe Economics, 1998–2006. *Publications*: Equity Issues and the London Capital Market (with A. J. Merrett and G. D. Newbould), 1967; Rockley Wilson: remarkable cricketer, singular man, 2008; Frank Sugg: a man for all seasons, 2011; Norman Yardley: Yorkshire's gentleman cricketer, 2015; articles on variety of topics in learned and professional jls; articles in cricket jls. *Recreations*: theatre (including amateur dramatics), cricket, gardening, bowls. *Address*: 6 Mansdale Road, Redbourn, Herts AL3 7DN. *T*: (01582) 792074. *E*: martinhowe1@sky.com.

**HOWE, Martin John**; Founding Partner and Senior Partner, Howe & Co. Solicitors, since 1991; *b* London, 12 Dec. 1958; *s* of Michael Howe and Margaret Howe (*née* O'Brien); *m* 1992, Guldil Dilmec; one *s* one *d*. *Educ*: Sheffield Univ. (BA Hons Law 1980). Admitted solicitor, 1983; in practice as solicitor, Sheffield, until 1986, London, 1986–91; estab. Howe & Co., specialising in human rights and personal injury cases. Exec. Dir, Liberty, 2012–. Founding Mem., HUSH, 1997; co-founder, Gurkha Justice Campaign, 2008. *Recreations*: travel (especially road trips), reading, playing the guitar, sport. *Address*: Howe & Co. Solicitors, 1010 Great West Road, Brentford TW8 9BA. *T*: (020) 8840 4688. *E*: law@howe.co.uk.

**HOWE, Martin Russell Thomson**; QC 1996; *b* 26 June 1955; *s* of late Colin Howe, FRCS and Dr Angela Howe, *d* of Baron Brock, surgeon; *m* 1989, Lynda Barnett; one *s* three *d*. *Educ*: Trinity Hall, Cambridge (BA, Pt I Engrg, Pt II Law; Baker Prize for Engrg, 1974; MA). Called to the Bar, Middle Temple, 1978 (Harmsworth Exhibnr), Bencher, 2013; in practice, specialising in intellectual property and European law, 1980–; Appointed Person for design appeals under Intellectual Property Act 2014, 2015–. Councillor (C), London Borough of Hammersmith and Fulham, 1982–86 (Chm., Planning Cttee, 1985–86). Contested (C) Neath (S Wales), 1987. Member: Coalition Govt Commn on a Bill of Rights for the UK, 2011–13; Cons. Party Commn on Human Rights and Eur. Convention, 2013–. Chm., Lawyers for Britain, 2016–; *Publications*: Europe and the Constitution after Maastricht, 1992; (ed) Russell-Clarke on Industrial Designs, 6th edn, 1998 to 9th edn, as Russell-Clarke & Howe on Industrial Designs, 2016; contrib. Halsbury's Laws of England, 1986, 1995, 2000; Tackling Terrorism: the European Human Rights Convention and the enemy within, 2001, 2nd edn 2003; A Constitution for Europe: a legal assessment of the Treaty, 2003, 2nd edn 2005; numerous articles in legal jls and pamphlets on European constitutional issues and intellectual property law. *Address*: 8 New Square, Lincoln's Inn, WC2A 3QP.
*See also R. P. T. Howe.*

**HOWE, Robert Paul Thomson**; QC 2008; *b* England, 12 May 1964; *s* of late Colin Howe and Hon. Angela Howe; *m* 1998, Rosella Albano; two *d*. *Educ*: Trinity Hall, Cambridge (BA 1986); St Edmund Hall, Oxford (BCL). Called to the Bar, Middle Temple, 1988. *Address*: Blackstone Chambers, Blackstone House, Temple, EC4Y 9BW.
*See also M. R. T. Howe.*

**HOWE, His Honour Ronald William**; Director of Appeals, General Dental Council, 1999–2004; a Circuit Judge, 1991–97 (Deputy Circuit Judge, 1997–2000); *b* 19 June 1932; *s* of William Arthur and Lilian Mary Howe; *m* 1956, Jean Emily Goodman; three *s* one *d*. *Educ*: Morpeth Sch.; Coll. of Law, London. Admitted Solicitor, 1966; partner with Ronald Brooke & Co., Ilford, then Brooke, Garland & Howe, 1966–75; Registrar of County Court, subseq. Dist Judge, 1975–91. Mem., Judicial Studies Bd, 1990–91 (Mem., Civil and Family Cttee, 1988–91; Tutor, 1987–91); Advocacy Trng Advr, Law Soc., 1998–2000. *Recreations*: gardening, an increasing use of my computer, golf (not as often as I would like), masonry.

**HOWE, Stephen Douglas**; Editor, Farmers Weekly, 1991–2005; Associate Publisher, Farmers Weekly Group, 2000–05; *b* 28 Feb. 1948; *m* 1971, Susan Jane Apps; one *s* one *d*. *Educ*: Brymore Sch., Somerset; Seale-Hayne Coll. (DipAgr); NDA, Dip Farm Management. Lectr in Crop Husbandry and Arable Manager, Lackham Coll. of Agric., Wilts, 1969–72; Power Farming magazine: Management Specialist, 1972–82; Managing Editor, 1982–85; Agricultural Machinery Jl, 1985–87; Editor, Crops, 1987–91. Dir, British Crop Protection Enterprises Ltd, 2005–08; Business Develt Advr, UBM/Farmers Guardian, 2007–12. Governor: Inst. of Grassland and Environmental Res., 1996–2000; Nat. Fedn of Young Farmers, 1999–2000. Pres., Eurofarm, 1999–2006. Member: Council, RASE, 2005– (Trustee, 2009–17); Exec., BCPC, 2008– (Trustee, 2014–18); Trustee, Guild of Agricultural Journalists' Charitable Trust, 2005– (Chm., 2008–). Fellow, Guild of Agricultural Journalists, 1991; FRAgS 2008 (ARAgS 2003). Hon. Life Mem., Royal Smithfield Club, 2004. Hon. DArts Plymouth, 2000. *Recreations*: gardening, sailing, farming. *Address*: Springfield Cottage, Byers Lane, South Godstone, Surrey RH9 8JH. *T*: (01342) 893018. *Club*: Farmers.

**HOWE, Timothy Jean-Paul**; QC 2008; *b* London, 12 June 1963; *s* of late Prof. Alan Howe and of Mireille Howe; *m* 1990, Katharine Jane Zisman; one *s* two *d*. *Educ*: St Paul's Sch., London (First Foundn Schol.); Magdalen Coll., Oxford (Anne Shaw Open Schol.; BA 1st Cl. Hons Lit.Hum.; Editor, Isis, 1983–84); City Univ. (Dip. Law with Dist. 1986). Called to the Bar, Middle Temple, 1987 (Queen Mother's Fund, Astbury and Harmsworth Scholarships); in practice as barrister, specialising in commercial law, 1988–. Sec. and Mem., Exec. Cttee, Commercial Bar Assoc., 1997–2008; Chm., Member Services Bd, Bar Council, 2008–11. CEDR Accredited Mediator, 2004. Trustee, BHF, 2018–. Gov., Godolphin and Latymer Sch., 2011–. *Publications*: (ed jtly) Commercial Court Procedure, (contrib.) Law of Bank Payments. *Recreations*: collecting modern British art, wine, travel, ballet and opera. *Address*: Fountain Court Chambers, Temple, EC4Y 9DH. *T*: (020) 7583 3335. *E*: th@fountaincourt.co.uk. *Club*: Hurlingham.

**HOWELL**, family name of **Baron Howell of Guildford**.

**HOWELL OF GUILDFORD**, Baron *cr* 1997 (Life Peer), of Penton Mewsey in the co. of Hampshire; **David Arthur Russell Howell**; PC 1979; journalist and economist; *b* 18 Jan. 1936; *s* of late Colonel A. H. E. Howell, DSO, TD, DL and Beryl Howell, 5 Headfort Place, SW1; *m* 1967, Davina Wallace; one *s* two *d*. *Educ*: Eton; King's Coll., Cambridge (BA 1st class hons 1959). Lieut Coldstream Guards, 1954–56. Joined Economic Section of Treasury, 1959; resigned, 1960. Leader-Writer and Special Correspondent, The Daily Telegraph, 1960–64; Chm. of Bow Gp, 1961–62; Editor of Crossbow, 1962–64; contested (C) Dudley, 1964. MP (C) Guildford, 1966–97. A Lord Comr of Treasury, 1970–71; Parly Sec., CSD, 1970–72; Parly Under-Sec.: Dept of Employment, 1971–72; NI Office, March–Nov. 1972; Minister of State: NI Office, 1972–74; Dept of Energy, 1974; Secretary of State: for Energy, 1979–81; for Transport, 1981–83. Chairman: Select Cttee on Foreign Affairs, 1987–97; H of L Sub-Cttee on EC Foreign and Security Policy, 1999–2000; H of L Internat. Relns Cttee, 2016–. H of L Opposition spokesman on foreign affairs, 2000–10; Dep. Leader of the Opposition, H of L, 2005–10; Minister of State, FCO, 2010–12. Chairman: Cons. One Nation Gp, 1987–97; UK-Japan 21st Century (formerly 2000) Group, 1990–2001. Sen. Vis. Fellow, PSI, 1983–85; Vis. Fellow, Nuffield Coll., Oxford, 1993–2001. Dir of Conservative Political Centre, 1964–66. Director: Jardine Insurance Brokers, 1991–97; Monks Investment Trust, 1993–2004; John Laing Plc, 1999–2002; Adv. Dir, UBS (formerly SBC Warburg), 1997–2000; Advisor: Japan Central Railway Co., 2001–10, 2013–; Mitsubishi Electric, Europe, BV, 2003–10, 2013–; Kuwait Investment Office, 2003–10, 2013–; Hermitage Global Fund, 2007–10. Mem., Internat. Adv. Council, Swiss Bank Corp., 1988–97. President: BIEE, 2006–13; Energy Industries Council, 2013–. Governor, Sadler's Wells Trust, 1995–98; Trustee: Shakespeare Globe Theatre, 2000–10; Duke of Edinburgh's Commonwealth Conferences, 2008–10; Chm. Council, Commonwealth Socs, 2013–; Pres., Royal Commonwealth Soc., 2013–. *Publications*: (co-author) Principles in Practice, 1960; The Conservative Opportunity, 1965; Freedom and Capital, 1981; Blind Victory: a study in income, wealth and power, 1986; The Edge of Now, 2000; Out of the Energy Labyrinth, 2007; Old Links and New Ties: power and persuasion in an age of networks, 2013; Empires in Collision: green versus black in our energy future, 2016; various pamphlets and articles. *Recreations*: writing, history, travel. *Address*: House of Lords, SW1A 0PW. *Club*: Beefsteak.
*See also Rt Hon. G. G. O. Osborne.*

**HOWELL, Anthony**; Chief Education Officer, 2002–11, Strategic Director, Children, Young People and Families (formerly Learning and Culture), 2003–11, Birmingham City Council; *b* 7 Jan. 1951; *s* of late Bernard Howell and Katherine Howell; *m* 1975, Hilary Helen Ellis; one *s* one *d*. *Educ*: Xaverian Coll., Manchester; Univ. of Liverpool (BSc Zool.); Univ. of Bristol. Teacher, 1975; Chief Advr, Derbys LEA, 1995–2002; Dep. Chief Educn Officer, Birmingham CC, 2002. Bd Mem., Birmingham and Solihull Connexions, 2002; Bd Mem. and Trustee, Acad. of Youth/Univ. of the First Age, 2002; BECTA Educn Cttee, 2002–11. Pres., Soc. of Chief Inspectors and Advrs, 1999.

**HOWELL, Gareth**, CBE 1993; PhD; CChem; Director, British Council, Malaysia, 1990–95; *b* 22 April 1935; *s* of Amwel John and Sarah Blodwen Howell; *m* 1957, Margaret Patricia Ashelford; one *s* two *d*. *Educ*: Ferndale Grammar Sch., Rhondda; University College London; Inst. of Education, Univ. of London. BSc, PhD; PGCE London. MRSC. Asst Master, Canford Sch., Wimborne, Dorset, 1957–61; Lectr, Norwich City Coll., 1961–65; British Council: Science Educn Officer, London, 1965–66; Science Educn Officer, Nigeria, 1966–70; Head, Science Educn Section, 1970–74; Director, Science and Technology Dept, 1974; Representative, Malawi, 1974–76; on secondment to Min. of Overseas Development as Educn Adviser, 1976–79; Counsellor and Dep. Educn Adviser, British Council Div., British High Commn, India, 1979–83; Controller: Sci., Technol. and Educn Div., 1983–87; Americas, Pacific and E Asia Div., 1987–90. *Recreations*: photography, philately, gardening, tennis, walking, travel. *Address*: 9 Alderway, West Cross, Swansea SA3 5PD.

**HOWELL, Gwynne Richard**, CBE 1998; Principal Bass, Royal Opera House, 1971; *b* Gorseinon, S Wales, 13 June 1938; *s* of Gilbert and Ellaline Howell; *m* 1968, Mary Edwina Morris; two *s*. *Educ*: Pontardawe Grammar Sch.; Univ. of Wales, Swansea (BSc; Hon. Fellow 1986); Manchester Univ. (DipTP); MRTPI 1966. Studied singing with Redvers Llewellyn while at UCW; pt-time student, Manchester RCM, with Gwilym Jones, during DipTP trng at Manchester Univ.; studied with Otakar Kraus, 1968–72. Planning Asst, Kent CC, 1961–63; Sen. Planning Officer, Manchester Corp., 1965–68, meanwhile continuing to study music pt-time and giving public operatic performances which incl. the rôle of Pogner, in Die Meistersinger, as a result of this rôle, apptd Principal Bass at Sadler's Wells, 1968; also reached final of BBC Opera Singers competition for N of Eng., 1967. In first season at Sadler's Wells, sang 8 rôles, incl. Monterone and the Commendatore; appearances with Hallé Orch., 1968 and 1969; Arkel in Pelleas and Melisande, Glyndebourne and Covent Garden, 1969; Goffredo, in Il Pirato, 1969. *Royal Opera House, Covent Garden*: début as First Nazarene, Salome, 1969–70 season; the King, in Aida; Timur, in Turandot; Mephisto, in Damnation of Faust; Prince Gremin, in Eugene Onegin; High Priest, in Nabucco; Reinmar, in Tannhauser, 1973–74 (later rôle, Landgraf); Colline, in La Bohème; Pimen, in Boris Godunov; Ribbing, Un ballo in maschera; Padre Guardiano, in La forza del destino; Hobson, in Peter Grimes, 1975; Sparafucile, in Rigoletto, 1975–76 season; Ramfis in Aida, 1977; Tristan und Isolde, 1978, 1982; Luisa Miller, 1978; Samson et Delilah, 1981; Fiesco in Simon Boccanegra, 1981; Pogner in Die Meistersinger, 1982; Arkel in Pelléas et Mélisande, 1982; Dossifei in Khovanshchina, 1982; Semele, 1982; Die Zauberflöte, 1983; Raimondo, in Lucia di Lammermoor, 1985; Rocco in Fidelio, 1986; Marcel in Les Huguenots, 1991; Daland in Der Fliegende Holländer, 1992; Katya Kabanova, 1994; Stiffelio, 1995; Mathis der Maler, 1995; The Bartered Bride, 1998; Greek Passion, 2000; The Tempest (world première), 2004; *English National Opera*: Don Carlos, Die Meistersinger, 1974–75; The Magic Flute, Don Carlos, 1975–76; Duke Bluebeard's Castle, 1978, 1991; The Barber of Seville, 1980; Tristan and Isolde, 1981; Hans Sachs in Die Meistersinger, 1984; Parsifal, 1986; Don Carlos, 1992; Banquo in Macbeth, 1993; Fidelio, 1996; Mary Stuart, 1998; Silver Tassie (world première), 2000; War and Peace, 2001; Lulu, 2002; Dansker in Billy Budd, 2005, 2012; Aida, 2007; *Metropolitan Opera House, New York*: début as Lódovico in Otello, and Pogner in Die Meistersinger, 1985; *Bastille, Paris*: début in Parsifal, 1997; *sacred music*: Verdi and Mozart Requiems, Missa Solemnis, St Matthew and St John Passions; sings in Europe and USA; records for BBC and for major recording companies. *Recreations*: tennis, golf, Rugby enthusiast, gardening. *Address*: 197 Fox Lane, N13 4BB. *T* and *Fax*: (020) 8886 1981.

**HOWELL, John Frederick**; Director, Overseas Development Institute, 1987–97 (Senior Research Associate, 1997–2016); *b* 16 July 1941; *s* of late Frederick Howell and Glenys Griffiths; *m* 1993, Paula Wade; two *s*, and one step *s*. *Educ*: Univ. of Wales (BA Hons 1963); Univ. of Manchester (MA Econ. Dist. 1965); Univ. of Reading (external; PhD). Lectr, Univ. of Khartoum, 1966–73; correspondent, Africa Confidential, 1971–75; Sen. Lectr,

Univ. of Zambia, 1973–77; Overseas Development Institute, 1977–2016; seconded as Advr, Min. of Agric. and Land Affairs, S Africa, 1997–2001. Vis. Lectr, Mananga Agric. Management Centre, Swaziland, 1978–80; Vis. Prof. in Agricl Develt, Wye Coll., Univ. of London, 1988–96. Consultant on aid and agricl develt: World Bank; EC; FAO; Commonwealth Secretariat; DFID in S Africa, India, Nepal, Nigeria, Brazil, Tanzania, Malawi, Sudan; Adviser: All-Party Parly Gp on Overseas Develt, 1985–86; Princess Royal's Africa Review Gp, 1987–89; Economic Advr, Chagos Refugees Gp, 2008–10. Mem. Council, VSO, 1991–97. Pres., UK Chapter, Soc. of Internat. Develt, 1991–93. *Publications:* Local Government and Politics in the Sudan, 1974; (ed) Borrowers and Lenders: rural financial markets and institutions in developing countries, 1980; Administering Agricultural Development for Small Farmers, 1981; (ed) Recurrent Costs and Agricultural Development, 1985; (ed) Agricultural Extension in Practice, 1988; (with Alex Duncan) Structural Adjustment and the African Farmer, 1992. *Address:* 3 Elers Road, Ealing, W13 9QA.

**HOWELL, John Michael**, OBE 2000; DPhil; MP (C) Henley, since June 2008; *b* London, 27 July 1955; *s* of Alexander J. Howell and Gladys S. Howell; *m* 1987, Alison Parker; one *s* two *d*. *Educ:* Battersea Grammar Sch.; Univ. of Edinburgh (MA 1978); St John's Coll., Oxford (DPhil 1981). Ernst & Young, 1987–96; Business Presenter, BBC World Service TV, 1996–97; Director: Fifth World Prodns Ltd, 1996–2003; Media Presentation Consultants Ltd, 2005–08. Mem. (C), Oxfordshire CC, 2004–09 (Cabinet Mem. for Change Mgt, 2005–08). PPS to Leader, H of C, 2010–14; to Minister of State, DCLG, 2010–12, to Sec. of State for Housing, Communities and Local Govt, 2018–. Member: Justice Select Cttee, 2014–; Executive, 1922 Cttee, 2014–16; Chairman, All-Party Parliamentary Group: for Alternative Dispute Resolutions, 2015–; for River Thames, 2016–; for Fusion Technol., 2017–; for Digital Currencies, 2017–; Mem., All Party Parly Gp for Design and Innovation, 2014– (Jt Chm., 2017–). Prime Minister's Trade Envoy to Nigeria, 2016–. Mem., Council of Europe, 2016–. Neighbourhood Planning Champion, 2016–. *Publications:* Neolithic Northern France, 1983; Understanding Eastern Europe: the context of change, 1994. *Recreations:* music, theatre. *Address:* House of Commons, SW1A 0AA. *T:* (020) 7219 4828, 7219 6676, *Fax:* (020) 7219 2606. *E:* howellJm@parliament.uk; PO Box 84, Watlington, Oxon OX49 5XD. *T:* (01491) 613072. *Club:* Leander (Henley).

**HOWELL, Leslie**, CBE 1996; Chairman, St Helens and Knowsley Teaching Hospital NHS Trust, 2008–13; *b* Liverpool, 11 Oct. 1943; *s* of Philip Leslie Howell and Gladys Howell; *m* 1969, Joan; one *s* one *d*. *Educ:* Liverpool Collegiate Sch.; Open Univ. (BA 1973); INSEAD (MBA Gen. Mgt Prog. 1986). FCII. Trainee, Liverpool and London Globe Insce Co., 1962; Royal Insurance, later Royal Sun Alliance: Claims Hd, 1965–68; Sen. Tutor, Trng Sch., 1968–70; Mktg Admin. Manager, 1970–72; Mgt Trng Officer, 1972–75; Mgt Trng Manager, 1975–78; HR Dir, British Engine Insce, 1978–81; on secondment to Govt Task Force, Liverpool, 1981–82; Trng and Develt Manager, 1982–83; BCG Consultants, 1984–85 (on secondment); Regl Manager, NW England, 1985–86; Dir and Gen. Manager, 1986–95; Gen. Manager, Gp Strategy, 1996–98; Sec. Gen., Comité Européen des Assurances, 1999–2002. Chairman: British Engine Insce, 1990–95; CIG Hldgs Ltd, 2002–06. Dir, Insce Ombudsman Bd, 1992–98; Chairman: Motor Insurers Bureau, 1994–98; Eur. Motor Cttee, Comité Européen des Assurances, 1994–98; Mem., British Insurers Internat. Cttee, 1993–98. Member: Nat. Council, TEC, 1996–98 (Chm., Merseyside TEC, 1995–98); Bd, NACETT, 1997–98. Member: Govt Task Force in Liverpool, 1981–82; Bd, Liverpool City Challenge, 1995–98. Vis. Prof., Business Sch., 1998–2008, Dir, 2002–, Liverpool John Moores Univ.; Director: Liverpool Univ., 1995–98; Liverpool Sch. of Tropical Medicine, 1996–98. Trustee, Lung Cancer Fund, 2001–04. *Recreations:* walking, music, family, cricket. *E:* les.howell1@btinternet.com. *Club:* Artists'.

**HOWELL, Margaret**, CBE 2007; RDI 2007; Designer and Creative Director, Margaret Howell Ltd, since 1986; *b* Tadworth, Surrey, 5 Sept. 1946; *d* of Edwin Harris Howell and Gladys Ivy Howell; *m* 1972, Paul Andrew Renshaw (marr. diss. 1987); one *d* (one *s* decd). *Educ:* Goldsmith's Coll., Univ. of London (DipAD). Self-employed clothes designer, 1970–86; founded Margaret Howell Ltd, 1986. Hon. Prof., Univ. of Creative Arts, 2013. Hon. Fellow, Goldsmith's, Univ. of London, 2015. Hon. Dr Univ. of Arts, London, 2010. *Recreations:* walking, swimming, photography, art exhibitions. *Address:* 6 Welbeck Way, W1G 9RZ. *T:* (020) 7009 9000, *Fax:* (020) 7009 9001. *E:* admin@margarethowell.co.uk.

**HOWELL, Michael Edward**, CMG 1989; OBE 1980; HM Diplomatic Service; High Commissioner, Mauritius, 1989–93; *b* 2 May 1933; *s* of Edward and Fanny Howell; *m* 1958, Joan Little; one *s* one *d*. *Educ:* Newport High Sch. Served RAF, 1951–53. Colonial Office, 1953; CRO, 1958; Karachi, 1959; 2nd Secretary: Bombay, 1962; UK Delegn to Disarmament Cttee, Geneva, 1966; 1st Sec. (Parly Clerk), FCO, 1969; Consul (Comm.), New York, 1973; ndc 1975; FCO, 1976; Hd of Chancery, later Chargé d'Affaires, Kabul, 1978; Consul-General: Berlin, 1981; Frankfurt, 1983; High Comr to Papua New Guinea, 1986. *Recreation:* golf. *Address:* c/o Foreign and Commonwealth Office, SW1A 2AH.

**HOWELL, Michael William Davis**; Director, Westinghouse Air Brake Technologies Corporation (USA) (Wabtec, Inc.), since 2003; *b* 11 June 1947; *s* of late Air Vice-Marshal Evelyn Michael Thomas Howell, CBE, and Helen Joan Hayes; *m* 1975, Susan Wanda Adie (marr. diss. 2017); two *s* one *d*. *Educ:* Charterhouse Sch., Godalming; Trinity Coll., Cambridge (BA 1968, MA 1969); INSEAD, Fontainebleau (MBA 1975); Harvard Business Sch. (MBA 1976). British Leyland Truck and Bus Division: Graduate Trainee, 1969–71; Personnel Manager, Leyland Nat., 1971–74; Cummins Engine Co. Inc.: Asst to Vice-Pres. Internat. (USA), 1976–77; Dir, European Mktg, Brussels, 1977–80; Vice-President: Europe (based in London), 1981–84; Corporate Strategy, 1984–88; Vice-Pres., GE Canada Inc., 1988–89; Gen. Manager, GE Transportation, 1989–91; Dir, Arlington Capital Partners (formerly Mgt) Ltd, 1991–96 (non-exec. Dir, 1996–2010); Commercial Dir, Railtrack Gp plc, 1996–97; Chm., FPT Gp Ltd, 1998–2002; Chief Exec., Transport Initiatives Edinburgh, subseq. tie ltd, 2002–06. Chm., Evo Electric Ltd, 2007–12; Dir, Hutchison China Meditech Ltd, 2006–17. Mem. Council, Univ. of Leeds, 2016–. City and Guilds of London Institute: Treas., 2003–06; Chm., 2006–12. Gov., Clothworkers' Foundn, 1999– (Master, 2014–15). *Recreations:* hill-walking, travel. *Address:* Cambridge CB21 5BL. *Club:* Oxford and Cambridge.

**HOWELL, Patrick Leonard**; QC 1990; *b* 4 Dec. 1942; *s* of Leonard Howell, MC, and Mary Isobel (*née* Adam); *m* 1966, Sandra Marie McColl; two *s* one *d*. *Educ:* Radley; Christ Church, Oxford (MA); London Sch. of Econs and Pol Science (LLM). Called to the Bar: Inner Temple, 1966; Lincoln's Inn, 1968. Teaching Fellow, Osgoode Hall Law Sch., Toronto, 1965–66. An Upper Tribunal Judge (Administrative Appeals, Tax and Chancery Chambers) (formerly Social Security Comr and Child Support Comr), 1994–2012; a Judge, Employment Appeal Tribunal, 1999–2012.

**HOWELL, Peter Adrian**; Senior Lecturer, Department of Classics, Royal Holloway and Bedford New College, University of London, 1994–99 (Lecturer, 1985–94), now Hon. Research Fellow; *b* 29 July 1941; *s* of Lt-Col Harry Alfred Adrian Howell, MBE and Madge Maud Mary, *d* of Major-Gen. R. L. B. Thompson, CB, CMG, DSO. *Educ:* Downside School; Balliol College, Oxford (BA 1963; MA; MPhil 1966). Asst Lectr and Lectr, Dept of Latin, Bedford Coll., Univ. of London, 1964–85. Dep. Chm., Jt Cttee, Nat. Amenity Socs, 1991–93; Member: Cttee, Victorian Soc., 1968–2005 (Chm., 1987–93); Westminster Cathedral Art Cttee, 1974–91, 1993–; Dept of Art and Architecture, Liturgy Commn, RC Bishops' Conf., 1977–84; Churches Cttee, English Heritage, 1984–88; RC Historic Churches Cttee for Wales and Herefordshire, 1995–2015; Westminster Diocesan Historic Churches Cttee, 1995–99. Hon. DPhil Uppsala, 2016. *Publications:* Victorian Churches, 1968; (with Elisabeth Beazley) Companion Guide to North Wales, 1975; (with Elisabeth Beazley) Companion Guide to South Wales, 1977; A Commentary on Book I of the Epigrams of Martial, 1980; (ed with Ian Sutton) The Faber Guide to Victorian Churches, 1989; (ed and trans.) Martial: the Epigrams Book V, 1995; Martial, 2009; articles in Architectural History, Country Life. *Recreations:* art, architecture, music. *Address:* 127 Banbury Road, Oxford OX2 6JX. *T:* (01865) 515050.

**HOWELL, Robert**; theatre designer; *b* Liverpool, 14 Nov. 1966; *s* of Stuart and Doreen Howell; *m* 1996, Gail Lonsdale; two *s*. *Educ:* John Hamden Grammar Sch.; Bucks Coll. of Higher Educn; Birmingham Poly. (BA 1st Cl. Hons). Resident Design Asst, RSC, 1989–91; freelance theatre designer, 1991–; *productions:* Relative Values, Chichester Fest. Th., 1993, then tour, transf. Savoy Th.; Eurovision, Sydmonton Fest. and Vaudeville Th., 1993; Oliver, Crucible Th., Sheffield, 1993; Private Lives, Dalateatern, Sweden, 1994; Julius Caesar, Royal Exchange, 1994; The Shakespeare Revue, RSC, 1994; True West, Donmar, 1994; Simpatico, Royal Ct, 1995; The Painter of Dishonour, RSC, 1995; The Glass Menagerie, Donmar, 1995; Tartuffe, Almeida, 1996; The Loves of Cass Maguire, Druid Th. Co., 1996; Habeas Corpus, Donmar, 1996; Peter Pan, W Yorks Playhouse, 1996; Little Eyolf, RSC, 1996; Tom and Clem, Aldwych, 1997; Chips with Everything, RNT, 1997; Entertaining Mr Sloane, Th. Clywd, 1997; The Government Inspector, Almeida, 1997; The Fix, Donmar, 1997; Eddie Izzard: Glorious Tour, 1997, 2000; How I Learned to Drive, Donmar, 1998; Richard III, RSC, 1998; Real Classy Affair, Royal Ct, 1998; Vassa, Almeida, 1999; Troilus and Cressida, Money, RNT, 1999; The Family Reunion, RSC, 1999; Betrayal, Th. d'Atelier, Paris, 1999; Battle Royal, RNT, 1999; Little Malcolm and his Struggle against the Eunuchs, Hampstead and West End, 1999; Eddie Izzard, UK Tour, 1999–2000; Hard Fruit, Royal Ct, 2000; Turn of the Screw, WNO, 2000; Conversations After a Burial, Almeida, 2000; The Caretaker, Guildford and Comedy Th., 2000; True West, Circle in the Sq., NY, 2000; Lulu, Almeida, transf. Kennedy Th., Washington, 2001; Howard Katz, RNT, 2001; Sunset Boulevard, UK tour, 2001; Faith Healer, Almeida, 2001, transf. West End, 2002; Proof, Donmar, 2002; Our House, West End, 2002; Sophie's Choice, ROH, 2002; The Graduate, Gielgud and Broadway, 2002 (UK tour, 2004); Simply Heavenly, Young Vic, 2003, transf. West End, 2004; The Lady from the Sea, Almeida, 2003; Tell Me on a Sunday, West End and UK tour, 2003; Endgame, West End, 2004; Buried Child, RNT, 2004; Hedda Gabler, Almeida, 2005 (Best Set Design, Olivier Awards, 2006); Lord of the Rings, Toronto, 2006, transf. Th. Royal Drury Lane, 2007 (Best Designer, What's On Stage Awards, Outstanding Costume Design, Dora Mavor Awards, 2006); Bash, Trafalgar Studios, 2007; The Reporter, RNT, 2007; Boeing Boeing, Comedy Th., 2007, transf. Broadway and UK tour, 2008; Speed-the-Plow, Old Vic, 2008; Our House, Birmingham Repertory and UK tour, 2008; Her Naked Skin, RNT, 2008; The Norman Conquests, Old Vic, 2008, transf. NY, 2009; Complicit, Old Vic, 2009; The Last Cigarette, Chichester and West End, 2009; The Observer, RNT, 2009; Inherit the Wind, Old Vic, 2009; Carmen, Metropolitan Opera, NY, 2009; Private Lives, The Prisoner of Second Avenue, Vaudeville, 2010; Deathtrap, Noel Coward, 2010; Matilda (The Musical), RSC, 2010, transf. NY, 2013, Australia, 2015, Korea, 2018, UK and US tours, 2018 (Best Set Design, Olivier Awards, 2012; Outstanding Set Design, Drama Desk Awards, Outer Critic Circle Awards, 2013; Helpmann Awards, 2016 and Green Room Awards, 2017, for Best Scenic Design and Best Costume Design); A Flea in her Ear, Old Vic, 2010; Ghost (The Musical), Manchester and London, 2011, transf. NY, 2012, UK and N American tours, 2013 (Outstanding Set Design, Drama Desk Awards, 2012); Philadelphia, Here I Come, Donmar, 2012; Stephen Ward, Aldwych, 2013; Fathers and Sons, Donmar Warehouse, 2014; Manon Lescaut, Baden Baden, 2014, Metropolitan Opera, NY, 2016; Le Nozze di Figaro, Metropolitan Opera, NY, 2014; The Lorax, Old Vic, 2015 and 2017, Minneapolis, 2018; Future Confidential, Old Vic, 2015; The Master Builder, The Caretaker, Old Vic, 2016; Groundhog Day, Old Vic, 2016, transf. NY, 2017; Long Day's Journey into Night, Bristol Old Vic, 2016, Wyndham's, 2018; Wild Honey, Hampstead, 2016; The Ferryman, Royal Court, then Gielgud, 2017; Venus in Fur, Th. Royal Haymarket, 2017; A Christmas Carol, Old Vic, 2017; Present Laughter, Old Vic, 2019; 8 Hotels, Minerva, Chichester, 2019. Best Set Designer for Troilus and Cressida, Vassa and Richard III, Olivier Awards, 2000; Best Designer, for Matilda (The Musical) and Ghost (The Musical), What's On Stage Awards, 2012. *Address:* c/o Judy Daish Associates, 2 St Charles Place, W10 6EG. *T:* (020) 8964 8811. *E:* judy@judydaish.com.

**HOWELL, Rupert Cortlandt Spencer**, FIPA; Group Development Director (formerly Group Transformation Director), Reach (formerly Trinity Mirror) plc, since 2013; *b* 6 Feb. 1957; *s* of late Lt Col F. R. Howell, MBE, RE, and S. D. L. Howell (*née* McCallum); *m* 1987, Claire Jane Ashworth; one *s* one *d*. *Educ:* Wellington Coll.; Univ. of Warwick (BSc Mgt Scis). FIPA 1995; Fellow, Marketing Soc., 2008. Mkting trainee, Lucas Service Overseas, 1978; Account Exec., Mathers Advertising, 1979–81; Account Supervisor, Grey Advertising, 1981–83; Young & Rubicam: Account Dir, 1983–84; New Business Dir, 1985–86; Hd, Client Services, 1987; Howell Henry Chaldecott Lury Ltd, subseq. HHCL & Partners; Founder, 1987; Man. Partner, 1987–97; Jt Chief Exec., 1997–98; Chm., 1999–2002; Jt Chief Exec., Chime Communications plc, 1997–2002; Chm., UK & Ireland, and Pres., Europe, Middle E and Africa, Interpublic Gp, subseq. McCann Worldgroup, 2003–07; Man. Dir, ITV Brand and Commercial, 2007–10; CEO, Phoenix Newspaper Publishing, 2011–13. Non-exec. Chm., Hey Human (formerly Billington Cartmell) Gp, 2012–17; non-exec. Chm., Matomy Media Ltd, 2015–17 (non-exec. Dep. Chm., 2014–15); Non-exec. Chair, Brave, Lagardere Sports and Entertainment, 2017–19. President: Inst. of Practitioners in Advertising, 1999–2001; Eur. Assoc. of Communication Agencies, 2006–07; Vice-Chm., Advertising Assoc., 2008–12. Trustee, Media Trust, 2008–19. Fellow, Mktg Soc. *Recreations:* theatre, travel, shooting; watching cricket, Rugby Union, soccer and golf. *Clubs:* MCC, Lord's Taverners, Thirty, Ivy (Founder Mem.).

**HOWELL, Prof. Simon Laurence**, PhD, DSc; Professor of Physiology, since 1985, Guy's Campus Dean, since 2005, and Director of Estates Strategy (Health), since 2015, King's College London (Director, Research and Development, 2007–15); *b* 29 June 1943; *s* of Laurence James Howell and Joan Kathleen Rosemary (*née* Wheelwright); *m* 1969, Linda Margaret Chapman (marr. diss. 2012); one *d*; partner, Rebecca Williams (*d* 2016). *Educ:* St John's Sch., Leatherhead; Chelsea Coll., London (BSc Hons 1964); KCL (PhD 1967); DSc London 1983. Res. Fellow, Univ. of Sussex, 1968–78; Lectr, Charing Cross Hosp. Med. Sch., London, 1978–80; Reader, Queen Elizabeth Coll., London, 1980–85; King's College London: Hd, Biomed. Scis Div., 1988–98; Hd, GKT Sch. of Biomed. Scis, 1998–2003; Dean, Faculty of Life Scis and Medicine, 2014–15. Chm., Diabetes UK, 2006–09 (Vice Chm., 2002–06). Dir, Sheffield Park Mgt Ltd, 2017–. Chair, Team London Bridge, 2017–. Chm., Lord Brock Meml Trust, 2011–. Minkowski Prize, Eur. Assoc. Study of Diabetes, 1983. *Publications:* (jtly) Biochemistry of the Polypeptide Hormones, 1985; (jtly) Diabetes and its Management, 5th edn 1996, 6th edn 2003; The Biology of the Pancreatic B Cell, 1999. *Recreations:* gardening, opera. *Address:* King's College London Faculty of Life Sciences and Medicine, Guy's Campus, SE1 1UL.

**HOWELL-JONES, Very Rev. Peter;** Dean of Blackburn, since 2017; *b* Liverpool, 15 March 1962; *s* of Eric Jones and Brenda Jones (*née* Penreth); *m* Siân Edwards; two *s* two *d*. *Educ:* Hillfoot Hey Sch., Liverpool; Huddersfield Sch. of Music (BMus 1984); Bretton Hall Coll. (PGCE 1985); St John's Coll., Nottingham (MA 1996). Festival Dir, Gower Music Internat., 1987–90; ordained deacon, 1993, priest, 1994; Asst Curate, St Matthew's, Walsall, 1993–98; Vicar, St Michael, Boldmere, 1998–2004; Chair, Birmingham House of Clergy, 2003–10; Dir for Mission, Dio. of Birmingham, 2005–11; Acting Dean, Birmingham Cathedral, 2008–10; Vice Dean, Chester Cathedral, 2011–17. Dir, Medic Malawi, 2017–. *Publications:* Pints of View, 2005. *Recreations:* cycling, ski-ing, hill-walking, cooking, international development. *Address:* The Deanery, Cathedral Close, Blackburn BB1 5AA. *T:* (01254) 277430. *E:* dean@blackburncathedral.co.uk.

**HOWELL WILLIAMS, Craig;** QC 2009; *b* Liverpool; *s* of late Peter and of Fiona Elizabeth Howell Williams; *m* 1994, Elizabeth Jill Ainger; one *s* one *d*. *Educ:* Univ. of Leeds (BA Hons); Council of Legal Educn. Called to the Bar, Gray's Inn, 1983; Accredited Mediator, CEDR, 2005; Accredited Evaluative Mediator, RICS, 2017. Jun. Counsel to Crown B Panel, 1993–99. Chm., London Luton Airport Consultative Cttee, 1999–2002; Lead Asst Comr, Boundary Commn for England, 2011–13; Member: RICS Mediation, later President's Panel, 2010–; Planning Mediation Panel, DCLG, 2012–15; Panel of Approved Counsel, Nat. Procurement Service for Wales, 2017–. MCIArb 2012. Trustee, Planning Aid for London, 2007–11; Associate Trustee, Lord Edmund-Davies Legal Educn Trust, 2019–. *Recreations:* music, theatre, books, films.

**HOWELLS,** family name of **Baroness Howells of St Davids**.

**HOWELLS OF ST DAVIDS,** Baroness *cr* 1999 (Life Peer), of Charlton in the London Borough of Greenwich; **Rosalind Patricia-Anne Howells,** OBE 1994; Chancellor, University of Bedfordshire, 2009–14; Vice Chair, London Voluntary Services Council, 1978–83; *b* Grenada, WI, 10 Jan. 1931; *m* 1955, John Charles Howells (*d* 2004); two *d*. *Educ:* St Joseph's Convent, Grenada; South West London Coll. (Cert. Welfare and Counselling); City Univ., Washington. Formerly Dep. High Comr for Grenada in London; Equal Opportunities Dir, Greenwich Council for Racial Equality, 1980–87; Chair, Lewisham Racial Equality Council, 1994–97; Mem., Commn on Future of Multi-Ethnic Britain, 1998–2000. Mem., H of L, 1999–2019. Governor, Avery Hill Coll., later Thames Poly., then Univ. of Greenwich, 1985–97. Trustee: West Indian Standing Conf.; City Parochial Foundn; Museum of Ethnic Arts; Women of the Year Cttee; Stephen Lawrence Charitable Trust; Pres., Windward Is Res. and Educn Foundn Trust, Univ. of St George's, Grenada, 2014–. Patron: Jason Roberts Foundn, 2012–; Greenwich and Bexley Hospice, 2014–16. DUniv Greenwich, 1998; Hon. DCL Northumbria, 2014. *Recreations:* travelling, adventurous food, all types of music.

**HOWELLS, Anne Elizabeth;** opera, concert and recital singer; Professor, Royal Academy of Music, since 1997; *b* 12 Jan. 1941; *d* of Trevor William Howells and Mona Hewart; *m* 1st, 1966, Ryland Davies, *qv* (marr. diss. 1981); 2nd, 1981, Stafford Dean (marr. diss. 1996); one *s* one *d*; 3rd, 1999. *Educ:* Sale County Grammar Sch.; Royal Manchester (subseq. Royal Northern) Coll. of Music (ARMCM; Hon. FRMCM); studied under Frederick Cox and Vera Rosza. Three seasons (Chorus), with Glyndebourne, 1964–66; at short notice given star rôle there in Cavalli's L'Ormindo, 1967; rôles there also include: Dorabella in Così fan Tutte; Cathleen in (world première of) Nicholas Maw's Rising of the Moon, 1970; the Composer in Ariadne; Diana in Calisto; under contract, 1969–71, subseq. Guest Artist, Royal Opera, Covent Garden; sings with Scottish Opera, ENO and major orchs in UK; recitals in Brussels and Vienna; operatic guest performances incl. La Scala (Milan), Chicago, Metropolitan (NY), San Francisco, Geneva, Brussels, Salzburg, Amsterdam, Hamburg (W German début), W Berlin, Paris. Rôles include: Lena in (world première of) Richard Rodney Bennett's Victory; Rosina in Barber of Seville; Cherubino in Marriage of Figaro; Zerlina in Don Giovanni; Giulietta in The Tales of Hoffmann; Orsini in Lucrezia Borgia; Ascanius in Benvenuto Cellini; Helen in King Priam; Judit in Bluebeard's Castle; Octavian in Der Rosenkavalier (video recording), 1985; Annius in La Clemenza di Tito (film of Salzburg prodn); Lady Hautdesert in (world première of) Gawain, 1994. Hon. RAM. *Recreations:* theatre, cinema, reading, writing (articles published in The Oldie Mag.). *Address:* c/o Royal Academy of Music, Marylebone Road, NW1 5HT.

**HOWELLS, Sir Eric (Waldo Benjamin),** Kt 1993; CBE 1986; farmer and landowner, since 1966; *b* 9 Aug. 1933; *s* of Vincent Vaughan Howells and Amy (*née* Jones); *m* 1960, Margaret Maisie Edwards; one *s* twin *d*. Sec. and Gen. Manager of a limited co., 1959–66; Director: Carmarthen and Pumsaint Farmers Ltd, 1997–2001; Welsh Milk Ltd, 2000–06. Chm., Whitland and Dist Abattoir Cttee, 2001–05; New Enterprise Timber Recycling Plant, 2007–. Former Chm., Pembrokeshire NFU. Mem., Llanddewi Velfrey Parish Community Council, 1967–2008 (Chm., 1967, 1974, 1981, 1988, 1995, 2001); Chm., 1978–87, Pres., 1987–90, Pembrokeshire Cons. and Unionist Assoc.; Wales Area Conservative Party: Treas., 1984–88; Dep. Chm., 1988–90; Chm., 1990–95; Pres., 1996–99; Life Vice-Pres. Chm., Wales Area Cons. European Co-ordinating Cttee, 1992–95; Mem. of numerous other local and nat. Cons. and other bodies; regular broadcaster on radio and television in English and Welsh. Deacon and Treas., Bethel Congregational Chapel, Llanddewi Velfrey, 1974–. *Recreations:* music, bee keeping, DIY, reading, writing. *Address:* Meadow View, Llanddewi Velfrey, Narberth, Pembrokeshire SA67 7EJ. *T:* (01994) 240205, 07754 124582. *E:* erichowells@rocketmail.com.

**HOWELLS, Gwyn;** Marketing and Communications Consultant, Gwyn Howells Marketing, since 2002; *b* 21 May 1949; *s* of late Emrys Howells and Edith Frances (*née* Taylor); *m* 1st, 1976, Margaret Anne Farrall (*d* 1995); one *s* one *d*; 2nd, 2003, Virginia Ann McCarthy. *Educ:* Lewis Sch. for Boys, Pengam; City of London Poly. (BSc Econs 1970). Sen. Brand Manager, Gallaher Ltd, 1971–82; Dir, Brand and Trade Mktg, Courage Ltd, 1982–89; Marketing Dir, Reebok UK Ltd, 1989–92; Marketing Dir, 1992–99, Dir Gen., 1999–2002, Meat and Livestock Commn. Liveryman, Butchers' Co., 2001 (Court Asst, 2013–; Warden, 2019–20). *Recreations:* Rugby football, tennis, theatre. *Address:* 30 Bewdley Street, N1 1HB. *Clubs:* Hampstead Rugby Football, Rhymney Rugby Football.

**HOWELLS, James Richard;** QC 2014; *b* Kent, 10 July 1971; *s* of Russell Mervyn Howells and Margaret Anne Howells; *m* 2001, Zoë Yasmin Khan; three *s*. *Educ:* Magdalene Coll., Cambridge (BA 1992; MA); Brasenose Coll., Oxford (BCL 1994). Called to the Bar, Middle Temple, 1995. *Recreations:* family, cinema, art and antiques, gym, obstacle course racing. *Address:* Boothby Graffoe; 1 Atkin Building, Gray's Inn, WC1R 5AT.

**HOWELLS, Rt Hon. Kim (Scott),** PC 2009; PhD; writer, painter and television presenter, since 2010; *b* 27 Nov. 1946; *s* of Glanville James and Joan Glenys Howells; *m* 1983, Eirlys Howells (*née* Davies); two *s* one *d*. *Educ:* Mountain Ash Grammar Sch.; Hornsey College of Art; Cambridge College of Advanced Technology (BA (Jt Hons)); Warwick Univ. (PhD). Steel-worker, 1969–70; Coal-miner, 1970–71; Lectr, 1975–79; Research Officer: Swansea Univ., 1979–82; NUM, S Wales Area, 1982–89. MP (Lab) Pontypridd, Feb. 1989–2010. Opposition Front bench spokesman on aid and develt, 1993–94, on foreign affairs, 1994, on home affairs, 1994–95, on trade and industry, 1995–97; Parliamentary Under-Secretary of State: DFEE, 1997–98; DTI, 1998–2001; DCMS, 2001–03; Minister of State: DfT, 2003–04; DfES, 2004–05; (Minister for the Middle East), FCO, 2005–08; Chm., Intelligence and Security Cttee, 2008–10. Pres., Sports Aid Cymru/Wales, 2017–. Mem., Chatham House, 2018–. Mem., British Mountaineering Council, 1993–. Presenter, The Miners' Strike: a personal memoir, BBC, 2014 (Gwyn Alf Williams Award, BAFTA Wales). *Recreations:* climbing, painting, jazz, cinema, literature, art, growing vegetables.

**HOWELLS, Philippa Mary;** see Hopkins, P. M.

**HOWELLS, Victoria, (Vikki);** Member (Lab) Cynon Valley, National Assembly for Wales, since 2016; *b* Cardiff, 7 June 1977; *d* of Clive and Lesley Munden; *m* 2004, Timothy Howells (marr. diss. 2018); one *d*. *Educ:* St John Baptist Ch in Wales High Sch., Aberdare; Univ. of Wales, Cardiff (BA Hons Internat. and Welsh Hist.; MA Modern Welsh Hist.); Univ. of Wales, Swansea (PGCE Secondary Hist.). Teacher of Hist., 2000–16, Asst Hd of Sixth Form, 2011–16, St Cenydd Community Sch., Caerphilly. *Address:* National Assembly for Wales, Cardiff Bay, Cardiff CF99 1NA. *T:* 0300 200 7163. *E:* vikki.howells@assembly.wales.

**HOWES, Maj. Gen. Buster;** see Howes, Maj. Gen. F. H. R.

**HOWES, Sir Christopher (Kingston),** KCVO 1999 (CVO 1997); CB 1993; Second Commissioner and Chief Executive of the Crown Estate, 1989–2001; Member: HRH Prince of Wales's Council, 1990–2011; Council, Duchy of Lancaster, 1993–2005; *b* 30 Jan. 1942; *yr s* of late Leonard Howes, OBE and Marion Howes (*née* Bussey); *m* 1967, Clare, *o d* of Gordon and Lilian Cunliffe; one *s* one *d* (and one *s* one *d* decd). *Educ:* Gresham's Sch.; Coll. of Estate Management, Univ. of London (BSc 1965); Univ. of Reading (MPhil 1976). ARICS 1967, FRICS 1977. Valuation and Planning Depts, GLC, 1965–67; Partner and Sen. Partner, Chartered Surveyors, Norwich, 1967–79; Department of the Environment: Dep. Dir, Land Economy, 1979–81; Chief Estates Officer, 1981–85; Dir, Land and Property Div., 1985–89. Sen. Vis. Fellow, Sch. of Envmtl Scis, UEA, 1975; Visiting Lecturer: Dept of Land Economy, Univ. of Cambridge, 1976–81; Univ. of Reading, 1974–80; Aberdeen 1982; UCLA and UCS Los Angeles, 1983; Harvard, 1985; Univ. N Carolina, Chapel Hill, 1985; Miami, 1985; Vis. Prof., Bartlett Sch. of Architecture and Planning, UCL, 1984–. Member: Sec. of State for the Envmt's Thames Adv. Cttee, 1995–98; CNAA Surveying Bd, 1978–82; OECD Urban Policy Gp, 1985–88; Planning and Develt Divl Council, RICS, 1983–92; Policy Review Cttee, RICS, 1984–90; RIBA Awards Gp, 1997–2002; Council: Norfolk Archaeol Trust, 1979–; British Property Fedn, 1992–2001. Jt Chm., World Land Policy Congress, London, 1986. Vis. Speaker, Commonwealth Assoc. of Surveying and Land Economy Conf., Trinidad, 1982 and Cyprus, 1984, 2009. Hon. Mem., Cambridge Univ. Land Soc., 1989–. Founder Mem., Norwich Third World Centre, 1970; dir of various housing assocs, 1970–80; Dep. Chm., Howard de Walden Estate, 2012– (non-exec. Dir, 2002–12); non-executive Director: Norwich & Peterborough Building Soc., 1998–2005; Compco Hldg Ltd, 2004–16; Dir, Colville Estates Ltd, 2003–12; non-exec. Chm., Barclays Real Estate (formerly Property Finance) Team, 2005–10; Member, Advisory Board: Barclays Private Banking, 2001–12; Three Delta LLP, 2006–11; Advr, Operational Efficiency Prog., HM Treasury, 2008–09; Sen. Advr, Barclays Wealth and Investment Mgt, 2013–17; Mem., Barclays Private Bank Adv. Cttee, 2008–13. Member: Bd, Norwich Theatre Royal Trust, 1969–79; Adv. Bd, Aldeburgh Music, 1998–2010. Steward and Hon. Surveyor to Dean and Chapter, Norwich Cathedral, 1973–79; Trustee: HRH The Prince of Wales's Inst. of Architecture, 1992–99; British Architectural Library Trust, 1997–2010; Suffolk Historic Churches Trust, 2009–14; Ore and Alde Estuary Trust, 2013–16; Britten-Pears Foundn, 2016–; Mem., British Archtl Trust Bd (formerly RIBA Trust), 2010–16. Member: Court of Advisers, 1980–99, Investment Adv. Cttee, 1999–2011, St Paul's Cathedral; Court, UEA, 1992–. Patron, Heatherley Sch. of Fine Art Chelsea, 2008–. Norwich CC, 1969–73; JP Norfolk 1973–80. Hon. FRIBA 1995. Hon. LittD E Anglia, 2000. Mem. of various editorial bds. *Publications:* (jtly) Acquiring Office Space, 1975; Value Maps: aspects of land and property values, 1979; Economic Regeneration (monograph), 1988; Urban Revitalization (monograph), 1988; papers on land and planning policy in learned jls. *Recreations:* music, art, architecture, sailing. *Address:* 8 Millennium House, 132 Grosvenor Road, SW1V 3JY. *T:* (020) 7828 9920; Westerly House, Aldeburgh, Suffolk IP15 5EL. *Clubs:* Athenæum, Garrick; Norfolk (Norwich); Aldeburgh Yacht; Aldeburgh Golf.

**HOWES, Maj. Gen. Francis Hedley Roberton, (Buster),** CB 2013; OBE 2003; consultant on resilience, leadership and the circular economy, since 2017; Chief Executive Officer, Here Be Dragons Príncipe, 2015–17; *b* Newcastle upon Tyne, 22 March 1960; *s* of Martin and Lolita Howes; three *d*. *Educ:* York Univ. (BA Chem.); City Univ. London (MA Strategic Studies). Joined RM, 1982; rcds 2002; CO, 42 Commando RM, 2003–05; Divl Dir, JCSC, 2005–06; HCSC, 2006; Dir, Naval Staff, MoD, 2007; Comdr, 3 Commando Bde, RM, 2008; Hd, Overseas Ops, MoD, 2008–09; Comdt Gen., RM and Comdr, UK Amphibious Forces, 2010–11; Defence Attaché and Hd of British Defence Staff, Washington, 2012–15. *Recreations:* art, bodging, growing vegetables, admiring trees, resurrection, poetry.

**HOWES, Rupert Spencer;** Chief Executive Officer, Marine Stewardship Council, since 2004; *b* London, 1 April 1963; *s* of Peter John Howes and Elizabeth Jane Howes; *m* 1995, Louise Ann Hulton (*d* 2017); three *s* one *d*. *Educ:* Haverstock Comprehensive Sch., N London; Sussex Univ. (BA (Econ) Hons 1985); Imperial Coll. London (MSc Envmtl Technol. 1992). ACA 1991. Trainee accountant, KPMG, 1987–91; Res. Officer, Internat. Inst. for Envmt and Develt, 1991–94; Sen. Res. Fellow, Sci. Policy Res. Unit, Sussex Univ., 1994–97; Dir, Sustainable Econ. Prog., Forum for the Future, 1997–2004. Social Entrepreneur Award, SKOLL Foundn, 2007; Leaders for a Living Planet Award, WWF, 2009; Schwab Foundn Social Entrepreneur of the Year, 2014. *Publications:* (jtly) Clean and Competitive?: motivating environmental performance in industry, 1997; (contrib.) The Triple Bottom Line: does it all add up?, 2004. *Recreations:* treasure hunting, fishing, occasional diver, country walks and time with family and dog. *Address:* Marine Stewardship Council, Marine House, 1 Snow Hill, EC1A 2DH. *T:* (020) 7246 8903. *E:* rupert.howes@msc.org.

**HOWES, Dr Sally,** OBE 2004; Strategic Adviser, Methods Ltd, since 2016; *b* Peterborough, 17 Jan. 1961; *d* of Stanley and Dorothy Howes; *m* 2003, Paul Becksmith. *Educ:* Fitzwilliam Coll., Cambridge (BA Geog. 1982; MA); Bristol Univ. (PhD 1985). Software engr, Logica Space & Defence Systems, 1985–90; Commercial Dir, 1990–99, Man. Dir, 1999–2002, Esys plc; Dir Gen., Soc. of British Aerospace Cos, 2003–07; Commercial Dir, MoD, 2008–10; Dir, 2010–13, Exec. Leader, Digital and Innovation, 2013–16, Nat. Audit Office. Non-exec. Dir, Copyright Licensing Agency, 2017–. Ind. Mem., It Investment Bd, H of C, 2017–. Chair, Steering Bd, UK Space Agency, 2019–. Vis. Prof., Surrey Univ., 2014–. Lay Mem. Council, Univ. of Surrey, 2015–. *Recreations:* gardening, reading, ski-ing, interior design. *Address:* Abergavenny Barn, Clipbush Lane, Scoulton, Norwich, Norfolk NR9 4BP. *E:* sally.howes1@outlook.com.

**HOWES, Sally Ann;** actress (stage, film and television); *b* 20 July; *d* of late Bobby Howes; *m* 1958, Richard Adler (marr. diss.); *m* 1969, Andrew Maree (marr. diss.). *Educ:* Glendower, London; Queenswood, Herts; privately. *Films include:* Thursday's Child, 1943; Halfway House, 1943; Dead of Night, 1945; Nicholas Nickleby, 1947; Anna Karenina, 1948; My

Sister and I; Fools Rush In; History of Mr Polly, 1949; Stop Press Girl; Honeymoon Deferred; The Admirable Crichton, 1957; Chitty, Chitty Bang Bang, 1968. First appeared West End stage in (revue) Fancy Free, at Prince of Wales's, and at Royal Variety Performance, 1950. *Stage Shows include:* Caprice (musical debut); Paint Your Wagon; Babes in the Wood; Romance by Candlelight; Summer Song; Hatful of Rain; My Fair Lady; Kwamina, NY; What Makes Sammy Run?, NY; Brigadoon (revival), NY City Center, 1962; Sound of Music, Los Angeles and San Francisco, 1972; Lover, St Martin's; The King and I, Adelphi, 1973, Los Angeles and San Francisco, 1974; Hans Andersen, Palladium, 1977; Hamlet (tour), 1983; The Dead, NY, 2000. Has appeared on television: in England from 1949 (Short and Sweet Series, Sally Ann Howes Show, etc); in USA from 1958 (Dean Martin Show, Ed Sullivan Show, Mission Impossible, Marcus Welby MD); Play of the Week; Panel Shows: Hollywood Squares; Password; Bell Telephone Hour; US Steel Hour, etc. *Recreations:* reading, riding, theatre.

**HOWES, Sally Margaret**; QC 2003; *b* 10 Sept. 1959; *d* of Patrick George Howes and Janet Howes. *Educ:* Polam Hall Sch., Co. Durham; Univ. of Newcastle upon Tyne (BA Hons (Classics); Dip. Law). Called to the Bar, Middle Temple, 1983; Judge Advocate (pt-time), 1993–. Specializes in criminal law. *Recreations:* polo, racing, walking the South Downs with my labrador Shamba. *Address:* 2KBW, 2 King's Bench Walk, Temple, EC4Y 7DE. *Clubs:* National Liberal; Cowdray Park Polo.

**HOWESON, Commodore Charles Arthur**, RNR; Chairman: Harvey Nash plc (SW), 2010–18; SPS (Pathology and Microbiology), 2012–14; Bristol Water plc, 2015–16; South West Water (Water Share), 2015–18; *b* 27 Nov. 1949; *s* of Arthur C. Howeson and Sheila B. Howeson; *m* 1978, Emma Jane Stevenson; one *s* two *d*. *Educ:* Uppingham Sch.; Royal Naval Coll. Dartmouth; Royal Naval Staff Coll. RN 1968–90, Chief of Allied Staffs and Dep. COS (Ops) to Comdr British Forces Gibraltar, 1990; retired in rank of Comdr, 1991; Hon. Cdre, RNR, 2015. Exec. Dir, Plymouth Area Groundwork Trust, 1991–93. Member: Nat. Consumer Council for Water, 2006–15 (Chm., Western Reg., 2006–15; Chm., Adv. Bd, 2009–14); Nat. Consumer Council for Postal Services (Chm., Western Reg.), 2000–07. Chairman: Horizon Roofing Ltd, 2004–10; UK Seafish Industry Authy, 2007–10; Coutts & Co. Private Bankers (SW), 2009–13; non-executive Chairman: Rowe Gp, 2003–10; St Piran Homes Ltd, 2004–10; Clearwood Joinery Ltd, 2004–10; First Great Western Trains, 2007–09 (Chm., Adv. Bd, 2009–); Crownhill Estates Ltd; Eko-Tek Gp of Cos; Buckland Corporate Finance Ltd; NHS Property Services Ltd, 2011–13; non-exec. Dir, Duchy of Somerset Estates Ltd. Chm., SW Strategic HA, 2009–11; NHS Lead for Veterans, 2009–13; Vice Chm., NHS South of England, 2011–12. Pres., Millfields Community Econ. Develt Trust; Vice-Pres., Plymouth Chamber of Commerce and Industry, 2006–10; Chairman: Plymouth Area Business Council (formerly Plymouth Econ. Develt Gp), 1999–2017 (Pres., 2017–18); Seaton Area Residents' Assoc., 2000–14; Plymouth Policing Adv. Bd, 2007–08; Plymouth Employment Action Zone Bd and Working Links Partnership Bd; Plymouth's Econ. Task Force; Vice-Chm. and Dir, City of Plymouth's Local Strategic Partnership; Vice Chm., Plymouth Sub-Regl Econ. Partnership of Local Authorities, 2000–09; Director: Millfields Estate Mgt Co. Ltd, 2000–18; London and West Country Estates Ltd; Frog Construction Ltd; Sailport plc and Solemeasure Ltd; Radio Plymouth Ltd, 2008–12; RNH (West End) Ltd, 2000–18; Plymouth Naval Base Visitors' Centre and Mus. Ltd, 2000–12. Gp Chm. Bd, Mount Batten Sailing and Water Sports Centre, 2000–07; Chm., Plymouth Branch, STA, later Tall Ships Youth Trust. President: Devon and Cornwall Business Council, 2015–18; Plymouth and Devon Chamber of Commerce, 2015–18. Patron, St Austell Br., Royal Naval Assoc., 1995–2010; Vice-Patron, Prowess's People; Pres., G-Scale Soc., SW; Chm. Trustees and Govs, Plymouth Drake Foundn, 2006–12, now Life Vice Pres.; Governor and Trustee: Plymouth Coll. Sch., 1997–2009; St Dunstan's Abbey Sch.; Gov., Plymouth Coll. of Further Educn; Trustee: Estates of 19th Duke of Somerset, 1995–2016; Bermuda Inst. for Oceanographic Sci., 2008–16; Hon. Sec. and Treas., 1999–2009, and Dep. Vice Patron, Britannia Assoc., 2010–18. Mem., RNSA, 1968–2018. MRIN; FInstD; FCMI; FRSA; FFB; FNI. Freeman, City of London; Liveryman, Shipwrights' Co.; Mem., Guild of Freemen; Younger Brother, Trinity House. Hon. DPhil (Mgt) Plymouth, 2009. SLJ (Brunei) 1983. *Recreations:* competent international cruising yachtsman, tennis, adequate but still improving jazz pianist, designing and operating substantial garden railway called Third Great Western, wine tasting in heavy seas on board friends' yachts. *Address:* Constance Cottage, 12 Constance Place, The Millfields, Plymouth PL1 3NN. *Clubs:* Army and Navy, Naval and Military, 1910 (Goring Hotel); Royal Yacht Squadron.

**HOWICK OF GLENDALE**, 2nd Baron *cr* 1960; **Charles Evelyn Baring**; a Director, Northern Rock plc (formerly Northern Rock Building Society), 1987–2001; a Managing Director, Baring Brothers & Co. Ltd, 1969–82; *b* 30 Dec. 1937; *s* of 1st Baron Howick of Glendale, KG, GCMG, KCVO, and Lady Mary Cecil Grey, *er d* of 5th Earl Grey; *S* father, 1973; *m* 1964, Clare Nicolette, *y d* of Col Cyril Darby; one *s* three *d*. *Educ:* Eton; New Coll., Oxford. Director: The London Life Association Ltd, 1972–82; Swan Hunter Group Ltd, 1972–79. Member: Exec. Cttee, Nat. Art Collections Fund, 1973–86; Council, Friends of Tate Gall., 1973–78; Adv. Cttee, Westonbirt Arboretum, 1995–2001; Adv. Cttee, Nat. Arboreta, 2001–17. Trustee: Chelsea Physic Garden, 1994–2012; Royal Botanic Gdns, Edinburgh, 2001–09; Pres., NE Div., Plant Heritage, 2009–. Chm., Botanics Foundn, 2010–13; Mem. Council, Baring Foundn, 1982–99; Trustee, Northern Rock Foundn, 1997–2007. *Heir: s* Hon. David Evelyn Charles Baring [*b* 26 March 1975; *m* 2003, Victoria Jane, *d* of Owen and Margaret Sutherland]. *Address:* Howick, Alnwick, Northumberland NE66 3LB. *T:* (01665) 577624.

*See also* Sir E. H. T. Wakefield.

**HOWIE, Prof. Archibald**, CBE 1998; PhD; FRS 1978; Professor of Physics, Cavendish Laboratory, University of Cambridge, 1986–2001, now Emeritus; Fellow of Churchill College, Cambridge, since 1960; *b* 8 March 1934; *s* of Robert Howie and Margaret Marshall McDonald; *m* 1964, Melva Jean Scott; one *d* (one *s* decd). *Educ:* Kirkcaldy High Sch.; Univ. of Edinburgh (BSc); California Inst. of Technology (MS); Univ. of Cambridge (PhD). English Speaking Union, King George VI Memorial Fellow (at Calif. Inst. of Technology), 1956–57; Cambridge University: Research Scholar, Trinity Coll., 1957–60; Research Fellow, Churchill Coll., 1960–61; Cavendish Laboratory: ICI Research Fellow, 1960–61; Demonstrator in Physics, 1961–65; Lecturer, 1965–79; Reader, 1979–86; Hd of Dept of Physics, 1989–97. Visiting Scientist, Nat. Research Council, Canada, 1966–67; Vis. Prof. of Physics, Univ. of Aarhus, Denmark, 1974. Dir, NPL Management Ltd, 1995–2001. Pres., Internat. Fedn of Socs for Electron Microscopy, 1999–2002. Hon. Prof., Univ. of York, 2008–. Hon. Member: Chinese Electron Microscopy Soc., 2000; Japanese Soc. of Microscopy, 2003. Hon. FRMS 1978 (Pres., 1984–86); Hon. FRSE 1995; Hon. FInstP 2015. Hon. Dr (Physics): Bologna, 1989; Thessaloniki, 1995; DUniv York, 2011. Distinguished Scientist Award, Electron Microscopy Soc. of America, 1991; Guthrie Medal, Inst. of Physics, 1992; Royal Medal, Royal Soc., 1999; (jtly with M. J. Whelan): C. V. Boys Prize, Inst. of Physics, 1965; Hughes Medal, Royal Soc., 1988; Gjønnes Medal, Internat. Union of Crystallography, 2012; Cowley Medal, Internat. Fedn of Socs for Microscopy, 2018. *Publications:* (co-author) Electron Microscopy of Thin Crystals, 1965, 2nd edn 1977; papers on electron microscopy and diffraction in scientific jls. *Recreations:* gardening, wine-making. *Address:* 194 Huntingdon Road, Cambridge CB3 0LB. *T:* (01223) 570977.

**HOWIE, Prof. John Garvie Robertson**, CBE 1996; MD; PhD; FRCGP, FRCPE, FMedSci; Professor of General Practice, University of Edinburgh, 1980–2000; *b* 23 Jan. 1937; *s* of Sir James Howie and Isabella Winifred Mitchell, BSc; *m* 1962, Elizabeth Margaret Donald; two *s* one *d*. *Educ:* High School of Glasgow; Univ. of Glasgow (MD); PhD Aberdeen. House officer, 1961–62; Laboratory medicine, 1962–66; General practitioner, Glasgow, 1966–70; Lectr/Sen. Lectr in General Practice, Univ. of Aberdeen, 1970–80. Founder FMedSci 1998. Hon. DSc Aberdeen, 2002. *Publications:* Research in General Practice, 1979, 2nd edn 1989; A Day in the Life of Academic General Practice, 1999; Academic General Practice in the UK Medical Schools 1948–2000, 2011; articles on appendicitis, prescribing and general medical practice and education, in various jls. *Recreations:* golf, gardening, music. *Address:* 4 Ravelrig Park, Balerno, Midlothian EH14 7DL. *T:* (0131) 449 6305. *E:* john.howie23@btinternet.com.

**HOWIE, Robert Bruce McNeill**; QC (Scot.) 2000; *b* 24 Aug. 1960; *s* of Dr William Bruce McNeill Howie, OBE, and Dr Theresa Grant or Howie; *m* 1996, Deirdre Elizabeth Hughes Clark or Haigh; one *s*. *Educ:* Aberdeen Grammar Sch.; Aberdeen Univ. (LLB, DLP). Admitted Advocate, 1986. *Address:* 41a Fountainhall Road, Edinburgh EH9 2LN.

**HOWITT, Richard Stuart**; Chief Executive Officer, International Integrated Reporting Council, since 2016; *b* 5 April 1961. *Educ:* Lady Margaret Hall, Oxford (BA); Univ. of Hertfordshire (DMS). Community worker, 1982–94. Mem. (Lab), Harlow DC, 1984–94 (Leader, 1991–94). Contested (Lab) Billericay, 1987. Hon. Pres., SE Econ. Develt Strategy Assoc., 1994– (Chm., 1986–94); Hon. Vice-President: ADC, 1994–97; LGA, 1997–; Trustee, Centre for Local Econ. Strategies, 1994–. Mem., Labour Party Nat. Policy Forum and NEC Local Govt sub-cttee, 1994–. MEP (Lab) Essex S, 1994–99, Eastern Reg., England, 1999–2016. European Parliament: First Vice-Pres., Regl Affairs Cttee, 1997–99 (Mem., 1994–96); Pres., All-Party Disability Gp, 1999–2016; Rapporteur: Europe and UN Social Summit, 1995; European Funding for Local and Regl Authorities, 1995; European Refugee Policy, 1996; Guidelines for Effective European Projects, 1998; European Code of Conduct for Enterprises, 1999; Corporate Social Responsibility, 2002–03, 2007; Budget, 2002; Participation of Non-state Actors in EC Develt Policy, 2003; Human Right Report, 2006. *Address:* International Integrated Reporting Council, The Helicon, Third Floor, 1 South Place, EC2M 2RB.

**HOWKER, Shani Estelle**; *see* Barnes, S. E.

**HOWKINS, John Anthony**; adviser and author; *b* 3 Aug. 1945; *s* of Col Ashby Howkins and Lesley (*née* Stops); *m* 1st, 1971, Jill Liddington; 2nd, 1977, Annabel Whittet. *Educ:* Rugby Sch.; Keele Univ.; Architectural Association Sch. of Architecture (Dip.). Marketing Manager, Lever Bros, 1968–70; founder, TV4 Gp, 1971; TV/Radio Editor, Books Editor, Time Out, 1971–74; Sec., Standing Conf. on Broadcasting, 1975–76; Editor, InterMedia, Journal of Internat. Inst. of Communications, 1975–84; Exec. Dir, Internat. Inst. of Communications, 1984–89. Gov., London Film Sch. (formerly London Internat. Film Sch.), 1976–2014 (Chm., 1979–84); Member: Interim Action Cttee on the Film Industry, DTI, 1980–84; British Screen Adv. Council, 1985– (Dep. Chm., 1991–2013); Vice-Chm. (New Media), Assoc. of Independent Producers, 1984–85. Exec. Editor, National Electronics Review, 1981–99; TV Columnist, Illustrated London News, 1981–83. Chairman: Tornado Productions, 2000–03; BOP Consulting, 2007–11; Director: Television Investments, 1993–; Equator Gp plc, 1999–2006; Howkins & Associates, 2006–; HandMade plc, 2006–10; Hotbed Media Ltd, 2006–16; Screen East, 2006–10; Albany Prodns, 2016–; Great Map Prodns, 2018–; Project Dir, World Learning Network, 1996–2005; Bd Dir, Norfolk and Norwich Festival, 2010–17 (Trustee, 2017–). Dir, Adelphi (formerly Intellectual Property) Charter, RSA, 2004–06. Mem., AHRC, 2008–13. Specialist Advr, Select Cttee on European Communities, House of Lords, 1985–87; Adviser: Broadcasting Reform Commn, Poland, 1989–90; Polish-Radio-and-Television, 1991–94; Minister of Film, Poland, 1991–92; Chm., Adv. Bd, Createc, 1996–2000; Co-ordinator, Eur. Audiovisual Conf., 1997–98. Associate, Coopers Lybrand Deloitte, 1990–91. Special European Consultant, HBO Inc. (and other Time Warner Inc. cos), 1981–85 and 1989–95. Visiting Professor: Lincoln Univ., 2003–13; City Univ., London, 2009–; Vis. Prof. and Internat. Vice-Pres., Sch. of Creativity, Shanghai, 2006–; Executive-in-Residence, Drucker Sch. of Mgt, LA, 2014–15. Chm., John Howkins Res. Centre on the Creative Economy, Shanghai, 2006–. UK Rep., Transatlantic Dialogue on Broadcasting and Information Soc., 1998–2008. *Publications:* Understanding Television, 1977; The China Media Industry, 1980; Mass Communications in China, 1982; New Technologies, New Policies, 1982; Satellites International, 1987; (with Michael Foster) Television in '1992': a guide to Europe's new TV, film and video business, 1989; Four Global Scenarios on Information and Communication, 1997; The Creative Economy, 2001, 2nd edn 2013; CODE, 2002; Creative Ecologies, 2009; Dutty's Dare, 2009; Invisible, 2020. *Address:* E6 Albany, Piccadilly, W1J 0AR. *T:* (020) 7434 1400. *E:* john@johnhowkins.com.

**HOWLETT, Ben**; Managing Director: Public Policy Projects, since 2017; Dorson West Ltd, since 2018; *b* Colchester, 21 Aug. 1986; *s* of Clive Howlett and Beverley Howlett; partner, Josh Jones. *Educ:* Manningtree High Sch.; Colchester Sixth Form Coll.; Durham Univ. (BA Hons Hist. and Politics 2007); Univ. of Cambridge (MA Econ. Hist. 2008). Recruitment Consultant, Venn Gp, 2008–10; Managing Consultant, Finegreen Associates, 2010–15. MP (C) Bath, 2015–17; contested (C) same seat, 2017. *Recreations:* running (half marathons), Bath Rugby fan, charity work (healthcare and mental health), cooking, socialising, school governor.

**HOWLETT, Elizabeth, (Elizabeth Robson)**; Professor of Singing, Royal College of Music, since 1989; *b* 17 Jan. 1938; *d* of Walter James Robson and Lizzie Mason Robson (*née* Houston); *m* 1962, Neil Baillie Howlett (marr. diss. 1987); two *d*. *Educ:* Royal Scottish Acad. of Music (Sir James Caird Jun. and Sen. Scholarships; DRSAMD). Leading Lyric Soprano, Sadler's Wells Opera Co., 1961–65; Leading Soprano, Royal Opera House, Covent Gdn, 1965–70; Soprano, Staatsoper, Hamburg, 1970–74; guest engagements in Europe, S Africa, Japan, Korea, Canada, USA, Scottish Opera, WNO, Opera North, ENO, 1974–. Nat. and Internat. Examr, 1997–; Adjudicator, Festivales Musicales, Buenos Aires, 1995–2004. Mem. (C) Wandsworth BC, 1986–2014 (Chairman: Social Services Cttee, 1989–92; Educn Cttee, 1992–98; Chief Whip, 1999–2000); Mayor of Wandsworth, 1998. Mem. (C) Merton and Wandsworth, London Assembly, GLA, 2000–08. Mem., Inner London Probation Bd, 1995–2001. Non-exec. Dir and Chm., Nat. Hosp. for Neurol. and Neurosurgery, 1990–96. Founder and Trustee, Margaret Dick Award for young Scottish singers, 1982–; Trustee, Foundn for Young Musicians, 1996–2007. Hon. Vice Patron, Ystradgynlais Male Voice Choir, 1985–. JP Wimbledon, 1985–2006. Freeman, City of London, 1999. Eschanson of Roi René Award, Aix-en-Provence, 1970. *Recreations:* walking, theatre, music. *E:* elizabethhowlett@btconnect.com.

**HOWLETT, Gen. Sir Geoffrey (Hugh Whitby),** KBE 1984 (OBE 1972); MC 1952; Chairman: Leonard Cheshire Foundation, 1990–95; Services Sound & Vision Corporation, 1991–99 (Vice-Chairman, 1989–91); *b* 5 Feb. 1930; *s* of Brig. B. Howlett, DSO*, and Mrs Joan Howlett (later Latham); *m* 1955, Elizabeth Anne Aspinal (*d* 2006); one *s* two *d*. *Educ*: Wellington Coll.; RMA, Sandhurst. Commnd Queen's Own Royal W Kent Regt, 1950; served, 1951–69: Malaya, Berlin, Cyprus and Suez; 3 and 2 Para, 16 Parachute Bde and 15 Para (TA); RAF Staff Coll. and Jt Services Staff Coll.; Mil. Asst to CINCNORTH, Oslo, 1969–71; CO 2 Para, 1971–73; RCDS, 1973–75; Comd 16 Parachute Bde, 1975–77; Dir, Army Recruiting, 1977–79; GOC 1st Armoured Div., 1979–82; Comdt, RMA, Sandhurst, 1982–83; GOC SE District, 1983–85; C-in-C Allied Forces Northern Europe, 1986–89, retd. Colonel Commandant: ACC, 1981–89; Parachute Regt, 1983–90. Comr, Royal Hosp., Chelsea, 1989–95. President: CCF, 1989–2000; Army Benevolent Fund for Dorset, 1992–2000; Regular Forces Employment Assoc., 1993–97 (Vice-Chm., 1989–90; Chm., 1990–93); Army Cricket Assoc., 1984–85; Combined Services Cricket Assoc., 1985; Stragglers of Asia Cricket Club, 1989–94. Visitor, Milton Abbey Sch., 2001–05 (Chm. of Govs, 1994–2000). Liveryman, Cooks' Co., 1991–2013. Cross of Merit, 1st cl. (Lower Saxony), 1982. *Recreations*: watching cricket, racing. *Address*: 58 Hascombe Court, Somerleigh Road, Dorchester DT1 1AG. *Club*: MCC.

**HOWLETT, Air Vice-Marshal Neville Stanley,** CB 1982; RAF retired, 1982; Member: Lord Chancellor's Panel of Independent Inquiry Inspectors, 1982–95; Pensions Appeal Tribunal, 1988–2000; *b* 17 April 1927; *s* of Stanley Herbert Howlett and Ethel Shirley Howlett (*née* Pritchard); *m* 1952, Sylvia (*d* 2005), *d* of J. F. Foster; one *s* one *d*. *Educ*: Liverpool Inst. High Sch.; Peterhouse, Cambridge. RAF pilot training, 1945–47; 32 and 64 (Fighter) Squadrons, 1948–56; RAF Staff Coll. Course, 1957; Comdr, 234 Sqn at 229 (Fighter) OCU, RAF Chivenor, 1958–59; flew Hunter in London-Paris Air Race, 1959; OC Flying Wing, RAF Coltishall, 1961–63; Directing Staff, RAF Staff Coll., 1967–69; Station Comdr, RAF Leuchars, 1970–72; RCDS, 1972; Dir of Operations (Air Defence and Overseas), 1973–74; Air Attaché, Washington DC, 1975–77; Dir, Management Support of Intelligence, MoD, 1978–80; Dir Gen. of Personal Services (RAF), MoD, 1980–82. Consultant, Defence Intelligence Staff, 1982–93. Vice-Pres., RAFA, 1984–2003 (Chairman: Exec. Cttee, 1990–97; Central Council, 1999–2001). *Recreations*: golf, fishing. *Address*: Milverton, Bolney Trevor Drive, Lower Shiplake, Oxon RG9 3PG. *Clubs*: Royal Air Force; Leander, Phyllis Court (Henley); Huntercombe Golf.

**HOWLETT, Stephen William,** CBE 2018; DL; Chief Executive, Peabody Trust, 2004–17 (Board Member, 2011–17); *b* 18 Nov. 1951; *s* of late Ivan William and Marjorie Elsie Howlett; *m* 1989, Jane Elizabeth Everton (CBE 2015); two *s* one *d*. *Educ*: King Edward VI Sch., Bury St Edmunds; West Suffolk Coll. of Further Educn; Thames Polytech. (BA Hons). Admin. Officer, Housing Corp., 1975–76; Housing Officer, Warden Housing Assoc., 1976–78; London Regl Officer, NFHA, 1978–82; Director: Croydon Churches Housing Assoc., 1982–88; Notting Hill Housing Trust, 1988–92; Chief Executive: Swale Housing Assoc., 1992–99; Amicus, 1999–2004. Advr to Mayor of London's Infrastructure 2050 Delivery Bd, 2014–16. Member: Bd, Asset Skills, 2004–13; Residential Cttee, British Property Fedn, 2005–15; Centre for London Commn on East River Crossings, 2014; Greenwich Fairness Commn, 2016–17; Commercial Develt Adv. Gp, TfL, 2018–. Mem. Bd, Orbit Housing Gp, 2018–; Chm., Orbit Customer and Communities Bd, 2019–. Chm., G15 London Housing Assocs, 2009–11. A London Leader, London Sustainable Develt Commn, 2007–17. Academician, Inst. of Urbanism 2009–17. Mem. Bd, 1995–2004, Vice-Chm., 1999–2004, Canterbury Coll.; Mem. Court, 2008– (Vice-Chm., 2010–13; Chm., 2013–17), Pro Chancellor, 2013–17, Univ. of Greenwich; Chair, London SE Coll., 2017–. Trustee, Ancient Egypt Soc., 2012–. DL Gtr London, 2017. FRSA 2018. Hon. FRIBA 2017. *Recreations*: family, cinema, opera, sport. *Clubs*: MCC; Blackheath Football.

**HOWLIN, Brendan;** Member (Lab) of the Dáil (TD) for Wexford, since 1987; Leader, Labour Party, Republic of Ireland, since 2016; *b* Wexford, Ireland, 9 May 1956; *s* of John Howlin and Molly Howlin (*née* Dunbar). *Educ*: Christian Brothers Secondary Sch., Wexford; St Patrick's Coll., Dublin. Mem., Seanad Éireann, 1983–87; Mayor of Wexford, 1986–87; Republic of Ireland: Minister: for Health, 1993–94; for Envmt, 1994–97; for Public Expenditure and Reform, 2011–16; Leas-Cheann Comhairle (Dep. Speaker), 2007–11. *Address*: Dáil Eireann, Leinster House, Kildare Street, Dublin 2, Republic of Ireland. *T*: 6183538. *E*: brendan.howlin@oir.ie.

**HOWLING, Rex Andrew;** QC 2011; a Recorder, since 2019; *b* Bromley, Kent, 15 June 1961; *s* of late Richard John Howling and Shirley Maureen Howling; *m* 1985, Carol Melanie Dell; two *s* two *d*. *Educ*: Charterhouse Sch.; Univ. of Sussex (BSc Biochem. 1982); Britannia Royal Naval Coll.; Poly. of Central London (DipLaw). Officer, Submarine Services, RN, 1980–89. Called to the Bar, Middle Temple, 1991; in practice as a barrister specialising in child care and matrimonial finance, Field Court Chambers, 1992–2007, 4 Paper Buildings, 2007–. Door tenant: 18 St John St Chambers, Manchester; Trinity Chambers, Chelmsford. Member: Family Law Bar Assoc., 1991–; Resolution, 2010–; Assoc. of Lawyers for Children, 2010–. Member: RYA; RNSA. *Publications*: contrib. to Family Law. *Recreations*: sailing, hockey, reading, ski-ing, family. *Address*: Old Hill, Sampford Road, Radwinter, near Saffron Walden, Essex CB10 2TL. *T*: (01799) 599674, 07973 623876. *E*: rexhowling@btinternet.com. *Clubs*: Bar Yacht; Helford River Sailing; Old Carthusian Yacht.

**HOWSON, Peter John,** OBE 2009; painter, since 1981; *b* 27 March 1958; *s* of Tom and Janet Howson; *m* 1983, Frances Nevay (marr. diss.); *m* 1989, Terry Cullen; one *d*. *Educ*: Glasgow Sch. of Art (BA Hons 1981). Official British War Artist in Bosnia, 1993–95; The Times War Artist, Kosovo, 1999. DUniv Strathclyde, 1996.

**HOY, Sir Christopher (Andrew),** Kt 2009; MBE 2005; Member, Great Britain Cycling Team, 1996–2013; Founder, Hoybikes, 2013; *b* 23 March 1976; *s* of David Hoy and Carol Jane Hoy (*née* Reid) (MBE 2009); *m* 2010, Sarra Kemp; one *s*. *Educ*: George Watson's Coll., Edinburgh; Univ. of Edinburgh (BSc Hons Sport Sci.). Olympic Games: Silver Medal, team sprint, 2000; Gold Medal, 1 km time trial cycling, 2004; Gold Medals, team sprint, keirin, and sprint, 2008; Gold Medals, team sprint and keirin, 2012; world champion: 1 km time trial and team sprint, 2002; team sprint, 2005; 1 km time trial, 2004, 2006, keirin and 1 km time trial, 2007; keirin and sprint, 2008; keirin, 2010, 2012; Commonwealth champion, 2002, 2006; world record holder, 500 m; Olympic record holder: 1000 m, 2004; 200 m time trial, 2008; team sprint, 2012. Dr *hc*: Edinburgh, 2005; St Andrews, 2009; Hon. Dr Heriot-Watt, 2005. BBC Sports Personality of the Year, 2008; Lifetime Achievement Award, BBC Sports Awards, 2014. *Publications*: Heroes, Villains and Velodromes, 2008; Chris Hoy: the autobiography, 2009. *W*: www.chrishoy.com.

**HOY, John Francis Dudley,** FRICS; Chief Executive Castle Howard, since 2018; independent heritage consultant, Hoy Consultancy, since 2018; *b* Cambridge, 19 Jan. 1957; *s* of Dudley and Joan Hoy; *m* 1998, Tracy Lorraine Rogers; two *d*. *Educ*: Leys Sch., Cambridge; Royal Agricl Coll., Cirencester (Dip. Rural Estate Mgt 1979). FRICS 1990. Asst Resident Land Agent, Goodwood Estate, 1979–84; Resident Agent and Gen. Manager, Knebworth Estate, 1985–97; Hd of Ops, Warwick Castle, 1997–2000; Gen. Manager, Madame Tussaud's, London, 2000–02; Commercial Project Manager, NMSI Trading Ltd, 2002–03; Chief Exec., Blenheim Palace, 2003–16; Partner and Hd of Rural, Bidwells LLP, 2017–18. Mem. Adv. Bd, VisitEngland, 2011–19. Trustee, Soldiers of Oxfordshire Trust, 2014–16. *Recreations*: theatre, historic houses, golf, tennis, cinema, family, heritage, leisure, travel and tourism. *Address*: Upper Campsfield Farm, Upper Campsfield Road, Woodstock, Oxon OX20 1QG. *T*: (01993) 810440, 07787 112804. *E*: JohnFDHoy@aol.com, john@hoyconsultancy.co.uk.

**HOYER, Dr Werner;** President, European Investment Bank, since 2012; *b* Wuppertal, 17 Nov. 1951; *m* Katja; one *s* one *d*. *Educ*: High Sch., Hannover; Univ. of Cologne (Dip. Econs 1974; PhD Econs 1977). University of Cologne: Sen. Res. Asst in Econs, 1974–84; Associate Lectr for Foreign Trade, 1978–93; Dir, Econs and Information Dept, Carl-Duisberg Soc., 1985–87. Mem., Bundestag, 1987–2011; Dep. Foreign Minister, 1994–98 and 2009–11. *Publications*: Vermögenseffekte des Geldes: theoretische Ansätze zur Rolle des geldes als Vermögensobjekt im Wirtschaftsprozeß, 1978; (with W. Eibner) Mikroökonomische Theorie, 1984, 4th edn 2011; (contrib.) Maastricht II: entwicklungschancen und Risiken der EU: ertweiterung, vertiefung oder stagnation?, 1996; (ed jtly) Der Vertrag von Amsterdam, 1997; (ed with G. F. Kaldrak) Europäische Sicherheits und Verteidigungspolitik (ESVP): der weg zu integrierten europäischen streitkräften?, 2002. *Address*: European Investment Bank, Office of the President, 98–100 Boulevard Konrad Adenauer, 2950 Luxemburg. *T*: 43791, *Fax*: 437704.

**HOYLAND, Jeremy Quentin;** Managing Partner, Simmons & Simmons, since 2011; *b* Sheffield, 25 April 1967; *s* of James Irwin Hoyland and Janet Elizabeth Hoyland (*née* Green); *m* 1997, Oonagh Anne MacNamara; two *s* one *d*. *Educ*: High Storrs Sch., Sheffield; St Aidan's Coll., Durham Univ. (BA Hons Law); Trent Poly. Admitted as solicitor, England and Wales, 1991, Hong Kong, 1998; joined Simmons & Simmons, 1989: Partner, Banking and Capital Mkts Dept, 1997; Head: of Finance, Hong Kong, 1998–2001; of Capital Mkts, London, 2002–05; of Financial Mkts, 2005–10. *Recreations*: family, walking, gardening, sport. *Address*: Simmons & Simmons, CityPoint, One Ropemaker Street, EC2Y 9SS. *T*: (020) 7628 2020. *E*: jeremy.hoyland@simmons-simmons.com.

**HOYLE,** family name of **Baron Hoyle**.

**HOYLE, Baron** *cr* 1997 (Life Peer), of Warrington in the co. of Cheshire; **Eric Douglas Harvey Hoyle;** consultant; *b* 17 Feb. 1930; *s* of late William Hoyle and Leah Ellen Hoyle; *m* 1953, Pauline Spencer (*d* 1991); one *s*. *Educ*: Adlington C of E Sch.; Horwich and Bolton Techn. Colls (HNC Mech. Engrg). Engrg apprentice, British Rail, Horwich, 1946–51; Sales Engr, AEI, Manchester, 1951–53; Sales Engr and Marketing Executive, Charles Weston Ltd, Salford, 1951–74. Mem., Manchester Regional Hosp. Bd, 1968–74; Mem., NW Regional Health Authority, 1974–75. Contested (Lab): Clitheroe, 1964; Nelson and Colne, 1970 and Feb. 1974; MP (Lab): Nelson and Colne, Oct. 1974–1979; Warrington, July 1981–1983; Warrington N, 1983–97. Chm., PLP, 1992–97 (Mem., Trade and Industry Cttee, 1987–92); Mem., Select Cttee on Trade and Industry, 1984–92. Mem. Nat. Exec., Labour Party, 1978–82, 1983–85. A Lord in Waiting (Govt Whip), 1997–99. Pres., ASTMS, 1977–81, 1985–88 (Vice-Pres., 1981–85), MSF, 1988–91 (Jt Pres., 1988–90; Pres., 1990–91); Chm., ASTMS Parly Cttee, 1975–76. Pres., Adlington Cricket Club, 1974–; Chm., 1999–2010, Pres., 2010–, Warrington Rugby League Club. JP Chorley, 1958. Freeman: Gibraltar, 2004; Warrington, 2005. Hon. DLitt Chester, 2010. *Recreations*: sport, cricket, theatre-going, reading. *Address*: House of Lords, SW1A 0PW.
*See also Rt Hon. Sir L. H. Hoyle.*

**HOYLE, Very Rev. Dr David Michael;** Dean of Westminster, since 2019; *b* Edgeside, Waterfoot, Lancs, 1957; *s* of Michael and Yvonne Hoyle; *m* 1981, Janet Susan; one *s* one *d*. *Educ*: Watford Boys' Grammar Sch.; Corpus Christi Coll., Cambridge (BA 1980; MA 1983; PhD 1991); Ripon Coll., Cuddesdon (Cert. Theol.). Ordained deacon, 1986, priest, 1987; Curate, Good Shepherd, Chesterton, 1986–88; Chaplain, 1988–91, Fellow, 1988–95, Dean, 1991–95, Magdalene Coll., Cambridge; Vicar, Christ Church, Southgate, 1995–2002; Dir, Post-ordination Trng, Edmonton Area, 2000–02; Diocesan Dir of Ministry and Residentiary Canon, Gloucester Cathedral, 2002–10; Dean of Bristol, 2010–19. Sec., Theol Gp, House of Bishops, 2002–06. *Publications*: (jtly) A History of Magdalene College Cambridge, 1994; Reformation and Religious Identity in Cambridge, 2007; (jtly) A Disciple Call, 2013; The Pattern of Our Calling, 2016; (jtly) Holy Ground, 2017; A Year of Grace, 2019. *Recreations*: hill-walking, company and conversation. *Address*: The Deanery, Dean's Yard, SW1P 3PA.

**HOYLE, Prof. Eric;** Professor of Education, 1971–96, now Professor Emeritus, and Senior Research Fellow, since 1996, Graduate School of Education, University of Bristol; *b* 22 May 1931; *s* of Percy and Bertha Hoyle; *m* 1954, Dorothy Mary Morley; one *s* two *d*. *Educ*: Preston Grammar Sch.; Univ. of London (BSc Sociology, MA). Taught, Harehills Secondary Sch., Leeds, 1953–58 (Head of English Dept, 1956–58); Head, English Dept, Batley High Sch., 1958–60; Lectr and Sen. Lectr in Educn, James Graham Coll., Leeds, 1961–64; Lectr and Sen. Lectr in Educn, Univ. of Manchester, 1965–71; Bristol University: Hd, Sch. of Educn, 1971–91; Dean, Faculty of Educn, 1974–77, 1983–86. Vis. Prof., Sch. of Management, Univ. of Lincs and Humberside, 1995–2000. Member: Avon Educn Cttee, 1977–80; Educnl Res. Bd, SSRC, 1973–78 (Vice-Chm., 1976–78); Bd of Management, NFER, 1976–94; Council, Exec. Council for Educn of Teachers, 1971 (Mem. Exec., 1978–81, 1987–90); Adviser to Public Schools Commn, 1968–70; consultant and advr on educnl mgt and professional develt of teachers to UNESCO, World Bank etc, SE Asia and Africa, 1972–. Editor, World Yearbook of Educn, 1980–86; founding Co-Editor, Research in Educn, 1969. *Publications*: The Role of the Teacher, 1969; (with J. Wilks) Gifted Children and their Education, 1974; The Politics of School Management, 1986; (with Peter John) Professional Knowledge and Professional Practice, 1995; (with Mike Wallace) Educational Leadership: ambiguity, professionals and managerialism, 2005; *festschrift*: Teaching: professionalization, development and leadership, ed D. Johnson and R. Maclean, 2008; contribs to professional jls. *Recreations*: music, reading, collecting first editions, cooking. *Address*: 42 Oakwood Road, Henleaze, Bristol BS9 4NT. *T*: (0117) 962 0614; Graduate School of Education, University of Bristol, 35 Berkeley Square, Bristol BS8 1JA. *T*: (0117) 928 3000.

**HOYLE, Rt Hon. Sir Lindsay (Harvey),** Kt 2018; PC 2013; MP (Lab) Chorley, since 1997; Chairman of Ways and Means and a Deputy Speaker, House of Commons, since 2010; *b* 10 June 1957; *s* of Baron Hoyle, *qv*; *m* 1st, Lynda Anne Fowler (marr. diss. 1982); 2nd, Catherine Swindley; one *d* (and one *d* decd). *Educ*: Adlington County Sch.; Lord's Coll., Bolton. Owner of building co.; Man. Dir, textile printing co. Mem. (Lab) Chorley BC, 1980–98 (Dep. Leader, 1995–97; Chair, Economic Develt and Tourist Cttee); Mayor, 1997–98. Member: Trade and Industry Select Cttee, 1998–2010; H of C Catering Cttee, 1997–2005; European Scrutiny Cttee, 2005–10; Finance Select Cttee, 2010–17; All Pty Rugby League Gp, 1997– (Vice-Chm., 1997–); All Pty Cricket Gp, 1997– (Treas., 1998–); All Pty Parly Gp on Financial Educn for Young People; Unite Parly Gp; Vice Chm., All Pty Tourism Gp, 1999–; Chm., All Pty BVI Gp, 2007–10; Pres., All Pty Gp on Gibraltar, 2001–. Member: Royal Lancs Agricl Show Soc.; Unite the Union. Hon. Colonel: C (64) Med. Sqdn (Vols); 5 Gen. Support Med. Regt. *Recreations*: Rugby League (former Chm., Chorley Lynx), cricket, football. *Address*: House of Commons, SW1A 0AA. *T*: (020) 7219 3000. *Clubs*: Adlington Cricket, Chorley Cricket.

**HOYLE, Martin Trevor William Mordaunt;** Television, Radio, Arts and Media Writer, Financial Times, since 1994; *s* of Capt. T. W. Hoyle and Dora Marie (*née* Muller). *Educ*: Egypt and Canada; Clifton Coll.; Wadham Coll., Oxford (BA); Bristol Old Vic Sch.; Poly. of Central London Business Sch. Music Critic, Bristol Evening Post, 1963–67; freelance researcher, BBC TV 1965–; Sub-editor, John Calder Publishers, 1979–82; Theatre Critic, Financial Times, 1983–90; Classical Music and Opera Editor, Time Out, 1988–2008; freelance writer on theatre, music, TV, film, books for Financial Times, Time Out, The Times, Mail on Sunday, Herald, The House, Independent on Sunday; reviews for Meridian (BBC World Service). *Publications*: The World of Opera: Mozart, 1996. *Recreation*: shouting at cyclists. *Address*: 22 Scotland Street, Edinburgh EH3 6PX. *T*: (0131) 556 6093.

**HOYLE, Prof. Richard William,** DPhil; FAcSS; Professor of Regional and Local History, and Director and General Editor, Victoria County History, Institute of Historical Research, University of London, 2014–16; *b* 4 Dec. 1958; *s* of C. and H. M. Hoyle; *m* 1st, 1981, Gillian M. Bishop (marr. diss. 2012); two *s*; 2nd, 2014, Catherine Glover. *Educ*: Univ. of Birmingham (BA 1981); Corpus Christi Coll., Oxford (DPhil 1987). Res. Fellow, Magdalen Coll., Oxford, 1985–87; Lectr, Univ. of Bristol, 1987–89; British Acad. Res. Fellow, Magdalen Coll., Oxford, 1989–92; University of Central Lancashire: Lectr, then Sen. Lectr, 1993–96; Reader, 1997; Prof. of Hist., 1998–2000; Prof. of Rural History, 2000–14, Dir, Rural Hist. Centre, 2000–03, Univ. of Reading. British Acad. Res. Reader, 2004–06. Vis. Prof., Univ. of Reading, 2014–. Vis. Fellow, Folger Shakespeare Liby, Washington DC, 2014. Mem., Res. Grants Bd, ESRC, 1997–2001. Sec., British Agricl Hist. Soc., 1996–98. Ed., Agricl Hist. Review, 1998–; Chm. and Ed., Victoria Co. Hist. Shropshire, 2015–. FAcSS (AcSS 2006). *Publications*: books include: (ed) The Estates of the English Crown 1558–1640, 1992; The Pilgrimage of Grace and the Politics of the 1530s, 2001; (ed) People, Landscape and Alternative Agriculture, 2004; (with H. French) The Character of English Rural Society: Earls Colne 1550–1750, 2007; (ed) Our Hunting Fathers: field sports in England since 1850, 2007; (ed) Custom, Improvement and Landscape in Early Modern Britain, 2011; (ed) The Farmer in England, 2013; contrib. articles to Past and Present, English Histl Review, Histl Jl, Econ. Hist. Review, Northern Hist., Yorks Archaeol Jl. *Recreations*: gardening, twentieth-century music, walking. *E*: r.w.hoyle@reading.ac.uk.

**HOYLE, Susan Linda,** OBE 2011; cultural consultant, since 2017; Director, Clore Leadership Programme, 2008–17 (Deputy Director, 2003–08); *b* 7 April 1953; *d* of Roland and Joan Hoyle; *m* 2005, Graham Thomas Devlin, *qv*. *Educ*: Univ. of Bristol (BA Drama and French). Education Officer, London Festival Ballet, 1980–83; Administrator, Extemporary Dance Th., 1983–86; Dance and Mime Officer, 1986–89, Dir of Dance, 1989–94, Arts Council of GB; Dep. Sec.-Gen., Arts Council of England, 1994–97; Head of Arts, British Council, France, 1997–98; Gen. Manager, then Exec. Dir, The Place, 1998–2003. Director: Shobana Jeyasingh Dance Co., 1998–2002; Ricochet Dance Co., 2001–03; DV8 Physical Th., 2003–09; LPO, 2003–05; Create KX, 2007–11; Fuel Productions Ltd, 2017–; Dir and Trustee, ROH Foundn, 2017–. Lay Comr, Judicial Appts Commn, 2019–. Trustee, British Council, 2008–14. Cultural Fellow, KCL, 2015. Hon. Fellow, Falmouth Univ., 2014. Chevalier, Ordre des Palmes Académiques, 2010.

**HOYLES, Dame Celia (Mary), (Dame Celia Noss),** DBE 2014 (OBE 2004); PhD; Professor of Mathematics Education, Institute of Education, University College London (formerly Institute of Education, University of London), since 1984; *b* London, 18 May 1946; *d* of Harold French and Elsie French (*née* Last); *m* 1st, Martin Hoyles (marr. diss.); 2nd, 1996, Prof. Richard Noss; one step *s* one step *d*. *Educ*: Univ. of Manchester (BSc 1st Cl. Hons Maths 1967); Chelsea Coll., Univ. of London (PGCE 1971; MEd 1973; PhD 1980). Teacher in London schs, 1967–72; Sen. Lectr, then Principal Lectr, Poly. of N London, 1972–84; Dean of Res. and Consultancy, Inst. of Educn, Univ. of London, 2002–04. Govt Chief Advr for Maths, 2004–07; Dir, 2007–13, Exec. Chair, 2013–14, Nat. Centre for Excellence in Teaching of Mathematics. Pres., Inst. of Mathematics and its Application, 2013–15. DUniv Open, 2006; Hon. DSc Loughborough, 2008; DUniv Sheffield Hallam, 2011. Hans Freudenthal Medal for res. in maths educn, Internat. Commn on Mathematical Instruction, 2004; Kavli Educn Medal, Royal Soc., 2011. *Publications*: (with R. Sutherland) Logo Mathematics in the Classroom, 1992; (ed with R. Noss) Learning Mathematics and Logo, 1992; (ed jtly) Computers for Exploratory Learning, 1995; (with R. Noss) Windows on Mathematical Meanings: learning cultures and computers, 1996; (ed jtly) Mathematics Education and Technology, 2009; (jtly) Improving Mathematics at Work: the need for techno-mathematical literacies, 2010; contrib. res. jls. *Recreations*: tennis, swimming, walking, reading. *Address*: UCL Institute of Education, 20 Bedford Way, WC1H 0AL. *T*: (020) 7612 6659. *E*: c.hoyles@ucl.ac.uk.

**HOYT, Hon. William Lloyd,** OC 2007; Chief Justice of New Brunswick, 1993–98; *b* 13 Sept. 1930; *m* 1954, Joan Millier; three *d*. *Educ*: Woodstock High Sch.; Acadia Univ. (BA, MA); Emmanuel Coll., Cambridge (BA, MA; Hon. Fellow, 2001). Called to New Brunswick Bar, 1957; QC (NB) 1972; Associate, Limerick & Limerick, 1957–59; Partner, Limerick, Limerick & Hoyt and successor firm, Hoyt, Mockler, Allen & Dixon, 1959–81; Judge, 1981–84, Court of Appeal, 1984–98, New Brunswick. Mem., Bloody Sunday Tribunal of Inquiry (UK), 1998–2010. Member: Fredericton Barristers' Soc., 1957–81 (Pres., 1970–71); New Brunswick Barristers' Soc., 1957–81 (Council, 1970–72, 1975–79); Cttee on Canadian Constitution, Canadian Bar Assoc., 1977–78; Director: Canadian Inst. for Admin of Justice, 1979–83; Canadian Judges' Conf., 1985–89; Canadian Inst. of Advanced Legal Studies, 1994–2008; Chm., New Brunswick Judicial Council, 1993–98 (Vice-Chm., 1988–93). Hon. LLD: St Thomas Univ., Fredericton, 1997; Univ. of New Brunswick, 1998; Hon. DCL Acadia Univ., 2001. *Publications*: Married Women's Property, 1961; Professional Negligence, 1973.

**HRUSKA, Dr Jan;** private investor; Managing Director, LogicIQ Ltd, 2006–17; *b* 22 April 1957; *s* of Ivan Hruska and Bozena Bozicek-Ferrari; *m* 2000, Regula Voellm. *Educ*: 1st Gymnasium, Zagreb; King's Sch., Canterbury; Downing Coll., Cambridge (BA 1978); Magdalen Coll., Oxford (DPhil 1984). Co-founder, and Technical Dir, 1985–2000, Jt Chief Exec. Officer, 2000–05, non-exec. Dir, 2006–15, Sophos Plc. *Publications*: The PC Security Guide, 1988; Computer Security Solutions, 1990; Computer Viruses and Anti-Virus Warfare, 1990, 2nd edn 1992; Computer Security Reference Book, 1992. *Recreations*: running, piano-playing, lock-picking, ex-flying (Private Pilots Licence, Instrument Meteorological Conditions, Night), ex-ski-ing, ex sub-aqua diving. *Address*: c/o Sophos Plc, The Pentagon, Abingdon, Oxon OX14 3YP. *T*: (01235) 559933, *Fax*: (01235) 559935. *E*: jan.hruska@logiciq.com.

**HTUT, U Kyaw Myo;** Ambassador of Myanmar to Canada, since 2016; *b* Meiktila, 9 Dec. 1957; *s* of U Tin Tut and Daw Yi Yi San; *m* 1984, Daw Khin Myint Kyi; one *s* two *d*. *Educ*: Basic Educn High Sch. I; Rangoon Univ. (Botany); Defence Service Acad. (BSc 1981); Nat. Defence Coll. (MA Defence Studies 2006). Served Defence Services to rank of Col, Myanmar, 1981–2008 (Mil. Meritorious Services Medal, 2nd and 3rd Cl.). Minister Counsellor, Min. of Foreign Affairs, 2008; Minister Counsellor, 2008–10, Ambassador, 2010–11, Perm. Mission of Myanmar to UN, Geneva; Ambassador to the Court of St James's, 2011–13; non-resident Ambassador to Sweden, 2012–13, and to Norway, 2013; Ambassador to the USA, 2013–16. *Recreations*: golf, football. *Address*: Embassy of Myanmar, 336 Island Park Drive, Ottawa, ON K1Y 0A7, Canada.

**HU JINTAO;** General Secretary, Communist Party of China, 2002–13; President, People's Republic of China, 2003–13 (Vice-President, 1998–2003); Chairman, Central Military Commission, 2004–13 (Vice-Chairman, 1999–2004); *b* 21 Dec. 1942; *m* Liu Yongqing; one *s* one *d*. *Educ*: Tsinghua Univ., Beijing. Engineer; joined Min. of Water Conservancy, 1968, Technician, 1969–74; Gansu Provincial Construction Committee: Sec., 1974–75; Dep. Dir of Design Mgt, 1975–80; Vice-Chm., 1980–82. Communist Youth League of China: Sec., Gansu Provincial Cttee, 1982; Sec., 1983–84; First Sec., 1984–85; Communist Party of China: Mem., Central Cttee, 1985–; Sec., Guizhou, 1985–88, Tibet, 1988–92; Mem., Standing Cttee, Political Bureau, 1992–2013. *Address*: c/o Office of the President, Zhong Nan Hai, Beijing, People's Republic of China.

**HUANG, Prof. Christopher Li-Hur,** FRSB, FESC; Professor of Cell Physiology, Cambridge University, since 2002; Fellow, Murray Edwards College (formerly New Hall), Cambridge, since 1979; *b* 28 Dec. 1951; *s* of late Rayson Lisung Huang, CBE. *Educ*: Methodist Boys' Sch., Kuala Lumpur; Nat. Jun. Coll., Singapore; Queen's Coll., Oxford (Singapore President's Scholar; Florence Heale Scholar; Benefactors Prize; BA, BM, BCh, MA; DM 1985; DSc 1995); Gonville and Caius Coll., Cambridge (MA; PhD 1980; MD 1986; ScD 1995). House Physician, Nuffield Dept of Medicine, Oxford Univ., 1977–78; Cambridge University: MRC Schol., Physiological Lab., 1978–79; Asst Lectr, 1979–84; Lectr in Physiol., 1984–96; Reader in Cellular Physiol., 1996–2002; Hon. Sen. Res. Fellow in Biochemistry, 2006–; New Hall, Cambridge: Fellow and Lectr in Physiol., 1979–2002; Dir of Studies in Med. Sci., 1981–; Professorial Fellow, 2002–. Hon. Res. Fellow, RCS, 1985–88; Hon. Sen. Res. Fellow, St George's Hosp. Med. Sch., London Univ., 1991–. Procultura Foundn Vis. Prof., Debrecen Univ., Hungary, 1996; Vis. Prof., 2001–04, Ext. Assessor, 2007, Mount Sinai Med. Sch., NY; Vis. Prof., 2005, Ext. Assessor, 2005–06 and 2008, Univ. of HK; Ext. Assessor, Univ. of Leeds, 2008; Adjunct Prof., First Affiliated Hosp., Med. Coll., Xi'an Jiaotong Univ. Med. Centre, China, 2008–11. Consulting Ed., John Wiley, 1986–2008; Mem. Editl Bd, 1990–96, Distributing Ed., 1991–94, Jl Physiol.; Chm., Editl Bd, Monographs of Physiol Soc., 1994–99; Member Editorial Board: BioMed Central Physiology, 2005–; Europace, 2008–; Biological Revs, 2009– (Chm., 2000–18). Mem. Ct of Examrs, RCSE, 1999–2004. Cambridge Philosophical Society: Council Mem., 1994–2018; Biol Sec., 2000–08; Adjudicator and convenor, 2008, Adjudicator, 2010, 2018, Wm Bate Hardy Prize; Vice-Pres., 2010–13, 2016–18; Pres., 2014–15. Manager, Prince Philip Scholarship Fund, 1986–. Dir, Aw Boon Haw Foundn, 2004–09; independent non-executive Director: Hutchison China Meditech Ltd, 2006–17; Hutchison Biofilm Medical Solutions Ltd, 2015–; Dir, Cambridge Cardiac Systems, 2009–14. Member: Fellowships Cttee, 2014–17, Adv. Council, 2015–17, British Heart Foundn UK; Prog. Approval and Rev. Panel, Univ. of Bradford, 2015–. FRSB (FSB 2011); FESC 2017; FPhysiol 2017. Brian Johnson Prize in Pathology, Univ. of Oxford, 1976; Lepra Award, Brit. Leprosy Relief Assoc., 1977; Rolleston Meml Prize for Physiological Res., Oxford Univ., 1980; Gedge Prize in Physiol., Cambridge Univ., 1981 (Adjudicator, 2007–). *Publications*: Companion to Neonatal Medicine, 1982; Companion to Obstetrics, 1982; Companion to Gynaecology, 1985; Research in Medicine: a guide to writing a thesis in the medical sciences, 1990, 3rd edn as Research in Medicine: planning a project - writing a thesis, 2010; Intramembrane Charge Movements in Striated Muscle, 1993; (ed jtly) Applied Physiology for Surgery and Critical Care, 1995; (ed jtly) Molecular and Cellular Biology of Bone, 1998; (ed jtly) Translational Models for Cardiac Arrhythmogenesis, 2008; Nerve and Muscle, 2011; (ed jtly) Sudden Arrhythmic Death: from basic science to clinical practice, 2013; Basic Physiology for Anaesthetists, 2015, 2nd edn 2019; 350 original scientific papers and reviews on striated muscle activation and homeostasis, peripheral nerve growth and repair, physiol magnetic resonance imaging, cellular triggering processes in osteoclasts and cardiac arrhythmogenesis. *Recreations*: music, playing the violin (Cambridge String Players, 2001–08; City of Cambridge SO, 2008–), reading Shakespeare plays, Impressionist and Post-Impressionist art history. *Address*: Murray Edwards College, Huntingdon Road, Cambridge CB3 0DF.

**HUANG, Sally-Anne;** Headmistress, James Allen's Girls' School, 2015–Sept. 2020; High Master, St Paul's School, from Sept. 2020; *b* Buxton, 30 Oct. 1971; *d* of Anthony Craig Blakemore and Anne Blakemore; *m* 1995, Alexis Huang; two *s*. *Educ*: Bolton Sch. Girls' Div.; Lady Margaret Hall, Oxford (MA Classics and English); Leicester Univ. (MSc Educnl Leadership and Mgt); Roehampton Univ. (MA Children's Lit.). Housemistress and teacher, Sevenoaks Sch., 1994–2000; Housemistress and Dep. Hd, Roedean Sch., 2000–08; Headmistress, Kent Coll., Pembury, 2008–15. Vice Chair, 2018–19, Chair Elect, 2019–20, HMC. Governor: Bedes Sch., 2003–15; Sevenoaks Prep. Sch., 2009–; Tonbridge Sch., 2016–; Bolton Sch., 2018–. Trustee, Dulwich Picture Gall., 2017–. *Recreations*: reading and writing about children's literature, Welsh Rugby, walking in Wales, pretending to be Welsh, owning two attention-seeking dogs, as much theatre as possible with an especial interest in immersive productions.

**HUBBARD,** family name of **Baron Addington**.

**HUBBARD, David;** *see* Hubbard, R. D. C.

**HUBBARD, Ven. Julian Richard Hawes;** Director, Ministry Division, Archbishops' Council, 2011–18; *b* 15 Feb. 1955; *m* 1984, Rachel (*née* Ashton); three *s* one *d*. *Educ*: Emmanuel Coll., Cambridge (BA 1976, MA 1981); Wycliffe Hall, Oxford (BA 1980, MA 1985). Ordained deacon, 1981, priest, 1982; Curate, St Dionis, Parsons Green, 1981–84; Tutor, Wycliffe Hall, Oxford, and Chaplain, Jesus Coll., Oxford, 1984–89; Selection Sec., ACCM, 1989–91, Sen. Selection Sec., ABM, 1991–93; Vicar, Bourne, 1993–99; RD, Farnham, 1996–99; Priest-in-charge, Tilford, 1997–99; Canon Residentiary, Guildford Cathedral, and Dir, Ministerial Trng, Dio. Guildford, 1999–2005; Archdeacon of Oxford and Residentiary Canon, Christ Church, Oxford, 2005–11.

**HUBBARD, (Richard) David (Cairns),** OBE 1995; Chairman: Powell Duffryn, 1986–96; London and Manchester Group, 1993–98 (Director, 1989–98); Exco plc, 1996–98 (Deputy Chairman, 1995); *b* 14 May 1936; *s* of late John Cairns Hubbard and Gertrude Emilie Hubbard; *m* 1964, Hannah Neale (*née* Dennison); three *d*. *Educ*: Tonbridge. FCA. Commissioned, Royal Artillery, 1955–57; Peat Marwick Mitchell & Co., 1957–65; Cape Asbestos Co., 1965–74; Bache & Co., 1974–76; Finance Dir, Powell Duffryn, 1976–86; Chm., Andrew Sykes Group, 1991–99; non-executive Director: Blue Circle Industries, 1986–96; City of London Investment Trust (formerly TR City of London Trust), 1989–2002; Slough Estates, 1994–2001; Medical Defence Union Ltd, 1998–2000; Mem., Southern Adv. Bd, Nat. Westminster Bank, 1988–91. Mem., Bd of Crown Agents for Oversea Govts and Admins, 1986–88. Mem. Council, Inst. of Dirs, 1991–97. Chm., CRC Council, 1996–98 (Council Mem., 1982–98). Liveryman, Skinners' Co.; Freeman, City of London. *Recreation*: golf. *Address*: Meadowcroft, Windlesham, Surrey GU20 6BJ. *T*: (01276) 472198. *Clubs*: Berkshire Golf (Pres., 1999–2004), Lucifer Golfing Society, Elders Golfing Society (Capt., 2002–04; Pres., 2007–10).

**HUBBLE, Benedict John Wakelin;** QC 2009; *b* Taplow; *s* of late John Clifford Hubble and Gillian Mary Hubble; *m* 1995, Zara Jane Sinclair; two *d*. *Educ:* University Coll., Oxford (BA Hons; Dip. Law). Called to the Bar, Middle Temple, 1992, Bencher, 2017; in practice as barrister specialising in professional liability and commercial law. *Recreations:* family, skiing, hiking. *Address:* 4 New Square, Lincoln's Inn, WC2A 3RJ. *T:* (020) 7822 2000, *Fax:* (020) 7822 2001. *E:* b.hubble@4newsquare.com.

**HUBER, Prof. Robert;** Director, Max-Planck-Institut für Biochemie, and Scientific Member, Max-Planck Society, 1972–2005, now Director Emeritus; *b* 20 Feb. 1937; *s* of Sebastian and Helene Huber; *m* 1960, Christa Essig; two *s* two *d*. *Educ:* Grammar Sch. and Humanistisches Gymnasium, München; Technische Univ., München (Dr rer. nat. 1963). Lecturer, 1968, Associate Prof., 1976–, Technische Univ., München. Scientific Mem., Max-Planck Soc. Editor, then Adv. Ed., Jl of Molecular Biology, 1976–. Visiting Professor: Univ. Autónoma de Barcelona, 2001; Nat. Univ. of Singapore, 2005; Univ. Duisburg-Essen, 2005; Cardiff Univ., 2007. Member: EMBO (also Mem. Council); Deutsche Chem. Ges.; Ges. für Biologische Chem.; Bavarian Acad. of Scis, 1988; Deutsche Akademie der Naturforscher Leopoldina; Accademia Nazionale dei Lincei, Rome; Orden pour le mérite für Wissenschaft und Künste; Corresp. Mem., Croatian Acad. of Scis and Arts; Fellow, Amer. Acad. of Microbiology, 1996; Associate Fellow, Third World Acad. of Scis, 1995; Foreign Associate, Nat. Acad. of Scis, USA, 1995; Foreign Mem., Royal Soc., 1999. Hon. Member: Amer. Soc. of Biolog. Chemists; Swedish Soc. for Biophysics; Japanese Biochem. Soc.; Sociedad Española de Bioquímica y Biología Molecular. Hon. Professor: Ocean Univ., Qingdao, 2002; Peking Univ., 2003; Sichuan Univ., Chengdu, 2003; Shanghai Second Med. Univ., 2004; Shanghai Jiao Tong Univ., 2005; Univ. de Sevilla, 2006; Lotte Dist. Prof., Seoul Nat. Univ., 2005. Dr *hc*: Catholic Univ. of Louvain, 1987; Univ. of Ljubljana, Jugoslavia, 1989; Univ. Tor Vergata, Rome, 1991; Univ. of Lisbon, 2000; Univ. of Barcelona, 2000; Tsinghua Univ., Peking, 2003. E. K. Frey Medal, Ges. für Chirurgie, 1972; Otto-Warburg Medal, Ges. für Biolog. Chem., 1977; Emil von Behring Medal, Univ. of Marburg, 1982; Keilin Medal, Biochem. Soc., 1987; Richard Kuhn Medal, Ges. Deutscher Chem., 1987; (jtly) Nobel Prize for Chemistry, 1988; E. K. Frey-E. Werle Gedächtnismedaille, 1989; Kone Award, Assoc. of Clin. Biochemists, 1990; Sir Hans Krebs Medal, FEBS, 1992; Linus Pauling Medal, 1993–94; Distinguished Service Award, Miami Winter Symposia, 1995; Max Tishler Prize, Harvard Univ., 1997; Max Bergmann Medal, 1997. Bayerischer Maximiliansorden für Wissenschaft und Kunst, 1993; Das Grosse Verdienstkreuz mit Stern und Schulterband (Germany), 1997; Röntgenplakette der Stadt Remscheid-Lennep, 2004; Premio Città di Firenze sulle Scienze Molecolari, 2004. *Publications:* numerous papers in learned jls on crystallography, immunology and structure of proteins. *Recreations:* cycling, hiking, ski-ing. *Address:* Max-Planck Institut für Biochemie, Am Klopferspitz 18a, 82152 Martinsried, Germany. *T:* (089) 85782677/8.

**HÜBNER, Danuta Maria,** PhD; Member (Christian Democrats), European Parliament, since 2009; *b* 8 April 1948; two *d*. *Educ:* Central Higher Sch. of Planning and Statistics, Warsaw (MSc (Econs) 1971; PhD 1974). Researcher, 1971–92, Prof. of Econs, 1992–, Central Higher Sch. of Planning and Statistics, Warsaw, subseq. Warsaw Sch. of Econs; Dep. Dir, Inst. of Develt and Strategic Studies, Warsaw, 1991–94; Under-Sec. of State, Min. of Industry and Trade, 1994–96; Sec. of State for European Integration, 1996–97; Hd, Chancellery of Pres. of Poland, 1997–98; Dep. Exec. Sec., 1998–2000, Exec. Sec., 2000–01, UN Econ. Commn for Europe, Geneva; Sec. of State, Min. of Foreign Affairs, 2001–03; Minister for European Affairs, 2003–04. Mem., Eur. Commn, 2004–09. *Publications:* books and scientific articles. *Address:* European Parliament, 60 rue Wiertz, 1047 Brussels, Belgium.

**HÜBSCHER, Prof. Stefan Georg,** FRCPath; Professor of Hepatic Pathology, since 2005, and Leith Professor, since 2011, University of Birmingham; Hon. Consultant Histopathologist, University Hospitals Birmingham NHS Foundation Trust, since 1989; *b* Birmingham, 6 Oct. 1956; *s* of Georg and Agnes Hübscher; *m* 1981, Dawn Emeny; three *s*. *Educ:* King Edward's Sch., Birmingham; Nottingham High Sch.; Univ. of Birmingham (MB ChB 1979). MRCPath 1985, FRCPath 1995. Hse Surgeon, Selly Oak Hosp., Birmingham, 1979–80; Hse Physician, Dudley Rd Hosp., Birmingham, 1980; Senior House Officer: in Histopathol., Queen Elizabeth Hosp., Birmingham, 1980–81; in Microbiol., Children's Hosp., Birmingham, 1981; University of Birmingham: Lectr in Pathol., 1981–89; Sen. Lectr in Pathol., 1989–2000; Reader in Hepatic Pathol., 2000–05. *Publications:* contrib. papers to peer-reviewed jls, review articles and book chapters. *Recreations:* swimming, gardening, cookery, season ticket holder and shareholder at West Bromwich Albion FC. *Address:* Department of Cellular Pathology, Level -1, Queen Elizabeth Hospital, Birmingham B15 2WB. *T:* (0121) 371 3345, *Fax:* (0121) 371 3333. *E:* s.g.hubscher@bham.ac.uk.

**HUCK, Prof. Steffen,** PhD; Director, Economics of Change, Wissenschaftszentrum Berlin für Sozialforschung, since 2012; Professor of Economics, University College London, since 2003; *b* Seligenstadt, 2 Oct. 1968; *s* of Jochen and Waltraud Huck; *m* 2010, Heike Harmgart. *Educ:* Goethe Univ., Frankfurt (Dip. Econs); Humboldt Univ. (PhD). Res. Fellow, Humboldt Univ., Berlin, 1995–97; Res. Scholar, German Sci. Foundn, 1998–99; Sen. Lectr in Econs, Royal Holloway, Univ. of London, 2000–01; Reader in Econs, 2002–03, Hd, Dept of Econs, 2008–11, UCL. *Publications:* (trans. and ed) Wilfred Owen, Gedichte aus dem Krieg; (ed) Das Narrenschiff, vol. 1 1993, vol. 2 1994; (ed as Julian Weiss) Pop, 1999; (ed) Advances in Understanding Strategic Behaviour, 2004; contribs to learned jls on econs, biol., physics, political sci. and opera. *Recreations:* opera and more opera, TV series binge watching. *Address:* c/o Department of Economics, University College London, Gower Street, WC1E 6BT. *T:* (Germany) (30) 25491421. *E:* s.huck@ucl.ac.uk.

**HUCKFIELD, Leslie (John);** Director, Leslie Huckfield Research (services for higher education and research for non profit organisations), since 1997; Lecturer in Business Management, Glasgow Caledonian University, since 2016; *b* 7 April 1942; *s* of Ernest Leslie and Suvla Huckfield. *Educ:* Prince Henry's Grammar Sch., Evesham; Keble Coll., Oxford; Univ. of Birmingham; Heriot Watt Univ.; Glasgow Caledonian Univ. Lectr in Economics, City of Birmingham Coll. of Commerce, 1963–67. Advertising Manager, Tribune, 1983; Co-ordinator, CAPITAL (transport campaign against London Transport Bill), 1983–84. Prin. Officer, External Resources, St Helen's Coll., Merseyside, 1989–93; European Officer, Merseyside Colls, 1994–95; Eur. Funding Manager, Wirral Metropolitan Coll., 1995–97. Contested (Lab) Warwick and Leamington, 1966; MP (Lab) Nuneaton, March 1967–1983. PPS to Minister of Public Building and Works, 1969–70; Parly Under-Secretary of State, Dept of Industry, 1976–79. MEP (Lab) Merseyside E, 1984–89. Member: Nat. Exec. Cttee, Labour Party, 1978–82; W Midlands Reg. Exec. Cttee, Labour Party, 1978–82; Political Sec., Nat. Union Lab. and Socialist Clubs, 1979–81. Chairman: Lab. Party Transport Gp, 1974–76; Independent Adv. Commn on Transport, 1975–76; Pres., Worcs Fedn of Young Socialists, 1962–64; Member: Birmingham Regional Hosp. Bd, 1970–72; Political Cttee, Co-op. Retail Soc. (London Regional), 1981–93; British Consultants and Construction Bd, 2003–04; Bd, Senscot (Scottish Social Entrepreneurs' Network), 2007–; Associate, W Midlands Office in Europe, 2004–07; community develt, HE and FE projects in W Midlands and Scotland, 2006–. Chartered Mem., RTPI, 2010–13 (Associate Mem., 2007–10). Vis. Fellow, Researcher and Lectr, Yunus Centre for Social Business and Health, Glasgow Caledonian Univ., 2012. *Publications:* various newspaper and periodical articles. *Recreation:* running marathons. *Address:* Glasgow School for Business and Society, Glasgow Caledonian University, Cowcaddens Road, Glasgow G4 0BA. *T:* 07796 266002. *E:* les@huckfield.com. *W:* www.huckfield.com.

**HUCKLE, Alan Edden;** HM Diplomatic Service, retired; Vice President, Falkland Islands Association, since 2019 (Chairman, 2011–14); *b* 15 June 1948; *m* 1973, Helen Gibson; one *s* one *d*. *Educ:* Univ. of Warwick (BA 1st Cl. Hons Hist. 1969; MA Renaissance Studies 1970). Leverhulme Trust Schol., 1971; British Sch. at Rome Schol., 1971; Personnel Mgt Div., CSD, 1971–74; Asst Private Sec. to Sec. of State for NI, Belfast, 1974–75; Machinery of Govt Div., CSD, 1975–78; Pol Affairs Div., NI Office, Belfast, 1978–80; FCO, 1980–83; Exec. Dir, British Inf. Services, NY, 1983–87; Hd of Chancery, Manila, 1987–90; Dep. Hd, Arms Control and Disarmament Dept, FCO, 1990–92; Counsellor and Dep. Hd of Delegn to CSCE, Vienna, 1992–96; Head: Dependent Territories Regl Secretariat, Bridgetown, 1996–98; OSCE/Council of Europe Dept, FCO, 1998–2001; Overseas Territories Dept, FCO, and Comr (non-resident), British Antarctic Territory and British Indian Ocean Territory, 2001–04; Gov. of Anguilla, 2004–06; Gov., Falkland Is and Comr for S Georgia and S Sandwich Is, 2006–10; re-employed as Res. Analyst, FCO, 2012–14. Chm., Chagos Conservation Trust, 2011–14; Trustee, Falkland Is Maritime Heritage Trust, 2015–18.

**HUCKLE, Theodore David;** QC 2011; *b* Blaenavon, Mon, 27 May 1962; *s* of Sylvia Huckle (*née* Lewis); *m* 1994, Alison Claire Bird; four *d*. *Educ:* Jones's West Mon Grammar Sch., Pontypool; Jesus Coll., Cambridge (Titular Exhibnr; BA 1983; LLM 1985; MA 1987). Called to the Bar, Lincoln's Inn, 1985 (Hardwicke & Megarry Schol.), Bencher, 2012. Counsel Gen. for Wales, 2011–16. Formerly Member: Treasury Panel of Counsel; Panel of Counsel, Nat. Assembly for Wales; Panel of Counsel, Serious Fraud Office. Vis. Prof. of Law, KCL, 2016–. Non-executive Director: Justice, 2016–; Welsh Amateur Rowing Assoc. Ltd, 2017–. Ed., Butterworth's Personal Injury Litigation Service, 2016–. *Publications:* (contrib.) Occupational Illness Litigation, 2005–15; Future Loss in Practice: periodical payments and lump sums, 2007; (contrib.) Munkman on Employer's Liability, 15th edn 2009, 16th edn 2013; Jordans Apil Guide to Noise Claims, 2015; contribs to New Law Jl, Jl Personal Injury Law, Personal Injury Law Jl, Personal Injury Focus. *Recreations:* sculling, karaoke, walking, drumming, opera, ski-ing. *Address:* Doughty Street Chambers, 54 Doughty Street, WC1N 2LS. *T:* (020) 7404 1313. *E:* t.huckle@doughtystreet.co.uk. *Club:* Llandaff Rowing.

**HUDD, Roy,** OBE 2004; actor; *b* 16 May 1936; *s* of Harold Hudd and Evalina Barham; *m* 1st, 1963, Ann Lambert (marr. diss. 1983); one *s*; 2nd, 1988, Deborah Flitcroft. *Educ:* Croydon Secondary Technical School. Entered show business, 1957, as half of double act Hudd & Kay; Butlin Redcoats; started as a solo comedian, 1959; first pantomime, Empire Theatre, Leeds, 1959; 4 years' concert party Out of the Blue, 1960–63; first radio broadcast Workers Playtime, 1960; *stage includes:* The Merchant of Venice, 1960; The Give Away, 1969; At the Palace, 1970; Young Vic Co. seasons, 1973, 1976, 1977; Oliver!, 1977; Underneath the Arches, 1982 (SWET Actor of the Year); Run For Your Wife, 1986, 1989; The Birth of Merlin, Theatre Clwyd, 1989; The Fantasticks, 1990; Midsummer Night's Dream, 1991; Friends Like This, 1998; A Funny Thing Happened on the Way to the Forum, 1999; Hard Times, Haymarket, 2000; Theft, 2001; Roy Hudd's Exceedingly Entertaining Evening, 2005–08; The Solid Gold Cadillac, Garrick, 2006; The Merry Widow, Coliseum, 2008; The Wizard of Oz, RFH, 2008; When We Are Married, Garrick, 2010–11; An Evening/Afternoon with Roy and Debbie Hudd, 2012–14; Dick Whittington, 2015, Mother Goose, 2016, Wilton's Music Hall; *films include:* Blood Beast Terror, 1967; Up Pompeii; The Seven Magnificent Deadly Sins; Up the Chastity Belt; The Garnet Saga; An Acre of Seats in a Garden of Dreams, 1973; The Sweet Life, 1998; Kind of Hush, 1998; Purely Belter, 2000; Our Robot Overlords, 2012; *television series include:* Not So Much a Programme, More a Way of Life, 1964; Illustrated Weekly Hudd, 1966–68; Roy Hudd Show, 1971; Comedy Tonight, 1970–71; Up Sunday, 1973; Pebble Mill, 1974–75; Hold the Front Page, 1974–75; The 60 70 80 show, 1974–77; Movie Memories, 1981–85; Halls of Fame, 1985; The Puppet Man, 1985; Cinderella, 1986; Hometown, 1987, 1988–89; What's My Line?, 1990; Lipstick On Your Collar, 1993; Common as Muck, 1994–96; What's My Line, 1994–96; Karaoke, 1996; The Quest, 2002; Coronation Street, 2002–04, 2006–09; The Quest 2, 2004; The Final Quest, 2005; In the City, 2006; *radio series:* The News Huddlines, 1975–2003; Like They've Never Been Gone, 2001–04; Tickling Tunes, 2006; *author of stage shows:* Victorian Christmas, 1978; Just a Verse and Chorus, 1979; Roy Hudd's Very Own Music Hall, 1980; Beautiful Dreamer, 1980; Underneath the Arches, 1982; While London Sleeps, 1983; They Called Me Al, 1987; numerous pantomimes, 1980–. Columnist, Yours magazine, 1991–. Chm., Entertainment Artistes Benevolent Fund, 1980–90. President: British Music Hall Soc., 1992–; TRIC, 2000–01. Trustee, British Actors Equity, 2007–. King Rat, Grand Order of Water Rats, 1989, 2000. Hon. DCL E Anglia, 2007; Hon. DLitt Westminster, 2010. Variety Club BBC Radio Personality, 1976, 1993; Gold Badge of Merit, BASCA, 1981; Sony Gold Award, 1990; British Comedy Lifetime Achievement, LWT, 1990; EMAP Columnist of the Year, 1995; Crystal Award for services to entertainment, Inst. of Entertainment & Arts Mgt, 1995; Roy Castle Award for outstanding services to variety, 2003; The Oldie Diamond Geezer of the Year, 2012; Lifetime Achievement Award, British Pantomime Awards, 2018. *Publications:* Music Hall, 1976; Roy Hudd's Book of Music Hall, Variety and Show Biz Anecdotes, 1993; Roy Hudd's Who's Who in Variety 1945–60, 1997; Twice Nightly, 2007; A Fart In a Colander (autobiog.), 2009. *Recreations:* collecting old songs, sleeping. *Address:* PO Box 604, Ipswich IP6 9WZ. *Club:* Garrick.

**HUDDART, Gabrielle Helen Louise;** Group Editorial Director, Lifestyle, Hearst UK, since 2017; Editor-in-Chief, Good Housekeeping, since 2017; *b* Taplow, 4 April 1966; *d* of Bruce Huddart and Brenda Huddart (later Rogers); *m* 1998, Moussa Ouabdesslam; two *d*. *Educ:* James Allen's Girls' Sch.; Bristol Univ. (BA Hons Hist.). Ed., Square Meal, Monomax, 2001–07; Dep. Ed., Woman & Home, Time Inc. UK, 2007–13; Ed.-in-Chief, Prima, Hearst UK, 2013–17. *Publications:* (ed.-in-chief) Good Housekeeping Christmas, 2018; (ed.-in-chief) Good Housekeeping Express, 2019. *E:* Gaby.Huddart@hearst.co.uk.

**HUDDERSFIELD, Area Bishop of,** since 2014; Rt Rev. Dr Jonathan Robert Gibbs; *b* Manchester, 6 May 1961; *s* of Phillip and Jean Gibbs; *m* 1986, Toni Millsted; two *s* one *d*. *Educ:* King's Sch., Chester; Jesus Coll., Oxford (MA 1989); Jesus Coll., Cambridge (PhD Theol. 1990); Ridley Hall, Cambridge. Ordained deacon, 1989, priest, 1990; Asst Curate, Stalybridge, 1989–92; Chaplain, Basle with Freiburg-im-Breisgau, 1992–98; Rector, Heswall, 1998–2014. Hon. Canon: Ripon Cathedral, 2015–; Bradford Cathedral, 2015–; Wakefield Cathedral, 2017–. *Recreations:* reading and cooking, wines and the culture of France, hill-walking. *Address:* Stone Royd, 9 Valley Head, Huddersfield, W Yorks HD2 2DH. *T:* (01484) 900656. *E:* bishop.jonathan@leeds.anglican.org.

**HUDDLESTON, Nigel Paul;** MP (C) Worcestershire Mid, since 2015; an Assistant Government Whip, since 2019; *b* Lincs, 13 Oct. 1970; *m* 1999, Melissa Peters; one *s* one *d*. *Educ:* Robert Pattinson Comprehensive Sch., N Hykeham; Christ Church, Oxford (BA Hons PPE 1992); Anderson Sch. of Mgt, Univ. of Calif, Los Angeles (MBA 1998). Sen. Manager, Arthur Andersen Business Consulting, 1993–2002; Dir, Strategy Practice,

Deloitte Consulting, 2002–10; Industry Hd of Travel, Google, 2011–15. Mem. (C) St Albans DC, 2011–15. Contested (C) Luton S, 2010. Vice Chair, Conservative Party, 2019. *Address:* House of Commons, SW1A 0AA.

**HUDGELL, Susan Alison**; *see* Pember, S. A.

**HUDGHTON, Ian Stewart**; Member (SNP) Scotland, European Parliament, 1999–2019 (Scotland North East, Nov. 1998–1999); *b* 19 Sept. 1951; *m* 1981, Lily M. Ingram; one *s* one *d* (and one *s* decd). *Educ:* Forfar Acad.; Kingsway Technical Coll., Dundee. Partner and Jt Proprietor, then Proprietor, F. Hudghton & Son, Painters and Decorators, 1971–95. Mem., Cttee of Regions, 1998. Member (SNP): Angus DC, 1986–96 (Housing Convener, 1988–96); Angus Council, 1995–99 (Leader, 1995–99); Tayside Regl Council, 1994–96 (Depute Leader, 1994–96). Pres., SNP, 2005–. *Recreations:* family, theatre, music, horse riding.

**HUDSON, Andrew Peter**, CB 2012; Director General, Public Services (formerly Managing Director, Public Services and Growth), HM Treasury, 2009–11; *b* 22 March 1958; *s* of late John Thomas David Hudson and of Margaret Hudson; *m* 2002, Judith Simpson. *Educ:* King Edward's Sch., Birmingham; New Coll., Oxford (BA Hons). Inland Revenue, 1980–82, 1984–86; HM Treasury: 1982–84; Chancellor of the Exchequer's Office, 1986–89; Local Govt Finance Div., 1989–91; seconded to Interconnection Systems Ltd, 1991–92; Press Sec. to Chancellor of the Exchequer and Hd of Communications, 1992–96; Hd, Health Team, 1996–99; Essex County Council: Asst Chief Exec., 1999–2002; Dep. Chief Exec. (Finance and Performance), 2002–04; Chief Exec., Valuation Office Agency, 2004–09. Sen. Advr, Big Lottery Fund, 2012–15. Chair: Circle 33 Housing Trust, 2012–16; Centre for Homelessness Impact, 2019–; non-exec. Dir, Clarion Housing Gp, 2016–. Chair, The Old Church, arts centre, Stoke Newington, 2012–17; Dir, What Works Centre for Wellbeing, 2015–. Trustee: Hackney Doorways, 2012–19 (Chair, 2014–19); Volunteering Matters, 2015–; Mayday Trust, 2016–. External Mem., Finance Cttee, Univ. of Oxford, 2018–. *Publications:* This Ancient Road: London to Holyhead: a journey through time, 2017; (with Judith Simpson) Wisdom and Wit: extracts from the parish magazine of St Mary's Stoke Newington, 2017. *Recreations:* running, walking, watching sport. *E:* ap.hudson@btinternet.com.

**HUDSON, Prof. Anne Mary**, DPhil; FRHistS; FBA 1988; Professor of Medieval English, Oxford, 1989–2003; Fellow of Lady Margaret Hall, Oxford, 1963–2003, now Hon. Fellow; *b* 28 Aug. 1938; *d* of late R. L. and K. M. Hudson. *Educ:* Dartford Grammar Sch. for Girls; St Hugh's Coll., Oxford (BA English cl. I; MA; DPhil 1964). FRHistS 1976. Lectr in Medieval English, 1961–63, Tutor, 1963–91, LMH, Oxford; Oxford University: CUF Lectr, 1963–81; Special Lectr, 1981–83; British Acad. Reader in the Humanities, 1983–86; Lectr in Medieval English, 1986–89. Early English Text Society: Exec. Sec., 1969–82; Mem. Council, 1982–; Dir, 2006–13. Sir Israel Gollancz Prize, British Acad., 1985, 1991. Dr Hist. *hc* Charles Univ. of Prague, 2010. *Publications:* (ed) Selections from English Wycliffite Writings, 1978; (ed) English Wycliffite Sermons, i, 1983, iii, 1990, iv and v (with P. Gradon), 1996; Lollards and their Books, 1985; (ed jtly) From Ockham to Wyclif, 1987; The Premature Reformation, 1988; (ed) Two Wycliffite Texts, 1993; (ed jtly) Heresy and Literacy 1000–1500, 1994; (ed) The Works of a Lollard Preacher, 2001; Studies in the Transmission of Wyclif's Writings, 2008; (ed) Two Revisions of Rolle's English Psalter Commentary and the Related Canticles, vol. 1, 2012, vol. 2, 2013, vol. 3, 2014; Doctors in English: a study of the Wycliffite Gospel commentaries, 2015. *Address:* Lady Margaret Hall, Oxford OX2 6QA.

**HUDSON, Anthony Sean**; QC 2015; *b* Gateshead, 23 Sept. 1969; *s* of Tony and Eva Hudson; *m* 2000, Shereener Browne; two *s* one *d*. *Educ:* Bedale Secondary Sch.; Univ. of Exeter (LLB Hons). Called to the Bar, Middle Temple, 1996; in practice as barrister, 1996–. *Recreations:* swimming, cycling, running, jazz. *Address:* Matrix Chambers, Griffin Buildings, Gray's Inn, WC1R 5LN. *T:* (020) 7404 3447. *E:* anthonyhudson@matrixlaw.co.uk.

**HUDSON, Barrie**; *see* Hudson, N. B.

**HUDSON, Dr Ian Robert Burton**, FRCP, FFPM; Chief Executive, Medicines and Healthcare Products Regulatory Agency, 2013–19; *b* Middlesbrough, 18 Sept. 1958; *s* of Eric Hudson and Matilda Hudson; *m* 1987, Denise; one *c*. *Educ:* Kingswood Sch., Bath; London Hosp. Med. Coll., Univ. of London (BSc 1979; MB BS 1982; DCH 1985; Dip. Pharm. Med. 1991; MD 1992). FFPM 2001; FRCP 2006. Mainly paediatrics, NHS, 1982–87; Res. Fellow, Univ. of Glasgow, 1987–89; various posts in R&D, SmithKline Beecham, 1989–2001; Dir, Licensing Div., Medicines and Healthcare Products Regulatory Agency, 2001–13. *Publications:* contrib. book chapters in pharmaceutical lit.; articles in jls on paediatrics, anti-infectives, oncology and pharmaceutical regulation. *Recreations:* hiking, kayaking, photography, theatre, opera, restaurants. *Club:* Athenæum.

**HUDSON, Isabel Frances**; Chairman, National House Building Council, since 2011 (Deputy Chairman, 2011); *b* Leicester, 8 Dec. 1959; *d* of Prof. Ronald Philip Draper, *qv*; *m* 1982, Adrian Hudson; two *d*. *Educ:* Collegiate Grammar Sch., Leicester; St Margaret's Sch., Aberdeen; Harlaw Acad., Aberdeen; Lady Margaret Hall, Oxford (MA 1st Cl. Modern Langs 1981). Corporate develt, Royal Internat. and Royal Global, with secondments to Germany and Italy, Royal Insce Gp, 1981–93; Hd, Eur. Develt and Ops, Lloyd's of London, 1993–95; Develt Dir, GE Insce, 1996–99; Chief Financial Officer, Eureko BV, 1999–2002; Exec. Dir, Prudential UK, 2002–06; CEO, Synesis Life, 2006–08. Non-executive Director: Fineos, Ireland, 2002–06; QBE Insce, Australia, 2005–14; Pensions Regulator, 2009–14; Phoenix Gp Hldgs, 2010–17; MGM Advantage, 2010–13; Standard Life, 2014–16; BT plc, 2014–; RSA, 2016– (Sen. Ind. Dir, 2017–). Chm., Business Develt Bd, 2008–11, Ambassador, 2013–, Scope. Mem., Adv. Council, Lady Margaret Hall, Oxford, 2011–. FCII 1985. Rutter Gold Medal, Chartered Insce Inst., 1985. *Recreations:* travel, restaurants, financing daughters' shopping, French DIY.

**HUDSON, Prof. John Geoffrey Henry**, DPhil; FBA 2016; FRSE; Professor of Legal History, University of St Andrews, since 2003; *b* Romford, 7 May 1962; *s* of Stephen Hudson and Rosamond Hudson; *m* 1992, Lise McAslan; two *d*. *Educ:* Brentwood Sch.; Worcester Coll., Oxford (BA 1983; DPhil 1988); Univ. of Toronto (MA 1984). Res. Fellow, Inst. of Histl Res., 1987–88; Jun. Res. Fellow, Worcester Coll., Oxford, 1987–88; University of St Andrews: Lectr in Medieval Hist., 1988–96; Reader in Medieval Hist., 1996–2003. William W. Cook Global Law Prof., Univ. of Michigan Law Sch., 2012–. FRSE 2014. *Publications:* Land, Law and Lordship in Anglo-Norman England, 1994; (ed with G. S. Garnett) Law and Government in Medieval England and Normandy, 1994; (ed) The History of English Law Before the Time of Edward I, 1996; The Formation of the English Common Law, 1996 (trans. Chinese 2006), 2nd edn 2017; The History of Abingdon Abbey, vol. II, 2002, vol. I, 2007; The Oxford History of the Laws of England, vol. II: 871–1216, 2012; (ed with A. Rodríguez) Diverging Paths?: the shapes of power and institutions in Medieval Christendom and Islam, 2014; (ed with G. S. Garnett) J. C. Holt, Magna Carta, 3rd edn, 2015; (ed with S. Crumplin) The Making of Europe, 2016. *Recreations:* music of all forms, sport, literature, conversation over beer or wine. *Address:* Department of Medieval History, University of St Andrews, 71 South Street, St Andrews, Fife KY16 9QW. *T:* (01334) 462888, *Fax:* (01334) 463334. *E:* jghh@st-andrews.ac.uk.

**HUDSON, Kathryn Margaret**; Parliamentary Commissioner for Standards, 2013–17; *b* 28 March 1949; *d* of William and Anne Stead; *m* 1971, Michael Hudson; two *s*. *Educ:* Univ. of Southampton (BSc Sociol./Law); Univ. of S Bank (MSc Public Sector Mgt 1994); letter of accreditation as Probation Officer, Home Office, 1971. Probation Officer, 1971–75; Youth Worker, ILEA, 1979–83; Social Worker, Bromley, 1983–86; Sen. Social Worker, Greenwich, 1986–90; Team Ldr, Adoption and Fostering, 1990–92, Principal Officer, 1992–94, Bexley; Assistant Director of Social Services: Bexley, 1994–98; Lewisham, 1998–2000 (Actg Dir, 2000); Dir, Social Services, Newham, 2001–04; Nat. Dir for Social Care, DoH, 2004–08; Dep. Parly and Health Service Ombudsman, 2008–12. *E:* kathryn@mandkhudson.net.

**HUDSON, Kirsty**; *see* McLeod, K.

**HUDSON, Lucian John**; Director of Public Affairs and Communications, University of Oxford, since 2019; Chair, Earthwatch Europe, since 2016; *b* 5 July 1960; *s* of late John and Vanda Hudson; *m* 1982, Margaret Prythergch. *Educ:* Ecole Montalembert, Paris; Lycée Français de Londres; St Catherine's Coll., Oxford (MA (Hons) PPE); exec. educn courses at London Business Sch., Judge Business Sch., Cambridge Univ. and Saïd Business Sch., Oxford Univ. Strategic communications specialist, with expertise in advocacy, negotiation, collaboration and mediation; BBC: producer and sen. producer, Nine O'Clock News, 1988–93; night editor, Breakfast News, news editor, party confs, 1993–94; strand editor, BBC World, 70 live events and breaking news specials inc. first 6 hrs of death of Diana, Princess of Wales, 1994–97; Hd of Programming and Chief Editl Advr, BBC Worldwide, 1997–99; Dir of e-Communications Gp, Cabinet Office, 2000–01; seconded to MAFF to run media ops during foot and mouth disease, 2001; Dir of Commns, DEFRA, 2001–04; Dir of Commns, DCA, 2004–06; Dir of Communication and Press Sec., FCO, 2006–08; special assignment: on collaborative partnerships, FCO, 2008 (report, The Enabling State: collaborating for success, 2009); MoJ, 2008–09; on secondment from MoJ as Interim Man. Dir, Cornerstone Global Associates and Sen. Advr to Chief Exec., Marie Curie Cancer Care, 2009–10; Partner and Man. Dir, Cornerstone Global Associates, 2010–11; Dir of Communications, Open Univ., 2011–18. Ind. Reviewer, No 10 and Cabinet Office communications review, 2013. Mem., Nat. Criminal Justice Bd, 2004–06. Expert Panel Mem., CEDR Panel on Inquiry into Public Inquiries, 2011, on Collaborative Working, 2011. Mem. Adv. Bd, Global Thinkers Forum, 2014–17. Founding editorial dir, Justpeople.com, 1999–2000. Chm., Liberal Judaism, 2009–15; Mem., 2009–, Chm., Strategic Communications Task Force, 2010–11, Jewish Leadership Council, 2009–16. Chm., Citizens MK Leadership Team, 2015–17. Chm., Rory Peck Trust, 1998–2000. Chm., Council, Tavistock Inst., 2003–07. Gov. and Trustee, Leo Baeck Coll., 2009–12. CEDR Accredited Mediator, 2010. MCIPR 2005. FInstD 2015; FRSA. Sen. Editor, Annual Rev. of Social Partnerships, 2016–. *Publications:* (contrib.) Corporate Responsibility: a research handbook, 2012; (contrib.) Social Partnerships and Responsible Business: a research handbook, 2013; (contrib. jtly) Sustainability, Accounting, Mgt and Policy Jl. *Recreations:* writing, reading, swimming, good conversation. *E:* lucian.hudson@admin.ox.ac.uk.

**HUDSON, Sir Mark (Henry)**, KCVO 2017; Managing Partner, Kinmel Home Farm Partnership, since 2015; *b* 27 Jan. 1947; *s* of Tom Hudson and Peggy Hudson (*née* Field); *m* 1970, Susan Gordon Russell; two *s*. *Educ:* Sedbergh Sch.; St Catharine's Coll., Cambridge (BA 1969, MA 1974); Wye Coll., Univ. of London (Dip. Farm Business Admin 1970). Dir, 1985–2017, Chm., 2006–17, NWF Gp plc; Principal, Mark Hudson Associates, 1991–; Chm., Game Conservancy Trust Ltd, later Game and Wildlife Conservation Trust, 2006–10. Panel Mem., Agricultural Land Tribunal, 1981–99, 2013–16. Pres., CLA, 2003–05. Mem. Council, Duchy of Lancaster, 2006–17 (Chm., 2015–17). Chm., Oxford Farming Conf., 1990–91. Trustee, Farming Community Network, 2018–. Author of report, Food, Flora and Fauna: can land managers deliver?, RICS/RAC, 2009. FRAgS 2015. *Recreations:* family, fishing, golf, travel. *Address:* Pen-y-Waen, Llanbedr DC, Ruthin, Denbighshire LL15 1SU. *Clubs:* Farmers (Chm., 1990), Boodle's, MCC.

**HUDSON, Michael William**; Director of Finance, Worcestershire County Council, since 2018; *b* Liverpool, 21 Jan. 1970; *s* of William Hudson and Norma Hudson; *m* 2010, Catriona Henderson; one *s* three *d*. *Educ:* Woodhey High Sch.; Holy Cross Coll.; Huddersfield Univ. (LLB Hons 1991); Univ. of Manchester (LLM 1992); Liverpool John Moores Univ. (CIPFA 1996). Sen. Auditor, Audit Commn, 1992–98; Dir, KPMG, 1998–2004; Hd of Finance, Oldham Council, 2004–06; Dir of Resources and Treas. to Humber Bridge, Hull CC, 2006–10; Dir of Finance, Wilts Council, 2010–18. Ind. Mem., Audit Cttee, NE Lincs Council, 2000–02. Chm. Govs, North Thoresby Sch., 2000–02. *Recreations:* sports including football, walking, climbing. *Address:* Worcestershire County Council, County Hall, Spetchley Road, Worcester WR5 2NP.

**HUDSON, Rt Rev. Nicholas Gilbert Erskine**; an Auxiliary Bishop of Westminster, (RC), since 2014; Titular Bishop of St Germans, since 2014; *b* Hammersmith, London, 14 Feb. 1959; *s* of Richard Hudson and Marie-Charlotte Hudson (*née* Valdelièvre). *Educ:* Wimbledon Coll.; Jesus Coll., Cambridge (BA 1981); Pontifical Gregorian Univ. (PhB 1982; BTh 1985; STL Fundamental Theol. 1987). Ordained priest, 1986; Asst Priest, St Thomas of Canterbury, Canterbury, 1987–92; Dir, Southwark Christian Educn Centre, 1992–2000; Vice-Rector, 2000–04, Rector, 2004–13, Venerable English Coll., Rome; Parish Priest, Sacred Heart, Wimbledon, 2013–14. *Recreations:* tennis, classical music, Italy. *Address:* Archbishop's House, Ambrosden Avenue, SW1P 1QJ. *T:* (020) 7798 9381, *Fax:* (020) 7798 9077. *E:* nicholashudson@rcdow.org.uk.

**HUDSON, (Norman) Barrie**, CB 1996; Director, International Development Affairs (formerly Under Secretary, International Division), Overseas Development Administration, 1993–97, retired; *b* 21 June 1937; *s* of William and Mary Hudson; *m* 1963, Hazel (*née* Cotterill); two *s* one *d*. *Educ:* King Henry VIII Sch., Coventry; Univ. of Sheffield (BA Hons 1958); University Coll., London (MScEcon 1960). Economist, Tube Investments Ltd, 1960; Economist, Economist Intell. Unit, 1962; National Accounts Statistician (UK Technical Assistance to Govt of Jordan), 1963; Statistician, ODM, 1966; Econ. Adviser, ME Develt Div., Beirut, 1967; Overseas Development Administration: Econ. Adviser, 1972, Sen. Econ. Adviser, 1973; Head, SE Asia Develt Div., Bangkok, 1974; Asst Sec., 1977; Under Sec. (Principal Establishments Officer), 1981; Under Sec. for Africa, 1986. Trustee, SCF, 1998–2005. *Recreations:* theatre, reading, music, watching football and cricket. *Address:* 2 Pine Rise, Meopham, Kent DA13 0JA. *T:* (01474) 814419.

**HUDSON, Pamela May**; *see* Hudson-Bendersky, P. M.

**HUDSON, Vice Adm. Peter Derek**, CB 2015; CBE 2005; Senior Naval Advisor to BAE Systems (Maritime), since 2018; *b* Manchester, 25 June 1961; *s* of Brian and Elizabeth Hudson; *m* 1997, Linda Williams; three *s*. *Educ:* Netherthorpe Grammar Sch., Staveley, Derbys; Britannia Royal Naval Coll.; Open Univ. (BSc Maths/Econs). Joined Royal Navy, 1980; in command: HMS Cottesmore, 1994–96; HMS Norfolk, 1996–98; Fleet Ops Officer, 1998–2000, Team Leader, Fleet Change Prog., 2000–02, Fleet HQ; in command, HMS Albion, 2002–04; Hd of Personnel, C-in-C Fleet, 2005; Dir, Naval Resources and Programming, MoD, 2005–07; Comdr, UK Amphibious Forces, 2008–09; Comdr, UK Maritime Forces, 2009–11; COS (Capability) to C-in-C Fleet, 2011–13; Comdr Maritime

Comd, NATO HQ Northwood, 2013–15. Dir, Internat. Maritime Progs, L3 Technologies, 2016–18. ADC to the Queen, 2008–09. Younger Brother, Trinity Hse, 2005. Freeman, City of London, 2003. *Recreations:* cricket, fly fishing, hill walking, entertaining my children. *Address:* Marchbank, Fordwater Road, Chichester, W Sussex PO19 6PS. *E:* Peter@bethwines.org.uk.

**HUDSON, Prof. Peter John,** DPhil; FRS 2008; Willaman Professor of Biology and Director, Huck Institutes of the Life Sciences, Pennsylvania State University, since 2002. *Educ:* Univ. of Leeds (BSc Zool.); Magdalen Coll., Oxford (DPhil). Hd, Upland Res. Gp, Game Conservancy Trust; Prof., Univ. of Stirling, 1995–2002. Corresp. FRSE 2010. Laurent Perrier Award, 1985; Carlton Herman Award, 2005. *Publications:* The Red Grouse: the biology and management of a wild gamebird, 1986; (with M. W. R. Rands) Ecology and Management of Gamebirds, 1988; Grouse in Space and Time, 1992; (with D. Newborn) A Handbook of Grouse and Moorland Management, 1995; (jtly) Ecology of Wildlife Diseases, 2001; contribs to jls incl. Nature, Science, Ecol., Amer. Naturalist, Internat. Jl Parasitol., Parasitol., Proc. Royal Soc., Jl Helminthol., Oikos, Jl Applied Ecol. *Address:* Huck Institutes of the Life Sciences, Pennsylvania State University, University Park, PA 16802, USA.

**HUDSON, Rachel Sophia Margaret; Her Honour Judge Hudson;** a Circuit Judge, since 2009; a Deputy High Court Judge, since 2008; Designated Family Judge for Northumbria and North Durham, since 2014; *b* Cranleigh, Surrey, 29 Jan. 1963; *d* of late Stuart Hudson and Olive Hudson; *m* 2013, Gary Stacey; one *s* by a previous marriage. *Educ:* Newcastle Church High Sch.; Queen Elizabeth Grammar Sch., Hexham; London Sch. of Econs (LLB). Called to the Bar, Middle Temple, 1985; in practice as a barrister, Trinity Chambers, Newcastle upon Tyne, 1985–2009; a Recorder, 2005–09. *Recreation:* family life. *Address:* Newcastle upon Tyne Combined Court Centre, Quayside, Newcastle upon Tyne NE1 3LA. *T:* (0191) 201 2000.

**HUDSON, Prof. Raymond,** PhD, DLitt, DSc; FBA 2006; Professor of Geography, 1990–2016, now Emeritus Professor, and Deputy Vice-Chancellor, 2012–14 and 2015–16, University of Durham (Acting Vice-Chancellor, 2014–15); *b* 7 March 1948; *s* of John and Jean Hudson; *m* 1975, Geraldine Holder Jones; one *s* one *d. Educ:* Bristol Univ. (BA 1st Cl. Hons 1969; PhD 1974; DSc 1996); DLitt Durham 2013. University of Durham: Lectr in Geog., 1972–83; Sen. Lectr, 1983–87; Reader, 1987–90; Head of Geog. Dept, 1992–97; Dir, Centre for European Studies, 1990–99; Chair, Internat. Centre for Regl Regeneration and Develt Studies, 1999–2005; Dir, Wolfson Res. Inst., 2003–07; Pro Vice-Chancellor, Partnerships and Engagement, 2007–12. Vis. Prof., UCD, 2017–; Hon. Prof., Cardiff Univ., 2017–. Chairman: Conf. of Heads of Geog. Depts in HE Instns in UK, 1995–99; Human Geog. Subject Area Panel, ESRC, 1999–2001; Member: Trng and Develt Bd, ESRC, 2002–06; Higher Educn Acad., 2007–; HEFCE Strategic Adv. Cttee for Enterprise and Skills, 2010–13, for Res. and Knowledge Exchange, 2013–14; Bd, Health and Educn Innovation Cluster North East, 2012–14. Vice-Pres., RGS with IBG, 1999–2004; Pres., Geog. Sect., BAAS, 2001–02. FAcSS (AcSS 2001); MAE 2007; FRSA 2009; Fellow, Regl Studies Assoc., 2010. Editor, European Urban and Regional Studies, 1994–2007. Hon. DSc Roskilde, 1987. Edward Heath Award, 1989, Victoria Medal, 2005, RGS; Sir Peter Hall Award, Regl Studies Assoc., 2014. *Publications:* (with D. Pocock) Images of the Urban Environment, 1978; (contrib. and ed, jtly) Regions in Crisis, 1980; (with D. W. Rhind) Land Use, 1980; (contrib. and ed, jtly) Regional Planning in Europe, 1982; (contrib. and ed, jtly) Redundant Spaces in Cities and Regions, 1983; (jtly) An Atlas of EEC Affairs, 1984; (contrib. and ed, jtly) Uneven Development in Southern Europe, 1985; (with A. Williams) The United Kingdom, 1986; Wrecking a Region, 1989; (with D. Sadler) The International Steel Industry, 1989; (with A. Williams) Divided Britain, 1989; (jtly) A Tale of Two Industries, 1991; (jtly) A Place called Teesside, 1994; (ed and contrib., jtly) Towards a New Map of Automobile Manufacturing in Europe?, 1995; (with M. Dunford) Successful European regions, 1996; (contrib. and ed jtly) Divided Europe, 1998; (jtly) Digging up Trouble: environment, protest and opencast coal mining, 2000; Production, Place and Environment: changing perspectives in economic geography, 2000; (jtly) Coalfields Regeneration: dealing with the consequences of industrial decline, 2000; Producing Places, 2001; (jtly) Placing the Social Economy, 2002; Economic Geographies: circuits, flows and spaces, 2005; Approaches to Economic Geography: towards a geographical political economy, 2016; (contrib. and ed jtly) Corrupt Places: the illicit and illegal in the governance and development of cities and regions, 2017; Co-Produced Economies: capital, collaboration, competition, 2019; numerous articles in scientific and scholarly jls. *Recreations:* reading, music, watching sport, travel. *Address:* 7 Oliver Place, Merryoaks, Durham DH1 3QS. *T:* (0191) 386 2963, 07793 903351.

**HUDSON, Prof. Richard Anthony,** FBA 1992; Professor of Linguistics, University College London, 1989–2004, now Emeritus; *b* 18 Sept. 1939; *s* of late Prof. John Pilkington Hudson, CBE, GM and Mary Gretta Hudson (*née* Heath); *m* 1970, Gaynor Evans; two *d. Educ:* Loughborough Grammar Sch.; Corpus Christi Coll., Cambridge (BA); Sch. of Oriental and African Studies, London (PhD). University College London: Research Asst, Linguistics, 1964–70; Lectr 1970, Reader 1980, Dept of Phonetics and Linguistics. *Publications:* English Complex Sentences: an introduction to systemic grammar, 1971; Arguments for a Non-Transformational Grammar, 1976; Sociolinguistics, 1980; Word Grammar, 1984; An Invitation to Linguistics, 1984; English Word Grammar, 1990; Teaching Grammar: a guide for the national curriculum, 1992; Word Meaning, 1995; English Grammar, 1998; Language Networks: the new word grammar, 2007; An Introduction to Word Grammar, 2010; articles in jls. *Recreations:* walking, cycling, music. *Address:* Research Department of Linguistics, University College London, Chandler House, 2 Wakefield Street, WC1N 1PF. *T:* (020) 7679 2000.

**HUDSON, Richard Bayliss,** RDI 1999; stage designer; *b* 9 June 1954; *s* of Peter Obank Hudson and Ella Joyce Bayliss. *Educ:* Peterhouse Sch., Rhodesia; Wimbledon Sch. of Art (BA Hons 1976). Designer of sets and costumes, 1986–, for major theatre companies in Britain, and for Royal Opera, ENO, Glyndebourne, Chicago Lyric Opera, La Fenice, Vienna State Opera, Bayerische Staatsoper; designs include: King Lear and Candide, Old Vic (Olivier award for season), 1988; A Night at the Chinese Opera, Kent Opera, 1990; The Queen of Spades, 1992, Eugene Onegin, 1994, Manon Lescaut, 1997, Le Nozze di Figaro and Don Giovanni, 2000, Glyndebourne; Die Meistersinger, Royal Opera, 1993; The Cherry Orchard, RSC, 1995; The Lion King, Broadway, 1997 (Tony Award, 1998), also London, Tokyo, Osaka, Toronto, Los Angeles, Hamburg; Samson et Dalila, Met. Opera, New York, 1998; Guillaume Tell and Ernani, Vienna State Opera, 1998; Peter Grimes, Amsterdam, 2000; Pique Dame, Chicago Lyric Opera, 2000; Tamerlano, Maggio Musicale Fiorentino, 2001; The Cunning Little Vixen, Opera North, 2001; Khovanshchina, Opéra de Paris, 2001; Doctor Faustus, Young Vic, 2002; Benvenuto Cellini, Zurich, 2002; Les Vêpres Siciliennes, Opéra de Paris, 2003; Ring Cycle, ENO, 2004–05; Emperor Jones, Gate, 2005; Women Beware Women, 2006, Coriolanus, 2007, RSC; L'après-midi d'un Faune, Jeux, Fall of the House of Usher, Bregenz Fest., 2006; The Makropulos Case, Royal Danish Opera, 2006; Death in Venice (costumes), Aldeburgh Fest., La Bohème, Greek Nat. Opera, 2007; La Forza del Destino, Vienna State Opera, Rushes, Royal Ballet, 2008; Divorzio all'Italiana, 2008, Kafka's Monkey, 2009, Young Vic; Goldberg Variations, ROH2, 2009; Rigoletto, Vienna Volksoper, 2009; Armida, Metropolitan Opera, NY, Tamerlano, Royal Opera, The Nutcracker, Amer. Ballet Th., 2010; Eidolon, Royal Danish Ballet, Invitus Invitam, Royal Ballet, 2010; Die Entführung aus dem Serail, Rome Opera, Romeo and Juliet, Nat. Ballet of Canada, 2011; La Nuit de Gutenberg, Opéra du Rhin (costumes), Terre et Cendres, Opéra de Lyon (costumes), Pêcheurs des Perles, Opéra Comique, Paris (costumes), La Bayadère and Le Coq d'Or, Royal Danish Ballet, 2012; Versailles, Donmar Warehouse, Peter Grimes, Opéra de Lyon (costumes), La Traviata, Grange Park Opera, 2014; Morgen und Abend, ROH, Roméo et Juliette, Nat. Opera of Korea, The Sleeping Beauty, Amer. Ballet Th. and La Scala, Milan, 2015; Das Rhinegold, Die Walküre, Siegfried and Götterdämmerung, Teatro Massimo, Palermo, Morgen und Abend, Deutsche Oper Berlin, 2016; Common, NT, Raymonda, Royal Danish Ballet, Romeo and Juliet, Bolshoi Ballet, Moscow, 2017; The Outsider, Print Room, 2018; Peter Gynt, NT, 2019. British Scenographic Comr, Orgn Internat. des Scénographes, Techniciens et Architectes de Théâtre, 1996–2011. Pres., Soc. of British Stage Designers, 2008–. Companion, Liverpool Inst. for Perf. Arts, 2009. FRWCMD 2010. DUniv Surrey, 2005. Gold Medal for set design, Prague Quadriennal, 2003. *Address:* c/o Judy Daish Associates, 2 St Charles Place, W10 6EG.

**HUDSON-BENDERSKY, Pamela May,** CBE 1988; JP; Regional Nursing Director, North West Thames Regional Health Authority, 1985–88, retired; *b* 1 June 1931; *d* of late Leonard Joshua Hudson and of Mabel Ellen Hudson (now Baker); *m* 1987, David Bendersky (*d* 2012), NY State and Kansas City. *Educ:* South West Essex High School. SRN. Nursing Officer, Charing Cross Hosp., 1966–67; Matron, Fulham Hosp., 1967–70; Principal Regl Nursing Officer, SE Thames RHB, 1970–73; Area Nursing Officer, Lambeth, Southwark and Lewisham AHA(T), 1973–82; Regional Nursing Officer, NW Thames RHA, 1982–85. Member, Alcohol Education and Research Council, 1982–87. JP: Inner London SE Div., 1983–88; N Glos (formerly Cheltenham) Petty Sessional Div., 1989–2001 (Chm., 1998–2001). *Publications:* contribs to nursing profession jls. *Recreations:* embroidery, theatre, gardening. *Address:* 15 Horsefair, Campden Road, Shipston on Stour CV36 4PD. *T:* (01608) 661158.

**HUDSON-SMITH, Prof. Andrew Paul,** PhD; Professor of Digital Urban Systems, University College London, since 2015 (Director, Bartlett Centre for Advanced Spatial Analysis, 2010–18); *b* Wokingham, Berks, 15 Oct. 1970; *s* of John and Barbara Smith; partner, Sonja K. Curtis. *Educ:* Plymouth Univ. (BSc Geog. 1992); Univ. of Wales Coll., Cardiff (MSc Town Planning 1996); University Coll. London (PhD Digital Planning 2003). Bartlett Centre for Advanced Spatial Analysis, University College London: res. asst, 1996–99; Res. Fellow, 2004–05; Sen. Res. Fellow, 2005–08; Lectr and Res. Manager, 2008–10; Reader in Digital Urban Systems, 2012–15; Dep. Academic Dir, UCL East, 2016–17. Vis. Prof., Univ. of Plymouth, 2018–. Ed.-in-Chief, Future Internet Jl, 2010–. Mem., All Party Parly Gp, Smart Cities, 2014–. Mem., Smart London Bd, GLA, 2013–. FRSA 2011. *Recreations:* meteorology, horology, 3D printing. *Address:* Bartlett Centre for Advanced Spatial Analysis, UCL Faculty of the Built Environment, 1st Floor, 90 Tottenham Court Road, W1T 4TJ. *T:* (020) 3108 3877. *E:* a.hudson-smith@ucl.ac.uk.

**HUDSON-WILKIN, Rt Rev. Rose Josephine;** *see* Dover, Bishop Suffragan of.

**HUEY, Robert John,** TD 2006; Chief Veterinary Officer for Northern Ireland and Deputy Secretary, Department of Agriculture, Environment and Rural Affairs, Northern Ireland, since 2013; *b* Magherafelt, Co. Londonderry, 9 April 1959; *s* of John Huey and Anna Huey (*née* Causey); *m* 2006, Jane Alison Virgoe; one *s* one *d. Educ:* Cookstown High Sch., University Coll. Dublin (MVB). RCVS Dip. Vet. Public Health (Meat Hygiene) 1996; FRCVS 2017. Gen. Vet. Practice, Maghera, Co. Londonderry, 1983–88; Department of Agriculture, then Department of Agriculture and Rural Development, later Department of Agriculture, Environment and Rural Affairs, Northern Ireland: Vet. Officer, 1988–95; Divl Vet. Officer, 1995–2002; Sen. Principal Vet. Officer, 2002–09; Dep. Chief Vet. Officer, 2009–13. President: Vet. Public Health Assoc., 1997; N of Ireland Vet. Assoc., 2003; Union of Eur. Vet. Hygienists, 2003–07; Vice Pres., Fedn of Vets of Europe, 2012–15. RAVC, 1989–2016, retd in rank of Lt Col. ARAgS 2017. Volunteer Medal, 2015. Freeman, City of London, 2014; Liveryman, Butchers' Co., 2014. *Publications:* Meat Hygiene, 10th edn 1999, 11th edn 2015. *Recreations:* breeding Irish Draught/Sport horses, cattle, sheep, gardening. *Address:* Cloonlara, 31a Knockaleery Road, Cookstown, Co. Tyrone BT80 9EG. *T:* 07764 204418. *E:* roberthuey@btinternet.com. *Club:* Farmers.

**HUEY EVANS, Gay Jeanette,** OBE 2016; Chair, London Metal Exchange, since 2019; *b* New York, 17 July 1954; *d* of late Clarence Calvin Huey and of Frances Huey; *m* (marr. diss.); one *d. Educ:* Bucknell Univ. (BA Econs). Sen. Man. Dir, Bankers Trust, NY and London, 1984–98; Dir, Mkts Div., FSA, 1998–2005; Pres., Tribeca Global Mgt and Hd of Governance, Citigroup Alternatives, 2005–08; Vice-Chm., Investment Banking and Investment Mgt, Barclays, 2008–10. Chm., 1994–98, Vice-Chm., 2011–12, non-exec. Chm. (Europe), 2011–12, Internat. Swaps and Derivatives Assoc., Inc. Non-executive Director: London Stock Exchange Gp, 2010–13; Itau BBA International, 2012–; Standard Chartered plc, 2015–; Independent non-executive Director: Aviva plc, 2011–15; ConocoPhillips, 2013–; HM Treasury, 2019–. Dep. Chair, Financial Reporting Council, 2014–19 (Mem., 2012–19). Mem., Lord Mayor's Appeal Cttee, 2009–10. Mem., Council of Foreign Relns, 2009–. Mem., Forum UK, 2010–19. Trustee: Wigmore Hall, 2005–13; Bucknell Univ., 2009–11; Wellbeing of Women, 2011–; Beacon Collaborative, 2018–; Chair, Beacon Fellowship Charitable Trust, 2014–18. FRSA. *Recreations:* tennis, music, cooking, trekking.

**HUFFINGTON, Arianna Stassinopoulos;** Founder and Chief Executive, Thrive Global, since 2016; *b* Athens, 15 July 1950; *d* of Kostantinos and Elli Stassinopoulos; *m* 1986, Michael Huffington (marr. diss. 1997); two *d. Educ:* Girton Coll., Cambridge (BA Econs 1972; MA). Pres., Cambridge Union. Co-founder: Detroit Project, 2003; Huffington Post, 2005; Pres. and Ed.-in-Chief, Huffington Post Media Gp, 2011–16. Board Member: El País; Cttee to Protect Journalists. Hon. Dr Brown, 2011. Awards include: Best Political Blog, Webby Awards, 2008; President's Award, LA Press Club, 2009; Oceana Partners Award, 2009; Fred Dressler Lifetime Achievement Award, 2009; Emery Award, Hetrick-Martin Inst., 2010; Media/Entertainment Design Award, Global Green Sustainable Design Awards, 2010; Online Commentary/Blogging Award, Online Journalism Awards, 2011; Forces for Nature Award, Natural Resources Defense Council, 2011; Aenne Burda Award, 2012. *Publications:* The Female Woman, 1974; After Reason, 1978; Maria Callas: the woman behind the legend, 1981, 2002; The Gods of Greece, 1983, 2000; Picasso: creator and destroyer, 1988, 1996; The Fourth Instinct: the call of the soul, 1994, 2003; Greetings from the Lincoln Bedroom, 1998, 1999; How to Overthrow the Government, 2000, 2001; Pigs at the Trough: how corporate greed and political corruption are undermining America, 2003, 2004; Fanatics and Fools: the game plan for winning back America, 2004; On Becoming Fearless… in Love, Work and Life, 2006, 2007; Right is Wrong: how the lunatic fringe hijacked America, shredded the Constitution and made us all less safe, 2008; Third World America: how our politicians are abandoning the middle class and betraying the American dream, 2010, 2011; Thrive: the third metric to redefining success and creating a life of well-being, wisdom and wonder, 2014; The Sleep Revolution, 2016. *Address:* Thrive Global, 599 Broadway, 6th Floor, New York, NY 10012, USA.

**HUFTON, Dame Olwen,** DBE 2004; PhD; FBA 1993; Professor of History, University of Oxford, 1997–2003 (Leverhulme Personal Research Professor, 1997–2002); Senior Research Fellow, Merton College, Oxford, 1997–2003, now Fellow Emeritus; *d* of Joseph Hufton and Caroline Hufton; *m* 1965, Brian Taunton Murphy; two *d*. *Educ*: Hulme Grammar Sch., Oldham; Royal Holloway Coll., Univ. of London (BA 1959; Hon. Fellow, 2000); UCL (PhD 1962; Hon. Fellow, 1999). Lectr, Univ. of Leicester, 1963–66; Reading University: Lectr, then Reader, 1966–75; Prof. of Modern Hist., 1975–88; Vis. Fellow, All Souls Coll., Oxford, 1986–87; Prof. of Modern Hist. and Women's Studies, Harvard Univ., 1987–91; Prof. of History, Eur. Univ. Inst., Florence, 1991–97. Hon. DLitt: Reading, 1999; Southampton, 2006. *Publications*: Bayeux in the Late Eighteenth Century, 1967; The Poor of Eighteenth Century France, 1974; Europe, Privilege and Protest 1730–1789, 1980, 2nd edn 2001; Women and the Limits of Citizenship in the French Revolution, 1992; The Prospect before Her: a history of women in Western Europe, vol. 1, 1500–1800, 1995; articles in Past and Present, Eur. Studies Rev., and French Hist. Studies.

**HUGGINS,** family name of **Viscount Malvern**.

**HUGGINS, Geoffrey Lawrence;** Director, NHS Education for Scotland Digital Service, since 2018; *b* Newtownards, 24 Sept. 1965; *s* of Reginald Lawrence Huggins and Kathleen Patricia Huggins; partner, Stella Smith; two *s* one *d*. *Educ*: Bangor Grammar Sch.; Queen's Univ., Belfast (LLB Hons 1988; MSSc 1998); Univ. of Edinburgh; European University Inst., Fiesole (Erasmus Scholarship 1989). NI Office, 1991–98; Hd, Schs Policy, Scottish Exec., 1998–2000; Scottish Government: Dep. Dir, Housing, 2000–04; Hd, Mental Health, 2004–13; Dir for Health and Social Care Integration, 2013–18. Director: EU Jt Action on Dementia, 2016–; Internat. Initiative for Mental Health Leadership, 2019–; Cornerstone, 2019–. Mem., Health Cttee, NESTA, 2018–. *Recreations*: photography, running, film. *Address*: NHS Education for Scotland Digital Service, Bayes Centre, 47 Potterrow, Edinburgh EH8 9BT. *E*: geoff.huggins@nes.scot.nhs.uk, geoffhuggins@gmail.com.

**HUGGINS, Rt Rev. Philip James;** an Assistant Bishop, Diocese of Melbourne (Bishop of the North & West Region (formerly Bishop of the Northern Region)), 2004–18; *b* 16 Oct. 1948; *s* of Alf Huggins and Mary Nutt; *m* 1976, Elizabeth Cuming; three *s*. *Educ*: Monash Univ. (BEcon, Grad. Dip. Welfare Admin, MA). Teaching Fellow, Univ. of New England, 1971–74; ordained priest, 1977; worked in parishes, Dio. of Bendigo, 1977–80; Industrial Chaplain, dio. Melbourne, 1980–83; Univ. Chaplain, Monash Univ., 1983–89; Exec. Officer, Archbishop of Melbourne's Internat. Develt Fund, 1990–91; Rector of Williamstown, 1991–95; Archdeacon of Essendon, 1994–95; Regl Bishop, Dio. of Perth, 1995–98; Bishop of Grafton, NSW, 1998–2003; Parish Priest, St Stephen's Anglican Church, Richmond, Vic, 2003–04. ChLJ 1997. *Recreations*: varied sports, poetry, the arts. *Address*: c/o The Anglican Centre, 209 Flinders Lane, Melbourne, Vic 3000, Australia.

**HUGH, Nicholas Daniel;** Chief Executive Officer, Telegraph Media Group, since 2017 (Chief Operating Officer, 2016–17); *b* London, 4 April 1975; *s* of Terence and Doris Hugh; *m* 2003, Jodi Marshall; two *s* one *d*. *Educ*: Haberdashers' Aske's Boys' Sch.; Univ. of Manchester (BA French and Italian 1998); INSEAD (Louis Frank Schol.; MBA Business Mgt 2004). Yahoo, 2008–16, Vice Pres., EMEA, 2015–16. Non-executive Director: Esure, 2018–19; Go Compare, 2019–. Mem. Bd, News Media Assoc., 2017–. Mem. Bd, Childline, 2018–. *Recreations*: football, ski-ing. *Address*: The Telegraph, 111 Buckingham Palace Road, SW1W 0DT. *Club*: Soho House.

**HUGH-JONES, George;** QC 2010; *b* London, 7 March 1958; *s* of late Kenneth Hugh-Jones and Denise Hugh-Jones; *m* 1993, Shelley North; one *s* one *d*. *Educ*: Downside Sch.; Downing Coll., Cambridge (BA Mod. Langs (French and Russian) 1979; MA); City Univ. (DipLaw 1982). Called to the Bar, Middle Temple, 1983; in practice as barrister, 1983–, specialising in clinical negligence and healthcare disciplinary work. *Recreations*: tennis, swimming. *Address*: Serjeants' Inn Chambers, 85 Fleet Street, EC4Y 1AE. *E*: ghughjones@serjeantsinn.com.

**HUGHES,** family name of **Baroness Hughes of Stretford** and **Baron Hughes of Woodside**.

**HUGHES OF STRETFORD,** Baroness *cr* 2010 (Life Peer), of Ellesmere Port in the County of Cheshire; **Beverley June Hughes;** PC 2004; Deputy Mayor for Policing, Criminal Justice and Fire, Greater Manchester, since 2017; *b* 30 March 1950; *d* of Norman Hughes and Doris Hughes (*née* Gillard); *m* 1973, Thomas K. McDonald; one *s* two *d*. *Educ*: Manchester Univ. (BSc Hons, MSc); Liverpool Univ. (DSA, DASS). Merseyside Probation Service, 1973; Manchester University: Res. Fellow, 1976; Lectr, Sen. Lectr and Head of Dept of Social Policy and Social Work, 1981–97. Mem. (Lab), Trafford MBC, 1986–97 (Leader, 1995–97). MP (Lab) Stretford and Urmston, 1997–2010. Parly Under-Sec. of State, DETR, 1999–2001, Home Office, 2001–02; Minister of State: Home Office, 2002–04; DFES, later DCSF, 2005–09; Minister for the NW, 2007–09. Non-exec. Dir, Gtr Manchester Chamber of Commerce, 2013–. Chair, Council, Salford Univ., 2014–17; Trustee, Lowry Co., 2012–. *Publications*: Community Care and Older People, 1995. *Recreations*: jazz, walking, family. *Address*: House of Lords, SW1A 0PW.

**HUGHES OF WOODSIDE,** Baron *cr* 1997 (Life Peer), of Woodside in the City of Aberdeen; **Robert Hughes;** *b* Pittenweem, Fife, 3 Jan. 1932; *m* 1957, Ina Margaret Miller; two *s* three *d*. *Educ*: Robert Gordon's Coll., Aberdeen; Benoni High Sch., Transvaal; Pietermaritzburg Tech. Coll., Natal. Emigrated S Africa, 1947, returned UK, 1954. Engrg apprentice, S African Rubber Co., Natal; Chief Draughtsman, C. F. Wilson & Co. (1932) Ltd, Aberdeen, until 1970. Mem., Aberdeen Town Council, 1962–70; Convener: Health and Welfare Cttee, 1963–68; Social Work Cttee, 1969–70. Mem., AMICUS (formerly AEU, then AEEU), 1952–97. Contested (Lab) North Angus and Mearns, 1959; MP (Lab) Aberdeen North, 1970–97. Member: Standing Cttee on Immigration Bill, 1971; Select Cttee, Scottish Affairs, 1971 and 1992–97; introd Divorce (Scotland) Bill 1971 (failed owing to lack of time); Parly Under-Sec. of State, Scottish Office, 1974–75; sponsored (as Private Member's Bill) Rating (Disabled Persons) Act 1978; Principal Opposition Spokesman: on agriculture, 1983–84; on transport, 1985–88 (Jun. Opp. Spokesman, 1981–83); Mem., PLP Shadow Cabinet, 1985–88. Chm., Aberdeen City Labour Party, 1961–69. Vice-Chm., Tribune Gp, 1984–85. Founder Mem. and Aberdeen Chm., Campaign for Nuclear Disarmament; Vice-Chm., 1975–76, Chm., 1976–94, Anti-Apartheid Movement; Member: GMC, 1976–79; Movement for Colonial Freedom, 1955 (Chm. Southern Africa Cttee); Scottish Poverty Action Group; Aberdeen Trades Council and Exec. Cttee, 1957–69; Labour Party League of Youth, 1954–57; Chm., 1994–99, Hon. Pres., 1999–, Action for Southern Africa; Hon. Pres., Mozambique Angola Cttee, 2001–; Trustee, Canon Collins Educn Trust for Southern Africa, 1997–2007. Grand Companion, Order of Oliver Tambo (SA), 2004. *Recreation*: fishing. *Address*: House of Lords, SW1A 0PW.

**HUGHES OF OMBERSLEY, Rt Hon. Lord;** **Anthony Philip Gilson Hughes,** Kt 1997; PC 2006; a Justice of the Supreme Court of the United Kingdom, 2013–18; *b* 11 Aug. 1948; *s* of late Patrick and Patricia Hughes; *m* 1972, Susan Elizabeth March; one *s* one *d*. *Educ*: Tettenhall Coll., Staffs; Van Mildert Coll., Durham (BA 1969; Hon. Fellow 2015). Sometime Lectr, Durham Univ. and QMC. Called to the Bar, Inner Temple, 1970, Bencher, 1997 (Treas. 2019); in practice at the Bar, 1971–97; a Recorder, 1988–97; QC 1990; a Judge of the High Court of Justice, Family Div., 1997–2003, QBD, 2004–06; a Lord Justice of Appeal, 2006–13; Vice-Pres., Court of Appeal (Criminal Div.), 2009–13. Presiding Judge, Midland (formerly Oxford and Midland) Circuit, 2000–03. Hon. LLD: Birmingham, 2009; Durham, 2019; Hon. DLitt Worcester, 2014. *Recreations*: garden labouring and mechanics, bellringing. *Clubs*: Athenæum; Worcester Rowing.

**HUGHES, Alan;** Managing Director, Whitechapel Bell Foundry Ltd (established 1570), since 1982; *b* 25 Aug. 1948; *s* of William A. Hughes and Florence I. Hughes; *m* 1985, Kathryn Smith; two *d*. *Educ*: Christ's Hosp. Church bell founder, 1966–. Freeman, City of London, 1984; Liveryman, Founders' Co., 2000. *Address*: Whitechapel Bell Foundry Ltd, 126 Queensway, West Wickham, Kent BR4 9DY.

**HUGHES, Prof. Alan;** Professor of Innovation, Imperial College Business School, Imperial College London, since 2014; Margaret Thatcher Professor of Enterprise Studies, Judge Business School (formerly Judge Institute of Management Studies), 1999–2013, now Emeritus, and Director, Centre for Business Research, 1994–2013, now Director Emeritus, University of Cambridge; Life Fellow, Sidney Sussex College, Cambridge, since 2013 (Fellow, 1973–2013); *b* 1 Aug. 1946; *s* of Benjamin Redshaw Hughes and Lilias Hughes; *m* 1968, Jean Braddock; two *s* one *d*. *Educ*: King's Coll., Cambridge (BA Econs 1968). Sen. Economic Asst, NEDO, 1971–73; University of Cambridge: Univ. Asst Lectr, then Univ. Lectr in Econs, 1973–94; Chm., Faculty Bd of Econs and Pols, 1983–88; Dir, ESRC Small Business Res. Centre, Dept of Applied Econs, 1989–93; Dir of Res., Judge Inst. of Mgt Studies, 2001–04; Dir, Nat. Competitiveness Network Prog., Cambridge-MIT Inst., 2000–03; Dir, ESRC Impact Acceleration Account Prog., 2013–. Distinguished Visiting Professor: Doshisha Univ., Kyoto, 2005–15; Lancaster Univ. Mgt Sch., 2016–; Hon. Prof., Univ. of Queensland Business Sch., 2012–; Sen. Res. Fellow, Nat. Centre for Univs and Business, 2013–16. Member: Commn on Public Policy and British Business, 1995–96; DfES Expert Panel on Educn, Learning and Lifelong Skills, 2000–05; Prime Minister's Council for Sci. and Technol., 2004–13; Expert Panel, Australian Nat. Innovation Rev., 2008–09; Adv. Panel, Excellence Initiative, Wissenschaftsrat, Germany, 2011–12; EPSRC Strategic Adv. Network, 2011–13; Lead Expert Gp, Foresight Future of Manufg Proj., 2012–14; Patents Expert Adv. Gp, IP Office, 2012; Ind. Sci. and Technol. Adv. Panel, MoD, 2017–. *Publications*: (ed with D. J. Storey) Finance and the Small Firm, 1994; (ed with S. Deakin) Enterprise and Community: new directions in corporate governance, 1997; edited with A. D. Cosh) The Changing State of British Enterprise: growth, innovation and competitive advantage in SMEs 1986–1995, 1996; Enterprise Britain: growth innovation and public policy in the small and medium sized enterprise sector 1994–1997, 1998; Takeovers, 3 vols, 1998; British Enterprise in Transition: growth innovation and public policy in the small and medium sized enterprise sector 1994–1999, 2000; Enterprise Challenge: policy and performance in the British SME Sector 1999–2002, 2003; British Enterprise: thriving or surviving, 2007; (jtly) Knowledge Exchange Between Academics and the Business, Public and Third Sectors, 2009; (jtly) Growing Value: business-university collaboration for the 21st century, 2012; (with M. Kitson) Connecting with the Ivory Tower: business perspectives on knowledge exchange in the UK, 2013; (jtly) Cultural Connections: the role of the arts and humanities in competitiveness and local development, 2014; (ed) The Future of UK Manufacturing: scenario analysis, capital markets and industrial policy, 2014; (jtly) The Economic Significance of the UK Science Base, 2014; over 200 articles in jls etc. *Recreations*: photography, birdwatching, golf, gardening, watching football and Rugby. *Address*: Centre for Business Research, Judge Business School, Trumpington Street, Cambridge CB2 1AG. *T*: (01223) 765335, *Fax*: (01223) 765338. *E*: a.hughes@cbr.cam.ac.uk.

**HUGHES, Ven. Dr Alexander James;** Archdeacon of Cambridge, since 2014; *b* Honiara, Solomon Islands, 3 Oct. 1975; *s* of John and Jill Hughes; *m* 1998, Sarah Newman; two *s*. *Educ*: Priory Sch., Lewes; Eton Coll.; Greyfriars, Oxford (BA 1997; MA 2004); St Edmund's Coll., Cambridge (MPhil 1999; PhD 2011). Ordained deacon, 2000, priest, 2001; Asst Curate, Headington Quarry, Oxford, 2000–03; Bishop's Domestic Chaplain, Portsmouth, 2003–08; Vicar, St Luke and St Peter, Southsea, 2008–14. Hon. Canon, Ely Cathedral, 2014–. *Publications*: Public Worship with Communion by Extension: some pastoral and theological issues, 2002; (contrib.) The Anglican Religious Communities Yearbook, 2005; (contrib.) Fear and Friendship: Anglicans engaging with Islam, 2012; Alexander J. Hughes, Oliver Quick and the Quest for a Christian Metaphysic, 2015; (jtly) For God's Sake: reimagining priesthood and prayer in a changing church, 2017; contrib. to jls incl. Third Millennium, Theology, Anaphora, Modern Believing. *Recreations*: running, music, reading, writing. *Address*: 1A Summerfield, Cambridge CB3 9HE. *T*: (01223) 355013. *E*: alexanderjameshughes@gmail.com. *Club*: Newnham Riverbank.

**HUGHES, Aneurin Rhys;** Ambassador and Head of Delegation of European Commission to Australia and New Zealand, 1995–2002; *b* 11 Feb. 1937; *s* of William and Hilda Hughes; *m*; two *s*; *m* 2001, Lisbeth Lindbaeck. *Educ*: University College of Wales, Aberystwyth (BA; Fellow, 2002). President, National Union of Students, 1962–64. Research in S America, 1964–66; HM Diplomatic Service, 1967–73: served, Singapore and Rome; Commission of the European Communities, 1973–2002: Head of Division for Internal Coordination in Secretariat-General, 1973–77; Adviser to Dir Gen. for Information, 1977–80; Chef de Cabinet to Mr Ivor Richard, Comr responsible for Employment, Social Affairs and Educn, 1981–85; Adviser to Dir Gen. for Information, and Chm., Selection Bd for Candidates from Spain and Portugal, 1985–87; Amb. and Head of Delegn in Norway, 1987–95. *Publications*: Billy Hughes – Founding Father of the Australian Labour Party, 2005. *Recreations*: golf, music.

**HUGHES, Anthony Philip Gilson;** see Hughes of Ombersley, Rt Hon. Lord.

**HUGHES, Antony;** see Hughes, M. A.

**HUGHES, Dr Antony Elwyn;** consultant, 1996–2003; Director, Engineering and Science, and Deputy Chief Executive, Engineering and Physical Sciences Research Council, 1994–96; *b* 9 Sept. 1941; *s* of Ifor Elwyn Hughes and Anna Betty Hughes (*née* Ambler); *m* 1963, Margaret Mary Lewis; one *s* two *d* (and one *s* decd). *Educ*: Newport High Sch., Gwent; Jesus Coll., Oxford (MA; DPhil). CPhys; FInstP. Harkness Fellow, Cornell Univ., 1967–69. United Kingdom Atomic Energy Authority, Atomic Energy Research Establishment (Harwell): Scientific Officer, 1963–67; Sen. Scientific Officer, 1969–72; Principal Scientific Officer, 1972–75; Leader: Defects in Solids Gp, 1973; Solid State Sciences Gp, 1978; Individual Merit Appointment, 1975–81; Sen. Personal Appointment, 1981–83; Head, Materials Physics Div., 1983–86; Dir, Underlying Res. and Non-Nuclear Energy Res., 1986–87; Authority Chief Scientist and Dir, Nuclear Res., 1987–88. Science and Engineering Research Council: Dir, Labs, 1988–91; Dir, Progs, and Dep. Chm., 1991–93; acting Chief Exec., 1993–94. Mem., NI Higher Educn Council, 1993–2001. Member Council: Royal Instn of GB, 1995–98; Careers Res. and Adv. Centre, 1994–2007. *Publications*: Real Solids and Radiation, 1975; (ed) Defects and their Structure in Non-Metallic Solids, 1976; review articles in Contemporary Physics, Advances in Physics, Jl of Materials Science, Jl of Nuclear Materials, Reports on Progress in Physics. *Recreations*: walking, watching Rugby and cricket, playing the trumpet, gardening. *Address*: Kingswood, King's Lane, Harwell, Didcot, Oxfordshire OX11 0EJ. *T*: (01235) 835301.

**HUGHES, Belinda Carol, (Bee);** Headmistress, Maynard School, Exeter, 2009–16; b Liverpool, 12 Dec. 1962; d of Derek Visick Hughes and Gillian Hughes. Educ: Helsby Grammar Sch.; Liverpool John Moores Univ. (BEd Hons); Univ. of Leicester (MBA); Nat. Coll. of Sch. Leaders (NPQH). Hd of House, Island Sch., Hong Kong, 1987–97; Hd, Lower Sch., West Island Sch., Hong Kong, 1997–2001; Dep. Headteacher, Hitchin Girls' Sch., 2001–08. Chair, GSA SW and Wales Reg., 2013; Ind. Sch. Rep., ASCL Nat. Council, 2013–16. Mem., CBI, 2014. Recreations: photography, tennis, theatre, international cinema, Renaissance Italy.

**HUGHES, Hon. Claudia Madeleine;** see Ackner, Hon. C. M.

**HUGHES, Colin;** Managing Director, Collins Learning, HarperCollins UK, since 2012; b Dunstable, Beds, 17 March 1958; s of Gerald Arthur Hughes and Edith Annalina Hughes (née Welsch); m 1st, 1981, Nicola Gerrard (marr. diss. 1990); one s one d; 2nd, 1992, Alexandra Smith (marr. diss. 2018); one s one d; one d by Fiona Lazenby. Educ: Bulmershe Sch., Reading; Hertford Coll., Oxford (MA English Lang. and Lit. 1979); Preston Coll. (NCTJ 1979); Wharton Coll., Univ. of Pennsylvania (AMP 2005). Reporter and municipal corresp., Sheffield Star, 1979–82; gen. reporter, Press Assoc., 1982; local govt and Whitehall corresp., The Times, 1983–86; The Independent: political corresp., 1986–89; US corresp., 1990; Educn and Policy Ed., 1991–93; Man. Ed., 1993–98, Dep. Ed., 1996–98; Associate Ed., Guardian, 1998–2000; Man. Dir, Learn.co.uk, 2000–06; Dir, Business and Professional, Guardian, 2006–12. Non-exec. Dir, Excelsoft Technologies (Mysore) Pty, 2010–. Mem., Technol. and Content Cttee, British Educnl and Communications Technol. Agency, 2004–05. Mem., Adv. Bd, The Rialto, 2016–. Chm., Educnl Publishers' Council, 2013–18; Mem. Council, Publishers' Assoc., 2013–17. Dep. Chm., Cttee of Univ. Chairs, 2015–17; Mem. Council, Coll. of Teachers, 2015–16. Chairman: of Govs, Gospel Oak Primary Sch., 1992; of Govs, Yerbury Primary Sch., 2001–06; Bd of Govs, Univ. of Middx, 2009–17. Trustee: PiXL Edge, 2015–17; WEA, 2016–18; Aldeburgh Cinema Trust, 2018–. Publications: (with P. Wintour) Labour Rebuilt: the new model party, 1990; (ed) What Went Wrong, Gordon Brown?, 2010. Recreations: writing mediocre poetry, reading better poetry, suffering the Arsenal's failings, delighting in my children's existence, walking too fast over hills, cycling too slowly up them, running too far everywhere, watching birds wherever, sailing my aged 32-footer onto sandbanks and into pontoons, playing my concert grand badly and hearing others play theirs gloriously as a Friend of the Wigmore. Address: HarperCollins UK, News Building, 1 London Bridge Street, SE1 9GF. T: (020) 8307 4120. E: colin.hughes@harpercollins.co.uk.

**HUGHES, His Honour Dafydd Lloyd;** a Circuit Judge, 2004–14; Deputy Designated Family Judge, Caernarfon and Rhyl, 2007–14; b 3 June 1947; s of Rev. Elwyn Morris Hughes and Gwen Mai Hughes (née Evans); m 1971, Ann Tegwen Davies; one s two d. Educ: Grove Park Grammar Sch. for Boys, Wrexham; University Coll. London (LLB Hons). Admitted solicitor, 1971; Asst Solicitor and Partner, Edmund Pickles & Upton, Solicitors, Wrexham, 1971–90; Co. Court Registrar, later Dist Judge, 1990–2004; Asst Recorder, 1994–98; Recorder, 1998–2004; Liaison Judge, N Wales Magistrates, 2007–14; Nominated Judge to hear Court of Protection cases for N Wales, 2012–. Mem., Ministerial Steering Gp on Childcare Proceedings Rev., Welsh Assembly Govt, later Welsh Govt, 2006–. Mem., Adv. Cttee, CAFCASS Cymru, 2006–14. Hon. Recorder of Caernarfon, 2012–15. Recreations: theatre, museums and galleries, travel, cookery, developing and refining grandparenting skills.

**HUGHES, (David Evan) Peter,** MA; Head of Science, Westminster School, 1984–89; b 27 April 1932; s of late Evan Gwilliam Forrest-Hughes, OBE; m 1956, Iris (née Jenkins); one s one d (and one d decd). Educ: St Paul's Sch.; St John's Coll., Oxford (Gibbs Schol. in Chemistry; MA). National Service, 5 RHA, 1954. Assistant Master, Shrewsbury School, 1956; Head of Chemistry, 1958, Science, 1965; Nuffield Foundation, 1967–68; Second Master, Shrewsbury Sch., 1972; Headmaster, St Peter's Sch., York, 1980–84; part-time teacher, Westminster Sch., 1994–2011; Dir, Understanding Science Project, and Leverhulme Res. Fellow, Imperial Coll. and Westminster Sch., 1989–94. Chief Examr, Univ. of Cambridge Local Exam. Syndicate, 1968–2006. Chm., Friends' Cttee, Imperial Coll., 1992–94. Publications: Advanced Theoretical Chemistry (with M. J. Maloney), 1964; Chemical Energetics, 1967; (ed) Awareness of Science, 4 vols, 1993–94; (with P. F. Cann) Chemistry for Advanced Level, 2002; (with P. F. Cann) Chemistry, 2015; contrib. Oxford DNB; articles in professional jls. Recreations: music, bridge, hill-walking. Address: 5 Woodbank Drive, Porthill, Shrewsbury SY3 8RW.

**HUGHES, Prof. David John,** CEng, FREng, FIMechE, CDir; Managing Director, Business Innovation Group LLP, since 2006; b 5 May 1947; m 1970, Dawn Anne Newman; two d. Educ: Royal Grammar Sch., High Wycombe; Aston Univ. (MSc 1970). CEng 1975, FREng 2001; FIMechE 1996; MIEEE 2000. Hd, Electrical/Electronic Systems, Ford Motor Co., 1970–91; Director: Advanced Vehicle Systems, Lucas plc, 1991–97; Technol. Planning, GEC plc, 1997–99; Exec. Vice Pres., Marconi plc, 1999–2001; Dir, Special Projects, BAE Systems, 2002; Dir Gen., Innovation Gp, and Chief Scientific Advr, DTI, 2002–06. Member: Technol. and Innovation Cttee, CBI, 1999–2003; EPSRC, 2003–06; Innovation and Engagement Bd, Cardiff Univ., 2005–11; Innovation Adv. Bd, Surrey Univ., 2006–11; Chairman: Industrial Partnership Panel, City Univ., 2009–12; Mgt Bd, Additive Manufacturing Centre, Loughborough Univ., then at Nottingham Univ., 2011–14; Member, Strategic Advisory Board: Wolfson Sch., Loughborough Univ., 2016–; Sch. of Maths, Computer Sci. and Engrg, City, Univ. of London, 2017–. Vis. Prof., Engrg Mgt, City, Univ. of London (formerly City Univ.), 2006–. Trustee: RAEng, 2016–; Engrs Trust, Engrs' Co., 2018–. CDir 2007; FInstD 2016. Hon. DTech Loughborough, 2008. Publications: articles for various jls and mgt confs. Recreations: walking, 20th century British art, antique metalware, African tribal art. Address: School of Mathematics, Computer Science and Engineering, City, University of London, EC1V 0HB.

**HUGHES, David Richard;** journalist; Chief Leader Writer, Daily Telegraph, 2006–13; b 3 April 1951; s of John Arfon Hughes and Lilian Elvira Hughes (née Jones); m 1973, Christine O'Brien; two s. Educ: Cowbridge Grammar Sch.; Univ. of Leicester (BA Hons Hist.). Reporter, Merthyr Express, 1973–76; Leader Writer, 1976–79, Political Corresp. 1979–84, Western Mail; Political Reporter, Daily Mail, 1984–86; Political Corresp. 1986–89, Chief Political Corresp., 1989–92, Sunday Times; Editor, Western Mail, 1992–94; Political Ed., 1994–2005, Leader Writer, 2005–06, Daily Mail. Recreations: Rugby, walking in Wales. Address: 7 Southfield Gardens, Strawberry Hill, Twickenham TW1 4SZ. T: (020) 8892 5726.

**HUGHES, Dr David Treharne Dillon,** FRCP; Consultant Physician, Royal London (formerly London) Hospital, 1970–96; Director, Respiratory Medicine, Royal Hospitals NHS Trust, 1994–96; Head, Department of Clinical Investigation, Wellcome Research Laboratories, 1978–93; b 31 Oct. 1931; s of Maj.-Gen. W. D. Hughes, CB, CBE; m 1959, Gloria Anna Bailey; one s two d. Educ: Cheltenham Coll.; Trinity Coll., Oxford (BSc, MA); London Hosp. Medical Coll. (BM BCh); RPMS. MRCP 1959, FRCP 1972. Jun. hosp. posts, London Hosp., 1957–59; Capt. RAMC, 1959–61 (jun. med. specialist, BMH Hong Kong); Res. Fellow, Univ. of Calif, 1963–64; jun. hosp. appts, London Hosp., 1964–70. Mem., GMC, 1993–96. Clinical Dir, Atos Origin Coalminers Medical Assessment Process for DTI, 1999–2010. Past President: Internat. Soc. Internal Medicine; Hunterian Soc.; Chm., Bd of Govs, Moving Theatre Trust, 1994–2000; Hon. Vice-Pres., Royal Theatrical Fund, 2010–. Master, Soc. of Apothecaries, 1992–93. Publications: Tropical Health Science, 1967; Human Biology and Hygiene, 1969; Lung Function for the Clinician, 1981; numerous scientific papers on respiratory function and chest disease. Recreations: cricket, rowing, horse racing, theatre. Address: Littleport Farm, Sedgeford, Norfolk PE36 5LR. T: (01485) 570955. Clubs: Savage, Garrick; Leander (Henley-on-Thames).

**HUGHES, Dr (Edgar) John,** CBE 2017; HM Diplomatic Service, retired; b 27 July 1947; s of William Thomas Hughes and Martha Hughes (née Riggs); m 1982, Lynne Evans; two s. Educ: Lewis Sch., Pengam, Wales; LSE (BSc Econ 1969); Lehigh Univ., USA (MA 1970); Pembroke Coll., Cambridge (Univ. of Cambridge Sara Norton Res. Prize in Amer. Hist., 1972; PhD 1973). FCO, 1973–79; on secondment to Cabinet Office, 1979–81; First Sec., UK Delegn to CSCE, Madrid, 1981–82; FCO, 1982–83; First Sec. and Head of Chancery, Santiago, 1983–85; First Sec. (Inf.), Washington, 1985–89; Counsellor and Hd of Aviation and Maritime Dept, FCO, 1990–93; Dep. Hd of Mission, Norway, 1993–97; Change Manager, FCO, 1997–99; on secondment to BAE Systems, 1999–2000; Ambassador to Venezuela, 2000–03; on secondment to Shell, 2003–04; Ambassador to Argentina, 2004–08; non-resident Ambassador to Paraguay, 2005–08. Robin Humphreys Fellow, Inst. for Study of the Americas, Univ. of London, 2008–10; Sen. Vis. Fellow, 2011–12, Vis. Prof. in Practice, 2016–, LSE (Mem. Adv. Bd, LSE Ideas, 2016–). Chm., Marshall Scholarships Commn, 2011–16 (Comr, 2009–16); Hon. Mem., Assoc. of Marshall Scholars, 2015–. Chm., Canning House, 2012–16 (Trustee, 2010–16). Chairman: LatAmConsult Ltd, 2009–; British Argentine Chamber of Commerce, 2017–. Trustee, Atlantic Coll., Wales, 2010–17. FRSA 2010. Mem., Gorsedd, Y Wladfa (Patagonia, Argentina), 2007–. Publications: The Historian as Diplomat (with P. A. Reynolds), 1976; articles in internat. affairs jls. Recreations: ski-ing, golf, watching Rugby, reading. Club: Rhymney Rugby Football.

**HUGHES, Edmund Francis;** MP (C) Walsall, since 2017; b Birmingham, 3 Oct. 1968; s of Tommie Hughes; m 2014, Clare; one s one d by a previous marriage. Educ: Handsworth Grammar Sch.; Univ. of Glamorgan (BSc Civil Engrg). Dir, Develt and Asset Mgt, 2014–17, Asst Chief Exec., 2017, YMCA Birmingham. Mem. Bd, 2012–16, Chm., 2016–, Walsall Housing Gp. Mem. (C), Walsall Council, 1999–2018. Contested (C) Birmingham Hall Green, 2005. Address: House of Commons, SW1A 0AA.

**HUGHES, Frances Mary Theresa;** Senior Partner, Hughes Fowler Carruthers, since 2001; b Richmond, Surrey, 15 June 1954; d of Noel and Joanna Hughes; m 2003, Jonathan Buckeridge; two s one d. Educ: Ursuline Convent, Wimbledon; St Anne's Coll., Oxford (BA 1976; MA 1981). Admitted solicitor, 1981; Solicitor: Theodore Goddard, 1981–83; Bates Wells & Braithwaite, 1983–2001. Vice Pres., Eur. Br., 2003–09, Gov. at Large, Internat. Br., 2005–11, Internat. Acad. of Matrimonial Lawyers. Mediator, 1990–. Gov., Hanover Primary Sch., 1993–98. Co-Founder, Poet in the City, 1999 (Mem., Steering Cttee, 1999–2002); Mem. Bd, Poetry Soc., 2001–05; Trustee: Shelter from the Storm, 2009–11; Arts Patrons Trust, 2010–; Complicité Th., 2014–. FRSA. Recreations: viola player, both orchestral and in string quartets, opera, theatre, poetry, Hampstead Ladies Pond. Address: Hughes Fowler Carruthers, Academy Court, 94 Chancery Lane, WC2A 1DT. T: (020) 7421 8383, Fax: (020) 7421 8384. E: f.hughes@hfclaw.com. Club: Union.

**HUGHES, Francine Elizabeth;** see Stock, F. E.

**HUGHES, Very Rev. Geraint Morgan Hugh;** Dean of Brecon, 1998–2000; b 21 Nov. 1934; s of late Ven. Hubert Hughes, Archdeacon of Gower, and late Blodwen Hughes; m 1959, Rosemary Criddle; one s one d. Educ: Brecon Grammar Sch.; Keble Coll., Oxford (BA 1958; MA 1963); St Michael's Coll., Llandaff. Nat. Service, RAF, 1953–55. Ordained deacon, 1959, priest, 1960; Curate: Gorseinon, 1959–63; Oystermouth, 1963–68; Rector: Llanbadarn Fawr Group, 1968–76; Llandrindod with Cefnllys, 1976–98; Canon of Brecon Cathedral, 1989–98; RD of Maelienydd, 1995–98. Chaplain, Mid and West Wales Fire Bde, 1996–2009 (Supervisory Chaplain, 2002–09); Mid Wales Regl Chaplain, SJAB, 2003–18. Pres., Llandrindod Hosp. Friends, 2002–19. Paul Harris Fellow, Rotary Club, 1991. OStJ 2004. Recreations: gardening, computing, sheep husbandry, wood turning, local history. Address: Hafod, Cefnllys Lane, Penybont, Llandrindod Wells, Powys LD1 5SW. T: (01597) 851830.

**HUGHES, Rev. Dr Gerard Joseph,** SJ; Tutor in Philosophy, since 1998, Master, 1998–2006, Campion Hall, University of Oxford; b 6 June 1934; s of Henry B. Hughes and Margaret (née Barry). Educ: Campion Hall, Oxford (MA Greats 1962); Heythrop Coll. (STL 1967); Univ. of Michigan (PhD 1970). Entered Society of Jesus, 1951; ordained priest, 1967; Heythrop College, University of London: Lectr in Philosophy, 1970–98; Head, Dept of Philosophy, 1974–96; Vice-Principal, 1984–98. Hon. DLit London, 2009. Publications: Authority in Morals, 1978; (ed) The Philosophical Assessment of Theology, 1987; The Nature of God, 1995; Aristotle on Ethics, 2001; Is God to Blame?, 2007; Fidelity without Fundamentalism, 2010. Recreations: classical music, gardening. Address: Campion Hall, Oxford OX1 1QS. T: (01865) 286111.

**HUGHES, Prof. Graham Robert Vivian,** MD; FRCP; Professor of Medicine, King's College London, since 2005; Head, London Lupus Centre, London Bridge Hospital, since 2005; b 26 Nov. 1940; s of G. Arthur Hughes and Elizabeth Emily Hughes; m 1966, Monica Ann Austin; one s one d. Educ: Cardiff High Sch. for Boys; London Hosp. Med. Coll. (MB BS 1967; MD 1973). Trng posts, London Hosp., 1967–69; Vis. Fellow, Columbia Univ., NY, 1969–70; Sen. Registrar, Hammersmith Hosp., 1970–73; Consultant, Univ. Hosp. of WI, Kingston, Jamaica, 1974; Consultant, and Reader in Medicine, Hammersmith Hosp., 1975–85; Consultant, and Hd, Lupus Arthritis Res. Unit, subseq. Lupus Unit, St Thomas' Hosp., 1985–2005. Ed., Lupus, 1991–; mem., editl bds of numerous jls. Consultant, RAF, 1985–. Life Pres., Lupus UK, 1985; Hughes Syndrome Foundn, 2001–; Patron, Arthritis Research UK, 2011–. Dr hc: Marseilles, 2001; Barcelona, 2004. Rheumatology World Prize, Internat. League against Rheumatism, 1993; Lifetime Achievement Award: Internat. Soc. for Immunology, 2006; European Lupus Soc., 2011; Master, Amer. Coll. of Rheumatol., 2006. Publications: Connective Tissue Diseases, 1977, 4th edn 1994; Modern Topics in Rheumatology, 1977; Clinics in Rheumatic Diseases: Systemic Lupus Erythematosus, 1982; Lupus: a guide for patients, 1985; Lecture Notes in Rheumatology, 1986; Problems in the Rheumatic Diseases: lessons from patients, 1988; Phospholipid Binding Antibodies, 1991; Autoimmune Connective Tissue Diseases, 1993; Antibodies to Endothelial Cells and Vascular Damage, 1993; Hughes Syndrome, 1998; Lupus: the facts, 2000; Hughes Syndrome: a patients' guide, 2001; Understanding Hughes Syndrome, 2009; The London Lupus Centre, Book of Lupus: a patients' guide, 2009; Tales of a Flying Doctor, 2011; Hughes Syndrome: highways and byways, 2013; Sjogren's Syndrome in Clinical Practice, 2014; contrib. numerous papers on lupus and related diseases. Recreations: tennis, golf, sailing, piano (classical and jazz). Address: London Lupus Centre, London Bridge Hospital, 27–29 Tooley Street, SE1 2PR. T: (020) 7234 2155. E: graham.hughes@hcaconsultant.co.uk.

**HUGHES, (Harold) Victor,** CBE 1989; FRAgS; Principal, Royal Agricultural College, Cirencester, 1978–90, Principal Emeritus 1990; b 2 Feb. 1926; s of Thomas Brindley Hughes and Hilda Hughes (née Williams). Educ: Tenby County Grammar Sch.; UCW,

Aberystwyth (BSc). FRAgS 1980. Lectr, Glamorgan Training Centre, Pencoed, 1947–49; Crop Husbandry Adv. Officer, W Midland Province, Nat. Agricultural Adv. Service, 1950; Lectr in Agric., RAC, 1950–54; Vice Principal, Brooksby Agricultural Coll., Leics, 1954–60; Royal Agricultural College: Farms Dir and Principal Lectr in Farm Management, 1960–76; Vice Principal and Farms Dir, 1976–78. Hon. MRICS (Hon. ARICS 1984). FIAgrM 1992. *Publications:* articles in learned jls and agric. press. *Recreation:* shooting. *Address:* Park House Court, Narberth Road, Tenby, Pembrokeshire SA70 8TJ.

**HUGHES, Helen Margaret;** *see* Mahy, H. M.

**HUGHES, Henry Andrew Carne M.;** *see* Meyric Hughes.

**HUGHES, Iain;** QC 1996; *His Honour Judge Iain Hughes;* a Circuit Judge, since 2002; Designated Civil Judge for Hampshire, Isle of Wight, Dorset and Wiltshire, since 2003; a Senior Circuit Judge, since 2010; *b* 7 Dec. 1950; *s* of late John Sidney Mather and of Jessica Mather; *m* 1978, Hon. Claudia Madeleine Ackner, *qv*; one *s* and (and one *s* decd). *Educ:* Moseley Hall Grammar Sch., Cheadle; Univ. of Bristol (LLB); King's Coll. London (MA Dist. War Studies 2011). Called to the Bar, Inner Temple, 1974; Bencher, 2001. Recorder, 2000–02. Chm., Professional Negligence Bar Assoc., 2000–01. *Publications:* (ed) Jackson and Powell on Professional Negligence, 3rd edn 1992, 4th edn 1997. *Recreations:* military history, opera, theatre. *Address:* c/o The Law Courts, Winchester SO23 9EL.

**HUGHES, Prof. Ian Edward,** PhD; Professor of Pharmacology, University of Leeds, 1999–2006, now Emeritus, and Visiting Professor, Institute of Membrane and Systems Biology, since 2010; *b* Southport, 9 Aug. 1941; *s* of late Lawrence Edward Hughes and Elizabeth Winifred Hughes (*née* Aspinwall); *m* 1966, Patricia Anne Frettsome (*d* 2003); two *s*. *Educ:* Worksop Coll.; Univ. of Leeds (BSc Pharmacy 1962; BSc Pharmacol. 1963; PhD Pharmacol. 1965). FBPhS (FBPharmacolS 2000). Asst Lectr in Pharmacol., Univ. of Leeds, 1966; Sen. Tutor in Pharmacol., Univ. of WA, 1966–68; University of Leeds: Lectr in Pharmacol., 1968–79; Sen. Lectr, 1979–99; Actg Hd of Dept, 1984–90. Dir, UK Centre for Biosci., Higher Educn Acad., 2000–07. Chair, 1998–2010, Mental Health Act Manager, 2010–, Leeds Partnerships NHS Foundn Trust. Panel Chair, Judicial Appts Commn, 2007–. Chair, Speciality Sch. Bds (Medicine, Pathol., Oncol., Radiol.), London Deanery, 2010–14. Member: Fitness to Practise panels, Gen. Social Care Council, 2007–12; Teaching Regulation Agency (formerly Teaching Agency, then Nat. Coll. for Teaching and Leadership), 2012–; HCPC, 2012–. Member: Gen. Osteopathic Council, 2003–13; GMC, 2004–08. Vice-Chm., Qualifications Cttee, Bar Council, 2006–11. Mem. and Vice-Chm., Wellcome Trust/MRC UK Biobank Ethics and Governance Council, 2004–11. UK Nat. Teaching Fellowship holder, 2001. Mem., Bd of Mgt, Richmond Fellowship, 2005–14. FHEA 2001. *Publications:* MCQ in Dental Pharmacology and Therapeutics, 1984; Learning Pharmacology through MCQ, 1985, 2nd edn 1990 (Japanese edn 1990); contribs to jls incl. British Jl Pharmacol., Eur. Jl Pharmacol., Jl Pharmacy and Pharmacol., Trends in Pharmacol Scis. *Recreations:* gardening, walking, wood turning. *Address:* Faculty of Biological Sciences, University of Leeds, Leeds LS2 9JT.

**HUGHES, Ian Noel,** CMG 2014; HM Diplomatic Service, retired; Ambassador to the Republic of South Sudan, 2013–15; *b* 5 Dec. 1951; *s* of Robert John Hughes and Sylvia Betty Hughes (*née* Lewis); *m* 1978, Tereasa June Tinguely; two *s* one *d*. *Educ:* Khormaksar, Aden; St John's, Singapore. FCO, 1971–74; Latin America Floater, 1974–76; Vice-Consul: Kabul, 1976–80; Warsaw, 1980–82; S Pacific Dept, FCO, 1982–85; Second Sec. and Vice-Consul, Tegucigalpa, 1985–88; First Sec. (Political), Berne, 1988–90; News Dept, FCO, 1991–93; First Sec. (Press/Information), New Delhi, 1993–97; Dep. Hd, Near East and N Africa Dept, FCO, 1997–2000; Dep. Hd of Mission and Consul-Gen., Mexico City, 2000–03; Dep. High Comr, Mumbai, 2003–05; Ambassador to Guatemala, El Salvador and Honduras, 2006–09; High Comr to Sierra Leone, and Ambassador (non-resident) to Liberia, 2009–13. *Recreations:* reading, history, travel, playing golf badly.

**HUGHES, Prof. Ieuan Arwel,** MD; FRCP, FRCPCH, FMedSci; FLSW; Professor and Head of Department of Paediatrics, 1989–2011, Foundation Professor, 2011, Emeritus Professor, 2012, University of Cambridge; Fellow, Clare Hall, Cambridge, 1994–2007, now Life Member; Member, Fitzwilliam College, Cambridge, since 2012 (Bye Fellow, 2007–12); Visiting Fellow, PHG Foundation (Foundation for Genomics and Population Health), since 2012; *b* 9 Nov. 1944; *s* of Arwel Hughes and Enid Phillips (*née* Thomas); *m* 1969, Margaret Maureen Davies; two *s* one *d*. *Educ:* Univ. of Wales Coll. of Medicine, Cardiff (MB, BCh, MD); MA Cantab, 1991. MRCP 1971, FRCP 1984; FRCPC 1974; FRCPCH 1997; MRSocMed. Medical Registrar, UCH, 1970–72; Senior Paediatric Resident, Dalhousie Univ., Canada, 1972–74; Endocrine Research Fellow, Manitoba Univ., Canada, 1974–76; MRC Fellow, Tenovus Inst., Cardiff, 1976–78; Consultant Paediatrician, Bristol, 1978–79; Senior Lectr in Child Health, 1979–85, Reader in Child Health, 1985–89, Univ. of Wales Coll. of Medicine, Cardiff. Chm., DoH Cttee on Toxicity of Chemicals in Food, Consumer Products and the Envmt (Phytoestrogen Working Gp), 2002–08. President: European Soc. for Paediatric Endocrinology, 1993– (Sec., 1987–92); Assoc. of Clinical Profs of Paediatrics, 1995–99; Section of Endocrinology, RSocMed, 2005–07; Chm., Clinical Cttee, British Soc. for Paediatric Endocrinology and Diabetes, 2009–12; Coordinator, Eur. Soc. of Paediatric Endocrinology-supported Paediatric Endocrine Trng Centres in Africa (Nairobi, Lagos), 2013–; Member: Council, Soc. for Endocrinology; Expert Gp on Androgens and Women in Sport, IAAF, 2010–; Cambridge-Africa Adv. Gp, 2014–. Trustee: Newlife the Charity for Disabled Children (formerly Newlife Foundn), 2011–; dsdfamilies, 2017–. Hon. Vis. Prof. of Paediatrics, NUS, 2012–. Sen. (formerly Perspectives) Ed., Archives of Disease in Childhood, 2003–11 (Chair, Nominations Cttee for Biomed. Scis, 2015–18; Mem. Council, 2018–). Member: Ralph Vaughan Williams Soc., 2000–; Wagner Soc., 2009–. Founder FMedSci 1998; FLSW 2012 (Chair, Nominations Cttee for Biomed. Scis, 2015–18). Andrea Prader Prize, European Soc. for Paediatric Endocrinology, 2006; James Spence Medal, RCPCH, 2014. *Publications:* Handbook of Endocrine Tests in Children, 1986; (ed) Elsevier Encyclopaedia of Paediatric Endocrinology, 2019; 350 articles on paediatric endocrine disorders, biochemistry and mechanism of steroid hormone action; 100 chapters in standard endocrine textbooks, incl. Williams Textbook of Endocrinology, 14th edn; medico-legal expert for paediatric endocrinology and case reviews for hospital trusts and Health Ombudsman. *Recreations:* music (choral singing, bassoon, piano, concert-going), travel, hill walking, cycling, ski-ing. *Address:* 4 Latham Road, Cambridge CB2 7EQ.

**HUGHES, Ignatius Loyola;** QC 2009; a Recorder, since 2005; *b* Liverpool, 1962; *s* of late Peter Hughes and Rose Mary Hughes; *m* 1994, Dagmar Steffens; one *s* one *d*. *Educ:* St Anselm's Coll., Birkenhead; Univ. of Newcastle upon Tyne (LLB Hons). Called to the Bar, Middle Temple, 1986; in practice as barrister specialising in criminal law. *Recreations:* ski-ing, surfing, real ale, football. *Address:* Albion Chambers, Broad Street, Bristol BS1 1DR. *T:* (0117) 927 2144, *Fax:* (0117) 926 2569. *E:* Ignatius.hughesqc@albionchambers.co.uk. *Club:* Liverpool Football.

**HUGHES, Isabel Anne;** *see* Lloyd-Jones, I. A.

**HUGHES, Janis;** Member (Lab) Glasgow Rutherglen, Scottish Parliament, 1999–2007; *b* 1 May 1958; *d* of Thomas Nish and Janet (*née* Cumming); *m* (marr. diss.). *Educ:* Queen's Park Sch., Glasgow; Western Coll. of Nursing, Glasgow. Nursing: Royal Hosp. for Sick Children, Glasgow, 1980–82; Victoria Infirmary, Glasgow, 1982–86; Belvidere Hosp., Glasgow, 1986–88; Health Service Adminr, Renal Unit, Glasgow Royal Infirmary, 1988–99. Steward, 1980–83, Sec., Glasgow Royal Infirmary Br., 1993–99, NUPE, then UNISON. *Recreations:* reading, cooking.

**HUGHES, Jeremy Michael,** CBE 2015; Chief Executive, Alzheimer's Society, since 2010; *b* 15 Aug. 1957; *s* of Rev. Martyn L. Hughes and Mary D. Hughes; *m* 1989, Caroline Anne Chappell; two *s*. *Educ:* Harrow Sch.; St Edmund Hall, Univ. of Oxford (BA 1st cl., MA). Man. Dir, LMS Public Relns Ltd, 1983–89; Asst Dir, Nat. Children's Home, 1989–92; Director: Muscular Dystrophy Gp, 1992–93; Leonard Cheshire, 1994–99; BRCS, 1999–2003; Hd, External Relns, Internat. Fedn of Red Cross and Red Crescent Socs, 2003–04; Chief Exec., Breakthrough Breast Cancer, 2005–10. Bd Mem., NCRI, 2007–10. Trustee: Ockenden Internat., 2002–06; Sightsavers Internat., 2006–14; AMRC, 2006–09; Chairman: Nat. Voices, 2009–14 (Jt Chm., 2008–09); Global Alzheimer's and Dementia Action Alliance, 2014–; Co-Chm., Prime Minister's Champion Gp on Dementia Friendly Communities, 2012–; Mem., World Dementia Council, 2016– (Vice-Chm., 2018–). Mem. Adv. Bd, Foundn for Excellence in Business Practice, Geneva, 2003–05. Hon. DSc Exeter, 2018. *Publications:* (contrib.) Sweet Charity: the role and workings of voluntary organisations, 1996. *Recreations:* hill-walking, house renovation. *Address:* Alzheimer's Society, 43–44 Crutched Friars, EC3N 2AE. *T:* (020) 7423 3507. *E:* jeremy.hughes@alzheimers.org.uk.

**HUGHES, John;** *see* Hughes, Edgar J. and Hughes, Robert J.

**HUGHES, Prof. John,** PhD; FRS 1993; FBPhS; Director, Parke-Davis Neuroscience Research Centre (formerly Parke-Davis Research Unit), Cambridge, 1983–2000; Chairman and Joint Founder, Cambridge Biotechnology Ltd, 2000–03; Senior Research Fellow, 1983–2009, Emeritus Fellow, 2010, Wolfson College, University of Cambridge; *b* London, 6 Jan. 1942; *s* of Joseph and Edith Hughes; *m* 1967, Madelaine Carol Jennings (marr. diss. 1981); one *d*; three *s* one *d*; *m* 1997, Ann Rosemary Elizabeth, *d* of Joseph and Norma Mutty; one step *s* one step *d*. *Educ:* Mitcham County Grammar Sch. for Boys; Chelsea Coll., London (BSc); Inst. of Basic Med. Sciences, London (PhD). MA Cantab, 1988. Res. Fellow, Yale Univ. Med. Sch., 1967–69; University of Aberdeen: Lectr in Pharmacology, 1969–77; Dep.-Dir, Drug Res. Unit, 1973–77; Imperial College, London University: Reader in Pharmacol Biochemistry, 1977–79; Prof. of Pharmacol Biochemistry, 1979–82; Vis. Prof., 1983–. Hon. Professor: of Pharmacol., Univ. of Cambridge, 1989–2000 (Vis. Res. Fellow, Dept Pharmacol., 2000–); of Pharmacol., Aberdeen Univ., 1998–. Vice-Pres., Drug Discovery Europe, Warner-Lambert Co., 1987; Vice-Pres. of Res., Warner-Lambert/Parke-Davis Co., 1988–2000; Chm., Scientific Adv. Bd, Synaptica Ltd, 2002–. Member: Substance Abuse Cttee, Mental Health Foundn, 1986–; Scientific Cttee, Assoc. of British Pharmaceutical Industry, 1990–95; Bd, Nat. Inst. for Biol Standards and Control, 1999–; Chm., Res. Cttee, Chronic Fatigue Syndrome (formerly Persistent Virus Disease) Res. Foundn, 1992– (Trustee of the Foundn, 1997–). Mem. Council, Internat. Soc. Neuroscience, 1988–. Editor: Brit. Jl Pharmacol., 1977–83; Brain Res., 1976–; Mem. Editl Bd, Neuropeptides, 2010– (Jt Chief Exec. Ed., 1980–2010). J. Y. Dent Meml Lectr, Soc. for Study of Drug Addiction, 1976; Oliver-Sharpey Lectr, RCP, 1980; Gaddum Lectr and Medal, British Pharmacol Soc., 1982. Mem., Royal Acad. of Medicine, Belgium, 1983. Fellow, Internat. Neuropeptide Soc., 2002; FBPhS (FBPharmacolS, 2008). DMed *hc* Univ. of Liège, 1978; Hon. DSc Aberdeen, 2010. Sandoz Prize, British Pharmacol Soc., 1975; Pacesetter Award, US Nat. Inst. on Drug Abuse, 1977; Lasker Prize, Albert and Mary Lasker Foundn, NY, 1978; Scientific Medal, Soc. for Endocrinology, 1980; W. Feldberg Foundn Award, 1981; Lucien Dautrebande Prize, Fondation de Pathophysiologie, Belgium, 1983; Lilly Award, European Coll. of Neuropsychopharmacology, 1992. *Publications:* Centrally Acting Peptides, 1978; Opioids Past, Present and Future, 1984; (ed jtly) The Neuropeptide Cholecystokinin (CCK), 1989; articles in Nature, Science, Brit. Jl Pharmacol., and Brain Res. *Recreations:* family, friends, gardening, golf. *Address:* Wolfson College, Barton Road, Cambridge CB3 9BB. *E:* john@sbulbeck.com.

**HUGHES, John Charles;** Managing Director and Political Engineer, JCH Global Consulting Ltd, since 2015; *b* 1961; *s* of Prof. Daniel R. Hughes and Carol M. Hughes; *m* 1997, Prof. Jenny L. N. Parkes; two *s*. *Educ:* Imperial Coll. London (BSc (Eng) Hons Electrical Engrg 1983); King's Coll., London (PGCE Sci. 1984; MA Sci. Educn 1993). MIET 2018. Teacher, then Hd of Physics, Highbury Grove Sch., London, 1984–89; Electronics Lectr and Industrial Liaison, Hendon Coll., 1989–90; Internat. Mentoring and Tutoring Project Manager, Imperial Coll. London, 1990–93; BP: Manager, Community and Public Affairs, 1993–97; Internat. Advr, Social Investment, 1997–98; Regl Advr, Russia and Central and Eastern Europe, 1998–2000; Regl Manager, Govt and Public Affairs, Southern Africa, 2000–01; Reputation Dir, USA, 2002–03; Strategy Dir, Communications and Ext. Affairs, 2003–05; Regl Dir, Asia Pacific, 2005–08; Ext. Affairs Dir, 2008–10; Gp Political Advr, 2010–15. Mem. Bd, OFSTED, 2015– (Chm., Strategic Risk Cttee, 2015–16; Chm., Audit Cttee, 2018–). Chair of Advisory Board: Assaye Risk Ltd, 2016–; Abkons, 2017–. Mem., Internat. Adv. Gp, Confucius Inst. for Business, LSE, 2009–15; Mem. Bd and Advr, GB China Centre, 2009–16; Advr, Internat. Conflict and Security Inst. Ltd, 2018–. Gov., LSE, 2011– (Mem. Council, 2015–; Chm., Audit Cttee, 2017–). FRSA. *Recreations:* growing vegetables, hill walking, bread-making. *E:* jch@johnchughesconsulting.com. *T:* 07833 570875.

**HUGHES, John Gerard,** PhD; FBCS; FLSW; Vice-Chancellor, Bangor University, 2010–18; *b* Belfast, 28 Aug. 1953; *s* of John Hughes and Mary Hughes; *m* 1975, Maura Smyth; two *s*; *m* 2007, Xinyu Wu; one *s*. *Educ:* Queen's Univ., Belfast (BSc 1st Cl. Maths 1975; PhD Theoretical Physics 1978). Lectr, QUB, 1980–84; Scientist, IAEA, 1984–86; Prof. of Information Systems Engrg, 1991–2004, Pro Vice-Chancellor, 2000–04, Univ. of Ulster; Pres., NUI, Maynooth, 2004–10. Chair, Higher Educn Wales, 2011–13; Vice-Chair, Universities UK, 2011–13. FBCS 1996; FLSW 2013. *Publications:* Database Technology, 1985; Object-Oriented Databases, 1991. *Recreations:* football, walking, gardening, history, music.

**HUGHES, John Winston,** FRICS; Founding Partner, Hemson Consulting Ltd, since 1983; President, Royal Institution of Chartered Surveyors, 2017–18; *b* Gerrards Cross, 4 June 1946; *s* of Eric Hughes and Winifred Hughes; *m* 1976, Thérèse Vié; one *s* one *d*. *Educ:* King's College Sch., Wimbledon; Coll. of Estate Mgt. FRICS 1987. Valuer, Ontario Min. of Revenue, 1970–74; Tax Manager, Commonwealth Holiday Inns, 1974–75; Vice Pres., Smith Donkin, 1975–79; Manager, Curry Coopers Lybrand, 1979–83. *Recreations:* sailing, travel. *Address:* Hemson Consulting Ltd, 30 St Patrick Street, Suite 1000, Toronto, ON M5T 3A3, Canada. *T:* (416) 5935090. *E:* jhughes@hemson.com. *Club:* Royal Canadian Yacht.

**HUGHES, Jonathan;** Chief Executive, WCMC United Nations Environment World Conservation Monitoring Centre, since 2019; *b* Wrexham; *s* of Gwynfor and Meryl Hughes; partner, Emmi Hartikainen; two *s* one *d*. *Educ:* Univ. of Wales, Bangor; Univ. degli Studi di Firenze, Italy (MSc Ecol. 1991). Policy Advr, Forestry Commn England,

2004–06; Scottish Wildlife Trust: Hd of Policy, 2006–08; Dep. Chief Exec., 2008–14; Chief Exec., 2014–19. Mem. Bd, Architecture and Design Scotland, 2010–. Sci. Advr, European Outdoor Conservation Assoc., 2012–; Global Councillor, IUCN, 2012–. Chm., Postcode Heroes Trust, 2013–. Hon. Fellow, Univ. of Edinburgh, 2015–. Contributor: Guardian; Scotsman; Huffington Post. *Publications*: contrib. papers to scientific jls. *Recreations*: tennis, theatre, architecture, Italian cinema, comics, squash, table-football. *Address*: WCMC UN Environment World Conservation Monitoring Centre, 219 Huntingdon Road, Cambridge CB3 0DL. *E*: Jonathan.Hughes@unep-wcmc.org.

**HUGHES, Jonathan Peter D.;** *see* Douglas-Hughes.

**HUGHES, Judith Caroline Anne;** QC 1994; **Her Honour Judge Judith Hughes;** a Circuit Judge, since 2001; a Deputy High Court Judge, since 1997; *b* 13 Oct. 1950; 3rd *d* of Frank and Eva Hughes; *m* 1st, 1977, Mark G. Warwick (marr. diss. 1998); two *d*; 2nd, 2004, Inigo Geoffrey Bing, *qv* (marr. diss.). *Educ*: Univ. of Leeds (LLB 1973). Called to the Bar, Inner Temple, 1974 (Bencher, 1994); Asst Recorder, 1991–95; a Recorder, 1995–2001; a judicial Mem., Parole Bd, 2002–09. Vice Chm., Legal Services Cttee, Bar Council, 1999. Trustee: Gilbert Place Centre, 1995–98; Children's Soc., 1996–2003; Help African Schs to Educate, 2000– (Chm., 2001–). Mem. Cttee, Bottoms Up, 2001–. Hon. Mem., Harrow Rotary Club, 2004. *Publications*: (jtly) Butterworths Guide to Family Law, 1996. *Recreations*: theatre, reading, handicrafts, travel, gardening, philately, opera. *Address*: Central Family Court, First Avenue House, High Holborn, WC1V 6NP.

**HUGHES, Warrant Officer Kim Spencer,** GC 2009; High Threat Counter Improvised Explosive Device Specialist, since 2010; *b* Münster, 12 Sept. 1979; *s* of Barry Melvin Hughes and Francis Mary Elizabeth Hughes (née Trask); one *s*. *Educ*: William Reynolds Jun. Sch.; Thomas Telford Sch.; Cranfield Univ. (Ammunition Technician course Cl. 2). Basic trng, Army Trng Regt Pirbright, 1997; driver, 8 Transport Regt RLC, 1997–2000; Ammunition Technician Cl. 2, 2000–01; Troop Corp., Fallingbostel, Germany, 2001–03; Troop Sgt, Bielefeld, Germany, 2003–07; Instructor: B Team (Jt Service), 2007–09; A Team (High Threat), 2009–10; High Threat IED Disposal Operator, 19 Light Bde, Helmand Province, Afghanistan, 2009; High Threat Counter Terrorist Bomb Disposal Instructor, 2009–10. Captain Webb Medal, Shropshire Soc. in London, 2011. *Publications*: Painting the Sand (autobiog.), 2017. *Recreations*: deer stalking, target shooting, practical shot gun, practical mini rifle, motorcycle.

**HUGHES, Lewis Harry,** CB 1996; consultant in public sector audit, 2004–10; Deputy Auditor General for Wales, 2000–04; *b* 6 March 1945; *s* of Reginald Harry Hughes, retired MoD official, and Gladys Lilian Hughes; *m* 1975, Irene June Nash, violinist and teacher; one *s*. *Educ*: Devonport High Sch. for boys; City of London Coll. CIPFA. Exchequer and Audit Dept, 1963–83 (Associate Dir, 1982–83); National Audit Office, 1983–2000: Dir of Health Audit and of Defence Audit to 1990; Asst Auditor Gen., 1991–2000. Chm., Harpenden Probus Club, 2017–. *Recreations*: golf, music, family life. *Address*: 1 Wood End Road, Harpenden, Herts AL5 3EB. *T*: (01582) 764992. *Club*: Harpenden Golf.

**HUGHES, Louis Ralph;** Chairman, Workplay Technology by InZero Systems (formerly GBS Laboratories LLC, later InZero Systems) (Chief Executive Officer, 2004); *b* Cleveland, Ohio, 10 Feb. 1949. *Educ*: General Motors Inst., Flint (BMechEng 1971); Harvard Univ. (MBA 1973). General Motors Corp., 1973–2000: financial staff, 1973; Asst Treasurer, 1982; Vice-Pres., of Finance, Gen. Motors of Canada, 1985; Vice-Pres. of Finance, General Motors Europe, Zürich, 1987; Chm. and Man. Dir, Adam Opel AG, Rüsselsheim, 1989; Pres., General Motors Europe, 1992; Exec. Vice Pres., 1992–2000; Pres., Internat. Ops, 1994–98; Pres. and Chief Operating Officer, Lockheed Martin Corp., 2000. C of S, Afghanistan Reconstruction Gp, US Embassy, Kabul, 2004–05. Non-exec. Chm., OutPerformance (formerly Maxager Technology Inc.), 2001–08; non-executive Director: ABB Ltd, 2003–; Nokia Corp., 2016–; Ind. Dir, AkzoNobel, 2014–18. *Recreations*: ski-ing, climbing, cuisine, antiques. *Address*: Workplay Technology by InZero Systems, 13755 Sunrise Valley Drive, #230, Herndon, VA 20171–4608, USA.

**HUGHES, Louise Joanne M.;** *see* Moelwyn-Hughes, L. J.

**HUGHES, Prof. Medwin,** DPhil; DL; FLSW; Vice Chancellor: University of Wales Trinity St David, since 2010; University of Wales, since 2011; *s* of Mildred Emily Hughes, MBE; *m* 1986, Fiona Campbell Gray; three *s*. *Educ*: Llangefni Secondary Sch.; Univ. of Wales, Aberystwyth (BA Hons 1st cl. 1983); Jesus Coll., Oxford (Meyrick Grad. Scholar; Sir John Rhys Scholar; DPhil 1987; Welsh Supernumerary Fellow, 2012–13). DPS. Researcher and lectr, NE Wales Inst. of Higher Educn, 1987–89; Sen. Lectr, Trinity Coll., Carmarthen, 1989–91; Lectr, Univ. of Wales, Cardiff, 1991–94; Trinity College, Carmarthen: Dean, 1994–97; Asst Principal, 1997–98; Dep. Principal, 1998–2000; Principal and Vice Chancellor, 2000–09; Vice Chancellor: Trinity UC, 2009–10; Univ. of Wales, Lampeter, 2009–10; Swansea Metropolitan Univ., 2013. Chairman: Citizenship 2000 Project, 1992–95; Kaleidoscope UK, 2006–12; Welsh Govt Rev. of Support for Literature and Publishing Panel, 2016–; Vice Chm., Higher Educn Wales, 2012–13. Welsh Language Board: Vice Chm., 1999–2003; Chm., Adv. Cttee, 2003; Chm., Jt Adv. Cttee, Welsh Language Bd and Nat. Assembly of Wales, 1999–2000; Mem., Statutory Welsh Language Bd, 1993–2003; Council of Europe: Mem., UK Intergovtl Educn Delegn, 1989; Project Dir, Minorities and Teacher Educn, 1990–95; Educnl Advr, Citizenship and Educn, 1996–; Rapporteur, Language Learning for Eur. Citizenship, 1997. Member: Wales Digital Coll., 2000–03; Governing Body, Ch in Wales, 2000–05; Nat. Soc. for Educn, C of E, 2000–; Wales Cttee, Duke of Edinburgh Award, 2000–04; Ct, Aberystwyth Univ., 2000–; Ct, Cardiff Univ., 2003–; Graham Commn, Nat. Assembly of Wales, 2005–07; Educn Commn, Ch in Wales, 2007–08; Founding Mem., Welsh American Acad., 2001–. Chair of Govs, Llandovery Coll., 2015–17. Trustee, Heritage Regeneration Trust, 2012–13. Mem., Swansea Bay City Reg. Bd, 2015–17. DL, 2011, High Sheriff, 2016–17, Dyfed. FRSA 2001; FLSW 2013. Hon. Fellow, Harris Manchester Coll., Oxford, 2018. Hon. DPA Univ. Rio Grande Ohio, 2001. *Recreations*: music, reading, walking. *Address*: University of Wales Trinity St David, College Road, Carmarthen Campus, Carmarthen SA31 3EP. *Club*: Oxford and Cambridge.

**HUGHES, Merfyn;** *see* Hughes, T. M.

**HUGHES, Michael,** CBE 1998; Chief Investment Officer, Baring Asset Management Ltd, 2000–07 (Director, 1998–2000); *b* 26 Feb. 1951; *s* of late Leonard and Gwyneth Mair Hughes; *m* 1978, Jane Ann Gosham (*d* 2016); two *d*. *Educ*: Univ. of Manchester (BA Econs); London School of Economics and Political Science (MSc Econs). Economist, BP Pension Fund, 1973–75; Partner and Chief Economist, de Zoete and Bevan, Stockbrokers, 1976–86; Dir, BZW Securities, 1986–89; Man. Dir, BZW Strategy, 1989–98; Chm., Barclays Capital Pension Fund, 1995–2000. Chm., Financial Panel, Foresight Prog., DTI, 1994–97; Mem., ESRC, 1995–98. Sen. Ind. Dir, 2005–, 2008–16, Chm., 2016–, JPMorgan Mid-Cap Investment Trust; non-executive Director: T Bailey Ltd, 2009–; Aberdeen New India Investment Trust, 2016–. Investment Consultant, Guide Dogs for the Blind, 1995–; Consultant: Seven Investment Mgt, 2008–14; Fiducia Wealth Mgt, 2008–; Sen. Advr, BT Pension Scheme, 2010–12. Mem. Council, Univ. of Essex, 1997–2006. Trustee: Littlegarth Sch., 2006–13; Duntons Charity, 2011–14. FRSA 2005. *Recreations*: horses, gardening. *Club*: National Liberal.

**HUGHES, (Michael) Antony; His Honour Judge Antony Hughes;** a Circuit Judge, South Eastern Circuit, since 2006; Designated Family Judge, Milton Keynes and Oxford, since 2007; Deputy High Court Judge, since 2007; *b* 26 May 1953; *s* of late Joseph Frederick Hughes, MA Oxon, BSc, and Doris Anne Hughes, MBE; *m* 1977, Ann Holdsworth; three *d*. *Educ*: King's Sch., Canterbury; Coll. of Law. Articled with Cole & Cole, Oxford, 1973–77; admitted as solicitor, 1977; Partner with Linnell & Murphy, then Linnells, subseq. Borneo Linnells, Solicitors, Oxford, 1979–2006; NP, 1985–2006; Dep. Metropolitan Stipendiary Magistrate, 1993–2000; a Recorder, 2000–06; Designated Family Judge, Northampton, 2014–16. Hon. Recorder of Milton Keynes, 2012. *Recreations*: walking, growing vegetables, fly fishing, shooting. *Address*: Milton Keynes County Court, 351 Silbury Boulevard, Milton Keynes MK9 2DT. *T*: (01908) 302810. *Club*: Lansdowne.

**HUGHES, Miranda,** PhD; CPsychol; Regional Commissioner, Northern and Yorkshire, Appointments (formerly NHS Appointments) Commission, 2004–12; *b* 18 Oct. 1952; *d* of John and Diana Hughes; *m* 1987, Paul Rayner; two *s* one *d*. *Educ*: Univ. of Keele (BA 1976; PhD 1981); Univ. of Stirling (MSc 1978). CPsychol 1988. Lectr in Psychol., Leeds Univ., 1979–84; Mgt Consultant, KPMG, 1984–87; consultancy and non-exec. appts in private and public sectors, 1987–2001. Chair, W Yorks Probation Bd, 2001–05.

**HUGHES, Nigel Howard,** FREng; Director of Technology, Smiths Industries Aerospace and Defence Systems Ltd, 1992–97; *b* 11 Aug. 1937; *s* of late William Howard Hughes and of Florence Hughes (née Crawshaw); *m* 1962, Margaret Ann Fairmaner; three *d*. *Educ*: St Paul's Sch.; Queen's Coll., Oxford (MA). CEng, FIMechE; FRAeS 1993; FREng (FEng 1995). Pilot Officer, RAF, 1956–58. RAE, Bedford, 1961–73; Head of Radio and Navigation Div., 1973–77, Head of Flight Systems Dept, 1977–80, RAE, Farnborough; MoD Central Staffs, 1980–82; Asst Chief Scientific Advr (Projects), MoD, 1982–84; Dep. Chief Scientific Advr, MoD, 1985–86; Dir, RSRE, 1986–89; Chief Exec., Defence Res. Agency, 1989–91. Mem., 1992–98, Chm., 1998–2003, Airworthiness Requirements Bd, CAA. *Recreations*: pre-1940 Rolls-Royce cars, model engineering, amateur radio, vintage radio and TV, music.

**HUGHES, Owain Arwel,** CBE 2009 (OBE 2004); orchestral conductor, since 1970; Principal Conductor, Aalborg Symphony Orchestra, Denmark, 1995–99; Principal Associate Conductor, Royal Philharmonic Orchestra, 2003–10; Professor of Music, University of Wales Trinity St David, since 2014; *b* 21 March 1942; *s* of Arwel Hughes and Enid Hughes (née Thomas); *m* 1966, Jean Lewis; one *s* (one *d* decd). *Educ*: Howardian High Sch., Cardiff; University Coll., Cardiff (BA Hons); Royal Coll. of Music. Has conducted all major UK orchs and their choirs and also orchs throughout Europe; Associate Conductor: BBC Welsh Symphony Orch., 1980–86; Philharmonia Orch., London, 1985–90; Musical Dir, Huddersfield Choral Soc., 1980–86; Founder, Artistic Dir and Conductor, Annual Welsh Proms, 1986–; Music Dir, NYO of Wales, 2003–10; Founder and Music Dir, Camerata, Wales, 2005–; Principal Guest Conductor, Cape Town Philharmonic Orch., S Africa, 2007–. Television: Blodeugerdd (series), BBC Wales, 1974–76; Development of English Choral Tradition, 1975; Walton Belshazzar's Feast, 1975; Music in Camera, 1976–86; Much Loved Music Show, 1977–83; Verdi Requiem, 1986; Requiem series, 1987; Easter series, 1988; Mahler Symphony No 8, 1990; Pantycelyn, 1995, Dewi Sant, 2002 (S4C oratorios); Divas, 2002, 2004; Codi Canu (3 series, 2006, 2008, 2010); documentaries: Remembering Wales, 2002; Maestro, 2005; Centenary documentary on Arwel Hughes, 2009. Has made numerous recordings for a range of companies. Vice-Pres., NCH Action for Children, 1988–; Founder, Lisa Crispin Charitable Foundn, 2017. Founding Fellow, George Thomas Soc., 1989. FRWCMD (FWCMD 1995). Mem., IAM. Hon. Fellow: Univ. of S Wales (formerly Poly. of Wales, then Univ. of Glamorgan), 1986; UC, Cardiff, 1991; Trinity Coll., Carmarthen, 2004; UC, Lampeter, 2007; UC, Bangor, 2007. Hon. DMus: CNAA, 1986; Wales, 1991. Gold Medal, Welsh Tourist Bd, 1988; Jubilee Award, Guild of Welsh Music, 2006; Sir Geraint Evans Meml Award, Welsh Music Guild, 2011. *Publications*: My Life in Music (autobiog.), 2012. *Recreations*: Rugby, cricket, golf. *E*: owainarwel@btinternet.com. *Clubs*: Lord's Taverners; London Welsh Rugby.

**HUGHES, Patrick Anthony;** Sheriff of North Strathclyde at Oban and Campbeltown, since 2017; *b* Irvine, 9 Aug. 1976; *s* of Patrick Hughes and Ann Hughes. *Educ*: St Michael's Acad., Kilwinning; Univ. of Strathclyde (LLB Hons European, DipLP); Univ. de Rouen; Coll. of Europe, Bruges (LLM Eur. Legal Studies). Trainee solicitor, MacRoberts, 2000–02; Solicitor, Brodies WS, 2002–03; Procurator Fiscal Depute, Glasgow, 2004–08; Sen. Procurator Fiscal Depute, Crown Office Appeals Unit, 2008–17; Hd, Wildlife and Envmtl Crime Unit, Crown Office and Procurator Fiscal Service, 2016. NP 2010; Solicitor-Advocate, 2016. Tutor, Strathclyde Univ. Law Sch., 2005–15. Nat. Pres., JCI Scotland, 2016. *Address*: Oban Sheriff Court House, Albany Street, Oban PA34 4AL.

**HUGHES, Paul Michael;** Director (formerly General Manager): BBC Symphony Orchestra, and BBC Symphony Chorus, since 1999; BBC Singers, since 2012; *b* Malvern, 16 June 1956; *s* of Charles Bernard Hughes and June Patricia Hughes. *Educ*: King's Sch., Worcester; Trinity Coll. of Music, London (LTCL; GTCL; FTCL; Hon. Fellow, Trinity Laban Conservatoire, 2012). Gen. Manager, Acad. of Ancient Music, 1985–89; Events Manager and Artist Manager, IMG Artists, 1989–93; Chief Exec., Royal Scottish Nat. Orch., 1993–96; Gen. Manager, Monteverdi Choir and Orch., 1997–98. Governor, Board: RSAMD, 1994–96; GSMD, 2007–. Hon. RCM 2012; Hon. FGS 2014. *Recreations*: cooking, hiking, attending the theatre. *Address*: 31 Sabine Road, SW11 5LN. *T*: 07799 625180. *E*: paulmh@me.com, paul.hughes-bbcso@bbc.co.uk. *Club*: Two Brydges.

**HUGHES, Ven. Paul Vernon;** Archdeacon of Bedford, 2003–18, now Archdeacon Emeritus; *b* 4 Aug. 1953; *s* of Reginald Harry Hughes and Eileen Mary Hughes; *m* 1984, Elizabeth Jane Hawkes, (Rev. Canon Liz Hughes, Lead Chaplain, London Luton Airport); one *s* one *d*. *Educ*: Ghyll Royd Prep. Sch., Ilkley; Pocklington Sch.; Central London Poly. (Dip. Urban Estate Mgt); Ripon Coll., Cuddesdon. Residential Property Surveyor, Chestertons, 1974–79. Ordained deacon, 1982, priest, 1983; Curate, Chipping Barnet with Arkley, 1982–86; Team Vicar, Dunstable, 1986–93; Vicar, Boxmoor, 1993–2003. RD Hemel Hempstead, 1996–2003. *Recreations*: music, amateur operatics, walking (country and coast), reading. *Club*: Lansdowne (Luton).

**HUGHES, Peter;** *see* Hughes, D. E. P.

**HUGHES, Peter John,** OBE 2012; HM Diplomatic Service; High Commissioner to Belize, 2013–18; *b* 14 Sept. 1953. Entered FCO, 1976; Caribbean Dept, FCO, 1976–78; Islamabad, 1978–80; Vice-Consul, Rome, 1980–83; Warsaw, 1983–85; Desk Officer, Defence Dept, FCO, 1985–87; Dep. Hd of Area, Personnel Ops Dept, FCO, 1987–89; Vice-Consul (Commercial), Sydney, 1989–94; Hd, Korea Section, Far East and Pacific Dept, FCO, 1994–98; Resident Comr, Castries, 1998–2001; Dep. High Comr, Colombo,

2001–05; First Sec. (Pol/Mil.), Kabul, 2005–08; Ambassador to the Democratic People's Republic of Korea, 2008–11; FCO, 2011–13. *Address:* c/o Foreign and Commonwealth Office, King Charles Street, SW1A 2AH.

**HUGHES, His Honour Peter Thomas;** QC 1993; a Circuit Judge, 2007–18; Judge of the Court of Protection, 2010–18; *b* 16 June 1949; *s* of late Peter Hughes, JP, and Jane Blakemore Hughes (*née* Woodward); *m* 1974, Christine Stuart Taylor; one *s* one *d*. *Educ:* Bolton Sch.; Bristol Univ. (LLB Hons). Called to the Bar, Gray's Inn, 1971, Bencher, 2001; Mem., Wales and Chester Circuit, 1971–2007 (Junior, 1991; Treas., 1999–2000), Northern Circuit, 2007–18; Asst Recorder, 1988–92; Recorder, 1992–2007; Deputy High Court Judge: Family Div., 2001–07; QBD, 2007–18; Liaison Judge: Cumbria Magistrates, 2012–18; between English and Scottish Judiciary, 2014–18. Tutor Judge, Judicial Studies Bd, 2008–12. Chairman: Medical Appeal Tribunals, 1988–93; Registered Homes Tribunals, 1993–2002 (Lead Chm., 2000–02); Mental Health Review Tribunals, 1999–. Member: Gen. Council of the Bar, 1993–98; Council of Circuit Judges, 2011–18. Trustee, Gardens' Trust, 2018–. Freeman, 2005, Liveryman, 2015, Clockmakers' Co.; Freeman, City of London, 2014. *Recreations:* taming an unruly garden and escaping to far away places. *Club:* Army and Navy.

**HUGHES, Philip;** *see* Hughes, R. P.

**HUGHES, Philip Arthur Booley,** CBE 1982; artist; Director, Thames and Hudson Publishing Ltd (formerly Thames and Hudson Ltd), since 1991; *b* 30 Jan. 1936; *s* of Leslie Booley Hughes and Elizabeth Alice Hughes (*née* Whyte); *m* 1964, Psiche Maria Anna Claudia Bertini; two *d*, and two step *d*. *Educ:* Bedford Sch.; Clare Coll., Cambridge (BA). Engineer, Shell Internat. Petroleum Co., 1957–61; Computer Consultant, SCICON Ltd (formerly CEIR), 1961–69; Co-Founder, Logica, 1969: Man. Dir, 1969–72; Chm., 1972–90; Dir, 1990–95. Vis. Prof., UCL, 1981–90. Member: SERC, 1981–85; Nat. Electronics Council, 1981–88. Governor, Technical Change Centre, 1980–88. Mem. Council, RCA, 1988–92. Trustee: Design Museum, 1990–96; Inst. for Public Policy Res., 1988–99; Nat. Gall., 1996–2002 (Chm., Bd of Trustees, 1996–99). Official Vis. Artist to Antarctica, British Antarctic Survey, 2001–02. Exhibn of paintings with Beryl Bainbridge, Monks Gall., Sussex, 1972; exhibited: Contemp. British Painting, Madrid, 1983; Contemp. Painters, Ridgeway Exhibn Museum and Art Gall., Swindon, 1986; exhibitions with: Philip Wolfhagen, Sherman Gall., Sydney, 2002; Keith Grant, Churchill Coll., Cambridge, 2003; with Antoine Poncet, Château la Nerthe, Châteauneuf-du-Pape, 2004; one-man exhibitions: Parkway Focus Gall., London, 1976; Angela Flowers Gall., London, 1977; Gal. Cance Manguin, Vaucluse, France, 1979, 1985, 2000; Francis Kyle Gall., London, 1979, 1982, 1984, 1987, 1989, 1992, 1994, 1997, 2000, 2003, 2007, 2010, 2012; Gal. La Tour des Cardinaux, Vaucluse, France, 1993; Mus. of Contemp. Art, Monterrey, Mexico, 1997; Mus. Rufino Tamayo, Mexico City, 1998; Tate St Ives, 2000; V&A Mus., 2001; Musée du Châtillonais, Châtillon-sur-Seine, 2002; Star Gall., Lewes, 2004; Watermill Gall., Aberfeldy, 2005, 2012, 2016; Rex Irwin Gall., Sydney, 2005, 2008; Galerie Pascal Lainé, Ménerbes, Vaucluse, France, 2007, 2010, 2014, 2018; Charleston, E Sussex, 2008, 2019; Pier Arts Centre, Stromness, Orkney, 2008; Galerie Gimpel et Müller, Paris, 2011; Brighton Mus. and Art Gall., 2012; Cromarty Arts Trust, 2012; Univ. of Stirling, 2012; Salisbury and S Wilts Mus., 2012; Jerwood Gall., Hastings, 2014; Gallery 3, Kent Univ., 2015, 2016; Pelican Gall., Cambridge, 2018; European Space Operations Centre, Darmstadt, 2018; retrospectives: Inverness Mus. and Art Gall., 1990; Ambassade d'Australie, Paris, 1995; Drill Hall Gall., Canberra, 1998, 2002, 2008; Volvo Gall., Sydney, George Adams Gall., Melbourne, 1999; Maison de la Truffe et du Vin, Ménerbes, 2007, 2018. CompOR 1985. Hon. Fellow, QMC, 1987. DUniv Stirling, 1985; Hon. DSc: Kent, 1988; London, 2000. *Publications:* Patterns in the Landscape, 1998; Tracks: walking the ancient landscapes of Britain, 2012, 2019; articles in nat. press and learned jls on management scis and computing. *E:* studio@philiphughesart.com.

**HUGHES, Dr Richard Alan,** FGS; Executive Secretary, Geological Society of London, since 2017; *b* Wrexham, Wales, 29 April 1959; *s* of Ifor and Doreen Hughes; *m* 1991, Catherine Goss; one *s* one *d*. *Educ:* Univ. of Wales, Cardiff (BSc Hons Geol. 1980); Darwin Coll., Cambridge (PhD Earth Sci. 1985). FGS 2000; CGeol 2002. British Geological Survey: geologist, 1985–2000; Internat. Business Develt, 2000–05; Hd, Inf. Delivery, 2005–07; Dir of Inf., 2007–13; Dir, Business Develt, Coal Authy, 2013–17. Member, Council: Geol Soc. of London, 2009–13; Commn for Application of Geosci. Inf., Internat. Union of Geol Scis, 2012–13. *Recreations:* cycling, sailing, ski-ing, spending time with family and friends. *Address:* Geological Society of London, Burlington House, Piccadilly, W1J 0BG. *T:* (020) 7434 9944.

**HUGHES, Prof. Richard Anthony Cranmer,** MD; FRCP; FMedSci; FEAN; Professor of Neurology, King's College London (formerly Guy's, King's and St Thomas's School of Medicine, King's College London), 1999–2007, now Emeritus; *b* 11 Nov. 1942; *s* of late Dr Anthony Chester Cranmer Hughes and Lilian Mildred Hughes; *m* 1968, Coral Stephanie Whittaker; one *s* two *d*. *Educ:* Marlborough Coll.; Clare Coll., Cambridge (BA Double First); Guy's Hosp. Med. Sch. (MB BChir (Dist. in Pathol.), MD). MRCP 1970, FRCP 1980. Sen. Lectr, Guy's Hosp. Med. Sch., 1975–87; Prof. of Neurol., UMDS, 1987–98, Hd, Div. of Clin. Neuroscis, GKT, 1999–2001. Hon. Prof., UCL, 2008–. Hon. Consultant Neurologist: Guy's Hosp., 1975–2007; KCH, 1995–2007. Ed., Jl Neurol., Neurosurgery and Psychiatry, 1989–96; Founding Co-ordinating Ed., Cochrane Neuromuscular Disease Gp, 1998–2010. Pres., Clinical Neuroscis Section, RSocMed, 2002–03. Mem. Council, Assoc. British Neurologists, 2001–03. Pres., Eur. Fedn of Neurol Socs, 2009–14 (Vice-Pres., 2001–05). Trustee, Muscular Dystrophy UK (formerly Muscular Dystrophy Campaign), 2011–14. Gov., Highgate Sch., 1991–95. Hughlings Jackson Lect., RSocMed, 2009. FMedSci 2000; FEAN 2015. Medal, Assoc. of British Neurologists, 2006; Gebhart Prize, Internat. Peripheral Nerve Soc., 2018. *Publications:* Guillain-Barré Syndrome, 1990; Neurological Emergencies, 1994, 4th edn 2003; European Handbook of Neurological Management, 2006; contrib. numerous articles to New England Jl of Medicine, Lancet, Annals of Neurol., Brain and other jls on neuroimmunol., multiple sclerosis and peripheral neuropathy. *Recreations:* botany, theatre, tennis. *Address:* PO Box 114, National Hospital, Queen Square, WC1N 3BG. *Clubs:* Athenæum, Royal Society of Medicine; Newport Boat.

**HUGHES, Richard John C.;** *see* Carey-Hughes.

**HUGHES, Robert Gurth;** Chief Executive, Sight for Surrey (formerly Surrey Association for Visual Impairment), since 2013; *b* 14 July 1951; *s* of late Gurth Martin Hughes and Rosemary Dorothy Hughes (*née* Brown), JP; *m* 1986, Sandra Kathleen (*née* Vaughan); four *d*. *Educ:* Spring Grove Grammar Sch.; Harrow Coll. of Technology and Art. Trainee, then Film Producer, BAC Film Unit, 1968–73; News Picture Editor, BBC Television News, 1973–87. Greater London Council: Mem., 1980–86; Opposition Dep. Chief Whip, 1982–86; Opposition spokesman on arts and recreation, 1984–86. MP (C) Harrow West, 1987–97; contested (C) same seat, 1997. PPS to Rt Hon. Edward Heath, 1988–90, to Minister of State, DSS, 1990–92; an Asst Govt Whip, 1992–94; Parly Sec., OPSS, Cabinet Office, 1994–95. Gen. Sec. (subseq. Exec. Dir), Fedn of Ophthalmic and Dispensing Opticians, 1997–2005; Chief Exec., Assoc. of Optometrists, 2005–11. Chm., Telephones for the Blind, 2018–. National Chm., Young Conservatives, 1979–80; Chm., Guildford Conservatives, 2017–. A Governor, BFI, 1990–92. Trustee, Gtr London Fund for the Blind, 2018–. Hon. DSc Anglia Poly. Univ., 1998. *Recreations:* photography, cricket, listening to music.

**HUGHES, (Robert) John;** Director, International Media Studies Program, 1991–97 (on leave of absence, 1997–2006), Professor of Communications, 2007–16, now Emeritus, Brigham Young University, Utah; *b* Neath, S Wales, 28 April 1930; *s* of Evan John Hughes and Dellis May Hughes (*née* Williams); *m* 1st, 1955, Vera Elizabeth Pockman (marr. diss. 1987); one *s* one *d*; 2nd, 1988, Peggy Janeane Chu; one *s*. *Educ:* Stationers' Company's Sch., London. Reporter, sub-editor, corresp. for miscellaneous London and S African newspapers and news agencies (Natal Mercury, Durban; Daily Mirror, Daily Express, Reuter, London News Agency), 1946–54; joined The Christian Science Monitor, Boston, USA, 1954: Africa Corresp., 1955–61; Asst Foreign Editor, 1962–64; Far East Corresp., 1964–70; Man. Editor, 1970; Editor, 1970–76; Editor and Manager, 1976–79; Pres. and Publisher, Hughes Newspapers Inc., USA, 1979–81, 1984–85; Associate Dir, US Information Agency, 1981–82; Dir, Voice of America, 1982; Asst Sec. of State for Public Affairs, USA, 1982–84; Pres., Concord Communications Inc., 1989–91; Asst Sec.-Gen., UN, 1995 (on leave of absence); special advr on communications to Sec.-Gen., UN, 1996–; Ed., 1997–2006, and Chief Operating Officer, 1999–2006, Deseret Morning News, Salt Lake City. Syndicated Columnist, The Christian Science Monitor, 1985–2012. Chairman: Presidential Commn on US Govt Internat. Broadcasting, 1991; Congressional Commn on Broadcasting to China, 1992. Nieman Fellow, Harvard Univ., 1961–62. Pres., Amer. Soc. of Newspaper Editors, 1978–79. Pulitzer Prize for Internat. Reporting, 1967; Overseas Press Club of America award for best daily newspaper or wire service reporting from abroad, 1970; Sigma Delta Chi's Yankee Quill Award, 1977. Hon. LLD Colby Coll., 1978; Hon. DH Southern Utah, 1995. *Publications:* The New Face of Africa, 1961; Indonesian Upheaval (UK as The End of Sukarno), 1967; Islamic Extremism and the War of Ideas: lessons from Indonesia, 2010; Paper Boy to Pulitzer, 2014; articles in magazines and encyclopaedias. *Recreations:* reading, walking. *Address:* 1645 Oak Lane, Provo, UT 84604–2142, USA. *Clubs:* Foreign Correspondents' (Hong Kong); Overseas Press (New York).

**HUGHES, His Honour (Robert) Philip;** a Circuit Judge, 1998–2015; Community Relations Judge (North Wales), 2007–15; *b* 4 June 1947; *s* of late Peredur and Myra Hughes; *m* 1973, Kathleen, (Katie), Dolan; two *s*. *Educ:* Valley Sch., Anglesey; Wrekin Coll., Shropshire; Inns of Court Sch. of Law. Called to the Bar, Gray's Inn, 1971; in practice at the Bar, 1971–98, Hd of Chambers, 1994–98; Asst Recorder, 1990–93, a Recorder, 1993–98, Wales and Chester Circuit; Designated Family Judge at Warrington, 2000–07; Liaison Judge, Powys Magistrates, 2007–13. Asst Boundary Comr, 1996–98. Mem. Cttee, Council of HM Circuit Judges, 2007–15. Mem., Bd of Govs, Glyndŵr Univ. (formerly NE Wales Inst. of Higher Educn), 2008–11 (Hon. Fellow, 2012). Member, Board of Trustees: Nightingale House Hospice, 2015–; Chariotts Community Transport, 2016–. *Recreations:* sailing, vegetable gardening, coarse cooking, theatre, singing. *Club:* Holyhead Sailing.

**HUGHES, Robert Valentine,** CBE 1999; Chairman, Horserace Betting Levy Board, 1998–2009; *b* 13 Feb. 1943; *s* of Robert Canning Hughes and Betty Bertha Hughes; *m* 1968, Eryl Lumley. *Educ:* Univ. of Birmingham (DMS 1976; MSocSc 1979). Review Leader (Performance Rev.), W Midlands Co. Transport and Engrg Dept, 1977–81; Birmingham District Council: Principal Asst to Chief Exec., 1981–83; Develt and Promotion Officer, 1983–84; Town Clerk and Chief Exec., Great Grimsby BC, 1984–88; Chief Exec., Kirklees Metropolitan Council, 1988–98. Pres., SOLACE, 1997–98. DUniv UCE, 1999. *Recreations:* playing the piano, accordion and melodian, cooking, watching Birmingham City FC. *Address:* Highbury, Parish Lane, King's Thorn, Herefordshire HR2 8AT.

**HUGHES, Rodger Grant,** FCA; Chairman, National Counties Building Society, since 2015 (non-executive Director, since 2013); Chairman, Audit Committee, 2013–15); *b* 24 Aug. 1948; *s* of Eric and Doreen Hughes; *m* 1973, Joan Clare Barker; two *s*. *Educ:* Rhyl Grammar Sch.; Queens' Coll., Cambridge (BA 1970; MA). FCA 1973. PricewaterhouseCoopers (formerly Price Waterhouse): joined 1970; Partner, 1982–2007: i/c Ind. Business Gp, 1988–91; i/c NW Reg., 1991–95; Mem., Supervisory Bd, 1991–95; Hd, Audit and Business Adv. Services, 1995–2002; Mem., Mgt Bd, 1995–2007; Managing Partner, Clients and Mkts, 2002–06; Sen. Ind. Dir, Chime Communications plc, 2007–15. Auditor to Duchy of Cornwall, 1998–2007. Mem., Steering Bd and Chm., Audit Cttee, Companies House, 2008–10; non-exec. Mem. Bd and Chm., Audit Cttee, Simmons & Simmons, 2008–; non-executive Director: Friends Provident plc, 2009; Bell Pottinger Communications USA LLC, 2010–12; Mem., UK Adv. Council, Raab Karcher AG, 1995–97. Mem., Educn Leadership Team, BITC, 2005–08.

**HUGHES, Rosemary Ann, (Rosemary, Lady Hughes);** DL; President, Special Educational Needs and Disability Tribunal, 2003–08; *b* 30 June 1939; *d* of Rev. John Pain and Barbara Pain; *m* 1964, Sir David Collingwood Hughes, 14th Bt (*d* 2003); three *s* (and one *s* decd). *Educ:* Girton Coll., Cambridge (BA 1960; LLB 1962). Dep. Metropolitan Stipendiary Magistrate, 1990–95. Chm. (pt-time), Special Educnl Needs and Disability Tribunal, 1995–2003. Lay Canon, Ely Cathedral, 2000–13, now Lay Canon Emerita. DL Cambs, 1997. *Recreations:* playing double bass, horse racing, bridge. *Address:* The Coach House, High Street, Wilburton, Ely, Cambs CB6 3RA.
*See also* Sir T. C. Hughes, Bt.

**HUGHES, Prof. Sean Patrick Francis,** MS; FRCS, FRCSEd, FRCSI, FRCSEd (Orth); Professor of Orthopaedic Surgery, Imperial College London (formerly at Royal Postgraduate Medical School), University of London, 1991–2006, now Emeritus; Medical Director, Ravenscourt Park Hospital, 2002–04; Hon. Consultant Orthopaedic Surgeon: Imperial College Healthcare NHS Trust (formerly Hammersmith Hospitals), 1991–2016; Medway Maritime Hospital NHS Trust, 2007–15; *b* 2 Dec. 1941; *s* of late Patrick Hughes and Kathleen Ethel Hughes (*née* Bigg); *m* 1972, Felicity Mary (*née* Anderson); one *s* two *d*. *Educ:* Downside Sch.; St Mary's Hospital, Univ. of London (MB BS, MS 1976); King's Coll. London (MA 2017). DHMSA 2014; DPMSA 2015. FRCSEd 1971; FRCS 1972; FRCSI 1972; FRCSEd (Orth) 1984. Senior Registrar in Orthopaedics, Middlesex and Royal National Orthopaedic Hosp., 1974–76; Research Fellow in Orthopaedics, Mayo Clinic, USA, 1975; Sen. Lectr, and Dir Orthopaedic Unit, RPMS, Hammersmith Hosp., 1977–79; George Harrison Law Prof. of Orthopaedic Surgery, Univ. of Edinburgh, 1979–91; Chief of Orthopaedic Service, 1995–98, Clin. Dir, Surgery and Anaesthesia, 1998–2002, Hammersmith Hosps NHS Trust; Hd of Surgery, Anaesthesia and Intensive Care, Imperial Coll. Faculty of Medicine, 1997–2004; Dir, Inst. of Musculoskeletal Surgery, Imperial Coll. London, 2004–06. Hon. Civilian Consultant, RN, 1985–2012; Hon. Consultant, Nat. Hosp. for Nervous Diseases, Queen Sq., 1994–2010. Non-exec. Dir, W Middlesex Univ. Hosp. NHS Trust, 1998–2006. Vice President: RCSE, 1994–97 (Mem. Council, 1984–97); Assoc. Res. Circulation Bone, 1994–97; Mem. Council, British Orthopaedic Assoc., 1989–92. Fellow: Brit. Orthopaedic Assoc.; Royal Soc. Med.; Member: Orthopaedic Research Soc.; British Orth. Res. Soc. (Pres., 1995–97); Soc. Internat. de Chirurgie Orth. et de Traumatologie; World Orth. Concern; Internat. Soc. for Study of the Lumbar Spine. Keats Lect., Apothecaries' Soc. and KCL, 2017. Primary Ed., Bone and Joint Jl, 2012–. *Publications:* Astons Short Text Book of Orthopaedics, 2nd edn

1976 to 5th edn (jtly) 1997; Basis and Practice of Orthopaedics, 1981; Basis and Practice of Traumatology, 1983; Musculoskeletal Infections, 1986; (ed jtly) Orthopaedics: the principles and practice of musculoskeletal surgery, 1987; (ed jtly) Orthopaedic Radiology, 1987; papers on blood flow and mineral exchange, fracture healing, bone scanning, antibiotics and infection in bone, external fixation of fractures, surgery of the lumbar and cervical spine, pathogenesis of disc regeneration and medical history. *Recreations*: walking, music. *Address*: 5 Meadow Place, Edensor Road, W4 2SY. *T*: (020) 8995 7708. *Club*: Athenæum.

HUGHES, Shirley, (Mrs J. S. P. Vulliamy), CBE 2017 (OBE 1999); FRSL; free-lance author/illustrator; *b* 16 July 1927; *d* of Thomas James Hughes and Kathleen Dowling; *m* 1952, John Sebastian Papendiek Vulliamy (*d* 2007); two *s* one *d*. *Educ*: West Kirby High Sch. for Girls; Liverpool Art Sch.; Ruskin Sch. of Art, Oxford. Illustrator/author; overseas edns or distribn in France, Spain, W Germany, Denmark, Holland, Sweden, Aust., NZ, Japan, USA, China and Canada. Lectures to Teacher Trng Colls, Colls of Further Educn, confs on children's lit. and to children in schs and libraries; overseas lectures incl. tours to Aust. and USA. Mem., Cttee of Management, 1983–86, Chm., Children's Writers and Illustrators Gp, 1994–96, Soc. of Authors; Member: Public Lending Right Registrar's Adv. Cttee, 1984–88; Library and Information Services Council, 1989–92. FRSL 2000. Hon. FCLIP (Hon. FLA 1997); Hon. Fellow, Liverpool John Moores Univ., 2004. Hon. LittD: UEA, 2004; Liverpool, 2004. Eleanor Farjeon Award for services to children's lit., 1984. *Publications*: illustrated about 200 books for children of all ages; written and illustrated: Lucy and Tom's Day, 1960, 2nd edn 1979; The Trouble with Jack, 1970, 2nd edn 1981; Sally's Secret, 1973, 3rd edn 1976; Lucy and Tom go to School, 1973, 4th edn 1983; Helpers, 1975 (Children's Rights Other Award, 1976), 2nd edn 1978; Lucy and Tom at the Seaside, 1976, 3rd edn 1982; Dogger, 1977 (Kate Greenaway Medal, 1978; Silver Pencil Award, Holland, 1980; Greenaway Picture Book of All Time, 2007), 4th edn 1980; It's Too Frightening for Me, 1977, 4th edn 1982; Moving Molly, 1978, 3rd edn 1981; Up and Up, 1979, 3rd edn 1983; Here Comes Charlie Moon, 1980, 3rd edn 1984; Lucy and Tom's Christmas, 1981, 2nd edn 1982; Alfie Gets in First, 1981, 2nd edn 1982; Charlie Moon and the Big Bonanza Bust-up, 1982, 2nd edn 1983; Alfie's Feet, 1982, 2nd edn 1984; Alfie Gives a Hand, 1983; An Evening at Alfie's, 1984; Lucy and Tom's abc, 1984; A Nursery Collection, 6 vols, 1985–86; Chips and Jessie, 1985; Another Helping of Chips, 1986; Lucy and Tom's 123, 1987; Out and About, 1988; The Big Alfie and Annie Rose Story Book, 1988; Angel Mae, 1989; The Big Concrete Lorry, 1989; The Snowlady, 1990; Wheels, 1991; The Big Alfie Out-of-Doors Story Book, 1992; Bouncing, 1993; Giving, 1993; Stories by Firelight, 1993; Chatting, 1994; Hiding, 1994; Rhymes for Annie Rose, 1995; Enchantment in the Garden, 1996; Alfie and the Birthday Surprise, 1997; The Lion and the Unicorn, 1998; (ed) Mother and Child Treasury, 1998; Abel's Moon, 1999; Alfie's Numbers, 1999; The Shirley Hughes Collection, 2000; Alfie Weather, 2001; A Life Drawing: recollections of an illustrator (memoirs), 2002; Annie Rose is My Little Sister, 2002; Olly and Me, 2003; Ella's Big Chance, 2003 (Kate Greenaway Medal, 2004); Alfie Wins a Prize, 2004; A Brush with the Past, 2005; Alfie's World, 2006; Alfie and the Big Boys, 2007; Jonadab and Rita, 2008; Olly and Me 1, 2, 3, 2009; Bye Bye Birdie, 2009; Don't Want to Go!, 2010; The Christmas Eve Ghost, 2010; All About Alfie, 2011; Hero on a Bicycle, 2012; Bobbo Goes to School, 2012; Alfie's Christmas, 2013; Dixie O'Day in the Fast Lane!, 2012; Dixie O'Day and the Great Diamond Robbery, 2014; Alfie Outdoors, 2015; Whistling in the Dark, 2015; Dixie O'Day, Up, Up and Away, 2015; Dixie O'Day and the Haunted House, 2015; Dixie O'Day on his bike, 2016; Alfie and his Very Best Friend, 2016; Alfie and Dad, 2017; Ruby in the Ruins, 2018; Snow in the Garden, 2018; Alfie at Nursery School, 2018; Alfie on Holiday, 2019; Angel on the Roof, 2019. *Recreations*: looking at paintings, dressmaking, writing books for children. *Address*: c/o Penguin Random House, 80 Strand, WC2R 0RL.
*See also* E. S. Vulliamy.

HUGHES, Rt Hon. Sir Simon (Henry Ward), Kt 2015; PC 2010; barrister; Chancellor, London South Bank University, since 2018; *b* 17 May 1951; *s* of late James Henry Annesley Hughes and of Sylvia (Paddy) Hughes (*née* Ward). *Educ*: Llandaff Cathedral Sch., Cardiff; Christ Coll., Brecon; Selwyn Coll., Cambridge (BA 1973, MA 1978). Inns of Court Sch. of Law; Coll. of Europe, Bruges (Cert. in Higher European Studies, 1975). Trainee, EEC, Brussels, 1975–76; Trainee and Mem. Secretariat, Directorate and Commn on Human Rights, Council of Europe, Strasbourg, 1976–77. Called to the Bar, Inner Temple, 1974; in practice, 1978–. MP: Southwark and Bermondsey, Feb. 1983–1997 (L, 1983–88, Lib Dem, 1988–97); (Lib Dem) Southwark N and Bermondsey, 1997–2010; (Lib Dem) Bermondsey and Old Southwark, 2010–15; contested (Lib Dem) same seat, 2015, 2017. Spokesman: (L), on the environment, 1983–Jan. 1987 and June 1987–March 1988; (Alliance), on health, Jan.–June 1987; (Lib Dem), on education and science, 1988–90, on envmt, 1988–94, on natural resources, 1992–94, on community and urban affairs and young people, 1994–95, on social welfare, 1995–97, on health, 1995–99, on home affairs, 1999–2003, on London, 2003–05, on ODPM affairs, 2005; Lib Dem shadow to Attorney-Gen., 2005–07, to Leader of H of C, 2007–09; Lib Dem spokesman on energy and climate change, 2009–10; Dep. Leader, Lib Dems, 2010–14; Minister of State, MoJ, 2013–15. Mem., Accommodation and Works Select Cttee, 1992–97; Co-Chair, All Party Gp on Youth Affairs. Advocate for Access to Education, 2011–15. Jun. Counsel, Lib. Party application to European Commn on Human Rights, 1978–79; Chm., Lib. Party Adv. Panel on Home Affairs, 1981–83; Vice-Chm., Bermondsey Lib. Assoc., 1981–83. Jt Pres., British Youth Council, 1983–84. President: Young Liberals, 1986–88 (Vice-Pres., 1983–86, Mem. 1973–78); Democrats Against Apartheid, 1988; Lib Dem Party, 2004–08. Hd of Public Affairs, Open Univ., 2016–17. Pres., Southwark Chamber of Commerce, 1984–87, 2004–07, 2013– (Mem., 1987–); Vice-President: Union of Liberal Students, 1983–88 (Mem., 1970–73); Student Democrats, 1988. Member: the Christian Church; Gen. Synod of Church of England, 1984–85; Southwark Area Youth Cttee; Council of Management, Cambridge Univ. Mission, Bermondsey; Anti-Apartheid Movement. Trustee: Salmon Youth Centre, Bermondsey; Rose Theatre Trust; Gov., St James C of E Sch., Bermondsey. Hon. Fellow, South Bank Univ., 1992. Member to Watch Award, 1985. *Publications*: pamphlets on human rights in Western Europe, the prosecutorial process in England and Wales, Liberal values for defence and disarmament. *Recreations*: music, theatre, listening to the radio, sport (Millwall and Hereford FC, Glamorgan CCC, Wales RFU), travel, the open air. *Address*: 6 Lynton Road, Bermondsey, SE1 5QR.

HUGHES, Stephen Edward; local government consultant, since 2014; *b* 18 Feb. 1954; *s* of Lawrence Edward Hughes and Dorothy Hughes (*née* Merricks); *m* 1991, Marian Nicholls (marr. diss. 2007); one step *s* one step *d*. *Educ*: Lincoln Grammar Sch.; Tettenhall Coll., Wolverhampton; Peterhouse, Cambridge (BA Hons Econs). CPFA 1997. Res. Officer, Internat. Wool Secretariat, 1976–79; Economist, Coventry CC, 1979–81; Principal Officer (Finance), AMA, 1981–84; Dep. Sec., ALA, 1984–90; seconded to Policy Unit, Islington LBC, 1990–92; Principal Asst Dir of Finance, 1992–97, Head of Finance and Property Services, 1997–98, Islington LBC; Divl Manager, Local Govt Taxation, DETR, 1998–99; Dir of Finance, London Bor. of Brent, 1999–2004; Birmingham City Council: Strategic Dir of Resources, 2004–05; Acting Chief Exec., 2005–06; Chief Exec., 2006–14; interim Exec. Dir, LGA, 2015; interim Strategic Dir, Resources, London Bor. of Brent, 2016; interim Chief Exec., Bristol CC, 2016–17. Strategic Advr on local govt, CIPFA, 2014–15; Assoc. Consultant, Bevan Brittan, 2014–15. Non-executive Director: Business Link W Midlands,

2008–09; Big Bang Ltd, 2013–19; Housing and Care 21, 2014– (Chm., 2018–); Valuation Office Agency, 2016–; High Speed Two (HS2) Ltd, 2019–. Dir, Walterton and Elgin Community Homes Ltd, 2001–04. Mem. (Lab), Didcot Town Council, 1987–95 (Chair, Finance Cttee, 1991–93; Dep. Leader, 1991–95). *Publications*: contribs to various local govt jls. *Recreations*: golf, ski-ing, sailing, chess, Go, surfing the net.

HUGHES, Stephen Skipsey; Member (Lab) North East Region, England, European Parliament, 1999–2014 (Durham, 1984–99); *b* 19 Aug. 1952; *m* 1988, Cynthia Beaver; one *s* one *d*, and one *s* twin *d* by previous marriage. *Educ*: St Bede's School, Lanchester; Newcastle Polytechnic (DMA). European Parliament: Dep. Ldr, Lab. Pty, 1991–93; Substitute Member: Legal Affairs Cttee, 1989–94; Citizens Rights Cttee, 1989–94; Mem., Environment Cttee, 1984–94; former Member: Rules Cttee; Security and Defence Cttee; Mem., Intergroup on Nuclear Disarmament, 1988–2014 (Chm., 1988–90); Chm., 1994–99, Socialist Co-ordinator, 1999–2014, Social Affairs and Employment Cttee; Vice-Pres., Progressive Alliance of Socialists and Democrats Gp, 2009–14. Vice-President: Fedn of Industrial Develt Authorities, 1990–; Assoc. of District Councils, 1990–. *Address*: 19 Oakdene Avenue, Darlington, Co. Durham DL3 7HR.

HUGHES, Sir Thomas (Collingwood), 15th Bt *cr* 1773, of East Bergholt, Suffolk; FRCEM; FRCSE; consultant in emergency medicine informatics and medical educator; Consultant in Emergency Medicine, John Radcliffe Hospital, Oxford, since 2005; Hon. Senior Lecturer in Emergency Medicine, University of Oxford, since 2008; Medical Director, L2S2 Ltd, since 2014; *b* 16 Feb. 1966; *s* of Sir David Collingwood Hughes, 14th Bt and of Rosemary Ann Hughes, *qv*; *S* father, 2003; *m* 1996, Marina Louise Barbour, MB BS, DPhil, MRCP, FRACP, consultant in paediatric cardiology, Gt Ormond St Hosp., *d* of Richard Barbour, Albany, WA; one *s* two *d*. *Educ*: Oundle; Soham Village Coll.; Hills Road Sixth Form Coll.; Univ. of Sheffield (MB ChB); Univ. of Wales Coll. of Medicine (MSc); Open Univ. (MBA). MRCP. PhD student, Univ. of Melbourne. Consultant in Emergency Medicine, Ballarat, 1999–2004; Dir of Acute Care, Hinchingbrooke Hosp., 2012–13. FRCEM (FCEM 2008). Major Educator Award, Univ. of Oxford, 2009; President's Medal, Royal Coll. of Emergency Medicine, 2015. *Publications*: Adult Emergency Medicine at a Glance, 2011. *Heir*: *s* Alfred Collingwood Hughes, *b* 24 May 2001. *E*: mail@berristead.com.

HUGHES, Thomas George; Sheriff of Tayside, Central and Fife at Dundee, since 2004; *b* 2 Jan. 1955; *s* of Thomas and Patricia Hughes; *m* 1995, Janice Owens; one *s* one *d*. *Educ*: Strathclyde Univ. (LLB). Admitted solicitor, 1979; in practice as solicitor, 1979–2003; pt-time Sheriff, 2003–04. *Recreations*: sport, reading. *Address*: Sheriff Court House, 6 West Bell Street, Dundee DD1 9AD. *T*: (01382) 229961. *E*: sheriffthughes@scotcourts.gov.uk.

HUGHES, Thomas Lowe; Trustee, since 1971, and President Emeritus, since 1991, Carnegie Endowment for International Peace, Washington (President, 1971–91); *b* 11 Dec. 1925; *s* of Evan Raymond Hughes and Alice (*née* Lowe); *m* 1st, 1955, Jean Hurlburt Reiman (*d* 1993); two *s*; 2nd, 1995, Jane Dudley Casey Kuczynski. *Educ*: Carleton Coll., Minn (BA); Balliol Coll., Oxford (Rhodes Schol., BPhil); Yale Law Sch. (LLB, JD). USAF, 1952–54 (Major). Member of Bar: Supreme Court of Minnesota; US District Court of DC; Supreme Court of US. Professional Staff Mem., US Senate Sub-cttee on Labour-Management Relations, 1951; part-time Prof. of Pol Sci. and Internat. Relations, Univ. of Southern California, Los Angeles, 1953–54, and George Washington Univ., DC, 1957–58; Exec. Sec. to Governor of Connecticut, 1954–55; Legislative Counsel to Senator Hubert H. Humphrey, 1955–58; Admin. Asst to US Rep. Chester Bowles, 1959–60; Staff Dir of Platform Cttee, Democratic Nat. Convention, 1960; Special Asst to Under-Sec. of State, Dept of State, 1961; Dep. Dir of Intelligence and Research, Dept of State, 1961–63; Dir of Intell. and Res. (Asst Sec. of State), 1963–69; Minister and Dep. Chief of Mission, Amer. Embassy, London, 1969–70; Mem., Planning and Coordination Staff, Dept of State, 1970–71. Vis. Sen. Res. Fellow, German Histl Inst., Washington, 1997–. Chm., Nuclear Proliferation and Safeguards Adv. Panel, Office of Technology Assessment, US Congress; Chm., Bd of Editors, Foreign Policy Magazine; Sec., Bd of Dirs, German Marshall Fund of US; Dir, Arms Control Assoc. Chairman: Oxford-Cambridge Assoc. of Washington; US-UK Bicentennial Fellowships Cttee on the Arts. Member Bds of Visitors: Harvard Univ. (Center for Internat. Studies); Princeton Univ. (Woodrow Wilson Sch. of Public and Internat. Affairs); Georgetown Univ. (Sch. of Foreign Service); Bryn Mawr Coll. (Internat. Adv. Bd.); Univ. of Denver (Soc. Sci. Foundn); Atlantic Council of US (Exec. Cttee). Member Bds of Advisers: Center for Internat. Journalism, Univ. of S Calif; Coll. of Public and Internat. Affairs, Amer. Univ., Washington, DC; Washington Strategy Seminar; Cosmos Club Jl (Chm.). Member Bds of Trustees: Civilian Military Inst.; Amer. Acad. of Political and Social Sci.; Amer. Cttee, IISS; Hubert H. Humphrey Inst. of Public Affairs; Amer. Inst. of Contemp. German Studies, Washington, DC; Arthur F. Burns Fellowship Program. Mem. Adv. Bd, Fundación Luis Munoz Marin, Puerto Rico. Member: Internat. Inst. of Strategic Studies; Amer. Assoc. of Rhodes Scholars; Amer. Political Sci. Assoc.; Amer. Bar Assoc.; Amer. Assoc. of Internat. Law; Amer. For. Service Assoc.; Amer. Acad. of Diplomacy; Internat. Studies Assoc.; Washington Inst. of Foreign Affairs (Pres.); Trilateral Commn; Assoc. for Restoration of Old San Juan, Puerto Rico; Soc. Mayflower Descendants. Arthur S. Flemming Award, 1965. Hon. LLD: Washington Coll., 1973; Denison Univ., 1979; Florida Internat. Univ., 1986; Hon. HLD: Carleton Coll., 1974; Washington and Jefferson Coll., 1979. KStJ 1984. *Publications*: Perilous Encounters: the Cold War collisions of domestic and world politics: oral history interviews with Thomas L. Hughes, 2011; Oxford After Dinner, 2011; Speaking Up and Speaking Out, 2013; Anecdotage: some authentic retrievals, 2014; occasional contribs to professional jls, etc. *Recreations*: swimming, tennis, music, 18th century engravings. *Address*: 5636 Western Avenue, Chevy Chase, MD 20815, USA. *T*: (301) 6561420. *Clubs*: Yale, Century Association, Council on Foreign Relations (New York); Cosmos, Chevy Chase (Washington).

HUGHES, His Honour (Thomas) Merfyn; QC 1994; a Circuit Judge, 2001–14; Resident Judge, North Wales Crown Courts, 2010–14; a Deputy Circuit Judge, 2014–19; *b* 8 April 1949; *s* of John Medwyn Hughes and Blodwen Jane Hughes (*née* Roberts); *m* 1977, Patricia Joan (DL; High Sheriff, Gwynedd, 2002–03), *d* of John Talbot, surgeon, Brentwood; two *s* one *d*. *Educ*: Rydal Sch., Colwyn Bay; Liverpool Univ. (LLB Hons 1970); Council of Legal Educn. Called to the Bar, Inner Temple, 1971; in practice at the Bar, Chester, 1971–94, Temple, 1994–2001; Asst Recorder, 1987–91; a Recorder, 1991–2001; Leading Counsel to Local Authorities, Waterhouse Tribunal on Child Abuse, 1996–98; Pres., Mental Health Review Tribunal, 1999–2011; Member: Parole Bd for England and Wales, 2004–11; Courts Bd for N Wales, 2005–14; N Wales Probation Bd, 2005–10. Chm., Chester Bar Cttee, 1999–2001; Mem., Wales and Chester Circuit Mgt Bd, 1999–2001. Mem., Beaumaris RNLI, 2014–. Contested (Lab) Caernarfon, 1979. *Recreations*: sailing, watching Rugby, golf. *Clubs*: Royal Anglesey Yacht; Bangor Rugby Union Football (Pres., 2012–).

HUGHES, Victor; *see* Hughes, H. V.

HUGHES, William Frederick, CBE 2009; QPM 2001; Director General, Serious Organised Crime Agency, 2006–10 (Director General designate, 2004–06); *b* Aug. 1950. *Educ*: Univ. of Aston in Birmingham (BSc Hons Mech. Engrg 1973). PC to Supt, Thames

Valley Police, 1975–91; Asst Chief Constable, W Yorks Police, 1991–97; Dep. Chief Constable, Herts Constabulary, 1997–2000; Dir Gen., Nat. Crime Squad, 2000–06; seconded to SOCA, 2004. Internat. Dir, Bluelight Global Solutions Ltd, 2010–12; CEO, Probimus Ltd, 2013–18. *Recreations:* aviation, personal computers, music.

**HUGHES, William Lloyd;** QC 2013; *b* 26 Nov. 1964; *s* of late Dr Gwilym Hughes and of Maureen Anne Hughes (*née* Day); *m* 1994, (Katharine) Louise D'Arcy, QC (*d* 2010); two *d. Educ:* Merchant Taylors' Sch., Northwood; Leicester Poly. (BSc Hons Law with Chem.); Inns of Court Sch. of Law. Called to the Bar, Gray's Inn, 1989; in practice as barrister, 1989–. Dir, Educn, SE Circuit. Chair, Kent Bar Mess; Mem. Cttee, Assoc. of London Welsh Lawyers. Freeman, City of London, 2013. *Recreations:* being a father to Daisy and Emily and enjoying their wonderful company, most sport, particularly Rugby Union (Welsh), football, cricket, kayaking, swimming, surfing, music of Bruce Springsteen, the Clash, the Ramones, Manic Street Preachers, alternative and indie music, attending concerts (eclectic), theatre, cinema, literature. *Address:* Foundry Chambers, 5–9 Quality Court, Chancery Lane, WC2A 1HP. *T:* (020) 7400 1800, *Fax:* (020) 7404 1405. *E:* w.hughes@foundrychambers.com; 9 Park Place, Cardiff CF10 3DP. *T:* (029) 2038 2731. *Clubs:* Watford Football, London Welsh Rugby Football, Surrey County Cricket; United Services Mess (Cardiff).

**HUGHES, William Young,** CBE 1987; Chairman, Aberforth Smaller Companies Trust plc, 1990–2005; Chief Executive, 1976–98, and Chairman, 1985–98, Grampian Holdings plc; *b* 12 April 1940; *s* of Hugh Prentice Hughes and Mary Henderson Hughes; *m* 1964, Anne Macdonald Richardson; two *s* one *d. Educ:* Firth Park Grammar Sch., Sheffield; Univ. of Glasgow (BSc Hons Pharmacy, 1963). MRPharmS (MPS 1964). Research, MRC project, Dept of Pharmacy, Univ. of Strathclyde, 1963–64; Lectr, Dept of Pharmacy, Heriot-Watt Univ., 1964–66; Partner, R. Gordon Drummond (group of retail chemists), 1966–70; Man. Dir, MSJ Securities Ltd (subsid. of Guinness Gp), 1970–76; Grampian Holdings, Glasgow, 1977–98 (holding co. in transport, tourism and retail). Non-executive Chairman: Fairfax I.S. plc, 2005–12; Palm Tree Technol. plc, 2007–14; non-executive Director: Cashbox plc, 2007–10; Frenkel Topping plc, 2007–10. Dir, Royal Scottish Nat. Hosp. and Community NHS Trust, subseq. Central Scotland Healthcare NHS Trust, 1992–97; Mem. Council, Strathcarron Hospice, 2000–06. Chairman: CBI Scotland, 1987–89; Prince's Scottish Youth Business Trust, 2000–07; Prince's Trust—Scotland, 2003–07; Trustee, Prince's Trust (UK), 2003–07. Hon. Chm., European Summer Special Olympic Games (1990), Strathclyde, 1988–91. Pres., Right Track (formerly Work Wise), 1994–. Treas., Scottish Conservative Party, 1993–98 (Dep. Chm., 1989–92).

**HUGHES HALLETT, Prof. Andrew,** DPhil; FRSE; Professor of Economics, Copenhagen Business School, since 2016; Senior Research Fellow in Economics and Finance, King's College London, since 2017; *b* London, 1 Nov. 1947; *s* of Vice-Adm. Sir (Cecil) Charles Hughes Hallett and Joyce Hughes Hallett; *m* 1982, Claudia Becker; two *s* one *d. Educ:* Radley Coll., Abingdon; Univ. of Warwick (BA Hons 1st Cl. 1969); London Sch. of Econs and Pol Sci. (MSc Econ. 1971); Nuffield Coll., Oxford (DPhil 1976). Associate Prof., Erasmus Univ., Rotterdam, 1977–85; David Dale Prof. of Econs, Univ. of Newcastle, 1985–89; Jean Monnet Prof. of Econs, Strathclyde Univ., Glasgow, 1989–2001; Prof. of Econs, Vanderbilt Univ., 2001–06; Prof. of Econs and Public Policy, George Mason Univ., 2006–18; Prof. of Econs, Univ. of St Andrews, 2007–16. Vis. Prof. of Econs and Fulbright Scholar, Princeton Univ., 1992–94; Visiting Professor: Univ. of Rome Sapienza, 1986–87, 2006, 2010–16; Univ. of Paris X, 2002; Univ. of Frankfurt, 2006; Bundesbank Prof., Free Univ. of Berlin, 2005; Faculty Associate, Kennedy Sch., Harvard Univ., 2012–13. Consultant: World Bank; IMF; UNDP; EC; Eur. Central Bank. Mem., Council of Econ. Advrs to Scottish Govt, 2007–15; Comr, Scottish Fiscal Commn, 2014–16; Mem., Scottish Growth Commn, 2016–. Advr, Econs and Monetary Cttee, Eur. Parlt, 2015–; consultant to various national central banks and govts; expert witness to UK, Scottish and Swedish Parlts. FRSE 2000. *Publications:* Quantitative Economic Policies and Interactive Planning, 1983; Stabilising Speculative Commodity Markets, 1987; Optimal Control, Expectations and Uncertainty, 1989; The Theory of Economic Policy in a Strategic Context, 2012; Macroeconomics Paradigms, 2016; 220 articles in learned jls on policy design, game theory and policy coordination, monetary union, fiscal policy frameworks, monetary policy and public debt management. *Recreations:* history, beer graduating to malt whisky, blues music. *Address:* Economics Department, Copenhagen Business School, Porcelaenshavn 16A, 2000 Fredericksberg, Denmark. *T:* 38152575. *E:* ahughes@gmu.edu.

**HUGHES-HALLETT, David John,** FRICS; chartered surveyor; consultant, 1999–2019; *b* 19 June 1947; *s* of Peter Hughes-Hallett and Pamela (*née* Marshall); *m* 1976, Anne Mary Wright; two *s* one *d. Educ:* Fettes Coll., Edinburgh; Coll. of Estate Mgt, Reading. FRICS 1982. Director: Scottish Landowners' Federation, 1982–89; Scottish Wildlife Trust, 1989–98; main Bd Mem., SEPA, 1995–2002; Bd Mem., 2002–10, Depute Convener, 2006–09, Loch Lomond and Trossachs Nat. Park Authy; Mem., East Areas Bd, 2005–07 Local Advr, 2007–12, SNH; Panel Mem., Waterwatch Scotland, 2006–09; Member: Bd, Office of Scottish Charity Regulator, 2008–16; Registration and Conduct Cttee, Scottish Social Services Council, 2010–17; adjudication panels, Gen. Teaching Council for Scotland, 2012–; Home Owners Housing Panel and Private Rented Housing Panel, Scottish Govt, 2012–; Ind. Mem. Bd, Public Prosecution Service NI, 2011–18. Chm., RICS in Scotland, 1987–88; Chm., Balerno High Sch. Bd, 1994–96. *Recreations:* cycling, choral singing, golf, Scottish countryside and its wildlife. *Address:* The Old School, Back Latch, Ceres, Fife KY15 5NT. *T:* (01334) 829333. *E:* david@hugheshallett.co.uk.

**HUGHES-HALLETT, James Wyndham John,** CMG 2012; FCA; Director: John Swire & Sons Ltd, since 2005 (Chairman, 2005–14); Clarkson plc, since 2015 (Chairman, 2015–19); *b* 10 Sept. 1949; *s* of late Michael Wyndham Norton Hughes-Hallett and Penelope Ann Hughes-Hallet (*née* Fairbairn); *m* 1st, 1991, Lizabeth Louise Hall (marr. diss. 2009); two *d*; 2nd, 2016, Katrina Elizabeth Repka. *Educ:* Eton Coll.; Merton Coll., Oxford (MA; Hon. Fellow 2007). FCA 1973. Articled Clerk, Dixon, Wilson, Tubbs and Gillett, 1970–73; chartered accountant, 1974–76; various posts in Japan, Taiwan, Hong Kong and Australia, Swire Gp, 1976–2000; Chairman: John Swire & Sons (HK) Ltd, 1999–2004; Cathay Pacific Ltd, 1999–2004; Swire Pacific Ltd, 1999–2004 (Dir, 1995–2014); Director: Cathay Pacific Airways Ltd, 1999–2014; HSBC Hldgs plc, 2005–14. Trustee: Esmée Fairbairn Foundn, 2005– (Chm., 2013–); Dulwich Picture Gall., 2005–12; China Now, 2006–09; Dep. Chm., Attingham Trust, 2013–. Governor: SOAS, Univ. of London, 2005–10; Courtauld Inst., 2008– (Chm., 2012–). Hon. Fellow, Univ. of Hong Kong, 2004. Silver Bauhinia Star (Hong Kong), 2003. *Address:* c/o John Swire and Sons Ltd, Swire House, 59 Buckingham Gate, SW1E 6AJ. *T:* (020) 7834 7717. *Clubs:* Brooks's; Hong Kong.

*See also* L. *Hughes-Hallett, Sir T. Hughes-Hallett.*

**HUGHES-HALLETT, Lucy,** FRSL; author; *b* London, 7 Dec. 1951; *d* of late Michael Wyndham Norton Hughes-Hallett and Penelope Ann Hughes-Hallett (*née* Fairbairn); *m* 1984, Dan Franklin; two *d*. FRSL 2011. *Publications:* Cleopatra, 1990; Heroes, 2004; The Pike: Gabriele d'Annunzio, 2013 (Samuel Johnson Non-Fiction Prize, 2013; Costa Biography Award, 2013; Duff Cooper Prize, 2013); Peculiar Ground, 2017. *Address:* c/o Lutyens & Rubinstein, 21 Kensington Park Road, W11 2EU. *T:* (020) 7792 4855. *E:* felicity@lutyensrubinstein.co.uk.

*See also* J. W. J. *Hughes-Hallett, Sir T. Hughes-Hallett.*

**HUGHES-HALLETT, Sir Thomas,** Kt 2012; DL; Chief Executive, Marie Curie Cancer Care, 2000–12; *b* 28 Aug. 1954; *s* of late Michael Wyndham Norton Hughes-Hallett and Penelope Ann Hughes-Hallet (*née* Fairbairn); *m* 1979, Juliet, *o d* of Col Anthony Rugge-Price; two *s* one *d. Educ:* Eton Coll.; Oriel Coll., Oxford (MA Modern Hist. 1974); Coll. of Law. Called to the Bar, Inner Temple, 1975. J. Henry Schroder Wagg & Co. Ltd, 1978–82; Enskilda Securities, 1982–93 (Chief Exec., Enskilda Corp., London, 1991–93); Robert Fleming & Co. Ltd, 1993–2000; Chm., Robert Fleming Securities, 1993–99; Chm., Fleming Private Asset Mgt, 1999–2000. Chairman: End of Life Care Implementation Adv. Bd, DoH, 2009; End of Life Palliative Care Funding Review, 2010–11; Chelsea and Westminster Hosp. NHS Foundn Trust, 2014–. Mem., Gen. Adv. Council, King's Fund, 2010–. Chairman: English Churches Housing Gp, 2000–04; Michael Palin Centre for Stammering Children, 2002–09. Co-founder and Chm., Marshall Inst. for Philanthropy and Social Entrepreneurship, LSE, 2015–; Co-founder and Exec. Chm., Helpforce, 2017–. Special Trustee, Great Ormond St Hosp. Children's Charity, 2004–08. DL Suffolk, 2013. *Recreations:* music, tennis, cooking, walking.

*See also* J. W. J. *Hughes-Hallett.*

**HUGHES JONES, Dr Nevin Campbell,** FRS 1985; on scientific staff, Medical Research Council, 1954–88; Fellow of Hughes Hall, Cambridge, 1987–90, now Emeritus; *b* 10 Feb. 1923; *s* of William and Millicent Hughes Jones; *m* 1952, Elizabeth Helen Dufty (*d* 2014); two *s* one *d. Educ:* Berkhamsted Sch., Herts; Oriel Coll., Univ. of Oxford; St Mary's Hosp. Med. School. MA, DM, PhD; FRCP. Medical posts held at St Mary's Hosp., Paddington, Radcliffe Infirmary, Oxford, and Postgrad. Med. Sch., Hammersmith, 1947–52; Member: MRC's Blood Transfusion Unit, Hammersmith, 1952–79 (Unit transferred to St Mary's Hosp. Med. Sch., Paddington, as MRC's Experimental Haematology Unit, 1960); MRC's Mechanisms in Immunopathology (formerly in Tumour Immunity) Unit, Cambridge, 1979–88. *Publications:* Lecture Notes on Haematology, 1970, 8th edn 2009. *Recreations:* making chairs, walking the Horseshoe Path on Snowdon. *Address:* 65 Orchard Road, Melbourn, Royston, Herts SG8 6BB. *T:* (01763) 260471.

**HUGHES-MORGAN, Sir (Ian) Parry (David),** 4th Bt *cr* 1925, of Penally, co. Pembroke; *b* 22 Feb. 1960; *e s* of His Honour Maj.-Gen. Sir David John Hughes-Morgan, 3rd Bt, CB, CBE and Isabel Jean Hughes-Morgan (*née* Lindsay); *S* father, 2006; *m* 1992, Julia Katrin, *er d* of R. J. S. Ward; three *d. Heir: b* Jonathan Michael Vernon Hughes-Morgan [*b* 19 Feb. 1962; *m* 1996, Gail Christine Melling; one *s* one *d*].

**HUGHES-PENNEY, Robert Charles;** Investment Director, Rathbone Brothers plc, since 1999; *b* Rio de Janeiro, 2 March 1968; *s* of Roger Hughes-Penney and Angela Hughes-Penney; *m* 1998, Elspeth Roare; two *s* one *d. Educ:* Haberdashers' Aske's Sch., Elstree; Manchester Poly. (BSc Hons); RMA Sandhurst. Chartered Fellow CISI 2010. Joined Army, 1990; Lieut 13th/18th Royal Hussars, QMO, 1990–92; Capt., Light Dragoons, 1993; Laurence Keen Ltd, 1993–95; Dir, Rathbone Investment Mgt Ltd, 2003–06. Mem. Council, C&G, 2006–11 (Hon. Mem., 2010–). Trustee: Mercy Ships UK, 1999–2004; City Parochial Foundn, 2004–10; Dir, Investing for Good, 2016–. Mem., Court of Common Council, 2004–12 (Member: Finance Cttee, 2006–12; Policy and Resources Cttee, 2007–12; Chairman: Investment Cttee, 2011–12; Financial Investment Bd, 2011–12). Mem. Court, Haberdashers' Co., 2008– (Third Warden, 2014–15); Upper Warden, Guild of Investment Managers, 2018–; Alderman, City of London, 2018–, Gov., Haberdashers' Aske's Sch., Elstree, 2009–16. *Recreations:* family, reading, walking, motor sport. *Address:* Rathbone Investment Management Ltd, 8 Finsbury Circus, EC2M 7AZ. *T:* (020) 7399 0000. *E:* Robert.Hughes-Penney@Rathbones.com. *Club:* Cavalry and Guards.

**HUGHES-YOUNG,** family name of **Baron St Helens.**

**HUGHESDON, John Stephen,** FCA; Partner, 1977–2004, Consultant, 2004–06, Mazars (formerly Neville Russell); *b* 9 Jan. 1944; *s* of Eric Hughesdon and Olive Mona (*née* Quirk); *m* 1970, Mavis June Eburne; one *s* one *d. Educ:* Eltham Coll. ACA 1967, FCA 1977. Articled Clerk, then Manager, Peat Marwick Mitchell, 1962–73; Manager, Neville Russell, 1973–76. Common Councilman, 1991–96, Alderman, 1997–2008, Sheriff, 2004–05, City of London. Liveryman: Co. of Coopers, 1992– (Master, 2006–07); Co. of Chartered Accountants, 2003–12; Freeman: Co. of Parish Clerks, 2001–; Co. of Watermen and Lightermen, 2005–. Trustee: Christ's Hosp. Foundn, 1993–2007 (Trustee, Pension Scheme, 2007–10); British and Foreign Bible Soc., 1997–2012 (Chm., 2010–12; Trustee, Pension Scheme, 2000–); Culham St Gabriel's Trust (formerly Culham Inst.), 2012–17. Chm., Southwark Dio. Welcare, 2005–07; Lay Chm., Newbury Deanery Synod, 2010–17; Pres., Boys' Bde London Dist, 2005–08; Hon. Treasurer: Girls' Bde Nat. Council for England and Wales, 1979–91; Tear Fund, 1992–96. Mem., Audit Cttee, Church House Corp., 2017–. *Recreations:* family, church, golf. *Address:* 44 Speen Lane, Speen, Newbury, Berks RG14 1RN. *T:* (01635) 43120. *E:* john.hughesdon@hotmail.com. *Club:* City Livery.

**HUGHFF, Victor William,** FIA; Chief General Manager, Norwich Union Insurance Group, 1984–89; *b* 30 May 1931; *s* of William Scott Hughff and Alice Doris (*née* Kerry); *m* 1955, Grace Margaret (*née* Lambert) one *s* one *d. Educ:* City of Norwich School. Served in RAF, 1951–53; commnd in Secretarial Br., National Service List. Joined Norwich Union Life Insce Soc., 1949; Assistant Actuary, 1966; General Manager and Actuary, 1975; Main Board Director, 1981–89. Director: Stalwart Assurance Group, 1989–93; Congregational & General Insurance, 1989–2001; United Reformed Church Ministers' Pension Trust Ltd, 1993–2005; Norwich Centre Projects Ltd, 1994–2006. Liveryman, Actuaries' Co., 1990–. Elder of United Reformed Church, 1972–. *Recreation:* bowls. *Address:* 18 Hilly Plantation, Thorpe St Andrew, Norwich NR7 0JN. *T:* (01603) 434517.

**HUHNE, Christopher Murray Paul;** energy and climate change consultant, since 2012; Adviser, Zilkha Biomass Energy, since 2016; Senior Adviser, Engaged Tracking, since 2018; *b* 2 July 1954; *s* of Peter Ivor Paul Huhne and Ann Gladstone Murray; *m* 1984, Vicky Pryce, *qv* (marr. diss. 2011); two *s* one *d*, and two step *d. Educ:* Université de Paris-Sorbonne (Certificat 1972); Magdalen Coll., Oxford (BA 1st Cl. Hons PPE 1975). Freelance and trainee journalist, 1975–77; Brussels Corresp., Economist, 1977–80; Economics Leader Writer, 1980–84, Economics Editor, 1984–90, Guardian; Business Editor and Asst Editor, Independent on Sunday, 1990–91; Economic Columnist and Business and City Editor, Independent and Independent on Sunday, 1991–94; Founder and Man. Dir, sovereign ratings div., Ibca Ltd, 1994–97; Gp Man. Dir, Fitch Ibca Ltd, 1997–99. Contested (SDP/Lib Dem Alliance): Reading E, 1983; Oxford W and Abingdon, 1987. MEP (Lib Dem) SE Reg., England, 1999–2005. European Parliament: spokesman: European Lib Dem and Reformist Gp, Econ. and Monetary Affairs Cttee, 1999–2004; Alliance of Liberals and Democrats for Europe, 2004–05. MP (Lib Dem) Eastleigh, 2005–Feb. 2013; PC 2010–13. Lib Dem dep. Treasury spokesman, 2005–06, spokesman on the envmt, 2006–07, on home affairs, 2007–10; Sec. of State for Energy and Climate Change, 2010–12. Vis. Fellow, Nuffield Coll., Oxford, 2009–12. Strategic Advr, Anaerobic Digestion and Biogas, later

Bioresources, Assoc., 2013–18. *Publications:* (jtly) Debt and Danger: the world financial crisis, 1984, 2nd edn 1987; Real World Economics, 1990; (jtly) The Ecu Report, 1991; Both Sides of the Coin: the case for the Euro, 1999, 2nd edn 2001. *E:* chris@chrishuhne.org.uk. *W:* www.chrishuhne.org.uk.

HUHNE, Vicky; *see* Pryce, V.

HUISMANS, Sipko; non-executive Director, Imperial Tobacco, 1996–2006; *b* 28 Dec. 1940; *s* of Jouko and Roelofina Huismans; *m* 1969, Janet; two *s* one *d*. *Educ:* primary sch., Holland; secondary sch., Standerton, S Africa; Stellenbosch Univ., S Africa (BA Com). Shift chemist, Usutu Pulp Co. Ltd, 1961–68; Gen. Man., Springwood Cellulose Co., 1968–74; Man. Dir, Courtaulds Central Trading, 1974–80; Dir, 1980–96, Man. Dir, 1982–84, Courtaulds Fibres; Dir, 1984–96, Man. Dir, 1990–91, Chief Exec., 1991–96, Courtaulds PLC; Chairman: Internat. Paints Ltd, 1987–90; Courtaulds Chemical and Industrial Exec., 1988–96; Special Advr to Chm., Texmaco, Indonesia, 1996–2000. Non-exec. Dir, Vickers, 1996; Mem., Supervisory Bd, Reemtsma, 2002. *Recreations:* motor racing, sailing, competition. *Clubs:* Royal Lymington Yacht, Royal Southampton Yacht.

HULANÌCKI, Barbara, OBE 2012; RDI 2009; Designer, Hu Design Inc., since 2004; *b* Warsaw, Poland, 8 Dec. 1936; *d* of late Witold Hulanìcki and Victoria Hulanìcki; *m* 1963, Stephen Charles Fitz-Simon (*d* 1997); one *s*. *Educ:* Brighton Sch. of Art (Fashion). Freelance fashion illustrator, incl. for Women's Wear Daily, Vogue, The Times, Sunday Times, Observer; Founder (with Stephen Fitz-Simon), Biba, London, 1964–76; Biba Cosmetics, 1964–76; opened shop, Barbara Hulanìcki, Brazil, 1978; fashion designer for: Cacharel, 1977–80; Fiorucci, 1977–80; Minirock, Japan, 1980–92; Barbara Hulanìcki, London, 1980–84; Barbara Hulanìcki Cosmetics, worldwide, 1985–87; Fitz & Fitz, NY, 1996; IslandLife Ministore, Miami Beach, 2002; B with G, Miami Beach, 2003; Coccinelle, Italy, 2007–; Topshop, UK and USA, 2008–10; George, Asda, UK, 2010–; interior designer, 1987–, projects include: Woody's on the Beach, Miami Beach, 1986; Who's in the Grove, Miami, 1988; Sempers, Miami Beach, 1988; Match Club, Bolera Restaurant, Miami Beach, 1989; Marlin Hotel, South Beach, 1990–92 (Miami Design Preservation League Award), 1996 and 1998; Gloria and Emilio Estefan Recording Studio, 1992–93 and Star Island, 1996–97, Miami; Cavalier Hotel, Leslie Hotel, South Beach, 1993; Compass Point Beach Club, Bahamas, 1994–95; The Netherlands, South Beach, 1995 (AIA award, Florida Architects Assoc. award, 1993); Pink Sands Hotel, Bahamas, 1998, 2004–06, 2010–; Coral Sands Hotel, Bahamas, 2004–05, 2006; Goldeneye Develt, Jamaica, 2004; product designer for: Habitat (textiles and wallpapers), 2005–; Graham & Brown (wallpaper and paint collection), 2007–; V&A Mus. (jewellery, scarves and cards), 2007–; Virago Press (book cover), 2008; French Sole (shoe collection), 2016; Peonie & Moore (handbag collection), 2016–17; Made.com, 2017–18. Fashion illustration exhibn, Conde Contemporary Gall., 2017. Hon. Dr Design: Wolverhampton, 2008; Heriot-Watt, 2009; Brighton, 2010. Dress of the Yr award, Bath Mus. of Costume, 1972; Cosmetic Achievement Lifetime Award, Cosmetic Exec. Women, 2005. *Publications:* From A to Biba (autobiog.), 1983; Disgrace, 1990; In Biba, 2004; Sinbiba: sin babe sister of 'In Biba' - a graphic romance, 2006; Seamless From Biba: a life in design, 2012; The Biba Years, 2014; Barbara Hulanìcki's Fashion Illustration Workbook, 2017. *Address:* Hu Design Inc., 1300 Collins Avenue #206, Miami Beach, FL 33139, USA. *T:* (786) 4852839. *E:* hula@barbarahulanickidesign.com.

HULL, Bishop Suffragan of, since 2015; Rt Rev. Alison Mary White; *b* 1956; *d* of late Dr Keith Rodney Dumbell; *m* 1982, Rt Rev. Francis, (Frank), White, *qv*. *Educ:* St Aidan's Coll., Durham (BA English 1978); Cranmer Hall, Durham; Leeds Univ. (MA Theol. 1994). Ordained deaconess, 1986, deacon, 1987, priest, 1994; non-stip. Minister, St Mary and St Cuthbert, Chester le Street, 1986–89; Hon. Parish Deacon, St John the Evangelist, Birtley, 1989–93; Diocesan Missioner, Dio. of Durham, 1989–93; Dir, Past Studies, Cranmer Hall, Durham, 1993–98; Dir of Ordinands, Durham, 1998–2000; Springboard Missioner, 2000–04; Adult Educn Officer, Dio. of Peterborough, 2005–10; Canon, Peterborough Cathedral, 2009–10; Hon. Canon Theologian, Sheffield Cathedral, 2010–15; Priest-in-charge, St James, Riding Mill, 2011–15; Advr for Spirituality and Spiritual Direction, Dio. of Newcastle, 2011–15. *Address:* Hullen House, Woodfield Lane, Hessle, E Yorks HU13 0ES.

HULL, Prof. Christopher Michael, FRS 2012; Professor of Theoretical Physics, Imperial College London, since 2003 (Head, Theoretical Physics Group, 2007–11); *b* London, 20 April 1957; *s* of Charles Hull and Margaret Hull (*née* Gordon); one *s* one *d*. *Educ:* Haberdashers' Aske's Sch., Elstree; King's Coll., Cambridge (BA 1st Cl. Maths 1979; PhD Maths 1983). Res. Fellow, MIT, 1983–85; Res. Fellow, King's Coll., Cambridge, 1985–87; SERC Advanced Res. Fellow, Imperial Coll. London, 1987–88; Queen Mary College, then Queen Mary and Westfield College, later Queen Mary, University of London: SERC Advanced Res. Fellow, 1988–92; Lectr in Physics, 1992–93; Reader in Theoretical Physics, 1993–95; Prof. of Theoretical Physics, 1995–2003. FInstP. Dirac Medal, Inst. of Physics, 2003. *Publications:* articles on theoretical physics in scientific jls. *Recreations:* music, theatre, cinema, art, hiking, cycling, guitar. *Address:* Blackett Laboratory, Imperial College London, Prince Consort Road, SW7 2AZ. *T:* (020) 7594 7867. *E:* c.hull@imperial.ac.uk.

HULL, Prof. Sir David, Kt 1993; FRCP, FRCPCH; Foundation Professor of Child Health, University of Nottingham, 1972–96; *b* 4 Aug. 1932; *s* of late William and Nellie Hull; *m* 1960, Caroline Elena Lloyd; two *s* one *d*. *Educ:* Univ. of Liverpool (BSc Hons, MB ChB). DCH, DObstRCOG; FRCP 1974; FRCPCH 1996. Lectr in Paediatrics, Oxford, 1963–66; Consultant Paediatrician, Hosp. for Sick Children, London, 1966–72; Sen. Lectr, Inst. of Child Health, Univ. of London, 1966–72. President: Neonatal Soc., 1987–91; British Paediatric Assoc., 1991–94. Hon. FFPH 2000. *Publications:* (with D. I. Johnston) Essential Paediatrics, 1981, 4th edn 1999; (with A. D. Milner) Hospital Paediatrics, 1984, 3rd edn 1997; (with E. F. St J. Adamson) Nursing Sick Children, 1984; (with L. Polnay) Community Paediatrics, 1984, 2nd edn 1993. *Recreations:* gardening, drawing.
*See also* Derek Hull.

HULL, Air Vice-Marshal David Hugill, FRCP; Dean of Air Force Medicine and Clinical Director, RAF, 1994–96, retired; *b* 21 Aug. 1931; *s* of late T. E. O. and M. E. Hull (*née* Dinsley); *m* 1957, Ann Thornton-Symington; two *d*. *Educ:* Rugby; Trinity Hall, Cambridge; St Thomas' Hosp. MA, MB BChir. Royal Waterloo and Kingston upon Thames Hosps, 1956–57; RAF 1957; Consultant in Medicine, PMRAF Hosp., Akrotiri, 1966–67; RAF Hosp., Cosford, 1967–74; Exchange Consultant, Aeromedical Consultation Service, USAF Sch. of Aerospace Medicine, 1974–77; PARAF Hosp., Wroughton, 1977–82; Consultant Advr in Medicine, RAF, 1983–93; Reader, Clinical Aviation Medicine, RAF IAM, 1981–93. QHS, 1991–96. Lady Cade Medal, RCS, 1973. Hon. Texas Citizen, 1977. OStJ 1997. *Publications:* chapters in books on aviation and aerospace medicine; papers in professional jls. *Recreations:* sailing, gardening, cross-country ski-ing. *Club:* Royal Air Force.

HULL, Prof. Derek, FRS 1989; FREng, FIMMM; Senior Fellow, University of Liverpool, since 1991; Goldsmiths' Professor of Metallurgy, University of Cambridge, 1984–91, now Professor Emeritus; Fellow, Magdalene College, Cambridge, 1984–91; *b* 8 Aug. 1931; *s* of late William and Nellie Hull (*née* Hayes); *m* 1953, Pauline Scott; one *s* four *d*. *Educ:* Baines Grammar School, Poulton-le-Fylde; Univ. of Wales (PhD, DSc). AERE, Harwell and Clarendon Lab., Oxford, 1956–60; University of Liverpool: Senior Lectr, 1960–64; Henry Bell Wortley Prof. of Materials Engineering, 1964–84; Dean of Engineering, 1971–74; Pro-Vice-Chancellor, 1983–84. Dist. Vis. Prof. and Senior Vis. NSF Fellow, Univ. of Delaware, 1968–69; Monash Vis. Prof., Univ. of Monash, 1981; Andrew Laing Lecture, NECInst, 1989. FREng (FEng 1986). Hon. Fellow, University Coll. Cardiff, 1985. Hon. DTech Tampere Univ. of Technology, Finland, 1987. Rosenhain Medal, 1973, A. A. Griffith Silver Medal, 1985, Inst. of Metals; Medal of Excellence in Composite Materials, Univ. of Delaware, 1990; Leslie Holliday Prize, IMMM, 2015. *Publications:* Introduction to Dislocations, 1966, 5th edn 2011; An Introduction to Composite Materials, 1981, 2nd edn 1996; Fractography: observing, measuring and interpreting fracture surface topography, 1999; Celtic and Anglo-Saxon Art: geometric aspects, 2003; A Blind Autobiography, 2018; numerous contribs to Proc. Royal Soc., Acta Met., Phil. Mag., Jl Mat. Sci., MetalScience, Composites. *Recreations:* golf, music, fell-walking, early Medieval art. *Address:* School of Engineering, University of Liverpool, Liverpool L69 3GH. *Club:* Heswall Golf.
*See also* Sir David Hull.

HULL, John Folliott Charles, CBE 1993; Chairman, 1997–98, Deputy Chairman, 1976–97 and 1998–99, Land Securities plc; *b* 21 Oct. 1925; *er s* of Sir Hubert Hull, CBE, and Judith, *e d* of P. F. S. Stokes; *m* 1951, Rosemarie Waring; one *s* three *d*. *Educ:* Downside; Aberdeen Univ.; Jesus Coll., Cambridge (Titular Schol.; 1st cl. hons Law; Keller Prize; MA). RA, 1944–48 (attached Royal Indian Artillery, 1945–48). Called to Bar, Inner Temple, 1952, *ad eund* Lincoln's Inn, 1954. J. Henry Schroder Wagg & Co. Ltd, 1957–72, 1974–85: a Man. Dir, 1961–72; Dep. Chm., 1974–77; Chm., 1977–83; Dir, 1984–85; Schroders plc: Dir, 1969–72, 1974–85; Dep. Chm., 1977–85. Director: Lucas Industries plc, 1975–90; Legal and General Assurance Soc., 1976–79; Legal & General Group plc, 1979–90; Goodwood Racecourse Ltd, 1987–93. Dir-Gen., City Panel on Take-overs and Mergers, 1972–74 (Dep. Chm., 1987–99); Chm., City Company Law Cttee, 1976–79. Lay Mem., Stock Exchange, 1983–84. Mem., Council, Manchester Business Sch., 1973–86. *Recreation:* reading 19th century novelists. *Address:* 33 Edwardes Square, W8 6HH. *T:* (020) 7603 0715. *Club:* MCC.
*See also* Duke of Somerset.

HULL, His Honour Leslie David; a Circuit Judge, 2001–16; *b* 7 Jan. 1950; *s* of Leslie and Irene Hull; *m* Susanna; two *s* one *d*. *Educ:* Cowley Sch., St Helens; Brasenose Coll., Oxford (MA Juris.). Called to the Bar, Middle Temple, 1972 (Harmsworth Schol.); a Recorder, 1988–2001. *Recreations:* sport, music, wine.

HULL, Robert; Director, Consultative Work, European Economic and Social Committee, 2002–06; *b* 23 Jan. 1947; *s* of John Whitfield Hull and Marguerite (*née* Stace); *m* 1972, Christine Elizabeth Biffin; one *s* two *d*. *Educ:* Dame Allan's Sch., Newcastle upon Tyne; Univ. of Leicester (BA Hist. 1968); Manchester Business Sch. (MBA 1973); King's Coll. London/RADA (MA Text and Performance Studies 2007). UKAEA, 1968–69; PO Telecommunications, 1969–71; North of England Develt Council, 1973–74; EC Commission, 1974–79: Customs Service, 1974–76; Ext. Relns, SE Asia, 1976–79; Civil Servant, Scottish Office, 1979–82; European Commission, 1982–98: Ext. Relns, ME, 1982–86; Asst to Dir Gen., Financial Instns and Co. Law, 1986–90; Head, Policy Co-ordination Unit for Envmt and Sustainable Develt, 1990–98; Dir, Common Services Orgn, subseq. Jt Services, Eur. Econ. and Social Cttee and Eur. Cttee of Regs, 1998–2002. Contested (C) Durham, EP elecn, 1989. Chm., Hexham Community Partnership, 2010–16; non-exec. Dir, Théâtre Sans Frontières, 2009–. Mem., Hexham Town Council, 2017– (Mayor, 2019–). Mem. Council, Newcastle Univ., 2006–15. FRSA. *Publications:* various articles on EU ext. relns, financial services, envmt and sustainable develt, lobbying the EU. *Recreations:* sailing, ski-ing, music, theatre, local history. *Address:* Maiden Cross, Allendale Road, Hexham, Northumberland NE46 2DH. *T:* (01434) 606192. *Club:* Travellers.

HULL, Robert David, (Rob), PhD; *b* 17 Dec. 1950; *s* of David Archibald Hull and late Rosalie Joy Hull (*née* Cave); *m* 1973, Sarah, (Sally), Ann, FRCGP, *d* of late Frank Bernard Cockett, FRCS; one *s* one *d*. *Educ:* Royal Grammar Sch., Guildford; Jesus Coll., Cambridge (BA 1st cl. Hons Mathematics; MA; PhD Linguistics 1975). Civil Service Dept, 1974–81; HM Treasury, 1981–82; Dept of Educn and Science, later Dept for Educn, 1982–94; Sec., HEFCE, 1994–98 (on secondment); Dir for Qualifications and Occupational Standards, subseq. for Qualifications and Young People, DFEE, subseq. DFES, 1998–2004. Mem., NIHEC, 1994–98. Chm., E London Advanced Technol. Trng, 2005–13. Chm., On Golden Lane, 2007–10; Mem. Bd, Islington Giving, 2012– (Chm., 2017–). Trustee, Education Action, 2008–10. Governor: Holloway Sch., 1999–2018 (Chm., 2010–18); Richard Cloudesley Sch., 2007–10; Prior Weston Sch., 2007–10; Cripplegate Foundn, 2008– (Chair, 2014–15); London Metropolitan Univ., 2010–17 (Dep. Chm., 2013–17); Chair, New City Coll., 2019–. FRSA 2007. Hon. PhD London Metropolitan, 2018. *Recreations:* chess, photography, theatre, cinema, walking. *Address:* 27 Myddelton Square, EC1R 1YE. *T:* (020) 7713 5343. *Clubs:* Surrey County Cricket; Cavendish Chess.

HULME, Prof. Charles, DPhil; FBA 2017; CPsychol, FBPsS; Professor of Psychology and Education, University of Oxford, since 2017; William Golding Senior Research Fellow, Brasenose College, Oxford, since 2017; *b* 12 Oct. 1953; *s* of Norman and Edith Hulme; *m* 1995, Margaret Jean Snowling, *qv*; three *d*, and one step *s*. *Educ:* Oriel Coll., Oxford (MA; DPhil 1979). CPsychol 1989; FBPsS 1990. University of York: Lectr in Psychology, 1978–88; Reader, 1988–92; Prof., 1992–2011; Prof. of Psychology, UCL, 2011–16. *Publications:* Reading Retardation and Multi-sensory Teaching, 1981; (with S. Mackenzie) Working Memory and Severe Learning Difficulties, 1992; (with M. Snowling) The Science of Reading, 2005; (with M. Snowling) Developmental Disorders of Language and Cognition, 2009; (jtly) Developing Language and Literacy: effective intervention for language and literacy in the early years, 2011; (jtly) Developing Reading Comprehension, 2013. *Recreations:* walking, music, wine. *Address:* Department of Education, University of Oxford, 15 Norham Gardens, Oxford OX2 6PY.

HULME, Margaret Jean; *see* Snowling, M. J.

HULME, Prof. Michael, PhD; Professor of Human Geography, University of Cambridge, since 2017; Fellow, Pembroke College, Cambridge, since 2018; *b* 23 July 1960; *s* of Ralph Hulme and Shelagh Mary Hulme (*née* Close); *m* 1987, Gillian Margaret Walker; one *d*. *Educ:* Madras Coll., St Andrews; Univ. of Durham (BSc); UC, Swansea (PhD 1985). Lectr in Geog., Univ. of Salford, 1984–88; Sen. Res. Associate, 1988–97, Reader, 1998–2002, Prof. of Climate Change (formerly Envmtl Sci.), 2002–13, UEA; Dir, Tyndall Centre for Climate Change Res., 2000–07; Prof. of Climate and Culture, KCL, 2013–17. Manager, Intergovtl Panel on Climate Change Data Distribution Centre, 1997–2002; Convening Lead Author, Lead Author and Review Ed., UN Intergovtl Panel on Climate Change, 3rd Assessment Report, 2001. Editor-in-Chief, Wiley Interdisciplinary Reviews: Climate Change, 2008–. *Publications:* (ed) Climates of the British Isles, 1997; Climate Change Scenarios for the United Kingdom, 1998, 2nd edn 2002; Imagined Memories and the Seductive Quest for a Family History, 2008; Why we Disagree about Climate Change, 2009; (ed) Making Climate Change Work For Us, 2010; Exploring Climate Change Through Science and In Society, 2013; Can Science Fix Climate Change: a case against climate engineering, 2014; (ed) Climates and Cultures, 6 vols, 2015; Weathered: cultures of climate, 2016; (ed) Companion to Environmental Studies, 2018; Contemporary Debates in Climate Change, 2020; contrib. numerous climate-related articles to acad., professional and popular jls. *Recreations:* cricket, modern history, genealogy. *Address:* Department of Geography, University of Cambridge, Downing Place, Cambridge CB2 3EN. *E:* mh903@cam.ac.uk. *W:* www.mikehulme.org.

HULME, Rev. Paul; Minister, Guildford Circuit, since 2012; *b* 14 May 1942; *s* of Harry Hulme and Elizabeth Hulme; *m* 1976, Hilary Frances Martin; three *s*. *Educ:* Hatfield House, Yorks; Didsbury Theological Coll., Bristol (BA). Minister: Bungay, Suffolk, 1968–70; Brighton, (also Chaplain, Sussex Univ.), 1970–75; Newquay, Cornwall, 1975–79; Taunton, 1979–86; Enfield, 1986–88; Supt Minister, Wesley's Chapel, London, 1988–96; Minister: New River Circuit, N London, 1997–2003; Orpington and Chislehurst Circuit, 2003–12; Wey Valley Circuit, 2012. Duty Chaplain, Westminster Abbey, 1996–. Mem., BBC Churches Religious Adv. Council, 1992–95. Trustee, Joseph Rank Trust, 1991. Freeman, City of London, 1990. *Recreations:* walking, music. *Address:* Epworth, Charterhouse Road, Godalming, Surrey GU7 2AL. *T:* (01483) 414709. *Club:* National Liberal.

HULME, Tom; General Partner, Google Ventures, since 2014; *b* London, 27 June 1976. *Educ:* Univ. of Bristol (BSc 1st Cl. Hons Physics); Harvard Business Sch. (MBA; Baker Schol. Award). Man. Dir, Marcos Sportscars, 1998–99; Founder and Man. Dir, Fluid Conditioning Systems, 2000; Design Dir, IDEO, 2008, later Sen. Advr; Founder and Man. Dir, openideo.com and oiengine.com, 2010. Hon. DDes Univ. of the Arts. Young Global Leader, World Econ. Foundn, 2012. *Address:* Google Ventures, 4th Floor, 146–148 Clerkenwell Road, EC1R 5DG.

HULME CROSS, Peter; Member, London Assembly, Greater London Authority, 2004–08 (UK Ind, 2004–05; One London, 2005–08). Computer engr, then trainer. Former Mem., London Fire and Emergency Planning Authy.

HULSE, Christopher, CMG 1992; OBE 1982; HM Diplomatic Service, retired; Ambassador to the Swiss Confederation, and concurrently (non-resident) to the Principality of Liechtenstein, 1997–2001; *b* 31 July 1942; *s* of late Eric Cecil Hulse and Joan Mary Hulse (*née* Tizard); *m* 1966, Dimitra (*d* 2010), *d* of Brig. and Mrs D. Karayannakos, Karayanneïka-Trypi, Sparta, Greece; one *d*. *Educ:* Woking Grammar Sch.; Trinity Coll., Cambridge (BA 1964). Entered Foreign Office, 1964; UN Dept, FO, 1964–67; Third Sec., later Second Sec., Prague, 1967–70; Eastern European and Soviet Dept, FCO, 1970–72; First Sec., Bangkok, 1973; Western European Dept, FCO, 1973–77; UK Delegn to NATO, Brussels, 1977–80; UK Delegn to CSCE Conf., Madrid, 1980–81; Asst Hd, Defence Dept, FCO, 1981–82; Counsellor, NATO Defence Coll., Rome, 1983; Political Counsellor and Consul-Gen., Athens, 1983–88; Hd of Eastern European, subseq. Central European Dept, FCO, 1988–92; Permt Rep., UN, Vienna, 1992–97. *Recreations:* books, music, walking, gardening, carpentry. *Address:* Karayanneïka-Trypi, near Sparta, 23100, Greece.

HULSE, Sir Edward (Jeremy Westrow), 10th Bt *cr* 1739, of Lincoln's Inn Fields; DL; *b* 22 Nov. 1932; *er s* of Sir Westrow Hulse, 9th Bt and his 1st wife Philippa Mabel Hulse (decd) (*née* Taylor, later Lamb); *S* father, 1996; *m* 1957, Verity Ann Pilkington; one *s* one *d*. *Educ:* Eton; Sandhurst. Late Captain, Scots Guards. High Sheriff, Hampshire, 1978; DL Hampshire, 1989. *Recreations:* tennis, shooting. *Heir: s* Edward Michael Westrow Hulse [*b* 10 Sept. 1959; *m* 1986, Doone Brotherton; three *s* three *d*]. *Address:* Topps Farm House, Breamore, Fordingbridge, Hampshire SP6 2BU. *T:* (01725) 512233.

HULSE, Dr Russell Alan; Regental Professor and Associate Vice President for Strategic Initiatives, since 2007, and Founding Director, Science and Engineering Education Center, since 2009, University of Texas at Dallas; *b* 28 Nov. 1950; *s* of Alan Earle Hulse and Betty Joan Hulse (*née* Wedemeyer); *m* 2010, Jeanne V. Kuhlman. *Educ:* The Cooper Union, NY (BS Physics 1970); Univ. of Massachusetts, Amherst (MS Physics 1972; PhD Physics 1975; DSc 1994). National Radio Astronomy Observatory, 1975–77; Plasma Physics Lab., Princeton Univ., 1977–2007, Principal Res. Physicist, 1992–2007, Dist. Res. Fellow, 1994. Vis. Prof. of Physics and Sci. Educn, Univ. of Texas at Dallas, 2004–07. Mem. Bd, Battelle Meml Inst., 2006–12. Fellow, Amer. Physical Soc., 1993. (Jtly) Nobel Prize in Physics, 1993. *Publications:* papers in professional jls and conf. procs in fields of pulsar astronomy, controlled fusion plasma physics and computer modeling. *Recreations:* nature photography, bird watching, clay target shooting, hunting, other outdoor activities. *Address:* University of Texas at Dallas, 800 West Campbell Rd, AD 15, Richardson, TX 75080–3021, USA.

HULYER, Douglas, FRSB; independent adviser on environment and heritage and on environmental communications and learning; artist and writer; Director, Naturalhistories (consultancy), since 2006; *b* 13 April 1952; *s* of Charles and Florence Hulyer; *m* 1975, Beth Woodward (*d* 2012); two *d*; *m* 2017, Ann Finlayson. *Educ:* Colfe's Sch.; Avery Hill Coll. of Educn (Cert Ed Dist.; BEd 1st Cl. Hons London). FRSB (FIBiol 2008). Educn Officer, Surrey Wildlife Trust, 1977–84; Wildfowl and Wetlands Trust: Educn Officer, 1984–88; Dir, Educn and Public Affairs, 1988–97; Dir, Conservation Progs, 1997–2005. Member: Council for Envmtl Educn, 1998–2002; Council, English Nature, 2002–06; Bd, Natural England, 2006–14. Mem., Commn on Educn and Communication, IUCN, 1996–. Mem., Learning Panel, 2008–15, Chm., SW Regl Adv. Bd, 2016–, NT. Trustee: Nat. Heritage Meml Fund, 2006–13; Heritage Lottery Fund, 2006–12; Earth Trust, 2012–17 (Chm., 2014–16); Woodchester Mansion Trust, 2012–16; Chairman: Jurassic Coast World Heritage Site Steering Gp, 2014–16; Jurassic Coast Trust, 2016–; Chair, Glos Local Nature Partnership, 2018–. Vice-Pres., Surrey Wildlife Trust, 2003–15. FRSA. *Recreations:* art, gardening, design, music. *Address:* Tranquility, Houndscroft, Rodborough, Stroud, Glos GL5 5DF. *E:* doug.hulyer@btinternet.com.

HUM, Sir Christopher (Owen), KCMG 2003 (CMG 1996); HM Diplomatic Service, retired; Master of Gonville and Caius College, Cambridge, 2006–12, now Life Fellow; *b* 27 Jan. 1946; *s* of late Norman Charles Hum and Muriel Kathleen (*née* Hines); *m* 1970, Julia Mary, second *d* of Hon. Sir Hugh Park; one *s* one *d*. *Educ:* Berkhamsted Sch.; Pembroke Coll., Cambridge (Foundn Scholar; 1st Cl. Hons; MA; Hon. Fellow 2004); Univ. of Hong Kong; Sch. of Oriental and African Studies, Univ. of London (Postgrad. Dip. in Asian Art 2015). Joined FCO, 1967; served in: Hong Kong, 1968–70; Peking, 1971–73; Office of the UK Perm. Rep. to the EEC, Brussels, 1973–75; FCO, 1975–79; Peking, 1979–81; Paris, 1981–83; Asst Head, Hong Kong Dept, FCO, 1983–85; Counsellor, 1985; Dep. Head, Falkland Is Dept, FCO, 1985–86; Head, Hong Kong Dept, FCO, 1986–89; Counsellor (Political) and Hd of Chancery, UK Mission to UN, New York, 1989–92; Asst Under-Sec. of State (Northern Asia), 1992–94; (Northern Asia and Pacific), 1994–95; Ambassador to Poland, 1996–98; Dep. Under-Sec. of State and Chief Clerk, FCO, 1998–2001; Ambassador to the People's Republic of China, 2002–05. Dir, Laird, plc, 2006–17. Adv. Cttee, China Policy Inst., Univ. of Nottingham, 2006–17; Exec. Cttee, GB-China Centre, 2006–17 (Vice-Chm., 2013–17). Gov., SOAS, 1998–2001; Mem. Council, Cambridge Univ., 2009–12; Syndic, Fitzwilliam Mus., 2008–14; Chm., Cambridge Assessment, 2010–12; Trustee, Young Classical Artists Trust, 2006–14; Co-Founder and Trustee, Viola Commissioning Circle, 2018–. Hon. Pres., China Assoc., 2014–. Hon. LLD Nottingham, 2006; Hon. PhD London Metropolitan, 2006. *Recreations:* all the arts, walking, Asia. *E:* ch407@cam.ac.uk. *Club:* Athenæum.

HUMBLE, James Kenneth, OBE 1996; fair trading consultant, since 1998; *b* 8 May 1936; *s* of Joseph Humble and Alice (*née* Rhodes); *m* 1962, Freda (*née* Holden); three *d*. Served RN, 1954–56. Weights and Measures, Oldham, 1952–62; Fed. Min. of Commerce and Industry, Nigeria, 1962–66; Chief Trading Standards Officer, Croydon, 1966–74; Asst Dir of Consumer Affairs, Office of Fair Trading, 1974–79; Dir of Metrication Bd, 1979–80; Dir, Nat. Metrological Co-ordinating Unit, 1980–87; Chief Exec., Local Authorities Co-ordinating Body on Food and Trading Standards, 1982–98. Non-exec. Dir, NCC, 1997–2002. Sec., Trade Descriptions Cttee, Inst. of Trading Standards, 1968–73; Examr, Dip. in Trading Standards, 1978–94; Vice Chm., Council of Europe Cttee of Experts on Consumer Protection, 1976–79. Member: Council for Vehicle Servicing and Repair, 1972–75; Methven Cttee, 1974–76; OECD Cttee, Air Package Tours, 1978–79; BSI Divl Council, 1976–79; Eden Cttee on Metrology, 1984; Food Codes Cttee, DoH, 1998; Group Chairman: World Conf. on Safety, Sweden, 1989; Yugoslavian Conf. on Fair Trading, 1992; Member: European Consumer Product Safety Assoc., 1987–97; W European Legal Metrology Co-operation, 1989–98; European Forum Food Law Enforcement Practitioners, 1990–98; Consumer Congress, 1998–2002. Non-executive Director: Wine Standards Bd, 1999–2003; Dignity in Dying, 2007– (Chm., Orgnl Develt Cttee, 2007–); Chm., Golden Leaves Funeral Planning, 2019. Organiser, First European Metrology Symposium, 1988. Conf. papers to USA Western States Conf. on Weights and Measures, 1989. FITSA 1974– (Vice Pres., 1997–); Orator, 1998–); FRSA 1996. Rugby, Devonport Services, 1954–56; Captain, Oldham Rugby Union, 1957–59; Professional Rugby, Leigh RFC, 1959–65. *Publications:* (contrib.) Marketing and the Consumer Movement, 1978; European Inspection, Protection and Control, 1990; A Grandad's Life, 2008; (jtly) A History of the Trading Standards Institute, 2014; contrib. to various jls. *Recreations:* bridge, golf, opera. *Address:* 153 Upper Selsdon Road, Croydon, Surrey CR2 0DU. *T:* (020) 8657 6170.

HUMBLE, (Jovanka) Joan; JP; *b* 3 March 1951; *d* of John and Dora Piplica; *m* 1972, Paul Nugent Humble; two *d*. *Educ:* Lancaster Univ. (BA Hons). DHSS, 1972–73; Inland Revenue, 1973–77. Mem. (Lab), Lancs CC, 1985–97. MP (Lab) Blackpool N and Fleetwood, 1997–2010. Chair, Blackpool Town FC, 2018–; Chm., Blackpool Civic Trust, 2013– (Treas., 2012–13); Member: Adv. Bd, Blackpool Salvation Army Bridge project, 2012–; Bd, Civic Voice, 2014– (Chm., 2016–); Bd, Blackpool Wyre and Fylde Volunteer Centre, 2015–. JP Preston, 1993. *Recreations:* gardening, cooking, reading.

HUME, Gary, RA 2001; artist; *b* 9 May 1962; *m* Georgie Hopton. *Educ:* Goldsmiths' Coll., Univ. of London (BA 1988). Prof. of Drawing, RA, 2004. *Solo exhibitions* include: Karsten Schubert Ltd, 1989, 1991; Galerie Tanja Grünert, Cologne, 1991, 1993; Matthew Marks Gall., NY, 1992, 1994, 1997, 1998, 2001, 2005, 2009; White Cube, ICA, Kunsthalle Bern, 1995; Galleria il Ponte, Rome, 1996; Hayward Gall., Sadler's Wells Th., 1998; Whitechapel Art Gall., Dean Gall., Edinburgh, 1999; La Caixa, Barcelona, 2000; White Cube, 2002; MOMA, Dublin, 2003; MOMA, Oxford, 2008; New Art Centre, Salisbury, 2010; White Cube, Leeds Art Gall., 2012; *group exhibitions* include: Karsten Schubert Ltd, 1990, 1992, 1993, 1995; British Art Show, McLellan Galls, Glasgow, Leeds City Art Gall. and Hayward Gall., 1990; Matthew Marks Inc., NY, 1991; Musée Nat. d'Histoire, Luxembourg, Times Sq., NY, 1993; Stedelijk Mus., Amsterdam, 1995; Venice Biennale, 1995, 1999; Saatchi Gall., 1997, 2000; White Cube$^2$, NPG, 2000; Tate Modern, 2001; Tate Liverpool, 2002; Tate Britain, 2004, 2013; *work in public collections* including Arts Council, British Council, Saatchi Collection, Tate Gall., Paine Webber Art Collection, NY, DESTE Foundn for Contemp. Art, Athens, and Art Inst. of Chicago. Jerwood Painting Prize, 1997. *Address:* c/o Royal Academy of Arts, Burlington House, Piccadilly, W1J 0BD.

HUME, James Robert, (Jim); Convener, National Rural Mental Health Forum, Scotland, since 2017; Director for Policy and Public Affairs, Support in Mind, Scotland, since 2018; *b* 4 Nov. 1962; *s* of Walter and Joyce Hume; two *s* one *d*. *Educ:* Selkirk High Sch.; East of Scotland Coll. of Agric. (Dip. Agric. 1982); Univ. of Edinburgh (MBA 1997). Farmer; Partner, John Hume & Son, 1988–2015. Dir, NFU Scotland, 2004–06 and 2007. Mem. (Lib Dem), Scottish Borders Council, 2007–12. Chm., Borders Foundn for Rural Sustainability, 2002–07; Mem. Bd, Scottish Enterprise Borders, 2002–07. Trustee, Borders Forest Trust, 2000–06. Mem. (Lib Dem) Scotland S, Scottish Parlt, 2007–16; contested (Lib Dem) Ettrick, Roxburgh and Berwickshire, Scottish Parlt, 2016. Non-exec. Dir, Scotland's Rural Coll., 2017–. Volunteering Director: Broomhouse Centre, 2016–18; Tweed Forum, 2016–18. MCIM 1997; ARAgS 2018. Hon. Associate, BVA, 2018. *Publications:* (contrib.) Shepherds, by Walter Elliot, 2000. *Recreations:* amateur radio, gardening, motorcycling, conservation work. *Address:* 8/11 Leslie Place, Edinburgh EH4 1NH. *E:* jim@hume.scot. *Clubs:* Victory Services; Cockenzie and Port Seton Amateur Radio; Royal Scots' (Edinburgh).

HUME, Prof. John; Tip O'Neill Professor of Peace Studies, Faculty of Social Sciences, University of Ulster, 2002–10, now Hon. Professor; *b* 18 Jan. 1937; *s* of Samuel Hume; *m* 1960, Patricia Hone; two *s* three *d*. *Educ:* St Columb's Coll., Derry; St Patrick's Coll., Maynooth, NUI (MA). Res. Fellow in European Studies, TCD; Associate Fellow, Centre for Internat. Affairs, Harvard, 1976. Pres., Credit Union League of Ireland, 1964–68; MP for Foyle, NI Parlt, 1969–73; Member (SDLP): Londonderry: NI Assembly, 1973–75; NI Constitutional Convention, 1975–76; NI Assembly, 1982–86; Foyle, NI Assembly, 1998–2000; Minister of Commerce, NI, 1974. Mem. (SDLP) NI, European Parlt, 1979–2004. Leader, SDLP, 1979–2001. Mem. (SDLP) New Ireland Forum, 1983–84. Contested (SDLP) Londonderry, UK elections, Oct. 1974. Member: Cttee on Regl Policy and Regl Planning, European Parlt, 1979–2004; ACP-EEC Jt Cttee, 1979–2004; Bureau of European Socialist Gp, 1979–2004. MP (SDLP) Foyle, 1983–2005. Mem., Irish T&GWU (now Services, Industrial, Professional & Technical Union). Hon. DLitt: Massachusetts, 1985; Catholic Univ. of America, 1986; St Joseph's Univ., Philadelphia, 1986; Tusculum Coll., Tennessee, 1988. St Thomas More Award, Univ. of San Francisco, 1991; (jtly) Nobel Peace Prize, 1998; Freedom of Londonderry, 2000. KCSG 2012. *Address:* c/o Faculty of Social Sciences, University of Ulster, Magee Campus, Londonderry BT48 7JL.

HUME, Dr Robert, FRCPE, FRCPGlas, FRCPI, FRCPath, FRCSE; Consultant Physician, Southern General Hospital, Glasgow, 1965–93; *b* 6 Jan. 1928; *m* 1958, Kathleen Ann Ogilvie; two *s* one *d*. *Educ:* Univ. of Glasgow (MB, ChB, MD, DSc). FRCPGlas 1968; FRCPE 1969; FRCPath 1992; FRCSE 1992; FRCPI 1993. Nat. Service in India and Germany, 1946–48, commnd into Gordon Highlanders. Glasgow University: Hutcheson Res. Scholar, 1955–56; Hall Fellow, 1956–58; Hon. Clinical Sub-Dean, 1985–93. Dir, HCI Internat. Med. Centre, 1996–2002. Pres., RCPSGlas, 1990–92. Chm., Jt Cttee on Higher Med. Trng for UK Colls, 1990–93. Member: Acad. of Medicine, Malaysia, 1991; Royal Philosophical Soc. of Glasgow; Glasgow Antiques and Fine Arts Soc.; NT for Scotland. Hon. FACP; Hon. FRACP; Hon. FCSSA; Hon. FRCP&S (Canada). *Publications:*

on haematological and vascular diseases. *Recreations:* hill-walking, swimming, reading, art appreciation, gardening, talking, golf. *Address:* 6 Rubislaw Drive, Bearsden, Glasgow G61 1PR. *T:* (0141) 586 5249. *Club:* Buchanan Castle Golf.

**HUMFREY, Charles Thomas William,** CMG 1999; HM Diplomatic Service, retired; *b* 1 Dec. 1947; *s* of Brian and Marjorie Humfrey; *m* 1971, Enid Thomas; two *s* one *d*. *Educ:* The Lodge Sch., Barbados (Barbados Scholar, 1966); St Edmund Hall, Oxford (Webb Medley Jun. Prize, 1968). FCO 1969; Tokyo, 1971–76; SE Asian Dept, FCO, 1976–79; Private Sec. to Minister of State, 1979–81; UK Mission, NY, 1981–85; Southern African Dept, FCO, 1985–87; Counsellor, Ankara, 1988–90; Counsellor (Econ.), Tokyo, 1990–94; Head of African Dept (Southern), FCO, 1994–95; Minister, Tokyo, 1995–99; Ambassador: Republic of Korea, 2000–03; Republic of Indonesia, 2004–08. Exec. Dir, UK-Japan 21st Century Gp, 2008–11. Chm., Anglo-Indonesian Soc., 2010–18; Mem. Council, RSAA, 2011–17. Chm., Welford Place Ltd, 2009–15. *Address:* 31 Welford Place, Wimbledon, SW19 5AJ.

**HUMM, Robert Peter,** CBE 2011; Head of Regulatory Development, General Pharmaceutical Council, 2014; *b* 8 June 1949; *s* of Joseph Robert Humm and Winifred Maud Humm (*née* Fox). Chartered Sec. Formerly Solicitor to HSC and HSE; Dir, Legal Services, DEFRA, 2004–09; Dir, Tax Litigation, then Legal Dir, HMRC, 2009–14. *Recreations:* opera, travel.

**HUMM, Roger Frederick;** Director: Andrew Macdonald (London) Ltd, since 2002; St James and Country Estates Ltd, since 2004; Mount Securities Ltd, since 2006; *b* 7 March 1937; *s* of Leonard Edward Humm, MBE, and Gladys Humm; *m* 1966, Marion Frances (*née* Czechman) (marr. diss.). *Educ:* Hampton Sch., Hampton, Middx; Univ. of Sheffield (BA Hons Econ). Graduate trainee, Ford Motor Co. Ltd (UK), 1960, Sales Manager, 1973; Marketing Dir, 1977, Internat. Gp Dir, N Europe, 1978, Ford of Europe Inc.; Exec. Dir of Sales, 1980, Man. Dir, 1986–90, Ford Motor Co. Ltd; Director: Henry Ford & Son Ltd (Cork), 1978–90; Ford Motor Credit Co. Ltd, 1980–90; Vice-Chm. and Chief Exec., 1992–2000, non-exec. Dir, 2000–02, Alexanders Holdings plc. FRSA 1987; FInstD; FIMI. Liveryman, Worshipful Co. of Carmen, 1986; Freeman, City of London, 1986. *Recreations:* golf, scuba diving, writing. *Address:* Shepley Wood, Shepley Drive, Ascot SL5 0LH. *Clubs:* Royal Automobile, Lord's Taverners, Variety Club of Great Britain.

**HUMPHERSON, Edward Allen;** Director General, Office for Statistics Regulation, UK Statistics Authority, since 2014; *b* Salisbury, 2 June 1970; *s* of late William Allen Humpherson and Rosemary Elizabeth Humpherson (*née* Arbuthnot); *m* 2004, Fiona Kathryn James; one *s* two *d*. *Educ:* Univ. of Edinburgh (MA 1st Cl. Hons Politics and Econ. Hist.). Chartered Accountant 1996. Nat. Audit Office, 1993–2007; Asst Auditor Gen., Nat. Audit Office, 2007–13. *Publications:* National Audit Office reports. *Recreations:* cricket, contemporary art. *Address:* UK Statistics Authority, 1 Drummond Gate, SW1V 2QQ. *T:* (020) 7592 8675.

**HUMPHERY-SMITH, Cecil Raymond Julian,** OBE 2004; FSA; Principal, 1983–2010, now Emeritus, and Trustee, since 1964, Institute of Heraldic and Genealogical Studies, Canterbury; *b* 29 Oct. 1928; *s* of Frederick Humphery-Smith, MBE and Agnes Violet (*née* Boxall); *m* 1951, Alice Elizabeth Gwendoline Cogle; one *s* five *d*. *Educ:* Hurstpierpoint Coll.; London Sch. of Hygiene and Tropical Medicine, Univ. of London (BSc 1950); Parma-Piacenza Dept of Agronomy; Univ. of Kent at Canterbury. Consumer Services Manager, H. J. Heinz Corp., 1955–60; UK Rep. and Internat. Consultant, DeRica SpA, 1961–74; Man. Dir, Achievements Ltd, 1961–91; script ed. and writer, Media Internat., 2001–04. Founder and Director: Sch. of Family History, 1957; Inst. of Heraldic and Genealogical Studies, 1961. Pt-time Extra Mural Lectr, Univs of Oxford, London and Kent, 1951–2000. Ed., Family History, 1962–. Vis. Prof., Univ. of Minho, 1975. Co-Founder, Fedn of Family Hist. Socs, 1974; formerly Mem. Cttees, Soc. of Genealogists (FSG 1970); Heraldry Society: Mem. Council, 1953–2003; Fellow, 1960; Vice-Pres., 1993; Vice-Pres., Cambridge Univ. Heraldry Soc., 1954; Hon. Vice Pres., Cambridge Univ. Heraldic and Genealogical Soc., 1994. Pres. Emeritus, Confedn Internat. des Sciences Généalogique et Héraldique (Pres., 1986–90); Mem., Bureau Perm. des Congrès internationaux, 1976–; Academician, 1976, Mem. Council, 1994–, Acad. Internat. d'Héraldique; Pres., Internat. Fedn of Schs of Family Hist. Studies, Bologna, 2001. Mem., Governing Council, Rutherford Coll., Univ. of Kent at Canterbury, 1992–2001. FSA 1982. Hon. Fellow, Canterbury Christ Ch Univ., 2008. Freeman, City of London, 1967; Liveryman: Co. of Broderers, 1973–; Co. of Scriveners, 1979– (Hon. Historian, 1983; Mem. Court, 1999). DLit Minho, 1975. Kt of Obedience, SMO Malta, 1977; Founding Co-ordinator, Order of Malta Volunteers, 1974. *Publications:* (jtly) The Colour of Heraldry, 1958; General Armory Two, 1973; Sonnets of Life, 1973; Anglo-Norman Armory, vol. 1, 1973, vol. 2, 1993; Atlas and Index of Parish Registers, 1974, as Phillimore's Atlas and Index of Parish Registers, 1995, 3rd edition 2003; A Genealogist's Bibliography, 1985; Hugh Revel, Master of the Hospital 1257–1277, 1994; Armigerous Ancestors, 1997; (jtly) A History of the Worshipful Company of Scriveners of London, 2001; A Tudor Armorial, 2004; several pamphlets and studies in the heraldry of Canterbury Cathedral; contrib. articles to proc. of internat. congresses and colloquia in genealogy and heraldry; contrib. encyclopedias, DNB, The Coat of Arms, Genealogists Mag., Family History, etc. *Recreations:* music, writing sonnets, enjoying four generations of family, now immobile and housebound. *Address:* Institute of Heraldic and Genealogical Studies, Northgate, Canterbury, Kent CT1 1BA; Saint Michael's, Allan Road, Seasalter, Whitstable, Kent CT5 4AH. *T:* (01227) 275791. *E:* scatterbr@sky.com.

**HUMPHREY, Dame Caroline, (Lady Rees of Ludlow),** DBE 2011; PhD; FBA 1998; Fellow, King's College, Cambridge, since 1978; Sigrid Rausing Professor of Collaborative Anthropology, University of Cambridge, 2006–10, now Emeritus; *b* 1 Sept. 1943; *d* of Prof. C. H. Waddington, CBE, FRS and M. J. Waddington; *m* 1st, 1967, Nicholas Humphrey (marr. diss. 1977); 2nd, 1986, Prof. Martin Rees (*see* Baron Rees of Ludlow). *Educ:* St George's High Sch., Edinburgh; Girton Coll., Cambridge (BA 1965; PhD 1973); Leeds Univ. (MA Mongolian Studies 1971). University of Cambridge: Research Fellow, Girton Coll., 1971–74; Sen. Asst in Res., Scott Polar Res. Inst., 1973–78; Asst Lectr, 1978–83; Lectr, 1983–95; Reader, 1995–98; Prof. of Asian Anthropology, 1998–2006; Dir of Res., Div. of Social Anthropology, 2010–15; Res. Dir, Mongolia and Inner Asia Studies Unit, 2016–. British Acad. Research Reader, 1990–92; Vis. Fellow, Inst. for Humanities, Univ. of Michigan, 1992. MAE 2007. Internat. Mem. (formerly Foreign Mem.), Amer. Philosophical Soc., 2004. Hon. Fellow, Robinson Coll., Cambridge, 2019. Hon. Dr: Mongolian State Univ.; Bolton. Staley Prize in Anthropology, Sch. of Amer. Res., USA, 1990; Burton Medal, Royal Asiatic Soc., 2014. Chevalier, Ordre des Palmes Académiques (France), 2004. *Publications:* Karl Marx Collective: economy, society and religion in a Siberian collective farm, 1983, rev. edn 1998; (with J. Laidlaw) The Archetypal Actions of Ritual, 1994; Shamans and Elders: experience, knowledge and power among the Daur Mongols, 1996; (with D. Sneath) The End of Nomadism?: pastoralism and the state in Inner Asia, 1998; The Unmaking of Soviet Life, 2002; (ed with R. Mandel) Markets and Moralities: ethnographies of postsocialism, 2002; (ed with K. Verdery) Property in Question: value transformation in the global economy, 2004; (ed with C. Alexander and V. Buchli) Urban Life in Post-Soviet Central Asia, 2007; Post-Soviet Transformations in Asian Russia: anthropological essays, 2009; (ed with F. Billé and G. Delaplace) Frontier Encounters: knowledge and practice at the Russian, Chinese and Mongolian border, 2012; (ed with V. Skvirskaja) Post-Cosmopolitan Cities: explorations of urban coexistence, 2012; (jtly) A Monastery in Time: the making of Mongolian Buddhism, 2013; (ed) Trust and Mistrust in the Economies of the Russia-China Borderlands, 2018. *Recreation:* classical music. *Address:* 5a Herschel Road, Cambridge CB3 9AG. *T:* (01223) 369043.

**HUMPHREY, John Eugene;** Group Chief Executive, Kent Holdco Ltd, since 2019; *b* Norwich, 12 Oct. 1962; *s* of John Edwin and Anne Theresa Humphrey; *m* 1991, Kathryn Anne; two *s*. *Educ:* Thornleigh Salesian Coll., Bolton; Univ. of Bradford (BA Hons Interdisciplinary Human Studies); Grad. DipM. Articled Clerk, Arthur Young, 1986–87; Grad. trainee, then Sales Exec., Unisys, 1987–90; Sales Exec., then Divl Mktg Manager, ICL plc, 1990–95; Sales and Mktg Dir, Seaward Electronic Ltd, 1995–96; Gen. Manager and Sales Dir, AlliedSignal Laminate Systems Ltd, 1996–98; Gp Man. Dir, Dedicated Micros Gp Ltd, 1999–2001; Man. Dir, Braddahead Ltd, 2001–04; Vice Pres., Infrastructure Solutions, Verint, Canada, 2004–07; Hd, Sales and Mktg, UK Hydrographic Office, 2007–08; Geschäftsführer, Admiralty Deutschland GmbH, 2008–12; UK Hydrographic Office: Interim Commercial Dir, 2012–14; Chief Commercial Officer and Dep. Chief Exec., 2014–15; Chief Exec. and Accounting Officer, 2015–19. Lay Trustee, Royal Coll. of Speech and Language Therapists, 2018–. Younger Brother, Trinity House, 2018–. *Recreations:* constantly twiddling with an old Porsche, watching amazingly good amateur shows at Farnworth Little Theatre, walking around the block endlessly. *Clubs:* Civil Service, Naval and Military.

**HUMPHREYS, Baroness** *cr* 2013 (Life Peer), of Llanrwst in the County of Conwy; **Christine Mary Humphreys;** President, Welsh Liberal Democrats, since 2007. Former teacher. Mem. (Lib Dem) Wales N, Nat. Assembly for Wales, 1999–2003.

**HUMPHREYS, Sir Colin (John),** Kt 2010; CBE 2003; FRS 2011; FREng, FIMMM, FInstP; Director, Cambridge Centre for Gallium Oxide, since 2000 and Director of Research, Department of Materials Science and Metallurgy, since 2008, University of Cambridge (Goldsmiths' Professor of Materials Science, 1992–2008); Professor of Experimental Physics, Royal Institution of Great Britain, 1999–2016; Director, Rolls-Royce University Technology Centre, since 1994; Fellow of Selwyn College, Cambridge, since 1990; *b* 24 May 1941; *s* of Arthur William Humphreys and Olive Annie (*née* Harton); *m* 1966, Sarah Jane Matthews; two *d*. *Educ:* Luton Grammar Sch.; Imperial Coll., London (BSc); Churchill Coll., Cambridge (PhD); Jesus Coll., Oxford (MA). Sen. Res. Officer 1971–80, Lectr 1980–85, in Metallurgy and Science of Materials, Univ. of Oxford; Sen. Res. Fellow, Jesus Coll., Oxford, 1974–85; Henry Bell Wortley Prof. of Materials Engrg and Hd of Dept of Materials Sci. and Engrg, Liverpool Univ., 1985–89; Prof. of Materials Sci., 1990–92, Hd, Dept of Materials Sci. and Metallurgy, 1991–95, Univ. of Cambridge. Visiting Professor: Univ. of Illinois, 1982–86; Arizona State Univ., 1979. Lectures: D. K. C. MacDonald Meml, Toronto, 1993; Hume-Rothery Meml, Oxford, 1997; Gladstone, London, 1999; Hatfield Meml, Sheffield, 2000; Royal Acad. of Engrg Sterling, Singapore and Malaysia, 2001; John Matthews Meml, Durban, 2002; Robert Warner, Founders' Co., London, 2002; Sigma Xi, McGill Univ., 2004; Golden Jubilee Oration, Defence Res. Develt Orgn, Delhi, 2008; IEEE Dist. Lect., IIT, Bombay, 2008; Sir D. Owen Evans Meml, Univ. of Wales, Aberystwyth, 2010; John Cowley Dist. Lect., Arizona State Univ., 2011; Winegard Lect., Guelph and Toronto, 2012; Finniston, IMMM, London, 2012; Armourers' and Brasiers' Kelly Lect., Cambridge, 2013; Walton, Cork, Dublin and Belfast, 2016. Chm., Commn on Electron Diffraction, and Mem. Commn on Internat. Tables, Internat. Union of Crystallography, 1984–87. Member: SERC, 1988–92 (Chm., Materials Sci. and Engrg Commn, 1988–92; Mem., Science Bd, 1990–92); Adv. Cttee, Davy-Faraday Labs, Royal Instn, 1989–92; Scientific Adv. Cttee on Advanced Materials for EC Internat. Scientific Co-opn Prog., 1990–2000; Metallurgy and Materials Panel, RAE 2001, HEFCE; BERR (formerly DTI) Nat. Adv. Cttee on Electronic Materials and Devices, 1999–2006; Internat. Adv. Panel, Etisalat, UAE, 2003–04; Adv. Panel, Leverhulme Trust, 2005–; Internat. Review Panel, Japan World Premier Res. Centre Initiative, 2008–; Res. Appt Panel, Royal Soc., 2010–12 (Co-Chm., 2013; Chm., 2014–16); External Adv. Bd, Energy Frontier Res. Center for Solid-State Lighting Sci., Sandia National Labs, 2010–14; Tribology Trust Awards Cttee, 2011–; Internat. Scientific Adv. Bd, Photon Sci. Inst., Manchester, 2012–15; Internat. Scientific Adv. Panel, Monash Centre for Electron Microscopy, Australia, 2013–16; Adv. Bd, Plessey, 2013–; Chairman: Internat. Adv. Bd, Nat. Inst. for Materials Sci., Tsukuba, Japan, 2003–; Internat. Review Panel, Dept of Materials, Technion, Israel, 2004. Member Council: RMS, 1988–89; Inst. of Metals, 1989–91; President: Physics sect., BAAS, 1998–99; Inst. of Materials, 2002 (Mem. Council, 1992–2002; Sen. Vice-Pres., 2000–01); Inst. of Materials, Minerals and Mining, 2002–03 (Chm., Managing Bd, 2004–05); Awards Cttee, Royal Acad. of Engrg, 2003–06; Victoria Inst., 2014–; Christians in Sci., 2015–. Director: Camgan Ltd, 2011–; Intellec Ltd, 2011–; Plessey Lighting Ltd, 2012–; 2D Technologies Ltd, 2016–. Fellow in Public Understanding of Physics, Inst. of Phys, 1997–98; Selby Fellow, Aust. Acad. of Scis, 1997; Fellow, Sch. of Engrg, Univ. of Tokyo, 2007; FCGI 2011. Hon. Pres., Canadian Coll. for Chinese Studies, 1996–2007; Member Court: Univ. of Bradford, 1990–92; Univ. of Cranfield, 1992–. Trustee, Link House Trust, Cambridge, 1994–. Member: Bd of Advrs, Templeton Religion Trust, 2014–; Templeton World Charity Foundn, 2014–; John Templeton Foundn, 2015–. Freeman, City of London, 1994; Liveryman: Goldsmiths' Co., 1997– (Freeman, 1992); Mem., Technology and Promotions Cttee, 2002–); Armourers' and Brasiers' Co., 2001– (Freeman, 1998; Mem., Ct of Assts, 2004–; Master, 2010–11). FREng (FEng 1996); MAE 1991. Hon. Fellow Royal Microscopical Soc., 2015. Hon. DSc Leicester, 2001. RSA Medal, 1963; Reginald Mitchell Meml Lecture and Medal, 1989; Rosenhain Medal and Prize, Inst. of Metals, 1989; Templeton Award, 1994; Elegant Work Prize, Inst. of Materials, 1996; Kelvin Medal and Prize, Inst. of Physics, 1999; Gold Medal, Fedn of Eur. Materials Socs, 2001; Robert Franklin Mehl Gold Medal, Minerals, Metals and Materials Soc., USA, 2003; Platinum Medal, IMMM, 2013; Henry Clifton Sorby Award, Internat. Metallographic Soc., 2017. Editor, Reports on Progress in Physics, 2001–06. *Publications:* (ed) High Voltage Electron Microscopy, 1974; (ed) Electron Diffraction 1927–77, 1978; Creation and Evolution, 1985 (trans. Chinese 1988); (ed) Understanding Materials, 2002; The Miracles of Exodus, 2003 (trans. German 2007, Portuguese 2004); The Mystery of the Last Supper: reconstructing the final days of Jesus, 2011 (trans. German, Japanese, Portuguese, Russian, 2012, Greek, 2013); patents and numerous sci. and tech. pubns mainly on electron microscopy, semiconductors, superconductors and nanometre scale electron beam lithography. *Recreations:* chronology of ancient historical events, contemplating gardening. *Address:* Department of Materials Science and Metallurgy, 27 Charles Babbage Road, Cambridge CB3 0FS. *T:* (01223) 334457.

**HUMPHREYS, Emyr Owen,** FRSL; author; *b* 15 April 1919; *s* of William and Sarah Rosina Humphreys, Prestatyn, Flints; *m* 1946, Elinor Myfanwy, *d* of Rev. Griffith Jones, Bontnewydd, Caerns; three *s* one *d*. *Educ:* University Coll., Aberystwyth; University Coll., Bangor (Hon. Fellow, Univ. of Wales, 1987). Gregynog Arts Fellow, 1974–75; Hon. Prof., English Dept, Univ. Coll. of N Wales, Bangor, 1988. FRSL 1993. Hon. DLitt Wales, 1990. Cymmrodorion Medal, 2003. *Publications:* The Little Kingdom, 1946; The Voice of a Stranger, 1949; A Change of Heart, 1951; Hear and Forgive, 1952 (Somerset Maugham

Award, 1953); A Man's Estate, 1955; The Italian Wife, 1957; Y Tri Llais, 1958; A Toy Epic, 1958 (Hawthornden Prize, 1959); The Gift, 1963; Outside the House of Baal, 1965; Natives, 1968; Ancestor Worship, 1970; National Winner, 1971 (Welsh Arts Council Prize, 1972); Flesh and Blood, 1974; Landscapes, 1976; The Best of Friends, 1978; Penguin Modern Poets No 27, 1978 (Soc. of Authors Travelling Award, 1979); The Kingdom of Brân, 1979; The Anchor Tree, 1980; Pwyll a Riannon, 1980; Miscellany Two, 1981; The Taliesin Tradition, 1983 (Welsh Arts Council Non-Fiction Prize, 1984); Jones: a novel, 1984; Salt of the Earth, 1985; An Absolute Hero, 1986; Darn o Dir, 1986; Open Secrets, 1988; The Triple Net, 1988; The Crucible of Myth, 1990; Bonds of Attachment, 1991 (Book of the Year, Welsh Arts Council, 1992); Outside Time, 1991; Brodyr a Chwiorydd, 1994; Unconditional Surrender, 1996; The Gift of a Daughter, 1998 (Book of the Year, Welsh Arts Council, 1999); Collected Poems, 1999; Dal Pen Rheswm, 1999; Ghosts and Strangers, 2001; Conversations and Reflections, 2002; Old People Are a Problem, 2003; The Shop, 2005; Welsh Time, 2009; The Woman at the Window, 2009; Shards of Light, 2018. *Recreation:* walking. *Address:* Llinon, Penyberth, Llanfairpwll, Ynys Môn, Gwynedd LL61 5YT.

**HUMPHREYS, Janet, (Mrs V. W. Humphreys);** *see* Anderson, Janet.

**HUMPHREYS, Kate;** *see* Priestley, K.

**HUMPHREYS, Richard William;** QC 2006; barrister; *b* 22 Feb. 1963; *s* of Ian Richardson Humphreys and Valerie Thursby Trewin; *m* 1988, Rosalind Julia Birley; one *s* two *d*. *Educ:* Aldwickbury Sch., Wheathampstead; Stowe Sch.; Nottingham Univ. (LLB); Gonville and Caius Coll., Cambridge (LLM 1985). Called to the Bar, Inner Temple, 1986. *Recreations:* history, tennis, ski-ing.

**HUMPHRIES, Barry;** *see* Humphries, J. B.

**HUMPHRIES, Chris,** CBE 1998; Chief Executive Officer, UK Commission for Employment and Skills, 2008–10; Pro Chancellor, University of West London, since 2012 (Chairman, Board of Governors, 2010–18); *b* 31 Aug. 1948; *s* of John Joseph Humphries and Berenice Mary Lee; *m* 1996, Hazel Maxwell Cross; one *s* two *d*. *Educ:* Univ. of NSW (BA 1972). Media Resources Officer, ILEA, 1975–79; Producer, Promedia, 1979–82; IT Prog. Manager, 1982–84, Asst Dir, 1984–87, CET; Production Manager, ICL Interactive Learning Services, 1987–88; Educn Business Unit Manager, Acorn Computers Ltd, 1988–91; Chief Exec., Hertfordshire TEC, 1991–94; Dir, then Chief Exec., TEC Nat. Council, 1994–98; Director General: British Chambers of Commerce, 1998–2001; City & Guilds of London Inst., 2001–07. Chairman: Nat. Skills Task Force, 1998–2000; UK Skills, 2000–13; WorldSkills London 2011, 2008–12; Nat. Numeracy, 2012–14 (Trustee, 2014–15); Member: Nat. Learning and Skills Council, 2000–02; Nat. Adult Learning Cttee, 2000–07; Council for Excellence in Leadership and Mgt, 2001–02; BBC Educn Adv. Gp, 2002–07; Skills Strategy Steering Gp, 2002–04. Mem. Council, Gresham Coll., 2003–07. Bd Mem., NHSU Trust, 2003–05. Hon. Mem., WorldSkills Internat., 2006–.

**HUMPHRIES, David Ernest;** defence science consultant; Director, Materials Research Laboratory, Defence Science and Technology Organisation, Melbourne, Australia, 1992–94; *b* 3 Feb. 1937; *er s* of late Ernest Augustus Humphries and Kathleen Humphries; *m* 1959, Wendy Rosemary Cook; one *s* one *d*. *Educ:* Brighton Coll.; Corpus Christi Coll., Oxford (Scholar; MA). RAE Farnborough: Materials Dept, 1961; Avionics Dept, 1966; Head of Inertial Navigation Div., 1974; Head of Bombing and Navigation Div., 1975; Head of Systems Assessment Dept, 1978; Dir Gen. Future Projects, MoD PE, 1981–83; Chief Scientist (RAF) and Dir Gen. of Res. (C), MoD, 1983–84; Dir Gen. Res. Technol., MoD (PE), 1984–86; Asst Chief Scientific Advr (Projects and Research), MoD, 1986–90; Dir, Australian Aeronautical Res. Lab., 1990–92. *Recreations:* music, theatre. *Address:* Lynmouth Cottage, 28 Howard Road, Dorking, Surrey RH4 3HP.

**HUMPHRIES, His Honour Gerard William;** a Circuit Judge, 1980–2003; *b* 13 Dec. 1928; *s* of late John Alfred Humphries and Marie Frances Humphries (*née* Whitwell), Barrow-in-Furness; *m* 1st, 1957, Margaret Valerie (*d* 1999), *o d* of late W. W. Gelderd and Margaret Gelderd (*née* Bell), Ulverston; four *s* one *d*; 2nd, 2007, Elizabeth Anne Swinburne. *Educ:* St Bede's Coll., Manchester; Manchester Univ. (LLB Hons). Served RAF, 1951–53, Flying Officer. Called to Bar, Middle Temple, 1952; admitted to Northern Circuit, 1954; Asst Recorder of Salford, 1969–71; a Recorder of the Crown Court, 1974–80. Chairman: Medical Appeals Tribunal, 1976–80; Vaccine Damage Tribunals, 1979–80. Charter Mem., Serra Club, N Cheshire, 1963– (Pres. 1968, 1973, 1995–96, 2003–04). Trustee: SBC Educnl Trust, 1979–2015 (Chm., 1979–90); Serra Foundn, 1998–2015. Foundn Governor, St Bede's Coll., Manchester, 1978–2008. KCHS 1996, with star 2003 (KHS 1986). *Publications:* The Stations of the Cross: stations for vocation, 1995. *Recreations:* holidays, reading, following Man City.

**HUMPHRIES, Prof. Jane;** *see* Humphries, K. J.

**HUMPHRIES, (John) Barry,** AO 1982; CBE 2007; music-hall artiste and dadaist; *b* 17 Feb. 1934; *s* of J. A. E. Humphries and L. A. Brown; *m* 1959, Rosalind Tong; two *d*; *m* 1979, Diane Millstead; two *s*; *m* 1990, Lizzie, *d* of Sir Stephen (Harold) Spender, CBE, CLit. *Educ:* Melbourne Grammar Sch.; Univ. of Melbourne. Repertory seasons, Union Theatre, Melbourne, 1953–54; Phillip Street Revue Theatre, Sydney, 1956; Demon Barber, Lyric, Hammersmith, 1959; Oliver!, New, 1960; Piccadilly, 1968, London Palladium, 1997; Treasure Island, Mermaid, 1968; Dick Whittington, New Wimbledon Th., 2011. One-man shows (author and performer): A Nice Night's Entertainment, 1962; Excuse I, 1965; Just a Show, Australia, 1968, Fortune Theatre, 1969; A Load of Olde Stuffe, 1971; At Least You Can Say That You've Seen It, 1974; Housewife Superstar, 1976; Isn't It Pathetic at His Age, 1979; A Night with Dame Edna, 1979; An Evening's Intercourse with Barry Humphries, 1981–82; Tears Before Bedtime, 1986; Back with a Vengeance, 1987; Look At Me When I'm Talking To You!, 1994; Rampant in Whitehall, Les Patterson Has a Stand Up, 1996; New Edna, the Spectacle, 1998; Edna's Royal Tour, 1998, NY, 2000 (Special Tony Award); Remember You're Out, 1999; Nat. American Tour, 2001; Back to My Roots and Other Suckers, Australia, 2003; Dame Edna Back With a Vengeance, NY, 2004 and US nat. tour, 2005; Back With a Vengeance, a New Effort, Australia, 2006; Last Night of the Poms, UK tour, 2009; All About Me, Broadway, 2010; Eat Pray Laugh!, farewell Australian tour, 2012–13, UK tour, 2013; Dame Edna's Glorious Goodbye, farewell US tour, 2015; Barry Humphries' Weimar Cabaret, Edinburgh Fest., 2016, Barbican, 2018; The Man Behind the Mask, Australia tour, 2018. TV series: The Dame Edna Experience, 1987; Ally McBeal, 2002; The Dame Edna Treatment, 2007; Passions: Weimar Art, 2017. Numerous plays, films, broadcasts and recordings. Exhibition: Wish You Were Here!: travels with a brush, Savill Galls, Melbourne, 2007. Patron of Honour, Internat. League of Antiquarian Booksellers, 2012–. Pres., Frans de Boever Soc. (Belgium). Hon. FKC 2017. DUniv: Griffith Univ., Qld, 1994; S Australia, 2016; Hon. DLaw Melbourne, 2003. Lifetime Achievement Award, Sydney Theatre Awards, 2012. *Publications:* Bizarre, 1964; Innocent Austral Verse, 1968; (with Nicholas Garland) The Wonderful World of Barry McKenzie, 1970; (with Nicholas Garland) Bazza Holds His Own, 1972; Dame Edna's Coffee Table Book, 1976; Les Patterson's Australia, 1979; Treasury of Australian Kitsch, 1980; A Nice Night's Entertainment, 1981; Dame Edna's Bedside Companion, 1982; The Traveller's Tool, 1985; (with Nicholas Garland) The Complete Barry McKenzie, 1988; My Gorgeous Life: the autobiography of Dame Edna Everage, 1989; The Life and Death of Sandy Stone, 1991; More Please (autobiog.), 1992; Women in the Background (novel), 1995; My Life As Me (autobiog.), 2002; Handling Edna: the unauthorised biography, 2010; Ednapedia: a history of Australia in a hundred objects, 2016. *Recreation:* drawing attention to himself. *Clubs:* Garrick, Beefsteak, Pratt's, Roxburgh; Savage (Melbourne).

**HUMPHRIES, John Charles Freeman;** Founder and Trustee, since 1987, and Director, 1993–2002, British Bone Marrow Donor Appeal; Chief Executive, Cymru Annibynnol Independent Wales Party, 2000–03; *b* 2 Jan. 1937; *s* of Charles Montague Humphries and Lilian Clara Humphries; *m* 1959, Eliana Paola Julia Mifsud; two *s* one *d*. *Educ:* St Julian's High Sch., Newport, Gwent. Western Mail: News Editor, 1966–73; Dep. Editor, 1973–80; Thomson Regional Newspapers: European Bureau Chief, 1980–86; London/City Editor, 1986–87; Editor, Western Mail, 1988–92; Launch Editor, Wales on Sunday, 1989. Mem., Wales Cttee, Consumer Council for Water, 2005–09. *Publications:* The Man From the Alamo: why the Welsh Chartist uprising of 1839 ended in a massacre, 2004; Gringo Revolutionary: the amazing adventures of Caryl ap Rhys Pryce, 2005; Freedom Fighters: Wales' forgotten 'war' 1963–1993, 2008; Spying for Hitler: the Welsh doublecross, 2012; Welsh Explorer of the Nile: the ruined reputation of John Petherick, nineteenth-century adventurer, 2013; Last Rites, 2018. *Recreations:* walking, opera, reading, Rugby, gardening. *Address:* Cwr y Coed, Usk Road, Tredunnoc, Gwent NP15 1PE.

**HUMPHRIES, Juliet Claire;** Chair, Girls' Day School Trust, since 2016 (Trustee, since 2015); *b* 15 July 1961; *d* of Nicholas John Hampton and Valerie Hampton; *m* 1989, Michael John Humphries, *qv*; one *s* two *d*. *Educ:* Wimbledon High Sch.; Univ. of Leicester (LLB); Coll. of Law (DipLP); Nottingham Trent Univ. (MBA). Admitted solicitor, 1985; Corporate Lawyer, Knapp-Fishers, 1985–87; Linklaters: Corporate Lawyer, 1987–91; Professional Support Lawyer, 1991–95; Dir of Knowledge, 1995–2004; Owner, Pierian Spring Consulting, 2004–09; Hd of Knowledge and Learning, Bird & Bird, 2009–11. Trustee, GDST Acad. Trust Bd, 2012–. *Publications:* Changing Role of the Professional Support Lawyer, 2008. *Recreations:* theatre, house in France, literature. *E:* juliet.humphries@btinternet.com. *Club:* Groucho.

**HUMPHRIES, Prof. (Katherine) Jane,** CBE 2018; PhD; FBA 2012; Centennial Professor, London School of Economics and Political Science, since 2019; Professor of Economic History, University of Oxford, 2004–17, now Emeritus; Fellow of All Souls College, Oxford, 1998–2017, now Emeritus; *b* Rotherham, Yorks, 9 Nov. 1948; *d* of John Humphries and Doris Humphries; *m* 1975, Michael Hepburn Best; one *s* one *d*, and four step *d*. *Educ:* Mexborough Grammar Sch.; Mexborough Sixth Form Coll.; Newnham Coll., Cambridge (BA 1st Cl. Econs 1970); Cornell Univ. (PhD Econs 1973). Asst Prof., Econs, 1973–79, Associate Prof., Econs, 1979–80, Univ. of Massachusetts; University of Cambridge: Lectr in Econs, 1980–95; Reader in Econs and Econ. Hist., 1995–98; Fellow, Newnham Coll., Cambridge, 1980–98; Reader in Econ. Hist., Univ. of Oxford, 1998–2004. Pres., Econ. Hist. Soc., 2010–13. Editor, Econ. Hist. Review, 2004–09. Hon. DLitt Uppsala, 2014; Hon. Dr Sheffield, 2019. *Publications:* Childhood and Child Labour in the British Industrial Revolution, 2010; papers in learned jls and edited collections. *Recreations:* family, tennis, walking, fiction, cinema. *Address:* All Souls College, Oxford OX1 4AL. *T:* (01865) 279346. *E:* jane.humpries@all-souls.ox.ac.uk.

**HUMPHRIES, Mark Julian;** Senior Partner, Humphries Kerstetter LLP, since 2009; *b* Bath, 5 Feb. 1962; *s* of Bernard and Diane Humphries; *m* 2008, Anne Elaine Edwards (*d* 2016). *Educ:* King Edward's Sch., Bath; St Catharine's Coll., Cambridge (BA 1983; MA 1987; Fellow Commoner, 2016); Coll. of Law, Guildford. Articled clerk, Winters Huntingdon, 1984–86; admitted solicitor, 1986; Linklaters: Associate Solicitor, 1986–93; Partner, 1993–2009; Solicitor/Advocate, 1994. Mem. Bd, Solicitors' Regulation Authy, 2010–12. Mem. Council, Law Soc., 2016–18. Lloyd's Members' Ombudsman, 2010–. *Publications:* contrib. articles concerning litigation, advocacy, litigation funding and professional ethics to jls incl. Law Soc. Gazette, The Lawyer, Legal Week and Solicitors' Jl. *Recreations:* walking, especially St James Camino and in Austria, singing, wine appreciation. *Address:* Humphries Kerstetter LLP, St Bartholomew House, 92 Fleet Street, EC4Y 1DH. *T:* (020) 7632 6900. *E:* mh@humphrieskerstetter.com.

**HUMPHRIES, Prof. Martin James,** PhD; FMedSci; FRSB; Professor of Biochemistry, University of Manchester, since 1995 (Vice-President and Dean, Faculty of Life Sciences, 2008–16); *b* 26 Nov. 1958; *s* of Terence and Kathleen Lesley Humphries; *m* 1982, Sandra Ceinwen Jones (marr. diss. 2015); two *d*; *m* 2016, Seena Patel. *Educ:* Nottingham High Sch.; Univ. of Manchester (BSc 1980; PhD 1983). Guest Researcher, Nat. Cancer Inst., NIH, Bethesda, Md, 1983–88; Postdoctoral Res. Associate, 1983–87, Associate Dir for Res., 1987–88, Howard Univ. Cancer Center, Washington; Wellcome Trust Sen. Res. Fellow, 1988–95, Principal Res. Fellow, 1995–2008, Univ. of Manchester; Dir, Wellcome Trust Centre for Cell-Matrix Research, 2000–10. Vice-Chm., 2005–07, Chm., 2008–10, Biochemical Soc.; Vice-Pres., Acad. of Med. Scis, 2012–17. Special Ind. Mem., UKRI-BBSRC, 2018–. FMedSci 2000; FRSB (FSB 2010). MAE 2006. *Publications:* The Extracellular Matrix Factsbook, 1993, 2nd edn 1998; contrib. numerous articles to learned jls. *Recreations:* golf, red wine. *Address:* Faculty of Biology, Medicine and Health, University of Manchester, Michael Smith Building, Oxford Road, Manchester M13 9PT. *E:* martin.humphries@manchester.ac.uk.

**HUMPHRIES, Michael John;** QC 2003; *b* 15 June 1959; *s* of Derek James Humphries and Joan Irene Humphries; *m* 1989, Juliet Claire Hampton (*see* J. C. Humphries); one *s* two *d*. *Educ:* Univ. of Leicester (BL). Called to the Bar, Inner Temple, 1982, Bencher, 2009. Sen. Vis. Fellow, Dept of Land Economy, Univ. of Cambridge, 2016– (Vis. Fellow, 2013–). Sen. Editor, later Consultant Editor, Bloomsbury's (formerly Butterworths, then Tottel's) Compulsory Purchase and Compensation Service, 1999–. *Publications:* (ed) National Infrastructure Planning Handbook, 3rd edn 2018. *Recreations:* house in France, music, literature. *Address:* Francis Taylor Building, Inner Temple, EC4Y 7BY. *T:* (020) 7353 8415. *Club:* Reform.

**HUMPHRYES, Jane Carole;** QC 2003; a Recorder, since 1999; *d* of Alan John Humphryes and Avril Pamela Gloria Humphryes; *m* Timothy Stephen Robert Wakefield; one *s* four *d*, and one step *s* one step *d*. *Educ:* Univ. of Kent at Canterbury; Council of Legal Educn. Called to the Bar, Middle Temple, 1983. *Recreations:* walking, watercolours, travel, cuisine, theatre, ski-ing. *Address:* 3 Raymond Buildings, Gray's Inn, WC1R 5BH. *T:* (020) 7400 6400.

**HUMPHRYS, John;** Presenter: Today Programme, Radio 4, 1987–2019; On the Ropes, Radio 4, since 1994; Mastermind, BBC TV, since 2003; *b* 17 Aug. 1943; *s* of George and Winifred Humphrys; *m* 1965, Edna Wilding (marr. diss. 1991; she *d* 1997); one *s* one *d*; one *s* with Valerie Sanderson. *Educ:* Cardiff High School. BBC TV: Washington Correspondent, 1971–77; Southern Africa Correspondent, 1977–80; Diplomatic Correspondent, 1980–81; Presenter: 9 O'Clock News, 1981–86; On the Record, 1993–2002. Hon. Fellow, Cardiff Univ., 1998. Hon. DLitt Abertay Dundee, 1996; Hon. MA Wales, 1998; Hon. LLD St Andrews, 1999. *Publications:* Devil's Advocate, 1999; The

Great Food Gamble, 2001; Lost for Words: the mangling and manipulation of the English language, 2004; Beyond Words: how language reveals the way we live now, 2006; In God We Doubt: confessions of a failed atheist, 2007; (with Dr Sarah Jarvis) The Welcome Visitor: living well, dying well, 2009; (with C. Humphrys) Blue Skies and Black Olives, 2009; A Day Like Today: memoirs, 2019. *Recreations:* music, attempting to play the 'cello, hill walking. *Address:* c/o BBC News Centre, New Broadcasting House 03B, Portland Place, W1A 1AA.

**HUNGIN, Prof. Amritpal Singh, (Pali),** OBE 2000; DL; MD; FRCGP, FRCP, FRCPE; Professor of General Practice and Primary Care, 1998–2017, and Founding Dean of Medicine and Head, School of Medicine, Pharmacy and Health, 2003–14, Durham University; Professor, Institute of Health and Society, Newcastle University, 2017–18, now Emeritus Professor, Faculty of Medical Sciences; President, British Medical Association, 2016–17; *b* Nairobi, Kenya, 2 Jan. 1952; *s* of Shanker Singh Hungin and Barbir Kaur Hungin; *m* 1976, Barbara Helen Munt; two *s* one *d*. *Educ:* Kongoni Primary Sch. and Highway Secondary Sch., Nairobi; Univ. of Newcastle upon Tyne (MB BS 1975; MD 1996). DRCOG 1979; MRCGP 1979, FRCGP 1991; FRCP 2006; FRCPE 2006. Vocational Trng in Gen. Practice, NE England, 1976–80; GP trng, Univ. of Western Ontario, 1977; GP, Eaglescliffe, Stockton on Tees, 1980–2004; Hosp. Practitioner in Gastrointestinal Endoscopy, James Cook Univ. Hosp., Middlesbrough, 1982–99. Founder and Dir, Northern Primary Care Res. Network, 1992–2000; Dir, NHS R&D Forum (England), 2001–05; Lead, Changing Face of Medicine Commn, Acad. of Med. Royal Colleges, 2014–. Trustee and Treas., Royal Med. Benevolent Fund, 2014–. FRSA. DL Co. Durham, 2008. John Fry Res. Medal, 1997, William Pickles Medal, 2015, RCGP; William Cullen Prize, RCPE, 2017. *Publications:* (ed jtly) Gastroenterology in Primary Care: an evidence-based guide to management, 2000; (ed jtly) Rome IV Functional Gastrointestinal Disorders for Primary Care and Non-GI Clinicians, 2016; contrib. research papers. *Recreations:* music, reading, cricket, motor sport. *Address:* 4 Butts Lane, Eaglescliffe, Stockton on Tees TS16 9BT.

**HUNJAN, Satinder Pal Singh;** QC 2002; a Recorder, since 2003; a Deputy High Court Judge, since 2008; *b* 5 Nov. 1960; *s* of Nasib Singh Hunjan and Rajinder Kaur Hunjan; two *s* one *d*. *Educ:* Univ. of Birmingham (LLB Hons). Called to the Bar, Gray's Inn, 1984; specialises in clinical negligence, personal injuries and general commercial law. *Recreations:* travelling, tennis, ski-ing, football, theatre. *Address:* Kings Chambers, Embassy House, 60 Church Street, Birmingham B3 2DJ.

**HUNKIN, Timothy Mark Trelawney;** artist, cartoonist, engineer; *s* of late Oliver John Hunkin and of Frances Elizabeth Hunkin; *m* 2005, Meg; one step *d*. *Educ:* St Paul's Sch., Hammersmith; Caius Coll., Cambridge (BA Engrg 1972). Launched Phlegethon Fireworks, staging public displays and building fireworks, 1971; cartoonist, Rudiments of Wisdom (cartoon strip), Observer, 1973–87; worked for Oxfam, Africa, 1980; Osher Fellow, Exploratorium Sci. Centre, San Francisco, 1993; British Council lect. tour, How to Cheat at Art, Australia and USA, 1997; Fellowship, Xerox Parc, 1998; Co-founder Mongrel Media, designing and building exhibns, 1999; Nesta Dreamtime Fellowship, 2004. Projects include: inflatable pigs and sheep shot from mortar shells, developed for Pink Floyd's Animal tour, 1977; designed and built 50-ft high water clock, Neal's Yd, Covent Gdn, 1982; designed How Television Works (gallery), Nat. Museum of Photography, Bradford, 1986; designed Ride of Life (ride), 1989; created The Secret Life of the Home (gallery), Sci. Mus., London, 1994–95; created, with Mongrel Media, visitor centre, Eden Project, 2000, Science in the Dock (sci. ethics automata show), Glasgow Sci. Centre, 2001; opened Under the Pier Show (amusement arcade of homemade slot machines), Southwold Pier, 2002; public clocks, Hawkins Bazaar and London Zoo, 2008; clock for The Exploratorium, San Francisco, 2013; opened Novelty Automation (amusement arcade), London, 2015. Exhibitions include: The Disgusting Spectacle (mechanical sculptures), ICA, London, 1981; The Art Gallery (mechanical art gall. spectators), tour of 20 provincial galls, 1983. Researcher, writer and presenter, Channel 4: Secret Life of Machines, series 1, 1988, series 2, 1990; Secret Life of the Office (series), 1992. *Publications:* Mrs Gronkwonk and the Post Office Tower (for children), 1973; Almost Everything There is to Know: the Rudiments of Wisdom cartoons, 1988; Hunkin's Experiments, 2003. *E:* hunkin@timhunkin.com.

**HUNNIFORD, (Mary Winifred) Gloria,** OBE 2017; television and radio presenter; *b* Portadown, NI, 10 April 1940; *d* of Charlie Hunniford and May Hunniford (*née* McCann); *m* 1st, 1961, Don Keating (marr. diss.; he *d* 1997); two *s* (one *d* decd); 2nd, 1998, Stephen Robert Way. *Educ:* Portadown Coll.; Portadown Tech. Coll. Singer, radio and TV progs, Kingston, Ont, 1958; prodn asst, Ulster Television First, 1959–61; local radio broadcaster, BBC, Belfast, 1961; presenter: BBC Radio, NI, 1969–81 (nightly news and current affairs prog., 1978–81); The Gloria Hunniford Show, BBC Radio 2, 1982–95; *television* includes: Songs of Praise, 1977–79; Good Evening, Ulster, 1977–81; Sunday, Sunday, 1982–91; Holiday, 1993; Open House with Gloria Hunniford, 1998–2005; Heaven and Earth with Gloria Hunniford, 2006–07; Cash in the Celebrity Attic, 2008–11; Rip Off Britain, 2009–; Three After Three, 2010; Rip Off Food, 2012–14; Loose Women, 2014–; Food: Truth or Scare, 2016–17; Springtime on the Farm, 2018. Pres., TRIC, 1999–2000. Patron: Caron Keating Foundn (set up in name of daughter); Action Cancer; Hope for Youth NI. BBC Radio Personality of Year, Royal Variety Club of GB, 1982; Top Female Personality, TV Times Awards, 1984; Special Award, TRIC, 2018. *Publications:* Next to You, 2005; Always with You, 2008; Glorious Grandparenting, 2010; My Life (autobiog.), 2017. *Recreations:* countryside, dog walks, tennis, theatre, travelling. *Address:* c/o Talent4Media, G9 Shepherds Buidling, Rockley Road, W14 0DA. *T:* (020) 7183 4334. *E:* enquiries@talent4media.com.

**HUNNINGS, Mary Rosa Alleyne;** *see* Berry, M. R. A.

**HUNSDON OF HUNSDON,** Baron; *see* Aldenham, Baron.

**HUNT,** family name of **Barons Hunt of Chesterton, Hunt of Kings Heath** and **Hunt of Wirral.**

**HUNT OF CHESTERTON,** Baron *cr* 2000 (Life Peer), of Chesterton in the co. of Cambridgeshire; **Julian Charles Roland Hunt,** CB 1998; PhD; FRS 1989; Professor in Climate Modelling, University College London, 1999–2008, now Emeritus; Visiting Fellow, Malaysian Commonwealth Studies Centre, University of Cambridge, since 2008; *b* 5 Sept. 1941; *s* of Roland Charles Colin Hunt, CMG and Pauline Hunt; *m* 1965, Marylla Ellen Shephard; one *s* two *d*. *Educ:* Westminster Sch.; Trinity Coll., Cambridge (BA 1963; PhD 1967); Univ. of Warwick. Post-doctoral res., Cornell Univ., USA, 1967; Res. Officer, Central Electricity Res. Labs, 1968–70; University of Cambridge: Fellow, 1966–, Sen. Res. Fellow, 1998–99, Trinity Coll.; Lectr in Applied Maths and in Engrg, 1970–78; Reader in Fluid Mechanics, 1978–90; Prof., 1990–92, Hon. Prof., 1992–, in Fluid Mechanics; Chief Exec., Meteorol Office, 1992–97. Hon. Dir, Lighthill Inst. for Math. Scis, 2003–06; Acad. Dir, Lighthill Risk Network, 2006–, UCL. Vis. Scientist, 1997, 1998, Pierre Fermat Vis. Prof., 2007, 2008, Cerfacs and Inst de Mécanique des Fluides de Toulouse; Visiting Professor: Colorado State Univ., 1975; NC State Univ., and Envmtl Protection Agency, 1977; Univ. of Colorado, 1980; Nat. Center for Atmospheric Res., Boulder, Colo, 1983; Arizona State Univ., 1997–98, 2007–; Stanford Univ., 1998; Univ. of Notre Dame, Indiana, 2011–; Hong Kong Univ., 2011–; J. M. Burgers Prof., Tech. Univ., Delft, 1998–; Mary B. Upson Vis. Prof., Cornell Univ., 2003–06; Sir Gilbert Walker Vis. Prof., Indian Inst. of Technol., Delhi, 2016–. Founder Dir, 1986–91, Dir and Chm., 1997–, Cambridge Envmtl Res. Consultants Ltd. President: IMA, 1993–95 (Hon. Sec., 1984–89); Vice-Pres., 1989–93; Hon. Fellow, 2003); Adv. Cttee on Protection of the Sea, 2003– (Chm., 2001–03); Nat. Soc. for Clean Air, 2006–07; Vice Pres., Globe Internat., 2006–14. Member: Mgt Bd, European Res. Community for Flow Turbulence and Combustion, 1988–95; Exec. Council, WMO, 1992–97; NERC, 1994–96; Stakeholder Adv. Panel, EDF Energy, 2006–09; Chair, Adv. Cttee, Tokamak Energy (formerly Tokamak Solutions) Ltd, 2010–; Co-Chair, Asian Network on Climate Science and Technol., 2013–. Hon. Chm., Just Ghana Ltd, 2010–. Councillor, Cambridge CC, 1971–74 (Leader, Labour Gp, 1972). Branch Sec., Electrical Power Engrs Assoc., 1970. Fellow, APS, 2003; Hon. FICE 2003. Hon. DSc: Salford, 1995; Bath, 1996; UEA, 1997; Grenoble, Uppsala, Warwick, 2000; Dundee, 2005; Western Univ., Ont, 2014. L. F. Richardson Medal, Eur. Geophysical Soc., 2001. *Publications:* (contrib.) New Applications of Mathematics, ed C. Bondi, 1991; (ed) London's Environment, 2005; scientific pubns in Jl of Fluid Mechanics, Atmospheric Envmt, Qly Jl of Royal Meteorol Soc., Proc. Royal Soc., Jl of the Atmospheric Scis, Jl Flow Turb Combustion. *Address:* Department of Earth Sciences, University College London, Gower Street, WC1E 6BT.

*See also* P. M. Hunt, Hon. T. J. W. Hunt.

**HUNT OF KINGS HEATH,** Baron *cr* 1997 (Life Peer), of Birmingham in the co. of West Midlands; **Philip Alexander Hunt,** OBE 1993; PC 2009; *b* 19 May 1949; *s* of Rev. Philip Lacey Winter Hunt and Muriel Hunt; *m* 1st, 1974 (marr. diss.); one *d*; 2nd, 1988, Selina Ruth Helen Stewart; three *s* one *d*. *Educ:* City of Oxford High Sch.; Oxford Sch.; Leeds Univ. (BA). Oxford RHB, 1972–74; Nuffield Orthopaedic Centre, 1974–75; Mem., Oxfordshire AHA, 1975–77; Sec. Edgware/Hendon Community Health Council, 1975–78; Asst Sec., 1978–79, Asst Dir, 1979–84, NAHA; Dir, NAHA, then NAHAT, 1984–97; Chief Exec., NHS Confedn, 1997. Chair, Nat. Patient Safety Agency, 2004–05. Sen. Policy Advr, Sainsbury Centre for Mental Health, 1997; Sen. Policy Associate, King's Fund, 1998. Member: Oxford City Council, 1973–79; Birmingham City Council, 1980–82. A Lord in Waiting (Govt Whip), 1998–99; Parly Under-Sec. of State, DoH, 1999–2003, DWP, 2005–06; Minister of State, DoH, 2006–07; Parly Under-Sec. of State, MoJ, 2007–08; Minister of State, DEFRA, 2008–09, DECC, 2008–10; Dep. Leader, 2009–10, Dep. Leader of Opposition, 2010–17, H of L; opposition spokesperson on Cabinet Office, 2010–12, 2017–18, on home affairs, 2010–12, on health, 2012–18, on higher education, 2017–18, on health and social care, 2018. Chm., H of L Select Cttee on Merits of Statutory Instruments, 2004; Co-Chm., All-Party Gp on Public Health and Primary Care, 1997–98. Chm., Heart of England NHS Foundn Trust, 2011–14; Member: Council, Internat. Hosp. Fedn, 1986–91; King's Fund Inst. Adv. Cttee, 1991–93; Council, Assoc. for Public Health, 1992 (Co-Chm., 1994); GMC, 2019–. President: FPA, 1998; RSPH, 2013–; Health Care Supplies Assoc., 2013–; GS1, 2013–. *Publications:* The Health Authority Member (discussion paper) (with W. E. Hall), 1978; articles in Health Service publications. *Recreations:* music, cycling, swimming, football. *Address:* House of Lords, SW1A 0PW.

**HUNT OF WIRRAL,** Baron *cr* 1997 (Life Peer), of Wirral in the co. of Merseyside; **David James Fletcher Hunt,** MBE 1973; PC 1990; Chairman, Financial Services and Partner, DAC Beachcroft LLP, solicitors; Chairman, Press Complaints Commission, 2011–14; *b* 21 May 1942; *s* of late Alan Nathaniel Hunt, OBE and Jessie Edna Ellis Northrop Hunt; *m* 1973, Patricia, (Paddy), Margery (*née* Orchard); two *s* two *d*. *Educ:* Liverpool Coll.; Montpellier Univ.; Bristol Univ. (LLB); Guildford Coll. of Law. Solicitor of Supreme Court of Judicature, admitted 1968; Stanley Wasbrough & Co., then Stanleys & Simpson North, then Beachcroft Stanleys, then Beachcroft Wansbroughs, then Beachcroft LLP, subseq. DAC Beachcroft LLP: joined, 1965; Partner, 1969–; Sen. Partner, 1995–2005; Chm., Financial Services, 2005–. Director: BET Omnibus Services Ltd, 1980–81; Solicitors Indemnity Mutual Insce Assoc. Ltd, 2001–05. Chartered Insurance Institute: Chm., Professional Standards Bd, 2004–06; Dep. Pres., 2006–07; Pres., 2007–08; Chairman: Assoc. of Ind. Financial Advisers, 1999–2002; BIBA, 2013–19. Contested (C) Bristol South, 1970, Kingswood, 1974; MP (C) Wirral, March 1976–1983, Wirral West, 1983–97; contested (C) Wirral West, 1997. PPS to Sec. of State for Trade, 1979–81, to Sec. of State for Defence, 1981; an Asst Govt Whip, 1981–83; a Lord Comr of HM Treasury, 1983–84; Parly Under-Sec. of State, Dept of Energy, 1984–87; Treasurer of HM Household and Dep. Chief Whip, 1987–89; Minister for Local Govt and Inner Cities, DoE, 1989–90; Secretary of State: for Wales, 1990–93; for Employment, 1993–94; Chancellor, Duchy of Lancaster and Minister for Public Service and Sci., 1994–95. Chm., Cons. Shipping and Shipbuilding Cttee, 1977–79; Vice-Chairman: Parly Youth Lobby, 1978–80; Parly War Crimes Gp, 2000–; Vice-Pres., Cons. Group for Europe, 1984–87 (Vice-Chm., 1978–81; Chm., 1981–82); Pres., All Party Parly Gp on Occupational Safety and Health, 1999–. Chm., Inter-Parly Council against Anti-Semitism, 1996–. Chm., Bristol Univ. Conservatives, 1964–65; winner of Observer Mace for British Universities Debating Competition, 1965–66; Nat. Vice-Chm., FUCUA, 1965–66; Chm., Bristol City CPC, 1965–68; Nat. Vice-Chm., YCNAC, 1967–69; Chm., Bristol Fedn of YCs, 1970–71; Chm., British Youth Council, 1971–74 (Pres., 1978–80); Vice-Pres., Nat. YCs, 1986–88 (Chm., 1972–73); Vice-Chairman: Nat. Union of Cons. and Unionist Assocs, 1974–76; Cons. Party, 1983–85. Pres., Tory Reform Gp, 1991–97. Vice-Pres., Nat. Playbus Assoc., 1981–. Member: South Western Economic Planning Council, 1972–76; CBI Council, 1999–2006; Chairman: McDonald's Educn Co. Ltd, 2009–15; Lending Standards Bd, 2011–17; non-exec. Dir, GRP MGA Holdco Ltd, 2017–; Sen. Ind. Dir, LINK Scheme Ltd, 2018–. Bd Mem., ICC Cricket World Cup 2019 (Chair, Risk and Finance Cttee). Mem. Adv. Cttee on Pop Festivals, 1972–75. Trustee, Holocaust Educnl Trust, 1998–; Chm., ESU, 2005–11 (Gov., 1999–2011); Dep. Chm., 2000–05). Bencher, Inner Temple, 2015. Mem., Rotary Club, London, 2000– (Dep. Pres., 2011–). Churchwarden, Parish of Chewton Mendip with Emborough, Somerset, 2007–17. Fellow, Internat. Inst. of Risk and Safety Mgt, 2002. Hon. FIA 2003; Hon. FCII 2004. Hon. DLitt Chester, 2013. *Publications:* pamphlets on political subjects. *Recreations:* cricket, walking. *Address:* DAC Beachcroft LLP, 100 Fetter Lane, EC4A 1BN. *T:* (020) 7894 6066, *Fax:* (020) 7894 6158. *E:* lordhunt@dacbeachcroft.com. *Club:* Hurlingham.

**HUNT, Alan Charles,** CMG 1990; HM Diplomatic Service, retired; trainer and consultant in diplomatic practice, since 2010; *b* 5 March 1941; *s* of John Henry Hunt and Nelly Elizabeth Hunt (*née* Hunter); *m* 1978, Meredith Margaret Claydon; two *d*. *Educ:* Latymer Upper School, Hammersmith; Univ. of East Anglia. First Cl. Hons BA in European Studies. Clerical Officer, Min. of Power, 1958–59; FO, 1959–62; Vice-Consul, Tehran, 1962–64; Third Sec., Jedda, 1964–65; floating duties, Latin America, 1965–67; University, 1967–70; Second, later First Sec., FCO, 1970–73; First Sec., Panama, 1973–76; FCO 1976–77; First Sec. (Commercial), Madrid, 1977–81; FCO, 1981–83; Counsellor (Econ. and Commercial), Oslo, 1983–87; Head of British Interests Section, subseq. Chargé d'Affaires, Buenos Aires, 1987–90; Counsellor, FCO, 1990–91; Consul-Gen., Düsseldorf, and Dir-Gen. of Trade and Investment Promotion in Germany, 1991–95; Sen. Directing Staff (Civilian), RCDS, 1995–96; Dir of Trade and Investment Promotion, FCO, and Dep. Dir-

Gen. for Export Promotion, DTI, 1996–97; High Comr, Singapore, 1997–2001. Dir, Oxford Univ. Foreign Service Prog., 2003–10. Vis. Prof., Coll. of Europe, 2012–. *Publications:* No Immunity, 2014; Public Diplomacy: what it is and how to do it, 2015; A Game That Must Be Lost, 2016; Unauthorised Action, 2017. *Recreations:* golf, bridge, travel, reading, music.

**HUNT, Anthony Blair,** DLitt; FBA 1999; Senior Research Fellow, St Peter's College, Oxford, 2009–11, now Emeritus Fellow (Fellow and Tutor in French, 1990–2009; Vice Master, 2007–09); Lecturer in Mediaeval French Literature, Oxford University, 1990–2009; *b* 21 March 1944; *s* of Norman Blair Hunt and Dorothy Gaskell Hunt (*née* Mottershead). *Educ:* Birkenhead Sch.; Worcester Coll., Oxford (BLitt, MA 1971); St Andrews Univ. (DLitt 1991). University of St Andrews: Asst Lectr, 1968–72; Lectr, 1972–79; Reader, 1979–90; British Acad. Res. Reader, 1986–88. Vis. Prof. of Mediaeval Studies, Westfield Coll., London Univ., 1986–88. Jt Pres., Anglo-Norman Text Soc., 2011–. FSA 1986–2009. Foreign Mem., Norwegian Acad. of Sci. and Letters, 1999; Officier, Ordre des Palmes Académiques, 2008. *Publications:* Rauf de Linham, Kalender, 1983; Chrétien de Troyes, Yvain, 1986; Les giupartiz des eschez, 1986; Plant Names of Medieval England, 1989; Popular Medicine in Thirteenth-Century England, 1990; Teaching and Learning Latin in Thirteenth-Century England, 1991; The Medieval Surgery, 1992; Anglo-Norman Medicine, vol. 1, 1994, vol. 2, 1997; Le Livre de Catun, 1994; Villon's Last Will, 1996; Sermons on Joshua, 1998; Three Receptaria from Medieval England, 2001; Le Chant des Chanz, 2004; Les Paraboles maistre Alain en Françoys, 2005; Les Cantiques Salomon, 2006, 2019; Les Proverbez d'Alain, 2006; Miraculous Rhymes: the writing of Gautier de Coinci, 2007; Ovide, Du remede d'amours, 2008; An Old French Herbal, 2009; Three Anglo-Norman Treatises on Falconry, 2009; Old French Medical Texts, 2011; Cher Alme: texts of Anglo-Norman piety, 2010; Les Paroles Salomon, 2012; Writing the Future: prognostic texts of Anglo-Norman England, 2013; An Anglo-Norman Medical Compendium, 2014; An Anglo-Norman Pharmacopoeia, 2017; Tiaudelet: Theodulus in medieval France, 2018; (with M. Coombe and A. Mouron) Reginald of Durham's Life of St Godric: an Anglo-Norman version, 2019; articles in learned jls, contribs to collective vols, etc. *Recreations:* fell-walking, playing the double bass, opera. *Address:* 140 Main Road, Long Hanborough, Witney OX29 8JY.

**HUNT, Anthony James,** CEng, FIStructE; Chairman: Anthony Hunt Associates, 1988–2002; YRM plc, 1993–94; *b* 1932; *s* of late James Edward Hunt and of Joan Margaret (*née* Cassidy); *m* 1st, 1957, Patricia Daniels (marr. diss. 1972; remarried 1975; marr. diss. 1982); one *s* one *d*; 3rd, 1985, Diana Joyce Collett (marr. diss. 2007); 4th, 2013, Hélène Moore (*née* Etchats). *Educ:* Salesian Coll., Farnborough; Westminster Tech. Coll. CEng 1961; FIStructE 1973. Articled via Founders' Co. to J. L. Wheeler Consulting Engr, 1948–51; F. J. Samuely and Partners, Consulting Engrs, 1951–59; Morton Lupton, Architects, 1960–62; founded Anthony Hunt Associates, Consulting Engrs, 1962; acquired by YRM plc, Bldg Design Consultants, 1988; became separate limited co., 1997. Major buildings: Sainsbury Centre for the Visual Arts, Norwich, 1978, 1993; Willis Faber Dumas HQ, Ipswich, 1975; Inmos Micro Electronics Factory, Gwent, 1982; Schlumberger Cambridge Research, 1985; Waterloo Internat. Terminal, 1993; Law Faculty, Cambridge, 1995; Nat. Botanic Gdn, Wales, 1998; New Mus. of Scotland, Edinburgh, 1998; Lloyd's Register of Shipping, London, 1998–99; Eden Project, Cornwall, 1998–99. Willis Vis. Prof. of Architecture, Sheffield Univ., 1994–; Graham Vis. Prof. of Architecture, Univ. of Penn, 2002; Velux Vis. Prof., KAA Sch. of Art and Architecture, Copenhagen, 2009–; Visiting Professor: Chinese Univ. of Hong Kong, 2004; Univ. du Québec, Montreal, 2004–; Inst. Superior Técnico, Lisbon, 2005–. FRSA 1989. Hon. FRIBA 1989. Hon. DLitt Sheffield, 1999; Hon. DEng Leeds, 2003; Hon. Dr RCA, 2012. Gold Medallist, IStructE, 1995. *Publications:* Tony Hunt's Structures Notebook, 1997, 2nd edn 2003; Tony Hunt's Sketchbook, 1999, vol. 2, 2003; *relevant publications:* The Engineer's Contribution to Contemporary Architecture—Anthony Hunt, by Angus Macdonald, 2000; Connexions: the unseen hand of Tony Hunt, by N. Dale, 2012. *Recreations:* furniture restoration, music, sailing, ski-ing, painting. *Address:* Dolphin House, Vicarage Street, Painswick, Stroud, Glos GL6 6XR. *Club:* Chelsea Arts.

**HUNT, Barbara L.;** *see* Leigh-Hunt.

**HUNT, Christopher H.;** *see* Holdsworth Hunt.

**HUNT, Christopher John,** FSA; Acting Director of Library Services, University of London, 2003–04; Director and University Librarian, John Rylands University Library of Manchester, 1991–2002, now University Librarian Emeritus; *b* 28 Jan. 1937; *s* of Richard John Hunt and Dorothy (*née* Pendleton); *m* 1963, Kathleen Mary Wyatt. *Educ:* Rutlish Sch., Merton; Univ. of Exeter (BA); King's Coll., Univ. of Durham (MLitt). FSA 1995. Asst Librarian, Univ. of Newcastle upon Tyne, 1960–67; Sub Librarian, Univ. of Manchester, 1967–74; University Librarian: James Cook Univ. of N Queensland, 1974–81; La Trobe Univ., 1981–85; Librarian, British Library of Political and Economic Science, LSE, 1985–91. Chairman: Internat. Cttee for Social Sci. Inf. and Documentation, 1989–92; Library Panel, Wellcome Trust, 1993–99 (Mem., 1988–99). Curator of Libraries, Univ. of Oxford, 2000–02; Acting Dir of Library Servs, London Univ., 2003. Academic Gov., LSE, 1989–91; Mem. Council, Univ. of Manchester, 2000–02; Feoffee of Chetham's Hosp. and Library, Manchester, 1993–2005. *Publications:* The Leadminers of the Northern Pennines, 1970; The Book Trade in Northumberland and Durham to 1860, 1975; papers in professional and learned jls. *Recreations:* book collecting, wine. *Address:* 35 South End, Longhoughton, Alnwick, Northumberland NE66 3AW.

**HUNT, David John;** HM Diplomatic Service; Consul General, Washington, since 2015; *m* Sarah; one *s* one *d*. *Educ:* Univ. of Hull (BA 1994). Entered FCO, 2001; Hd, US Section, N America Dept, 2001–03, Hd, Sanctions Unit, UN Dept, 2003–04, FCO; Deputy Head: of Mission and Consul Gen., Zagreb, 2005–08; Conflict Dept, FCO, 2008–11; Ambassador to Lithuania, 2011–15. *Address:* c/o Foreign and Commonwealth Office, King Charles Street, SW1A 2AH.

**HUNT, His Honour (David) Peter;** a Circuit Judge, 1997–2017; Designated Family Judge for West Yorkshire, Leeds County Court (formerly Care Centre), 2000–17; a Senior Circuit Judge, 2010–17; *b* 25 April 1951; *s* of late Rev. Charles Christopher Hunt and of Edna Hunt; *m* 1984, Cherryl Janet Nicholson; two *s*. *Educ:* Grangefield Grammar Sch., Stockton-on-Tees; Keble Coll., Oxford (MA). Called to the Bar, Gray's Inn, 1974; in practice at the Bar, 1974–97; Junior, North Eastern Circuit, 1981–82; a Recorder, 1993–97. Mem., Gen. Council of the Bar, 1981–84. Chm., Inquiry into multiple abuse of nursery sch. children, Newcastle, 1993–94. Dep. Chancellor, Diocese of Ripon and Leeds, 2011–. *Publications:* (with M. L. Rakusen) Distribution of Assets on Divorce, 1979, 3rd edn 1990.

**HUNT, David Roderic Notley;** QC 1987; a Recorder, 1991; Commissioner of the Royal Court of Jersey, 2012–18; *b* 22 June 1947; *s* of Dr Geoffrey Notley Hunt and Deborah Katharine Rosamund Hunt; *m* 1974, Alison Connell Jelf; two *s*. *Educ:* Charterhouse Sch.; Trinity Coll., Cambridge (MA Hons). Called to the Bar, Gray's Inn, 1969, Bencher, 1996 (Vice-Treas., 2015; Treas., 2016). *Recreations:* sailing, ski-ing, golf. *Address:* Blackstone Chambers, Blackstone House, Temple, EC4Y 9BW. *T:* (020) 7583 1770.

**HUNT, Jacqueline Leigh, (Jay);** Creative Director, Worldwide Video (Europe), Apple Inc., since 2018; *b* Sydney, Australia, 20 Jan. 1967; *d* of late John Hunt and Wendy Hunt (*née* Smith); *m* 2005, Ian Blandford; one *s* one *d*. *Educ:* St John's Coll., Cambridge (BA English). Joined BBC, 1989; Assistant Editor: Breakfast News, 1990–95; Newsnight, 1995–98; Panorama, 1999; Editor: One O'Clock News, 2000–03; Six O'Clock News, 2003–05; Controller, Daytime, 2005–07; Hd of Progs, Five, 2007–08; Controller, BBC One, 2008–10; Chief Creative Officer, Channel 4, 2011–17. *Recreations:* travel, running, cycling.

**HUNT, Rt Hon. Jeremy;** PC 2010; MP (C) South West Surrey, since 2005; *b* 1 Nov. 1966; *s* of Adm. Sir Nicholas John Streynsham Hunt, GCB, LVO; *m* 2009, Lucia Guo; one *s* two *d*. *Educ:* Charterhouse; Magdalen Coll., Oxford (BA 1st Cl. Hons PPE 1988). Co-Founder and Man. Dir, Hotcourses, 1991–2005; Co-Founder, Hotcourses Foundn, 2004. Shadow Sec. of State for Culture, Media and Sport, 2007–10; Sec. of State for Culture, Olympics, Media and Sport, 2010–12; Sec. of State for Health, then for Health and Social Care, 2012–18; Sec. of State for Foreign and Commonwealth Affairs, 2018–19. *Recreation:* Latin music and dancing. *Address:* House of Commons, SW1A 0AA. *E:* huntj@parliament.uk.

**HUNT, John Michael Graham,** OBE 2000; Chief Executive and Secretary, British Dental Association, 1993–2001; Director, Smile-on Ltd, 2001–11; *b* 5 Feb. 1942; *s* of Robert Graham Hunt and Patricia Mary Hunt; *m* 1966, Jill Mason Williams; one *s* two *d*. *Educ:* Guy's Hosp. Dental Sch., Univ. of London (BDS 1965). LDS RCS 1965. Resident House Officer, Guy's Hosp., 1965; Fulbright Travelling Schol., Clinical Dental Fellow, Eastman Dental Centre, NY, 1966–67; London Hospital Dental Institute: Registrar, Conservative Dentistry, 1967–70; Lectr in Oral Surgery, 1968–70; General Dental Practice, Torquay, 1970–80; Clinical Dental Surgeon, Prince Philip Dental Hosp., Univ. of Hong Kong, 1980–84; Dental Officer, 1984–89, Sen. Dental Officer, 1989–93, DoH. Hon. Lectr, London Hosp. Med. Coll., 1989–93; Speaker, FDI, World Dental Fedn, 1999–2005. FRSA. Hon. FFGDP(UK) 2001. *Recreations:* walking, ski-ing, sailing. *Address:* Ryden, Paternoster Lane, Ipplepen, Totnes, Devon TQ12 5RY.

**HUNT, Rt Hon. Jonathan (Lucas),** ONZ 2005; PC 1987; High Commissioner for New Zealand in the United Kingdom, and Ambassador to Eire, 2005–08; *b* 2 Dec. 1938; *s* of Henry Lucas Hunt and Alison Zora Hunt. *Educ:* Auckland Grammar Sch.; Univ. of Auckland (MA Hons). Teacher, Kelston Boys' High Sch., 1961–66; MP NZ, 1966–2005 (MP (Lab) New Lynn, Auckland, 1966–96). New Zealand Parliament: Dep. Speaker, 1974–75; Sen. Opposition Whip, 1980–84; Minister of Broadcasting and Communications, 1984–90; Leader of the House, 1987–90; Speaker, 1999–2005. *Recreations:* music, cricket, wine appreciation, reading. *Club:* Wellington (New Zealand).

**HUNT, Judith Anne,** OBE 1999; consultant and executive coach, since 1999; *b* 13 Sept. 1945; *d* of late Philip E. Riley and Amy Riley; *m* 1st, 1967, Alan J. Hunt (marr. diss. 1979); two *d*; 2nd, 1988, Daniel W. Silverstone, *qv*. *Educ:* Cheadle Hulme Sch.; Leeds Univ. (BA Hons). Lectr, Stockport Coll. and Salford Coll. of Technology, and teacher, Salford, 1967–74; Nat. Organiser, 1974–80 and Asst Gen. Sec., 1980–82, AUEW (TASS); Equal Opportunities Advr and Dep. Head, Personnel Services, GLC, 1982–84; Dir of Personnel (Staffing), GLC, 1984–86; Acting Dir of Personnel, ILEA, 1986–87; Chief Executive: London Borough of Ealing, 1987–93; Local Govt Mgt Bd, 1993–99. Special Advr, LGA, 1999–2000. CS Comr, 1995–98; Mem. Adv. Council, CS Coll., 1995–99. Non-exec. Dir, CPS, 2002–05. Chairman: Camden and Islington HA, 2000–02; London Health Observatory, 2002–06; Lay Mem., Camden CCG, 2013–17. Bd Mem., TfL, 2006–12 (Chm., Audit Cttee, 2006–12). Parent Governor, ILEA; Member: Governing Body, Ruskin Coll.; Exec. Council, Solace; Women's Nat. Commn, 1976–82; ESRC Res. Priorities Bd, 1995–99; W London TEC; W London Leadership, 1989–93; London First, 1992–95. Trustee, Common Purpose, 1994–2004. FRSA 1990. *Publications:* Organising Women Workers, 1985; (ed) Jackie West: work, women and the labour market; contribs to jls. *Recreations:* books, gardening, opera, etching and painting.

**HUNT, Rev. Canon Dr Judith Mary;** Rector, St Alkmund's Parish Church, Whitchurch, since 2012; interim Minister, Fauls, Holy Immanuel and Tilstock, Christ Church since 2018; *b* Darwen, Lancs, 16 April 1957. *Educ:* Bristol Univ. (BVSc 1980); London Univ. (PhD 1985); Ridley Hall, Cambridge; Fitzwilliam Coll., Cambridge (BA 1990). MRCVS 1980. House Surgeon, 1980–82, Res. Scholar, 1982–85, Royal Vet. Coll., London; Lectr in Equine Vet. Sci., Univ. of Liverpool, 1985–88; ordained deacon, 1991, priest, 1994; Parish Deacon, 1991–94, Asst Curate, 1994–95, St Peter's and Church of the Good Shepherd, Heswall; Priest-in-charge, St Mary's, Tilston and Shocklach, 1995–2003; Diocese of Chester: Bishop's Advr for Women in Ministry, 1995–2000; Dir of Mission and Ministry, 2003–09; Archdeacon of Suffolk, 2009–12. Canon Res., 2003–09, Canon Emeritus, 2012–, Chester Cathedral.

**HUNT, Maj.-Gen. Malcolm Peter John,** OBE 1984; Royal Marines retired, 1992; General Secretary, Association of British Dispensing Opticians, 1995–99; *b* 16 Nov. 1938; *s* of Peter Gordon Hunt and Rachel Margaret Hunt (*née* Owston); *m* 1st, 1962, Margaret Peat (*d* 1996); two *s*; 2nd, 2004, Angela Jean Payne (*née* Oats), *widow* of Capt. R. N. E. Payne, RN. *Educ:* St John's Sch., Leatherhead; Staff Coll., Camberley. Joined Royal Marines, 1957; service in Malta, Aden and NI; OC RM Detachment, HMS Nubian, 1966–68; Instructor, Army Staff Coll., 1979–81; CO, 40 Commando RM, 1981–83 (Falklands, NI); Internat. Mil. Staff, HQ NATO, 1984–87; Dir, NATO Defence Commitments Staff, MoD, 1987–90; Comdr, British Forces Falkland Islands, 1990–91. Exec. Dir, Nat. Back Pain Assoc., 1993–94. Member: Metropolitan Police Cttee, 1995–2000; Gen. Optical Council, 1999–2001. Pres., S Atlantic Medal Assoc. 1982, 2002–11. Gov., St John's Sch., Leatherhead, 1993–2007 (Vice-Chm., 1997–2006). FRSA 1993. Freeman, City of London, 1999; Liveryman, Co. of Spectacle Makers, 2000. *Recreations:* politics, reading, theatre. *Address:* 6 Court View, Chapel Road, South Cadbury, Somerset BA22 7FG. *T:* (01963) 440929.

**HUNT, Margaret Corinna;** *see* Phillips, M. C.

**HUNT, Air Cdre Mark,** OBE 2015; CEng, FIMechE, FRAeS; Head, Air ISTAR, Defence Equipment and Support, since 2019; President, Institution of Mechanical Engineers, 2014–15 (Deputy President, 2012–14); *b* Shoreham-by-Sea, 9 Sept. 1971; *s* of Robert Henry Hunt and Angela Gillian Hunt; *m* 1996, Lisa Rogers; three *s*. *Educ:* Cardinal Newman Sch., Hove; Univ. of Brighton (BEng Mech. Engrg 1993); RAF Coll., Cranwell; Cranfield Univ. (MBA (Def) 2004); UK Defence Acad. (Staff Coll.); King's Coll. London (MA Defence Studies 2009); Open Univ. (Foundn French 2009); Windsor Leadership Prog., 2012, 2016; Exeter Univ. (RAF Strategic Leadership Develt Prog. 2015). CEng 1999; FIMechE 2004; FRAeS 2015. Jun. Engr Officer, 20 Sqdn, RAF Wittering, 1997–99; Sen. Engr Officer, IV (AC) Sqdn, RAF Cottesmore, 2005–07; Chief Air Engr, RAF Brize Norton, 2010–12; Sentinel and Sentry Type Airworthiness Authy, ISTAR Force, RAF Waddington, 2012–15; Comdt, Defence Sch. of Aeronautical Engrg and Station Comdr, RAF Cosford, 2015–17; Dir Ground Trng and Dep. AOC, 22 Gp, RAF High Wycombe, 2017–19. RAF Social Mobility Advocate, 2018–; Pres., RAF Ice Hockey, 2019–. RAEng Arkwright Schol. Mentor, 2009–. Registered with Internat. Project Mgt Assoc., 2014.

Trustee, IMechE, 2007–15. Freeman, City of London, 2005; Liveryman, Engineers' Co., 2005 (Mem., Ct of Assts, 2015–; Trustee, Engineers' Trust, 2017–). FCMI 2006. *Publications:* (contrib.) RAF Engineer Yearbook, 2005, 2007, 2018; contrib. articles to IMechE Jl. *Recreations:* practising heartily to become a Master of Wines, investing in sons' early adoption of mobile technology, rescuing chocolate labradors, fusion cooking, watching cricket and Rugby, marathons (personal best 3 hours 29 minutes) and sprint triathlons (1 hour 10 minutes). *Club:* Royal Air Force.

**HUNT, Maurice William;** Deputy Director-General, 1989–97, and Secretary, 1986–97, Confederation of British Industry; *b* 30 Aug. 1936; *s* of Maurice Hunt and Helen Hunt (*née* Andrews); *m* 1960, Jean Mary Ellis; one *s* one *d. Educ:* Selhurst Grammar School, Croydon; LSE (BSc Econ). ACIB. Nat. Service, RAF, 1955–57. ANZ Bank, 1953–66; Joint Iron Council, 1966–67; Board of Trade, 1967; Asst Sec., DTI, 1974; RCDS 1982; Dir, Membership, CBI, 1984; Exec. Dir (Ops), CBI, 1987. Dir, Pool Reinsurance Co. Ltd, 1994–2002. *Recreations:* walking, gardening, sailing. *Address:* 12 Savill Road, Lindfield, Haywards Heath, W Sussex RH16 2NX. *T:* (01444) 482687.

**HUNT, Neil Philip;** Chief Executive, Royal College of General Practitioners, 2011–17; *b* 2 May 1954; *s* of Keith Hunt and Doreen Hunt; *m* Tracey Ellen Hassell; two *s* (twins). *Educ:* Univ. of Sussex (BA Hons); Goldsmiths Coll., London (PGCE); Croydon Coll. (DipASS; CQSW). Social worker, 1977–84; Team/Area Manager, London Borough of Lewisham, 1984–89; Divl Manager, Kent CC, 1989–91; NSPCC: Regl Dir, 1991–97; Dir of Child Protection, 1997–2003; on secondment to Home Office, then to DfES, 2002–03; Chief Exec., Alzheimer's Soc., 2003–10. *Recreations:* still marvelling at Bob Dylan, endeavouring to exist as a balanced adult around two charming, very lively and increasingly independent sons, forcing an absurd quantity of plants into the garden.

**HUNT, Prof. Nigel Peter,** OBE 2017; PhD; FRCS; FDSRCS, FDSRCPSGlas, FDSRCSE, FGDP(UK), FHEA; Clinical Professor of Orthodontics and Head, Division of Craniofacial Development, UCL Eastman Dental Institute (formerly Eastman Dental Institute), University College London, since 1998; Honorary Consultant in Orthodontics, Eastman Dental Hospital, University College London Hospital, since 1984; *b* Horbury, Yorks, 21 May 1952; *s* of Ralph Hunt and Vera Hunt (*née* Phelps); *m* 1st, 1980, Gillian von Klemperer (marr. diss. 2001); one *s* one *d;* 2nd, 2002, Susan Cochrane; one *s* one *d. Educ:* Queen Elizabeth Grammar Sch., Wakefield; Guy's Hosp. Dental Sch., Univ. of London (BDS 1974; MSc 1980; PhD 1992). FDSRCPSGlas 1978; DOrthRCS 1980, MOrthRCS 1988; FDSRCSE 1994; FDSRCS 2001; FGDP(UK) 2014; FRCS 2017. Hse Surgeon, SHO and Registrar, Guy's Hosp., 1975–78; Clinical Asst, Eastman Dental Hosp., 1978–80; Sen. Registrar, Guy's Hosp. and Orpington Hosp., 1980–84; Sen. Lectr and Hon. Consultant, Inst. of Dental Surgery, London, 1984–90; Consultant Orthodontist, Eastman Dental Hosp., London and Regl Plastic Surgery Unit, Queen Victoria Hosp., E Grinstead, 1990–92; Consultant, Sen. Lectr and Dir, Orthodontic Res., Eastman Dental Inst. and Hosp., 1992–96; Hd, Orthodontics Unit, Eastman Dental Inst. and Consultant in Orthodontics, UCL Hosps Trust, 1996–98. Royal College of Surgeons: Trustee, 2012–17; Mem. Council, 2012–17; Dean, Faculty of Dental Surgery, 2014–17 (Hon. Vice-Dean, 2010–12). Pres., British Orthodontic Soc., 2015–16 (Chm., 2011–14; Hon. Life Mem., 2014); Hon. Life Mem., World Fedn of Orthodontists, 2015. FHEA 2002. Mem., Council Club, RCS. Bradshaw Medal, RCS, 2016. *Publications:* (with M. Harris) Fundamentals of Orthognathic Surgery, 2008; contrib. scientific articles to peer-reviewed jls. *Recreations:* ski-ing, walking, cricket. *Address:* Department of Orthodontics, UCL Eastman Dental Institute, 256 Grays Inn Road, WC1X 8LD. *T:* (020) 3456 1239, *Fax:* (020) 3456 1238. *E:* n.hunt@ucl.ac.uk. *Club:* MCC.

**HUNT, Paula,** MNZM 2015; Artistic Director, Royal Academy of Dance, 2017–18. *Educ:* ARAD. Royal Academy of Dance: an examiner, 1985–; Chair, Panel of Examiners, 2005–17 (Consultant, 2018–). *E:* phunt@rad.org.uk.

**HUNT, Perdita Mary, (Mrs Gilles Gergaud),** OBE 2015; DL; Director, Watts Gallery Trust, 2004–17; *b* Cape Town, SA, 27 Sept. 1953; *d* of Roland Charles Colin Hunt, CMG, and Pauline Hunt; *m* 1981, Gilles Gergaud; two *s* one *d. Educ:* Downe House, Newbury; Univ. of Sussex (BA French Studies); City Univ. (Dip. Arts Admin). Theatre co-ordinator, Chapter Arts Centre, 1979–81; Mktg and Develt Dir, Aldeburgh Music, 1981–90; Sponsorship Manager and Dir, Ext. Relns, Arts Council, 1990–93; Director of Communications: NHMF, 1993–97; WWF, 1997–2004. Consultant, Leadership Insight, 2016–; Volunteer Specialist Advr, Nat. Trust, 2016–. Tutor, 2008–, Exec. Dir, 2017–18, Recess Coll.; Chm., Surrey Hills Arts Adv. Cttee. Trustee: Baynards Zambia Trust, 2000–; NHMF, 2014–; Foundling Mus., 2016–. DL Surrey, 2011. Hon. DArts Surrey, 2018. *Recreations:* wild swimming, opera, theatre. *Address:* 9 St John's Street, Godalming, Surrey GU7 3EH. *T:* (01483) 416629.
*See also Baron Hunt of Chesterton.*

**HUNT, Peter;** *see* Hunt, D. P.

**HUNT, Peter Lawrence,** CMG 2001; HM Diplomatic Service, retired; Chief Operating Officer, Magrath Sheldrick (formerly Magrath) LLP, since 2012; *b* 10 June 1945; *s* of late Lawrence Hunt and Catherine Hunt (*née* Bree); *m* 1972, Anne Langhorne Carson; two *s* two *d. Educ:* St Anselm's Coll.; Birkbeck Coll., Univ. of London (BA Hons). Joined HM Diplomatic Service, 1962: African floater duties, 1967–69; Managua, 1970–73; FCO, 1973–78; Second Sec., (Commercial), Caracas, 1978–82; First Secretary: FCO, 1982–87; Dep. Head of Mission and Consul, Montevideo, 1987–90; Dep. Head, S Atlantic and Antarctic Dept and Dep. Comr, British Antarctic Territory, 1990–93; Minister-Counsellor, Dep. Head of Mission, and Consul-Gen., Santiago, 1993–96; Consul-General: Istanbul, 1997–2001; Los Angeles, 2001–05. Man. Dir, London, BritishAmerican Business Council, 2005–12. *Recreations:* chess, golf, tennis, hill-walking. *Address:* Magrath Sheldrick LLP, 22 Chancery Lane, WC2A 1LS.

**HUNT, Richard Bruce;** Chairman, R. B. Hunt and Partners Ltd, 1966–95; Deputy Chairman, Howe Robinson and Co. Ltd, 1990–97; *b* 1927; *s* of Percy Thompson Hunt and Thelma Constance Hunt; *m* 1972, Ulrike Dorothea Schmidt; two *d. Educ:* Christ's Hospital. FICS. Served Royal Signals, 1946–48; joined Merchant Bankers Ralli Brothers, 1949–66; formed own company, R. B. Hunt and Partners, 1966. Chm., Baltic Exchange Ltd, 1985–87 (Dir, 1977–80, re-elected, 1981–87). Liveryman, Shipwrights' Co. *Recreations:* golf, ski-ing. *Clubs:* Hurlingham, Royal Wimbledon Golf; Royal Lymington Yacht.

**HUNT, Sir Richard Timothy;** *see* Hunt, Sir Tim.

**HUNT, Sally Colette;** General Secretary, University and College Union, 2007–19 (Joint General Secretary, 2006–07); *b* 14 July 1964; *d* of Barry Hunt and Catherine Hunt (*née* Cox); one *d. Educ:* Univ. of Sussex (BA Hons Internat. Relns 1987). Researcher, Ind. Union of Halifax Staff, 1990–91; Asst Gen. Sec., Nationwide Gp Staff Union, 1991–95; Association of University Teachers: London Regl Official, 1995–97; Asst Gen. Sec., 1997–2002; Gen. Sec., 2002–06. Mem., Gen. Council, 2002–19, Exec. Cttee, 2008–19, Pres., 2017–18, TUC; Member: Gen. Council, ITUC (formerly Exec. Bd, ICFTU), 2004–19; Exec., European TUC, 2005–19; Council, ACAS, 2015–.

**HUNT, Simon John;** Chief Executive, William Grant & Sons Ltd, since 2016; *b* Sydney, Australia, 9 July 1971; *s* of Prof. John Wallace Hunt and Wendy Ellen Hunt; *m* 2002, Carol Lee Meadows; one *s* two *d. Educ:* London Sch. of Econs and Pol Sci. (BSc Sociol.); London Business Sch. (MBA). 2nd Lieut RM Commandos, 1989–90. Vice Pres., Global Mktg, Smirnoff, Diageo, 2000–01; Sen. Vice Pres., Global Innovation, 2001–04, Exec. Vice Pres., Mktg, N America, 2004–05, Allied Domecq; CEO and Pres., Malibu-Kahlua Internat., 2005–07; Pres. and Man. Dir, N America, 2007–13, Chief Commercial Officer, 2013–16, William Grant & Sons Ltd. Liveryman, Distillers' Co., 2013–. A Keeper of the Quaich, 2010–. *Recreations:* ski-ing, swimming, Rugby, theatre.

**HUNT, Terence,** CBE 1996; Chief Executive (formerly National Director), NHS Supplies, 1991–2000; *b* 8 Aug. 1943; *s* of Thomas John Hunt and Marie Louise Hunt (*née* Potter); *m* 1967, Wendy Graeme George; one *s* one *d. Educ:* Huish's Grammar Sch., Taunton. Associate Mem. Inst. of Health Service Management. Tone Vale Group HMC, 1963–65; NE Somerset HMC, 1965–67; Winchester Gp HMC, 1967–69; Lincoln No 1 HMC, 1969–70; Hosp. Sec., Wycombe General Hosp., 1970–73; Dep. Gp Sec., Hillingdon Hosp., 1973–74; Area General Administrator, Kensington and Chelsea and Westminster AHA(T), 1974–77; District Administrator: NW Dist of KCW AHA(T), 1977–82; Paddington and N Kensington, 1982–84; Regl Gen. Manager, NE Thames RHA, 1984–91. Member: Steering Gp on Undergrad. Med. and Dental Educn and Res., 1987–91; NHS Central R&D Cttee, 1991–94; Hosp. Cttee, EEC, 1991–93; Med. Cttee, UFC, 1989–91. Member: Twyford & Dist Round Table, 1975–84 (Chm., 1980–81; Pres., 1988–89); Cttee, Reading Town Regatta, 1984–95 (Treas., 1984–86; Chm., 1989–93); Rotary Club of Reading Maiden Erlegh, 2004–11. Church Warden, St Andrew's Ch, Sonning, Berks, 2010–17. Member: Council of Govs, London Hosp. Med. Coll., 1985–91; Council, UCL, 1985–91. CCMI. Freeman, 1991, Liveryman, 1998, Barbers' Co. Knight's Cross, Order of Falcon (Iceland), 2001. *Recreations:* walking, clockmaking. *Address:* 36 Old Bath Road, Charvil, Reading, Berks RG10 9QR. *T:* (0118) 934 1062. *Club:* Royal Society of Medicine.

**HUNT, Sir Tim,** Kt 2006; PhD; FRS 1991; Principal Scientist, Cancer Research UK, Francis Crick Institute, London (formerly Senior Scientist, Imperial Cancer Research Fund), 1990–2010, Emeritus Researcher, 2011; Visiting Researcher, Okinawa Institute of Science and Technology, Japan, since 2016; *b* 19 Feb. 1943; *s* of Richard William Hunt and Katherine Eva Rowland; christened Richard Timothy, name changed by Deed Poll to Tim, 2004; *m* 1st, 1971, Missy Cusick (marr. diss. 1974); 2nd, 1995, Prof. Mary Katharine Levinge Collins; two *d. Educ:* Dragon Sch.; Magdalen Coll. Sch., Oxford; Clare Coll., Cambridge (BA Nat. Sci. 1964; PhD 1968; Hon. Fellow, 2002). University of Cambridge: Fellow, Clare Coll., 1968–2002; Univ. Lectr in Biochem., 1981–90; Junior Proctor, 1982–83. Mem., Scientific Council, European Res. Council, 2011–15. Mem., EMBO; MAE 1998. Founder FMedSci 1998. Foreign Hon. Mem., Amer. Acad. of Arts and Scis, 1997; Foreign Associate, US Nat. Acad. of Scis, 1999. (Jtly) Nobel Prize for Physiology or Medicine, 2001. Officier, Légion d'Honneur (France), 2002. *Publications:* Molecular Biology of the Cell: the problems book (with John Wilson), 1989, 6th edn 2014; The Cell Cycle: an introduction (with Andrew Murray), 1993; articles in cell and molecular biology jls. *Recreations:* cooking, eating, photography. *Address:* Seaside Faculty House H, 7543 Onna, Kunigamigun, Okinawa 904–0411, Japan. *E:* rtimhunt@gmail.com.

**HUNT, Hon. Tristram Julian William,** PhD; FRHistS; Director, Victoria and Albert Museum, since 2017; *b* 31 May 1974; *s* of Baron Hunt of Chesterton, *qv*; *m* 2004, Juliet Thornback; one *s* two *d. Educ:* University Coll. Sch.; Trinity Coll., Cambridge (BA 1995; PhD 2000); Univ. of Chicago (Exchange Fellow). FRHistS 2005. Sen. researcher, Labour Party election campaign, 1997; Special Advr to Parly Under-Sec. of State, DTI, 1998–2001; Res. Fellow, IPPR, 2001; Associate Fellow, Centre for Hist. and Econs, King's Coll., Cambridge, 2001–02; Lectr, 2003–10, Sen. Lectr, 2010–17, QMUL. Vis. Prof., Arizona State Univ., 2004–05. Author and presenter, television: Civil War (series), 2002; Isaac Newton: Great Briton, 2002; British Middle Class, 2005; The Protestant Revolution (series), 2007. MP (Lab) Stoke-on-Trent Central, 2010–Jan. 2017. Shadow Sec. of State for Educn, 2013–15. Trustee: Heritage Lottery Fund, 2005–10; Nat. Heritage Meml Fund, 2005–10; History of Parliament Trust, 2011–17. *Publications:* The English Civil War, 2002, 3rd edn 2006; Building Jerusalem: the rise and fall of the Victorian city, 2004, 2nd edn 2005; Friedrich Engels: the frock-coated communist, 2009 (Elizabeth Longford Histl Biog. Prize, 2010); Ten Cities that made an Empire, 2014; contribs to History Today, Jl Social Hist. *Recreations:* Victorian urban architecture, fresh-water swimming, ceramics, book-browsing. *Address:* Victoria and Albert Museum, Cromwell Road, SW7 2RL.

**HUNT, Dame Vivian (Yvonne),** DBE 2018; Managing Partner, UK and Ireland, McKinsey & Company, since 2014. *Educ:* Harvard Univ. (AB 1989; MBA 1995). US Peace Corps, 1989–91; McKinsey & Company, 1996–: Partner, 2001–08, Sen. Partner, 2008–; Leader, Pharmaceuticals and Med. Products Practice, EMEA, 2009–13. Chair, London Council, CBI, 2016–; Mem. Bd, BritishAmerican Business. Trustee: Henry Smith Charity; Action on Addiction; British Mus., 2019–. Mem. Adv. Council, Tate Modern. *Address:* McKinsey & Company, Post Building, Museum Street, WC1A 1AP.

**HUNT, William George,** TD 1988 (and Clasp 1994); Research Assistant, College of Arms, since 2017 (Registrar, 2007–14); Windsor Herald of Arms, 1999–2017; Genealogist, Order of St John, 2010–17; HM Lieutenant, City of London, since 2012; *b* 8 Dec. 1946; *s* of late Frank Williams Hunt, TD, MA, and Mary Elizabeth Leyland Hunt (*née* Orton), JP; *m* 1998, Michaela Wedel; two *s. Educ:* Liverpool Coll.; Univ. of Southampton (BA); Univ. of Constance; Univ. of Lausanne; Univ. of Caen (Dip.). FCA 1979. Mentor, Salem Sch., 1967–69; Audit Manager, Arthur Young McClelland Moores, 1970–83; Financial Controller and Partnership Sec., Frere Cholmeley, 1983–92; Finance Dir, Hopkins & Wood, 1993–95; Portcullis Pursuivant of Arms, 1992–99. Clerk, HM Commn of Lieutenancy for City of London, 1990–2013; Mem., Ct of Common Council, City of London, 2004–13. Dir, Heraldry Soc., 1997–2006, 2016–17. Treas., HAC Biographical Dictionary (1537–1914) Trust, 1993–. Gov., City of London Sch., 2009–13. Mem., RFCA, 1990– (Exec. Mem., City of London Assoc., 2007–15). Freeman, City of London; Founder Mem., Treas., 1976–78, Chm., 1978–79, Soc. of Young Freemen of City of London; Maj. and Mem., Ct of Assts, 1988–2000, HAC; Mem., Ct of Assts, 1996–, Master, 2000–01, Co. of Makers of Playing Cards. CStJ 2011 (SBStJ 1999). *Publications:* Guide to the Honourable Artillery Company, 1987; (ed jtly) Dictionary of British Arms, Vol. 1, 1992. *Recreation:* orders and decorations. *Address:* College of Arms, 130 Queen Victoria Street, EC4V 4BT. *T:* (020) 7329 8755.

**HUNTER, Air Vice-Marshal Alexander Freeland Cairns,** CBE 1982 (OBE 1981); AFC 1978; Deputy Chairman, Annington Holdings plc, 1996–2013; *b* 8 March 1939; *s* of late H. A. C. and L. E. M. Hunter; *m* 1964, Wilma Elizabeth Bruce Wilson. *Educ:* Aberdeen Grammar Sch.; Aberdeen Univ. (MA 1960, LLB 1962). Commissioned RAFVR 1959; RAF 1962; flying training 1962; Pilot, 81 (PR) Sqn, FEAF, 1964–67; Central Flying Sch., 1967–68; Instructor, Northumbrian Univ. Air Sqn, 1968–69; Asst Air Attaché, Moscow, 1971–73; RAF Staff Coll., 1974; Flight Comdr, 230 Sqn, 1975–77; OC 18 Sqn, RAF Germany, 1978–80; Air Warfare Course, 1981; MoD (Air), 1981; OC RAF Odiham, 1981–83; Gp Captain Plans, HQ Strike Comd, 1983–85; RCDS 1986; Dir of Public

Relations (RAF), 1987–88; Comdt, RAF Staff Coll., 1989–90; Comdr British Forces Cyprus and Adminr of Sovereign Base Areas, 1990–93. Chm., Home Housing Assoc., 1995–98; Member, Board: North Housing Assoc. Ltd, 1993–95 (Vice Chm. (NE), 1994); Warden Housing Assoc., 1996–98. Chairman: Home in Scotland Ltd, 1998–2000; Home Gp, 1998–2003; Paramount Homes Ltd, 1998–2003; Kenton Bar Bunker Co. Ltd, 1999–2004; UK Haptics Ltd, 2006–07; Chm., Annington Trust, 2008–16 (Dep. Chm., 1996–2008); Dep. Chm., Urban Housing Trust Ltd, 2001–03; Director: Clyde Helicopters Ltd, 1993–95; Newcastle Bldg Soc., 1993–2004; Newcastle Bank (Gibraltar), 1995–99; Great NE Air Ambulance Trading Co. Ltd, 2000–01. Vice-Pres., HMS Trincomalee Trust, 2007–17. Chm., N of England, RFCA, 2003–06 (Vice Chm. (Air), 1996–2003); Vice Chm. (Air), Council of RFCAs (formerly TAVRAs), 1999–2004. Hon. Col, Tyne-Tees Regt, 1999–2006; Hon. Air Cdre, No 609 (W Riding) Sqdn, RAuxAF, 2001–06. Gentleman of the Four and Twenty, Rothbury, 2002–. DL Northumberland, 1994. OStJ 1994 (Chm. Council, Northumbria, 1998–2000). *Recreations:* shooting, fishing, hill-walking, military history, living in Germany. *Address:* c/o Clydesdale Bank, Business Banking Centre, Wakefield Road, Carlisle CA3 0HE. *Clubs:* Royal Air Force; Northern Counties (Newcastle upon Tyne).

**HUNTER, Sir Alistair (John),** KCMG 1994 (CMG 1985); DL; HM Diplomatic Service, retired; *b* 9 Aug. 1936; *s* of Kenneth Clarke Hunter and Joan Tunks; *m* 1st, 1963, Gillian Bradbury; one *s* two *d*; 2nd, 1978, Helge Milton (*née* Kahle); two step *s. Educ:* Felsted; Magdalen Coll., Oxford. Royal Air Force, 1955–57; CRO, 1961–65; Private Sec. to Permanent Under-Sec., 1961–63; 2nd Sec., Kuala Lumpur, 1963–65; 1st Sec. (Commercial), Peking, 1965–68; seconded to Cabinet Office, 1969–70; FCO, 1970–73; 1st Sec., Rome, 1973–75; FCO, 1975–80; Hd of Chancery, Bonn, 1980–85; seconded to DTI as Under Sec., Overseas Trade, 1985–88; Consul-Gen., Düsseldorf, and Dir-Gen. of British Trade and Investment Promotion in FRG, 1988–91; Consul-Gen., NY, and Dir-Gen. of Trade and Investment, USA, 1991–96. Exec. Chm., British-Amer. Chamber of Commerce, London, 1996–98. Chairman: British Music Rights, 1998–2005; E Kent Forum, 1998–2001; Manston Airport Consultative Cttee, 1999–2006; Margate Th. Royal Trust, 2000–07. Dir, PRS, 1996–2002; Dep. Chm., Locate in Kent, 1996–2005. Trustee, Horniman Mus. and Gdns, 1996–99. DL Kent, 2001. *Address:* Bay View House, 2A Bay View Road, Broadstairs CT10 2EA.

**HUNTER, Allison;** *see* Hunter, J. A.

**HUNTER, Andrew Reid;** Headmaster, Merchiston Castle School, 1998–2018; *b* Nairobi, 28 Sept. 1958; *s* of John Horatio Hunter and Irene Hunter (*née* Fish); *m* 1981, Barbara Gandy Bradford; two *s* one *d. Educ:* Kenton Coll., Nairobi; Aldenham Sch., Elstree; Univ. of Manchester (BA Hons); St Luke's Coll., Exeter. PGCE. Westbrook Hay Prep. Sch., 1978–79; Teacher of English, 1983–91, Housemaster, 1987–91, Worksop Coll.; Teacher of English and Religious Studies, 1991–98, Housemaster, 1992–98, Bradfield Coll. Member: HMC, 1998– (Mem., Wellbeing Wkg Gp, 2015–). Governor: Ardveck Prep. Sch., Crieff, 2008–; Laidlaw Schs Trust (formerly Excelsior Acad.), Newcastle upon Tyne, 2009–; RNCF/Springboard Bursary Foundn, 2012. Former Chm., Public Schs Hockey Fest., Oxford; Former Mem. Cttee, Public Schs Lawn Tennis Assoc. *Recreations:* reading, attending theatre, former county player of tennis, squash and hockey (spectator these days), international cuisine and culture. *Address:* 10A Redhall House Drive, Graysmill Dell, Edinburgh EH14 1JE.

**HUNTER, Andrew Robert Frederick Ebenezer;** *b* 8 Jan. 1943; *s* of late Sqdn Leader Roger Edward Hunter, MBE, DFC and Winifred Mary Hunter (*née* Nelson); *m* 1972, Janet (*d* 2002), *d* of late Samuel Bourne of Gloucester; one *s* one *d. Educ:* St George's Sch., Harpenden; Durham Univ.: Jesus Coll., Cambridge; Westcott House, Cambridge. In industry, 1969; Asst Master, St Martin's Sch., Northwood, 1970–71; Asst Master, Harrow Sch., 1971–83. Contested: (C) Southampton, Itchen, 1979; (DemU) Lagan Valley, NI Assembly, 2003. MP (C, 1983–2002, Ind C, 2002–04, DemU, 2004–05) Basingstoke. PPS to Minister of State, DoE, 1985–86. Member: NI Select Cttee, 1994–2001; NI Grand Cttee, H of C, 1996–2005; Chm., Cons. NI Cttee, 1992–97. Chm., Monday Club, 2006–15. Mem., NFU, 1984–2005. Vice-Pres., Nat. Prayer Book Soc., 1987–97. Mem. Ct, Univ. of Southampton, 1983–2005. Commnd TAVR (resigned comm as Major, 1984). Hon. Mem., Soc. of the Sealed Knot, 1987–. *Recreations:* watching cricket and Rugby football, collecting model soldiers, reading. *Address:* 21 Manor Court, Meeting Street, Moira, Co. Down BT67 0TL. *Club:* Carlton.

**HUNTER, Angela Margaret Jane, (Anji);** Senior Adviser, Edelman, since 2013; *b* 29 July 1955; *d* of Arthur John, (Mac), Hunter and Joy Lorraine Hunter; *m* 1st, 1980, Nick Cornwall (marr. diss. 2004); one *s* one *d*; 2nd, 2006, (Thomas) Adam (Babington) Boulton, *qv. Educ:* St Leonard's Sch., St Andrews, Fife; St Clare's Hall, Oxford; Brighton Poly. (BA 1987). Teacher of English as a Foreign Language, Academia Británica, Córdoba, Spain, 1976–78; Legal Asst, Hodge Jones & Allen, then Offenbach & Co., 1978–80; Res. Asst to Tony Blair, MP, 1986–90, Head of Office, 1990–97; Special Asst to Prime Minister, 1997–2001; Dir of Govt Relations, Prime Minister's Office, 2001–02; Dir of Communications, BP plc, 2002–07; Gp Hd of Govt Relations and Social Affairs, Anglo American plc, 2009–11; Dir, Queen Elizabeth Prize for Engrg, RAEng, 2011–13. Member: UK Adv. Bd, All Nippon Airways, 2004–; Bd of Dirs, Arab-British Chamber of Commerce, 2013–. Trustee: Snowdon Awards Scheme; Three Faiths Forum. Mem., Bd of Govs, Birmingham Business Sch., 2005–. DUniv: Birmingham, 2013; Brighton, 2014. *Recreations:* diving, ski-ing, horse-riding.

**HUNTER, Prof. (Ann) Jacqueline,** CBE 2010; PhD; FMedSci; FZS, FRBS; Professor of Life Science Innovation, St George's Hospital Medical School, since 2013; Chief Executive, Benevolent Bio Ltd (formerly Stratified Medical Ltd), since 2016; Director, Benevolent AI, since 2016; *m*; one *d* and two step *d. Educ:* Selwyn Sch.; Kings Secondary Sch.; Bedford Coll., Univ. of London (BSc Jt Hons Physiol. and Psychol. 1977; PhD 1980). Wellcome Trust Post-doctoral Res. Fellow, St George's Hosp. Med. Sch., 1982–83; Sen. Pharmacologist, Dept of Neuropharmacol., Glaxo Gp Res., 1983–86; Hd of Behavioural Pharmacol., Astra Neurosci. Res., 1986–89; Asst Dir, Pharmacol., SmithKline and French, 1989–90; Prog. Manager, SmithKline Beecham Pharmaceuticals, 1990–92; Dir, Neurol. Res., 1992–97, Gp Dir, Neurobehavioural Res., 1997–2000, SmithKline Beecham; GlaxoSmithKline: Vice Pres., Biol., 2000–02; Sen. Vice Pres. and Hd, Neurol. and G1 Centre of Excellence for Drug Discovery, 2002–08; Sen. Vice Pres. and Hd, Sci. Envmt Develt, 2008–10; Founder and CEO, OI Pharma Partners Ltd, 2010–; CEO, NeuroSymptomatix Ltd, 2010–13; Chief Exec., BBSRC, 2013–16 (Mem, 2004–16). Non-executive Director: Proximagen Neuroscience Gp plc, 2010–12; Chiltern plc, 2016–17. Mem. Bd, Bioindustry Assoc., 2017–. Trustee, Age Care, 2010–13. Member, Council: RHUL, 2011–13; Univ. of Herts, 2013–. FBPhS (FBPharmacolS 2012), Hon. FBPhS 2017; FMedSci 2014; FZS 2015; FRBS 2016. Hon. DSc: Brunel, 2016; UEA, 2017. *Publications:* (ed jtly) Memory: neurochemical and abnormal perspectives, 1991; (ed jtly) Neurodegeneration, 1992; (ed jtly) Inflammatory Cells and Mediators in CNS Diseases, 1999; (ed jtly) Antisense Technology in the Central Nervous System, 1999; contribs to scientific jls. *Address:* Benevolent Bio Ltd, 4–8 Maple Street, W1T 5HD. *E:* jackie.hunter@benevolent.ai.

**HUNTER, Anthony John,** OBE 2010; Chief Executive, Social Care Institute for Excellence, since 2014; *b* 9 March 1954; *s* of Robert and Elizabeth Hunter; *m* 1986, Tatyana Fomina; one *s* one *d. Educ:* Doncaster Grammar Sch.; Queen's Coll., Oxford (MA PPE 1976); Nottingham Univ. (MA Applied Social Studies, CQSW, 1980); Sheffield Poly. (DMS 1984). Social Worker and Social Services Manager, Doncaster MBC, 1976–84; Day and Home Services Manager, Barnsley MBC, 1985–86; Res. and Develt Manager, Barnardo's, 1986–89; Health and Social Care Consultant, Price Waterhouse, 1989–95; Dir of Social Services, Housing and Public Protection, ER of Yorks Council, 1995–2003; Exec. Dir, Community Services, Liverpool CC, 2004–08; Chief Exec., NE Lincs Council, 2008–13. Pres., Assoc. of Dirs of Social Services, 2004–05. *Publications:* articles on social care, local govt develt and change mgt issues. *Recreations:* football, rock'n'roll singing, comedy. *E:* tony.hunter@scie.org.uk.

**HUNTER, Anthony Rex;** *see* Hunter, Tony.

**HUNTER, Archibald Sinclair;** DL; CA; Chairman, Macfarlane Group PLC, 2004–12 (Director, since 1998); *b* 20 Aug. 1943; *s* of late John Lockhart Hunter and Elizabeth Hastings (*née* Sinclair); *m* 1969, Patricia Ann Robertson; two *s* one *d. Educ:* Queen's Park Sch., Glasgow. CA 1966. With Mackie & Clark, Glasgow, 1966; joined Thomson McLintock, 1966: Partner, 1974–87; Glasgow Managing Partner, 1983–87; Glasgow Managing Partner, KPMG Peat Marwick, 1987–92; Sen. Partner, Scotland, KPMG, 1992–99. Pres., ICAS, 1997–98. Non-executive Director: Clydeport plc, 1999–2002; N American Income Trust (formerly Edinburgh US Tracker Trust), 2003–; Royal Bank of Scotland, 2004–10; Chm., Le Chardon d'Or Ltd, 2001–. Dir, Beatson Inst., 1999–2010; Treas., Scottish Cancer Foundn, 2003–15. Mem. Court, Univ. of Strathclyde, 1999–2007 (Chm., 2002–07). DL Renfrewshire, 1995. DUniv Strathclyde, 2006. *Recreations:* golf, swimming, hill-walking. *Address:* Macfarlane Group, Clansman House, 21 Newton Place, Glasgow G3 7PY. *T:* (0141) 314 3979. *Clubs:* Williamwood Golf (formerly Capt.) (Glasgow); Western Gailes Golf (Ayrshire).

**HUNTER, Prof. Christopher Alexander,** FRS 2008; Herchel Smith Professor of Organic Chemistry, University of Cambridge, since 2014; *b* Dunedin, NZ, 19 Feb. 1965; *s* of John Alexander Hunter and Alice Mary Hunter; *m* 2008, Rosaleen Theresa McHugh; two *s* one *d. Educ:* Churchill Coll., Cambridge (BA 1986; PhD 1989). Lectr, Dept of Chem., Univ. of Otago, NZ, 1989–91; Lectr, 1991–94, Reader, 1994–97, Prof. of Chemistry, 1997–2014, Dept of Chem., Univ. of Sheffield; Lister Inst. Res. Fellow, 1994–99. EPSRC Sen. Res. Fellow, 2005–10. Hon. DSc Ulster, 2013. Hon. MRIA 2015. Meldola Medal, 1992, Corday Morgan Medal, 1999, Tilden Prize, 2009, Physical Organic Chem. Award and Ingold Lectr, 2011, RSC. *Publications:* contrib. papers to scientific jls. *Address:* Department of Chemistry, University of Cambridge, Lensfield Road, Cambridge CB2 1EW. *T:* (01223) 336710. *E:* ch664@cam.ac.uk.

**HUNTER, Craig;** *see* Hunter, J. C.

**HUNTER, Prof. David James,** PhD; FRCPE; Professor of Health Policy and Management, Institute of Health and Society, Newcastle University, 2017–18, now Emeritus; *b* Irvine, Ayrshire, 17 April 1950; *s* of Thomas Drummond Hunter and Peggie Hunter; *m* 1994, Jacqueline Floyd; one *s* one *d. Educ:* Rudolf Steiner Sch., Edinburgh; Univ. of Edinburgh (MA Social Sci. 1st Cl. Hons (Political Sci.) 1974; PhD Social Policy 1979). FRCPE 1992. Health Policy Analyst, King's Fund Inst., London, 1987–88; Prof. of Health Policy and Mgt, and Dir, Nuffield Inst. for Health, Univ. of Leeds, 1989–99; Durham University: Prof. of Health Policy and Mgt, 1999–2017, Dir, Centre for Public Policy and Health, 2002–17 (a WHO Collaborating Centre on Complex Health Systems Res. Knowledge and Action, 2014–17); Fellow, Wolfson Res. Inst. for Health and Wellbeing, 2002–17. Dep. Dir, Fuse, UK Clin. Res. Collaboration Centre for Transitional Res. in Public Health, 2008–. Non-exec. Dir, NICE, 2009–16. Gov., S Tees Hosp. NHS Foundn Trust, 2009–. Hon. MFPH 1990. *Publications:* Coping with Uncertainty: policy and politics in the National Health Service, 1980; Desperately Seeking Solutions: rationing health care, 1997; Public Health Policy, 2003; The Health Debate, 2008, 2nd edn 2016; (jtly) The Public Health System in England, 2010; (jtly) Reforming Healthcare: what's the evidence?, 2014; (with N. Perkins) Partnership Working in Public Health, 2014. *Recreations:* walking and mountain biking in the Yorkshire dales, listening to jazz. *Address:* Institute of Health and Society, Newcastle University, Level 4, Sir James Spence Institute, Royal Victoria Hospital, Queen Victoria Road, Newcastle upon Tyne NE2 4LP. *T:* (0191) 282 1320. *E:* david.hunter2@newcastle.ac.uk.

**HUNTER, David Peter;** Director, Department for Environment, Food and Rural Affairs, 1996–2007; *b* 31 Dec. 1948; *o s* of Mr and Mrs D. Hunter, Southampton; *m* 1973, Judith, *d* of Mr and Mrs G. A. Baker, Worcester; two *s* two *d. Educ:* Regent's Park Sch.; Shirley Sch.; King Edward VI Sch., Southampton; Magdalen Coll., Oxford (MA). MAFF, 1972–82; Cabinet Office, 1982–83; rejoined MAFF, 1983: Head: Beef Div., 1983–87; Trade Policy and Tropical Products Div., 1987–93; Agencies and Citizen's Charter Div., 1993–96; EU and Livestock Gp, 1995–98; Agricl Gp, MAFF, subseq. DEFRA, 1998–2001; Dir, EU and Internat. Policy Directorate, 2001–06, Review of Rural Payments Agency, 2006–07, DEFRA. *Recreations:* theatre, vegetables, Soton FC, country walks, churches.

**HUNTER, Rear-Adm. Ian Alexander,** CB 1993; Chief of Naval Staff, New Zealand, 1991–94; *b* 23 Oct. 1939; *s* of late A. A. Hunter and O. R. Hunter; *m* 1965, Hilary R. Sturrock; two *s. Educ:* Christchurch Boys' High Sch.; BRNC Dartmouth. Joined RNZN 1957; served HMNZS Otago, HMS Tabard, USS Arneb, HMNZS Rotoiti (Antarctic), N Ireland Anti-Submarine Sch., HM Ships Torquay and Eastbourne, HMNZ Ships Taranaki, Blackpool, Canterbury, Waikato (Command), Southland (Command); posts with Chief of Naval Staff; RCDS 1985; ACDS (Develt Plans), 1987–88; Commodore Auckland, 1988–91 (concerned with Govt financial reforms for RNZN, restructuring Dockyard, orgn of Whitbread Round the World Yacht Race). Pres., Sea Cadet Assoc. of NZ, 1998. Trustee, United Services Medal Collection Trust, 2006; Patron, Wellington Returned Services Assoc., 2001–13. *Address:* 108B Messines Road, Karori, Wellington, New Zealand.

**HUNTER, Prof. Ian Charles,** PhD; FREng, FIET, FIEEE; Radio Design/Royal Academy of Engineering Professor of Microwave Signal Processing, since 2012, and Deputy Head, School of Electronic and Electrical Engineering, since 2013, University of Leeds; *b* Fleetwood, Lancs, 1 Sept. 1957; one *s* two *d. Educ:* Univ. of Leeds (BSc 1st Cl. Hons 1978; PhD 1981). FIET 2000; FIEEE 2007; FREng 2013. With Aercom Industries, Inc., Sunnyvale, Calif; KW Engrg, San Diego; Principal Engr, Filtronic Components Ltd, UK; Fellow Engr, Filtronic Comtek, 1995–2001; Mem., academic staff, Univ. of Bradford, 1991–97 (Sen. Lectr, 1995–97); Sen. Res. Fellow (pt-time), 1999–2001, Reader, 2001–03, Prof., 2003–12, Univ. of Leeds. Ed-in-Chief, Internat. Jl Electronics, 2006–. *Publications:* (jtly) Practical Microstrip Circuit Design, 1991; Theory and Design of Microwave Filters, 2001; The Story of Filtronic, 2003; contrib. papers to IEEE and IEE jls. *Recreations:* walking, sailing. *Address:* School of Electronic and Electrical Engineering, University of Leeds, Woodhouse Lane, Leeds LS2 9JT. *E:* i.c.hunter@leeds.ac.uk.

**HUNTER, Ian Gerald Adamson**; QC 1980; SC (NSW) 1994; a Recorder, 1986–2000; *b* 3 Oct. 1944; *s* of late Gerald Oliver Hunter and Jessie Hunter; *m* 1975, Maggie (*née* Reed) (marr. diss. 1999); two *s*; *m* 2000, Jill (*née* Nichols). *Educ*: Reading Sch.; Pembroke Coll., Cambridge (Open Scholar, Squire Univ. Law Scholar, Trevelyan Scholar, BA (double first in Law), MA, LLB); Harvard Law Sch. (Kennedy Memorial Scholar, LLM). Called to the Bar, Inner Temple, 1967 (Duke of Edinburgh Entrance Scholar, Major Scholar), Bencher, 1986; Mem. Bar, NSW, 1993; Avocat à la cour de Paris, 1995–2010. CEDR Accredited Mediator, 1998–. Chm., Consolidated Regulations and Transfer Cttee, Senate of Inns of Court, 1986–87 (Mem., 1982–85); Member: International Relations Cttee, Bar Council, 1982–90; Exec. Cttee, Bar Council, 1985–86. Mem. and Rapporteur, Internat. Law Assoc. Anti-Trust Cttee, 1968–72; Pres., Union Internat. des Avocats, 1989 (UK Vice-Pres., 1982–86; first Vice Pres., 1986–; Dir of Studies, 1990–91); Vice Pres., Franco-British Lawyers Soc., 1996–99; Pres., Anglo-Australasian Lawyers Soc., 1998–; Treas., Bar Pro Bono Unit, 1997–99; Hon. Mem., Canadian Bar Assoc., 1990. FCIArb. *Publications*: articles on public international law. *Recreations*: bebop, other good music, French cooking. *Address*: Essex Court Chambers, 24 Lincoln's Inn Fields, WC2A 3EG. *T*: (020) 7813 8000.

**HUNTER, Jacqueline**; *see* Hunter, A. J.

**HUNTER, James**, CBE 2001; PhD; FRSE; Director, Centre for History, UHI Millennium Institute, Dornoch, 2005–10, now Emeritus Professor of History, University of the Highlands and Islands; *b* 22 May 1948; *s* of Donald and Jean Hunter; *m* 1972, Evelyn Ronaldson; one *s* one *d*. *Educ*: Oban High Sch.; Aberdeen Univ. (MA Hons 1971); Edinburgh Univ. (PhD 1974). Res. Fellow, Aberdeen Univ., 1974–76; journalist: Press and Jl, 1976–81; Sunday Standard, 1981–82; freelance journalist and broadcaster, 1982–85; Founding Dir, Scottish Crofters' Union, 1985–90. Chairman: Skye and Lochalsh Enterprise, 1995–98; Highlands and Is Enterprise, 1998–2004 (Bd Mem., 1991–95); Isle of Eigg Heritage Trust, 2004–07; Member: Scottish Tourist Bd, 1995–98; Council, NT for Scotland, 1995–98; Convention of the Highlands and Is, 1996–2004; Bd, Scottish Natural Heritage, 2004–10 (Mem., N Areas Bd, 1992–98); Bd, Community Land Scotland, 2016–18; Vice-Chair, Land Reform Rev. Gp, Scottish Govt, 2012–13. Mem., BBC's Broadcasting Council for Scotland, 1999–2002. FRSE 2007. *Publications*: The Making of the Crofting Community, 1976; For the People's Cause, 1986; Skye: the island, 1986; The Claim of Crofting, 1991; Scottish Highlanders: a people and their place, 1992; A Dance Called America: the Scottish Highlands, the United States and Canada, 1994; On the Other Side of Sorrow: nature and people in the Scottish Highlands, 1995; Glencoe and the Indians, 1996 (US edn as Scottish Highlanders, Indian Peoples); Last of the Free: a millennial history of the Highlands and Islands of Scotland, 1999; Culloden and the Last Clansman, 2001; Scottish Exodus: travels among a worldwide clan, 2005; From the Low Tide of the Sea to the Highest Mountain Tops: community ownership of land in the Scottish Highlands and Islands, 2012; Set Adrift Upon the World: the Sutherland clearances, 2015. *Recreations*: walking, keeping in touch with family, being with grandchildren. *Address*: 19 Mansefield Park, Kirkhill, Inverness IV5 7ND. *T*: (01463) 831228. *E*: jameshunter22548@btinternet.com.

**HUNTER, (Jane) Allison**; QC 2017; a Recorder, since 2018; *b* England, 25 Sept. 1962; *d* of Walker Hunter and Elizabeth Hunter; *m* 1990, Tarek Ismail; two *s* one *d*. *Educ*: Dahran Acad., Saudi Arabia; Bede Sch., Sunderland; Harrogate Ladies' Coll.; Poly. of North London (LLB Hons); Queen Mary Coll., Univ. of London (LLM (Merit)); Council of Legal Educn (Bar Finals). Called to the Bar, Lincoln's Inn, 1986; in practice as a barrister, 1986–, specialising in criminal law incl. murder, rape, human trafficking, serious and complex fraud and money laundering, and serious organised crime and criminal networks. *Recreation*: travel. *Address*: 23 Essex Street, WC2R 3AA. *T*: 07900 214300, *Fax*: (020) 7413 0353. *E*: allisonhunterqc@23es.com.

**HUNTER, Jean McLaren**; Vice Lord-Lieutenant for Clackmannanshire, 2014–17; *b* Alva, Clackmannanshire, 20 June 1943; *d* of John Graham Wright and Jeanie Wright (*née* MacCallum); *m* 1978, Dr Kenneth W. Hunter; two *s*. *Educ*: Alva Primary Sch.; Alloa Acad.; Sch. of Radiography, Edinburgh Royal Infirmary (MSR 1963). Radiographer: Victoria Infirmary, Kirkcaldy, 1963–64; Commune Hosp., Aarhus, Denmark, 1964; Stirling Royal Infirmary, 1965; VSO, BVI, 1967–68; Girl Guide Trainer, Scotland, 1969–70; Sen. Radiographer, Stirling Royal Infirmary, 1970–71; Superintendent Radiographer, X-Ray Dept, Stirling and Alloa Hosps, 1971–79. Member: Muckhart Coronation Hall Cttee, 1998–2008; Muckhart Community Council. DL Clackmannanshire, 2002–14. *Address*: Grange Cottage, Pool of Muckhart, Dollar FK14 7JW. *T*: (01259) 781338. *E*: jeanmhunter@gmail.com.

**HUNTER, Prof. John Angus Alexander**, OBE 1997; MD; Grant Professor of Dermatology, University of Edinburgh, 1981–99, now Emeritus; *b* 16 June 1939; *s* of Dr John Craig Alexander Hunter and Alison Hay Shand Alexander; *m* 1968, Ruth Mary Farrow; one *s* two *d*. *Educ*: Loretto Sch., Musselburgh; Pembroke Coll., Cambridge (BA 1960); Univ. of Edinburgh (MB ChB 1963; MD 1977 (Gold Medal)). FRCPE 1978. Gen. med. posts, Edinburgh, 1963–66; Research Fellow in Dermatology: Inst. of Dermatology, London, 1967; Univ. of Minnesota, 1968–69; Lectr, Dept of Dermatology, Univ. of Edinburgh, 1970–74; Consultant Dermatologist, Lothian Health Bd, 1974–80. Chm., Specialist Adv. Cttee (Dermatol.), JCHMT, 1986–90. President: Section of Dermatol., RSocMed, 1993–94; Scottish Dermatol Soc., 1994–97; Hon. Member: British Assoc. of Dermatologists, 1999 (Pres., 1998–99); Dermatological Socs of N America, Greece, Germany, Poland, Austria and USA. *Publications*: (jtly) Common Diseases of the Skin, 1983; (jtly) Clinical Dermatology, 1989, 4th edn 2008; (jtly) Skin Signs in Clinical Medicine, 1997; (ed jtly) Davidson's Principles and Practice of Medicine, 18th edn 1999 to 20th edn 2006; (ed jtly) Davidson's Clinical Cases in Medicine, 2008, 2nd edn as Davidson's 100 Clinical Cases, 2012; numerous articles in dermatol jls. *Recreations*: family archives, golf, gardening, music. *Address*: Sandy Lodge, Nisbet Road, Gullane, E Lothian EH31 2BQ. *E*: jaa.hunter@virgin.net. *Clubs*: Hawks (Cambridge); Hon. Company of Edinburgh Golfers.

**HUNTER, (John) Craig**; Founder Director and Managing Director, VERSEC Ltd, since 1998; *b* Hitchin, Herts, 16 Jan. 1961; *s* of Ronald Hunter and Hazel Hunter; civil partnership 2010, Nick Hazell. *Educ*: Hitchin Boys' Grammar Sch.; Sheffield City Poly. (BA Hons Business Studies with Law 1983). Fellow, ICSA, 1998; Chartered Sec. in Public Practice 1998. Dep. Company Sec., NFC plc, 1991–98. Specialist Dir (non-exec.), British Swimming, 2007–; Mem., 2008–16, Vice Chm., Technical Swimming Cttee, Ligue Européenne de Natation, 2008–; Member: Mission Control Panel, UK Sport, 2011–13; Tech. Swimming Cttee, Fédération internat. de natation, 2017–; Ind. Dir, English Inst. of Sport, 2014–18; Ind. Mem., Audit Cttee, UK Sport Gp, 2014–. Chef de Mission, Commonwealth Games England: Commonwealth Games, 2010, Commonwealth Youth Games, 2011; Chef de Mission, Eur. Youth Olympic Fest., British Olympic Assoc., 2011; Chef de Mission, ParalympicsGB, London 2012, 2011–12. Ext. Examr, MSc Finance and Corporate Governance, Univ. of Hertfordshire, 2007–11. President: Herts Amateur Swimming Assoc., 1991–92; Hatfield Swimming Club, 2008–. Outstanding Achievement Award, ICSA 2013. *Recreations*: ski-ing, yoga, theatre, French conversation. *Address*: 39 Alma Road, St Albans, Herts AL1 3AT. *T*: (01727) 855512, 07771 814929. *E*: craighunter1601@gmail.com.

**HUNTER, John Garvin**, CB 2004; Permanent Secretary, Department of Finance and Personnel, Northern Ireland Civil Service, 2003–07; *b* 9 Aug. 1947; *s* of Garvin and Martha Hunter; *m* 1976, Rosemary Alison Haire; one *s* two *d*. *Educ*: Merchant Taylors' Sch., Liverpool; Queen's Univ., Belfast (BA); Cornell Univ., NY (MBA). Asst Principal, NICS, 1970; Department of Health and Social Services: Dep. Principal, 1973; Harkness Fellow, 1977–79; Principal Officer, 1979; Asst Sec., 1982; Dir Gen., Internat. Fund for Ireland, 1986; Under Sec., 1988; Chief Exec., Mgt Exec., Health and Personal Social Services, NI, 1990–96; Dir of Personnel, NICS, 1997–99; Perm. Sec., Dept for Social Develt, NICS, 1999–2003. Chm., Chief Executives' Forum, 2008–14. University of Ulster: Mem. Council, 2008– (Chair, 2015–); Pro-Chancellor, 2015–. Mem., Bd of Finance and Personnel, Presbyterian Church in Ireland, 2009–; Chm. Council, Corrymeela Community, 2011–16. Trustee, Age NI, 2009–13. *Publications*: contribs to conf. papers on the conflict in NI and on health service planning. *Recreations*: Corrymeela Community, Abbey Singers, Ulster Historical Foundation, U3A.

**HUNTER, Prof. John Rotheram**, OBE 2011; PhD; FSA, FSAScot, FCSFS; Professor of Ancient History and Archaeology, University of Birmingham, 1996–2010, now Emeritus; *b* 4 Jan. 1949; *s* of William Rotheram Hunter and Stella Maud Hunter (*née* Atthill); *m* 1971, Margaret Suddes; three *s* one *d*. *Educ*: Merchant Taylors' Sch., Crosby; Univ. of Durham (BA 1970; DipArch 1971; PhD 1977); Univ. of Lund. FSAScot 1980; MCIfA (MIFA 1985); FSA 1986. Lectr, 1974–83, Sen. Lectr, 1983–95, Reader, 1995–96, in Archaeology, Univ. of Bradford. Vis. Prof. of Archaeol., Univ. of Oxford, 2010–. Cathedral Archaeologist, Bradford Cathedral, 1990–99. Registered Forensic Practitioner, 2003–; Dir, Centre for Internat. Forensic Assistance, 2003–05. Mem., Royal Commn on Ancient and Histl Monuments of Scotland, 2004–15. FCSFS (FFSSoc 2007). *Publications*: Rescue Excavations on the Brough of Birsay, Orkney, 1986; (with I. B. M. Ralston) Archaeological Resource Management in the UK, 1993; (with C. Roberts and A. Martin) Studies in Crime: an introduction to forensic archaeology, 1996; Fair Isle: the archaeology of an island community, 1996; (with I. B. M. Ralston) The Archaeology of Britain: an introduction, 1998, 2nd edn 2010; (with M. Cox) Advances in Forensic Archaeology, 2005; Investigations in Sanday, Orkney: vol. 1, Excavations at Pool, Sanday, 2007; (with A. Woodward) An Examination of Prehistoric Stone Bracers from Britain, 2011; (with B. Simpson and C. Sturdy Colls) Forensic Approaches to Buried Remains, 2013; (with A. Woodward) Ritual in Early Bronze Age Grave Goods, 2015; The Small Isles, 2016. *Recreations*: rowing, watching football, walking the dog. *Address*: School of Classics, Ancient History and Archaeology, Arts Building, University of Birmingham, Birmingham B15 2TT. *T*: (0121) 414 5497.

**HUNTER, Keith Robert**, OBE 1981; British Council Director, Italy, 1990–96; *b* 29 May 1936; *s* of Robert Ernest Williamson and Winifred Mary Hunter; *m* 1st, 1959, Ann Patricia Fuller (marr. diss. 1989); one *s* two *d*; 2nd, 1991, Victoria Solomonidis. *Educ*: Hymers Coll., Hull; Magdalen Coll., Oxford (MA); Sch. of African and Oriental Studies, Univ. of London; Chinese Univ. of Hong Kong; Inst. of Educn, Univ. of London. Joined British Council, 1962; Lectr, Royal Sch. of Admin, Phnom Penh, 1960–64; Schs Recruitment Dept, 1964–66; SOAS, 1966–67; Asst Rep., Hong Kong, 1967–69; Dir, Penang, 1970–72; Dep. Rep., Kuala Lumpur, 1972–74; London Univ. Inst. of Educn, 1974–75; Rep., Algeria, 1975–78; First Sec. (Cultural), subseq. Cultural Counsellor (British Council Rep.), China, 1979–82; Sec. of Bd, and Hd of Dir-Gen.'s Dept, 1982–85; Controller, Arts Div., 1985–90. Trustee, British Sch. at Rome, 1997–2001. Chm., Parkhouse Arts Trust, 1999–. *Recreations*: music, printmaking, restoration. *Address*: 15 Queensdale Road, W11 4SB.

**HUNTER, Sir Laurence (Colvin)**, Kt 1995; CBE 1987; FRSE 1986; Professor of Applied Economics, University of Glasgow, 1970–2003, now Professor Emeritus; *b* 8 Aug. 1934; *s* of Laurence O. and Jessie P. Hunter; *m* 1958, Evelyn Margaret (*née* Green); three *s* one *d*. *Educ*: Hillhead High Sch., Glasgow; Univ. of Glasgow (MA); University Coll., Oxford (DPhil). Asst, Manchester Univ., 1958–59; National Service, 1959–61; Post-Doctoral Fellow, Univ. of Chicago, 1961–62; University of Glasgow: Lectr, 1962; Sen. Lectr, 1967; Titular Prof., 1969; Vice-Principal, 1982–86; Dir of External Relations, 1987–90; Dir, Business Sch., 1996–99. Member: Ct of Inquiry into miners' strike, 1972; Council, Advisory, Conciliation and Arbitration Service, 1974–86; Royal Commn on Legal Services in Scotland, 1976–80; Council, ESRC, 1989–92; Chairman: Post Office Arbitration Tribunal, 1974–92; Police Negotiating Bd, 1987–99 (Dep. Chm., 1980–86). Pres., Scottish Econ. Soc., 1993–96; Treas., RSE, 1999–2004. DUniv Paisley, 1999. *Publications*: (with G. L. Reid) Urban Worker Mobility, 1968; (with D. J. Robertson) Economics of Wages and Labour, 1969, 2nd edn (with C. Mulvey), 1981; (with G. L. Reid and D. Boddy) Labour Problems of Technological Change, 1970; (with A. W. J. Thomson) The Nationalised Transport Industries, 1973; (with R. B. McKersie) Pay, Productivity and Collective Bargaining, 1973; (with L. Baddon *et al.*) People's Capitalism, 1989; other pubns in economics and industrial relations. *Recreations*: golf, painting. *Address*: 7 Boclair Crescent, Bearsden, Glasgow G61 2AG. *T*: (0141) 563 7135.

**HUNTER, Mack Robert**; a District Judge (Magistrates' Courts), since 2004; *b* 21 Oct. 1954; *s* of Mack and Joan Hunter; *m* 1996, Margaret (*née* Campbell); one *s* one *d*. *Educ*: Sevenoaks Sch.; Worcester Coll., Oxford (MA). Called to the Bar, Gray's Inn, 1979; in practice as barrister, 1979–2004; Actg Stipendiary Magistrate, then Dep. Dist Judge, 1998–2004. *Recreations*: swimming, walking, history, spending time with family and friends. *Address*: c/o Chief Magistrates' Office, Westminster Magistrates' Court, 181 Marylebone Road, NW1 5BR.

**HUNTER, Mark James**; *b* 25 July 1957; *s* of Arthur Brian Hunter and Betty Elizabeth Mary Hunter; *m* 1st, 1997, Lesley Graham (*d* 2013); one *s* one *d*; 2nd, 2017, Rachel Wood. *Educ*: Audenshaw Grammar Sch. Employed in newspaper advertising industry, latterly as business develt manager, local newspaper div., Guardian Media Gp. Member (Lib Dem): Tameside MBC, 1980–89; Stockport MBC, 1996–2005, 2016– (Chm., Educn Cttee; Dep. Leader, 2001–02; Leader, 2002–05). Contested: (Liberal SDP Alliance) Ashton under Lyne, 1987; (Lib Dem) Stockport, 2001. MP (Lib Dem) Cheadle, July 2005–2015; contested (Lib Dem) same seat, 2015, 2017. Lib Dem spokesman on foreign affairs, 2007, dep. spokesperson on transport and PPS to Lib Dem Leader, 2007–10; Lib Dem Dep. Chief Whip, 2010–15; an Asst Govt Whip, 2010–14. Member: Nat. Trust; Amnesty Internat.; CAMRA.

**HUNTER, Prof. Michael Cyril William**, FSA; FRHistS; FBA 2007; Professor of History, Birkbeck College, University of London, 1992–2011, now Emeritus; *b* 22 April 1949; *s* of Francis Hunter and Olive Hunter (*née* Williams). *Educ*: Christ's Hospital; Jesus Coll., Cambridge (BA 1971, MA 1975); Worcester Coll., Oxford (DPhil 1975). Research Fellow: Worcester Coll., Oxford, 1972–75; Univ. of Reading, 1975–76; Birkbeck College, University of London: Lectr in History, 1976–84; Reader in History, 1984–92. Longstanding activist on issues concerning historic preservation; also involved in projects for making digital resources available online. *Publications*: John Aubrey and the Realm of Learning, 1975; Science and Society in Restoration England, 1981; The Victorian Villas of Hackney, 1981; (with Annabel Gregory) An Astrological Diary of the Seventeenth Century, 1988; Establishing the New Science, 1989; (jtly) Avebury Reconsidered, 1991; The Royal Society and its Fellows 1660–1700, 1982, rev. edn 1994; Robert Boyle by

Himself and his Friends, 1994; Science and the Shape of Orthodoxy, 1995; (ed) Preserving the Past, 1996; (ed) Archives of the Scientific Revolution, 1998; (ed with Edward B. Davis) The Works of Robert Boyle, vols 1–7, 1999, vols 8–14, 2000; Robert Boyle: scrupulosity and science, 2000; (ed jtly) The Correspondence of Robert Boyle, 6 vols, 2001; The Occult Laboratory, 2001; (jtly) London's Leonardo, 2003; The Boyle Papers, 2007; Editing Early Modern Texts, 2007; Boyle: between God and science, 2009 (Samuel Pepys Award, 2011; Roy G. Neville Prize, 2011); (ed) Printed Images in Early Modern Britain, 2010; Boyle Studies, 2015; (with J. Bennett) The Image of Restoration Science, 2017; The Decline of Magic, 2020. *Recreations:* book-collecting, motorcycling, historic buildings. *Address:* Exmouth House, Exmouth Place, Hastings, East Sussex TN34 3JA. *T:* (01424) 430727.

**HUNTER, Paul Anthony**, FRCS, FRCP, FRCOphth; Consultant Ophthalmic Surgeon, King's College Hospital, 1982–2013, Honorary Consultant, 2013–14; President, Royal College of Ophthalmologists, 2000–03; *b* 22 Nov. 1944; *s* of Gordon Nicholson Hunter and Kathleen Margaret (*née* Tyldesley); *m* 1971, Elizabeth Alex Pearse; one *s* one *d*. *Educ:* Leys Sch., Cambridge; Queens' Coll., Cambridge (BA Hons 1966; MB BChir 1969); Middlesex Hosp. Med. Sch. DO RCP&RCS 1974. FRCS 1977; FRCOphth 1993; FRCP 2002. Resident Surgical Officer, Moorfields Eye Hosp., 1976–79; Sen. Registrar, Middx Hosp., 1980–81; Hon. Lectr, King's Coll. Med. Sch., London Univ., 1982–2013. Chm., Bd of Trustees, British Council for Prevention of Blindness, 2015–. *Publications:* (ed jtly) Atlas of Clinical Ophthalmology, 1988, 3rd edn 2005; contribs on cornea and external eye disease to professional jls. *Recreations:* travel, ski-ing, gardening, grandchildren.

**HUNTER, Prof. Peter John**, DPhil; FRS 2006; FRSNZ; Professor of Engineering Science, since 1997, and Director, Bioengineering Institute, since 2001, University of Auckland; *b* Auckland, NZ, 30 July 1948. *Educ:* Univ. of Auckland (BE 1971; ME 1972); Univ. of Oxford (DPhil 1975). Res. Fellow, Rutherford Lab., 1975–77; Fellow, St Catherine's Coll., Oxford, 1975–77; Lectr in Engrg Sci., Univ. of Auckland, 1978–97. Dir of Computational Physiol., Univ. of Oxford. Co-Chm., Physiome Cttee, IUPS. FRSNZ 1994. Rutherford Medal, Royal Soc. of NZ, 2009. *Publications:* articles in learned jls. *Address:* Bioengineering Institute, Faculty of Engineering, University of Auckland, Private Bag 92019, Auckland Mail Centre, Auckland 1142, New Zealand.

**HUNTER, Sir Philip (John)**, Kt 2008; CBE 1999; PhD; Chief Schools Adjudicator, 2002–09; Chair, North Staffordshire Combined Healthcare Trust, 2009–12; *b* 23 Nov. 1939; *m* Ruth Bailey; two *s* one *d*. *Educ:* Univ. of Durham (BSc 1962); Univ. of Newcastle upon Tyne (PhD 1965). Lectr, Univ. of Khartoum, 1965–67; Senior Scientific Officer: ARC, Cambridge, 1967–69; DES, 1969–71; Course Dir, CS Staff Coll., 1971–73; posts at DES, including science, schools, finance and Private Office, 1973–79; Dep. Chief Educn Officer, ILEA, 1979–85; Chief Educn Officer, then Dir of Educn, Staffs, 1985–2000. Dir, Staffs TEC, 1990–2001; Member of Council: Keele Univ., 1987–99; BTEC, 1990–95; Member: Nat. Council for Educnl Technol., 1986–91; Nat. Curriculum Wkg Gp on Design and Technol., 1988–89; Design Council Educn Cttee, 1990–94; Qualifications and Curriculum Authy, 1997–2001. Chm., West Midlands Chief Educn Officers, 1995–97; Pres., Soc. of Educn Officers, 1998–99 (Vice-Pres., 1997). Vis. Prof. of Educn, Keele Univ., 1998–2005. Trustee, Staffs Wildlife Trust, 2012–19. Chm., Little Eaton Neighbourhood Plan Steering Gp, 2018–. Hon. DTech Staffs, 1999. *Publications:* (jtly) Terrestrial Slugs, 1970; (jtly) Pulmonates, 1978; (ed) Developing Education: fifteen years on, 1999; papers on ecology of invertebrates; contrib. educnl jls on educn policy matters. *Recreation:* gardening. *Address:* Park Farm, Vicarage Lane, Little Eaton, Derbyshire DE21 5EA.

**HUNTER, Prof. Richard Lawrence**, PhD; FBA 2013; Regius Professor of Greek, Cambridge University, since 2001; Fellow, Trinity College, Cambridge, since 2001; *b* 30 Oct. 1953; *s* of John Lawrence Hunter and Ruth Munro Hunter; *m* 1978, Iris Temperli; one *s* one *d*. *Educ:* Cranbrook Sch., Sydney; Univ. of Sydney (BA Hons 1974); Pembroke Coll., Cambridge (PhD 1979). University of Cambridge: Fellow, 1977–2001, Dir of Studies in Classics, 1979–99, Asst Tutor, 1985–87, Tutor for Admissions, 1987–93, Pembroke Coll.; Univ. Lectr in Classics, 1987–97; Reader in Greek and Latin Lit., 1997–2001; Chm., Sch. of Arts and Humanities, 2007–08. Visiting Professor: Princeton Univ., 1991–92, 2012–13; Univ. of Virginia, 1979, 1984. Pres., Council, Aristotle Univ. of Thessaloniki, 2013–16. MAE 2013. Fellow, Alexander S. Onassis Public Benefit Foundn, 2006. Ed., Jl of Hellenic Studies, 1995–2000. Corresp. Fellow, 2001, Foreign Fellow, 2014, Acad. of Athens; Hon. Fellow, Aust. Acad. of Humanities, 2005. Hon. Dr Phil.: Thessaloniki, 2004; Ioannina, 2016. Premio Anassilaos, Reggio Calabria, 2006. *Publications:* Eubulus: the fragments, 1983; A Study of Daphnis and Chloe, 1983; The New Comedy of Greece and Rome, 1985; Apollonius of Rhodes, Argonautica III, 1989; The Argonautica of Apollonius, Literary Studies, 1993; trans., Jason and the Golden Fleece (The Argonautica), 1993; Theocritus and the Archaeology of Greek Poetry, 1996; (ed) Studies in Heliodorus, 1998; Theocritus: a selection, 1999; Theocritus, Encomium of Ptolemy, 2003; Plato's Symposium, 2004; (with M. Fantuzzi) Tradition and Innovation in Hellenistic Poetry, 2004 (Italian edn 2002); (ed) The Hesiodic Catalogue of Women: constructions and reconstructions, 2005; The Shadow of Callimachus, 2006; On Coming After (collected papers), 2008; (ed with I. Rutherford) Wandering Poets in Ancient Greek Culture, 2009; Critical Moments in Classical Literature, 2009; (ed with K. Carvounis) Signs of Life?: studies in later Greek poetry, 2009; (with D. Russell) Plutarch: how to study poetry (De audiendis poetis), 2011; Plato and the Traditions of Ancient Literature, 2012; Hesiodic Voices, 2014; Apollonius of Rhodes, Argonautica IV, 2015; (ed with S. Oakley) Latin Literature and its Transmission, 2017; (ed with A. Uhlig) Imagining Reperformance in Ancient Culture, 2017; The Measure of Homer, 2018; (ed with C. de Jonge) Dionysius of Halicarnassus and Augustan Rome, 2019; articles and reviews in learned jls. *Recreation:* travel. *Address:* Faculty of Classics, Sidgwick Avenue, Cambridge CB3 9DA. *T:* (01223) 335152.

**HUNTER, Robert Walter**; Lord-Lieutenant for Shetland, since 2011; *b* 1949; *m* 1971, Mabel Joan Hawick; two *s* one *d*. *Educ:* Strathclyde Univ. (BSc Naval Architecture). Work in shipbuilding and marine electrical equipment supply, then fish processing industry; Manager: Shetland Oil Industries Gp, 1990–2002; Grimista Property Ltd, 2003–04; Electrical Manager, Camvo 86 Ltd, 2004–06. Chairman: Shetland Charitable Trust; Hjaltland Housing Assoc. DL Shetland, 2002. *Address:* Millburn, Bridge End, Shetland ZE2 9LD.

**HUNTER, Prof. Rosemary Claire**, JSD; FAcSS; Professor of Law and Socio-Legal Studies, University of Kent, since 2018; *b* Sydney, Australia, 28 Feb. 1962; *d* of Cornelius Newbold Hunter and Jean Elizabeth Hunter; *m* 1987, Laurence James Duggan. *Educ:* Presbyterian Ladies' Coll., Melbourne; Univ. of Melbourne (LLB Hons, BA Hons); Stanford Univ. (JSM; JSD). Lectr, Sen. Lectr, then Associate Prof., Univ. of Melbourne, 1989–99; Principal Researcher, Justice Res. Centre, Sydney, 1998–99; Professor of Law: Griffith Univ., Brisbane, 2000–06; Univ. of Kent, 2008–14; Prof. of Law and Socio-Legal Studies, QMUL, 2014–18. Sen. Associate Res. Fellow, Inst. of Advanced Legal Studies, 2016–; Hon. Adjunct Prof., Univ. of Technol., Sydney, 2018–. Academic Mem., Family Justice Council, 2016–. Pt-time Hearing Comr, Aust. Human Rights and Equal Opportunity Commn, 1994–97; Mem., Qld Cttee, Aust. Fulbright Commn, 2000–04. Chair: Wkg Gp on Gender and Law, Res. Cttee on Sociol. of Law, Internat. Sociol Assoc., 2003–10; Socio-Legal Studies Assoc., 2011–17. Member: Council, JUSTICE, 2012–18; Governing Bd, Oñati Internat. Inst. for Sociol. of Law, 2018–; Private Law Wkg Gp, 2019–; MoJ Expert Panel on Domestic Abuse in Private Law Children Cases, 2019. FAcSS 2012. Academic Editor, Feminist Legal Studies jl, 2006–10; Founding Editor, feminists@law jl, 2011–. *Publications:* Indirect Discrimination in the Workplace, 1992; (ed jtly) Thinking About Law, 1995; (ed jtly) Changing Law: rights, regulation and reconciliation, 2005; (ed jtly) Choice and Consent: feminist engagements with law and subjectivity, 2007; (ed) Rethinking Equality Projects in Law, 2008; Domestic Violence Law Reform and Women's Experience in Court, 2008; (ed jtly) Feminist Judgments: from theory to practice, 2010; (with Beth Gaze) Enforcing Human Rights in Australia, 2010; (ed jtly) Australian Feminist Judgments, 2014; (ed jtly) Feminist Judgments of Aotearoa New Zealand, 2017; (jtly) Mapping Paths to Family Justice, 2017. *Address:* Kent Law School, Eliot College, University of Kent, Canterbury CT2 7NS.

**HUNTER, Sir Thomas (Blane)**, Kt 2005; Chairman: West Coast Capital, since 1998; Hunter Foundation, since 1998; *b* 6 May 1961; *m* 1990, Marion McKillop; two *s* one *d*. *Educ:* Strathclyde Univ. (BA Mktg and Econs). Founder: Sports Div., 1984, sold 1998; Hunter Foundn, 1998; West Coast Capital, 2001. Founder and Mem. Bd, Clinton-Hunter Develt Initiative, 2005–. Beacon Prize, 2004; Carnegie Medal of Philanthropy, 2004. *Recreations:* ski-ing, water sports, music. *Address:* Marathon House, Olympic Business Park, Drybridge Road, Dundonald KA2 9AE. *T:* (01563) 852226, *Fax:* (01563) 850091.

**HUNTER, Dr Tony, (Anthony Rex Hunter)**, FRS 1987; Professor, since 1982, and Renato Dulbecco Chair, since 2011, Molecular and Cell Biology Laboratory, Salk Institute, La Jolla, California; concurrently Adjunct Professor of Biology and Pharmacology, University of California, San Diego; *b* 23 Aug. 1943; *s* of Ranulph Rex Hunter and Nellie Ruby Elsie Hunter (*née* Hitchcock); *m* 1969, Philippa Charlotte Marrack (marr. diss. 1974); *m* 1992, Jennifer Ann Maureen Price; two *s*. *Educ:* Felsted Sch., Essex; Gonville and Caius Coll., Cambridge (BA, MA, PhD). Research Fellow, Christ's Coll., Cambridge, 1968–71 and 1973–74; Salk Inst., La Jolla: Res. Associate, 1971–73; Asst Prof., 1975–78; Associate Prof., 1978–82; Dir, Salk Inst. Cancer Centre, 2008–16. American Cancer Soc. Res. Prof., 1992–2008. Einstein Prof., Chinese Acad. of Scis, 2013. Assoc. Mem., EMBO, 1992. FRSA 1989; FAACR 2013; Fellow, Amer. Acad. of Arts and Scis, 1992; For. Associate, US Nat. Acad. of Scis, 1998; Member: Nat. Acad. of Medicine (formerly Inst. of Medicine), US Nat. Acads, 2004; Amer. Philos. Soc., 2006. Katharine Berkan Judd Award, Meml Sloan-Kettering Cancer Center, 1992; Gairdner Foundn Internat. Award, 1994; Hopkins Meml Medal, Biochemical Soc., 1994; Mott Prize, Gen. Motors Cancer Res. Foundn, 1994; Feodor Lynen Medal, Univ. of Miami, 1999; J. Allyn Taylor Internat. Prize in Medicine, John P. Robarts Res. Inst. and C. H. Stiller Meml Foundn, 2000; Keio Med. Sci. Prize, Keio Univ. Med. Sci. Fund, Tokyo, 2001; Sergio Lombroso Award in Cancer Res., Weizman Inst. Sci., 2003; Amer. Cancer Soc. Medal of Honor, 2004; Kirk A. Landon Amer. Assoc. for Cancer Res. Prize, 2004; Prince of Asturias Award, 2004; Louis Gross Horowitz Prize, 2004; Wolf Prize in Medicine, 2005; Daniel Nathans Meml Award, Van Andel Inst., 2005; Pasarow Award in Cancer, Robert J. and Claire Pasarow Foundn, 2007; Herbert Tabor Award, Amer. Soc. of Biochem. and Molecular Biol., 2007; Clifford Prize for Cancer Res., Inst. of Med. and Veterinary Sci., Adelaide, 2007; Signal Transduction Soc. Hon. Medal, 2011; Royal Medal, Royal Soc., 2014; BBVA Foundn Frontiers of Knowledge Award in Biomedicine, 2014; Sjöberg Prize for Cancer Res., Swedish Acad. of Scis, 2017; Internat. Award for Extraordinary Achievement in Cancer Res., Pezcoller Foundn-Amer. Assoc. for Cancer, 2018; Tang Prize for Biopharmaceutical Sci., 2018; Triumph Award, Amer. Cancer Soc., 2018. *Publications:* numerous, in leading scientific jls. *Recreations:* white water rafting, exploring the Baja peninsula. *Address:* Molecular and Cell Biology Laboratory, The Salk Institute, 10010 North Torrey Pines Road, La Jolla, CA 92037, USA. *T:* (858) 4534100, ext. 1385, *Fax:* (858) 4574765. *E:* hunter@salk.edu.

**HUNTER, William John**, MB, BS; FRCP, FRCPE, FFOM; Director, Public Health, European Commission, 1999–2000; *b* 5 April 1937; *m*; two *s* one *d*. *Educ:* Westminster Medical Sch. (MB, BS). LRCP 1961, FRCP 1995; FRCPE 1999; MRCS 1961; FFOM 1978. Commission of the European Communities: Principal Administrator, 1974–82; Hd of Div., Industrial Medicine and Hygiene, 1982–88; Dir, Public Health and Safety at Work, 1988–99. Hon. DG, EC, 2000–. Permt Mem., Caducée Gp, Commissariat Gén. du Plan advising Prime Minister of France, 2004–. Internat. Advr, 1998–2007, Mem., European Wkg Gp, 2001–07, RCP. Member: Admin. Bd, Assoc. Internat. des Anciens des Communautés Européennes, 2001–12; Adv. Bd, Inst des Scis de la Santé, 2004–06; Admin. Bd, Ribérac Hosp., 2006–15; Admin. Bd, Centre Hospitalier Intercommunal Ribérac Dronne Double, 2016. Member, Administrative Board: Cercle d'Histoire et de Généalogie du Perigord, 1998–2005; Ensemble Vocal Arnaut de Mareuil, 2004–05. Hon. FFPH (Hon. FFPHM 1997). OStJ 1993. Ed., Internat. Jl of Integrated Care, 1999–2002. *Publications:* over 400 pubns on public health and safety at work. *Recreations:* swimming, diving, music.

**HUNTER, Winston Ronald O'Sullivan**; QC 2000; a Recorder, since 2000; *b* 7 Sept. 1960; *m* 1988, Louise Mary Blackwell; three *s*. *Educ:* Leeds Univ. (LLB 1st Cl. Hons). Called to the Bar, Lincoln's Inn, 1985, Bencher, 2011. *Recreations:* cricket, shooting, antiques. *Address:* 12 Byrom Street, Manchester M3 4PP. *T:* (0161) 829 2100.

**HUNTER BLAIR, Sir Patrick (David)**, 9th Bt *cr* 1786, of Dunskey; owner, Milton of Blairquhan, Ayrshire; *b* 12 May 1958; *s* of Francis John Hunter Blair and of Joyce Adeline Mary (*née* Graham); *S* cousin, 2006; *m* 1984, Marguerite Catherine O'Neill; three *s* (incl. twins) two *d*. *Educ:* Edinburgh Acad.; Univ. of Aberdeen (BSc Forestry). FICFor. Dir of Policy Standards, NI Forest Service, 1998–2005. Non-exec. Dir, Scottish Natural Heritage, 2007–13. Chm., S Scotland Regl Forestry Forum, 2010–; Pres., Royal Scottish Forestry Soc., 2015–17. *Recreations:* family, friends, forestry and fishing. *Heir:* *s* Ronan Patrick Hunter Blair, *b* 10 Feb. 1995. *Address:* Milton of Blairquhan, Maybole, Ayrshire KA19 7LY.

**HUNTING, Richard Hugh**, CBE 2010; Chairman, Hunting plc, 1991–2017 (Deputy Chairman, 1989–91); *b* 30 July 1946; *s* of late Charles Patrick Maule Hunting, CBE, TD and Diana, *d* of Brig. A. B. P. Pereira, DSO; *m* 1970, Penelope, *d* of Col L. L. Fleming, MBE, MC; one *s* two *d*. *Educ:* Rugby Sch.; Sheffield Univ. (BEng); Manchester Business Sch. (MBA). Joined Hunting Gp, 1972; worked at Hunting Surveys and Consultants, Field Aviation, E. A. Gibson Shipbrokers, Hunting Oilfield Services, Hunting Engineering; Director: Hunting Associated Industries, 1986–89 (Chm., 1989); Hunting Petroleum Services, 1989; Hunting plc, 1989– (non-exec. Dir, 2011–). Dir, Yule Catto & Co. plc, 2000–09. Non-exec. Dir, Royal Brompton and Harefield NHS Foundn Trust (formerly NHS Trust), 2007–15. Mem. Council, CBI, 1992–97. Comr, Royal Hosp., Chelsea, 2002–08; Mem., Adv. Bd, Greenwich Hosp., 2011–. Trustee: Geffrye Mus., 1995–2009 (Chm., 2000–09); Battle of Britain Meml Trust, 1998– (Chm., 2000–); Chm., Royal Brompton and Harefield Hosps Charity, 2012–. Mem. Court, Ironmongers' Co., 1986– (Master, 1996). *Recreations:* arts, ski-ing, family history. *Address:* (office) 5 Hanover Square, W1S 1HQ. *T:* (020) 7321 0123. *Clubs:* Boodle's, Chelsea Arts, Hurlingham.

**HUNTINGDON**, 17th Earl of, *cr* 1529 (by some reckonings 16th Earl of); **William Edward Robin Hood Hastings Bass**, LVO 1999; farmer and consultant; *b* 30 Jan. 1948; *s* of Capt. Peter Robin Hood Hastings Bass (who assumed additional surname of Bass by deed poll, 1954) (*d* 1964); *g s* of 13th Earl and Priscilla Victoria, *d* of Capt. Sir Malcolm Bullock, 1st Bt, MBE; *S* kinsman, 1990; *m* 1989, Sue Warner (marr. diss. 2001). *Educ:*

Winchester; Trinity Coll., Cambridge. Began as racehorse trainer, 1976; Trainer, West Ilsley Stables, Berks, 1989–98. *Heir: b* Hon. John Peter Robin Hood Hastings Bass [*b* 1954; *m* 1982, Sophie, *d* of Peter Ewald Scarisbrick; one *d* (and one *d* decd)]. *Address:* Wells Head House, Kingsclere, near Newbury, Berks RG20 5PX.

**HUNTINGDON AND WISBECH, Archdeacon of;** *see* McCurdy, Ven. H. K.

**HUNTINGFIELD,** 7th Baron *cr* 1796 (Ire.); **Joshua Charles Vanneck;** Bt 1751; Lecturer, Cambridge Enterprise Agency, since 1999; Development Manager, Young Enterprise Cambridgeshire, 2001–08; *b* 10 Aug. 1954; *o s* of 6th Baron Huntingfield and Janetta Lois, *er d* of Captain R. H. Errington, RN; *S* father, 1994; *m* 1982, Arabella Mary (*d* 2011), *d* of A. H. J. Fraser, MC; four *s* one *d* (incl. twin *s*). *Educ:* West Downs, Winchester; Eton; Magdalene Coll., Cambridge (MA). ACA. With Gerald Eve & Co., London, 1976, Chestertons, London, 1977–82; Highland Wineries, Inverness, 1982–87; accountant: Deloitte Haskin & Sells, later Coopers & Lybrand, Cambridge, 1987–91; NFU Mutual, Cambridge, 1993–96; Stafford & Co., Cambridge, 1996–2001. *Recreations:* family, history, writing. *Heir: s* Hon. Gerard Charles Alastair Vanneck, *b* 12 March 1985. *Address:* 69 Barrons Way, Comberton, Cambridge CB23 7EQ. *Club:* Pratt's.

**HUNTINGFORD, Richard Norman Legh;** Chairman: Future plc, since 2017; Prince's Trust Trading Ltd, since 2010; *b* Winchester, 14 May 1956; *s* of Jonathan and Joanna Huntingford; *m* 1996, Nicky; one *s* two *d* and one step *s*. *Educ:* Radley Coll. FCA 1979. With Peat Marwick, subseq. KPMG, 1975–87; Dir, 1987–2000, Chief Exec., 2000–07, Chrysalis plc; Chairman: Virgin Radio, 2007–08; Boomerang Plus plc, 2008–12; UTV Media plc, subseq. Wireless Gp plc, 2012–16. Non-executive Director: JP Morgan Mid Cap Investment Trust plc, 2013–; Bankers Investment Trust plc, 2018–. *Recreations:* tennis, cricket, Rugby, travel, food. *Clubs:* MCC, Queen's, Garrick.

**HUNTINGTON-WHITELEY, Sir Leopold Maurice,** 5th Bt *cr* 1918, of Grimley, Worcester; *b* 15 July 1965; *s* of Lt Comdr Sir (John) Miles Huntington-Whiteley, 4th Bt and HIllH Countess Victoria zu Castell-Rüdenhausen; *S* father, 2019, but his name does not appear on the Official Roll of the Baronetage.

**HUNTINGTOWER, Lord; James Patrick Grant of Rothiemurchus;** *b* 14 Sept. 1977; *s* and heir of Earl of Dysart, *qv*; *m* 2009, Daisy Sandi Ziani, *d* of Mark de Ferranti; two *s*. *Educ:* Eton; Edinburgh Univ. (BSc 2003). ACA 2004. *Heir: s* Hon. John Peter Grant, yr of Rothiemurchus, Master of Huntingtower, *b* 13 July 2011.

**HUNTLEY, Andrew John Mack,** FRICS; Chairman, Insignia Richard Ellis (formerly Richard Ellis, Chartered Surveyors), 1993–2001; *b* 24 Jan. 1939; *s* of William Mack Huntley and Muriel Huntley (*née* Akehurst); *m* 1963, Juliet Vivien Collum; three *d*. *Educ:* Monkton Combe Sch., Bath. FRICS 1963. Davis & Son, Bristol, 1956–58; D. Ward & Son, Plymouth, 1958–61; Davige & Partners, London, 1961–65; with Richard Ellis, subseq. Insignia Richard Ellis, 1965–2001. Director: Pillar Property, 2002–05; Miller Gp, 2002–; Charities Official Investment Fund, 2004–08. Chairman: Pancetltica Hldgs Ltd, 2007–09; Metric Property Investments plc, 2010–13; Dir, Capital & Counties plc, 2010–; Sen. Ind. Dir, Intu Properties plc (formerly Capital Shopping Centres), 2010–. *Recreations:* shooting, tennis. *Address:* Meadow Hills, Stedham, W Sussex GU29 0PT. *Club:* Boodle's.

**HUNTLEY, Gillian Lesley;** *see* Slater, G. L.

**HUNTLEY, Maj. Gen. Michael,** CB 2005; Director General Logistics (formerly Equipment Support) (Land), 2002–06; Defence Analyst, Louisburg Keane Ltd, since 2006; *b* 24 Dec. 1950. *Educ:* BSc. Commnd REME, 1972; psc; hcsc; rcds; Dep. COS 1st (UK) Armoured Div.; Dir Equipment Support (Army); Comdr Equipment Support, HQ Land Comd; Dir Support Ops, Equipment Support (Land), until 2002. Col Comdt, REME, 2004–10. *Address:* c/o Army Personnel Centre, Kentigern House, 65 Brown Street, Glasgow G2 8EX.

**HUNTLY,** 13th Marquess of, *cr* 1599 (Scot.); **Granville Charles Gomer Gordon;** Earl of Huntly, 1450; Earl of Aboyne, Baron Gordon of Strathavon and Glenlivet, 1660; Baron Meldrum (UK), 1815; Premier Marquess of Scotland; Chief of House of Gordon; *b* 4 Feb. 1944; *s* of 12th Marquess of Huntly and Hon. Mary Pamela Berry (*d* 1998), *d* of 1st Viscount Kemsley; *S* father, 1987; *m* 1st, 1972, Jane Elizabeth Angela (marr. diss. 1990), *d* of late Col Alistair Gibb and Lady McCorquodale of Newton; one *s* two *d*; 2nd, 1991, Mrs Catheryn Millbourn; one *d*. *Educ:* Gordonstoun. Chm., Cock o' the North Liqueur Co. Ltd, 1998–; Dir, Hintlesham Hldgs Ltd, 1987–2005. *Heir: s* Earl of Aboyne, *qv*. *Address:* Aboyne Castle, Aberdeenshire AB34 5JP. *T:* (01339) 887778.
*See also* Baron Cranworth.

**HUNTON, Christopher John;** Global Managing Partner, WPP, since 2007; *b* 12 Aug. 1961; *s* of Thomas and Elsie Hunton; *m* 1992, Dr Sara Hunton; one *s* one *d*. *Educ:* Bedford Coll., London (BA Hons); Hughes Hall, Cambridge (PGCE 1983). Teacher, Knox Sch., NY, 1984–85; Asst Housemaster, Wellingborough Sch., Northants, 1985–86; Account Manager, Foote, Cone & Belding, 1986–88; Account Dir, Ayer Barker, 1988–90; Bd Account Dir, Young & Rubicam, 1990–94; Gp Account Dir, Lowe Howard-Spink, 1994–98; CEO, McCann-Erickson, 1998–2004; Man. Dir, Lowe London, 2005–07. *Recreations:* family, sport, musical theatre, fishing.

**HUNTSMAN, Peter William,** FRICS; FAAV; Principal, College of Estate Management, University of Reading, 1981–92, Hon. Fellow, 1993; *b* 11 Aug. 1935; *s* of late William and Lydia Irene Huntsman (*née* Clegg); *m* 1st, 1961, Janet Mary Bell (marr. diss.); one *s* one *d*; 2nd, 1984, Cicely Eleanor (*née* Tamblin) (*d* 2013). *Educ:* Hymers Coll., Hull; Coll. of Estate Management, Univ. of London (BSc Estate Man.). Agricultural Land Service, Dorset and Northumberland, 1961–69; Kellogg Foundn Fellowship, Cornell Univ., USA, 1969–70; Principal Surveyor, London, ADAS, 1971–76; Divl Surveyor, Surrey, Middx and Sussex, 1976–81. Liveryman, Chartered Surveyors' Co., 1985; Freeman, City of London, 1985. Hon. FSVA 1993. *Publications:* (contrib.) Walmsley's Rural Estate Management, 6th edn 1978; contribs to professional jls. *Recreations:* sport, Sussex countryside, reading. *Address:* 8 Durrants House, Durrants Drive, Faygate, W Sussex RH12 4GB. *T:* (01293) 851198.

**HUOT, Prof. Sylvia,** PhD; FBA 2011; Professor of Medieval French Literature, University of Cambridge, 2007–20; Fellow, Pembroke College, Cambridge, since 1996. *Educ:* Univ. of Calif, Santa Cruz (BA 1976); Princeton Univ. (PhD 1982). William Rainey Harper Post-doctoral Teaching Fellow, Univ. of Chicago, 1982–84; Asst Prof. of French, later Assoc. Prof., then Presidential Res. Prof., Dept of Foreign Langs and Lits, Northern Illinois Univ., 1986–95; Lectr, 1996–99, Reader in Medieval French Lit., 1999–2007, French Dept, Univ. of Cambridge. *Publications:* From Song to Book, 1987; (ed jtly) Rethinking the Romance of the Rose, 1992; The Romance of the Rose and its Medieval Readers, 1993; Allegorical Play in the Old French Motet, 1997; Madness in Medieval French Literature, 2003; Postcolonial Fictions in the Roman de Perceforest, 2007; Dreams of Lovers and Lies of Poets: poetry, knowledge and desire in the Roman de la Rose, 2010; Outsiders: the humanity and inhumanity of giants in medieval French prose romance, 2016.

**HUPPERT, Prof. Herbert Eric,** ScD; FRS 1987; FRSN; Professor of Theoretical Geophysics and Foundation Director, Institute of Theoretical Geophysics, Cambridge University, 1989–2011, now Professor Emeritus; Leverhulme Emeritus Research Fellow, 2013–15; Fellow of King's College, Cambridge, since 1970; Dean of Science Professor, University of Bristol, since 2012; Professor, School of Mathematics and Statistics, University of New South Wales, since 2012 (Visiting Professor, 1991–96); *b* 26 Nov. 1943; *er c* of Leo Huppert and Alice Huppert (*née* Neuman); *m* 1966, Felicia Adina Huppert (*née* Ferster), PhD; two *s*. *Educ:* Sydney Boys' High Sch.; Sydney Univ. (BSc 1963); ANU (MSc 1964); Univ. of California at San Diego (MS 1966, PhD 1968); Univ. of Cambridge (MA 1971, ScD 1985). ICI Research Fellow, 1968–70; University of Cambridge: Asst Dir of Research, 1970–81; Lectr in Applied Maths, 1981–88; BP Venture Unit Sen. Res. Fellow, 1983–89; Reader in Geophysical Dynamics, 1988–89. Visiting research scientist: ANU; Univ. of California, San Diego; Canterbury Univ.; Caltech; MIT; Univ. of NSW; Univ. of WA; Univ. of Sydney; Tata Inst., Mumbai; Weizmann Inst. of Sci., Rehovot; Woods Hole Oceanographic Inst. Member: NERC, 1993–98; Council, Royal Soc., 2001–03. Adv. Bd, MATRIX, 2016–. MAE 2011. Fellow: Amer. Geophysical Union, 2002; APS, 2004. FRSN 2018. Lectures: Evnin, Princeton, 1995; Midwest Mechanics, 1996–97; Henry Charnock Dist., Southampton Oceanography Centre, 1999; Smiths Industries, Oxford Univ., 1999; Arthur L. Day (also Prize), Nat. Acad. of Sci., USA, 2005; Dist. Israel Pollak, Technion, 2005; Bakerian (also Prize), Royal Soc., 2011. Associate Editor, Jl Fluid Mechanics, 1971–90; Editor, Jl of Soviet Jewry, 1985–; Member, Editorial Board: Philosophical Trans of Royal Soc. (series A), 1994–99; Reports on Progress in Physics, 1997–2003; Geomechanics and Geophys for Geo-Energy and Geo-Resources, 2014–; Subject Editor, Proc. Royal Soc. A, 2016–. William Hopkins Prize, Cambridge Philos. Soc., 2005; Wolfson Merit Award, Royal Soc., 2006; Murchison Medal, London Geol Soc., 2007. *Publications:* approximately 265 papers on applied mathematics, crystal growth, fluid mechanics, geology, geophysics, oceanography and meteorology. *Recreations:* my children, squash, tennis, mountaineering, cycling. *Address:* Institute of Theoretical Geophysics, Department of Applied Mathematics and Theoretical Physics, Centre for Mathematical Sciences, Wilberforce Road, Cambridge CB3 0WA. *T:* (office) (01223) 337853, *Fax:* (01223) 765900. *E:* heh1@esc.cam.ac.uk.
*See also* J. L. Huppert.

**HUPPERT, Julian Leon,** PhD; FRSC; Fellow, and Director, Intellectual Forum, Jesus College, Cambridge, since 2016; *b* 21 July 1978; *s* of Prof. Herbert Eric Huppert, *qv*; partner, Dr Caroline Wright. *Educ:* Trinity Coll., Cambridge (MSci 2000; PhD 2005). FRSC 2013. Business Analyst, Monis Software Ltd, 2000–01; CEO, Cambridge Laboratory Innovations Ltd, 2003–05. Fellow: Trinity Coll., Cambridge, 2004–08; Clare Coll., Cambridge, 2009–16; RCUK Fellow, Cavendish Lab., 2009–12, Lectr, 2012–16, Univ. of Cambridge. Vis. Prof., KCL. Mem. (Lib Dem) Cambridgeshire CC, 2001–09 (Leader, Lib Dem Gp, 2004–07). Contested (Lib Dem) Huntingdon, 2005. MP (Lib Dem) Cambridge, 2010–15; contested (Lib Dem) same seat, 2015, 2017. Mem. Council, Liberty, 2009–10. Lay Mem. (Governance) and Audit Chair, 2015–, Vice-Chair, 2018–, Cambs and Peterborough CCG. Dir, Joseph Rowntree Reform Trust Ltd, 2016–. Sen. Ind. Trustee, Cycling UK, 2017–. FRSA 2017. *Publications:* various scientific papers and political articles. *Recreations:* cycling, hiking. *E:* jlh29@cam.ac.uk.

**HUQ, Dr Rupa Asha;** MP (Lab) Ealing Central and Acton, since 2015; *b* Ealing, 2 April 1972; *d* of late Muhammad Huq and of Roshan Huq. *Educ:* Montpelier Primary Sch.; Notting Hill and Ealing High Sch.; Newnham Coll., Cambridge (BA Hons Social and Pol Scis with Law 1993); Univ. of E London (PhD Cultural Studies 1999). Asst to Carole Tongue, MEP, Strasbourg, 1996; Lectr, Manchester Univ., 1998–2004 (Leverhulme Trust Fellow); Sen. Lectr in Sociol. and Criminol., Kingston Univ., 2004–15. Dep. Mayoress of Ealing, 2010–11. Shadow Minister for Crime and Prevention 2016–17. Member: Regulatory Reform Cttee, 2015–17; Public Affairs and Constitl Reform Cttee, 2017–. Contested (Lab): North West, EP, 2004; Chesham and Amersham, 2005. *Publications:* Beyond Subculture, 2006; On the Edge: the contested cultures of English suburbia, 2013; Making Sense of Suburbia Through Popular Culture, 2013; contrib. articles to Guardian, Tribune, THES. *Address:* House of Commons, SW1A 0AA.

**HURD,** family name of **Baron Hurd of Westwell**.

**HURD OF WESTWELL,** Baron *cr* 1997 (Life Peer), of Westwell in the co. of Oxfordshire; **Douglas Richard Hurd,** CH 1996; CBE 1974; PC 1982; Deputy Chairman, Coutts & Co., 1998–2009; *b* 8 March 1930; *e s* of Baron Hurd (*d* 1966) and Stephanie Corner (*d* 1985); *m* 1st, 1960, Tatiana Elizabeth Michelle (marr. diss. 1982), *d* of A. C. Benedict Eyre, Westburton House, Bury, Sussex; three *s*; 2nd, 1982, Judy (*d* 2008), *d* of Sidney and Pamela Smart; one *s* one *d*. *Educ:* Eton (King's Scholar and Newcastle Scholar; Fellow, 1981–96); Trinity Coll., Cambridge (Major Scholar). Pres., Cambridge Union, 1952. HM Diplomatic Service, 1952–66; served in: Peking, 1954–56; UK Mission to UN, 1956–60; Private Sec. to Perm. Under-Sec. of State, FO, 1960–63; Rome, 1963–66. Joined Conservative Research Dept, 1966; Head of Foreign Affairs Section, 1968; Private Sec. to Leader of the Opposition, 1968–70; Political Sec. to Prime Minister, 1970–74. MP (C): Mid-Oxon, Feb. 1974–1983; Witney, 1983–97. Opposition Spokesman on European Affairs, 1976–79; Minister of State, FCO, 1979–83; Minister of State, Home Office, 1983–84; Sec. of State for NI, 1984–85, for Home Dept, 1985–89; Sec. of State for Foreign and Commonwealth Affairs, 1989–95. Mem., H of L, 1997–2016. Dir, NatWest Gp, 1995–99; Dep. Chm., NatWest Markets, 1995–98; Chm., British Invisibles, 1997–2000; Sen. Advr, Hawkpoint, 2000–11. Member: Royal Commn on H of L reform, 1999; H of L Appointments Commn, 2000–10. Chairman: Prison Reform Trust, 1997–2001 (Hon. Pres., 2001–); CEDR, 2001–04; Canterbury Review Gp, 2000–01. Co-Pres., RIIA, 2001–07. Chm., German British Forum, 2000–05. Vis. Fellow, Nuffield Coll., Oxford, 1978–86. Chm. Booker Prize Judges, 1998. High Steward, Westminster Abbey, 2000–11. *Publications:* The Arrow War, 1967; An End to Promises, 1979; The Search for Peace (televised), 1997; Ten Minutes to Turn the Devil (short stories), 1999; Memoirs, 2003; Robert Peel, 2007; Choose Your Weapons, 2010; (with Edward Young) Disraeli: the two lives, 2013; Elizabeth II: the steadfast, 2015; *novels:* Truth Game, 1972; Vote to Kill, 1975; The Shape of Ice, 1998; Image in the Water, 2001; (with Andrew Osmond: Send Him Victorious, 1968; The Smile on the Face of the Tiger, 1969, repr. 1982; Scotch on the Rocks, 1971; War Without Frontiers, 1982; (with Stephen Lamport) Palace of Enchantments, 1985. *Recreation:* writing. *Clubs:* Pratt's, Travellers, Beefsteak.
*See also* Rt Hon. N. R. Hurd.

**HURD, Rt Hon. Nicholas (Richard);** PC 2017; MP (C) Ruislip, Northwood and Pinner, since 2010 (Ruislip Northwood, 2005–10); Minister of State, Northern Ireland Office, since 2019; *b* 13 May 1962; *s* of Baron Hurd of Westwell, *qv* and Tatiana Elizabeth Michelle Hurd; *m* 1st, 1988, Kim Richards (marr. diss.); two *s* two *d*; 2nd, 2010, Lady Clare Kerr, *d* of Marquess of Lothian, *qv* and Lady Herries of Terregles, *qv*; one *s* one *d*. *Educ:* Eton Coll.; Exeter Coll., Oxford (BA Classics 1985). Investment Manager, Morgan Grenfell, 1985–90; Corporate Finance Exec., Crown Communications, 1990–92; Managing Director: Passport Magazine Directories, 1992–94; Robert Fleming Do Brasil, 1994–2000; Business Develt Dir, Band-X Ltd, 2000–04; COS to Tim Yeo, MP, 2004–05. Shadow Minister for Charities, Social Enterprise and Volunteering, 2008–10; Parly Sec., Cabinet

Office, 2010–14; Parly Under-Sec. of State, DFID, 2015–16; Minister of State, BEIS, 2016–17, Home Office, 2017–19. Trustee, Greenhouse Sports Charity, 2004–. *Recreations:* sport, music. *Address:* House of Commons, SW1A 0AA. *T:* and *Fax:* (020) 7219 1053. *E:* nick.hurd.mp@parliament.uk.

**HURFORD, Prof. James Raymond,** PhD; FBA 2015; Professor of General Linguistics, University of Edinburgh, 1979–2008, now Emeritus; *b* Reading, 16 July 1941; *s* of James H. Hurford and Muriel K. L. W. Crocker; *m* 1964, Sue Ann Davis; one *d* (and one *d* decd). *Educ:* Exeter Sch.; St John's Coll., Cambridge (BA 1963); University Coll. London (PhD 1967). Post Doctoral Fellow, Systems Develt Corp., 1967–68; Asst Prof., Univ. of Calif at Davis, 1968–71; Lectr, 1972–76, Sen. Lectr, 1976–79, Univ. of Lancaster. *Publications:* The Linguistic Theory of Numerals, 1975; (with B. Heasley) Semantics: a coursebook, 1983; Language and Number, 1987; Grammar: a student's guide, 1994; The Origins of Meaning, 2007; The Origins of Grammar, 2011; The Origins of Language, 2014. *Recreations:* gardening, squash, hiking. *Address:* Linguistics and English Language, University of Edinburgh, Dugald Stewart Building, 3 Charles Street, Edinburgh EH8 9AD. *T:* (0131) 650 3959. *E:* jim@ling.ed.ac.uk.

**HURLES, Dr Matthew,** FMedSci; FRS 2019; Group Leader, since 2003, and Head, Human Genetics, since 2017, Wellcome Sanger Institute; *b* Hammersmith, 8 May 1974; *s* of Jeremy and Helene Hurles; *m* 2002, Elizabeth Aust; one *s* two *d*. *Educ:* Hampton Sch.; Lincoln Coll., Oxford (BA 1st Cl. Biochem.); Univ. of Leicester (PhD Genetics 2000). Post-doctoral Fellow, McDonald Inst. of Archaeological Res., Univ. of Cambridge, 1999–2003. FMedSci 2019. *Publications:* (jtly) Human Evolutionary Genetics, 2004; contrib. peer-reviewed articles to learned jls. *Recreations:* family, gardening, cycling, Fortnite. *Address:* Wellcome Sanger Institute, Wellcome Genome Campus, Hinxton, Cambridge CB10 1SA. *T:* (01223) 495377. *E:* meh@sanger.ac.uk.

**HURLSTON, Malcolm,** CBE 2013; social entrepreneur; Founding Chairman: Malcolm Hurlston Corporate Consultancy, since 1980; Registry Trust, since 1985; Employee Share Ownership Centre, since 1986; *b* Southport, Lancs, 7 July 1938; *s* of Robert Hurlston and Alice Mary Hurlston (*née* Taylor); three *s* two *d*; *m* 2002, Linda Wilbert. *Educ:* Sunnymede, Southport; Magdalene Coll., Cambridge (Open Maj. Schol.; BA 1961; MA). Nat. Service, Jt Services Sch. for Linguists (Flying Officer). Reporter, City Press; Dir, London Press Exchange; DJ, BBC Serbo Croat Service; Chairman: Open Shop; Euroshop; Student Loans Co.; Irish Judgements; Financial Inclusion Centre; Founding Chairman: Foundn for Credit Counselling, 1992–2010 (Pres., 2010–); StepChange (formerly CCCS); Proof of Age Standards Scheme; devised Unity Trust Bank (co-operative and trade union bank); Founder: Retail Credit Gp; Standing Cttee on Reciprocity; Credit Card Res. Gp; Office of Travel Charter. Campaigner: *for:* opening shops on Sundays; Co-operative Bank into clearing; liberalisation of pharmacies; tax simplification of share schemes; Company Share Option Plan; *against:* insce nationalisation; takeover of Cooperative Wholesale Soc. by City interests. Mentor, Univ. of Westminster. Remy Schlumberger Award, Internat. Assoc. for Financial Participation, 2012. *Publications:* Samovar (poems); *translations:* L'art de la drague, by Alain Krief; Leda, by Miroslav Krleža; monographs. *Recreations:* Eton fives (Cambridge 2nd VI), tennis, dining, reading, humming, this transitory life. *Address:* Maida Vale, London and La Napoule, France. *E:* mhurlston@hurlstons.com. *Clubs:* Royal Air Force; Omnisport de Tanneron.

**HURN, Sir (Francis) Roger,** Kt 1996; Chairman, Prudential plc, 2000–02; Deputy Chairman, Cazenove Group plc, 2003–09 (Director, 2001–09); *b* 9 June 1938; *s* of Francis James Hurn and Joyce Elsa Hurn (*née* Bennett); *m* 1980, Rosalind Jackson; one *d*. *Educ:* Marlborough Coll. Engrg apprentice, Rolls Royce Motors, 1956; joined Smiths Industries, 1958. National Service, 1959–61. Smiths Industries: Export Dir, Motor Accessory Div., 1969; Man. Dir, Internat. Operations, 1974; Exec. Dir, 1976; Man. Dir, 1978; Chief Exec., 1981–96; Chm., 1991–98; Chm., GEC, subseq. Marconi, 1998–2001; Dep. Chm., Glaxo Wellcome, 1997–2000, GlaxoSmithKline, 2000–03. Non-executive Director: Ocean Transport & Trading, 1982–88; Pilkington, 1984–94; S. G. Warburg Gp, 1987–95; ICI, 1993–2001. Gov., Henley Mgt Coll., 1986–2004 (Chm. Govs, 1996–2004). Liveryman, Coachmakers and Coach Harness Makers' Co., 1979–. *Recreations:* outdoor pursuits, travel. *Address:* Stonesdale, Bulstrode Way, Gerrards Cross, Bucks SL9 7QT.

**HURRELL, Prof. Andrew James,** DPhil; FBA 2011; Montague Burton Professor of International Relations, University of Oxford, since 2008; Fellow, Balliol College, Oxford, since 2008; *b* 2 Feb. 1955; *s* of late William Palmer Hurrell and Brenda Joan Hurrell (*née* Batch); *m* 1977, Yasmin Ahmed; one *s* one *d*. *Educ:* Gresham's Sch.; St John's Coll., Cambridge (BA 1977); St Antony's Coll., Oxford (MPhil 1982; DPhil 1986). Lloyds Bank Internat., London and Brazil, 1978–80; Res. Fellow, Christ Church, Oxford, 1983–86; Asst Prof. of Internat. Relns, Bologna Center, Sch. of Advanced Internat. Studies, Johns Hopkins Univ., 1986–89; Lectr in Internat. Relns, Oxford Univ., 1989–2008; Fellow, Nuffield Coll., Oxford, 1989–2008, now Emeritus. Visiting Professor: Univ. of São Paulo, 1994, 1997; Univ. of Brasilia, 2005; Fundação Getúlio Vargas, Rio de Janeiro, 2009; Inaugural Fellow, Straus Inst. for Advanced Study of Law and Justice, NYU Law Sch., 2009–10. Delegate, OUP, 2010– (Mem., Finance Cttee). Mem., Soc. of Scholars, Johns Hopkins Univ., 2010. Susan Strange Award, Internat. Studies Assoc., 2015. *Publications:* (ed with L. Fawcett) Regionalism in World Politics, 1995; (ed with N. Woods) Inequality, Globalisation and World Politics, 1999; (with K. Alderson) Hedley Bull on International Society, 2000; (ed jtly) Order and Justice in International Relations, 2003; On Global Order: power, values and the constitution of international society, 2007; contribs to jls incl. Internat. Affairs, Rev. Internat. Studies, Metaphilosophy. *Recreations:* theatre, cooking, travel, books. *Address:* Balliol College, Oxford OX1 3BJ. *E:* andrew.hurrell@politics.ox.ac.uk.

**HURST, Alan Arthur;** Partner, Law Hurst & Taylor, since 1980; *b* 2 Sept. 1945; *s* of George Arthur Hurst and Eva Grace Hurst; *m* 1976, Hilary Caroline Burch; two *s* one *d*. *Educ:* Westcliff High Sch.; Univ. of Liverpool (BA Hons). Admitted Solicitor, 1975. Member (Lab): Southend BC, 1980–96; Essex CC, 1993–98. MP (Lab) Braintree, 1997–2005; contested (Lab) same seat, 2005. Pres., Southend-on-Sea Law Soc., 1992–93. *Recreations:* bird watching, local history, canvassing. *Address:* 28 Whitefriars Crescent, Westcliff-on-Sea, Essex SS0 8EU. *T:* (01702) 337864.

**HURST, Andrew Robert; His Honour Judge Andrew Hurst;** a Circuit Judge, since 2019; *b* Cambridge, 4 Feb. 1965; *s* of John Hurst and Molly Hurst (*née* Carr); *m* 1995, Teresa Buckpitt; one *s* one *d*. *Educ:* Coleridge Community Coll.; Hills Road Sixth Form Coll.; Mansfield Coll., Oxford (BA Juris. 1987). Admitted solicitor, 1991; called to the Bar, Inner Temple, 1992; in practice as a barrister, 36/23 Essex St, 1993–2013, 2 Hare Court, 2013–19; a Recorder, 2009–19. *Recreations:* The Hebrides, reading, Church of England, family and friends. *Address:* c/o Basildon Crown Court, The Gore, Basildon SS14 2EW.

**HURST, Sir Geoffrey Charles,** Kt 1998; MBE 1977; Director, Aon Warranty Group (formerly London General Insurance), 1995–96; Director of Football, McDonald's, UK, since 2002; professional football player, 1957–76; *b* 8 Dec. 1941; *s* of Charles and Evelyn Hurst; *m* 1964, Judith Helen Harries; three *d*. Professional Football Player: West Ham United, 1957–72; Stoke City, 1972–75; West Bromwich Albion, 1975–76; Player-Manager, Telford United, 1976–79; Manager, Chelsea, 1979–81; English Football International, 1966–72. Joined London General Insurance, 1981. *Publications:* The World Game, 1970; (with Michael Hart) 1966 and All That, 2001; World Champions, 2006. *Recreations:* sport in general, family.

**HURST, (Jonathan) Martin (Stuart),** PhD; Chairman, Southern Regional Flood and Coastal Committee, since 2018; *b* 7 Sept. 1960; *s* of John Stuart Hurst and Jeanette Rose Hurst; *m* 2007, Stephanie (*née* Cottrill); one *d*, and one step *d*. *Educ:* Queens' Coll., Cambridge (BA 1982); Univ. of Southampton (MSc 1983; PhD 1989). Economist, HM Treasury, 1985–95; Divl Manager, DETR, 1995–2002; Sen. Policy Advr (envmt, farming, housing, planning), 10 Downing Street, 2002–05; Transformation Dir, Natural England, 2005; Department for Environment, Food and Rural Affairs: Dir, Regulation, 2006–07; Water, 2007–10; Arms Length Bodies and Estates, 2010–11; Commercial Dir, 2011–15. Associate Partner, Cadence Innova, 2015–. Vice Chm., Wandle Housing Assoc., 2008–14; Chairman: Finance and Treasury Cttee, bpha, 2015–; Treasury and Investment Cttee, Radian Housing, 2017–. Vis. Sen. Lectr, UCL, 2017–. Trustee: Groundwork SE London, 2005–11; SE Rivers Trust, 2018–. *Recreations:* hill walking, cricket, choral singing, bird watching. *Address:* Oakleigh, Peaches Close, Cheam, Sutton SM2 7BL. *E:* martinhurst7@btinternet.com.

**HURST, Prof. Laurence Daniel,** DPhil; FMedSci; FRS 2015; Professor of Evolutionary Genetics, since 1997, Director, Genetics and Evolution Teaching Project, since 2012 and Director, Milner Centre for Evolution, since 2015, University of Bath; President, Genetics Society, since 2018; *b* Ilkley, Yorks, 6 Jan. 1965; *s* of John Stuart Hurst and Jeanette Rose Hurst; *m* 1999, Clair Florence Ann Brunton; two *d*. *Educ:* Truro Sch.; Churchill Coll., Cambridge (BA Nat. Scis (Zool.) 1987); University Coll., Oxford (DPhil 1991). Henry Fellowship, Harvard Univ., 1987–88; Browne Res. Fellow, Queen's Coll., Oxford, 1991–93; University of Cambridge: Res. Fellow, Dept of Genetics, 1994–97; Sen. Res. Fellow, Churchill Coll., 1995–97. Horace le Marquand and Dudley Bigg Res. Fellow, Royal Soc., 1993–2001. Professorial Res. Fellow, Inst. for Advanced Study, Collegium Budapest, 1995; External Faculty, John Innes Centre, Norwich, 2010–14. Mem., EMBO, 2004; FMedSci 2015. Charles Darwin Award, BAAS, 1999; Scientific Medal, Zool Soc., 2003; Medal, Genetics Soc., 2010. *Publications:* papers on evolution, genetics and genomics in Nature, Nature Genetics, Public Liby of Sci. Biol. *Recreations:* music (listening), collecting antique maps, walking (especially with dogs), attempting but failing to perfect lemon tart. *Address:* Department of Biology and Biochemistry, University of Bath, Bath BA2 7AY. *T:* (01225) 386424, *Fax:* (01225) 386779. *E:* l.d.hurst@bath.ac.uk.

**HURST, Peter Thomas;** Arbitrator and Mediator, 39 Essex Chambers, since 2015; Senior Costs Judge of England and Wales (formerly Chief Master of the Supreme Court Taxing Office), 1992–2014 (Master, 1981–92); a Recorder, 2000–12; *b* Troutbeck, Westmorland, 27 Oct. 1942; *s* of Thomas Lyon Hurst and Nora Mary Hurst; *m* 1968, Diane Irvine; one *s* two *d*. *Educ:* Stonyhurst College; LLB 1973, MPhil 2000, London. Admitted as Solicitor of the Supreme Court, 1967; Partner: Hurst and Walker, Solicitors, Liverpool, 1967–77; Gair Roberts Hurst and Walker, Solicitors, Liverpool, 1977–81; Judicial Taxing Officer: H of L, 2002–09; Privy Council, 2002–14; Supreme Court of UK, 2009–14. Greffier Substitute, Royal Court of Jersey, 2005–. Assessor to Lord Justice Jackson's Rev. of Civil Costs, 2009. Chair, Ind. Rev. Panel, NHS Continuing Healthcare, 2014; Member; Panel, Kuala Lumpur Regl Centre for Arbitration, 2015–; Users Council, Singapore Internat. Arbitration Centre, 2015–. Accredited Mediator, 2014; FCIArb 2015; Mem., Expert Witness Inst., 2015 (Mem., Editl Bd, 2016–). Hon. Bencher, Gray's Inn, 2007. Mem. Gen. Editl Bd, Civil Procedure (The White Book) (formerly The Supreme Court Practice), 2000–15 (contrib., 1986–2014; Advisory Ed., 2014–). *Publications:* (ed jtly) Butterworth's Costs Service, 1986–2017; (contrib.) Cordery on Solicitors, 8th edn 1988; (ed jtly) Legal Aid, 1994, Solicitors, 1995, Halsbury's Laws of England, 4th edn; Civil Costs, 1995, 6th edn 2018; (ed jtly) Legal Aid Practice 1996–97, 1996; (ed jtly) The New Civil Costs Regime, 1999; Criminal Costs, 2007; (contrib.) Civil Procedure Rules Ten Years On, 2009; (contrib.) Civil Justice Qly; (contrib.) European Business Law Rev. (Special Edn), 2014; Costs and Funding Following the Civil Justice Reforms, 2015, 5th edn 2019. *Recreation:* music. *Address:* 39 Essex Chambers, 81 Chancery Lane, WC2A 1BQ. *Club:* Athenæum.

**HURST, Rachel Catherine,** FIET, FREng; Chief Operating Officer and Executive Director, Domino Printing Sciences plc, since 2014; *b* Bath, 18 June 1971; *d* of Richard Belringer and Christine Belringer; *m* 1999, Michael Hurst; one *s*. *Educ:* Anglia Poly. (HNC Electrical and Electronic Engrg); Warwick Business Sch. (MSc Engrg Mgt). FIET 2016; FREng 2017. Domino Printing Sciences plc: Manufg Engr, 1994–97; Product Manager, 1997–2001; UK Ops Dir, 2001–06; Gp Ops Dir, 2006–14. Viscount Nuffield Silver Medal, IET, 2015. *Recreations:* cycling, horse riding, scuba diving. *Address:* Domino Printing Sciences plc, Bar Hill, Cambs CB23 8TU. *T:* 07775 824095. *E:* rachel.hurst@domino-printing.com.

**HURWITZ, Michael;** Director, Transport Innovation, Transport for London, since 2016; *b* Leeds, 25 April 1971; *s* of His Honour Vivian Ronald Hurwitz and of Dr Ruth Hurwitz; *m* 1999, Anna Turner; one *s* two *d*. *Educ:* Leeds Grammar Sch.; Univ. of Manchester (BA 1st Cl. Psychol.; MSc Psychol.). Andersen Business Consulting, 1998–2000; Deloitte MCS Ltd, 2000–04; Hd, Planning and Performance, 2004–06, Envmt Policy, 2006–09, DfT; Dir, Office for Low Emission Vehicles, BIS, 2009–11; Dir, Analysis and Strategy, 2012–13, Dir, Greener Transport and Internat., then Energy, Technol. and Internat., 2013–16, DfT. *Address:* Transport for London, Windsor House, 42–50 Victoria Street, W1H 0TL.

**HUSAIN, Saleem, (Sam);** Managing Director, HEP Holdings Ltd, since 1987 (consultancy appointments, 2004–07 and since 2015); Chief Executive Officer, W & G Foyle Ltd, 2007–15 (non-executive Director, 2015); *b* New Delhi, 27 April 1947; *s* of late Dr Mumtaz Husain and Mary Husain; *m* 1977, Lesley Mary Todd (marr. diss. 2005). *Educ:* St Mary's Acad., Pakistan; Open Univ. (MBA 1993). ACA 1972, FCA 1979. Articled clerk, David J. Jones & Co., Manchester, 1965–70; Audit Senior: Mann Judd & Co., Manchester, 1970–73; Tansley Witt & Co., 1973–74; Hudson Group Ltd: Mgt Accountant, 1974; Gp Mgt Accountant, 1975; Gp Chief Accountant, 1976–78; Finance Dir, 1978–82; Dep. Chm., 1982–87; Ascent Media Group (formerly Liberty Livewire): UK Gp Chief Finance Officer and Dir, Corporate Affairs, 2001; UK Gp Man. Dir, Corporate and Finance, 2002–04. Mem. Council, 2009–15, Vice Pres., 2012–15, Bookseller Assoc. FInstD 1986. Pres.'s Award, 1995, Roland Chase Award, 1997, BKSTS; Outstanding Contribn to Book Trade, Bookseller Assoc., 2015. *Recreations:* golf, motor boating, bridge. *Address:* 4 Waters Edge, Maidstone, Kent ME15 6SG. *T:* (020) 8368 1005. *E:* shusain@btclick.com. *Clubs:* Hadley Wood Golf (Captain, 2011; Country Mem., 2018–), Bearsted Golf, Littlestone Golf (Associate Mem.).

**HUSBAND, Dame Janet (Elizabeth Siarey),** DBE 2007 (OBE 2002); FRCP, FRCR, FMedSci; Professor of Diagnostic Imaging, Institute of Cancer Research, University of London, 1996–2007, now Emeritus; Consultant Radiologist, Royal Marsden NHS Foundation Trust (formerly Royal Marsden Hospital), 1980–2007 (non-executive Director, since 2014); *b* 1 April 1940; *d* of late Ronald Howard Siarey and Clarissa Marian Siarey; *m* 1963, Peter Husband; three *s*. *Educ:* Headington Sch., Oxford; Guy's Hosp. Med. Sch., Univ. of London (MB BS 1964). MRCS, LRCP 1964; DCH 1966; DObstRCOG

1967; DMRD 1974; FRCR 1976; FRCP 1987. Registrar in Diagnostic Radiol., Guy's Hosp. and KCH (pt-time), 1971–76; Clinical Scientist, MRC Div. of Radiol., Northwick Park Hosp., 1976; Royal Marsden Hospital, later Royal Marsden NHS Foundation Trust: Radiol. Res. Fellow, 1977–80; Hd, Academic Dept of Radiol., 1985–2007; Med. Dir, 2003–06; Chm., Nat. Cancer Res. Inst., 2010–12. Co-dir, CRUK (formerly CRC) Clinical Magnetic Resonance Res. Gp, Inst. Cancer Res., London Univ., 1986–2005. Special Comr, Royal Hosp. Chelsea, 2007–13. Non-executive Director: Nuada Medical Gp, 2009–15; Spire Healthcare plc, 2014–. Member: Cooperation and Competition Panel, Monitor, 2009–14; Health Honours Cttee, 2009–15. Co-founder and Trustee, Internat. Cancer Imaging Soc., 2000–; President: BIR, 2003–04; RCR, 2004–07. Hon. Mem., 5 internat. med. socs. FMedSci 2001. Hon. DSc Inst. of Cancer Res., London 2013. Gold Medal: Eur. Congress of Radiology, 2006; RCR, 2009; Internat. Cancer Imaging Soc., 2009. *Publications:* (ed) Computed Tomography Review, 1989; (ed jtly) Imaging in Oncology, 2 vols, 1998, 3rd edn 2009; (jtly) Guide to the Practical Use of MRI in Oncology, 1999; articles in learned jls. *Recreations:* walking, opera. *Address:* Nuffield Hill Cottage, Nuffield, Henley on Thames RG9 5SN. *Club:* Sloane.

**HUSBAND, Prof. Thomas Mutrie**, PhD; FREng, FIMechE; Chairman: UKERNA, 1997–2000; East and North Herts NHS Trust, 2000–01; Vice-Chancellor, University of Salford, 1990–97; *b* 7 July 1936; *s* of Thomas Mutrie Husband and Janet Clark; *m* 1st, 1962, Pat Caldwell (*d* 2001); two *s*; 2nd, 2003, Gwen Fox. *Educ:* Shawlands Acad., Glasgow; Univ. of Strathclyde (BSc(Eng), MA, PhD). Weir Ltd, Glasgow: Apprentice Fitter, 1953–58; Engr/Jun. Manager, 1958–62; sandwich degree student (mech. engrg), 1958–61; various engrg and management positions with ASEA Ltd in Denmark, UK and S Africa, 1962–65; postgrad. student, Strathclyde Univ., 1965–66; Teaching Fellow, Univ. of Chicago, 1966–67; Lectr, Univ. of Strathclyde, 1967–70; Sen. Lectr, Univ. of Glasgow, 1970–73; Prof. of Manufacturing Organisation, Loughborough Univ., 1973–81; Prof. of Engrg Manufacture, 1981–90, Dir of Centre for Robotics, 1982–90, Hd of Dept of Mech. Engrg, 1983–90, Imperial Coll., London Univ. Member: Standing Cttee for Educn, Training and Competence to Practise, Royal Acad. of Engrg (formerly Fellowship of Engrg), 1989–93; Engrg Technol. Adv. Cttee, DTI, 1990–93; Council, Engrg Council, 1992–95; Manufacturing Div. Bd, IEE, 1992–95; McRobert Award Cttee, Royal Acad. of Engrg, 2000–05. Mem., Univ. Bd, Bournemouth Univ., 2003–09. Non-executive Director: Royal Exchange Theatre, Manchester, 1993–97; Univs and Colls Employers Assoc., 1994–97. FREng (FEng 1988). Hon. DSc: Manchester, 1997; Salford, 1998. *Publications:* Work Analysis and Pay Structure, 1976; Maintenance and Terotechnology, 1977; Education and Training in Robotics, 1986; articles in Terotechnica, Industrial Relations Jl, Microelectronics and Reliability, etc. *Recreations:* watching Arsenal FC, music, theatre. *Address:* 12 Roscrea Drive, Wick Village, Bournemouth BH6 4LU.

**HUSBAND, William Anthony, (Tony);** freelance cartoonist and writer; *b* 28 Aug. 1950; *s* of Henry Ronald and Vera Husband; *m* 1976, Carole Garner; one *s*. *Educ:* Holy Trinity Primary Sch., Hyde; Greenfield Secondary Sch., Hyde. Full-time cartoonist, 1984–; works for Private Eye, The Spectator, The Oldie, Playboy, Punch, Golf International, Nursing Standard, The Idler, TES, The Dalesman, The Cumbrian, Down Your Way, Practical Caravan and many more; campaign work with Envmtl Investigation Agency; co-devised and co-wrote: Oink (comic), 1985–88; Round the Bend (children's TV prog.), 1988–90; co-wrote: (with David Wood) Save The Human (play), UK tour, 1991; Hanger 17 (children's TV series), 1993; episode of Chucklevision, 1994; series of greetings cards, Camden, Carlton, Hallmark Cards and Paperhouse; (with Ian McMillan, poet) performs cartoon/poetry event in front of live audiences. Several solo exhibns, incl. Ruby Lounge, Temple, Richard Goodhall Gall. and Jackalope, Manchester; exhibn accompanying Lowry's paintings, The Lowry, Salford, 2001; Cartoonist in Residence, The Lowry, 2006–. Edited and helped create first prison comic 'The Bird'. Awards: Cartoonist Club of GB: Gag Cartoonist, 1985, 1986, 1988; Strip Cartoonist, 1987; Cartoon Arts Trust: Sports Cartoonist, 1995, 2001; Gag Cartoonist, 2000, 2002; Strip Cartoonist, 2000; Pont Award, 2005. *Publications:* Use Your Head, 1985; Bye Bye Cruel World, 1986; Animal Husbandry, 1987; 102 Uses for a Black Lace Album, 1988; The Greatest Story Never Told, 1988; Yobs 1, 1989; Another Pair of Underpants, 1990; Yobs 2, 1993; (with David Day) True Tales of Environmental Madness, 1993; (with David Wood) Save The Human, 1993; (with David Day) The Complete Rhino, 1994; Football Food Guide, 1995; Reduced History of Football, 2004; Reduced History of Cricket, 2005; Reduced History of Golf, 2005; Reduced History of Rugby, 2006; Reduced History of Britain, 2006; The World's Worst Jokes, 2006; Reduced History of Tennis, 2006; (illus.) Private Eye's Coleman Balls, 2006; Reduced History of Sex, 2007; Reduced History of Cats, 2007; Reduced History of Dogs, 2007; The Calmer Sutra, 2008; (with Deborah Hudson) Sing Your Heart Out, 2010; I Nearly Died Laughing, 2012; It's Only a Game, 2012; (with Dan Cockrill) Sellotaping Rain to my Cheek, 2013; (ed) Propaganda Cartoons of World War II, 2013; Take Care, Son: the story of my dad and his dementia, 2014; with Ian McMillan: Yorkshire Humour, 2009; Daft Yorkshire Customs, 2010; Yorkshire T'Olympics, 2011; 100 Uses for a Yorkshire Pudding, 2011; The Tale of Walter the Pencil Man, 2013; 101 Uses for a Flat Cap, 2013; 10 books pubd in Germany. *Recreations:* golf (10 handicap), music, photography (Mem., Hyde Photographic Soc.), Manchester United, playing the drums, wine and good food. *Address:* Hicroft, 132 Joel Lane, Gee Cross, Hyde, Cheshire SK14 5LN. *T:* (0161) 366 0262, *Fax:* (0161) 368 8479. *E:* toonyhusband@hotmail.com. *W:* www.tonyhusband.co.uk. *Clubs:* Groucho; Werneth Low Golf (Hyde).

**HUSBANDS, Prof. Sir Christopher (Roy),** Kt 2018; PhD; Vice-Chancellor, Sheffield Hallam University, since 2016; *b* Nuneaton, Warwickshire, 29 May 1959; *s* of Humphrey Roy and Pearl Husbands; *m* 1983, Nicola Owen-Jones; four *d*. *Educ:* King Edward VI Sch., Nuneaton; Nuneaton Sixth Form Coll.; Emmanuel Coll., Cambridge (BA 1980; PhD 1985; Hon. Fellow 2016); Inst. of Educn, Univ. of London (PGCE 1984). Teacher: Heartsease Sch., 1984–88; Fearnhill Sch., 1988–90; Lectr, 1991–93, Sen. Lectr, 1993–95, in Educn, UEA; University of Warwick: Reader, 1995–98; Prof., 1998–2003; Dir, Inst. of Educn, 2001–03; Dean of Educn and Lifelong Learning, UEA, 2003–07; Prof. of Educn and Dean of Faculty, 2007–10, Dir, 2011–15, Inst. of Educn, Univ. of London, subseq. UCL; Vice Provost (Academic Develt), UCL, 2014–15. Hon. Prof., E China Normal Univ., Shanghai, 2013. Member: Bd, TDA, 2006–12; RSA/Pearson Academies Commn, 2012–13; Chairman: Teaching Excellence and Student Outcomes (formerly Teaching Excellence) Framework, 2016–; Higher Educn Statistics Agency, 2017–. Non-exec. Dir, Edexcel, 2000–04. Trustee, AQA, 2005–08. Mem., Learning Panel, Nat. Trust, 2007–15. *Publications:* What is History Teaching?, 1995; Professional Learning, 1998; The Performing School, 2001; Understanding History Teaching, 2003; (jtly) Transforming Education for All, 2013; Voices in the Air, 2016; Policy Learning and Educational Change, 2016. *Recreations:* reading, writing, cycling, walking, playing the piano badly. *Address:* Sheffield Hallam University, City Campus, Howard Street, Sheffield S1 1WB. *T:* (0114) 225 2050.

**HUSEYIN, Martin Trevor; His Honour Judge Huseyin;** a Circuit Judge, since 2018; *b* Croydon, 27 May 1963. *Educ:* Sussex Univ. (BA Hons English 1986); Poly. of Central London (DipLaw 1987); Inns of Court Sch. of Law. Called to the Bar, Inner Temple, 1988; in practice as barrister, 1989–2017; a Recorder, 2012–17. *Recreations:* walking, cinema, music. *Address:* Maidstone Combined Court Centre, Barker Road, Maidstone, Kent ME16 8EQ. *T:* (01622) 202000. *E:* hhj.martin.huseyin@ejudiciary.net.

**HUSH, Prof. Noel Sydney**, AO 1993; DSc; FRS 1988; FAA; Foundation Professor and Head of Department of Theoretical Chemistry, University of Sydney, 1971–92, now Professor Emeritus, and Hon. Associate, Chemistry School and School of Molecular and Microbial Biosciences, since 1990; *b* 15 Dec. 1924; *s* of Sidney Edgar Hush and Adrienne (*née* Cooper); *m* 1949, Thea L. Warman (decd), London; one *s* one *d*. *Educ:* Univ. of Sydney (BSc 1946; MSc 1948); Univ. of Manchester (DSc 1959). FAA 1977. Res. Fellow in Chemistry, Univ. of Sydney, 1946–49; Lectr in Phys. Chem., Univ. of Manchester, 1950–54; Lectr, subseq. Reader in Chem., Univ. of Bristol, 1955–71. Visiting Professor: ANU, 1960; Florida State Univ., 1965; Case Western Reserve Univ., 1968; Cambridge Univ., 1981; Stanford Univ., 1987; Vis. Fellow, Cavendish Lab., 1971; Vis. Sen. Scientist, Brookhaven Nat. Lab., USA, 1959–. Mem., Aust. Res. Grants Cttee, 1984–90 (Chm., Chem. Cttee, 1987–90). Director: Molecular Electronics Res. Ltd, 1997–; Quadrant Ltd, 2009–. Adv. Editor, Chemical Physics, 1973–; Mem. Bd of Mgt, Quadrant Magazine, 2002–08. Foreign Member: Amer. Acad. of Arts and Scis, 1999; US NAS, 2011. Fellow, Royal Soc. of NSW, 2011. Hon. DSc Sydney, 2009. Centenary Medal, Royal Soc. of Chem., 1990; Flinders Medal, 1994, Inaugural Award, David Craig Medal, 2000, Australian Acad. of Science; Centenary Medal, Australia, 2004; Physical Chem. Medal, RACI, 2006; Robert A. Welch Award in Chem., Welch Foundn, USA, 2007; Ahmed Zewail Prize, Elsevier, 2013. *Publications:* (ed) Reactions of Molecules at Electrodes, 1971; *c* 350 papers in Jl of Chemical Physics, Chemical Physics, Jl of Amer. Chemical Soc., etc. *Recreations:* literature, music, travel. *Address:* 170 Windsor Street, Paddington, Sydney, NSW 2021, Australia. *T:* (2) 93281685; School of Molecular Bioscience, University of Sydney, Sydney, NSW 2006, Australia. *T:* (2) 96923330. *Clubs:* Athenæum; Union, University and Schools (Sydney).

**HUSKINSON, His Honour (George) Nicholas (Nevil);** a Circuit Judge, 2003–18; a Member, Upper Tribunal (Lands Chamber) (formerly Lands Tribunal), 2006–18; *b* 7 Dec. 1948; *s* of Leonard and Margaret Huskinson; *m* 1972, Pennant Elfrida Lascelles Iremonger; two *s*. *Educ:* Eton (King's Schol.); King's Coll., Cambridge (MA). Called to the Bar, Gray's Inn, 1971 (Arden Schol.); Asst Recorder, 1995–99; a Recorder, 1999–2003; a Vice Pres., Immigration Appeal Tribunal, subseq. a Sen. Immigration Judge and Mem., Asylum and Immigration Tribunal, 2003–05. Asst Ed., Woodfall's Law of Landlord and Tenant, 28th edn, 1978–89. *Recreations:* bridge, gardening, walking, cooking. *Clubs:* MCC, Garrick.

**HUSKISSON, Edward Cameron,** MD; FRCP; Consultant Rheumatologist, King Edward VII's Hospital Sister Agnes (formerly King Edward VII Hospital for Officers), since 1982; *b* 7 April 1939; *s* of Edward William Huskisson, Northwood, Middx and late Elinor Margot Huskisson (*née* Gibson); *m* 1990, Janice Elizabeth Louden; three *s* one *d*. *Educ:* Eastbourne Coll.; King's Coll., London (BSc); Westminster Hosp. Med. Sch. (MB BS 1964); MD London 1974. MRCS 1964; LRCP 1964, MRCP 1967, FRCP 1980. Consultant Physician and Head of Rheumatology, St Bartholomew's Hosp., 1976–93. *Publications:* (jtly) Joint Disease: all the arthropathies, 1973, 4th edn 1988; Repetitive Strain Injury, 1992. *Address:* 14A Milford House, 7 Queen Anne Street, W1G 9HN. *T:* (020) 7636 4278, *Fax:* (020) 7323 6829. *E:* edwardhuskisson@aol.com.

**HUSSAIN,** Baron *cr* 2011 (Life Peer), of Luton in the County of Bedfordshire; **Qurban Hussain;** *b* Kashmir, 27 March 1956; *m*; six *c*. *Educ:* Rochdale Coll.; Bedford Coll., Univ. of London; Luton Univ. Came to live in UK, 1971. Partner, BMQ Properties. Sec., Luton TUC, 1994–96. Member: Labour Party, 1996–2003; Lib Dem Party, 2003–. Mem. (Lib Dem), Luton BC, 2003–10 (Dep. Leader, 2005–07; Dep. Leader, Lib Dem Gp). Contested (Lib Dem) Luton S, 2005, 2010. *Address:* House of Lords, SW1A 0PW.

**HUSSAIN, Altaf;** Member (C) South Wales West, National Assembly for Wales, May 2015–2016; *b* Srinagar, 31 July 1944; *s* of Mohamed Saiyed and Amira Saiyed; *m* 1973, Khalida Sultan; one *s* one *d*. *Educ:* Med. Coll. Srinagar, Kashmir, India (MB BS 1966); Kashmir Univ. (MS 1973); Liverpool Univ. (MChOrth 1982). FICS 1985. Resident, 1967–70, Registrar of Orthopaedics, 1970–74, Lectr in Orthopaedics, 1974–81, SMHS Hosp. and Med. Coll., Srinagar; Resident, then Registrar, Royal Liverpool Hosp., 1979–83; Consultant Orthopaedic Surgeon: Al Zulfi Hosp., Riyadh, 1983–86; Prince Salman Hosp., Riyadh, 1986–92; various NHS hospitals, 1992–2000; Prince Charles Hosp., Merthyr Tydfil, 2000–10. Tutor, RCS, 2004–. Consultant Ed., Internat. J&K Practitioner. Invented Notch Trial in total knee replacement and Thumb Index Reference in total hip replacement. Shadow Minister for Social Services, Nat. Assembly for Wales, 2015–16. Mem., Bridgend CBC, 2017–. Dep. Chm., Bridgend Cons. Assoc., 2009–11; Chm., S Wales W, Cons. Party, 2011–15. Member: New Castle Higher Community Council, 2012–; Cwm Taf Morgannwg Community Council, 2019–. Governor: St Robert's Catholic Sch., Aberkenfig, 2013–18; Pen y Fai CIW Sch., Bridgend, 2017–. Trustee, Age Cymru Swansea Bay, 2016–18; Chm., Brynawel Rehab, 2018–. Life Member: Indian Orthopaedic Soc., UK; Indian Orthopaedic Assoc.; Member: British Orthopaedic Assoc.; Western Orthopaedic Assoc.; Amnesty Internat. UK. Best Practice Team Award, CamTaf Health Bd, 2007; Glory of India Award, 2008, Lifetime Achievement Award, 2009, India Internat. Friendship Soc.; Bharat Gaurav Award, 2009. *Publications:* contrib. articles to internat. professional jls. *Recreations:* golf, swimming, keep fit, South East politics. *Address:* 20 Plas Ty Mawr, Penyfai, Bridgend CF31 4NH. *T:* (01656) 660483, 07817 506004. *E:* draltafhussain1@gmail.com.

**HUSSAIN, Rear Adm. Amjad Mazhar,** CB 2011; CEng; Executive Director, Jacobs (UK), since 2012; *b* Rawalpindi, Pakistan, 15 May 1958; *s* of Mazhar Hussain and Tahira Hussain (*née* Begum); *m* 1983, Wendy Downer; one *s* two *d*. *Educ:* Downer Grammar Sch.; Harrow Weald 6th Form Coll.; Univ. of Durham (BSc Engrg Sci. and Mgt 1979); Cranfield Univ. (MSc 1987); London Business Sch. (MSc 2002). MIET. Joined RN, 1976; served: HMS Dido, 1982–83; HMS Cornwall, 1989–91; HMS Invincible, 1995–97; Integrated Project Team Leader, 1997–99; Naval Base Comdr, Portsmouth, 2002–05; Director General: Logistics (Fleet), 2007–09; Weapons, 2007–09; Dir, Precision Attack, 2009–12; Controller of the Navy, 2009–12. Chairman: SQR Systems Ltd, 2012–16; Cura Systems Internat. Ltd, 2016–17; Dir, Places for People Gp Ltd, 2018–. Trustee: Imperial War Mus., 2015–; HMS Victory Preservation Trust, 2017–. FCGI 2012 (Mem. Council, 2015–). Freeman, City of London, 2006; Liveryman, Lightmongers' Co., 2006. Hon. DCL Durham, 2011. *Recreations:* family life, all sports. *Address:* 1180 Eskdale Road, Winnersh, Wokingham RG41 5TU. *Clubs:* Army and Navy.

**HUSSAIN, Gul Nawaz Mahboob;** QC 2018; *b* Sheffield, 15 Dec. 1975; *s* of Mahboob Hussain and Zahida Parveen; *m* 2003, Hiba Amin-Uddin; one *s* two *d*. *Educ:* Firth Park Sch.; Nene Coll., Northampton (LLB); Nottingham Trent Univ. (BVC). Called to the Bar, Gray's Inn, 2000; in practice as a barrister, specialising in criminal defence, 2000–; Jt Hd, Bank House Chambers, 2018–. *Recreations:* Muay Thai, shooting, cinema, theatre, Brazilian jiu-jitsu. *Address:* Bank House Chambers, Old Bank House, Hartshead, Sheffield S1 2EL. *T:* (0114) 275 1223. *E:* gn.hussain@bankhousechambers.co.uk.

**HUSSAIN, Imran**; MP (Lab) Bradford East, since 2015; b 7 June 1978. Educ: Univ. of Huddersfield (LLB). Called to the Bar, Lincoln's Inn. Mem. (Lab), City of Bradford MDC, 2002– (Dep. Leader, 2010–15). Shadow Minister for Internat. Devlt, 2016–17, for Justice, 2017. Address: House of Commons, SW1A 0AA. T: (020) 7219 8636. E: imran.hussain.mp@parliament.uk.

**HUSSAIN, Mamnoon**; President of Pakistan, 2013–18; b Agra, India, 23 Dec. 1940; s of Haji Azhar Hussain and Siraj Begum; m 1970, Mehmooda Kamil; three s. Educ: Karachi Secondary Educn Bd; Karachi Univ. (BCom Hons 1963); Inst. of Business Admin, Karachi (MBA 1965). Advr to Chief Minister of Sindh, 1997–98; Gov. of Sindh, 1999. Pres., Chamber of Commerce and Industry, Karachi, 1999. Hon. PhD Inst. of Business Admin, Karachi, 2014; Hon. Dr Bako Siaje, 2015; Hon. FRCPE 2018. Recreations: games, cricket, reading. Club: Karachi Gymkhana.

**HUSSAIN, Mukhtar**; QC 1992; a Recorder of the Crown Court, since 1989; b 22 March 1950; s of late Karam Dad and Rehmi Bi; m 1972, Shamim Akhtar Ali; three d. Educ: William Temple Secondary School. Came to UK, 1964. Called to the Bar, Middle Temple, 1971, Bencher, 2000; Asst Recorder, 1986–89; Head of Chambers, 1992–2012. Chm., Police Discipline Appeals Tribunal, 1997–; Member: Mental Health Review Tribunal, 2000–; CICB, 2000–; Bar Council, 2001. Presenter, Granada TV, 1982–87. Recreations: cricket, squash, bridge, golf, reading. Address: Tower 12, Bridge Street, Spinningfields, Manchester M3 3BZ.

**HUSSAIN, Nasser**, OBE 2002; columnist, Daily Mail, since 2003; cricket commentator, Sky Sports, since 2004; b Madras, India, 28 March 1968; s of Joe Hussain and Shireen Hussain (née Price); m Karen Birch; two s one d. Educ: Univ. of Durham (BSc). Essex County Cricket Club: first-class début, 1987; county cap, 1989; Vice-Captain, 1995–99; Captain, 1999–2004, retired; England: début, 1990; Vice-Captain, 1998–99; Captain, 1999–2003; toured India, W Indies, Zimbabwe, NZ, Aust., S Africa, Pakistan, Sri Lanka; highest test score 207 vs Aust., Edgbaston, 1997. Player of the Series, England vs India, 1996. Publications: (with Steve Waugh) An Ashes Summer, 1997; Playing with Fire (autobiog.), 2004. Address: The Old Rectory, Colam Lane, Little Baddow, Chelmsford, Essex CM3 4SY.

**HUSSEIN-ECE**, Baroness cr 2010 (Life Peer), of Highbury in the London Borough of Islington; **Meral Hussein Ece**, OBE 2009; Member, Equality and Human Rights Commission, 2009–12; b Islington, 10 Oct. 1953; one s two d. Educ: BA (Hons). Mem. (Lab) 1994–96, (Lib Dem) 1997–2002, Hackney LBC (Dep. Leader, 1995–96); Mem. (Lib Dem) Islington LBC, 2002–10 (Cabinet Mem. for Health and Social Care, 2002–06). Chm., Islington Health Partnership Bd, 2004–06; Mem. Bd, Islington PCT, 2002–06. Non-exec. Dir, Camden and Islington Mental Health and Social Care Trust, 2004–06. Chair, Ethnic Minority Liberal Democrats, 2006–10; Special Advr to Nick Clegg, MP, on community cohesion and black and minority ethnic communities, 2008. Mem., Black, Asian and Minority Ethnic Women Councillors' Govt Taskforce, 2008–09. Mem., Lib Dem Federal Exec., 2005–10. Hon. DLitt Coventry, 2012. Address: House of Lords, SW1A 0PW.

**HUSSELL, Prof. Tracy**, PhD; FRSB; FMedSci; Director, Manchester Collaborative Centre for Inflammation Research, and Professor of Inflammatory Disease, since 2012, and Director of Infection, Immunity, Inflammation and Repair, since 2016, University of Manchester; b Kidderminster, 14 April 1967; d of Roger Joiner Hussell and Hilda Carol Paget (née Starr); m 1994, Nicholas Beesley; two d and two step s. Educ: Worcester Tech. Coll. (OND Sci. 1985); Nottingham Univ. (BSc Hons Applied Biol. 1989); Med. Sch., University Coll. London (PhD Immunol. 1994); Imperial Coll. London (Cert. Advanced Studies in Learning and Teaching 2002). FRSB 2016. Res. asst, Dept of Immunol., UCL and Middx Sch. of Medicine, 1989–90; Postdoctoral Research Fellow: Dept of Histopathol., UCL Med. Sch., 1994; in Respiratory Medicine, Imperial Sch. of Medicine, St Mary's Hosp., Paddington, 1994–98; Hon. non-clin. Lectr in Respiratory Medicine, Nat. Heart and Lung Inst., St Mary's Hosp., Imperial Coll. Sch. of Medicine, 1998–2000; non-clin. Lectr in Biochem., 2000–02, Sen. Lectr in Biol Scis, 2002–04, Dept of Biochem., Imperial Coll. London; Reader in Immunol., Kennedy Inst. for Rheumatol., Charing Cross Hosp., London, 2004–06; Prof. of Inflammatory Disease, Imperial Coll. London, 2006–12. FMedSci 2017. Mem., Med. Res. Club. Publications: contribs to learned jls. Recreations: reading, making mischief, sailing. Address: Manchester Collaborative Centre for Inflammation Research, Division of Infection, Immunity and Respiratory Medicine, University of Manchester, Core Technology Facility, 146 Grafton Street, Manchester M13 9PL. T: (0161) 275 1537. E: tracy.hussell@manchester.ac.uk.

**HUSSEY, Ann Elizabeth, (Mrs Alastair Sharp)**; QC 2009; b London, 5 March 1959; d of Arnold Hussey and Jean Hussey; m 1984, Alastair Sharp; one s three d. Educ: St Albans Girls Sch.; Univ. of Kent (BA Hons Law). Called to the Bar, Middle Temple, 1981 (Blackstone Law Scholar), Bencher, 2012; in practice as barrister specialising in matrimonial finance. Recreations: riding, showing native ponies, ski-ing. Address: 1 Hare Court, Temple, EC4Y 7BE. E: hussey@1hc.com.

**HUSSEY, Derek Robert**; Member (UU) Tyrone West, Northern Ireland Assembly, 1998–2007; b 12 Sept. 1948; s of Sydney Robert Hussey and Rachel Hussey (née Maguire); m 1st (marr. diss.); one s; 2nd, Karen (née Vaughan); one s one d. Educ: Model Sch., Omagh; Omagh Acad.; Stranmillis Coll., Belfast (Cert Ed). Head of Business Studies, Castlederg High Sch., 1972–98, retired. Member: Strabane DC, 1989–2015 (Ind. U 1989–97, UU 1997–2015); (UU) Derry City and Strabane DC, 2015– (Alderman; Vice Chm., Business and Culture Cttee, 2017–18; Dep. Mayor, 2018–19). Mem., N Ireland Forum, 1996–98. Dep. Whip, UUP, NI Assembly, 1998–99; former UU spokesman on victims' issues. Contested (UU) Tyrone West, NI Assembly, 2007. Londonderry Port and Harbour Comr, 2015–; Mem., Derry City and Strabane Police and Community Partnership, 2015– (Chm., 2018–19). Recreations: country and western music, soccer, Rugby, ski-ing, Ulster-Scots history and culture, church choir, Castlederg Young Loyalists' Old Boys' Flute Band. E: drhussey@hotmail.com.

**HUSSEY, Hon. James Arthur**; Advisor to Chairman, Oberthur Fiduciaire, since 2011; b 15 Aug. 1961; s of Baron Hussey of North Bradley and of Lady Susan Katharine Hussey, qv; m 1994, Emma Betty Shelley; one s two d. Educ: Harrow Sch.; Trinity Coll., Oxford (BA Hons Modern Hist.). De La Rue PLC, 1983–2010: Commercial Dir, Thomas De La Rue, 1990–95; Managing Director: Portals Ltd, 1995–98; Currency Div., 1998–2006; Security and Paper Div., 2006–08; Chief Exec., 2009–10. Dir, Camelot, 2006–09. Bd Advr, Currency Res., 2013–. Trustee, Ruffer CP, 2011–; Trustee and Vice Chm., Friends of the Elderly, 2012–. Recreations: shooting, football, Rugby, cricket. Address: Old Rectory, Wylye, Warminster BA12 0RN. T: (01985) 248280. Clubs: Brooks's; MCC.

**HUSSEY, Ross Michael**; Member (UU) West Tyrone, Northern Ireland Assembly, 2011–17; b Omagh, 25 Feb. 1959; s of Sydney Robert Hussey and Rachel Hussey. Educ: Omagh Co. Primary Sch.; Omagh Acad.; Omagh Technical Coll.; Open Univ. (BA Hons); Nat. Univ. of Ireland, Galway (Dip. Community Develt); Queen's Univ. Belfast (Cert. Effective Mgt of Volunteers). Pearl Assurance plc, 1976–2002. Reserve Constable (pt-time), RUC GC, 1977–2001; Police Service, NI, 2001–02. Mem., Omagh DC, 2005–12 (Vice Chm., 2011–12). Mem., Finance and Personnel Cttee, 2011–12, Public Accounts Cttee, 2011–16, NI Assembly; Mem., NI Assembly Commn, 2016–17. Contested (UU) W Tyrone, 2015. Mem., NI Policing Bd, 2011–17; Chm., Part-time Officers Welfare Gp, RUC GC Assoc., 2002–; Trustee: NI Assembly Pension Fund, 2011–17; RUC GC Foundn, 2015–. Recreations: historical research, First World War.
See also D. R. Hussey.

**HUSSEY, Lady Susan Katharine**, GCVO 2013 (DCVO 1984; CVO 1971); Lady-in-Waiting to the Queen, since 1960; b 1 May 1939; 5th d of 12th Earl Waldegrave, KG, GCVO; m 1959, Marmaduke Hussey (later Baron Hussey of North Bradley) (d 2006); one s one d. Address: 18 Lochmore House, Cundy Street, SW1W 9JX.
See also Sir Francis Brooke, Bt, Hon. J. A. Hussey.

**HUSTLER, Dr Margaret Joan**; Headmistress, Harrogate Ladies' College, 1996–2007; Director, International School of Choueifat-Amman, Jordan, since 2007; b 1 Nov. 1949; d of Harry Hustler and Dorothy (née Kaye); m 1976, David Thomas Wraight; three s five d. Educ: Marist Convent, London; Westfield Coll., London Univ. (BSc Hons); Royal Holloway Coll., London Univ. (PhD Biochem). Teacher, Lady Eleanor Holles Sch., Hampton, 1977–85; Dep. Headmistress, Atherley Sch., Southampton, 1985–89; Headmistress, St Michael's Sch., Limpsfield, 1989–96. Recreations: walking, sewing, knitting, reading.

**HUSTON, Felicity Victoria**; political commentator, public affairs and recruitment consultant, since 2011; Partner, Huston & Co., Tax Consultants, since 1994; b May 1963; d of Jim McCormick and Joy McCormick (née Day); m 1992, Adrian Robert Arthur Huston, JP; two s. Educ: Strathearn Sch., Belfast; Campbell Coll., Belfast; Nottingham Univ. (BA Hons 1985). HM Inspector of Taxes, 1988–94. Commissioner: H of L Appts Commn, 2000–08; Public Appts for NI, 2005–11. Director: Cassandra Consulting (NI) Ltd, 2003–07; Moyle Interconnector (Financing) plc, 2003–10; Moyle Interconnector plc; NI Energy Hldgs Ltd and gp cos, 2005–10. Gen. Comr of Income Tax, 2002–09 (Chm., NI Reg., Assoc. of Gen. Comrs of Income Tax, 2005–07). Mem., Industrial Tribunals Panel, 1999–2000. Member: Consumer Panel, PIA, 1996–98; PO Users' Council, NI, 1996–2000; Gen. Consumer Council, 1996–2000 (Dep. Chm., 1999–2000); Chm., NI Consumer Cttee for Electricity, 2000–03. Chm., Selection Panel, Ind. Parly Standards Authy, 2009; Ind. Mem., QC Selection Panel, England and Wales, 2011–13, NI, 2011–. Member Board: NI Charities Adv. Cttee, 1998–2000; Clifton House (Belfast Charitable Soc.), 1995–2007 (Hon. Treas., 2000–05). Dir, Team NI Ltd, 2004–06. Chm., Point Fields Th. Co., 1996. Trustee, Assisi Animal Sanctuary, 2006–11. Recreations: cookery, family, pets. Address: c/o Huston & Co., 13 Cabin Hill Gardens, Belfast BT5 7AP. T: (028) 9080 6080. E: felicity@huston.co.uk.

**HUTCHEON, Joy Louise**, CB 2017; Director General, Finance and Corporate Performance, Department for International Development, 2015–18; b 26 Feb. 1965; d of Keith Hutcheon and Margaret (née Swindells); partner, Christopher Peter Nuttall, qv. Educ: University Coll. London (BA English). Home Office: Private Sec. to Minister of State, 1991–92; Hd, Sentencing Policy, 1992–95; Private Sec. to Perm. Sec., 1995–97; Franchising Exec., Office of Passenger Rail Franchising, 1997–99; Team Leader, Performance and Innovation Unit, Cabinet Office, 1999–2000; Consultant, Caribbean, 2000–03; Department for International Development: Hd, Western Asia Dept, 2003–05; Dir, Communication and Knowledge Sharing, 2005–07; Hd, Zambia, 2007–09; Dir, E and Central Africa, 2009–11; Dir Gen., Country Progs (formerly Africa, S and E Asia and Western Hemisphere), 2011–15. Publications: Winning the Generation Game, 2000; Prime Minister's Review of Adoption, 2000; Sentencing for Drug and Drug Related Cases in OECS Magistrates' Courts, 2005. Recreations: weekends in Suffolk, playing the saxophone, California.

**HUTCHEON, William Robbie**; Editor, The Courier and Advertiser, 2002–11 (Deputy Editor, 2001); b 19 Jan. 1952; s of Alexander Hutcheon and Williamina Hutcheon (née Robbie); m 1974, Margo Martin; one s two d. Educ: Aberdeen Acad. D. C. Thomson & Co. Ltd: joined as reporter, Aberdeen, 1969; Sports Sub-ed., Dundee, 1970; various posts, The Courier and Advertiser, inc. Sports Ed., Chief Sub-ed., Night News Ed., to 2001. Mem., Editors' Cttee, Scottish Daily Newspapers Soc., 2002–11 (Chm., 2007–08). Recreations: sport, music, travel, computing. Address: 42 Ferndale Drive, Broughty Ferry, Dundee DD5 3DF. T: (01382) 774552. E: hutcheonbill@gmail.com.

**HUTCHESON, Linda Dolores**; see Cardozo, L. D.

**HUTCHINGS, Prof. Graham John**, CBE 2018; PhD, DSc; FRS 2009; FRSC, FIChemE; FInstP; FLSW; Regius Professor of Chemistry, Cardiff University, since 2016 (Professor of Physical Chemistry, 1997–2016; Director, Cardiff Catalysis Institute, 2008–19; Pro-Vice-Chancellor Research, 2010–12); b Weymouth, 3 Feb. 1951; s of Duncan Herbert and Celia Doris Hutchings; m 1973, Sally Joanna Dalton; one s three d. Educ: Weymouth Grammar Sch.; University Coll. London (BSc 1st Cl. Hons; PhD Chem. 1975; DSc 2002). FRSC 1987; FIChemE 2006; FInstP 2009. SO, 1975–79, Res. and Prodn Manager, 1979–81, ICI Petrochem. Div.; CSO, AECI, S Africa, 1981–84; Lectr, Sen. Lectr, then Prof., Dept of Chem., Univ. of Witwatersrand, Johannesburg, 1984–87; Asst Dir, 1987–94, Prof. and Dep. Dir, 1994–97, Leverhulme Centre for Innovative Catalysis, Univ. of Liverpool. MAE 2010. Founding FLSW 2010 (Menelaus Medal, 2017). Ed., Jl Catalysis, 1999–. Treas., Internat. Catalysis Socs, 2000–08. Davy Medal, Royal Soc., 2013; ENI Award for Advanced Envmtl Soc., 2017. Publications: contrib. papers to scientific jls, incl. Nature and Science, on subject of heterogeneous catalysis; more than 30 patents on subject of catalysis. Recreations: walking, sketching landscapes. Address: Cardiff Catalysis Institute, School of Chemistry, Cardiff University, Park Place, Cardiff CF10 3AT. T: (029) 2087 4059, Fax: (029) 2087 4030. E: hutch@cf.ac.uk.

**HUTCHINGS, Gregory Frederick**; Chairman, GCH Corporation (formerly GCH Capital) Ltd, since 2010. Educ: Uppingham Sch.; University of Aston (BSc); MBA Aston Mgt Centre. Dir, 1983–2000, Chief Exec., 1984–95, Chm., 1995–2000, Tomkins plc; Exec. Chm., Lupus Capital plc, 2004–09. Bd Mem., RNT, 1996–2002; Gov., Mus. of London, 1999–2008. Team Mem., England veterans' hockey teams, 1998–. Hon. DBA Sunderland, 2000.

**HUTCHINGS, Prof. Ian Michael**, PhD; FInstP, FIMMM; FREng; GKN Professor of Manufacturing Engineering, University of Cambridge, 2001–17, now Emeritus Professor; Fellow, St John's College, Cambridge, since 1975; Chairman, St John's Innovation Centre Ltd, Cambridge, since 1996; b 6 May 1950; s of Douglas and Sheila Hutchings; m 1973, Jennifer Farrant; three s one d. Educ: Rugby Sch.; Trinity Coll., Cambridge (BA 1971; MA; PhD 1975). FIMMM 1993; FInstP 1994; FREng 2002. Department of Materials Science, University of Cambridge: demonstrator, 1977–82; Lectr, 1982–97; Reader in Tribology, 1997–2000; St John's College, Cambridge: Lectr, 1978–2001; Dir of Studies in Materials Sci. and Metallurgy, 1990–2000. Hon. Prof., China Univ. of Mining and Technol., Beijing, 1999; Vis. Prof., Xi'an Univ. of Architecture and Technol., China, 2004; Adjunct Prof., Xi'an Jiaotong Univ., China, 2004. Ed.-in-Chief, Wear, 1998–2012. Tribology Silver

Medal, 1994, Donald Julius Groen Prize, 2000, IMechE; NPL Award for Materials Metrol., Inst. of Materials, 2000; Staudinger-Durrer Prize and Medal, ETH Zürich, 2007. *Publications:* Tribology: friction and wear of engineering materials, 1992, 2nd edn 2017; contrib. papers to scientific and engrg jls on tribology, materials engrg and manufg engrg incl. engrg aspects of ink-jet printing and history of tribology. *Recreation:* not gardening. *Address:* St John's College, Cambridge CB2 1TP. *E:* imh2@cam.ac.uk.

**HUTCHINGS, Martin Anthony**; QC 2011; *b* Farnborough, Kent, 14 July 1959; *s* of Donald Hutchings and Mary Hutchings; *m* 1990, Claudia Dalton; one *s* one *d. Educ:* Ravensbourne Sch.; St Catherine's Coll., Oxford (BA). Called to the Bar, Middle Temple, 1986; in practice as barrister, specialising in property litigation; Mem., Wilberforce Chambers, 2006–. *Recreations:* walking, cinema, swimming. *Address:* Wilberforce Chambers, 8 New Square, Lincoln's Inn, WC2A 3QP. *T:* (020) 7306 0102. *E:* mhutchings@wilberforce.co.uk.

**HUTCHINGS, Matthew Howard Olsen**; QC 2017; *b* Peterborough, 3 Feb. 1969; *s* of Paul Hutchings and Myra Hutchings; two *s* two *d. Educ:* King's Sch., Worcester; Worcester Sixth Form Coll.; Pembroke Coll., Oxford (BA PPE 1991); City Univ. (GDL 1992). Called to the Bar, Inner Temple, 1993. *Recreations:* books, music, long walks, art and films. *Address:* Cornerstone Barristers, 2–3 Gray's Inn Square, WC1R 5JH. *T:* (020) 7242 4986. *E:* matth@cornerstonebarristers.com.

**HUTCHINS, Bonnie**; *see* Greer, B.

**HUTCHINSON**; *see* Hely-Hutchinson.

**HUTCHINSON, Alison Elizabeth**, CBE 2016; Chief Executive, Pennies Foundation, since 2009; *b* Dumbarton, Scotland, 5 Feb. 1967; *d* of Charles and Elizabeth McCrea; *m* 1995, David John Hutchinson; one *s* two *d. Educ:* Strathclyde Univ. (BSc Technol. and Business Studies). IBM Corporation: Systems Engr, 1986–89; Software Sales Manager, 1989–91; Sales Exec., 1991–93; Eur. Customer Progs Manager, 1993–95; Global Manager, Smart Cards, 1995–97; Chief Exec., E-Net, 1997–99; Dir, Global Financial Solutions, 1999–2000; CEO, Barclays B2B, 2000–01, Mktg Dir, Barclaycard, 2002–03, Barclays Bank plc; Man. Dir, Kensington Mortgages, 2003–07, Gp CEO, 2007–08, Kensington Gp plc. Independent non-executive Director: LMAX Ltd, 2010–15; Aviva Life Hldgs UK Ltd, 2014–; Yorkshire Building Soc. Gp, 2015–; Liverpool Victoria Insurance; DFS plc. Trustee, CAF, 2010–16. *Recreations:* variety of sports, including cross country running and fitness training, sampling wine of many different varieties. *Address:* Beacon Underwood, Wood Road, Hindhead, Surrey GU26 6PX. *T:* 07917 064176. *E:* alison.hutchinson3@btinternet.com.

**HUTCHINSON, Anne-Marie**, OBE 2002; Partner, Dawson Cornwell, since 1998; *b* Donegal, 1 Aug. 1957; *d* of Samuel Gerald Hutchinson and Catherine Hutchinson; one *s* one *d. Educ:* St Peter's Sch., Huntingdon; Univ. of Leeds (BA Internat. Hist. and Politics). Admitted solicitor, 1985; Partner, Beckman and Beckman, 1988–98. Member: Nat. Commn on Forced Marriage, H of L, 2013–; Panel, Rev. on Sharia Law in England and Wales, 2016–18. Chair, Family Law Cttee, 2007–10, Chair, Women Lawyers' Interest Gp, 2011–13, Internat. Bar Assoc.; Gov. at Large, 2011–16, Parliamentarian, 2016–, Internat. Acad. of Family Lawyers (formerly Internat. Acad. of Matrimonial Lawyers). Trustee, Reunite, 1990–; Ambassador, Sharan Proj., 2014–. Hon. QC 2016. Hon. DLaws Leeds, 2016. *Publications:* (jtly) International Parental Child Abduction, 2003. *Recreations:* travel, reading, charity work. *Address:* Dawson Cornwell, 11 Staple Inn, WC1V 7QH. *T:* (020) 7242 2556, *Fax:* (020) 7539 4841. *E:* amh@dawsoncornwell.com.

**HUTCHINSON, David**; Co-Founder and Chief Executive Officer, Selladoor Worldwide (formerly Sell a Door Theatre Company), since 2009; *b* Stirling, 28 May 1988; *s* of Martin Hutchinson and Nuala Hutchinson. *Educ:* Liverpool Inst. of Performing Arts (BA Hons Acting 2009). Man. Dir, I AM Marketing, 2016–; Director: Pulse Artist Mgt, 2015–; Desktidy Design, 2018–; Prime Pantomimes, 2018–. Internat. Associate, Brooklyn Youth Co. Mem. Bd, New Wolsey Th., Ipswich. *Recreations:* running, travelling, film, tennis. *Address:* Selladoor Worldwide, 1 Creek Road, SE8 3BT. *T:* (020) 3355 8567. *E:* david@selladoor.com.

**HUTCHINSON, Elisabeth Helen**; *see* Wicksteed, E. H.

**HUTCHINSON, (George) Malcolm**, CB 1989; CEng, FIET; Director, Malcolm Hutchinson Ltd, since 1992; *b* 24 Aug. 1935; *s* of Cecil George Hutchinson and Annie Hutchinson; *m* 1958, Irene Mary Mook (*d* 2015); four *d. Educ:* Pocklington Sch.; Queens' Coll., Cambridge (MA). Develt Engr, Metropolitan Vickers, 1957; short service commn, 1958, regular commn, 1961, REME; RMCS, 1967; sc Camberley, 1968; CO 12 Armd Workshop, REME, 1968–70; Staff appts, 1970–74; British Liaison Officer, USA Army Materiel Comd, 1974–76; Comdr REME 1 British Corps troops, 1977–79; REME staff, 1979–82; Project Man., Software Systems, 1982–85; Dep. to DGEME, 1985–86; Dir Procurement Strategy MoD(PE), 1986–88; Vice Master-Gen. of the Ordnance, 1988–90. Mem., Defence Prospect Team, 1990. Procurement and logistic consultant, 1991–92. Managing Director: DLR, 1992–97; Docklands Rly Mgt Ltd, 1997–99; Chm., Atomic Weapon Estabt Mgt Ltd, 1999–2003; Exec. Chm., Atomic Weapon Estabt plc, 2002–05. Chm., Serco Docklands Ltd, 2006–10. Mem., Engrg Council, 1993–99. Pres., IEEIE, 1990–94. Col Comdt, REME, 1991–96. *Recreations:* Rugby, cricket, sailing. *Address:* Rectory Cottage, Little Ann Road, Little Ann, Andover, Hants SP11 7SN.

**HUTCHINSON, Prof. Gregory Owen**, DPhil; Regius Professor of Greek, University of Oxford, since 2015; Student of Christ Church, Oxford, since 2015; *b* London, 5 Dec. 1957; *s* of Jeremy Hutchinson and Daphne Hutchinson; *m* 1979, Yvonne Downing; one *d. Educ:* City of London Sch.; Balliol Coll., Oxford (BA 1979); Christ Church, Oxford (DPhil 1983). University of Oxford: Res. Lectr, Christ Church, 1981–84; Fellow and Tutor in Classics, Exeter Coll., 1984–2015; Reader in Classical Lit., 1996–98; Prof. of Greek and Latin Langs and Lit., 1998–2015. *Publications:* Aeschylus, Septem contra Thebas, 1985; Hellenistic Poetry, 1988; Latin Literature from Seneca to Juvenal: a critical study, 1993; Cicero's Correspondence: a literary study, 1998; Greek Lyric Poetry: a commentary on selected larger pieces, 2001; Propertius: Elegies Book IV, 2006; Talking Books: readings in Hellenistic and Roman books of poetry, 2008; Greek to Latin: frameworks and contexts for intertextuality, 2013; Plutarch's Rhythmic Prose, 2018. *Recreations:* playing the piano, reading literature in various languages, washing up to music. *Address:* Christ Church, Oxford OX1 1DP. *E:* gregory.hutchinson@classics.ox.ac.uk.

**HUTCHINSON, Henry**; *see* Hutchinson, M. H. R.

**HUTCHINSON, (John) Maxwell**, PPRIBA; architect, writer, broadcaster; *b* 3 Dec. 1948; *s* of late Frank Maxwell Hutchinson and Elizabeth Ross Muir (*née* Wright); marr. diss. *Educ:* Wellingborough Prep. Sch.; Oundle; Scott Sutherland Sch. of Arch., Aberdeen; Architectural Assoc. Sch. of Arch. (AA Dip. 1972); RIBA 1972. Founder, Hutchinson and Partners, Chartered Architects, 1972, Chm., 1987–93; Dir, The Hutchinson Studio Architects, 1993–. Chairman: Permarock Products Ltd, Loughborough, 1985–95; Holland, Hannen and Cubitts, 2010; non-exec. Dir, Archial Gp plc, 2005–10. Royal Institute of British Architects: Mem. Council, 1978–93, Sen. Vice Pres., 1988–89, Pres., 1989–91;

Chairman: East Midlands Arts Bd Ltd, 1991–95; Industrial Bldg Bureau, 1987–89; Vice-Chm., Construction Industry Council, 1990–92. Vis. Prof., Architecture, QUB, 1989–93; Special Prof. of Architecture, Nottingham Univ., 1993–96; Vis. Prof., Westminster Univ., 1998–2000. Founder and Chm., Article 25 (Architects for Aid), 2005–. Chm., British Architectural Library Trust, 1991–99; Mem. Council, RSCM, 1997–2000. Associate Mem., PRS, 1988. Trustee: Univ. of London; Univ. of London Inst. in Paris. Fellow, Chartered Inst. of Building, 2011. Hon. Fellow: Greenwich Univ., 1990; Royal Soc. of Ulster Architects, 1991; UCL, 2008. Hon. DDes, Robert Gordon, 2007. Church Warden Emeritus, Our Most Holy Redeemer, Clerkenwell; ordained deacon, 2014; Asst Curate, St John on Bethnal Green, 2014–16; Curate, All Saints, Chingford, 2016–. *Compositions:* The Kibbo Kift, Edinburgh Fest., 1976; The Ascent of Wilberforce III, Lyric Hammersmith, 1982; Requiem in a Village Church (choral), 1986; St John's Cantata, 1987. *Publications:* The Prince of Wales: right or wrong?, 1989; Number 57: the storey of a house, 2003. *Recreation:* jazz piano.

**HUTCHINSON, Ven. Karen Elizabeth**; Archdeacon of Norwich and Warden of Readers, Diocese of Norwich, since 2016; *b* 1964. *Educ:* Lady Margaret Hall, Oxford (BA 1985); Univ. of Kent (MA 2006); Wycliffe Hall, Oxford. Admitted as solicitor, 1989; ordained deacon, 2001, priest, 2002; Curate, St Lawrence, Alton, 2001–06; Vicar: All Saints, Crondall, 2006–12; St Thomas, Bourne and Tilford, 2012–16. Mem., Gen. Synod, 2013–16. Hon. Canon, Guildford Cathedral, 2013–16. *Address:* c/o Diocesan House, 109 Dereham Road, Easton, Norwich NR9 5ES.

**HUTCHINSON, Malcolm**; *see* Hutchinson, G. M.

**HUTCHINSON, Prof. (Marcus) Henry (Ritchie)**, PhD; Director, Central Laser Facility, CCLRC Rutherford Appleton Laboratory, 1997–2005; *b* 2 Dec. 1945; *s* of Marcus Henry McCracken Hutchinson and Maud Hutchinson; *m* 1973, Gillian Ruth Harris; one *s* two *d. Educ:* Coleraine Academical Instn; Queen's Univ. of Belfast (BSc 1st cl. Hons Physics 1968; PhD Physics 1971). FInstP 1998. Imperial College, London: Lectr in Physics, 1973–83; Sen. Lectr, 1983–86; Reader in Optics, 1986–89; Prof. of Laser Physics, 1989–2002; Dir, Blackett Lab. Laser Consortium, 1986–97; Associate Dir, Centre for Photomolecular Scis, 1992–97. Chief Scientist, CCLRC, 2004–07. Chief Scientific Advr, PETAL (Petawatt Aquitaine Laser) Prog., 2009–11. Vis. Res. Prof., Univ. of Illinois at Chicago, 1986; Vis. Prof., Univ. of Oxford, 2003–11; Invited Prof., Univ. of Bordeaux 1, 2009–11. Member: SERC Physics Cttee, 1990–92; Wissenschaftliche Rat, Gesellschaft für Schwerionenforschung mbH, Darmstadt, 2001–05 (Chm., Plasma Physics Adv. Cttee, 2004–10); UK Mem., European Strategy Forum for Res. Infrastructures, 2005–07. FRSA 2007. *Publications:* contrib. numerous scientific papers and articles in physics. *Recreations:* walking, gardening. *Address:* 16 Chiltern Hills Road, Beaconsfield, Bucks HP9 1PL.

**HUTCHINSON, Maxwell**; *see* Hutchinson, J. M.

**HUTCHINSON, Prof. Peter John Ashton**, PhD; FRCS; Professor of Neurosurgery, University of Cambridge, since 2014; Director of Clinical Studies and Fellow, Robinson College, Cambridge, since 2008; Hon. Consultant Neurosurgeon, Cambridge University Hospitals NHS Foundation Trust, since 2003; *b* Plymouth, 16 Dec. 1965; *s* of David and Rosalind Hutchinson; *m* 1998, Elizabeth Barr; two *s. Educ:* Judd Sch., Tonbridge; St Bartholomew's Hosp. Med. Sch., Univ. of London (BSc Hons; MB BS); Robinson Coll., Cambridge (PhD 2001). FRCS 1994 (FRCS (Surg. Neurol. 2002)). Hse Officer, St Bartholomew's and Homerton Hosps, 1990–91; SHO, St Bartholomew's and Oxford rotation, 1991–94; Registrar: St Bartholomew's, 1994; Addenbrooke's Hosp., Cambridge, 1994–2002; Acad. of Med. Scis/Health Foundn Sen. Fellow, 2003–13; Reader in Neurosurgery, Univ. of Cambridge, 2008–13. Mem., Sec. of State for Transport's Hon. Med. Adv. Panel on Driving and Disorders of the Nervous System, 2008–. Speciality Lead for Neurosurgery, RCS Academic and Res. Bd, 2013–. Chair, Trauma Gp, Soc. of British Neurol Surgeons, 2010–. Vice Pres., Eur. Assoc. of Neurosurgeons, 2010–; Treas., Internat. Neurotrauma Soc., 2013–. FMedSci 2018. *Publications:* (jtly) Intracranial Pressure and Brain Biochemical Monitoring XI, 2002; (jtly) Intracranial Pressure and Brain Biochemical Monitoring XII, 2005; (ed jtly) Head Injury: a multidisciplinary approach, 2009; contribs to learned jls, incl. Lancet. *Recreation:* Chief Medical Officer of Formula One British Grand Prix. *Address:* Box 167, Academic Division of Neurosurgery, University of Cambridge, Addenbrooke's Hospital, Cambridge CB2 0QQ. *T:* (01223) 336946, *Fax:* (01223) 216926. *E:* pjah2@cam.ac.uk.

**HUTCHINSON, Prof. Philip**; DL; FREng; CPhys; Principal, Royal Military College of Science, Cranfield University, 1996–2006, now Emeritus Professor; Chairman, Letcombe Technology Ltd, 2006–13; *b* 26 July 1938; *s* of George and Edna Hutchinson; *m* 1960, Joyce Harrison; one *s* one *d. Educ:* King James 1st Grammar Sch., Bishop Auckland, Co. Durham; King's Coll., Univ. of Durham (BSc); Univ. of Newcastle upon Tyne (PhD). MInstP. SO and SSO, Theoretical Phys. Div., AERE, Harwell, 1962–69; Vis. Fellow, Chem. Engrg Dept, Univ. of Houston, Texas, 1969–70; AERE, Harwell: SSO and PSO, Theoretical Phys Div., 1970–75; Hd of Thermodynamics and Fluid Mechanics Gp, Engrg Scis Div., 1975–80; Hd of Engrg Phys Br., Engrg Scis Div., 1980–85; Hd of Engrg Scis Div., 1985–87; Hd, Harwell Combustion Centre, 1980–87; Cranfield Institute of Technology, then Cranfield University: Head, Sch. of Engrg, 1987–2002; Pro Vice-Chancellor, 1996–99; Dep. Vice Chancellor, 1996–2003. Visiting Professor: Imperial Coll., London, 1980–85; Univ. of Leeds, 1985–. Chairman: Exec. Cttee on Fundamental Res. in Combustion, 1977–81, Exec. Cttee on Energy Efficiency and Emissions Reduction in Combustion, 1997–98, Internat. Energy Agency; Combustion Phys Gp of InstP, 1985–89; MRI 1989; Mem., Combustion Inst., 1977–2003; Past Mem., Watt Cttee on Energy, representing InstP and Combustion Inst. respectively; Founding Bd Mem., Eur. Research Community on Flow Turbulence and Combustion, 1988 (Chm., 1994–2000; Treas., 2000–02). 27th Leonardo da Vinci Lectr for IMechE, 1983. Liveryman, Engineers' Co., 2004–. DL Oxon, 2003. FREng (FEng 1997). Hon. DTech Lund, 1999. *Publications:* papers in learned jls on statistical mechanics, fluid mechanics, combustion and laser light scattering. *Recreations:* music, reading, Go, gadgets.

**HUTCHISON**, family name of **Baroness Kennedy of the Shaws**.

**HUTCHISON, Most Rev. Andrew Sandford**; Primate of the Anglican Church of Canada, 2004–07; *b* 19 Sept. 1938; *s* of Ralph Burton Hutchison and Kathleen Marian (*née* Van Nostrand); *m* 1960, Lois Arlene Knight; one *s. Educ:* Lakefield Coll. Sch.; Upper Canada Coll.; Trinity Coll. Toronto (LTh). Ordained deacon, 1969, priest, 1970; served fifteen years in the dio. of Toronto; Dean of Montreal, 1984–90; Bp of Montreal, 1990–2004, Archbishop, 2002–04; Metropolitan, Ecclesiastical Province of Canada, 2002–04. Pres., Montreal Diocesan Theol Coll., 1990–2004; Visitor, Bishops Univ., Lennoxville, 1990–2004; Chaplain: Canadian Grenadier Guards, 1986–90 (Hon. Chaplain, 1990–2004); 6087 and 22 CAR, 1986–2004; Order of St John of Jerusalem, Quebec, 1987–2004; Bishop Ordinary, Canadian Forces, 1997–2004. Pres., Fulford Residence, Montreal, 1990–2004. Trustee, Lakefield Coll. Sch., 1997–2000. Hon. DD: Montreal Diocesan Theol Coll., 1993; Trinity Coll., Toronto, 1994; Huron Univ. Coll., London, Ont, 2007; Hon. DCL Bishop's Univ., Lennoxville, 2003. OStJ 1991. Ecclesiastical Grand Cross, Order of St Lazarus, 1992.

**HUTCHISON, Geordie Oliphant;** Managing Director, Calders & Grandidge, timber importers and manufacturers, 1974–96; *b* 11 June 1934; *s* of late Col Ronald Gordon Oliphant Hutchison and of Ruth Gordon Hutchison-Bradburne; *m* 1964, Virginia Barbezat; two *s* one *d*. *Educ:* Eton Coll. Served RN, 1952–54: commnd as aircraft pilot, 1953. Calders Ltd, 1954–59; Calders & Grandidge Ltd, 1959–96: Dir, 1969. Comr, Forestry Commn, 1981–89. High Sheriff, Lincs, 1998. *Recreations:* golf, shooting. *Address:* Collairnie House, Cupar, Fife KY15 7RX. *T:* (01337) 810309. *Club:* Royal and Ancient Golf (St Andrews).

**HUTCHISON, Sir James Colville,** 3rd Bt *cr* 1956; *b* 7 Oct. 1967; *s* of Sir Peter Craft Hutchison, 2nd Bt and Virginia Hutchison (*née* Colville); *S* father, 2019, but his name does not appear on the Official Roll of the Baronetage; *m* 1996, Jane Frances Elizabeth, *d* of Peter Laidlaw; one *s* one *d*. *Heir: s* Harry Leo Peter Hutchison, *b* 23 Aug. 1998.

**HUTCHISON, Prof. James Douglas,** PhD; FRCSE, FRCS, FRCSGlas; Regius Professor of Surgery, since 2000 and Sir Harry Platt Professor of Orthopaedics, since 1995, University of Aberdeen; Hon. Consultant Orthopaedic Surgeon, Aberdeen Royal Infirmary, since 1991; *b* 8 Oct. 1955; *s* of James Hutchison, FRCS and Grace J. J. Holloway, MA; *m* 1985, Catherine, (Kate), MacLeod Douglas; two *s* one *d*. *Educ:* High Sch. of Dundee; Univ. of Dundee (MB ChB 1979); Univ. of Aberdeen (PhD 1988). FRCSE 1984; FRCS 2000; FRCSGlas 2002. Orthopaedic Registrar and Sen. Registrar, Royal Infirmary, Edinburgh, and Princess Margaret Rose Orthopaedic Hosp., 1986–90; Sen. Lectr in Orthopaedics, Univ. of Aberdeen, 1991–95. Speciality Advr in Orthopaedics and Trauma to CMO (Scotland), 1998–2007. Chairman: Scottish Cttee for Orthopaedics and Trauma, 2000–04; Scottish Hip Fracture Audit, 2004–06; Hip Fracture Delivery Team for Scottish Exec. Health Dept, 2005–09; Scottish Orthopaedic Services Develt Gp, Scottish Govt, 2010–; Scottish Surgical Mortality Audit, 2011–14. Chairman: Intercollegiate Specialty Bd in Trauma and Orthopaedic Surgery, 2005–08; Specialty Exams Quality Assce Cttee, FRCS, 2009–11; Royal College of Surgeons of Edinburgh: Trustee (Mem. Council), 2008–12; Vice-Pres., 2012–15; Mem., Specialty Adv. Bd in Orthopaedics, 1997–2015 (Chm., 2007–11); Chm., Heritage Cttee, 2009–15. Member: Harveian Soc., 1997 (Pres., 2008); Moynihan Chirurgical Club, 2005; President: Aberdeen Medico-Chirurgical Soc., 2005–06; Assoc. of Profs of Orthopaedic Surgery, 2010–14; ex officio Mem. Council, British Orthopaedic Assoc., 2010–12. Chm., Bd of Govs, Surgeons' Hall Trust, 2007–09; Pres., Dundee High Sch. Old Boys' Club, 2007–08; Mem., Bd of Govs, Robert Gordon's Coll., Aberdeen, 2011– (Chm., 2013–). *Publications:* contribs to scientific and clinical jls incl. Lancet, BMJ, Jl Bone and Joint Surgery. *Recreations:* family, dogs, shooting, art, curling. *Address:* Cowiehillock Cottage, Echt, Skene, Aberdeenshire AB32 6XD. *T:* (01330) 860716. *E:* j.d.hutchison@abdn.ac.uk. *Clubs:* Royal Northern and University (Aberdeen); Aesculapian (Edinburgh).

**HUTCHISON, Sir Robert,** 3rd Bt *cr* 1939, of Thurle, Streatley, co. Berks; independent financial adviser, since 1978; *b* 25 May 1954; *er s* of Sir Peter Hutchison, 2nd Bt and Mary-Grace (*née* Seymour); *S* father, 1998; *m* 1987, Anne Margaret, *e d* of Sir (Godfrey) Michael (David) Thomas, 11th Bt; two *s*. *Educ:* Orwell Park Sch., Ipswich; Marlborough Coll. With J. & A Scrimgeour Ltd, 1973–78. *Recreations:* golf, tennis, watching Association Football, family life. *Heir: s* Hugo Thomas Alexander Hutchison, *b* 16 April 1988. *Address:* Hawthorn Cottage, Lower Road, Grundisburgh, Woodbridge, Suffolk IP13 6UQ. *Clubs:* Ipswich & Suffolk (Ipswich), Woodbridge Golf.

**HUTH, Angela Maureen, (Mrs J. D. Howard-Johnston);** writer; *b* 29 Aug. 1938; *d* of late Harold Edward Strachan Huth and Bridget Huth (*née* Nickols); *m* 1961, Quentin Hugh Crewe (marr. diss. 1970; he *d* 1998); one *d* (one *s* decd); *m* 1978, James Douglas Howard-Johnston; one *d* (one *s* decd). *Educ:* Lawnside, Gt Malvern, Worcs; Beaux Arts, Paris; Annigoni Sch. of Painting, Florence; Byam Shaw Art Sch., London. Harpers Bazaar, 1957–58; Art dept, J. Walter-Thompson, 1958–59; Queen mag., 1959–61; reporter, Man Alive, BBC, 1965–67; BBC TV presenter, How It Is, 1969–70; Kaleidoscope, Radio 4, 1970; freelance, 1968–. Radio and TV: plays: The Drip (radio); I didn't take my mother (radio); Past Forgetting (radio), 2001; Special Co-respondent; The Emperor's New Hat; The Summer House; Virginia Fly is Drowning; Sun Child; documentaries: The English Woman's Wardrobe, 1987; Land Girls, 1995; stage plays: The Understanding, 1982; The Trouble with Old Lovers, 1995. FRSL 1975. *Publications:* Nowhere Girl, 1970; Virginia Fly is Drowning, 1972; Sun Child, 1975; South of the Lights, 1977; Monday Lunch in Fairyland and Other Stories, 1978; The Understanding (play), 1982; Wanting, 1984; The English Woman's Wardrobe (non-fiction), 1986; Eugenie in Cloud Cuckoo Land (for children), 1986; Such Visitors and Other Stories, 1989; Invitation to the Married Life, 1991; Land Girls, 1994; The Trouble with Old Lovers (play), 1995; Another Kind of Cinderella, 1996; Wives of the Fishermen, 1998; Easy Silence, 1999; Of Love and Slaughter, 2002; The Collected Stories of Angela Huth, 2003; (ed) Well Remembered Friends: eulogies on celebrated lives, 2004; Once a Land Girl, 2010; Colouring In, 2015; Not the Whole Story: a memoir, 2018. *Recreations:* collecting antique paste jewellery, re-visiting favourite places in Britain, tap dancing. *Address:* c/o Caroline Michel, PFD, 55 New Oxford Street, WC1A 1BS.

**HUTH, Johannes Peter;** Managing Director, Kohlberg Kravis Roberts & Co. Partners LLP (formerly Ltd), since 1999; *b* Heidelberg, Germany, 27 May 1960; *s* of Prof. Karl Otto Huth and Dr Brigitte Marielouise Soergel; *m* 1st, 1991, Leili (marr. diss. 2008); two *s* three *d*; 2nd, 2011, Helene. *Educ:* London Sch. of Econs and Pol Sci. (BSc Econ. 1984); Univ. of Chicago (MBA 1986). Vice Pres., Mergers and Acquisitions Dept, NY, Salomon Brothers, 1986–91; Mem., Mgt Cttee, Investcorp, 1991–99. Chm. Trustees, Private Equity Foundn, then Impetus - Private Equity Foundn, 2011–; Trustee: Design Mus., 2011– (Vice Chm.); Staedel Mus.; Educnl Endowment Foundn. Gov., LSE, 2002–. Vis. Fellow, Oxford Univ. FRSA. *Recreations:* cycling, ski-ing. *Address:* Kohlberg Kravis Roberts & Co. Partners LLP, Stirling Square, 7 Carlton Gardens, SW1Y 5AD. *E:* huthj@kkr.com.

**HUTSON, Prof. Jeremy Mark,** DPhil; FRS 2010; CChem, FRSC; FInstP; Professor of Chemistry and Physics (formerly Chemistry), University of Durham, since 1996; *b* 7 May 1957; *s* of James Murray Hutson and Margaret Joyce Hutson (*née* Pearson). *Educ:* Brentwood Sch.; Wadham Coll., Oxford (MA); Hertford Coll., Oxford (DPhil 1981). CPhys, MInstP 1994; FInstP 2004; MRSC, CChem 1988; FRSC 1999. NATO/SERC Res. Fellow, Univ. of Waterloo, Canada, 1981–83; Drapers' Co. Res. Fellow, 1983–84, Stokes Res. Fellow, 1984–86, Pembroke Coll., Cambridge; Lectr, 1987–93, Reader, 1993–96, Hd, Dept of Chem., 1998–2001, Univ. of Durham. JILA Vis. Fellow, Univ. of Colo, Boulder, 2001–02. Chairman: EPSRC Collaborative Computational Project on Molecular Quantum Dynamics, 2000–05; ESF Sci. Cttee, EuroQUAM, 2007–10. Member: EPSRC Peer Review College, 1994–; Bd, Atomic Molecular and Optical Physics Div., European Physical Soc., 2004–07. Ed., Internat. Rev. in Physical Chem., 2000–. Corday-Morgan Medal, 1991, Tilden Prize, 2011, RSC; Kolos Medal, Univ. of Warsaw and Polish Chemical Soc., 2007; Computational Chem. Award, RSC, 2007; Humboldt Prize, Alexander von Humboldt Foundn, 2010; Thomson Medal, InstP, 2016. *Publications:* numerous contribs to jls incl. Jl Chem. Physics, Physical Rev. *Recreations:* hiking, paddling, photography, local history. *Address:* Department of Chemistry, University of Durham, South Road, Durham DH1 3LE. *E:* J.M.Hutson@durham.ac.uk.

**HUTSON, John Whiteford,** OBE 1966; HM Diplomatic Service, retired; Consul-General, Casablanca, 1984–87; *b* 21 Oct. 1927; *s* of John Hutson and Jean Greenlees Laird; *m* 1954, Doris Kemp (*d* 2014); one *s* two *d*. *Educ:* Hamilton Academy; Glasgow Univ. (MA (Hons)). MCIL (MIL 1987). HM Forces, 1949–51; Foreign Office, 1951; Third Secretary, Prague, 1953; FO, 1955; Second Sec., Berlin, 1956; Saigon, 1959; First Sec., 1961; Consul (Commercial) San Francisco, 1963–67; First Sec. and Head of Chancery, Sofia, 1967–69; FCO, 1969; Counsellor, 1970; Baghdad, 1971–72; Inspector, FCO, 1972–74; Head, Communications Operations Dept, FCO, 1974–76; Counsellor (Commercial), Moscow, 1976–79; Consul-Gen., Frankfurt, 1979–83. *Recreations:* British diplomatic oral history project, church yesterday and today, elementary bridge.
See also L. M. Hutson.

**HUTSON, Prof. Lorna Margaret,** DPhil; FBA 2016; Merton Professor of English Literature, University of Oxford, since 2016; Fellow of Merton College, Oxford, since 2016; *b* Berlin, 27 Nov. 1958; *d* of John Whiteford Hutson, *qv*; civil partnership 2005, Catherine M. Sprent (*d* 2011); partner, 2013, Linda R. Hardy; one adopted *d*. *Educ:* St Hilary's Sch., Edinburgh; Tormead Sch., Guildford; Somerville Coll., Oxford (MA Hons 1st Cl.; DPhil 1983). Lectr, 1985–95, Reader in English Lit., 1995–98, QMC; Prof. of English Lit., Univ. of Hull, 1998–2000; Prof., Univ. of California at Berkeley, 2000–04; Berry Prof. of English Lit., 2004–16, Hd of Sch., 2008–11, Univ. of St Andrews. John Simon Guggenheim Meml Fellowship, 2004; Leverhulme Trust Major Res. Fellowship, 2014–17. *Publications:* Thomas Nashe in Context, 1989; The Usurer's Daughter, 1994; (with V. Kahn) Rhetoric and Law in Early Modern Europe, 2000; The Invention of Suspicion, 2007; Circumstantial Shakespeare, 2015; The Oxford Handbook of English Law and Literature, 1500–1700, 2017; articles in Representations, English Lit. Hist., Texas Studies in Lit. and Lang., Huntington Library Qly. *Recreations:* walking, swimming, cooking, art galleries. *Address:* Merton College, Oxford OX1 4JD. *E:* lorna.hutson@ell.ox.ac.uk.

**HUTSON, Robin Charles;** Chairman and Chief Executive Officer: Lime Wood Group Ltd, since 2009; Home Grown Hotels Ltd, since 2011; *b* Beckenham, Kent, 9 Jan. 1957; *s* of Derek and Eileen Hutson; *m* 1983, Judith Alison Hill; two *s*. *Educ:* Godalming Grammar Sch.; Brooklands Tech. Coll. Mgt trainee, Savoy Hotel Gp, 1975–78; Trainee, Le Crillon, Paris, 1978–79; Front Office Manager, Berkeley Hotel, 1979–84; Ops Manager, Elbow Beach, Bermuda, 1984–86; Gen. Manager, then Man. Dir, Chewton Glen Hotel, 1986–94; Co-Founder, Chm. and CEO, Hotel du Vin Gp Ltd, 1994–2004; Chm., Soho Hse Gp, 2004–08. Non-exec. Chm., Belstaff Ltd, 2018–. Hon. DBus Southampton Solent, 2015. Outstanding Contribution Award, Hotel Cateys, 2014; Lifetime Achievement Award, AA, 2015. *Recreations:* fly-fishing, motorcycling, food, wine, travel. *Address:* Lime Wood Group Ltd, Clayhill, Beechen Lane, Lyndhurst, Hants SO43 7DD. *E:* robin@robinhutson.com. *Clubs:* Soho House, Groucho.

**HUTT, Ven. David Handley;** Canon, 1995–2005, now Emeritus, and Archdeacon, 1999–2005, of Westminster; Steward, 1995–2005, and Sub-Dean, 1999–2005, Westminster Abbey; *b* 24 Aug. 1938; *s* of late Frank and of Evelyn Hutt. *Educ:* Brentwood; RMA Sandhurst; King's College London (Hanson Prize for Christian Ethics; Barry Prize for Theology; AKC). Regular Army, 1957–64. KCL, 1964–68. Deacon 1969, priest 1970: Curate: Bedford Park, W4, 1969–70; St Matthew, Westminster, 1970–73; Priest Vicar and Succentor, Southwark Cathedral, 1973–78; Sen. Chaplain, King's Coll., Taunton, 1978–82; Vicar: St Alban and St Patrick, Birmingham, 1982–86; All Saints, Margaret St, 1986–95. Mem. Court, Sion Coll., 2005–07 (Pres., 1996–97; Fellow, 2007–). Nat. Co-ordinator, Affirming Catholicism, 1998–. Mem. Council, ALVA, 2000–05. Trustee, Utd Westminster Schs' Foundn, 2006–14; Governor: Westminster City Sch., 1995–2005; Sutton Valence Sch., 2007–13. Patron, London Parks and Gardens Trust, 2003–. MA Lambeth, 2005. *Publications:* miscellaneous theol articles and reviews. *Recreations:* reading, reflection, the enjoyment of fine wine. *Address:* 14 Up The Quadrangle, Morden College, Blackheath, SE3 0PW.

**HUTT, Sir Dexter (Walter),** Kt 2004; Chief Executive (formerly Executive Head), Ninestiles Federation of Schools, Birmingham, 2004–11; Executive Leader, Hastings Schools Federation, 2008–11; *b* Georgetown, Guyana, 25 July 1948; *s* of Walter and Binks Hutt; *m* 1976, Rosemary Lyn Jones; two *s* one *d*. *Educ:* Birmingham Univ. (BScSoc). Hd, Middle Sch., Holte Sch., Birmingham, 1978–82; Dep. Hd and Actg Hd, Sidney Stringer Sch., Coventry, 1982–88; Headteacher, Ninestiles Sch., Birmingham, 1998–2004. Chief Exec., Ninestiles Plus, 2003–11. Mem., Ninestiles Acad. Trust, 2013–19. Member: DFE Reference Gp, 1998–2011; Bd, Young People's Learning Agency, 2010–12; Bd, CBSO, 2014–17; Chair, Corp., Birmingham Metropolitan Coll. 2019–. Comr, Commn for Racial Equality, 2004–07. Trustee, Villiers Park, 2005–11. *Recreations:* current affairs, reading novels and biographies, horse–racing, golf. *Address:* Orchard House, 7 Hole Farm Road, Birmingham B31 2BS. *T:* (0121) 477 4385. *E:* dexterhutt@gmail.com.

**HUTT, Jane Elizabeth;** Member (Lab) Vale of Glamorgan, National Assembly for Wales, since 1999; Deputy Minister and Chief Whip, since 2018; *b* 15 Dec. 1949; *d* of late Prof. Michael Stewart Rees Hutt and of Elizabeth Mai Hutt; *m* 1984, Michael John Hillary Trickey; two *d*. *Educ:* Highlands Sch., Eldoret, Kenya; Rosemead Sch., Littlehampton; Univ. of Kent (BA Hons 1970); London Sch. of Econs (CQSW 1972); Bristol Univ. (MSc Mgt Develt and Social Responsibility 1995). Community worker: IMPACT (Town Planners & Architects), Wales, 1972–74; Polypill (Community Projects Foundn), Wales, 1975–77; Co-ordinator, Welsh Women's Aid, 1978–88; Director: Tenant Participation Adv. Service, (Wales), 1988–92; Chwarae Teg (Wales), 1992–99. National Assembly for Wales: Sec., then Minister, for Health and Social Services, 1999–2005; Business Minister and Minister for Children, 2005–07; Minister for Children, Educn, Lifelong Learning and Skills, 2007–09; Minister for Business and Budget, 2009–11; Minister for Finance and Leader of the House, 2011–14; Minister for Finance and Govt Business, 2014–16; Leader of the House and Chief Whip, 2016–17. Hon. Fellow, UWIC, 1996. *Publications:* Opening the Town Hall: an introduction to local government, 1989; Making Opportunities: a guide for women and employers, 1992. *Recreations:* music, reading. *Address:* National Assembly for Wales, Cardiff Bay, Cardiff CF99 1NA. *T:* 0300 200 7110.

**HUTTER, Prof. Otto Fred,** PhD; Regius Professor of Physiology, University of Glasgow, 1971–90, now Emeritus; *b* 29 Feb. 1924; *s* of Isak and Elisabeth Hutter; *m* 1948, Yvonne T. Brown; two *s* two *d*. *Educ:* Chajes Real Gymnasium, Vienna; Bishop's Stortford Coll., Herts; University Coll., London (BSc, PhD). Univ. of London Postgrad. Student in Physiology, 1948; Sharpey Scholar, UCL, 1949–52; Rockefeller Travelling Fellow and Fellow in Residence, Johns Hopkins Hosp., Baltimore, 1953–55; Lectr, Dept of Physiology, UCL, 1955–61; Hon. Lectr, 1961–70. Visiting Prof., Tel-Aviv Univ. 1968, 1970; Scientific Staff, Nat. Inst. for Medical Research, Mill Hill, London, 1961–70. Hon. Mem., Physiological Soc., 1992. Hon. DSc Glasgow Caledonian, 1994. *Publications:* papers on neuromuscular and synaptic transmission, cardiac and skeletal muscle, in physiological jls. *Address:* 60 Browning Avenue, Bournemouth BH5 1NW.

**HUTTON,** family name of **Barons Hutton** and **Hutton of Furness**.

**HUTTON,** Baron *cr* 1997 (Life Peer), of Bresagh in the county of Down; **James Brian Edward Hutton,** Kt 1988; PC 1988; a Lord of Appeal in Ordinary, 1997–2004; *b* 29 June 1931; *s* of late James and Mabel Hutton, Belfast; *m* 1st, 1975, Mary Gillian Murland (*d* 2000); two *d*; 2nd, 2001, Lindy, *widow* of Christopher H. Nickols; two step *s* one step *d*. *Educ:* Shrewsbury Sch.; Balliol Coll., Oxford (1st Cl. final sch. of Jurisprudence; Hon. Fellow, 1988); Queen's Univ. of Belfast. Called to the Northern Ireland Bar, 1954; QC (NI) 1970; Bencher, Inn of Court of Northern Ireland, 1974; called to English Bar, 1972. Junior Counsel to Attorney-General for NI, 1969; Legal Adviser to Min. of Home Affairs, NI, 1973; Sen. Crown Counsel in NI, 1973–79; Judge of the High Court of Justice (NI), 1979–88; Lord Chief Justice of NI, 1988–97. Mem., H of L, 1997–2018. Hon. Bencher: Inner Temple, 1988; King's Inns, Dublin, 1988. Mem., Jt Law Enforcement Commn, 1974; Dep. Chm., Boundary Commn for NI, 1985–88. Chm., Inquiry into death of Dr David Kelly, 2003–04. Visitor, Univ. of Ulster, 1999–2004. Hon. LLD: QUB, 1992; Ulster, 2004.

**HUTTON OF FURNESS,** Baron *cr* 2010 (Life Peer), of Aldingham in the County of Cumbria; **John Matthew Patrick Hutton;** PC 2001; Chairman: Independent Public Service Pensions Commission, since 2010; MyCSP Ltd, since 2012; *b* 6 May 1955; *m* (marr. diss.); three *s* one *d* (and one *s* decd); *m* 2004, Heather Rogers, OBE. *Educ:* Magdalen Coll., Oxford (BA, BCL). Research Associate, Templeton Coll., Oxford, 1980–81; Sen. Lectr, Newcastle Poly., 1981–92. Contested (Lab): Penrith and Borders, 1987; Cumbria and Lancs N, European Parlt, 1989. MP (Lab) Barrow and Furness, 1992–2010. Parly Under-Sec. of State, 1998–99, Minister of State, 1999–2005, DoH; Chancellor, Duchy of Lancaster, 2005; Secretary of State: for Work and Pensions, 2005–07; for Business, Enterprise and Regulatory Reform, 2007–08; for Defence, 2008–09. Chm., RUSI, 2010–15. *Publications:* Kitchener's Men, 2008; August 1914: surrender at St Quentin, 2010; (with Sir Leigh Lewis) How to be a Minister: a 21st-century guide, 2014; The Gunners of August 1914, 2014; articles on labour law in Industrial Law Jl. *Recreations:* football, cricket, cinema, music, First World War history. *Address:* House of Lords, SW1A 0PW.

**HUTTON, Alasdair Henry,** OBE 1990 (MBE 1986); TD 1977; writer and narrator of public events, UK and overseas; Member (C), Scottish Borders Council, 2002–12 (Convener, 2003–12); *b* 19 May 1940; *s* of Alexander Hutton and Margaret Elizabeth (*née* Henderson); *m* 1975, Deirdre Mary Cassels (*see* Dame D. M. Hutton); two *s*. *Educ:* Dollar Academy; Brisbane State High Sch., Australia. Radio Station 4BH, Brisbane, 1956; John Clemenger Advertising, Melbourne, 1957–59; Journalist: The Age, Melb., 1959–61; Press and Journal, Aberdeen, Scotland, 1962–64; Broadcaster, BBC: Scotland, N Ireland, London, Shetland, 1964–79. MEP (C) S Scotland, 1979–89; European Democratic Gp spokesman on regional policy, 1983–87, on budgetary control, 1987–89; contested (C) S Scotland, EP elecn, 1989 and 1994. Contested (C) Roxburgh and Berwickshire, Scottish Parly elecn, 1999. Sen. Consultant, Coutts Career Consultants, Scotland, 1994–97; Sen. Advr, Career Associates, 1998–2003. European Adviser: Royal Bank of Scotland, 1989–94; IOM Parlt, 1989–94; Scottish Police Coll., 1989–94. Board Mem., Scottish Agricl Coll., 1992–95. Chm., Crime Concern, Scotland, 1990–95. Member: Internat. Relns Cttee, Law Soc. of Scotland, 1991–99; Church and Nation Cttee, Church of Scotland, 1992–96; Social Security Adv. Cttee, 1996–99. Presenter, The Business Programme, BBC Radio Scotland, 1989–90; Narrator, Edinburgh Mil. Tattoo, later Royal Edinburgh Mil. Tattoo, 1992–. Mem., Queen's Body Guard for Scotland, Royal Co. of Archers; Pres., Scotland and NI Br., Parachute Regl Assoc., 2016–. Hon. Col, Lothian and Borders Bn, ACF, 2006–09. Former Vice Pres., John Buchan Soc.; Life Mem., Edinburgh Sir Walter Scott Club (former Chm.). Scottish Chm. and Trustee, Community Service Volunteers, 1985–2010. President: RBL Scotland, Kelso, 2000–, Border Area, 2014–16, Edinburgh, Lothian and Borders Area, 2016–; Kelso Farmers' Mkt, 2006–12. Patron: Overseas Projects, ROKPA UK, 1997–2016; Borders Ind. Advocacy Service, 2001–; Borders Talking Newspaper, 2008–. Chm., SE Scotland Br., Order of St John, 2012–. Elder, Kelso N, Church of Scotland. MStJ 2013. *Publications:* 15 Para 1947–1993, 1997; The Tattoo Fox, 2013; The Tattoo Fox Makes New Friends, 2014; The Greatest Show on Earth, 2016; (ed) Luath Treasury of Scottish Nursery Rhymes, 2016; Mustard and Pepper, 2019. *Address:* 4 Broomlands Court, Kelso, Roxburghshire TD5 7SR. *T:* (01573) 224369, 07753 625734. *E:* AlasdairHutton@yahoo.co.uk. *Clubs:* New, Royal Scots (Edinburgh).

**HUTTON, Anthony Charles,** CB 1995; Executive Director, OECD, Paris, 2001–07; *b* 4 April 1941; *s* of Charles James Hutton and Athene Mary (*née* Hastie); *m* 1963, Sara Flemming; two *s* one *d*. *Educ:* Brentwood School; Trinity College, Oxford (MA). HM Inspector of Taxes, 1962; joined Board of Trade, 1964; Private Sec. to 2nd Perm. Sec., 1967–68; Principal Private Sec. to Sec. of State for Trade, 1974–77; Asst Sec., DoT, 1977, DTI, 1983; Under Sec., 1984–91; Dep. Sec., 1991–96; Principal Estabt and Finance Officer, 1991–97; Dir Gen., Resources and Services, 1996–97; Dir Gen., Trade Policy, DTI, 1997–2000; Dir, Public Mgt Service, OECD, 2000–01. *Recreations:* music, reading, 20th century history.

**HUTTON, Brian Gerald,** PhD; Secretary, 1976–88, Deputy Librarian, 1983–88, National Library of Scotland (Assistant Keeper, 1974–76); *b* Barrow-in-Furness, 1 Nov. 1933; *s* of James and Nora Hutton; *m* 1958, Serena Quartermaine May; one *s* one *d*. *Educ:* Barrow Grammar Sch.; Nottingham Univ. (BA Hons Hist. 1955); University Coll. London (Dip. Archive Admin and Churchill Jenkinson prizeman, 1959); Oxford Brookes Univ. (LLB 1st Cl. 1996); PhD Brunel 2002. National Service as Russian Linguist, RN, 1955–57. Asst Archivist, Herts County Record Office, 1959–60; Asst Keeper and Dep. Dir, Public Record Office, N Ireland, also Administrator, Ulster Hist. Foundn and Lectr in Archive Admin, Queen's Univ., Belfast, 1960–74; Stagiaire, Archives Nationales, Paris, 1970. County Sec., Bucks CPRE, 1990–93. Chm., Friends of Oxfordshire Museums, 1991–96; Member: Exec. Cttee, Bucks Record Soc., 1999–; Cttee, Bucks Br., Histl Assoc., 2010– (Chm., 2005–10). Lectr in local history studies and on legal topics. Commissioned, Kentucky Colonel, 1982. *Publications:* contribs to library, archive and legal hist. jls. *Recreations:* visiting art galleries, listening to music, enjoying the company of grandsons in Scotland and Italy. *Address:* Robin Cottage, The Green, Kingston Blount, Oxon OX39 4SE. *T:* (01844) 354173.

**HUTTON, Dame Deirdre (Mary),** DBE 2004 (CBE 1998); Chairman, Civil Aviation Authority, 2009–Aug. 2020; *b* 15 March 1949; *d* of Kenneth Alexander Home Cassels and Barbara Kathleen Cassels; *m* 1975, Alasdair Henry Hutton, *qv* (marr. diss. 2010); two *s*. *Educ:* Sherborne Sch. for Girls; Hartwell House Coll. Researcher, Glasgow Chamber of Commerce, 1975–80; freelance researcher, 1980–86; Scottish Consumer Council: Mem. Council, 1987–89; Vice Chm., 1990–91; Chm., 1991–99; Vice-Chm., 1997–2000, Chm., 2001–05, Nat. Consumer Council. Dep. Chm., Financial Services Authy, 2004–07 (non-exec. Dir, 1998–2007); Chm., Food Standards Agency, 2005–09. Vice Chm., Borders Local Health Council, 1991–94; Chairman: Enterprise Music Scotland Ltd, 1992–95 (also Founder); Rural Forum (Scotland) Ltd, 1992–99; Council, PIA Ombudsman, 1997–2000 (Dep. Chm., 1995–97); DTI Foresight Panel on Food Chains and Crops for Industry, 1999–2000; Steering Gp, Food Chain Centre, 2002–05; Vice-Chm., Scottish Envmt Protection Agency, 1999–2002; Dep. Chm., European Food Safety Authy, 2003–08; Member: Music Cttee, Scottish Arts Council, 1985–91; Scottish Consultative Council on the Curriculum, 1987–91; Parole Bd for Scotland, 1993–97; Minister's Energy Adv. Panel, DTI, 1997–99; Sec. of State for Scotland's Constitutional Steering Gp on Scottish Parliament, 1998; Sec. of State's Competitiveness Council, DTI, 1999–2000; Better Regulation Task Force, 1999–2005; Sustainable Develt Commn, 2000–01; Curry Commn on Future of Agriculture and Food, 2001; non-exec. Mem. Bd, HM Treasury, 2008–13. Board Member: Picker Inst. Europe, 2003–06; Castle Trust, 2011–16; Chair, Trustees, London Youth Choir, 2018–. Non-executive Director: Edinburgh Festival Theatres Ltd, 1997–99; Borders Health Bd, 1997–2002; Thames Water Utilities Ltd, 2010–19. Honorary Vice-President: Inst. of Food Sci. and Technol., 2007; Trading Standards Inst., 2007. FCGI 2010. Pro-Chancellor, Cranfield Univ., 2012–. DUniv Stirling, 2000; Hon. DSc: Loughborough, 2005; Cranfield, 2007. *Recreations:* reading, eating, talking, music. *Address:* Civil Aviation Authority, CAA House, 45–59 Kingsway, WC2B 6TE.

**HUTTON, His Honour Gabriel Bruce;** a Circuit Judge, 1978–2003; *b* 27 Aug. 1932; *y s* of late Robert Crompton Hutton, and Elfreda Bruce; *m* 1st, 1963, Frances Henrietta Cooke (*d* 1963); 2nd, 1965, Deborah Leigh Windus; one *s* two *d*. *Educ:* Marlborough; Trinity Coll., Cambridge (BA). Called to Bar, Inner Temple, 1956; Dep. Chm., Glos QS, 1971. A Recorder of the Crown Court, 1972–77. Liaison Judge for Glos, 1987–2003, and Resident Judge for Gloucester Crown Court, 1990–2003. Chairman: Glos and Wilts Area Criminal Justice Liaison Cttee, 1992–2000; Glos Criminal Justice Strategy Cttee, 2001–03. Chm., Glos Br., CPRE, 1993–2005. *Recreations:* hunting (Chm., Berkeley Hunt, 1973–2005), shooting, fishing. *Address:* Chestal House, Chestal, Dursley, Glos GL11 5AA. *T:* (01453) 543285.

**HUTTON, Janet;** nursing/management adviser, self-employed consultant, 1988–99; *b* 15 Feb. 1938; *d* of Ronald James and Marion Hutton. *Educ:* Gen. Infirmary at Leeds Sch. of Nursing. SRN 1959. Ward Sister, Leeds Gen. Infirmary, 1962–64, 1966–68; Nursing Sister, Australia, 1964–66; Commng Nurse, Lister Hosp., Stevenage, 1968–71; Planning and Develts Nurse, N London, 1971–73; Divl Nursing Officer, Colchester, 1973–79; Dist Nursing officer, E Dorset, 1979–83; Regl Nursing Officer, 1983–88, Quality Assurance Manager, 1986–88, Yorks RHA. Trustee, Sue Ryder Care (formerly Sue Ryder Foundn), 1998–2017 (Vice Chm., 2004–07). *Recreations:* music, needlework, walking, gardening, tennis (spectator). *Club:* Soroptimist International of Harrogate and District (Harrogate).

**HUTTON, Prof. John Philip,** MA; Emeritus Professor of Economics, since 2013, Professor of Economics and Econometrics, 1982–2004, and Head of Department of Economics and Related Studies, 2001–04, University of York; *b* 26 May 1940; *s* of Philip Ernest Michelson Hutton and Hester Mary Black Hutton; *m* 1964, Sandra Smith Reid (*d* 2009); one *s* one *d*. *Educ:* Daniel Stewart's Coll., Edinburgh; Edinburgh Univ. (MA 1st Cl.). York University: Junior Research Fellow, 1962; Lecturer, 1963; Sen. Lectr, 1973; Reader, 1976. Economic Adviser, HM Treasury, 1970, 1971; Advr to Malaysian Treasury, 1977, Mem., Technical Assistance Mission, Kenya, 1990, IMF; Consultant to: NEDO, 1963; Home Office, 1966; Royal Commission on Local Govt in England and Wales, 1967; NIESR, 1980. Chairman, HM Treasury Academic Panel, 1980, 1981; Mem. Council, Royal Economic Soc., 1981–86. Jt Managing Editor, Economic Journal, 1980–86; Jt Editor, Bulletin of Economic Research, 1986–91 (Chm., Bd of Trustees, 2000–); Associate Editor, Applied Economics, 1986–2004. *Publications:* contribs to learned jls, incl. Economic Jl, Rev. of Economic Studies, Oxford Economic Papers. *Recreations:* golf, modern fiction, cinema, music, especially cello playing. *Address:* 1 The Old Orchard, Fulford, York YO10 4LT. *T:* (01904) 638363.

**HUTTON, Prof. Peter,** PhD; FRCP, FRCA, CEng, FIMechE; Professor of Anaesthesia, 1986–2009, and Head, Department of Anaesthesia and Intensive Care, 1986–2001, University of Birmingham; Hon. Consultant Anaesthetist, University Hospital Birmingham NHS Trust, since 1986; President, Royal College of Anaesthetists, 2000–03; *b* 9 Nov. 1947; *s* of Peter Hutton and Lily Hutton (*née* Draper); *m* 1973, Barbara Meriel Johnson; two *s* two *d*. *Educ:* Morecambe GS; Birmingham Univ. (BSc 1st Cl. Hons Mech. Engrg 1969, PhD 1973; MB ChB 1978). FRCA 1982; FRCP 2001; CEng, FIMechE 2003; FRCS 2004. SERC Res. Fellow, Birmingham Univ., 1969–72; jun. doctor trng posts in anaesthesia and medicine, Birmingham and Bristol, 1978–82; Clinical Lectr in Anaesthesia, Univ. of Bristol and Hon. Sen. Registrar, Avon AHA, 1982–86. Mem., Jt Cttee for Higher Trng in Anaesthesia, 1988–92; Chm., Nat. Clinical Adv. Bd, 2003–04. Pres., Anaesthetic and Recovery Nurses Assoc., 1989–90; Council Member: Assoc. Anaesthetists of GB and Ireland, 1989–92; RCAnaes, 1993– (Sen. Vice Pres., 1999–2000); Chm., Acad. of Med. Royal Colls, 2002–04 (Vice-Chm., 2001–02). Founder FMedSci 1998; FRCPGlas (*ad eundem*) 2003; Hon. FRCEM (Hon. FFAEM 2003); Hon. FCA(SA) 2003; Hon. Fellow, Coll. of Anaesthetists, RCSI, 2003. *Publications:* (with G. M. Cooper) Guidelines in Clinical Anaesthesia, 1985; (ed. with C. Prys-Roberts) Monitoring in Anaesthesia and Intensive Care, 1994; (ed jtly) Fundamental Principles and Practice of Anaesthesia, 2001; contrib. numerous scientific and rev. papers. *Recreations:* family, woodwork, fell-walking. *Address:* University Department of Anaesthesia, North 5, Queen Elizabeth Hospital, University Hospital Birmingham NHS Trust, Edgbaston, Birmingham B15 2TH. *T:* (0121) 627 2060, *Fax:* (0121) 627 2062. *Club:* Athenæum.

**HUTTON, Dr Roger Martin Stanley;** Director, International Security, Ministry of Defence, since 2018; *b* Broxbourne, Herts, 24 Oct. 1960; *s* of Stanley and Pamela Hutton; *m* 1990, Karen Applegate; two *d*. *Educ:* Kingsbridge Sch., Devon; Sussex Univ. (BSc Hons Physics with Eur. Studies 1983; MSc Sci., Technol. and Industrialisation 1984); Lancaster Univ. (MA Sci. and Technol. in Internat. Affairs 1985); European University Inst., Florence (PhD Political and Social Sci. 1989). Joined MoD as admin fast streamer, 1988; Asst Dir, Defence Policy, 1992–93; househusband, 1993–96; Asst Dir, Resources and Progs (Navy), 1996–99; Hd, Arts Funding and Orgn Br., DCMS (on secondment), 1999–2000; Dep. Dir, NATO and Eur. Policy Gp, MoD, 2000–03; on secondment: Dir, Corporate Affairs, Bromley PCT, 2003; Project Manager, Efficiency Study into Criminal Injuries Compensation Authy and Appeals Panel, Home Office, 2003; Dir, Jt Commitments Policy, MoD, 2003–06; Head: of Defence Resources and Plans, 2006–09; of Strategy Develt, 2009–11; Hd, Defence Transformation Unit, then Dir, Defence Transformation, 2011–13; Dir Defence Strategy, then Dir Corporate Strategy, 2013–15; Dir, PricewaterhouseCoopers (on secondment), 2015–16; Dir Chilcot, MoD, 2016–18. Hon. Associate Prof., Strategy and Security Inst., Univ. of Exeter, 2016–. *Recreations:* family, ski-ing, singing, classical music, Charlton Athletic FC. *Address:* Ministry of Defence, Main Building, Whitehall, SW1A 2HB.

**HUTTON, Prof. Ronald Edmund,** DPhil; FBA 2013; FRHistS, FSA, FLSW; Professor of History, University of Bristol, since 1996; *b* 19 Dec. 1953; *s* of Geoffrey Edmund Hutton and late Elsa Edwina (*née* Hansen); *m* 1988, Lisa Radulovic (marr. diss. 2003); one *d*. *Educ:* Pembroke Coll., Cambridge (BA 1976; MA 1980); St John's Coll., Oxford (DPhil 1980). FRHistS 1981; FSA 1993; FLSW 2011. Prize Fellow, Magdalen Coll., Oxford, 1979–81; University of Bristol: Lectr, 1981–89; Reader, 1989–96. Comr, English Heritage, 2009–14. *Publications:* The Royalist War Effort 1642–1646, 1981, 2nd edn 1999; The Restoration, 1985; Charles II, 1989; The British Republic, 1990, 2nd edn 2000; The Pagan Religions of the Ancient British Isles, 1991; The Rise and Fall of Merry England, 1994; The Stations of the Sun, 1996; The Triumph of the Moon, 1999; Shamans, 2001; Witches, Druids and King Arthur, 2003; Debates in Stuart History, 2004; The Druids, 2007; Blood and

Mistletoe, 2009; A Short History of Britain 1485–1660, 2011; Pagan Britain, 2013; The Witch, 2017. *Recreation:* conviviality. *Address:* Department of Historical Studies, University of Bristol, 13 Woodland Road, Bristol BS8 1TB. *T:* (0117) 928 7595, *Fax:* (0117) 928 8276. *E:* r.hutton@bristol.ac.uk.

HUTTON, Tracy Jane; *see* Ayling, T. J.

HUTTON, William Nicholas; Principal, Hertford College, Oxford, since 2011; *b* 21 May 1950; *s* of late William Thomas Hutton and Dorothy Anne (*née* Haynes); *m* 1978, Jane Anne Elizabeth Atkinson (*d* 2016); one *s* two *d*. *Educ:* Chislehurst and Sidcup GS; Bristol Univ. (BSocSc); INSEAD (MBA). With Phillips & Drew, Stockbrokers, 1971–77; Sen. Producer, Current Affairs, BBC Radio 4, 1978–81; Dir and Producer, Money Programme, BBC 2, 1981–83; econs corresp., Newsnight, BBC 2, 1983–88; Ed., European Business Channel, 1988–90; The Guardian: Econs Ed., 1990–95; Asst Ed., 1995–96; The Observer: Ed., 1996–98; Ed.-in-Chief, 1998–99; Contributing Ed. and columnist, 2000–; Chief Exec., 2000–08, Vice-Chm., 2008–11, Industrial Soc., later The Work Foundn; Chm., Big Innovation Centre, 2011–. Rapporteur, Kok Gp, 2004; Chairman: Review into Fair Pay in Public Sector, 2011; Ind. Univ. Tuition Fees Commn, 2012. Vis. Fellow, Nuffield Coll., Oxford, 1995; Visiting Professor: Manchester Business Sch., 1996–99; Bristol Univ., 1996–; Univ. of the Arts, 2006. Fellow, Sunningdale Inst., 2006. Chm., Employment Policy Inst., 1995–2002. Hon. Fellow, Mansfield Coll., Oxford. Hon. DLitt: Kingston, 1995; De Montfort, 1996; Strathclyde, London Guildhall, UCE, 1997; Bristol, Glasgow, 2003; Greenwich, 2013; York St John, 2014; DUniv Open, 2001. Political Journalist of Year, What The Papers Say, 1993. *Publications:* The Revolution That Never Was: an assessment of Keynesian economics, 1986; The State We're In, 1995; The State To Come, 1997; The Stakeholding Society, 1998; (with Anthony Giddens) On the Edge: living with global capitalism, 2000; The World We're In, 2002; The Writing on the Wall, 2007; Staying Ahead: the economic performance of the UK's creative industries, 2007; Them and Us: changing Britain - why we need a fair society, 2010; How Good We Can Be: ending the mercenary society and building a great country, 2015; (with A. Adonis) Saving Britain, 2018. *Recreations:* family, reading, eating, tennis, cinema, writing. *Address:* Hertford College, Cattle Street, Oxford OX1 3BW. *T:* (01865) 279407.

HUXLEY, Air Vice-Marshal Brian; CB 1986; CBE 1981; Deputy Controller, National Air Traffic Services, 1985–86; retired 1987; *b* 14 Sept. 1931; *s* of Ernest and Winifred Huxley; *m* 1955, Frances (*née* Franklin) (*d* 2007); two *s*. *Educ:* St Paul's Sch.; RAF College, Cranwell. Commissioned 1952; No 28 Sqdn, Hong Kong, 1953–55; qual. Flying Instructor, 1956; Cranwell, Central Flying Sch. and No 213 Sqdn, 1956–65; MoD, 1966–68; Chief Flying Instr, Cranwell, 1969–71; Commanding RAF Valley, 1971–73; RAF Staff Coll., 1973–74; RCDS 1975; Defence Intelligence Staff, 1976–77; AOC Mil. Air Traffic Ops, 1978–80; Dir of Control (Airspace Policy), and Chm., Nat. Air Traffic Management Adv. Cttee, 1981–84. Mem., CAA Ops Adv. Cttee, 1987–99. Chm., Review of Helicopter Offshore Safety and Survival, 1993–94. *Publications:* contribs to Children's Encyclopaedia Britannica, 1970–72, and to Railway Modeller, 1974–83. *Recreations:* flying, model-making. *Club:* Royal Air Force.

HUXLEY, Prof. George Leonard, FSA; MRIA; Hon. Professor, Trinity College Dublin, since 1989 (Research Associate, 1983–89); Professor Emeritus, Queen's University, Belfast, since 1988; Adjunct Professor in Mathematics and Ancient Classics, National University of Ireland, Maynooth, since 2007; *b* Leicester, 23 Sept. 1932; *s* of late Sir Leonard Huxley, KBE and Ella M. C., *d* of F. G. and E. Copeland; *m* 1957, Davina, *d* of L. W. H. D. Best, ICS; three *d*. *Educ:* Blundell's Sch.; Magdalen Coll., Oxford (Demy; 2nd Mods, 1st Greats, Derby Scholar 1955). Commnd in RE, 1951, Actg Op. Supt, Longmoor Mil. Rly. Fellow of All Souls Coll., Oxford, 1955–61; Asst Dir, British School at Athens, 1956–58; Prof. of Greek, QUB, 1962–83; Dir, Gennadius Library, Amer. Sch. of Classical Studies, Athens, 1986–89. Harvard University: Vis. Lectr, 1958 and 1961; Loeb Lectr, 1986; Leverhulme Fellow, European Sci. Foundn, 1980–81; Vis. Lectr, St Patrick's Coll., Maynooth, 1984–85 and 1993; Faber Lectr, Princeton Univ., 1987; Vis. Prof., UCSD, 1990. Examiner for Newcastle Award, Eton, 1960. Mem. of Exec., NI Civil Rights Assoc., 1971–72. Member: Irish Nat. Cttee, Greek and Latin Studies, 1972–86, 1991–99 (Chm., 1976–79); Irish Adv. Cttee, Liverpool Univ. Inst. of Irish Studies, 1996–2004; Exec., Nat. Library of Ireland Soc., 1997–2000; Member, Managing Committee: British Sch. at Athens, 1967–79; Amer. Sch. of Classical Studies, Athens, 1991–; Irish Mem., Standing Cttee on Humanities, European Science Foundn, Strasbourg, 1978–86. Royal Irish Academy: Sec., Polite Literature and Antiquities Cttee, 1979–86; Sen. Vice-Pres., 1984–85 and 1999–2000; Vice-Pres., 1997–98; Hon. Librarian, 1990–94; Special Envoy, 1994–97; Hon. Pres., Classical Assoc. of Ireland, 1999; Mem., Bureau, Fédn Internat. d'Etudes Classiques, 1981–89 (Senior Vice-Pres. 1984–89); Mem., Internat. Commn, Thesaurus Linguae Latinae, Munich, 1999–2001; MAE 1990. Patron, Irish Inst. of Hellenic Studies, Athens, 1998–. Hon. Mem., Friends of Museums of Kythera, 2016. Hon. Freeman of Kythera, 2012. Hon. LittD TCD, 1984; Hon. DLit: QUB, 1996; NUI Maynooth, 2013. Irish citizen, 2018. Cromer Greek Prize, British Acad., 1963. *Publications:* Achaeans and Hittites, 1960; Early Sparta, 1962; The Early Ionians, 1966; Greek Epic Poetry from Eumelos to Panyassis, 1969; (ed with J. N. Coldstream) Kythera, 1972; Pindar's Vision of the Past, 1975; On Aristotle and Greek Society, 1979; Homer and the Travellers, 1988; articles on Hellenic, Byzantine, mathematical and railway subjects. *Recreation:* siderodromophilia. *Address:* Department of Classics, Trinity College, Dublin 2, Ireland; Forge Cottage, Church Enstone, Oxfordshire OX7 4NN. *Club:* Athenæum.

HUXLEY, Paul, RA 1991 (ARA 1987); artist; Professor of Painting, Royal College of Art, 1986–98, now Emeritus; Treasurer, Royal Academy, 2000–14; *b* 12 May 1938; *m* 1st, 1957, Margaret Doria Perryman (marr. diss. 1972); two *s*; 2nd, 1990, Susan Jennifer Metcalfe. *Educ:* Harrow Coll. of Art; Royal Acad. Schs (Cert.). Harkness Fellow, 1965–67; Vis. Prof., Cooper Union, New York, 1974; Vis. Tutor, RCA, 1974–85. Member: Serpentine Gallery Cttee, 1971–74; Art Panel and Exhibns Sub-Cttee, Arts Council of GB, 1972–76; Trustee, Tate Gall., 1975–82. Mem. Council, British Sch. at Rome, 2000–05. Commnd by London Transport to design 22 ceramic murals for King's Cross Underground Stn, 1984; commnd by Rambert Dance Co. to design sets and costumes for Cat's Eye, 1992. *One-man exhibitions:* Rowan Gall., London, 1963, 1965, 1968, 1969, 1971, 1974, 1978, 1980; Juda Rowan Gall., London, 1982; Kornblee Gall., New York, 1967, 1970; Galeria da Emenda, Lisbon, 1974; Forum Kunst, Rottweil, W Germany, 1975; Mayor Rowan Gall., 1989; Galerie zur alten deutschen Schule, Switzerland, 1992; Gillian Jason Gall., 1993; Gardner Art Centre, Sussex Univ., 1994; Jason & Rhodes Gall., London, 1998; Rhodes & Mann Gall., London, 2001; Watergate Gall., Seoul and Chang Art Gall., Beijing, 2009; Gall. Reis, Singapore, 2011; Mark Rothko Art Centre, Daugavpils, 2016; David Richard Gall., Santa Fé, 2016; *group exhibitions:* Whitechapel Art Gall., London, and Albright-Knox Gall., Buffalo, NY, 1964; Paris Biennale, and Marlborough-Gerson Gall., New York, 1965; Galerie Milano, Milan, 1966; Carnegie Inst., Pittsburgh, 1967; UCLA, Calif (also USA tour), and touring show of Mus. of Modern Art, New York, 1968; Mus. am Ostwall, Dortmund (also Eur. tour), and Tate Gall., 1969; Walker Art Gall., Liverpool, 1973; Hayward Gall., 1974; São Paulo Bienal, and Forum Gall., Leverkusen, 1975; Palazzo Reale, Milan, 1976; Royal Acad., 1977; Nat. Theatre, 1979; Arts Council tour, Sheffield, Newcastle upon Tyne and Bristol, 1980; Museo Municipal, Madrid, and Eastern Arts 4th Nat. Exhibn and British tour, 1983; Juda Rowan Gall., 1985; Künstlerhaus, Vienna, 1986; Mappin Art Gall., Sheffield, 1988; British Council tour, Eastern Europe, 1990–93; South Bank Centre, and Arts Council tour, 1992–93; Barbican Gall., London, 1993; British Council tour, Africa, 1994–96; Gallery 7, HK, 1996; Gulbenkian Foundn Center for Modern Art, Lisbon, 1997; Pallant House Gall., Chichester, 1998; Kettle's Yard, Cambridge, 1999; Rhodes+Mann, London, 2000; Kunstmus., Wolfsburg, 2002; Mus. of Contemp. Art, Andros, Greece and China Nat. Mus. of Fine Arts, Beijing, 2005; Falmouth and Hayward Gall., London, 2006; Centre Culturel Calouste Gulbenkian, Paris, 2010; *works in public collections:* Tate Gall., V&A Mus., Arts Council of GB, British Council, Royal Acad., RCA, Contemp. Arts Soc., Camden Council, Govt Art Collection, Nuffield Foundn, London; Whitworth Art Gall., Manchester; Graves Art Gall., Sheffield; Walker Art Gall., Liverpool; City Art Gall., Leeds; Creasey Collection of Modern Art, Salisbury; Leics Educn Authority; Fitzwilliam Mus., Cambridge; Ulster Mus., Belfast; Art Gall. of NSW, and Mus. of Contemp. Art, Sydney; Art Gall. of SA, Adelaide; Albright-Knox Gall., Buffalo, Neuberger Mus., Purchase, and MOMA, NY; Centro Cultural Arte Contemporáneo, Mexico City; Art Gall. of Ontario, Toronto; Moroccan Royt Collection, Asilah; Szépmüvészeti Mus., Budapest; Technisches Mus., Vienna; Seoul Mus. of Art, and Bukchon Mus., Seoul; Mark Rothko Art Centre, Daugavpils; Nat. Mus., Gdansk. Ed., Artists' Laboratory series, 01–06, 2010–12. *Publications:* (ed) Exhibition Road: painters at the Royal College of Art, 1988. *Address:* 2 Dalling Road, W6 0JB.

HUXLEY, Dr Peter Arthur, PhD; CBiol; FRSB; agroforestry education consultant, 1992–2002; *b* 26 Sept. 1926; *s* of Ernest Henry Huxley and Florence Agnes (*née* King); *m* 1st, 1954, Betty Grace Anne Foot (marr. diss. 1980); three *s* one *d*; 2nd, 1980, Jennifer Margaret Bell (*née* Pollard); one *s* one *d*. *Educ:* Alleyn's Sch.; Edinburgh Univ.; Reading Univ. (BSc, PhD). FRSB (FIBiol 1970). RNVR, 1944–46. Asst Lectr to Sen. Lectr, Makerere University Coll., Uganda, 1954–64; Dir of Res., Coffee Res. Foundn, Kenya, 1965–69; Prof. of Horticulture, Univ. of Reading, 1969–74; Prof. of Crop Science, Univ. of Dar es Salaam/FAO, 1974–76; Agric. Res. Adviser/FAO, Agric. Res. Centre, Tripoli, 1977–78; International Council for Research in Agroforestry, Nairobi, 1979–92: Dir, Res. Develt Div., 1987–90; Principal Res. Advr, 1991–92. *Publications:* (ed jtly) Soils Research in Agroforestry, 1980; (ed jtly) Plant Research and Agroforestry, 1983; (ed) Manual of Research Methodology for the Exploration and Assessment of Multipurpose Trees, 1983; (ed jtly) Multipurpose trees: selection and testing for agroforestry, 1989; (ed jtly) Tree-crop Interactions: a physiological approach, 1996; (ed jtly) Agroforestry for Sustainable Development in Sri Lanka, 1996; (ed jtly) Glossary for Agroforestry, 1997; (compiled and ed jtly) Tropical Agroforestry, 1999; approx. 135 pubns in agric., horticult., agroforestry, meteorol and agricl botany jls. *Recreations:* music, philosophy. *Address:* 84a Five Mile Drive, Oxford OX2 8HN.

HUYGELEN, Rudolf; Ambassador of Belgium to the Court of St James's, since 2017; *b* Duffel, Belgium, 29 Dec. 1961; *s* of Constant Huygelen and Liane Boeykens; *m* 2017, Marianne Lesceu; two *s* one *d*. *Educ:* Grad. in Law, Master's degree Moral Sci. Central Admin, Min. of Foreign Affairs, Belgium, 1989–91; Attaché, Political Sect., Bonn, 1991–94; Central Admin, Min. of Foreign Affairs, 1994–97; First Sec., Political Sect., Washington, 1997–2002; Counsellor and Chargé d'Affaires, Pretoria, 2002–03; Spokesman and Hd, Press Office, Min. of Foreign Affairs, 2003–07; Ambassador of Belgium to Portugal, 2007–10; Perm. Rep. of Belgium to NATO, 2010–14; Chief of Protocol, Min. of Foreign Affairs, 2014–16; Hd, Private Office of Belgian Minister of Foreign Affairs, 2016–17. *Address:* Embassy of Belgium, 17 Grosvenor Crescent, SW1X 7EE. *T:* (020) 7470 3700. *Clubs:* Hurlingham, Travellers.

HYAM, Jeremy Rupert Daniel; QC 2016; a Recorder, since 2018; *b* London, 1970; *s* of late Michael Joshua Hyam (His Honour Judge Hyam) and Diana Hyam; *m* 2002, Rebecca; one *s* one *d*. *Educ:* Westminster Sch.; King's Coll. London. Called to the Bar, Gray's Inn, 1995. *Recreations:* reading, cricket, music. *Address:* One Crown Office Row, Temple, EC4Y 7HH. *T:* (020) 7797 7500. *E:* Jeremy.Hyam@1cor.com. *Club:* Garrick.

HYAMS, Edward Barnard; non-executive director and business advisor, since 2011; Owner, Lexdenergy Ltd, 2012–16; Chairman, Tevva Motors, since 2017 (Member, Advisory Board, 2016); *b* London, 1951; *s* of Leonard Hyams and Jean Hyams; *m* 1974, Janet; two *s* one *d*. *Educ:* Ipswich Sch., Ipswich; Imperial Coll., London (BSc Eng Electrical Engrg); CDipAF 1979. CEng 1981. Dir, Engrg, Southern Electric plc, 1992–96; Man. Dir, Eastern Gp plc, 1996–2000; CEO, BizzEnergy Ltd, 2000–02; Chm., Ergo Services, Beaufort, 2003–08; Investment Partner, Englefield Capital LLP, 2005–12; Founding Partner, Rockfield Energy Partners, 2012–14. Chm., Energy Saving Trust, 2005–12; Dir, Carbon Trust, 2005–11. Member: Adv. Bd, Estover Ltd, 2011–; Bd, CPREL Ltd, 2012–; Adv. Gp, Lymphoma Assoc., 2015–. Trustee, Ipswich Sch. Foundn, 2011–14; Gov., Ipswich Sch., 2014–. *Recreations:* classical music, ski-ing, music, art.

HYAMS, Maj. Gen. Timothy David, OBE 2011; Military Secretary, since 2019; General Officer Scotland, since 2019; *b* Banbury, 13 Aug. 1966; *s* of David Hyams and Penelope Hyams; *m* 1994, Catherine Mary Everard; two *s*. *Educ:* Cranfield Univ. (MA). 5th Royal Inniskilling Dragoon Guards: commnd, 1986; Troop Leader, 1986–89; Close Recce Troop Leader, 1990–92; Adjutant, 5th Royal Inniskilling Dragoon Guards/Royal Dragoon Guards, 1992–94; Instructor, RMA Sandhurst, 1994–95; SO3 G2 NI, 1995–97; student, Staff Coll., 1997–99; Sqdn Leader, Royal Dragoon Guards, 1999–2001; Military Asst to Comdr Field Army, 2001–03; SO2 Brigadiers, Sen. Officers' Career Mgt, 2003–04; SO1 Policy, Gen. Staff, 2004–05; CO, Royal Dragoon Guards, 2005–08; Comdr, Comd, Staff and Tactical Trng Gp, 2008–10; Col, Sen. Officers Career Mgt, 2011; Dir, Personnel Services (Army), 2011–12; Chief, Insider Threat Mitigation, HQ ISAF, Kabul, 2012–13; Dir, Personnel Capability, 2013–14; Comdr, Collective Trng Gp, 2014–16; GOC, Recruiting and Trng Div., 2016–18; Dir, Land Warfare, 2018–19. Col of Regt, Royal Dragoon Guards, 2019–; Hon. Col, QOY, 2019–. Trustee: Regtl Charity of the Royal Dragoon Guards, 2013–; RAC War Meml Benevolent Fund, 2014–; Pres., RAC Sport, 2016–. Gov., St George's Catholic Primary Sch., Warminster, 2015–. *Recreations:* Rugby, cricket, dog walking, history. *E:* thehyams56@btinternet.com. *Club:* Cavalry and Guards.

HYDE, Lord; Edward George James Villiers; *b* 17 April 2008; *s* and *heir* of Earl of Clarendon, *qv*.

HYDE, Charles Gordon; QC 2006; a Recorder, since 2004; a Deputy High Court Judge, since 2011; *b* 27 Feb. 1963; *s* of Gordon and Ann Hyde; *m* 2001, Liz Cunningham; two *s* one *d*. *Educ:* Rugby Sch.; Manchester Univ. (LLB Hons). Called to the Bar, Middle Temple, 1988. Mem., Family Procedure Rule Cttee, 2004. *Recreations:* fly fishing, walking, watching sport, natural history. *Address:* Albion Chambers, Broad Street, Bristol BS1 1DR.

HYDE, Daniel Stephen, FRCO; Director of Music, King's College, Cambridge, since 2019; *b* Matlock, 24 April 1980; *s* of Nigel and Susan Hyde; *m* 2005, Salima Virji (marr. diss. 2012). *Educ:* Durham Cathedral Choir Sch.; Oakham Sch.; King's Coll., Cambridge (MA). Dir, Chapel Music, Jesus Coll., Cambridge, 2004–09; Informator Choristarum, Tutorial Fellow and Organist, Magdalen Coll., Oxford, 2009–16; Organist and Dir of

Music, St Thomas Ch, Fifth Ave, NY, 2016–19. *Recreations:* opera, reading, food and wine. *Address:* King's College, Cambridge CB2 1ST. *E:* choir@kings.cam.ac.uk. *W:* www.danielhyde.co.uk.

**HYDE, Dame Helen (Yvonne),** DBE 2013; MA; Headmistress, Watford Grammar School for Girls, 1987–2016; *b* 11 May 1947; *d* of Henry and Tilly Seligman; *m* 1968, Dr John Hyde; two *d*. *Educ:* Parktown Girls' High Sch., Johannesburg; Witwatersrand Univ. (BA 1967; BA Hons 1969); King's Coll., London (MA 1974). Teacher of French, 1970; Head of Modern Languages, 1978, Acland Burghley; Dep. Headmistress, Highgate Wood, 1983. Student of Yad Vashem in Holocaust Studies, 2007–10; Fellow of Imperial War Mus. in Holocaust Studies, 2008; Mem., Holocaust Commn, 2014. Pres., Freedom and Autonomy - Nat. Schs Assoc. (formerly Assoc. of Heads of Grant Maintained Schs, later Assoc. of Heads of Foundn and Aided Schs, subseq. Foundn and Aided Schs Nat. Assoc., then Freedom and Autonomy for Schs - Nat. Assoc.), 2006– (Treas., 1995–2006). Patron: Rwandan Sisterhood Assoc., 2016– (Dir); Religious Educn Council, 2016–; Chair, Bd of Trustees, Foundn for Jewish Heritage, 2018–; Trustee: Holocaust Educnl Trust; Nat. Holocaust Centre and Mus.; Anne Frank Trust UK, 2017–19. Leads working visits to Rwanda; Holocaust educator and leader of adult Holocaust study trips. Accredited Trainer: Edward de Bono Thinking Skills, 2003; Mind Mapping (Buzan), 2004; Mentor to secondary headteachers. Hon. DEd Hertfordshire, 2018. *Recreations:* reading, exercise, crochet and knitting for Rwandan Sisterhood clinic, travel. *E:* dhh@damehelenhyde.com.

**HYDE, Margaret Sheila,** OBE 2006; Director, Esmée Fairbairn Foundation (formerly Esmée Fairbairn Charitable Trust), 1994–2005; *b* 11 Sept. 1945; *er d* of late Gerry Tomlins and Sheila (*née* Thorpe); *m* 1966, Derek Hyde (marr. diss. 1976); civil partnership 2017, Barbara Nancy Hosking, *qv*. *Educ:* Watford Grammar Sch. for Girls; London Sch. of Econs and Political Science (DSA 1969; BSc Hons Social Admin 1971; Mostyn Lloyd Meml Prize, 1969; Janet Beveridge Award, 1971). Blackfriars Settlement, 1965–67; Home Office, 1972–77: served in Probation, Prison and Gen. Depts, 1972–76; Private Sec. to Perm. Under Sec. of State, 1976–77; Head of Information, NCVO, 1977–85; Chief Exec., Action Resource Centre, 1985–91 (Trustee, 1992–94); Dep. Sec. Gen., Arts Council of GB, 1991–92; Prog. Consultant, Internat. Save the Children Alliance and Save the Children UK, 1992–94. Mem., Exec. Cttee, 300 Gp, 1984–87 (Treas., 1985–87). Member: Exec. Cttee, Assoc. of Charitable Foundns, 1995–99 (Vice Chm., 1997–99); Venturesome Investment Cttee, 2005–10; Futurebuilders Adv. Panel, 2005–07; England Cttee, Big Lottery Fund, 2007–11; Charity Tribunal, 2008–15; Trustee: Peter Bedford Trust, 1983–92 (Chm., 1985–87); Charities Effectiveness Review Trust, 1986–91; New Econs Foundn, 2005–14; Hammersmith United Charities, 2012–14; Allen Lane Foundn, 2013–. Mem. Ct of Govs, LSE, 1987–2014, now Emeritus Gov. FRSA 1991 (Mem. Council, 1994–99). *Recreation:* hill walking.

**HYDE, Matthew Thomas;** Chief Executive, Scout Association, since 2013; *b* Peterborough, 22 Feb. 1975; *s* of Richard and Diana Hyde; *m* 2005, Laura Bates; one *s*. *Educ:* Queen Mary and Westfield Coll., Univ. of London (BA 1st Cl. Hons English); Univ. of Westminster (MBA Dist.). President: Students' Union, QMW, 1996–98; Univ. of London Union, 1998–99; Dep. Gen. Manager, Students' Union, KCL, 1999–2001; Gen. Manager, Students' Union, Goldsmiths' Coll., 2001–06; Chief Exec., NUS, 2006–13. Trustee: NCVO, 2011–17; Step up to Serve, 2014–; Comic Relief, 2019–. Hon. Fellow, QMUL, 2012. *Recreations:* family, football (supporting Peterborough United), cricket, art, food, travel. *Address:* Scout Association, Gilwell Park, Chingford, E4 7QW. *T:* (020) 8433 7105. *E:* matt.hyde@scouts.org.uk.

**HYDE-CHAMBERS, Fredrick Rignold,** OBE 2003; Executive Chairman, Enterprise and Parliamentary Dialogue International (formerly International Association of Business and Parliament), since 2012 (Secretary-General, 1997–2012); *b* 12 May 1944; *s* of late Derek Christie Hyde-Chambers and Margaret M. Rignold; *m* 1976, Audrey Christine Martin (*née* Smith) (separated 2008); two *s*; partner, 2009, Fuad Janmohamed. *Educ:* Buckingham Coll., Harrow; Arts Educnl Sch. Child actor, TV and stage, 1958–64; The Tibet Relief Fund, UK, 1965–68; Gen. Sec., Buddhist Soc., 1968–72; Private Sec. to MPs, 1974–80; Industry and Parliament Trust, 1980–, Dir, 1987–2003. Co-Founder and Hon. Advr, All-Party Parly Tibet Gp. Member: Adv. Bd, State Legis. Leaders' Foundn, USA; Bd, Crystal Fund, Georgia, 2014– (Vice Chair); Chairman: Tibet Soc. of UK, 2004–19 (Hon. Pres., 2019); Tibet Relief Fund, 2007–17 (Hon. Pres., 2017–); Buddhist Chaplaincy Support Gp, 2009–; Hon. Advr, Nepalese Buddhist Community Centre, 2012–. Co-Founder and Co-Dir, Tanzanian Fine Art Project, 2014–. Dir, Funeralsafe Ltd, 2017–. Script writer and consultant, BBC TV and Channel 4 documentaries. First Novel Award, Authors' Club, 1988; Airey Neave Trust Human Rights Scholarship, 1989. *Publications:* The Mouse King, 1976; (with Audrey Hyde-Chambers) Tibetan Folktales, 1979, repr. 2002 (Japan, 1997); Tibet and China, 1988; Lama, 1988 (also USA, Germany, Sweden, Argentina and France). *Recreation:* carriage driving. *Address:* Enterprise and Parliamentary Dialogue International, 14 Great College Street, SW1P 3RX. *T:* 07812 691071. *E:* frhc@epdi.eu, frhc@enterpriseparliament.org; 12 Gloucester Court, Swan Street, SE1 1DQ.

**HYDE-PARKER, Sir Richard William;** *see* Parker.

**HYDON, Kenneth John;** *b* Leicester, 1944; *s* of John Thomas and Vera Hydon; *m* 1966, Sylvia Sheila Johnson (decd); one *s* one *d*. FCMA 1970; FCCA 1983; FCT 1997. Financial Director: Racal Electronics subsids, 1979–85; Vodafone Gp plc, 1985–2005. Non-executive Director: Cellco Partnership (dba Verizon Wireless USA), 2000–05; Tesco plc, 2004–13; Mem., Supervisory Bd, Vodafone Deutschland (formerly Mannesmann), 2000–03. Non-executive Director: Reckitt Benckiser plc, 2003–18; Royal Berks NHS Foundn Trust, 2005–12; Pearson plc, 2006–15; Merlin Entertainments plc, 2013–18. Patron, Dixie GS, 2000–. FRSA. *Recreations:* dinghy sailing, golf, track days, gym, cycling, watching Rugby and horse-racing. *Address:* Oxon. *Clubs:* Royal Automobile; Leander (Henley-on-Thames).

**HYETT, Paul David Etheridge,** PPRIBA; Principal, HKS Inc. (Architects), since 2008; *b* 18 March 1952; *s* of Derek James and Josephine Mable Hyett (*née* Sparks); *m* 1976, Susan Margaret Beavan; three *s*. *Educ:* Architectural Assoc. (AA Dip.); Bartlett Sch. of Planning (MPhil Planning). Career Assistant: Cedric Price Architects, 1974–78; Alan Baxter Associates, 1978–80; Partner: Arno Jobst & Paul Hyett Architects, 1981–82; Nicholas Lacey, Jobst and Hyett Architects, 1982–87; Paul Hyett Architects, 1987–97; Hyett Salisbury Whiteley, 1997–2001; Chm., Ryder, later Ryder HKS, then Principal, HKS Architects Ltd, 2001–. Dir, Building Centre, 2004–08. Tutor: Dusseldorf Fachhochschule (Architecture), 1987–90; Bartlett Sch. of Planning, 1996–98. Chm., Carbon Trust Res. Prog., 2004–08. Royal Institute of British Architects: Vice Pres., Educn, 1998–2001; Pres., 2001–03; Vice Pres., Internat. Affairs, 2003–05. Mem., Architectl Assoc., 1972–. Columnist: Architects Jl; RIBA Jl. Trustee: British Architectural Liby Trust, 2004–06; Civic Trust, 2004–07. Hon. FAIA 2005; Hon. Fellow, Royal Soc. of Architects of Wales, 2006. Hon. DArt Lincoln, 2004. *Publications:* In Practice, 2000; (with B. Edwards) Rough Guide to Sustainability, 2001; (contrib.) Sustaining Architecture in the Anti-Machine Age, 2001; (with John Jenner) Tomorrow's Hospitals, 2004; Changing Hospital Architecture, 2008; contribs to Building Design, Architects' Jl, RIBA Jl, Moscow DOM. *Recreations:* trekking,

political biographies, history, writing. *Address:* HKS Inc. (Architects), Elsley House, 24–30 Great Titchfield Street, W1W 8BF. *T:* (020) 7292 9494, *Fax:* (020) 7292 9495. *E:* phyett@hksinc.com.

**HYLAND, Susan Margaret;** Political Counsellor, Islamabad, 2011–14; *b* 30 Oct. 1964; *d* of Alan and Joan Frances Hyland (*née* Beddow). *Educ:* Somerville Coll., Oxford (MA; BPhil; Nuffield Exhibn Grad. Scholarship); Yale Univ. (Henry Fellowship); Ecole Nationale d'Admin, France (diplôme). Joined HM Diplomatic Service, 1990; Second Sec., Oslo, then UK Mission to the UN, NY, 1992; Second Sec., UK Delegn to the OECD, 1993; Ecole Nationale d'Admin, 1994–95; First Secretary: FCO, 1996; Moscow, 2000; Private Sec. to Perm. Under-Sec., FCO, 2001; seconded to Westminster Foundn for Democracy, 2004; First Sec., Paris, 2005; Head, Human Rights, Democracy and Governance Gp, subseq. Human Rights and Democracy Dept, FCO, 2006–11. *Recreations:* theatre, travel, reading. *Address:* 47A The Cut, SE1 8LF.

**HYLTON,** 5th Baron *cr* 1866; **Raymond Hervey Jolliffe,** MA; *b* 13 June 1932; *er s* of 4th Baron Hylton and Perdita Rose Mary (*d* 1996), *d* of late Raymond Asquith and *sister* of 2nd Earl of Oxford and Asquith, KCMG; *S* father, 1967; *m* 1966, Joanna Ida Elizabeth, *d* of late Andrew de Bertodano; four *s* one *d*. *Educ:* Eton (King's Scholar); Trinity Coll., Oxford (MA). ARICS. Lieut R of O, Coldstream Guards. Asst Private Sec. to Governor-General of Canada, 1960–62; Trustee, Shelter Housing Aid Centre, 1970–76; Chairman: Catholic Housing Aid Soc., 1972–73; Nat. Fedn of Housing Assocs, 1973–76; Housing Assoc. Charitable Trust; Help the Aged Housing Trust, 1976–82; Hugh of Witham Foundn, 1978–; Vice-Pres., Age Concern (Nat. Old People's Welfare Council), 1971–77; President: SW Reg. Nat. Soc. for Mentally Handicapped Children, 1976–79; NI Assoc. for Care and Resettlement of Offenders, 1989–2010. An indep. mem. of H of L; Member, All Party Parliamentary Group: on Penal Affairs; on Human Rights; British-Russian; British-Armenian; British-Albanian; British-Palestine; elected Mem., H of L, 1999. Founder and Mem., Mendip and Wansdyke Local Enterprise Gp, 1979–85. Hon. Treas., Study on Human Rights and Responsibilities in Britain and N Ireland, 1985–88. Mem., Nat. Steering Gp, Charter '87, 1987–99; Signatory of Charter '88 and of Charter '99. Trustee: Christian Internat. Peace Service, 1977–82; Acorn Christian Healing Trust, 1983–98; Action around Bethlehem among Children with Disabilities, 1993–2000; Forward Thinking, 2004–; Chairman: Moldovan Initiatives Cttee of Mgt, 1993–; Adv. Council, Foundn for Reconciliation and Relief in Middle East, 2006–16; Mem., Council for Advancement of Arab-British Understanding; Patron, Soul of Europe Trust, 2009–. Gov., Ammerdown Centre, Bath, 1972–. Mem., Frome RDC, 1968–72. DL Somerset, 1975–90. Hon DSc (SocSci) Southampton, 1994. *Heir: s* Hon. William Henry Martin Jolliffe [*b* April 1967; *m* 2015, Dr Pia M. Vogler; one *s* one *d*]. *Address:* c/o House of Lords, SW1A 0PW.

**HYMAN, Prof. Anthony Arie,** PhD; FRS 2007; Research Group Leader and Director, Max Planck Institute of Molecular Cell Biology and Genetics, since 1999 (Managing Director, 2011–13); *b* Haifa, Israel, 27 May 1962. *Educ:* University Coll. London (BSc 1984); King's Coll., Cambridge (PhD 1988). Res. Asst, Dept of Zool., UCL, 1981; Gp Leader, 1993–97, Vis. Sen. Scientist, 1998–99, Eur. Molecular Biol. Lab., Heidelberg. Prof. of Molecular Cell Biol., Dresden Univ. of Technol., 2002. Lucille P. Markey Vis. Fellow, 1988–90, Sen. Fellow, 1991–94; Amer. Cancer Soc. Fellow, 1990. Mem., EMBO, 2000– (Gold Medal, 2003); Gottfried Wilhelm Leibniz Prize, German Res. Foundn, 2011; Schleiden Medal, German Nat. Acad. of Scis Leopoldina, 2017. *Publications:* contribs to jls incl. Cell Biol., Current Biol., Methods in Cell Biol., Nature, Science, Natural Cell Biol., Cell, EMBO, Development. *Address:* Max Planck Institute of Molecular Cell Biology and Genetics, Pfotenhauerstrasse 108, 01307 Dresden, Germany.

**HYMAN, Howard Jonathan;** Chairman: Hyman Associates, since 1997; Hyman Developments Ltd, since 2011; VinoVeritas Asia Ltd, since 2012; *b* 23 Oct. 1949; *s* of late Joe Hyman and Corrine Irene (*née* Abrahams); *m* 1972, Anne Moira Sowden; two *s* one *d*. *Educ:* Bedales Sch., Hants; Manchester Univ. (BA Hons Econs 1972); Sch. of Oriental and African Studies, Univ. of London; Beijing Normal Univ. ACA 1975, FCA 1982. Price Waterhouse: articled clerk, 1972–75; Partner, 1984; seconded to HM Treasury as specialist privatisation adviser, 1984–87; Founder and Partner i/c of Privatisation Services Dept, 1987–90; Head of Corporate Finance, Europe, 1990; Member: E European Jt Venture Bd, 1990–94; European Mgt Bd, 1991–94; China Bd, 1993–94; World Gen. Council, 1992–94; World Head, Corporate Finance, 1994; Dep. Chm., Charterhouse Bank Ltd, 1994–96; Man. Dir, Charterhouse plc, 1994–96. Dir, Kingstream Steel plc, Perth, Australia, 2000–02. Mem., Chartered Accountants' Co. *Publications:* Privatisation: the facts, 1988; The Implications of Privatisation for Nationalised Industries, 1988; chapters in: Privatisation and Competition, 1988; Privatisation in the UK, 1988; articles in Electrical Rev., Equities Internat., Public Finance and Accountancy, Business and Govt, Administrator. *Recreations:* Chinese culture and language, walking, watching cricket, reading, gardening, classical music. *Address:* Turners, Duntisbourne Leer, Cirencester, Glos GL7 7AS. *Clubs:* Reform, MCC; Minchinhampton Golf.

**HYMAN, Peter Jonathan;** Founder and Headteacher, School 21, since 2012; Co-Director, Big Education, since 2018; *b* London, 23 Nov. 1968; *s* of late Robin Philip Hyman; *m* 1999, Corinna Little; one *s* two *d*. *Educ:* University Coll. Sch.; Bristol Univ. (BA 1st Cl. Hons Hist. 1991); City Univ. (Dip. Journalism 1992). QTS 2006; NPQH 2010. Researcher, Behind the Headlines prog., BBC, 1992–93; Advisor: Shadow Chancellor, 1993; Shadow Social Security Sec., 1993–94; Advr and speechwriter to Leader of the Opposition, later Prime Minister, 1994–2001; Hd, Prime Minister's Strategic Communication Unit, 2001–03; teaching asst, 2004–05, trainee hist. teacher, 2005–06, Islington Green Sch.; hist. teacher, Seven Kings High Sch., 2006–07; Dep. Headteacher and on Future Leaders Headship Prog., Greenford High Sch., 2007–11. *Publications:* 1 Out of 10: from Downing Street vision to classroom reality, 2005. *Recreations:* family, cooking, reading, politics, writing, Arsenal FC. *Address:* School 21, Pitchford Street, E15 4RZ. *T:* (020) 8262 2121. *E:* phyman@school21.org.uk.

**HYMAN, Richard Allan;** Founder, 2012, and Retail Advisor, since 2012, RAH Advisory Ltd; Founder, richardtalksretail.com, 2014; *b* Ilford, Essex, 6 Aug. 1951; *s* of David and Rose Hyman; *m* 1st, 1976, Sandra Levy (marr. diss. 1993); two *d*; 2nd, 1998, Debbie Grant (*d* 2008); one *d*. *Educ:* Shoreditch Sch. Researcher, Financial Times, 1972–78; Editl and Mktg Dir, Mintel, 1979–84; Verdict Research: Founder and Chm., 1984–2005; Man. Dir, 2005–08; Strategic Adviser: Deloitte, 2008–12. Pres., PatelMiller, 2012–13. *Recreations:* jazz, football, tennis, current affairs, business, visiting shops. *Address:* RAH Advisory Ltd, 10 Northaw Place, Coopers Lane, Northaw, Potters Bar, Herts EN6 4NQ. *E:* richard.hyman@btconnect.com. *Clubs:* Home House, Ronnie Scott's.

**HYMAN, Timothy James,** RA 2011; painter and writer; *b* Hove, 17 April 1946; *s* of Alan Hyman and Noreen Hyman; *m* 1982, Judith Ravenscroft. *Educ:* Hall Sch., Hampstead; Charterhouse; Slade Sch. of Fine Art, London (Dip. 1967). Curator, Narrative Paintings, ICA and tour, 1979–80; solo exhibitions include: Blond Fine Art, London, 1981, 1983, 1985; Usher Gall., Lincoln, Ferens Art Gall., Hull and tour, 1984; Westfield Coll., London, 1985; Contemporary Art Gall., Ahmedabad, 1988; Austin/Desmond Fine Art, London, 1990; Castlefield Gall., Manchester, 1993; Gall. M, London, 1994; Gall. Chemould, Bombay, 1994; Mid River: Paintings and Drawings of a Decade, 2000, London Mappings and

Panoramas, 2006, Austin/Desmond Fine Art, London; The Man Inscribed with London, Gall. of the Artists' Studios, Tel Aviv, 2006, Austin/Desmond Fine Art, London, 2009; A Year with Maggie's, RA, 2015; *works in public collections* include: Arts Council; British Mus.; British Council; Contemporary Art Soc.; Deutsche Bank; Mus. of London; LA County Mus.; lead curator, Stanley Spencer, Tate Britain, 2001; co-curator, British Vision, Ghent, 2007–08. Artist-in-Residence: Lincoln Cath., 1983–84; Westfield Coll., 1984–85; Sandown Racecourse, 1992; Maggie Cancer Caring Centres, 2011–12. Mem., Powys Soc., 1970– (Chm., 2010–). *Publications:* Bonnard, 1998; Bhupen Khakhar, 1998; Carnivalesque, 2000; Sienese Painting, 2003; Timothy Hyman: fifty drawings, 2010; A Year at Maggie's, 2015; The World New Made: figurative painting in the twentieth century, 2016; contrib. TLS, London Mag., Artscribe, etc. *Recreations:* novels of John Cowper Powys, cinema, walking, travel, looking at paintings, Italian cinema. *Address:* 62 Myddelton Square, EC1R 1XX. T: (020) 7837 1933.

**HYNARD, Andrew James,** FRICS; Chief Executive, Howard de Walden Estate, since 2016; *b* St Leonards-on-Sea, 27 Jan. 1960; *s* of Ralph Hynard and Maureen Hynard; *m* 1986, Deborah Rosa; one *s* one *d*. *Educ:* King's Sch., Canterbury; Hastings Grammar Sch.; Oxford Poly. (BSc Real Estate Mgt 1983). FRICS 1984. Graduate, Edward Erdman, 1981–83; Jones Lang LaSalle, 1984–2016: Chm., England, 2009–11; UK Dep. Chm., 2011–16. Hon. DSc Oxford Brookes, 2013. *Recreations:* cycling, squash, golf, interest in the Olympics and motor racing. *Address:* Howard de Walden Estate, 27 Baker Street, W1U 8EQ. T: (020) 7580 3163. *E:* andrew.hynard@hdwe.co.uk. *Clubs:* Royal Automobile, Alfred's; Littlestone Golf, Rye Golf.

**HYND, Ronald;** choreographer; Ballet Director, National Theater, Munich, 1970–73 and 1984–86; *b* 22 April 1931; *s* of William John and Alice Louisa Hens; *m* 1957, Annette Page (*d* 2017); one *d*. *Educ:* erratically throughout England due to multiple wartime evacuation. Joined Rambert School, 1946; Ballet Rambert, 1949; Royal Ballet (then Sadler's Wells Ballet), 1952, rising from Corps de Ballet to Principal Dancer, 1959; danced Siegfried (Swan Lake), Florimund (Sleeping Beauty), Albrecht (Giselle), Poet (Sylphides), Tsarevitch (Firebird), Prince of Pagodas, Moondog (Lady and Fool), Tybalt (Romeo), etc; produced first choreography for Royal Ballet Choreographic Group followed by works for London Festival Ballet, Royal Ballet, Dutch National Ballet, Munich Ballet, Houston Ballet, Australian Ballet, Tokyo Ballet, Nat. Ballet of Canada, Grands Ballets Canadiens, Santiago Ballet, Cincinnati Ballet, Pact Ballet, Malmö Ballet, Ljubljana Ballet, Northern Ballet, Ballet of La Scala, Milan, Bonn Ballet, Vienna State Ballet, Amer. Ballet Theatre, New London Ballet, Deutsche Oper Berlin, Hungarian Na. Ballet, Royal Danish Ballet, Chicago Joffrey Ballet, Tulsa Ballet Theater, Texas Ballet Theater, Sodre Ballet, Uruguay, Argentine Nat. Ballet. *Ballets include:* Le Baiser de la Fée, 1968, new production 1974; Pasiphaë, 1969; Dvorak Variations, 1970; Wendekreise, 1972; In a Summer Garden, 1972; Das Telefon, 1972; Mozartiana, 1973; Charlotte Brontë, 1974; Mozart Adagio, 1974; Galileo (film), 1974; Orient/Occident, 1975; La Valse, 1975; Valses Nobles et Sentimentales, 1975; The Merry Widow, 1975, 17 subseq. prodns incl. Amer. Ballet Th. at Met. Opera, NY, 1997 and Royal Danish Ballet, 1998; L'Eventail, 1976; The Nutcracker (new version for Festival Ballet), 1976, new prodns for Ballet de Nice, 1997, La Scala, 2000; ice ballets for John Curry, 1977; Rosalinda, 1978, eleven subseq. prodns incl. Berlin, 1998; La Chatte, 1978; Papillon, 1979; The Seasons, 1980; Alceste, 1981; Scherzo Capriccioso, 1982; Le Diable a Quatre, 1984; Fanfare für Tänzer, 1985; Coppelia (new prodn for Festival Ballet), 1985, new prodns for Santiago and Berlin, 2000, Hong Kong Ballet, 2008, Estonian Nat. Ballet, 2010; Ludwig-Fragmente Eines Rätsels, 1986; The Hunchback of Notre Dame, 1988; Ballade, 1988; Liaisons Amoureuses, 1989; Sleeping Beauty (new prodn for English Nat. Ballet), 1993 and Pacific Northwest Ballet, 2001; *musicals:* Sound of Music, 1981; Camelot, 1982; *TV productions:* The Nutcracker, The Sanguine Fan (Fest. Ballet); The Merry Widow (Nat. Ballet of Canada and Aust. Ballet); operas, La Traviata and Amahl and the Night Visitors. *Recreations:* the gramophone, garden, travel.

**HYNES, Dame Ann Patricia;** *see* Dowling, Dame A. P.

**HYNES, Paul Richard;** QC 2010; *b* London, 17 Dec. 1963; *s* of Patrick Hynes and Joan Hynes (*née* Pritchard); *m* 1992, Michelle Simpson; two *d*. *Educ:* Forest Sch.; North East London Poly. (BA Hons Law). Called to the Bar, Lincoln's Inn, 1987; in practice as a barrister, 1987–, specialising in criminal defence. Hon. LLD UEL, 2011. *Publications:* (contrib.) Abuse of Process: a practical approach, 2006, 2nd edn 2011; (jtly) International Money Laundering and Terrorist Financing: a UK perspective, 2009. *Recreation:* being grumpy. *Address:* 25 Bedford Row, WC1R 4HD. T: (020) 7067 1500, *Fax:* (020) 7067 1507. *E:* phynes@25bedfordrow.com.

**HYNES, Prof. Richard Olding,** FRS 1989; Daniel K. Ludwig Professor for Cancer Research, Massachusetts Institute of Technology, since 1999; Investigator, Howard Hughes Medical Institute, since 1988; *b* 29 Nov. 1944; *s* of late Hugh Bernard Noel Hynes and Mary Elizabeth Hynes; *m* 1966, Fleur Marshall; two *s*. *Educ:* Trinity Coll., Cambridge (BA 1966; MA 1970); MIT (PhD Biology 1971). Res. Fellow, Imperial Cancer Res. Fund, 1971–74; Massachusetts Institute of Technology: Asst Prof., 1975–78, Associate Prof., 1978–83, Prof., 1983–, Dept of Biology and Center for Cancer Res.; Associate Hd, 1985–89, Head, 1989–91, of Biology Dept; Dir, Center for Cancer Res., 1991–2001. Gov., Wellcome Trust, 2007–16. Hon. Res. Fellow, Dept of Zoology, UCL, 1982–83. Guggenheim Fellow, 1982. Pres., Amer. Soc. for Cell Biol., 2000. Mem., Inst. of Medicine, US NAS, 1995; Mem., US NAS, 1996. FAAAS, 1987; Fellow, Amer. Acad. of Arts and Scis, 1994; FAACR 2014; Inaugural Fellow, Amer. Soc. for Cell Biol., 2016. Gairdner Internat. Award, Gairdner Foundn, Toronto, 1997; E. B. Wilson Medal, Amer. Soc. for Cell Biol., 2007; Pasarow Med. Res. Award, Robert J. and Claire Pasarow Foundn, 2008; David Rall Medal, Nat. Acad. of Medicine, 2017; Drexel Prize in Cancer Biol., Drexel Univ., 2017; Paget-Ewing Award, Metastasis Res. Soc., 2018. *Publications:* (ed) Surfaces of Normal and Malignant Cells, 1979; (ed) Tumor Cell Surfaces and Malignancy, 1980; Fibronectins, 1990; (ed with K. Yamada) Extracellular Matrix Biology, 2012; over 390 articles in professional jls. *Recreations:* reading, music, gardening, ski-ing, travel. *Address:* 76–361D, Koch Institute for Integrative Cancer Research, Massachusetts Institute of Technology, Cambridge, MA 02139–4307, USA. T: (617) 2536422, *Fax:* (617) 2538357.

**HYNES, Prof. Samuel,** DFC 1945; PhD; Woodrow Wilson Emeritus Professor of Literature, Princeton University, since 1990; *b* 29 Aug. 1924; *s* of Samuel Hynes and Margaret Turner Hynes; *m* 1944, Elizabeth Igleheart (*d* 2008); two *d*. *Educ:* Univ. of Minnesota (AB 1947); Columbia Univ. (PhD 1956). Pilot, US Marine Corps: 2nd Lieut, 1943–46; Capt., then Major, 1952–53. Instructor to Prof. of English, Swarthmore Coll., 1949–52 and 1954–68; Professor: Northwestern Univ., 1968–76; Princeton Univ., 1976–90. Woodrow Wilson Prof. of Literature, 1977–90. FRSL 1978. Air Medal, 1945. *Publications:* (ed) Further Speculations by T. E. Hulme, 1955; The Pattern of Hardy's Poetry, 1961; The Edwardian Turn of Mind, 1962; William Golding, 1964; (ed) The Author's Craft and Other Critical Writings of Arnold Bennett, 1968; (ed) Romance and Realism, 1970; Edwardian Occasions, 1972; The Auden Generation, 1976; (ed) Complete Poetical Works of Thomas Hardy, Vol. I 1982, Vol. II 1984, Vol. III 1985, Vols IV and V 1995; (ed) Thomas Hardy, 1984; Flights of Passage: reflections of a World War II aviator, 1988; A War Imagined, 1990; (ed) Joseph Conrad: complete short fiction, 4 vols, 1992–93; The Soldiers' Tale: bearing witness to modern war, 1997; The Growing Seasons, 2003; The Unsubstantial Air: American fliers in the First World War, 2014; On War and Writing, 2018. *Address:* 130 Moore Street, Princeton, NJ 08540, USA. T: (609) 9211930.

**HYSLOP, Fiona Jane;** Member (SNP) Linlithgow, Scottish Parliament, since 2011 (Lothians, 1999–2011); Cabinet Secretary for Culture, Tourism and External Affairs (formerly Culture, Europe and External Affairs), since 2014; *b* 1 Aug. 1964; *d* of Thomas Hyslop and Margaret Birrell; *m* 1994; two *s* one *d*. *Educ:* Ayr Acad.; Glasgow Univ. (MA Hons 1985); Scottish Coll. of Textiles (Post Grad. Dip. 1986). Mkting Manager, Standard Life, 1986–99. Scottish Parliament: Cabinet Sec. for Educn and Lifelong Learning, 2007–09; Minister for Culture and External Affairs, 2009–11; Cabinet Sec. for Culture and External Affairs, 2011–14. Mem., SNP, 1986– (Mem., Nat. Exec., 1990–). Contested (SNP): Edinburgh Leith, 1992; Edinburgh Central, 1997. *Address:* Scottish Parliament, Edinburgh EH99 1SP. T: (0131) 348 5920.

**HYSLOP, Peter Henry St G.;** *see* St George-Hyslop.

**HYTNER, Benet Alan;** QC 1970; a Recorder of the Crown Court, 1972–97; a Deputy High Court Judge, 1974–97; Judge of Appeal, Isle of Man, 1980–97; Expert to Asbestos Trust, 2006–12; *b* 29 Dec. 1927; *s* of late Maurice and Sarah Hytner, Manchester; *m* 1954, Joyce Myers (OBE 2004); three *s* one *d*. *Educ:* Manchester Grammar Sch.; Trinity Hall, Cambridge (Exhibr; MA). National Service, RASC, 1949–51 (commnd). Called to Bar, Middle Temple, 1952, Bencher, 1977, Reader, 1995; in practice as barrister, 1952–2010; Leader, Northern Circuit, 1984–88. Member: Gen. Council of Bar, 1969–73, 1986–88; Senate of Inns of Court and Bar, 1977–81, 1984–86. Volunteer worker, British Museum, 2010–16. *Recreations:* music, theatre, reading. *Address:* 12 Byrom Street, Manchester M3 4PP.
*See also* J. E. Hytner, Sir N. R. Hytner.

**HYTNER, James Edward;** Global Chief Operating Officer, IPG Mediabrands, since 2015 (Chief Executive Officer, G14 and President, Global Clients, 2013–15); *b* Manchester, 22 July 1964; *s* of Benet Alan Hytner, *qv*; *m* 2008, Joanna; two *s* two *d*. *Educ:* Oxford Poly.; Wharton Business Sch. Marketing Director: Coca-Cola, 1991–95; Sky TV, 1995–2001; ITV, 2001–05; Barclays, 2005–09; Universal McCann: Chief Executive Officer: EMEA, 2009–11; G14, 2011–12; Worldwide CEO, Initiative, 2012–13. Trustee, Comic Relief, 2006–; Mem., Commercial Bd, BAFTA, 2012. *Recreations:* Manchester United, ski-ing, wine, theatre. *Address:* IPG Mediabrands, 42 St John's Square, EC1M 4EA. T: (020) 7073 7333. *E:* jim.hytner@mbww.com. *Club:* Thirty.
*See also* Sir N. R. Hytner.

**HYTNER, Sir Nicholas (Robert),** Kt 2010; theatre and film director; Founder and Artistic Director, London Theatre Company, since 2015; *b* 7 May 1956; *s* of Benet Alan Hytner, *qv*. *Educ:* Manchester Grammar School; Trinity Hall, Cambridge (MA; Hon. Fellow, 2003). Associate Director: Royal Exchange Theatre, Manchester, 1985–89; NT, 1989–97; Dir, Nat. Theatre, 2003–15. Vis. Prof. of Contemporary Theatre, Oxford Univ., 2000–01; Emeritus Fellow, St Catherine's Coll., Oxford, 2003. Trustee, ROH, 2008–; non-exec. Dir, BBC, 2014–15. Director of many theatre and opera productions including: *theatre:* As You Like It, 1985, Edward II, 1986, The Country Wife, 1986, Don Carlos, 1987, Royal Exchange; Measure for Measure, 1987, The Tempest, 1988, RSC; Ghetto, National Theatre, 1989; Miss Saigon, Drury Lane, 1989, Broadway, 1991; Volpone, Almeida, 1990; King Lear, RSC, 1990; The Wind in the Willows, NT, 1990; The Madness of George III, NT, 1991; The Recruiting Officer, NT, 1992; Carousel, NT, 1992, Shaftesbury, 1993, NY, 1994; The Importance of Being Earnest, Aldwych, 1993; The Cripple of Inishmaan, NT, 1997; Twelfth Night, NY, 1998; Lady in the Van, Queen's 1999; Cressida, Albery, 2000; Orpheus Descending, Donmar Warehouse, 2000; The Winter's Tale, Mother Clapp's Molly House, NT, 2001; Sweet Smell of Success, NY, 2002; National Theatre: Henry V, His Dark Materials, 2003; The History Boys, 2004, NY, 2006; Stuff Happens, 2004; Henry IV, Pts 1 and 2, 2005; Southwark Fair, The Alchemist, 2006; The Man of Mode, The Rose Tattoo, Rafta, Rafta, Much Ado About Nothing, 2007; Major Barbara, 2008; England People Very Nice, Phèdre, The Habit of Art, 2009; London Assurance, Hamlet, 2010; One Man, Two Guvnors (transf. Adelphi), Collaborators, 2011; Travelling Light, Timon of Athens, People, Cocktail Sticks, 2012; Great Britain, 2014; The Hard Problem, 2015; Bridge Theatre: Young Marx, 2017; Julius Caesar, Allelujah!, 2018; Alys, Always, A Midsummer Night's Dream, Two Ladies, 2019; *opera:* English National Opera: Rienzi, 1983; Xerxes, 1985 (Laurence Olivier and Evening Standard Awards); The Magic Flute, 1988; The Force of Destiny, 1992; King Priam, Kent Opera, 1983; Giulio Cesare, Paris Opera, Houston Grand Opera, 1987; Le Nozze di Figaro, Geneva Opera, 1989; La Clemenza di Tito, Glyndebourne, 1991; Don Giovanni, Bavarian State Opera, 1994; The Cunning Little Vixen, Paris, 1995; Così fan tutte, Glyndebourne, 2006, 2017; Don Carlo, Covent Garden, 2008, 2013, 2017, Metropolitan Opera, NY, 2010; *films:* The Madness of King George, 1994 (Evening Standard and BAFTA Awards for Best British Film); The Crucible, 1997; The Object of My Affection, 1998; The History Boys, 2006; The Lady in the Van, 2015. Awards for Best Director: Evening Standard, 1989, 2012; Critics Circle, 1989; Olivier, 1993, 2005; Tony, 1994, 2006; Lebedev Special Award, London Evening Standard Theatre Award, 2012; Trailblazer in Theatre and Dance Award, Internat. Inst. of Dance and Theatre, 2018. Hon. FKC 2012. Hon. DLit London, 2009; Hon. DFA Juilliard Sch., NY, 2015; Hon. DLitt Cambridge, 2016. Freeman, City of London, 2015. Chevalier, Ordre des Arts et des Lettres (France), 2009. *Publications:* Balancing Acts: behind the scenes at the National Theatre, 2017.
*See also* J. E. Hytner.

# I

**IACOBESCU, Sir George**, Kt 2012; CBE 2003; Executive Chairman, Canary Wharf Group plc, since 2019 (Chief Executive Officer, 1997–2019; Chairman, 2011–19); *b* 9 Nov. 1945; *m* 1976, Gabriela; one d. *Educ*: Lyceum D. Cantemir (BSc 1963); Univ. of Civil & Industrial Engrg, Bucharest (Masters degree in professional engrg 1968). Construction Dir, Homeco Invst, Montreal and Toronto, 1975–78; Project Dir, Olympia Center and Neiman Marcus Bldgs, Chicago, 1981–84; Vice-Pres., Devet and Construction, World Financial Center, 1984–87; Vice-Pres., Construction, 1987–92; Dir, CWL, 1993–95; Dep. CEO, Canary Wharf Gp plc, 1995–97. Co-Chm., Teach First; Director: London First; Gateway to London; Wood Wharf (Gen. Partners) Ltd. Member: Adv. Bd, UK Acad. of Finance; Defence Reform Unit, MoD, 2010–; Adv. Bd, The CityUK, 2012–; Brexit Adv. Gp for Mayor of London, 2016–; Develt Bd, Chelsea and Westminster Hosp. Comr, Thames Estuary Growth Commn, 2015–. Trustee, British Mus., 2007–15 (Mem., Major Projects Delivery Cttee, 2019–); Vice Patron, Royal British Soc. of Sculptors, 2009–; Mem. Council, RCM, 2016–; Mem., Hon. Adv. Council, Art Acad. CCMI. Hon. Mem., Lightmongers' Co., 2010–. Hon. DBA East London, 2007. Commander: Nat. Order of Merit (Romania), 2004; Order of the Star (Romania), 2012; Order of the Crown (Romania), 2016. *Recreations*: jazz, opera, antiques, football. *Address*: Canary Wharf Group plc, 1 Canada Square, E14 5AB. *T*: (020) 7418 2209.

**IAN, David;** *see* Lane, D. I.

**IANNUCCI, Armando Giovanni**, OBE 2012; freelance writer, director and comedy producer; *b* 28 Nov. 1963; *s* of Armando and Gina Iannucci; *m* 1990, Rachael Jones; two s one d. *Educ*: St Peter's Primary Sch., Glasgow; St Aloysius Coll., Glasgow; Glasgow Univ.; University Coll., Oxford (MA English Lang. and Lit. 1986). *Writer for television*: and performer, The Friday Night Armistice (2 series), 1996–98; and producer, The Day Today, 1995; and director, The Armando Iannucci Shows, 2001; and producer, I'm Alan Partridge (2 series), 1997–2002; and presenter/producer, GASH, 2003; and director/co-producer, The Thick of It, 2005–07, 2009 and 2012; and director/performer: Time Trumpet, 2006; 2004—The Stupid Version, 2004–05; and director/producer, Veep (4 series), 2012–15; also exec. producer. *Films*: (dir) In the Loop, 2009; (writer) Alan Partridge: Alpha Papa, 2013; (dir and screenplay) The Death of Stalin, 2017; (dir and screenplay) The Personal History of David Copperfield, 2019. Operas: Skin Deep, Opera North, 2009. Columnist: Daily Telegraph, 1998–2005; Sunday Observer, 2006–; Gramophone mag., 2006–. Writers' Guild of Britain Award, British Comedy Awards, 2011. *Publications*: Facts and Fancies, 2000; Alan Partridge: every ruddy word, 2005; The Audacity of Hype: bewilderment, sleaze and other tales of the 21st century, 2009; Hear Me Out: all my music, 2017. *Recreations*: prevaricating, bad piano, astronomy, fearing, re-assuring, theology. *Address*: c/o PBJ Management, 22 Rathbone Street, W1T 1LG. *T*: (020) 7287 1112. *E*: general@pbjmanagement.co.uk; c/o CAA, 2000 Avenue of the Stars, Los Angeles, CA 90067, USA. *T*: 4242882000.

**IBBETSON, Prof. David John**, DPhil, FBA 2003; Regius Professor of Civil Law, University of Cambridge, since 2000; President, Clare Hall, Cambridge, 2013–Sept. 2020. *Educ*: Corpus Christi Coll., Cambridge (BA 1976; PhD 1980); DPhil Oxon. Formerly Lectr in Law, Univ. of Oxford, and Fellow of Magdalen Coll., Oxford; Fellow of Corpus Christi Coll., Cambridge, 2000–13. Hon. Bencher, Gray's Inn, 2008. *Publications*: (ed with A. D. E. Lewis) Roman Law Tradition, 1994; Historical Introduction to the Law of Obligations, 1999; Common Law and Ius Commune, 2001; (jtly) European Legal Development: the case of tort, 2012; (ed jtly) Oxford International Encyclopedia of Legal History, 2009; (jtly) Law and Legal Process: substantive law and procedure in English legal history, 2013. *Address*: Clare Hall, Herschel Road, Cambridge CB3 9AL.

**IBBOTSON, Peter Stamford;** broadcasting and media consultant; *b* 13 Dec. 1943; *s* of Arthur Ibbotson and Ivy Elizabeth (*née* Acton); *m* 1975, Susan Mary Crewdson; two s (one d decd). *Educ*: Manchester Grammar Sch.; St Catherine's Coll., Oxford (BA Modern History). BBC: Editor, Newsweek, 1978–82; Editor, Panorama, 1983–85; Asst Head, Television Current Affairs, 1985–86; Chief Asst to Dir of Programmes, Television, 1986–87; Dep. Dir of Progs, TV, 1987–88; Dir of Corporate Affairs, Carlton Television Ltd, 1991–94. Director: UK Radio Develts Ltd, 1990–94; Film and Television Completions PLC, 1990–98. Corporate Consultant, Channel 4, 1988–91 and 1994–2004; Consultant: to BBC Govs, 2004–06; to Chm., ITV plc, 2007–09. Dir, BARB, 1987–88. Gov., ESU, 2000–05. FRTS 1994. *Publications*: (jtly) The Third Age of Broadcasting, 1978. *Recreations*: silviculture, reading, photography. *Address*: Newnham Farm, Wallingford, Oxon OX10 8BW. *T*: (01491) 833111.

**IBBOTSON, Vice Adm. Sir Richard (Jeffery)**, KBE 2011; CB 2008; DSC 1992; DL; Deputy Commander-in-Chief Fleet and Chief Naval Warfare Officer, 2009–11; *b* 27 June 1954; *s* of Jeffrey Ibbotson and Joan Ibbotson; *m* 1975, Marie; two d. *Educ*: Univ. of Durham (BSc); RNEC Manadon (MSc). CGIA. Capt., First Frigate Sqdn and HMS Boxer, 1998–99; Asst Dir, MoD, 1999–2001; Comdr, British Forces Falkland Is, 2001–02; Comdr, Standing Naval Forces Atlantic, 2003–04; CO, Britannia RNC, 2004–05; Naval Sec. and Dir Gen. Human Resources Navy, 2005–07; Flag Officer Sea Training, 2007–09. Mem., Armed Forces Pay Rev. Body, 2011–. Chm., S Devon Healthcare NHS Foundn Trust, 2014–. President: Officers' Assoc., 2012–; Historical Diving Soc., 2014–. DL Devon, 2011. Hon. DTech Plymouth, 2008. *Recreations*: water sports, classic cars.

**IBBOTSON, His Honour Roger;** a Circuit Judge, 2001–13; *b* 2 Jan. 1943; *s* of Harry and Lily Ibbotson; *m* 1967, Susan Elizabeth Dalton; three d. *Educ*: Cockburn High Sch., Leeds; Univ. of Manchester (LLB). Articled clerk, Burton and Burton, Leeds, 1963–66; admitted solicitor, 1966; Asst Solicitor, 1966–70, Partner, 1970–2001, Booth & Co., later Addleshaw Booth & Co.; Asst Recorder, 1994–98; Recorder, 1998–2001. Pres., Leeds Law Soc., 1996–97; Council Mem., Law Soc., 1997–2001. *Recreations*: walking, reading, the language and modern history of France.

**IBBOTT, Alec**, CBE 1988; HM Diplomatic Service, retired; *b* 14 Oct. 1930; *m* 1964, Margaret Elizabeth Brown; one s one d. Joined Foreign (subseq. Diplomatic) Service, 1949; served in HM Forces, 1949–51; FCO, 1951–54; ME Centre for Arab Studies, 1955–56; Second Secretary and Vice Consul, Rabat, 1956–60; Second Secretary, FO, 1960–61; Second Sec. (Information), Tripoli, 1961; Second Sec., Benghazi, 1961–65; First Sec. (Information), Khartoum, 1965–67; First Sec., FO (later FCO), 1967–71; Asst Political Agent, Dubai, 1971; First Secretary, Head of Chancery and Consul: Dubai, 1971–72; Abu Dhabi, 1972–73; First Secretary and Head of Chancery: Nicosia, 1973–74; FCO, 1975–77; Carácas, 1977–79; Counsellor, Khartoum, 1979–82; seconded to IMS Ltd, 1982–85; Ambassador to Liberia, 1985–87; High Comr to the Republic of The Gambia, 1988–90. Chief Exec., Southern Africa Assoc., 1992–95; Gen. Manager, UK Southern Africa Business Assoc., 1994–95. Mem. Council, Anglo-Arab Assoc., 1992–2003. Trustee, Charlton Community Develt Trust, 1995–2003.

**IBELL, Prof. Timothy James**, PhD; FREng, FIStructE, FICE; Professor of Structural Engineering, University of Bath, since 2018; *b* Cape Town, 25 Feb. 1967; *s* of Anthony James Ibell and Elizabeth Diane Ibell (*née* Hall); partner, Jacqueline Ann Hatton; one s. *Educ*: Western Province Prep. Sch., Cape Town; Diocesan Coll. (Bishops), Cape Town; Univ. of Cape Town (BScEng 1st Cl. Hons 1988); Univ. of Cambridge (PhD 1992). FREng 2013; FIStructE 2007; FICE 2013. Sen. Civil Engr, Sasol Technol., 1993–94; Sen. Res. Associate, Univ. of Cambridge, 1994–97; Department of Architecture and Civil Engineering, University of Bath: Lectr, 1997–2000; Sen. Lectr, 2000–03; Prof. of Civil Engrg, 2003–17; Hd of Dept, 2005–08 and 2010–13; Associate Dean, Faculty of Engrg and Design, 2008–17; Sir Kirby Laing Prof. of Civil Engrg, Univ. of Cambridge, 2017–18. Pres., IStructE, 2015. FHEA 1998. *Publications*: contribs to peer-reviewed jls. *Recreations*: cricket, killer sudoku, swimming. *Address*: Department of Architecture and Civil Engineering, University of Bath, Claverton Down, Bath BA2 7AY.

**ICHIOKA, Sarah Mineko;** Director, Desire Lines Pte Ltd, since 2017; *b* Berkeley, Calif, 9 Feb. 1979; *d* of Victor Masaru Ichioka and Marilyn Jane Ichioka; *m* 2012, Jack Stiller; two d. *Educ*: Berkeley High Sch.; Univ. of Paris; Yale Univ. (BA Hist. 2001); London Sch. of Econs and Pol Sci. (MSc City Design and Social Sci. 2003). Housing and Community Develt Fellow, NY City Dept of Housing Preservation and Develt, 2001–02; Associate, Enterprise LSE Cities Ltd, 2003–05; Exhibn Content Coordinator and Catalogue Ed., 10th Venice Architecture Biennale, 2005–06; Founding Res. Associate, Urban Age Project, 2004–07; Consultant Curator, Tate Modern, 2006–07; Dep. Dir, 2007–08, Co-Dir, 2009–14, London Fest. of Architecture; Dir, Architecture Foundn, 2008–14; Principal, New Intentional Communities Project, 2014–15; Centre for Urban Greenery and Ecology Res. Fellow, Nat. Parks Bd of Singapore, 2015–17. Bd Mem., London Sch. of Architecture, 2013–14. Member: Curatorial Cttee, Design Mus., 2013–14; Adv. Bd, Woolf Works, 2015–17. World Cities Summit Young Leader, 2017. Pres., Jury, XXII Triennale Milano, 2019. Hon. FRIBA 2013. Cultural Leadership Internat. Grant Recipient, British Council, 2009. *Publications*: (contrib.) The Endless City, 2008; (contrib.) In Favour of Public Space: ten years of the European Prize for Urban Public Space, 2010; (contrib.) The Union Street Urban Orchard, 2011; (ed jtly) South Kilburn Studios: notes on an experiment, 2012; (contrib.) Constructing Europe: 25 years of architecture, 2013; (contrib.) Constructing Worlds: photography and architecture in the modern age, 2014; (contrib.) The Seoul Experiment, 2015; (contrib.) The Monocle Guide to Cosy Homes, 2015; (contrib.) Imminent Commons: the expanded city, 2017. *Recreations*: travel, reading, cycling, gardening, walking, contemporary art, environmental campaigning, Yale Alumni Schools Committee member. *Address*: Desire Lines Pte Ltd, The Great Room Offices, One George Street #10–01, Singapore 049145. *T*: 91815546; Brendon Cottage, Henshaw Lane, Siddington near Macclesfield, Cheshire SK11 9JW. *T*: 07791 732478. *E*: mail@sarahichioka.com.

**ICKE, Robert William**, FRSL; freelance writer and director; *b* Stockton-on-Tees, 29 Nov. 1986; *s* of Stephen William Icke and Morag Mackenzie. *Educ*: Ian Ramsey C of E Comp. Sch., Stockton-on-Tees; King's Coll., Cambridge (BA; Scholar). Artistic Dir, Arden Theatre Co., 2003–07; Associate Director: Headlong, 2010–13; Almeida Th., 2013–19. Productions include: Romeo and Juliet, nat. tour, Boys, Soho Th. and tour, Headlong, 2012; The Alchemist, Liverpool Playhouse, 2012; 1984, Headlong, tours 2013, transf. Almeida Th., 2014 (Best Director: Liverpool Arts Awards, 2013; UK Th. Awards, 2014), NY, 2017; Almeida Theatre: Mr Burns, 2014; The Fever, 2015; Oresteia, 2015 (Best Director: Critics' Circle and Evening Standard Th. Awards, 2015; Olivier Awards 2016; Kurt-Hübner-Regiepreis, 2018); Uncle Vanya, 2016; Mary Stuart, 2016, transf. Duke of York's, 2018; Hamlet, 2017, transf. Harold Pinter Th., 2017, televised, 2018; The Wild Duck, 2018; The Doctor, 2019; The Red Barn, NT, 2016; Oedipus, Toneelgroep Amsterdam, 2018; The Crucible, Theater Basel, 2019. FRSL 2018. *Publications*: adaptations for theatre: 1984, by George Orwell (with Duncan Macmillan), 2013; Oresteia, by Aeschylus, 2015; Uncle Vanya, by Chekhov, 2016; Mary Stuart, by Schiller, 2016; Hamlet, by Shakespeare, 2017; The Wild Duck, by Ibsen, 2018; Professor Bernhardi, by Schnitzler, 2019. *E*: roberticke@gmail.com.

**IDDESLEIGH, 5th Earl of**, *cr* 1885; **John Stafford Northcote**; Bt 1641; Viscount St Cyres, 1885; *b* 15 Feb. 1957; *s* of 4th Earl of Iddesleigh, and of Maria Luisa Alvarez-Builla y Urquijo (Condesa del Real Agrado in Spain), OBE, DL; S father, 2004; *m* 1983, Fiona Caroline Elizabeth (marr. diss. 1999; she *d* 2006), *d* of P. Wakefield, Barcelona, and Mrs M. Hattrell, Burnham, Bucks; one s one d; *m* 2000, Maria Ann Akaylar. *Educ*: Downside Sch.; RAC Cirencester. *Heir*: *s* Viscount St Cyres, *qv*.

**IDDON, Dr Brian**, CChem, FRSC; *b* 5 July 1940; *s* of John Iddon and Violet (*née* Stazicker); *m* 1st, 1965, Merrilyn Ann Muncaster (marr. diss. 1989); two d; 2nd, 1995, Eileen Harrison; two step s. *Educ*: Univ. of Hull (BSc Chem. 1961; PhD Organic Chem. 1964; DSc 1981). FRSC (FCS 1959), Hon. FRSC 2010; CChem 1980. Temp. Lectr in Organic Chem., 1964–65, Sen. Demonstrator, 1965–66, Univ. of Durham; University of Salford: Lectr in Organic Chem., 1966–78; Sen. Lectr, 1978–86; Reader, 1986–97. Vis. Prof., Dept of Chemistry, Liverpool Univ., 2002–07. Has lectured worldwide, incl. lect. The Magic of Chemistry presented to schs and univs in UK and Europe, 1968–98. Chm., Bolton Technical Innovation Centre Ltd, 2003–08. Has made TV and radio broadcasts. Mem. (Lab) Bolton MDC, 1977–98, Hon. Alderman, 1998 (Vice-Chm., 1980–82, Chm., 1986–96, Housing Cttee). MP (Lab) Bolton SE, 1997–2010. Mem., Ext. Adv. Bd, Sch. of Chemistry, Univ. of Manchester, 2006–15. Chm., Govt Affairs Cttee, RSC, 2012–15. Chm., Care Not Killing Alliance Ltd, 2006–10 and 2012–15. Trustee, SCI, 2011–15 (Hon. Mem., 2003). Hon. Fellow, Univ. of Bolton, 2005. Hon. FIChemE 2010. Hon. Dr Bolton, 2010. President's Award, RSC, 2006; Citizens Advice Parliamentarian of the

Year Award, 2010. *Publications:* (jtly) Radiation Sterilization of Pharmaceutical and Biomedical Products, 1974; The Magic of Chemistry, 1985; James Lawrence Isherwood (1917–1989), 2013; Science and Politics: an unlikely mixture (autobiog.), vol. 1, 2014, vol. 2, 2017; A Timeline of Political and Social Events in Bolton 1970–2014, 6 vols, 2016, abridged version, 2018; contrib. chapters in books; numerous papers and reviews and articles in learned jls incl. Jl Chem. Soc., Perkin Trans, Tetrahedron, Chem. Comm., Sch. Sci. Rev., Heterocycles. *Recreations:* gardening, philately, local history. *Address:* 3 Avoncliff Close, Bolton BL1 8BD. *T:* (01204) 491785. *E:* iddonb@hotmail.co.uk.

**IDIENS, Dale;** Depute Director, National Museums of Scotland, 2000–01 and Acting Director, 2001–02; Vice-Chair, Scottish Arts Council, 2002–05 (Member, 1998–2005; Acting Chair, 2004–05); *b* 13 May 1942; *d* of Richard Idiens and Ruth Christine Idiens (*née* Hattersley). *Educ:* High Wycombe High Sch.; Univ. of Leicester. BA (Hons); DipEd. Department of Art and Archaeology, Royal Scottish Museum, later National Museums of Scotland: Asst Keeper in charge of Ethnography, 1964; Dep. Keeper, 1979; Keeper, Dept of Hist. and Applied Art, 1983; Depute Dir (Collections), 1992. Mem. Council, Architectural Heritage Soc. of Scotland, 2003–06; Ind. Mem., Conservation Cttee, NT for Scotland, 2007–11. *Publications:* Traditional African Sculpture, 1969; Ancient American Art, 1971; (ed with K. G. Ponting) African Textiles, 1980; The Hausa of Northern Nigeria, 1981; Pacific Art, 1982; (contrib.) Indians and Europe, an Interdisciplinary Collection of Essays, 1987; Cook Islands Art, 1990; (contrib.) No Ordinary Journey: John Rae, Arctic explorer 1813–1893, 1993; articles and papers in Jl of the Polynesian Soc., African Arts, Textile History, Jl History of Collections, Mus. Ethnographers Gp Occasional Papers; reviews and lectures. *Recreations:* travel, film, wine. *Address:* 97/10 East London Street, Edinburgh EH7 4BF. *T:* (0131) 557 8481. *Club:* Naval and Military.

**IDLE, Eric;** actor and writer; *b* 29 March 1943; *m* 1st, Lynn Ashley (marr. diss.); one *s*; 2nd, Tania Kosevich; one *d*. *Educ:* Royal Sch., Wolverhampton; Pembroke Coll., Cambridge (BA 1965; Pres., Cambridge Footlights, 1964–65). Pres., Prominent Features. *Stage* includes: I'm Just Wild About Harry, Edinburgh Fest., 1963; Monty Python Live at Drury Lane, 1974; Monty Python Live at the Hollywood Bowl, 1980; The Mikado, ENO, 1987, Houston Opera House, 1989; writer: Spamalot (musical), Chicago, 2004, NY, 2005, Palace Th., 2007; (with J. Du Prez) Not the Messiah, (He's a Very Naughty Boy) (comic oratorio), Toronto, 2007, toured Australia, NZ and USA, 2008, Royal Albert Hall, 2009; What About Dick?, LA, 2008; Rutlemania! The Tribute Concert, 2008; Monty Python Live (Mostly), 02 Arena, 2014; concert tours: Eric Idle Exploits Monty Python, USA, 2000; The Greedy Bastard Tour, USA, 2003; co-creator, Seussical the Musical, Southwark Playhouse, 2018; *television* includes: joint writer: The Frost Report, 1967; Marty Feldman, 1968–69; joint writer and actor: Monty Python's Flying Circus, 4 series, 1969–74; Rutland Weekend Television, 1978; actor: Do Not Adjust Your Set, 1968–69; Around the World in 80 Days, 1989; Nearly Departed, 1989; *films* include: joint writer and actor: And Now for Something Completely Different, 1970; Monty Python and the Holy Grail, 1974; Life of Brian, 1978; The Rutles, 1978; The Meaning of Life, 1982; Splitting Heirs, 1993; actor: The Adventures of Baron Munchausen, 1988; Nuns on the Run, 1990; Casper, 1995; Wind in the Willows, 1996. *Publications:* The Greedy Bastard Diary, 2005; *novels:* Hello Sailor, 1975; The Road to Mars, 1999; The Pythons Autobiography by the Pythons, 2003; Always Look on the Bright Side of Life (autobiog.), 2018.

**IDLE, Prof. Jeffrey Robert,** PhD; CSci; CChem, FRSC, EurChem; CBiol, FRSB, EurProBiol; FBPhS; Director and Endowed Professor, Arthur G. Zupko's Systems Pharmacology and Pharmacogenomics, Arnold and Marie Schwartz College of Pharmacy and Health Sciences, Long Island University, Brooklyn, New York, since 2018; Scientific Contractor and Consultant, Laboratory of Metabolism, Center for Cancer Research, National Cancer Institute, National Institutes of Health, USA, since 2002; *b* 17 Sept. 1950; *s* of Robert William Idle and Margaret Joyce Idle (*née* Golightly). *Educ:* Hatfield Polytechnic (BSc 1972, BSc Hons 1973); St Mary's Hosp. Med. Sch. (PhD 1976). CChem 1987; FRSC 1987; CBiol 1999; FRSB (FIBiol 1999); EurChem 2000; EurProBiol 2000; CSci 2004; FBPhS (FBPharmacolS 2005). St Mary's Hospital Medical School, London: Lectr in Biochem., 1976; Lectr in Biochemical Pharmacol., 1976–83; Wellcome Trust Sen. Lectr, 1983–88; Reader in Pharmacogenetics, 1985–88; University of Newcastle upon Tyne: Prof. of Pharmacogenetics, 1988–95; Hd, Sch. of Clinical Med. Scis, 1992–95; Hd, Dept of Pharmacol. Scis, 1992–95; Consultant in Med. Genetics, Regl Hosp., Trondheim, 1996–99; Prof. in Medicine and Molecular Biol., Norwegian Univ. of Sci. and Technol., 1996–2004; Prof. of Pharmacology, Charles Univ., Prague, 2004–10. Vis. Prof. and Res. Fellow, Hepatology Res. Gp, Dept of Clinical Res., Univ. of Bern, 2003–16. Founding Editor and Editor-in-Chief, Pharmacogenetics, 1991–98. Chief Executive: Genotype Ltd, 1993–95; VitOmega Internat., 1995–98; Pres., Radka LLC, 2009–10. Dir, Nivy Blacksmith Music sro, 1999–2010; Exec. Producer, Sixth Ave Records LLC, 2009–10. *Publications:* over 300 peer reviewed articles, reviews and chapters in internat. scientific and med. jls and books in the fields of pharmacogenetics, drug metabolism and metabolomics. *Recreations:* music and film.

**IDRIS, Kamil El Tayeb,** PhD; Member, Permanent Court of Arbitration, The Hague, since 2013; *b* 26 Aug. 1954. *Educ:* Univ. of Cairo (BA); Univ. of Geneva (PhD Internat. Law); Univ. of Ohio (Master Internat. Affairs); Inst. of Public Admin, Khartoum (DPA); Univ. of Khartoum (LLB). Part-time Journalist, El-Ayam and El-Sahafa (newspapers), Sudan, 1971–79; Lecturer: in Philosophy and Jurisp., Univ. of Cairo, 1976–77; in Jurisp., Ohio Univ., 1978; Asst Dir, Res. Dept, subseq. Dep. Dir, Legal Dept, Min. of Foreign Affairs, Sudan, 1978; Vice-Consul in Switzerland, and Legal Advr, Sudan Perm. Mission to UN Office, Geneva, 1979–82; World Intellectual Property Organization: Sen. Prog. Officer, Develt Co-operation and External Relns Bureau for Africa, 1982–85; Dir, Develt Co-operation and External Relns Bureau for Arab and Central and European Countries, 1985–94; Dep. Dir Gen., 1994–97; Dir Gen., 1997–2008; Sec. Gen., Internat. Union for Protection of New Varieties of Plants, 1997–2008. Prof. of Public Internat. Law, Univ. of Khartoum. Advocate and Comr of Oaths, Republic of Sudan. Member: UN Internat. Law Commn, 1992–96, 2000–01; Sudan Bar Assoc.; African Jurists Assoc. Comdr, Ordre Nat. du Lion (Senegal), 1998. *Publications:* articles on law, econs, jurisp. and aesthetics in jls.

**IDRIS JONES, Denise;** *see* Jones, Denise I.

**IEMMA, Hon. Morris;** MP (ALP) Lakemba, New South Wales, 1999–2008; Premier of New South Wales, 2005–08; Chairman, Greyhound Racing NSW, since 2017; *b* July 1961; *s* of George and Maria Iemma; *m* 1997, Santina Raiti; three *s* one *d*. *Educ:* Narwee Boys' High Sch.; Univ. of Technology, Sydney (LLB); Univ. of Sydney (BEc). Industrial Officer, Commonwealth Bank Officers Assoc., 1984–86; Advr to Senator Graham Richardson, Minister for Envmt, Arts, Sport, Tourism and Territories, Australian Nat. Parlt, 1986–91. Government of New South Wales: MP (ALP) Hurstville, 1991–99; Member: Parly Constitutional Fixed Terms Cttee, 1991–92; Parly Regulation Rev. Cttee, 1991–95; Parly Sec. to the Premier, 1995–99; Minister: for Public Works and Services, 1999–2003; Assisting the Premier on Citizenship, 1999–2003; for Sport and Recreation, 2001–03; for Health, 2003–05; for Citizenship, 2005–08; for State and Regl Develt, 2006–07; Treasurer, 2005–06. Dist. Comr, Greater Sydney Commn, 2016–19. Mem., ALP, 1977–. President: Kingsgrove Cricket Club, 2012–; Campbelltown Camden District Cricket Club, 2017–. *Recreations:* all sports, particularly Australian Rules, league and soccer, blues music, cinema.

**IFE, Prof. Sir Barry (William),** Kt 2017; CBE 2000; PhD; Principal, 2004–17, Hon. Senior Research Fellow, since 2017, Guildhall School of Music & Drama; *b* 19 June 1947; *s* of Bernard Edward Ife and Joan Mary (*née* Thacker); *m* 1st, 1968, Anne Elizabeth Vernon (marr. diss. 1985); 2nd, 1986, Christine Mary Whiffen (marr. diss. 1998); two *s*; 3rd, 2012, Dr Trudi Laura Darby. *Educ:* King's Coll., London (BA Hons 1968; FKC 1992); Birkbeck Coll., London (PhD 1984). ALCM 1965. Asst Lectr in Spanish, 1969–71, Lectr, 1971–72, Univ. of Nottingham; Lectr in Spanish, Birkbeck Coll., London, 1972–88; King's College, London: Cervantes Prof. of Spanish, 1988–2004, now Emeritus; Hd, Sch. of Humanities, 1989–96; Vice-Principal, 1997–2003; Actg Principal, 2003–04. Leverhulme Res. Fellow, 1983–85. Trustee: Boise Foundn, 2004–12; Mendelssohn Scholarship Foundn, 2004–12; Chm., Mendelssohn Boise Foundn, 2013–14; City Arts Trust, 2004–15; Chm., Culture Capital Exchange, 2011–17; Member, Board: Universities UK, 2010–13; Incorporated Soc. of Musicians, 2015–18 (Pres., 2014–15); Creative Industries Fedn, 2016–18; Performance Arts Lab, 2017–; Saffron Hall Trust, 2017–. Gov., RAM, 1998–2004. Pres., British Harpsichord Soc., 2009–. Fellow, Birkbeck, Univ. of London, 2007. FRCM 2013; FGS 2016; PFHEA 2018. Hon. FRAM 2001. *Publications:* Dos Versiones de Piramo y Tisbe, 1974; Francisco de Quevedo: La Vida del Buscón, 1977; Anthology of Early Keyboard Methods, 1981, 2nd edn 2019; Domenico Scarlatti, 1985; Reading and Fiction in Golden-Age Spain, 1985; Early Spanish Keyboard Music, 1986; Antonio Soler: Twelve Sonatas, 1989; Christopher Columbus: Journal of the First Voyage, 1990; Lectura y Ficción, 1992; Letters from America, 1992; Miguel de Cervantes: Exemplary Novels, 1993, new edn 2013; Corpus of Contemporary Spanish, 1995; Don Quixote's Diet, 2000; Domenico Scarlatti: 39 sonatas, 2015; Novel as Drama/Drama as Novel, 2017; From Stage to Page: Don Quixote as performance, 2019; contrib. articles and reviews to Bull. Hispanic Studies, Bull. Spanish Studies, MLR, Jl Inst. Romance Studies, TLS, Music and Letters, Eighteenth Century Music, Early Music and others. *Recreations:* music, literature, sorting things out. *Address:* Hasketon Grange, Grundisburgh Road, Hasketon, Woodbridge, Suffolk IP13 6HN. *E:* barry.ife@gsmd.ac.uk.

**IGGULDEN, Conn Francis Harry Nicholls;** author, since 2002; *b* Hillingdon, London, 24 Feb. 1971; *s* of late Henry and Kathy Iggulden; *m* 1997, Ella D'Urso; two *s* two *d*. *Educ:* Merchant Taylors' Sch., Middx; Queen Mary and Westfield Coll., London Univ. (BA Hons); Univ. of Greenwich (PGCE). Hd of English, St Gregory's RC High Sch., Kenton, Middx, 1999–2001. *Publications:* The Gates of Rome, 2003; The Death of Kings, 2004; The Field of Swords, 2005; The Gods of War, 2006; The Dangerous Book for Boys, 2006; Blackwater, 2006; The Dangerous Book for Boys Yearbook, 2007; Wolf of the Plains, 2007; Lords of the Bow, 2008; Bones of the Hills, 2008; The Dangerous Book of Heroes, 2009; Tollins, 2009; Empire of Silver, 2010; Conqueror, 2011; Quantum of Tweed, 2012; Emperor: the blood of gods, 2013; Wars of the Roses: Stormbird, 2013, Trinity, 2014, Bloodline, 2015, Ravenspur, 2016, Dunstan, 2017, Darien, 2017; The Falcon of Sparta, 2018; Shiang, 2018; The Sword Saint, 2019; The Double Dangerous Book for Boys, 2019. *Recreations:* carpentry, reading, copying out poems by hand. *Address:* c/o A. M. Heath, 6 Warwick Court, WC1R 5DJ. *W:* www.conniggulden.com.

**IGNARRO, Prof. Louis J.,** PhD; Professor, Department of Molecular and Medical Pharmacology, University of California, Los Angeles, 1985–2013, now Emeritus; *b* 31 May 1941; *m* 1997, Sharon Elizabeth Williams. *Educ:* Long Beach High Sch.; Columbia Univ. (BA 1962); Univ. of Minnesota (PhD 1966). Post-doctoral Fellow, NIH, 1966–68; Hd, Biochem. and Anti-inflammatory Prog., Geigy Pharmaceuticals, 1968–73; Asst Prof., 1973–79, Prof., 1979–85, Dept of Pharmacol., Sch. of Medicine, Tulane Univ. Mem., US Nat. Acad. of Scis. Nobel Prize for Medicine (jtly), 1998. *Publications:* articles in scientific jls. *Address:* 269 South Beverly Drive, Unit 288, Beverly Hills, CA 90212, USA.

**IGNATIEFF, Prof. Hon. Michael,** CM 2016; PC (Can.) 2010; PhD; writer; President and Rector, Central European University, since 2016; *b* 12 May 1947; *s* of George Ignatieff and Alison (*née* Grant); *m* 1st, 1977, Susan Barrowclough (marr. diss. 1998); one *s* one *d*; 2nd, 1999, Suzanna Zsohar. *Educ:* Upper Canada Coll., Toronto; Univ. of Toronto (BA 1969); Cambridge Univ. (MA 1978); Harvard Univ. (PhD 1976). Asst Prof. of History, Univ. of BC, 1976–78; Sen. Res. Fellow, King's Coll., Cambridge, 1978–84; Vis. Fellow, Ecole des Hautes Etudes, Paris, 1985; Alistair Horne Fellow, St Antony's Coll., Oxford, 1993–95; Visiting Professor: Univ. of Calif, Berkeley, 1997; LSE, 1998–2000; Carr Prof. of Human Rights Policy, Kennedy Sch. of Govt, Harvard Univ., 2000–06; Sen. Resident, Massey Coll., Toronto, 2011–12; Prof., Munk Sch. of Global Affairs, Univ. of Toronto, 2011–14; Edward R. Murrow Prof. of Press, Politics and Public Policy, Kennedy Sch. of Govt, Harvard Univ., 2014–16. MP (L) Etobicoke-Lakeshore, Canada, 2006–11; contested (L) same seat, 2011. Leader, Liberal Party of Canada and of the Opposition, 2009–11. Presenter: Voices, Channel 4, 1986; Thinking Aloud, BBC TV Series, 1987–88; The Late Show, BBC TV, 1989–95; Blood and Belonging, BBC, 1993; Trial of Freedom, C4, 1999; The Future of War, BBC, 2000. Editorial Columnist, The Observer, 1990–93. Hon. DPhil Stirling, 1996; Hon. Dr: Bishop's, 1995; Trinity Coll., Toronto, 1999; New Brunswick, 2001; Queen's, 2001; Western Ontario, 2001; McGill, 2002; Regina, 2003; Whitman Coll., 2004; Niagara, 2008; Tilborg, 2009. *Publications:* A Just Measure of Pain, 1978; The Needs of Strangers, 1984; The Russian Album, 1987 (Canadian Governor General's Award, 1988; Heinemann Prize, RSL, 1988); Asya, 1991; Scar Tissue, 1993; Blood and Belonging, 1993; The Warrior's Honour: ethnic war and the modern conscience, 1998; Isaiah Berlin: a life, 1998; Virtual War: Kosovo and beyond, 2000; The Rights Revolution, 2000; Human Rights as Politics and Idolatry, 2001; Empire Lite, 2003; Charlie Johnson in the Flames, 2003; The Lesser Evil: political ethics in an age of terror, 2004; True Patriot Love, 2009; Fire and Ashes: success and failure in politics, 2013; The Ordinary Virtues: moral order in a divided world, 2017. *Recreations:* walking, talking, wine, theatre, music. *Address:* Central European University, Nador u. 9, 1051 Budapest, Hungary.

**IKRAM, Tanweer;** Deputy Senior District Judge (Chief Magistrate), since 2017; Deputy Lead Diversity and Community Relations Judge, since 2013; Associate Judge, HM Court, Sovereign Base Areas, Cyprus, since 2015; *b* Taplow, Bucks, 1965; *s* of Mohammed Ikram and Azmat Sultana. *Educ:* Univ. of Wolverhampton (LLB 1988); Nottingham Trent Univ. (Postgrad. Dip. Mgt of Legal Practice 2003). Called to the Bar, Inner Temple, 1990, Bencher, 2017; Partner, IBB Solicitors, 1993–2007; Consultant, ABV Solicitors, 2007–09; District Judge (Magistrates' Courts), 2009–17. Vis. Prof., Univ. of W London, 2017–. Hon. Pres., London Criminal Courts Solicitors' Assoc., 2007–08. Hon. LLD: West London, 2012; Wolverhampton, 2015. *Publications:* (Contributing Ed.) Archbold Magistrates' Court Criminal Practice, 2013, 2014, 2015, 2016, 2017, 2018, 2019; (Consultant Ed.) Archbold Criminal Pleading, Evidence and Practice, 2019. *Recreations:* classic cars, travel. *Address:* Westminster Magistrates' Court, 181 Marylebone Road, NW1 5BR. *T:* (020) 3126 3050. *E:* tan@ikram.eu.

**ILCHESTER,** 10th Earl of, *cr* 1756; **Robin Maurice Fox-Strangways;** Baron Ilchester of Ilchester, Somerset, and Baron Strangways of Woodsford, Dorset, 1741; Baron Ilchester and Stavordale of Redlynch, Somerset, 1747; *b* 2 Sept. 1942; *s* of Hon. Raymond Fox-

Strangways, 2nd s of 8th Earl of Ilchester and Margaret Vera (née Force); S uncle, 2006; m 1969, Margaret Elizabeth, d of late Geoffrey Miles; one d (one s decd). *Educ:* Loughborough Coll. *Heir: b* Hon. Paul Andre Fox-Strangways, *b* 2 Nov. 1950.

**ILES, Adrian;** Legal Adviser, Legal Office of the Church of England, since 2004; Chancellor and Vicar-General, Diocese of Durham, since 2018; *s* of Arthur Iles and Joan Iles; *m* 1985, Helen Singleton; two *d. Educ:* Buckhurst Hill County High Sch., Chigwell; Jesus Coll., Cambridge (MA). Called to the Bar, Inner Temple, 1980; a Dep. District Judge, 2000–. Dep. Chancellor, Dio. of Durham 2014–18. *Address:* Church House, Great Smith Street, Westminster, SW1P 3AZ.

**ILES, Isobel Christine, (Chrissie);** Anne and Joel Ehrenkranz Curator, Whitney Museum of American Art, New York, since 1997; *b* Beirut, Lebanon, 30 Nov. 1957; *d* of Albert Ronald Iles and Isobel Campbell Iles. *Educ:* Univ. of Bristol (BA Jt Hons Hist. of Art and Political Hist. 1979); City Univ., London (Post-grad. Dip. Arts Admin 1980). Curator, Waterloo Gall., London, 1980–82; Curatorial Asst, B2 Gall., London, 1982–84; freelance curator, London, 1984–86; Curatorial Asst, Matt's Gall., London, 1986–88; Hd of Exhibns, MOMA, Oxford, 1988–97. Hon. DLitt Bristol, 2015. *Publications:* monographs and exhibn catalogues; contribs to jls incl. Frieze Mag., Artforum, Parkett, Coil Mag. of the Moving Image, Performance Mag. *Recreations:* contemporary art, medieval, renaissance and eighteenth century art and architecture. *Address:* Whitney Museum of American Art, 99 Gansevoort Street, New York, NY 10014, USA. *T:* (212) 5703600. *E:* chrissie_iles@whitney.org.

**ILEY, Jason;** Chairman and Chief Executive Officer, Sony Music UK and Ireland, since 2014; *b* Farnborough, 15 Jan. 1969; *s* of Michael and Zandra Iley; *m* 1997, Nadia Adorni; two *s. Educ:* Trent Poly. (BA Hons Modern Eur. Studies). Product Manager: Epic, 1995–97; Polydor, 1997–2000; Gen. Manager, Island Records, 2000–05; Man. Dir, 2005–06, Pres., 2006–13, Mercury Records; Pres., ROC Nation Records, 2013–14. *Recreations:* cycling, running. *Address:* Sony Music Entertainment, 9 Derry Street, W8 5HY. *T:* (020) 7361 8000.

**ILIC, Fiona Jane;** *see* Alexander, F. J.

**ILIESCU, Ion;** Member of Senate, Romania, 1996–2000 and 2004–08; President of Romania, 1990–96 and 2000–04; *b* 3 March 1930; *s* of Alexandru and Maria Iliescu; *m* 1951, Elena Șerbănescu. *Educ:* Bucharest Poly. Inst.; Moscow Energy Inst. Design Engr and Researcher, Energy Engrg Inst., Bucharest, 1955–56; Chm., Nat. Water Resources Council, 1979–84; Dir, Tech. Publishing House, 1984–89. President: Council, Nat. Salvation Front, 1989–90; Provisional Council for Nat. Unity, 1990; Pres. of Romania, 1990–92, then, on first constitutional mandate, 1992–96; Pres., Social Democratic Party (formerly Party of Social Democracy) of Romania, 1996–2000, now Hon. Pres. *Publications:* Global Issues: Creativity, 1992; Revolution and Reform, 1993; Romania in Europe and in the World, 1994; The Revolution as I lived it, 1995; Diplomatic Autumn, 1995; Moments of History, vol. I 1995, vols II and III 1996; Romanian-American Dialogues, 1998; Political Life Between Dialogue and Violence, 1998; Where to? - Romanian Society, 1999; Hope Reborn, 2001; Romanian Revolution, 2001; Integration and Globalisation, 2003; The Great Shock at the End of a Short Century, 2004; Romanian Culture and European Identity, 2005; For Sustainable Development, 2005; Romania and the World at the Crossroad of XX and XXI Centuries, 2009; After 20 Years, 2010; Fragments of Life and Lived History, 2011. *Recreations:* reading, theatre, opera, classical music concerts. *Address:* Str. Molière 3, Bucharest, Romania.

**ILIFFE,** family name of **Baron Iliffe**.

**ILIFFE, 3rd Baron** *cr* 1933, of Yattendon; **Robert Peter Richard Iliffe;** DL; Chairman, Yattendon Group (formerly Investment Trust) PLC, since 1984; *b* Oxford, 22 Nov. 1944; *s* of late Hon. W. H. R. Iliffe and Mrs Iliffe; *S* uncle, 1996; *m* 1966, Rosemary Anne Skipwith; three *s* one *d* (of whom one *s* one *d* are twins). *Educ:* Eton; Christ Church, Oxford. Subsidiary cos of Yattendon Group (formerly Investment Trust): Marina Developments Ltd; Iliffe News & Media Ltd; Iliffe Print Cambridge Ltd; Yattendon Estates Ltd; Dir, Scottish Provincial Press. Former Chairman: Birmingham Post and Mail Ltd; West Midlands Press Ltd; Dillons Newsagents; Coventry Newspapers Ltd; Cambridge Newspapers Ltd; Herts & Essex Newspapers Ltd; Staffs Newspapers Ltd. Member of Council, RASE, 1972– (Chm., 1994–98). Pres., Rare Breeds Survival Trust, 1999–2003. Mem., Governing Body, Bradfield Coll., 1996–2008 (Warden, 2001–06). High Sheriff of Warwicks, 1983–84; DL Berks, 2007. *Recreations:* yachting, shooting, fishing, old cars. *Heir: s* Hon. Edward Richard Iliffe, *b* 13 Sept. 1968. *Address:* Barn Close, Yattendon, Thatcham, Berks RG18 0UX. *Clubs:* Boodle's; Royal Yacht Squadron (Cdre, 2005–09).

**ILIFFE, Prof. John;** Professor of African History, University of Cambridge, 1990–2006, now Emeritus; Fellow of St John's College, Cambridge, since 1971; *b* 1 May 1939; 2nd *s* of late Arthur Ross Iliffe and Violet Evelyn Iliffe. *Educ:* Framlingham Coll.; Peterhouse, Cambridge (BA 1961; MA; PhD 1965; LittD 1990). Lectr, then Reader, in History, Univ. of Dar-es-Salaam, 1965–71; University of Cambridge: Asst Dir of Res. in Hist., 1971–80; Reader in African Hist., 1980–90. FBA 1989–2006. *Publications:* Tanganyika under German Rule, 1969; A Modern History of Tanganyika, 1979; The Emergence of African Capitalism, 1983; The African Poor: a history, 1987; Famine in Zimbabwe, 1989; Africans: the history of a continent, 1995, 3rd edn 2017; East African Doctors: a history of the modern profession, 1998; Honour in African History, 2005; The African Aids Epidemic: a history, 2006; Obasanjo, Nigeria and the World, 2011. *Address:* St John's College, Cambridge CB2 1TP. *T:* (01223) 338714.

**ILLINGWORTH, David Jeremy,** FCA; Partner, 1975–2001, Senior Adviser, 2001–04, KPMG (formerly KMG Thomson McLintock); President, Institute of Chartered Accountants in England and Wales, 2003–04; *b* Stockport, Cheshire, 28 April 1947; *s* of late Prof. Charles Raymond Illingworth and Joan Ellen Mary Illingworth; *m* 1968, Annie Vincenza Bailey; two *d. Educ:* Stockport Sch.; Emmanuel Coll., Cambridge (BA 1968). ACA 1971, FCA 1972. Trainee, KMG Thomson McLintock, 1968–71. Non-exec. Dir, Nuclear Decommng Authy, 2004–11 (Chm., Audit Cttee). Independent Chairman: Trinity Retirement Benefit Scheme, 2006–18; Places for People Retirement Benefit Scheme, 2011–16; Wolseley plc Pension Scheme, 2011–. Mem., Cttee, Manchester Soc. of Chartered Accountants, 1983–2004 (Pres., 1992–93); Institute of Chartered Accountants in England and Wales: Mem. Council, 1997–2006; Vice-Pres., 2001–02; Dep. Pres., 2002–03; Chairman: NW Regl Bd, 2004–07; Staff Pension Fund, 2007–14; Foundn charity, 2007–13; Ind. Chm., Combined Nuclear Pension Plan, 2014–17. NW Regl Council Mem., CBI, 1993–2003. Mem. Council, C&G, 2006– (Trustee and Mem. Exec. Cttee, 2007–18; Chm., Audit Cttee, 2009–18). Governor: Oldham Hulme Grammar Sch. (formerly Hulme Grammar Sch., Oldham), 1992–2015 (Chm., 2008–15); Withington Girls Sch., 2006– (Treas., 2007–). FRSA; FCGI 2017. Liveryman, Co. of Chartered Accountants, 2002– (Mem. Court, 2007–; Master, 2014–15). *Recreations:* travel, golf, music, theatre, opera, walking. *Address:* Alphin, 7 Park Lane, Greenfield, Oldham OL3 7DX. *T:* (01457) 875971. *Clubs:* St James' (Manchester); Saddleworth Golf (Oldham).

**ILLINGWORTH, Raymond,** CBE 1973; cricketer; Manager, Yorkshire County Cricket Club, 1979–84; Chairman of Selectors, Test and County Cricket Board, 1994–96; and Manager, England Cricket Team, 1995–96; *b* 8 June 1932; *s* of late Frederick Spencer Illingworth and Ida Illingworth; *m* 1958, Shirley Milnes; two *d. Educ:* Wesley Street Sch., Farsley, Pudsey. Yorkshire County cricketer; capped, 1955. Captain: MCC, 1969; Leics CCC, 1969–78; Yorks CCC, 1982–83. Toured: West Indies, 1959–60; Australia twice (once as Captain), 1962–63 and 1970–71. Played in 66 Test Matches (36 as Captain). President: Farsley CC, 1991–96, 2008–19; Yorks CCC, 2010–12. Hon. MA Hull, 1983; Hon. Dr Leeds Metropolitan, 1997. *Publications:* Spinners Wicket, 1969; The Young Cricketer, 1972; Spin Bowling, 1979; Captaincy, 1980; Yorkshire and Back, 1980; (with Kenneth Gregory) The Ashes, 1982; The Tempestuous Years 1977–83, 1987; One Man Committee, 1996; (with G. Boycott) Fire and Ashes, 2009. *Recreations:* golf, bridge. *Address:* The Mistle, 4 Calverley Lane, Farsley, Pudsey, West Yorkshire LS28 5LB.

**ILLSLEY, Anthony Kim;** *b* 8 July 1956. *Educ:* Loughborough Grammar Sch.; Bath Univ. (BSc Business Admin). Mktg and Sales Trainee, subseq. Gp Brand Manager, Colgate Palmolive, 1979–84; joined Pepsico, 1984: European Mktg Manager, subseq. Ops Dir, Pepsicola International; resp. for business in France, Belgium and Scandinavia, Pepsi-Cola; President: Pepsicola Japan; Asia Pacific Div., Hong Kong; Walkers Snack Foods UK Ltd, 1995–98; CEO, Telewest Communications, 1998–2000. Non-executive Chairman: Power Paper Ltd, 2005–06; Plastic Logic Ltd, 2006–15; Velocix Ltd, 2007–09; non-executive Director: EasyJet, 2000–05; GCap Media plc (formerly Capital Radio), 2000–08; Northern Foods plc, 2006–11; Sepura plc, 2007–13; KCOM Gp plc, 2009–16; Datalase Ltd, 2009–13; Camelot UK Lotteries Ltd, 2011–18; Watchstone (formerly Quindell) plc, 2015–17.

**ILLSLEY, Eric Evlyn;** *b* 9 April 1955; *s* of John and Maude Illsley; *m* 1978, Dawn Webb; two *d. Educ:* Barnsley Holgate Grammar Sch.; Leeds Univ. (LLB Hons 1977). NUM, Yorkshire Area: Compensation Officer, 1978–81; Asst Head of General Dept, 1981–84; Head of Gen. Dept and Chief Admin. Officer, 1984–87. MP Barnsley Central, 1987–Feb. 2011 (Lab, 1987–2010, Ind, 2010–11). An Opposition Whip, 1991–94; Opposition spokesperson: on health, 1994–95; on local govt, April–Oct. 1995; on NI, 1995–97. Member, Select Committee: on televising proceedings of H of C, 1988–91; on Energy, 1987–91; on Procedure, 1991–2010; on Foreign Affairs, 1997–2010; Mem., Speaker's Panel of Chairmen, 1999–2010; Chm., All Party Parly Packaging Manufg Industry Gp, 2005–10; Jt Chm., All Party Parly Glass Gp, 1992–2002; Vice Chm., All Party Parly Gp on Occupnl Pensions, 1997–2011 (Treas., 1993–97); Mem., Party and Scientific Cttee, 1987–2011 (Jt Hon. Sec., 1994–95; Jt Dep. Chm., 1995–98; Vice-Pres., 1998–2001). Sec., Barnsley Constit. Lab. Pty, 1980–83 (Treas., 1979–80); Sec. and Election Agent, Yorks S Eur. Constit. Lab. Pty, 1983–87; Treas., Yorks Gp of Lab. MPs, 1988–2010. Member Executive Committee: CPA, 1997–2010; IPU, 1997–2010. *Recreation:* golf.

**ILLSTON, Prof. John Michael,** CEng, FICE; Director of the Hatfield Polytechnic, 1982–87, Professor and Professor Emeritus, 1987, Fellow, 1991; *b* 17 June 1928; *s* of Alfred Charles Illston and Ethel Marian Illston; *m* 1951, Olga Elizabeth Poulter; one *s* two *d. Educ:* Wallington Country Grammar Sch.; King's Coll., Univ. of London (BScEng, PhD, DScEng; FKC 1985). CEng, FICE 1975. Water engr, then schoolmaster, 1949–59; Lectr, Sen. Lectr and Reader in Civil Engrg, King's Coll., London, 1959–77; Dir of Studies in Civil Engrg, Dean of Engrg, and Dep. Dir, Hatfield Polytechnic, 1977–82. Member: Commonwealth Scholarships Commn, 1983–92; Engrg Bd, SERC, 1983–86; Engrg Council, 1984–90; Council, BTEC, 1986–89; Chm., CNAA Cttee for Engrg, 1987–91; Visitor, Building Res. Stn, 1989–95. Chairman: Govs, Bishop Wordsworth Sch., 1994–98; Salisbury Br., CRUSE Bereavement Care, 1998–2001; Salisbury and Dist, Univ. of Third Age, 2002–05. *Publications:* (with J. M. Dinwoodie and A. A. Smith) Concrete, Timber and Metals, 1979; (ed) Construction Materials, 2nd edn 1994, 3rd edn 2001; contrib. Cement and Concrete Res. and Magazine of Concrete Res. *Address:* 10 Merrifield Road, Ford, Salisbury, Wilts SP4 6DF.

**ILVES, Toomas Hendrik,** Hon. GCB 2006; President of Republic of Estonia, 2006–16; *b* Stockholm, 26 Dec. 1953; *m* Ieva Kupce; one *s* two *d* by previous marriages. *Educ:* Columbia Univ., USA (BA Psychol. 1976); Pennsylvania Univ. (MA Psychol. 1978). Res. Asst, Dept of Psychol., Columbia Univ., 1974–79; Asst Dir and English teacher, Open Educn Center, Englewood, NJ, 1979–81; Dir, Literary Storefront Soc., Vancouver, 1981–83; Lectr in Estonian Lit. and Linguistics, Dept of Interdisciplinary Studies, Simon Fraser Univ., Vancouver, 1983–84; analyst and researcher, res. unit, 1984–88, Hd, Estonian desk, 1988–93, Radio Free Europe, Munich; Ambassador of Estonia to USA, Canada and Mexico, 1993–96; Minister of Foreign Affairs, 1996–98; Chm., N Atlantic Inst., 1998; Minister of Foreign Affairs, 1999–2002; MP (Moderate People's Party) Estonia, 2002–04; MEP (Socialist Gp), 2004–06. Co-Chm., Adv. Panel, World Develt Report 2016 on Digital Dividends, World Bank, 2014–16. Chairman: EU Task Force on e-Health, 2011–12; Steering Bd, Eur. Cloud Computing, 2012–14; High-Level Panel on Global Internet Cooperation and Governance Mechanisms, Internat. Corp. for Assigned Names and Numbers, 2013; Global Agenda Council on Cyber Security, WEF, 2014. Democracy Award, Nat. Democratic Inst., 2013; Freedom Award, Atlantic Council Expert Assignments, 2014. Knight First Cl., Royal Norwegian Order of Merit, 1999; Grand Cross, Order of Honour (Greece), 1999; Grand Comdr, Légion d'Honneur (France), 2001; Third Cl. Order of the Seal (Estonia), 2004; Three Star Order of Republic (Latvia), 2004; Collar: Order of Cross of Terra Mariana (Estonia), 2006; Order of Nat. Coat of Arms (Estonia), 2008; Order of White Rose (Finland), 2007; Golden Fleece Order (Georgia), 2007; Collar, Order of Isabel la Católica (Spain), 2007; Order of Vytautas the Gt with the Golden Chain (Lithuania), 2008; Grand Cross, Order of Netherlands Lion, 2008; Grand Cordon, Leopold of Belgium, 2008; Chain, Three Star Order of Republic (Latvia), 2009; Grand Cross, Order of Merit of Republic (Hungary), 2009; Order of St George (Georgia), 2011; Collar, Nat. Order Star (Romania), 2011; Dostyk, Star of Award 1 (Kazakhstan), 2012; Grand Collar, Nat. Order of Merit of Republic (Malta), 2012; Cross of Recognition 1 Cl. (Lativa), 2012; Grand Cross, Special Cl. Order of Merit (Germany), 2013; Order of White Eagle (Poland), 2013; Grand Cross, Order of St Olav (Norway), 2014. *Publications:* Eesti jõudmine: compilation of speeches and writings from 1986–2006, 2006; A nagy európai fal?, 2007; Atvērtā pasaule un nacionālās vērtības: runas, raksti, viedokļi, 2010; Omalla äänellä, 2011; Suurem Eesti: a selection of the President's speeches and essays from 2006–2011, 2011; In Our Own Voice, 2012; The Head of State Speaking, 2014. *Address:* c/o Office of the President, A. Weizenbergi 39, 15050 Tallinn, Estonia.

**IMAFIDON, Anne-Marie Osawemwenze Ore-Ofe,** MBE 2017; Co-Founder and Chief Executive Officer, Stemettes, since 2013; *b* Barking, London, 24 June 1989; *d* of Chris and Anne Imafidon. *Educ:* Keble Coll., Oxford (MMathsCompsci Maths and Computer Sci. 2010; Hon. Fellow 2017). Intern, Goldman Sachs, 2008; Asst Vice Pres., Deutsche Bank, 2010–13. Member: Digital Skills Partnership Bd, DCMS, 2017–; Adv. Council, British Liby, 2018–. Mem. Council, RCA, 2019–. Hon. DSc: Glasgow Caledonian, 2017; Kent, 2018; Bristol, 2019. *Recreations:* eating, cooking, watching TV. *Address:* Stemettes HQ, Studio 409, Pelican House, 144 Cambridge Heath Road, E1 5QJ. *T:* 07908 071304. *E:* team@stemettes.org. *Club:* Soho House.

**IMBERT-TERRY, Sir Michael Edward Stanley**, 5th Bt *cr* 1917, of Strete Ralegh, Whimple, Co. Devon; *b* 18 April 1950; *s* of Major Sir Edward Henry Bouhier Imbert-Terry, 3rd Bt, MC, and Jean (who *m* 1983, 6th Baron Sackville), *d* of late Arthur Stanley Garton; *S* brother, 1985; *m* 1975, Frances Dorothy, *d* of late Peter Scott, Ealing; two *s* two *d*. *Educ:* Cranleigh. *Heir: s* Brychan Edward Imbert-Terry, *b* 1975.

**IMBODEN, Dr Christoph Niklaus**; consultant ecologist; *b* 28 April 1946; *s* of Max Imboden and Elisabeth Imboden-Stahel; one *s* one *d*; *m* 2009, Maria Reich-Rohrwig. *Educ:* Univ. of Basel (PhD). New Zealand Wildlife Service: Sen. Scientist, 1977; Asst Dir (Research), 1978; Dir-Gen., ICBP, later BirdLife Internat., 1980–96; Interim CEO, WWF Switzerland, 2002–03. Former Mem., Bd of Dirs, Plantlife International. Premio Gaia, Sicily, 1993; RSPB Conservation Medal, 1993. Officer, Order of the Golden Ark (Netherlands), 1996. *Publications:* papers on ornithology, ecology, conservation. *Recreations:* classical music, birdwatching, hill-walking, travelling.

**IMERY, Gillian Anne**, QPM 2017; HM Chief Inspector of Constabulary in Scotland, since 2018; *b* Bridge of Allan, Scotland, 4 Nov. 1965; *d* of David Gow and Kathleen Gow; *m* 2009, Douglas Imery; two *s*, and one step *d*. *Educ:* Dollar Acad.; Univ. of Edinburgh (MA 1986). Joined Lothian and Borders Police, 1986; worked through ranks in uniform and detective posts; Chief Superintendent in Charge of Policing Edinburgh, 2010–12; Detective Chief Superintendent and Hd of CID, Lothian and Borders Police, 2012–13; Detective Chief Superintendent, Specialist Crime Div., 2013–14, Divl Comdr, Lothians and Borders Div., 2014–16, Police Scotland; Asst Inspector of Constabulary, HM Inspectorate of Constabulary in Scotland, 2016–18. *Recreations:* avid reader, especially Victorian literature. *Address:* HM Inspectorate of Constabulary, 1st Floor, St Andrew's House, Regent Road, Edinburgh EH1 3DG. *T:* (0131) 244 5610. *E:* gill.imery@gov.scot.

**IMPEY, Dr Edward Alexander**, FSA, FRHistS; Director-General and Master of the Royal Armouries, since 2013; *b* 28 May 1962; *s* of late Oliver Richard Impey and Jane Impey (*née* Mellanby); *m* 2008, Karen Lundgren; two *d*. *Educ:* Dragon Sch., Oxford; Bedales Sch. (Schol.); Oriel Coll., Oxford (BA; MA; MPhil; DPhil 1991). FRHistS 2011. British Acad. Post-doctoral Res. Fellow, Oriel Coll., Oxford, 1992–95; Asst Curator, Historic Bldgs, 1995–97, Curator, 1997–2002, Historic Royal Palaces; English Heritage: Dir of Res. and Standards, 2002–09; Dir, Conservation and Protection, 2009–10; Dir, Heritage Protection and Planning, 2010–13. Chercheur Associé, Univ. of Caen, 1992–. Trustee, Ancient Monuments Soc., 1994–. FSA 1996; MCIfA (MIFA 2003). *Publications:* (jtly) The Tower of London, 2000, rev. edn 2009; Kensington Palace, 2003, rev. edn 2012; (ed and contrib.) The White Tower, 2008; The Great Barn of 1425–7 at Harmondsworth, Middlesex, 2017; contrib. articles and guidebooks on architecture and hist. *Recreations:* castle studies, antiquarianism. *Address:* Royal Armouries, Armouries Drive, Leeds LS10 1LT. *T:* (0113) 220 1830. *E:* edward.impey@armouries.org.uk. *Club:* Athenæum.

**IMRAN KHAN, (Imran Ahmad Khan Niazi)**; *see* Khan.

**IMRAY, Prof. Christopher Henry Ernest**, PhD; FRCP, FRCS; Consultant Vascular and Renal Transplant Surgeon, University Hospitals Coventry and Warwickshire NHS Trust, since 1995; *b* Canberra, 10 Feb. 1959; *s* of Sir Colin Henry Imray, *qv*; *m* 1988, Sylvia Yarwood Brown; two *s* one *d*. *Educ:* Rugby Sch.; Charing Cross Hosp., Univ. of London (MB BS; PhD 2004); Univ. of Leicester (Dip. Mountain Medicine 2005). FRCS 1986; FRCP 2007. Honorary Professor: Warwick Med. Sch., 2009–; Coventry Univ., 2016–; Univ. of Exeter, 2016–. Hon. Advr to Army for vascular surgery, 2012–. Mem. Council, Vascular Soc. of GB and Ire., 2013– (Chm., Res. Cttee, 2016–18; Vice Pres., 2018–19; Pres., 2019–Nov. 2020). Gov., Rugby Sch., 2006–17. FRGS. *Publications:* Oxford Handbook of Expedition and Wilderness Medicine, 2008, 2nd edn 2015; over 160 articles in learned jls; areas of interest in carotid surgery, fitness for surgery and altitude. *Recreations:* travel, mountaineering (incl. summiting Everest and Cho Oyu; completed Seven Summits, Jan. 2019 on Mount Vinson, Antarctica), sailing, walking, family. *Address:* Department of Specialist Surgery, University Hospitals Coventry and Warwickshire NHS Trust, Clifford Bridge Road, Coventry CV2 2DX. *T:* (024) 7696 5222, *Fax:* (024) 7696 5265. *Clubs:* Alpine, Climbers.

**IMRAY, Sir Colin (Henry)**, KBE 1992; CMG 1983; HM Diplomatic Service, retired; *b* 21 Sept. 1933; *s* of late Henry Gibbon Imray and Frances Olive Imray; *m* 1957, Shirley Margaret Matthews; one *s* three *d*. *Educ:* Highgate Sch.; Hotchkiss Sch., Conn; Balliol Coll., Oxford (2nd cl. Hons PPE, MA). Served in Seaforth Highlanders and RWAFF, Sierra Leone, 1952–54. CRO, 1957; Canberra, 1958–61; CRO, 1961–63; Nairobi, 1963–66; FCO, 1966–70; British Trade Comr, Montreal, 1970–73; Counsellor, Head of Chancery and Consul-Gen., Islamabad, 1973–77; RCDS, 1977; Commercial Counsellor, Tel Aviv, 1977–80; Rayner Project Officer, 1980; Dep. High Comr, Bombay, 1980–84; Asst Under-Sec. of State (Dep. Chief Clerk and Chief Inspector), FCO, 1984–85; High Commissioner: Tanzania, 1986–89; Bangladesh, 1989–93. Order of St John: Sec. Gen., 1993–97; Dir, Overseas Relns, 1997–98. Vice Pres., Royal Over-Seas League, 2005– (Mem., Central Council, 1998–2005; Mem., Exec. Council, 1999–2005; Chm., 1999–2005); Trustee, Jt Commonwealth Societies Trust, 2000–05; Patron, Wallingford Chameleon Arts, 2010– (Chm., 2008–10). Freeman, City of London, 1994. High Steward, Wallingford, 2002–15. KStJ 1993. *Publications:* Remember and Be Glad, 2009. *Address:* 1A St John's Road, Wallingford, Oxon OX10 9AD. *Club:* Royal Over-Seas League.
*See also* C. H. E. Imray, F. King.

**IMRIE, Celia Diana Savile**; actress; *b* 15 July 1952; *d* of David and Diana Imrie; one *s*. *Educ:* Guildford High Sch. Advanced Greek Dancing Cert. *Theatre* includes: The Sea, National Th., 1992 (Clarence Derwent Award for Best Supporting Actress); Acorn Antiques, Theatre Royal, Haymarket, 2005 (Olivier Award for Best Musical Supporting Actress); Unsuspecting Susan, East 59th Street Th., New York, 2005; Plague Over England, Duchess, 2009; Mixed Up North, Wilton's Music Hall, 2009; Noises Off, Old Vic, 2011, Novello, 2012; King Lear, Old Vic, 2016; Pinter Six, Harold Pinter Th., 2018; *films* include: Highlander, 1986; Frankenstein, In the Bleak Midwinter, 1995; The Borrowers, 1997; Hilary and Jackie, 1998; Star Wars: Episode 1, 1999; Bridget Jones's Diary, Lucky Break, 2001; Calendar Girls, 2003; Wimbledon, Bridget Jones: The Edge of Reason, 2004; Nanny McPhee, 2005; The Best Exotic Marigold Hotel, 2012; Love Punch, What We Did on Our Holiday, Nativity 3: Dude, Where's my Donkey?!, 2014; The Second Best Exotic Marigold Hotel, 2015; Absolutely Fabulous: the movie, Bridget Jones's Baby, 2016; A Cure for Wellness, 2017; Monster Family, Malevolent, Finding Your Feet, Mamma Mia! Here We Go Again, Nativity Rocks!, 2018; *television* includes: Acorn Antiques, 1986; Oranges are not the Only Fruit, 1990; The Riff Raff Element, 1993; Dark Adapted Eye, 1994; Blackhearts in Battersea, 1996; The History of Tom Jones, 1997; dinnerladies, 1998; Gormenghast, 2000; Love in a Cold Climate, 2001; Gathering Storm, Doctor Zhivago, Daniel Deronda, 2002; After You've Gone, 2007; Cranford, 2009; Titanic, 2012; Dr Who, Love and Marriage, The Blandings, 2013; Vicious, 2015; Better Things, 2016–17; Hang Ups, 2018. *Publications:* The Happy Hoofer (autobiog.), 2011; novels: Not Quite Nice, 2015; Nice Work (If You Can Get It), 2016; Sail Away, 2018; A Nice Cup of Tea, 2019. *Recreations:* biking by the sea, going to Nice. *Address:* c/o Clare Eden, 194 Amyand Park Road, Twickenham TW1 3HY.

**INCH, Thomas David**, OBE 2000; CChem, FRSC; Secretary-General, Royal Society of Chemistry, 1993–2000; *b* 25 Sept. 1938; *s* of Thomas Alexander Inch and Sarah Lang Graves Inch; *m* 1964, Jacqueline Vivienne Pudner; one *d*. *Educ:* St Austell Grammar Sch.; Univ. of Birmingham (BSc 1st Cl. Hons Chem. 1960; PhD 1963; DSc 1971). Salters Fellow, Univ. of Birmingham, 1963–64; Vis. Fellow, NIH, USA, 1964–65; Chemical Defence Estabt, MoD, 1965–87 (RCDS 1985); Gen. Manager, Research Business Development, BP Research, 1987–90; Vice-Pres., R&D, BP America, 1990–93. Director: BP Ventures, 1987–89; Edison Polymer Innovation Corp., 1990–92; Ohio Science and Technology Commn, 1992. Chm., Nat. Adv. Cttee, Chemical Weapons Convention, 1997–2005. *Publications:* papers and reviews on chemistry and related topics. *Recreation:* golf. *Address:* 16 Ashlands, Ford, Salisbury SP4 6DY. *Club:* High Post Golf.

**INCHCAPE, 4th Earl of**, *cr* 1929; **Kenneth Peter Lyle Mackay**, AIB; Viscount Glenapp 1929; Viscount Inchcape 1924; Baron Inchcape 1911; Director: Glenapp Estate Co. Ltd, since 1980 (Chairman, since 2002); Inchcape Family Estates (formerly Investments) Ltd, since 1980 (Chairman, since 2002); Gray Dawes Travel Ltd, since 1996 (Chairman, 2002); Duncan MacNeill & Co. Ltd, since 1986; Assam Oil and Gas, since 2006; farmer in Wiltshire; *b* 23 Jan. 1943; *er s* of 3rd Earl of Inchcape, and of his 1st wife, Mrs Aline Thorn Hannay, *d* of Sir Richard Pease, 2nd Bt; *S* father, 1994; *m* 1966, Georgina, *d* of late S. C. Nisbet and Mrs G. R. Sutton; one *s* two *d*. *Educ:* Eton. Late Lieut 9/12th Royal Lancers. Inchcape PLC, 1970–91. Master, Grocers' Co., 1993–94; Prime Warden, Shipwrights' Co., 1998–99. *Recreations:* shooting, fishing, golf, travel, ski-ing. *Heir: s* Viscount Glenapp, *qv*. *Address:* Manor Farm, Clyffe Pypard, Swindon SN4 7PY. *Clubs:* White's, Oriental, Pratt's; New (Edinburgh); Prestwick (Ayrshire); Royal Sydney (Sydney, NSW).
*See also* Baron Camoys.

**INCHIQUIN, 18th Baron of**, *cr* 1543; **Conor Myles John O'Brien**; (The O'Brien); Bt 1686; Prince of Thomond; Chief of the Name; *b* 17 July 1943; *s* of Hon. Fionn Myles Maryons O'Brien (*d* 1977) (*y s* of 15th Baron) and Josephine Reine (*d* 2011), *d* of late Joseph Eugene Bembaron; *S* uncle, 1982; *m* 1988, Helen, *d* of Gerald Fitzgerald O'Farrell; two *d*. *Educ:* Eton. Served as Captain, 14th/20th King's Hussars. *Heir: cousin* Conor John Anthony O'Brien, *b* 24 Sept. 1952. *Address:* Thomond House, Dromoland, Newmarket on Fergus, Co. Clare, Ireland.

**INCHYRA, 3rd Baron** *cr* 1962, of St Madoes, Co. Perth; **Christian James Charles Hoyer Millar**; *b* 12 Aug. 1962; *o s* of 2nd Baron Inchyra and of Fiona Mary (*née* Sheffield); *S* father, 2011; *m* 1992, Caroline Jane, *d* of late Robin Swan; one *s* two *d*. *Educ:* Eton; Edinburgh Univ. *Heir: s* Hon. Jake Christian Robert Hoyer Millar, *b* 10 July 1996.

**IND, Hugh Timothy**; Chief Executive, British Transport Police Authority, since 2019; *b* Pembury, Kent, 13 July 1969; *s* of Jack Kenneth Ind, *qv*; *m* 2003, Jo Grinter; one *s* one *d*. *Educ:* Tonbridge Sch., Kent; St John's Coll., Oxford (BA PPE 1991). Various roles, Home Office, 1991–99; Bill Manager, Regulation of Investigatory Powers Act, 1999–2000; Principal Private Sec., DCMS, 2001–04; Dir of Ops, Nat. Asylum Support Service, 2005–06; Strategic Dir Asylum, 2007–10, Regl Dir, 2010–12, UK Border Agency; Dir, Crime and Enforcement, UK Border Agency, then Dir, Compliance and Returns, later Casework and Returns, Immigration Enforcement, Home Office, 2012–16; Director General: Immigration Enforcement, Home Office, 2016–18; Cabinet Office, 2018–19. *Recreations:* reading, cricket, walking, football. *Address:* British Transport Police Authority, 74–80 Camden Street, NW1 0EG.

**IND, Jack Kenneth**; Headmaster, Dover College, 1981–91; *b* 20 Jan. 1935; *s* of late Rev. William Price Ind and Mrs Doris Maud Ind (*née* Cavell); *m* 1964, Elizabeth Olive Toombs; two *s* two *d*. *Educ:* Marlborough Coll.; St John's Coll., Oxford (BA Hons Mods, 2nd Cl. Class. Lit. and Lit. Hum.). Teacher: Wellingborough Sch., 1960–63; Tonbridge Sch., 1963–81 (Housemaster, 1970–81) and 1991–92; Eastbourne Coll., 1992–93; Gymnásium, Nové Zámky, Slovakia, 1994; Talbot Heath Sch., Bournemouth, 1996–97; Eastbourne Coll., 1997–98; Prior Park Coll., Bath, 1999–2001; Eastbourne Coll., 2001–02; (part time) Brighton Coll., 2002–04; Guildford High Sch., 2004–05 and 2009–10; St Catherine's Sch., Bramley, 2006–07 and 2008–09. Trustee, HMC projects in Central and Eastern Europe, 1997–2003. Reader in Ch of England, 1963–. *Recreations:* tennis, Rugby football, music, reading. *Address:* 68 Whitelake Road, Tonbridge, Kent TN10 3TJ. *T:* (01732) 300367.
*See also* H. T. Ind.

**IND, Rt Rev. William**; Bishop of Truro, 1997–2008; Assistant Bishop, Diocese of Salisbury, since 2009; *b* 26 March 1942; *s* of William Robert and Florence Emily Ind; *m* 1967, Frances Isobel Bramald; three *s*. *Educ:* Univ. of Leeds (BA); College of the Resurrection, Mirfield. Asst Curate, St Dunstan's, Feltham, 1966–71; Priest in charge, St Joseph the Worker, Northolt, 1971–74; Team Vicar, Basingstoke, 1974–87; Director of Ordinands, dio. of Winchester, 1982–87; Hon. Canon of Winchester, 1985–87; Bishop Suffragan of Grantham, 1987–97; Dean of Stamford, 1988–97. Hon. DD Exeter, 2009. *Recreations:* bird watching, cricket watching, orchid finding. *Address:* 15 Dean Close, Melksham, Wilts SN12 7EZ. *T:* (01225) 340979.

**INDIAN OCEAN, Archbishop of the**, since 2017; **Most Rev. James Richard Wong Yin Song**; Bishop of the Seychelles, since 2009; *b* Rodrigues Island, Mauritius, 13 Jan. 1960; *s* of Maxime and Louisa Wong Yin Song; *m* 1982, Doreen Kuin Fong; one *s* one *d*. *Educ:* St Paul's Theol Coll., Mauritius; Selly Oak Colls, Birmingham. Ordained deacon and priest, 1983; Canon, St James Cathedral, Mauritius, 2002; Archdeacon of Mauritius, 2003. *Address:* Bishop's House, Bel Eau, PO Box 44, Victoria, Mahé, Seychelles. *T:* (office) 4323879, 4321977, (mobile) 2813177. *E:* bp.james.wong@gmail.com.

**INGE**, family name of **Baron Inge**.

**INGE, Baron** *cr* 1997 (Life Peer), of Richmond in the co. of North Yorkshire; **Field Marshal Peter Anthony Inge**, KG 2001; GCB 1992 (KCB 1988); PC 2004; DL; Chief of the Defence Staff, 1994–97; Constable, HM Tower of London, 1996–2001; *b* 5 Aug. 1935; *s* of late Raymond Albert Inge and Grace Maud Caroline Inge (*née* Du Rose); *m* 1960, Letitia Marion Beryl, *yr d* of late Trevor and Sylvia Thornton-Berry; two *d*. *Educ:* Summer Fields; Wrekin College; RMA Sandhurst. Commissioned Green Howards, 1956; served Hong Kong, Malaya, Germany, Libya and UK; ADC to GOC 4 Div., 1960–61; Adjutant, 1 Green Howards, 1963–64; student, Staff Coll., 1966; MoD, 1967–69; Coy Comdr, 1 Green Howards, 1969–70; student, JSSC, 1971; BM 11 Armd Bde, 1972; Instructor, Staff Coll., 1973–74; CO 1 Green Howards, 1974–76; Comdt, Junior Div., Staff Coll., 1977–79; Comdr Task Force C/4 Armd Bde, 1980–81; Chief of Staff, HQ 1 (BR) Corps, 1982–83; GOC NE District and Comdr 2nd Inf. Div., 1984–86; Dir Gen. Logistic Policy (Army), MoD, 1986–87; Comdr 1st (Br.) Corps, 1987–89; Comdr Northern Army Gp, and C-in-C, BAOR, 1989–92; CGS 1992–94. ADC Gen. to the Queen, 1991–94. Colonel, The Green Howards, 1982–94. Col Comdt: RMP, 1987–92; APTC, 1988–97. Mem., H of L, 1997–2016. Non-exec. Dir, Racal Electronics plc, 1997–2000. Comr, Royal Hosp. Chelsea, 1998–2004; Trustee, Historic Royal Palaces, 1999–2007. President: Army Benevolent Fund, 1998–2002; The Pilgrims, 2002–; Member Council: St George's House, Windsor Castle, 1998–2006, 2010–; Marlborough Coll., 1998–2006. Mem., Hakluyt

Foundn, 1999–2004; Chm., King Edward VII's Hosp. Sister Agnes, 2004–12. DL N Yorks, 1994. Hon. DCL Newcastle, 1995. *Recreations:* cricket, walking, music and reading, especially military history. *Clubs:* Boodle's, Beefsteak, Army and Navy, Travellers, MCC.

INGE, George Patrick Francis; Chairman: Savills plc, 1987–95; FPD Savills (formerly Savills Land & Property) Ltd, 1992–2000; *b* 31 Aug. 1941; *s* of late John William Wolstenholme Inge and Alison Lilias Inge; *m* 1977, Joyce (*née* Leinster); one *s* one *d. Educ:* Old Malthouse Prep. Sch., Dorset; Sherborne Sch. Joined Alfred Savill & Sons, 1960; Partner, 1968; Man. Partner, Savills, 1985; Chief Exec., Savills plc, 1987–91. Non-exec. Chm., Severn Trent Property Ltd, 1995–2006; non-exec. Dir, Westbury plc, 1995–2003. Governor: Old Malthouse Sch., Dorset, 1977–98 (Chm., 1986–98); Cothill House Sch., 1989–2013; Nottingham Trent Univ., 1994–96; Downe House Sch., 1996–2004 (Chm., 1999–2004). *Recreations:* shooting, fishing, golf. *Address:* The Old Vicarage, Little Milton, Oxford OX44 7QB. *T:* (01844) 279538.

INGE, Rt Rev. John Geoffrey; *see* Worcester, Bishop of.

INGESTRE, Viscount; James Richard Charles John Chetwynd-Talbot; *b* 11 Jan. 1978; *s* and *heir* of 22nd Earl of Shrewsbury and Waterford, *qv*; *m* 2006, Polly Elizabeth, *d* of Henry Blackie; one *s* three *d. Educ:* Shrewsbury Sch.; Royal Agricl Coll. MRICS 2002. *Heir:* s Hon. George Henry Charles John Alton Chetwynd-Talbot, *b* 3 May 2013.

INGHAM, Sir Bernard, Kt 1990; Secretary, Supporters of Nuclear Energy, 1998–2008 and 2010–14; *b* 21 June 1932; *s* of Garnet and Alice Ingham; *m* 1956, Nancy Hilda Hoyle (*d* 2017); one *s. Educ:* Hebden Bridge Grammar Sch., Yorks. Reporter: Hebden Bridge Times, 1948–52; Yorkshire Post and Yorkshire Evening Post, Halifax, 1952–59; Yorkshire Post, Leeds, 1959–61; Northern Industrial Correspondent, Yorkshire Post, 1961; Reporter, The Guardian, 1962–65; Labour Staff, The Guardian, London, 1965–67; Press and Public Relns Adviser, NBPI, 1967–68; Chief Inf. Officer, DEP, 1968–73; Director of Information: Dept of Employment, 1973; Dept of Energy, 1974–77; Under Sec., Energy Conservation Div., Dept of Energy, 1978–79; Chief Press Sec. to Prime Minister, 1979–90; Head, Govt Inf. Service, 1989–90. Chm., Bernard Ingham Communications, 1990–2011. Columnist: The Express (formerly Daily Express), 1991–98; PR Week, 1994–2001; Yorkshire Post, 2003–. Non-executive Director: McDonald's Restaurants Ltd, 1991–2005 (Mem. Adv. Bd, 2005–10); Hill and Knowlton (UK) Ltd, public relations counsel, 1991–2002. Mem. Exec. Cttee, Meml to Women of WWII, 2004–05. Vis. Fellow, Univ. of Newcastle, 1989–2004; Vis. Prof., Middlesex Univ. Business Sch., 1998–. President: British Franchise Assoc., 1993–2012; Hardcastle Crags Preservation Cttee, Hebden Bridge. Mem. Council Univ. of Huddersfield, 1994–2000. Hon. DLitt: Buckingham, 1997; Bradford, 2004; DUniv Middlesex, 1999. *Publications:* Kill The Messenger, 1991; Yorkshire Millennium, 1999; Yorkshire Castles, 2001; Yorkshire Villages, 2001; The Wages of Spin, 2003; Yorkshire Greats, 2005; The Slow Downfall of Margaret Thatcher, 2019. *Recreations:* watching sport, reading, writing. *Address:* 9 Monahan Avenue, Purley, Surrey CR8 3BB. *T:* (020) 8660 8970, 07860 535962. *E:* bernardinghamcom@aol.com. *Clubs:* Reform; Midgehole Working Men's, Pennine (Hebden Bridge).

INGHAM, Christopher John, CMG 2002; HM Diplomatic Service, retired; Ambassador to Republic of Uzbekistan and (non-resident) to Republic of Tajikistan, 1999–2002; *b* 4 June 1944; *s* of Dr Roland Ingham and Dorothy Ingham; *m* 1968, Jacqueline Anne Clarke; one *s* two *d. Educ:* St John's Coll., Cambridge (MA). Mgt trainee, Cadbury Bros Ltd, 1966–68; joined HM Diplomatic Service, 1968; Moscow, 1972–74; Calcutta, 1974; Kuwait, 1974–76; FCO, 1976–80; Dep. Perm. Rep. to IAEA/UNIDO, Vienna, 1980–85; FCO, 1985–87; Hd, Commercial Section, Mexico City, 1987–89; FCO, 1989–91; Counsellor and Dep. Hd of Mission, Bucharest, 1991–95; Counsellor, EU and Economic, Madrid, 1995–99. Parish Councillor, Little Chalfont, 2015–. *Recreations:* hill-walking, choral singing.

INGHAM, Rt Rev. Michael; Bishop of New Westminster, 1994–2013; *b* 25 Aug. 1949; *s* of Herbert and Dorothy Ingham. *Educ:* Univ. of Edinburgh (MA 1970; BD 1973 (First Class Hons)). Ordained deacon and priest, 1974; Asst Curate, St John the Evangelist, Ottawa, Ontario, 1974–76; Rector: Christ the King, Burnaby, BC, 1976–80; St Francis-in-the-Wood, W Vancouver, 1980–89; Principal Sec. to the Primate, Toronto, 1989–92; Dean of Christ Church Cathedral, Vancouver, 1992–94. Hon. DD: Vancouver Sch. of Theol., 1998; Episcopal Divinity Sch., Cambridge, MA, 2009; Hon. LLD Simon Fraser, 2013. Queen Elizabeth II Diamond Jubilee Medal, 2012. *Publications:* Rites for a New Age, 1985, 2nd edn 1990; Mansions of the Spirit, 1997; More Than I can Say: Michael Peers: a memoir, 2014. *Recreations:* sailing, golf.

INGHAM, Prof. Philip William, DPhil; FMedSci; FRS 2002; Professor of Developmental Biology, since 2013 and Toh Kian Chui Distinguished Professor, since 2014, Lee Kong Chian School of Medicine, Nanyang Technological University, Singapore (Vice Dean, Research, 2014–16); *b* 19 March 1955; *s* of late George Philip Ingham and Dorothy Ingham; *m* 1993, Anita Maria Taylor; one *s* two *d. Educ:* Queens' Coll., Cambridge (BA, MA); Univ. of Sussex (DPhil 1981). Res. Scientist, MRC, 1986; Imperial Cancer Research Fund: Res. Scientist, 1986–91; Sen. Scientist, 1991–94; Principal Scientist, 1994–96; Prof. of Develtl Genetics and Dir, MRC Centre for Develtl and Biomed. Genetics (formerly Centre for Develtl Genetics), Univ. of Sheffield, 1996–2009; Prof. of Develtl Biol., Imperial Coll. London, 2013–16; Dir, Living Systems Inst., Univ. of Exeter, 2016–18, now Hon. Prof. Dep. Dir, then Res. Dir, Inst. of Molecular and Cell Biol., Singapore, 2006. Chm., British Soc. for Develtl Biol., 1999–2004. Mem., EMBO, 1995. FRSB (FIBiol 2000); FMedSci 2001. Hon. FRCP 2007. Genetics Soc. Medal, 2005; Waddington Medal, British Soc. for Develtl Biol., 2014. *Publications:* contrib. scientific papers to Cell, Nature, Science, Genes and Develt, Develt, Develtl Biol. *Recreations:* music, playing tennis, walking, ski-ing, travelling, reading.

INGHAM, Stuart Edward; Chief Executive, United Leeds Teaching Hospitals NHS Trust, 1991–98; *b* 9 Oct. 1942; *s* of Edward Ingham and Dorothy Mary (*née* Pollard); *m* 1969, Jane Stella Wilkinson; one *s* one *d. Educ:* Canon Slade Grammar Sch., Bolton. AHSM 1970. Bolton and District HMC: Trainee in Hosp. Admin, 1965–66; HCO, 1966–67; Dep. Gen. Supt, Ancoats Hosp., 1967–69; Sen. Admin. Asst, Royal Bucks and Associated HMC, 1969–70; Hospital Secretary: Harefield Hosp., 1970–73; St James's Univ. Hosp., Leeds, 1973–74; Leeds Area Health Authority (Eastern): General Administrator, 1974–77; Dist Administrator, 1977–82; York Health Authority: Dist Administrator, 1982–84; Dist Gen. Manager, 1985–88; Dist Gen. Manager, Leeds Western HA, 1988–90. *Recreations:* equestrian sports, bad golf. *Address:* The Turnings, Woodacre Crescent, Bardsey, Leeds LS17 9DQ.

INGILBY, Sir Thomas (Colvin William), 6th Bt *cr* 1866; managing own estate; *b* 17 July 1955; *s* of Sir Joslan William Vivian Ingilby, 5th Bt, DL, JP, and Diana, *d* of late Sir George Colvin, CB, CMG, DSO; *S* father, 1974; *m* 1984, Emma Clare Roebuck, *d* of Major R. R. Thompson, Whinfield, Strensall, York; four *s* one *d. Educ:* Aysgarth Sch., Bedale; Eton Coll.; Royal Agricultural Coll., Cirencester. MRAC; MRICS; FAAV. Joined Army, May 1974, but discharged on death of father; Assistant: Stephenson & Son, York, 1978–80; Strutt & Parker, Harrogate, 1981–83. Chairman: Harrogate Mgt Centre Ltd, 1991–99; Action Harrogate Ltd, 1992–98. Dir, Yorks Tourist Bd, 1997–2009 (Dep. Chm., 2005–09); Dir, Welcome to Yorkshire, 2014–. Founder and Nat. Co-ordinator, Stately Homes Hotline, 1988–; Pres., Council for Prevention of Art Theft, 1991–2001; Chm., Yorkshire's Great Houses, Castles and Gardens, 1995–; Fest. Dir, World Golden Oldies Cricket Fest., Harrogate, 2020. Chm., Bd of Govs, Cundall Manor Sch., Helperby, 2007–. President: Nidderdale Amateur Cricket League, 1979–; Harrogate Gilbert and Sullivan Soc., 1988–. Internat. Hon. Citizen, New Orleans, 1979; Lifetime Achievement Award, Harrogate Business Awards, 2011. *Publications:* Yorkshire's Great Houses: behind the scenes, 2005. *Recreations:* cricket, tennis, reading, writing, public speaking, historical research, walking. *Heir:* s James William Francis Ingilby [*b* 15 June 1985; *m* 2014, Sara Nicholson]. *Address:* Ripley Castle, Ripley, near Harrogate, North Yorkshire HG3 3AY. *T:* (01423) 770152. *E:* sirthomas@ripleycastle.co.uk.

INGLE, Alan Richmond, CMG 2000; HM Diplomatic Service, retired; *b* 16 Oct. 1939; *s* of late Henry Ingle and of Helen Ingle (*née* Keating); *m* 1963, Gillian Hall; one *s* one *d. Educ:* Stand Grammar Sch. and Prince Rupert Sch., Wilhelmshaven. Entered BoT, 1957; Accra (Trade Commn Service), 1961–65; FO, 1965–66; Kingston, 1966–70; Third Sec., Christchurch, 1970–74; Second Secretary: FCO, 1974–77; (Commercial), Singapore, 1977–81; First Sec., FCO, 1981–83; Consul and Dir, British Inf. Services, NY, 1983–88; First Sec., FCO 1988–93; Counsellor (Mgt), Lagos and Abuja, 1993–96; Hd of Delegn, Jt Mgt Office, Brussels, 1996–99; Counsellor: FCO, 2000; UK Mission to UN, NY, 2001. *Address:* Chaseley, Higher Broad Oak Road, West Hill, Ottery St Mary, Devon EX11 1XJ. *Club:* Royal Over-Seas League.

INGLEDOW, Anthony Brian, OBE 1969; HM Diplomatic Service, retired; Counsellor, Foreign and Commonwealth Office, 1983–93; *b* 25 July 1928; *s* of Cedric Francis Ingledow and Doris Evelyn Ingledow (*née* Worrall); *m* 1956, Margaret Monica, *d* of Sir Reginald Watson-Jones, FRCS; one *s* one *d. Educ:* St Bees School; London Univ. Served HM Forces, 1947–49. Joined Colonial Administrative Service, Nigeria, 1950; District Officer: Auchi, 1954; Oyo, 1956; Secretariat, Ibadan, 1958, retired 1960; joined HM Diplomatic Service, 1961; 2nd Secretary, Khartoum, 1962; FO, 1964; 1st Secretary, Aden, 1966; Lagos, 1967; FCO, 1970; Dakar, 1972; FCO, 1975. *Recreations:* reading, travel. *Address:* c/o Lloyds Bank, Box 3, BX1 1LT. *Club:* Athenæum.

INGLEHEARN, Catherine Mary, (Mrs Christopher Jarratt), MBE 2016; HM Diplomatic Service; Ambassador to the Republic of Guinea, 2015–19; *b* St Albans, 15 May 1965; *d* of Francois Inglehearn and Maureen Hillam; *m* 2012, Christopher Jarratt; one step *s* one step *d. Educ:* Bar Convent Grammar Sch., York; Bath Univ. (BA Hons Modern Langs and Eur. Studies 1988). Joined FCO, 1990; Third Sec., Rome, 1992–95; Consul, Ljubljana, 1996–99; Desk Officer: for Serbia, 1999–2000, for Stability Pact for Eur., 2000–01, Eastern Adriatic Dept, FCO; for former Soviet Union, EU Dept, FCO, 2001–03; Dep. Hd of Mission, Kazakhstan, 2003–07; Head: Nigeria and Central Africa Sect., E and W Africa Dept, FCO, 2007–09; Energy Security, Climate Change and Energy Dept, FCO, 2009–12; Dep. Hd, E and W Africa Dept, Africa Directorate, FCO, 2012–14. *Recreations:* gardening, travel, sport (running, hiking, tennis), music. *Address:* c/o Foreign and Commonwealth Office, King Charles Street, SW1A 2AH. *E:* Catherine.Inglehearn@fco.gov.uk.

INGLESE, Anthony Michael Christopher, CB 2008; General Counsel and Solicitor, HM Revenue and Customs, 2008–14; *b* 19 Dec. 1951; *s* of Angelo Inglese and Dora Inglese (*née* Di Paola); *m* 1974, Jane Elizabeth Kerry Bailes; one *s* one *d. Educ:* Salvatorian Coll., Harrow Weald; Fitzwilliam Coll., Cambridge (MA, LLB). Called to the Bar, Gray's Inn, 1976, Bencher, 2002; Legal Advr's Br., Home Office, 1975–86; Legal Secretariat to Law Officers, 1986–88; Legal Advr's Br., Home Office, 1988–91; Legal Dir, OFT, 1991–95; Legal Advr, MoD (Treasury Solicitor's Dept), 1995–97; Dep. Treasury Solicitor, 1997–2001; Solicitor and Dir Gen., Legal Services, DTI, later BERR, 2002–08. *E:* anthony.inglese@btinternet.com.

INGLEWOOD, 2nd Baron *cr* 1964; (William) Richard Fletcher-Vane; farmer, landowner and businessman; Vice Lord-Lieutenant of Cumbria, since 2012; *b* 31 July 1951; *e s* of 1st Baron Inglewood, TD and Mary (*d* 1982), *e d* of Major Sir Richard George Proby, 1st Bt, MC; *S* father, 1989; *m* 1986, Cressida, *y d* of late Desmond Pemberton-Pigott, CMG; one *s* two *d. Educ:* Eton; Trinity Coll., Cambridge (MA); Cumbria Coll. of Agriculture and Forestry. MRICS. Called to the Bar, Lincoln's Inn, 1975. Member: Lake Dist Special Planning Bd, 1984–90 (Chm., Develt Control Cttee, 1984–89); NW Water Authority, 1987–89. Pres., Cumbria Tourist Bd, 2004–. Non-executive Director: CN Group, 1997–2018 (Chm., 2002–16); Carr's Milling Industries, 2004–13 (Chm., 2005–13); Chm., Gen2, 2016–. Chm., Reviewing Cttee on Export of Works of Art, 2002–14; Pres., British Art Market Fedn, 2014–. Contested (C) Houghton and Washington, 1983; Durham, EP elecns, 1984; MEP (C) Cumbria and Lancashire N, 1989–94; contested (C) same reg., 1994; MEP (C) NW Reg., England, 1999–2004. Cons. spokesman on legal affairs, EP, 1989–94 and 1999–2004, on constitutional affairs, 2001–04; Dep. Whip, EDG, 1992–94; Chief Whip, 1994. A Lord in Waiting (Govt Whip), 1994–95; Captain of HM Yeomen of the Guard (Dep. Govt Chief Whip), 1995; Parly Under-Sec. of State, DNH, 1995–97; elected Mem., H of L, 1999. Chm., H of L Select Cttee on Communications, 2011–13, on Extradition, 2013–14. Mem., Delegn to Parly Assembly, Council of Europe, 2010–11. Vis. Parly Fellow, St Antony's Coll., Oxford, 2014–15. Mem., Adv. Bd, Reuters Inst., Univ. of Oxford, 2015–. FSA 2002. Chairman: Cumbria Local Nature Partnership, 2013–17; Cumbria LEP, 2018–; Pres., Uplands Alliance, 2015–. DL Cumbria, 1993. *Heir:* s Hon. Henry William Frederick Fletcher-Vane, *b* 24 Dec. 1990. *Address:* Hutton-in-the-Forest, Penrith, Cumbria CA11 9TH. *T:* (01768) 484500. *Clubs:* Pratt's, Travellers.
See also Hon. C. J. Fletcher-Vane.

INGLIS, George Bruton; Senior Partner, Slaughter and May, 1986–92; *b* 19 April 1933; *s* of late Cecil George Inglis and Ethel Mabel Inglis; *m* 1968, Patricia Mary Forbes; three *s. Educ:* Winchester College; Pembroke College, Oxford (MA). Solicitor. Partner, Slaughter and May, 1966–92. *Recreation:* gardening.

INGLIS, Heather Hughson; *see* Swindells, H. H.

INGLIS, Ian Grahame, CB 1983; Chairman, State Grants Commission, Tasmania, 1990–2001; *b* 2 April 1929; *s* of late William and Ellen Jean Inglis; *m* 1952, Elaine Arlene Connors; three *s* one *d. Educ:* Hutchins Sch., Hobart; Univ. of Tasmania (BCom). Agricl Economist, Tasmanian Dept of Agric., 1951–58; Economist, State Treasury, 1958–69; Chairman: Rivers and Water Supply Commn, and Metropolitan Water Bd, 1969–77; NW Regl Water Authority, 1977; State Under Treasurer, Tas, 1977–89. Dir, TGIO Ltd (formerly Tasmanian Govt Insce Bd), 1989–96. Chm., Retirement Benefits Fund Investment Trust, 1989–95. Member: Ambulance Commn of Tasmania, 1959–65; Tasmanian Grain Elevators Bd, 1962–65; Clarence Municipal Commn, 1965–69; Motor Accidents Insurance Bd, 1991–95. Dir, Comalco Aluminium (Bell Bay) Ltd, 1980–95. *Recreations:* yacht-racing, gardening, bridge. *Address:* 5 Sayer Crescent, Sandy Bay, Hobart, Tas 7005, Australia. *T:* (3) 62231928. *Clubs:* Tasmanian, Royal Yacht of Tasmania (Hobart).

**INGLIS of Glencorse, Sir Ian Richard,** 11th Bt *cr* 1703 (then Mackenzie of Gairloch); *b* 9 Aug. 1965; *s* of Sir Roderick John Inglis of Glencorse, 10th Bt and Rachel Inglis (*née* Morris); *S* father, 2018, but his name does not appear on the Official Roll of the Baronetage; *m* 1st, 1990, Lesley Margaret Moss (marr. diss. 1994); one *s*; 2nd, 2000, Yvonne Rossina Hird; one *s* one *d*. *Heir: s* Joshua Ben Mackenzie Inglis, *b* 21 Nov. 1990.

**INGLIS, His Honour Richard Anthony Girvan;** a Circuit Judge, 1996–2014; *b* 28 Dec. 1947; *s* of Angus Inglis and Kathleen Flora Inglis; *m* 1976, Heather Hughson Swindells, *qv*; one *s*. *Educ:* Marlborough Coll.; Selwyn Coll., Cambridge (BA 1969). Called to the Bar, Middle Temple, 1971; Jun., Midland and Oxford Circuit, 1984; Recorder, 1993–96; Hon. Recorder of Newark, 2002–14. *Recreations:* garden, music, church bell ringing.

**INGLIS, Dr Stephen Charles,** CBE 2017; Director, National Institute for Biological Standards and Control, 2002–16 (a Health Protection Agency centre, 2009–13; a Medicines and Healthcare products Regulatory Agency centre, 2013–16); *b* 1 Sept. 1952; *s* of John Reid Inglis and Joan Inglis (*née* Devear); *m* 1975, Moira Margaret Hunter; two *s* one *d*. *Educ:* Aberdeen Grammar Sch.; Aberdeen Univ. (BSc Hons Biochem. 1974); Churchill Coll., Cambridge (PhD 1978). University of Cambridge: Res. Fellow, Churchill Coll., 1978–80; Demonstrator, 1979–84, Lectr, 1984–90, Dept of Pathol.; Fellow, Darwin Coll., 1984–90; Hd, Molecular Scis, 1990–95, Res. Dir, 1995–2001, Cantab Pharmaceuticals, subseq. Xenova PLC. Chm., Phogen, 1997–2001. Dir, WHO Collaborating Lab. for Standards, 2002–16. Member, Corporate Executive Team: HPA, 2005–09; MHRA, 2012–. Member: Scientific Pandemic Influenza Adv. Cttee, 2005–16, Expert Scientific Gp on Phase One Clin. Trials, 2006–07, DoH; Bd, Nat. Measurement Systems, DIUS, then BIS, 2007–14; UK Vaccine R&D Network, 2015–; Scientific Adv. Bd, Pirbright Inst. 2016–. Chm., MRC/HFEA Wkg Party on evaluation of clin. procedures for assisted reprodn, 2003–; Member: Molecular and Cellular Medicine Bd, MRC, 1996–2000; Scientific Adv. Cttee, CRC Ventures, 2000–01; Scientific Adv. Cttee, Edward Jenner Inst. Vaccine Res., 2000–12; Jt Professional Adv. Cttee on Blood Safety, 2002–; Biologicals Subcttee, Cttee for Safety of Medicines, 2002–05; Jt Cttee on Vaccines and Immunisation, 2002–09 (Chm., sub-gp on varicella-zoster, 2007–08); Nat. Biol Standards Bd, 2002–09; Biologicals and Vaccines Expert Adv. Gp, Commn for Human Medicines, 2006–13; Steering Cttee, Nat. Genetics Ref. Lab., 2007–09; Steering Bd, Health Tech. and Medicines Knowledge Transfer Network, 2010–13. Mem., Governing Body, Lister Inst. of Preventative Medicine, 2003–10. Hon. Prof., Div. of Infection and Immunity, Faculty of Med. Scis, UCL, 2016. FRSB 2016. MInstD 1997. *Publications:* contrib. scientific papers to professional jls in fields of virology, molecular biol., vaccine develt. *Recreations:* music: jazz piano, saxophone, sport: ski-ing, cycling, hillwalking, swimming.

**INGLIS-JONES, Nigel John;** QC 1982; Barrister-at-Law; *b* 7 May 1935; 2nd *s* of Major John Alfred Inglis-Jones and Hermione Inglis-Jones; *m* 1st, 1965, Lenette Bromley-Davenport (*d* 1986); two *s* two *d*; 2nd, 1987, Ursula Culverwell; one *s*. *Educ:* Eton; Trinity Coll., Oxford (BA). Nat. Service with Grenadier Guards (ensign). Called to the Bar, Inner Temple, 1959, Bencher, 1981. A Recorder, 1976–93. Dep. Social Security Comr, 1993–2002; Gen. Comr of Income Tax, 1992–2005. *Publications:* The Law of Occupational Pension Schemes, 1989. *Recreations:* gardening, fishing, collecting English drinking glass. *Address:* Woolston Manor Farm House, Woolston, North Cadbury, Yeovil BA22 7BL. *T:* (01963) 441031.

**INGMAN, David Charles,** CBE 1993; Chairman, British Waterways Board, 1987–93; *b* 22 March 1928; *s* of Charles and Muriel Ingman; *m* 1951, Joan Elizabeth Walker; two *d*. *Educ:* Grangefield Grammar Sch., Stockton-on-Tees; Durham Univ. (BSc, MSc). Imperial Chemical Industries, 1949–85: Dir, then Dep. Chm., Plastics Div., 1975–81; Gp Dir, Plastics and Petrochemicals Div., 1981–85; Chm. and Chief Exec., Bestobell, 1985–86. Dir, Engineering Services Ltd, 1975–78; Alternative Dir, AECI Ltd, SA, 1978–82; non-exec. Dir, Negretti-Zambra, 1979–81. Mem., Nationalised Industries Chairmen's Gp, 1987–93. *Recreations:* golf, walking, travel.

**INGOLD, Dr Keith Usherwood,** OC 1994; FRS 1979; FRSC 1969; Distinguished Research Scientist, National Research Council, Canada, since 1991; *b* Leeds, 31 May 1929; *s* of Christopher Kelk Ingold and Edith Hilda (*née* Usherwood); *m* 1956, Carmen Cairine Hodgkin; one *s* one *d* (and one *s* decd). *Educ:* University Coll. London (BSc Hons Chem., 1949; Fellow, 1987); Univ. of Oxford (DPhil 1951). Emigrated to Canada, 1951; Post-doctorate Fellow (under Dr F. P. Lossing), Div. of Pure Chem., Nat. Res. Council of Canada, 1951–53; Def. Res. Bd Post-doctorate Fellow (under Prof. W. A. Bryce), Chem. Dept, Univ. of BC, 1953–55; National Research Council of Canada: joined Div. of Appl. Chem., 1955; Head, Hydrocarbon Chem. Section of Div. of Chem., 1965; Associate Dir, Div. of Chemistry, 1977–90. Adjunct Professor: Brunel Univ., 1983–94; Univ. of Guelph, 1985–87; Carleton Univ., 1991–; Van Arkel Vis. Prof., Leiden Univ., Holland, 1992; Vis. Lectr, Japan Soc. for Promotion of Science, 1982. Hon. Treas., RSC, 1979–81; Canadian Society for Chemistry: Vice-Pres., 1985–87, Pres., 1987–88. Hon. Mem., Argentinian Soc. for Res. in Organic Chem., 1997. Lectures: Frontiers in Chem., Case Western Res. Univ. and Frank Burnett Dains Meml, Univ. of Kansas, 1969; J. A. McRae Meml, Queen's Univ., Ont, 1980; Canadian Industries Ltd, Acadia Univ., NS, Imperial Oil, Univ. of Western Ont, and Douglas Hill Meml, Duke Univ., NC, 1987; Rayson Huang, Univ. of Hong Kong, 1988; 3M University, Univ. of Western Ont, Peter de la Mare Meml, Univ. of Auckland, and Gilman, Iowa State Univ., 1993; Marjorie Young Bell, Mount Allison Univ., NB, and Bergman, Yale Univ., 1994; Weissberger-Williams, Kodak Res. Center, Rochester, NY, and Stanley J. Cristol, Univ. of Colorado, 1995; (first) Cheves Walling, Gordon Res. Conf., 1997; Max T. Rogers, Michigan State Univ., 2000. Hon. FRSE 2001. Hon. DSc: Univ. of Guelph, 1985; St Andrews, 1989; Carleton, 1992; McMaster, 1995; Hon. LLD: Mount Allison, New Brunswick, 1987; Dalhousie, 1996; Dr *hc* Ancona, 1999. Awards: American Chemical Society: Award in Petroleum Chem., 1968; Pauling Award, 1988; Arthur C. Cope Scholar Award, 1992; James Flack Norris Award in Physical Organic Chem., 1993; Award in Kinetics and Mechanism, Chem. Soc., 1978; Chemical Institute of Canada: Medal, 1981; Syntex Award for Physical Organic Chem., 1983; Royal Society of Canada: Centennial Medal, 1982; Henry Marshall Tory Medal, 1985; Humboldt Res. Award, Alexander von Humboldt Foundn, W Germany, 1989; Alfred Bader Award in Organic Chem., Canadian Soc. for Chem., 1989; Sir Christopher Ingold Lectureship Award, 1989, Sir Derek Barton Gold Medal, 2016, Royal Soc. of Chem.; VERIS Award, Vitamin E Res. Inf. Services, 1989; Lansdowne Visitor Award, Univ. of Victoria, Canada, 1990; Mangini Prize in Chem., Univ. of Bologna, 1990; Royal Society: Davy Medal, 1990; Royal Medal A, 2000; Izaak Walton Killam Meml Prize, Canada Council, 1992; Angelo Mangini Medal, Italian Chem. Soc., 1997; Canada Gold Medal for Sci. and Engrg, Natural Scis and Engrg Res. Council of Canada, 1998. Silver Jubilee Medal, 1977; Golden Jubilee Medal, 2002; Gold Medal, Professional Inst. of Public Service, Canada, 2009; Diamond Jubilee Medal, 2012. *Publications:* over 500 scientific papers in field of physical organic chemistry, partic. free-radical chemistry. *Recreation:* ski-ing. *Address:* 72 Ryeburn Drive, Ottawa ON K1V 1H5, Canada. *T:* (613) 8221123, (office) (613) 9900938.

**INGOLD, Prof. Timothy,** PhD; FBA 1997; FRSE; Professor of Social Anthropology, University of Aberdeen, 1999–2018, now Emeritus (Head, School of Social Science, 2008–11); *b* 1 Nov. 1948; *s* of late Cecil Terence Ingold, CMG and Leonora Mary Ingold (*née* Kemp); *m* 1972, Anna Kaarina Väli-Kivistö; three *s* one *d*. *Educ:* Churchill Coll., Cambridge (BA 1st cl. Hons 1970; PhD Social Anthropol. 1976). Department of Social Anthropology, University of Manchester: Lectr, 1974–85; Sen. Lectr, 1985–90; Prof., 1990–99 (Max Gluckman Prof. of Social Anthropology, 1995–99); Hd of Dept, 1993–97. British Academy Res. Readership, 1997–99; ESRC Professorial Fellowship, 2005–08; Adjunct Prof., Univ. of Tromsø, Norway, 1997–2000. Corresp. Mem., Finnish Literary Soc., 1993. FRSE 2000. Hon. Dr: Leuphana Univ., Germany, 2015; Univ. of Lapland, 2019. Rivers Meml Medal, RAI, 1989; Jean-Marie Delwart Foundn Award, Royal Belgian Acad. of Scis, 1994; Anders Retzius Gold Medal, Swedish Soc. for Anthropol. and Geog., 2004; Huxley Meml Medal, RAI, 2014. Kt, 1st Class, Order of White Rose (Finland), 2014. *Publications:* The Skolt Lapps today, 1976; Hunters, pastoralists and ranchers, 1980; Evolution and social life, 1986; The appropriation of nature, 1986; (ed) What is an animal?, 1988; (ed jtly) Hunters and gatherers, 2 vols, 1988; (ed jtly) Tools, language and cognition in human evolution, 1993; (ed) Companion encyclopedia of anthropology, 1994; (ed) Key debates in anthropology, 1996; The Perception of the Environment, 2000; (ed jtly) Creativity and Cultural Improvisation, 2007; Lines, 2007; (ed jtly) Ways of Walking, 2008; Being Alive, 2011; Redrawing Anthropology, 2011; (ed jtly) Imagining Landscapes, 2012; (ed jtly) Biosocial Becomings, 2013; Making, 2013; (ed jtly) Making and Growing, 2014; The Life of Lines, 2015; Anthropology and/as Education, 2017; Anthropology: why it matters, 2018; articles in academic books and learned jls. *Recreation:* music ('cello and piano). *Address:* Department of Anthropology, University of Aberdeen, Aberdeen AB24 3QY. *T:* (01224) 272726.

*See also* P. Healey.

**INGRAHAM, Rt Hon. Hubert Alexander;** PC 1993; Prime Minister, Commonwealth of the Bahamas, 1992–2002 and 2007–12; Member, National Assembly, 1977–2012 (PLP, 1977–86, Ind, 1987–90, FNM, 1990–2012); *b* 4 Aug. 1947; *m* Delores Velma Miller; five *c*. *Educ:* Cooper's Town Public Sch.; Southern Senior Sch.; Govt High Sch. Evening Inst., Nassau. Called to Bahamas Bar, 1972; Sen. Partner, Christie, Ingraham & Co. Formerly: Mem., Air Transport Licensing Authy; Chm., Real Property Tax Tribunal. Chm., Bahamas Mortgage Corp., 1982. Mem., Progressive Liberal Party, 1975–86; Minister of Housing, Nat. Insurance and Social Services, 1982–84; Leader, Free National Movement, 1990–2012; Leader of Opposition, 1990–92, 2005–07. *Address:* c/o Free National Movement, PO Box N–10713, Nassau, Bahamas.

**INGRAM, Adam Hamilton;** Member (SNP) Carrick, Cumnock and Doon Valley, Scottish Parliament, 2011–16 (South of Scotland, 1999–2011); *b* 1 May 1951; *m* 1977, Gerry; three *s* one *d*. *Educ:* Kilmarnock Acad.; Paisley Coll. (BA Hons Business Economics, 1980). Family bakery business, 1971–76; Sen. Economic Asst, Manpower Services Commn, 1985–86; Researcher and Lectr, Paisley Coll., 1987–88; Hd of Res., Development Options Ltd; Economic Develt consultant, 1990–99. Minister for Children and Early Years, Scottish Parlt, 2007–11. Joined SNP, 1983 (Mem., Nat. Exec. Cttee, 1994–99).

**INGRAM, Rt Hon. Adam (Paterson);** PC 1999; *b* 1 Feb. 1947; *s* of Bert Ingram and Louisa Paterson; *m* 1970, Maureen Georgina McMahon. *Educ:* Cranhill Secondary School. Commercial apprentice, 1965, computer programmer, 1966–69, J. & P. Coats, Glasgow; programmer/analyst, Associated British Foods, 1969–70; programmer/systems analyst, SSEB, 1970–77; Trade Union Official, NALGO, 1977–81. Chair, East Kilbride Constituency Labour Party, 1981–85; Councillor, E Kilbride DC, 1980–87, Leader, 1984–87. MP (Lab) E Kilbride, 1987–2005, E Kilbride, Strathaven and Lesmahagow, 2005–10. An Opposition Whip, Feb.–Nov. 1988 (responsible for Scottish business and Treasury matters); PPS to Leader of the Opposition, 1988–92; front bench spokesman on social security, 1993–95, on sci. and technol., 1995–97; Minister of State: NI Office, 1997–2001; MoD, 2001–07. Mem., Select Cttee on Trade and Industry, 1992–93; Vice-Chm., British-Japanese All-Party Parly Gp, 1992–97; Sec., British-Singapore All-Party Parly Gp, 1992–97; Vice-Chm., All-Party Parly Gp on Nuclear Energy, 2007–10; Sec., All-Party Parly Gp on Iraq, 2008–10. Head, Study Team on Defence role in counter-terrorism and resilience, 2007–09. Dir, Kilbryde Hospice, 2010–. JP E Kilbride, 1980–2008. Hon. Col, 154 Scottish Regt, RLC, 2013–17. Hon. Pres., E Kilbride Sea Cadets, 2017–. *Recreations:* fishing, cooking, reading, golf. *E:* adam_ingram@compuserve.com.

**INGRAM, Christopher John;** Partner, Ingram Enterprise Investors LLP, since 2008; *b* 9 June 1943; *s* of Thomas Frank Ingram and Gladys Agnes Ingram; *m* 1964, Janet Elizabeth Rye; one *s* one *d*. *Educ:* Woking Grammar Sch. KMP, 1970–72; Man. Dir, TMD Advertising, 1972–76; Founder Chris Ingram Associates (CIA), later Tempus Group plc, 1976, Chm., 1976–2002; Partner, Genesis Investments, 2002–08; Founder, The Ingram Partnership Ltd, 2003–07. Owner, Woking FC, 2002–12. Chm., Vitesse Media, 2014–. Dep. Chm., Foundn for Entrepreneurial Mgt, 2003–07, Chm., Centre for Creative Business, 2005–08, London Business Sch. Exec. Chm., Sports Revolution, 2009–13. Mem., Vice-Chancellor's Adv. Council, Univ. of Arts London, 2012–. Vice Pres., Shelter, 2001–08. Trustee, Ingram Trust, 1997–. Hon. Fellow, London Business Sch., 2007–. *Recreations:* theatre, football, modern British art, eating out, travel in cold climates.

**INGRAM, Prof. David Stanley,** OBE 1999; botanist, plant pathologist and horticulturist; Hon. Professor: University of Edinburgh, since 1992; Lancaster Environment Centre, University of Lancaster, since 2009; Hon. Fellow: Royal Botanic Garden, Edinburgh, since 1998 (Regius Keeper, 1990–98); St Catharine's College, Cambridge, since 2006 (Master, 2000–06); *b* 10 Oct. 1941; *s* of Stanley Arthur Ingram, toolmaker and Vera May Ingram (*née* Mansfield); *m* 1965, Alison Winifred Graham; two *s*. *Educ:* Yardley Grammar School, Birmingham; Univ. of Hull (BSc, PhD); MA, ScD Cantab. CBiol, FRSB (FIBiol 1986); FLS 1991; FRSE 1993; FCIHort (FIHort 1997); FRCPE 1998. Research Fellow, Univ. of Glasgow Dept of Botany, 1966–68; ARC Unit of Develt Botany, Cambridge, 1969–74; University of Cambridge: Research Fellow, Botany Sch., 1968–69; Univ. Lectr, 1974–88; Reader in Plant Pathology, 1988–90; Mem. Gen. Board, 1984–88; Fellow, Downing Coll., Cambridge, 1974–90 (Dean, 1976–82; Tutor for Graduate Students, 1982–88; Dir of Studies in Biology, 1976–89; Hon. Fellow, 2000); Advr to Univ. of Edinburgh on public engagement with science, 1998–2006 (Mem. Adv. Cttee, Div. of Biol Scis, 1991–98); Cambridge University: Chairman: Cttee for Interdisciplinary Envmtl Studies, 2001–03; Colls Cttee, 2003–05; Mem., Council, 2003–05. Visiting Professor: Univ. of Glasgow, 1991–2005 (Hon. Prof., 2005–10); of Envmtl Sci. and Horticulture, Napier Univ., 1998–2005; Glyndwr Univ., 2012–; Prof. of Horticulture, RHS, 1995–2000; Vis. Sen. Res. Fellow, ESRC Genomics Forum, Edinburgh, 2006–09 (Mem. Adv. Cttee, 2005–); Hon. Professorial Fellow, Sci., Technol. and Innovation Studies, 2012–, Hon. Associate, Innogen, 2015–, Univ. of Edinburgh; Fellow, Ruskin Foundn, 2014–. Chairman: Scientific Council, Sainsbury Lab. for Plant Pathology, 1990–92; Science and Plants for Schools Trust, 1991–98; Science and Plants for Schs, Scotland, 1998–2000; Scientific and Horticultural Advice Cttee, RHS, 1995–2000 (Mem., Scientific Cttee, 1992–95); Adv. Cttee, Darwin Initiative for Survival of the Species, 1999–2005; Prog. Convener and Chair, Sci. and Soc. Steering Gp, RSE, 2005–09; Chair, Biodiversity Adv. Gp, Ruskin Land, Wyre Forest, Guild of St George, 2017–; Member: Adv. Cttee, St Andrews Botanic Garden, 1990–95; Exec. Cttee, Scotland's Nat. Gardens Scheme, 1990–96; Adv Cttee on SSSI in Scotland, 1992–98; Council, Linnean Soc., 1992–95 (Vice Pres., 1993–94); Council, Internat. Assoc. of Botanic Gardens; Main Bd and Scientific Adv. Cttee, Scottish Natural Heritage,

1999–2000; Jt Nature Conservation Cttee, 1999–2000 and 2002– (Dep. Chm., 2006–); Forestry Commn Adv. Panel, 2004–06. Member: Editl Cttee, Flora of China, 1992–98; Editorial Board: Biol Revs, 1993–98, 2001–05; Annals of Botany, 1992–2001; Advances in Plant Path., 1992–95; Food Security, 2009–18 (Mem., Adv. Bd, 2006–). Companion, Guild of St George, 2015. Hon. Mem., Inst. of Analytical Plant Illustration, 2016–. Trustee: Grimsthorpe and Drummond Castle Trust, 1990–98; John Fife Meml Trust, 1990–98; Younger Botanic Garden Trust, 1990–2000; Royal Botanic Garden (Sibbald) Trust, 1990–98; Botanic Gardens Conservation International, 1991–98; Scottish Sci. Trust, 1998–99 (Mem. Scientific Adv. Cttee, 1999–2002); Dynamic Earth Proj., 1998–2000; World Conservation Monitoring Centre 2000, 2001–04. President: 7th Internat. Congress of Plant Pathology, 1994–98; British Soc. for Plant Pathology, 1998 (Hon. Mem., 2008); Hon. Vice-Pres., Royal Caledonian Horticultural Soc., 1990. Hon. Fellow: Myerscough Coll., 2001; Worcester Coll., Oxford, 2003; St Catharine's Coll., Cambridge, 2006. Hon. FRSGS 1998. DUniv Open, 2000. VMH 2004. *Publications:* (with D. N. Butcher) Plant Tissue Culture, 1974; (with J. P. Helgeson) Tissue Culture Methods for Plant Pathologists, 1980; (with A. Friday) Cambridge Encyclopedia of Life Sciences, 1985; (with P. H. Williams) Advances in Plant Pathology, vol. 1, 1982 to vol. 9, 1993; (with A. Hudson) Shape and Form in Plants and Fungi, 1994; (with A. Karp and P. G. Isaac) Molecular Tools for Screening Biodiversity, 1998; (with N. F. Robertson) Plant Disease, 1999; (with D. Vince-Prue and P. J. Gregory) Science and the Garden, 2002, 3rd edn 2015; The Flora of Blackwell, 2011; (with S. Wildman) Ruskin's Flora: the botanical drawings of John Ruskin, 2011; (with E. House) Painting Flowers: Fantin-Latour and the Impressionists, 2011; The Gardens at Brantwood: evolution of John Ruskin's Lakeland paradise, 2014; Ruskin's Botanical Books: re-ordered and annotated editions of Baxter and Sowerby, 2016; (with R. Roberts) Spinning the colours of Lakeland: Annie Garnett's spinnery, textiles and garden, 2017; (with S. Wildman) John Ruskin's Flora of Chamouni, 2019; contrib. papers dealing with research in plant pathology, plant tissue culture, botany, horticultural science, garden history and history of art to learned jls; contrib. articles to magazines and newspapers dealing with horticulture and sci. *Recreations:* listening to classical music and jazz, theatre, ceramics and other decorative arts, gardening, reading, strolling around cities. *Address:* c/o Royal Society of Edinburgh, 22–26 George Street, Edinburgh EH2 2PQ. *Club:* New (Edinburgh).

**INGRAM, Edward John W.;** *see* Winnington-Ingram.

**INGRAM, Sir James (Herbert Charles),** 4th Bt *cr* 1893; *b* 6 May 1966; *s* of (Herbert) Robin Ingram (*d* 1979) and of Shiela, *d* of late Charles Peczenik; *S* grandfather, 1980; *m* 1998, Aracea Elizabeth (marr. diss. 2014), *d* of Graham Pearce; one *s*. *Educ:* Eton; Cardiff Univ. *Heir: s* Herbert Rufus Ingram, *b* 12 Aug. 2010.

**INGRAM, Paul;** Head of Agricultural Services, Barclays Bank plc, 1988–94; *b* 20 Sept. 1934; *s* of John Granville Ingram and Sybil Ingram (*née* Johnson); *m* 1st, 1957, Jennifer Gillian (*née* Morgan) (*d* 1988); one *s* one *d*; 2nd, 2013, Janet Elizabeth Farmer. *Educ:* Manchester Central High School; University of Nottingham (BSc 1956). Dept of Conservation and Extension, Fedn of Rhodesia and Nyasaland, 1956–63; Nat. Agricl Adv. Service, later ADAS, MAFF, 1965–88; County Livestock Officer, Lancs, 1969–70; Policy Planning Unit, MAFF, 1970–72; Farm Management Adviser, Devon, 1972–76; Regional Farm Management Adviser, Wales, 1976–77; Dep. Sen. Livestock Advr, 1977–79, Sen. Agricl Officer, 1979–85, Chief Agricl Officer, 1985–87, Dir of Farm and Countryside Service, 1987–88, ADAS. *Address:* 36 Ceylon Road, W14 0PY.

**INGRAM, Robert Alexander;** General Partner, Hatteras Venture Partners, since 2007; Chairman, Elan Corporation plc, 2011–13 (Director, 2010–13); *b* 6 Dec. 1942; *s* of Myra L. Ingram; *m* 1962, Carolyn Jean Hutson; three *s*. *Educ:* Eastern Illinois Univ. (BSc Business Admin); Lumpkin Coll. of Business. Sales rep., 1965; Merrell Dow Pharmaceuticals: various sales mgt, then govt and public affairs posts; Vice Pres., Public Affairs, until 1985; Vice Pres., Govt Affairs, Merck & Co. Inc., 1985–88; Pres., Merck Frosst Canada Inc., 1988–90; joined Glaxo Inc., 1990: Exec. Vice Pres., Admin and Regulatory Affairs, 1990–93; Exec. Vice Pres., then Pres. and Chief Operating Officer, 1993–94; Pres. and CEO, 1994–99; Chm., Glaxo Wellcome Inc., and Chief Exec., Glaxo Wellcome plc, 1997–2000; Chm., Glaxo Inc., 1999–2000; GlaxoSmithKline: Chief Operating Officer and Pres., Pharmaceutical Ops, 2000–02; Vice Chm., Pharmaceuticals, 2003–09; Strategic Advr to CEO, 2010–. Director: Wachovia Corp., 1997; TheraCom, 1998; Northern Telecom Ltd (NORTEL), 1999–2006; Valeant Pharmaceuticals Internat., 2003–. Hon. LLD: Eastern Illinois, 1988; Univ. of Scis, Philadelphia, 1999. *Recreations:* Formula One motor racing, Porsche restoration. *Address:* Hatteras Venture Partners, 280 S Mangum Street, Suite 350, Durham, NC 27701, USA. *Club:* Royal Automobile.

**INGRAM, Tamara,** OBE 2011; Chairman, Wunderman Thompson, since 2018 (Chief Executive, J. Walter Thompson, 2016–18); *b* 1 Oct. 1960; *d* of John Ingram and Sonia (*née* Bolson); *m* 1989, Andrew Millington; one *s* one *d*. *Educ:* Queen's Coll., Harley St; Univ. of E Anglia (BA Hons Eng.). Joined Saatchi & Saatchi, 1985: Account Exec., 1985–87; Bd Account Dir, 1989–90; Gp Account Dir, 1990–93; Exec. Bd Dir, 1993–95; Saatchi & Saatchi Advertising Ltd: Jt CEO, 1995–99; Chief Exec., 1999–2001; Chm., 2001; Chm. and Chief Exec., McCann-Erickson London, 2002; Global CEO, Added Value, Henley Centre, and Fusion5, Kantar Div., WPP, 2003–05; CEO, Grey Gp UK, 2005–07, Pres. and CEO, Team P&G, 2007–16, WPP. Non-exec. Dir, Serco, 2014–. Chm., Visit London, 2002–09; Mem. Bd, London Develt Agency, 2000–06. Chm., Develt Bd, Royal Court Th., 2004–08. Board Member: Sage Gp, 2005–13; Almeida Th., 2008–13. Member Council: IPA, 1995–; Mktg Soc., 1995–. *Recreations:* theatre, football, tennis, family.

**INGRAM, Timothy Charles William;** Chairman: Wealth Management Association, since 2012; Greencoat UK Wind plc, since 2012; QBE European Operations plc, since 2014; *b* 18 June 1947; *s* of Stanley Ingram and Sheila Ingram; *m* 1975, Christine Cooper; three *s*. *Educ:* Harrow Sch.; Churchill Coll., Cambridge (MA Econs); INSEAD Business Sch. (MBA). Gen. Manager, ANZ Bank, 1985–91; First National Finance Corporation: Finance Dir, 1992–94; Chief Exec., 1994–2002; Man. Dir, Abbey National plc, 1996–2002; Chief Exec., Caledonia Investments plc, 2002–10; Chairman: Collins Stewart plc, 2010–12; RSM Tenon plc, 2012–13. Non-executive Director: Hogg Robinson plc, 1999–2000; Sage Group plc, 2002–11; Savills plc, 2002–12; ANZ Bank (Europe) Ltd, 2004–10; Alliance Trust plc, 2010–12. *Recreations:* ski-ing, opera, travel. *Clubs:* Reform, Hurlingham.

**INGRAMS,** family name of **Baron Darcy de Knayth**.

**INGRAMS, Richard Reid;** journalist; Editor: Private Eye, 1963–86; The Oldie, 1992–2014; *b* 19 Aug. 1937; *s* of late Leonard St Clair Ingrams and Victoria (*née* Reid); *m* 1st, 1962, Mary Morgan (marr. diss. 1993; she *d* 2007); one *s* (and one *s* one *d* decd); 2nd, 2011, Sara Soudain. *Educ:* Shrewsbury; University Coll., Oxford. Joined Private Eye, 1962; columnist: Observer, 1988–90, 1992–2005; The Independent, 2005–11. *Publications:* (with Christopher Booker and William Rushton) Private Eye on London, 1962; Private Eye's Romantic England, 1963; (with John Wells) Mrs Wilson's Diary, 1965; Mrs Wilson's 2nd Diary, 1966; The Tale of Driver Grope, 1968; (with Barry Fantoni) The Bible for Motorists, 1970; (ed) The Life and Times of Private Eye, 1971; (as Philip Reid, with Andrew Osmond) Harris in Wonderland, 1973; (ed) Cobbett's Country Book, 1974; (ed) Beachcomber: the works of J. B. Morton, 1974; The Best of Private Eye, 1974; God's Apology, 1977; Goldenballs, 1979; (with Fay Godwin) Romney Marsh and the Royal Military Canal, 1980; (with John Wells) Dear Bill: the collected letters of Denis Thatcher, 1980; (with John Wells) The Other Half: further letters of Denis Thatcher, 1981; (with John Wells) One for the Road, 1982; (with John Piper) Piper's Places, 1983; (ed) The Penguin Book of Private Eye Cartoons, 1983; (with John Wells) My Round!, 1983; (ed) Dr Johnson by Mrs Thrale, 1984; (with John Wells) Down the Hatch, 1985; (with John Wells) Just the One, 1986; John Stewart Collis: a memoir, 1986; (with John Wells) The Best of Dear Bill, 1986; (with John Wells) Mud in Your Eye, 1987; The Ridgeway, 1988; You Might As Well Be Dead, 1988; England (anthology), 1989; (with John Wells) Number 10, 1989; On and On…, 1990; (ed) The Oldie Annual, 1993; (ed) The Oldie Annual 2, 1994; Malcolm Muggeridge: the authorized biography, 1995; (ed) I Once Met, 1996; (ed) The Oldie Annual 3, 1997; (ed) Jesus: authors take sides (anthology), 1999; (ed) The Oldie Annual 4, 1999; The Life and Adventures of William Cobbett, 2005; My Friend Footy: a memoir of Paul Foot, 2005; Quips & Quotes: a journalist's commonplace book, 2012; Ludo and the Power of the Book, 2017. *Recreation:* piano. *Address:* Forge House, Downs Road, Aldworth, Reading, Berks RG8 9TU.

**INJIA, Hon. Sir Salamo,** GCL 2014; Kt 2005; Chief Justice of Papua New Guinea, 2008–18 (Deputy Chief Justice, 2003–08); *b* 12 Sept. 1958; *s* of Kapo Injia and Anna Injia; *m* 1994, Peam; three *s* two *d*. *Educ:* Univ. of Papua New Guinea (LLB 1982); Harvard Law Sch. (LLM). Dep. Public Solicitor, 1989–90; private legal practice, 1991–93; a Judge of the Nat. and Supreme Courts, PNG, 1993–2003. *Publications:* (jtly) Criminal Law and Practice in Papua New Guinea, 3rd edn, 2001; Injia on: Criminal Offences in Papua New Guinea and the Pacific, 2013; Practice and Procedure in Papua New Guinea and the Pacific, 2013; Investigatory practice in Papua New Guinea and the Pacific, 2013; Evidence in Papua New Guinea and the Pacific, 2013; Sentencing in Papua New Guinea and the Pacific, 2013; Contempt of Court in Papua New Guinea and the Pacific, 2013; Statutory Interpretation in Papua New Guinea and the Pacific, 2013; Coronial Proceedings in Papua New Guinea and the Pacific, 2013. *Recreation:* social golf. *Address:* PO Box 1300, Waigani, Papua New Guinea. *T:* 3245715, *Fax:* 3257732.

**INKSTER, Nigel Norman,** CMG 2003; Counsellor, Foreign and Commonwealth Office, 1998. Entered FCO, 1975; Third Secretary: FCO, 1975; Kuala Lumpur, 1976; Third, later Second Sec., FCO, 1976–79; Second, later First Sec., Bangkok, 1979–82; First Secretary: FCO, 1982–83; Peking, 1983–85; Buenos Aires, 1985–89; FCO, 1989–92; Counsellor: Athens, 1992–94; Hong Kong, 1994–98. *Publications:* China's Cyber Power, 2016.

**INMAN, Edward Oliver,** OBE 1998; FRAeS; Chair, Jubilee Gardens Trust, since 2010; *b* 12 Aug. 1948; *s* of late John Inman and Peggy Inman (*née* Beard); *m* 1st, 1971, Elizabeth (*née* Douglas) (marr. diss. 1982); one *s* one *d*; 2nd, 1984, Sherida (*née* Sturton) (marr. diss. 2005); one *d*; 3rd, 2009, Julia Heasman. *Educ:* King's College Sch., Wimbledon; Gonville and Caius Coll., Cambridge (MA); School of Slavonic and East European Studies, London (MA). FRAeS 1999. Joined Imperial War Museum as Res. Asst, 1972; Asst Keeper 1974; Dir, Imperial War Mus., Duxford, 1978–2004; Chief Exec., S Bank Employers' Gp, 2004–15. Trustee, American Air Mus. in Britain, 2004–. *Address:* Jubilee Gardens Trust, Elizabeth House, 39 York Road, SE1 7NQ. *T:* (020) 7202 6900, *Fax:* (020) 7202 6904. *E:* jubileegardens@southbanklondon.com.

**INMAN, Melbourne Donald,** QC 1998; **His Honour Judge Melbourne Inman;** a Circuit Judge, since 2007; a Senior Circuit Judge, since 2014; Recorder of Birmingham, since 2014; *b* 1 April 1957; *s* of Melbourne and Norah Inman. *Educ:* Bishop Vesey's Grammar Sch.; Regent's Park Coll., Oxford (MA). Called to the Bar, Inner Temple, 1979, Bencher, 2002. Asst Recorder, 1996–99; Recorder, 1999–2007. Hd of Advocacy Trng and Continuing Professional Develt, Midland Circuit, 1998–2007. *Recreations:* ski-ing, listening to the piano. *Address:* Queen Elizabeth II Law Courts, 1 Newton Street, Birmingham B4 7NA.

**INNES of Coxton, Sir Alastair (Charles Deverell),** 13th Bt *cr* 1686 (NS), of Coxton, co. Moray; *b* 17 Sept. 1970; *o s* of Sir David Innes of Coxton, 12th Bt and of Marjorie Alison (*née* Parker); *S* father, 2010; *m* 2008, Sarah Louise, *d* of Robin and Carolyn Jones, Chester; one *s* two *d*. *Educ:* Haileybury; Southampton Univ. Admitted Solicitor, 1999; Solicitor, 2010–, Legal Dir, Amey plc, 2013–. *Recreations:* golf, tennis, running and walking. *Heir: s* Alexander David Carwyn Innes, *b* 7 Sept. 2017.

**INNES, Alistair Campbell M.;** *see* Mitchell-Innes.

**INNES of Edingight, Sir Malcolm (Rognvald),** KCVO 1990 (CVO 1981); Orkney Herald of Arms Extraordinary, since 2001; *b* 25 May 1938; 3rd *s* of late Sir Thomas Innes of Learney, GCVO, LLD, and Lady Lucy Buchan, 3rd *d* of 18th Earl of Caithness; *m* 1963, Joan (*d* 2013), *o d* of Thomas D. Hay, CA, Edinburgh; three *s*. *Educ:* Edinburgh Acad.; Univ. of Edinburgh (MA, LLB). WS 1964. Falkland Pursuivant Extraordinary, 1957–58; Carrick Pursuivant, 1958–71; Lyon Clerk and Keeper of the Records, 1966–81; Marchmont Herald, 1971–81; Lord Lyon King of Arms, 1981–2001; Sec., Order of the Thistle, 1981–2001. Mem., Queen's Body Guard for Scotland (Royal Company of Archers), 1971. Fellow, Heraldry Socs of NZ, 1978, Canada, 1982, and Scotland, 2001. Grand Officer of Merit, SMO Malta. *Recreation:* visiting places of historic interest. *Clubs:* New, Puffin's (Edinburgh).

**INNES, Sir Peter (Alexander Berowald),** 17th Bt *cr* 1628, of Balvenie; *b* 6 Jan. 1937; *s* of Lt-Col Sir (Ronald Gordon) Berowald Innes, 16th Bt, OBE and Elizabeth Haughton (*d* 1958), *e d* of late Alfred Fayle; *S* father, 1988; *m* 1959, Julia Mary, *d* of A. S. Levesley; two *s* one *d*. *Educ:* Prince of Wales School, Nairobi, Kenya; Bristol Univ. (BSc). Scott Wilson Kirkpatrick and Partners, then Scott Wilson Kirkpatrick & Co. Ltd, Consulting Engineers, 1964–2000: Associate, 1982–87; Partner, 1987–95; Dir, 1995–2000; responsible for several airport projects in UK, Africa and Middle East, including major military airbases. Lt-Col Engr and Logistic (formerly Transport) Staff Corps, RE (TA). Voluntary guide, Winchester Cathedral, 2001–. *Heir: s* Alexander Guy Berowald Innes, *b* 4 May 1960. *Club:* S Winchester Golf.

**INNES, Peter Maxwell;** HM Diplomatic Service, retired; Consul-General, Melbourne, 1998–2001; *b* 9 Aug. 1941; *s* of James Innes and Agnes Margaret Innes (*née* Dea); *m* 1965, Robina Baillie Walker; one *s* one *d*. *Educ:* Morrison's Acad., Crieff; Open Univ. (BA Hons Hum 2011). Min. of Aviation, 1960–72; Department of Trade and Industry, 1972–77; Asst Airport Manager, Aberdeen Airport, 1972–73; on secondment to British Embassy, Washington, 1973–76; joined FCO, 1977; Seoul, 1979–83; FCO, 1983–85; First Sec. (Agric.), Dublin, 1985–89; FCO, 1989–92 (EC Monitoring Mission in Bosnia, 1991); Dir, British Information Services, NY, 1992–97; FCO, 1997–98. *Recreations:* reading, walking, travel, watching most sports. *Address:* Alberton, South Crieff Road, Comrie, Perthshire PH6 2HF. *Clubs:* Royal Over-Seas League; Probus (Comrie); 30 (Crieff); Comrie Golf.

**INNES, Rt Rev. Dr Robert Neil;** *see* Gibraltar in Europe, Bishop of.

**INNES, Ruth Margaret**; QC (Scot.) 2018; *b* Aberdeen, 12 Sept. 1976; *d* of George and Catherine Strachan; *m* 2002, Gregor J. Innes. *Educ:* Dingwall Acad.; Univ. of Aberdeen (LLB Hons 1st Cl. 1999; DipLP 2000). Admitted as solicitor, 2002; solicitor, 2002–04; called to the Scottish Bar, 2005.

**INNES, Sheila Miriam**; consultant (education and media); *b* 25 Jan. 1931; *d* of late Dr James Innes, MB, ChB, MA and of Nora Innes. *Educ:* Talbot Heath School, Bournemouth; Lady Margaret Hall, Oxford (Exhibnr; BA Hons Mod. Langs; MA). BBC Radio Producer, World Service, 1955–61; BBC TV producer: family programmes, 1961–65; further education, 1965–73; exec. producer, further education, 1973–77; Head, BBC Continuing Educn, TV, 1977–84; Controller, BBC Educnl Broadcasting, 1984–87; Dir, BBC Enterprises Ltd, 1986–87; Chief Exec., 1987–89, Dep. Chm., 1989–92, Open Coll. Non-exec. Dir, Brighton Health Care NHS Trust, 1993–96. Chairman: Cross-Sector Cttee for Development and Review, BTEC, 1986–87; Cross-Sector Cttee for Product Develt, BTEC, 1989–92; British Gas Training Awards, 1988–92. Member: Gen. Board, Alcoholics Anonymous, 1980–; Board of Governors, Centre for Information on Language Teaching and Research, 1981–84; Council, Open Univ., 1984–87; Council for Educational Technology, 1984–87; EBU Educational Working Party, 1984–87; Educn Cttee, 1990–95, Women's Adv. Gp, 1992–95, RSA; Standing Conf. on Schools' Science and Technol., 1990–93 (Mem. Council, 1993–98); Age Concern Training Validation (later Quality) Cttee, 1992–94; IMgt Management Develt Proj., 1992–95. Vice-Pres., Educn Sect., British Sci. Assoc. (formerly BAAS), 1990–. Mem., Clothing and Allied Products ITB Management 2000 Cttee of Enquiry, 1989. Patron, One World Broadcasting Trust, 1988–98. Gov., Talbot Heath Sch., Bournemouth, 1989–95 (Patron. 2017–). Vice-Pres., Abbeyfield Eastbourne Soc., 2005–. Mem., RTS, 1986; FRSA 1986; FITD 1987; CCMI (CIMgt 1987). Hon. DLitt South Bank, 1992. *Publications:* BBC publications; articles for language jls and EBU Review. *Recreations:* music (classical and jazz), country pursuits, sketching, photography, travel, languages. *Address:* Wychwood, Barcombe, East Sussex BN8 5TP. *T:* (01273) 400268. *Clubs:* Reform; Oxford Society.

**INNES-KER**, family name of **Duke of Roxburghe**.

**INSALL, Sir Donald (William)**, Kt 2010; CBE 1995 (OBE 1981); FSA, RWA, FRIBA, architect and planning consultant; Founder, Donald Insall Associates Ltd (formerly Donald W. Insall & Associates), 1958 (Principal, 1958–81; Chairman, 1981–98, now Consultant); *b* 7 Feb. 1926; *o s* of late William R. Insall and Phyllis Insall, Henleaze, Bristol; *m* 1964, Amy Elizabeth, MA, *er d* of Malcolm H. Moss, Nanpantan, Leics; two *s* one *d*. *Educ:* Bristol Univ.; RA Sch. of Architecture; Sch. of Planning, London (Dip. (Hons)); SPAB Lethaby Schol. 1951. FRIBA 1968, FRTPI 1973. Coldstream Guards, 1944–47. Architectural and Town-Planning Consultancy has included town-centre studies, civic and univ., church, domestic and other buildings, notably in conservation of historic towns and buildings (incl. restoration of ceiling, House of Lords, and Windsor Castle after fire, 1992); Medal (Min. of Housing and Local Govt), Good Design in Housing, 1962. Visiting Lecturer: RCA, 1964–69; Coll. d'Europe, Bruges, 1976–81; Catholic Univ. of Leuven, 1982–2003; Adjunct Prof., Univ. of Syracuse, 1971–81. Mem., Council of Europe Working Party, 1969–70; Nat. Pilot Study, Chester: A Study in Conservation, 1968; Consultant, Chester Conservation Programme, 1970–87 (EAHY Exemplar; European Prize for Preservation of Historic Monuments, 1981; Europa Nostra Medals of Honour, 1983 and 1989). Member: Historic Buildings Council for England, 1971–84; Grants Panel, EAHY, 1974; Council, RSA, 1976–80 (FRSA, 1948); Council, SPAB, 1979–2007; Ancient Monuments Bd for England, 1980–84; UK Council, ICOMOS, 1998–2014; Royal Parks Adv. Bd, 2000–02; Comr, Historic Bldgs and Monuments Commn, 1984–89; Member: Standing Adv. Cttee, Getty Grant Program, 1988–92; EC Expert Cttee on Architectl Heritage, 1990, 1993–; DNH Inquiry into Fire Protection at Royal Palaces, 1993; Architectl Adv. Cttee, World Monuments Fund in Britain, 1996–; Vice-Chm., Conf. on Trng in Architectural Conservation, 1990–2000 (Hon. Sec., 1959–89); Vice-President: Bldg Crafts and Conservation Trust, 1994–2010; City of Winchester Trust, 2002–. Member: Architectl Adv. Cttee, Westminster Abbey, 1993–98; Fabric Adv. Cttee, Southwark Cathedral, 1992–2016, Canterbury Cathedral, 1997–2016. Patron: Kew Soc., 2001–; Envmtl Trust for Richmond-on-Thames, 2001–; Bedford Park Soc., 2001–. RIBA: Banister Fletcher Medallist, 1949; Neale Bursar, 1955; Examr, 1957; Competition Assessor, 1971. Conferences: White House (Natural Beauty), 1965; Historic Architectural Interiors, USA, 1988, 1993; Singapore, 1994. Lecture tours: USA, 1964, 1972 (US Internat. Reg. Conf. on Conservation), 2003; Mexico, 1972; Yugoslavia, 1973; Canada, 1974, 1999; Argentina, 1976; India, 1979; Portugal, 1982. Liveryman, Goldsmiths' Co., 1998 (Freeman, 1996). Hon. Freeman, City of Chester, 2000. Hon. LLD Bristol, 2004; Hon. DArch Chester, 2012. European Architectural Heritage Year Medal (for Restoration of Chevening), 1973; Harley J. McKee Award, Assoc. for Preservation Technol. Internat., 1999; People in Conservation Award, RICS, 1999; Europa Nostra Medal of Honour, 2000; Plowden Medal, Royal Warrant Holders' Assoc., 2001. Silver Jubilee Medal, 1977. *Publications:* (jtly) Railway Station Architecture, 1966; (jtly) Conservation Areas 1967; The Care of Old Buildings Today, 1973; Historic Buildings: action to maintain the expertise for their care and repair, 1974; Conservation in Action, 1982; Conservation in Chester, 1988; Living Buildings, Architectural Conservation: philosophy, principles and practice, 2008; contrib. to Encyclopædia Britannica, professional, environmental and internat. jls. *Recreations:* visiting, sketching, photographing and enjoying places; appreciating craftsmanship; Post-Vintage Thoroughbred Cars (Mem., Rolls Royce Enthusiasts' Club). *Address:* 73 Kew Green, Richmond, Surrey TW9 3AH; (office) 12 Devonshire Street, W1G 7AB. *T:* (020) 7245 9888. *Club:* Athenæum.

**INSCH, Elspeth Virginia**, OBE 1998; Headmistress, King Edward VI Handsworth School, Birmingham, 1989–2012; *b* 21 Aug. 1949; *d* of John Douglas Insch and Isabella Elizabeth Campbell (née Brodie). *Educ:* Newarke Girls' Sch., Leicester; Birkbeck Coll., Univ. of London (BSc); Univ. of Edinburgh (MPhil, DipEd, PGCE). CGeog 2002. Demonstrator, Univ. of Edinburgh, 1970–73; Teacher: Abington High Sch., Leics, 1974–77; Nottingham High Sch. for Girls (GPDST), 1977–84; Dep. Head, Kesteven and Sleaford High Sch. for Girls, 1984–89. Consultant, Springbank Sand and Gravel Co. Ltd, 1970–79. Pres., Assoc. of Maintained Girls' Schools, 1999–2000; Mem. Cttee, Nat. Grammar Schools Assoc., 1990–2006. FRGS 1968 (Mem., 1994–, Chm., 2003–06, Educn Cttee; Vice Pres., 2003–06). Fellow, Winston Churchill Meml Trust, 1980; Trustee, Grantham Yorke Trust, 1990–2005. DL W Midlands, 2008–12. Hon. DSc Aston, 2006. *Address:* 14 Ormsby Court, Richmond Hill Road, Edgbaston, Birmingham B15 3RJ.

**INSHAW, Maj. Gen. Timothy Gordon**, CB 2011; Head, Strategy and Policy, London Operations, L-3 Technologies (formerly Communications), 2014–17; *b* Hong Kong, 14 Aug. 1957; *s* of Gordon Henry William Inshaw and Rita Inshaw; *m* 1982, Sally Patricia Roe; three *s*. *Educ:* Wilsthorpe Comp. Sch.; Welbeck Coll.; RMA Sandhurst; RMCS (BSc 1981). CE; MIET 2000, FIET 2009; CITP 2008; FBCS 2009. SO3 Comms HQN1, 1985–86; Instructor, Sch. of Signals, 1987; Army Staff Coll., 1988–89; OC 212 (12 Armoured Bde) Signal Sqn, 1990–92; Instructor, Jun. Div. of Staff Course, 1992–93; SO2 Operational Requirements, 1994; SO1 Mgt Plans, Directorate Gen. CIS, 1995; CO 9th Signal Regt (Radio), 1995–98; Dep. Dir Defence Resources and Plans, 1998–2000; rcds 2001; Comdr 1st Signal Bde, 2002–04; Dir Capability Integration (Army), 2004–07; Dir Gen. Trng and Educn, 2007–10; Dir, Inf. Systems and Services, Defence Equipment and Support, 2010–13. Controller, Royal Signals Trustees Ltd, 2014–; non-executive Dir, Harris Defence Ltd, 2018. *Recreations:* cricket, gardening, walking, DIY, voluntary work in education and local community.

**INSKIP**, family name of **Viscount Caldecote**.

**INSTANCE, Caroline Mary**; Chief Executive, Institute and Faculty of Actuaries (formerly Actuarial Profession), 2002–11; *b* 4 May 1957; *d* of William Henry and late Hilary Willatt; *m* 1st (marr. diss. 1995); one *s* one *d*; 2nd, 1998, John Instance; two step *d*. *Educ:* Henley Grammar Sch.; Sheffield Univ. (BSc Hons Psychol. 1978). MIPD. With Rank Orgn, 1978–82; United Friendly, 1982–96 (Human Resources Dir, 1993–96); Chief Exec., OPRA, 1996–2002. Non-exec. Dir, Omnilife, 2015–; Dir, RLGPS Trustee Ltd, 2016–18. Trustee: ShareAction, 2011–17; Age UK (Horsham Dist), 2015–. Mem., Thakeham Parish Council, 2014– (Chm., 2019–). *Recreations:* theatre, opera, enjoying countryside, voluntary work with the elderly and Pallant Gallery.

**INSTONE, Daniel Richard**; independent environmental advisor, since 2013; *b* London, 17 Dec. 1947; *s* of Ralph and Sybil Instone; *m* 1986, Anne Scrope; two *d*. *Educ:* Westminster Sch.; Christ Church, Oxford (MA Hons Classics). Ministry of Technology, later Department of Trade and Industry: Asst Principal, 1970–73; Asst Pte Sec. to Minister of Industrial Develt, 1973; Pte Sec. to Minister of State for Industry, 1974; Grade 7, 1975–83 (seconded to Econ. Secretariat, Cabinet Office, 1978–80); Department of Transport: Dep. Dir, 1983–91 (seconded to HM Treasury, 1985–88); Hd, Transport Policy Unit, 1991–98; Team Leader, Prime Minister's Strategy Unit, 1998–2001; Department for Environment, Food and Rural Affairs: Hd, Water Quality Div., 2001–05; Waste Strategy Div., 2005–08; Sen. Responsible Owner, Waste Prog., 2008–09; Prog. Dir, Atmosphere and Local Envmt Prog., 2009–13. *Recreations:* walking, music, literature, interesting ideas.

**INVERDALE, John Ballantyne**; sports presenter, BBC; *b* 27 Sept. 1957; *s* of Capt. John Ballantyne Inverdale, CBE, RN and Stella Norah Mary Westlake (née Richards); *m* Jacqueline Elizabeth Knight; two *d*. *Educ:* Clifton Coll.; Univ. of Southampton (BA Hons). Journalist, Lincolnshire Echo, 1979–82; BBC Radio Lincs, 1982–85; BBC Radio 2, 1985–88; presenter: Sport on 5 (formerly Sport on 2), BBC Radio, 1988–94; Drivetime, BBC Radio 5 Live, 1994–97, and Rugby Special, BBC TV, 1994–; Onside, 1997–2001, Grandstand, 1999–2004, BBC TV. President: Surrey Br., Wooden Spoon, 1998–; British Univs and Colls Sport, 2005–; Aspire Spinal Injuries Charity, 2008–; Chm., Esher Rugby FC, 1998–. Hon. Fellow, UWIC, 2009. Hon. DLitt Soton, 2001; Hon. DArts Lincoln, 2006. *Address:* c/o BBC News Centre, Broadcasting House, Portland Place, W1A 1AA.

**INVERFORTH**, 4th Baron *cr* 1919, of Southgate; **Andrew Peter Weir**; *b* 16 Nov. 1966; *s* of 3rd Baron Inverforth and of Jill Elizabeth, *o d* of late John W. Thornycroft, CBE; *S* father, 1982; *m* 1992, Rachel Sian Shapland Davies. *Educ:* Marlborough College; Trinity Coll., Cambridge; London Hosp. Med. Coll. MB BS 1994.

**INVERNE, James Allan Marshall**; journalist, author, playwright and artist manager; Managing Director, James Inverne Music Consultancy, since 2015 (Co-Managing Director, Inverne Price Music Consultancy, 2012–15); Founder and Editor-in-Chief, www.thepianoforum.org, 2014; *b* Bournemouth, 5 May 1975; *s* of Richard Inverne and late Susan Inverne; *m* 2004, Kareen Cartier; one *s*. *Educ:* Bournemouth Grammar Sch.; Queen Mary and Westfield Coll., Univ. of London (BA Hons). Arts Ed., Performance TV, 1996–2001; Classical CD reviewer, Mail on Sunday, 1996–98; Eur. Performing Arts corresp., Time mag., 1999–2005; London Th. corresp., Playbill Online, 2003–05; Ed., Gramophone mag., 2005–11; Founder Ed., Inside Sundance Institute mag., 2009–; Contributing Editl Dir, programmes, Delfont Mackintosh Theatres, 2013–; contrib. Wall St Jl, Sunday Telegraph, The Times and Jerusalem Report. Dir and Co-Founder, Interact: Interfaith Action, 2007–. Playwright, A Walk with Mr Heifetz, NY, 2018. *Publications:* Jack Tinker: a life in review, 1997; The Impresarios, 2000; Wrestling with Elephants: the authorised biography of Don Black, 2003; Inverne's Stage and Screen Trivia, 2004; The Faber Pocket Guide to Musicals, 2009. *Recreations:* theatre, concert and cinema-going, reading (especially biographies), museums. *T:* 07870 203181. *E:* james.inverne@gmail.com.

**INVERNESS (St Andrew's Cathedral), Provost of**; *see* Murray, Very Rev. S. E.

**INVERURIE, Lord; Tristan Michael Keith**; *b* 28 May 2010; *s* and *heir* of Earl of Kintore, *qv*.

**INYUNDO, (Richard) Kwame (Swake)**; a District Judge (Magistrates' Courts), since 2014; *b* Nairobi, 15 Sept. 1972; *s* of Weboko Inyundo and Jill Inyundo; *m* 2001, Lucette Fogarty; two *s* one *d*. *Educ:* Starehe Boys Centre, Nairobi; St Andrew's Sch., Turi; Christ's Hospital Sch.; Univ. of Liverpool (MA Hons); Inns of Court Sch. of Law (DipLaw). Called to the Bar, Gray's Inn, 1997; a barrister, 6KBW College Hill, London, 1997–2014. *Recreations:* football (Tottenham Hotspur FC), travel, film, family, city cycling by Brompton.

**ION, Dame Susan (Elizabeth)**, DBE 2010 (OBE 2002); PhD; FRS 2016; FREng, FIMMM, FNucI; consultant; Vice-President, Royal Academy of Engineering, 2002–08; *b* 3 Feb. 1955; *d* of Lawrence James Burrows and Doris Burrows (née Cherry); *m* 1980, John Albert Ion. *Educ:* Penwortham Girls' Grammar Sch., Preston, Lancs; Imperial Coll., London (BSc 1st Cl. Hons, DIC; PhD Materials Sci./Metallurgy 1979). FREng (FEng 1996). British Nuclear Fuels ltd; Hd, R & D, Fuel Div., 1990–92; Dir, Technol. Develt, 1992–96; Dir of Technol., 1996–2006; Mem., Company Executive, 1996–2006. Member: PPARC, 1994–2000; Council for Sci. and Technol., 2004–11; EPSRC, 2005–10. Chairman: UK Fusion Adv. Bd, 2006–12; Nuclear Innovation Res. Adv. Bd, 2014–16. Non-exec. Dir, Health and Safety Lab., HSE, 2005–15. Visiting Professor: Imperial Coll. London, 2006–; London Southbank Univ., 2011–; Hon. Prof., Univ. of Central Lancs, 2007–. Pres., British Nuclear Soc., 2004–06. Gov., Univ. of Manchester, 2004–18; Mem., Bd of Trustees, Univ. of Central Lancs, 2018–. Hinton Medal for Outstanding Contribn to Nuclear Engrg, INucE, 1993; President's Medal, RAEng, 2014. *Recreations:* ski-ing, fell walking, playing the violin.

**IPGRAVE, Rt Rev. Michael Geoffrey**; *see* Lichfield, Bishop of.

**IPSWICH, Bishop of**; *see* St Edmundsbury and Ipswich.

**IQBAL, Abdul Shaffaq**; QC 2014; a Recorder, since 2008; *b* Wolverhampton, 3 Aug. 1969; *s* of Mohammed Iqbal and Zubaida Bibi; *m* 1996, Rifat Parveen; one *s* one *d*. *Educ:* Moor End High Sch., Huddersfield; Univ. of Bradford (BPharm Hons 1991); Univ. of Northumbria (DipLaw 1993); Inns of Court Sch. of Law. Pharmacist, 1991–92; called to the Bar, Gray's Inn, 1994; in practice as criminal barrister, 1994–. *Recreations:* football, cricket, motorsport, travel, family. *Address:* 6 Park Square, Leeds LS1 2LW. *T:* (0113) 245 9763, *Fax:* (0113) 242 4395. *E:* iqbalqc@psqb.co.uk. *Clubs:* Huddersfield Town Football, Wolverhampton Wanderers Football.

**IRBY**, family name of **Baron Boston**.

**IREDALE, Prof. John Peter,** DM; FRCP, FRCPE; FRSE; FMedSci; Pro Vice-Chancellor Health and Life Sciences, University of Bristol, since 2016; Honorary Consultant Physician: North Bristol NHS Trust, since 2016 (non-executive Director, since 2017); University Hospitals Bristol NHS Foundation Trust, since 2016; *b* Oxford, 9 Nov. 1960; *s* of late Peter Iredale and of Judith Margaret Iredale; *m* 1990, Dr Catriona Jean Gunn; two *s* one *d*. *Educ*: City of Oxford Sch. for Boys; Univ. of Southampton (BM Hons 1985; DM 1995). MRCP 1988, FRCP 1999; FRCPE 2007. Vis. Clin. Scientist, UCL, 1994–98; University of Southampton: MRC Clinician Scientist, 1994–98; MRC Sen. Clin. Fellow, 1998–2004; Prof. of Hepatol., 2000–04; of Medicine, 2004–06; University of Edinburgh: Prof. of Medicine, 2006–13; Regius Prof. of Med. Sci., 2013–16; Dir, MRC Centre for Inflammation Res., 2009–15; Dean of Clin. Medicine, 2010–16; Vice Principal, Health Services, 2014–16; Consultant Hepatologist, Edinburgh Royal Infirmary, 2006–16. Non-exec. Dir, NHS Lothian, 2010–16. Mem. Council, UKRI-MRC (formerly MRC), 2017–. Med. Trustee, BHF, 2016–. MAE. FMedSci 2003; FRSE 2011. *Publications:* contribs to learned jls on tissue scarring and regeneration, incl. Science, Jl Clin. Investigation, Procs NAS, Nature Medicine, Nature Cell Biology. *Recreations:* family, cycling, watercolour painting, fishing. *Address:* University of Bristol, Senate House, Tyndall Avenue, Bristol BS8 1TH. *T:* (0117) 928 7609. *E:* pa-pvchealth@bristol.ac.uk.

**IREDALE, Prof. Roger Oliver,** PhD; Professor of International Education, 1993–96, now Professor Emeritus, and Director (formerly Dean), Faculty of Education, 1994–96, University of Manchester; *b* 13 Aug. 1934; *s* of Fred Iredale and Elsie Florence (*née* Hills); *m* 1968, Mavis Potter; one *s* one *d*. *Educ:* Harrow County Grammar Sch.; Univ. of Reading (BA 1956, MA 1959, PhD 1971; Hurry Medal for Poetry; Early English Text Soc.'s Prize; Seymour-Sharman Prize for Literature; Graham Robertson Travel Award); Peterhouse Coll., Univ. of Cambridge (Cert. Ed. 1957). Teacher, Hele's Sch., Exeter, 1959–61; Lectr and Senior Lectr, Bishop Otter Coll., Chichester, 1962–70; British Council Officer and Maître de Conférences, Univ. of Algiers, 1970–72; Lectr, Chichester Coll. of Further Educn, 1972–73; British Council Officer, Madras, 1973–75; Dir of Studies, Educnl Admin, Univ. of Leeds, 1975–79; Educn Adviser, 1979–83, Chief Educn Advr, 1983–93, ODA. Sen. Consultant, Iredale Develt Internat., 1996–2003. Member: Commonwealth Scholarship Commn, 1984–93; Unesco-Unicef Jt Cttee, 1991–96; VSO Educn Adv. Cttee, 2002–04; Comr, Sino-British Friendship Scholarship Scheme Commn, 1986–96. Hon. Leader Writer, Western Daily Press, 2011–13. Governor: Sch. of Oriental and African Studies, 1983–95; Queen Elizabeth House, Oxford, 1986–87; Commonwealth of Learning, 1988–93; Sidcot Sch., 2001–03. Trustee, 1993–98, non-exec. Dir, 1998–2007, CfBT Educn Services, subseq. CfBT Educn Trust; Chm., CfBT LLC, Abu Dhabi, 2006–08. Trustee: War on Want, 1998–2000; BookPower, 1999–2006. Hon. FCP 1995. Poetry Society's Greenwood Prize, 1974; First Prize for Poetry, Sherborne Literary Fest., 2013. *Publications:* Turning Bronzes (poems), 1974; Out Towards the Dark (poems), 1978; An Inventory of Time (poems), 2010; articles in The Times, Guardian, Western Daily Press, Comparative Education and other jls; poems for BBC Radio 3 and in anthologies and jls. *Recreations:* poetry writing, championing the oppressed, journalism. *Address:* Northsyde House, 17 High Street, West Coker, Yeovil BA22 9AP. *T:* (01935) 864422.

**IRELAND, Ven. Mark Campbell;** Archdeacon of Blackburn, since 2016; *b* Aylesbury, 5 April 1960; *s* of Donald Ireland and Jean Ireland; *m* 2001, Gillian Thatcher. *Educ:* Bromsgrove Sch.; Oban High Sch.; St John's Sch., Marlborough; Univ. of St Andrews (MTheol 1981); Wycliffe Hall, Oxford (CTh 1984); Univ. of Sheffield (MA 2001). Teacher, Murree Christian Sch., Pakistan, 1981–82; ordained deacon, 1984, priest, 1985; Curate, St Gabriel, Blackburn, 1984–87; Curate, Lancaster Priory and Chaplain, HM Prison Lancaster, 1987–89; Vicar, St John the Baptist, Baxenden, 1989–98; Diocesan Missioner, Dio. of Lichfield and Team Vicar, St Matthew, Walsall, 1998–2007; Vicar, All Saints, Wellington and St Catherine, Eyton, 2007–16. Mem., Archbishops' Council, 2010–15. *Publications:* (with M. Booker) Evangelism - Which Way Now?, 2003, 2nd edn 2005; (jtly) Evangelism in a Spiritual Age, 2005; (jtly) Renewing the Eucharist, vol. 1: journey, 2008; (with M. Chew) How to Do Mission Action Planning, 2009, 2nd edn 2016; (with M. Booker) Making New Disciples: explaining the paradoxes of evangelism, 2015. *Recreations:* ski-ing, walking, learning to sail. *Address:* 19 Clarence Park, Blackburn BB2 7FA. *T:* (01254) 262571. *E:* mark.ireland@blackburn.anglican.org.

**IRELAND, Mary Elizabeth;** Head, Bancroft's School, 2008–16; *b* Dumbarton, 5 April 1956; *d* of Denis Ferguson and Elizabeth Ferguson (*née* Gilchrist); *m* 1979, Simon Ireland; one *s*. *Educ:* Notre Dame High Sch.; Univ. of St Andrews (BSc Biochem.); Univ. of Dundee (DipEd). CBiol 1994; MBS 1994. Manufacturing Exec., Procter and Gamble, 1977–79; Hd, Sci. and Technol., King's Hall Sch., Taunton, 1985–89; Housemistress, Ardingly Coll., 1991–2000; Dep. Hd, Christ's Hospital, 2000–07. Gov., Ardingly Coll., 2016– (Chair, Educn Cttee, 2017–). FRSA 2012. Trustee, Sue Thompson Foundn, 2013–. Freeman: City of London, 2011; Drapers' Co., 2016–. *Recreations:* dogs, music (particularly early music and opera), Italy, theatre, cricket, science fiction. *E:* meiard@sky.com. *Club:* Lansdowne.

**IRELAND, Patrick Gault de C.;** *see* de Courcy-Ireland.

**IRELAND, Prof. Peter Thomas,** DPhil; CEng; FIMechE; Donald Schultz Professor of Turbomachinery, and Head, Osney Thermo-Fluids Laboratory, University of Oxford, since 2011 (Director, Rolls-Royce University Technology Centre, 2011); Fellow of St Catherine's College, Oxford, since 2011; *b* Coventry, 23 April 1962; *s* of John Ireland and Edna Merry; *m* 2004, Melanie Rigby; one *d*. *Educ:* St John's Coll., Oxford (BA Engrg Sci.; DPhil Turbine Cooling 1987). CEng 1995; FIMechE 2004. Tutorial Fellow in Engrg Sci., St Anne's Coll., Oxford, 1989–2007; UK Corporate Specialist in Heat Transfer, Rolls-Royce Aerospace, Derby, 2007–11. Dir, Fire Precautions Ltd, 2006–. *Publications:* over 120 papers in heat transfer, turbine cooling and heat transfer measurement method. *Address:* Department of Engineering Science, University of Oxford, Thermo-Fluids Laboratory, Southwell Building, Osney Mead Industrial Estate, Oxford OX2 0ES. *T:* (01865) 288723. *E:* peter.ireland@eng.ox.ac.uk.

**IRELAND, Seith;** *see* Ireland, W. S. S.

**IRELAND, Susan Jean;** consultant on landscape management; Director of Open Spaces, City of London Corporation, 2008–17; *b* Hertford, 9 May 1956; *d* of late Prof. Geoffery Dowrick and of Pamela Dowrick; *m* 1980, Clive Ireland (marr. diss. 1991). *Educ:* Ashford Grammar Sch.; Newton Abbot Grammar Sch.; University Coll. Wales, Aberystwyth (BSc Hons Geog. 1977); Wye Coll., Univ. of London (MSc Landscape Ecol., Design and Maintenance 1978). Tech. Officer, Ashford BC, 1978–82; Chelmsford Borough Council: Sen. Tech. Officer, 1982–86; Inf. and Support Services Manager, 1986–88; Asst Dir, Leisure Services, 1988–2002; Hd of Parks, 2002–04; Dir, Parks and Heritage Services, 2005–08. Vice Chair, Parks Alliance, 2015–17; Chm., Parks for London, 2016–17. FLI 2018. Liveryman, Gardeners' Co., 2010. *Recreations:* reading, using my 'Jubilacion' to re-landscape my garden and travel (having explored a little of Easter Island, French Polynesia and New Zealand, the challenge is to decide where next), still studying landscapes and communities, volunteer witness support. *E:* africasuenew@gmail.com. *Club:* Guildhall.

**IRELAND, (William) Seith (Stanners);** Sheriff of North Strathclyde at Paisley, since 2014; *b* 5 April 1956; *s* of Samuel Ireland and Isobel Ireland (*née* Stanners); *m* 2006, Elizabeth Crombie. *Educ:* High Sch. of Glasgow; Univ. of Glasgow (LLB Hons 1979). Pres., Students' Rep. Council, Univ. of Glasgow, 1977–78. Admitted as solicitor, 1982; asst solicitor, 1982–85; founded own practice, Ireland & Co., 1986–2003. Temp. Sheriff, 1999; Sheriff (pt-time), 2000–03; Floating Sheriff, 2003–04; Sheriff of N Strathclyde at Kilmarnock, 2004–14. Pres., Glasgow Bar Assoc., 1993–94; Member, Council: Law Soc. of Scotland, 1995–98; Sheriffs' Assoc., 2009–13 (Hon. Sec. and Treas., 2010–12); Scottish Assoc. for the Study of Offending, 2013–. Mem. Business Cttee, Gen. Council, Univ. of Glasgow, 2005–09 and 2019–. Mem., Scottish Bd, Phoenix Futures, 2013–. *Recreations:* golf, cinema, cooking. *Address:* Sheriff's Chambers, Sheriff Court House, Paisley, Renfrewshire PA3 2HW. *T:* (0141) 887 5291, *Fax:* (0141) 887 6702. *E:* sheriffwsireland@scotcourts.gov.uk.

**IRENS, Nicholas James;** Treasurer, Benefice of Hever, Four Elms and Mark Beech, since 2015; *b* 6 Oct. 1946; *s* of late Gp Capt. Henry James Irens and of Helen Margaret Irens; *m* 1972, Fiona Mary Walker; three *s* one *d*. *Educ:* Blundell's Sch., Tiverton. FCA 1970. Partner, Turner Easdale & Co., Chartered Accountants, 1970–78; Finance Director: Juliana's Hldgs plc, 1979–87; First Leisure Corp. plc, 1988–92; Chm., Cannons Gp plc, 1992–2001. Chm., Esporta Gp Ltd, 2002–06; Dir, Sporting Index Ltd, 2006–15. *Recreations:* bridge, cricket, racing, Chelsea FC. *Address:* Saxby's Mead, Cowden, Kent TN8 7DR. *T:* (01342) 850520. *E:* nirens@btopenworld.com. *Club:* MCC.

**IRETON, Barrie Rowland,** CB 2000; Director, Copperbelt Development Foundation, 2002; *b* 15 Jan. 1944; *s* of Philip Thomas Ireton, CBE, and Marjorie Rosalind Ireton; *m* 1965, June Collins; one *s* one *d* (and one *s* decd). *Educ:* Alleyne's Grammar Sch., Stevenage; Trinity Coll., Cambridge (MA); London School of Economics (MSc 1970). Economic Statistician, Govt of Zambia, 1965–68; Economist, Industrial Develt Corp., Zambia, 1968–69; Development Sec., The Gambia, 1970–73; Overseas Development Administration: Economic Advr, 1973–76; Sen. Economic Advr, 1976–84; Asst Sec., 1984–88; Under Sec., 1988–96; Principal Finance Officer, 1988–93; Dir, Africa Div., 1993–96; Dir-Gen., Progs, subseq. Internat. and Resources, ODA, FCO, then DFID, 1996–2003. Sen. Fellow, Inst. of Commonwealth Studies, 2005. Director: Zambia Copper Investments, 2002–05; European Investment Bank, 2002–05; Dir, 2002–05, Business Advr, 2006, Konkola Copper Mines. *Publications:* Britain's International Development Policies: a history of DFID and overseas aid, 2013. *Recreations:* tennis, gardening, walking.

**IRONS, Jeremy;** actor; *b* 19 Sept. 1948; *s* of late Paul Dugan Irons and of Barbara Anne Brereton (*née* Sharpe); *m* 1st (marr. diss.); 2nd, 1978, Sinead Cusack; two *s*. *Educ:* Sherborne; Bristol Old Vic Theatre Sch. *Theatre* appearances include: Bristol Old Vic Theatre Co., 1968–71; Godspell, Round House, transf. Wyndham's, 1971; The Taming of the Shrew, New Shakespeare Co., Round House, 1975; Wild Oats, RSC, 1976–77; The Rear Column, Globe, 1978; The Real Thing, Broadway, 1984 (Tony Award for Best Actor); The Rover, Mermaid, 1986; A Winter's Tale, RSC, 1986; Richard II, RSC, 1986; A Little Night Music, NY, 2003; Camelot, Hollywood Bowl, 2004; Embers, Duke of York, 2006; Never So Good, Lyttelton, 2008; The Gods Weep, Hampstead, 2010; Long Day's Journey into Night, Bristol Old Vic, 2016, transf. Wyndham's Th., 2018; *television* appearances include: The Pallisers; Love for Lydia; Brideshead Revisited, 1981; The Captain's Doll, 1983; Longitude, 2000; Elizabeth I, 2005 (Best Supporting Actor, Emmy Awards, 2006, Golden Globe Awards, 2007); The Borgias, 2011, 2012, 2013; Henry IV, 2012; *films* include: The French Lieutenant's Woman, 1981; Moonlighting, 1982; Betrayal, 1982; Swann in Love, 1983; The Wild Duck, 1983; The Mission, 1986; A Chorus of Disapproval, 1988; Dead Ringers, 1988 (Best Actor, New York Film Critics Circle Awards, 1988, Genie Awards, 1989); Danny Champion of the World, 1988; Reversal of Fortune, 1990 (Academy Award for Best Actor, 1991); Australia, 1991; Kafka, 1992; Waterland, 1992; Damage, 1993; M. Butterfly, 1994; The House of the Spirits, 1994; Die Hard: with a vengeance, 1995; Stealing Beauty, 1996; Lolita, 1997; The Man in the Iron Mask, 1998; Chinese Box, 1998; Dungeons and Dragons, And Now Ladies and Gentlemen, Callas Forever, Last Call, 2001; The Time Machine, 2002; Being Julia, 2004; Merchant of Venice, 2004; Kingdom of Heaven, 2005; Casanova, Eragon, Inland Empire, 2006; Appaloosa, 2008; The Pink Panther 2, 2009; Beautiful Creatures, 2013; Night Train to Lisbon, 2013; The Man Who Knew Infinity, High-Rise, Batman v Superman, 2016; Red Sparrow, 2018. Member: Gaia Foundn; European Film Acad.; Patron: Prison Phoenix Trust; Archway Foundn. Chancellor, Bath Spa Univ., 2017–.

**IRONS, Norman MacFarlane,** CBE 1995; DL; CEng; Lord Provost and Lord Lieutenant of Edinburgh, 1992–96; Partner, IFP Consulting Engineers, 1983–2006; *b* 4 Jan. 1941; *s* of Dugald Paterson Irons and Anne Galbraith Irons (*née* Rankin); *m* 1966, Anne Wyness Buckley; one *s* one *d*. *Educ:* George Heriot's Sch.; Borough Road Coll.; Napier Tech. Coll. CEng; MCIBSE 1968; MIMechE 1973. Building Services Engr, 1962–. Mem. (SNP) City of Edinburgh Council, 1976–96. JP 1983–2008, DL 1988, Edinburgh. Pres., Lismore RFC, 1989–94. Hon. Consul: for Denmark, 1999–2011; for Hungary, 2013–. Dean of Consular Corps, Edinburgh and Leith, 2010–11. Paul Harris Fellow, Rotary Internat., 1996; Hon. Mem. Rotary Club of Edinburgh, 2007. Hon. FRCSE 1994. Hon. DLitt Napier, 1993; DUniv Heriot-Watt, 1997. Royal Order of Merit (Norway), 1994; Kt, Order of Dannebrog (Denmark), 2008. *Recreations:* enjoying life with his wife, Rugby. *Address:* 141 Saughtonhall Drive, Edinburgh EH12 5TS. *T:* (0131) 337 6154. *Club:* New (Edinburgh).

**IRONSIDE,** family name of **Baron Ironside**.

**IRONSIDE, 2nd Baron** *cr* 1941, of Archangel and of Ironside; **Edmund Oslac Ironside;** Defence Consultant, Rolls-Royce Industrial Power Group, 1989–95; *b* 21 Sept. 1924; *o s* of 1st Baron Ironside, Field Marshal, GCB, CMG, DSO, and Mariot Ysabel Cheyne (*d* 1984); *S* father, 1959; *m* 1950, Audrey Marigold (*d* 2015), *y d* of late Lt-Col Hon. Thomas Morgan-Grenville, DSO, OBE, MC; one *s* one *d*. *Educ:* Tonbridge Sch. Joined Royal Navy, 1943; retd as Lt, 1952. Marconi Co., 1952–59; English Electric Leo Computers, 1959–64; Cryosystems Ltd, 1964–68; International Research and Development Co., 1968–84; Market Co-ordinator (Defence), NEI plc, 1984–89. Mem., EC Select Cttee, H of L, 1974–90; Vice-Pres., Parly and Scientific Cttee, 1977–80 and 1983–86 (Dep. Chm., 1974–77); Treas., All Party Energy Studies Gp, 1979–92; Chm., All Party Defence Study Gp, 1994–99 (Hon. Sec., 1992–94). Mem., Organising Cttee, British Library, 1972–74. President: Electric Vehicle Assoc., 1975–83; European Electric Road Vehicle Assoc., 1980–82; Vice-Pres., Inst. of Patentees and Inventors, 1976–90; Chm., Adv. Cttee, Science Reference Lib., 1975–85. Member: Court, 1975–94, Council, 1986–88, City Univ.; Court, 1982–, Council, 1984–87, Essex Univ. Pres., Sea Cadet Corps, Chelmsford, 1959–88. Mem. Ct Assts, Skinners' Co. (Master, 1981–82). Hon. FCGI (CGIA 1986). *Publications:* (ed) High Road to Command: the diaries of Major-General Sir Edmund Ironside, 1920–22, 1972; Ironside: the authorised biography of Field Marshal Lord Ironside, 2018. *Heir: s* Hon. Charles Edmund Grenville Ironside [*b* 1 July 1956; *m* 1st, 1985, Hon. Elizabeth Law (marr. diss. 2000), *e d* of Lord Coleraine, *qv*; one *s* two *d*; 2nd, 2001, Katrina Rowley; one *d*]. *Address:* Sutton Manor, Sutton Scotney, Hants SO21 3JX.

**IRONSIDE, Gordon Douglas;** Headmaster, Sutton Grammar School, since 1990; *b* 11 Aug. 1955; *s* of Douglas William Ironside and Doreen Grant Ironside; *m* 1979, Rachael Elizabeth Ann Golder; two *s* one *d*. *Educ:* Pembroke Coll., Cambridge (BA 1977; Scholar);

Durham Univ. (PGCE). CMath; FIMA. Hd of Maths, 1983–89, Dep. Headmaster, 1987–90, Sutton Grammar Sch. *Recreations:* tennis, golf, Rotary, mathematics. *Address:* Sutton Grammar School, Manor Lane, Sutton SM1 4AS. *T:* (020) 8642 3821. *E:* gironside@aol.com. *Clubs:* Sutton Rotary (Pres., 1998–2000); Cuddington Golf; Surrey Racquets.

**IRONSIDE, Prof. James Wilson,** CBE 2006; MD; FRCPath; FRSE; Professor of Clinical Neuropathology, National CJD Research and Surveillance Unit, University of Edinburgh, 2000–17, now Emeritus; *b* 18 Nov. 1954; *s* of James F. Ironside and Jessie C. Ironside (*née* Moir); *m* 1979, Janet A. D. Cruickshank (marr. diss. 1992); one *s* one *d*. *Educ:* Univ. of Dundee (BMSc, MB ChB); Univ. of Edinburgh (MD 2017). FRCPath 1997. Lectr in Pathology, Univ. of Leeds, 1986–90; Consultant Neuropathologist, Western Gen. Hosp., Edinburgh, 1990; Sen. Lectr in Pathology, 1994–98, Reader, 1998–2000, Univ. of Edinburgh. Hon. Consultant Neuropathologist, Western Gen. Hosp., Lothian Univ. Hosps NHS Trust, 1994–2017. FMedSci 2002; FRSE 2011. *Publications:* (jtly) Neuropathology: a color atlas and text, 1994; (jtly) Intraoperative Diagnosis of CNS Tumours, 1997; (jtly) Diagnostic Pathology of Nervous System Tumours, 2002; (ed jtly) Greenfield's Neuropathology, 9th edn, 2015; numerous contribs to scientific jls. *Recreations:* opera, early music, piano, choral singing, visual arts. *Address:* c/o National CJD Research and Surveillance Unit, Western General Hospital, Crewe Road, Edinburgh EH4 2XU.

**IRONSIDE, Leonard,** CBE 2003; JP; Scottish Manager for Information and Support (formerly Information and Support Manager for Scotland), Parkinson's Disease Society, 2007–15; *b* Aberdeen; *b* 16 Feb.; *s* of Alexander and Olive Ironside; *m* 1992, Wendy Anita Cook (marr. diss. 2011); two *d*. *Educ:* Hilton Acad., Aberdeen. Professional Lightweight Wrestler, 1973–91 (Commonwealth Middleweight Champion, 1979–81, 1981–91; European Lightweight title, 1985–89). Department of Social Security, Aberdeen: Welfare Benefits Manager, 1976–79; Manager, Pensions Section, 1980–85; Adjudication Officer, 1985–87; Nat. Insce Inspector, 1987–99; Nat. Minimum Wage Officer, 1999–2000. Area Develt Officer, N of Scotland, Parkinson's Disease Soc., 2003–07. Convention of Scottish Local Authorities: social works spokesman, 1997–99; Chm., Urban Affairs, 1999–2001. Freelance feature writer, Aberdeen Independent Newspapers and Evening Express, 2000–; freelance columnist, Press and Jl. Mem., Grampian Regl Council, 1982–96. Mem. (Lab) Aberdeen CC, 1995– (Convener: Social Work Cttee, 1995–97; Social Care and Well Being Cttee, 2012–; Leader, 1999–2003). Chm., Grampian Initiative, 1990–94 (Founder Mem., 1988). Mem. Bd, NHS Grampian, 2001–03. Member: Bd, Aberdeen Exhibn and Conf. Centre, 1986–96; Aberdeen Voluntary Service, 1995–99; Bd of Govs, Robert Gordon Univ., 1999–2008. Chm., Aberdeen Internat. Youth Fest., 1995–2003. Patron, Grampian Special Olympics, 1988–; Athletics Coach, Bon Accord (Special Needs), 1987–. Chairman: Horizon Rehabilitation Centre, 1997–2004; Aberdeen Health and Social Care Partnership Bd, 2015–17; Dir, Albyn Hse, Alcohol Support Orgn, Aberdeen, 2013–; Mem. Bd, NE Sensory Services, 2017–. Director: Scottish Sub-Sea Technol. Gp, 1988–92; Grampian Food Resource Centre Ltd, 1990–96; Grampian Enterprise Ltd, 1990–94; Mem., Grampian Racial Equality Commn, 1986–90; Member, Board: Aberdeen Sports Council, 1986–94; Club Sport Aberdeen, 2018–. Chair, Befriend a Child, 2018–. FRSA 2003. JP Aberdeen, 1995. Rose Bowl Award for services to disabled sport, Scottish Sports Council, 1990; Veteran of Year in Sport Award, Aberdeen Sports Council, 2014. *Publications:* When You're Ready Boys… Take Hold, 2008; articles in local govt mags, local press, etc. *Recreations:* Granite City Chorus (barbershop harmony) (Chm., 2011–), yoga teacher, plays tennis, squash, badminton, cycling, after-dinner speaking, coaching wrestling. *Address:* (home) 42 Hillside Terrace, Portlethen, Aberdeen AB12 4QG. *T:* (01224) 780929, 07802 332656; (office) 239 North Anderson Drive, Aberdeen AB16 7GR. *E:* Lenironside@outlook.com, lenironside65@gmail.com.

**IRRANCA-DAVIES, (Ifor) Huw;** Member (Lab) Ogmore, National Assembly for Wales, since 2016; *b* 22 Jan. 1963; *s* of Gethin Davies and Anne Teresa Davies; *m* 1991, Joanna Teresa Irranca; three *s*. *Educ:* Crewe and Alsager Coll. (BA Hons Combined Studies); Swansea Inst. of Higher Educn (MSc Eur. Leisure Resource Mgt (Univ. of Wales Study)). Recreation Asst, then Duty Manager, Lliw Valley BC, 1986–89; Manager, CLM Ltd and Serco Ltd, 1989–92; Facilities Manager, Swansea Coll., 1994–96; Sen. Lectr, Swansea Inst. of Higher Educn, 1996–2002. MP (Lab) Ogmore, Feb. 2002–March 2016. An Asst Govt Whip, 2006–07; Parly Under-Sec. of State, Wales Office, 2007–08, DEFRA, 2008–10; Shadow Minister for Energy, 2010–11, for Food and Farming, 2011–15. Chairman: Envmtl Audit Select Cttee, 2015–16; Constitutional and Legislative Affairs Cttee, 2016–17. Formerly: All-Party Parliamentary Groups: Chm., Recognition of Munitions Workers; Co-Chm., Patient and Public Involvement in Health and Social Care; Vice Chairman: Energy Intensive Industries; British Council; University. Minister for Children, Older People and Social Care, Welsh Govt, 2017–18. *Recreations:* family activities, hill-walking, cycling, reading biographies and historical fiction, Rugby. *Address:* National Assembly for Wales, Cardiff Bay, Cardiff CF99 1NA.

**IRVIN, Joseph David;** Chief Executive, Living Streets, since 2014; *b* Fleetwood, Lancs, 25 Dec. 1955; *s* of Thomas Irvin and Mabel Irvin; *m* 2011, Diana Holland; one *s* one *d*. *Educ:* St Edmund's Infants Sch., Fleetwood; St Mary's Primary Sch., Fleetwood; St Joseph's Secondary Sch., Blackpool; Catholic Coll., Preston; Brasenose Coll., Oxford (BA Hons PPE); Birkbeck Coll., London (MSc British Politics and Govt). Industrial Policy Officer, TUC, 1977–80; Dir, Educn and Res., TGWU, 1980–95; Dir, Political Affairs, RSPB, 1995–96; Special Advr to Dep. Prime Minister, 1997–2001; Dir, Policy, TGWU, 2003–06; Dir, Public Affairs, BAA, 2006–07; Political Sec., Policy Unit, Prime Minister's Office, 10 Downing St, 2007–10; Consultant, Keep the Post Public, 2010–11; CEO, NAVCA, 2012–14. Mem. Adv. Gp, Cycling and Walking Investment Strategy, DfT, 2012–. Trustee, ACEVO, 2012–18 (Hon. Vice Chm., 2012–18; Hon. Chm., 2018). Mem. Bd, Centre for British Politics, Birkbeck, Univ. of London, 2012–. Trustee, Voluntary Action Islington, 2014–. Judge, Guardian Charity Awards, 2014–. FRSA. *Recreations:* walking, music, film, reading, football, birdwatching. *Address:* Living Streets, 2 America Square, EC3N 2LU. *T:* (020) 7377 4900. *E:* joe.irvin@livingstreets.org.uk.

**IRVINE,** family name of **Baron Irvine of Lairg**.

**IRVINE OF LAIRG, Baron** *cr* 1987 (Life Peer), of Lairg in the District of Sutherland; **Alexander Andrew Mackay Irvine;** PC 1997; Lord High Chancellor of England and Wales, 1997–2003; *b* 23 June 1940; *s* of Alexander Irvine and Margaret Christina Irvine; *m* 1974, Alison Mary, *y d* of Dr James Shaw McNair, MD, and Agnes McNair, MA; two *s*. *Educ:* Inverness Acad.; Hutchesons' Boys' Grammar Sch., Glasgow; Glasgow Univ. (MA, LLB); Christ's Coll., Cambridge (Scholar; BA 1st Cl. Hons with distinction; LLB 1st Cl. Hons; George Long Prize in Jurisprudence; Hon. Fellow, 1996). Called to the Bar, Inner Temple, 1967, Bencher, 1985; QC 1978; a Recorder, 1985–88; Dep. High Court Judge, 1987–97. Univ. Lectr, LSE, 1965–69. Contested (Lab) Hendon North, 1970. Opposition spokesman on legal and home affairs, 1987–92; Shadow Lord Chancellor, H of L, 1992–97. Joint President: Industry and Parlt Trust, 1997; British-Amer. Parly Gp, 1997; IPU, 1997; CPA, 1997; Pres., Magistrates' Assoc., 1997–2003. Church Comr, 1997–2003. Trustee, John Smith Meml Trust, 1992–97; Foundn Trustee, Whitechapel Art Gall., 1990–97; Trustee, Hunterian Collection, 1997–. Mem. Cttee, Friends of the Slade, 1990–. Vice-Patron, World Fedn of Mental Health, 1998–. Hon. Bencher, Inn of Court of NI, 1998. Fellow, US Coll. of Trial Lawyers, 1998; Hon. Fellow: Soc. for Advanced Legal Studies, 1997; LSE, 2000. Hon. Mem., Polish Bar, 2000. Hon. LLD: Glasgow, 1997; Siena, 2000. *Recreations:* cinema, theatre, collecting paintings, reading, travel. *Address:* House of Lords, SW1A 0PW. *Club:* Garrick.

**IRVINE, Alan Montgomery,** RDI 1964; DesRCA, ARIBA; architect in private practice; *b* 14 Sept. 1926; *s* of Douglas Irvine and Ellen Marler; *m* 1st, 1955; (one *s* decd); 2nd, 1966, Katherine Mary Buzas; two *s*. *Educ:* Regent Street Polytechnic, Secondary Sch. and Sch. of Architecture; Royal College of Art. RAF (Aircrew), 1944–47. Worked in Milan with BBPR Gp, 1954–55. In private practice since 1956, specialising in design of interiors, museums and exhibitions; partnership Buzas and Irvine, 1965–85. Work has included interior design for Schroder Wagg & Co., Lazards, Bovis, S Australian Govt, Nat. Enterprise Bd; Mem. of design team for QE2, 1966. Various exhibns for V&A Museum, Tate Gallery, Royal Academy, Imperial War Museum, RIBA, British Council, British Museum, Wellcome Inst., Olivetti, Fiat etc including: Cartier Bresson Photographs, 1958; Treasures of Cambridge, 1959; Book of Kells, 1961; Internat. Exhibn of Modern Jewellery, 1961; Architecture of Power, 1963; Mellon Collection, 1969; Art and the E India Trade, 1970; Age of Charles I, 1972; Internat. Ceramics, 1972; Pompeii AD79, 1976; Gold of El Dorado, 1978; The Medal: Mirror of History, 1979; Horses of San Marco (London, NY, Milan, Berlin), 1979–82; Great Japan Exhibition, 1981; Art and Industry, 1982; Cimabue Crucifix (London, Madrid, Munich), 1982–83; Treasures of Ancient Nigeria, 1983; The Genius of Venice, 1983; Leonardo da Vinci: studies for the Last Supper (Milan, Sydney, Toronto, Barcelona, Tokyo), 1984; Art of the Architect, 1984; Re dei Confessori (Milan, Venice), 1985; C. S. Jagger: War and Peace Sculpture, 1985; Queen Elizabeth II: portraits of 60 years, 1986; Eye for Industry, 1986; Glass of the Caesars (London, Cologne, Rome), 1988; Michelangelo Drawings, Louvre, 1989; Conservation Today, 1989; Paul de Lamerie, 1990; Lion of Venice (London, Amsterdam), 1991; David Smith Medals, Imperial War Mus., 1991; Leonardo and Venezia, Venice, 1992. Museum work includes: Old Master Drawings Gallery, Windsor Castle, 1965; New Galleries for Royal Scottish Museum, 1968; Crown Jewels display, Tower of London, 1968; Heinz Gallery for Architectural Drawings, RIBA, London, 1972; War Meml, Winchester Coll., 1973; Museum and Art Gallery for Harrow School, 1975; Internat. Mus. of Contemp. Art, Villa Strozzi, Milan, 1976; Heralds' Museum, London, 1980; Housesteads Roman Fort Mus., 1982; Al Shaheed Museum, Baghdad, 1983; Cabinet War Rooms, London, 1984; West Wing Galls, Nat. Maritime Mus., Greenwich, 1986; Beatrix Potter Museum, Cumbria, 1988; George III Gall., Science Mus., 1993; English Sculpture Gall., V&A Mus., 1999; Fleming Collection Gall., London, 2001; Project, Monumental Tower, Bologna Airport, 2003; Treasuries at: Winchester Cathedral, 1968; Christ Church, Oxford, 1975; Winchester Coll., 1982; Lichfield Cath., 1993. Retrospective personal exhibitions: RIBA Heinz Gall., 1989; Portraits from Detroit: US cars 1940s–60s, photographs by Alan Irvine, RCA, 1996. Accredited corresp. to NASA, Apollo 13 Mission, 1970. Consultant designer to Olivetti, Italy, 1979–89; Consultant architect to British Museum, 1981–84. Mem., Crafts Council, 1984–86. Liveryman, Worshipful Co. of Goldsmiths. Hon. Fellow, RCA. *Recreations:* travel, photography. *Address:* 1 Aubrey Place, St John's Wood, NW8 9BH.

**IRVINE, Rev. Canon Christopher Paul;** Priest-in-Charge, Ewhurst Green and Bodiam, and Rural Dean of Rye, since 2017; Canon Librarian, Canterbury Cathedral, 2007–17; *b* 17 Dec. 1951; *s* of Joseph Ernest Irvine and Phyllis Irvine; *m* 1978, Rosemary Hardwicke; two *d*. *Educ:* Univ. of Nottingham (BTh); Univ. of Lancaster (MA); Kelham Theol Coll.; St Martin's Coll., Lancaster (PGCE). Ordained deacon and priest, 1976; Asst Curate, St Mary, Stoke Newington, 1977–80; Anglican Chaplain, Sheffield Univ., 1980–85; Chaplain, St Edmund Hall, Oxford, 1985–90; Tutor, 1985–90, Vice-Principal, 1991–94, St Stephen's House, Oxford; Vicar, Cowley St John, Oxford, 1994–98; Principal, Coll. of the Resurrection, Mirfield, 1998–2007. Hon. Sen. Res. Fellow, Sch. of History, Univ. of Kent, 2009–18; Hon. Teaching Fellow, St Augustine's Coll. of Theology, 2018–. Chm., Soc. of Liturgical Study, 1998–2002; Member: C of E Liturgical Commn, 2011– (Consultant, 2006–10); Cathedrals Fabric Commn for England, 2011–. Trustee and Christianity Enquiry, 2008–18; Chm. of Trustees, Alcuin Club, 2015–. Mem., Soc. of Resurrection, 2018. *Publications:* Worship, Church and Society, 1993; (ed) Celebrating the Easter Mystery, 1996; (ed) They shaped our Worship, 1998; (with Anne Dawtry) Art and Worship, 2002; The Art of God: the making of Christians and the meaning of worship, 2005; (ed) The Use of Symbols in Worship, 2007; (ed) Anglican Liturgical Identity, 2008; (contrib.) Anglican Words for Worship, 2012; (contrib.) The Study of Liturgy and Worship, 2013; The Cross and Creation in Christian Liturgy and Art, 2013; (contrib.) The Edinburgh Companion to the Bible and the Arts, 2014; (contrib.) Holy Ground: cathedrals in the twenty-first century, 2017; (contrib.) Oneness: the dynamics of monasticism, 2017. *Recreations:* art galleries and exhibitions, poetry, gardening, film. *Address:* The Rectory, Ewhurst Green, Robertsbridge TN32 5TB. *E:* canonchristopher@outlook.com.

**IRVINE, Hazel Jane;** broadcast journalist and television presenter, BBC Sport, since 1990; *b* 26 May 1965; *d* of William and Norma Irvine; *m*; one *d*. *Educ:* St Andrews Univ. (MA Hons Art Hist.). Prodn asst, Radio Clyde, 1986–87; sports broadcaster and journalist: Scottish Television, 1987–90; BBC Scotland, 1990–99; based in London, 1999–. Best Regl Presenter/Reporter, 1999, Sports Presenter of the Year, 2006, RTS. *Recreations:* golf, hill-walking, travelling, playing piano. *Address:* c/o Jane Morgan Management, Argentum, 2 Queen Caroline Street, W6 9DX. *T:* (020) 3178 8071.

**IRVINE, Very Rev. John Dudley;** Associate Vicar, Holy Trinity, Cambridge, 2012–16; *b* 2 Jan. 1949; 3rd *s* of Rt Hon. Sir Arthur Irvine, QC, MP and Eleanor Irvine; *m* 1972, Andrea Mary Carr; three *s* one *d*. *Educ:* Haileybury Coll. (Hd of Sch.); Sussex Univ. (BA (Hons) Law, 1970); Wycliffe Hall, Oxford (BA (Hons) Theol., 1980; MA 1985). Called to the Bar, Middle Temple, 1973; in practice, Inner Temple, 1973–78. Ordained deacon, 1981, priest, 1982; Curate, Holy Trinity, Brompton with St Paul's, Onslow Sq., 1981–85; Priest i/c, 1985–95, Vicar, 1995–2001, St Barnabas, Kensington; Dean of Coventry, 2001–12, now Dean Emeritus; Priest-in-charge, St Francis's, North Radford, 2006–12. *Recreations:* travel, film, theatre, walking.
*See also* M. F. *Irvine.*

**IRVINE, John Jeremy;** Senior International Correspondent, ITN, since 2014; *b* 2 June 1963; *s* of Dr Kenneth Irvine and Jacqueline Irvine; *m* 1992, Libby McCann; one *s* one *d*. *Educ:* Brackenber House Prep. Sch., Belfast; Campbell Coll., Belfast. Reporter: Tyrone Constitution, Omagh, 1983–87; Ulster TV, Belfast, 1987–94; ITN: Ireland Corresp., 1994–2000; Middle East Corresp., 2000–03; Asia Corresp., 2003–06; Washington Corresp., 2006–10; Internat. Corresp., 2010–14. DLitt Ulster, 2017. *Recreation:* golf. *Address:* c/o ITN, 200 Gray's Inn Road, WC1X 8XZ. *Club:* Royal County Down Golf (Newcastle).

**IRVINE, Air Vice-Marshal Lindsay John,** CB 2014; FRAeS; Director of Legal Services, Royal Air Force, 2009–17; *b* Aberdeen, 5 Nov. 1959; *s* of late Jack Irvine and Christine Irvine; *m* 1981, Claire Negus; one *s* one *d*. *Educ:* Robert Gordon's Coll., Aberdeen; University Coll., Oxford (MA Classics); City Univ., London (Dip. Law); King's Coll. London (MA Internat. Relns). Called to the Bar, Middle Temple, 1983; in practice as barrister, 1983–86; commnd Legal Br., RAF, 1986; MoD, 1986–89; HQ British Forces, Cyprus, 1989–93; HQ PTC, 1994–96; PJHQ, 1996–99; HQ STC, 1999–2000; MoD, 2000–02; Dep. Dir, Legal Services (RAF), 2003–09; rcds 2006. Legally Qualified Chair, Med. Practitioners Tribunal Service, 2017–. FRAeS 2009. Hon. LLD City, 2017. *Recreations:* running, ski-ing, old cars, flying old de Havilland aeroplanes, playing clarinet and saxophone. *Club:* Royal Air Force.

**IRVINE, Michael Fraser;** *b* 21 Oct. 1939; *s* of Rt Hon. Sir Arthur Irvine, PC, QC, MP, and Eleanor Irvine. *Educ:* Rugby; Oriel College, Oxford (BA). Called to the Bar, Inner Temple, 1964; in practice as barrister, 1964–2004. Sen. Legal Assessor, NMC, 2004–06. Contested (C): Bishop Auckland, 1979; Ipswich, 1992; MP (C) Ipswich, 1987–92. PPS to Attorney-Gen., 1990–92. Pres., Ipswich Cons. Assoc., 1998–2011. *Recreation:* hill walking in Scotland. *Address:* 13 East Sheen Avenue, SW14 8AR. *T:* (020) 8392 9337.
See also Very Rev. J. D. Irvine.

**IRVINE, Oliver Henry U.;** *see* Urquhart Irvine.

**IRVINE, Prof. Robin Francis,** FRS 1993; Royal Society Research Professor of Molecular Pharmacology, University of Cambridge, 1996–2016, now Emeritus; *b* 10 Feb. 1950; *s* of Charles Donald Irvine and June (*née* Ievers); *m* 1973, Sandra Jane Elder; two *s. Educ:* Stroud Sch., Romsey; Sherborne Sch., Dorset; St Catherine's Coll., Oxford (MA Biochem. 1972); Corpus Christi Coll., Cambridge (PhD Botany 1976). SRC Res. Student, ARC Unit of Developmental Botany, Cambridge, 1972–75; Beit Meml Fellow, ARC Inst. of Animal Physiol., Babraham, 1975–78; Mem. of Scientific Staff, 1978–95, UG5, 1993–95, AFRC Inst. of Animal Physiol. and Genetics Res., subseq. AFRC Babraham Inst., Cambridge. Mem., Wellcome Trust Cell and Molecular Panel, 1989–92. Mem. Council, Royal Soc., 1999–2001. Morton Lectr, Biochem. Soc., 1994. FRSB (FIBiol 1998); Founder FMedSci 1998. Member Editorial Board: Biochemical Jl, 1988–96; Cell, 1994–2008; Current Biology, 1994–2014; Molecular Pharmacology, 2000–09. J. R. Vane Medal, British Pharmacol Soc., 2010; Van Deenan Medal, Utrecht Univ., 2013. *Publications:* (ed) Methods in Inositide Research, 1990; contribs to Nature, Biochem. Jl and other scientific jls. *Recreations:* playing the lute and guitar, music (especially pre-1650), ornithology, reading.

**IRVINE, Sarah Frances;** *see* Beamish, S. F.

**IRVINE-CAPEL, Ven. Luke Thomas;** Archdeacon of Chichester, since 2019; *b* Dover, 27 Sept. 1975; *s* of John Capel and Margaret Capel (*née* Barley); *m* 2002, Ruth Sarah Irvine; one *s* two *d. Educ:* Caerleon Comp. Sch.; Crosskeys Coll., Newport; Greyfriars, Univ. of Oxford (BA 1997; MA 2001); Coll. of the Resurrection, Mirfield; Univ. of Leeds (MA 1999). Ordained deacon, 1999, priest, 2000; Asst Curate, Abertillery with Cwmtillery and Six Bells, 1999–2001; Minor Canon, St Woolos Cathedral, Newport, 2001–03; Rector, Cranford, St Dunstan with Holy Angels, 2003–08; Vicar, St Gabriel's, Warwick Square, Pimlico, 2008–13; Rector, Christ Church, St Leonards, 2013–19. Chair, Diocesan Bd of Educn, Dio. of Chichester, 2019–. *Publications:* (contrib.) Rightly Dividing the Word of Truth: essays in honour of Bishop David Thomas, 2007. *Recreations:* music, reading, walking, hospitality and entertaining. *Address:* The Palace, Chichester PO19 1PY. *E:* archchichester@chichester.anglican.org.

**IRVING, Dotti;** Founder and Chief Executive Officer, Four Culture (formerly Colman Getty, then Four Colman Getty), since 1987; *b* Annan, Scotland; *d* of Alex and Sheila Irving; *m* 1981, Alasdair J. Riley (marr. diss. 2004); one *d. Educ:* Esdaile Sch.; St George's Sch.; Edinburgh Univ. (MA Hons); Moray Hse Teacher Trng Coll. Penguin Books: Asst, Schs Unit, 1975; Schs Advr, 1976, PR/Marketing Asst, 1977, Hd of PR, 1978–80, Puffin Books; PR Officer, 1980–82; PR Dir, 1982–86. *Recreations:* swimming, reading, gardening. *Address:* Woodstock House, Woodstock Road, Bedford Park, W4 1DR. *T:* (020) 8747 0381, 07850 122428. *E:* dotti.irving@gmail.com. *Club:* Groucho.

**IRVING, Gillian;** QC 2006; *b* 1 Nov. 1958; *d* of Roger Irving and Mary Holliday Irving; *m* 1988, Peter Cadwallader. *Educ:* Caldew Comprehensive Sch., Dalston; Trent Poly., Nottingham (BA Hons Law); Inns of Court Sch. of Law. Called to the Bar, Inner Temple, 1984; in practice specialising in family law, Court of Protection, and community and mental health law. Part-time Judge of First-tier Tribunal (Health, Educn and Social Care Chambers). *Recreations:* gardening, racing (flat and National Hunt), country pursuits. *Address:* 15 Winckley Square, Preston PR1 3JJ; Dere Street Barristers, 33 Broad Chare, Newcastle upon Tyne NE1 3DQ; Broadway House Chambers, 1 The Square, Leeds LS1 2ES.

**IRVING, Prof. John Alan,** PhD; fortepianist and harpsichordist; Professor of Music, Guildhall School of Music and Drama, since 2019; *b* Rotherham, S Yorks 30 May 1959; *s* of Alan Arthur Irving and Iris June Irving (*née* Cartright); *m* 2006, Jane Booth. *Educ:* Old Hall Comp. Sch.; Thomas Rotherham Coll.; Univ. of Sheffield (BMus Hons 1980; PhD 1985). LRAM 1978; ARCM Hons 1981. Ida Carroll Res. Fellow, RNCM, 1984–86; Temp. Lectr in Music, Univ. of Birmingham, 1986–87; Stipendiary Music Lectr, New Coll., Oxford, 1987–88; University of Bristol: Lectr, 1988–99; Sen. Lectr, 1999–2003; Reader, 2003–07; Prof. of Music Hist. and Performance Practice, 2007–11; Dir, Inst. of Musical Res., Sch. of Advanced Study, Univ. of London, 2009–11 (on secondment), Associate Fellow, 2011–; Prof. of Music Hist. and Performance Practice, Canterbury Christ Ch Univ., 2011–12; Prof. of Music, Trinity Laban Conservatoire of Music and Dance, 2013–19. Trustee: Royal Musical Assoc., 2009–14 (Vice Pres., 2009–14); Horniman Mus., 2010–14. FRSA 2011; FRHistS 2011; Sen. FHEA 2014. *Publications:* Mozart's Piano Sonatas: contexts, sources, style, 1997; Mozart: the 'Haydn' Quartets, 1998; Mozart's Piano Concertos, 2003; The Treasures of Mozart, 2009; Understanding Mozart's Piano Sonatas, 2010; The Mozart Project, 2014; book chapters; articles in specialist jls on Mozart, and performance practice. *Recreations:* concert-going, reading, British church architecture. *E:* johnirvingimr@googlemail.com. *Club:* Athenæum.

**IRVING, John Winslow;** novelist; *b* Exeter, New Hampshire, 2 March 1942; *s* of Colin Franklin Newell Irving and Frances Winslow Irving; *m* 1st, 1964, Shyla Leary (marr. diss. 1981); two *s*; 2nd, 1987, Janet Turnbull; one *s. Educ:* Phillips Exeter Acad., USA; Univ. of New Hampshire (BA 1965); Univ. of Iowa (MFA 1967). Professor of English: Windham Coll., 1967–72; Univ. of Iowa, 1972–75; Mount Holyoke Coll., 1975–78; Brandeis Univ., 1978–79. Wrestling Coach: Northfield Mt Hermon Sch., 1981–83; Fessenden Sch., 1983–86; Vermont Acad., 1987–89. Rockefeller Foundn grantee, 1971–72; Nat. Endowment for the Arts Fellow, 1974–75; Guggenheim Fellow, 1976–77. Mem., AAAL, 2001. *Publications:* Setting Free the Bears, 1968; The Water-Method Man, 1972; The 158-Pound Marriage, 1974; The World According to Garp, 1978 (Nat. Book Award, USA, 1979); The Hotel New Hampshire, 1981; The Cider House Rules, 1985 (screenplay, 1999; Best Screenplay Award, Nat. Bd of Review, 1999; Academy Award for best adapted screenplay, 2000); A Prayer for Owen Meany, 1989; A Son of the Circus, 1994; Trying to Save Piggy Sneed, 1996; A Widow for One Year, 1998; My Movie Business: a memoir, 1999; The Fourth Hand, 2001; Until I Find You, 2005; Last Night in Twisted River, 2009; In One Person, 2012; Avenue of Mysteries, 2015.

**IRVING, Prof. Malcolm,** PhD; FRS 2003; Professor of Biophysics, King's College London, since 1998; Associate Research Director, Francis Crick Institute, since 2016; *b* 23 July 1953. *Educ:* Emmanuel Coll., Cambridge (BA 1974); University Coll. London (MSc 1976; PhD 1979). Research Fellow: UCLA, 1979–80; Yale Univ., 1980–81; King's College London: Res. Asst, 1982–83; Royal Soc. Univ. Res. Fellow, 1983–91; Lectr in Biophysics, 1991–94; Reader in Biophysics, 1994–98; Dir, Randall Div. of Cell and Molecular Biophysics, 2003–16. FMedSci 2006. *Address:* Randall Centre for Cell and Molecular Biophysics, King's College London, New Hunt's House, Guy's Campus, SE1 1UL.

**IRVING, Sir Miles (Horsfall),** Kt 1995; MD; FRCS; FMedSci; Professor of Surgery, University of Manchester, 1974–99, now Emeritus; Chairman: Newcastle upon Tyne NHS Hospitals Trust, 1998–2006; Northeast Health Innovation and Education Cluster, 2010–13; *b* 29 June 1935; *s* of Frederick William Irving and Mabel Irving; *m* 1965, Patricia Margaret Blaiklock; two *s* two *d. Educ:* King George V Sch., Southport; Liverpool Univ. (MB, ChB 1959; MD 1962; ChM 1968); Sydney Univ., Australia; MSc Manchester Univ., 1977. FRCS 1964; FRCSE 1964. Robert Gee Fellow, Liverpool Univ., 1962; Phyllis Anderson Fellow, Sydney Univ., 1967; St Bartholomew's Hospital, London: Chief Asst in Surgery, 1969–71; Reader in Surgery, Asst Dir of Professorial Surgical Unit, and Hon. Consultant Surgeon, 1972–74. Hon. Consultant Surgeon: Hope Hosp., Salford, 1974–99; Manchester Royal Infirmary, 1993–2005; to the Army, 1989–2002. Hunterian Prof., 1967, Hunterian Orator, 1993, RCS; Sir Gordon Bell Meml Orator, NZ, 1982. Regl Dir of R&D, N Western RHA, 1992–94; Chm., Standing Gp on Health Technol., DoH, 1993–99; Nat. Dir, NHS Health Technol. Prog., 1994–99; Chm., NHS Innovations (N), 2004–10. Member: Expert Adv. Gp on AIDS, DoH, 1991–96; MRC Health Services and Public Health Res. Bd, 1993–96. Member: Council, RCS, 1984–95; GMC, 1989–92; President: Ileostomy Assoc. of GB and Ireland, 1982–92; Assoc. of Surgeons of GB and Ireland, 1995–96; Internat. Surgical Gp, 1995–96; Section of Coloproctology, RSM, 1997–98; Assoc. of Coloproctology of GB and Ireland, 1998–99; Manchester Med. Soc., 1999–2000. Mem. Bd, Imperial War Mus., 2006–14; Dir, Imperial War Mus. Trading Co., 2012–14. Mem. Council, Newcastle Univ., 2001–11. Chm. Council, Northumbria, Order of St John, 2007–14. Founder FMedSci 1998. Hon. Fellow: Amer. Assoc. for Surgery of Trauma, 1985; Amer. Surgical Assoc., 2000; Barbers' Co., 2014; Hon. FRCEM (Hon. FFAEM 1995); Hon. FRCSCan; FRCSGlas *ad eund*; Hon. FACS 2000. Hon. Member: Assoc. Française de Chirurgie, 1996; Romanian Soc. of Surgeons. Hon. DSc Salford, 1996; DSc (*hc*) Sibiu Univ., Romania, 1997; Hon. DCL Northumbria, 2007; Dr *hc* Univ. of Medicine and Pharmacy, Iasi, Romania, 2014. Moynihan Medal, Assoc. of Surgeons of GB and Ire., 1968; Pybus Medal, N of England Surgical Soc., 1986; John Loewenthal Medal, Sydney Univ., 1993; Canet Medal, Inst. of Mech. Incorp. Engrs, 1995; Bryan Brooke Medal, Ileostomy Assoc. of GB and Ire., 1996; Presidents Medal, British Soc. of Gastroenterology, 1999; Guthrie Medal, RAMC, 2005. Hon. Col 201 (Northern) Fd Hosp. Vol., 1999–2006. MStJ (SBStJ 2009). *Publications:* Gastroenterological Surgery, 1983; Intestinal Fistulas, 1985; ABC of Colorectal Diseases, 1993; Introduction to Minimal Access Surgery, 1995; 100 Years of the RVI, 2006. *Recreations:* thinking about and occasionally actually climbing mountains, reading, opera. *Address:* 12 Ashford Close, Woodstock, Oxon OX20 1FF. *T:* (01993) 811761.

**IRWIN, Lord; James Charles Wood;** Managing Director, The Handy Squad, 2005; *b* 24 Aug. 1977; *s* and *heir* of 3rd Earl of Halifax, *qv*; *m* 2006, Georgia Emily, *d* of Patrick Robert James Clarkson; one *s* one *d. Educ:* Eton; Keble Coll., Oxford. *Heir: s* Hon. Rex Hunter Wood, *b* 12 Aug. 2010. *Address:* Garrowby, York YO41 1QD.

**IRWIN, Alan;** *see* Irwin, G. A.

**IRWIN, Lt Gen. Sir Alistair (Stuart Hastings),** KCB 2002; CBE 1994 (OBE 1987); Adjutant General, 2003–05; Director, Balhousie Publications Ltd, 2008–15; *b* 27 Aug. 1948; *s* of late Brig. Angus Digby Hastings Irwin, CBE, DSO, MC and of Elizabeth Bryson Irwin (*née* Cumming); *m* 1972, Nicola Valentine Blomfield Williams; one *s* two *d. Educ:* Wellington Coll.; St Andrews Univ. (MA); Univ. of Balochistan (BSc Hons 1980). Commnd The Black Watch (RHR), 1970; Staff Coll., Quetta, Pakistan, 1980; CO 1st Bn, The Black Watch, 1985–88 (despatches, 1987); Instructor, Staff Coll., Camberley, 1988–92; Comd, 39 Inf. Bde, 1992–94; Dir Land Warfare, MoD, 1994–95; Prog. Dir, PE, MoD, 1996; Comdt, RMCS, 1996–99; Military Sec., 1999–2000; GOC NI, 2000–03. Member: Commonwealth War Graves Commn, 2006–13 (Vice-Chm., 2011–13); Scottish Govt Great War Commemoration Adv. Panel, 2013–19. Mem., Adv. Bd, Inst. of Continuing Professional Develt, 2004–. Strategic Advr, Eruma plc, 2008–14. President: Quetta Assoc., 2004–18; RBL Scotland, 2006–; Earl Haig Fund for Scotland, 2006–; Officers' Assoc. Scotland, 2006–18; Officers' Assoc., 2006–15; Veterans Scotland, 2006–11; Chairman: Christina Mary Hendrie Trust, 2006–11; Black Watch Heritage Appeal, 2007–13. Trustee, Queen Mother Meml Fund for Scotland, 2003–08. Col, The Black Watch, 2003–06; Chm., Black Watch Castle and Museum Trust, 2013–16. Col Comdt, Scottish Div., 2000–04; Hon. Col Tayforth Univs OTC, 1998–2009. Officer, Royal Co. of Archers (Queen's Bodyguard for Scotland), 2007– (Mem., 1989–2007). Pres., Army Angling Fedn, 1997–2005; Mem., Atlantic Salmon Trust, 2008–. Life Mem., Highland Soc. of London, 2003–. Vice-Pres., Royal Caledonian Educn Trust (formerly Royal Caledonian Schs Trust), 2007–; Patron: Annan Juvenile Pipe Band, 2007–; Dundee Fest. of Remembrance, 2015–; Hon. Pres., Dundee Ex-Servicemen's Assoc., 2010–. FCMI 2005. Hon. Keeper of the Quaich, 2007–. Hon. Mem., Incorporation of Dundee Weavers, 2012–. *Recreations:* shooting, fishing, photography, small scale farming, writing. *Address:* c/o Adam & Co. plc, 25 St Andrew Square, Edinburgh EH2 1AF. *Clubs:* Boodle's; Highland and Lowland Brigade, Royal Scots.

**IRWIN, David;** Partner, Irwin Grayson Associates (consultants in enterprise and economic development), since 2002; *b* 5 Sept. 1955; *s* of Hew Irwin and Ann (*née* Tattersfield); *m* 1st, 1983, Jane Christine Kinghorn (marr. diss. 2008); one *s* one *d*; 2nd, 2013, Penny Hawley; two *s. Educ:* Worksop Coll.; Durham Univ. (BSc (Hons) Engrg Sci and Mgt 1977); Cambridge Univ. (Adv. Course Prodn Methods and Mgt 1978); Newcastle Univ. (MBA 1986; PhD 2019). Develt Engr, Hydraulic Hose Div., Dunlop, 1978–80; Co-founder and Dir, Project North East, 1980–2000; Chief Exec., Small Business Service, 2000–02; Chm., Cobweb Information Ltd, 2002–. Chm., Internat. Assoc. for Enterprise Promotion, 2009–15. Trustee, Speakers' Corner Trust, 2010–18. Vis. Fellow, Northumbria Univ., 2018–. FRSA 1993. Queen's Award for Enterprise Promotion, 2009. *Publications:* Financial Control, 1991; Planning to Succeed in Business, 1995; Financial Control for Non Financial Managers, 1995; Make Your Business Grow, 1998; On Target, 1999; Advocacy for Business Associations, 2012. *Recreations:* squash, photography. *Club:* Northern Rugby Football (Newcastle upon Tyne).

**IRWIN, Prof. (George) Alan,** PhD; Professor, Department of Organization, Copenhagen Business School, since 2015 (Dean of Research, 2007–14; Vice President, 2015–18); *b* Sunderland, 16 July 1955; *s* of late George William Irwin and of Doreen Irwin (*née* Payne, now Bittlestone); *m* 2008, Maja Horst; one *s* two *d. Educ:* St Aidan's Grammar Sch., Sunderland; Univ. of Salford (BSc); Univ. of Manchester (MSc; PhD 1980). Lectr in Sci. and Technol. Policy and Sociol., Univ. of Manchester, 1981–91; Brunel University: Sen.

Lectr, 1991–94, Reader, 1994–98, Prof., 1998–2004, Hd of Dept, 1998–2001, Dept of Human Scis; Dean of Arts and Social Scis, 2001–04; Pro-Vice-Chancellor for Res. and Enterprise, 2004; Dean, Social and Envmtl Studies, Univ. of Liverpool, 2004–07; Acting Pres., Copenhagen Business Sch., 2011. Vis. Prof., Dept of Mgt, Univ. of Glasgow, 2010–15; Carl and Thecla Lamberg Guest Prof., Faculty of Social Sci., Univ. of Gothenburg, 2015; Sir Frederick McMaster Fellowship, CSIRO, Australia, 2018. Hon. Prof., Alliance Manchester Business Sch., Univ. of Manchester, 2018–. Mem., 2005–07, Chair, 2008–10, Biosci. for Society Strategy Panel, BBSRC; panel mem./chair, Eur. Res. Council, 2013–. Member: Public Engagement Strategy Adv. Gp, Wellcome Trust, 2002–04; R&D Steering Cttee, Eur. Foundn for Mgt Develt, 2011–15; Strategy Adv. Bd for Global Food Security Prog., 2011–16; Scientific Adv. Bd, Faculty of Social Scis, Univ. of Vienna, 2016–; Chair, Internat. Adv. Bd, Wageningen Sch. of Social Scis, 2017–. Foreign Mem., Royal Danish Acad. of Scis and Letters, 2013. FAcSS (AcSS 2014). Hon. Fellow, British Assoc. for Advancement of Sci., 2008. Hon. Dr Gothenburg, 2017. Knight, Order of Dannebrog (Denmark), 2014. *Publications:* Risk and Control of Technology, 1985; Citizen Science, 1995; (ed with B. Wynne) Misunderstanding Science?, 1996; Sociology and the Environment, 2001; (with M. Michael) Science, Social Theory and Public Knowledge, 2003; (ed with J. Molin) The Distinctiveness of Diversity, 2009; (with Maja Horst) Hvad vil vi med universiteterne? (What will we do with the universities?), 2018. *Recreations:* music, literature, Sunderland FC, good company, fresh air. *Address:* Department of Organization, Copenhagen Business School, Kilevej 14a, Frederiksberg 2000, Denmark. *T:* 38153815. *E:* ai.ioa@cbs.dk.

IRWIN, Dr Gregor, CMG 2014; Chief Economist, Global Counsel, since 2014; *b* Glasgow, 26 Jan. 1971; *s* of Robert and Anne Irwin; *m* 2002, Dr Kersti Berge; one *s*. *Educ:* Thomas Muir High Sch., Bishopbriggs, Glasgow; Glasgow Univ. (BAcc Econs and Accountancy 1991); Balliol Coll., Oxford (MPhil Econs 1994; DPhil Econs 1996). Strategy Consultant, Marakon Associates, 1996–97; Fellow in Economics: Lady Margaret Hall, Oxford, 1997–2000; University Coll., Oxford, 2000–02; Econ. Advr, Internat. Debt and Capital Mkts, HM Treasury, 2002–04; Hd of Res., 2004–06, Hd of Policy, 2006–08, Internat. Finance Div., Bank of England; Chief Economist, 2008–14, Dir for Economics, 2011–14, FCO. *Publications:* contrib. papers to jls incl. Internat. Jl Finance and Econs, Econs Jl, Oxford Econ. Papers, Rev. Internat. Econs, Develt Policy Rev. *Address:* 5 Huntly Gardens, Glasgow G12 9AS. *T:* 07729 420518. *E:* gregor.irwin@icloud.com.

IRWIN, Helen Elizabeth; Clerk of Committees, House of Commons, 2005–08; *b* 21 April 1948; *d* of late Walter William Taylor and Kathleen Taylor (*née* Moffoot); *m* 1972, Robert Graham Irwin; one *d*. *Educ:* Whalley Range Grammar Sch., Manchester; King's Coll., London (BA Hons Hist. 1969); SSEES, Univ. of London (MA Soviet Studies 1970). Asst Clerk, H of C, 1970–72; Admin. Asst, Univ. of St Andrews, 1972–75; a Clerk, House of Commons, 1977–2008: Cttee of Public Accounts, 1977–81; served in Table Office, 1981–85; Social Services Cttee, 1985–89; Health Cttee, 1989–91; Foreign Affairs Cttee, 1991–94; Principal Clerk, Committee Office, 1994–99; Clerk of Bills, 1999–2001; Principal Clerk, Table Office, 2001–05. Mem. Council, Hansard Soc., 1990–99. Life Mem., Study of Parlt Gp. Fellow, Industry and Parlt Trust. Hon. Res. Fellow, UCL, 2009–11. *Publications:* occasional contribs to books on parliamentary practice and procedure. *Recreations:* family, friends, travel, Vauxhall. *E:* helenirwin@aol.com.

IRWIN, Dr Michael Henry Knox; Chairman, Voluntary Euthanasia Society, 1996–99 and 2001–03 (Vice-Chairman, 1995 and 1999–2001); *b* 5 June 1931; *s* of late William Knox Irwin, FRCS and of Edith Isabel Mary Irwin; *m* 1st, 1958, Elizabeth Naumann (marr. diss. 1982); three *d*; 2nd, 1983, Frederica Harlow (marr. diss. 1991); 3rd, 1994, Patricia Walters (marr. diss. 2000); partner, Angela Farmer. *Educ:* St Bartholomew's Hosp. Med. Coll., London (MB, BS 1955); Columbia Univ., New York (MPH 1960). House Phys. and House Surg., Prince of Wales' Hosp., London, 1955–56; MO, UN, 1957–61; Dep. Resident Rep., UN Technical Assistance Bd, Pakistan, 1961–63; MO, 1963–66, SMO, 1966–69, and Med. Dir, 1969–73, United Nations; Dir, Div. of Personnel, UNDP, 1973–76; UNICEF Rep., Bangladesh, 1977–80; Sen. Advr (Childhood Disabilities), UNICEF, 1980–82; Sen. Consultant, UN Internat. Year of Disabled Persons, 1981; Med. Dir, UN, UNICEF and UNDP, 1982–89; Director: Health Services Dept, IBRD, 1989–90; Westside Action, 1991–93. Founder, Doctors for Assisted Dying, 1998. Pres., Assistance for Blind Children Internat., 1978–84. Consultant, Amer. Assoc. of Blood Banks, 1984–90; Advr, ActionAid, 1990–91; Vice Pres., UNA, 1999–2013 (Vice-Chm., 1995–96; Chm., 1996–98); Chm., UK Cttee, UNHCR, 1997–2002; Vice Pres., Nat. Peace Council, 1996–2000. Director: World Fedn of Right-to-Die Socs, 2004–06 (Vice-Pres., 2000–02; Pres., 2002–04; Treas., 2008–12); Right-to-Die Europe, 2011–13. Co-ordinator, Secular Med. Forum, 2006–08. Hon. Associate, Nat. Secular Soc., 2011; Hon. Med. Advr, Friends at the End, 2004–16. Patron: Humanists UK (formerly British Humanist Assoc.), 2015–; My Death My Decision (formerly Soc. for Old Age Rational Suicide), 2015– (Founder and Co-ordinator, 2009–15). Contested (Living Will Campaign) Kensington and Chelsea, Nov. 1999. Mem. Editl Adv. Panel, Medicine and War, 1985–95. Officer Cross, Internat. Fedn of Blood Donor Organizations, 1984; Tenrei Ohta Award, World Fedn of Right-to-Die Socs, 2014. *Publications:* Check-ups: safeguarding your health, 1961; Overweight: a problem for millions, 1964; Travelling without Tears, 1964; Viruses, Colds and Flu, 1966; Blood: new uses for saving lives, 1967; The Truth About Cancer, 1969; What Do We Know about Allergies?, 1972; A Child's Horizon, 1982; Aspirin: current knowledge about an old medication, 1983; Can We Survive Nuclear War?, 1984; Nuclear Energy: good or bad?, 1985; Peace Museums, 1991; Pro-Choice Living Will, 2003; Psyche-Anima, 2004; What Survives?, 2005; Tilting at Windmills, 2007; Irish Living Will, 2008; Old Age Rational Suicide, 2009; Approaching Old-Old, 2014; I'll See Myself Out, Thank You, 2015; A Completed Life, 2017; Preparing to Leave, 2018; Departing at Ninety?, 2019; *novel:* Talpa, 1990. *Recreations:* politics, metaphysics. *Address:* 9 Waverleigh Road, Cranleigh, Surrey GU6 8BZ.

IRWIN, Rear-Adm. Richard Oran, CB 1995; Member, Tribunal (Criminal Injuries Compensation) (formerly Criminal Injuries Compensation Appeals Panel), 2000–12; *b* 3 Sept. 1942; *s* of Lt Col Richard Arthur Irwin, TD and Catherine Millicent (*née* Palmer); *m* 1st, 1965, Coreen Jill Blackham (marr. diss. 2005), *d* of Rear-Adm. J. L. Blackham, CB; one *s* one *d*; 2nd, 2006, Rosemary Sylvia Helen Groves, PhD, *widow* of Richard Groves, and *d* of R. E. Storrar. *Educ:* Sherborne; Dartmouth; RN Engrg Coll., Manadon (BSc Engrg). FIEE 1986. Served in 7th, 3rd and 10th Submarine Sqdns, 1968–78; on Naval Staff, 1978–81; on staff of Flag Officer, Submarines, 1981–83; on staff, Strategic Systems Exec., 1983–86; RCDS, 1987; Dir, Nuclear Systems, 1988–91; Captain, HMS Raleigh, 1991–92; Chief, Strategic Systems Exec., MoD, 1992–95; RN retd, 1996. Mem., DFEE Panel of Ind. Assessors, 1996–2008; Panel of Ind. Assessors, DCMS, 2004–08. Ind. Investigator, Financial Services Compensation Scheme, 2002–08. Chm., W Sussex HA, 1996–2000. Non-exec. Dir, Halmatic Ltd, 1996–98. Chm., Queen Alexandra Hosp. Home, 1998–2011. Trustee, 2003–08, Vice Pres., 2008–18, Royal Naval Mus. (Chm., Friends of RN Mus. and HMS Victory, 1999–2010). Member: RNSA; Assoc. of Retired Naval Officers. Chairman: Selborne Assoc., 2010–Feb. 2020; Selborne PCC, 2010–; Friends of Gilbert White's House and Garden and Oates Collections, 2014–19. Gov., Kingsham Primary Sch., 1996–2004; Pres., Old Shirburnian Soc., 1999–2000. Officer, Legion of Merit (US), 1996. *Recreations:* tennis, bridge. *Address:* Deep Thatch, Gracious Street, Selborne, Hants GU34 3JB.

IRWIN, Rt Hon. Sir Stephen (John), Kt 2006; PC 2016; Rt Hon. Lord Justice Irwin; a Lord Justice of Appeal, since 2016; *b* 5 Feb. 1953; *s* of late John McCaughey Irwin and of Norma Gordon Irwin; *m* 1978, Deborah Rose Ann Spring; one *s* two *d*. *Educ:* Methodist Coll., Belfast; Jesus Coll., Cambridge (BA Hons 1975; Hon. Fellow, 2017). Called to the Bar: Gray's Inn, 1976, Bencher, 2002 (Treas., 2020); Northern Ireland, 1997; QC 1997; a Recorder, 2000–06; a Judge of the High Ct, QBD, 2006–16; Presiding Judge, N Circuit, 2008–12. Chm., Bar Council, 2004; Mem., Special Immigration Appeals Commn, 2012–16 (Chm., 2013–15); Pres., Personal Injury Bar Assoc., 2018–. Chm., Trustees, Poetry Soc., 2011–14. *Publications:* Medical Negligence: a practitioner's guide, 1995; legal articles in learned jls. *Recreations:* walking, Irish history, music, verse. *Address:* Royal Courts of Justice, Strand, WC2A 2LL.

IRWIN, Prof. Terence Henry, PhD; FBA 2010; Professor of Ancient Philosophy, University of Oxford, 2007–17, now Emeritus; Fellow, Keble College, Oxford, 2007–17; *b* Enniskillen, NI, 21 April 1947. *Educ:* Magdalen Coll., Oxford (BA 1969); Princeton Univ. (PhD 1973). Loeb Fellow in Classical Phil., 1971–72, Asst Prof. of Phil. and Classics, 1972–75, Santayana Fellowship, 1975, Harvard Univ.; Cornell University: Associate Prof. of Phil., 1975–82; Prof. of Phil., 1982–94; Prof. of Classics, 1994–95; Susan Linn Sage Prof. of Phil. and Humane Letters, 1995–2008, now Emeritus. Mem., Amer. Acad. of Arts and Scis, 1995. *Publications:* Plato's Moral Theory, 1977; Plato's Gorgias, 1979; Aristotle's Nicomachean Ethics, 1985, 2nd edn, 1999; Aristotle's First Principles, 1988 (trans. Italian); Classical Thought, 1988 (trans. Chinese, Japanese, Greek); Plato's Ethics, 1995 (trans. Spanish); (jtly) Aristotle: selections, 1995; Oxford Reader in Classical Philosophy, 1999; The Development of Ethics, vol. 1, Socrates to the Reformation, 2007, vol. 2, Suarez to Rousseau, 2008, vol. 3, Kant to Rawls, 2009; (ed) Classical Philosophy, 8 vols, 1995.

IRWIN-GIBSON, Rt Rev. Mary; *see* Montreal, Bishop of.

ISAAC, Anthony Eric; Chief Executive, The BOC Group, 2000–06; *b* 24 Nov. 1941; *m* Janice Donovan; one *s* one *d*. Finance Director: GEC Plessey Telecommunications, 1988–90; Arjo Wiggins Appleton plc, 1990–94; BOC Gp, 1994–2000. Non-executive Director: GDF SUEZ Energy Internat. (formerly Internat. Power plc), 2000–13; Schlumberger plc, 2003–15 (Chm., 2012–15); Hogg Robinson Gp plc, 2006–15.

ISAAC, Anthony John Gower, CB 1985; fiscal consultant; a Deputy Chairman, Board of Inland Revenue, 1982–91 (a Commissioner of Inland Revenue, 1973–77 and 1979–91); *b* 21 Dec. 1931; *s* of Ronald and Kathleen Mary Gower Isaac; *m* 1963, Olga Elizabeth Sibley; one *s* two *d* (and two *d* decd). *Educ:* Malvern Coll.; King's Coll., Cambridge (BA). HM Treasury, 1953–70: Private Sec. to Chief Sec. to Treasury, 1964–66; Inland Revenue, 1971; on secondment to HM Treasury, 1976–78. Mem., Tax Law Rev. Cttee, Internat. 1994–2006. *Publications:* A Local Income Tax, 1992; A Comment on the Viability of the Allowance for Corporate Equity, 1997. *Recreations:* gardening, grandchildren.

ISAAC, David, CBE 2011; Partner, since 2000, and Head, Advanced Manufacturing and Technology Sector, since 2012, Pinsent Masons LLP; Chairman, Equality and Human Rights Commission, since 2016; *b* Johannesburg, SA, 31 March 1958; *s* of Glen Isaac and Jill Isaac (*née* Edge); civil partnership 2005, Paul John Thornton Keene. *Educ:* King Henry VIII Sch., Abergavenny; Trinity Hall, Cambridge (BA 1979); Wolfson Coll., Oxford. Admitted as solicitor, 1985; Solicitor: Morgan Cole, 1984–2000; Pinsent Masons, 2000–. Mem. Bd, Big Lottery Fund, 2014–18. Chairman: Modern Art Oxford, 2001–18; Stonewall, 2003–12; Dir, 14–18 Now, 2015– (Chm., Develt Adv. Gp, 2015–19). Chm. Trustees, UAL, 2018–. Trustee: Diana, Princess of Wales Meml Fund, 2007–13; British Future, 2011–14; Black Mountains Coll., 2018–. *Recreations:* visual arts, walking, bee keeping. *Address:* Pinsent Masons LLP, 30 Crown Place, EC2A 4ES. *T:* (020) 7490 6375. *E:* david.isaac@pinsentmasons.com.

ISAAC, Nicholas Dudley; QC 2019; *b* Boston, Lincs, 21 July 1968; *s* of Adrian Isaac and Rosemary Isaac; *m* 1997, Sophie Garner; one *s* one *d*. *Educ:* Bootham Sch., York; Univ. of Leeds (BA Hons 1st Cl. 1990). Called to the Bar, Gray's Inn, 1993; in practice as a barrister, 1993–. *Publications:* The Law and Practice of Party Walls, 2014; Where is My Boundary?, 2018. *Recreations:* ski-ing, golf, cycling, hillwalking, rock climbing. *Address:* Tanfield Chambers, 2–5 Warwick Court, WC1R 5DJ. *T:* (020) 7421 5300. *E:* nisaac@tanfieldchambers.co.uk.

ISAACS, family name of Marquess of Reading.

ISAACS, Dr Anthony John; Consultant Endocrinologist, London Medical (formerly London Diabetes and Lipid Centre, then London Medical London Diabetes), 2002–13; *b* 22 Oct. 1942; *s* of late Benjamin H. Isaacs, BSc and Lily Isaacs (*née* Rogol); *m* 1st, 1971, Jill Kathleen Elek; three *s*; 2nd, 1986, Dr Edie Friedman; one *d*. *Educ:* Wanstead County High Sch.; Hertford Coll., Oxford (Open Exhibnr; Domus Scholar; BA Animal Physiology, 1st Cl. Hons 1965; MA 1968; BM, BCh 1968); Westminster Med. Sch. (Barron Schol.); MSc (Public Health Medicine), London, 1992. MRCP 1971, FRCP 1997. House posts, Westminster, Whittington and Hammersmith Hosps, 1968–70; Med. Registrar, Westminster Hosp., 1971–73; Research Fellow (Endocrinology), Royal Free Hosp., 1973–75; Sen. Med. Registrar, Westminster Hosp., 1975–84; SMO, Medicines Div., 1984–85, PMO, and Med. Assessor, Cttee on Safety of Medicines, 1985–86, SPMO/Under Sec., and Hd, Med. Manpower and Educn Div., 1986–91, DHSS, subseq. DoH; Regl Consultant (Service Policy and Clinical Audit), NE Thames, later N Thames RHA, 1993–95; Consultant Endocrinologist: Charing Cross Hosp., 1993–95; Chelsea & Westminster Hosp., 1993–2003, Emeritus, 2003–. Sen. Med. Assessor, Medicines and Healthcare products Regulatory (formerly Medicines Control) Agency, 2002–08. Consultant in Clinical Audit, Educn and Trng, Barnet HA, 1995–2001; Hon. Consultant Physician, Barnet, Enfield and Haringey HA, 2001–02. Hon. Consultant Phys. (Endocrinology), UC and Middx Hosps, 1986–96. Vice-Chm., Jt Planning Adv. Cttee, 1986–91; Member: Steering Gp for Implementation of Achieving a Balance (and Co-Chm., Technical sub-gp), 1986–91; 2nd Adv. Cttee on Med. Manpower Planning, 1986–89; Steering Gp on Undergrad. Med. and Dental Educn and Res., 1987–91 (Chm., Implementation Task Gp, 1989–90 and Working Gp, 1990–91); Ministerial Gp on Junior Doctors' Hours, 1990–91; GMC Associate, Fitness to Practise Panels, GMC, 2006–12; Tribunal Mem. (formerly Med. Panellist), MPTS, 2012–16; Partner and Lay Panel Mem., Health and Care Professionals Council, 2014–. Chairman: Barnet Health Promoting Schs, later Barnet Healthy Schs Scheme, Steering Gp, 1995–2002; Barnet Cardiovascular Strategy Steering Gp (formerly Barnet Coronary Heart Disease, Stroke and Smoking Focus Gp), 1995–2001; Barnet Adv. Gp on Palliative Care Services, 1996–2000. Gov., Royal Free Hampstead NHS Trust, 2012–. Hon. Vis. Fellow, LSHTM, 1992–93; Associate Prof., Sch. of Health, Biol and Envmtl Scis, subseq. of Health and Social Scis, Middlesex Univ. 2002–05 (Hon. Vis. Prof., 2001–02, 2006–07). Chm., New End Sch. PTA, 1983–85; Parent Governor, 1987–92, Partnership (formerly First) Gov., 1992–2010, Chm. Governing Body, 2002–10, Hendon Sch. Mem., Soc. for Endocrinology, 1998–2012.

Chm., Friends of Belsize Community Library, 2012–. DFPHM 1999. FRSocMed 1971 (Hon. Treas., 2001–03, Hon. Sec., 2003–05, Vice-Pres., 2005–07, Section of Endocrinol. and Diabetes). *Publications*: Anorexia Nervosa (with P. Dally and J. Gomez), 1979; papers in med. jls on rheumatol and endocrinol topics. *Recreations*: music, cinema, table tennis, chess, travel.

**ISAACS, Barry Russell;** QC 2011; *b* London, 27 Oct. 1964; *s* of Sam Isaacs and Rita Isaacs; *m* 1995, Deborah De Groen; one *s* two *d*. *Educ*: Ilford Co. High Sch. for Boys; Oriel Coll., Oxford (BA 1987); Harvard Univ. (AM 1989). ASA 1989. Mgt Consultant, Bain & Co., 1987–90; Investment Manager, Venture Capital, Touche Remnant, 1990–91; called to the Bar, Inner Temple, 1994; in practice as a barrister, specialising in insolvency, banking and commercial law, South Square, 1994–. *Recreation*: tennis. *Address*: 3–4 South Square, Gray's Inn, WC1R 5HP. *T*: (020) 7696 9900. *E*: practicemanagers@southsquare.com. *Club*: Chandos Lawn Tennis.

**ISAACS, Elizabeth;** QC 2013; a Recorder, since 2009; a Deputy High Court Judge, since 2016; *b* London, 8 March 1963; *d* of Eliot and Gloria Isaacs; *m*; one *d*. *Educ*: Sponne Sch., Towcester; Univ. of Durham (BA Hons Psychol. 1984); Univ. of Leicester (MA Social Work 1989); Univ. of Coventry (LLB Hons 1997); Inns of Court Sch. of Law. Social worker, Warks CC, 1990–97; called to the Bar, Lincoln's Inn, 1998; in practice as family barrister, 1998–. Mem., Family Justice Council, 2015–18. *Publications*: (jtly) Social Work Decision Making: a guide for childcare lawyers, 2008, 2nd edn 2012; (jtly) Challenging and Defending Local Authority Childcare Decisions, 2013; (contrib.) The Family Court Practice, 2014–; (contrib. Ed.) Clarke Hall & Morrison on Children, 2014–. *Recreations*: writing, cinema, theatre, art, swimming. *Address*: St Ives Chambers, Whittall Street, Birmingham B4 6DH. *T*: (0121) 236 0863. *E*: elizabeth.isaacs@stiveschambers.co.uk.

**ISAACS, Jane;** *see* King, Jane.

**ISAACS, Sir Jeremy (Israel),** Kt 1996; General Director, Royal Opera House, Covent Garden, 1988–97 (Member, Board of Directors, 1985–97); Chief Executive, Jeremy Isaacs Productions, 1998–2008; *b* 28 Sept. 1932; *s* of Isidore Isaacs and Sara Jacobs; *m* 1st, 1958, Tamara (*née* Weinreich) (*d* 1986), Cape Town; one *s* one *d*; 2nd, 1988, Gillian Mary Widdicombe. *Educ*: Glasgow Acad.; Merton Coll., Oxford (MA; Hon. Fellow 2006). Pres. of the Union, Hilary, 1955. Television Producer, Granada TV (What the Papers Say, All Our Yesterdays), 1958; Associated-Rediffusion (This Week), 1963; BBC TV (Panorama), 1965; Controller of Features, Associated Rediffusion, 1967; with Thames Television, 1968–78: Controller of Features, 1971–74; Producer, The World at War, 1974; Director of Programmes, 1974–78; Chief Exec., Channel Four TV Co., 1981–87; TV programmes: A Sense of Freedom, STV; Ireland, a Television History, BBC; Cold War, CNN; Millennium, CNN; Millennium Minds, Channel 4; Artists At Work, Artsworld, 2001; interviewer, Face to Face, BBC. Chm., Artsworld Channels Ltd, 2000–03. Dir, Glasgow 1999, 1996–99. Chairman: DCMS Adv. Panel, European Capital of Culture UK Nomination for 2008, 2002–03; EU Selection Panel, European Capitals of Culture 2010, 2006, and Eur. Capitals of Culture 2016, 2011–13. Chm., Salzburg Festival Trust, 1997–2001; Trustee, IPPR, 1989–99. Member: Somerset House Trust, 1997–2003; Council, UEA, 1997–2000; Trustee: European Opera Centre, 1996–2008; Children's Music Workshop, 1997–2007; 2011 Trust, 2009–. Dir, Open College, 1987–92. Governor, BFI, 1979–84 (Chm., BFI Production Bd, 1979–81). President: RTS, 1997–2000; Merton Soc., 2005–07; Merton Founder's Soc., 2009–15. Organised A Statue for Oscar Wilde, Adelaide Street, 1998. James MacTaggart Meml Lectr, Edinburgh TV Fest., 1979; Jonathan Dennis Meml Lectr, Giornate del Cinema Muto, Pordenone, 2010. FRSA 1983; Fellow: BAFTA, 1985; BFI, 1986; FRSAMD 1989; FGS (FGSM 1989). Hon. FRIBA 2004. Hon. DLitt: Strathclyde, 1984; CNAA, 1987; Bristol, 1988; Hope, Liverpool, 2009; Hon. LLD Manchester, 1999. Desmond Davis Award for outstanding creative contrib. to television, 1972; George Polk Meml Award, 1973; Cyril Bennett Award for outstanding contrib. to television programming, RTS, 1982; Lord Willis Award for Distinguished Service to Television, 1985; Bidlake Meml Prize for services to cycling, 1986; Directorate Award, Internat. Council of Nat. Acad. of TV Arts and Scis, NY, 1987; Lifetime Achievement Award, Banff, 1988; BAFTA Scotland Award, 2009. Commandeur de l'Ordre des Arts et des Lettres (France), 1988; Mem., Ordre pour le Mérite (France), 1993. *Publications*: Storm over Four: a personal account, 1989; (jtly) Cold War, 1998, 2nd edn 2008; Never Mind the Moon: my time at the Royal Opera House, 1999; Look Me in the Eye: a life in television, 2006. *Recreations*: reading, walking, cooking, drinking, watching TV sport. *Club*: Garrick.

**ISAACS, Jeremy Michael,** CBE 2015; Founding Partner, JRJ Group, since 2009; *b* London, 1964; *s* of Vincent Isaacs and Pauline Isaacs; *m* 1988, Joanne; one *s* one *d*. Exec. Dir, Goldman Sachs, 1989–96; Lehman Brothers, 1996–2008: Co-Chief Operating Officer, Eur. Equities, 1996; Head: global equity derivative activities, 1996; overall equity activities in Europe, 1997; Chief Exec., Eur. activities, 1999; responsible for Asian ops, 2000–08; CEO, Eur., Middle E and Asia-Pacific, until 2008. Non-executive Director: Marex Spectron Gp Ltd, 2010– (non-exec. Chm., 2010–16); Food Freshness Technol. Hldgs Ltd, 2013–; Nomad Foods, 2016–; Landscape Acquisition Hldgs Ltd, 2017–. Mem., Adv. Bd, Bridges Ventures LLP, 2008–18. Mem. Adv. Bd, British Olympic Assoc., 2007–12. Non-exec. Dir, Imperial Coll. Healthcare NHS Trust, 2003–16. Trustee: J. Isaacs Charitable Trust, 1996–; Noah's Ark Children's Hospice, 2009– (Chair, 2017–). Hon. Fellow, London Business Sch., 2005. Hon. DPhil Haifa, 2019. *Recreations*: shooting, art, golf. *Club*: Arts.

**ISAACS, Stuart Lindsay;** QC 1991; a Recorder, since 1997; a Deputy High Court Judge, since 2004; *b* 8 April 1952; *s* of late Stanley Leslie Isaacs and of Marquette Isaacs; *m* 2000, Melodie, *e d* of Mannie and Judy Schuster; two *s* one *d*. *Educ*: Haberdashers' Aske's Sch., Elstree; Downing Coll., Cambridge (Law, Double 1st cl. Hons); Univ. Libre de Bruxelles (Licence spéciale en droit européen, grande distinction). Called to the Bar, Lincoln's Inn, 1975, Bencher, 1999; admitted NY Bar, 1985. An Asst Recorder, 1992–97. Member, International Panel of Arbitrators: Singapore Internat. Arbitration Centre, 1998–; Hong Kong Internat. Arbitration Centre, 2006–; Korean Commercial Arbitrators Bd, 2010–; Kuala Lumpur Regl Centre for Arbitration, 2010–; Vietnam Internat. Arbitration Centre, 2016–; Member: Restricted Patients Panel, Mental Health Review Tribunal, 2000–04; Internat. Panel of Mediators, Singapore Mediation Centre, 2007–. Mem. Law Adv. Cttee, British Council, 1996–99. Formerly Consultant Ed., Butterworth's EC Case Citator; Consultant Ed., Banking Law Reports, 1996–98. *Publications*: EC Banking Law, 1985, 2nd edn 1994; Banking and the Competition Law of the EEC, 1978; (ed jtly) The EC Regulation on Insolvency Proceedings, 2003, 3rd edn 2016. *Recreations*: family, travel, languages. *Address*: King & Spalding, 125 Old Broad Street, EC2N 1AR. *E*: sisaacsqc@kslaw.com, stuart@stuartisaacsqc.com.

**ISAACS, Tamara Margaret;** *see* Finkelstein, T. M.

**ISAACSON, Prof. Peter Gershohn,** DM, DSc; FRCPath; FRS 2009; Professor of Morbid Anatomy, University College London, 1982–2002, now Emeritus; Consultant Histopathologist, University College London Hospitals NHS Foundation Trust, 2002–15; *b* 24 Nov. 1936; *s* of Robert and Freda Isaacson; *m* 1959, Maria de Lourdes Abranches Pinto; one *s* three *d*. *Educ*: Prince Edward Sch., Salisbury, Rhodesia; Univ. of Cape Town (MB ChB); DM Southampton, 1980; DSc London, 1992. FRCPath 1972. Sen. Lectr, then Reader, Southampton Univ. Med. Sch., 1974–82. Founder FMedSci 1998. Hon. MD: Free Univ. of Berlin, 1998; Universidade Nova de Lisboa, 2005. San-Salvatore Prize, Lugano, 1999. *Publications*: Biopsy Pathology of the Lymphoreticular System, 1983; Oxford Textbook of Pathology, 1993; Extranodal Lymphoma, 1994; numerous contribs to med. jls. *Address*: 3 Owen's Row, EC1V 4NP. *T*: 07752 635090.

**ISCHINGER, Prof. Wolfgang Friedrich;** Chairman, Munich Security Conference, since 2008; Senior Professor for Security Policy and Diplomatic Practice, and Director, Centre for International Security Policy, Hertie School of Governance, Berlin, since 2015; *b* 6 April 1946; *s* of Karl and Margarete Ischinger; *m* 2002, Jutta Falke; one *s* two *d* (and one *s* decd). *Educ*: German Law Sch.; Fletcher Sch. of Law and Diplomacy, Medford, Mass. (MA 1973); Harvard Law Sch., Cambridge, Mass. Joined German Foreign Service, 1975; Policy Planing Staff, Foreign Ministry, Bonn, 1977–79; Washington, 1979–82; Pvte Sec. to Foreign Minister, 1982–90; Minister, Paris, 1990–93; Dir, Policy Planning Staff, 1993–95, Political Dir, 1995–98, State Sec., 1998–2001, Foreign Ministry; Ambassador to USA, 2001–06; Ambassador to UK, 2006–08. Holds numerous foreign decorations incl. Comdr, Légion d'Honneur (France), 1999. *Publications*: numerous contribs on foreign and security policy issues. *Recreations*: mountaineering, ski-ing. *Address*: Munich Security Conference, Prinzregentenstrasse 7, 80538 Munich, Germany. *E*: office@securityconference.de.

**ISENBERG, Prof. David Alan,** MD; FRCP, FMedSci; Arthritis Research UK (formerly Arthritis Research Campaign) Diamond Jubilee Professor of Rheumatology and Academic Director of Rheumatology, University College London, since 1996; *b* 20 Oct. 1949; *s* of late Dr Harry and of Sheila Isenberg; *m* 1975, Lucy Fischel; one *s* one *d*. *Educ*: St Bartholomew's Hosp. Med. Coll. (MB BS 1973); MD London 1984. MRCS 1973; LRCP 1973, MRCP 1976, FRCP 1990. Various trng posts in internal medicine, N London hosps, 1976–79; Sir Jules Thorn Res. Fellow, UCL, 1979–81; Sir Stanley Thomas Johnson Res. Fellow, Tufts-New England Med. Center, Boston, 1982–83; University College London: Consultant Rheumatologist, Middlesex Hosp., 1984–; Sen. Lectr, Middlesex Hosp., 1984–92; Prof. of Rheumatology, 1992–95. Non-exec. Dir, Royal Nat. Orthopaedic Hosp., Stanmore, 2011–. Pres., British Soc. of Rheumatology, 2004–06. FMedSci 2006. Founder, Lupus Acad., 2012. Evelyn Hess Award, Lupus Foundn of America, 2010; Roger Demers Award, 2012; Master Award, Amer. Coll. of Rheumatology, 2016. *Publications*: (jtly) Autoimmune Rheumatic Disease, 1987, 2nd edn 1999; (ed jtly) Oxford Textbook of Rheumatology, 1993, 3rd edn 2004; (jtly) Friendly Fire: explaining autoimmune disease, 1995; (ed jtly) Controversies in Rheumatology, 1997; (ed jtly) Adolescent Rheumatology, 1998; (ed jtly) Imaging in Rheumatology, 2002; Lupus: the facts, 2008; 540 res. papers; 290 reviews and chapters. *Recreations*: playing tennis and guitar (founder of rheumatology rock band, Lupus Dave and the Davettes), writing short stories, watching football, going to the theatre and classical music concerts. *Address*: Room 424, The Rayne Building, University College London, 5 University Street, WC1E 6JF. *T*: (020) 3108 2150, 2148. *E*: d.isenberg@ucl.ac.uk.

**ISH-HOROWICZ, Prof. David,** FRS 2002; PhD; Professor of Cell and Developmental Biology, University College London, since 2013; *b* 2 Aug. 1948; *s* of Moshe Ish-Horowicz and Hava Ish-Horowicz (*née* Berman); *m* 1988, Rosamund Diamond. *Educ*: Manchester Grammar Sch.; Pembroke Coll., Cambridge (BA 1969); Darwin Coll., Cambridge/MRC Lab. of Molecular Biol. (PhD 1973). Post-doctoral Res. Fellow, Basel Univ., Switzerland, 1973–76; Imperial Cancer Research Fund, later Cancer Research UK: Res. Scientist, 1977–81; Sen. Res. Scientist, 1981–87; Principal Scientist, 1987–2013. Hon. Prof., UCL, 1997–2013. Mem., EMBO, 1985. *Publications*: contrib. papers to research jls. *Recreations*: music, swimming, ski-ing, eating.

**ISHAM, Sir Norman (Murray Crawford),** 14th Bt *cr* 1627, of Lamport, Northamptonshire; OBE 1988; Chartered Architect, now retired; *b* 28 Jan. 1930; *yr s* of Lt-Col Vere Arthur Richard Isham, MC (*d* 1968) and Edith Irene (*d* 1973), *d* of Harry Brown; *S* brother, 2009; *m* 1956, Joan, *d* of late Chief Inspector Leonard James Genet, BEM, BSAP; two *s* one *d*. *Educ*: Stowe; Univ. of Cape Town (BArch Dist.). ARIBA 1958. Study Bursary, Italian Govt, 1958–59. Projects include Browning Barracks, Parachute Regiment Depot, Aldershot, 1968 (Civic Trust Award, 1968; Concrete Soc. Award, 1969). Former Mem. Cttee, Alton Soc.; Pres., Orton Trust, Northants; establd Anglo-American Isham Ancestry Assoc., 2012. *Heir*: *s* Richard Leonard Vere Isham [*b* 30 Dec. 1958; *m* 1990, Julia Claire Mary (marr. diss. 2017), *d* of David Frost Pilkington, CBE; two *s*].

**ISHERWOOD, John David Gould,** CMG 2001; Chairman, Hampshire Archives Trust, 2001–11; consultant solicitor, 1991–2002; *b* 8 Feb. 1936; *s* of Frank Hilton Isherwood and Beatrice Marion Isherwood (*née* Gould); *m* 1967, Anne Isobel Inglis; one *s* one *d*. *Educ*: Cheltenham Coll.; Merton Coll., Oxford (MA 1963; MSt 1997); Stanford Univ., California. Lieut, RA, 1954–56. Admitted Solicitor, 1964; VSO, 1964–68; Solicitor, 1969, Sen. Partner, 1985–91, Barker, Son & Isherwood, Andover. Mem., Law Soc. Trustee: Oxfam, 1968–98 (Chm., Exec. Cttee, 1979–85); Wateraid, 1981–2001 (Chm., 1995–2001); NCVO, 1996–2003. Trustee, SE Museums, Libraries and Archives Council, 2003–08. Hon. Sec., Hants New Victoria Co. Hist. Project, 2008–. *Recreations*: local history, theatre, travel. *Address*: Chalcot, Penton Mewsey, Andover, Hants SP11 0RQ.

**ISHERWOOD, Mark;** Member (C) Wales North, National Assembly for Wales, since 2003; *b* 21 Jan. 1959; *s* of late Rodney Isherwood and of Patricia McLean; *m* 1985, Hilary Fleming; two *s* four *d*. *Educ*: Univ. of Newcastle-upon-Tyne (BA Hons Politics). Trainee Manager, subseq. Br. Manager, Cheshire Building Soc., 1981–89; Commercial Business Develt Manager, NWS Bank, 1989–90; Wirral Area Manager, 1990–94, N Wales Area Manager, 1994–2003, Cheshire Building Soc. Mem., Treuddyn Community Council, 1999–2004 (Vice-Chm., 2002–03). Bd Mem., Venture Housing Assoc., 1992–2003. Gov., Ysgol Parc-y-Llon, 1996–2004. Contested (C): Alyn and Deeside, 2001; Delyn, 2015. Mem., Mold Round Table, 1984–2009. ACIB. *Recreations*: sailing, spending time with family. *Address*: National Assembly for Wales, Cardiff Bay, Cardiff CF99 1NA. *T*: 0300 200 7219. *E*: mark.isherwood@assembly.wales; (constituency office) 5 Halkyn Street, Holywell, Flintshire CH8 7TX.

**ISHIGURO, Sir Kazuo,** Kt 2018; OBE 1995; FRSL; author; *b* 8 Nov. 1954; *s* of Shizuo and Shizuko Ishiguro; *m* 1986, Lorna Anne MacDougall; one *d*. *Educ*: Univ. of Kent (BA English/Philosophy); Univ. of East Anglia (MA Creative Writing). Began publishing short stories, articles, in magazines, 1980; writer of TV plays, 1984–; filmscripts: (jtly) The Saddest Music in the World, 2004; The White Countess, 2006. Mem. Jury, Cannes Film Festival, 1994. FRSL 1989. Hon. DLitt: Kent, 1990; UEA, 1995; St Andrews, 2003. Hon. Citizen, Nagasaki, 2018. Premio Scanno for Literature, Italy, 1995; Premio Mantova, Italy, 1998; Peggy V. Helmerich Distinguished Author Award, 2013; Sunday Times Award for Literary Excellence, 2014; Lion Medal, NY Public Liby, 2014; Golden Plate Award, Amer. Acad. of Excellence, 2017; Nobel Prize in Literature, 2017; Bodley Medal, Bodleian Liby, Oxford, 2019. Chevalier de l'Ordre des Arts et des Lettres (France), 1998; Gold and Silver Star, Order of the Rising Sun (Japan), 2018. *Publications*: A Pale View of Hills, 1982 (Winifred Holtby Prize, RSL); An Artist of the Floating World, 1986 (Whitbread Book of the Year, Whitbread Fiction Prize); The Remains of the Day, 1989 (Booker Prize; filmed 1993; adapted for stage, 2019); The Unconsoled, 1995 (Cheltenham Prize, 1995); When We Were Orphans, 2000; Never Let Me Go, 2005 (Premio Serono, Italy, Corine Internat.

Book Prize, Germany, Casino de Santiago Eur. Novel Award, Spain, 2006; filmed 2010); Nocturnes: five stories of music and nightfall, 2009 (Giuseppe Tomasi di Lampedusa Internat. Literary Prize); The Buried Giant, 2015; My Twentieth Century Evening and Other Small Breakthroughs, 2017. *Recreations:* music; playing piano and guitar. *Address:* c/o Faber & Faber, Bloomsbury House, 74–77 Great Russell Street, WC1B 3DA.

**ISLE OF MAN, Archdeacon of;** *see* Brown, Ven. A.

**ISLE OF WIGHT, Archdeacon of;** *see* Leonard, Ven. P. P.

**ISLINGTON, Bishop Suffragan of,** since 2015; **Rt Rev. Richard Charles Thorpe;** an Honorary Assistant Bishop, Diocese of Southwark, since 2018; *b* 3 Feb. 1965; *s* of Anthony Lawrence Thorpe and late Wendy Thorpe; *m* 1993, Louise Rachel Arden-White; two *s* one *d*. *Educ:* Birmingham Univ. (BSc 1987); Wycliffe Hall, Oxford (BTh 1996). Ordained deacon, 1996, priest, 1997; Curate, Holy Trinity, Brompton, with St Paul's, Onslow Square, 1996–2005; Priest-in-charge, 2005–10, Rector, 2010–15, St Paul's, Shadwell, with Ratcliffe St James; Priest-in-charge, All Hallows, Bromley-by-Bow, 2010–14. *E:* bishop.islington@london.anglican.org.

**ISMAIL, (Jane) Allison;** *see* Hunter, J. A.

**ISON, Very Rev. David John,** PhD; Dean of St Paul's, since 2012; *b* 15 Sept. 1954; *s* of Richard Lea Ison and Maureen Jean Ison; *m* 1977, Hilary Margaret Powell; two *s* two *d*. *Educ:* Univ. of Leicester (BA 1976); Univ. of Nottingham (BA 1978); St John's Coll., Nottingham (DPS 1979); King's Coll. London (PhD 1985). Ordained deacon, 1979, priest, 1980; Asst Curate, St Nicholas and St Luke, Deptford, 1979–85; Tutor, Church Army Trng Coll., 1985–88; Vicar, Potters Green, Coventry, 1988–93; Officer for Contg Ministerial Educn, Dio. Exeter, 1993–2005; Dean of Bradford, 2005–12. FKC 2016. *Publications:* (ed) Pilgrim Guide to Exeter Cathedral, 1999; (ed) The Vicar's Guide, 2005. *Recreation:* bodgery. *Address:* The Chapter House, St Paul's Churchyard, EC4M 8AD. *T:* (020) 7246 8360. *E:* deanspa@stpaulscathedral.org.uk.

**ISRAEL, Prof. Jonathan Irvine,** DPhil; FBA 1992; Professor of Modern History, Institute for Advanced Study, Princeton, 2000–16, now Emeritus; *b* 22 Jan. 1946; *s* of David and Miriam Israel; *m* 2009, Annette Munt; one *s* one *d* by a previous marriage. *Educ:* Kilburn Grammar Sch.; Queens' Coll., Cambridge; St Antony's Coll., Oxford (DPhil 1972). Lectr, Hull Univ., 1972–74; Lectr, 1974–81, Reader, 1981–84, Prof. of Dutch History and Instns, 1985–2000, UCL. *Publications:* Race, Class and Politics in Colonial Mexico, 1975; The Dutch Republic and the Hispanic World, 1982; European Jewry in the Age of Mercantilism 1550–1750, 1985; Dutch Primacy in World Trade 1585–1740, 1989; Empires and Entrepots: the Dutch, the Spanish monarchy and the Jews 1585–1713, 1990; (ed) The Anglo-Dutch Movement: essays on the Glorious Revolution and its world impact, 1991; The Dutch Republic, 1995; Conflicts of Empires: Spain, the Low Countries and the struggle for world supremacy 1585–1713, 1997; Radical Enlightenment: philosophy and the making of modernity 1650–1750, 2001; Enlightenment Contested, 2006; A Revolution of the Mind: radical enlightenment and the intellectual origins of modern democracy, 2010; Democratic Enlightenment: philosophy, revolution, and human rights, 1750–1790, 2011; Revolutionary Ideas: an intellectual history of the French Revolution from The Rights of Man to Robespierre, 2014. *Address:* School of Historical Studies, Institute for Advanced Study, 1 Einstein Drive, Princeton, NJ 08540, USA.

**ISRAEL, Prof. Werner,** OC 1994; FRS 1986; Adjunct Professor of Physics, University of Victoria, since 1997; *b* 4 Oct. 1931; *s* of Arthur Israel and Marie Kaufpauf; *m* 1958, Inge Margulies; one *s* one *d*. *Educ:* Cape Town High Sch.; Univ. of Cape Town (BSc 1951, MSc 1954); Dublin Inst. for Advanced Studies; Trinity Coll., Dublin (PhD 1960). Lectr in Applied Maths, Univ. of Cape Town, 1954–56; University of Alberta: Asst Prof., 1958; Associate Prof., 1964; Prof. of Maths, 1968–71; Prof. of Physics, 1972–96; Univ. Prof., 1985–96. Sherman Fairchild Dist. Schol., CIT, 1974–75; Vis. Prof., Dublin Inst. for Advanced Studies, 1966–68; Sen. Visitor, Dept of Applied Maths and Theoretical Physics, Univ. of Cambridge, 1975–76; Maître de Recherche Associé, Inst. Henri Poincaré, Paris, 1976–77; Visiting Professor: Berne, 1980; Kyoto, 1986, 1998; Vis. Fellow, Gonville and Caius Coll., Cambridge, 1985. Fellow, Canadian Inst. for Advanced Research, 1986–. Pres., Internat. Soc. of Gen. Relativity and Gravitation, 1998–2001. Hon. DSc: Queen's, Kingston, Ont, 1987; Victoria, BC, 1999; Dr *hc* Tours, 1994. *Publications:* (ed) Relativity, Astrophysics and Cosmology, 1973; (ed with S. W. Hawking) General Relativity: an Einstein centenary survey, 1979; (ed with S. W. Hawking) 300 Years of Gravitation, 1987; numerous papers on black hole physics, general relativity, relativistic statistical mechanics. *Recreation:* music. *Address:* Department of Physics and Astronomy, University of Victoria, Victoria, BC V8W 2Y2, Canada.

**ISSA, Caroline;** Chief Executive Officer, Tank Publications Ltd, since 2002; Tank Form Ltd, since 2004; *b* Montreal, 18 April 1977; *d* of Farah Issa and Lee Chin Lim. *Educ:* Royal West Acad., Montreal; Marianopolis Coll., Westmount, Quebec; Wharton Sch., Univ. of Pennsylvania (BScEcon). Analyst, Marakon Associates, San Francisco, 1999–2002. *Address:* Tank, 91–93 Great Portland Street, W1W 7NX. *T:* (020) 7637 0303. *E:* caroline@tankmagazine.com.

**ISSERLIS, Steven John,** CBE 1998; 'cellist; *b* 19 Dec. 1958; *s* of late George and Cynthia Isserlis; partner, Pauline Mara (*d* 2010); one *s*. *Educ:* City of London School; International 'Cello Centre; Oberlin College. London recital début, Wigmore Hall, 1977; concerts in Europe, Asia, N America, Australia, 1978–; tours in USSR, later Russia, 1984–; débuts, 1990–, in New York, Paris, Berlin, Vienna, Tokyo, Sydney, Seoul, Taipei, etc; numerous recordings. Hon. Fellow, St Hilda's Coll., Oxford, 2018. Awards for recordings include: Gramophone Award (Contemporary Music), for John Tavener's The Protecting Veil, 1992; Deutsche Schallplattenpreis, for Schumann Cello Concerto, 1998; Classic CD Award, for Haydn Concertos, 1999; Gramophone Award (Instrumental Recording), Critics' Award, Classical Brits and CD of the Year, BBC R3 CD Review, for Bach Cello Suites, 2007. Piatigorsky Artist Award, USA, 1993; Instrumentalist Award, Royal Philharmonic Soc., 1993; Schumann Prize, City of Zwickau, 2000; Red F Award, Classic FM, 2002; Classical Artist of the Year, Time Out, 2002; Gramophone Hall of Fame, 2013; Glashütte Original Music Fest. Award, Dresden, 2017; Wigmore Hall Gold Medal, 2017; Walter Willson Cobbett Medal, 2017. *Publications:* Cello World, 1999; Beethoven: mandolin variations (arr. violin or cello and piano), 1990; (with Sabina Teller Ratner) Saint-Saens Complete Shorter Works for cello and piano, 1998; Unbeaten Tracks (short pieces for cello by various contemporary composers), 2000; for children: Why Beethoven Threw the Stew, 2001; Why Handel Waggled His Wig, 2006; (with A. Dudley) Little Red Violin (musical story), 2008; (with A. Dudley) Goldiepegs and the 3 Cellos, 2010; (with A. Dudley) Cindercella, 2012; Robert Schumann's Advice to Young Musicians, 2016. *Recreations:* talking on the telephone, e-mailing everybody I know (usually for no good reason), eating too much, regretting it, watching videos, reading, panicking about upcoming concerts, sleeping, jet-lag, telling people how tired I am, wondering if I should have any more worthwhile recreations. *Address:* c/o IMG Artists, Capital Tower, 91 Waterloo Road, SE1 8RT. *T:* (020) 7957 5800.

**ISSING, Dr Otmar;** President, Center for Financial Studies, Goethe University, Frankfurt, since 2006; Member, Executive Board, European Central Bank, 1998–2006; *b* 27 March 1936. *Educ:* Univ. of Würzburg (BA Econs; PhD 1961). Res. Asst, Inst. of Econs and Social Scis, 1960–66, Lectr, 1965–66, Univ. of Würzburg; Temp. Prof., Univ. of Marburg, 1965–66; Professor: Faculty of Econs and Social Scis, and Dir, Inst. for Internat. Econ. Relns, Univ. of Erlangen-Nuremberg, 1967–73 (Temp. Prof., 1966–67); of Econs, Monetary Affairs and Internat. Econ. Relns, Univ. of Würzburg, 1973–90 (Hon. Prof., 1991–); Mem. Directorate, Deutsche Bundesbank, 1990–98. Co-founder and Jt Ed., WiSt (scientific jl), 1972–90. Hon. doctorates from: Bayreuth, 1996; Constance, 1998; Frankfurt am Main, 1999; Laurea *hc* in Internat. Econ. Integration, Univ. of Pavia, 2010. Internat. Prize, Friedrich August von Hayek Stiftung, 2004; Bernhard Harms Medal, Inst. for World Econs, Kiel, 2004; Hans Möller Medal, Univ. of Munich, 2005; Ludwig Erhard Prize (for econ. writing), 2006. Grand Cross, Order of Merit (Germany), 2006; Grand Officer, Order of Merit (Luxemburg), 2006; Silver Insignia, Würzburg, 2007. *Publications* include: Leitwährung und internationale Währungsordnung, 1965; Indexklauseln und Inflation, 1973; Einführung in die Geldtheorie, 1974, 15th edn 2011 (trans. Chinese and Bulgarian); Investitionslenkung in der Marktwirtschaft?, 1975; (jtly) Kleineres Eigentum: Grundlage unserer Staats- und Wirtschaftsordnung, 1976; Einführung in die Geldpolitik, 1981, 6th edn 1996; Internationale Währungsordnung, 1991; Von der D-Mark zum Euro, 1998; (jtly) Monetary Policy in the Euro Area, 2001; Der Euro: Geburt, Erfolg, Zukunft, 2008 (The Birth of the Euro, 2008; trans. Chinese, 2011); contrib. learned jls. *Address:* Georg Sittig Strasse 8, 97074 Würzburg, Germany.

**IVANYI, Prof. Juraj,** MD; PhD; Director, Tuberculosis and Related Infections Unit, MRC Clinical Sciences Centre, Hammersmith Hospital, 1984–97; Hon. Professor of Immunology of Infectious Diseases, Guy's Campus of King's College London (formerly Guy's, King's and St Thomas's Hospital Medical and Dental School), 1998–2019, now Emeritus Professor; *b* 20 June 1934; *s* of Dr Arnold Ivanyi and Maria (*née* Keszner); *m* 1st, 1960, Dr Ludmila Svobodova (*d* 2002); 2nd, 2009, Katharine Mary Honey. *Educ:* Charles Univ., Prague (MD); Acad. of Scis, Prague (PhD 1963). Czechoslovak Acad. of Scis, Prague, 1961–68 (Hd, Dept of Immunochem., Inst. of Experimental Biol. and Genetics, 1966–68); Head, Dept of Immunobiol., Wellcome Res. Labs, Beckenham, 1970–84; Prof. of Mycobacteriological Immunol., RPMS, Univ. of London, 1990–97. Founding Mem., Comenius Academic Club, 2012. Fellow, Learned Soc. of Czechia, 2017. Hon. Mem., Slovak Soc. for Immunology, 1995. Garnet Immunoglobulin Award, Czech Immunology Soc., 2006. *Publications:* over 300 in field of immunology. *Address:* 3 Grotes Place, Blackheath, SE3 0QH. *T:* (020) 8318 1088.

**IVE, Sir Jonathan (Paul),** KBE 2012 (CBE 2006); RDI 2003; Chief Design Officer, Apple, 2015–19 (Senior Vice President and Head of Design, 1996–2015; Head of Human Interface, 2012–15); *b* London, 1967; *m*; twin *s*. *Educ:* Newcastle upon Tyne Poly. (BA 1st Cl. Hons Industrial Design 1989). Partner, Tangerine, design consultancy, London, 1989–92; joined Apple, 1992. *Designs* include: ceramic-ware, electrical appliances; consumer electronics, computers (incl. iMac, PowerBook, iBook, iPod, iPhone, iPad). Chancellor, RCA, 2017–. Hon. Dr: Newcastle Poly.; Univ. of the Arts, London; RCA. Inaugural medal, RSA, 1999; Designer of Year, Design Museum, 2003; Benjamin Franklin Medal, RSA, 2004; President's Award, D&AD, 2005, and Royal Acad. of Engrs, 2005.

**IVEAGH, 4th Earl of,** *cr* 1919; **Arthur Edward Rory Guinness;** DL; Chairman, Elveden Farms; Bt 1885; Baron Iveagh 1891; Viscount Iveagh 1905; Viscount Elveden 1919; *b* 10 Aug. 1969; *s* of 3rd Earl of Iveagh and Miranda Daphne Jane, *d* of Maj. Michael Smiley; *S* father, 1992; *m* 2001, Clare Hazell; two *s*. Dir, Burhill Estates. Mem. Bd, Iveagh Trust; Chm., Chadacre Agricl Trust; Trustee: Robert Black Meml Fund; East Anglian Air Ambulance. DL Suffolk, 2008. FIAgrM 2008; ARAgS 2018. Hon. Fellow, Royal Agricultural Univ., 2017. *Heir: s* Viscount Elveden, *qv*. *Address:* The Estate Office, Elveden, Thetford, Norfolk IP24 3TQ.

**IVENS, Anne;** *see* McElvoy, A.

**IVENS, Martin Paul;** Editor, Sunday Times, since 2013 (Deputy Editor, 1996–2013); *b* London, 29 Aug. 1958; *s* of Michael William and Rosalie Joy Evans; *m* 1994, Anne McElvoy, *qv*; two *s* one *d*. *Educ:* Finchley Catholic High Sch.; St Peter's Coll., Oxford (BA 1st Cl. Modern Hist.). Foreign Ed., Sunday Telegraph, 1986–88; The Times: Foreign News Ed., 1988–90; Foreign Ed., 1990–94; Exec. Ed. (News and Comment), 1994–96. Directory Trustee, Social Mkt Foundn. *Recreations:* medieval and modern history, running, classical music. *Address:* The Sunday Times, 1 London Bridge Street, SE1 9GF. *Club:* Garrick.

**IVERS, Michael Joseph;** QC 2016; *b* London, 27 Dec. 1966; *s* of Henry James Ivers and Kathleen Jean Ivers. *Educ:* Finchley RC High Sch.; Queen Mary Coll., Univ. of London (LLB Hons). Called to the Bar, Middle Temple, 1991; in practice as barrister, specialising in criminal law and internat. human rights law. Chm., Kurdish Human Rights Project, 2009–11. Membership Sec., Bar Human Rights Cttee, 2019– (Treas., 2010–16; Sec., 2016–18). *Recreations:* travel and food, preferably combined! *Address:* Garden Court Chambers, 57–60 Lincoln's Inn Fields, WC2A 3LJ. *T:* (020) 7993 7600. *E:* michaeli@gclaw.co.uk.

**IVERSEN, Prof. Leslie Lars,** CBE 2013; PhD; FRS 1980; Professor of Pharmacology and Director, Wolfson Centre for Age-Related Diseases, King's College London, 1999–2004; Visiting Professor of Pharmacology, University of Oxford, since 2007; *b* 31 Oct. 1937; *s* of Svend Iversen and Anna Caia Iversen; *m* 1961, Susan Diana (*née* Kibble) (*see* S. D. Iversen); one *s* one *d* (and one *d* decd). *Educ:* Trinity Coll., Cambridge (BA Biochem., PhD Pharmacol). Harkness Fellow, United States: with Dr J. Axelrod, Nat. Inst. of Mental Health, and Dr E. Kravitz, Dept of Neurobiology, Harvard Med. Sch., 1964–66; Fellow, Trinity Coll., Cambridge, 1964–84; Locke Research Fellow of Royal Society, Dept of Pharmacology, Univ. of Cambridge, 1967–71; Dir, MRC Neurochemical Pharmacology Unit, Cambridge, 1971–82; Dir, Merck, Sharp & Dohme Neurosci. Res. Centre, Harlow, 1982–95; Sen. Vis. Scientist, Dept of Pharmacology, 1995–96, Vis. Prof. of Pharmacol., 1996–2007, Oxford Univ. Chm., Adv. Council on Misuse of Drugs, 2011–16 (interim Chm., 2010). Foreign Associate, Nat. Acad. of Scis (USA), 1986. *Publications:* The Uptake and Storage of Noradrenaline in Sympathetic Nerves, 1967; (with S. D. Iversen) Behavioural Pharmacology, 1975, 2nd edn 1981; The Science of Marijuana, 2000; Drugs: a very short introduction, 2001, 2nd edn 2016; Speed, Ecstasy, Ritalin: the science of amphetamines, 2007; (jtly) Introduction to Neuropsychopharmacology, 2009. *Recreations:* reading, gardening. *Address:* Department of Pharmacology, University of Oxford, Mansfield Road, Oxford OX1 3QT.

**IVERSEN, Prof. Susan Diana,** CBE 2005; PhD, ScD; FMedSci; Professor of Psychology, 1993–2005, now Emeritus, and Pro-Vice-Chancellor, (Planning and Resource Allocation), 2000–05, (Special Projects), 2005–12, Oxford University; Fellow of Magdalen College, Oxford, 1993–2005, now Emeritus; *b* 28 Feb. 1940; *d* of Jack Bertram Kibble and Edith Margaret Kibble; *m* 1961, Leslie Lars Iversen, *qv*; one *s* one *d* (and one *d* decd). *Educ:* Girton Coll., Cambridge (BA Zoology, PhD Exp. Psych, ScD). NATO Science Fellow, Nat. Inst. Mental Health and Dept of Pharmacology, Harvard Med. Sch., 1964–66; Fellow: Girton Coll., Cambridge, 1964–75; Jesus Coll., Cambridge, 1981–93; Dept of Exp. Psychology,

Cambridge, 1966–83; Merck Sharp & Dohme, Neuroscience Research Centre, Harlow, 1983–93; Oxford University: Prof. and Head of Dept of Experimental Psychol., 1993–2000; Pro-Vice-Chancellor (Res.), 1998–2000. Oxford University Press: Psychology Delegate, 1994–2005; Chm., Finance Cttee, 2001–05. Member: Council, SERC, 1991–94; BBSRC, 1994–97. Member: Animal Procedures Cttee, Home Office, 1989–98; Mental Health and Neurosci. Grant Cttee, Wellcome Trust, 1990–98 (Chm. Panel, 1995–98); Health and Life Scis Panel, 1993–98, Brain Sci., Addiction and Drug Project Panel, 2004, Foresight. President: British Assoc. of Psychopharmacol., 1984–86; Experimental Psychol. Soc., 1988–90; Med. Sect., 1989, Psychol. Sect., 1997, BAAS; Chm., Brain Res. Assoc., 1994–96. Mem. Council, Bioscis Fedn, 2004–08; Trustee, Inst. for Animal Health, 2004–09; Trustee and Mem. Council, GDST, 2005–14 (Chm., Acad. Trust Bd, 2007–14); Mem. Council, 2004–07, Treas., 2010–14, Acad. of Med. Scis. Chm., Internat. Adv. and Scientific Bd, Inst. of Neurosci., TCD; Mem. Adv. Bd, Brain, Mind and Behavior Prog., J. S. McDonnell Foundn, St Louis, USA, 1999–2008. Gov., Sevenoaks Sch., 2016–. A. Vibert Douglas Fellow, Internat. Fedn of Univ. Women, 1964–65. FMedSci 1999. Hon. Fellow, Cardiff Univ., 1999. Hon. DSc St Andrews, 2005. K. M. Stott Prize, Newnham Coll., Cambridge, 1972; Spearman Medal, BPsS, 1974; Lifetime Achievement Award, British Assoc. for Psychopharmacol., 2003. Receiving Ed., Science, 1994–99; Chief Ed., Neuropsychologia, 1997–2000. *Publications:* (with L. L. Iversen) Behavioural Pharmacology, 1975, 2nd edn 1981; (ed with L. L. Iversen and S. H. Snyder) Handbook of Psychopharmacology, 20 vols; (jtly) Introduction to Neuropsychopharmacology, 2008. *Recreations:* history, wildlife, modern art, theatre. *Address:* Magdalen College, Oxford OX1 4AU.

**IVES, Charles John Grayston, (Bill);** Informator Choristarum, Organist, and Tutor in Music, Magdalen College, Oxford, 1991–2009; Fellow of Magdalen College, 1991–2009, now Emeritus; *b* 15 Feb. 1948; *s* of Harold James Ives and Catherine Lilla Ives; *m* 1st, 1972, Bethan Eleri Jones (marr. diss. 1986); one *s* one *d*; 2nd, 1988, Janette Ann (*née* Buqué) (separated 2017). *Educ:* King's Sch., Ely; Selwyn Coll., Cambridge. Asst Dir of Music, Reed's Sch., Cobham, 1971–76; Lectr in Music, Coll. of Further Educn, Chichester, 1976–78; tenor, The King's Singers, 1978–85; freelance composer, 1985–91. Examr, Associated Bd of Royal Schs of Music, 1988–2006. Hon. FRSCM 2008. DMus Lambeth 2008. *Publications:* (as Grayston Ives) musical compositions of sacred choral music, including Canterbury Te Deum (commnd for Enthronement of Archbishop George Carey, Canterbury Cathedral, 1991), The Gift of Grace (commnd for Nat. Commemoration Service, Westminster Abbey, 2007) and Requiem (commnd for 550th anniv. of Magdalen Coll., Oxford, 2008). *Recreations:* books, wine, travel. *Address:* 4a East View Close, Radwinter, Essex CB10 2TZ. *T:* (01799) 599443. *W:* www.graystonives.com.

**IVISON, David Malcolm;** Director, British Metallurgical Plant Constructors' Association, 1994–2002; *b* 22 March 1936; *s* of John and Ruth Ellen Ivison; *m* 1961, Lieselotte Verse; one *s* one *d*. *Educ:* King Edward VI School, Lichfield; RMA Sandhurst; Staff College, Camberley. Army, Gurkha Transport Regt, 1955–83 (Lt-Col). Tate & Lyle, 1984–85; Chief Exec., Inst. of Road Transport Engrs, 1985–89. Mem. (C) Surrey CC, 2005–18. *Recreations:* learning languages, tennis, reading. *Address:* 1 Dundaff Close, Camberley, Surrey GU15 1AF. *T:* (01276) 27778.

**IVORY, Sir Brian (Gammell),** Kt 2006; CVO 2018; CBE 1999; CA; FRSE; Chairman, Marathon Asset Management LLP, since 2011; *b* 10 April 1949; *s* of late Eric James Ivory and Alice Margaret Joan, *d* of Sir Sydney James Gammell; *m* 1981, Oona Mairi Macphie Bell-MacDonald (*see* O. M. M. Ivory); one *s* one *d*. *Educ:* Eton College; Magdalene College, Cambridge (MA). The Highland Distilleries Co., subseq. Highland Distillers plc: Dir, 1978–99; Man. Dir, 1988–94; Gp Chief Exec., 1994–97; Exec. Chm., 1997–99. Executive Chairman: Macallan Glenlivet plc, 1996–99; Scottish American Investment Co. plc, 2001–16; Retec Digital plc, 2006–13; Arcus Eur. Infrastructure Fund, 2010–; Deputy Chairman: Shawbrook Bank Ltd, 2011–15; IPSX Ltd, 2015–; Director: Rémy Cointreau SA, 1991–2014; Bank of Scotland, 1998–2007; HBOS plc, 2001–07; Orpar SA, 2003–13; Insight Investment Mgt Ltd, 2003–; Synesis Life Ltd, 2007–08. Vice-Chm., Scottish Arts Council, 1988–92; Mem., Arts Council of GB, 1988–92; Mem., Scottish Economic Council, 1996–98; Chm. of Trustees, Nat. Galleries of Scotland, 2001–09; Chm. of Trustees, Gt Steward of Scotland's Dumfries House Trust, 2010–17. Chair, Governance and Nominations Cttee, St Andrews Univ., 2007–16. Founder and Chm., Nat. Piping Centre, 1996–2018 (Jt Chm., 2018–). Mem., Royal Co. of Archers (Queen's Body Guard for Scotland), 1996–. FRSA 1993; FRSE 2001. Freeman, City of London, 1996. Paolozzi Gold Medal, Nat. Galls of Scotland, 2009. *Recreations:* the arts, travel, wild places. *E:* judy@enitar.co.uk. *Club:* New (Edinburgh).

**IVORY, James Francis;** film director; Partner in Merchant Ivory Productions, since 1961; *b* 7 June 1928; *s* of Edward Patrick Ivory and Hallie Millicent De Loney. *Educ:* Univ. of Oregon (BA Fine Arts); Univ. of Southern California (MFA Cinema). Guggenheim Fellow, 1974. Collaborator with Ruth Prawer Jhabvala and Ismail Merchant on the following films: The Householder, 1963; Shakespeare Wallah, 1965; The Guru, 1969; Bombay Talkie, 1970; Autobiography of a Princess, 1975; Roseland, 1977; Hullabaloo over Georgie and Bonnie's Pictures, 1978; The Europeans, 1979; Jane Austen in Manhattan, 1980; Quartet, 1981; Heat and Dust, 1983; The Bostonians, 1984; A Room With a View, 1986; Mr and Mrs Bridge, 1990; Howards End, 1992; The Remains of the Day, 1993; Jefferson in Paris, 1995; Surviving Picasso, 1996; A Soldier's Daughter Never Cries, 1998; The Golden Bowl, 2000; Le Divorce, 2003; The City of Your Final Destination, 2008; collaborator with Ismail Merchant (producer) on: (with Nirad Chaudhuri) Adventures of a Brown Man in Search of Civilization, 1971; (with George W. S. Trow and Michael O'Donoghue) Savages, 1972; (with Walter Marks) The Wild Party, 1975; (with Kit Hesketh-Harvey) Maurice, 1987; (with Tama Janowitz) Slaves of New York, 1989; (with Kazuo Ishiguro) The White Countess, 2006; other films: (with Terrence McNally) The Five Forty Eight, 1979; documentaries: Venice, Theme and Variations, 1957; The Sword and the Flute, 1959; The Delhi Way, 1964; (screenplay) Call Me By Your Name, 2017 (Best Adapted Screenplay, BAFTA and Academy Awards, 2018). D. W. Griffith Award, Directors Guild of America, 1995. Commandeur, Ordre des Arts et des Lettres (France), 1996. *Publications:* Autobiography of a Princess (Also Being the Adventures of an American Film Director in the Land of the Maharajas), 1975. *Recreations:* looking at pictures, Ancient Egypt and Rome. *Address:* PO Box 93, Claverack, NY 12513, USA. *T:* (office) (212) 5828049.

**IVORY, Oona Mairi Macphie, (Lady Ivory);** DL; Founder and Director, since 1996 and Joint Chairman, since 2017, National Piping Centre (Deputy Chairman, 1999–2017); *b* 21 July 1954; *d* of late Archibald Ian Bell-Macdonald and Mary Rae (*née* Macphie); *m* 1981, Brian Gammell Ivory (*see* Sir B. G. Ivory); one *s* one *d*. *Educ:* Royal Scottish Acad. of Music and Drama; King's Coll., Cambridge (MA); Royal Acad. of Music. ARCM. Dir, 1988–97, Chm., 1995–97, Scottish Ballet; Dir, RSAMD, 1989–2002. Dir, Glasgow Internat. Piping Fest., 2004–. Trustee, Sri Lanka Reconciliation Music Trust, 2010–15. FRSA 1993. DL Edinburgh, 1998. *Recreations:* the arts, sailing, wild places. *E:* judy@enitar.co.uk.

**IWAN, Dafydd;** President, Plaid Cymru, 2003–10 (Vice-President, 2001–03); *b* 24 Aug. 1943; *s* of Rev. Gerallt Jones and Elizabeth Jane Jones; *m* 1988, Bethan; two *s*; two *s* one *d* from previous marriage. *Educ:* Welsh Sch. of Architecture, Cardiff (BArch 1968). Chair, Cymdeithas yr Iaith Gymraeg, 1968–71; Dir, 1969–, Man. Dir, 1982–2004, Sain Recording Co. Organiser, Tai Gwynedd Housing Assoc., 1974–82. Mem., Gwynedd Council, 1996–2008 (Leader, Develt Portfolio, 2004–08). Hon. Fellow: Univ. of Wales, Bangor, 1998; Univ. of Wales, Aberystwyth, 1998. Hon. Mem., Gorsedd of Bards. Hon. LLD Wales, 2004. *Publications:* First Autobiography, 1983; Holl Ganeuon (song collection), 1992; Cân Dros Gymru (autobiog.), 2002; Pictorial Biography, 2005; Pobol, 2015. *Recreations:* writing, composing, art, Rugby. *Address:* Carrog, Caeathro, Caernarfon, Gwynedd LL55 2TF. *T:* (01286) 676004. *E:* dafyddiwan2@gmail.com.

**IYER, Kumar Sabapathy;** HM Diplomatic Service; Chief Economist, and Director for Economics, Foreign and Commonwealth Office, since 2019; *b* London; *s* of Sabapathy Iyer and Mahalakshmi Iyer; *m* 2004, Kathryn Ann Worth; one *s* one *d*. *Educ:* Blurton High Sch.; Stoke-on-Trent Sixth Form Coll.; University Coll., Durham Univ. (BA Hons 1st Cl. Econs); Corpus Christi Coll., Cambridge (MPhil Econs; Bank of England Schol.); Harvard Univ. (Kennedy Schol.). Teaching Fellow, Harvard Univ.; Boston Consulting Gp, until 2008; Dep. Dir, Prime Minister's Strategy Unit, No 10 Downing St, 2008–10; Dep. Dir, Strategy, Planning and Budget, 2010–12, Hd, Financial Sector Interventions, 2012–13, HM Treasury; Dep. High Comr, Mumbai and Dir Gen., Economics, Trade and Investment, India, 2013–17; Sen. Partner, Oliver Wyman, 2017–19. Vis. Academic, Hertford Coll., Oxford, 2017–19. *Publications:* (contrib.) The Internet Revolution: a global perspective, 2003. *Recreations:* cricket, chess. *Address:* c/o Foreign and Commonwealth Office, King Charles Street, SW1A 2AH.

**IZZA, Michael Donald McCartney,** FCA; Chief Executive, Institute of Chartered Accountants in England and Wales, since 2006; *b* 13 Dec. 1960; *s* of late Salvatore Izza and of Jean Izza (*née* McCartney); *m* 1991, Gillian Johnston; one *s* one *d*. *Educ:* Thornleigh Salesian Coll., Bolton; Durham Univ. (BA Hons Law). ACA 1987, FCA 2007. Coopers & Lybrand, 1983–89; John Labatt Ltd, 1989–96 (Man. Dir, John Labatt Retail, 1992–96); Spring Group plc, 1996–2000: Man. Dir, Spring Skills, 1996–97; Divl Man. Dir, 1997–98; Actg Gp Finance Dir, 1999–2000; Divl Dir, Professional Services and Exec. Dir, Support Services, Carlisle Support Services, 2001; Institute of Chartered Accountants in England and Wales, 2002–: Exec. Dir, Finance and Ops, 2002–03; Chief Operating Officer, 2004–06. Chm., HM Treasury cttees to appoint ind. valuers for financial instns; mem., Govt cttees and gps. Trustee, Moorfields Eye Charity. *Recreations:* running, hill walking, gardening, Bolton Wanderers FC, history, philately. *Address:* Institute of Chartered Accountants in England and Wales, Chartered Accountants' Hall, PO Box 433, Moorgate Place, EC2P 2BJ. *T:* (020) 7920 8419. *E:* michael.izza@icaew.com.

# J

**JABALÉ, Rt Rev. (John) Mark,** OSB; Bishop of Menevia, (RC), 2001–08, now Bishop Emeritus; Parish Priest, Holy Trinity Catholic Church, Chipping Norton, 2008–14; *b* 16 Oct. 1933; *s* of John and Arlette Jabalé. *Educ:* Belmont Abbey Sch.; Fribourg Univ. (LèsL); St Mary's Coll., London (DipEd). Belmont Abbey School: Games Master and House Master, 1963–69; Headmaster, 1969–83; built Monastery of the Incarnation, in Tambogrande, Perú; Prior, 1986–93, Abbot, 1993–2000, Belmont Abbey; Bp Coadjutor of Menevia, 2000–01. Steward, Henley Royal Regatta, 1985–. *Recreations:* computers, rowing. *Address:* 14 Egerton Gardens, NW4 4BA. *Club:* Leander (Henley-on-Thames).

**JACK, Rt Hon. Alister (William);** PC 2019; DL; MP (C) Dumfries and Galloway, since 2017; Secretary of State, Scotland Office, since 2019; *b* Dumfries, 1963; *s* of David Jack and Jean Jack; *m* 1987, Ann Hodgson; one *s* two *d*. *Educ:* Glenalmond Coll. Dir, Field and Lawn Ltd, 1986–2017; Man. Dir, Aardvark Self Storage, 1995–2002; Partner, Courance Farms and Dairy, 2003–; Director: Armadillo Self Storage, 2003–08; Alligator Self Storage, 2008–14; Chairman: Edinburgh Self Storage Ltd, 2006–17; Galloway Woodlands, 2012–17; Fulling Mill Ltd, 2013–. Non-exec. Dir, James Gordon (Engrs) Ltd, 2003–08. PPS to Leader, H of L, 2018–19; an Asst Govt Whip, 2019; a Lord Comr of HM Treasury (Govt Whip), 2019. Mem., Treasury Select Cttee, 2017–18. Contested (C) Tweeddale, Ettrick and Lauderdale, 1997. Vice-Chm., Scottish Cons. Party, 1997–2001. Chairman: River Annan and Dist Salmon Fishery Bd, and River Annan Trust, 2013–; Fisheries Mgt Scotland, 2016–18; non-exec. Dir, Atlantic Salmon Trust, 2016–. Mem., Queen's Bodyguard for Scotland (Royal Co. of Archers), 2007–. *Recreations:* shooting, fly fishing, music, fine wine. *Address:* House of Commons, SW1A 0AA. *T:* (020) 7219 2994. *E:* alister.jack.mp@parliament.uk.

**JACK, David M.;** *see* Morton Jack.

**JACK, Ian Grant;** writer and editor; columnist, Guardian, since 2001; *b* 7 Feb. 1945; *s* of Henry Jack and Isabella Jack (*née* Gillespie); *m* 1st, 1979, Aparna Bagchi (marr. diss. 1992); 2nd, 1998, Rosalind Sharpe; one *s* one *d*. *Educ:* Dunfermline High School, Fife. Trainee journalist, Glasgow Herald, 1965; reporter, Cambuslang Advertiser and East Kilbride News, 1966; journalist, Scottish Daily Express, 1966–70; Sunday Times, 1970–86; Observer and Vanity Fair (NY), 1986–88; Dep. Editor, 1989–91, Exec. Editor, 1991–92, Editor, 1992–95, Independent on Sunday; Editor, Granta, 1995–2007. FRSL 2009. Journalist of the Year, Granada TV What The Papers Say award, 1985; Colour Magazine Writer of the Year, 1985, Reporter of the Year, 1988, British Press Awards; Nat. Newspaper Editor of the Year, Newspaper Focus Awards, 1992; Edgar Wallace Award, London Press Club, 2019. *Publications:* Before the Oil Ran Out, 1987; The Crash That Stopped Britain, 2001; The Country Formerly Known as Great Britain, 2009; Mofussil Junction, 2013. *Address:* c/o Rogers, Coleridge and White, 20 Powis Mews, W11 1JN. *Clubs:* Academy; India International Centre (New Delhi).

**JACK, Prof. (James) Julian (Bennett),** PhD; FRS 1997; Professor of Physiology, University of Oxford, 1996–2003; Fellow of University College, Oxford, 1968–2018, now Emeritus; *b* Invercargill, NZ, 25 March 1936. *Educ:* Univ. of Otago (MMedSci, PhD); Magdalen Coll., Oxford (BM 1963) MA). Rhodes Scholarship, 1960–63; House Officer, Radcliffe Infirmary, Oxford, 1963–64; Foulerton Gift Res. Fellow, Royal Soc., 1964–68; University of Oxford: Weir Jun. Res. Fellow in Natural Sci., UC, 1966; Lectr in Physiology, 1970–94; Reader in Cellular Neurosci., 1994–96. Visiting Professor: UCL, 2003–10; KCL, 2012–. Chm., Sci. Adv. Bd, Syntaxin plc, 2005–14; Member, Scientific Advisory Board: Rose Kennedy Center, NY, 2002–; OXION, Oxford, 2006–13; Coco Therapeutics, 2013–14. Mem. Council, Action Res., 1988–91; Chm. Res. Panel, Multiple Sclerosis Soc., 2001–10; Gov., Wellcome Trust, 1987–2004 (Dep. Chm. of Govs, 1994–99); Trustee, Brain Res. Trust, 2006–13. Founder FMedSci 1998; FRCP 1999. Hon. FRSNZ 1999. Hon. DSc Otago. *Address:* 24 Claylands Road, SW8 1NZ. *T:* (020) 7582 3085.

**JACK, Rt Hon. (John) Michael,** CBE 2015; PC 1997; Chairman: G's Fresh, since 2017; Topps Tiles plc, 2011–15 (non-executive Director, 2000–15); *b* 17 Sept. 1946; *m* 1976, Alison Jane Musgrave; two *s*. *Educ:* Bradford Grammar Sch.; Bradford Tech. Coll.; Leicester Univ. BA(Econs); MPhil. Shipping, subseq. Advertising, Depts, Procter & Gamble, 1970–75; PA to Sir Derek Rayner, Marks & Spencer, 1975–80; Sales Dir, L. O. Jeffs Ltd, 1980–87. Mem., Mersey RHA, 1984–87. Contested (C) Newcastle upon Tyne Central, Feb. 1974. MP (C) Fylde, 1987–2010. PPS to Minister of State, DOE, 1988–89, to Minister of Agric., Fisheries and Food, 1989–90; Parly Under Sec. of State, DSS, 1990–92; Minister of State: Home Office, 1992–93; MAFF, 1993–95; Financial Sec. to HM Treasury, 1995–97; Opposition front bench spokesman on health, 1997, on agric., fisheries and food, 1998. Member: Agriculture Select Cttee, 2000–01; Envmt, Food and Rural Affairs Select Cttee, 2001–07 (Chm., 2003–10); Tax Law Rewrite Steering Cttee, 1999–2010; Exec., 1922 Cttee, 2000–03. Sec., Cons. Back-bench Transport Cttee, 1987–88; Chm., Cons. Back-bench sub-cttee on Horticulture and Markets, 1987–88; Sec., Cons. NW Members Gp, 1988–90. Nat. Chm., Young Conservatives, 1976–77. Chm., Office of Tax Simplification, 2010–15. Agric. and Food Advr, HSBC Bank, 2010–16. Lay Canon, Blackburn Cathedral, 2008–. Trustee: MedAlert, 1990–2015; Lytham Community Sports Assoc., 1997; Linking Envmt and Farming, 2014–17. Vice-Pres., Think Green, 1989–90; Pres., Nat. Fruit Show, 2009–; Judge, BBC Food and Farming Awards, 2010–11. Chair, Govs, RAU, 2018–. *Recreations:* cycling, mountain biking, olive tree cultivation, vegetable growing, motor sport, boules. *E:* michaeljack17@gmail.com.

**JACK, Julian;** *see* Jack, J. J. B.

**JACK, Lorna Burn,** CA; Chief Executive, Law Society of Scotland, since 2009; *b* Fraserburgh, 20 Aug. 1962; *d* of George Buchan Jack and Mary Strachan Jack; *m* Lucas Hooijenga. *Educ:* Univ. of Aberdeen (MA Accountancy and Econs); Harvard Business Sch.; Exec. Develt Prog., Inst. of Chartered Accountants. CA 1984. Audit Senior, Arthur Andersen & Co., 1982–85; Finance Dir, Aberdeen Cable Services Ltd, 1985–89; Scottish Enterprise: Hd of Food Sector Team, 1989–97; Hd of Global Companies Research, 1997–98; Dir of Ops and Dep. Chief Exec., 1998–2000, Chief Exec., 2000–02, Scottish Enterprise Forth Valley; Pres. Americas, Scottish Develt Internat., 2002–08. Non-exec. Dir, Highlands and Islands Airport Ltd, 2014– (Chair, 2017–). Trustee and Treas., McConnell Internat. Foundn, 2013–. Ind. Mem. Court, Univ. of Aberdeen, 2017–. *Recreations:* ski-ing, reading, music. *Address:* Law Society of Scotland, Atria One, 144 Morrison Street, Edinburgh EH3 8EX. *T:* (0131) 226 7411, *Fax:* (0131) 225 2934.

**JACK, Sir Malcolm (Roy),** KCB 2011; PhD; FSA; FRAS; author, historian and lecturer; Clerk and Chief Executive of the House of Commons, 2006–11; *b* 17 Dec. 1946; *s* of late Iain Ross Jack and Alicia Maria Eça da Silva, Hong Kong. *Educ:* school in Hong Kong; Univ. of Liverpool (Hong Kong Govt Scholar; BA Hons 1st Class); LSE, Univ. of London (PhD). A Clerk, House of Commons, 1967–; Private Sec. to Chm. of Ways and Means, 1977–80; Clerk to Agriculture Select Cttee, 1980–88; Clerk of Supply, 1989–91; Clerk of Standing Cttees, 1991–95; Sec. to H of C Commn, 1995–2001; Clerk of the Journals, 2001–03; Clerk to Jt Cttee on H of L Reform, 2002–03; Clerk of Legislation, 2003–06. Presidential Advr, OSCE Parly Assembly, 1992–96. Vis. Prof. (Enlightenment Studies), Nanyang Technol Univ., Singapore, 2015. President: Beckford Soc., 2015– (Chm., 1996–2015); Johnson Club, 2016– (Sec., 1998–2016); Constitution Soc., 2017– (Mem., Adv. Bd, 2013–17). FSA 2012; FRAS 2018. *Publications:* The Social and Political Thought of Bernard Mandeville, 1987; Corruption and Progress: the eighteenth-century debate, 1989; (ed with Anita Desai) The Turkish Embassy Letters of Lady Mary Wortley Montagu, 1993; (ed) Vathek and Other Stories: a William Beckford Reader, 1993; (ed) The Episodes of Vathek of William Beckford, 1994; William Beckford: an English Fidalgo, 1996; Sintra: a glorious Eden, 2002; Lisbon: city of the sea, 2007; (ed) Erskine May's Parliamentary Practice, 24th edn, 2011; To the Fairest Cape: European encounters in the Cape of Good Hope, 2019; articles and essays in books, learned and literary jls; reviews in TLS, APN Lisbon, NLB S Africa. *Recreations:* thinking for oneself (Enlightenment), empires adrift, Johnsoniana, oriental ceramics, Africana, escaping southwards. *E:* Malcolm.Jack@btinternet.com. *Club:* East India.

**JACK, Rt Hon. Michael;** *see* Jack, Rt Hon. J. M.

**JACK, Sir Raymond (Evan),** Kt 2001; a Judge of the High Court, Queen's Bench Division, 2001–11; *b* 13 Nov. 1942; *s* of Evan and Charlotte Jack; *m* 1976, Elizabeth Alison, *d* of Rev. Canon James Seymour Denis Mansel, KCVO; one *s* two *d*. *Educ:* Rugby; Trinity Coll., Cambridge (MA). Called to Bar, Inner Temple, 1966, Bencher, 2000; QC 1982; a Recorder, 1989–91; a Circuit Judge, 1991–2001; Judge of the Bristol Mercantile Court, 1994–2001. Gov., Salisbury NHS Foundn Trust, 2012–. *Publications:* Documentary Credits, 1991, 4th edn 2009. *Recreations:* horses, words and wood. *Address:* Serle Court, 6 New Square, Lincoln's Inn, WC2A 3QS.

**JACK, Simon Michael; His Honour Judge Jack;** a Circuit Judge, North Eastern Circuit, since 2004; *b* 29 Oct. 1951; *s* of Donald Fingland Jack and Hilary Jack (*née* Gresham); *m* 1st, 1973, Christine Anne King (separated 2004; marr. diss. 2010); one *s* two *d*; 2nd, 2013, Sarah Louise Fearon. *Educ:* Richard Hale Sch., Hertford; Winchester Coll.; Trinity Coll., Cambridge (BA (Langs and Law) 1973). Called to the Bar, Middle Temple, 1974; in practice as barrister, N Eastern Circuit, 1975–2003 (specialised in criminal and family law, and civil actions involving police). *Recreations:* triathlon, sailing, ski-ing, cinema. *Address:* Kingston upon Hull Combined Court Centre, Lowgate, Hull HU1 2EZ. *Clubs:* Barracuda Triathlon; Hull Thursday Road.

**JACK, Stuart Duncan Macdonald,** CVO 1994; HM Diplomatic Service, retired; Governor, Cayman Islands, 2005–09; *b* 8 June 1949; *s* of William Harris Jack and Edith Florence Jack (*née* Coker); *m* 1977, Mariko Nobechi; one *s* two *d*. *Educ:* Westcliff High Sch. for Boys; Merton Coll., Oxford (BA 1971). VSO, Laos, 1971; joined HM Diplomatic Service, 1972: Eastern European and Soviet Dept, FO, 1972–73; Tokyo, 1974–79; Far Eastern Dept, FCO, 1979–81; Moscow, 1981–84; on secondment with Bank of England, 1984–85; Tokyo, 1985–89; Overseas Inspector, 1989–92; Consul Gen., St Petersburg, 1992–95; Hd of Research and Analysis, FCO, 1996–99; Minister, Tokyo, 1999–2003; FCO, 2003–05. *Recreations:* reading, photography, music.

**JACK, Dr William Hugh,** CB 1988; management consultant, 1994–2005; Comptroller and Auditor General, Northern Ireland Audit Office, 1989–94; *b* 18 Feb. 1929; *s* of John Charles Jack and Martha Ann Jack; *m* 1953, Beatrice Jane Thompson; three *s* one *d*. *Educ:* Ballymena Acad.; Univ. of Edinburgh (BSc(For); PhD); Queen's Univ., Belfast (BScEcon). MICFor 1959. Min. of Agriculture for NI, 1948–49; Colonial Forest Service, Gold Coast/Ghana, 1949–59 (Conservator of Forests, 1957); Dept of Agriculture for NI, 1959–89 (Permanent Sec., 1983). CCMI. *Publications:* various articles in forestry research and economic jls. *Recreations:* walking, reading. *Address:* 22 Viewfort Park, Belfast BT17 9JY.

**JACKAMAN, Michael Clifford John;** Chairman of Grand Appeal, Royal Hospital for Sick Children, Bristol, 1995–2001; Chairman, Allied Domecq (formerly Allied-Lyons) plc, 1991–96 (Vice-Chairman, 1988–91); *b* 7 Nov. 1935; *s* of Air Cdre Clifford Thomas Jackaman, OBE and Lily Margaret Jackaman (*née* Turner); *m* 1960, Valerie Jane Pankhurst; one *s* one *d*. *Educ:* Felsted Sch., Essex; Jesus Coll., Cambridge (MA Hons). Lieut RA, 1955–56. Dep. Man. Dir, Harveys of Bristol, 1976–78; Marketing Dir, Allied Breweries, 1978–83; Dir, Allied Domecq (formerly Allied Lyons) plc, 1978–96; Chairman: Showerings Vine Products and Whiteways, 1983–86; Hiram Walker Allied Vintners, 1986–91; John Harvey & Sons Ltd, 1983–93; Mem., Council of Admin, Château Latour, 1983–93; Director: Fintex of London Ltd, 1986–92; Rank Orgn, 1992–97; Kleinwort Benson Gp, 1994–98. Governor, Bristol Polytechnic, 1988–91. Dir, Th. Royal, Bath, 1999–2005. Founder Mem., Wine Guild of UK. Vice Pres., Internat. Wine and Spirits Comp. Liveryman, Distillers' Co.; Grand Master, Keepers of the Quaich (Scotland), 1996; Commanderie des Bontemps du Médoc et des Graves (France); Confraria do Vinho do Porto (Portugal). Hon. DBA UWE, 1993. *Publications:* contribs to periodicals, incl. Arts Review. *Recreations:* Budleigh Salterton Literary Festival, Iford Arts, thrown and handmade pottery, opera, walking. *Club:* Army and Navy.

**JACKLIN, Anthony,** CBE 1990 (OBE 1970); professional golfer, 1962–85 and 1988–99; Director of Golf, San Roque Club, 1988–90; golf course designer, since 2002; *b* 7 July 1944; *s* of Arthur David Jacklin; *m* 1st, 1966, Vivien (*d* 1988); two *s* one *d*; 2nd, 1988,

Astrid May Waagen; one s, one step s one step d. Successes include: British Assistant Pro Championship, 1965; Pringle Tournament, 1967; Dunlop Masters, 1967; Greater Jacksonville Open, USA, 1968; British Open Championship, 1969; US Open Championship, 1970; Benson & Hedges, 1971; British Professional Golfers Assoc., 1972, 1982; Gtr Jacksonville Open, 1972; Bogota Open, 1973 and 1974; Italian Open, 1973; Dunlop Masters, 1973; Scandinavian Open, 1975; Kerrygold International, 1976; English National PGA Championship, 1977; German Open, 1979; Jersey Open, 1981; PGA Champion, 1982; Ryder Cup player, 1967–80, Team Captain, Europe, 1983–89; Champion Tour wins: First of America Classic, 1994; Franklin Quest, 1995. Life Mem., PGA (Hon. Life Mem., European Tournament Players Div.). Inducted, World Golf Hall of Fame, 2002. *Publications:* Golf with Tony Jacklin, 1969; The Price of Success, 1979; (with Peter Dobereiner) Jacklin's Golfing Secrets, 1983; Tony Jacklin: the first forty years, 1985; (with Bill Robertson) Your Game and Mine, 1990; Tony Jacklin: my autobiography, 2006. *Recreations:* shooting, marquetry. *Clubs:* Royal & Ancient Golf (Hon. Mem., 2002); Potters Bar Golf; Hon. Mem. of others.

**JACKLIN, Susan Elizabeth;** QC 2006; **Her Honour Judge Jacklin;** a Circuit Judge, since 2018; b 4 Aug. 1958; d of Joseph and Alice Jacklin. *Educ:* Winckley Sq. Convent Sch., Preston; Univ. of Durham (BA Hons Law); Inns of Court Sch. of Law. Called to the Bar, Inner Temple, 1980, Bencher, 2011; in practice at the Bar, 1982–2018; a Recorder, 1998–2018. Advocacy Trainer, Inner Temple and Western Circuit, 1996–. Ext. Examr, Bar Vocational Course, UWE, 2002–06. Chm., Access to the Bar Cttee, 2011–13, Mem., 2012, Co-Chair, Remuneration Cttee, 2016–17, Bar Council; Vice-Chm., 2012–13, Chm., 2014–15, Family Law Bar Assoc. *Recreations:* international travel, walking, cooking and entertaining. *Address:* Barnet Civil and Family Courts Centre, St Mary's Court, Regents Park Road, N3 1BQ. *Club:* Athenæum.

**JACKLIN, William, (Bill),** RA 1991 (ARA 1989); b 1 Jan. 1943; s of Harold and Alice Jacklin; m 1st, 1979, Lesley Sarina Berman (marr. diss. 1993); 2nd, 1993, Janet Ann Russo. *Educ:* Walthamstow Sch. of Art; Royal College of Art (NDD, MARCA). Part-time Lectr at various art colleges, 1967–75; Arts Council Bursary, 1975; lives and works in New York and Newport, RI, 1985–; Artist in Residence, British Council, Hong Kong, 1993–94. One man exhibns, London galleries, 1970– (incl. Marlborough Fine Art, 1980, 1983, 1988, 1992, 1994, 1995, 1997, 2000, 2004, 2005, 2007, 2008, 2013, 2016, 2019), USA, 1985– (incl. Marlborough Gall., NY, 1985, 1987, 1990, 1997, 1999, 2002, 2003, 2007, 2012, 2017, 2018), Hong Kong, 1995, Marlborough Gall., Monaco 2009; retrospective exhibn, Mus. of Modern Art, Oxford, 1992; graphic retrospective, RA, 2016; frequent shows in internat. exhibns; works in major collections including Arts Council, British Mus., Metropolitan Mus. NY, Mus. of Modern Art NY, Tate Gall., V&A. *Publications:* catalogues to one man exhibns, London and New York; *relevant publication:* Bill Jacklin (monograph), by John Russell-Taylor, 1997; Bill Jacklin: graphics 1961–2016 (monograph), by Nancy Campbell, 2016; Bill Jacklin: New York (monograph), by Michael Peppiatt, 2016; *Recreation:* planting trees. *Address:* c/o Marlborough Fine Art, 6 Albemarle Street, W1S 4BY. *T:* (020) 7629 5161, (Bill Jacklin) 4016626582. *Clubs:* Arts, Chelsea Arts.

**JACKLING, Sir Roger Tustin,** KCB 2001 (CB 1995); CBE 1982; Director, Defence Academy of the UK, 2002–05; b 23 Nov. 1943; s of Sir Roger Jackling, GCMG and late Joan (née Tustin) (Lady Jackling); m 1976, Jane Allen Pritchard; two s. *Educ:* Wellington Coll.; New York Univ. (BA); Jesus Coll., Oxford. Asst Principal, MoD, 1969, Principal, 1972; London Executive Prog., London Business Sch., 1974; Sec. of State's Office, MoD, 1976–79; Asst Sec. and Hd of DS11, 1979–82; Prime Minister's Office, 1983; Head of DS7/Resources and Programmes (Army), MoD, 1983–85; Fellow, Center for Internat. Affairs, Harvard Univ., 1985–86; Principal, CS Coll., 1986–89; Asst Under-Sec. of State (Progs), MoD, 1989–91; Dep. Under-Sec. of State (Resources, Progs and Finance), MoD, 1991–96; Second Perm. Under Sec. of State, MoD, 1996–2002. Visiting Professor: War Studies Dept, KCL, 2002–12; Durham Business Sch., 2003–13; Cranfield Univ. at Shrivenham, 2003–10. Trustee: Imperial War Mus., 1997–2003; RAF Mus., 2002–11. Member Council: RIPA, 1987–92; RUSI, 1993–2005; Chairman: Toc H, 2004–06; Internat. Military Services, 2005–; Council of Voluntary Welfare Work, 2005–15; non-exec. Dir, Moorfield Eye Hosp., 2008–15. Member, Advisory Board: Durham Business Sch., 1999–2010; Kent Business Sch., 2005–15 (Chm., 2008–15). Chm. Govs, Purcell Sch., 2012–. Liveryman, Tallow Chandlers' Co., 2011. *Recreations:* books, theatre, opera, playing golf, watching cricket. *Clubs:* Garrick; Highgate Golf, Faversham Golf.

**JACKSON, Adam Edward;** Director, Public Affairs and Brexit Advisory (formerly Head, Public Affairs, then Director Public Affairs and Policy) Grant Thornton UK LLP, since 2014; b 5 March 1969; s of Michael and Patricia Jackson; m 2011, Holly Hodges. *Educ:* University Coll. London (BA Modern Hist.; MA Legal and Pol Theory). Industry and Consumer Affairs Attaché, UK Perm. Repn to EU, Brussels, 1994–96; Number Portability Manager, Oftel, 1996–97; Department of Trade and Industry: Asst Dir, Regl Policy, 1997–99; Hd, Strategic Communications and Speechwriting, 2000–02; Dep. Dir, Sen. Staff Mgt, 2002–03; Dir, Business Planning, 2003–05; Dir of Finance, 2005–06; Tesco: Dir of Public Policy, 2006–08; Dir, Climate Change Prog., 2008; Dir, Enterprise, BERR, then BIS, 2008–13; led review of DfT Rail Gp, 2013; Dir, Change and Capability, Rail Exec., DfT, 2013–14. Mem. Bd, London Retail Consortium, 2007–08. Trustee, Watermans Arts Centre, 2014–. MCIPR 2014. *Recreations:* cooking and eating, real ale, gardening, walking Dolly and Spud the dogs. *Address:* Grant Thornton UK LLP, 30 Finsbury Square, EC2A 1AG. *T:* (020) 7728 2385. *E:* adam.e.jackson@uk.gt.com.

**JACKSON, Alison Mary;** artist, photographer, film-maker; b 15 May 1960; d of George Hulbert Mowbray Jackson and Catherine Mary Jackson (née Harvey Kelly). *Educ:* Chelsea Coll. of Art (BA Hons Fine Art Sculpture); Royal Coll. of Art (MA Fine Art Photography). *Solo art exhibitions* include: Richard Salmon Gall., London, 1999, 2000, 2003; Jerwood Space, London, 2001; Musée de la Photographie à Charleroi, Brussels, 2002; Le Mois de la Photo, Montreal, Photo London, Pro-gram Gall., 2004; Julie Saul Gall., NY, 2005; M&B Gall., Los Angeles, 2007; Hamiltons Gall., London, 2008; Mitchell Liby, Glasgow, 2009; Ben Brown Fine Arts, 2011; *group art exhibitions* include: Edinburgh Fest., Art 2000, London, 2000; Paris Photo, Louvre, Photographers' Gall./Julie Saul Gall., NY, 2002–05; Internat. Center of Photography (ICP), NY, Musée de l'Elysée, Lausanne, 2003; Photo London, Hayward Gall., London, 2004; KunstForum, Vienna, 2005–06; Liverpool Biennial, Tate, 2008; New Art Gall. Walsall, 2008; Tate Britain, 2010; MOMA, San Francisco, 2010; Tate Modern, 2010; RA Summer Exhibn, 2018. *Television:* creator, writer, dir, Doubletake, 2001–03 (BAFTA Award for Innovation, 2002); producer/dir, Saturday Night Live, USA, 2004–05; writer and director: Royal Wedding Special, 2005; The Secret Election, 2005; Sven: the coach, the cash and his lovers, 2006; Blaired Vision, 2007; The South Bank Show: Alison Jackson on Andy Warhol, 2009; dir, Tony Blair Rock Star, 2006; The Alison Jackson Review, 2011; Private Lies, 2012. Schweppes advertising campaign, 2001–03 (Best of the Best Award for Photography, IPA, 2003; Creative Circle Award, 2002) and 2007. Ambassador, Spinal Injuries Assoc. Photographers' Gall. Award, London, 1999; Infinity Award for Photography, ICP, NY, 2004. *Publications:* Private, 2003; Confidential, 2007; Up the Aisle, 2011; Exposed! 2011, 2011. *Recreation:* tennis. *Address:* c/o Kevin Cooper, CAA, 2000 Avenue of the Stars, Los Angeles, CA 90212, USA. *T:* (424) 2884545.

**JACKSON, Alison Muriel;** Team Leader, Public Issues, Methodist Church, 2005–08; Director, Wales Office, 1999–2005; b 24 Sept. 1947; d of John McIntyre and Muriel McIntyre (née Brookes); m 1970, Alan D. Jackson; one s. *Educ:* Sydenham High Sch., GPDST; St Anne's Coll., Oxford (BA (Lit. Hum.) 1970, MA 1976); Bristol Univ. (Dip. Adult Educn (ext.) 1982). Land Registry, Gloucester, 1983–86; Welsh Office: Local Govt Finance, 1986–88; Private Sec. to Perm. Sec., 1988–90; Urban Affairs Div., 1990–93; Agric. Div., 1993–98. Panel Chair, Judicial Appts Commn, 2005–17. Chm., Church Action on Poverty, 2015–. Methodist Local Preacher, 1976–. *Recreations:* walking, cooking.

**JACKSON, (Ann) Mererid;** see Edwards, A. M.

**JACKSON, Sir Barry (Trevor),** Kt 2001; MS, FRCS; Serjeant Surgeon to the Queen, 1991–2001; Consultant Surgeon: St Thomas' Hospital, 1973–2001; Queen Victoria Hospital, East Grinstead, 1977–98; King Edward VII Hospital for Officers, 1983–2002; President, Royal Society of Medicine, 2002–04; b 7 July 1936; er s of Arthur Stanley Jackson and Violet May (née Fry); m 1962, Sheila May Wood; two s one d. *Educ:* Sir George Monoux Grammar Sch.; King's College London (FKC 2012); Westminster Med. Sch. (Entrance Scholar). MB, BS 1963; MRCS, LRCP 1963; MS 1972; FRCS 1967; FRCP 1999; FRCSGlas 1999. Down Bros Ltd, 1952–54; RAF 1954–56; junior surgical appts, Gordon Hosp.; St James' Hosp., Balham, St Peter's Hosp., Chertsey, St Helier Hosp., Carshalton, St Thomas' Hosp. Surgeon to the Royal Household, 1983–91; Hon. Consultant in Surgery to the Army, 1990–2006. Royal College of Surgeons: Arris & Gale Lectr, 1973; Vicary Lectr, 1994; Bradshaw Lectr, 1998; Examr Primary FRCS, 1977–83; Mem. Court of Examrs, 1983–89; Mem. Council, 1991–2001; Pres., 1998–2001; Mem., Court of Patrons, 2008–; Asst Editor 1984–91, Editor, 1992–97, Annals RCS; Pres., Assoc. of Surgeons of GB and Ireland, 1994–95 (Mem. Council, 1982–85; Hon. Sec., 1986–91; Vice Pres., 1993–94); Mem. Council, RSocMed, 1987–92 (Pres., Sect. of Coloproctology, 1991–92); Steven's Lect. for the Laity, 2001; Stuart Lectr, 2005); Mem., GMC, 1999–2003. Pres., British Acad. Forensic Scis, 2005–07. External examr in surgery: Khartoum, 1981, 1997; Ibadan, 1982; Colombo, 1984, 1988; Abu Dhabi, 1989. Mem., W Lambeth HA, 1982–83; Special Trustee: St Thomas' Hosp., 1982–84, 1994–99; Guy's Hosp., 1996–99; Trustee: Smith & Nephew Foundn, 1995–2002; Hunterian Collection, 2004– (Chm., 2008–14); Refresh, 2005–16 (Chm., 2006–16); Surgical Foundn, 2009–13; Bowel and Cancer Res., 2012–16 (Chm., 2012–15; Patron, 2016–). Chm., SE Thames Regional Med. Adv. Cttee, 1983–87. Mem. Council of Govs, UMDS of Guy's and St Thomas' Hosps, 1989–94. Mem. Council, Imperial Soc. of Kts Bachelor, 2012–16. President: Royal Med. Benevolent Fund, 2002–08; Med. Artists Assoc. of GB, 2005–; Patron, Bowel Disease Res. Foundn, 2010–. Liveryman, Barbers' Co. (Master, 2003–04; Charles Bernard Lectr, 2007). Hon. FRCSI, 1999; Hon. FRCSEd, 1999; Hon. FDSRCS, 1999; Hon. FACS, 2000; Hon. FRACS, 2000; Hon. FRCSCan, 2003; Hon. FRSocMed 2005. Hon. DSc Hull, 2001. *Publications:* contribs to surgical jls and textbooks (surgery of gastro-intestinal tract). *Recreations:* book collecting, reading, medical history, music, especially opera, cryptic crosswords. *T:* (020) 8399 3157. *E:* barryjck7@aol.com. *Club:* Garrick.

**JACKSON, Betty,** CBE 2007 (MBE 1987); RDI 1988; Design Director, Betty Jackson Ltd, since 1981; b 24 June 1949; d of Arthur and Phyllis Gertrude Jackson; m 1985, David Cohen; one s one d. *Educ:* Bacup and Rawtenstall Grammar Sch.; Birmingham Coll. of Art (DipAD fashion and textiles). Freelance fashion illustrator, 1971–73; design asst, 1973–75; chief designer, Quorum, 1975–81. Part-time Tutor, 1982–90, Vis. Prof., 1998–, RCA. Fellow: Birmingham Polytechnic, 1989; Univ. of Central Lancs, 1992. Trustee: V&A Mus., 2005–12; Intoart, 2014–. Mem. Bd, Creative Skillset, 2010–. Patron, Smartworks, 2010–. Master, Faculty of RDI, 2015–. Hon. Fellow: RCA, 1989; Univ. of Bournemouth, 2017. DUniv Huddersfield, 2012; Hon. Dr: Norwich Univ. of Arts, 2017; Univ. of the Arts London. Awards include: British Designer of the Year, Harvey Nichols and British Fashion Council, 1985; Viyella, 1987; Fil d'Or, Internat. Linen, 1989; Contemporary Designer of the Year, British Fashion Awards, 1999; Lifetime Achievement Award, Drapers Record, 2015. *Address:* Betty Jackson Ltd, 30 Ashchurch Park Villas, W12 9SP. *T:* (020) 8354 0145. *E:* info@bettyjackson.com. *Clubs:* Groucho, Chelsea Arts, Soho House, Ivy.

**JACKSON, Very Rev. Brandon Donald;** Dean of Lincoln, 1989–97, now Emeritus; b 11 Aug. 1934; s of Herbert and Millicent Jackson; m 1958, Mary Lindsay, 2nd d of John and Helen Philip; two s one d. *Educ:* Stockport School; Liverpool Univ.; St Catherine's Coll. and Wycliffe Hall, Oxford (LLB, DipTh). Curate: Christ Church, New Malden, Surrey, 1958–61; St George, Leeds, 1961–65; Vicar, St Peter, Shipley, Yorks, 1965–77; Provost of Bradford Cathedral, 1977–89. Mem., Gen. Synod, 1970–77, 1980–89. Religious Adviser to Yorkshire Television, 1969–79; Church Commissioner, 1971–73; Mem., Marriage Commn, 1975–78; Examining Chaplain to Bishop of Bradford, 1974–80. Chm., Wensleydale CPRE, 1998–2005. Mem., Ind. Monitoring Bd, HM Prison Gartree, 2008–13. Member Council: Wycliffe Hall, Oxford, 1971–85; St John's Coll., Nottingham, 1987–89; Governor: Harrogate College, 1974–86; Bradford Girls' GS, 1977–81; Bradford Grammar Sch., 1977–89; Bishop Grosseteste Coll., Lincoln, 1989–97; Lincoln Christ's Hosp. Sch., 1989–97. Hon. DLitt Bradford, 1990. *Recreations:* sport (mainly watching), Sale RFC (former playing member), long suffering supporter of Man. City, cycling, fell-walking, fishing, enjoying grandchildren, reading, playing the cornet in brass bands (Mem., 60s Club Band). *Address:* 1 Kingston Way, Market Harborough, Leics LE16 7XB. *T:* (01858) 462425. *E:* brandon.j1@btinternet.com.

**JACKSON, Caroline Frances;** historian, environmental consultant and speaker, since 2009; Member (C) South West Region, England, European Parliament, 1999–2009 (Wiltshire, 1984–94; Wiltshire North and Bath, 1994–99); b 5 Nov. 1946; d of G. H. Harvey; m 1975, Robert Victor Jackson, qv; one s decd. *Educ:* School of St Clare, Penzance; St Hugh's and Nuffield Colleges, Oxford. MA, DPhil. Elizabeth Wordsworth Research Fellow, St Hugh's College, Oxford, 1972. Oxford City Councillor, 1970–73; contested (C) Birmingham, Erdington, 1974. European Parliament: Secretariat of Cons. Group, 1974–84; Chm., Envmt, Consumer Protection and Public Health Cttee, 1999–2004. Chm., Inst. for European Envmt Policy, 2006–10; Pres., Envmtl Protection UK, 2010–12; Mem., Foresight Adv. Council, GDF Suez Envmt (formerly SITA), 2009–13. Dir, Peugeot Talbot (UK) Ltd, 1987–99. Mem., Nat. Consumer Council, 1982–84. *Publications:* A Student's Guide to Europe, 1988; Europe's Environment, 1989; The End of the Throwaway Society, 1998; Playing by the Green Rules, 2000; Britain's Waste: the lessons we can learn from Europe, 2006; Diary of Captain Primrose, South Africa 1851–53, 2016. *Recreations:* golf, playing the piano, painting. *Address:* New House, Hanney Road, Southmoor, Abingdon, Oxon OX13 5HR. *T:* (01865) 821243. *E:* contactcfjackson@gmail.com. *W:* www.drcarolinejackson.com.

**JACKSON, Christopher Murray;** Partner, Christopher Jackson Associates, since 1994; Chairman: CJA Consultants Ltd, 1995–2002 (Director, since 1995); Member of Council, Bethany School Ltd, Goudhurst, since 2011 (Chairman, 1999–2009; Director, 1999–2011); b 24 May 1935; s of Rev. Howard Murray Jackson and Doris Bessie Jackson (née Grainger); m 1971, Carlie Elizabeth Keeling; one s one d. *Educ:* Kingswood Sch., Bath; Magdalen Coll., Oxford (Open Exhibnr, BA Hons (Physics) 1959, MA 1964); Goethe Univ., Frankfurt; London Sch. of Economics. National Service, commnd RAF, Pilot, 1954–56. Unilever, 1959–69, Sen. Man., 1967; Save and Prosper Gp, 1969–71; D. MacPherson Gp,

1971–74; Dir of Corporate Development, Spillers Ltd, 1974–80; Chairman: Wellmeade Ltd, 1998–2010; Natural Resources Internat. Ltd, 1997–2003; European Broadcasting Network plc, 1997–99. Contested (C): East Ham South, 1970; Northampton North, Feb. 1974. MEP (C) Kent E, 1979–94; contested (C) Kent E, EP elecns, 1994; Hon. MEP, 1994–; European Parliament: spokesman, on develt and co-op., 1981–87, on foreign affairs, 1991–92, on econ. affairs, 1992–94; Cons. spokesman on agric., 1987–89; Chm., Intergroup on Frontier Controls, 1987–94; Co-Pres., Working Gp on Population and Develt, 1990–94; Mem., Bureau of EDG, 1984–91; Dep. Ldr, Cons. MEPs, 1989–91; Rapporteur-General, ACP-EEC Jt Assembly, 1985–86. Nat. Chm., Cons. Countryside (formerly Nat. Agricl and Countryside) Forum, 1995–98. Mem., Cons. Nat. Union Exec. Cttee, 1995–98; Mem. Council, Cons. Gp for Europe, 2017–. Dir, Politics International Ltd, 1995–98. Vice President: Assoc. of Dist Councils, 1980–95; Assoc. of Local Councils, 1984–95; Assoc. of Port Health Authorities, 1989–99. Member: Chatham Hse (RIIA); Inst. of Dirs, 1998–2008. Treas., St Martin-in-the-Fields, 1975–77. Pres., Kent Hotels and Restaurants Assoc., 1988–94. *Publications:* Towards 2000—People Centred Development, 1986 (major report); (ed) Your European Watchdogs, 1990; Shaking the Foundations: Britain and the New Europe, 1991; The Maastricht Summit, 1992; Whose Job is it Anyway?—decentralisation (or subsidiarity) and the EC, 1992; Working for the European Community, 1990, 2nd edn 1992; (ed) Industrial Property Rights, 1997 (official EC pubn); (with B. Patterson) Both Sides of the Coin: arguments for and against UK membership of the EU, 2016; pamphlets on Britain and Europe. *Recreations:* music, tennis, walking, travel. *Address:* Flackley Ash Farmhouse, Peasmarsh, Rye, E Sussex TN31 6TB. *T:* (01797) 230660. *E:* flackley.ash2@btinternet.com. *Clubs:* Athenæum; Rye Lawn Tennis.

**JACKSON, Colin Ray**, CBE 2003 (OBE 2000; MBE 1990); former athlete; broadcaster and television presenter; *b* Cardiff, 18 Feb. 1967. *Educ:* Llanederyn High Sch., Cardiff. Gold Medals won in 110m hurdles: European Cup, 1989, 1993, 1998; Commonwealth Games, 1990, 1994; European Championships, 1990, 1994, 1998, 2002; World Cup, 1992; World Championships, 1993, 1999; also Silver Medal, Olympic Games, 1988; Gold Medals won in 60m hurdles: European Indoor Championships, 1989, 1994, 2002; World Indoor Championships, 1999; set world record for 110m hurdles (12.91 secs), 1993, and 60m indoor hurdles (7.30 secs), 1994. Silver Medal for 4 × 100m relay, World Championships, 1993. *Publications:* Colin Jackson: the autobiography, 2003; Life's New Hurdles, 2008. *Address:* c/o MTC (UK) Ltd, 71 Gloucester Place, W1U 8JW.

**JACKSON, Daphne Diana;** Assistant Personnel Officer, City Engineer's Department, City of Birmingham, 1986–93; *b* 8 Oct. 1933; *d* of Major Thomas Casey, MC, South Lancs Regt, and Agnes Nora Casey (*née* Gradden); *m* 1953, John Hudleston Jackson (*d* 2014). *Educ:* Folkestone County Grammar School for Girls; South West London College. ACIS. Westminster Bank, 1951–53; Kent Educn Cttee, 1953–57; Pfizer Ltd, Sandwich, 1957–67; Southern Transformer Products, 1967–68; Borough of Hounslow, 1968–86, Personnel and Central Services Officer, Borough Engr and Surveyor's Dept, 1978–86. Mem., NACRO Employment Adv. Cttee, 1984–86; Chm., Gen. Adv. Council to IBA, 1985–89 (Mem., 1980). Mem., Soroptimists International (Pres., Stratford-upon-Avon, 1995–96). Mem., Cleeve Prior PCC, 1991–; Gov., Cleeve Prior C of E Controlled First Sch., 1989–2005; Chm. Mgt Cttee, Cleeve Prior Meml Village Hall, 1994–97. Freeman, City of London, 1980; Liveryman, Chartered Secretaries and Administrators Co., 1980. *Recreations:* bereavement counselling, learning about antiques, reading. *Address:* 3 Manor Court, Bidford Road, Cleeve Prior, Evesham, Worcs WR11 8HZ. *T:* (01789) 772817.

**JACKSON, Prof. David Cooper;** Chairman, Immigration Appeal Tribunal, 1996–2003 (Vice-President, 1984–96); Professor of Law (part time), 1984–98, now Emeritus, and Director, Institute of Maritime Law, 1987–90, University of Southampton; *b* 3 Dec. 1931; *s* of late Rev. James Jackson and Mary Emma Jackson; *m* Roma Lilian (*née* Pendergast) (decd). *Educ:* Ashville Coll., Harrogate; Brasenose Coll., Oxford. MA, BCL; Senior Hulme Scholar, 1954; LLD Southampton, 1997. Called to the Bar, Inner Temple, 1957, and Victoria, Australia, 1967. Bigelow Fellow, Univ. of Chicago, 1955; Fellow, Assoc. of Bar of City of New York, 1956; National Service, 1957–59; Senior Lectr, Univ. of Singapore, 1963–64; Sir John Latham Prof. of Law, Monash Univ., 1965–70 (Carnegie Travelling Fellow, 1969); Prof. of Law, Southampton Univ., 1970–83 (Dean of Law, 1972–75, 1978–81; Dep. Vice-Chancellor, 1982–83); Consultant, UNCTAD, 1980, 1983. Visiting Professor: Queen Mary Coll., London, 1969; Arizona State Univ., 1976; Melbourne Univ., 1976. JP Hants 1980–84. Editor, World Shipping Laws, 1979–89 (and contrib.). *Publications:* Principles of Property Law, 1967; The Conflicts Process, 1975; Enforcement of Maritime Claims, 1985, 4th edn 2005; Civil Jurisdiction and Judgments: maritime claims, 1987; Immigration Law and Practice, 1996, 4th edn (jtly) 2008; articles in legal jls, Australia, UK, USA. *Recreations:* walking, travel, theatre.

**JACKSON, David Richard Holmes**, CBE 2004; JP; Chief Executive, Bradford Teaching Hospitals NHS Foundation Trust (formerly Bradford Hospitals NHS Trust), 1992–2005; *b* 24 Sept. 1948; *s* of Samuel Horace Jackson and Pauline Jackson (*née* Blockey); *m* 1973, Frances Bush; two *s* two *d*. *Educ:* Kingswood Sch., Bath; Univ. of Leeds (LLB). DipHSM 1978. Trainee and Dep. Hosp. Sec., Leeds (St James) Univ. HMC, 1970–73; Sen. Adminr, Hull A Gp HMC, 1973–74; Dep. Dist Adminr, Gen. Infirmary, Leeds, 1974–78; Dist Adminr, Beverley Health Dist, 1978–82; Grimsby Health Authority: Dist Adminr, 1982–85; Dist Gen. Manager, 1985–92. JP Bradford, 1998. *Recreations:* walking, travelling, good living. *Address:* 10 Southway, Ilkley LS29 8QG. *T:* (01943) 609521. *E:* davidrhjackson@hotmail.com. *Club:* Ilkley Bowling.

**JACKSON, Donald**, MVO 1985; artist calligrapher; Scribe to Crown Office, since 1964 (Senior Illuminator, 1974–2014); *b* 14 Jan. 1938; *s* of Wilfred Jackson and Helena Ruth Jackson (*née* Tolley); *m* 1962, Mabel Elizabeth Morgan; one *s* one *d*. *Educ:* Bolton Sch. of Art; City & Guilds, London; Central Sch. of Art; Goldsmiths' Coll. FSSI 1960 (Chm., 1973). Preparer of Letters Patent and Royal Charters under Great Seal, 1964, incl. redesignated Royal Cities, towns and boroughs in England and Wales, 1974; Dir, Calligraphy Centre, 1984–97; Artistic Director: The St John's Bible (handwritten and illuminated Bible in seven vols to mark Millennium, for St John's Univ. and Benedictine Abbey, Minn), 1997–2011; Heritage Series of Fine Art Facsimile Reproductions, 2007–12. Vis. Lectr, Camberwell Sch. of Art, 1958–75; Distinguished Vis. Prof. of Art, California State Univ., 1976–77; lectr in USA and Australia. 30-year personal retrospective exhibn, Painting with Words, in USA, Puerto Rico, Hong Kong, Europe, 1988–91; internat. exhibition series, Illuminating the Word: the St John's Bible, incl. Minneapolis Inst. of Arts, 2005, Joslyn Mus., Omaha, V&A, Mus. of Biblical Image and Art, NY, Liby of Congress, Washington, 2006, Naples Art Mus., Fla, and Phoenix Art Mus., Arizona, 2007, Winnipeg Art Gall., Canada, and Mobile Mus. of Art, Alabama, 2008, Walters Art Mus., Baltimore, 2009; Sci. Mus. of Minnesota (with Dead Sea Scrolls exhibn), 2010; Minneapolis Inst. of Arts, 2011; New Mexico History Mus., Sante Fe, 2011–12, ongoing; work in internat. public and private collections, incl. Vatican Liby and Mus., Liby of Congress, Washington DC, Pierpont Morgan Liby, NY, perm. display at St Martin-in-the-Fields, London and St John's Univ., Collegeville, Minn. Founding Trustee, Irene Wellington Educnl Trust, 1987. Presenter, and producer with Jeremy Bennett: Alphabet (documentary film series), 1979; The Illuminator (documentary), BBC Wales, 2005. Liveryman, Scriveners' Co., 1973 (Master, 1997–98). KSG 2016. *Publications:* The Story of Writing, 1980, 3rd edn 1994; (jtly) The Calligraphers' Handbook, 1985; (jtly) More than Fine Writing, 1986; Gospel and Acts (facsimile edn), 2005; Psalms (facsimile edn), 2006; Pentateuch (facsimile edn), 2006; Prophets (facsimile edn), 2007; Wisdom (facsimile edn), 2007; (jtly) The Lion Companion to Christian Art, 2008; Historical (facsimile edn), 2010; Letters and Revelation (facsimile edn), 2012. *Recreations:* friends, family, other people's art, country sports. *Address:* The Scriptorium, The Hendre, Monmouth NP25 5HG. *T:* (01600) 714222.

**JACKSON, Prof. Emily Meg**, OBE 2017; FBA 2016; Professor of Law, London School of Economics and Political Science, since 2007; *b* London, 28 Dec. 1966; *d* of Douglas Jackson and Lesley Jackson. *Educ:* Bushey Meads Sch.; Brasenose Coll., Oxford (BA Juris. 1989). Fellow and Lectr in Law, St Catharine's Coll., Cambridge, 1991–93; Lectr in Law, Birkbeck Coll., Univ. of London, 1993–97; Sen. Lectr in Law, LSE, 1998–2004; Prof. of Medical Law, QMUL, 2004–07. Dep. Chm., Human Fertilisation and Embryology Authy, 2008–12 (Mem., 2003–12). Mem., Judicial Appointments Commn, 2014–17. *Publications:* Regulating Reproduction, 2001; Medical Law, 2006, 5th edn 2019; Debating Euthanasia, 2011; Law and the Regulation of Medicines, 2012. *Recreations:* art, architecture, music, walking, food. *Address:* Law Department, London School of Economics and Political Science, Houghton Street, WC2A 2AE. *T:* (020) 7955 6368. *E:* e.jackson@lse.ac.uk.

**JACKSON, Ven. Frances Anne, (Peggy);** Archdeacon of Llandaff, since 2009; Priest-in-charge, St Fagans and Michaelston-super-Ely, since 2014; *b* Loughborough, 1 Aug. 1951; *d* of Wilfrid Ernest, (Bill), Pegg and Eileen Florence Pegg; *m* 1972, Tony Jackson (marr. diss. 1981); one *d*. *Educ:* Somerville Coll., Oxford (BA Modern History 1972; MA 1976); Ripon Coll., Cuddesdon. FCA 1981 (ACA 1976). Chartered Accountant: Robson Rhodes, 1973–76; Deloitte, Haskins & Sells, 1976–85; ordained deacon, 1987, priest, 1994; Asst Curate, St Mary the Virgin, Ilkeston, Derbyshire, 1987–90; Team Vicar, St Paul's, Highfield, Hemel Hempstead, 1990–98; Team Rector, Mortlake with E Sheen, 1998–2009; Area Dean, Richmond and Barnes, 2000–05; Dean, Women's Ministry, Dio. of Southwark, 2004–09; Priest-in-charge, Penmark with Llancarfan with Llantrithyd, 2009–14. Member: WATCH, 1994–; Gp for Rescinding the Act of Synod, 2000–14; elected Mem., Governing Body, Church in Wales, 2012– (co-opted Mem., 2010–12). Member: Amnesty Internat., 1987–; Fawcett Soc., 2005–; Friends of Llandaff Cath., 2009–. Trustee: Cardiff Women's Aid, 2013–; MAECymru, 2016–. *Recreations:* flying (private pilot's licence, 2008–), circle dancing, bell-ringing, singing. *Address:* The Rectory, Greenwood Lane, St Fagans, Cardiff CF5 6EL. *T:* (029) 2056 7393. *E:* archdeacon.llandaff@churchinwales.org.uk. *Clubs:* Oxford Union; Soroptimist Internat. (Glamorgan).

**JACKSON, Francis Alan**, CBE 2007 (OBE 1978); Organist and Master of the Music, York Minster, 1946–82, Organist Emeritus, since 1988; *b* 2 Oct. 1917; *s* of W. A. Jackson; *m* 1950, Priscilla, *d* of Tyndale Procter; two *s* one *d*. *Educ:* York Minster Choir Sch.; Sir Edward Bairstow. Chorister, York Minster, 1929–33; ARCO, 1936; BMus Dunelm 1937; FRCO (Limpus Prize), 1937; DMus Dunelm 1957. Organist Malton Parish Church, 1933–40. Served War of 1939–45, with 9th Lancers in Egypt, N Africa and Italy, 1940–46. Asst Organist, York Minster, 1946; Conductor York Musical Soc., 1947–82; Conductor York Symphony Orchestra, 1947–80. Pres. Incorp. Assoc. of Organists, 1960–62; Pres., RCO, 1972–74. Hon. FRSCM 1963; Hon. Fellow, Westminster Choir Coll., Princeton, NJ, 1970; Hon. FRNCM, 1982; Hon. FGCM 2005; Hon. FGMS; Hon. FNMSM 2015. DUniv York, 1983; DMus Lambeth, 2012. Medal, RCO, 2012. Order of St William of York, 1983. *Publications:* Blessed City: the life and works of Sir Edward C. Bairstow 1874–1946, 1996; Piano Trio, 2001; Fantasy for Two Organs, 2014; Music for a Long While (autobiog.), 2014; organ music, including 6 sonatas and 40 organ pieces, 3 duets, symphony, organ concerto, church music, including 80 anthems, songs, monodramas. *Recreation:* gardening. *Address:* Nether Garth, East Acklam, Malton, N Yorks YO17 9RG. *T:* (01653) 658395.

**JACKSON, Prof. Frank Cameron**, AO 2006; Distinguished Professor, 2003–15, and Fractional Professor of Philosophy, 2011–15, Australian National University, now Professor Emeritus (Professor of Philosophy, 1986–90 and 1992–2007); *b* 31 Aug. 1943; *s* of Allan Cameron Jackson and Ann Elizabeth Jackson; *m* 1966, Morag Elizabeth Fraser; two *d*. *Educ:* Melbourne Univ. (BA, BSc, 1966); La Trobe Univ. (PhD 1975). Temp. Lectr, Adelaide Univ., 1967; Lectr, Sen. Lectr, then Reader, La Trobe Univ., 1968–77; Prof., Monash Univ., 1978–86 and 1991; Australian National University: Dir, Inst. of Advanced Studies, 1998–2001; Dir, Res. Sch. of Soc. Scis, 2004–07; Fractional Prof. of Philosophy, La Trobe Univ., 2008–10. Vis. Prof., Princeton Univ., 2007–14. Corresp. FBA 2000. *Publications:* Perception, 1977; Conditionals, 1987; (with D. Braddon-Mitchell) Philosophy of Mind and Cognition, 1996; From Metaphysics to Ethics, 1998; Mind, Method, and Conditionals, 1998; Language, Names, and Information, 2010. *Recreations:* reading, tennis. *Address:* 33 David Street, O'Connor, ACT 2602, Australia.

**JACKSON, Glenda May**, CBE 1978; *b* Birkenhead, 9 May 1936; *d* of Harry and Joan Jackson; *m* 1958, Roy Hodges (marr. diss. 1976); one *s*. *Educ:* West Kirby Co. Grammar Sch. for Girls; RADA. Actress, 1957–92; with various repertory cos, 1957–63, stage manager, Crewe Rep.; joined Royal Shakespeare Co., 1963. Dir, United British Artists, 1983. Pres., Play Matters (formerly Toy Libraries Assoc.), 1976. *Plays:* All Kinds of Men, Arts, 1957; The Idiot, Lyric, 1962; Alfie, Mermaid and Duchess, 1963; Royal Shakespeare Co.: Theatre of Cruelty Season, LAMDA, 1964; The Jew of Malta, 1964; Marat/Sade, 1965, NY and Paris, 1965; Love's Labour's Lost, Squire Puntila and his Servant Matti, The Investigation, Hamlet, 1965; US, Aldwych, 1966; Three Sisters, Royal Ct, 1967; Fanghorn, Fortune, 1967; Collaborators, Duchess, 1973; The Maids, Greenwich, 1974; Hedda Gabler, Australia, USA, London, 1975; The White Devil, Old Vic, 1976; Stevie, Vaudeville, 1977; Antony and Cleopatra, Stratford, 1978; Rose, Duke of York's, 1980; Summit Conference, Lyric, 1982; Great and Small, Vaudeville, 1983; Strange Interlude, Duke of York's, 1984; Phedra, Old Vic, 1984, Aldwych, 1985; Across from the Garden of Allah, Comedy, 1986; The House of Bernarda Alba, Globe, 1986; Macbeth, NY, 1988; Scenes from an Execution, Almeida, 1990; Mother Courage, Mermaid, 1990; King Lear, Old Vic, 2016 (Best Actress, Evening Standard Theatre Awards, 2017); Three Tall Women, NY, 2018 (Best Actress, Tony Awards, 2018); *films:* This Sporting Life, 1963; Marat/Sade, 1967; Negatives, 1968; Women in Love (Oscar Award, 1971), 1970; The Music Lovers, 1971; Sunday, Bloody Sunday, 1971; The Boyfriend, 1972; Mary, Queen of Scots, 1972; Triple Echo, 1972; Il Sorviso de Grande Tentatore (The Tempter), 1973; Bequest to the Nation, 1973; A Touch of Class (Oscar Award, 1974), 1973; The Maids, 1974; The Romantic Englishwoman, 1974; Hedda Gabler, 1975; The Incredible Sarah, 1976; House Calls, 1978; Stevie, 1978; The Class of Miss MacMichael, 1978; Lost and Found, 1979; Hopscotch, 1980; Return of the Soldier, 1982; Health, 1982; Giro City, 1982; Sacharov, 1983; Turtle Diary, 1985; Business as Usual, 1987; Beyond Therapy, 1987; Salome's Last Dance, 1988; The Rainbow, 1989; The Secret Life of Sir Arnold Bax, 1992; *TV:* Elizabeth in Elizabeth R, 1971; The Patricia Neal Story (Amer.); *radio:* Blood, Sex and Money, Radio 4, 2015. Best film actress awards: Variety Club of GB, 1971, 1975, 1978; NY Film Critics, 1971; Nat. Soc. of Film Critics, US, 1971. MP (Lab) Hampstead and Highgate, 1992–2010, Hampstead and Kilburn, 2010–15. Parly Under-Sec. of State, DETR, 1997–99. *Recreations:* cooking, gardening, reading Jane Austen.

**JACKSON, Gordon;** see Jackson, W. G.

**JACKSON, Helen Margaret,** CBE 2010; Member, Women's Budget Group (formerly Women and Pensions Network) (voluntary outreach worker on women and pensions, Equal Opportunities Commission, 2005–06); *b* 19 May 1939; *d* of Stanley Price and Katherine (*née* Thornton); *m* 1960, Keith Jackson (marr. diss. 1998); two *s* one *d*. *Educ:* St Hilda's Coll., Oxford (BA Hons Mod. Hist., MA); C. F. Mott Coll. of Educn, Prescot (Cert Ed 1972). Asst Librarian, 1961; mother, housewife and voluntary worker, 1961–72; teacher, 1972–80; City Cllr, Sheffield, 1980–91 (Chm., Public Works and Econ. Develt Cttees). Founder Mem. and Chair, Centre for Local Economic Strategies, 1986–91. MP (Lab) Sheffield, Hillsborough, 1992–2005. PPS to Sec. of State for NI, 1997–2001. Member: Envmt Select Cttee, 1992–97; Modernisation of H of C Select Cttee, 1997–2001; Transport, Local Govt and the Regions Select Cttee, 2001–03; Chair: All-Party Parly Water Gp, 1993–97; Parly Envmt Gp, 1997–2005; All-Party Parly Gp on S Africa, 1997–2005; Founder and Chair, All-Party Parly Steel Gp, 2002–05; Co-Chair, PLP Women's Gp, 1992–97; Sec., PLP Gp on Envmtl Protection, 1995–97; Vice-Chair, PLP, 2001–02 (Mem., Party Cttee, Labour Party, 2001–05); Mem., NEC, Labour Pty, 1999–2005. UK Parly Rep., Assoc. of Eur. Parliamentarians for Africa, 1997–2005. Vice Chair, Fawcett Soc., 2007–10; Comr, Women's Nat. Commn, 2008–10. Pres., Sheffield Homestart, 2005–; Trustee: S Yorks Women's Develt Trust, 2005–10; Age UK (formerly Age Concern), Sheffield, 2005–12; Grandparents Plus (incorp. The Grandparents' Assoc.), 2011– (Co-Chm., 2015–17). *Publications:* The Active Citizen, 2007; (ed) The Journal of Elizabeth Anne Saville, 2011; (ed) Life Long Labour: a local history chronicle of life in South Yorkshire - Frank Rodgers 1916–2012, 2015. *Recreations:* walking, music, grandchildren. *Address:* 2 Topside, Grenoside, Sheffield S35 8RD.

**JACKSON, Prof. James Anthony,** CBE 2015; PhD; FRS 2002; Professor of Active Tectonics, Cambridge University, since 2002 (Head, Department of Earth Sciences, 2008–16); Fellow, Queens' College, Cambridge, since 1979; *b* 12 Dec. 1954; *s* of Richard Owen Jackson and Honor (*née* Thomason); *m* 1984, Susan Elliott; one *s* one *d*. *Educ:* Cranleigh Sch.; Queens' Coll., Cambridge (BA 1976, PhD 1980). Res. Fellow, NERC, 1979–82; Asst Lectr, 1984–88, Lectr, 1988–96, Reader, 1996–2002, Dept of Earth Scis, Cambridge Univ. Allan Cox Vis. Prof., Stanford Univ., 1990–91; Visiting Professor: CIT, 2006; CNRS Grenoble, 2006; Indian Inst. of Sci. Educn and Res. Kolkata, 2016. Royal Instn Christmas Lects, Planet Earth: an Explorer's Guide, 1995. Fellow, Amer. Geophys. Union, 2003. Pres.'s Award, 1985, Bigsby Medal, 1997, Wollaston Medal, 2015, Geol. Soc. London. *Publications:* contribs to professional jls in earth scis. *Recreations:* swimming, tandeming. *Address:* Bullard Laboratories, Madingley Road, Cambridge CB3 0EZ. *T:* (01223) 337197, *Fax:* (01223) 360779.

**JACKSON, Jane Thérèse, (Tessa),** OBE 2011; curator, writer and cultural adviser, International Cultural Development, since 2015 (curator and consultant, 2002–10; Owner, 2002–10 and since 2015); *b* 5 Nov. 1955; *d* of John Nevill Jackson and Viva Christian Thérèse Jackson (*née* Blomfield). *Educ:* Univ. of East Anglia (BA Hons Fine Art); Univ. of Manchester (Dip. Museum Studies); Univ. of Bristol (MA Film and TV Prodn 1998). Art Editor, OUP, 1979–80; Exhibns Organiser, SPAB, 1981–82; Curator: Eyemouth Museum, 1982; Collins Gallery, Univ. of Strathclyde, 1982–88; Visual Arts Officer, Glasgow 1990— European City of Culture, 1988–91; Director: Arnolfini, Bristol, 1991–99; Scottish Arts Council, 1999–2001; Chief Exec. and Founding Artistic Dir, Artes Mundi Prize, 2002–10; Chief Exec., Inst. of Internat. Visual Arts, 2009–15. Trustee: Centre for Chinese Contemporary Art, 2015–; Spike Island, 2016–; Art Fund, 2018–. FRSA 2000. Ed., Artes Mundi, 2004–10. *Publications:* (with John R. Hume) George Washington Wilson and Victorian Glasgow, 1983; (jtly) Signs of the Times: art and industry in Scotland 1750–1985, 1985; (ed jtly) A Platform for Partnership (Glasgow City Council), 1991; contrib. exhibn catalogues. *Recreations:* travel, walking, architecture. *E:* jtessajackson@gmail.com.

**JACKSON, John Bernard Haysom;** Chairman: Xenova Group plc, 1990–2005; Oxford Technology Venture Capital Trusts plc, 1997–2014; *b* 26 May 1929; *m* 1st, 1955, Ann Nichols (marr. diss. 1984); one *s* two *d*; 2nd, 1984, Rowena Thomas. *Educ:* King's School, Canterbury; Queens' Coll., Cambridge (BA, LLB). Called to the Bar, Inner Temple, 1954. Philips Electronics, 1952–80 (Dir, 1966–94); Dir, 1980–2001, Vice-Chm., 1991–94, Chm., 1994–2001, Hilton Gp. Non-solicitor Chm., Mishcon de Reya, 1992–2015, now Chm. Emeritus; Chairman: Celltech Gp, 1982–2003; Wyndeham Press Gp plc, 1990–2003; Dep. Chm., BHP Billiton plc, 2001–02; Director: WPP Group plc, 1993–2004 (Founding Mem., Adv. Bd, 2004–); Instore (formerly Brown & Jackson) plc, 1994–2013; Billiton plc, 1997–2001; Opendemocracy Ltd, 2000–14. Chairman: Countryside Alliance, 1999–2005; Rural Regeneration Unit, 2003–06; Trustee, One World Action, 1998–2005. Co-owner, History Today magazine, 1981– (Chm., 1981–2014). *Publications:* A Bucket of Nuts and a Herring Net, 1979, 3rd edn as A Little Piece of England: a tale of self-sufficiency, 2011; (contrib.) Even Paranoids have Enemies, 1998; Tales for Great Grandchildren, 2011; Brahma Dreaming, 2013. *Recreations:* growing rare plants, breeding butterflies, fishing, painting, writing.

**JACKSON, John Henry;** Clerk to the Governors, Dulwich College, 1998–2007; Company Secretary, BG plc (formerly British Gas), 1990–97; *b* 7 Aug. 1948; *s* of late John and May Jackson; *m* 1975, Patricia Mary Robinson; one *s* one *d*. *Educ:* Trinity School, Croydon; St Catherine's College, Oxford (MA). FCIS. Joined SE Gas Board, 1970; Asst Sec., 1977, Sen. Asst Sec., 1983, British Gas Corp., later British Gas plc. Mem., Solicitors Disciplinary Tribunal, 2002–12. Assessor, Nat. Clinical Assessment Service (formerly Authy), 2003–07. Mem., Ind. Monitoring Bd, HMP High Down, 2004–05; Independent Member: Parole Bd, 2005–14; CIPFA Disciplinary Cttee, 2007–10. Mem. UK and Internat. Councils, ICSA, 1996–2002 (a Chief Examr, 1997–2000). Non-exec. Dir, Queen Victoria Hosp. NHS Trust, E Grinstead, 1996–98. Chm., Horsham and Crawley Samaritans, 2008–10. Clerk to Govs, Alleyn's Sch., 1998–2004.

**JACKSON, (John) Patrick;** Director, Portugal, British Council, 1993–96; *b* 18 Sept. 1940; *s* of Godfrey Jackson and Mary Jackson (*née* Worthington); *m* 1st, 1963, Marieliese de Vos van Steenwyk (marr. diss.); three *d* (and one *d* decd); 2nd, 1978, Hélène Mellotte; two *d*. *Educ:* Worksop Coll.; Midhurst Grammar Sch.; New Coll., Oxford (MA); Moscow Univ. (postgrad. studies); London Univ. Inst. of Educn (postgrad. Cert Ed). British Council, 1963–96: English Language Teaching Inst., London, 1964–66; Asst Dir, Bahrain, 1966–69; Asst Cultural Attaché, Moscow, 1969–71; Dep. Dir, Higher Educn Dept, 1971–73; Regl Dir, Calcutta, 1973–75; Dir, N Europe Dept, 1975–79; Rep., Senegal, 1979–83; Regl Dir, São Paulo, 1983–88; Dep. Controller, Home Div., 1988–91; Dir, Exchanges and Training Div., 1991–93; early retirement, 1996; kidney transplant, 1997; Baggage Agent, Gatwick Handling Ltd, 1997–2000; Homesearch consultant, 2000–04; retd, 2004. *Recreations:* birdwatching, languages, IT, crosswords. *Address:* The Two Houses, Hollow Lane, East Grinstead, W Sussex RH19 2JP.

**JACKSON, Judith Mary;** QC 1994; *b* 18 Sept. 1950; *d* of Thomas Worthington Jackson and Betty Jackson (*née* Kinsey); one *d*. *Educ:* Queen Mary College, London (LLB, LLM); Birkbeck, Univ. of London (MRes (Dist.) Spanish and Latin American Cultural Studies 2012). Called to the Bar, Inner Temple, 1975; Bencher, Lincoln's Inn, 2001–15. Dir, Bar Mutual Insce Fund Ltd, 1999–2009. Chm., Young Barristers' Cttee, 1984–85. *Recreations:* music, cycling, trekking in the Andes and Andean culture. *Address:* Maitland Chambers, 7 Stone Buildings, Lincoln's Inn, WC2A 3SZ. *T:* (020) 7406 1200.

**JACKSON, Prof. Julian Timothy,** PhD; FBA 2003; FRHistS; Professor of Modern French History, Queen Mary, University of London, since 2003; *b* 10 April 1954; *s* of Edward Francis Jackson and Marion Marianne Marris (*née* Ellinger). *Educ:* Peterhouse, Cambridge (BA 1976; PhD 1982). Res. Asst to Robert Rhodes James, MP, for biog. of Eden, 1983; University College of Swansea, subseq. University of Wales, Swansea: Lectr, 1983–90, Sen. Lectr, 1990–95, Reader, 1995–2000, in Hist.; Prof. of Hist., 2000–03. FRHistS 1985. Commandeur, Ordre des Palmes Académiques (France), 2010. *Publications:* The Politics of Depression in France, 1985 (trans. Japanese 2001); The Popular Front in France: defending democracy, 1988 (trans. Japanese 1992); De Gaulle, 1990, rev. edn 2003 (trans. French 2004, Portuguese 2010); France: the dark years 1940–44, 2001 (trans. French 2004, Czech 2006); (ed) Europe 1900–1945, 2002 (trans. Spanish 2003); The Fall of France, 2003 (trans. Czech 2006); Living in Arcadia: homosexuality, politics and morality in France from the Liberation to Aids, 2010 (trans. French 2010); Jean Renoir, 2010; A Certain Idea of France: a life of Charles De Gaulle, 2018. *Recreations:* cinema, theatre, travel, food. *Address:* School of History, Queen Mary, University of London, Mile End Road, E1 4NS. *T:* (020) 7727 9930, *Fax:* (020) 8980 8400. *E:* j.t.jackson@qmul.ac.uk.

**JACKSON, Kathryn Elizabeth;** see Major, K. E.

**JACKSON, Sir Kenneth Joseph, (Sir Ken),** Kt 1999; Chairman, Nirex Ltd, 2001–05. *Educ:* St Joseph's Sch., Wigan. Electrical technician, RAF, 1956–61; joined ETU, 1966: Br. Sec., Wigan; area officer, Preston; officer, Merseyside and NW; Exec. Councillor, EETPU, 1987; Pres., EETPU section, 1992–96, Gen. Sec., 1996–2003, AEEU.

**JACKSON, (Kenneth) Robin,** CBE 2014; PhD; Chief Executive and Secretary, British Academy, 2006–15 (Interim Chief Executive, since 2019); *b* 7 Oct. 1949; *s* of Kenneth and Lily Jackson; *m* 1985, Joanna Motion; one *s*. *Educ:* RGS Newcastle upon Tyne; Pembroke Coll., Oxford (MA Lit.Hum. 1973); Princeton Univ. (PhD Classical Philos. 1982). Classics Fellow, Marlboro Coll., Vermont, 1973–75; Seymour Reader in Greek Philos., Ormond Coll., and Lectr, then Sen. Lectr, in Classics, Univ. of Melbourne, 1977–94; Associate Dir, QAA, 1995–98; Res. Policy Advr, UUK, 1998–2002; Regl Consultant, London, 2002–06, Actg Dir, Corporate Resources, 2006, HEFCE. Mem. Bd, Sch. of Advanced Studies, Univ. of London, 2008–17 (Dep. Chair, 2016–17). Chair, Humanities and Social Scis Panel, Irish Res. Council, 2016–. Hon. DCL East Anglia, 2016. *Publications:* Olympiodorus: commentary on Plato's Gorgias, 1998; articles on Greek philosophy; policy papers on higher educn funding and res. policy. *Recreations:* listening to music, reading, walking in London. *Address:* The Secret Garden, Back Street, Reepham, Norfolk NR10 4SJ. *T:* 07470 472370. *E:* krobinj2015@yahoo.co.uk. *Clubs:* Athenæum; Newcastle United Football.

**JACKSON, (Kevin) Paul;** freelance consultant, since 2014; Creative Director, Houghton Street Media, Beijing, 2012–14; *b* 2 Oct. 1947; *s* of late T. Leslie Jackson and of Jo (*née* Spoonley); *m* 1981, Judith Elizabeth Cain; two *d*. *Educ:* Gunnersbury Grammar Sch.; Univ. of Exeter (BA 1970); Stanford Univ. (Exec. Program 1993). Stage manager: Marlowe Theatre, Canterbury, 1970; Thorndike Theatre, Leatherhead, 1971. BBC Television: Production Assistant, 1971–79; Producer, 1979–82: programmes include: The Two Ronnies, Three of a Kind (BAFTA Award 1982), Carrot's Lib, The Young Ones (BAFTA Award 1984), Happy Families; freelance producer and director, 1982–84: programmes include: Cannon & Ball, Girls On Top; Producer and Chm., Paul Jackson Prodns Ltd, 1984–86: programmes include: Red Dwarf, Don't Miss Wax, Saturday Live; Man. Dir, Noel Gay TV, 1987–91: progs include The Appointments of Dennis Jennings (Oscar for Best Live Action Short, 1989); Dir of Progs, 1991–93, Man. Dir, 1993–94, Carlton TV; Man. Dir, Carlton UK Productions, 1994–96; Head, then Controller, BBC Entertainment, 1997–2000; Man. Dir, Granada Media Australia and Chief Exec., Red Heart Prodns, 2000–02; Dir, Internat. Prodn and Entertainment, Granada, London, 2002; CEO, Granada America, 2002–06; Chm., Granada Productions (Australia), 2002–06 (CEO, 2000–02); Dir, Entertainment and Comedy, ITV plc, 2006–09; CEO, 2009–12, Consultant, 2012, Eyeworks UK; progs with Houghton Street Media, Beijing incl. Mama Mia, Chinese Gadget Show. Chairman: RTS, 1994–96; Comic Relief, 1985–98; Charity Projects, 1992–98; Trustee, Pilotlight, 1996–2003 (Chm., 1996–2000); Chm. Trustees, 1999–2012, Patron, 2000–12, Timebank. Academic Visitor, 1996–2004, Vis. Prof., 2004–, Exeter Univ. FInstD 1992; FRTS 1993. Hon. LLD Exeter, 2004. *Recreations:* my family, theatre, Rugby, travel, food and wine. *Address:* c/o Anita Land Ltd, 10 Wyndham Place, W1H 2PU. *Club:* Groucho.

**JACKSON, Prof. Mark Andrew,** PhD; Professor of the History of Medicine, since 2003, and Director, Wellcome Centre for Cultures and Environments of Health, since 2017, University of Exeter; *b* Horley, 10 Sept. 1959; *s* of Richard and Valerie Jackson; *m* 1993, Siobhan Deehan; two *s* one *d*. *Educ:* Reigate Grammar Sch.; St Thomas' Hosp., Univ. of London (BSc 1983; MB BS 1985); Univ. of Leeds (PhD 1992). Res. Fellow, Univ. of Manchester, 1992–98; University of Exeter: Sen. Lectr, 1998–2000; Reader, 2000–03. Co-Dir, WHO Collaborating Centre on Culture and Health, 2016–. Wellcome Trust: Chair: Hist. of Medicine Panel, 2003–08; Res. Resources in Med. Hist. Panel, 2008–13; Sen. Acad. Advr (Med. Humanities), 2013–16. Mem., Hist. Sub-Panel, REF 2014, 2011–14; Chair, Hist. Sub-Panel, REF 2021, 2017–. Dir, Medical Humanities Consultancy Ltd, 2013–16. Gov., Colyton GS, 2011–14. Wilkins-Bernal-Medawar Medal, Royal Soc., 2018. *Publications:* (with G. Feinberg) The Chain of Immunology, 1983 (trans. Italian, Spanish and Japanese, 1985); New-Born Child Murder: women, illegitimacy and the Courts in Eighteenth-Century England, 1996; (ed jtly) Forgotten Lives: exploring the history of learning disability, 1997; The Borderland of Imbecility: medicine, society and the fabrication of the feeble mind in late Victorian and Edwardian England, 2000; (ed jtly) Crossing Boundaries: change and continuity in the history of learning disability, 2000; (ed) Infanticide: historical perspectives on child murder and concealment, 1520–2000, 2002; Allergy: the history of a modern malady, 2006 (trans. German, Japanese, Korean, 2007); (ed) Health and the Modern Home, 2007; Asthma: the biography, 2009; (ed) Oxford Handbook of the History of Medicine, 2011; The Age of Stress: science and the search for stability, 2013; History of Medicine: a beginner's guide, 2014; (ed) Stress in Post-War Britain, 1945–85, 2015; (ed) The Routledge History of Disease, 2016; (ed) The Global History of Medicine, 2018; contribs to jls incl. Social Hist. of Medicine, British Jl for Hist. of Sci., Studies in Hist. and Philosophy of Biol and Biomed. Scis, Hist. of the Human Scis, Lancet. *Recreations:* family, Queens Park Rangers FC, classical music. *Address:* Wellcome Centre for Cultures and Environments of Health, Queen's Building, The Queen's Drive, Exeter EX4 4QH. *T:* (01392) 723003. *E:* m.a.jackson@exeter.ac.uk.

**JACKSON, Michael;** Founder, and Chairman, Shaping Tomorrow Ltd, since 2003; *b* 12 March 1948; *s* of Stanley Jackson and Maisie Joan Jackson. *Educ:* Salford Univ. (BSc Electronics). Hawker Siddeley, 1970–73; Vice Pres., Citibank NA, 1973–86; Sen. Vice Pres., Bank of America, 1986–90; Chief Exec., Birmingham Midshires Bldg Soc., 1990–98; Chm., Results Plus Ltd, 1998–2004. Non-exec. Dir, GallifordTry plc, 1997–2004. Hon. DBA Wolverhampton, 1997. *Recreations:* genealogy, music, sport. *Address:* 41 Summerfield Avenue, Kingswinford, W Midlands DY6 9AS.

**JACKSON, Gen. Sir Michael David, (Sir Mike)**, GCB 2005 (KCB 1998; CB 1996); CBE 1992 (MBE 1979); DSO 1999; DL; *b* 21 March 1944; *s* of George Jackson and Ivy (*née* Bower); *m* 1985, Sarah Coombe; two *s* one *d*. *Educ*: Stamford Sch.; RMA Sandhurst; Birmingham Univ. (BSocSc 1967). Commnd Intelligence Corps, 1963; transf. to Parachute Regt, 1970; Staff Coll., 1976; Bde Major, Berlin, 1977–78; ndc 1981; Directing Staff, Staff Coll., 1981–83; Comd 1st Bn Parachute Regt, 1984–86; Sen. DS, Jt Service Defence Coll., 1986–88; Services Fellow, Wolfson Coll., Cambridge, 1989; Comdr, 39 Inf. Bde, 1990–92; Dir Gen. Personal Services (Army), MoD, 1992–94; GOC 3 (UK) Div., 1994–95; Comdr, Implementation Force Multinat. Div. SW, Bosnia Herzegovina, 1995–96; Dir Gen., Develt and Doctrine, MoD, 1996–97; Comdr, ACE Rapid Reaction Corps, 1997–2000; Comdr, Kosovo Force, March–Oct. 1999; C–in–C, Land Comd, 2000–03; ADC Gen. to the Queen, 2001–06; CGS, 2003–06. Non-exec. Dir, ForceSelect, 2010–; Sen. Advr, PA Consulting Gp, 2007–13; Mem. Internat. Adv. Bd, Rolls-Royce, 2007–12. Col Comdt, Parachute Regt, 1998–2004; Hon. Colonel: Rifle Vols, TA, 1999–2007; Bristol Univ., 2010–. DL Wilts, 2007. Hon. LLD: Birmingham, 2000; Sheffield, 2005. Freeman, City of London, 1988. *Publications*: Soldier: the autobiography, 2007. *Recreations*: travel, music, skiing, tennis. *Address*: Regimental Headquarters, Parachute Regiment, Merville Barracks, Colchester, Essex CO2 7UT. *Clubs*: Army and Navy, Buck's, Garrick; St Moritz Tobogganing.

**JACKSON, Most Rev. Michael Geoffrey St Aubyn;** *see* Dublin, Archbishop of, and Primate of Ireland.

**JACKSON, Michael Richard;** television executive and producer; Co-Chief Executive Officer, Two Cities Television, since 2017; *b* 11 Feb. 1958; *s* of Ernest Jackson and Margaret (*née* Kearsley). *Educ*: King's Sch., Macclesfield; Poly. of Central London (BA (Hons) Media Studies). Organiser, Channel Four Gp, 1979; Producer, The Sixties, 1982; Independent Producer, Beat Productions Ltd, 1983–87, produced Whose Town is it Anyway?, Open the Box, The Media Show; joined BBC Television; Editor: The Late Show (BFI Television Award), 1988–90; Late Show Productions, 1990–91, progs incl. The Nelson Mandela Tribute, Tales from Prague (Grierson Documentary Award), Moving Pictures, The American Late Show (PBS), Naked Hollywood (BAFTA Award, Best Factual Series); Head of Music and Arts, BBC Television, 1991–93; Controller, BBC 2, 1993–96; Controller, BBC 1 and BBC Dir of Television, 1996–97; Dir of Progs, 1997–98, Chief Exec., 1997–2001, C4; Chm., Film Four Ltd, 1997–2001; Pres. and Chief Exec., USA Entertainment, 2001–02; Chm., Universal Television Gp, 2002–04; Pres. of Programming, IAC, 2006–09; Sen. Advr, Lepe Partners, 2012–14. Executive Producer: The Genius of Photography (series), BBC, 2007; America: the Story of Us (series), 2010; Civilisations (series), BBC, 2018; Patrick Melrose (series), Sky Atlantic, 2018. Co-Founder, veryshortlist.com, 2007–. Non-executive Director: EMI Gp, 1999–2002; Scottish TV, 2009–; Nutopia, 2011–; Peters, Fraser and Dunlop, 2015–; Dir, DIC Entertainment, 2006–09. Chm., Photographers' Gall., 2001–02. FRTS 1997. Hon. DLitt Westminster, 1995. *Recreations*: reading, films, collecting photography, walking.

**JACKSON, Air Vice-Marshal Michael Richard,** CB 1998; independent consultant, since 2004; Director General, Intelligence Staff, Ministry of Defence, 1996–98; *b* 28 Dec. 1941; *s* of Felix Ralph Jackson and Margaret Jackson (*née* Marshall); *m* 1967, Kay Johnson; two *s*. *Educ*: Cardinal Vaughan Sch.; RAF Coll., Cranwell. Joined RAF, 1965: sqdn flying duties, 1965–69; navigation instructor, 1969–70; Exchange Officer, USA, 1971–74; RAF Staff Coll., 1974; Sqdn Comdr, 1975–77; Mem., Directing Staff, Army Staff Coll., Camberley, 1977–80; Ops Wing Comdr, 1981–84; Defence and Air Attaché, Warsaw, 1985–87; Unit Comdr, 1987–89; Defence Fellow, Rand Corp. and Cambridge Univ., 1989–90; Dir, MoD Central Staffs, 1991–95. Exec. Dir, Oracle Corp., 1998–2004; Dir, Market Develt, Silicon Graphics, 2002–04; Dep. Chm., Alpha Intelligence Mgt Ltd, 2007–09. Fellow, Centre for Security and Intelligence Studies, Buckingham Univ., 2009–10. Trustee and Project Dir, Bury St Edmunds Heritage Trust, 2011–17. *Recreations*: music, walking, gardening. *Address*: c/o RAF Record Office, High Wycombe, Bucks HP14 4UE. *Club*: Royal Air Force.

**JACKSON, Sir Neil Keith,** 9th Bt *cr* 1815, of Arsley, Bedfordshire; *b* 12 May 1952; *s* of Sir Keith Arnold Jackson, 8th Bt and of Pauline Mona (*née* Climo); S father, 2000, but his name does not appear on the Official Roll of the Baronetage; *m* 1973, Sandra Whitehead (marr. diss.); two *s*. *Heir*: *s* Stephen Keith Jackson, *b* 27 Sept. 1973.

**JACKSON, Sir Nicholas (Fane St George),** 3rd Bt *cr* 1913; organist, harpsichordist and composer; Director, Concertante of London, since 1987; *b* 4 Sept. 1934; *s* of Sir Hugh Jackson, 2nd Bt, and Violet Marguerite Loftus (*d* 2001), *y d* of Loftus St George; *S* father, 1979; *m* 1972, Nadia Françoise Geneviève (*née* Michard); one *s*. *Educ*: Radley Coll.; Wadham Coll., Oxford; Royal Acad. of Music. LRAM; ARCM. Organist: St Anne's, Soho, 1963–68; St James's, Piccadilly, 1971–74; St Lawrence, Jewry, 1974–77; Organist and Master of the Choristers, St David's Cathedral, 1977–84. Musical Dir, St David's Cathedral Bach Fest., 1979; Dir, Bach Festival, Santes Creus, Spain, 1987–89. Organ recitals and broadcasts: Berlin, 1967; Paris, 1972, 1975; USA (tour), 1975, 1978, 1980 and 1989; Minorca, 1977; Spain, 1979; Madrid Bach Festival, 1980; RFH, 1984; Croatia (tour), annually, 2002–08; France, 2009–12; concert tours of Spain and Germany, annually 1980–. Début as harpsichordist, Wigmore Hall, 1963; directed Soho Concertante, Queen Elizabeth Hall, 1964–72. Mem. Music Cttee, Welsh Arts Council, 1981–84. Examiner, Trinity Coll. of Music, 1985–99. Lectr on work of Sir Thomas Graham Jackson incl. Venice, 2008. Recordings: Mass for a Saint's Day, 1971; organ and harpsichord music, incl. works by Arnell, Bach, Couperin, Langlais, Mozart, Vierne and Walther; Spanish organ music; own organ music, recorded at Chartres Cath., 2000; Requiem and other choral music, 2006; own instrumental works, 2012. Hon. Patron: Hertford Coll. Music Soc., 1996–; British Croatian Soc., 2002–. Master, Drapers' Co., 1994–95; Liveryman, Musicians' Co., 1985. Hon. Fellow, Hertford Coll., Oxford, 1995. *Publications*: (ed) Sir Thomas Graham Jackson. Recollections: the life and travels of a Victorian architect, 2003; Requiem, 2007; *compositions*: Mass for a Saint's Day, 1966; 20th Century Merbecke, 1967; 4 Images (for organ), 1971; Divertissement (organ), 1983; Organ Mass, 1984; 2 Organ Sonatas, 1985; Suite, for brass quintet and organ, 1986; The Reluctant Highwayman (opera), 1992 (world première, 1995); (completed) Bach's Fugue, BWV 906, 1996; Missa Cum Jubilo, 1998; Venetian Serenade, 2008; The Four Temperaments, 2009; Six Elizabethan Songs, 2010; Piano Trio, 2011; The Rose and the Ring (opera), 2016. *Recreations*: sketching, writing. *Heir*: *s* Thomas Graham St George Jackson, *b* 5 Oct. 1980.

**JACKSON, Patrick;** *see* Jackson, J. P.

**JACKSON, Paul;** *see* Jackson, K. P.

**JACKSON, Paul Edward;** Managing Director (International) (Amex), Ogilvy Group, 2006–07; *b* 8 July 1953; *s* of George Edward Jackson and Joan (*née* Barry); *m* 2000, Elaine Claire Adams; two *s*. *Educ*: Taunton Sch.; Watford Sch. of Art; Canterbury Coll. of Art (BA Hons Graphic Design); Bradford Univ. Mgt Centre. MIPA 1987. Account Executive: Saatchi & Saatchi, 1978–80; Mathers, 1980–81; Account Supervisor, Fletcher Shelton Delaney, 1981–83; Account Manager, Publicis, 1983–85; Bd Dir, BSB Dorland, 1985–92; Man. Dir, Kevin Morley Mktg, 1992–95; Exec. Man. Partner and Vice Chm., Ammirati Purlis Lintas, 1995–97; Client Service Dir, Dewe Rogerson, 1997–99; Ogilvy & Mather: Exec. Mgt Dir, 1999–2002; CEO, 2002–06. Non-exec. Dir, Aga Rangemaster Gp (formerly AGA Foodservice) plc, 2005–15. Dep. CEO and Trustee, Listening Place, 2016–. MInstD 1992. FRSA 1993. *Recreations*: sailing, fly fishing.

**JACKSON, Ven. Peggy;** *see* Jackson, Ven. F. A.

**JACKSON, Prof. Peter,** PhD; FBA 2012; Professor of Medieval History, Keele University, 2002–11, now Emeritus; *b* Rochdale, Lancs, 27 Jan. 1948; *s* of Frank Jackson and Dorothy Jackson; *m* 1990, Rebecca Oswald. *Educ*: Northern Grammar Sch., Portsmouth; St John's Coll., Cambridge (BA 1st Cl. Hist. 1971; PhD 1977). Jun. Res. Fellow, Churchill Coll., Cambridge, 1975–79; Keele University: Lectr in Hist., 1979–91; Sen. Lectr in Hist., 1991–2000; Reader in Hist., 2000–02. Vis. Fellow, Inst. for Advanced Studies, Hebrew Univ. of Jerusalem, 2000. *Publications*: (ed) The Cambridge History of Iran, vol. 6, 1986; (trans. and ed jtly) The Mission of Friar William of Rubruck, 1990; The Delhi Sultanate, 1999; The Mongols and the West 1221–1410, 2005, 2nd edn 2018; The Seventh Crusade, 1244–1254: sources and documents, 2007; Studies on the Mongol Empire and Early Muslim India, 2009; The Mongols and the Islamic World from Conquest to Conversion, 2017.

**JACKSON, Prof. Peter,** DPhil; FBA 2017; FAcSS; Professor of Human Geography, University of Sheffield, since 1993; *b* Stoneleigh, Surrey, 22 July 1955; *s* of (Lewis) Malcolm Stanley Jackson and Nancy May Irene Jackson (*née* Abbnett); *m* 1998, (Margaret) Deborah Lee; one *s* one *d*. *Educ*: Glyn Grammar Sch., Epsom; Keble Coll., Oxford (BA Hons Geog. 1976; Dip. Social Anthropol. 1977; DPhil Geog. 1980). Lectr in Geog., 1980–92, Sen. Lectr in Geog., 1992–93, UCL. FAcSS (AcSS 2001). Victoria Medal, RGS, 2007. *Publications*: Maps of Meaning, 1989; Changing Families, Changing Food, 2009; Food Words, 2013; Anxious Appetites, 2015. *Address*: Department of Geography, University of Sheffield, Sheffield S10 2TN. *T*: (0114) 222 7908. *E*: p.a.jackson@sheffield.ac.uk.

**JACKSON, Rt Hon. Sir Peter (Arthur Brian),** Kt 2010; PC 2017; **Rt Hon. Lord Justice Peter Jackson;** a Lord Justice of Appeal, since 2017; *b* 9 Dec. 1955; *s* of late Guy Jackson and of Amanda Jackson (now Park); *m* 1983, Deborah Sanderson; two *d*. *Educ*: Marlborough Coll.; Brasenose Coll., Oxford (BA Hons; Hon. Fellow, 2017). Called to the Bar, Inner Temple, 1978, Bencher, 2010; barrister specialising in family law, 1978–2010; QC 2000; Recorder, 2000–10; Family Div; a Judge of the High Court of Justice, Family Div., 2010–17. Liaison Judge, Northern Circuit, 2011–17. Chair, Trustee Bd, RCJ Advice, 2019–. Gov., 2000–13, Trustee, 2013–15, Camden Sch. for Girls. *Address*: Royal Courts of Justice, Strand, WC2A 2LL.

**JACKSON, Peter John;** Chairman, Kingfisher plc, 2006–09; *b* 16 Jan. 1947; *s* of Jack and Joan Jackson; *m* 1974, Anne Campbell; two *s* one *d*. *Educ*: Leeds Univ. (BA Econs). Industrial Relations Officer, BSC, 1968–71; Res. Officer, Commn on Industrial Relns, 1971–73; Personnel Manager, Guthrie Industries Europe, 1973–76; Perkins Engines: Indust. Relns Manager, 1976–80; Personnel Dir, 1980–83; Man. Dir, Rolls Royce Diesels, 1983–84; Dir and Gen. Manager, Gp Parts and Distribn, 1985–87; joined Associated British Foods, 1987; British Sugar plc: Exec. Dir, 1987–88; Dep. Man. Dir, 1988–89; Chief Exec., 1989–99; Chief Exec., Associated British Foods, 1999–2005. Non-exec. Dir, Smiths Group plc, 2003–09. Chm. Trustees, Disabilities Trust, 2007–17. *Recreations*: garden, golf, Sheffield United.

**JACKSON, Peter (Michael);** Senior Lecturer in Industrial Studies, Institute of Extra-mural Studies, National University of Lesotho, 1980; *b* 14 Oct. 1928; *s* of Leonard Patterson Jackson; *m* 1961, Christine Thomas. *Educ*: Durham Univ.; University Coll., Leicester. Lecturer, Dept of Sociology, University of Hull, 1964–66; Fellow, Univ. of Hull, 1970–72; Tutor, Open Univ., 1972–74; Senior Planning Officer, S Yorks CC, 1974–77. MP (Lab) High Peak, 1966–70; contested (Lab) Birmingham North, European Parly elecns, 1979. Member: Peak Park Jt Planning Bd, 1973–77, 1979–82; Derby CC, 1973–77. *Recreations*: numismatics, book collecting, ski-ing. *Address*: 82 Vandon Court, 64 Petty France, SW1H 9HG. *Club*: Maseru (Lesotho).

**JACKSON, Sir Peter (Robert),** ONZ 2012; KNZM 2010 (CNZM 2002); film producer, director, writer and actor; *b* Pukerua Bay, NZ, 31 Oct. 1961; *s* of late Bill and Joan Jackson; *m* 1987, Frances Walsh; one *s* one *d*. Formerly photographer, Evening Post, Wellington, NZ; Founder and Partner: WingNut Films Ltd (acquired Nat. Film Unit, NZ, 2000); Weta Ltd; Three Foot Six Ltd, 1999–. *Films*: producer, director, co-writer and actor: Bad Taste, 1987; Braindead, 1992; Heavenly Creatures, 1994; Forgotten Silver, 1995; The Frighteners, 1997; The Lord of the Rings trilogy: The Fellowship of the Ring, 2001 (BAFTA Awards for Best Film and Best Dir, 2002); The Two Towers, 2002; The Return of the King, 2003 (Acad. Awards for Best Dir, Best Picture and Best Adapted Screenplay, 2004); prod., dir and co-writer: Meet the Feebles, 1989; King Kong, 2005; The Lovely Bones, 2010; The Adventures of Tintin, 2011; The Hobbit Trilogy: An Unexpected Journey, 2012; The Desolation of Smaug, 2013; The Battle of the Five Armies, 2014; They Shall Not Grow Old, 2018; producer and co-writer: Jack Brown Genius, 1994; Mortal Engines, 2018; prod. and actor, The Long and Short of it, 2003; producer: Valley of the Stereos, 1992; District 9, 2009.

**JACKSON, Philip Henry Christopher,** CVO 2009; DL; FRSS; sculptor; *b* 18 April 1944; *s* of Humphrey Hoskins Jackson and Margaret Jackson (*née* Edwards); *m* 1979, Jean Barbara Welch; two *s* one *d*, and one step *s* one step *d*. *Educ*: Farnham Sch. of Art. Vice Pres., RBS, 1991–93; Pres., W Sussex Art Soc., 2001–; Member: Art Workers Guild, 1988; Fabric Adv. Cttee, Chichester Cath., 2006–; Lambert Barnard Paintings Steering Gp, 2009–. *Major commissions* include: Manchester Peace Gp, St Peters Sq., Manchester, 1988; Falklands War Monument, Portsmouth, 1992; The Young Mozart, Orange Sq., London, 1994; Liberation Sculpture Jersey, St Helier, 1995; Sir Matt Busby, Manchester United FC, Manchester, 1996; Wallenberg Monument, Great Cumberland Place, London, 1997; Minerva Sculpture, Chichester Fest. Th., 1997; Gurkha Monument, Horse Guards Ave., London, 1997; Constantine the Great, York Minster, 1998; Christ in Judgement, 1998, St Richard, 2000, Chichester Cath.; Empress Elizabeth of Austria, Geneva, 1998; Wallenberg Monument, Buenos Aires, 1998; The In Pensioner, Royal Hosp. Chelsea, London, 2000; King George VI, RNC, Dartmouth, 2002; Champions, the World Cup Sculpture, West Ham, London, 2003; equestrian sculpture of HM the Queen, Windsor Great Park, 2003; Terence Cuneo, Waterloo Station, London, 2003; Bobby Moore Sculpture, new Wembley Stadium; Queen Mother Meml, The Mall, London, 2008; United Trinity sculpture, Manchester United FC, 2008; Sir Alf Ramsey sculpture, New Wembley Stadium, 2008; British Diplomats commemorative sculpture, FCO, London, 2008; Lord Glenconner sculpture, Mustique, 2009; Archangel Gabriel sculpture, S Harting Church, W Sussex, 2009; St John the Evangelist, Portsmouth RC Cathedral, 2010; Peter Osgood sculpture, Chelsea FC, 2010; Bomber Command Meml, Green Park, 2012 (Marsh Award for Excellence in Public Sculpture, Public Monuments and Sculpture Assoc., 2013); Sir Alex Ferguson, Manchester United FC, 2012; HRH Prince Philip, Windsor Great Park, 2013; Joan Littlewood, Stratford East, 2013; Korean War Meml, Victoria Embankment, London, 2014 (Stone Award, 2016); Mahatma Gandhi sculpture, Parliament Sq., London, 2015; Sir Simon Milton, Tower Bridge, London, 2016; Brighton Coll. War Meml, Brighton, 2016;

Muhammad Ali Jinnah, Lincoln's Inn, London, 2017; Sir Simon Milton relief sculpture, Sutherland St, London, 2018; Lloyd George, Danny House, Hurstpierpoint, 2018. DL W Sussex, 2008. Hon. MA UC Chichester. Silver Medal, 1990, Sir Otto Beit Medal for Sculpture, 1991, 1992 and 1993, RBS. *Publications:* Philip Jackson: sculptures since 1987, 2002. *Recreations:* messing about in boats, Real tennis. *Address:* The Sculpture Studio, Mill Lane, Cocking, West Sussex GU29 0HJ. *T:* (01730) 812586, *Fax:* (01730) 812618. *E:* pj@sculpturestudio.co. *Clubs:* Athenæum, Sloane.

**JACKSON, Ralph S.;** *see* Seymour-Jackson.

**JACKSON, Rt Rev. Richard Charles;** *see* Lewes, Bishop Suffragan of.

**JACKSON, Prof. Richard James,** PhD; FRS 2006; Professor of RNA Biochemistry, University of Cambridge, 2000–07, now Emeritus; Fellow of Pembroke College, Cambridge, 1967–2007, now Emeritus; *b* 1 July 1940; *s* of James Rufus Jackson and Edith Winifred Jackson (*née* Clark); *m* 1967, Wiltrud Elfriede Klippel; two *d. Educ:* Bryanston Sch., Blandford Forum; Pembroke Coll., Cambridge (BA Natural Scis (Biochem.) 1962; PhD 1966). Res. Fellow, Dept of Molecular Biol., Univ. of Geneva, 1966–67; University of Cambridge: Res. Fellow, Pembroke Coll., 1967–70; Univ. Demonstrator, 1970–73; Lectr, 1973–94; Reader in the Biochem. of Nucleic Acids, 1994–2000. Roche Res. Fellow, Dept of Molecular Biol., Univ. of Geneva, 1977 (on sabbatical). Mem. EMBO, 1990. Jubilee Lect. and Harden Medal, Biochem. Soc., 2005. *Publications:* articles, esp. on the mechanism and regulation of mammalian protein biosynthesis, in scientific jls. *Recreations:* walking, bird watching, travel, music, reading. *Address:* Department of Biochemistry, University of Cambridge, Tennis Court Road, Cambridge CB2 1QW. *T:* (01223) 333682, *Fax:* (01223) 333345. *E:* rjj1000@cam.ac.uk.

**JACKSON, Robert Victor;** *b* 24 Sept. 1946; *m* 1975, Caroline Frances Harvey (*see* C. F. Jackson); one *s* decd. *Educ:* Falcon Coll., S Rhodesia; St Edmund Hall, Oxford (H. W. C. Davis Prize, 1966; 1st Cl. Hons Mod. Hist. 1968); President Oxford Union, 1967. Prize Fellowship, All Souls Coll., 1968 (Fellow, 1968–86). Councillor, Oxford CC, 1969–71; Political Adviser to Sec. of State for Employment, 1973–74; Member, Cabinet of Sir Christopher Soames, EEC Commn, Brussels, 1974–76; Chef de Cabinet, President of EEC Economic and Social Cttee, Brussels, 1976–78; Mem. (C) Upper Thames, European Parlt, 1979–84; Special Adviser to Governor of Rhodesia (Lord Soames), 1979–80; European Parlt's Rapporteur-Gen. on 1983 European Community Budget. MP Wantage, 1983–2005 (C, 1983–2005, Lab, 2005). Parly Under Sec. of State, DES, 1987–90, Dept of Employment, 1990–92, Office of Public Service and Sci., 1992–93. Mem., Select Cttee on Sci. and Technol., 1999–2001. Mem., Adv. Cttee on Works of Art, H of C; Treas., Cons. Mainstream Parly Gp. Mem., UK Delegn, Council of Europe and WEU, 2000–01. Contested (C) Manchester Central Div., Oct. 1974. Co-Chm., CAABU, 2001. Founder Trustee: Hattori Foundn, 1992–2018; Hattori Trust Co. Ltd, 1992–2018. Editor: The Round Table: Commonwealth Jl of Internat. Relations, 1970–74; International Affairs (Chatham House), 1979–80. *Publications:* South Asian Crisis: India, Pakistan, Bangladesh 1972, 1975; The Powers of the European Parliament, 1977; The European Parliament: Penguin Guide to Direct Elections, 1979; Reforming the European Budget, 1981; Tradition and Reality: Conservative philosophy and European integration 1982; From Boom to Bust?—British farming and CAP reform, 1983; Political Ideas in Western Europe Today, 1984. *Recreations:* reading, music, walking. *Address:* New House, Hanney Road, Southmoor, Abingdon OX13 5HR.

**JACKSON, Ven. Robert William;** Archdeacon of Walsall, 2004–09; freelance church growth consultant, since 2009; *b* 21 June 1949; *s* of Joseph William and Mary Edith Jackson; *m* 1973, Anne Christine Day; one *s* one *d* (and one *s* decd). *Educ:* King's Coll., Cambridge (MA 1973); Univ. of Manchester (MA 1973); Univ. of Nottingham (DipTh). Govt Economic Advr, 1972–78. Ordained deacon, 1981, priest, 1982; Curate, Christ Church, Fulwood, 1981–84; Vicar: St Mark's, Grenoside, 1984–92; St Mary, Scarborough, 1992–2001; Springboard Res. Missioner, 2001–04. *Publications:* Matthew, 1987, 2nd edn 1993; Godspeed, 1994; Till the Fat Lady Sings, 1996; Higher than the Hills, 1999; Hope for the Church, 2002; The Road to Growth: towards a thriving church, 2005; Going for Growth, 2006; (jtly) Everybody Welcome: the course where everybody helps grow their church, 2009; Growing Through a Vacancy, 2013; (jtly) LyCiG Local Course, 2013; What Makes Churches Grow?, 2015; Peat Pilgrimage Guide, 2015. *Recreations:* tennis, cricket, walking, trains. *Address:* 4 Glebe Park, Eyam, Hope Valley S32 5RH. *E:* venerablebob@gmail.com.

**JACKSON, Robin;** *see* Jackson, K. R.

**JACKSON, Sir Roland;** *see* Jackson, Sir W. R. C.

**JACKSON, Rosemary Elizabeth;** QC 2006; full-time mediator, since 2014; *b* 16 April 1958; *d* of Douglas and Pauline Jackson; *m* (marr. diss. 2010); one *s* one *d. Educ:* King's Coll. London (LLB Hons 1980; AKC 1980). Called to the Bar, Middle Temple, 1981; Accredited Mediator, 2001; a Recorder, 2002–15. *Address:* Keating Chambers, 15 Essex Street, WC2R 3AA. *T:* (020) 7544 2600, *Fax:* (020) 7544 2700.

**JACKSON, Prof. Roy,** DSc; FRS 2000; Class of 1950 Professor of Engineering and Applied Science, Princeton University, 1983–98, now Professor Emeritus; *b* 6 Oct. 1931; *s* of Harold and Ellen Jackson; *m* 1957, Susan Margaret Birch (*d* 1991); one *s* one *d. Educ:* Trinity Coll., Cambridge (BA 1954, MA 1959); Univ. of Edinburgh (DSc 1968). ICI Ltd, 1955–61; Reader in Chemical Engrg, Univ. of Edinburgh, 1961–68; A. J. Hartsook Prof. of Chemical Engrg, Rice Univ., 1968–77; Prof. of Chemical Engrg, Univ. of Houston, 1977–82; Sherman Fairchild Dist. Schol., CIT, 1982–83. Alpha Chi Sigma Award, 1980, Thomas Baron Award, 1993, AIChE. *Publications:* Transport in Porous Catalysts, 1977; The Dynamics of Fluidized Particles, 2000; articles in learned jls; more than 100 tech. papers. *Recreations:* sailing, water colour painting. *Address:* 311 Johnson Street, New Bern, NC 28560, USA. *T:* (252) 5142493.

**JACKSON, Rt Hon. Sir Rupert (Matthew),** Kt 1999; PC 2008; a Lord Justice of Appeal, 2008–18; arbitrator, since 2018; a Judge (part time), Astana International Financial Centre Court, Kazakhstan, since 2018; *b* 7 March 1948; *s* of late George Henry Jackson and Nancy Barbara Jackson (*née* May); *m* 1975, Claire Corinne Potter; three *d. Educ:* Christ's Hospital; Jesus College, Cambridge (MA, LLB; Hon. Fellow, 2009). Pres., Cambridge Union, 1971. Called to the Bar, Middle Temple, 1972, Bencher, 1995; QC 1987; a Recorder, 1990–98; a Dep. High Court Judge, 1993–98; a Judge of the High Court of Justice, QBD, 1999–2008; Judge in charge of Technol. and Construction Ct, 2004–07. Conducted Rev. of Civil Litigation Costs, 2009–10 (reported 2010), further Rev. of Civil Litigation Costs, 2017 (Supplemental Report, 2017). Chm., 1993–95, Pres., 2010–, Professional Negligence Bar Assoc.; Pres., Soc. of Construction Law, 2012–18. Ed., 1982–99, consultant ed., 2000–, Jackson and Powell on Professional Liability (formerly Jackson and Powell on Professional Negligence); Ed., 2000–10, Ed.-in-Chief, 2011–17, Civil Procedure (The White Book). *Publications:* The Reform of Civil Litigation, 2016, 2nd edn as The Reform of Civil Justice, 2018. *Recreations:* bridge, chess, gardening, walking, Roman history, playing with grandchildren. *Address:* 4 New Square, Lincoln's Inn, WC2A 3RJ. *Club:* Reform.

**JACKSON, Prof. Stephen Philip,** PhD; FRS 2008; Frederick James Quick and Cancer Research UK Professor of Biology, Department of Biochemistry, Cambridge University, since 2009 (Frederick James Quick Professor of Biology, Department of Zoology, 1995–2009); Senior Scientist, since 1996, Head, Cancer Research UK Laboratories, since 2004, Wellcome Trust/Cancer Research UK Gurdon Institute (formerly Wellcome/CRC Institute of Cancer and Developmental Biology), Cambridge University; Fellow of St John's College, Cambridge, since 1995; *b* 17 July 1962; *s* of Philip George Jackson and Marian Margaret (*née* Smith); *m* 1991, Teresa Margaret Clarke; two *s. Educ:* Univ. of Leeds (BSc 1st Cl. Hons Biochem. 1983); Univ. of Edinburgh (PhD Molecular Biol. 1987). Postgraduate research: Imperial Coll., London, 1983–85; Univ. of Edinburgh, 1985–87; Postdoctoral Fellow, Univ. of Calif, Berkeley, 1987–91; Research Gp Leader, 1991–95, Dep. Dir, then Dep. Chm., 2001–04, Wellcome/CRC Inst., subseq. Wellcome Trust/CRUK Gurdon Inst., Univ. of Cambridge. Founder, and Chief Scientific Officer: KuDOS Pharmaceuticals Ltd, 1997–2008; Mission Therapeutics Ltd, 2011–18 (Chair, Scientific Adv. Bd, 2018–); Co-Founder, Adrestia Therapeutics Ltd, 2018–. Lectures: Tenovus Medal, Tenovus-Scotland, 1997; Sackler, Univ. of Cambridge and Acad. of Med. Scis, 2015; J. Gregor Mendel Medal, Czech Republic, 2016; John J. Ryan Dist. Medal, RCSI, 2016; Sir Anthony Epstein Annual, Univ. of Bristol, 2017. FMedSci 2001. Mem. EMBO, 1997–. Hon. DSc Leeds, 2016. Eppendorf European Investigator Award, 1995; Colworth Medal, 1997, GlaxoSmithKline Award, 2008, Biochemical Soc.; Anthony Dipple Carcinogenesis Young Investigator Award, 2002; Innovator of Year Award, BBSRC, 2009; Buchanan Medal, Royal Soc., 2011; Gagna A. and Ch. Van Heck Prize, Fonds de la Recherche Scientifique, Brussels, 2015; King Faisal Internat. Prize for Sci., 2016; Impact Award, Sch. of Biol Scis, Univ. of Cambridge, 2016; Dr A. H. Heineken Prize for Medicine, Royal Netherlands Acad. of Arts and Scis, 2016; Genome Stability Network Medal, 2017; Léopold Griffuel Award, Fondation ARC, 2019. *Publications:* over 200 research papers and review articles in leading scientific jls, particularly in areas of DNA repair. *Recreations:* my children, gardening, travel. *Address:* Wellcome Trust/Cancer Research UK Gurdon Institute, University of Cambridge, Tennis Court Road, Cambridge CB2 1QN. *T:* (office) (01223) 334102.

**JACKSON, Stewart James;** Chief of Staff and Special Advisor to Secretary of State for Exiting the European Union, 2017–18; Strategic Counsellor, CTF Partners, since 2018; *b* 31 Jan. 1965; *s* of Raymond Thomas Jackson and late Sylvia Alice Theresa Jackson; *m* 1999, Sarah O'Grady; one *d. Educ:* Royal Holloway Coll., Univ. of London (BA Hons (Econs and Public Admin) 1988); Thames Valley Univ. (MA Human Resource Mgt). MCIPD 2001. Pres., Univ. of London, 1988–89. Retail Banker, Lloyds TSB, 1993–98; Business Services Manager, AZTEC (Trng and Enterprise Council for SW London), 1998–2000; Business Advr, Human Resources, Business Link for London, 2000–05. Mem. (C) Ealing BC, 1990–98. Contested (C) Brent S, 1997, Peterborough, 2001. MP (C) Peterborough, 2005–17; contested (C) same seat, 2017. *Recreations:* family, cinema, travel, biographies, local history. *Clubs:* Carlton; Peterborough Conservative.

**JACKSON, Dr Sylvia;** Member (Lab) Stirling, Scottish Parliament, 1999–2007; *b* 3 Dec. 1946; *d* of Herbert Edward Woodforth and Lucy Franklin; *m* 1970, Michael Peart Jackson (*d* 2001); one *s* one *d. Educ:* Brigg Girls' High Sch.; Univ. of Hull (BSc Hons Chemistry; PGCE; BPhil Educn); Univ. of Stirling (PhD Educn). Teacher of chemistry and physics, schools in Hull, Alva, Stirling, Cumbernauld and Kirkintilloch; Asst Sci. Advr, Edinburgh CC and Lothian Regl Council; Res. Fellow, Univ. of Stirling; Lectr, Moray House Inst. of Educn, Univ. of Edinburgh. Scottish Parliament: Dep. Convenor, Local Govt Cttee, 2000; Convenor, Subordinate Legislation Cttee, 2003–07; Mem., Local Govt and Transport Cttee, 2003–07; Cross Party Groups: Convenor, Animal Welfare; Co-Convenor, Affordable Housing; Vice Convenor, Drugs and Alcohol, 2004–07. Exec. Mem., CPA, 2003–07. *Publications:* Introducing Science (series of 12 pupil books and 6 teacher guides); contribs to jls, mainly dealing with professional develt of teachers. *Recreations:* walking, photography.

**JACKSON, Tessa;** *see* Jackson, J. T.

**JACKSON, Sir Thomas St Felix,** 6th Bt *cr* 1902; *b* 27 Sept. 1946; *s* of Sir Michael Roland Jackson, 5th Bt and Hilda Margaret Jackson (*née* Richardson); *S* father, 2016; *m* 1st, 1980, (Georgina) Victoria, *d* of late George Scatliff (marr. diss. 2009); two *d*; 2nd, 2013, Ann Margaret von Brockdorff, *d* of late Frank Gleave. *Educ:* Stowe Sch.; Univ. of Southampton (BA). Former Dep. Chm., Billington Jackson Advertising Ltd. *Heir:* none.

**JACKSON, Vanessa,** RA 2015; painter; *b* Guildford, 6 June 1953; *d* of Keith Jackson and Hilary Jackson; *m* 1993, John Dougill (*d* 2015), artist. *Educ:* Dorking Grammar Sch.; St Martin's Sch. of Art (BA 1st Cl. Hons 1975); Painting Sch., Royal Coll. of Art (MA 1978). FRCA 2004. Pres., New Contemporaries, 1974–75; Winchester School of Art: Vis. Fellow, Painting, 1978–80; Sen. Lectr, Fine Art Painting, 1980–87; Hd, Painting, 1988–97; MA and Res. Tutor, Painting, RCA, 1993–2007; Sen. Tutor, Fine Art, RA Schs, 1998–2013. Yaddo Fellowship, 1985, 1991; Edwin Austin Abbey Fellowship, British Sch. at Rome, 1995. Mem. Council, Incorporated Edwin Austin Abbey Meml Scholarship, 1995– (Chair, 2013–). External Examr incl. Glasgow, Middx, Chelsea Sch. of Arts, Wimbledon, Ecole Cantonale d'Art du Valais, UEA, Bergen Archtl Sch., C&G, Manchester Poly., Humberside. *Solo exhibitions* include: AIR Gall., London, 1981; Cubitt Gall. Gasworks, London, 1992; Art Inc., NYC, 2003; Studio 1.1, London, 2005; Sadler's Wells, 2008; CGP, 2010; *group exhibitions* include: New Contemporaries, London, 1974, 1975, 1976; John Moores 18 (prizewinner), 1993; Gall. Thomas Jaeckel, NYC, 2017; works in public and private collections internationally. *Address:* Bermondsey, London.

**JACKSON, (William) Gordon;** QC (Scot) 1990; Member (Lab) Glasgow Govan, Scottish Parliament, 1999–2007; *b* 5 Aug. 1948; *s* of Alexander Jackson and Margaret Shillinglaw or Jackson; *m* 1972, Anne Stevely; one *s* two *d. Educ:* Ardrossan Academy; St Andrews Univ. (LLB). Advocate, 1979; called to the Bar, Lincoln's Inn, 1989; Advocate Depute, Scotland, 1987–90.

**JACKSON, Sir (William) Roland (Cedric),** 9th Bt *cr* 1869, of The Manor House, Birkenhead; DPhil; science historian, policy adviser and writer; *b* 9 Jan. 1954; *s* of Sir (William) Thomas Jackson, 8th Bt and Gillian Malise (*née* Stobart); *S* father, 2004; *m* 1977, Nicola Mary, MA, DPhil, *yr d* of Prof. Peter Reginald Davis, PhD, FRCS; three *s. Educ:* Wycliffe Coll.; St Peter's Coll., Oxford (MA); Exeter Coll., Oxford (DPhil). Hd of Science, Backwell Sch., 1986–89; Educn Advr, ICI, 1989–93; Science Museum: Hd of Learning, 1993–2002; Hd of Mus., 2001–02; Chief Exec., BAAS (British Sci. Assoc.), 2002–13. Res. Associate, UCL, 2014–. Dir, Big Bang Educn CIC, 2010–13. Chair, Biosci. for Society Strategy Panel, BBSRC, 2011–14; Exec. Chair, Sciencewise, 2012–16. Member: Nuffield Council on Bioethics, 2013–19; Mgt Bd, Industrial Biotechnol. Catalyst, 2014–16. Vis. Fellow, Royal Instn, 2013– (Trustee, 2019–). Trustee: Mather-Jackson Library, 2007–; Lowther Castle and Gardens Trust, 2014–. Sec., Alpine Club Library, 2011–16. Gen. Ed., Correspondence of John Tyndall, 2016–. Hon. DSc Aston, 2011; DHC Aberdeen, 2012. *Publications:* The Ascent of John Tyndall, 2018. *Recreation:* collecting and reading mountaineering and rock-climbing literature and occasionally repeating some of the feats described therein. *Heir: s* Adam William Roland Jackson, *b* 19 May 1982. *Clubs:* Athenæum, Alpine.

**JACKSON-NELSON, Hon. Marjorie,** AC 2001; CVO 2002; MBE 1953; Governor, South Australia, 2001–07; *b* 13 Sept. 1931; *d* of William Alfred Jackson and Mary Jackson; *m* 1953, Peter Nelson (*d* 1977); one *s* two *d*. *Educ*: Lithgow High Sch., NSW. Athlete (the Lithgow Flash): holder, Australian 100 yards, 100 metres, 220 yards and 200 metres sprint titles, 1950–54; broke world sprint records on ten occasions; Olympic Gold Medals for 100m and 200m, Helsinki, 1952; 7 Commonwealth Games Gold Medals. Australian Commonwealth Games teams: Women's Section Manager, Auckland, 1982, Edinburgh, 1986, Auckland, 1990; Gen. Team Manager, Victoria, Canada, 1994; Athletes' Liaison Officer, Malaysia, 1998. Member Board: S Australian Govt's Sports Inst., 1985–90; Sydney Organising Cttee for 2000 Olympic Games, 1998–2000. Launched Peter Nelson Leukaemia Res. Fellowship, 1977; has raised over Aust. 6 million to sponsor research into fighting leukaemia; funds raised have sponsored a leukaemia lab. in Adelaide. Freedom of City of London, 2006. Hon. Dr: Charles Sturt, NSW, 2001; Flinders, SA, 2018. Australian Sports Medal, 2000; Olympic Order, IOC, 2008; IAAF Hall of Fame, Monaco, 2013.

**JACKSON-STOPS, Timothy William Ashworth,** FRICS; Chairman, 1978–98, Consultant, since 1998, Jackson-Stops & Staff; *b* 1942; *s* of late Anthony and Jean Jackson-Stops; *m* 1987, Jenny MacArthur; two *s*. *Educ*: Eton; Agricultural Coll., Cirencester. Jackson-Stops & Staff, 1967–: Dir, 1974. *Recreations*: ski-ing, sailing, shooting. *Address*: Wood Burcote Court, Towcester, Northants NN12 6JP. *T*: (01327) 350443.

**JACOB, Rt Hon. Sir Robert Raphael Hayim, (Sir Robin),** Kt 1993; PC 2003; a Lord Justice of Appeal, 2003–11; Sir Hugh Laddie Professor in Intellectual Property and Director, Institute of Brand and Innovation Law, University College London, since 2011; *b* 26 April 1941; *s* of Sir Isaac Hai, (Sir Jack) Jacob, QC and Rose Jacob; *m* 1967, Wendy Jones; three *s*. *Educ*: King Alfred Sch., Hampstead; Mountgrace Secondary Comprehensive Sch., Potters Bar; St Paul's Sch.; Trinity Coll., Cambridge (BA, MA); LSE (LLB; Hon. Fellow, 2005). Called to the Bar, Gray's Inn, 1965 (Atkin Scholar; Bencher, 1989; Vice-Treas., 2006; Treas., 2007); teacher of law, 1965–66; pupillage with Nigel Bridge (later Lord Bridge of Harwich), 1966–67, with A. M. Walton, 1967; entered chambers of Thomas Blanco White, 1967; Junior Counsel to Treasury in Patent Matters, 1976–81; QC 1981; a Judge of the High Court of Justice, Chancery Div., 1993–2003. Judge, Astana Internat. Financial Centre Court, 2018–. Dep. Chm., Copyright Tribunal, 1989–93; apptd to hear appeals to Sec. of State under the Trade Marks Acts, 1988–93. Member: Adv. Bd, Centre for European Law, KCL, 2002–; Adv. Council on Intellectual Property Law, Osgoode Hall Law Sch., 2009–; Econ. and Scientific Adv. Bd, Eur. Patent Office, 2012–. Governor: LSE, 1994–; Expert Witness Inst., 1996–2006, 2011–. Hon. Vis. Prof. of Law, Univ. of Birmingham, 1999–; Dist. Judicial Visitor, UCL, 2002–11. Pres., Intellectual Property Judges' Assoc., 2013–; Hon. President: Assoc. of Law Teachers, 2002–; Licensing Exec. Soc., 2003–. Hon. Fellow, St Peter's Coll., Oxford, 1998. Hon. LLD Wolverhampton, 2009. Jt Editor, Encyclopedia of UK and European Patent Law, 1977–. *Publications*: Kerly's Law of Trade Marks (ed jtly), 1972, 1983 and 1986 edns; Patents, Trade Marks, Copyright and Designs (ed jtly), 1970, 1978, 1986; Editor, Court Forms Sections on Copyright (1978), Designs and Trade Marks (1975–86); section on Trade Marks (ed jtly), 4th edn, Halsbury's Laws of England, 1985, 1995; Guidebook to Intellectual Property, 1993, 6th edn 2013; IP and Other Things, 2015; articles and lectures. *Recreations*: Arsenal FC, photography, country garden. *Address*: Faculty of Laws, University College London, Bentham House, Endsleigh Gardens, WC1H 0EG. *E*: rjacob@ucl.ac.uk.

**JACOB, Ven. William Mungo,** PhD; FRHistS; Archdeacon of Charing Cross, 1996–2015, now Archdeacon Emeritus; Rector, St Giles-in-the-Fields, 2000–15; Priest-in-charge: St Anne's, Soho with St Thomas and St Peter, 2011–13; St John's, East Dulwich, 2015–16; *b* 15 Nov. 1944; *s* of John William Carey Jacob and Mary Marsters Dewar. *Educ*: King Edward VII School, King's Lynn; Hull Univ. (LLB); Linacre Coll., Oxford (MA); Exeter Univ. (PhD). FRHistS 2013. Deacon 1970, priest 1971; Curate of Wymondham, Norfolk, 1970–73; Asst Chaplain, Exeter Univ., 1973–75; Lecturer, Salisbury and Wells Theological Coll., 1975–80, Vice-Principal, 1977–80; Sec. to Cttee for Theological Education, ACCM, 1980–86; Warden, Lincoln Theol Coll., 1986–96; Canon of Lincoln Cathedral, 1986–96. D. J. James Prof. of Pastoral Theol., Univ. of Wales, Lampeter, 2006–09. Vis. Res. Fellow, KCL, 2011–. Trustee: Lincoln Theol Inst. for Theol Study of Religion and Soc., 1996–; Paddington Develt Trust, 2016–; Soc. of the Faith, 2017–. Pres., Chapels Soc., 2019–. Great Ringstead Parish Council, 2016–. Ed., Theology, 1998–2008. *Publications*: (ed with P. Baelz) Ministers of the Kingdom, 1985; (contrib.) Religious Dissent in East Anglia, 1991; (contrib.) The Weight of Glory, 1991; (ed with N. Yates) Crown and Mitre, 1993; Lay People and Religion in the Early Eighteenth Century, 1996; The Making of the Anglican Church Worldwide, 1997; (contrib.) The National Church in Local Perspective, 2003; (contrib.) Studies in Church History, vols 16, 28, 31, 38, 40, 42, 50, 51; (contrib.) Anglicanism and the Western Christian Tradition, 2003; (contrib.) The Pastor Bonus, 2004; (contrib.) St Paul's: the Cathedral Church of London 604–2004, 2004; (contrib.) Cambridge History of Libraries in Britain and Ireland, vol. 2, 2006; The Clerical Profession in the Long Eighteenth Century, 1680–1840, 2007; (contrib.) The Welsh Church from Reformation to Disestablishment 1603–1920, 2007; (contrib.) Treasures of the English Church, 2008; (contrib.) Lambeth Palace Library: treasures from the collections of the Archbishops of Canterbury, 2010; (contrib.) Comfortable Words: polity, piety and the Book of Common Prayer, 2012; (contrib.) The Oxford History of Anglicanism, vol. 2, 2017; contribs to Jl Anglican Studies, Liby and Information Studies, Studies in Church History. *Address*: 4 St Mary's Walk, SE11 4UA. *T*: (020) 7735 8201.

**JACOBI, Sir Derek (George),** Kt 1994; CBE 1985; actor; *b* 22 Oct. 1938; *s* of Alfred George Jacobi and Daisy Gertrude Masters. *Educ*: Leyton County High Sch.; St John's Coll., Cambridge (MA Hons; Hon. Fellow, 1987). Artistic Associate, Old Vic Co. (formerly Prospect Theatre Co.), 1976–81; associate actor, RSC; Artistic Dir, Chichester Fest. Th., 1995–96. Vice-Pres., Nat. Youth Theatre, 1982–. *Stage*: Birmingham Repertory Theatre, 1960–63 (first appearance in One Way Pendulum, 1961); National Theatre, 1963–71; Prospect Theatre Co., 1972, 1974, 1976, 1977, 1978; Hamlet (for reformation of Old Vic Co., and at Elsinore), 1979; Benedick in Much Ado About Nothing (Tony Award, 1985), title rôle in Peer Gynt, Prospero in The Tempest, 1982, title rôle in Cyrano de Bergerac, 1983 (SWET Award; Plays and Players Award), RSC; Breaking the Code, Haymarket, 1986, Washington and NY 1987; Dir, Hamlet, Phoenix, 1988; title rôle in Kean, Old Vic, 1990; title rôle in Becket, Haymarket, 1991; Byron, in Mad, Bad and Dangerous to Know, Ambassadors, 1992; Macbeth, RSC, 1993; title rôle in Hadrian VII, Playing the Wife, Chichester, 1995; Uncle Vanya, Chichester, 1996, NY, 2000; God Only Knows, Vaudeville, 2001; The Tempest, Old Vic, 2003; Don Carlos, Gielgud, 2005; A Voyage Round My Father, Wyndham's, 2006; Malvolio in Twelfth Night, Wyndham's, 2008 (Olivier Award, Best Actor); title rôle in King Lear, Donmar Warehouse, 2010; Heartbreak House, Chichester, 2012; Romeo and Juliet, Garrick, 2016; *appearances include*: *TV*: She Stoops to Conquer, Man of Straw, The Pallisers, I Claudius, Philby, Burgess and Maclean, Richard II, Hamlet, Inside the Third Reich, Mr Pye, Cadfael; The Gathering Storm, 2002; The Jury, 2002; The Long Firm, 2004; The Old Curiosity Shop, 2007; Last Tango in Halifax, 2012–17; Vicious, 2013, 2015, 2016; Les Misérables, 2018; *films*: 1971–: Odessa File; Day of the Jackal; The Medusa Touch; Othello; Three Sisters; Interlude; The Human Factor; Charlotte; The Man Who Went Up in Smoke; Enigma; Little Dorrit (Best Actor Award, Evening Standard); Henry V; The Fool; Dead Again; Hamlet; Love is the Devil (Best Actor Award, Evening Standard); Gladiator; The Body; Gosford Park; A Revenger's Tragedy; Nanny McPhee; The Golden Compass; A Bunch of Amateurs; The King's Speech; Anonymous; Grace of Monaco; Cinderella; Murder on the Orient Express; Tolkien; Horrible Histories: The Movie. *Awards*: BAFTA Best Actor, 1976–77; Variety Club TV Personality, 1976; Standard Best Actor, 1983. *Publications*: As Luck Would Have It, 2013. *Address*: c/o Independent Talent Group Ltd, 40 Whitfield Street, W1T 2RH.

**JACOBS, Alexander Marc;** a District Judge (Magistrates' Courts), since 2018; a Recorder, since 2019; *b* Liverpool, 9 Oct. 1972; *s* of late David Jacobs and of Barbara, (Bobby), Jacobs (*née* Myers); *m* 2002, Donna Deena Abudarham; one *s* two *d*. *Educ*: King David Sch., Liverpool; Manchester Metropolitan Univ. (LLB Hons 1995); Inns of Court Sch. of Law. Called to the Bar, Gray's Inn, 1997; in practice as barrister, Lion Court, 1997–2000, St Ives Chambers, Birmingham, 2000–18. Fee-paid Social Security Tribunal Judge (Social Entitlement Chamber), 2011–18; a Dep. Dist Judge (Magistrates' Courts), 2012–18. Legally qualified Chair and Legal Adviser/Assessor: Med. Practitioners Tribunal Service, 2010–18; NMC, 2010–18; Health and Care Professions Tribunal Service, 2012–18; Gen. Chiropractic Council, 2015–18; GDC, 2016–18. Barrister Mem., Professional Conduct Cttee, Bar Standards Bd, 2008–13. *Recreations*: singing - synagogue cantor/chazan, family time. *Address*: c/o Westminster Magistrates' Court, 181 Marylebone Road, NW1 5BR.

**JACOBS, Edward John;** an Upper Tribunal Judge (Administrative Appeals Chamber) (formerly Social Security and Child Support Commissioner), since 1998; *b* 20 Nov. 1952; *m* Jill, *d* of W. J. Langford. *Educ*: Paston Sch.; Univ. of Southampton. Called to the Bar, Inner Temple, 1976. *Publications*: Effective Exclusion Clauses, 1990; (with M. Jones) Company Meetings: law and procedure, 1991; Child Support: the legislation, 1993, 14th edn 2019; Tribunal Practice and Procedure, 2009, 5th edn 2019; (ed and contrib.) Jowitt's Dictionary of English Law, 3rd edn 2010; contrib. articles to legal jls. *Recreations*: ancient and medieval murder, cross-country ski-ing. *Address*: Upper Tribunal, Administrative Appeals Chamber, 5th Floor, Rolls Building, 7 Rolls Buildings, Fetter Lane, EC4A 1NL.

**JACOBS, Rt Hon. Sir Francis (Geoffrey),** KCMG 2006; PC 2005; Professor of Law, since 2006, and President, Centre of European Law, since 2007; King's College London; an Advocate General, Court of Justice of the European Communities, 1988–2006; *b* 8 June 1939; *s* of late Cecil Sigismund Jacobs and Louise Jacobs (*née* Fischhof); *m* 1st, 1964, Ruth (*née* Freeman); one *s*; 2nd, 1975, Susan Felicity Gordon (*née* Cox); one *s* three *d*. *Educ*: City of London Sch.; Christ Church, Oxford; Nuffield Coll., Oxford. MA, DPhil. Called to the Bar, Middle Temple, 1964, Bencher, 1990, Reader, 2009; in part-time practice, 1974–88, 2006–; QC 1984; Lectr in Jurisprudence, Univ. of Glasgow, 1963–65; Lectr in Law, LSE, 1965–69; Secretariat, European Commn of Human Rights, and Legal Directorate, Council of Europe, Strasbourg, 1969–72; Legal Sec., Court of Justice of European Communities, Luxembourg, 1972–74; Prof. of European Law, Univ. of London, 1974–88; Dir, Centre of Eur. Law, 1981–88, Vis. Prof., 1989–2006, KCL. Pres., UK Assoc. for European Law, 2009–13 (Hon. Sec., 1974–81; a Vice-Pres., 1988–2009); Trustee, British Inst. of Internat. and Comparative Law, 2006–09, 2010–16. Chm., Eur. Maritime Law Orgn, 2005–12; Pres., Admin. Tribunal, Internat. Inst. for Unification of Private Law, 2009–; Founding Pres., 2011–13, Mem. Senate, 2013–, European Law Inst. Cooley Lectr, 1983; Bishop Lectr, 1989, LeRoy Fellow, 1993, 2002, Jean Monnet Fellow, 2006, Univ. of Mich.; Hamlyn Lectr, 2006; British Acad. Law Lect., 2008. Marcel Storme Prof., Univ. of Ghent, 2005–06; Jean Monnet Prof., KCL, 2006–; Prof., Coll. of Europe, Bruges, 2006–09. Governor: British Inst. of Human Rights, 1985–; Inns of Court Sch. of Law, 1996–2001. Patron, UK Envmtl Law Assoc., 2007–; Pres., 2007–13, Patron, 2013–, Missing Children Europe. FKC, 1990. Hon. Fellow, Soc. for Advanced Legal Studies, 1998; Hon. Mem., Soc. of Legal Scholars, 2003; Foreign Mem., Royal Flemish Acad. of Belgium for Sci. and Arts, 2005. Hon. LLD: Birmingham, 1996; Glasgow, 2006; Kingston, 2012; Hon. DCL City, 1997; Hon. Dr Ghent, 2007; Hon. DLaws, Groningen, 2014. Hon. Texan, 2000. Commandeur de l'Ordre de Mérite, Luxembourg, 1983. Founding Editor, Yearbook of European Law, 1981–88; Mem. Editl Bd, Yearbook of European Law and many law reviews. Gen. Ed., Oxford EC Law Library (formerly Oxford European Community Law series), 1986–2010. *Publications*: Criminal Responsibility, 1971; The European Convention on Human Rights, 1975, 7th edn (jtly), 2017; (jtly) References to the European Court, 1975; (ed) European Law and the Individual, 1976; (jtly) The Court of Justice of the European Communities, 1977; (jtly) The European Union Treaty, 1986; (joint editor): The European Community and GATT, 1986; The Effect of Treaties in Domestic Law, 1987; Liber Amicorum Pierre Pescatore, 1987; European Community Law in English Courts, 1998; (contrib.) de Smith, Woolf and Jowell, Judicial Review of Administrative Action, 1995; The Sovereignty of Law: the European way, 2007; *relevant publications*: Continuity and Change in EU Law: essays in honour of Sir Francis Jacobs, 2008; Making Community Law: the legacy of Advocate General Jacobs at the European Court of Justice, 2008. *Recreations*: family life, books, music, nature, travel. *Address*: Wayside, 15 St Alban's Gardens, Teddington, Middx TW11 8AE. *T*: (020) 8943 0503. *E*: francis.jacobs@kcl.ac.uk; Fountain Court, Temple, EC4Y 9DH.

**JACOBS, Prof. Ian Jeffrey,** MD; FRCOG; President and Vice-Chancellor, UNSW Sydney (formerly UNSW Australia), since 2015; *b* 6 Oct. 1957; *s* of Sidney and Shirley Jacobs; *m* 1988, Chris Steele; two *s* one *d*. *Educ*: Trinity Coll., Cambridge (BA 1980, MA 1983); London Univ. (MB BS 1983; MD 1991). FRCOG (MRCOG 1990). Consultant Gynaecological Oncologist, Bart's and the London NHS Trust, 1996–2004; Prof. of Gynaecological Oncology, 1999–2004, and Dir, Cancer Inst., 2002–04, Bart's and the London, Queen Mary's Sch. of Medicine; Hd of Res., Dept. of Gynaecological Cancer, UCL, 2004–11; Gynaecol Oncologist, UCLH, 2004–11; Director: Inst. for Women's Health, UCL, 2004–09; UCLH/UCL Comprehensive Biomed. Res. Centre, 2007–10; Dean of Biomed. Scis, UCL, 2009–10; Res. Dir, UCL Partners Academic Health Sci. Centre, 2009–10; Prof. of Women's Health and Cancer, UCL, 2004–11; Sen. Investigator, NIHR, 2009–14; Vice Pres. and Dean, Faculty of Med. and Health Scis, Manchester Univ., 2010–15; Hd, Manchester Academic Health Sci. Centre, 2011–15. Hon. Consultant: Royal Marsden Hosp., 1996–2010; Central Manchester NHS Trust, Manchester, 2011–14. Chair, Gp of 8 Univs Australia, 2018–19. Non-exec. Dir, Abcodia Ltd, 2012–. Founder, Gynaecology Cancer Res. Fund/Eve Appeal charity, 1985 (Scientific Dir, 1985–2015; Emeritus Trustee, 2015–); Founder and Mem. Bd, Uganda Women's Health Initiative, 2005– (Chm., 2005–15); Member, Board: Research Australia, 2017–; The Conversation, 2018–; Ovarian Cancer Australia, 2018–. *Publications*: over 200 articles on Ovarian Cancer; numerous contribs to med. and scientific jls, incl. Lancet, BMJ and Cancer Res. *Recreations*: Arsenal football fan, dogs, family life, running, charitable work. *Address*: Office of the President and Vice-Chancellor, UNSW Sydney, Sydney, NSW 2052, Australia.

**JACOBS, Rabbi Irving,** PhD; Principal, Jews' College, London, 1990–93; *b* 2 Aug. 1938; *s* of Solomon Jacobs and Bertha (*née* Bluestone); *m* 1963, Ann Klein; one *s* three *d*. *Educ*: Jews' Coll., London; Univ. of London (BA, PhD); Rabbinical Dip. Jews' College, London: Res. Fellow, 1966–69; Lectr, 1969–75; Sen. Lectr, 1975–84; Dean, 1984–90. *Publications*: The Midrashic Process, 1995; The Impact of Midrash, 2006; articles on Midrash Apocryphal lit. and Jewish liturgy in scholarly jls. *Address*: 28 Elmstead Avenue, Wembley, Middx HA9 8NX. *T*: (020) 8248 5777.

**JACOBS, Jeffrey,** CB 2002; Head of Paid Service and Director of Communities and Intelligence, 2011–18, and Greater London Returning Officer, 2014–18, Greater London Authority; b 20 July 1949; s of late Sydney and Jane Jacobs; m 1974, Mary Jane Whitelegg; one s one d. Educ: Enfield Grammar Sch. Joined Ministry of Housing and Local Government, later Department of the Environment, 1965: Asst Private Sec. to Sec. of State for Envmt, 1979–82; Head: Housing Policies Studies Div., 1987–90; Envmt Agency Project Team, 1990–92; Manchester Olympic Unit, 1992–94; Regeneration Div., 1994–97; Principal Private Sec. to Dep. Prime Minister, 1997–98; Dir, Planning Directorate, DETR, 1998–2001; Exec. Dir, Policy and Partnerships, GLA, 2001–04; Dir Gen., Children and Young People and Communities, 2004–06, Chief Exec., Govt Olympic Exec., 2006–07, DCMS; Sen. Advr to Mayor of London, 2007–08; Exec. Dir and Dep. Chief Exec., GLA, 2008–11. Fellow, Hubert H. Humphrey Inst., Minneapolis, 1986–87. Recreations: sport, walking. E: jacobs116@sky.com.

**JACOBS, Laurence Warren;** Partner, Milbank Tweed, since 2004; b London, 21 March 1960; s of Sidney and Shirley Jacobs; m 1984, Ann Gainsford; one s three d. Educ: Haberdashers' Aske's Sch., Elstree; Queens' Coll., Cambridge (BA Hist. 1982); King's Coll., Cambridge. Admitted Solicitor, 1990; Articled Clerk, 1988–90, Associate, 1990–92, Clifford Chance; Associate, 1992–98, Partner, 1998–2004, Allen & Overy. Recreations: reading, hiking, grandchildren, living in Jerusalem. Address: Milbank Tweed, 10 Gresham Street, EC2V 7JD. T: (020) 7615 3000, Fax: (020) 7615 3100. E: ljacobs@milbank.com.

**JACOBS, Sir Michael (Graham),** Kt 2016; PhD; Consultant in Infectious Diseases, Royal Free London NHS Foundation Trust, since 2000; b London, 18 Jan. 1964; s of Alan and Eva Jacobs; m 1st, 1995, Kate Cwynarski (marr. diss. 2009); one s one d; 2nd, 2010, Suzanne; one d. Educ: University Coll. Sch.; St John's Coll., Oxford (BA 1985); St Bartholomew's Hosp. Med. Sch., London (MB BS 1988); PhD London 2000. MRCP 1991, FRCP 2005; DTM&H 1995. Hse Physician, Whipps Cross Hosp., 1988–89; Hse Surgeon, St Bartholomew's Hosp., 1989; SHO, Royal Free Hosp., 1989–90; Rotating Med. SHO, Addenbrooke's and Hinchingbrooke Hosps, Cambridge, 1990–91; Med. Registrar, Ealing and Hammersmith Hosps, 1991–94; Wellcome Res. Trng Fellow, 1994–98, Locum Clin. Lectr, 1998, Imperial Coll. London; Specialist Registrar: Infectious and Tropical Diseases, Northwich Park Hosp., 1998–99; Infectious Diseases and Gen. Medicine, Hammersmith Hosp., 1999–2000; Dept of Infection, Guy's and St Thomas's Hosps, 2000; Wellcome Advanced Fellow, UCL, 2001–04. Publications: contribs in field of infectious diseases. Recreations: fitness training, walking, cinema, modern literature. Address: Royal Free London NHS Foundation Trust, Pond Street, NW3 2QG. E: michael.jacobs@ucl.ac.uk.

**JACOBS, Michael Upton;** Professorial Research Fellow in Political Economy, Sheffield Political Economy Research Institute, University of Sheffield, since 2018; b London, 3 Dec. 1960; s of Arthur Jacobs and Betty Upton Hughes; m 1997, Catherine McKenzie; one s two d. Educ: Woodhouse Sch.; Wadham Coll., Oxford (BA Hons PPE); Middlesex Poly. (Postgrad. Dip. Employment and Planning). Coordinator, Tools for Self Reliance, 1983–84; Community Educn Worker, Hampshire CC, 1985–88; Adult Educn Lectr, Southampton Univ., 1985–89; freelance journalist, 1985–92; Dir, then Man. Dir, CAG Consultants, 1990–94; ESRC Res. Fellow, Centre for Study of Envmtl Change, Lancaster Univ., and Dept of Geog., LSE, 1994–97; Gen. Sec., Fabian Soc., 1997–2003; Mem., Council of Econ. Advrs, HM Treasury, 2004–07; Special Advr to Prime Minister, 10 Downing St, 2007–10; Climate Change Advr, Children's Investment Fund Foundn, 2010–13; Senior Adviser: Inst. du Développement Durable et des Relations Internationales, 2013–14; Global Commn on the Economy and Climate, 2013–16; Dir, IPPR Commn on Econ. Justice, 2016–18 (Final Report, 2018). Visiting Professor: Grantham Res. Inst. on Climate Change and Envmt, LSE, 2010–16; Dept of Political Sci., UCL, 2011–; Associate Fellow, 2011–, Vis. Fellow, 2016, IPPR. Mem., Editl Bd, 2002–, Co-Ed., 2012–14, Political Qly. Member: Climate Change Adv. Bd, Children's Investment Fund Foundn, 2010–15; Supervisory Bd, Eur. Climate Foundn, 2011–13. Trustee: Action Aid, 2004–07. Gov., Sir Thomas Abney Primary Sch., Hackney, 2010–. Publications: The Green Economy: environment, sustainable development and the politics of the future, 1991; The Politics of the Real World, 1996; (ed) Greening the Millennium: the new politics of the environment, 1997; Paying for Progress: a new politics of tax for public spending, 2000; (ed jtly) Rethinking Capitalism: economics and policy for sustainable and inclusive growth, 2016. Recreations: art, theatre, cycling, 5-a-side football, sailing, school governor. Address: Sheffield Political Economy Research Institute, University of Sheffield, ICOSS Building, 219 Portobello, Sheffield S1 4DP.

**JACOBS, Nigel Robert;** QC 2006; barrister and arbitrator; b 31 May 1960; m 1993, Suzanne Tanchan; two d. Educ: Highgate Sch.; Pembroke Coll., Cambridge (BA 1982); Trinity Coll., Cambridge (LLM 1984). Called to the Bar, Middle Temple, 1983. Recreations: tennis, theatre, cinema. Address: Quadrant Chambers, 10 Fleet Street, EC4Y 1AU. T: (020) 7583 4444, Fax: (020) 7583 4455.

**JACOBS, Prof. Patricia Ann,** OBE 1999; FRS 1993; Co-Director of Research, Wessex Regional Genetics Laboratory, 1990–15 (Director, 1988–2001); b 8 Oct. 1934; d of Cyril Jacobs and Sadie Jacobs (née Jones); m 1972, Newton Ennis Morton (d 2018); three step s two step d. Educ: St Andrews Univ. (BSc 1st Cl. Hons 1956; D'Arcy Thomson Medal 1956; DSc 1966; Sykes Medal 1966). FRSE 1977; FRCPath 1987; FRCPE 1998; FRCOG 1999. Res. Asst, Mount Holyoke Coll., USA, 1956–57; Scientist, MRC, 1957–72; Prof., Dept of Anatomy and Reproductive Biology, Univ. of Hawaii Sch. of Medicine, 1972–85; Prof. and Chief of Div. of Human Genetics, Dept of Pediatrics, Cornell Univ. Med. Coll., 1985–87. Hon. Prof. of Human Genetics, Univ. of Southampton Med. Sch., 1993–. Mem., MRC, 1996–98. Founder FMedSci 1998; FRSA 1993. Foreign Associate, NAS, 2009. Hon. DSc St Andrews, 2002. Allan Award, Amer. Soc. of Human Genetics, 1981; Regents Medal, Univ. of Hawaii, 1983; Premio Phoenix Anni-Verdi, 1998; Mauro Baschirotto Award, European Soc. of Human Genetics, 1999; March of Dimes Prize in Develtl Biol., 2011. Publications: numerous articles in learned jls. Recreations: walking, botany, gardening.
See also Peter A. Jacobs.

**JACOBS, Peter Alan;** non-executive Chairman: L. A. Fitness (formerly L. A. Leisure), 1999–2005; W. T. Foods, 2002–05; b 22 Feb. 1943; s of Cyril and Sadie Jacobs; m 1966, Eileen Dorothy Naftalin; twin s one d. Educ: Glasgow Univ. (BSc Hons MechEng); Aston Univ. (Dip. Management Studies). Tube Investments: grad. trainee, 1965–67; Production Controller, Toy Div., 1968–70; Pedigree Petfoods: Production Shift Manager, 1970–72; Purchasing Dept, 1972–81; Production Manager, 1981–83; Sales Dir, Mars Confectionery, 1983–86; Berisford International: Man. Dir, British Sugar, 1986–89; Chief Exec., Berisford and Chm., British Sugar, 1989–91; Chief Exec., BUPA, 1991–98; non-executive Chairman: Healthcall Ltd, 1998–2001; Hillsdown Holdings plc, 1999–2000; abc Media, 2005–10; non-executive Director: Allied Domecq, 1998–2004; Bank Leumi (UK), 1999–2003; Virtual Communities Inc., 1999–2000; RAF Air Command (formerly RAF Strike Command), 2002–09. Recreations: tennis, theatre, music. Address: Garden Flat, 29 Daleham Gardens, NW3 5BY.
See also Patricia A. Jacobs.

**JACOBS, His Honour Peter John;** a Circuit Judge, 1997–2013; b 16 April 1943; s of Herbert Walter Jacobs and Emma Doris Jacobs; m 1975, Dr Ruth Edwards; two s. Educ: King Edward VII Sch., King's Lynn; University Coll., Cardiff (BA Hons 1964). Schoolmaster: Barry Boys' Grammar Sch., 1965–68; Cathays High Sch., 1968–72; called to the Bar, Gray's Inn, 1973; practice, 1973–97; Standing Counsel to Inland Revenue, 1995–97; Resident Judge, Norwich Crown Court, 2004–13. Mem. (L), Barry Borough Council, 1966–69. Pres., Old Lennensians Assoc., 2006–. Hon. Recorder of Norwich, 2008–13. Recreations: watching Norwich City Football Club, fine art, Norfolk railways and churches. Address: White Lodge, 133 Lower Street, Horning, Norwich, Norfolk NR12 8PF. Club: Norwich City Football.

**JACOBS, Hon. Sir Richard David,** Kt 2018; **Hon. Mr Justice Jacobs;** a Judge of the High Court of Justice, Queen's Bench Division, since 2018; b 21 Dec. 1956; s of late Elliott Jacobs, chartered accountant, and of Ruth Jacobs (née Ellenbogen); m 1990, Pamela Fine; one s two d. Educ: Highgate Sch.; Pembroke Coll., Cambridge. Called to the Bar, Middle Temple, 1979, Bencher, 2011; QC 1998; a Recorder, 2002–18. Vis. Fellow, LSE, 2003. Publications: (jtly) Liability Insurance in International Arbitration: the Bermuda form, 2004, 2nd edn 2011. Recreations: tennis, Arsenal FC, theatre, piano. Address: Royal Courts of Justice, Strand, WC2A 2LL. Clubs: MCC, Royal Automobile.

**JACOBSON, Howard Eric,** FRSL; novelist; critic; b 25 Aug. 1942; s of Max Jacobson and Anita (née Black); m 1st, 1964, Barbara Starr (marr. diss.); one s; 2nd, 1978, Rosalin Sadler (marr. diss.); 3rd, 2005, Jenny De Yong. Educ: Stand Grammar Sch., Whitefield; Downing Coll., Cambridge (BA, MA; Hon. Fellow, 2012). Lectr in English Lit., Univ. of Sydney, Australia, 1965–67; Tutor in English, Selwyn Coll., Cambridge, 1968–72; Sen. Lectr, Wolverhampton Poly., 1974–80. Vis. Prof., New Coll. of Humanities, 2012–. Writer and presenter, TV documentaries: Into the Land of Oz, 1991; Yo, Mrs Askew, 1991; Roots Schmoots, 1993; Sorry, Judas, 1993; Seriously Funny, 1997; Howard Jacobson Takes on the Turner, 2000; Why the Novel Matters: a South Bank Show Special, 2002; Jesus the Jew, 2009; Creation, 2010; Flesh, 2010; Rebels of Oz, 2014; contrib. to Late Show, 1989–, Late Rev., 1995–. TV critic, The Correspondent, 1989–90; columnist, The Independent, 1998–2016. Mem., Editl Bd, Modern Painters, 1990–2005. FRSL 2012. Hon. DArts Wolverhampton, 2018. Publications: (with W. Sanders) Shakespeare's Magnanimity, 1978; In the Land of Oz, 1987; Roots Schmoots, 1993; Seeing with the Ear (Peter Fuller Meml Lecture), 1993; Seriously Funny, 1997; Whatever It Is, I Don't Like It, 2011; The Dog's Last Walk, 2017; novels: Coming from Behind, 1983; Peeping Tom, 1984; Redback, 1986; The Very Model of a Man, 1992; No More Mister Nice Guy, 1998; The Mighty Walzer, 1999 (Everyman Bollinger Wodehouse Prize for Comic Writing, Jewish Qly Wingate Prize, 2000); Who's Sorry Now?, 2002; The Making of Henry, 2004; Kalooki Nights, 2006 (Jewish Qly Wingate Prize, 2007); The Act of Love, 2008; The Finkler Question, 2010 (Man Booker Prize, 2010); Zoo Time, 2012 (Everyman Bollinger Wodehouse Prize for Comic Writing, 2013); J, 2014; Shylock is My Name, 2016; Pussy, 2017; Live a Little, 2019. Address: c/o Curtis Brown, Haymarket House, 28–29 Haymarket, SW1Y 4SP. T: (020) 7393 4400. Clubs: Chelsea Arts, Groucho.

**JACOBUS, Prof. Mary Longstaff,** CBE 2012; DPhil; FBA 2009; Professor of English (Grace 2), 2000–11, now Emerita, and Director, Centre for Research in the Arts, Social Sciences and Humanities, 2006–11, University of Cambridge; Fellow of Churchill College, Cambridge, 2000–18 (Hon. Fellow, 2018); b 4 May 1944; d of Marcus Jacobus and Diana (née Longstaff); m 1981, A. Reeve Parker; one s one d. Educ: Oxford High Sch. for Girls, GPDST; Lady Margaret Hall, Oxford (BA 1st Cl. Hons English 1965, MA; DPhil 1970; Hon. Fellow, 2000). Oxford University: Randall McIver Jun. Res. Fellow, 1968–70, Fellow and Tutor in English, 1971–80, Lady Margaret Hall; CUF Lectr, English Faculty, 1972–80; Lectr, Manchester Univ., 1970–71; Cornell University: Associate Prof. of English, 1980–82; Prof. of English, 1982–89, now Emerita; John Wendell Anderson Prof. of English and Women's Studies, 1989–2000. Hon. Res. Fellow, LMH, Oxford, 1980–2000. Guggenheim Fellow, 1988–89. M. H. Abrams Distinguished Vis. Prof., Cornell Univ., 2011–12; Distinguished Scholar Award, Keats-Shelley Assoc. of America, 2015; Bogliasco Foundn Residency, 2017. Publications: Tradition and Experiment in Wordsworth's Lyrical Ballads (1798), 1976; (ed) Women Writing and Women Writing About Women, 1979; Reading Woman: essays in feminist criticism, 1986; (ed jtly) Body/Politics: women and the discourse of science, 1989; Romanticism, Writing and Sexual Difference: essays on The Prelude, 1989; First Things: the maternal imaginary in literature, art and psychoanalysis, 1996; Psychoanalysis and the Scene of Reading, 1999; The Poetics of Psychoanalysis: in the wake of Klein, 2005; Romantic Things: a tree, a rock, a cloud, 2012; Reading Cy Twombly: poetry in paint, 2016. Address: Faculty of English, University of Cambridge, 9 West Road, Cambridge CB3 9DP. T: (01223) 335070.

**JACOBY, Stefan;** Executive Vice President, Consolidated International Operations, and President, GM International, General Motors Corp, since 2013; b Hannover, Germany, 10 April 1958; s of Hans Albin Jacoby and Anne Marie Jacoby; m 2006, Roberta Bantel; two s one d. Educ: Univ. of Cologne (Dip. KFM; MBA). Analyst, Industrial Sales and Controlling Dept, Volkswagen AG, 1985–88; Pricing Manager, Product and Mktg Depts, Volkswagen of America, 1988–90; Manager, Pricing Dept, Commercial Vehicle Div., Volkswagen AG, 1989–90; Gen. Manager of Controlling, Volkswagen Audi Nippon KK, Japan, 1990–92; Volkswagen AG: Gen. Manager, Export Sales Planning Dept, 1992–95; Hd, Gen. Office of Chm., Bd of Mgt, 1995–97; Vice Pres., Asia-Pacific, Volkswagen Asia-Pacific Ltd, 1997–2001; Pres. and CEO Europe, Mitsubishi Motors Europe BV (Amsterdam), 2001–04; Exec. Vice Pres. and Gen. Rep., Mktg and Sales, Volkswagen AG, 2004–07; Pres. and CEO, Volkswagen Gp of America Inc., 2007–10; Pres. and CEO, Volvo Car Corp., 2010–12.

**JACOMB, Sir Martin (Wakefield),** Kt 1985; Chairman: Share plc, 2001–13; Canary Wharf Group PLC, 2003–11 (Director, 1999–2011); Pension Insurance Corporation Ltd, 2006–12; b 11 Nov. 1929; s of Hilary W. Jacomb and Félise Jacomb; m 1960, Evelyn Heathcoat Amory (MBE 2007); two s one d. Educ: Eton Coll.; Worcester Coll., Oxford (MA Law 1953; Hon. Fellow, 1994). 2nd Lieut, RA, 1948–49. Called to the Bar, Inner Temple, 1955 (Hon. Bencher, 1987); practised at the Bar, 1955–68. Kleinwort Benson Ltd, 1968–85; Dep. Chm., Barclays Bank PLC, 1985–93; Chairman: Barclays de Zoete Wedd, 1986–91; Postel Investment Management, 1991–95; Delta plc, 1993–2003; Prudential Corp., 1995–2000 (Dir, 1994–2000); Director: The Telegraph plc (formerly Daily Telegraph), 1986–2000; Rio Tinto plc (formerly RTZ Corp.), 1988–2000; Marks and Spencer, 1991–2000; Director: Mercantile Credit Co. Ltd, 1969–75; John Mowlem and Co. Ltd, 1969–77; Australian and NZ Bank, 1970–80; Hudson's Bay Co., 1972–86; Merchants Trust plc, 1974–85 (Chm., 1980–85); Christian Salvesen, 1974–88; British Gas, 1981–88; SIB, 1985–91; Royal Opera House, 1988–91. A Dir, Bank of England, 1986–95. Chm., British Council, 1992–98. Mem., Internat. Adv. Cttee, New York Federal Reserve, 1994. Chm., Internat. Adv. Bd, First Avenue Partners, 2006–. External Mem., Finance Cttee, OUP, 1971–95. Mem., Nolan Cttee on Standards in Public Life, 1994–97. Director, Oxford Playhouse Trust, 1999–2006. Trustee, Nat. Heritage Meml Fund, 1982–97. Chancellor, Univ. of Buckingham, 1998–2010. Hon. FKC 2007. Hon. Dr: Humberside, 1993; Buckingham, 1997; Hon. DCL Oxford, 1997. Recreations: theatre, family bridge, visual arts, the outdoors.

**JACOVIDES, Mario;** Global Head of Structured and Asset Finance, Allen & Overy LLP, since 2009 (Partner, since 1999); *b* London, 1964; *s* of Christakis and Yiannoulla Jacovides; *m* 1995, Maria Pieretti; two *s*. *Educ*: Chace Sch.; Univ. of E Anglia (LLB Hons). Admitted solicitor, 1989. Wilde Sapte: trainee, 1987, then solicitor; Partner, 1995–99. *Recreations*: ornithology, fishing, golf, tennis. *Address*: Allen & Overy LLP, One Bishops Square, E1 6AB. *T*: (020) 3088 2659. *E*: mario.jacovides@allenovery.com.

**JACQUES, Dr David Lawson;** garden historian; owner, Sugnall Estate, since 2003; *b* 29 Sept. 1948; *s* of late Greville Lawson Jacques and Anne Grace Jacques; *m* 1st, 1973, Rosalind Catherine Denny (marr. diss. 1993); two *d*; 2nd, 2004, Karen Sims-Neighbour (marr. diss. 2016). *Educ*: Univ. of Leeds (MSc Transportation Engrg 1972); Poly. of N London (DipTP 1977); Courtauld Inst., Univ. of London (PhD 1999). MCIHT (MIHT 1977); MRTPI 1981. Land Use Consultants, 1973–76; Jacques Miller Partnership, 1977–78; Associate, Travers Morgan Planning, 1978–87; Inspector of Historic Parks and Gardens, English Heritage, 1987–93; Consultant on historic landscapes, parks and gardens, 1993– (e.g. Privy Garden, Hampton Court; Tudor Garden, Kenilworth Castle); Lectr (pt-time) Landscapes and Gardens, Dept of Archaeol., Univ. of York, 1994–98; Prog. Dir, MA in Landscape Conservation and Change, Architectural Assoc., 2000–06. Vis. Prof., De Montfort Univ., 1999–2003. Mem. Council, 1975–2001, Chm., 1998–2000, Garden Hist. Soc.; International Council on Monuments and Sites: Co-ordinator, Landscapes Wkg Gp, 1991–95; Corresp. Mem., Internat. Scientific Cttee for Cultural Landscapes (formerly for Historic Gdns and Sites), 1991– (Mem. Bd, 2017–); Chm., UK Historic Gdns and Landscapes Cttee, 1993–98. Trustee and Chm., Gdns Cttee, Castle Bromwich Hall Gdns Trust, 1985–87; Chm., Bishop's Park Co-ordinating Gp, 1985–87; Trustee: Landscape Design Trust, 1994–2018; Chiswick House & Garden Trust, 2005–. Chairman: Staffs Gdns and Parks Trust, 1994–97; Friends of the William Salt Liby, 2004–. Chm., Hammersmith and Fulham Liberal Democrats, 1987–93. *Publications*: Georgian Gardens: the reign of nature, 1983, repr. 1990; (with A. J. Van der Horst) The Gardens of William and Mary, 1988; Strategic Guidance for Heritage Land in London, 1988; Essential to the practtick part of phisick: the London apothecaries 1540–1617, 1994; Landscape Modernism Renounced: the career of Christopher Tunnard, 2009; Gardens of Court and Country: English design, 1630s to 1730s, 2017; Landscape Appreciation: theories since the cultural turn, 2019; contrib. chapters in books and articles to jls incl. Jl Gdn Hist. Soc., Landscape Design, Country Life, Jl Envmtl Mgt, Jl RTPI, Monuments Historiques, English Heritage Conservation Bull., Die Gartenkunst, Arte dei Giardini, Internat. Jl Heritage Studies, Jl Architectural Conservation, Schriftenreihe des Deutschen Rates für Landespflege, Tuinjournaal and Architectural Hist. *Recreations*: local history, croquet, visiting historic gardens. *Address*: Sugnall Hall, Sugnall, Stafford ST21 6NF. *T*: (01785) 851711. *Club*: Farmers.

**JACQUES, Peter Roy Albert,** CBE 1990; Secretary, TUC Social Insurance and Industrial Welfare Department, 1971–2000; *b* 12 Aug. 1939; *s* of George Henry Jacques and Ivy Mary Jacques (*née* Farr); *m* 1965, Jacqueline Anne Sears; one *s* one *d*. *Educ*: Archbishop Temple's Secondary Sch.; Newcastle upon Tyne Polytechnic (BSc Sociology); Univ. of Leicester. Building labourer, 1955–58; market porter, 1958–62; Asst, TUC Social Insce and Industrial Welfare Dept, 1968–71. Member: Industrial Injuries Adv. Council, 1972; Nat. Insce Adv. Cttee, 1972–78; Health and Safety Commn, 1974–95; Royal Commn on the Nat. Health Service, 1976–79; EEC Cttee on Health-Safety, 1976; NHS London Adv. Cttee, 1979; Social Security Adv. Cttee, 1980–95; Health Educn Council, 1984–87; Civil Justice Review Adv. Cttee, 1985–; Royal Commn on Envmtl Pollution, 1989–95; Employment Appeal Tribunal, 1996–2009. Jt Sec., BMA/TUC Cttee, 1972; Secretary: TUC Social Health and Envmt Protection Cttee (formerly Social Insurance and Industrial Welfare Cttee), 1972–93; TUC Health Services Cttee, 1979–2000; TUC Special Advr, 1992–95. Vice-Chm., Redbridge and Waltham Forest HA, 1996–99. Mem. Exec. Cttee, Royal Assoc. for Disability and Rehabilitation, 1975. *Publications*: responsible for TUC pubns Health-Safety Handbook; Occupational Pension Schemes. *Recreations*: reading, yoga, walking, camping, vegetable growing. *Address*: 8 Osborne Road, Buckhurst Hill, Essex IG9 5RR. *T*: (020) 8257 7757.

**JAFFÉ, David Andrew,** FSA; Senior Curator, National Gallery, 1998–2012; art consultant, since 2012; *b* 7 July 1953; *s* of Peter John Jaffé and Patricia Willis Jaffé (*née* Andrew); *m* 1988, Elizabeth Kate Stephen (marr. diss. 2018); two *s*. *Educ*: Geelong Grammar Sch.; Melbourne Univ. (BSc); Courtauld Inst. of Art, Univ. of London (MA). Lectr, Univ. of Qld, 1979–81; Curator, Australian Nat. Gall., 1982–90; engaged in research, 1990–94; Curator of Paintings, J. Paul Getty Mus., 1994–98. FSA 1989. Hon. Life Mem., Art Exhibns Australia, 2005. Commendatore, Stella della Solidarietà (Italy), 2004. *Publications*: Rubens: self portrait in focus, 1988; Rubens and the Italian Renaissance, 1992; Titian, 2003; Rubens: the making of a master, 2005; Rubens: Massacre of the Innocents, 2009; contrib. articles to jls incl. Apollo, Burlington mag., Jl Warburg and Courtauld Insts. *Recreations*: tennis, gymnastics. *Address*: Flat 2, 39 Belsize Park Gardens, NW3 4JJ. *E*: davidjaffe7@gmail.com. *Club*: Melbourne (Melbourne).

**JAFFERJEE, Aftab Asger;** QC 2008; Senior Treasury Counsel, Central Criminal Court, 2001–11; *b* 25 June 1956; *s* of Asger Jafferjee and Tara Kajiji; *m* 2001, Nazli Javeri; two *d*. *Educ*: St Paul's Sch., Darjeeling; Rugby Sch.; Durham Univ. (BA Hons). Called to the Bar, Inner Temple, 1980, Bencher, 2011; Jun. Treasury Counsel, 1997–2001. Member: Professional Conduct Cttee of Bar (of England and Wales), 1994–96; Cttee, Criminal Bar Assoc., 1995–97. Criminal Lawyer of Year Award, Soc. of Asian Lawyers, 2012. *Recreations*: cuisine, travel, theatre (Founder, Castle Th. Co., Durham, 1977). *Address*: 6KBW, 21 College Hill, EC4R 2RP. *E*: AJafferjee@6kbw.com.

**JAFFRAY, Alistair Robert Morton,** CB 1978; Deputy Under-Secretary of State, Ministry of Defence, 1975–84; *b* 28 Oct. 1925; *s* of late Alexander George and Janet Jaffray; *m* 1st, 1953, Margaret Betty Newman (decd); two *s* one *d*; 2nd, 1980, Edna Mary (decd), *e d* of late S. J. Tasker, Brasted Chart. *Educ*: Clifton Coll.; Corpus Christi Coll., Cambridge. BA First Cl. Hons, Mod. Langs. Served War, RNVR, 1943–46. Apptd Home Civil Service (Admty), 1948; Private Sec. to First Lord of Admty, 1960–62; Private Sec. to successive Secretaries of State for Defence, 1968–70; Asst Under-Sec. of State, MoD, 1971, Dep. Sec. 1975; Sec. to Admty Bd, 1981–84. Governor, Clifton Coll., 1980–; Chm. Management Cttee, Royal Hospital Sch., Holbrook, 1985–91. *Address*: Okeford, 10 Lynch Road, Farnham, Surrey GU9 8BZ.

**JAFFRAY, Sir William Otho,** 5th Bt *cr* 1892; *b* 1 Nov. 1951; *s* of Sir William Edmund Jaffray, 4th Bt, TD, JP, DL and of Anne, *d* of Captain J. Otho Paget, MC, Thorpe Satchville, Leics; *S* father, 1953; *m* 1st, 1981, Cynthia Ross Corrington (marr. diss. 1997); three *s* one *d*; 2nd, 2009, Constance Haynes Latshaw (marr. diss. 2018). British Rep. for investors in litigation against Lloyd's insce markets in High Court, Court of Appeal, H of L and ECHR, 1997–2003. *Publications*: (ed) Memories of the Shires, 2nd edn 2012. *Heir*: *s* Nicholas Gordon Alexander Jaffray, *b* 18 Oct. 1982. *Address*: c/o Flat A9, Sloane Avenue Mansions, Sloane Avenue, SW3 3JF.

**JAGDEO, Bharrat;** MP (People's Progressive/Civic), Republic of Guyana, since 2015; *b* 23 Jan. 1964; *m* 1998, Varshnie Jagdeo. *Educ*: Gibson Primary Sch.; Mahaica Multilateral Sch.; Univ. of Moscow (MSc Econs 1990). Economist, Macro-economic Planning Div., State Planning Secretariat, 1990–92; Special Advr to Minister of Finance, 1992–93; Jun. Minister of Finance, 1993–95; Minister of Finance, 1995–2001; Pres. and Comdr-in-Chief of the Armed Forces, Republic of Guyana, 1999–2011; High Level Envoy for Sustainable Develt in Forest Countries and Patron of Nature, IUCN, 2012. Director: Guyana Water Authy; Nat. Bank of Industry and Commerce; Governor: IMF; World Bank; Caribbean Develt Bank (Dir); Inter American Develt Bank (Chm., Caribbean Gp of Govs). Nat. Authorising Officer, EU. *Address*: Parliament of the Republic of Guyana, Parliament Building, Georgetown, Guyana.

**JAGGER, Bianca;** Founder, President and Chief Executive, Bianca Jagger Human Rights Foundation, since 2005; Senior Fellow, Centre for International Governance Innovation, Waterloo, Ontario, since 2015; *b* Managua, Nicaragua, 2 May 1950; *d* of Carlos Pérez-Mora and Dora Macias; *m* 1971, Michael Philip Jagger (*see* Sir M. P. Jagger) (marr. diss. 1979); one *d*. *Educ*: La Immaculada, Managua; Univ. Sciences Po, Paris. Actress: *films*: The Rutles: All You Need is Cash, 1978; Flesh Colour, 1978; The American Success Company, 1980; Cannonball Run, 1981; C.H.U.D II, 1989; *television*: Street Hawk, 1985; Miami Vice, 1986; Hotel, 1986; The Colbys, 1987. Writer of blog for Huffington Post, USA. Chair, World Future Council, 2007–09. Member: Coalition for Internat. Criminal Court; Exec. Dir's Leadership Council, Amnesty Internat., USA; Adv. Cttee, Human Rights Watch America; Adv. Bd, Creative Coalition; Women and Girls' Lead Initiative, Ind. Television Service, 2013–. Former Member: Adv. Bd, Coalition for Internat. Justice; Bd, People for the American Way; Twentieth Century Task Force to Apprehend War Criminals. Council of Europe Goodwill Ambassador, 2003–; Bonn Challenge Ambassador, IUCN, 2012–. Patron: Circle of Conscience, Amnesty Internat., 2014–; Global Network for Study of Human Rights and the Envmt, 2014–. Hon. DHum Stonehill Coll., Mass, 1983; Hon. Dr Human Rights Simmons Coll., Boston, 2008; Hon. LLD E London, 2010. Earth Day Internat. Award, UN, 1994; USA Media Spotlight Award for Leadership, Amnesty Internat., 1997; Green Globe Award, Rainbow Alliance, 1997; American Civil Liberties Union Award, 1998; Right Livelihood Award, 2004; World Achievement Award, Mikhail Gorbachev's World Awards, 2004; World Citizenship Award, Nuclear Age Peace Foundn, 2006; Latin American UK Award for Lifetime Achievement, Latin-UK Awards, 2014; Nuestra Madre Award, Americas Latino Eco Fest., 2015. *Publications*: contribs to newspapers incl. NY Times, Washington Post, Dallas Morning News, Columbus Dispatcher, Guardian, Observer, Independent, Mail on Sunday, Sunday Express, New Statesman, Der Spiegel, Süddeutsche Zeitung, European, Libération, Le Journal du Dimanche, Le Juriste Internat., Panorama. *Recreations*: family, music, opera, art, theatre, cinema, photography, outdoor activities, walking in the rainforest, horseback riding, yoga. *Address*: Unit 246, 272 Kensington High Street, W8 6ND. *E*: biancajagger1@gmail.com. *W*: www.biancajagger.com, www.twitter.com/BiancaJagger.

**JAGGER, Ven. Ian;** Archdeacon of Durham and Canon Residentiary of Durham Cathedral, 2006–19; *b* 17 April 1955; *m* 1993, Ruth Green; one *s*. *Educ*: Huddersfield New Coll.; King's Coll., Cambridge (BA 1977, MA 1981); St John's Coll., Durham (BA 1980, MA 1987). Ordained deacon, 1982, priest, 1983; Curate, St Mary, Twickenham, 1982–85; Team Vicar, Willen, Milton Keynes, 1985–94; Team Rector, Fareham, 1994–98; RD Fareham, 1996–98; Canon Residentiary, Portsmouth Cathedral, 1998–2001; Archdeacon of Auckland, Dio. Durham, 2001–06.

**JAGGER, Jonathan David,** CVO 2018 (LVO 2012); FRCS, FRCOphth; Surgeon-Oculist to the Queen, 2002–18; Consultant Ophthalmologist: Royal Free Hospital, 1986–2018; King Edward VII's Hospital for Officers, since 1995; St Luke's Hospital for the Clergy, since 2000; *b* 12 April 1951; *s* of Lt-Col Derek Bourne Jagger and Pamela (*née* Jarratt); *m* 1977 Sarah Elisabeth Lee; one *s* one *d*. *Educ*: Uppingham; St Thomas' Hosp., London (MB, BS 1974); DO 1979. FRCS 1981; FRCOphth 1989. Registrar, Westminster Hosp., 1979–80; Resident Surgical Officer, 1980–83, Sen. Resident, 1983, Moorfields Eye Hosp.; Sen. Registrar, Western Ophthalmic Hosp. and Moorfields Eye Hosp., 1983–86; Cons. Ophthalmic Surgeon, UCH and Middx Hosp., 1986–89; Surgeon-Oculist to HM Household, 1999–2002. Cons. Ophthalmologist, Assoc. of Royal Naval Officers, 1998–2015. Mem. Council, RCOphth, 1990–94; Mem., Ophthalmic Qualifications Cttee, 1993–. FRSocMed. *Publications*: articles on cataract surgery, lasers, retinal disorders. *Recreations*: travel, ski-ing, DIY. *Address*: 119 Harley Street, W1G 6AU.

**JAGGER, Sir Michael Philip, (Sir Mick),** Kt 2002; singer, songwriter and film producer; *b* Dartford, Kent, 26 July 1943; *s* of late Basil Fanshawe, (Joe), Jagger and Eva Jagger; *m* 1st, 1971, Bianca Rose Pérez Morena de Macías (*see* Bianca Jagger) (marr. diss. 1979); one *d*; 2nd, 1990, Jerry Hall (marr. diss. 1999); two *s* two *d*; one *d* by Marsha Hunt; one *s* by Luciana Gimenez Morad; one *s* by Melanie Hamrick. *Educ*: Dartford Grammar Sch.; LSE. Lead singer, Rolling Stones, 1962–; tours worldwide, 1964–. *Records include*: *albums*: The Rolling Stones, 1964; The Rolling Stones No 2, 1965; Out of Our Heads, 1965; Aftermath, 1966; Between the Buttons, 1967; Their Satanic Majesties Request, 1967; Beggars' Banquet, 1968; Let It Bleed, 1969; Get Yer Ya-Ya's Out!, 1970; Sticky Fingers, 1971; Exile on Main Street, 1972; Goat's Head Soup, 1973; It's Only Rock 'n' Roll, 1974; Black and Blue, 1976; Some Girls, 1978; Emotional Rescue, 1980; Tattoo You, 1981; Still Life, 1982; Undercover, 1983; Dirty Work, 1986; Steel Wheels (also prod.), 1989; Flashpoint, 1991; Voodoo Lounge, 1994; Bridges to Babylon, 1997; Bent, 1997; No Security, 1998; Forty Licks, 2002; A Bigger Bang, 2005; GRRR!, 2012; Blue & Lonesome, 2016; *solo albums*: She's the Boss, 1985; Primitive Cool, 1987; Wandering Spirit, 1993; Goddess in the Doorway, 2001; album with SuperHeavy, SuperHeavy, 2011. *Films include*: Performance, 1970; Ned Kelly, 1970; Freejack, 1992; Shine a Light, 2008; producer: Enigma, 2001; Get On Up, 2014. Co-creator, TV series, Vinyl, 2016. Founded film prodn co., Jagged Films.

**JAGLAND, Thorbjørn;** Secretary General, Council of Europe, since 2009; *b* 5 Nov. 1950; *m* 1975, Hanne Grotjord; two *s*. *Educ*: Univ. of Oslo. Leader, Labour Youth League, 1977–81; Labour Party of Norway: Res. and Analysis Sec., 1981–86; Party Sec., 1986–92; Leader, 1992–2002. MP (Lab) Buskerud County, Norway, 1993–2009. Prime Minister of Norway, 1996–97; Minister of Foreign Affairs, 2000–01; Pres. of Storting, 2005–09. Chm., Standing Cttee on Foreign Affairs, 2001–05. Chm., Norwegian Nobel Cttee, 2009–15. Chm., Bd of Dirs, Oslo Centre for Peace and Human Rights, 2006–09. *Publications*: My European Dream, 1990; New Solidarity, 1993; Letters, 1995; Our Vulnerable World, 2001; Ten Theses on the EU and Norway, 2003. *Recreations*: ski-ing, outdoor activities, literature. *Address*: Council of Europe, Avenue de l'Europe, 67075 Strasbourg Cedex, France.

**JAGO, Daniel Alexander;** Chairman, Wine and Spirit Trade Association, 2016–19 (Member, Board, 1998–2019); *b* London, 28 May 1961; *s* of late Tom Jago and Penelope Jago; *m* 1991, Geraldine Mary Drayson; two *d*. *Educ*: Frensham Heights Sch.; Richmond Coll.; BRNC Dartmouth. Lieut, RN, 1980–88. Sales Manager, Laytons Wine Merchants, 1988–90; Sales Manager, then Sales Dir, later Agency Dir, subseq. Man. Dir, Bibendum Wine Merchants, 1990–2006; Gp Wine Dir, Tesco Stores plc, 2006–15; Chief Exec., Berry Bros & Rudd Ltd, 2015–19. *Recreations*: golf, shooting, wine and food, boats. *Clubs*: 67 Pall Mall; Royal Wimbledon Golf.

**JAGO, David Edgar John**; Communar of Chichester Cathedral, 1987–92; *b* 2 Dec. 1937; *s* of late Edgar George Jago and of Violet Jago; *m* 1st, 1963, Judith Lissenden, DPhil (*d* 1995); one *s* one *d*; 2nd, 1997, Gertraud Marianne, (Gerty), Apfelbeck. *Educ*: King Edward's Sch., Bath; Pembroke Coll., Oxford (MA). National Service, RA, 1956–58. Asst Principal, Admiralty, 1961; Private Sec. to Permanent Under Sec. of State (RN), 1964–65; Principal 1965; Directing Staff, IDC, 1968–70; Private Sec. to Parly Under Sec. of State for Defence (RN), 1971–73; Ministry of Defence: Asst Sec., 1973; Asst Under Sec. of State: Aircraft, 1979–82; Naval Staff, 1982–84; Under Sec., Cabinet Office, 1984–86. Gov., Bedgebury Sch., 1996–2000. *Recreations:* theatre, opera, military history, supporting Arsenal FC. *Club:* Oxford and Cambridge.

**JAGPAL, Jagdip**; Fair Director, India Art Fair, since 2017; *b* London, 22 Nov. 1964; *d* of late Darshan Singh and of Jaswant Kaur. *Educ:* London Sch. of Econs and Pol Sci. (LLB Hons); Coll. of Law; London Business Sch. Man. Ed., Butterworths Ltd, 1986–91; Solicitor, Rubinstein Callingham Polden & Gale, 1992–95; BBC Radio: lawyer, 1995–96; Chief Asst to Controller, Radio 4, 1996–99; Man. Dir, Network Television Prodn, SMG plc, 1999–2002; Associate, 2002–04, non-exec. Dir, 2004–11, Franklin Rae Communications, 2002–04; Chief Exec., Cloisters, 2004–07; exec. search consultant, 2007–09; Man. Dir, Anareva, 2009–14; Manager, Internat. Progs, Tate, 2014–15; arts consultant, 2015–16; Project Co-ordinator, Whitworth Art Gall., Manchester Art Gall. and Manchester Mus., 2016–17. Advr, New Art Exchange, 2017. Non-executive Director: Noel Gay Artists Ltd, 2004–08; Bend It Networks Gp, 2015. Mem Bd, Almeida Theatre, 2009–14. Trustee, Wallace Collection, 2007–15. Mem., Ct of Govs, LSE, 2011–. *Recreations:* art, theatre, travel, London, watching television, south asian contemporary art. *E:* jagdip@mac.com. *Clubs:* Soho House, Every House.

**JAGUARIBE, Roberto**; President, Apex-Brasil (Brazilian Trade and Investment Promotion Agency), 2016–19; *b* Rio de Janeiro, 27 Dec. 1952; *s* of Hélio Jaguaribe and Maria Lúcia Jaguaribe; *m* Cinara Lima (marr. diss.); two *d* and two step *s*. *Educ:* Pontifical Catholic Univ. of Rio de Janeiro (BE Systems Engrg). Public Entry Exam Diplomat, Brazil, 1978; Mission to UN, NY, 1983–87; Montevideo, 1987–90; Head: Div. for Intellectual Property and Sensitive Technologies, 1990–93; Intellectual Property Sect. and Disarmament Sect., Internat. Orgns, Mission in Geneva, 1993–95; Sec. for Internat. Affairs, Min. of Planning and Budget, 1995–98; Dir-Gen. for Trade Promotion, Min. of Ext. Relns, 1998–2000; Dep. Hd of Mission, Washington, 2000–03; Sec. for Industrial Technol., Min. of Develt, Industry and Foreign Trade, 2003–05; Pres., Nat. Inst. of Industrial Property of Brazil, 2005–06; Under Sec.-Gen. for Political Affairs, Min. of Ext. Relns, 2007–10; Ambassador: to the Court of St James's, 2010–15; to China, 2015–16. *Recreations:* music, reading, outdoors, golf, biking.

**JAGUSCH, Stephen Richard**; QC 2016; Global Chair of International Arbitration, Quinn Emanuel Urquhart & Sullivan, since 2012; *b* Auckland, NZ, 31 May 1967; three *d*. *Educ:* Auckland Univ. (BCom 1989; LLB 1989; MCom Law 1st Cl. Hons 1994). Called to the Bar and solicitor, High Court of NZ, 1989; Associate: Simpson Grierson Butler White, Auckland, 1989–94; Freshfields Bruckhaus Deringer LLP, London and Paris, 1994–2000; admitted as solicitor, England and Wales, 1995; Sen. Associate, 2000–02, Partner, 2002–12, Allen & Overy LLP, London. *Publications:* (ed with E. Triantafilou) Getting the Deal Through: investment treaty arbitration, annually, 2014–17; (Gen. Ed. and contrib.) The Guide to Advocacy, 2016; *contributed chapters to:* Arbitration World, 2003, 3rd edn 2010; Towards a Uniform International Arbitration Law, 2005; Investment Arbitration and the Energy Charter Treaty, 2006; Pervasive Problems in International Arbitration, 2006; Electronic Disclosure in International Arbitration, 2008; Investment Protection and the Energy Charter Treaty, 2008; Enforcement of Arbitral Awards Against Sovereigns, 2009; The Backlash Against Investment Arbitration: perception and reality, 2010; The Art of Advocacy in International Arbitration, 2010; Energy Dispute Resolution: investment protection, transit and the Energy Charter Treaty, 2011; The International Arbitration Review, 2011; The Leading Arbitrators' Guide to International Arbitration, 3rd edn 2014; Choice of Venue in International Arbitration, 2014; International Financial Disputes, 2015; Building International Investment Law: the first 50 years of ICSID, 2016; The Guide to Energy Arbitrations, 2nd edn 2016; contribs to Arbitration Internat., Jl World Investment and Trade, Global Arbitration Rev., Jl Chartered Inst. Arbitrators, Stockholm Internat. Arbitration Rev., Eur. and Middle Eastern Arbitration Rev. *Address:* Quinn Emanuel Urquhart & Sullivan LLP, 90 High Holborn, WC1V 6LJ. *T:* (020) 7653 2050. *E:* stephenjagusch@quinnemanuel.com.

**JAINE, Tom William Mahony**; freelance writer; Proprietor, Prospect Books, 1993–2014; *b* 4 June 1943; *s* of William Edwin Jaine and Aileen (*née* Mahony); *m* 1st, 1965, Susanna F. Fisher; 2nd, 1973, Patience Mary Welsh (decd); two *d*; 3rd, 1983, Sally Caroline Agnew; two *d*. *Educ:* Kingswood Sch., Bath; Balliol Coll., Oxford (BA Hons). Asst Registrar, Royal Commn on Historical Manuscripts, 1967–73; Partner, Carved Angel Restaurant, Dartmouth, 1974–84; publisher, The Three Course Newsletter (and predecessors), 1980–89; Editor: Good Food Guide, 1989–94; Petits Propos Culinaires, 2000–. Wine and Food Writer of the Year, Glenfiddich Awards, 2000; Derek Cooper Lifetime Achievement Award, BBC Food and Farming Awards, 2014. *Publications:* Cooking in the Country, 1986; Cosmic Cuisine, 1988; Making Bread at Home, 1995; Building a Wood-Fired Oven, 1996; (ed) Oxford Companion to Food, 2nd edn 2006, 3rd edn 2014; trans., Millet-Robinet, The French Country Housewife, 2017; contribs Guardian, etc. *Recreations:* baking, buildings. *Address:* Allaleigh House, Blackawton, Totnes, Devon TQ9 7DL.

**JAKEMAN, Prof. Eric**; FRS 1990; Professor of Applied Statistical Optics, University of Nottingham, 1996–2004, now Professor Emeritus; *b* 3 June 1939; *s* of Frederick Leonard Jakeman and Hilda Mary Hays; *m* 1968, Glenys Joan Cooper; two *d*. *Educ:* Brunts Grammar Sch., Mansfield; Univ. of Birmingham (BSc, PhD). FInstP 1979. Asst Res. Physicist, UCLA, 1963–64. DRA (formerly RRE, subseq. RSRE), 1964–95 (DCSO, 1985–95). Hon. Sec., Inst. of Physics, 1994–2003 (Vice-Pres. for Publications, 1989–93); Mem. Exec. Cttee, European Physical Soc., 1990–94. Fellow, Optical Soc. of America, 1988. Maxwell Medal and Prize, Inst. of Physics, 1977; (jtly) MacRobert Award, 1977; (jtly) Instrument Makers' Co. Award. *Publications:* numerous contribs to learned jls. *Recreations:* gardening, music, beekeeping. *Address:* University of Nottingham, University Park, Nottingham NG7 2RD.

**JAKENS, Claire; Her Honour Judge Jakens**; a Circuit Judge, since 2010; *b* Brighton, 23 May 1952; *d* of Arthur George Jakens and Frances Bell Jakens; *m* 1984, Prof. Nicholas Hamlyn; one *s*. *Educ:* Reading Univ. (BA Hons Italian); Warburg Inst., London Univ. (MPhil Combined Histl Studies; Dip. Law 1987). Various posts in UK and Italy; Lectr (pt-time) in Italian, Reading Univ., 1975–77; teacher of Italian, St Paul's Girls' Sch., 1977–87; called to the Bar, Middle Temple, 1988; in practice as barrister, 1988–2010. FRSA. *Recreations:* walking, travel, opera and theatre, friends and family.

**JAKOBSDÓTTIR, Katrín**; MP (Left-Green Movement), Reykjavík North, since 2007; Prime Minister of Iceland, since 2017; *b* Reykjavík, 1 Feb. 1976; *d* of Jakob Ármannsson and Signý Thoroddsen; *m* 2007, Gunnar Sigvaldason; three *s*. *Educ:* Univ. of Iceland (BA Icelandic and French 1999; MA Icelandic Lit. 2004). Minister of Educn, Sci. and Culture, 2009–13, for Nordic Cooperation, 2009–13. Leader, Left-Green Movement, 2013– (Mem., 2002–; Dep. Leader, 2003–13). *Publications:* Glæpurinn sem ekki fannst: saga og þróun íslenskra glæpasagna (The Undiscovered Crime: the history of Icelandic crime novels), 2001; *contributions to:* Þjóðerni í þúsund ár? (National Identity for a Thousand Years?), 2003; Í Guðrúnarhúsi (In Gudrun's House), 2005; Scandinavian Crime Fiction, 2011; Ísland: atvinnuhættir og menning 2010 (Iceland: industries and culture 2010), 2012. *Recreations:* reading fiction (especially crime fiction - wrote thesis for MA on work of popular Icelandic crime writer Arnaldur Indriðason), enthusiastic runner and hiker, social justice, future of the environment and gender equality issues. *E:* lara.bjorg.bjornsdottir@for.is.

**JAKOBSEN, Dr Bent Karsten**, FMedSci; Founder, Director and Chief Scientific Officer, Immunocore Ltd, since 2008; Founder, 2008, and Chief Scientific Adviser, since 2014, Adaptimmune Ltd, Oxford (Director, 2008–14); *b* Aarhus, Denmark, 21 Aug. 1959; *s* of Dr Bent Erik Jakobsen and Edith Jakobsen (*née* Mygind); three *s* by Bente Helkjaer Jakobsen. *Educ:* Foraeldreskolen, Aarhus; Marselisborg Gymnasium, Aarhus; Aarhus Univ. (Cand. Scient. 1987); Univ. of Cambridge (PhD 1990). Sen. Res. Fellow, Aarhus Univ., Denmark, 1990–93; Oxford University: Lectr, and Hd, Immune Receptor Gp, Inst. of Molecular Medicine, Nuffield Dept of Clin. Medicine, 1993–98; Tenured Hd, Immune Receptor Gp, MRC Human Immunol. Unit, 1998–2000; Founder, 1999, and CSO, 2000–06, Avidex Ltd, Oxford; Sen. Vice Pres. of Res., MediGene AG, Oxford, 2006–08. FMedSci 2015. *Publications:* contribs to internat. peer-reviewed scientific and med. jls incl. Nature, Jl Exptl Medicine, Nature Medicine, Nature Biotechnol., Immunity, Jl Immunol., EMBO Jl, Molecular and Cellular Biol., Molecular Cell, Immunol., Protein Sci., Protein Engrg, Jl Biol Chem., Immunol. Today; more than 100 patents and patent filings relating to immune receptors as biol, particularly monoclonal TCRs, phage display of TCRs. *Recreations:* classic cars, tennis, squash. *Address:* Immunocore Ltd, 101 Park Drive, Milton Park, Abingdon, Oxon OX14 4RY. *T:* (01235) 438600.

**JAKUB, Claire**; *see* Curtis-Thomas, C.

**JAMAN, Poppy Sultana**, OBE 2018; Chief Executive Officer (formerly Programme Director), City Mental Health Alliance, since 2015; *b* Bangladesh, 4 Sept. 1976; *d* of Abdul Rahman and Jubada Rahman; partner, Jaan Madan; two *d* and two step *s*. *Educ:* City of Portsmouth Girls' Sch.; Univ. of Portsmouth (Exec. MBA 2008). Support Worker, CAB Portsmouth, 1996–97; Project Manager, Mental Health Support Service, Portsmouth CC, 1998–99; Strategic Business Manager, Portsmouth City PCT, 2003–04; Regl Prog. Leader, Nat. Inst. for Mental Health England, 2004–09; CEO, Mental Health First Aid England, 2009–18. Non-exec. Dir, Public Health England, 2014–. Hon. DPhil Glos, 2019. *Recreations:* hiking, yoga, cooking. *Address:* c/o Mental Health First Aid England, 4th Floor, 21 Prescot Street, E1 8BB. *T:* 07795 298944. *E:* poppy@citymha.org.uk.

**JAMES;** *see* Streatfeild-James.

**JAMES**, family name of **Baron Northbourne**.

**JAMES OF BLACKHEATH**, Baron *cr* 2006 (Life Peer), of Wildbrooks in the County of West Sussex; **David Noel James**, CBE 1992; Chairman, Litigation Control Group Ltd, 2002–06; *b* 7 Dec. 1937; *m* 2004, Caroline Webster. Lloyds Bank, 1959–64; Chairman: Eagle Trust plc, 1989–97; Davies & Newman, 1990–92; New Millennium Experience Co., 2000–01; Racecourse Holdings Trust, 2003–05. *Address:* House of Lords, SW1A 0PW.

**JAMES, Alex**; *see* James, S. A.

**JAMES, Christopher John**; Deputy Chairman, R. Griggs Group Ltd, 1994–2000 (Director, 1993–2000); *b* 20 March 1932; *s* of John Thomas Walters James, MC and Cicely Hilda James; *m* 1958, Elizabeth Marion Cicely Thomson (*d* 2019); one *s* one *d*. *Educ:* Clifton Coll., Bristol; Magdalene Coll., Cambridge (MA). Served RA, 2nd Lieut, 1951–52; TA, 1952–60. Admitted Solicitor, 1958; Partner, Johnson & Co., Birmingham, 1960–87 (Sen. Partner, 1985–87); Dep. Senior Partner, Martineau Johnson, 1987–89, Sen. Partner, 1989–94. Director: Birmingham Building Soc., then Birmingham Midshires Building Soc., 1980–96 (Dep. Chm., 1988–90; Chm., 1990–96); Police Mutual Assurance Soc., 1996–2001. Gen. Comr for Income Tax, 1974–82. Pres., Birmingham Law Soc., 1983–84. Chm., Kalamazoo Trust, 1997–2001. Mem. Council, Edgbaston High Sch. for Girls, 1980–90 (Chm., 1988–90); Gov., Clifton Coll., 1980–99. *Recreations:* photography, railways, trying to get the better of my computer, water colour painting.

**JAMES, Christopher Noel Mackworth**, OBE 1987; Vice Lord-Lieutenant of Herefordshire, since 2014; Adviser, YLR Group Ltd, since 2018; *b* Jubblepore, India, 28 Jan. 1946; *s* of Lt Col Noel James and Ann James; *m* 1970, Charlotte Elizabeth Shepley-Cuthbert; two *s*. *Educ:* Eastbourne Coll.; RMA, Sandhurst. Commnd Welsh Guards, 1965–70. 22nd SAS Regt, 1971–74. Joined FCO, 1975; Second Sec., Nairobi, 1976–79; First Secretary: Lagos, 1979–80; Zimbabwe, 1980–81; Delhi, 1983–86; Counsellor, Cyprus, 1988–92; founded Hakluyt and Co., 1995–2006; Sen. Advr, Crosby Textor, 2006–08; Chairman: Malachite, 2007–11; Longbow NXG, 2014–17; Linguistica Global, 2015–18. Director: Communicaid Global Communications, 2007–17; Inter Mediate, 2011–14. Chm., Hereford Cath. Perpetual Trust, 2009–16. Trustee: Sandy and Zorica Glen Charitable Settlement, 2004–; Sultan's Fund, 2012–. Mem., SAS Assoc. DL Herefordshire, 2010. *Recreations:* tennis, interesting people, bucking the system, military history, good conversation, good food, excellent wine, watching Rugby. *Address:* Glan Arrow, Eardisland, Leominster, Herefordshire HR6 9BW. *T:* (office) (01544) 388751. *Club:* Boodle's.

**JAMES, His Honour Christopher Philip**; a Circuit Judge, 1980–97; *b* 27 May 1934; *yr s* of late Herbert Edgar James, CBE, and Elizabeth Margaret James. *Educ:* Felsted School; Magdalene Coll., Cambridge (MA). Commnd RASC, 1953. Called to the Bar, Gray's Inn, 1959; a Recorder of the Crown Court, 1979; Judge of Woolwich County Court, 1982–92, of Lambeth County Court, 1992–97. *Address:* Flat 8, 93 Elm Park Gardens, SW10 9QW. *Club:* Oxford and Cambridge.

**JAMES, Clive Vivian Leopold**, CBE 2012; AO 2013 (AM 1992); FRSL; poet, writer and broadcaster; Director, clivejames.com, since 2005; *b* 7 Oct. 1939; *s* of Albert Arthur James and Minora May (*née* Darke). *Educ:* Sydney Technical High Sch.; Sydney Univ. (BA Hons); Pembroke Coll., Cambridge (MA; Hon. Fellow). President of Footlights when at Cambridge. Dir, Watchmaker Prodns, 1994–99. Record albums as lyricist for Pete Atkin: Beware of the Beautiful Stranger; Driving through Mythical America; A King at Nightfall; The Road of Silk; Secret Drinker; Live Libel; The Master of the Revels; Touch has a Memory, 1991; Midnight Voices, the Clive James-Pete Atkin Songbook Vol. 1, 2008. Song-book with Pete Atkin: A First Folio. Television series: Cinema, Up Sunday, So It Goes, A Question of Sex, Saturday Night People, Clive James on Television; Postcard series, 1989–: Rio, Chicago, Paris, Miami, Rome, Shanghai, Sydney, London, Cairo, New York, Bombay, Berlin, Buenos Aires, Nashville, Hong Kong, Mexico City, Las Vegas, Havana. FRSL. Hon. Mem., Australian Acad. of the Humanities, 2006. Hon. DLitt: Sydney, 1999; UEA, 2006. Philip Hodgins Meml Medal, 2003; George Orwell Special Prize, 2008; NSW Premier's Award, 2012; British Academy President's Medal, 2014; Special Award, BAFTA, 2015. *Publications: non-fiction:* The Metropolitan Critic, 1974, 2nd edn 1994; The Fate of

Felicity Fark in the Land of the Media, 1975; Peregrine Prykke's Pilgrimage through the London Literary World, 1976; Britannia Bright's Bewilderment in the Wilderness of Westminster, 1976; Visions Before Midnight, 1977; At the Pillars of Hercules, 1979; First Reactions, 1980; The Crystal Bucket, 1981; Charles Charming's Challenges on the Pathway to the Throne, 1981; From the Land of Shadows, 1982; Glued to the Box, 1982; Flying Visits, 1984; Snakecharmers in Texas, 1988; On Television, 1991; The Dreaming Swimmer, 1992; Fame, 1993; Reliable Essays, 2001; Even As We Speak, 2001; The Meaning of Recognition: new essays 2001–2005, 2005; Cultural Amnesia, 2007; The Revolt of the Pendulum, 2009; A Point of View, 2011; Poetry Notebook: 2006–2014, 2014; Latest Readings, 2015; Play All: a bingewatcher's notebook, 2016; *fiction*: Brilliant Creatures, 1983; The Remake, 1987; Brrm! Brrm!, 1991; The Silver Castle, 1996; *verse*: Fan-Mail, 1977; Poem of the Year, 1983; Other Passports: poems 1958–85, 1986; The Book of my Enemy: collected verse 1958–2003, 2003; Opal Sunset: selected poems 1958–2008, 2008; Angels Over Elsinore: collected poems 2003–2008, 2008; Nefertiti in the Flak Tower, 2012; (trans.) Dante, The Divine Comedy, 2013; Sentenced to Life, 2015; Gates of Lilac, 2016; Collected Poems: 1958–2015, 2016; Injury Time, 2017; The River in the Sky, 2018; *autobiography*: Unreliable Memoirs, 1980; Falling Towards England: Unreliable Memoirs II, 1985; May Week Was in June: Unreliable Memoirs III, 1990; Always Unreliable, 2001; North Face of Soho: Unreliable Memoirs IV, 2006; The Blaze of Obscurity, 2009.

**JAMES, Colin John Irwin**, FCIPD; Chief Executive, Roads Service, Northern Ireland, 1999–2002; *b* 17 Sept. 1942; *s* of William and Evelyn James; *m* 1968, Monica Jean Patston; one *s* one *d*. *Educ*: Royal Belfast Academical Instn; Queen's Univ., Belfast (BSc Hons 1965); University Coll. London (MPhil 1967). FCIPD (FIPD 1988); MCIH 1992; MCIHT (MIHT 1999). GLC, 1967–71; DoE (NI), 1971–73; NI Housing Exec., 1973–94; joined Defence Housing Exec., 1994, Chief Exec., 1995–99. Dir, Waldovision Ltd, 2012–14. *Recreations:* local history, photography, walking, home cinema. *Address:* 10 Fort Road, Helens Bay, Co. Down BT19 1LA.

**JAMES, Darius**, OBE 2019; Artistic Director, Ballet Cymru, since 1986; *b* Newport, 18 Feb. 1966; *s* of Bernard Williams and Yvonne Williams (*née* Greenleaf); *né* Darius James Williams; *m* 2012, Amy Doughty; one *s* one *d*. *Educ*: Royal Ballet Sch. Dancer: Northern Ballet Th., 1984–86; Alexander Roy London Ballet Th., 1987–92. Dir, Community Dance Wales, 2008–10. Vice Pres., London Ballet Circle, 2016. Creative Wales Major Award, Arts Council of Wales, 2008. *Recreations:* theatre, ballet, dance, surfing. *Address:* Ballet Cymru, Unit 1, Wern Industrial Estate, Rogerstone, Newport, S Wales NP10 9FQ. *E:* dariusjames@welshballet.co.uk.

**JAMES, Rt Rev. David Charles**, PhD; Bishop of Bradford, 2002–10; an Honorary Assistant Bishop, Diocese of York, since 2010; *b* 6 March 1945; *s* of Charles George Frederick James and Cecilia Lily James; *m* 1971, Gillian Patricia Harrop; four *d*. *Educ*: Nottingham High Sch.; Exeter Univ. (BSc 1966; PhD 1971); Nottingham Univ. (BA 1973); St John's Theol Coll., Nottingham. Asst Lectr in Chemistry, Southampton Univ., 1969–70. Ordained deacon, 1973, priest, 1974; Curate: Highfield Church, Southampton, 1973–76; Goring by Sea, Worthing, 1976–78; Anglican Chaplain, UEA, 1978–82; Vicar of Ecclesfield, Sheffield, 1982–90; RD, Ecclesfield, 1987–90; Vicar of Highfield, Southampton, 1990–98; Bp Suffragan of Pontefract, 1998–2002. Hon. Canon of Winchester, 1998. Took seat in H of L, 2009. Gov., King Alfred's UC, Winchester, 1992–97. *Address:* 7 Long Lane, Beverley, E Yorks HU17 0NH.

**JAMES, Prof. David Edward**; Professor (formerly Director) of Adult Education, 1969–2002, University Professor, and Special Adviser to the Vice-Chancellor on Regional Academic Affairs, 2002–05, University of Surrey; *b* 31 July 1937; *s* of Charles Edward James and Dorothy Hilda (*née* Reeves); *m* 1963, Penelope Jane Murray; two *s* one *d*. *Educ*: Universities of Reading, Oxford, Durham, London (Bsc Hons Gen., BSc Hons Special, MEd, DipEd, DipFE); FRSPH; FITD 1992; FRSB. Lectr in Biology, City of Bath Tech. Coll. 1961–63; Lectr in Sci. and Educn, St Mary's Coll. of Educn, Newcastle upon Tyne, 1963–64; University of Surrey: Lectr in Educnl Psych., 1964–69; Hd, Dept of Educnl Studies, 1982–93; Dean of Associated Instns, 1996–2002. FRSA. *Publications:* A Student's Guide to Efficient Study, 1966, Amer. edn 1967; Introduction to Psychology, 1968, Italian edn 1972. *Recreation:* farming. *Address:* 30 Glendale Drive, Burpham, Guildford, Surrey GU4 7HZ.

**JAMES, (David) Keith (Marlais)**, OBE 2005; Chairman: Julian Hodge Bank Ltd, 2012–17; Hodge Life Assurance Co. Ltd, 2012–17; *b* Carmarthen, 16 Aug. 1944; *s* of James Lewis James and Margaret Evelyn James; *m* 1973, Kathleen Linda Marrs; one *s* two *d*. *Educ*: Cardiff High Sch.; W Monmouth Sch.; Queens' Coll., Cambridge (MA). Admitted as solicitor, 1969; Partner, Phillips and Buck Solicitors, 1969–95; Chairman: Eversheds LLP, 1995–2004; Admiral Inscce Co. Ltd, 2003–; Internat. Greetings plc, 2006–11. Non-executive Director: Bank of Wales plc, 1988–2001; Axa Insce Co. Ltd, 1992–99; HTV Gp Ltd, 1997–98 and 1999–2006. Dep. Chm., Inst. of Welsh Affairs, 1987–2007 (Hon. Fellow, 2009). Trustee, Nat. Trust, 2011–14. *Recreations:* hill walking, theatre, golf. *Address:* Trehedyn Cottage, Peterston-super-Ely, Vale of Glamorgan CF5 6LG. *T:* (029) 2078 7674. *Clubs:* Oxford and Cambridge; Cardiff and County.

**JAMES, Diane Martine**; Member for South East Region, European Parliament, 2014–19 (UK Ind, 2014–16, Ind, 2016–19); *b* 20 Nov. 1959; *d* of Edwin James and Margaret James; *m* 1st, John Stuart Smith (marr. diss. 2000); 2nd, John Richard Forrest (*d* 2019). *Educ*: Ealing Coll. of Higher Educn. Non-exec. Dir, ProVen Health VCT; Commercial Advr, Healthcare Financial Mgt Assoc. Chair, Surrey and Sussex CLRN. Mem. (UK Ind) Waverley BC, 2006–15. Leader, UKIP, 2016. Mem., Brexit Party. Vice Chair and Trustee, Red Ribbon Internat. Charity. *Recreations:* travel, fitness, antiques, animal rescue (volunteer, Hydestile and Wildlife Aid animal rescue centres).

**JAMES, Hon. Edison Chenfil**; MP (UWP) Marigot, Dominica, 1990–2014; Leader, United Workers' Party, 2012–13; *b* 18 Oct. 1943; *s* of David and Patricia James; *m* 1970, Wilma; one *s* two *d*. *Educ*: North East London Poly. (BSc Hons); Univ. of Reading (MSc); Imperial Coll., London (Dip. Pest Management). Teacher, St Mary's Acad., 1973; Agronomist, Min. of Agriculture, Dominica, 1974–76; Farm Improvement Officer, Caribbean Develt Bank and Agric. and Indust. Develt Bank, 1976–80; Project Co-ordinator, Coconut Rehabilitation; Gen. Manager, Dominica Banana Marketing Corp., 1980–87; Man. Dir, Agric. Managing Corp., 1987–95. Prime Minister, Dominica, 1995–2000; Leader of the Opposition, 2000–07. *Recreations:* cricket, football, table tennis, politics, international affairs. *Club:* Rotary Club of Dominica.

**JAMES, Erwin**; *see* Monahan, E. J.

**JAMES, Prof. Frank Arthur John Lord**, PhD; FRAS; Professor of the History of Science, 2004–March 2020, and Head, Collections and Heritage, 1998–March 2020, Royal Institution; Professor of History of Science, University College London, since 2013; *b* 7 March 1955; *s* of Arthur Montague James and Mary Patricia James (*née* Lord); *m* 1986, Joasia Hermaszewska; two *s* one *d*. *Educ*: Chelsea Coll. (BSc); Imperial Coll., London (MSc, DIC, PhD 1981). FRAS 1981. Associate, Univ. of London Inst. of Educn, 1981–82; Royal Institution: Res. Fellow, 1982–86; seconded to Marine Soc. serving in S Atlantic, 1984; Lectr, 1986–97; Reader in Hist. of Sci., 1997–2004. Vis. Res. Fellow, Sci. Studies Centre, Univ. of Bath, 1998–; Visiting Professor: UCL, 2007–13; Centro Simão Mathias, São Paulo, 2008. Earnshaw Lectr, QUB, 2004. Mem., Exec. Cttee, COPUS, 1989–97. British Society for History of Science: Officer and Council Mem., 1989–2005; Vice-Pres., 2005–06, 2008–09; Pres., 2006–08; Newcomen Society for History of Engineering and Technology: Mem. Council, 1991–94, 1996–99, 2005–07, 2010–Feb. 2020; Vice Pres., 1999–2003; Pres., 2003–05; Treas., 2011–Feb. 2020; British Association for Advancement of Science, later British Science Association: Recorder of Hist. of Sci. Section, 1992–97; Mem. Council, 1995–2000; Pres., 2009–10; Member, Council: Div. of Hist. of Sci. Technol., Internat. Union for the Hist. and Philosophy of Sci., 2009–17; Soc. for Hist. of Alchemy and Chem., 2010– (Chm., 2017–). MAE 2012. Chm., Nat. Organising Cttee, 24th Internat. Congress for Hist. of Sci. and Technol., 2009–13. Jt Ed., History of Technol., 1989–96. Liveryman, Scientific Instrument Makers' Co., 2010–. Corresp. Mem., 2011, Membre Effectif, 2014, Acad. internat. d'histoire des scis. *Publications:* (ed jtly) Faraday Rediscovered: essays on the life and work of Michael Faraday, 1791–1867, 1985; Chemistry and Theology in mid-Victorian London: The Diary of Herbert McLeod 1860–1870, 1987; (ed) The Place of Experiment: essays on the development of laboratories in industrial civilisation, 1989; (jtly) Faraday, 1991; (ed) The Correspondence of Michael Faraday, vol. 1 1991, vol. 2 1993, vol. 3 1996, vol. 4 1999, vol. 5 2008, vol. 6 2012; (ed jtly) Renaissance and Revolution: humanists, scholars, craftsmen and natural philosophers in early modern Europe, 1993; (jtly) Science in Art: works in the National Gallery that illustrate the history of science and technology, 1997; (ed) Semaphores to Short Waves, 1998; Guide to the Microfilm edition of the Manuscripts of Michael Faraday (1791–1867) from the Collections of the Royal Institution, Institution of Electrical Engineers and Guildhall Library, 2000–01; (ed) The Common Purposes of Life: science and society at the Royal Institution of Great Britain, 2002; Guide to the Microfilm edition of the Letters of John Tyndall (1820–1893) from the Collections of the Royal Institution, 2003; Christmas at the Royal Institution: an anthology of lectures, 2007; Michael Faraday: a very short introduction, 2010; (ed) Faraday's Chemical History of a Candle, 2011; (ed jtly) Being Modern: the cultural impact of science in the early twentieth century, 2018; contrib. many articles on nineteenth century science in its social, religious, military and cultural contexts. *Recreations:* walking in the country, visiting historic buildings, browsing in second hand bookshops. *Address:* Department of Science and Technology Studies, University College London, Gower Street, WC1E 6BT. *T:* (020) 7679 7713. *E:* frank.james@ucl.ac.uk.

**JAMES, Geraldine**, OBE 2003; actress; *b* 6 July 1950; *d* of Gerald Trevor Thomas and Annabella Doogan Thomas; adopted stage name, Geraldine James, 1972; *m* 1984, Joseph Sebastian Blatchley; one *d*. *Educ*: Downe House, Newbury; Drama Centre London Ltd. *Stage:* repertory, Chester, 1972–74; Exeter, 1974–75; Coventry, 1975; Passion of Dracula, Queen's, 1978; The White Devil, Oxford, 1981; Turning Over, Bush, 1984; When I was a Girl I used to Scream and Shout, Whitehall, 1987; Cymbeline, National, 1988; Merchant of Venice, Phoenix, 1989, NY (Drama Desk Best Actress Award), 1990; Death and the Maiden, Duke of York's, 1992; Lysistrata, Old Vic and Wyndham's, 1993; Hedda Gabler, Royal Exchange, Manchester, 1993; Give Me Your Answer Do!, Hampstead, 1998; Faith Healer, Almeida, 2001; The Cherry Orchard, 2003, Home, 2004, Oxford Stage Co.; UN Inspector, RNT, 2005; The Exonerated, Riverside Studios, 2006; Victory, Arcola, 2009; Hamlet, Donmar on Broadway, 2009; The Seagull, Arcola, 2011; 13, NT, 2011; Lawrence After Arabia, Hampstead Th., 2016; *TV series include:* The History Man, 1980; Jewel in the Crown, 1984; Blott on the Landscape, 1985; Echoes, 1988; Band of Gold, 1994, 1995; Kavanagh QC, 1994, 1995, 1997, 1998; Drovers' Gold, 1996; Seesaw, 1998; The Sins, 2000; White Teeth, State of Play, 2002; Jane Hall, 2004; The Amazing Mrs Pritchard, 2006; Time of your Life, 2007; The Last Enemy, City of Vice, 2008; Utopia, 2012, 2013; Black Work, 2015; The Five, 2016; Anne with an E, 2017, 2018, 2019 (Best Supporting Actress, Canadian Screen Awards); Back to Life, 2019; *TV films include:* Dummy (Best Actress, BPG), 1977; A Doll's House, 1992; Doggin' Around, 1994; Crime and Punishment, 2001; Hound of the Baskervilles, 2002; Hex, 2004; Poirot, 2005; A Harlot's Progress, 2006; The Heist, Rapunzel, Caught in a Trap, 2008; The Other Woman, 2012; *films include:* Sweet William, Night Cruiser, 1978; Gandhi, 1981; The Storm, 1985; Wolves of Willoughby Chase, 1988; The Tall Guy, She's Been Away, (Best actress, Venice Film Festival, 1989), 1989; If Looks Could Kill, The Bridge, 1990; Prince of Shadows, 1991; No Worries Australia, 1993; Words on the Window Pane, 1994; Moll Flanders, 1995; The Man Who Knew Too Little, 1998; All Forgotten, The Testimony of Taliesin Jones, The Luzhin Defence, 2000; An Angel for May, 2001; Calendar Girls, 2002; The Fever, 2003; Sherlock Holmes, 2009; Alice in Wonderland, Made in Dagenham, 2010; Arthur, Sherlock Holmes 2, The Girl with the Dragon Tattoo, 2011; Diana, 2013; Robot Overlords, 45 Years, 2015; Alice Through the Looking Glass, Rogue One: A Star Wars Story, 2016; Daphne, 2017; Beast, 2018; Downton Abbey, 2019; *radio includes:* The Hours, 2000; The Raj Quartet, 2006; The Waves, 2007; Dombey and Son, 2007; Sacred Hearts, 2009; The Carhullan Army, 2010. *Recreation:* music. *Address:* c/o Julian Belfrage Associates, 3rd Floor, 9 Argyll Street, W1F 7TG.

**JAMES, Rt Rev. Graham Richard**; Bishop of Norwich, 1999–2019; *b* 19 Jan. 1951; *s* of late Rev. Lionel Dennis James and Florence Edith May James (*née* James); *m* 1978, Julie Anne Freemantle; one *s* one *d* (and one *d* decd). *Educ*: Northampton Grammar Sch.; Univ. of Lancaster (BA 1972); Univ. of Oxford (DipTh 1974); Cuddesdon Theological Coll. Deacon 1975, priest 1976; Asst Curate, Christ the Carpenter, Peterborough, 1975–78; Priest-in-charge, later Team Vicar, Christ the King, Digswell, 1979–83; Selection Sec. and Sec. for Continuing Ministerial Educn, ACCM, 1983–85; Sen. Selection Sec., ACCM, 1985–87; Chaplain to Archbishop of Canterbury, 1987–93; Bishop Suffragan of St Germans, 1993–99. Hon. Canon: St Matthew's Cathedral, Dallas, Texas, 1989–; Truro Cathedral, 1993–99. Vice-Moderator, Churches Commn on Inter-Faith Relations, 1993–99; Chm., Rural Bishops Panel, C of E, 2001–06; Member: Gen. Synod of C of E, 1995–2019; Archbps' Council, 2006–10 (Chm., Ministry Div., 2006–12). Took seat in H of L, 2004. Mem., H of L Select Cttee on Communications, 2011–15. Chairman: Central Religious Adv. Cttee, BBC, 2004–08; Standing Conf. on Religion and Belief, BBC, 2009–11. Chair, Paterson Ind. Inquiry, 2018–. Mem. Bd, Countryside Agency, 2001–06; Chm., Norfolk Community Foundn, 2005–08; Pres., Royal Norfolk Agric. Assoc., 2005. Hon. DCL: UEA, 2015; Norwich Univ. of Arts, 2016. *Publications:* (contrib.) Say One for Me, 1992; (ed) New Soundings, 1997; Changing Rural Life, 2004; A Fallible Church, 2008; A Place for God, 2017; contribs to Theology; The Lent Factor, 2014. *Recreations:* theatre, discovering secondhand bookshops, cricket. *Address:* 31 Knoll Park, Truro TR1 1FF. *E:* grj51@icloud.com. *Club:* Athenæum.

**JAMES, Hamilton E.**; Executive Vice Chairman, Blackstone Group, since 2018 (President, 2006–18; Vice Chairman, 2002–06); *b* 3 Feb. 1951; *s* of Hamilton R. James and Waleska Bacon Evans; *m* 1973, Amabel G. Boyce; one *s* two *d*. *Educ*: Harvard Coll. (AB *magna cum laude* 1973); Harvard Business Sch. (MBA with High Dist., Baker Schol. 1975). Chairman: Banking Gp, Donaldson, Lufkin & Jenrette, 1975–2000; Global Investment Banking and Private Equity, Credit Suisse First Boston, 2000–02. Dir, Costco Corp., 1988– (Chm. Bd, 2017–); has served on other corporate bds. Former Mem., Subcttee on Technology and Competitiveness, US President's Export Council. Vice Chm., Coldwater Conservation

Fund, Trout Unlimited. Trustee: (and Chm. Emeritus) American Ballet Th., 1992–2000; (and Mem., Exec. Cttee) Second Stage Th., 1995–2015; (and Chm., Finance Cttee) Metropolitan Mus. of Art; (and Vice Chm., Bd of Trustees) Wildlife Conservation Soc.; Brearley Sch., 1996–2001; Member, Board of Trustees: Mount Sinai Health System (Chm., Finance Cttee); Centre for American Progress. Chm., Educn Finance Inst.; Member: Adv. Bd, Max S. Baucus Inst., Univ. of Montana; Adv. Council, Monetary Authy of Singapore; Adv. Bd, Montana Land Reliance. *Publications:* (jtly) Rescuing Retirement, 2016, 2nd edn 2018. *Recreations:* fly-fishing, hunting, soccer, cycling, ski-ing, racquet sports. *Address:* Blackstone Group, 345 Park Avenue, New York, NY 10154, USA. *T:* (212) 5835455, *Fax:* (212) 5835460. *E:* James@Blackstone.com. *Clubs:* Links (New York); Wee Burn Country (Darien, Conn.); Little Harbor (Harbor Springs, MI).

**JAMES, Howell Malcolm Plowden,** CBE 1997; non-executive Chairman, Radiocentre, since 2018; Chief Executive, Quiller Consultants, 2014–17, now Senior Advisor; *b* 13 March 1954; *s* of late T. J. and Virginia James. *Educ:* Mill Hill Sch., London. Head of Promotions, Capital Radio, 1978–82; Organiser, Help a London Child Charity, 1979–82; Head of Press and Publicity, TV-am, 1982–85; Special Adviser: Cabinet Office, 1985; Dept of Employment, 1985–87; DTI, 1987; Dir of Corporate Affairs, BBC, 1987–92; Dir of Corporate and Govt Affairs, Cable and Wireless, 1992–94; Pol Sec. to Prime Minister, 1994–97; Dir, Brown Lloyd James, 1997–2004; Permanent Sec., Govt Communications, 2004–08; Barclays Bank plc: Gp Corporate Affairs Dir, 2008–11; Vice Chm., Corporate Affairs, 2011–12; Global Hd, Corporate Communications, Christie's, 2012–14. Mem., Review of Govt Communication, 2003. Dir, Broadcast Audience Res. Bd, 1987–92. Dir, Equilibrium Hotels (Riad El Fenn), 2003–. Director: English Nat. Ballet Sch., 1990–96; Chichester Fest. Th., 2005–14; Trustee, British Council, 2010–16. Gov., George Eliot Sch., 1989–92; Mem., Ct of Govs, Mill Hill Sch., 1996–2003. Trustee, Queen Elizabeth's Foundn for Disabled People Develt Trust, 1992–96; Trustee and non-exec. Dir, Employers' Forum on Disability, 2012–13. *Recreations:* theatre, movies, food. *Address:* Quiller Consultants, 8th Floor, Holborn Gate, 26 Southampton Buildings, WC2A 1AN. *T:* (020) 7233 9444. *E:* james@quillerconsultants.com. *Clubs:* Garrick, Groucho.

**JAMES, Prof. Ioan Mackenzie,** FRS 1968; MA, DPhil; Savilian Professor of Geometry, Oxford University, 1970–95, Professor Emeritus, since 1995; Fellow of New College, Oxford, 1970–95, Emeritus Fellow, 1995, Leverhulme Emeritus Fellow, 1996–98, Hon. Fellow, 1999; *b* 23 May 1928; *o s* of Reginald Douglas and Jessie Agnes James; *m* 1961, Rosemary Gordon Stewart (*d* 2015); no *c*. *Educ:* St Paul's Sch. (Foundn Schol.); Queen's Coll., Oxford (Open Schol.; Hon. Fellow, 2017). Commonwealth Fund Fellow, Princeton, Berkeley and Inst. for Advanced Study, 1954–55; Tapp Res. Fellow, Gonville and Caius Coll., Cambridge, 1956; Reader in Pure Mathematics, Oxford, 1957–69, and Senior Research Fellow, St John's Coll., 1959–69, Hon. Fellow, 1988. Hon. Prof., Univ. of Wales, 1989; Vis. Prof., Univ. of Paris, 1995–97. Ed., Topology, 1962–90. London Mathematical Society: Treasurer, 1969–79; Pres., 1985–87; Whitehead Prize and Lectr, 1978. Mem. Council, Royal Soc., 1982–83. Gov., St Paul's Sch, 1970–99. Hon. DSc Aberdeen, 1993. *Publications:* The Mathematical Works of J. H. C. Whitehead, 1963; The Topology of Stiefel Manifolds, 1976; Topological Topics, 1983; General Topology and Homotopy Theory, 1984; Aspects of Topology, 1984; Topological and Uniform Spaces, 1987; Fibrewise Topology, 1988; Introduction to Uniform Spaces, 1990; Handbook of Algebraic Topology, 1995; Fibrewise Homotopy Theory, 1998; Topologies and Uniformities, 1999; History of Topology, 1999; Remarkable Mathematicians, 2002; Remarkable Physicists, 2003; Asperger's Syndrome and High Achievement, 2006; The Mind of the Mathematician, 2007; Remarkable Biologists, 2009; Driven to Innovate, 2009; Remarkable Engineers, 2010; papers in mathematical, medical and historical jls. *Address:* Mathematical Institute, Radcliffe Observatory Quarter, Woodstock Road, Oxford OX2 6GG.

**JAMES, Irene;** Member (Lab) Islwyn, National Assembly for Wales, 2003–11; *b* 1952. Formerly special needs teacher, Risca Primary Sch. Agent to Don Touhig, MP, gen. election, 2001.

**JAMES, Isabella Garden;** *see* McColl, I. G.

**JAMES, Jason Charles;** Director General, Daiwa Anglo-Japanese Foundation, since 2011; *b* Edinburgh, 15 Feb. 1965; *s* of Donald William James and Lorna Constance James (*née* Dunford); *m* 1992, Kyoko Igarashi; two *s* one *d*. *Educ:* King's Coll., Cambridge (BA 1987; MA 1990). Gaimuin, Tokyo Stock Exchange; Associate, Soc. of Investment Analysts. Sec. to Principal, Ueno Gakuen Coll., Tokyo, 1983; analyst, Nat. Securities, Tokyo, 1985–86; Japanese Equity Fund Manager, Robert Fleming Asset Mgt, 1987–89; HSBC, Tokyo: Japanese Equity Strategist, 1989–96; Head: Japanese Equity Strategy, 1990–96; Japanese Equity Res., 1996–98; HSBC, London: Global Strategist, 1998–99; Head: Eur. Equity Strategy, 1999–2002; Global Equity Strategy, 2002–04; Dir, Japan, British Council, 2007–11. *Publications:* (contrib.) British Youths: messages from Cambridge, 1985; (jtly) The Political Economy of Japanese Financial Markets: myths versus reality, 1999; (trans.) HSBC's Challenge, by Kazuo Tatewaki, 2006; (contrib.) Britain and Japan: biographical portraits, vol. VIII, 2013; (contrib.) Japanese Studies in Britain: a survey and history, 2016; academic papers in DBJ Discussion Paper Series and Trans of Asiatic Soc. of Japan. *Recreations:* singing, piano, cryptic crosswords. *Address:* Daiwa Anglo-Japanese Foundation, Daiwa Foundation Japan House, 13/14 Cornwall Terrace (Outer Circle), NW1 4QP. *Clubs:* Reform; Tokyo (Tokyo).

**JAMES, Jeffrey Daniel Dominic;** Chief Executive, Keeper of Public Records and Historical Manuscripts Commissioner, since 2014; Controller, HM Stationery Office, since 2017; Queen's Printer of Acts of Parliament, Queen's Printer for Scotland, and Government Printer for Northern Ireland, since 2017; *b* Solihull, 11 March 1968; *né* Walker; adopted *s* of late Edwin and Edith James; *m* 2010, Joanne Knight; three *s* (incl. twin *s*). *Educ:* Open Univ. (BSc Hons 2001); Univ. of Hertfordshire (MA Hist. 2010). Electronic technician, 1984–92, Chief Petty Officer, 1992–98, RN. Network Gp Manager, Univ. of Leeds, 1998–2003; Ops Manager, Swift Res. Ltd, 2003–04; Hd of Ops, BL, 2004–07; Dir of Ops and Services, Nat. Archives, 2007–13; Dep. Chief Exec., Chartered Inst. of Housing, 2013–14. *Address:* National Archives, Kew, Richmond, Surrey TW9 4DU. *T:* (020) 8392 5220. *E:* jeff.james@nationalarchives.gov.uk.

**JAMES, Sir Jeffrey (Russell),** KBE 2001; CMG 1994; HM Diplomatic Service, retired; UK Special Representative for Nepal, 2003–05; *b* 13 Aug. 1944; *s* of Lewis Charles James and Ruth James; *m* 1965, Mary Longden; two *d*. *Educ:* Whitgift Sch.; Keele Univ. (BA Hons Internat. Relations). FCO 1967; served Tehran and Kabul; Dep. Political Advr, BMG Berlin, 1978; FCO 1982; Counsellor on loan to Cabinet Office, 1984; Counsellor and Head of Chancery, Pretoria/Cape Town, 1986; Counsellor (Economic and Commercial), New Delhi, 1988; Head, Edinburgh European Council Unit, FCO, 1992; Chargé d'Affaires, Tehran, 1993; High Comr, Nairobi, 1997–2001. Lay Mem., Asylum and Immigration Tribunal, 2005–14. Dir, Eastern Africa Assoc., 2006–; Member, Council: British Inst. in Eastern Africa, 2012–; British Inst. of Persian Studies, 2016–. Mem., Chatham House (RIIA), 2002– (Assoc. Fellow, 2006–11). Mem. Governing Council, Keele Univ., 2006–14. *Recreations:* birding, golf, hill walking. *Address:* 7 Rockfield Close, Oxted, Surrey RH8 0DN. *Club:* Tandridge Golf.

**JAMES, Jennifer Rosemary;** Costs Judge and Taxing Master, Senior Court Costs Office, since 2015; *b* Livingston, Scotland, 23 June 1967; *d* of late John James and of Barbara Joyce James; *m* 2014, Liberato Cestaro. *Educ:* Balshaw's High Sch., Leyland; Runshaw Tertiary Coll., Leyland; Univ. of Lancaster (LLB Hons); Univ. of Edinburgh (LLM). Admitted as solicitor, 1992; in private practice as solicitor, 1992–2007; a Dep. Costs Judge and Taxing Master, 2003–15; a Dep. Dist Judge, 2003–; Attorney-at-Law (NY State Bar), 2007; Sen. Lectr, Univ. of Law (formerly Coll. of Law), 2007–15; called to the Bar, Lincoln's Inn, 2016. Mem., Amer. Bar Assoc., 2000. Fellow, Assoc. Law Costs Draftsmen, 1999. *Recreations:* reading, travel, illustration, bears. *Address:* Senior Court Costs Office, Thomas More Building, Royal Courts of Justice, Strand, WC2A 2LL.

**JAMES, John Christopher Urmston,** OBE 2003; Honorary Life President, European Tennis Federation, since 2008 (President, 2002–08); Life Vice-President, Lawn Tennis Association, since 2007 (Vice-President, 2003–07); Chairman, British Olympic Foundation, 1989–2017; *b* 22 June 1937; *s* of John Urmston James and Ellen Irene James; *m* 1st, 1959, Gillian Mary Davies (marr. diss. 1982); two *s*; 2nd, 1982, Patricia Mary, *d* of late Arthur Leslie Walter White and Mary Nicol White. *Educ:* St Michael's, Llanelli; Hereford Cathedral Sch. Harrods, 1954; Jaeger, 1961; Pringle, 1972; Asst Sec., 1973–81, Sec., 1981–2002, LTA. Pres., Middx Tennis Assoc., 2003–. Mem., Internat. Council, Tennis Hall of Fame, 2003–18. Vice Chm., British Olympic Assoc., 2001–04 (Hon. Life Vice-Pres., 2017). Mem., Olympic Cttee, ITF, 1991–2009. Trustee: Tennis Foundn (formerly British Tennis Foundn), 2003–10; Dan Maskell Trust, 2003–. Member: NT; Ealing NT; Friends of Osterley Park (Chm., 2012–); Wildfowl & Wetlands Trust, Barnes. Lay Vice Chm., St Mary's, Osterley PCC; Lay Mem., Hounslow Deanery Synod, 2004–; Mem. House of Laity, London Diocesan Synod, 2010–. Mem., Lib Dem Party (Pres., Hounslow Lib Dems, 2005–). *Recreations:* tennis, Rugby football, walking, architecture, the countryside, gardening, theatre. *Address:* Parkfield Cottage, Osterley Road, Isleworth, Middx TW7 4PF. *T:* (020) 8232 8683. *Clubs:* All England Lawn Tennis and Croquet, Queen's, International of GB; Cambridge University Tennis (Hon. Vice Pres.); Llanelli Lawn Tennis and Squash; Isleworth Probus (Vice Chm., 2013–).

**JAMES, John Douglas,** OBE 1996; conservationist and environmental arts consultant; *b* 28 July 1949; *s* of late William Antony James, ERD, MA and Agnes Winifred James (*née* Mitchell); *m* 1971, Margaret Patricia Manton. *Educ:* Spalding Grammar School; Dip. in Co. Direction, Inst. of Dirs, 1994; MBA Nottingham Univ. 1999. Articled pupil, William H. Brown & Son, 1967–68; Marketing Dept, Geest Industries, 1969–71; Marketing Dept, John Player & Sons, 1971–77; Woodland Trust: Nat. Develt Officer, 1977; (first) Director, 1980; Exec. Dir, 1985; Chief Exec., 1992–97. Forestry Comr, 1998–2004 (Mem. Nat. Cttee for England, 2003–04). Co-owner: Focus Gall., Nottingham, 1995–2004; Church Street Gall., Cromer, 2004–12; Cromerart, 2012–. Nottingham Roosevelt Scholar, 1975 (Trustee, Nottingham Roosevelt Scholarship, 1997–2004); Churchill Fellow, 1980. Founder Mem., S Lincs Nature Reserves Ltd, 1968. FRSA 1995. *Recreations:* woodland walks, writing about natural history.

**JAMES, John Henry;** Chief Executive, Kensington & Chelsea and Westminster Health Authority (formerly Commissioning Agency), 1992–2002; *b* 19 July 1944; step *s* of late George Arthur James and *s* of late Doris May James; *m* 3rd, 1987, Anita Mary Stockton, *d* of late Brian Scarth, QPM and Irene Scarth. *Educ:* Ludlow Grammar Sch.; Keble Coll., Oxford (BA Mod. Hist. 1965; postgrad. dip. in Econ. and Pol Sci. 1966). AHSM 1991 (LHSM 1989). Entered Home Civil Service 1966; Asst Principal, Min. of Pensions and Nat. Insurance; Private Sec. to First Perm. Sec., 1969–71, Principal, 1971–74, DHSS; seconded to HM Treasury, 1974–76; Principal, 1976–78, Asst Sec., 1978–86, Under Sec., 1986–91, DHSS, later Dept of Health; Dir of Health Authority Finance, NHS Management Bd, 1986–89; General Manager: Harrow DHA, 1990–92; Parkside DHA, 1991–93. Chm. of reviews and dir of projects, DoH, 2002–05. Co-ordinator, London Cardiac Specialty Rev., 1993. Non-exec. Dir, Laing Homes Ltd, 1987–89. Member: Adv. Council, King's Fund Inst., 1990–93; NHS Res. Task Force, 1993; NHS Central R&D Council, 1994–99; MRC Health Services and Public Health Res. Bd, 1995–99; NHS Adv. Cttee on Resource Allocation, 1997–99; Accessible Transport Commn for London, 1998–2002; Nat. Strategic Gp tackling Racial Harassment in NHS, 1999–2001. Mem. Editl Bd, Milbank Foundn, NY, 2000–12. Mem. Bd, Enfield Healthwatch, 2013–17. FRSA 1994. *Publications:* Transforming the NHS, 1994; contributed: Oxford Textbook of Public Health, 1985, 2nd edn 1991; Health Care UK, 1993; Rationing of Health and Social Care, 1993; Information Management in Health Services, 1994; articles in jls. *Recreations:* chess, watching cricket, travel, food and wine, collecting edible fungi. *E:* anj.james@btinternet.com. *Club:* Athenæum.

**JAMES, Sir John (Nigel Courtenay),** KCVO 1997; CBE 1990; FRICS; Secretary and Keeper of the Records, Duchy of Cornwall, 1993–97; Trustee of the Grosvenor Estate, 1971–2000; a Crown Estate Commissioner, 1984–99; *b* 31 March 1935; *s* of Frank Courtenay James and Beryl May Wilford Burden; *m* 1961, Elizabeth Jane St Clair-Ford (*d* 2018); one *s* one *d*. *Educ:* Sherborne Sch., Dorset. Chief Agent and Estate Surveyor, Grosvenor Estate, 1968–71. Director: Sun Alliance & London Insurance Gp, 1972–93 (a Vice-Chm., 1988–93); Woolwich Equitable Building Soc., 1982–89; Williams & Glyn's Bank plc, 1983–85; Royal Bank of Scotland, 1985–93. Member: Commn for the New Towns, 1978–86; Cttee of Management, RNLI, 1980–2005 (Dep. Chm., 1999–2005); Council, Architectural Heritage Fund, 1983–2001 (Chm., 1999–2001); Prince of Wales' Council, 1984–97. Pres., RICS, 1980–81. Trustee, Henry Smith's Charity, 1991–2005. Gov., Sherborne Sch., 1990–2002. *Recreation:* sailing. *Club:* Brooks's.

**JAMES, Jonathan Elwyn Rayner;** QC 1988; a Recorder, 1998–2002; *b* 26 July 1950; *s* of late Basil James and of Moira James; *m* 1981, Anne Henshaw (*née* McRae); one *s*. *Educ:* King's College Sch., Wimbledon; Christ's Coll., Cambridge (MA, LLM); Brussels Univ. (Lic. Spécial en Droit Européen 1973). Called to Bar, Lincoln's Inn (Hardwicke Schol.), 1971, Bencher, 1994. Asst Recorder, 1994–98. Mem. Editl Bd, Entertainment Law Rev., 1990. *Publications:* (co-ed) EEC Anti-Trust Law, 1975; (co-ed) Copinger and Skone James on Copyright, 12th edn 1980–14th edn 1998; (jt consulting editor) Encyclopaedia of Forms and Precedents, Vol. 15 (Entertainment), 1989. *Recreations:* DIY, opera, 007, squash, France. *Address:* Hogarth Chambers, 5 New Square, Lincoln's Inn, WC2A 3RJ. *T:* (020) 7404 0404.

**JAMES, Julie;** Member (Lab) Swansea West, National Assembly for Wales, since 2011; Minister for Housing and Local Government, since 2018; *b* Swansea, 25 Feb. 1958; *d* of Derek James and Lorna James; *m* 1988, David Flatt; two *s* one *d*. *Educ:* Penzance Girls' Grammar Sch.; Univ. of Sussex (BA Hons 1980); Poly. of Central London (DipLaw 1982); Inns of Court Sch. of Law. Called to the Bar, 1983. Policy Lawyer, London Bor. of Camden, 1986–93; Asst County Sec., West Glamorgan CC, 1993–96; Asst Chief Exec. (Governance), City and Co. of Swansea, 1996–2005; Consultant, Clarkslegal LLP, 2005–11. Dep. Minister for Skills and Technol., 2014–16, Minister for Skills and Sci., 2016–17, Leader of the House and Chief Whip, 2017–18, Welsh Govt. *Recreations:* swimming, ski-ing, gardening, family. *Address:* (office) 1st Floor, 11 Wind Street, Swansea SA1 1DP. *T:* (01792) 460836. *E:* julie.james@assembly.wales.

**JAMES, Most Rev. Kay Maree;** *see* Goldsworthy, Most Rev. K. M.

**JAMES, Keith;** see James, D. K. M.

**JAMES, Lawrence Edwin;** historian and journalist, since 1985; b 26 May 1943; s of Arthur and Laura James; m 1967, Mary Charlotte Williams; two s. Educ: Weston-super-Mare GS; York Univ. (BA 1966); Merton Coll., Oxford (MLitt 1979). Schoolmaster: Merchant Taylors' Sch., Northwood, 1969–76; Sedbergh Sch., Cumbria, 1976–85. Publications: Crimea: the war with Russia in contemporary photographs, 1981; The Savage Wars: the British conquest of Africa 1870–1920, 1985; Mutiny, 1987; Imperial Rearguard: wars of empire 1919–1985, 1988; The Golden Warrior: the life and legend of Lawrence of Arabia, 1990, 3rd edn 2005, repr. 2018; The Iron Duke: a military biography of the Duke of Wellington, 1992, 2nd edn 2001; Imperial Warrior: the life and times of Field-Marshal Viscount Allenby, 1993; The Rise and Fall of the British Empire, 1994, 2nd edn 1997; Raj: the making and unmaking of British India, 1997; Warrior Race: the British experience of war, 2001; The Middle Class: a history, 2006; Aristocrats, 2009; Churchill and Empire: portrait of an Imperialist, 2013; Empires in the Sun: the struggle for the mastery of Africa, 2016. Recreations: bird watching, pipe smoking, maintenance of a Springer spaniel. Address: 4 Lechlade Road, Langford, Glos GL7 3LE.

**JAMES, Linda Elizabeth Blake;** see Sullivan, L. E.

**JAMES, Margot;** MP for Stourbridge, since 2010 (C, 2010–19; Ind, since 2019); b Coventry, 1957; d of Maurice and Cathleen James; partner, Jay. Educ: Millfield Sch., Som; London Sch. of Econs and Pol Sci. (BSc Econs and Govt). Work in sales and mktg for Maurice James Industries; consulting firm; Co-founder, Shire Health Communications, 1986–98; Hd, Eur. Healthcare, 1998, Regl Pres., Pharmaceutical Div., 2005, Ogilvy & Mather. Non-exec. Dir, Parkside NHS Trust, 1998–2003. Mem. (C) Kensington and Chelsea LBC, 2006–08. Contested (C) Holborn and St Pancras, 2005. PPS to Minister for Trade and Investment, BIS and FCO, 2012, to Leader of H of C, 2014–15; an Asst Govt Whip, 2015–16; Parly Under-Sec. of State, BEIS, 2016–18; Minister of State, DCMS, 2018–19. Mem., Business, Innovation and Skills Select Cttee, 2010–12. Address: House of Commons, SW1A 0AA.

**JAMES, Marlon,** V; novelist, short story writer and essayist; Professor of English, Macalester College, Minnesota, since 2007; b St Andrew, Jamaica, 1970. Educ: Wolmer's Boys' High Sch.; Univ. of the West Indies (BA); Wilkes Univ. (MA). Writer: New York Times, 2015–16; GQ, 2016. Publications: novels: John Crow's Devil, 2005; The Book of Night Women, 2009; A Brief History of Seven Killings, 2014 (Man Booker Prize, 2015); Black Leopard, Red Wolf, 2019; contributor: Kingston Noir, 2012; The Book of Men, 2013. Recreation: cycling. Address: 2 East Franklin Avenue, Suite #5, Minneapolis, MN 55404, USA. E: marlonjameswriter@gmail.com.

**JAMES, Prof. Mary Elizabeth,** PhD; FAcSS; Professor, Faculty of Education, University of Cambridge, 2008–13, now Professor Emerita; b Dorking, 21 March 1946; d of Robert Henry James and Florence Edna James; m 2013, David Peter Ebbutt; one s. Educ: Brighton Coll. of Educn (Teachers' Cert. 1967); Univ. of Sussex (BEd 1968); Inst. of Educn, Univ. of London (MA 1979); Open Univ. (PhD 1990); MA Cantab 1992. Teacher of RE, Park Barn Secondary Sch., Guildford, 1968–70; Hd of Yr and English Teacher, Portsmouth Southern Grammar Sch. for Girls, 1970–74; Hd of Social Studies and Sociol., Hatch End High Sch., Harrow, 1974–79; Res. Asst in Curriculum, Faculty of Educnl Studies, Open Univ., 1979–82; Sen. Res. Associate, Dept of Educn, Univ. of Cambridge, 1982–85; Res. Fellow, Sch. of Educn, Open Univ., 1985–89; Tutor in Educn, Cambridge Inst. of Educn, 1989–92; University of Cambridge: Lectr in Educn, 1992–2000; Sen. Lectr, 2000–02; Reader in Educn, 2002–04; Associate Dir of Res., Faculty of Educn, 2008–13; Fellow, Lucy Cavendish Coll., Cambridge, 1996–2004, Fellow Commoner, 2004–; Chair in Educn, Inst. of Educn, London Univ., 2005–07, 2008; Chair, Scientific Adv. Panel for NordForsk Prog., 2012–17; Mem., Scientific Adv. Bd, NordForsk Educn for Tomorrow Phase 2 Prog., 2018–. Non-exec. Dir, Bell Educnl Services Ltd, 2013–15. Mem., Expert Panel for Nat. Curriculum Rev., 2010–11. Overseas Mem., Curriculum Develt Council, Educn Bureau, Govt of Hong Kong, 2004–07. Pres., British Educnl Res. Assoc., 2011–13 (Vice Pres., 2010–11, 2013–14). FAcSS (AcSS 2006). Publications: (ed jtly) Calling Education to Account, 1982; (with R. McCormick) Curriculum Evaluation in Schools, 1983, 2nd edn 1988 (trans. Spanish, 1996), reissued 2019; Using Assessment for School Improvement, 1998; (jtly) Learning How to Learn: tools for schools, 2006; (jtly) Improving Learning How to Learn, in classrooms, schools and networks, 2007; (contrib. ed.) International Encyclopedia of Education, 3rd edn 2010; (with A. Pollard) Principles for Effective Pedagogy, 2012; Educational Assessment, Evaluation and Research: the selected works of Mary E. James, 2013; (jtly) Reflective Teaching in Schools, 4th edn 2014, 5th edn 2019; contribs to jls. Recreations: walking, horse-riding, book club, visiting gardens, houses, galleries, theatre, cinema, making things with textiles, travel (especially on horse-back). T: 07714 652809. E: mej1002@cam.ac.uk. Club: Farmers.

**JAMES, Dr Matthew Clive Campbell;** Commercial Director, Cabinet Office, since 2018; b Gloucester, 6 Dec. 1971; s of Clive James and Ruth James; two s one d; m 2018, Canna Grindley. Educ: Univ. of Leeds (BA Music, MMus); Univ. of Bath (MBA, PhD 2011). Qualified Commercial Mediator, Centre for Dispute Resolution, 2014. Joined Civil Service, 1995; Commercial Manager, DWP, 1995–2006; Dir of Procurement, Personal Accounts Delivery Authy, 2006–10; Commercial Dir, Cabinet Office, 2010–15; Man. Dir, Commercial, UKTI, subseq. DIT, 2015–18. Trustee, Aim for Change, 2013–. E: mattccjames1971@gmail.com. T: 07738 697372.

**JAMES, Michael;** see James, R. M. and Jayston, M.

**JAMES, Michael Francis;** a District Judge (Magistrates' Courts) (formerly Stipendiary Magistrate), West Midlands, 1991–2002; b 30 Oct. 1933; s of Francis and Eveline James; m 1958, Lois Joy Elcock. Educ: King Charles I Grammar Sch., Kidderminster. Admitted solicitor, 1956. National Service: commnd RAF, 1957; qualified as air navigator, 1958. Partner, Ivens Morton & Greville-Smith (later Morton Fisher), 1959–86; Sen. Partner, 1986–91. Part-time ind. prison adjudicator, 2002–08. Vis. Fellow, UWE, 1996–99. Recreations: books, wine, walking, music.

**JAMES, Michael Leonard, (Michael Hartland),** MBE 2012; writer and broadcaster, since 1983; b 7 Feb. 1941; m 1975, Jill Tarján (marr. diss. 1992); two d. Educ: Latymer Upper Sch.; Christ's Coll., Cambridge (Holland Rose Prize; Wren Prize). Entered British govt service, 1963; Private Sec. to Rt Hon. Jennie Lee, MP, Minister for the Arts, 1966–68; DES, 1968–71; Planning Unit of Rt Hon. Margaret Thatcher, MP, Sec. of State for Educn and Science, 1971–73; Asst Sec., 1973; DCSO 1974; served London, Milan, Paris, Tokyo, 1973–78; Director, IAEA, Vienna, 1978–83; Advr on Internat. Relations, CEC, Brussels, 1983–85. Member: CSSB, 1983–93; Immigration Appeal Tribunal, 1987–2005; Asylum and Immigration Tribunal, 2005–13; a Chm., Fitness to Practise Cttee, GMC, 2000–06. Governor: Colyton Grammar Sch., 1985–90; Sidmouth Community Coll., 1988–2004 (Chm., 1998–2001). Chm., 2001–11, Pres., 2011–, Kennaway House Trust. Feature writer and book reviewer for The Times (thriller critic, 1989–90; travel correspondent, 1993–2003), Daily Telegraph (thriller critic, 1993–), Sunday Times and Guardian, 1986–2014. Television and radio include: Sonja's Report (ITV), 1990; Masterspy,

interviews with Oleg Gordievsky (BBC Radio 4), 1991. FRSA 1982. Hon. Fellow, Univ. of Exeter, 1985. Publications: as M. L. James: (jtly) Internationalization to Prevent the Spread of Nuclear Weapons, 1980; as Michael Hartland: Down Among the Dead Men, 1983; Seven Steps to Treason, 1985 (SW Arts Lit. Award; dramatized for BBC Radio 4, 1990); The Third Betrayal, 1986; Frontier of Fear, 1989; The Year of the Scorpion, 1991; The Verdict of Us All (short stories), 2006; Masters of Crime: Lionel Davidson and Dick Francis, 2006; as Ruth Carrington: Dead Fish, 1998. Address: Kennaway House Trust, Sidmouth, Devon EX10 8NG. Clubs: Athenæum, PEN, Detection.

**JAMES, Prof. Michael Norman George,** DPhil, FRS 1989; FRS(Can) 1985; Professor of Biochemistry, 1978–2014, and Distinguished University Professor of Biochemistry, 1993–2014, University of Alberta, now Emeritus Distinguished Professor; b 16 May 1940; s of Claud Stewart Murray James and Mimosa Ruth Harriet James; m 1961, Patricia McCarthy; one s one d; m 1977, Anita Sielecki; m 1996, Deborah Brown; one d. Educ: Univ. of Manitoba (BSc, MSc); Linacre Coll., Oxford (DPhil). University of Alberta: Asst Prof., then Associate Prof., 1968–78; Canada Res. Chair in Protein Structure and Function, 2001–08. Mem., MRC of Canada Group in Protein Structure and Function, 1974. Hon. DSc Manitoba, 2010. Publications: over 300 contribs to learned jls. Address: Department of Biochemistry, University of Alberta, Edmonton, AB T6G 2H7, Canada. T: (780) 4924550, (780) 6412978.

**JAMES, Dame Naomi (Christine),** DBE 1979; PhD; author and philosopher; former yachtswoman; b 2 March 1949; d of Charles Robert Power and Joan Power; m 1st, 1976, Robert Alan James (d 1983); one d; 2nd, 1990, Eric G. Haythorne (marr. diss.), o s of G. V. Haythorne, Ottawa, Canada. Educ: Rotorua Girls' High Sch., NZ; UC, Cork (BA Philosophy and Eng. Lit. 1997; MA Philosophy 1999); Milltown Inst. of Theology and Philosophy (PhD Philosophy 2005). Hair stylist, 1966–71; language teacher, 1972–74; yacht charter crew, 1975–77. Sailed single handed round the world via the three great Capes, incl. first woman solo round Cape Horn, on 53 ft yacht, Express Crusader, Sept. 1977–June 1978; sailed in 1980 Observer Transatlantic Race, winning Ladies Prize and achieving women's record for single-handed Atlantic crossing, on 53 ft yacht Kriter Lady; won 1982 Round Britain Race with Rob James, on multihull Colt Cars GB. Trustee, Nat. Maritime Museum, 1985–92; Council Mem., Winston Churchill Meml Trust, 1986–93. Royal Yacht Sqdn Chichester Trophy, 1978; NZ Yachtsman of the Year, 1978. Publications: Woman Alone, 1978; At One with the Sea, 1979; At Sea on Land, 1981; Courage at Sea, 1987. Recreations: literature, philosophy, walking. Address: Shore Cottage, Currabinny, Carrigaline, Co. Cork, Ireland. Clubs: Royal Dart Yacht (Dartmouth); Royal Lymington Yacht (Lymington); Royal Western Yacht (Plymouth).

**JAMES, Prof. Oliver Francis Wintour,** FRCP, FMedSci; Medical Director, North East and North Cumbria Academic Health Science Network; President, British Liver Trust; b 23 Sept. 1943; s of Baron James of Rusholme and Cordelia Mary (née Wintour); m 1965, Rosanna Foster; one s one d. Educ: Winchester; Balliol Coll., Oxford (MA 1964; BM BCh 1967); Middlesex Hosp. Med. Sch. Registrar and Fellow, Royal Free Hosp., 1971–74; University of Newcastle upon Tyne: First Asst in Medicine, 1974–75; Reader in Medicine (Geriatrics), 1975–85; Prof. of Geriatric Medicine, 1985–2008; Hd, Sch. of Clin. Med. Scis, 1994–2004; Pro Vice Chancellor, 2004–08. Consultant Physician, Freeman Hosp., Newcastle, 1977. Vis. Prof., Univs of Hong Kong, Indianapolis and St Louis. Chairman: Liver Section, EC Concerted Action on Cellular Aging, 1982–86; Jt Cttee for Higher Med. Trng, SAC in Geriatrics, 1992–95. Pres., Brit. Assoc. for Study of Liver, 1992–94. Royal College of Physicians: Censor, 1994–96; Sen. Vice Pres., 1997–2001. Non-exec. Bd Mem., North of England Strategic HA (formerly NE Strategic HA), 2009–13. Chair, Sir James Knott Charitable Trust, 2006–. Trustee, Help the Aged, 2001–. Medical Assessor, Penrose Inquiry, 2015. Founder FMedSci 1998. Publications: numerous papers and chapters on aspects of liver disease, geriatric medicine and training of physicians. Recreations: vegetable growing, wine, golf, long distance cycling. Address: Aumery Park, Fadmoor, York YO62 7JG.

**JAMES, Peter John,** CBE 2011; Principal, London Academy of Music and Dramatic Art, 1994–2010, now Emeritus; Head, Department of Theatre Directing MA, Mountview Academy, since 2012; b 27 July 1940; s of Arthur Leonard James and Gladys (née King); m 1st, 1964, Anthea Olive (marr. diss. 1972); one d; one s by Bernadette McKenna; 2nd, 1999, Alexandra Paisley. Educ: Birmingham Univ. (BA Hons English, Philosophy); Bristol Univ. (Postgrad. Cert. Drama). Founder Dir, Liverpool Everyman Theatre, 1964–71; Associate Dir, NT at Young Vic, 1971–73; Director: Crucible Theatre, Sheffield, 1974–81; Lyric Theatre, Hammersmith, 1981–94 (numerous first productions; Theatre Awards, 1986, 1992). Dir of plays, UK and overseas, incl. Russia. Chair of Trustees, Diorama Arts, 1992–. Former cttee memberships incl. Arts Council, European Theatre Convention, Internat. Theatre Inst. (Award for Excellence, 1990). Recreations: cooking, watching boxing and football matches. Address: 68a Springfield Road, Tottenham, N15 4AZ. T: 07784 245563.

**JAMES, Peter John;** author; b Hove, 22 Aug. 1948; s of John James and Cornelia James (née Katz). Educ: Charterhouse; Ravensbourne Film Sch. Director: Quadrant Prodn Ltd, Toronto, 1971–76; Yellowbill Prodn Ltd, 1976–85; Cornelia James Ltd, 1977–95; Ministry of Vision, 1990–; CEO, Movision Ltd, 2001–05. Film productions: The Corpse Grinders, 1971; Blood Orgy of the She-Devils, Under Milk Wood, 1972; Blue Blood, Children Shouldn't Play with Dead Things, The Blockhouse, 1973; Deranged, Dead of Night, Sunday in the Country, 1974; It Seemed Like a Good Idea at the Time, Shivers, 1975; Spanish Fly, Find the Lady, 1976; Biggles, 1986; Jericho Mansions, 2003; A Different Loyalty, The Merchant of Venice, Head in the Clouds, The Bridge of San Luis Rey, 2004; The Last Sign, Bailey's Billions, Guy X, Beowulf & Grendel, The River King, 2005; Perfect Creature, 2006. Stage adaptation: The Perfect Murder, UK tour, 2014, 2016; Dead Simple, UK tour, 2015; Not Dead Enough, UK tour, 2017. Hon. Chair, CWA, 2011, 2012. Chair, Brighton Drugs Commn, 2012–. Patron, Sussex Crimestoppers, 2009–; Co-Patron, Sussex Police Charitable Trust. Hon. DLitt Brighton, 2009; MUniv Open., 2015. Best Crime Author of All Time, WHSmith, 2015; Diamond Dagger Prize, CWA, 2016; First Rheinbach Glass Dagger Award, 2017. Publications: Dead Letter Drop, 1981; Atom Bomb Angel, 1982; Billionaire, 1983; Possession, 1988; Dreamer, 1989; Twilight, 1991; Sweet Heart, 1991; Prophecy, 1993; Host, 1994; Alchemist, 1996; The Truth, 1997; Denial, 2000; Faith, 2000; Dead Simple, 2005; Looking Good Dead, 2006; Not Dead Enough, 2007; Dead Man's Footsteps, 2008; Dead Tomorrow, 2009; The Perfect Murder, 2010; Dead Like You, 2010; Dead Man's Grip, 2011; Perfect People, 2011; Not Dead Yet, 2012; Dead Man's Time, 2013; Want You Dead, 2014; A Twist of the Knife, 2014; You Are Dead, 2015 (Dr Lecter Award for Scariest Villian, Dead Good Readers, 2015); The House on Cold Hill, 2015; Love You Dead, 2016; Need You Dead, 2017; Death Comes Knocking, 2017; Dead If You Don't, 2018; Absolute Proof, 2018; Dead At First Sight, 2019. Recreations: motor racing, ski-ing, tennis, running, fine wine, food, animals. Address: c/o Isobel Dixon, Blake Friedmann Literary, TV and Film Agency, First Floor, Selous House, 5–12 Mandela Street, NW1 0DU. T: (020) 7387 0842. E: isobel@blakefriedmann.co.uk. Clubs: Ivy, Groucho, Annabel's, British Automobile Racing, 5 Hertford Street.

**JAMES, Philip;** see James, W. P. T.

**JAMES, Richard**, OBE 2018; Co-Founder and Director, Richard James, tailor, 1992–2015; *b* Ely, 9 Jan. 1953; *s* of Clifford James and Jean James. *Educ:* Brighton Coll. of Art. *Publications:* (contrib.) Richard James Savile Row, 2018. *Recreation:* the V&A. *Address:* Richard James, 19 Clifford Street, W1S 3RH. *T:* (020) 7434 0171. *E:* rohan@richard-james.com.

**JAMES, (Robert) Michael**; UK Trade Adviser, International Tropical Timber Organisation, 1998–2000; *b* 2 Oct. 1934; *s* of late Rev. B. V. James and Mrs D. M. James; *m* 1959, Sarah Helen (*née* Bell); two *s* one *d*. *Educ:* St John's, Leatherhead; Trinity Coll. Cambridge (BA Hons History). Schoolmaster: Harrow Sch., 1958–60; Cranleigh Sch., 1960–62; joined CRO, 1962; 3rd Sec., Wellington, NZ, 1963–65; 1st Sec., Colombo, Sri Lanka, 1966–69; FCO, 1969–71; Dep. High Comr and Head of Chancery, Georgetown, Guyana, 1971–73; Econ. Sec., Ankara, Turkey, 1974–76; FCO, 1976–80; Commercial Counsellor and Deputy High Commissioner: Accra, 1980–83; Singapore, 1984–87; Dep. High Comr, Bridgetown, Barbados, 1987–90. Exec., Timber Trade Fedn, 1990–98; Dir, Forests Forever Campaign, 1990–98. *Recreations:* sport (cricket Blue, 1956–58), drawing, travel. *Address:* 17 North Grove, Highgate, N6 4SH. *T:* (020) 8245 3763. *Clubs:* MCC; Hawks (Cambridge); Hunstanton Golf, Highgate Golf.

**JAMES, Roy Lewis**, CBE 1998; independent educational consultant, since 1997; HM Chief Inspector of Schools in Wales, 1992–97; *b* 9 Feb. 1937; *s* of David John and Eleanor James; *m* 1962, Mary Williams; one *d*. *Educ:* Llandysul Grammar School; University College of Wales, Aberystwyth (BSc Hons, DipEd). Asst Master, Strode's Grammar Sch., Egham, 1959–60; Head of Maths Dept, Lampeter Comp. Sch., 1960–62; Head of Maths Dept, Cyfarthfa Castle Sch., Merthyr Tydfil, 1962–70; HM Inspector of Schs, 1970–84, seconded as Sec., Schs Council Cttee for Wales, 1975–77; Staff Inspector, 1984–90; Chief Inspector of Schs (Wales), 1990–97. External Prof., Univ. of Glamorgan, 1997–2002. Hon. Res. Fellow, UWIC, 1999–2004. Chairman: Techniquest (Wales) Educn Adv. Gp, 1997–2002; Awards Panel Wales (Teaching Awards), 2000–06; Chair: Denbighshire Educn Recovery Bd, 2007–11; Welsh for Adults Mid-Wales Centre Strategic Bd, 2013–16. Trustee, Welsh Dyslexia Proj., 2004–11. Admitted to Gorsedd of Bards, Nat. Eisteddfod of Wales, 1997. *Publications:* numerous res. reports and articles on educn policy, curriculum and assessment, and initial trng and continuous professional develt of teachers. *Recreations:* travel, walking, reading, wine, chess, snooker, eating out. *Address:* Bryn Cemais, Llanfarian, Aberystwyth SY23 4BX.

**JAMES, Hon. Sebastian Richard Edward Cuthbert**; Senior Vice President, Walgreens Boots Alliance, and President and Managing Director, Boots, since 2018; *b* London, 11 March 1966; *s* of 5th Baron Northbourne and Aliki Louise Hélène Marie Sygne (*née* Claudel); *m* 1998, Anna Katherine Gregory; three *s* one *d*. *Educ:* Eton Coll.; Magdalen Coll., Oxford (BA Hons Law 1987); INSEAD (MBA 1991). Associate, Bain & Co., 1987–90; Case Leader, Boston Consulting Gp, 1991–94; Man. Dir, Longwall Hldgs Ltd, 1995–2001; Partner, iFormation Gp, 2001–02; Strategy Dir, Mothercare plc, 2002–03; Founder and Chief Exec., Silverscreen Ltd, 2004–06; CEO, Synergy Insce Services, 2006–08; Dixons Retail plc: Transformation Dir, 2008–12; Gp Services Dir, 2008–12; Gp Ops Dir, 2008–12; Gp CEO, 2012–14; Gp CEO, Dixons Carphone, 2014–18. Chm., Ink Publishing, 2001–12; Ind. Dir, Direct Line, 2014–. Advr DFE, 2010–11. Trustee, Save the Children, 2014–. *Recreations:* ski-ing, scuba diving, playing guitar. *Address:* Boots, 1 Thane Road, Beeston, Nottingham NG2 3AA. *E:* sebastian@james.net. *Club:* Soho House.

**JAMES, Shani R.**; *see* Rhys-James.

**JAMES, Siân Catherine**; *b* 24 June 1959; *d* of Melbourne Griffiths and Martha Griffiths (*née* Morgan); *m* 1976, Martin R. James; one *s* one *d*. *Educ:* University Coll. of Wales, Swansea (BA Hons Welsh). Field Officer, Wales, Nat. Fedn of Young Farmers Clubs, 1990–91; Fundraiser, Wales, SCF, 1991–95; Dep. Public Affairs Manager, Wales, NT, 1995–98; Communications Manager, Securicor, HMP Parc, 1998–99; Assembly Liaison Manager, ATOL, 1999–2003; Dir, Welsh Women's Aid, 2003–05. MP (Lab) Swansea E, 2005–15. *Recreations:* dolls houses, model railways, antiques, spending quality time with family.

**JAMES, Simon John; His Honour Judge Simon James**; a Circuit Judge, since 2010; Resident Judge, Canterbury Crown Court, since 2019; *b* Plymouth, 24 Jan. 1966; *s* of Comdr David John Dicks James, RN and Anne James; *m* 1991, Dawn Hilditch; one *s* one *d*. *Educ:* Brookfield Comprehensive Sch.; Leeds Univ. (LLB Hons); Inns of Court Sch. of Law. Called to the Bar, Lincoln's Inn, 1988; in practice at the Bar on Northern Circuit, specialising in crime, 1988–2010; Recorder, 2005–10. Hon. Recorder of Canterbury. *Recreations:* family, friends, food and wine, watching sport, cycling. *Address:* The Law Courts, Chaucer Road, Canterbury, Kent CT1 1ZA.

**JAMES, Stephen Howard George Thompson B.**; *see* Bellamy-James.

**JAMES, Stephen Lawrence**; Consultant, Simmons & Simmons, Solicitors, 1992–2002 (Partner, 1961; Senior Partner, 1980–92); *b* 19 Oct. 1930; *s* of Walter Amyas James and Cecile Juliet (*née* Hillman); *m* 1st, 1955, Patricia Eleanor Favell James (marr. diss. 1986); two *s* two *d*; 2nd, 1998, Monique Whittome (Dame, Order of Royal Crown of Crete), *d* of Count Dom Joseph Borda of Kalkara, Malta. *Educ:* Clifton Coll.; St Catharine's Coll., Cambridge (BA History and Law). Mem., Gray's Inn, 1953, Bar finals, 1956; admitted Solicitor: England and Wales, 1959; Hong Kong, 1980. Director: Horace Clarkson PLC (formerly H. Clarkson (Holdings) PLC), 1975–2002; Shipping Industrial Holdings Ltd, 1972–82; Tradinvest Bank & Trust Co. of Nassau Ltd, 1975–85; Nodiv Ltd, 1975–78; Silver Line Ltd, 1978–82; Thompson Moore Associates Ltd, 1984–88; Greycoat PLC, 1994–99; Kiln Capital PLC, 1994–99. Mem., Law Soc., 1961–. *Recreations:* yachting, gardening. *Address:* 6 Elystan Place, SW3 3LF; Widden, Shirley Holms, Lymington, Hants SO41 8NL. *Clubs:* Royal Yacht Squadron; Royal Thames Yacht.

**JAMES, Steven Alexander, (Alex)**; musician, journalist, cheesemaker; *b* Bournemouth, 21 Nov. 1968; *s* of Jason Bernard James and Kelly Joyce James; *m* 2003, Claire Louise Neate; three *s* two *d*. *Educ:* Bournemouth Sch.; Goldsmiths Coll., Univ. of London (Hon. Fellow, 2008). Bass guitarist in Blur, 1989–; other musical projects incl. Me, Me, Me (with Stephen Duffy) and band, Fat Les; writer and producer with Marianne Faithfull, Sophie Ellis-Bextor, Florence and the Machine, Bernard Sumner and Kevin Rowland (Dexys); Contributing Ed. Food, Fabulous mag.; weekly columnist: Alex James on Food, The Sun, 2010–14; Mucking In..., The Sunday Telegraph, 2011–16; weekly radio show, Date Night, Classic FM, 2008–17; producer of award-winning artisan cheeses; host, annual food and music festival, The Big Feastival, 2011–. Hon. DArts: Bournemouth, 2010; Gloucestershire, 2013. *Publications:* Bit of a Blur (autobiog.), 2007; All Cheeses Great and Small (autobiog.), 2012. *Recreations:* building, napping. *E:* kate@alexjames.co. *Clubs:* Groucho, 5 Hertford Street.

**JAMES, Steven Wynne Lloyd**; Circuit Administrator, North-Eastern Circuit, Lord Chancellor's Department, 1988–94; *b* 9 June 1934; *s* of Trevor Lloyd James and Olwen James; *m* 1962, Carolyn Ann Rowlands (*d* 1995), *d* of James Morgan Rowlands and Mercia Rowlands; three *s*. *Educ:* Queen Elizabeth Grammar Sch., Carmarthen; LSE. LLB 1956. Admitted solicitor, 1959. Asst Solicitor in private practice, 1959–61; Legal Asst, HM Land Registry, 1961; Asst Solicitor, Glamorgan CC, 1962–70; Asst Clerk of the Peace, 1970–71; Lord Chancellor's Dept, 1971–94: Wales and Chester Circuit: Courts Administrator, (Chester/Mold), 1971–76; Asst Sec., 1976; Dep. Circuit Administrator, 1976–82; Under Sec., 1982; Circuit Administrator, 1982–88. *Address:* Westlake, 2 Heol-y-Bryn, The Knap, Barry, Vale of Glamorgan CF62 6SY. *T:* (01446) 420677. *Club:* Civil Service.

**JAMES, Air Vice-Marshal Warren Austin William**, CBE 2012 (MBE 2000); FRAeS; Chief of Staff Training and Air Officer Commanding No 22 Group, since 2017; *b* Cheadle, Cheshire, 11 March 1967; *s* of Captain Ian William James, MN, and Pauline Ann James; *m* 1991, Jane Elizabeth Thomas; two *s*. *Educ:* King Ecgbert Secondary Sch., Sheffield; Lochgilphead High Sch.; Jt Services Comd and Staff Coll./King's Coll. London (MA with Merit Internat. Studies 2002); Jt Services Comd and Staff Coll. (Postgrad. Dip. Strategic Leadership and Mgt 2012). CMgr 2009; FRAeS 2016. Joined RAF, 1985; officer cadet, RAF Cranwell, 1985; trainee pilot, RAF Linton on Ouse, 1986–87; trainee helicopter pilot, RAF Shawbury, 1987–88; Sqn pilot, 72 Sqn, 1988–90 (mentioned in dispatches, 1989); Helicopter instructor (A2), RAF Shawbury, 1990–95; Helicopter Instructor, 28 (AC) Sqn, Hong Kong, 1995–97; Ops Co-ordination, HQ Strike Comd, High Wycombe, 1997–99; OC, Central Flying Sch. (Helicopters), 1999–2001; acsc 2002; Ops Plans, HQ US Central Comd, Florida, 2002; Ops, UK Perm. Jt HQ, Northwood, 2003–04; OC No 202 Sqn, 2004–07; Air Ops COS, NATO HQ, Kabul, 2007; JSSC, 2007–08; Dir of Ops, Jt Helicopter Comd, 2008–09; Station Comdr, RAF Shawbury, Shropshire, 2009–11; hcsc 2012; Directorate COS, HQ US Central Comd, Florida, 2012–13; Dir, Air Infrastructure, HQ Air Comd, 2013; Hd of Trng, Educn, Skills, Recruiting and Resettlement, MoD, 2013–16; Dir, Ground Trng, RAF, 2016–17. Member, Executive Board: Apprenticeship Ambassador Network, 2014–16; Skills Sector Council, then Skills for Justice, 2014–15 (Mem., Risk and Remuneration and Finance Sub-cttees, 2014–15); Bd Advr, People Director Partnership, 2017–. Mem., Talent Cttee, Nat. Centre for Univs and Business, 2015–16. Trustee, RAF Sports Fedn, 2016–. Pres., RAF Basketball, 2010–. CCMI 2016. *Recreations:* digital photography, walking/outdoors, bass guitar, basketball, life member of NT and RAF Association. *Address:* HQ 22 Group, Hunter Block, RAF High Wycombe, Bucks HP14 4UE.

**JAMES, Prof. Wendy Rosalind, (Mrs D. H. Johnson)**, CBE 2011; DPhil; FBA 1999; Professor of Social Anthropology, University of Oxford, 1996–2007, now Emeritus; Fellow, St Cross College, Oxford, 1972–2007, now Emeritus; President, Royal Anthropological Institute, 2001–04; *b* 4 Feb. 1940; *d* of William Stanley James and Isabel James (*née* Lunt); *m* 1977, Douglas Hamilton Johnson; one *s* one *d*. *Educ:* Kelsick Grammar Sch., Ambleside; St Hugh's Coll., Oxford (BA 1962; BLitt 1964; DPhil 1970). Lectr in Social Anthropol., Univ. of Khartoum, 1964–69; Leverhulme Res. Fellow, St Hugh's Coll., Oxford, 1969–71; Lectr in Social Anthropol., Univ. of Oxford, 1972–96. Vis. Lectr, Univ. of Bergen, 1971–72. Vice-Pres., British Inst. in Eastern Africa, 2001–11. Hon. Dr Scientiarum Anthropologicarum Copenhagen, 2005. Rivers Meml Medal for anthropological res., RAI, 2009. *Publications:* (ed with I. G. Cunnison) Essays in Sudan Ethnography: presented to Sir Edward Evans-Pritchard, 1972; 'Kwanim Pa: the making of the Uduk people, 1979; (ed with D. L. Donham) The Southern Marches of Imperial Ethiopia, 1986; The Listening Ebony: moral knowledge, religion and power among the Uduk of Sudan, 1988; (ed with D. H. Johnson) Vernacular Christianity, 1988; (ed) The Pursuit of Certainty: religious and cultural formulations, 1995; (ed jtly) Juan Maria Schuver's Travels in North East Africa 1880–1883, 1996; (ed with N. J. Allen) Marcel Mauss: a centenary tribute, 1998; (ed jtly) Anthropologists in a Wider World: essays on field research, 2000; (ed jtly) Remapping Ethiopia: socialism and after, 2002; The Ceremonial Animal: a new portrait of anthropology, 2003; (ed with D. Mills) The Qualities of Time: anthropological approaches, 2005; (ed jtly) R. G. Collingwood, The Philosophy of Enchantment: studies in folktale, cultural criticism and anthropology, 2005; War and Survival in Sudan's Frontierlands: voices from the Blue Nile, 2007; (ed jtly) Early Human Kinship: from sex to social reproduction, 2008; (contrib.) An Autobiography and Other Writings: with essays on Collingwood's life and work, 2013; contrib. Jl of Classical Sociol. *Recreations:* travel, vegetarian cookery, gardening. *Address:* c/o Institute of Social and Cultural Anthropology, 51 Banbury Road, Oxford OX2 6PE. *T:* (01865) 559041.

**JAMES, Prof. (William) Philip (Trehearne)**, CBE 1993; MD, DSc; FRCP, FMedSci; FRSE; FRSB; President, World Obesity Federation (formerly International Association for the Study of Obesity), 2009–14 (Senior Vice-President, 2004–06; President Elect, 2006–09; Past President, 2014–16); public health researcher, since 1983; *b* 27 June 1938; *s* of Jenkin William James and Lilian Mary James; *m* 1961, Jean Hamilton (*née* Moorhouse); one *s* one *d*. *Educ:* Ackworth Sch., Pontefract, Yorks; University Coll. London (BSc Hons 1959; DSc 1983); University Coll. Hosp. (MB, BS 1962; MD 1968). FRCP 1978; FRCPE 1983; FRSE 1986; FRSB (FIBiol 1988). Sen. House Physician, Whittington Hosp., London, 1963–65; Clin. Res. Scientist, MRC Tropical Metabolism Res. Unit, Kingston, Jamaica, 1965–68; Harvard Res. Fellow, Mass Gen. Hosp., 1968–69; Wellcome Trust Res. Fellow, MRC Gastroenterology Unit, London, 1969–70; Sen. Lectr, Dept of Human Nutrition, London Sch. of Hygiene and Trop. Medicine, and Hon. Consultant Physician, UCH, 1970–74; Asst Dir, MRC Dunn Nutrition Unit, and Hon. Consultant Physician, Addenbrooke's Hosp., Cambridge, 1974–82; Dir, Rowett Res. Inst., Aberdeen, 1982–99. Res. Prof., Aberdeen Univ., 1983–; Hon. Prof. of Nutrition, LSHTM, 2004–. Dir, Public Health Policy Gp, 1999–2010. Chairman: FAO Consultation on internat. food needs, 1987; Nat. Food Alliance, 1988–90 (Pres., 1990–98); Coronary Prevention Gp, 1988–95 (Pres., 1999–); WHO Consultation on world food and health policies, 1989; DoH Panel on Novel Foods, 1992–98; DoH Task Force on Obesity, 1994; RCPE Wkg Pty on Mgt of Obesity in NHS, 1994–97; Eur. Panel, Eur. Heart Foundn's Analysis of Cardiovascular Risk, 1994; Planning Gp, Eur. Young Nutrition Leadership Courses, 1994–2001; Internat. Obesity Task Force, 1995–2009; UN Commn on Food and Health, later Nutrition Needs in new Millennium, 1997–99; Assoc. of Profs of Human Nutrition, 1994–97; Member: MAFF Adv. Cttee on Novel Foods and Processes, 1986–88; EC Scientific Cttee for Food, 1992–95; DoH (formerly MAFF) Nutrition Task Force, 1992–95; DoH Cttee on Med. Aspects of Food Policy, 1990–99; Internat. Panel on Diet and Cancer, World Cancer Res. Fund, 1994–97, 2004–09; WHO Non-communicable Diseases Internat. Adv. Council, 2010–14; Independent Member: Scientific Steering Cttee, DGXXIV, Brussels, 1997–2000; BSE Cttee, 2001–02. Advr, Eur. Dirs of Agricl Res. on Diet and Health, 1995–2000; Principal Advr on Nutrition and Public Health, 2002, Chief Advr on non-communicable diseases, 2012–, WHO Eastern Mediterranean Region Office. Author, proposals on Food Standards Agency for Prime Minister, 1997 and EU, 1999; new criteria for limits on sugar intake accepted by WHO, 2015. Vice-Pres., Internat. Union of Nutritional Scis, 2001–05. Founder FMedSci 1998. Hon. MFPHM 1994. FRSA 1988. Hon. MA Cantab, 1977; Hon. DSc: City, 2000; Buckingham, 2012; Aberdeen, 2013. Life Achievement Award, Internat. Union of Nutritional Scis, 2017. *Publications:* The Analysis of Dietary Fibre in Food, 1981; The Body Weight Regulatory System: normal and disturbed mechanisms, 1981; Assessing Human Energy Requirements, 1990; (ed) Human Nutrition and Dietetics, 1992, 2nd edn 1999; documents on European national nutrition policy and energy needs for Scottish Office, DoH, FAO, NACNE and WHO; scientific pubns on energy metabolism, salt handling, obesity and heart disease in Lancet, Nature, Clin. Science, New England Jl of Medicine; policy commentaries in World Nutrition for the World Public Health Nutrition Assoc. *Recreations:* talking, writing reports; eating, preferably in France. *Address:* 1 Gatti's Wharf, 5 New Wharf Road, N1 9RS. *E:* jeanhjames@aol.com. *Club:* Athenæum.

**JAMESON, (David) Neil,** CBE 2016; Founder, 1988, and Executive Director, 2002–18, Citizens UK, now Emeritus Director; Director, UK Centre for Civil Society, since 2019; *b* Tynemouth, 25 Nov. 1946; *s* of Eric Jameson and Violet Jameson; *m* 1970, Jean Bird; three *s* one *d*. *Educ:* Solihull Sch.; Univ. of Bristol (BSocSci 1969; Cert. Applied Soc. Sci. 1971). Social worker, Somerset CC, 1972–76; Proj. Dir, Coventry Council, 1976–79; Regl Dir, Save the Children Fund, 1979–83; Regl Dir, Wales and West, Children's Soc., 1983–89; Community Organiser, Bristol, 1989–94, E London Citizens, 1994–96, Lead in London, 1996–2009, Citizens UK. Mem., Soc. of Friends. Hon. Fellow, QMUL, 2012. DUniv Open, 2014. *Recreations:* strengthening civil society, promoting democracy, tennis, optimism. *T:* 07710 468930.

**JAMESON, Prof. (Guy) Antony,** PhD; FRS 1995; FREng, FRAeS; Thomas V. Jones Professor of Engineering, 1997–2014, Professor (Research), since 2015, Stanford University; *b* 20 Nov. 1934; *s* of Brig. Guy Oscar Jameson and late Olive Maud Helen Jameson (*née* Turney); *m* 1st, 1964, Catharina Selander (marr. diss.); one *s* one *d*; 2nd, 1985, Charlotte Ansted. *Educ:* Trinity Hall, Cambridge (MA; PhD 1963). FRAeS 2004; FREng 2005. Nat. Service, 2nd Lieut, RE, 1953–55. Research Fellow, Trinity Hall, Cambridge, 1960–63; Economist, TUC, 1964–65; Chief Mathematician, Hawker Siddeley Dynamics, Coventry, 1965–66; Aerodynamics Engineer, Grumman Aerospace, Bethpage, NY, 1966–72; Courant Institute of Mathematical Sciences, New York University: Research Scientist, 1972–74; Prof. of Computer Sci., 1974–80; Prof. of Aerospace Engrg, 1980–82, James S. McDonnell Dist. Univ. Prof. of Aerospace Engrg, 1982–96, Princeton Univ. John von Neumann Medal, Assoc. for Computational Mechanics, 2015; Daniel Guggenheim Medal, 2015. *Publications:* numerous articles in jls and conference proceedings. *Recreations:* squash, tennis, ski-ing. *Address:* Department of Aeronautics and Astronautics, Stanford University, Durand Building, Stanford, CA 94305, USA.

**JAMESON, Brig. Sir Melville (Stewart),** KCVO 2018; CBE 1994; Lord-Lieutenant for Perth and Kinross, 2006–19; *b* 17 July 1944; *s* of Melville Stewart Jameson and Mary Bowring Jameson; *m* 1973, Sarah Amy Walker-Munro; two *s*. *Educ:* Glenalmond; RMA Sandhurst. Commnd Royal Scots Greys, 1965; CO, Royal Scots Dragoon Guards, 1986–88; Comdr, 51 Highland Bde, 1993–96; Col, Royal Scots Dragoon Guards, 2003–09. Chief Exec. and Producer, 1995–2007, Sen. Advr, 2012–, Royal Edinburgh Mil. Tattoo; consultant to Basel Tattoo, 2007–. Patron: Perth and Kinross Assoc. of Voluntary Services, 2007–; Pitlochry Fest. Th., 2010–. Officer, Royal Co. of Archers, Queen's Body Guard for Scotland, 1983–. Mem., Royal Caledonian Hunt. CStJ 2010. *Recreations:* shooting, music, Highland bagpipes, gardening, trees. *Address:* Easter Logie, Blairgowrie, Perthshire PH10 6SL. *T:* (01250) 884258, *Fax:* (01250) 884351. *E:* production@melvillejameson.co.uk. *Club:* Cavalry and Guards.

**JAMESON, Michael Peter;** Strategic Director, Bradford City Council, 2014–18; *b* Blackburn, Lancs, 26 June 1961; *s* of Peter and Patricia Jameson; *m* 1994, Deborah Harrison; one *s* two *d*. *Educ:* St Mary's Coll., Blackburn; Hull Univ. (BA Hons Hist. 1983); Manchester Univ. (MA Econ. and Social Studies 1988; CQSW 1988). Social work and mgt posts, Lancs CC, 1984–86; Bolton MBC, 1988–96; Resource Manager, Wigan MBC, 1996–98; Gp Manager, Blackburn with Darwen BC, 1998–2002; Service Dir, Stockport MBC, 2002–09; Exec. Dir and Dir of Children's Services, Oldham MBC, 2009–14. *Recreations:* golf, football, Rugby, walking, family, fine wines. *Address:* 21 Knowsley Road West, Clayton-Le-Dale, Blackburn, Lancs BB1 9PW. *T:* (01254) 245592. *E:* michael_jameson@btinternet.com. *Club:* Wilpshire Golf (Blackburn).

**JAMESON, Neil;** *see* Jameson, D. N.

**JAMESON, Rodney Mellor Maples;** QC 2003; **His Honour Judge Jameson;** a Circuit Judge, since 2012; *b* 22 Aug. 1953; *s* of late Denys and of Rosemary Jameson; *m* 1977, Clare Fiona Mary Agius; two *s*. *Educ:* Charterhouse; Univ. of York (BA Hons). Called to the Bar, Middle Temple, 1976; a Recorder, 2001–12; Hd of Chambers, No 6 Park Square, Leeds, 2009–12. *Recreations:* opera, wine, ski-ing, golf, tennis. *Address:* Leeds Combined Court Centre, The Courthouse, 1 Oxford Row, Leeds LS1 3BG.

**JAMIESON, Brian George,** PhD; FRSB; FGS; research management consultant, 1997–2013; *b* 7 Feb. 1943; *s* of late George and Amy Jamieson; *m* 1966, Helen Carol Scott. *Educ:* Boroughmuir Sch.; Edinburgh Univ. (BSc, PhD); Dip. WSET. FRSB (FSB 2010); FGS 2019. Research Assistant: Brigham Young Univ., Utah, 1967–68; Edinburgh Univ., 1968–70; Natural Environment Res. Council, 1970–73 and 1975–77; Principal, ARC, 1973–75; Cabinet Office, 1977–78; Agricultural and Food Research Council: Asst Sec., 1978–87; Dir, Central Office, 1987–91; Acting Sec., Oct.–Dec. 1990; Dir of Admin, 1991–94; Dep. Chief Exec., BBSRC, 1994–97. Mem., Univ. of Bristol Agriculture Cttee, 1997–2001. Mem., Remuneration Cttee, Royal Soc., 1995–2000. Chm., Silbury Housing Ltd, 2012–15; Member: Bd, Sarsen Housing Assoc., 1997–2012 (Vice-Chm., 2004–08; Chm., 2008–12); Bd, Mendip Housing Ltd, 2005–06; Bd, Aster Communities, 2012–14. Mem. Court, Univ. of Salford, 1996–98. Associate Mem., Inst. of Wines and Spirits, 2015. *Publications:* papers on igneous petrology and research management. *Recreations:* croquet, keeping fit, travelling, family history, studying and tasting wine. *Address:* 8 Orwell Close, Caversham, Reading, Berks RG4 7PU. *T:* (0118) 954 6652.

**JAMIESON, Cathy;** Chief Executive Officer, Care Visions Children's Services, since 2017 (Managing Director, 2015–17); *b* 3 Nov. 1956; *d* of Robert and Mary Jamieson; *m* 1976, Ian Sharpe; one *s*. *Educ:* James Hamilton Acad., Kilmarnock; Glasgow Art Sch. (BA Hons Fine Art); Goldsmiths' Coll. (Higher Dip. Art); Glasgow Univ. (CQSW); Glasgow Caledonian Univ. (Cert. Management). Social Worker, Strathclyde Regl Council, 1980–92; Principal Officer, Who Cares? Scotland, 1992–99. MSP (Lab and Co-op) Carrick, Cumnock and Doon Valley, 1999–2011. Scottish Executive: Minister: for Educn and Young People, 2001–03; for Justice, 2003–07. MP (Lab and Co-op) Kilmarnock and Loudoun, 2010–15; contested (Lab and Co-op) same seat, 2015. Dep. Leader, Scottish Labour Party, 2000–08. Mem., Scottish Exec. Cttee, 1996–2008, NEC, 1998–99, Labour Party. Dir, Scotwest Credit Union, 2017–. Dir, Kilmarnock FC Supporters Assoc. (Killie Trust), 2017–; Mem. Bd, Scottish Football Supporters Assoc., 2017–.

**JAMIESON, David Charles;** Police and Crime Commissioner (Lab) for West Midlands, since Aug. 2014; *b* 18 May 1947; *s* of Frank and Eileen Jamieson; *m* 1971, Patricia Hofton; one *s* one *d* (and one *s* decd). *Educ:* Tudor Grange Sch., Solihull; St Peter's, Birmingham; Open Univ. (BA). Teacher, Riland Bedford Sch., 1970–76; Head, Maths Dept, Crown Hills Sch., Leicester, 1976–81; Vice-Principal, John Kitto Community Coll., Plymouth, 1981–92. MP (Lab) Plymouth Devonport, 1992–2005. An Asst Govt Whip, 1997–98; a Lord Comr of HM Treasury (Govt Whip), 1998–2001; Parly Under-Sec. of State, DTLR, subseq. DfT, 2001–05. Mem., Select Cttee on Educn, 1992–97. Sponsored Private Mem.'s Bill for Activity Centres (Young Persons' Safety) Act, 1995. Mem. (Lab), Solihull BC, 1970–74; Mem. (Lab), Solihull MBC, 2010–14. Member: Bd, Roadsafe, 2007–; IAM, 2007–11 (Vice Chm., 2010–11). Trustee, Road Safety Trust, 2016–. Fellow, Inst. of Couriers, 2007. *Recreations:* music, classic cars, gardening. *E:* davidcj@hotmail.co.uk.

**JAMIESON, George;** Sheriff of South Strathclyde, Dumfries and Galloway at Dumfries, since 2009; *b* Paisley, 21 Aug. 1961; *s* of George Jamieson and Isabella Jamieson. *Educ:* Paisley Grammar Sch.; Univ. of Strathclyde (LLB Hons, DipLP). Trainee Solicitor, Hart, Abercrombie Caldwell & Co., 1984–86; admitted Solicitor, Scotland, 1985, England and Wales, 2002; Asst Solicitor, 1986–90, Partner, 1990–2001, Walker Laird; Consultant, Pattison & Sim, Solicitors, 2001–08; Immigration Adjudicator, then Immigration Judge, 2002–09; pt-time Sheriff, 2006–09. *Publications:* Parental Responsibilities and Rights, 1995; Summary Applications and Suspensions, 2000; Family Law Agreements, 2005. *Recreations:* swimming, walking, history, travel, Dutch language, culture and history. *Address:* Sheriff Court House, Buccleuch Street, Dumfries DG1 2AN. *T:* (01387) 262334. *E:* sheriffgjamieson@scotcourts.gov.uk.

**JAMIESON, Rt Rev. Hamish Thomas Umphelby;** Bishop of Bunbury, 1984–2000; *b* 15 Feb. 1932; *s* of Robert Marshall Jamieson and Constance Marzetti Jamieson (*née* Umphelby); *m* 1962, Ellice Anne McPherson (*d* 2013); one *s* two *d*. *Educ:* Sydney C of E Grammar Sch.; St Michael's House, Crafers (ThL); Univ. of New England (BA). Deacon 1955; Priest 1956. Mem. Bush Brotherhood of Good Shepherd, 1955–62. Parish of Gilgandra, 1957; Priest-in-Charge, Katherine, NT, 1957–62; Rector, Darwin, 1962–67; Canon of All Souls Cathedral, Thursday Island, 1963–67; Royal Australian Navy Chaplain, 1967–74; HMAS Sydney, 1967–68; HMAS Albatross, 1969–71; Small Ships Chaplain, 1972; HMAS Cerberus, 1972–74; Bishop of Carpentaria, 1974–84. Liaison Bp to the West and Chm. Australian Council, Mission to Seafarers (formerly to Seamen), 1992–2000. Chm. Nat. Exec., Anglican Renewal Ministries of Australia, 1984–2000; Exec. Mem., Internat. Charismatic Consultation on World Evangelisation, 1994–2002; Member: Anglican Bd of Mission, 1977–98; Bd of Reference, Christian Solidarity Australasia, 1990–99; Internat. Bd, Sharing of Ministries Abroad, 1998–2008; Bd, People Alive Prayer Ministry, 2001–08; Advr, Fremantle Aglow, 2000–16; Nat. Advr, Aglow Australia, 2005–07. Mem. Bd, Australian Coll. of Theology, ACT, 1993–97. *Recreations:* reading, music, cricket. *Address:* Villa 339 Springfields, 17 Hefron Street, Rockingham, WA 6168, Australia.

**JAMIESON, Margaret;** *see* Wallace, M.

**JAMIESON, Rt Rev. Penelope Ann Bansall,** DCNZM 2004; PhD; Bishop of Dunedin, 1990–2004; *b* Chalfont St Peter, Bucks, 21 June 1942; *m* 1964, Ian William Andrew Jamieson; three *d*. *Educ:* St Mary's Sch., Gerrards Cross; High Sch., High Wycombe; Edinburgh Univ. (MA 1964); Victoria Univ., Wellington (PhD 1977); Otago Univ. (BD 1983). Ordained deacon 1982; priest 1983; Asst Curate, St James', Lower Hutt, 1982–85; Vicar, Karori West with Makara, dio. Wellington, 1985–90. *Publications:* Living at the Edge, 1997. *Address:* c/o Diocesan Office, PO Box 13–170, Green Island, 9052, Dunedin, New Zealand.

**JAMIESON, Peter Nicholas;** Executive Chairman, British Phonographic Industry, 2002–07; *b* 4 April 1945; *s* of William Herbert Jamieson and Mary Elaine Jamieson; *m* 1989, Jane Elinor Dalzell; one *s* two *d*. *Educ:* St George's Coll., Buenos Aires; Eastbourne Coll. Managing Director: EMI-AL Greece, 1972–75; EMI NZ, 1977–79; EMI Australia, 1979–83; EMI Records UK, 1983–86; Chm., RCA BMG UK, 1986–89; Vice-Pres., BMG Asia Pacific, 1989–95; Pres., MTV Asia, 1995–98; CEO, Linguaphone Gp, 1998–2002. Director: Combe House Hotel, Devon, 1998–2015; pjams Ltd, 2009–; Bat out of Hell Hldgs, 2009–; The Dots Global, 2014–. *Recreations:* tennis, golf. *Address:* Newlands, South Road, St George's Hill, Surrey KT13 0NA. *T:* (01932) 855822. *E:* pj@jamiesonslive.com. *Clubs:* Hurlingham, Royal Automobile; St George's Hill Lawn Tennis (Chm., 2011–18); St George's Hill Golf.

**JAMIESON, William Bryce;** commentator and policy analyst; Executive Editor, The Scotsman, 2000–12; Director, The Policy Institute, 2000–08; *b* 9 June 1945; *s* of John Bryce Jamieson and Anne Jamieson (*née* Leckie); *m* 1971, Elaine Margaret Muller; one *s*. *Educ:* Sedbergh Sch., Yorks; Manchester Univ. (BA Econs). Sub-Editor, Gwent Gazette, 1969–70; Chief Sub-Editor, Celtic Press, 1970–71; Sub-Editor, Western Mail, 1971–73; Thomson Regional Newspapers: City Reporter, 1973–75; Economics Correspondent, 1975–76; City Reporter, Daily Express, 1976–78; City Editor, 1978–86; Dep. City Editor, Today, 1986; Dep. City Editor, 1986–95, Econs Editor, 1995–2000, Sunday Telegraph. Ed., Scot-Buzz, 2013–17. Business Journalist of the Year, Overall Journalist of the Year, 2009, Lifetime Achievement Award, 2012, Scottish Press Awards. *Publications:* Goldstrike: Oppenheimer empire in crisis, 1989; Britain Beyond Europe, 1994; UBS Guide to Emerging Markets, 1997; EU Enlargement: a coming home or poisoned chalice?, 1998; Britain: free to choose, 1998; Illustrated Guide to the British Economy, 1998; Illustrated Guide to the Scottish Economy, 1999; A Constitution to Destroy Europe, 2003; Scotland's Ten Tomorrows, 2005. *Recreations:* reading, opera, gardening. *Address:* Invergle, Lochearnhead, Stirlingshire FK19 8PR. *T:* 07771 800587.

**JAMISON, Abbot (Peter) Christopher,** OSB; Abbot President, English Benedictine Congregation, since 2017; *b* 26 Dec. 1951; *s* of John Warren Jamison and Mary Beverley (*née* Allen). *Educ:* Downside Sch.; Oriel Coll., Oxford (MA Mod. Langs 1973); Heythrop Coll., Univ. of London (BA Theol. and Philos. 1977). Entered Worth Abbey, 1973; ordained priest, 1978; Worth School: Head of RE and Housemaster, 1979–93; Headmaster, 1994–2002; Abbot of Worth, 2002–10; Dir, Nat. Office for Vocation of the Catholic Church in England and Wales, 2010–17. Pres., Internat. Commn on Benedictine Educn, 2002–13. Mem., Mgt Cttee, CTVC Ltd, 2015–. Hon. Fellow, Rank Foundn, 2012. *Publications:* (with D. Lundy and L. Poole) To Live is to Change: a way of reading Vatican II, 1994; (with R. Steare) Integrity in Practice, 2003; Finding Sanctuary, 2006; Finding Happiness, 2008; (ed) The Disciples' Call, 2013; articles in The Tablet. *Address:* Douai Abbey, Upper Woolhampton, Reading, Berks RG7 5TQ. *T:* (0118) 207 3020. *E:* president@benedictines.org.uk.

**JAMMEH, Alhaji Yahya Abdulaziz Jemus Junkung;** President, Republic of the Gambia, 1996–2017; *b* 25 May 1965; *m* 1998, Zineb Yahya Souma. *Educ:* Gambia High Sch. Joined Gambia Nat. Gendarmerie, 1984; commnd 1989; served: Special Intervention Unit, 1984–86; Mobile Gendarmerie Special Guards Unit, 1986–87; Gendarmerie Trng Sch., 1987–89; 2nd Lieut, 1989; OC, Mobile Gendarmerie, Jan.–June 1991; OC, Mil. Police Unit, June–Aug. 1991; Gambia Nat. Army, 1991–93; Lieut, 1992; Mil. Police Officers' Basic Course, Alabama, 1993–94; Capt., 1994; Chm., Armed Forces Provisional Ruling Council and Hd of State, 1994–96; Col, 1996; retd from Army, 1996. Chm., CILLS (Inter-states cttee for control of drought in Sahel), 1997–2000; Vice-Chm., Orgn of Islamic Conf., 2000–. Hon. DCL St Mary's, Halifax, Canada, 1999. Has received numerous awards and decorations from USA, Libya, China, Liberia and Senegal. *Recreations:* tennis, soccer, hunting, reading, correspondence, driving, riding motorcycles, music, movies, world events, animal rearing.

**JANDRELL, Steven Richard;** Principal, Queen Ethelburga's Collegiate (formerly Queen Ethelburga's Collegiate Foundation), since 2006; *b* Llanidloes, Powys, 25 Nov. 1957; *s* of Donald and Patricia Jandrell; *m* 1991, Margaret Healey; one *s*. *Educ:* Univ. of Sussex (BA Hons Music 1979); University Coll. of N Wales, Bangor (PGCE Music and Drama 1980). ARCM (Organ) 1987; ARCO 1987. Organist and Choirmaster, Parish of Holyhead, freelance musician, actor and teacher, 1980–83; Organist and Choirmaster, Cath. of St Mary the Crowned, Gibraltar, and music teacher, 1983–85; music teacher, Sandwell, 1985–86; Organist and Choirmaster, Parish of Holyhead and Choirmaster, UC of N Wales Choir, 1986–90; Dir of Music, Penrhos Coll., 1990–95; Dir of Music, 1995–99, Vice Principal, 1999–2001, Dep. Hd and Hd of Sen. Sch., 2001–06, Area Co-ord. for N and Exec. Council, 2014–16, Queen Ethelburga's Coll. Mem., Ind. Schs Assoc., 2014–. *Recreations:* music of all genres, early church music, theatre, travelling, swimming, walking, chocolate tasting, avoiding management speak. *Address:* Queen Ethelburga's Collegiate, Thorpe Underwood Estate, Ouseburn, York YO26 9SS. *T:* (01423) 333300. *E:* sj@qe.org.

**JANIS SMITH, Niove Rachel, (Nia Janis);** Director, Playful Productions, since 2010; *b* London, 18 Feb. 1977; *d* of Nikolas Janis and Roberta Aarons; *m* 2010, Richard Smith; one *d*. *Educ:* Godolphin and Latymer Sch.; Univ. of Bristol (BA Hons). Prodn Asst, Upstairs at the Gatehouse, 1998–99; Asst Producer, The Connection Ltd, 1999–2000; Prodn Asst, RSC, 2000–01; Administrator, Royal Court, 2001–05; Gen. Manager, Act Productions, 2005–10. Member, Board: Paines Plough, 2012–; Bush Th., 2019–. Member: Soc. of London Th., 2011–; Bd, Stage One Council, 2017–; Bd, League of Ind. Producers, 2017–. *Recreations:* reading, pilates, running. *Address:* Playful Productions, 4th Floor, 41–44 Great Queen Street, WC2B 5AD. *T:* (020) 7811 4600. *E:* annie@playfuluk.com.

**JANKE,** family name of **Baroness Janke**.

**JANKE,** Baroness *cr* 2014 (Life Peer), of Clifton in the City and County of Bristol; **Barbara Lilian Janke;** *b* Liverpool, 5 June 1947; *m* John Janke; one *s* one *d*. Former teacher. Mem. (Lib Dem) Bristol CC, 1995–2015 (Leader, 2003–07 and 2009–12). Contested (Lib Dem) Surbiton, 1992. *Address:* House of Lords, SW1A 0PW.

**JANKOVIĆ, Dr Vladeta;** Ambassador of Serbia to the Holy See, 2007–12; *b* 1 Sept. 1940; *s* of Dr Dragoslav and Bosiljka Janković; *m* 1970, Slavka Srdić; one *s* one *d*. *Educ:* Univ. of Belgrade (BA 1964; MA 1967; PhD Lit. 1975). University of Belgrade, Faculty of Philology: Asst Lectr, 1970–78; Lectr, 1978–83; Prof. of Classical Lit. and Comparative Hist. of Eur. Drama, 1983–2000; Hd, Dept of Comparative Lit. and Theory of Lit., 1992–2000. Lectr, Univ. of Ann Arbor, and Univ. of Columbia (Fulbright Schol.), 1987–88. Co-founder (with Vojislav Kostunica), Democratic Party of Serbia, 1992 (Pres., Political Council, 2012–). MP Serbia, 1992–93 and Jan.–June 2007; Mem., Fed. Parlt of Yugoslavia, 1996–2000; Chm., Foreign Affairs Cttee, Upper Chamber of Parlt, 2000–01. Ambassador of Federal Republic of Yugoslavia, then Serbia and Montenegro, to UK, 2001–04; Diplomatic Advr to Prime Minister of Serbia, 2004–07. *Publications:* Menander's Characters and the European Drama, 1978; Terence, Comedies, 1978; The Laughing Animal: on classical comedy, 1987; Comedies of Hroswitha, 1988; Who's Who in Classical Antiquity, 1991, 2nd edn 1996; Myths and Legends, 1995, 5th edn 2006; The Link (essays), 2011. *Recreation:* tennis. *Address:* 16 Vlajkovićeva, 11000 Belgrade, Serbia.

**JANMAN, Timothy Simon;** Senior Consultant, Hoggett Bowers, 2003–16; *b* 9 Sept. 1956; *s* of Jack and Irene Janman; *m* 1990, Shirley Buckingham (marr. diss. 2000). *Educ:* Sir William Borlase Grammar Sch., Marlow, Bucks; Nottingham Univ. (BSc Hons Chemistry). Ford Motor Co., 1979–83; IBM UK Ltd, 1983–87; Manpower PLC: Nat. Account, subseq. Public Sector Business, Manager, 1993–95; Sen. Nat. Account Manager, 1995–97; Dir, Boyden Internat. Ltd, 1997–2003. Nat. Sen. Vice-Chm., FCS, 1980–81; Vice-President: Selsdon Gp, 1988– (Chm., 1983–87); Jordan is Palestine Cttee, 1988–. Mem., Southampton City Council, May–July 1987. MP (C) Thurrock, 1987–92; contested (C) Thurrock, 1992. Mem., Select Cttee on Employment, 1989–92. Vice-Chm., Cons. Backbench Employment Cttee, 1988–92 (Sec., 1987–88); Sec., Cons. Backbench Home Affairs Cttee, 1989–92. Pres., Thurrock Cons. Assoc., 2002–. *Publications:* contribs to booklets and pamphlets. *Recreations:* restaurants, theatre. *Address:* 35c Weltje Road, Hammersmith, W6 9LS.

**JANNER, Hon. Daniel (Joseph Mitchell);** QC 2002; *b* 27 April 1957; *s* of Baron Janner of Braunstone, QC and Myra Janner, JP; *m* 1983, Caroline Gee; three *d*. *Educ:* University College Sch.; Trinity Hall, Cambridge (MA; Pres., Cambridge Union Soc., 1978; Dr Cooper's Law Studentship, 1979). Called to the Bar, Middle Temple (Jules Thorn Scholar), 1980, Bencher, 2009. Accredited Mediator, CIArb, 2004. Dir of Res., Soc. of Conservative Lawyers, 1996–99. Mem., Cttee, Criminal Bar Assoc., 1999–2005. Founder and Chm., Falsely Accused Individuals for Reform, 2018–. Member: Bd of Deputies of British Jews, 2000–05; Cttee, Dermatrust, 2005–. Contested (Lab) Bosworth, 1983. Trustee, Cambridge Union Soc., 2010–. Gov., The Hall Sch., Hampstead, 2005–10; Chm. Govs, Immanuel Coll., Herts, 2007–09. Editor: Litigation Law Jl, 1986–90; Criminal Appeal Reports, 1994–. Mem., Cambridge Union Soc. *Recreations:* walking in the Cotswolds, swimming, ski-ing, Arsenal Football Club. *Address:* 187 Fleet Street, EC4A 2AT. *Club:* Garrick.

**JANNER-KLAUSNER, Rabbi Laura Naomi;** Senior Rabbi to Reform Judaism, since 2011; *b* London, 1 Aug. 1963; *d* of Baron Janner of Braunstone, QC and Myra Janner (*née* Sheink), JP; *m* 1988, Dr David Klausner; one *s* one *d* one non-binary *c*. *Educ:* South Hampstead High Sch.; Trinity Hall, Cambridge (BA Divinity 1985); Hebrew Univ. (Dip. Community Centre Mgt); Brandeis Univ. (MA Jewish Communal Service); Leo Baeck Coll. (BA, MA). Teacher, 1985–98, English-Speaking Dir, 1991–94, Inst. of Youth Leaders; trng tour educators, 1992–98, Dir, Centre for Christian Encounters with Israel, 1994–95, Melitz. Rabbinic ordination, Leo Baeck Coll., 2004; Rabbi, Alyth Synagogue, 2003–11. Chair, British Friends of Rabbis for Human Rights, 2006–11. *Publications:* A New Soul: an anthology of birth liturgy, 1998. *Recreations:* running, weight training, singing, quilting. *Address:* c/o Sternberg Centre, 80 East End Road, N3 2SY. *T:* (020) 8349 5674. *E:* rabbilaura@rjuk.org.
See also Hon. D. J. M. Janner.

**JANŠA, Janez;** MP (Soc Dem), Slovenia, 2008–12; Prime Minister of Slovenia, 2004–08 and 2012–13; President, Slovene Social Democratic Party; *b* 17 Sept. 1958; one *s* one *d*; *m* 2009, Urška Bačkovnik; one *s*. *Educ:* Univ. of Ljubljana (Defence Studies). Trainee, Republican Secretariat for Defence, 1982; Pres., Cttee for Basic People's Defence and Social Self-Protection, 1983–89; Ed.-in-Chief, Democracy, 1989–90. Minister of Defence and MP (SDZ), Slovenia, 1990–94; MP (Soc. Dem.), 1994–2004; Leader of the Opposition, 1994–2000; Minister of Defence, 2000. Vice Pres., later Pres. Council, Slovene Democratic Alliance (SDZ), 1989–91; Mem., 1992–, Pres., 1993–2012, Social Democratic Party. *Publications:* On My Own Side, 1988; Movements, 1992; The Barricades, 1994; (jtly) Seven Years Later, 1995.

**JANSEN, Elly, (Mrs Elly Whitehouse-Jansen),** OBE 1980; Founder and Chief Executive Officer: The Richmond Fellowship for Community Mental Health, 1959–91; The Richmond Fellowship International, 1981–2000; Fellowship Charitable Foundation, 1983–93; Richmond Psychosocial Foundation International (formerly Richmond Fellowship Foundation International), 2006–10 (Consultant, 2010–18); *b* 5 Oct. 1929; *d* of Jacobus Gerrit Jansen and Petronella Suzanna Vellekoop; *m* 1969, Alan Brian Stewart Whitehouse (known as George); two *d* (and one *d* decd). *Educ:* Paedologisch Inst. of Free Univ., Amsterdam; Boerhave Kliniek (SRN); London Univ. Founded: Richmond Fellowship of America, 1968, of Australia, 1973, of New Zealand, 1978, of Austria, 1979, of Canada, 1981, of Hong Kong, of India, of Israel, 1984, and of the Caribbean, 1987; Richmond Fellowship Internat., 1981; Richmond Fellowship branches in France, Malta, Peru, Bolivia, Uruguay, Costa Rica, Mexico, Ghana, Nigeria, Zimbabwe, Pakistan, Philippines, Nepal and Bangladesh, 1981–93; Richmond Companions Internat., 2015. Organised internat. confs on therapeutic communities, 1973, 1975, 1976, 1979, 1984, 1988 and 1999; acted as consultant to many govts on issues of community care. Fellowship, German Marshall Meml Fund, 1977–78. Templeton Award, 1985. *Publications:* (ed) The Therapeutic Community Outside the Hospital, 1980; (contrib.) Mental Health and the Community, 1983; (contrib.) Towards a Whole Society: collected papers on aspects of mental health, 1985; (contrib.) R. D. Laing: creative destroyer, 1997; contribs to Amer. Jl of Psychiatry, L'Information Psychiatrique, and other jls. *Recreations:* literature, music, interior design. *Address:* 21 Thames Eyot, Cross Deep, Twickenham TW1 4QL. *T:* (020) 8891 3643.

**JANSON-SMITH, (Peter) Patrick;** Chairman, Kingsford Campbell Literary and Marketing Agency, since 2014; *b* 28 July 1949; *s* of late (John) Peter Janson-Smith and (Diana) Mary Janson-Smith (*née* Whittaker); *m* 1st, 1972, Lavinia Jane Priestley (marr. diss.); one *s* one *d*; 2nd, 1987, Pamela Jean Gossage (marr. diss.); two *s*; 3rd, 2006, Anne-Louise Fisher. *Educ:* Cathedral Sch., Salisbury; Cokethorpe Park Sch., Witney. Asst to Export Publicity Manager, Univ. of London Press Ltd, 1967–69; Granada Publishing: asst to Publicity Manager, Panther Books Ltd, 1969–70; ed., 1970–71, 1973–74, press officer, 1971–72, Mayflower Books; Publicity Manager, Octopus Books, 1972; Transworld Publishers: ed., 1974–78, Associate Editl Dir, 1978–79, Corgi Books; Editl Dir, Nationwide Book Service, 1979–81; Publisher: Corgi and Black Swan Books, 1981–95; Adult Trade Div., 1995–2005; Literary Agent, Christopher Little Literary Agency, 2005–07; Publisher, Blue Door, HarperCollins, 2008–14. Member: Bd, Edinburgh Book Fest., 1994–97; Soc. of Bookmen, 1998–; Cttee, Imaginative Book Illustration Soc., 2010–. *Recreations:* book collecting, late 19th and early 20th century illustrations, wine, food. *Clubs:* Beefsteak, Century.

**JANSONS, Mariss;** conductor; Music Director, Bavarian Radio Symphony Orchestra, Munich, since 2003; *b* Riga, Latvia, 14 Jan. 1943; *s* of late Arvid Jansons; *m* 1998, Irina; one *d* from previous marr. *Educ:* Leningrad Conservatory; studied in Vienna with Prof. Hans Swarowsky and in Salzburg with Herbert von Karajan. Leningrad Philharmonic (later renamed St Petersburg Philharmonic): Associate Conductor, 1973–85; Associate Principal Conductor, 1985–; Music Director: Oslo Philharmonic Orch., 1979–2002; Pittsburgh SO, 1997–2004; Principal Guest Conductor, LPO, 1992–; Principal Conductor, Royal Concertgebouw Orch., Amsterdam, 2004–15. Has conducted leading orchestras of Europe and America incl. Boston and Chicago Symphony Orchestras, Berlin and Vienna Philharmonic, Royal Concertgebouw, etc; conductor, Vienna New Year's concert, Vienna Philharmonic Orch., 2006, 2012. Has toured extensively in Europe, America and Japan. Prof. of Conducting, St Petersburg Conservatoire, 1992–2000. Numerous recordings. Hon. RAM 1999; Hon. Member: Ges. der Musikfreunde, Vienna, 2001; Koninklijk Concertgebouworkest, 2015. Hon. Dr: Oslo, 2006; Riga, 2006. Eddison Award for recording of Shostakovich's 7th Symphony, Holland, 1989; Dutch Luister Award for recording of Berlioz Symphonie fantastique with Royal Concertgebouw Orch., 1982; Norwegian Culture Prize of Anders Jahre, 1991; Artist of the Year, EMI Classics, 1996, MIDEM, 2006; Grammy Award for Shostakovich's 13th Symphony, 2006; Conductor of Yr, Opernwelt, 2011; Ernst von Siemens Music Prize, 2013; Latvian Great Music Award, 2015; Gold Medal, Royal Philharmonic Soc., 2017. Comdr with Star, Royal Norwegian Order of Merit, 1995; Three Stars Medal (Latvia), 2006; Medal of Merit of St Petersburg, 2013; German Federal Cross of Merit with Star, 2013; Knight of Lion (Netherlands), 2013; Commandeur des Arts et des Lettres (France), 2015. *Address:* c/o Bavarian Radio Symphony Orchestra, Rundfunkplatz 1, 80335 Munich, Germany. *T:* (89) 590034120.

**JANUARY, Peter,** PhD; HM Diplomatic Service, retired; *b* 13 Jan. 1952; *s* of late Eric Frank January and Hetty Amelia January (*née* Green); *m* 2000, Catherine Helen Courtier Jones, MBE. *Educ:* Sexey's Sch., Bruton; Univ. of Reading (BA 1st Cl. Hons History and Italian 1974); University Coll. London (PhD Italian History 1983). Asst Master, Chatham Grammar Sch. for Girls, 1975–80; joined FCO, 1983; First Sec. (Commercial), Hungary, 1985–88; FCO, 1988–91; Dep. Head of Mission, Mozambique, 1991–93; FCO, 1993–99; Ambassador to Albania, 1999–2001; Hd, OSCE and Council of Europe Dept, FCO, 2001–04; Hd of Private Military/Security Co. policy rev. team, Internat. Security Directorate, FCO, 2004–08. *Recreations:* spending time with my wife and golden retriever, watching and reading about cricket, Shakespeare, Elizabethan and Jacobean tragedy, cinema, European (esp. Italian) and Levantine history (article on military history of the Venetian Republic in Ateneo Veneto, 2008), medieval English churches, travel in Italy and elsewhere in the Mediterranean, Roman and Byzantine mosaics and frescoes, poetry, English detective and spy novels, British coins, Falkland Island and other Commonwealth stamps, Times crossword, English countryside, political discussion, supporting African wildlife, daydreaming. *Address:* 8 New Road, Trull, Taunton TA3 7NJ. *Club:* Somerset County Cricket (Chm., Taunton Area Cttee, 2009–).

**JANVRIN,** family name of **Baron Janvrin**.

**JANVRIN,** Baron *cr* 2007 (Life Peer), of Chalford Hill in the County of Gloucestershire; **Robin Berry Janvrin,** GCB 2007 (KCB 2003; CB 1997); GCVO 2007 (KCVO 1998; CVO 1994; LVO 1983); QSO 2007; PC 1998; Senior Advisor, HSBC Private Bank (UK) Ltd, since 2016 (Deputy Chairman, 2008–16); *b* 20 Sept. 1946; *s* of Vice Adm. Sir Richard Janvrin, KCB, DSC; *m* 1977, Isabelle de Boissonneaux de Chevigny; two *s* two *d*. *Educ:* Marlborough Coll.; Brasenose Coll., Oxford (BA 1970; Hon. Fellow, 1999). Royal Navy, 1964–75; joined Diplomatic Service, 1975; First Secretary: UK Delegn to NATO, 1976–78; New Delhi, 1981–84; Counsellor, 1985; Press Sec. to the Queen, 1987–90; Asst Private Sec. to the Queen, 1990–95; Dep. Private Sec. to the Queen, 1996–99; Private Sec. to the Queen and Keeper of the Queen's Archives, 1999–2007. Prime Minister's Trade Envoy to Turkey, 2015–. Mem. Bd, British Lib., 2017–. Trustee: Entente-Cordiale Scholarship Scheme, 2008–17 (Chm., Entente-Cordiale Scholarship Trust, 2008–17); Nat. Portrait Gall., 2008–16; Gurkha Welfare Trust, 2009–16; Royal (formerly Charitable) Foundn of the Duke and Duchess of Cambridge and Prince Harry, 2009–16 (Chm., 2011–16). *Recreations:* family, painting, gardening. *Address:* House of Lords, SW1A 0PW.

**JAPAN, Emperor of,**
See under Akihito.

**JARAY, Tess,** RA 2010; artist; *b* Vienna, 31 Dec. 1937; *d* of Francis Ferdinand Jaray and Pauline Jaray; two *d* by Marc Vaux. *Educ:* Alice Ottley Sch., Worcester; St Martin's Sch. of Art, London; Slade Sch. of Fine Art, University Coll. London (Slade Dip.). Teacher: Hornsey Sch. of Art, 1964–68; Slade Sch. of Fine Art, UCL, 1968–99; Emeritus Reader in Fine Art, UCL, 2000–. First solo exhibn, Grabowski Gall., London, 1963; *solo exhibitions* include: Whitechapel Gall., 1973; Ashmolean Mus., Oxford, Whitworth Art Gall., Manchester, 1984; Serpentine Gall., London, 1988; Djanogly Gall., Nottingham, 2013; *work in public collections* including: British Mus., Arts Council, V&A Mus., Tate Gall.; *public commissions* include: Centenary Sq., Birmingham, 1992; Wakefield Cathedral Precinct,

1992; forecourt of new British Embassy, Moscow, 2000; paving for St Mary's Church, Nottingham, 2012. Hon. FRIBA 1995. *Publications:* For Years Now: poems by W. G. Sebald, images by Tess Jaray, 2001; Painting: mysteries and confessions, 2010; (with Richard Davey) Thresholds, 2012; The Art of Tess Jaray, 2014; The Blue Cupboard: inspirations and recollections, 2014; Desire Lines: the public work of Tess Jaray, 2016. *Address:* Lion East Apartment, 24 North Road, N7 9EA. *T:* (020) 7607 1263. *E:* email@tessjaray.com.

**JARDINE, Sir Andrew (Colin Douglas),** 5th Bt *cr* 1916; charity trustee and property consultant, since 2014; Estates Bursar and Fellow, Worcester College, Oxford, 2010–14; *b* 30 Nov. 1955; *s* of Brigadier Sir Ian Liddell Jardine, 4th Bt, OBE, MC, and Priscilla Daphne, *d* of Douglas Middleton Parnham Scott-Phillips; *S* father, 1982; *m* 1997, Dr Claire Vyvien Griffith, *d* of Dr William and Dr Vyvien Griffith; one *s* two *d*. *Educ:* Charterhouse; Royal Agricultural Coll., Cirencester; Reading Univ. (BSc Hons 1996). MRICS (ARICS 1998). Commissioned Royal Green Jackets, 1975–78. With C. T. Bowring & Co. Ltd, 1979–81; with Henderson Administration Gp, 1981–92; Dir, Gartmore Investment Trust Management Ltd, 1992–93; with Strutt & Parker, 1996–99; resident land agent, 2000–10. MCSI (MSI 1993). Mem., Queen's Body Guard for Scotland, Royal Company of Archers, 1990–2007. *Heir: s* Guy Andrew Jardine, *b* 15 March 2004. *Address:* Caudle Farm, Caudle Green, near Cheltenham, Glos GL53 9PR.

See also Sir J. A. G. Baird, Bt.

**JARDINE, Christine;** MP (Lib Dem) Edinburgh West, since 2017; *d* of William and Nessie Jardine; *m* 1987, Calum Macdonald (*d* 2017); one *d*. *Educ:* Braidfield High Sch.; Univ. of Glasgow (MA Hons Modern Hist. and Politics 1982). Sen. production journalist, BBC, 1991–97; Lectr and Tutor in Journalism, Univ. of Strathclyde, 1997–2002; Ed., Scotland, Press Assoc., 2002–04; freelance consultant, 2004–09; Project Manager, Internat. Progs, TRC Media, 2009–11; Scotland Media Advr, 10 Downing St, 2011–12; media consultant and political commentator, Scottish Lib Dems, 2012–17. Mem., Scottish Affairs Cttee, H of C, 2017–. *Address:* House of Commons, SW1A 0AA.

**JARDINE, Edgar Frederick,** CB 2012; independent consultant, since 2012; Interim Chief Executive, Northern Ireland Policing Board, 2011–12 and 2015–16; *b* Dungannon, Co. Tyrone, 19 March 1951; *s* of late James and Rachael Jardine; *m* 1972, Sandra Givans; one *s* one *d*. *Educ:* Royal Sch., Dungannon; Queen's Univ., Belfast (BSc, MSc). Statistician/Researcher, Policy, Planning and Res. Unit, Dept of Finance and Personnel, NI, 1979–96; Chief Exec., NI Stats and Res. Agency, 1996–2002; Dep. Sec., Office of First Minister and Dep. First Minister, NI, 2002–04; Dep. Sec., Dept of Culture, Arts and Leisure, NI, 2004–11. Mem. Bd, NI Educn Authy, 2015–. Gov., Stranmillis Univ. Coll., 2014–. *Recreation:* Ulster Rugby.

**JARDINE, Dr Ian William,** OBE 2018; National Advisor on Environmental Policy, Scottish Government, 2017–19; *b* 22 May 1959; *s* of William Laing Jardine and Isabel Dakers Jardine (*née* Ferguson); *m* 1986, Anne Scott Daniel; three *s*. *Educ:* Royal High Sch., Edinburgh; Univ. of Durham (BSc Biol. (Ecol.) 1980); Univ. of Leeds (PhD Zool. 1984). Various posts, mainly in urban renewal, housing and industry, Scottish Office, 1984–91; Dir, NE Scotland, Nature Conservancy Council for Scotland, 1991–92; Scottish Natural Heritage: Director: NE Scotland, 1992–97; Strategy and Ops, 1997–2002; Chief Exec., 2002–17; Nat. Expert, European Commn (on secondment), 2015–16. Pres., Eurosite, 2007–10. Trustee, Royal Botanic Gardens Edinburgh, 2019–. Mem. Council, RZSScot, 2005–08. *Recreations:* natural history, walking, reading (fiction, science, history), theatre.

**JARDINE, Sir John Christopher Rupert B.;** see Buchanan-Jardine.

**JARDINE, Prof. Nicholas,** PhD; FBA 2004; Professor of History and Philosophy of the Sciences, University of Cambridge, 1991–2010, now Emeritus; Fellow, Darwin College, Cambridge, since 1975; *b* 4 Sept. 1943; *s* of Michael James Jardine and Jean Caroline (*née* Crook); *m* 1992, Marina Frasca-Spada; two *s* two *d* from previous marriages. *Educ:* Monkton Combe; King's Coll., Cambridge (BA 1965; PhD 1969). Jun. Res. Fellow, 1967–71, Sen. Res. Fellow, 1971–75, King's Coll., Cambridge; Royal Soc. Res. Fellow, 1968–73; University of Cambridge: Lectr, 1975–86; Reader, 1986–91. Dir, Cambridge Scientific Heritage Project, 2010–13. Mem., Internat. Acad. of Hist. of Sci., 1991–. Editor: Studies in Hist. and Philosophy of Sci., 1982–2012; Studies in Hist. and Philosophy of Biol and Biomedic. Scis, 1998–2012. *Publications:* (with R. Sibson) Mathematical Taxonomy, 1971; The Birth of History and Philosophy of Science, 1984, rev. edn 1988; The Fortunes of Inquiry, 1986; (ed jtly) Romanticism and the Sciences, 1990; The Scenes of Inquiry, 1991, 2nd edn 2000; (ed jtly) Cultures of Natural History, 1996; (ed jtly) Books and Sciences in History, 2000; (with A. Segonds) La guerre des astronomes, 2 vols, 2008; (with M. Granada and A. Mosley) Christoph Rothmann's Discourse on the Comet of 1585, 2014; (ed jtly) Observing the World through Images, 2014; (ed jtly) Worlds of Natural History, 2018. *Recreation:* plant hunting. *Address:* 83 Alpha Road, Cambridge CB4 3DQ. *T:* (01223) 313734.

**JARDINE of Applegirth, Sir William Murray,** 13th Bt *cr* 1672 (NS); 24th Chief of the Clan Jardine; *b* 4 July 1984; *s* of Sir Alec Jardine of Applegirth, 12th Bt and of Mary Beatrice, posthumous *d* of Hon. John Cross, 3rd *s* of 2nd Viscount Cross; *S* father, 2008; *m* 2011, Gemma, *d* of Maurice Clish; two *s*. *Educ:* Strathallan Sch., Perthshire. Outdoor sports educator. *Recreations:* windsurfing, sailing. *Heir: s* Alexander Jardine, *b* 5 May 2012. *Address:* Ash House, Millom, Cumbria LA18 5HY. *E:* jardinesglobal@aol.com.

**JARDINE-YOUNG, Eve;** DL; Principal, Cheltenham Ladies' College, since 2011; *b* Malawi, 1972; *d* of Ian and Anne Jardine-Young; *m* 2008, James Postle. *Educ:* St Andrew's Sch., Malawi; Cheltenham Ladies' Coll.; Pembroke Coll., Cambridge (BA Engrg Sci. 1994). Teacher of Econs, Radley Coll., 1994–95; Founding Housemistress, Raven House, and Hd of Sixth Form, Epsom Coll., 1995–2005; Dir of Studies, Blundell's Sch., 2005–11. Chair, World Leading Schs Assoc. Gov., Barnwood Trust. DL Glos, 2017. *Recreations:* music, drama, literature, conservation and sustainability initiatives, architecture and design. *Address:* Cheltenham Ladies' College, Bayshill Road, Cheltenham, Glos GL50 3EP. *T:* (01242) 520691, *Fax:* (01242) 227882. *E:* principal@cheltladiescollege.org.

**JARMAN, Andrew Miles,** MA; Teacher of Mathematics, Ripley St Thomas Church of England Academy, 2012; *b* 16 May 1957; *s* of Basil Jarman and Josephine Mary Jarman (*née* Lockyer); *m* 1980, Kerstin Maria Bailey; one *s* two *d*. *Educ:* Hertford Coll., Oxford (PGCE 1979; MA 1992); NPQH 2000. Mathematics teacher: Aylesbury GS, 1979–80; Portsmouth GS, 1980–84; Haberdashers' Aske's Sch., Elstree, 1984–88; Cheltenham College, 1988–2001: Hd of Maths, 1988–92; Dir of Studies, 1992–2001; Headmaster, Lancaster Royal GS, 2001–12. OMLJ 2008. *Recreations:* golf, family. *Address:* Westwood, Westbourne Drive, Lancaster LA1 5EE. *T:* (01524) 35524. *E:* jarman67@yahoo.com.

**JARMAN, Sir Brian,** Kt 1998; OBE 1988; PhD; FRCP, FRCGP, FFPH, FMedSci; Professor of Primary Health Care, Imperial College School of Medicine (formerly St Mary's Hospital Medical School), 1984–98, now Emeritus; President, British Medical Association, 2003–04; *b* 9 July 1933; *m* 1963, Marina Juez Uriel; three *s*. *Educ:* Barking Abbey Sch.; St Catharine's Coll., Cambridge (Open Exhibn; BA Nat. Sci. 1954; MA 1957); Imperial Coll., London (DIC 1957, PhD 1960, Geophysics); St Mary's Hosp. Med. Sch., London Univ. (MB BS 1st Cl. Hons 1969). MRCP 1972, FRCP 1988; MRCGP (Hons) 1978, FRCGP 1984; MFPHM 1994, FFPH (FFPHM 1999). National Service, 2nd Lt, 19 Field Regt, RA, 1954–55, Army Opnl Res. Gp, 1955–56. Geophysicist: Royal Dutch Shell Oil Co., 1960–63; Geophysical Services Inc., 1963–64; House appts: St Mary's Hosp., London, 1969; St Bernard's Hosp., Gibraltar, 1970; Beth Israel Hosp., Harvard Med. Sch., 1970; Clin. Fellow, Harvard Univ., 1970; GP, London, 1971–99; St Mary's Hospital Medical School, later Imperial College School of Medicine: pt-time Sen. Lectr, Dept of Gen. Practice, 1973–83; Hd of Community Health Scis Div., 1995–97; Hd, Div. of Primary Care and Population Health Scis, 1997–98; Dir, Dr Foster Unit, 2001–. Med. Advr and Cons., Barnet FHSA, 1991–95. Member: Sci. Consultative Gp, BBC, 1983–89; Health Services Res. Cttee, MRC, 1987–89; Requirements Bd, Advanced Informatics in Medicine, EC, 1989–90; Kensington, Chelsea & Westminster FHSA, 1990–96; Standing Med. Adv. Cttee, 1998–2005. Chm., BMA NHS IT Gp, 2010–12. Mem. Council, RCP, 1995–98. Med. Mem., Bristol Royal Infirmary Inquiry, 1999–2001. Sen. Fellow, Inst. for Healthcare Improvement, Boston, USA, 2001–. Trustee, Wytham Hall Unit for the Homeless, 1979–; Chm., Trustees, Anna Freud Centre, 1995–2003. Founder FMedSci 1998. President's Medal, RCGP, 2014. *Publications:* (ed and contrib.) Primary Care, 1988; contribs to books, papers, reviews, articles in med. jls, conf. proceedings. *Recreations:* music, reading, family, travel, squash, friends. *Address:* 62 Aberdare Gardens, NW6 3QD. *T:* (020) 7624 5502.

**JARMAN, (John) Milwyn;** QC 2001; His Honour Judge Jarman; a Specialist Chancery Circuit Judge, since 2007; *b* 30 April 1957; *s* of Thomas Jarman and Mary Elizabeth Jarman; *m* 1983, Caroline Anne Joyce Newman (marr. diss.); two *s* one *d*. *Educ:* UCW, Aberystwyth (LLB 1st Cl. Hons); Sidney Sussex Coll., Cambridge (LLM). Called to the Bar, Gray's Inn, 1980, Bencher, 2006; in practice, Cardiff, 1981–2007, specialising in chancery, planning and local government, and personal injuries law; Recorder, 2002–07; Principal Technol. and Construction Ct Judge for Wales, 2008–12; Additional Judge, Upper Tribunal (Lands, Immigration and Asylum, Property and Tax and Chancery Chambers) (formerly Lands Tribunal), 2009–; Diversity and Community Relations Judge, 2009–; authorised to sit in Administrative Ct, 2009–, Planning Ct, 2014–. Mem., Civil Procedure Rules Cttee, 2018–. Treasurer: Wales and Chester Circuit, 2006–07; Assoc. of Judges of Wales. An Asst Boundary Comr. Hon. Counsel, Welsh Books Council, 2002–07. Chm., Legal Wales Foundn Bd, 2011–18. Fellow, Aberystwyth Univ., 2017. Gov., Christ Coll., Brecon, 2017–. Adv. Ed., Civil Procedure, 2016–. *Recreations:* ski-ing, Welsh affairs and sport. *Address:* Civil Justice Centre, 2 Park Street, Cardiff CF10 1ET.

**JARMAN, Pauline;** Member (Plaid Cymru), Rhondda Cynon Taff County Borough Council, since 1995 (Leader, 1999–2004); *b* 15 Dec. 1945; *m* Colin Jarman; two *s*. *Educ:* Mountain Ash Grammar Sch. Export Officer, AB Metals, 1962–65; Export/Import Officer, Fram Filters, 1965–68; self-employed retailer, 1976–88. Member: Cynon Valley BC, 1976–96 (Leader, Plaid Cymru Gp; Mayor, 1987–88); Mid-Glamorgan CC, 1981–96 (Leader, Plaid Cymru Gp; Leader of Council); (Plaid Cymru) S Wales Central, Nat. Assembly for Wales, 1999–2003. *Address:* 3 Middle Row, Mountain Ash, Aberdare CF45 4DN.

**JARMAN, Richard Neville;** author; consultant, retired; General Director, Britten-Pears Foundation and Britten Estate, 2002–15; *b* 24 April 1949; *s* of late Dr Gwyn Jarman and Pauline (*née* Lane). *Educ:* King's Sch., Canterbury; Trinity Coll., Oxford (MA Engls). Sadler's Wells Opera and ENO, 1971–76; Touring Officer, Dance, Arts Council, 1976–77; Edinburgh International Festival: Artistic Asst, 1978–82; Fest. Adminr, 1982–84; Gen. Adminr, London Fest. and English Nat. Ballet, 1984–90; Gen. Dir, Scottish Opera, 1991–97; Interim Gen. Manager, Arts Theatre, Cambridge, 1997–98; Artistic Dir, Royal Opera House, 1998–2000; Interim Gen. Dir, Scottish Opera, 2005–06; Interim Chief Exec., Nat. Dance Co. Wales, 2014–15. Chm., Dance Umbrella, 1997–2000; Dir, Canterbury Fest., 2001–05. Artistic Assessor, Arts Council, 2010–12. Gov., Central Sch. of Speech and Drama, 2000–05. Trustee: British Performing Arts Medicine Trust, 1999–2004; Music Preserved, 2014– (Chm., 2015–). *Publications:* History of Sadler's Wells Opera, 1974; History of London Coliseum Theatre, 1979. *Recreations:* listening to music, going to the theatre, gardening, food and drink, travel, reading. *Address:* Quartier Les Crucifix, Route de la Loubière, 84120 Pertius, France. *T:* (6) 72267615.

**JAROSZEK, Jeremy;** Chief Executive, Erewash Borough Council, since 2006; *b* 5 Dec. 1951; *s* of Walenty Jaroszek and Sylvia Jaroszek (*née* Stanley); *m* 1989, Rosemary Moony; one *s* one *d*. *Educ:* Vyners Sch.; Selwyn Coll., Cambridge (MA); Imperial Coll., London (MSc 1974). CPFA 1982. Greater London Council, 1974–85; Camden LBC, 1985–86; Dep. Dir of Finance, London Borough of Hillingdon, 1986–89; Dir of Finance, 1990–99, Strategic Dir of Resources, 1999–2002, London Borough of Barnet; Dir, J. J. Global Ltd, financial consultancy and mgt for local govt, 2002–06. Treas., Middlesex Probation Service, 1990–2001. *Recreations:* ski-ing, stargazing, family pursuits.

**JARRATT, Sir Alexander Anthony, (Sir Alex),** Kt 1979; CB 1968; DL; Chancellor, University of Birmingham, 1983–2002; Chairman, Centre for Dispute Resolution, 1990–2000, Life President, since 2000; *b* 19 Jan. 1924; *o s* of Alexander and Mary Jarratt; *m* 1946, Mary Philomena Keogh (*d* 2018); one *s* two *d*. *Educ:* Royal Liberty Gram. Sch., Essex; University of Birmingham, BCom, 1946–49. Asst Principal, Min. of Power, 1949, Principal, 1953, and seconded to Treas., 1954–55; Min. of Power: Prin. Priv. Sec. to Minister, 1955–59; Asst Sec., Oil Div., 1959–63; Under-Sec., Gas Div., 1963–64; seconded to Cabinet Office, 1964–65; Secretary to the National Board for Prices and Incomes, 1965–68; Dep. Sec., 1967; Dep. Under Sec. of State, Dept of Employment and Productivity, 1968–70; Dep. Sec., Min. of Agriculture, 1970. Man. Dir, IPC, 1970–73; Chm. and Chief Executive, IPC and IPC Newspapers, 1974; Chm. and Chief Exec., Reed Internat., 1974–85 (Dir, 1970–85); Chm., Smiths Industries, 1985–91 (Dir, 1984–96); a Dep. Chm., Midland Bank, 1980–91; Jt Dep. Chm., Prudential Corp. plc, 1987–91, 1992–94 (Dir, 1985–94); Director: ICI, 1975–91; Thyssen-Bornemisza Group, 1972–89; Mem., Ford European Adv. Council, 1983–88. Confederation of British Industry: Mem., Council, 1972–92; Mem., President's Cttee, 1983–86; Chairman: Economic Policy Cttee, 1972–74; Employment Policy Cttee, 1983–86; Mem., NEDC, 1976–80. President: Advertising Assoc., 1979–83; PPA 1983–85; Age Concern, Essex, 2000–17. Chairman: Industrial Soc., 1975–79; Henley: The Management Coll., 1977–89; Gov., Ashridge Management Coll., 1975–91. Vice-Pres., Inst. of Marketing, 1982–92. FRSA. DL Essex, 1995. Hon. CGIA 1990. Hon. DSc Cranfield, 1973; DUniv: Brunel, 1979; Essex, 1997; Hon. LLD Birmingham, 1982. *Recreations:* the countryside, reading, music.

**JARRATT, Catherine Mary;** see Inglehearn, C. M.

**JARRATT, Prof. Peter,** CEng; FBCS; FSS; FIMA; CITP; Professor of Computing, University of Birmingham, 1975–2000, now Emeritus; *b* 2 Jan. 1935; *s* of Edward Jarratt and Edna Mary Jarratt; *m* 1972, Jeanette Debeier; one *s* two *d*. *Educ:* Univ. of Manchester (BSc, PhD). Programmer, Nuclear Power Plant Co. Ltd, 1957; Chief Programmer, Nuclear Power Gp, 1960; Lectr in Mathematics, Bradford Inst. of Technology, 1962; Asst Dir, Computing Lab., Univ. of Bradford, 1966; Dir, Computing Lab., Univ. of Salford, 1972; University of Birmingham: Dir, Computer Centre, 1975–91; Dep. Dean, Faculty of Science and Engrg, 1984; first Dean of Faculty of Science, 1985–88; Develt Advr to Vice-

Chancellor, 1988–93. Director: Birmingham Res. and Develt Ltd, 1986–88; BISS Ltd, 1993–96; Carma Ltd, 1993–2008; Wang-Inet Ltd, 1996–97; Wang Global Ltd, 1997–99. Chm., Birmingham Inst. for Conductive Educn, 1987–90. Member: Birmingham Lunar Soc., 1991–93; Anglo-Belgian Soc., 2009–. Gov., Royal Nat. Coll. for the Blind, 1986–95; Patron, Henshaw's Soc. for the Blind, 1993–. *Publications:* numerous res. papers on mathematics, computer sci. and risk mgt. *Recreations:* classical music, mountain walking, gardening, chess. *Address:* c/o The University of Birmingham, Edgbaston, Birmingham B15 2TT. *Club:* Athenæum.

**JARRAUD, Michel**; Secretary-General, World Meteorological Organization, 2004–15, now Emeritus; *b* 31 Jan. 1952; *s* of René Jarraud and Simone Blanchet; *m* 1975, Martine Camus; one *s* one *d. Educ:* Ecole Polytechnique, Paris; Ecole de la Météorologie Nationale, Paris (Ingénieur de la Météorologie 1976). Researcher in Numerical Weather Prediction: Météo France, Paris, 1976–78; Eur. Centre for Medium-range Weather Forecast, Reading, 1978–85; Dir, French Nat. Forecasting, Météo France, Paris, 1986–89; Hd, Ops Dept, 1990–94, Dep. Dir, 1991–94, ECMWF, Reading; Dep. Sec.-Gen., WMO, 1995–2003. *Address:* Chemin de la Bassire 37, 1267 Vich, Switzerland. *E:* mic.jarraud@bluewin.ch.

**JARRETT, Keith**; pianist and composer; *b* Allentown, Penn, 8 May 1945; *s* of Daniel and Irma Jarrett; *m* Margot (marr. diss.); two *s. Educ:* Berklee Sch. of Music. Pianist with jazz gps led by Art Blakey, 1965, Charles Lloyd, 1966–69, Miles Davis, 1970–71; tours of Europe and numerous recordings; soloist and leader of own gps, 1969–. Concert soloist with various US orchs; numerous recordings of classical music. *Albums include:* Life Between the Exit Signs, 1968; Restoration Ruin, 1968; Birth, 1971; Expectations, 1971; Facing You, 1972; In the Light, 1973; Belonging, 1974; Treasure Island, 1974; Death and the Flower, 1974; Personal Mountains, 1979; Nude Arts, 1979; Invocations, 1981; Standards, 1983; The Cure, 1990; Bye Bye Black Bird, 1991; At the Deer Head Inn, 1992; Bridge of Light, 1993; At the Blue Note, 1994; La Scala, 1995; Tokyo '96, 1998; Expectations, 1999; Melody at Night with You, 1999; Whisper Not, 2000; Inside Out, 2001; Always Let Me Go, 2002; Yesterdays, 2009; Hamburg '72, 2014; Creation, 2015; A Multitude of Angels, 2016; After the Fall, 2018; La Fenice, 2018. *Compositions include:* Celestial Hawk, 1980; Sonata for Violin and Piano, 1985; Elegy for Violin and String Orchestra, 1985; Sacred Ground, 1985.

**JARRETT, Rt Rev. Martyn William**; Bishop Suffragan of Beverley, 2000–12; Episcopal Visitor for the Northern Province, 2000–12; *b* 25 Oct. 1944; *s* of Frederick and Ivy Jarrett, Bristol; *m* 1968, Betty, *d* of Frank and Mabel Wallis, Bristol; two *d. Educ:* Cotham GS, Bristol; King's Coll., London (BD 1967; AKC 1967); Hull Univ. (MPhil 1991); St Boniface, Warminster. Ordained deacon, 1968, priest, 1969; Curate: St George, Bristol, 1968–70; Swindon New Town, 1970–74; St Mary, Northolt, 1974–76; Vicar: St Joseph the Worker, Northolt West End, 1976–81; St Andrew, Hillingdon, 1981–83; Priest-in-charge, Uxbridge Moor, 1982–83; Vicar, St Andrew with St John, Uxbridge, 1983–85; Selection Sec., 1985–88, Sen. Selection Sec., 1989–91, ACCM; Vicar, Our Lady and All Saints, Chesterfield, 1991–94; Suffragan Bp of Burnley, 1994–2000; Hon. Assistant Bishop: Ripon and Leeds, 2000–12; Durham, 2000–12; Sheffield, 2000–12; Manchester and Wakefield, 2001–12; Southwell and Nottingham (formerly Southwell), 2001–; Bradford, 2002–12; Liverpool, 2003–12; Newcastle, 2010–12. Member: Bishops' Urban Panel, 1998–2010; Gen. Synod, 2000–12; Churches Commn for Inter-Faith Relations, 2000–06; Council for Christian Unity, 2001–10; C of E and C of S Jt Study Gp, 2006–10; Church Union Council, 2011–. Chm., Worksop Priory and Gatehouse Trust, 2012–17. Vice Chm., Internat. Bps' Conf. on Faith and Order, 1998–2013. Vice-Pres., Soc. for the Maintenance of the Faith, 2011–. Patron, Coll. of Readers, 2003–12 (Co-Patron, 2012–). *Recreations:* psephology, reading, bird watching. *Address:* 91 Beaumont, Worksop, Notts S80 1YG. *T:* (01909) 477847. *E:* martyn.jarrett@yahoo.co.uk.

**JARROLD, Kenneth Wesley**, CBE 1997; Director, Other People's Shoes Ltd, since 2017; *b* 19 May 1948; *s* of William Stanley Jarrold and Martha Hamilton Jarrold (*née* Cowan); *m* 1973, Patricia Hadaway (marr. diss. 2010); two *s*; partner 2011, Robert Attenborough. *Educ:* St Lawrence Coll., Ramsgate; Sidney Sussex Coll., Cambridge (Whittaker Schol.; BA Hons Hist. 1st cl.; Pres., Cambridge Union Soc.) Dip. IHSM (Hons Standard). E Anglian RHB, 1969–70; Briggs Cttee on Nursing, 1970–71; Dep. Supt, Royal Hosp., Sheffield, 1971–74; Hosp. Sec., Derbyshire Royal Infirmary, 1974–75; Sector Administrator, Nottingham Gen. and Univ. Hosps, 1975–79; Asst Dist Administrator (Planning), S Tees HA, 1979–82; Dist Administrator, 1982–84, Dist Gen. Manager, 1984–89, Gloucester HA; Regl Gen. Manager, Wessex RHA, 1990–94; Dir of Human Resources and Dep. Chief Exec., NHS Exec., 1994–97; Chief Executive: Co. Durham HA, 1997–2002; Co. Durham and Tees Valley Strategic HA, 2002–05; Sen. Consultant, 2006–07, Dir, 2007–09, Chm., 2009–11, Dearden Consulting; Partner, Dearden Partnership LLP, 2012–16; Consultant, Dearden HR, 2016–17. Non-exec. Dir, Serious Organised Crime Agency, 2005–09. Chm., Co. Durham Econ. Partnership, 2006–12. Member: NHS Training Authy (and Chm., Training Cttee), 1984–87; Nat. Adv. Gp, NHS Leadership Centre, 2002–04; Nat. Mental Health Taskforce, 2003–05; Govt Programme Bd on Health Inequalities, 2004–05; Chairman: Management Educn System by Open Learning Project Group, 1986–89, and 1991–93; Durham and Teesside Workforce Develt Confedn, 2001–02; DoH Wkg Party on Code of Conduct of NHS Managers, 2002; NHS Reference Gp on Health Inequalities, 2003–05; DoH Task Gp on maximising NHS contrib. to Public Health, 2004; Pharmacy Regulation and Leadership Oversight Gp, 2007–09; Partnership Cttee, Child Exploitation and Online Protection Centre, 2009–12; N Staffordshire Combined Healthcare NHS Trust, 2011–16; Prog. Bd for Govts work on rebalancing of medicines legislation and pharmacy regulation, 2013–; Bd of Mgt, Brighter Futures Stoke on Trent, 2016–18. Chm., Northumberland Tyne and Wear NHS Foundn Trust, 2018–. Patron: NHS Retirement Fellowship, 2009–; Cavell Nurses Trust, 2013–. Pres., IHSM, 1985–86 (Mem., Nat. Council, 1977–89). Hon. Visiting Professor: York Univ., 1998–2006; Salford Univ., 1998–2004; Durham Univ., 2005–07, 2013–16. Hon. Fellow, John Snow Coll., Durham Univ., 2006. DUniv Open, 1999. *Publications:* Challenges for Health Services in the 1990s, 1990; (contrib.) Health Care Systems in Canada and the UK, 1994; Minding Our Own Business: healing division in the NHS, 1995; Servants and Leaders, 1998; Other People's Shoes: leadership and management, 2018; articles in professional jls. *Address:* 75 Beechwood Road, Eaglescliffe, Stockton-on-Tees TS16 0AE; Butterlands Farm, Top Road, Biddulph Moor, Staffordshire Moorlands ST8 7LF. *Club:* Athenæum.

**JARROLD, Nicholas Robert**; HM Diplomatic Service, retired; Director, British Association for Central and Eastern Europe, 2004–09; *b* 2 March 1946; *s* of late Albert and Dawn Jarrold; *m* 1972, Anne Catherine Whitworth; two *s. Educ:* Shrewsbury Sch.; Western Reserve Acad., Ohio (ESU Scholar); St Edmund Hall, Oxford (Exhibnr, MA). Entered Diplomatic Service, 1968: FCO, 1968–69; The Hague, 1969–72; Dakar, 1972–75; FCO, 1975–79; 1st Sec. and Hd of Chancery, Nairobi, 1979–83; FCO, 1983–89; Counsellor and Dep. Head of Mission, Havana, 1989–91; Vis. Fellow, St Antony's Coll., Oxford, 1991–92; Counsellor (Economic and Commercial), Brussels and Luxembourg, 1992–96; Ambassador to: Latvia, 1996–99; Croatia, 2000–04. Chairman: British-Latvian Assoc., 2009–14; British-Croatian Soc., 2014–. *Recreations:* reading history, cricket, the theatre. *Address:* 9 Park Drive, SW14 8RB. *Club:* Athenæum.

**JARROW, Bishop Suffragan of**, since 2019; **Rt Rev. Sarah Elizabeth Clark**; *b* S Wales, 21 April 1965; *d* of Kenneth Clark and Shirley Fletcher (*née* Morton). *Educ:* Abersychan Grammar Sch.; Loughborough Univ. of Technol. (BA Jt Hons PE, Sports Sci. and Hist. 1986); Keele Univ. (MBA 1994); St John's Coll., Nottingham (MA Theol Studies 1997). Civil Servant, Dept of Employment, 1987–95; ordained deacon, 1998, priest, 1999; Asst Curate, Porchester, Nottingham, 1998–2002; Rector of Carlton-in-Lindrick and Langold with Oldcotes, 2002–09; Area Dean of Worksop, 2006–09; Team Rector, Clifton, Nottingham, 2009–14; Dean of Women's Ministry, Dio. of Southwell and Nottingham, 2011–14. Hon. Canon, Southwell Minster, 2011–. *Recreations:* sport, walking, bird-watching, history. *Address:* Bishop's House, 25 Ivy Lane, Low Fell, Gateshead NE9 6QD. *T:* (0191) 491 0917. *E:* bishop.of.jarrow@durham.anglican.org.

**JÄRVI, Neeme**; Chief Conductor, Residentie Orkest, The Hague, since 2005; Conductor Laureate and Artistic Advisor, New Jersey Symphony Orchestra (Principal Conductor and Music Director, 2005–09); Music Director, Estonian National Symphony Orchestra, since 2010; *b* Tallinn, Estonia, 7 June 1937; *s* of August and Elss Järvi; *m* 1961, Liilia Järvi; two *s* one *d. Educ:* Estonia-Tallinn Conservatory of Music; Leningrad State Conservatory. Chief Conductor: Estonian Radio Symphony Orch., 1963–77 (Conductor, 1960–63); Estonia opera house, Tallinn, 1963–77; toured USA with Leningrad Phil. Orch., 1973 and 1977; Chief Conductor, Estonian State Symph. Orch., 1976–80; since emigration to USA in 1980 has appeared as Guest Conductor with New York Phil. Orch., Philadelphia Orch., Boston Symph., Chicago Symph., Los Angeles Phil., Met. Opera (New York) and in San Francisco, Cincinnati, Indianapolis, Minneapolis and Detroit; has also given concerts in Vienna, London, Canada, Sweden, Finland, Norway, Denmark, Holland, Switzerland and W Germany; Principal Guest Conductor, CBSO, 1981–84; Chief Conductor, Gothenburg SO, Sweden, 1982–2004, now Principal Conductor Emeritus; Musical Dir and Principal Conductor, Royal Scottish Nat. Orch., 1984–88, Conductor Laureate, 1989; Music Dir, Detroit SO, 1990–2005, now Music Dir Emeritus; First Principal Guest Conductor, Japan Philharmonic SO. 1st Prize, Internat. Conductors Competition, Accademia Santa Cecilia, Rome, 1971. Over 310 CDs including: works by Bartok, Dvorak, Medtner, Barber, Prokofiev (symphonic cycle), Shostakovich; complete works of Sibelius and all symphonies of Nielsen and Mahler (Toblach Prize for best recording, 1993, for No 3); Saul and David, opera by Nielsen; Don Giovanni; Schmidt symphonies. *Recreation:* traveller. *Address:* c/o HarrisonParrott International Artists Management Ltd, The Ark, 201 Talgarth Road, W6 8BJ.

**JARVIE, Elizabeth (Marie-Lesley)**; QC (Scot.) 1995; Sheriff of Lothian and Borders at Edinburgh, 1997–2013; *b* 22 Jan. 1952; *d* of Dr James Leslie Rennie and Marie-Thérèse (*née* Loyseau de Mauléon); *m* 1976, John Jarvie; one *s* four *d. Educ:* Larbert High Sch., Stirlingshire; Univ. of Edinburgh (MA Hons, LLB). Apprentice, Biggert Baillie & Gifford WS, 1978–79; admitted to Scots Bar, 1981; Advocate-Depute, 1991–94. Part-time Chm., Social Security Appeal Tribunal, 1986–89. *Recreations:* ski-ing, music, lunching, news. *Address:* Rowallan, Barnton Avenue, Edinburgh EH4 6JJ. *T:* (0131) 336 2117.

**JARVIS, Alison**; freelance management consultant, since 1998; *b* Barnstaple, N Devon, 11 March 1966; *d* of late Adrian John Wilson Jarvis and of Stella Christine Jarvis (now Philp); civil partnership 2006, *m* 2016, Madeline Jane Smith. *Educ:* Univ. of Bristol (BA Modern Langs 1988). Graduate Trainee, Lyons Tetley, 1988–90; Mktg Manager, Ind Coope Retail, 1990–94; Dir of Change, Allied Domecq, 1994–99; Dir, Stonewall Scotland, 2000–04; Dir of Countries, Regions and Communities and Dir of Scotland, CRE, 2005–07. Assessor, Office of Comr for Public Appts Scotland, 2008–. Member: SFC, 2008–15; NHS Health Scotland, 2011–. Interim Chair, Glasgow Colls Regl Bd, 2015–16. *Address:* NHS Health Scotland, Gyle Square, 1 S Gyle Crescent, Edinburgh EH12 9EB.

**JARVIS, Anne Elizabeth**; University Librarian, Princeton University, since 2016; *b* Dublin, 31 July 1962; *d* of late P. J. Murray and Maeve Keelan; *m* 2007, David Jarvis. *Educ:* Our Lady's Sch., Terenure, Dublin; Univ. of Dublin (BA 1984); Dublin City Univ. (MA 1997); Univ. of Cambridge (MA 2003). Asst Librarian, Coopers & Lybrand, London, 1989–92; Asst Librarian, 1992–97, Sub-Librarian, 1997–98, Dublin City Univ.; Sub-Librarian, TCD, 1998–2000; Dep. Librarian, 2000–09, University Librarian, 2009–16, Univ. of Cambridge; Fellow, Wolfson Coll., Cambridge, 2000–16. Member: Legal Deposit Adv. Panel, DCMS, 2009–10; Bd, Res. Libraries UK, 2010–16. Vice-Pres., Wolfson Coll., Cambridge, 2005–07. *Recreations:* cinema, theatre, reading, travel. *Address:* Princeton University Library, One Washington Road, Princeton, NJ 08544–2098, USA. *Club:* Grolier (New York).

**JARVIS, Anthony**, MA; Headmaster, St Olave's and St Saviour's Grammar School, 1994–2010; Chairman, Council of Governors, Hurstpierpoint College, since 2013; *b* Oxford, 30 March 1945; *s* of Donald Anthony Jarvis and Ida Jarvis (*née* Allmond); *m* Brigit Mary, *d* of Baillie Andrew Convery and Elizabeth Convery; one *s* one *d. Educ:* City of Oxford High Sch.; Brighton Coll. of Educn (Cert Ed); Univ. of Sussex (BEd Hons; MA). Haywards Heath County School: Asst Master, 1968–71; Librarian, 1971–72; Hd, Social Studies, 1972–73; Housemaster, Beckworth Boarding Hse, Lindfield, 1969–72; Oathall School: Hd of Year, 1973–74; Hd, Social Studies and Curriculum Co-ordinator, 1974–79; Hd of English, 1979–84; Dep. Principal and Headmaster of Secondary Sch., St George's English Sch., Rome, 1984–90 (Acting Principal, 1987–88); Headmaster, Sir Thomas Rich's Sch., Gloucester, 1990–94. PGCE teacher and tutor, Univ. of Sussex, 1975–79. Educn consultancies in UK and Europe, 2004–. Addnl Mem., HMC, 1996–2010. Mem., Nationally Recognised Outstanding Leaders in Educn, 2008–; Chartered London Teacher, 2008–; Leadership Pathways Coach, Nat. Coll. of Sch. Leadership, 2009–. Headteacher Mem., Army Scholarship Bd, 1997–2001. Woodard Corporation: Fellow, 2002–; Dir, 2006–12; Chm., Educn Cttee, 2006–12. Governor: Hurstpierpoint Coll., 2001–; Christ's Hosp., Horsham, 2007–12. Dir, The Severals Freehold Ltd, 2016– (Vice Chm., 2017; Chm., 2019–). FRSA 1993. Hon. Mem., East India and Public Schs Club, 1996–2010. *Recreations:* travel and restaurants, books and newspapers, Rugby Union, Italy, art and antiques. *Address:* The Severals, Bury Road, Newmarket, Suffolk CB8 7YN. *Club:* Sir Thomas Rich's Bowling.

**JARVIS, Carolyn Hayley Jane**; see Hilder, C. H. J.

**JARVIS, Catriona, (Mrs P. St J. Bolton)**; a Judge of the Upper Tribunal (Immigration and Asylum Chamber) (formerly a Vice-President, Immigration Appeal Tribunal, later a Senior Immigration Judge, Asylum and Immigration Tribunal), 2004–13; writer; *b* 16 April 1950; *d* of late Stanley and Isabella Jarvis; *m* 1996, Philip St John Bolton; one *s. Educ:* Manresa House Coll. of Educn (Cert Ed 1972); Univ. of Paris, Sorbonne (Cert. de Langue Française Degré Supérieur 1975); Univ. of E London (LLM Dist. 2000); Univ. of London (MA Merit 2009). Admitted solicitor, 1985; solicitor in private practice and local govt, 1985–92; Immigration Adjudicator (pt-time), 1992–96; Immigration Adjudicator, Immigration Appellate Authy, 1996–2004. Founder Mem., 1997, Dep. Pres., 1997–98, Council of Immigration Judges. Chair, Unaccompanied Migrant Children's Court Steering Gp, 2014–. Pro bono legal and policy work internationally, in relation to refugee and migrant rights, esp. following journeys incl. on Lesbos and in Greece, 2015– (Co-Convenor, Last Rights, 2015–). Mem., Internat. Assoc. of Refugee Law Judges, 1999– (Mem. Council, 2005–11; Rapporteur, Vulnerable Persons Working Party, 2007–14).

Member, Board of Trustees: Inderpal Rahal Meml Trust, 1998–; English PEN, 2012–13; Prisoners of Conscience, 2013– (Vice-Chair, 2016; Chair, 2016–18); Founding Mem., Refugee Initiative, 2016–. Fellow, Centre for Social Policy, Dartington Social Res. Unit, 2015–. *Publications:* (contrib.) Security of Residence and Expulsion: protection of aliens in Europe, 2001; (contrib.) Protecting Migrant Children: in search of best practice, 2018; contrib. to Statewatch, Immigration Asylum and Nationality Law Jl; contrib. papers and articles on internat. refugee, immigration and human rights law. *Recreations:* creative writing, literary debate, theatre and cinema, yoga, swimming, walking. *Club:* Highbury Group.

JARVIS, Daniel Owen Woolgar, MBE 2011; MP (Lab) Barnsley Central, since March 2011; Mayor, Sheffield City Region, since 2018; *b* Nottingham, 30 Nov. 1972; *m* 2001, Caroline (*d* 2010); one *s* one *d*; *m* 2013, Rachel Jarvis; one *d*. *Educ:* Aberystwyth Univ.; RMA Sandhurst. Served Parachute Regt; deployed to Kosovo, Sierra Leone, NI, Iraq and Afghanistan; ADC to Gen. Sir Mike Jackson; Adjutant, 3 Para; Staff Planner, Perm. Jt HQ Northwood and Army HQ, Salisbury; Co. Comdr, Special Forces Support Gp. Shadow Culture Minister, 2011–13; Shadow Justice Minister, 2013–15; Shadow Foreign Office Minister, 2015. Mem., Business, Innovation and Skills Select Cttee, 2011–12. *Address:* House of Commons, SW1A 0AA.

JARVIS, Frederick Frank, (Fred), CBE 2015; General Secretary, National Union of Teachers, 1975–89; Member of General Council, 1974–89, President, 1987, Trades Union Congress (Chairman, 1986–87); *b* 8 Sept. 1924; *s* of Alfred and Emily Ann Jarvis; *m* 1954, Elizabeth Anne Colegrove (*d* 2007), Stanton Harcourt, Oxfordshire; one *s* one *d*. *Educ:* Plaistow Secondary Sch., West Ham; Oldershaw Grammar Sch., Wallasey; Liverpool Univ. (Dip. in Social Science with dist.); St Catherine's Society, Oxford (BA Hons PPE; MA). Contested (Lab) Wallasey, Gen. Elecn, 1951; Chm., Nat. Assoc. of Labour Student Organisations, 1951; Pres., Nat. Union of Students, 1952–54 (Dep. Pres., 1951–52); Asst Sec., Nat. Union of Teachers, 1955–59; Head of Publicity and Public Relations, 1959–70; Dep. Gen. Sec., NUT, 1970–74 (apptd Gen. Sec. Designate, March 1974). Pres., Eur. Trade Union Cttee for Educn, 1983–84, 1985–86 (Vice-Pres., 1981–83); Chairman, TUC Cttees: Local Govt, 1983–88; Educn Training, 1985–88; Chm., TUC Nuclear Energy Review Body, 1986–88. Member: Central Arbitration Cttee, 1985–94; Franco-British Council, 1986–98. Mem. Council, Nat. Youth Theatre; Trustee, Trident Trust; Mem. Bd, Univ. of First Age, Birmingham. *Photographic exhibitions:* Days of Rallies and Roses, London, Manchester, Norwich and Grantham, 1997; Politicians, Poppies and other Flowers, London, 1998; Monet's Garden and the lesser known Provence, London, Birmingham, 2000, Poole, Edinburgh, Alton, Provence, Oxford, 2001; Homage to the Hammers, London, 2001; Market Day, Provence, 2002; Forty Years On: a year in the life of St Catherine's College, Oxford, 2002; London's Future: the spirit of its schools, London, 2004; Photo Opportunities, London, 2004; Pictures for a Hospice, London, 2010; In the Days Before Selfies, 2018. FRSA. Hon. FEIS 1980; Hon. FCP 1982. DUniv UCE, 2004. Nat. Merit Award, Labour Party, 2008; Lifetime Contribution Award, NUS, 2009; Lifetime Achievement Award, TES Awards, 2013; Lifetime Contribution to Educn, Pearson Teaching Awards, 2018. *Publications:* The Educational Implications of UK Membership of the EEC, 1972; Education and Mr Major, 1993; (autobiog.) You Never Know Your Luck: reflections of a Cockney campaigner for education, 2014; Before Selfies, 2018; Ed, various jls including: 'Youth Review', NUT Guide to Careers; NUT Univ. and Coll. Entrance Guide. *Recreations:* swimming, cycling, gardening, cinema, theatre, photography. *Address:* 92 Hadley Road, New Barnet, Herts EN5 5QR.

JARVIS, His Honour (James) Roger; a Circuit Judge, 2000–14; *b* 7 Sept. 1944; *s* of late Flt Lieut Douglas Bernard Jarvis, DFC, RAF (retd), and Elsie Vanessa Jarvis; *m* 1972, Kerstin Marianne Hall; one *s* two *d*. *Educ:* Latymer Upper Sch.; Brockenhurst County Grammar Sch.; Peter Symonds. Articled Clerk, Bernard Chill & Axtell; admitted Solicitor, 1969; joined Andrews McQueen, later McQueen Yeoman, 1972; Asst Solicitor, 1972–73; Partner, 1973–2000. *Recreations:* jogging, walking, reading.

JARVIS, John Francis, CVO 2001; CBE 1993; Chairman, Jarvis Hotels Ltd, 1990–2011 (Chief Executive, 1990–2002); *b* 15 Feb. 1943; *s* of Thomas Jarvis and Mary Jarvis; *m* 1984, Sally Ann Garrod; one *s* two *d*. *Educ:* Scarborough Grammar Sch.; S Devon Hotel Coll. FIH (FHCIMA 1975). With Rank Orgn, 1965–75; Ladbroke Gp plc, 1975–90: Chairman: Ladbroke Hotels, Holidays and Entertainment, 1975–87; Texas Homecare, 1985–87; Hilton Internat., 1987–90; Prince's Trust-Action, 1993–98; Prince's Trust Trading, 1998–2000; Prince's Foundn, 2001–03: Director: Shepperton Hldgs Ltd, 1995–2001; Apollo Leisure Gp, 1998–99; non-exec. Dir, Ladbrokes plc, 2006–14; non-executive Chairman: On Board Services Ltd, later Eur. Rail Catering (Hldgs) Ltd, 1995–97; Sandown Park, 2003–12. Member: English Tourist Bd, 1983–96; BTA, 1995–2000; Chm., British Hospitality Assoc. Council, 2000–01. Mem., Exec. Bd, Variety Club of GB, 1986–98. Mem., Jockey Club, 2005–. *Recreation:* tennis.

JARVIS, Dr John Herbert; Senior Vice President Advisor, John Wiley & Sons Inc., 2007–09 (Senior Vice President, John Wiley and Sons - Europe, 1997–2007); *b* 16 May 1947; *s* of Herbert Henry Wood Jarvis and Mabel (*née* Griffiths); *m* 1970, Jean Elizabeth Levy; one *s* one *d*. *Educ:* UC of Swansea (BSc; PhD 1972). Research Fellow: Welsh Nat. Sch. of Medicine, 1972–75; Univ. of Bristol, 1975–77; Ed., Elsevier Sci. Pubns, 1977–79; John Wiley Publishers, 1979–2009: Publishing Dir, 1987–93; Man. Dir, 1993–2007. Director: STM Publishing Gp, 1999–2005; Royal Pharmaceutical Soc. Publishing; Maney Publishing. Mem. Council, Publishers' Assoc., 1998–2005. Mem. Bd, Chichester Fest. Th., 2001–10. Gov., Chichester Coll., 2005–11. Trustee Dir, Weald and Downland Open Air Mus., 2010–. *Publications:* contrib. articles to various med. and biomed. jls on aspects of cancer. *Recreations:* boating, walking, guitar, reading, theatre, hypochondria. *Address:* Chilgrove Barn, Chilgrove, Chichester, West Sussex PO18 9HX. *T:* (01243) 535323, *Fax:* (01243) 770122. *E:* johnhjarvis@btinternet.com. *Clubs:* Groucho; Goodwood (Sussex).

JARVIS, John Manners; QC 1989; a Recorder, since 1992; a Deputy High Court Judge, since 1998; *b* 20 Nov. 1947; *s* of late Donald Edward Manners Jarvis and Theodora Brixie Jarvis; *m* 1972, Janet Rona Kitson; two *s*. *Educ:* King's Coll. Sch., Wimbledon; Emmanuel Coll., Cambridge (MA (Law)). Called to Bar, Lincoln's Inn, 1970, Bencher, 1998; practising barrister specialising in Commercial Law, particularly banking; Jt Hd of Chambers, 1999–2009. An Asst Recorder, 1987–92. CEDR Mediator, 2000–. Chm., Commercial Bar Assoc., 1995–97 (Treas., 1993–95); Mem., Bar Council, 1995–97. Governor: King's Coll. Sch., Wimbledon, 1987– (Chm., 2008–13); King's Coll. Sch. Chinese Schs, 2018–. Trustee, World Horse Welfare Trust, 2017– (Vice Chm., 2018–). Overseas Editor, Jl of Banking and Finance—Law and Practice, 1990–; Consultant Editor, Jl of Internat. Banking and Finance, 2006–. *Publications:* (jtly) Lender Liability, 1993; (contrib.) Banks, Liability and Risk, 2nd edn 1995. *Recreations:* tennis, horse-riding, sailing, ski-ing, cycling, music. *Address:* 3 Verulam Buildings, Gray's Inn, WC1R 5NT. *T:* (020) 7831 8441, *Fax:* (020) 7831 8479. *E:* jjarvis@3vb.com. *Club:* Hurlingham.

JARVIS, Surg. Rear Adm. Lionel John, CBE 2012; DL; FRCR; Prior, England and The Islands, Order of St John of Jerusalem and Chair, St John Ambulance, since 2016; *b* Windsor, 13 May 1955; *s* of Steve and Eileen Jarvis; *m* 1998, Dr Penelope Gordon; one *s* one *d*. *Educ:* Wellington Coll., Berks; Guy's Hosp., London (MB BS 1977). MRCS, LRCP 1977; FRCR 1988; MIET 2003. Defence consultant advr in radiol., 1995–2000; Cons. Radiologist and CO, Royal Hosp., Haslar, 2001–03; rcds 2004; Dir, Med. Policy, MoD, 2005–08; ACDS (Health), 2008–11; Chief Naval Med. Officer and Med. Dir Gen. (Naval), 2009–12. Chief Exec., Qatar Heart Hosp., Hamad Medical Corp., Doha, 2012–15. QHS, 2006–12. Pres., Royal Navy Cresta, 2010–12. Vice Patron, 2012–18, Pres., 2018–, Poppy Factory. Gov., Royal Star and Garter Homes, 2009–12. DL Hants, 2018. Freeman, City of London, 2018. Diagnostic Imaging Dr of Year, 1999; Crookshank Medal, RCR, 2007. Gulf War Medal (with clasp), 1991; Queen's Jubilee Medal, 2002, 2012; Iraq War Medal (with clasp), 2003. KStJ 2016 (OStJ 2012); Comdr of Merit (with swords), SMHO, 2019. *Publications:* contribs to med. jls, incl. Lancet, American Jl Radiol., Clinical Radiol., BMJ. *Recreations:* sailing, ski-ing, cresta, riding. *Address:* Midlington Farmhouse, Droxford, Hants SO32 3PU. *Clubs:* Army and Navy; Royal Naval Sailing Association.

JARVIS, Martin, OBE 2000; actor, director, writer and producer; *b* 4 Aug. 1941; *s* of late Denys Jarvis and Margot Jarvis; *m*; two *s*; *m* 1974, Rosalind Ayres. *Educ:* Whitgift School; RADA (Hons Dip., 1962, Silver Medal, 1962, Vanbrugh Award, 1962; RADA Associate, 1980). Nat. Youth Theatre, 1960–62; played Henry V, Sadler's Wells, 1962; Manchester Library Theatre, 1962–63; *stage:* Life of Galileo, Mermaid, 1963; Cockade, Arts, 1963; Poor Bitos, Duke of York's, 1963; Man and Superman, Vaudeville, 1966; The Bandwagon, Mermaid, 1970; The Rivals, USA, 1973; Hamlet (title rôle), Fest. of British Th., 1973; The Circle, Haymarket, 1976; She Stoops to Conquer, Canada, and Hong Kong Arts Festival, 1977; Caught in the Act, Garrick, 1981; Importance of Being Earnest, NT, 1982; Victoria Station, NT, 1983; The Trojan War Will Not Take Place, NT, 1983; Woman in Mind, Vaudeville, 1986; The Perfect Party, Greenwich, 1987; Henceforward, Vaudeville, 1989; Exchange, Vaudeville, 1990, Los Angeles, 1992; You Say Potato, Los Angeles, 1990; Twelfth Night, Playhouse, 1991; Leo in Love, Southampton, 1992; Just Between Ourselves, Greenwich, 1992; Make and Break, 1993, Man of the Moment, 1994, Los Angeles; On Approval, Playhouse, 1994; Table Manners, LA, 1995; The Doctor's Dilemma, Almeida, 1998; Skylight, LA, 1999; Passion Play, Donmar, 2000; By Jeeves, NY, 2001; recitals of Paradise Lost, Old Vic, Chichester and QEH, 1975–77; The Queen's Birthday Concert, Royal Festival Hall, 1996; narrator, Peter and the Wolf, Barbican, 1997; An Audience with Martin Jarvis, RNT, 2003; Gielgud Centenary Gala, Gielgud, 2004; Twelfth Night, Regent's Pk, 2005; Honour, Wyndham's, 2006; Dir, The Life of Galileo, LA, 2008; recitals of Beloved Clara and Odyssey of Love, Chichester, Wigmore Hall, Kings Place, St John Smith's Square and Los Angeles, 2007–15; The Importance of Being Earnest, Harold Pinter Th., 2014; Racing Demon, LA, 2014; The Guilty Mother, LA, 2015; (narrator) Hallelujah!, Salt Lake City, 2016; Whither Would You Go? (UN refugee concert), LA, 2017; Just William, Orange Tree Th., 2017; Orpheus - The Mythical, Other Palace, 2018; *films:* The Last Escape, Ike, The Bunker, Taste the Blood of Dracula, Buster; The Fool of the World and the Flying Ship, 1991 (Emmy Award); Emily's Ghost, 1992; Calliope; Absence of War, 1995; Titanic, 1997; The X-Ray Kid, Sex 'n' Death, 1999; Mrs Caldicot's Cabbage War, By Jeeves, 2002; Much Ado About Nothing, 2005; Framed, 2006; The Legend of Spyro, 2007; Return of the Neanderthal Man, 2009; Neander Jin, 2010; Cars 2, The Girl with the Dragon Tattoo, 2011; Wreck-It Ralph, 2013; Phil Spector (USA), 2013; United Passions, 2014; *television series:* The Forsyte Saga, 1967; Nicholas Nickleby, 1968; Little Women, 1969; The Moonstone, 1971; The Pallisers, 1974; David Copperfield, 1975; Killers, 1976; Rings on Their Fingers, 1978–80; Breakaway, 1980; The Black Tower, 1985; Chelworth, 1988; Countdown, 1990–; Murder Most Horrid, 1991; The Good Guys, 1992; Woof!, 1992; Library of Romance, 1992; Girl from Ipanema (British Comedy Award); Scarlet and Black, 1993; Brillat Saverin, 1994; Lovejoy, 1994; Murder She Wrote, 1995; Supply and Demand, 1998; Space Island One, 1998; Lorna Doone, 2000; Micawber, 2001; Bootleg, 2002; Psi-Kix (USA), 2003; Doctors, 2004, 2009; Numb3rs (USA), 2007; The Bill, 2008; Stargate Atlantis (USA), 2008; Taking the Flak, 2009; Eastenders, 2010; Marple: The Mirror Crack'd From Side to Side, 2010; Just William, 2011; Funny or Die (USA), 2011; Endeavour; By Any Means, 2013; Poirot: Dead Man's Folly, 2013; Law and Order UK, 2014; Cosmos, 2014; A Year in the Life of a Year, 2017; Election Spy, 2017; New Chilling Tales, 2019; *radio:* numerous performances, incl. oneman series, Jarvis's Frayn; as Charles Dickens in series, The Best of Times; Gush, 1994; (and prod.) Speak After the Beep, 2 series, 1997; Spies, 2002; Ring for Jeeves, 2014; Jefferson's Garden, 2017; (dir) Fathers and Sons, 2017; (dir) Lady Windermere's Fan, 2018; (dir) Moonraker, 2018; (dir) An Enemy of the People, 2018; (dir) Live and Let Die, 2019; (codir with Rosalind Ayres) The School for Scandal (played Sir Peter Teazle), 2019; Michael Frayn's Magic Mobile, 2020; productions of plays; script writing and adaptations (many under pseudonym Archie Scottney); prod. and dir dramas, 2002–, incl. Dr No, 2008; Jeeves Live, BBC and Cheltenham Fest., 2008; Dir, A Small Family Business, 2009; Man of the Moment, 2009; Dir, Goldfinger, 2010 (Earphones Award, 2010); Dir, Widowers' Houses, The Browning Version, England, Their England, 2011; Henceforward…, From Russia With Love, 2012; Dir, Skios, You Never Can Tell, Air Force One, 2013, On Her Majesty's Secret Service, 2014; Dir, A Midsummer Night's Dream, The Liar (Corneille), 2013; Dir, Diamonds Are Forever, Michael Frayn's Matchbox Th., A View from the Bridge, Thunderball, 2015; Director, for LATW-NPR (USA): The Rivals, Macbeth, Hamlet, Romeo and Juliet, Copenhagen, 2011–12; An Enemy of the People, 2014; God of Carnage, 2015; commentaries for TV and film documentaries and for arts programmes; has adapted and read over 100 of Richmal Crompton's Just William stories for radio, TV and CD; Just William Live!, Best of British Fest., Th. Royal Winchester and radio, 2012; Jeeves Live and Just William Live, BBC Radio and Cheltenham Fest., 2014, 2019; Just William, Jeeves and Jarvis, Kings Place, Boswell Book Fest., 2015; recitals of Beloved Clara and Odyssey of Love, Chichester, Wigmore Hall, Kings Place, St John Smith's Square, LA, 2007–17; recital, The Life of Beatrix Potter, Stratford Literary Fest., 2015; recorded oneman performance of David Copperfield for cassette, 1991; one-man perf., Oscar Wilde, 1996; co-produced cassette 2nd World War Poetry, 1993; produced and directed cassettes, Lord of the Flies; Tales from Shakespeare; P. G. Wodehouse recordings, Peter Pan, 2007–; Voice of God, OT CD recordings (USA), 2009. Writer/presenter, Concorde Playhouse, 1994–97. Dir, Children's Film Unit, 1993–2000. Co-founder (with Rosalind Ayres), Jarvis & Ayres Productions, 2000–. Mem., Artist Adv. Council, LA Theatre Works, 2000–. Vice-Pres., Salamander Oasis Trust, 1990–2007. Mem., BAFTA. Sony Silver Award, 1991; NY Internat. Award, for contribn to broadcasting, 1994; British Talkies award, 1995, 1997, 1998; US Audie Award, 1999; Theatre World Award for Outstanding Broadway Debut, 2002; US Earphones Award, 2003, 2005, 2007, 2009, 2015, 2017; Radio Independents Gp Award, for outstanding contribn to broadcasting, 2007. *Publications:* Bright Boy, 1977; William Stories: a personal selection, 1992; Meet Just William, 1999; Acting Strangely (autobiog.), 1999; Broadway, Jeeves?, 2003; short stories for radio; contribs to many anthologies; articles in The Listener, Punch, Tatler, The Times, Daily Express, Daily Telegraph and Daily Mail. *Recreations:* Beethoven, Mozart, Schumann, growing lemons, grandchildren. *Address:* c/o AHA Talent, 2 Percy Street, W1T 1DD. *Club:* Ivy.

JARVIS, Prof. Martin John, OBE 2002; DSc; Principal Scientist, Cancer Research UK (formerly Imperial Cancer Research Fund), 1991–94; Professor of Health Psychology, University College London, 1999–2004, now Emeritus; *b* 30 June 1939; *s* of Richard William Jarvis and Mary May Jarvis (*née* Utting); *m* 1969, Muriel Richardson; one *s* one *d*. *Educ:* Watford Grammar Sch.; Corpus Christi Coll., Cambridge (MA); Birkbeck Coll.,

London (BA Psychol.); Inst. of Psychiatry (MPhil Clin. Psychol); UCL (DSc Medicine 1997). Res. worker, 1978–89, Sen. Lectr, 1986–89, Addiction Res. Unit, Inst. Psychiatry; Sen. Scientist, Health Behaviour Unit, ICRF, 1989–91; Reader in Health Psychol., UCL, 1996–99. Mem., CMO's Scientific Cttee on Tobacco and Health, 1994–. Dir, ASH, 1996–. Mem., Scientific Cttee on Tobacco Product Regulation, WHO, 2000–. *Publications:* numerous res. papers on tobacco smoking and nicotine addiction. *Recreations:* growing vegetables, bee-keeping, walking, gym. *Address:* Department of Epidemiology and Public Health, University College London, 1–19 Torrington Place, WC1E 6BT; 118 Woodwarde Road, SE22 8UT. *T:* (020) 8693 3508. *E:* martin.jarvis@ucl.ac.uk.

**JARVIS, Richard James;** Consultant in Communicable Disease Control, Public Health England (formerly Health Protection Agency), since 2003; *b* Stoke-on-Trent, 28 March 1966; *s* of Victor and Doroteamaria Jarvis; *m* 1996, Kathryn Simpson; one *s* one *d*. *Educ:* Cotton Coll., N Staffs; King's Coll. London (BSc Immunol. and Basic Med. Scis 1988; MB BS Medicine and Surgery 1991); Univ. of Birmingham (MPH 1998); Univ. of Salford (Postgrad. Envmtl Protection 2006). MFPH 2001, FFPH 2005. Jun. med. posts, N Staffs Hosp., 1991–93, Trent Postgrad. Hosp., 1993–95; GP registrar, Bath Rd Surgery, Buxton, 1995–96; specialist registrar, W Midlands Public Health Trng Scheme, 1996–2001; Consultant in communicable disease control, Liverpool HA, 2001–03; Hd of Sch., NW Sch. of Public Health, 2013–19. Hon. Clin. Lectr, Liverpool Univ., 2011–. Chm., Public Health Medicine Cttee, BMA, 2008–12. *Recreations:* photography, astronomy, amateur meteorology, walking, cinema. *Address:* Public Health England North West, Suite 3B, 3rd Floor, Cunard Building, Water Street, Liverpool L3 1DS. *T:* 0344 225 0562. *E:* richard.jarvis@phe.gov.uk.

**JARVIS, Roger;** see Jarvis, J. R.

**JARVIS, Sian Elizabeth,** CB 2010; Managing Director, Jarvis & Bo Communications Ltd, since 2013; *b* Bromsgrove, 11 April 1963; *d* of Anthony and Marjorie Jarvis; twin *s* and *d*. *Educ:* Loughborough Univ. (BA Hons). With BBC, 1986–92: Current Affairs, Radio 4, 1986–88; news trainee, 1988–89; reporter/presenter, Look East, 1989–92; Political Corresp., GMTV, 1992–99; Hd of News, 1999–2001, Dir-Gen. Communications, 2001–11, DoH; Dir, Corporate Relns, Asda, 2012–13. Partner, African Horseback Safaris, 2007–. *Recreations:* opera and theatre, horseback riding, ski-ing.

**JARY, Michael Keith,** FRAS; Founder Member, 1987, and Senior Partner, OC&C Strategy Consultants (Partner, since 1993); *b* Cambridge, 15 June 1963; *s* of late Keith Jary and Jacqueline Ann Jary (*née* Pogue); *m* 2015, Jonathan Jimenez Ferrer. *Educ:* Berkhamsted Sch. (Schol.); Merton Coll., Oxford (Postmaster 1982; BA Hons Physics 1985; MA 1989); INSEAD (Louis Franck Schol.; Kitchener Schol.; MBA Dist. 1989); Sch. of Oriental and African Studies, Univ. of London (Postgrad. Cert. Asian Art (Dist.) 2008). Associate, Booz Allen & Hamilton, 1985–87; OC&C Strategy Consultants: Man. Partner, London and Hd, Worldwide Retail Practice, 2000–05; Worldwide Man. Partner and Chm. Internat. Exec. Cttee, 2005–11. Mem., Investment Cttee, Web-Angel plc, 1999–2001; non-executive Chairman: Duchy Originals Ltd, 2008–; The Prince's Social Enterprises, 2010–15; ITAD Ltd, 2016–; AG Carrick Ltd, 2018–; Highgrove Enterprises Ltd, 2018–; lead non-exec. Dir, MHCLG, 2019–; non-executive Director: Wax Lyrical Ltd, 1995–96; Nationwide Building Soc., 2009–15; Barclays Bank UK plc, 2017–; Barclays Investment Solutions Ltd (Chm., 2018–19). Member: Adv. Bd, World Retail Congress, 2009–12; Exec. Sub-cttee, The Prince's Charities, 2010–13; Adv. Bd, Fashion Retail Acad., 2016–; Adv. Council, These Islands, 2017–. Chair: Bd of Trustees, Fairtrade Foundn, 2013–18; Commercial Cttee, The Prince of Wales's Charitable Foundn, 2015–; Trustee, Opera Holland Park, 2018–. Ambassador, Retail Trust, 2014–. FRAS 2011. *Publications:* (jtly) Retail Power Plays, 1997; (jtly) Markenpower, 1998; (jtly) Brands: the new wealth creators, 1998; (contrib.) Market Leader, 2009; In the Footsteps of a Himalayan Pilgrimage, 2013. *Recreations:* collecting Indian and South East Asian art and cultural artefacts, organic farming (pigs, sheep, poultry, bees and vegetables), opera-going, playing croquet, classic cars, cooking, Himalayan trekking. *Address:* c/o OC&C Strategy Consultants, 6 New Street Square, EC4A 3AT. *T:* (020) 7010 8024, *Fax:* (020) 7010 8100. *Club:* Royal Automobile.

**JASON, Sir David,** Kt 2005; OBE 1993; actor; *b* 2 Feb. 1940; *s* of Arthur and Olwyn White; adopted stage name, David Jason, 1965; *m* 2005, Gill Hinchcliffe; one *d*. Stage career began with a season in repertory, Bromley Rep.; *theatre includes:* Under Milk Wood, Mayfair, 1971; The Rivals, Sadler's Wells, 1972; No Sex Please … We're British!, Strand, 1972; Darling Mr London, tour, 1975; Charley's Aunt, tour, 1975; The Norman Conquests, Oxford Playhouse, 1976; The Relapse, Cambridge Theatre Co., 1978; Cinderella, 1979; The Unvarnished Truth, Mid/Far East tour, 1983; Look No Hans!, tour and West End, 1985; *films:* Under Milk Wood, 1970; Royal Flash, 1974; The Odd Job, 1978; Only Fools and Horses; Wind in the Willows, 1983; *television includes:* Do Not Adjust Your Set, 1967; The Top Secret Life of Edgar Briggs, 1973–74; Mr Stabbs, 1974; Ronnie Barker Shows, 1975; Open All Hours, 1975; Porridge, 1975; Lucky Feller, 1975; A Sharp Intake of Breath, 1978; Del Trotter in Only Fools and Horses, 1981–91 (Best Light Entertainment Perf., BAFTA, 1990); Porterhouse Blue, 1986; Jackanory, 1988; A Bit of A Do, 1988–89; Single Voices: The Chemist, 1989; Amongst Barbarians, 1989; Pa Larkin in The Darling Buds of May, 1990–93; A Touch of Frost, 1992–2010; The Bullion Boys, 1993; All the King's Men, 1999; Micawber, 2001; The Quest (also dir), 2002; The Hogfather, 2006; The Colour of Magic, 2008; The Royal Bodyguard, 2011; Still Open All Hours, 2015–17; David Jason's Secret Service, 2017; David Jason: planes, trains and automobiles, 2019; *voice work:* Dangermouse, Count Duckula, The Wind in the Willows. Awards include Best Actor Award, BAFTA, 1988; Special Recognition Award for Lifetime Achievement in Television, Nat. Television Awards, 1996; Best Comedy Perf. Award, BAFTA, 1997; BAFTA Fellowship, 2003. *Publications:* David Jason: my life, 2013; Only Fools and Stories, 2017. *Recreations:* diving, flying, motorcycles. *Address:* c/o Meg Poole, 191 Kingston Road, Teddington, Middx TW11 9JN; c/o Conway van Gelder Grant, Third Floor, 8/12 Broadwick Street, W1F 8HW.

**JASPAN, Andrew;** Director and Editor-in-Chief, Global Academy, since 2017; Adjunct Professor, School of Media and Communications, since 2011, and Professorial Fellow, since 2017, RMIT University, Melbourne; *b* 20 April 1952; *s* of Mervyn and Helen Jaspan; *m* 1991, Karen Jane Grant; two *s*. *Educ:* Beverley GS; Manchester Univ. (BA Hons Politics). Co-Founder, New Manchester Review, 1976–79; Daily Telegraph features, 1979; Fellowship, Journalists in Europe, Paris, 1980–81; freelance journalist, Daily Mirror and Daily Telegraph, 1982; News Sub-Ed., The Times, 1983–85; Asst News Ed., Sunday Times, 1985–88; Editor: Sunday Times Scotland, 1988–89; Scotland on Sunday, 1989–94; The Scotsman, 1994–95; The Observer, 1995–96; Publr and Man. Dir, The Big Issue, 1996–98; Ed., Sunday Herald, 1999–2004; Ed.-in-Chief, The Age, 2004–08; Founder, Exec. Dir and Ed., The Conversation website, Melbourne, 2010–17; Ed.-in-Chief and Trustee, The Conversation website, UK, 2012–17; Ed.-in-Chief and Bd Mem., The Conversation website, USA, 2013–17; Editor-in-Chief: The Conversation, Africa, 2015–17; The Conversation, France, 2015–17; The Conversation, Global, 2016–17. Consultant, 2008–10, Sen. Res. Fellow, Faculty of Engrg and Infrastructure, 2011–, Univ. of Melbourne; Bd Mem. and Adjunct Prof., Global Studies Inst., Royal Melbourne Inst. of Technol., 2008–11. Asia-Pacific Dir, Innovation Media Consultancy, 2008–. Media appearances and contribs to radio, TV, online and print outlets. *Publications:* Exams and Assessment, 1975; Preparing for Higher Education, 1975; Media Innovation and Disruption, 2016. *Recreations:* keeping across the topsy turvy world of media, travelling, reading, gardening. *Address:* Global Academy, RMIT University, GPO Box 2476, Melbourne, Vic 3001, Australia. *E:* andrew.jaspan@rmit.edu.au.

**JASPERT, Augustus James Ulysses;** Governor, British Virgin Islands, since 2017; *m* Amelia; two *s*. *Educ:* Univ. of Edinburgh (MA 1st Cl. German and Hist. 2001); Kingston Univ. (Postgrad. Dip. Mgt Studies 2003); King's Coll. London (MA Internat. Relns and Security Strategy 2015). Lead Manager, Children's Services, Surrey CC, 2001–07; Delivery Manager, Prime Minister's Delivery Unit, HM Treasury, 2007–09; Hd, Drugs and Alcohol and Hd, Policing, Home Office, 2009–12; Private Sec. to the Prime Minister, No 10 Downing St, 2012–14; Mem., RCDS, 2014–15; Dir, Security and Intelligence, National Security Secretariat, Cabinet Office, 2015–17. *Address:* Office of the Governor, PO Box 702, Road Town, Tortola VG1110, British Virgin Islands. *T:* 4683501. *E:* govoffice.tortola@fco.gov.uk.

**JASUDASEN, Thambynathan;** Ambassador (non-resident) for Singapore to the African Union and to Ethiopia, since 2014; Independent Chairman, Zico Holdings Inc., since 2015; *b* Malaysia, 20 June 1952; *m* 1980, Patricia Ibbotson; one *s* twin *d*. *Educ:* Raffles Instn; Nat. Jun. Coll., Singapore; Nat. Univ. of Singapore (LLB Hons 1977); Ecole Nat. d'Admin, Paris. Nat. Service as Armour Officer, Singapore Armed Forces, 1971–73. Joined Min. of Foreign Affairs, Singapore, 1977; served: Singapore Perm. Mission to UN, NY, 1979–81: Manila, 1988–90; Kuala Lumpur, 1991–94; Dir, ASEAN Directorate and Dir, Policy, Planning and Analysis Directorate IV, Min. of Foreign Affairs; Ambassador: to France, 1997–2004; to Myanmar, 2004–06; High Commissioner: in Malaysia, 2006–11; in UK, 2011–14. Freeman, City of London, 2013. Public Admin Medal, Silver, 1990, Gold, 2011 (Singapore); Comdr, Palmes Académiques (France), 2002; Officer, Légion d'Honneur (France), 2004; Darjah Sultan Ahmad Shah of Pahang (Malaysia), 2010. *Clubs:* Travellers, Royal Over-Seas League, Mosimann, Caledonian; Wentworth; Brocket Hall.

**JAUNZENS, Serena Michelle;** see Best, S. M.

**JAVACHEFF, Christo;** see Christo and Jeanne-Claude.

**JAVID, Rt Hon. Sajid;** PC 2014; MP (C) Bromsgrove, since 2010; Chancellor of the Exchequer, since 2019; *b* Rochdale, 5 Dec. 1969; *m* 1997, Laura; one *s* three *d*. *Educ:* Univ. of Exeter (BA Hons Econs and Politics 1991). Analyst and Associate, 1991–94, Vice Pres., 1994–2000, Chase Manhattan Bank, N. A.; Dir, 2000–04, Man. Dir, 2004–09, Deutsche Bank AG; Mem. Bd, Deutsche Bank Internat. Ltd, 2007–09. Economic Sec., 2012–13, Financial Sec., 2013–14, HM Treasury; Minister for Equalities, 2014; Sec. of State for Culture, Media and Sport, 2014–15; Sec. of State for Business, Innovation and Skills and Pres., Bd of Trade, 2015–16; Sec. of State for Communities and Local Govt, then for Housing, Communities and Local Govt, 2016–18; Sec. of State for the Home Dept, 2018–19. *Address:* House of Commons, SW1A 0AA. *T:* (020) 7219 7027. *E:* sajid.javid.mp@parliament.uk.

**JAVORCIK, Prof. Beata Katarzyna,** PhD; Chief Economist, European Bank for Reconstruction and Development, since 2019; Professor of Economics, University of Oxford, since 2014 (on leave); Fellow, All Souls College, Oxford, since 2014; *b* Krakow, Poland, 19 Aug. 1971; *d* of Stanislaw Smarzynski and Anna Smarzynska; *m* 2001, William Javorcik; one *d*. *Educ:* Univ. of Rochester, USA (BA Econs 1994); Yale Univ. (PhD Econs 1999). Economist, 1999–2004, Sen. Economist, 2004–07, World Bank; Reader in Econs, 2007–10, Prof. of Internat. Econs, 2010–14, Univ. of Oxford. *Publications:* contribs to jls incl. Amer. Econ. Rev., Jl Eur. Econ. Assoc., Econ. Jl. *Recreation:* collecting frequent flyer miles. *Address:* European Bank for Reconstruction and Development, Chief Economist Office, One Exchange Square, EC2A 2JN. *T:* (020) 7338 6000. *E:* beata.javorcik@economics.ox.ac.uk.

**JAY,** family name of **Baroness Jay of Paddington**.

**JAY OF EWELME,** Baron *cr* 2006 (Life Peer), of Ewelme, in the County of Oxfordshire; **Michael Hastings Jay,** GCMG 2006 (KCMG 1997; CMG 1992); HM Diplomatic Service, retired; Chairman, House of Lords Appointments Commission, 2008–13; *b* 19 June 1946; *s* of late Alan David Hastings Jay, DSO, DSC, RN and Vera Frances Effa Vickery, MBE; *m* 1975, Sylvia Mylroie (see Lady Jay of Ewelme). *Educ:* Winchester Coll.; Magdalen Coll., Oxford (MA; Hon. Fellow, 2004); School of Oriental and African Studies, London Univ. (MSc 1969). ODM, 1969–73; UK Delegn, IMF-IBRD, Washington, 1973–75; ODM, 1976–78; First Sec., New Delhi, 1978–81; FCO, 1981–85; Counsellor: Cabinet Office, 1985–87; (Financial and Commercial), Paris, 1987–90; Asst Under-Sec. of State for EC Affairs, FCO, 1990–93; Dep. Under-Sec. of State (Dir for EC and Economic Affairs), FCO, 1994–96; Ambassador to France, 1996–2001; Prime Minister's Personal Rep. for G8 Summits, 2005–06; Perm. Under-Sec. of State, FCO and Head of the Diplomatic Service, 2002–06. Non-executive Director: Associated British Foods, 2006–15; Credit Agricole SA, 2007–11; Valeo SA, 2007–15; Candover Investments plc, 2008–14; EDF SA, 2009–14. Chairman: Merlin, 2007–13; Culham Langs and Scis, 2009–11. Vice Chairman: Business for New Europe, 2006–16; European Policy Forum, 2017–; Assoc. Mem., BUPA, 2006–11. Mem., Adv. Council, 2011–14, Chm., 2014–17, BL. Sen. Associate Mem., St Antony's Coll., Oxford, 1996. *Address:* House of Lords, SW1A 0PW.

**JAY OF EWELME, Lady; Sylvia Jay,** CBE 2005; Chairman, L'Oréal UK and Ireland, 2011–13 (Vice-Chairman, L'Oréal (UK) Ltd, 2005–11); *b* 1 Nov. 1946; *d* of William Edwin Mylroie and Edie Mylroie (*née* Chew); *m* 1975, Michael Hastings Jay (see Baron Jay of Ewelme). *Educ:* Nottingham Univ. (BA (Hons) Soc. Sci.); London Sch. of Econs. Home Civil Service: Admin. grade, ODA, 1971–87; secondments to French Ministère de la Coopération, 1988–89, to French Trésor, Paris, 1990, to EBRD, London, 1990–93; Clerk to European Union Sub-cttee A, H of L, 1994–96; accomp. husband, Ambassador to France, Paris, 1996–2001; Dir Gen., Food and Drink Fedn, 2001–05. Non-executive Director: Saint-Gobain, 2001–16; Carrefour, 2003–05; Lazard Ltd, 2006–; Alcatel-Lucent, 2006–14; Casino Supermarket Gp, 2012–. Chm., Food from Britain, 2006–09 (Mem., 2003–). Chm., Pilgrim Trust, 2005–14; Trustee: Entente Cordiale Scholarships Scheme, 2001–14; Prison Reform Trust, 2006–14; Body Shop Foundn, 2006–11. High Sheriff, Oxfordshire, 2019–20. Hon. DLaws Nottingham, 2009. Chevalier, Légion d'Honneur (France), 2008. *Address:* 38 Markham Street, SW3 3NR.

**JAY OF PADDINGTON,** Baroness *cr* 1992 (Life Peer), of Paddington in the City of Westminster; **Margaret Ann Jay;** PC 1998; Leader of the House of Lords, 1998–2001; Minister for Women, 1998–2001; *b* 18 Nov. 1939; *er d* of Baron Callaghan of Cardiff, KG, PC and late Audrey Elizabeth (*née* Moulton); *m* 1961, Peter Jay, *qv* (marr. diss. 1986); one *s* two *d*; *m* 1994, Prof. M. W. Adler, *qv*. Principal Opposition Spokesman on Health, H of L, 1995–97; Minister of State, DoH, 1997–98. Chm., H of L Select Cttee on Constitution, 2010–14. Dir, Nat. Aids Trust, 1988–92. Non-executive Director: Carlton Television, 1996–97; Scottish Power, 1996–97; Independent Media Gp, 2001–; BT Gp, 2002–08. Mem., Kensington, Chelsea & Westminster HA, 1992–97; Chm., Nat. Assoc. of Leagues of Hosp. Friends, 1994. Chm., ODI, 2002–08 (Mem. Council, 2008–); Jt Pres., Foreign

Policy Centre, 2009–17. Mem. Bd, Hansard Soc., 2013–. Sen. Fellow, Somerville Coll., Oxford; Mem., Alumni Bd, Oxford Univ., 2016–. *Address:* c/o House of Lords, SW1A 0PW.

JAY, Alexandrina, (Alexis), OBE 2012; Chair, Independent Inquiry into Child Sexual Abuse, since 2016 (Panel Member, 2015–16); *b* Edinburgh, 1949; *d* of Joseph and Margaret Deas; *m* 1978, Christopher Jay. *Educ:* CQSW; MBA. Reg. Social Worker. Social work posts, Strathclyde Reg., 1975–96; Hd, Social Work Services, N Lanarks Council, 1996–2000; Dir of Social Work, W Dunbartonshire Council, 2000–05; Chief Inspector of Social Work, 2005–11, Chief Social Work Advr, 2011–13, Scottish Govt. Chair, Centre for Excellence for Looked After Children, Strathclyde Univ., 2013–. Vis. Prof., Univ. of Strathclyde, 2014–. Ind. Inquiry into Child Sexual Exploitation in Rotherham, 2014; Rev. of Safeguarding Bd of NI, 2016. Chm., Life Changes Trust. DUniv Strathclyde, 2015. *Recreations:* cinema, cooking, music, patchwork. *Address:* Independent Inquiry into Child Sexual Abuse, Millbank Tower, Millbank, SW1P 4QP. *E:* alexis.jay@iicsa.org.uk.

JAY, John Philip Bromberg; Business Development Partner, Brompton Asset Management, since 2009; *b* 1 April 1957; *s* of late Alec Jay and June (*née* Bromberg); *m* 1st, 1987, Susy Streeter (marr. diss. 1992); 2nd, 1992, Judi Bevan (*née* Leader); one *d. Educ:* University Coll. Sch.; Magdalen Coll., Oxford (BA Hons Mod. Hist.). Journalist, Western Mail, 1979–81; financial journalist: Thomson Regl Newspapers, 1981–84; Sunday Telegraph, 1984–86; City Editor, Sunday Times, 1986–89; City and Business Editor, Sunday Telegraph, 1989–95; Man. Ed., Business News, Sunday Times, 1995–2001; Dir, New Star Asset Mgt, 2001–09. *Publications:* (with Judi Bevan) The New Tycoons, 1989; Facing Fearful Odds: my father's story of captivity, escape and resistance, 1940–45, 2014. *Recreations:* ski-ing, cinema, theatre, walking. *Address:* Brompton Asset Management, 1 Knightsbridge Green, SW1X 7QA. *T:* (020) 7045 0600.

JAY, Hon. Martin, CBE 2000; DL; Chairman: VT Group (formerly Vosper Thornycroft Holdings) plc, 2002–05 (Chief Executive, 1989–2002); Invensys plc, 2003–09; Oxsensis Ltd, since 2009; *b* 18 July 1939; *s* of Baron Jay, PC and Margaret Christian Jay; *m* 1969, Sandra Mary Ruth Williams; one *s* two *d. Educ:* Winchester Coll.; New Coll., Oxford (MA). With BP, 1962–69; GEC plc, 1969–85 (Man. Dir, GEC Inf. Services, and Mem., Mgt Bd, 1980–85); Man. Dir, Lewmar plc, 1985–87; Man. Dir, Electronics Components Div., GEC plc, 1987–89. Chm., EADS UK Ltd, 2005–06. Advr to HM Treasury, to lead collaborative procurement strand of operational efficiency prog., 2008–11. Mem., Nat. Defence Industries Council, 1997–2005; Pres., British Maritime Equipment Council, subseq. Soc. for Maritime Industries, 1997–2003. DL Hants, 2001. Chairman: Rose Rd Children's Appeal, 1997–2003; Tall Ships Youth Trust, 2005–10; Vice Pres., RNLI, 2010–. Hon. DBA Southampton Inst., 2001; Hon. LLD Portsmouth, 2004. *Recreations:* sailing, gardening, tennis. *Address:* Bishops Court, Bishops Sutton, Alresford, Hants SO24 0AN. *T:* (01962) 732193. *Club:* Garrick.

*See also* C. I. Arney, P. Jay.

JAY, Peter; writer and broadcaster; *b* 7 Feb. 1937; *s* of Baron Jay, PC and Margaret (Peggy) Christian Jay; *m* 1st, 1961, Margaret Ann (*see* Baroness Jay of Paddington) (marr. diss. 1986), *d* of Baron Callaghan of Cardiff, KG, PC; one *s* two *d*; one *s*; 2nd, 1986, Emma, *d* of late P. K. Thornton, CBE; three *s. Educ:* Winchester Coll.; Christ Church, Oxford (MA 1st cl. hons PPE, 1960). President of the Union, 1960. Nuffield Coll., 1960. Midshipman and Sub-Lt RNVR, 1956–57. Asst Principal 1961–64, Private Sec. to Jt Perm. Sec. 1964, Principal 1964–67, HM Treasury; Economics Editor, The Times, 1967–77, and Associate Editor, Times Business News, 1969–77; Presenter, Weekend World (ITV Sunday morning series), 1972–77; The Jay Interview (ITV series), 1975–76; Ambassador to US, 1977–79; Dir Economist Intelligence Unit, 1979–83. Consultant, Economist Gp, 1979–81; Chm. and Chief Exec., TV-am Ltd, 1980–83 and TV-am News, 1982–83, Pres., TV-am, 1983; Presenter, A Week in Politics, Channel 4, 1983–86; COS to Robert Maxwell (Chm, Mirror Gp Newspapers Ltd), 1986–89; Supervising Editor, Banking World, 1986–89 (Editor, 1984–86); Economics and Business Editor, BBC, 1990–2001. Publisher and Ed., Woodstock & Bladon News, 2017–. Non-exec. Dir, Bank of England, 2003–09. Presenter, The Road to Riches, BBC TV series, 2000. Chairman: NACRO Working Party on Children and Young Persons in Custody, 1976–77; NCVO, 1981–86 (Vice-Pres., 1986–92); Trustee, Charities Aid Foundn, 1981–86; Chm., Charities Effectiveness Review Trust, 1986–87. Vis. Scholar, Brookings Instn, Washington, 1979–80; Wincott Meml Lectr, 1975; Copland Meml Lectr, Australia, 1980; MacTaggart Meml Lectr, 1981; Shell Lectr, Glasgow, 1985. Hon. Prof., Univ. of Wales, Aberystwyth, 2001–; Exec. Prof. of Political Economy, Henley Business Sch. (formerly Henley Mgt Coll.), 2006–10. Governor, Ditchley Foundn, 1982–2015; Mem. Council, St George's House, Windsor, 1982–85. Mem., Woodstock Town Council, 2004– (Dep. Mayor, 2004–06; Mayor, 2008–10). Dir, New Nat. Theater, Washington, DC, 1979–81. Political Broadcaster of Year, 1973; Harold Wincott Financial and Economic Journalist of Year, 1973; RTS Male Personality of Year (Pye Award), 1974; SFTA Shell Internat. TV Award, 1974; RTS Home News Award, 1992. FRGS 1977. Hon. DH Ohio State Univ., 1978; Hon. DLitt Wake Forest Univ., 1979; Berkeley Citation, Univ. of Calif, 1979. *Publications:* The Budget, 1972; (contrib.) America and the World 1979, 1980; The Crisis for Western Political Economy and other Essays, 1984; (with Michael Stewart) Apocalypse 2000, 1987; Road to Riches, or The Wealth of Man, 2000; contrib. Foreign Affairs jl. *Recreations:* sailing, bridge. *Address:* The Retreat, Woodstock, Oxon OX20 1LJ. *T:* (01993) 811222, 07860 355557, *Fax:* (01993) 812861. *E:* thepeterjay@btinternet.com. *Clubs:* Garrick; Royal Naval Sailing Association, Royal Cork Yacht.

*See also* Hon. M. Jay.

JAY, Hon. Sir Robert Maurice, Kt 2013; Hon. Mr Justice Jay; a Judge of the High Court of Justice, Queen's Bench Division, since 2013; *b* 20 Sept. 1959; *s* of late Prof. Barrie Samuel Jay and of Marcelle Ruby Jay; *m* 1997, Deborah Jacinta Trenner; one *d. Educ:* King's Coll. Sch. (Open Schol.); New Coll., Oxford (Open Schol.; BA 1st cl. Hons Jurisp. 1980). Called to the Bar, Middle Temple, 1981, Bencher, 2007; in practice at the Bar, 1981–2013; QC 1998; a Recorder, 2000–13; a Dep. High Ct Judge, 2008–13. Jun. Counsel to the Crown (Common Law), 1989–98. Gov., King's Coll. Sch., 2012–. *Recreations:* history, cooking, opera, classical music, Italy. *Address:* Royal Courts of Justice, Strand, WC2A 2LL. *T:* (020) 7947 6387.

JAY, Rosemary Patricia; Senior Consultant Attorney, Hunton Andrews Kurth (UK) LLP (formerly Hunton & Williams, Solicitors), since 2014; *b* Salford, Lancs, 13 Oct. 1951; *d* of Thomas Patrick and Bridget Irene Collins; *m* 1977, George Neville Jay; one *s* one *d. Educ:* Adelphi Salford Girls Grammar Sch.; Hull Univ. (BA Hons English 1972); Chester Coll. (PGCE 1974); Law Faculty, Manchester Poly. Teacher, Manchester, 1974–77; trainee and Solicitor, Stockport MBC, 1979–84; admitted Solicitor, 1981; Sen. Solicitor, Vale Royal DC, 1984–87; Legal Advr, Office of Data Protection Registrar, 1987–99; Solicitor, Pinsent Masons, 1999–2011 (Partner, 2003–11); Sen. Attorney, Hunton & Williams, Solicitors, 2011–14. FBCS 2010. *Publications:* Data Protection Law and Practice, 1999, 4th edn 2012, Supplement, 2014; Ed., Encyclopedia of Data Protection, 2000–16; Guide to the General Data Protection Regulation, 2017. *Recreations:* gardening, including allotment, reading, walking, family. *Address:* Hunton Andrews Kurth (UK) LLP, 30 St Mary Axe, EC3A 8EP. *T:* (020) 7220 5700, *Fax:* (020) 7220 5772. *E:* rjay@hunton.com.

JAY-O'BOYLE, Fionnuala Mary, CBE 2008 (MBE 2000); Founder and Principal, Jay Associates Public and Government Affairs, since 1991; Lord-Lieutenant, County Borough of Belfast, since 2014; *b* Londonderry, 22 March 1960; *d* of Thomas Boyle and Elizabeth Boyle (*née* McGrory); *m* 1989, Richard Jay. *Educ:* Thornhill Coll., Londonderry; Queen's Univ., Belfast (BA Hons Pol Sci. and Ancient Hist. 1982). Communications and PR Manager, Bryson House, 1986–90; Dir, PR and Mktg, Andras House Ltd, 1990–91. Founder and Working Dir, Belfast Buildings Preservation Trust, later Belfast Buildings Trust, 1995–. Former Chm., Belfast Civic Trust. Former Mem. Council, Architectural Heritage Fund. Founder, NI Schs Debating Competition. Vice Chair, NI Opera. Ind. Mem., H of L Appts Commn, 2019–. Trustee: Prince's Regeneration Trust, 2003–; Prince's Foundn for Building Communities, 2016–17; Founding Trustee, Teachers of Singers in Ireland, 2006–. Hon. RSUA 2008. DL Belfast 2009. *Recreations:* opera, theatre, food and wine, travel, history. *Address:* Elderslie House, 18 Ashley Avenue, Belfast, Northern Ireland BT9 7BT. *T:* (028) 9066 5630. *E:* jay.associates@btconnect.com.

JAYARATNE, Dissanayake Mudiyanselage; Prime Minister of Sri Lanka, 2010–15; Minister of Buddhist and Religious Affairs, 2010–15; *b* Gampola, Ceylon, 4 June 1931; *s* of Dissanayake Mudiyanselage Punchirala and Dissanayake Mudiyanselage Bandaramenika; *m* 1981, Dona Anula Yapa; one *s* two *d. Educ:* Gampola Zahira Vidyalaya; Gampola Gandhi Vidyalaya. Postmaster. Mem., Doluwa Village Council, Gampola, 1959; Chm., Pahala Korale Village Council, 1961. MP (Sri Lanka Freedom Party) Gampola, 1970–77 and 1989–2015; Minister: of Lands, Agric. and Envmt, 1994–2000; of Agric., Food and Co-operatives, 2000–01; of Post, Telecommunication and Rural Develt, 2004–07; of Plantation Industries, 2008–10. Exec. Mem., Telecommunication Commn. Founder Mem., Sri Lanka Freedom Party, 1951 (Vice Pres.); Gen. Sec., United People's Alliance. President: Fedn of Village Councils of Kandy Dist, 1965; Fedn of All Village Councils, 1965. Pres., Internat. Youth Conf. *Address:* c/o Parliament of Sri Lanka, Sri Jayewardenepura Kotte, Colombo, Sri Lanka.

JAYASINGHE, Nihal; Justice Jayasinghe; Judge, Supreme Court of Extraordinary Chamber of Courts of Cambodia, United Nations, since 2006; *m* 1977, Indira Wickremasinghe; one *s* one *d. Educ:* Univ. of Colombo (LLB 1969). State Counsel, Attorney Gen's Dept, Sri Lanka, 1975–83; Sen. State Counsel, 1983–94; Dep. Solicitor Gen., 1994–97; Judge, 1997–2002, Pres., 2002, Court of Appeal; Judge, 2002–06, Sen. Presiding Judge, 2006–08, Supreme Court of Sri Lanka; High Comr for Sri Lanka in the UK, and concurrently Ambassador to Ireland, 2008–10. Vis. Schol., Univ. of Illinois at Chicago, 1989–90. *Recreations:* music, cricket. *Address:* No 12 De Soyza Mawatha, Templars Road, Mount Lavinia, Sri Lanka. *T:* 112726880.

JAYAWARDENA, Ranil Malcolm; MP (C) North East Hampshire, since 2015; *b* London, 3 Sept. 1986; *s* of Nalin Mahinda Jayawardena and Indira Maureen Jayawardena; *m* 2011, Alison Lyn Roberts; two *d. Educ:* Robert May's Sch., Odiham; Alton Coll., Alton; London Sch. of Econs and Political Sci. (BSc Hons); Royal Coll. of Defence Studies. Various roles, from commercial banking to gp exec. functions, Lloyds Banking Gp, 2008–15. Mem., Basingstoke and Deane BC, 2008–15 (Dep. Leader, 2012–15). Member: Home Affairs Select Cttee, 2015–17; Internat. Trade Cttee, 2016–; Procedure Cttee, 2017–. Vice Chm., Cons. Party, 2019–. *Recreations:* cricket, golf, tennis, shooting, walking, local history, film, theatre. *Address:* House of Commons, SW1A 0AA. *T:* (020) 7219 3637. *E:* ranil.jayawardena.mp@parliament.uk.

JAYNE, Prof. David Roland Walker, MD; FRCP, FRCPE, FMedSci; Professor of Clinical Autoimmunity, University of Cambridge, since 2017; *b* Sutton, Surrey, 19 Jan. 1957; *s* of Freeman Oliver Jayne and Ruth Margaret Jayne; *m* 1982, Lucinda Higson Smith; two *s* one *d. Educ:* King's Sch., Canterbury; Corpus Christi Coll., Cambridge (BA 1978; BChir 1981; MB 1981; MD 1993). MRCP 1985, FRCP 1999; FRCPE 2009. Hse Surgeon, Royal Northern Hosp., 1981–82; Hse Physician, St Peter's Hosp., Chertsey, 1982; Senior House Officer: UCH, 1982–83; St Thomas' Hosp., 1983–84; Nat. Heart Hosp., 1984–85; Registrar, St Mary's Hosp., 1985–87; Clinical Research Fellow: Addenbrooke's Hosp., Cambridge, 1987–90; Gonville and Caius Coll., Cambridge, 1990–95; Sen. Lectr, St George's Hosp., London, 1996–2001; Consultant in Nephrology and Vasculitis, Addenbrooke's Hosp., Cambridge, Cambridge Univ. Hosps NHS Foundn Trust, 2001–13; Reader in Vasculitis, Dept of Medicine, Univ. of Cambridge, 2013–17. NIHR Senior Investigator, 2016–. Pres., Eur. Vasculitis Soc., 2011–. FMedSci 2013. *Recreation:* horse riding. *Address:* Department of Medicine, Addenbrooke's Hospital, Cambridge CB2 2SP. *T:* (01223) 336816. *E:* dj106@cam.ac.uk.

JAYSON, Prof. Malcolm Irving Vivian, MD; FRCP; Professor of Rheumatology and Director, University Centre for the Study of Chronic Rheumatism, University of Manchester, 1977–96, now Emeritus Professor; *b* 9 Dec. 1937; *s* of Joseph and Sybil Jayson; *m* 1962, Judith Tauber; two *s. Educ:* Middlesex Hosp. Med. Sch., Univ. of London (MB, BS 1961); MD Bristol, 1969; MSc Manchester, 1977. FRCP 1976. House Physician, 1961, House Surgeon, 1962, Middlesex Hosp.; House Physician: Central Middlesex Hosp., 1962; Brompton Hosp., 1963; Sen. House Officer, Middlesex Hosp., 1963; Registrar: Westminster Hosp., 1964; Royal Free Hosp., 1965; Lectr, Univ. of Bristol, Royal Nat. Hosp. for Rheumatic Diseases, Bath, and Bristol Royal Infirmary, 1967; Sen. Lectr, Univ. of Bristol, and Consultant, Royal Nat. Hosp. for Rheumatic Diseases, Bath, and Bristol Royal Infirmary, 1970. Visiting Professor: Univ. of Iowa, 1984; Univ. of Queensland, 1985; Univ. of Cairo, 1992. Gen. Sec., Internat. Back Pain Soc., 1986–; President: Soc. of Chiropodists, 1984; Arachnoiditis Self-Help Gp, 1989–; Pres., Internat. Soc. for Study of the Lumbar Spine, 1995–96. *Publications:* (with A. St J. Dixon) Rheumatism and Arthritis, 1974, 8th edn 1991; The Lumbar Spine and Back Pain, 1976, 4th edn 1992; Back Pain: the facts, 1981, 3rd edn 1992; (with C. Black) Systemic Sclerosis: Scleroderma, 1988; Understanding Back Pain, 2001, 8th edn 2009; contribs to Lancet, BMJ and other med. jls. *Recreations:* antiques (especially sundials), trout fishing. *Address:* The Gate House, 8 Lancaster Road, Didsbury, Manchester M20 2TY. *T:* (0161) 445 1729.

JAYSTON, Michael, (Michael James); actor; *b* 29 Oct. 1935; *s* of Aubrey Vincent James and Edna Myfanwy Llewelyn; *m* 1st, 1965, Lynn Farleigh (marr. diss. 1970); 2nd, 1970, Heather Mary Sneddon (marr. diss. 1977); 3rd, 1978, Elizabeth Ann Smithson; three *s* one *d. Educ:* Becket Grammar School, Nottingham; Guildhall Sch. of Music and Drama (FGS). *Stage:* Salisbury Playhouse, 1962–63 (parts incl. Henry II, in Becket); Bristol Old Vic, 1963–65; RSC, 1965–69 (incl. Ghosts, All's Well That Ends Well, Hamlet, The Homecoming (NY), The Relapse); Equus, NT, 1973, Albery, 1977; Private Lives, Duchess, 1980; The Sound of Music, Apollo, 1981; The Way of the World, Chichester, 1984, Haymarket, 1985; Woman in Mind, Vaudeville, 1987; Dancing at Lughnasa, Garrick, 1992; The Wind in the Willows, NT, 1994; Easy Virtue, Chichester, 1999; Wild Orchids, Chichester, 2001; The Rivals, Moment of Weakness, tour, 2002; The Marquise, tour, 2004; Heroes, tour, 2006; Last Confession, Haymarket, 2007; Quartet, Yvonne Arnaud Th., 2010; *films include:* Midsummer Night's Dream, 1968; The Power Game, 1968; Cromwell, 1969; Nicholas and Alexandra, 1970; *television includes:* Beethoven, 1969; Mad

Jack, 1970; Wilfred Owen, 1971; Tinker, Tailor, Soldier, Spy, 1979; Dr Who, 1986; A Bit of a Do, 1988, 1989; Haggard, 1990; Darling Buds of May, 1992; Outside Edge, 1995, 1996; Only Fools and Horses, 1996; Eastenders, 2001; Doctors, 2003, 2011, 2013, 2015; The Bill, 2005; Emmerdale, 2008–09; Holby City, 2010; Casualty, 2011, 2015. Life Mem., Battersea Dogs and Cats Home. *Recreations:* cricket, darts, chess. *Address:* c/o Diamond Management, 31 Percy Street, W1T 2DD. *Clubs:* MCC, Lord's Taverners, Cricketers'; Sussex CC, Gedling Colliery CC (Vice-Pres.); Rottingdean CC (Pres.).

**JEAN, Rt Hon. Michaëlle**, CC 2005; CMM 2005; CD 2005; PC (Can.) 2012; Governor General of Canada, 2005–10; Secretary-General, Organisation internationale de la Francophonie, 2014–18; *b* Port au Prince; *m* Jean-Daniel Lafond (CC 2005); one *d*, and two step *d*. *Educ:* Univ. of Montreal (BA Italian and Hispanic Langs and Lit; MA Comparative Lit); Univ. of Perouse; Univ. of Florence; Catholic Univ. of Milan. Worked with Québec shelters for battered women, 1979–86; taught at Faculty of Italian Studies, Univ. of Montreal, 1984–86; Employment and Immigration Canada; Conseil des Communautés culturelles du Québec; joined Radio-Canada, 1988; reporter and host on news and public affairs progs incl. Actuel, Montréal ce soir, Virages and Le Point; presenter of several Réseau de l'Information à Radio-Canada progs, 1995; presenter: The Passionate Eye and Rough Cuts, CBC Newsworld, 1999; weekend edns of Le Téléjournal, 2001, daily edn of Le Téléjournal, Le Midi, 2003, Radio-Canada; own show, Michaëlle, 2004. Co-Founder and Co-Chm., Michaëlle Jean Foundn, 2009–. UNESCO Special Envoy to Haiti, 2010–14. Chancellor, Univ. of Ottawa, 2012–. *Address:* Michaëlle Jean Foundation, 143 Séraphin-Marion Street, Ottawa, ON K1N 6N5, Canada.

**JEANES, Ronald Eric;** Deputy Director, Building Research Establishment, 1981–86; *b* 23 Sept. 1926; *s* of Edwin and Eunice Jeanes; *m* 1951, Helen Field (*née* Entwistle); one *s* one *d*. *Educ:* University Coll., Exeter (BSc 1951). Served HM Forces, 1945–48. Royal Naval Scientific Service, 1951–62; BRE, 1962–86. *Publications:* DoE and BRE reports. *Recreation:* amateur theatre. *Address:* 10 Whybrow Gardens, Berkhamsted, Herts HP4 2GU. *T:* (01442) 870242.

**JEANNERET, Marian Elizabeth;** *see* Hobson, M. E.

**JEANNIOT, Pierre Jean;** OC 1988; CQ 2002; Director General and Chief Executive Officer, International Air Transport Association, 1993–2002, now Director General Emeritus; Chairman and Chief Executive Officer, Jinmag Inc., since 1990; *b* Montpellier, France, 9 April 1933; *s* of Gaston and Renée Jeanniot; *m* 1979, Marcia David; two *s* one *d*. *Educ:* Sir George Williams Univ. (BSc); McGill Univ. (Management Prog.). Sperry Gyroscope, 1952–55; Air Canada, 1955–90: jun. technician; sen. posts in tech. services; Vice-Pres., Computer and Systems Services, 1970–76; Exec. Vice Pres., Sales, Mktg and Planning; Exec. Vice-Pres. and Chief Operating Officer, 1980; Pres. and CEO, 1984–90. Chm. and CEO, Revue Commerce Mag., 1977–82. Pres., Canadian OR Soc., 1966; Chm., Air Transport Assoc. of Canada, 1984; Mem., Exec. Cttee and Chm., Strategic Planning Sub-Cttee, IATA, 1988–90. Founding Dir, Edmonton Regl Airports Authy, 1991–92. Mem. Bd, Nat. Air Transport System, 2000–02. Bank of Nova Scotia: Mem. Bd, 1990–2004; Mem., Exec. Cttee, 1991–2004; Member, Board: McGraw Hill Pubns, 1989–92; Engenuity Technologies Inc., 2002–05; Jet Airways, 2005–09; Argo Consulting Inc., 2018–; Chairman: Thales Canada Inc., 2003–09; Laurentian Aerospace Inc., 2006–15; Luxell Inc., 2009–11; Adv. Bd, Star Navigation Inc., 2006–16. Internat. Aviation Consultant, Gerson Lehrman Gp, 2010–. Chm., Council for Canadian Unity, 1991–94. University of Québec: Chm. Bd, 1972–78; Pres., Foundn, 1978–92; Chancellor, 1995–2008; Sen. Aviation Advr to Pres., 2016–, Chm., Aviation Think Tank, 2016–, Concordia Univ. Chm. and participant, numerous charitable bodies. FRAeS 2007. Hon. Dr Quebec, 1988; Hon. Dr Internat. Law Concordia, 1997; Hon. DSc McGill, 2006. Roger Demers Prize, Gens de l'Air du Québec, 1991; Airline Business Strategy Award, Airline Business Magazine, 2002; Canadian Aviation Hall of Fame, 2012. Officier, Légion d'Honneur (France), 2017; Independence Medal (First Order) (Kingdom of Jordan), 1995. *Address:* 1010 de la Gauchetière West #960, Montreal, QC H3B 2N2, Canada. *T:* (514) 8680880. *W:* www.pierrejeanniot.com.

**JEANS, Ven. Alan Paul;** Archdeacon of Sarum, since 2003; *b* 18 May 1958; *s* of Brian Edward and Jacqueline Rosemary Jeans; *m* 1981, Anita Gail (*née* Hobbs); two *d*. *Educ:* Bournemouth Sch.; Bournemouth and Poole Coll. (MIAS, MIBC 1983); Southampton Univ. (BTh 1989); Salisbury and Wells Theol Coll.; Univ. of Wales, Lampeter (MA 2002). Building Surveyor, 1976–86. Ordained deacon, 1989, priest, 1990; Curate, Parkstone with Branksea, 1989–93; Priest i/c, Bishop's Cannings, All Cannings and Etchilhampton, 1993–98; Advr for Parish Develt, 1998–2005, Diocesan Dir of Ordinands, 2007–12, Dio. of Salisbury; Rural Dean, Alderbury, 2005–07. Canon, Salisbury Cathedral, 2002–. Asst Chaplain, Dauntsey's Sch., 1995–2007; Chaplain to the Forces (Reserves), 2002–. Mem., Gen. Synod of C of E, 2000–05 and 2010–. *Recreations:* food, architectural history, classic motor cars. *Address:* Ramsbury Office, Church House, Crane Street, Salisbury SP1 2QB. *T:* (01722) 438662. *E:* adsarum@salisbury.anglican.org.

**JEANS, Christopher James Marwood;** QC 1997; a Recorder, since 2009; *b* 24 Jan. 1956; *s* of late David Marwood Jeans and Rosalie Jean Jeans; *m* 1998, Judith Mary Laws; one *d*. *Educ:* Minchenden Sch.; King's Coll. London (LLB 1977); St John's Coll., Oxford (BCL 1979). Called to the Bar, Gray's Inn, 1980, Bencher, 2007; Lectr, City of London Poly., 1981–83; in practice at the Bar, 1983–. Part-time Employment Judge (formerly part-time Chm.), Employment Tribunals, 1998–2008. Mem., Law Panel, The Times, 2007–08. Pres. (pt-time), Commonwealth Secretariat Arbitral Tribunal, 2011–17 (Mem., 2008–17). FICPD 1998. *Recreations:* football (Spurs), cricket, walking, swimming, cinema, theatre, arctic and world travel. *Address:* 11 King's Bench Walk, Temple, EC4Y 7EQ.

**JEAPES, Maj.-Gen. Anthony Showan,** CB 1987; OBE 1977; MC 1960; retired; Consultant Inspector, Lord Chancellor's Panel of Independent Inspectors, 2003–05 (Member, 1991–2003); *b* 6 March 1935; *s* of Stanley Arthur Jeapes; *m* 1959, Jennifer Clare White; one *s* one *d*. *Educ:* Raynes Park Grammar Sch.; RMA Sandhurst. Commissioned Dorset, later Devonshire and Dorset, Regt, 1955; joined 22 SAS Regt, 1958; attached US Special Forces, 1961; Staff College, 1966; Brigade Major, 39 Inf. Bde, NI, 1967; Sqn Comdr, 22 SAS Regt, 1968; Nat. Defence Coll., 1971; Directing Staff, Staff Coll., Camberley, 1972; CO 22 SAS Regt, 1974; Mem., British Mil. Adv. Team, Bangladesh, 1977; Dep. Comdr, Sch. of Infantry, 1979; Comdr, 5 Airborne Brigade, 1982; Comdr, Land Forces NI, 1985–87; GOC, SW Dist, 1987–90. Vice-Chairman: Romanian Orphanage Trust, 1991–99; European Children's Trust, 1995–99. Vice-Patron, Poppy Factory, 2015–. *Publications:* SAS Operation Oman, 1980; SAS Secret War, 1996. *Recreation:* country pursuits. *Address:* c/o National Westminster Bank, 62 Fore Street, Trowbridge, Wilts BA14 8EX.

**JEARY, Anthony John P.;** *see* Pye-Jeary, A. J.

**JEAVONS, Richard Matthew,** CBE 2015; Chief Executive, Independent Reconfiguration Panel, since 2008; *b* Birmingham, 4 Aug. 1957; *s* of Garth and Mary Jeavons; *m* 1986, Helen Christie; two *s* one *d*. *Educ:* King Edward VI Sch., Birmingham; Univ. of Edinburgh (MA Econs 1980); Univ. of York (MSc Health Econs 1982). Res. economist, Leeds West HA, 1982–84; economist, Mersey RHA, 1984–86; Res. Fellow, Univ. of York, 1986–89; Dir, Northern Gen. Hosp., Sheffield, 1990–94; Chief Executive: Sheffield Children's Hosp., 1994–97; Lincs HA, 1998–2002; W Yorks SHA, 2002–05; Dir, DoH, 2005–08; Dir of Commng, Specialised Services, NHS England, 2014–15. Sen. Partner, NHS Interim Mgt and Support, 2010–. Dir, Health Data Insights CIC, 2015–. *Recreations:* family, friends, the outdoors, supporting cricket - England, Yorkshire and Horsforth. *Address:* Independent Reconfiguration Panel, 6th Floor, 157–197 Buckingham Palace Road, SW1W 9SP.

**JEAVONS, (Robert) Clyde (Scott);** Curator, National Film and Television Archive, British Film Institute, 1990–97; *b* 30 June 1939; *s* of Frank Rechab Scott-Jeavons and Olive Edith (*née* Robins); *m* 1st, 1963, Hilary Coopey (marr. diss.); one *d*; 2nd, 1977, Orly Yadin (marr. diss.); 3rd, 2007, Shirley Ann Tait. *Educ:* St Lawrence Coll.; Royal Russell Sch.; University Coll. London (BA Hons Scandinavian Studies). Asst Stage Manager, Det Norske Rikstreatret, Norway, 1963; financial journalist, Investors' Rev., 1964; Chief Sub, Features Ed. and book reviewer and film critic, SHE mag., 1964–69; Dep. Curator and Hd, Film and TV Acquisitions, Nat. Film Archive, BFI, 1969–85; freelance author and film programmer, 1986–90. Archive Consultant, London Film Fest., 1997–2016. Member: Satyajit Ray Foundn (Vice-Chair, 2010–14); BAFTA; Critics' Circle; British Cinema and TV Veterans. Hon. Mem., BFI. Mem., Islington Choral Soc. FRSA 1992–2002. Hon. FBKS 1994. *Publications:* (with Michael Parkinson) A Pictorial History of Westerns, 1974; A Pictorial History of War Films, 1975; (with Jeremy Pascall) A Pictorial History of Sex in the Movies, 1976; British Film-Makers of the Eighties, 1990; contrib. Sight & Sound, Monthly Film Bull., Guardian, Sunday Times, Jl of Film Preservation, etc. *Recreations:* cricket, golf, travel, cooking and dining, music, film, choral singing, reading the New Yorker. *Address:* Garden Flat, 110A Highbury New Park, N5 2DR. *T:* (020) 7226 6778. *Clubs:* Union; Middlesex CC, Brondesbury Cricket, Barnes Cricket (Hon. Mem.), Bertie Joel Net XI, Bushmen Cricket and Dining; Surrey Seniors Cricket; Kent Golf Union.

**JEEVES, Prof. Malcolm Alexander,** CBE 1992; FMedSci, FBPsS; PPRSE; Professor of Psychology, University of St Andrews, 1969–93, Hon. Research Professor, since 1993; *b* 16 Nov. 1926; *s* of Alderman Alexander Frederic Thomas Jeeves and Helena May Jeeves (*née* Hammond); *m* 1955, Ruth Elisabeth Hartridge; two *d*. *Educ:* Stamford Sch.; St John's Coll., Cambridge (MA, PhD). Commissioned Royal Lincs Regt, served 1st Bn Sherwood Foresters, BAOR, 1945–48. Cambridge University: Exhibnr, St John's Coll., 1948, Res. Exhibnr, 1952; Burney Student, 1952; Gregg Bury Prizeman, 1954; Kenneth Craik Res. Award, St John's Coll., 1955. Rotary Foundn Fellow, Harvard, 1953; Lectr, Leeds Univ., 1956; Prof. of Psychology, Adelaide Univ., 1959–69, and Dean, Faculty of Arts, 1962–64; Vice-Principal, St Andrews Univ., 1981–85; Dir, MRC Cognitive Neuroscience Res. Gp, St Andrews, 1984–89. Lectures: Abbie Meml, Adelaide Univ., 1981; Cairns Meml, Aust., 1986; New Coll., Univ. of NSW, 1987; Boyle, St Mary le Bow, Cheapside, 2008. Member: SSRC Psych. Cttee, 1972–76; Biol. Cttee, 1980–84, Science Bd, 1985–89, Council, 1985–89, SERC; MRC Neuroscience and Mental Health Bd, 1985–89; Council, 1984–88, Exec., 1985–87, Vice-Pres., 1990–93, Pres., 1996–99, RSE; ABRC Manpower Sub-Cttee, 1991–93; Pres., Section J, BAAS, 1988. Founder FMedSci 1998. Hon. Sheriff, Fife, 1986–. Hon. DSc: Edinburgh, 1993; St Andrews, 2000; DUniv Stirling, 1999. Editor-in-Chief, Neuropsychologia, 1990–93. *Publications:* (with Z. P. Dienes) Thinking in Structures, 1965 (trans. French, German, Spanish, Italian, Japanese); (with Z. P. Dienes) The Effects of Structural Relations upon Transfer, 1968; The Scientific Enterprise and Christian Faith, 1969; Experimental Psychology: an introduction for Biologists, 1974; Psychology and Christianity: the view both ways, 1976 (trans. Chinese); (with G. B. Greer) Analysis of Structural Learning, 1983; (with R. J. Berry and D. Atkinson) Free to be Different, 1984; Behavioural Sciences: a Christian perspective, 1984; (with D. G. Myers) Psychology—through the eyes of faith, 1987, 2nd edn 2002; Mind Fields, 1994; Human Nature at the Millennium, 1997; (with R. J. Berry) Science, Life and Christian Belief, 1998; (ed and contrib.) From Cells to Souls, 2004; (ed and contrib.) Human Nature, 2005; (with W. S. Brown) Neuroscience, Psychology and Religion, 2009 (trans. Spanish, Greek and Chinese); (ed and contrib.) Rethinking Human Nature, 2011; Minds, Brains, Souls and Gods, 2013; The Emergence of Personhood - a quantum leap?, 2015; Psychological Science and Christian Faith, 2018; papers in sci. jls, mainly on neuropsychology and cognition. *Recreations:* music, fly fishing, walking. *Address:* Psychology Laboratory, The University, St Andrews KY16 9JU. *T:* (01334) 462057.

**JEEWOOLALL, Sir Ramesh,** GCSK 2007; Kt 1979; Speaker, Mauritius Parliament, 1979–82 and 1996–2000; *b* 20 Dec. 1940; *s* of Shivprasad Jeewoolall; *m* 1971, Usweenee (*née* Reetoo); two *s*. *Educ:* in Mauritius; Inns of Court Sch. of Law. Called to the Bar, Middle Temple, 1968; practising at the Bar, 1969–71; Magistrate, 1971–72; practising at the Bar and Chm., Mauritius Tea Develt Authority, 1972–76. Mem., Mauritius Parlt, 1976–82 and 1987–91; Minister of Housing, Lands, Town and Country Planning and the Envmt, 1987–90; Dep. Speaker, 1977–79. Pres., CPA, 1996–97 (Vice-Pres., 1995–96). Chancellor, Univ. of Mauritius, 2006–. *Publications:* Who Owns Your Agenda?, 2013; The Passing Away of a Gentleman, 2015; The Politician for Whom the Party Does Not Matter, 2017. *Recreations:* reading, conversation, chess. *Address:* 92 Belle Rose Avenue, Quatre Bornes, Mauritius. *T:* 4645371.

**JEFFCOTT, Prof. Leo Broof,** PhD, DVSc; FRCVS; Professor of Veterinary Science, University of Sydney, 2004–12, now Emeritus (Dean, Faculty of Veterinary Science, 2004–09); *b* 19 June 1942; *s* of late Edward Ian Broof Jeffcott and Pamela Mary (*née* Hull); *m* 1969, Tisza Jacqueline (*née* Hubbard); two *d*. *Educ:* Univ. of London (BVetMed 1967, PhD 1972); Univ. of Melbourne (DVSc 1989); MA Cantab 1994. FRCVS 1978. Animal Health Trust, Newmarket: Asst Pathologist, 1967–71; Clinician, 1972–77; Head, Clinical Dept, 1977–81; Professor: of Clinical Radiology, Swedish Univ. of Agricl Scis, Uppsala, 1981–82; of Veterinary Clinical Sciences, Univ. of Melbourne, 1982–91; Prof. of Vet. Clin. Studies and Dean of Vet. Sch., 1991–2004, Fellow of Pembroke Coll., 1993–2004, Cambridge Univ. Mem. Council, RCVS, 1992–2004. Chm., Internat. Cttee for 5th Internat. Conf. on Equine Exercise Physiology, 1994–98; Mem. Bureau, FEI, 1998–2006 (Hon. Mem., 2006; Chm., Vet. Cttee, 1998–2006). Lectures: Sir Frederick Hobday Meml, BEVA, 1977; Peter Hernqvist, Swedish Univ. of Agricl Scis, Skara, 1991; Share-Jones, RCVS, 1993; J. D. Stewart Address, Univ. of Sydney, 2004; R. R. Pascoe Peroration, Australian Equine Vet. Assoc., 2005; John Hickman Meml, 50th BEVA Congress, 2011. FEI Official Veterinarian: Seoul Olympics, 1988; World Equestrian Games, Stockholm, 1990, The Hague, 1994, Rome, 1998; Jerez, Spain, 2002; Barcelona Olympics, 1992; Atlanta Olympics, 1996; Sydney Olympics, 2000; Athens Olympics, 2004; Beijing Olympics, 2008; Beijing Paralympics, 2008. Hon. FRVC 1997. VetMedDr *hc* Swedish Univ. of Agricl Scis, 2000. Norman Hall Medal for Research, RCVS, 1978; Internat. Prize of Tierklinik Hochmoor, Germany, 1981; Equine Veterinary Jl Open Award, BEVA, 1982; John Hickman Orthopaedic Prize, BEVA, 1991; Internat. Hall of Fame Award for Equine Res., Univ. of Kentucky, 1991; UK Equestrian Award for Scientific Achievement, 1994; Sefton Award for Services to Equestrian Safety, 1997; Dalrymple-Champneys Cup and Medal, 2001. Hon. Order of Kentucky Cols, Gov. of Kentucky, 2011. *Publications:* (with R. K. Archer) Comparative Clinical Haematology, 1977; (ed jtly) Equine Exercise Physiology 3, 1991; (with G. Dalin) Osteochondrosis in the 90s, 1993; (with A. F. Clarke)

On to Atlanta '96, 1994; (with A. F. Clarke) Progress towards Atlanta '96: thermoregulatory responses during competitive exercise with performance horse, Vol. I 1995, Vol. II 1996; Equine Exercise Physiology 5, 1999; (ed jtly) Osteochondrosis and Musculoskeletal Development in the Foal Under the Influence of Exercise, 1999; (ed with P. D. Rossdale) A Tribute to Colonel John Hickman, 2001; 350 articles in equine veterinary sci. jls. *Recreations:* swimming, photography, equestrian sports. *Address:* Sydney School of Veterinary Science, University Veterinary Teaching Hospital Camden, University of Sydney, 410 Werombi Road, Camden, NSW 2570, Australia.

**JEFFERIES, Andrew;** QC 2009; **His Honour Judge Jefferies;** a Circuit Judge, since 2018; *b* 18 April 1968; *s* of Alan Jefferies and Ann Jefferies (*née* Shearden); one *s* one *d*; *m* 2015, Georgina Meikle; one step *s*. *Educ:* Priestley Sixth Form Coll.; Univ. of E Anglia (LLB Hons); Inns of Court Sch. of Law. Called to the Bar, Middle Temple, 1990; in practice as barrister specialising in criminal defence; a Recorder, 2016–18. *Recreations:* reading, languages, music, travelling. *Address:* Preston Combined Court Centre, The Law Courts, Openshaw Place, Ring Way, Preston PR1 2LL.

**JEFFERIES, Roger David;** Independent Housing Ombudsman, 1997–2001; *b* 13 Oct. 1939; *s* of George Edward Jefferies and Freda Rose Jefferies (*née* Marshall); *m* 1st, 1962, Jennifer Anne Southgate (marr. diss.); one *s* two *d*; 2nd, 1974, Margaret Sealy (marr. diss.); 3rd, 1984, Pamela Mary Elsey (*née* Holden); one *s*. *Educ:* Whitgift School; Balliol College, Oxford. BA, BCL; solicitor. Member: Law Society, 1965–; British and Irish Ombudsman Assoc., 1997–. Asst Solicitor, Coventry Corporation, 1965–68; Asst Town Clerk, Southend-on-Sea County Borough Council, 1968–70; Director of Operations, London Borough of Hammersmith, 1970–75; Chief Exec., London Borough of Hounslow, 1975–90; Under Secretary, DoE, 1983–85 (on secondment); Chief Exec., London Bor. of Croydon, 1990–93; Housing Assoc. Tenants' Ombudsman, 1993–97. Chm., Discipline Cttees, Lambeth, Southwark and Lewisham HA, 1998–2004. Non-executive Director: Nat. Clinical Assessment Authy, 2001–05; Financial Ombudsman Service, 2002–08; Telecommunications Ombudsman Service, 2002–07. Ind. Adjudicator for Lewisham LBC, 2006–07; Ind. Assessor for Telecommunications and Energy Ombudsman, 2007–11. Member: Regl Planning Bd, Arts Council of GB, 1986–88; Adv. Bd, Lewisham Theatre, 1994–99; Council, RIPA, 1982–88; Bd, Public Finance Foundn, 1987–93; Pres., SOLACE, 1990–91. Clerk: Mortlake Crematorium Bd, 1973–90; W London Waste Authy, 1986–90. Director: Extemporary Dance Co., 1989–91; Croydon Business Venture, 1991–93; Solotec, 1992–93. Hon. Sec., Commn for Local Democracy, 1993–96. Trustee: S African Advanced Educn Project, 1989–96; Barnes Workhouse Fund, 2002–10. *Publications:* Tackling the Town Hall, 1982; Ursula's Secrets (novel), 2014; (ed) I Remain Your Loving Wife Lizzie: letters in a skip 1917–19, 2018. *Recreations:* the novel, genealogy, the Languedoc.

**JEFFERIES, Stephen;** freelance teacher and choreographer, since 2008; international ballet competition judge, since 2014; *b* 24 June 1951; *s* of George and Barbara Jefferies; *m* 1972, Rashna Homji; one *s* one *d*. *Educ:* Turves Green Sch., Birmingham; Royal Ballet Sch. ARAD (Advanced Hons). Joined Sadler's Wells Royal Ballet, 1969; created 10 leading roles whilst with Sadler's Wells; Principal Dancer, 1973–76 and 1977–79, Sen. Principal Dancer, 1979–95, Character Principal, 1994–95, Royal Ballet; joined National Ballet of Canada as Principal Dancer, 1976; created role of Morris, in Washington Square, 1977; returned to Royal Ballet at Covent Garden, 1977; Rehearsal Dir, Rambert Dance Co., Jan.–July 1995 (on leave of absence); Artistic Dir, Hong Kong Ballet, 1996–2006; Artistic Dir and Choreographer, Suzhou Kewen Promotion Co., 2007–08; co-choreographer (with Wayne Eagling), Beauty and the Beast, Kremlin Ballet, 2013. Gov., Royal Ballet, Birmingham Royal Ballet and Royal Ballet Sch., 2016–. *Major roles include:* Prince in Sleeping Beauty, Swan Lake and Giselle, Prince Rudolf in Mayerling, Petruchio in Taming of the Shrew, Romeo and Mercutio in Romeo and Juliet, Lescaut in Manon; lead, in Song and Dance, 1982; *roles created:* Yukinojo (mime role), in world première of Minoru Miki's opera An Actor's Revenge, 1979; male lead in Bolero, Japan (chor. by Yashiro Okamoto), 1980; Antonio in The Duenna, S Africa (chor. by Ashley Killar), 1980; lead, in Dances of Albion (chor. by Glen Tetley), 1980; Esenin in Kenneth Macmillan's ballet, Isadora, Covent Garden, 1981; lead, in L'Invitation au Voyage, Covent Garden (chor. by Michael Corder), 1982; Consort Lessons, and Sons of Horos, 1986, Still Life at the Penguin Café, and The Trial of Prometheus, 1988 (chor. by David Bintley); title role in Cyrano (chor. by David Bintley), 1991. Choreographed ballets: Bits and Pieces, in Canada, 1977; Mes Souvenirs, in London, 1978; Magic Toyshop, 1987; *for Hong Kong Ballet:* Swan Lake, 1996; Giselle, Nutcracker, 1997; Tango Ballet Tango, 2000; Sleeping Beauty, 2002; (and designed) The Legend of the Great Archer, 2004; Suzie Wong, 2006. *Film:* Anna, 1988. *Recreations:* golf, football, gardening, swimming and various other sports. *Address:* Flat 37, Regatta Point, 38 Kew Bridge Road TW8 0EB.

**JEFFERISS, Dr Paul Howard;** Head of Policy, BP, since 2010 (Director of Environmental Policy, 2006–09; Head of Energy, Climate and Environmental Policy, 2009–10); *b* 29 Oct. 1955; *s* of Leonard James Jefferiss and Elsie Jefferiss (*née* Shenton). *Educ:* Peterhouse, Cambridge (BA Hons Anglo-Saxon, Norse and Celtic 1977, MA 1990); Harvard Univ. (MA Celtic Langs and Lit. 1980; PhD 1991); Tufts Univ. (Cert. Envmtl Mgt 1992; MA Envmtl (and Urban) Policy 1994). Publicity Asst, OUP, 1978–79; Harvard University: Hd Teaching Fellow, 1982–91; Lectr, 1988–91; Asst Sen. Tutor, 1988–91, Tutor, 1991–93, Dunster House; Lectr in Envmtl Mgt, UNEP at Tufts Univ., 1995–97; Dir of Energy, Union of Concerned Scientists, 1994–98; Hd, Envmtl Policy, RSPB, 1998–2000 and 2001–06; Dir, Green Alliance, 2000–01. Member: Renewables Wkg Gp, US President's Initiative on Climate Change Technol. Strategy, 1997; Energy Adv. Panel, 1999–2003, Renewables Adv. Bd, 2006–10, DECC (formerly DTI); Envmtl Adv. Gp, Ofgem, 2002–10; Envmtl Innovations Adv. Gp, BERR (formerly DTI)-DEFRA, 2003–08; Sustainable Develt Task Force, DEFRA, 2003–05; Bd, Renewable Fuels Agency, 2007–10; World Business Council on Sustainable Develt, 2015–; Exec. Cttee, Oil and Gas Climate Initiative, 2015–. Non-executive Director: Renewable Energy Policy Project, 1997–98; Carbon Trust, 2001–; Carbon Trust Investments Ltd, 2003–12; SITA Trust, 2005–08; Mem., Adv. Bd, SITA UK, 2009–11. Member: Adv. Bd and Annual Assessment Panel, Tyndall Centre for Climate Change Res., 2000–06; Steering Bd, (Univ. of) Sussex Energy Gp, 2005–10. Member: Green Globe Network, 2000; Bd, Eur. Envmtl Bureau, 2000–01 (Chm., EEB-UK, 2000–01); Bd, Low-Carbon Vehicle Partnership, 2003–08. Trustee, Nat. Energy Foundn, 2005–08. *Publications:* (ed with W. J. Mahon) Proceedings of the Harvard Celtic Colloquium, Vol IV 1984, Vol V 1985; reports, briefing papers and articles on sustainable develt, envmt, energy and transport policy, incl. contribs to Science jl. *Recreations:* reading, running, travelling, maintaining a listed building. *Address:* The Mill House, 61 Mill Street, Gamlingay, Cambs SG19 3JS. *T:* 07770 342123. *E:* paul.jefferiss@bp.com.

**JEFFERSON, Prof. Ann Margaret,** FBA 2004; Fellow and Tutor in French, New College, Oxford, 1987–2015, now Emeritus Fellow; Professor of French, University of Oxford, 2006–15; *b* 3 Nov. 1949; *d* of Antony and Eirlys Jefferson; *m* 1st, 1971, Anthony Glees (marr. diss. 1992); two *s* one *d*; 2nd, 2011, Michael Holland. *Educ:* St Anne's Coll., Oxford (BA Hons 1971; MA); Wolfson Coll., Oxford (DPhil 1976). University of Oxford: Jun. Res. Fellow, 1978–82, Lectr in French, 1982–87, St John's Coll.; CUF Lectr in French, Fac. of Mod. Langs, 1987–2006. Visiting Professor: Columbia Univ., 2006; (Chaire Dupront), Sorbonne, Univ. Paris IV, 2008. Fellow, Paris Inst. of Advanced Studies, 2016. Commandeur, Ordre des Palmes Académiques (France), 2012 (Officière, 2001). *Publications:* The Nouveau Roman and the Poetics of Fiction, 1980; (with D. Robey) Modern Literary Theory: a comparative introduction, 1982, rev. edn 1986; Reading Realism in Stendhal, 1988; Nathalie Sarraute, Fiction and Theory: questions of difference, 2000; Stendhal: La Chartreuse de Parme, 2003; Biography and the Question of Literature in France, 2007; (trans.) Le Défi biographique, 2012; Genius in France: an idea and its uses, 2015. *Address:* New College, Oxford OX1 3BN. *E:* ann.jefferson@new.ox.ac.uk.

**JEFFERSON, Joan Ena;** see Appleyard, J. E.

**JEFFERSON, Sir John Alexander D.;** see Dunnington-Jefferson.

**JEFFERSON, William Hayton,** OBE 1985; Director, Portugal, British Council, and Cultural Counsellor, Lisbon, 1996–98; *b* 29 July 1940; *s* of late Stanley Jefferson and Josephine (*née* Hayton); *m* 1st, 1963, Marie-Jeanne Mazenq (marr. diss. 1986); three *s*; 2nd, 1986, Fadia Georges Tarraf; one *s*. *Educ:* Nelson-Thomlinson Grammar Sch., Wigton, Cumbria; Wadham Coll., Oxford (MA 1966). Russian teacher, 1963–66; with British Council, 1967–98: Tripoli, 1967–70; Kuwait, 1970–72; Algeria, 1972–75; Director: Qatar, 1975–79; Overseas Co-operation, London, 1979–82; United Arab Emirates, 1982–85; Algeria, 1985–90; Dir, Czechoslovakia, and Cultural Counsellor, Prague, 1990–96. Mem. (Ind) Allerdale Borough Council, Cumbria, 1999–; Chairman: N Allerdale Regeneration Gp, 2001–06; Jt Adv. Cttee, Solway Coast Area of Outstanding Natural Beauty, Cumbria, 2002–; Lake Dist Nat. Park Authy, 2008–14 (Mem., 2007–). Pres., Cumbria Co. Bowling Assoc., 2005–07. Gold Medal: Czech Scientific Univ., 1995; Palacky Univ., Olomouc, 1996; Silver Medal: Charles Univ., Prague, 1996; Masaryk Univ., Brno, 1996. *Recreation:* Cumbrian local history and dialect. *Address:* 3 Marine Terrace, Silloth, Cumbria CA7 4BZ. *T:* (01697) 332526.

**JEFFERTS SCHORI, Most Rev. Katharine,** PhD; Assisting Bishop, Episcopal Diocese of San Diego, 2017–19; *b* 26 March 1954; *m* 1979, Richard Miles Schori; one *d*. *Educ:* Stanford Univ. (BS 1974); Oregon State Univ. (MS Oceanography 1977; PhD 1983); Church Divinity Sch. of the Pacific (MDiv 1994). Ordained deacon and priest, 1994; Pastoral Associate, then Asst Rector, Episcopal Ch of the Good Samaritan, Corvallis, Oregon, and Priest-in-charge, El Buen Samaritano, Corvallis, 1994–2001; Bishop of Nevada, 2001–06; Presiding Bishop, Episcopal Church in the USA, 2006–15. *Publications:* A Wing and a Prayer: a message of faith and hope, 2007; The Gospel in the Global Village: seeking God's dream of Shalom, 2009; Gathering at God's Table: the five marks of mission in the feast of faith, 2012; The Heartbeat of God: finding the sacred in the middle of everything, 2015.

**JEFFERY, Prof. Charles Adrian,** CBE 2016; PhD; Vice Chancellor and President, University of York, since 2019; *b* 27 July 1964; *yr s* of late Frank Jeffery and June Jeffery (now Addington); *m* 1998, Elke Lieve Versmessen; one *s* two *d*. *Educ:* Univ. of Loughborough (BA 1985; PhD 1990). Lecturer: in Eur. Hist., N Staffs Poly., 1988–89; in W Eur. Politics, Leicester Univ., 1989–94; Institute for German Studies, University of Birmingham: Sen. Res. Fellow, 1994–96; Reader, 1996–99; Prof. of German Politics and Dep. Dir, 1999–2004; University of Edinburgh: Prof. of Politics, 2004–19; Vice Principal, 2011–14; Sen. Vice Principal, 2014–19. Joint Editor: Regl and Fed. Studies, 1995–2012; German Politics, 2001–05. Member: Res. Adv. Bd, Cttee on Standards in Public Life, 2001–06; Commn on Consequences of Devolution for H of C, 2012–13. Specialist Advr, Select Cttee on ODPM, 2004–05. Director: ESRC Res. Prog. on Devolution and Const. Change, 2000–06; ESRC Future of the UK and Scotland Prog., 2013–15. Mem., ESRC, 2005–11. Chairman: Assoc. for Study of German Politics, 1999–2000 and 2005–08; Political Studies Assoc., 2011–14 (Pres., 2014–15; Vice Pres., 2015–). FAcSS (AcSS 2004). FRSE 2007. *Publications:* (jtly) German Federalism Today, 1991; Social Democracy in the Australian Provinces 1918–1934, 1995; The Regional Dimension of the European Union, 1997; Recasting German Federalism, 1998; (jtly) Germany's European Diplomacy, 2000; Verfassungspolitik und Verfassungswandel: Deutschland und Grossbritannien im Vergleich, 2001; (jtly) Devolution and Electoral Politics, 2006; (jtly) The Scottish Parliament, The First Decade, 2009; (jtly) Rethinking Germany and Europe, 2010; (jtly) Citizenship after the Nation-State, 2013. *Recreations:* food and cooking, rock music, running. *Address:* University of York, York YO10 5DD. *T:* (01904) 322009. *E:* vc@york.ac.uk.

**JEFFERY, David John,** CBE 2000; Chief Executive, British Marine Equipment Council, 2000–01; *b* 18 Feb. 1936; *s* of late Stanley John Friend Jeffery and Sylvia May (*née* Mashford); *m* 1959, Margaret (*née* Yates); one *s* two *d*. *Educ:* Sutton High Sch., Plymouth; Croydon Coll. of Technology. Nat. Service, RAOC, 1954–56; Admiralty Dir of Stores Dept, 1956–66; RN Staff Coll., 1967; MoD, 1968–70; on secondment, 1970–76: Treasury Centre for Admin. Studies, 1970–72; Management Science Training Adviser, Malaysian Govt, Kuala Lumpur, 1972–74; Civil Service Dept, 1974–76; MoD, 1976–83; RCDS, 1983; Dir, Armaments and Management Services, RN Supply and Transport Service 1984–86; Chief Exec. and Bd Mem., PLA, 1986–99. Chm., Estuary Services Ltd, 1988–99. Director: UK Major Ports Ltd, 1993–99; British Ports Industry Trng Ltd, 1993–99 (Chm., 1998–99); Trustee Dir, Pilots' Nat. Pension Fund, 1987–95; Vice-Pres. of Conf., Internat. Assoc. of Ports and Harbors, 1995–97; Chairman: European Sea Ports Orgn, 1997–99; DTI Ports Sector Gp, 1998–2002; Mem., European Maritime Industries High Level Panel, 1994–95, Marine Foresight Panel, 1997–99. Orgnl Develt Advr, VSO, Kathmandu, 2004–06. Chm., Frome CAB, 2001–04. Governor: Selwood Middle Sch., Frome, 2001–04; Trinity Sch., Frome, 2014–15. Freeman, City of London, 1987; Mem., Co. of Watermen and Lightermen of River Thames, 1987. *Recreations:* theatre, music, travel, trekking. *Address:* Apartment 9, West Hill House, West End, Frome, Somerset BA11 3AD.

**JEFFERY, Prof. Nicholas David,** PhD; FRCVS; Professor of Neurology and Neurosurgery, College of Veterinary Medicine, Texas A&M University, since 2016; *b* 1 May 1958; *s* of John and Jill Jeffery; *m* 2005, Kat (marr. diss. 2010); three *s*; *m* 2011, Unity Locke. *Educ:* Bristol Univ. (BVSc); Wolfson Coll., Cambridge (PhD); London Sch. of Hygiene and Tropical Medicine. FRCVS; Dip. ECVN; Dip. ECVS; Dip. SAS. Veterinary Officer, PDSA, 1981–83; Veterinary Surgeon: Citivet, E1, 1983–90; Animal Health Trust, 1990–93; Wellcome Trust Scholarship, Cambridge Univ., 1993–97; Wellcome Trust Fellowship, UCL, 1997–2000; Lectr in Veterinary Neurol., 2000–06, Prof. of Veterinary Clinical Studies, 2006–10, Univ. of Cambridge; Prof. of Neurol. and Neurosurgery, Lloyd Vet Med. Center, Iowa State Univ., 2010–16. *Publications:* Handbook of Small Animal Spinal Surgery, 1995; contrib. veterinary and neurosci. jls. *Recreations:* dog walking, TV, crosswords, reading the newspaper. *Address:* College of Veterinary Medicine, Texas A&M University, 4474 College Station, TX 77843, USA.

**JEFFERY, Maj.-Gen. the Hon. (Philip) Michael,** AC 1996 (AO (mil.) 1988); CVO 2000; MC 1971; Governor-General of Australia, 2003–08; *b* 12 Dec. 1937; *s* of Philip Frederick Jeffery and Edna Mary Jeffery (*née* Johnson); *m* 1967, Marlena Joy Kerr; three *s* one *d*. *Educ:* Kent Street High Sch., WA; Royal Mil. Coll., Duntroon. Served Infantry, 1958–93: jun. regtl appts, 17 Nat. Service Trng Co. and SAS Regt, 1959–62; Operational Service, Malaya, Borneo and Vietnam, 1962–72; psc 1972; Commanding Officer: 2nd Bn

Pacific Islands Regt, PNG, 1974–75; SAS Regt, Perth, 1976–77; jssc 1978; Dir, Special Forces, 1979–81; Comd, 1 Bde, Sydney, 1983–84; rcds 1985; comd, 1 Div., Brisbane, 1986–88; DCGS, Canberra, 1990–91; ACGS Materiel, 1991–93. Gov., WA, 1993–2000. Founding Chm. and Patron, Future Directions Internat. Ltd, 2001–03 and 2008–. Chairman: Outcomes Australia, 2008–17; Royal Flying Doctor Service of Australia, 2009–12; Global Foundn, 2009–12; Diamond Jubilee Trust of Australia, 2012; Soils for Life, 2012–; Constitution Educn Fund Australia, 2015–; Nat. Advocate for Soil Health, 2012–. Mem., United Services Inst., Canberra, 1978–. Hon. DTech Curtin, 2000. Citizen of WA, 2000. KStJ 1995. Grand Companion, Order of Logohu (PNG), 2005. *Recreations:* golf, fishing, music. *Address:* 18 Hampton Circuit, Yarralumla, ACT 2600, Australia. *Clubs:* Commonwealth (Canberra); Royal Canberra Golf.

**JEFFERY, Sir Thomas (Baird),** Kt 2015; CB 2006; Director General, Children Services and Departmental Strategy (formerly Children, Young People and Families), Department for Education (formerly Director General, Children, Young People and Families, Department for Education and Skills, then Director General, Children and Families, Department for Children, Schools and Families), 2003–14; *b* 11 Feb. 1953; *s* of Herbert George, (Jeff), Jeffery and Margaret (*née* Thornton); *m* 1987, Alison Nisbet; one *s* one *d*. *Educ:* King's Sch., Canterbury; Jesus Coll., Cambridge (MA Eng. Lit.); Centre for Contemporary Cultural Studies, Univ. of Birmingham. Joined DES, 1981; Private Sec. to Perm. Sec., 1984–85; Principal Private Sec. to Sec. of State, 1987–89; Dir, Student Loans Co., 1989–92; Head: Special Educnl Needs Div., 1992–95; Personnel and Related Roles, 1995–98; on secondment to DoH as Hd, Children's Services, 1998–2001; Dir, Children and Families Group, DfES, 2001–03. Mem. Bd, Nat. Develt Team for Inclusion, 2015–. *Publications:* (contrib.) Impacts and Influences, 1987; (contrib.) Metropolis London, 1989; (contrib.) Splintered Classes, 1990; Mass-Observation: a short history, 1999. *Recreations:* family, walking, cricket, modern history and literature. *Club:* MCC.

**JEFFERYS, Dr David Barrington,** FFPM, FRCP, FRCPE; Senior Vice President, Global Regulatory Affairs, Government Relations and Patient Safety, Eisai Europe Ltd, since 2011; *b* 1 Aug. 1952; *s* of Godfrey B. Jefferys and Joyce E. Jefferys; *m* 1985, Ann-Marie Smith; one *s* one *d*. *Educ:* St Dunstan's Coll.; Guy's Hosp. Med. Sch., Univ. of London (BSc Hons; MB BS 1976; MD 1983). FFPM 1990; FRCPE 1990; FRCP 1992. Medical posts at Guy's and St Thomas' Hosps, 1976–83; locum consultant physician, Tunbridge Wells, 1983–84; SMO, DoH, 1984–86; PMO and Principal Assessor to Cttee on Safety of Medicines, 1986; Medicines Control Agency: Business Manager, Eur. and New Drug Licensing, 1986–94; Dir, Licensing Div., 1994–2000; Chief Exec. and Dir, Medical Devices Agency, 2000–03; Actg Hd, Med. Devices Sector, Medicines and Healthcare products Regulatory Agency, 2003. Sen. Strategic Regulatory Advr, Eisai Europe, 2005–06; Vice Pres., 2006–08, Sen. Vice Pres., Global Regulatory Affairs, 2008–11, Eisai Research and Develt Co. Ltd, subseq. Eisai Europe Ltd. Vis. Prof. in Medicine, Univ. of Newcastle upon Tyne, 1994. UK Deleg. to Cttee on Proprietary Medicinal Products, 1995–2000. Chm., Mutual Recognition Facilitation Gp, EU, 1997–98. Member: EU Med. Device Expert Gp; Global Harmonisation Task Force Steering Cttee. Pres., Regulatory Affairs Professional Soc., 2008–10 (Chm. Bd, 2009–10); Pres. and Chm., Orgn for Professionals in Regulatory Affairs, 2011–12; Co-Chm., Regulatory Policy and Tech. Standards Cttee, 2013–, Chm., Regulatory Sci. Cttee, 2018–, Internat. Fedn of Pharmaceutical Manufrs and Assocs. Mem. Bd and Trustee, Faculty of Pharmaceutical Medicine, 2017–. Chm., Health and Wellbeing Bd, Bromley, 2015–; Mem., President's Cttee, Young Epilepsy, 2012–. Mem. (C), Bromley LBC, 2011–. Public Gov., KCH Foundn Trust, 2017–. Pres., Old Dunstonian Assoc., 2013–14. Church Warden, St Mary's Shortlands, 2009–16. FRSocMed 2004. Freeman, City of London, 2002–; Liveryman: Soc. of Apothecaries, 2008–; Glovers' Co. 2017–. *Publications:* chapters in books and articles on medicines regulation, regulatory policy and quality assurance. *Recreations:* sport, ski-ing, theatre, music, art. *Club:* Surrey County Cricket.

**JEFFERYS, Judith Patricia;** see Armitage, J. P.

**JEFFORD, Andrew Christopher;** author, journalist and broadcaster, since 1988; *b* Berkeley, 14 March 1956; *s* of Peter and Celia Jefford; *m* 1st, 1980, Bogumila Magdalena Kaczanowska (marr. diss. 2006); 2nd, 2008, Paula Tracy Grech; two *s*. *Educ:* Gresham's Sch., Norfolk; Reading Univ. (BA 1st Cl. Hons English Lit.); Univ. of E Anglia (MA with dist. 19th and 20th Century Novel 1980). Ed., Octopus Books, 1983–88; Wine Corresp., Evening Standard, 1992–2002; columnist: Decanter mag., 1998–; Waitrose Food Illustrated mag., 2000–10; World of Fine Wine mag., 2003–; travel and drink writer, FT, 2004–; Wine Writer-in-Residence, Wine 2030 Res. Network, 2009–10. Occasional presenter, Food Prog., BBC Radio 4, 1995–2008. Sen. Res. Fellow, Univ. of Adelaide, 2009–10. *Publications:* Port: an essential guide to the classic drink, 1988; Which? Wine Guide, 1991; The Wines of Germany, 1994; The Evening Standard Wine Guide, 1996, 1997; Smokes, 1997; One Hundred and One Things You Need to Know About Wine, 1998; Wine Tastes, Wine Styles, 2000; The New France, 2002; After-Dinner Drinks, 2003; Choosing Wine, 2003; Peat Smoke and Spirit: a portrait of Islay and its whiskies, 2004, republd as Whisky Island, 2019; Andrew Jefford's Wine Course, 2008; contributor: Robert Louis Stevenson, 1983; (with P. Draper) Questions of Taste: the philosophy of wine, 2007; Whiskey and Philosophy: a small batch of spirited ideas, 2009. *Recreations:* music, swimming, walking, reading, thinking. *Address:* c/o Watson Little, Suite 315, Screenworks, 22 Highbury Grove, N5 2ER. *E:* andrewjefford@gmail.com. *W:* www.andrewjefford.com.

**JEFFORD, Barbara Mary,** OBE 1965; actress; *b* Plymstock, Devon, 26 July 1930; *d* of late Percival Francis Jefford and Elizabeth Mary Ellen (*née* Laity); *m* 1953, Terence Longdon (marr. diss. 1961); *m* 1967, John Arnold Turner. *Educ:* Weirfield Sch., Taunton, Som. Studied for stage, Bristol and Royal Academy of Dramatic Art (Bancroft Gold Medal). *Royal Shakespeare Co.:* Stratford-on-Avon, 1950–54: Isabella in Measure for Measure; Anne Bullen in Henry VIII; Hero in Much Ado About Nothing; Lady Percy in Henry IV parts I and II; Desdemona in Othello; Rosalind in As You Like It; Helena in A Midsummer Night's Dream; Katharina in The Taming of the Shrew; Patsy Newquist in Little Murders, Aldwych, 1967; Volumnia in Coriolanus, 1989 and 1990; Tatyana in Barbarians, 1990; Countess in All's Well That Ends Well, Mistress Quickly in The Merry Wives of Windsor, 1992; Katia in Misha's Party, 1993; Countess Terzky in Wallenstein, 1993–94; *Old Vic Company:* (1956–62) Imogen in Cymbeline; Beatrice in Much Ado About Nothing; Portia in The Merchant of Venice; Julia in Two Gentlemen of Verona; Tamora in Titus Andronicus; Lady Anne in Richard III; Queen Margaret in Henry VI parts I, II and III; Isabella in Measure for Measure; Regan in King Lear; Viola in Twelfth Night; Ophelia in Hamlet; Rosalind in As You Like It; St Joan; Lady Macbeth; Gwendoline in The Importance of Being Earnest; Beatrice Cenci; Lavinia in Mourning Becomes Electra; *for Prospect, at Old Vic:* (1977–79) Gertrude in Hamlet; Cleopatra in All for Love; Cleopatra in Antony and Cleopatra; Nurse in Romeo and Juliet; Anna in The Government Inspector; RSC Nat. Tour, 1980, Mistress Quickly in Henry IV pts 1 and 2; *National Theatre:* Gertrude in Hamlet, Zabina in Tamburlaine the Great, 1976; Mother in Six Characters in Search of an Author, Arina Bazarov in Fathers and Sons, Salathiel in Ting Tang Mine (Clarence Derwent Award, 1988), 1987; Sanctuary, 2002; Anne of Austria in Power, 2003. *Other London stage appearances include:* Andromache in Tiger at the Gates, Apollo, 1955, NY, 1956; Lina in Misalliance, Royal Court and Criterion, 1963; step-daughter in Six Characters in Search of an Author, Mayfair, 1963; Nan in Ride a Cock Horse, Piccadilly, 1965; Mother Vauzou in Mistress of Novices, Piccadilly, 1973; Filumena, Lyric, 1979; Duchess of York in Richard II, and Queen Margaret in Richard III, Phoenix, 1988–89; Oenone in Phèdre, Albina in Britannicus, Albery, 1998, NY, 1999; Duchess of York in Richard II, and Volumnia in Coriolanus, Almeida at Gainsborough Studios, NY and Tokyo, 2000; Mary in The Old Masters, Comedy, 2004; Hanna in Mary Stuart, Donmar, 2005; *other stage appearances include:* Hedda Gabler, Medea; Phaedra, Oxford Playhouse, 1966; Lady Sneerwell in The School for Scandal, toured UK, 1995; Our Betters, Chichester, 1997; Queen Margaret in Richard III, Crucible Th., Sheffield, 2002; Mrs Higgins in Pygmalion, Th. Royal Bath and tour, 2007, transf. Old Vic, 2008; has toured extensively in UK, Europe, USA, Near East, Far East, Africa, Australia, Russia, Poland and Yugoslavia. *Films:* Ulysses, 1967; A Midsummer Night's Dream, 1967; The Shoes of the Fisherman, 1968; To Love a Vampire, 1970; Hitler: the last ten days, 1973; And the Ship Sails On, 1983; Why the Whales Came, 1988; Reunion, 1988; Where Angels Fear to Tread, 1991; The Ninth Gate, 1999; The Deep Blue Sea, 2011; Philomena, 2012. Has appeared in numerous television and radio plays. Hon. DLitt Exeter, 2004. Pragnell Shakespeare Award, 1994. Silver Jubilee Medal, 1977. *Recreations:* music, swimming, gardening. *Address:* c/o United Agents Ltd, 12–26 Lexington Street, W1F 0LE.

**JEFFORD, Hon. Dame Nerys (Angharad),** DBE 2016; **Hon. Mrs Justice Jefford;** a Judge of the High Court of Justice, Queen's Bench Division, since 2016; Presiding Judge, Wales Circuit, from Jan. 2020; *b* Swansea, 25 Dec. 1962; *d* of John Keith Jefford and late Eirlys Rona Jefford. *Educ:* Olchfa Comprehensive Sch.; Lady Margaret Hall, Oxford (Schol.; BA 1984); Univ. of Virginia (Fulbright Schol.; LLM 1985). MCIArb 2006. Called to the Bar, Gray's Inn, 1986 (Lord Justice Holker Schol.; Karmel Schol.), Bencher, 2007; in practice at the Bar, 1988–2016; a Recorder, 2007–16; QC 2008. Bar Standards Board: Mem., Educn and Trng Cttee, 2007–15 (Vice Chm., 2013–15); Mem., Professional Conduct Cttee, 2016. Mem. Council, Soc. of Construction Law, 2002–09 (Chm., 2007–08). Mem., Adv. Council, Lady Margaret Hall, Oxford, 2006–. Trustee, Tech 4 All, 2013–. Sec., London Welsh Chorale, 2011–14. *Publications:* Keating on Construction Contracts, 8th edn 2016 to 10th edn 2016; (contrib.) Keating on Building Contracts, 5th edn 1991 to 8th edn 2006; (ed) Bullen, Leake and Jacob's Precedents of Pleadings, HK edn, 2013. *Recreation:* choral singing (London Welsh Chorale; Gray's Inn Chapel Choir; The Harry Ensemble). *Address:* Royal Courts of Justice, Strand, WC2A 2LL.

**JEFFREY, Dianne Michele,** CBE 2011; DL; Chairman: Age UK, 2009–18; Age International, 2012–18 (Trustee, since 2018); *b* Sheffield, 23 Nov. 1944; *d* of Cyril and Eve Cantor; *m* 1965, Nicholas Jeffrey; two *s* two *d*. *Educ:* Sheffield High Sch.; Badminton Sch., Bristol; Sheffield Univ. (BA). Chm., Digital Outreach Ltd, 2007–15. Chm., Community Healthcare (N Derbys) NHS Trust, 1994–2002. Chm., NHS Confedn, 2000–03. Mem., Regl Cttee, HLF, 2007–13. Vice Chm., Derwent Valley Mills World Heritage Site, 2011–14; Chair, Strategic Adv. Gp, Peak Nat. Park, 2012–. Chm., Malnutrition Task Force, 2013–. Chm., Anchor Trust, 2003–08; Trustee, Devonshire Educnl Trust, 2013–. Chm., Governing Council, Univ. of Derby, 2002–11. Chm., Derbys Armed Forces Covenant, 2018–. Hon. Col, Derbys Army Cadet Force, 2004–14. High Sheriff, 2002–03, DL 2004, Derbys. DUniv Derby, 2012; Hon Dr Sheffield Hallam, 2014. *Recreations:* music, ski-ing, opera, gardening, walking. *Address:* Eyam, Derbyshire. *E:* diannejeffrey@gmail.com. *Clubs:* Royal Automobile, Royal Society of Medicine.

**JEFFREY, Joan;** see MacNaughton, J.

**JEFFREY, Sir William Alexander,** KCB 2008 (CB 2001); Permanent Secretary, Ministry of Defence, 2005–10; *b* 28 Feb. 1948; *s* of Alexander and Joyce Jeffrey; *m* 1979, Joan MacNaughton, *qv*. *Educ:* Allan Glen's, Glasgow; Univ. of Glasgow (BSc Hons). Home Office, 1971–94: Private Sec. to Permanent Under Sec. of State, 1975–76; Principal, 1976–84; Assistant Secretary: Criminal Policy Dept, 1984–88; HM Prison Service, 1988–91; Asst Under Sec. of State, Immigration and Nationality Dept, 1991–94; Under Sec., Economic and Domestic Affairs Secretariat, Cabinet Office, 1994–98; Dep. Sec., NI Office, 1998–2002; Dir Gen., Immigration and Nationality, Home Office, 2002–05; Security and Intelligence Co-ordinator and Permanent Sec., Cabinet Office, 2005. Chm. of Trustees, Police Foundn, 2011–; Chm., Civil Service Healthcare, 2011–15; Chair, Implementation Bd for successor to ACPO, 2014–15. Reviewer, Rev. of Ind. Advocacy in Criminal Courts, 2013–14. DUniv Strathclyde, 2008. *Recreations:* reading, hill-walking, watching football.

**JEFFREYS,** family name of **Baron Jeffreys**.

**JEFFREYS,** 3rd Baron *cr* 1952, of Burkham; **Christopher Henry Mark Jeffreys;** stockbroker, since 1992; *b* 22 May 1957; *s* of 2nd Baron Jeffreys and of Sarah Annabelle Mary, *d* of late Major Henry Garnett; *S* father, 1986; *m* 1985, Anne Elisabeth Johnson; one *s* one *d*. *Educ:* Eton. With: GNI Ltd, 1985–90; Raphael Zorn Hemsley, 1992–2000; Savoy Investment Mgt, 2000–12; Ashcourt Rowan Asset Mgt, 2012–15; Towry Asset Mgt, 2015–16; Tilney Investment Mgt, 2016–. *Recreation:* country sports. *Heir: s* Hon. Arthur Mark Henry Jeffreys, *b* 18 Feb. 1989. *Address:* Bank House, 3 Main Street, Sproxton, Leics LE14 4QS. *T:* (01476) 861008.

**JEFFREYS, Alan Howard,** QC 1996; a Recorder, 1993–2004; *b* 27 Sept. 1947; *s* of late Hugh and Rachel Jeffreys; *m* 1975, Jane Olivia Sadler; one *s* one *d*. *Educ:* Ellesmere Coll.; King's College, London (LLB Hons). Called to the Bar, Gray's Inn, 1970; South Eastern Circuit; Asst Recorder, 1989–93. Mem., Criminal Injuries Compensation Appeals Panel (formerly Criminal Injuries Compensation Bd), 1999–2002. Mem., Exec. Cttee, Personal Injuries Bar Assoc., 2006–09. *Recreations:* fishing, chess, music. *Address:* Farrar's Building, Temple, EC4Y 7BD. *T:* (020) 7583 9241. *Club:* Hurlingham.

**JEFFREYS, Sir Alec John,** CH 2017; Kt 1994; FRS 1986; Wolfson Research Professor of the Royal Society, University of Leicester, 1991–2012 (Professor of Genetics, 1987–2012, now Emeritus); *b* 9 Jan. 1950; *s* of Sidney Victor Jeffreys and Joan (*née* Knight); *m* 1971, Susan Miles; two *d*. *Educ:* Luton Grammar School; Luton VIth Form College; Merton College, Oxford (Postmaster; Christopher Welch Schol.). BA, MA, DPhil 1975; Hon. Fellow, 1990). EMBO Research Fellow, Univ. of Amsterdam, 1975–77; Leicester University: Lectr, Dept of Genetics, 1977–84; Reader, 1984–87; Lister Inst. Res. Fellow, 1982–91. Member: EMBO, 1983; Human Genome Orgn, 1989. Editor, Jl of Molecular Evolution, 1985. FRCPath 1991; FLS 1994; Founder FMedSci 1998. Hon. FRCP 1993; Hon. FIBiol 1998; Hon. FRSocMed 2001. Fellow, Forensic Sci. Soc. of India, 1989; Hon. Mem., Amer. Acad. of Forensic Scis, 1998. Hon. Fellow, Univ. of Luton, 1995. DUniv Open, 1991; Hon. DSc: St Andrews, 1996; Strathclyde, 1998; Hull, 2004; Oxford, 2004. Colworth Medal for Biochemistry, Biochem. Soc., 1985; Carter Medal, Clinical Genetics Soc., 1987, 2003; Davy Medal, Royal Soc., 1987; Linnean Soc. Bicentenary Medal, 1987; Analytika Prize, German Soc. for Clin. Chem., 1988; Press, Radio and TV Award, Midlander of the Year, 1989; Linnean Medal, 1994; Sir Frederick Gowland Hopkins Meml Medal, Biochem. Soc., 1996; Albert Einstein World of Science Award, World Cultural Council, 1996; Baly Medal, RCP, 1997; SCI Medal, 1997; Sir George Stokes Medal, RSC, 2000; Gold Medal, RCS, 2004; Copley Medal, Royal Soc., 2014. Hon. Freeman, City of

Leicester, 1993. UK Patents on genetic fingerprints. *Publications:* research articles on molecular genetics and evolution in Nature, Cell, etc. *Recreations:* walking, swimming, postal history, reading unimproving novels.

**JEFFREYS, Annabel Kate;** *see* Arden, A. K.

**JEFFREYS, David Alfred;** QC 1981; a Recorder of the Crown Court, 1979–99; *b* 1 July 1934; *s* of late Coleman and Ruby Jeffreys; *m* 1964, Mary Ann Elizabeth Long; one *s* one *d*. *Educ:* Harrow; Trinity Coll., Cambridge (BA Hons). Served, Royal Signals, 1952–54; City, 1958. Called to the Bar, Gray's Inn, 1958, Bencher, 1989; Junior Prosecuting Counsel to the Crown, Central Criminal Court, 1975; Sen. Prosecuting Counsel to the Crown, CCC, 1979–81; Jt Head, Hollis Whiteman Chambers, 1995–99, retd. Mem., Bar Council, 1977–80. *Address:* c/o 1–2 Laurence Pountney Hill, EC4R 0EU.

**JEFFREYS, Prof. Elizabeth Mary;** Bywater and Sotheby Professor of Byzantine and Modern Greek Language and Literature, University of Oxford, 1996–2006; Fellow of Exeter College, Oxford, since 1996; *b* 22 July 1941; *d* of Lawrence R. Brown and Veronica Thompson; *m* 1965, Michael J. Jeffreys; one *d*. *Educ:* Blackheath High Sch. for Girls (GPDST); Girton Coll., Cambridge (MA (Class. Tripos)); St Anne's Coll., Oxford (BLitt; Hon. Fellow, 1997). Classics Mistress, Mary Datchelor Girls' Sch., 1965–69; Sen. Res. Fellow, Warburg Inst., London Univ., 1969–72; Vis. Fellow, Dumbarton Oaks Centre for Byzantine Studies, 1972–74, 1984; Res. Fellow, Ioannina Univ., Greece, 1974–76; part-time Lectr, univs in Sydney, Australia, 1976–86; Vis. Fellow, Humanities Centre, Canberra, 1978; Res. Fellow, Melbourne Univ., 1987–89; Res. Fellow, 1990–92, Australian Sen. Res. Fellow, 1993–95, Sydney Univ. Fellow, Australian Acad. of Humanities, 1993. *Publications:* Byzantine Papers, 1981; Popular Literature in Late Byzantium, 1983; The Chronicle of John Malalas: a translation, 1986; Studies in John Malalas, 1990; The War of Troy, 1996; Digenis Akritis, 1998; Through the Looking Glass, 2000; Rhetoric in Byzantium, 2003; The Age of the Dromon, 2006; Oxford Handbook of Byzantine Studies, 2008; Iacobi Monachi Epistulae, 2009; Four Byzantine Novels, 2012. *Recreation:* walking. *Address:* Exeter College, Oxford OX1 3DP.

**JEFFREYS, Louise;** Artistic Director (formerly Director of Programming, then Director of Arts), Barbican Centre, since 2010; *b* Whitstable, Kent; *d* of Peter Jeffreys and Sylvia Taylor. *Educ:* City of London Freemen's Sch.; Univ. of Manchester (BA Hons Drama 1978). Tech. Dir, ENO, 1990–94; Hd of Prodn, Bavarian State Opera, Munich, 1994–96; Admin. Dir, Nottingham Playhouse, 1996–98; Hd of Theatre, Barbican, London, 1999–2010. Chm., Assoc. of British Theatre Technicians, 2014–. Member, Board: Told by an Idiot, 2011–; ENO, 2016– (Vice Chair, Artistic Cttee, 2019). Mentor and exec. coach. Excellence in Internat. Theatre Award, Internat. Inst. of Dance and Theatre, 2018. FGS 2019. Freeman, City of London, 2019. *Recreations:* reading, walking, gardening. *Address:* Barbican Centre, Silk Street, EC2Y 8DS. *T:* (020) 7382 7381. *E:* louise.jeffreys@barbican.org.uk.

**JEFFREYS, Prof. Paul William,** PhD; CPhys; Professor of Computing, since 2002, Director, IT Risk Management, 2012–15, and Fellow, e-Research Centre, since 2006, University of Oxford; Fellow, Keble College, Oxford, 2001–15, now Emeritus; Information Governance Risk Manager, Diamond Light Source, since 2019; *b* 4 July 1954; *s* of George Lewis Jeffreys and Naomi Emily Jeffreys; *m* 1985, Linda Christine Pay; two *s* one *d*. *Educ:* Drayton Manor Grammar Sch., Hanwell; Univ. of Manchester (BSc Hons); Univ. of Bristol (PhD 1980). MA Oxon. CPhys 1982; MInstP 1982. CERN Fellow, Geneva, 1979–82; Rutherford Appleton Laboratory: physicist, 1982–95; Hd, Computing and Resource Mgt Div., Particle Physics Dept, 1995–2001; Leader, CCLRC e-Science Centre, 2000–01; University of Oxford: Dir, Oxford Univ. Computing Services, 2001–05; Dir, e-Science Centre, 2001–06; Dir, e-Horizons Inst., 2005–10; Acting Dir, 2005–07, Dir, 2007–12, Inf. and Communications Technol.; Vice-Pres., Sen. Common Room, Keble Coll., 2013–. Dir, Digitalspires, 2006–08; Digital Ops Prog. Lead, Inst. of Cancer Res., Univ. of London, 2015–19. Mem., FCO Academic Expert Network for internat. cyber security policy, 2014–. Trustee, Jisc, 2012–14. Mem., Editl Bd, British Jl of Interdisciplinary Studies, 2014–. *Recreations:* family life, ski-ing, squash, running, Real tennis. *Address:* Keble College, Oxford OX1 3PG. *T:* (01865) 273229, *Fax:* (01865) 283346.

**JEFFRIES, Michael Makepeace Eugene,** RIBA; FICE; Chairman: Civica Group Ltd, 2010–16; Mouchel Group plc, 2013–15; *b* 17 Sept. 1944; *s* of William Eugene Jeffries and Margaret Jeffries (*née* Makepeace); *m* 1966, Pamela Mary Booth; two *s* two *d*. *Educ:* Poly. of North London (DipArch Hons). RIBA 1973; FICE 2003. Architectural Assistant: John Laing & Sons Ltd, 1963–67; Surrey CC, 1967–68; Gillespie & Steele, Trinidad, 1968–69; Deeks Bousell Partnership, London, 1969–73; Senior Architect: Bradshaw Gass & Hope, Lancs, 1973–75; W. S. Atkins Ltd, 1975–78; Man. Dir, ASFA Ltd, 1978; Dir, W. S. Atkins Gp Consultants Ltd, 1979–92; Mkting and Business Develt Dir, W. S. Atkins Ltd, 1992–95; W. S. Atkins plc: Chief Exec., 1995–2001; Chm., 2001–04. Non-executive Director: De La Rue, 2000–07; Worksmart Ltd, 2013–; Tenderspace, 2016–. Chairman: Wembley Nat. Stadium Ltd, 2002–08; Parking Internat. Hldgs Ltd (NCP), 2005–07; NCP Services Ltd, 2008–10; VT Group plc, 2005–10; Priory Group, 2011–14; Purpose Hldgs Ltd, 2018–. Chm., Poole Arts Trust, 2016–. Governor: RNLI, 2007–14; Canford Sch., 2014–. *Publications:* various technical papers in jls. *Recreations:* sailing, golf, water colour painting, antiquarian horology. *Address:* Seaspray, 1 Gardens Road, Poole, Dorset BH14 8JF. *T:* (01202) 706051. *Club:* Royal Motor Yacht (Poole).

**JEFFRIES, Neil,** RA 2013; sculptor; Lecturer, Slade School of Fine Art, University College London; *b* Bristol, 7 Oct. 1959. *Educ:* St Martin's Sch. of Art; Slade Sch. of Fine Art. Exhibitions include: Riverside Studios, London, 1997; Flowers East, London, 1998; Oldham Art Gall., 1998; Flowers West, Santa Monica, 1999; Brighton Mus. and Art Gall., 2000; The Gallery, Gildenburgh Complex, Peterborough, 2001; Jeffrey Charles Gall., London, 2001; Flowers Central, London, 2003; Mall Galls, 2007; Art Space Gall., London, 2008, 2013; Summer Exhibn, RA, 2008, 2010, 2012.

**JEFFS, Julian;** QC 1975; author; *b* 5 April 1931; *s* of Alfred Wright Jeffs, Wolverhampton, and Janet Honor Irene (*née* Davies); *m* 1966, Deborah, *d* of Peter James Stuart Bevan; three *s*. *Educ:* Wrekin Coll.; Downing Coll., Cambridge (MA; Associate Fellow, 1986; Emeritus Associate Fellow, 2015). Nat. Service, Naval rating, 1949–50. Sherry Shipper's Asst, Spain, 1956. Barrister, Gray's Inn, 1958 (Bencher 1981), Inner Temple, 1971; Midland and Oxford Circuit; Hong Kong Bar; retired from practice, 1991; a Recorder, 1975–96; a Dep. High Court Judge, Chancery Div., 1981–96. Chm., Patent Bar Assoc., 1980–89; Member: Senate of Inns of Court and Bar, 1984–85; Bar Council, 1988–89. Gen. Comr of Income Tax, 1983–91. Editor, Wine and Food, 1965–67; Mem., Cttee of Management, International Wine & Food Soc., 1965–67, 1971–82; Chm., 1970–72, Vice-Pres., 1975–91, Pres., 1992–96, Life Trustee, 2014, Circle of Wine Writers. Gen. Editor, Faber's Wine Series, 1985–2002. Dep. Gauger, City of London, 1979. Freeman, City of London. Lauréat de l'Office International de la Vigne et du Vin, 1962 and 2001; Glenfiddich wine writer awards, 1974 and 1978. Mem., Gran Orden de Caballeros del Vino. Encomienda, Orden de Isabel la Católica (Spain), 2004. *Publications:* Sherry, 1961, 6th edn 2015; (an editor) Clerk and Lindsell on Torts, 13th edn 1969 to 16th edn 1989; The Wines of Europe, 1971; Little Dictionary of Drink, 1973; (jtly) Encyclopedia of United Kingdom and European Patent Law, 1977; The Wines of Spain, 1999, 2nd edn 2006; A Short History of

the Lodge of Antiquity No 2, 2007; (ed with Jocelyn Hillgarth) Maurice Baring: letters, 2007. *Recreations:* freemasonry, wine, old cars, musical boxes, follies, Iberian things. *Address:* Church Farm House, East Ilsley, Newbury, Berks RG20 7LP. *T:* (01635) 281216. *E:* julian.jeffs@btopenworld.com. *Clubs:* Beefsteak, Garrick, Reform, Saintsbury.

**JEHANGIR, Sir Cowasji,** 4th Bt *cr* 1908, of Bombay; *b* 23 Nov. 1953; *er s* of Sir Hirji Jehangir, 3rd Bt and of Jinoo, *d* of K. H. Cama; *S* father, 2000; *m* 1988, Jasmine, *d* of Beji Billimoria; one *s* one *d*. *Educ:* Cathedral and John Connon Sch., Bombay; Elphinstone Coll., Bombay (BA Econ). National Radio and Electronics Co. Ltd, Bombay, 1976–80. Chairman: Jehangir Hosp., Pune, 1989–; Hirabai C Jehangir Medical Res. Inst., Pune, 1995–; Jehangir Clinical Develt Centre Ltd, Pune, 2006–. Hon. Dir, Centre for Photography as an Art Form, Bombay, 1986–. Mem. Senate, Univ. of Pune, 1992–95. Trustee: Sir Cowasji Jehangir Sch., Bombay, 1976–; Jehangir Art Gall., Bombay, 2000–; Sir Ratan Tata Trust, Bombay, 2019–. *Recreations:* wildlife, photography, jazz, squash. *Heir: s* Cowasji Jehangir, *b* 28 March 1990. *Clubs:* Willingdon Sports, Bombay Gymkhana (Mumbai); Royal Western India Turf (Mumbai and Pune); Poona (Pune).

**JEJEEBHOY, Sir Jamsetjee,** 8th Bt *cr* 1857, of Bombay; *b* 16 Nov. 1957; *o s* of Sir Jamsetjee Jejeebhoy, 7th Bt and Shirin J. H. Cama; *S* father, 2006, and assumed name of Jamsetjee Jejeebhoy in lieu of Rustom Jejeebhoy; *m* 1984, Delara Jal Bhaisa; one *s*. *Educ:* Bombay Univ. (BCom 1979; LLM 1984). Dep. Man., Legal, Tata Exports Ltd, 1983–98; Vice Pres., India, Quantum Technologies Inc., 1998–2004. Dir, Beaulieu Investment Pvt. Ltd, 1975. Chairman: Parsi Dhandha Rojgar Fund, 2004; Sett Rustomjee Jamsetjee Jejeebhoy Gujarati Sch. Fund, 2006; Sir Jamsetjee Jejeebhoy Parsee Benevolent Institution, 2006; Sir Jamsetjee Jejeebhoy Charity Fund, 2006; Parsi Surat Charity Fund, 2013. Trustee: Destitute Eranis Charity Fund, 1990; Zoroastrian Building Fund, 2004; K. N. Bahadurji Meml Sanatorium for Parsis, 2014. Hon. Freeman and Liveryman, Clockmakers' Co., 2008. *Recreation:* collecting antiques. *Heir: s* Jehangir Jejeebhoy [*b* 20 Jan. 1986; *m* 2012, Naira Sam Variava]. *Address:* (residence) Beaulieu, 95 Worli Seaface, Mumbai 400030, India. *T:* 24938517; (office) Sir J J Charity Fund, Kalpataru Heritage Building, 5th Floor, 127 Mahatma Gandhi Road, Mumbai 400001, India. *T:* 22673843. *E:* jj@sjjcf.org. *Clubs:* Willingdon Sports, Royal Western India Turf, Ripon (Mumbai).

**JELINEK, Elfriede;** writer; *b* Mürzzuschlag, Austria, 20 Oct. 1946; *m* 1974, Gottfried Hüngsberg. *Educ:* Vienna Conservatory; Albertsgymnasium, Vienna; Univ. of Vienna. Writer of plays for radio, and for theatre incl. Raststätte, Das Werk, Jackie; screenplays: Die Ausgesperrten (TV), 1982; Malina (film), 1991; Das Werk (TV), 2004; opera libretto, Lost Highway, 2003. Nobel Prize for Literature, 2004. *Publications:* Lisas Schatten (poems), 1967; ende: Gedichte von 1966–1968, 1980; Die endlose Unschuldigkeit (essays), 1980; Was geschah, nachdem Nora ihren Mann verlassen hatte oder Stützen der Gesellschaften, 1980; Theaterstücke, 1984; Oh Wildnis, oh Schutz vor ihr, 1985; Krankheit oder moderne Frauen, 1987; Isabelle Huppert in Malina, 1991; Sturm und Zwang, 1995; Stecken, Stab und Stangl, 1997; er nicht als er, 1998; Macht nichts: eine kleine Trilogie des Todes, 1999; Der Tod und das Mädchen I–V: Prinzessinnendramen, 2003; Einar, 2006; Rein Gold, 2013; *novels:* wir sind lockvögel baby!, 1970; Michael: ein Jugendbuch für die Infantilgesellschaft, 1972; Die Liebhaberinnen, 1975 (Women as Lovers, 1994); bukolit, 1979; Die Ausgesperrten, 1980 (Wonderful, Wonderful Times, 1990); Die Klavierspielerin, 1983 (The Piano Teacher, 1988) (filmed, 2001); Lust, 1989 (Lust, 1992); Die Kinder der Toten, 1995; Gier: ein Unterhaltungsroman, 2000 (Greed, 2006); *plays:* Wolken. Heim, 1990; Totenauberg: ein Stück, 1991; Ein Sportstück, 1998 (Sports Play, 2012); Das Lebewohl, 2000; In den Alpen, 2002; Bambiland, Babel, 2004; Ulrike Maria Stuart, 2007; Drei Theaterstücke, 2009; Winterreise: ein Theaterstück, 2011; also translations of other writers' works. *Address:* c/o Serpent's Tail, 3 Holford Yard, Bevin Way, WC1X 9HD.

**JELLICOE,** family name of **Earl Jellicoe**.

**JELLICOE, 3rd Earl** *cr* 1925; **Patrick John Bernard Jellicoe;** Viscount Jellicoe of Scapa, 1918; Viscount Brocas of Southampton, 1925; *b* 29 Aug. 1950; *s* of 2nd Earl Jellicoe, KBE, DSO, MC, PC, FRS and his 1st wife, Patricia Christine (*née* O'Kane) (*d* 2012); *S* father, 2007; *m* 1971, separated 1971, marr. diss. 1981; two *s* (*b* 1970, 1977). *Educ:* Eton. Profession, engineer. *Heir: b* Hon. Nicholas Charles Joseph John Jellicoe [*b* 23 March 1953; *m* 1982, Patricia, *d* of late Count Arturo Ruiz de Castilla; two *d*].

**JENCKS, Charles Alexander,** PhD; landscape architect, designer and writer; *b* 21 June 1939; *s* of Gardner Platt Jencks and Ruth Pearl Jencks; *m* 1st, 1960, Pamela Balding (marr. diss. 1973); two *s*; 2nd, 1978, Margaret Keswick (*d* 1995); one *s* one *d*; 3rd, 2006, Louisa Lane Fox. *Educ:* Harvard University (BA Eng. Lit. 1961; BA, MA Arch. 1965); London University (PhD Arch. Hist., 1970). Joined Architectural Association, 1968: Lectr in Architecture, 1970–91; Lectr in Arch., 1974–85, Vis. Prof. of Arch., 1985–94, Univ. of Calif at LA Sch. of Arch. Writer on Post-Modern architecture, 1975–, Late-Modern architecture, 1978–; designer of furniture, gardens, and sculpture, incl. DNA sculpture for James Watson, Kew Gardens, and Landform for Scottish Nat. Gall. of Modern Art (Gulbenkian Prize 2004); Parco Portello, Milan, 2002–11; various landforms, 2005–, including: Doublewalk, Midpark Hosp., Dumfries, 2010–12; Holding the Eco-Line, Suncheon, S Korea, 2011–13; What is Life?, Dublin Botanic Gdn, 2013; Crawick Multiverse, 2015–; numerous Univ. lectures, incl. Peking, Warsaw, Tokyo, USA, Paris; house designs incl. The Garagia Rotunda, 1976–77, The Elemental House, 1983, The Thematic House, 1984. Fulbright Schol., Univ. of London, 1965–67; Melbourne Oration, Australia, 1974; Bossom Lectr, RSA, 1980; Mem., Cttee for selection of architects, Venice Biennale, 1980; Curator, Post-Modern London, exhibn, 1991. Editor at Academy Editions, 1979–; Editl Consultant, Architectural Design, 1979–. Co-Founder, Maggie Centres, 1995. Member: Architectural Assoc.; RSA. Gold Medal for Architecture, Nara, Japan, 1992; Gardener of the Year, Country Life, 1998. *TV films:* (wrote) Le Corbusier, BBC, 1974; (wrote and presented) Kings of Infinite Space (Frank Lloyd Wright and Michael Graves), 1983. *Publications:* Meaning in Architecture, 1969; Architecture 2000, 1971; Adhocism, 1972; Modern Movements in Architecture, 1973, 2nd edn 1985; Le Corbusier and the Tragic View of Architecture, 1974, 2nd edn 1987; The Language of Post-Modern Architecture, 1977, 6th edn 1991; Late-Modern Architecture, 1980; Post-Modern Classicism, 1980; Free-Style Classicism, 1982; Architecture Today (Current Architecture), 1982, 2nd edn 1988; Abstract Representation, 1983; Kings of Infinite Space, 1983; Towards a Symbolic Architecture, 1985; What is Post-Modernism? 1986, 3rd edn 1989; Post-Modernism—the new classicism in art and architecture, 1987; The Architecture of Democracy, 1987; The Prince, The Architects and New Wave Monarchy, 1988; The New Moderns, 1990; (ed) The Post Modern Reader, 1992; Heteropolis, Los Angeles, the Riots and the Strange Beauty of Heteroarchitecture, 1993; The Architecture of the Jumping Universe, 1995, 2nd edn 1997; Frank O. Gehry: cultural conservation and individual imagination, 1995; (ed jtly) Theories and Manifestos of Contemporary Architecture, 1997; Ecstatic Architecture, 1999; Le Corbusier and the Continual Revolution in Architecture, 2000; Architecture 2000 and Beyond, 2001; The New Paradigm in Architecture, 2002; The Garden of Cosmic Speculation, 2003; Scottish Parliament, 2005; The Iconic Building, 2005; Critical Modernism, 2007; (with E. Heathcote) The Architecture of Hope, Maggie Cancer Caring Centres, 2010, 2nd edn 2015; The Universe in the Landscape, 2011; The Story of Post-Modernism: five decades of ironic, iconic and critical architecture, 2011;

articles in professional jls incl. Architecture Forum, Architecture Rev., Domus, A&U, Architectural Design; occasional contrib. Sunday Times Mag., Encounter, TLS, The Observer, The Independent, Prometheus. *Recreations:* travel, collecting Chinese (bullet-hole) rocks. *Address:* 19 Lansdowne Walk, W11 3AH.

**JENKIN,** family name of **Baroness Jenkin of Kennington**.

**JENKIN OF KENNINGTON,** Baroness *cr* 2011 (Life Peer), of Hatfield Peverel in the County of Essex; **Anne Caroline Jenkin;** *b* 8 Dec. 1955; *d* of late Hon. Charles Richard Strutt and of Hon. Jean Elizabeth, *d* of 1st Viscount Davidson, GCVO, CH, CB, PC; *m* 1988, Hon. Bernard Christison Jenkin (see Hon. Sir B. C. Jenkin); two *s.* Vice Chairman: All Party Women in Parlt Gp, 2011–; All Party Agroecology Gp, 2012–; Co-chair: Cons. Friends of Internat. Develt, 2011–; Associate Parly Sustainable Resource Gp, 2012–. Pres., Harwich and North Essex Cons. Women's Gp, 1992–. Co-Founder, 2005, Co-Chair, 2011–, Women2Win. Mem., Adv. Bd, Global Poverty Project, 2011–. Patron: Soham for Kids, 2011–; Restless Development, 2011–; Trustee: UNICEF (UK), 2013–16; Feeding Britain; Cool Earth; WRAP. Chancellor, Writtle Univ. Coll., 2016–. *Address:* House of Lords, SW1A 0PW.

*See also Baron Rayleigh.*

**JENKIN, Hon. Sir Bernard Christison,** Kt 2018; MP (C) Harwich and North Essex, since 2010 (Colchester North, 1992–97; North Essex, 1997–2010); *b* 9 April 1959; *s* of Baron Jenkin of Roding, PC; *m* 1988, Anne Caroline Strutt (*see* Baroness Jenkin of Kennington); two *s. Educ:* Highgate Sch.; William Ellis Sch.; Corpus Christi Coll., Cambridge (BA Hons Eng. Lit., MA). Ford Motor Co., 1983–86; 3i, 1986–88; Hill Samuel Bank, 1988–89; Legal & General Ventures, 1989–92. Contested (C) Glasgow Central, 1987. PPS to Sec. of State for Scotland, 1995–97; Opposition spokesman on constitutional affairs, 1997–98, on transport, 1998–99; Shadow Minister for Transport, and for London, 1999–2001; Shadow Defence Sec., 2001–03; Shadow Sec. of State for the Regions, 2003–04; Shadow Minister for Energy, 2005; Dep. Chm., Conservative Party (Candidates), 2005–06. Chairman: Select Cttee on Public Admin, 2010–15; Select Cttee on Public Admin and Constitutional Affairs, 2015–; Member: Select Cttee on Social Security, 1992–97; Select Cttee on Defence, 2006–10; Sec., Cons. Backbench Small Business Cttee, 1992–97; Jt Sec., Cons. Backbench Foreign Affairs Cttee, 1994–95; Mem. Exec., 1922 Cttee, 2010–. Vis. Fellow, Henley Business Sch., Univ. of Reading, 2016–. Founder and Dir, Vote Leave, 2015–16. Vice Pres., Combat Stress, 2009–. Mem., St Paul's Cathedral Council, 2005–15. Pres., Cambridge Union Soc., 1982. Life Mem., Eur Acad. of Sci. and Arts, 2016. *Publications:* (jtly) Defence Acquisition for the Twenty-First Century, 2015. *Recreations:* family, music (esp. opera), fishing, shooting, sailing, DIY, arguing the Conservative cause. *Address:* House of Commons, SW1A 0AA. *T:* (020) 7219 3000. *Clubs:* Pratt's; Colchester Conservative.

*See also Baron Rayleigh.*

**JENKIN, Rear Adm. (David) Conrad,** CB 1983; Commandant, Joint Service Defence College (formerly National Defence College), 1981–84, retired; *b* 25 Oct. 1928; *s* of Mr and Mrs C. O. F. Jenkin; *m* 1958, Jennifer Margaret Nowell; three *s* one *d. Educ:* Dragon Sch., Oxford; RNC, Dartmouth. Entered RN at age of 13½, 1942; qual. in Gunnery, 1953; commanded: HMS Palliser, 1961–63; HMS Cambrian, 1964–66; HMS Galatea, 1974–75; HMS Hermes (aircraft carrier), 1978–79; Flag Officer, First Flotilla, 1980–81. President: Hong Kong Flotilla Assoc., 1999–2012; HMS Cambrian Assoc., 2005–13. *Recreations:* sailing, scale model-making. *Address:* Knapsyard House, West Meon, Hants GU32 1LF. *T:* (01730) 829227.

**JENKIN, Guy Arthur Allen;** writer, director and producer for television and film; *b* Carmarthen, 27 April 1955; *s* of Allen and Hazel Jenkin; *m* 2010, Bernadette Davis; two *s* one *d. Educ:* King Edward's Sch., Bath; Trinity Coll., Cambridge (BA English Lit. 1978). Television: contributor: Weekending, 1978–82; Not the Nine O'Clock News, 1979; Spitting Image, 1984; Who Dares Wins, 1982–86; writer: Shelley, 1983–89; Rebecca's Daughters (film), 1992; The Private Life of Samuel Pepys, 2004; co-writer and producer, Drop the Dead Donkey, 1990–98; writer and director: A Very Open Prison, 1995; Lord of Misrule, 1996; Crossing the Floor, 1997; Sex 'n' Death, 2001; The Sleeping Dictionary (film), 2002; Jeffrey Archer: the truth, 2003; Hacks, 2012; Election Spy, 2017; co-writer, director and producer, Outnumbered, 2007–11; co-writer and dir, Just Around the Corner, 2012; co-writer and co-director: What We Did on Our Holiday (film), 2014; Ballot Monkeys, 2015; Power Monkeys, 2016; writer, Fighting for the Dunghill (theatre), 1992; writer and dir, Bugsplat!, 2015.

**JENKIN, Simon William Geoffrey,** OBE 2006; education consultant, retired; Chief Education Officer, Devon County Council, 1989–98; *b* 25 July 1943; *s* of Dudley Cyril Robert Jenkin and Muriel Grace (*née* Mather); *m* 1973, Elizabeth Tapsell; two *d. Educ:* Univ. of London (BSc Econs); Jesus Coll., Oxford (DipEd). Lectr, 1967–72, Sen. Lectr, 1972–75, Bournemouth Coll. of Technology; Educn Officer, Essex CC, 1975–80; Area Educn Officer, NE Essex, 1980–83; Principal Educn Officer, Derbys CC, 1983–87; Dep. Chief Educn Officer, Devon CC, 1988–89. Mem., SW Regl Cttee, FEFCE, 1993–98. Director: Cornwall and Devon Careers Co. Ltd, 1995–98; Cambridge Education, 2001–09. Advr, LGA, 1991–98. Gov., United World Coll. of the Atlantic, 1991–98. Trustee, Bath Technology Centre, 2006–09. FRSA 1992. *Recreation:* my wife. *Address:* Grainge House, 10 Matford Avenue, Exeter EX2 4PW. *T:* (01392) 499798.

**JENKINS,** family name of **Baroness Morgan of Ely**.

**JENKINS, Adrian Richard;** Director, Bowes Museum, Barnard Castle, since 2001; *b* 23 Jan. 1965; *s* of George and Mary Jenkins; *m* 2006, Lucy Whetstone; one *s* one *d. Educ:* Tasker Milward Comp. Sch.; Univ. of Leicester (BA Hons Ancient Hist. 1986); Barber Inst. of Fine Arts, Univ. of Birmingham (MPhil Art Hist. 1990); Bolton Business Sch. (MBA 2001). Curatorial Asst, English Heritage, 1990–92; Asst Keeper of Art, Laing Art Gall., Newcastle upon Tyne, 1992–96; Sen. Keeper of Fine and Applied Art, Bolton Mus. and Art Gall., 1996–2001. Hon. Fellow, Inst. of Advanced Study, Univ. of Durham, 2013–16. *Publications:* catalogues: (with Lucy Whetstone) Expressionism in Germany 1905–1925, 1999; Painters and Peasants: Henry La Thangue and British Rural Naturalism 1880–1905, 2000; (ed) The Road to Impressionism: Josephine Bowes and painting in nineteenth century France, 2002; (jtly) Creative Tension: British art 1900–1950, 2005; Goya's Prison: the year of despair, 2009; various contribs to jls. *Recreations:* looking at paintings, drainage issues, enjoying Upper Teesdale, celebrating the flair of Welsh Rugby. *Address:* c/o The Bowes Museum, Barnard Castle, Co. Durham DL12 8NP. *T:* (01833) 690606, *Fax:* (01833) 637163. *E:* adrian.jenkins@thebowesmuseum.org.uk.

**JENKINS, Alan Dominique;** Chairman, Eversheds, solicitors, 2004–11; *b* 27 May 1952; *s* of Ian Samuel and Jeannette Juliette Jenkins; *m* 1979, Caroline (*née* Treverton Jones); one *s* three *d. Educ:* Clifton Coll., Bristol; New Coll., Oxford (MA Jurisprudence). Admitted solicitor, 1977; Partner, 1983–98, Man. Partner, 1996–98, Frere Cholmeley Bischoff; Eversheds: Partner, 1998–2011; Hd of Internat., 2002–09. Non-executive Member, Board: UK Trade and Investment, 2009–15; CPS, 2011–17; non-executive Director: Financial Ombudsman Service, 2011–; Northcourt Ltd, 2011–; Sydney and London Properties Ltd, 2011–; Pension Protection Fund, 2013– (Sen. Ind. Dir, 2016–). Trustee: Foundn for Internat. Envmtl Law and Develt, 1998–2011 (Chm., 2003–05); Internat. Inst. for Envmt and Develt, 2005–13 (Vice-Chm., 2005–13); London Middle East Inst., 2011–17; Chm., Mencap Trust Co. Ltd, 2009–17. FInstD (Mem., Council, 2007–16). *Publications:* (contrib.) International Commercial Fraud, 2002. *Recreations:* ski-ing, tennis, golf, watching sport in general (especially cricket and Rugby), theatre, music. *Clubs:* MCC, Roehampton.

**JENKINS, Alun;** *see* Jenkins, T. A.

**JENKINS, Antony Peter;** Founder and Executive Chairman, 10x Future Technologies, since 2016; *b* Blackburn, Lancs, 11 July 1961; *s* of Peter Jenkins and Patricia Jenkins (*née* Salter); *m* 1984, Amanda Mary Benson; one *s* one *d. Educ:* Malbank Sch., Nantwich; University Coll., Oxford (BA PPE 1982); Cranfield Inst. of Technol. (MBA 1988). Barclays plc, 1983–89; Citigroup, 1989–2005: Hd of Product Develt, 1989–91, Regl Product Manager, 1991–93, Eur. Securities Services; Dir of Strategic Implementation, Worldwide Securities Services/Global Transaction Services, 1993–95; Exec. Dir, N America Cash Mgt, 1995–98; Head, College Strategic Business Unit, 1998–99, Internet Initiatives, 1999–2000, Citi Cards; Chief Executive: c2it, 2000–02; eConsumer, 2002; Executive Vice President: US Hispanic, Global and Strategic Delivery Strategic Business Unit, 2002–04; Citibrands, 2004–05; Chief Executive Officer: Barclaycard, 2006–09; Global Retail Banking, Barclays Bank plc, 2009–12; Group Chief Exec., Barclays Bank plc, 2012–15. Chairman: BITC, 2015–17 (Dir, 2014–17); Currencies Direct, 2016–; Mem. Bd, Blockchain, 2016–. Chair, Inst. for Apprenticeships, then Inst. for Apprenticeships and Tech. Educn, 2017– (Shadow Chair, 2016–17). ACIB 1986; ACIM 1987. *Recreations:* family, running and fitness, ski-ing. *Club:* New York Road Runners.

**JENKINS, (Archibald) Ian;** *b* 18 March 1941; *s* of Archibald Jenkins and Margaret (*née* Duncan); *m* 1967, Margery MacKay. *Educ:* Rothesay Acad., Isle of Bute; Glasgow Univ. (MA 1963; DipEd 1964). Teacher of English, Clydebank High Sch., 1964–70; Principal Teacher of English, Peebles High Sch., 1970–99. Mem. (Lib Dem) Tweeddale, Ettrick and Lauderdale, Scottish Parlt, 1999–2003; Lib Dem spokesman on educn, culture and sport, 2000–03. *Recreations:* jazz, reading. *Address:* 1 South Park Drive, Peebles EH45 9DR. *T:* (01721) 720528.

**JENKINS, Prof. Aubrey Dennis;** Professor of Polymer Science, University of Sussex, 1971–92, now Emeritus; *b* 6 Sept. 1927; *s* of Arthur William Jenkins and Mabel Emily (*née* Street); *m* 1st, 1950, Audrey Doreen Middleton (marr. diss. 1987); two *s* one *d*; 2nd, 1987, Jitka Horská, er *d* of late Josef Horský and Anna Horská, Hradec Králové, Czechoslovakia. *Educ:* Dartford Grammar Sch.; Sir John Cass Technical Inst.; King's Coll., Univ. of London. BSc 1948, PhD 1951; DSc 1961. FRIC 1957. Research Chemist, Courtaulds Ltd, Fundamental Research Laboratory, Maidenhead, 1950–60; Head of Chemistry Research, Gillette Industries Ltd, Reading, 1960–64 (Harris Research Labs, Washington, DC, 1963–64); University of Sussex, 1964–92: Sen. Lectr in Chemistry, 1964–68; Reader, 1968–71; Dean, Sch. of Molecular Scis, 1973–78. Visiting Professor: Inst. of Macromolecular Chemistry, Prague, 1978 and 1986; Univ. of Massachusetts, Amherst, 1979; ETH Zürich, 2002. Mem. Council, RSC, 2003–05. Member: Internat. Union of Pure and Applied Chemistry, Commn on Macromolecular Nomenclature, 1974– (Chm., 1977–85; Sec., Macromolecular Div., 1985–93); British Assoc. for Central and Eastern Europe (formerly GB/E Europe Centre), 1975–2005; British, Czech and Slovak Assoc., 1990–. Mem., Brighton HA, 1983–90. Examining chaplain to Bishop of Chichester, 1980–90. Hon. Fellow, Soc. of Organic Chemistry of Argentina, 1993. Geza Zemplen Medal, Budapest, 1984; Heyrovský Gold Medal for Chemistry, Czechoslovak Acad. of Scis, 1990. *Publications:* Kinetics of Vinyl Polymerization by Radical Mechanisms (with C. H. Bamford, W. G. Barb and P. F. Onyon), 1958; Polymer Science, 1972; (with A. Ledwith) Reactivity, Mechanism and Structure in Polymer Chemistry, 1974; (with J. F. Kennedy) Macromolecular Chemistry, Vol. I 1980, Vol. II 1982, Vol. III 1984; Progress in Polymer Science (12 vols), 1967–85; (with J. N. Murrell) Properties of Liquids and Solutions, 1994; papers in learned jls. *Recreations:* music, travel, photography. *Address:* Vixen's, 22A North Court, Hassocks, West Sussex BN6 8JS. *T:* (01273) 845410. *E:* polygon@vixens.eclipse.co.uk.

**JENKINS, Bethan Maeve;** *see* Sayed, B. M.

**JENKINS, Brian David;** *b* 19 Sept. 1942; *s* of Hiram Jenkins and Gladys (*née* Morgan); *m* 1963, Joan Dix; one *s* one *d. Educ:* Aston Coll.; Coventry Coll.; Coleg Harlech; London Sch. of Econs (BSc Econ); Wolverhampton Poly. (PGCE). With CEGB, 1963–68; Jaguar Cars, 1968–73; Percy Lane, 1973–75; Lecturer: Isle of Man Coll., 1981–83; Tamworth Coll., 1983–96. Mem., USDAW. Tamworth Borough Council: Mem. (Lab), 1985–96; Dep. Mayor, 1992–93; Mayor, 1993–94; Leader, 1995–96. Contested (Lab) SE Staffs, 1992. MP (Lab) SE Staffs, April 1996–1997, Tamworth, 1997–2010; contested (Lab) same seat, 2010. Mem., Tamworth Br., RBL. *Recreations:* music, reading, watching sport.

**JENKINS, Sir Brian (Garton),** GBE 1991; FCA; Deputy Chairman, Barclays Bank plc, 2000–04; Prior, England and the Islands, Order of St John of Jerusalem, 2004–10; Lord Mayor of London, 1991–92; *b* 3 Dec. 1935; *s* of late Owen Garton Jenkins and Doris Enid (*née* Webber); *m* 1967, (Elizabeth) Ann Prentice; one *s* one *d. Educ:* Tonbridge; Trinity Coll., Oxford (State Scholar; MA; Hon. Fellow, 1992). FCA 1974. Served RA, Gibraltar, 1955–57 (2nd Lieut). With Cooper Brothers & Co., later Coopers & Lybrand, 1960–95; Chm., Woolwich Bldg Soc., later Woolwich plc, 1995–2000. Pres., ICAEW, 1985–86. Pres., London Chamber of Commerce, 1996–98. Chm., 1998–2003, Pres., 2003–08, Charities Aid Foundn. Alderman, City of London (Ward of Cordwainer), 1980–2004 (Sheriff, 1987–88); Liveryman: Chartered Accountants' Co., 1980– (Master, 1990–91); Merchant Taylors' Co., 1984– (Master, 1999–2000); Information Technologists' Co., 1985– (Master, 1994–95). Dep. Pres., 1996–97, Pres., 1997–98, BCS. Hon. Bencher, Inner Temple, 1992; Hon. Mem., Baltic Exchange, 1993. Hon. DSc City Univ., 1991; Hon. DLitt London Guildhall Univ., 1991; Companion, De Montfort Univ., 1993; Hon. Fellow, Goldsmiths Coll., London, 1998. FBCS. CCMI. FRSA. Centenary Award, Chartered Accountants Founding Socs, 1993. KStJ 1991. *Publications:* An Audit Approach to Computers, 1978, 4th edn 1992. *Recreations:* walking, reading, ephemera. *Clubs:* Brooks's, City of London, City Livery.

**JENKINS, Sir Christopher;** *see* Jenkins, Sir J. C.

**JENKINS, David Edward Stewart;** Managing Consultant, Lateral Research Consultants, since 2003 (Senior Partner, 1994–2003); *b* 9 May 1949; *s* of late William Stephen Jenkins and of Jean Nicol Downie; *m* 1972, Maggie Steele, *d* of Dr C. H. and Mrs J. D. Lack; two *s* one *d. Educ:* Univ. of London Goldsmiths' College (BA(Soc) 1977); LSE. Warden, Ellison Hse Adult Probation Hostel, SE17, 1973–74; Lecturer: (part-time) in Sociology, Brunel Univ., 1980–81; (part-time) in Social Administration, LSE and Goldsmiths' Coll., 1980–81; in Criminology, Univ. of Edinburgh, 1981; Dir, Howard League, 1982–86; Res. Fellow, PSI, 1986–87; Res. Consultant to HM Chief Inspector of Prisons, 1987–95. Morris Ginsburg Fellow in Sociology, LSE, 1986–87. *Recreations:* music, swimming, cycling.

**JENKINS, Ven. David Harold,** PhD; FRHistS; Archdeacon of Sudbury, since 2010; *b* Belfast, 19 Oct. 1961; *s* of Joseph Jenkins and Janet Jenkins; *m* 1997, Sarah Gillian Benjamin; two *s* one *d. Educ:* Belfast Royal Acad.; Sidney Sussex Coll., Cambridge (BA 1984; MA

1987); Ripon Coll., Cuddesdon (BA 1989, MA 1994, Oxon); Univ. of Wales, Lampeter (MA 2001; PhD 2008). Ordained deacon, 1989, priest, 1990; Vicar: St Michael and All Angels, Blackpool, 1994–99; St John the Baptist, Broughton, 1999–2004; Rural Dean, Preston, 2004; Diocesan Dir of Educn, Dio. of Carlisle, 2004–10; Asst Curate, St Thomas a Becket, Great Whelnetham, 2016–18. Canon, Carlisle Cathedral, 2004–10; Hon. Canon, St Edmundsbury Cathedral, 2010–. FRHistS 2011. *Publications:* Holy, Holier, Holiest: the sacred topography of the early medieval church, 2010; (contrib.) English Cathedrals and Monasteries through the Ages, 2013. *Recreations:* reading, music, jogging, my family! *Address:* Sudbury Lodge, Stanningfield Road, Great Whelnetham, Bury St Edmunds IP30 0TL. *T:* (01284) 386942. *E:* archdeacon.david@cofesuffolk.org.

JENKINS, David Hugh; DL; Chief Executive, Dorset County Council, 1999–2012; Deputy Chairman, NHS Dorset Clinical Commissioning Group, 2013–19; *b* 28 April 1952; *s* of David Lyndhurst Jenkins and Charlotte Elizabeth Jenkins; *m* 1980, Ethna Geraldine Trafford; one *d*. *Educ:* Barry Boys' Comprehensive Sch.; Jesus Coll., Oxford (MA); Coll. of Law, Chester. Asst Master, Fairfield GS, Bristol, 1973–74; admitted solicitor (Hons), 1977; Articled Clerk then Asst Solicitor, Oxon CC, 1975–79; Solicitor, Commn for Local Admin in Wales, 1979–84; Asst Co. Sec., Hants CC, 1984–89; Dorset County Council: Dep. Co. Solicitor, 1989–91; Asst Chief Exec., 1991–93; Co. Solicitor, 1993–96; Dir, Corporate Services, 1996–99. Pres., Dorset Law Soc., 1993–94. Clerk to: Dorset Fire Authy, 1999–2008; Dorset Lieutenancy, 1999–2012; Secretary: Dorset Probation Cttee, 1999–2009; Dorset Strategic Partnership, 2002–12. Chairman: Wessex Regl Flood and Coastal Cttee, 2015–; Inquiry into Infant Cremations in Shropshire, 2014–15. Dep. Chair, Nat. Efficiency Taskforce, 2008–10. Board Member: Dorset TEC, 1999–2001; Dorset Business Link, 1999–2001; Bournemouth SO, 2000–13 (Trustee, 2013–, Chm., 2014–18, Bournemouth SO Endowment Trust); Dorset Connexions Partnership, 2001–06 (Chair, 2005–06); Somerset Rivers Authy, 2015–; Assoc. of Drainage Authorities, 2016–. Pres., Dorset Assoc. of Parish and Town Councils, 2013–18 (Vice Pres., 2018–). Ind. Chair, Glos CC Waste Working Gp, 2013–14. Chair: SW Comm for Excellence Bd, 2004–07; Bd, SW Regl Improvement and Efficiency Partnership, 2007–12. Chm., Dorset Working Gp for 2012 Games, 2003–12; Mem., SW Bd for 2012 Games, 2011–12. Chm., ACCE, 2006–07; Mem. Council, SOLACE, 2005–07. Trustee: Burton Bradstock Fest., 2012–; Richard Ely Trust, 2012–15; Minerva Learning Trust, 2016–. Patron, Bridport Arts Centre, 2009–. DL Dorset, 2012. *Recreations:* music, theatre, travel, family. *Address:* Bucklers Bid, Shipton Lane, Burton Bradstock, Bridport DT6 4NQ.

JENKINS, David John, OBE 2004 (MBE 1993); Chairman, Aneurin Bevan University (formerly Local) Health Board, 2009–17; *b* 21 Sept. 1948; *s* of William and Dorothy Jenkins; *m* 1976, Felicity Anne (*née* Wood); two *s* one *d*. *Educ:* Canton High Sch., Cardiff; Liverpool Univ. (BA Hons); Garnett Coll., London (CertEd). Industrial Sales Organiser, ITT (Distributors), 1970–74; social worker, GKN, 1974; Lectr, Peterborough Tech. Coll., 1975–78; Wales Trades Union Congress: Research and Admin. Officer, 1978–83; Gen. Sec., 1983–2004. Chairman: Health Professions Wales, 2004–06; Nat. Leadership and Innovation Agency for Healthcare in Wales, 2007–09. Chm., Wales Co-op. Develt Centre, 1994–. Pt-time Mem., Competition (formerly Monopolies and Mergers) Commission, 1993–2002; Member: Employment Appeal Tribunal, 1994–2019; Fitness to Practise Panel, GMC, 2006–14. *Recreations:* walking, fishing, family. *Address:* Ty Brith Cottage, Twyn Square, Usk, Monmouthshire NP15 1BH. *T:* (01291) 673570.

JENKINS, Maj.-Gen. David John Malcolm, CB 2000; CBE 1994; Under-Treasurer, Honourable Society of Gray's Inn, 2000–08; *b* 2 Jan. 1945; *m* 1969, Ann Patricia Sharp; one *s* two *d*. *Educ:* Sherborne Sch.; Reading Univ. (BA Hons); Magdalene Coll., Cambridge (MPhil). Commissioned The Queen's Own Hussars, 1964; regimental service, 1964–75; RMCS and Staff Coll., 1976–77; Allied Staff, Berlin, 1983–85; CO, The Queen's Own Hussars, 1985–87; COS, 3 Armd Div., 1988–90; Comdr Armd 1 (Br) Corps, 1990–91; Dir, Military Ops, 1991–93; Commandant, RMCS, 1994–96; DG Land Systems, MoD, 1996–2000; Master Gen. of the Ordnance, 1998–2000. Col Comdt, REME, 1997–2002; Col, Queens Royal Hussars, 1999–2004; Hon. Col, Inns of Court and City Yeomanry, 2003–10. Mem. Council, Cranfield Univ., 2005–15. Order of Merit (1st Class), Jordan, 1994. *Recreations:* ski-ing, country sports, music, military history. *Club:* Garrick.

JENKINS, Deborah Mary, (Mrs Ivor Stolliday), MBE 1995; DL; Director and owner, Kindling Ltd, since 1997; Chief Executive Officer, since 1993, and Chairman, since 2006, The Derwent Initiative; *b* Oxford, 14 July 1959; *d* of late Rt Rev. David Edward Jenkins; *m* 1997, Ivor Stolliday. *Educ:* LTCL, piano, 1976; Brasenose Coll., Oxford (BA 1981); Durham Univ. Business Sch. (MBA 1995). Tutor, Tübingen Univ., and British Council Student, Budapest, 1981–83; Manager, Caravanserai, Bishop Auckland, 1983–85; Owner, The Silver Swan, 1985–88; Personnel Dir, Impasse, 1986–87; Project Dir, Inner Cities Unit, Industrial Soc., 1987–89; Regl Dir, Common Purpose, 1989–95. Vice Chair, Mental Health Act Commn, 2001–08. Vice Chair, Newcastle City Health NHS Trust, 1995–97; Chm., S Tees Hosps NHS Foundn Trust, 2008–17. Non-executive Director: Northern Arts, 1992–95; NE SHA, 2006–08. Chair: Barnard Castle Vision, 2006–15; Northern Neonatal Network, 2009–; Northern Council for Further Educn, 2017–; Together for Children Sunderland, 2017–; Brighter Futures for Children, 2018–. Trustee, N of England Civic Trust, 2018–. Gov., Newcastle Coll., 1993–95. DL Tyne and Wear, 2017. *Recreations:* domesticity, lustreware, pretending to be Niçoise. *Address:* 28 The Bank, Barnard Castle, Co. Durham DL12 8PQ. *E:* kindlingltd@msn.com.

JENKINS, Prof. Edgar William, CChem, FRSC; FRSB; JP; Professor of Science Education Policy, University of Leeds, 1993–2000, now Emeritus; *b* 7 Jan. 1939; *s* of Lewis Morgan Jenkins and Eira Gwyn (*née* Thomas); *m* 1961, Isobel Harrison; two *d*. *Educ:* Univ. of Leeds (BSc, MEd). CChem, FRSC 1974; FRSB (FSB 2010). Teacher: Keighley Grammar Sch., 1961–62; Leeds Grammar Sch., 1962–67; University of Leeds: Lectr and Sen. Lectr, 1967–76; Reader in Science Education, 1980–92; Head, Sch. of Education, 1980–84, 1991–95; Dir, Centre for Studies in Science Educn, 1997–2000. Chm., Bd, Grad. Teacher Trng Registry, 1995–2001. JP W Yorks, 1977. FRSA. Editor: Studies in Science Education, 1986–98; Internat. Jl of Technology and Design Education, 1994–2000. *Publications:* A Safety Handbook for Science Teachers, 1973, 4th edn 1991; From Armstrong to Nuffield, 1979; Inarticulate Science?, 1983; Technological Revolution?, 1985; A Magnificent Pile, 1985; Policy, Practice and Professional Judgement, 1993; Investigations by Order, 1996; Junior School Science Education since 1900, 1998; Learning from Others, 2000; Policy, Professionalism and Change, 2001; Innovations in Science and Technology Education, 2003; Guidelines for Policy-making in Secondary School Science and Technology Education, 2003; 75 Years and more: the ASE in Yorkshire, 2009; Advancing Science Education: the first fifty years of the Association for Science Education, 2013; E. J. Holmyard and the Historical Approach to Science Teaching, 2014; Science for All: the struggle to establish school science in England, 2019; books for schools. *Recreations:* choral music, walking, lay administration of justice.

JENKINS, Edward Nicholas; QC 2000; a Recorder, since 2000; *b* 27 July 1954; *m* 1979; one *s* one *d*. *Educ:* Trinity Hall, Cambridge (BA Hons). Called to the Bar, Middle Temple, 1977; Asst Recorder, 1999–2000. *Address:* 5 Paper Buildings, Temple, EC4Y 7HB. *T:* (020) 7583 6117.

JENKINS, Emyr; *see* Jenkins, J. E.

JENKINS, Ffion Llywelyn; *see* Hague, F. L.

JENKINS, Prof. George Charles, MB, BS, PhD; FRCPE; FRCPath; Consultant Haematologist, The Royal London (formerly London) Hospital, 1965–92, now Hon. Consulting; Hon. Consultant, St Peter's Hospitals, 1972–86; Professor of Haematology in the University of London, 1974–92, now Emeritus; Consultant to the Royal Navy, now Emeritus; *b* 2 Aug. 1927; *s* of late John R. Jenkins and Mabel Rebecca (*née* Smith); *m* 1956, Elizabeth (*d* 2014), *d* of late Cecil J. Welch, London; one *s* two *d*. *Educ:* Wyggeston, Leicester; St Bartholomew's Hosp. Med. Coll. MB, BS, PhD; MRCS 1951; LRCP 1951; FRCPath 1975 (MRCPath 1964); FRCPE; FRSocMed. House Phys. and Ho. Surg., St Bart's Hosp., 1951–52. Sqdn Ldr, RAF Med. Br., 1952–54. Registrar in Pathology, St Bart's Hosp., 1954–57; MRC Research Fellow, Royal Postgraduate Med. Sch., 1957–60; Sen. Registrar, Haematology, London Hosp., 1960–63; Cons. Haematologist, N Middlesex Hosp., 1963–65. Examiner: Univ. of London, 1971–95; Univ. of Cambridge, 1984–95; Sen. Examiner, RCPath, 1971–92, Mem. Council, 1979–84, Vice-Pres., 1981–84. Member, sub-cttee on biologicals, 1976–86, cttee on dental and surgical materials, 1988–92, Cttee on Safety of Medicines. Pres., British Acad. of Forensic Scis, 1990–91 (Mem., 1977–; Chm. Exec. Council, 1985–89); Member: British Soc. for Haematology, 1962– (formerly Hon. Sec.; Pres., 1988–89); Internat. Soc. of Haematology, 1975–95; Assoc. of Clinical Pathologists, 1958–92. Gov. and Mem. Council, Home Farm Trust, 1993–2002. *Publications:* (jtly) Advanced Haematology, 1974; (jtly) Infection and Haematology, 1994; papers and contribs to med. and sci. books and jls. *Recreations:* theatre, music, art, talking to people, attempting to paint pictures. *Address:* 3 Lambert Jones Mews, Barbican, EC2Y 8DP.

JENKINS, Prof. Geraint Huw, PhD, DLitt; FBA 2002; FLSW; Director, University of Wales Centre for Advanced Welsh and Celtic Studies, 1993–2008, Hon. Senior Fellow, 2009; Professor Emeritus, University of Wales, 2009; *b* 24 Jan. 1946; *s* of David Hugh Jenkins and Lilian Jenkins (*née* Phillips); *m* 1972, Ann Ffrancon; three *d*. *Educ:* Ardwyn Grammar Sch., Aberystwyth; UCW, Swansea (BA 1st Cl. Hons 1967; Hon. Fellow, Univ. of Wales Swansea, 2004); UCW, Aberystwyth (PhD 1974); DLitt Wales 1994. University of Wales, Aberystwyth: Lectr in Welsh Hist., 1968–81; Sen. Lectr, 1981–88; Reader, 1988–90; Prof. of Welsh Hist., 1990–93; Head of Welsh History, 1991–93. Vis. Prof., UCLA, 2003. Member: Univ. of Wales Bd of Celtic Studies, 1985– (Chm., 1993–2007); Council and Court, Univ. of Wales, Aberystwyth, 1991–2006; Cardiganshire Historical (formerly Antiquarian) Soc. (Chm., 1998–2019; Pres., 2019–); Council, British Acad., 2007–09; Univ. of Wales Press Bd, 2009–12. Founding FLSW 2010. Hon. Fellow: Swansea Univ., 2004; Swansea Metropolitan Univ., 2010. Editor: Ceredigion, 1985–95; Cof Cenedl, 1986–2009. *Publications:* Cewri'r Bêl-droed yng Nghymru, 1977; Literature, Religion and Society in Wales 1660–1730, 1978; Thomas Jones yr Almanaciwr, 1980; Hanes Cymru yn Cyfnod Modern Cynnar, 1983, rev. edn 1988 (Welsh Arts Council Prize, 1989); The Foundations of Modern Wales, 1987, rev. edn 1993; (ed jtly) Politics and Society in Wales 1840–1922, 1988; Llunio Cymru Fodern, 1989; The Making of Modern Wales, 1989; Cymru Ddoe a Heddiw, 1990; Wales Yesterday and Today, 1990; Cadw Tŷ mewn Cwmwl Tystion, 1990 (Welsh Arts Council Prize, 1991); Protestant Dissenters in Wales 1639–1689, 1992; The Illustrated History of the University of Wales, 1993; (ed jtly) Merêd: Casgliad o'i Ysgrifau, 1995; (ed) Y Gymraeg yn ei Disgleirdeb, 1997; (ed) The Welsh Language before the Industrial Revolution, 1997; (ed jtly) Cardiganshire in Modern Times, 1998; (ed) Iaith Carreg fy Aelwyd, 1998; (ed) Language and Community in the Nineteenth Century, 1998; (ed) Gwnewch Bopeth yn Gymraeg, 1999; Doc Tom: Thomas Richards, 1999; (ed) Welsh and its Social Domains 1801–1911, 2000; (ed jtly) Eu Hiaith a Gadwant?, 2000; (ed jtly) Let's Do Our Best for the Ancient Tongue, 2000; (ed) Cymru a'r Cymry 2000, 2001; (ed jtly) From Medieval to Modern Wales, 2004; A Rattleskull Genius: the many faces of Iolo Morganwg, 2005; A Concise History of Wales, 2007; (ed jtly) The Correspondence of Iolo Morganwg, 2007; (ed jtly) Degrees of Influence, 2008; Iolo Morganwg y Gwerinaiethwr, 2010; The Swans Go Up, 2011; Yr Elyrch: Dathlu'r Cant, 2012; Bard of Liberty: the political radicalism of Iolo Morganwg, 2012; Proud to be a Swan: the centenary history of Swansea City FC, 2012; (ed jtly) The Welsh Language in the Twentieth Century, 2015; Y Digymar Iolo Morganwg, 2018; (ed jtly) Cardiganshire County History: medieval and early modern Cardiganshire, 2019. *Recreations:* music, sport, gardening. *Address:* Llain Wen, Blaenplwyf, Aberystwyth, Ceredigion SY23 4QJ. *T:* (01970) 612024.

JENKINS, Hugh Royston, CBE 1996; FRICS, FPMI; Chairman and Chief Executive, Prudential Portfolio Managers, and Director, Prudential Corporation, 1989–95; Chairman: Falcon Property Trust, 1995–2003; Development Securities plc, 1999–2003; *b* 9 Nov. 1933; *m* 1988, Mrs Beryl Kirk. *Educ:* Llanelli Grammar Sch. National Service, Royal Artillery, 1954–56. Valuer, London County Council, 1956–62; Assistant Controller, 1962–68, Managing Director, 1968–72, Coal Industry (Nominees) Ltd; Dir Gen. of Investments, NCB, 1972–85. Vice Chm., National Assoc. of Pension Funds, 1979–80; Chief Exec. Officer, Heron Financial Corp., 1985–86; Gp Investment Dir, Allied Dunbar Assce, 1986–89; Dep. Chm. and Chief Exec., Allied Dunbar Unit Trusts, 1986–89; Chm., Dunbar Bank, 1988–89; Chm. and Chief Exec., Allied Dunbar Asset Management, 1987–89. Dep. Chm., 1996–97, Chm., 1997–98, Thorn plc; Director: Unilever Pensions Ltd, 1985–89; IBM Pensions Trust PLC, 1985–89; Heron International, 1985–89; EMI, 1995–2003; Rank Gp plc, 1995–2001; Johnson Matthey, 1996–2003. Chm., Property Adv. Gp, DoE, 1990–96; Member: The City Capital Markets Cttee, 1982; Private Finance Panel, 1994–95; Lay Mem. of the Stock Exchange, 1984–85. *Address:* Flat 3, 36 Sloane Court West, SW3 4TB.

JENKINS, Ian; *see* Jenkins, A. I.

JENKINS, Sir (James) Christopher, KCB 1999 (CB 1987); First Parliamentary Counsel, 1994–99; *b* 20 May 1939; *s* of Percival Si Phillips Jenkins and Dela (*née* Griffiths); *m* 1962, Margaret Elaine Edwards, yr *d* of Rt Hon. L. John Edwards and Dorothy (*née* Watson); two *s* one *d*. *Educ:* Lewes County Grammar Sch.; Magdalen Coll., Oxford (Mackinnon Schol.; BA 1st class Hons Jurisprudence 1961; MA 1968). With Slaughter and May, 1962–67, solicitor, 1965. Joined Office of Parly Counsel, 1967; at Law Commn, 1970–72 and 1983–86; Parly Counsel, 1978–91; Second Parly Counsel, 1991–94. Adv. Council, Citizenship Foundn, 1989–2010; Adv. Law Cttee, British Council, 1998–2001; Adv. Council, Constitution Unit, UCL, 1999–2010; Council, Statute Law Soc., 2000–02. Hon. QC 1994.

*See also* O. J. Jenkins.

JENKINS, Jeremy David; His Honour Judge Jenkins; a Circuit Judge, since 2016; *b* Aberdare, S Wales; *s* of John Leslie and Jacqueline Elizabeth Jenkins; *m* 1990, Annie; one *s* one *d*. *Educ:* Aberdare Boys' Grammar Sch.; City of Birmingham Poly. (BA Hons Law 1980). Called to the Bar, Inner Temple, 1984; pupillage, 34 Park Place, Cardiff, 1985–86; Attorney-at-Law, Truman Bodden & Co., Georgetown, Grand Cayman, 1986–90; in practice as a barrister, Apex Chambers, Cardiff, 1990–2016; a Recorder, 2008–16. *Recreations:* golf, travel, Rugby football, watching my son play football. *Address:* 25 Church Road, Whitchurch, Cardiff CF14 2DX. *T:* (029) 2061 0576. *E:* jeremyjenkins1958@yahoo.com. *Clubs:* Aberdare Golf, Whitchurch Golf (Cardiff).

**JENKINS, Sir John,** KCMG 2011 (CMG 2003); LVO 1989; HM Diplomatic Service, retired; Associate, Policy Exchange, London, since 2017; *b* 26 Jan. 1955; *s* of John Malsbury Jenkins and Mabel Lilleen Norah Jenkins (*née* Gardiner); *m* 1982, Nancy Caroline Pomfret. *Educ:* St Philip's Grammar Sch., Birmingham; Becket Sch., Nottingham; Jesus Coll., Cambridge (BA 1977; PhD 1980). Joined FCO, 1980; full-time lang. trng, SOAS, Univ. of London and London Centre for Arabic Studies, 1981–83 and 1998–99; Second, later First, Sec., Abu Dhabi, 1983–86; First Sec., FCO, 1986–89; Head of Chancery, Kuala Lumpur, 1989–92; First Sec., FCO, 1992–95; Counsellor and Dep. Head of Mission, Kuwait, 1995–98; lang. trng, SOAS, Univ. of London, 1998–99; Ambassador to Burma (Union of Myanmar), 1999–2002; Consul-Gen., Jerusalem, 2003–06; Ambassador to Syria, 2006–07; Dir, Middle East and N Africa, FCO, 2007–09; Ambassador to Iraq, 2009–11; UK Special Rep. to Nat. Transitional Council, Benghazi, 2011; Ambassador to Libya, 2011; Ambassador to Saudi Arabia, 2012–15. Exec. Dir, Middle E, IISS, 2015–17. Sen. Fellow, Jackson Inst. for Global Affairs, Yale Univ., 2017. *Recreations:* Nottingham Forest FC, walking, theatre, films and books, the ancient world, drumming, the Middle East. *Clubs:* Oxford and Cambridge, Two Brydges.

**JENKINS, John David;** QC 1990; a Recorder, 1990–2016; *b* 7 Dec. 1947; *s* of late Vivian Evan Jenkins, MBE and of Megan Myfanwy Evans; *m* 1972, Susan Elizabeth Wilkinson; two *s. Educ:* Ashville Coll., Harrogate; King's Coll. London (LLB Hons). Called to the Bar, Gray's Inn, 1970; in practice at the Bar, Wales and Chester Circuit, 1970–2008. *Recreations:* football, cricket, psephology. *Address:* (office) 30 Park Place, Cardiff CF10 3BS. *T:* (029) 2039 8421. *Club:* Pentyrch Cricket.

**JENKINS, (John) Emyr;** Chief Executive, Arts Council of Wales, 1994–98; *b* 3 May 1938; *s* of Llewellyn Jenkins and Mary Olwen Jenkins; *m* 1964, Myra Bonner Samuel; two *d. Educ:* Machynlleth County Sch.; UCW, Aberystwyth (BSc Physics). BBC Studio Manager, 1961–63; BBC Announcer and Newsreader, 1963–71; Anchorman, Heddiw (Daily TV Mag.), 1968–69; BBC Wales Programme Organiser, 1971–77; First Dir, Royal Nat. Eisteddfod of Wales, 1978–93; Dir, Welsh Arts Council, 1993–94. Mem., IBA Welsh Adv. Cttee, 1986–90. Foundn Chm., Mudiad Ysgolion Meithrin (Assoc. of Welsh Playgroups), 1971–73; Member: Welsh Lang. Educn Develt Cttee, 1987–88; Council, UCW Aberystwyth, 1982–86; Steering Cttee/Council, Voluntary Arts Network, 1988–94; Voluntary Arts Wales Cttee, 1999–2001; Bd, Univ. of Wales Press, 1999– (Chm., 2003–06). Chm., Welsh Music Inf. Centre, 2000–05; Foundn Chm., Sherman Cymru Th., 2006–12. Gov., RWCMD, 1998– (Dep. Chm., 2000–06). FRSA 1992. Hon. FRWCMD (Hon. FWCMD 1997). Hon. MA Wales, 1993. Hon. Mem., Gorsedd of Bards, 1982. Elder, Crwys Presbyterian Church of Wales, Cardiff, 1984 (Treas., 2009–19). *Recreations:* music, theatre, walking, sport.
See also F. L. Hague, M. B. Antoniazzi.

**JENKINS, Sir Karl (William Pamp),** Kt 2015; CBE 2010 (OBE 2005); DMus; FRAM; composer; *b* 17 Feb. 1944; *s* of late David and Lily Jenkins; *m* 1973, Carol Barratt, composer; one *s. Educ:* Gowerton Grammar Sch.; University Coll. of Wales, Cardiff (BMus); DMus Wales 2006; Royal Acad. of Music (LRAM 1966; ARAM 2001; FRAM 2003). Played saxophone, keyboards and oboe with Ronnie Scott's jazz band, Nucleus (co-founder) and Soft Machine (1972–80); composer of advertising music for Levi's, British Airways, Pepsi, etc (D&AD award for best music, 1985, 1989; Creative Circle Gold Award, 1986). *Compositions:* Adiemus: Songs of Sanctuary, 1995; Cantata Mundi, 1997; Dances of Time, 1998; The Journey, 1999; The Eternal Knot, 2000; Vocalise, 2003; Diamond Music/ Palladio, 1996; Imagined Oceans, 1998; Eloise (opera), 1999; The Armed Man: A Mass for Peace (for soloists, chorus and orch.) (commnd by Royal Armouries), 2000; Dewi Sant, 2000; Over the Stone (harp concerto), 2002; In These Stones Horizons Sing, 2004; Requiem, 2005; Quirk (concertante), 2005; Tlep, 2006; Stabat Mater, 2008; Joy to the World, Stella Natalis, 2009; Gloria, 2010; The Healer - A Cantata For St Luke, 2014; Cantata Memoria: for the children, 2016; Miserere: songs of mercy and redemption, 2019; film score: River Queen, 2005. FRWCMD (FWCMD 2003); Fellow: Cardiff Univ., 2004; Trinity Coll., Carmarthen, 2005; Swansea Inst., 2005. *Publications:* Still with the Music: my autobiography, 2015. *Recreations:* travel, food, sport. *Address:* c/o Karl Jenkins Music Ltd, 3rd Floor, Paternoster House, 65 St Paul's Churchyard, EC4M 8AB. *E:* info@karljenkins.com.

**JENKINS, Katharine Mary;** Visiting Professor, Department of Government, London School of Economics and Political Science, since 2002; *b* 14 Feb. 1945; *d* of late Rev. Dr Daniel Thomas Jenkins and Nell Jenkins; *m* 1967, Euan Sutherland, *qv* (marr. diss. 1995); one *s* one *d. Educ:* South Hampstead High Sch.; St Anne's Coll., Oxford (BA Hons); London School of Economics (MScEcon). Called to Bar, Inner Temple, 1971. Asst Principal, 1968, Principal, 1973, Dept of Employment; Central Policy Review Staff, Cabinet Office, 1976; Asst Sec., Dept of Employment, 1979; Dep. Head of Efficiency Unit, 1984; Dir, Prime Minister's Efficiency Unit, and Under Sec., Cabinet Office, 1986–89; Dir, Personnel, Royal Mail, 1989–91; Chm., Kate Jenkins Associates, 1991–2008. Dir, Carrenza Ltd, 2003–16; Chm., Carrenza Consulting Ltd, 2007–14. Chair, Internat. Women's Forum UK, 2014–16. Member: NHS Policy Bd, 1992–95; Audit Commn, 1993–99; Council, Hansard Soc., 2003–10 (Vice Chm., 2005–10). Dir, London and Manchester Gp, 1989–97. Special Trustee, St Thomas' Hosp., 1992–95. Member: Barbican Centre Cttee, 2000–06; Council, Spitalfields Fest., 2003–06; St Bartholomew's Hosp. Trust Med. Coll., 2003–12 (Vice Chm., 2006–12). London School of Economics and Political Science: Mem., Ct of Govs, 1990–2016 (Vice Chm., 2009–14); Mem. Council, 2000–03, 2008–14 (Vice Chm., 2009–14). *Publications:* (with W. Plowden) Governance and Nationbuilding: the failure of international intervention, 2006; Politicians and Public Services: a clash of cultures, 2008; reports: Making Things Happen: the implementation of government scrutinies, 1985; Improving Management in Government: the next steps, 1988; (with W. Plowden) Keeping Control: the management of public sector reform programmes, 1995. *Address:* 513 Gilbert House, Barbican, EC2Y 8BD.
See also Sir S. D. Jenkins, B. J. Mack.

**JENKINS, Sir Michael (Nicholas Howard),** Kt 1997; OBE 1991; *b* 13 Oct. 1932; *s* of C. N. and M. E. S. Jenkins; *m* 1957, Jacqueline Frances Jones; three *s. Educ:* Tonbridge School; Merton College, Oxford (MA Jurisp.). Shell-Mex & BP, 1956–61; IBM UK, 1961–67; Partner, Robson, Morrow, Management Consultants, 1967–71; Technical Dir, Stock Exchange, 1971–77; Man. Dir, European Options Exchange, Amsterdam, 1977–79; Chief Executive, LIFFE, 1981–92; Chairman: London Commodity Exchange, 1992–96; Futures and Options Assoc., 1993–99; Dir, 1991–2003, Chm., 1996–2003, London Clearing House Ltd. Chm., E-Crossnet Ltd, 1999–2005; Director: Tradepoint Financial Networks plc, 1995–99; British Invisibles, 1998–2001; EasyScreen plc, 1999–2005. Trustee: Brain and Spine Foundn, 1993–2010; Physics Partners (formerly Success in Shortage Subjects), 2007–. Pres., Merton Soc., 2007–10. Gov., Sevenoaks Sch., 1993–2007. Liveryman: Information Technologists' Co., 2004–; World Traders' Co., 2009–. *Recreations:* golf, music, wood turning. *Club:* Wildernesse (Sevenoaks).

**JENKINS, Neil Martin James;** opera singer; tenor; music editor; choral conductor; music adjudicator; *b* 9 April 1945; *s* of Harry James Jenkins and Mary Morrison Jenkins (*née* Terry); *m* 1st, 1969, Sandra Wilkes; one *s*; 2nd, 1982, Penny (*née* Underwood); one *s*, and two step *s* one step *d. Educ:* Westminster Abbey Choir School; Dean Close School (music Scholar); King's College Cambridge (Choral Scholar; MA). Recital début, Kirkman Concert Series, Purcell Room, 1967; operatic début, Menotti's The Consul, Israel Festival, 1968; major rôles with English Music Theatre, Glyndebourne Fest. Opera, Kent Opera, New Sussex Opera, Scottish Opera, WNO; ENO; numerous recordings, film sound tracks and videos. Prof. of Singing, RCM, 1975–76; teacher, summer schools, incl. Canford, AIMS (formerly Ardingly) and Dartington, 1989–. Cummins Harvey Vis. Fellow, Girton Coll., Cambridge, 2003. President: Grange Choral Soc., Hants; Haywards Heath Music Soc., 2000–; Shoreham Oratorio Choir, 2003–; Basildon Choral Soc., 2008–; Kent Chorus, 2011–; Vice-President: Hunts Philharmonic; Brighton Competitive Music Festival; Patron: Goldsmith's Choral Union, 2011–; New Sussex Opera, 2017–. Geoffrey Tankard Lieder Prize, 1967; NFMS Award, 1972; Sir Charles Santley Award, Musicians' Co., 2004. *Publications:* choral music (edited and arranged): The Carol Singer's Handbook, 1993; O Praise God, 1994; O Holy Night, 1994; Sing Solo Sacred, 1997; works by J. S. Bach: St Matthew Passion, 1997; St John Passion, 1998; Christmas Oratorio, 1999; Magnificat, 2000; B Minor Mass, 2002; Easter Oratorio, 2003; Haydn The Seasons, 2003; Ascension Oratorio, 2004; The Creation, 2005; Handel The Passion of Christ, 2014; Haydn The Seven Last Words, 2015; Schutz: The Christmas Story, 2000; The Seven Last Words, 2015; The Resurrection Story, 2015; articles in: Haydn Soc. of Great Britain Jl, 2005; Göttinger Händel-Beiträge XII, 2008; (contrib.) Handel, 2011; John Beard, Handel and Garrick's Favourite Tenor, 2012. *Recreations:* visiting ancient monuments, 18th century music research. *Address:* c/o Music International, 13 Ardilaun Road, N5 2QR. *T:* (020) 7359 5813.

**JENKINS, Owen John;** HM Diplomatic Service; Ambassador to Indonesia and (non-resident) to Timor-Leste, since 2019; *b* London, 21 Aug. 1969; *s* of Sir (James) Christopher Jenkins, *qv*; *m* 1998, Catherine Baker; two *s* one *d. Educ:* Highgate Sch.; Univ. of Sheffield (BA Hons 1st cl. English Lit.). Entered FCO, 1991; Third, later Second, Sec., Ankara, 1994–97; First Secretary: FCO, 1998–2002; Buenos Aires, 2002–06; UK Representation to EU, Brussels, 2006–09; Counsellor: New Delhi, 2009–12; FCO, 2012–14; Dir, S Asia and Afghanistan, FCO, 2014–17; UK Special Rep. for Afghanistan and Pakistan, 2015–17; on secondment to Aberdeen Standard Life, 2018. *Address:* Foreign and Commonwealth Office, King Charles Street, SW1A 2AH.

**JENKINS, Paul,** OBE 2001; Chief Executive, Tavistock and Portman NHS Foundation Trust, since 2014; *b* 11 Feb. 1963; *s* of late Ifor and of Sheila Jenkins; *m* 1989, Catherine Bannister; two *s. Educ:* Solihull Sch.; Balliol Coll., Oxford (MA Ancient and Modern Hist.); Manchester Business Sch. (MBA). Admin. trainee, DoH, 1985; Project Manager, DoH, 1998–2004: Next Steps Proj. Team, Cabinet Office, 1988–91; Policy Lead for NHS Community and Continuing Care, 1991–96; Dir, Service Develt, NHS Direct, 2004–07; Chief Exec., Rethink, later Rethink Mental Illness, 2007–14. Chair, Mental Health UK, 2016–; Trustee: Joseph Rowntree Foundn, 2017– (Chm., Audit and Risk Cttee); NHS Confederation, 2018– (Chair, Mental Health Network, 2018–). *Recreations:* Welsh language and culture, Rugby, cricket, history, archaeology, hill-walking. *Address:* Tavistock and Portman NHS Foundation Trust, Tavistock Centre, 120 Belsize Lane, NW3 5BA. *E:* PJenkins@tavi-port.nhs.uk.

**JENKINS, Peter Redmond,** CMG 2005; HM Diplomatic Service, retired; Partner, Ambassador Partnership (formerly ADRg Ambassadors), since 2010; *b* 2 March 1950; *s* of late Denys Arthur Reali Jenkins and Monique Marie-Louise Jenkins; *m* 1990, Angelina Chee-Hung Yang; one *s* one *d. Educ:* Downside Sch.; Corpus Christi Coll., Cambridge (BA Hons, MA); Harvard Univ. Graduate Sch. of Arts and Scis (Harkness Fellow). Joined HM Diplomatic Service, 1973: FCO, 1973–75; UK Mission to Internat. Orgns, Vienna, 1975–78; FCO, 1978–82; Private Sec. to HM Ambassador, Washington, 1982–84; FCO, 1984–87; Paris, 1987–91; Minister-Counsellor and Consul Gen., Brasilia, 1992–95; Dep. Perm. Rep., 1996–2001, and Minister, 1998–2001, UK Mission to UN, Geneva; Perm. Rep. to UN and other Internat. Orgns, Vienna, 2001–06; Special Rep. for the Renewable Energy and Energy Efficiency Partnership, 2006–08. Special Advr to Dir, Internat. Inst. for Applied Systems Analysis, 2006–08. Associate Fellow, Geneva Centre for Security Policy, 2010–12. Non-exec. Dir, Ecoenergen, 2009–16. Chm., IAEA Conference on Illicit Trafficking of Nuclear Materials, 2007. Vis. Lectr, Univ. of Bath, 2009–. Gov., Downside Sch., 2012–19. Member: Cttee, Harkness Fellows Assoc., 2012–; Exec. Cttee, British Pugwash Gp, 2014– (Chm., 2016–). *Publications:* many articles on nuclear issues, esp. the problem posed by Iran's nuclear prog. *Recreations:* ski-ing, hill/mountain walking, reading, travelling. *Address:* 14 Great Bedford Street, Bath BA1 2TZ. *E:* prjs@post.harvard.edu. *Clubs:* Brooks's, Beefsteak.

**JENKINS, Peter White,** MBE 2007; County Treasurer, Merseyside County Council, 1973–84; *b* 12 Oct. 1937; *s* of John White Jenkins, OBE, and Dorothy Jenkins; *m* 1961, Joyce Christine Muter; one *s* one *d. Educ:* Queen Mary's Grammar Sch., Walsall; King Edward VI Grammar Sch., Nuneaton. CIPFA. Local govt service in Finance Depts of Coventry, Preston, Chester, Wolverhampton; Dep. Treasurer, Birkenhead, 1969–73; Dir of Finance, Welsh Water Authority, 1984–87. Hon. Treas., 1994–98, Chapter Clerk, 2006–15, Brecon Cathedral. Treas., Brecknock Soc. and Mus. Friends, 2013–19. *Recreations:* walking, gardening, local history, reading, Rotary since 1986. *Address:* 9 Camden Crescent, Brecon, Powys LD3 7BY.

**JENKINS, Richard David;** Chief Executive, Bath Building Society, since 2013; Chairman, Building Societies Association, 2015–17; *b* Stourbridge, 25 Sept. 1957; *s* of Jack Jenkins and Mary Jenkins; *m* 1981, Sally Maiden; one *s* one *d. Educ:* King Edward VII Sch., King's Lynn; Trinity Coll., Cambridge (BA Geog.). Gen. Manager, Audits of Great Britain, 1981–89; Dir, Res., Management Horizons, 1989–92; CEO, Bank of Ireland Mortgages, 1996–99; Exec. Dir, Bristol and West, 1999–2003; Chief Exec., Bath Building Society, 2003–. *Recreations:* gardening, guitar, golf (badly), choir. *Address:* Frocester Cottage, Frocester, Stonehouse, Glos GL10 3TE. *T:* (01453) 825416. *E:* dickjenkins@btconnect.com.

**JENKINS, Richard Thomas,** OBE 1986; HM Diplomatic Service, retired; Ambassador to Georgia, 1998–2001; *b* 19 Aug. 1943; *s* of Vincent Arthur Wood Jenkins and Edna Jenkins (*née* Frith); *m* 1976, Maurizia Marantonio; two *s. Educ:* Plaistow Co. GS; Nottingham Univ. (BA Hons 1964); Warsaw Univ.; Glasgow Univ. Entered HM Diplomatic Service, 1967; FCO, 1967–70; Warsaw, 1970; FCO, 1970–76; Second, subseq. First Sec., E Berlin, 1976–79; Res. Dept, FCO, 1979–83; First Sec. (Commercial), Warsaw, 1983–85; Head, Central European Sect., 1985–89, Dep. Head, Jt Assistance Unit (Know How Fund), 1989–94, FCO Res. Dept; Dep. Head of Mission and Consul-Gen., Kiev, 1994–97. Election monitoring for OSCE Office for Democratic Instns and Human Rights: Albania, 2003; Georgia, Macedonia, 2004; Belarus, Tajikistan, Kazakhstan, 2005; Kosovo (Council of Europe), 2006. Mem., Fabian Soc. Freeman, City of London, 1998. Hon. Fellow, Univ. of E London, 1995.

**JENKINS, (Sir) Simon David,** Kt 2004; author; columnist, The Guardian, since 2005; Chairman, National Trust, 2008–14; *b* 10 June 1943; *s* of late Rev. Dr Daniel Thomas Jenkins and Nell Jenkins; *m* 1st, 1978, Gayle Hunnicutt (marr. diss. 2008); one *s*, and one step *s*; 2nd, 2014, Hannah Kaye. *Educ:* Mill Hill Sch.; St John's Coll., Oxford (BA Hons; Hon. Fellow 2004). Country Life magazine, 1965; Univ. of London Inst. of Educn, 1966;

Times Educational Supplement, 1966–68; Evening Standard, 1968–74; Insight Editor, Sunday Times, 1974–75; Editor, Evening Standard, 1976–78; Political Editor, The Economist, 1979–86; The Sunday Times: columnist, 1986–90; editor, Books Section, 1988–89; The Times: Editor, 1990–92; columnist, 1992–2005. Member: British Railways Bd, 1979–90; LRT Bd, 1984–86; South Bank Bd, 1985–90; Calcutt Cttee on Privacy, 1989–90; Grade Cttee on Fear of Crime, 1989; Runciman Cttee on Misuse of Drugs Act 1971, 1998–2000; HFEA, 2001–06. Chm., Commn for Local Democracy, 1994–95. Director: Municipal Journal Ltd, 1980–90; Faber & Faber, 1980–90. Chm., Booker Prize 2000. Mem. Council, Bow Group, and Editor of Crossbow, 1968–70; Member: Cttee, Save Britain's Heritage, 1976–; Historic Buildings and Monuments Commn, 1985–90 (Dep. Chm., 1988–90); Millennium Commn, 1994–2000; Churches Conservation Trust, 2016–; Mem. Council, Old Vic Co., 1979–81; Chm., Pevsner Books Trust, 1994–2011; Dep. Chm., Thirties Soc., 1979–85; Founder and Dir, Railway Heritage Trust, 1985–90; Trustee: World Monuments Fund, 1995–98; Somerset House Trust, 2003–09. Guv., Mus. of London, 1985–87. FSA 2004; FRSL 2004; Hon. RIBA, 1997. Hon. Dr UCE, 1998; Hon. DLitt: London, 2000; City, 2001; Univ. of Wales, Lampeter, 2001; Exeter, 2003; Univ. of London Inst. of Educn, 2005; Kent, 2008; Sussex, 2015. What The Papers Say Journalist of the Year, 1988; Columnist of the Year, British Press Awards, 1993; Edgar Wallace Trophy for Outstanding Reporting, London Press Club, 1997; David Watt Meml Prize, FT, 1998; Commentariat of the Year, Comment Awards, 2010; Columnist of the Year, Editorial Intelligence, 2015. *Publications:* A City at Risk, 1971; Landlords to London, 1974; (ed) Insight on Portugal, 1975; Newspapers: the power and the money, 1979; The Companion Guide to Outer London, 1981; (with Max Hastings) The Battle for the Falklands, 1983; Images of Hampstead, 1983; (with Anne Sloman) With Respect Ambassador, 1985; The Market for Glory, 1986; The Times Guide to English Style and Usage, 1992; The Selling of Mary Davies, 1993; Against the Grain, 1994; Accountable to None: the Tory nationalization of Britain, 1995; England's Thousand Best Churches, 1999; England's Thousand Best Houses, 2003; Big Bang Localism, 2005; Thatcher and Sons, 2006 (Political Book of the Year, Channel 4, 2007); Wales: churches, houses, castles, 2009; A Short History of England, 2011; England's Hundred Best Views, 2013; Mission Accomplished, 2015; England's Cathedrals, 2016; Britain's 100 Best Railway Stations, 2017; A Short History of Europe, 2018; A Short History of London, 2019. *Address:* c/o The Guardian, King's Place, 90 York Way, N1 9GU. *Club:* Garrick.
See also K. M. Jenkins.

**JENKINS, Stephen Lewis;** public relations consultant, since 2013; Head of Media Relations, Archbishops' Council of the Church of England, 1999–2013 (Acting Head of Communications, 2002–04; Acting Director of Communications, 2011–12; Acting Head of Media, 2016); *b* 1 Dec. 1955; *s* of Charles Lewis Jenkins and Marjorie Jenkins (*née* Negus); *m* 1979, Susan Jane Varley; two *s. Educ:* Reading Sch.; UCNW, Bangor (BSc Hons (Agric. with Agricl Econs)). Technical and news reporter, Big Farm Weekly, 1977–80; Dep. Ed., Big Farm Management, subseq. Farm Business, 1980–84; freelance, 1984–85; tech. journalist, Farm Contractor Mag., 1985–87; Press Officer: Children's Soc., 1987–90; Gen. Synod of C of E, 1991–99. Develt Officer, Mothers' Union, Dio. of Oxford, 2015–16. *Recreation:* family life and the search for time in the busy life of a churchwarden. *Address:* 34 Dickens Close, Caversham, Reading RG4 5LZ. *T:* 07768 764783. *E:* stevejenkins100@gmail.com.

**JENKINS, Prof. Stephen Pryse,** DPhil; Professor of Economic and Social Policy, London School of Economics and Political Science, since 2011; *b* 11 June 1956; *s* of David W. P. Jenkins and Katherine E. Jenkins (*née* Gillingham). *Educ:* Univ. of Otago, Dunedin (BA 1977); Univ. of York (DPhil 1983). Jun. Lectr, Massey Univ., 1978; Res. Fellow, Univ. of York, 1979–80, 1981–83; Lectr, Univ. of Bath, 1983–91; Prof. of Applied Econs, Univ. of Wales, Swansea, 1991–94; Prof. of Econs, 1994–2011, Dir, 2006–09, Inst. for Social and Economic Res., Univ. of Essex. *Publications:* (ed jtly) The Distribution of Household Welfare and Household Production, 1998; (ed jtly) The Dynamics of Child Poverty in Industrialized Countries, 2001; Changing Fortunes: income mobility and poverty dynamics in Britain, 2011 (ed jtly) The Great Recession and the Distribution of Household Income, 2013; numerous articles in learned jls. *Recreations:* music, running, cycling. *Address:* Department of Social Policy, London School of Economics and Political Science, Houghton Street, WC2A 2AE. *T:* (020) 7955 6527. *E:* s.jenkins@lse.ac.uk.

**JENKINS, (Thomas) Alun;** QC 1996; Advocate, Public Defender Service, 2014–18; *b* 19 Aug. 1948; *s* of Seward Thomas Jenkins and Iris, *d* of Alderman W. G. H. Bull, miner and sometime Chm. of Monmouthshire CC; *m* 1971, Glenys Maureen Constant; one *s* two *d. Educ:* Ebbw Vale Tech. Sch.; Bristol Univ. (LLB Hons 1971). Called to the Bar, Lincoln's Inn, 1972, Bencher, 2008; in private practice, Bristol, 1972–2014, and London, 1996–2014, specialising in law of serious crime, esp. large diversion frauds, large scale drug importations, organised crime, and conspiracies; Head of Chambers, Queen Square, Bristol, 1995–2014. Asst Recorder, 1992–2000; Recorder, 2000–14. *Recreations:* cultural: opera, Shakespeare and literature generally; sport: horse riding, Rugby, motor cars, point to point.

**JENKINS, Thomas Lawrence;** Sports Photographer: The Guardian, since 1990; Observer, since 1993; *b* 1 Jan. 1968; *s* of Richard and Mary Jenkins; *m* 2003, Rosamund Harris; one *s* one *d. Educ:* Sevenoaks Sch.; Gwent Coll. of Higher Educn (BTEC HND Documentary Photography 1989). Freelance sports photographer: Allsport, 1989; Sunday Telegraph, 1989; Sunday Express, 1990. Young Photographer of the Year, 1990, Sports Photographer of the Year, 2004, 2006, 2007, 2015, British Press Awards; Sports Photographer of the Year, 2000, Photograph of the Year, 2004, What the Papers Say; Sports Photographer of the Year, Nikon, 2002, Sports Journalists Assoc., 2003, 2004; Barclays Football Photographer of the Year, 2008–09; 4 awards, Press Photographer's Year, 2009; Sports Portfolio of the Year, Sports Journalists Assoc., 2011; Sports Photographer of the Year, UK Picture Editors Guild, 2015; First Prize, sports singles, World Press Photo Contest, 2017. *Publications:* In the Moment: the sports photography of Tom Jenkins, 2012. *Recreation:* spending time with my family. *E:* tom.jenkins@theguardian.com.

**JENKINS, Victor,** CEng; Director ISTAR, Defence Equipment and Support, Ministry of Defence, 2007–11; *b* Cardiff, 17 April 1950; *s* of Roy and Hazel Jenkins; *m* 1995, Sheila Lonsdale (*née* Richardson); one step *d. Educ:* Paston Sch., Norfolk; Univ. of Kent at Canterbury (BSc Hons Electronics). CEng 1991; Certificated Project Manager, 1994. Systems Engr, Cossor Electronics Ltd, 1972–76; Manager, res. and projects, 1976–90, Dir, Procurement Policy for Project Mgt, 1990–92, PE, MoD; rcds 1993; Dir of Projects, Al Yamamah Prog., MoD, 1994–98; Dir of Ops and Dep. Chief Exec., UK Hydrographic Office, 1998–2004; Dir of Ops and Actg Chief Exec., HM Govt Communications Centre, 2004–07. *Recreations:* cycling, walking, dining.

**JENKINSON, Eric,** CVO 2009; OBE 2003; HM Diplomatic Service, retired; Information Management Department, Foreign and Commonwealth Office, 2011; *b* 13 March 1950; *s* of Horace and Bertha Jenkinson; *m*; two *s*; *m* 2004, Máire Donnelly. Joined FCO, 1967; Protocol Div., FCO, 1967–70; Brussels, 1971–73; Islamabad, 1973–76; full-time language training, 1976–77; temp. duty, then Third Sec., Commercial, Jedda, 1978–80; Second Sec., Commercial, Riyadh, 1980–82; Sci., Energy and Nuclear Dept, FCO, 1982–84; Asst Private Sec., FCO, 1984–86; First Sec., Econ., Bonn, 1986–90; Dep. Consul General, Frankfurt, 1990–91; full-time language training, 1991–92; Dep. Head of Mission, Bahrain, 1992–95; Head, Parly Relns Dept, FCO, 1995–98; First Sec., Commercial/Econ., then Dep. Head of Mission, Tehran, 1999–2002; High Commissioner: The Gambia, 2002–06; Trinidad and Tobago, 2007–11. *Recreations:* cooking, photography, Rugby, cricket, reading.

**JENKINSON, Jeffrey Charles,** MVO 1977; Chief Executive, Harwich Haven Authority, 1992–97; *b* 22 Aug. 1939; *s* of late John Jenkinson and Olive May Jenkinson; *m* 1962, Janet Ann (*née* Jarrett); one *s* two *d. Educ:* Royal Liberty Sch., Romford; City of London Coll. National Service, RN, 1957–59. Port of London Authority: Port operations and gen. management, 1959–71; British Transport Staff Coll., 1972; PLA Sec., 1972–81; Dir of Admin, 1982–86; Bd Mem., 1982–92; Chief Exec., Property, 1987–92; Dir, Placon Ltd and other PLA gp subsid. cos, 1978–92. Dir, E London Small Business Centre Ltd, 1977–92; Mem. Bd, Globe Centre Ltd, 1992–96. Envmt Agency Chm., Essex Area Envmt Gp, 1996–2002; Mem., Anglian (Eastern) Regl Flood Defence Cttee, 2003–11 (Vice Chm., 2005–11). Member: Bd, and Council, London Chamber of Commerce and Industry, 1989–92; Council, British Ports Assoc., 1993–96; Chm., Thames Riparian Housing Assoc., 1986–92; Member: Newham CHC, 1974–80; Committee of Management: Seamen's Gp of Hosps, 1972–74; Seafarers (formerly Seamen's) Hosp. Soc., 1974– (Hon. Treas., 1998–2002). Mem. Bd, Colne Housing Soc., 2009–14. Freeman, City of London, 1975; Mem. Ct, Co. of Watermen and Lightermen of River Thames, 1990– (Master, 1997–98). *Recreations:* sailing, walking, music.

**JENKINSON, Sir John (Banks),** 14th Bt *cr* 1661; *b* 16 Feb. 1945; *o s* of Sir Anthony Banks Jenkinson, 13th Bt and Frances (*d* 1996), *d* of Harry Stremmel; *S* father, 1989; *m* 1979, Josephine Mary Marshall-Andrew; one *s* one *d. Educ:* Eton; Univ. of Miami. *Heir: s* George Samuel Anthony Banks Jenkinson, *b* 8 Nov. 1980.

**JENKINSON, Kenneth Leslie;** Headmaster, Colchester Royal Grammar School, 2000–15 (Deputy Headmaster, 1994–2000); *b* 4 Oct. 1955; *s* of Reginald and Margaret Jenkinson; *m* 1979, Jacqueline Anne Loose; two *d. Educ:* Danum Grammar Sch., Doncaster; Univ. of Leeds (BA, PGCE); Univ. of Sheffield (MA); NPQH. Teacher, Modern Languages, Hayfield Sch., Doncaster, 1979–88; Head, Modern Languages, Blundell's Sch., Tiverton, 1988–94. Nat. Leader of Educn, 2013. *Recreations:* family, travel, sport.

**JENKINSON, Nigel Harrison;** Division Chief, Financial Supervision and Regulation, Monetary and Capital Markets Department, International Monetary Fund; *b* 18 June 1955; *s* of Alan and Jean Jenkinson; two *s. Educ:* Birmingham Univ. (BSocSc 1st cl. Hons Mathematics, Econs and Statistics); London Sch. of Economics (MSc Econometrics and Mathematical Econs (Dist)). Bank of England: Economist, 1977–90; Mem., Economic Unit, Secretariat of Cttee of Govs, European Union Central Banks, 1990–93 (on secondment); Dep. Head, Reserves Mgt, 1993–94; Head, Structural Economic Analysis Div., 1994–98; Dep. Dir, Monetary Analysis and Statistics, 1999–2003; Exec. Dir, Financial Stability, 2003–09; Advr to Gov., 2009; Advr, Financial Stability Bd, Bank for Internat. Settlements, 2009–14; Asst Dir, Monetary and Capital Mkts Dept, IMF. Mem., REconS. *Recreations:* football, cricket, reading. *Club:* Colchester United Supporters Association.

**JENKINSON, Philip,** DL; Chairman, Active Devon Sports Partnership, 2005–15; *b* 2 June 1948; *s* of Harold Jenkinson and Edith Florence Jenkinson (*née* Phillipson); *m* 1970, Sandra Elizabeth Cornish; four *s. Educ:* Manchester Grammar Sch.; Univ. of Exeter (LLB 1st Cl. Hons); Liverpool Poly. Trainee solicitor, Gillingham Bd, Kent, 1970–72; admitted solicitor, 1972; Asst Solicitor, Bath CC, 1972–74; Devon County Council: Solicitor, 1974–95; Chief Exec., and Clerk to the Lieutenancy, 1995–2006. Director: Prosper (formerly Devon and Cornwall TEC), 1995–2002; Cornwall and Devon Connexions, 2001–12. Governor: Exeter Coll., 2005–13 (Chm., 2008–10); Southbrook Special Sch., 2010–; Exeter Mathematics Sch., 2014–. DL Devon, 2006. FRSA. *Recreations:* walking designated footpaths, music.

**JENKINSON, Prof. Timothy John,** DPhil; Professor of Finance, Saïd Business School, University of Oxford, since 2006; Fellow, Keble College, Oxford, since 1987; *b* Hockley, Essex, 12 April 1961; *s* of John and late Jean Jenkinson; *m* 1986, Rebecca Priestman; two *s. Educ:* Greensward Sch.; Churchill Coll., Cambridge (BA Econs 1982); Univ. of Pennsylvania (MA Econs 1983); Christ Church, Oxford (DPhil Econs 1986). Lectr in Econs, 1987–2000; Reader in Business Econs, 2000–05, Oxford Univ.; Dir, Oxford Private Equity Inst., 2009–. Dir and Partner (formerly Chm.), Oxera Ltd, then Oxera Consulting, 2008–. *Publications:* Going Public, 1996, 2nd edn 2001; Readings in Microeconomics, 1996, 2nd edn 2000; Readings in Macroeconomics, 1996, 2nd edn 2000; Competition in Regulated Industries, 1998; contrib. articles to internat. academic jls. *Recreations:* travel, cycling, family, theatre, watching football and Rugby. *Address:* Saïd Business School, University of Oxford, Park End Street, Oxford OX1 1HP. *T:* (01865) 288916. *E:* tim.jenkinson@sbs.ox.ac.uk.

**JENKS, Prof. Christopher,** FAcSS; sociologist; Vice-Chancellor and Principal, Brunel University, 2006–12, now Emeritus Professor; *b* 12 June 1947; *y s* of late Arthur Jenks and Alice Elizabeth Jenks; *m* Barbara Read; two *d. Educ:* Westminster City Sch.; Univ. of Surrey (BSc 1969); Univ. of London; PGCE 1970, MSc Econ 1971, London Univ. Goldsmiths' College, London University: Lectr, 1971–76, Sen. Lectr, then Reader, 1976–94, in Sociology; Prof. of Sociology, 1995–2004; Pro-Warden, 1995–2000; Prof. of Sociology and Pro-Vice-Chancellor, Brunel Univ., 2004–06. Hon. Prof., E China Normal Univ., 2007–. Ed., Childhood jl, 1995–. Member, Council: Chartered Instn for Further Educn, 2015–; City, Univ. of London, 2017–. FAcSS (AcSS 2000). FRSA 2006; FRSocMed 2008; FCGI 2011; FGCL 2012. Hon. Freeman, Water Conservators' Co., 2011. Hon. PhD Univ. of Sci. and Technol., Trondheim, 2005. *Publications:* Rationality, Education and the Social Organization of Knowledge, 1976; (ed jtly) Worlds Apart, 1977; (jtly) Toward a Sociology of Education, 1977; (ed) The Sociology of Childhood, 1982; Culture, 1993, 2nd edn 2005; Cultural Reproduction, 1993; Visual Culture, 1995; Childhood, 1996, 2nd edn 2005; (jtly) Theorizing Childhood, 1998; (ed) Core Sociological Dichotomies, 1998; (jtly) Images of Community: Durkheim, social systems and the sociology of art, 2000; Aspects of Urban Culture, 2001; Culture, 4 vols, 2002; Transgression, 2003; Urban Culture, 4 vols, 2004; Subculture: the fragmentation of the social, 2004; Childhood, 3 vols, 2005; (jtly) Qualitative Complexity, 2006; Transgression, 4 vols, 2006; (jtly) Sociology and Human Ecology, 2018; articles in British Jl of Sociology, Theory, Culture and Society, Cultural Values and others. *Recreations:* cricket, art and literature, previously rock climbing and mountaineering. *Address:* c/o Brunel University, Uxbridge, Middx UB8 3PH. *Clubs:* Athenæum, Chelsea Arts, MCC.

**JENKS, Sir (Richard) Peter,** 4th Bt *cr* 1932; of Cheape in the City of London; FCA; *b* 28 June 1936; *yr s* of Sir Richard Atherley Jenks, 2nd Bt and of Marjorie Suzanne Arlette Jenks (*née* du Cros); *S* brother, 2004; *m* 1963, Juniper Li-Yung Foo; one *s* two *d. Educ:* Charterhouse; Grenoble Univ. FCA 1959. Lieut, Royal Inniskilling Dragoon Guards, 1959–61. Articled chartered accountancy clerk, 1954–59; stockbroking, 1961–88; Partner, Govett Sons & Co.; Partner and Finance Dir, Hoare Govett; Dir, Security Pacific Bank Ltd. *Recreations:* ski-ing, mountaineering, olive farming, butterflies, wine, travel, astronomy, charity work. *Heir:* s Richard Albert Benedict Jenks, b 27 Feb. 1965. *Address:* 81 Onslow Square, SW7 3LT. *T:* (020) 7589 6295. *E:* sirpeterjenks@gmail.com; Sornanino, Loc. Casafrassi, 53011 Castellina in Chianti, Siena, Italy.

**JENKYNS, Andrea Marie;** MP (C) Morley and Outwood, since 2015; b Beverley, 16 June 1974; d of late Clifford Jenkyns; m 2017, Jack Lopresti, qv; one s. *Educ:* Marton Primary Sch., Holderness; Open Univ. (Dip. Econs); Univ. of Lincoln (BA Internat. Relns and Politics 2014). Soprano singer and songwriter; music tutor in secondary schs, Lincs CC; musical theatre dir, two children's performing arts academies. PPS, MHCLG, 2018. Member: Health Select Cttee, 2015–17; Cttee for Exiting the EU, 2016–. Mem. (C), Lincs CC, 2009–13. Trustee, MRSA Action UK. *Address:* House of Commons, SW1A 0AA.

**JENNER, Ann Maureen;** freelance ballet teacher; Ballet Teacher, Australian Ballet School, 1999–2008; Guest Ballet Teacher: Royal Ballet School; Australian Ballet; Queensland Ballet, and many other schools in Sydney and Melbourne; also guest choreographer; retired; b 8 March 1944; d of Kenneth George Jenner and Margaret Rosetta (née Wilson); m 1980, Dale Robert Baker; one s. *Educ:* Royal Ballet Junior and Senior Schools. Royal Ballet Co., 1961–78: Soloist 1964; Principal Dancer 1970. Australian Ballet, 1978–80. Associate Dir, 1987, Dir, 1988–94, Nat. Theater Ballet Sch., Melbourne. Roles include: Lise, Fille Mal Gardée, 1966; Swanhilda, Coppelia, 1968; Cinderella, 1969; Princess Aurora, Sleeping Beauty, 1972; Giselle, 1973; Gypsy, Deux Pigeons, 1974; White Girl, Deux Pigeons, 1976; Juliet, Romeo and Juliet, 1977; Countess Larisch, Mayerling, 1978; Flavia, Spartacus, 1979; Kitri, Don Quixote, 1979; Anna, Anna Karenina, 1980; Poll, Pineapple Poll, 1980; one-act roles include: Symphonic Variations, 1967; Firebird, 1972; Triad, 1973; Les Sylphides; Serenade; Les Patineurs; Elite Syncopations, Concert, Flower Festival Pas de Deux, etc. Guest Teacher, San Francisco Ballet Co. and San Francisco Ballet Sch., 1985.

**JENNER, Prof. Peter George,** PhD, DSc; FRPharmS; Professor of Pharmacology, King's College London School of Biomedical Sciences (formerly Guy's, King's, and St Thomas' School of Biomedical Sciences), King's College London, 1989–2008, now Emeritus Professor; b 6 July 1946; s of late George Edwin Jenner and Edith (née Hallett); m (marr. diss. 2003); one s; m 2014, Melanie Gardner. *Educ:* Chelsea Coll., London Univ. (BPharm Hons 1967; PhD 1970; DSc 1987). FRPharmS 1994; FBPhS (FBPharmacolS 2005). Post-doctoral Fellow, Dept of Pharmacy, Chelsea Coll., London, 1970–72; Lectr in Biochem., 1972–78, Sen. Lectr, 1978–85, Dept of Neurol., Inst. of Psychiatry, Univ. of London, 1972–78; King's College, London University: Reader in Neurochem. Pharmacol., Inst. of Psychiatry and KCH Med. Sch., 1985–89; Hon. Sen. Lectr, Inst. of Neurol., 1988–2000; Prof. of Pharmacology and Head, Dept of Pharmacology, 1989–98, Head, Div. of Pharmacology and Therapeutics, GKT Sch. of Biomed. Scis, 1998–2004; FKC 2006. Director: Exptl Res. Labs, Parkinson's Disease Soc., 1988–99; Neurodegenerative Diseases Res. Centre, 1993–. Dir, Primagen Ltd, 1999–; Dir and CSO, Proximagen Ltd, 2005–10; CSO, Chronos Therapeutics, 2015–17 (Chm., Scientific Adv. Bd, 2017–). Adjunct Prof. of Neurology, Univ. of Miami, USA, 1997–99. Parkinson's Disease Society: Mem. Council, 1993–99 (Hon. Sec. to Council, 1996–99); Mem., Med. Adv. Panel, 1993–99. Mem., Molecular and Cellular Pharmacol. Gp Cttee, Biochem. Soc., 1993–2000. Mem., Bd of Mgt, Inst. of Epileptology, KCL, 1994–2003. Vice-Pres., Eur. Soc. for Clin. Pharmacol., 2001–08. Mem., Med. Adv. Bd, Bachman-Strauss Foundn, 2000–05. FRSocMed 2011. European Ed., Synapse, 1990–2015; Series Editor: Neurosci. Perspectives, 1991–96; (jtly) Internat. Review of Neurobiol., 1996–; Handling Editor: Jl of Neurochemistry, 1998–2008; Neuropharmacology, 2002–10; Jl of Neural Transmission; Member, Editorial Board: Jl of Pharmacy and Pharmacology; Polish Jl of Pharmacology, 2002–. *Publications:* (with B. Testa) Drug Metabolism: chemical and biochemical aspects, 1976; (ed with B. Testa) Concepts in Drug Metabolism, Part A 1980, Part B 1981; (ed jtly) Approaches to the Use of Bromocriptine in Parkinson's Disease, 1985; (ed jtly) Neurological Disorders, 1987; (ed) Neurotoxins and their Pharmacological Implications, 1987; (ed jtly) Disorders of Movement, 1989; (ed jtly) Neuroprotection in Parkinson's Disease, vol. 3: beyond the decade of the brain, 1998; (ed jtly) Biomedical and Health Research, vol. 19: dopamine receptor subtypes, 1998; contrib. Lancet, Jl Neurochem.; Annals Neurol., Biochem. Pharmacol., Brain Res., Psychopharmacol., Neurosci.; Exptl Neurol.; Jl Pharmacol Exptl Therapeutics; Pharmacol. & Therapeutics; Eur. Jl of Pharmacol.; Clinical Neuropharmacol.; Jl of Neurochem. *Recreations:* gardening, driving. *Address:* Walnut Tree Farm, Long Green, Wortham, Diss, Norfolk IP22 1PU. *T:* (01379) 890533. *Club:* Athenæum.

**JENNER, Air Marshal Sir Timothy (Ivo),** KCB 2000 (CB 1996); FRAeS; Chairman, Board of Trustees, Thames Valley Air Ambulance (formerly Thames Valley and Chiltern Air Ambulance), 2011–19; b 31 Dec. 1945; s of Harold Ivo Jenner and Josephine Dorothy Jenner; m 1968, Susan Lesley Stokes; two d. *Educ:* Maidstone Grammar Sch.; RAF Coll., Cranwell. Wessex Sqdn Pilot and Instructor, UK, ME and Germany, 1968–75; Puma Pilot and Instructor, 1976–78; MoD Desk Officer, Helicopter, 1979–80; Army Staff Coll., Camberley, 1981; OC 33 Sqdn, 1982–84; Military Assistant to: ACDS (Commitments), 1985; DCDS (Programmes & Personnel), 1986; OC, RAF Shawbury, 1987–88; RCDS 1989; Dep. Dir, Air Force Plans, 1990–91; Dir, Defence Progs, 1992–93; AO Plans, HQ Strike Command, 1993; Asst Chief of Defence Staff (Costs Review), 1993–95; ACAS, 1995–98; COS and Dep. C-in-C, Strike Comd, 1998–2000; Comdr, NATO Combined Air Ops Centre 9, 2000; Dir, European Air Gp, 2000; Strategic Advr, Serco Gp, 2001–03; Chm., Serco Defence, then Serco Defence and Aerospace, 2003–05; Sen. Advr, Serco Defence, Sci. and Nuclear (formerly Sen. Military Advr, Serco Defence and Aerospace, then Sen. Advr, Serco Defence, Sci. and Technol.), 2005–11. Advr, Atmaana Ltd, 2006–10. Non-exec. Dir, NATS, 1996–98. FRAeS 1997 (Mem. Council, 2001–03; Pres., Coventry Br., 2002–16). *Recreations:* old cars, photography, mountain walking. *Address:* c/o Lloyds, Coxs & Kings, 39 Piccadilly, W1V 0AA. *Club:* Royal Air Force.

**JENNINGS, Alex Michael;** actor; b 10 May 1957; s of Michael Thomas Jennings and Peggy Patricia Jennings (née Mahoney); partner, Lesley Moors; one s one d. *Educ:* Abbs Cross Tech. High Sch., Hornchurch; Univ. of Warwick (BA); Bristol Old Vic Theatre Sch. *Theatre:* début, Orchard Theatre Co., 1980; The Country Wife, Royal Exchange, Manchester, 1986; seasons at York, Cambridge Th. Co., Bristol Old Vic; Associate Actor with RSC, Stratford and London: Measure for Measure, Taming of the Shrew, Hyde Park, 1987–88; Richard II, 1991–92; Peer Gynt (Olivier Award for Best Actor, 1996), Measure for Measure, A Midsummer Night's Dream, 1994–96; Hamlet (also in NY and Washington) (Helen Hayes Award for Best Actor, 1999), Much Ado About Nothing, 1996–98; Associate Actor with Royal National Theatre: Ghetto, 1989; The Recruiting Officer, 1992; The Winter's Tale, The Relapse (Evening Standard Award for Best Actor), 2001; Albert Speer, 2000; His Girl Friday, 2003; Stuff Happens, 2004; The Alchemist, 2006; Present Laughter, 2007; The Habit of Art, 2009; Collaborators, 2011; Hymn, 2012; Cocktail Sticks, 2012; Hansard, 2019; other London appearances include: Too Clever By Half, 1988 (Olivier Award for Best Comedy Performance, London Theatre Critics' Award for Best Actor, 1987), The Liar, 1987, Old Vic; The Wild Duck, Peter Hall Co., 1990; The Importance of Being Earnest, Aldwych, 1993; My Fair Lady, Th. Royal, Drury Lane (Olivier Award for Best Actor in a Musical), 2002; Candide, ENO, 2008, Japan, 2010; My Fair Lady, Théâtre du Châtelet, 2010, 2013; Charlie and the Chocolate Factory, Th. Royal, Drury Lane, 2014; My Fair Lady, Sydney Opera Hse, 2016; The Light in the Piazza, RFH, 2019; *films:* War Requiem, 1988; A Midsummer Night's Dream, 1995; Wings of the Dove, 1996; The Four Feathers, 2002; Five Children and It, 2004; Bridget Jones: The Edge of Reason, 2004; The Queen, 2006; Babel, 2007; Trap for Cinderella, 2013; Belle, 2014; The Lady in the Van, 2015; Denial, 2017; *television:* Ashenden, 1992; Bad Blood, 1999; Riot at the Rite, 2005; A Very Social Secretary, 2005; State Within, 2006; Cranford, 2007; 10 Days to War, 2008; Hancock and Joan, 2008; Whitechapel, 2009, 2010; Return to Cranford, 2009; On Expenses, 2010; Silk, 2011–14; We'll Take Manhattan, 2012; The Lady Vanishes, 2013; Castles in the Sky, 2014; Foyle's War, 2015; Churchill's Secret, 2015; The Crown, 2016, 2017; Victoria, 2016–18; The Halcyon, 2017; A Very English Scandal, 2018; Unforgotten, 2018; Four Weddings and a Funeral, 2019; Gold Digger, 2019; *concert work:* Peer Gynt (with Gothenberg SO), 1993; with London Mozart Players: The Soldier's Tale, 2001; The Crocodiamond, 2004; Tamos, King of Egypt, 2006; with Medici Quartet, Hymn, 2011; extensive radio work. Hon. DLitt Warwick, 1999; Hon. DA West of England, 2017. *Recreations:* books, painting, shopping. *Address:* c/o Independent Talent Group Ltd, 40 Whitfield Street, W1T 2RH. *T:* (020) 7636 6565.

**JENNINGS, Audrey Mary;** see Frisby, A. M.

**JENNINGS, Colin Brian;** Chief Executive, Wilton Park Conference Centre, Foreign and Commonwealth Office, 1996–2006; b 27 Nov. 1952; s of Brian Jennings and Jean (née Thomas); m 1978, Jane Barfield. *Educ:* Hereford Cathedral Sch.; Univ. of Leicester (BA 1975; MA 1976). Joined MoD, 1976; Procurement Executive, 1976–78; Defence Secretariat, 1979; Second Sec., UK Delegn to NATO, 1980–81 (on secondment); Principal Defence Secretariat, 1982–83; HM Diplomatic Service, 1983–2006; Policy Planning Staff, FCO, 1983–86; First Sec. (Economic), Lagos, 1986–89; Asst, Central and Southern Africa Dept, FCO, 1990–92; Dep. High Comr, Nicosia, 1992–96. Vice Chair, Diplomatic Service Appeal Bd, 2007–11. Special Prof. of Diplomacy, Univ. of Nottingham, 2006–15; Vis. Lectr, Inst. of Policy Studies, Rennes and Univ. of Rennes, 2007–10. Internat. Advr, Electoral Reform Internat. Services, 2009–11. West Cornwall Rep., Cornwall Homeseekers Ltd, 2011–13. *Recreations:* walking the fox terrier, enjoying living in France. *Address:* c/o Wilton Park, Wiston House, Steyning, W Sussex BN44 3DZ.

**JENNINGS, Rt Rev. David Willfred Michael;** Bishop Suffragan of Warrington, 2000–09; an Honorary Assistant Bishop: Diocese of Gloucester, since 2010; Diocese of Oxford, since 2013; b 13 July 1944; s of late Rev. Willfred Jennings and Nona Jennings (née de Winton); m 1969, Sarah Catherine Fynn, d of late Dr Robert Fynn of Harare, Zimbabwe; three s. *Educ:* Summer Fields, Oxford; Radley Coll.; King's Coll., London (AKC 1966). Ordained deacon, 1967, priest, 1968; Assistant Curate: St Mary, Walton on the Hill, Liverpool, 1967–69; Christchurch Priory, Christchurch, Hants, 1969–73; Vicar: Hythe, Southampton, 1973–80; St Edward, Romford, 1980–92; Rural Dean of Havering, 1985–92; Archdeacon of Southend, 1992–2000. Commissary for Bishop of Bahamas, 1986–; Commissary (Acting Bishop), Dio. of Sodor and Man, 2007–08; non-residentiary Canon, Chelmsford Cathedral, 1987–92. Chair, Retired Clergy Assoc., 2012–17. Mem., Governing Council, Liverpool Hope Univ. (formerly UC), 2000–09 (Vice Chm., 2007–09); Gov., Summer Fields, Oxford, 2010–19. *Recreations:* exploring the buildings of the British Isles, walking, reading, listening to music. *Address:* Laurel Cottage, East End, Northleach, near Cheltenham, Glos GL54 3ET. *T:* (01451) 860743. *E:* bishopdavidjennings@gmail.com.

**JENNINGS, Sir John (Southwood),** Kt 1997; CBE 1985; PhD; FRSE; Director, Shell Transport and Trading Company plc, 1987–2001 (Chairman, 1993–97); Vice Chairman, Committee of Managing Directors, Royal Dutch/Shell Group of Companies, 1993–97; Managing Director, Royal Dutch/Shell Group of Companies, 1987–97; b 30 March 1937; s of George Southwood Jennings and Irene Beatrice Jennings; m 1961, Gloria Ann Griffiths (marr. diss. 1996); one s one d; m Linda Elizabeth Baston. *Educ:* Oldbury Grammar Sch.; Univ. of Birmingham (BSc Hons Geology, 1958); Univ. of Edinburgh (PhD Geology, 1961); London Business Sch. (Sloan Fellow, 1970–71). Various posts, Royal Dutch/Shell Group, 1962–2001, including: Gen. Man. and Chief Rep., Shell cos in Turkey, 1976–78; Man. Dir, Shell UK Exploration and Prodn, 1979–84; Exploration and Prodn Co-ordinator, Shell Internationale Petroleum Mij., The Hague, 1985–90. Non-executive Director: Robert Fleming Holdings, 1997–2000; Det Norske Veritas, 1997–2001; MITIE Gp, 1997–2007 (Dep. Chm., 1997–2007); Bechtel Gp Internat., 2002–08; Nexant Inc., 2002–09 (Mem., Adv. Cttee, 2009–11); Xyleco Inc. (Chm., 2007–10; Dep. Chm.); Mem., Internat. Adv. Bd, Toyota, 1997–2005; Chairman: Spectron Gp, 2000–05; Intelligent Energy, 2001–05; Ida Tech plc, 2007–11. Vice Chm., Governing Body, London Business Sch., 1993–97 (Mem., 1992–); Vice Pres., Liverpool Sch. of Tropical Medicine, 1991–97; Member Council: RIIA, 1994–97; Exeter Univ., 1997–99. Chancellor, Loughborough Univ., 2003–10. FRSE 1992. Hon. FGS 1992. Hon. DSc: Edinburgh, 1991; Birmingham, 1997. Commandeur de l'Ordre National du Mérite (Gabon), 1989. *Recreations:* fly fishing, travel, reading. *Clubs:* Brooks's, Flyfishers'.

**JENNINGS, Rev. Jonathan Peter;** Assistant Priest, St Margaret's, Rainham, Kent, since 2016; b 6 March 1961; s of John Harold Jennings and Margaret Jennings (née Amps); m 1998, Helen Jarvis; two s one d. *Educ:* Grangefield Grammar Sch., Stockton-on-Tees; Stockton 6th Form Coll.; KCL (BD); Westcott House, Cambridge. Ordained deacon, 1986, priest, 1987; Curate: St Cuthbert Peterlee, 1986–89; St Cuthbert Darlington, 1989–92; Press and Communications Officer, Dio. Manchester, 1992–95; Broadcasting Officer, Gen. Synod of C of E, 1995–98; Hd of Broadcasting, Archbps' Council, 1998–2001; Press Sec. to Archbp of Canterbury, 2001–08; Priest-in-Charge, St Augustine's, Gillingham, 2008–16; Rural Dean of Gillingham, 2010–11. Producer, religious progs, and news and sports journalist, 1987–2000. Chaplain to HM Forces (V), 1993–. *Recreations:* early music, Middlesbrough FC, cricket, table tennis, sea fishing, steam railways. *Address:* 7 Elmstone Road, Rainham, Kent ME8 9BD.

**JENNINGS, Martin;** sculptor; b Arundel, 31 July 1957; s of Michael Jennings and Mariella Jennings; one s one d. *Educ:* Ampleforth Coll., York; St Benet's Hall, Oxford (MA Hons Eng. Lang. and Lit.). Sculptures include: 3 portrait sculptures for NPG, 2008–11; statues of: Sir John Betjeman, St Pancras Station, 2007; Philip Larkin, Paragon Interchange, Hull, 2010; Charles Dickens, Guildhall Sq., Portsmouth, 2014; Sir Archibald McIndoe, East Grinstead, 2014; Women of Steel, Sheffield, 2016; Mary Seacole, by Westminster Bridge, 2016; George Orwell, BBC Broadcasting House, 2017; John Radcliffe, next to Radcliffe Observatory, Oxford, 2018; Stanley Baldwin, Bewdley, Worcs, 2018. FRSS (FRBS 2000). *Recreations:* books, art, family. *Address:* 7 Welbeck House, 19 Hadow Road, Oxford OX3 0JW. *T:* 07765 117964. *E:* mj@martinjennings.com.

**JENNINGS, Prof. Nicholas Robert,** CB 2016; PhD; FREng; FIEEE; FIET; FBCS; Professor of Artificial Intelligence and Vice-Provost (Research and Enterprise), Imperial College London, since 2016; b London, 15 Dec. 1966; s of Robert George and Valerie Ann Jennings; m 1993, Dr Joanne Smith; one s one d. *Educ:* Univ. of Exeter (BSc 1st Cl. Hons Computer Sci. 1988); Queen Mary and Westfield Coll., Univ. of London (PhD Artificial Intelligence 1992). FBCS 2003; FIET 2004; FREng 2005; FIEEE 2008. Queen Mary College, later Queen Mary and Westfield College, University of London: Res. Asst, Electronic Engrg, 1988–89; Lectr in Electronic Engrg, 1989–95; Reader, 1995–98; Prof. of Electronic Engrg, 1998–99; University of Southampton: Prof. of Electronics and Computer

Sci., 1999–2014; Associate Dean (Res. and Enterprise), Faculty of Engrg, Sci. and Maths, 2008–10; Regius Prof. of Computer Sci., 2014–16; Hd, Electronics and Computer Sci. Dept, 2015–16; Chief Scientific Advr for Nat. Security to UK Govt, 2010–15. Dist. Adjunct Prof., King Abdulaziz Univ., Saudi Arabia, 2011–17. Founding Dir, Internat. Foundn on Autonomous Agents and Multi-Agent Systems, 1998–2012. Scientific Advr, Lost Wax/Aerogility, 2000–; Senior Advisor: Crossword Cybersecurity, 2016–; Contact Engine, 2017–. Mem. Bd, CERT-UK, 2014–16; Mem., UKRI-EPSRC, 2018–. Trustee, BRE, 2015–18. FCGI; FRSA. *Publications:* contrib. scientific articles on artificial intelligence, autonomous systems and agent-based computing. *Recreations:* football, cricket, travel. *Address:* Faculty Building, Room 4.10, Imperial College London, South Kensington Campus, SW7 2AZ. *T:* (020) 7594 2638. *E:* n.jennings@imperial.ac.uk.

**JENNINGS, Rev. Peter;** educational and interfaith consultant; *b* 9 Oct. 1937; *s* of Robert William Jennings and Margaret Irene Jennings; *m* 1963, Cynthia Margaret Leicester; two *s*. *Educ:* Manchester Grammar Sch.; Keble Coll., Oxford (MA); Hartley Victoria Methodist Theological Coll.; Manchester Univ. (MA). Ordained 1965. Minister: Swansea Methodist Circuit, 1963–67; London Mission (East) Circuit, 1967–78, and Tutor Warden, Social Studies Centre, 1967–74; Gen. Sec., Council of Christians and Jews, 1974–81; Associate Minister, Wesley's Chapel, 1978–81; Asst Minister, Walthamstow and Chingford Methodist Circuit, 1981–82; Superintendent Minister: Whitechapel Mission, 1982–91; Barking and Ilford Methodist Circuit, 1991–93; Dir, N E London Religious Educn Centre, 1993–98; Associate Minister: Cambridge Methodist Circuit, 1998–2003; Welshpool and Bro Hafren Methodist Circuit, 2003–06; retired to Wales Circuit, Synod Cymru, 2006. Pastoral Tutor, Centre for Jewish-Christian Relns, Wesley House, Cambridge Univ., 1999–2003. *Publications:* papers and articles on aspects of Christian-Jewish relations. *Recreations:* photography, being educated by Tim and Nick and now by their respective children, Dan, Leah, Dillon and Rosie. *Address:* 5 Cuffnell Close, Liddell Park, Llandudno LL30 1UX. *T:* (01492) 860449.

**JENNINGS, Sir Peter (Nevile Wake),** Kt 2000; CVO 1999; Serjeant at Arms, House of Commons, 1995–99; *b* 19 Aug. 1934; *s* of late Comdr A. E. de B. Jennings, RN and Mrs V. Jennings, MBE; *m* 1958, Shirley Anne (*d* 2012), *d* of late Captain B. J. Fisher, DSO, RN and Mrs C. C. Fisher; one *s* two *d*. *Educ:* Marlborough College; psc (m)†, osc (US). Commissioned 2/Lt, RM, 1952; retired, 1976. Appointed to staff of House of Commons, 1976. Chairman: Central London Br., SSAFA Forces Help, 2001–12; St Martin-in-the-Fields Almshouse Charity, 2004–10; Bowles (formerly Bowles Outdoor Centre), 2004–10; Dep. Chm., 2011–14, Chm., 2014–15, ESU. *Address:* Cross Farm, Chilmark, Salisbury SP3 5AR.

**JENNINGS, Robert Samuel,** MBE 2003; DPhil; Principal, Slemish College, Ballymena, 1996–2010; *b* 29 Aug. 1949; *s* of James and Elizabeth Jennings; *m* 1978, Jennifer Titterington; one *s* one *d*. *Educ:* Stranmillis Coll., Belfast (Cert Ed); London Bible Coll. (BA Hons Theol.); Queen's Univ., Belfast (MTh); Univ. of Ulster (DPhil); Open Univ. (MA). Head of physical educn, 1971–73, and of RE, 1973–75, Antrim High Sch.; Asst Teacher of RE, Wallace High Sch., Lisburn, 1978–80; Head of RE, Rainey Endowed Sch., Magherafelt, 1980–94; Asst Adv. Officer for RE, Western Educn and Library Bd, 1994–96. Pt-time Lectr, Post Grad. Cert. in Expert Teaching, Univ. of Ulster, 1999–. *Publications:* (contrib.) New International Version Thematic Study Bible, 1996. *Recreations:* golf, walking.

**JENNINGS, Saira Kabir;** *see* Sheikh, S. K.

**JENNINGS, Air Vice-Marshal Tamara Nancy,** OBE 2015; Director Legal Services, Royal Air Force, since 2018; *b* Akrotiri, Cyprus, 27 Aug. 1973; *d* of Nigel John Quincey and Janet Mary Quincey; *m* 2002, John Reginald Jennings; one *s* one *d*. *Educ:* Kesteven and Sleaford High Sch.; Lady Manners Sch.; Univ. of Northumbria at Newcastle (LLB Hons); King's Coll. London (MA). Commnd RAF, 2000; Dep. Dir Legal Services, RAF, 2017–18. *Recreations:* hill walking, spinning, theatre.

**JENNINGS, Thomas James,** CBE 2004; CEng, FIMechE; Chairman, Ducales Capital Ltd, since 2013; *b* 1 March 1954; *s* of Gerald and Dorithia Jennings; *m* 1978, Jane Speers; two *s* one *d*. *Educ:* Queen's Univ. of Belfast (BSc). CEng, FIMechE. Grad. engr, 1975; subseq. held mgt posts; Chm. and Man. Dir, Rotary Gp Ltd, 1997–2009; Chm., Ballyrogan Hldgs Ltd, 2008. FRSA 2004. *Recreation:* country sports. *T:* (028) 9181 1361.

**JENNY, Prof. Frédéric,** PhD; Professor of Economics, Business School, since 1972, and Co-director, European Centre for Law and Economics, since 2010, École Supérieure des Sciences Économiques et Commerciales, Paris; *b* Geneva, 29 Sept. 1943; *s* of Frederic Marc Jenny and Madeleine Jenny (*née* Permezel); *m* 1984, Sarah Harrison Beers. *Educ:* Business Sch., École Supérieure des Scis Écon. et Commerciales, Paris (MBA 1966); Harvard Univ. (PhD Econs 1975); Univ. of Paris (Dr Econs 1977). Judge, French Supreme Court, 2004–12. Visiting Professor: Keio Univ., Tokyo, 1984; UCL, 2005–; Faculty of Law, Haifa Univ., Israel, 2012; Global Prof. of Antitrust, New York Univ. Law Sch., NY, 2014; Vis. Lectr, Cape Town Business Sch., SA, 1991. French Competition Authority: Rapporteur, 1978–84, Rapporteur Gen., 1984–93; Vice-Chm., 1993–2004. Mem. Bd, OFT, 2007–14. Chm., Competition Cttee, OECD, 1994–; Pres., Wkg Gp on Trade and Competition, WTO, 1994–2003; Mem., Adv. Bd, Interdisciplinary Centre for Competition Law and Initiative, Middle East Initiative, 2010–. Chm., Scientific Bd, Consumer Unity Trust of India (CUTS), 2009–. Member, Editorial Board: Concurrences, 2008–; World Competition, 2009–; Jl Competition Law and Econs, 2012–. Officier de la Légion d'honneur (France); 2003 (Chevalier, 1992); Officier de l'Ordre du Mérite (France), 1999 (Chevalier, 1988). *Publications:* book chapters; contribs to jls incl. Actualité Juridique, Droit Administratif, Antitrust Bull., Competition Policy, Concurrences, Economia Industrial, Eur. Business Orgn Law Rev., Eur. Econ. Rev., Eur. Merger Control Reporter, Fordham Internat. Law Jl, Internat. Antitrust Law and Policy, Internat. Business Lawyer, Jl Econ. Literature, OECD Jl Competition Law and Policy, Oxera, Rev. d'Economie Industrielle, Rev. française de gestion, Semaine Juridique, Rev. des Affaires Européennes, Rev. de la Concurrence et de la Consommation, Rev. de jurisprudence commerciales, Rev. Lamy de la Concurrence, World Competition Law and Econs Rev. *Recreations:* hiking, sailing. *Address:* 19 rue de l'Estrapade, 75005 Paris, France. *T:* 674654437. *E:* frederic.jenny@gmail.com.

**JENRICK, Rt Hon. Robert;** PC 2019; MP (C) Newark, since June 2014; Secretary of State for Housing, Communities and Local Government, since 2019; *b* Wolverhampton, 1982; *m* 2009, Michal Berkner; three *d*. *Educ:* Wolverhampton Grammar Sch.; St John's Coll., Cambridge (BA 1st Cl. Hist. 2003); Univ. of Pennsylvania (Thouron Fellow 2004); Coll. of Law (Grad. Dip. Law 2005); BPP Law Sch. (Legal Practice Course 2006). Trainee solicitor, Skadden Arps, Slate, Meagher & Flom LLP, 2006–08; admitted as solicitor, 2008; Solicitor, Sullivan & Cromwell LLP, 2008–10; Sen. Exec. and Internat. Man. Dir, Christie's, 2010–14. PPS to Parly Under-Sec. for Energy and Climate Change, 2014–15, to Employment Minister, 2015, to Lord Chancellor and Justice Sec., 2015–18, to Home Sec., 2017–18; Exchequer Sec. to HM Treasury, 2018–19. Mem., Health Select Cttee, 2014–15. Mem. Bd, Cons. Party, 2017–18. Contested (C) Newcastle-under-Lyme, 2010. *Address:* House of Commons, SW1A 0AA; Belvedere, 29a London Road, Newark-on-Trent NG24 1TN.

**JENSEN, Elisabeth, (Liz),** FRSL; writer; *b* Oxon, 26 Nov. 1959; *d* of Niels Rosenvinge Jensen and Valerie Jensen (*née* Corcos); *m* 2010, Carsten Jensen; two *s*. *Educ:* Oxford High Sch.; Somerville Coll., Oxford (BA Hons Eng. Lang. and Lit.). Journalist, South China Morning Post, Hong Kong, 1979–80; radio journalist, ICRT, Taiwan, 1982–83; news reporter and documentary producer, BBC, 1983–87; freelance radio producer and journalist, 1987–95; novelist, critic and creative writing teacher, 1995–. Writer in Residence, Kingston Univ., 2006–12; Course Dir, Creative Writing, Danish Inst. for Study Abroad, Copenhagen, 2016. FRSL 2005. *Publications:* Egg Dancing, 1995; Ark Baby, 1998; The Paper Eater, 2000; War Crimes for the Home, 2002; The Ninth Life of Louis Drax, 2004; My Dirty Little Book of Stolen Time, 2006; The Rapture, 2009; The Uninvited, 2012. *Address:* c/o Aitken Alexander Associates, 291 Gray's Inn Road, WC1X 8EB. *E:* liz.jensen@rocketmail.com.

**JENSEN, Rt Rev. Peter;** Archbishop of Sydney, and Metropolitan of the Province of New South Wales, 2001–13; *b* 11 July 1943; *s* of Arthur Henry Jensen and Dorothy Lake Jensen (*née* Wilins); *m* 1968, Christine Willis Jensen (*née* O'Donell); three *s* two *d*. *Educ:* Univ. of London (BD 1970); Sydney Univ. (MA 1976); Magdalen Coll., Oxford (DPhil 1980). Ordained deacon, 1969, priest, 1970, Anglican Ch of Australia; Curate, Broadway, 1969–76; Asst Minister, St Andrew, N Oxford, 1976–79; Moore College: Lectr, 1973–76 and 1980–84; Principal, 1985–2001. *Publications:* The Quest for Power, 1973; At the Heart of the Universe, 1991; The Revelation of God, 2002; The Future of Jesus, 2005; Power and Promise, 2014. *Recreations:* golf, reading. *Address:* 102/7 Karrabee Avenue, Huntleys Cove, NSW 2111, Australia.

**JENSEN, Tom Risdahl;** Ambassador of Denmark to Russia, 2010–13; *b* 28 Sept. 1947; *s* of Laust and Eva Jensen; *m* 2001, Helle Bundgaard. *Educ:* Univ. of Aarhus, Denmark (BA Scand. Lit. and Langs; MSc Political Sci.). Ministry of Foreign Affairs, Copenhagen, 1977–2015: First Sec., Danish Perm. EU Repn, 1981–84; Hd of Section, 1984–88; Econ. Counsellor, Bonn, 1988–92; Hd of Dept, 1992–97; Under-Sec., 1997–2001; Ambassador: to UK, 2001–06; to Sweden, 2006–10.

**JEPHCOTT, Sir David Welbourn,** 4th Bt *cr* 1962, of East Portlemouth, Devon; *b* 9 Aug. 1952; *er s* of Sir Neil Welbourn Jephcott, 3rd Bt and Mary Denise (*née* Muddiman); *S* father, 2012; *m* 1977, Madeleine Ann, *d* of Maurice Arthur Burridge (marr. diss. 2018); one *d*. *Heir:* *b* Mark Lanwer Jephcott [*b* 23 Feb. 1957; *m* 1st, 1983, Lysa Ann Rigden; one *s* one *d*; 2nd, 2010, Dr Sarah Brigitte Vardy].

**JEPSON, Martin Clive;** President and Chief Operating Officer, Brookfield Office Properties, Europe, 2013–17; *b* Leeds, 6 April 1962; *s* of Donald Jepson and Mildred Jepson; *m* 1988, Anne Cleaver; one *s* one *d*. *Educ:* Garforth Comp. Sch.; Bristol Poly. (BSc Hons Valuation and Estate Mgt 1983). ARICS 1986, FRICS 1999. Director: Sinclair Goldsmith, 1987–93; Conrad Ritblat, 1993–95; Milner Estates, 1995–98; Delancey, 1998–2000; London Regl Dir, Taylor Woodrow Property Co., 2000–03; Chief Exec., Southside Capital, 2003–05; UK Man. Dir, Howard Hldgs, 2005–08; Man. Dir, London Gp, Hammerson plc, 2008–11; Sen. Vice Pres., Brookfield Office Properties, 2011–13. Trustee and Dir, Sparks, 2012–17. *Recreations:* golf, Rugby, cricket, football, walking, cinema, family, reading. *Clubs:* Arts; Walton Heath Golf.

**JEREMIAH, Melvyn Gwynne,** CB 1994; Chairman, Wages and Salary Commission, Republic of Namibia, 1995–97; *b* 10 March 1939; *s* of Bryn Jeremiah and Evelyn (*née* Rogers); *m* 1960, Lilian Clare (*née* Bailey) (marr. diss. 1966). *Educ:* Abertillery County Sch. Apptd to Home Office, 1958; HM Customs and Excise, 1963–75; Cabinet Office, 1975–76; Treasury, 1976–79; Principal Finance Officer (Under Sec.), Welsh Office, 1979–87; Under Sec., DHSS, later DoH, 1987–95; Chief Exec., Disablement Services Authy, 1987–91, on secondment from DoH. Special Advr to Govt of Repub. of Namibia, 1995–97. Sec., Assoc. of First Div. Civil Servants, 1967–70. Pres., Internat. Assoc. of Amateur Heralds, 2006–10 (Sec., 2002–04); Hon. Secretary: Heraldry Soc., 2002–09 (Vice-Pres., 2013; Hon. Fellow, 2014); Friends of City Churches, 2006–11; Chm., White Lion Soc., 2008–16. Churchwarden, 2009–15, Parish Clerk, 2011–, St Stephen Walbrook. Gov., Chelsea and Westminster Hosp. Foundn Trust, 2010–16. Life FRSA 2005. Freeman, City of London, 2002; Liveryman: Co. of Scriveners, 2002; Parish Clerks' Co., 2012. JP Inner London, 2002–09. St Mellitus Medal, Dio. London, 2015. *Recreations:* heraldry, genealogy, ecclesiology. *Club:* Reform.

**JEREMY, David Hugh Thomas;** QC 2006; a Recorder, since 1999; *b* 3 March 1955; *s* of Tom and Sarah Jeremy; *m* 1991, Caroline Jacobs (*d* 2015); three *s* one *d*. *Educ:* Cheltenham Coll.; Exeter Univ. (LLB). Called to the Bar, Middle Temple, 1977; in practice at the Bar specialising in criminal law. *Recreations:* reading newspapers, studying maps, watching my children play sport, camping, researching cheap red wines. *Address:* QEB Hollis Whiteman Chambers, 1–2 Laurence Pountney Hill, EC4R 0EU. *T:* (020) 7933 8855, *Fax:* (020) 7929 3732. *E:* david.jeremy@qebhw.co.uk.

**JERMEY, Dominic James Robert,** CVO 2010; OBE 2001; Director General, Zoological Society of London, since 2017; *b* 26 April 1967; *s* of Kevin Jermey and Maureen Jermey; *m* 2003, Clare Judith Roberts; one *s* one *d*. *Educ:* Tonbridge Sch.; Clare Coll., Cambridge (BA Hons 1989). Corp. Finance Dept, J. H. Schroder Wagg & Co. Ltd, 1990–93; Foreign and Commonwealth Office, 1993–: Second Sec. (Pol), then First Sec. (Afghanistan), Islamabad, 1995–99; First Sec., Skopje, 1999; British Rep., East Timor, 2000; peacekeeping and crisis related roles, London and Kabul, 2000–03; Hd, British Embassy Office (Tsunami Crisis), Phuket, Jan.–Feb. 2005; Dir of Trade and Investment, 2004–06, and Dep. Hd of Mission, 2006–07, Madrid; Man. Dir, Sectors Gp, UK Trade & Investment, 2007–10 (Actg Chief Exec., 2009); Ambassador to the UAE, 2010–14; Chief Exec., UKTI, 2014–15; Internat. Counter-Extremism Coordinator, FCO, 2015–16; Ambassador to Afghanistan, 2016–17. Trustee and Mem. Bd, CAFOD, 2008–. Freeman, 2002, Liveryman, 2009–, Cutlers' Co. *Recreations:* slow triathlete, adventure travel, diving, Hospitalité Notre Dame de Lourdes. *Address:* Zoological Society of London, Regent's Park, NW1 4RY.

**JERMEY, Michael Francis;** Director of News and Current Affairs, ITV, since 2009 (Director of Sport, 2009–12); *b* London, 24 March 1964; *s* of late Clifford George Gray Jermey and Patience Jermey (*née* Hughes); *m* 2003, Caroline, *d* of Baron Taverne, *qv*; one *s*. *Educ:* City of London Sch.; Brasenose Coll., Oxford (BA PPE 1985). Current affairs journalist, Central Television, 1985–86; ITN: trainee, 1986–87; prodn journalist, News, 1987–90; Prog. Ed., News at Ten, 1990–91; Hd, Foreign News, 1991–93; Associate Ed., 1993–95, Dep. Ed., 1995–99, News; Dir of Develt, 1999–2004; Launch Man. Dir, News Channel, 2000–01; Man. Dir, ITN Internat., 2002–04; ITV plc: Ed., Regl News, 2004–07; Dir, Regions and Network News Ops, 2007–09. Commissioning Editor: First Election Debate, ITV, 2010; The Royal Wedding, ITV, 2011; Leaders' Debate, ITV, 2015; Eur. Referendum debates, 2016; Leaders' Debate, 2017; ITV series: Tonight, 2009; Exposure, 2011; The Agenda, 2012; On Assignment, 2014; Peston on Sunday, 2016. Non-exec. Dir, Parliamentary Broadcasting Unit Ltd, 2007–11. Chm., Creative Diversity Network's News

Wkg Gp, 2013–17; Member: Defence Press and Broadcasting Adv. Cttee, 2007–15; Defence and Security Media Adv. Cttee, 2015–. Mem., TV Cttee, BAFTA, 2009–12. Trustee, Rory Peck Trust, 2002–14 (Chm., 2011–14). Ext. Examr, Cardiff Sch. of Journalism, Cardiff Univ., 2013–15; Hon. Prof., Cardiff Univ. Sch. of Journalism, Media and Culture, 2018–. *Recreations:* family, reading, supporting Arsenal FC. *Address:* ITV plc, 2 Waterhouse Square, 140 Holborn, EC1N 2AE. *T:* (020) 7157 6425. *E:* Michael.Jermey@itv.com.

**JERRAM, (Jeremy) James,** CBE 1995; Chairman, Railways Pension Scheme, 1996–2007; *b* 7 Aug. 1939; *s* of Lionel Jerram and Kathleen (*née* Cochrane); *m* 1965, Ruth Middleton; four *d. Educ:* Selwyn Coll., Cambridge (MA). FCA 1966. Arthur Andersen & Co., 1963–71; Standard Telephones & Cables, 1971–87; finance dir, computer software cos, 1987–90; Bd Mem. for Finance, then Vice-Chm., BRB, 1991–2000; Dir, Railways (formerly British Rail) Pension Trustee Co. Ltd, 1991–2010.

**JERSEY,** 10th Earl of, *cr* 1697; **George Francis William Child Villiers;** Viscount Grandison of Limerick (Ire.), 1620; Viscount Villiers of Dartford and Baron Villiers of Hoo, 1691; actor; *b* 5 Feb. 1976; *s* of George Henry Child Villiers, Viscount Villiers (*d* 1998), and of his 2nd wife, Sacha Jane Hooper Valpy (now Mrs Raymond Marshall); *S* grandfather, 1998; *m* 2003, Marianne Simonne, *d* of Peter and Jeannette De Guelle; one *s* three *d. Educ:* Canford Sch.; Birmingham Sch. of Speech and Drama. Patron: Jersey RFC; Macmillan Cancer Support, Jersey; Relate, Jersey. *Recreations:* Rugby, squash, tennis, cricket, sailing, shooting. *Heir: s* Viscount Villiers, *qv. Club:* Royal Automobile.

**JERSEY, Dean of;** *see* Keirle, Very Rev. M. R.

**JERVIS,** family name of **Viscount St Vincent.**

**JERVIS, Simon Swynfen,** FSA; Director of Historic Buildings (formerly Historic Buildings Secretary), National Trust, 1995–2002; *b* 9 Jan. 1943; *s* of late John Swynfen Jervis and Diana (*née* Marriott); *m* 1969, Fionnuala MacMahon; one *s* one *d. Educ:* Downside Sch.; Corpus Christi Coll., Cambridge (schol.). Student Asst, Asst Keeper of Art, Leicester Mus. and Art Gall., 1964–66; Department of Furniture, Victoria and Albert Museum: Asst Keeper, 1966–75; Dep. Keeper, 1975–89; Actg Keeper, 1989; Curator, 1989–90; Dir, Fitzwilliam Mus., Cambridge, 1990–95. Guest Schol., J. Paul Getty Mus., 1988–89, 2003; Ailsa Mellon Bruce Sen. Fellow, Center for Advanced Study in Visual Arts, Nat. Gall. of Art, Washington, 2006–07. Mem., Reviewing Cttee on Export of Works of Art, 2007–15. Chairman: Nat. Trust Arts Panel, 1987–95; Furniture Hist. Soc., 1998–2013 (Ed. Furniture Hist., 1987–92); Walpole Soc., 2003–13. Dir, Burlington Magazine, 1993– (Trustee, 1996–). Trustee: Royal Collection Trust, 1993–2001; Leche Trust, 1995–2013 (Chm., 2007–13); Sir John Soane's Mus., 1999–2002 (Life Trustee, 2002–13; Chm., 2008–13); Emery Walker Trust, 2003–12; Mem., Adv. Council, NACF, 2002–. FSA 1983 (Pres., 1995–2001). Iris Foundn award, Bard Center, NY, 2003. *Publications:* Victorian Furniture, 1968; Printed Furniture Designs Before 1650, 1974; High Victorian Design, 1983; Penguin Dictionary of Design and Designers, 1984; British and Irish Inventories, 2010; (with Dudley Dodd) Roman Splendour, English Arcadia, 2015; many articles in learned jls. *Address:* 45 Bedford Gardens, W8 7EF. *T:* (020) 7727 8739.

**JESKY, John Sydney;** Chair, Pennine Acute Hospitals NHS Trust, 2006–16; *b* London, 12 Dec. 1945; *s* of Isaac and Elizabeth Joan Jesky; *m* 1st, 1972, Lynne Behrens (marr. diss.); twin *s*; 2nd, 2008, Christine Knight. *Educ:* William Ellis Grammar Sch.; London Univ. (BSc (Econ) Hons). Econ. and Mkt Res. Exec., Food Manufacturers' Fedn, 1969–72; Strategic Planning Exec., 1973–76, Business Develt Manager, 1976–77, Mktg and Business Develt Dir, 1977–83, Rank Hovis Ltd; Dep. Man. Dir, Campbell's Foods Ltd, 1984–88; Man. Dir, Crossley Carpets & Yarns Ltd, 1988–90; Gp Man. Dir, Waterford Foods (UK) Ltd, 1992–96; Chief Exec., Lyndale Foods Ltd, 1996–2001; Exec. Chm., FHSC Ltd, 2002–06. Chm., Organisation Development Services Ltd, 2010–11. Non-exec. Dir, Gtr Manchester Strategic HA, 2002–06. Trustee: Princess Royal Trust for Carers, 1999–2009; Music in Hospitals, 2009–13 (Chm., NW Cttee, 2009–13). Mem. Bd, Buxton Fest., 2015–. Gov., RNCM, 2000–09. Freeman, City of London, 2003. *Recreations:* opera, cricket, collecting cricket prints and forgetting their names, collecting clocks and watches. *E:* johnsjesky@gmail.com. *Club:* MCC.

**JESSEL, Sir Charles (John),** 3rd Bt *cr* 1883; farmer; nutrition consultant, since 1987; *b* 29 Dec. 1924; *s* of Sir George Jessel, 2nd Bt, MC, and Muriel (*d* 1948), *d* of Col J. W. Chaplin, VC; *S* father, 1977; *m* 1st, 1956, Shirley Cornelia (*d* 1977), *o d* of John Waters, Northampton; two *s* one *d*; 2nd, 1979, Gwendolyn Mary (marr. diss. 1983), *d* of late Laurance Devereux, OBE, and *widow* of Charles Langer, MA. *Educ:* Eton; Balliol College, Oxford; Northants Inst. of Agric., Moulton, 1952 (Dip with distinction); Dip., Inst. for Optimum Nutrition, 1987. Served War of 1939–45, Lieut 15/19th Hussars (despatches). Chm., Ashford Br., NFU, 1963–64; Mem., Exec. Cttee, Kent Br., NFU, 1960–73; Pres., Kent Br., Men of the Trees, 1979–85, and 1995–2016. Life Vice Pres., British Soc. of Dowsers, 1994 (Pres., 1987–93). Gov., Inst. for Optimum Nutrition, 1994–98 (Chm., 1997–98). Life Mem., British Inst. for Allergy and Envmtl Therapy; Mem., British Assoc. of Nutritional Therapists, 1997–2008 (Fellow, 2008). Patron, Nutritional Cancer Therapy Trust, 1998–2005. Hon. Fellow, Psionic Med. Soc., 1977 (Pres., 1995–2002; Vice Pres., 2003–16); Hon. Mem., Inst. of Psionic Med., 2008. JP Kent 1960–78. *Publications:* (ed) An Anthology of Inner Silence, 1990; Memories by Request, 2011, rev. edn, 2017. *Recreations:* gardening, planting trees, opera, choral works. *Heir: s* George Elphinstone Jessel [*b* 15 Dec. 1957; *m* 1st, 1988, Rose (marr. diss. 1993), *yr d* of James Coutts-Smith; 2nd, 1998, Victoria, *y d* of Captain A. J. B. Naish, CBE, RN]. *Address:* South Hill Farm, Hastingleigh, near Ashford, Kent TN25 5HL. *T:* (01233) 750325. *Club:* Cavalry and Guards.

**JETHWA, Shruti;** *see* Ajitsaria, S.

**JEVANS, Deborah Ann,** CBE 2013; sports consultant; Member of Board, since 2013, and Vice Chair, since 2014, Sport England; *b* London, 20 May 1960; *d* of Reginald Thomas George Jevans and Leslie Isobel Jevans. *Educ:* Loughton County High Sch. Professional tennis player, 1977–83; International Tennis Federation: Dir, Women's Tennis, 1987–91; Gen. Sec., 1991–2001; owner, sports consultancy co., 2001–03; Dir, Sport and Venues, 2012 Olympic Bid, 2003–05; Dir, Sport, LOCOG, 2006–12; CEO, England Rugby 2015, 2012–15. Member: Bd, WTA Tour, 1990–2000; Women in Sport Commn, IOC, 2000–03. Director: All England Lawn Tennis and Croquet Club Ltd, 2008–14; All England Lawn Tennis Championships Ltd, 2008–14; non-exec. Dir, Football League, 2014–. Trustee: Invictus Foundn, 2014–; Fields in Trust, 2016–. *Recreations:* playing and watching sport, history and art, particular interest in sports participation. *Club:* All England Lawn Tennis.

**JEVON, Louise Mary;** *see* Richardson, L. M.

**JEWELL, Prof. Derek Parry,** DPhil; FRCP, FMedSci; Professor of Gastroenterology, University of Oxford, 1999–2008, now Emeritus; Fellow, Green Templeton College (formerly Green College), Oxford, since 1995; Consultant Physician, John Radcliffe Hospital, Oxford, since 1980; *b* 14 June 1941; *s* of Ralph Parry Jewell and Eileen Rose Jewell; *m* 1974, Barbara Margaret Lockwood; one *s* one *d. Educ:* Bristol Grammar Sch.; Pembroke Coll., Oxford (MA, DPhil 1972). FRCP 1979. Radcliffe Travelling Fellow, 1973; Associate Prof. in Medicine, Stanford Univ., USA, 1973–74; Sen. Lectr in Medicine, Royal Free Sch. of Medicine, 1974–80; Sen. Lectr, 1980–97, Reader, 1997–99, Univ. of Oxford. Pres., British Soc. of Gastroenterology, 2001–02. Pres., Oxford Medical Alumni, 2007–10. FMedSci 1999. *Publications:* (with H. C. Thomas) Clinical Gastrointestinal Immunology, 1979; Challenges in Inflammatory Bowel Disease, 2001; (contrib.) Topics in Gastroenterol., 1972, 1980–90; over 400 original papers. *Recreations:* music, reading, gardening. *Address:* Nuffield Department of Medicine, John Radcliffe Hospital, Oxford OX3 9DU.

**JEWELL, John Anthony, (Tony),** FRCGP; Chief Medical Officer for Wales, 2006–12; *b* 6 May 1950; *s* of late John Jewell and Madelon Jewell; *m* 1978, Jane Rickell; two *s. Educ:* Christ's Coll., Cambridge (BA 1972; MB BChir 1976); London Hosp. Med. Coll. DRCOG 1977, DCH 1979; MA Cantab 1996. FFPH 1998, Hon. FFPH 2012; FRCGP 2001. Principal in gen. practice, 1980–90; Consultant, 1994; Director of Public Health: Peterborough, 1996–98; NW Anglia, 1996–98; Cambridgeshire, 1998–2002; Clin. Dir and Dir, Public Health, Norfolk, Suffolk and Cambs SHA, 2002–06. Mem., Tower Hamlets HA, 1982–88. Pres., UK Assoc. of Dirs of Public Health, 2001–06 (Hon. Mem., 2013). Hon. Sen. Vis. Fellow, Cambridge Inst. of Public Health, Univ. of Cambridge, 2013; Associate, Moller Inst., Cambridge, 2018. Hon. Fellow, UWIC, 2007. Hon. DSc Glamorgan, 2011. Alwyn Smith Prize, 2011; President's Award, Chartered Inst. of Envmtl Health, 2012. *Publications:* (with S. Hillier) Healthcare and Traditional Medicine in China 1800–1982, 1984, 2nd edn 2005; (ed) On Call in Africa: in war and peace 1910–1932, 2016; (contrib.) Oxford Handbook of Public Health; (contrib.) Perspectives in Public Health; contribs to jls on road traffic injuries, primary care, counselling and politics of the NHS. *Recreation:* travelling with Dorling Kindersley (DK) guidebooks. *Address:* 34 Marlow House, Kingsley Walk, Cambridge CB5 8NY.

**JEWITT, (Anselm) Crispin;** historian of cartography; Specialist Adviser to British Library on British military cartography, since 2011; Director, National Sound Archive, British Library, 1992–2007; *b* 30 July 1949; *s* of Vivian Henry Anselm Jewitt and Helen Phyllis Jewitt (*née* Charles); *m* 1970, Mary Lee Lai-ling; two *s* one *d. Educ:* Skinners' Sch., Tunbridge Wells; Polytech. of N London. ALA 1974. Curator, Map Liby, 1980–83, Nat. Conspectus Officer, 1984–88, BL; Asst Dir, Nat. Sound Archive, 1988–92. Pres., Internat. Assoc. of Sound and Audiovisual Archives, 1999–2002; Convenor, Co-ordinating Council of Audiovisual Archives Assocs, 2003–07; specialist in 19th and 20th century British mil. cartography, 2011–. Advisor: Arkivet för Ljud och bild, 1998; ScreenSound Australia, 2001. Trustee: Nat. Life Stories Collection, 1992–2007; Wildlife Sound Trust, 1992–2017; Saga Trust, 1999–2007; Bridges, 2008–11. *Publications:* Maps for Empire, 1992; Intelligence Revealed, 2011; book reviews and articles in professional jls. *Recreations:* dogs, trees, whisky. *Address:* Edenbridge, Kent. *E:* crispinjewitt@hotmail.com.

**JEWKES, Sir Gordon (Wesley),** KCMG 1990 (CMG 1980); HM Diplomatic Service, retired; Director, Slough Estates plc, 1992–2002; *b* 18 Nov. 1931; *er s* of late Jesse Jewkes; *m* 1954, Joyce Lyons (*d* 2005); two *s*; *m* 2008, Estelle Heime (*née* Houghton). *Educ:* Barrow Grammar Sch.; Magnus Grammar Sch., Newark-on-Trent, and elsewhere. Colonial Office, 1948; commnd HM Forces, Army, 1950–52; Gen. Register Office, 1950–63; CS Pay Res. Unit, 1963–65; Gen. Register Office, 1965–68; transf. to HM Diplomatic Service, 1968; CO, later FCO, 1968–69; Consul (Commercial), Chicago, 1969–72; Dep. High Comr, Port of Spain, 1972–75; Head of Finance Dept, FCO, and Finance Officer of Diplomatic Service, 1975–79; Consul-General: Cleveland, 1979–82; Chicago, 1982–85; Gov., Falkland Is and High Comr, British Antarctic Territory, 1985–88; Dir-Gen. of Trade and Investment, USA, and Consul-Gen., NY, 1989–91. Dir, Hogg Group, 1992–94; Exec. Dir, Walpole Cttee, 1992–96. Member: Council, Univ. of Buckingham, 1996–2001; Marshall Aid Commemoration Commn, 1996–99; London Metropolitan Adv. Bd, Salvation Army, 1996–2002. DUniv Buckingham, 2007. *Recreations:* music, travel, walking. *Address:* 53 Woodside Avenue, Beaconsfield, Bucks HP9 1JH. *T:* (01494) 678564.

**JEWSON, Sir Richard (Wilson),** KCVO 2019; Lord-Lieutenant of Norfolk, 2004–19; Chairman, Tritax Big Box REIT plc, since 2013; *b* 5 Aug. 1944; *s* of Charles Boardman and Joyce Marjorie Jewson; *m* 1965, Sarah Rosemary Spencer; one *s* three *d. Educ:* Rugby; Pembroke Coll., Cambridge (MA). Joined Jewson & Sons, 1965, Man. Dir, 1974–86; Meyer International: Dir, 1983–93; Group Man. Dir, 1986–91; Dep. Chm., 1990–91; Chm., 1991–93; Chairman: Danogue (formerly Ideal Hardware, then Inter X) plc, 1994–2002; Anglian Housing Gp Ltd, 1996–2001; Eastern Counties Newspapers Gp Ltd, then Archant, 1997–2014 (Dir, 1982–2014); Octagon Healthcare (Holdings) Ltd, 1998–2006; Hy-phen.com Ltd, 2000–01; East Port Great Yarmouth Ltd, 2000–07; PFI Infrastructure plc, 2004–07; Raven Russia Ltd, 2007–; Dep. Chm., Anglian Water, 1994–2002 (Dir, 1991–2002); non-executive Director: Pro Share (UK), 1992–95; Building Centre Gp Ltd, 1992–95; Delian Lloyds Investment Trust, 1993–95; Savills plc, 1994–2004 (Chm., 1995–2004); Queens Moat Houses, 1994–2003 (Chm., 2001–03); Grafton Gp plc, 1995–2013; Miller Insurance Group Ltd, 1995–96; Angerstein Underwriting Trust, 1995–96; Taverham Hall Educnl Trust Ltd, 1998–2004; Temple Bar Investment Trust plc, 2001–; Anglian Water Services Ltd, 2002–04; Jarrold and Sons Ltd, 2003–13; Watts, Blake, Bearne & Co. plc, 2004–07; Clean Energy Brazil plc, 2007–09. Mem., CBI London Region Cttee, 1986–93. CCMI. DL Norfolk, 2000. *Recreations:* golf, sailing, Real tennis, horse trials, gardening, opera, visual arts. *Address:* Dades Farm, Barnham Broom, Norfolk NR9 4BT. *T:* (01603) 757909, *Fax:* (01603) 757909. *Clubs:* Boodle's; Royal West Norfolk Golf; Brancaster Staithe Sailing.

**JEZZARD, Prof. Peter Hamish,** PhD; FInstP; Herbert Dunhill Professor of Neuroimaging, University of Oxford, since 2003; Fellow, since 2003, and Vice-Master, since 2018, University College, Oxford; *b* Middlesbrough, 6 Nov. 1965; *s* of Frank Ernest Jezzard and Kathleen May Jezzard; *m* 2000, Helen Rachel Simms; two *s* one *d. Educ:* Univ. of Manchester (BSc Physics 1987); Darwin Coll., Cambridge (PhD MRI Physics 1991). FInstP 2007. National Institutes of Health, USA: Vis. Fellow, 1991–95; Unit Chief, Unit on MRI Physics, 1995–97; MRC Ext. Scientific Staff, Univ. of Oxford, 1998–2003; Res. Fellow, Wolfson Coll., Oxford, 2000–03. Pres., Internat. Soc. for Magnetic Resonance in Medicine, 2013–14 (Fellow, 2008). Ed.-in-Chief, Magnetic Resonance in Medicine, 2020–. *Publications:* (jtly) Functional MRI: an introduction to methods, 2001; (contrib.) Quantitative Magnetic Resonance in the Brain: monitoring disease progression and treatment response, 2003; (contrib.) MR Imaging in White Matter Diseases of the Brain and Spinal Cord, 2005; (contrib.) Handbook of Medical Image Processing, 2nd edn 2008; (contrib.) Clinical MR Neuroimaging, 2nd edn 2010; (contrib.) Clinical Perfusion MRI, 2013; (contrib.) Brain Mapping: an encyclopedic reference, 2014; contribs to scientific jls incl. Radiol., Proc. NAS, Neuroimage, Neurol., Magnetic Resonance in Medicine. *Recreations:* walking, pottering in my woodshop, making furniture. *Address:* Oxford Centre for Functional Magnetic Resonance Imaging of the Brain, John Radcliffe Hospital, Oxford OX3 9DU. *T:* (01865) 611452. *E:* peter.jezzard@univ.ox.ac.uk.

**JHOTI, Dr Harren,** FMedSci; FRS 2018; Chief Executive Officer, Astex Therapeutics Ltd, since 2007; *b* India, 1962; *s* of Dilbag Singh and Surinder Kaur; *m* Kate Hilyard; two *d. Educ:* Queen Mary Coll., Univ. of London (BSc Hons Biochem. 1985); Birkbeck Coll., Univ. of

London (PhD 1989). Postdoctoral scientist, Univ. of Oxford, 1989–91; Scientist/Manager, Glaxo, subseq. Glaxo Wellcome, 1991–99; Chief Scientific Officer, Astex Therapeutics Ltd, 1999–2007. FMedSci 2015. *Publications:* articles in jls incl. Nature and Science. *Recreations:* opera, punk-rock music, Formula One, dancing. *E:* jhoti@astx.com.

**JI Chaozhu;** Under-Secretary General of the United Nations, 1991–96; *b* Shanxi Province, 30 July 1929; *s* of Dr Chi Kung-Chuan, Commissioner of Education, and Chang Tao-Jan; *m* 1957, Wang Xiangtong; two *s*. *Educ:* Primary and secondary schools in Manhattan; Harvard Univ. (reading Chemistry); Tsinghua Univ. (graduated 1952). English stenographer at Panmunjom, Korea, for Chinese People's Volunteers, 1952–54; English interpreter for Chinese leaders, incl. Chairman Mao, Premier Chou En-Lai, 1954–73; Dep. Dir, Translation Dept, Foreign Ministry, 1970–73; Counsellor, Liaison Office, Washington DC, 1973–75; Dep. Dir, Dept of Internat. Organisations and Confs, Foreign Min., 1975–79; Dep. Dir, Dept of American and Oceanic Affairs, Foreign Min., 1979–82; Minister-Counsellor, US Embassy, 1982–85; Ambassador to Fiji, Kiribati and Vanuatu, 1985–87; Ambassador to UK, 1987–91. Vice Pres., All China Fedn of Returned Overseas Chinese, 1996–2005. *Publications:* The Man on Mao's Right: from Harvard Yard to Tiananmen Square, my life inside China's foreign ministry (autobiog.), 2008. *Recreations:* swimming, music.

**JIANG ENZHU;** Chairman, Foreign Affairs Committee, National People's Congress, China, 2003–08; *b* 14 Dec. 1938; *s* of Jiang Guohua and Yu Wen Guizhen; *m* 1967, Zhu Manli; one *s*. *Educ:* Beijing Foreign Languages Inst. Teacher, Beijing Foreign Languages Inst., 1964; London Embassy, People's Republic of China, 1964–77; Ministry of Foreign Affairs: Dep. Dir, 1978, Dir, 1983, Dep. Dir-Gen. and Dir-Gen., 1984–90, Dept of W European Affairs; Asst Minister, 1990–91; Vice Foreign Minister, 1991–95; Chinese Ambassador to UK, 1995–97; Dir, Xinhua News Agency (Hong Kong Br.), 1997–2000; Minister, Liaison Office of Central People's Govt, HKSAR, 2000–02. Chief Negotiator for People's Republic of China in Sino-British talks over future of Hong Kong, 1993; a Dep. Hd, Prelim. Wkg Cttee of Preparatory Cttee, HKSAR, 1993–95. Res. Fellow, Center for Internat. Affairs, Harvard Univ., and Sen. Vis. Scholar, Brookings Inst., USA, 1981–82. *Address:* Foreign Affairs Committee, National People's Congress, 23 XI Jiao Min Xiang, Beijing 100805, People's Republic of China.

**JIANG ZEMIN;** President, People's Republic of China, 1993–2003; Chairman, Central Military Commission, 1990–2004; *b* Yangzhou City, Aug. 1926. *Educ:* Jiaotong Univ., Shanghai. Participated in student movement led by underground Party orgns, 1943; joined Communist Party of China, 1946. Associate engr, section chief and power workshop dir, factory Party sec., then First Dep. Dir, Shanghai Yimin No 1 Foodstuffs Factory; First Dep. Dir, Shanghai Soap Factory; Section Chief of electrical machinery, Shanghai No 2 Designing Sub-bureau, First Min. of Machine-building Industry; trainee, Stalin Automobile Plant, Moscow, 1955; Dep. Chief, Power Div., Dep. Chief Power Engr, and Dir, Power Plant, Changchun No 1 Auto Works, 1956–62; Dep. Dir, Shanghai Electric Equipt Res. Inst., 1962; Dir and actg Party sec., Wuhan Thermo-Tech. Machinery Res. Inst.; Dep. Dir, and Dir, Foreign Affairs Bureau, First Min. of Machine-building Industry; Vice-Chm. and Sec.-Gen., State Commns on Admin of Imports and Exports and on Admin of Foreign Investment, 1980–82; Vice Minister and Dep. Sec., Party Gp, later Minister and Sec., Party Gp, Min. of Electronics Industry, 1982–85. Mayor of Shanghai and Dep. Sec., later Sec., Shanghai Municipal Party Cttee, 1985. Communist Party of China Central Committee: Mem., 1982; Mem., Political Bureau, 1987 (Mem., Standing Cttee, 1989, Gen. Sec.); Chm., Military Cttee, 1989. *Address:* 25 Huangsi Dajie, Beijing 100011, People's Republic of China.

**JICKELLS, Prof. Timothy David,** PhD; CChem, FRSC; Professor of Environmental Sciences, University of East Anglia, 1998–2018; *b* Cardiff, 18 June 1953; *s* of John and Noreen Jickells; *m* 1976, Susan Baker. *Educ:* Barry Comprehensive Sch.; Univ. of Reading (BSc 1st Cl. Chem. 1974); Univ. of Southampton (MSc Oceanography 1975; PhD Oceanography 1986). CChem 2012, FRSC 2012. Asst Marine Chemist, Clyde River Purification Bd, 1975–79; Res. Associate, Bermuda Biol Station, 1979–85; Lectr, 1985–93, Reader, 1993–98, UEA. Theme Leader, NERC, 2007–12. Mem., Scientific Adv. Council, DEFRA, 2016–. Mem., Broads Authy, England's Nat. Park Authorities, 2019–. Trustee, Plymouth Marine Lab., 2014–. Fellow, Amer. Geophysical Union, 2016. *Publications:* (jtly) An Introduction to Environmental Chemistry, 2004; (with R. Chester) Marine Geochemistry, 2012; contrib. scientific papers. *Recreations:* walking and cycling, gardening, cinema, cricket. *Address:* School of Environmental Sciences, University of East Anglia, Norwich Research Park, Norwich NR4 7TJ.

**JILANI, Asaf;** journalist and broadcaster; a pioneer of Urdu journalism in the UK; Senior Producer, South Asia Region (formerly Eastern) Service, BBC World Service, 1983–2010; *b* 24 Sept. 1934; *s* of Abdul Wahid Sindhi and Noor Fatima Jilani; *m* 1961, Mohsina Jilani; two *s* one *d*. *Educ:* Jamia Millia, Delhi; Sindh Madrasa, Karachi; Karachi Univ. (MA, Economics). Sub-Editor, Daily Imroze, Karachi (Progressive Papers Ltd), 1952; Political Corresp., Daily Imroze, 1954; Special Corresp., Daily Jang, Karachi (posted in India), 1959–65; first Urdu journalist to be posted as a foreign correspondent; held prisoner in Delhi during India/Pakistan War, 1965; London Editor: Daily Jang (Karachi, Rawalpindi, Quetta); Daily News, Karachi, and Akhbar-e-Jehan, Karachi, 1965–73; Editor, Daily Jang, London (first Urdu Daily in UK), 1973–82; writer: London Letter for Akhbar-e-jahan, Karachi, 2009–; columns for Daily Jehan Pakistan, Karachi, Lahore and Islamabad, 2013–14; columns for Daily Jasarat, Karachi and Lahore, 2014–; columns for Daily Aag, Lucknow, 2013–; columns for Daily Ausaf, London and Nia Zamana online, 2010–. Iqbal Medal (Pakistan), for journalistic contribution to exposition of Islamic poetic philosopher Dr Mohammed Iqbal, during his centenary celebrations, 1979. *Publications:* Wast Asia, Nai Azadi Nay Challenge (Central Asian Journey, in Urdu; based on 21 prog. series for BBC World Service), 1994; Gaon Gaon Badalti Dunia (Changing Villages, in Urdu; based on 36 prog. series for BBC Urdu Service), 1998; Saghar Shishay Lalo Gohar: a collection of articles, 2009; Shehar e Bekaran (Problems and Challenges Faced by the Large Cities of the India/Pakistan Subcontinent, in Urdu; based on 30 prog. series for BBC Urdu Service), 2009, 2nd edn 2015; Europe Ke Asiai (Asians in Europe), 2012. *Recreations:* walking, swimming, painting. *Address:* 17 Leys Gardens, Cockfosters, Herts EN4 9NA.

**JILES, Prof. David Collingwood,** PhD, DSc; CEng, FREng, FInstP, FIEEE, FIET, FIMA, FIMMM; Anson Marston Distinguished Professor of Engineering, 2003–05 and since 2010, and Palmer Endowed Chair in Electrical and Computer Engineering, since 2010, Iowa State University, Ames (Chairman, Department of Electrical and Computer Engineering, 2010–16); *b* London, 28 Sept. 1953; *s* of Kenneth Gordon Jiles and Vera Ellen Jiles (*née* Johnson); *m* 1979, Helen Elizabeth Graham; two *s* two *d*. *Educ:* Univ. of Exeter (BSc 1975); Univ. of Birmingham (MSc 1976; DSc 1990); Univ. of Hull (PhD 1979). FInstP 1988; CEng 1989; Registered Professional Engr, USA, 1989; FIEEE 1994; FIET (FIEE 1995); FIMA 1999; FIMMM 2007; FREng 2014. Postdoctoral Fellow, Phys Dept, Victoria Univ., NZ, 1979–81; Res. Associate, Phys Dept, Queen's Univ., Kingston, Canada, 1981–84; Ames Laboratory, US Dept of Energy: Res. Fellow, 1984–86; Associate Physicist, then Physicist, 1986–90; Sen. Scientist, 1990–2005, Iowa State University: Asst Prof., then Associate Prof., 1986–90; Prof. of Materials Sci. and Engrg, 1990–2005; Prof. of Electrical and Computer Engrg, 1992–2005; Prof., Dir and Royal Soc. Res. Fellow, Wolfson Centre for Magnetics, Cardiff Univ., 2005–10 (Hon. Prof., 2010–). Visiting Professor: Dept of Applied Phys, Univ. of Hull, 1991, 1994; Fraunhofer Inst., Univ. of the Saarland, 1992, 1997; Vienna Univ. of Technol., 2000, 2003, 2007; Wolfson Centre for Magnetics, Cardiff Univ., 2004; Univ. of Sheffield, 2010; Vis. Scientist, Inst. of Phys, Czech Acad. of Scis, 1999. Fellow: Magnetics Soc., 1994; APS 1997; Japanese Soc. for the Promotion of Sci., 2006. Hon. Fellow, Indian Soc. for Nondestructive Testing, 2011. Member: Eta Kappa Nu, IEEE, 2011–; Tau Beta Pi, 2011–. Editor-in-Chief, IEEE Trans. on Magnetics, 2005–11. *Publications:* Introduction to Magnetism and Magnetic Materials, 1991, 3rd edn 2015; Introduction to the Electronic Properties of Materials, 1994, 2nd edn 2001; Introduction to the Principles of Materials Evaluation, 2007; over 600 scientific papers in learned jls and confs; 18 patents. *Recreations:* classical music, opera, chess, running, soccer, squash. *Address:* Department of Electrical and Computer Engineering, Iowa State University, Ames, IA 50011, USA. *T:* (515) 2941097, *Fax:* (515) 2943637.

**JILLINGS, Godfrey Frank;** Deputy Chairman, Gladedale Holdings plc, 2000–09; *b* 18 May 1940; *s* of late Gerald Frank Jillings and Dorothy Marjorie Jillings; *m* 1967, Moira Elizabeth McCoy (*d* 1986); one *s*; civil partnership 2006, *m* 2015, Ian Mitchell Takats, *s* of late Tibor Lajos Takats and of Constance Elizabeth Takats. *Educ:* Tiffin Sch., Kingston; Inst. of Personnel Management. DMS; FCIB. S. G. Warburg & Co. Ltd, 1956–58; National Westminster Bank Ltd, 1958–90: Head of Industrial Section, 1983; Sen. Project Manager, 1985–86; Director: County Unit Trust Managers Ltd, 1986–87; Natwest Stockbrokers Ltd, 1986–89; Chief Exec., Natwest Personal Financial Management Ltd, 1987–89; Senior Exec., Group Chief Exec.'s Office, 1989–90; Chief Exec., FIMBRA, 1990–94; Dir, Financial Services Initiative, later Dir, London Office, WDA, 1994–97. A Dep. Chief Exec., PIA, 1992–94. Chm., John Gater Holdings Ltd, 1994–95; Director: DBS Mgt plc, 1994–2001 (Dep. Chm., 1996–2001); Baronsmead VCT plc, 1995–2014; DBS Financial Management plc, 1997–2001; Baronsmead VCT 2 plc, 1998–2010; Spring Studios Ltd, 2004–14 (Chm., 2006–13); Chm., Ma Potter's plc, 2002–07. *Recreations:* travel, chess, golf. *Address:* 1 Fairacres, Roehampton Lane, SW15 5LX. *Club:* Royal Automobile.

**JINGA, Ion,** PhD; Ambassador and Permanent Representative of Romania to the UN, New York, since 2015; *b* Daneasa, Romania, 1 Sept. 1961; *s* of Ion Jinga and Viorica Jinga; *m* 1987, Daniela Doina; one *d*. *Educ:* Dinicu Golescu High Sch., Câmpulung-Muscel; Univ. of Bucharest (BSc Physics 1986; BA Law 1992); National Sch. for Pol and Admin. Studies, Bucharest (MA Public Admin 1992); College of Europe, Bruges (MA Eur. Admin 1992); Inst. for Internat. Studies, Univ. of Leeds, 1993; Al. I. Cuza Acad., Bucharest (PhD Law 1999). Teacher: Economic High Sch. no. 4, Bucharest, 1984–85; Secondary Sch. no. 127, Bucharest, 1985–86; Physicist Engr, Nuclear Energy Reactors Inst., Pitesti, 1986–91; Hd of Protocol, Mass Media and External Rels Office, Arges Co. Govt, Pitesti, 1991–92; Third Sec., Directorate for EU Affairs, 1992–94, Second Sec., Minister's Office, 1994–95, Min. of Foreign Affairs, Bucharest; First Sec., 1995–98, Dep. Hd of Mission, 1998–99, Mission of Romania to the EU, Brussels; Counsellor, Directorate for EU Affairs, Min. of Foreign Affairs, 1999–2000; Dep. Hd of Mission, then Chargé d'Affaires ai, Mission of Romania to the EU, Brussels, 2000–01; Mem., Romanian Delegn, and Coordinator of Nat. Secretariat, Convention on the Future of Europe, 2002; Dir Gen. for EU Affairs, Min. of Foreign Affairs, Bucharest, 2002–03; Ambassador of Romania to Belgium, 2003–08, to the UK, 2008–15. NATO Res. Fellow, 1997–99. Member: Scientific Council, Romanian Magazine for Community Law, 2003–; Eur. Gp for Evaluation and Prospective, 2005–; Founder Mem., Romanian Soc. for Eur. Law, 2009–. Co-Patron, Scottish Romanian Univs Exchange, 2010–; Member: Bd, Mid-Atlantic Club, London, 2010–15; Atlantic Council of UK, 2011–15; Life Mem., Manchester Debating Union, Manchester Univ., 2011–. Freeman: City of London, 2014; City of Glasgow, 2014. Patriarchal Cross, Romanian Orthodox Church, 2005; Hon. Citizen, Câmpulung-Muscel, 2007; Dip. of Excellence and Son of the Arges County, 2007; Medal of Excellence, Nat. Sch. for Pol and Admin. Studies, Bucharest, 2012; Hon. Award of Achievement, Romanian Nat. Union of Students UK, 2014; Diplomat of Year, Belgium, 2008; Eur. Diplomat of Year, 2012, Diplomat of Year, UK, 2015, Tata/Diplomat Mag. Officer, Nat. Order for Merit (Romania), 2000; Cross, Romanian Royal House, 2008; Officier, l'Ordre national du mérite (France), 2003; Grand Cross, Order of the Crown (Belgium), 2008; Silver Medal (State of Jersey), 2014. *Publications:* over 100 articles and interviews published in British media, mainly on Romanians living in UK, free movement of people, Romania's economy and British-Romanian relations, UN policies, Romania at the UN. *Recreations:* literature, history, travelling, tennis, ski-ing, swimming. *Address:* Permanent Mission of Romania to the UN, 573–577 Third Avenue, New York, NY 10016, USA.

**JINKINSON, Alan Raymond;** General Secretary, UNISON, 1993–96; *b* 27 Feb. 1935; *s* of Raymond and Maggie Jinkinson; *m* 1968, Madeleine Gillian Douglas (*d* 1995). *Educ:* King Edward VII Sch., Sheffield; Keble Coll., Oxford (BA Hons). National and Local Government Officers' Association: Education Dept, 1960; District Officer, 1967; District Orgn Officer, 1973; National Officer (Local Govt), 1976; Asst Gen. Sec., 1981; Dep. Gen. Sec., 1983; Gen. Sec., 1990. *Recreations:* cinema, opera, theatre, walking, watching cricket. *Address:* 10 Princethorpe Road, SE26 4PF. *T:* (020) 8778 1098.

**JIRIČNA, Eva Magdalena,** CBE 1994; RA 1997; RDI 1991; architect; Principal of own practice, 1984–2017; President, Architectural Association, 2003–05; *b* 3 March 1939; *d* of Josef Jiričny and Eva (*née* Svata); *m* 1963, Martin Holub (marr. diss. 1973). *Educ:* Coll. of Architecture and Town Planners, Univ. of Prague (Engr Architect 1962); Acad. of Fine Arts, Prague (Acad. Architect 1967). Professional practice and management examination, RIBA, 1973. Main projects include: AMEC plc, London HQ; Boodle & Dunthorne (later Boodles), Jewellers, Dublin, London, Chester, Manchester and Liverpool; Prague HQ, Andersen Consulting; Canada Water Bus Stn, Jubilee Line Extension; Orangery, Prague Castle; Hotel Josef, Prague; RA shop, London; V&A Museum: masterplan; Modernism Exhibn; Jewellery Gall.; Canary Wharf penthouses; Selfridges shopfronts, London; Faith Zone, Millennium Dome. Hon. Prof. of Architecture and Design, Univ. of Applied Arts, Prague, 2002. Mem. AIA 2006.

**JOACHIM, Rev. Dr Margaret Jane;** Operations Manager, Fujitsu Services Ltd, 2011–14; Minister in Secular Employment, Diocese of London, since 1997; *b* 25 June 1949; *d* of late Reginald Carpenter and Joyce Margaret Carpenter; *m* 1970, Paul Joseph Joachim (*d* 2011); one *d*. *Educ:* Brighton and Hove High School; St Hugh's College, Oxford (MA Geology); Univ. of Birmingham (PhD Geology); Southern Dioceses Ministerial Trng Scheme; Sch. of Advanced Study, Univ. of London (MA History of the Book 2016). FRES 1983; FGS 1991. Grammar school teacher, 1971–76; post-doctoral research Fellow, Univ. of Birmingham, 1976–79; computer consultant, 1979–84; Futures Database Manager, Rudolf Wolff & Co., 1984–87; EDS (Electronic Data Systems) Ltd: Manager, UK Insurance Services, 1988–91; Leadership and Professional Develt Instr, 1991–93; Sen. Relationship Manager (Insce), 1994–96; Manager, EMEA Year 2000 Services, 1997–2000; Client Delivery Manager, 2000–02; Global Support Manager, 2002–03; UK Applications Prog. Manager, ABN Amro Account, 2003; Prog. Dir, 2003–04, EMEA Applications Delivery Manager (Insce), 2004–05, Applications Develt Manager, EMEA Financial Services Applications Industry Unit, 2005–06, EDS Credit Services Ltd; Prog. Manager, 2006–10, Hd, Progs, Information and Technol. Gp, 2010–11, Fujitsu Services Ltd. Asst Dir,

Taskforce 2000, 1997 (on secondment). Training Officer, Liberal Party Assoc., 1979–84; Mem., Exec. Cttee, Women's Liberal Fedn, 1984–85; Chair, Fawcett Soc., 1984–87 (Vice-Chair, 1993–95; Mem. Exec. Cttee, 1990–95); Trustee, Fawcett Trust, 1995–2005; Chair, internat. working gp to set up EEC Women's Lobby, 1988–90; Chair, 1989–90, Vice-Chair, 1990–92, WLD (formerly SLD Women's Orgn). Co-ordinator, Women into Public Life Campaign, 1987–88; Vice-Chair, 1989, Mem. Exec. Cttee, 1989–91, 300 Gp. Contested: (L) West Gloucestershire, 1979; (L/Alliance) Finchley, 1983; (L/Alliance) Epsom and Ewell, 1987. Chair: Lib Dem London Region Candidates' Cttee, 2007–10; Lib Dem English Candidates' Cttee, 2011–14; Regl Parties Cttee, 2015–; Vice-Chair, Lib Dem English Pty, 2015–. Ordained deacon, 1994, priest, 1995; Asst Curate (non-stipendiary), St Barnabas, Ealing, 1994–97, St Peter's, Mount Park, Ealing, 1998–. Moderator, 1999–2002, 2007–09, Sec., 2009–16, CHRISM (Christians in Secular Ministry). Trustee: Christians in Secular Employment Trust, 2003–; Royal Assoc. for Deaf People, 2007–13 and 2016–. Mem., Exec. Cttee, Nat. Traction Engine Club, 1976–79; Founder, Steam Apprentice Club, 1978; Founder, Oxford Univ. Gilbert and Sullivan Soc., 1968. *Publications:* papers in: Studies in the Late-Glacial of North-West Europe, 1980; Holocene Palaeoecology and Palaeohydrology, 1986; Jl of the Edinburgh Bibliographical Soc., 2019; Edinburgh History of Reading, 2019. *Recreations:* walking, reading, making jam, gardening, research into heraldry in medieval manuscripts (studying for PhD), household servant to two cats. *Address:* 8 Newburgh Road, W3 6DQ. *T:* (020) 8723 4514. *E:* margaret.joachim@london.anglican.org. *Club:* Reform.

**JOB, Sir Peter James Denton,** Kt 2001; Chief Executive, Reuters Group PLC, 1991–2001; *b* 13 July 1941; *s* of late Frederick Job and of Marion Job (*née* Tanner); *m* 1966, Christine Cobley, *d* of Frederick Cobley; one *s* one *d*. *Educ:* Clifton College; Exeter College, Oxford (BA). Trainee Reuter journalist, 1963; reporter then manager in Paris, New Delhi, Kuala Lumpur, Jakarta and Buenos Aires, 1963–78; Man. Dir, Reuters Asia, based in Hong Kong, 1978–90; Dir, Reuters Gp, 1989–2001; Chm., Visnews Ltd, 1991–92. Non-executive Director: Grand Metropolitan, 1994–97; Glaxo Wellcome, 1997–99; Diageo, 1997–99; Schroders, 1999–2010 (Sen. Ind. Dir, 2004–10); GlaxoSmithKline, 2000–04; Instinet, 2000–05; TIBCO Software Inc., 2000–14 (Presiding Dir, 2007–14); Royal Dutch Shell (formerly Shell Transport & Trading), 2001–10. Member Supervisory Board: Deutsche Bank AG, 2001–11; Bertelsmann AG, 2002–05. Chm., Internat. Adv. Council, NASDAQ, 1999; Member: DTI Multimedia Adv. Gp, 1994–97; DTI Japan Trade Gp, 1994–98; HM Treasury Adv. Panel, 1995; High Level Adv. Gp on Information Society, EU, 1996; FCO Business Panel, 1998; INSEAD UK Nat. Council, 1993–2001. Trustee, Action on Hearing Loss (formerly RNID), 2010–14. Hon. Fellow, Green Coll., Oxford, 1995. Hon. DLitt Kent, 1998; Hon. DLaws Exeter, 2008. Comdr, Order of the Lion (Finland), 2001. *Recreations:* boating, golf, tennis, early choral music, gardening, theatre, country sports. *Address:* 701 Rowan House, 9 Greycoat Street, SW1P 2QD. *Clubs:* Garrick, Oriental; Hong Kong (Hong Kong); Tadmarton Golf.

**JOBBINS, Robert,** OBE 2001; PhD; media consultant, since 2001; Director of News, BBC World Service, 1996–2001; *b* 2 Nov. 1941; *s* of Henry Robert Jobbins and Miriam Jeffrey Jobbins; *m* 1st, 1962, Jenifer Ann Rowbotham (marr. diss. 1991); two *s*; 2nd, 1992, Jacqueline Duff. *Educ:* Rickmansworth Grammar Sch.; Univ. of Essex (MA Art History, 2005; PhD 2015). BBC Foreign Correspondent: Cairo, 1977–83; Singapore, 1983–86; Head of BBC Arabic Service, 1986–89; Editor, BBC World Service News and Current Affairs, 1989–96. Ind. Mem., Essex Police Authy, 2001–05. Chm., Rory Peck Trust, 2001–10. Chm., Media Legal Defence Initiative, 2017– (Trustee, 2013–). *Recreations:* art history, opera, walking. *Address:* 11 North End, Bassingbourn, Cambs SG8 5NX. *T:* (01763) 242931.

**JOBLING, Karen Elizabeth;** *see* Todner, K. E.

**JOBSON, Roy;** Director of Children and Families Department, Edinburgh City Council, 2005–07; *b* 2 June 1947; *s* of James Jobson and Miriam H. Jobson; *m* 1971, Maureen Scott; one *s* two *d*. *Educ:* Bedlington Grammar Sch.; Univ. of Durham; Newcastle and Sunderland Polytechnics. Teacher: King's Sch., Tynemouth, 1970–73; Norham High Sch., 1973–74; Asst Sec., E Midland Regional Examining Bd, 1974–80; Asst Dir of Educn, Gateshead Metropolitan Borough Council, 1980–84; Dep. Chief Educn Officer, 1984–88, Chief Educn Officer, 1988–98, Manchester City Council; Dir of Education, Edinburgh CC, 1998–2005. Adviser: AMA, 1993–97; LGA, 1997–98. Member: Jt Council for GCSE, 1989–93; NEAB, 1992–93; Soc. of Educn Officers, 1988–2007; Chm., ACEO, 1997–98; Pres., Assoc. of Dirs of Educn in Scotland, 2004–05 (Vice-Pres., 2003–04). FRSA 1994. Hon. DS Heriot-Watt, 2010. *Recreations:* children, family, church, music, dogs. *Address:* 4 Buckstone View, Edinburgh EH10 6PE. *T:* (0131) 469 3322.

**JOCELYN,** family name of **Earl of Roden.**

**JOCELYN, Viscount; Shane Robert Henning Jocelyn;** Investment Analyst, Institutional Clients Group, Citi, since 2014; *b* 9 Dec. 1989; *s* and *heir* of Earl of Roden, *qv*. *Educ:* London Business Sch.; Harvard Univ. CFA. Intern: Hiscox, 2006; Brewin Dolphin, 2006; Summer Analyst: BCM & Partners, 2007; Key Capital (Deutsche Bank), 2008; Asset Mgt, Union Investment Mgt/Dollarhane, 2008–11; Special Situations, TLG Capital, 2011–13. *Recreations:* business, ice hockey, travelling, Rugby.

**JODRELL, Prof. Duncan Ian,** DM; FRCPE; Professor of Cancer Therapeutics, University of Cambridge, since 2008; Researcher, Cancer Research UK Cambridge Institute, since 2008; *b* Warrington, 8 Oct. 1958; *s* of Ian and Joyce Jodrell. *Educ:* Univ. of Southampton (BM 1982; DM 1990); Univ. of London (MSc 1989). FRCPE 1999. Registrar, Royal Marsden Hosp., London, 1986–87; Clinical Fellow, Inst. of Cancer Res., Univ. of London, 1987–90; Vis. Asst Prof., Univ. of Maryland at Baltimore, 1990–91; Sen. Registrar and Lectr, Beatson Oncol. Centre, Univ. of Glasgow, 1991–94; University of Edinburgh: Sen. Lectr, 1994–98, Reader, 1998–2006; Prof. of Cancer Therapeutics, 2006–08. *Recreations:* golf, hill-walking. *Address:* Cancer Research UK Cambridge Institute, Li-Ka Shing Centre, University of Cambridge, Robinson Way, Cambridge CB2 0RE. *T:* (01223) 769750. *E:* dij21@cam.ac.uk. *Club:* Gog Magog (Cambridge).

**JOEL, William Martin, (Billy);** singer, pianist and songwriter, since 1972; *b* 9 May 1949; *s* of Howard Joel and Rosalind Joel (*née* Nyman); *m* 1st, 1971, Elizabeth Weber (marr. diss. 1982); 2nd, 1985, Christie Brinkley (marr. diss. 1994); one *d*; 3rd, 2004, Kate Lee; 4th, 2015, Alexis Roderick; two *d*. Albums include: Cold Spring Harbor, 1972; Piano Man, 1973; Streetlife Serenade, 1974; Turnstiles, 1976; The Stranger, 1977; 52nd Street, 1978; Glass Houses, 1980; The Nylon Curtain, 1982; An Innocent Man, 1983; The Bridge, 1986; Storm Front, 1989; River of Dreams, 1993; Fantasies and Delusions, 2001. *Publications:* Goodnight, My Angel: a lullabye, 2004; New York State of Mind, 2005. *Address:* c/o Maritime Music, 34 Audrey Avenue, Oyster Bay, NY 11771–1559, USA.

**JOFFE, Chantal,** RA 2013; painter; *b* St Albans, Vermont, USA, 1969. *Educ:* Camberwell Sch. of Arts and Crafts (Foundn Course); Glasgow Sch. of Art (BA Hons Fine Art 1991); Royal Coll. of Art (MA Painting 1994). *Solo exhibitions* include: Victoria Miro Gall., London, 1997, 2000, 2003, 2005, 2008, 2011, 2016; Il Capricorno, Venice, 1999, 2000, 2004, 2011; Regen Project, LA, 2006; Cheim & Read, NY, 2009, 2012, 2015; Jerwood Gall., Hastings, 2015; Jewish Mus., NY, 2015; *group exhibitions* include: Whitworth Gall., Manchester, 1993; Tate Gall., London, 1996; Whitechapel Art Gall., 1998; Pallant Hse Gall., Chichester, 1998, 2006; British Sch. at Rome, 1999; Victoria Miro Gall., London, 1998, 2000, 2001, 2010, 2013; Royal Acad., 2002, 2017, Summer Exhibn, 2006; Cheim & Read, NY, 2008, 2009, 2011; Turner Contemp., Margate, 2011; Saatchi Gall., London, 2013–14; NPG, 2015; Lowry, Salford, 2018; Compton Verney, 2019; *work in public collections:* Mus. of Fine Arts, Boston, Mass; Metropolitan Mus. of Art, NY; UK Govt Art Collection; RCA; Scottish Nat. Gall. of Modern Art; Saatchi Collection; Fonds Nat. d'Art Contemporain, France, Arts Council England. Charles Wollaston Award, Royal Acad., 2006. *Address:* c/o Victoria Miro Gallery, 16 Wharf Road, N1 7RW.

**JÓHANNSSON, Kjartan,** PhD; Icelandic Ambassador to the European Union, 2002–05; *b* 19 Dec. 1939; *s* of Jóhann and Astrid Dahl Thorsteinsson; *m* 1964, Irma Karlsdottir; one *d*. *Educ:* Reykjavík Coll.; Royal Inst. of Technol., Sweden; Univ. of Stockholm; Illinois Inst. of Technol., Chicago. Consulting Engr, Reykjavik, 1966–78; University of Iceland: Teacher, Faculty of Engrg and Sci., 1966–74; Prof., Faculty for Econs and Business Admin, 1974–78 and 1980–89. Mem., Municipal Council, Hafnarfjördur, 1974–78; Mem. (SDP), Althing (Parlt of Iceland), 1978–89; Speaker, Lower Hse, 1988–89; Minister of Fisheries, 1978–80, also of Commerce, 1979–80; Ambassador and Perm. Rep. to UN and other internat. orgns, Geneva, 1989–94; Sec. Gen., EFTA, 1994–2000; Ambassador, Ministry for Foreign Affairs, Reykjavik, 2000–02. Social Democratic Party: Mem., Party Council and Exec. Council, 1972–89; Vice-Chm., 1974–80; Chm., 1980–84.

**JOHANSEN-BERG, Rev. John;** Founder Member, since 1984, and International Director, since 2001, Community for Reconciliation (Leader, 1986–2001); Moderator, Free Church Federal Council, 1987–88; *b* 4 Nov. 1935; *s* of John Alfred and Caroline Johansen-Berg, Middlesbrough; *m* 1971, Joan, *d* of James and Sally Ann Parnham, Leeds; two *s* one *d*. *Educ:* Acklam Hall Grammar Sch., Middlesbrough; Leeds Univ. (BA Hons Eng. Lit., BD); Fitzwilliam Coll., Cambridge Univ. (BA Theol Tripos, MA); Westminster Theol Coll. (Dip. Theol.). Tutor, Westminster Coll., Cambridge, 1961; ordained, 1962; pastoral charges: St Ninian's Presbyterian Church, Luton, 1962–70 (Sec., Luton Council of Churches); Founder Minister, St Katherine of Genoa Church, Dunstable (dedicated 1968); The Rock Church Centre, Liverpool (Presbyterian, then United Reformed), 1970–77, work begun in old public house, converted into Queens Road Youth Club, new Church Centre dedicated 1972, a building designed for youth, community and church use; Minister: St Andrew's URC, Ealing, 1977–86; Rubery URC, 1992–2001. Convener, Church and Community Cttee of Presbyterian C of E, 1970–72; Chm. Church and Society Dept, URC, 1972–79; Moderator of the Gen. Assembly of the URC, 1980–81. British Council of Churches: Mem., Assembly, 1987–90; formerly Member: Div. of Internat. Affairs; Div. of Community Affairs; Chm. Gp on Violence, Non-violence and Social Change (for Britain Today and Tomorrow Programme, 1977); Convenor, Commission on Non-Violent Action (report published 1973); Mem., Forum of Churches Together in England, 1990–97; Chairman: Reflection Gp, 2000–05, Mgt Gp, 2003–05, Project Gp, 2005–10, CTBI Living Spirituality Network. Chm., Christian Fellowship Trust, 1981–87; Trustee, Nat. Assoc. of Christian Communities and Networks, 1989–2001; Mem., Exec., CCJ, 1989–97; Mem. Council, Centre for Study of Judaism and Jewish Christian Relns, 1989–96; Trustee, Fellowship of Reconciliation, England, 2000– (Chm., 2005–12). Co-Convenor, Methodist/URC Gp Report, Peacemaking: A Christian Vocation, 2005–06. Founder Mem. and Sponsor, Christian Concern for Southern Africa, 1972–94; Founder Sponsor, Clergy Against Nuclear Arms, 1982– (Chm., 1986–90); Founder: Romania Concern, 1990; United Africa Aid, 1996; Ecumenical Order of Ministry, 1990; initiated Village India Aid, 2006; Jt Leader, Ecumenical Festivals of Faith in: Putney and Roehampton, 1978; Stroud, 1980; Banstead, 1983; North Mymms, 1985; Guildford, 1986; Jesmond, 1987; Worth Abbey, 1988; Palmers Green, 1990; Poole, and Ballyholme, 1991; Finchley, 1992; South Wallasey, 1994; Rye, 2003. Jt Editor, Jl of Presbyterian Historical Soc. of England, 1964–70. Pro Ecclesia Millennium Award, 2001. *Publications:* Arian or Arminian? Presbyterian Continuity in the Eighteenth Century, 1969; Prayers of the Way, 1987, rev. edn 1992; Prayers of Pilgrimage, 1988; Prayers of Prophecy, 1990; Prayers for Pilgrims, 1993; A Celtic Collection, 1996; Pilgrims on the Edge, 1997. *Recreations:* mountain walking, golf, drama. *Address:* 3 Collinwood Road, Oxford OX3 8HH.

**JOHANSON, Capt. Philip,** OBE 2002; International Secretary, Church Army International, 2007–12; Chaplain to Mayor of Bournemouth, 2014–15; *b* 10 April 1947; *s* of late Stanley Theodore Johanson and Betty Johanson. *Educ:* Alderman Cogan Sch., Hull; Wilson Carlile Coll. of Evangelism, London. Missioner, dio. of Coventry, 1972–75; Church Army: Head of Missions, 1975–83; Dir of Evangelism, 1983–90; Chief Sec., 1990–2006. Patron, African Pastors Trust, 2000–12 (Chm., 1981–97); Member: C of E Partnership for World Mission Cttee, 1990–2006; Portman House Trust, 1990–2006; Council, Evangelical Alliance, 1991–2003; C of E Board of Mission, 1997–2003; Council, Wilson Carlile Coll. of Evangelism, 2002–06; Council, Christian Enquiry Agency, 2003–07. Chm., Bournemouth Nightclub Outreach Work Trust, 2012–. Mem., Royal Commonwealth Soc., 1980–; Mem., Boscombe and Southbourne Rotary Club, 2011–. *Recreations:* theatre, music, travel, reading. *Address:* 10 Ditton Lodge, 8 Stourwood Avenue, Bournemouth BH6 3PN. *T:* (01202) 416917. *E:* p.johanson@btinternet.com. *Clubs:* Royal Over-Seas League, Nikaean.

**JOHN, Rt Rev. Andrew Thomas Griffith;** *see* Bangor, Bishop of.

**JOHN, Sir David (Glyndwr),** KCMG 1999; Chairman: BSI Group (formerly British Standards Institution), 2002–12; Royal Society for Asian Affairs, 2009–17 (Hon. Vice-President, 2017); *b* 20 July 1938; *o s* of William Glyndwr John and Marjorie John (*née* Gaze); *m* 1964, Gillian Edwards; one *s* one *d*. *Educ:* Llandovery Coll., Carms; Christ's Coll., Cambridge (MA); Columbia Univ., NY (MBA); Harvard Univ. (ISMP). 2nd Lieut, RA, 1957–59. United Steel Co., 1962–64; Rio Tinto Zinc Corp., 1966–73 (RTZ Consultants, Hardman & Holden); Redland plc, 1973–81 (Land Reclamation Co., Redland Indust. Services, Redland Purle); Inchcape, 1981–95: Main Bd Dir, 1988–95; Develt Dir, later Chief Exec., Gray Mackenzie & Co., Middle East, 1981–87; Chairman: Inchcape Bhd, Singapore, 1990–95 (Chief Exec., 1987–90); Inchcape Middle East, 1991–94; Inchcape Toyota, 1994–95; BOC Group, 1996–2002 (non-exec. Dir, 1993–96); Premier Oil plc, 1998–2009; Balfour Beatty, 2003–08 (non-exec. Dir, 2000–03). Non-executive Director: British Biotech plc, 1996–99; The St Paul Cos Inc., Minn, USA, 1996–2003. Dir, WDA, 2001–02; Vice Chm., British Trade Internat., 1999–2002. Vice Pres. and Mem. Bd, POW Business Leaders Forum, 1996–99; Member: President's Cttee, and Chm. Internat. Cttee, CBI, 1996–2002; CBI Internat. Adv. Bd, 2002–11; Dir and Trustee, Council for Industry and Higher Educn, 1996–2002; Mem., Wilson Cabinet Cttee on Export Promotion, 1998–99. Gov., SOAS, 1993–2008; Mem. Bd of Overseers, Columbia Business Sch., NY, 1996–2002; Trustee: Asia House, 2000–04; Llandovery Coll., Carms, 2003–11. Chm., Cotswold Water Park Trust, 2011–. Freeman, City of London, 1997; Liveryman, Scientific Instrument Makers' Co., 1997–. DUniv Glamorgan, 2003. *Recreations:* walking, gardening, reading. *Address:* c/o C. Hoare & Co., 37 Fleet Street, EC4P 4DQ. *Clubs:* Oxford and Cambridge, Oriental, Travellers.

**JOHN, Dr David Thomas, (Dai),** PhD; Vice Chancellor, University of Luton, 1998–2003; *b* 31 Oct. 1943; *s* of Trevor John and Violet Gwyneth; *m* 1966, Jennifer Christine Morris; one *s* two *d*. *Educ:* Portsmouth (BSc ext. London Univ.); Birkbeck Coll., London (PhD). Kingston Polytechnic: Asst Lectr, 1966–67; Lectr, 1967–70; Sen Lectr, 1970–74; Principal Lectr, 1974–84; Hd of Applied Sci. and Associate Dean of Sci., 1984–86; Vice Principal, NE Surrey Coll. of Technology, 1987–89; Dep. Dir, Luton Coll. of Higher Educn, 1989–93, Dep. Vice-Chancellor, Univ. of Luton, 1993–98. *Publications:* several books and chapters on geology and geomorphology; various sci. papers on Tertiary and Quaternary history of SE England and on soils. *Recreations:* music, reading, travel, squash, Rugby, fly-fishing, painting. *E:* johndaijen@btinternet.com.

**JOHN, Sir Elton (Hercules),** Kt 1998; CBE 1996; musician; *b* Pinner, Middlesex, 25 March 1947; *s* of late Stanley Dwight and Sheila (later Farebrother); *né* Reginald Kenneth Dwight; changed name to Elton Hercules John; *m* 1984, Renate Blauel (marr. diss. 1988); civil partnership 2005, *m* 2014, David Furnish; two *s*. *Educ:* Pinner County Grammar Sch.; Royal Acad. of Music, London. Singer, songwriter, musician, began playing piano 1951; joined group, Bluesology, 1965; since 1969 has toured across the world consistently as solo performer and with the Elton John Band; played to over 2 million people across 4 continents, 1984–86; first popular Western singer to perform in USSR, 1979. Appeared: (film) Tommy, 1975; Live Aid, 1985; Freddie Mercury Tribute concert, 1992; Live 8, 2005. Voice (films): The Lion King, 1994; The Road to El Dorado, 2000. Pres., Watford Football Club, (Chm., 1976–90). Established Elton John AIDS Foundn, 1992; Patron: Amnesty International, 1997–; Internat. AIDS Vaccine Initiative, 1999–; Terrence Higgins Trust; Globe Theatre; Elton John Scholarship Fund, RAM, 2004–. Chm., Old Vic Trust, 2000–. *Composer:* albums: Empty Sky, 1969; Elton John, Tumbleweed Connection, 1970; 11.17.70, Friends, Madman Across the Water, 1971; Honky Chateau, 1972; Don't Shoot Me, I'm Only the Piano Player, Goodbye Yellow Brick Road, 1973; Caribou, Greatest Hits, 1974; Captain Fantastic and the Brown Dirt Cowboy, Rock of the Westies, 1975; Here and There, Blue Moves, 1976; Greatest Hits vol. II, 1977; A Single Man, 1978; Victim of Love, 1979; 21 at 33, 1980; The Fox, 1981; Jump Up, 1982; Too Low for Zero, 1983; Breaking Hearts, 1984; Ice on Fire, 1985; Leather Jackets, 1986; Live in Australia, 1987; Reg Strikes Back, 1988; Sleeping with the Past, 1989; To Be Continued, 1990; The One, 1992; Duets, 1993; Made in England, 1995; Love Songs, 1996; The Big Picture, 1997; Elton John and Tim Rice's Aida, The Muse, 1999; One Night Only, 2000; Songs From the West Coast, 2001; Greatest Hits—1970–2002, 2002; Peachtree Road, 2004; The Captain & the Kid, 2006; (with Leon Russell) The Union, 2010; The Diving Board, 2013; Wonderful Crazy Night, 2016; *musical scores:* (film) The Lion King, 1994 (Acad. Award for Best Original Song—Can You Feel the Love Tonight?); Broadway musicals: The Lion King, 1998 (6 Tony Awards); Aida, 2000 (Tony Award for Best Original Score); Lestat, 2006; (West End) Billy Elliot the Musical, 2005; *singles:* co-writer of many international hit songs with Bernie Taupin (and others) including Your Song, Rocket Man, Crocodile Rock, Daniel, Goodbye Yellow Brick Road, Candle in the Wind, Don't Let the Sun Go Down On Me, Philadelphia Freedom, Someone Saved My Life Tonight, Don't Go Breaking My Heart (duet with Kiki Dee), Sorry Seems to be the Hardest Word, The Bitch is Back, Song for Guy, I Guess that's Why They Call It the Blues, I'm Still Standing, Nikita, Sacrifice, Blue Eyes, Circle of Life, Are You Ready for Love?, I Want Love, Electricity. Biggest selling single of all time, Candle in the Wind, re-released 1997 (over 33,000,000 copies sold). Fellow, British Acad. of Songwriters and Composers, 2004. Hon. RAM 1997; Hon. Dr RAM, 2002. Awards include: 11 Ivor Novello Awards, 1973–2000; Brit Award (Best British Male Artist), 1991; inducted into Rock 'n Roll Hall of Fame, 1994; 5 Grammy Awards, 1986–2000; Grammy Legend Award, 2001; Kennedy Center Honor, 2004; Brits Icon Award, 2013. *Publications:* Love is the Cure: on life, loss and the end of AIDS, 2012; Me, 2019. *Address:* Rocket Music Entertainment LLP, 1 Blythe Road, W14 0HG. *T:* (020) 7348 4800.

**JOHN, Very Rev. Jeffrey Philip Hywel,** DPhil; Dean of St Albans, since 2004; *b* 10 Feb. 1953; *s* of late Howell John and Dulcie John; civil partnership 2006, Rev. Grant Holmes. *Educ:* Tonyrefail Grammar Sch.; Hertford Coll., Oxford (BA Classics and Modern Langs 1975; Hon. Fellow, 2017); St Stephen's House, Oxford (BA Theol. 1977, MA 1978); Brasenose Coll., Oxford; DPhil Oxon 1984. Ordained deacon, 1978, priest, 1979; Curate, St Augustine, Penarth, 1977–80; Asst Chaplain, Magdalen Coll., Oxford, 1980–82; Chaplain and Lectr, Brasenose Coll., Oxford, 1982–84; Fellow and Dean of Divinity, Magdalen Coll., Oxford, 1984–91; Vicar, Holy Trinity, Eltham, 1991–97; Canon Theologian and Chancellor, Dio. of Southwark, 1997–2004; nominated Bishop Suffragan of Reading, 2003. Hon. DLitt Hertfordshire, 2015. *Publications:* Living Tradition, 1990; Living the Mystery, 1995; This is Our Faith, 1995, 2nd edn 2001; Permanent, Faithful, Stable, 2000, extended edn as Permanent, Faithful, Stable: Christian same-sex marriage, 2012; The Meaning in the Miracles, 2002; Going for Growth, 2017. *Recreation:* modern European languages. *Address:* The Deanery, Sumpter Yard, St Albans, Herts AL1 1BY.

**JOHN, Lindsey Margaret;** see Bareham, L. M.

**JOHN, Maldwyn Noel,** FREng, FIEEE, FIET; Consultant, Kennedy & Donkin, 1994–97 (Chairman, 1987–94); *b* 25 Dec. 1929; *s* of Thomas Daniel John and Beatrice May John; *m* 1953, Margaret Cannell; two *s*. *Educ:* University College Cardiff. BSc 1st Cl. Hons, Elec. Eng. Metropolitan Vickers Elec. Co. Ltd, Manchester, 1950–59; Atomic Energy Authy, Winfrith, 1959–63; AEI/GEC, Manchester, as Chief Engineer, Systems Dept, Chief Engineer, Transformer Div., and Manager, AC Transmission Div., 1963–69; Chief Elec. Engineer, 1969–72, Partner, 1972–86, Kennedy & Donkin. President: IEE, 1983–84; Convention of Nat. Socs of Elec. Engineering of Western Europe, 1983–84; Dir Bd, Nat. Inspection Council for Electrical Installation Contractors, 1988–91; Mem., Overseas Projects Bd, 1987–91. FIEE 1969, Hon. FIET (Hon. FIEE 1998); FIEEE 1985; FREng (FEng 1979). Freeman, City of London, 1987. *Publications:* (jtly) Practical Diakoptics for Electrical Networks, 1969; (jtly) Power Circuit Breaker Theory and Design, 1975, 2nd edn 1982; papers in IEE Procs. *Recreation:* golf. *Address:* 65 Orchard Drive, Horsell, Woking, Surrey GU21 4BS. *T:* (01483) 825755.

**JOHN, Martin Anthony;** Deputy Director, Operations, Infrastructure and Projects Authority (formerly Major Projects Authority), Cabinet Office, since 2015; *b* Kingston-upon-Thames, 15 Aug. 1970; *s* of Tony and Monika John; *m* 2007, Lisa Sadler (*née* Ennis); one *s* one *d*. *Educ:* Open Univ. (MBA). Sen. Policy Asst, DSS, 1998–2000; Planning and Corporate Services Manager, 2000–01, Expansion Programme Manager, 2001–02, Court Service, Immigration Appellate Authy; Director: Tribunal Ops, 2002–05; Asylum and Immigration Tribunals Service, 2005–07; Business Develt Tribunals Service, 2007–08; Public Guardian and Chief Exec., Office of the Public Guardian, MoJ, 2008–12; Hd of Civil Family and Tribunals, HM Courts and Tribunals Service, 2012–14; Dep. Dir, Programme, Assurance and Testing, Transforming Rehabilitation, MoJ, 2014–15.

**JOHN, Peter Charles,** OBE 2016; Chairman, London Councils, since 2018; *b* Weston-super-Mare, 26 Oct. 1966; *s* of Leonard Francis John and Pauline John; *m* 2017, Symon Lee Smith. *Educ:* Queen Mary Coll., Univ. of London (LLB Hons 1988). Called to the Bar, Inner Temple, 1989; in practice as a barrister, 5 Paper Bldgs, Temple, 1989–. Mem. (Lab), Southwark LBC, 2002– (Leader, 2010–). Chair, Govs, Riverside Primary Sch., London, 2006–. Mem. Bd, St Olave, St Thomas and St John United Charity, 2007–. *Recreations:* reading, music, theatre, cities, TV box sets, thinking big, feeding the cats. *Address:* c/o 5 Paper Buildings, Temple, EC4Y 7HB. *T:* (020) 7815 3200. *E:* peterjohn@fivepaper.com; c/o Southwark Council, Cabinet Suite, 160 Tooley Street, SE1 2QH. *T:* (020) 7525 7158. *E:* peter.john@southwark.gov.uk.

**JOHN, Prof. Peter David,** PhD; Vice-Chancellor and Chief Executive, University of West London (formerly Thames Valley University), since 2007; *b* Bridgend, S Wales, 15 Aug. 1957; *s* of Douglas and Pamela John; *m* 1984, Lydia Jones; three *d*. *Educ:* University Coll., Swansea (BA Hons Hist. 1978); Univ. Coll. of Wales, Aberystwyth (PGCE 1980); Birkbeck Coll., London (MA Victorian Studies 1988); Jesus Coll., Oxford (MSc Educn); Univ. of Bristol (PhD 1998). Lectr, Univ. of Reading, 1989–90; Lectr, 1990–96, Sen. Lectr, 1996–2003, Univ. of Bristol; University of Plymouth: Prof. and Dean, Faculty of Education, 2004–06; Pro Vice-Chancellor, 2005–06; Dep. Vice-Chancellor, 2006–07. FHEA; FRSA; MInstD. Hon. DEd Plymouth, 2008. Global Excellence Award, Amity Univ. *Publications:* (with P. Lurbe) Civilization Britannique, 1992, 8th edn 2010; Lesson Planning for Teachers, 1993, 2nd edn 1997; (with E. Hoyle) Professional Knowledge and Professional Practice, 1996; (with S. Wheeler) The Digital Classroom, 2006; (jtly) Interactive Education, 2008; (jtly) Improving Classroom Learning with ICT, 2009; (ed) Dimensions of Marketisation in Higher Education, 2015. *Recreations:* painting, reading, Rugby Union, France and French life, politics. *Address:* Somerset Villa, 33 Bloomfield Road, Bath BA2 2AD. *Club:* Oxford and Cambridge.

**JOHN, Sarah;** Chief Cashier and Director of Notes, Bank of England, since 2018; *b* Oldham, 8 Oct. 1976; *d* of Keith and Barbara Wharmby; two *s*. *Educ:* Corfe Hills Sch., Broadstone, Dorset; King's Coll., Cambridge (BA Econs). Bank of England: Risk and Statistical Analyst, 1999–2005; Sen. Manager, Sterling Operations, 2005–12; Hd, European Systemic Risk Bd Unit, 2012–14; Hd of Risk, Mgt Div., 2014–15; Hd of Sterling, Mkts Div., 2015–18. *Address:* Bank of England, Threadneedle Street, EC2R 8AH. *E:* Sarah.John@bankofengland.co.uk.

**JOHN, Stephen Alun; His Honour Judge John;** a Circuit Judge, since 2008; *b* London, 1 Feb. 1953; *s* of late S. Beynon John and A. Sybil John; *m* 1985, Fiona Rosalind Neale; two *d*. *Educ:* Varndean Grammar Sch., Brighton; Jesus Coll., Oxford (Open Exhibnr 1971; Viscount Sankey Schol. 1972; BA Juris. 1974; MA 1979). Called to the Bar, Middle Temple, 1975; practised in common law and crime, 1975–2001; specialised in criminal law, 2001–08; Asst Recorder, 1999–2000; Recorder, 2000–08. *Recreations:* music, history (especially biography), Burgundy (the area and the wine). *Address:* Kingston Crown Court, 6–8 Penrhyn Road, Kingston-upon-Thames, Surrey KT1 2BB. *T:* (020) 8240 2500. *E:* HHJ.Stephen.John@ejudiciary.net.

**JOHN, Stewart Morris,** OBE 1992; FREng, FRAeS; Director, Taikoo Aircraft Engineering Company, Xiamen, China, 1992–2013; *b* 28 Nov. 1938; *s* of Ivor Morgan John and Lilian John; *m* 1961, Susan Anne Cody; one *s* one *d*. *Educ:* Porth Co. Grammar Sch.; N Staffs Tech. Coll.; Southall Tech. Coll. CEng 1977; FREng (FEng 1990); FRAeS 1977. BOAC: apprentice, 1955–60; on secondment to: Kuwait Airways, 1960–63; Malaysia-Singapore Airlines, as Chief Engr, Borneo, 1963–67; Develt Engr, 1967–70; Workshop Superintendent/Manager, 1970–73; Manager Maintenance, American Aircraft Fleet, 1973–77; Cathay Pacific Airways: Dep. Dir, Engrg, Hong Kong, 1977–80; Engrg Dir (Main Bd Mem.), 1980–94; Dep. Chm., Hong Kong Aircraft Engrg Co., 1982–94; Director: Rolls-Royce Commercial Aero Engines Ltd, 1994–98; British Aerospace Aviation Services, 1994–98; British Midland Aviation Services, 1995–2000; Hong Kong Aero Engine Services Ltd, 1996–98. Non-executive Director: Green Dragon Gas, 2006–18; Greka Drilling Ltd, 2011–15; Mem., Adv. Bd, Kingfisher Airlines, 2006–09. President: Internat. Fedn of Airworthiness, 1993–96; RAeS, 1997–98 (Pres., Weybridge Br., 2004–). Trustee, Brooklands Mus., 1994–. Pres., Rolls-Royce Enthusiasts' Club, 2009–17 (Chm., Surrey Sect., 2000–09). Liveryman, GAPAN, 1996–2008. *Recreations:* golf, classic cars, Rugby. *Address:* Taipan, 5 Pond Close, Burwood Park, Walton-on-Thames, Surrey KT12 5DR. *Club:* Burhill Golf.

**JOHN, Dame Susan (Elizabeth),** DBE 2011; Headteacher, Lampton School, 1997–2015 (Deputy Headteacher, 1987–97); *b* 1953; *m* 1975, Richard John. Dir, London Leadership Strategy. Non-exec. Dir, DfE. Mem., Future Leaders' Project Bd. Hon. Fellow, Brunel Univ., 2000.

**JOHN, His Honour Terence Aneurin;** a Circuit Judge, 2009–14; a Designated Family Judge, Swansea Civil Justice Centre, 2012–14; *b* Wolf's Castle, Pembrokeshire; *s* of Joseph Aneurin John and Elizabeth May John; *m* 1971, Susan Helen Jones; one *s* one *d*. *Educ:* Haverfordwest Grammar Sch.; Univ. of Wales Inst. of Sci. and Technol. (BSc Econ.); Crewe Coll. of Educn (Cert Ed 1971). Solicitor, Eaton, Evans and Morris, Haverfordwest, 1976–94; Dep. District Judge, 1992–94; District Judge, 1994–2009. President: Pembrokeshire Law Soc., 1984–85; West Wales Law Soc., 1988–89; Assoc. of District Judges, 2006–07.

**JOHNS, Vice Adm. Sir Adrian (James),** KCB 2008; CBE 2001; DL; Governor and Commander-in-Chief, Gibraltar, 2009–13; *b* 1 Sept. 1951; *m* 1976, Susan Lynne; one *s* three *d*. *Educ:* Imperial Coll., London (BSc). In command: HMS Yarnton, 1981–83; HMS Juno and HMS Ariadne, 1989–90; HMS Campbeltown, 1995–96; Captain, RN Presentation Team, 1996–97; Asst Dir, Naval Plans, 1997–98; Principal Staff Officer to CDS, 1998–2000; i/c HMS Ocean, 2001–03; ACNS, MoD, 2003–05; Head, FAA, 2003–08; Second Sea Lord and C-in-C Naval Home Comd, 2005–08; Flag ADC to the Queen, 2005–08. Mem., Sen. Salaries Rev. Body, 2015–; non-exec. Mem., CS Pensions Bd, 2017–. Younger Brother, Trinity Hse, 2007–. Freeman, City of London, 2002; Liveryman, Hon. Co. of Air Pilots (formerly GAPAN), 2006–; Freeman, Co. of Farriers, 2002. DL Gtr London, 2015. QCVS 2003. KStJ 2011. *Recreations:* music, reading.

**JOHNS, Alan Grant;** QC 2016; **His Honour Judge Johns;** a Specialist Civil Circuit Judge (Chancery), since 2018; *b* Truro, 26 May 1972; *s* of Frederick Alan and Paula Johns; *m* 2005, Katharine Gorsuch; two *s*. *Educ:* Helston Sch.; Magdalen Coll., Oxford (MA Juris.). Called to the Bar, Gray's Inn, 1994; in practice as barrister, specialising in property litigation, 1994–2016; a Judge of the First-tier Tribunal, 2011–; a District Judge, 2016–18. *Recreations:* sport, music. *Address:* Central London County Court, Royal Courts of Justice, Thomas More Building, Strand, WC2A 2LL.

**JOHNS, Prof. David John,** CBE 1998; CEng, FREng, FRAeS; Vice Chairman, Lay Advisory Group, Faculty of General Dental Practice, Royal College of Surgeons of England, 2008–13 (Lay Member, Executive Committee for e-learning in Dentistry, 2008–15); *b* 29 April 1931. *Educ:* Univ. of Bristol (BSc Eng, MSc Eng, Aeronautical Engineering); Loughborough Univ. of Technology (PhD, DSc). CEng 1964; FRAeS 1969; FCIT 1977; FIOA 1977; FHKIE 1984; FAeSI 1986; FREng (FEng 1990). Bristol Aeroplane Co., 1949–57 (section leader); Sen. Tech. Officer, Sir W. G. Armstrong Whitworth Co., 1957–58; Lectr, Cranfield Coll. of Aeronautics, 1958–64; Loughborough University of Technology: Reader, 1964–68; Prof. in Aeronautics, 1968–72; Hd, Dept of Transport Technology, 1972–82; Dean, Sch. of Engrg, 1975–78; Senior Pro-Vice-

Chancellor, 1982–83; (Foundation) Dir, City Polytechnic of Hong Kong, 1983–89; Vice-Chancellor and Principal, Univ. of Bradford, 1989–98. Chairman: Loads and Dynamics Cttee, ARC, 1976–79; Envmtl Pollution Adv. Cttee, 1994–96; Prescription Pricing Authy, NHS, 1998–2001; N and E Yorks and Northern Lincs Strategic HA, 2002–06; Adv. Cttee for Clin. Excellence Awards, 2005–08; Genetics and Insce Cttee, DoH, DIUS, HM Treasury, 2006–09; Lay Mem., Exec. Cttee, e-learning for Dental Health, DoH, 2008–13. Chm., Bradford Business Link, 1994–96. Dir, British Bd of Agrément, 1997–2006. Comr, Commonwealth Scholarships Commn, 2002–08. Member, Council: British Acoustical Soc., 1980–83; Hong Kong Instn of Engrs, 1985–88; RAEng, 2000–03; RAeS, 2002–05. Unofficial JP Hong Kong, 1986–89. *Publications:* Thermal Stress Analyses, 1965; 126 tech. articles and papers on educn and training in learned jls. *Recreations:* bridge, theatre, music, art appreciation. *Clubs:* Harrogate; Harrogate Men's Forum; Harrogate Men's Probus; Harrogate Rugby Union Football; Hong Kong; Hong Kong Jockey.

**JOHNS, Derek Ernest;** art dealer; *b* 22 July 1946; *s* of late Ernest Edward Johns and Evelyn May Johns (*née* Pays); *m* 1st, 1971, Annie Newman; one *s* one *d*; 2nd, 1981, Daphne Ellen Hainworth; one *s* one *d*. *Educ:* City of London Freemen's Sch., Ashtead Park. Dir, and Hd Old Master Paintings, Sotheby's, London, 1966–81; Chm., Derek Johns Ltd, Fine Paintings, 1981–. Winner, Masterchef, BBC, 1997. Mem., Chirton Parish Council, Wilts, 2003–07. *Recreations:* horticulture, shooting, travel, languages, opera. *Address:* Conock Old Manor, Devizes, Wilts SN10 3QQ; Derek Johns Ltd, 27 Georgian House, 10 Bury Street, SW1Y 6AA. *T:* (020) 7839 7671, *Fax:* (020) 7930 0986. *E:* fineart@derekjohns.co.uk. *Clubs:* East India, Garrick.

**JOHNS, Glynis;** actress; *b* Pretoria, South Africa; *d* of late Mervyn Johns and Alice Maude (*née* Steel-Payne); *m* 1st, Anthony Forwood (marr. diss.) (one *s* decd); 2nd, David Foster, DSO, DSC and Bar (marr. diss.); 3rd, Cecil Peter Lamont Henderson; 4th, Elliott Arnold. *Educ:* Clifton and Hampstead High Schs. First stage appearance in Buckie's Bears as a child ballerina, Garrick Theatre, London, 1935. Parts include: Sonia in Judgement Day, Embassy and Strand, 1937; Miranda in Quiet Wedding, Wyndham's, 1938 and in Quiet Weekend, Wyndham's, 1941; Peter in Peter Pan, Cambridge Theatre, 1943; Fools Rush In, Fortune; The Way Things Go, Phœnix, 1950; Gertie (title role), NY, 1952; Major Barbara (title role), NY, 1957; The Patient in Too True to Be Good, NY, 1962; The King's Mare, Garrick, 1966; Come as You Are, New, 1970; A Little Night Music, New York, 1973 (Tony award for best musical actress); Ring Round the Moon, Los Angeles, 1975; 13 Rue de l'Amour, Phœnix, 1976; Cause Célèbre, Her Majesty's, 1977 (Best Actress Award, Variety Club); Hayfever, UK; The Boy Friend, Toronto; The Circle, NY, 1989–90. Entered films as a child. *Films include:* South Riding, 49th Parallel, Frieda, An Ideal Husband, Miranda (the Mermaid), State Secret, No Highway, The Magic Box, Appointment with Venus, Encore, The Card, Sword and the Rose, Personal Affair, Rob Roy, The Weak and the Wicked, The Beachcomber, The Seekers, Poppa's Delicate Condition, Cabinet of Dr Caligari, Mad About Men, Josephine and Men, The Court Jester, Loser Takes All, The Chapman Report, Dear Bridget, Mary Poppins, Zelly and Me, Nuki, While You Were Sleeping, Superstar. Also broadcasts; television programmes include: Star Quality; The Parkinson Show (singing Send in the Clowns); Mrs Amworth (USA); All You Need is Love; Across a Crowded Room; Little Gloria, Happy at Last; Sprague; Love Boat; Murder She Wrote; The Cavanaughs; starring role, Coming of Age (series). *Address:* Catalyst Group, 715 Navy Street, Santa Monica, CA 90405, USA.

**JOHNS, Jasper;** painter; *b* 15 May 1930; *s* of Jasper Johns and Jean Riley. *Educ:* Univ. of South Carolina. Works in collections of Tate Gall., NY Mus. of Modern Art, Buffalo, Cologne, Washington, Amsterdam, Stockholm, Dallas, Chicago, Baltimore, Basle, Cleveland, Minneapolis; one-man exhibitions principally in Leo Castelli Gallery, NY; others in UK, USA, Canada, France, Germany, Italy, Japan, Switzerland; retrospective exhibns, NY Mus. of Modern Art, 1996, Scottish Nat. Gall. of Modern Art, 2004; RA, 2017; The Broad, LA 2018. Hon. RA; Mem., Amer. Acad. of Arts and Letters (Gold Medal, 1986); Pittsburgh Internat. Prize, 1958; Wolf Foundn Prize, 1986; Venice Biennale, 1988; Nat. Medal of Arts, 1990; Praemium Imperiale Award, Japan, 1993. Officier, Ordre des Arts et des Lettres (France), 1990. *Address:* c/o Matthew Marks Gallery, 523 West 24th Street, New York, NY 10011, USA.

**JOHNS, Michael Alan,** CB 2000; Chief Executive, Valuation Office Agency and a Commissioner of Inland Revenue, 1997–2004; *b* 20 July 1946; *s* of John and Kathleen Johns. *Educ:* Judd School, Tonbridge; Queens' College, Cambridge (MA Hist.). Inland Revenue, 1967–79; Central Policy Review Staff, 1979–80; Inland Revenue, 1980–84; seconded to Orion Royal Bank, 1985; Inland Revenue, 1986–; Under Sec., 1987; Dir, Oil and Financial Div., 1988–91; Dir, Central Div., 1991–93; Dir, Business Ops Div., 1993–97. Treasurer, Working Men's College, 1986–90. Hon. RICS 2003. *Recreations:* trekking, teaching adults, moral philosophy.

**JOHNS, Rev. Patricia Holly,** MA; Headmistress, St Mary's School, Wantage, 1980–94; Priest in charge, Mildenhall, Marlborough, 1996–99; *b* 13 Nov. 1933; *d* of William and Violet Harris; *m* 1958, Michael Charles Bedford Johns (*d* 1965), MA; one *s* one *d*. *Educ:* Blackheath High Sch.; Girton Coll., Cambridge (BA 1956, MA 1959, CertEd with distinction 1957). Assistant Maths Mistress: Cheltenham Ladies' Coll., 1957–58; Macclesfield Girls' High Sch., 1958–60; Asst Maths Mistress, then Head of Maths and Dir of Studies, St Albans High Sch., 1966–75; Sen. Mistress, and Housemistress of Hopeman House, Gordonstoun, 1975–80. Ordained deacon, 1990, priest, 1994; non-stipendiary Curate, Marlborough Team Ministry, 1994–99. *Recreations:* choral singing, walking, travel, reading, cookery, music. *Address:* Flat 1, Priory Lodge, 93 Brown Street, Salisbury, Wilts SP1 2BX. *T:* (01722) 328007.

**JOHNS, Paul;** public speaker; Co-founder, 1994, and Director, since 1998, SANA, development agency in Bosnia and Herzegovina; *b* 13 March 1934; *s* of Alfred Thomas Johns and Margherita Johns; *m* 1st, 1956, Ruth Thomas (marr. diss. 1973); two *s* one *d*; 2nd, 1984, Margaret Perry (marr. diss. 1986). *Educ:* Kingswood School, Bath; Oriel College, Oxford (MA Hons Modern Hist.); Univ. of Wales (MTh 2010). Personnel Management, Dunlop Rubber Co., 1958–63 and Northern Foods Ltd, 1963–68; Senior Partner, Urwick Orr & Partners, 1968–83; Dir, Profile Consulting, 1983–89; Man. Dir, Traidcraft, 1988–91; Chief Exec., Fairtrade Foundn, 1992–94. Chairperson, 1985–87, Vice-Chairperson, 1987–88, CND. Consultant, FA Premier League, 1994–2000. Dir, Coll. of Preachers, 2007–14. Lay preacher, Methodist Church. *Recreations:* story telling, listening to music, watching football (keen supporter of Nottingham Forest). *Address:* 33 Burleigh Road, West Bridgford, Nottingham NG2 6FP.

**JOHNS, Air Chief Marshal Sir Richard (Edward),** GCB 1997 (KCB 1994; CB 1991); KCVO 2007 (LVO 1972); CBE 1985 (OBE 1978); FRAeS; Chief of Air Staff, 1997–2000; Constable and Governor of Windsor Castle, 2000–08; *b* Horsham, 28 July 1939; *s* of late Lt-Col Herbert Edward Johns, MBE, RM and of Marjory Harley Johns (*née* Everett); *m* 1965, Elizabeth Naomi Anne Manning; one *s* two *d*. *Educ:* Portsmouth Grammar Sch.; RAF College, Cranwell. FRAeS 1997. Commissioned 1959; Night Fighter and Fighter/ Reconnaissance Sqns, UK, Cyprus, Aden, 1960–67; Flying Instructional duties, 1968–71; Flying Instructor to Prince of Wales, 1970–71; OC 3 (Fighter) Sqn (Harrier), 1975–77; Dir, Air Staff Briefing, 1979–81; Station Comdr and Harrier Force Comdr, RAF Gütersloh, 1982–84; ADC to the Queen, 1983–84; RCDS 1985; SASO, HQ RAF Germany, 1985–88; SASO, HQ Strike Comd, 1989–91; AOC No 1 Gp, 1991–93; COS and Dep. C-in-C, Strike Comd and UK Air Forces, 1993–94; AOC-in-C Strike Comd, 1994; C-in-C, Allied Forces NW Europe, 1994–97; Air ADC to the Queen, 1997–2000. Hon. Col, 73 Engr Regt (V), 1994–2002; Hon. Air Cdre, RAF Regt, 2000–13. Patron, Labrador Lifeline Trust, 2001–; Pres., Hearing Dogs for Deaf People, 2005–16. Vice-Pres., Royal Windsor Horse Show, 2000–; Pres., Windsor Fest., 2000–08. Chm., Bd of Trustees, RAF Mus., 2000–06; Pres., RAF Histl Soc., 2016–. Pres., Chitterne Cricket Club, 2012–; Vice-Pres., Royal Household Cricket Club, 2006–. Hon. Pres., Aviation Focus Gp, 2004–17. Governor: Portsmouth GS, 1996–2009; Dauntsey's Sch., 2008–. Freeman, City of London, 1999; Liveryman, Hon. Co. of Air Pilots (formerly GAPAN), 1999–. *Recreations:* military history, Rugby, cricket, equitation. *Address:* Dolphin House, Warminster Road, Chitterne, Wilts BA12 0LH. *T:* (01985) 850039. *Club:* Royal Air Force.

**JOHNSON, Adam Martin;** QC 2017; Partner, Herbert Smith Freehills (formerly Herbert Smith) LLP, since 1997; a Deputy High Court Judge, since 2018; *b* Sheffield, 4 Oct. 1965; *s* of Raymond and Sheila Johnson; *m* 1996, Jennifer; one *s* two *d*. *Educ:* Beaver Hill Comprehensive Sch., Sheffield; Churchill Coll., Cambridge (BA 1987; MA 1991). Admitted as solicitor, Herbert Smith, 1990; Asst Solicitor, Herbert Smith, 1990–97. *Recreations:* family, cycling, cricket, golf, literature, theatre, music, Sheffield Wednesday FC (WAWAW). *Address:* Herbert Smith Freehills LLP, Exchange House, Primrose Street, EC2A 2EG. *T:* (020) 7374 8000, *Fax:* (020) 7374 0888. *E:* adam.johnson@hsf.com.

**JOHNSON, Rt Hon. Alan (Arthur);** PC 2003; Chairman: Citycare, since 2017; Shared Agenda, since 2017; *b* 17 May 1950; *s* of late Lillian May and Stephen Arthur Johnson; *m* 1st, 1968, Judith Elizabeth Cox (marr. diss.); one *s* one *d* (and one *d* decd); 2nd, 1991, Laura Jane Patient (marr. diss.); one *s*; 3rd, Carolyn Burgess. *Educ:* Sloane Grammar School, Chelsea. Postman, 1968; UCW Branch Official, 1976; UCW Exec. Council, 1981; UCW National Officer, 1987–93; Gen. Sec., UCW, 1993–95; Jt Gen. Sec., CWU, 1995–97. MP (Lab) Kingston-upon-Hull W and Hessle, 1997–2017. PPS to Financial Sec. to the Treasury, 1997–99, to Paymaster General, 1999; Parly Under-Sec. of State, 1999–2001, Minister of State, 2001–03, DTI; Minister of State, DFES, 2003–04; Secretary of State: for Work and Pensions, 2004–05; for Trade and Industry, 2005–06; for Educn and Skills, 2006–07; for Health, 2007–09; for Home Dept, 2009–10; Shadow Sec. of State for Home Dept, 2010; Shadow Chancellor of the Exchequer, 2010–11. Mem., Trade and Industry Select Cttee, 1997. Mem. Gen. Council, TUC, 1994–95; Exec. Mem., Postal, Telegraph and Telephone Internat., 1994–97; Mem., Labour Party NEC, 1995–97; Dir, Unity Trust Bank plc. Duke of Edinburgh Commonwealth Study Conf., 1992. Gov., Ruskin Coll., 1992–97. Presenter, Alan Johnson: The Post Office and Me, 2015. *Publications:* This Boy: a memoir of a childhood, 2013 (Orwell Prize, 2014; Ondaatje Prize, 2014); Please, Mister Postman: a memoir, 2014 (Autobiog. of the Year, Nat. Book Awards, 2014); The Long and Winding Road: a memoir, 2016 (Winner, Parly Book Awards, 2017); In My Life: a music memoir, 2018. *Recreations:* music, tennis, reading, football, cookery, radio.

**JOHNSON, Air Vice-Marshal Alan Taylor,** FRAeS; Director of Occupational Health and Chief Medical Officer, Metropolitan Police, 1991–96; *b* 3 March 1931; *s* of Percy and Janet Johnson; *m* 1954, Margaret Ellen Mee; two *s* three *d* (and one *s* decd). *Educ:* Mexborough Grammar Sch.; Univ. of Sheffield (MB, ChB); FFOM, MFCM; DAvMed. Commnd RAF, 1957; MO, RAF Gaydon, 1957–59; Princess Mary's RAF Hosp., Akrotiri, Cyprus, 1959–61; No 1 Parachute Trng Sch., RAF Abingdon, 1961–65; RAF Changi, Singapore, 1965–67; RAF Inst. of Aviation Medicine, 1967–71; RAF Bruggen, Germany, 1971–74; Med. SO (Air) HQ RAF Support Comd, 1974–77; RAF Brize Norton, 1977–78; Chief of Aerospace Medicine HQ SAC Offutt AFB, USA, 1978–81; Dep. Dir of Health and Res. (Aviation Medicine), 1981–84; OC Princess Alexandra Hosp., RAF Wroughton, 1984–86; Asst Surg.-Gen. (Environmental Medicine and Res.), MoD, 1986; PMO, HQ RAF, Germany, 1986–88; PMO, HQ Strike Comd, RAF High Wycombe, 1988–91; retired. QHS 1986–91. OStJ 1976. Hon. MD Sheffield, 2017. *Recreations:* sport parachuting, music, cricket. *Address:* 6 Ivelbury Close, Buckden, St Neots, Cambs PE19 5XE. *Club:* Royal Air Force.

**JOHNSON, Rt Hon. (Alexander) Boris (de Pfeffel);** PC 2016; MP (C) Uxbridge and South Ruislip, since 2015; Prime Minister and First Lord of the Treasury, since 2019; *b* 19 June 1964; *s* of Stanley Patrick Johnson, *qv* and Charlotte Maria Johnson (*née* Fawcett); *m* 1st, 1987, Allegra Mostyn-Owen (marr. diss. 1993); 2nd, 1993, Marina Wheeler; two *s* two *d*; one *d* by Helen Macintyre. *Educ:* Eton (King's Schol.); Balliol Coll., Oxford (BA Classics; Brackenbury Schol.; Pres., Oxford Union). LEK Partnership, one week, 1987; The Times, 1987–88; Daily Telegraph, 1988–99: EC Correspondent, 1989–94; Asst Ed. and Chief Pol Columnist, 1994–99; Ed., The Spectator, 1999–2005. MP (C) Henley, 2001–June 2008. Opposition frontbench spokesman on higher educn, 2005–07; Sec. of State for Foreign and Commonwealth Affairs, 2016–18. Jt Vice-Chm., Cons. Party, 2003–04. Mayor of London (C), 2008–16. Commentator of the Year, 1997; Columnist of the Year, 2005, What the Papers Say Awards, 1997; Editors' Editor of the Year, 2003; Columnist of the Year, British Press Awards, 2004; Politician of the Year, Spectator Parliamentarian of the Year Awards, 2008, 2012; Politician of the Year, Political Studies Assoc., 2008; Politician of the Year, GQ Men of the Year Awards, 2008, 2012; Irving Kristol Award, Amer. Enterprise Inst., 2018. *Publications:* Friends, Voters, Countrymen, 2001; Lend Me Your Ears: the essential Boris Johnson, 2003; Seventy Two Virgins (novel), 2004; The Dream of Rome, 2006; Life in the Fast Lane: the Johnson guide to cars, 2007; The Perils of the Pushy Parents, 2007; Johnson's Life of London, 2011; The Churchill Factor: how one man made history, 2014. *Recreations:* painting, cricket. *Address:* 10 Downing Street, SW1A 2AA. *Club:* Beefsteak.
*See also* Rt Hon. J. E. Johnson, L. F. Johnson, R. S. Johnson.

**JOHNSON, Andrew Robert;** Headmaster, St Benedict's School, Ealing, since 2016; *b* Lytham St Annes, 1 April 1967; *s* of Robert and Josephine Johnson; *m* 1993, Dawn Bridger; two *s*. *Educ:* Univ. of Bristol (BA Hons Mod. Langs). Asst Teacher, Douai Sch., 1991–93; Winchester College: Asst Teacher, 1993–98; Hd, Mod. Langs, 1998–2002; Dep. Headmaster, Birkdale Sch., Sheffield, 2002–06; Headmaster, Stonyhurst Coll., 2006–16. *Recreations:* hill-walking, theatre, music. *Address:* St Benedict's School, 54 Eaton Rise, Ealing, W5 2ES. *Club:* Lansdowne.

**JOHNSON, Anna S.;** *see* Sylvester Johnson.

**JOHNSON, Prof. Dame Anne (Mandall),** DBE 2013; MD; FFPH, FRCP, FRCGP, FMedSci; Professor of Infectious Disease Epidemiology (formerly of Epidemiology), UCL Medical School (formerly University College London Medical School, then Royal Free and University College Medical School), since 1996, and Vice Dean for External Relations, Faculty of Population Health Sciences, since 2014, University College London; *b* 30 Jan. 1954; *d* of Gordon Trevor Johnson and Helen Margaret Johnson; *m* 1996, John Martin Watson; one *s* one *d*. *Educ:* Newnham Coll., Cambridge (BA 1974; MA 1979; Associate, 1996–); Univ. of Newcastle upon Tyne (MB BS 1978; MD with commendation 1992); LSHTM (MSc 1984); MRCGP 1982, FRCGP 2002; FFPH (FFPHM 1993); MRCP 1998, FRCP 2005. House Officer, Newcastle upon Tyne, 1978–79; Sen. House Officer, vocational trng in Gen. Practice, Northumbria, 1979–83; Registrar in Community Medicine, NE Thames RHA, 1983–84; Lectr, Middlesex Hosp. Med. Sch., 1985–88;

University College London Medical School, subseq. Royal Free and University College Medical School, University College London: Sen. Lectr in Epidemiology and Hon. Consultant in Public Health Medicine, 1988–94; Reader in Epidemiology, 1994–96; Hd, Dept of Primary Care and Population Studies, 2002–07; Dir, Div. of Popn Health, UCL, 2007–10; Co-Dir, Institute for Global Health, UCL, 2008–13; Chair: UCL Populations and Lifelong Health Domain, 2011–12; UCL Grand Challenge for Global Health, 2012–14. Hon. Sen. Lectr, 1990–99, Vis. Prof., 1999–, LSHTM; Hon. Consultant in Public Health Medicine, Central and NW London NHS Trust (formerly Camden and Islington, subseq. Camden Primary Health Care) NHS Trust, 1995–. Non-exec. Dir, Whittington Hosp. NHS Trust, 2005–08. Dir, MRC UK Co-ordinating Centre for Epidemiol Study of HIV and AIDS, 1989–99. Chm., Prison Health Res. Ethics Cttee, 1999–2001 (Mem., 1996–); Member: Council, Inst. of Drug Dependency, London, 1990–98; Specialist Adv. Cttee on antimicrobial resistance, 2001–06, Expert Adv. Gp on AIDS, 2013–17, DoH; MRC Physiological Medicine and Infections Bd, 2002–04; MRC Infections and Immunity Bd, 2004–06; Public Health Ethical Issues Wkg Party, Nuffield Council on Bioethics, 2006–07; Populations and Public Health Funding Cttee, 2008–, Bd of Govs, 2011–18, Wellcome Trust; Adaptation Sub-cttee, Climate Change Cttee, DEFRA, 2009–18; Chairman: MRC Population Health Scis Gp, 2009–10; Health of the Public 2040 Working Gp, Acad. of Med. Scis, 2014–. Sen. Investigator, NIHR, 2009–. Vis. Scholar, Univ. of Sydney, 1998. Vice Pres., Internat. Acad. Med. Scis, 2018–. Editor, AIDS, 1994–2000. FMedSci 2001. *Publications:* (jtly) Sexual Attitudes and Lifestyles, 1994; Sexual Behaviour in Britain, 1994; articles on HIV/AIDS, sexually transmitted diseases and infectious disease epidemiology. *Recreation:* singing. *Address:* Faculty of Population Health Sciences, University College London, Mortimer Market Centre, off Capper Street, WC1E 6JB.

**JOHNSON, Anthony Smith Rowe;** High Commissioner of Jamaica in the United Kingdom, 2010–12; *b* St Andrew, Jamaica, 14 June 1938; *s* of Cecil T. Johnson and Grethel Hairs (née Monfries); *m* 1969, Pamela Rosalie Casserly; one *s* two *d*. *Educ:* Kingston Coll.; Univ. of Calif, Los Angeles (BA Econs 1964; MA Internat. Trade and Finance 1965). Senior Economist: Min. of Finance, Jamaica, 1965–67; Central Planning Unit, 1967–70; Gen. Manager and Dir, Jamaica Frozen Food, 1970–75; Exec. Dir, Private Sector Orgn of Jamaica, 1976–80. Lectr, 1989–93, Sen. Lectr, 1993–2008, UWI. Parliament of Jamaica: Senator, 1980–83 and 1993–2008; Minister of State, 1983–89; MP, 1983–93. Ambassador of Jamaica to USA, 2008–10. *Publications:* The Economy: how it works, 1976; J. A. G. Smith, 1988; Kingston: portrait of a city, 1993; Jamaican Leaders, 1995; Ocho Rios: portrait of the garden parish, 1997; Ethical Business, 1997. *Recreation:* historical research. *Address:* 23 Plymouth Avenue, Kingston 6, Jamaica, West Indies. *T:* 9278001. *E:* ajohnson566@ gmail.com.

**JOHNSON, (Arthur) Keith;** Vice Lord-Lieutenant for Orkney, 2014–19; *b* Kirkwall, Orkney, 1 Feb. 1944; *s* of Robert Johnson and Lalla Johnson; *m* 1967, Jean Flett. *Educ:* Kirkwall Grammar Sch.; Aberdeen Nautical Coll. (Master Mariner); Glasgow Nautical Coll. (Extra Master Mariner). Ben Line Steamers, 1962–67; Shell Tankers UK, 1968–75; Shell International Marine: Asiatic Petroleum Corp., 1976–78; Qatar General Petroleum Corp., 1978–82; various posts with Shell, UK, 1982–93. Mem., Orkney Is Council, 1994–2007. Mem., Climatological Observers Link, 2004–. Chm., Birsay Heritage Trust, 2010–18. Mem., RMetS 2004. Trustee, Orkney Historic Boat Soc., 2013–. *Recreations:* gardening, walking, voluntary work, climate observer for Met Office, researching the Orkney climate. *Address:* Hundasaeter, Twatt, Orkney KW17 2JD. *T:* (01865) 771328, 07788 418396. *E:* ak.johnson@btinternet.com.

**JOHNSON, WO1 Barry,** GC 1990; RAOC; Warrant Officer 1 (Staff Sergeant Major), 1986, retired 1992; *b* 25 Jan. 1952; *s* of Charles William Johnson and Joyce Johnson; *m* 1971, Linda Maria Lane; one *s* one *d*. Mem., Inst. of Explosives Engineers. Army Apprentices College, Chepstow, 1967; Royal Army Ordnance Corps, 1970; served in UK, BAOR, NI, Canada and Belize. *Club:* Victoria Cross and George Cross Association.

**JOHNSON, Rt Hon. Boris;** *see* Johnson, A. B. de P.

**JOHNSON, Prof. Brian Frederick Gilbert,** PhD; FRS 1991; FRSE; FRSC; Professor of Inorganic Chemistry, University of Cambridge, 1995–2005; Master of Fitzwilliam College, Cambridge, 1999–2005; *b* 11 Sept. 1938; *s* of Frank and Mona Johnson; *m* 1962, Christine Draper; two *d*. *Educ:* Northampton Grammar Sch.; Univ. of Nottingham (BSc, PhD). FRSE 1992; FRSC 1992. Lecturer: Univ. of Manchester, 1965–67; UCL, 1967–70; Cambridge University: Lectr, 1970–78; Reader, 1978–90; Fitzwilliam College: Fellow, 1970–90, and 1995–99, Hon. Fellow, 2005; Pres., 1988–89; Vice Master, 1989–90; Crum Brown Prof. of Inorganic Chem., Univ. of Edinburgh, 1991–95. Mem., EPSRC, 1994–99 (Chm., Public Understanding of Sci., Engrg and Technol. Steering Gp, 1998–). Fellow, European Soc. *Publications:* Transition Metal Clusters, 1982. *Recreations:* chemistry, walking, cycling, travel.

**JOHNSON, Caroline Elizabeth;** MP (C) Sleaford and North Hykeham, since Dec. 2016; Consultant Paediatrician, since 2013; *b* Middlesbrough, 31 Dec. 1977; *d* of Len and Lynda Burton; *m* 2001, Nik Johnson; one *s* two *d*. *Educ:* Nunthorpe Comprehensive Sch.; Gordonstoun; Newcastle Univ. (MB BS 2001). MRCPCH 2004. Jun. House Officer, Medicine and Surgery, 2001–02; SHO, Paediatrics, 2002–05; Specialist Registrar, Paediatrics, 2005–13. Mem., Envmt, Food and Rural Affairs Cttee, 2017–, Health Cttee, 2017–, H of C. Contested (C) Scunthorpe, 2010. *Recreations:* cooking, running, family. *Address:* House of Commons, SW1A 0AA.

**JOHNSON, Christopher Edmund;** Director General, Defence Accounts, Ministry of Defence, 1984–89; *b* 17 Jan. 1934; *s* of late Christopher and Phyllis Johnson; *m* 1956, Janet Yvonne Wakefield (*d* 2007); eight *s* three *d*. *Educ:* Salesian Coll., Chertsey; Collyer's Sch., Horsham. Sub Lt, RNVR, 1952–54. Exec. Officer, 1954–58, Higher Exec. Officer, 1959–65, War Office; Principal, MoD, 1965–71; UK Jt Comd Sec., ANZUK Force, Singapore, 1971–74; Ministry of Defence: Asst Sec., 1974–84; Asst Under Sec. of State, 1984. *Recreations:* gardening, reading. *Address:* 3 Cedric Close, Bath BA1 3PQ. *T:* (01225) 314247.

**JOHNSON, Most Rev. Colin Robert;** Bishop of Toronto, 2004–18; Metropolitan of Ontario and Archbishop of Toronto, 2010–18; Bishop of Moosonee, 2014–18; *b* 6 Nov. 1952; *s* of John McLellan Johnson and Marie Lynn (née Johnston); *m* 1976, (Margaret) Ellen Johnson (née Smith); one *s* two *d*. *Educ:* Univ. of Western Ont (BA 1974); Trinity Coll. Toronto (MDiv 1977; DD 2005). Ordained deacon, 1977, priest, 1978; Asst Curate, Ch of St Simon-the-Apostle, Toronto, 1977–79; Incumbent, Parish of Georgina, 1979–83; Regional Dean, Deanery of the Holland, 1980–83; Incumbent, Ch of the Holy Trinity, Ajax, 1983–92; Exec. Asst to Archbishop of Toronto, and Hon. Asst, St Martin's Bay Ridges, Pickering, and Assisting Priest, St James' Cathedral, Toronto, 1992–2003; Archdeacon of York, 1994–2003; Acting Dir of Communications, Dio. Toronto, 1994–97 and 2001–03; a Bp Suffragan of Toronto, and Area Bp of Trent Durham, 2003–04. Hon. Sen. Fellow, Renison Univ. Coll., Waterloo, 2017–. Hon. DD: Wycliffe Coll., Toronto, 2005; Huron University Coll., 2016. *Recreations:* music, mystery novels, movies, cooking.

**JOHNSON, Sir (Colpoys) Guy,** 8th Bt *cr* 1755, of New York in North America; Director, ClearLine Communications Ltd, since 2002; *b* 13 Nov. 1965; *s* of Sir Peter Colpoys Paley Johnson, 7th Bt and his 1st wife, Clare (née Bruce); *S* father, 2003; *m* 1990, Marie-Louise, *d* of John Holroyd; three *s*. *Educ:* Winchester Coll.; King's Coll., London (BA Hons); Henley Mgt Coll. (MBA). Midland Bank plc, 1988–90; HSBC Capital Markets, 1990–98; Eurospend.com Ltd, 1999–2001. Hon. Col Comdt, King's Royal Yorkers, Canada, 2003. FRGS. *Recreations:* yacht racing, fly fishing. *Heir: s* Colpoys William Johnson, *b* 28 Dec. 1993. *Address:* Hollygate, Sleepers Hill, Winchester, Hants SO22 4ND. *Club:* Royal Ocean Racing.

**JOHNSON, Daniel,** GOQ 2008; PhD; Counsel, McCarthy Tétrault, Barristers and Solicitors LLP, 1998–2019; Chairman, Walter Global Asset Management, since 2019; *b* Montreal, 24 Dec. 1944; *s* of Daniel Johnson (Premier of Quebec, 1966–68) and Reine (née Gagné); *m* 1993, Suzanne Marcil; one *s* one *d* from former marriage. *Educ:* Stanislas Coll., Montreal; Saint-Laurent Coll. (BA Univ. of Montreal); Univ. of Montreal (LLL); University Coll. London (LLM, PhD); Harvard Business Sch. (MBA). A lawyer. Corp. Sec., 1973–81, Vice-Pres., 1978–81, Power Corp. of Canada. Director: Bombardier Inc., 1999–2017; IGM Financial Inc., 1999–2017; Investors Gp, 2003–; Mackenzie Financial, 2003–; Bank of Canada, 2008–13; exp Global Inc. (formerly TROW Global Hldgs Inc.), 2009–14; Ezeflow Inc., 2014–16; Dir and Chm., C Series Aircraft Managing Gp Inc., 2016–18; Mem., Adv. Bd, J. Walter Co. Gp, 2002–19. Mem. (L) Vaudreuil, Quebec Nat. Assembly, 1981–98; Minister of Industry and Commerce, 1985–88; Dep. House Leader, 1985–94; Chm., Treasury Bd, 1988–94; Minister responsible for Admin, 1988–89, for Admin and CS, 1989–94; Prime Minister and Pres. Exec. Council, Jan.–Sept. 1994; Leader of Official Opposition, 1994–98. Leader, Quebec Liberal Party, 1993–98. Chm., Quebec Judges Remuneration Cttee, 2007–10. Hon. Consul for Sweden in Montreal, 2002–. Ordre de la Pléiade (Francophonie), 2000, 2010; Order of the North Star (Sweden), 2011. *Address:* (office) Suite 1850, 1 Westmount Square, Westmount, QC H3Z 2P9, Canada. *E:* djohnson@walter-gam.com.

**JOHNSON, Daniel Benedict;** Editor, TheArticle, since 2018; *b* 26 Aug. 1957; *s* of Paul Bede Johnson, *qv*; *m* 1988, Sarah Thompson, *d* of late John William McWean Thompson, CBE; two *s* two *d*. *Educ:* Langley Grammar Sch.; Magdalen Coll., Oxford (BA 1st Cl. Hons Hist.). Res. Student, Peterhouse, Cambridge, 1978–81; Shakespeare Scholar, Berlin, 1979–80; taught German hist., QMC, 1982–84; Dir of Pubns, Centre for Policy Studies, 1983–84; Daily Telegraph: Leader Writer, 1986–87; Bonn Corresp., 1987–89; Eastern Europe Corresp., 1989; The Times: Leader Writer, 1990–91; Literary Editor, 1991–95; an Asst Editor, 1995–98; an Associate Editor, Daily Telegraph, 1998–2005; a Contrib. Editor, NY Sun, 2005–08; Founding Ed., Standpoint, 2008–19. *Publications:* White King and Red Queen: how the Cold War was fought on the chessboard, 2007; co-edited: German Neo-Liberals and the Social Market Economy, 1989; Thomas Mann: Death in Venice and other stories, 1991; Collected Stories, 2001; contrib. to Amer. and British newspapers and jls. *Recreations:* family, antiquarian book-collecting, music, chess. *Address:* c/o Georgina Capel Associates Ltd, 29 Wardour Street, W1D 6PS.
*See also* L. O. *Johnson*.

**JOHNSON, Daniel Guy;** Member (Lab) Edinburgh Southern, Scottish Parliament, since 2016; *b* Edinburgh, 3 Sept. 1977; *s* of John Christopher Herbert and Alison Frances Johnson; *m* Jacqueline Elizabeth Cook; two *d*. *Educ:* Stewart's Melville Coll., Edinburgh; St Andrews Univ. (MA Hons); Strathclyde Univ. (MSc). Researcher to Nigel Griffiths, MP, 1997–2000; Mgt Consultant, Accenture, 2001–08; Man. Dir, Studio One and Paper Tiger Retail Gp, 2008–15. *Recreations:* reading, ski-ing, playing guitar. *Address:* Scottish Parliament, Holyrood, Edinburgh EH99 1SP. *T:* (0131) 348 6462. *E:* Daniel.Johnson.msp@parliament.scot.

**JOHNSON, Darren Paul;** freelance PR, campaigns and communication work, since 2016; Campaigns Co-ordinator, Stay Up Late, since 2019; *b* 20 May 1966; *s* of late Alan Johnson and of Joyce Johnson (née Abram, now Reynolds). *Educ:* Goldsmiths' Coll., Univ. of London (BA 1st Cl. Hons Politics and Econs 1997). Finance and admin posts, 1987–93. Mem. (Green) London Assembly, GLA, 2000–16; Envmt Advr to Mayor of London, 2000–01; Chm., Envmt Cttee, 2004–08, Housing Cttee, 2013–15, London Assembly, GLA; Dep. Chair, 2008–09 and 2012–13, Chair, 2009–10 and 2013–14, GLA. Mem. (Green) Lewisham BC, 2002–14 (Leader, Green Gp, 2006–10). Contested (Green) Lewisham Deptford, 2001, 2005, 2010. Mem., Green Party, 1987–; Elections Co-ordinator, Nat. Exec., 1993–95; Principal Speaker, 2001–03. *Recreations:* walking, cycling, music.

**JOHNSON, Ven. David Allan G.;** *see* Gunn-Johnson.

**JOHNSON, David Gordon,** CBE 2003; Director of Financial Planning and Analysis, Defence Equipment and Support, since 2013; *b* 1 Aug. 1966; *s* of Gordon Alexander Johnson and Margaret Edith Johnson (née Bangay); *m* 1995, Salimata Ouattara; two *s* one *d*. *Educ:* Chesterfield Sch.; Pembroke Coll., Oxford (BA Hons Classics, MA 1992). Ministry of Defence: various posts, 1989–95; Assistant Director: Housing Project Team, 1995–97; Defence Policy, 1997–98; Defence and Overseas Secretariat, Cabinet Office, 1998–2001; Asst Dir, Defence Resources and Plans, 2001–02; Director: Iraq, 2002–04; Human Resources Develt, 2004–06; Dir-Gen., Logistics (Resources), 2006–07; Dir, later Dep. Command Sec. (Secretariat), 2007–10, Command Sec. (Secretariat), 2010, HQ Land Forces; Hd, Plans and Progs, then Resources and Plans, Defence Equipment and Support, 2011–13. *Recreations:* studying and teaching karate, coaching young cricketers. *Address:* Defence Equipment and Support, Maple 2C #2219, Ministry of Defence, Abbey Wood, Bristol BS34 8JH.

**JOHNSON, Dr David Michael,** FREng; Technical Director, DGauge Ltd, since 2008; *b* Aldershot, 24 Jan. 1956; *s* of Dennis Johnson and Vera Virtue Johnson; *m* 2009, Marilyn Wedgwood; three *s* one *d*. *Educ:* Univ. of Leeds (BSc Hons 1977); Imperial Coll., London (PhD 2008; DIC 2008). CEng 1985; FICE 2001; FIET 2018. British Rail, 1977–89; Founder and CEO, Laser Rail Ltd, 1989–2007. Hon. Vis. Prof., City Univ., London. FPWI 1978; FREng 2018. Master, Engineers' Co., 2018–19. *Recreation:* walking. *Address:* Cumhill House, Pilton, Somerset BA4 4BG. *T:* (01749) 899487. *E:* davidm.johnson@ btinternet.com. *Club:* Royal Air Force.

**JOHNSON, David Robert W.;** *see* Wilson-Johnson.

**JOHNSON, David Timothy;** Vice-President for Strategic Development and Washington Operations, Janus (formerly Sterling) Global Operations Inc., since 2014; *b* 28 Aug. 1954; *s* of Weyman T. Johnson and Dixie P. Johnson; *m* 1981, Scarlett M. Swan; one *s* two *d*. *Educ:* Emory Univ. (BA Econs 1976); Nat. Defence Coll. of Canada. United States Foreign Service, 1977–2011: Consul Gen., Vancouver, 1990–93; Dir, State Dept Press Office, 1993–95; Dep. Press Sec., The White House, and Spokesman for Nat. Security Council, 1995–97; Ambassador to OSCE, 1998–2001; Afghan Co-ordinator for US, 2002–03; Chargé d'affaires, 2003–05, Dep. Chief of Mission, 2005–07, US Embassy, London; Asst

Sec. of State, Bureau of Internat. Narcotics and Law Enforcement Affairs, US, 2007–11. Sen. Advr (non-resident), Americas Prog., Center for Strategic and Internat. Studies, 2011–14. Mem., Internat. Narcotics Control Bd, 2012–.

JOHNSON, Diana Ruth; MP (Lab) Kingston upon Hull North, since 2005; *b* 25 July 1966; *d* of late Eric Johnson and Ruth Johnson. *Educ:* Northwich Co. Grammar Sch. for Girls, later Leftwich High Sch.; Sir John Deane's Sixth Form Coll., Cheshire; Queen Mary Coll., Univ. of London (LLB 1988). Volunteer/locum lawyer, Tower Hamlets Law Centre, 1991–94; lawyer: N Lewisham Law Centre, 1995–99; Paddington Law Centre, 1999–2002. Member (Lab): Tower Hamlets LBC, 1994–2002; London Assembly, GLA, March 2003–2004. Mem., Metropolitan Police Authy, 2003–04. Non-executive Director: Newham Healthcare Trust, 1998–2001; Tower Hamlets PCT, 2001–05. Vis. Legal Mem., Mental Health Act Commn, 1995–98; Mem., CWGC, 2019–. Contested (Lab) Brentwood and Ongar, 2001. PPS to Minister of State, DWP, 2005–06, to Chief Sec. to HM Treasury, 2006–07; an Asst Govt Whip, 2007–10; Parly Under-Sec. of State, DCSF, 2009–10; Shadow Minister for Health, 2010, for Home Office, 2010–15, for FCO, 2015–16. Mem., Health and Social Care (formerly Health) Select Cttee, 2017–. Backbencher of Year, Political Studies Assoc., 2018. *Recreations:* cinema, books, theatre, fan of Hull City Football Club, walking. *Address:* (office) Rooms 0–031 – 0–035, The Avenues Centre, Park Avenue, Hull HU5 4DA. *E:* johnsond@parliament.uk. *W:* www.dianajohnson.co.uk, www.twitter.com/DianaJohnsonMP; House of Commons, SW1A 0AA.

JOHNSON, Edwin Geoffrey; QC 2006; barrister; a Deputy High Court Judge, since 2017; *b* 11 May 1963; *s* of Colin Johnson and Fiona Johnson; *m* 1991, Mary Ann Thorne; two *s* one *d*. *Educ:* Lancing Coll.; Christ Church Coll., Oxford (BA Hons Jurisprudence 1986). Called to the Bar, Lincoln's Inn, 1987; in practice as a barrister, 1988–, specialising in real property and professional negligence. *Publications:* (ed) Snell's Equity, 31st edn 2005. *Recreations:* travel, running, hill walking, scuba diving, ski-ing, reading. *Address:* Maitland Chambers, 7 Stone Buildings, WC2A 3SZ. *T:* (020) 7406 1200, *Fax:* (020) 7406 1300. *E:* ejohnson@maitlandchambers.com.

JOHNSON, Emma Louise, MBE 1996; solo clarinettist; *b* 20 May 1966; *d* of Roger and Mary Johnson; *m* 1997, Chris West; one *d* (one *s* decd). *Educ:* Newstead Wood Sch.; Sevenoaks Sch.; Pembroke Coll., Cambridge (MA English Lit. and Music 1992; Hon. Fellow, 1999). Concerts and tours in Europe, USA, Far East, Australia and Africa; guest appearances with major orchestras world-wide; compositions commnd from several leading British composers. Dir, chamber music gp; Prof. of Clarinet, RCM, 1997–2002. Numerous recordings, including the concertos of Mozart, Crusell, Weber, Finzi, Arnold and Berkeley. Winner, BBC Young Musicians, 1984; Bronze Medal, Eurovision Young Musicians Competition, 1984; Winner, Young Concert Artists Auditions, NY, 1991. *Publications:* "Encore!": compositions and transcriptions for clarinet and piano, 1994; The Emma Johnson Collection, 2008; Songs of Celebration for Clarinet and Choir, 2018. *Recreations:* theatre, literature, art, gardening, bird watching, travel. *Address:* c/o Upbeat Classical Management, 170 Thirlmere Gardens, Northwood, Middx HA6 2RU. *T:* (01923) 836220.

JOHNSON, Frederick James Maugham M.; *see* Marr-Johnson.

JOHNSON, Gareth Alan; MP (C) Dartford, since 2010; *b* Bromley, 12 Oct. 1969; *s* of Alan and Ruth Johnson; *m* 1997, Wendy Morris; one *s* one *d*. *Educ:* Dartford Grammar Sch.; Coll. of Law. Admitted solicitor, 1997; Solicitor, Thomas Boyd Whyte, Solicitors, 1997–2003. Contested (C): Lewisham W, 2001; Dartford, 2005. PPS to Sec. of State for Exiting the EU, 2017; an Asst Govt Whip, 2018–19. *Recreation:* cricket. *Address:* House of Commons, SW1A 0AA. *E:* gareth.johnson.mp@parliament.uk.

JOHNSON, Gen. Sir Garry (Dene), KCB 1990; OBE 1977 (MBE 1971); MC 1965; Chairman, International Security Advisory Board, since 1995; *b* 20 Sept. 1937; *m* 1962, Caroline Sarah Frearson; two *s*. *Educ:* Christ's Hospital. psc, ndc, rcds. Commissioned 10th Princess Mary's Own Gurkha Rifles, 1956; Malaya and Borneo campaigns, 1956–67; Royal Green Jackets, 1970; command, 1st Bn RGJ, 1976–79; Comdr, 11 Armoured Brigade, 1981–82; Dep. Chief of Staff, HQ BAOR, 1983; ACDS (NATO/UK), 1985–87; Comdr, British Forces Hong Kong, and Maj.-Gen., Bde of Gurkhas, 1987–89; MEC, Hong Kong Govt, 1987–89; Comdr Trng and Arms Dirs, 1989–91; Inspector Gen. Doctrine and Trng, 1991–92; C-in-C, AFNORTH, 1992–94. Colonel, 10th PMO Gurkha Rifles, 1985–94; Col Comdt, Light Div., 1990–94. Chm., TEC Nat. Council, 1995–99; Vice-Pres., Nat. Fedn of Enterprise Agencies, 1996–99. Chairman: Ogilby Trust, 1991–2009; Need in Nepal, 1997–2005; Trustee, Gurkha Welfare Trust, 1985–2007 (Chm., 1987–89). Patron, Nat. Malaya & Borneo Veterans Assoc., 2002–. Pres., De Burght Foundn, 2001–07; Member: NACETT, 1995–99; Adv. Council, Prince's Youth Business Trust, 1995–99; NCIHE, 1996–99; Adv. Bd, Centre for Leadership Studies, Exeter Univ., 1998–2005; Chm., Adv. Bd, Internat. Centre for Defence Studies, Tallinn, 2008–. Treas. and Chm., Christ's Hosp. Foundn, 2007–13. FRGS 1993; FRAS 1994; FRSA 1994; FRUSI 1999. Hon. DSc Soton 1999. Order of Terra Mariana (Estonia), 1997; Order of Grand Duke Gediminas (Lithuania), 1999; Medal of Merit (Latvia), 2000; Order of Orange Nassau (Netherlands), 2008; Order of Honour (Georgia), 2010. *Publications:* Brightly Shone the Dawn, 1979; Inland from Gold Beach, 1999. *Club:* Army and Navy.

JOHNSON, Prof. Garth Roston, PhD; FREng, FIMechE; Professor of Rehabilitation Engineering, University of Newcastle upon Tyne, 1995–2008, now Emeritus; *b* 23 Jan. 1945; *s* of Daniel Cowan Johnson and Vera Olive Johnson; *m* 1978, Katherine Zaida Cooke; one *s*. *Educ:* Univ. of Leeds (BSc Hons; PhD 1974). CEng 1991, FIMechE 1991; FREng 2000. Res. engr, Adcock & Shipley, machine tool manufrs, Leicester, 1961–71; Res. Fellow, Rheumatology Res. Unit, Dept of Medicine, Univ. of Leeds, 1971–75; Tech. Dir, Orthotics and Disability Res. Centre, Derbys Royal Infirmary, 1975–81; University of Newcastle upon Tyne: William Leech Reader in Biomed. Engrg, Dept of Mechanical, Materials and Manufg Engrg, 1981–95; Tech. Dir, Centre for Rehabilitation and Engrg Studies, 1991–2008. Head of Res., ADL Smartcare Ltd, 2008–13. *Publications:* (ed with M. P. Barnes) Upper Motor Neurone Syndrome and Spasticity, 2001; contrib. to learned jls incl. Proc. IMechE, Jl Biomechanics, Clin. Biomechanics. *Recreation:* music. *Address:* c/o Centre for Rehabilitation and Engineering Studies, University of Newcastle upon Tyne, Stephenson Building, Newcastle upon Tyne NE1 7RU. *T:* (0191) 222 6196.

JOHNSON, Dr Gordon; President, Wolfson College, Cambridge, 1993–2010 (Hon. Fellow 2010); Deputy Vice-Chancellor, University of Cambridge, 2002–10; *b* 13 Sept. 1943; *s* of Robert Johnson and Bessie (née Hewson); *m* 1973, Faith Sargent Lewis, New Haven, Conn; three *s*. *Educ:* Richmond Sch., Yorks; Trinity Coll., Cambridge (BA 1964; MA, PhD 1968). Fellow, Trinity Coll., Cambridge, 1966–74; Selwyn College, Cambridge: Fellow, 1974–93; Tutor, 1975–92; Hon. Fellow, 1994; University of Cambridge: Lectr in History of S Asia, 1974–2005; Dir, Centre of S Asian Studies, 1983–2001; Chairman, Faculty of: Oriental Studies, 1984–87; Architecture and History of Art, 1985–2008; Educn, 1994–2005; Member: Library Syndicate, 1978–2008; Press Syndicate, 1981–2010 (Chm., 1993–2009; Chm., Publishing Cttee, 2009–10); Syndicate on Govt of Univ., 1988–89; Statutes and Ordinances Revision Syndicate, 1990; Gen. Bd of Faculties, 1979–82 and 1985–90; Council, Senate, 1985–92 and 1999–2000; Sandars Reader in Bibliography, 2010. Lady Margaret Preacher, Univ. of Cambridge, 2006. Provost, Gates Cambridge Trust, 2000–10; Trustee: Cambridge Commonwealth Trust, 1983–2015; Cambridge Overseas Trust, 1989–2015; Malaysian Commonwealth Studies Centre, 1999–2011; Cam (formerly Comberton) Acad. Trust (Chm., 2011–18). Pres., RAS, 2009–12, 2015–18. Governor: Comberton Village Coll., 1991–2001 (Chm., 1992–2001; Chm., Comberton Educnl Trust, 2008–18); Gresham's Sch., 2006–10; Stephen Perse Foundn, 2012–19. Liveryman, Stationers' Co., 2003–. Editor, Modern Asian Studies, 1971–2008; Gen. Editor, The New Cambridge History of India, 1979. *Publications:* Provincial Politics and Indian Nationalism, 1973; University Politics: F. M. Cornford's Cambridge and his advice to the young academic politician, 1994; Cultural Atlas of India, 1995; Printing and Publishing for the University: three hundred years of the press syndicate, 1999. *Recreations:* reading, taking exercise. *Address:* Wolfson College, Cambridge CB3 9BB.

JOHNSON, Gordon Arthur; DL; Chief Executive, Lancashire County Council, 1998–2000; *b* 30 Aug. 1938; *y s* of Annie Elizabeth Johnson and William Johnson; *m* 1963, Jennifer Roxane Bradley (*d* 2016); two *d*. *Educ:* Bournemouth Sch.; University College London (BA Hons Hist.). Solicitor. Kent CC, 1962–64; Staffs CC, 1964–73; Dep. Dir of Admin, W Yorks MCC, 1973–76; Dep. Clerk, 1977–90, Chief. Exec. Clerk, 1991–98, Lancs CC. Lancs County Electoral Returning Officer, 1991–2000; Clerk: Lancs Lieutenancy, 1991–2000; Lancs Police Authy, 1995–2000; Lancs Combined Fire Authy, 1998–2000; Secretary: Lancs Adv. Cttee, 1991–2000; Lord Chancellor's Adv. Cttee on Gen. Comrs of Income Tax, 1991–2000; Lancs Probation Cttee; Lancs Cttee, Prince's Trust-Action; Co. Sec., Lancs County Enterprises Ltd, 1991–2000; Mem., MSC Area Manpower Bd, 1986–88; Chm., Soc. of County Secretaries, 1987–88 (Hon. Treasurer, 1977–86); Dir, LAWTEC, 1991–98. Adviser: LGA Policy and Strategy Cttee, 1997–2000; Assoc. of Police Authorities, 1997–2000. Mem. Court, 1991–2000, Dep. Pro-Chancellor, 2002–10, Univ. of Lancaster. Constable, Lancaster Castle, 2004–13. DL Lancs, 2000. *Recreations:* travel, reading. *Address:* Beech House, 72 Higher Bank Road, Fulwood, Preston, Lancs PR2 8PH.

JOHNSON, Graham Rhodes, OBE 1994; concert accompanist; Senior Professor of Accompaniment, Guildhall School of Music, since 1986; *b* 10 July 1950; *s* of late John Edward Donald Johnson and Violet May Johnson (née Johnson). *Educ:* Hamilton High Sch., Bulawayo, Rhodesia; Royal Acad. of Music, London. FRAM 1984; FGS (FGSM 1988). Concert début, Wigmore Hall, 1972; has since accompanied Elisabeth Schwarzkopf, Jessye Norman, Victoria de los Angeles (USA Tour 1977), Dame Janet Baker, Sir Peter Pears, Dame Felicity Lott, Dame Margaret Price (USA Tour 1985), Peter Schreier, John Shirley Quirk, Mady Mesplé, Thomas Hampson, Robert Holl, Tom Krause, Sergei Leiferkus, Brigitte Fassbaender, Matthias Goerne, Christine Schäfer. Work with contemporaries led to formation of The Songmakers' Almanac (Artistic Director); has devised and accompanied over 150 London recitals for this group since Oct. 1976. Tours of US with Sarah Walker, Richard Jackson, and of Australia and NZ with The Songmakers' Almanac, 1981. Writer and presenter of major BBC Radio 3 series on Poulenc songs, and BBC TV programmes on Schubert songs (1978) and the songs of Liszt (1986). Lectr at song courses in Savonlinna (Finland), US and at Pears-Britten Sch., Snape; Artistic advr and accompanist, Alte Oper Festival, Frankfurt, 1981–82; Song Adviser, Wigmore Hall, 1992–; Chm. Jury, Wigmore Hall Internat. Singing Competition, 1997, 1999 and 2001. Festival appearances in Aldeburgh, Edinburgh, Munich, Hohenems, Salzburg, Bath, Hong Kong, Bermuda. Many recordings incl. those with Songmakers' Almanac, Martyn Hill, Elly Ameling, Arleen Auger, Janet Baker, Philip Langridge, Marjana Lipovsek, Ann Murray, Sarah Walker, Anthony Rolfe Johnson, and of complete Schubert, Schumann and Brahms Lieder and Fauré and Poulenc mélodies, with various artists, 1987–. Hon. Member: Royal Swedish Acad. of Music, 2000; Royal Philharmonic Soc., 2010. Hon. DMus: Durham, 2013; New England Conservatory, Boston, USA 2013. Gramophone Award, 1989, 1996, 1997 and 2001; Royal Philharmonic Prize for Instrumentalist, 1998; Edison Prize, 2006; Walter Wilson Cobbett Chamber Music Medal, 2009; Wigmore Hall Medal, 2013; Hugo Wolf Medal, Stuttgart, 2015. Chevalier, Ordre des Arts et des Lettres (France), 2002. *Publications:* (contrib.) The Britten Companion, ed Christopher Palmer, 1984; (contrib.) Gerald Moore, The Unashamed Accompanist, rev. edn 1984; (contrib.) The Spanish Song Companion, 1992; The Songmakers' Almanac: reflections and commentaries, 1996; A French Song Companion, 2000; Britten, Voice and Piano, 2003; Gabriel Fauré: the songs and their poets, 2009; Franz Schubert: the complete songs (3 vols), 2014. *Address:* c/o Askonas Holt Ltd, 15 Fetter Lane, EC4A 1BW.

JOHNSON, Sir Guy; *see* Johnson, Sir C. G.

JOHNSON, Heather Jean; *see* Mellows, H. J.

JOHNSON, Hugh Eric Allan, OBE 2007; author, editor and broadcaster; *b* 10 March 1939; *s* of late Guy Francis Johnson, CBE and Grace, (Enid), Kittel; *m* 1965, Judith Eve Grinling; one *s* two *d*. *Educ:* Rugby Sch.; King's Coll., Cambridge (MA; Fellow Commoner, 2001). Staff writer, Condé Nast publications, 1960–63; Editor, Wine & Food, and Sec., Wine and Food Soc., 1963–65; Wine Corresp., 1962–64, and Travel Editor, 1967, Sunday Times; Editor, Queen, 1968–70; Wine Editor, Gourmet, NY, 1971–72. President: The Sunday Times Wine Club, 1973–; Circle of Wine Writers, 1997–2006. Founder Mem., Tree Council, 1974. Chairman: Saling Hall Press, 1975–2013; Conservation Cttee, Internat. Dendrology Soc., 1979–86 (Vice Chm., 2014–); Winestar Productions Ltd, 1984–2006; The Hugh Johnson Collection Ltd, 1985–2014; Director: Société Civile de Château Latour, 1986–2001; Coldstream Winemakers Ltd, 1991–94; Exbury Gardens Ltd, 2013–18. Editorial Director: Jl of RHS, 1975–89, Editl Cons., 1989–2006; The Plantsman, 1979–94. Wine Editor, Cuisine, New York, 1983–84; Wine Consultant: to Jardine Matheson Ltd, Hong Kong and Tokyo, 1985–2001; to British Airways, 1987–2002; to the Royal Tokaji Wine Co., 1990–; Hon. Trustee, Amer. Center for Wine, Food and the Arts, Calif, 2000–11; Hon. Pres., Internat. Wine and Food Soc., 2002–08; Hon. Pres., Wine and Spirit Educn Trust, 2009–11. Gardening Correspondent, New York Times, 1986–87; Columnist, Trad's Diary, 1975– (www.tradsdiary.com), Hortus mag. Editl Advr, The World of Fine Wine, 2004–. Video, How to Handle a Wine, 1984 (Glenfiddich Trophy, 1984; reissued as Understanding Wine, 1989); TV series: Wine—a user's guide (KQED, San Francisco), 1986; Vintage—a history of wine (Channel 4 and WGBH, Boston), 1989. Hon. Chm., Wine Japan (Tokyo exhibn), 1989–94. Pres., Metropolitan Public Gardens Assoc., 2012–; Vice-Pres., Essex Gardens Trust, 1997–2013. Hon. Liveryman, Vintners' Co., 2003. Docteur ès Vins, Acad. du Vin de Bordeaux, 1987. DUniv Essex, 1998. Hon. Citizen of Hungary, 2014. Carl-Friedrich von Rumor Gold Award, German Gastronomical Acad., 1998; Veitch Meml Medal, RHS, 2000; Lifetime Achievement Award, Inst. of Masters of Wine, 2015; Walter Scheel Medaille, Germany, 2016. Chevalier, Ordre Nat. du Mérite (France), 2003; Knight's Cross of the Order of Merit (Hungary), 2017. *Publications:* Wine, 1966, rev. edn 1974; (ed) Frank Schoonmaker's Encyclopedia of Wine, English edn, 1967; The World Atlas of Wine, 1971, 8th edn (with Jancis Robinson) 2019; The International Book of Trees, 1973, 2nd edn as Trees: a lifetime's journey through forests, woods and gardens, 2010; (with Charles Mozley) The Chateaux of Bordeaux, 1975; (with Bob Thompson) The California Wine Book, 1976; Hugh Johnson's Pocket Wine Book, annually 1977–; The Principles of Gardening, 1979, rev. edn as Hugh Johnson's Gardening Companion, 1996; Understanding Wine, 1980; (with Paul Miles) The Pocket Encyclopedia of Garden Plants, 1981; Hugh Johnson's Wine

Companion, 1983, 6th edn (with Stephen Brook), 2009; How to Enjoy Your Wine, 1985, 2nd edn 1998; The Hugh Johnson Cellar Book, 1986; The Atlas of German Wines, 1986, rev. edn (with Stuart Pigott) 1995; Hugh Johnson's Wine Cellar, (US) 1986; (with Jan Read) The Wine and Food of Spain, 1987; (with Hubrecht Duijker) The Wine Atlas of France, 1987, rev. edn 1997; The Story of Wine, 1989 (ten awards, incl. Glenfiddich Wine Award, 1990, Grand Prix de la Communication de la Vigne et du Vin, 1992), new illus. edn, 2004; Hugh Johnson's Pop-up Wine Book, 1989; (with James Halliday) The Art and Science of Wine, 1992, new edn 2006; Hugh Johnson on Gardening: the best of Tradescant's Diary, 1993; Tuscany and its Wines, 2000; Wine: a life uncorked, 2005; Hugh Johnson in The Garden, 2009; Wine Journal, 2011; Hugh Johnson on Wine: good bits from 55 years of scribbling, 2016; articles on gastronomy, travel and gardening. *Recreations:* trees, staying at home, gardening, wine, lunch and dinner, writing. *Address:* 70 Scarsdale Villas, W8 6PP. *Clubs:* Garrick, Brooks's, Saintsbury, Beefsteak.

**JOHNSON, Rt Rev. James Nathaniel;** Bishop of St Helena, 1985–91, now Bishop Emeritus; Hon. Assistant Bishop, Diocese of Oxford, since 2004; *b* 28 April 1932; *s* of William and Lydia Florence Johnson; *m* 1953, Evelyn Joyce Clifford; one *s* one *d*. *Educ:* Primary and Secondary Selective School, St Helena; Church Army College; Wells Theol Coll. Ordained deacon 1964, priest 1965; Curate of St Peter's, Lawrence Weston, Dio. of Bristol, 1964–66; Priest-in-charge of St Paul's Cathedral, St Helena, 1966–69, Vicar 1969–71; Domestic Chaplain to Bishop of St Helena, 1967–71; USPG Area Sec. for Dio. of Exeter and Truro, 1972–74; Rector of Combe Martin, Dio. of Exeter, 1974–80; Hon. Canon of St Helena, 1975–; Vicar of St Augustine, Thorpe Bay, Dio. of Chelmsford, 1980–85; Rector of Byfield with Boddington and Aston-le-Walls, and Hon. Asst Bishop, Dio. of Peterborough, 1991–92; Vicar of Hockley, Essex, 1992–97; Asst Bishop, 1992–97, Hon. Asst Bishop, 1997–2004, Dio. of Chelmsford. Non-residentiary Canon, Chelmsford Cathedral, 1994–97, Canon Emeritus, 1997. Permission to officiate, Dio. of Europe, 1998. *Recreations:* music, gardening, walking, cycling. *Address:* St Helena, 28 Molyneux Drive, Bodicote, Oxon OX15 4AP. *T:* (01295) 255357.

**JOHNSON, James North,** MD; FRCS, FRCP; FDSRCS; Consultant Surgeon: Halton General Hospital, Runcorn, 1985–2010; Royal Bolton Hospital, 2011–12; Betsi Cadwaladr University Health Board, Wales, since 2013; *b* 13 Nov. 1946; *s* of Edwin Johnson and Elizabeth Marjorie Johnson (née North); *m* 1st, 1972, Dr Gillian Christine Markham (marr. diss. 2002); one *s* one *d*; 2nd, 2006, Fiona Helen Simpson. *Educ:* Liverpool Univ. Med. Sch. (MB ChB 1970, MD 1980). FRCS 1977; FRCP 2000; FDSRCS 2000. Demonstrator, then Lectr in Anatomy, Univ. of Liverpool, 1971–74; Fellow, Merseyside Assoc. for Kidney Res., 1974–75; Registrar and Sen. Registrar trng posts, Mersey Reg., 1975–85; Clinical Lectr in Surgery, Liverpool Univ., 1987–. Vis. Prof. in Anatomy, Univ. of Texas, 1973. British Medical Association: Mem. Council, 1975–80 and 1992–2007; Chm. Council, 2003–07; Chairman: Hosp. Jun. Staffs Cttee, 1979–80; Central Consultants and Specialists Cttee, 1994–98 (Vice-Chm., 1990–94). Chm., Jt Consultants Cttee, 1998–2003 (Vice-Chm., 1994–98); Mem., Standing Med. Adv. Cttee, DoH, 1998–2004. Mem., Mgt Cttee, Nat. Counselling Service for Sick Doctors, 1985–2004. Hon. Consultant Surgeon, Guy's and St Thomas' NHS Trust, 2009–10. *Publications:* contrib. articles on surgical, vascular surgical and medico-political topics, incl. the future rôle of consultant, hospital configuration and appraisal. *Recreations:* travel, fine wine, medical politics, modern languages. *Address:* Talgarth, 66 View Road, Rainhill, Prescot, Merseyside L35 0LS. *T:* (0151) 426 4306, *Fax:* (0151) 493 0024. *E:* jnjohnson33@hotmail.com. *Clubs:* Athenæum; XX, Artists (Liverpool).

**JOHNSON, Rt Hon. Joseph (Edmund);** PC 2019; MP (C) Orpington, since 2010; *b* London, Dec. 1971; *s* of Stanley Patrick Johnson, *qv* and Charlotte Maria Fawcett; *m* 2005, Amelia Gentleman; one *s* one *d*. *Educ:* Eton Coll.; Balliol Coll., Oxford (MA 1st cl. Mod. Hist.); Inst. d'Etudes Européennes, Brussels (Licence Spéciale); INSEAD, Fontainebleau (MBA 2000). Corporate financier, Investment Banking Div., Deutsche Bank, 1996–97; Financial Times: Lex columnist, 1997–99; Paris corresp., 2001–05; S Asia Bureau Chief, 2005–08; Associate Ed. and Ed., Lex column, 2008–10. PPS to Mark Prisk, Minister of State for Business and Enterprise, 2010–12; an Asst Govt Whip, 2012–14; Hd of No 10 Policy Unit, and Chair, Prime Minister's Policy Bd, 2013–15; Parly Sec., 2013–14, Minister of State, 2014–15, Cabinet Office; Minister of State (Minister for Univs and Sci.), BIS, then Minister of State (Minister for Univs, Sci., Res. and Innovation), BEIS, 2015–18; Minister of State, DFE, 2016–18; Minister of State (Minister for London), and Minister of State, DfT, 2018; Minister of State, BEIS and DfE, 2019. *Publications:* (with Martine Orange) The Man Who Tried to Buy the World, 2003; (ed jtly) Reconnecting Britain and India: ideas for an enhanced partnership, 2011. *Recreations:* trekking, writing, tennis. *Address:* House of Commons, SW1A 0AA. *E:* jo.johnson.mp@parliament.uk.
*See also Rt Hon. A. B. de P. Johnson, L. F. Johnson, R. S. Johnson.*

**JOHNSON, Prof. Julian Michael,** DPhil; FBA 2017; Regius Professor of Music, Royal Holloway, University of London, since 2013 (Professor of Music, since 2007); *b* Macclesfield, 1 July 1963; *s* of Simon Johnson and Ann Johnson; *m* 1989, Julia Canneaux; two *s*. *Educ:* Reading Sch.; Pembroke Coll., Cambridge; Dartington Coll. of Arts (BA Hons); Univ. of Sussex (MA; DPhil 1994). Lectr, Univ. of Sussex, 1994–2001; Fellow, St Anne's Coll., Oxford, 2001–07; Reader, Faculty of Music, Univ. of Oxford, 2001–07. Dent Medal, Royal Musical Assoc., 2005. *Publications:* Webern and the Transformation of Nature, 1999; Who Needs Classical Music?, 2002; Classical Music: a beginner's guide, 2009; Mahler's Voices: expression and irony in the songs and symphonies, 2009; Out of Time: music and the making of modernity, 2015. *Recreations:* mountaineering, cycling, gardening, music. *Address:* Department of Music, Royal Holloway, University of London, Egham TW20 0EX. *T:* (01784) 443540, *Fax:* (01784) 414490. *E:* julian.johnson@rhul.ac.uk.

**JOHNSON, Keith;** *see* Johnson, A. K.

**JOHNSON, Leo Fenton;** Partner and Disruption Lead, PricewaterhouseCoopers (Partner, Sustainability and Climate Change, 2008); *b* London, 26 Sept. 1967; *s* of Stanley Patrick Johnson, *qv* and Charlotte Maria Johnson (née Fawcett); *m* 1996, Taies Nezam, *d* of Amanullah Nezam and Malal Moosa; two *d*. *Educ:* New Coll., Oxford (Stephens Schol.; BA); University Coll. London (MSc Resource and Envmtl Econs); INSEAD (MBA). Consultant, Envmt Dept, IFC, 1993–2003; Co-Founder and Dir, Sustainable Finance Ltd, 2003–08. Dir, Handbag Pictures, 1997–2003. Vis. Business Fellow, Smith Sch. of Enterprise and Envmt, Univ. of Oxford, 2010–. Presenter: Down to Business prog., BBC World News; FutureProofing, BBC Radio 4. Sustainability Advr and Judge, Prix Pictet for photography on sustainability; Judge, FT Boldness in Business Awards. Writer and dir, film, Eating and Weeping, 2002. Trustee: New Econs Foundn; Green Alliance. *Publications:* Beyond Risk, 2002; (jtly) Turnaround Challenge: business and the City of the future, 2013; contribs to FT, Wall St Jl. *Recreation:* time with my wife and daughters. *Address:* c/o JLA Agency, 14 Berners Street, W1T 3LJ. *T:* (020) 7907 2800. *E:* leojohnson1@gmail.com.
*See also Rt Hon. A. B. de P. Johnson, Rt Hon. J. E. Johnson, R. S. Johnson.*

**JOHNSON, Luke Oliver;** Chairman: Risk Capital Partners, since 2001; StartUp Britain, since 2012; Brainspark, since 2012; TellTheChef, since 2014; Co-founder and Chairman, Centre for Entrepreneurs, since 2013; *b* 2 Feb. 1962; *s* of Paul Bede Johnson, *qv*; *m* 2004, Liza Pickrell; two *s* one *d*. *Educ:* Langley Grammar Sch.; Magdalen Coll., Oxford. Stockbroking Analyst, Grieveson Grant, then Kleinwort Benson, 1983–88; Director: AoD, 1989–92; ICD, 1989–92; Crabtree Gp, 1992–94; PizzaExpress, 1992–95 and 1998–99 (Chm., 1996–98); My Kinda Town, 1994–96; American Port Services, 1995–98; Abacus Recruitment, 1995–99; Integrated Dental Hldgs, 1996–2006; Whittards of Chelsea, 1998–2001; NewMedia SPARK, 1999–2001; Nightfreight, 1999–2001; Acquisitor, 1999–2004; Manager, Intrinsic Value, 1999–2001; Chairman: Belgo Gp, subseq. Signature Restaurants Ltd, 1997–2005; Grand Union, 2013–; Red Hot World Buffet, 2013–; Gaucho Gp, 2016–17; Arden Partners, 2016–18 (non-exec. Dir, 2015–18). Chairman: Channel 4 TV, 2004–09; Royal Soc. of Arts, 2009–12. Mem., Govt Adv. Panel on public library service in England, 2014–. Chm. of Trustees, Action on Addiction, 2012–. Gov., Univ. of the Arts, London (formerly London Inst.), 2000–06. Columnist: Sunday Telegraph, 1997–2006; FT, 2007–. *Publications:* How to Get a Highly Paid Job in the City, 1987; Betting to Win, 1990, 2nd edn 1997; The Maverick: dispatches from an unrepentant capitalist, 2007; Start It Up: why running your own business is easier than you think, 2011. *Recreations:* writing, tennis, swimming. *Address:* Risk Capital Partners, 31 North Row, W1K 6DA. *T:* (020) 7016 0700. *Clubs:* Royal Automobile, Groucho, Lansdowne.
*See also D. B. Johnson.*

**JOHNSON, Prof. Margaret Anne,** MD, FRCP; Consultant Physician in Thoracic Medicine and HIV Medicine, since 1989, and Clinical Director, HIV/AIDS, since 1992, Royal Free Hampstead NHS Trust; Professor of HIV Medicine, University College London, since 2005; *b* 7 Feb. 1952; *d* of Dr Frederick W. Johnson and Dr Margaret Rosemary Johnson; *m* 1980, Prof. John William Winston Studd, *qv*; one *s* two *d*. *Educ:* Convent of the Sacred Heart, Woldingham; Royal Free Hosp. Sch. of Medicine, Univ. of London (MD 1987). FRCP 1993. House Physician, 1976, House Surgeon, 1976–77, Royal Free Hosp.; Senior House Officer: Postgrad. Trng Scheme in Medicine, Whittington Hosp., 1977–78; London Chest Hosp., 1978; Nat. Hosp. for Nervous Diseases, 1978–79; Registrar Rotation in Gen. Medicine, St Mary's Hosp., W2, 1979–81; Res. Registrar, Royal Brompton Hosp., 1981–83; Sen. Registrar Rotation in Gen. Medicine and Thoracic Medicine, Royal Free Hosp./Royal Brompton Hosp., 1983–89; Med. Dir, Royal Free Hampstead NHS Trust, 2002–06. Academic Vice-Pres., RCP, 2015–. Chm., British HIV Assoc., 2004–08. *Publications:* An Atlas of HIV and AIDS, 1995, 2nd edn 2004; articles concerning clinical mgt of HIV in learned jls. *Address:* UCL Institute of Immunity and Transplantation, Royal Free Hospital, Pond Street, NW3 2QG. *T:* (020) 7941 1820, *Fax:* (020) 7941 1830. *Club:* Athenæum.

**JOHNSON, Prof. Mark Henry,** PhD; FBA 2011; Professor of Experimental Psychology, University of Cambridge, since 2017; *b* London, 4 June 1960; *s* of James Johnson and Krystyna Johnson; *m* 2001, Prof. Annette Dionne Karmiloff-Smith, CBE, FBA (*d* 2016). *Educ:* Univ. of Edinburgh (BSc Biol Scis 1981); King's Coll., Cambridge (PhD Zool. 1985). Res. Scientist, MRC Cognitive Develt Unit, London, 1985–90; Associate Prof. of Psychol., Carnegie-Mellon Univ., 1991–95; Sen. Res. Scientist, MRC Cognitive Develt Unit, London, 1994–98; Prof. of Psychol., and Dir, Centre for Brain and Cognitive Develt, Birkbeck, Univ. of London, 1997–2017. *Publications:* (with J. Morton) Biology and Cognitive Development: the case of face recognition, 1991; Brain Development and Cognition: a reader, 1993, 2nd edn (jtly) 2002; (jtly) Rethinking Innateness: a connectionist perspective on development, 1996; Developmental Cognitive Neuroscience: an introduction, 1997, 4th edn (with Michelle de Haan) 2015; (ed jtly) The Cognitive Neuroscience of Development, 2003; (ed jtly) Attention and Performance XXI: processes of change in brain and cognitive development, 2006; (jtly) Neuroconstructivism, vol. 1: how the brain constructs cognition, 2007, vol. 2: perspectives and prospects, 2007; (ed jtly) The Handbook of Face Perception, 2011. *Recreations:* gardening, whisky, science. *Address:* Department of Psychology, University of Cambridge, Downing Street, Cambridge CB2 3EB. *Club:* Hanbury Manor (Ware, Herts).

**JOHNSON, Martin;** Sports Feature Writer, Sunday Times, since 2008; *b* 23 June 1949; *s* of late Basil Johnson and of Bridget Johnson; *m* 1985, Teresa Mary Wright; one *s* one *d*. *Educ:* St Julian's High Sch., Newport, Mon.; Monmouth Sch. Ronald French Advertising Agency, Liverpool, 1970; South Wales Argus, Newport, 1970–73; Leicester Mercury, 1973–86; Cricket Corresp., The Independent, 1986–95; Sports Feature Writer, Daily Telegraph, 1995–2008. *Publications:* (ed) The Independent World Cup Cricket, 1987; (jtly) Gower: the autobiography, 1992; Rugby and All That: an irreverent history, 2000. *Recreation:* golf. *Address:* The Old Chapel House, Chapel Road, Ross-on-Wye HR9 5PR. *Club:* Ross on Wye Golf.

**JOHNSON, Prof. Martin Hume,** PhD; FMedSci; FRS 2014; Professor of Reproductive Sciences, University of Cambridge, 1992–2012, now Emeritus; Life Fellow, Christ's College, Cambridge, since 1969 (Vice-Master, 2007–09; President, 2009–10; Tutor, 2013–14); *b* 19 Dec. 1944; *s* of late Reginald Hugh Ben Johnson and Joyce Florence Johnson. *Educ:* Cheltenham Grammar Sch.; Christ's Coll., Cambridge (MA, PhD). Jun. Res. Fellow, Christ's Coll., Cambridge, 1969; MRC Jun. Res. Fellow, 1970; Harkness Fellow, 1971; University of Cambridge: Lectr in Anatomy, 1974–84; Reader in Exptl Embryology, 1984–92; Head of Dept of Anatomy, 1995–99. Hon. Sen. Lectr in Obstetrics and Gynaecology, UMDS, 1991–95; Distinguished Vis. Fellow, La Trobe Univ., 1993, 2006; Vis. Prof., Sydney Univ., 1999–2004; Hon. Academic Fellow, St Paul's Coll., Sydney Univ., 2005. Chm., Brit. Soc. for Developmental Biol., 1984–89; Mem., HFEA, 1994–99. Special Advr to Jt Lords and Commons Inquiry Cttee on the Human Tissue and Embryos (Draft) Bill, 2007. Chief Exec., Edwards and Steptoe Charitable Trust, 2010. Ed., Reproductive Medicine OnLine, 2010. Lectures: Hammond, Soc. for Study of Fertility, 1992; Haliburton, Dept of Physiol., KCL, 1994; S. T. Huang-Chan Meml, Hong Kong Univ., 1997; Ver Heyden de Lancey, Univ. of Cambridge, 2007; A. E. Szulman, Univ. of Pittsburg, 2007, 2015; Robert G. Edwards Nobel, Lisbon, 2012; Historical Lectr, Eur. Soc. for Human Reproduction, Istanbul, 2012; R. G. Edwards, Acad. of Clinical Embryologists, Jaipur, 2016. Co-Chief Ed., Reproductive BioMedicine and Society Online, 2015–. FMedSci 2012. Hon. FRCOG (FRCOG 2005); Hon. Fellow: Soc. for Reproduction Fertility, 2014; Physiol Soc., 2014. Albert Brachet Prize, Belgian Royal Acad. Scis, Letters and Fine Arts, 1989; Prize for Innovation in Med. Educn, King's Fund, 1993; Marshall Medal, Soc. for Reproduction and Fertility, 2014. *Publications:* Essential Reproduction, (with B. J. Everitt) 1980, 8th edn (sole author) 2018 (BMA Book Prize in Obstetrics and Gynaecol., 2008); (ed jtly) Sexuality Repositioned: diversity and the law, 2004; (ed jtly) Death Rites and Rights, 2007; (ed jtly) Birth Rites and Rights, 2011; contrib. to numerous scientific pubns. *Recreations:* opera, music, theatre, travel. *Address:* Anatomy School, Department of Physiology, Development and Neuroscience, Downing Street, Cambridge CB2 3DY. *T:* (01223) 333777.

**JOHNSON, Martin Osborne,** CBE 2004 (OBE 1998); Rugby Union football player, retired; Team Manager, England Rugby Football Union Team, 2008–11; *b* Solihull, 9 March 1970; *s* of David Johnson and late Hilary Johnson; *m* 2000, Kay Gredrig; one *s* one *d*. *Educ:* Robert Smyth Sch., Market Harborough. Joined Leicester RFU Club Youth team, 1988; played for College Old Boys, King Country, NZ and NZ Under 21s, 1989–90; joined Leicester Tigers, 1989: Captain, 1997–2003, 2004–05; Premiership Champions, 1999, 2000, 2001, 2002; winners, European Cup, 2001, 2002. 1st cap for England, 1993;

Capt., 1999–2003; 84 caps, 39 as Capt.; captained Grand Slam side, 2003; has played in 3 World Cup teams, two as Capt.; winners, Rugby World Cup, Australia, 2003; Member, British Lions tours: NZ, 1993; S Africa, 1997 (Capt.); Australia, 2001 (Capt.). *Publications*: Agony and Ecstasy, 2001; Martin Johnson: the autobiography, 2003.

**JOHNSON, Matthew Alfred;** Head, Mediterranean Migration Unit, Foreign and Commonwealth Office, since 2019; *b* Rochford, Essex, 11 June 1970; *s* of late Alfred Henry James Johnson and Mary Theresa Johnson (*née* Slattery); *m* 1993, Heidi Suzanne Burton; one *s* one *d*. *Educ*: Westcliff High Sch. for Boys. Joined FCO, 1988; FCO, 1988–90; Pretoria and Cape Town, 1990–93; Third Sec., Middle E Dept, FCO, 1993; Vice-Consul, Osaka, 1994–96; Third Sec., Eastern Dept, FCO, 1996–98; Second Sec., Cultural Relns Dept, FCO, 1998–99; Private Sec. to Hd of Policy Unit, Prime Minister's Office, 10 Downing St, 1999–2000; Second Sec., UK Mission to UN, NY, 2000–03; First Sec., Afghanistan Gp, FCO, 2003–06; First Sec. and Dep. Hd, Conflict Gp, FCO, 2006–08; Counsellor and Dep. High Comr, Accra, 2008–12; UK Perm. Rep. (with personal rank of Ambassador) to Council of Europe, Strasbourg, 2012–16; Dir, Democratic Citizenship and Participation, Council of Europe, 2016–18; Dep. Migration Envoy, FCO, 2018–19. *Recreations*: sports (cricket, tennis, Rugby), history, music (piano and singing), films. *Address*: Foreign and Commonwealth Office, King Charles Street, SW1A 2AH. *E*: matthew.johnson@fco.gov.uk.

**JOHNSON, Melanie Jane;** JP; Chair, Pay.UK (formerly New Payment System Operator), since 2017; *b* 5 Feb. 1955; *d* of David Guyatt Johnson and Mary Angela Johnson; one *s* twin *d* by William Jordan. *Educ*: University Coll. London (BA Jt Hons Phil. and Ancient Greek); King's Coll., Cambridge (postgrad. res.). Mem. Relns Officer, 1981–88, Retail Admin Manager, 1988–90, Cambridge Co-op. Soc.; Asst Gen. Manager (Quality Assurance), Cambs FHSA, 1990–92; Schools Inspector, 1993–97. Mem. (Lab) Cambs CC, 1981–97. MP (Lab) Welwyn Hatfield, 1997–2005; contested (Lab) same seat, 2005. PPS to Financial Sec., HM Treasury, 1999; Economic Sec., HM Treasury, 1999–2001; Parly Under-Sec. of State, DTI, 2001–03; Parly Under-Sec. of State (Minister for Public Health), DoH, 2003–05. Member: Public Admin. Select Cttee, 1997–98; Home Affairs Select Cttee, 1998–99; Chm., All Party Parenting Gp, 1998–2005. Chairman: Customer Impact Panel, ABI, 2006–11; UK Cards Assoc., 2009–17. Mem. Bd, Newta, 2016–17. Contested (Lab) Cambs, EP elecn, 1994. JP Cambridge, 1994. *Recreations*: family, films, gardening. *E*: melaniejohnson@ntlworld.com.

**JOHNSON, Melinda Jane;** Commercial Director, Department of Health and Social Care (formerly Department of Health), since 2017; *b* Wakefield, 13 Nov. 1965; *d* of Henry and June Johnson; *m* 2004, Philip James Considine. *Educ*: Univ. of York (BSc Hons Psychol. 1988); Univ. of Durham (MBA (Dist.) 1996). DipM, MCIM 2003. Product buyer, BT, 1988–89; buyer, GSPK Electronics, 1989–90; Sen. Buyer, IT, Nat. Power plc, 1990–93; Head: Procurement, Univ. of Durham, 1993–99; Policy and Representation, Chartered Inst. of Purchasing and Supply, 1999–2003; Principal Procurement Consultant, Improvement and Develt Agency, 2003–05; Deputy Director: Centre for Procurement Performance, DfES, subseq. DCSF, 2005–08; Commercial, DCSF, subseq. DFE, 2008–11; Dep. Finance and Commercial Dir, DFE, 2011–12; Dir, Gp Procurement and Property, DfT, 2012–15; Dir of Gp Commercial Services, DfT, 2015–17. Non-executive Director: British Quality Foundn, 2016–; NHS Supply Chain Coordination Ltd, 2017–. Chartered Institute for Purchasing and Supply: Member: Council, 2008–11; Bd of Mgt, 2010–11; Disciplinary Cttee, 2011–14; Global Bd of Trustees, 2012–14; Chm., Global Congress, 2012–14. Mem. Council, 1995–98, Chair, 1998, Assoc. of Univ. Purchasing Officers. FCIPS 2003 (MCIPS 1992); MCMI 1996; MBPsS 2010. *Recreations*: travel, art, cinema, reading. *Address*: Department of Health and Social Care, 39 Victoria Street, SW1H 0EU. *T*: 07920 266375.

**JOHNSON, Michael Robert;** graphic designer; Founder, 1992, and Creative Director, since 1992, Johnson Banks Design, graphic design consultancy; *b* 26 April 1964; *s* of late Charles Beverley Johnson and of Shirley Anne Johnson (*née* Fowler); *m* 1995, Elisabeth Schoon; one *s* one *d*. *Educ*: Ecclesbourne Sch., Duffield, Derby; Univ. of Lancaster (BA 1st Cl. Jt Hons Design and Mktg 1985). Junior consultant, Wolff Olins, London, 1985–86; designer, Billy Blue Gp, Sydney, 1986–87; freelance designer, Tokyo, 1987; designer, Emery Vincent Design, Melbourne and Sydney, 1988; Art Dir, Omon Advertising, Sydney, 1988; Sen. Designer, Sedley Place Design, London, 1988–89; Gp Art Dir, Smith and Milton, London, 1990–92. D&AD: Mem., 1991–; Cttee Mem., 1999–2003; Educn Chm., 2001–02; Pres., 2003; Chm., Design Week Awards, 1989, 1999. External Examiner: Glasgow Sch. of Art, 2001–04; Kingston Univ., 2006–; Mem., Re-validation Cttee, Communications course, RCA, 1998. Visiting Lecturer: Kingston Univ.; Nottingham Univ.; Northumbria Univ.; Middlesex Univ.; Falmouth Coll. of Art; Glasgow Sch. of Art; Central St Martins. *Exhibitions* include: *group*: The Power of the Poster (contrib. curator), 1998, Rewind: 40 Years of Design and Advertising (co-curator), 2002, V&A; European Design Biennial, Design Mus., 2003, 2005; Communicate: Independent British Graphic Design since the Sixties, Barbican Gall., 2004–05; *solo*: Words & Pictures, the design work of Michael Johnson + johnson banks, 2004, Jeans Shop Ginza, 2005, Creation Gall., Tokyo. Seven Silver Awards, one Gold Award, President's Award, 2017, D&AD; 13 Design Week Awards; Gold Award, 1991, 2008, Silver Award, 2004, NY Art Dirs. *Publications*: Problem Solved: a primer in design and communication, 2002, 2nd edn 2012; (contrib.) Rewind: 40 years of design and advertising, 2002; (contrib.) The Education of a Typographer, 2004; Branding: in five and a half steps, 2016; Now Try Something Weirder: how to keep having great ideas and survive in the creative business, 2019. *Recreations*: playing and collecting guitars, music. *Address*: Johnson Banks Design Limited, Crescent Works, Crescent Lane, SW4 9RW. *T*: (020) 7587 6400, *Fax*: (020) 7587 6411. *E*: Michael@johnsonbanks.co.uk.

**JOHNSON, Michael York-;** *see* York, M.

**JOHNSON, Neil Anthony,** OBE (mil.) 1989; TD 1985, bar 1992; DL; Chairman, Electra Private Equity plc, since 2016; *b* 13 April 1949; *s* of Anthony and Dilys Johnson, Glamorgan; *m* 1st, 1971 (marr. diss. 1996); three *d*; 2nd, 1996, Elizabeth Jane Hunter Johnston (*née* Robinson); one *d*, and three step *d*. *Educ*: Canton High Sch., Cardiff; RMA Sandhurst. Graduate Trainee, Lex Gp, 1971–73; British Leyland Motor Corp., 1973–82; Dir, Sales and Marketing, Jaguar Cars, 1982–86; MoD, 1986–89; Main Bd Dir, Rover Gp, British Aerospace, resp. for European Ops, 1989–92; Dir-Gen., EEF, 1992–93; Gen. Sec., 1994–99, Chief Exec., 1996–99, RAC; Chief Exec., British and Amer. Chamber of Commerce, 2000–01. Chairman: Hornby plc, 2000–13; Motability Finance Ltd, then Motability Operations Gp plc, 2001–19; Cybit plc, 2001–10; Tenon plc, 2003–06 (Dir, 2000–06); Umeco plc, 2009–12; Synthomer (formerly Yule-Catto) plc, 2011–; e2v plc, 2013–17; Centaur Media plc, 2018–19; QinetiQ plc, 2019– (Dir, 2019–); Sen. Ind. Dir, Business Growth Fund, 2013– (Dep. Chm., 2011–13). Territorial Army: Pembroke Yeomanry, 1971; 4th Bn RGJ, 1973; CO, 1986–89; ADC to the Queen, 1990; Hon. Col, 157 Transport Regt, RLC, 1993–2001; Trustee, Rifles Volunteer Trust (formerly RGJ TA Trust), 1994– (Chm., 2015–); Hon. Col, F Co., London Regt, RGJ, 2000–07. Member: Prime Minister's Panel of Advrs on Citizen's Charter, Cabinet Office, 1995–2003; UK Round Table on Sustainable Develt, 1997–98; Cleaner Vehicles Task Force, 1997–99. Member: Nat. Employers' Liaison Cttee for the Reserve Forces, 1992–98; Nat. Employers'

Adv. Bd, 2006–15. Ind. Mem., Metropolitan Police Authy, 2008–12. UK Rep. Mem., FIA, 1994–99. Trustee, Jaguar Daimler Heritage Trust, 1994–99. FIMI; CCMI (CIMgt 1995); FRSA. Freeman, City of London, 1985. DL Greater London, 1993; Rep. DL, City of Westminster, 1993–2007. Ordre de l'Encouragement Publique (France), 1987. *Recreations*: town and country pursuits, fast British cars, slow Italian lunches. *Address*: Electra Private Equity plc, First Floor, 50 Grosvenor Hill, W1K 3QT. *Clubs*: Army and Navy, Royal Green Jackets, Royal Automobile, Beefsteak, Cavalry and Guards; Cardiff and County (Cardiff); Woodroffe's; Midland Automobile (Shelsley Walsh); Arlberg Ski.

**JOHNSON, Prof. Newell Walter,** CMG 2011; MDSc, PhD; FDSRCS, FRACDS, FRCPath, FMedSci, FFOP (RCPA), FICD, FHEA; Honorary Professor of Dental Research, Menzies Health Institute Queensland at Griffith University (formerly Griffith Institute for Health and Medical Research, then Griffith Health Institute), Queensland, 2009–12, now Emeritus Professor; Professor of Oral Health Sciences, GKT Dental Institute, King's College London, 2003–05, now Emeritus; specialist in oral medicine, oral pathology and periodontics; *b* 5 Aug. 1938; *s* of Otto Johnson and Lorna (*née* Guy); *m* 1st, 1965, Pauline Margaret Trafford (marr. diss. 1984); two *d*; 2nd, 2003, Jeannette Giblin. *Educ*: University High Sch., Melbourne; Univ. of Melbourne (BDSc Hons 1960; MDSc 1963); Univ. of Bristol (PhD 1967). FDSRCS 1964; FRACDS 1966; FRCPath 1982; FMedSci 1995; FFOP (RCPA) 1996; FICD 2006. Res. Fellow in Pathology, Univ. of Melbourne, 1961–63; Lectr in Dental Surgery, UCL, 1963–64; Scientific Officer, MRC Dental Res. Unit, Bristol, 1964–67; London Hospital Medical College: Reader in Experimental Oral Path., 1968–76; Prof. of Oral Path., 1976–83; Hon. Dir, MRC Dental Res. Unit, 1983–93; Governor, 1983 (Chm., Academic Div. of Dentistry, 1983); Chm., London Hosp. Div. of Dentistry, 1981–83; Nuffield Res. Prof. of Dental Science, RCS, 1984–2003; Dir of Res. and Univ. Postgrad. Educn, Dental Inst., KCL, 1994–95; Prof. of Oral Pathology, King's Coll. Sch. of Medicine and Dentistry, subseq. GKT Dental Inst. of KCL, Univ. of London, 1994–2003; Foundn Dean and Hd, Sch. of Dentistry and Oral Health, Griffith Univ., Qld, 2005–09. Hon. Consultant Surgeon: Royal London (formerly London) Hosp., 1968–; King's Healthcare NHS Trust, 1993–2005. Consultant, Fédération Dentaire Internationale, 1984– (Comr, 1996–); Academician, Argentine Acad. of Medicine, 2004. Consultant in Oral Health, WHO, 1984–; Dir, WHO Collaborating Centre for Oral Cancer and Precancer, 1995–2005. Pres., British Soc. of Periodontology, 1992–93. Chairman: UK Cttee, Royal Australasian Coll. of Dental Surgeons, 1981–83; Australasian Council of Dental Schs, 2006–10; Faculty of Oral Pathology, Royal Coll. of Pathologists, Australasia, 2008–10; FRSocMed (Mem. Council, 2001–; Mem. Council, Section of Odontology, 1972–91 (Pres., 1988–89 and 2004–05)); Founder FMedSci 1998; Fellow, Acad. of Oral Medicine, Acad. of Australasia, 2007; Fellow, NH&MRC, 2009. Member, Editorial Board: Jl of Oral Pathology, 1982–93; Jl of Periodontal Research, 1986–96 (Associate Ed., 1993–); Jl of Clin. Periodontology, 1990–; Oral Oncology, 1992–; Editor in Chief, Oral Diseases, 1994–2005. Hon. Mem., British Soc. for Oral Medicine, 2011. John Tomes Medal, BDA, 2005; Dist. Scientist Award, Oral Medicine and Pathology, IADR, 2005. *Publications*: (jtly) The Oral Mucosa in Health and Disease, 1975; (jtly) The Human Oral Mucosa: structure, metabolism and function, 1976; (jtly) Dental Caries: aetiology, pathology and prevention, 1979; (ed jtly) Oral Diseases in the Tropics, 1992; (ed) Detection of High Risk Groups for Oral Diseases, 3 vols, 1991; Oral Cancer, 2000; (ed jtly) Oral Cancer, 2003, 2nd edn 2018; (contrib.) Head and Neck Cancer: multimodality management, 2011, 2nd edn 2015; (contrib.) Oral Cancer: a comprehensive approach, 2016; articles in scientific jls. *Recreations*: music, theatre, visual arts, the environment, global health inequalities, multicultural studies. *E*: n.johnson@griffith.edu.au.

**JOHNSON, Nichola,** OBE 2013; FSA; Director of Museology, 1993–2010, Director, Museum Leadership Programme, 1994–2012, and Director, Sainsbury Centre for Visual Arts, 1996–2010, University of East Anglia; *b* 21 May 1945; *d* of John Nicholas Healey and Jessica (*née* Horrocks); *m* 1965, M. D. Johnson (marr. diss. 1971); one *s* one *d*. *Educ*: Ipswich High Sch.; Univ. of Sheffield (BA); Univ. of Essex (MA). FSA 2011. Lectr, Dept of Art History, Univ. of Essex, 1980–83; Hd, Dept of Later London History, Mus. of London, 1983–93. Chair: mda, 1998–2003; Univ. Museums Gp, 2003–09; Clore Leadership Prog., 2004–09 (Trustee, 2009–); Ruskin Foundn, 2009–12; E Anglia Art Fund, 2013–. Trustee: Dulwich Picture Gall., 2006–17; Norfolk and Norwich Fest., 2009–16; Brantwood Trust, 2009–; Pallant House Gall., 2010–14; Sir John Soane's Mus., 2014–; Mem. Council, Nat. Trust, 2016–18 (Trustee, 2010–16). Vis. Prof., Norwich Univ. of Arts, 2014–. Mem., Bd of Dirs, Guild of St George, 2018–. *Publications*: University Museums in the United Kingdom, 2004; contribs to professional jls and edited volumes. *Recreations*: music-making, lurcher shows, long-distance walking. *Address*: The Lodging House, Church Street, Reepham, Norfolk NR10 4JW.

**JOHNSON, Nicholas;** Deputy Chief Executive, Urban Splash Group Ltd, 1999–2012; *b* Bolton, 10 Jan. 1966; *s* of Derek Johnson and Valerie Johnson; partner, Jenny; four *d*. *Educ*: Sheffield Hallam Univ. (BSc Hons). Principal, Johnson Urban Develt Consultants, 1991–99. Chm., Marketing Manchester, 2006–13; Dir, Market Ops Ltd, 2013–. Mem., CABE, 2007–11. Dist. Vis. Fellow, Yale Sch. of Architecture, 2007–08. FRSA. *Recreations*: cycling, canal boats.

**JOHNSON, Nicholas James;** QC 2016; *b* London, 15 May 1970; *s* of Rev. Michael Johnson and Barbara Johnson; *m* 1st, 1996, Josephine Laura Butler (marr. diss. 2015); two *d*; 2nd, 2017, Stephanie Alwyn Raine; four step *d*. *Educ*: Swanley Comprehensive Sch.; Univ. of York (BA 1st Cl. English); Coll. of Law; Inns of Court Sch. of Law. Asst lang. teacher, JET Prog., Miyazaki Prefecture, Japan, 1991–92; called to the Bar, Inner Temple, 1994; in practice as barrister, specialising in financial, corporate and organised crime, commercial and regulatory work, 1994–. Member: Internat. Cttee, Bar Council, 2019–; Internat. Bar Assoc. *Recreations*: contemporary photography, walking, ski-ing, anything Japanese, Ronnie Scott's. *Address*: Exchange Chambers, Oxford House, Oxford Road, Leeds LS1 3BE. *T*: (0113) 203 1970. *E*: johnsonqc@exchangechambers.co.uk; Bright Line Law, Central Court, 25 Southampton Buildings, WC2A 1AL. *T*: (020) 3917 4682.

**JOHNSON, Nicholas Robert;** QC 2006; a barrister, since 1987; *b* 28 Aug. 1964; *s* of late Rev. Robin E. H. Johnson and of Joyce Verry Johnson; *m* 2001, Jane Woodfine; one *s* two *d*. *Educ*: St Paul's Cathedral Choir Sch.; Manchester Grammar Sch.; Leeds Univ. (BA Hist. 1985; played Rugby League for British Students, 1985); Poly. of Central London (Dip. Law 1986). Called to the Bar, Inner Temple, 1987. *Recreation*: catching up. *Address*: 7 Harrington Street, Liverpool L2 9YH. *T*: (0151) 236 0707.

**JOHNSON, Sir Patrick Eliot,** 8th Bt *cr* 1818, of Bath; *b* 11 June 1955; *s* of Sir Robin Eliot Johnson, 7th Bt and of Barbara Alfreda, *d* of late Alfred T. Brown; *S* father, 1989, but his name does not appear on the Official Roll of the Baronetage; *m* 1980, Rose (marr. diss. 1989), *d* of Olav Alfhein; twin *s*. *Heir*: *s* Richard Eliot Johnson, *b* 8 Jan. 1983.

**JOHNSON, Prof. Paul A.,** DPhil; Warden of Forrest Hall, University of Western Australia, since 2017; *b* Bath, 26 Nov. 1956; *s* of Alan and Joyce Johnson; *m* Dr Susannah Morris; one *s* one *d*. *Educ*: St John's Coll., Oxford (BA); Nuffield Coll., Oxford (DPhil). Res. Fellow, Nuffield Coll., Oxford, 1981–84; London School of Economics: Lectr in Social Hist., 1984–94; Reader in Econ. Hist., 1994–99; Prof. of Econ. Hist., 1999–2007; Dep. Dir, 2004–07; Vice-Chancellor and Pres., La Trobe Univ., Australia, 2007–11; Vice-

Chancellor, Univ. of Western Australia, 2012–16. Gov., Forrest Res. Foundn, 2014–. *Publications:* Saving and Spending, 1985; Ageing and Economic Welfare, 1992; Twentieth Century Britain, 1994; Old Age: from antiquity to post-modernity, 1998; (ed jtly) Cambridge Economic History of Modern Britain, 2004, 2nd edn 2014; Making the Market, 2010. *Recreation:* my family. *Address:* Forrest Hall, M441, University of Western Australia, 35 Stirling Highway, Crawley, WA 6009, Australia.

**JOHNSON, Paul Antony;** Deputy Editor, Guardian News and Media, since 2008; *b* Aldershot, 21 Nov. 1953; *s* of Alfred Johnson and Myrtle Johnson; *m* 2007, Fionnuala Cosgrove; one *s* one *d*. *Educ:* Cardiff Univ. (BSc; Postgrad. Dip. Journalism). The Guardian: reporter, 1979–87; News Ed., 1987–92; Asst Ed., 1992–95; Dep. Ed., 1995–2008; Sports Ed., Guardian News and Media, 2010–13. *Recreations:* football, running, cinema, cooking. *Address:* Guardian News and Media, Kings Place, 90 York Way, N1 9GU. *T:* (020) 3353 3802. *E:* paul.johnson@guardian.co.uk. *Clubs:* Middlesex County Cricket; Wolverhampton Wanderers Football.

**JOHNSON, Paul (Bede),** CBE 2016; author; *b* 2 Nov. 1928; *s* of William Aloysius and Anne Johnson; *m* 1957, Marigold Hunt, MBE; three *s* one *d*. *Educ:* Stonyhurst; Magdalen Coll., Oxford. Asst Exec. Editor, Réalités, 1952–55; Editorial Staff, New Statesman, 1955, Dir, Statesman and Nation Publishing Co., 1965, Editor of the New Statesman, 1965–70. Member: Royal Commn on the Press, 1974–77; Cable Authority, 1984–90. *Publications:* The Suez War, 1957; Journey into Chaos, 1958; Left of Centre, 1960; Merrie England, 1964; Statesmen and Nations, 1971; The Offshore Islanders, 1972; (with G. Gale) The Highland Jaunt, 1973; Elizabeth I, 1974; A Place in History, 1974; Pope John XXIII, 1975 (Yorkshire Post Book of the Year Award, 1975); A History of Christianity, 1976; Enemies of Society, 1977; The National Trust Book of British Castles, 1978; The Recovery of Freedom, 1980; British Cathedrals, 1980; Ireland: Land of Troubles, 1980; Pope John Paul II and the Catholic Restoration, 1982; A History of the Modern World from 1917 to the 1980s, 1983, rev. edn 1991; The Pick of Paul Johnson, 1985; Oxford Book of Political Anecdotes, 1986; A History of the Jews, 1987; Intellectuals, 1988; The Birth of the Modern: world society 1815–30, 1991; Wake Up Britain! A Latterday Pamphlet, 1994; The Quest for God: a personal pilgrimage, 1996; To Hell With Picasso!: essays from the Spectator, 1996; A History of the American People, 1997; The Renaissance, 2000; Napoleon, 2002; Art: a new history, 2003; Washington, 2003; The Vanished Landscape: a 1930s childhood in the Potteries, 2004; Heroes: from Alexander the Great to Mae West, 2008; Churchill, 2009; Brief Lives, 2010; Darwin, 2010; Stalin, 2012; Socrates, 2013; Mozart, 2013; Eisenhower, 2014. *Recreation:* painting. *Address:* 29 Newton Road, W2 5JR.
*See also* D. B. Johnson, L. O. Johnson.

**JOHNSON, Paul Gavin,** CBE 2018; Director, Institute for Fiscal Studies, since 2011 (Research Fellow, 2007–11); *b* 5 Jan. 1967; *s* of Robert and Joy Johnson; partner, Lorraine Dearden; four *s*. *Educ:* Keble Coll., Oxford (BA 1st Cl. Hons PPE); Birkbeck Coll., London (MSc Econs). Inst. for Fiscal Studies, 1988–98 (Dep. Dir, 1996–98); Hd, Econs of Financial Regulation, FSA, 1999–2000; Chief Economist, and Dir, Analytical Services, DFEE, subseq. DFES, 2000–04; Dir, Public Services, and Chief Micro-Economist, HM Treasury, 2004–07; Dep. Hd, Govt Econ. Service, 2005–07; Sen. Associate, Frontier Economics Ltd, 2007–11. Vis. Prof., Dept of Econs, UCL, 2013–. Member: ESRC, 2002–07; Committee on Climate Change, 2012–; Actuarial Council, 2012–. Trustee, King's Fund. *Publications:* (jtly) Inequality in the UK, 1996; (jtly) Pension Systems and Retirement Incomes Across OECD Countries, 2001; (ed) Tax by Design: the Mirrlees review, 2011; contrib. numerous articles to econs jls and in press. *Address:* Institute for Fiscal Studies, 7 Ridgmount Street, WC1E 7AE. *E:* pjohnson@ifs.org.uk.

**JOHNSON, Penelope Jane,** CBE 2010; Director, Government Art Collection, since 1997; *b* Wimbledon, 23 June 1956; *d* of Dennis George Johnson and June Anne Johnson (*née* Wilkinson). *Educ:* St Helen's Sch., Northwood, Middx; Univ. of E Anglia (BA Fine Arts 1978); Univ. of Manchester (Postgrad. Dip. Gall. and Mus. Studies 1980); Dip. Mus Assoc. 1984. Catalogue asst and researcher, Art Nouveau Collection, Sainsbury Centre for Visual Arts, UEA, 1978–79; Asst Keeper of Fine Art, Stoke-on-Trent City Mus. and Art Gall., 1981–86; Curator, Towner Art Gall. and Local Mus., Eastbourne, 1987–97. Tutor (pt-time), UEA, 1981; asst (pt-time), Communications Dept, Mus. of London, 1981. *Publications:* (contrib.) Art Power Diplomacy. Government Art Collection: the untold story, 2011. *Recreations:* theatre, literature, film, walking, travel. *Address:* Government Art Collection, Queen's Yard, 179a Tottenham Court Road, W1T 7PA. *T:* (020) 7211 2425, *Fax:* (020) 7580 9130. *E:* penny.johnson@culture.gov.uk. *Club:* Chelsea Arts.

**JOHNSON, Peter Michael;** Chairman, Electrocomponents plc, since 2010; *b* 3 July 1947; *s* of late James and Nancy Johnson; *m* 1972, Janet Esther Ashman (*d* 2012); two *s* one *d*; *m* 2018, Diana Celia Joan Lidderdale. *Educ:* Bromley Grammar Sch.; St Edmund Hall, Oxford (MA PPE, BPhil Econs). With Unilever PLC, 1970–73; Redland PLC, 1973–96: Gp Treas., 1978–81; Dir of Planning, 1981–84; Man. Dir, Redland Bricks Ltd, 1984–88; Dir, Redland PLC, 1988–96; Chief Executive: Rugby Gp PLC, 1996–2000; George Wimpey Plc, 2000–06. Chm., David S. Smith Hldgs, later DS Smith plc, 2007–12 (Dir, 1999–2012); Mem., Supervisory Bd, Wienerberger AG, 2005– (Vice-Chm., 2013–); Dir, SSL International Plc, 2008–10. President: Fédération Européene des Fabricants de Tuiles et de Briques, 1994–96; Nat. Council of Building Material Producers, 1997–2000; Mem., Council for Industry and Higher Educn, 2001–06. *Recreations:* music, tennis, cricket, sailing.

**JOHNSON, Peter Michael;** Headmaster, Millfield School, 1998–2008; *b* 21 Dec. 1947; *s* of Joseph William (Johnnie) Johnson and Dorothy Johnson; *m* 1969, Christine Anne Rayment; two *s*. *Educ:* Bec Grammar Sch.; Mansfield Coll., Oxford (Army Scholarship; MA Geog.; PGCE; Rugby Blue, 1968, 1969, 1970, Judo Blue, 1968, 1969). Commnd Royal Army Educn Corps, 1970; transf. to RA, 1972; served 7 Parachute Regt, RHA, 1971–76 (emergency tours in NI, 1972 and 1974 (GSM)); retd in rank of Captain, Radley College: Asst Master, 1976–91; Housemaster, 1983–91; Headmaster, Wrekin Coll., 1991–98. Ambassador, London Chamber Orch., 2016– (Educn Advr, 2011–16). Oxford Univ. Rep. on RFU Council, 1987–98; Trustee: Nat. Centre for Schs and Youth Rugby, 1992–98; Raleigh Internat., 2003–05; Wells Cathedral, 2004–18 (Chm. Trustees, 2009–18); Millfield Foundn, 2018–. Pres., England Rugby Football Schs' Union, 2009–12. Governor: Blundell's Sch., 2008–; Sherborne Girls, 2008–12; Christ's Hospital, 2011–16. Capt., Northampton FC, 1978–79. FRSA. *Recreations:* gardening, music, oenology, writing, cooking. *Address:* Borrowdale, Mill Hill, Stoke Gabriel, Devon TQ9 6RY. *Clubs:* East India; Vincent's (Oxford); Free Foresters.

**JOHNSON, Peter William;** Chairman, Retail Motor Industry Federation, since 2015; *b* 2 Nov. 1947; *s* of Alfred and Emily Johnson; *m* 1973, Ann Gillian Highley; one *s* one *d*. *Educ:* Hull Univ. (BSc Hons Econs). Mgt trainee, 1969, sen. mgt posts, 1970–79, British Leyland; Sales Dir, Austin-Morris, 1980–84; Export Dir, Austin-Rover, 1984–86; Sales Dir, Rover Gp, 1986–88; Chief Executive: Applied Chemicals, 1988–90; Marshall Gp, 1990–94; Inchcape Motors International, 1994–99; Chief Exec., 1999–2005, Chm., 2006–09, Inchcape plc. Non-executive Director: Wates Gp, 2002–06, 2011–13; Bunzl plc, 2006–15; Chairman: Automotive Skills Ltd, 2003–06; Rank plc, 2007–11; Marshall Motor Hldgs, 2015–18. Vice Pres., Motor Agents Assoc., 1992–95. Pres., Ben, 2016–. FIMI 1984 (Chm., 1991–95); MInstD 1990. *Recreations:* golf, reading, travel. *Clubs:* Royal Automobile; Redditch Golf.

**JOHNSON, Prof. Peter William Montague,** CBE 2016; MD; FRCP; FMedSci; Professor of Medical Oncology, University of Southampton, since 1998; *b* Walton-on-Thames, 4 May 1961; *s* of Alan Montague and Bobbie Johnson; *m* 1987, Maria Susanna Alkema; one *s* one *d*. *Educ:* Sherborne Sch., Dorset; Gonville and Caius Coll., Cambridge (BA 1982; MB BChir 1985; MA 1986; MD 1994); St Thomas's Med. Sch., London. FRCP 1998. ICRF Clin. Res. Fellow, St Bartholomew's Hosp., London, 1989–94; Sen. Lectr, Univ. of Leeds, 1994–98; Chief Clinician, CRUK, 2008–18. FMedSci 2014. *Publications:* contrib. papers on cancer res., malignant lymphoma, cancer immunol. *Recreations:* theatre, opera, wine, sleeping through the news. *Address:* Centre for Cancer Immunology, Southampton General Hospital, Tremona Road, Southampton SO16 6YD. *T:* (023) 8120 6186. *E:* johnsonp@soton.ac.uk.

**JOHNSON, Rachel Sabiha;** journalist and novelist; broadcaster and presenter; *b* London, 3 Sept. 1965; *d* of Stanley Patrick Johnson, *qv* and Charlotte Maria Johnson (*née* Fawcett); *m* 1992, Ivo Nicholas Payan Dawnay; two *s* one *d*. *Educ:* Winsford First Sch., Exmoor; Primrose Hill Primary Sch., Camden; European Sch., Brussels; Ashdown Hse, Sussex; Bryanston Sch., Dorset (Schol.); St Paul's Girls' Sch., London; Davidson Coll., N Carolina (Dean Rusk Schol., 1984); New Coll., Oxford (MA Lit.Hum. 1988). Financial Times: grad. trainee, 1989–90; reporter, 1990–94; on secondment to FCO, 1992–93; sen. broadcast journalist, BBC Radio Four, 1994–96; columnist: Sunday Telegraph, 1996–98 FT, 1998–2000; Daily Telegraph and Evening Standard, 2000–06; contributing ed., Spectator, 2006–07; columnist, Sunday Times, 2007–09; Ed., 2009–12, Ed.-in-Chief, 2012, The Lady mag. Panellist, The Pledge, Sky News, 2016–. Contested (Change UK) SW, EP, 2019. *Publications:* (ed) The Oxford Myth, 1988; The Mummy Diaries, 2005; Notting Hell, 2006; Shire Hell, 2008; The Diary of a Lady: my first year as Editor, 2010; The Diary of a Lady: my first year and a half, 2011; Winter Games, 2012; Notting Hell, Actually, 2013; Fresh Hell, 2015. *Recreations:* tennis, Exmoor, ski-ing. *Address:* 1 Rosmead Road, W11 2JG. *E:* racheljohnson11@btinternet.com. *Clubs:* Electric House; Campden Hill Lawn Tennis.
*See also* C. J. P. Dawnay, C. M. Dawnay, Rt Hon. A. B. de P. Johnson, Rt Hon. J. E. Johnson, L. F. Johnson.

**JOHNSON, Richard,** OBE 2019; National Hunt jockey; *b* 21 July 1977; *m* 2007, Fiona, *d* of Noel Chance; two *s* one *d*. Equal 10th in list of winning jockeys while still an apprentice, 1995–96; 2nd, 1996–97, 1997–98, 1998–99, 1999–2000, 2000–01, 2001–02, 2002–03, 2005–06, 2006–07, 2007–08, 2008–09, 2009–10, 2010–11, 2011–12, 2013–14, 2014–15 and 2015–16 seasons; 3rd, 2012–13 season; 1st, 2016–17 season; winner: Cheltenham Gold Cup, on Looks Like Trouble, 2000, on Native River, 2018; Queen Mother Champion Chase on Flagship Uberalles, 2002; Champion Hurdle on Rooster Booster, 2003; Hennessy Gold Cup on Native River, 2016. Rode 2,000th winner, Newbury, 2009. *Publications:* (with Alan Lee) Out of the Shadows, 2002. *Address:* c/o Nicholas Whittle, Bucklow Hill, Knutsford, Cheshire WA16 6PP.

**JOHNSON, Richard John M.;** *see* McGregor-Johnson.

**JOHNSON, Sir Robert (Lionel),** Kt 1989; a Justice of the High Court, Family Division, 1989–2004; *b* 9 Feb. 1933; *er s* of late Edward Harold Johnson, MSc, FRIC, and of Ellen Lydiate Johnson, Cranleigh; *m* 1957, Linda Mary, *er d* of late Charles William Bennie and Ena Ethel Bennie, Egglescliffe; one *d* (and one *s* one *d* decd). *Educ:* Watford Grammar Sch. (1940–51); London Sch. of Econs and Pol Science. 5th Royal Inniskilling Dragoon Guards, 1955–57, Captain; ADC to GOC-in-C Northern Comd, 1956–57; Inns of Court Regt, 1957–64. Called to the Bar, Gray's Inn, 1957, Bencher, 1986; QC 1978; a Recorder, 1977–89. Jun. Counsel to Treasury in Probate Matters, 1975–78; Legal Assessor, GNC, 1977–82. Chairman: Bar Fees and Legal Aid Cttee, 1984–86 (Vice-Chm., 1982–84); Family Law Bar Assoc., 1984–86; Family Law Cttee, Justice, 1990–93; Mem., Bar Council, 1981–88; Vice Chm., 1987, Chm., 1988, Gen. Council of Bar. Member: Supreme Court Procedure Cttee, 1982–87; Law Soc. Legal Aid Cttee, 1981–87; No 1 Legal Aid Area Cttee, 1980–87; Co-Chm., Civil and Family Cttee, Judicial Studies Bd, 1989–94. Pres., English Chapter, Internat. Acad. of Matrimonial Lawyers, 1986–89. Sec., Internat. Cystic Fibrosis Assoc., 1984–90; Trustee: Cystic Fibrosis Res. Trust, 1964–2009; Robert Luff Charitable Foundn, 1977–2017. *Publications:* (with James Comyn) Wills & Intestacies, 1970; Contract, 1975; (with Malcolm Stitcher) Atkin's Trade, Labour and Employment, 1975. *Address:* Forest Gate, Pluckley, Kent TN27 0RU.

**JOHNSON, Robin Peter; His Honour Judge Johnson;** a Circuit Judge, since 2009; *b* London, 28 Jun 1954; *s* of Peter and Kathleen Joan Johnson. *Educ:* Exeter Univ. (BA). Called to the Bar, Gray's Inn, 1979; Recorder, 2003–09. *Address:* Isleworth Crown Court, 36 Ridgeway Road, Isleworth, Surrey TW7 5LP.

**JOHNSON, Prof. Roger Paul,** FREng; Professor of Civil Engineering, University of Warwick, 1971–98, now Emeritus; *b* 12 May 1931; *s* of Norman Eric Ernest Johnson and Eleanor Florence (*née* Paul); *m* 1958, Diana June (*née* Perkins); three *s*. *Educ:* Cranleigh Sch., Surrey; Jesus Coll., Cambridge (BA 1953; MA 1957). FIStructE 1972; FICE 1979; FREng (FEng 1986). Holloway Bros (London), Civil Engineering Contractor, 1953–55; Ove Arup and Partners, Consulting Engineers, 1956–59; Lectr in Engineering, Cambridge Univ., 1959–71. Visiting Professor: Univ. of Sydney, 1982–83; Univ. of Adelaide, 1995, 1999. Gold Medal, IStructE, 2006. *Publications:* Structural Concrete, 1967; Composite Structures of Steel and Concrete, vol. 1, 1975, 4th edn 2018, vol. 2 (with R. J. Buckby), 1979, 2nd edn 1986; (with D. Anderson) Designers' Handbook to Eurocode 4, 1994; Designers' Guide to Eurocode 4, Pt 1-1 (with D. Anderson), 2004, 2nd edn 2012, Pt 2 (with C. R. Hendy), 2006; contribs to learned jls. *Recreations:* music, gardening, mountain walking. *Address:* School of Engineering, University of Warwick, Coventry CV4 7AL. *T:* (024) 7652 3129.

**JOHNSON, Samantha T.;** *see* Taylor-Johnson.

**JOHNSON, Stanley Patrick;** author and environmentalist; *b* 18 Aug. 1940; *s* of Wilfred Johnson and Irène (*née* Williams); *m* 1st, 1963, Charlotte Offlow Fawcett (marr. diss.): three *s* one *d*; 2nd, 1981, Mrs Jennifer Kidd; one *s* one *d*. *Educ:* Sherborne Sch.; Exeter Coll., Oxford (Trevelyan Schol., Sen. Classics Schol.; Newdigate Prize for Poetry, 1962; MA 1963; Dip. Agric. Econs 1965). Harkness Fellow, USA, 1963–64; World Bank, Washington, 1966–68; Project Dir, UNA-USA Nat. Policy Panel on World Population, 1968–69; Mem. Conservative Research Dept, 1969–70; Staff of Internat. Planned Parenthood Fedn, London, 1971–73; Consultant to UN Fund for Population Activities, 1971–73; Mem. Countryside Commn, 1971–73; Head of Prevention of Pollution and Nuisances Div., EEC, 1973–77; Adviser to Head of Environment and Consumer Protection Service, EEC, 1977–79; MEP (C) Wight and Hants E, 1979–84; Advr to Dir Gen. for Envmt, Civil Protection and Nuclear Safety, EEC, 1984–90; Dir for Energy Policy, EEC, 1990; Special Advr, Coopers & Lybrand, Deloitte, 1991; Dir, Envmtl Resources Mgt, 1992–94. Contested (C) Teignbridge, 2005. Hon. Ambassador, UNEP

Convention on Migratory Species, 2005–. Chm., Gorilla Orgn, 2010–14. Richard Martin Award, RSPCA, 1982; Greenpeace Award, 1984; Silver Medal, WWF, 2013; RSPB Medal, 2015; Leaders for a Living Planet Award, WWF, 2015. *Publications:* Life Without Birth, 1970; The Green Revolution, 1972; The Politics of the Environment, 1973; (ed) The Population Problem, 1973; The Pollution Control Policy of the EEC, 1979, 3rd edn 1989; Antarctica—the last great wilderness, 1985; (jtly) The Environmental Policy of the EEC, 1989, 2nd edn 1995; The Earth Summit: the United Nations Conference on Environment and Development, 1993; World Population—turning the tide, 1994; The Politics of Population, 1995; Stanley I Presume, 2009; (jtly) Survival: saving endangered migratory species, 2010; Where the Wild Things Were: travels of a conservationist, 2012; UNEP: the first forty years, 2013; Stanley I Resume, 2014; *novels:* Gold Drain, 1967; Panther Jones for President, 1968; God Bless America, 1974; The Doomsday Deposit, 1980; The Marburg Virus, 1982; Tunnel, 1984; The Commissioner, 1987; Dragon River, 1989; Icecap, 1999; Kompromat, 2017. *Recreations:* writing, travel. *Clubs:* Beefsteak, Garrick.

See also Rt Hon. A. B. de P. Johnson, Rt Hon. J. E. Johnson, L. F. Johnson, R. S. Johnson.

**JOHNSON, Terry;** playwright and director; *b* 20 Dec. 1955; *s* of Harry Douglas Johnson and Winifred Mary Johnson (*née* Wood); one *d* by Marion Bailey. *Educ:* Birmingham Univ. (BA 2nd cl. Drama and Th. Arts). Actor, 1971–75; *playwright:* Amabel, Bush Th., 1972; Insignificance, Royal Court (Most Promising Playwright, Evening Standard Award), 1982 (screenplay, 1985); Unsuitable for Adults, Bush, Cries from the Mammal House, Royal Ct, 1984; (jtly) Tuesday's Child, Stratford Th. Royal, 1986; Imagine Drowning, Hampstead (John Whiting Award), 1991; Hysteria, Royal Ct, 1993 (Meyer–Whitworth Award, 1993; Best Comedy, Olivier Award, and Best Play, Writers' Guild, 1994); (also dir.) Dead Funny, Savoy, 1994 (Best Play, Writers' Guild, 1994; Best New Play, Critics' Circle, and Playwright of the Year, Lloyds Pvte Banking, 1995), Vaudeville, 2016; Prism, Hampstead, 2017; adaptation (also dir.), The London Cuckolds, 1997, (also dir.) Cleo, Camping, Emmanuelle and Dick, 1998 (Best Comedy, Olivier Award, 1999), RNT; adaptation (also dir.), The Graduate, Gielgud, 2000; Hitchcock Blonde, Royal Court, 2003; (also dir.) Hysteria, Th. Royal, Bath, 2012, Hampstead Th., 2013; (also dir.) Mrs Henderson Presents, Th. Royal, Bath, 2015, transf., Noël Coward Th., 2016; (also dir.) Uncle Vanya, Hampstead Th., 2018; plays also performed in USA, Europe, Australia, Canada and NZ; other *plays directed* include: The Memory of Water, Vaudeville, 1996; The Libertine, Chicago, 1996, Th. Royal Haymarket, 2016; Elton John's Glasses, Queen's, 1997; Sparkleshark, RNT, 1999; Entertaining Mr Sloane, Arts, 2001; One Flew Over the Cuckoo's Nest, Gielgud, 2004; Dumb Show, Royal Court, 2004; Piano/Forte, 2006; Whipping It Up, 2006; La Cage aux Folles, Menier Chocolate Factory, transf. Playhouse, 2008, NY, 2010 (Best Dir, Tony Awards, 2010); The Prisoner of Second Avenue, Vaudeville, 2010; End of the Rainbow, Trafalgar Studios, 2010; La Cage aux Folles, US tour, 2012; Race, Hampstead Th., 2013; The Duck House, Vaudeville, 2013; Oh What a Lovely War, Th. Royal, Stratford E, 2014; Fings Ain't Wot They Used T'Be, Th. Royal, Stratford E, 2014; Seminar, Hampstead Th., 2014; (also actor) Ken, Bunker Th., 2018; *television:* (dir.) Way Upstream, 1988; wrote and directed: Blood and Water, 1995; Cor Blimey!, 2000; Not Only But Always, 2004; The Man Who Lost His Head, 2007; screenplay, The Bite, 1994. *Publications:* Insignificance, 1982; Cries from the Mammal House, 1984; Unsuitable for Adults, 1985; Tuesday's Child, 1987; Imagine Drowning, 1991; Hysteria, 1993; Dead Funny, 1994; Johnson: Plays One, 1993; The London Cuckolds, 1997; Johnson: Plays Two, 1998; Cleo, Camping, Emmanuelle and Dick, 1998; The Graduate, 2000; Hitchcock Blonde, 2003; Piano/Forte, 2006.

**JOHNSON, Timothy Brett;** Partner, More Partnership, since 2019; *b* Wallingford, Oxon, 21 Dec. 1965; *s* of Raymond Sidney Johnson and Patricia Mary Johnson; *m* 1995, Sarah Jones; two *s* one *d*. *Educ:* Wallingford Sch.; Bristol Poly. (BA Hons Social Scis 1988). Publicity Officer, Castle Priory Coll., Spastics Soc., 1984–85; Appeals Officer: Mencap, 1989–91; BTCV, 1991–92; Corporate Devel Officer, 1994–96, Hd of Fundraising, 1996–98, CSV; Hd of Fundraising, UCL, 1998–2002; Great Ormond Street Hospital Children's Charity: Dep. Dir (Hd, Major Donor Develt), 2002–06; Dir, Major Gift Fundraising, 2006–08; Exec. Dir, 2008–12; Chief Exec., 2012–19. Trustee: Jeans for Genes Campaign, 2009–11; Costa Foundn, 2013–. *Recreations:* family, cooking, wine, walking, travel. *E:* tjohnson@morepartnership.com.

**JOHNSON, Wendy Rosalind;** *see* James, W. R.

**JOHNSON, Zoe Elisabeth;** QC 2012; a Recorder, since 2010; *b* Poole, 27 March 1967; *d* of William Clifford Johnson and Jean Violetta Johnson; *m* 2014, Peter Eric Kyte, *qv*. *Educ:* Corfe Hills, Corfe Mullen; St Hilda's Coll., Oxford (BA Hons Eng. Lit.); City Univ. (DipLaw). Called to the Bar, Inner Temple, 1990; Jun. Treasury Counsel, 2004–11, Sen. Treasury Counsel, 2011–15, Central Criminal Court. *Recreations:* travel to South East Asia, theatre, gardens, reading novels and comparative history. *Address:* QEB Hollis Whiteman Chambers, 1–2 Laurence Pountney Hill, EC4R 0EU. *T:* (020) 7933 8855, *Fax:* (020) 7929 3732. *E:* zoe.johnson@qebhw.co.uk.

**JOHNSON-FERGUSON, Lt-Col Sir Mark (Edward),** 5th Bt *cr* 1906, of Springkell, Dumfries, of Kenyon, Newchurch-in-Culceth, Lancaster, and of Wiston, Lanark; Overseas Manager, Infrastructure, Joint Forces Command, Northwood HQ, since 2018; *b* Surrey, 14 Aug. 1965; *e s* of Sir Ian Edward Johnson-Ferguson, 4th Bt and of Rosemary Teresa (*née* Whitehead); *S* father, 2015; *m* 1995, Dr Julia Catherine Getley; three *d*. *Educ:* Ampleforth Coll.; Trinity Coll., Cambridge (MA). CEng; MICE, MInstRE. Royal Engrs, 1987–; served in NI, Germany, Cyprus, Kosovo, Bosnia and Afghanistan; comdr 65 Field Support Sqn, 1999–2001; SO 1, Estate Requirements, HQ British Forces Cyprus, 2015–18. *Recreations:* offshore and dinghy sailing, ski-ing, cycling. *Heir: b* Paul Duncan Johnson-Ferguson [*b* 20 Aug. 1966; *m* 1990, Maria Barbara Antonette Menke; three *d* (incl. twins)]. *Address:* Joint Forces Command, Northwood HQ, Sandy Lane, Northwood HA6 3HP. *Club:* Royal Engineer Yacht (Cdre).

**JOHNSON-LAIRD, Prof. Philip Nicholas,** FRS 1991; FBA 1986; Stuart Professor of Psychology, Princeton University, 1994–2012, now Emeritus (Professor of Psychology, 1989–2012); Visiting Scholar, New York University, since 2012; *b* 12 Oct. 1936; *s* of Eric Johnson-Laird and Dorothy (*née* Blackett); *m* 1959, Maureen Mary Sullivan; one *s* one *d*. *Educ:* Culford Sch.; University Coll. London (Rosa Morison Medal, 1964; James Sully Schol., 1964–66; BA (Hons) 1964; PhD 1967; Fellow, 1994). MBPsS 1962. 10 years of misc. jobs, as surveyor, musician, hosp. porter (alternative to Nat. Service), librarian, before going to university. Asst Lectr, then Lectr, in Psychol., UCL, 1966–73; Reader, 1973, Prof., 1978, in Exptl Psychol., Univ. of Sussex; Asst Dir, MRC Applied Psychology Unit, Cambridge, 1983–89; Fellow, Darwin Coll., Cambridge, 1984–89. Vis. Mem., Princeton Inst. for Advanced Study, 1971–72; Vis. Fellow, Stanford Univ., 1980; Visiting Professor: Stanford Univ., 1985; Princeton Univ., 1986. Member: Psychol. Cttee, SSRC, 1975–79; Linguistics Panel, SSRC, 1980–82; Adv. Council, Internat. Assoc. for Study of Attention and Performance, 1984. Member: Linguistics Assoc., 1967; Exptl Psychol. Soc., 1968; Cognitive Sci. Soc., 1980; Assoc. for Computational Linguistics, 1981; Amer. Philosophical Soc. 2006; Nat. Acad. of Scis, 2007. Fellow, Assoc. of Psychol Sci., 2007. Hon. DPhil: Göteborg, 1983; Padua, 1997; Madrid, 2000; Dublin, 2000; Ghent, 2002; Palermo, 2005; Hon. DSc Sussex, 2007; Laurea *hc* Univ. Ca' Foscari, Venice, 2008. Spearman Medal, 1974,

President's Award, 1985, BPsS; International Prize, Fondation Fyssen, 2002; William James Fellow Award, Assoc. of Psychol Sci., 2011. *Publications:* (ed jtly) Thinking and Reasoning, 1968; (with P. C. Wason) Psychology and Reasoning, 1972; (with G. A. Miller) Language and Perception, 1976; (ed jtly) Thinking, 1977; Mental Models, 1983; The Computer and the Mind, 1988; (with Ruth Byrne) Deduction, 1991; Human and Machine Thinking, 1993; How We Reason, 2006; contribs to psychol, linguistic and cognitive sci. jls, reviews in lit. jls. *Recreations:* talking, arguing, laughing, composing music.

**JOHNSON SIRLEAF, Ellen Eugenia;** President of Liberia, 2006–18; *b* Monrovia, Liberia, 29 Oct. 1938; *née* Johnson; *m* James Sirleaf (marr. diss.); four *s*. *Educ:* Coll. of W Africa, Monrovia; Madison Business Coll., Wisconsin (accounting degree); Univ. of Colorado; Kennedy Sch. of Govt, Harvard Univ. (MPA 1971). Joined Treasury Dept, Liberia, 1965; Asst Minister of Finance, 1972–73; Minister of Finance, 1979–80; Pres., Liberian Bank for Develt and Investment, 1980; forced to flee Liberia and travelled to Kenya, 1980; Vice-Pres., Africa Regl Office, Citicorp, Nairobi, 1980–85; Sen. Loan Officer, World Bank; Vice Pres., Equator Bank; Asst Adminr and Dir, Regl Bureau for Africa, UNDP, 1992–97; returned to Liberia, 1997; contested Presidential election, 1997; self-imposed exile in Côte d'Ivoire, 1997–2003; estabd Kormah Develt and Investment Corp., Abidjan; Chair, Governance Reform Commn, Nat. Transitional Govt of Liberia, 2003–05. Founding Mem., Internat. Inst. for Women in Political Leadership. Mem. Cttee to investigate Rwanda genocide, Orgn for African Unity, 1999. Former Member, Advisory Board: Internat. Crisis Gp; Women Waging Peace; Synergos Inst.; Open Soc. Inst. for W Africa (Chair); Chair, African Peer Rev. Mechanism, African Union Summit, 2013. Freedom Award, Internat. Republican Inst., 2006; Gold Medal, Pres. of Italian Republic, 2006; Freedom Award, Nat. Civil Rights Mus., 2007; Presidential Medal of Freedom, USA, 2007; Internat. Women's Leadership Award, 2008; CERES Medal, FAO, 2008; African Gender Award, PanAfrican Center for Gender, Peace and Develt, 2011; (jtly) Nobel Prize for Peace, 2011; Martin Luther King Peace Medal and Alpha Award of Honor, 2012; Indira Gandhi Prize for Peace, Disarmament and Develt, 2012; Grand Croix, Légion d'Honneur (France), 2012; Lifetime Humanitarian Award for Healthcare, Nat. Med. Assoc. of USA, 2013; Mo Ibrahim Prize for African Leadership, 2018. *Publications:* This Child Will be Great (memoir), 2008.

**JOHNSTON;** *see* Campbell-Johnston.

**JOHNSTON;** *see* Lawson Johnston.

**JOHNSTON, Alexander Dewar Kerr, (Alistair),** CMG 2011; UK Vice Chairman, KPMG, 2004–10 (Partner, 1986–2010, General Partner, UK, 1996); *b* Giffnock, Scotland, 28 June 1952; *s* of Kerr Johnston and Elizabeth Alexandra Johnston (*née* Dewar); *m* Christina Maria Nijman. *Educ:* Hutchesons' Sch., Glasgow; Trinity Sch. of John Whitgift; London Sch. of Econs and Pol Sci. (BSc Hons Econs 1973). Chartered Accountant 1976; FCA 1976; CPA Calif 1979 (non-practising). Peat Marwick Mitchell, later KPMG: joined, 1973; San Francisco, 1977–79; Internat. Office, 1987–89; Partner in Charge, UK Mktg, 1990–93; Hd, UK Insce Practice, 1994–97; Internat. Man. Partner, Global Mkts, 1998–2003; Global Vice Chm., 2007–10. Mem. Bd, FCO, 2005–10. Non-exec. Dir, Prudential plc, 2012–16. Trustee: Design Mus., 2012–17; Create, 2014–17; Kate's Home Nursing, 2014–15; Royal Acad. Develt Trust (formerly Royal Acad. Trust), 2014–19. Vis. Prof., Cass Business Sch., 2005–19 (Mem., Strategy and Develt Bd, 2009–14). Create Ambassador, 2018–. *Recreations:* design, restoration, art, music, tennis. *T:* 07802 610102. *E:* adkjohnston@gmail.com. *Club:* Athenæum.

**JOHNSTON, (Alexander) Graham;** Sheriff of Strathkelvin at Glasgow, 1985–2005; part-time Sheriff, 2005–13; *b* 16 July 1944; *s* of Hon. Lord Kincraig; *m* 1st, 1972, Susan (marr. diss. 1982); two *s*; 2nd, 1982, Angela; two step *d*. *Educ:* Edinburgh Acad.; Strathallan Sch.; Univ. of Edinburgh (LLB); University Coll., Oxford (BA). Admitted as solicitor and Writer to the Signet, 1971; Partner, Hagart and Burn-Murdoch, Solicitors, Edinburgh, 1972–82. Sheriff of Grampian, Highland and Isles, 1982–85. Editor, Scottish Civil Law Reports, 1987–92. *Recreations:* photography, computing and IT, bridge, puzzles. *Address:* 1 The Courtyard, Elie House, Elie, Fife KY9 1ER. *E:* ag_johnston@btinternet.com. *Clubs:* Oxford and Cambridge Golfing Society; Vincent's (Oxford); Elie Golf House.

**JOHNSTON, Alistair;** *see* Johnston, A. D. K.

**JOHNSTON, Angela Maureen Howard-;** *see* Huth, A. M.

**JOHNSTON, Callum William;** Secretary and Chief Executive, Central Arbitration Committee, 1999–2002; *b* 15 Sept. 1946; *s* of James Johnston, OBE, and Mary Johnston; *m* 1974, Sarah Motta; one *s* one *d*. *Educ:* Westcliff High Sch.; King Edward VII Sch., Lytham; Durham Univ. (BA Econs and Law 1968); Indiana Univ. (MBA 1970). Financial journalist and broadcaster, 1970–73; DTI, 1973–80 (Private Sec., 1975–77); Cabinet Office, 1980–82; Department of Trade and Industry, 1982–99: British Steel privatisation, 1986–89; EU Co. Law Policy, 1989–90; on secondment to Leyland DAF plc, 1990–92; Dir, UK and EU Technol. and IT Security Policy, 1992–95; Pay Dir, 1995–98; Dir, Small Business Policy, 1998–99. *Recreations:* playing piano and listening to music, walking, cycling, volunteering. *Address:* 10 Wontner Road, SW17 7QT.

**JOHNSTON, Carey Ann;** QC 2003. *Educ:* Univ. of Warwick (LLB, LLM). Called to the Bar, Middle Temple, 1977, Bencher, 2009. Specializes in criminal law. *Address:* Red Lion Chambers, 18 Red Lion Court, EC4A 3EB. *T:* (020) 7520 6000.

**JOHNSTON, Catherine Elizabeth,** CB 2000; Parliamentary Counsel, 1994–2015; *b* 4 Jan. 1953; *d* of Sir Alexander Johnston, GCB, KBE and Betty Joan Johnston (*née* Harris), CBE; *m* 1989, Brendan Patrick Keith; one *s* one *d*. *Educ:* St Paul's Girls' Sch.; St Hugh's Coll., Oxford (Scholar 1970; BA 1974). Admitted as solicitor, 1978; joined Parliamentary Counsel Office, 1980; with Law Commn 1983–85 and 1990–92; on secondment to Office of Parly Counsel, Canberra, 1987–88.

**JOHNSTON, Christopher George;** QC 2011; *b* Ballymena, 1967; *s* of Harry and Isobel Johnston; *m* 1996, Joanna Warwick; two *d*. *Educ:* Ballymena Acad.; Trinity Hall, Cambridge (BA Law 1989). Called to the Bar, Gray's Inn, 1990; in practice as a barrister, specialising in clinical negligence, medical ethics and product liability. Ed., Medical Law Reports. *Publications:* (ed) Medical Treatment Decisions and the Law, 2001, 3rd edn 2016. *Recreations:* watching Rugby, playing football, reading Tintin. *Address:* Serjeants' Inn Chambers, 85 Fleet Street, EC4Y 1AE. *T:* (020) 7427 5000. *E:* cjohnstonqc@serjeantsinn.com.

**JOHNSTON, Claire Lizbeth,** CB 2014; Director General, Government Legal Department (formerly Treasury Solicitor's Department), 2014–18; *b* Edinburgh, 19 Feb. 1960; *d* of Ronald Johnston and Margaret Johnston (*née* Rae); *m* 1991, Chris Miele; one *d*. *Educ:* Clare Coll., Cambridge (BA Hons English 1981); Columbia Univ., NY (MA English and Comparative Lit. 1982); City of London Poly. (CPE and Law Soc. Finals). Admitted as solicitor: England and Wales, 1987; Scotland, 1993; Solicitor, T. V. Edwards & Co., 1985–92; Lawyer: Law Commn, 1992–96; Official Solicitor's Office, 1997–2001; Sen.

Civil Service Lawyer, Lord Chancellor's Dept, 2001–06; Gp Hd, HMRC, 2006–07; Legal Dir, DFE, 2007–14. Trainee teacher of English, Now Teach, 2018–19. *Recreations:* dance, hill walking.

**JOHNSTON, Prof. Clare Frances**; Professor and Course Director of Textiles, 2000–15, now Emeritus Professor, and Senior Research Fellow, 2015–19, Royal College of Art (Business Fellow of Innovation, 2004–12); *b* Whitby, Yorks, 7 Aug. 1951; *d* of Rev. Alan and Joan Johnston; partner, Paul Notley. *Educ:* Birmingham Coll. of Art (DipAD Textile Design). Design asst to Pat Albeck, 1973–74; design partnership with Veronica Marsh, 1974–78; own design co. working with internat. fashion cos, 1978–80; Sen. Designer, Walker & Rice Fabrics, 1980–82; Design Consultant, Nigel French Enterprises, 1982–86; Principal Lectr, Brighton Coll. of Art, 1986–90; colour and textiles designer, Marks & Spencer, 1990–98; Hd of Design, Liberty of London, 1998–2003. Vis. Prof., Swedish Sch. of Textiles, Univ. of Borås, 2015–17. Hon. Dr Borås, 2017. *Recreations:* Ecole de Dance Francoise Chantraine, pilates, reading, walking. *W:* www.clarejohnston.com.

**JOHNSTON, Prof. David,** MD, ChM; FRCS, FRCSE, FRCSGlas; Professor of Surgery and Head of Department, University of Leeds at Leeds General Infirmary, 1977–98, now Professor Emeritus; *b* Glasgow, 4 Sept. 1936; *s* of Robert E. and Jean Johnston; *m* (marr. diss.); three *s* one *d*; *m* 1987, Dr Maureen Teresa Reynolds; two *s*. *Educ:* Hamilton Acad.; Glasgow Univ. (MB, ChB Hons; MD Hons, ChM). FRCSE 1963; FRCSGlas 1964; FRCS 1979. House Surgeon, Western Infirmary, Glasgow, 1961–62; Res. Asst and Registrar, Univ. Dept of Surg., Leeds Gen. Infirm., 1962–64; Lectr in Surg., Univ. of Sheffield, 1965–68; Sen. Lectr, then Reader, and Consultant, Univ. Dept of Surg., Leeds Gen. Infirm., 1968–75; Prof. of Surg. and Head of Dept, Univ. of Bristol (Bristol Royal Infirm.), 1975–77. *Publications:* papers on physiology and surgery of the stomach, colon and rectum, and on obesity. *Recreations:* reading, walking, tennis, fishing. *Address:* 3 The Coppice, Middleton, Ilkley, W Yorks LS29 0EZ. *T:* (01943) 816349, 07799 791545.

**JOHNSTON, David Carr**; education consultant, since 2002; Chief Education Officer, Manchester City Council, 1998–2002; *b* 18 March 1944; *s* of William and Sarah Johnston; *m* 1969, Jennifer Anne Hopkinson; two *d*. *Educ:* Didsbury Coll. of Educn (Teacher's Cert. 1965); Sheffield Univ. (DipASE 1971); Sheffield Poly. (Dip Educn Mgt 1975); Leicester Univ. (MEd 1982). Asst Teacher, Trafford, Lancs, 1965–67, Sheffield primary schs, 1967–69; Dep. Hd, Park Hill Jun. Sch., Sheffield, 1969–72; Headteacher: Shirebrook Middle Sch., Sheffield, 1972–74; Ballifield Nursery, First and Middle Sch., Sheffield, 1974–79; School Advr, Derbys CC, 1979–84; Sen. Sch. Inspector, 1984–88, Dep. Chief Educn Officer, 1988–92, Manchester City Council; Dir of Educn and Leisure, Salford City Council, 1992–98. *Publications:* Managing Primary Schools, 1985; Managing Primary Schools in the 1990s, 1990. *Recreations:* music appreciation, fell walking, supporting Manchester City FC. *Address:* Totley Hall Croft, Totley, Sheffield S17 4BE.

**JOHNSTON, Dr David Eric Lothian**; QC (Scot.) 2005; advocate, since 1992; *b* 10 March 1961; *e s* of late Thomas Lothian Johnston and of Joan (*née* Fahmy). *Educ:* Daniel Stewart's and Melville Coll., Edinburgh; St John's Coll., Cambridge (BA 1982; MA 1986; PhD 1986; LLD 2001). Research Fellow, 1985–89, Fellow, 1993–99, Christ's Coll., Cambridge; Regius Prof. of Civil Law, Univ. of Cambridge, 1993–99. Visiting Fellow: Univ. of Freiburg, 1985–86; Univ. of Michigan Law Sch., 1987; Univ. of Calif, Berkeley, Law Sch., 1996, 1998, 2019; Univ. Cattolica del Sacro Cuore, Milan, 2020; Visiting Professor: Paris I, 1999; Paris V, 2000–3; Univ. of Osaka, 2000; Hon. Prof., Edinburgh Univ. Law Sch., 2000–. Comr (pt-time), Scottish Law Commn, 2015–20. FRSE 2016. *Publications:* On a Singular Book of Cervidius Scaevola, 1987; The Roman Law of Trusts, 1988 (trans. Chinese 2017); Roman Law in Context, 1999; Prescription and Limitation, 1999, 2nd edn 2012; (ed with R. Zimmermann) Unjustified Enrichment: key issues, 2002; (contrib.) Gloag and Henderson, The Law of Scotland, 11th edn 2001; (ed with A. Burrows and R. Zimmermann) Judge and Jurist: essays in memory of Lord Rodger of Earlsferry, 2013; (ed) The Cambridge Companion to Roman Law, 2015; articles in learned jls mainly on Roman law and legal history. *Recreations:* music, travel, wine and food. *Address:* Advocates' Library, Parliament House, Edinburgh EH1 1RF. *T:* (0131) 226 5071.

**JOHNSTON, David Lawrence**, OBE 1997; CEng, FIET; RCNC; Director General, National Inspection Council for Electrical Installation Contracting, 1989–2001; Chairman, National Quality Assurance Ltd, 1993–2001 (Director, 1989–93); *b* 12 April 1936; *s* of late Herbert David Johnston and Hilda Eleanor Johnston (*née* Wood); *m* 1959, Beatrice Ann Witten; three *d*. *Educ:* Lancastrian Sch., Chichester; King's Coll., Durham (BSc). FIET (FIEE 1980). Electrical Engineering Apprentice, HM Dockyard, Portsmouth, 1951–56; Short Service Commn (Lieut), RN, 1959–62; joined Ministry of Defence, 1962; Overseeing, Wallsend, 1962–63; switchgear design, Bath, 1963–66; Production and Project Mgt, Devonport Dockyard, 1966–73; Dockyard Policy, Bath, 1973–76; Warship System Design, Bath, 1976–79; Production and Planning, Portsmouth Dockyard, 1979–81; Planning and Production, Devonport Dockyard, 1981–84; Asst Under-Sec. of State, and Man. Dir, HM Dockyard, Devonport, 1984–87; Chm., Devonport Dockyard Ltd, Mgt Buy-out Co., 1985–87; Dep. Chm., Devonport Mgt Ltd, 1987–88; mgt consultant, 1988–89. Dep. Chm., NQA, USA Inc., 1998–2001 (Dir, 1993–98); Dir, UK Accreditation Service, 2000–06. Dir, Nat. Supervisory Council, Intruder Alarms Ltd, subseq. Nat. Approval Council, Security Systems Ltd, 1989–96. Chairman: BASEEFA Adv. Council, subseq. Electrical Equipment Certification Service Product Adv. Cttee, HSE, 1990–2002; Adv. Bd, BASEEFA 2001 Ltd, 2003–; Member: HSE Open Govt Complaints Panel, 1995–2002; IEE Wiring Regulations Policy Cttee, 2001–04. *Recreations:* home, hearth and garden, novice golf, watercolour painting. *Address:* Weirside Mill, 8 Greenland Mills, Bradford-on-Avon, Wilts BA15 1BL. *T:* (01225) 542268. *E:* davidandbeatrice08@icloud.com.

**JOHNSTON, Rt Hon. David Lloyd**, CC 1997 (OC 1988); CMM 2010; Governor General of Canada, 2010–17; Executive Adviser, Deloitte, Kitchener, Ont, since 2017; *b* 28 June 1941; *s* of Lloyd Johnston and Dorothy Stonehouse Johnston; *m* 1963, Sharon Downey; five *d*. *Educ:* Harvard Univ., Cambridge, Mass; Cambridge Univ.; Queen's Univ. at Kingston, Ont. Asst Prof., Faculty of Law, Queen's Univ., Kingston, 1966–68; Faculty of Law, Univ. of Toronto: Asst Prof., 1968–69; Associate Prof., 1969–72; Prof., 1972–74; Dean and Prof., Faculty of Law, Univ. of Western Ont, 1974–79; Prof. of Law, 1979–99, Principal and Vice-Chancellor, 1979–94, McGill Univ.; Pres. and Vice-Chancellor, Univ. of Waterloo, 1999–2010. Chairman: Nat. Round Table on Envmt and the Economy, 1988–92; Information Highway Adv. Council, 1994–97; Canadian Inst. for Advanced Res., 1994–99; NeuroScience Network, 1994–98. LLD *hc* Law Soc. of Upper Canada, 1980. *Publications:* Computers and the Law (ed), 1968; Canadian Securities Regulation, 1977; (jtly) Business Associations, 1979, 2nd edn 1989; (with R. Forbes) Canadian Companies and the Stock Exchange, 1980; (jtly) Canadian Securities Regulation, Supplement, 1982; (jtly) Partnerships and Canadian Business Corporations, 1989; (jtly) If Quebec Goes, 1995; (jtly) Getting Canada Online: understanding the information highway, 1995; (jtly) Cyberlaw and Communication Law, 1997; articles and reports. *Recreations:* jogging, ski-ing, tennis. *Clubs:* University (Toronto); University (Waterloo); Westmount Golf.

**JOHNSTON, Hon. Donald (James)**; PC (Can.) 1980; OC 2008; QC (Can.) 1985; Secretary-General, Organisation for Economic Co-operation and Development, 1996–2006; *b* 26 June 1936; *s* of Wilbur Austin Johnston and Florence Jean Moffat Tucker; *m* 1965, Heather Bell Maclaren; four *d*. *Educ:* McGill Univ. (BA, BCL; Gold Medallist 1958); Univ. of Grenoble (schol.). Joined Stikeman & Elliott, 1961; founder of law firm, Johnston, Heenan and Blaikie; Counsel, Heenan Blaikie, 1988–96; Lectr, Fiscal Law, McGill Univ., 1963–76; MP (L) St Henri-Westmount, 1978–88; Pres., Treasury Bd of Canada, 1980–82; Minister for Econ. Develt, and Minister of State for Sci. and Tech., 1982–83; Minister of State for Econ. Develt and Tech., 1983–84; Minister of Justice and Attorney-Gen., Canada, 1984. Pres., Liberal Party, 1990–94. Chair, Internat. Risk Governance Council, 2006–10. Vis. Prof., Yonsei Univ., Seoul, S Korea, 2006–10. Hon. dr: King's Coll., Halifax, 1999; Econs Univ. of Bratislava, 2000; McGill, 2003; McMaster, 2008; Bishop's, 2010. Grand Cordon, Order of the Rising Sun (Japan), 2006; Commander's Cross with Star of the Order of Merit (Hungary), 2006; Order of White Double Cross, First Class (Slovak Republic), 2006; Grand-Croix de l'Ordre de Léopold II (Belgium), 2007; Officier, Légion d'Honneur (France), 2011. *Publications:* How to Survive Canada's Tax Chaos, 1974; Up the Hill (political memoirs), 1986; (ed) With a Bang, Not a Whimper: Pierre Trudeau speaks out, 1988; Missing the Tide, 2017. *Recreations:* writing, tennis, piano. *Club:* Mount-Royal (Montreal).

**JOHNSTON, Frederick Patrick Mair,** CBE 1993; Chairman, Johnston Press plc (formerly F. Johnston & Co. Ltd), 1973–2001 (Director, 1959–2010); *b* Edinburgh, 15 Sept. 1935; *e s* of late Frederick M. Johnston and Mrs M. K. Johnston, Falkirk; *m* 1961, Elizabeth Ann Jones; two *s*. *Educ:* Morrison's Acad., Crieff; Lancing Coll., Sussex; New Coll., Oxford (MA, Mod. Hist.). Commissioned in Royal Scots Fusiliers, 1955; served in E Africa with 4th (Uganda) Bn, KAR, 1955–56. Joined Editorial Dept of Liverpool Daily Post & Echo, 1959; joined The Times Publishing Co. Ltd, as Asst Sec., 1960–62; F. Johnston & Co. Ltd, subseq. Johnston Press plc: Asst Manager, 1962; Company Sec., 1969–73; Managing Dir, 1973–80; Chief Exec., 1980–91; Exec. Chm., 1991–97. Chm., Dunn & Wilson Ltd, 1976–97; Director: Scottish Mortgage and Trust plc, 1991–2002; Lloyds TSB Bank Scotland plc, 1996–2003; The Press Association Ltd, 1997–2001. Dir, FIEJ, 1990–96. President: Young Newspapermen's Assoc., 1968–69; Forth Valley Chamber of Commerce, 1972–73; Scottish Newspaper Proprietors' Assoc., 1976–78; Newspaper Soc., 1989–90; Chm., Newspapers Press Fund Appeal, 1995; Chm., Central Scotland Manpower Cttee, 1976–83; Mem., Press Council, 1974–88; Treasurer: Soc. of Master Printers of Scotland, 1981–86; CPU, 1987–91. Chm., Edinburgh Internat. Book Fest. (formerly Edinburgh Book Fest.), 1996–2001. Chm., Scotland in Europe, 2001–04. Regent, RCSE, 2001–10. FRSA 1992. Liveryman, Stationers' and Newspapermakers' Co., 2004–. *Recreations:* reading, travelling. *Clubs:* Caledonian; New (Edinburgh).

**JOHNSTON, Graham;** *see* Johnston, A. G.

**JOHNSTON, Lt Col Grenville Shaw,** CVO 2018; OBE 1986; TD (2 clasps) 1975; CA; farmer, since 2005; Lord-Lieutenant of Moray, 2005–Jan. 2020 (Vice Lord-Lieutenant, 1996–2005); *b* 28 Jan. 1945; *s* of Lt Col William Dewar Johnston, OBE, TD, CA and Margaret Raynor Adeline Johnston (*née* Shaw); *m* 1972, Marylyn Jean Picken; two *d*. *Educ:* Seafield Primary Sch., Elgin; Blairmore Prep. Sch., Huntly; Fettes Coll., Edinburgh. CA 1968. Apprentice with Scott-Moncrieff Thomson & Sheils, Edinburgh, 1963–68; Asst, Thomson McLintock & Co., Glasgow, 1968–70; with W. D. Johnston & Carmichael, 1970–2005, Sen. Partner, 1975–2001, Consultant, 2001–05. Mem. Council, ICA Scotland, 1993–98 (Jun. Vice Pres., 1998; Sen. Vice Pres., 1999–2000; Pres., 2000–01). Chm., Grampian & Shetland Cttee, Royal Jubilee and Prince's Trusts, 1980–91; Mem., Grampian Cttee, Prince's Scottish Youth Business Trust, 1989–97. Sec., Moray Local Health Council, 1975–91; Board Member: Moray Enterprise Trust, 1985–93; Moray Badenoch & Strathspey Local Enterprise Co. Ltd, 1990–93; Cairngorm Mountain Ltd, 1999–2014 (Chm., 2008–14); Highlands and Is Airports Ltd, 2001–08 (Chm., 2009–16); Chairman: Caledonian Maritime Assets Ltd, 2007–14; Calmac Pension Fund, 2015–. Trustee: Nat. Museums of Scotland, 1998–2006; Knockando Woolmill Trust, 2004–14; Chm., Fresson Trust, 2010–. Vice-Chm., Gordonstoun Sch., 1985–99. Highland Area, TAVRA Association, later Highland Reserve Forces and Cadets Association: Mem., 1980–; Chm., Northern Area, 1999–2001; Chm., 2001–05; Vice Pres., 2005–06 and 2012–; Pres., 2007–12; Vice Chm. (Army), RFCA, 2003–07. Lt Col, TA, 1982; Hon. Col, 3rd Highlanders, 1997–99. Pres., Moray Scouts, 2005–; Hon. Pres., Moray Soc., 2009–. DL Moray, 1979. KCSG 1982; OStJ 2011. *Recreations:* fishing, ski-ing, shooting, singing tenor. *Address:* Spynie Kirk House, Quarrywood, Elgin, Moray IV30 8XJ. *T:* (01343) 542578, 07774 120202. *Clubs:* New, Royal Scots (Edinburgh); Elgin Rotary (Hon. Mem., 2008–).

**JOHNSTON, Henry Butler M.;** *see* McKenzie Johnston.

**JOHNSTON, Sir Ian;** *see* Johnston, Sir W. I. R.

**JOHNSTON, Ian Alistair,** CB 1995; PhD; Vice Chancellor and Principal, Glasgow Caledonian University, 1998–2006; *b* 2 May 1944; *s* of late Donald Dalrymple Johnston and Muriel Joyce Johnston; *m* 1973, Mary Bridget Lube; one *s* one *d*. *Educ:* Royal Grammar Sch., High Wycombe; Birmingham Univ. (BSc, PhD). Joined Dept of Employment as Assistant Principal, 1969; Private Sec. to Permanent Secretary, Sir Denis Barnes, 1972–73; Principal, 1973; First Sec. (Labour Attaché), British Embassy, Brussels, 1976–77; Asst Sec. (Director, ACAS), 1978; Under-Sec. (Dir of Planning and Resources, MSC), 1984; Chief Exec., Vocational Educn Trng Gp, MSC, 1985; Dep. Dir Gen., MSC, subseq. Training Commn, then Training Agency, then Training Enterprise and Education Directorate of Department of Employment, 1987–92; Dir of Resources and Strategy (Dep. Sec.), Dept of Employment, 1992; Dir Gen., TEED, Dept of Employment, 1992–95; Dep. Principal, Sheffield Hallam Univ., 1995–98. Director: Glasgow Chamber of Commerce, 1998–2005; CAPITB plc, 1999–2002. Hon. Treas. and Council Mem., Industrial Soc., 1991–2002. Mem., European Commn Expert Study Gp on Educn and Trng, 1995–2000. Member, Council: BTEC/Univ. of London Exam. Bd, 1995–98; Council for Industry and Higher Educn, 2001–06; Mem., Jt Nat. Council for Higher Educn Staff, 2002–06. Director: Qualification for Industry, 1996–99; Univs and Colls Employers Assoc., 2001–06; Board Member: Scottish Enterprise Glasgow, 2004–06; Lifelong Learning UK, 2005–06. Consultant, Young Foundn, 2008–10. Gov. and Dep. Chm., Sheffield Hallam Univ. (formerly Sheffield City Poly.), 1988–95; Chief. Exec., Transition, 1998, Bd Mem., then Dep. Chm., 1998–2003, Univ. for Industry; Trustee, Carnegie Trust for Univs of Scotland, 1998–2006. Trustee, Buxton Fest. Foundn, 2008– (Chm., 2010–15). Mem., Merchants House of Glasgow, 2005. Hon. Life Mem., Work Foundn, 2002. DL City of Glasgow, 2004–06. CCMI (CIMgt 1993); FCIPD (FIPD 1993); FRSA 1995. DUniv: Glasgow Caledonian, 2006; Sheffield Hallam, 2010. Lord Provost's Medallist for Educn, 2005. *Publications:* contribs to learned jls on atomic structure of metals, 1966–69, and subseq. on public admin and educn and trng strategy, incl. virtual educn and apprenticeships; contrib. New DNB. *Recreations:* birding, fishing, travel, cooking, bridge, gardening. *Address:* Stonecroft, 18 Eaton Drive, Baslow, Bakewell, Derbys DE45 1SE.

**JOHNSTON, Prof. Ian Alistair,** PhD; FRSE; Professor of Biology, University of St Andrews, since 2016 (Chandos Professor, School of Biology, 1997–2016; Director, Scottish Oceans Institute, 2012–15); Co-founder and Chief Executive Officer, Xelect Ltd, since

2013; *b* 13 April 1949. *Educ*: Univ. of Hull (BSc 1st cl. Hons Biological Chem. and Zoology 1970; PhD 1973). NERC Res. Fellow, Univ. of Bristol, 1973; University of St Andrews: Lectr, 1976–84, Reader, 1984, in Physiology; Prof., 1985–95; Dir, Gatty Marine Lab., 1985–2008; Founding Chm., Dept of Biology and Preclin. Medicine, 1987–91; Head, Sch. of Biological and Med. Scis, 1991–92; Mem. Court, 1997–2002; Founding Head, Div. of Envmtl and Evolutionary Biol., Sch. of Biology, 1997–2004; Dir of Res., Sch. of Biology, 2003–06. Vis. Prof., Univ. of Nairobi, 1993. Mem. Council, NERC, 1995–2000. Pres., Soc. for Experimental Biol., 2007–09. FRSE 1987. Scientific Medal, Zool Soc., 1984. *Publications*: (contrib.) Essentials of Physiology, 3rd edn 1991 (trans. Spanish 1987, trans. Italian 1989, trans. French 1990); (ed jtly) Phenotypic and Evolutionary Adaptation of Animals to Temperature, 1996; (jtly) Environmental Physiology of Animals, 2000. *Address*: Xelect Ltd, Horizon House, Abbey Walk, St Andrews, Fife KY16 9LB. *T*: (01334) 845357.

**JOHNSTON, James William H.;** *see* Halcro Johnston.

**JOHNSTON, Jennifer, (Mrs David Gilliland),** FRSL; author; *b* 12 Jan. 1930; *d* of late (William) Denis Johnston, OBE; *m* 1st, 1951, Ian Smyth; two *s* two *d*; 2nd, 1976, David Jervois Thetford Gilliland (*d* 2019). *Educ*: Park House Sch., Dublin; Trinity Coll., Dublin. FRSL 1979. Mem., Aosdána. Plays: Indian Summer, performed Belfast, 1983; The Porch, prod Dublin, 1986. Hon. DLitt: Ulster, 1984: TCD, 1992; QUB, 1993; UCD 2005. Irish PEN Award, 2006; Lifetime Achievement Award, Irish Book Awards, 2012. *Publications*: The Captains and the Kings, 1972; The Gates, 1973; How Many Miles to Babylon?, 1974; Shadows on Our Skin, 1978 (dramatised for TV, 1979); The Old Jest, 1979 (Whitbread Novel Award; filmed as The Dawning, 1988); (play) The Nightingale and not the Lark, 1980; The Christmas Tree, 1981; The Railway Station Man, 1984; Fool's Sanctuary, 1987; The Invisible Worm, 1991; The Illusionist, 1995; (contrib.) Finbar's Hotel, 1997; Two Moons, 1998; The Gingerbread Woman, 2000; This Is Not a Novel, 2002; Grace & Truth, 2005; Foolish Mortals, 2007; Truth or Fiction, 2009. *Recreations*: theatre, cinema, gardening, travelling. *Address*: Brook Hall, 65 Culmore Road, Derry, N Ireland BT48 8JE. *T*: (028) 7135 1297.

**JOHNSTON, Mark Steven;** racehorse trainer, since 1987; Trainer and Managing Director, Johnston (formerly Mark Johnston) Racing Ltd, since 1988; *b* 10 Oct. 1959; *s* of Ronald and Mary Johnston; *m* 1985, Deirdre Ferguson; two *s*. *Educ*: Glasgow Univ. Vet. Sch. (BVMS 1983). MRCVS 1983. Veterinary practice, 1983–86. MRSocMed 1999. *Recreation*: cycling. *Address*: Kingsley House, Middleham, Leyburn, N Yorks DL8 4PH. *T*: (01969) 622237, *Fax*: (01969) 622484. *E*: mark@johnston.racing.

**JOHNSTON, Lt-Gen. Sir Maurice (Robert),** KCB 1982; CVO 2005; OBE 1971; Lord-Lieutenant of Wiltshire, 1996–2004; Deputy Chief of Defence Staff, 1982–83, retired 1984; *b* 27 Oct. 1929; *s* of late Brig. Allen Leigh Johnston, OBE, and Gertrude Geraldine Johnston (*née* Templer); *m* 1960, Belinda Mary Sladen; one *s* one *d*. *Educ*: Wellington College; RMA Sandhurst. rcds, psc. Commissioned RA, 1949; transf. The Queen's Bays, 1954; served in Germany, Egypt, Jordan, Libya, N Ireland, Borneo. Instr, Army Staff Coll., 1965–67; MA to CGS, 1968–71; CO 1st The Queen's Dragoon Guards, 1971–73; Comdr 20th Armoured Brigade, 1973–75; BGS, HQ UKLF, 1977–78; Senior Directing Staff, RCDS, 1979; Asst Chief of Gen. Staff, 1980; Dep. Chief of Defence Staff (Op. Reqs), 1981–82. Col, 1st The Queen's Dragoon Guards, 1986–91. Chairman: Secondary Resources plc, 1988–91; Detention Corp., 1988–94; Managing Director: Freshglen Ltd, Wraxall Gp, 1984–85; Unit Security Ltd, 1985–88; Director: HIAB (formerly Partek Cargotec), 1984–2010; Shorrock Guards Ltd, 1988–91. Governor: Dauntsey's Sch., Wilts 1987–2004, St Mary's Sch., Calne, 1988–94. DL Wilts, 1990, High Sheriff, 1993–94. *Recreations*: fishing, shooting, gardening, music, glass engraving. *Address*: The Paddock, Reeves Piece, Bratton, Wilts BA13 4TH.

**JOHNSTON, Nicholas;** *see* Johnston, P. N.

**JOHNSTON, Paul Charles;** HM Diplomatic Service; Ambassador to Political and Security Committee, European Union, since 2017; *b* 29 May 1968; *s* of late Charles Johnston and of Muriel (*née* Hall); *m* 2004, Nicola Carol Maskell. *Educ*: Galashiels Acad.; Univ. of Glasgow (MA Hons). MoD, 1990–93; HM Diplomatic Service, 1993–: Desk Officer, Eastern Adriatic Unit, 1993–95 (Private Sec. to Lord Owen at Internat. Conf. on Former Yugoslavia, 1994); Private Sec. to Ambassador to France, 1995–97; 2nd Sec. (Political), Paris, 1997–99; Foreign and Commonwealth Office: Head: Kosovo Policy Section, 1999–2000; European Defence Section, 2000–01; Dep. Hd, EU Ext. Dept, 2001–02; Hd, Security Policy Dept, FCO, 2002–04; Counsellor (Political), UK Mission to the UN, NY, 2005–08; Dir, Internat. Security, FCO, 2008–11; Ambassador to Sweden, 2011–15; Dep. Perm. Rep. to NATO, 2015–17. *Recreations*: cinema, music, walking, idling. *Address*: c/o Foreign and Commonwealth Office, King Charles Street, SW1A 2AH.

**JOHNSTON, (Paul) Nicholas,** FIMI; *b* 5 Jan. 1948; *s* of Joseph Leo Johnston and Winifred Vera Neale or Johnston; *m* 1st, 1972, Catherine MacPhee (marr. diss. 1993); one *s* two *d*; 2nd, 1993, Anna Jiménez-Olive; two *s*. *Educ*: North Kesteven Grammar Sch.; RMA Sandhurst. Dir, Eastern Hldgs Ltd, 1972. Mem. (C) Scotland Mid and Fife, Scottish Parlt, 1999–2001. *Recreations*: cookery, history, gardening.

**JOHNSTON, Peter Henry;** Director (formerly Controller), BBC Northern Ireland, since 2006; *b* 20 Jan. 1966; *s* of Tommy and Edna Johnston; *m* 1991, Jill McAlister; one *s* one *d*. *Educ*: Imperial College, London (MEng Chem. Engrg 1988). Business Consultant, Shell Internat., London, 1988–90; Sen. Associate, Price Waterhouse Coopers Mgt Consultants, Belfast, 1990–94; BBC Northern Ireland, Belfast: Res. and Special Projs Exec., 1994–97; Hd, Mktg and Develt, 1997–2001; Hd, New Media, BBC Nations and Regions, London, 2001–03; Hd, Broadcasting, BBC NI, Belfast, 2003–06. *Recreations*: no longer playing but watching Rugby, being at the North Coast of Northern Ireland, socialising, playing golf badly. *Address*: BBC Northern Ireland, Broadcasting House, Ormeau Avenue, Belfast BT2 8HQ. *T*: (028) 9033 8200, *Fax*: (028) 9033 8800. *E*: peter.johnston@bbc.co.uk.

**JOHNSTON, Peter William;** consultant to World Bank and International Federation of Accountants, 2005–14; *b* 8 Feb. 1943; *s* of late William Johnston and of Louisa Alice Johnston (*née* Pritchard); *m* 1967, Patricia Sandra Macdonald; one *s* one *d*. *Educ*: Univ. of Glasgow (MA, LLB). Partner, MacArthur & Co., Solicitors, Inverness, 1971–76; Procurator Fiscal Depute, Dumfries, 1976–78; Procurator Fiscal, Banff, 1978–86; Senior Procurator Fiscal Depute, Crown Office, Edinburgh, 1986–87; Asst Solicitor, Crown Office, 1987–89; Chief Exec. and Sec., ICAS, 1989–99; Chief Exec., 1999–2002, Dir, 2002–03, Advr, 2003–05, IFAC. Mem. Bd, Risk Management Authy, 2006–16 (Convenor, 2008–16). Trustee: Friends of Duff House, 2006–15; Friends of Chalmers Hospital, 2011–. *Recreations*: music, foreign languages. *Address*: 13 Scotstown, Banff AB45 1LA.

**JOHNSTON, Robert Alan,** AC 1986; Governor, Reserve Bank of Australia, 1982–89; *b* 19 July 1924; *m* 1st, 1948, Verna (*d* 1999), *d* of H. J. Mullin; two *s* two *d*; 2nd, 2000, Judith Ann, *d* of P. A. Lazzarini. *Educ*: Essendon High School; University of Melbourne. BCom. Commonwealth Bank of Australia, 1940–60; RAAF, 1943–46; Reserve Bank of Australia, 1960–89: Dep. Manager and Manager, Investment Dept, 1964–70; Chief Manager, Internat. Dept, 1970–76; Adviser, 1973–82; Chief Representative, London, 1976–77; Exec. Dir, World Bank Group, Washington, 1977–79; Secretary, Reserve Bank of Aust., 1980–82. Director: Australian Mutual Prov. Soc., 1989–97; John Fairfax Gp Pty, 1989–90; Westpac Banking Corp., 1992–96. Pres., Cttee for Econ. Develt of Australia, 1990–94. Hon. DCom Melbourne, 1992.

**JOHNSTON, Robert Gordon Scott,** CB 1993; Executive Director, United Kingdom Major Ports Group, 1993–99; *b* 27 Aug. 1933; *s* of late Robert William Fairfield Johnston, CMG, CBE, MC, TD; *m* 1960, Jill Maureen Campbell; one *s* (and one *d* decd). *Educ*: Clifton; Clare Coll., Cambridge (1st Cl. Hons Classical Tripos, MA). 2/Lieut Scots Guards (National Service), 1955–57. Entered Air Min. as Asst Principal, 1957; Private Sec. to Parly Under Sec. of State for Air, 1959–62; transf. to MPBW, Def. Works Secretariat, 1963; Sec., Bldg Regulation Adv. Cttee, 1964; Principal Private Sec. to successive Ministers of Public Bldg and Works, 1965–68; seconded to Shell Internat. Chemical Co., Finance Div., 1968–70; Asst Dir of Home Estate Management, Property Services Agency, 1970–73; seconded to Cabinet Office, 1973–75; Asst Sec., Railways Directorate, Dept of Transport, 1975–79; Under Sec., DoE, 1979–93; seconded to Price Commn, 1979; Dir of Civil Accommodation, 1979–88, Dir, Defence Services, 1988–90, PSA; Man. Dir, PSA Internat., 1990–93. Rep. of Sec. of State for Envmt on Commonwealth War Graves Commn, 1988–93. Lay Chm., NHS Complaints Panels, 2000–05; Mem., Ind. Review Panel, Healthcare Commn, 2004–07. Coronation Medal, 1953. *Address*: 5 Methley Street, SE11 4AL.

**JOHNSTON, Prof. Ronald John,** OBE 2011; PhD; FBA 1999; FAcSS; Professor of Geography, Bristol University, since 1995; *b* 30 March 1941; *s* of Henry Louis Johnston and Phyllis Joyce (*née* Liddiard); *m* 1963, Rita Brennan; one *s* one *d*. *Educ*: Commonweal County Secondary Grammar Sch., Swindon; Univ. of Manchester (BA 1962; MA 1964); Monash Univ. (PhD 1967). Department of Geography, Monash University: Teaching Fellow, 1964; Sen. Teaching Fellow, 1965; Lectr, 1966; University of Canterbury, New Zealand: Lectr, 1967–68; Sen. Lectr, 1969–72; Reader, 1973–74; University of Sheffield: Prof. of Geography, 1974–92; Pro-Vice-Chancellor for Acad. Affairs, 1989–92; Vice-Chancellor, Essex Univ., 1992–95. FAcSS (AcSS 1999). DU Essex, 1996; Hon. LLD Monash, 1999; Hon. DLitt: Sheffield, 2002; Bath 2006. Murchison Award, 1985, Victoria Medal, 1990, RGS; Honors Award for Distinction in Res., Assoc. Amer. Geographers, 1991; Prix Vautrin Lud, Fest. Internat. de Geographie, 1999; Lifetime Achievement Award, Assoc. Amer. Geographers, 2010; Political Communicator of the Year, Political Studies Assoc., 2011. *Publications*: (with P. J. Rimmer) Retailing in Melbourne, 1970; Urban Residential Patterns: an introductory review, 1971; Spatial Structures: an introduction to the study of spatial systems in human geography, 1973; The New Zealanders: how they live and work, 1976; The World System: some enquiries into its spatial structure, 1976; (with B. E. Coates and P. L. Knox) Geography and Inequality, 1977; Multivariate Statistical Analysis in Geography: a primer on the general linear model, 1978; Political, Electoral and Spatial Systems, 1979; (with P. J. Taylor) Geography of Elections, 1979; Geography and Geographers: Anglo-American human geography since 1945, 1979, 6th edn 2004; City and Society: an outline for urban geography, 1980; The Geography of Federal Spending in the United States of America, 1980; The American Urban System: a geographical perspective, 1982; Geography and the State, 1982; Philosophy and Human Geography: an introduction to contemporary approaches, 1983, 2nd edn 1986; Residential Segregation, the State and Constitutional Conflict in American Urban Areas, 1984; The Geography of English Politics: the 1983 General Election, 1985; On Human Geography, 1986; Bell-Ringing: the English art of change-ringing, 1986; Money and Votes: constituency campaign spending and election results, 1987; (jtly) The United States: a contemporary human geography, 1988; (with C. J. Pattie and J. G. Allsopp) A Nation Dividing?: the electoral map of Great Britain 1979–1987, 1988; Environmental Problems: nature, economy and state, 1989, 2nd edn 1996; (jtly) An Atlas of Bells, 1990; A Question of Place: exploring the practice of human geography, 1991; (ed) The Dictionary of Human Geography, 1989, 4th edn 2000; (with D. J. Rossiter and C. J. Pattie) The Boundary Commissions, 1999; (jtly) From Votes to Seats, 2001; (with C. J. Pattie) Putting Voters in Their Place, 2006; (with S. Hix and I. McLean) Choosing an Electoral System, 2010; (jtly) Drawing a New Constituency Map for the United Kingdom, 2010; (with C. J. Pattie) Money and Electoral Politics: local parties and funding in general elections, 2014; contrib. chapters in ed vols and numerous papers in learned jls. *Recreation*: bell-ringing. *Address*: School of Geographical Sciences, University of Bristol, Bristol BS8 1SS. *T*: (0117) 928 9116, *Fax*: (0117) 928 7878. *E*: r.johnston@bristol.ac.uk.

**JOHNSTON, Prof. Sebastian Lennox,** PhD; FRCP; FRSB; FMedSci; FERS; Asthma UK Clinical Professor, National Heart and Lung Institute, Imperial College London, since 2011; Director, MRC and Asthma UK Centre in Allergic Mechanisms of Asthma, since 2011 (Deputy Director, 2010–11); *b* London, 30 March 1959; *s* of Ivor Johnston and Marlo Johnston; *m* 1997, Dr Tea Endeladze; four *s* two *d*. *Educ*: Guy's Hosp., London (MB BS 1982); Univ. of Southampton (PhD 1993). MRCP 1985, FRCP 2000; FRSB (FSB 2011). MRC Travelling Res. Fellow, Univ. of Iowa, 1994–95; University of Southampton: Lectr in Medicine and Respiratory Medicine, 1992–96; Sen. Lectr in Medicine, Respiratory Medicine and Respiratory Infection, 1996–99; National Heart and Lung Institute, Imperial College London: Professorial Fellow in Respiratory Medicine, 1999–2000; Prof. of Respiratory Medicine, 2000–11. NIHR Sen. Investigator, 2009–13, 2015–18; Eur. Res. Council Advanced Investigator, 2009–13. Member: BMA, 1982; British Thoracic Soc., 1988; Amer. Thoracic Soc., 1995; Assoc. of Physicians of GB and Ire., 2000; British Soc. of Allergy and Clin. Immunol., 2000; Eur. Acad. of Allergology and Clin. Immunol., 2001; Amer. Acad. of Asthma, Allergy and Immunol., 2002. FMedSci 2014; FERS 2014. *Publications*: (ed jtly) Asthma: critical debates, 2001; (ed jtly) Respiratory Infections in Allergy and Asthma, 2003; (jtly) Medicine and Surgery: a concise textbook, 2005; (ed jtly) Asthma Exacerbations, 2006; (ed) An Atlas of Asthma, 2007; contrib. book chapters and approx. 370 papers in jls. *Recreations*: opera, football, Rugby. *Address*: National Heart and Lung Institute, Imperial College London, Norfolk Place, W2 1PG.

**JOHNSTON, Sir Thomas Alexander,** 14th Bt *cr* 1626, of Caskieben; *b* 1 Feb. 1956; *s* of Sir Thomas Alexander Johnston, 13th Bt, and of Helen Torry, *d* of Benjamin Franklin Du Bois; *S* father, 1984. *Heir*: *cousin* William Norville Johnston, *b* 25 Dec. 1955.

**JOHNSTON, Ven. William Francis,** CB 1983; Rector, Winslow with Great Horwood and Addington, Diocese of Oxford, 1991–95; *b* 29 June 1930; *m* 1963, Jennifer Morton; two *s* one *d*. *Educ*: Wesley Coll., Dublin; Trinity Coll., Dublin (BA 1955; MA 1969). Ordained 1955; Curate of Orangefield, Co. Down, 1955–59; commissioned into Royal Army Chaplains Dept, 1959; served, UK, Germany, Aden, Cyprus; ACG South East District, 1977–80; Chaplain-Gen. to the Forces, 1980–86; QHC 1980–86; Priest-in-charge, Winslow with Addington, 1987–91. *Recreations*: golf, fishing, gardening. *Address*: Lower Axehill, Chard Road, Axminster, Devon EX13 5ED. *T*: (01297) 33259.

**JOHNSTON, Sir (William) Ian (Ridley),** Kt 2009; CBE 2001; QPM 1995; DL; non-executive Director, Security Industry Authority, since 2013; Member, Regulatory Authority, Football Association, since 2016; *b* 6 Sept. 1945; *s* of late William and Alice Johnston; *m* 1968, Carol Ann Smith; two *s*. *Educ*: Enfield Grammar Sch.; LSE (BSc 1st Cl. Hons). Joined Metropolitan Police 1965; ranks of PC to Chief Supt, 1965–88; Staff Officer to Sir Peter Imbert, 1988–89; Senior Command Course, 1989; Asst Chief Constable, Kent,

1989–92; Dep. Asst Comr, 1992–94, Asst Comr, 1994–2001, Met Police; Chief Constable, British Transport Police, 2001–09; Dir of Security, London Organising Cttee of the Olympic and Paralympic Games, 2009–12. Mem., Audit Cttee, British Mus., 2011–. Mem. Bd, Canterbury Christ Church Univ., 2014–. Trustee, Suzy Lamplugh Trust, 2004–. Gov., Riverside Special Needs Sch., 2018–. DL Gtr London, 2007. *Recreations:* walking, jogging, foreign travel, grandchildren. *E:* carolian.johnston@me.com. *Club:* Orpington Rovers Football.

**JOHNSTON, Sir William Robert Patrick K.;** *see* Knox-Johnston.

**JOHNSTONE;** *see* Hope Johnstone, family name of Earl of Annandale and Hartfell.

**JOHNSTONE, VANDEN-BEMPDE-,** family name of **Baron Derwent**.

**JOHNSTONE, Lord; David Patrick Wentworth Hope Johnstone;** Master of Annandale and Hartfell; *b* 13 Oct. 1971; *s* and *heir* of Earl of Annandale and Hartfell, *qv*; *m* 2001, Penny, *d* of late John Macmillan; one *s* two *d. Educ:* Stowe; St Andrews Univ. (BSc 1994). Chairman: Moffat Town Hall Redevelt Trust, 2013–16; Scottish Land & Estates, 2014–; Johnstonebridge Develt Trust, 2016– (Vice-Chm., 2012–16); Dir, Dumfries & Galloway Small Community Housing Trust, 2007–. *Heir: s* Percy John Wentworth Hope Johnstone, Master of Johnstone; *b* 16 Feb. 2002.

**JOHNSTONE, Catherine, (Mrs Martin Holt),** CBE 2016; Chief Executive Officer, Royal Voluntary Service, since 2017; *b* Beckenham, Kent, 6 June 1964; *d* of Ernest Arthur and Mavis Ann Clemson; *m* 2008, Martin Holt; two *s* three *d. Educ:* Highams Park Sen. Sch.; Highams Park 6th Form Coll.; W Essex Sch. of Nursing (RGN 1985). Nursing posts with NHS, 1986–96; Chief Executive: Crossroads Caring for Carers, 1996–2000; Bucks Community Action, 2000–03; Regl Action and Involvement SE, 2003–07; Capacitybuilders, 2007–09; Chief Exec., Samaritans, 2009–15; Chief Exec., Migrant Help UK, 2016–17. Lay Rep., Aylesbury Vale Primary Care Gp, 1999–2001. Accredited Nat. Social Enterprise Advr, Small Firms Enterprise Develt Initiative, 1985–2000; non-deptl public body Accounting Officer, 2007–09.

**JOHNSTONE, Vice Adm. Sir Clive (Charles Carruthers),** KBE 2019 (CBE 2007); CB 2015; Commander Maritime Command HQ Northwood, 2015–19; *b* Kampala, Uganda, 6 Sept. 1963; *s* of Charles and Patricia Johnstone; *m* 1990, Alison Duguid; two *d* (one *s* decd). *Educ:* Royal Shrewsbury Sch.; Durham Univ. (BA Hons Anthropology); Britannia Royal Naval Coll. Joined RN, 1985; Commanding Officer: HMS Iron Duke, 1998–99; HMS Bulwark, 2005–06; Director: Naval Personnel Strategy, 2007; Naval Staff, 2008; HCSC, 2008; Principal Staff Officer to CDS, 2008–10; rcds, 2011; FOST, 2011–13; ACNS (Policy), 2013–15. Younger Brother, Trinity House, 2009–. *Recreations:* swimming, fishing, gardening, wine, enjoying family time in our cottage in Argyll. *Club:* Naval.

**JOHNSTONE, David;** Interim Director of Health and Social Care, Bristol City Council, 2010–11; *b* 9 May 1951; *s* of David Armour Johnstone and Veronica Johnstone; *m* 1974, Andra Newton; one *s* two *d. Educ:* Middlesex Poly. (BA Hons Social Sci.); Newcastle upon Tyne Univ. (MBA). Joined Social Services Dept, Newcastle upon Tyne, 1974, Asst Dir, 1990–95; Director of Social Services: Stockton on Tees, 1995–99; Devon CC, 1999–2009; Dir of Ops, Care Quality Commn, 2009. *Recreations:* sport, rare breed animal husbandry. *Club:* Teign Corinthian Yacht.

**JOHNSTONE, Debbie;** *see* Alder, D.

**JOHNSTONE, Prof. Eve Cordelia,** CBE 2002; MD; FRCPsych, FRCPGlas, FRCPE, FMedSci; FRSE; Professor of Psychiatry, 1989–2010, now Emeritus, and Honorary Assistant University Principal for Mental Health Research and Development, since 2010, University of Edinburgh (Head, Department of Psychiatry, 1989–2010); *b* 1 Sept. 1944; *d* of late William Gillespie Johnstone and Dorothy Mary Johnstone. *Educ:* Park Sch., Glasgow; Univ. of Glasgow (MB ChB 1967; DPM 1970; MD 1976). MRCP 1971; MRCPsych 1972, FRCPsych 1984; FRCPE 1992. House officer posts, 1967–68, trng posts in Psychiatry, 1968–72, Glasgow Hosp.; Lectr in Psychological Medicine, Glasgow Univ., 1972–74; Mem., Scientific Staff, MRC, Clin. Res. Centre and Northwick Park Hosp., Harrow, 1974–89 (Hon. Consultant, 1979–89). Mem., MRC, 1996–2002 (Chm., Neuroscience and Mental Health Bd, 1999–2002). Founder FMedSci 1998; FRSE 2005. *Publications:* Searching for the Causes of Schizophrenia, 1994; (ed) Biological Psychiatry, 1996; (ed jtly) Schizophrenia: concepts and management, 1999; (ed jtly) Companion to Psychiatric Studies, 6th edn 1998 to 8th edn 2010; (with C. Frith) Schizophrenia: a very short introduction, 2003; (ed jtly) Schizophrenia: from neuroimaging to neuroscience, 2004; numerous contribs to learned jls mainly relating to schizophrenia and other serious psychiatric disorders. *Recreations:* card-playing, gardening, listening to opera, foreign travel. *Address:* Department of Psychiatry, University of Edinburgh, Kennedy Tower, Royal Edinburgh Hospital, Edinburgh EH10 5HF. *T:* (0131) 650 9221.

**JOHNSTONE, Sir (George) Richard (Douglas),** 11th Bt *cr* 1700, of Westerhall, Dumfriesshire; *b* 21 Aug. 1948; *er s* of Sir Frederic Allan George Johnstone, 10th Bt and of Doris Johnstone (*née* Shortridge); *S* father, 1994; *m* 1976, Gwyneth Susan Bailey (marr. diss. 2003); one *s* one *d. Educ:* Leeds Grammar Sch.; Magdalen Coll., Oxford (MA; Dip. Physical Anthropology). *Recreations:* travel, computing. *Heir: s* Frederic Robert Arthur Johnstone, *b* 18 Nov. 1981.

**JOHNSTONE, Iain Gilmour;** author and broadcaster; *b* 8 April 1943; *s* of Jack and Gilly Johnstone; *m* 1980, Mo Watson; one *s* two *d. Educ:* Campbell College, Belfast; Bristol Univ. (LLB Hons). Newscaster, ITN, 1966–68; Producer, BBC TV, 1968–74; Prof. of Broadcasting, Boston Univ., 1975; Man. Dir, DVD Prodns Ltd (formerly Kensington TV), 1977–2015; BBC presenter, Film 1983, 1984; film critic, The Sunday Times, 1983–93. Accredited Mediator, ADR Gp. Screenplays: Fierce Creatures (with John Cleese), 1996; The Evening News, 2001; The Bank of San Benedetto, 2002; Elsinore: The Year Before; documentaries: John Wayne and his films, 1969; Muhammad Ali, 1977; The Pythons, 1979; Snowdon on Camera, 1981; Steven and Stanley, 2001; Making Connections: the Weizmann Institute, 2010; (play) St Etheldreda's Day, 2018. Mem., BAFTA, 1998–. *Publications:* The Arnhem Report, 1977; The Man With No Name, 1980; Cannes: The Novel, 1990; Wimbledon 2000, 1992; The James Bond Companion, 1999; (contrib.) British Comedy Greats, 2003; Tom Cruise: all the world's a stage, 2006; (with Kathryn Apanowicz) Richard by Kathryn, 2006; Streep: a life in film, 2009; Pirates of the Mediterranean, 2009; Close Encounters: a media memoir, 2013; Get Carman!, 2020. *Recreations:* lawn tennis, theatre, grandchildren. *Address:* 16 Tournay Road, SW6 7UF. *E:* iain.j@uk.com. *Clubs:* Garrick, Queen's; Campden Hill Lawn Tennis.
*See also* Baron Tollemache.

**JOHNSTONE, Isobel Theodora,** PhD; painter and art consultant; Curator, Arts Council Collection, 1979–2004; *b* 1944. *Educ:* James Gillespie's High School; Edinburgh Univ.; Edinburgh Coll. of Art (MA Hons Fine Art); Glasgow Univ. (PhD). Lectr in History of Art, Glasgow School of Art, 1969–73; Scottish Arts Council, 1975–79. Painter. *Publications:* (as Isobel Spencer): Walter Crane, 1975; articles on late 19th century and 20th century British art. *Address:* 50A Hammersmith Grove, W6 7HA. *W:* www.isobeljohnstone.co.uk.

**JOHNSTONE, Sir (John) Raymond,** Kt 1993; CBE 1988; Managing Director, Murray Johnstone Ltd, Glasgow, 1968–89 (Chairman, 1984–94; President, 1994–97); Chairman, Forestry Commission, 1989–94; *b* 27 Oct. 1929; *s* of Henry James Johnstone of Alva, Captain RN and Margaret Alison McIntyre; *m* 1979, Susan Sara Gore, DL; five step *s* two step *d. Educ:* Eton Coll.; Trinity Coll., Cambridge (BA Maths). CA. Apprenticed Chiene & Tait, Chartered Accts, Edinburgh, 1951–54; Robert Fleming & Co. Ltd, London, 1955–59; Partner in charge of investment management, Brown Fleming & Murray CA (becoming Whinney Murray CA, 1965), Glasgow, 1959–68; a Founder of Murray Johnstone Ltd, Glasgow to take over investment management dept of Whinney Murray, 1968. Chairman: Summit Gp, 1989–98; Atrium (formerly Lomond) Underwriting plc, 1994–2003; Director: Shipping Industrial Holdings, 1964–75; Scottish Amicable Life Assce Soc., 1971–97 (Chm., 1983–85); Dominion Insurance Co. Ltd, 1973–95 (Chm., 1978–95); Scottish Financial Enterprise, 1986–91 (Chm., 1989–91); Kiln plc, 1995–2002. Hon. Pres., Scottish Opera, 1986–98 (Dir, 1978–86; Chm., 1983–85); Chm., Patrons, Nat. Galls of Scotland, 1996–2003. Member: Scottish Adv. Cttee, Nature Conservancy Council, 1987–89; Scottish Econ. Council, 1987–95; Chm., Historic Buildings Council for Scotland, 1995–2002. Trustee, Nuclear Trust, 1996–2007; Dir, Nuclear Liabilities Fund (formerly Nuclear Generation Decommissioning Fund) Ltd, 1996–2007 (Chm., 1996–2003). *Recreations:* fishing, music, farming. *Address:* 32 Ann Street, Edinburgh EH4 1PJ. *T:* (0131) 311 7100.

**JOHNSTONE, Paul William,** FFPH; Regional Director, North, Public Health England, since 2013; Regional Director of Public Health, NHS North East and Yorkshire; *b* 12 Feb. 1960; *s* of Peter and Pamela Johnstone; *m* Caroline; one *s* two *d. Educ:* Southampton Univ. (BM); Liverpool Univ. (DTM&H); LSHTM (MSc Public Health); Glasgow Univ. (DCH). MRCGP 1990; FFPH (FFPHM 2001). Overseas health volunteer, 1988–90; Officer, ODA, 1991–93; public health consultant, 1996–99; Dir of Public Health, Teesside, 2002; Medical Dir, Co. Durham Tees Valley, 2002; Regl Dir of Public Health, Yorks and Humberside, 2002–11; Dir of Public Health, NHS N of England, 2011–13. Visiting Professor: Nuffield Inst. for Health, Univ. of Leeds, 2002–; Leeds Beckett (formerly Leeds Metropolitan) Univ., 2004–. MRSocMed 1990. *Publications:* Management Support for Primary Care, 1994; around 40 peer reviewed articles and monographs. *Recreations:* ski-ing, walking. *Address:* 16 Almsford Avenue, Harrogate, N Yorks HG2 8HD.

**JOHNSTONE, Peter,** CMG 2004; HM Diplomatic Service, retired; Governor of Anguilla, 2000–04; *b* 30 July 1944; *m* 1969, Diane Claxton; one *s* one *d.* Joined FO, 1962; served: Berne, 1965–66; Benin City, 1966–68; Budapest, 1968–69; Maseru, 1969–72; FCO, 1973–77; Dacca, 1977–79; First Sec., Dublin, 1979–82; FCO, 1983–86; First Sec. (Commercial), Harare, 1986–89; Consul Gen., Edmonton, 1989–91; FCO, 1991–95; Counsellor (Commercial Develt), Jakarta, 1995–98; FCO, 1999.

**JOHNSTONE, Sir Raymond;** *see* Johnstone, Sir J. R.

**JOHNSTONE, Sir Richard;** *see* Johnstone, Sir G. R. D.

**JOHNSTONE, Rev. Prof. William,** DLitt; Professor of Hebrew and Semitic Languages, University of Aberdeen, 1980–2001; *b* 6 May 1936; *s* of Rev. T. K. Johnstone and Evelyn Hope Johnstone (*née* Murray); *m* 1964, Elizabeth Mary Ward; one *s* one *d. Educ:* Hamilton Academy; Glasgow Univ. (MA 1st Cl. Hons Semitic Langs, BD Distinction in New Testament and Old Testament; DLitt 1998); Univ. of Marburg. University of Aberdeen: Lectr 1962, Sen. Lectr 1972, in Hebrew and Semitic Languages; Dean, Faculty of Divinity, 1984–87; Hd of Dept, Divinity with Religious Studies, 1998–2000. Member, Mission archéologique française: Ras Shamra, 1963, 1964, 1966; Enkomi, 1963, 1965, 1971; Member, Marsala Punic Ship Excavation, 1973–79. Pres., SOTS, 1990. *Publications:* Exodus, 1990; 1 and 2 Chronicles, 1997; Exodus and Chronicles, 1998; Exodus (2 vols), 2014; (ed and contrib.) William Robertson Smith: essays in reassessment, 1995; (ed and contrib.) The Bible and the Enlightenment: a case study - Dr Alexander Geddes (1737–1802), 2004; *translation:* Fohrer: Hebrew and Aramaic Dictionary of the Old Testament, 1973; *contributions to:* Ugaritica VI, 1969, VII, 1978, Alasia I, 1972; Dictionary of Biblical Interpretation, 1990; Cambridge Companion to Biblical Interpretation, 1998; Eerdmans Commentary on the Bible, 2003; New Interpreter's Dictionary of the Bible, 2006; Festschriften for: W. McKane, 1986; R. Davidson, 1992; G. W. Anderson, 1993; C. H. W. Brekelmans, 1997; E. W. Nicholson, 2003; A. G. Auld, 2006; G. I. Davies, 2011; articles in Aberdeen Univ. Review, Atti del I Congresso Internazionale di Studi Fenici e Punici, Bibliotheca Ephemeridum Theologicarum Lovaniensium, Expository Times, Kadmos, Notizie degli Scavi, Palestine Exploration Qly, Trans. Glasgow Univ. Oriental Soc., Scottish Jl of Theology, Studia Theologica, Theology, Vetus Testamentum, Zeitschrift für die Alttestamentliche Wissenschaft, etc. *Recreation:* alternative work. *Address:* 9/5 Mount Alvernia, Edinburgh EH16 6AW; Makkevet Bor, New Galloway, Castle Douglas DG7 3RN.

**JOHNSTONE, William Neill,** RDI 1989; Founder Chairman: Neill Johnstone Ltd, 1986–2009; Fabric Design Consultants International, 1988–2009; *b* 16 May 1938; *s* of Harry McCall Johnstone and Ethel Mary Neill; *m* 1st, (marr. diss.); two *d*; 2nd, 1991, Mara Lukic; one *s* one *d. Educ:* Forfar Acad.; Edinburgh Acad.; Univ. of Edinburgh; Scottish Coll. of Textiles; RCA. Designer, then Design Dir, R. G. Neill & Son, 1961–70; Man. Dir and Design Dir, Neill of Langholm, 1970–85; Design Dir, Illingworth Morris Gp and Co-ordinator of design training programme, 1982–85; Internat. Wool Secretariat Design Consultant, 1978–90. Chm., Confedn of British Wool Textiles Ltd Steering Cttee, 1982–85; Industrialist on Selection Panel, Designer Graduate Attachment Scheme, 1982–85. *Recreations:* climbing, hill walking, collecting Inuit carvings, painting.

**JOHNSTONE-BURT, Vice Adm. Charles Anthony, (Tony),** CB 2013; OBE 1997; DL; Master of HM Household, since 2013; *b* 1 Feb. 1958; *s* of Comdr Charles Leonard Johnstone-Burt, OBE, RN and Margaret Hilary Johnstone-Burt; *m* 1981, Rachel Ann Persson; three *s* two *d. Educ:* Wellington Coll.; Durham Univ. (BA Jt Hons Psychol. and Anthropol. 1980); US Naval War Coll., Rhode Is (MA Internat. Relns and Strategic Studies 1997; UK Res. Fellow). Chartered FCIPD 2002; CCMI 2012. HMS Active, Falklands War, 1982; helicopter pilot, Fleet Air Arm, and Anti-submarine Warfare Officer; CO HMS Brave, 1994–96; Captain 6th Frigate Sqdn and CO HMS Montrose, 2000–02; Cdre, BRNC, 2002–04; CO HMS Ocean, 2004–05; Dep. Comdr and COS, Jt Helicopter Comd, 2005–06; FO Scotland, England, Wales and NI and FO Reserves, 2006–08; Comdr, Jt Helicopter Comd, 2008–11; ISAF Dir of Counter Narcotics, Kabul, 2011; COS to Supreme Allied Comdr Transformation, 2011–13. Mem., Windsor Leadership Trust, 1999–. Mem., Royal Co. of Archers, 2010. Younger Brother, Trinity House, 2005–. Freeman: City of London, 1998; Haberdashers' Co., 1998 (Liveryman, 2015–); City of Glasgow, 2007; Mem., Incorporation of Wrights, Trades House, Glasgow, 2007. DL Dorset, 2016. *Recreations:* all sports, reading, hill walking, fly fishing, running, longbow archery. *Address:* Buckingham Palace, SW1A 1AA.

**JOICEY,** family name of **Baron Joicey**.

**JOICEY, 5th Baron** cr 1906, of Chester-le-Street, Co. Durham; **James Michael Joicey**; DL; Bt 1893; b 28 June 1953; s of 4th Baron and Elisabeth Marion Joicey, MBE (née Leslie Melville); S father, 1993; m 1984, Agnes Harriet Frances Mary, yr d of Rev. and Mrs W. M. D. Thompson; two s two d. Educ: Eton Coll.; Christ Church, Oxford. DL Northumberland, 2006. Heir: s Hon. William James Joicey, b 21 May 1990. Address: Etal Manor, Etal, Cornhill-on-Tweed TD12 4TL.

**JOICEY, Nicholas Beverley**, CB 2019; Director General, Finance, Department for Work and Pensions, since 2018; b Guisborough, 11 May 1970; s of Harold Beverley and Wendy Joicey. Educ: Wintringham Sch., Grimsby; Univ. of Bristol (BA Hons Hist.); Peterhouse, Cambridge (PhD 1996). Journalist, The Observer, 1995–96; HM Treasury: Asst Private Sec. to Chief Sec., 1996–98; Hd, Internat. Instns Br., 1998–99; Private Sec. and Speechwriter to Chancellor of the Exchequer, 1999–2001; Advr, UK Delegn to IMF and World Bank, Washington, 2001–03 (on secondment); Head: EU Policy Team, 2004–06; EU Coordination and Strategy, 2006–07; Dir, Europe, 2007–08; Dir, Internat., 2008–12; Dir Gen., Strategy, Internat. and Biosecurity, then Strategy, Internat. and EU Exit, later Strategy, Europe and Finance, DEFRA, 2014–18. Recreations: modern history, film. Address: Department for Work and Pensions, Caxton House, Tothill Street, SW1H 9NA.

**JOINER, Hon. Sarah Louise**; Deputy Chairman, Multiple Sclerosis Trust, since 2012 (Patron, 2007–12); Chairman of Trustees, Gardening for the Disabled Trust, 2009–17 (Trustee, since 2006); b London, 3 March 1960; d of late Kevin Gardner and of Baroness Gardner of Parkes, qv; m 1991, Timothy M. Joiner (marr. diss. 2003). Educ: City of London Sch. for Girls; Birkbeck, Univ. of London (CertHE 2013). Jun. Sec., Cons. Central Office, 1979; PA to Dir, Saatchi & Saatchi Garland Compton Ltd, 1979–86; PA to Chief Exec., C F Anderson & Son Ltd, 1986–89; Business Manager, S Thames RHA, 1991–94; Hd, Office of Chm., SE NHS Exec., 1994–2001; Hd, Office of Chm., NHS Appts Commn, 2001–05, Hd, Private Office for Dir of Develt, 2005–07, DoH. Lady Mayoress of Westminster, 2005–06. Mem., All Party Osteoporosis Gp, 1996–2000. Member: N Westminster Lay (Police) Visitors Panel, 1987–94; Bd of Visitors, HMP Wormwood Scrubs, 1995–98. Member: Westminster Youth Cttee, 1978–85; Mgt Cttee, Nat. Youth Agency, 1989–93. Various county rôles, Girl Guides Assoc., 1979–91. Mem., N London Regl Steering Cttee, MS Soc., 1997–2002. Member: Access Focus Gp, Royal Opera Hse, 1996–2000; Self-Help Panel, Thames TV Trust, 1985–86; Bd, Habinteg Housing Assoc., 2014–. Mem. Cttee, RHS, 2013– (Trustee, 2010–13). Chm., Cook Soc., 2009–10. Gov., St Edward's Primary Sch., London, 1984–90. Volunteer counsellor, St John and St Elizabeth Hospice, London, 1987–90. Recreations: gardening, the arts, entertaining at home, garden history.

**JOLL, James Anthony Boyd**, FSA; Chairman: Pearson Group Pension Trustee, since 1988; Advisory Board, White Cloud Capital Advisors, since 2009; b 6 Dec. 1936; s of late Cecil Joll, FRCS and Antonia (née Ramsden); m 1st, 1963, Thalia Gough (marr. diss. 1973); one s two d; 2nd, 1977, Lucilla Kingsbury (marr. diss. 2007); two s. Educ: Eton (Oppidan Scholar); Magdalen Coll., Oxford (BA 1st Class Hons PPE 1960/MA); Chelsea Coll. of Art. FSA 2000. 2nd Lieut, 4th Queen's Own Hussars, 1955–57. Editorial staff, Financial Times, 1961–68, Jt Ed., Lex column, 1965–68; N. M. Rothschild & Sons, 1968–80, Dir, 1970–80; Exec. Dir, 1980–96, Finance Dir, 1985–96, Pearson plc; Partner, Lazard Partners, 1984–95. Chairman: AIB Asset Mgt Hldgs, 1997–2004; Atrium Underwriting plc, 2006–07; Dep. Chm., Jarvis Hotels, 1990–2004; Director: The Economist Newspaper, 1995–99; Equitas Hldgs, 1996–2007. Chm., Museums and Galls Commn, 1996–2000; Mem., Urgent Issues Task Force, Accounting Standards Bd, 1991–95. Chairman: Sir Winston Churchill Archive Trust, 2000–10; S. J. Noble Trust, 2004–13. Trustee: Wallace Collection, 1999–2000; Design Museum, 1992–2005; Henry Moore Foundn, 2003–11; Royal Sch. of Needlework, 2006–11. Mem. Council, RCM, 2000–07. Robinson Medallist, V&A Museum, 2004. Recreations: painting, learning, the gothic revival. Address: White Cloud Capital Advisors, Henry Wood House, 2 Riding House Street, W1W 5BT. Club: Boodle's.

**JOLLEY, Ven. Dr Andrew John**; Archdeacon of Bradford, since 2016; b Nottingham, 21 March 1961; s of Dennis Jolley and Margaret Jolley; m 1992, Ricky Takes; one s one d. Educ: Loughborough Grammar Sch.; Univ. of Nottingham (BSc Mechanical Engrg 1983; BTh 1997; PhD 2006); Univ. of Warwick (MBA 1988); St John's Coll., Nottingham. MIMechE 1988. Project Manager, Ford Motor Co., 1983–87; Mgt Consultant, Deloitte Haskins and Sells, then Coopers and Lybrand, 1988–95; ordained deacon, 1998, priest, 1999; Asst Curate, St John's Church, Sparkhill, Birmingham, 1998–2002; Vicar, Aston and Nechells, 2002–16; Area Dean of Aston, 2005–12. Hd of Urban Ministry, New Wine, 2014–. Chair: Can Do 4:13, 2011–16; Sorted, 2017–. Mem. Council, St Hild Coll., 2017–; Dir, Fountains Ch, Bradford, 2019–. Trustee, Lee Abbey Small Missional Communities, 2009–. Publications: Growing Different Leaders: leadership in a multicultural church, 2015; contrib. Jl of Adult Theol Educn, Anvil, Voluntary Sector Rev. Recreations: cycling, ski-ing, cinema, walking, spectator sports. Address: 1 Selborne Grove, Bradford BD9 4NL. T: (01274) 405720. E: andy.jolley@leeds.anglican.org.

**JOLLIFFE**, family name of **Baron Hylton**.

**JOLLIFFE, Sir Anthony (Stuart)**, GBE 1982; Senior Partner, Cork Gully LLP, 2012–15; b Weymouth, Dorset, 12 Aug. 1938; s of late Robert and Vi Dorothea Jolliffe. Educ: Portchester Sch., Bournemouth. Qualified chartered accountant, 1964; articled to Morison Rutherford & Co.; commenced practice on own account in name of Kingston Jolliffe & Co., 1965, later, Jolliffe Cork & Co., Sen. Partner, 1976. Chairman: Jolliffe Internat.; CMS Ltd, 2005–; Dir, General Mediterranean Holdings. Chm., Stoke Mandeville NHS Trust, 1994–95. Alderman, Ward of Candlewick, 1975–84; Sheriff, City of London, 1980–81; Lord Mayor of London, 1982–83. Pres., London Chamber of Commerce, 1985–88. Treasurer: Britain in Europe, 1970–76; Relate, 1971–76. Pres., Soc. of Dorset Men, 1982–2011, Dep. Pres., 2011–. DL Dorset, 2006–13. KStJ 1983. Recreations: yachting, classic cars. Clubs: Garrick, City Livery (Pres., 1979–80), Saints and Sinners (Chm., 2011); Phyllis Court (Henley).

**JOLLIFFE, Maj.-Gen. David Shrimpton**, CB 2003; FRCP; Director General, Army Medical Services, 2000–03; b 20 March 1946; s of John Hedworth Jolliffe and Gwendoline Florence Angela Jolliffe (née Shrimpton); m 1969, Hilary Dickinson; two d. Educ: Ratcliffe Coll., Leicester; King's Coll. Hosp., London (MB). FRCP 1987. Regl MO, 22 Para Field Amb., 1971–73, 2 Para, 1973–74; Cons. Dermatologist, Queen Elizabeth Mil. Hosp., 1980–82; Consultant Advr in Dermatology to the Army, 1982–86; Commanding Officer: British Mil. Hosp., Hong Kong, 1986–89; Cambridge Mil. Hosp., Aldershot, 1993–94; COS, Army Medical Directorate, 1996–99; Comdr, Med. HQ, Land Command, 1999–2000. QHP 1999–2003. Hon. Med. Advr, Royal Commonwealth Ex-Services League, 2003–. Trustee: Hong Kong Locally Enlisted Personnel Trust, 2001– (Chm., 2001–11); Blind Veterans UK (formerly St Dunstan's), 2004–16; RBL, 2012–. Gov., Ratcliffe Coll., Leicester, 2001–08; Mem., Council and Ct, LSHTM, 2006–14 (Chairman: Audit Cttee, 2001–12; Ct, 2009–14). Mem., Yorks and Humber Veterans Adv. and Pensions Cttee, 2010–. Hon. Col, 207 (Manchester) Field Hosp. (V), 2003–09. Pres., Yorks Reg., Parachute Regtl Assoc., 2012–. Publications: contrib. papers on general and tropical dermatology to professional jls. Recreations: carpentry, computer technology. Address: Ness House, 75 Eastgate, Pickering, North Yorkshire YO18 7DY. E: red@pennswood.demon.co.uk.

**JOLLY, Baroness** cr 2010 (Life Peer), of Congdon's Shop in the County of Cornwall; **Judith Anne Jolly**; b Leamington Spa; m; two s. Educ: Univ. of Leeds; Univ. of Nottingham (PGCE). Teacher of Maths and IT, 1974–97; Chief of Staff to MEP for Cornwall, 1997–99; teacher of English with British Council Oman. Chm., Digital Services Cornwall CIC, 2009–13. Chm., Exec. Cttee, Lib Dems, Devon and Cornwall, 2007–10. A Baroness in Waiting (Govt Whip), 2013–15; Lib Dem spokesperson on Health, 2017–. Chm. Trustees, Hft, 2016–; Trustee, Orthopaedic Res. UK, 2019–. Address: House of Lords, SW1A 0PW.

**JOLLY, Sir (Arthur) Richard**, KCMG 2001; PhD; development economist; Hon. Professorial Fellow, Institute of Development Studies, University of Sussex; b 30 June 1934; s of late Arthur Jolly and Flora Doris Jolly (née Leaver); m 1963, Alison Bishop, PhD (d 2014); two s two d. Educ: Brighton Coll.; Magdalene Coll., Cambridge (BA 1956, MA 1959; Hon. Fellow, 2001); Yale Univ. (MA 1960, PhD 1966). Community Develt Officer, Baringo Dist, Kenya, 1957–59; Associate Chubb Fellow, Yale Univ., 1960–61; Res. Fellow, E Africa Inst. of Social Res., Makerere Coll., Uganda, 1963–64; Res. Officer, Dept of Applied Econs, Cambridge Univ., 1964–68 (seconded as Advr on Manpower to Govt of Zambia, 1964–66); Fellow, 1968–71, Professorial Fellow, 1971–81, Dir, 1972–81, Inst. of Develt Studies, Univ. of Sussex; Dep. Exec. Dir, Programmes, 1982–95, Actg Exec. Dir, 1995, UNICEF, NY; Special Advr to Adminr, UNDP, NY, 1996–2000; Co-Dir, UN Intellectual History Project, Graduate Center, City Univ., NY, 2000–10. Advr on Manpower Aid, ODM, 1968; Sen. Economist, Min. of Develt and Finance, Zambia, 1970; Advr to Parly Select Cttee on Overseas Aid and Develt, 1974–75; ILO Advr on Planning, Madagascar, 1975; Member: Triennial Rev. Gp, Commonwealth Fund for Tech. Co-operation, 1975–76; UK Council on Internat. Develt, 1974–78; UN Cttee for Develt Planning, 1978–81; Special Consultant on N-S Issues to Sec.-Gen., OECD, 1978; UN Sec.-Gen.'s Eminent Persons Gp Panel on Least Developed Countries, 2011; sometime member and chief of ILO and UN missions, and consultant to various governments and international organisations. Hon. Chairman: Water Supply and Sanitation Collaborative Council, 1997–2005 (Hon. Lifetime Patron, 2005); UNA-UK, 2001–05. Trustee, Oxfam, 2001–06. Pres., British Assoc. of Former UN Civil Servants, 2007–11. Sec., British Alpine Hannibal Expedn, 1959. Member: Founding Cttee, European Assoc. of Develt Insts, 1972–75; Governing Council, 1976–85, and N-S Round Table, SID, 1976– (Vice-Pres., 1982–85; Chm., N-S Round Table, 1988–96). Mem., Editorial Bd, World Development, 1973–90. Master, Curriers' Co., 1977–78. Hon. LittD E Anglia, 1988; Hon. DLitt Sussex, 1992; Hon. Dr Inst. of Social Studies, The Hague, 2007. Publications: (jtly) Cuba: the economic and social revolution, 1964; Planning Education for African Development, 1969; (ed) Education in Africa: research and action, 1969; (ed jtly) Third World Employment, 1973; (jtly) Redistribution with Growth, 1974 (trans. French 1977); (ed) Disarmament and World Development, 1978, 3rd edn 1986; (ed jtly) Recent Issues in World Development, 1981; (ed jtly) Rich Country Interests in Third World Development, 1982; (ed jtly) The Impact of World Recession on Children, 1984; (ed jtly) Adjustment with a Human Face, 1987 (trans. French 1987, Spanish 1987); (ed jtly) The UN and the Bretton Woods Institutions, 1995; (ed jtly) Human Development Report, annually 1996–2000 (trans. French, Spanish); (ed jtly) Development with a Human Face, 1998; (jtly) Ahead of the Curve, 2001; (ed) Jim Grant - UNICEF visionary, 2001; (jtly) UN Contributions to Development Thinking and Practice, 2004; (jtly) UN Ideas that Changed the World, 2009; (jtly) Be Outraged: there are alternatives, 2012; UNICEF: global governance that works, 2014; articles in professional and develt jls. Recreations: billiards, croquet, nearly missing trains and planes. Address: Institute of Development Studies, University of Sussex, Brighton, Sussex BN1 9RE. T: (01273) 606261. E: r.jolly@ids.ac.uk.

**JOLLY, James Falcon**; Editor-in-Chief, Gramophone, since 2006 (Editor, 1989–2005); freelance broadcaster and journalist; b 12 Feb. 1961; s of late Gordon Jolly, FRCOG and Enid Jolly; m 2006, Christopher Peter Davies. Educ: Pinewood Sch., Bourton; Bradfield Coll.; Univ. of Bristol (BA Hons); Univ. of Reading (MA). Asst Editor, Gramophone, 1985–88; Producer, 1988–89, Presenter, 2007–18, BBC Radio 3. Publications: contrib. British Music Yearbook, 1986–88, Good CD Guide, Gramophone, Independent, Le Monde de la Musique, New Grove Dictionary of Opera. Recreations: food, wine, travel, cinema, gardening. Address: Downs Farm Barn, Baunton, Cirencester, Glos GL7 7BB. T: (01285) 654865; Mark Allen Group, St Jude's Church, Dulwich Road, SE24 0PB.

**JOLLY, Michael Gordon**, CBE 2001; Director, Bluestone National Park Resort, Wales, 2009–13; b 21 Sept. 1952; s of Ron and Joy Jolly; m 1975, Julia Catherine Gordon Sharp; one s one d. Educ: Henley-on-Thames Grammar Sch. Marketing and other positions, Cadbury-Schweppes plc, 1972–83; Tussaud's Group: Head, Marketing, 1983–87; Bd Dir, 1987–91; Chief Operating Officer, 1991–94; CEO, 1994–2001; Chm., 1994–2001; Chief Exec., Penna Consulting plc, 2001–03; Chairman: Star Parks SA Europe, 2004–06; Park Holidays UK (formerly Cinque Ports Leisure Ltd), 2006–12. Comr, English Heritage, 2002–10. Trustee, Alnwick Garden Trust, 2009–12. Recreations: golf, the Arts.

**JOLLY, Sir Richard**; see Jolly, Sir A. R.

**JOLLY, Schona Kaur**; QC 2017. Educ: Magdalen Coll., Oxford (BA Juris.); Université Libre de Bruxelles (Licence spéciale en droit européen). Called to the Bar, Gray's Inn, 1999; in practice as a barrister, Cloisters Chambers, 1999–, specialising in discrimination, human rights and employment law. Chm., Bar Human Rights Cttee, 2019– (Jt Vice-Chm., 2015–18). Mem., Council, Justice, 2014–16; Trustee, ROLE UK, 2015–17. Publications: (jtly) Age Discrimination Handbook, 2006; (contrib.) Discrimination in Employment, 2013; articles in internat. news pubns. Address: Cloisters Chambers, 1 Pump Court, EC4Y 7AA. T: (020) 7827 4000.

**JONAH, Samuel Esson**, Hon. KBE 2003; Chairman, Jonah Capital; b 19 Nov. 1949; s of Thomas Jonah and Beatrice Sampson; m 1973, Theodora (marr. diss.); three s two d; m 2009, Giselle. Educ: Camborne Sch. of Mines (ACSM 1973); Imperial Coll. of Sci. and Technol. (MSc Mine Mgt). CEO, Ashanti Goldfields Co. Ltd, 1986–2005 (non-exec. Dir, AngloGold Ashanti, 2004–07). Exec. Chm., Equator Exploration Co., 2005–07; Director: Lonmin plc, 1992–2004; Anglo American Corp. of SA; Amplats; Standard Banking Gp. Member, International Advisory Council: Pres. of S Africa; Pres. of Ghana; Pres. of Nigeria; Member: Adv. Council of Pres. of African Develt Bank; Adv. Council, IFC; Global Compact Adv. Council of UN Sec.-Gen.; Togo Presidential Adv. Council; Global Adv. Council, Bank of America, 2013–; Co-Chm., World Econ. Forum, Durban, 2003. Vis. Prof. of Business, Univ. of Witwatersrand Business Sch. of Johannesburg. Trustee, Nelson Mandela Legacy Trust, UK. Hon. DSc Camborne Sch. of Mines and Univ. of Exeter, 1994. Lifetime Achievement Award, Mining Jl, 2004. Relevant publication: Sam Jonah and the Re-making of Ashanti, by A. A. Taylor. Publications: Mine Management into the 21st Century: perspective from Ashanti, 1993. Recreations: fishing, golfing. Address: 21B Drake Close, Airport Residential Area, Accra, Ghana. T: 202112003. E: sam.jonah@jonahcapital.com.

**JONAS, Christopher William**, CBE 1994; FRICS; quotidien documentary photographer, since 2015; President, Royal Institution of Chartered Surveyors, 1992–93; Chairman, Henderson International Income Trust plc, 2011–17; b 19 Aug. 1941; s of late Philip Griffith Jonas, MC and Kathleen Marjory Jonas (née Ellis); m 1st, 1968, Penny Barker (marr. diss. 1997); three s one d; 2nd, 2003, Dame Judith Mayhew (see Dame Judith Mayhew Jonas). Educ: Charterhouse; Coll. of Estate Management; London Business Sch. (Sloan

Fellow). TA Inns of Court Regt, 1959–66. Jones Lang Wootton, 1959–67; Drivers Jonas: Partner, 1967–82; Managing Partner, 1982–87; Sen. Partner, 1987–95. Property Adviser, Staffs County Council, 1982–2005. Director: SFA, 1988–91; BITC, 1999–2006; Railtrack Gp plc, 1994–2001; Canary Wharf Gp plc, 1994–2004; England Bd, Bank of Scotland, 1998–2000; Sunrise Senior (formerly Assisted) Living, 1998–2012; ECNlive (formerly Executive Channel Europe) Ltd, 2011–14; Chairman: Tate Modern develt, 1997–2000, and 2nd stage develt, 2006–16; Education Capital Finance plc, 2000–03; Glasgow Harbour Ltd, 2001–03; Henderson Global Property Cos Ltd, 2006–11; Sen. Advr, Lazard & Co., 2007–17; Board Member: PLA, 1985–99; British Rail Property Bd, 1991–94; BR, 1993–94. Founder, ProHelp, 1989; Mem., FEFC, 1992–98. Chm., Economics Research Associates, USA, 1987–93; Mem., Counselors of Real Estate, USA, (Gold Medal 2007). Dir, ENO, 1999–2007; Trustee, Westminster Abbey Pension Fund, 2001–; Chm. Trustees, Contemporary Art Soc., 2014–17. Governor: Charterhouse, 1995–2006; UCL, 1997–2005 (Vice-Chm., 2000–04); Chairman of Council: Roedean, 2004–11; Goldsmiths Univ. of London (formerly Goldsmiths Coll.), 2006–12. Second career as documentary photographer (www.cwjpix.org); everyday life photo-documentaries for Westminster Abbey, 2016, Westminster Sch., 2017 (publd as Ad Te Levavi, 2018), Metropolitan Police centenary of Women in the Met, 2018 (book publd, 2019), 45 Commando Royal Marines, 2018, Adam Internat. Chamber Fest., Nelson, NZ, 2019; exhibitions of photographs: Goldsmiths 2012; Tate Modern, 2013; RA, 2013; Garsington Opera, Wormsley, 2013; Nat. Churches Trust, 2013; Canary Wharf Gp Atrium, 2014; Peltz Gall., 2015; Bristol, 2017; Met series at City Hall, London, 2019. Liveryman, Clothworkers' Co. (Master, 2007–08). Hon. DSc De Montfort, 1997. *Recreations:* cathedral music, lieder, opera. *Address:* 25 Victoria Square, SW1W 0RB. *T:* (020) 7828 9977. *E:* cwj@kingslodge.com. *Club:* Queen's.
*See also* R. W. Jonas.

JONAS, Dame Judith M.; *see* Mayhew Jonas.

JONAS, Sir Peter, Kt 2000; CBE 1993; opera company and orchestra director; university lecturer; General Director (Staatsintendant), Bavarian State Opera, 1993–2006 (Hon. Life Member (Ehrenmitglied), 2006); *b* 14 Oct. 1946; *s* of late Walter Adolf Jonas and Hilda May Jonas; *m* 1st, 1989, Lucy (marr. diss. 2001), *d* of Christopher and Cecilia Hull; 2nd, 2012, Barbara, *d* of Eckhard and Karin Burgdorf. *Educ:* Worth School; Univ. of Sussex (BA Hons); Royal Northern Coll. of Music (LRAM; FRNCM 2000); Royal Coll. of Music (CAMS; Fellow, 1989); Eastman Sch. of Music, Univ. of Rochester, USA. Asst to Music Dir, 1974–76, Artistic Administrator, 1976–85, Chicago Symphony Orch.; Dir of Artistic Admin, Orchestral Assoc. of Chicago (Chicago Symph. Orch., Chicago Civic Orch., Chicago Symph. Chorus, Allied Arts Assoc., Orchestra Hall), 1977–85; Man. Dir, subseq. Gen. Dir, ENO, 1985–93. Member: Adv. Bd, Hypo-Vereinsbank, 1994–2005; Bd of Governors, Bayerische Rundfunk, 1999–2006; Adv. Bd, Actori GmbH Munich, 2004–; Chm., German Speaking Opera Intendants Conf., 2000–06; Lectr, Faculty, Univ. of St Gallen, Switzerland, 2003–; Lectr, Master's Prog., Univ. of Zürich, 2004–; Vis. Lectr, Bavarian Theatre Acad., Munich, 2006–14. Mem., Adv. Bd, Tech. Univ., Munich, 2006–12. Member: Bd of Management, Nat. Opera Studio, 1985–93; Council, RCM, 1988–95; Council, London Lighthouse, 1990–94; Supervisory Bd, City of Berlin Opera Trust, 2005–12; Supervisory Bd, Netherlands Nat. Opera and Ballet (formerly Netherlands Opera), Amsterdam, 2009–18; Governing Bd, Univ. of Lucerne, 2009–16; Kuratorium and Governing Bd, Wissenschaftszentrum für Sozialforschung, Berlin, 2015–. FRSA 1989. Fellow, Bavarian Acad. of Fine Arts, 2005; 50th Anniv. Fellow, Univ. of Sussex, 2012. Hon. DMus Sussex, 1994. Munich Prize for Culture, 2003; German-British Forum Award, 2006. Bavarian Constitutional Medal, 2001; Bayerische Verdienstorden, 2001, Maximiliansorden, 2008. *Publications:* (with Mark Elder and David Pountney) Power House, 1992; (jtly) Eliten und Demokratie, 1999; Wenn Musik der Liebe Nahrung ist, spielt weiter…, 2006. *Recreations:* cinema, old master paintings, cricket, long-distance hiking, Crystal Palace FC, epic TV series, Greek and Roman antiquities. *Address:* Scheuchzerstrasse 36, 8006 Zürich, Switzerland. *Clubs:* Athenæum; Surrey County Cricket.

JONAS, Richard Wheen, FRICS; Senior Partner, Cluttons, 1992–2003; *b* 10 April 1943; *s* of late Philip Griffith Jonas, MC and of Kathleen Marjory (*née* Ellis); *m* 1973, Bettina Banton; two *d*. *Educ:* Charterhouse; Royal Agricl Coll. Strutt & Parker, 1965–70; Carter Jonas, 1970–73; Cluttons, 1973–2003: Partner, 1978–2003. Dir, Babraham Bioscience Technologies Ltd, 2003–16. Mem. Council, Roedean Sch., 2000–05; Gov., Sutton's Hospital in Charterhouse, 2002–13. Liveryman, Clothworkers' Co., 1965– (Master, 2010). Gold Medal, RASE, 1967. *Recreations:* shooting, golf, ornithology.
*See also* C. W. Jonas.

JONES; *see* Allen-Jones.

JONES; *see* Armstrong-Jones, family name of Earl of Snowdon.

JONES; *see* Clement-Jones, family name of Baron Clement-Jones.

JONES; *see* Duncan-Jones.

JONES; *see* Garel-Jones.

JONES; *see* Griffith-Jones.

JONES; *see* Gwynne Jones, family name of Baron Chalfont.

JONES; *see* Idris Jones.

JONES; *see* Lloyd Jones and Lloyd-Jones.

JONES; *see* Neville-Jones.

JONES; *see* Owen-Jones.

JONES; *see* Rhys Jones.

JONES, family name of Barons Jones and Jones of Cheltenham.

JONES, Baron *cr* 2001 (Life Peer), of Deeside in the County of Clwyd; **Stephen Barry Jones**; PC 1999; Chancellor, Glyndŵr University, 2008–12; *b* 1937; *s* of late Stephen and Grace Jones, Mancot, Flintshire; *m* Janet Jones (*née* Davies); one *s*. MP (Lab): Flint East, 1970–83; Alyn and Deeside, 1983–2001. PPS to Rt Hon. Denis Healey, 1972–74; Parly Under-Sec. of State for Wales, 1974–79; Opposition spokesman on employment, 1980–83; Chief Opposition spokesman on Wales, 1983–87, 1988–92; Mem., Labour Shadow Cabinet, 1983–87 and 1988–92. Member: Speaker's Panel of Chairmen, 1993–2001; Prime Minister's Intelligence and Security Cttee, 1994–2001; Dep. Speaker, Westminster Hall, 2001–; Chm., Speaker's Adv. Cttee on political parties, 1999; Mem., Speaker's Cttee on Electoral Commn, 2001. Mem., WEU and Council of Europe, 1971–74. Member: Govs, Nat. Mus., Wales, 1992–; Court, Univ. of Wales, 1992–; Nat. Liby of Wales, 1992–; Bd, Clwyd Theatr Cymru, 2012–. Chm., St Asaph Diocesan Bd of Educn and Lifelong Learning, 2004–; President: Deeside Hosp., 2000–; Flintshire Br., Alzheimer's Soc., 2001–; Wrexham-Birkenhead Rail Users Assoc., 2001–; Chester and E Clwyd Advanced Motorists, 2003–; Arthritis Care Flintshire, 2006–; NE Wales Inst. for Higher Educn, 2007–08; Flintshire Neighbourhood Watch Assoc., 2008–; Deeside Industrial Park Forum, 2011–; Army Cadet Forces Assoc. Wales, 2012–; Sain Clwyd Sound, 2013–; N Wales Exporters' Council, 2014–; Training Ship Tuscan (Flintshire), 2014–; Vice Pres., Attend (League of Friends) UK, 2013–. Trustee, Bodelwyddan Castle Trust, 2008–. Patron: Gap Quay Nomads AFC, 1985–; Brain Injury Rehabilitation and Develt Learning Centre, 1990–; Welsh Assoc. of ME and CFS Support, 2011–; N Wales and Chester Neuro Centre, 2014–. A Dementia Champion Wales, 2013. Hon. Fellow: Gladstone Liby, 2000–; Bangor Univ., 2012. *Address:* House of Lords, SW1A 0PW.

JONES OF BIRMINGHAM, Baron *cr* 2007 (Life Peer), of Alvechurch and of Bromsgrove in the county of Worcestershire; **Digby Marritt Jones**, Kt 2005; broadcaster, business adviser and author; *b* 28 Oct. 1955; *s* of late Derek Alwyn Jones and of Bernice Joyce Jones; *m* 1990, Patricia Mary Moody. *Educ:* Alvechurch Primary Sch.; Bromsgrove Sch. (Foundn Scholar); UCL (LLB Hons 1977; Fellow, 2004). Midshipman, RN, 1974–77. Admitted Solicitor, 1980. Joined Edge & Ellison, Solicitors, 1978; articled clerk, 1978–80; Asst Solicitor, 1980–81; Associate, 1981–84; Partner, 1984–98; Head of Corporate, 1987; Dep. Sen. Partner, 1990–95; Sen. Partner, 1995–98; Vice-Chm., Corporate Finance, KPMG Business Advisors, 1998–99; Dir Gen., CBI, 2000–06; Minister of State, UK Trade and Investment, BERR and FCO, 2007–08; Business Ambassador, UK Trade and Investment, 2008–12. Mem., CRE, 2003–07. Senior Advr to Exec., Deloitte, Barclays Capital, JCB, 2006–07; Corporate Advr to Ford of Europe, 2006–07; Corporate Affairs Advr to Bucknall Austin Ltd, 2006–07; Special Advisor: Monitise plc (formerly Monitise Ltd), 2006–07 (Global Ambassador, 2011–14); Harvey Nash, 2009–17; Mem., Adv. Bd, Thales (UK) Ltd, 2006–07; Chairman: Internat. Business Adv. Bd, HSBC, 2009–11 (Sen. Advr, 2012); Internat. Business Adv. Bd, British Airways, 2011–12; Grove Industries Ltd, 2012–16 (Business Advr, 2009–11); Business Advr, Barberry Develts Ltd, 2009–14; Adviser: Birmingham Assay Office, 2009–18; Babcock Internat. Gp plc, 2010–18 (Chm., Emergency Services Bd, 2012–14); BP plc, 2013–15; G-Labs Ltd, 2015–17. Non-executive Director: Alba plc, 2004–07; Leicester Tigers Rugby Club plc, 2005–; Flybe plc, 2012–13; Spicers Ltd, 2012–14; Grafton Fields Ltd, 2013–16; Urica Ltd, 2014–18; Croft Property Develt Ltd, 2017–; Dep. Chm., Unipart Expert Practices, 2013–17; Chairman: Triumph Motorcycles Ltd, 2009–; Neutrino Concepts Ltd, 2009–15; SHP Ltd, 2014–16; Cell Therapy Ltd, 2015–18; On-Logistics Ltd, 2015–; Thatchers Cider Ltd, 2016–; ProBuild 360 Ltd, 2018–; Elonex, 2018–; Argentex LLP, 2019– (Chm., Adv. Bd, 2012–19). Chm., Tourism Alliance, 2001–05; Dir, VisitBritain, 2003–06. Dir, BITC, 2000–06; Mem., Nat. Learning and Skills Council, 2003–06. UK Skills Envoy, 2006–07. Corporate Ambassador: Jaguar Cars, 2009–17; JCB, 2009–15; Cancer Res. UK, 2010–17; Aon, 2014–; Ravenscroft Investment Advrs, 2015–16. Vice-Pres., UNICEF, 2002–06 (Fellow, 2006). Special Advr to the Duke of York, 2006–07 and 2009–10. Chm., Adv. Bd, Birmingham Univ. Business Sch., 2005–16. Trustee: Millennium Point, Birmingham, 2009–11; UK Community Foundn, 2014–15; Temple Grafton Village Hall Trust, 2014–18. Mem., RSC, 2012–. Patron: Ladies Fighting Breast Cancer, 2010–16; CBSO, 2014–. Chm. of Govs, Stratford-upon-Avon Coll. of Educn., 2015–18. Presenter, BBC TV series, The New Troubleshooter, 2014; winner, Celebrity Mastermind, 2010. CCMI. DUniv: UCE, 2002; Birmingham, 2002; Herts 2004; Hon. DLitt UMIST, 2003; Hon. Dr: London; Cardiff; Manchester; Middlesex; Sheffield Hallam; Aston; Hull; Warwick; Bradford; Thames Valley; Wolverhampton; QUB; Loughborough; Nottingham. *Publications:* Fixing Britain: the business of reshaping our nation, 2011; Fixing Business: making profitable business work for the good of all, 2017. *Recreations:* Rugby, ski-ing, military history, keeping fit by cycling (cycled from John O'Groats to Lands End in June 1998) and running (London Marathon in 5 hours 58 minutes and 26 seconds, 2005), theatre, Aston Villa FC. *Address:* House of Lords, SW1A 0PW.

JONES OF CHELTENHAM, Baron *cr* 2005 (Life Peer), of Cheltenham in the county of Gloucestershire; **Nigel David Jones**; *b* 30 March 1948; *m* 1981, Katy Grinnell; one *s* twin *d*. *Educ:* Prince Henry's Grammar Sch., Evesham. With Westminster Bank, 1965–67; computer programmer, ICL Computers, 1967–70; systems analyst, Vehicle and Gen. Insce, 1970–71; systems programmer, Atkins Consulting, 1971; systems designer and consultant, ICL Computers, 1971–92. Contested (L) Cheltenham, 1979. MP (Lib Dem) Cheltenham, 1992–2005. Lib Dem spokesman on England, local govt and housing, 1992–93, science and technology, 1993–99, consumer affairs, 1995–97, culture, media and sport, 1997–99, internat. devlt, 1999–2005. Mem., H of L Information Cttee, 2006–09. *Address:* House of Lords, SW1A 0PW.

JONES OF MOULSECOOMB, Baroness *cr* 2013 (Life Peer), of Moulsecoomb, in the County of East Sussex; **Jennifer, (Jenny), Helen Jones**; *b* 23 Dec. 1949; *d* of Percy and Christine Jones; *m* (marr. diss.); two *d*. *Educ:* Westlain Grammar Sch., Brighton; Inst. of Archaeol., Univ. of London (BSc Envmtl Archaeol.). Archaeologist, 1990–99; Financial Controller, Metro Inspection Services, 1999–2000. Mem. (Green), London Assembly, GLA, 2000–16; Dep. Mayor of London, 2003–04; Greater London Authority: Chm., Standards Cttee, 2000–03; London Mayor's Road Safety Ambassador, 2002–08; London Mayor's Green Transport Advr, 2006–08; Chm., Planning and Housing Cttee, 2009–10, 2011–12; Dep. Chm., Police and Crime Cttee, 2012–16; Mem., Metropolitan Police Authy, 2000–12; Chair: London Food, 2004–08; Mayor of London's Walking Adv. Panel (formerly Walking Forum), 2003–08. Mem. (Green), Southwark LBC, 2006–10. Contested (Green) Camberwell and Peckham, 2010; London Mayoral candidate, 2012. *Recreations:* yoga, cinema, family and friends. *Address:* House of Lords, SW1A 0PW. *W:* jennyjones.org.

JONES OF WHITCHURCH, Baroness *cr* 2006 (Life Peer), of Whitchurch in the County of South Glamorgan; **Margaret Beryl Jones**; Director of Policy and Public Affairs, UNISON, 1995–2006; *b* 22 May 1955; *d* of Bill and Audrey Jones. *Educ:* Whitchurch High Sch., Cardiff; Sussex Univ. (BA Hons Sociol. 1976). Regl Official, 1979–89, Nat. Officer, 1989–95, NUPE, later UNISON. Member, Board: Circle (formerly Circle Anglia), 2006–15; Waste and Resources Action Prog., 2007–15; Ombudsman Services, 2013–. Mem., Fitness to Practise Panel, GMC, 2006–13. Chm., RICS Ombudsman Scheme, 2007–13. Contested (Lab) Blaenau Gwent, 2005. *Address:* House of Lords, SW1A 0PW.

JONES, Adam M.; *see* Mars-Jones.

JONES, Adrianne Shirley, (Ann), CBE 2014 (MBE 1969); Women's Team Captain, Lawn Tennis Association, 1990–97; BBC tennis commentator, since 1970; *b* 17 Oct. 1938; *d* of Adrian Arthur Haydon and Doris (*née* Jordan); *m* 1962, Philip Frank Jones (*d* 1993); two *s* one *d*. *Educ:* King's Norton Grammar Sch., Birmingham. Finalist, World Table Tennis Championships: Ladies Doubles, 1954; Singles, Ladies Doubles, Mixed Doubles, 1957; Tennis Championships: Winner, French Open, 1961, 1966; Winner, Italian Open, 1966; Finalist, US, 1961, 1967; Wimbledon: Finalist, Ladies Singles, 1967; Winner, 1969; semi-finalist nine times. Chm., Women's Internat. Professional Tennis Council, 1977–84; Dir, European Ops, Women's Tennis Assoc., 1976–84. Member: Cttee of Mgt, Wimbledon Championships, 1991–2015; Bd, AELTC, 1991–2015 (Vice-Pres., 2015–; Chm., Order of Play Cttee, later Tennis Cttee, 2005–14); Internat. and Professional Tennis Bd, LTA, 1993–2004. *Publications:* Tackle Table Tennis My Way, 1957; Tennis: a game to love, 1970. *Recreations:* all sports, reading, music. *Address:* 101 Knightlow Road, Harborne, Birmingham B17 8PX. *T:* (0121) 247 5644. *Clubs:* All England Lawn Tennis; Edgbaston Priory.

**JONES, Alan;** consultant; Chief Executive, Somerset County Council, 2003–09; *b* 22 Sept. 1952; *s* of Thomas Jones and Ellen Jones; *m* 1974, Susan Fiona Dawn Lovell; two *d*. *Educ:* Univ. of Kent at Canterbury (BA 1st cl. Hons (Sociol.) 1974); Univ. of Liverpool (MCD 1st cl. 1976); Kent Coll. (Dip. Mgt Studies (Distn) 1982). Res. Asst, Merseyside MCC, 1975–76; Area Planning Officer, Maidstone BC, 1976–83; Prin. Planner, Gravesham BC, 1983–84; Develt Control Manager, Reading BC, 1984–86; Hd, Develt and Planning, Stevenage BC, 1986–88; Corporate Dir, Develt Services, Newbury DC, 1988–96; Chief Exec., Test Valley BC, 1996–2003; Interim Change Manager, Watford Council, 2002–03. Founder and Owner: Future Communities Ltd; AJAPlanning.com; Civic Cloud Ltd; non-exec. Dir, Public-i Gp Ltd, 2009–. *Recreations:* cycling, golf, canoeing, watercolour painting, photography, gardening.

**JONES, Alan David,** CVO 2016; OBE 1996; Founder Chairman, Team Excellence Ltd, 2004–15; *b* 16 June 1947; *s* of late Sydney Jones and Yvette Jones; *m* 1996, Juliet Louise Nance-Kivell Berrisford (marr. diss. 2015); one *s* three *d*. *Educ:* Holly Lodge Grammar Sch. for Boys; Staffordshire Coll. of Commerce. CTA 1968; FCCA 1973; FCILT (FCIT 1990); FCIPS 1992. Man. Dir, TNT UK Ltd, 1984–99; Gp Man. Dir, TNT Express, 1999–2003; Mem. Bd of Mgt, TPG NV, 1999–2003; Chief Exec., GSL, 2005–08. Founder Chairman, Midlands Excellence, 1996–2011; Chm., Investors in Excellence, 2011–18. Director: Ardent Productions Ltd, 1994–2002; British Quality Foundn, 1995–99; Services Bd, DTI, 2001–04. Member: Ministerial Adv. Bd for Defence Procurement, 1996–2006; Employment Tribunal System Taskforce, 2002–04. Special Prof., Nottingham Univ. Business Sch., 2003–09. Founder, Faculty of Freight, Chartered Inst. of Transport, 1990, Chm., 1990–91, CIT; Mem. Council, Inst. of Logistics, 1992–94. Mem., Eastern Reg. Council, 1977–78, Nat. Council, 1989–91, CBI; Dep. Chm., Coventry and Warwicks TEC, 1992–99. Freeman, City of London, 1994; Liveryman, Co. of Carmen, 1994–2012. Guardian, Assay Office, Birmingham, 1998–2000. Chm., In Kind Direct, 1997–2004; Chm., European, Mediterranean and Arab States Regl Adv. Bd, and Trustee, Duke of Edinburgh's Award Internat. Foundn, 2004–15 (World Fellow, 2013–). Mem. Ct, Warwick Univ., 1992–96. Invited Gov., European Foundn for Quality Mgt, 2000–09. CCMI (CIMgt 1993); CCQI (CIQA 2004). Chm., Upper Glyme Valley Br., W Oxfordshire Cons. Assoc., 2013–15. Hon. MA Coventry, 1996; Hon. DSc Aston, 2002; DUniv UCE 2004. *Recreations:* reading, walking, jazz, voluntary work. *Address:* Avenida Marginal 8023B, Hotel Atlantico Residences, Apartment 405, Monte Estoril 2765–249, Portugal.

**JONES, Sir Alan (Jeffrey),** Kt 2005; CEng; Chairman, Toyota Motor Manufacturing (UK) Ltd, 2003–06, now Chairman Emeritus; Executive Vice-President, Toyota Motor Engineering and Manufacturing Europe, 2003–06, now Senior Executive Adviser. *Educ:* Luton Coll. of Higher Educn. Manufacturing Dir, Vauxhall Motors, 1987–90; Dir of Manufacturing, 1990–96, Dep. Man. Dir, 1996–2001, Man. Dir, 2001–03, Toyota Motor Manufacturing (UK) Ltd. Chairman: SMMT Industry Forum, 2002 (Founder Mem. Bd, 1997); Sci., Engrg and Manufg Technologies Alliance, 2006–10, now Chm. Emeritus; Mem. Bd, EngineeringUK.

**JONES, Alan John P.;** see Pateman-Jones.

**JONES, Aled,** MBE 2013; singer; television and radio presenter; musical theatre performer; *b* 29 Dec. 1970; *s* of Derek Jones and Nêst Jones; *m* 2001, Claire Fossett; one *s* one *d*. *Educ:* Royal Acad. of Music (ARAM); Bristol Old Vic Theatre Sch. Presenter: Songs of Praise, Escape to the Country, Cash in the Attic, BBC TV; Daybreak, 2012–14, Weekend, 2014–, ITV1; various progs on BBC Radio 2, Radio 3, Radio Wales, Classic FM. Musical theatre lead roles: Joseph and the Amazing Technicolour Dreamcoat, 2001; Chitty Chitty Bang Bang, Cardiff, 2008; White Christmas, Plymouth and Manchester, 2009; Southampton, Dublin and Liverpool, 2011, Dominion Th., London, 2014. UK concert tour, 2013. Recordings include: Walking in the Air, 1985; 30 albums include: Aled Jones; Ave Maria; Hear My Prayer; Whenever God Shines His Light, 2002; From the Heart, 2002; Aled, 2002; Higher, 2003; Morning Has Broken, 2003; Sacred Songs, 2004; The Christmas Album, 2004; New Horizons, 2005; You Raise Me Up: the best of Aled Jones, 2006; Forever, 2011; The Heart of It All, 2014; One Voice, 2016; One Voice at Christmas, 2016; (with Russell Watson) In Harmony, 2018. *Publications:* Aled: the autobiography (with Darren Henley), 2005; Forty Favourite Hymns, 2009; Favourite Christmas Carols, 2010; My Story (autobiog.), 2013. *E:* wendi.batt@sky.com. *W:* www.twitter.com/realaled, www.facebook.com/realaledjones.

**JONES, Dr Aled Gruffydd;** Chief Executive and Librarian, National Library of Wales, 2013–15; *b* Bangor, Gwynedd, 9 Aug. 1955; *s* of John Edwin Jones and Ellen Jones; *m* 1994, Yasmin Ali. *Educ:* Ysgol Ardudwy, Harlech; Univ. of York (BA 1st Cl. Hist. 1977); Univ. of Warwick (MA 1978; PhD 1982). Aberystwyth University: Lectr, 1979–92; Sen. Lectr, 1992–95; Hd, Dept of Hist. and Welsh Hist., 1994–2002; Sir John Williams Prof. of Welsh Hist., 1995–2013; Dean, Faculty of Arts, 2004–05; Pro Vice-Chancellor, 2005–13. Prof. of Internat. History, Northwest Univ., Xi'an, China, 2016–17; Vis. Prof. of Cultural History, Panteion Univ. of Social and Political Sci., Athens, 2017–18. Joint Editor: Llafur, Jl of Welsh Labour Hist., 1985–92; Welsh Hist. Rev., 2003–11; Literary Dir (Modern), RHistS, 2000–04. *Publications:* Press, Politics and Society: a history of journalism in Wales, 1993; Powers of the Press: newspapers, power and the public in nineteenth-century England, 1996. *Recreations:* mountains, visual art. *Address:* Gwynfa, Heol y Llan, Llanbadarn Fawr, Aberystwyth, Ceredigion SY23 3SA. *T:* (01970) 612836. *E:* aledgjones@yahoo.co.uk.
See also R. M. Jones.

**JONES, Alexander Martin, (Sandy);** Executive President, Professional Golfers' Association, since 2017 (Chief Executive, 1991–2017); *b* 9 Dec. 1946; *s* of Henry and Catherine Jones. *Educ:* Stow Coll., Glasgow (qualif. Structl Engr 1968). Structural engineer/computer programmer, 1969–80; Scottish Regl Sec., PGA, 1980–91; Director: Ryder Cup, 1991–; Golf Foundn, 1991–2016 (Pres., 2016–); Chm., PGA of Europe, 1995–2017. CCMI 2006. DUniv Birmingham, 2009. *Recreations:* golf, football (watching). *Address:* Professional Golfers' Association, Centenary House, The Belfry, Sutton Coldfield, W Midlands B76 9PT. *T:* (01675) 470333. *E:* sandy.jones@pga.org.uk. *Clubs:* Caledonian; Loch Lomond Golf, Little Aston Golf, Royal and Ancient Golf (St Andrews).

**JONES, Allan William,** MBE 2000; Owner and Director, Allan Jones Energy and Climate Change, 2008–09 and since 2014; President and Chair, International Energy Advisory Council, since 2014; *b* 23 Dec. 1948; *s* of Leonard John William Jones and Joan Violet Jones; *m* 1989, Margaret Jane Drury (*née* Deeks); one *s* one *d*, and one step *s*. *Educ:* Guildford County Coll. of Technology (CNAA HNC Electrical and Electronic Engrg). IEng; MIET 1977, FIET 1990. From Design Engr to Sen. Manager, Dept of Mech. and Elec. Engrg, GLC, 1971–86; Sen. Manager, Dept of Bldg and Property Services, ILEA, 1986–89; Energy Services Manager, Woking BC, 1989–2004; Dir, Thamesway Ltd (Woking BC's energy and envmtl services co.), 1999–2004; Chief Develt Officer, then CEO, London Climate Change Agency, 2004–08; Chief Technologist, London Develt Agency, 2007–08; Dir and Trustee, Sustainable Envmt Foundn, 2007–09; Mem. Bd, Nat. Climate Change Adaption Res. Facility, 2011–13; Chief Develt Officer, Energy and Climate Change, City of Sydney, 2009–14. Director: London ESCO Ltd, 2006–08; Better Building Partnership, 2008. Mem., Seoul Internat. Energy Adv. Council, 2013–. Mem., Inst. for Strategic Develt, 2015–. *Publications:* Woking Park - fuel cell combined heat and power system, 2003; (contrib.) Moving London towards a Sustainable Low-carbon City, 2007; (contrib.) Cut Carbon, Grow Profits, 2007; (contrib.) Planning for Climate Change, 2009; (contrib.) City of Sydney Decentralised Water Master Plan, 2013; (contrib.) City of Sydney Decentralised Energy Master Plan - Renewable Energy, 2013; (contrib.) City of Sydney Decentralised Energy Master Plan - Advanced Waste Treatment, 2014; (contrib.) One Less Nuclear Power Plant: reframing urban energy policy - challenges and opportunities in the city Seoul, 2017; numerous papers incl. for IEE, IMechE, CIBSE, Combined Heat and Power Assoc., Fuel Cell Europe, Renewable Power Assoc., Connecticut Clean Energy Fund, Forum for the Future, Parly Renewable and Sustainable Energy and Warm Homes Gps, London Hydrogen Partnership, Australian Prime Minister's Task Force on Energy Efficiency, NSW Govt. *Recreations:* nature, the environment, walking, photography, the family.

**JONES, Allen,** RA 1986 (ARA 1981); artist; *b* 1 Sept. 1937; *s* of William Jones and Madeline Jones (*née* Aveson); *m* 1st, 1964, Janet Bowen (marr. diss. 1978); two *d*; 2nd, 1994, Deirdre Morrow. *Educ:* Ealing Grammar Sch. for Boys; Hornsey Sch. of Art (NDD; ATD); Royal Coll. of Art. Teacher of Lithography, Croydon Coll. of Art, 1961–63; Teacher of Painting, Chelsea Sch. of Art, 1966–68; Tamarind Fellow in Lithography, Los Angeles, 1968; Guest Professor: Hochschule für Bildenden Kunst, Hamburg, 1968–70; Univs of S Florida, 1970, Calif at Irvine, 1973, Los Angeles, 1977; Hochschule für Kunst Berlin, 1983; has travelled extensively. Sec., Young Contemporaries exhibn, London, 1961. First internat. exhibn, Paris Biennale, 1961 (Prix des Jeunes Artistes); first professional exhibn (with Howard Hodgkin), Two Painters, ICA, 1962; first UK mus. exhibn, Decade of Painting and Sculpture, Tate Gall., 1964; *museum and group exhibitions* in UK and abroad include: New Generation, Whitechapel, 1964; London, The New Scene, Minneapolis, 1965; British Drawing/New Generation, NY, 1967; Documenta IV, Kassel, 1968; Pop Art Redefined, Hayward Gall., 1969; British Painting and Sculpture, Washington, 1970; Metamorphosis of Object, Brussels, and tour, 1971; Seibu, Tokyo, 1974; Hyperealist/Realistes, Paris, 1974; Arte Inglese Oggi, Milan, 1976; El color en la pintura británica, British Council S American tour, 1977; British Painting 1952–77, Royal Academy, 1977; Arts Council sponsored exhibn tour, UK, 1978, Wales, 1992; British Watercolours, British Council tour, China, 1982; The Folding Image, Washington and Yale, 1984; Pop Art 1955–1970, NY, then Aust. tour, 1985; 40 Years of Modern Art, Tate Gall., 1986; British Art in the Twentieth Century, Royal Academy, then Stuttgart, 1987; Pop Art, Tokyo, 1987; Picturing People, British Council tour, Hong Kong, Singapore, Kuala Lumpur, 1990; New Acquisitions, Kunstmus., Dusseldorf, 1990; Seoul Internat. Art Fest., 1991; BM, 1991, 1997; Pop Art, Royal Academy, 1991, then Cologne, Madrid and Montreal, 1992; From Bacon to Now, Florence; Nat. Portrait Gall., 1994; Centre Georges Pompidou, Paris, 1995; Treasure Island, Gulbenkian Foundn, Lisbon, 1997; The Pop '60s, Centro Cultural de Belém, Lisbon, 1997; Pop Impressions Europe/USA, MoMA NY, 1999; Pop Art: US/UK Connections 1956–1966, Menil Foundn, Houston, 2001; Les années pop, Centre Georges Pompidou, Paris, 2001; Transition: the London art scene in the Fifties, Barbican, 2002; Out of Line: drawings from the Arts Council collection, 2002; Den Haag Sculptuur, 2002; Blast to Freeze, Wolfsburg, 2002; Thinking Big: concepts for 21st century British Sculpture, Peggy Guggenheim Collection, Venice, 2002; Phantom der Lust, Stadtmus., Graz, 2002; Mike Kelley - The Uncanny, Tate Liverpool, 2004; Art and the Sixties: This Was Tomorrow, Tate Britain, 2004 and Birmingham Mus. and Art Gall., 2004–05; Pop Art Portraits, NPG, 2007; Gagosian Gall., London, 2007, 2010; Kunsthalle Vienna, 2007–08; Raue, 2008; Grand Théâtre, Angers, 2008; Tate Liverpool, 2009; Musée D'Orsay, Paris, 2009–10; Samuel Freeman Gall., Los Angeles, 2009; Crash, Gagosian Gall., 2010; 60's Design, Möbelmuseum, Vienna, 2012; Glam, Tate Liverpool, 2012; You Inspire Me, Wolverhampton Art Gall. and Cartwright Hall, Bradford, 2012; Pop to Popism, Art Gall. of NSW, Sydney, 2012; Pop Art Design, Vitra Design Mus., Germany, 2012; Louisiana MOMA, Denmark, 2013; Moderna Museet, Stockholm, 2013; Oltre l'Informale verso la Pop Art, Guggenheim Collection, Vercelli, 2013; Pop Culture, Mana Fine Arts, Jersey City, 2013; Pop Art Myth, Museo Thyssen-Bornemissza, Madrid, 2014; The Wish List, London Design Fest., V&A Mus., 2014; The Artist's Eye, LWL-Museum für Kunst und Kultur, Münster, 2014; Ludwig Goes Pop, Museum Ludwig, Cologne, 2014; Pop Europe!, Wolverhampton Art Gall., 2014–15; Hyperrealistic Sculptures, Institut for Kulturaustausch (touring), Nat. Gall. of Australia, Kunsthal Rotterdam, Arken Copenhagen, 2017–18; exhibited annually at Royal Acad., 1981–; *one-man exhibitions* include: Arthur Tooth and Sons, London, 1963, 1964, 1967, 1970; Richard Feigen Gall., NY, Chicago and LA, 1964, 1965, 1970; Marlborough Fine Art, London, 1972, 2015; Arts Council sponsored exhibn tour, UK, 1974; Waddington Galls, London, 1976, 1980, 1982, 1983, 1985, 1993; James Corcoran Gall., LA, 1977, 1987; UCLA Art Galls, LA, 1977; Graphic Retrospective 1958–78, ICA, 1978; first Retrospective of Painting, 1959–79, Walker Art Gall., Liverpool, and tour of England and Germany, 1979; Thorden Wetterling, Gothenburg, 1983; Gall. Kammer, Hamburg, 1983, 1984; Gall. Wentzel, Cologne (sculpture), 1984; Gall. Patrice Trigano, Paris, 1985, 1986, 1989, 1998; Gall. Kaj Forsblom, Helsinki, 1985, 1999; Gall. Hete Hunermann, Dusseldorf, 1987, 1994; Charles Cowles Gall., NY, 1988; Heland Wetterling Gall., Stockholm, 1989; Gall. Wentzel, Cologne, 1992; Gall. Punto, Valencia, 1992; Gall. Levy, Hamburg and Madrid, 1993, 1995, 1997, 1999, 2003; Galerie Hilger, Vienna, 2004; Galerie Terminus, Munich, 2004, 2010; Print Retrospective, Barbican Centre and tour, 1995–98; Kunsthalle, Darmstadt, 1996; Galeria Civica, Modena, 1996; Thomas Gibson Fine Art, London, 1997; Trussardi, Milan, 1998; Ars Nova Mus. of Contemp. Art, Turku, 1999; Summerstage (sculpture), Vienna, 1999; Gall. d'Arte Maggiore, Bologna, 1999; Palazzo dei Sette, Orvieto, 2002; Norddeutschen Landesbank, Hanover, 2002; Landeshauptstadt, Schwerin, 2003; Galerie Trigano, Paris, 2006; Galerie Levy, Hamburg, 2006; Lorenzelli Arte, Milan, 2010; Wetterling Gall., Stockholm and Gothenburg, 2011–12; Off The Wall, Tübingen, Chemnitz and Völklinger Hutte, Ruhr, 2012–13; Galerie Terminus, 2014; Kunsthaus Hannover, 2014; Royal Acad., 2014–15; Gibson Fine Arts, 2014; Galerie Forsblom, Helsinki, 2014; Colour Matters, Marlborough Gall., 2015; Baur au Lac, Zurich, 2015; Galerie Gmurzynska, St Moritz, 2015; Maitresse, Michael Werner, London, 2016, New York, 2016, Galerie Levy, Hamburg, 2016, Galerie Hilger, Vienna, 2017; 'Allen Jones: Thrill Me' prints from 1959–2007, Sims Reed Gall., London, 2017; 80 Not Out, Wetterling Gall., Stockholm, 2017; Galerie Levy, Hamburg, 2018; Bystander, Marlborough Contemp., NY, 2018; Sign Lang., Galerie Levy, Hamburg, 2019, Marlborough, London, 2019; *dedicated rooms:* RA Summer Exhibn, 2002; paintings and drawings, Tate Britain, 2007–08; water colours, Royal Acad., 2007–08; Galeria Prates, Lisbon, 2007; Alan Cristea Gall., London, 2007; Marlborough Fine Art, London, 2008; Galerie Hilger, Vienna, 2008; *murals and sculptures for public places* include: Fogal, Basel and Zurich; Liverpool Garden Fest., 1984; Citicorp/Canadian Nat. Bank, London Bridge City, 1987; Milton Keynes, 1990; BAA, Heathrow, 1990; Ivy Restaurant, London, 1990; Chelsea/Westminster Hosp., 1993; LDDC, 1994; Swire Properties, Hong Kong, 1997; Sculpture at Goodwood, 1998; Chatsworth House, 2000; GlaxoSmithKline, London, 2001; Swire Properties, Hong Kong, 2002; Yuzi Paradise Sculpture Parks, Guilin and Shanghai, China, 2006; Greenwich Peninsula, London, 2019; television and stage sets include: O Calcutta!, for Kenneth Tynan, London and Europe, 1970; Manner Wir Kommen, WDR, Cologne, 1970; Understanding Opera, LWT, 1988; Cinema/Eric Satie, for Ballet Rambert, 1989; Signed in Red, for Royal Ballet, 1996. Television films have been made on his work. Trustee, British Mus., 1990–99. Hon. DArts Southampton Solent, 2007. *Publications:* Allen Jones Figures, 1969; Allen Jones Projects, 1971; Waitress, 1972; Sheer Magic, 1979, UK 1980; Allen Jones, 1993; Allen Jones Prints, 1995; Allen Jones, 1997; Allen Jones Works, 2005; articles in various jls. *Recreation:* gardening. *Address:* 41 Charterhouse Square, EC1M 6EA. *E:* aj@allenjonestheartist.com.

**JONES, Alun;** *see* Jones, R. A.

**JONES, Dr Alun Denry Wynn,** OBE 2001; FInstP; Chief Executive, Institute of Physics, 1990–2002; *b* 13 Nov. 1939; *s* of Thomas D. and Ray Jones; *m* 1964, Ann Edwards; two *d.* *Educ:* Amman Valley Grammar Sch.; Christ Church, Oxford (MA, DPhil). FInstP 1973; CSci 2004–10. Sen. Student, Commission for Exhibn of 1851, 1964–66; Sen. Research Fellow, UKAEA, 1966–67; Lockheed Missiles and Space Co., California, 1967–70; Tutor, Open Univ., 1971–82; joined Macmillan and Co., Publishers, 1971; Dep. Editor, Nature, 1972–73; British Steel Corp., 1974–77; British Steel Overseas Services, 1977–81; Asst Dir, Technical Change Centre, 1982–85; Dep. Dir, 1986–87, Dir, 1987–90, Wolfson Foundn. British Association for Advancement of Science, later British Science Association: Sec. of working party on social concern and biological advances, 1972–74; Mem., Section X Cttee, 1981–92; Council Mem., 1999–2005; Mem., Exec. Cttee, 2001–05; Mem., Audit Cttee, 2005–14. British Library: Adv. Council, 1983–85; Document Supply Centre Adv. Cttee, 1986–89; Mem. Council, Nat. Library of Wales, 1987–94 (Gov., 1986–94). Dir, Sci. Council (formerly Council for Sci. and Technol. Insts), 1990–2002 (Chair, Registration Authority, 2005–09); Mem. Council, Assoc. of Schs' Sci., Engrg & Technol. (formerly Standing Conf. on Schs' Sci. & Technol.), 1992–2000 (Dep. Chm., 1996–2000). Gov., 1990–92 and 2002–05, Council Mem., 2002–05, UCW, Aberystwyth; Governor: City Univ., 1991–2001; Sir William Perkins's Sch., Chertsey, 2002–12 (Chair of Govs, 2005–12). Fellow, Univ. of Wales, Aberystwyth, 2000. *Publications:* (with W. F. Bodmer) Our Future Inheritance: choice or chance, 1974. *Recreations:* gardening, theatre, cricket. *Address:* 4 Wheatsheaf Close, Woking, Surrey GU21 4BP.

**JONES, Alun Ffred;** Member (Plaid Cymru) Arfon, National Assembly for Wales, 2007–16 (Caernarfon, 2003–07); *b* 29 Oct. 1949; *s* of Rev. Gerallt and Elizabeth Jane Jones; *m* 1981, Alwen Roberts (*d* 2005); two *s* one *d. Educ:* University Coll. of N Wales, Bangor (BA). Teacher: Deeside High Sch., 1971–75; Alun High Sch., Mold, 1975–79 (Head of Dept); TV journalist, 1979–81; TV director/producer, 1981–2003. Member: Arfon Borough DC, 1992–96; Gwynedd Council, 1996–2004; Leader, Gwynedd UA, 1996–2003. National Assembly for Wales: Minister for Heritage, 2008–11; Chairman: Envmt, Agric. and Planning Cttee, 2003–07; Envmt and Sustainability Cttee, 2014–16.

**JONES, Alun Rhys;** Co-Founder and Director, Dow Jones Architects, since 2000; *b* Caerphilly, 15 Dec. 1966; *s* of Brynmor Jones and Ann Jones; *m* 1996, Elizabeth Clare, (Biba), Dow, *qv*; one *s* two *d. Educ:* St Martin's Sch., Caerphilly; Univ. of Bath (BSc 1st Cl. Hons 1989; MPhil 1991); Darwin Coll., Cambridge (DipArch 1992). ARB 1993. Project Architect: Evans and Shalev Architects, 1993–95; Caruso St John Architects, 1995–2000. Projects include: Christ Church Spitalfields, 2015; Garden Mus., 2017; St Mary Magdalene, Paddington, 2018; Maggie's Centre, Cardiff, 2018. Diploma Studio Master: Univ. of Bath, 1994–95; AA, 1995–96; London Metropolitan Univ., 2007–13; Sen. Lectr, Kingston Univ., 2000–03; external examiner: Univ. of Glasgow, 2011–14; Univ. of Leicester, 2014–17; UEL, 2017–20; Dublin Inst. of Technol., 2019–. Mem., South Downs Nat. Park Design Rev. Panel, 2012–. *Recreations:* art, theatre, cinema, opera, cycling, gardening, walking, food, music. *Address:* Dow Jones Architects, 10 Station Parade, Balham High Road, SW12 9AZ. *T:* (020) 8675 2544. *E:* alun@dowjonesarchitects.com.

**JONES, Alun Selwyn;** Principal, Chetham's School of Music, Manchester, since 2016; *b* Mid-Glamorgan, 23 May 1961; *s* of Selwyn and Mary Jones; *m* 1984, Judith Gilpin; one *d. Educ:* Bryntirion Comprehensive Sch., Bridgend; Royal Welsh Coll. of Music and Drama (Licentiate). Dir of Vocal Studies, Cathedral Sch., Llandaff, 1983–91; Dir of Studies, Music Master and Choirmaster, Howell's Sch., 1992–97; Dep. Headmaster, St Mary's Wantage, 1997–2001; Principal, St Gabriel's Sch., Newbury, 2001–16. Team Inspector, ISI, 2002–. Pres., GSA, 2015. *Recreations:* adjudicating, speeches, presentations, family, good food and wine. *Address:* Chetham's School of Music, Long Millgate, Manchester M3 1SB. *T:* (0161) 838 7214. *E:* alunjones@chethams.com.

**JONES, Ven. Andrew David W.;** *see* Wooding Jones.

**JONES, Andrew Hanson;** MP (C) Harrogate and Knaresborough, since 2010; *b* Leeds, 28 Nov. 1963; *s* of Richard and Jean Jones. *Educ:* Bradford Grammar Sch.; Leeds Univ. (BA English 1985). Marketing Manager: Kingfisher plc, 1985–88, 1996–98; Going Places, 1989–96; Account Dir, M&C Saatchi, 1998–2000; The Mktg Store, Leeds, 2000–05; Mktg consultant, 2005–10, incl. Bettys and Taylors of Harrogate, 2006–08. Mem. (C) Harrogate BC, 2003–11 (Cabinet Mem., Finance and Resources, 2006–10). Contested (C) Harrogate and Knaresborough, 2001. Parly Under-Sec. of State, DfT, 2015–17; Exchequer Sec. to HM Treasury, 2017–18; Parly Under-Sec. of State, DfT, 2018–19. Member: Regulatory Reform Select Cttee, 2010–15; Public Accounts Cttee, 2017–. Apprenticeship Ambassador, 2012–15. Chm., Bow Gp, 1999–2000. *Recreations:* cricket, walking. *Address:* 57 East Parade, Harrogate, N Yorks HG1 5LQ. *T:* (01423) 529614. *E:* andrew.jones.mp@parliament.uk. *Clubs:* Carlton, MCC; Yorkshire CC.

**JONES, Prof. Andrew Malcolm,** PhD; FRGS; Professor of Economic Geography, since 2012, and Vice-President (formerly Pro-Vice Chancellor) for Research and Enterprise, since 2016, City, University of London (formerly City University London) (Dean, School of Art and Social Sciences, 2012–16); *b* Chester, 3 Nov. 1973; *s* of Radleigh and Pauline Jones; *m* 2011, Fay Sullivan; two *d. Educ:* King's Sch., Chester; St John's Coll., Cambridge (BA Geog. 1995; PhD Geog. 2001); Bristol Univ. (MSc Society and Space); Inst. of Educn, Univ. of London (Postgrad. DipEd). Birkbeck College, University of London: Lectr, 2000–06; Hd, Dept of Geog., Envmt and Develt Studies, 2006–12. Mem. (Lab), Hammersmith and Fulham LBC, 2002–06 and 2010– (Cabinet Mem. for Economy and Arts, 2014–). Contested (Lab) Eastbourne, 2005. FAcSS (AcSS 2011); FRSA 2015. *Publications:* Management Consultancy and Banking in an Era of Globalization, 2003; Dictionary of Globalization, 2006; (ed with N. Coe) The Economic Geography of the UK, 2010; Globalization: key thinkers, 2010; Human Geography: the basics, 2012; (ed jtly) Services and the Green Economy, 2016. *Recreations:* politics, ski-ing, rowing coach. *Address:* City, University of London, Northampton Square, EC1V 0HB. *T:* (020) 7040 3123. *E:* andrew.jones@city.ac.uk.

**JONES, Angela;** *see* Jones, S. A. M.

**JONES, Ann;** *see* Jones, Adrianne S.

**JONES, Ann;** Member (Lab) Vale of Clwyd, National Assembly for Wales, since 1999; *b* 4 Nov. 1953; *d* of Charles and Helen Sadler; *m* 1973, Adrian Jones; two *c. Educ:* Rhyl Grammar, then High, Sch. Fire Service Emergency Call Operator, 1976–99. Nat. Official, Fire Brigades Union, 1982–99. Member (Lab): Rhyl Town Council, 1991–99 (Mayor of Rhyl, 1996–97); Denbighshire CC, 1995–99 (Lab spokesman on educn, 1995–98). Mem., N Wales Fire Authy, 1995–99. National Assembly for Wales: Dep. Presiding Officer, 2016–; Chm., Lab Mems, 1999–2000; Member: Econ. Develt Cttee, 1999–2003; N Wales Regl Cttee, 1999–2007; Health and Social Services Cttee, 2000–03; Finance Cttee, 2011–16; Chair: Equality of Opportunity Cttee, 2007–11; Communities, Equality and Local Govt Cttee, 2011–13; Assembly Labour Gp, 2011–; Children, Young People and Educn Cttee, 2013–16. *Address:* The Hub, 69–75 Wellington Road, Rhyl LL18 1BE. *T:* (01745) 332813.

**JONES, (Ann) Camilla;** *see* Toulmin, A. C.

**JONES, Anna Louise;** *see* Bradley, A. L.

**JONES, Prof. Anne;** Professor of Lifelong Learning, Brunel University, 1995–2001, now Professor Emeritus; *b* 8 April 1935; *d* of Sydney Joseph and Hilda Pickard; *m* 1958, C. Gareth Jones (marr. diss. 1989); one *s* one *d* (and one *d* decd). *Educ:* Harrow Weald County Sch.; Westfield Coll., London (BA; Fellow, QMW, 1992); DipSoc, PGCE London. Assistant Mistress: Malvern Girls' Coll., 1957–58; Godolphin and Latymer Sch., 1958–62 (Hd of Sixth Form); Dulwich Coll., 1964; Sch. Counsellor, Mayfield Comprehensive Sch., 1965–71; Dep. Hd, Thomas Calton Sch., 1971–74; Head: Vauxhall Manor Sch., 1974–81; Cranford Community Sch., 1981–87; Under Sec. (Dir of Educn), Dept of Employment, 1987–91; management consultant, 1991–93; Brunel University: Prof. of Continuing Educn, 1991–97; Dir of Contg Educn, 1991–93; Hd of Dept of Contg Educn, 1993–97; Dir, Centre for Lifelong Learning, 1995–2001; Mem. of Ct, 2001–; Founder and Man. Dir, Lifelong Learning Systems Ltd, 2000–07. Vis. Prof. of Educn, Sheffield Univ., 1989–91. Chm., W London Area Manpower Bd, Manpower Services Commn, 1983–87. Chairman: SHA, 1986; Parents in a Learning Soc., RSA, 1992–95. Director: CRAC, 1983–94; Grubb Inst. of Behavioural Studies, 1987–94; TVEI, 1987–95. Occasional Mem., Selection Panel, Cabinet Office, 1993–. Advr, European Trng Foundn, 1995–2002. Ind. Lay Chair, Complaints, NHS, 1996–2003. Member Council: QMW, 1992–2002; W London Inst. of Higher Educn, 1991–95; NICEC, 1991–95. Chm., Boathouse Reach Mgt, 2005–10. Gov., Abbey Sch., Reading, 2004–12. Trustee: The Westfield Trust, 1992–2010; Menerva Educnl Trust, 1993–2004 (Chm., 1993–99). FRSA 1984 (Mem. Council, 1986–94); FCMI (FIMgt 1992) (Chm., Reading Br., 2004–08); FICPD 1998. Hon. FCP 1990. *Publications:* School Counselling in Practice, 1970; Counselling Adolescents in School, 1977, 2nd edn as Counselling Adolescents, School and After, 1984; Leadership for Tomorrow's Schools, 1987; The Education Roundabout, 2015; (with Jan Marsh and A. G. Watts): Male and Female, 1974, 2nd edn 1982; Living Choices, 1976; Time to Spare, 1980; contribs to various books. *Recreations:* travel, boating, gardening, theatre, opera, singing in Henley Choral Society (Chm., 2005–08). *Address:* 8 Boathouse Reach, Henley-on-Thames, Oxfordshire RG9 1TJ. *T:* (01491) 578672. *E:* annepickardjones@googlemail.com. *Club:* Phyllis Court (Henley-on-Thames) (Dir, 2009–15).

**JONES, Prof. Anthony Edward,** CBE 2003; FRCA; President, School of the Art Institute of Chicago, 1986–92 and 1996–2012, now Chancellor and President Emeritus (Co-Chief Executive Officer, Corporation of the Art Institute of Chicago, 1996–2012); President, Kansas City Art Institute, since 2015 (Interim President, 2014–15); *b* 3 Aug. 1944; *s* of late Edward and Violet Jones; *m* 1st, 1972, Gwen Brandt (marr. diss. 1978); one *s*; 2nd, 1989, Patricia Jon Carroll. *Educ:* Goldsmiths' Coll., Univ. of London; Newport Coll. of Art, Newport (DipAD, BA); Tulane Univ., New Orleans (MFA). Artist-in-Residence, Loyola Univ., 1967–68; Teaching Fellow, Gloucester Coll. of Art, Cheltenham, 1968–69; Sen. Lectr and Dep. Head of Sculpture, Glasgow Sch. of Art, 1969–72; Chm., Dept of Art and Art Hist., Texas Christian Univ., 1972–80; Dir, Glasgow Sch. of Art, 1980–86 (Hon. Vice-Chm. of Govs, 2009); Rector, Royal Coll. of Art, 1992–96. Fulbright Scholar, USA, 1966–68. Hon. Prof., Univ. of Wales, 2000; Hon. Dir, Osaka Univ. of the Arts, 2002. Exhibn, Liberty Style, Japan tour, 1999–2000, and catalogue, 1999; Exhibn, Painting the Dragon, Nat. Mus. of Wales, 2000 (presenter, BBC TV series, 2001). Chm., James Dyson America Foundn, 2011–; Co-Chm., Amer. Friends of RCA. FRCA 1993; FRSA 1994; Hon. AIA 1991; Hon. Fellow, Univ. of Wales, 2012. Hon. DFA Memphis Coll. of Art, 2002; Hon. Dr: Maryland Inst., 2009; Art Inst. of Chicago, 2011; LLD Lincoln, 2008; DLitt Glasgow, 2010. Newbery Medal, Glasgow Univ., 1986; US Nat. Council of Art Administrators Award, 2001; Austrian Cross of Honour for Sci. and the Arts, 2002. *Publications:* Chapel Architecture in the Merthyr Valley, 1964; Welsh Chapels (Capeli Cymru), 1984, 1996; Charles Rennie Mackintosh, 1990; Painting the Dragon, 2000; Living in Wales: David Hurn, 2003; Archibald Knox (essays), 2003; Robert Stewart Design (essays), 2003. *Recreation:* travel, reluctantly! *Address:* Kansas City Art Institute, 4415 Warwick Boulevard, MO 64111–1820, USA.

**JONES, His Honour Anthony Graham Hume;** a Circuit Judge, 1993–2015; Deputy Senior Judge, Sovereign Base Areas, Cyprus, 1999–2015; *b* 16 Aug. 1942; *s* of Rt Hon. Sir Edward Jones, PC and Margaret Anne Crosland (*née* Smellie); *m* 1966, Evelyn Ann Brice Smyth (*d* 1998), *o d* of Brice Smyth, Belfast; two *s* one *d. Educ:* Trinity Coll., Glenalmond; Trinity Coll., Dublin (BA 1966). Mardon, Son & Hall Ltd, 1966–71; called to the Bar, Gray's Inn, 1971; called to the Bar, NI, 1981; a Recorder, 1990–93; Resident Judge, Taunton Crown Court, 2003–13. Vice-Pres., Avon Br., SSAFA, 1993–; County Pres., Avon, St John Ambulance, 2016–18. Trustee, Hardman Trust, 2017–. Mem. Council, RNLI, 2003–13. Master, Antient Soc. of St Stephen's Ringers, 1999–2000. *Recreations:* sailing, golf. *Address:* Yeowood, Wrington, Bristol BS40 5NS; Craig-y-Mor, Trearddur Bay, Holyhead, Anglesey LL65 2UP. *Clubs:* Royal Ocean Racing; Trearddur Bay Sailing (Cdre, 1994–96); Royal County Down Golf, Burnham and Berrow Golf, Holyhead Golf.

**JONES, Anthony W.;** *see* Whitworth-Jones.

**JONES, Antony Gerald Morrell;** QC (Scot.) 2017; Partner and Queen's Counsel, Brodies LLP, since 2018; *b* Edinburgh, 9 May 1966; *s* of Gerald N. L. Jones and Grace W. R. Jones (*née* Morrell); *m* 2000, Ashley H. Mawby; two *s* one *d. Educ:* George Watson's Coll.; Edinburgh Univ. (MA 1987); Dundee Univ. (LLB 1989; DipLP 1990). Admitted as solicitor, 1991; Solicitor Advocate, 1999; WS 1999; Partner and Solicitor Advocate, Kercher & Stevens WS, 1999–2003; Partner and Sen. Solicitor Advocate, BTO Solicitors LLP, 2003–18 Trustee: Scottish Veterans Residences, 2010–; Royal Scots (Royal Regt) Club, 2013–. *Address:* Brodies LLP, Capital House, 2 Festival Square, Edinburgh EH3 9SU. *T:* (0131) 228 3777. *E:* tony.jones@brodies.com. *Club:* Royal Scots (Edinburgh).

**JONES, Anushka;** *see* Asthana, A.

**JONES, Rt Rev. Arthur Lucas Vivian,** OAM 2006; PhD; Interim Rector, then Rector, Holy Trinity Episcopal, Makati City, Manila, 2008–14; *b* 11 Dec. 1934; *s* of Arthur Edmond Jones and Mona Emily Jones; *m* 1979, Valerie Joan Maxwell; one *s* three *d. Educ:* St John's Coll., Morpeth, NSW (ThL); ACT (ThSchool); London Univ. (BD ext); Deakin Univ.; Newcastle Univ., NSW (MA Classics); Adelaide Coll. of Adv. Educn (Grad. DipRE); Geneva Theol Coll. (ThD); Lambeth Diploma; La Trobe Univ. (PhD 1998; MCounsHS 2003). Ordained deacon 1966, priest 1967; Curate, Holy Trinity, Orange, NSW, 1966–69; Missionary, Panama, 1970–73 and 1977–80; Rector, St Barnabas, Orange,

NSW, 1973–77; Vicar, Corangamite, Vic, 1980–82; Lectr in NT, St John's Coll., Morpeth, 1982–85; Rector, Woy Woy, NSW, 1985–89; Dean, St Paul's Cathedral, Sale, 1989–94; Diocesan Theologian, Gippsland, 1989–94; Bishop of Gippsland, 1994–2001; Rector, Holy Trinity, Dubbo, NSW, 2004–07. Lectr in New Testament, Singapore, India, Manila, Peru, PNG, 2001–14. Hon. Res. Associate, Monash Univ., Vic, 2003. *Recreations:* golf, writing. *Address:* 151 Phillip Street, Orange, NSW 2800, Australia; 48 McKinley Road, Makati City 1219, Metro Manila, Philippines.

**JONES, Prof. Arthur Stanley,** CBE 1997; CBiol, FRSB; consultant to agricultural and food industries, since 1997; Principal, Royal Agricultural College, Cirencester, 1990–97; *b* 17 May 1932; *s* of John Jones and Anne Jones (*née* Hamilton); *m* 1962, Mary Margaret Smith; three *s* one *d*. *Educ:* Gosforth Grammar Sch.; Durham Univ. (BSc); Aberdeen Univ. (PhD). Commnd Army, 2nd Lieut, 1955–57; Pilot Officer, RAFVR, 1958–62. Rowett Research Institute: Res. Scientist, 1959; Hd, Applied Nutrition Dept, 1966; Chm., Applied Scis Div., 1975; Dep. Dir, 1983; Governor, 1986–90; Strathcona-Fordyce Prof. of Agriculture, Univ. of Aberdeen, 1986–90; Head, Sch. of Agriculture, Aberdeen, and Principal, N of Scotland Coll. of Agriculture, 1986–90; Gov., Aberdeen Centre for Land Use, 1987–90. Mem., House of Lords Rural Econ. Gp, 1992–94. Chairman: Scottish Beef Develts Ltd, 1988–91; RAC Enterprises Ltd, 1992–97; Member: Council, RASE, 1991–97; Bd, Arable Res. Centres, 1992–96. Gov., Henley Coll. of Management, 1996–2003 (Chm. Acad. Adv. Council, 1996–2001). Dir, Clan Grant Centre Trust Ltd, 1998–2006; Mem. Council and Hon. Treas., Clan Grant Soc., 1998–2006. Trustee: Trehane Trust, 1993–2007; Geoffrey Cragghill Meml Scholarship Trust, 1993–99; Ceres Foundn, 1996–2008. Hon. Prof., Univ. of Prague, 1994–2012. FRSA; FCMI; FIAgrM; FRAgS. *Publications:* Nutrition of Animals of Agricultural Importance (vol. 17, Internat. Encyc. of Food and Nutrition) (ed D. P. Cuthbertson), 1967; 115 articles in learned jls. *Recreations:* yachting, flying, gardening. *Address:* Begsdell, Caskieben, Kinellar, Aberdeenshire AB21 0TB. *Club:* Royal Air Force.

**JONES, Benedict L.;** *see* Llewellyn-Jones.

**JONES, Benjamin Timothy D.;** *see* Douglas-Jones.

**JONES, Brinley;** *see* Jones, Robert B.

**JONES, Sir Bryn Terfel, (Sir Bryn Terfel),** Kt 2017; CBE 2003; opera singer; bass baritone; *b* 9 Nov. 1965; *s* of Hefin and Nesta Jones; *m* Lesley Halliday (marr. diss. 2014); three *s*. *Educ:* Guildhall Sch. of Music and Drama (AGSM). Opera performances in major venues: WNO, 1990–; ENO, 1991–; Salzburg, 1992–; Covent Garden, 1992–; Vienna State Opera, 1993–; NY Metropolitan, 1994–; La Scala, Milan, 1997–; Sydney Opera House, 1999–; rôles include: Guglielmo in Così fan tutte, Speaker in Die Zauberflöte, Jochanaan in Salome, Balstrode in Peter Grimes, Figaro, Falstaff, title rôle and Leporello in Don Giovanni, Nick Shadow in The Rake's Progress, Wolfram in Tannhauser, Four Villains in Les Contes d'Hoffmann, Dulcamara in L'Elisir d'Amore, Méphistophélès in Gounod's Faust, Wotan in Der Ring des Nibelungen, The Flying Dutchman, Scarpia in Tosca, Sweeney Todd, Gianni Schicchi, Hans Sachs in Die Meistersinger von Nürnberg, Tevye in Fiddler on the Roof, Boris Godunov. Hon. Mem., Gorsedd, Royal Nat. Eisteddfod of Wales, 1992; Hon. RAM 2000. Hon. Fellow, Univ. of Wales, Bangor, 1994, Aberystwyth, 1995, Cardiff, 2009; Hon. FRWCMD (Hon. FWCMD, 1995). Hon. DMus: Glamorgan, 1997; Univ. of Wales, Cardiff, 2000. Queen's Medal for Music, 2006. *Recreations:* golf, supporting Manchester United, collecting fob watches. *Address:* c/o Harlequin Agency, 5th Floor, Gloworks, Porth Teigr, Cardiff CF10 4GA. *T:* (029) 2075 0821.

**JONES, Dame Caroline;** *see* Dean, Dame C.

**JONES, Caroline Yvonne;** Member for South Wales West, National Assembly for Wales (UK Ind, 2016–18, Ind, since 2018); *b* Llwynypia, 1 April 1955; *d* of Ernest Jones and Lorraine Jones (*née* Speed); *m* 2011, Alun Williams. *Educ:* Y Pant Secondary Sch.; Glamorgan Coll. of Educn (HNC Law/Econs and Applied Econs Univ. of Wales). Supply teacher, 1977–80; Local Govt Officer, 1980–86; self-employed, 1986–90; Area Retail Manager, 1990–97; Hd of Dept, Prison Service, 1997–2005; self-employed, 2005–16. *Recreations:* voluntary work, animal fostering, socialising with friends, involvement in the arts. *Address:* National Assembly for Wales, Cardiff Bay, Cardiff CF99 1NA. *T:* 0300 200 7259. *E:* caroline.jones@assembly.wales.

**JONES, Rt Hon. Carwyn (Howell);** PC 2010; Member (Lab) Bridgend, National Assembly for Wales, since 1999; First Minister of Wales, 2009–18; *b* 21 March 1967; *s* of Caron Wyn Jones and late (Katherine) Janice Jones; *m* 1994, Lisa Josephine Murray; one *s* one *d*. *Educ:* Aberystwyth Univ. (LLB). Called to the Bar, Gray's Inn, 1989. Tutor, Centre for Professional Legal Studies, Cardiff, 1997–99. National Assembly for Wales: Sec. for Agric. and Rural Develt, 2000; Minister: for Rural Affairs, 2000–02; for Open Govt and Assembly Business, 2002–03; for Envmt, Planning and Countryside, 2003–07; for Educn, Culture and the Welsh Language, 2007; Counsel Gen., Leader of the House and Minister for Assembly Business and Communications, 2007–09. Mem., Cardiff Business Club. *Recreations:* sport, reading, travel. *Address:* National Assembly for Wales, Cardiff Bay, Cardiff CF99 1NA. *T:* 0300 200 7095. *Clubs:* Bridgend United Services; Brynamman Rugby, Bridgend Rugby.

**JONES, Ceri Jayne, (Mrs T. C. Cuthbert);** business and financial journalist; *b* 3 July 1958; *d* of David and Julie Jones; *m* 1984, Thomas Charles Cuthbert; three *s* one *d*. *Educ:* Keele Univ.; Liverpool Univ. (BA Hons 1982). Ed., Pensions & Employees Benefits, 1986; Ed., Pensions Management, 1986–87, Financial Advr, 1987–94, Financial Times magazines; Ed., Investors Chronicle, 1994–2002; Ed.-in-Chief, Personal Finance Div., Financial Times Business, 1997–2002. *Publications:* Guide to Alternative Investments, 2006; business and financial commentary in various newspapers and magazines. *Recreations:* natural history, travel.

**JONES, Ceri Windsor;** Headmaster, Caterham School, since 2015; *b* Plymouth, 9 Nov. 1968; *s* of Howard and Patricia Jones; *m* 1997, Kay Moxon; two *d*. *Educ:* Nab Wood Grammar Sch.; Fitzwilliam Coll., Cambridge (BA Hist. 1991); Univ. of Buckingham (MEd Educnl Leadership 2016). Teacher of Hist., Bancroft's Sch., 1992–96; Hd of Hist., Caterham Sch., 1996–2004; Housemaster and Teacher of Hist., Tonbridge Sch., 2004–15 (Second Master, 2009–15); Principal, Marsh Acad., New Romney, 2013–15. Dir, Accelerate and Access Foundn, 2015–. Governor: London Acad. of Excellence, 2015–; Banstead Prep. Sch., 2017–; former Governor: Hazelwood Prep. Sch.; Slade Primary Sch. FRSA 2018. *Recreations:* history, social mobility, sport. *Address:* Caterham School, Harestone Valley Road, Caterham, Surrey CR3 6YA. *T:* (01883) 343028. *E:* headmaster@caterhamschool.co.uk. *Clubs:* Lansdowne; Hawks (Cambridge).

**JONES, Chris;** Director-General, City & Guilds, since 2008; *b* Berks, 15 July 1965; *s* of Phillip and Barbara Jones; *m* 1989, Judi Dixon; one *s* one *d*. Reed Business Publishing and EMAP plc, 1986–96; Gp Dir, FT Electronic Publishing, 1997–99; Senior Vice-President: LexisNexis Gp, 2000–01; LexisNexis Risk Mgt Gp, 2001–04; CEO, Harcourt Educn Internat., Reed Elsevier, later Pearson plc, 2004–08. Mem., Talent and Skills Leadership Team, BITC, 2011–. Gov., Activate Learning Gp, 2011– (Chm., 2016–). Mem., Tallow Chandlers' Co. *Recreations:* keen reader and sports enthusiast, travel, music and film. *Address:* City & Guilds, 1 Giltspur Street, EC1A 9DD. *T:* (020) 7294 2569. *E:* chris.jones@cityandguilds.com.

**JONES, Christine L.;** *see* Lee-Jones.

**JONES, Sir Christopher L.;** *see* Lawrence-Jones.

**JONES, Cliff;** *see* Jones, J. C.

**JONES, Clive Lawson,** CBE 1997; Secretary General, European Energy Charter Conference, 1991–95; *b* 16 March 1937; *s* of Celyn John Lawson Jones and Gladys Irene Jones; *m* 1961, Susan Brenda (*née* McLeod); one *s* one *d*. *Educ:* Cranleigh School; University of Wales. BSc (Chemistry). With British Petroleum, 1957–61; Texaco Trinidad, 1961–68; Principal, Min. of Power, 1968–69; Min. of Technology, 1969–70; DTI, 1970–73; Asst Sec., Oil Emergency Group, 1973–74; Department Energy: Asst Sec., 1974–77; Under Sec., Gas Div., 1981–82; Counsellor (Energy), Washington, 1977–81; Dir for Energy Policy, EC, 1982–86; Dep. Dir Gen. for Energy, EC, 1987–94. Chm., European Consultative Cttees on Electricity and Gas Markets, 1990–91. *Recreation:* ephemera.

**JONES, Sir Clive (William),** KCMG 2019; CBE 2007; Chairman: Runnymede Trust, since 2009 (Trustee, since 2004); Procam TV, since 2013; National Theatre Wales, since 2016; Sightsavers International, since 2019; *b* 10 Jan. 1949; *s* of Kenneth David Llewellyn Jones and Joan Muriel Jones (*née* Withers); *m* 1st, 1971, Frances Mawer (marr. diss. 1988); two *s* one *d*; 2nd, 1988, Fern Britton (marr. diss. 2000); two *s* one *d*; 3rd, 2004, Victoria Mary Taylor Heywood, *qv*. *Educ:* Newbridge Grammar Sch.; LSE (BSc Econ.). Journalist, until 1978; with Yorks TV, 1978–82; Man. Editor, Editor, then Editor-in-Chief, TV-am Ltd, 1982–84; TVS: Controller, News, Current Affairs and Sport, 1984–87; Dep. Dir of Programmes, 1987–91; Dep. Man. Dir, 1991–92; Founding Man. Dir, London News Network, 1992–94; Man. Dir, Central Independent Television PLC, April–Dec. 1994; Man. Dir, Carlton UK Broadcasting Ltd, 1995; Chief Exec., Carlton Television, 1996–2004; Chairman: Westcountry Television, 1998–2001 (Dir, 1998–2007); HTV, 2000–07; GMTV, 2005–10 (Dir, 2001–10); Two Way TV, 2007–09 (Dir, 2007–09); Netplay TV, 2009–14; Jt Man. Dir, ITV, 2002–04; Chief Exec., ITV News and Regions, 2004–07; Dir, S4C, 2007–12. Chm., Energetic Communications, NY, 2007–. Chm., Disasters Emergency Cttee, 2011–18. Chairman: ITV Pension Fund, 2016– (Trustee, 2005–); ITV Pension Scheme, 2018–; ITV Pension Plan, 2018–. Dir, Skills Develt Agency, 2006–08. Dir, Ladies Who Learn, 2015–18. Chairman: Skillset, 2002–10; YCTV, 2002–08; Wales IP Fund, 2005–11; Mediabox, 2007–. Director: Young Vic Th., 2003–16; Provenance Pictures, 2015–; Lake End Films, 2015–. Chm., London Metropolitan Univ., 2010–16. Trustee, Thomson Foundn, 2017–. Gov., Nat. Film and Television Sch., 1998–2012. FRTS 2000; FRSA 2000. *Recreations:* Rugby, golf, films, theatre. *Address:* 48 Church Crescent, N10 3NE. *Club:* Reform.

**JONES, Prof. Colin David Hugh,** CBE 2014; DPhil; FBA 2008; FRHistS; Professor of History, Queen Mary University of London, since 2006; *b* Isleworth, 12 Dec. 1947; *s* of Lawrence and Frances Joyce Jones; *m* 1996, Josephine McDonagh; three *s* one *d* from previous marriage. *Educ:* St Mary's C of E Primary Sch., Twickenham; Hampton Grammar Sch.; Jesus Coll., Oxford (Edwin Jones Schol.; BA Modern Hist. and Modern Langs (French) 1971); St Antony's Coll., Oxford (DPhil 1978). Temp. Lectr in Hist., Univ. of Newcastle upon Tyne, 1972–73; University of Exeter: Lectr in Hist., 1974–87; Sen. Lectr, 1987–90; Prof. of Hist., 1991–95; Prof. of Hist., Univ. of Warwick, 1996–2006. Fellow, Columbia Univ. Inst. of Scholars at Reid Hall (Paris), 2001–02; Kratter Vis. Prof. in Eur. Hist., Stanford Univ., 1993–94, 2000, 2005; Vis. Prof., Coll. de France, Paris, 2003; Visiting Fellow: Shelby Cullom Davis Center for Histl Studies, Princeton Univ., 1986; Nat. Liby of Medicine, Washington, 2004. Member: Steering Cttee, Hist. at Univ. Defence Gp, 1995–2001; Hist. of Medicine Panel, Wellcome Trust, 1999–2003 (Vice-Chm., 2001–03); Res. Panel for Hist., AHRC, 2004–08 (Convenor, 2006–08). Royal Historical Society: Fellow 1984; Vice Pres., 2000–03; Pres., 2009–12. Officier, Ordre des Palmes académiques (France), 2008. *Publications:* Charity and Bienfaisance: the treatment of the poor in the Montpellier Region, 1740–1815, 1982; The Longman Companion to the French Revolution, 1988; The Charitable Imperative: hospitals and nursing in Ancien Régime and Revolutionary France, 1989; (with J. Ardagh) Cultural Atlas of France, 1991; Cambridge Illustrated History of France, 1994; (with L. Brockliss) The Medical World of Early Modern France, 1997; The Great Nation: France from Louis XV to Napoleon (1715–99), 2002; Madame de Pompadour and her Image, 2002; Paris: biography of a city, 2004; The Smile Revolution in Eighteenth Century Paris, 2014; edited books, articles and book chapters on French hist., esp. 17th–19th centuries, incl. French Revolution and hist. of medicine. *Recreations:* music, wine, cooking, cycling, Paris. *Address:* History Department, Queen Mary University of London, Mile End Road, E1 4NS. *E:* c.d.h.jones@qmul.ac.uk.

**JONES, Courtney John Lyndhurst,** OBE 1989 (MBE 1980); President, National Ice Skating Association, 1987–95; *b* 30 April 1933; *s* of Reginald Jones and Inez Jones (*née* Wilsher). *Educ:* Ringwood Grammar Sch.; Bournemouth Coll. of Art (NDD). NSA Gold Medals for Ice Dance and for Pair Skating, 1957; British Ice Dance Champion, with June Markham, 1956–57, with Doreen Denny, 1958–60; European Ice Dance Champion, with June Markham, 1957–58, with Doreen Denny, 1959–61; World Ice Dance Champion, with June Markham, 1957–58, with Doreen Denny, 1959–60. Free-lance fashion designer, 1977–96. Hon. Mem., Internat. Skating Union, 2010– (Mem., Council, 2002–10). Mem., US Figure Skating Hall of Fame, 1987; George Hasler Medal, Internat. Skating Union, 1991; Lifetime Achievement Award, British Ice Teachers Assoc., 2017. *Recreations:* reading, music, the arts. *Address:* c/o International Skating Union, Avenue Juste-Oliver 17, 1006 Lausanne, Switzerland. *T:* (21) 6726677. *E:* courtandbobskate@hotmail.com.

**JONES, Darren Paul;** MP (Lab) Bristol North West, since 2017; *b* Bristol, 13 Nov. 1986; *s* of Alan and Susan Jones; *m* 2017, Lucy Elizabeth Symons; two *d*. *Educ:* Univ. of Plymouth (BSc Hons Human Biosci.); Univ. of W of England (Grad. DipLaw); Univ. of Law (Legal Practice course). Admitted solicitor, 2013; Bond Dickinson LLP, 2012–16, Solicitor, 2013–16; Legal Counsel, BT Gp plc, 2015–17. Mem., Sci. and Technol. Cttee, 2017–; European Scrutiny Select Cttee, 2017–, H of C. *Address:* House of Commons, SW1A 0AA. *T:* (020) 7219 2302. *E:* darren.jones.mp@parliament.uk.

**JONES, Prof. David,** OBE 1986; FRCN; Professor, School of Nursing and Midwifery, University of Sheffield, 1995–2000, now Emeritus Professor (Foundation Dean, 1995–98); *b* 27 July 1940; *s* of John Evan Jones and Edith Catherine (*née* Edwards); *m* 1962, Janet Mary Ambler; two *s* two *d*. *Educ:* Boys' Grammar Sch., Bala, N Wales; Univ. of Wales (BEd). SRN; RMN; RNT; FRCN 1998. Divl Nursing Officer, Gwynedd, 1974–78; Chief Admin. Nursing Officer, Gwynedd HA, 1979–87; first Chm., Welsh Nat. Bd for Nursing, Midwifery and Health Visiting, 1979–86; Chief Exec., English Nat. Bd for Nursing, Midwifery and Health Visiting, 1987–89; Principal, Sheffield and N Trent Coll. of Nursing and Midwifery, 1990–95. Board Mem., Clwyd Alyn Housing Assoc. Ltd, 2006–12. Hon. DSc Sheffield, 2005. *Recreations:* public affairs, countryside, family. *Address:* 7 Afon Glas, Llangollen, Denbighshire LL20 8AZ. *T:* (01978) 253081.

**JONES, Sir David A.**; see Akers-Jones.

**JONES, Sir David (Charles)**, Kt 2009; CBE 1999; FCCA, FCIS; Chairman, CWM 2001 Ltd, since 2001; b 2 Feb. 1943; s of Frederick Charles Thomas Jones and Annie Marcella Jones; m 1968, Jeanette Ann Crofts; two s one d. Educ: King's Sch., Worcester. FCIS 1974; FCCA 1975. Joined Kays Mail Order Co. (part of Great Universal Stores), 1960, Finance Dir, 1971–77; Man. Dir, BMOC, 1977–80; Chief Exec., Grattan Plc, 1980–86; Next Plc: Dep. Chief Exec., 1986–88; Chief Exec., 1988–2001; Dep. Chm., 2001–02; Chm., 2002–06. Dir, JJB Sports plc, 2007–10 (Dep. Chm., 2008–09; Chm., 2009–10). *Publications*: Next to Me (autobiog.), 2005. *Recreations*: bridge, chess.

**JONES, David George**; Director General (formerly Assistant Under-Secretary of State), Financial Management, Ministry of Defence, 1996–2001; b 31 May 1941; s of Frederick George Jones and Dorothy Jones (née Steele); m 1962, Leonie Usherwood Smith; three s. Educ: High Storrs Grammar Sch., Sheffield. Joined War Office as Exec. Officer, 1960; Asst Private Sec. to Army Minister, 1970–71; Principal, MoD Central Financial Planning Div., 1973–77; Private Sec. to Minister of State for Defence, 1977–80; Regl Marketing Dir, Defence Sales Organisation, 1980–84; Asst Sec., Air Systems Controllerate, 1984–85; Dep. Dir Gen., Al Yamamah Project Office, 1985–88; Dir Gen. Aircraft 2, Air Systems Controllerate, MoD (PE), 1988–89; Civil Sec., British Forces Germany, 1989–92; Dir Gen. Supplies and Transport (Naval), 1993–95, Dir Gen. Naval Bases and Supply, 1995–96, MoD. FCILT (FILog 1994). *Recreations*: gardening, travel.

**JONES, (David) Huw**; Chairman, S4C Authority (Welsh Fourth Channel), since 2011; b 5 May 1948; s of Idris Jones and Olwen Mair Lloyd Jones; m 1972, Sian Marylka Miarczynska; one s one d. Educ: Cardiff High Sch. for Boys; Jesus Coll., Oxford (BA, MA). Singer and TV presenter, 1968–76; Dir, Sain (Recordiau) Cyf, 1969–81; Man. Dir, Teledu'r Tir Glas, 1982–93; Chief Exec., S4C (Welsh Fourth Channel), 1994–2005; Dir, SDN Ltd, 1999–2005. Chairman: Barcud Cyf, 1981–93; TAC, 1984–86; Arianrhod Cyf, 1988–93; Celtic Film and TV Fest. Ltd, 2001–04; Portmeirion Ltd, 2007–; Cyfle Cyf, 2007–11; Ymdd: Nant Gwrtheyrn, 2018– (Dir, 2007–18). Mem. Adv. Bd, Pontio, Bangor Univ., 2014–. Member: FEFC for Wales, 1992–95; Investors in People Adv. Bd, UK Commn for Employment and Skills, 2010–11; Dir, Skillset Ltd, 2001–05 (Patron, 2006–08); Chair, Skillset Cymru Cyf, 2002–05; Vice-Chm., Wales Employment and Skills Bd, 2008–12. Welsh Government (formerly Welsh Assembly Government): Chm., Broadcasting Adv. Gp, 2008; Mem., Digital Wales Adv. Bd, 2010–11; Welsh-lang. educn strategy Ministerial Adv. Gp, 2011. Member: Welsh Lang. Bd, 2007–12; Adv. Cttee for Wales, RSPB, 2007–12; Council, RSPB, 2008–13. Trustee, RTS, 2012–16. FRTS 1999. Hon. Fellow: Univ. of Wales, Aberystwyth, 1997; Bangor Univ., 2013. Gov., Coleg Llandrillo Cymru, 2010–12. *Recreations*: reading, cycling, walking, ski-ing, languages. Address: Y Bwlan, Llandwrog, Caernarfon, Gwynedd LL54 5SR.

**JONES, Rev. Dr (David) Huw**, FRCR, FRCP; Dean, Postgraduate Medical and Dental Education for East of England, 2002–09; b 20 Feb. 1949; s of David and Nansi Jones; m 1984, Siân Davies; two d. Educ: Welsh Nat. Sch. of Medicine (MB BCh Hons 1972; MD 1979); MSc London 1978; MA Cantab 1987; E Anglian Ministerial Trng Course. FRCR 1983; FRCP 1996. Univ. Hosp. of Wales, Cardiff, 1972–75; MRC Fellow in Clin. Pharmacol., RPMS, Hammersmith Hosp., 1975–79; MRC Clin. Scientist, Clin. Oncology Unit, Cambridge, 1979–84; Consultant in Clinical Oncol., Addenbrooke's Hosp., Cambridge, 1984–2002; Associate Dean, Postgrad. Med. Educn, E Anglian Reg., 1998–2002. Vis. Prof. in Med. Educn, Anglia Ruskin Univ., 2003–09. Bye-Fellow, Gonville and Caius Coll., Cambridge, 2015–18. Ordained deacon 1998, priest 1999; NSM, Trumpington, 1998–2002; permission to officiate, dio. Ely, 2002–07; Dean's Vicar, Gonville and Caius Coll., Cambridge, 2006–18; Rural Dean, Cambridge South, 2011–15; Hon. Canon, Ely Cathedral, 2014–19. Hon. FFPM 2007. *Publications*: contribs on clinical pharmacol. and oncol. to peer-reviewed med. jls. *Recreations*: classical music, organ, gardening, carpentry.

**JONES, Rt Hon. David (Ian)**; PC 2012; MP (C) Clwyd West, since 2005; b 22 March 1952; s of Bryn and Elspeth Savage Jones; m 1982, Sara Eluned Tudor; two s. Educ: Ruabon Grammar Sch.; University Coll. London (LLB); Coll. of Law. Admitted Solicitor, 1976; Sen. Partner, David Jones & Co., Llandudno, 1985–2009. Mem. (C) N Wales, Nat. Assembly for Wales, 2002–03. Parly Under-Sec. of State, Wales Office, 2010–12; Sec. of State for Wales, 2012–14; Minister of State, DExEU, 2016–17. Contested (C): Conwy, 1997; City of Chester, 2001. *Recreation*: travel. Address: House of Commons, SW1A 0AA. T: (020) 7219 8070. E: david.jones.mp@parliament.uk.

**JONES, Rev. David Ian Stewart**; Headmaster, Bryanston School, 1974–82; b 3 April 1934; s of Rev. John Milton Granville Jones and Evelyn Moyes Stewart Jones (formerly Chedburn); m 1967, Susan Rosemary Hardy Smith; twin s and d. Educ: St John's Sch., Leatherhead; Selwyn Coll., Cambridge (MA); Westcott House, Cambridge. Commnd Royal Signals, 1952–54. Curate at Oldham Parish Church, 1959–62; Vicar of All Saints, Elton, Bury, 1963–66; Asst Conduct and Chaplain of Eton Coll., 1966–70; Conduct and Sen. Chaplain of Eton Coll., 1970–74; Rector-designate of Bristol City, 1982–85; Dir, 1985–97, Consultant, 1997–99, Lambeth Endowed Charities; Hon. Priest Vicar, Southwark Cath., 1985–94. Chm., Inner Cities Young People's Proj., 1988–98. *Recreations*: reading, music, politics. Address: 33 St Lucian's Garden, St Lucian's Lane, Wallingford, Oxon OX10 9ER.

**JONES, Maj. Gen. David John R.**; see Rutherford-Jones.

**JONES, Sir David John Walter P.**; see Prichard-Jones.

**JONES, David le Brun**, CB 1975; Director, Long Term Office, International Energy Agency, 1982–88; b 18 Nov. 1923; s of Thomas John Jones and Blanche le Brun. Educ: City of London Sch.; Trinity Coll., Oxford. Asst Principal, Min. of Power, 1947; Principal, MOP, 1952; Asst Sec., Office of the Minister for Science, 1962; Asst Sec., MOP, 1963; Under-Sec., MOP, later Min. of Technology and DTI, 1968–73; Dep. Sec., DTI, later DoI, 1973–76; Cabinet Office, 1976–77; Dept of Energy, 1978–82. Trustee, Nat. Energy Foundn, 1989–99. *Recreations*: reading, chess. Club: Oxford and Cambridge.

**JONES, David Lloyd**; see Lloyd-Jones, Rt Hon. Lord.

**JONES, David M.**; see Mansel-Jones.

**JONES, David Martin**, FRSB; Director, North Carolina Zoological Park, 1994–2015, now Director Emeritus; b 14 Aug. 1944; s of John Trevor Jones and Mair Carno Jones; m 1969, Janet Marian Woosley; three s. Educ: St Paul's Cathedral Choir Sch.; St John's Sch., Leatherhead; Royal Veterinary Coll., London (BSc, BVetMed). MRCVS. Veterinary Officer, Whipsnade, 1969; Sen. Veterinary Officer, 1975, Asst Dir of Zoos, 1981, Dir of Zoos, 1984, Gen. Dir, 1991, Dir, Conservation and Consultancy Div., 1992, Zoological Soc. of London. Trustee, WWF UK, 1986–92, 1993–96 (Chm., Conservation Review Gp, subseq. Conservation Cttee, 1990–94); Member Council: WWF UK, 1994–2005; WWF US, 1996–2002; Chm., Fauna and Flora Internat., 1987–94. Chairman: Brooke Hosp. for Animals, 1990–98, 2000–02 (Vice-Chm., 1973–90); Central Park NC (formerly Yadkin Pee-Dee Lakes Project), 1998–; Brooke USA, 2013–; Wild Welfare, 2015–; Board Member: Uwharrie Capital Corps, 1998–2004; Nat. Audubon (N Carolina), 2002–07; Environmental Defense Fund (formerly Environmental Defense) (N Carolina), 2003– (Vice-Chm., 2012–14; Chm., 2015–19); Pfeiffer Univ., 2004–10; Governor of N Carolina's Adv. Council on China, 2010–; Mem., Uwharrie Regl Resources Commn, 2010–13. Order of the Long Leaf Pine (NC, USA), 2015. *Publications*: over 100 papers on wildlife medicine, management and conservation, in veterinary, medical and zoological jls. *Recreations*: field conservation, travel, antiquarian books, driving, gardening. Address: 1688 Sylvan Way, Asheboro, NC 27205, USA.

**JONES, David Robert**; Co-Founder, One Young World, 2009; Founder and Chief Executive Officer, You & Mr Jones, since 2015; b Altrincham, Cheshire, 9 Nov. 1966; s of Robert Cyril Jones and Jennifer Ann Denise Studley Jones; m 1997, Karine Marie Bernard; two s one d. Educ: Middlesex Business Sch. (BA Hons Eur. Business Admin); Reutlingen Fachhochschule (Dip. Europaische Betriebswirtschaftslehre). Bd Account Dir, Abbott Mead Vickers BBDO, 1994–98; Euro RCSG: CEO, Partnership Sydney, 1998–2002; Pres., Global Brands, Worldwide, 2002–04; CEO, NY, 2004–05. Young Global Leader, WEF, 2008; Global Chief Executive Officer: Havas Worldwide (formerly Euro RSCG Worldwide), 2005–14; Havas, 2011–14. *Publications*: Who Cares Wins: why good business is better business, 2011. *Recreations*: family, tennis, Rugby, wine. Clubs: Soho House, Stone.

**JONES, Prof. David Simon**, PhD, DSc; FRSC; FREng; FIMMM; FSS; Professor of Biometric Science, since 1999, and Pro-Vice-Chancellor (Education and Students), since 2014, Queen's University Belfast; b Portadown, Co. Armagh, 1 May 1963; s of Frederick and Mary Emily Jones; m 1988, Linda Maureen Crooks; one s one d. Educ: Royal Sch., Dungannon; Queen's Univ. Belfast (BSc 1st Cl. Hons Pharmacy 1985; PhD Pharmaceutics 1988; DSc Biomaterial Sci. 2006); Open Univ. (BA 1st Cl. Hons Maths and Stats 2014). CChem 1998; FSS 2000; FIMMM 2001; CEng 2001; FRSC 2016; CStat 2016. Lectr in Pharmaceutical Technol., Univ. of Otago, NZ, 1988–92; Hd, Formulations, Norbrook Labs, Newry, NI, 1992–94; Queen's University Belfast: Lectr in Pharmaceutics, 1994–97; Sen. Lectr in Pharmaceutics, 1997–99; Hd, Sch. of Pharmacy, 2012–13. Royal Soc. Industrial Fellow, 2009–13. Hon. Professor: Univ. of Otago, NZ, 2011–; Univ. of Auckland, NZ, 2013–; China Med. Univ., Shenyang, China, 2018–. Ed., Jl Pharmacy and Pharmacol., 2000–. Fellow, Pharmaceutical Soc. of NI, 2013; Eminent Fellow, Acad. of Pharmaceutical Scis, 2016; FIAE 2018; FREng 2018. *Publications*: Pharmaceutical Statistics, 2002; Pharmaceutics: dosage, form and design, 2008, 2nd edn 2016; contrib. refereed jl articles, reviews, book chapters, patents and conf. proceedings. *Recreations*: music (ABRSM Grade 8 saxophone), listening and playing, reading, running. Address: Vice-Chancellor's Office, Queen's University Belfast, University Road, Belfast, Northern Ireland BT71 1NN. T: (020) 9097 5220. E: d.jones@qub.ac.uk.

**JONES, Dr (David) Timothy**; Deputy Chairman, Education and Learning Wales (formerly Education and Training Wales), 2001–06; non-executive Director: Orpar SA, since 2002; Rémy-Cointreau, 2008–15; b 21 Aug. 1944; s of David Percy Jones and Elvair (née Evans); m 1968, Jean Margaret Whitehead; four d. Educ: Leeds Univ. (PhD Physical Chem.); INSEAD, Fontainebleau (MBA with Dist.). MRSC 1967. Gen. Manager, Deutsche BP, 1985–88; Dir, BP France, 1988–89; Chief Exec., BP Oil Supply and Trading, 1990; Dir, BP Oil Europe, 1990–93; Dep. Chm., 1993–2000, Chief Exec., 1996–2000, Lloyd's Register. Chm., Marine Panel, Foresight Initiative, DTI, 1999–2002. Mem. Exec. Cttee, Envmt, Sustainability and Energy Div., RSC, 2010. *Recreations*: watching Rugby, walking, golf.

**JONES, Deborah Elizabeth Vavasseur B.**; see Barnes Jones.

**JONES, Deborah Mary**, PhD; author of fiction; b 5 April 1948; d of Thomas Jones and Glenys Jones. Educ: W Kirby Grammar Sch. for Girls; University Coll. of S Wales, Cardiff (BA Gen. Hons); Leeds Univ. (PGCE); Regina Mundi Pontifical Inst., Rome; Margaret Beaufort Inst. of Theol.; Anglia Poly. Univ. (MA); Univ. of Wales, Lampeter (PhD 2008). Teacher of English and Classical Studies, Clacton Co. High Sch., 1972–78; Dir, Adult Educn, Dio. of E Anglia, 1980–96 (pt-time, 1992–96); Lectr in Religious Studies, Suffolk Coll., 1987–92; Dep. Ed., Priests & People, 1991–96, 1999–2004; Editor, Catholic Herald, 1996–98; Gen. Sec., Catholic Concern for Animals, and Ed., The Ark, 1998–2015. *Publications*: Focus on Faith, 1987, 2nd edn 1996; This is My Body, 1989; The School of Compassion: a Roman Catholic theology of animals, 2009; *novels*: The World According to Julia, 2015; Julia's World goes West, 2017; Julia's World in Tune, 2018. *Recreations*: Baroque opera, playing 'cello, 18th century women's literature.

**JONES, Della Louise Gething**; mezzo-soprano; d of Eileen Gething Jones and late Cyril Vincent Jones; m 1988, Paul Vigars; one s. Educ: Neath Girls' Grammar School; Royal College of Music. GRSM; LRAM (singing), ARCM (piano); Kathleen Ferrier Scholarship. Mem., ENO, 1977–82, leading roles, 1982–; guest artist, ENO and Royal Opera House; sings with major British opera companies; overseas concert and operatic appearances in all major European countries, also Russia, Japan and USA; radio and TV; prolific recordings with all major recording cos. Hon. FRWCMD (Hon. FWCMD 1995). Hon. Fellow, Univ. of Wales Swansea, 1999. *Recreations*: writing cadenzas, art galleries, animal welfare, reading, piano. Address: c/o Music International, 13 Ardilaun Road, Highbury, N5 2QR. T: (020) 7359 5183.

**JONES, Denise**; Director: Eastside Arts and Eastside Books, since 1983; Brick Lane Bookshop, since 2004; b Farnham, 18 April 1945; d of Leslie William Turner and Stella Ethel May Turner (née Wright); m 1967, Daniel Elwyn Jones, MBE; two s one d. Educ: Rye Grammar Sch.; Brighton Coll. of Art; Avery Hill Coll., London (Teachers Cert. 1969). Primary sch. teacher, E London, 1970–76; community publisher, Stepney Books, 1974–2001. Mem. (Lab) Tower Hamlets LBC, 1994– (Chm., Culture, 1994–99; Mayor, 1999–2000; Dep. Leader, 2002–06; Leader, 2006–08; Scrutiny Lead, 2008–; Cabinet Mem., Adults Health and Wellbeing, 2017–; Older Persons Champion, 2017–). Chm. Bd, Mile End Partnership, 1997–; Vice Chm., NHS Tower Hamlets, 2006–11; Dir, Tower Hamlets Homes, 2008–10. Director: Arts Council London Regl Bd, 1998–2006; Trinity Buoy Wharf Trust, 1998–; Aldgate and Allhallows Foundn, 1998–; Wellclose Square Bldg Preservation Trust, 2000–08; Wilton's Music Hall, 2000–16; (Founder Mem.) Rich Mix Cultural Foundn, 2002–; V&A Nat. Mus. of Childhood, 2002–; Greenwich & Docklands Fest., 2002–06; VisitLondon, 2003–11; Heritage of London Trust, 2003–15; TourEast London, 2004–10; Half Moon Young People's Theatre, 2004–06; Mus. of London and Mus. of London Docklands, 2005–09; St Katharine's & Shadwell Trust, 2006–08; 5 Borough Leaders' Olympics 2012 Bd, 2006–08; Whitechapel Art Gall., 2008–12; Cultural Industries Develt Agency, 2009–13; East End Community Trust, 2009–13; Lee Valley Regl Park Authy, 2010–; Mem. Council, Women's Liby, 2008–13; Trustee: Create London, 2016–; Sir John Cass Foundn, 2018–. Governor: Mulberry Sch. for Girls, 2002–; Mulberry Acad. Trust, 2016–. FRSA 2014. Freeman, City of London, 2002. Hon. DLitt East London, 2008. *Recreations*: arts and heritage, visiting galleries, theatre, cinema, reading, gym, swimming. Address: 196 Cable Street, E1 0BL. T: and Fax: (020) 7790 6420. E: denisejones196@hotmail.com.

**JONES, Denise Idris**; Member (Lab) Conwy, National Assembly for Wales, 2003–07; *b* 7 Dec. 1950; *d* of James and Rhona Woodrow; *m* 1984, John Idris Jones; two *s*. Teacher in English and French, Grango Secondary Sch., Rhos, Wrexham, 1972–2003. Contested (Lab) Aberconwy, Nat. Assembly for Wales, 2007. *Recreations:* travelling, literature, arts, golf. *Address:* Borthwen, Llanfair Road, Ruthin, Denbs LL15 1DA.

**JONES, Derek**; Chief Executive Officer, DER Touristik UK, since 2011; Managing Director, Kuoni UK, since 2011; *b* Liverpool, 12 Dec. 1963; *s* of Alfred Jones and Kathleen Jones (*née* Rogers); *m* 2018, Natalie Hufton; three *s* two *d*. *Educ:* W Derby Comprehensive Sch.; W Derby Sixth Form Coll. Exec. Asst to Chief Inspector of Factories, 1983–88; Thomson Holidays: Area Sales Manager, Spain, 1988–90; Nat. Account Manager, Manchester, 1990–93; Hd of New Product Delivery, 1993–97; Nat. Sales Manager, 1998–99; Hd of Trading, Lunn Poly Ltd, 1999–2001; TUI UK Ltd: Commercial Dir, 2001–04; Retail and Commercial Dir, 2004–06; Distribution Dir, TUI Travel PLC (UK and Ireland), 2006–08; Vice Pres., Distribution and Ops, Kuoni Travel, 2009–11. Dir, ABTA, 2006–07 and 2018–; Mem. Bd, Fedn of Tour Operators, 2015–. Chm., ABTA Lifeline, 2006–07, 2018–. FInstTT, 2017; FRSA 2019. Columnist, Travel Trade Gazette, 2015–. *Recreations:* hiking, camping, ski-ing, cycling. *Address:* DER Touristik UK Ltd, Touristik House, One Dorking Office Park, Station Road, Dorking, Surrey RH4 1HJ. *T:* (01306) 744535. *E:* derek.jones@kuoni.co.uk.

**JONES, Sir Derek (William)**, KCB 2014 (CB 2009); Permanent Secretary, Welsh Government, 2012–17; Chair, Prince's Trust Wales, since 2017; *b* 8 Dec. 1952; *s* of William Jones and Patricia Mary Jones (*née* Gill); *m* 1976, Fiona Christine Anne Laidlaw; two *s*. *Educ:* UC Cardiff, Univ. of Wales (BA Hons). Regional policy, company law and privatisation, DTI, 1977–82; HM Treasury: Public Expenditure Control, 1982–84; Head, Financial Instns and Markets, 1984–87; Head, Japan Desk and Overseas Trade Policy Div., DTI, 1987–89; Welsh Office: Asst Sec., 1989; Head, Industrial Policy Div., 1989–92; Head, Finance Progs Div., 1992–94; Under Sec., 1994; Dir, Industry and Trng Dept, 1994–99; Dir, Economic Affairs, 1999–2003, Sen. Dir, 2003–08, Welsh Assembly Govt; Dir, Business and Strategic Partnerships, Cardiff Univ., 2008–12. Chairman: Membership Selection Panel, Welsh Water, 2011–12 (Mem., 2010–12); SE Wales Econ. Forum, 2011–12. Member: Bd, EADS Foundn Wales, 2011–12; Ministerial Adv. Bd (Business, Enterprise, Technology and Sci.), Welsh Govt, 2012; Civil Service Bd/Sen. Leadership Cttee, 2015–17. Non-exec. Dir, IQE plc, 2017–. Ind. Advr, Cardiff Univ., 2017–. Chm. and Mem., Royal Anniversary Trust Awards Council for Queen's Anniversary Prizes. Pres., Civil Service Sports and Social Cttee. Hon. Prof., Cardiff Univ., 2008 (Hon. Fellow, 2017). *Recreations:* reading, blues guitar, surfing, watching Rugby. *Club:* Reform.

**JONES, Diane C.**; *see* Cellan-Jones.

**JONES, Dylan**, OBE 2013; Editor, GQ magazine, since 1999; Editor-in-Chief, GQ Style, since 2005; *b* 18 Jan. 1960; *s* of Michael and Audrey Jones; *m* 1997, Sarah Walter; two *d*. *Educ:* Chelsea Sch. of Art; St Martin's Sch. of Art (BA Hons Design and Photography). Ed., i-D mag., 1984–87; Contributing Ed., The Face, 1987–88; Ed., Arena, 1988–92; Associate Editor: Observer Mag., 1992–93; Sunday Times Mag., 1993–96; Gp Ed., The Face, Arena, Arena Homme Plus, 1996–97; Ed.-at-Large, Sunday Times, 1997–99. Chm., BSME, 2005. Chm., Fashion Rocks for Prince's Trust, 2005; Vice Pres., Hay Fest.; Member, Board: Norman Mailer Center; Norman Mailer Writers Colony. Editor of Year Award, BSME, 1993, 2001, 2002, 2004, 2007, 2008. *Publications:* Dark Star, 1990; Sex, Power and Travel, 1996; Meaty, Beaty, Big and Bounty, 1997; iPod, Therefore I Am, 2005; Mr Jones' Rules, 2006; (with David Cameron) Cameron on Cameron: conversations with Dylan Jones, 2008; (with David Bailey) British Heroes in Afghanistan, 2010; When Ziggy Played Guitar, 2012; (ed) The Biographical Dictionary of Popular Music, 2012; The Eighties: one day, one decade, 2013; Elvis Has Left the Building: the day the king died, 2014; David Bowie: a life, 2017; The Wichita Lineman: searching in the sun for the world's greatest unfinished song, 2019. *Address:* GQ Magazine, Vogue House, Hanover Square, W1S 1JU. *T:* (020) 7499 9080. *E:* dylan.jones@condenast.co.uk. *Clubs:* Chelsea Arts, Groucho, Soho House, Ivy, George.

**JONES, Prof. (Edith) Yvonne**, DPhil; FRS 2017; FMedSci; Professor of Protein Crystallography, since 1999, Joint Head of Structural Biology, since 2008, and Interim Director, since 2018, Wellcome (formerly Wellcome Trust) Centre for Human Genetics, University of Oxford; Fellow, Jesus College, Oxford, since 2006; *b* Oswestry, 22 Sept. 1960; *d* of David Iorwerth Jones and Eluned Jones (*née* Evans). *Educ:* Bwlch-y-cibau Primary Sch.; Llanfechain Jun. Sch.; Llanfyllin High Sch. (Ysgol Uwchradd Llanfyllin); Jesus Coll., Oxford (BA Physics 1982; DPhil Molecular Biophysics 1985). Postdoctoral Fellow, Edinburgh Univ., 1985–86; University of Oxford: Postdoctoral Fellow, 1986–91; Royal Soc. Univ. Res. Fellow, 1991–2001; CRUK Principal Res. Fellow, 2001–11; Dep. Dir, 2010–17, Actg Dir, 2017–18, Wellcome (formerly Wellcome Trust) Centre for Human Genetics, Univ. of Oxford. Mem., EMBO, 2007–. FMedSci 2003. *Publications:* contribs to learned jls. *Recreation:* the Montgomeryshire countryside. *Address:* Division of Structural Biology, Wellcome Centre for Human Genetics, University of Oxford, Roosevelt Drive, Oxford OX3 7BN. *T:* (01865) 287547. *E:* yvonne@strubi.ox.ac.uk.

**JONES, Edward David Brynmor**, CBE 2011; RIBA; architect in private practice, since 1973; Principal, Dixon Jones Ltd (formerly Jeremy Dixon·Edward Jones), since 1989; *b* 20 Oct. 1939; *s* of David Jones and Margot Derricourt; *m* 1st; one *s* two *d*; 2nd, Margot Griffin; one *s* two *d*. *Educ:* Haileybury and ISC; AA Sch. of Architecture (AADip Hons 1963); RIBA 1968; RAIC and Ont Assoc. of Architects, Canada, 1983–89. Tutor, AA, PCL and UC Dublin, 1968–72; Sen. Tutor, Sch. of Environmental Design, RCA, 1973–83; Vis. Prof., 1973–82, Adjunct Prof., 1983–89, Univ. of Toronto; Visiting Professor: Cornell, Harvard, Princeton, Yale, Pennsylvania, Rice, Syracuse, Waterloo and Kent State (Florence) Univs, 1973–; Portsmouth Univ., 1994–98; Hon. Prof., Cardiff Univ. (formerly Univ. of Wales, Cardiff), 2003–. RIBA External Examiner: AA 1985; Portsmouth Univ.; Kingston Univ., Heriot-Watt Univ., 1990–93; Univ. of Wales, 1995–97; Univ. of Technol., Kingston, Jamaica, 1997–2000; Mackintosh Sch., Glasgow, 2007–10. Member: RIBA President's Gold Medal Cttee, 1993, 1994; AA Council, 1993–99 (Vice Pres., 1995); RIBA Stirling Interim Award Cttee, 2004–08; RIBA Stirling Final Cttee, 2010; Hon. Librarian, AA, 1994–95. Competitions, first prize: Northampton County Offices, 1973; Mississauga City Hall, Canada, 1982–87; Bus Stn, Venice, 1990; other projects include: Royal Opera House, Covent Garden, 1983–99; buildings for: Henry Moore Foundn at Leeds, 1989–93 and Perry Green, 1989–; Darwin Coll., Cambridge, 1989, 1994; Robert Gordon Univ., Aberdeen, 1991; superstore for J. Sainsbury at Plymouth, 1991–94; Portsmouth Univ. (Dept of Sci.), 1992–96; housing in New Delhi, 1994; Nat. Portrait Gall., 1994–2000; Saïd Business Sch., Oxford Univ., 1996–2001, Phase 2, Centre for Exec. Educn, 2007–12; Somerset House, south terrace and central courtyard, 1998–2000; Kensington and Chelsea Coll., 2000–11; Student Centre, QUB, 2001; Panopticon Bldg, UCL, 2001–; Magna Carta Bldg, Salisbury Cathedral, 2001–; Portrait Gall. of Canada, 2003–; Marlborough Primary Sch., RBKC, 2012–17; Westgate Shopping Centre, Oxford, 2013–17; private houses in Bargemon, France, 2003, W London, 2012, and Georgian Bay, Canada, 2013; master plans for: Nat. Gall., 1998–2006; Somerset House, 1998–; Exhibition Road, 2008–11; Chelsea Barracks Housing, 2009–; Olympic Way, Wembley Stadium, 2016–; College Green, Dublin, 2017; office developments: King's Cross for Parabola, 2001; Regent's Palace for Crown Estates, 2005–12; 5–6 St James's Square for Rio Tinto, 2006–; Edinburgh Park for Parabola, 2017–; housing developments: 35 Marylebone High St for Royalton Estates, 2011–; Chelsea Apartments for Manhattan lofts, 2003–11; Cheval properties, 55–91 Knightsbridge, 2006–; Moxon Street and Beaumont Street for Howard de Walden Estate, 2010, 2015–; Royalton Estates, 2018. Rep. Britain at Biennale: Venice, 1980, 2002; Paris, 1981; Santiago, 1982. Chairman Jury: Laban Dance Sch. Competition, Deptford, 1987; Google's Line of Site Competition, 2008, 2009; Jury Member: Diana Princess of Wales Fountain Competition, London, 2002; new Parliament Bldg, Ottawa, 2003; Barbara Hepworth Gall. Competition, Wakefield, 2003; Univ. Boulevard Competition, UBC, 2005; Victoria Embankment Competition, 2005–; Europan Ireland, 2009; Mem., Design Review Panel, 2012 Olympics, 2006–; Vice Chair, Quality Review Panel, London Legacy Devcelt Corp., 2012. Trustee, Portsmouth Naval Base Property Trust, 2005–08. FRSA. Hon. FRIAI 2011. Hon. Fellow, Cardiff Univ., 2001; Hon. DLitt Portsmouth, 2001. Governor-General's Award for Architecture (Canada), 1988. *Publications:* A Guide to the Architecture of London (with C. Woodward), 1983, 5th edn 2013; Jeremy Dixon·Edward Jones Buildings and Projects, vol. I, 1959–2002, 2002, vol. II, 1998–2019, 2019; contribs to arch. jls. *Recreations:* drawing, planting trees, looking out of the window in France, Staffordshire bull terriers. *Address:* 41 Gloucester Crescent, NW1 7DL. *T:* (020) 7267 7015.
*See also* B. J. Goldsmith.

**JONES, Edward W.**; *see* Wilson Jones.

**JONES, Edwina Currie**; *see* Currie, E.

**JONES, Eleri Wynne**; Member, Independent Television Commission, with special responsibility for Wales, 1990–98; *b* 9 Aug. 1933; *d* of Ellis Edgar and Elen Mary Griffith; *m* 1960, Bedwyr Lewis Jones (*d* 1992); two *s* one *d*. *Educ:* Howell's Sch., Denbigh (Foundn Schol.); University Coll. of Wales, Aberystwyth; University Coll., Cardiff. BA (Wales); DipIPM. Journalist, Canada, 1956–57; Careers Officer, Gwynedd, 1957–64; Tutor, Marr. Guidance Council, 1978–87; Lectr, Gwynedd Technical Coll., 1980–84; Member: Welsh Fourth Channel Authy, 1984–91; Bd of Channel Four, 1987–90. Dir, Cais Ltd, 1993–2001. Member: Staff Commn for Local Govt Reorgn (Wales), 1994–97; HEFCW, 2000–05; Rees Review into Devolution of Student Support System and Tuition Fees in Wales, 2004–05. Mem., Council, Univ. of Wales, Aberystwyth, 1995–98, Univ. of Wales, Bangor, 1998–2002 (Hon. Fellow, 2001). Formerly trainer and practitioner in psychotherapy and counselling. *Recreations:* walking, travel, television, films. *Address:* 60 Y Bae, Beach Road, Bangor LL57 2BH. *T:* (01248) 371370.

**JONES, Elin**; Member (Plaid Cymru) Ceredigion, since 1999, and Presiding Officer, since 2016, National Assembly for Wales; *b* 1 Sept. 1966; *d* of John and Avril Jones. *Educ:* Llanwnnen Primary Sch.; Lampeter Comprehensive; UC Cardiff (BScEcon); Univ. of Wales, Aberystwyth (MSc). Research Officer, Dept of Agric. Econs, UCW, Aberystwyth, 1988–91; Econ. Devclt Officer, Devclt Bd for Rural Wales, 1991–98; Regl Devclt Manager, WDA, 1998–99. Mayor of Aberystwyth, 1997–98. Chm., Plaid Cymru, 2000–02. Minister for Rural Affairs, Nat. Assembly for Wales, 2007–11. *Recreations:* music, Welsh culture. *Address:* (constituency office) Ty Goronwy, 32 Heol y Wig, Aberystwyth, Ceredigion SY23 2LN.

**JONES, Elisabeth A.**; *see* Arfon-Jones.

**JONES, Elizabeth Clare, (Biba)**; *see* Dow, E. C.

**JONES, Elizabeth Jane**; *see* Butler, E. J.

**JONES, Elizabeth Sian**; QC 2000; *b* 24 March 1960; *d* of John Oswald Jones and Margrette Rachel Jones; *m* 1997, John Clark; one *s* two *d*. *Educ:* Howell's Sch., Llandaff; Ryde Sch., IoW; King's Coll., Cambridge. Called to the Bar, Middle Temple, 1984; Bencher, Lincoln's Inn, 2007; in practice at the Bar, 1984–. *Recreations:* singing, opera, yoga, family. *Address:* Serle Court, 6 New Square, Lincoln's Inn, WC2A 3QS. *T:* (020) 7242 6105.

**JONES, Prof. (Elphin) Wynne**, OBE 2009; PhD; FRAgS, FIAgrE, FIAgrM, FCGI, FRSB; Principal, Harper Adams University College (formerly Harper Adams Agricultural College), 1996–2009; *b* 29 March 1949; *s* of Elphin and Eluned Jones; *m* 1977, Irfana Siddiqi; two *d*. *Educ:* University Coll. of N Wales, Bangor (BSc Hons); Univ. of Reading (PhD 1976). MIBiol 1978; FRAgS 1994; FIAgrE 2003; FIAgrM 2008; FCGI 2009; FRSB (FIBiol 2009). Lectr in Animal Prodn, 1975–78, Hd, Dept of Animal Prodn, 1978–88, Welsh Agricl Coll.; Vice Principal and Dir, Acad. Affairs, Harper Adams Agricl Coll., 1988–96. Mem., Bd of Mgt, BASIS, 2004–07. Chm., Trehane Trust, 2007–; Member, Board: of Trustees, Lantra, 2001–09; of Mgt, AMTRA, 2007–10; of Mgt, Shrewsbury Sch., 2007–; Mem. Council, Aberystwyth Univ., 2009–15. Pres., Future Farmers of Wales, 2009–. Fellow, Inst. of Welsh Affairs, 2006. Hon. DSc Cranfield, 2006. Nat. Agricl Award, RASE, 2005. *Recreations:* travel, walking, reading. *Club:* Farmers.

**JONES, Emma Louise**, MBE 2012; Founder, Enterprise Nation, since 2007; *b* Wellington, Shropshire, 28 March 1972; *d* of Richard Faughey Jones and Fay Shirley Easton (*née* Goulding). *Educ:* Shrewsbury High Sch.; Concord Coll.; Univ. of Wales, Cardiff (LLB Law and Japanese). Manager, Arthur Andersen, 1995–2000; Co-founder, Techlocate.com, 2000–04. Govt Business Ambassador, 2015–; Small Business Crown Rep., 2016–. Co-Founder and ran, StartUp Britain, 2011–14. *Publications:* Spare Room Start Up, 2008; Working 5 to 9, 2010; Go Global, 2012; Going for Growth, 2014. *Recreations:* travel, exercise (although latter more of a chore!). *Address:* Enterprise Nation, 133 Whitechapel High Street, E1 7QA. *E:* emma@enterprisenation.com.

**JONES, Eurfron Gwynne**; Director of Education, BBC, 1992–94; *b* 24 Sept. 1934; *d* of William Gwynne Jones and Annie (*née* Harries); *m* 1968, Michael Coyle; one *s*. *Educ:* Aberdare Girls' Grammar Sch.; University Coll., Cardiff, Univ. of Wales (BSc (Zoology); PhD). Teaching Asst, Mount Holyoke Coll., Mass, 1955–56; joined BBC as gen. trainee, 1959; Producer, BBC Sch. Radio, Sch. Television and Continuing Educn, TV, 1959–75; freelance broadcaster, writer and cons., Media Cons. Internat. Children's Centre, Educn Commn of the States, 1975–83; Asst Hd, Sch. Radio, 1983–84; Hd of Sch. Television, 1984–87; Controller, Educnl Broadcasting, BBC, 1987–92. Member: Wyatt Commn on Violence, 1986; OU Council, 1987–94; Open Coll. Council, 1987–89; Council, Royal Instn, 1989–92, and 1994–97; COPUS, 1992–94; Educn Adv. Cttee, Nat. Museums and Galls of Wales, 1995–99; Res. Panel, Inst. of Welsh Affairs, 1996–2002; Chm., Digital Coll. for Wales, 1997–2001. Vis. Prof., Inst. of Educn, Univ. of London, 1994–97. Chm., Friends of Glynn Vivian Art Gall., 2006–08. FRTS 1994 (Mem., 1984–94; Vice Pres., 1996–2002). Fellow, Univ. of Wales Cardiff, 1996. Hon. LLD Exeter, 1990; DUniv Open, 1996. *Publications:* Children Growing Up, 1973; The First Five Years, 1975; How Did I Grow?, 1977; Television Magic, 1978; Lifetime I, Lifetime II, 1982; numerous articles on children and educn. *Recreations:* photography, swimming, twin grandchildren.

**JONES, Felicity**; actress; *b* Bournville, Birmingham, 17 Oct. 1983; *d* of Gareth Jones and Julia Hadley; *m* 2018, Charles Guard. *Educ:* Wadham Coll., Oxford (BA Eng. Lit. and Lang. 2006). *Films:* The Treasure Seekers, 1996; Northanger Abbey, 2007; Brideshead Revisited,

2008; Soulboy, 2010; The Tempest, 2010; Like Crazy, 2011; Chalet Girl, 2011; Breathe In, 2013; The Invisible Woman, 2013; The Theory of Everything, 2014; Inferno, 2016; Rogue One: A Star Wars Story, 2016; A Monster Calls, 2017; On the Basis of Sex, 2019; The Aeronauts, 2019; *television series:* The Worst Witch, 1998–99; Weirdsister College, 2001–02; The Diary of Anne Frank, 2009; *theatre:* That Face, Royal Court, 2007; The Chalk Garden, Luise Miller, Donmar Warehouse, 2008. *Recreations:* reading, theatre, cinema, family, friends, swimming.

**JONES, Fielding;** *see* Jones, Norman F.

**JONES, Gareth;** *see* Jones, John Gareth.

**JONES, Gareth,** OBE 1991; Commissioner, Isle of Anglesey County Council, 2011–12; Chairman, C6 Creative Industries North Wales, 2013–17; *b* 14 May 1939. *Educ:* UC, Swansea (BA Hons Geography). Former Headmaster; educnl consultant. Chm., Univ. of Wales Bd for Welsh Lang. Teaching, 2003–06. National Assembly for Wales: Mem. (Plaid Cymru) Conwy, 1999–2003; contested same seat, 2003; Mem. (Plaid Cymru) Aberconwy, 2007–11. Chm., Enterprise and Learning Cttee, Nat. Assembly for Wales, 2007–11. Mem. (Plaid Cymru), Conwy CBC, 1997–2008, 2012– (Leader, 2017–). *Address:* Dolarfon, 21 Roumania Drive, Craig y Don, Llandudno LL30 1UY.

**JONES, Gareth,** OBE 2003; Vice President, Enterprise Registry Solutions, since 2016; *b* 13 Aug. 1957; *s* of late Hubert John Jones and Audrey Margaret Jones; *m* 1979, Susan (*née* Brown); one *s* one *d*. *Educ:* Open Univ. (BA Hons Hist.). Civil Servant, 1979–2015; Private Sec. to Sec. of State for Trade and Ind., 1988–90; Welsh Assembly Government: Hd, CAP Mgt Div., Agric. and Rural Affairs Dept, 1999–2003; Dir, Dept for Envmt, Planning and Countryside, 2003–07; Registrar of Cos and Chief Exec., Companies House, 2007–12; Dir Gen. for Natural Resources (formerly Sustainable Futures), Welsh Govt, 2012–15. Chm., Assoc. of Co. Registration Agents, 2018–. CCMI 2011. FRSA. *Recreations:* Freemasonry (Provincial Grand Master for South Wales, 2013–; Third Grand Principal, 2016–), ski-ing, shooting. *Address:* Cyncoed, Cardiff. *Club:* Cardiff and County.

**JONES, Gareth Daryl; His Honour Judge Gareth Jones;** a Circuit Judge, since 2009; a Deputy High Court Judge, Family Division, since 2008; Designated Family Judge for North Wales, since 2011; *b* Swansea, 24 Nov. 1961; *s* of late Marshall Stanley Jones and of Esther Elizabeth Avril Jones; *m* 1989, Rosamund Ann, *d* of late Thomas Richard Lloyd and Marion Lloyd. *Educ:* Ysgol Gyfun Ystalyfera; University Coll. of Wales, Aberystwyth (LLB Hons 1983). Called to the Bar, Gray's Inn, 1984; Recorder, Wales and Chester Circuit, 2003–09. *Address:* Wrexham County and Family Court, The Law Courts, Bodhyfryd, Wrexham LL12 7BP.

**JONES, Gareth S.;** *see* Stedman Jones.

**JONES, Gemma;** *see* Jones, Jennifer.

**JONES, Geoffrey M.;** *see* Melvill Jones.

**JONES, George H.;** *see* Hugh-Jones.

**JONES, George Quentin;** freelance broadcaster and writer; Multi-media Political Correspondent, Press Association, 2007–10; *b* 28 Feb. 1945; *s* of (John) Clement Jones, CBE; *m* 1st, 1972, Diana Chittenden (marr. diss. 1989); one *s* one *d*; 2nd, 1990, Teresa Grace Rolleston. *Educ:* Highfields Sch., Wolverhampton. Trainee journalist, Eastern Daily Press, 1963–67; journalist, S Wales Argus and Western Mail, 1967–69; Reuters, London, 1969; Parly Staff, The Times, 1969–73; Parly and Political Corresp., Scotsman, 1973–82; Political Correspondent: Sunday Telegraph, 1982–85; Sunday Times, 1985–86; Political Corresp., 1986–88, Political Ed., 1988–2007, Daily Telegraph. Regular broadcaster, BBC News and current affairs programmes, Sky News. Chairman: Parly Lobby Journalists, 1987–88; Parly Press Gallery, 1996–97. Assessor, Leveson Public Inquiry into Culture, Practices and Ethics of the Press, 2011–13. Judge, Spectator Parliamentarian of the Year Awards, 1993–2006. Dir, North Curry Community Ltd, 2011–13. Mem., North Curry Parish Council, 2011–14. *Recreations:* walking (Offa's Dyke and other long distance paths), vegetable gardening, mastering change ringing, time with family, enjoying a long-awaited escape to the country after 40 years reporting parliament and politics. *Address:* Helland House, Helland, North Curry, Taunton, Som TA3 6DU. *T:* (01823) 491035.

**JONES, Geraint Anthony;** QC 2001; a Recorder, since 2009; *b* 5 April 1953; *s* of John and Lydia Jones; *m* 1976, Pauline Julia Gibson; two *d*. *Educ:* Christ Coll., Brecon; Jesus Coll., Cambridge (MA). MCIArb 2002. Called to the Bar, Middle Temple, 1976; in practice as barrister, specialising in chancery, commercial and professional negligence law, Cardiff, 1976–, and London, 2001–. Mem., Judicial Panel, World Rugby (formerly Internat. Rugby Bd), 2002–. *Recreations:* hill walking, sailing.

**JONES, Dr Gerald;** FRCP; Senior Principal Medical Officer, Department of Health (formerly of Health and Social Security), 1984–95; *b* 25 Jan. 1939; *s* of John Jones and Gladys Jones (*née* Roberts); *m* 1st, 1964, Anne Heatley (*née* Morris) (marr. diss. 1987); one *s* two *d*; 2nd, 1990, Jutta Friese. *Educ:* Swansea Grammar School; Merton College, Oxford; London Hosp. Med. Coll. (BA, BM, BCh, PhD, MSc). Appointments in hosp. medicine, 1965–69; research with MRC, 1969–73; pharmaceutical industry, 1974–75; medical staff, DHSS, later DoH, 1975–95. *Publications:* papers on cardiopulmonary physiology, respiratory medicine, cellular immunology and drug regulation. *Recreations:* music, gardening, mathematics. *Address:* 58 Palace Road, N8 8QP.

**JONES, Gerald;** MP (Lab) Merthyr Tydfil and Rhymney, since 2015; *b* Caerphilly, 21 Aug. 1970; *s* of Colin and Patricia Jones; partner, Tyrone Powell. *Educ:* Bedwellty Comprehensive Sch.; Ystrad Mynach Coll. Grants Liaison Officer, Cardiff CC, 1990–2000; Community Develt Officer, Gwent Assoc. of Voluntary Orgns, 2001–05 and 2008–15. Mem. (Lab) Caerphilly CBC, 1995–2015 (Dep. Leader, 2004–08 and 2012–15). Shadow Minister for Wales, 2016–17, for Defence, 2017–. *Recreations:* cinema, reading, music. *Address:* House of Commons, SW1A 0AA. *T:* (020) 7219 5874; (office) Oldway House, Castle Street, Merthyr Tydfil CF47 8UX. *T:* (01685) 383739. *E:* gerald.jones.mp@parliament.uk.

**JONES, Gerald Kenneth;** Chief Executive, Wandsworth Borough Council, 1986–2010; *b* 16 June 1943; *s* of Sir Kenneth Jones, CBE, QC and of Menna (*née* Jones); *m* 1976, Janet Norma Dymock; three *s* one *d*. *Educ:* Royal Grammar Sch., Guildford; St John's Coll., Cambridge (MA 1965); Brunel Univ. (MTech 1972). Operational Res. Scientist, NCB, 1966–69; Mgt Consultant, RTZ Corp., 1969–72; Corporate Planner, Haringey Council, 1972–74; Wandsworth Council: Asst Dir, Admin, 1974–81; Dir, Admin, 1981–83; Dep. Chief Exec., 1983–86. *Publications:* contrib. technical and professional jls. *Recreations:* collecting antiquarian books, cycling, swimming, running. *Address:* 9 McKay Road, Wimbledon, SW20 0HT.

**JONES, Gillian Hunter;** QC 2017; a Recorder, since 2012; *b* Newcastle-under-Lyme, 13 April 1973; *d* of Lawrence Jones and Theresa Jones; *m* 2002, Daniel Gordon; one *d*. *Educ:* Univ. of Leicester (LLB EC); Modena Univ. (DipLaw). Called to the Bar, Lincoln's Inn, 1996. Mem., Develtd Bd, Clean Break, 2014–. *Publications:* (contrib.) Fraud: law, practice and procedure; (contrib.) Rook and Ward, Sexual Offences, Law and Practice. *Recreations:* theatre, music, art. *Address:* Red Lion Chambers, 18 Red Lion Court, EC4A 3EB. *T:* (020) 7520 6000. *E:* gillian.jones@18rlc.co.uk.

**JONES, Rev. Canon Glyndwr;** Secretary General, Mission to Seafarers (formerly Missions to Seamen), 1990–2000; a Chaplain to the Queen, 1990–2005; *b* 25 Nov. 1935; *s* of late Bertie Samuel Jones and of Elizabeth Ellen Jones; *m* 1st, 1961, Cynthia Elaine Jenkins (*d* 1964); 2nd, 1966, (Marion) Anita Morris; one *s* one *d*. *Educ:* Dynevor Sch., Swansea; St Michael's Theol Coll., Llandaff, Univ. of Wales (DipTh); MA Wales 2005. Nat. Service, 1954–56: RAPC, attached 19 Field Regt RA; served Korea, Hong Kong; demobbed Sgt AER. Deacon 1962, priest 1963; Curate: Clydach, 1962–64; Llangyfelach with Morriston, 1964–67; Sketty, 1967–70; Rector, Bryngwyn with Newchurch and Llanbedr, Painscastle with Llanddewi Fach, 1970–72; The Missions to Seamen: Port Chaplain, Swansea and Port Talbot, 1972–76; Sen. Chaplain, Port of London, 1976–81; Auxiliary Ministries Sec., Central Office, 1981–85; Asst Gen. Sec., 1985–90. Hon. Chaplain, Royal Alfred Seafarers Soc., 1987–93; Chaplain to Lay Sheriff of London, 1993–94, 1999–2000; Hon. Canon, St Michael's Cathedral, Kobe, Japan, 1988–. Commissary to Bp of Cyprus in the Gulf, 1996–2000. Mem., Eddie Baird Meml Trust, 2003–08 (Treas., 2007–08). Gov., Treetops Sch., Grays, 2008–12. Hon. Mem., Co. of Master Mariners, 1990–2000; Freeman, City of London, 1990; Chaplain: Co. of Information Technologists, 1989–2000; Co. of Innholders, 1990–2002; Co. of Farriers, 1990–2004 (Liveryman, 1999–); Co. of Carmen, 1990–2004 (Liveryman, 1995–). Sec. to Trustees, Orsett Churches Centre, 2003–07. President: Probus Club, Grays Thurrock, 2005–06; Batti-Wallahs' Soc., 2006–07; Rotary Club, Grays Thurrock, 2007–08 (Mem., 2003–; Sec., 2009–12). *Recreations:* sport, music, reading, theatre, travel. *Address:* 5 The Close, Grays, Essex RM16 2XU. *Clubs:* Little Ship (Hon. Chaplain, 1996–2000); Thurrock Rugby Football (Chaplain, 1999).

**JONES, Prof. Glynis Eleanor May,** PhD; FBA 2013; Professor of Archaeology, University of Sheffield, since 2004; *b* Kenfig Hill, 4 Feb. 1950; *d* of Cyril Nelson and Phyllis Nelson (*née* Powell); one *s* by a previous marriage. *Educ:* Cynffig Comprehensive Sch.; University Coll. of Cardiff (BSc Hons Zool.; Cert Ed); Darwin Coll., Cambridge (MPhil Archaeol. 1979; PhD 1984). Teacher of Biol., Barry Comprehensive Sch., 1972–73; res. asst, Fitch Lab., British Sch. at Athens, 1974–78; Envmtl Archaeologist, Dept of Urban Archaeol., Mus. of London, 1983–84; Lectr, 1984–93, Sen. Lectr, 1993–2000, Reader, 2000–04, Dept of Archaeol., Univ. of Sheffield. *Publications:* (ed jtly) Fodder: archaeological, historical and ethnographic studies, 1998; (ed jtly) Archaeology of Plants, 2001; contrib. papers to learned jls. *Recreations:* walking, theatre, local conservation group. *Address:* Department of Archaeology, University of Sheffield, Minalloy House, 10–16 Regent Street, Sheffield S1 3NJ. *T:* (0114) 222 2904. *E:* g.jones@sheffield.ac.uk.

**JONES, Gordon Frederick;** architect; *b* 25 Aug. 1929; *s* of Harold Frederick and Rose Isabel Jones; *m* 1954, Patricia Mary (*née* Rowley); one *s* one *d*. *Educ:* Saltley Grammar Sch.; The School of Architecture, Birmingham (DipArch 1950), and subseq. by BBC; Sch. of Planning, UCL (Cert. Landscape Design, 1963). RIBA 1950. FRSA. Architect: in local government, 1952; War Office, 1959; Asst City Architect, Sheffield, 1966; private practice, London, 1968; Property Services Agency, DoE: Architect, 1970; Head of Student Training Office, 1976; Head of Architectural Services, 1979–85; Res. Dir, 1985–90, Editor, 1990–93, Product Design Review. Dir, Building Centre, London, 1984–87. Chm. of Standards, BDB/–, BSI, 1984–87. *Recreations:* watching cats, listening to music, re-building houses. *Address:* Cartref, Monkleigh, Bideford, Devon EX39 5JT.

**JONES, Graham Edward,** MA; Headmaster, Repton School, 1987–2003; *b* 22 Sept. 1944; *s* of late Edward Thomas Jones and Dora Rachel Jones; *m* 1976, Vanessa Mary Heloise (*née* Smith). *Educ:* Birkenhead Sch.; Fitzwilliam Coll., Cambridge (schol.; 1st cl. Hons Econs Tripos 1966). Asst Master, Hd of Economics and Politics, Housemaster, Charterhouse, 1967–87; secondment to British Petroleum, 1981. Awarder in Economics, Oxford and Cambridge Schs Examination Bd, 1979–91; Reviser in Economics, JMB, 1981–91; Chm. Examrs, Oxford and Cambridge and RSA Examinations, 1996–2001; Chm., Ind. Schs Examinations Bd, 1998–2006. Governor: Birkenhead Sch., 2004–16; Royal GS, Worcester, 2004–07; Malvern Coll., 2005– (Vice-Chm., 2011–18). FRSA 1988. *Publications:* various articles on economics and teaching economics. *Recreations:* painting, travel, music, cooking, the classics. *Address:* Tilton House, Sutton St Nicholas, Hereford HR1 3BB. *T:* (01432) 882075.

**JONES, His Honour Graham Julian;** a Senior Circuit Judge, 2002–05 (a Circuit Judge, 1985–2005; authorised to sit as a Judge of the High Court, 1994–2005); a Judge of Technology and Construction Court (formerly a Circuit Official Referee), 1993–2005; Resident and Designated Judge, Cardiff County Court, 1994–98; Designated Civil Judge, Cardiff, 1998–2000, South and West Wales, 2000–05; Deputy High Court Judge, 2005–11; acting Designated Civil Judge for Wales, 2008; *b* 17 July 1936; *s* of late David John Jones, CBE, and Edna Lillie Jones; *m* 1961, Dorothy, *o d* of late James Smith and Doris Irene Tickle, Abergavenny; two *s* one *d*. *Educ:* Porth County Grammar Sch. (state scholarship); St John's Coll., Cambridge. MA, LLM (Cantab). Admitted Solicitor, 1961; Partner, Morgan Bruce and Nicholas, 1961 (represented Parents and Residents Assoc., Aberfan Disaster, 1966). Dep. Circuit Judge, 1975–78; a Recorder, 1978–85. Pres., Pontypridd Rhondda and Dist Law Soc., 1973–75; Member Council: Cardiff Law Soc., 1975–78, 1984–85; Associated Law Socs of Wales, 1974–85 (Pres., 1982–84); Member: Lord Chancellor's Legal Aid Adv. Cttee, 1980–85; Adv. Bd, Centre for Professional Legal Studies, Cardiff Law Sch., 1995–; Civil Justice Council, 2004–12 (Chm., Comparative Law Cttee and Collective Redress Working Gp, 2006–11); Judicial Estates Adv. Gp, 2004–10. Chairman: Swansea Intervention Bd, Welsh Assembly Govt, 2009–10; Pembrokeshire Ministerial Bd, 2011–13. Mem. Court, UWCC, 1995–98; Gov., Univ. of Glamorgan, 1999–2006. Council Mem., RNLI, 2002–05 (Vice Pres., 2005–). *Publications:* papers and presentations in Europe on collective redress. *Recreations:* golf, boats. *Clubs:* Cardiff and County (Cardiff), Radyr Golf, Royal Porthcawl Golf.

**JONES, Graham Peter;** MP (Lab) Hyndburn, since 2010; *b* 2 March 1966; partner, Kimberley Whitehead; one *s* one *d*. *Educ:* BA (Hons) Applied Social Studies. Graphic Designer, 1992–2010. Member (Lab): Hyndburn BC, 2002–10; Lancs CC, 2009–10. An Opposition Asst Whip, 2010–15. Mem., Defence Select Cttee, 2017–. *Address:* House of Commons, SW1A 0AA.

**JONES, Gregory Dennis T.;** *see* Treverton-Jones.

**JONES, Gregory Percy;** QC 2011; *b* Dartford, Kent, 4 Jan. 1968; *s* of late Colin Frederick Jones and of Jeannette Bridget Jones (*née* McDonald); *m* 1997, Rosali Margaretha Pretorius; two *d*. *Educ:* Colfe's Sch.; New Coll., Oxford (MA; Pres., Oxford Univ. Law Soc. 1986; Treas., Oxford Union Soc. 1986; New Coll. 1st XV Rugby); University Coll. London (LLM). ESU debating tour, USA, 1989; Stagiaire, EC, Brussels, 1990. Called to the Bar: Lincoln's Inn, 1991 (Hardwicke Schol.; Thomas More Bursar); King's Inns, Dublin, 1997; Inn of Court, NI, 2008; Inner Temple (ad eundem), 2016; in practice as a barrister, 1993–. Pt-time Sen. Lectr in EU Law, South Bank Univ., 1993–97; Jean Pierre Warner Scholar, Eur. Court of Justice, Luxembourg, 1995; Fellow, Centre for Eur. Law, KCL, 2008–. Legal Associate, RTPI 2003. Deputy Chancellor: Dio. of Truro, 2008–; Dio. of Exeter, 2008–;

Dio. of Ely, 2010–12. Governor: Colfe's Sch., 2008–13; Leathersellers' Fedn of Schs, 2012–17 (Associate Gov., 2017–). Member: Bar Council, 2008–16; House Council, St Stephen's House, Univ. of Oxford, 2011–; Common Councilman, 2013–17, Alderman, 2017–, City of London (Farringdon Without); Chm., Ind. Orgnl Rev. of An Bord Pleanála, 2015–16. FRSA 2013; FRGS 2014; FLS 2015. Freeman, City of London, 1999; Liveryman: Leathersellers' Co., 2003; Butchers' Co., 2017. *Publications:* (jtly) Statutory Nuisance, 2001, 3rd edn 2011; (jtly) Environmental Law in Property Transactions, 4th edn 2016; (ed and contrib.) The Habitats Directive: a developer's obstacle course?, 2012; (ed jtly and contrib.) The Strategic Environmental Assessment Directive: a plan for success?, 2017; (Asst Ed.) National Infrastructure Planning Articles, 2013–. *Recreations:* history (esp. military and Irish), 20th century South African art, scuba diving, watching Rugby, cricket and football. *Address:* Francis Taylor Building, Temple, EC4Y 7BY. *T:* (020) 7353 8415. *E:* clerks@ftbchambers.co.uk. *Clubs:* Athenæum, Brooks's, Oxford and Cambridge; Surrey County Cricket; Old Colfeians Rugby Football.

**JONES, Guy Charles L.;** *see* Lloyd-Jones.

**JONES, Gwilym Haydn;** management consultant, 1997–2007; *b* 20 Sept. 1947; *s* of late Evan Haydn Jones and Mary Elizabeth Gwenhwyfar Jones (*née* Moseley); *m* 1974, Linda Margaret (*née* John); one *s* one *d*. Dir, Bowring Wales Ltd, 1980–92. Councillor, Cardiff CC, 1969–72 and 1973–83. MP (C) Cardiff North, 1983–97; contested (C) same seat, 1997. PPS to Minister of State, Dept of Transport, 1991–92; Parly Under-Sec. of State, Welsh Office, 1992–97. Secretary: Welsh Cons. Members Gp, 1984–92; All Party Gp for Fund for Replacement of Animals in Medical Experiments, 1987–92. Fellow, Industry and Parlt Trust, 1986. Mem. Exec. Cttee, Assoc. of Former Members of Parlt, 2001–10. Founder Chm., Friendship Force in Wales, 1978–81; Chm., St John Ambulance Council for Cardiff and Vale of Glamorgan, 2013–19; Vice Pres., Kidney Res. Unit for Wales Foundn, 1986–92. Rowed for Wales in Speaker's Regatta, 1986. Liveryman, Welsh Livery Guild, 1993–2010. Officer: United Grand Lodge of England, 2010–; Supreme Grand Chapter of England, 2012–; Grand Lodge of Mark Master Masons, 2015–; District Grand Master for S Wales, Order of Royal and Select Masters, 2015–. CStJ 2019 (OStJ 1997). *Recreation:* watching Wales win at Rugby. *Clubs:* County Conservative, Cardiff and County (Cardiff).

**JONES, Gwyn;** *see* Jones, Miah G.

**JONES, Gwyn;** a District Judge (Magistrates' Courts), since 2013; *b* Trawsfynydd, 22 July 1960; *s* of Edgar and Lowri Jones; *m* 1986, Margaret Macmillan; one *s* one *d*. *Educ:* Ysgol y Moelwyn, Blaenau Ffestiniog; Liverpool Poly. (BA Hons Law); Coll. of Law, Chester. Leo Abse & Cohen Solicitors: articled clerk, 1982–84; asst solicitor, 1984–86; Partner, 1986–96; Partner, Gamlins Solicitors, 1996–2013; Dep. Dist Judge (Magistrates' Courts), 2000–13. Chair, Llamau Housing Soc. Ltd, 1989–92. *Recreations:* gardening, mountain biking, travelling, eating out. *Address:* Llandudno Magistrates' Court, The Court House, Conwy Road, Llandudno, Conwy LL30 1GA. *T:* (01492) 863854.

**JONES, Gwyn,** FRAgS; farmer; Member, since 2014, and Chairman, Dairy Board (formerly DairyCo), since 2014, Agriculture and Horticulture Development Board; *b* Dolgellau, 10 March 1954; *s* of Humphrey Lloyd Jones and Eirlys Lloyd Jones; *m* 1973, Lorayne; two *d*. *Educ:* Ysgol y Gader, Dolgellau. Engrg apprentice, Rolls Royce, 1970. Chm., Dairy Bd, 2004–10, Vice Pres., 2010–12, NFU. Chairman: Eur. Platform for Responsible Use of Medicines in Animals, 2012–; Responsible Use of Medicines in Agric., 2013–; Vice Chm., COPA-Gogeca Animal Health and Welfare Wkg Gp, 2010–. Dir, Anaerobic Digestion and Bioresources Assoc., 2010–14. Nuffield Scholar. *Address:* Moores Green Cottage, Kirdford, Billingshurst, W Sussex RH14 0LE. *T:* 07730 001387. *E:* wealdclay@btinternet.com. *Club:* Farmers.

**JONES, Gwyn Idris M.;** *see* Meirion-Jones.

**JONES, Dame Gwyneth,** DBE 1986 (CBE 1976); a Principal Dramatic Soprano: Royal Opera House, Covent Garden, since 1963; Vienna State Opera, since 1966 (Hon. Member, 1989); Deutsche Oper Berlin, since 1966; Bavarian State Opera, since 1967; *b* 7 Nov. 1936; *d* of late Edward George Jones and late Violet (*née* Webster); one *d*; *m* 2008, Adrian Mueller. *Educ:* Twmpath Sec. Mod. Sch., Pontypool, Mon; Royal College of Music, London; Accademia Chigiana, Siena; Zürich Internat. Opera Studio. Maria Carpi Prof., Geneva. Guest Artiste: La Scala, Milan; Berlin State Opera; Munich State Opera; Bayreuth Festival; Salzburg Festival; Verona; Orange; Tokyo; Zürich; Metropolitan Opera, New York; Paris; Geneva; Dallas; San Francisco; Los Angeles; Teatro Colon, Buenos Aires; Edinburgh Festival; Welsh National Opera; Rome; Hamburg; Cologne; Maggio Musicale, Florence; Chicago; Seoul; Peking; Hong Kong. Many opera roles including: Leonora in Il Trovatore; Desdemona in Otello; Aida; Leonore in Fidelio; Senta in The Flying Dutchman; Medea (Cherubini); Sieglinde in Die Walküre; Lady Macbeth; Elizabeth in Don Carlos; Madame Butterfly; Tosca; Donna Anna in Don Giovanni; Salome/Herodias; Kundry in Parsifal; Isolde; Helena in Die Ägyptische; Färberin/Kaiserin in Die Frau ohne Schatten; Chrysothemis/Elektra/Klytaemnestra in Elektra; Elizabeth/Venus in Tannhäuser; Octavian/Marschallin in Der Rosenkavalier; Sieglinde/Gutrune/Brünnhilde in Der Ring des Nibelungen; Ortrud in Lohengrin; Minnie in Fanciulla del West; Norma; Erwartung (Schoenberg); La voix humaine (Poulenc); Esmeralda in Notre Dame (Schmidt); Leokadia Begvick in Aufstieg und Fall der Stadt Mahagonny (Brecht/Weil); Kusterin Buryja in Jenufa (Janáček); Kabanicha in Katia Kabanowa (Janáček); Queen of Hearts in Alice in Wonderland (Unsuk Chin); Claire Zachanassian in Der Besuch der alten Dame (Gottfried von Einem); Cosima Wagner in Wagnerin; The Countess in Pique Dame; Enoch Arden, Tennyson/Richard Strauss; oratorio and recitals. Numerous recordings, radio and TV appearances; film, Quartet, 2013. Début as Opera Dir, Der Fliegende Holländer, Deutsches Nat. Th., Weimar, 2003. Pres., Richard Wagner Soc., 1990–. FRCM. Kammersängerin, Austria and Bavaria. Hon. Member: RAM, 1980; Vienna State Opera, 1989; Hon. FRWCMD 1992. Hon. DMus: Wales. Glamorgan. Shakespeare Prize, FVS Hamburg, 1987; Premio Puccini, 2003; Cymru for the World Honours, 2004. Verdienstkreuz, Klasse 1 (FRG), 1988; Golden Medal of Honour (Austria), 1991; Comdr, Ordre des Arts et des Lettres (France), 1992; Ehrenkreuz für Wissenschaft und Kunst, 1 Klasse (Austria), 1998. *Address:* PO Box 2000, 8700 Küsnacht, Switzerland.

**JONES, Gwynoro Glyndwr;** Director, EPPC Severn Crossing Ltd, 1999–2012; Lay Inspector of Schools, 1994–2012; *b* 21 Nov. 1942; *s* of late J. E. and A. L. Jones, Minyrafon, Foelgastell, Cefneithin, Carms; *m* 1967, A. Laura Miles (marr. diss. 1991); two *s* one *d*. *Educ:* Gwendraeth Grammar Sch.; Cardiff Univ. BSc Econ (Hons) Politics and Economics. Market Research Officer, Ina Needle Bearings Ltd, Llanelli, 1966–67; Economist Section, Wales Gas Bd, 1967–69; Public Relations Officer, Labour Party in Wales, March 1969–June 1970; West Glamorgan County Council: Dir of Res., 1974–77; Asst Educn Officer, Develt Forward Planning, 1977–92. Advr/Assessor, Investors in People, 1999–2007; External Assessor: Performance Mgt of Headteachers, 2000–06; for EFQM and Lexcel standards, 2003–06; Best Value Assessor, Audit Commn, 2003–05. Vice-Pres., Dist Council Assoc., 1974; Mem., Council of European Municipalities, 1975–77; first Chm., Welsh Council of European Movt, 1995–97 (Vice Chm., 2015–). Broadcaster and television interviewer, S4C, 1993–95. MP (Lab) Carmarthen, 1970–Oct. 1974; Member: House of Commons Expenditure Cttee, 1972–74; Council of Europe and WEU, 1974; PPS to Home Sec., 1974. Pres., Nat. Eisteddfod of Wales, 1974. Co-ordinator, Wales in Europe campaign, 1975; Sponsor, Wales Lab and TU Cttee for Europe, 1975; joined SDP, May 1981; contested: (SDP) Gower, Sept. 1982; (SDP/Alliance) Carmarthen, 1987; (Lib Dem) Hereford, 1992; (Ind) Mid and W Wales, Nat. Assembly for Wales, 2007. Chairman: SDP Council for Wales, 1982–85, 1987–88; Alliance Cttee for Wales, 1983–88; Interim Chm., Welsh Soc & Lib Dem Exec., 1988; Member: Council for Social Democracy, 1982–88; SDP Nat. Cttee, 1982–85; SDP Orgn Cttee, 1987–88; Lib Dem Federal Exec., 1988–90; Vice Chm., Lib Dem Policy Cttee, 1988–89; rejoined Labour Party, 1997. Mem., Electoral Reform Soc., 2015–. *Publications:* booklets: The Record Put Straight, 1973; SDP and the Alliance in Wales 1981–1986, 1986; SLD Golden Opportunities, 1988; A Movement in Crisis, 1989; Gwynoro a Gwynfor, 2019. *Recreation:* sport (played Rugby for both 1st and 2nd class teams). *Address:* 180 West Street, Gorseinon, Swansea SA4 4AQ. *W:* http://gwynorojones.blogspot.co.uk, www.twitter.com/Gwynoro, www.facebook.com/Gwynoro Jones.

**JONES, Sir Harry (George),** Kt 2000; CBE 1995; Member (Lab), Newport County Borough Council, since 1995 (Leader of Council, 1995–2003); *b* 29 April 1927; *s* of Edward and Alice Jones; *m* 1956, Hazel Kembrey; three *s*. *Educ:* St Woolos Sch.; Newport Tech. Coll. Officer, Merchant Navy, 1948. Apprentice engr, 1943; worked in aluminium ind., 1970s. Member (Lab), Newport DC, 1973–96 (Shadow Mem., 1973–74; Leader of Council, 1987–96; Mayor, 1990–91). Leader, Welsh LGA, 1986–; Vice-Chm., LGA, 1995–; Chm., Local Govt Mgt Bd, 1994. Mem., Welsh NEC, 1990–, and Nat. Policy Forum, 1997–, Labour Party. Hon. Mem. Council, NSPCC, 1993–; Patron, Prince's Trust, 1995–; Trustee, Firebrake Wales, 2005–. Freeman, Newport City and County, 2003. Hon. Mem., RSA, 2000. Hon. Fellow, UCW, Newport, 1999. *Recreations:* swimming, art, gardening. *Address:* 8 Beaufort Place, Newport, S Wales NP19 7NB. *T:* (01633) 769538, (office) (01633) 232121.

**JONES, Helen Mary;** MP (Lab) Warrington North, since 1997; *b* 24 Dec. 1954; *d* of late Robert Edward Jones and of Mary Scanlan; *m* 1988, Michael Vobe; one *s*. *Educ:* Ursuline Convent, Chester; UCL; Chester Coll.; Univ. of Liverpool; Manchester Metropolitan Univ. BA, PGCE, MEd, CPE, LSF. Teacher of English; Develt Officer, Mind; Justice and Peace Officer, Liverpool; Solicitor. Contested (Lab): Shropshire N, 1983; Lancashire Central, EP elecn, 1984; Ellesmere Port and Neston, 1987. An Asst Govt Whip, 2008–09; Vice-Chamberlain of HM Household, 2009–10. Chm., Petitions Select Cttee, 2015–. *Address:* House of Commons, SW1A 0AA; 67 Bewsey Street, Warrington, Cheshire WA2 7JQ.

**JONES, Helen Mary;** Member (Plaid Cymru) Mid and West Wales, National Assembly for Wales, since 2018; *b* 29 June 1960; *d* of late John Mervyn Jones and Daphne Lyle Stuart; one *d*. *Educ:* Colchester County High Sch. for Girls, Essex; Llanfair Caereinion High Sch.; UCW Aberystwyth (BA Hist.). Special Educn Teacher, Gwent, 1982–87; Orgnr for Wales, ActionAid, 1987–91; various positions in youth, community and social work, 1991–96; Sen. Develt Manager (Dep. Dir), EOC, Wales, 1996–99. Public affairs consultant, 2011–17. Former Mem., Nat. Assembly Adv. Gp. National Assembly for Wales: Mem. (Plaid Cymru) Llanelli, 1999–2003 and 2007–11, Mid and W Wales, 2003–07; Plaid Cymru spokesman on educn and equality, 2002–03, on the environment, planning and countryside, 2003–05, on educn, 2005–07, on health and social services, 2007–11; Chair, Children and Young People's Cttee, 2007–11. Contested (Plaid Cymru): Islwyn, 1992; Montgomery, 1997; Llanelli, Nat. Assembly for Wales, 2011, 2016. Chair, Plaid Cymru, 2011–13. Mem. Bd, Ministerial Intervention Pembrokeshire, Welsh Govt, 2011–13. Chief Exec., Youth Cymru, 2011–17. Associate Prof., Swansea Univ., 2017–18. Hon Dr Swansea, 2017. *Address:* National Assembly for Wales, Cardiff Bay, Cardiff CF99 1NA.

**JONES, His Honour Hugh Duncan Hitchings,** DL; a Circuit Judge, 1991–2004; a Deputy Circuit Judge, 2004–12; *b* 25 May 1937; *s* of Norman Everard Jones and Ann Jones (*née* Hitchings); *m* 1966, Helen Margaret Payne; three *d*. *Educ:* Mountain Ash Grammar School (State Scholarship); University College London (LLB). Admitted Solicitor, 1961; Registrar, Cardiff County Court and Dist Registrar of the High Court, Cardiff Dist Registry, 1978; a Recorder, 1988–91; Designated Family Judge, 1996–2004. Mem., County Court Rules Cttee, 1994–97. Vice-Pres., Disciplinary Tribunal, Church in Wales, 1996–2004. DL Mid Glamorgan, 2007. *Recreations:* cricket, gardening, holidays in France. *Address:* The Cottage, Cwmpennar, Mountain Ash, Mid Glamorgan CF45 4DB. *Clubs:* MCC; Cardiff and County; Mountain Ash Golf.

**JONES, Huw;** *see* Jones, David H.

**JONES, Rev. Huw;** *see* Jones, Rev. David H.

**JONES, Hywel Ceri,** CMG 1999; Chairman of Board, Wales Governance Centre, University of Cardiff, 2012–15; *b* 22 April 1937; *m* 1967, Morwenna Armstrong; one *s* one *d*. *Educ:* UCW, Aberystwyth (BA French and Classics, DipEd; Hon. Fellow, 1990). Admin. appts, Sussex Univ., 1962–73; joined EC, 1973; Head, Dept for Educn and Youth Policies, 1973–79; Dir for Educn, Vocational Trng and Youth Policy, 1979–88; Dir, Task Force for Human Resources, Educn, Trng and Youth, 1989–93; Acting Dir-Gen., 1993–95, Dep. Dir-Gen., 1995–98, Employment, Social Policy and Indust. Relns. Vis. Fellow in Educn and Contemp. European Studies, Sussex Univ., 1973–80. Eur. Advr to Sec. of State for Wales, 1998–99. Chm., Governing Bd, European Policy Centre, Brussels, 2000–07; Dir, Network of European Foundns, 2004–09; Governor: Eur. Cultural Foundn, Amsterdam, 1999–2007; Federal Trust for Educn and Research, 2004–; Eur. Funding Ambassador to Welsh Govt, 2014–. Board Member: Franco-British Council, 2004–10; Supervisory Bd, ECORYS Gp, 2006–14. Trustee: Tomorrow's Wales, 2008–; Equal Rights Trust, 2011–; Nat. Mus. of Wales, 2014–. Hon. Fellow: NE Wales Inst. of Higher Educn, 1992; Swansea, 1992; Aberystwyth, 1993; Glamorgan, 1994; Westminster, 1994; Trinity Univ. Coll., Carmarthen, 2008. DUniv: Sussex, 1991; Leuven, 1992; Open, 2000; Free Univ. Brussels, 2002; Univ. of Wales, 2013; Hon. LLD NCEA, Ireland, 1992. Gold Medal, Republic of Italy, 1987. *Recreations:* Rugby, cricket, snooker, theatre, travel, golf. *Address:* 38 Plymouth Road, Penarth CF64 3DH. *Clubs:* Reform; Fondation Universitaire (Brussels); Glamorganshire Golf.

**JONES, Hywel Rhys;** Deputy Director of Education, Astrea Academies, since 2018; *b* Newport, Gwent, 26 June 1978; *s* of Alun and Rosemarie Jones; partner, Fiona Murray; one *s* one *d*. *Educ:* London Sch. of Econs and Pol Sci. (BSc Internat. Relns); Pembroke Coll., Cambridge (MPhil Internat. Relns; PGCE Secondary Educn). Consultant, Deloitte, 2000–04; teacher, City of Ely Community Coll., 2005–07; teacher, 2007–10, Asst Headteacher, 2010–14, St Mary's Catholic Sch., Bishop's Stortford; Headteacher, W London Free Sch., Hammersmith, 2014–18; Primary Dir, Inspiration Trust, 2018. Non-exec. Dir, Ofqual, 2017–. *Recreation:* cycling. *Address:* Astrea Academy Trust, 28 Leman Street, E1 8ER. *E:* hywel.jones@astreaacademytrust.org.

**JONES, Ian;** media consultant, since 2017; Chief Executive Officer, S4C, 2012–17; *b* Swansea, 14 Jan. 1959; *s* of Lyle Jones and Margaret Jones; two *s*. *Educ:* Ysgol Gyfun Ystalyfera; University Coll. of Wales, Aberystwyth (BSc Econ). Commng Exec., S4C,

1982–85; Unit Manager, Entertainment, ITV, 1986–87; Ind. Prod., 1987–89; Dir Business and S4C Internat., 1990–96; Dir, Internat., STV, 1997–99; Chief Operating Officer, ITEL, 2000; Dep. Man. Dir, Internat., Granada, 2000–04; Pres., Internat., National Geographic TV, 2004–07; Man. Dir, Target, 2007–09; Man. Dir, Content Distribution and Commercial Develt, A&E TV Networks Internat., 2010–11. Pres., Latitude Quest. Hon. DLitt Swansea, 2018. *Recreation:* all forms of sport.

**JONES, Ian Michael**; Director, Office of Manpower Economics, 2007–10; *b* 5 Sept. 1949; *s* of Derek and Jean Jones; *m* 1976, Vivien Hepworth; two *s*. *Educ:* St Bartholomew's Grammar Sch., Newbury; Fitzwilliam Coll., Cambridge (BA Econs and Politics 1972). Home Office, 1972–83; DTI, 1983–85, Grade 5, 1985; Dept of Employment, 1985–89; Sec., BOTB, 1989–90; Department of Trade and Industry, 1989–2000: Regl Dir, SE Reg., 1990–94; Leader, London City Action Team, 1992–94; Grade 3, 1994; Head, Textiles and Retail Div., 1994–96; Head, Post, Retail and Textiles Directorate, 1996; Chief Exec., Employment Tribunals Service, 1997–2000; Dir, Regl Gp, British Trade Internat., 2000–01; Dep. Chief Exec., British Trade Internat., subseq. UK Trade and Investment, 2001–04; Dir, Efficiency Prog., 2004–05, Ops Directorate, 2005–07, DTI. Director: Lingfield and Dormansland Community Centre 2014– (Chm., 2015–); Pennies from Heaven Distribn, 2015– (Chm., 2015–). Trustee, William Buckwell Almshouses, 2011–18; Chairman: Lingfield Guest House Trustee Ltd, 2015–; Lingfield and Dormansland Bridge Club, 2016–. *Recreations:* cricket, bridge. *T:* (01342) 832907. *E:* ian@cyderbarn.com.

**JONES, Rt Rev. Dr Idris**; Bishop of Glasgow and Galloway, 1998–2009; Primus of the Episcopal Church in Scotland, 2006–09; *b* 2 April 1943; *s* of Edward Eric Jones and Alice Gertrude (*née* Burgess); *m* 1973, Alison Margaret Williams; two *s*. *Educ:* St David's Coll., Lampeter, Univ. of Wales (BA; Hon. Fellow 2007); Univ. of Edinburgh (LTh); NY Theol Seminary (DMin 1987); Dip. Person Centred Therapy 1994. Curate, St Mary, Stafford, 1967–70; Precentor, Dundee Cathedral, 1970–73; Team Vicar, St Hugh, Gosforth, 1973–80; Chaplain, St Nicholas Hosp. (Teaching), 1975–80; Rector, Montrose with Inverbervie, 1980–89; Canon, St Paul's Cathedral, Dundee, 1984–92; Anglican Chaplain, Dundee Univ. and Priest-in-Charge, Invergowrie, 1989–92; Team Rector, Ayr, Girvan, Maybole, 1992–98; Dir, Pastoral Studies, Theol Inst., Edinburgh, 1995–98. Nat. Spiritual Dir, Anglican Cursillo UK, 2011–14; Dir, Scottish Episcopal Church, 2014–17. Lay Psychotherapist: Dundee, 1990–92; Ayr, 1995–98. Dir, Merchants House of Glasgow, 2010–16; Collector, Trades House of Glasgow, 2012–13; Convenor, Incorporated Trades of Glasgow, 2014–15. Gov., Hutcheson's Educnl Trust, 2002–09; Patron, Hutcheson's Hosp., Glasgow, 2002–09. Mem., Incorpn of Skinners & Glovers of Glasgow, 1999– (Hon. Master, 2016). Paul Harris Fellow, Rotary Internat., 2011. *Recreations:* walking, golf, music. *Address:* 27 Donald Wynd, The Rise, Largs KA30 8TH.

**JONES, Ieuan Wyn**; Adviser, Menai Science Park, since 2018 (Executive Director, 2013–18); *b* 22 May 1949; *s* of late John Jones and of Mair Elizabeth Jones; *m* 1974, Eirian Llwyd (*d* 2014); two *s* one *d*. *Educ:* Pontardawe Grammar School; Ysgol-y-Berwyn, Y Bala, Gwynedd; Liverpool Polytechnic. LLB Hons. Qualified Solicitor, 1973; Partner in practice, 1974–87. Plaid Cymru: National Vice-Chm., 1975–79; National Chm., 1980–82, 1990–92; Pres., 2000–03; Leader, Assembly Gp, 2003–12. MP (Plaid Cymru) Ynys Môn, 1987–2001. Mem. Select Committee: on Welsh Affairs, 1990–92, 1997–2001; on Agriculture, 1992–97. Contested (Plaid Cymru) Ynys Môn (Anglesey), 1983. Mem. (Plaid Cymru) Ynys Môn, Nat. Assembly for Wales, 1999–2013. Dep. First Minister and Minister for the Economy and Transport, Nat. Assembly for Wales, 2007–11. Leader, Plaid Cymru, 2000–12. Contested (Plaid Cymru) Ynys Môn, 2017. Hon. Fellow: Bangor Univ., 2001; Univ. of Wales Trinity St David, 2008. Hon. DLaws Swansea, 2015. *Publications:* Europe: the challenge for Wales, 1996; Thomas Gee (biog.), 1998. *Recreations:* sport, local history. *Address:* Tŷ Newydd, Rhosmeirch, Llangefni, Ynys Môn LL77 7RZ. *T:* (01248) 722261. *E:* ieuanwjones@gmail.com.

**JONES, Iona Elisabeth Lois, (Mrs Timothy Wilson)**; Chief Executive, S4C, 2005–10; *b* 15 Jan. 1964; *d* of John Stuart Roberts and Verina Roberts (*née* Gravelle); *m* 1st, 1990, Wynford Jones (marr. diss. 2008); one *s* two *d*; 2nd, 2013, Timothy Wilson. *Educ:* Ysgol Gyfun Llanhari; Univ. of Exeter (BA Hons Econ. and Social Hist.); Cardiff Univ. (Postgrad. Dip. Journalism). Journalist, BBC Wales, 1986–95; Director, Corporate Affairs: S4C, 1995–2000; HTV Gp, 2000–03; Dir of Progs, S4C, 2003–05.

**JONES, Jacqui**; *see* Lait, J.

**JONES, Sir James (Peter Martin Benton)**, 5th Bt *cr* 1919; *b* Ipswich, 1 Jan. 1973; *s* of Sir Simon Warley Frederick Benton Jones, 4th Bt and Margaret Fiona Benton Jones, OBE (*née* Dickson); *S* father, 2016, but his name does not appear on the Official Roll of the Baronetage; *m* 2008, Leila Joelle Reuter; one *s* one *d*. *Educ:* Milton Abbey Sch., Dorset. Dir, JBJ Construction, 1993–. *Recreations:* natural world, entomology, taxidermy, shooting, skiing, lepidoptery, historical buildings. *Heir: s* Blake Alexander Benton Jones, *b* 30 Oct. 2009. *Address:* Irnham Hall, Irnham, Grantham, Lincs NG33 4JD. *T:* 07973 168452. *E:* jbentonjones@gmail.com.

**JONES, (James) Roger**; Head of Antiques Department, since 1994, and Director, since 1996, Sibyl Colefax & John Fowler; *b* 30 May 1952; *s* of late Albert James Jones and Hilda Vera Jones (*née* Evans); civil partnership 2007, Gregory John Ellis Chambers. *Educ:* Shrewsbury; St Catharine's Coll., Cambridge (Sen. Schol.; Double First, History and Law Triposes; MA). Called to the Bar, Middle Temple, 1974 (Lloyd Jacob Meml Exhibnr; Astbury Schol.); practised Oxford and Midland Circuit, 1975–83. Joined Office of Parly Counsel, 1983; with Law Commn, 1988–91; Dep. Parly Counsel, 1991–94. *Recreation:* walking the dog. *Address:* Sibyl Colefax & John Fowler, 89–91 Pimlico Road, SW1W 8PH.

**JONES, Rt Rev. James Stuart**, KBE 2017; Bishop of Liverpool, 1998–2013; an Hon. Assistant Bishop, Diocese of York, since 2014; *b* 18 Aug. 1948; *s* of Major James Stuart Anthony Jones and Helen Jones; *m* 1980, Sarah Caroline Rosalind Marrow; three *d*. *Educ:* Duke of York's Royal Mil. Sch., Dover; Exeter Univ. (BA Hons Theol.); Wycliffe Hall, Oxford. Teacher, Sevenoaks Sch., 1970–74; Producer, Scripture Union, 1975–81; ordained deacon, 1982, priest, 1983; Curate, Christ Church, Clifton, 1982–90; Vicar, Emmanuel Church, S Croydon, 1990–94; Bishop Suffragan of Hull, 1994–98; Bishop to HM Prisons, 2007–13. Took his seat in H of L, 2003. Visitor, St Peter's Coll., Oxford, 2007–13. Chairman: Hillsborough Ind. Panel, 2009–12; Ind. Panel on Future of Forestry, 2011–12; Gosport Ind. Panel, 2013–18; Co-Chair of Corporate Social Responsibility, Waitrose, 2013–19. Advr to Home Sec. on Hillsborough, 2013–18. Vice Pres., TCPA, 2008–. Fellow: Inst. of Chartered Foresters, 2014; Soc. of the Envmt, 2016. Ambassador, WWF, 2006–14 (Fellow, 2014–); Patron, UK Envmtl Law Assoc., 2016. Hon. Fellow, Liverpool John Moores, 2013. Hon. DD Hull, 1999; Hon. DLitt Lincolnshire and Humberside, 2001; Hon PhD: Liverpool Hope, 2009; Liverpool, 2013; Exeter, 2013; Gloucester, 2013. Freedom, City of Liverpool, 2016. Trustee, Athenæum Club, 2019–. *Publications:* Finding God, 1987; Why do people suffer?, 1993; The Power and the Glory, 1994; A Faith that touches the World, 1994; People of the Blessing, 1999; The Moral Leader, 2002; Jesus and the Earth, 2003; With My Whole Heart, 2012. *Address:* Mount Pleasant Cottage, Burythorpe, Malton YO17 9LJ.

**JONES, Jennifer, (Gemma)**; actress; *b* 4 Dec. 1942; *d* of late Griffith Jones and Irene Jones (*née* Isaac); one *s* by Sebastian Graham Jones. *Educ:* Royal Acad. of Dramatic Art (Gold Medal). *Theatre* includes: Hamlet, Birmingham Rep., 1968; Getting On, Queen's, 1972; A Streetcar Named Desire, Nottingham Playhouse, 1978; Unfinished Business, 1994; The Master Builder, Haymarket, 1995; Cat on a Hot Tin Roof, Lyric, 2001; And Then There Were None, Gielgud, 2005; On Religion, Soho Th., 2006; The Family Reunion, Donmar Warehouse, 2008; Richard III, Old Vic, 2011; The Turn of the Screw, Almeida, 2013; The Rivals, Arcola, 2014; Royal Shakespeare Co.: Julius Caesar, Twelfth Night, Henry VIII, The Winter's Tale; A Midsummer Night's Dream, 1970; *films* include: The Devils, 1971; Sense and Sensibility, 1995; Wilde, 1997; The Theory of Flight, 1998; The Winslow Boy, 1999; Captain Jack, 1999; Cotton Mary, 1999; Bridget Jones's Diary, 2001; Harry Potter and the Chamber of Secrets, 2002; Shanghai Knights, 2003; Kiss of Life, 2003; Bridget Jones: The Edge of Reason, 2004; Harry Potter and the Half-Blood Prince, 2009; You Will Meet a Tall Dark Stranger, 2011; Harry Potter and the Deathly Hallows, Pt 2, 2011; Bridget Jones's Baby, 2016; Rocketman, 2019; *television* includes series: The Duchess of Duke Street, 1976; Chelworth, 1989; Devices and Desires, 1991; The Phoenix and the Carpet, 1997; Spooks, 2007, 2008; The Lady Vanishes, 2013; Marvellous, 2014 (Best Supporting Actress, BAFTA, 2015); Unforgotten, 2015; Capital, 2015; God's Own Country, 2016 (Best Supporting Actress, Evening Standard British Film Awards, 2017). *Recreation:* hill-walking. *Address:* c/o Conway van Gelder Grant Ltd, 8–12 Broadwick Street, W1F 8HW. *T:* (020) 7287 0077, *Fax:* (020) 7287 1940.

**JONES, Jennifer Grace**; international election adviser and observer, 2003–08; *b* 8 Feb. 1948; *d* of Ernest Bew and Ivy Blake; *m* 1974, John Alun Charles Jones; one *s*. *Educ:* Bradford Univ. (BA Hons, CQSW 1972); Birmingham Univ. (MSocSc 1987); Wolverhampton Univ. (ITD). Legal Sec., ICI, 1968–69; Social Worker, Oxford CC, 1972–74; Housing Advr, Oxford Housing Aid Centre and Birmingham Housing Dept, 1974–77; Trng Officer, Birmingham Housing Co-op., 1980–85; Researcher, Wolverhampton Council, 1985–87; Business Advr, Black Country CDA, 1987–97. Trng Manager and Co. Dir, 1995–97. Mem. (Lab) Wolverhampton BC, 1991–97. MP (Lab) Wolverhampton SW, 1997–2001. Election advr, OSCE/UN Mission in Kosovo, 2002–03. Tutor, Open Univ., 2003–. *Recreations:* swimming, gardening, keeping cats, writing, walking.

**JONES, Jessica Leigh**; Engineer, Sony Europe BV, since 2016; *b* Cardiff, 22 July 1994; *d* of Gary Collins and Hayley Anne Jones. *Educ:* Cardiff Univ. (BSc Astrophysics 2015). Apprentice installation electrician, Edgenet Engineering Ltd, 2008–11. Res. and Develt Advr to CEO, Maplin Electronics Ltd, 2011–14; Sci. Champion, Chwarae Teg, 2012–14; Technol. Translator, Cardiff Univ., 2014–16; Lectr in Engrg, Cardiff and Vale Coll., 2015. Non-executive Director: Engineering Educn Scheme Wales Ltd, 2017–; WJEC CBAC Ltd, 2018– (Chair, WHEC CBAC (Services) Ltd, 2019–); Inst. for Apprenticeships and Tech. Educn, 2018–. MInstP. Freeman, City of London, 2017; Liveryman, Scientific Instrument Makers' Co., 2017. *Recreations:* karate, hiking, adventure, discovery, continual learning. *Address:* Sony UK Technology Centre, Pencoed Technology Park, Pencoed, Bridgend CF35 5HZ. *T:* (01656) 867266. *E:* jessicaleigh.jones@sony.com.

**JONES, Joanne**; *see* Elvin, J.

**JONES, Prof. John Clifford, (Cliff)**, PhD; FREng, FInstP, FRSC; Professor of Physics, University of Leeds, since 2015; *b* Bolton, 6 April 1964; *s* of David Jones and Joan Jones (*née* Whitaker); *m* 1999, Dr Rebecca Wilson; one *s*. *Educ:* Queen Elizabeth's Grammar Sch., Tamworth; Poly. of Wolverhampton (BSc Hons 1st Cl. Applied Phys 1985); Univ. of Hull (PhD Chem. 1990). FInstP 2000; FREng 2013; FRSC 2019. Res. Physicist, GEC Hirst Res. Centre, 1985–89, Jun. Res. Fellow, BDH Chemicals, 1989–90, on secondment to RSRE Malvern, 1985–90; RSRE Malvern, subseq. DRA, then DERA: SSO, 1991–94; PSO, 1994–97; SPSO with Individual Merit, subseq. DERA Fellow, 1997–2000; Displaydata (formerly ZBD Displays) Ltd: Founder, 2000; Dir of Res., 2000–03; CSO, 2003–05; Chief Technol. Officer, 2005–13; Chief Scientific Advr, 2013–; Prof. of Physics, Univ. of Manchester, 2013–15. FRSA 2007. *Publications:* four book chapters on liquid crystals and displays; 150 articles; 60 granted patents. *Recreations:* family and friends, family history, weight lifting, mountaineering, goal to publish a successful novel. *Address:* School of Physics and Astronomy, University of Leeds, Woodhouse Lane, Leeds LS2 9JT. *E:* j.c.jones@leeds.ac.uk.

**JONES, John Elfed**, CBE 1987; DL; CEng, FIET; Chairman: International Greetings plc, 1996–2006; Eclectica Ltd, since 2007; *b* 19 March 1933; *s* of Urien Maelgwyn Jones and Mary Jones; *m* 1957, Mary Sheila (*née* Rosser); two *d*. *Educ:* Blaenau Ffestiniog Grammar Sch.; Denbighshire Technical Coll., Wrexham; Heriot-Watt Coll., Edinburgh. Student apprentice, 1949–53, graduate trainee, 1953–55, CEGB; National Service, RAF, 1955–57 (FO); Rock Climbing Instr, Outward Bound Sch., Aberdyfi, 1957; Technical Engr with CEGB, 1957–59; Dep. Project Manager, Rheidol Hydro-Electric Project, 1959–61; Sen. Elec. Engr, Trawsfynydd Nuclear Power Station, 1961–63; Deputy Manager: Mid Wales Gp of Power Stations, 1963–67; Connah's Quay Power Station, 1967–69; Anglesey Aluminium Metal Ltd: Engrg Manager, 1969–73; Production Manager, 1973–76; Admin. Director, 1976–77; Dep. Man. Dir, 1977–79; Industrial Dir, Welsh Office (Under Sec. rank), 1979–82. Chairman: Welsh Water Authy, later Welsh Water plc, 1982–93; British Water International Ltd, 1983–88. Dep. Chm., HTV Gp, 1991–96; Director: HTV Cymru/Wales Ltd, 1990–96 (Chm., 1992–96); W Midlands and Wales Regl Adv. Bd, National Westminster Bank, 1990–91; BMSS plc, 1993–96; Cwmni Rheilffordd Beddgelert Cyf., 1994–98; Cwmni Rheilffordd Caernarfon Cyf., 1994–99; Chairman: Menter Mantis Cyf., 1999–2004; Awen Cymru Ltd, 2009–12. Chm. Adv. Gp, Nat. Assembly of Wales, 1997–99. Treasurer, Urdd Gobaith Cymru, 1964–67; Chm., Welsh Language Bd, 1988–93; Mem., Royal National Eisteddfod of Wales, 1981–90; Member: BBC Broadcasting Council for Wales, 1979–83; Council, Food from Britain, 1985–87; Prince of Wales Cttee, 1986–90. Mem., British/Irish Encounter, 2000–05. Pres., Univ. of Wales, Lampeter, 1992–98; Member: Court and Council: UCNW, Bangor, 1978–89; Nat. Library of Wales, 1983–88; Coleg Harlech, 1983–88; Court, Univ. Coll., Aberystwyth, 1984–93. Mem., Civic Trust for Wales, 1982–88; President: CPRW, 1995–2001; Cwlwm Busnes Caerdydd a'r Cylch, 2009–; Cantorian Coety, 2009–. FRSA 1984; CCMI (CBIM 1990). DL Mid Glam, 1989. Hon. Fellow: Univ. of Wales, Aberystwyth, 1990; NE Wales Inst., 1996; Trinity St Davids Univ. (Trinity Univ. Coll.), 2007); Glyndwr Univ., 2009. Hon. Dr Glamorgan, 1997; Hon. LLD Wales, 2000. Hon. Col, Commonwealth of Kentucky, 1976. *Recreations:* fishing for salmon and trout, reading, attending Eisteddfodau, golf. *Address:* Ty Mawr, Coity, Bridgend, Mid Glamorgan CF35 6BN.

**JONES, Sir John (Francis)**, Kt 2003; author, educational commentator and motivational speaker; Managing Director, JFJ Training Ltd; *b* 20 Nov. 1950; *s* of late Thomas Jones and of Joan Jones (now Hogg); two *s* one *d*; *m* 2015, Rachel Glazebrook; one *d*. *Educ:* Univ. of Wales, Bangor (BA Hons French and Latin; PGCE); Liverpool Univ. (MEd). Teacher, 1974–89; Res. Fellow, Lancaster Univ., 1988–89; Headteacher: Rivington High Sch., St Helens, 1989–91; Ruffwood Sch., Knowsley, 1991–99; Maghull High Sch., Sefton, 1999–2004. Member: Policy Action Team, Social Exclusion Unit, 1998–99; Task Gp, Truancy and Exclusion in Cities, DFES, 1998–2002; Leadership Develt Unit, Manchester

Univ., DFES and Nat. Coll. for Sch. Leadership, 2002–03. Chancellor, Sefton Children's Univ., 2010–. Non-exec. Dir, Aintree Hospls Trust, 1994–98. Chm., Everton in the Community, 2010–17. Chair of Govs, Everton Free Sch. and Sixth Form Coll., 2016–. *Recreations:* reading, keeping fit, golf, playing guitar, theatre, fell-walking, watching Everton FC, gardening. *Address:* Waterside House, 135A The Green, Worsley, Manchester M28 2PA. *E:* sirjj3@hotmail.co.uk.

**JONES, John Francis A.;** *see* Avery Jones.

**JONES, Prof. (John) Gareth,** MD; FRCP; FRCA; Professor of Anaesthesia, Cambridge University, 1990–99; *b* 20 Aug. 1936; *s* of late Dr John and Catherine Jones; *m* 1964, Susan Price; three *d*. *Educ:* Canton High Sch., Cardiff; Welsh Nat. Sch. of Medicine, Univ. of Wales (MB BCh 1960); MD Birmingham, 1967. MRCP 1963, FRCP 1983; FRCA (FFARCS 1970). Res. Fellow, Dept of Medicine, 1964–68, Lectr, Anaesthesia, 1968–70, Univ. of Birmingham; North Sen. Fellow, Cardiovascular Res. Inst., Univ. of California, San Francisco, 1970–74; Scientific Staff, MRC, Northwick Park, 1974–86; Prof. of Anaesthesia, Univ. of Leeds, 1986–91. Vis. Scientist, Chest Service, Univ. of California, San Francisco, 1977–78; Consultant, Baragwanath Hosp., Soweto, South Africa, 1986. Royal College of Anaesthetists: Mem. Council, 1996–99; Ed., Bulletin, 1997–99. Ed., Cardiff Med. Grads Jl, 1999–2001. Ext. Examr, Center for Sensory-Motor Interaction, Aalborg Univ., Denmark, 2010–11. Member: York Model Engrg Soc., 1999–2009; Crusoe Soc., 2003–; Yorks Philosophical Soc., 2005–12 (Mem. Council, 2006–09); History of Medicine Soc. of Wales, 2007–18. Hon. FANZCA 1992. *Publications:* Effects of Anaesthesia and Surgery on Pulmonary Mechanisms, 1984; (jtly) Aspects of Recovery from Anaesthesia, 1987; Depth of Anaesthesia, 1989, 2nd edn 1993; (jtly) The Upper Airway, 1995; Thomas Graham Brown (1882–1965): behind the scenes at the Cardiff Institute of Physiology, 2011; (jtly) The Brenva Feud: Graham Brown vs Frank Smythe, 2014; (jtly) Sacking the Editor: the Alpine journal, 2015; (jtly) An Anaesthetist at Belsen, 2016; res. papers on hypoxaemia at altitude, oxygen delivery in neonates, the effect of gen. anaesthetics on cognitive function, the effect of fatigue and sedation on saccadic eye movements, and computer methods for non-invasive measurement of oxygen exchange in oxygen dependent pre-term infants. *Recreations:* writing, aeroplanes, gyrocopters, model engineering (building a driveable ½ scale replica Bugatti 35 grand prix racer). *Address:* Woodlands, Rufforth, York YO23 2QF. *Clubs:* Royal Society of Medicine; Sherburn Aero.

**JONES, John Knighton C.;** *see* Chadwick-Jones.

**JONES, John Lloyd,** OBE 1995; DL; farmer; Chairman, National Infrastructure Commission for Wales, since 2018; *b* 10 Nov. 1949; *s* of late Arthur Egryn Jones and Elizabeth Jones (*née* Owen); *m* 1972, Anne Tudor Lewis; three *d*. *Educ:* Tywyn Primary Sch.; Llandovery Coll. Chairman: NFU Wales, 1993–98; NFU Parly Land Use and Envmt Cttee, England and Wales, 1998–2000. Examng Inspector for Nationally Significant Infrastructure Projects, Planning Inspectorate (formerly Infrastructure Planning Commn), 2010–18. Chairman: Welsh Adv. Cttee, Forestry Commn, 1994–2000; Countryside Council for Wales, 2000–10; Member: Bd, Inst. of Grassland and Envmtl Res., 2002–08; Rural Economy and Land Use Prog. Adv. Cttee, 2004–12; Welsh Nat. Cttee, Forestry Commn, 2009–13; Ext. Adv. Bd, Inst. of Biol, Envmtl and Rural Scis, 2009–17; Bd, Cambrian Mountains Initiative, 2010–17; Welsh Designated Landscapes Review Panel, 2014–15. Mem. Council, National Trust, 2009–15. Pres., Snowdonia Soc., 2013–18. Trustee, Campaign for Nat. Parks, 2016–18. Lay Mem. for Disciplinary Hearings, Councils of Inns of Court, 2005–07. Mem., Gorsedd of Bards, 2002. DL Gwynedd, 2013. FRSA 1995; FRAgS 2016 (ARAgS 2009). Hon. Fellow, Univ. of Wales, Bangor, 2003; Hon. FLI 2015. *Recreations:* woodland creation, gardening, seeking to find wisdom before it's too late. *Address:* Hendy, Tywyn, Gwynedd LL36 9RU. *T:* (01654) 710457.

**JONES, (John) Lynton;** Chairman, Bourse Consult LLP, 2002–13, now Emeritus; *b* Prestatyn, N Wales, 12 Nov. 1944; *s* of Frank and Eileen Jones; *m* 1968, Judith Mary Coop; one *s* two *d*. *Educ:* Rhyl Grammar Sch.; University Coll. of Wales, Aberystwyth (BSc Econ 1st Cl. Hons Internat. Politics). VSO, India, 1963–64; HM Diplomatic Service: Third Secretary: FCO, 1968–69; Lusaka, 1969–70; Second Secretary: Bangkok, 1970–74; SE European Dept, FCO, 1974–76; Pte Sec. to Minister of State, FCO, 1976–79; First Sec., Commercial and Financial, Paris, 1979–83; Hd of Public Affairs, London Stock Exchange, 1983–87; Man. Dir, NASDAQ Internat., 1987–92; Chief Executive: OM London Exchange, 1992–96; Internat. Petroleum Exchange, 1996–99; Chairman: Jiway Hldgs Ltd, 2000–01; Dubai Internat. Financial Exchange, 2003–05; DSX Cloud Ltd (formerly Digiservex Ltd), 2014–19. Board Member: Futures & Options Assoc., 1995–97; London Clearing House, 1996–99; Kenetics Gp Ltd, 2006–11; Aseana plc, 2007–18. Trustee, Horniman Mus., 2005–13. Mem., Develt Bd, Aberystwyth Univ., 2011– (Chm., 2015–19). FCSI (Fellow, Securities and Investment Inst., 2008). MInstD 1996. Freeman, City of London, 2005. *Publications:* contribs to City of London Corporation research reports and to financial pubns. *Recreations:* photography, astronomy, Darwinism, secularism and the promotion of rationality. *E:* jlj@bourse-consult.com.

**JONES, John Richard;** QC 2002; a Recorder, since 1999; *b* 8 Feb. 1959; *s* of late Harold Jones and of Barbara Jones (*née* Jerstice); *m* 2000, Heather Billam; one *s*. *Educ:* Shevington High Sch.; Upholland Grammar Sch.; Liverpool Univ. (LLB Hons); Inns of Court Sch. of Law. Called to the Bar, Middle Temple (Winston Churchill Scholar), 1981. Mem., Very High Cost Cases Appeals Panel, Legal Services Commn, 2009–. Mem., Criminal Law Bar Assoc., 2009–17. Co-founding Mem., Scarisbrick Hall Sch. Law Soc., 2018–. *Recreations:* golf, fell-walking, music, classic cars, walking in the New Forest. *Address:* Exchange Chambers, 1 Derby Square, Liverpool L2 9XX. *T:* (0151) 236 7747. *E:* johnrjonesqc@exchangechambers.co.uk; Exchange Chambers, 5th Floor, 201 Deansgate, Manchester M3 3NW. *T:* (0161) 833 2722. *Clubs:* Royal Lytham and St Annes Golf; Formby Golf; Hindley Hall Golf; St Andrews Golf; Phoenician Golf (Arizona, USA).

**JONES, (John) Stanley,** MBE 2009; Director, Curwen Studio, 1959–2012; President and Director, Curwen Print Study Centre, since 2013; *b* 10 June 1933; *s* of George White Jones and Elizabeth Jones; *m* 1961, Jennifer Frances Stone; one *s* one *d*. *Educ:* Wigan Grammar Sch.; Wigan Art Sch. (NDD); Slade Sch. of Fine Art, UCL (Dip. Fine Art). Lectr in Lithography, Slade Sch. of Fine Art, 1958–98. Pres., Printmakers' Council, 1981–96. Hon. RE 2004. Hon. DLitt Southampton, 1999. *Publications:* Lithography for Artists, 1967 (Italian edn 1981); (contrib.) Elizabeth Frink Original Prints, ed C. Wiseman, 1998; (autobiog.) Stanley Jones and the Curwen Studio, 2010; contribs to Printmaking Today, Graphion. *Recreations:* black and white photography (analogue), country walking, weather observation, appreciation of music (contemporary). *Address:* Curwen Print Study Centre, Chilford Hall, Linton, Cambs CB21 4LE. *T:* (01223) 892380, *Fax:* (01223) 893638. *E:* enquiries@curwenprintstudy.co.uk. *Club:* Double Crown.

**JONES, Prof. (John) Stephen,** PhD, DSc; FRS 2012; Professor of Genetics, University College London, 1992–2011, now Senior Research Fellow (Head, Department of Genetics, Evolution and Environment, 2008–10); *b* 24 March 1944; *s* of Thomas Gwilym Jones and Lydia Anne Jones; *m* 2004, Norma Percy. *Educ:* Wirral Grammar Sch.; Univ. of Edinburgh (BSc, PhD 1971, DSc 2005). Postdoctoral Fellow, Univ. of Chicago, 1969–71; Lectr in Genetics, Royal Free Hosp. Med. Sch., 1971–78; Lectr then Reader in Genetics, UCL, 1978–92; Head of Dept of Genetics and Biometry, 1989–94. Reith Lectr, 1991. Columnist, Daily Telegraph, 1992–. Trustee, British Council, 2007–13. Pres., Assoc. for Sci. Educn, 2011. FRSL 2011; FLSW 2011; Fellow, Amer. Philosophical Soc., 2011. Faraday Medal, Royal Soc., 1996; Charter Medal, Inst. of Biology, 2002; Tercentenary Medal, Linnean Soc., 2007. *Publications:* (ed) Cambridge Encyclopedia of Human Evolution, 1992; The Language of the Genes, 1993 (Science Book Prize, 1994); In the Blood, 1996; Almost Like a Whale: the origin of Species updated, 1999; Y: The Descent of Men, 2002; The Single Helix, 2005; Coral: a pessimist in paradise, 2007; Darwin's Island: the Galapagos in the garden of England, 2009; The Serpent's Promise: the Bible retold as science, 2013; No Need for Geniuses: revolutionary science in the age of the guillotine, 2016; The Ladybird Book of Evolution, 2017; Here Comes the Sun: how it feeds us, kills us, heals us and makes us what we are, 2019; scientific papers in learned jls. *Recreations:* not administrating, speaking bad French. *Address:* Department of Genetics, Evolution and Environment, University College London, Gower Street, WC1E 6BT. *T:* (020) 3108 4095.

**JONES, Jonathan Arthur David;** QC 2013; *b* Cardiff, 12 March 1970; *s* of Peter Wingate Jones and Mary Catherine Jones; *m* 1998, Sally Ann Tudor; three *d*. *Educ:* Bedford Sch.; Univ. of St Andrews (MA Econs); City Univ. (Dip. Law); Inns of Court Sch. of Law. Called to the Bar, Gray's Inn, 1994. *Recreations:* tennis, ski-ing, sailing, golf. *Address:* No 5 Chambers, Fountain Court, Steelhouse Lane, Birmingham B4 6DR. *T:* (0121) 606 0500. *E:* jjo@no5.com.

**JONES, Jonathan D.;** *see* Davies-Jones.

**JONES, Jonathan Dallas George,** PhD; FRS 2003; Senior Scientist, since 1988, and Professor, since 1998, Sainsbury Laboratory, Norwich; *b* 14 July 1954; *s* of George Ronald Jones and Isabel Dallas Orr (*née* Pinkney); one *d*; *m* 1991, Caroline Dean (*see* Dame C. Dean); one *s* one *d*. *Educ:* Univ. of Cambridge (BSc Nat. Scis 1976; PhD 1980). Postdoctoral Fellow, Harvard, 1981–82; Res. Scientist, Advanced Genetic Scis Inc., Oakland, Calif, 1983–88. Mem., EMBO, 1998. Foreign Mem., US NAS, 2015. *Publications:* contribs to Cell, Science, Plant Cell, Plant Jl, Genetics, Plant Physiol., etc. *Recreations:* sailing, children, grandchildren. *Address:* Sainsbury Laboratory, Norwich Research Park, Colney Lane, Norwich NR4 7UH. *T:* (01603) 450327.

**JONES, Jonathan Guy;** HM Procurator General, Treasury Solicitor and Permanent Secretary, Government Legal Department, since 2014; *b* 21 May 1962; *s* of Leonard Martell Jones and Margaret Eleanor Jones (*née* Jones). *Educ:* Llandovery Coll.; Univ. of Durham (BA Law 1984). Called to the Bar: Middle Temple, 1985, Bencher, 2007; NI, 2006. Legal Advr, Motor Agents Assoc., 1986–89; Legal Div., OFT, 1989–93; Dept of Transport Adv. Div., Treasury Solicitor's Dept, 1993–94; Attorney General's Chambers, Legal Secretariat to the Law Officers, 1994–98; Dep. Legal Advr, HM Treasury, 1998–2002; Legal Dir, DFES and Dir, Treasury Solicitor's Dept, 2002–04; Dir Gen., Attorney General's Office, 2004–09; Dep. Treasury Solicitor, Treasury Solicitor's Dept, 2009–12; Dir Gen., Legal, Home Office, 2012–14. Hon. QC 2019. *Recreation:* music. *Address:* Government Legal Department, 102 Petty France, SW1H 9AJ.

**JONES, Jonathan Owen;** *b* 19 April 1954; *s* of Gwynfor Owen Jones and Dorothy Mary (*née* Davies); *m* 1989, Allison Clement; two *s* one *d*. *Educ:* Univ. of East Anglia (BSc Hons Ecology); Cardiff Univ. (PGCE). Science and biology teacher, 1977–92. MP (Lab and Co-op) Cardiff Central, 1992–2005; contested (Lab and Co-op) same seat, 2005. An Opposition Whip, 1993–97; a Lord Comr of HM Treasury (Govt Whip), 1997–98; Parly Under-Sec. of State, Welsh Office, 1998–99. A Forestry Comr, 2007–13. *Recreations:* cooking, walking, watching Rugby, my family, caravanning. *Address:* 19 Ty Draw Road, Roath, Cardiff CF23 5HB. *Club:* Roath Labour.

**JONES, Dame Julia P.;** *see* Peyton-Jones.

**JONES, Julie,** CBE 2010 (OBE 2003); Chairman, Look Ahead Care, Support and Housing, since 2017 (non-executive Director, since 2012); *b* 17 March 1948; *d* of Peter and Kitty Clark; *m* 1970, Alan Richard Watson Jones; two *d*. *Educ:* Benenden C of E Primary Sch.; Tunbridge Wells Grammar Sch. for Girls; University Coll., Cardiff (BSc Econ. Hons Sociology 1969); Brunel Univ. (MA Public and Soc. Admin 1980). Dep. Hd, Soc. Services Planning Unit, Camden, 1972–76; Westminster City Council: Principal Res. and Planning Officer for Soc. Services, 1982–85; Dep. Dir, 1992–96, Dir, 1996–2005, Soc. Services; Dep. Chief Exec., 2000–07; Dir, Children and Community Services, 2005–07; Chief Exec., Social Care Inst. for Excellence, 2007–12. Non-exec. Dir, Open Door, Barnet Homes Gp, 2016–. Pres., Assoc. of Dirs of Social Services, 2005–06 (Vice Pres., 2004–05); Chm., London Assoc., 2001–04). Mem., Governance Bd, Centre for Workforce Intelligence, 2012–13. Lay Mem. Council, Inst. of Educn, 2007–14 (Vice Chair, Council and Chair, Audit Cttee, 2013–14); Comr, Future of Social Services in Wales, 2009–10. Mem., C of E Nat. Safeguarding Panel, 2014–18. Mem. Council, Queen's Coll., London, 1993–98. Trustee, Sir Simon Milton Foundn, 2013–. FRSA 2006; FCGI 2009 (Mem., Fellowship Adv. Cttee, 2013–18). *Recreations:* reading, travel, opera, theatre, family and friends (3 granddaughters). *Address:* 18 The Grove, N3 1QL. *T:* (020) 8349 1359, 07850 548755. *E:* juliejonesuk@hotmail.co.uk.

**JONES, Karen Elisabeth Dind, (Mrs Hamish Easton),** CBE 2006; company director; Executive Chairman, Prezzo Ltd, since 2018; *b* Billinge, 29 July 1956; *d* of Eric and Margaret Jones; *m* 1990, Hamish Easton; one *s* two *d*. *Educ:* Univ. of E Anglia (BA 1st Cl. English and American Lit.); Wellesley Coll., Mass. Account planner, Boase Massimi Pollitt, 1980–81; Ops Dir, Theme Hldgs plc, 1981–88; Man. Dir and Co-Founder, Pelican Gp plc, 1989–97; Punch Group Ltd: CEO, Punch Retail, 2000–02; Chief Exec., Spirit Gp Ltd, 2002–06; Co-Founder, Food and Fuel Ltd, 2006–18. Chm., Hawksmoor, 2013–; non-executive Director: EMAP, 1997–2006; Gondola Hldgs plc, 2005–07 (Chm., Remuneration Cttee); HBOS plc, 2006–08 (Chm., Remuneration Cttee, 2007–08); Virgin Active Gp, 2008–11 (Chm., Remuneration Cttee, 2009–11); ASOS plc, 2009–15 (Chm., Remuneration Cttee; Mem., Audit Cttee); Booker plc, 2009–18 (Chm., Remuneration Cttee; Mem., Audit Cttee, 2009–12); Cofra Hldg AG, 2008–17, then Advr (Chm., HR Cttee; Chm., Audit Cttee); Firmenich Internat. SA, 2011– (Chm., Governance and Compensation Cttee); Corbin and King Restaurants Ltd, 2012–17 (Chm., Remuneration Cttee); Mowgli Street Food Ltd, 2017– (Chm., 2017–). Member: Bd, RNT, 1996–2002; Bd, RNT Enterprises, 2004–; Industrial Develt Adv. Bd, DTI, 2004–10. Mem., Rebuilding Childhoods Bd, NSPCC, 2006–13 (Chm., 2007–12). Gov., Ashridge Business Sch., 2005–15; Chancellor, UEA, 2016–. Hon. DCL East Anglia, 2013. *Recreations:* my children, food and wine, theatre, contemporary American and English literature, art. *Address:* Paddock House, 9 Spencer Park, SW18 2SX. *T:* 07768 010030. *E:* karen@pioneerhospitality.co.uk. *Clubs:* Hurlingham, Groucho, House of St Barnabas.

**JONES, Kathryn P.;** *see* Pritchard-Jones.

**JONES, Very Rev. Kathy Louise;** Dean of Bangor, since 2016; Team Rector, Bro Deiniol Ministry Area, since 2016; *b* 1968. *Educ:* Queen's Coll., Birmingham; Univ. of Wales, Bangor (BTh 1996); Northumbria Univ. (PGCE 2011); Univ. of Leeds (MA 2013). Ordained deacon, 1992, priest, 1997; Curate, Holyhead, 1992–94; Curate, 1994–95, Priest-in-charge, 1995–99, St Deiniol, Bangor; Vicar, St Mary, Betws-y-Coed, 1999–2006;

Chaplain, Newcastle upon Tyne Hosps NHS Foundn Trust, 2006–12; Chaplain Team Leader, Northumbria Healthcare NHS Foundn Trust, 2012–16. *Address*: Erw Fach, Hwfa Road, Bangor LL57 2BN.

**JONES, Very Rev. Keith Brynmor;** Dean of York, 2004–12, now Emeritus; permission to officiate, Diocese of St Edmundsbury and Ipswich, since 2013; *b* 27 June 1944; *s* of John Brynmor Jones and Mary Emily Jones; *m* 1973, Viola Mary, *d* of late Henry Leigh Jenkyns; three *d*. *Educ*: Selwyn Coll., Cambridge (BA 1965; MA 1969); Cuddesdon Coll., Oxford. Ordained deacon, 1969, priest, 1970; Asst Curate, Limpsfield with Titsey, Surrey, 1969–72; Dean's Vicar, Cathedral and Abbey Church of St Alban, 1972–76; Priest-in-charge, 1976–79, Team Vicar, 1979–82, St Michael's, Boreham Wood; Vicar of St Mary-le-Tower, Ipswich, 1982–95; Rural Dean of Ipswich, 1992–95; Hon. Canon, St Edmundsbury Cathedral, 1993–95; Dean of Exeter, 1996–2004. Mem., Gen. Synod of C of E, 1999–2005. Chm., Pilgrims Assoc., 2001–08. Affiliated to Order of Carmelites, 2011. *Publications*: Adam's Dream, 2008; (with L. Hampson and R. Shephard) York Minster: a living legacy, 2008. *Recreations*: playing the piano, looking out of the window. *Address*: 7 Broughton Road, Ipswich, Suffolk IP1 3QR. *Club*: Army and Navy.

**JONES, Dr Keith Howard,** CB 1997; FRCP, FRCPE; Chairman, European Medicines Evaluation Agency, 2000–03 (Member, 1995–2000); Chief Executive, Medicines Control Agency, Department of Health, 1989–2002; retired; *b* 14 Oct. 1937; *s* of Arthur Leslie Jones and Miriam Emily Jones; *m* 1962, Dr Lilian, (Lynne), Pearse; three *s*. *Educ*: Welsh Nat. Sch. of Medicine, Cardiff (MB, BCh 1960; MD 1966). FFPM 1989; FRCPE 1990; FRCP 1993. Posts in clinical and academic medicine, Cardiff, Edinburgh and Cambridge, 1960–67; Chief Toxicologist, Fisons Agrochemicals, 1967–70; Head, Safety Assessment, Beecham Res. Labs, 1970–79; Exec. Dir, Medical Affairs, Merck & Co., USA, 1979–89. Adjunct Prof. of Medicine, Thomas Jefferson Med. Sch., Philadelphia, 1985–89; Vis. Prof. of Pharmacology, Sch. of Pharmacy, Univ. of London, 1995–2002. UK Representative: EC Cttee for Pharmaceutical Medical Products, 1989–95; EC Pharmaceutical Cttee, 1989–2003; Chairman: EC Scientific Cttee for Medicinal Products and Med. Devices, 1997–2000; Expert Mem., EC Scientific Steering Cttee on Consumer Health and Food Safety, 1997–2003. *Publications*: contribs to learned jls on issues of metabolic medicine, toxicology, drug develt and regulatory matters. *Recreations*: sailing, tennis. *Address*: Shelford, Headley Road, Leatherhead, Surrey KT22 8PT. *T*: (01372) 376747.

**JONES, Keith O.;** *see* Orrell-Jones.

**JONES, Prof. Kelvyn,** PhD; FBA 2016; FLSW, FAcSS; Professor of Quantitative Human Geography, University of Bristol, since 2000; *b* Rhondda, 31 Oct. 1953; *s* of Alexander and Glenys May Jones; *m* 1979, Christina Thrush; one *s*. *Educ*: Rhondda Co. Grammar Sch. for Boys, Porth; Univ. of Southampton (BSc 1st Cl. Hons Geog. 1975; PhD Geog. 1980). CGeog 2002. Lecturer: Univ. of Newcastle, 1978–79; UC Swansea, 1979–80; SSRC Res. Fellow, Univ. of Reading, 1980–82; Portsmouth Polytechnic, subsequently University of Portsmouth: Lectr, 1982–94; Prof., 1994–2001; Hd, Dept of Geog., 1997–99; Hd, Dept of Geographical Scis, 2005–09, Dir, Centre for Multilevel Modelling, 2014, Univ. of Bristol. Lectr, Summer Sch. in Social Sci. Data Analysis, Univ. of Essex, 1992–; Docent, Univ. of Leuven, 1996–. Mem. Panel, HEFCE RAE, 2001 and 2008. FAcSS (AcSS 2008); FLSW 2013. Murchison Award, RGS, 2013. *Publications*: Health, Disease and Society: a critical medical geography, 1987; Multilevel Models in Geographical Research, 1991; Epidemiology, 2000; Social Capital, Place and Health, 2004; Developing Multilevel Models for Analyzing Contextuality, Heterogeneity and Change, Vols 1 and 2, 2014; contribs to professional social sci. and health jls. *Recreations*: watching Rugby Union, opera, wine, gardening, reading non-fiction. *Address*: School of Geographical Sciences, University of Bristol, University Road, Clifton, Bristol BS8 1SS. *T*: (0117) 928 7509. *E*: kelvyn.jones@bristol.ac.uk. *Club*: Bristol Rugby.

**JONES, Sir Kenneth Lloyd, (Sir Ken),** Kt 2009; QPM 2000; global counter terrorism, policing and cyber security consultant, since 2015; *b* Welshpool, 13 June 1952; *s* of John and Joan Jones; *m* 1985, Kaye Firth; three *d*. *Educ*: Welshpool High Sch.; Univ. of Sheffield (BA Hons, MBA); Univ. of Leeds (Dip. Company Direction). Joined Sheffield and Rotherham Constabulary, 1971; served ICAC, Hong Kong, 1985–88; Chief Constable, Sussex Police, 2001–06; Pres., ACPO, 2006–09; Dep. Comr, Victoria Police, Australia, 2009–11; Counter Terrorism Advr, ITN London, 2012; Defence and Security Advr, British Embassy, Washington DC, 2013–14. Fulbright Scholar, UCLA, 1996. *Recreations*: reading, cycling, running, aviation (glider and helicopter). *E*: homeward1@hotmail.com.

**JONES, Rt Hon. Kevan (David);** PC 2018; MP (Lab) North Durham, since 2001; *b* 25 April 1964. *Educ*: Univ. of Southern Maine, USA; Newcastle upon Tyne Poly. (BA). Political Officer, 1989–2001, Regl Organiser, 1992–99, Sen. Organiser, 1999–2001, GMB. Newcastle upon Tyne City Council: Mem. (Lab), 1990–2001; Chair of Public Health, 1993–97; Chief Whip, 1994–2000; Chair and Cabinet Mem. for Develt and Transport, 1997–2001. Parly Under-Sec. of State and Minister for Veterans, MoD, 2008–10; Shadow Minister for Armed Forces, 2010–16. Member: Select Cttee on Defence, 2001–08; Intelligence and Security Cttee, 2017–. Chair, 1998–2000, Vice-Chair, 2000–01, Northern Regl Lab. Party. Mem., Commonwealth War Graves Commn, 2010–. *Address*: c/o House of Commons, SW1A 0AA; (office) Fulforth Centre, Front Street, Sacriston, Co. Durham DH7 6JT. *T*: (0191) 371 8834. *Club*: Sacriston Workmen's.

**JONES, Prof. Kevin David,** PhD; Professor of Computing Science, and Executive Dean, Science and Engineering, University of Plymouth, since 2014; *b* Wales, 2 Aug. 1960; *s* of Waunford Jones and Dilys Jones; *m* 2000, Colette Campbell. *Educ*: Univ. of Reading (BSc Hons 1981); St Catherine's Coll., Oxford (MSc 1982); Univ. of Manchester (PhD 1985). FBCS 2011; CITP 2011; FIET 2012; CEng 2013; CSci 2014; FIMarEST 2017. Technical staff, Imperial Coll. London, 1984–85; Res. Associate, Univ. of Manchester, 1986–89; res. staff, Digital Equipment Corp. Systems Res. Center, 1989–93; Engrg Dir, Rambus, 1993–2008; Chief Scientist, Green Plug, Calif, 2008–10; City University, London: Prof. of Security, 2010–12; Dep. Dean, Sch. of Informatics, 2012–14. Trustee, Engrg Council, 2015–. Liveryman, Information Technologists' Co., 2015. Pres. and Kaicho, Shugenkai, 2000–. *Recreations*: aikido, instrument rated pilot, kayaking. *Address*: University of Plymouth, Drake Circus, Plymouth PL4 8AA. *T*: (01752) 584504, *Fax*: (01752) 548540. *E*: kevin.jones@plymouth.ac.uk.

**JONES, Kim Niklas;** menswear designer; Artistic Director, Dior Homme, since 2018; *b* London, 11 Sept. 1979. *Educ*: Central St Martins Sch. of Art and Design (MA Menswear). First catwalk collection, London Fashion Week, 2003; Paris collections, 2004–08; Creative Dir, Alfred Dunhill, 2008–11 (presented 8 collections, incl. NY Men's Collection, 2007); Men's Artistic Dir, Louis Vuitton Malletier, 2011–18; has designed for cos incl. Uniqlo, Topman, Umbro, Mulberry, Alexander McQueen, Hugo Boss and Iceberg; has presented short films, incl. Everywhere, with Alasdair McLellan, for London Fashion Week, 2006. Exhibn, Mus. of London, 2004. Menswear Designer of Year Award, British Fashion Council, 2006, 2009, 2011; Menswear Designer of Year, British Fashion Awards, 2012. *Relevant publication*: Kim Jones, by Luke Smalley, 2004. *Address*: Christian Dior Couture, 11 bis rue François 1er, 75008 Paris, France.

**JONES, Kirsty Jackson;** *see* Young, K. J.

**JONES, Laura Anne;** Member (C), Monmouthshire County Council, since 2017; *b* 21 Feb. 1979; *d* of John Dilwyn Jones and Penelope Anne Jones. *Educ*: Univ. of Plymouth (BSc Politics). Chm., SE Wales Cons. Future Area, 2000–02. Mem. (C) S Wales E, Nat. Assembly for Wales, 2003–07. Opposition spokesman on Sports, Nat. Assembly for Wales, 2003–07. Girl Guiding Ambassador, 2004–. Trustee, Usk Park Project. Hon. Mem., Cardiff Business Club. Contested (C): Islywn, 2015; S Wales E, Nat. Assembly for Wales, 2016. *Recreations*: swimming, ski-ing, horse riding, cycling, Girl Guides, walking, countryside pursuits.

**JONES, Luke B.;** *see* Bradley-Jones.

**JONES, Sir Lyndon (Hugh),** Kt 1999; Principal and Chief Executive, Harris City Technology College, 1990–99; *b* 2 Feb. 1943; *s* of late David Hugh Jones and Victoria Maud (*née* Elias); *m* 1st, 1965, Gillian Fortnum (marr. diss. 1981); two *s* one *d*; 2nd, 1990, Sandra Lees; two step *d*. *Educ*: Cardiff High Sch. for Boys; UC Cardiff (BA); Univ. of Reading (Postgrad. DipEd); Birmingham Univ. (MEd). Hd of Music Dept, Pool Hayes Comprehensive Sch., 1965–70; Sen. Lectr in Music and Educn, Bingley Teacher Trng Coll., 1970–76; Hd, Arts Faculty, Doncaster Inst. Higher Educn, 1976–78; Dir of Arts, Richmond Tertiary Coll., 1978–82; Dep. Principal, Westminster Further Educn Coll., 1982–85; Principal, S London Further Educn Coll., 1985–90. Chief Examr, GCE Music, London Univ., 1978–83. Tutor, Nat. Professional Qualification for Headship, 1998; Trainer, Leadership Prog. for Serving Head Teachers, 1999; Sch. Improvement Partner, Nat. Coll. for Sch. Leadership, 2006. Chm., E Surrey Carers Support Assoc., 2015–16. Volunteer interviewer, Pecan jobs project; Volunteer: Crawley Open House, 2013; Sutton Youth Offending Team, 2013–15. Life Mem., NAHT. Composer, The Prince and the Pauper, 1992. *Recreations*: playing the piano, composing, Rugby, mountaineering, opera, amateur chef and wine taster.

**JONES, Dr Lynne Mary;** Vice President, British Association for Counselling and Psychotherapy, 2009–16; *b* 26 April 1951; two *s*. *Educ*: Birmingham Univ. (BSc, PhD Biochem.); Birmingham Polytechnic (Dip. Housing Studies). Joined Labour Party, 1974; ASTMS, then MSF, later Amicus, subseq. Unite, 1972–. Mem. (Lab) Birmingham City Council, 1980–94 (Chair, Housing Cttee, 1984–87). Former Exec. Mem., Labour Housing Gp. MP (Lab) Birmingham, Selly Oak, 1992–2010. Member: Select Cttee on science and technology, 1992–2001; Select Cttee on envmt, food and rural affairs, 2005–10. *W*: www.lynnejones.org.uk.

**JONES, Lynton;** *see* Jones, J. L.

**JONES, Prof. Malcolm Lang,** PhD; FDSRCSE, FDSRCS; Professor of Child Dental Health and Orthodontics, Cardiff University (formerly University of Wales College of Medicine), 1992–2010, Emeritus Professor, 2011 (Pro-Vice-Chancellor (Health and Estates), 2006–10); Hon. Consultant in Orthodontics, Dental Hospital, Cardiff and Vale NHS Trust, 1987–2010; *b* Surbiton, 28 June 1950; *s* of Derek Lang Jones and Ellen Joan Jones; *m* 1976, Rhona Marie Logue; one *s* one *d*. *Educ*: King's Coll. Sch., Wimbledon; Welsh Nat. Sch. of Medicine (BDS 1973; PhD 1987); Univ. of London (MSc 1979). DOrthRCS 1979; FDSRCSE 1980; FDSRCS 2003. Community Dental Officer, Derbys, 1973–74; Resident Hse Officer, Oral and Maxillofacial Surgery, Cardiff Dental Hosp., 1974–75; SHO, Chepstow Hosp., 1975; Registrar, Middlesex Hosp., 1976–77; Registrar, Orthodontics, Royal Dental Hosp., 1977–79; Lectr, 1979–84, Sen. Lectr, 1984–92, in Orthodontics; Head, Child Dental Health, Univ. of Wales Coll. of Medicine, 1992–99; Dean and Hd of Sch. of Dentistry, Cardiff Univ., 1999–2006; Gen. Manager, Dental Services, Cardiff & Vale NHS Trust, 1999–2006. Non-exec. Dir, Swansea NHS Trust, 2004–08; Ind. Mem. Bd, Cardiff and Vale NHS Trust, 2009–10. Ed., British Jl Orthodontics, subseq. Jl Orthodontics, 1995–2000. Exec. Sec., UK Council of Deans and Heads of Dental Schs, 2005–08; Founder Chm., Forum of Eur. Heads and Deans of Dental Schs, 2007–08; Pres., Assoc. for Dental Educn in Europe, 2008–09. Mem., Dental Council, RCSE, 2005–09 (Dental Faculty Gold Medal, 2009). Hon. Fellow, Hong Kong Coll. of Surgeons, 2007. Hon. MD Riga Stradins, Latvia, 2002; Hon. DDS Malmo 2004. Special Service Award, British Orthodontic Soc., 2002. *Publications*: (with K. G. Isaacson) Orthodontic Radiography Guidelines, 1994; (with R. G. Oliver) Walther and Houston's Orthodontic Notes, 5th edn, 1995, 6th edn, 2000; (with J. Middleton and G. N. Pande) Computer Methods in Biomechanics and Biomedical Engineering, 1996; (with J. Middleton and N. G. Shrive) Computer Methods in Biomechanics and Biomedical Engineering: book 4, 2003; numerous contribs to scientific jls mostly in areas of clinical trials, applied computational biomechanics and dental education. *Recreations*: sailing, Morgan sports cars, reading as widely as time allows. *Address*: Vice Chancellor's Office, Cardiff University, Main Building, Park Place, Cardiff CF10 3AT. *T*: (029) 2074 2075, *Fax*: (029) 2074 5306. *E*: JonesML@cf.ac.uk.

**JONES, Marcus Charles;** MP (C) Nuneaton, since 2010; an Assistant Government Whip, since 2019; *b* 5 April 1974; *s* of Brian and Jean Jones; *m* 2004, Suzanne Clarke; one *s* one *d*. *Educ*: St Thomas More Sch., Nuneaton; King Edward VI Coll., Nuneaton. Conveyancing Manager, Tustain Jones & Co., Solicitors, 1999–2010. Mem. (C) Nuneaton and Bedworth BC, 2005–10 (Leader, 2008–09). Parly Under-Sec. of State, DCLG, 2015–18. *Address*: House of Commons, SW1A 0AA.

**JONES, Dr Margaret Anne,** OBE 2001; Chief Executive, Brook Advisory Centres, 1988–2001; *b* 30 Oct. 1940; *d* of Cecil Newton Collard and Rita Ross Collard (*née* White); *m* 1974, Hugh Vaughan Price Jones. *Educ*: Methodist Ladies' Coll., Burwood, Australia; Univ. of New South Wales (BSc, MSc); University College London (PhD); Dip. Mus. Open 2004. Postdoctoral Res. Fellow, Univ. of Cambridge, 1970–71; Res. Fellow, Univ. of Bath, 1971–74; Resources Officer, Health Education Council, 1974–88. Lay Mem., Chiltern and S Bucks Primary Care Gp, 1999–2002; non-exec. Dir, Chiltern and S Bucks Primary Care Trust, 2002–06. Mem., Ind. Adv. Gp, Teenage Pregnancy Unit, DoH, 2000–03. Hon. DSc Southampton, 2000. *Recreations*: music, cooking.

**JONES, Sir Mark (Ellis Powell),** Kt 2010; bookseller, Golden Hare Books, Edinburgh, since 2012; Master, St Cross College, Oxford, 2011–16; *b* 5 Feb. 1951; *s* of John Ernest Powell-Jones, CMG and of Ann Paludan; *m* 1983, (Ann) Camilla Toulmin, *qv*; two *s* two *d*. *Educ*: Eton College; Worcester College, Oxford (MA; Hon. Fellow, 2015); Courtauld Inst. of Art. Asst Keeper, 1974–90, Keeper, 1990–92, Dept of Coins and Medals, BM; Dir, Nat. Mus of Scotland, 1992–2001; Dir, V&A Mus., 2001–11. Scottish Cultural Resources Access Network: Co-Founder, 1994–96; Mem. Bd, 1996–2003, 2013–16; Chm., 2004–06. Director: Scottish Museums Council, 1992–2001; Edinburgh and Lothians Tourist Bd, 1998–2000. Member: Royal Mint Adv. Cttee, 1994–2006; Arts and Humanities Data Service Steering Cttee, 1997–99; Bd, MLA, 2000–05; Council, RCA, 2001–13 (Hon. Sen. Fellow, 2014); Chancellor's Forum, Univ. of the Arts, London, 2002–06; Council, Crafts Council, 2002–06; Chm., Nat. Mus. Dirs' Conf., 2006–09; Oxford Univ. Mus Bd, 2013–16; Bd of Visitors, Ashmolean Mus., 2014–. President: Fédn Internat. de la Médaille, 1994–2000; British Art Medal Soc., 1998–2004 (Sec., 1982–94). Trustee: Gilbert Collection, 2001–11; NT, 2005–12; Pilgrim Trust, 2006– (Chm., 2015–); Design Council,

2011–12; Tullie House Mus. and Art Gall., 2011–; Auckland Castle Trust, 2012–15; Grimsthorpe and Drummond Trust, 2012–; Watts Gall., 2012–18; Historic Scotland Trust, 2017– (Chm., 2019–); York Museums Trust, 2018–; Chair, Hospitalfield, 2016–; Hon. Chair, Sarikhani Collection, 2017–. Gov., Compton Verney, 2013–16. Hon. Prof., Univ. of Edinburgh, 1997 and 2017. Editor, The Medal, 1983–97. FSA 1992; FRSE 1999. Hon. DLit London, 2002; Hon. DArts Abertay, 2009; Hon. LLD Dundee, 2012; Hon. DLitt UEA, 2012. Chevalier, Ordre des Arts et des Lettres (France), 2005. *Publications:* The Art of the Medal, 1977; Impressionist Painting, 1979; Catalogue of French Medals in the British Museum, I, 1982, II, 1988; Contemporary British Medals, 1986; (ed) Fake?: the art of deception, 1990; (ed) Why Fakes Matter, 1992; (ed) Designs on Posterity, 1994; contrib. Sculpture Jl and Museums Jl. *Address:* 31/4 India Street, Edinburgh EH3 6HE.

**JONES, Prof. Martin Kenneth,** DPhil; FBA 2018; FSA; George Pitt-Rivers Professor of Archaeological Science, University of Cambridge, 1990–2018; Vice Master, Darwin College, Cambridge, 2012–18; *b* 29 June 1951; *s* of John Francis Jones and Margaret Olive (*née* Baldwin); *m* 1985, Lucy Walker; one *s* one *d*. *Educ:* Eltham Coll.; Univ. of Cambridge (MA); Univ. of Oxford (DPhil 1985). FSA 1991. Oxford Archaeological Unit, 1973–79; Res. Asst, Oxford Univ., 1979–81; Lectr, 1981–89, Sen. Lectr, 1989–90, Durham Univ. MAE 2013. DUniv Stirling, 1999. *Publications:* The Environment of Man: the Iron Age to the Anglo-Saxon period, 1981; Integrating the Subsistence Economy, 1983; England before Domesday, 1986; Archaeology and the Flora of the British Isles, 1988; Molecular Information and Prehistory, 1999; The Molecule Hunt: archaeology and the search for ancient DNA, 2001; Conflict, 2006; Feast: why humans share food, 2007; Archaeology Meets Science, 2008; Unlocking the Past: how archaeologists are rewriting human history with ancient DNA, 2016. *Recreation:* dancing. *Address:* Department of Archaeology, Downing Street, Cambridge CB2 3DZ.

**JONES, Martin William;** Chief Executive, Parole Board for England and Wales, since 2015; *b* Erith, Kent, 31 Dec. 1971; *s* of Terence Jones and Linda Jones; *m* 1995, Nicola; two *d*. *Educ:* Univ. of Kent (BA Hons Eng. Lit.). Policy Officer, Home Office, 1993–98; Policy Manager, Lord Chancellor's Dept, 1998–2003; HM Courts Service: Hd, Courts Innovation, 2004–06; Hd, Criminal Justice Improvement Prog., 2006–07; Dep. Dir and Hd of Crime, 2007–11; Dep. Dir for Sentencing Policy, MoJ, 2012–15. *Recreation:* tennis. *Address:* Parole Board for England and Wales, Floor 3, 10 South Colonnade, Canary Wharf, E14 4PU. *E:* martin.jones@paroleboard.gov.uk.

**JONES, Martyn David;** *b* 1 March 1947; *m* 1974, Rhona Bellis (marr. diss. 1991); one *s* one *d*. *Educ:* Liverpool and Trent Polytechnics. MRSB. Microbiologist, Wrexham Lager Beer Co., 1968–87. Mem., Clwyd CC, 1981–89. MP (Lab) Clwyd SW, 1987–97, Clwyd S, 1997–2010. An Opposition Whip, 1988–92; Opposition spokesman on food, agric. and rural affairs, 1994–95; Mem., Chairmen's Panel, 1992–94, 2005–10. Member: Select Cttee on Agriculture, 1987–94 and 1997–99; Select Cttee on Welsh Affairs, 1997–2010 (Chm., 1997–2005); Chm., Parly Labour Party Agriculture Cttee, 1987–94. Hon. Pres., Wrexham Lager Beer Co., 2010–. *E:* jonesm47@hotmail.com.

**JONES, Martyn Eynon,** FCA; pro bono work on leadership and employability skills at various universities and business schools, since 2014; President and Chairman of Board, Institute of Chartered Accountants in England and Wales, 2013–14 (Vice President, 2011–12; Deputy President, 2012–13); *b* Gower, Wales, 1951; *s* of James Cledwyn Jones and Megan Jones; *m* 1973, Doreen Judith Long; two *s*. *Educ:* Dynevor Grammar Sch., Swansea; Denbigh Grammar Sch.; Denbigh High Sch.; Swansea Univ. (BSc Hons). ACA 1976, FCA 1981. Chartered Accountant, Robson Rhodes, W Yorks and Deloitte Haskins & Sells, 1972–77; Lectr in Accounting and Auditing, then Hd, Accountancy Tuition Centre, Newcastle upon Tyne, 1977–81; Under-Sec., then Sec., Auditing Practices Cttee, Consultancy Cttee of Accounting Bodies, 1981–84; Sen. Manager, 1984–87, Nat. Audit Tech. Partner, 1987–2012, Nat. Accounting and Auditing, Nat. Audit Tech. Dept, Touche Ross & Co., subseq. Deloitte LLP. Member: Deloitte Touche Tohmatsu Global Service Innovation Adv. Bd, 1999–2002; Deloitte Touche Tohmatsu Global Tech. Policy and Methodol. Gp, then Audit Task Force Leaders, later Audit Tech. Adv. Bd, 1999–2012; Deloitte LLP: Chm., Corporate Governance Services Gp, 2007–12; Chm., Quality of Assce Services on sustainability and greenhouse gas emissions, 2010–12. Provision of adv. services on risk mgt, internal control and governance to entities incl. H of C, H of L, public sector bodies, corporate bodies and mutuals, 1998–2012; provision of advice to Sen. Policy Advr, 10 Downing St on going concern, 2009. UK and Irish Tech. Advr to Internat. Auditing Practices Cttee, 1983–84. Auditing Practices Board: Mem., Internat. Cttee, 2002–12; Mem., Working Gp on going concern issues during current econ. conditions, 2008. CCAB Ltd (Consultative Committee of Accounting Bodies): Chm., Ethics Standards Gp, 2006–11; Mem. Bd, 2013–14; Mem., Takeover Panel, 2013–14. Institute of Chartered Accountants in England and Wales: Mem., Business Law Cttee, 1993–2006; Chairman: Special Reports of Accountants Sub-Cttee, then Panel, 1993–2000; Accountants Reports on Internal Controls over Financial Service Orgns, 1997–2013; Centre for Business Perf., 2002–06; Internat. Standards on Auditing Implementation Sub-Gp, 2003–11; Ethics Standards Cttee, 2006–11; Wkg Gp developing audit insights on manufg sector, 2013; Vice Chm., Tech. and Practical Auditing Cttee, 1995–2006; Member: Res. Bd, 1995–99; Tech. Strategy Bd, 2002–11; Corporate Governance Cttee, 2005–06; Council, 2006–14; Nominating Cttee, 2011–13; Bd, 2011–14. Confederation of British Industry: Member: City Regulatory Panel, 1993–96; Corporate Law Panel, 1996–2003; Companies Cttee, 2003–12. Mem., Adv. Bd, 2009–12, Hon. Lectr, 2010–12, Swansea Univ. Sch. of Business and Econs; Chm., Adv. Bd, Dept of Econs and Finance, Brunel Univ. London, 2014–. *Publications:* (jtly) Safely Past the Perils: the new investment business accounting requirements, 1987; (jtly) The Finance Director and the Audit Committee, 1992; (jtly) The Audit Committee and its Chairman, 1993; (Consultant Ed.) Corporate Governance Handbook, 1996–2003; (jtly) Taking Fraud Seriously, 1996; (jtly) Implementing Turnbull: a boardroom briefing, 1999; (jtly) Audit Committees: a framework for assessment, 1997. *Recreations:* gardening, appreciating Georgian architecture, watching Rugby, relaxing in Gower, S Wales and Cumbria, local health walk leader. *E:* martyneynonjones@gmail.com.

**JONES, Medwyn;** Partner, Wiggin, since 2014; *b* Bangor, 13 Sept. 1955; *s* of Ieuan Glyn du Platt Jones and Margaret Jones; *m* 1990, Rita Bailey; one *s* one *d*. *Educ:* Scorton Grammar Sch.; Chester Grammar Sch.; Univ. of Sheffield (LLB Hons); Coll. of Law. Articled clerk, 1978–80, solicitor, 1980–81, Theodore Goddard; solicitor, 1981–92, Partner, 1983–92, Walker Martineau; Partner, Cameron Markby Hewitt, 1992–94; Partner, 1994–2013, Hd, Television Gp, 1998–2013, Harbottle & Lewis LLP. Dir, Overmorrow Partners Ltd, 2018–. Trustee, BAFTA, 2010–16 (Mem., 2002); Chm., BAFTA Mgt Ltd, 2016–. *Recreations:* skiing, gym, cycling.

**JONES, Merfyn;** *see* Jones, Richard M.

**JONES, Mervyn C.;** *see* Colenso-Jones.

**JONES, Mervyn Thomas;** HM Diplomatic Service, retired; Partnership Development Officer, Diocese of Winchester, 2004–10; *b* 23 Nov. 1942; *s* of William Clifford Jones and Winifred Mary Jones (*née* Jenkins); *m* 1965, Julia Mary Newcombe; two *s*. *Educ:* Bishop Gore Grammar Sch., Swansea; University Coll., Swansea (BA Hons Eng.). Entered HM Diplomatic Service, 1964: FCO, 1964–66; Calcutta, 1966; Bonn, 1966–70; Warsaw, 1970–73; FCO, 1973–77; Oslo, 1977–80; First Sec. (Mgt), then Hd of Chancery, Bangkok, 1981–85; jsdc, RNC Greenwich, 1985; on secondment to Commonwealth Secretariat as Asst Dir, Internat. Affairs Div., 1985–90; Dep. Consul Gen. and Consul (Commercial), LA, 1990–94; Asst Hd, Migration and Visa Dept, FCO, 1994–96; Counsellor (Commercial and Econ.), Brussels, and co-accredited to Luxembourg, 1996–99; Consul-Gen. and Dep. Head of Mission, Brussels, 1999–2000; Governor, Turks and Caicos Is, 2000–02. *Recreations:* reading, cinema, music, walking, Rugby (Welsh).

**JONES, Miah Gwynfor, (Gwyn Jones),** PhD; Director, Corporate Technologies, 1989–2017; Dean of Business, Enterprise and Employability, University of Gloucestershire, 2017–18; *b* 2 Dec. 1948; *s* of Robert Jones and Jane Irene Jones (*née* Evans); *m* 1976, Maria Linda Johnson; two *d*. *Educ:* Ysgol Eifionydd, Porthmadog; Univ. of Manchester (BSc 1st Cl. Hons); Univ. of Essex (PhD). FBCS 1987. British Steel Corp., 1974–77; ICL, 1977–81; Chm., Business Micro Systems, 1981–85; Chm. and Chief Exec., Corporate Technology Gp plc, 1985–87; Chm., L. G. Software, 1985–87; Director: ACT Computers PLC, 1989–95; Welsh Water Enterprises Ltd, 1990–93; Tesco plc, 1992–98; Invesco English and Internat. Trust plc, 1993–2010; HBO (formerly HBOL) (UK) Ltd, 1996–97; Real Radio Ltd, 2000–02; RMR plc, 2001–02; Si Corporate Develt Ltd, 2004–07 (Chm., 2006–07); Unit Superheaters Ltd, 2005–10; Dep. Chm., Agenda Television Ltd, 1997–2000; Partner, Quayside Properties, 1997–; Chairman: Agenda Multimedia Ltd, 2000–01; Press Red Ltd, 2003–05; Oxford English Trng Ltd, 2004–06; RogenSi, 2006–10. Chm., Adv. Cttee, NW Equity Fund, 2005–08. Chm., Welsh Develt Agency, 1988–93; BBC Nat. Gov. for Wales, 1992–96; Dir, S4C Authy, 1992–96; Pres., Royal Welsh Agric. Soc., 1993. Director: Univ. of Essex Knowledge Gateway Ltd, 2013–15; Univ. of Essex Knowledge Gateway Hldgs Ltd, 2013–15. Member: Council, Univ. of Wales, 1989–95; Court, UC of Swansea, 1989–95; Prince of Wales Cttee, 1989–92; Prince's Youth Business Trust, 1989–92. Chm., Adv. Bd, 2009–13, Vis. Prof., 2010–15, Dir, 2013–15, Essex Business Sch., Univ. of Essex; External Academic: Global MBA, Manchester Business Sch., 2012–; Strathclyde Business Sch., 2013–; Dean: of Business, 2015–16, of Business, Computing and Applied Sciences, 2016–17, of Business, Enterprise and Employability, 2017–18, Univ. of Gloucestershire. Sheffield Motor Neurone Disorder Res. Adv. Gp, 2019–; Sheffield Tissue Bank, 2019–. Hon. Fellow, Poly. of Wales, 1991. *Recreations:* tennis, cycling, reading, boats, mountain walking, reading.

**JONES, Michael Abbott;** communications consultant, 1998–2009; *b* 3 May 1944; *s* of Ronald and Irene Jones; *m* 1973, Wendy (*née* Saward); twin *d*. *Educ:* Felsted; Magdalen Coll., Oxford (BA, DipEd). Joined Life Offices' Assoc., 1968, Jt Sec. 1982; transf. to Assoc. of British Insurers on its formation, as Manager, Legislation, 1985, Chief Exec., 1987–93, Hd of Corporate Affairs, Sun Alliance, 1993–96; Hd of Gp Corporate Affairs, Royal & Sun Alliance Insurance Gp plc, 1996–98. *Recreations:* reading, photography, theatre. *Address:* 10 Parkhill Road, E4 7ED. *Club:* Oxford and Cambridge.

**JONES, Michael Frederick;** Associate Editor (Politics), The Sunday Times, 1995–2002; *b* 3 July 1937; *s* of late Glyn Frederick Jones and of Elizabeth (*née* Coopey); *m* 1959, Sheila Joan Dawes; three *s*. *Educ:* Crypt Grammar Sch., Gloucester. Reporter: Maidenhead Advertiser, 1956–59; Northern Echo, Darlington, 1959–61; Manchester Evening News, 1961–64; Labour reporter, Financial Times, 1964–65; Industrial reporter, Daily Telegraph, 1965–67; News Editor, later Asst Editor, Times Business News, 1967–70; Managing Editor, The Asian, Hong Kong, 1971; Sunday Times: Associate News Editor, 1972–75; political correspondent, 1975–84; Political Editor, 1984–95; Associate Editor, 1990–2002. Chm., Parly Press Gallery, 1989–91. Parly Researcher to Baroness Boothroyd, 2002–. Vis. Fellow, Goldsmiths Coll., London, 2000–02. Exec. Mem., Meml to Women of World War 2 Fund, 2004–05. *Publications:* (jtly) Strike: Thatcher, Scargill and the miners, 1985; (with Betty Boothroyd) Betty Boothroyd: the autobiography, 2001.

**JONES, Rt Rev. Michael Hugh Harold B.;** *see* Bedford-Jones.

**JONES, Michael Selwyn Tudor;** QC 2018; Prosecution Counsel, Crown Prosecution Service, Cardiff, since 2009; *b* Caerphilly, 23 March 1970; *s* of Arthur Tudor Jones, MBE and Patricia Margaret Jones (*née* Caswell); *m* 1995, Charis Anne Brooks; twin *d*. *Educ:* St Martin's Comprehensive Sch., Caerphilly; New Coll., Cardiff; Univ. of Greenwich (BA Hons Econs 1992); Univ. of Glamorgan (CPE 1993); Inns of Court Sch. of Law (BVC 1994). Called to the Bar, Middle Temple, 1995; in practice as a barrister, specialising in criminal law, Swansea, then Cardiff, 1995–. Ind. Assessor, CPS Advocacy Panel, 2018–. Associate Mem., Cardiff and Dist Law Soc., 2018–; Hon. Sec., Middle Temple Wales Circuit Soc., 2019–. Vice Pres. Mem., Wrexham RFC, 2010–16; Chm., Welsh Assembly Parly Rugby XV, 2015–. Gov., Ysgol Gyfun Gymraeg Plasmawr, Cardiff, 2011–16. *Recreation:* going for a pint with my dog. *Address:* Crown Prosecution Service, 21st Floor, Capital Tower, Greyfriars Road, Cardiff CF10 3HH. *E:* mike.jones@cps.gov.uk.

**JONES, Dr Nevin Campbell H.;** *see* Hughes Jones.

**JONES, Nicholas Keith Arthur,** MBE 2017; restaurateur; Chief Executive Officer (formerly Managing Director), Soho House, since 1991; *b* 22 Sept. 1963; *s* of Keith and Anna Jones; *m* 1999, Kirsty Jackson Young, *qv*; two *d*, and one *s* one *d* from former marriage. *Educ:* Shiplake Coll. Opened: Café Bohème, London W1, 1992; Soho House, 1995; Babington House, Som, 1998; Bohème Kitchen Bar, London W1, 1999; Electric Cinema, House and Brasserie, London W11, 2002; Soho House New York, 2003; Balham Kitchen and Bar, 2003; Cecconi's, London W1, 2005; Cowshed, Clarendon Cross, 2005; High Road House, Chiswick, 2006; Shoreditch House, 2007; Pizza East, London E1, 2009; Dean Street Townhouse, 2009; Cecconi's, LA, 2009; Soho House West Hollywood, 2010; Soho House Berlin, 2010; Soho Beach House, and Cecconi's, Miami, 2010; Pizza East, London W10, 2011; UK Little House, 2012; Soho House Berlin Apartments, 2012; Soho House Toronto, 2012; Pizza East, Chicken Shop, and Dirty Burger, London NW5, 2012; Soho House Chicago, 2014; Soho House Istanbul, 2015; Soho Farmhouse, Oxon, 2015; Ludlow Hse, NYC, Little Beach Hse Malibu, Soho Hse Barcelona, 2016; The Ned, London EC2, 2017; Cecconi's Dumbo NY, 2017; Kettner's Townhouse, London, 2018; White City House, W London, 2018; Dumbo House, Brooklyn, NY, 2018; Mollie's Motel and Diner, Oxon, 2019. *Publications:* (jtly) Eat, Drink, Nap: bringing the house home, 2014; Morning, Noon, Night, 2016. *Recreations:* cooking, eating, drinking, napping. *Address:* Soho House, Royalty House, 72–74 Dean Street, W1D 3SG. *T:* (020) 7851 1171, *Fax:* (020) 7851 1198.

**JONES, Nicholas Michael Houssemayne,** FCA; Director, British Horseracing Authority, 2011–14; Steward, Jockey Club, 2010–16; *b* London, 27 Oct. 1946; *s* of Henry and Patricia Jones; *m* 1st, 1971, Veronica Anne Hamilton-Russell (marr. diss. 1999); one *s* one *d*; 2nd, 2002, Cherry Victoria Smart. *Educ:* Winchester Coll.; London Business Sch. (MBA). FCA 1969. Peat, Marwick, Mitchell & Co., 1965–73; J. Henry Schroder Wagg & Co. Ltd: Exec., 1975–83; Dir, 1983–87; Lazard: Man. Dir, 1987–2010; Vice-Chm., 1999–2010. Chm., Nat. Stud, 1991–2000. Director: Hilton Gp plc, 2002–06; Ladbroke Gp plc, 2006–10 (Dep. Chm., 2009–10); Newbury Racecourse plc, 2007–10; Candover Investments plc, 2008–10. Dir, Thoroughbred Breeders Assoc., 2016–; Trustee, Retraining of Racehorses, 2016–. Mem., Adv. Bd, London Business Sch., 1996–2010. Governor: James Allen Girls' Sch.,

1989–93; Birkbeck Coll., Univ. of London, 1996–99. *Recreations:* racing, bridge, tennis, gardening, stalking. *Address:* The Manor, Coln St Dennis, Cheltenham, Glos GL54 3JU. *E:* colnvalleystud@hotmail.com. *Clubs:* Turf, Jockey (Dir, 2010–16).

**JONES, (Nicholas) Rory C.;** *see* Cellan-Jones.

**JONES, Prof. Nicholas Spencer,** MD; FRCS; Consultant Ear, Nose and Throat Surgeon, Queen's Medical Centre, Nottingham, 1991–2013; Honorary Professor, University of Nottingham, 1999–2013; *b* Davos, Switzerland, 12 Sept. 1953; *s* of John Spencer Jones and Philis Helen Jones (*née* Gibson); *m* 1984, Jean Margaret Shaw; two *s. Educ:* Epsom Coll.; Guy's Hosp. Dental Sch. (BDS 1975); Guy's Hosp. Med. Sch. (MB BS 1982); Univ. of London (MD 1997). FRCSEd 1986; FRCS 1986; FRCS (Otol) 1987. Sen. Registrar, Royal Nat. Throat, Nose and Ear Hosp., Gt Ormond St Hosp. and Royal Berks Hosp., 1989–91. Platinum Clin. Excellence Award, 2010. *Publications:* (with D. Simmen) A Manual of Endoscopic Sinus Surgery, 2005 (trans German, Spanish, Portuguese, Greek, Turkish, Mandarin), 2nd edn 2013; (ed jtly) Scott-Brown's Otorhinolaryngology, 7th edn 2008; Practical Rhinology, 2010; *poetry:* Encounter, 2017; Night Journey, 2018; Still Life, 2019. *Recreations:* poetry, etching, golf. *Address:* 5 Carisbrooke Drive, Nottingham NG3 5DS. *T:* (0115) 9245329.

**JONES, Nicola; Her Honour Judge Nicola Jones;** a Circuit Judge, since 2019; *b* 15 Aug. 1969; *d* of Francis Hadfield and Patricia McNally; *m* (marr. diss.); four *c. Educ:* Cardinal Langley Catholic High Sch., Middleton, Manchester; Hull Univ. (LLB Hons); Chester Coll. of Law. Admitted as solicitor, 1992; Consultant Solicitor, Strain & Co., Solicitors, 2009–19; Assistant Coroner: NW Wales, 2000–13; NE/Central Wales, 2013–18. Legal Member: Mental Health Rev. Tribunal Wales, 2014–; Welsh Lang. Tribunal, 2016–. *Address:* Cardiff Crown Court, The Law Courts, Cathays Park, Cardiff CF10 3PG. *T:* 07845 004588. *E:* hhj.nicola.jones@ejudiciary.net.

**JONES, Nigel John I.;** *see* Inglis-Jones.

**JONES, Nigel Michael;** Global Chief Strategy Officer, FCB (Foote, Cone & Belding) (formerly Draftfcb), since 2013; *b* Wolverhampton, 23 Sept. 1960; *s* of Ralph Michael Jones and Patricia May Jones; *m* (marr. diss.); two *s* one *d. Educ:* Wolverhampton Grammar Sch.; Keble Coll., Oxford (BA Hons Maths). BMP DDB, 1984–99, Hd, Account Planning, 1991–99; Founder, Jones Mason Barton Antenen, 1999–2001; CEO, Claydon Heeley Jones Mason, 2001–05; CEO, FCB London, later Draft FCB, 2005–08; CEO and Chm., Publicis Gp UK, 2008–13. *Recreations:* music, www.abarrelofnails.com, Wolverhampton Wanderers FC. *Address:* 33 Mount Pleasant Road, NW10 3EG. *T:* 07979 808771. *E:* nmjonesuk@yahoo.co.uk.

**JONES, Dr (Norman) Fielding,** FRCP; Consultant Physician, St Thomas' Hospital, London, 1967–93, now Emeritus; *b* 3 May 1931; *s* of William John and Winifred Jones; *m* 1958, Ann Pye Chavasse; three *s. Educ:* Christ Coll., Brecon; King's Coll., Cambridge (MA 1957; MD 1966); St Thomas' Hosp., London. FRCP 1970. Rockefeller Fellow, Univ. of N Carolina, 1963–64. Physician, King Edward VII's Hosp. for Officers, 1977–95; Consulting Physician, Metropolitan Police, 1980–92; Hon. Consulting Physician: to the Army, 1980–93; to Royal Hosp., Chelsea, 1987–93; CMO, Equitable Life Assurance Soc., 1985–97. Vice Chm., West Lambeth HA, 1989–93. Royal College of Physicians: Sen. Censor and Vice Pres., 1989–90; Treasurer, 1991–96; Chm., Cttee on Renal Disease, 1980–92; Chm., Cttee on Legal Aspects of Medicine, 1990–93. Medical Mem., Ind. Public Inquiries: Gulf War Illnesses, 2004; NHS Supplied Blood and Blood Products, 2007–09. Special Trustee, St Thomas' Hosp., 1990–94; Treas., Royal Medical Benevolent Fund, 1996–2002. Member: Med. Res. Soc., 1962–2011; Assoc. of Physicians of GB and Ire., 1968–. *Publications:* (ed) Recent Advances in Renal Disease, 1975; (ed with Sir Douglas Black) Renal Disease, 1979; (ed with D. K. Peters) Recent Advances in Renal Medicine, 1982. *Recreations:* icons, music. *Address:* The Old Coach House, Forest Park Road, Brockenhurst, Hants SO42 7SW.

**JONES, His Honour Norman Henry;** QC 1985; a Circuit Judge, 1992–2007 (a Senior Circuit Judge, 2000–07); *b* 12 Dec. 1941; *s* of late Henry Robert Jones and Charlotte Isabel Scott Jones; *m* 1970, Trudy Helen Chamberlain; two *s* one *d. Educ:* Bideford Grammar School; North Devon Tech. Coll.; Univ. of Leeds (LLB, LLM). Called to the Bar, Middle Temple, 1968 (Harmsworth Schol.). A Recorder, 1987–92. Recorder of Leeds and Resident Judge at Leeds, 2001–07; Asst Surveillance Comr, 2007–18. *Recreations:* reading, walking, boating. *Address:* c/o The Crown Court, Oxford Road, Leeds LS1 3BG.

**JONES, Owen Griffith Ronald, (Ron),** CBE 2012; Founder and Executive Chairman, Tinopolis Ltd (formerly Agenda Television Ltd), since 1990; *b* Carmarthen, 11 Dec. 1948; *s* of William Tascar Jones and Eirlys Jones (*née* Jenkins); *m* 1970, Cheryl Noble (*d* 2009); one *d; m* 2015, Kim Morgans; one *s. Educ:* Amman Valley Grammar Sch.; Cardiff Univ. (BSc Econ 1970). FCA 1975. Joined Arthur Andersen as trainee, 1970, Partner, 1983–89. Chm., Real Radio Ltd, 1998–2000. Hon. Treas., Glamorgan CCC, 1989–97; Dir, Llanelli RFC, – (Chm., 1997–98). Mem., Sports Council for Wales, 1994–2004; Chm., Sportlot Wales, 2000–04. Mem., Welsh Lang. Bd, 1985–2001. Chm., Welsh Govt Creative Industries Panel, 2010–. Former Mem. Council and Ct of Govs, Swansea Univ. Hon. Fellow: Univ. of Wales Trinity St David, 2009; Swansea Univ., 2011. *Address:* Coed, Ferryside, Carmarthen SA17 5TP. *T:* (01554) 880880. *E:* ron.jones@tinopolis.com.

**JONES, Peter,** CBE 2009; entrepreneur, philanthropist and author; Founder: Peter Jones Foundation, 2005; Peter Jones Enterprise Academy (formerly National Enterprise Academy), 2009; *b* 18 March 1966; *s* of David and Eileen Jones; five *c. Educ:* Haileybury Jun. Sch.; Windsor Boys' Sch. Dir, Siemens Nixdorf, 1996–97. Founder, Peter Jones TV Ltd, 2006; investor, various industries ranging from telecoms and fast moving consumer goods brands to property and publishing. Appeared in BBC TV business series, Dragons' Den, 10 series, 2005–12; creator, presenter and judge, American Inventor, US, 2006, 2007; creator, presenter and mentor, Tycoon, 2007; Peter Jones Meets..., 2012. Emerging Entrepreneur of Year, Ernst & Young/Times Nat. Awards, 2001. *Publications:* Tycoon: how to turn dreams into millions, 2006. *Recreations:* tennis, golf, karate. *Address:* Network House, Globe Park, Marlow, Bucks SL7 1EY. *E:* enquiries@peterjones.tv.

**JONES, Peter Anthony;** Chairman: Port of Milford Haven, 2013–17; Henderson Opportunities Trust, since 2016; *b* 8 Jan. 1955. The Mersey Docks and Harbour Co.: Dir, 1993; Port Ops Dir, 1997–99; Dep. Chief Exec., 1999–2000; Chief Exec., 2000–06; Gp Chief Exec., Associated British Ports Hldgs Ltd, 2007–13.

**JONES, Peter B.;** *see* Bennett-Jones.

**JONES, Peter Benjamin Gurner,** CB 1991; Under Secretary; Director of Personnel, Board of Inland Revenue, 1984–92; *b* 25 Dec. 1932; *s* of Gurner Prince Jones and Irene Louise Jones (*née* Myall); *m* 1962, Diana Margaret Henly; one *s* one *d. Educ:* Bancroft's Sch.; St Catherine's Society, Oxford (BA (Hons) English Language and Literature). Inspector of Taxes, 1957; Inspector (Higher Grade), 1963; Sen. Inspector, 1969; Principal Inspector, 1975; Sen. Principal Inspector, 1980; Dir of Data Processing, Bd of Inland Revenue, 1981–84. Hon. Nat. Chm., CS Retirement Fellowship, 1994–2000 (Vice-Pres., 2001–). *Clubs:* Hampshire Rugby Union, Swanage and Wareham RFC.

**JONES, Prof. Peter Brian,** PhD; FMedSci; Professor of Psychiatry, since 2000, and Deputy Head, School of Clinical Medicine, since 2014, University of Cambridge (Head, Department of Psychiatry, 2000–14); *b* 24 Jan. 1960; *s* of Owen Trevor Jones and Amy M. Anita Jones; *m* 1986, Caroline Lea-Cox; two *s. Educ:* Northampton Grammar Sch.; King's Coll., London (BSc Neuroanatomy); Westminster Med. Sch. (MB BS); London Sch. of Hygiene and Tropical Medicine (MSc Dist.); Inst. of Psychiatry (PhD 1997). MRCP 1987, FRCP 2002; MRCPsych 1990, FRCPsych 2007. House physician, Westminster Hosp., 1984; house surgeon, E Surrey Hosp., 1985; Casualty Officer, Westminster Hosp., 1985; SHO, Whittington Hosp., 1986–87; Med. Registrar, KCH, 1987; Registrar, Bethlem Royal and Maudsley Hosps, 1987–90; Sen. Registrar in Psychiatry, KCH, 1991; MRC Trng Fellow, 1991–93; Sen. Lectr, Inst. of Psychiatry, 1993–95 (Hon. Lectr, 1991–93); Hon. Consultant Psychiatrist, Bethlem Royal and Maudsley Hosps, 1993–95; University of Nottingham: Sen. Lectr in Psychiatric Epidemiol., 1995–96; Prof. of Psychiatry and Community Mental Health, 1997–2000; Head, Div. of Psychiatry, 1997–2000. SMO (part-time), R&D Div., DoH, 1994–96. Hon. Consultant Psychiatrist: and Dir, R&D, Nottingham Healthcare Trust, 1995–2000; Addenbrooke's NHS Trust, 2000–; Cambs and Peterborough NHS Foundn Trust (formerly Cambs and Peterborough Mental Health Partnership NHS Trust), 2002– (Dir, 2003–05; non-exec. Dir, 2017–). Sen. Investigator, NIHR, 2010–18, now Emeritus (Director: NIHR Collaboration in Applied Health Res. and Care, 2008–19); Applied Res. Collaboration E of England, 2019–); Dir, Cambridge Univ. Health Partners, 2009–. Hon. Prof., UEA, 2019–. FMedSci 2003. Hon. MD Oulu, Finland, 2006. *Publications:* contribs to learned jls on causation, clinical features, epidemiology and treatment of mental illness, the psychoses, in particular. *Recreations:* growing it, cooking it, walking it off. *Address:* Department of Psychiatry, University of Cambridge, Herchel Smith Building, Robinson Way, Cambridge Biomedical Centre, Cambridge CB2 0SZ. *T:* (01223) 336960.

**JONES, Peter Derek;** Deputy Chairman, Civil Service Appeal Board, 1992–2001; Secretary: Council of Civil Service Unions, 1980–92; Civil Service National Whitley Council (Trade Union Side), 1963–92; *b* 21 May 1932; *s* of Richard Morgan Jones and Phyllis Irene (*née* Lloyd); *m* 1st, 1962, Noreen Elizabeth (*née* Kemp) (*d* 2001); 2nd, 2006, Delwin Ann Kirkstone Hunter (*née* Wood); one step *d. Educ:* Wembley County Grammar School. National Service and TA, Green Jackets/Parachute Regt, 1950–56; Civil Service, Nat. Assistance Bd, 1952–59; Asst Sec., Civil Service Nat. Whitley Council, 1959–63. Chm., Civil Service Housing Assoc. Ltd, 1988–97 (Dir, 1963–81; Vice Chm., 1981–88, 1997–99); Dir, Civil Service Building Soc., 1963–87. Vice-Pres., RIPA, 1991–92 (Chm., 1987–90; Vice-Chm., 1986–87; Mem. Exec. Council, 1981–85); Member: Adv. Council, Civil Service Coll., 1982–92; Tourism and Leisure Industries EDC, 1987–92; Adv. Council, CS Occupational Health Service, 1988–92; Employment (formerly Industrial) Tribunals, 1992–2002; Security Vetting Appeals Panel, 1997–2009; Chm., CIPFA Disciplinary Investigations Cttee, 2001–08. Trustee: Inst. of Contemporary Brit. History, 1985–; CS Benevolent Fund, 1992–99. Editor: Whitley Bulletin, 1963–83; CCSU Bulletin, 1984–92. *Publications:* articles in RIPA and personnel management jls; contrib. Oxford DNB. *Recreations:* relaxing, reading, painting. *Address:* Chaseview, Rowlands Hill, Wimborne, Dorset BH21 2QQ. *T:* (01202) 888824; Fern Cottage, Paradise Road, Lower Rowe, Holt, Wimborne, Dorset BH21 7DZ. *T:* (01202) 883578. *Clubs:* Belfry; Mansion House (Poole); Wimborne Cricket.

**JONES, Peter Edward,** CMG 2018; HM Diplomatic Service; Chief Operating Officer, Foreign and Commonwealth Office, since 2017; *b* Liverpool, 28 Aug. 1961; *s* of William Jones and Dorothy Jones; *m* 1998, Sumita Biswas. *Educ:* King Edward VI Sch., Southampton; Pembroke Coll., Oxford (MA Mod. Hist.). IBM UK Ltd, 1983–85; joined FCO, 1985; Second, then First Sec., UK Delegn to Vienna, 1989–92; First Sec., Bonn, 1994–98; Asst Dir, Personnel, 1998–2001, Afghanistan Emergency Unit, 2001, FCO; Counsellor, Rome, 2002–07; Dep. Dir, 2007–09, Dir, 2009–11, Migration, FCO; High Comr to Ghana, and Ambassador (non-res.) to Togo and Burkina Faso, 2011–14; Dir, Defence and Internat. Security, 2014–17. *Recreations:* football and cricket (watching), cycling and walking (doing), history. *Address:* c/o Foreign and Commonwealth Office, King Charles Street, SW1A 2AH.

**JONES, Peter H.;** *see* Heaton-Jones.

**JONES, His Honour Peter Henry Francis;** a Circuit Judge, 2001–17; *b* 25 Feb. 1952; *s* of late Eric Roberts Jones, MBE and Betty Irene Jones (*née* Longhurst); *m* 1978, Anne Elizabeth (*née* Jones); two *d. Educ:* Bishop Gore Grammar Sch., Swansea; Newport High Sch., Gwent; Balliol Coll., Oxford (MA (Hons) Lit.Hum.). Admitted Solicitor of Supreme Court, 1977. Partner: Darlington and Parkinson, Solicitors, London, 1978–87; J. Howell and Co., Solicitors, Sheffield, 1987–95; Asst Recorder, 1993–97; a Stipendiary Magistrate, then Dist Judge (Magistrates' Courts), S Yorks, 1995–2001; a Recorder, 1997–2001. Member: Lord Chancellor's Legal Aid Adv. Cttee, 1983–92; Legal Aid Bd, 1992–95; Sentencing Adv. Panel, 1999–2005; Magistrates' Cts Rules Cttee, 2001–04; Parole Bd, 2018–. Course Dir, Family Law Trng, Judicial Coll. (formerly Judicial Studies Bd), 2004–11. *Recreations:* tennis, books, watching Rugby Union, petanque, golf. *Clubs:* Dethreau Boat; Scorpions Cricket; Druidstone (Dyfed).

**JONES, Prof. Peter (Howard),** FRSE, FSAScot; Director and Trustee, Foundation for Advanced Studies in the Humanities, 1997–2002; Professor of Philosophy, 1984–98, now Emeritus, and Director, Institute for Advanced Studies in the Humanities, 1986–2000, University of Edinburgh; *b* 18 Dec. 1935; *s* of Thomas Leslie Jones and Hilda Croesora (*née* Parkinson); *m* 1st, 1960, (Elizabeth) Jean (*d* 2009), *yr d* of R. J. Roberton, JP; two *d*; 2nd, 2011, Lt Col Diana M. Henderson (*d* 2019), *yr d* of Edna Henderson. *Educ:* Highgate Sch.; Queens' Coll., Cambridge. Nat. Service (Intelligence Corps), 1955–57. British Council, 1960–61; Asst Lectr in Philosophy, Univ. of Nottingham, 1963–64; Lectr, then Reader in Philosophy, 1964–84, Associate Dean of Arts, 1975–78 and 1986–89, Univ. of Edinburgh. Visiting Professor of Philosophy: Univ. of Rochester, NY, 1969–70; Dartmouth Coll., NH, 1973, 1983; Carleton Coll., Minn, 1974; Oklahoma Univ., 1978; Baylor Univ., 1978; Univ. of Malta, 1993; Belarusian State Univ., 1997; Jagiellonian Univ., Cracow, 2001–13; Mid-America Dist. Vis. Prof., 1978; Visiting Fellow: Humanities Res. Centre, ANU, 1984, 2002; Calgary Inst. for Humanities, 1992. Lothian Lectr, Edinburgh, 1993; Gifford Lectr, Univ. of Aberdeen, 1994–95; Loemker Lectr, Emory Univ., 1995–96; Lectures: Swiss Acad. of Humanities and Social Scis, 1994; Yalta Malta Yalta, 1995; Windsor Meetings, 1996–2001; Polish Acad. of Arts and Scis, 1998, 2013; St Petersburg Acad. of Scis, 1999; RCDS, 1999–2001; Hungarian Acad. of Sci., 2000; British Council Lectr, India, Pakistan, Japan, Taiwan, Poland, Czech Republic and Hungary. Member: Planning Cttee, Commonwealth Heads of Govt Meeting, Malta, 1990; UK Spoliation Adv. Panel, 2000–18. Trustee: Nat. Museums of Scotland, 1987–99 (Chm., Mus. of Scotland Client Cttee, 1991–99); Univ. of Edinburgh Develt Trust, 1990–98; AMAR Internat. Charitable Foundn, 1994–99; Charlemagne Inst., 1995–99; Policy Inst., 1999–2008; Scots at War, 1999–2014; Morrison's Acad., 1984–98; Fettes Coll., 1995–2005; MBI Al Jaber Foundn, 2005–19. Member: UNESCO forum on tolerance, Tbilisi, 1995; UNESCO dialogue on Europe and Islam, 1997. Member: Court, Univ. of Edinburgh, 1987–90; Council, RSE, 1992–95. Founder Mem., Hume Soc., 1974. FRSE 1989; FSAScot 1993. *Publications:* Philosophy and the Novel, 1975; Hume's Sentiments, 1982; (ed) A Hotbed of Genius,

1986, 2nd edn 1996; (ed) Philosophy and Science in the Scottish Enlightenment, 1988; (ed) The Science of Man in the Scottish Enlightenment, 1989; Revolutions in Science 1789–1989, 1989; (ed) Adam Smith Reviewed, 1992; Family Values in the Mediterranean, 1994; (ed) Commonwealth Lectures, 1997; (ed) Investigation of the Principles of Knowledge, by James Hutton, 1999; (contrib.) National Heritage - National Canon, 2001; (ed) The Enlightenment World, 2004, 2nd edn 2006; (ed) The Reception of David Hume in Europe, 2005, 2nd edn 2012; (ed) Elements of Criticism, by Henry Home, Lord Kames, 2005; Ove Arup Master Builder of the Twentieth Century, 2006, 2nd edn 2018, Japanese edn 2017; Conversation: and the reception of David Hume, 2011; (contrib.) New Essays on Adam Smith's Moral Philosophy, 2012; (ed) The Reception of Edmund Burke in Europe, 2016; over 150 articles on philosophy, literature and culture. *Recreations:* opera, 18th century music and culture, conversation, gardens, clavichords. *Club:* Army and Navy.

**JONES, Peter Ivan,** CBE 2008; Director, Goodwood Racecourse, 2008–18; *b* 14 Dec. 1942; *s* of Glyndwr and Edith Evelyn Jones; *m* 1st, 1964, Judith Watson (marr. diss. 1969); one *s* one *d*; 2nd, 1970, Elizabeth Gent; one *s* one *d*. *Educ:* Gravesend Grammar Sch.; London School of Economics (BSc Econs 1964). MIPA 1967. Chief Executive: Boase Massimi Pollitt, 1988–89; Omnicom UK plc, 1989–93 (Dir, Omnicom Inc., 1989–97); Pres., Diversified Agency Services, 1993–97. Dir, Sutton Gp Hldgs, 2005–. Dir, British Horseracing Bd, 1993–97; Mem., Horserace Betting Levy Bd, 1993–95; Chm., Horserace Totalisator Bd, 1997–2007 (Dir, 1995–97). Chm., Dorset Police Authy, 1997–2003. Chm., Goodwood Estate Pension Fund, 2010–18. Pres., Racehorse Owners Assoc., 1990–93. Gov., LSE, 2007–18, now Emeritus; Chm., LSE Annual Fund, 2010–15. Trustee, Animal Health Trust, 2010–15. Contrib., The Scout, Daily Express, 2015–. *Publications:* Trainers Record, annually 1973 to 1987 (Editor, 1982–87); (ed) Ed Byrne's Racing Year, annually 1980 to 1983. *Recreations:* horse racing, computer programming, watching sport, theatre. *Address:* Melplash Farmhouse, Melplash, Bridport, Dorset DT6 3UH. *T:* (01308) 488383. *Club:* Bridport and West Dorset Golf.

**JONES, Maj.-Gen. (Peter) John R.;** *see* Russell-Jones.

**JONES, Prof. Philip Alan;** Vice-Chancellor, Sheffield Hallam University, 2007–16; *b* 26 Nov. 1950; *s* of Jean Keir; partner, Hilary Bloor. *Educ:* Poly. of Central London (LLB Hons (ext.) 1972); London Sch. of Econs (LLM 1973); Univ. of Essex (MA Sociol. 1979); Univ. of Surrey (Postgrad. Dip. Practice of Higher Educn). Lectr, Manchester Poly., 1973–75; Polytechnic of Central London, later University of Westminster: Lectr, then Sen. Lectr, 1975–87; Principal Lectr, 1987–91; Dep. Hd and Actg Hd, 1991–92; University of Sheffield: Dir, Legal Practice Course, 1993–97; Dean, Faculty of Law, 1996–98; Pro Vice Chancellor, 1998–2004; Dep. Vice-Chancellor and Sub-Warden, Durham Univ., 2004–07. Vis. Lectr, Brunel Univ., 1988; Vis. Prof., DC Sch. of Law, Washington, 1991. Ed.-in-Chief, Legal Practice Guides, 1993–2000; Exec. Ed., Internat. Jl Legal Profession, 1993–2004; Mem., Editl Bd, Jl Professional Legal Educn, 1995–2004. Member: Bd of Studies and Consultant, Council of Legal Educn, 1993–96; NCVQ Policy Cttee, 1996–98; S Yorks Learning and Skills Council, 2001–04; Quality Assce Cttee, UK eUniv., 2001–04; Quality Assce, Learning and Teaching Cttee, HEFCE, 2003–08; All Party Parly Univ. Gp, 2007–; Univ. Alliance, 2007–; Teacher Educn Adv. Gp, UUK, 2007–; Student Policy Network (formerly Student Experience Policy Cttee, then Students, Quality and Participation Policy Network), UUK, 2008–; Chm., Quality Assce System in Higher Educn Gp, UUK/GuildHE/HEFCE/Dept for Employment and Learning NI, 2010–; Advr to Higher Educn Quality Council, 1996–97; various QCA posts, 1998–2003, incl. Mem., Vocational Qualifications and Occupational Standards Cttee, 1998–2000 and Qualification Cttee, 2000–03. Director: Creative Sheffield, 2007–11; Nat. Sci. Learning Centre (Myscience), 2007–; Yorkshire Univs, 2007. Mem., Sheffield City Region LEP, 2010. Trustee, ENTHUSE Charitable Trust, 2008. Hon. LittD Sheffield, 2014. *Publications:* (ed jtly) Politics and Power, vol. 1 1980, vol. 2 1980, vol. 3 1981; (contrib.) Problems in Labour Politics, 1980; (contrib.) Law, Politics and Justice, 1982; Lawyers' Skills, 1993, 4th edn 1996, then reprints annually; (contrib.) Examining the Law Syllabus: beyond the core, 1993; Competences, Learning Outcomes and Legal Education, 1994; (contrib.) Teaching Lawyers' Skills, 1996; (contrib.) An Agenda for Comparative Legal Skills Research: the European Community and the Commonwealth, 1996; (contrib.) The Development of the NVQ Framework at the Higher Levels, 1997; (contrib.) NVQs and Higher Education, 1997; contribs to jls incl. Law Teacher, Modern Law Rev., Jl Law and Soc., New Law Jl, Internat. Jl Legal Profession; numerous conf. papers and res. reports. *Recreations:* rock climbing and biking, road and mountain. *Clubs:* Dark Peak Fell Running; Crosstrax Cycling.

**JONES, Adm. Sir Philip (Andrew),** KCB 2014 (CB 2012); DL; First Sea Lord and Chief of the Naval Staff, 2016–19; First and Principal Naval Aide-de-Camp to the Queen, 2016–19; *b* 14 Feb. 1960; *s* of Edgar Jones and Edna Lilian Jones (*née* Peers); *m* 1987, Elizabeth Collins; one *s* two *d*. *Educ:* Birkenhead Sch.; Mansfield Coll., Oxford (BA Geog. 1981; MA 1985). HMS Fearless, Falklands War, 1982; Watchkeeping and Navigation Officer, Frigates and HMY Britannia, 1983–88; Prin. Warfare Officer, Frigates and Maritime Battle Staff, 1989–93; CO HMS Beaver, 1994–96; Directorate Navy Plans and Progs, MoD, 1997–99; CO HMS Coventry, 1999–2001; Chief of Defence Logistics Office, MoD, 2002–03; Dir, Jt Maritime Operational Trng Staff, 2003–04; ACOS C4ISTAR Fleet HQ, 2004–06; Comdr Amphibious Task Gp, 2006–08; FO Scotland, England, Wales and NI, and FO Reserves, 2008; Comdr UK Maritime Forces and Rear Adm., Surface Ships, 2008–09; Asst Chief of Naval Staff, 2009–11; Dep. C-in-C Fleet, COS Navy Comd HQ, and Chief Naval Warfare Officer, 2011–12; Fleet Comdr and Dep. Chief of Naval Staff, 2012–16. Mem., Windsor Leadership Trust, 2008–. President: RN Rugby Union, 2012–17 (Vice-Pres., 2008–12); RN Polo, 2013–19; RN Tennis, 2017–19. Younger Brother, Trinity House, 2009. Freeman: City of Glasgow, 2009; City of London, 2019; Co. of Shipwrights, 2017. DL Hants, 2019. *Recreations:* watching and following most sports (especially Rugby Union), supporting Liverpool FC, reading, hill walking.

**JONES, Lt Gen. Philip David,** CB 2015; CBE 2012 (MBE 1994); DL; Chief of Staff to Supreme Allied Commander Transformation, 2013–15; Managing Director, Othrys Ltd, since 2017; *b* Maldon, Essex, 23 July 1961; *s* of Michael York Jones and Vivien Jones; *m* 1984, Denise Anne Spong; one *s* one *d*. *Educ:* King Edward VI Grammar Sch., Chelmsford; RMA, Sandhurst. Royal Anglian Regiment: Platoon Comdr, 3rd Bn, 1981–83, Inf. Jun. Leaders Bn, 1983–85; Anti-Tank Platoon Comdr, 3rd Bn, 1985–87; Adjt, 1st Bn, 1987–89; SO3 G3 Ops HQ, 8th Inf. Bde, Londonderry, 1989–92; Army Staff Coll., 1993; Comdr, Rifle Co., 1st Bn, Royal Anglian Regt, 1993–95; COS, HQ 24 Airmobile Bde, 1995–97; MA to C-in-C Allied Forces Northwest Europe, 1997–99; CO, 1st Bn, Royal Anglian Regt, 1999–2003; Chief of Plans: Combined Jt Task Force 180, Afghanistan, 2003; HQ ARRC, 2003–05; Comdr, 8th Inf. Bde, NI, 2005–06; MA to Special Rep. of Sec. Gen., UN Assistance Mission Afghanistan, 2006–07; Mil. Attaché, Washington DC, 2007–10; Dir Force Reintegration, HQ ISAF, Afghanistan, 2010–11; COS Jt Forces Comd, 2011–13. Chm., Army Benevolent Fund, 2016–. Trustee, Tsavo Conservation Trust, 2016–. MInstD 1992. DL Suffolk, 2018. QCVS 2002. *Recreations:* family, dogs, reading, running, cycling.

**JONES, Philip David Simon;** Editor, The Bookseller, since 2012; *b* Manchester, 12 Oct. 1971; *s* of Barrie Jones and Jean Wright (*née* Healy); *m* 2005, Amy Lankester-Owen; three *s*. *Educ:* Wem Adams Sch.; Univ. of Reading (BA Hons Eng. Lang. and Lit.). The Bookseller: Financial Reporter, 1996–99; Web Ed., 2002–08; Man. Ed., 2008–10; Dep. Ed., 2010–12; Ed., Futurebook.net, 2010–. *Recreations:* cricket, reading, family. *Address:* The Bookseller, Floor 10, Westminster Tower, 3 Albert Embankment, Lambeth, SE1 7SP. *T:* (020) 3358 0364. *E:* philip.jones@thebookseller.com. *Club:* h.

**JONES, Prof. Philip Douglas,** PhD; FRMetS; Professor, since 1998, and Director, since 2003, Climatic Research Unit, School of Environmental Sciences, University of East Anglia; *b* 22 April 1952; *s* of late Douglas Idris Jones and Peggy Rita Yvonne Jones; *m* 1973, Ruth Anne Shackleton; one *s* one *d*. *Educ:* Univ. of Lancaster (BA Envmtl Scis 1973); Univ. of Newcastle upon Tyne (MSc Engrg Hydrol. 1974; PhD Hydrol. 1977). FRMetS 1992, Hon. FRMetS 2018. Sen. Res. Associate, 1976–94, Reader, 1994–98, Co-Dir, 1998–2003, Climatic Res. Unit, Sch. of Envmtl Scis, UEA. Member, Editorial Board: Internat. Jl Climatol., 1989–94; Climatic Change, 1992–. Sec., Internat. Commn for Climatol., 1987–95. MAE 1998; Mem., 2001, Fellow, 2006, Amer. Meteorol. Soc.; Fellow, Amer. Geophys. Union, 2009. Hon. Dr Univ: Rovira i Virgili, Tarragona, Spain, 2012; Stockholm, 2016. Hugh Robert Mill Medal, 1995, Internat. Jl Climatol. Prize, 2002, RMetS; Hans Oeschger Medal, Eur. Geophysical Soc., 2002. *Publications:* (ed with R. S. Bradley) Climate since AD 1500, 1992, 2nd edn 1995; (ed Jtly) Climatic Variations and Forcing Mechanisms of the Last 2000 Years, 1996; (contrib.) Climate and Climate Impacts: the last 1000 years, 2001; (ed with D. Camuffo) Improved Understanding of Past Climatic Variability from Early Daily European Instrumental Sources, 2002; chapters in peer reviewed in books; contrib. Climate Change. *Recreation:* playing bridge for local club and for Norfolk. *Address:* Climatic Research Unit, University of East Anglia, Norwich NR4 7TJ. *T:* (01603) 592090, *Fax:* (01603) 507784. *E:* p.jones@uea.ac.uk.

**JONES, Philip E.;** *see* Edgar-Jones.

**JONES, Ven. Philip Hugh;** Archdeacon of Hastings (formerly of Lewes and Hastings), 2005–16, now Emeritus; Rector, Slindon, Eartham and Madehurst, since 2019 (Priest-in-charge, 2016–19); *b* 13 May 1951; *m* 1979, Anne Atkinson; two *s* two *d*. *Educ:* Leys Sch., Cambridge; Chichester Theol Coll. Admitted solicitor, 1975; in private practice, 1975–92. Ordained deacon, 1994, priest, 1995; Curate, Horsham, 1994–97; Vicar, Southwater, 1997–2005. RD Horsham, 2002–05. *Recreations:* ornithology, medieval history, music (esp. choral). *Address:* The Rectory, Dyers Lane, Slindon, Arundel BN18 0RE. *T:* (01243) 814275.

**JONES, Philip John;** QC 2006; *s* of Colin and Sally Jones; *m* 1990, Philippa Seal; one *s* one *d*. *Educ:* Ynysawdre Comprehensive Sch.; Hertford Coll., Oxford (BCL, MA); Dalhousie Univ., Canada (LLM). Called to the Bar, Lincoln's Inn, 1985, Bencher, 2013; Jun. Counsel to the Crown, 1994–2006. Mem., YMCA. *Address:* 6 New Square, Lincoln's Inn, WC2A 3QS. *T:* (020) 7242 6105, *Fax:* (020) 7405 4004. *E:* pjones@serlecourt.co.uk.

**JONES, (Piers) Nicholas L.;** *see* Legh-Jones.

**JONES, Raymond Francis,** OBE 1986; HM Diplomatic Service, retired; Chairman, CPM Ltd, 2010–12; *b* 15 Nov. 1935; *s* of late Hugh and Jessie Jones; *m* 1957, Maurag Annat (*d* 1994); two *d*. *Educ:* Liverpool Collegiate Sch. Nat. Service, RAF, 1954–56. Joined Foreign Office, 1953; served Amman, Tokyo, Cairo, Accra, 1956–70; Second Sec., FCO, 1970–73; Consul, Seattle, 1973–78; First Sec., 1978; on loan to DoI, 1978–82; New Delhi, 1982–86; Dep. Consul-Gen., Chicago, 1986–91; High Comr, Honiara, Solomon Is, 1991–95. Dir, 1996–2002, Chm., 2001–02, Holywell Hook Heath Ltd. *Recreations:* music, sport, reading. *Address:* Flat 168, Centrium, Station Approach, Woking, Surrey GU22 7PE.

**JONES, Prof. Raymond Leonard,** PhD; FAcSS; Professor of Social Work, Kingston University and St George's, University of London, 2008–15, now Emeritus; *b* 21 Oct. 1949; *s* of Leonard and Pauline Jones; *m* 1973, Mary Elaine Abbott; one *s* one *d*. *Educ:* Redruth Grammar Sch.; Univ. of Bath (BSc 1st Cl. Hons Sociol. 1972; MSc 1981; PhD 1983). CQSW 1972. Asst Warden, Mental Health Hostel, Cornwall CC, 1967–68; Social Worker, then Sen. Social Worker, Social Services, Berks CC, 1972–75; Lectr in Social Work, Univ. of Bath, 1975–80; Area Team Leader, Social Services, Wilts CC, 1981–84; Asst Divl Dir, Barnardo's, 1984–87; Divl Dir, Social Services, Surrey CC, 1987–89; Dep. Dir, Social Services, Berks CC, 1989–92; Chief Exec., Social Care Inst. for Excellence, 2001–02; Dir, Social Services, 1992–2001 and 2002–06, Adult and Community Services, 2002–06, Wiltshire CC. Chm., Marlborough Brandt Gp, 2003–07. Dep. Chm., then Chm., BASW, 2005–06. Chairman: Bristol Safeguarding Children Bd, 2009–13; Salford Safeguarding Children Improvement Bd, 2010–13; Torbay Safeguarding Children Improvement Bd, 2012–14; IoW Safeguarding Children Bd, 2013–15; Devon Safeguarding Children Bd, 2013–15; Sandwell Children's Performance Accountability Bd, 2013–15. Vis. Prof. (formerly Vis. Fellow), Univ. of Bath, 1993–2011; Vis. Prof. (formerly Univ. Fellow), Univ. of Exeter, 1997–2004. Trustee: Quarriers, 2006–11; Wytham Hall, 2011–14. FCMI (FIMgt 1992); FRSA 1996; FAcSS (AcSS 2002). Hon. Fellow, Univ. of Glos (formerly Cheltenham and Gloucester Coll.), 1995. Chm., Social Worker of the Year Awards, 2014–17 (Outstanding Contribn to Social Work Award, 2017). *Publications:* Fun and Therapy, 1979; Intermediate Treatment and Social Work, 1979; Social Work with Adolescents, 1980; From Resident to Community Worker, 1983; Like Distant Relatives, 1987; The Story of Baby P: setting the record straight, 2014, 2nd edn 2017; In Whose Interest?: the privatisation of child protection and social work, 2018; chapters in books and papers on social work and social policy. *Recreations:* Rugby, fell walking. *Club:* Redruth Rugby Football.

**JONES, Rhiannon;** QC 2015; *b* Stockport, Cheshire, 7 April 1970; *d* of Geraint and Nina Jones; *m* 1996, Dominic Happé; two *s*. *Educ:* King's Coll. London (BMus; AKC; MA Med. Law and Ethics). Called to the Bar, Inner Temple, 1993; in practice as barrister, 1993–. *Recreations:* sport, music. *Address:* Bryom Street Chambers, 12 Byrom Street, Manchester M3 4PP. *E:* rhiannon.jones@byromstreet.com.

**JONES, Richard,** CBE 2015; operatic and theatrical director; *b* London. *Opera productions* include: English National Opera: The Love for Three Oranges, Die Fledermaus, 1993; Pelleas and Melisande (also for Opera North), 1995; From Morning to Midnight (David Sawer), 2001; Lulu, 2002; The Trojans, 2003 (Olivier Award); The Bitter Tears of Petra von Kant, 2005; Cavalleria Rusticana, Pagliacci, 2008; The Tales of Hoffman, 2012; Julietta, 2012; Rodelinda, 2014; The Girl of the Golden West, 2014; The Mastersingers of Nuremberg, 2015 (Best New Opera Production, Olivier Awards, 2015); Don Giovanni, 2016; Royal Opera: Der Ring des Nibelungen, 1994–95 (Evening Standard Award); Lady Macbeth of Mtsensk, 2004 (Olivier Award); L'Heure Espagnol, and Gianni Schicchi, 2007; The Gambler, 2010; Anna Nicole, 2011; Il Trittico, 2011; Gloriana, 2013; Boris Godunov, 2016; La Bohème, 2017; Katya Kabanova, 2019; Welsh National Opera: Hansel and Gretel, 1998 (Olivier Award); The Queen of Spades, 2000; Wozzeck, 2005; Die Meistersinger, 2010; Glyndebourne: Flight (Jonathan Dove), 1998; Euryanthe, 2002; Macbeth, 2007; Falstaff, 2009; Der Rosenkavalier, 2014; Der fliegende Holländer, 1993, Jenufa, 1997, The Cunning Little Vixen, 2006, Amsterdam; Julius Caesar (Opernwelt Prodn of Year), 1994,

The Midsummer Marriage, 1998, The Cunning Little Vixen, 2006, Lohengrin, 2009, The Tales of Hoffman, 2011, Ariodante, 2017, Munich; L'enfant et les Sortilèges, and Der Zweig, 1998, Julietta, 2012, Paris; Un ballo in maschera, 1999 ((jtly) Designer of the Year, 2000), La Bohème, 2001, Bregenz Fest.; The Fiery Angel, Brussels, 2007; Billy Budd, 2007, Makropulos Case, 2012, Frankfurt; Hansel and Gretel, Metropolitan Opera, 2007; Rusalka, Copenhagen, 2008; Skin Deep, Opera North, 2009; Peter Grimes, Milan, 2012; Gloriana, Hamburg, 2013; Ariodante, Aix-en-Provence Fest., 2015; Don Giovanni, Basle, 2017; theatre productions include: Too Clever by Half (Olivier Award); The Illusion (Evening Standard Award), A Flea in Her Ear, 1989, Old Vic; Into the Woods, Phoenix, 1990 (Olivier and Evening Standard Awards); Le Bourgeois Gentilhomme, 1992, Tales from the Vienna Woods, 2003, NT; Holy Mothers, Royal Court, 1999; Six Characters Looking for an Author, 2001, Hobson's Choice, 2003, The Good Soul of Szechuan, 2008, Annie Get Your Gun, 2009, Government Inspector, 2010, Public Enemy, 2013, The Trial, 2015, Once in a Lifetime, 2016, Young Vic; A Midsummer Night's Dream, RSC, 2002; David Sawer's Rumpelstiltskin, Birmingham Contemporary Music Gp, 2009; The Hairy Ape, Old Vic, 2015, NY, 2017; The Twilight Zone, Almeida Th., 2017; in New York: La Bête, 1991; Black Snow, 1992; All's Well That Ends Well; Titanic, 1997; Wrong Mountain, 1999. *Address*: c/o Judy Daish Associates, 2 St Charles Place, W10 6EG.

**JONES, Prof. Richard Anthony Lewis**, PhD; FRS 2006; Professor of Physics, University of Sheffield, since 1998; *b* 7 March 1961; *s* of Rev. Robert Cecil Jones and Sheila Howell Jones; *m* 1998, Dulcie Anne Jordan; one *s* one *d*. *Educ*: Denstone Coll.; St Catharine's Coll., Cambridge (BA Natural Scis 1983; PhD Physics 1987). Postdoctoral Res. Associate, Cornell Univ., 1987–89; Asst Lectr, 1989–94, Lectr, 1994–98, Univ. of Cambridge. *Publications*: Polymers at Surfaces and Interfaces (with R. W. Richards), 1999; Soft Condensed Matter, 2002; Soft Machines: nanotechnology and life, 2004; more than 150 papers in learned jls. *Recreations*: rock climbing, mountain walking. *Address*: Department of Physics and Astronomy, University of Sheffield, Hicks Building, Hounsfield Road, Sheffield S3 7RH. *T*: (0114) 222 9820. *E*: r.a.l.jones@sheffield.ac.uk.

**JONES, Rev. Richard Granville**; Chairman of East Anglia District, Methodist Church, 1983–93; President of the Methodist Conference, 1988–89; *b* 26 July 1926; *s* of Henry William and Ida Grace Jones; *m* 1955, Kathleen Stone; three *d*. *Educ*: Truro School, Cornwall; St John's Coll., Cambridge (MA); Manchester Univ. (BD). Instructor Officer, RN, 1947–49. Methodist Minister in Plymouth East, 1949–50; Area Sec., SCM, 1953–55; Minister: Sheffield North Circuit, 1955–59; Sheffield Carver Street, 1959–64; Birkenhead, 1964–69; Tutor, Hartley Victoria Coll., Manchester, 1969–78, Principal 1978–82; Minister, Fakenham and Wells Circuit, 1982–83. Editor, Epworth Review, 1991–2005. Hon. DD Hull, 1988. *Publications*: (ed) Worship for Today, 1968; (with A. Wesson) Towards a Radical Church, 1972; How goes Christian Marriage?, 1978; Groundwork of Worship and Preaching, 1980; Groundwork of Christian Ethics, 1984; What to Do?: Christians and ethics, 1999; Michael's War, 2010. *Recreations*: walking, reading, writing. *Address*: 35 Davies Road, West Bridgford, Nottingham NG2 5JE. *T*: (0115) 914 2352.

**JONES, Richard Henry**; QC 1996; a Recorder, since 2000; *b* 6 April 1950; *s* of Henry Ingham Jones and Betty Marian Jones; *m* 1989, Sarah Jane Wildsmith; one *s* one *d*. *Educ*: Moseley Grammar Sch., Birmingham; St Peter's Coll., Oxford (MA Jurisp.). Called to the Bar, Inner Temple, 1972; in practice, 1973–80; Legal Adviser: Crown Life Insurance Gp, 1980–82; Financial Times Gp, 1982–86; in practice, 1986–. *Publications*: Investigations and Enforcement, 2001. *Recreations*: cricket and Rugby (spectating), reading, walking. *Address*: 5 Fountain Court, Steelhouse Lane, Birmingham B4 6DR. *T*: (0121) 606 0500. *Clubs*: Royal Automobile, MCC; London Scottish Football.

**JONES, Richard Hugh Francis**; HM Diplomatic Service; Deputy Director, Human Rights and Democracy, Foreign and Commonwealth Office, since 2017; *b* 28 Sept. 1962; *s* of late Lynn and Audrey Jones. *Educ*: Dulwich Coll.; Merton Coll., Oxford (MA). Joined FCO, 1983; Arabic lang. trng, 1984–86; Third, later Second Sec., Abu Dhabi, 1986–89; FCO, 1989–94; First Sec., UK Perm. Rep. to EU, Brussels, 1994–98; Dep. Hd, Common Foreign and Security Policy Dept, FCO, 1998–2000; Counsellor, Dep. Hd, EU Dept (Internal), FCO, 2000–03; Albanian lang. trng, 2003; Ambassador to Albania, 2003–06; Consul-Gen., Basra, 2007–08; Political Counsellor and Dep. Hd of Mission, UK Perm. Rep. to EU, Brussels, 2008–11; European External Action Service, Hd of European Union Delegn to Switzerland and Principality of Liechtenstein, 2012–16. *Recreations*: music, places, words, the past, food. *Address*: c/o Foreign and Commonwealth Office, King Charles Street, SW1A 2AH.

**JONES, Richard Mansell M.**; *see* Mansell-Jones.

**JONES, Prof. R(ichard) Merfyn**, CBE 2011; PhD; FRHistS; Professor of Welsh History, 1994–2010, Vice-Chancellor, 2004–10, Bangor University (formerly University of Wales, Bangor); *b* 16 Jan. 1948; *s* of John Edwin Jones and Ellen Jones; *m* 1st, 1969, Dr Jill Lovecy (marr. diss. 2003); two *s*; 2nd, 2004, Dr Nerys Patterson (*née* Thomas) (*d* 2007); 3rd, 2009, Dr Catrin Hughes (*née* Richards). *Educ*: Univ. of Sussex (BA 1st cl. Hons 1968); Univ. of Warwick (MA; PhD 1976). Sen. Researcher, ESRC Coalfield Hist. Project, UC, Swansea, 1971–74; Lectr, then Sen. Lectr in Mod. Hist., Dept of Continuing Educn, Univ. of Liverpool, 1975–90; Sen. Lectr, Dept of Hist. and Welsh Hist., Univ. of Wales, Bangor, 1990–94. Chairman: Higher Educn Wales, 2006–08; Review of Higher Educn in Wales Task and Finish Gp (Jones Review), 2008–09; N Wales Branch, Inst. of Welsh Affairs, 2009–14; Vice-Press., UUK, 2006–08. Ind. Mem., Betsi Cadwaladr Univ. Health Bd, 2009–13 (Chm., 2011–13). Writer and presenter of TV historical documentaries. Gov., BBC, 2002–06. Trustee: Sir Clough William-Ellis Foundn, 2010–; Friends of Lloyd George Mus., 2018–; Chm., Coleg Cymraeg Cenedlaethol (Nat. Welsh Coll.) 2011–14. Hon. Patron, Bevan Foundn, 2005–. FRHistS 1996. *Publications*: The North Wales Quarrymen 1874–1922, 1981; Cymru 2000: Hanes Cymru yn yr Ugeinfed Ganrif (History of Wales in the Twentieth Century), 1999; numerous articles in specialist jls. *Recreations*: mountaineering, cooking, Rugby. *Club*: Athenæum.
*See also* A. G. Jones.

**JONES, Riel Meredith K.**; *see* Karmy-Jones.

**JONES, (Robert) Alun**; QC 1989; *b* 19 March 1949; *s* of late Owen Glyn Jones and Violet Marion Jones (*née* Luxton); *m* 1974, Elizabeth Clayton; one *s* three *d*. *Educ*: Oldershaw Grammar Sch., Wallasey, Cheshire; Bristol Univ. (BSc 1970). Called to the Bar, Gray's Inn, 1972. Asst Recorder, 1988–92; Recorder, 1992–96. *Publications*: Jones on Extradition, 1995, 2nd edn 2001, (jtly) 3rd edn, as Jones and Doobay on Extradition and Mutual Assistance, 2005. *Recreations*: gardening, rural conservation, local history, chess. *Address*: 37 Great James Street, WC1N 3HB. *T*: (020) 7440 4919.

**JONES, Dr (Robert) Brinley**, CBE 2000; FSA; President: National Library of Wales, 1996–2007 (Member, Court and Council, 1974–82); University of Wales Trinity Saint David (formerly University of Wales, Lampeter); *b* 27 Feb. 1929; *yr s* of John Elias Jones and Mary Ann Jones (*née* Williams); *m* 1971, Stephanie Avril Hall; one *s*. *Educ*: Tonypandy Grammar Sch.; University Coll. Cardiff (BA Wales 1st cl. Hons 1950; DipEd 1951; Fellow 1984); Jesus Coll., Oxford (DPhil 1960); Internat. Inst. for Advanced Studies,

Clayton, Mo (MA 1984). FSA 1971. Commissioned RAF, 1955; Educn Officer, RAF Kidlington and Bicester, 1955–58. Asst Master, Penarth Grammar Sch., 1958–60; Lectr, UC Swansea, 1960–66; Asst Registrar, Univ. of Wales, 1966–69; Dir, Univ. of Wales Press, 1969–76; Warden, Llandovery Coll., 1976–88. Member: Literature Cttee, Welsh Arts Council, 1968–74, 1981–87; Bd, British Council, 1987–96 (Chm., Welsh Cttee, 1987–96); Broadcasting Standards Council, 1988–91. Chairman: European Assoc. of Teachers, 1965; Dinefwr Tourism Gp, 1988–96; Carmarthenshire Tourist Forum, 1998–2007. Chm., Mgt Cttee, Univ. of Wales Centre for Advanced Welsh and Celtic Studies, 2002–07. Member: Council: St David's UC (later Univ. of Wales), Lampeter, 1977–95 (Hon. Fellow 1987); Trinity Coll., Carmarthen, 1984–2003 (Vice-Chm., 1998–2003; Hon. Fellow, 2003); Court: UC Swansea (later Univ. of Wales, Swansea), 1983–2007 (Hon. Fellow 2002); Univ. of Wales, 1997–2007; Univ. of Wales, Aberystwyth, 1997–2007; Univ. of Wales, Cardiff, 1997–2007; Governing Body, Church in Wales, 1981–2004 (Chairman: Provincial Validating Bd for Ministerial Educn, 1990–2012; Cathedrals and Churches Commn, 1994–2004; Church in Wales Publications, 1998–2001); Managing Trustee, St Michael's Theol Coll., 1982–94. Chm., Physicians of Myddfai Soc., 2014–. Hon. Mem., Druidic Order, Gorsedd of Bards, 1979–; Mem., Welsh Acad., 1981–; Vice-Pres., Llangollen Internat. Musical Eisteddfod, 1989–. Hon. Pres., Assoc. of Friends of Nat. Liby of Wales, 2011–. Fellow, Royal Commonwealth Soc., 1988–91. Editor, The European Teacher, 1964–69. Hon. Series Editor, Writers of Wales, 2009–. Hon. DD Faraston Theol Seminary, Longview, WA, 1993; Hon. DLitt: Greenwich, 1997; Glamorgan, 2008; DUniv Wales, 2006. *Publications*: The Old British Tongue, 1970; (ed and contrib.) Anatomy of Wales, 1972; (ed with M. Stephens) Writers of Wales, 1970–2008 (100 titles published); (ed with R. Bromwich) Astudiaethau ar yr Hengerdd: studies in old Welsh poetry, 1978; Introducing Wales, 1978, 3rd edn 1988; Prifysgol Rhydychen a'i Chysylltiadau Cymreig, 1983; Certain Scholars of Wales, 1986; (ed with D. Ellis Evans) Cofio'r Dafydd, 1987; (contrib.) C. N. D. Cole, The New Wales, 1990; (introd.) Songs of Praises: the English hymns and elegies of William Williams Pantycelyn 1717–1791, 1991, 2nd edn 1995; Prize Days: a headmaster remembers his school 1976–1987, 1993; William Salesbury, 1994; A Lanterne to their Feete: remembering Rhys Prichard 1579–1644, 1994; Floreat Landubriense, 1998; The Particularity of Wales, 2001; World-Wide Wales, 2005; Sir John Williams Bart, MD, 1840–1926, 2007; Rhamant Rhydychen, 2016; Scolares Cambrenses M. A. (Oxon), 2018; articles and reviews in learned jls. *Recreations*: music, farming, writing. *Address*: Drovers Farm, Porthyrhyd, Llanwrda, Dyfed SA19 8DF. *T*: (01558) 650649.

**JONES, Robert David T.**; *see* Trevor-Jones.

**JONES, Sir Robert (Edward)**, Kt 1989; author; sporting and political commentator; Founder, Robt Jones Holdings Ltd, 1961 (Chairman, 1982–92); *b* 24 Nov. 1939; *s* of Edward Llewyllan and Joyce Lillian Jones; three *s* five *d*. *Educ*: Victoria Univ. of Wellington. Leader, New Zealand Party, Gen. Elect., 1984. Chm., NZ Winter Olympics Cttee, 1988. New Zealand Commemoration Medal, 1990. *Publications*: New Zealand Boxing Yearbooks, 1972 and 1973; Jones on Property, 1977, 6th edn 1979; NZ The Way I Want It, 1978; Travelling, 1980; Letters, 1981; Wimp Walloping, 1989; Prancing Pavonine Charlatans, 1990; 80's Letters, 1990; Punchlines, 1991; A Year of It, 1992; Wowser Whacking, 1993; Prosperity Denied—How the Reserve Bank Harms New Zealand, 1996; Memories of Muldoon, 1997; My Property World, 2005; Jones on Management, 2008; Fighting Talk: boxing and the modern lexicon, 2013; No Punches Pulled, 2013; *novels*: The Permit, 1984; Full Circle, 2000; Ogg, 2002; True Facts, 2003; Degrees For Everyone, 2004. *Recreations*: reading, writing, gardening, trout-fishing, tennis, travel, golf, wind-surfing. *Address*: Melling, Lower Hutt, New Zealand; Darling Point, Sydney, Australia; Glasgow, Scotland.

**JONES, Ven. Robert George**; Archdeacon of Worcester, since 2014; *b* Birmingham, 30 Oct. 1955; *s* of Kenneth and Dorothy Jones. *Educ*: King Edward's Sch., Birmingham; Hatfield Coll., Durham (BA Modern Langs 1977); Ripon Coll., Cuddesdon, Oxford (MA Theol. 1987); Ecumenical Inst., Geneva. Ordained deacon, 1980, priest, 1981; Curate, Holy Innocents, Kidderminster, 1980–84; Vicar, St Francis, Dudley, 1984–92; Rector, St Barnabas with Christ Church, Worcester, 1992–2006; Proctor in Convocation, 1995–2005; Rural Dean, Worcester East, 1999–2006. Hon. Canon, 2003–; Diocesan Dir of Develt and Training, 2006–14, Worcester Cathedral. Mem., Meissen Commn, 2002–. *Recreations*: walking, choral singing, friends, German culture. *Address*: Archdeacon's House, Walkers Lane, Whittington, Worcester WR5 2RE. *T*: (01905) 773301. *E*: archdeacon.worcester@cofe-worcester.org.uk.

**JONES, Roger**; *see* Jones, James R.

**JONES, Rear-Adm. Roger Charles M.**; *see* Moylan-Jones.

**JONES, Prof. Roger Hugh**, DM; FRCP, FRCGP, FRCPE, FMedSci; Editor, British Journal of General Practice, since 2010; Wolfson Professor of General Practice, 1993–2010, now Emeritus, and Head, Department of General Practice and Primary Care, 1993–2010, King's College London School of Medicine (formerly Guy's, King's and St Thomas's Medical School, King's College London); *b* 11 Nov. 1948; *s* of (Sydney Elsom) Vernon Jones and Phyllis Marion Elsie Jones (*née* Yemm); *m* 1998, Prof. Janice Rymer; one *s* one *d* (and one *s* decd). *Educ*: Monmouth Sch.; St Peter's Coll., Oxford (MA 1973); St Thomas's Hosp. Med. Sch. (BM BCh 1973); Univ. of Southampton (DM 1990). MRCP 1976, FRCP 2000; FRCGP 1990; FRCPE 1992. House Surgeon and House Physician, St Richard's Hosp., Chichester, 1973–74; Registrar and Res. Fellow, Royal Sussex Co. Hosp., Brighton, and KCH, London, 1974–79; GP, Andover, 1979–84; Sen. Lectr in Primary Health Care, Univ. of Southampton, 1984–91; William Leech Prof. of Primary Health Care, Univ. of Newcastle upon Tyne, 1991–93; Dean for Ext. Affairs, 2001–07, Dean for Teaching, 2002–06, KCL. Provost, S London Faculty, RCGP, 2013–16. Chair, Royal Medical Benevolent Fund, 2013–17. FMedSci 1998; FHEA 2007. FRSA 1996. Editor, Family Practice, 1990–2004. *Publications*: (Ed. in Chief) Oxford Textbook of Primary Medical Care, 2003. *Recreations*: literature, travel, golf, bridge. *Address*: 56 Scotts Sufferance Wharf, 5 Mill Street, SE1 2DE. *T*: (020) 7394 9586. *E*: roger.jones@kcl.ac.uk. *Club*: Athenæum.

**JONES, Roger Kenneth**; Secretary, Co-operative Wholesale Society, 1996–98; *b* 10 Sept. 1947; *s* of George Ephraim Jones and Winifred Annie Jones; *m* 1972, Caroline Ruth Proctor; three *d*. *Educ*: Abbeydale Grammar Sch., Sheffield; Manchester Univ. (BA Hons Econs 1969). Called to the Bar, Gray's Inn, 1977; Asst Sec., Manchester Ship Canal Co., 1977–83; Dep. Sec., CWS Ltd, 1983–96; Secretary: Unity Trust Bank, PLC, 1984–92; Co-operative Bank PLC, 1992–96. Mem., UK Co-operative Council, 1991–98. Hon. Pres., Co-operative Law Assoc., 1999–2007. Hon. Chm., Manchester Cathedral Country Home, 2002–07.

**JONES, Sir Roger (Spencer)**, Kt 2005; OBE 1996; Chairman, ZooBiotic Ltd, since 2005; *b* 2 July 1943; *s* of Richard David Jones and Gwladys Jones; *m* 1970, Ann Evans; one *s* one *d*. *Educ*: Bala Boys' Grammar Sch.; Univ. of Wales (BPharm); Univ. of Bradford (MSc). FRPharmS 2009 (MRPharmS 1968). Area Manager, then Marketing Planning Manager, Wellcome Foundn Ltd, 1968–82; Man. Dir, Nigeria, Smith Kline & French Ltd, 1982–83; with Penn Pharmaceuticals Ltd, 1983–2000 (Chm., 1986–2000). Nat. Gov. for Wales,

BBC, 1997–2003; Mem., S4C Broadcasting Authy, 2004–11. Chairman: Gwent TEC, 1993–98; TEC SE Wales, 1998–2000; Council of Welsh TECs, 1995–2001; Welsh Develt Agency, 2002–06. Non-exec. Dir, Powys Healthcare NHS Trust, 1993–2000. Chm., Wales Inst. of Dirs, 1995–2002. Chairman: Children in Need, 1999–2003; Carmarthen Heritage Regeneration Trust, 2004–11; Chm., Nat. Trust Wales Cttee, 2006–12 (Dep. Chm., 2005–06); Bd Mem., Botanic Gdns of Wales, 2005–. Pres., YMCA Wales, 2000–. Chm. Council, Swansea Univ. (formerly Univ. of Wales, Swansea), 2005– (Pro-Chancellor, 2009–). DUniv Glamorgan, 1997; Hon. DSc Wales, 2000. *Recreations:* salmon and trout fishing, shooting, nature conservation. *Address:* Battle House, Battle, Brecon LD3 9RW. *T:* (01874) 611777. *Club:* Athenæum.

**JONES, Ron;** *see* Jones, O. G. R.

**JONES, Prof. Ronald Mervyn,** MD; FRCA; Director of Continuing Education and Professional Development, and Editor of Bulletin, Royal College of Anaesthetists, 1999–2002; *b* 24 April 1947; *s* of Comdr Glyn Owen Jones, RN and Doris Woodley Jones; *m* 1st, 1970, Angela Christine Parsonage (marr. diss.); one *s* one *d*; 2nd, 1989, Caroline Ann Marshall; two *d*. *Educ:* Devonport High Sch., Plymouth; Univ. of Liverpool (MB ChB 1971; MD 1990). FRCA 1978. Karolinska Inst., Stockholm, 1978; Univ. of Michigan, 1979–80; Consultant, Nottingham Hosps, 1981–82; Sen. Lectr and Hon. Consultant, Guy's Hosp. and Med. Sch., 1982–90; Foundn Prof. of Anaesthetics and Hd of Dept, ICSM at St Mary's, London, 1990–99. Mem. Council, Royal Coll. of Anaesthetists, 1997–2002. Academician, European Acad. Anaesthesiologists, 1984; Hon. Life Mem., Australian Soc. Anaesthetists, 1988. *Publications:* (ed jtly) Medicine for Anaesthetists, 3rd edn 1989; (ed jtly) Clinical Anaesthesia, 1996. *Recreations:* art history, sailing. *Club:* Royal Naval Sailing Assoc.

**JONES, Prof. Ronald Samuel,** OBE 1998; DVSc; FRCVS; FRSB; JP; Professor of Veterinary Anaesthesia, 1991–2001, now Emeritus, and Head of Department of Anaesthesia, 1995–2000, University of Liverpool; *b* 29 Oct. 1937; *s* of Samuel and Gladys Jane Jones; *m* 1962, Pamela Evans; two *d*. *Educ:* High Sch. for Boys, Oswestry; Univ. of Liverpool (BVSc 1960; MVSc; DVA); DVetMed Berne, 1980; DVSc Pretoria, 1991. FRCVS 1981; FRSB (FIBiol 1987). University of Glasgow: house surgeon, 1960–61; Asst, 1961–62; University of Liverpool: Lectr, 1962–77; Sen. Lectr, 1977–86; Reader, 1986–90; Dean, Faculty of Vet. Sci., 1989–93. Visiting Professor: Univ. of Zurich, 1975; Cornell Univ., 1980, 1993; Univ. of Pretoria, 1994; Univ. of Valdivia, 2001, 2002, 2003; Univ. of Vienna, 2002, 2003. Member: Home Office Adv. Council on the Misuse of Drugs, 1994–2001; Medicines Commn, 1997–2005; Chm., Farriers' Registration Council, 2010–12. Royal College of Veterinary Surgeons: Mem. Council, 1986–98; Treas., 1993–95; Jun. Vice-Pres., 1995–96; Pres., 1996–97; Sen. Vice-Pres., 1997–98. Mem., EC Adv. Cttee of Vet. Trng, 1990–93. FLS 2003; FRSA 1996. JP Liverpool City, 1981–2007. Hon. FRCA 2001. John Henry Steele Medal, RCVS, 1989; Coll. Medal, Royal Coll. Anaesthetists, 1996. *Publications:* (jtly) Principles of Veterinary Therapeutics, 1994; contrib. chapters to books and vet. and med. jls. *Recreations:* horse-racing, fly-fishing, vegetable gardening, philately. *Address:* 7 Birch Road, Prenton, Merseyside CH43 5UF. *T:* (0151) 653 9008. *Clubs:* Farmers, Royal Society of Medicine.

**JONES, Maj. Gen. Rupert Timothy Herbert,** CBE 2014 (MBE 2000); Standing Joint Force Commander, since 2018; *b* Münster, W Germany, 29 April 1969; *s* of Lt Col Herbert, ('H'), Jones, VC, OBE and Sara Jones; *m* 1997, Lucinda Jane Brasher; two *s* one *d*. *Educ:* Sherborne Sch.; Reading Univ. (BA Hons Hist.); RMA, Sandhurst; Defence Acad. (MA). Commnd Army, 1991; CO, 4th Bn, Rifles, 2008–10; Military Advr, Defence Reform, MoD, 2010–11; Comdr, 1st Armd Infantry Bde, 2012–14; Dep. Comdr, Combined Jt Task Force, Operation Inherent Resolve, Iraq/Kuwait, 2016–17; Asst Chief of Gen. Staff, MoD, 2018; Dir, Engagement and Communication, 2018. Liveryman, Carpenters' Co. Legion of Merit (USA), 2017. Asst Col Comdt, The Rifles, 2019–. *Recreations:* sailing, ski-ing, our labrador Bentley. *Clubs:* Farmers; Royal Dart Yacht.

**JONES, Ruth Lorraine,** FCSP; MP (Lab) Newport West, since April 2019; *b* Newport, S Wales, 23 April 1962; *d* of Keith and Hazel Jones; *m* 1988, David Jones; one *s* one *d*. *Educ:* Duffryn Comprehensive Sch., Newport; Cardiff Univ. (Dip. Physiotherapy 1983; MEd 1998). FCSP 2009. Physiotherapy posts in fields of neurorehabilitation and paediatrics, 1983–2016; Sen. Negotiating Officer, CSP, 2016–19. Pres., Wales TUC, 2007–08. Contested (Lab) Monmouth, 2015, 2017. Member: Cambrensis, S Wales Baptist Choir; Bethesda Baptist Ch, Rogerstone, Newport. *Recreations:* singing, keeping fit. *Address:* Ground Floor Office, The Stables, 25–26 Gold Tops, Newport NP20 4PG. *T:* (01633) 256268. *E:* Ruth.jones.mp@parliament.uk.

**JONES, Samantha, (Mrs Joseph Harrison);** Chief Executive and President, Centene UK, since 2019; *b* London, 25 Feb. 1971; *d* of Robert Jones and late Vivienne Jones (née Bloom); *m* 2007, Joseph Harrison; one *s* one *d* (twins). *Educ:* Gt Ormond St Hosp. (RGN/RSCN 1992); Open Univ. (Postgrad. Dip. (Health) 1998); Middlesex Univ. (MA Leadership 2005). Gen. Manager, Surgery and Paediatrics, Central Middx Hosp., 1998–99; Project Manager, Nat. Clinical Governance Support Team, 1999–2000; Asst Dir of Ops, Barnet and Chase Farm Hosps NHS Trust, 2000–03; Dir of Ops and Dep. Chief Exec., Ealing Hosp. NHS Trust, 2003–04; Dir of Ops and Dep. Chief Exec., 2004–06, Acting Chief Exec., 2006–07, N Middx Univ. Hosp.; Chief Exec., Epsom and St Helier Univ. Hosps NHS Trust, 2007–10; Dir, Care UK, 2011–13; Chief Exec., W Herts NHS Trust, 2013–15; Dir, New Care Models, NHS England, 2015–17. *Recreations:* spending time with family, cycling, holidays. *E:* samantha.jones@centene.com.

**JONES, Samuel,** CBE 1996; DL; Chairman, Heathrow Airport Consultative Committee, 1997–2014; *b* 27 Dec. 1939; *s* of late Samuel Jones and Sarah Johnston Jones (née McCulloch); *m* 1964, Jean Ann Broadhurst; two *d*. *Educ:* Morpeth Grammar Sch.; Manchester Univ. (LLB); Kent Univ. (MA). Admitted Solicitor, 1964. Asst Solicitor, Macclesfield Bor. Council, 1964–67; Asst Town Clerk, Bedford Bor. Council, 1967–71; Head of Legal Div., Coventry CBC, 1971–73; Head of Admin and Legal Dept, Sheffield Dist Council, 1973–76; Chief Exec. and County Clerk, Leics CC, and Clerk of Lieutenancy, 1976–91; Town Clerk, Corp. of London, 1991–96. Mem., Council on Tribunals, 1996–2002. Chairman: N Devon Marketing Bureau, 1996–98; Westcountry Ambulance Service NHS Trust, 1996–2004; N Devon NHS PCT, 2004–06; non-exec. Dir, Northern Devon Healthcare NHS Trust, 2006–10. Mem., Adjudication Panel for England, 2002–09. DL Leics, 1992. *Recreation:* dog walking. *Address:* Glenfield, Raleigh Park, Barnstaple, Devon EX31 4JD. *T:* (01271) 345010.

**JONES, Sandy;** *see* Jones, Alexander M.

**JONES, Sarah;** MP (Lab) Croydon Central, since 2017; *b* Croydon, 20 Dec. 1972; *d* of David Jones and Rosemary Jones; one *s*; *m* Ian Lloyd; twin *s* one *d*. *Educ:* Old Palace Sch.; Durham Univ. (BA Hist. 1995). Researcher for Rt Hon. Marjorie Mowlam, MP, 1996–97; Public Affairs and Campaigns Manager, Shelter UK, 2000–04; Dep. Dir of Communications, NHS Confedn, 2004–08; Sen. Civil Servant, Govt Olympic Communications, 2008–12; Consultant and Dir, Lloyd-Jones Communications, 2013–17 (clients incl. Bond, Cambridge Univ. Hosps, Gatwick Airport). Dir, Wandle Housing Assoc., 2013–17. Mem., Home Affairs Cttee, H of C, 2017–. Contested (Lab) Croydon Central, 2015. *Address:* House of Commons, SW1A 0AA.

**JONES, Sarah Frances;** QC 2019; *b* Nottingham, 15 May 1974; *d* of Alan Jones and Valerie Jones; *m* 2005, Russell Tyner; one *d*. *Educ:* Nottingham High Sch. for Girls; University Coll., Oxford (MA Hons Juris.). Called to the Bar, Lincoln's Inn, 1996; in practice as a barrister, 2 King's Bench Walk, 1996–2013, Pump Court Chambers, 2013–. Mem., Criminal Bar Assoc. Gov., Holy Trinity Sch., East Finchley, 2001–. *Recreations:* theatre, reading, preserves. *Address:* Pump Court Chambers, Temple, EC4Y 7AJ. *T:* (020) 7353 0711. *E:* clerks@pumpcourtchambers.com.

**JONES, Sarah Jane V.;** *see* Vaughan Jones.

**JONES, Sarah Louise R.;** *see* Rowland-Jones.

**JONES, Schuyler,** CBE 1998; DPhil; Director (formerly Curator and Head of Department of Ethnology and Prehistory), Pitt Rivers Museum, 1985–97, and Fellow of Linacre College, 1970–97, now Emeritus Professor, Oxford University; *b* 7 Feb. 1930; *s* of Schuyler Jones, Jr and Ignace Mead Jones; *m* 1st, 1955, Lis Margit Søndergaard Rasmussen; one *s* one *d*; 2nd, 1998, Dr Lorraine Christine Da'Luz Vieira. *Educ:* Edinburgh Univ. (MA Hons Anthropology); Oxford Univ. (DPhil Anthropology). Anthropological expeditions to: Atlas Mountains, Southern Algeria, French West Africa, Nigeria, 1951; French Equatorial Africa, Belgian Congo, 1952; East and Southern Africa, 1953; Morocco High Atlas, Algeria, Sahara, Niger River, 1954; Turkey, Iran, Afghanistan, Pakistan, India, Nepal, 1958–59; ten expeditions to Nuristan in the Hindu Kush, 1960–70; to Chinese Turkestan, 1985; Tibet and Gobi Desert, 1986; Southern China, Xinjiang, and Pakistan, 1988; Western Greenland, 1991; Greenland and E Africa, 1993. Asst Curator, Pitt Rivers Mus., 1970–71; Asst Curator and Univ. Lectr in Ethnology, 1971–85. Mem. Council, Royal Anthropological Inst., 1986–89. Trustee, Horniman Mus., 1989–94. *Publications:* Sous le Soleil Africain, 1955 (Under the African Sun, 1956); Annotated Bibliography of Nuristan (Kafiristan) and The Kalash Kafirs of Chitral, pt 1 1966, pt 2 1969; The Political Organization of the Kam Kafirs, 1967; Men of Influence in Nuristan, 1974; (jtly) Nuristan, 1979; Afghanistan, 1992; Tibetan Nomads: environment, pastoral economy and material culture, 1996; A Stranger Abroad: a memoir, 2007; numerous articles. *Recreation:* travel in remote places. *Address:* The Prairie House, 1570 N Ridgewood Drive, Wichita, KS 67208, USA.

**JONES, Simon Alan,** LVO 1998; Senior Partner, Gardiner & Theobald LLP, 2001–18; Managing Director, Gardiner & Theobald Management Services, since 1986; *b* 28 March 1956; *s* of Alan Reginald Walter Jones, MBE and Kathleen Jones; *m* 1998, Hon. Caroline Lucy, *d* of Baroness Billingham, *qv*; two *s*. *Educ:* King Edward VII Sch., Lytham; Reading Univ. (BSc Quantity Surveying). Joined Gardiner & Theobald, 1977: Project Dir on behalf of the Royal Household, Windsor Castle Fire Restoration, 1993–97. Trustee, Historic Royal Palaces, 1998–2004. Lt Col, Engrg and Logistics Staff Corp., 2001–10. *Recreations:* tennis, golf, squash. *Address:* 10 South Crescent, WC1E 7BD. *T:* (020) 7209 3000. *E:* s.jones@gardiner.com. *Clubs:* All England Lawn Tennis (Mem. Cttee, 2012–); Cumberland Lawn Tennis (Chm., 2004–15); Highgate Golf.
*See also* Z. A. Billingham.

**JONES, Rt Rev. Simon David B.;** *see* Burton-Jones, Rt Rev. S. D.

**JONES, Simon Martin Dedman;** Director of Policy and Public Affairs, Marie Curie, since 2015; *b* 10 June 1958; *s* of Rev. Canon William David Jones and late Sheila Mary Jones; *m* 2005, Lesley Ann Bird; one *s* two *d*. *Educ:* Mexborough Grammar Sch.; Durham Wearside Secondary Sch.; Exeter Univ. (BA Hons Politics). Business Manager, Rebecca, News Mag. of Wales, 1982–83; Research officer: TGWU, 1985–89; Wales TUC, 1989–93; Chief Exec., Wales Co-op. Centre, 1994–2004. Chair: Cardiff and Vale NHS Trust, 2003–08; NHS Wales Confedn, 2006–08; Lead Chair, NHS Trusts in Wales, 2004–07. Hd of Public Sector, Wales, Odgers Berndtson, 2009–12; Hd of Policy and Public Affairs, Wales, Marie Curie, 2012–15. Mem. Bd, Charities Commn, 2007–12. Member: S Glamorgan HA, 1989–96; Bro Taf HA, 1996–2003 (Chm., 2000–03). Chm., Welsh Assembly and Govt Commn to Review Voluntary Sector Scheme, 2003–04. Ind. Mem. Bd, RCT Homes, 2007–. Presenter, On the Fly, Radio Wales, 2005, 2006, 2007. *Recreations:* fly fishing and fly tying, cooking, gardening. *Address:* Marie Curie, 89 Albert Embankment, SE1 7TP. *E:* simon.jones57@ntlworld.com.

**JONES, Dr Simon Richard,** CEng, FIET; Vice Chancellor, National University of Science and Technology, Oman, since 2018; *b* Llanelli, 19 July 1958; *s* of Oliver and Barbara Jones; *m* 1997, Archontia Mexi; two *d*. *Educ:* Hatfield Poly. (BSc Computer Sci. 1981); Brunel Univ. (PhD 1986); Univ. of Herts (DSc 2003). CEng 1990; SMIEE 1990; FIET 1991. ARM/RAEng Prof., Loughborough Univ., 1992–2002; Dean, Engrg and Design, Univ. of Bath, 2002–03; CEO, MIT Media Lab. (Europe), Ireland, 2003–05; Lab. Dir and Prof., Univ. of Amsterdam, 2005–08; Pres., Higher Colls of Technol. (Abu Dhabi), UAE, 2008–12; Provost, Nazarbayev Univ., Kazakhstan, 2012–15; Pro-Vice Chancellor, and Head, Cranfield Defence and Security, Cranfield Univ., 2016–18. *Recreation:* uxory. *Address:* National University Headquarters, Bousher, Muscat PC130, Sultanate of Oman. *E:* Simon-Jones@Simon-Jones.com. *Club:* Naval and Military.

**JONES, Stanley;** *see* Jones, John Stanley.

**JONES, Stephen;** *see* Jones, John Stephen.

**JONES, Stephen Charles Ion;** Warden, St Edward's School, Oxford, since 2011; *b* Shropshire, 11 Feb. 1959; *s* of Alfred Jones and Ann Jones (née Duff-Jones, now Clements); *m* 1983, Katie Ann Hannam; one *s* two *d*. *Educ:* Hurstpierpoint Coll.; Lord Wandsworth Coll.; Univ. of Durham (BA 1981; MLitt 1997); Open Univ. (BA 1987; MSc 1991). Assistant Master: Orley Farm Sch., 1981–82; Dragon Sch., 1983–85; Cheltenham Coll., 1985–90; Hd of Maths, Berkhamsted Sch., 1990–94; Housemaster, Radley Coll., 1994–2004; Headmaster, Dover Coll., 2004–11. *Recreations:* fives, sailing. *Address:* St Edward's School, Woodstock Road, Oxford OX2 7NN. *T:* (01865) 319323, *Fax:* (01865) 319242. *E:* warden@stedwardsoxford.org. *Clubs:* East India, Lansdowne, Jesters; Royal Cinque Ports Yacht; Band of Brothers.

**JONES, Stephen John Moffat,** OBE 2010; RDI 2009; milliner; Designer, Stephen Jones Millinery Ltd, since 1980; *b* W Kirby, Cheshire, 31 May 1957; *s* of John Gordon Jones and Margaret Jones (née Moffat). *Educ:* Liverpool Coll.; St Martin's Sch. of Art (BA Hons Fashion Design). Hon. Prof., Univ. of the Arts, 2008–. Collaborations with Comme des Garçons, John Galliano and Christian Dior; hats in permanent collections: V&A Mus.; La Louvre; Metropolitan Mus. of Art, NY; Kyoto Costume Inst., Japan; Australian Nat. Gall., Canberra; curator: Hats: an anthology by Stephen Jones, V&A Mus., 2009; Stephen Jones Hats at the Royal Pavilion, 2019. FRSA. Outstanding Achievement in Fashion Design Award, British Fashion Awards, 2008. *Publications:* (jtly) Hats: an anthology by Stephen Jones, 2009; *relevant publication:* Stephen Jones and the Accent of Fashion, by Hamish Bowles, 2010; Stephen Jones: souvenirs, 2016. *Recreations:* adventure, Rococo. *Address:* Stephen Jones Millinery, 36 Great Queen Street, WC2B 5AA.

**JONES, Stephen Morris**, CBE 2005; Senior Partner, The In Practice Partnership, management consultants, since 2005; *b* 12 March 1948; *s* of late Owain Morus Jones and Sylvia Blanche Jones (*née* Moss); *m* 1970, Rosemary Diana Pilgrim; one *s* two *d*. *Educ:* Univ. of Manchester (BA Hons Town Planning, 1970). MRTPI 1972. Asst Chief Exec., Bolton MBC, 1978–85; Chief Executive: Blackburn BC, 1985–90; Wigan MBC, 1990–2005. Chairman: Leigh Sports Village Co., 2005–16; Shop 4 Support, 2008–14; Lancs Care NHS Foundn Trust, 2010–13; My Life, 2015–. Director: iMPOWER, 2006–19; Alocura Care Ltd, 2016–. Mem., Soc. of Local Govt Chief Execs, 1985–. *Recreations:* family, walking, sport, reading, S Africa, New Hall Monday Club. *Address:* The In Practice Partnership, Moorside, Plumley Moor Road, Plumley, Knutsford, Cheshire WA16 9RX.

**JONES, Stephen O.;** *see* Oliver-Jones.

**JONES, Stephen Roger Curtis;** Chairman of Governors, Centre for Information on Language Teaching and Research, 1996–2003; *b* 31 March 1944; *s* of Roger Henry Curtis Jones and Kate Alice Jones (*née* Pearson); *m* 1973, Janet Corkett; two *d*. *Educ:* Brentwood Sch., Essex; Univ. of Southampton (BA Hons French 1967; MA French 1968); Cambridge/ RSA Cert. TEFLA, 1996. MoD, 1968–71; UK Delegn to NATO, 1971–73; DES, 1973–81 (Private Sec. to Sec. of State, Rt Hon. Shirley Williams, 1976–78); Asst Dir, City of London Poly., 1982–85; Department of Education and Science: Staff Inspector, HM Inspectorate, 1986–88; Head, Internat. Relations Div., 1988–92; Head of Internat. Relns, Youth and Gen. Br., DFE, 1992–94. Trustee, Employability Forum, 2003–09. Mem., Guild of Voluntary Guides, Winchester Cath., 2010–. Comenius Fellow, CILT, the Nat. Centre for Langs, 2004. *Recreations:* walking, choral singing. *Address:* Hussle Cottage, Winton Hill, Stockbridge, Hants SO20 6HL. *T:* (01264) 810935. *E:* stephen22jones@btinternet.com.

**JONES, Stephen William**, CB 2007; Director of Finance and Resources (formerly Director, Finance and Performance, then Group Finance Director), Local Government Association, 2007–12. *Educ:* King's Sch., Macclesfield; Balliol Coll., Oxford (BA 1976). FCMA 2006; CPFA 2008. Inland Revenue, subseq. HM Revenue & Customs, 1976–2006: Dir, Large Business Office, 2000–03; Finance Dir, 2003–06. Chm., Adv. Bd, Public Sector Deposit Fund, 2011.

**JONES, Stewart Elgan**; QC 1994; a Recorder, since 1990; *b* 20 Jan. 1945; *s* of late Gwilym John Jones and Elizabeth (*née* Davies); *m* 1979, Jennifer Anne (*née* Syddall); two *d*, and one step *s* one step *d*. *Educ:* Cheltenham Coll.; Queen's Coll., Oxford (MA Mod. Langs). Called to the Bar, Gray's Inn, 1972, Bencher, 2002; Mem., Western Circuit. *Recreations:* painting, home, hearth, the great outdoors. *Address:* 3 Paper Buildings, Temple, EC4Y 7EU. *T:* (020) 7583 8055. *W:* www.stew-art.fr.

**JONES, Rev. Canon Stewart William;** Vicar, St John the Baptist, Barlaston, since 2017; *b* 17 March 1957; *s* of William Jones and Nettie Jean Jones; *m* 1st, 1982, Susan Kathleen Griffith (*d* 1990); one *d*; 2nd, 1992, Julie Marie Perkin; one *s* one *d*. *Educ:* Heriot-Watt Univ. (BA Hons Business Orgn); Bristol Univ. (Dip. Social Admin); Trinity Coll., Bristol (BA Hons Theol.). Grad. mgt trainee, National Westminster Bank, 1979–80; worker, Bristol Cyrenians, 1980–81; Supervisor, Bristol Churches Community Prog., 1983–85; ordained deacon 1988, priest 1989; Curate, St Mary's, Stoke Bishop, Bristol, 1988–92; Priest-in-charge, St Luke's, Brislington, Bristol, 1992–97; Archbp of Canterbury's Diocesan Chaplain and Tait Missioner, 1997–2003; Priest-in-charge, All Saints', Canterbury, 2001–05; Area Dean, Canterbury, 2002–05; Rector, St Martin-in-the-Bullring, Birmingham, with St Andrew's, Bordesley, 2005–17. Hon. Provincial Canon, Canterbury Cathedral, 2002–06; Hon. Canon, Birmingham Cathedral, 2011–17. *Publications:* The Teaching of Jesus, 1994; The Touch of Jesus, 1995; Albert the Forgetful Angel, 2011; The Amazing Kindness of Obadiah, 2013. *Recreations:* cooking, sport on TV, films, reading. *Address:* The Vicarage, 2 Longton Road, Barlaston, Stoke-on-Trent ST12 9AA.

**JONES, Susan Elan;** MP (Lab) Clwyd South, since 2010; *b* Wrexham, 1 June 1968; *d* of Richard James and Margaret Eirlys Jones. *Educ:* Grango Comprehensive Sch., Rhosllannerchrugog; Ruabon Comprehensive Sch.; Univ. of Bristol (BA 1989); Univ. of Wales, Cardiff (MA 1992). English teacher: Tomakomai English Sch., Japan, 1990–91; Atsuma Bd of Educn, Japan, 1992–94; Corporate Develt Fundraiser, Muscular Dystrophy Campaign, 1995–96; fundraiser, USPG, 1997–2002; Dir, CARIS Haringey, 2002–05; Fundraising Exec., Housing Justice, 2005–10. Mem. (Lab) Southwark LBC, 2006–09 (Dep. Opposition Leader, 2007–09). Co-Chair, All Party Parly Gp for Charities and Volunteering, 2012–. Mem., Church in Wales. *Publications:* (contrib.) The Red Book of the Voluntary Sector, 2014. *Recreation:* classical music. *Address:* House of Commons, SW1A 0AA. *E:* susan.jones.mp@parliament.uk.

**JONES, Susan Elizabeth;** *see* Marks, S. E.

**JONES, Very Rev. Dr Susan Helen;** Dean of Liverpool, since 2018; *b* Barry, S Wales, 29 Oct. 1960; *d* of Gwylim Jones and Joan Jones. *Educ:* Trinity Coll., Carmarthen (BEd 1992; MPhil 1994); Ripon Coll., Cuddesdon (Dip. Min. 1995); Univ. of Wales, Bangor (PhD 2002). Bank Clerk, Midland Bank; ordained deacon, 1995, priest, 1997; Chaplain, Univ. of Wales Swansea, 1995–98; Hon. Curate, Sketty, Swansea, 1995–98; Dir of Pastoral Studies, St Michael's Coll., Llandaff, 1998–2000; Lectr, Univ. of Wales, Cardiff, 1998–2000; Team Vicar, Rectorial Benefice of Bangor, 2000–10; Dir, Ministry Course, Bangor Dio., 2000–09; Area Dean, Ogwen, 2007–10; Dean of Bangor, 2011–15, now Dean Emeritus; Dir of Mission and Ministry, Dio. of Derby, 2015–18. Dir, St Seiriol Centre, Bangor, 2009–12; Canon Missioner and Cursal Canon, Bangor Cathedral, 2010–11; Canon Residentiary, Derby Cathedral, 2015–18. Mem., Presidium and Central Cttee, Conf. of Eur. Churches, 1997–2009. Hon. Lectr, Univ. of Wales, Bangor, 2000–09; Vis. Res. Fellow, Glyndwr Univ., 2009–; Res. Associate, Religion and Psychol., Albert and Jesse Danielson Inst., Boston Univ., 2009–. *Publications:* (ed jtly) Psychological Perspectives on Christian Ministry, 1996; Listening for God's Call, 2014; Everyday Public Worship, 2019. *Address:* Liverpool Cathedral, St James Mount, Liverpool L1 7AZ.

**JONES, Dr (Sybil) Angela (Margaret), (Mrs Michael Pearson)**, FFPH; Consultant in Public Health Medicine, North (formerly North West) Thames Regional Health Authority, 1985–96; *b* 23 Aug. 1940; *d* of Cyril and Ida Jones; *m* 1964, Dr Michael Pearson; three *s* one *d*. *Educ:* Cranford House Sch.; King's College London (AKC); King's Coll. Hosp. (MB BS). Dist MO, Victoria Health Authy, 1985–92. Member: Tech. Sub-Gp of Achieving a Balance, 1988–92; Standing Cttee on Postgrad. Med. Educn, 1989–96 (Chm., working gp on Health of the Nation); Jt Planning Adv. Cttee, 1988–92; Chm., Regl Med. Manpower and Personnel Gp, 1988–92. *Publications:* articles on med. manpower and public health issues in learned jls. *Recreations:* opera, dining with friends.

**JONES, Tecwyn**, CMG 2002; OBE 1974; FRES, CBiol, FRSB; Chairman, BioNET-INTERNATIONAL Consultative Group, 2000; Life President, BioNET-INTERNATIONAL, 2002; consultant; *b* 7 Feb. 1929; *s* of Owen and Lily Jones; *m* 1952, Joan Peggy, (Joy), Edwards; three *s*. *Educ:* Aberaeron Co. Sch.; Imperial Coll., London (BSc Hons; ARCS). FRES 1952 (Hon. FRES 2001); FRSB (FIBiol 1974); CBiol 1979. Entomologist i/c W African Timber Borer Res. Unit, Gold Coast/Ghana, 1952–59; Hd, Biol. and Forestry Divs, Dep. Dir, then interim Dir, E African Agric. and Forestry Res. Orgn, Kenya, 1959–74; Dep. Dir, Centre for Overseas Pest Res. and Natural Resources Inst., ODA, 1974–89; pest mgt and quarantine consultant, FAO, Africa and Asia, 1989–92; Dir, Internat. Inst. of Entomol., CAB Internat., UK, 1992–95; Founder and Dir, Technical Secretariat, BioNET-INTERNAT., 1993–2000. Ed., E African Agric. and Forestry Jl, 1963–74. Chm. Council, Internat. Bee Res. Assoc., 1977–90. Hon. Prof. of Entomol., Sch. of Pure and Applied Biol./Bioscis, Univ. of Cardiff (formerly UC, Cardiff), 1987–2002. Trustee, 2003–, Vice-Pres., 2004–07, Royal Entomol Soc. of London; Mem., Internat. Trust for Zool Nomenclature, 2006– (Mem., Mgt Cttee, 2006–). Trustee, Age Cymru (formerly Age Concern), Ceredigion, 2003–11 (Chm., 2003–10); Chairman: Chairs and Vice-Chairs Cttee, Age Concern, All Wales, 2005–07; Age Concern Partnership, Wales, 2006–09 (Mem., 2004–06, Chm., 2006–09, Exec. Cttee). Chairman: Senior Citizens' Club, Aberaeron, 2001–; Cross Inn and Maenygroes Retirement Assoc., 2004–10. *Publications:* contrib. numerous scientific and technical papers, reports and bulletins on tropical pests of agric. and forestry, plant quarantine and R&D, incl. networking; conceptual papers on BioNET-INTERNAT., a global network for taxonomy to support sustainable develt and implement the Convention on Biol Diversity. *Recreations:* amateur dramatics, the countryside, gardening, walking. *Address:* Weston, South Road, Aberaeron, Ceredigion SA46 0DP. *T:* and *Fax:* (01545) 571208.

**JONES, Terry, (Terence Graham Parry Jones);** writer, film director and occasional performer; *b* 1 Feb. 1942; *s* of Alick George Parry Jones and Dilys Louisa Newnes; *m* 1st, Alison Telfer (marr. diss.); one *s* one *d*; 2nd, 2012, Anna Söderström; one *d*. *Educ:* Esher C of E Primary Sch.; Royal Grammar Sch., Guildford; St Edmund Hall, Oxford. *Television and radio:* wrote for various TV shows, 1966–68; wrote and performed in series: Do Not Adjust Your Set, 1968–69; The Complete and Utter History of Britain, 1969; Monty Python's Flying Circus, 1969–75; wrote (with Michael Palin): Secrets (play), 1974; Ripping Yarns, 1976–79; presented: Paperbacks; Victorian Values, (radio); wrote and directed The Rupert Bear Story (documentary), 1981; wrote, directed and presented, So This Is Progress, 1991; co-wrote and presented: Crusades, 1995; Ancient Inventions, 1999; Gladiators, the Brutal Truth, 2000; Hidden History of Ancient Egypt/Ancient Rome, 2002/03; The Anti-Renaissance Show (radio), 2002; wrote and presented: Terry Jones's Medieval Lives, 2004; The Story of One, 2005; Terry Jones' Barbarians, 2006; In Charlie Chaplin's Footsteps, 2015. *Films:* And Now For Something Completely Different, 1971; directed (with Terry Gilliam), co-wrote and performed, Monty Python and the Holy Grail, 1975; directed, co-wrote and performed: Monty Python's Life of Brian, 1978; Monty Python's Meaning of Life, 1983 (Grand Prix Spécial du Jury, Cannes); directed Personal Services, 1986; wrote, directed and performed: Erik the Viking, 1989; The Wind in the Willows, 1996; Asterix and Obelix (English version), 2000; wrote (with Gavin Scott) and directed, Absolutely Anything, 2015. *Live show:* Monty Python Live (Mostly), 02 Arena, 2014. Wrote libretto and directed: musical play, Evil Machines, São Luiz, Lisbon, 2008; The Doctor's Tale, Royal Opera House, 2011; wrote libretto, The Owl and the Pussycat, ROH2 (touring), 2012; dir, Jeepers Creepers, Leicester Square Th., 2016. BAFTA Cymru award, 2016. *Publications:* Chaucer's Knight, 1980, 3rd edn 1984; Fairy Tales, 1981, 4th edn 1987; The Saga of Erik the Viking, 1983, 3rd edn 1986; Nicobobinus, 1985, 2nd edn 1987; Goblins of the Labyrinth, 1986; The Curse of the Vampire's Socks, 1988; Attacks of Opinion, 1988; Fantastic Stories, 1992; (with Brian Froud) Lady Cottington's Pressed Fairy Book, 1994; (with Alan Ereira) Crusades, 1994; The Knight and the Squire, 1997; (with Brian Froud) Lady Cottington's Pressed Fairy Journal, 1998; The Lady and the Squire, 2000; Who Murdered Chaucer?, 2003; (with Alan Ereira) Medieval Lives, 2004; Terry Jones' War on the War of Terror, 2005; (with Alan Ereira) Terry Jones' Barbarians, 2006; (contrib.) Fourteenth Century England, 2008; Animal Tales, 2011; Trouble on The Heath, 2011; Evil Machines (short stories), 2011; The Tyrant and the Squire, 2018; (with Michael Palin) Dr Fegg's Encyclopeadia (sic) of all World Knowledge, etc; Ripping Yarns, etc; contrib. to the various Monty Python books. *Recreation:* sleeping.

**JONES, Terry**, MBE 2017; Founding Editor-in-Chief, Creative Director and Publisher, i-D magazine, 1980–2013; *b* Northampton, 1945; *m* 1968, Patricia Sandra, (Tricia); one *s* one *d*. *Educ:* West of England Coll. of Art, Bristol (Nat. Dip. Graphics). Asst to Ivan Dodd, 1965–68; Asst Art Dir, Good Housekeeping, 1968–70; Art Director: Vanity Fair, 1970–71; British Vogue, 1972–77; Sportswear Europe, 1978–80. Advertising Consultant, Lurzep/Conrad Agency, 1978–80; Consultant Art Director: German Vogue, 1979–80; DONNA, 1979–80; Vogue Gioello, 1979–80; Music Video Co-Dir, Careless Memories, Duran Duran, 1981; Image Dir, Fiorucci, 1982–85; Image Consultant, Mexx, 1985–89; Ad Campaign and Catalogue Consultant, Charro, Fila, Mexx mag., Lorenzini, St Moritz, Fooks, Neos, Fiorucci, Swatch, Brylcreem and Mr Joe, 1985–88; Ad Campaign Consultant, Chipie, 1989–90. Eur. Art Dir, Espirit, 1989–90; Art Dir, Fire and Ice. Smile i-D exhibn, Wapping Project, London, 2000, then NY, Paris, Tokyo, Milan, Moscow; Identity exhibn, Fashion and Textile Mus., London, 2005, then touring in Europe, S America, NY and Beijing. (Jtly) Outstanding Achievement in Fashion Award, British Fashion Awards, 2013. *Publications:* Masterpieces of Erotic Photography, 1977; The MGM Story, 1978; Women on Women, 1978; Not Another Punk Book, 1980; The Tree; Wink; Private Viewing, 1983; A Decade of Ideas, 1990; Instant Design: a manual of graphic techniques, 1990; Catching the Moment, 1997; SMILE i-D, Fashion and Style: the best from 20 years of i-D, 2001; (ed) Fashion Now, 2003; (ed) Fashion Now II, 2005; SOUL i-D, 2008 (Chinese edn 2012); (ed) 100 Contemporary Fashion Designers, 2009; i-D Covers: 1980–2010, 2010; Vivienne Westwood, 2012; Rei Kawakubo, 2012; Yohji Yamamoto, 2012; Rick Owens, 2013; Raf Simons, 2013.

**JONES, Tia Catherine;** Lord-Lieutenant of Powys, since 2018; *b* London, 7 July 1954; *d* of Philip Loscombe Wintringham Owen, TD, QC and Elizabeth Jane Owen (*née* Widdicombe, later Kelsey); *m* 1974, John Athelstan Jones; two *s* two *d*. *Educ:* St Mary's Sch., Shaftesbury; Kingston Tech. Coll. Journalist and writer, incl. for Country Times, The Field, Window on Wales, Cambrian News, Daily Post; writer, TV drama, Llety Piod, 1995; Advertising and Sponsorship Manager, Welsh Internat. Film Fest., 1990–99; Sponsorship and Develt Manager, Aberystwyth Arts Centre, Univ. of Wales, Aberystwyth, 1999–2007. *Publications:* On Open Ground, 2008; The Moss Gatherers, 2013; The Curlew's Cry, 2016. *Recreations:* horses, dogs, wildlife, the countryside, coastal Britain. *Address:* Fferm Pwlliwrch, Darowen, Machynlleth, Powys SY20 8NS. *T:* (01650) 511379. *E:* tiajones007@gmail.com.

**JONES, Timothy;** *see* Jones, David T.

**JONES, Timothy Aidan;** *see* Marschall Jones, T. A.

**JONES, Timothy John;** Co-Founder and Chairman, CH&Co Catering Ltd (formerly Charlton House Catering), since 1991; *b* Newport, Gwent, 17 Nov. 1959; *s* of John Samuel Jones and Margaret Rose Jones (*née* Bull); *m* 1986, Robyn Anne Lardge (Robyn Jones, OBE) (*d* 2015); one *s* one *d*. *Educ:* Croesyceiliog Sch.; Univ. of Bristol (BSc Hons Econs). ACA 1985. Asst Manager, Price Waterhouse, 1981–85; Financial Controller, Marvel Comics, 1985–90; Finance Dir, RWS Gp plc, 1990–2000. *Recreations:* golf, cycling, swimming, food and wine, travel, jukeboxes. *Address:* CH&Co Catering Ltd, 550 Thames Valley Park, Reading, Berks RG6 1PT. *T:* 0333 014 1777. *E:* tim.jones@chandcogroup.com. *Club:* Huntercombe Golf.

**JONES, Prof. Timothy Rhys;** continuo player, pianist and musicologist; Deputy Principal (Programmes and Research), Royal Academy of Music, since 2008; Professor of Music, University of London, since 2016; b Cardiff, 18 Jan. 1967; s of Wyndham Jones and Florence Jones (née Thomas). Educ: Porth Co. Comprehensive Sch.; Christ Church, Oxford (BA 1988; MA 1992; DPhil 1992). LTCL 1984. Lecturer: in Music, St Peter's Coll., Oxford, 1992–95; St Edmund Hall, Oxford, 1992–95; Keble Coll., Oxford, 1994–95; Univ. of Exeter, 1995–2005; RNCM, 2005–08; Reader, Univ. of London, 2009–16. Trustee, Eur. String Teachers' Assoc., 2010–13. Hon. RAM 2014. Presenter and writer, First Class Series on Music and Society, NHK (Japan), 2016. *Publications*: Beethoven: The Moonlight and other sonatas Op. 27 and Op. 31, 1999; (contrib.) The Oxford Companion to Music, 2002; (contrib.) French Music since Berlioz, 2006; completion of fragments by Mozart, including: Concerto for piano and violin, 2008; Requiem, 2010; String Quintets, 2013; String Quartets, 2013; String Trio, 2013; Clarinet Quintets, 2014; Violin Sonatas, 2014; C minor Mass, 2016; Sinfonia concertante for violin, viola and cello, 2017; Horn Concertos, 2018. *Recreations*: cricket, Scrabble, Anglican liturgy. *Address*: Royal Academy of Music, Marylebone Road, NW1 5HT. *T*: (020) 7873 7309. *E*: t.jones@ram.ac.uk. *Club*: Athenæum.

**JONES, Sir Tom;** see Woodward, Sir T. J.

**JONES, Tracey Anne;** see Angus, T. A.

**JONES, Trevor;** Deputy Chairman, NHS Direct NHS Trust, 2008–13 (Director, 2007–13); b 23 Dec. 1950; s of John Jones and Florence Mary Jones (née Rogerson); m 1974, Hazel Oliver. Local Govt Finance, 1969–78; Sen. Asst Regl Treas., Northern RHA, 1978; Dep. Treas., S Manchester HA, 1983; Waltham Forest Health Authority: Dir of Finance, 1986; Dist Gen. Manager, 1989–92; Chief Exec., Forest Healthcare NHS Trust, 1992–95; Gen. Manager, then Chief Exec., Lothian Health Bd, 1995–2000; Chief Exec., NHS Scotland and Hd of Health Dept, Scottish Exec., 2000–04; Chief Exec., Avon, Glos and Wilts Strategic HA, 2004–06. Chm., Gen. Managers' Gp, Scottish Health Bd, 1998–2000. Director: Pinnacle Staffing Gp plc, 2006–08; Patient Safety Agency, 2007–. Dir, Sport England SW, 2005–09. Trustee: WellChild, 2006–; Royal Voluntary Service, 2009–15. Regl FRSocMed, 2004. CPFA, FCCA, CCMI. *Recreations*: golf, photography. *Address*: The Granary, Culkerton, Tetbury, Glos GL8 8SS. *Clubs*: Royal Society of Medicine; Durham CC.

**JONES, Trevor Charles B.;** see Bish-Jones.

**JONES, Trevor David K.;** see Kent-Jones.

**JONES, Trevor Mervyn,** CBE 2003; Chairman, Simbec-Orion Group, since 2013; b 19 Aug. 1942; s of Samuel James Jones and Hilda May Jones (née Walley); m 1966, Verity Ann Bates; one s one d. *Educ*: Wolverhampton Grammar Sch.; King's Coll. London (BPharm Hons 1964; PhD 1967; FKC 1994). CChem 1975; FRSC 1978; FPS 1987; MCPP 1982. Lectr, Univ. of Nottingham, 1967–72; Hd of Pharmaceutical Develt, Boots Co. Ltd, 1972–76; Develt Dir, Wellcome Foundation Ltd, 1976–87; R&D Dir and Mem. Bd, Wellcome plc, 1987–94; Dir-Gen., Assoc. of British Pharmaceutical Industry, 1994–2004. Director: Wellcome Biotechnology Ltd, 1983–93; Wellgen Inc. USA, 1990–93; Merlin Partners, 1996–2012 (Chm., Scientific Adv. Bd, 1996–2012); Sen. R&D Advr, Esteve SA, 2004–08. Visiting Professor: KCL, 1984– (Vice Chm. Council, 2001–08); Univ. of Strathclyde, 1988–93; Adjunct Prof., Univ. of N Carolina, 1985–90. Non-executive Chairman: Health Reform Investment Trust plc, 1996–98; ReNeuron, 2000–11; Synexus Ltd, 2008–11; Simbec Res. Ltd, 2013–19; Chairman: Kinetique Biomedical Seed Fund, 2001–08; Director: Next Pharma Ltd, 2004–11; Allergan Inc., 2004–15; BAC bv, 2005–08; People in Health, 2006–09; Verona Pharma plc, 2007–15; Sigma-Tau Finanziaria SpA, 2008–13; Sigma-Tau SpA, 2010–11; Tecnogen SpA, 2010–11; Aegate Ltd, 2010–13; e-Therapeutics, 2015–; Arix Bioscience plc, 2016–; Pres., Sigma-Tau Pharmaceuticals Inc., 2012–14. Member: Expert Cttees, British Pharmacopoeia, 1976–89; Pharmacy Res. Bd, CNAA, 1978–83; UK Govt Medicines Commn, 1982–94; Adv. Bd on Human Genome, Cabinet Office, 1991–96; Expert Wkg Party on Use of Tissues, Nuffield Council for Bioethics, 1992–97; Exec. Cttee, Internat. Fedn of Pharmaceutical Manufrs, 1994–2004; Bd of Mgt, European Fedn of Pharmaceutical Industry Assoc., 1994–2004; Nat. Biological Standards Bd Review, 1995–97; Advisory Board: MRC, 2001–04; MRC Social, Genetic and Develtl Psychiatric Res. Centre, Inst. of Psych., 2002–; MRC Centre for Neurodegeneration Res., 2006–; Prime Minister's Task Force on Competitiveness of Pharmaceutical Industry, 2001; Bevan Commn, Welsh Govt, 2014–; Chm., Adv. Gp on Genetics Res., 2003–07. Pres., Internat. Commn on Technology, 1979–83, Member: Pharmaceut. Scis Bd, 1980–84, 1996–, Fédn Internat. Pharmaceutique; WHO Commn on Intellectual Property Rights, Innovation and Public Health, 2004–06; Senate, Eur. Fedn for Pharmaceutical Scis, 2014–. Founder and Mem. Bd, Medicines for Malaria Venture, 1999–2007. Trustee: Epilepsy Res. Foundn, 1996–2004; Northwick Park Inst. of Med. Res., 1998–2004; British Urological Foundn, 2005–07. Life Sci. Advr, Fleming Family and Partners, 2006–08. Liveryman, Co. of Apothecaries, 1989–. FRSocMed 2007; FMedSci 2016; FLSW 2018. Hon. FFPM 1995; Hon. FRCP 2005; Hon. Fellow: London Sch. of Pharmacy, 1998; British Pharmacol. Soc., 2005. For. Mem., Acad. Nat. de Pharmacie, 2005–. Hon. PhD Athens, 1993; Hon. DSc: Strathclyde, 1994; Nottingham, 1998; Bath, 2000; Bradford, 2003. Harrison Meml Medal, 1987, Charter Gold Medal, 1996, RPSGB; Gold Medal, Comenius Univ., 1992. *Publications*: Drug Delivery to the Respiratory Tract, 1987; Advances in Pharmaceutical Sciences, 1993. *Recreations*: golf, gardening, Wales RU. *Address*: Woodhyrst House, Friths Drive, Reigate, Surrey RH2 0DS. *Club*: Athenæum.

**JONES, Ven. Dr Trevor Pryce;** Archdeacon of Hertford, 1997–2016, now Archdeacon Emeritus; b 24 April 1948; s of John Pryce Jones and Annie (née Jepson); m 1976, Susan Diane Pengelley; one s one d. *Educ*: Dial Stone Sch., Stockport; St Luke's Coll., Exeter; Univ. of Southampton (BEd, BTh); Salisbury and Wells Theol Coll.; Univ. of Wales, Cardiff Law Sch. (LLM); St John's Coll., Univ. of Durham (DThMin). Asst Teacher and Lay Chaplain, Shaftesbury Grammar Sch., 1969–73; ordained deacon, 1976, priest, 1977; Asst Curate, Gloucester St George, Lower Tuffley, 1976–79; Warden, Bishop Mascall Centre, Ludlow, and Mem., Hereford Diocesan Educn Team, 1979–84; Diocesan Communications Officer, Hereford, 1981–86; Team Rector, Hereford S Wye Team Ministry, 1984–97. OCF, 1985–97. Prebendary, Hereford Cathedral, 1993–97; Hon. Canon, Cathedral and Abbey Church of St Alban, 1997; Chapter Canon, Exeter Cathedral, 2017–. Chm., St Alban's at Oxford Ministry Course, 1998–2007; Vice-Chairman: E Anglia Ministerial Trng Course, 2005–07; Eastern Reg. Ministerial (formerly E Anglia Ministerial Trng) Course, 2007–16. Bishops' Selector, 2001–08. Mem., Gen. Synod of C of E, 2000–05 and 2005–10 (Mem., Legal Adv. Commn, 2006–11; Mem., Rule Cttee, 2013–16). Chairman: Reach Out Plus (formerly Reach Out Projects), 1998–2012; Rural Strategy Gp, Dio. of St Albans, 2001–16. Chm., Hockerill Educnl Foundn, 2005–12; Trustee, St Luke's Foundn, Exeter, 2017–. Mem., Royal Commonwealth Soc. Hon. LLM Herts. *Recreations*: country walks, vintage buses and trains, film and theatre, biography. *Address*: 3 South Terrace, Longmeadow Road, Lympstone, Devon EX8 5LN. *T*: (01395) 268745. *E*: tprycejones@gmail.com. *Club*: Royal Over-Seas League.

**JONES, Prof. Tudor Bowden,** MBE 2011; DSc; FInstP; Professor of Ionospheric Physics, 1980–98, Head of Department of Physics and Astronomy, 1993–98, University of Leicester, now Professor Emeritus; b 8 Nov. 1934; s of Idris Jones and Tydvil Ann Jones (née Bowden); m 1960, Patricia Brown; two s. *Educ*: County Grammar Sch., Ystradgynlais; University Coll. of Wales, Swansea (BSc Hons, PhD, DSc). FInstP 1975; CEng 1987; FIET (FIEE 1987). Res. Asst, UCW, Aberystwyth, 1959; University of Leicester: Lectr in Physics, 1960–69; Sen. Lectr, 1969–75; Reader, 1975–80. PPARC Nat. Co-ordinator for Solar Terrestrial Physics, 1998–2001. Guest Res. Scientist at various Govt estabts in UK and overseas, 1970–; Sen. Resident Associate, Nat. Oceanic and Atmospheric Admin Lab., Boulder, Colo, 1971–72. Leverhulme Emeritus Fellowship, 2001–02. Appleton Lectr, IEE, 1997. Appleton Prize, Internat. Union of Radio Sci. and Royal Soc., 1993; Charles Chree Prize and Medal, Inst. of Physics, 1995. *Publications*: (ed) Oblique Incidence Radio Wave Propagation, 1966; numerous papers in scientific jls on ionospheric physics and radio wave propagation. *Recreation*: classical music. *Address*: Department of Physics and Astronomy, University of Leicester, University Road, Leicester LE1 7RH. *T*: (0116) 252 3561.

**JONES, Prof. Vaughan Frederick Randal,** DCNZM 2002; FRS 1990; Professor of Mathematics, University of California, Berkeley, 1985–2011, now Emeritus; Distinguished Professor of Mathematics, Vanderbilt University, Nashville, since 2011; b Gisborne, NZ, 31 Dec. 1952; s of J. H. Jones and J. A. Goodfellow (née Collins); m 1979, Martha Weare Jones (née Myers); one s two d. *Educ*: St Peter's Sch., Cambridge, NZ; Auckland Grammar Sch.; Univ. of Auckland (schol.; Gillies schol.; Phillips Industries Bursary; BSc, MSc 1st Cl. Hons); Ecole de Physique, Geneva (Swiss Govt schol.; F. W. W. Rhodes Meml schol.); Ecole de Mathématiques, Geneva (DèsSc Mathematics); Vacheron Constantin Prize, Univ. de Genève. Asst, Univ. de Genève, 1975–80; E. R. Hedrick Asst Prof., UCLA, 1980–81; University of Pennsylvania: Vis. Lectr, 1981–82; Asst Prof., 1981–84; Associate Prof., 1984–85. Alfred P. Sloan Res. Fellowship, 1983; Guggenheim Fellowship, 1986. Hon. Vice Pres., Internat. Guild of Knot-tyers, 1991. Fields Medal, 1990. *Publications*: Coxeter graphs and Towers of algebras, 1989. *Recreations*: music, tennis, squash, ski-ing. *Address*: Department of Mathematics, 1326 Stevenson Center, Vanderbilt University, Nashville, TN 37240, USA.

**JONES, Very Rev. Sarah Caroline R.;** see Rowland Jones.

**JONES, Victoria Mary Taylor, (Lady Jones);** see Heywood, V. M. T.

**JONES, Walter;** see Jones, William W. A.

**JONES, William George Tilston;** independent telecommunications consultant, 1990–2004; b 7 Jan. 1942; s of late Thomas Tilston Jones and Amy Ethel Jones; m 1965, Fiona Mary; one d. *Educ*: Portsmouth Grammar School; Portsmouth Polytechnic (BSc; Hon. Fellow 1989). Post Office Engineering Dept, 1960; Head, Electronic Switching Gp, 1969; Head, System X Develt Div., 1978; Dir, System Evolution and Standards, 1983; Chief Exec., Technology, BT, 1984; seconded as Exec. in Residence, Internat. Management Inst., Geneva, 1987; Sen. Strategy Adviser, BT, 1988. Member: IEE Electronics Divl Bd, 1984–89; Parly IT Cttee, 1985–87; Chairman: IT Adv. Bd, Polytechnic of Central London, 1984–87; Adv. Gp, Centre of Communication and Information Studies, 1988–89; SE Centre, IEE, 1989–90; Dir, Technology Studies, British Telecom, 1988–90. Governor, Polytechnic of Central London, 1985–89. *Publications*: contribs on telecommunications to learned jls. *Recreations*: theatre, camping, making furniture, landscape gardening.

**JONES, William Michael Roger B.;** see Bankes-Jones.

**JONES, William Pearce A.;** see Andreae-Jones.

**JONES, (William) Walter (Alexander);** Principal, Kolej Tuanku Ja'afar, Malaysia, 2005–11; b 11 Sept. 1949; s of Rev. Eric Jones and Elizabeth Jones; m 1974, Frances Linda Grant; one s two d. *Educ*: Campbell Coll., Belfast; Queens' Coll., Cambridge (MA; PGCE); Inst. of Education, Univ. of London (MA). Asst Teacher, St Edward's C of E Comprehensive, Romford, 1973–75; Head of Economics, King's Coll. Sch., Wimbledon, 1976–87; Second Master, King's Sch., Bruton, 1987–93; Headmaster, Royal Grammar Sch., Worcester, 1993–2005. *Publications*: contrib. to British Economic Survey. *Recreations*: Rugby, walking. *Address*: 4 Padwick's Field, Fittleworth, W Sussex RH20 1HJ.

**JONES, Wynne;** see Jones, Elphin W.

**JONES, Yvonne;** see Jones, E. Y.

**JONES-EVANS, Prof. Dylan,** OBE 2013; PhD; Professor of Entrepreneurship and Assistant Pro-Vice Chancellor, University of South Wales, since 2017; b Bangor, Gwynedd, 16 May 1966; s of Cyril Jones-Evans and Carys Jones-Evans; m 1993, Dr Angela Sullivan (marr. diss. 2018); two s. *Educ*: Ysgol Glan y Mor, Pwllheli; University Coll. Cardiff (BSc Hons Physics 1987); Univ. of Manchester (MSc Tech. Change and Industrial Strategy 1988); Aston Univ. (PhD Entrepreneurship 1994). Res. Fellow, Durham Univ., 1992–94; Marie Curie Postdoctoral Res. Fellow, UCD, 1994–96; Prof. of Entrepreneurship and Small Business Mgt, Univ. of Glamorgan, 1996–2000; Dep. Dir, Sch. of Business and Regl Develt, Univ. of Wales, Bangor, 2000–04; Dir, Enterprise, NE Wales Inst. of Higher Educn, 2004–05; Dep. Dir, Centre for Advanced Studies, Cardiff Univ., 2005–08; Dir, Enterprise and Innovation, Univ. of Wales, 2008–13; Prof. of Entrepreneurship and Strategy, UWE, 2013–17. Chm., Outlook Expeditions, 2001–08. Chm., Community Enterprise Wales, 1999–2003; Dir, Wales Fast Growth 50, 1999–. Chairman: Star for Burton Appeal, 2012–13; Town Square Spaces, 2018–; Trustee, Prime Cymru, 2012–18; Fabric, 2018–. Mem., Cardiff Business Club; MInstD. Columnist: Daily Post, 2003–; Western Mail, 2004–; Bristol Post, 2015–. FRSA 2002. *Publications*: Technology, Enterprise and Innovation: the European experience, 1997; Creating an Entrepreneurial Wales, 2001; Enterprise and Small Business: principles, policy and practice, 2012; articles in jls on entrepreneurship, innovation and business. *Recreations*: reading biographies, walking, cinema, supporting Cardiff Blues. *Address*: University of South Wales, Treforest, Pontypridd CF37 1DL. *T*: 07776 166361. *E*: prof@talk21.com. *Clubs*: Cardiff and County; Rygbi Pwllheli; Crawshays Rugby.

**JONES PARRY, Sir Emyr,** GCMG 2007 (KCMG 2002; CMG 1992); PhD; FInstP; HM Diplomatic Service, retired; President, Learned Society of Wales, since 2014; b 21 Sept. 1947; s of Hugh Jones Parry and Eirwen Jones Parry (née Davies); m 1971, Lynn Noble; two s. *Educ*: Gwendraeth Grammar Sch.; University Coll. Cardiff (BSc, Dip Crystallography); St Catharine's Coll., Cambridge (PhD; Hon. Fellow, 2008). FInstP 2004. FO, 1973–74; First Sec., Ottawa, 1974–79; FO, 1979–82; First Sec., UK Rep. to EC, Brussels, 1982–86; Dep. Head, Office of Pres. of European Parlt, 1987–89; Head, EC Dept (External), FCO, 1989–93; Minister, British Embassy, Madrid, 1993–96; Dep. Pol Dir, FCO, 1996–97; Dir, EU, FCO, 1997–98; Political Dir, FCO, 1998–2001; UK Perm. Rep., UK Delegn to NATO, 2001–03; UK Perm. Rep. to UN, 2003–07. Chairman: All Wales Convention, 2007–09; Redress, 2008–16; Wales Millennium Centre, 2010–16. Mem., McKay Commn, 2012–13. Pres., 2008–14, Chancellor, 2014–17, Aberystwyth Univ. Hon. Fellow: Univ. of Cardiff, 2003; Univ. of Wales Aberystwyth, 2006; Trinity Coll., Carmarthen, 2007. Hon. Dr Laws Wales, 2005; Hon. DSc S Wales, 2016. *Publications*: (contrib.) Satow's Diplomatic

Practice, 7th edn, 2017; various scientific articles. *Recreations:* gardening, theatre, reading, sport. *Address:* c/o Learned Society of Wales, University Registry, Cathays Park, Cardiff CF10 3NS. *Club:* Glamorgan County Cricket.

**JONES-PARRY, Tristram**, MA; Head Master, Westminster School, 1998–2005; *b* 23 July 1947; *s* of Sir Ernest Jones-Parry and late Mary (*née* Powell). *Educ:* Westminster Sch.; Christ Church, Oxford (MA). Operational Researcher, NCB, 1968–70; Maths Teacher, Dulwich Coll., 1970–73; Head of Maths, Housemaster and Under Master, Westminster Sch., 1973–94; Headmaster, Emanuel Sch., 1994–98. *Recreations:* reading, walking, cycling, travelling. *Address:* 4 Bainton Road, Oxford OX2 7AF. *Club:* Athenæum.

**JONSSON, Lars Ossian;** artist, author, ornithologist; *b* 22 Oct. 1952; *s* of Sven and May Jonsson; *m* 1985, Ragnhild Erlandson; two *s* two *d*. *Educ:* autodidact. Wildlife artist, mainly specialising in birds; debut show at age 15, Nat. Mus. of Natural Hist., Stockholm, 1968; solo exhibitions: Prins Eugens Waldemarsudde, Stockholm, 2002, 2012; Stockholm Cultural House, 2009; Millesgarden Stockholm, 2017; permanent exhibn, Museum Lars Jonsson, Vamlingbo Vicarage, Gotland, 2004–. Hon. Dr Uppsala, 2002. Master Wildlife Artist, Leigh Yawkey Wordson Art Mus., Wis, USA, 1988. *Publications:* Birds of Sea and Coast, 1978; Birds of Lake, River, Marsh and Field, 1978; Birds of Wood, Park and Garden, 1978; Birds of Mountain Regions, 1980; Bird Island, 1984; Birds of Europe: with North Africa and the Middle East, 1992; Birds and Light: the art of Lars Jonsson, 2002; Birds: paintings from a near horizon, 2009; Winter Birds, 2017. *Recreations:* guitar music, travelling, art. *Address:* Hamra, Norrgårde 311, 620 10 Burgsvik, Sweden.

**JOPLING,** family name of **Baron Jopling**.

**JOPLING, Baron** *cr* 1997 (Life Peer), of Ainderby Quernhow in the co. of N Yorkshire; **Thomas Michael Jopling;** PC 1979; farmer; *b* 10 Dec. 1930; *s* of Mark Bellerby Jopling, Masham, Yorks; *m* 1958, Gail, *d* of Ernest Dickinson, Harrogate; two *s*. *Educ:* Cheltenham Coll.; King's Coll., Newcastle upon Tyne (BSc Agric. Durham). Mem., Thirsk Rural District Council, 1958–64; Mem. National Council, National Farmers' Union, 1962–64. Contested (C) Wakefield, 1959. MP (C): Westmorland, 1964–83; Westmorland and Lonsdale, 1983–97. PPS to Minister of Agriculture, 1970–71; an Asst Govt Whip, 1971–73; a Lord Comr, HM Treasury, 1973–74; an Opposition Whip, March–June 1974; an Opposition spokesman on agriculture, 1974–79; Shadow Minister of Agriculture, 1975–76; Parly Sec. to HM Treasury, and Chief Whip, 1979–83; Minister of Agriculture, Fisheries and Food, 1983–87. Mem., Select Cttee on Foreign Affairs, 1987–97; Chm., Select Cttee on Sittings of the House (Jopling Report), 1991–92; Member: H of L Select Cttee on European Legislation, 2000–04, 2007–12 (Mem. Sub-Cttee (D) Agric., 1998–2000, (C) Defence and Foreign Policy, 2000–04, 2010–15 (Chm., 2001–04), (F) Home Office, 2006–10 (Chm., 2007–10)); H of L Select Cttee on Merits of Statutory Instruments, 2003–07; Select Cttee on Internat. Relations, 2016–; Jt Sec., Cons. Parly Agric. Cttee, 1966–70. Hon. Sec., British Amer. Parly Gp, 1987–2001 (Vice Chm., 1983–86). Mem., UK Delegn to NATO Assembly, 1987–97, 2001– (Chairman: Civilian Aspects of Security Cttee, 2011–14; Democratic Governance Cttee, 2014–17; Vice Pres., 2014–16). Member, UK Executive: CPA, 1974–79, 1987–97 (Vice Chm., 1977–79); IPU, 1997–. Pres. Councils, EEC Agric. and Fishery Ministers, July–Dec. 1986; Leader, 1990–97, Mem., 2000–01, UK Delegn to OSCE Parly Assembly. Mem. Cttee, Assoc. of Cons. Peers, 1997–2000. Pres., Auto Cycle Union, 1989–2004. DL Cumbria, 1991–97, N Yorks, 1998–2005. Hon. DCL Newcastle, 1992. *Address:* Ainderby Hall, Thirsk, North Yorks YO7 4HZ. *T:* (01845) 567224. *Clubs:* Buck's (Hon.); Royal Automobile (Hon.).

*See also* J. Jopling.

**JOPLING, Jeremy Michael Neal, (Jay);** Founder, White Cube, art gallery, 1993; *s* of Lord Jopling, *qv*; *m* 1997, Samantha Taylor-Wood (*see* S. Taylor-Johnson) (marr. diss. 2009); two *d*. *Educ:* Eton; Univ. of Edinburgh (MA Art Hist. 1984). *Address:* White Cube, 144–152 Bermondsey Street, SE1 3TQ. *T:* (020) 7930 5373, *Fax:* (020) 7749 7480.

**JORDAN,** family name of **Baron Jordan**.

**JORDAN, Baron** *cr* 2000 (Life Peer), of Bournville in the co. of West Midlands; **William Brian Jordan,** CBE 1992; General Secretary, International Confederation of Free Trade Unions, 1995–2001; *b* 28 Jan. 1936; *s* of Walter and Alice Jordan; *m* 1958, Jean Ann Livesey; three *d*. *Educ:* Secondary Modern Sch., Birmingham. Convener of Shop Stewards, Guest Keen & Nettlefolds, 1966; full-time AUEW Divl Organiser, 1976; Pres., AEU, then AEEU, 1986–95. Mem., TUC General Council, 1986–95 (Chm., Cttee on European Strategy, 1988–95). A Gov., BBC, 1988–98. Member: NEDC, 1986–92; Engrg Industry Training Bd, 1986–91; Council, Industrial Soc., 1987–95; RIIA, 1987–; ACAS, 1987–95; Nat. Trng Task Force, 1989–92; Engrg Trng Authy, 1991–95; NACETT, 1993–95; English Partnerships, 1993–2002 (Chm., Pension Scheme, Homes and Communities Agency, 2004–); President: European Metal-Workers Fedn, 1986–95; Exec., Internat. Metalworkers Fedn, 1986–95; RoSPA, 2009–. Member: UN High Level Panel on Youth Employment; UN Global Compact Adv. Council; Victim Support Adv. Bd, 1990–2007; Steering Bd, Nat. Contact Point, 2007–. Fellow, World Econ. Forum. Governor: London School of Economics, 1987–2002; Manchester Business School, 1987–92; Ashridge Management Coll., 1992–; Mem. Ct of Govs, Henley Coll., 1991–. Hon. CGIA 1989. DUniv Central England, 1993; Hon. DSc Cranfield, 1995. *Recreations:* reading, keen supporter of Birmingham City FC. *Address:* 352 Heath Road South, Northfield, Birmingham B31 2BH.

**JORDAN, Andrew;** a Judge of the Upper Tribunal (Immigration and Asylum Chamber) (formerly a Vice President, Immigration Appeal Tribunal, later a Senior Immigration Judge, Asylum and Immigration Tribunal), 2003–18; *b* 30 Nov. 1949; *s* of Norman and Muriel Jordan; *m* 1978, Susan Jennifer Young; one *s* two *d*. *Educ:* Univ. of Warwick (LLB); Univ. of Wales, Cardiff (LLM Canon Law). Called to the Bar, Lincoln's Inn, 1973; in practice as barrister, 1973–2000 (specialised in gen. common law); Immigration Adjudicator, 2000–03. Dep. Chancellor, 2001–02, Chancellor, 2002–, Dio. Guildford. *Recreations:* music, London.

**JORDAN, Anthony;** television script writer and producer; Chief Executive Officer, Red Planet Pictures, since 2016 (Managing Director, 2005–16); *b* Southport, Merseyside, 21 July 1957; *s* of Anthony and Lily Jordan; *m* 1995, Tracy Tyler; two *s* four *d*. *Educ:* Broadlands, Bristol. Lead writer, Eastenders, 1990–2007; series creator: City Central, 1995; Hustle, 2002–12; Moving Wallpaper, 2007; series co-creator, Life on Mars, 2005; writer: Nativity, 2011; Death in Paradise, 2011–; The Passing Bells, 2014; The Ark, 2015; Dickensian, 2015; Hooten & The Lady, 2016. *Recreations:* music, swimming, boating, golf, hiking. *Address:* Red Planet Pictures Ltd, Corinthian House, 279 Tottenham Court Road, W1T 7RJ. *E:* tonyjordan@redplanetpictures.co.uk. *Club:* Century.

**JORDAN, Dame Carole,** DBE 2006; PhD; FRS 1990; Professor of Physics, University of Oxford, 1996–2008, now Emeritus; Wolfson Tutorial Fellow in Natural Science, Somerville College, Oxford, 1976–2008, now Emeritus Fellow; *b* 19 July 1941; *d* of Reginald Sidney Jordan and Ethel May Jordan. *Educ:* Harrow County Grammar School for Girls; University College London (BSc 1962; PhD 1965; Fellow 1991). FInstP 1973, Hon. FInstP 2011. Post-Doctoral Research Associate, Jt Inst. for Lab. Astrophysics, Boulder, Colorado, 1966; Asst Lectr, Dept of Astronomy, UCL, attached to Culham Lab., UKAEA, 1966–69; Astrophysics Research Unit, SRC, 1969–76; Oxford University: Lectr in Physics, 1976–94; Reader, Dept of Physics (Theoretical Physics), 1994–96. Member: SERC, 1985–90 (Chm., Solar System Cttee, 1983–86); Mem., Astronomy, Space and Radio Bd, 1979–86; Mem., Astronomy and Planetary Sci. Bd, 1986–90); PPARC, 1994–97. Pres., Royal Astronomical Soc., 1994–96 (Sec., 1981–90; Vice-Pres., 1990–91, 1996–97). DUniv Surrey, 1991; Hon. DSc QUB, 2008. *Publications:* scientific papers on astrophysical plasma spectroscopy and structure and energy balance in cool star coronae, in learned jls. *Address:* Department of Physics, University of Oxford, Clarendon Laboratory, Rudolf Peierls Centre for Theoretical Physics, Parks Road, Oxford OX1 3PU. *T:* (01865) 273997.

**JORDAN, Craig;** *see* Jordan, V. C.

**JORDAN, Edmund Patrick, (Eddie),** Hon. OBE 2012; Formula 1 commentator, Channel 4, since 2016; Chief Executive Officer, Jordan Grand Prix, 1991–2004; *b* 30 March 1948; *s* of Patrick Jordan and Eileen Jordan; *m* 1979, Marie McCarthy; two *s* two *d*. *Educ:* Synge Street Sch., Dublin; Coll. of Commerce, Dublin. Winner, Irish Kart Championship, 1971; single seater racing in FF1600, 1974; winner, Irish Formula Atlantic Championship, 1978; teamed up with Stefan Johannson, Marlboro Team Ireland, for British Formula 3 Championship, 1978; Formula 2, 1979; test drove McLaren F1 car, 1979; retired from single seater racing, 1980; Founder: Eddie Jordan Racing, 1979; Jordan Grand Prix, 1991. Formula 1 commentator, BBC, 2009–15; presenter, Top Gear, BBC, 2016–. Irish Sporting Ambassador, 1999. Patron: CLIC Sargent; Amber Foundn. *Publications:* An Independent Man: the autobiography, 2007. *Recreations:* golf, music, ski-ing. *Clubs:* Sunningdale Golf, Oxfordshire Golf, Wentworth.

**JORDAN, Graham Harold Ben,** CB 2004; Science and Technology Director, Ministry of Defence, 2001–03; Senior Science and Technology Adviser, 2004–15, and Associate Fellow, 2007–18, Royal United Services Institute; *b* 1 April 1945; *s* of Harold Jordan and Violet Emily Jordan (*née* Wakefield); *m* 1977, Jean Anne Swale. *Educ:* Chislehurst and Sidcup Grammar Sch.; Downing Coll., Cambridge (Schol.; BA 1966 Nat. Scis and Chem. Eng; MA 1970); Brunel Univ. (MTech 1974 Op. Res.). DOAE, 1967–77; Dept of Chief Scientist, RAF, 1977–78; Supt, Land Air Studies Div., DOAE, 1978–82; Royal Aircraft Establishment: Supt, Air to Air Weapons Div., 1982–85; Head, Defensive Weapons Dept, 1985–87; Head, Civil Service Personnel Policy Div., HM Treasury, 1987–90; Scientific Advr (Command Inf. Systems), MoD, 1990–91; Asst Chief Scientific Advr (Capabilities), MoD, 1991–95; Dep. Chief Scientist (Scrutiny and Analysis), MoD, 1995; Dir of Central IT Unit, Cabinet Office (OPS), 1995–97; Dep. Under-Sec. of State (Science and Technol.), MoD, 1997–2001. Member: Technol. Bd, DSAC, 2004–07; European Security Res. Adv. Bd, 2005–07; NATO Sci. Cttee, 2006–13. MIET 2019. *Publications:* RUSI reports and articles in RUSI Jl and RUSI Defence Systems. *Recreations:* small scale farming, home maintenance, music, walking.

**JORDAN, Marc Lewis Aron,** FSA; Founder and Chief Executive, Creative Education Trust, since 2010; *b* 12 July 1955; *s* of late Philip Jordan, MICE and Dr Louise Jordan (*née* Jackson); *m* 2000, Olivia, *d* of late Terence Kilmartin, CBE and Joanna Kilmartin; one *s*. *Educ:* William Ellis Sch.; Univ. of Exeter (BA Hons English Lit.); Courtauld Inst. of Art (MA Hist. of Art); London Business Sch. (MBA). Res. Assistant, Nat. Portrait Gallery, 1979–80; Cataloguer, Dept of Watercolours and Drawings, Phillips Auctioneers, 1981–82; Grove Dictionary of Art: Area Editor, 1985–88; Dep. Editor, 1988–92; Commissioning Editor, Phaidon Press, 1992–95; Publisher, Harvey Miller Publishers, 1998–99; Man. Dir, Acoustiguide Ltd, 1999–2003; Mgt Consultant, AEA Consulting, 2003–06; Interim Dir, Contemporary Art Soc., 2006–07; mgt consultant, 2007–10. Trustee: Hackney Historic Buildings Trust, 2000–04; Bishopsgate Foundn, 2009–15; Member: London Regl Cttee, Heritage Lottery Fund, 2001–07; Adv. Panel on European Capital of Culture 2008, 2002–03. Mem. Council, Univ. of Exeter, 2007–13; Gov., Midhurst Rother Coll., 2008–12. Jt author, Arts Council England Rev. of Presentation of Contemporary Visual Arts, 2005. FSA 2007. *Publications:* contribs to Apollo, Burlington Magazine, The Times, NY Times, TLS. *Recreations:* gardening, old houses, sailing. *Address:* Creative Education Trust, Sicilian House, Sicilian Avenue, WC1A 2QR. *Clubs:* Athenæum; Beaulieu River Sailing.

**JORDAN, Michael Anthony;** Chairman and Senior Partner, Cork Gully, Chartered Accountants, 1983–93; Partner, Coopers & Lybrand, Chartered Accountants, 1980–93; *b* 20 Aug. 1931; *s* of Charles Thomas Jordan and Florence Emily (*née* Golder); *m* 1st, 1956, Brenda Gee (marr. diss. 1989); one *s* one *d*; 2nd, 1990, Dorothea Rosine Estelle Coureau (*d* 2000). *Educ:* Haileybury. FCA 1956. Joined R. H. March Son & Co., 1958, Partner, 1959–68; Partner: Saker & Langdon Davis, 1963–93; W. H. Cork Gully & Co., 1968–80. Principal insolvency appointments: Acrow, Barlow Clowes, Capper Neill, Homfray Carpets, Learfan, Lines Bros, Lyon Gp, Mitchell Construction, Norton Villiers Triumph Manufacturing, Norvic Shoes, Polly Peck, Savings & Investment Bank, Wolverhampton Wanderers FC; Jt Inspector for High Court of IoM into the affairs of the Savings & Investment Bank, 1983. Gen. Comr of Income Tax, City of London, 1970–2006 (Chm., 1998–2006). Gov., Royal Shakespeare Co., 1979–2001. Freeman, City of London; Master, Tower Ward, 1979–80; Liveryman, Bakers' Co. *Publications:* (jtly) Insolvency, 1986. *Recreations:* opera, DIY, gardening. *Address:* 8 Clifton Place, W2 2SN.

**JORDAN, Richard James;** theatrical producer, since 1998; Director, Richard Jordan Productions Ltd, since 2001; *b* Norwich, 28 Oct. 1974; *s* of Anthony Frederick Richard Jordan and Diane Jane Jordan (*née* Wiley); *m* 2005, Tammy Dale. *Educ:* Cringleford First and Middle Sch., Norfolk; Hethersett High Sch., Norfolk; Oxford Sch. of Drama (Stage Mgt and Th. Admin). Wanted to be a producer from age 12; wrote to Cameron Mackintosh for advice, encouraged by his reply, began career in theatre at age 16 as stagehand on West End musical, Cats, 1990; joined tech. team, Stephen Joseph Th., Scarborough, 1993; mgt team, Wycombe Swan Th., High Wycombe, Nederlander Theatres (London), Michael Codron Ltd, 1994–97; Line Manager, Cottesloe Th. for RNT, 1997–98. Creative Consultant, Teatros Artes, Brazil, 2001–11; Director: New Wolsey Th., Ipswich, 2003–11; Oxford Playhouse, 2008–11; Associate: Theatre Royal Haymarket, London, 2005– (Creative Dir, 2006–09); Perry St Theater, NYC, 2005–11; UK Associate, Primary Stages, NYC, 2007–09; Associate Artist, Bush Th., London, 2006–13; Internat. Associate, Illawarra Performing Arts Centre, Wollongong, Australia, 2009–; Internat. Producing Partner, Chicago Shakespeare Th., 2011–. Artistic Consultant for creation and inaugural season of Theatre Royal Haymarket Co., 2007–08. Trustee, Youth Music Th. UK, 2003–11; Patron: Norwich Theatre Royal 250 Appeal; Norwich Playhouse; Brighton Fringe. Voting Mem., BAFTA, 2002–. Columnist, Stage newspaper; theatre contributor for BBC and ABC. First London prodn, Shylock, Hampstead Th., 1999; first NY prodn, Rum and Vodka, Ohio Th., 2002. Other productions include: Of Thee I Sing, Anna Weiss, 1999; Sweeney Todd – Demon Barber of Fleet St, God's Official, Troilus and Cressida, Rum and Vodka, The Good Thief, Almost Forever But, 2000; Kissing Sid James, St Nicholas, 2001; Smoking with Lulu, Love Songs, The Life of Galileo, Dust to Dust, Single Spies, 2002; Miriam Margolyes: Dickens' Women, 2002, 2012; Larkin with Women, 2002, 2003, 2005; The Lady in the Van, 2002, 2009, 2010, 2011, 2012; Protection, This Lime Tree Bower, Nine Parts of Desire, Miguel Street, Roald Dahl's The Twits, 2003; Third Finger Left Hand, Ladies and Gents, 2004; Dylan Thomas: Return

Journey, A Mobile Thriller, The Broken Road, 2005; Monsieur Ibrahim and the Flowers of the Qur'an, Lunch with the Hamiltons, Killing Castro, Marlon Brando's Corset, Insomnobabble, Bussmann's Holiday, In the Continuum, The Truman Capote Talk Show, Goodness, an Oak Tree, 2006; Believe, Victor Spinetti: A Very Private Diary… Revisited!, Exits and Entrances, Get Your War On, Hamlet (solo), 2007; Life and Beth, Haunting Julia, Snake in the Grass, Falstaff, Once and For All We're Gonna Tell You Who We Are so Shut Up and Listen, Itsoseng, Berkoff's Women, Basic Training, 2008; Dumbshow, Under the Influence, Stefan Golaszewski is a Widower, Internal, The Smile Off Your Face, East 10th Street, Edwyn Collins - A Casual Introduction, Stefan Golaszewski Speaks about a Girl He Once Loved, Die Roten Punkte, Impressionism, MacHomer: the Simpsons do Macbeth!, 2009; Heroin(e) for Breakfast, 2009, 2019; A Game of You, Teenage Riot, Double Edged, Jordan, The Friendship Experiment, The Über Hate Gang, en route, 2010; Roadkill, 2010, 2011, 2013, A Behanding in Spokane, 2010; Funk It Up About Nothin', Audience, Alphonse, Kafka and Son, Penny Dreadful's Etherdome, Bette and Joan, My Filthy Hunt, Laundry Boy, Bigger Than Jesus, 2011; Midsummer (a play with songs), A History of Everything, All That is Wrong, XXXO, Othello: The Remix, Razing Eddie, 2012; Glasgow Girls, 2012, 2014, An Audience with the Duke of Windsor, 2012; Cadre, Bitch Boxer, Chapel Street, BigMouth, Beeston Rifles, The Vanish Inquisition, Vanya and Sonia and Masha and Spike, Fight Night, Ali J, Whatever Gets You Through the Night, Hirsch, Bonanza, Tourniquet, Freeze, Parkin'Son, 2013; The Adventure, 2013, 2015; Q Brothers, A Christmas Carol, 2013, 2014, 2015, 2017, 2018; Landscape with Skiproads, Looking for Paul, Sirens, Where the World is Going, That's Where We're Going, Live Forever, The Art of Falling Apart, Small War, Since I Suppose, GRIT - the Martyn Bennett Story, Mush and Me, 2014; La Merda, 2014, 2015, 2016, 2018, 2019; Janis Joplin: Full Tilt, 2014, 2016; a Brimful of Asha, Night + Daze, The History of the World Based on Banalities, Mark Thomas: Bravo Figaro!, Pardon/In Cuffs, The Great Downhill Journey of Little Tommy, A Reason to Talk, Gommar Trilogy, On Track, Gary Busey's One-man Hamlet, Forever Young, A Piece of Time, 2015; Are We Not Drawn Onward to New Era, 2015, 2019; UpsideDownInsideOut, 2015, 2016, 2018; Us/Them, Century Song, On Track, A World Without Us, One Hundred Homes, Unpathed Waters Undreamed Shores, Mr Kingdom's Queen Victoria, Hamlet in Bed, Krapp 39, My Name is Gideon, Intergalactic Nemesis, Macbain, Bildraum, Last Call, 2016; Room, Three Tales of Life and Death, Ivona: Princess of Burgundia, Bombastic Declaration of Love, Arm, 2017; £¥€$ (LIES) 2017, 2019; Naughty, 2017, 2018; On Ice, 2017, 2019; Working Method, 2017, 2019; Trump/Lear, Loopstation, A Piece of Two, Another One, Unsung, European Citizen PopSong, Nele Needs a Holiday: the Musical, De Fuut, Circolombia's Acelere, 2018; Happy Hour, 2018, 2019; Penny Arcade: Bitch! Dyke! Faghag! Whore!, Buzz, 2019. Co-creator and producer, Big in Belgium season at Edinburgh Fest. Fringe, 2012. Has also produced and presented prodns worldwide; associations with many of world's leading theatres and producing orgns. Lucille Lortel Award; John Gassner Award for Best New American Play; 2 Herald Angel Awards; 2 Helen Hayes Awards; 3 Obie Awards; 2 Jeff Awards; 17 Scotsman Fringe First Awards; Carol Tambor Award; 10 Total Theatre Awards; 3 Musical Th. Matters UK Awards; Spirit of the Fringe Award; Icelandic Mask Theatre Award; Tap Award; US Black Alliance Award; Time Out Lisbon Award; Adelaide Fest. Award; Off West End Award; Stage Award; Drama Desk Award; Outer Critics Circle Award; Drama League Award; TheaterMania Award; Emmy Award; Norfolk Outstanding Contribution to the Arts Award; TIF/Soc. of London Th. Producers Award; Laurence Olivier Award; Tony Award. In 2013 became first British producer to have won every Best Play award on and off Broadway. *Recreations:* going to the theatre, collecting theatrical memorabilia and musical cast recordings, cinema, playing tennis, travelling. *Address:* Richard Jordan Productions Ltd, Mews Studios, 16 Vernon Yard, W11 2DX. *T:* (020) 7243 9001, *Fax:* (020) 7313 9667. *E:* info@richardjordanproductions.com. *Club:* Groucho.

**JORDAN, Robert Anthony; His Honour Judge Jordan;** a Circuit Judge, since 2015; *b* Dewsbury, 16 Aug. 1952; *s* of Neil Jordan and Maureen Jordan; *m* 1984, Helen Dorothy (*née* Kay); three *s* two *d. Educ:* St Thomas Aquinas Grammar Sch., Leeds; Park Lane Coll., Leeds; Anglia Ruskin Univ.; Coll. of Law, London. Admitted solicitor, 1978; NP 1981; solicitor: Joynson-Hick, 1978–81; Jordans, 1981–99; Dep. Dist Judge, 1995–99; Dist Judge, 1999–2015; Recorder, 2008–15; Dep. High Court Judge, 2015–. Mem., Civil Justice Council, 2006–12. Pres., Assoc. of HM's District Judges, 2014–15. *Recreations:* sailing, fly fishing, hill walking, family, cycling. *Address:* Manchester County Court and Family Court Hearing Centre, Manchester Civil and Family Justice Centre, 1 Bridge Street West, Manchester M60 9DJ.

**JORDAN, Prof. (Virgil) Craig,** CMG 2019; OBE 2002; PhD, DSc; Professor of Breast Medical Oncology and Molecular and Cellular Oncology, since 2014, and Dallas/Fort Worth Living Legend Chairman of Cancer Research, since 2015, M. D. Anderson Hospital and Cancer Center, University of Texas; *b* New Braunfels, Texas, 25 July 1947; *s* of Geoffrey Webster Jordan and Sybil Cynthia Jordan (*née* Mottram); two *d* by a previous marriage. *Educ:* Moseley Hall Grammar Sch., Cheadle; Leeds Univ. (BSc 1969; PhD 1972; DSc 1984). FMedSci 2009; FRSB (FSB 2009). Vis. Scientist, Worcester Foundn for Experimental Biol., Mass, 1972–74; Lectr in Pharmacol., Leeds Univ., 1974–79; Hd, Endocrine Unit, Ludwig Inst., Univ. of Berne, 1979–80; University of Wisconsin: Asst Prof. of Human Oncol., 1980–82; Associate Prof., 1982–85; Prof., 1985–93; Dir, Breast Cancer Res. and Treatment Prog., Wisconsin Comprehensive Cancer Center, 1988–93; Prof. of Cancer Pharmacol., 1993–2004, Diana Princess of Wales Prof. of Cancer Res., 1999–2004, Northwestern Univ. Med. Sch., Ill, and Dir, Breast Cancer Res., Lurie Cancer Center, Chicago, 1993–2004; Alfred G. Knudson Prof. of Cancer Res., and Res. Dir for Med. Scis, Fox Chase Cancer Center, Philadelphia, 2004–09; Scientific Dir, Vincent T. Lombardi Prof. of Translational Cancer Res. and Prof. of Oncol. and Pharmacol., and Vice Chm., Dept of Oncol., Lombardi Comprehensive Cancer Center, Georgetown Univ. Med. Center, Washington DC, 2009–14. Vis. Prof. in Molecular Medicine, Leeds Univ., 2012–. Pres., RSocMed Foundn, USA, 2010–. Commnd Leeds Univ. OTC, 1969; Captain: Intelligence Corps TAVR, 1970–75; 23 SAS TAVR, 1975–79; SAS RARO, 1980–97; SAS Reg. Assoc., 2007–; Hon. Col, Leeds Univ. OTC, 2014–16. MNAS 2009; MNAM 2017. Fellow: Deutsche Gesellschaft für Senologie, 2016; German Soc. of Gynaecology and Obstetrics, 2016. Hon. Mem., RPSGB, 2008. Hon. Faculty Fellow, Univ. Coll., Dublin, 2000; Hon. FRSocMed 2009; FAACR 2013; FCGI 2013. Hon. DM: Leeds, 2001; Crete, 2009. Hon. DSc: Mass, 2001; Bradford, 2005. Caine Award, Amer. Assoc. for Cancer Res., 1989; 1st Brinker Internat. Breast Cancer Award for Basic Sci., Susan G. Komen Foundn, 1992; Award for Experimental Therapeutics, Amer. Soc. for Pharmacol. and Experimental Therapeutics, 1993; Cameron Prize for Therapeutics, Edinburgh Univ. Med. Sch., 1993; Gaddum Meml Award, British Pharmacol. Soc., 1993; 12th Award for Scientific Excellence in Medicine, Amer. Italian Foundn for Cancer Res., 1995; Laureate of 6th Cino del Duca Award for Oncol., Paris, 1997; Bristol-Myers Squibb Award for Cancer Res., 2001; 3rd Annual Breast Cancer Award, Eur. Inst. of Oncol., 2001; Medal of Honor, Amer. Cancer Soc., 2002; Avon Med. Advancement Award, Avon Foundn, 2002; Landon Prize, Amer. Assoc. for Cancer Res., 2002; Kettering Prize, Gen. Motors Cancer Res. Foundn, 2003; N Amer. Menopause Soc. and Eli Lilly SERM Res. Award, 2003; 3rd George and Christine Sosnovsky Award, RSC, 2004; Amer. Cancer Soc. Award for Chemoprevention, Amer. Soc. of Clin. Oncol., 2006; Gregory J. Pincus Award and Medal, Worcester Foundn for Biomed. Res., 2007; Karnofsky Award, Amer. Soc. of Clin. Oncol., 2008; Jephcott Medal, RSocMed, 2009; Investigator Hall of Fame and Susan G. Komen for the Cure Scientific and Medical Dist. Award, Susan G. Komen Foundn, 2010 (Komen Schol., 2010–16); St Gallen Breast Cancer Award, 2011; Goodman and Gilman Award, Amer. Soc. for Pharmacol and Exptl Therapeutics, 2012; 50 Luminaries, Amer. Soc. of Clin. Oncol., 2014; Sir James Black Award for Contribns to Drug Discovery, British Pharmacol Soc., 2015; Gerald D. Aurbach Award for Translational Res., Endocrine Soc., 2018; Reynold Spector Award in Clinical Pharmacology, Amer. Soc. for Pharmacology and Experimental Therapeutics, 2019; Amer. Cancer Soc./Soc. Surgical Oncology Basic Sci. in Medicine Award, 2019. *Publications:* Estrogen and Antiestrogen Action and Breast Cancer Therapy, 1985; Long Term Adjuvant Tamoxifen Therapy, 1992; Tamoxifen for the Treatment and Prevention of Breast Cancer, 1999; Tamoxifen: a pioneering medicine for breast cancer, 2013; Estrogen Action SERMs and Women's Health, 2013; over 750 res. articles in professional med. jls on receptor pharmacol. and breast cancer. *Recreations:* London, Germany, collecting mountains, English longbow, target pistol, military history, antique weapons collecting, my library, bookshops, Falkland Island stamps. *E:* VCJordan@mdanderson.org. *Clubs:* Royal Society of Medicine; Union League (Philadelphia).

**JORDANOVA, Prof. Ludmilla Jane,** PhD; FRHistS; Professor of History and Visual Culture, Durham University, 2013–19, now Emeritus; *b* 10 Oct. 1949; *d* of Ivan Nicholov Jordanov and Phyllis Elizabeth Jordanova (*née* Brown); *m* 1970, Simon Thomas Emmerson (marr. diss. 1974); two *d* by Karl Michael Figlio. *Educ:* Oxford High Sch. for Girls; New Hall, Cambridge (BA 1971; MA, PhD 1977); Univ. of Essex (MA 1987). FRHistS 1989. Res. Fellow, New Hall, Cambridge, 1975–78; Res. Officer, Wellcome Unit for History of Medicine, Univ. of Oxford, 1978–79; Lectr, 1980–88, Sen. Lectr, 1988–91, Prof., 1991–93, Dept of Hist., Univ. of Essex; Prof., Dept of Hist., Univ. of York, 1993–96; Prof. of Visual Arts, 1996–2005 and Dean, Schs of World Art Studies and Music, 1999–2002, UEA; Dir, Centre for Res. in the Arts, Social Scis and Humanities, Univ. of Cambridge and Fellow, Downing Coll., Cambridge, 2003–05 (on secondment); Prof. of Modern Hist., KCL, 2006–13. Mem., Educn Honours Cttee, 2005–07. President: British Soc. for Hist. of Sci., 1998–2000; Hist. of Sci. Sect., BAAS, 2006; Mem. Council, 1993–97, Vice-Pres., 2001–04, RHistS. Trustee, Science Mus. Gp, 2011–. FRSocMed 1999. Trustee, Nat. Portrait Gall., 2001–09. *Publications:* Lamarck, 1984; Sexual Visions: images of gender in science and medicine between the Eighteenth and Twentieth Centuries, 1989; Nature Displayed: gender, science and medicine 1760–1820, 1999; Defining Features: scientific and medical portraits 1660–2000, 2000; History in Practice, 2000, 3rd edn 2019; The Look of the Past, 2012; Physicians and their Images, 2018; several edited vols, book reviews, contribs to learned jls. *Recreations:* grandparenting, friendship, Scotland, travel, listening to music, art, museums, galleries. *Address:* Bewlie Lodge, Bewlie, Melrose TD6 9ER. *E:* ludmilla.jordanova@durham.ac.uk.

**JORDON, William Eddy,** CBE 2004; Executive Director, Northern Education Trust, since 2016; *b* 17 Dec. 1947; *s* of John and Kathleen Jordon; *m* 1971, Doreen Thompson; one *s. Educ:* Newcastle upon Tyne Univ. (BPhil, MEd, DAES); Sunderland Polytech. (Teachers' Cert.). Hd, Phys. Educn, Marton Boarding Sch., Cheshire, 1969–73; Community Tutor and Dep. Hd (Community), Blyth Ridley High Sch., 1973–78; Hd, Referral Unit, 1978–81, Hd of House, 1981–83, Slatyford Comprehensive Sch., Newcastle upon Tyne; Sen. Teacher, Redewood Comprehensive Sch., 1983–89; Dep. Hd, Ralph Gardner High Sch., N Tyneside, 1989–93; Headteacher, 1993–2011, Exec. Headteacher, 2011–12, Dyke House Sch., Hartlepool; Exec. Headteacher, Brierton Community Sch., Hartlepool, 2007–09; Principal, North Shore Acad., Stockton, 2012–14; Exec. Dir, North Shore and Grangefield Acads, Stockton, 2014–16. Regl Dir, NE, Future Leaders Charitable Trust, 2012–15. FRSA 2004. *Recreations:* running, walking the dog, reading, fell-walking, listening to music. *Address:* Rosemount, Ovingham, Prudhoe, Northumberland NE42 6DE. *T:* (01661) 832431.

**JORY, Richard Norman;** QC 2013; *b* Bristol, 22 April 1967; *s* of late William and of Carolyn Jory; *m* 2002, Stephanie Suzanne Evans; two *s* one *d. Educ:* Sherborne Sch.; Reading Univ. (BA Hons Modern Hist. and Internat. Relns). Called to the Bar, Middle Temple, 1993; in practice as barrister, specialising in serious crime and fraud; Standing Counsel to Revenue and Customs Prosecutions Office, 2008–11; QC list for SFO Prosecutions, 2013–. Mem., Conduct Cttee, Bar Standards Bd, 2006–12. *Recreations:* theatre, cricket, competing in marathons and triathlons, dancing with my children, impersonating Elvis, badger conservation. *Address:* Foundry Chambers, Quality House, 5–9 Quality Court, Chancery Lane, WC2A 1HP. *T:* (020) 7400 1800. *E:* r.jory@foundrychambers.com. *Club:* MCC.

**JOSCELYNE, Richard Patrick;** British Council Director, Japan, 1991–94; *b* 19 June 1934; *s* of Dr Patrick C. Joscelyne and Rosalind Whitcombe; *m* 1st, 1961, Vera Lucia Mello (marr. diss. 1988); one *s* one *d;* 2nd, 1988, Irangani Dias. *Educ:* Bryanston; Queens' Coll., Cambridge. Teaching posts in France, Brazil and Britain, 1958–62. British Council: Montevideo, 1962; Moscow, 1967; Madrid, 1969; Director, North and Latin America Dept, 1973; Representative, Sri Lanka, 1977; Controller, Overseas Div. B (America, Pacific and Asia Div.), 1980; Controller, Finance Div., 1982; Representative, Spain, 1987. *Address:* 4 Alexandra Close, Cam, Glos GL11 4GN.

**JOSEPH, Alison Jane;** *see* Kirkham, A. J.

**JOSEPH, Cedric;** *see* Joseph, His Honour T. J. C.

**JOSEPH, David Philip;** QC 2003; *b* 22 April 1961; *s* of late Dr Joe Joseph and of Judith Joseph (*née* Lobl); *m* 1990, Denise Bass; three *s. Educ:* St Paul's Sch., London; Pembroke Coll., Cambridge (BA 1982). Called to the Bar, Middle Temple, 1984, Bencher, 2018; in practice specialising in internat. arbitration and commercial law. *Publications:* Jurisdiction and Arbitration Agreements and their Enforcement, 2005. *Recreations:* tennis, opera, singing, mountain walking. *Address:* Essex Court Chambers, 24 Lincoln's Inn Fields, WC2A 3ED. *E:* djoseph@essexcourt.net.

**JOSEPH, (Hon. Sir) James Samuel,** (3rd Bt *cr* 1943, of Portsoken, City of London); musician; *b* 27 Jan. 1955; *o s* of Baron Joseph, CH (Life Peer) and Hellen Louise (*née* Guggenheimer); *S* to baronetcy of father, 1994, but does not use the title and his name does not appear on the Official Roll of the Baronetage; *m* 1990, Sarah Jane Thwaites; two *s. Heir: s* Sam Nathan Joseph, *b* 7 Aug. 1991.

**JOSEPH, Julian,** OBE 2018; jazz pianist and composer; Founder and Artistic Director, Julian Joseph Jazz Academy, since 2013; *b* London, 11 May 1966. *Educ:* Berklee Sch. of Music, Boston, Mass (BA). Founder: own quartet, 1990; Julian Joseph Trio; Forum Project (8 piece); Electric Project; All Star Big Band; tours of Europe, USA, Canada, Asia, Australia and appearances at festivals. Presenter, TV series, Jazz with Julian Joseph, 1999, 2000; writer and presenter, Jazz Legends, Radio 3, 2000–07. Composer: Bridgetower - A Fable of 1807 (jazz opera), UK tour, 2007; Shadowball (children's jazz opera), 2010. Patron, Jazz Develt Trust, 1998. *Recordings:* The Language of Truth, 1991; Reality, 1993; Universal Traveller, 1996. *Address:* c/o James Joseph Music Management, 85 Cicada Road, SW18 2PA.

**JOSEPH, Rt Rev. Keith Ronald;** see Queensland, North, Bishop of.

**JOSEPH, Leslie;** QC 1978; b 13 Aug. 1925; s of Benjamin Francis Joseph and Sarah Edelman; m 1st, 1964, Ursula Mary Hamilton (d 1988); one s two d; 2nd, 2001, Hedwig Erna Lydia Swan (née Pesendorfer). Educ: Haberdashers' Aske's, Hampstead; University Coll. London (LLB Hons). Served Army, 1943–47: Infantry, 1943–45 (Sgt); Chindits, Jan. 1945; AEC, 1945–47. Called to the Bar, Middle Temple, 1953, Bencher, 1986; Master of the Revels, 1989–2000; Autumn Reader, 2003. Mem., Common Professional Examn Bd, 1989–2001 (Chm., 1996–98); Chairman: Bar Vocational Stage Sub-Cttee, 1996; Bar Vocational Course Validation Panel, 1996–97. Gov., Inns of Court Sch. of Law, 1994–96. Recreations: wine, water, cooking for friends. Address: Rose Lodge, 1b Southway, Totteridge, N20 8EB. T: (020) 8445 3681; Church Cottage, Buckhorn Weston, Dorset SP8 5HS.

**JOSEPH, Richard David;** Chief Executive Officer, Nextone Inc., since 2018; b 6 June 1956; s of late Philip and Pamela Joseph; m 1987, Nicole Beauchamp; three s. Educ: King Edward VII Sch., Johannesburg; Univ. of Witwatersrand (BCom). Higher Dip. in Accountancy, Public Accountants and Auditors Bd, SA. Articled clerk, Coopers & Lybrand, SA, 1978–80; Man. Dir, Books Etc Ltd, 1981–97; CEO, Borders (UK) Ltd, 1997–2000; Officer, Borders Gp Inc., 1997–2000; CEO, Arcadia Publishing Internat. Inc. and Arcadia Publishing Inc., 2002–18. Member: Soc. of Bookmen, London, 1980–2008; Cttee, Book Sellers' Assoc. of GB and Ireland, 1983–2000. Recreations: family, vacation, swimming, books, flying, boating. Address: 420 Wando Park Boulevard, Mount Pleasant, SC 29464, USA. E: rjoseph@nextoneinc.com. Club: Groucho.

**JOSEPH, Robert Edward;** Editorial Consultant, Meininger's Wine Business International (Editor-at-Large, 2005); Co-owner: Le Grand Noir, since 2005; Greener Planet Wines, since 2005; commentator, consultant and speaker; b London, 15 Feb. 1955; s of Alfred and Vivienne Joseph; partner, Catharine Lowe; one s one d. Educ: St Paul's Sch., London. Ed., 1983–85, Publishing Ed., 1985–2005, Wine Internat. mag.; Wine corresp., Sunday Telegraph, 1984–99; Partner, Hugh, Kevin & Robert, 2005–. Publisher, Joseph Report, 2005–. Chairman, International Wine Challenge: London, 1984–2005; China, 1997–2009. Chm., Wine Inst. of Asia, 1997–. Dir, DoILikeIt? Ltd, 2010–; Partner, Winestars World, 2013–. Chevalier du Tastevin, 2004; Mem., Commanderie du Bontemps de Médoc et des Graves, Sauternes et Barsac. Publications: The Wine Lists, 1985; The Art of the Wine Label, 1987; The Good Wine Guide, annually, 1988–2004; The White Wines of France, 1989; The Essential Guide to Wine, 1989; The Wines of the Americas, 1990; Complete Encyclopedia of Wine, 1996, 2nd edn 2006; French Wines, 1999, 2nd edn 2005; (with M. Rand) Kiss Guide to Wine, 2000; Bordeaux and Its Wines, 2003; Wine Buyer's Guide, 2005, 2nd edn 2006; The Wine Travel Guide to the World, 2006; The Wine Sales and Marketing Toolkit, 2015. Recreations: travel, photography, cooking, collecting irony, tortoise husbandry. Address: 8 Herndon Road, Wandsworth, SW18 2DG. T: (020) 8870 2094. E: robertjoseph@unforgettable.com. Club: Chelsea Arts.

**JOSEPH, Stephen Francis Waley,** OBE 1996; Chief Executive (formerly Executive Director), Campaign for Better Transport (formerly Transport 2000), 1988–2018; b London, 20 April 1956; s of Peter and Margaret Joseph; m 1986, Dr Jill Bartlett; three d. Educ: University Coll. Sch., Hampstead; Queen's Coll., Oxford (BA Hons Modern Hist.). Co-ordinator, Youth Envmtl Action, 1977–78; Director: Youth Unit, Council for Envmtl Conservation, 1978–82; Youth Participation Unit, British Youth Council, 1982–85; Jt Co-ordinator, London Planning Aid Service, TCPA, 1986–88. Member: Standing Adv. Cttee on Trunk Rd Assessment, 1996–99; Commn for Integrated Transport, 1999–2005. Vis. Prof., Univ. of Hertfordshire, 2019. FRSA. Hon. DSc Hertfordshire, 2010. Lifetime Achievement Award, Nat. Transport Awards, 2018. Publications: Waking up Dormant Land, 1981; Urban Wasteland Now, 1989; contrib. articles and papers on aspects of transport to jls and newspapers. Recreations: family life, music, walking, exploring cities. E: stephenfwjoseph@gmail.com.

**JOSEPH, His Honour (Thomas John) Cedric;** a Circuit Judge, 1994–2008; b 25 Aug. 1938; s of Thomas Rees Joseph and Katherine Ann Joseph; m 1960 Mary Weston; three d. Educ: Cardigan GS; LSE (LLB). Called to the Bar, Gray's Inn, 1960; Crown Counsel, Nyasaland, 1962–64; practised at the Bar, 1964–94; Asst Recorder, 1987–92; Recorder, 1992–94; Resident Judge, Croydon Crown Court, 1998–2006. Mem., Adv. Council on Misuse of Drugs, 2001–07. Recreations: music, travel, collecting old wine glasses and using them. Address: c/o Lewes Crown Court, The Law Courts, High Street, Lewes, East Sussex BN7 1YB.

**JOSEPH, Wendy Rose;** QC 1998; Her Honour Judge Wendy Joseph; a Senior Circuit Judge, since 2012; b 11 March 1952; d of late Norman Joseph and Carole Joseph (née Marks). Educ: Cathays High Sch., Cardiff; Westridge Sch. for Girls, Pasadena, Calif; New Hall, Cambridge (MA). Called to the Bar, Gray's Inn, 1975, Bencher, 2003; Asst Recorder, 1995–99; Recorder, 1999–2007; a Circuit Judge, 2007–12. A Pres., Mental Health Review Tribunal, 2001–12. Recreations: gardening, reading, Tudor history. Address: Central Criminal Court, Old Bailey, EC4M 7EH.

**JOSEPHSON, Prof. Brian David,** FRS 1970; Professor of Physics, Cambridge University, 1974–2007, now Emeritus; Fellow of Trinity College, Cambridge, since 1962; b 4 Jan. 1940; s of Abraham Josephson and Mimi Josephson; m 1976, Carol Anne Olivier; one d. Educ: Cardiff High School; Cambridge Univ. BA 1960, MA, PhD 1964, Cantab. FInstP. Asst Dir of Res. in Physics, 1967–72, Reader in Physics, 1972–74, Univ. of Cambridge. Res. Asst Prof., Illinois Univ., 1965–66; Vis., Fellow, Cornell Univ., 1971; Vis. Faculty Mem., Maharishi European Res. Univ., 1975; Visiting Professor: Wayne State Univ., 1983; Indian Inst. of Sci., Bangalore, 1984. Fellow, Sci. Mus., 2009. Hon. MIEEE, 1982; For. Hon. Mem., Amer. Acad. of Arts and Scis, 1974. Hon. DSc: Wales, 1974; Exeter, 1984. Awards: New Scientist, 1969; Research Corp., 1969; Fritz London, 1970; Nobel Prize for Physics, 1973; Casys, 2000. Medals: Guthrie, 1972; van der Pol, 1972; Elliott Cresson, 1972; Hughes, 1972; Holweck, 1973; Faraday, 1982; Sir George Thomson, 1984. Publications: Consciousness and the Physical World, 1980 (ed jtly); The Paranormal and the Platonic Worlds (in Japanese), 1997; research papers on physics and theory of intelligence, paranormal phenomena, Platonism, the convergence of science and religion; musical composition, unification of mind and matter, Sweet and Sour Harmony, 2005. Recreations: mountain walking, ice skating, music, astronomy. Address: Cavendish Laboratory, J. J. Thomson Avenue, Cambridge CB3 0HE. T: (01223) 337260. E: bdj10@cam.ac.uk. W: www.tcm.phy.cam.ac.uk/~bdj10, www.youtube.com/user/cogito2.

**JOSHI, Bharat Suresh;** HM Diplomatic Service; Deputy High Commissioner, Chennai, India, 2013–18; b Croydon, 23 Aug. 1969; s of Suresh Kantilal Joshi and Geeta Suresh Joshi; m 1997, Bhakti, d of Navinchandra Umashankar Oza and Pravina Navinchandra Oza; two d. Educ: Middlesex Univ. (BSc Hotel and Restaurant Admin). Dep. High Comr, Gambia, 1999–2001; Team Leader, Policy Sect., then Hd, Correspondence Sect., UK Visas, 2001–04; Private Sec. to Parly Under-Sec. of State, FCO, 2004–06; Dir, Visa Services, Dhaka, 2006–07; Regl Manager for Gulf and Iran, Qatar, Doha, UK Border Agency, 2007–09; High Comr to Cameroon and Ambassador (non-resident) to Chad, Gabon, Equatorial Guinea and Central African Republic, 2009–13. Recreations: cricket, reading, watching old musicals, jogging, swimming, cooking, listening to motown, playing piano. Address: c/o Foreign and Commonwealth Office, King Charles Street, SW1A 2AH. E: bharat.joshi@fco.gov.uk, beebeeje@yahoo.com.

**JOSHI, Prof. Heather Evelyn,** CBE 2015 (OBE 2002); FBA 2000; FAcSS; Professor of Economic and Developmental Demography in Education, Institute of Education, London University, 1998–2011, now Emeritus (Director (formerly Principal Investigator), Millennium Cohort Study, 2000–11; Director, Centre for Longitudinal Studies, 2003–10); Research Professor, UCL Institute of Education, since 2016; b 21 April 1946; d of Guy Malcolm Spooner, MBE and Molly Florence Spooner, MBE; m 1st, 1969, Vijay Ramchandra Joshi (marr. diss. 1977); 2nd, 1982, Gregory Hans David Martin; one d (one s decd), and two step d. Educ: St Hilda's Coll., Oxford (BA 1967, MA); St Antony's Coll., Oxford (MLitt 1970). Jun. Res. Officer, Oxford Inst. of Econs and Statistics, 1969–73; Econ. Advr, Govt Econ. Service, 1973–79; Res. Fellow, 1979–83, Sen. Res. Fellow, 1983–88, LSHTM; Sen. Res. Fellow, Birkbeck Coll., 1988–90; Sen. Lectr, LSHTM, 1990–93; Sen. Res. Fellow, subseq. Prof., City Univ., 1993–98; Dep. Dir, Centre for Longitudinal Studies, Inst. of Educn, London Univ., 1998–2003. Co-Dir, Eur. Child Cohort Network, 2008–13. President: Eur. Soc. for Population Econs, 1996; British Soc. for Population Studies, 1999–2001; Soc. for Longitudinal and Lifecourse Studies, 2010–12. Ed., Longitudinal and Life Course Studies, 2017–. Publications: (with V. R. Joshi) Surplus Labour and the City, 1976; (ed) The Changing Population of Britain, 1989; (with P. Paci) Unequal Pay for Women and Men, 1998; Children of the 21st Century: vol. 1, from birth to nine months (ed with S. Dex), 2005; vol. 2, the first five years (ed with K. Hansen and S. Dex), 2010; articles in economics, demography and social policy jls. Recreations: family life, listening to classical music, walking. Address: Centre for Longitudinal Studies, UCL Institute of Education, 20 Bedford Way, WC1H 0AL. T: (020) 7612 6874.

**JOSIPOVICI, Prof. Gabriel David,** FRSL; FBA 2001; Research Professor, School of Graduate Studies, University of Sussex, since 1998; b 8 Oct. 1940; s of Jean Josipovici and Sacha (née Rabinovitch) (d 1996). Educ: Victoria Coll., Cairo; Cheltenham Coll.; St Edmund Hall, Oxford (BA 1st Cl. Hons 1961). FRSL 1998. School of European Studies, University of Sussex: Asst Lectr in English, 1963–65; Lectr, 1965–74; Reader (part-time), 1974–84; Prof. of English, 1984–98. Lord Northcliffe Lectr, UCL, 1980–81; Weidenfeld Vis. Prof. in Eur. Comparative Lit., Univ. of Oxford, 1996–97. Plays: Dreams of Mrs Fraser, 1972; Evidence of Intimacy, 1973; Playback, 1973; A Life, 1974; Vergil Dying, 1976; A Moment, 1977; AG, 1977; Kin, 1982; Mr Vee, 1987; A Little Personal Pocket Requiem, 1989. Publications: fiction: The Inventory, 1968; Words, 1971; Mobius the Stripper, 1974; The Present, 1975; Migrations, 1977; The Air We Breathe, 1981; Conversations in Another Room, 1984; Contre-Jour, 1987; The Big Glass, 1989; In the Fertile Land, 1991; Steps, 1992; In a Hotel Garden, 1993; Moo Pak, 1994; Now, 1998; Goldberg: Variations, 2002; Everything Passes, 2006; After, 2009; Making Mistakes, 2009; Heart's Wings, 2010; Only Joking, 2010; Infinity: the story of a moment, 2012; Hotel Andromeda, 2014; The Cemetery in Barnes, 2018; non-fiction: The World and the Book, 1971, 3rd edn 1994; The Lessons of Modernism, 1977, 2nd edn 1986; Writing and the Body, 1982; The Mirror of Criticism, 1983; The Book of God, 1988, 2nd edn 1989; Text and Voice, 1992; Touch: an essay, 1996; On Trust, 1999; A Life, 2001; The Singer on the Shore, 2006; Whatever Happened to Modernism?, 2010; Hamlet: fold on fold, 2016; The Teller and the Tale, 2017. Recreations: walking, swimming. Address: 60 Prince Edward's Road, Lewes, Sussex BN7 1BH.

**JOSLIN, Peter David,** QPM 1983; DL; Chief Constable of Warwickshire, 1983–98; b 26 Oct. 1933; s of Frederick William Joslin and Emma Joslin; m 1960, Kathleen Josephine Monaghan; one s one d (and one s decd). Educ: King Edward VI Royal Grammar School, Chelmsford; Essex University. BA Hons. Joined Essex Police, 1954–74 (Police Constable to Superintendent; Chief Superintendent, Divl Comdr, Leicestershire Constabulary, 1974–76; Asst Chief Constable (Operations), Leics Constab., 1976–77; Dep. Chief Constable, Warwicks Constabulary, 1977–83. Chm., Traffic Cttee, ACPO, 1989–92. Pres., Warwickshire Assoc. for the Blind, 1993–. DL Warwickshire, 1999. Recreations: sport (now mainly as a spectator), house renovation, good wines, after dinner speaking. Address: Nash House, 41 High Street, Kenilworth, Warks CV8 1LY. T: (01926) 511517.

**JOSPIN, Lionel Robert;** Prime Minister of France, 1997–2002; Member, Constitutional Council of France, 2014–19; b 12 July 1937; s of late Robert Jospin and Mireille Jospin (née Dandieu); m; one s one d; m 1994, Prof. Sylviane Agacinski; one step s. Educ: Institut d'Etudes Politiques, Paris; Ecole Nationale d'Administration. French Foreign Office, 1965–70; Prof. of Economics, Technical Univ. Inst., Paris-Sceaux, 1970–81; MP 1981–88; MEP 1984–88; French Socialist Party: Nat. Sec., various divs, 1973–81; First Sec., 1981–88 and 1995–97; Minister of State, Nat. Educn and Sports, 1988–92; Minister plenipotentiary, Foreign Office, 1992. Member: Conseil général, Haute-Garonne, 1988–2002; Conseil régional, Midi-Pyrénées, 1992–97. Grand-Croix, Ordre National du Mérite (France), 1997; Grand Officier, Légion d'Honneur (France), 2008. Publications: L'invention du Possible, 1991; Propositions pour la France 1995–2000, 1995; Le Temps de Répondre, 2002; Le Monde comme je le vois, 2005; L'Impasse, 2007; Lionel raconte Jospin, 2010. Recreation: tennis. Address: c/o Parti Socialiste, 10 Rue de Solferino, 75007 Paris, France.

**JOSS, Vivienne Mary Hunt;** see Parry, V. M. H.

**JOSSE, David Benjamin;** QC 2009; b London, 22 July 1961; s of S. E. Josse, OBE and Lea Harris; m 1995, Natalie Poplar. Educ: King's Coll. London (BA Hist.); City Univ. (Dip. Law). Called to the Bar, Middle Temple, 1985; in practice at Criminal Bar, specialising in extradition, 1985–2005, 2010–; Defence Counsel, Internat. Criminal Tribunal for former Yugoslavia, 2005–09. Recreations: watching most sports (in particular cricket), politics, Scotland. Address: 5 St Andrew's Hill, EC4V 5BZ. T: (020) 7332 5400. E: davidjosse@5sah.co.uk. Clubs: MCC; Middlesex CC.

**JOUGHIN, Prof. John Joseph;** Vice-Chancellor and Chief Executive, University of East London, 2013; b July 1958. Formerly Prof. of Shakespeare Studies; Dean and Actg Pro Vice-Chancellor (Res.), Univ. of Central London, until 2010; Dep. Vice-Chancellor, Univ. of E London, 2010–13. Mem., Nat. Refugees Welcome Bd, Citizens UK, 2015–. Founding Mem., British Council of Undergrad. Res., 2011–. Mem., Exec. Bd, British Shakespeare Assoc. (Founding Chm., 2002–08; Hon. Fellow, 2010). Mem., Internat. Shakespeare Conf., 2000–15. A Founding Ed., Shakespeare jl, 2005. Publications: (ed) Shakespeare and National Culture, 1997; Philosophical Shakespeares, 2000; (ed with S. Malpas) The New Aestheticism, 2004.

**JOULWAN, Gen. George Alfred;** Adjunct Professor, National Defense University, 2000–01; Olin Professor of National Security Studies, United States Military Academy, West Point, 1998–2000; Supreme Allied Commander, Europe, 1993–97; Commander-in-Chief, United States European Command, 1993–97; b 16 Nov. 1939; m Karen E. Jones; three d. Educ: US Mil. Acad., West Point (BS 1961); Loyola Univ. (Master of Pol Sci. 1968); US Army War Coll., Washington. Joined US Army, 1961; served Europe, US and Vietnam, 1962–73; Special Assistant: to the Pres., 1973–74; to Supreme Allied Comdr, SHAPE, 1974–75; Bn Comdr, Europe, 1975–77; US Army War College: student, 1977–78; Dir, Pol and Econ. Studies, 1978–79; Bde Comdr, Europe, 1979–81; COS, 3 Inf.

Div., Europe, 1981–82; Exec. Officer to Chm., Jt Chiefs of Staff, Washington, 1982–86; US Army Europe and Seventh Army: DCS for Ops, 1986–88; Commanding General: 3rd Armored Div., 1988–89; V Corps, 1989–90; C-in-C, US Southern Comd, Quarry Heights, Panama, 1990–93. Pres., One Team Inc. Defense Distinguished Service Medal, with two Oak Leaf Clusters (USA); Distinguished Service Medal (USA); Silver Star (with Oak Leaf Cluster) (USA). Foreign orders include: Grand Cross, Order of Merit, Hessian Order of Merit (Germany); Legion of Honour, Legion of Merit (France); Cross of Gallantry with three Gold Stars (Vietnam). *Address:* 2107 Arlington Ridge Road, Arlington, VA 22202–2120, USA.

**JOURDAN, Dr Martin Henry,** FRCS; Consultant Surgeon, Guy's Hospital, 1977–2011, and St Thomas' Hospital, 1982–2011; Reader in Surgery, University of London, 1982–2011; *b* 7 Oct. 1941; *s* of Henry George Jourdan and Jocelyn Louise (*née* Courteney); *m* 1966, May McElwain (*d* 2012); two *s* two *d*. *Educ:* Bishopshalt Sch., Hillingdon; Guy's Hosp. Med. Sch. (MB BS; PhD 1970; MS 1980). LRCP 1966; FRCS 1974. Lectr in Physiol., Guy's Hosp., 1967–70; MRC Travelling Fellow, Univ. of Calif, Berkeley, 1971–72; Registrar, then Sen. Registrar in Surgery, Guildford, Norwich and Guy's Hosp., 1974–77. Chm., Examrs in Surgery, Univ. of London, 1989–91; Mem., Court of Examrs, RCS, 1987–2000. Master, Soc. Apothecaries, 2001–02. *Publications:* (contrib.) The New Aird's Companion in Surgical Studies, 2000; papers on surgical nutrition and bowel disease. *Recreations:* tennis, theatre, gardening, opera. *Address:* 55 Shirlock Road, Hampstead, NW3 2HR. *T:* (020) 7267 1582.

**JOURDAN, Stephen Eric;** QC 2009; a Recorder, since 2010; a Deputy High Court Judge, since 2013; Judge First-tier Tribunal (Property Chamber), since 2013; *b* Hammersmith, 13 Nov. 1962; *s* of Werner Jourdan and Rita Jourdan; *m* 1986, Nicola Ann Gamble (marr. diss. 2011); one *s* two *d*. *Educ:* Haberdashers' Aske's Sch., Elstree; Trinity Coll., Cambridge (BA Law 1984; MA). Solicitor, Theodore Goddard, 1985–89; called to the Bar, Gray's Inn, 1989. Dep. Adjudicator, HM Land Registry, 2008–13. *Publications:* Adverse Possession, 2002, 2nd edn 2010. *Recreations:* jazz, walking, sailing. *Address:* Falcon Chambers, Falcon Court, EC4Y 1AA. *T:* (020) 7353 2484, *Fax:* (020) 7353 1261. *E:* jourdan@falcon-chambers.com.

**JOUYET, Jean-Pierre;** Officier, Légion d'honneur; Officier, l'Ordre national du Mérite; Permanent Representative of France to the Organisation for Economic Co-operation and Development, since 2019; *b* Montreuil-sous-Bois, France, 13 Feb. 1954; *s* of Paul Jouyet and Hélène Jouyet (*née* Lavalette); *m* 2006, Brigitte Taittinger; one *d*; four *c* from a former marriage (one *s* decd). *Educ:* Ecole nat. d'admin; Inst. d'études politiques, Paris (Dip.); Advanced Dip. in Public Law. Inspecteur des finances (auditor), with special resp. for inspection of public finances, 1980, Bureau Chief, then Principal, Service de la législation fiscale, 1981–88, Min. for Economy and Finance; Dir of Studies, Paris Inst. d'études politiques, 1981–88; Principal Private Sec. to Minister of Industry, Foreign Trade and Town and Country Planning (Regl Develt), then Minister of Industry and Town and Country Planning (Regl Develt), 1988–91; Dep. Principal Private Sec., 1991–94, Principal Private Sec., 1994–95, to Pres. of EC; Partner, Jeantet Associés Law Firm, 1995–97; Dep. Principal Private Sec. to Prime Minister, 1997–2000; Hd, Agence France Trésor, and Ambassador for Internat. Econ. Affairs, Min. of Foreign Affairs, 2000–04; Chm., Barclays Bank France, 2004–05; Hd, Service de l'inspection générale des finances, Min. of Economy, Finance and Industry, 2005–07; Minister of State resp. for Eur. Affairs, 2007–08; Chm., Autorité des Marchés Financiers (Financial Mkts Regulator), 2008–12; Dir-Gen., Caisse des Dépôts et Consignations, and Chm., Public Investment Bank, 2012–14; Sec.-Gen. to Pres. of the Republic, 2014–17; Ambassador of France to the Court of St James's 2017–19. Hon. Chm., Aspen Inst.; Chm., Bd of Dirs, Inst. Pasteur. *Publications:* (with P. Mabille) N'enterrez pas la France, 2007; (jtly) Une Présidence de crises, 2009; Nous les avons tant aimés, 2010. *Recreations:* tennis, cycling. *Address:* Organisation for Economic Co-operation and Development, 2 rue André Pascal, 75775 Paris Cedex 16, France. *Club:* Le Siècle (Paris).

**JOVINE, Dame Nemat;** *see* Shafik, Dame N.

**JOWELL, Sir Jeffrey (Lionel),** KCMG 2011; barrister, Blackstone Chambers; Director, Bingham Centre for the Rule of Law, British Institute of International and Comparative Law, 2010–15; Professor of Law, University College London, 2006–10, now Emeritus (Professor of Public Law, 1975–2006); *b* 4 Nov. 1938; *s* of Jack and Emily Jowell, Cape Town; *m* 1963, Frances Barbara, *d* of late Dr M. M. Suzman and Helen Suzman, OM, Hon. DBE; one *s* one *d*. *Educ:* Cape Town Univ. (BA, LLB 1961); Hertford Coll., Oxford (BA 1963, MA 1969; Hon. Fellow, 2018), Pres., Oxford Union Soc., 1963; Harvard Univ. Law Sch. (LLM 1966, SJD 1971). Called to Bar, Middle Temple, 1965 (Hon. Bencher, 1999, Bencher 2013). Research Asst, Harvard Law Sch., 1966–68; Fellow, Jt Center for Urban Studies of Harvard Univ. and MIT, 1967–68; Associate Prof. of Law and Admin. Studies, Osgoode Hall Law Sch., York Univ., Toronto, 1968–72; Leverhulme Fellow in Urban Legal Studies, 1972–74, and Lectr in Law, 1974–75, LSE; University College London: Dean, Faculty of Laws, 1979–89 and 1998–2000; Head of Dept, 1982–89 and 1998–2002; Vice Provost, 1992–99; Hon. Fellow, 1997. Chm., Rev. into Devolution in UK, 2015. Mem., Foreign Sec.'s Adv. Cttee on Human Rights, 2015–. UK Mem., 2000–11 and Mem., Governing Bd, 2001–11, Venice Commn (Eur. Commn on Democracy through Law) (Vice-Pres., 2003–05). Chairman, Social Sciences and The Law Cttee, 1981–84, and Vice-Chm., Govt and Law Cttee, 1982–84, Social Science Res. Council; Asst Boundary Comr, 1976–85; Chm., Cttee of Heads of University Law Schools, 1984–86; Member: Cttee of Management, Inst. of Advanced Legal Studies, 1978–89; Standing Cttee, Oxford Centre for Socio-Legal Studies, 1980–84; Gp for Study of Comparative European Admin, 1978–86; Nuffield Cttee on Town and Country Planning, 1983–86; Council, Justice, 1997–2013; Lord Chancellor's Review of Crown Office List, 1999–2000; Internat. Adv. Bd, Freedom Under Law, 2008–; Council of Advrs, Great Britain China Centre, 2016–; Experts Panel, Clooney Foundn for Justice, 2019–. UK deleg., Cttee of Experts, CSCE, Oslo, 1991. Mem., Royal Commn on Envmtl Pollution, 2003–10. Convenor of numerous internat. workshops and confs on constitutional law and human rights. Assisted with drafting of various nat. constitutions. Non-executive Director: UCL Press, 1993–95; Camden and Islington Community Health Services NHS Trust, 1994–97; Bd, Office of Rail Regulation, 2004–07; Chm., British Waterways Ombudsman Cttee, 2004–13. Trustee: John Foster Meml Trust, 1986–; Internat. Centre for Public Law, 1992–98; Bd, Inst. of Commonwealth Studies, 1994–99; Prince of Wales's Foundn (formerly Inst. of Architecture), 1997–99; S African Constit. Court Trust, 2003–; Sigrid Rausing Trust, 2019– (Internat. Bd, 2016–19); Chm., Inst. of Philanthropy, 2000–04. Patron, Public Law Project, 2017–. Lionel Cohen Lect., Jerusalem, 1988; JUSTICE, Tom Sargent Meml Lect., Judicial Studies Bd of NI, 2008; Annual Lect., Constitutional and Admin. Law Bar Assoc., 2010; Eason Weinmann Lect., Univ. of Tulane, 2010; Annual UK Supreme Court Review Lect., 2018; Visiting Professor: Univ. of Paris II, 1991; Univ. of Aix-Marseilles, 2002; Columbia Law Sch., NY, 2002; Hon. Prof., 1999–2005, Vis. Prof. and Rabinowitz Fellow, 2010, Univ. of Cape Town. Corresp. Mem., Acad. of Athens, 2009. Hon. QC 1993. Hon. DJur Athens, 1987; Hon. LLD: Ritsumeikan, 1988; Cape Town, 2000; Hon. Dr Univ. of Paris II, 2010. Commander, Nat. Order of Southern Cross (Brazil), 2016. Member Editorial Bds: Public Law, 1977–93; Policy and Politics, 1976–83; Urban Law and Policy, 1978–83; Jl of Environmental Law, 1988–92; Public Law Review, 1995–; Judicial Review, 1996–; S African Law Jl, 2003–; Jt Editor, Current Legal Problems, 1984–89. *Publications:* Law and Bureaucracy, 1975; (ed jtly) Welfare Law and Policy, 1979; (ed jtly) Lord Denning: the Judge and the Law, 1984; (ed jtly) The Changing Constitution, 1985, 9th edn 2019; (ed jtly) New Directions in Judicial Review, 1988; (ed with H. Woolf) de Smith, Judicial Review of Administrative Action, 5th edn 1995 to 8th edn (jtly) as de Smith's Judicial Review, 2018; (ed jtly) Principles of Judicial Review, 1999; (ed jtly) Understanding Human Rights Principles, 2001; (ed jtly) Delivering Rights, 2003; articles and reviews on public law, human rights and planning law. *Recreations:* tennis, London, Exmoor. *Address:* Blackstone Chambers, Middle Temple, EC4Y 9BW. *T:* (020) 7583 1770.

**JOWETT, Dame Susan,** DBE 2016; education adviser; Chief Executive Officer, Spencer Academies Trust, 2012–17; Principal, George Spencer Academy, Nottingham, 2004–15; *b* 21 Sept. 1952; *d* of Eric and Ida Longhurst; *m* 1973, John Jowett; two *d*. *Educ:* City Grammar Sch., Sheffield; Univ. of London (BA 1975); Univ. of Birmingham (PGCE 1976); Univ. of Manchester (MEd 1988). Teaching posts, Birmingham, Salford and Tameside, 1976–84; Hd, Faculty of Communication and Langs, Westhoughton High Sch., 1984–88; Dep. Headteacher, Siddal Moor High Sch., 1988–96; Headteacher, Holly Lodge Girls' Coll., Liverpool, 1996–2004. *Recreations:* theatre, walking and backpacking, travel.

**JOWITT, Sir Edwin (Frank),** Kt 1988; a Justice of the High Court, Queen's Bench Division, 1988–2000; *b* 1 Oct. 1929; *s* of Frank and Winifred Jowitt; *m* 1959, Anne Barbara Dyson (*d* 2008); three *s* two *d*. *Educ:* Swanwick Hall Grammar Sch.; London Sch. of Economics. LLB London 1950. Called to Bar, Middle Temple, 1951, Bencher 1977; Member Midland and Oxford Circuit, 1952–80. Dep. Chm. Quarter Sessions: Rutland, 1967–71; Derbyshire, 1970–71; QC 1969; a Recorder of the Crown Court, 1972–80; a Circuit Judge, 1980–88; a Sen. Circuit Judge, 1987–88; Hon. Recorder, Birmingham, 1987–88; Presiding Judge, Midland and Oxford Circuit, 1996–99. Chm., Robert Hamill Inquiry, 2004–11. *Recreations:* walking, cycling. *Address:* Church House, Desborough, Northants NN14 2NP.

**JOWITT, Juliet Diana Margaret, (Mrs Thomas Jowitt);** DL; Member, Independent Broadcasting Authority, 1981–86; Director, Yorkshire Television, 1987–94; *b* 24 Aug. 1940; *yr d* of late Lt-Col Robert Henry Langton Brackenbury, OBE and Eleanor Trewlove (*née* Springman); *m* 1963, Frederick Thomas Benson Jowitt; one *s* one *d*. *Educ:* Hatherop Castle; Switzerland and Spain. Associate Shopping Editor, House and Garden and Vogue, 1966–69; Proprietor, Wood House Design (Interior Design) (formerly Colour Go Round), 1971–2002. Director: YTV Holdings PLC, 1988–92; Dancers Career Develt Trust Ltd, 2005–09; Northern Ballet Theatre, 2001–10. Member: Domestic Coal Consumers' Council, 1985–95; Potato Marketing Bd, 1986–90. Fellow, IDDA, 1995 (Mem., 1985; Mem. Council, 1989). Trustee, Great North Art Show, 2010–. Gov., Barnardo's, Ripon, 2002–10. JP North Yorks, 1973–89; DL N Yorks, 2004. *Address:* Thorpe Lodge, Littlethorpe, Ripon, N Yorkshire HG4 3LU.

**JOWITT, Prof. Paul William,** CBE 2011; PhD; CEng, FICE, CEnv, FREng; FRSE; Professor of Civil Engineering Systems, Heriot Watt University, since 1987; Executive Director, Scottish Institute of Sustainable Technology, 1999–2014; *b* Doncaster, 3 Aug. 1950; *s* of Stanley Jowitt and Joan Jowitt (*née* Goundry); *m* 1973, Jane Urquhart; one *s* one *d*. *Educ:* Maltby Grammar Sch.; Imperial Coll., London (BSc (Eng); PhD; DIC). CEng 1988; MICE 1988, FICE 1994; CEnv 2005. Lectr, Imperial Coll., London, 1974–86; Hd, Dept of Civil and Offshore Engrg, 1989–99, Dir, Inst. of Offshore Engrg, 1996–99, Heriot-Watt Univ. CEO and Chm., Tynemarch Systems Engrg Ltd, 1983–86. Mem. Bd, Edinburgh Envmtl Partnership Grants Scheme Ltd, 2000–04; non-executive Board Member: E of Scotland Water Authy, 1999–2002; Scottish Water, 2002–08; non-exec. Mem., E Regl Bd, Scottish Envmt Protection Agency, 2000–04. Non-exec. Dir, United Utilities Water, 2009–11. Warden, Falmouth-Keogh Hall, Imperial Coll., London, 1980–86. Pres., ICE, 2009–10. FRSE 2005; FCGI 2005; FIPENZ 2008; FREng 2012. FRSA 1996. Trustee: Forth Bridges Visitor Centre Trust, 2003–12; Steamship Sir Walter Scott Trust, 2005–14; Engrs Against Poverty, 2005– (Chm., 2011–); Engrs for Change, Sierra Leone, 2016–. *Publications:* Bootstrapping Infrastructure: the driving forces for sustainable development, 2008; A Systems Journey - with the Systems Boys, 2010; Now is the Time, 2010; Decisions, Decisions, 2013; contribs to Proc. ICE. *Recreations:* Morgan and Jowett cars, sculpture, painting, digging at the allotment (Dean Gallery allotments), making cider, canal cruising on a narrow boat. *Address:* 14 Belford Mews, Edinburgh EH4 3BT; Heriot Watt University, Edinburgh EH14 4AS. *E:* p.w.jowitt@hw.ac.uk. *Clubs:* Morgan Three Wheeler, Morgan Sports Car, Jowett Car.

**JOXE, Pierre Daniel,** Hon. KBE; lawyer at the Bar, Paris, since 2010; *b* 28 Nov. 1934; *s* of Louis Joxe and Françoise-Hélène Joxe (*née* Halévy); *m* 4th, Laurence Fradin; two *s* two *d* from previous marriages. *Educ:* Lycée Henri-IV; Faculté de droit de Paris; Ecole Nat. d'Administration. Started career in Audit Office, 1962; elected Deputy for Saône-et-Loire, 1973, 1978, 1981, 1986, 1988; Mem., European Parlt, 1977–79; Minister of Industry, 1981; Minister of the Interior, 1984–86, 1988–91; Minister of Defence, 1991–93; Auditor General, Audit Office, Paris, 1993–2001; Mem., Constitutional Court, Paris, 2001–10. Mem. Exec., Socialist Party, 1971–. *Publications:* Parti socialiste, 1973; A propos de la France, 1997; L'Edit de Nantes: une histoire pour aujourd'hui, 1998; Pourquoi Mitterrand?, 2006; Cas de conscience, 2010; Pas de Quartier?, 2012; Soif de Justice, 2014. *Address:* (office) 39 Quai de l'Horloge, 75001 Paris, France.

**JOY, David,** CBE 1983; HM Diplomatic Service, retired; *b* 9 Dec. 1932; *s* of late Harold Oliver Joy and Doris Kate Buxton; *m* 1957, Montserrat Morancho Saumench, *o d* of late Angel Morancho Garreta and Josefa Saumench Castells, Zaragoza, Spain; one *s* one *d*. *Educ:* Hulme Grammar Sch., Oldham, Lancs; St Catharine's Coll., Cambridge (MA). Colonial Service Trng Course, 1955–56; HMOCS, Northern Rhodesia, 1956–64; Zambia, 1964–70; Cabinet Office, 1964; Under Sec. (Cabinet), 1968–70; joined HM Diplomatic Service, 1971; FCO, 1971–73; First Sec. (Inf.), Caracas, 1973–75; Head of Chancery, Caracas, 1975–77; Asst Head, Mexican and Caribbean Dept, FCO, 1977–78; Counsellor and Head of Chancery, Warsaw, 1978–82; Counsellor and Head of British Interests Section, Buenos Aires, 1982–84; Head of Mexico and Central America Dept, FCO, 1984–87; Ambassador to Honduras and El Salvador, 1987–89; Consul Gen., Barcelona, 1989–92. *Recreations:* golf, tennis, music, reading. *E:* dmmjoy@mac.com. *Clubs:* Oxford and Cambridge; Cercle del Liceu (Barcelona); Rotary, La Peñaza Golf (Zaragoza); Key Biscayne Yacht (Florida).

**JOY, His Honour (Henry) Martin;** a Circuit Judge, 2007–18; *b* Fleet, Hants, 18 April 1948; *s* of Henry and Margaret Joy; *m* 1977, Hilary Ann Smyth; one *s* one *d*. *Educ:* Bradfield Coll., Berks; Univ. of Southampton (LLB Hons). Called to the Bar, Lincoln's Inn, 1971; in practice as barrister, 1971–2007; Recorder, 1993–2007. *Recreations:* family, gardening, golf, Catholicism.

**JOY, Larissa;** Chair, Foundling Museum, since 2016; *b* Brentwood, Essex, 1968; *d* of B. K. Joy and R. M. Joy; *m* 2008, Jonathan Mark Morran Page; one *s* two *d*. *Educ:* Sidney Sussex Coll., Cambridge (BA Law 1990); London Business Sch. (MBA 2009); Coll. of Law, London. FTCL 1985; LRAM 1987. Trainee solicitor, Addleshaw Goddard, 1992–94;

Lawyer, IMG Artists and TWI, 1994–96; Commercial Dir and Hd of Legal, TBWA, 1996–99; Vice Chm., Ogilvy Gp UK, 1999–2002; Chief Operating Officer, Weber Shandwick, 2002–06; Chief Operating Officer and Partner, Actis LLP, 2007–09; Chm., House of Illustration, 2009–15. Sen. Ind. Dir, East Thames Ltd, 2014–16; non-executive Director: Saxton Bampfylde, 2016–; L&Q Gp, 2016–; Charles Russell Speechlys LLP, 2017–. FRSA. *Recreations:* music, family, art, theatre. *Club:* Arts.

**JOY, Rupert Hamilton Neville;** Ambassador and Head, European Union Delegation to Morocco, 2013–17; *b* London, 5 Sept. 1963; *s* of late Peter Joy, OBE; *m* 2004, Kirsteen Hall; two *s* one *d*. *Educ:* New Coll., Oxford (BA Modern Hist. 1985); Dijon Business Sch. (Master's Dip. in Internat. Wine and Spirits Trade 2004). English teacher, British Council, Hong Kong, 1986–87; editor: Macmillan Publishers, Hong Kong, 1987–88; Mitchell Beazley Publishers, 1988–90; entered FCO, 1990; Soviet Dept, FCO, 1990–91; Arabic lang. trng, 1991–93; Second Sec., Sana'a, 1994–95; First Sec., Riyadh, 1995–96; Counter-Terrorism Dept, FCO, 1996–99; Kosovo Unit, FCO, 1999; Dep. Hd of Mission, Rabat, 2000–03; Dep. Consul-Gen., Basra, 2005; S America Team, FCO, 2005–08; Ambassador to Uzbekistan, 2009–12. *Publications:* contribs to UK wine mag., Decanter. *Recreations:* wine, archaeology, Islamic history, tennis.

**JOYCE, Prof. Bruce Arthur,** DSc; FRS 2000; CPhys, FInstP; Professor of Semiconductor Materials, Department of Physics, 1988–2000, now Emeritus Professor of Physics, and Distinguished Research Fellow, since 2016, Imperial College London; *b* 17 Oct. 1934; *s* of Frederick Charles James Joyce and Dorothy Joyce (*née* Crouch); *m* 1956, Beryl Ann Mead; three *s* one *d*. *Educ:* Birmingham Univ. (BSc 1956; DSc 1973). CPhys, FInstP 1973. Nat. Service Commn, RAF, 1956–58. Sen. Scientist, Allen Clark Res. Centre, Plessey Co., 1958–69; Sen. Principal Scientist, Philips Res. Labs, Redhill, 1969–88; Dir, Univ. of London IRC for Semiconductor Materials, ICSTM, 1988–99. *Publications:* contrib. over 360 original papers to learned jls. *Recreations:* hill-walking, athletics (track and road running), Rugby football and cricket (now as a spectator), crosswords, gardening. *Address:* 15 Tennyson Rise, East Grinstead, W Sussex RH19 1SQ. *T:* (01342) 323059.

**JOYCE, Prof. Dominic David,** DPhil; FRS; Professor of Mathematics, University of Oxford, since 2006; Senior Research Fellow, Lincoln College, Oxford, since 2006; *b* Cambridge, 8 April 1968; *s* of David Joyce and Dawn Joyce; *m* 1994, Jayne Clare Douglas; three *d*. *Educ:* Queen Elizabeth's Hospital Sch., Bristol; Merton Coll., Oxford (BA Maths 1989; DPhil Maths 1992). Jun. Res. Fellow, Christ Church Coll., Oxford, 1992–95; Lectr in Maths, Univ. of Oxford, 1995–2006; Tutorial Fellow in Pure Maths, Lincoln Coll., Oxford, 1995–2006; EPSRC Advanced Res. Fellow, 2001–06. *Publications:* Compact Manifolds with Special Holonomy, 2000; (jtly) Calabi-Yau Manifolds and Related Geometries, 2003; Riemannian Holonomy Groups and Calibrated Geometry, 2007. *Recreations:* family, walking, gardening. *Address:* Mathematical Institute, University of Oxford, Andrew Wiles Building, Radcliffe Observatory Quarter, Woodstock Road, Oxford OX2 6GG.

**JOYCE, Eric Stuart;** *b* 13 Oct. 1960; *s* of Leslie Joyce and Sheila Joyce (*née* Christie); *m* 1991, Rosemary Jones; twin *d*. *Educ:* Univ. of Stirling (BA Hons 1986); W London Inst. (PGCE 1987); Univ. of Bath (MA 1994); Univ. of Keele (MBA 1995). Served Army, 1978–99: Black Watch, 1978–81; RMA Sandhurst, 1987; commnd RAEC, 1987; served AGC; Maj. 1992. Public Affairs Officer, CRE, 1999–2000. MP Falkirk W, Dec. 2000–2005, Falkirk, 2005–15 (Lab, 2000–12, Ind 2012–15). PPS to Minister for Trade, Investment and Foreign Affairs, 2003–05, to Minister of State for Work, 2005–07, to Sec. of State for Business, Enterprise and Regulatory Reform, 2007–08, to Sec. of State for Defence, 2008–09, to Shadow Sec. of State for NI, 2010. *Publications:* Arms and the Man: renewing the armed services, 1997; (ed) Now's the Hour!: new thinking for Holyrood, 1999. *Recreations:* climbing, judo, most sports. *Club:* Camelon Labour (Falkirk).

**JOYCE, Lucy Rebecca,** OBE 2012; HM Diplomatic Service; Ambassador to the Republic of Moldova, 2016–19; *d* of Philip Joyce and (Gloria) Barbara Joyce. *Educ:* Hereford Cathedral Sch.; Bristol Grammar Sch.; Univ. of Warwick (BA Hons 1992); Open Univ. (MBA 2011). Joined FCO, 1992; S Asian Dept, FCO, 1992–94; Chancery, Sofia, 1995–96; Central Eur. Dept, FCO, 1997–99; Hd, Press and Public Affairs, Brussels, 2000–04; Internat. Policy Section, Paris, 2004–08; Hd, London 2012 Unit, FCO, 2008–12; Counsellor, Brasilia, 2012–13; Hd, N America Dept, FCO, 2013–15; High Comr, Lusaka, 2015–16. Fellow, British Amer. Proj., 2014. *Address:* c/o Foreign and Commonwealth Office, King Charles Street, SW1A 2AH. *E:* lucy.joyce@fco.gov.uk.

**JOYCE, Peter Robert,** CB 2000; FCCA; Director General, Insolvency Practitioners Association, 2003–10; *b* 14 Jan. 1942; *s* of George Henry Joyce and Edith Doris Joyce; *m* 1st, 1965 (marr. diss. 1988); one *s* one *d*; 2nd, 1988, Marian Neal. *Educ:* Westwood's Grammar Sch., Northleach, Glos. FCCA 1970. Insolvency Service, Board of Trade, subseq. Department of Trade and Industry, 1960–2001: Examr, 1960–69; Sen. Examr, 1969–76; Asst Official Receiver and Chief Examr, 1976–82; Official Receiver and Principal Examr, 1982–85; Dep. Inspector General, 1985–89; Inspector General and Agency Chief Exec., 1989–2001. Consultant, World Bank, 2004–08. Chm., 1995–2001, Exec. Dir, 2002–08, Internat. Assoc. of Insolvency Regulators; World Bank Wkg Gp on Insolvency Regulatory Frameworks, 1999–2001. Mem. Council, Central Govt NTO, 1999–2001. Hon. FCICM (Hon. FICM 2000); Hon. FIPA 2010. *Recreations:* watching cricket, theatre, dining out. *Club:* Gloucestershire County Cricket.

**JOYCE, Robert,** FREng, FIMechE; Executive Director, Product Creation and Delivery, Jaguar Land Rover, 2013–16; *b* Littlehampton, 24 May 1958; *s* of Charles and Audrey Joyce; *m* 1981, Amanda West; two *s* one *d*. *Educ:* Leicester Univ. (BSc Hons Engrg 1979); Warwick Univ. (MBA 1992). FIMechE 1991; FREng 2013. Austin Rover Group, then Rover Group: Manager: Engrg Performance Develt, 1987–90; Petrol Engine Design, 1990–91; Chief Engr, Small Engines, 1991–94; Director: Vehicle Engrg, 1994–95; Body and Trim, 1996–97; Dir, Prodn Engrg, 1997–98, Sen. Vice Pres., Mini Rover, 1998–2000, BMW; Jaguar Land Rover: Dir, Prodn Engrg, 2000–03; Gp Dir, Engrg, 2003–13. Hon. DSc Leicester, 2015. *Recreations:* motorbikes, Rugby.

**JOYCE, Lt-Gen. Sir Robert John H.;** see Hayman-Joyce.

**JOYCE, Robert Sean D.;** *see* Dwyer-Joyce.

**JOYNSON-HICKS,** family name of **Viscount Brentford**.

**JUBB, David;** Artistic Director and Chief Executive Officer, Battersea Arts Centre, 2004–19 (Joint Artistic Director and Joint Chief Executive Officer, 2008–12); *b* Newport Pagnell, 14 June 1969; *s* of John Jubb and Audrey Jubb; *m* 2010, Allegra Galvin; one *s* two *d*. *Educ:* Bedford Modern Sch.; Bretton Hall Coll. (Theatre Arts); Univ. of Bristol (MA Film); Central Sch. of Speech and Drama (MA Advanced Theatre Practice (Distinction)). Teacher, Duston Upper Sch., 1991–92; Dir, Economical Truth, 1997–2001; Producer, Battersea Arts Centre, 1999–2001; Dir, Me and Him, subseq. Your Imagination, 2001–04. Chair: Kneehigh Th., 2008–13; London Th. Consortium, 2012–15; Mem., Adv. Council, Creative Industries Fedn, 2015–16. *Publications:* (contrib.) The Producers: alchemists of the impossible, 2007 (contrib.) Proximo Ato, 2011; articles in The Stage, Evening Standard. *E:* mrdavidjubb@gmail.com.

**JUCKES, Robert William Somerville;** QC 1999; **His Honour Judge Juckes;** a Circuit Judge, 2007–April 2020; Resident Judge, Worcester Crown Court, 2011–April 2020; *b* 1 Aug. 1950; *s* of late Dr William Renwick Juckes and Enid Osyth Juckes (*née* Hankinson); *m* 1974, Frances Anne MacDowel; three *s*. *Educ:* Marlborough Coll.; Exeter Univ. (BA Hons Sociol. and Law 1972). Called to the Bar, Inner Temple, 1974; in practice, Birmingham, 1975; Hd of Chambers, 2000–03. Asst Recorder, 1992–95; Recorder, 1995–2007; Hon. Recorder of Worcester, 2012–. *Recreations:* golf, tennis, cricket, novels of Patrick O'Brian, culturing three sons, two grandsons and three granddaughters. *Address:* Worcester Combined Court, The Shirehall, Foregate Street, Worcester WR1 1EQ.

**JUDD,** family name of **Baron Judd**.

**JUDD, Baron** *cr* 1991 (Life Peer), of Portsea in the County of Hampshire; **Frank Ashcroft Judd;** Trustee, Saferworld, 2002–15 (Senior Fellow, 1994–2002); Member, Advisory Board, Centre for Human Rights, since 2007, and Commission on Diplomacy, 2014–15, London School of Economics; *b* 28 March 1935; *s* of late Charles Judd, CBE and Helen Judd, JP; *m* 1961, Christine Elizabeth Willington; two *d*. *Educ:* City of London Sch.; London Sch. of Economics. Short Service Commn, RAF (Educn Br.), 1957–59; Sec.-Gen., IVS, 1960–66. Contested (Lab): Sutton and Cheam, 1959; Portsmouth West, 1964; MP (Lab) Portsmouth W, 1966–74, Portsmouth N, 1974–79; PPS: to Minister of Housing and Local Govt, 1967–70; to the Leader of the Opposition, 1970–72; Mem., Opposition's Front Bench Defence Team, 1972–74; Parliamentary Under-Secretary of State: for Defence (Navy), MoD, 1974–76; ODM 1976; Minister of State: for Overseas Develt, 1976–77; FCO, 1977–79; Mem., British Parly Delegn to Council of Europe and WEU, 1970–73, 1997–2005; Rapporteur to Parly Assembly of Council of Europe on Chechnya, 1999–2004; Opposition front bench spokesperson, H of L, on for. affairs, 1991–92, on defence, 1995–97; principal spokesperson, on educn, 1992–94, on overseas develt co-operation, 1994–97; Member: Procedure Cttee, H of L, 2001–04; Ecclesiastical Cttee, H of C and H of L, 2001–; Human Rights Cttee, H of C and H of L, 2003–07; Sub Cttee F (Home Affairs, later Home Affairs, Health and Educn), 2010–15, EU Justice Sub Cttee, 2015–, H of L Select Cttee on EU; IPU Middle East Cttee, 2012–16. Ind. Advr to UK Delegn to UN Special Session on Disarmament, 1982. Associate Dir, Internat. Defence Aid Fund for Southern Africa, 1979–80; Director: VSO, 1980–85; Oxfam, 1985–91. Sen. Fellow, De Montfort Univ., 1999 (Professional Advr, 1993–2012). Chairman: Centre for World Development Educn, 1980–85; Internat. Council of Voluntary Agencies, 1985–90; World Econ. Forum Conf., Geneva, on the future of S Africa, 1990 and 1991; Member: Steering Cttee, World Bank—NGO Cttee, 1989–91; Internat. Commn on Global Governance, 1992–2001; WHO Task Force on Health and Develt, 1994–98; Internat. Working Gp on Human Duties and Responsibilities in the New Millennium, 1997–99. Pres., European-Atlantic Gp, 1999–2001. Past Chm., Fabian Soc. Chm., Oxford Diocesan Bd for Social Responsibility, 1992–95; Convenor, Social Responsibility Forum, Churches Together in Cumbria, 1999–2005. Mem., NW Regl Cttee, Nat. Trust, 1996–2003; Dir (non-exec.), Portsmouth Harbour Renaissance Bd, 1998–2006; Vice-President: Campaign (formerly Council) for Nat. Parks, 1998–; Lakeland Housing Trust, 2007–; UNA-UK (formerly UN Assoc.); Nat. Pres., YMCA England, 1996–2005; Pres., Friends of RN Mus., 2002–12, now Hon. Life Vice-Pres.; Pres., 2005–12, Patron, 2012–, Friends of the Lake Dist.; Hon. Pres., Hospice at Home, W Cumbria, 2008–15, now Hon. Vice-Pres. Trustee: Internat. Alert, 1994–2000 (Chm., 1997–2000); Selly Oak Colls Birmingham, 1994–97 (Chm. Council, 1994–97); Ruskin Foundn, 2002–11. University of Lancaster: Mem. Council, 1996–2002; Mem. Court, 2002–11; Life Mem., 2011; Mem. Court, Univ. of Newcastle upon Tyne, 2004–13, Life Mem., 2013; Governor: LSE, 1982–2012, now Gov. Emeritus; Westminster Coll., Oxford, 1991–98. Member: Unite; GMB. Freeman, City of Portsmouth, 1995. Hon. Fellow: Univ. of Portsmouth (formerly Portsmouth Poly.), 1978; Univ. of Lancaster, 2015. Hon. DLitt: Bradford Univ., 1987; Portsmouth, 1997; De Montfort, 2006; Hon. LLD Greenwich, 1999. FRSA 1988. *Publications:* (jtly) Radical Future, 1967; Fabian International Essays, 1970; Purpose in Socialism, 1973; (jtly) Our Global Neighbourhood, 1995; (jtly) Imagining Tomorrow: rethinking the global challenge, 2000; various papers and articles on current affairs. *Recreations:* relaxing in the countryside, family holidays, enjoying music, opera, theatre and film. *Address:* House of Lords, SW1A 0PW. *Club:* Royal Over-Seas League.

**JUDD, Clifford Harold Alfred,** CB 1987; Under Secretary, HM Treasury, 1981–87; *b* 27 June 1927; *s* of Alfred Ernest and Florence Louisa Judd; *m* 1951, Elizabeth Margaret Holmes; two *d*. *Educ:* Christ's Hospital; Keble Coll., Oxford. National Service, RA, 1946–48 (to 2/Lt). HM Treasury: Executive Officer, 1948, through ranks to Principal, 1964, Sen. Prin., 1969, Asst Sec., 1973. *Recreations:* cricket, golf, do-it-yourself. *Address:* 17 Elgin Road, Lilliput, Poole, Dorset BH14 8QT. *Clubs:* Forty; Sevenoaks Vine (Vice-Pres.).

**JUDD, Lt-Gen. David Leslie,** CB 2003; CEng, FIMechE; Deputy Commander Allied Joint Force Command Brunssum (formerly Deputy Commander-in-Chief, Allied Forces North), 2004–07; *b* 26 Jan. 1950; *s* of Leslie and Jean Judd; *m* 1973, Margot Hazell Patterson; one *s* one *d*. *Educ:* RMCS (BSc Hons Engrg). CEng 1976, MIMechE 1976, FIMechE 2006. Commnd 13th/18th Royal Hussars (Queen Mary's Own), 1970; 22 Air Defence Regt RA Workshop, REME, 1974; Life Guards, 1976; Adjt Comd, Maintenance Corps Troops, REME, 1978–81; Army Staff Coll., 1981–83; Dep. COS, 33 Armd Bde, 1983–85; OC, 5 Armd Workshop, REME, 1985–87; SO1 Directing Staff, Staff Coll., 1987–88; Comdr Maintenance, 1st Armd Div., 1988–90; Col QMG, 1990–92; Chief Maintenance, HQ ARRC, 1992–94; rcds 1994; Dep. COS, G1/G4 HQ ARRC, 1994–98; Dir, Equipt Support Change Mgt Prog., 1998–99; Dir Gen., Equipt Support (Land), 1999–2002, and QMG, 2000–02; GOC 4th Div., 2003–04. *Recreations:* anything mechanical, Rugby, furniture restoration. *Club:* Army and Navy.

**JUDD, Prof. Denis,** PhD; FRHistS; Professor of British and Imperial History, London Metropolitan University (formerly North London Polytechnic, then University of North London), 1990–2004, now Emeritus; Professor of British Imperial History, New York University in London, since 2006; *b* 28 Oct. 1938; *s* of Denis and Joan Judd; *m* 1964, Dorothy Woolf; three *s* one *d*. *Educ:* Magdalen Coll., Oxford (BA Hons Mod. Hist.); Birkbeck Coll., London (PhD; PGCE). Poly., then Univ., of N London, later London Metropolitan Univ., 1964–2004. Visiting Professor: Univ. of California, 2002–05; NY Univ., 2007–. Series Editor, Traveller's History Series, 1989–; Advr, BBC History Mag., 2000–; writer and presenter, BBC Radio. *Publications:* Balfour and the British Empire, 1968, 2nd edn 2015; The Victorian Empire, 1970; Posters of World War Two, 1972; Livingstone in Africa, 1973; George V, 1973, 5th edn 1993; The House of Windsor, 1973; Someone has Blundered: calamities of the British army in the Victorian age, 1973, 3rd edn 2007; Edward VII, 1975; Palmerston, 1975, 2nd edn 2015; The Crimean War, 1976; Eclipse of Kings, 1976; Radical Joe: a life of Joseph Chamberlain, 1977, 3rd edn 2010; The Adventures of Long John Silver, 1977 (Russian edn 2015); Return to Treasure Island, 1978 (Russian edn 2015); Prince Philip, 1980, 3rd edn 1991; (with Peter Slinn) The Evolution of the Modern Commonwealth 1902–80, 1982; Lord Reading, 1982, 2nd edn 2013; King

George VI, 1982, 2nd edn 2012; Alison Uttley: the life of a country child, 1986, 3rd edn 2010; Jawaharlal Nehru, 1993; Empire: the British imperial experience from 1765 to the present, 1996, 4th edn 2012; (with Keith Surridge) The Boer War, 2002, 3rd edn 2013; The Lion and the Tiger: the rise and fall of the British Raj, 2004, 2nd edn 2005; (ed) The Diaries of Alison Uttley, 2009, 2nd edn 2011; regular contribs and reviews for nat. press. *Recreations:* reading, writing, film, theatre, sport (supports QPR), talking, listening, food and wine, travel, the Suffolk coast, playing with and looking after grandchildren, fixing things. *Address:* 20 Mount Pleasant Road, Brondesbury Park, NW10 3EL. *T:* and *Fax:* (020) 8459 1118. *E:* denisjudd@ntlworld.com. *W:* www.denisjudd.com.

**JUDD, Hon. Dame Frances (Jean), (Hon. Dame Frances Pritchard),** DBE 2019; **Hon. Mrs Justice Judd;** a Judge of the High Court, Family Division, since 2019; *b* 13 Feb. 1961; *d* of Christopher and Jean Judd; *m* 1985, David Pritchard; two *s*. *Educ:* King's Sch., Canterbury; New Hall, Cambridge (BA Hons Hist. 1982). Called to the Bar, Middle Temple, 1984, Bencher, 2014; in practice at the Bar, 1984–, specialising in family law; Recorder, 2002–19; QC 2006; Dep. High Court Judge, 2011–19. Hd, Harcourt Chambers, Oxford, 2009–18. Chm., Family Law Bar Assoc., 2018 (Vice-Chm. 2016). *Publications:* (jtly) Contact: The New Deal, 2006; Relocation: a practical guide, 2013, 2016. *Recreations:* cycling, walking, swimming outdoors. *Address:* Royal Courts of Justice, Strand, WC2A 2LL.

**JUDD, Judith Margaret;** Editor-at-Large, Times Educational Supplement, 2007–09 (Associate Editor, 2001–05; Editor, 2005–07); *b* 18 April 1949; *d* of John Berry and Joan Berry (*née* Edge); *m* 1973, Very Rev. Peter Somerset Margesson Judd, *qv*; one *s* one *d*. *Educ:* Bolton Sch.; St Anne's Coll., Oxford (BA Modern History). Reporter, 1972–74, Educn Reporter, 1974–75, Birmingham Post and Birmingham Mail; joined THES, 1975, News Editor, 1977–79; Reporter, 1979–82, Educn Correspondent, 1982–90, Observer; Education Correspondent: Independent on Sunday, 1990–93; Independent, 1991–93; Educn Ed., The Independent and The Independent on Sunday, 1993–2001. Mem. Council, Essex Univ., 2010– (Chm. Council, 2018–; Pro-Chancellor, 2012–). Mem., Adv. Council, Whole Educn, 2010–12 (Mem. Bd, 2012–17). *Recreations:* gardening, reading, walking, singing.

**JUDD, Very Rev. Peter Somerset Margesson;** Dean (formerly Provost) of Chelmsford Cathedral, 1997–2013; *b* 20 Feb. 1949; *s* of William Frank Judd and Norah Margesson Judd (*née* Margesson); *m* 1973, Judith Margaret Berry (*see* J. M. Judd); one *s* one *d*. *Educ:* Charterhouse Sch.; Trinity Hall, Cambridge (MA Architecture); Cuddesdon Coll., Oxford (Cert. Theol.). Ordained deacon, 1974, priest, 1975; Asst Curate, St Philip with St Stephen, Salford, 1974–76; Chaplain, 1976–81, Fellow, 1980–81, Clare Coll., Cambridge; Team Vicar of Hitcham and Dropmore, Burnham Team Ministry, Dio. of Oxford, 1981–88; Vicar, St Mary the Virgin, Iffley, 1988–97; Rural Dean of Cowley, 1995–97. DL Essex, 2009–13. *Recreations:* architecture, art, listening to music, literature, drawing, cooking, fell walking. *Address:* 18 Baycliffe Close, Cambridge CB1 8EE.

**JUDGE,** family name of **Baron Judge**.

**JUDGE,** Baron *cr* 2008 (Life Peer), of Draycote in the County of Warwickshire; **Igor Judge,** Kt 1988; PC 1996; Chief Surveillance Commissioner, 2015–17; Lord Chief Justice of England and Wales, 2008–13; *b* 19 May 1941; *s* of Raymond and Rosa Judge; *m* 1965, Judith Mary Robinson; one *s* two *d*. *Educ:* Oratory Sch., Woodcote; Magdalene Coll., Cambridge (Exhbnr, MA; Hon. Fellow). Harmsworth Exhibnr and Astbury Scholar, Middle Temple. Called to the Bar, Middle Temple, 1963, Bencher, 1987 (Treas., 2014); a Recorder, 1976–88; Prosecuting Counsel to Inland Revenue, 1977–79; QC 1979; a Judge of the High Court, QBD, 1988–96; Leader, 1988, Presiding Judge, 1993–96, Midland and Oxford Circuit; a Lord Justice of Appeal, 1996–2005; Sen. Presiding Judge for England and Wales, 1998–2003; Dep. Chief Justice of England and Wales, 2003–05; Pres., QBD, High Ct of Justice, 2005–08. Vis. Prof. and Distinguished Visitor, KCL, 2013–. Member: Senate, Inns of Court and the Bar, 1980–83, 1984–86; Bar Council, 1987–88; Judicial Studies Bd, 1984–88, 1991–94 and 1996–98 (Chm. Criminal Cttee, 1991–93 and 1996–98). Commissary, Univ. of Cambridge, 2016–. Pres., Selden Soc., 2009–15. Hon. LLD Cantab, 2012. *Publications:* (with Anthony Arlidge) Magna Carta Uncovered, 2014; The Safest Shield, 2015. *Recreations:* history, music, cricket. *Address:* House of Lords, SW1A 0PW.

**JUDGE, Hon. Barbara Singer T.;** *see* Thomas Judge.

**JUDGE, Ian;** international opera and theatre director; *b* 21 July 1946; *s* of Jack and Marjorie Judge. *Educ:* King George V Grammar Sch., Southport; Guildhall Sch. of Music and Drama (Prodn Prize). Joined RSC as an asst dir, 1975; productions include: The Wizard of Oz, 1987; The Comedy of Errors, 1990; Love's Labour's Lost, 1993; Twelfth Night, 1994; A Christmas Carol, 1994; The Relapse, 1995; Troilus and Cressida, 1996; The Merry Wives of Windsor, 1996; *opera:* English National Opera: Faust, 1985; Cavalleria Rusticana and Pagliacci, 1987; Don Quichotte, 1994; La Belle Vivette, 1995; Mephistopheles, 1999; Sir John in Love, 2006; Opera North: Macbeth, 1987; Tosca, 1988; Boris Godunov, 1989; Attila, 1990; Show Boat, 1990 (also at London Palladium); Scottish Opera: Falstaff, 1991; Norma, 1993; Royal Opera House: The Flying Dutchman, 1992; Simon Boccanegra (1857), 1997; Simon Boccanegra (1881), 2008; Los Angeles: Tosca, 1989; Madama Butterfly, 1991; Le Nozze di Figaro, 2004, 2014–15; Roméo et Juliette, 2005; Don Carlo, 2006; Tannhäuser, 2007; Die Gezeichneten, 2010; Melbourne and Sydney: Faust, 1990; Tales of Hoffman, 1992; Kirov, St Petersburg: La Bohème, 2001; Der fliegende Holländer, 2008; Macbeth, Cologne, 1992; Così Fan Tutte, Garsington, 1997; Eugene Onegin, Grange Park Opera, 2000; Falstaff, Paris, 2001; Ernani, Holland, 2002; Salome, NY, 2002; Tannhäuser, Teatro Real, Madrid, 2009; Simon Boccanegra, Canadian Opera Co., Toronto, 2009; A Midsummer Night's Dream, Britten Th., 2009; *theatre:* The Rivals and King Lear, Old Vic, 1977; Chichester: Henry VIII, 1991; Love for Love, 1996; Macbeth, Sydney Th. Co., 1999; *musical:* Merrily We Roll Along, London, Bloomsbury, 1983; Chichester: Oh! Kay, 1984; A Little Night Music, 1990 (also Piccadilly Theatre); West Side Story (Sydney and Melbourne), 1994–96; The Mikado, Savoy Theatre, 2000. *E:* ijudge1@mac.com.

**JUDGE, Richard,** PhD; CEng, FIMechE; CDir; Chief Executive, Health and Safety Executive, 2014–18; *b* 2 Nov. 1962; *s* of Peter Judge and Elspeth Judge; *m* 1998, Susan Thompson; one *d*. *Educ:* Elizabeth Coll., Guernsey; Durham Univ. (BSc Hons Engrg Sci. 1984; PhD 1987). CEng 1990, FIMechE 2006. Various roles, AEA Technology, 1987–2000; Man. Dir, AEA Technol. Rail BV, 2000–03; Gp Dir, AEA Envmt, 2003–05; an Interim Manager, 2005–07; Chief Exec., CEFAS, 2007–12; Inspector Gen. and Chief Exec., Insolvency Service, 2012–14. CDir 2011. FInstD 2011.

**JUDGE, Simon Patrick;** Director, Cabinet Office, 2018–19; *b* 10 Nov. 1959; *s* of late Harry George Judge and of Elizabeth Mary Judge; *m* 1985, (Isobel) Jane Cox; three *s*. *Educ:* Banbury Sch.; Oxford Sch.; Clare Coll., Cambridge (BA 1981; MMath 2011). Warwick Business Sch. (Dip. 2008). CPFA 2009. Joined HM Treasury, 1985; Private Sec. to Paymaster Gen., 1987–88; Asst Sec., 1994; various posts, incl. Hd of Inf. Systems, 1995–97; Planning and Finance Div., DSS, subseq. Welfare to Work Directorate, DWP, 1999–2005; Dir of Financial Strategy, DCA, later MoJ, 2005–08; Finance Director: DCMS, 2009–12; DfE, 2012–16; Dir, People and Capability, Govt Finance Function, 2017–18. *Recreations:* canal boating, choral singing. *E:* simon@judgefamily.org.uk.

**JUDSON, Air Vice-Marshal Robert William;** Managing Director, Bob Judson Consulting Ltd, since 2019; *b* Harlington, Middx, 4 June 1962; *s* of Alan Sheffield Judson and Brenda Jane Judson; *m* 2006, Saab Benning. *Educ:* Christ's Hosp., Horsham. Officer Cadet, RAF Coll., Cranwell, 1980; jsdc 1997; Officer Commanding: No 6 Sqdn, 1992–2002; RAF Coningsby, 2004–06; HCSC 2007; rcds 2007; Comdr, Kandahar Airfield, Afghanistan, 2008; Hd, Targeting and Information Ops, MoD, 2008–10; Liaison Officer of CDS to US Chm., Jt Chiefs, 2011; ACDS (Ops), 2011–13; Dir, Jt Warfare, 2013–14; Dir, Deloitte LLP, 2015–19. FRAeS 2007; FCMI 2014; MInstD 2015. *Recreations:* ski-ing, scuba diving, poor quality golf!, motor cycling. *Address:* Carabrae, Tottingworth Park, Broad Oak, Heathfield, East Sussex TN21 8XJ. *Club:* Royal Air Force.

**JUGNAUTH, Rt Hon. Sir Aneerood,** GCSK 2003; KCMG 1988; PC 1987; Grand Comdr, Order of Star and Key of Indian Ocean, 2003; QC (Mauritius) 1980; Prime Minister of Mauritius, 1982–95, 2000–03 and 2014–17; Minister of Defence and Minister for Rodrigues and National Development Unit, since 2014; Minister Mentor, since 2017; *b* 29 March 1930; *m* Sarojni Devi Ballah; one *s* one *d*. *Educ:* Roman Catholic Aided Sch., Palma, Mauritius; Regent Coll., Quatre Bornes. Called to the Bar, Lincoln's Inn, 1954 (Hon. Bencher, 2011). Teacher, New Eton Coll., 1948; worked in Civil Service, 1949. MLA Rivière du Rempart, 1963–67, Piton-Rivière du Rempart, 1976, 1982, 1983, 1987, 1991 and 2000; Town Councillor, Vacoas-Phoenix, 1964; Minister of State for Develt, 1965–67; Minister of Labour, 1967; Leader of the Opposition, 1976–82; Minister of Finance, 1983–84 and 1990–91; Pres. of Mauritius, 2003–12; Minister of Home Affairs, 2014–17. Dist Magistrate, 1967–69; Crown Counsel, 1969; Sen. Crown Counsel, 1971. Attended London Constitutional Conf., 1965. Pres., Mouvement Militant Mauricien, 1973–82; Leader, Mouvement Socialiste Militant, 1983–2003. Dr *hc* Aix-en-Provence, 1985; Hon. DCL Mauritius, 1985; Dr of Law *hc* Chennai, 2001; Hon. Dr Middx, 2009. Grand Prix, Order of La Pléiade, Assemblée parlementaire de la Francophonie, 1984. Order of Rising Sun (1st cl.) (Japan), 1988; Grand Officier, Ordre de la Légion d'Honneur (France), 1990. *Address:* La Caverne No 1, Vacoas, Mauritius.

**JUKES, Paul;** Chief Executive, North Lanarkshire Council, 2015–18; *b* Gateshead, 17 Oct. 1958; *s* of John and Mary Jukes; *m* 1978, Maureen Bartley; two *s*. *Educ:* St Oswald's Primary Sch., Gateshead; St Aidan's Secondary Sch., Gateshead; Newcastle Poly. (Dip.); Strathclyde Univ. (MSc). Tech. Advr, British Seed Houses, 1985–87; Asst Dir, Leisure Services, Motherwell DC, 1987–95; Hd of Service, 1995–99, Dir, Community Services, 1999–2015, N Lanarks Council. *Recreations:* squash, badminton, road cycling.

**JULIAN, Prof. Desmond Gareth,** CBE 1993; MD, FRCP; Consultant Medical Director, British Heart Foundation, 1987–93; *b* 24 April 1926; *s* of Frederick Bennett Julian and Jane Frances Julian (*née* Galbraith); *m* 1st, 1956, Mary Ruth Jessup (decd); one *s* one *d*; 2nd, 1988, Claire Marley. *Educ:* Leighton Park Sch.; St John's Coll., Cambridge; Middlesex Hosp. MB BChir (Cantab) 1948; MA 1953; MD 1954; FRCPE 1967; FRCP 1970; FRACP 1970; FACC 1985. Surgeon Lieut, RNVR, 1949–51. Med. Registrar, Nat. Heart Hosp., 1955–56; Res. Fellow, Peter Bent Brigham Hosp., Boston, 1957–58; Sen. Reg., Royal Inf., Edinburgh, 1958–61; Cons. Cardiologist, Sydney Hosp., 1961–64, Royal Inf., Edinburgh, 1964–74; Prof. of Cardiology, Univ. of Newcastle upon Tyne, 1975–86. Mem., MRC Systems Bd, 1980–84. Pres., British Cardiac Soc., 1985–87; Second Vice-Pres., RCP, 1990–91. Hon. MD: Gothenburg, 1987; Edinburgh, 1997. Gold Medal, European Soc. of Cardiology, 1998; Mackenzie Medal, British Cardiac Soc., 2003; Internat. Service Award, Amer. Coll. of Cardiol., 2005. Editor, European Heart Jl, 1980–88. *Publications:* Cardiology, 1972, 8th edn 2004; (ed) Angina Pectoris, 1975, 2nd edn 1984; Acute Myocardial Infarction, 1967; (ed) Diseases of the Heart, 1989, 2nd edn 1995; Coronary Heart Disease: the facts, 1991; contribs to med. jls, particularly on coronary disease. *Recreation:* writing. *Address:* Flat 1, 7 Netherhall Gardens, NW3 5RN. *T:* (020) 7435 8254.

**JULIEN, Isaac,** CBE 2017; RA 2017; artist; Distinguished Professor of the Arts, University of California, Santa Cruz, since 2019; *b* London, 21 Feb. 1960; *s* of Austin and Rose Julien; *m* 2007, Mark Nash. *Educ:* Central St Martin's Sch. of Art (BA Fine Art Film 1984). Postdoctoral res., Les Entrepreneurs de L'Audiovisuel Européen, Brussels. Vis. Lectr, Schs of Afro-American and Visual Envmtl Studies, Harvard Univ., 1998–2002; Res. Fellow, Goldsmiths' Coll., Univ. of London, 1998–2003; Faculty Mem., Ind. Study Prog., Whitney Mus. of American Art, NY, 2006–13. *Works* include: film/audiovisual installations: Looking for Langston, 1989; The Long Road to Mazatlán, 1999; Vagabondia, 2000; Baadasssss Cinema, 2002; Paradise Omeros, 2002; Lost Boundaries, 2003; Baltimore, 2003; True North, 2004; Fantôme Afrique, 2005; Fantôme Créole, 2005; Western Union: Small Boats, 2007; Derek, 2008; Dungeness, 2008; Ten Thousand Waves, 2010; Kapital, 2013; Playtime, 2013; Stones Against Diamonds, 2015; Lessons of the Hour, 2019: Lina Bo Bardi: A Marvellous Entanglement, 2019; solo exhibitions include: Victoria Miro Gall., London, 1999, 2000, 2003, 2005, 2010, 2014, 2017, 2019; Mus. of Contemp. Art, Miami, Pompidou Centre, Paris, 2005; Nat. Mus. of Contemp. Art, Lisbon, 2008; Mus. Brandhorst, Munich, 2009; Bass Mus., Miami, 2010; Mus. of Contemp. Art, San Diego, 2012; Art Inst., Chicago, MOMA, NY, 2013; De Pont Mus., Netherlands, 2015; Univ. Mus. of Contemp. Art, Mexico City, MAC, Niterói, Rio de Janeiro, 2016; Royal Ontario Mus., Toronto, 2017; Mori Art Mus., Tokyo, 2018; gp exhibns include RA Summer Exhibn, 2017 (Charles Wollaston Award), 2018, 2019. Mem. Bd, Parasol Unit, 2015–. Trustee, Art Place Foundn, San Antonio, USA, 1999–; Zeitz Mus. of Contemp. Art Africa, Cape Town, SA, 2015–; Art Monthly, 2016–; Art Fund, 2016–. Hon. DA Sch. of Art Inst., Chicago, 2019. *Publications:* The Film Art of Isaac Julien, 2000; Isaac Julien: True North, 2005; Isaac Julien: Love/Hate, 2005; Isaac Julien: True North/Fantôme Afrique, 2006; Western Union: Small Boats, 2009; Ten Thousand Waves, 2020; Isaac Julien: Riot, 2013; Isaac Julien: Looking for Langston, 2017. *Recreations:* theatre, opera, art, dance, cinema. *Address:* Isaac Julien Studio, Ground Floor Hutley Wharf, 29 Branch Place, N1 5PW. *T:* (020) 7837 7097. *E:* info@isaacjulien.com.

**JULIEN, Michael Frederick,** FCA; FCT; Chairman, First Choice Holidays PLC (formerly Owners Abroad Group plc), 1993–97; *b* 22 March 1938; *s* of late Robert Auguste François and Olive Rita (*née* Evans); *m* 1963, Ellen Martinsen; one *s* two *d*. *Educ:* St Edward's Sch., Oxford. Price Waterhouse & Co., 1958–67; other commercial appts, 1967–76, incl. Gp Finance Dir, Lloyds Insurance Brokers and Underwriters, Willis Faber and CE Heath; Gp Finance Dir, BICC, 1976–83; Exec. Dir, Finance and Planning, Midland Bank, 1983–86; Man. Dir, Finance and Administration, Guinness PLC, 1987–88 (non-exec. Dir, 1987–88); Gp Chief Exec., Storehouse PLC, 1988–92. Director (non-executive): Littlewoods Orgn plc, 1981–86; Medeva PLC, 1993–98. *Recreations:* family, travel. *E:* michael@julienco.com.

**JULIUS, Prof. Anthony Robert,** PhD; Deputy Chairman, Mishcon de Reya, since 2009 (Consultant, 1998–2009); Professor of Law and the Arts, University College London, since 2017; *b* 16 July 1956; *s* of Morris and Myrna Julius; *m* 1st, 1979, Judith Bernie (marr. diss. 1998); two *s* two *d*; 2nd, 1999, Dina Rabinovitch (*d* 2007); one *s*; 3rd, 2009, Katarina Lester; one *s*. *Educ:* City of London Sch.; Jesus Coll., Cambridge (MA); University Coll. London (PhD 1992). Admitted Solicitor, 1981; Mishcon de Reya: Partner, 1984–98; Head of Litigation, 1988–98; Dir, Mishcon Acad., 2015–17. Institute of Jewish Policy Research: Dir, 1996–2000; Mem. Council, 2000–04; Chair, Law Cttee, 1998–2000; Mem., Appeals Cttee, Dermatrust, 1999–2004; foreword, report on holocaust denial and UK law, 2000; Member: Adv. Bd, Community Security Trust, 2007–; Mayor of London's Race and Faith Inquiry, 2009–10; Advancing Human Rights, 2011–16. Chairman: London Consortium, 2005–13; Jewish Chronicle, 2011–13; City and Guards Gp, 2012–; Oxera LLP, 2014–. Chair, Diana, Princess of Wales Meml Fund, 1997–99, Vice Pres., 2002–13; Mem., Fest. Council, The Word. Vis. Prof., Birkbeck, Univ. of London, 2005–17. Chm. Mgt Bd, Centre for Cultural Analysis, Theory and History, Univ. of Leeds, 2001–05. Trustee: Beit Halochem, 2012–17; Swarowski Foundn, 2013–16; Phenomen Trust, 2015–; PEN, 2017–. Hon. PhD Haifa, 2005. *Publications*: T. S. Eliot, anti-Semitism, and literary form, 1995, 2nd edn 2002; (contrib.) Law and Literature, 1999; Idolizing Pictures, 2001; Transgressions: the offences of art, 2002; Trials of the Diaspora: a history of anti-Semitism in England, 2010. *Address*: (office) Africa House, 70 Kingsway, WC2B 6AH. *T*: (020) 3321 7000.

**JULIUS, Dame DeAnne (Shirley),** DCMG 2013; CBE 2002; PhD; Chairman: Council, University College London, since 2014; Royal Institute of International Affairs, 2003–12 (Member Council, 2000–03); *b* 14 April 1949; *d* of Marvin G. Julius and Maxine M. Julius; *m* 1976, Ian Harvey; one *s* one *d*. *Educ*: Iowa State Univ. (BSc Econs 1970); Univ. of Calif at Davis (MA 1974; PhD Econs 1975). Economic Analyst, US CS, 1970–71; Lectr, Univ. of Calif at Santa Barbara, 1975; project economist, then econ. advr, World Bank, 1975–82; Man. Dir, Logan Associates Inc., 1983–86; Prog. Dir for Econs, RIIA, 1986–89; Chief Economist: Shell Internat., 1989–93; British Airways, 1993–97; Chm., British Airways Pension Investment Mgt Ltd, 1995–97. Mem., Monetary Policy Cttee, 1997–2001, Mem. of Court, 2001–04, Bank of England. Chairman: Banking Code Review Gp, 2006–07; Public Services Industry Review, 2007–08. Non-executive Director: BP, 2001–11; Lloyds TSB, 2001–07; Serco, 2001–07; Roche, 2002–16; Jones Lang LaSalle, 2008–; Deloitte LLP, 2011–14; Intercontinental Exchange Benchmark Administration, 2016–; Sen. Advr, Fathom Financial Consultants, 2008–11; Member: Internat. Panel, Temasek, 2010–17; Internat. Panel, China Investment Corp., 2016–. Vice Chm., Inst. Develt Studies, 2000–03. Vice Pres., Soc. of Business Economists, 2002–17. Lady Usher of the Blue Rod, Order of St Michael and St George, 2016–. *Publications*: (jtly) Appropriate Sanitation Alternatives: a technical and economic appraisal, 1982; (jtly) The Monetary Implications of the 1992 Process, 1990; Global Companies and Public Policy: the growing challenge of foreign direct investment, 1990; (with A. Mashayekhi) Economics of Natural Gas: pricing, planning and policy, 1990; (contrib.) Beyond the Dollar, 2010. *Recreations*: ski-ing, sailing, tending bonsai. *Address*: University College London, Gower Street, WC1E 6BT.

**JULLIEN, Beverley Gail;** Chief Executive, Mothers' Union, since 2015; *b* Walton-on-Thames, 31 Jan. 1958; *d* of Robert William Salt and Olive Salt; *m* 1991, Paul Jullien; one *s* one *d*. *Educ*: St George's Sch., Harpenden; United World Coll. of Atlantic; Selwyn Coll., Cambridge (BA Mod. Langs 1980); McGill Univ. (Masters Internat. Mgt 2000). CDir 2007. ICI Pharmaceuticals: Mkt Res. Exec., 1980–81; Sales Exec., 1982–83; Mktg Asst, 1984–87; Product Manager, Germany, 1988–89; Mktg Manager, UK, 1989–91; Business Develt, Central and E Europe, 1991–92; Zeneca, later AstraZeneca: Gen. Manager, Portugal, 1993–95; Hd, Global Health Econs, 1995–96; Hd, Urol. Global Business Unit, 1997–99; Mktg Co. Pres., UK, 1999–2001; Vice Pres. Strategic Planning, Emerging Mkts, 2002–06; on secondment to British Olympic Assoc., FTSE-BOA Partnerships, 2007–10; Pro-Vice-Chancellor (Ext.), London Southbank Univ., 2010–14; sabbatical, 2014–15. Non-executive Director: Lambeth Conference Co., 2018–; Anglican Communion Fund, 2018–; Five Talents UK, 2019–. *Recreations*: family, running (London Marathon), cycling (Ride London100), swimming, dog walking, cinema. *Address*: Mothers' Union, Mary Sumner House, 24 Tufton Street, SW1P 3RB. *T*: (020) 7222 5533. *E*: bev.jullien@mothersunion.org.

**JUMAN, Curtis Mark;** Finance Director, Ofcom, since 2018; *b* London, 28 March 1968; *s* of Christopher and Nazina Juman; *m* 1990, Heather Revnell; one *s* two *d*. *Educ*: Kingsmead Comprehensive Sch.; Univ. of Birmingham (BSc Hons Chem.). CPFA 1994, FCPFA. Sen. Auditor, Nat. Audit Office, 1989–97; Sen. Manager, Deloitte, 1997–2000; Dep. Dir, Finance, Ofgem, 2000; Audit Dir, 2000–02, Dir, Finance Strategy, 2002–04, DTI; Change Dir, Finance, DWP, 2004–06; Dir, Finance Control, DTI, subseq. BERR, 2006–07; Dir of Finance, UKTI, 2007–12; Chief Resources Officer, Equality and Human Rights Commn, 2012–16; Dir of Finance and Dep. Receiver Gen., Westminster Abbey, 2016–18. Mem. Bd and Chm., Gp Audit Cttee, LHA-ASRA Housing Gp, 2006–12; Mem., Audit Cttee, Open Univ., 2010–12. Mem. Council, 2004–10, Chm., Central Govt Panel, 2005–10, CIPFA. *Recreations*: spending time with my young family, contributing to the life of Warlingham Methodist Church, watching sci-fi movies. *Address*: Ofcom, Riverside House, 2a Southwark Bridge Road, SE1 9HA.

**JUNCKER, Dr Jean-Claude;** President, European Commission, 2014–19; *b* Redange-Attert, 9 Dec. 1954; *m* 1979, Christiane Frising. *Educ*: Secondary Sch., Clairefontaine, Belgium; Univ. of Strasbourg (Dr Public Law 1979). Parly Sec., Christian Social Party, 1979–82; State Sec. for Labour and Social Affairs, 1982–84; Mem., Chamber of Deputies, Luxembourg, 1984; Minister of: Labour and Minister i/c Budget, 1984–89; Labour and of Finance, 1989–95; Labour and Employment, 1995–99; Prime Minister, Minister of State and Minister for the Treasury (formerly Minister of Finance), 1995–2013. Pres., Christian Social Party, 1990–95. Pres., Eurogroup, 2005–13.

**JUNG, Prof. Roland Tadeusz,** MD; FRCP, FRCPE; Consultant Physician in Endocrinology and Diabetes, Ninewells Hospital, Dundee, 1982–2008; Chief Scientist, Scottish Government (formerly Executive) Health Department, 2001–07; *b* 8 Feb. 1948; *s* of Tadeusz Jung and Margaret (Pearl) Jung; *m* 1974, Felicity Helen King; one *d*. *Educ*: Pembroke Coll., Cambridge (BA 1969, MA 1972; MB, BChir 1972, MD 1980); St Thomas's Hosp. Med. Sch., London. FRCPE 1985; FRCP 1989. MRC Clinical Scientific Officer, Dunn Nutrition Unit, Cambridge, 1977–79; Sen. Registrar in Endocrinol. and Diabetes, RPMS, Hammersmith Hosp., 1980–82. Ext. Examr in Medicine, Univ. of Oxford, 2002–08. Rowett Institute of Nutrition and Health, University of Aberdeen: Mem., Prog. Mgt Cttee, 2007–12 (Chm., 2010–12); Mem., Scientific Consultative Gp, 2010–12. Hon. Prof. of Medicine, Univ. of Dundee, 1998–; Vis. Prof., Univ. of Southampton, 2009–. *Publications*: Colour Atlas of Obesity, 1990; chapters in books, original papers and reviews. *Recreations*: gardening, walking, volunteer guide for NT and HHA.

**JUNGELS, Dr Pierre Jean Marie Henri,** Hon. CBE 1989; Chairman, Velocys (formerly Oxford Catalysts) plc, since 2006; *b* 18 Feb. 1944; *s* of Henri and Jeanne Jungels; *m* 1988, Caroline Benc; one step *s* one step *d*; one *s* one *d* from former marriage. *Educ*: Univ. of Liège (Ing. Civ. 1967); California Inst. of Technology (PhD 1973). Petroleum Engr, Shell, 1973–74; Dist Manager, 1975–77, General Manager and Chief Exec., 1977–80, Petrangol (Angola); Man. Dir and Chief Exec., Petrofina UK, 1980–89; Exec. Dir, Downstream, Petrofina Gp, 1989–92; Exec. Dir, Exploration and Production, Petrofina Group, 1992–95; Man. Dir, Exploration and Production, British Gas, 1996; Chief Exec., Enterprise Oil plc, 1997–2001. Chairman: OHM plc, 2003–08; Rockhopper Exploration plc, 2005–16; Director: Imperial Tobacco plc, 2002–12; Woodside Petroleum Ltd, 2002–12; Baker Hughes Inc., 2006–17. Pres., Inst. of Petroleum, 1986–88 and 2002–03 (Jt Pres., Energy Inst., 2003). *Recreations*: tennis, shooting. *Address*: Enborne Chase, Enborne, Newbury, Berks RG20 0HD.

**JUNGIUS, Vice-Adm. Sir James (George),** KBE 1977; Supreme Allied Commander Atlantic's Representative in Europe, 1978–80, retired; Vice Lord-Lieutenant of Cornwall, 1995–98; *b* 15 Nov. 1923; *s* of Major E. J. T. Jungius, MC; *m* 1949, Rosemary Frances Turquand Matthey (*d* 2005); two *s* (and one *s* decd). *Educ*: RNC, Dartmouth. Served War of 1939–45 in Atlantic incl. Northern Patrol and passage to Archangel, and Mediterranean; Malta convoys and Commando Ops in Adriatic (despatches). Specialised in Navigation in 1946, followed by series of appts as Navigating Officer at sea and instructing ashore. Comdr, Dec. 1955; CO, HMS Wizard, 1956–57; Admty, 1958–59; Exec. Officer, HMS Centaur, 1960–61; Captain, 1963; Naval Staff, 1964–65; CO, HMS Lynx, 1966–67; Asst Naval Attaché, Washington, DC, 1968–70; CO, HMS Albion, 1971–72; Rear-Adm., 1972; Asst Chief of Naval Staff (Operational Requirements), 1972–74; Vice-Adm., 1974; Dep. Supreme Allied Comdr Atlantic, 1975–77. County Pres., Cornwall, RBL, 1995–2004. Vice-Chm., SW War Pensions Cttee, 1996–2000. Fellow, Woodard Corp., 1988–95. Gov., Grenville Coll., 1981–96. CCMI. DL Cornwall, 1982. CStJ 1995 (Chm., St John Council for Cornwall, 1987–95); Ushakov Medal (Russia), 2015.

**JUNIPER, Anthony Thomas,** CBE 2017; Chair, Natural England, since 2019; Fellow, University of Cambridge Institute (formerly Programme) for Sustainability Leadership (formerly for Industry), since 2013 (Senior Associate, 2008–13); *b* 24 Sept. 1960; *s* of late Austin Wilfred Juniper and Constance Margaret Juniper; *m* 1990, Susan Jane Sparkes; two *s* one *d*. *Educ*: Bristol Univ. (BSc Zool./Psychol. 1983); University Coll. London (MSc Conservation 1988). Worked with school children on nature conservation, S Oxon Countryside Educn Trust, 1984–85; Parrot Conservation Officer, Internat. Council for Bird Preservation, 1989–90; Friends of the Earth: Sen. Tropical Rainforest Campaigner, 1990–93; Sen. Biodiversity Campaigner, 1993–97; Campaign Dir, 1997–98; Policy and Campaigns Dir, 1998–2003; Exec. Dir, England, Wales and NI, 2003–08; Vice Chm., Friends of the Earth Internat., 2000–08; Ed.-in-Chief, GREEN Mag. (formerly Nat. Geographic Mag. Green Supplement), 2009–12; Founding Mem., Robertsbridge Gp, 2010–19; Exec. Dir for Advocacy and Campaigns, WWF UK, 2018–19. Mem., ACEVO, 2001–08. Special Adviser: Prince of Wales' Rainforests Project, 2008–10; Prince of Wales' Internat. Sustainability Unit, 2010–18. Member, Advisory Board: BBC Wildlife mag., 1998–; NCC, 2002–05; Ecologist mag., 2008–; Sandbag, 2008–. Columnist, Sunday Times, 2009–10; regular contributor: The Guardian, 1995–; The Independent, 1995–; Resurgence and Ecologist, 2000–. Advr on Climate Change, Sci. Mus., 2009–; Chm., Adv. Bd, Action for Renewables, 2011–. Mem. Council, FFI, 2013–. President: Soc. for the Envmt, 2012–; Wildlife Trusts, 2015–19. Founding Trustee and Bd Mem., Stop Climate Chaos, 2005–08; Mem. Bd, Climate for Ideas, 2008–12; Trustee: Beds, Cambs and Northants Wildlife Trust, 2009–15; Ecologist-Resurgence Mag., 2012–. Patron, Inst. for Ecology and Envmtl Mgt, 2012–. Contested (Green) Cambridge, 2010. FRSA 2013. Hon. FIEnvSc 2009. Hon. DSc: Bristol, 2013; Plymouth, 2013. Rothschild Medal, 2009. *Publications*: (with Mike Parr) Parrots: a guide to the parrots of the world, 1998 (McColvin Medal, LA, 1999); Spix's Macaw, 2002; How many light bulbs does it take to change a planet?, 2007; Saving Planet Earth, 2007; (with HRH The Prince of Wales and Ian Skelly) Harmony, 2010; What Has Nature Ever Done For Us?: how money really does grow on trees, 2013; What Nature Does for Britain, 2015; What's Really Happening to Our Planet?, 2016; (with HRH The Prince of Wales and Emily Shuckburgh) Climate Change, 2017; Rainforest: dispatches from Earth's most vital frontlines, 2018; contrib. to various scientific pubns. *Recreations*: natural history, fishing. *Address*: University of Cambridge Institute for Sustainability Leadership, 1 Trumpington Street, Cambridge CB2 1QA; Peters, Fraser and Dunlop, 55 New Oxford Street, WC1A 1BS. *E*: tdavid@pfd.co.uk. *W*: www.tonyjuniper.com.

**JUNKIN, (William) Roy,** CB 2008; Deputy Director of Public Prosecutions for Northern Ireland, 1998–2008 (Acting Director, Jan.–July 2007); *b* 29 May 1948; *o s* of William John Junkin and Elizabeth Margaret Junkin (*née* Parker); *m* 1972, Valerie Ann Elizabeth Barbour; two *s*. *Educ*: Rainey Endowed Sch.; Queen's Univ. Belfast (LLB); Univ. of Ulster (BA Public Sector Mgt). Called to the Bar of NI, 1971 (Jt 1st, Bernard J. Fox Prize); called to the Bar, Gray's Inn, 1985, Bencher, 2006. Tutor in Law, QUB, 1970; Lectr in Law and Jurisp., QUB, and Asst Parly Draftsman, Parlt of NI, 1971–72; Lectr in Law, Univ. of Ulster, 1973; Government Legal Service, Northern Ireland, Department of Public Prosecutions: Professional Officer, 1974; Asst Sec., 1977; Under Sec., 1989. Part-time Vis. Lectr, Sch. of Public Admin, Univ. of Ulster, 1981–82. Mem., Exec. Bureau, Consultative Council of Prosecutors Gen. of Europe, Council of Europe, 2006–08. Member: Internat. Bar Assoc.; Human Rights Inst., Internat. Bar Assoc., 1998–2008; Eurojustice, 1998–2008; Internat. Assoc. of Prosecutors, 1998–2008 (Mem., Rev. Gp on Standards for Prosecutors, 2006–08); Statutory Cttee, Pharmaceutical Soc. of NI, 2008–12. Gov., Castlereagh Coll. of Further Educn, 2002–07. *Publications*: (jtly) Council of Europe, Budapest Guidelines: European guidelines on ethics and conduct for Public Prosecutors; contribs to Eurojustice and CCPE, notes and reviews in legal periodicals. *Recreations*: fly fishing, golf, cooking. *Address*: c/o Public Prosecution Service, 93 Chichester Street, Belfast BT1 3JR.

**JUNOR, Penelope Jane, (Penny);** journalist, writer and broadcaster; *b* 6 Oct. 1949; *d* of Sir John Junor and Pamela Mary (*née* Welsh); *m* 1970, James Stewart Leith; three *s* one *d*. *Educ*: Benenden Sch.; Univ. of St Andrews. Feature writer, 19 mag., 1970–71; reporter, Londoner's Diary, Evening Standard, 1971–74; freelance, 1974–; columnist, Private Eye, 1977–82; television: reporter, Collecting Now, 1981; Presenter: 4 What It's Worth, 1982–89; The Afternoon Show, 1984–85; The Travel Show, 1988–97. Gen. Ed., John Lewis Partnership, 1993–99. Patron: Women's Health Concern, 2002–; Cirencester beat Self-Help Gp, 2005–. Trustee: beat, 2006–12; Central London Samaritans, 2008–10. *Publications*: Newspaper, 1979; Diana, Princess of Wales, 1982; Babyware, 1982; Margaret Thatcher: wife, mother, politician, 1983; Burton, the Man Behind the Myth, 1985; Charles, 1987; (ed) What Every Woman Needs to Know, 1988; Queen Elizabeth II: a pictorial celebration of her reign, 1991; Charles and Diana: portrait of a marriage, 1991; The Major Enigma, 1993; Charles: victim or villain?, 1998; Home Truths: life around my father, 2002; The Firm: the troubled life of the House of Windsor, 2005; Pattie Boyd: wonderful today, 2007; (with Sir Cliff Richard) My Life, My Way, 2008; The Man Who Lives With Wolves, 2010; Prince William: born to be King, 2012; Prince Harry: brother, soldier, son, 2014; The Duchess: the untold story, 2017; All the Queen's Corgis: the story of Elizabeth II and her most faithful companions: corgis, dorgis and gundogs, 2018. *Recreations*: walking, dogs and cats. *Address*: c/o Jane Turnbull, Barn Cottage, Veryan, Truro, Cornwall TR2 5QA. *T*: (01872) 501317. *E*: jane.turnbull@btinternet.com; Hilary Knight Management, Grange Farm, Church Lane, Old, Northants NN6 9QZ. *T*: (01604) 781818. *E*: hilary@hkmanagement.co.uk.

**JUPE, George Percival;** Under Secretary, Ministry of Agriculture, Fisheries and Food, 1979–90; *b* 6 April 1930; *s* of Frederick Stuart Jupe and Elizabeth (*née* Clayton); unmarried. *Educ*: Sandown Grammar Sch., IoW; Hertford Coll., Oxford. Ministry of Agriculture, Fisheries and Food: Asst Principal, 1955; Principal, 1960; Asst Sec., 1970–79: Eggs and Poultry, and Potatoes Divs, 1970–74; Internat. Fisheries Div., 1975–78; Emergencies, Food

Quality and Pest Controls Gp, 1979–85; Dir, ADAS Admin, 1985–88; Horticulture, Seeds, Plant Health and Flood Defence Gp, 1988–90. *Recreations:* hill walking, gardening, music. *Address:* 29 Belmore Road, Lymington, Hants SO41 3NU.

**JUPP, Elisabeth Anne;** an Upper Tribunal Judge (Administrative Appeals Chamber) (formerly a Social Security and Child Support Commissioner), 2001–11; a Deputy Upper Tribunal Judge (part-time) (Administrative Appeals Chamber), 2012–17; *b* 4 April 1944; *d* of Alfred Barrett Tebb and Sarah Tebb (*née* Burnham); *m* 1968, Rev. Dr Peter Creffield Jupp; two *s*. *Educ:* Easingwold Sch.; King's Coll. London (LLB 1966). Admitted Solicitor, 1969; Partner, Alexanders, London, 1972–2001. Dep. Social Security and Child Support Comr, 1997–2001; Chm. (pt-time), Pensions Appeal Tribunal, 2001–14. Chm., Ministerial Trng Cttee, URC, 1987–92. Member: Council, Mansfield Coll., Oxford, 1984–88; Mgt Cttee, Westminster Coll., Cambridge, 2010–13; Trustee: Homerton Coll., Cambridge, 1992–2010; Hospital of St John the Evangelist and St Anne in Okeham, 2018–. *Recreations:* gardening, reading, poetry, theatre.

*See also* M. H. B. Jupp.

**JUPP, Miles Hugh Barrett;** actor and writer; *b* London, 8 Sept. 1979; *s* of Rev. Dr Peter Creffield Jupp and Elisabeth Anne Jupp, *qv*; *m* 2008, Rachel Boase; four *s* one *d*. *Educ:* Univ. of Edinburgh (MA Hons Divinity 2005). *Television* includes: Rev, 2010–14; The Thick of It, 2009, 2012; In and Out of the Kitchen, 2015; Howard's End, 2017; The Crown, 2017; Bad Move, 2017–18; The Durrells, 2018–19; *films* include: Made in Dagenham, 2010; The Monuments Men, 2013; The Look of Love, 2014; Rosewater, 2015; Journey's End, 2017; The Man Who Invented Christmas, 2017; *radio* includes: In and Out of the Kitchen, 2011–15; host, The News Quiz, Radio 4, 2015–19; *theatre* includes: A Day in the Death of Joe Egg, Citizen's, Glasgow, 2011; People, NT, 2012–13; Neville's Island, Duke of York's, 2014; Rules for Living, NT, 2015; Miles Jupp: Songs of Freedom, UK tour, 2017; The Life I Lead, Park Th. and UK tour, 2019. *Publications:* Fibber in the Heat, 2012, 2nd edn 2014; Egg and Soldiers, 2017, 2nd edn 2018. *Recreations:* reading, walking, generally faffing about. *Address:* c/o Molly Wansell, 42 Management, 8 Flitcroft Street, WC2H 8DL. *T:* (020) 7292 0554.

**JUPPÉ, Alain Marie;** Minister of Foreign and European Affairs, France, 2011–12; Mayor of Bordeaux, 1995–2004 and 2006–19; Member, Constitutional Council of France, since 2019; *b* 15 Aug. 1945; *s* of Robert Juppé and Marie Darroze; *m* 1st, 1965, Christine Leblond (marr. diss.); one *s* one *d*; 2nd, 1993, Isabelle Bodin; one *d*. *Educ:* Lycées Victor-Duruy, Mont-de-Marsan and Louis-le-Grand, Paris; Ecole Normale Supérieure (Dr in Classical Langs); Inst. of Political Studies; Nat. Sch. of Admin. Finance Inspector, 1972; Asst to Prime Minister Jacques Chirac, 1976; Advr to Minister for Co-operation, 1976–78; MEP, 1984–86; Deputy for Paris, 1988–93, for Bordeaux, 1997–2004, National Assembly; Dep. Minister of Finance, and Govt Spokesman, 1986–88; Minister of Foreign Affairs, France, 1993–95; Prime Minister of France, 1995–97; Minister of Environment, Energy and Transport, 2007; Minister of Defence and Veterans Affairs, 2010–11. Rassemblement pour la République: Nat. Deleg., 1976–78; Nat. Sec., 1984–86; Gen. Sec., 1988–95; Pres., 1995–97. Adviser to Mayor of Paris, 1978; Dir of Finance and Economic Affairs, City of Paris, 1980–81; Mem., Paris City Council, 1983–95; Dep. Mayor of Paris, i/c Finance, 1983–95. Chm., Union for a Popular Movt, 2002–04. *Publications:* La Tentation de Venise, 1993; Entre Nous, 1996; Montesquieu le Moderne, 1999; Entre Quatre-Yeux, 2001; France mon pays: lettres d'un voyageur, 2006; Je ne mangerai plus de cerises en hiver, 2009; La Politique, telle qu'elle meurt de ne pas être, 2011; Mes chemins pour l'école, 2015; Pour un Etat fort, 2016; Cinq ans pour l'emploi, 2016; Dictionnaire amoureux de Bordeaux, 2018. *Address:* Constitutional Council, 2 rue de Montpensier, 75001 Paris, France.

**JURATOWITCH, Benjamin;** QC 2017; Arbitration Partner, since 2013, and Head, Public International Law Practice, since 2016, Freshfields Bruckhaus Deringer LLP (Co-Head, Public International Law Practice, 2014–16); *b* Brisbane, 1978; *s* of Timothy Juratowitch and Michele Juratowitch; *m* 2004, Ingrid Barnsley; one *s* three *d*. *Educ:* St Joseph's Coll., Brisbane; Univ. of Queensland (BA, LLB); New Coll., Oxford (BCL; DPhil 2007). Admitted solicitor: Qld, Australia, 2003; England and Wales, 2010. Joined Freshfields Bruckhaus Deringer, 2008. Lectr, Univ. of Paris V, 2009–; Vis. Fellow, LSE, 2013–14. *Publications:* (contrib.) British Yearbook of International Law, 2004, 2010; Retroactivity and the Common Law, 2008. *Recreations:* hiking, kayaking. *Address:* Freshfields Bruckhaus Deringer, 2 rue Paul Cézanne, 75008 Paris, France. *T:* (1) 44564456. *E:* ben.juratowitch@freshfields.com.

**JUROWSKI, Vladimir;** conductor; Chief Conductor, London Philharmonic Orchestra, since 2007; Artistic Director, Russian State Academic Symphony Orchestra, since 2011; Chief Conductor and Artistic Director, Rundfunk-Sinfonieorchester Berlin, since 2017; *b* Moscow, 1972; *s* of Mikhail Jurowski, conductor. *Educ:* Music Coll., Moscow Conservatory; High Sch. of Music, Dresden; High Sch. of Music, Berlin. Internat. début, Wexford Fest., 1995; débuts: Royal Opera Hse, Covent Gdn, 1995; Metropolitan Opera, NY, 1999; joined Komische Oper, Berlin, 1996, First Kapellmeister, 1997–2001; Music Dir, Glyndebourne Fest. Opera, 2001–13. Principal Guest Conductor: Orch. Sinfonica Verdi, Milan; Teatro Comunale, Bologna, 2000–03; LPO, 2003–06; Russian Nat. Orch., 2005–09; Principal Artist, Orch. of the Age of Enlightenment, 2006–. Guest Conductor: Royal Opera Hse, Covent Gdn; Teatro La Fenice, Venice; Opéra Bastille, Paris; Th. de la Monnaie, Brussels; Maggio Music Fest., Florence; Rossini Opera Fest., Pesaro; Edinburgh Fest.; Semperoper, Dresden; WNO; Metropolitan Opera, NY; Berlin Philharmonic; Royal Concertgebouw Orch.; Philadelphia Orch.; LA Philharmonic; Chamber Orch. of Europe; Chicago Symphony; Tonhalle Orchester, Zurich; Dresden Staatskapelle. *Address:* c/o IMG Artists, Capital Tower, 91 Waterloo Road, SE1 8RT.

**JUSS, Prof. Satvinder Singh,** PhD; Professor of Law, King's College London, since 2008; Deputy Judge of the Upper Tribunal (Immigration and Asylum Chamber), since 2010 (Immigration Judge, since 2000); *b* Moshi, Tanzania, 11 May 1958; *s* of Sardar Dhian Singh Juss and Sardarni Joginder Kaur Juss; *m* 1990, Ravinder Kaur; two *s*. *Educ:* Emmanuel Coll., Cambridge (PhD Law 1986); Harvard Law Sch. (Harkness Fellow 1996). Fellow and Coll. Lectr, Emmanuel Coll., Cambridge, 1985–88; called to the Bar, Gray's Inn, 1989; in practice as barrister, 1989–; pupillage at 4–5 Gray's Inn Sq., 1990; Law Lectr, Univ. of Wales Coll., Cardiff, 1991–93; Human Rights Fellow, Harvard Univ., 1997; Vis. Prof. of Law, Indiana Univ., Bloomington, 1998; Certified Lectr for Law Soc. of England and Wales, and Consultant, Coll. of Law, 1998–2001; Lectr in Law. 2000–03, Reader in Law, 2003–08, KCL. Vis. Fellow, Georgetown Univ., 1996–97. Alice Tay Lect., ANU, 2013; Annual Human Rights Lect., NZ Centre of Human Rights, 2014. Advocate: for Govt of Wales, Panel A, 2012–16; for Equality and Human Rights Commn of England and Wales, 2015–. Mem. Council, 2004, Migration Comr, 2005, RSA. Life Mem. and Mem. Council, Indian Council of Arbitration, 2010–. FRSA. *Publications:* Immigration, Nationality and Citizenship, 1993; Discretion and Deviation in the Administration of Immigration Control, 1998; International Migration and Global Justice, 2007; Contemporary Issues in Refugee Law, 2013; Ashgate Research Companion on Migration Law, Theory and Policy, 2014; Toward a Refugee Oriented Reform of Refugee Law, 2015; (ed with M. Sunkin) Landmark Cases in Public Law, 2017; (ed) Human Rights and America's War on Terror, 2018; (ed) Beyond Human Rights and the War on Terror, 2018; (ed) India and Human Rights, 2018; (ed) Research Handbook on International Refugee Law, 2019; Human Rights in India, 2019; contrib. King's Law Jl, Public Law Jl. *Recreations:* cricket, tennis, swimming, long-distance walking, running, ghazal singing, delving in dusty shelves of arcane bookstores, keeping up with my children. *Address:* Dickson Poon School of Law, Somerset House, East Wing, King's College London, Strand, WC2R 2LS. *T:* (020) 7848 1189. *E:* satvinder.juss@kcl.ac.uk; 3 Hare Court, Temple, EC4Y 7BJ. *T:* (020) 7415 7800, 07931 728328, *Fax:* (020) 7415 7811. *E:* simonhamilton@3harecourt.com.

# K

**KABERRY, Hon. Sir Christopher Donald, (Hon. Sir Kit),** 2nd Bt cr 1960, of Adel cum Eccup, City of Leeds; FCA; Director and Company Secretary, London & Continental Railways Ltd, 2011–14; b 14 March 1943; s of Lord Kaberry of Adel (Life Peer) and Lily Margaret (d 1992), d of Edmund Scott; S to baronetcy of father, 1991; m 1967, Gaenor Elizabeth Vowe, d of C. V. Peake; two s one d. Educ: Repton Sch. FCA 1967. Various overseas positions, Costain Group PLC, 1969–80; Financial Manager, United Buildings Factories, Bahrain, 1980–82; Resources Manager, Balfour Beatty Group, Indonesia and Bahamas, 1983–90; Hd of Finance, Union Railways, and CTRL Project, 1990–2007. Director: HSI (formerly Union Railways (North)) Ltd, 2004–10; CTRL (UK) Ltd, 2004–10; Channel Tunnel Rail Link Ltd, 2005–11. Trustee: Rhino Ark (UK), 2011–; Zamcog, 2018–. Recreations: walking, gardening, Land Rover driving, overseas travel. Heir: s James Christopher Kaberry [b 1 April 1970; m 1989, Juliet Clare Hill (marr. diss. 1995); two s one d]. Address: Rock View, Chiddingstone Hoath, Kent TN8 7BT.

**KABUI, Sir Frank (Utu Ofagioro),** GCMG 2009 (CMG 1996); CSI 2002; OBE 1988; Governor General, Solomon Islands, 2009–19; b Suluagwari, North Malaita, Solomon Is, 20 April 1946; s of late Michael Frank Kabui and Namaah Angialatha; m 1st, 1978, Maryanne (marr. diss. 1993; she d 2005); three s three d; 2nd, 1993, Grace Delight; one s one d. Educ: Elementary Sch., Malu'u, N Malaita; Aligegeo Sen. Prim. Sch., Auki, Malaita; King George VI Nat. Sec. Sch.; Univ. of Papua New Guinea (LLB 1974); Australian National Univ. (Grad. Dip. Internat. Law 1985). Joined Solomon Is Public Service as Crown Counsel, 1975; Asst Attorney-Gen., 1977–80; Attorney-Gen., 1980–94; first Chm., Law Reform Commn, 1995–98; a Puisne Judge, High Court, Solomon Is, 1998–2006; Chm., Law Reform Commn, 2006–09. Jt Sec., Constitutional Cttee, 1976; former mem. of numerous govt cttees. Mem., Investment Corp. of Solomon Is, 1979–94. Former Director: Solomon Taiyo Ltd; Sasape Marina Ltd; Solomon Airlines Ltd; Mendana Hotel Ltd; Nat. Bank of Solomon Is. Pres., Solomon Is Bar Assoc., 2007–09. Chancellor, Univ. of S Pacific, Suva, 2011–12. KStJ 2018. Hon. LLD South Pacific, 2019. Publications: contrib. to Jl of Pacific Studies. Recreations: table tennis, lawn tennis, squash, soccer, darts, golf.

**KACELNIK, Prof. Alejandro,** DPhil; FRS 2011; Professor of Behavioural Ecology, University of Oxford, 1997–2017, now Emeritus; E. P. Abraham Fellow of Pembroke College, Oxford, 1990–2017, now Emeritus; b Buenos Aires, 14 Dec. 1946; s of Meyer Kacelnik and Lisa Kacelnik (née Kogan); m 1971, Lidia Estela Rapaport; one s. Educ: Univ. of Buenos Aires (Licenciado en Ciencias Biológicas); Wolfson Coll., Oxford (DPhil 1979). Post Doctoral Researcher: Univ. of Groningen, 1980–82; Univ. of Oxford, 1982–86; Sen. Res. Fellow, King's Coll., Cambridge, 1986–90; University of Oxford: Lectr in Zool., 1990–97; Founder and Dir, Behavioural Ecol. Res. Gp, 1990–. Fellow, Inst. for Advanced Studies, Berlin, 2001–03. Visiting Professor: Univ. of Leiden, 1988; Indiana Univ., 1995; Univ. Claude Bernard, Lyon, 1997; Univ. of Buenos Aires, 1999; Princeton Univ., 2005; Univ. Pompeu Fabra, Barcelona, 2009; Hon. Prof., Univ. of Buenos Aires, 2016–. MAE 2003. Cogito Prize (jtly), Cogito Foundn, 2004; Eduardo de Robertis Prize, Argentinian Soc. for Res. in Neuroscis, 2009; Raíces Prize, Argentinian Govt, 2011; Tinbergen Medal, Assoc. for Study of Animal Behaviour, 2019. Publications: (ed jtly) Quantitative Analyses of Behavior, vol. 6, Foraging, 1987; over 200 articles in major scientific jls. Recreations: cycling, rowing in the Paraná Delta, reading, cooking, gardening. Address: Department of Zoology, University of Oxford, Oxford OX1 3PS. T: (01865) 271164. E: alex.kacelnik@zoo.ox.ac.uk.

**KADOORIE, Hon. Sir Michael (David),** Kt 2005; GBS 2003; Chairman: CLP Holdings Ltd (formerly China Light & Power Co. Ltd), since 1996 (Director, 1967–96); Hongkong & Shanghai Hotels Ltd, since 1985 (Director, 1964–85); b Hong Kong, 19 July 1941; s of Baron Kadoorie, CBE and Muriel Kadoorie (née Gubbay); m 1984, Betty Tamayo; one s two d. Educ: King George V Sch., Hong Kong; Le Rosey, Switzerland. Chairman: Heliservices (Hong Kong) Ltd, 1979–; Metrojet Ltd, 1996–; Dir, Sir Elly Kadoorie & Sons Ltd, 1988–; chairman, director and trustee of many other cos. Hon. LLD Hong Kong, 2004; Hon. DSc Imperial Coll. London, 2007. Commandeur: Ordre de Léopold II (Belgium), 1995; Ordre des Arts et des Lettres (France), 1998; Légion d'Honneur (France), 2014 (Chevalier, 1995; Officier, 2003); Ordre de la Couronne (Belgium), 2014. Recreations: world travel, flying, motor cars, photography. Address: 24th Floor, St George's Building, 2 Ice House Street, Central, Hong Kong SAR. T: 25249221, Fax: 28459133. Clubs: Hong Kong, Hong Kong Aviation, Hong Kong Jockey (Hong Kong).

**KADRI, Sibghatullah;** QC 1989; barrister-at-law; President, Standing Conference of Pakistani Organisations in UK, 1978–90 (Secretary General, 1975–78); b 23 April 1937; s of Haji Maulana Firasat Ullah Kadri and Begum Tanwir Fatima Kadri; m 1963, Carita Elisabeth Idman; one s one d. Educ: S. M. Coll., Karachi; Karachi Univ. Called to the Bar, Inner Temple, 1969, Bencher, 1997. Sec. Gen., Karachi Univ. Students Union, 1957–58; jailed without trial, for opposing military regime of Ayub Khan, 1958–59; triple winner, All Pakistan Students Debates, 1960; Gen. Sec., Pakistan Students' Fedn in Britain, 1961–62, Vice Pres., 1962–63; Pres., Inner Temple Students Assoc., 1969–70. Producer and broadcaster, BBC Ext. Urdu Service, 1965–68, and Presenter, BBC Home Service Asian Prog., 1968–70. In practice at the Bar, 1969– (former Hd of Chambers, 6 King's Bench Walk; former Hd of Chambers, 2 King's Bench Walk). Chm., Soc. of Afro-Asian and Caribbean Lawyers, UK, 1979–83. Vis. Lectr in Urdu, Holborn Coll., London, 1967–70. Org. Pakistani Def. Cttees during wave of 'Paki-bashing', 1970; active in immigrant and race-relations activities, 1970–; led Asian delegn to Prime Minister, June 1976; attended UN Conf., Migrant Workers in Europe, Geneva, 1975; led Pakistan delegn to 3rd Internat. Conf., Migrant Workers in Europe, Turin, 1977; Mem., Race Relations Cttee of the Bar, 1983–85, 1988, 1989; Chm., UK Lawyers Cttee of Human Rights and Justice in Pakistan, 2007–14. Gen. Sec., Pakistan Action Cttee, 1973; Convenor, Asian Action Cttee, 1976. Vice Chm., All Party Jt Cttee Against Racism, 1978–80. Publisher, Scopo News, London, until 1984. FRSA 1991. Lifetime Achievement Award, Soc. of Asian Lawyers, 2008; Lifetime Achievement Award, Third World Solidarity, 2008; Role Model of the Year, Pakistan Achievement Award UK and Europe, 2012; Life Mem., Karachi Press Club for service to freedom of press and civil liberties, 2019. Publications: Bikhri Yadein aur Baten (autobiog.), 2019. Recreations: family, reading. Address: 3 Paper Buildings, Temple, EC4Y 7EU.

**KAESER, Joe;** President and Chief Executive Officer, Siemens AG, since 2013; b Arnbruck, Germany, 23 June 1957; m Rosemarie; two d. Educ: degree in business admin; Dip. Betriebswirt. Joined Siemens AG, 1980; Components Group, 1980–87: Hd, Business Admin, Discrete Components Div.; Finance Dir, Semiconductor Plant, Regensburg, Germany; Hd, Accounting and Planning, Semiconductors Gp; Hd, Business Admin Projects, Siemens Semiconductors, Malacca, Malaysia, 1987–88; Head, Business Administration: Discrete Semiconductors Div., Siemens AG, Semiconductors Gp, 1988–90; Opto Semiconductors Div., 1990–95; Exec. Vice Pres. and Chief Financial Officer, Siemens Microelectronics Inc., San José, Calif, 1995–99; Accounting Unit, Controlling and Taxes, Siemens AG, Corporate Finance, 1999–2001; Mem., Gp Exec. Mgt, Information and Communication Mobile Gp, 2001–04; Chief Strategy Officer, 2004–06; Mem., Man. Bd, 2004; Chief Financial Officer, 2006–13. Non-exec. Dir, NXP Semiconductors NV, Netherlands, 2010–; Member, Supervisory Board: Allianz Deutschland AG, Munich; Daimler AG, Stuttgart, 2014–. Address: Siemens AG, Wittelsbacherplatz 2, 80333 Munich, Germany.

**KAHN, (Jacob) Meyer;** Group Chairman, SABMiller (formerly South African Breweries) plc, 1999–2012; b 29 June 1939; s of late Ben and Sarah Kahn; m 1968, Lynette Sandra Asher; two d. Educ: Univ. of Pretoria (BA, MBA). Joined South African Breweries Ltd, 1966; Man. Dir, Amrel, 1972–77; Man. Dir, 1977–80, Chm., 1980–83, OK Bazaars (1929) Ltd; Dir, 1981–2012, Man. Dir, 1983–90, Exec. Chm., 1990–97, South African Breweries, later SABMiller plc; Chief Exec., South African Police Service, 1997–99 (on secondment). Non-executive Director: AfroCentric Gp, 2005–; Comair Ltd.

**KAHN, Paul Emmanuel,** CEng, FIET, FRAeS, FIMechE, FAPM; President, Communications and Connectivity, Cobham plc, since 2017; b of Robert E. Kahn and Sylvia M. Kahn; m 1990, Sarah Burland; two s one d. Educ: Cardinal Vaughan Memorial Sch., Kensington; Brunel Univ. (BSc Hons, MEng Engrg and Mgt Systems); London Business Sch. (MBA). CEng 1992; FIET 2002; FRAeS 2004; FIMechE 2013; FAPM 2013. Undergrad., Ford Motor Co., 1984–88; Principal, MoD, 1988–95; Vice Pres., Thales (formerly Thomson-CSF), 1995–2014; President and Chief Executive Officer: Thales Canada Inc., 2010–14; Airbus Gp UK, 2014–17. UK Business Ambassador, 2015–18; Pres., UK Aerospace, Defence, Security Organisation (ADS), 2016–18. Prince of Wales Ambassador for Industrial Cadets, 2016–. Recreations: family, ski-ing, running, hill walking, canoeing, cycling. Club: Royal Automobile.

**KAHN, Paula;** Chair, MTVH (formerly Metropolitan Housing Trust), since 2013; b 15 Nov. 1940; d of Cyril Maurice Kahn and Stella Roscoe. Educ: Chiswick County High Sch.; Bristol Univ. (BA Hons). Teacher, administrator, 1962–66; Longman Group, 1966–94: editor, publisher, Publishing Director, Divl Man. Dir, 1966–79; Managing Director: ELT Div., Dictionaries Div. and Trade and Ref. Div., 1980–85; Internat. Sector, 1986–88; Chief Exec. (Publishing), 1988–89; Chief Exec. and Chm., 1990–94; Vice-Pres., Publishers Assoc., 1994–95; Project Dir, World Learning Network, 1995–96; Man. Dir, Phaidon Press, 1996–97. Non-executive Director: Inst. of Internat. Visual Arts, 1994–2008; Focus Central London, TEC, 1998–2001; English Languages Services Internat. Ltd, 1998–2006; New Ways to Work, 1998–2001; ITDG Publishing, 1999–2004; Stonewall, 2000–06; Chairman: Equality Works, 2000–08; Hidden Art, 2007–12. Member: English Teaching Adv. Cttee, British Council, 1990–98; Educn and Training Sector Gp, DTI, 1993–98. Mem., Islington CHC and PCG, 1998–2001; Chair: Islington PCT, 2002–13; North Central London NHS Cluster, 2011–13. Mem., Governing Body, SOAS, 1993–95. Chm., Camden Arts Centre, 2008–14. Governor: Elizabeth Garrett Anderson Sch., Islington, 1997–2000; Cripplegate Foundn, 2000– (Chair, 2005–07); Trustee, Assoc. of Charitable Foundns, 2012–18 (Treas., 2016–18); Treas., Stuart Hall Foundn, 2016–. FRSA 1993; CCMI (CIMgt 1992). Recreations: visual arts, cinema, theatre, reading.

**KAHNEMAN, Prof. Daniel,** PhD; Eugene Higgins Professor of Psychology, and Professor of Public Affairs, Woodrow Wilson School, Princeton University, 1993–2007, now Emeritus and Senior Scholar; b 1934; m 1st, Irah; 2nd, 1978, Prof. Anne Marie Treisman, FRS (d 2018). Educ: Hebrew Univ. (BA 1954); Univ. of Calif, Berkeley (PhD 1961). Lectr 1961–66, Sen. Lectr, 1966–70, Associate Prof., 1970–73, Prof. of Psychol., 1973–78, Hebrew Univ.; Professor of Psychology: Univ. of BC, 1978–86; Univ. of Calif, Berkeley, 1986–94. Corresp. FBA 2008. Nobel Prize in Econ. Scis (jtly), 2002; Presidential Medal of Freedom (USA), 2013. Publications: Attention and Effort, 1973; (ed jtly) Well-Being: foundations of hedonic psychology, 1999; (ed jtly) Choices, Values and Frames, 2000; (ed jtly) Heuristics and Biases: the psychology of intuitive judgement, 2002; Thinking, Fast and Slow, 2011; contrib. learned jls. Address: 229 Corwin Hall, Woodrow Wilson School of Public and International Affairs, Princeton University, Princeton, NJ 08544–1013, USA.

**KAIN, Prof. Roger James Peter,** CBE 2005; PhD, DLit; FSA; FBA 1990; Professor of Humanities, School of Advanced Study, University of London, since 2017 (Dean and Chief Executive, 2010–17); b 12 Nov. 1944; s of Peter Albert Kain and Ivy Kain; m 1970, Annmaree Wallington; two s. Educ: Harrow Weald County Grammar Sch.; University College London (BA; PhD 1973; DLit 1998; Fellow 2002). FSA 1992. Tutor, Bedford Coll., London, 1971–72; Exeter University: Lectr, 1972–88; Montefiore Reader in Geography, 1988–91; Montefiore Prof. of Geography, 1991–2010; Hd, Sch. of Geog. and Archaeol., 1999–2001; Dep. Vice-Chancellor, 2002–10. British Academy: Vice-Pres., 1997–99; Chm. Grants Cttee, 1999–2002; Treas., 2002–10; Vice Pres., Res. and Higher Educn Policy, 2014–. Mem., AHRC, 2008–14. Gill Meml Medal, RGS, 1990; Kenneth Nebenzahl Prize, Newberry Liby, Chicago, 1991. Publications: Planning for Conservation: an international perspective, 1984; The Tithe Surveys of England and Wales, 1985, repr. 2006; An Atlas and Index of the Tithe Files of Mid-Nineteenth-Century England and Wales, 1986; (jtly) Cadastral Mapping in the Service of the State: a history of property mapping, 1992; (jtly) The Tithe Maps of England and Wales: a cartographic analysis and county-by-county catalogue, 1995 (McColvin Medal, LA, 1996), repr. 2011; (jtly) English Cartography, 1997; (jtly) English Maps: a history, 1999; (ed) Historical Atlas of South-West England, 1999; (jtly) Tithe Surveys for Historians, 2000; Historic Parishes of England and Wales, 2001; (jtly) Enclosure Maps of England and Wales, 2004, repr. 2011; (ed) England's Landscape: the South-West, 2006; (jtly) British Town Maps: a history, 2015. *Recreations:* mountain walking, gardening. *Address:* School of Advanced Study, University of London, Senate House, Malet Street, WC1E 7HU. *T:* (020) 7862 8736. *Club:* Athenæum.

**KAISER, Martin S.;** *see* Seeleib-Kaiser, M.

**KAISER, Michael Martin;** Co-Chairman, IMG Artists, since 2014; Strategic Consulting Partner and Founding Artistic Director, Great Lakes Centre for the Arts, since 2016; *b* 27 Oct. 1953; *s* of Harold and Marion Kaiser. *Educ:* Brandeis Univ. (BS); Sloan Sch., MIT (MSM). Pres., Kaiser Associates, 1981–85; Exec. Dir, Kansas City Ballet, 1985–87; Associate Dir, Pierpoint Morgan Library, 1987–91; Exec. Dir, Alvin Ailey American Dance Theatre, 1991–93; Pres., Kaiser-Engler Gp, 1994–95; Executive Director: American Ballet Theatre, 1995–98; Royal Opera House, 1998–2000; Pres., John F. Kennedy Center for Performing Arts, Washington, 2001–14, now Pres. Emeritus. Founder and Chm., Kennedy Center Arts Mgt Inst., later DeVos Inst. of Arts Mgt, Univ. of Maryland, 2001–. *Address:* IMG Artists, 7 West 54 Street, New York, NY 10019, USA.

**KAISER, Prof. Michel Josef,** PhD, DSc; Professor of Fisheries Conservation, Heriot-Watt University, since 2019; *b* Stoke-on-Trent, 30 Jan. 1967; *s* of Michel and Margaret E. Kaiser; *m* 1993, Diane Angela Brown; two *d. Educ:* Birkenhead Sch.; Univ. of Liverpool (BSc Hons Marine Biol. 1988); Univ. of Wales, Bangor (PhD 1991); Univ. of Liverpool (DSc 2003). SSO, Centre for Envmt, Fisheries and Aquaculture Sci., Conwy Lab., 1991–98; Bangor University: Lectr, 1998–2001; Sen. Lectr, 2001–04; Reader, 2004–06; Prof. of Marine Conservation Ecology, 2006–18; Science and Standards Dir, Marine Stewardship Council, 2018–19. Sen. Res. Fellow, Marine Policy Centre, Woods Hole Oceanographic Inst., 2004. Hon. Lectr, Univ. of Manchester, 1996–99. Member: Bd, Seafish, 2008–15; Jt Nature Conservation Cttee, 2012–17; Marine Sci. Coordination Cttee, 2014–. Dir, P&O Maritime Ocean Scis Ltd, 2001–18. Member: Council, Fisheries Soc. of British Isles, 2017– (Vice-Pres., 2007–10); Fisheries Expert Gp, Internat. Union for Conservation of Nature, 2017–. Vice-Pres., 6th World Fisheries Congress, 2012. Fisheries Soc. of British Isles Medal 2004. *Publications:* (ed with S. J. De Groot) The effects of trawling on non-target species and habits: biological, conservation and socio-economic issues, 2000; (jtly) Marine Fisheries ecology, 2001; (jtly) Marine Ecology: processes, systems and impacts, 2005, 2nd edn 2011; (ed jtly) Fisheries for Global Welfare and Environment, 2008. *Address:* Lyell Centre, Institute of Life and Earth Sciences, Heriot-Watt University, Edinburgh EH14 4AS. *T:* 07733 138737. *E:* m.kaiser@hw.ac.uk.

**KAISER, Prof. Nicholas,** PhD; FRS 2008; Professor, Ecole Normale Supérieure, Paris, since 2017; *b* 15 Sept. 1954; *s* of late Prof. Thomas Reeve Kaiser and of Pamela Kaiser. *Educ:* Leeds Univ. (BSc Physics 1978); Clare Coll., Cambridge (Pt III Maths Tripos 1979; PhD Astronomy 1982). Lindemann Fellow, Univ. of Calif, Berkeley, 1983; Post Doctoral Fellow: UCSB, 1984; Univ. of Calif, Berkeley, 1984; SERC Sen. Visitor, Univ. of Sussex, 1985; Post Doctoral Fellow, 1985–86, SERC Advanced Fellow, 1986–88, Univ. of Cambridge; Prof., Canadian Inst. for Theoretical Astrophysics, Univ. of Toronto, 1988–97; Astronomer, Inst. for Astronomy, Univ. of Hawaii, 1997–2017. Ontario Fellow, Canadian Inst. Advanced Res. Cosmol. Prog., 1988; Steacie Fellow, NSERC, 1991–92. Helen Warner Prize, Amer. Astronomical Soc., 1989; Herzberg Medal, Canadian Assoc. Physicists, 1993; Rutherford Medal, RSC, 1997; Gold Medal, RAS, 2017; (jtly) Gruber Cosmology Prize, Gruber Foundn, 2019. *Publications: contributor:* Inner Space - Outer Space, 1986; Large Scale Motions in the Universe, 1989; The Epoch of Galaxy Formation, 1989; After the First 3 Minutes, 1991; contribs to learned jls incl. Astrophysical Jl, Bull. AAS, Monthly Notices of RAS, Nature, Contemporary Physics. *Address:* Ecole Normale Supérieure, 45 rue d'Ulm, 75230 Paris, France.

**KAJUMBA, Ven. Daniel Steven Kimbugwe;** Archdeacon of Reigate, 2001–16, now Emeritus; *b* 20 Nov. 1952; *s* of Prince Adonia Kajumba, Buganda royal clan, and Lady Esther Kajumba; family exiled to UK, 1971; *m* 1974, Tina Carole Hewlett; one *s* one *d. Educ:* school in Uganda; Southwark Ordination Course; HND 1977; Dip. Inst. Municipal Bldg Mgt, 1981; DipTh London 1985; BA (Open) 1987; Postgrad. Cert. Preaching (Univ. of Wales), 2007. Employment before ordination included: Auxiliary Nurse, Bournemouth; Youth Officer, West Cliff Baptist Ch; Dep. Warden, Christian Alliance Centre; Prop., Poole Parkside and Edward Russell Residential Homes for the Elderly. Ordained deacon, 1985, priest, 1986; Curate, Goldington, Dio. St Albans, 1985–87; employment in Uganda, 1987–98, included: Man. Dir, Transocean; Gen. Mgr, Rio Hldgs Internat.; Kingdom of Buganda: Sec. Gen.; Minister for Public Relns, Functions and Protocol, and Foreign Affairs; Team Vicar, Horley St Francis, Dio. Southwark, 1999–2001. *Address:* 84 Higher Drive, Purley, Surrey CR8 2HJ. *T:* (020) 8660 9276.

**KAKABADSE, Prof. Andrew,** PhD; Professor of Governance and Leadership, Henley Business School, University of Reading, since 2013; *b* Athens, 30 March 1948; *s* of George Kakabadse and Elfrieda Kakabadse; *m* 1st, 1979, Patricia Sweetman (*d* 1991); one *d;* 2nd, 1995, Nada Korac (*see* N. Kakabadse); one *s. Educ:* Altrincham Grammar Sch.; Salford Univ. (BSc 1970); Brunel Univ. (MA 1973); Manchester Univ. (PhD 1977). Derbyshire CC, 1970–71; RBK&C, 1971–73; Dept of Mgt, Manchester Univ., 1973–77; WS Atkins Gp of Internat. Consultants, 1977–78; Prof. of Internat. Mgt Develt, Cranfield Univ., 1978–2012, now Emeritus. Vis. Professor: Sorbonne, 2009–; Univ. of Ulster, 2010–; Hon. Prof., Coll. of Social Scis, Kazakhstan, 2011–. Specialist Advr, Public Admin Select Cttee, 2011–. FBPsS; Fellow, Soc. of Internat. Business Leaders. Fellow, Windsor Leadership Trust, 2010–. *Publications:* (ed jtly) Leadership and Organisation Development, 1980; Culture of the Social Services, 1982; People and Organisations, 1982; Stress, Change and Organisation, 1982; Politics of Management, 1983; (ed jtly) Power, Politics and Organisations, 1984; (ed jtly) Future of Management Education, 1984; (jtly) Privatisation and the NHS, 1985; (with S. Tyson) Cases in Human Resource Management, 1987, 2nd edn 1994; Working in Organisations, 1988, 2nd edn 2004; Management Development and the Public Sector, 1989; The Wealth Creators, 1991; (with F. Analoui) Sabotage, 1991; (jtly) Japanese Business Leaders, 1996; (jtly) Success in Sight: visioning, 1998; (jtly) Designing World Class Corporate Strategies, 2005; (with L. Okazaki-Ward) Corporate Governance in Japan, 2005; (ed jtly) Corporate Social Responsibility, 2006; (jtly) Extraordinary Performance from Ordinary People, 2007; (jtly) Spiritual Motivation, 2007; (jtly) Leading for Success, 2008; (jtly) The Elephant Hunters, 2008; (jtly) Leadership Teams, 2009; (jtly) Citizenship, 2009; (jtly) Leading Smart Transformation, 2011; (jtly) Bilderberg People, 2011; (jtly) From Battlefield to Boardroom, 2012; (with N. Korac-Kakabadse: Leadership in Government, 1998; Essence of Leadership, 1999; Creating Futures, 2000; The Geopolitics of Governance, 2001; Smart Sourcing, 2002; Intimacy, 2004; Governance, Strategy and Policy, 2005; CSR in Practice, 2007; Leading the Board, 2008; Global Boards, 2009; Rice Wine with the Minister, 2010; Global Elites, 2012; The Success Formula, 2015;

(jtly) Leadership Intelligence: the 5Qs for thriving as a leader, 2019; over 220 articles. *Recreation:* walking. *Address:* Henley Business School, University of Reading, Greenlands, Henley-on-Thames, Oxon RG9 3AU. *T:* (01491) 418770. *E:* a.kakabadse@henley.ac.uk. *Club:* Athenæum.

**KAKABADSE, Prof. Nada,** PhD; Professor of Policy, Governance and Ethics, Henley Business School, University of Reading, since 2013; *b* 31 Jan. 1953; *d* of Dmitar and Mila Lisa Korac; *m* 1995, Prof. Andrew Kakabadse, *qv;* one *s. Educ:* Univ. of Canberra (BSc Maths and Computing; Grad. Dip. Mgt Sci.; MPA); Univ. of Western Sydney Nepean (PhD 1998); Inst. of Learning and Teaching, UK (Cert.). Cartographer/programmer, Australian Public Service, Dept of Minerals and Resources, Canberra, 1973–78; Regl Manager, Alfa-Laval AB, Lund, Sweden, 1978–84; Sen. IT Officer, Australian Public Service, Dept of Employment, Educn and Trng, 1985–95; on leave as Financial Officer, Dept of Ext. Affairs and Trade, Ottawa, 1989–91; Cranfield School of Management: Res. Fellow, HR Gp, 1995–97; Sen. Res. Fellow, Information Systems Res. Centre, 1997–2002; Northampton Business School, University of Northampton: Prof. of Mgt and Business Res., Hd, Doctoral Prog. and Res. Leader, 2002–13. Mem., Governing Council, Empress Theophano Foundn, 2019–. Mem., Eur. Acad. Scis and Arts, 2012 (UK Rep., 2015–). *Publications:* Overload: explaining, diagnosing and dealing with techno-addiction, 2007; (jtly) Leading for Success: seven sides to leadership, 2008; (jtly) The Elephant Hunters: chronicles of the moneymen, 2008; (jtly) Leadership Teams: developing and sustaining high performance, 2009; (ed jtly) Citizenship: a reality far from ideal, 2009; Leadership in the Public Sector, 2010; (jtly) Bilderberg People: inside the exclusive global elite, 2011 (trans. Mandarin, Chinese edn 2013); (jtly) Public-Private Partnerships, 2017; with A. Kakabadse: Leadership in Government: study of the Australian Public Service, 1998; Essence of Leadership, 1999; Creating Futures: leading change through information systems, 2000; Geopolitics of Governance, 2000; Smart Sourcing: international best practice, 2001; Intimacy: international survey of the sex lives of people at work, 2004; Governance, Strategy and Policy: seven critical essays, 2006; (ed) CSR in Practice: delving deep, 2007; Leading the Board: the six disciplines of world-class chairmen, 2008; (ed) Global Boards: one desire, many realities, 2009; Rice Wine with the Minister: distilled wisdom to manage, lead and succeed on the global stage, 2010; (ed) Global Elites: the opaque nature of transnational policy determination, 2012; contrib. chapters to internat. vols and articles. *Recreations:* long walks, swimming, classical music. *Address:* Henley Business School, University of Reading, Greenlands, Room EH 500, Henley-on-Thames, Oxon RG9 3AU. *T:* (01491) 418786. *E:* n.kakabadse@henley.ac.uk.

**KAKKAR,** family name of **Baron Kakkar.**

**KAKKAR,** Baron *cr* 2010 (Life Peer), of Loxbeare in the County of Devon; **Ajay Kumar Kakkar;** PC 2014; PhD; FRCS, FRCP; Professor of Surgery, University College London, since 2011; Consultant Surgeon, University College London Hospitals NHS Foundation Trust, since 2006; Director, Thrombosis Research Institute, London, since 2009; *b* Dartford, Kent, 28 April 1964; *s* of late Prof. Vijay Vir Kakkar, OBE, FRCS, FRCSE; *m* 1993, Nicola Susan Lear; two *d. Educ:* Alleyn's Sch., Dulwich; King's Coll., Univ. of London (BSc 1985; MBBS (Hons) 1988); Imperial Coll. London (PhD 1998). FRCS 1992; FRCP 2015. Jun. surgical trng, King's Coll. Hosp., Brompton Hosp., Hammersmith Hosp. and Royal Sussex County Hosp., Brighton, 1988–92; Hammersmith Hospital, London: Registrar in Surgery, 1992–93; MRC Clinical Trng Fellow, 1993–96; MRC Clinician Scientist and Hon. Sen. Registrar, 1996–99; Sen. Lectr and Consultant Surgeon, Hammersmith Hosp. and Imperial Coll. London, 1999–2004; Prof. of Surgical Scis, Barts and the London Sch. of Medicine and Dentistry, QMUL, 2004–11; Consultant Surgeon, St Bartholomew's Hosp., 2004–11; Chm., UCL Partners Academic Health Scis System, 2014–. (Chm., Clin. Quality Directorate, 2009–14). Chairman: Health Honours Cttee, 2013–; H of L Appts Commn, 2013–18; Judicial Appts Commn, 2016–. UK Business Ambassador, Healthcare and Life Sci., 2013–. Mem., GMC, 2013–18. Com., Royal Hosp. Chelsea, 2012–18. Trustee and Gov., King Edward VII Hosp. for Officers Sister Agnes, 2014–. Bencher, Middle Temple, 2019. Fellow, S African Soc. on Thrombosis and Haemostasis, 2009; FKC 2016; Hon. Fellow, Assoc. of Surgeons of India, 2010. Hon. Fellow, Harris Manchester Coll., Oxford, 2010. Hunterian Prof., RCS, 1996; Wellcome Lectr, RSM, 2009; 12th Varma Lect., St George's, Univ. of London, 2011. James IV Assoc. of Surgeons Fellowship, 2006. David Patey Prize, Surgical Res. Soc., 1996; Knoll William Harvey Prize, Internat. Soc. on Thrombosis and Haemostasis, 1997. *Publications:* articles on prevention and treatment of venous thromboembolism and cancer associated thrombosis. *Recreation:* family. *Address:* House of Lords, SW1A 0PW. *T:* (020) 7351 8309, *Fax:* (020) 7351 8317. *E:* kakkara@parliament.uk. *Club:* Athenæum.

**KALAMBEKOVA, Baktygul R.;** Ambassador of the Kyrgyz Republic to the Court of St James's, 2010–12; *b* Batken, Kyrgyzstan, 18 Oct. 1961; *d* of Rysbay and Minavar; one *s. Educ:* Kyrgyz State Univ. (BA 1982); High Komsomol Sch.; Moscow Inst. of Youth (PhD Econs 1993); Inst. of Diplomacy, Turkey; Inst. of Internat. Relns and Diplomacy, Malaysia. Sen. Economist, Batken State Exec. Admin Agricl Sector, 1982–84; Sec., State Special Farm's Komsomol Cttee, 1984–85; First Sec., Batken Br., Leninist Young Communist League of the Soviet Union, 1985–90; First Sec., Central Asia and Caucasus Dept, and Mem., negotiation gp on border problems, Min. of Foreign Affairs, Kyrgyz Republic, 1993–95; Third Sec., Kyrgyz Embassy, Turkey, 1995–97; Second Sec., 1997–98, First Sec., 1998–2001, Western Countries Dept, Min. of Foreign Affairs, Kyrgyz Republic; Minister Counsellor, Kyrgyz Embassy, Turkey, 2001–04; Dep. Hd, Foreign Policy Planning and Multilateral Econ. Cooperation Dept, 2004–05, Advr to Minister, 2005–09, Vice-Minister, 2009–10, Min. of Foreign Affairs, Kyrgyz Republic; Foreign Policy Advr to Hd of Interim Govt and to Pres. of Kyrgyz Republic, 2010. Hon. Diploma, Foreign Min., Kyrgyzstan; Laureate of Internat. Award for merits before the Turkic World; Gold Medal and Diploma, Internat. Fund of Sci. and Culture Mustafa Kemal Ataturk. *Publications:* Agrarian Overpopulation in Kyrgyzstan (monograph), 2004; trans. six books from Kyrgyz, Russian and Turkish langs; 40 articles on regl and world econs. *Address:* c/o Embassy of the Kyrgyz Republic, 119 Ascot House, Crawford Street, W1U 6BJ.

**KALETSKY, Anatole;** Columnist, Reuters, since 2012; Co-Founder and Chief Economist, GaveKal Research, since 2001; Vice-Chairman and Chief Economist, GaveKal Dragonomics, Hong Kong; *b* Moscow, 1 June 1952; *s* of Jacob and Esther Kaletsky; *m* 1985, Fiona Murphy; two *s* one *d. Educ:* Melbourne High Sch., Australia; Westminster City Sch.; King's Coll., Cambridge (BA Maths). Harvard Univ. (MA Econs). Financial Writer, The Economist, 1976–79; Financial Times: Leader Writer, 1979–81; Washington Corresp., 1981–83; Internat. Econs Corresp., 1984–86; NY Bureau Chief, 1986–90; Moscow Assignment, 1990; The Times: Econs Ed., 1990–96; Associate Ed., 1992–2009; Ed. at Large, 2009–12. Hon. Sen. Scholar, King's Coll., Cambridge, 1973–74; Kennedy Scholar, Harvard Univ., 1974–76. Mem., Adv. Bd, UK Know-How Fund for E Europe and former Soviet Union, 1991–; Dir, Kaletsky Economic Consulting, 1997–2003. Mem. Council, REconS, 1999–2004. Trustee, New Europe Res. Trust, 1999–. Hon. DSc Buckingham, 2007. Specialist Writer of Year, British Press Awards, 1980, 1992; Commentator of the Year, What the Papers Say, 1996; Financial Journalist of the Year, Wincott Foundn Award, 1997. *Publications:* The Costs of Default, 1985; In the Shadow of Debt, 1992; Capitalism 4.0: the birth of a new economy, 2010. *Recreations:* playing the violin, cinema, family life.

**KALLAGHE, Peter Allan;** Senior Consulting Officer for Foreign Affairs, National Defence College, Tanzania, since 2016; *b* Korogwe, Tanzania, 31 Aug. 1959; *m* Joyce Daniel; two *s* two *d. Educ:* Kiev State Univ. (MA Internat. Relns 1982). Min. of Foreign Affairs, Tanzania, 1983–97; Dep. Private Sec. to President of Tanzania, 2001–06; Dir of Communications, President's Office, 2003–07; High Comr to: Canada and Cuba, 2007–10; UK, 2010–16. *T:* 07500 703388. *E:* pkallaghe@gmail.com.

**KALLAS, Siim;** MP (Reform) Estonia, since 2019; *b* 2 Oct. 1948; *s* of Udo Kallas and Rita Kallas; *m* 1972, Kristi Kartus; one *s* one *d. Educ:* Tartu State Univ. Chief Specialist, Min. of Finance, Estonia, 1975–79; Gen. Manager, Estonian Savings Bank, 1979–86; Dep. Ed., Rahva Hääl, 1986–89; Chm., Estonian Assoc. of Trade Unions, 1989–91; Pres., Bank of Estonia, 1991–95. MP, Estonia, 1995–2004; Minister: of Foreign Affairs, 1995–96; of Finance, 1999–2002; Prime Minister, 2002–03. Mem. and a Vice Pres., EC, 2004–14. Municipal Mayor of Viimsi, 2017–19. Founder and Chm., Estonian Reform Party, 1994–2004. Vis. Prof. of Internat. Econs, Univ. of Tartu, 2015–. *Publications:* Kallas: esseed, mõtted ja päevakaja 2004–2015, 2016; articles on econ. affairs, foreign policy and politics. *Address:* Parliament of Estonia, Lossi plats 1a, 15165 Tallinn, Estonia.

**KALLASVUO, Olli-Pekka;** President and Chief Executive Officer, 2006–10, Chairman of the Group Executive Board, 2006–10 (Member, 1990–2010) and Member of the Board of Directors, 2007–10, Nokia; *b* Lavia, Finland, 13 July 1953. *Educ:* Univ. of Helsinki (LLM). Various positions, Union Bank of Finland; Nokia: joined as Corporate Counsel, 1980; Asst Vice Pres., Legal Dept, 1987–88; Asst Vice Pres., 1988–90, Sen. Vice Pres., 1990–92, Finance; Exec. Vice Pres. and Chief Financial Officer, 1992–97; Corp. Exec. Vice Pres., Nokia Americas, 1997–98; Chief Financial Officer, 1999–2004; Exec. Vice Pres. and Gen. Manager, Mobile Phones, 2004–05; Pres. and Chief Operating Officer, 2005–06; Chm., Bd of Dirs, Nokia Siemens Networks, 2007–11. Chm., World Design Capital Helsinki 2012 Cttee, 2011–13. Member, Board: SRV Group plc, 2011– (Vice-Chm., 2012–); TeliaSonera, 2012– (Vice-Chm., 2013–); Chm., Zenterio, 2013–. Member: Bd, Confedn of Finnish Industries, 2009; Eur. Round Table of Industrialists, 2009; EU-Russia Industrialists' Round Table, 2010. Hon. LLD Helsinki, 2010. *Recreations:* golf, tennis, reading about political history.

**KALLIPETIS, Michel Louis;** QC 1989; a Recorder, 1989–2006; a Deputy High Court Judge, 1990–2006; independent civil and commercial mediator, Independent Mediators Ltd, since 2006; *b* 29 Aug. 1941; *s* of late Takis George Kallipetis and Sheila Gallally; *m* 2009, Caroline Sarah (*née* Ball). *Educ:* Cardinal Vaughan Sch.; University Coll., London. FCIArb; Chartered Arbitrator, 2002. Exchequer and Audit Dept, 1960–66. Called to the Bar, Gray's Inn, 1968, Bencher, 1997. Registered and accredited mediator, 1996. *Recreations:* opera, cooking, travel. *Clubs:* Reform, Garrick.

**KALMS, Baron** *cr* 2004 (Life Peer), of Edgware in the London Borough of Barnet; **Harold Stanley Kalms,** Kt 1996; President, Dixons Retail (formerly Dixons Group, then DSG International) plc, 2002–14 (Chairman, 1972–2002); Treasurer, Conservative Party, 2001–03; *b* 21 Nov. 1931; *s* of Charles and Cissie Kalms; *m* 1954, Pamela Jimack (MBE 1995); three *s. Educ:* Christ's College, Finchley. Whole career with Dixons Group: started in 1948 in one store owned by father; went public, 1962; Man. Dir, 1962–72; Dir, British Gas, 1987–97. Chairman: Volvere plc, 2002–11; NMT Gp plc, 2005–08; Acorn Brands, 2006–07. Chm., King's Healthcare NHS Trust, 1993–96. Director: Centre for Policy Studies, 1991–2001 (Treas., 1993–98); Business for Sterling, 1998–2001; Founder, Centre for Social Cohesion, 2007. Vis. Prof., Business Sch., Univ. (formerly Poly.) of N London, 1991–. Mem., Funding Agency for Schs, 1994–97. Governor: Dixons Bradford City Technol. Coll., 1988–2002; NIESR, 1995–2001. Trustee: Industry in Educn, 1993–2003; Economic Educn Trust, 1993–2002. Hon. FCGI 1991; Hon. Fellow, London Business Sch., 1995. Hon. DLitt: CNAA, 1991; Sheffield 2002; DUniv N London, 1994; Hon. DEcon Richmond, 1996; Hon. DSc Buckingham, 2002. *Recreations:* politics, opera, ballet, bridge. *Address:* House of Lords, SW1A 0PW. *T:* (020) 7629 1427.

**KALMUS, Prof. George Ernest,** CBE 2000; FRS 1988; Associate Director, 1986–94, Director, 1994–97, Particle Physics, Rutherford Appleton Laboratory; Visiting Professor, Physics and Astronomy Department, 1984–2000, Fellow, 1998, University College London; *b* 21 April 1935; *s* of late Hans Kalmus and Anna Kalmus; *m* 1957, Ann Christine Harland; three *d. Educ:* St Albans County Grammar Sch.; University Coll. London (BSc Hons, PhD). Res. Asst, Bubble Chamber Gp, UCL, 1959–62; Research Associate, Powell-Birge Bubble Chamber Gp, Lawrence Radiation Lab., Univ. of California, Berkeley, 1962–63 and 1964–67; Lectr, Physics Dept, UCL, 1963–64; Sen. Physicist, Lawrence Rad. Lab., 1967–71; Gp Leader, Bubble Chamber and Delphi Gps, Rutherford Appleton Lab., 1971–86. Mem., various Programme Cttees at CERN, 1974–; Mem., CERN Scientific Policy Cttee, 1990–96 (Chm., 1999–2001). *Publications:* numerous articles on experimental particle physics in Phys. Rev., Phys. Rev. Letters, Nuclear Phys., etc. *Recreations:* ski-ing, reading. *Address:* 16 South Avenue, Abingdon, Oxon OX14 1QH. *T:* (01235) 523340.
*See also* P. I. P. Kalmus.

**KALMUS, Prof. Peter Ignaz Paul,** OBE 2001; PhD; CPhys; Professor of Physics, 1978–98, and Head of Physics Department, 1992–97, Queen Mary and Westfield (formerly Queen Mary) College, University of London, now Emeritus Professor, Queen Mary University of London (Hon. Fellow 2003); *b* 25 Jan. 1933; *s* of late Hans and Anna Kalmus; *m* 1957, Felicity (Trixie) Barker (*d* 2018); one *s* one *d. Educ:* University Coll. London (BSc, PhD; Hon. Fellow 2001). CPhys, FInstP 1967 (Hon. FInstP). Res. Associate, University Coll. London, 1957–60; Lectr (part-time), Northern Poly. and Chelsea Poly., 1955–60; Physicist, Argonne Nat. Lab., USA, 1960–64; Queen Mary College, University of London: Lectr, 1964–66; Reader, 1966–78. Visiting Scientist: CERN, Geneva, 1961–62, 1970–71, 1981–82; Univ. of Chicago, 1965. Scientific Advr, UK Delegn to CERN, 1978–81; Member: SERC Nuclear Physics Bd, 1979–82, 1989–93; SERC Astronomy and Planetary Sci. Bd, 1990–93; PPARC Educn & Trng Cttee, 1994–98; PPARC Public Understanding of Sci. Panel, 1994–98. Member Council: Inst. of Physics, 1993–2000 (Vice-Pres., 1996–2000; Chairman: High Energy Physics Gp, 1989–93; London & SE Br., 2005–09; Hon. Fellow, 2010); Royal Instn, 1996–99 (MRI 1989–; Vice-Pres., 1997–99; Chm., Davy Faraday Lab. Res. Cttee, 1998–99); Member: Amer. Phys. Soc., 1963 (Fellow, 1995); European Phys. Soc., 1970 (Mem., High Energy Particle Physics Bd, 1994–98); BAAS, 1986 (Pres., Physics Sect., 1990–91; Hon. Fellow, 2002); International Union of Pure and Applied Physics: Vice Pres., 1999–2002; Mem., 1993–2002, Hon. Sec., 1996–99, Chm., 1999–2002, Commn on Particles and Fields. Active in physics outreach to schs and public. Rutherford Medal and Prize, 1988, Kelvin Medal and Prize, 2002, Branches Prize, 2010, Inst. Physics. Outreach Prize, Eur. Physical Soc., 2005. *Publications:* numerous papers in scientific jls. *Recreations:* photography, swimming, listening to traditional jazz. *Address:* School of Physics and Astronomy, Queen Mary University of London, Mile End Road, E1 4NS. *T:* (020) 7882 6168. *E:* p.i.p.kalmus@qmul.ac.uk.
*See also* G. E. Kalmus.

**KALVĪTIS, Aigars;** Chief Executive, Latvijas Gāze, since 2015; Prime Minister of the Republic of Latvia, 2004–07; *b* Riga, 27 June 1966; *s* of Edmunds Kalvītis and Velta Kalvite; *m* Kristine Kalvite; three *s. Educ:* Riga Sec. Sch. No 41; Latvia Univ. of Agriculture (Bachelors degree 1992, Masters degree Agricl Economy 1995); University Coll. Cork (Masters course Food Ind. Bus. Admin, 1993). Milkman and tractor driver on farm, Sweden, 1990–91; Dir, Agro Bizensa Centrs, 1992–94; Chm. Bd, Zemgales Piens, jt stock co., 1994; Chm. Commn, Central Union of Latvian Dairying, 1994–98; in-service training, Holstein Assoc., Univ. of Wisconsin, 1995. Mem., 7th Saeima, 1998–99, Member: Budget and Finance (Taxation) Cttee; Public Expenditure and Audit Cttee; Minister: for Agriculture, 1999–2000; for Economics, 2000–02; Mem., 8th Saeima, 2002–04; Chm., parly gp of People's Party, 2002–04; Mem., 9th Saeima, 2007–09. Chairman: Supervisory Bd, Latvijas Balzams, 2009–15; Bd, Dinamo Riga, 2010–15. *Address:* Latvijas Gāze, Vagonu Street 20, Riga 1009, Latvia.

**KALYVAS, Prof. Stathis N.,** PhD; Gladstone Professor of Government, University of Oxford, since 2018; Fellow, All Souls College, Oxford, since 2018; *b* Corfu, Greece, 7 March 1964; *s* of Nikolaos Kalyvas and Marguerite-Fernande Gérard; partner, Angeliki Louvi. *Educ:* Lycée Léonin, Athens; Univ. of Athens (BA Political Scis 1986); Univ. of Chicago (MA 1989; PhD Political Sci. 1993). Assistant Professor: Ohio State Univ., 1993–94; New York Univ., 1994–2000; Associate Prof., Univ. of Chicago, 2000–03; Arnold Wolfers Prof. of Political Sci., Yale Univ., 2003–14. Fellow, Amer. Acad. of Arts and Scis, 2008. *Publications:* The Rise of Christian Democracy in Europe, 1996; The Logic of Violence in Civil War, 2006; Modern Greece, 2015. *Address:* All Souls College, Oxford OX1 4AL.

**KAMALL, Syed Salah,** PhD; Member (C) London Region, European Parliament, May 2005–2019; *b* 15 Feb. 1967; *m* Sandira Beekoo; two *c. Educ:* Latymer Sch.; Univ. of Liverpool (BEng 1988); London Sch. of Econs and Pol Sci. (MSc 1989); City Univ. (PhD 2004). Business systems analyst, NatWest Bank Overseas Dept, 1989–91; Mgt Fellow, Sch. of Mgt, Univ. of Bath, 1994–96; Mgt Res. Fellow, Business Sch., Univ. of Leeds, 1996–97; Associate Dir and Consultant, Omega Partners, 1997–2001; Consultant, SSK Consulting, 2001–05. Contested (C): West Ham, 2001; London Reg., EP, 2019. *Publications:* Telecommunications Policy, 1996.

**KAMASA, Zygi;** Chief Executive Officer, Lionsgate UK and Europe, since 2015 (Chief Executive Officer, Lionsgate UK, 2005–15); *b* Stockholm, 12 Nov. 1969; *s* of Zygi and Kerstin Kamasa; *m* 2000, Eugenie; one *s* one *d. Educ:* Highgate Sch.; City Poly. (BA Hons Business Studies). CEO, Kamco Computers, 1990–94; Man. Dir, CCL Ltd, 1994–96; Founder and Man. Dir, Scorpio Prodns Ltd, 1996–99; Jt Founder and Pres., Redbus Film Distributions Ltd, 1999–2005. *Address:* Lionsgate UK, 45 Mortimer Street, W1W 8HJ. *T:* (020) 7299 8807. *E:* zkamasa@lionsgate.com.

**KAMEN, Ruth H(ope),** MBE 2007; Director, and Sir Banister Fletcher Librarian, British Architectural Library, Royal Institute of British Architects, 1988–2004; *b* NYC, 19 April 1944; *d* of Markus M. Epstein and Hilda W. Epstein (*née* Winner); *m* 1964, Dr Robert I. Kamen (marr. diss. 1985). *Educ:* Univ. of Wisconsin (BA 1964); Smith Coll., Northampton, Mass (MAT 1965); Simmons Coll., Boston (MSLS 1967). FCLIP (FLA 1993; ALA 1986). Ref. Librarian, Fine Arts Dept, Res. Div., Boston Public Liby, 1965–70; Royal Institute of British Architects, British Architectural Library: Cataloguer, Handley-Read Collection, 1973; Loans, Serials and Ref. Librarian, 1974; Sen. Inf. Librarian, 1974–76; Hd of Liby Inf. Services, 1976–88. Sec., British Architectural Liby Trust, 1988–2001, 2003–04. Chm., ARLIS UK and Ireland, 1982–86 (Hon. Mem., ARLIS, 2005). FRSA 1989. Hon. FRIBA 2002. *Publications:* British and Irish Architectural History: a bibliography and guide to sources of information, 1981 (Besterman Award, LA); contrib. to books, jls and websites on architecture and librarianship. *Recreations:* art and architecture, painting, theatre, photography, shopping (especially antiques). *Address:* 15 Bingham Place, W1U 5AZ. *T:* (020) 7935 8975. *Club:* Architecture.

**KAMIL, His Honour Geoffrey Harvey,** CBE 2009; a Circuit Judge, 1993–2010; *b* 17 Aug. 1942; *s* of Peter and Sadie Kamil; *m* 1968, Andrea Pauline Kamil (*née* Ellis); two *d. Educ:* Leeds Grammar Sch.; Leeds University (LLB). Admitted as solicitor of the Supreme Court, 1968; Partner with J. Levi & Co., solicitors, Leeds, 1968–87; Asst Stipendiary Magistrate, 1986–87; Stipendiary Magistrate, W Midlands, 1987–90, W Yorks, 1990–93; Asst Crown Court Recorder, 1986–91; Recorder, 1991–93; Ethnic Minority Liaison Judge, Leeds and Bradford, 1998–2006; Liaison Judge, Wakefield and Pontefract, 1998–2007; Chm., Immigration Appeals Tribunal, 1998–2000; Lead Diversity and Community Relations Judge, 2006–10. Judicial Studies Board: Member: Magisterial Cttee, 1991–93; Equal Treatment Adv. Cttee, 2000–10; Family Cttee, 2004–10. Member: Centre for Criminal Justice Studies, Leeds Univ., 1992–; W Yorks Race Issues Adv. Gp, 1998–; Parole Bd, 2000– (Mem., Learning and Develt Cttee, 2012–15); Race Issues Adv. Cttee, NACRO, 2003–10; Equality and Diversity Cttee, Law Soc., 2009–10. Leeds Law Society: Mem. Cttee, 1983–87; Chm., Courts Cttee, 1983–87; Mem., Duty Solicitor Cttee, 1986–87; Mem., Leeds Bar/Law Soc. Liaison Cttee, 1983–87. Sec., Kirkstall Lodge Hostel for Ex-Offenders, 1987–97. *Recreations:* golf, swimming, the Dales, classic cars, TV soap addict. *Address:* 52 High Ash Avenue, Alwoodley, Leeds, W Yorks LS17 8RG. *Club:* Moor Allerton Golf (Leeds) (Captain, 2015–16).

**KAMILL, Louise Naima Rachelle, (Mrs Max Lightwood); Her Honour Judge Kamill;** a Circuit Judge, since 2008; *b* London, 9 March 1951; *d* of Dr Mostapha Kamill, GM and Joan Mary Kamill (*née* Hirst); *m* 1978, Max Lightwood; two *d. Educ:* St Paul's Girls' Sch.; University Coll. London (LLB Hons). Called to the Bar, Inner Temple, 1974; Recorder, 1986–2008. Mem., Parole Bd, 2010–. Unit Pres., St John Ambulance, 2009–. *Recreations:* chamber music, birdwatching, painting, golf, tennis, cycling. *Address:* Snaresbrook Crown Court, 75 Hollybush Hill, E11 1QW. *Clubs:* Sunningdale Golf, Campden Hill Lawn Tennis.

**KAMIT, Sir (Leonard) Wilson (Fufus),** Kt 2009; CBE 2002; Governor and Chairman of Board, Bank of Papua New Guinea, 1999–2009; Registrar, Savings and Loan Societies, Papua New Guinea, 1999–2009; Director, Kamchild Ltd; *b* Tufi, PNG, 19 Nov. 1953; *s* of John Caswell Kamit and Naomi Taroben Kamit; *m* 1976, Winifred Pakalmat Tare; one *s* one *d. Educ:* Univ. of Papua New Guinea (BEc 1975); Univ. of New England (Dip. Corp. Dirs). Bank of Papua New Guinea: sponsored scholarship student, 1972–75; res. officer, 1975–80; various mgt roles, 1980–90; Dep. Gov., 1991–99. Alternate Exec. Dir, Asian Development Bank, 2010–13. Non-executive Director: InterOil Corp., 2013–17; Credit Corporation (PNG) Ltd, 2013–18 (Chm., 2015–18); PNG Sustainable Develt Prog. Ltd, 2013–. Trustee: Anglican Ch of PNG; Sir Anthony Siaguru Foundn. *Address:* Kamchild Ltd, PO Box 1569, Port Moresby, National Capital District 121, Papua New Guinea.

**KAMPFNER, John Paul;** author and broadcaster; Senior Associate Fellow, Royal United Services Institute; *b* 27 Dec. 1962; *s* of Dr Fred Kampfner and Betty Kampfner (*née* Andrews); *m* 1992, Lucy Ash; two *d. Educ:* Westminster Sch.; Queen's Coll., Oxford (BA Hons Modern Hist. and Russian). Reuters, 1984–89 (Correspondent, Moscow, 1985–86, Bonn, 1987–89); Daily Telegraph: Berlin and Eastern Europe corresp., 1989–91; Moscow corresp., 1991–94; Chief Political Corresp., Financial Times, 1995–98; Political Corresp., Today prog., BBC Radio, 1998–2000; documentary maker, BBC, 2000–02; Political Ed., 2002–05, Ed., 2005–08, New Statesman; Chief Exec., Index on Censorship, 2008–12 (Trustee, 2012–13); Ext. Advr on freedom of expression and culture for EMEA, Google, 2012–14; Chief Exec., Creative Industries Fedn, 2014–18. Columnist: Daily Telegraph,

2007–08; Independent, 2012–13. Chairman: Turner Contemporary, 2008–15; Clore Social Leadership Prog., 2014–18; Culture Conf., Frankfurt Book Fair. Mem. Council, KCL, 2012–15. FRSA 2003. Hon. DArts Bath Spa, 2019. Journalist of Year, For. Press Assoc., 2002; Ed. of Year, Current Affairs, BSME, 2006. *Publications:* Inside Yeltsin's Russia, 1994; Robin Cook, 1998; Blair's Wars, 2003; Freedom for Sale, 2009; The Rich: from slaves to super-yachts, a 2000-year history, 2014; Why the Germans Do it Better, 2020. *Recreations:* tennis, theatre, travel. *E:* john@jkampfner.net. *W:* www.jkampfner.net.

**KAN, Prof. Yuet Wai,** FRCP 1983; FRS 1981; Louis K. Diamond Professor of Hematology, University of California, San Francisco, since 1984; *b* 11 June 1936; *s* of Kan Tong Po and Kan Li Lai Wan; *m* 1964, Alvera L. Limauro; two *d*. *Educ:* Univ. of Hong Kong (MB, BS, DSc). Research Associate, Children's Hosp. Medical Center, Dept of Pediatrics, Harvard Medical Sch., Boston, Mass; Asst Prof. of Pediatrics, Harvard Medical Sch., 1970–72; Associate Prof. of Medicine, Depts of Medicine and Laboratory Medicine, Univ. of California, San Francisco, 1972–77; Chief, Hematology Service, San Francisco General Hospital, 1972–79; Investigator, Howard Hughes Med. Inst. Lab., 1976–2003; Prof. of Lab. Medicine and Medicine, 1977–, Hd of Div. of Molecular Medicine and Diagnostics, Dept of Lab. Medicine, 1989–2003, Univ. of California. Dir, Molecular Biology Inst., Univ. of Hong Kong, 1990–94 (Hon. Dir, 1988–90). Trustee, Croucher Foundn, 1992–2011 (Chm., 1997–2011). Member: Nat. Acad. of Scis, USA, 1986; Academia Sinica, Taiwan, 1988; Foreign Mem., Chinese Acad. of Scis, 1996. Hon. MD Univ. of Cagliari, Sardinia, 1981; Hon. DSc: Chinese Univ. of Hong Kong, 1981; Univ. of Hong Kong, 1987; Open Univ. of Hong Kong, 1998. *Publications:* contribs to: Nature, Genetics, Proc. of Nat. Academy of Sciences, Jl of Clinical Investigation, Blood, British Jl of Haematology, and others. *Address:* HSW 901, University of California, 513 Parnassus Avenue, San Francisco, CA 94143–0793, USA. *T:* (415) 4765841, *Fax:* (415) 4762956.

**KANANI, Dr Nikita,** MBE 2017; General Practitioner, Bellegrove Surgery, Welling, since 2012; Acting Medical Director for Primary Care, NHS England and NHS Improvement, since 2018 (Deputy Medical Director for Primary Care, NHS England, 2018); *b* London, 18 Aug. 1980; *d* of Jagdish Kanani and Keerti Kanani; *m* 2005, Chrisanthan Ferdinand; one *s* one *d*. *Educ:* Guy's, King's and St Thomas' Medical Sch. (BSc Hons Neurosci. 2001; MB BS 2004); King's Coll. London (Postgrad. Cert. Managing in Health and Social Care 2008); Univ. of Birmingham (MSc Healthcare Commng 2014). DRCOG 2009; Dip. FSRH 2010; MRCGP 2012. Voluntary jun. doctor work in Kampala, Uganda and Negombo, Sri Lanka, 2004–06; Dartford and Gravesham NHS Trust: SHO, 2006–07; Service Modernisation Lead and Trust Grade Dr, 2007–09; GP Registrar, Sidcup Vocational Trng Scheme, 2009–12; NHS Bexley Clinical Commissioning Group: Clin. Vice-Chair, then Clin. Chair, 2012–17; Chief Clin. Officer, 2015–18. Member: CCG Adv. Council, NHS England; Gen. Adv. Council, King's Fund. Jt Chair, The Network. Hon. Sec., Nat. Assoc. of Primary Care. Editor, NHS England and NHS Improvement Gen. Practice Bulletin. *Recreations:* running with/around/after children, powerlifting, hot yoga, family time.

**KANDEL, Prof. Eric Richard,** MD; University Professor, since 1983, Fred Kavli Professor, Director, Kavli Institute for Brain Science, since 2004, and Co-Director, Mortimer B. Zuckerman Mind Brain Behavior Institute, Columbia University; Senior Investigator, Howard Hughes Medical Institute, since 1984; *b* 7 Nov. 1929; *s* of Herman and Charlotte Kandel; *m* 1956, Denise Bystryn; one *s* one *d*. *Educ:* Harvard Coll. (BA 1952); New York Univ. Sch. of Medicine (MD 1956). Intern, Montefiore Hosp., NY, 1956–57; Associate in Res., Lab. of Neurophysiol., Nat. Inst. of Mental Health, Bethesda, 1957–60; Resident in Psychiatry, 1960–64, Staff Psychiatrist, 1964–65, Massachusetts Mental Health Center, Harvard Med. Sch., Boston (Milton Res. Fellow, 1961–62); Instructor, Dept of Psychiatry, Harvard Med. Sch., 1963–65; Associate Prof., then Prof., Depts of Physiol. and Psychiatry, NY Univ. Sch. of Medicine, 1965–74; Chief, Dept of Neurobiol. and Behavior, Public Health Res. Inst. of City of NY, 1968–74; College of Physicians and Surgeons, Columbia University: Prof., Depts of Physiol. and Psychiatry, 1974–, and Dept of Biochem. and Molecular Biophysics, 1992–; Dir, Center for Neurobiol. and Behavior, 1974–83. Associate Editor: Annual Rev. of Neurosci., 1977–82; Jl Neurophysiol., 1977–80; Jl Neurosci., 1981–83; Learning and Memory, 1993–; Reviews Ed., Neuron, 1988–; Mem., Editl Bd, Proc. NAS, 1991–97. Pres., Soc. for Neurosci., 1980–81. Member: Bd of Trustees, Cold Spring Harbor Labs, 1985–90; Bd of Dirs, McKnight Foundn, 1986–98; Bd of Scientific Advrs, Merck Foundn, 1991–94. Mem., numerous professional socs. For. Mem., Royal Soc., 2013. Hon. FRSE 2018. Holds numerous hon. degrees, including: Hon. DSc: Edinburgh, 1999; (Medicine) UCL, 2001. Numerous prizes and awards, including: Internat. Award for Outstanding Achievement in Med. Sci., Gairdner Foundn, Canada, 1987; Nat. Medal of Sci., NAS, 1988; NY Acad. of Medicine Award, 1996; Gerard Prize, Soc. of Neurosci., 1997; Wolf Prize in Biol. and Medicine, Israel, 1999; (jtly) Nobel Prize for Physiol. or Medicine, 2000. *Publications:* Cellular Basis of Behavior: an introduction to behavioral neurobiology, 1976; (ed) Handbook of Physiology: The Nervous System, Vol. 1, Cellular Biology of Neurons, 1977; A Cell-Biological Approach to Learning, 1978; The Behavioral Biology of Aplysia: a contribution to the comparative study of opisthobranch molluscs, 1979; (ed jtly) Principles of Neural Science, 1981, 5th edn 2012; (ed jtly) Molecular Aspects of Neurobiology, 1986; (ed) Molecular Neurobiology in Neurology and Psychiatry, 1987; (ed jtly) Essentials of Neural Science and Behavior, 1995; (with L. Squire) From Mind to Molecules, 1999; In Search of Memory, 2006; The Age of Insight; the quest to understand the unconscious in art, mind and brain, from Vienna 1900 to the present, 2012; Reductionism in Art and Brain Science: bridging the two cultures, 2016; contrib. numerous papers to learned jls incl. Jl Neurophysiol., Amer. Jl Physiol., Jl Physiol., Nature, Science, Brain Res., Scientific American. *Recreations:* tennis, opera. *E:* erk5@Columbia.edu.

**KANE, Adam Vincent;** QC 2015; *b* Cardiff, 19 June 1969; *s* of Vincent Kane, OBE and Mary Kane; *m* 2000, Emma Nott; one *s* two *d*. *Educ:* De La Salle Sch.; Radyr Sch.; University Coll., Oxford (BA); Wolverhampton Univ. (CPE). Called to the Bar, Gray's Inn, 1993; in practice as barrister, specialising in civil and criminal fraud, and commercial crime, 1993–. *Recreations:* extreme gardening, vintage champagne. *Address:* Voronzoff Gate, Savernake Forest, Marlborough, Wilts SN8 3HT. *T:* (020) 7936 6300. *E:* avkane@hotmail.com.

**KANE, Archie Gerard,** CA; Governor, Bank of Ireland, 2012–18; non-executive Chairman, ReAssure Group plc, since 2019; *b* 16 June 1952; *s* of Archie and Rose Kane; *m* 1986, Diana Muirhead; two *d*. *Educ:* Glasgow Univ. (BAcc); City Univ. (MBA); Harvard Business Sch. (AMP). CA 1977. FCIBS 2005. Student CA, Mann Judd, 1974–77; Asst Manager, Price Waterhouse, 1978–80; General Telephone & Electronics Corporation, 1980–85: Sen. Mgt Auditor, Sylvania, 1980–82; Asst Financial Controller, 1982–83, Finance Dir, 1983–85, Directories Corp.; Finance Dir, British Telecom Yellow Pages Sales Ltd, 1986; Gp Finance Controller, TSB Commercial Hldgs Ltd, 1986–89; TSB Bank plc: Financial Controller, then Dir, Financial Control, Retail Banking Div., 1989–91; Dir, Financial Control, 1991–92, Ops Dir, 1992–94, Retail Banking and Insce; Gp Strategic Develt Dir, 1994–96; Lloyds TSB Group, later Lloyds Banking Group plc: Project Dir, Post-Merger Integration, then Retail Financial Services Dir, 1996; Dir, Gp IT and Ops, 1997–99; Dir, 2000–11; Gp Exec. Dir, IT and Ops, 2000–03; Gp Exec. Dir, Insurance and Investments, 2003–11; Chief. Exec., Scottish Widows plc, 2003–11; Gp Exec. Dir, Insce and Scotland, 2009–11; Dir of various cos in the Lloyds Banking (formerly Lloyds TSB) and Scottish Widows Gp, 2000–11. Chm., APACS (Admin) Ltd, 2001–03; Dir, Hill Samuel Asset Mgt Internat. Ltd, 2003–06. Chm., ABI, 2007–10 (Mem. Bd, 2004); Member: Takeover Panel, 2007; Retail Financial Services Gp, 2007–09; Insce Industry Working Gp, 2008–09; Financial Services Adv. Bd, 2009; TheCityUK, 2010–17. FCIBS 2005. *Recreations:* golf, tennis, ski-ing.

**KANE, Christopher John;** Creative Director, Christopher Kane, since 2006; *b* Bellshill, N Lanarkshire, 26 July 1982; *s* of Thomas Kane and Christine Kane. *Educ:* Central Saint Martin's Coll. of Art and Design (BA Womenswear; MA Womenswear). Launched Christopher Kane label, 2006; womenswear designer for Versus, Versace, 2009. Lancôme Colour Award, 2005; Young Designer of the Yr, Scottish Fashion Awards, 2006; New Generation Designer, 2007, British Collection of the Yr, 2009, Designer of the Year, 2013, British Fashion Awards; British Designer of the Yr, Elle Style Awards, 2011. *Recreations:* drawing, going to exhibitions, music concerts, theatre, travel, collecting books. *Address:* The Communications Store, 2 Kensington Square, W8 5EP. *T:* (020) 7938 1010.

**KANE, Michael Joseph Patrick;** MP (Lab) Wythenshawe and Sale East, since Feb. 2014; *b* Wythenshawe, 9 Jan. 1969; *s* of Joseph Kane and Kathleen Kane (*née* McGirl); *m* 1996, Sandra Bracegirdle. *Educ:* St Paul's RC High Sch.; Manchester Metropolitan Univ. (BA Social Scis 1997; PGCE 1999). Teacher, Springfield Primary Sch., 2000–08; Parliamentary Assistant: to Rt Hon. James Purnell, MP, 2008–10; to Jonathan Reynolds, MP, 2010–11; Sen. Exec. Asst, Tameside Council, 2011–14. Mem. (Lab) Manchester CC, 1991–2008. Nat. Chair, 2010–13, Actg Chief Exec., 2014, Movement for Change. *Recreations:* playing flute and bagpipes, Manchester City FC. *Address:* House of Commons, SW1A 0AA. *T:* (constituency office) (0161) 499 7900. *E:* mike.kane.mp@parliament.uk. *Club:* Stretford Wheelers.

**KANE, Peter Ronald,** PhD; Chamberlain, City of London Corporation, since 2014; *b* 24 Nov. 1956; *s* of Ronald Kane and Katherine Kane; *m* 1989, Jan Evans; two *d*. *Educ:* St Edmund Hall, Oxford (BA 1st Cl. Hons PPE); London Sch. of Econs (MSc Econs 1979; PhD Econs 1982). Economist, TUC, 1981–88; Chief Econ. Advr, London Bor. of Hackney, 1988–92; Principal, 1992–99, Team Leader, 1999–2001, HM Treasury; Director: Office of Public Service Reform, Cabinet Office, 2002–05; Finance and Performance, Home Office, 2006–14. *Recreations:* travelling the globe, ski-ing, tennis, cinema, reading, current affairs. *Address:* City of London Corporation, Guildhall, PO Box 270, EC2P 2EJ. *E:* peter.kane@cityoflondon.gov.uk.

**KANE, Rosie;** Member (Scot Socialist) Glasgow, Scottish Parliament, 2003–07. Scot Socialist spokesman for envmt and transport, Scottish Parlt, 2003–07. Contested: (Scot Socialist Alliance) Glasgow, Rutherglen, 1997; (Scot Socialist) Glasgow Shettleston, Scottish Parlt, 1999.

**KANI, Wasfi,** OBE 2001; Founder and Chief Executive Officer: Grange Park Opera, since 1998; Pimlico Opera, since 1987; *b* Cable Street, London, 7 March 1956; *d* of Khawaja Mohammed Kani and Jaria Kani. *Educ:* Burlington Grammar Sch., Shepherds Bush; St Hilda's Coll., Oxford (MA Hons; Hon. Fellow, 2017). Computer programmer, then systems analyst, specialising in financial systems, 1980–90; initiated prog. of work in prisons, 1991; CEO, Garsington Opera, 1992–97. BBC TV and radio appearances and presenter. Trustee: Royal Court Th., 2008–14; Mayor's Fund for London, 2008–10; British Mus., 2013–17. Hon. FRIBA 2017; Hon. DMus Southampton Solent; Hon. Dr Winchester, 2016. *Recreations:* stopping time fly, collecting rainwater, growing roses, sewing, the Ancient World. *Address:* Grange Park Opera, Sutton Manor Farm, Bishops Sutton SO24 0AA. *E:* info@grangeparkopera.co.uk.

**KAO, Prof. Rowland Raymond,** PhD; Sir Timothy O'Shea Professor of Veterinary Epidemiology and Data Science, University of Edinburgh, since 2017; *b* Toronto, 7 Dec. 1964; *s* of Raymond Wen Yuan Kao and Flora Maria Kao (*née* Con Wong); *m* 2000, Eleanor Fiona Houston; two *d*. *Educ:* Univ. of Toronto (BASc Engrg Physics 1986); Univ. of Guelph (MSc Physics 1989; PhD Physics 1993). Res. Scientist, AgResearch, NZ, 1995–99; Postdoctoral Res. Scientist, Inst. for Animal Health, 1999–2001; University of Oxford: Postdoctoral Res. Asst, 2001–03; Wellcome Trust Res. Career Develt Fellow, 2003–07; University of Glasgow: Wellcome Trust Sen. Res. Fellow, 2007–14; Prof. of Mathematical Population Biol., 2009–17; Dir, Boyd Orr Centre for Population and Ecosystem Health, 2011–14. Mem., Sci. Adv. Council, DEFRA, 2017–. *Publications:* (jtly) Entrepreneurism: a philosophy and a sensible alternative for the market economy, 2002; (jtly) An Entrepreneurial Approach to Stewardship Accountability: corporate residual and global poverty, 2004; articles in Science, Nature Revs, Microbiol., PLoS Pathogens, PLoS Computational Biol., Procs of Biol Scis. *Recreations:* cycling, running, canoeing and (formerly) hockey (the Canadian type), boardgames, wargames, science fiction and fantasy, history, Star Trek, Advanced Squad Leader, Dungeons and Dragons. *Address:* Royal (Dick) School of Veterinary Studies and the Roslin Institute, Easter Bush Campus, University of Edinburgh EH25 9RG. *T:* (0131) 651 9114. *E:* rowland.kao@ed.ac.uk, rowland.kao@gmail.com.

**KAPLAN, Neil Trevor,** CBE 2001; QC (Hong Kong) 1982; arbitrator, mediator; *b* 1 Sept. 1942; *s* of Leslie Henry Kaplan and Sybil Sylvia Kaplan (*née* Gasson); *m* 1st, 1971, Barbara Jane Spector (marr. diss. 1997); one *s* one *d*; 2nd, 1998, Paula White (marr. diss. 2009); 3rd, 2013, Sue Lesser. *Educ:* St Paul's Sch.; King's College London (LLB). FCIArb. Called to the Bar, Inner Temple, 1965, Bencher 1991; practised London, 1965–80; Dep. Principal Crown Counsel, Hong Kong, 1980, Principal Crown Counsel, 1982; private practice, Hong Kong Bar, 1984–90; Solicitor-barrister, Victoria, NSW, 1983; NY Bar, 1986; High Court Judge, Hong Kong, 1990–94; Judge in charge of Construction and Arbitration List, 1990–94. Vis. Prof., City Univ. of Hong Kong, 1995–97 (Hon. Prof., 2001–). Pres., CIArb, 1999–2000 (Chm., Hong Kong Branch, 1984–87 and 1989–90); Chairman: Hong Kong Internat. Arbitration Centre, 1991–2004; Disputes Rev. Bd, new Hong Kong airport, 1995–99; Post-Release Supervision Bd, 1996–2006; WTO Rev. Body, Hong Kong, 2000–04; Hong Kong Telecommunications Appeal Tribunal, 2007–13 (Dep. Chm., 2001–07); Deputy Chairman: Justice, Hong Kong, 1988–90; Mem., Judicial Studies Bd, 1994–. Member: Council, ICCA, 1995–; Court of Arbitration, ICC, 2012–. Liveryman, Arbitrators' Co., 1982–. JP Hong Kong, 1984. Silver Bauhinia Star (HKSAR), 2007. *Publications:* (jtly) Hong Kong Arbitration—Cases and Materials, 1991; (jtly) Arbitration in Hong Kong and China, 1994; (jtly) Model Law Decisions, 2002; articles on arbitration. *Recreations:* golf, travel, food and wine, films, theatre, walking. *Address:* Arbitration Chambers Hong Kong, Chinachem Hollywood Centre, Suite 803, 1 Hollywood Road, Central, Hong Kong. *E:* neilkaplan@btconnect.com. *Clubs:* Athenæum, Oriental, Old Pauline; Hong Kong, Hong Kong Cricket.

**KAPOOR, Sir Anish,** Kt 2013; CBE 2003; Padma Bhushan 2012; RA 1999; artist and sculptor; *b* Bombay, 12 March 1954; *s* of Rear Adm. D. C. Kapoor and Mrs H. Kapoor; *m* 1995, Susanne Spicale; one *s* one *d*. *Educ:* Hornsey Coll. of Art; Chelsea Sch. of Art. Lectr, Wolverhampton Polytechnic, 1979–83. Artist in Residence, Walker Art Gall., Liverpool, 1982–83. Mem., Arts Council England (formerly Arts Council of England), 1998–; Trustee, Tate Britain, 2006–09. One-man exhibitions include: Lisson Gall., London, 1982, 1984,

1985, 1988, 1989–90, 1993, 1998, 2000, 2003, 2006; Walker Art Gall., Liverpool, 1982, 1983; Gladstone Gall., NY, 1984, 1986, 1989, 1990, 1998, 2001, 2004, 2007; Tate Gall., London, 1990–91; Tate Modern, 2002; San Diego Mus. Contemporary Art, 1992; Tel Aviv Mus. of Art, 1993; Nat. Gall. of Canada, Ottawa, 1993; Rockefeller Center, NY, 2006; RA, 2009; Manchester Art Gall., 2011; Pinchuk Art Centre, Kiev, 2012; retrospective exhibitions: Hayward Gall., 1998; Lisson Gall., 2015; and others in Europe, USA, Australia, Japan and India; contrib. numerous group exhibns in Britain, Europe, USA, Canada, Australia and Japan, incl. Tate Gall., London, 1983, 1991, 1994; Art Inst., Chicago, 1990; Expo '92, Seville, 1992; public works include: Sky Mirror, Nottingham, 2001; Sky Mirror, Rockefeller Center, NY, 2006; Cloud Gate, Millennium Park, Chicago, 2006; Turning the World Upside Down, Israel Mus., Jerusalem, 2010; (with C. Balmond and A. Agu) Orbit, Olympic Tower, London, 2012. Set designer, Tristan and Isolde, ENO, 2016. Hon. Fellow, Univ. of Wolverhampton, 1999; Hon. FRIBA 2001. Hon. Dr: London Inst., 1997; Leeds, 1997. Premio Duemila, Venice Biennale, 1990; Turner Prize, 1991; Praemium Imperiale, 2011. *Address:* c/o Lisson Gallery, 67 Lisson Street, NW1 5DA.

**KAPPLER, David John;** Senior Independent Director, Flybe plc, 2015–18; *b* Winchester, 24 March 1947; *s* of Alec and Hilary Kappler; *m* 1970, Maxine Lea; three *d. Educ:* Lincoln Sch. FCMA 1975. Finance Director: Jeyes Gp, 1977–85; Trebor Gp, 1985–89; Cadbury Ltd, 1989–91; Cadbury Confectionery, 1991–93; Cadbury Schwepppes plc: Corporate Finance Dir, 1993–94; Chief Financial Officer, 1995–2004. Chm., Premier Foods plc, 2004–10; non-executive Director: Camelot plc, 1995–2001; HMV plc, 2001–06; Intercontinental Hotels plc, 2004–14; Shire plc, 2004–16 (Dep. Chm., 2008–16). *Recreations:* playing golf, watching other sports, wine. *Address:* Willow House, 147 High Street, Old Amersham, Bucks HP7 0EB. *E:* djkappler@icloud.com. *Clubs:* Royal Automobile, MCC (Associate); Harewood Downs Golf; Barton-on-Sea Golf.

**KAPUR, (Arvind) Michael,** OBE 2017; Lord-Lieutenant of Leicestershire, since 2018; *b* Ludhiana, India, 1962; *s* of Chaman Lal Kapur and Sudesh Kapur; *m* 1987, Rita Mehan; two *s* two *d. Educ:* Leicester Poly. (BSc Hons Combined Studies 1985). ACA 1990. KPMG, 1985–96, Sen. Manager, 1993–96; Dir, Entrepreneurial Services, Ernst & Young, 1996–99; Finance Dir, Parker Plant, 1999–2001; Founder and Dir, Signum Corporate Communications, 2002–. Chm., Enterprise Council, CBI, 2013–17. Non-executive Director: Leicester Royal Infirmary, 1995–2000; Univ. Hosps of Leicester NHS Trust, 2000–09. Pro Chancellor, De Montfort Univ., 2012– (Gov. and Dep. Chm., 2009–18); Chairman: Nat. Space Centre, 2009–; Leicester City FC Trust, 2017–. Trustee: Nat. Learning and Work Inst., 2013–18; Warning Zone, 2016–18; Nat. Forest Co., 2018–. Gov., Derby Coll. Gp, 2017–. *Recreations:* listening to music, reading, watching any sport, foreign travel, supporting my children's ambitions. *Address:* Leicestershire Lieutenancy Office, County Hall, Glenfield, Leicester LE3 8RA. *T:* (0116) 305 6002. *E:* lieutenancyoffice@leics.gov.uk.

**KARABITS, Kirill;** Principal Conductor, Bournemouth Symphony Orchestra, since 2009; Artistic Director, I, Culture Orchestra, since 2014; General Music Director and Principal Conductor, Deutsches Nationaltheater and Staatskapelle, Weimar, since 2016; *b* Kiev, Ukraine, 26 Dec. 1976; *s* of Ivan Karabits and Marianna Kopytsa; partner, Coline Vandenberghe; one *s* one *d. Educ:* Lysenko Music Sch., Kiev; Tchaikovsky Nat. Acad. of Music, Kiev; Hochschule für Musik, Vienna. Asst Conductor, Budapest Fest. Orch., 1996–99; Associate Conductor, Orchestre Philharmonique de Radio France, 2002–05; Principal Guest Conductor, Orchestre Philharmonique de Strasbourg, 2005–07. *Address:* c/o Askonas Holt Ltd, 15 Fetter Lane, EC4A 1BW.

**KARAMANLIS, Konstantinos A., (Kostas);** MP (NDP) Thessaloniki A, Greece, since 1989; Prime Minister of Greece, 2004–09; President, New Democracy Party, 1997–2009; *b* 14 Sept. 1956; *s* of Alexandros and Ageliki Karamanlis; *m* 1998, Natasa Pazaiti; one *s* one *d* (twins). *Educ:* Sch. of Law, Univ. of Athens; Fletcher Sch. of Law and Diplomacy, Tufts Univ., Boston, USA. In practice as lawyer, 1984–89. Minister of Culture, 2004–06. Vice-President: EPP, 1999–2009 (Hd, Western Balkan Democracy Initiative, 2001–03); Chm., SE European Forum, 2003–05); Internat. Democrat Union, 2002; Co-Chm., Party Leaders Conf., European Democrat Union, 2003. *Publications:* Eleftherios Venizelos and Greek Foreign Relations, 1986; (ed) Spirit and Era of Gorbachev, 1987. *Address:* Hellenic Parliament, Vas. Sophias 2, 100 21 Athens, Greece.

**KARAS, Jonathan Marcus;** QC 2006; *b* 18 Sept. 1961; *s* of Arie Karas and Enid Novello Karas (*née* Owens); *m* 1989, Tracey Ann Elliott (marr. diss. 2012); three *d. Educ:* Brentwood Sch.; Trinity Coll., Oxford (Ford Student; MA Hons Lit.Hum.); City Univ. (Dip. Law). Called to the Bar, Middle Temple, 1986; Supplementary Panel, 1995–99, B Panel, 1999–2000, A Panel, 2000–06, of Jun. Counsel to the Crown. Subject Ed., Hill & Redman's Law of Landlord and Tenant, 1987–. *Publications:* (jtly) Elvin & Karas's Unlawful Interference with Land, 1995, 2nd edn 2002; (jtly) Commonhold and Leasehold Reform Act 2002, 2002; (jtly) Swinesend: Britain's greatest public school, 2006; Halsbury's Laws of England, 4th edn: (jtly) Compulsory Purchase, 1996 (reissue); Distress, 2000 (reissue, consultant ed.), 2007 (reissue); Forestry, 2007 (reissue, consultant ed.); (jtly and consultant ed.) Perpetuities, 2013; Rights of Light, 2016. *Recreations:* writing, embarrassing my daughters. *Address:* Falcon Chambers, Falcon Court, EC4Y 1AA. *T:* (020) 7353 2484, *Fax:* (020) 7353 1261. *Club:* Travellers.

**KARASIN, Grigory Borisovich;** State Secretary and Deputy Minister of Foreign Affairs, Russian Federation, since 2005; *b* 23 Aug. 1949; *m* 1971, Olga V. Karasina; two *d. Educ:* Coll. of Oriental Langs, Moscow State Univ. Joined USSR Diplomatic Service, 1972: served: Senegal, 1972–76; Australia, 1979–85; UK, 1988–92; Dir, Dept of Africa, 1992–93, Dept of Inf. and Press, 1993–96, Min. of Foreign Affairs; Dep. Minister of Foreign Affairs, Russian Fedn, 1996–2000; Ambassador to UK, 2000–05.

**KARET, Ian Albert Nathan;** Partner, Linklaters LLP, since 1997; *b* London, 3 April 1963; *s* of Jerome Karet and Patricia Karet; *m* 1993, Sara Hoffbrand; three *d. Educ:* University College Sch., Hampstead; Worcester Coll., Oxford (MA Chem.). Linklaters LLP, London: articled clerk, 1987–89; admitted solicitor, 1990; Asst Solicitor, 1990–97. Mem., Civil Justice Council, 2016–. Mem., Charity Commn, 2019–. Trustee: Leo Baeck Coll., 2009–14; Royal Botanic Gardens, Kew, 2014–. *Publications:* (contrib.) The Modern Law of Patents, 2010. *Recreations:* singing, cooking. *Address:* Linklaters LLP, One Silk Street, EC2Y 8HQ. *T:* (020) 7456 5800. *E:* ian.karet@linklaters.com.

**KARIA, Chirag Vrajlal;** QC 2012; *b* Nakuru, Kenya, 26 May 1965; *s* of Vrajlal Vallabhdas Karia and Vimlaben Vrajlal Karia; *m* 1995, Jagruty Topan; twin *s* one *d. Educ:* Sidney Sussex Coll., Cambridge (BA 1st Cl. Hons Law 1987; Slaughter & May Prize); Boalt Hall Sch. of Law, Univ. of Calif, Berkeley (LLM 1990). Denning Schol., Lincoln's Inn, 1987; Council of Legal Educn Studentship, 1987; Harkness Fellow, Commonwealth Fund of NY, 1989–90. Called to the Bar, Lincoln's Inn, 1988; called to State Bar of Calif as Attorney at Law, 1991; in practice as Attorney in commercial litigation and corporate law, Calif, 1991–2000; in practice as barrister, specialising in commercial law, London, 2000–. Examr of the Court, 2004–. *Publications:* (Jt Gen. Ed.) Butterworths Commercial Court and Arbitration Pleadings, 2005. *Recreations:* reading, music, ski-ing, theatre. *Address:* Quadrant Chambers, Quadrant House, 10 Fleet Street, EC4Y 1AU. *T:* (020) 7583 4444, *Fax:* (020) 7583 4455. *E:* chirag.karia@quadrantchambers.com.

**KARIM, Sheikh Mohammed Samiul, (Sam);** QC 2017; *b* Sutton-in Ashfield, 9 Sept. 1978; *s* of Dr Sheikh Mohammed Rezaul Karim and Hasina Karim; *m* 2008, Nadia Nooshin Mustafa Karim. *Educ:* Nottingham High Sch.; Birmingham City Univ. (LLB Hons); King's Coll. London (LLM); City Univ. (DipLaw). MCIArb. Called to the Bar, Gray's Inn, 2002; in practice as barrister, 2002–. Member: Attorney Gen.'s Panel of Regl Counsel, 2005–17; Attorney Gen.'s Regl Panel of Queens Counsel, 2017. Dir, Manchester Public Law Pro Bono Scheme, 2012–. Chair, Northern Admin. Law Assoc., 2010–. *Publications:* Judicial Review: law and practice, 2010, 2nd edn 2015; A Human Rights Perspective on Reducing Restraint Practices, 2015; (contrib.) Bullen & Leake & Jacob's Precedents of Pleading, 18th edn 2016; Finance and the Law for the Older Client, 71st edn, 2018. *Recreations:* classic cars, swimming. *Address:* Kings Chambers, 36 Young Street, Manchester M3 3PT. *T:* 0345 034 3444. *E:* skarimqc@kingschambers.com. *Clubs:* Aston Martin Owners; Old Nottinghamian.

**KARIM, Sajjad Haider;** Partner, Marsdens Solicitors, since 2001; *b* 11 July 1970; *s* of Fazal Karim and Shamshad Karim; *m* 1997, Zahida Chaudhary; one *s* one *d. Educ:* London Guildhall Univ. (LLB Hons Business Law); Coll. of Law, Chester. Admitted solicitor, 1997. Mem. (Lib Dem) Pendle BC, 1994–2002. MEP NW England, 2004–19 (Lib Dem, 2004–07; C, 2007–19); contested (C) same seat, 2019. *Address:* 442 Barlow Moor Road, Manchester M21 0BQ.

**KARIM, Sam;** *see* Karim, M. S.

**KARK, Thomas Victor William;** QC 2010; a Recorder, since 2000; *b* London, 12 Dec. 1960; *s* of Leslie and Evelyn Kark; *m* 1989, Judith Cornes; one *s* one *d. Educ:* Eton Coll.; Univ. of Buckingham (LLB). Called to the Bar, Inner Temple, 1982, Bencher, 2016; in practice as barrister specialising in crime, inquiries, inquests and professional regulation; Standing Counsel to HM Customs and Excise, 2002–10; Asst Recorder, 1999–2000. Lead Counsel, Mid Staffs NHS Foundn Trust Public Inquiry, 2010–13. Led govt review of Fit and Proper Person Test, 2019. *Recreations:* martial arts, cooking. *Address:* QEB Hollis Whiteman Chambers, 1–2 Laurence Pountney Hill, EC4R 0EU. *Clubs:* 606 Jazz, Ronnie Scott's.

**KARMAN, Tawakkol;** journalist and human rights activist; *b* Taiz, Yemen, 7 Feb. 1979; *m* Mohamed al-Nahmi; three *c. Educ:* Univ. of Sci. and Technol., Sana'a; Univ. of Sana'a. Co-founder, Women Journalists Without Chains, 2005; organized weekly protests in Sana'a against government repression, corruption, and social and legal injustice, 2007–11. Sen. Mem., Al-Islah party. (Jtly) Nobel Peace Prize, 2011. *Address:* Women Journalists Without Chains, 12702 Daeery Street, Sana'a, Yemen.

**KARMY-JONES, Riel Meredith;** QC 2015; *b* 16 Dec. 1965; *d* of Prof. William John Jones and Leila Karmy; *m* 1990, Mark Major, *qv*; one *s* one *d. Educ:* Tempo Sch., Edmonton; Univ. of Alberta, Edmonton (BA Drama and Eng. 1986); Drama Studio, London (Dip. Theatre Directing 1987); University Coll. London (LLB Hons 1994). Called to the Bar, Lincoln's Inn, 1995; in practice as a criminal barrister. Sen. Counsel, Inquiry into Child Sexual Abuse leading investigation into RC Church, 2017–19. Trustee, Pan Intercultural Arts, 2015–. *Publications:* (contrib.) Rook and Ward on Sexual Offences, 5th edn, 2016, supplement vol. 2018; (contrib.) Archbold Criminal Pleading, Evidence and Practice, 2019–. *Recreations:* theatre, cinema, walking, gardening, family, reading, art. *Address:* c/o Red Lion Chambers, 18 Red Lion Court, EC4A 3EB. *T:* (020) 7520 6000. *E:* clerks@18rlc.co.uk.

**KARP, Rachel Vivienne; Her Honour Judge Karp;** a Circuit Judge, since 2013; *b* Liverpool, 4 June 1961; *d* of David Karp and Shirley Karp; *m* Stephen Adler; one *s* two *d. Educ:* King David High Sch., Liverpool; Univ. of Bristol. Partner, Daniel and Harris Solicitors, 1986–2004; a District Judge, 2004–13. *Address:* Willesden County Court, 9 Acton Lane, NW10 8SB. *T:* (020) 8963 8200.

**KARPINSKI, Marek Romuald K.;** *see* Korab-Karpinski.

**KARPLUS, Prof. Martin,** PhD; Theodore William Richards Research Professor, Harvard University, 1999–2004, now Professor Emeritus of Chemistry; Professeur Conventionné, Université de Strasbourg (formerly Université Louis Pasteur), since 1995; *b* Vienna, 15 March 1930; moved to USA, 1938; naturalized US citizen, 1945; *m* Marci; one *s* one *d. Educ:* Harvard Coll. (BA 1950); California Inst. of Technol. (PhD 1953). NSF Postdoctoral Fellow, Oxford Univ., 1953–55; instructor, 1955–57, Asst, then Associate Prof., 1957–60, Univ. of Illinois; Associate Prof., 1960–63, Prof., 1963–66, Columbia Univ.; Prof., 1966–79, Theodore William Richards Prof. of Chem., 1979–99, Harvard Univ. Professeur Associé: Univ. de Paris-Sud, 1972–73 and 1980–81; Univ. Louis Pasteur, Strasbourg, 1992, 1994–95; Professeur: Univ. de Paris VII, 1974–75; Coll. de France, Paris, 1980–81, 1987–88; Eastman Prof., Oxford Univ., 1999–2000; Linnett Vis. Prof., Cambridge Univ. 2003. Member: Amer. Acad. Arts and Scis; NAS; Internat. Acad. Quantum Molecular Sci.; Foreign Member: Netherlands Acad. Arts and Sci.; Royal Soc.; Hon. Mem., Austrian Acad. of Sci., 2015. Dr *hc:* Sherbrooke, 1998; Ehrendoktorat Zurich, 2006; Bar-Ilan, 2014; Hon. Dr Vienna, 2015; Hon. MA Oxon, 1999. Hon. Citizen of Vienna, 2015. American Chemical Society: Harrison Howe Award, Rochester Section, 1967; Theoretical Chem. Award, 1993; Computers in Chem. and Pharmaceutical Res. Award, 2001; Pauling Award, Northwest Section, 2004; Award for Outstanding Contribn to Quantum Biol., Internat. Soc. for Quantum Biol., 1979; Irving Langmuir Award, Amer. Physical Soc., 1987; Anfinsen Award, Protein Soc., 2001; Lifetime Achievement Award in Theoretical Biophysics, Internat. Assoc. of Schs and Insts of Admin, 2008; Antonio Feltrinelli Internat. Prize for Chem., Accademia Nazionale dei Lincei, 2011; (jtly) Nobel Prize in Chemistry, 2013. Commandeur, Légion d'Honneur (France), 2014. *Publications:* (with R. N. Porter) Atoms & Molecules: an introduction for students of physical chemistry, 1970; (with O. M. Becker) A Guide to Biomolecular Simulations, 2006; Images of the 1950s (photography), 2011; Martin Karplus, La Couleur des Années 1950 (photography), 2013; contribs to scientific jls incl. Advanced Chem. Physics. *Recreations:* photography, cooking. *Address:* Department of Chemistry and Chemical Biology, Harvard University, 12 Oxford Street, Cambridge, MA 02138, USA.

**KARRAN, Graham,** QFSM 1985; Managing Director, Blundell, Benson & Co. Ltd, planning and safety consultants, 2004–07; *b* 28 Nov. 1939; *s* of Joseph Karran and Muriel Benson; *m* 1960, Thelma Gott (*d* 2010); one *s* one *d. Educ:* Bootle Grammar Sch.; Liverpool College of Building. Estate Management, 1958–60; Southport Fire Bde, 1960–63; Lancashire County Fire Bde, 1963–74; Greater Manchester Fire Service, 1974–78; Cheshire County Fire Service, 1978–80; Chief Fire Officer, Derbyshire Fire Service, 1980–83; Chief Fire Officer, W Yorks Fire Service, and Chief Exec., W Yorks Fire and Civil Defence Authy, 1983–90. FIFireE 1980. *Publications:* articles in English and Amer. Fire jls. *Recreations:* music, beachcombing, sailing.

**KARSTEN, His Honour Ian George Francis**; QC 1990; a Circuit Judge, 1999–2014; b 27 July 1944; s of late Dr Frederick Karsten and Edith Karsten; m 1984, Moira Elizabeth Ann O'Hara (marr. diss. 2002); one s two d. Educ: William Ellis School, Highgate; Magdalen College, Oxford (MA, BCL); Diplômé, Hague Acad. of Internat. Law. Called to the Bar, Gray's Inn, 1967; Midland and Oxford Circuit; commenced practice 1970; Lectr in Law, Southampton Univ., 1966–70, LSE, 1970–88; a Recorder, 1994–99. UK Deleg. to Hague Conf. on Private Internat. Law (Convention on the Law Applicable to Agency) (Rapporteur), 1973–77; Leader, UK Delegn to Unidroit Conf. on Agency in Internat. Sale of Goods, Bucharest, 1979, Geneva, 1983. Recreations: opera, travel, chess. Address: QEB, Queen Elizabeth Building, Temple, EC4Y 9BS.

**KARSTEN, Rear Adm. Thomas Michael**, CBE 2016; Chief Executive, Centre for Environment, Fisheries and Aquaculture Science, since 2015; b Gorseinon, 22 Sept. 1961; s of Peter Karsten and Barbara Karsten; m 1993, Sarah Rees; one s two d. Educ: Charterhouse; Univ. of Exeter (BA Hist.). FRICS 2012. Entered RN, 1979; Commands: HMS Bicester, 1993–94; HMS Sheffield, 1995–96; HMS Endurance, 2003–05; Dir, Maritime Warfare Centre, 2005–07; Dep. Comdr Ops, Navy Comd, 2007; RN Sen. Hudson Fellow, Univ. of Oxford, 2009; Comdr British Forces Gibraltar, 2010–12; Nat. Hydrographer and Dep. Chief Exec., UK Hydrographic Office, 2012–15. Recreation: sport.

**KARUNAIRETNAM, Nadesalingam, (Lee Karu)**; QC 2010; b Sri Lanka, 1 July 1954; s of Tharmalingam Karunairetnam and Malar Karunairetnam; m 1987, Usha Gupta (see U. Karunairetnam); two s. Educ: St Michael's Coll.; Univ. of Westminster (BA Hons Social Scis; DipLaw). Called to the Bar, Lincoln's Inn, 1985. Recreations: marlin fishing, cricket, tennis, golf, dining. Address: 9 Bedford Row, WC1R 4AZ. T: (020) 7489 2727. E: leekaru@9bedfordrow.co.uk.

**KARUNAIRETNAM, Usha; Her Honour Judge Karu**; a Circuit Judge, since 2005; Resident Judge, Inner London Crown Court, since 2017; Hon. Recorder of Southwark, since 2017; b 18 Dec. 1958; d of Dharamchandra Gupta and Saroj Gupta; m 1987, Nadesalingam Karunairetnam, (Lee Karu), qv; two s. Called to the Bar, Middle Temple, 1984, Bencher, 2012 (Autumn Reader, 2019); specialist criminal practitioner, SE Circuit; Asst Recorder, 1998–2000; Recorder, 2000–05; Judicial Mem., Mental Health Rev. Tribunal, 2010–; Circuit Judge Comr, Judicial Appts Commn, 2014–18. Hon. LLD London South Bank, 2018. Recreations: gardening, spending time with family, theatre. Address: Inner London Crown Court, Sessions House, Newington Causeway, SE1 6AZ. T: (020) 7234 3100, Fax: (020) 7234 3203.

**KASER, Prof. Arthur**, MD; Professor of Gastroenterology, University of Cambridge, since 2011; Hon. Consultant Physician, Cambridge University Hospitals NHS Foundation Trust, since 2011; b 1 May 1973; s of Dr Artur Kaser and Eva Kaser; m 2005, Dr Nicole C. Kaneider; one s two d. Educ: Anton-von-Eiselsberg Prim. Sch., Steinhaus bei Wels, Austria; Anton Bruckner Bundesrealgymnasium, Wels; Leopold-Franzens Univ., Innsbruck (MD 1996); Medical Univ. Innsbruck (Univ.-Doz. 2003). Postdoctoral Fellow, Dept of Medicine, 1996–98, Univ. Asst, 1998–2003, Leopold-Franzens Univ., Innsbruck; Consultant Physician, Innsbruck Univ. Hosp., 2002–10; Associate Prof. of Medicine, Medical Univ. Innsbruck, 2003–10. Max Kade Fellow, Mucosal Immunol. Lab., Brigham and Women's Hosp., Harvard Med. Sch., 2003–06. Vis. Prof. (pt-time), Dept of Medicine, Univ. of Oslo, 2009–12. FMedSci 2017. Publications: articles on immunology and medicine. Recreations: reading, music, hiking, ski-ing. Address: Division of Gastroenterology and Hepatology, Department of Medicine, Addenbrooke's Hospital, Level 5, Box 157, Hills Road, Cambridge CB2 0QQ. T: (01223) 768308, Fax: (01223) 336846. E: ak729@cam.ac.uk.

**KASER, Prof. Michael Charles**, DLitt; Hon. Professor and Senior Research Fellow, Institute for German Studies, University of Birmingham, since 1994; Reader in Economics, University of Oxford, and Professorial Fellow of St Antony's College, 1972–93 (Sub-Warden, 1986–87), now Reader Emeritus and Emeritus Fellow; b 2 May 1926; e s of Charles Joseph Kaser and Mabel Blunden; m 1954, Elisabeth Anne Mary, er d of Cyril Gascoigne Piggford; four s one d. Educ: King's Coll., Cambridge (Exhibr); DLitt Oxon 1993. Economic Sect., Min. of Works, 1946–47; Foreign Service, London and Moscow, 1947–51; UN Secretariat, Econ. Commn for Europe, Geneva, 1951–63; Faculty Fellow, St Antony's Coll., Oxford, 1963–72; Institute of Slavonic Studies (formerly Institute of Russian, Soviet and East European Studies), University of Oxford: Dir, 1988–93; Sen. Res. Assoc., 1997–2004; Mem., Cttee on SE European Studies (formerly Prog. on Contemporary Turkey) in Oxford, 2000–. Associate Fellow, Green Templeton Coll. (formerly Templeton Coll.), Oxford, 1983–. Hon. Fellow, Divinity Faculty, Univ. of Edinburgh, 1993–96. Visiting Professor of Economics: Inst. Universitaire des Hautes Etudes Internats, Geneva, 1959–63; Univ. of Michigan, 1966; Vis. Faculty (formerly Fellow), Henley Management Coll., 1987–2002; Vis. Lectr, Cambridge Univ., 1967–68, 1977–78 and 1978–79; Vis. Lectr, INSEAD, Fontainebleau, 1959–82, 1988–92. Gen. Ed. Internat. Econ. Assoc., 1986–2007. Specialist Advr, Foreign Affairs Cttee, H of C, 1985–87. Oxford Univ. Latin Preacher, 1982. Convenor/Chm., Nat. Assoc. for Soviet and East European Studies, 1965–73, Chm., Jt Cttee with BUAS, 1980–84; Vice-Chm., Internat. Activities Cttee (Vice-Chm., Area Studies Panel, SSRC) ESRC, 1980–84; Chm., Co-ordinating Council, Area Studies Assocs, 1986–88 (Mem., 1980–93 and 1995; Sec., 1980–84, Vice-Chm., 1984–86); Governor, Plater Coll., Oxford, 1968–95, Emeritus Governor, 1995–2006; Chairman: Acad. Council, Wilton Park (FCO), 1986–92 (Mem., 1985–2001); Acad. Cttee, St Catharine's, Cumberland Lodge, 1991–2001 (Mem., 1973–2001); Sir Heinz Koeppler Trust, 1992–2001 (Mem., 1987–2001). President: British Assoc. for Slavonic and East European Studies, 1988–91 (Vice-Pres., 1991–93); British Assoc. of Former UN Civil Servants, 1994–2001; Chairman: Standing Cttee on E European Affairs, European Econ. Assoc., 1990–93; Keston Inst., 1994–2002. Member: Council, Royal Econ. Soc., 1976–86, 1987–90; Council, RIIA, 1979–85, 1986–92; Internat. Soc. Sci. Council, UNESCO, 1980–91; Council, SSEES, 1981–87; E Europe Cttee, CAFOD, 2001–05; Project Evaluation Gp, Univ. of Halle, 2002–05. Sec., British Acad. Cttee for SE European Studies, 1988–93 (Mem., 1970–75, 1983–93). Steering Cttee, Königswinter Anglo-German Confs, 1969–90 (Chm., Oxford Organizing Cttee, 1975–78). Hon. Mem., Eur. Assoc. Comparative Econs, 2006. Pres., Albania Soc. of Britain, 1992–95; Trustee, King George VI and Queen Elizabeth Foundn, 1987–2006. Missions for various internat. agencies, 1955–, incl. EC to Moscow, 1991, UNICEF to Albania, 1991, Turkmenistan and Uzbekistan, 1992, and IMF to Kyrgyzstan, 1998. Editorial Boards: Member: Central Asian Survey; Slavonic and East European Rev.; former Member: Econ. Jl; Jl of Industrial Econs; Soviet Studies; Oxford Rev. of Educn; CUP E European Monograph Series; World Develt; European Econ. Rev.; Energy Econs. Hon. DSocSc Birmingham, 1994. KSG 1990. Knight's Cross, Order of Merit (Poland), 1999; Order of Naim Frashëri (Albania), 1999. Publications: Comecon: integration problems of the planned economies, 1965, 2nd edn 1967; (ed) Economic Development for Eastern Europe, 1968; (with J. Zielinski) Planning in East Europe, 1970; Soviet Economics, 1970; (ed, with R. Portes) Planning and Market Relations, 1971; (ed, with H. Höhmann and K. Thalheim) The New Economic Systems of Eastern Europe, 1975; (ed, with A. Brown) The Soviet Union since the Fall of Khrushchev, 1975, 2nd edn 1978; Health Care in the Soviet Union and Eastern Europe, 1976; (ed with A. Brown) Soviet Policy for the 1980s, 1982; (ed jtly) The Cambridge Encyclopaedia of Russia and the Soviet Union, 1982, revd edn as The Cambridge Encyclopaedia of Russia and the Former Soviet Union, 1994; Gen. Ed., The Economic History of Eastern Europe 1919–1975, vols I and II (1919–49), vol. III (1949–75), 1985–86; (ed with E. A. G. Robinson) Early Steps in Comparing East-West Economies, 1992; (ed with D. Phillips) Education and Economic Change in Eastern Europe and the Former Soviet Union, 1992; (with S. Mehrotra) The Central Asian Economies after Independence, 1992; Privatization in the CIS, 1995; The Economies of Kazakhstan and Uzbekistan, 1997; papers in economic jls and symposia. Address: 31 Capel Close, Oxford OX2 7LA. T: (01865) 515581. E: michael.kaser@economics.ox.ac.uk. Club: Reform.

**KASMIN, John**; art dealer, since 1960; b 24 Sept. 1934; s of Vera d'Olszewski and David Kosminsky (known as Kaye); m 1959, Jane Nicholson (marr. diss.); two s. Educ: Magdalen College School, Oxford. Adventurous and varied jobs in New Zealand, 1952–56; art gallery assistant, London, 1956–60; Founder Director: Kasmin Ltd, 1961– (in partnership with late Marquess of Dufferin and Ava); Knoedler Kasmin Ltd, 1977–92. Publisher of books, Trivia Press. Recreations: reading, walking in landscapes, museums, cities, collecting old postcards. Address: c/o Kasmin Ltd, 34 Warwick Avenue, W9 2PT.

**KASPAROV, Garry Kimovich**; chess player, retired; public speaker on strategy, decision-making, innovation and geopolitics, since 2004; b Baku, Azerbaijan, 13 April 1963; né Garry Weinstein; s of Kim Moiseyevich Weinstein and Klara Kasparova; m 1st, 1989, Maria Arapova (marr. diss. 1994); one d; 2nd, 1996, Yulia Vovk; one s; 3rd, 2005, Daria; one s one d. Youngest world chess champion, 1985; retained title, 1986, 1987, 1990, 1993, 1995; lost title, 2000. Introduced (with Nigel Short) Rapid Chess, 1987; won first title, 1993; won PCA World Championship, NY, 1995. Played supercomputer Deep Blue, Philadelphia, 1996 and NY, 1997, series drawn; played first Advanced chess against Topalov, Spain, 1998; played The World, 1999. Founded Kasparov Chess Foundn USA, 2002, Europe, 2011, Africa, 2012, Asia-Pacific, 2013, Latin America, 2014, Adriatic, 2016, Francophone, 2017. Russian Opposition Leader. Chm., Human Rights Foundn, NYC, 2012–. Publications: Kasparov Teaches Chess, 1985; New World Chess Champion, 1985; Fighting Chess, 1985; The Test of Time, 1986; London-Leningrad Championship Games, 1987; (with Donald Trelford) Child of Change, 1987; Unlimited Challenge, 1990; (with Daniel King) Kasparov Against the World, 2000; Garry Kasparov on My Great Predecessors: Part I and Part II, 2003, Part III and Part IV, 2004, Part V, 2006; Checkmate: my first chess book, 2004; How Life Imitates Chess, 2007; Garry Kasparov on Modern Chess: Part I, 2007, Part II, 2008, Part III, 2009, Part IV, 2010; Garry Kasparov on Garry Kasparov, Part 1, 2011, Part II, 2013, Part III, 2014; Trading in Fear (in Russian), 2015; Winter is Coming, 2015; (with Mig Greengard) Deep Thinking, 2017. E: office@kasparov.com. W: www.kasparov.com.

**KASPI, Prof. Victoria Michelle**, CC 2016; PhD; FRS 2010; FRSC; Professor of Physics, since 2006, and Director, McGill Space Institute, since 2015, McGill University; b Austin, Texas, 30 June 1967; m; three c. Educ: McGill Univ. (BSc Hons Physics 1989); Princeton Univ. (MA Physics 1991; PhD 1993). Higgins Instructor, Physics Dept, Princeton Univ., 1994; Vis. Associate, Astronomy Dept, CIT, 1994–96; Hubble Postdoctoral Fellow: Jet Propulsion Lab., Infrared Processing and Analysis Center, CIT, 1994–96; Center for Space Res., MIT, 1997; Asst Prof., Physics Dept, MIT, 1997–2002; Associate Prof., Physics Dept, McGill Univ., 1999–2006. Alfred P. Sloan Res. Fellow, 1998. Vis. Scientist, Space Scis Div., Canadian Space Agency, 2008–09. FRSC 2008; Fellow: American Phys. Soc., 2014; American Acad. of Arts and Scis, 2015. Rutherford Medal in Physics, Royal Soc. of Canada, 2007; John C. Polanyi Award, NSERC, 2011; Diamond Jubilee Medal, 2013; Killam Prize, 2015. Address: Department of Physics, McGill University, Rutherford Physics Building, 3600 University Street, Montreal, QC H3A 2T8, Canada.

**KASTRATI, Emma Rebecca**; see Deacon, E. R.

**KATAINEN, Jyrki**; Member, and a Vice-President, European Commission, 2014–19; b Siilinjärvi, Finland, 14 Oct. 1971; m Mervi; two c. Educ: MScS 1998. Mem., Siilinjärvi Municipal Council, 1993; Vice-Chair, Pohjois-Savo Regl Council, 1994–95; Vice-Pres., Northern Savonia Regl Council, 2001–04. MP (Nat. Coalition) Northern Savonia, Finland, 1999–2014; Finance Minister and Dep. Prime Minister, 2007–11; Prime Minister of Finland, 2011–14. Vice-Pres., 2001–04, Pres., 2004–14, Finnish Nat. Coalition Party. Vice-Pres., Youth, 1999–2000, Vice-Pres., 2006–12, Eur. People's Party.

**KATKHUDA, His Honour Samih Suleiman**; a Circuit Judge, 1995–2010; b 15 Dec. 1941; s of Dr S. M. Katkhuda and U. Katkhuda (née Ciĉić); m 1968, Suzanne Gundred de Warrenne Crews; two s. Educ: King's Sch., Bruton, Som; Inns of Court Sch. of Law. Court Admin, CCC, Old Bailey, 1964–73; called to the Bar, Gray's Inn, 1974; in practice as barrister, 1974–95; a Recorder, 1994–95. Publications: Forms of Indictment, 1990; (jtly) Crown Court Index, 2005–10; (contrib.) Witness Testimony, 2006. Recreations: music, travel, reading. Club: Savage.

**KATKOWSKI, Christopher Andrew Mark**; QC 1999; b 16 Jan. 1957; s of Edward and Maria Katkowski; m 1976, Anna Thérèse Louise Gunstone. Educ: Fitzwilliam Coll., Cambridge (BA Law 1978; LLB 1979). Lectr in Law, City of London Poly., 1979–83; called to the Bar, Gray's Inn, 1982, Bencher, 2007; in practice at the Bar, 1984–; Jun. Counsel to the Crown (Common Law), 1992–99; Hd of Chambers, 2006–09. Mem., Attorney-Gen.'s Supplementary Panel, 1988–92. Recreation: spending time with Anna and our dogs. Address: Landmark Chambers, 180 Fleet Street, EC4A 2HG. T: (020) 7430 1221.

**KATONA, Nisha Sujata**, MBE 2019; food writer and restaurateur; b 23 Oct. 1971; d of Dr Nityendra Mohan Biswas and Dr Meena Biswas (née Chakrabarty); m 1999, Zoltan Katona; two d. Educ: Scarisbrick Hall Sch., Lancs; Liverpool John Moores Univ. (LLB Hons); Inns of Court Sch. of Law. Called to the Bar, Lincoln's Inn, 1996; in practice as barrister, specialising in family law, 1996–2015. Trustee, Nat. Museums Liverpool, 2008–15. Ambassador for Diversity in Public Appts, 2009–. Founder and CEO, Mowgli Street Food restaurants, 2014–. Founder, Mowgli Street Food Trust. Television presenter. Publications: Pimp My Rice, 2015; The Spice Tree, 2017; Mowgli Street Food, 2018. Recreations: horse-riding, theatre, reading, classical music, opera, gardening, teacher of Indian cookery. Address: Mowgli Street Food, 69 Bold Street, Liverpool L1 4EZ. E: info@mowglistreetfood.com.

**KATSAV, Moshe**; President of the State of Israel, 2000–07; b Iran, 5 Dec. 1945; emigrated to Israel, 1951; m Gila; four s one d. Educ: Hebrew Univ. of Jerusalem. Newspaper reporter, Yediot Aharonot, 1966–68; Member of Knesset, 1977–2000; Mem., Interior and Educn Cttees, Knesset, 1977–81; Dep. Minister of Housing and Construction, 1981–84; Minister: of Labour and Social Affairs, 1984–88; of Transportation, and Mem., Ministerial Cttee on Defence, 1988–92; Chm., Parly Cttee of Chinese-Israeli Friendship League, 1992–96; Dep. Prime Minister, Minister of Tourism, and Minister for Israeli-Arab Affairs, 1996–99; Chm., Ministerial Cttee for Nat. Events and Mem., Ministerial Cttee on Defence, 1996–99; Mem., Foreign Affairs and Defence Cttee, 1999–2000. Mem., Commn on adoptive children, 1978; Chm., Commn to determine higher educn tuition, 1982. Chairman, Likud Party: at Hebrew Univ., Jerusalem, 1969; in Knesset, 1992–96. Pres., B'nai B'rith Youth, 1968. Mayor, Kiryat Malachi, 1969 and 1974–81. Mem., Bd of Trustees, Ben-Gurion Univ., 1978. Hon. Dr: Nebraska, 1998; George Washington, 2001; Hartford, Connecticut,

2001; Yeshiva, 2002; Bar Ilan, 2003; China Agricl Univ., Beijing, 2003; Sorbonne, 2004; ELTE Univ. of Budapest, 2004. Bene Merito Medal, Acad. of Sci., Australia, 2004. *Publications:* contrib. articles in newspapers, Maariv and Yediot Aharonot. *Address:* c/o Office of the President, 3 Hanassi Street, Jerusalem, 92188 Israel.

**KATZ, Ian Alexander;** Director of Programmes, Channel 4, since 2018; *b* 9 Feb. 1968; *s* of John Katz and Adrienne (*née* Karnovsky); *m* 1997, Justine Roberts; two *s* two *d*. *Educ:* University College Sch., London; New Coll., Oxford (BA PPE 1989). Reporter, Sunday Correspondent, 1989–90; The Guardian: reporter, 1991–94; NY Corresp., 1994–97; Internet Editor, 1997–98; Features Ed., 1998–2006; Saturday Ed., 2006–08; Dep. Ed. and Hd of News, 2008–13; Ed., Newsnight, BBC, 2013–17. *Recreation:* sailing. *Address:* Channel 4, 124 Horseferry Road, SW1P 2TX.

**KATZ, Dr Jonathan Bernard;** Public Orator, University of Oxford, since 2016; Fellow, St Anne's College, Oxford, since 2013; *b* Harrow, 26 May 1950; *s* of Sir Bernard Katz, FRS and Marguerite Katz (*née* Penly); *m* 1979, Mangal Narayan Katti; one *s*. *Educ:* University Coll. Sch.; Richard-Strauss-Konservatorium, Munich; Pembroke Coll., Oxford (BA; MA 1977); Queens' Coll., Cambridge (PGCE 1975); Wolfson Coll., Oxford (DPhil 1987). Asst Master, Westminster Sch., 1974–77; Hd, Indian Inst. Liby, then Sen. Asst Librarian, Bodleian Liby, Univ. of Oxford, 1977–87; Jun. Res. Fellow, then Res. Fellow, Wolfson Coll., Oxford, 1981–87; Master of Queen's Scholars, 1987–2003, Hd of Classics, 2003–10, Westminster Sch.; Lecturer: in Classics and Sanskrit, St Anne's Coll., Oxford, 2010–; in Classics, Brasenose Coll., Oxford, 2011–; Fellow, All Souls Coll., Oxford, 2014–17. Vis. Fellow, Humanities Council and Perkins Fellow in Music, Princeton Univ., 1991; Vis. Fellow, All Souls Coll., Oxford, 2005. *Publications:* books; articles and reviews in classical and S Asian studies and musicology; translations from German and Italian. *Recreations:* walking, travel, reading. *Address:* St Anne's College, 56 Woodstock Road, Oxford OX2 6HS. *Club:* Athenæum.

**KATZ, Philip Alec Jackson;** QC 2000; **His Honour Judge Katz;** a Circuit Judge, since 2014; a Permanent Judge, Central Criminal Court, since 2017; *b* 8 May 1953; *s* of Stanley Zeb Jackson (*née* Katz) and Anita Jackson; adopted patronymic Katz, 1976. *Educ:* Roundhay Grammar Sch., Leeds; University Coll., Oxford (MA). Called to the Bar, Middle Temple, 1976, Bencher, 2008; a Recorder, 2000–14; Hd of Chambers, 9–12 Bell Yard, 2008–11. *Address:* Central Criminal Court, Old Bailey, EC4M 7EH.

**KATZMAN, Silvia Suzen Giovanna;** *see* Casale, S. S. G.

**KAUFFMANN, Prof. C. Michael,** MA, PhD; FBA 1987; FMA; FSA; Professor of History of Art and Director, Courtauld Institute of Art, University of London, 1985–95, now Professor Emeritus; *b* 5 Feb. 1931; *s* of late Arthur and late Tamara Kauffmann; *m* 1954, Dorothea (*née* Hill); two *s*. *Educ:* St Paul's Sch.; Merton Coll., Oxford (Postmaster); Warburg Inst., London Univ. (Jun. Research Fellow). Asst Curator, Photographic Collection, Warburg Inst., 1957–58; Keeper, Manchester City Art Gall., 1958–60; Victoria and Albert Museum: Asst Keeper, 1960–75, Keeper, 1975–85, Dept of Prints & Drawings and Paintings; Asst to the Director, 1963–66; Visiting Associate Prof., Univ. of Chicago, 1969. Mem. Exec. Cttee, NACF, 1987–2005; Trustee, Nat. Museums and Galls on Merseyside, 1986–99. *Publications:* The Baths of Pozzuoli: medieval illuminations of Peter of Eboli's poem, 1959; An Altar-piece of the Apocalypse, 1968; Victoria & Albert Museum: Catalogue of Foreign Paintings, 1973; British Romanesque Manuscripts 1066–1190, 1975; Catalogue of Paintings in the Wellington Museum, 1982; John Varley, 1984; Studies in Medieval Art, 1992; Biblical Imagery in Medieval England 700–1550, 2003; Eve's Apple to the Last Supper: picturing food in the Bible, 2017.

**KAUFMANN, Julia Ruth,** OBE 1997; freelance consultant for voluntary sector, since 2000; *b* 29 March 1941; *d* of Prof. Felix Kaufmann and Ruth (*née* Arnold); marr. diss.; two *s* one *d*. *Educ:* St George's Hosp., London (SRN); Sidney Webb Coll. (BEd London); Brunel Univ. (Dip. Social Policy and Admin). Advisory teacher, ILEA, 1974–76; Dir, Centre for Social Educn, 1976–78; Press Officer, 1978–79, Dir, 1979–87, Gingerbread; Dir, BBC Children in Need Appeal, 1987–2000. Mem., Employment Relns Adv. Panel on Public Appts, 2001–04; Comr, Postcomm, 2000–05. Chairman: Nat. Assoc. of Toy and Leisure Libraries, 2000–04; Whizz Kidz, 2006–08; Bd Mem., Capacity Builders, 2006–09; Vice-Pres., DEAFAX, 2000; Trustee, Community Network, 2000–07. *Address:* 2 Carberry Road, SE19 3RU. *T:* (020) 8653 3877.

**KAUL, Kalyani;** QC 2011; **Her Honour Judge Kaul;** a Circuit Judge, since 2015; *b* New Delhi, 11 Dec. 1960; *d* of late Mahendra Nath Kaul, OBE; *m* 1988, Martin Lee (marr. diss.); one *s* one *d*. *Educ:* Heathfield Sch., Harrow; London Sch. of Econs and Pol Sci. (LLB Hons). Called to the Bar, Middle Temple, 1983; a Recorder, 2009–15. *Recreations:* travel, work, hot air ballooning. *Address:* Wood Green Crown Court, Woodall House, Lordship Lane, N22 5LF.

**KAUNDA, Kenneth David;** President of Zambia, Oct. 1964–1991 (Prime Minister, N Rhodesia, Jan.–Oct. 1964); Chancellor of the University of Zambia, 1966–91; *b* 28 April 1924; *s* of late David Julizgia and Hellen Kaunda, Missionaries; *m* 1946, Betty Banda (*d* 2012); five *s* two *d* one adopted *s* (and two *s* decd). *Educ:* Lubwa Training Sch.; Munali Secondary Sch. Teacher, Lubwa Training Sch., 1943–44, Headmaster, 1944–47; Boarding Master, Mufulira Upper Sch., 1948–49. African National Congress: District Sec., 1950–52; Provincial Organising Sec., 1952–53; Sec.-Gen., 1953–58; Nat. Pres., Zambia African Nat. Congress, 1958–59; founded United Nat. Independence Party, 1958, Nat. Pres., 1960–91, re-elected, 1995–2000; Chm., Pan-African Freedom Movement for East, Central and South Africa, 1962; Minister of Local Government and Social Welfare, N Rhodesia, 1962–63. Chairman: Organization of African Unity, 1970, 1987; Non-aligned Countries, 1970. Hon. Doctor of Laws: Fordham Univ., USA, 1963; Dublin Univ., 1964; University of Sussex, 1965; Windsor Univ., Canada, 1966; University of Chile, 1966; Univ. of Zambia, 1974; Univ. of Humboldt, 1980; DUniv York, 1966. *Publications:* Black Government, 1961; Zambia Shall Be Free, 1962; Humanist in Africa, 1966; Humanism in Zambia and its implementation, 1967; Letter to My Children; Kaunda on Violence, 1980. *Recreations:* golf, music, table tennis, football, draughts, gardening and reading. *Address:* c/o UNIP, POB 30302, 10101 Lusaka, Zambia.

**KAUR-STUBBS, Sukhvinder;** Managing Director, Engage, since 2012; *b* Punjab, India, 25 Oct. 1962; *d* of S. Inderjit Singh Thethy and Charanjit Kaur; *m* 1985, David Brian Stubbs (marr. diss. 2008); one *d*. *Educ:* Hertford Coll., Oxford (MA Geography); Henry Oliver Becket Meml Prize). MCIM 1992. Lectr, Orpington Coll., 1984–85; Graduate Manager, British Telecom, 1985–86; Mkting Exec., Prisoners Abroad, 1986–87; Appeals Dir, British Dyslexia Assoc., 1987–90; Dir of Corporate Affairs, Community Develt Foundn, 1990–94; Community Develt Manager, English Partnerships, 1994–96; Chief Executive: Runnymede Trust, 1996–2000; Barrow Cadbury Trust, 2001–09. Chair: European Network Against Racism, 1998–2002; Young Enterprise (WM), 2002–05; Volunteering Britain, 2009–14; Taylor Bennett Foundn, 2015–. Non-executive Director: W Midlands Regl Develt Agency (Advantage W Midlands), 1998–2003; CPS, 2000–02; Severn Trent Water, 2002–06; Home Gp Housing Assoc., 2013–; Lewisham and Greenwich NHS Trust, 2015–; Swan Housing Assoc., 2015–; London Legacy Develt Corp., 2018–. Member:

Learning and Skills Res. Develt Unit, 2001–03; Cabinet Office Better Regulation Taskforce, 2002–06; Consumer Focus (formerly National Consumer Council), 2007–13; Land and Society Commn, 2011; Director: Office for Public Mgt, 2009–; Bd, Admin. Justice and Tribunals Council, 2010–13; Trustee, Social Care Inst. for Excellence, 2009–15 (Chm., Audit Cttee, 2009–). Council Mem., Britain in Europe Trust, 2000–05; Steering Gp Mem., UN Cttee on World Conf. against Racism, 2001. Chm., Birmingham Secondary Educn Commn, 1998; Mem., Birmingham Democracy Commn, 2000–01; Council Mem., Univ. of Birmingham, 2013–16 (Hon. Fellow, 2016–18). Gov., Leathersellers' Fedn of Schools, 2017–. Trustee, Demos, 1998–2006. Mem., Lunar Soc., 1999. FRSA 1996; MInstD; Mem., ACEVO, 2002–; MCMI 2009. *Publications:* (contrib.) Renewing Citizenship and Democracy, 1997; (contrib.) Mindfields, 1998; Fear and Loathing in the EU, 2000; Participation in Social Care Regulation, 2004; Islam, Race and Being British, 2005; Better Regulation for Civic Society, 2005; (with Joel Anderson) Engaged Europe - developing full, free and equal participation, 2010; Building Contingent Capacity, 2015; papers, articles in jls. *Recreations:* singing, gardening, school fundraising. *Address:* (office) 629 Kings Road, Birmingham B44 9HW.

**KAVANAGH, David Edward;** QC 2017; Partner, Skadden, Arps, Slate, Meagher & Flom LLP, since 2009; *b* London, 19 March 1967; *s* of Michael and Joan Kavanagh; *m* 1996, Harriet Mellor; three *s*. *Educ:* St Ignatius Coll.; Durham Univ. (BA Hons Law 1988). Admitted solicitor, 1992; Watson Farley & Williams, 1992–2007; O'Melveny & Myers, 2007–09. *Recreations:* holidaying in West Cork, sharing wine, walking, cycling, game shooting, sea fishing, cooking, Arsenal FC. *Address:* Skadden, Arps, Slate, Meagher & Flom LLP, 40 Bank Street, E14 5DS. *T:* (020) 7519 7000. *E:* david.kavanagh@skadden.com. *Club:* 67 Pall Mall.

**KAVANAGH, Prof. Dennis Anthony;** Professor of Politics, 1996–2006, Emeritus Professor and Research Fellow in Politics and Communications, since 2007, University of Liverpool; *b* 27 March 1941; *s* of Patrick Kavanagh and Agnes Kavanagh; *m* 1966, Monica Anne Taylor; three *s* three *d*. *Educ:* St Anselm's Coll., Birkenhead; Univ. of Manchester (BA, MA Econ). Asst Lectr, Univ. of Hull, 1965–67; Lectr, then Sen. Lectr, Univ. of Manchester, 1967–81; Prof. of Politics, Univ. of Nottingham, 1982–95. Ford Foundn Fellow, Univ. of Stanford, Calif, 1969–70; Visiting Professor: European Univ. Inst., Florence, 1977; Univ. of Calif, San Diego, La Jolla, 1979; Hoover Instn, Stanford Univ., 1985. Mem. Council, 1991–94, Mem. Res. Grants Bd, 1994–97, ESRC; Aurora, 1999–2000. Mem. Editl Bd, political jls. FRSA. *Publications:* Constituency Electioneering in Britain, 1970; Political Culture, 1972; (with R. Rose) New Trends in British Politics: contemporary issues for research and discussions, 1977; The Politics of the Labour Party, 1982; Political Science and Political Behaviour, 1983; (ed) Comparative Politics and Government: essays in honour of S. E. Finer, 1984; British Politics, continuities and change, 1985, 4th edn 2000; Thatcherism and British Politics: the end of consensus?, 1987, 2nd edn 1990; Consensus Politics from Attlee to Thatcher, 1989, 2nd edn 1994; The Thatcher Effect, 1989; Personalities and Politics, 1990; Electoral Politics, 1992; (ed with A. Seldon) The Major Effect, 1995; Election Campaigning: the new marketing of politics, 1995; The Reordering of British Politics, 1997; (ed) Oxford Dictionary of Political Leadership, 1998; (with A. Seldon) The Powers Behind the Prime Minister, 1999; (ed with A. Seldon) The Blair Effect, 2005; (with P. Cowley) The British General Election of 2010, 2010; Philip Gould: an unfinished life, 2012; (with P. Cowley) The British General Election of 2015, 2016; (with P. Cowley) The British General Election of 2017, 2018; with David Butler: The British General Election of October 1974, 1975; The British General Election of 1979, 1980; The British General Election of 1983, 1984; The British General Election of 1987, 1988; The British General Election of 1992, 1992; The British General Election of 1997, 1997; The British General Election of 2001, 2002; The British General Election of 2005, 2006; over 100 contribs to jls and books. *Recreations:* running, tennis, music, obituaries. *Address:* Lynton, Belgrave Road, Bowdon, Altrincham, Cheshire WA14 2NZ. *E:* dennis.kavanagh@talktalk.net. *Clubs:* Bowdon Lawn Tennis, Hale Lawn Tennis.

**KAVANAGH, George Collins;** Sheriff, Sheriffdom of North Strathclyde, 2010 (Sheriff of North Strathclyde at Paisley, 1999–2010); *b* 29 May 1940; *s* of George and Mary Kavanagh (*née* Donagher); *m* 1967, Rosaleen Anne-Marie McCrudden or Kavanagh; two *s* two *d*. *Educ:* St John's Sch., Cumnock; St Joseph's High Sch., Kilmarnock; Univ. of Glasgow. Home Office, 1961–71; Hughes Dowdall, Solicitors, 1971–99, Sen. Partner, 1991–99. Examr, Soc. of Apothecaries, 2000–. KCHS 2000 (KHS 1995). *Recreations:* reading, cricket, sailing.

**KAVANAGH, Trevor Michael Thomas;** Associate Editor and Chief Political Columnist, The Sun, since 2006; *b* 19 Jan. 1943; *s* of Bernard George Kavanagh and Alice Rose (*née* Thompson); *m* 1967, Jacqueline Gai Swindells; two *s*. *Educ:* Reigate Grammar Sch. The Sun, 1978–: Industrial Corresp., 1981–83; Political Ed., 1983–2006. Chairman: Parly Lobby Journalists, 1990; Parly Press Gall., 2000. Journalist of the Year, Specialist Reporter of the Year, 1997, Reporter of the Year, 2005, British Press Awards; Scoop of the Year, What the Papers Say, 2000, 2004; Print Story of the Year, For. Press Assoc., 2004; Political Journalist of the Year, Pol Studies Assoc., 2004. *Recreations:* golf, swimming, travel, drawing. *Address:* Press Gallery, House of Commons, SW1A 0AA. *Club:* Royal Automobile.

**KAWCZYNSKI, Daniel;** MP (C) Shrewsbury and Atcham, since 2005; *b* 24 Jan. 1972; *s* of Leonard and Halina Kawczynski; *m* 2000, Kate Lumb (marr. diss. 2011); one *d*. *Educ:* Univ. of Stirling (BA Hons Business Studies with French 1994). Internat. export consultant in telecommunications industry, Middle E, 1994–2004. Contested (C) Ealing Southall, 2001. PPS to Minister of State for Agriculture and Food, 2010–12, to Sec. of State for Wales, 2012–14. Member: Envmt, Food and Rural Affairs Select Cttee, 2005–07; Justice Select Cttee, 2007–09; Internat. Develt Select Cttee, 2008–10; Foreign Affairs Select Cttee, 2015–17; Chairman: All Party Gp for Dairy Farmers, 2006–15; All Party Parly Gp for Saudi Arabia, 2007–15; All Party Parly Gp for Libya, 2008–15; British Middle E and N Africa Council, 2012–15. *Publications:* Seeking Gaddafi, 2010. *Address:* House of Commons, SW1A 0AA. *E:* kawczynskid@parliament.uk.

**KAY, Anne Jacqueline;** *see* Ridley, A. J.

**KAY, Prof. Anthony Barrington, (Barry),** PhD, DSc; FRCPE, FRCP, FRCPath, FMedSci; FRSE; Professor of Clinical Immunology and Head, Department of Allergy and Clinical Immunology, Imperial College, London University, 1980–2004, now Professor Emeritus; Senior Research Investigator, National Heart and Lung Institute Division, Imperial College London, 2004–17; Hon. Consultant Physician, Royal Brompton Hospital, 1980–2009; Consultant Physician (Allergy), The London Clinic, 2005–12; *b* 23 June 1939; *s* of Anthony Chambers and late Eva Gertrude (*née* Pearcey; she *m* 2nd H. Kay; later Mrs E. G. Reuben); *m* 1966, Rosemary Margaret Johnstone; three *d*. *Educ:* King's Sch., Peterborough; Edinburgh Univ. (MB, ChB 1963; DSc 1976); Jesus Coll., Cambridge (MA 1966; PhD 1970). Harvard Med. Sch. FRCPE 1975; FRCP 1980; FRCPath 1989. T. K. Stubbins Res. Fellow, RCP, 1969; Res. Fellow, Harvard Med. Sch., 1970–71; Lectr in Respiratory Diseases, Univ. of Edinburgh, 1972–74; Dep. Dir and Consultant, Immunology Div., Blood Transfusion Service, Royal Infirmary, Edinburgh, 1974–76; Sen. Lectr, then Reader, in Exptl Pathology, Dept of Pathology, Univ. of Edinburgh, 1977–79. Specialist Advr, H of L Select Cttee Enquiry into Allergy, 2006–07. Co-founder and

Consultant, Circassia Ltd, 1999–. President: European Acad. of Allergology and Clinical Immunology, 1989–92; Brit. Soc. of Allergy and Clinical Immunology, 1993–96 (Hon. Mem., 2009). Jt Editor, Clinical and Exptl Allergy, 1984–2007. FRSE 1993; FMedSci 1999. Hon. Fellow: Amer. Coll. of Allergy, 1986; Amer. Acad. of Allergy, Asthma and Immunology, 2004; Hon. Member: Amer. Assoc. of Physicians, 1988; Hungarian Soc. of Allergology and Clinical Immunology, 1990; Swiss Soc. of Allergology and Clinical Immunology, 1991; Belgian Soc. for Allergol. and Clin. Immunol., 1999. Hon. Dr Medicine and Surgery, Ferrara, 2000. Scientific Achievement Award, Internat. Assoc. of Allergology and Clinical Immunology, 1991; Paul Ehrlich Medal, Eur. Acad. of Allergology and Clin. Immunol., 2005. *Publications:* edited: Asthma: clinical pharmacology and therapeutic progress, 1986; Allergy and Inflammation, 1987; Allergic Basis of Asthma, 1988; Allergy and Asthma: new trends and approaches to therapy, 1989; Eosinophils, Allergy and Asthma, 1990; Eosinophils in Allergy and Inflammation, 1993; Allergy and Allergic Diseases, 1997, 2nd edn 2008; numerous scientific articles on allergy and asthma. *Recreations:* Baroque and modern bassoon, tennis, country walks. *Address:* 58 Madrid Road, Barnes, SW13 9PG. *Clubs:* Chelsea Arts, Hurlingham.

KAY, Brian Christopher; broadcaster and musician; *b* 12 May 1944; *s* of Noel Bancroft Kay and Gwendoline Mary (*née* Sutton); *m* 1st, 1970, Sally Lyne; one *s* one *d*; 2nd, 1983, Gillian Fisher. *Educ:* Rydal Sch.; King's Coll., Cambridge (MA 1966); New Coll., Oxford (DipEd 1967). Bass Singer: Westminster Abbey Choir, 1968–71; King's Singers, 1968–82; Chorus Master, Huddersfield Choral Soc., 1983–93; Conductor: Cecilian Singers of Leicester, 1984–92; Cheltenham Bach Choir, 1989–97; Leith Hill Musical Fest., 1996–2016; Mary Wakefield Westmorland Fest., 1996–2003; Burford Singers, 2002–; Musical Dir, Bradford Fest. Choral Soc., 1998–2002; Principal Conductor, The Really Big Chorus, 2010– (Associate Conductor, 2005–10). Presenter: Music in Mind, Radio 4, 1989–98; Brian Kay's Sunday Morning, Radio 3, 1992–2001; Comparing Notes, Radio 4, 1996–98; Brian Kay's Light Programme, Radio 3, 2001–07. Friday Night is Music Night, Radio 2, 1998–2007. President: Nottingham Choral Trust; Harrogate Choral Soc.; Market Harborough Singers; Derbys Singers; Bristol Bach Choir; English Arts Chorale; Joyful Co. of Singers; Cambridge Concert Orch.; Promenade Concert Orch. of Morecambe. Vice-Pres., Assoc. of British Choral Dirs; Patron, Stars Orgn for Scope. Vice-Pres., RSCM, 2005–. Hon. FTCL 2004. Music Presenter of the Year, Sony Gold Award, 1996. *Recreations:* gardening, reading. *Address:* Bell Cottage, Church Lane, Fulbrook, Burford, Oxon OX18 4BA.

KAY, Prof. Elizabeth Jane, MBE 2017; PhD; FDSRCPSGlas; Professor of Dental Public Health and Hon. Academic Consultant in Dental Public Health (Public Health England, formerly NHS Plymouth), 2012–19, now Emeritus Professor, and Foundation Dean, Dental School, Plymouth University Peninsula Schools of Medicine and Dentistry, since 2012; *b* 10 March 1959; *d* of late Robert Brian Kay and Cynthia Kay (*née* Bianchi); partner, Stella Ruth Tinsley. *Educ:* Univ. of Edinburgh (BDS 1982); Univ. of Glasgow (MPH 1984; PhD 1991). FDSRCPSGlas 1988; FDSRCS *ad eundem* 2002; FFGDP *ad eundem* 2010. Res. Fellow in Dental Epidemiology, Univ. of Edinburgh, 1982–86; Lectr in Community Dental Health, Univ. of Glasgow, 1986–90; Sen. Lectr in Dental Public Health, Univ. of Dundee, 1990–92; Sen. Registrar in Dental Public Health, South Glamorgan HA, 1992–94; University of Manchester: Sen. Lectr in Dental Health Services Res., 1994–98; Prof. of Dental Health Services Res., 1998–2006; Prof. of Oral Health and Dean, Peninsula Dental Sch., 2006–12. Member: Expert Cttee, NICE, 2013–17; Med. and Dental Adv. Cttee, Equality Challenge Unit, 2013–16; Chairman: Jt Trust Univ. Res. Cttee, 2012–; NICE Guidelines Cttee, 2018–. Associate non-exec. Dir, Plymouth Hosps Trust, 2017–. Pres. and Chm. Bd, Oral Health Foundn, 2017–19. Mem., Platform for Better Oral Health in Europe, 2017–. Editor, Evidence Based Dentistry, 2019–. *Publications:* (jtly) Communication for the Dental Team, 1996, 2nd edn 2004; (jtly) Clinical Decision Making: an art or a science, 1997; (jtly) A Review of Effectiveness of Oral Health Promotion, 1997; (ed) A Guide to Prevention in Dentistry, 2004; (jtly) Integrated Dental Treatment Planning, 2005; (ed) Dentistry at a Glance, 2016; 201 learned papers in acad. and professional jls. *Recreations:* all things equine, rural or historical. *Address:* Peninsula Dental School, Portland Square, Plymouth University, Drake Circus, Plymouth PL4 8AA. *T:* (01752) 586800.

KAY, Prof. Helen Sheppard, (Sarah), DPhil, LittD; Professor of French, New York University, since 2011; *b* 12 Nov. 1948; *d* of Brian Wilfrid Kay and Dorothea Sheppard Kay; *m* John Williamson (marr. diss.); one *s* two *d*. *Educ:* Somerville Coll., Oxford (BA 1st cl. (Mod. Langs (French)) 1971; DPhil 1976); Univ. of Reading (MA (Linguistics) 1972); LittD Cantab 2005. Kathleen Bourne Res. Fellow, St Anne's Coll., Oxford, 1973–75; Lectr in French, Univ. of Liverpool, 1975–84; University of Cambridge: Lectr, Dept of French, 1984–95; Reader, 1995–2001; Prof. of French and Occitan Lit., 2001–05; Fellow, 1984–2005, Life Fellow, 2005, Girton Coll.; Prof., Dept of French and Italian, Princeton Univ., 2006–11. Visiting Professor: Dept of Romance Langs, Univ. of Pennsylvania, 1993; Centre for Medieval and Renaissance Studies, QMW, 1996–99; Center for Medieval and Renaissance Studies, UCLA, 1999; Dept of Comparative Lit., Stanford Univ., 2004; Prof. invité, Univ. d'Artois, 1999. Guggenheim Fellow, 2014–15. FBA 2004–15. Chevalier, Ordre des Palmes Académiques (France). *Publications:* Subjectivity in Troubadour Poetry, 1990; (ed) Raoul de Cambrai, 1992; (ed with Miri Rubin) Framing Medieval Bodies, 1994; The Chanson de geste in the Age of Romance: political fictions, 1995; The Romance of the Rose, 1995; (ed with S. Gaunt) The Troubadours: an introduction, 1999; Courtly Contradictions: the emergence of the literary object in the twelfth century, 2001; Zizek: a critical introduction, 2003; (jtly) A Short History of French Literature, 2003; The Place of Thought: the complexity of one in late Medieval French didactic poetry, 2007; (ed with S. Gaunt) The Cambridge Companion to Medieval French Literature, 2008; (with A. Armstrong) Knowing Poetry: verse in medieval France from the Rose to the rhetoriqueurs, 2011; (jtly) Thinking Through Chrétien de Troyes, 2011; Parrots and Nightingales: troubadour quotations and the development of European poetry, 2013; Animal Skins and the Reading Self, 2016; numerous articles and chapters in books. *Recreations:* walking, contemporary classical music, reading, travel. *Address:* 4 Washington Square Village, Apt 17G, New York, NY 10012, USA. *E:* hsk8@nyu.edu.

KAY, Prof. Janice Margaret, CBE 2017; PhD; Professor of Cognitive Neuropsychology, Senior Deputy Vice-Chancellor and Provost, since 2014, University of Exeter; *b* Solihull, 25 Jan. 1956; *d* of Thomas Crump and Iris Crump; *m* 1979, Dr Peter Kay; one *s* one *d*. *Educ:* Tudor Grange Sch., Solihull; Newcastle Univ. (BA Hons); Darwin Coll., Cambridge (PhD 1982). MRC Post-Doctoral Res. Fellow, 1981–89; Univ. of York, 1989–90; University of Exeter: Wellcome Trust Univ. Lectureship, 1990; Prof. of Cognitive Psychol., 2004; Dep. Vice Chancellor (Educn), 2004–14. *Publications:* Psycholinguistic Assessments of Language Processing in Aphasia: a test battery, 1992 (numerous trans); numerous articles in Cognitive Neuropsychology, Brain. *Recreations:* cooking, walking in Devon and Cornwall, house restoration, art history, passionate about European cities.

KAY, Jervis; *see* Kay, R. J.

KAY, Jillian Gray; Director, Recovery and Resilience, Ministry of Housing, Communities and Local Government (formerly Department for Communities and Local Government), since 2017; *b* East Kilbride, 28 Feb. 1976; *d* of John Brodie Kay and Christine Graham Kay; partner, Paul Michael Kett, *qv*. *Educ:* Carluke High Sch.; Robert Schuman Univ. (Dip. French Legal Studies 1996); Univ. of Glasgow (LLB Hons 1st Cl. Public Law 1997); École nationale d'administration, Paris (Dip. Public Admin 2001); Open Univ. (Grad. Dip. (distinction) Psychol. 2009). Joined Civil Service, 1997; various policy and private office roles, Lord Chancellor's Dept and DCA, 1997–2006; Dep. Dir, Strategy, MoJ, 2006–08; Principal Pvte Sec. and Dep. Hd, Scotland Office, 2008–10; Deputy Director: Sentencing Reform, MoJ, 2010–12; Econ. and Domestic Affairs Secretariat, Cabinet Office, 2012; Chief Exec., Judicial Office of England and Wales, 2013–16; Dir, Local Govt Policy, DCLG, 2016–17. Trustee, Lambeth Elfrida Rathbone Soc., 2018–. *Recreations:* travel, swimming, crafting with my nieces. *Address:* Ministry of Housing, Communities and Local Government, 2 Marsham Street, SW1P 4DF. *T:* 0303 444 1818. *E:* jillian.kay@communities.gsi.gov.uk. *W:* www.twitter.com/jilliangkay.

KAY, Prof. John Anderson, CBE 2014; FBA 1997; FRSE; economist; *b* 3 Aug. 1948; *s* of late James Scobie Kay and of Allison (*née* Anderson); *m* 1st, 1986, Deborah Freeman (marr. diss. 1995); 2nd, 2009, Mika Oldham. *Educ:* Royal High Sch., Edinburgh; Univ. of Edinburgh (MA). Nuffield Coll., Oxford. Fellow of St John's Coll., 1970–, and Lectr in Econs, 1971–79, Univ. of Oxford; Res. Dir, 1979–81, Dir, 1981–86, Inst. for Fiscal Studies; London Business School: Prof., 1986–96; Dir, Centre for Business Strategy, 1986–91; Prof. of Mgt and Dir, Saïd Business Sch., Univ. of Oxford, 1997–99. Vis. Prof. LSE, 2000–16. Chairman: Undervalued Assets Trust, then SVM UK Active Fund, 1994–2005; Clear Capital Ltd, 2004–08; Director: London Econs Ltd, 1986–2000 (Chm., 1986–96); Halifax plc (formerly Halifax Building Soc.), 1991–2000; Foreign & Colonial Special Utilities Investment Trust Plc, 1993–2003; Value and Income Trust plc, 1994–; Law Debenture Corp. plc, 2004–14; Scottish Mortgage Investment Trust, 2008–; Buddi, 2012–17. Member: Council and Exec. Cttee, NIESR, 1989–97; Council of Econ. Advrs, Scottish Govt, 2007–10. Mem., Corporate Governance Adv. Bd, Norges Bank Investment Mgt, 2013–18. Vice-Pres., Econs & Business Educn Assoc., 1996–. FRSE 2007. *Publications:* (with L. Hannah) Concentration in Modern Industry, 1977; (with M. A. King) The British Tax System, 1978, 5th edn 1997; (jtly) The Reform of Social Security, 1984; (jtly) The Economic Analysis of Accounting Profitability, 1987; Foundations of Corporate Success, 1993; Why Firms Succeed, 1995; The Business of Economics, 1996; The Truth about Markets, 2003; Culture and Prosperity, 2004; Everlasting Light Bulbs, 2004; The Hare and the Tortoise, 2006; The Long and the Short of It, 2009, 2nd edn 2016; Obliquity, 2010; Other People's Money, 2015; (with M. A. King) Radical Uncertainty, 2020; contrib. articles in learned jls and columns in Financial Times. *Recreation:* walking, especially in France. *Address:* 87 Dorset House, Gloucester Place, NW1 5AF. *T:* (020) 7224 8797.

KAY, Jolyon Christopher; HM Diplomatic Service, retired; *b* 19 Sept. 1930; *s* of Colin Mardall Kay and Gertrude Fanny Kay; *m* 1956, Shirley Mary Clarke; two *s* two *d*. *Educ:* Charterhouse; St John's Coll., Cambridge (BA 1953; MEng 1993); Rose Bruford Coll. (BA Theatre Studies 2012). Chemical Engr, Albright and Wilson, 1954; UKAEA, Harwell, 1958; Battelle Inst., Geneva, 1961; Foreign Office, London, 1964; MECAS, 1965; British Interests Section, Swiss Embassy, Algiers, 1967; Head of Chancery and Information Adviser, Political Residency, Bahrain, 1968; FCO, 1970; Economic Counsellor, Jedda, 1974–77; Consul-Gen., Casablanca, 1977–80; Science, later Commercial, Counsellor, Paris, 1980–84; Counsellor and Consul-Gen., Dubai, 1985–90. Editl Dir, London Insurance Insider, 1996–98. Convenor, Transport Gp, Oxfordshire CPRE, 1995–97. Chm., Cyprus Third Age, 2011–13 (Vice Chm., Limassol Br., 2009–10). Chm., Southern Croquet Fedn, 1999–2003; Mem. Council, Croquet Assoc., 2001–04. *Recreations:* theatre, croquet, Go, Bananagrams. *Address:* 1 Anexartisias Street, 4603 Anogyra, Limassol District, Cyprus.

KAY, Prof. Lewis Edward, OC 2016; PhD; FRS 2010; FRSC; Professor of Biochemistry, Molecular Genetics and Chemistry, University of Toronto, since 1995 (Assistant Professor, 1992–94). *Educ:* Univ. of Alberta (BSc 1983); Yale Univ. (PhD 1988). Lab. of Chem. Physics, NIH, 1988–92. Internat. Scholar, Howard Hughes Med. Inst., 1997–2001. FRSC 2006. Steacie Prize, NRCC, 1999; Favelle Medal, Royal Soc. of Canada, 2002; Khorana Prize, Royal Soc. of Chem., 2012; Gairdner International Award, 2017. *Publications:* contribs to jls incl. Science, Jl Magnetic Resonance, Biochem., Jl Molecular Biol., Jl Phys. Chem. B, Jl Amer. Chem. Soc. *Address:* Department of Biochemistry, University of Toronto, 1 King's College Circle, Toronto, ON M5S 1A8, Canada.

KAY, Rt Hon. Sir Maurice (Ralph), Kt 1995; PC 2004; a Lord Justice of Appeal, 2004–14; President, Court of Appeal of Gibraltar, since 2015; *b* 6 Dec. 1942; *s* of Ralph and Hylda Kay; *m* 1968, Margaret Angela Alcock; four *s*. *Educ:* William Hulme's Grammar Sch., Manchester; Sheffield Univ. (LLB, PhD). Called to the Bar, Gray's Inn, 1975; Bencher, 1995 (Vice-Treas., 2012; Treas., 2013). Lecturer in Law: Hull Univ., 1967–72; Manchester Univ., 1972–73; Prof. of Law, Keele Univ., 1973–82. Practising barrister, 1975–95; an Asst Recorder, 1987–88; a Recorder, 1988–95; QC 1988; a Judge of the High Ct of Justice, QBD, 1995–2003; Judge, Employment Appeal Tribunal, 1995–2003; Lead Judge, Administrative Ct, 2002–03. Vice Pres., Court of Appeal Civil Div., 2010–14. Chm., Judicial Studies Bd, 2007–10. Judicial Visitor, UCL, 2006–. Hon. Fellow, Robinson Coll., Cambridge, 2007. Hon. LLD: Sheffield, 2003; Keele, 2005. *Publications:* (author, contributor) numerous legal books and jls. *Recreations:* music, theatre, sport. *Club:* Reform.

KAY, Michael Jack David; QC 2002; His Honour Judge Kay; a Circuit Judge, since 2004; a Deputy High Court Judge, since 2007; *b* 13 Oct. 1959; *m* 1984, Victoria Reuben; two *s* one *d*. *Educ:* Manchester Grammar Sch.; Christ's Coll., Cambridge. Called to the Bar, Lincoln's Inn, 1981; an Assistant Recorder, 1998–2000, Recorder, 2000–04; pt-time Chm., Employment Tribunals, 2001–04. *Recreations:* theatre, sports, baby-sitting.

KAY, Sir Nicholas (Peter), KCMG 2016 (CMG 2007); HM Diplomatic Service; Senior Civilian Representative in Afghanistan, National Atlantic Treaty Organisation, since 2019; *b* 8 March 1958; *s* of Ralph Peter Kay and Josephine Alice Kay (*née* Poyner); *m* 1986, Susan Ruth Wallace; one *s* two *d*. *Educ:* Abingdon Sch., Oxon; St Edmund Hall, Oxford (BA Hons English Lang. and Lit.); Univ. of Reading (MA Applied Linguistics). English lang. teacher, Spain, Peru, Brazil, Saudi Arabia, Cyprus and UK, 1980–94; entered FCO, 1994; Hd, Pakistan and Afghanistan Section, FCO, 1994–96; 1st Sec. and Dep. Hd of Mission, Havana, 1997–2000; Dep. Hd, Policy Planning Staff (later Directorate for Strategy and Innovation), FCO, 2000–02; Counsellor and Dep. Hd of Mission, Madrid, 2002–06; UK Regl Co-ordinator, Southern Afghanistan, 2006–07; Ambassador: to the Democratic Republic of the Congo and to the Republic of Congo, 2007–09; to Sudan, 2010–12; Dir, Africa, FCO, 2012–13; UN Sec.-Gen.'s Special Rep. for Somalia, 2013–16; UK Special Envoy for Horn of Africa, 2016–17; Ambassador to Afghanistan, 2017–18. *Recreations:* sailing, vegetarian cookery, travel. *Address:* c/o Foreign and Commonwealth Office, King Charles Street, SW1A 2AH. *E:* nicholas.kay@fco.gov.uk.

KAY, (Robert) Jervis; QC 1996; Admiralty Registrar, since 2009, and Deputy Master of the Senior Court, Queen's Bench Division, since 2019 (Master of the Senior (formerly Supreme) Court, 2009–19); *b* 25 Feb. 1949; *s* of late Philip Jervis Kay, VRD and Pamela Kay; *m* 1988, Henrietta Kathleen Ward (*d* 2011); one *s* three *d*; *m* 2019, Emma Louise

Rattrie (née Thorman). Educ: Wellington Coll.; Nottingham Univ. (LLB Hons). Called to the Bar, Lincoln's Inn, 1972 (Bencher 2005); in practice at the Bar, 1973–2009. Publications: (Ed.) Atkins Court Forms, Vol. 3 Admiralty, 1979, 1990, 1994, 2000, 2004, 2008. Recreations: reading, racing, sailing, golf. Address: Rolls Building, Fetter Lane, EC4A 1NL. Clubs: Turf, MCC, Royal Ocean Yacht, Bar Yacht, Ocean Cruising, Old Wellingtonian Sailing Assoc.

**KAY, Sarah;** see Kay, H. S.

**KAY, Prof. Simon Peter Jabir,** OBE 2019; FRCS; Consultant in Plastic and Reconstructive Surgery and Surgery of the Hand, since 1989, and Director of UK Hand Transplant Programme, since 2016, Leeds Teaching Hospitals NHS Trust; Professor of Hand Surgery, University of Leeds, since 2001; b Kuwait, 14 Jan. 1952; s of Fergus Milton Kay and Jessica Valerie Kay (née Ball); m 1986, Dr Ronan Clare Wilson; two s. Educ: Elizabeth Coll., Guernsey; Royal Shrewsbury Sch.; Christ Church, Oxford (BA Animal Physiol. 1973; BM BCh 1976). FRCS 1981; FRCS (Plastic Surgery) 1989. Trng posts in plastic surgery, Slough, Birmingham, Manchester, Adelaide, Australia and Louisville, USA; Sen. Clin. Lectr in Plastic Surgery, Univ. of Leeds. Visiting Professor: S African Soc. for Surgery of the Hand, Johannesburg, 1996; NSW Hand Surgery Soc., Sydney, 1999; Hon. Vis. Prof. of Plastic Surgery, Umeå Univ., Sweden, 1998–; CC Wu Prof. of Plastic Surgery, Univ. of Hong Kong, 2008; Vis. Guest Prof., Univ. of Milan, 2000. Ed., British Jl Plastic Surgery, 2002–06; Jt Ed.-in-Chief, Jl Brachial Plexus and Peripheral Nerve Injury, 2010–. President: British Soc. for Surgery of the Hand, 2007; British Assoc. of Plastic Reconstructive and Aesthetic Surgeons, 2009. Hon. FRCSE 2001. Hon. DSc Bradford, 2015. Publications: The Growing Hand, 2007; (ed) Oxford Textbook of Plastic Surgery, 2018; contribs to peer-reviewed jls. Recreations: sailing, outdoor pursuits, surgery. Address: Spire Hospital, Jackson Avenue, Roundhay, Leeds LS8 1NT. T: (0113) 268 8788, Fax: (0113) 269 0003. E: spjkay@gmail.com. Club: Oxford and Cambridge.

**KAY, Steven Walton;** QC 1997; b 4 Aug. 1954; s of late John Walton Kay and Eunice May Kay; m 1st (marr. diss.); one s; 2nd, 2000, Valerie (née Logan); one d. Educ: Epsom Coll.; Leeds Univ. (LLB). Called to the Bar, Inner Temple, 1977, Bencher, 2010. Asst Recorder, 1997–2000; Recorder, 2000–; Head of Chambers, 2015–. Defence Counsel, first trial, Internat. Criminal Tribunal for former Yugoslavia, 1996; Amicus Curiae, 2001–04, Assigned Defence Counsel, 2004–06, trial of ex-Pres. Milosevic; Defence Counsel: Internat. Criminal Tribunal for Rwanda, trial of Musema, 1997–2001; Internat. Criminal Tribunal for former Yugoslavia, trial of Gotovina et al, 2007–11; Internat. Criminal Ct, case of Pres. of Kenya, Uhuru Kenyatta, 2010–15. Co-Chair, War Crimes Cttee, IBA, 2012–16. Sec., Criminal Bar Assoc., 1993–96. Founder: Eur. Criminal Bar Assoc., 1998; Internat. Criminal Law Bureau, 2008. Director: Melbury House Music Ltd, 2012–16; Chm., Oculus Financial Intelligence Ltd, 2016–. Drafted: legal test, 100 Series Rules for Use of Force at Sea, 2012; training manual for Bahrain defence lawyers, 2012. Publications: (contrib.) The Rome Statute of the International Criminal Court, ed Casese, Gaeta and Jones, 2002; (contrib.) Cases That Changed Our Lives, vol. 2, 2014. Recreations: golf, gardening, music, sailing. Address: 9 Bedford Row, WC1R 4AZ. T: (020) 7489 2727. Clubs: Hurtwood Park Polo; Drift Golf.

**KAY, William John;** writer and journalist; Obituarist, The Times, since 2011; b 12 Sept. 1946; s of William Jarvie Kay and Agnes Sutherland Walker; m 1968 (marr. diss. 1986); two s; partner, 1987, Lynne Bateson. Educ: Westminster City Sch.; The Queen's Coll., Oxford (MA); Univ. of Calif, Los Angeles (Professional and Advanced Screenwriting). London Evening News, 1968; London Evening Standard, 1972; Daily Telegraph, 1977; Features Editor, Financial Weekly, 1979; Dep. Business Editor, Now!, 1979; Sen. Writer, Sunday Times Business News, 1981; City Editor, The Times, 1984; freelance, 1986–95; Financial Editor, Independent on Sunday, 1995; City Editor, Mail on Sunday, 1995–99; freelance, 1999–2001; Personal Finance Ed., Independent, 2001–05; Money columnist, Sunday Times, 2005–13 (Money Editor, 2005–06). Member: American Cinematheque, 2007–; Huntington Liby, 2007–; Hollywood Heritage, 2010–. Writer of screenplays, 2009–. Wincott Foundn Personal Finance Journalist of the Year, 2002; Headlinemoney Columnist of the Year, 2005; Lifetime Achievement Award, ABI, 2005. Publications: A–Z Guide to Money, 1983; Tycoons, 1985; Big Bang, 1986; (ed) The Stock Exchange: a market place for tomorrow, 1986; Battle for the High Street, 1987; (ed) Modern Merchant Banking, 1988; The Bosses, 1994; Lord of the Dance: the story of Gerry Robinson, 1999; Pasadena Parade, 2019. Recreations: football, cricket, travel, cheese, ice cream, Chelsea FC. E: billkay111@gmail.com. Club: MCC.

**KAY-SHUTTLEWORTH,** family name of **Baron Shuttleworth.**

**KAYE, Rev. Dr Bruce Norman,** AM 2005; General Secretary, The Anglican Church of Australia General Synod, 1994–2004; b 30 June 1939; s of John Harold Kaye and Elsie Evelyn Kaye; m 1st, 1965, Rosemary Jeanette Hutchison (d 1979); one s one d; 2nd, 1983, Margaret Louise Mathieson. Educ: Sydney Boys' High Sch.; Moore Theol Coll. (ThL 1963); Univ. of London (BD 1964); Univ. of Sydney (BA 1966); Univ. of Basel (Dr Theol 1976). Professional Officer, Sydney Water Bd, NSW, 1955–60. Deacon 1964; priest 1965; Curate, St Jude's, Dural, NSW, 1964–66; St John's College, University of Durham: Asst Tutor, 1968; Tutor, 1969; Tutor-Librarian, 1970–75; Sen. Tutor, 1975–82; Vice-Principal, 1979–82; Lectr, Faculty of Divinity, Univ. of Durham, 1970–82; Master, New Coll., Univ. of NSW, 1983–94; Founding Dir, New Coll. Inst. for Values Research, 1987–92. Visiting Fellow: Deutsche Akademische Austauschdienst, Freiberg, 1974; Sch. of Sci. and Technol. Studies, 1984–94; Sch. of Hist., 2005–19, Univ. of NSW; Fellow Commoner, Churchill Coll., and Vis. Schol., Faculty of Divinity, Univ. of Cambridge, 1991–92; Vis. Schol., Sch. of Theol. and Ministry, Seattle Univ., 2003; Professorial Associate, 2007–12, Adjunct Res. Prof., 2012–, Charles Sturt Univ. Founding Ed., 2002–13, Consulting Ed., 2013–, Jl of Anglican Studies. Hon. ThD Australian Coll. of Theol., 2006. Publications: Using the Bible in Ethics, 1976; The Supernatural in the New Testament, 1977; (ed) Obeying Christ in a Changing World, 1977; (ed) Law, Morality and the Bible, 1978; The Argument of Romans with Special Reference to Chapter 6, 1979; (ed) Immigration: what kind of Australia do we want?, 1989; A Church Without Walls: being Anglican in Australia, 1995; (ed) Authority and the Shaping of Tradition, 1997; Godly Citizens, 1999; Web of Meaning, 2000; (Gen. Ed.) Anglicanism in Australia, 2002; Reinventing Anglicanism, 2003; Introduction to World Anglicanism, 2008; Conflict and the Practice of Christian Faith: the Anglican experiment, 2009; The Rise and Fall of the English Christendom, 2017; contrib. numerous articles to theological and other learned jls. Recreations: theatre, golf, walking, reading. Address: 217 Hopetown Avenue, Watson's Bay, NSW 2030, Australia. Club: Australian (Sydney).

**KAYE, Geoffrey John;** President, Animal Shelter AC, Mexico, 2001; b 14 Aug. 1935; s of Michael and Golda Kaye; two d. Educ: Christ's College, Finchley. Started with Pricerite Ltd when business was a small private company controlling six shops, 1951; apptd Manager (aged 18) of one of Pricerite Ltd stores, 1953; Supervisor, Pricerite Ltd, 1955; Controller of all stores in Pricerite Ltd Gp, 1958; Director, 1963; Chairman and Man. Dir, 1966–73. Pres., Allied Automotive Inc., 1992. Recreations: tennis, golf.

**KAYE, Sir John Phillip Lister L.;** see Lister-Kaye.

**KAYE, Lindsey Joy, (Mrs D. N. Kaye);** see Kushner, L. J.

**KAYE, Maj. Sir Paul (Henry Gordon),** 5th Bt cr 1923, of Huddersfield, Co. York; Australian Army, retired 2001; Assistant Funeral Director, since 2017; b 19 Feb. 1958; s of Sir David Alexander Gordon Kaye, 4th Bt and of Adelle Francis Kaye (née Thomas); S father, 1994; m 1st, 1984, Sally Ann Louise Grützner (marr. diss. 2000); 2nd, 2005, Bonita Bonife Yang (marr. diss. 2007); 3rd, 2010, Marlyn Bancure Arambala; one s. Educ: Downlands Coll., Toowoomba; Univ. of Queensland (Dip. Applied Science (Rural Technol.) 1978). Lieut, Australian Regular Army, 1982; Captain, 1986; Major, 1991. Australian Service Medal, 1995; Multi-National Force and Observers Medal, 1995; Defence Force Service Medal, 1998. Recreations: bookbinding, reading, trap and skeet shooting, travel. Heir: s Lionel Gordon Arambala Kaye, b 6 Sept. 2012.

**KAYE, Prof. Paul Martin,** PhD; FRCPath, FMedSci; Professor of Immunology, University of York, since 2004; b London, 20 Oct. 1959; s of Jozef Kaye and Annie Kaye (née Bernor); m 1985, May Wood. Educ: Battersea Grammar Sch.; Imperial Coll. London (BSc 1981); University Coll. London (PhD 1985). FRCPath 2004. London School of Hygiene and Tropical Medicine, University of London: postdoctoral res., 1985–88; Lectr, 1988–91; Sen. Lectr, 1991–95; Reader, 1995–98; Hd, Immunol. Unit, 1997–2000; Prof. of Cellular Immunol., 1998–2004; Co-Dir, Wolfson Centre for Cell Biol., 1999–2004; University of York: Dir, Immunol. and Infection Unit, 2004–10; Dir, Centre for Immunol. and Infection, 2010–15; Dep. Dean (Res.) Hull York Med. Sch., 2011–13. Chm., MRC Infections and Immunity Bd, 2018– (Mem., 2011–15); Mem., Royal Soc. Newton Fellowship Panel, 2009–. FMedSci 2015. Publications: contribs to jls incl. Jl Clin. Investigation, Immunity, Nature Medicine. Recreations: hiking, travel. Address: York Biomedical Research Institute, Hull York Medical School, University of York, Heslington YO10 5DD. E: paul.kaye@york.ac.uk.

**KAYE, His Honour Roger Godfrey,** TD 1980 and Bar 1985; QC 1989; a Circuit Judge, 2005–16; Specialist Senior Chancery/Mercantile Judge, North Eastern Circuit, 2005–16; b 21 Sept. 1946; s of late Anthony Harmsworth Kaye and Heidi Alice (née Jordy); m 1974, Melloney Rose (marr. diss. 2017), d of late Rev. H. M. Westall. Educ: King's Sch., Canterbury; Birmingham Univ. (LLB 1968). FCIArb 2004. Lectr in Law, Kingston Poly., 1968–73. Called to the Bar, Lincoln's Inn, 1970, Bencher, 1997; Jun. Treasury Counsel in Insolvency Matters, 1978–89; Dep. High Court Registrar in Bankruptcy, 1985–2001; Dep. High Court Judge, Chancery Div., QBD and Family Div., 1990–2016; a Recorder, 1994–2005. Acting Judge, Commercial Div., High Court, Eastern Caribbean Supreme Court, 2017. Dep. Chancellor, dio. of Southwark, 1995–99; Chancellor: dio. of Hereford, 2000– (Dep. Chancellor, 1997–2000); dio. of St Albans, 2002–18 (Dep. Chancellor, 1995–2002). Judicial Mem., Parole Bd, 2018–. Chairman: Fees Collection Cttee, Bar Council, 1991–93 (Dep. Chm., 1990–91); Bristol & Cardiff Chancery Bar Assoc., 1990–95. Member: Professional Conduct Cttee, Bar Council, 1995–97; Panel of Chairmen, City Disputes Panel, 1997–2005. Varied TA service in Europe, 1967–97; Hon. Colonel: Intelligence and Security Gp (Volunteers), 1998–99; 3rd (Volunteer) Mil. Intelligence Bn, 1999–2011; 5th (Volunteer) Mil. Intelligence Bn, 2008–11. FRSA 1995. Recreation: going home. Clubs: Athenæum, Army and Navy, Royal Automobile, Special Forces.

**KAYE, Rosalind Anne, (Mrs J. A. Kaye);** see Plowright, R. A.

**KAYE, Prof. Stanley Bernard,** MD; FRCP; FRSE; FMedSci; Cancer Research UK (formerly Cancer Research Campaign) Professor of Medical Oncology, 2000–13, now Emeritus, and Senior Research Fellow, since 2013, Institute of Cancer Research and Royal Marsden NHS Foundation Trust (formerly Hospital); b 5 Sept. 1948; s of Peter Kaye and Dora Kaye (née Thomas); m 1975, Anna Catherine Lister; two s one d. Educ: Charing Cross Hosp. Med. Sch., London (BSc Biochem. 1969); Univ. of London (MB BS 1972; MD 1980). FRCP 1990. University of Glasgow: Sen. Lectr in Med. Oncology, 1980–85; Prof. of Med. Oncology, 1985–2000; Hd, Div. of Clin. Studies (formerly Sect. of Medicine), 2000–13, Hd, Drug Develt Unit, 2000–12, Inst. Cancer Res., London. FRSE 2001; FMedSci 2004. Publications: (ed jtly) Textbook of Medical Oncology, 1997, 4th edn 2009; (ed jtly) Emerging Therapeutic Targets in Ovarian Cancer, 2011. Recreations: playing squash, tennis and golf to varying degrees of indifference. Address: Royal Marsden Hospital, Downs Road, Sutton, Surrey SM2 5PT. T: (020) 8661 3539, Fax: (020) 8661 3541. E: stan.kaye@rmh.nhs.uk; (home) 44 Burdon Lane, Sutton, Surrey SM2 7PT. Club: Royal Automobile.

**KAYE, (William) John H.;** see Holland-Kaye.

**KEABLE-ELLIOTT, Dr (Robert) Anthony,** OBE 1988; FRCGP; general practitioner, 1948–87; b 14 Nov. 1924; s of Robert Keable and Jolie Buck; m 1953, Gilian Mary Hutchison (d 2011); four s. Educ: Sherborne Sch., Dorset; Guy's Hosp., London, 1943–48 (MB BS London). FRCGP 1966. Founder Mem., Chiltern Medical Soc., 1956, Vice-Pres. 1958, Pres. 1964; Member, Faculty Board of Thames Valley, Faculty of Royal Coll. of General Practitioners, 1960; Upjohn Travelling Fellowship, 1962; Member: Bucks Local Med. Cttee, 1958–75 (Chm., 1964–68; Hon. Life Mem., 1975–); GMC, 1989–94. British Medical Association: Mem., 1948–; Mem. Council, 1974–94; Treasurer, 1981–87; Chm., Journal Cttee, 1987–93; Chm., Gen. Med. Services Cttee, 1966–72. Mem., Finance Corp. of General Practice, 1974–79. Mem., Soc. of Apothecaries, 1985–; Freeman, City of London, 1986. Asst Editor, Guy's Hospital Gazette, 1947–48. BMA Gold Medal, 1994. Recreations: sailing, golf, gardening. Address: Peels, Ibstone, near High Wycombe, Bucks HP14 3XX. T: (01491) 638385.

**KEAL, Anthony Charles;** Partner, Simpson Thacher & Bartlett LLP, 2005–09; b Aldershot, 12 July 1951; s of Kitchener Keal and Joan Marjorie Keal; m 1979, Janet Michele King; four s. Educ: New Coll., Oxford (BA Juris.). Admitted solicitor, 1976; Partner, Allen & Overy, 1982–2005. Recreations: sailing, ski-ing, walking, opera, theatre. Address: c/o Simpson Thacher & Bartlett LLP, CityPoint, One Ropemaker Street, EC2Y 9HU. T: (020) 7275 6500, Fax: (020) 7275 6502.

**KEALEY, Gavin Sean James;** QC 1994; a Deputy High Court Judge, Queen's Bench Division (Commercial Court), since 2002; b 2 Sept. 1953; s of Paul and Evelyn Kealey; m 1981, Karen Elizabeth Nowak; three d. Educ: Charterhouse; University Coll., Oxford (BA Jurisp.). Lectr in Law, King's Coll. London, 1976–77; called to the Bar, Inner Temple, 1977, Bencher, 2002; Commercial Barrister, 1978; Recorder, 2000–10; Head of Chambers, 2003–. Address: 7 King's Bench Walk, Temple, EC4Y 7DS. T: (020) 7910 8300.
See also G. T. E. Kealey.

**KEALEY, Prof. (George) Terence (Evelyn),** DPhil; Professor of Clinical Biochemistry, University of Buckingham, 2011 (Vice-Chancellor, 2001–14); b 16 Feb. 1952; s of Paul and Evelyn Kealey; m 1989, Sally Harwood Gritten, d of late Donald Meredith Gritten and of Stella Harwood Gritten (now Huber); one s one d. Educ: Charterhouse Sch.; St Bartholomew's Hosp. Med. Sch. (MB BS 1975; BSc Biochem. 1976); Balliol Coll., Oxford (DPhil 1982); MA Cantab 1995. House physician, St Bartholomew's Hosp., 1976–77; MRC Trng Fellow, Nuffield Dept of Clinical Biochem., Oxford, 1977–82; Jun. Dean, Balliol Coll., Oxford, 1980–81; Sen. Registrar in Clinical Biochem. and Metabolic Medicine, Royal Victoria Infirmary, Newcastle upon Tyne, 1982–86; Wellcome Sen. Res.

Fellow in Clinical Sci., Nuffield Dept of Clinical Biochem., Univ. of Oxford, 1986–88; Lectr, Dept of Clinical Biochem., Univ. of Cambridge, 1988–2001. Member, Academic Advisory Council: Globalization Inst., 2005–; Global Warming Policy Foundn, 2009–; Sen. Fellow in Educn, Adam Smith Inst., 2008–; Adjunct Scholar, Center for Study of Sci., Cato Inst., Washington, 2014–. Trustee, Buckingham Centre for the Arts, 2005–; Gov., Royal Latin Sch., Buckingham, 2011. Hon. Consultant Chemical Pathologist: Oxford HA, 1986–88; Cambridge HA, 1988–2001. Lectures incl. 16th Annual IEA Hayek Meml Lect., 2007. Caldwell Prize, Pope Center for Higher Educn Policy, USA, 2001; Free Enterprise Award, IEA, 2004. *Publications:* The Economic Laws of Scientific Research, 1996; Sex, Science and Profits, 2008; Breakfast is a Dangerous Meal, 2016; contrib. papers in the molecular cell biol. of human skin develt. *Address:* Cato Institute, 1000 Massachusetts Avenue NW, Washington, DC 20001, USA. *Club:* Athenæum.
*See also G. S. J. Kealey.*

**KEALY, Robin Andrew,** CMG 1991; HM Diplomatic Service, retired; consultant, since 2004; *b* 7 Oct. 1944; *s* of Lt-Col H. L. B. Kealy, Royal Signals and Mrs B. E. Kealy; *m* 1987, Annabel Jane Hood; two *s. Educ:* Harrow Sch.; Oriel Coll., Oxford (Open Scholar; BA Lit. Hum. (1st Cl. Hons Mods); MA). Joined HM Diplomatic Service, 1967; FO, 1967; MECAS, 1968; Tripoli, 1970; Kuwait, 1972; ME Dept, FCO, 1975; Port of Spain, 1978; Commercial Sec., Prague, 1982; Asst, Aid Policy Dept, FCO, 1985; Counsellor and Consul Gen., Baghdad, 1987–90; Dir of Trade Promotion and Investment, Paris, 1990–95; Head, Aviation and Maritime Dept, FCO, 1995–97; Consul-Gen., Jerusalem, 1997–2001; Ambassador to Tunisia, 2002–04. Chairman: Welfare Assoc. (UK), 2006–09; Med. Aid to Palestinians, 2008–13 (Mem. Bd, 2004–13; Vice-Chm., 2006–08); Dir, Sir Harold Hillier Gardens, Romsey, 2006–08. Trustee, Arab-British Chamber Charitable Foundn, 2007–13. *Recreations:* music, theatre, ski-ing, cooking, gardening. *Club:* Travellers.

**KEANE, Prof. Adrian Nigel;** Professor of Law, City University London, 2001–15; now Emeritus; *b* Arundel, W Sussex, 12 July 1955; *s* of Michael and Mildred Keane; *m* 1st, 1981, Angela Stewart (marr. diss. 1990); 2nd, 1994, Rosemary Simon (*d* 2010). *Educ:* Chichester High Sch. for Boys; Univ. of Hull (LLB). Called to the Bar, Inner Temple, 1978; Lectr, Sch. of Law, Univ. of Hong Kong, 1981–82; Inns of Court School of Law: Lectr, 1984–87; Sen. Lectr, 1987–90; Reader, 1990–2001; Dean, 2001–08; Dir, Professional Progs, City Univ. London, 2008–11. Vis. Tutor, Wadham Coll., Oxford, 1987–88; Guest Lectr, Dept of Law, LSE, 1989–90. Consultant, Centre for Criminal Procedure Reform, Renmin Univ., Beijing, 2011. Chm. (pt-time), Employment Tribunals, 1996–2001. Mem., Educn and Trng Wkg Party, Bar Council, 1992, 2002–03. *Publications:* The Modern Law of Evidence, 1985, 12th edn 2018; (jtly) Blackstone's Criminal Practice, 1991, 30th edn 2019; (jtly) Advocacy, 1996, 10th edn 2005; (jtly) Blackstone's Civil Practice, 2000, 19th edn 2019; contrib. articles on evidence law to learned jls. *Recreations:* music, gardening, cooking, Arsenal FC. *Address:* City Law School, City, University of London, Northampton Square, EC1V 0HB. *T:* (020) 7404 5060. *E:* a.n.keane@city.ac.uk.

**KEANE, Sir Charles;** *see* Keane, Sir J. C.

**KEANE, Fergal Patrick,** OBE 1997; Special Correspondent, since 1997, and Africa Editor, since 2017, BBC News; *b* 6 Jan. 1961; *s* of Eamon Patrick Keane and Maura Theresa (*née* Hassett); *m* 1986, Anne Frances Flaherty; one *s* one *d. Educ:* Terenure Coll., Dublin; Presentation Coll., Cork. Reporter: Limerick Leader, 1979–82; Irish Press, 1982–84; RTE, 1984–88; joined BBC, 1988. Ireland Corresp., 1988–90; Southern Africa Corresp., 1990–94; Asia Corresp., 1994–97. Writer and presenter, TV series, Story of Ireland, 2011. Professorial Fellow, Inst. of Irish Studies, Univ. of Liverpool, 2013–. Radio Journalist of Year, Sony, 1994; Journalist of Year, RTS, 1994. BAFTA award, TV documentary, 1997. *Publications:* The Bondage of Fear, 1994; Season of Blood, 1995; Letter to Daniel, 1996; Letters Home, 1999; A Stranger's Eye, 2000; All of These People, 2005; Road of Bones: the siege of Kohima 1944, 2010 (British Army Mil. Book of Year, 2011); Wounds: a memoir of war and love, 2017. *Recreations:* fishing, sailing, reading. *Address:* c/o BBC News Centre, Broadcasting House, Portland Place, W1A 1AA. *Clubs:* Foreign Correspondents' (Hong Kong); Royal Cork Yacht (Cork).

**KEANE, Sir (John) Charles,** 7th Bt *cr* 1801, of Cappoquin, Co. Waterford; *b* UK, 16 Sept. 1941; *er s* of Maj. Sir Richard Keane, 6th Bt and Olivia Dorothy (*née* Hawkshaw); *S* father, 2010; *m* 1977, Corinne Everard de Harzir; two *s* one *d. Educ:* Christ Church, Oxford (BA 1963; MA 1967). ACA. *Recreations:* farming, forestry, gardening. *Heir: er s* Richard Christopher Keane, *b* 21 Aug. 1981. *Address:* Cappoquin House, Cappoquin, Co. Waterford, Ireland. *T:* 54290; 26 avenue d'Hougoumont, 1180 Brussels, Belgium. *T:* (2) 3755464. *E:* charles-keane@skynet.be. *Club:* Kildare Street and University.

**KEANE, John Granville Colpoys;** artist; *b* 12 Sept. 1954; *s* of Granville Keane and Elaine Violet Meredith Keane (*née* Doubble); *m* 1996, Rosemary Anne McGowan; one *s* one *d. Educ:* Hardenwick Sch., Harpenden; Cheam Sch., Berks; Wellington Coll.; Camberwell Sch. of Art, London (BA Fine Art). Over 60 solo exhibns in UK, Europe and USA, 1980–; official British War Artist, Gulf War, 1991; Artist in Residence: Independent on Sunday, 2000–01; Sch. of Internat. Relns, St Andrews Univ., 2014–17; commnd portrait of Kofi Annan for UN, 2010. Vis. Fellow, London Inst., 2000; Vis. Res. Fellow, Camberwell Coll. of Arts, 2000–11. FRSA 2005. Aesthetica Art Prize, 2015. *Publications:* Gulf, 1992; (with Duncan Green) Guatemala: burden of paradise, 1992; (with Mark Lawson) Conflicts of Interest, 1995; (with Mark Lawson) Troubles My Sight, 2015. *Recreations:* tennis, unpopular music, snooker. *Address:* c/o Flowers East, 82 Kingsland Road, E2 8DP. *T:* (020) 7920 7777, *Fax:* (020) 7920 7770. *E:* gallery@flowerseast.com. *Clubs:* Groucho, Chelsea Arts; Thorpeness Country.

**KEANE, Ronan;** Chief Justice of Ireland, 2000–04; *b* 20 July 1932; *s* of John Patrick Keane and Katherine Gertrude Keane (*née* Boylan); *m* 1st, 1962, Ann Therese O'Donnell (*d* 2008); one *s* two *d*; 2nd, 2010, Irene Garavan. *Educ:* Blackrock Coll., Co. Dublin; University Coll., Dublin (BA 1953). Called to the Irish Bar, King's Inns, Dublin, 1954 (Bencher, 1979); in practice at the Bar, 1954–79; Jun. Counsel, 1954–70; Sen. Counsel, 1970–79; Judge: High Court of Ireland, 1979–96; Supreme Court of Ireland, 1996–2000. Chm., Irish Bar Council, 1974–75; Pres., Law Reform Commn, 1987–92. Hon. Bencher: Lincoln's Inn, 2000; NI Inn of Court, 2000. Hon. Fellow, Univ. of Dublin, 2008. Hon. LLD UC Dublin, 2003. *Publications:* The Law of Local Government in the Republic of Ireland, 1982; Company Law in the Republic of Ireland, 1985, 5th edn 2016; Equity and the Law of Trusts in the Republic of Ireland, 1988, 3rd edn 2017. *Recreations:* music, theatre, reading. *Address:* 13 Leeson Park Avenue, Dublin 6, Ireland. *T:* (1) 6697008.

**KEARL, Guy Alexander;** QC 2002; **His Honour Judge Kearl;** a Circuit Judge, since 2011; a Senior Circuit Judge, since 2018; *b* 29 Sept. 1959; *s* of Ian Alexander Kearl and Sheila Kearl; *m* 1985, Anea Jayne Ellison; two *s. Educ:* Millfield Sch.; Univ. of Central Lancashire (BA Hons Law); Inns of Court Sch. of Law. Called to the Bar, Middle Temple, 1982; in practice, specialising in serious crime law; Recorder, 2001–11. *Recreations:* ski-ing, marathon running, tennis, cycling. *Address:* Leeds Combined Court Centre, Court House, 1 Oxford Row, Leeds LS1 3BG.

**KEARLEY,** family name of **Viscount Devonport.**

**KEARNEY, Brian;** Sheriff of Glasgow and Strathkelvin, 1977–2007; Temporary Sheriff Principal, South Strathclyde, Dumfries and Galloway, 2007–08; *b* 25 Aug. 1935; *s* of late James Samuel and Agnes Olive Kearney; *m* 1965, Elizabeth Mary Chambers; three *s* one *d. Educ:* Largs Higher Grade Sch.; Greenock Academy; Glasgow Univ. (MA, LLB). Qualified solicitor, 1960; Partner, Biggart, Lumsden & Co., Solicitors, Glasgow, 1965–74. Sheriff of N Strathclyde at Dumbarton (floating sheriff), 1974–77. Sometime tutor in Jurisprudence, and external examr in legal subjects, Glasgow Univ.; Hon. Lectr, Social Work Dept, Dundee Univ., 1995–. Chm., Inquiry into Child Care Policies in Fife, 1989–92 (report published, 1992). Mem., Judicial Studies Cttee (Scotland), 1997–2005. Pres., Glasgow Juridical Soc., 1964–65; Chm., Glasgow Marriage Guidance Council, 1977–90; Hon. President: Glasgow Marriage Counselling Service, 1990–; Family Law Assoc., Scotland, 1999–. *Publications:* An Introduction to Ordinary Civil Procedure in the Sheriff Court, 1982; Children's Hearings and the Sheriff Court, 1987, 2nd edn 2000; (ed jtly) Butterworths' Scottish Family Law Service, 1995; The Scottish Children's Hearings System in Action, 2007; articles in legal jls. *Recreations:* cutting sandwiches for family picnics, listening to music, reading, writing and resting. *Club:* Glasgow Art.

**KEARNEY, Martha Catherine;** BBC broadcaster; presenter, Today Programme, BBC Radio 4, since 2018; *b* 8 Oct. 1957; *d* of late Hugh Kearney and of Catherine Kearney; *m* 2001, Christopher Thomas Shaw, *qv. Educ:* George Watson's Ladies' Coll., Edinburgh; St Anne's Coll., Oxford. LBC Radio, 1981–87; A Week in Politics, Channel Four, 1987–88; BBC, 1988–: reporter, On the Record, 1988–94; Panorama, 1993; reporter, 1994–2000, Political Ed., 2000–07, Newsnight; presenter: Woman's Hour, Radio 4, 1999–2007; The Review Show (formerly Newsnight Review), BBC2, later BBC4, 2005–14; The World at One, BBC Radio 4, 2007–18. Year back packing, 1989–90. Hon. DLit Keele, 2007. *Recreations:* reading, cooking, travel, beekeeping. *Address:* c/o BBC News Centre, Broadcasting House, Portland Place, W1A 1AA. *T:* (020) 9743 8000. *E:* martha.kearney@bbc.co.uk. *Clubs:* Royal Over-Seas League, Soho House.

**KEARNEY, Prof. Michael John,** PhD; FInstP, FIET, FIMA; Professor of Electronic Device Engineering, since 2002, and Provost and Executive Vice President, since 2016, University of Surrey; *b* Crawley, Sussex, 7 Nov. 1962; *s* of Anthony and Jean Kearney; *m* 1988, Sally Smart; one *s. Educ:* St John's Coll., Oxford (BA 1985; MA 1990); Warwick Univ. (PhD 1988). CEng 1999; FIET 1999; CPhys 1999; FInstP 1999; FIMA 2003. Res. Scientist and Gp Leader, 1988–94, Lab. Manager, 1994–95, Long Range Res. Lab, Hirst Res. Centre, GEC-Marconi Ltd; Prof. of Electronic Device Engrg, 1995–2002, Hd of Dept, 1997–2000, Dept of Electronic and Electrical Engrg, Loughborough Univ.; University of Surrey: Dir, Advanced Technol. Inst., 2002–05; Hd, Sch. of Electronics and Physical Scis, 2005–07; Dean, Faculty of Engrg and Physical Scis, 2007–11; Pro-Vice-Chancellor (REF), 2011–13; Dep. Vice-Chancellor, Res. and Innovation, 2013–16; Actg Vice-Chancellor, 2015–16. *Publications:* contribs to jls. *Recreations:* travel, guitar. *Address:* University of Surrey, Guildford, Surrey GU2 7XH. *T:* (01483) 686481. *E:* m.j.kearney@surrey.ac.uk.

**KEARNEY, Hon. Sir William (John Francis),** Kt 1982; CBE 1976; Judge of the Supreme Court of the Northern Territory, 1982–99; *b* 8 Jan. 1935; *s* of William John Kilbeg Kearney and Gertrude Ivylene Kearney; *m* 1959, Jessie Alice Elizabeth Yung; three *d. Educ:* Univ. of Sydney (BA, LLB); University Coll. London (LLM). Legal Service of Papua New Guinea, 1963–75; Sec. for Law, 1972–75; dormant Commn as Administrator, 1972–73, and as High Comr, 1973–75; Judge, Supreme Ct of PNG, 1976–82; Dep. Chief Justice, 1980–82. Aboriginal Land Comr, 1982–86. *Recreations:* travelling, literature.

**KEARNS, Dr William Edward,** FFPH; consultancy in health policy and public health, 1993–2000; *b* 10 July 1934; *s* of William Edward Kearns and Kathleen Wolfenden; *m* 1954, Beryl Cross (decd); three *s* one *d* (and two *s* decd). *Educ:* Liverpool Coll.; Univ. of Liverpool (MB ChB); Univ. of London (MSc; DipTh 1995). MRCS, LRCP. Hosp. posts in cardiorespiratory physiology, gen. medicine and pathology, United Liverpool Hosps, 1958–70; NW Metropolitan Regional Hospital Board: Asst SMO, 1970–73; Regional Sci. Officer, 1973–74; Dist Community Physician, Kensington and Chelsea and Westminster AHA (Teaching), 1974–82; Hon. Sen. Lectr in Community Medicine, St Mary's Hosp. Med. Sch., 1975–86; Dist MO, Paddington and N Kensington HA, 1982–86; Regional MO and Dir of Health Care Policy, 1986–90, Dir of Public Health, 1990–92, CMO, 1990–93, NE Thames RHA. Reader, Neasden Parish Church (S Catherine), Reader Emeritus, 2015; Sec. for Readers, dio. of London, 1996–2003; Oblate Novice, Monastery of Our Lady and St Benedict, Elmore Abbey, 1996–98; Oblate, Monastery of St Mary at the Cross, Edgware Abbey, 1998–. Order of St Mellitus, dio. of London, 2015. FRSA 1997. *Publications:* The Health Report, North East Thames Health Region, 1990, 1991; contribs to med. jls. *Recreations:* gardening for wild life conservation, grandparenting. *Address:* 12 Windsor House, Pynnacles Close, Stanmore, Middx HA7 4FE. *T:* (020) 8954 3757. *Club:* Royal Society of Medicine.

**KEARON, Rt Rev. Kenneth Arthur;** *see* Limerick and Killaloe, Bishop of.

**KEATES, Jonathan Basil;** writer; teacher of English, City of London School, 1974–2013; *b* 7 Nov. 1946; *s* of Herbert Richard Basil Keates and Evangeline Sonia Wilcox. *Educ:* Bryanston Sch., Dorset (Schol.); Magdalen Coll., Oxford (MA); Exeter Univ. (PGCE). FRSL 1993; FSA 2009. Chm., Venice in Peril Fund, 2013–. *Publications:* The Companion Guide to the Shakespeare Country, 1979; Allegro Postillions (James Tait Black Prize; Hawthornden Prize), 1984; Handel: the man and his music, 1985, 2nd edn 2008; The Strangers' Gallery, 1987; Italian Journeys, 1991; Stendhal, 1994 (Enid McLeod Prize, 1995); Henry Purcell, 1995; Soon To Be a Major Motion Picture, 1997; Smile Please, 2000; The Siege of Venice, 2005; The Portable Paradise, 2011; Robert Browning, 2012; William III and Mary II: partners in revolution, 2015; Messiah: the composition and afterlife of Handel's masterpiece, 2016. *Recreations:* Venice, libraries, music, friendship. *Address:* 5 Houblon Road, Richmond, Surrey TW10 6DB. *T:* (020) 8940 9679. *Club:* Athenæum.

**KEATING, Prof. Jonathan Peter,** PhD; FRS 2009; Sedleian Professor of Natural Philosophy, University of Oxford, since 2019; Fellow, Queen's College, Oxford, since 2019; *b* Salford, 20 Sept. 1963; *s* of Albert Edward Keating and Sheila Keating; *m* 2009, Prof. Heidy Marita Mader; one *s* one *d* (and one *s* decd). *Educ:* New Coll., Oxford (BA 1st Cl.); Univ. of Bristol (PhD 1989). Lectr in Applied Maths, Univ. of Manchester, 1991–95; University of Bristol: Reader in Applied Maths, 1995–97; Prof. of Mathematical Physics, 1997–2012; Henry Overton Wills Prof. of Maths, 2012–19; Hd, Dept of Maths, 2001–04; Dean of Sci., 2009–13. EPSRC Sen. Res. Fellow, 2004–09. *Publications:* contrib. papers to mathematical and scientific jls. *Recreations:* cooking, cricket, running and (most importantly) my family. *Address:* Mathematical Institute, University of Oxford, Andrew Wiles Building, Radcliffe Observatory Quarter, Woodstock Road, Oxford OX2 6GG.

**KEATING, Kay Rosamond Blundell;** a District Judge (Magistrates' Courts) (formerly Metropolitan Stipendiary Magistrate), 1987–2004; *b* 3 Oct. 1943; *d* of Geoffrey Blundell Jones and Avis Blundell Jones; *m* 1st, 1965, Edmund Deighton (decd); one *d* decd; 2nd, 1978, Donald Norman Keating, QC (*d* 1995); one *s. Educ:* St Hugh's College, Oxford (BA Jurisp. 1965; MA 1968). Called to the Bar, Gray's Inn, 1966. *Recreations:* travel, walking, tennis, riding, opera.

**KEATING, Prof. Michael,** PhD; FBA 2012; FRSE; FAcSS; Professor of Politics, University of Aberdeen, since 1999; Director, Centre on Constitutional Change (formerly ESRC Scottish Centre on Constitutional Change), since 2013; *b* Hartlepool, 2 Feb. 1950; *s* of Michael Joseph Keating and Margaret Keating (*née* Lamb); *m* 1975, Patricia Ann McCusker; one *s*. *Educ*: St Aidan's Grammar Sch., Sunderland; Pembroke Coll., Oxford (BA 1971; MA 1975); Glasgow Coll. of Technol. (PhD 1975). Sen. Res. Officer, Univ. of Essex, 1975–76; Lectr, N Staffs Poly., 1976–79; Lectr, 1979–86, Sen. Lectr, 1986–88, Univ. of Strathclyde; Professor: Univ. of Western Ontario, 1988–99; European Univ. Inst., Florence, 2000–10; (pt-time) Univ. of Edinburgh, 2012–. MAE 2013. FRSE 2005; FAcSS (AcSS 2009). Hon. Dr Louvain. *Publications*: Labour and Scottish Nationalism, 1979; The Government of Scotland, 1983; Labour and the British State, 1985; Decentralisation in Contemporary France, 1986; Remaking Urban Scotland, 1986; Glasgow: the politics of urban regeneration, 1988; State and Regional Nationalism, 1988; Politics and Public Policy in Scotland, 1991; Comparative Urban Politics, 1992; The Politics of Modern Europe, 1993, 2nd edn 1999; Nations against the State, 1996, 2nd edn 2001; The New Regionalism in Western Europe, 1998; Plurinational Democracy, 2001; (jtly) Culture, Institutions and Economic Development, 2003; The Government of Scotland, 2005, 2nd edn 2010; The Independence of Scotland, 2009; Rescaling the European State, 2013; (jtly) Small Nations in a Big World, 2014; (jtly) Small States in the Modern World, 2015; (ed) Debating Scotland, 2017; (ed) A Wealthier, Fairer Scotland, 2017; (ed jtly) Constitutional Politics and the Territorial Question in Canada and the UK, 2018; (ed jtly) Changing Borders in Europe, 2019. *Recreations*: hill walking, sailing, traditional music. *Address*: 27 Dundas Street, Edinburgh EH3 6QQ. *T*: 07758 329876. *E*: m.keating@abdn.ac.uk.

**KEATING, Michael Matthew,** CMG 2019; Executive Director, European Institute of Peace, since 2018; *b* Kampala, 22 April 1959; *s* of Matthew Keating and Otylka Keating; *m* 1989, Kim Lowes; four *d*. *Educ*: Clare Coll., Cambridge (BA Hist. 1980). Exec. Trainee, Macmillan Publishers, 1980–82; Publishing Asst, Euromoney Publications, 1982–85; Exec. Asst to Prince Sadruddin Aga Khan, 1985–88; UN assignments, Afghanistan, 1988–90; Associate Producer, Barraclough-Casey (TV), 1990–92; Dir, Media Natura, 1992–96; UN assignments, Afghanistan, 1996–99; Sen. Advr to Adminr, UNDP, NY, 1999–2001; Dir, Socio-Econ. Affairs, UN Assistance Mission to Afghanistan, Jerusalem, 2001–04; UN Resident Coordinator, Malawi, 2004–08; Exec. Dir, Africa Progress Panel, 2008–10; Dep. Special Rep. of UN Sec. Gen. to Afghanistan, 2010–12; Associate Dir, Res. Partnerships, RIIA (Chatham House), 2014–15; Special Rep. of UN Sec. Gen. to Somalia, 2016–18. *Publications*: (ed jtly) Aid, Diplomacy and Facts on the Ground: the case of Palestine, 2005; (ed jtly) War and Peace in Somalia, 2018; academic papers on human rights, humanitarian affairs and develt issues. *Recreations*: trekking, tennis, bicycling. *Address*: European Institute of Peace, Rue des Deux Eglises 25, Brussels 1000, Belgium. *E*: keatingandco@gmail.com.

**KEATING, Michael Ray;** Director, Education and Lifelong Learning, Rhondda Cynon Taff County Borough Council, 2005–11; *b* 31 Aug. 1946; *s* of Raymond and Marion Keating; *m* 1967, Jacqueline Ann Pope; two *s*. *Educ*: Ifield Grammar Sch., Crawley; Nottingham Coll. of Educn (Teachers Cert. 1967); Univ. of Newcastle upon Tyne (BEd Hons 1976); Univ. of Warwick (Advanced Dip. Educn 1987). Primary sch. teacher, Breaston, Derbys, then St Albans, and Newcastle upon Tyne, 1967–78; Headteacher, S Benwell Jun. Sch., 1978–80, S Benwell Primary Sch., 1980–88, Newcastle upon Tyne; Primary Advr, 1988–91, Sen. Advr, 1991–96, Mid Glamorgan CC; Asst Dir, Educn, Rhondda Cynon Taff CBC, 1996–2005. Lectr (pt-time), Univ. of Newcastle upon Tyne, 1984–86; External Examr, Manchester Metropolitan Univ., 1990–94. *Recreations*: football, supporting Newcastle United, Alfa Romeo cars, steam trains, modern jazz and blues music, food and wine, caravanning. *Address*: Holly House, 1 Farfield Manor, Sedgefield, Stockton-on-Tees TS21 3NR.

**KEATING, Dr Michael Stockton,** AC 1996 (AO 1990); Director, Insight Economics, 2011–17; *b* 25 Jan. 1940; *s* of Russell James Keating and Alice (*née* Skinner); *m* 1962, Rosemary Gardner; four *s*. *Educ*: Geelong Coll.; Univ. of Melbourne (BCom Hons); ANU (PhD). Hd, Growth Studies and Resource Allocation Div., OECD, 1976–78; First Asst Sec., Econ. Div., Dept of Prime Minister and Cabinet, Australia, 1979–82; Dep. Sec., Dept of Finance, 1982–83; Secretary: Dept of Employment and Industrial Relns, 1983–86; Dept of Finance, 1986–91; Dept of the PM and Cabinet, 1991–96. Adjunct Prof., Griffith Univ., 1997–2004; Fellow, Econs Dept, Res. Sch. of Soc. Scis, ANU, 1997–2008. Chm., Ind. Pricing and Regulatory Tribunal, NSW, 2004–09. Member: Econ. Develt Bd, SA, 2005–14; Trng and Skills Commn, SA, 2008–14; Bd, Australian Workforce and Productivity Agency (formerly Skills, Australia), 2008–14. Chm., Community and Clinical Experts Adv. Council, Health NSW, 2009–10. Board Member: Australia Post, 1996–2001; Fujitsu Australia, 1998–2003. Mem. Council, ANU, 1996–2004. DUniv Griffith, 2000; Hon. DCom Melbourne, 2016. Centenary Medal (Australia), 2001. *Publications*: The Australian Workforce 1910–1911 to 1960–61, 1973; (jtly) The Making of Australian Economic Policy: 1983–88, 1989; (jtly) The Future of Governance, 2000; (jtly) Institutions on the Edge, 2000; Who Rules?: how government retains control of a privatised economy, 2004; (jtly) Fair Share: competing claims and Australia's economic future, 2018. *Recreations*: bushwalking, reading, golf. *Address*: 11/7 Bowen Drive, Barton, ACT 2600, Australia. *T*: (2) 62739405.

**KEATING, Hon. Paul John;** Prime Minister of Australia, 1991–96; *b* 18 Jan. 1944; *s* of Matthew and Minnie Keating; *m* 1975, Annita Johanna Maria Van Iersel; one *s* three *d*. *Educ*: De La Salle College, Bankstown, NSW. Research Officer, Federated Municipal and Shire Council Employees Union of Australia, 1967. MP (ALP) Blaxland, NSW, 1969–96; Minister for Northern Australia, Oct.–Nov. 1975; Shadow Minister for Agriculture, Jan.–March 1976, for Minerals and Energy, 1976–80, for Resources and Energy, 1980–83; Shadow Treasurer, Jan.–March 1983; Federal Treas. of Australia, 1983–91; Dep. Prime Minister, 1990–91. Member: Cabinet Expenditure Review Cttee (Dep. Chm.), 1987–91; Parly Structural Adjustment Cttee, 1987; Parly Social and Family Policy Cttee, 1983. Chm., Australian Loan Council, 1983–91. Hon. LLD: Keio, Tokyo, 1995; Nat. Univ. of Singapore, 1999; NSW, 2003; Hon. DLit Macquarie, 2012. *Publications*: Engagement: Australia faces the Asia Pacific, 2000; After Words: the post Prime Ministerial speeches, 2011. *Recreations*: classical music, architecture, fine arts, swimming. *Address*: PO Box 1265, Potts Point, NSW 1335, Australia.

**KEATING, Roland Francis Kester, (Roly);** Chief Executive, British Library, since 2012; *b* 5 Aug. 1961; *s* of Donald Norman Keating and Betty Katharine Keating (*née* Wells); *m* 1989, Caroline Marguerite Cumine Russell; one *s* two *d*. *Educ*: Westminster Sch.; Balliol Coll., Oxford (BA Hons). Joined BBC as gen. trainee, 1983: attachments to Radio Ulster, Kaleidoscope, Everyman, Newsnight progs; producer and dir, Music and Arts Dept, 1985–89; Editor: The Late Show, 1990–92; Bookmark, 1992–97; Executive Producer: (also devised and launched) One Foot in the Past, 1992; A History of British Art, 1996; The House Detectives, 1997; How Buildings Learn, 1997; Hd of Develt, Music and Arts, with special resp. for New Services, 1995; on secondment (part-time) to BBC Broadcast to develop new channel propositions for BBC Worldwide/Flextech jt venture, UKTV, 1996; Hd of Programming, UKTV, 1997–99; Controller, Digital Channels, 1999–2000, Controller of Arts Commissioning and Digital Channels, 2000–01, BBC TV; Controller, BBC4, 2001–04, on secondment as Jt Leader, BBC Charter Review, 2003; Controller, BBC2, 2004–08; Actg Controller, BBC1, 2007–08; Dir, Archive Content, BBC, 2008–12. Non-exec. Dir, Channel 4, 2016–. Member: Govt Adv. Panel on public library service in England, 2014–; Adv. Bd, Inst. for Innovation and Public Purpose, UCL, 2017–. Mem. Bd, Barbican Centre, 2009–17; Chm., Knowledge Quarter, 2015–19. Trustee: Turner Contemporary, Margate, 2009–17; Clore Leadership Prog., 2017–. Pres., Conf. of European Nat. Libraries, 2015–. Mem., BAFTA. Hon. FRSL 2018. Hon. DLitt: Lincoln, 2013; Warwick, 2015; Hon. DUniv. York, 2014. *Recreations*: family, friends, reading, walking, being by the seaside. *Address*: British Library, 96 Euston Road, NW1 2DB. *Club*: Soho House.

**KEATLEY, Robert Leland;** Editor, The Hong Kong Journal, 2005–11; Consultant, National Committee on US-China Relations, since 2013; *b* 14 Feb. 1935; *s* of Robert L. Keatley and Eva S. Keatley; *m* 1st, 1970, Anne Greene (marr. diss.); one *s*; 2nd, 1982, Catharine Williams; two *d*. *Educ*: Univ. of Washington (BA); Stanford Univ. (MA). Diplomatic Corresp., Wall St Jl, Washington, 1969–77; Foreign Ed., Wall St Jl, NY, 1978; Editor: Asian Wall St Jl, Hong Kong, 1979–84; Wall St Jl Europe, Brussels, 1984–92; columnist and feature editor, Wall St Jl, Washington, 1992–98; South China Morning Post: Sen. Associate Editor, 1998–99; Editor, 1999–2001. Consultant, Nat. Cttee on US-China Relns, 2011–. Mem., Washington Inst. Foreign Affairs, 2004– (Mem. Bd, 2006–10). Contrib., www.nationalinterest.org, 2012–. *Publications*: China: behind the mask, 1974. *Recreations*: hiking, golf. *Address*: 3109 Cathedral Avenue NW, Washington, DC 20008, USA. *Clubs*: Hong Kong, China, Ladies Recreation (Hong Kong); Cosmos (Washington).

**KEAVENY, Vincent Thomas;** Partner, DLA Piper UK LLP, since 2015; *b* Dublin, 1 July 1965; *s* of (Thomas) Vincent Keaveny, FRCSI and Phylomena Keaveny; *m* 1993, Amanda Powell. *Educ*: St Michael's Coll., Dublin; University Coll. Dublin (BCL 1986); Trinity Coll., Dublin (MLitt 1989). Called to the Bar, King's Inns, Dublin, 1988; admitted solicitor, England and Wales, 1992; Legal Dept, Bankers Trust Co., 1990–92; Solicitor: Slaughter and May, 1992–95; Wilde Sapte, 1995–97; Sen. Associate, Cadwalader, Wickersham & Taft, 1997–99; Partner, Norton Rose LLP, 1999–2005; Partner, 2005–15, Jt Deptl Manager, Banking and Finance, 2011–15, Baker & McKenzie LLP. Pres., City of London Law Soc., 2014–15. City of London: Alderman, 2013–; Sheriff, 2018–19. Liveryman: City of London Solicitors' Co., 2001– (Master, 2014–15); Woolmen's Co., 2007– (Upper Warden 2019–); Distillers' Co., 2016–; Spectacle Makers' Co., 2017–; Stationers' Co., 2019–. Chm., Bd of Trustees, EXAUDI, 2011–; Dir/Trustee, Actors Touring Co., 2014–; Trustee, Sir John Soane's Mus., 2015–. KC*HS 2016; MStJ 2018. *Recreations*: opera, theatre, tennis, riding, reading biographies, walking the labrador. *Address*: DLA Piper UK LLP, 160 Aldersgate Street, EC1A 4HT. *E*: vincent.keaveny@dlapiper.com; Members' Room, PO Box 270, Guildhall, EC2P 2EJ. *E*: vincent.keaveny@cityoflondon.gov.uk. *Clubs*: Carlton, Queen's, Mark's, City Livery; Royal St George Yacht; Guards Polo.

**KEAY, Dr Anna Julia,** OBE 2019; Director, Landmark Trust, since 2012; *b* Oban, Argyll, 22 Aug. 1974; *d* of John Stanley Melville Keay, *qv*; *m* 2008, Simon John Thurley, *qv*; one *s* one *d* (twins). *Educ*: Bedales Sch., Hants; Magdalen Coll., Oxford (BA Hons Modern Hist. 1995); Queen Mary and Westfield Coll., Univ. of London (PhD 2004). Asst Curator, Historic Royal Palaces, 1995–2002; Curatorial Dir, English Heritage, 2002–12. Presenter, TV progs and history documentaries. Mem., Collections and Interpretation Adv. Gp, Nat. Trust, 2016–. Trustee: Leeds Castle Foundn, 2009–17; The Royal Collections Trust, 2017–. Non-exec. Dir, Big Yellow Self Storage Co., 2017–. Gov., Bedales Sch., 2013–. *Publications*: The Elizabethan Tower of London: the Haiward and Gascoyne plan, 2001; The Magnificent Monarch: Charles II and the ceremonies of power, 2008; (jtly) The White Tower, 2009; The Crown Jewels, 2011; The Elizabethan Garden at Kenilworth, 2013; (jtly) Landmark: a history of Britain in 50 buildings, 2015; The Last Royal Rebel: the life and death of James, Duke of Monmouth, 2016; contrib. articles to jls. *Recreation*: picnics. *Address*: Landmark Trust, Shottesbrooke, Maidenhead, Berks SL6 3SW. *T*: (01628) 825920. *E*: akeay@landmarktrust.org.uk.

**KEAY, John Stanley Melville;** author and history writer, since 1971; *b* 18 Sept. 1941; *s* of Capt. Stanley Walter Keay and Florence Jessie Keay (*née* Keeping); *m* 1st, 1972, Julia Margaret Atkins (*d* 2011); two *s* two *d*; 2nd, 2014, Amanda Jane Douglas. *Educ*: Ampleforth Coll.; Magdalen Coll., Oxford (BA Hons Modern Hist.). Various jobs in advertising, printing, journalism (freelance, mostly as special corresp. on India for The Economist), 1963–71; writer and presenter of radio documentaries, mainly on Asia, 1981–95. Sykes Meml Medal, RSAA, 2009. *Publications*: Into India, 1973, 3rd edn 1999; When Men and Mountains Meet, 1977, The Gilgit Game, 1979, combined as The Explorers of the Western Himalayas, 1996; India Discovered, 1981, 3rd edn 2001; Eccentric Travellers, 1983, 2nd edn 2001; Highland Drove, 1984; Explorers Extraordinary, 1985, 2nd edn 2001; (Gen. Ed.) The Royal Geographical Society History of World Exploration, 1991; The Honourable Company: a history of the East India Company, 1991; (ed with Julia Keay) Collins Encyclopaedia of Scotland, 1994, 2nd edn 2000; Indonesia: from Sabang to Merauke, 1995; Last Post: the end of Empire in the Far East, 1997, 2nd edn 2000; India: a history, 2000; The Great Arc, 2000; Sowing the Wind: the seeds of conflict in the Middle East, 2003; Mad About the Mekong: exploration and empire in South East Asia, 2005; The Spice Route: a history, 2005; (ed with Julia Keay) The London Encyclopaedia, 3rd edn 2008; China: a history, 2008; Midnight's Descendants: South Asia from partition to the present day, 2014; The Tartan Turban: in search of Alexander Gardner, 2017. *Recreations*: weeding, walking, the warmer parts of Asia. *Address*: Succoth, Dalmally, Argyll PA33 1BB. *T*: (01838) 200250.
See also A. J. Keay.

**KEAY, Prof. Simon James,** PhD; FBA 2016; FSA; Professor of Roman Archaeology, University of Southampton, since 1998; *b* London, 21 May 1954; *s* of Anthony Keay and Lorelei Keay (*née* Shiel); *m* 1986, Nina Inzani; two *s*. *Educ*: Downside Sch.; Inst. of Archaeol., University Coll. London (BA 1977; PhD 1982). University of Southampton: Department of Archaeology: Lectr, 1985–94; Sen. Lectr, 1994–96; Reader, 1996–98; Hd of Dept, 2005–06 and 2012–14; Associate Dean for Res., Faculty of Humanities, 2014–18. Res. Prof., British Sch. at Rome, 2006–11, pt-time, 2011–17. Member: Internat. Scientific Adv. Panel, Inst. Català d'Arqueologia Clàssica, Tarragona, 2009–; Comitato Scientifico Internazionale, Parco Archeologico di Ostia Antica, 2017–. Corresponding Member: Inst. d'Estudis Catalans, 2009–; Reial Acadèmia de Bones Lletres, Barcelona, 2017–. FSA 1986. *Publications*: Late Roman Amphorae in the Western Mediterranean, 1984; Roman Spain, 1988; (jtly) La Villa Romana de Vilauba, 1988; Hispania Romana, 1992; (with M. Millett) A Roman Provincial Capital and its Territory: the survey of the territory of Tarragona, 1985–1990, 1995; (with B. Cunliffe) Social Complexity and the Development of Towns in Iberia, 1995; (ed with M. Diaz-Andreu) The Archaeology of Iberia: the dynamics of change, 1996; (ed) The Archaeology of Early Roman Baetica, 1998; (jtly) Celti: the archaeology of a Hispano-Roman town in Baetica, 2000; (ed with N. Terrenato) Italy and the West: comparative issues in Romanization, 2001; (jtly) Portus: an archaeological survey of the Port of Imperial Rome, 2005; (ed jtly) The Early Roman Towns of Hispania Tarraconensis, 2006; (ed jtly) Portus and its Hinterland, 2011; (ed) Rome, Portus and the Mediterranean, 2012; (ed jtly) Urban Landscape Survey in Italy and the Mediterranean, 2012; (jtly) Archaeological Survey Work at Ocriculum, 2014; contribs to learned jls incl. Antiquaries Jl, Antiquity, Archivo Español de Arqueologia, Empúries, Geophysical Prospection, Hyperborea, Jl Archaeol Sci., Jl Roman Archaeol., Jl Roman Studies,

PlosOne, Mélanges de l'École française de Rome, Oxford Jl Archaeol., Papers of British Sch. at Rome, Proc. NAS. *Recreations:* swimming, travelling, opera, contemporary music. *Address:* Department of Archaeology, University of Southampton, Southampton SO17 1BF. *T:* (023) 8059 2244, *Fax:* (023) 8059 3032. *E:* sjk1@soton.ac.uk.

**KEBEDE, Susan Michelle;** a Judge of the Upper Tribunal, Immigration and Asylum Chamber, since 2011; *b* Hull, 2 July 1964; *d* of Ronald Gordon Field and late Esther Judith Field; *m* 1998, Dr Zelalem Kebede; one *s* one *d*. *Educ:* Wolfreton Comprehensive Sch.; Leeds Univ. (LLB Hons 1986). Articled clerk, Saunders, Sobell, Leigh & Dobin; admitted as solicitor, 1991; Caseworker, Refugee Legal Centre, 1993–2001; non-salaried Immigration Adjudicator, later Judge, 2001–03; Salaried Immigration Judge, 2003–11. *Recreations:* mother of two (therefore not much time for recreations), spending time with children, walking in countryside. *Address:* Upper Tribunal (Immigration and Asylum Chamber), Field House, 15 Breams Buildings, EC4A 1DZ.

**KEDDIE, Dr Alistair William Carnegie,** CB 2003; FRAS; Deputy Director General, Innovation Group, Department of Trade and Industry, 2002–03 (Acting Director General, 2002); part-time Principal Fellow, Warwick Manufacturing Group, University of Warwick, 2003–18; *b* 1 Jan. 1943; *s* of late Stuart Keddie and Ethel Carnegie Keddie; *m* 1966, Marjorie Scott Masterton (*d* 2016); one *s* one *d*. *Educ:* Breadalbane Acad., Aberfeldy; Univ. of Glasgow (BSc Hons; PhD 1970). FRAS 1969. Res. Asst, then Asst Lectr, Dept of Astronomy, Univ. of Glasgow, 1967–70; res. mgt posts, 1970–77; Hd, Air Pollution Div., Warren Spring Lab., Stevenage, 1977–84; Department of Trade and Industry: Mem., Policy Planning Unit, 1984–85; Dir, Sci. and Technol. Policy, 1985–89; Dir, Single Market Unit, 1989–91; Hd, Innovation Unit, 1991–99; Dir, Envmt, Innovation, 1999–2002. Member: EPSRC, 2001–03; Bd, Carbon Trust, 2001–04. Trustee, Green Alliance, 2003–15. *Recreations:* walking, bird watching, music, gardening, voluntary work. *Address:* Pitully, Dull, Aberfeldy, Perthshire PH15 2JQ.

**KEEBLE, Dame Reena (Kapur),** DBE 2011; EdD; Headteacher, Cannon Lane First School, Harrow, 1992–2014; *b* New Delhi, 21 July 1955; *d* of Rabinder Nath Kapur and Enakshi Kapur; *m* 1980, Peter Weimer Keeble; one *s* one *d*. *Educ:* City of London Poly. (BSc Psychol. 1977); Roehampton Inst., Univ. of London (PGCE 1978); Inst. of Educn, Univ. of London (MSc Psychol. of Educn 1983); Univ. of Hull (EdD Educnl Leadership and Mgt 2006). Nursery teacher, 1981–84; Early Years Teacher, Brent Council, 1984–87; Hd of Nursery, Elsley Primary Sch., Harrow, 1987–89; Dep. Headteacher, Glebe Primary Sch., Harrow, 1989–92. Regl Leader for London, 2006–08. (Pt-time) Nat. Coll. for Sch. Leadership, 2006–08. *Recreations:* family, theatre, art, cooking, knitting. *E:* rkeeble@btinternet.com.

**KEEBLE, Sally Curtis;** Director, The Anglican Alliance: Development, Relief, Advocacy, 2010–13; *b* 13 Oct. 1951; *d* of Sir (Herbert Ben) Curtis Keeble, GCMG and Margaret Keeble; *m* 1990, Andrew Porter; one *s* one *d*. *Educ:* St Hugh's Coll., Oxford (BA Hons); Univ. of S Africa (BA Hons). Journalist, Daily News, Durban, SA, 1974–79; Reporter, Birmingham Post, 1979–83; Press Officer, Labour Party, 1983–84; Asst Dir, Ext. Relns, ILEA, 1984–86; Hd of Communications, GMB, 1986–90; Public Affairs Consultant, 1994–97. MP (Lab) Northampton N, 1997–2010; contested (Lab) same seat, 2010, 2015, 2017. Parly Under-Sec. of State, DTLR, 2001–02; DFID, 2002–03. Mem. (Lab) Southwark BC, 1986–94 (Leader, 1990–93). Hon. Fellow, S Bank Univ. *Publications:* Collectors' Corner, 1984; Conceiving Your Baby: how medicine can help, 1995. *Recreations:* walking, antiques, reading. *Address:* 8 Oakpark Close, Northampton NN3 5JG. *T:* (01604) 646310.

**KEEFE, Denis Edward Peter Paul,** CMG 2016; HM Diplomatic Service; Ambassador to Serbia, 2014–19; *b* 29 June 1958; *s* of late Dr John Victor Keefe and Dr Oonagh Rose Keefe (*née* McAleer); *m* 1983, Catherine Ann Mary Wooding; three *s* three *d*. *Educ:* Campion Sch., Hornchurch; Churchill Coll., Cambridge (MA Classics); Hertford Coll., Oxford; Malmö Univ. Joined HM Diplomatic Service, 1982; FCO, 1982–84; Second Sec., Prague, 1984–88; First Secretary: FCO, 1988–92; Nairobi, 1992–95; Dep. Hd, S Asian Dept, FCO, 1996–97; Hd, Asia-Europe Meeting Unit, 1997–98; Dep. Hd of Mission, Prague, 1998–2002; on secondment as Counter Terrorism Strategy Team Leader, Cabinet Office, 2002–03; Head, China Hong Kong Dept, 2003–04, Far Eastern Gp, 2004–06, FCO; Ambassador to Georgia, 2007–10; Dep. Head of Mission, Moscow, 2010–14. *Recreations:* singing, sailing, walking, learning languages. *Address:* c/o Foreign and Commonwealth Office, King Charles Street, SW1A 2AH. *E:* denis.keefe@fco.gov.uk.

**KEEFFE, Barrie Colin;** dramatist; *b* 31 Oct. 1945; *s* of late Edward Thomas Keeffe and Constance Beatrice Keeffe (*née* Marsh); *m* 1st, 1969, Dee Sarah Truman (marr. diss. 1979); 2nd, 1981, Verity Eileen Proud (*née* Bargate) (*d* 1981); Guardian of her sons *s*; 3rd, 1983, Julia Lindsay (marr. diss. 1993); 4th, 2012, Jacky Stoller. *Educ:* East Ham Grammar School. Formerly actor with Nat. Youth Theatre; began writing career as journalist; Thames Television Award writer-in-residence, Shaw Theatre, 1977; Resident playwright, Royal Shakespeare Co., 1978; Associate Writer, Theatre Royal, Stratford East, 1986–91. Member: Board of Directors: Soho Theatre Co., 1978–95; Theatre Royal, Stratford E, 1988–91; Tutor, City Univ., London, 2002–05; Dir and Tutor, Colladra Sch. of Writing, Venice, 2008–; Resident Writer, Kingston Univ., 2011–. Patron, Writing for Performance, Ruskin Coll., Oxford, 2010–. Edith J. Wilson Fellow, Christ's Coll., Cambridge, 2003–04. UN Ambassador, 1995. Hon. DLitt Warwick, 2010. French Critics Prix Revelation, 1978; Giles Cooper Best Radio Plays, 1980; Mystery Writers of America Edgar Allan Poe Award, 1982. *Theatre plays:* Only a Game, 1973; A Sight of Glory, 1975; Scribes, 1975; Here Comes the Sun, 1976; Gimme Shelter, 1977; A Mad World My Masters, 1977, 1984; Barbarians, 1977; Frozen Assets, 1978; Sus, 1979; Bastard Angel, 1980; She's So Modern, 1980; Black Lear, 1980; Chorus Girls, 1981; Better Times, 1985; King of England, 1988; My Girl, 1989; Not Fade Away, 1990; Wild Justice, 1990; I Only Want to Be With You, 1995; The Long Good Friday, 1997; Shadows on the Sun, 2001; Still Killing Time, 2006; My Girl 2, 2014; *television plays:* Substitute, 1972; Not Quite Cricket, 1977; Gotcha, 1977; Nipper, 1977; Champions, 1978; Hanging Around, 1978; Waterloo Sunset, 1979; King, 1984; *television series:* No Excuses, 1983; *films:* The Long Good Friday, 1981; SUS, 2010; also radio plays. *Publications: novels:* Gadabout, 1969; No Excuses, 1983; *plays:* Gimme Shelter, 1977; A Mad World My Masters, 1977; Barbarians, 1977; Here Comes the Sun, 1978; Frozen Assets, 1978; Sus, 1979; Bastard Angel, 1980; The Long Good Friday, 1984, new edn 1998; Better Times, 1985; King of England, 1988; My Girl, 1989; Wild Justice, Not Fade Away, Gimme Shelter, 1990; Barrie Keeffe Plays 1, 2001; My Girl 2, 2014. *Recreation:* origami. *Address:* 33 Brookfield, Highgate West Hill, N6 6AT.

**KEEGAN, Sir Donal (Arthur John),** KCVO 2012; OBE 1999; DPhysMed; FRCP, FRCPE, FRCPI; Lord-Lieutenant of Londonderry, 2002–13; *b* 8 Oct. 1938; *s* of Daniel McManus Keegan and Geraldine Keegan (*née* Halpin); *m* 1973, Doreen Elizabeth Nelson; one *d*. *Educ:* St Columb's Coll., Londonderry; Queen's Univ., Belfast (BSc Hons, MB BCh, BAO); DPhysMed. FRCPI 1973; FRCPE 1989; FRCP 1990. Consultant Physician: Highland and Western Isles Health Bd Areas, 1970–75; Altnagelvin Hosp., Londonderry, 1975–2003, now Emeritus. Chairman: Regl Adv. Cttee on Cancer, 1997–2005; NI Council for Postgrad. Med. and Dental Educn, 1998–2004; Central Med. Adv. Cttee, NI, 1999–2003; Mem., Cttee on Higher Med. Trng, RCPI, 2004. Med. Dir, Distinction and Meritorious Service Awards Cttee, NI, 2001–04. Vis. Prof., Univ. of Ulster, 2009–13. Pres., RFCA for NI, 2009–13. Hon. Col, 204 (N Irish) Field Hosp. (V), 2004–11. Freeman, City of London, 2013. *Publications:* articles on cardiology and musculoskeletal disease. *Recreations:* fishing, shooting, bird migration. *Address:* Auskaird, 5 Greenwood, Culmore, Londonderry BT48 8NP. *T:* (028) 7135 1292. *Club:* Royal Society of Medicine.

**KEEGAN, Dame (Elizabeth) Mary,** DBE 2007; FCA; non-executive Director, Met Office, 2015–18; *b* 21 Jan. 1953; *d* of Michael Keegan and Elizabeth Keegan (*née* Sarginson); *m* 2011, Albert Prangnell. *Educ:* Brentwood County High Sch. for Girls; Somerville Coll., Oxford (Caroline Haslett Meml Scholar, Coombs Exhibitioner; rowing blue; BA Natural Sci. 1974; MA 1977; Hon. Fellow 2008). ACA 1977, FCA 1983. Price Waterhouse, subseq. PricewaterhouseCoopers: articled London, 1974; Paris, 1979; Chicago, 1982; Partner, 1985–2001; Nat. Technical Partner, 1991–96; Dir Professional Standards Europe, 1994–98; Hd Global Corporate Reporting Gp, 1998–2001; Mem. Supervisory Bd, European Financial Reporting Adv. Gp, 2001–04; Finance Dir, 2004–07, Hd Govt Finance Profession and Mem. Bd, 2004–08, HM Treasury. Chm., Accounting Standards Bd, 2001–04. Non-exec. Dir, Nat. Audit Office, 2009–14. Member: Urgent Issues Task Force, Accounting Standards Bd, 1993–99; Standing Interpretations Cttee, Internat. Accounting Standards Cttee, 1997–2001; Internat. Forum on Accountancy Develt, 1999–2001; Chm., Financial Reporting Cttee, 1994–97, Mem. Council, 1994–97, ICAEW; Vice-Pres. and Mem. Council, Chm. Auditing Working Party, FEE, 1997–2001; Mem., Financial Reporting Rev. Panel, Financial Reporting Council, 2007–13. Mem. Adv. Cttee, Univ. of Exeter Business Sch., 2009–16. Mem. Council, RHS, 2016–19 (Mem., 2009–19, Chm., 2016–19, Audit Cttee). Gov., University Coll. Falmouth, 2007–12. FRSA. Hon. DBA Oxford Brookes, 2005; Hon. LittD Manchester, 2006; Hon. LLD Exeter, 2008. Outstanding Achievement Award, ICAEW, 2014. *Publications:* (jtly) The ValueReporting Revolution: moving beyond the earnings game, 2001. *Recreations:* gardening, classical music, walking. *Address:* Old Matthews Farm, Kerswell, Cullompton, Devon EX15 2EL. *E:* mary.keegan@btinternet.

**KEEGAN, Dame Geraldine (Mary Marcella),** DBE 2000 (OBE 1995); part-time management consultant; Headmistress, St Mary's College, Londonderry, 1987–2006; *b* 17 Jan. 1941; *d* of Daniel Anthony McManus Keegan and Geraldine Catherine Veronica (*née* Halpin). *Educ:* St Mary's UC, Belfast (Cert Ed 1963); Univ. of Ulster (DipEd 1972); Univ. of Manchester (MEd 1975). Secondary sch. teacher of music, history and English, 1963–75; Sen. Lectr in Educnl Psychology, St Mary's UC, Belfast, 1975–85; Dep. Dir, NI Centre for Educn Mgt, 1985–87. Pro-Chancellor, 1997–2001, Vis. Prof., 2001–, Univ. of Ulster. Mem. Cttee, European Foundn for Quality Mgt, 2001–06; Board Member: Community of Practice (Educn) SENTINUS, 1996–2007; Mellon Centre for Migration Studies (formerly Centre for Migration Studies), 1997–; Museums and Art Galls of NI, 2002–12; Optimus Approvals Cttee, Fáilte Ireland, 2005–; NW Regional Bd, 2007–15; non-exec. Dir, Ilex Urban Regeneration Co., 2010–16 (NI representative: UK Bd, Investors in People, 2002–08; Leadership and Mgt Adv. Panel, 2007). Member: Bd, President's Award, Ireland, 2002–; RUC George Cross Foundn, 2002–; Bd, Spirit of Enniskillen Trust, 2005–13; Trustee, Scotch Irish Trust, 1994–. FRSA 1995. DUniv Ulster, 2006. *Recreations:* classical music, travel, fishing. *Address:* 7 Locarden, Culmore Point Road, Londonderry BT48 8RP.

**KEEGAN, Gillian;** MP (C) Chichester, since 2017; *m* Michael Keegan; two step *s*. *Educ:* Liverpool John Moores Univ. (BA Hons Business Studies 1990); Instituto de Empresa, Madrid (Exec. Develt Prog. 2004); London Business Sch. (MSc Leadership and Strategy 2010). Commercial mgt apprentice, 1984–89, buyer, 1989–91, Sen. Buyer, 1992, Gen. Motors Inc.; Purchasing Manager (IT), National Westminster Bank plc, 1992–96; Hd, Strategic Alliances and Partnerships, 1996–99, Commercial Dir, 1999–2001, Mondex Internat. Ltd; Amadeus IT Group, Madrid: Dir, Business Travel, 2001–02; Gp Dir, Global Customer Gp, 2002–07; Gp Vice Pres., Multinat. Customer Gp, 2007–09; Sloan Fellow, London Business Sch., 2009–10; Exec. Vice Pres. and Chief Mktg Officer, Travelport, 2011–12. Mem. (C) Chichester DC, 2014–. Mem., Public Accounts Cttee, H of C, 2017–. Contested (C) St Helens S and Whiston, 2015. *Address:* House of Commons, SW1A 0AA.

**KEEGAN, James Douglas;** QC (Scot.) 2009; solicitor advocate; Senior Partner, Keegan Smith SSC, 1998; *b* Glasgow; *s* of James Keegan and Susan Keegan; *m* Karen; three *d*. *Educ:* Our Lady's High Sch., Motherwell; Univ. of Strathclyde (LLB 1973); Univ. of Glasgow (DipFM 1994; MPhil 1998). FCIArb 1994; WS 2008. Notary Public, 1977; Partner, Drummond & Co., Edinburgh, 1978–87; Sen. Partner, Keegan Walker SSC, 1987–97. FRSA 2000. *Recreations:* football, music, Rugby. *E:* jdKeegan1@msn.com. *Club:* Livingston Rugby.

**KEEGAN, (Joseph) Kevin,** OBE 1982; professional footballer, 1966–84; *b* 14 Feb. 1951; *s* of late Joseph Keegan; *m* 1974, Jean Woodhouse; two *d*. Professional footballer with: Scunthorpe Utd, 1966–71; Liverpool, 1971–77; Hamburg, 1977–80; Southampton, 1980–82; Newcastle Utd, 1982–84. Internat. appearances for England, 1973–82, Captain, 1976–82. Manager, Newcastle Utd FC, 1992–97 and 2008; Chief Operating Officer, Fulham FC, 1997–99; Coach, England Football Team, 1999–2000; Manager, Manchester City FC, 2001–05. Formerly football expert, Thames TV. Winners' medals: League Championships, 1973, 1976; UEFA Cup, 1973, 1976; FA Cup, 1974; European Cup, 1977. European Footballer of the Year, 1978, 1979. *Publications:* Kevin Keegan, 1978; Against the World: playing for England, 1979; Kevin Keegan: my autobiography, 1997; My Life in Football, 2018.

**KEEGAN, Dame Mary;** *see* Keegan, Dame E. M.

**KEEGAN, William James Gregory,** CBE 2009; Senior Economics Commentator, The Observer, since 2003 (Economics Editor, 1977–2003); *b* 3 July 1938; *s* of William Patrick Keegan and Sheila Julia Keegan (*née* Buckley); *m* 1st, 1967, Tessa (*née* Young, *widow* of John Ashton) (marr. diss. 1982); two *s* two *d*, 1992, Hilary, *d* of late Maurice Frank Stonefrost, CBE; one *s* two *d*. *Educ:* Wimbledon Coll.; Trinity Coll., Cambridge (MA). National Service (Army), 1957–59 (commissioned). Journalist, Financial Times, Daily Mail and News Chronicle, 1963–67; Economics Correspondent, Financial Times, 1967–76; Economic Intell. Dept, Bank of England, 1976–77; The Observer: Asst Editor and Business Editor, 1981–83; Associate Editor, 1983–2003. Member: BBC Adv. Cttee on Business and Indust. Affairs, 1981–88; Council, Employment Inst., 1987–92; Adv. Bd, Dept of Applied Economics, Cambridge, 1988–92; Cttee for Soc. Scis, CNAA, 1991–92; Nat. Council, The Catalyst Forum, 1998–; Adv. Bd, Mile End Gp, QMUL, 2011–; Chm., Editl Bd, OMFIF, 2010–. Gov., NIESR, 1998–. Vis. Prof. of Journalism, 1989–, Hon. Res. Fellow, 1990–, Sheffield Univ.; Visiting Professor: of Econs and Finance, QMUL, 2012–15; Policy Inst., KCL, 2015–. Hon. LittD Sheffield, 1995; Hon. DLitt City, 1998. *Publications:* Consulting Father Wintergreen, 1974; A Real Killing, 1976; (jtly) Who Runs the Economy?, 1978; Mrs Thatcher's Economic Experiment, 1984; Britain Without Oil, 1985; Mr Lawson's Gamble, 1989; The Spectre of Capitalism, 1992; 2066 and All That, 2000; The Prudence of Mr Gordon Brown, 2003; 'Saving the World'?: Gordon Brown reconsidered, 2012; Mr Osborne's Economic Experiment: austerity 1945–51 and 2010–, 2015, Nine Crises, 2019; contribs to The Tablet. *Address:* 76 Lofting Road, Islington, N1 1JB. *T:* (020) 7607 3590; The Observer, Kings Place, 90 York Way, N1 9GU. *Clubs:* Garrick, MCC.

**KEEHAN, Hon. Sir Michael (Joseph),** Kt 2013; **Hon. Mr Justice Keehan**; a Judge of the High Court of Justice, Family Division, since 2013; *b* 31 March 1960; *s* of Michael and Alice Keehan; *m* 1988, Sarah Elizabeth Monk; two *d*. *Educ*: Birmingham Univ. (LLB). Called to the Bar, Middle Temple, 1982, Bencher, 2013; QC 2001; a Recorder, 2000–13. *Recreations*: family life, gardening, walking. *Address*: Royal Courts of Justice, Queen's Building, Strand, WC2A 2LL.

**KEEL, Aileen Margaret, (Mrs Paul Dwyer),** CBE 2008; FRCPath; FRCPGlas, FRCPE, FRCSE, FRCGP; Director, Innovative Healthcare Delivery Programme, Usher Institute, University of Edinburgh, since 2015 (on secondment to Farr Institute, 2015–18); *b* Glasgow, 23 Aug. 1952; *d* of Walter and Everina Keel; *m* 1995, Paul Dwyer (*d* 2010); one *s*. *Educ*: Univ. of Glasgow (MB ChB 1976). MRCP 1979; MRCPath 1986, FRCPath 1995; FRCPGlas 1992; FRCPE 2005; MFPH 2004; FRCSE *ad hominem* 2013; FRCGP *ad hominem* 2014. Trng in gen. medicine and haematol., Glasgow Royal Infirmary, Royal Hosp. for Sick Children, Glasgow, Aberdeen Royal Infirmary, 1976–84; Consultant Haematologist and Dir of Pathol., Cromwell Hosp., London, 1987–89; Hon. Consultant Haematologist and Hon. Res. Fellow, Central Middx and Middx Hosp., London, 1988–92; SMO, 1992–98, PMO, 1998–99, Scottish Office; Dep. Chief Med. Officer, 1999–2014, Acting Chief Med. Officer, 2014–15, Scottish Exec., later Scottish Govt. Hon. Prof., Univ. of Edinburgh, 2016–. *Recreations*: the arts in general, music, particularly opera, current affairs, good food and wine, evidence based arguing! *Address*: Usher Institute, University of Edinburgh, Nine Edinburgh Bioquarter, 9 Little France Road, Edinburgh EH16 4UX. *T*: (0131) 651 7866. *E*: aileen.keel@ed.ac.uk.

**KEELER, Walter Charles John;** self-employed potter, since 1965; *b* 22 April 1942; *s* of Walter Stanley Keeler and Iris Eileen Keeler (*née* Callaghan); *m* 1964, Madoline; two *s* one *d*. *Educ*: Harrow Sch. of Art (Intermediate NDD); Hornsey Coll. of Art (Art Teachers Cert). Sen. Lectr in Studio Pottery, Harrow Sch. of Art, 1964–78; Bristol Polytechnic, subseq. University of West of England: Sen. Lectr in Ceramics, 1978–94; Reader, 1994–98; Prof. of Ceramics, 1998–2002. Pottery Studio: Bledlow Ridge, Bucks, 1965–76; Moorcroft Cottage, Penallt, Mons, 1976–. Associate Dir, Nat. Electronic and Video Archive of the Crafts, 1992–2002. Exhibitions include: Craft Potters Assoc., London, 1982; Contemp. Applied Arts, London, 1989, 1999; Leeds City Art Gall., 1993; Contemp. Ceramics, London, 2002; Ruthin Craft Centre Galls, 2009; The Scottish Gall., Edinburgh, 2012; Oxford Ceramics Gall., 2013; Contemp. Ceramics Gall., London, 2015; Goldmark Gall., Uppingham, 2017; work in public collections including: V&A Mus.; Crafts Council Collection; Nat. Mus. of Wales, Cardiff; Fitzwilliam Mus., Cambridge, and worldwide. Fellow, Craft Potters Assoc., 1967; Mem., Contemp. Applied Arts (formerly British Crafts Centre), 1969–. Hon. Pres., South Wales Potters, 2014–. *Relevant publication*: Walter Keeler, by E. Cooper and A. Fielding, 2004. *Recreations*: gardening, music, travel, cooking and eating. *Address*: Moorcroft Cottage, Penallt, Monmouthshire NP25 4AH. *T*: (01600) 713946. *E*: penalltpottery@gmail.com.

**KEELEY, Barbara Mary;** MP (Lab) Worsley and Eccles South, since 2010 (Worsley, 2005–10); *b* 26 March 1952; *d* of late Edward and Joan Keeley; *m* Colin Huggett. *Educ*: Univ. of Salford (BA 1st Cl. Hons Pols and Contemp. Hist.). Field Systems Engr and Systems Engrg Manager, IBM UK, until 1989; community regeneration advr, 1989–94; Area Manager, BITC, 1994–95; local govt and voluntary sector, 1995–2001; Consultant, researching policy issues, Princess Royal Trust for Carers, 2001–05. PPS to Parly Sec., Cabinet Office, then Minister of State, DWP, 2006–07, to Minister for Women and Equality, 2007–08; an Asst Govt Whip, 2008–09; Parly Sec., Leader of H of C, 2009–10; Shadow Minister: for Care Services, 2010; for Communities and Local Govt, 2010–11; for Treasury, 2015; for Health, 2015–16; for Mental Health and Social Care, 2016–. Mem., Health Select Cttee, 2011–15. Chair, PLP Women's Cttee, 2007–08. Mem., Trafford MBC, 1995–2004 (Cabinet Mem., 1999–2004); Dir, Pathfinder Children's Trust, 2002–04. *Recreations*: running, watching cricket, listening to live music. *Address*: c/o House of Commons, SW1A 0AA. *T*: (020) 7219 8025. *W*: www.barbarakeeley.co.uk.

**KEELING, Maj.-Gen. Andrew Myles,** CB 1994; CBE 1992 (OBE 1988); self-employed consultant, 1996–2013; *b* 4 July 1943; *s* of late Richard George Maynard Keeling, OBE and Audrey Stuart Baxter (*née* Frederick); *m* 1st, 1965, Ann Margaret Grey Dudley (*d* 2001); one *s* two *d*; 2nd, 2003, Woppy (*née* Brittan). *Educ*: Rugby School. Commissioned 2nd Lieut RM, 1961; served 41, 42 and 45 Commandos, and training jobs at BRNC, Dartmouth and RMA, Sandhurst, 1963–75; student, Canadian Forces Command and Staff Coll., 1975–76; HQ 3 Cdo Bde RM, 1976–78; 41 Cdo, 1978–80; Bde Major, HQ 3 Cdo Bde, 1980–81; Directing Staff, NDC and JSDC, 1982–83; Jt Force HQ, 1984–85; CO 45 Cdo, 1985–87; MoD, 1987–89; Comd, 3 Cdo Bde, 1990–92; COS to Comdt-Gen. RM, 1992–93; Maj.-Gen., RM, 1993–95, retired. Rep. Col Comdt, RM, 1998–2002. UK Rep., Saab Microwave Systems (formerly Ericsson Microwave Systems AB), 1997–2008. Sec., Salisbury Dio. Sudan Link, 2001–05; Lay Canon, Salisbury Cathedral, 2003–. Specialist Advr, Defence Select Cttee, H of C, 1997–98. Dir of Humanitarian Affairs, AMAR Internat. Charitable Foundn, 1995–96. Freeman, City of London, 1993. President: City of Winchester Br., RMA, 1996–2004; SBS Assoc., 2001–17; Devon County RBL, 2005–08; Naval Vice-Pres., CCF Assoc., 1995–2001; Mem. Council, Blind Veterans UK (formerly St Dunstan's), 1995–2013 (Vice-Chm., 2004–08; Chm., 2008–13; Vice-Pres., 2014–); Vice-Pres., 2006–, Pres., 2012–18, St George's Day Club; Sen. Patron, 65 Degrees North, 2014–; Trustee, Overlord Embroidery Trust, 2015–. *Recreations*: family, walking. *Clubs*: Special Forces; Royal Marines Sailing (Hon. Life Vice-Commodore).

**KEEMER, Peter John Charles;** Assistant Auditor General, National Audit Office, 1989–93; *b* 27 Jan. 1932; *s* of late Frederick and Queenie Keemer; *m* 1954, Yvonne Griffin (*d* 2002); one *s* one *d* (and one *s* decd). *Educ*: Price's Sch., Fareham; Univ. of Bath (MPhil). Exchequer and Audit Department: Asst Auditor and Auditor, 1950–62; Private Sec. to Comptroller and Auditor Gen., 1962–65; seconded to Parly Comr for Administration as Chief Exec. Officer, 1966–70; Chief Auditor, 1970; Dep. Dir, 1973; Dir, 1978–89 (seconded to European Court of Auditors as Director, 1978–86). External Auditor, European Univ. Inst., Florence, 1994–97. Mem., Conciliation Cttee, EC, 2001–06. Fellow, CIPFA, 2018 (Mem., 1982). Chm., 1995–2001, Trustee, 1995–2009, Dir, 1997–2009, Breakthrough Breast Cancer; Mem. Council, Inst. of Cancer Res., 1994–2000 (Hon. Treas., 1996–2000). *Address*: Highfield, Hazelwood Lane, Chipstead, Coulsdon CR5 3QW. *T*: (01737) 553711. *E*: pjckeemer@gmail.com. *Club*: Royal Thames Yacht.

**KEEN,** family name of **Baron Keen of Elie**.

**KEEN OF ELIE, Baron** *cr* 2015 (Life Peer), of Elie in Fife; **Richard Sanderson Keen;** PC 2017; QC (Scot.) 1993; Advocate General for Scotland, since 2015; *b* 29 March 1954; *s* of Derek Michael Keen and Jean Sanderson Keen; *m* 1978, Jane Carolyn Anderson; one *s* one *d*. *Educ*: King's Sch., Rochester; Dollar Acad.; Edinburgh Univ. (LLB Hons 1976; Beckman Schol.). Admitted Faculty of Advocates, 1980 (Treas., 2006–07; Dean, 2007–14); Standing Jun. Counsel in Scotland to DTI, 1986–93. Called to the Bar, Middle Temple, 2009, Bencher, 2011; Mem., Blackstone Chambers, London, 2011–. Chairman: Appeals Cttee, ICAS, 1996–2001; Police Appeals Tribunal, 2004–10. Chm., Scottish Cons. and Unionist Party, 2014–15. Spokesperson for Home Office, 2016, for MoJ, 2016–, H of L. *Recreations*: golf, ski-ing, shooting, opera. *Address*: The Castle, Elie, Fife KY9 1DN; 27 Ann Street, Edinburgh EH4 1PL. *Clubs*: Beefsteak; New (Edinburgh); Golf House (Elie); Hon. Co. of Edinburgh Golfers (Muirfield); Royal and Ancient (St Andrews).

**KEEN, Ann Lloyd;** *b* 26 Nov. 1948; *d* of late John Fox and Ruby Fox; one *s*; *m* 1980, (David) Alan Keen, MP (*d* 2011); one step *s* one step *d*. *Educ*: Elfed Secondary Modern Sch., Clwyd; Univ. of Surrey (PGCE). Formerly: Hd, Faculty of Advanced Nursing, Queen Charlotte's Coll., Hammersmith; Gen. Sec., Community and District Nursing Assoc. Contested (Lab) Brentford and Isleworth, 1987, 1992. MP (Lab) Brentford and Isleworth, 1997–2010; contested (Lab) same seat, 2010. Parly Under-Sec. of State, DoH, 2007–10. Prof. of Innovation Policy Practice and Health, Univ. of Bedfordshire, 2012–; Sen. Scholar, Hartford Inst. for Geriatric Nursing, NY Univ., 2013–; Vis. Prof., London South Bank Univ., 2015–; Hon. Professor of Nursing: Thames Valley Univ.; Florence Nightingale Sch. of Nursing, KCL. Hon. Sec., Imperial Coll. Global Initiative. Trustee: Florence Nightingale Foundn, 2010–; Katie Piper Foundn, 2010–14. Hon. LLD Beds.

**KEEN, Graeme Terence;** QC 2018; *b* Crayford, 10 Aug. 1965; *s* of Roy Keen and Marion Keen; *m* 1994, Alison Jones; one *s* two *d*. *Educ*: Dulwich Coll.; King's Coll. London (LLB). Called to the Bar, Middle Temple, 1995. *Recreations*: outdoor swimming, walking, Fulham FC, family time. *Address*: Landmark Chambers, 180 Fleet Street, EC4A 2HG. *T*: (020) 7430 1221.

**KEEN, His Honour Kenneth Roger;** QC 1991; a Circuit Judge, 2001–13; *b* 13 May 1946; *s* of Kenneth Henry Keen and Joan Megan Keen (*née* Weetman); *m* Mary Lorraine Raeburn; one *s* one *d* by previous marriage. *Educ*: Doncaster Grammar School. Qualified Solicitor, 1968; called to the Bar, Gray's Inn, 1976; practice on NE circuit; a Recorder, 1989. Former Member: Mental Health Tribunal; Boundary Commn; Complaints and Disciplinary Cttee, Bar Council; Mem., Parole Bd, 2010–13. *Recreations*: tennis, travel, golf.

**KEEN, Laurence John,** OBE 2000; FSA, FRHistS; President, British Archaeological Association, 1989–2004; County Archaeological Officer, Dorset County Council, 1975–99; Consultant, John Stark & Crickmay Partnership, architects, 1999–2003; *b* 11 July 1943; *er s* of late John William Frederick Keen and Dorothy Ethel Keen (*née* French). *Educ*: Kilburn GS; St John's Coll., York (Cert Ed (Music) 1966); Inst. of Archaeology, Univ. of London (Postgrad. Dip. in European Archaeol. 1969; Gordon Childe Meml Prize); UCL (MPhil 1978). FRHistS 1974; FSA 1979; MCIfA (MIFA 1985); FSAScot 1995. Répétiteur, Lycée Mohammed V, Marrakech, 1962–63; Asst Master, Cundall Manor Sch., York, 1966–67; Dir, Southampton Archaeol Res. Cttee, 1972–75. Archaeol Cons., MPBW, then DoE, then English Heritage, now Historic England, 1964–. Dir, Census of Medieval Tiles in Britain, 2004–. Director of excavations: Wardour Castle, Wilts; Blackfriars, Gloucester; Kingswood Abbey, Glos; Tattershall Coll., Lincs; Mountgrace Priory, Yorks; Beeston Castle, Cheshire; Prudhoe Castle, Northumberland; Sherborne Abbey, Dorset. Vis. Lectr in Archaeology, Univ. of Southampton, 1973–75. Winston Churchill Fellow, 1970; Hon. Research Fellow: Centre for South-Western Hist. Studies, Univ. of Exeter, 1995–98; York St John Univ. (formerly UC of Ripon and York St John, then York St John Coll.), 1995–. Member: DAC for Faculties, 1977–77, Re-use of Closed Churches Working Gp (formerly Diocesan Redundant Churches Cttee), 1985–97, 2005–, Salisbury; Paintings Cttee, Council for the Care of Churches, 1979–96; Fabric Advisory Committee: Gloucester Cath., 1991–; St George's Chapel, Windsor Castle, 1998–2013 (Chm., 1999–2009); Exeter Cath., 2006–16 (Chm., 2011–16). Chairman: Dorset Local Hist. Gp, 1985–99; Dorset Archaeol Cttee, Dorset Nat. Hist. and Archaeol Soc., 2002–15; Member, Council: Soc. for Medieval Archaeology, 1973–76; British Archaeol Assoc., 1973–76, 1978–81, 1984–87 (Vice-Pres., 1988, 2004–); Reginald Taylor Essay Prize, 1969); Royal Archaeol Inst., 1982–85. Trustee, Oxford Archaeol., 2004–17. Foreign Corresp. Associate Mem., Société Nat. des Antiquaires de France, 1990. Freeman, City of London, 1991; Freeman and Liveryman, Co. of Painter-Stainers, 1991. *Publications*: (jtly) William Barnes: the Dorset engravings, 1986 ((jtly) Mansel-Pleydell Essay Prize, Dorset Nat. Hist. & Archaeol. Soc., 1985), 2nd edn 1989; William Barnes: the Somerset engravings, 1989; (ed jtly) Historic Landscape of the Weld Estate, 1987; Dorset Domesday: an introduction, 1991; (ed jtly) Medieval Art and Architecture at Salisbury Cathedral, 1996; (ed) Almost the Richest City: Bristol in the Middle Ages, 1997; (jtly) Dorset from the Air, 1998; (ed) Studies in the Early History of Shaftesbury Abbey, 1999; (ed jtly) Windsor Castle: medieval archaeology, art and architecture of the Thames Valley, 2002; (jtly) Sherborne Abbey and School: excavations 1972–76 and 1990, 2005; (jtly) Mount Grace Priory: excavations of 1957–92, 2019; articles and reviews in nat. and county jls. *Recreations*: making music, entertaining, perfecting bread and butter pudding. *Address*: Hardye Chambers, 7 Church Street, Dorchester, Dorset DT1 1JN. *T*: (01305) 265460.

**KEEN, Lady Mary;** see Keen, Lady P. M. R.

**KEEN, Nigel John,** FCA, FIET; Chairman: Deltex Medical Group plc, since 1996; Syncona Investment Management Ltd (formerly Syncona Partners), since 2013; Oxford Academic Health Science Network, since 2013; Oxford University (formerly Isis) Innovation Ltd, since 2014; MedAccess (formerly CFAM) Ltd, since 2018; *b* 21 Jan. 1947; *s* of Peter and Margaret Keen; *m* 1972, Caroline Jane Cumming; two *s*. *Educ*: Charterhouse; Peterhouse, Cambridge (MA). FCA 1979; FIET 2012. Auditor, Touche Ross & Co., 1968–74; Dir, Eur. Banking Co. Ltd, 1974–83; Chm., Cygnus gp of cos, 1983–2001; Dep. Chm., 1999–2000, Chm., 2000–14, Laird (formerly Laird Gp) plc; Chairman: Axis-Shield plc, 1999–2010; Oxford Instruments plc, 1999–2016. Dir, Channel Is Develt Corp., 1996–2007; non-exec. Dir, 2008–09, Chm., 2009–16, Bioquell plc. Trustee: David Shepherd Wildlife Foundn, 1999–; UCL Hospitals Charity, 2017–. *Recreations*: opera, golf. *Address*: 19 Pembroke Square, W8 6PA. *T*: (020) 7937 6008. *Clubs*: Brooks's, HAC; Royal Mid Surrey Golf.

**KEEN, Lady (Priscilla) Mary (Rose);** garden designer, writer and lecturer; *b* 12 Feb. 1940; *d* of 6th Earl Howe and Priscilla (*née* Weigall, who *m* 2nd, Harold Coriat); *m* 1962, Charles Keen; one *s* three *d*. *Educ*: Lawnside, Malvern; Lady Margaret Hall, Oxford. Gardening Columnist: Evening Standard, 1980–88; Perspectives, 1988–98; Independent on Sunday, 1988–98; freelance journalist: Gardening; Daily Telegraph; designed Glyndebourne Opera House new gardens, 1992–93, and many large private commissions, as Mary Keen and Pip Morrison, Designed Landscapes. National Trust: Member: Gardens Panel, 1982–2006; Thames and Chilterns Regl Cttee, 1982–92; Severn Regl Cttee, 1996–2002. Inspirational Garden Journalist of the Year, Garden Writer's Guild Awards, 1999. *Publications*: The Garden Border Book, 1987; The Glory of the English Garden, 1989; Colour Your Garden, 1991; Decorate Your Garden, 1993; Creating a Garden, 1996; Paradise and Plenty: a Rothschild family garden, 2015. *Recreation*: gardening.

**KEENAGHAN, Fiona Therese;** Controller, Daytime and Lifestyle Features, ITV, 2008–13; *b* St Helens, Merseyside, 23 June 1969; *d* of James Keenaghan and Patricia Catherine Anne Keenaghan; partner, Paul Anthony Mottram; one *s* one *d*. *Educ*: Thames Valley Univ. (BA Hons Design and Media Mgt). Ed., Tonight with Trevor McDonald, 2005–06, Exec. Producer, 2006–08, ITV. *Recreations*: my children, theatre, opera, travel, books.

**KEENAN, Rt Rev. John;** see Paisley, Bishop of, (RC).

**KEENAN, Paul;** Chief Executive, Bauer Media UK and European Radio (formerly Bauer Media UK and Nordic), since 2016 (Chief Executive, Bauer Media UK, 2008–16); b Shrewsbury, 29 Dec. 1963; s of Thomas Keenan and Bridget Keenan; m 1990, Sandra Scase. *Educ:* St Ignatius Coll., London. Reporter, Local Government Chronicle, 1986; joined Emap, 1992; Managing Director: Emap Fashion, 1995–98; Emap Elan, 1998–2000; Dir, Emap Digital, 2000–01; Chief Exec., Emap Consumer, 2001–08. Dir, PPA, 2002–15 (Chm., Mktg Bd, 2005–09). *Address:* Bauer Media, Academic House, 24–28 Oval Road, NW1 7DT. *T:* (020) 7295 5000.

**KEENE, Rt Hon. Sir David (Wolfe),** Kt 1994; PC 2000; a Lord Justice of Appeal, 2000–09; Arbitrator, Kuala Lumpur Regional Centre for Arbitration, since 2014; b 15 April 1941; s of Edward Henry Wolfe Keene and Lilian Marjorie Keene; m 1965, Gillian Margaret Lawrance; one s one d. *Educ:* Hampton Grammar Sch.; Balliol Coll., Oxford (Winter Williams Prizewinner, 1962; BA 1st Cl. Hons Law, 1962; BCL 1963; Hon. Fellow, 2004). ACIArb 2010. Called to the Bar, Inner Temple, 1964 (Eldon Law Scholar, 1965; Bencher, 1987; Treas., 2006); QC 1980; a Recorder, 1989–94; a Dep. High Court Judge, 1993–94; a Judge of High Court of Justice, QBD, 1994–2000; a Judge, Employment Appeal Tribunal, 1995–2000; Dep. Pres., Qatar Internat. Court, 2011–13; Chm., Qatar Financial Centre Regulatory Tribunal, 2013–19. Chm. of Panel, Cumbria Structure Plan Examination in Public, 1980; conducted County Hall, London, Inquiry, 1987; Chairman: Planning and Envmtl Law Reform Working Gp, 1997–2009; Judicial Studies Bd, 2003–07 (Chm., Adv. Cttee on Equal Treatment, 1998–2003); Mem., QC Selection Panel, 2010–12. Mem., Arbitrators Panel, Sports Resolutions, 2011–. Chm., Planning Bar Assoc., 1994 (Vice-Chm., 1990–94). Non-exec. Chm., Argentum Capital Ltd, 2011–14. Mem. Bd, Sch. of Advanced Study, Univ. of London, 2008–10. Visitor, Brunel Univ., 1995–2000. Trustee: Oxford Philomusica, 2009–16; Slynn Foundn, 2010–. Hon. Fellow, Soc. of Advanced Legal Studies, 1998. Hon. LLD Brunel, 2001. *Recreations:* walking, opera, jazz, gardening. *Address:* 39 Essex Chambers, 81 Chancery Lane, WC2A 1DD. *Clubs:* Athenæum, Garrick.

**KEENE, Prof. Derek John,** DPhil; Leverhulme Professor of Comparative Metropolitan History, Institute of Historical Research, 2001–08, now Honorary Fellow and Professor Emeritus; b 27 Dec. 1942; s of Charles Henry Keene and Edith Anne Keene (née Swanston); m 1969, Suzanne Victoria Forbes (see S. V. Keene); one s one d. *Educ:* Ealing Grammar Sch.; Oriel Coll., Oxford (MA, DPhil). FRHistS. Researcher, 1968–74, Asst Dir, 1974–78, Winchester Research Unit; Institute of Historical Research: Dir, Social and Economic Study of Medieval London, 1987–99; Dir, Centre for Metropolitan History, 1987–2002; Actg Dir, 2008. Internat. Advr to Urban Society in the Low Countries, Belgian Sci. Policy Office, 2002–. Member: RCHM, 1987–99; Commn internat. pour l'histoire de villes, 1990–; Fabric Adv. Cttee, St Paul's Cathedral, 1991–; London Adv. Cttee, 1998–2004, Urban Panel, 2000–15, English Heritage. *Publications:* Winchester in the Early Middle Ages (jtly), 1976; Survey of Medieval Winchester, 1985; Cheapside Before the Great Fire, 1985; (with V. Harding) A survey of documentary sources for property holding in London before the Great Fire, 1985; (with V. Harding) Historical Gazetteer of London before the Great Fire, 1987; (ed with P. J. Corfield) Work in Towns 850–1850, 1990; (jtly) A Medieval Capital and its Grain Supply: agrarian production and distribution in the London region c 1300, 1993; (ed jtly) St Paul's: the cathedral church of London 604–2004, 2004; (ed jtly) Integration—Assimilation: religious and ethnic groups in the medieval towns of Central and Eastern Europe, 2009; (ed jtly) Cities into Battlefields: metropolitan scenarios, experiences and commemorations of total war, 2011; (ed jtly) The Singularities of London, 1578, 2014; contribs to learned jls and to collections of essays. *Recreations:* metropolises, walking uphill, making and repairing things, wood-turning, woodland management. *Address:* 162 Erlanger Road, SE14 5TJ. *T:* (020) 7639 5371.

**KEENE, Dr Suzanne Victoria,** FIIC; Course Director, Museum Studies, Institute of Archaeology, University College London, 2001–09, now Reader Emeritus in Museum Studies; b 21 July 1944; d of late Lt-Comdr Lachlan Andrew Forbes, RN and Adelaide Talbot Suzanne Forbes; m 1969, Derek John Keene, qv; one s one d. *Educ:* various schools; University Coll. London (Dip. Archaeol Conservation; Gordon Childe Prize, Inst. of Archaeol., 1969; PhD 1993). FIIC 1985. Archaeol Asst, British Sch. at Rome, 1964–66; Winchester Research Unit: Archaeol Conservator, 1969–75; Ed., Medieval Finds pubn, 1975–77; Museum of London: Hd of Section, Archaeol Conservation, 1979–86; Hd of Conservation, 1986–92; Hd of Collections Mgt, Science Mus., 1992–2000. Member: Exec. Cttee, 1970–74, Gen. Sec., 1972–76, UK Inst. for Conservation; Panel on Archaeol Collections, Area Mus. for S Eastern England, 1976–90; UK Nat. Cttee, ICOM, 1993–99; Bd, Textile Conservation Centre, 1993–2000. Member: Working Parties, English Heritage and Mus and Galls Commn, 1988–90 and 1992; Working Gp on Mus and Nat. Grid for Learning, DCMS, 1998–99; Bd, London Museums Agency, 2001–04; Bd, Collections Trust (formerly Mus Documentation Assoc.), 2006–12. Mem. Cttee, S Wilts and N Dorset Gps, 2011– (Hon. Chm., S Wilts, 2018–), Mem., Dorset Countryside Forum, 2013–, CPRE. Trustee: Tank Mus., 1998–2005; CPRE Wilts, 2018–. *Publications:* Managing Conservation in Museums, 1996, 2nd edn 2002; Digital Collections: museums in the information age, 1998; Fragments of the World, 2005; Collections for People, 2008; (with Francesca Monti) Museums and Silent Objects, 2013; (ed) Museums and the Second World War, 2017; contrib. numerous articles on museum digitisation, conservation and the countryside. *Recreations:* beautiful country-side, reading novels, films, the internet.

**KEENEN, Winton Laurence;** Chief Constable, Northumbria Police, since 2018; b Newcastle upon Tyne, 4 Feb. 1965; s of Laurence Keenen and Patricia Blanche Keenen. *Educ:* King's Sch., Tynemouth. Roles in uniformed, plain-clothed and covert policing, Northumbria Police, 1985–2007; on secondment to FCO as First Contingent Comdr for UK Police Officers deployed to Iraq, 2003; Northumbria Police: Superintendent, incl. Sen. Investigating Officer, Homicide Dept and Regl Kidnap and Extortion Lead, 2007–12; Detective Chief Superintendent, Hd of Crime Dept, 2012–14; Asst Chief Constable, Crime and Ops, 2014–17; Dep. Chief Constable, 2015–17; Temp. Chief Constable, 2017–18. *Recreations:* kayaking, triathlon, open-water swimming, skydiving. *Address:* Northumbria Police Force Headquarters, Middle Engine Lane, Wallsend, Newcastle upon Tyne, Tyne and Wear NE28 9NT. *T:* (0191) 437 5024. *E:* winton.keenen.7238@northumbria.pnn.police.uk.

**KEENLYSIDE, Hilary Anne;** Co-Founder and Director, Bonnar Keenlyside, since 1991; b Crawley, Sussex, 18 April 1955; d of Frederick Keenlyside and Hazel Keenlyside. *Educ:* Thomas Bennett Sch., Dartington Coll. of Arts (BA Hons); City Univ. (Dip Arts Admin); London Business Sch. (Sloan Fellow); Univ. of London (MSc Mgt). Executive Director: Acad. of St Martin in the Fields, 1985–90; Almeida Th., 1990–91. Gov., City Literary Inst., 1999–2009 (Dep. Chm., 2007–09). Trustee: Barnardo's, 2001–13 (Chm., 2011–13); St Wilfrid's Hospice, Chichester, 2017–. *Recreations:* sailing, Nordic walking. *Address:* Bonnar Keenlyside, Toynbee Studios, 28 Commercial Street, E1 6AB. *E:* england@b-k.co.uk. *Club:* Dell Quay Sailing.

**KEENLYSIDE, Sir Simon (John),** Kt 2018; CBE 2003; baritone; b London, 3 Aug. 1959; s of Raymond Keenlyside and Ann Leonie Hirsch; m 2006, Zenaida Yanowsky, ballerina; one s one d. *Educ:* St John's Coll., Cambridge (BA Zoology 1983; Hon. Fellow, 2008); Royal Northern Coll. of Music. With Scottish Opera, 1989–94 (rôles incl. Marcello, Danilo, Guglielmo, Figaro in Barber of Seville, Billy Budd, Papageno and Belcore); *débuts:* Royal Opera, Covent Garden, 1989 (Silvio in Pagliacci); ENO, 1990 (Guglielmo in Così fan tutte); WNO, 1991 (Falke); San Francisco, 1993 (Olivier in Capriccio); Geneva, 1993 (Papageno in Die Zauberflöte); Paris Opéra (Papageno), Australian Opera (Figaro) and La Scala, Milan, 1995; Glyndebourne, 1996 (Guglielmo); Metropolitan Opera, NY (Belcore in L'elisir d'amore); other rôles incl. Count Almaviva, Don Giovanni, Orfeo, Pelléas, Dandini in La Cenerentola, Wolfram in Tannhäuser, Yeletski in Queen of Spades, Oreste in Iphigénie en Tauride, Ubalde in Armide, Ford in Falstaff, title rôle in Hamlet, Prospero in The Tempest, Valentin in Gounod's Faust, Winston in 1984, title rôle in Eugene Onegin, title rôle in Wozzeck; Fagin in Oliver! Frequent concerts and recitals; recordings incl. operas, recitals of Schubert, Strauss and Mahler, and Schumann lieder. *Recreations:* a passion for all things zoological, diving, walking, painting, fly fishing. *Address:* c/o Askonas Holt, 15 Fetter Lane, EC4A 1BW. *T:* (020) 7400 1700.

**KEEP, Charles Reuben;** Chairman and Managing Director, Resource Management Associates Ltd, since 1992; Chairman, Towergate Securities, since 1978; b 1932; m; one d. *Educ:* Haverstock Central Sch., Hampstead. Joined Lloyds & Scottish Finance Ltd, 1956, Director, 1969; Man. Dir, International Factors Ltd, 1970; Group Man. Dir, Tozer Kemsley & Millbourn (Holdings) Ltd, 1973–77; Chm., Tozer Kemsley & Millbourn Trading Ltd, 1978–80; Director: Tozer Standard & Chartered Ltd, 1973–77; Barclays Tozer Ltd, 1974–77; Manufacturers Hanover Credit Corp., 1977–80; Chm., Export Leasing Ltd, Bermuda, 1974–77; Pres., France Motors sa Paris, 1974–81. *Address:* 23 Grovewood Place, Chigwell, Essex IG8 8PX. *T:* (020) 8504 3897. *Club:* Chigwell Golf.

**KEEP, Prof. Ewart John,** PhD; Professor of Education, Training and Skills, since 2013, and Director, Centre on Skills, Knowledge and Organisation Performance, since 2014, University of Oxford; b Worcester, 20 Jan. 1958; s of Frederick and Irene Keep. *Educ:* Ledbury Grammar Sch.; Royal Holloway Coll., Univ. of London (BA Modern Hist., Econ. Hist. and Politics 1979); Univ. of Warwick (PhD Industrial Relns 1992). Res. and Admin. Asst, CBI, 1979–82; researcher, Industrial Relns Unit, Warwick Univ., 1985–98; Professorial Fellow, and Dep. Dir, Centre on Skills, Knowledge and Orgn Perf., Warwick Business Sch., 1998–2006; Prof., and Dep. Dir, Centre on Skills, Knowledge and Orgn Perf., Cardiff Univ., 2006–13. Member: Skills Cttee, SFC, 2009–; Skills Policy Analysis Acad. Panel, BIS, then DFE, 2011–; Policies and Standards Cttee, Quality and Qualifications Ireland, 2013–; Vocational Adv. Gp, Ofqual, 2014–; Student Opportunity and Achievement Cttee, HEFCW, 2016–. FRSA. *Publications:* (jtly) A British Baccalaureate, 1990; (jtly) Higher Education: expansion and reform, 1992; (jtly) Education for All: the future of education and training for 14–19 year olds, 2009. *Recreations:* gardening, cinema, history, reading. *Address:* Department of Education, University of Oxford, 15 Norham Gardens, Oxford OX2 6PY. *T:* (01865) 274045. *E:* ewart.keep@education.ox.ac.uk.

**KEHOE, Paul,** CBE 2017; Chief Executive Officer, Gulf Air Group, Manama, Bahrain, since 2018; b Liverpool, 21 April 1959; s of Reginald and Mary Kehoe; m 1983, Lesley Powell; one s one d. *Educ:* Univ. of Leicester (BSc Hons 1981); Warwick Business Sch., Univ. of Warwick (MBA 1990). Served RAF, Flt Lieut, Air Traffic Control, 1979–87. Manager, Airports, BAE Systems, 1990–93; Man. Dir, Serco-IAL Ltd, Serco Gp, 1993–97; TBI plc: Man. Dir, Belfast Internat. Airport, 1997–2000; Dir, Eur. Airports, 1999–2001; Man. Dir, London Luton Airport, 2001–05; Gp Ops Dir, 2001–05; Chief Executive Officer: DX Services plc, 2005–06; Bristol Internat. Airport, 2007–08; Internat. Airport, then Birmingham Airport Ltd, 2008–17. Chm., Marketing Birmingham, then W Midlands Growth Co., 2009–18. Pres., Birmingham Chamber of Commerce, 2016–. Hon. DBus Birmingham City, 2012. *Recreations:* flying (Private Pilots Licence), sailing (day skipper), reading. *E:* paul.kehoe1@btopenworld.com.

**KEIGHLEY, Prof. Michael Robert Burch,** FRCS, FRCSE; Barling Professor of Surgery, University of Birmingham, 1988–2004, now Professor Emeritus; Managing Director, Keighleycolo Ltd, since 2009; b 12 Oct. 1943; s of late Dr Robert Arthur Spink Keighley and of Dr Jacqueline Vivian Keighley; m Dr Dorothy Margaret, MBE; one s one d. *Educ:* Monkton Combe Sch.; St Bartholomew's Hosp., Univ. of London (MB BS 1967; MS 1976); Durham Univ. (MA Theol. and Health 2016). FRCS 1970; FRCSE 1970. Prof. of Surgery, General and Dental Hosps, Univ. of Birmingham, 1984–88. Boerhaave Prof. of Surgery, Univ. of Leiden, 1985; Eyber's Vis. Prof., Univ. of OFS, 1987; Vis. Prof., Harvard Univ., 1990; Penman Vis. Prof., Univ. of Cape Town, 1992; Vis. Prof., St Mark's Hosp., London, 1995; Rupert Turnbull Prof., Washington Univ., 1996; Vis. Prof., Karolinska Inst., 2000; Hon. Prof., Christian Med. Coll., Vellore, India, 2004–16. Chairman: Public Affairs, United European Gastroenterol Fedn, 2000–05; Public Relns and Ethics, 2002–06, Assoc. of Coloproctol. of GB and Ire. (Pres., Res. Foundn, 2005–09). Pres., MASIC Foundn Charity, 2016–. Expert medico-legal witness. Trustee, Bowel Disease Res. Foundn (formerly Colon and Rectal Disease Res. Foundn), 2009– (Pres., 2004–09). Mem., Christian Med. Fellowship, 1967–. Hon. Fellow: Brazilian Coll. of Surgeons, 1991; Sri Lankan Coll. of Surgeons, 2015; Hon. FRACS 1992; Hon. Mem., Portuguese Soc. of Surgery, 2004. Jacksonian Prize, RCS, 1979; Hunterian Prof., RCS, 1979. *Publications:* Antimicrobial Prophylaxis in Surgery, 1979; Inflammatory Bowel Diseases, 1981, 3rd edn 1995; Gastrointestinal Haemorrhage, 1983; Textbook of Gastroenterology, 1985, 2nd edn 1994; Surgery of the Anus, Rectum and Colon, 1994, 4th edn 2018; Atlas of Colorectal Surgery, 1996. *Recreations:* painting, music, sailing, climbing. *Address:* Whalebone Cottage, Vicarage Hill, Tanworth in Arden, Warwicks B94 5AN. *T:* (01564) 741865. *E:* keighleycolo@btinternet.com. *Clubs:* Athenæum, Royal Society of Medicine; Aston Martin Owners.

**KEIGHLEY, Rev. Dr Thomas Christopher,** TSSF; FRCN; independent health care consultant, since 2001; Associate Priest, Hornchurch St Nicholas, Elm Park, since 2012; b 4 May 1951; s of late John Charles Keighley and Frances Louise Keighley (née Leary); m 1st, 1974, Anne Gibson (marr. diss. 1978); 2nd, 1979, Elizabeth Redfern (marr. diss. 1989); 3rd, 1990, Amanda Gunner; one step s one step d. *Educ:* St Michael's Coll., Kirkby Lonsdale; Preston Sch. of Nursing (SRN 1974; RMN 1976); Charles Frear Sch. of Nursing (NDN Cert. 1976); Huddersfield Polytechnic (RCNT 1979); Dip. Nursing, London Univ., 1981; BA Hons Open Univ. 1985; NE Oecumenical Course, Ushaw Coll., Durham (DipHE (Theol) 2003); Kings Coll. London (PhD 2016). FRCN 2004. Aux. Nurse, Deepdale Hosp., Preston, 1970; Staff Nurse, Preston Royal Infirmary, 1974; Community Charge Nurse, NW Leics, 1976; Clinical Teacher: Maidstone, 1977; Cambridge HA, 1979; RCN Adviser, Research, 1982; Dist Dir of Nursing, 1986, of Nursing and Quality, 1988, Waltham Forest; Regl Dir of Nursing, Yorkshire Health, 1990–95; Dir, Inst. of Nursing, Univ. of Leeds, 1993–96; Dir of Internat. Develt, Sch. of Healthcare Studies, Univ. of Leeds, 1997–2001. Associate Researcher, Lincoln Theol Inst., Sheffield Univ., 1998–2002. Lawrence S. Bloomberg Vis. Prof., Faculty of Nursing, Univ. of Toronto, 2012–13. Mem., EU Adv. Cttee on Training for Nursing, 1990–2000. Ordained deacon, C of E, 2003; priest, 2004; Curate, Upper Nidderdale, 2003–06; Assistant Priest: Dacre with Hartwith and

Darley with Thornthwaite, dio. Ripon and Leeds, 2006–07; Christchurch and St John with St Luke, Isle of Dogs, 2007–12; Dean, Coll. of Self Supporting Ministers: Stepney Area, Dio. of London, 2008–12; Barking Area, Dio. of Chelmsford, 2015–; Anglican Chaplain, St Joseph's Hospice, London, 2009–10. Winifred Raphael Meml Lecture, RCN Res. Soc., 1988; Ven. Catherine McAuley Meml Lecture, Mater Misericordiae Hosp., Dublin, 2002. TSSF, 2001–. Hon. Mem., American Orgn of Nurse Execs, 2010. Gran Cruz, Asociación Colombiana de Facultades de Medicina, 2001. Editor, Nursing Management, 1997–2004. *Publications:* articles on nursing, health care and theology. *Recreations:* opera, art, walking, rug making. *Address:* The Vicarage, 17 St Nicholas Avenue, Elm Park, Hornchurch RM12 4PT. *T:* (01708) 474639.

**KEIGHTLEY, Maj.-Gen. Richard Charles,** CB 1987; Chairman, Southampton University Hospitals NHS Trust, 2002–08; *b* 2 July 1933; *s* of General Sir Charles Keightley, GCB, GBE, DSO, and Lady (Joan) Keightley (*née* Smyth-Osbourne); *m* 1958, Caroline Rosemary Butler, *er d* of Sir Thomas Butler, 12th Bt, CVO, DSO, OBE; three *d. Educ:* Marlborough Coll.; RMA, Sandhurst. Commissioned into 5th Royal Inniskilling Dragoon Guards, 1953; served Canal Zone, BAOR, N Africa, Singapore, Cyprus; sc Camberley, 1963; comd 5th Royal Inniskilling Dragoon Guards, 1972–75; Task Force Comdr, 3 Armd Div., 1978–79; RCDS 1980; Brigadier General Staff HQ UKLF, 1981; GOC Western Dist, 1982–83; Comdt, RMA Sandhurst, 1983–87. Col, 5th Royal Inniskilling Dragoon Guards, 1986–91. Defence Consultant, Portescap (UK), 1987–92. Chairman: W Dorset, subseq. Dorset, HA, 1988–95, 1998–2002; Dorset Healthcare NHS Trust, 1996–98. President: Dorset Br., Royal British Legion, 1990–2012; Dorset Relate, 2001–14; St John Ambulance Dorset, 2008–12 (Chm., St John Priory Gp, 2012–16). Chm., Combined Services Polo Assoc., 1982–86. CStJ 2013 (OStJ 2004). *Recreations:* field sports, cricket, farming, horse racing. *Address:* Kennels Farmhouse, Tarrant Gunville, Blandford, Dorset DT11 8JQ. *Club:* Cavalry and Guards.

**KEIR, Colin;** Member (SNP) Edinburgh Western, Scottish Parliament, 2011–16; *b* 9 Dec. 1959; *s* of John Keir and Catherine Keir (*née* Bonnar). *Educ:* Craigmount High Sch., Edinburgh. Mem. (SNP), Edinburgh CC, 2007–12 (Convener: Regulatory Cttee, 2007–11; Mgt Cttee, Pentland Hills Regl Park, 2007–11). Scottish Parliament: Member: Justice Cttee, 2011–13; Public Audit Cttee, 2012–16; Health and Sport Cttee, 2013–16; Cross Party Gp on Germany, 2012–16; Co-convener, Cross Party Gp on Taiwan, 2011–16; Convener, Cross Party Gp on Aviation, 2012–16; Dep. Convener, Cross Party Gp on China, 2014–16. *Recreations:* golf, fly fishing, Rugby. *Club:* RHC Cougars Rugby Football.

**KEIR, Jane;** Partner, Kingsley Napley LLP, since 1992 (Senior Partner, 2013–18); *b* Skelton, Cumbria, 4 March 1962; *d* of Ronald John Keir, OBE and Audrie Jill Keir (*née* Curtis). *Educ:* Queen Elizabeth Grammar Sch., Penrith; Newcastle Poly. (LLB Hons); Coll. of Law, Chester. Admitted Solicitor, 1987; Asst Solicitor, Alexanders, 1987–89; Kingsley Napley LLP, 1989–: Sen. Equity Partner, 1997; Jt Man. Partner, 2004–07. Member: Law Soc., 1989–; Internat. Acad. of Family Lawyers (formerly of Matrimonial Lawyers), 2006–. Trustee, Racing Foundn, 2016–. Mem., Thoroughbred Breeders' Assoc., 2011–. *Recreations:* horseracing - breeding and owning, owner of Elkington Stud, Oxon. *Address:* Kingsley Napley LLP, Knights Quarter, 14 St John's Lane, EC1M 4AJ. *T:* (020) 7814 1273, 07887 571050. *E:* jkeir@kingsleynapley.co.uk.

**KEIRLE, Very Rev. Michael Robert;** Dean of Jersey, since 2017; *b* St Albans, 3 March 1962; *s* of Alan Keirle and Frances Windsor Keirle; *m* 1990, Emma Louise Ruddle; one *s* one *d. Educ:* St Albans Grammar Sch. for Boys; Trinity Theol Coll., Bristol (BA Hons Theology and Pastoral Studies 1989). Ordained deacon, 1989, priest, 1990; Curate, Christ Church, Orpington, 1989–92; Rector: St Paul's, Harare, 1992–95; Keston Parish Church, Bromley, 1995–2003; St Martin's, Guernsey, 2003–17. Trustee: IcFEM Mission, Kimilili, Kenya, 2006–; Channel Is Air Search, 2007–. *Recreations:* photography, music, ornithology, mineral collecting. *Address:* The Deanery, David Place, St Helier, Jersey, Channel Islands JE2 4TE. *T:* (01534) 720001. *E:* dean@jerseydeanery.je.

**KEITH,** family name of **Earl of Kintore**.

**KEITH, Hon. Sir Brian (Richard),** Kt 2001; a Judge of the High Court, Queen's Bench Division, 2001–14; *b* 14 April 1944; *s* of late Alan Keith, OBE, broadcaster, and Pearl Keith (*née* Rebuck); *m* 1978, Gilly (*d* 2017), *d* of late Air Cdre Ivan de la Plain, CBE; one *s* one *d. Educ:* University College School, Hampstead; Lincoln College, Oxford (MA). John F. Kennedy Fellow, Harvard Law School, 1966–67; called to the Bar, Inner Temple, 1968, Bencher, 1996; in practice, 1969–91; Assistant Recorder, 1988; QC 1989; a Recorder, 1993–2001. A Judge of the Supreme Court of Hong Kong, 1991–97; a Judge of the Court of First Instance, High Court of Hong Kong, 1997–99; Presiding Judge, Admin. Law List, High Court of Hong Kong, 1997–99; a Judge of the Court of Appeal, Hong Kong, 1999–2001; Judge of the Supreme Court of Fiji, 2015–. Hon. Lectr, Univ. of Hong Kong, 1994–2001. Mem., Judicial Studies Bd, Hong Kong, 1994–2001. Chm., Zahid Mubarek Inquiry, 2004–06. *Recreations:* travel, golf, cinema. *E:* brkeith@blueyonder.co.uk. *Club:* Hong Kong.

**KEITH, Hon. Deborah Jane, (Mrs R. S. Steedman),** PhD; Head, Global Research and Development External Collaborations, Syngenta, 2011–14; *b* Edinburgh, 3 Sept. 1957; *d* of Baron Keith of Kinkel, GBE, PC and of Alison Hope Alan Keith; *m* 2005, (Robert) Scott Steedman, *qv*; one step *s* one step *d. Educ:* St Leonard's Sch., St Andrews; Univ. of Edinburgh (BSc Hons Botany 1980); Wye Coll., Univ. of London (MSc Applied Plant Sci. 1982); Univ. of East Anglia (PhD 1995). Consultant, Basagene Ltd and Royal Govt of Bhutan, 1983–88; John Innes Centre, 1989–94; Volunteer, Farm Africa, 1996; Res. Fellow, Univ. of Reading, 1997–98; Syngenta: R&D, 1998–2006; Hd, Global R&D Crop Protection Res. Portfolio, 2006–11. Mem., UKRI-BBSRC (formerly BBSRC), 2015–. Non-executive Director: James Hutton Inst., 2014– (Chm., James Hutton Ltd, 2017–); Aerospace Technology Inst., 2015–; John Innes Centre, 2015–; Redag Crop Protection Ltd, 2016–. Trustee, Univ. of Warwick, 2015–. *Club:* New (Edinburgh).
See also Hon. H. G. Keith.

**KEITH, Hon. Hugo George;** QC 2009; barrister; *b* Edinburgh, 6 Feb. 1967; *twin s* of Baron Keith of Kinkel, GBE, PC and of Alison Hope Alan Keith (*née* Brown); *m* 1999, Lottie Bulwer-Long; one *s* three *d. Educ:* Winchester Coll.; Magdalen Coll., Oxford (BA Juris.). Called to the Bar, Gray's Inn, 1989, Bencher, 2013; Treasury Counsel: Supplementary Panel, 1994–95; B Panel Civil, 1995–2000; A Panel Civil, 2000–08. Mem., Bar Council, 1995–98. *Recreation:* sailing. *Address:* 3 Raymond Buildings, Gray's Inn, WC1R 5BH. *T:* (020) 7400 6400, *Fax:* (020) 7400 6464.
See also Hon. D. J. Keith.

**KEITH, Rt Hon. Sir Kenneth (James),** ONZ 2007; KBE 1988; PC 1998; a Judge of the International Court of Justice, 2006–15; Distinguished Fellow, Victoria University of Wellington, since 2015; *b* 19 Nov. 1937; *s* of Patrick James Keith and Amy Irene Keith (*née* Witheridge); *m* 1961, Jocelyn Margaret Buckett; two *s* two *d. Educ:* Auckland Grammar Sch.; Auckland Univ.; Victoria Univ. of Wellington (LLM); Harvard Law Sch. Barrister and Solicitor, High Court of New Zealand; QC (NZ) 1994. NZ Dept of External Affairs, 1960–62; Victoria Univ. of Wellington, 1962–64, 1966–91, Prof. of Law, 1974–91, now Emeritus; UN Secretariat, NY, 1968–70; NZ Inst. of Internat. Affairs, 1972–74; Pres., NZ Law Commn, 1991–96; a Judge of NZ Court of Appeal, 1996–2003; a Judge of Supreme Ct and Ct of Appeal, Fiji, 2003, NZ, 2004–05; a Judge of Court of Appeal: Western Samoa, 1982; Cook Is, 1982; Niue, 1995. Permanent Ct of Arbitration, 1985–2008. Mem., 1991–2006, Pres., 2002–06, Internat. Fact Finding Commn (Geneva Conventions). Mem., Inst de Droit Internat., 2003– (Assoc. Mem., 1997–2003). Hon. LLD: Auckland, 2001; Victoria, Wellington, 2004. *Publications:* (ed) Human Rights in New Zealand, 1968; The Extent of the Advisory Jurisdiction of the International Court, 1971; contrib. to Amer. Jl of Internat. Law, Internat. and Comparative Law Qly, NZ Univs Law Rev., etc. *Recreations:* walking, reading, music. *Address:* 11 Salamanca Road, Wellington 6012, New Zealand.

**KEITH, Larry Bacon;** Head of Conservation and Keeper, National Gallery, since 2010; *b* San Jose, Costa Rica, 18 April 1960; *s* of Clifford Keith and Shirley Keith; *m* 2006, Marie Louise Juel Sauerberg; one *s. Educ:* Oberlin Coll. (BA Art Hist. 1982); Royal Coll. of Music (LRCM 1988); Hamilton Kerr Inst., Univ. of Cambridge (DipCons 1988). Intern: with Herbert Lank, London, 1988–89; Metropolitan Mus., 1989–91; Conservator, Nat. Gall., 1991–. Mem. and ext. examnr, Internat. Adv. Bd of Studies, Dept of Conservation and Technol., Courtauld Inst. of Art, Univ. of London; ext. examnr, post-grad. easel painting conservation course, Hamilton Kerr Inst., Cambridge. Advisor: Bank of America Conservation Prog.; Heritage Conservation Trust; Mem., Adv. Bd, Reynolds Res. Proj., Wallace Collection. *Recreations:* music, cinema, sport. *Address:* National Gallery, Trafalgar Square, WC2N 5DN. *E:* larry.keith@ng-london.org.uk. *Club:* Blacks.

**KEITH, Dame Penelope (Anne Constance), (Dame Penelope Timson),** DBE 2014 (CBE 2007; OBE 1989); DL; actress; *b* 2 April; *d* of Frederick A. W. Hatfield and Constance Mary Keith; *m* 1978, Rodney Timson. *Educ:* Annecy Convent, Seaford, Sussex; Webber Douglas Sch., London. First prof. appearance, Civic Theatre, Chesterfield, 1959; repertory, Lincoln, Salisbury and Manchester, 1960–63; RSC, Stratford, 1963, and Aldwych, 1965; rep., Cheltenham, 1967; Maggie Howard in Suddenly at Home, Fortune Theatre, 1971; Sarah in The Norman Conquests, Greenwich, then Globe Theatre, 1974; Lady Driver in Donkey's Years, 1976; Orinthia in The Apple Cart, Chichester, then Phoenix Theatre, 1977; Epifania in The Millionairess, Haymarket, 1978; Sarah in Moving, Queen's Theatre, 1981; Maggie in Hobson's Choice, Haymarket, 1982; Lady Cicely Waynflete in Captain Brassbound's Conversion, Haymarket, 1982; Judith Bliss in Hay Fever, Queen's, 1983; The Dragon's Tail, Apollo, 1985; Miranda, Chichester, 1987; The Deep Blue Sea, Haymarket, 1988; Dear Charles, Yvonne Arnaud, Guildford, 1990; The Merry Wives of Windsor, Chichester, 1990; Lady Bracknell in The Importance of Being Earnest, UK tour, 1991; On Approval, UK tour, 1992; Glyn and It, Richmond, 1994; Monsieur Amilcar, Chichester, 1995; Mrs Warren's Profession, Richmond, 1997; Good Grief, nat. tour, 1998; Star Quality, Apollo, 2001; Time and the Conways, nat. tour, 2003; Madame Arcati in Blithe Spirit, Th. Royal, Bath, transf. Savoy Th., 2004; Entertaining Angels, Chichester, 2006; The Importance of Being Earnest, Vaudeville, 2008; Mrs Malaprop in The Rivals, Th. Royal, Haymarket, 2010; The Chalk Garden, Chichester, 2018; directed: Relatively Speaking, nat. tour, 1992; How the Other Half Loves, nat. tour, 1994; The Way of the World, Chichester, 2012; Mrs Pat, Chichester, 2015; *film:* The Priest of Love, 1980. Television plays and series include: The Good Life, 1974–77; Private Lives, 1977; The Norman Conquests, 1977; To the Manor Born, 1979, 1980 and 1981; Sweet Sixteen, 1983; Waters of the Moon, 1983; Moving, 1985; Executive Stress, 1986–88; No Job for a Lady, 1990–92; Next of Kin, 1995–97; Margery and Gladys, 2003; presenter: What's My Line?, 1988; Growing Places, 1989; The Manor Reborn, 2011; Penelope Keith's Hidden Villages, 2014, 2015; Village of the Year, 2018. Mem., HFEA, 1990–96. President: The Actors' Benevolent Fund, 1990–; Surrey Gardens Trust, 2007–; KeepOut, 2011–18; S of England Agricultural Soc., 2012–13. Patron, Yvonne Arnaud Theatre, 1992–. Trustee, King George V Fund for Actors and Actresses, 2010–. High Sheriff, Surrey, 2002–03; DL Surrey, 2004. Awards: BAFTA, 1976 and 1977; SWET, 1976; Variety Club of GB, 1976 and 1979. *Recreation:* gardening. *Address:* c/o The Actors' Benevolent Fund, 6 Adam Street, WC2N 6AA. *T:* (020) 7836 6378.

**KEITH, Shona;** see McIsaac, S.

**KEKIĆ, Dr Razia;** a Judge of the Upper Tribunal (Immigration and Asylum Chamber) (formerly a Senior Immigration Judge, Asylum and Immigration Tribunal), since 2008; *b* London, 7 July 1956; *d* of Abdur Razzak Dada and Diane Dada; *m* 1983, Laza Kekić (marr. diss. 1996); two *d. Educ:* Convent of Jesus and Mary, Karachi; Karachi Grammar Sch.; Univ. of Kent, Canterbury (BA Hons Social Anthropol.); London Sch. of Econs (MSc; PhD Social Anthropol. 2000). Counsellor, 1978–83, Sen. Counsellor, 1983–88, UK Immigrants Adv. Service, Harmondsworth; caseworker, 1992–2000, Team Leader, 2001, Refugee Legal Centre; Immigration Judge (pt-time), 2001–02, (full-time), 2002–05; Designated Immigration Judge, 2005–08. *Recreations:* walking, exploring, travel, reading, particularly travel books, Scandinavian crime and ethnic books, cinema, painting, photography, vegetarian cookery and juicing. *Address:* Upper Tribunal (Immigration and Asylum Tribunal), Field House, 15–25 Breams Building, EC4A 1DZ. *T:* (020) 7073 4249, *Fax:* (020) 7073 4004. *E:* UpperTribunalJudge.Kekic@eJudiciary.net.

**KELBURN, Viscount of;** courtesy title of heir of Earl of Glasgow, not used by current heir.

**KELEHER, Paul Robert;** QC 2009; a Recorder, since 2018; *b* Ilford, Essex; *s* of Roy and Margaret Keleher; *m* 2001, Barbara Grzybowska; one *s* one *d. Educ:* Chigwell Sch.; Gonville and Caius Coll., Cambridge (BA 1978); Inns of Court Sch. of Law. Called to the Bar, Gray's Inn, 1980, Bencher, 2013. *Recreations:* walking, cycling, gardening, fine wine and real ale. *Address:* 25 Bedford Row, WC1R 4HD. *T:* (020) 7067 1500. *E:* paul.keleher@25bedfordrow.com.

**KELL, Prof. Douglas Bruce,** CBE 2014; DPhil; FRSB; FLSW; FAAAS; Professor of Bioanalytical Science, University of Manchester (formerly University of Manchester Institute of Science and Technology), since 2002; *b* 7 April 1953; *s* of William Howard Kell and Nancy Kell (*née* Finniston); *m* 1989, Dr Antje Wagner; one *s* two *d. Educ:* Bradfield Coll., Berks (Top Schol.); St John's Coll., Oxford (BA Hons Biochem. Upper 2nd Cl. with Dist. in Chem. Pharmacol.; Sen. Schol., 1975–76; MA, DPhil 1978). FRSB (FIBiol 1999). UCW, Aberystwyth, then University of Wales, Aberystwyth: SRC Postdoctoral Res. Fellow, 1978–80; SERC Advanced Fellow, 1981–83; New Blood Lectr, 1983–88; Reader, 1988–92; Prof. of Microbiology, 1992–2002, Dir of Res., 1997–2002, Inst. of Biol Scis; Dir, Manchester Centre for Integrative Systems Biology, 2005–08; Chief Exec. and Dep. Chm., BBSRC, 2008–13 (on secondment). Fleming Lectr, Soc. for Gen. Microbiol., 1986. Founding Director: Aber Instruments, 1988–2008 (Queen's Award for Export Achievement 1998); Predictive Solutions Ltd (formerly Aber Genomic Computing), 2000–08. Dir, Chirkwell Consulting, 2017–. Member: Council, 2000–06, Strategy Bd, 2001–06, BBSRC; numerous scientific cttees of SRC, SERC and BBSRC, incl.: Plant Scis and Microbiol., 1985–88, Biotech. Directorate, 1992–94, Chemicals and Pharmaceuticals Directorate, 1994–96, Engrg and Biol Systems, 1999–2000; Biosci. for Industry Panel, 2007–08; DTI LINK Prog. Mgt Cttees for Technol. for Analytical and Physical Measurement, 1992–94, Biochem. Engrg, 1994–98, Analytical Biotech. (Chm., 1995–99); Basic Technol. Strategic Adv. Cttee, Res. Councils UK, 2001–04; Sci. Bd, STFC, 2007–08; Adv. Bd, UK PubMed Central, 2007–08. Member, Scientific Advisory Board:

Eagle Genomics, 2017; Eight Great Technologies, 2017–; Optalysys, 2018–. Assoc. Scientific Dir, Novo Nordisk Foundn Centre for Biosustainability, Technical Univ. of Denmark, 2018–. FLSW 2012; FAAAS 2012. Fellow, Aberystwyth Univ., 2013. Hon. DSc: Cranfield, 2012; Aberdeen, 2015; UEA, 2015. Interdisciplinary Award, 2004, Chem. Biol. Award, 2005, SAC Gold Medal, 2006, RSC; Theodor Bücher Medal, FEBS-IUBMB, 2005; Royal Soc./Wolfson Merit Award, 2005. *Publications:* numerous scientific pubns. *Recreation:* family. *Address:* School of Chemistry and Manchester Institute of Biotechnology, University of Manchester, 131 Princess Street, Manchester M1 7DN.

**KELL, Michael Stuart;** Advisor, Independent Evaluation Office, International Monetary Fund, Washington, DC, since 2019; *b* 27 Jan. 1965; *s* of Malcolm Kell and Jill Kell (*née* Wood); *m* 1995, Jane Morris; three *d*. *Educ:* St Edmund Hall, Oxford (BA Hons PPE 1986); Nuffield Coll., Oxford (MPhil Econs 1991). Res. Officer, Inst. for Fiscal Studies, 1986–89; Econ. Advr, HM Treasury, 1991–96; Advr to UK Exec. Dir, IMF and World Bank, 1996–98; Sen. Economist, Fiscal Affairs Dept, IMF, 1998–2002; Hd, Central Econ. Analysis, 2002–03, Chief Economist, 2003–07, ODPM, subseq. DCLG; Dir, Econ. Consulting, Deloitte and Touche LLP, 2008–10; Dir, Value for Money, DECC, 2010–16; Chief Economist, Nat. Audit Office, 2010–18. *T:* (USA) (202) 6237715. *E:* mkell@imf.org.

**KELLAND, John William,** LVO 1977; QPM 1975; Overseas Police Adviser and Inspector General of Dependent Territories' Police, Foreign and Commonwealth Office, 1985–91; *b* 18 Aug. 1929; *s* of William John Kelland and Violet Ethel (*née* Olsen); *m* 1963, Brenda Nancy (*née* Foulsham) (decd); *m* 1986, Frances Elizabeth (*née* Byrne); one step *d*; two *s* from a former marriage. *Educ:* Sutton High Sch.; Plymouth Polytechnic. FIMgt. RAF, 1947–49. Constable, later Insp., Plymouth City Police, 1950–67; Insp., later Supt, Devon & Cornwall Constabulary, 1968–72; Asst Chief Constable, Cumbria Constabulary, 1972–74; Dir, Sen. Comd Courses, Nat. Police Coll., Bramshill, 1974–75 and 1978–80; Comr, Royal Fiji Police, 1975–78; 1981–85: Management Consultant and Chm., CSSBs; Sen. Consultant, RIPA; Sen. Lectr, Cornwall Coll.; Facilitator, Interpersonal Skills, Cornwall CC Seminars. Mem., Cornwall & Isles of Scilly FHSA, 1992–93. Chm., Old Suttonian Assoc., 1993–2011 (Vice Pres., 2011–). *Publications:* various articles in learned jls. *Recreations:* Rugby football, choral singing. *Clubs:* Civil Service; Ferndown Probus (Pres., 2017–).

**KELLAWAY, Richard Edward,** CBE 2005; FRGS; Director General, Commonwealth War Graves Commission, 2000–10; *b* 13 Aug. 1946; *s* of late Edward John Kellaway and Elsie May Kellaway (*née* Judd); *m* 1968, Ann Clarke; two *d*. *Educ:* Poole Grammar Sch. FRGS 2010. Commnd as Officer of Customs and Excise, 1966: Sen. Investigation Officer, 1975–79; Principal, VAT Admin, 1979–80; Asst Chief Investigation Officer, 1980–84; Chief Staff Inspector, 1984–87; Head: Customs Dept, Bermuda, 1987–90; Estates and Security, 1990–94; Chief Investigation Officer, 1994–99; on secondment as Drugs and Serious Crime Advr, FCO, 1999–2000. Trustee, The Remembrance Trust, 2018–. *Recreations:* industrial archaeology, cooking, gardening. *Address:* Cranford, Ridge Langley, Sanderstead, Surrey CR2 0AR. *E:* rekellaway@blueyonder.co.uk. *Clubs:* Royal Air Force; Automobile de l'Ouest (France).

**KELLEHER, Benedict Peter John; His Honour Judge Kelleher;** a Circuit Judge, since 2018; *b* London, 1970. *Educ:* Wimbledon Coll.; Bristol Univ. (LLB; MSc 1993). Called to the Bar, Inner Temple, 1994; in practice as barrister, 1994–2018; a Recorder, 2012–18. *Address:* c/o Inner London Crown Court, Sessions House, Newington Causeway, SE1 6AZ.

**KELLEHER, Patricia Mary;** Principal, Stephen Perse Foundation (formerly Perse School for Girls and Stephen Perse Sixth Form College), since 2001; *b* 17 March 1962; *d* of Liam and Margaret Kelleher. *Educ:* Lady Margaret Hall, Oxford (MA Modern Hist. 1984); Univ. of Sussex (MA Renaissance Theory and Culture 1995); Univ. of Nottingham (PGCE 1985). History Teacher, Haberdashers' Aske's Sch. for Girls, Elstree, 1985–88; Hd of History and Hd of Year 7, Brighton and Hove High Sch. (GDST), 1988–97; Dep. Headmistress, Brentwood Sch., Essex, 1997–2001. *Recreations:* walking, travel, reading. *Address:* Stephen Perse Foundation, Union Road, Cambridge CB2 1HF. *T:* (01223) 454700, *Fax:* (01223) 467420. *E:* principal@stephenperse.com.

**KELLENBERGER, Dr Jakob;** President, International Committee of the Red Cross, 2000–12; *b* 19 Oct. 1944; *s* of Jakob and Klara Kellenberger; *m* 1973, Elisabeth Kellenberger-Jossi; two *d*. *Educ:* High Sch., Zurich; Univ. of Zurich (PhD 1975). Joined Swiss Diplomatic Service, 1974: served Madrid, EU (Brussels), London, 1974–84; Hd, Dept for European Integration, Berne, 1984–92 (Minister, 1984–88; Ambassador, 1988–92); State Sec. for Foreign Affairs, Switzerland, 1992–99. Teaching posts: Univ. of Salamanca; Grad. Inst., Geneva. Member, Board: Council for Future of Europe, 2011–; Centre for Humanitarian Dialogue, Geneva, 2012–; Pres., Swisspeace, 2013–. Hon. Councillor, Swiss Fed. Inst. of Technology, Zurich, 2007; Hon. Mem., Amer. Soc. of Internat. Law, 2012. Dist. Fellow, Graduate Inst. Geneva, 2014; Dr *hc* Basle, 2003; Catania, 2006. Grosses Verdienstkreuz mit Stern (Germany), 2012; Commandeur, Légion d'Honneur (France), 2013. *Publications:* Calderón de la Barca und das Komische, 1975; Humanitäres Völkerrecht, 2010; Wo liegt die Schweiz?, 2014; numerous articles, particularly on Swiss–EU relations. *Recreations:* reading (literature, philosophy), cross country ski-ing, jogging, tennis.

**KELLETT, Sir Stanley Charles,** 7th Bt *cr* 1801; *b* 5 March 1940; *s* of Sir Stanley Everard Kellett, 6th Bt, and of Audrey Margaret Phillips; *S* father, 1983, but his name does not appear on the Official Roll of the Baronetage; *m* 1st, 1962, Lorraine May (marr. diss. 1968), *d* of F. Winspear; 2nd, 1968, Margaret Ann (marr. diss. 1974), *d* of James W. Bofinger; 3rd, 1982, Catherine Lorna (marr. diss. 1991), *d* of W. J. C. Orr; two *d*; 4th, 1991, Yvonne Patricia (*d* 2001), *d* of Alan Blogg. Heir: cousin Maxwell Rex Kellett [*b* 1947; *m* 1968, Jennifer Maher; one *d*]. *Address:* 21 Debussy Place, Cranebrook, NSW 2749, Australia.

**KELLETT-BOWMAN, Edward Thomas;** JP; business and management consultant in private practice, since 1974; *b* 25 Feb. 1931; *s* of late R. E. Bowman and M. Bowman (*née* Mathers); *m* 1st, 1960, Margaret Patricia Blakemore (*d* 1970); three *s* one *d*; 2nd, 1971, (Mary) Elaine Kellett (Dame Elaine Kellett-Bowman, DBE). *Educ:* Reed's Sch.; Slough Coll. of Technol. (DMS 1973); Cranfield Inst. of Technol. (MBA 1974). Technical and management trng in textiles, 1951–53; textile management, 1953–55; pharmaceutical man., 1955–72. Mem. (C) Lancs East, European Parlt, 1979–84; contested same seat, 1984; MEP (C) Hampshire Central, Dec. 1988–1994, Itchen, Test and Avon, 1994–99; contested (C) SE Region, 1999. Freeman: City of London, 1978; Wheelwrights' Co., 1979. Hon. Citizen, New Orleans, 1960. FCMI. JP Middx, 1966. *Recreations:* shooting, tennis, swimming. *Address:* 6 Abbey Water, Romsey, Hants SO51 8EJ.

**KELLEY, Joan,** CB 1987; Member, Official Side Panel, Civil Service Appeal Board, 1987–96; *b* 8 Dec. 1926; *er d* of late George William Kelley and Dora Kelley. *Educ:* Whalley Range High Sch. for Girls, Manchester; London Sch. of Econs and Pol Science (BScEcon 1947). Europa Publications Ltd, 1948; Pritchard, Wood & Partners Ltd, 1949; joined Civil Service as Econ. Asst in Cabinet Office, 1949; admin. work in Treasury, 1954; Principal, 1956; Asst Sec., 1968; Under Sec., 1979; on secondment to NI Office, 1979–81; Under Sec., 1979–86, Principal Estabt Officer and Principal Finance Officer, 1984–86, HM Treasury. Mem. Council, Univ. of London Inst. of Educn, 1992–98. *Recreations:* gardening, map reading, drinking wine, foreign travel. *Address:* The Nook, The Street, Little Chart, Ashford, Kent TN27 0QB.

**KELLNER,** family name of **Baroness Ashton of Upholland**.

**KELLNER, Peter Jon;** President, YouGov, online polling and market research company, 2007–16 (Chairman, 2001–07); *b* 2 Oct. 1946; *s* of Michael Kellner and Lily Agnes Samson Kellner (*née* McVail); *m* 1st, 1972, Sally Collard (marr. diss. 1988); one *s* two *d*; 2nd, 1988, Catherine Margaret Ashton (*see* Baroness Ashton of Upholland); one *s* one *d*. *Educ:* Minchenden Grammar Sch., Southgate, London; Royal Grammar Sch., Newcastle upon Tyne; King's Coll., Cambridge (BA 1st Cl. Hons 1969). Journalist, Sunday Times, 1969–80; Political Ed., New Statesman, 1980–87; political columnist: Independent, 1986–92; Sunday Times, 1992–96; Observer, 1996–97; Evening Standard, 1997–2003. TV political analyst and commentator: A Week in Politics, 1982–88; Newsnight and election progs, 1990–97; Powerhouse, 1999–2003; radio presenter, Analysis, 1995–98. Vis. Scholar, Carnegie Europe, 2017–. Trustee: Royal Commonwealth Soc., 2007–13 (Chm., 2009–13); ASH, 2009–17; Hansard Soc., 2012–15; UpRising, 2013–19. Mem. Council, NIESR, 2013–17. Chm., NCVO, 2016–19. Journalist of Year, BPA, 1978; Chairman of the Year, Quoted Company Awards, 2007; Special Recognition Award, Political Studies Assoc., 2011. *Publications:* (with C. Hitchens) Callaghan: the road to Number Ten, 1976; (with Lord Crowther-Hunt) The Civil Servants, 1980; Democracy, 2009; contribs to various jls, incl. Parly Affairs, Political Qly, British Journalism Rev., Internat. Jl Mkt Res. *Recreations:* reading, arguing, travel.

**KELLS, Ronald David,** OBE 1999; DL; Group Chief Executive, Ulster Bank Ltd, 1994–98; *b* 14 May 1938; *s* of Robert Kells and Frances Elizabeth Kells; *m* 1964, Elizabeth Anne Kells; one *s* one *d*. *Educ:* Bushmills Grammar Sch.; Sullivan Upper Sch.; Queen's Univ., Belfast (BSc Econ). FCIS 1979; FIB 1985. Joined Ulster Bank, 1964; Investments Manager, 1969–76; Dep. Head, Related Banking Services, 1976–79; Head of Planning and Marketing, 1972–82; seconded to National Westminster Bank, 1982–84; Dir and Head, Retail Services (formerly Branch Banking Div.), 1984–94. Chm., Cunningham Coates Ltd, stockbrokers, 1998–2002; non-executive Director: United Drug Plc, 1999– (Chm., 2005–12); Readymix PLC, 1999–2009; Qubis Ltd, 2000–16. Pres., Confedn of Ulster Socs, 1999–2004. Gov., BFI, 1998–2003. DL Belfast, 1998. Hon. DEcon QUB, 2012. *Recreations:* golf, ski-ing. *Address:* The Moyle, 10 Upper Knockbreda Road, Belfast BT6 9QA. *T:* (028) 9079 7912. *Clubs:* Ulster Reform (Belfast); Royal County Down Golf, Royal Belfast Golf, Portmarnock Golf.

**KELLY, Amanda Jane;** a District Judge (Magistrates' Courts), since 2018; *b* Brighton, 9 Oct. 1973; *d* of Alan Kelly and Christine Kelly; *m* 2007, Michael Atkins; one *s* one *d*. *Educ:* Brighton and Hove High Sch.; Lancing Coll.; Brasenose Coll., Oxford (BA Hons Theol. 1995). Journalist: Mirror Gp Newspapers, 1997–2000; The Times, Independent and TES, 2000–02; called to the Bar, Lincoln's Inn, 2003; in practice as barrister specialising in criminal law, 2003–17; Crown Advocate, 2007–14; a fee-paid Judge, First-tier Tribunal, Social Entitlement Chamber, 2013–; an Immigration Judge, 2014–17. *Publications:* (jtly) Stone's Justices' Manual, 2018–. *Recreations:* tennis, cinema, dining. *Address:* c/o Chief Magistrate's Office, Westminster Magistrates' Court, 181 Marylebone Road, NW1 5BR.

**KELLY, Dame Barbara (Mary),** DBE 2007 (CBE 1992); DL; Convenor, Crichton Foundation, 2003–14; *b* 27 Feb. 1940; *d* of John Maxwell Prentice and Barbara Bain Adam; *m* 1960, Kenneth Archibald Kelly; one *s* two *d* (and two *s* decd). *Educ:* Dalbeattie High Sch.; Kirkcudbright Academy; Moray House Coll., Edinburgh. DipEd. Partner in mixed farming enterprise. Dir, Clydesdale Bank, 1994–98; Member: Scottish Adv. Bd, BP plc, 1990–2003; Scottish PO Bd, 1997–2003. Chairman: Area Manpower Bd, MSC, 1987–88; Scottish Consumer Council, 1985–90; Rural Forum, 1988–92 (Hon. Pres., 1992–99); Training 2000, 1991–97; Architects Registration Bd, 1997–2002; Member: Nat. Consumer Council, 1985–90; Scottish Enterprise Bd, 1990–95; Priorities Bd, MAFF, 1990–95; BBC Rural Affairs and Agric. Adv. Cttee, 1991–97; Scottish Econ. Council, 1991–98; Scottish Tourist Bd, 1993–97; Rathbone Community Industry Bd, 1993–98; Scottish Nat. Heritage Bd, 1995–2001; BBC Broadcasting Council for Scotland, 1997–2002; Comr, EOC, 1991–95. Convener, Millennium Forest for Scotland Trust, 1995–2008. Nat. Vice-Chm., Scottish Women's Rural Insts, 1983–86; Chm., Peter Pan Moat Brae Trust, 2008–. Hon. Pres., Scottish Conservation Projects Trust. Chm., Scottish Adv. Cttee, and Mem., Nat. Adv. Cttee, Duke of Edinburgh's Award Scheme, 1980–85. Trustee: Scottish Community (formerly Caledonian) Foundn, 1995–2002; Strathclyde Foundn, 1997–2002; Robertson Trust, 2002– (Chm., 2014–17); Royal Botanic Gdn, Edinburgh, 2002–11. Freeman, City of London, 2002. DL Dumfries, 1998. Fellow, Bell Coll., 2006; Hon. Fellow, Queen Margaret UC, 2005. FRSE 2017. Hon. FRIAS 2008; Hon. FRSGS 2008. Hon. LLD: Strathclyde, 1995; Aberdeen, 1997; DUniv: Glasgow, 2002; W of Scotland, 2010. *Recreations:* home and family, music, painting, the pursuit of real food, gardening of necessity. *Address:* Barncleugh, Irongray, Dumfries DG2 9SE. *T:* (01387) 730210.

**KELLY, Prof. Ben,** RDI 2007; interior designer, artist; Principal, Ben Kelly Design, since 1976; Professor of Interior Design, Kingston University, since 2017 (Research Fellow, 2013–16); *b* Welwyn Garden City, 1 April 1949; *s* of Herbert and Doreen Kelly; two *s*; *m* 2008, Clare Cumberlidge. *Educ:* Appletreewick Prim. Sch., N Yorks; Ermysted's Grammar Sch., Skipton; Lancaster Coll. of Art; Royal Coll. of Art (MA 1974). Notable projects include: Howie Shop, Covent Garden, 1977; Seditionaries, King's Rd, London, 1977; Sex Pistols rehearsal studio, Denmark St, London, 1978; The Haçienda, Manchester, 1982; Smile, King's Rd, London, 1983; DRY 201, Manchester, 1989; Factory Records HQ, 1990, and conversion into nightclub, FAC 251 The Factory, 2010; BAR TEN, Glasgow, 1991; The Basement, Sci. Mus., London, 1995; Design Council offices, Bow St, London, 1997; Borough Hotel, Edinburgh, 2001; Gymbox, St Martin's Lane, London, 2006; The Public, West Bromwich, 2008; Gymbox, Cornhill, City of London, 2008–09; Gymbox, Westfield, London, 2010; BIMM Manchester, 2013; exhibn design for V&A Mus., British Design 1948–2012 (incl. part re-build of Haçienda nightclub), 2012; Gymbox, Farringdon, 2012; Media Space, Sci. Mus., 2013; exhibn design for Mus. of London, Cheapside Hoard London's Lost Jewels, 2013; (with Virgil Abloh) Ruin (ruined nightclub installation), 2017, Columns, 2018, 180 The Strand. Solo exhibitions: International Orange, Kingston Univ., 2008; International Orange: Please Shut the Gate, Glasgow Sch. of Art, 2010. Chair, Interior and Spatial Design, Univ. of Arts London, 2014–17; Vis. Prof. of Interior Design, RCA, 2015–17. Hon. DDes Kingston, 2000. *Publications:* (contrib.) Plans and Elevations: Ben Kelly Design, 1990; (cover design) Cut & Shut, 2012. *Recreations:* walking, looking at art, making art, studying the work of Marcel Duchamp, watching Finbar (my younger son) grow up, Pop culture, looking at the colour orange, looking out of my window at the sea, looking out of my window at the stars, making coracles, stiles, gates and dry-stone walls. *Address:* 28 Claylands Road, SW8 1NZ. *E:* ben@bkduk.co.uk.

**KELLY, Bernadette Mary,** CB 2010; Permanent Secretary, Department for Transport, since 2017; *b* 10 March 1964; *d* of Edward Kelly and Teresa Bridget Kelly (*née* Garvey); *m* 1998, Howard Ewing; one *s*. *Educ:* King Edward VI Camp Hill Sch. for Girls, Birmingham; Hull Univ. (BA Hons); Imperial Coll., London (MBA 1997). Department of Trade and

Industry: Admin. trainee, 1987–91; Grade 7, 1991–97; Sen. Civil Servant, HM Treasury, 1998–2000 (on secondment); Principal Private Sec. to Sec. of State for Trade and Industry, 2000–02; on secondment to ICI, 2002–03; Dir, Corporate Law and Governance, DTI, 2003–05; Sen. Policy Advr, Policy Directorate, Prime Minister's Office, 2005–06; Dir, Planning Reform, Cabinet Office, 2006–07; Exec. Dir, Planning, 2007–09, Housing, 2009–10, DCLG; Dir Gen., Market Frameworks (formerly Fair Markets), 2010–12, Mkts and Local Growth, 2012–13, Business and Local Growth, 2013–15, BIS; Dir Gen., Rail Gp, DfT, 2015–17. Civil Service Champion for Social Mobility, 2018–. Trustee, Whitehall and Industry Gp. *Address:* Department for Transport, Great Minster House, 33 Horseferry Road, SW1P 4DR. *Clubs:* Goodwood, Midhurst Cricket, Midhurst Rugby (Sussex).

KELLY, Most Rev. Brendan; *see* Galway and Kilmacduagh, Bishop of, (R.C.).

KELLY, Brendan Damien; QC 2008; barrister; a Recorder, since 2002; *b* Manchester, 14 Oct. 1965; *s* of John Bosco Kelly and Maureen Olive Kelly; *m* 1992, Sallie Ann Bennett-Jenkins, QC; six *c*. *Educ:* Leeds Poly. Called to the Bar, Gray's Inn, 1988. *Recreations:* Rugby, golf, fishing. *Address:* 2 Hare Court, Temple, EC4Y 7BH. *T:* (020) 7353 5324. *E:* brendankelly@2harecourt.com.

KELLY, Prof. Catriona Helen Moncrieff, DPhil; FBA 2007; Professor of Russian, University of Oxford, since 2002; Fellow, New College, Oxford, since 1996; *b* 6 Oct. 1959; *d* of late Alexander Kelly and (Helen) Margaret Kelly (*née* Moncrieff); *m* 1993, Prof. Ian Thompson. *Educ:* St Hilda's Coll., Oxford (BA 1st cl. Hons Mod. Langs (German and Russian)); DPhil Oxon 1986. Christ Church, Oxford: Sen. Schol., 1983–87; Jun. Res. Fellow, 1987–90; British Acad. Post-Doctoral Fellow, 1990–93; Lectr, SSEES, Univ. of London, 1993–96; University of Oxford: Lectr in Russian, 1996–2002; Co-Dir, European Humanities Res. Centre, 2005–11. Member, Judging Panel: Rossica Prize, 2007; Independent Prize for Foreign Fiction, 2011; Joseph Brodsky/Stephen Spender Prize, 2011, 2012. Gen. Ed., Cambridge Studies in Russian Lit., 1995–2000; Member, Editorial Board: Antropologicheskii forum (Forum for Anthropol. and Culture) (St Petersburg); Kritika; Slavic Review; Eurasia Past and Present. Pres., Assoc. for Slavic, E Eur., and Eurasian Studies, USA, 2015. *Publications:* (ed jtly) Discontinuous Discourses in Modern Russian Literature, 1989; Petrushka, the Russian Carnival Puppet Theatre, 1990; A History of Russian Women's Writing 1820–1992, 1994; (ed) An Anthology of Russian Women's Writing 1777–1992, 1994; (ed with D. Shepherd) Constructing Russian Culture in the Age of Revolution, 1998; (ed with D. Shepherd) Russian Cultural Studies: an introduction, 1998; (ed) Utopias: Russian modernist texts 1905–1940, 1999; (ed with S. Lovell) Russian Literature, Modernism and the Visual Arts, 2000; Refining Russia: advice literature, polite culture and gender from Catherine to Yeltsin, 2001; Russian Literature: a very short introduction, 2001; Comrade Pavlik: the rise and fall of a Soviet boy hero, 2005; Children's World: growing up in Russia 1890–1991, 2007 (Grace Abbott Prize, Soc. for History of Childhood and Youth, USA, 2009); (ed with V. Bezrogov) The Little Town in a Snuffbox: documents on the history of Russian childhood from Nicholas II to Boris Yeltsin, 2 vols, 2008; (ed with M. Bassin), Soviet and Post-Soviet Identities, 2012; (ed jtly) Russian Cultural Anthropology after the Collapse of Communism, 2012; St Petersburg: shadows of the past, 2014; Socialist Churches: radical secularization and the preservation of the past in Petrograd and Leningrad, 1918–1988, 2016; *translations:* Leonid Borodin, The Third Truth, 1989; (contrib.) New Russian Fiction, ed O. Chukhontsev, 1989; Sergei Kaledin, The Humble Cemetery, 1990; (contrib.) Paradise, 1993; (contrib.) The Silk of Time, 1994; (contrib.) An Anthology of Contemporary Russian Women Poets, 2005; (contrib.) The Ties of Blood: Russian literature from the 21st century, 2008; contrib. numerous articles to professional jls and edited books, and reviews in TLS, Guardian, Evening Standard, etc. *Recreations:* freezing in the Atlantic, walking in St Petersburg. *Address:* New College, Oxford OX1 3BN. *T:* (01865) 279502. *E:* catriona.kelly@new.ox.ac.uk.

KELLY, Chris; Chairman, Keltruck Ltd, since 2015; *b* Wolverhampton, 1978; *s* of Chris Kelly and Sonia Kelly. *Educ:* Wolverhampton Grammar Sch.; Oxford Brookes Univ. (BA Hons 1999); Imperial Coll., London (MBA 2003). Keltruck Ltd: Sales and Mktg Exec., 1999–2000; Mktg Manager, 2000–02; non-exec. Dir, 2004–06 and 2010–13; Mktg Dir, 2006–10. MP (C) Dudley S, 2010–15. *Recreations:* swimming, squash, tennis, golf, ski-ing, running. *Address:* Keltruck Ltd, Kenrick Way, West Bromwich, W Midlands B71 4JW.

KELLY, Sir Christopher (William), KCB 2001; Chairman, The King's Fund, since 2010; Senior Independent Director, Co-operative Group, since 2014; *b* 18 Aug. 1946; *s* of late Reginald and Peggy Kelly; *m* 1970, Alison Mary Collens Durant; two *s* one *d*. *Educ:* Beaumont College; Trinity College, Cambridge (MA); Manchester University (MA Econ)). HM Treasury, 1970; Private Sec. to Financial Sec., 1971–73; Sec. to Wilson Cttee of Inquiry into Financial Instns, 1978–80; Under Sec., 1987–97; Dir of Fiscal and Monetary Policy, 1994–95; Dir of Budget and Public Finances, 1995; Hd of Policy Gp, DSS, 1995–97; Permanent Sec., DoH, 1997–2000. Chm., Financial Ombudsman Service, 2005–12 (non-exec. Dir, 2002–12). Chairman: Cttee on Standards in Public Life, 2008–13; Rev. of Co-operative Bank, 2013–14; non-exec. Mem., Office for Budget Responsibility, 2017–. Chairman: NSPCC, 2002–10; TPO Foundn, 2012–17. Mem. Bd, NCC, 2001–08. Trustee, Canal and River Trust, 2017–. Gov., Acland Burghley Sch., 1991–98. *Recreations:* walking, grandchildren.

KELLY, Daniel; QC (Scot.) 2007; Sheriff of South Strathclyde, Dumfries and Galloway at Hamilton, since 2015 (at Airdrie, 2011–15); *b* Dunfermline, 22 Jan. 1958; *s* of Daniel and Madeline Kelly; *m* 1985, Christine Marie MacLeod; three *s* one *d*. *Educ:* Univ. of Edinburgh (LLB Hons); Coll. of Europe, Bruges (Cert. de Hautes Études Européennes). Solicitor, 1981–90; lawyer, Brussels, 1983–84; Procurator Fiscal Depute, 1984–90; Advocate, 1991–2007; Temp. Sheriff, 1997–99; Pt-time Sheriff, 2005–11. Chair, Scottish Child Law Centre, 2007–09. Pres., Sheriffs' Assoc., 2019– (Vice-Pres., 2017–19). Ed., Scots Law Times Sheriff Court Reports, 1992–. *Publications:* Criminal Sentences, 1993; (contrib.) Green's Litigation Styles, 1994; (ed) Scottish Family Law Service, 2010–; various legal articles. *Recreations:* literature, travel, cycling, golf. *Address:* Hamilton Sheriff Court, 4 Beckford Street, Hamilton ML3 0BT. *T:* (01698) 282957, *Fax:* (01698) 201366. *E:* hamilton@scotcourts.gov.uk.

KELLY, Sir David (Robert Corbett), Kt 1996; CBE 1991; Chairman, Kelly Packaging Limited, 1962–99 (Managing Director, 1962–85); Chairman, Conservative Party Committee on Candidates, 1995–2000; *b* 10 Dec. 1936; *s* of late Col Robert Cecil Kelly, TD, DL, JP and Jean Haswell Kelly (*née* Bowran), JP; *m* 1969, Angela Frances Taylor; four *d*. *Educ:* Sedbergh; St John's Coll., Cambridge (Lamor Award; MA). Farm labourer, 1955–56; Nat. Service, Cane of Honour, Mons OCS, 1960; 2nd Lt, 2nd Bn, 7th DEO Gurkha Rifles, 1960–61; 17th (later 4th) Bn, Parachute Regt (9 DLI), TA, 1962–69 (Major); Mil. Mem., TA&VRA for N of England, 1969–75. Board Member: Regl Bd, Brit. Technol. Gp, 1980–84; Northumbrian Water Authy, 1983–89; Washington Develt Corp., 1984–88; NE Industrial Develt Bd, 1989–97. Chm., NE Reg., 1966–67, Industrial Relns Cttee, 1968–71, British Box and Packaging Assoc. Confederation of British Industry: Member: Smaller Firms Council, 1977–83; Regl Council, 1979–86; Council, 1981–83; Industrial Policy Cttee, 1981–83; Mem., Lord Chancellor's Adv. Cttee on Tax Comrs, Tyne and Wear, 1981–93. Contested (C) Gateshead W, 1979. Chm., Northern Area Conservatives, 1990–93; Vice Pres., 1992–95, Pres., 1995–96, Nat. Union of Cons. and Unionist Assocs; Chm., Cons. Pty Conf., 1995; Chm. Trustees, Cons. Agents Benevolent Fund, 2000–15; Trustee, Cons. Agents Superannuation Fund, 2000–15. Mem., Gateshead CHC, 1975–77. President: Gateshead Dispensary Housing Assoc., 1992–2011 (Chm., 1982–92 and 1993–2011); Craigielea Community Nursing Home, 1992–2011 (Chm., 1988–92, and 1993–2011); Gateshead Dispensary Nursing Home (Craigielea) Ltd, 2011–13; Chm., Gateshead Dispensary Trust, 1999–2011 (Trustee, 1965–2011); Trustee, Northumbrian Educnl Trust, 1981–2001 (Chm., 1983–93). Vice Pres., Cancer Bridge, 1999–2001. Exec. Vice Chm., SCF Newcastle City Appeal, 1996–98; Patron, Spirit of Enterprise Appeal, 1997–2000. Chm. Govs, Westfield Sch., 1983–93. *Recreations:* family, country living. *Address:* Stanton Fence, Morpeth, Northumberland NE65 8PP. *T:* (01670) 772236. *E:* stantonfence@hotmail.com. *Club:* Northern Counties (Newcastle upon Tyne).

KELLY, Prof. Deirdre Anne, (Lady Byatt), CBE 2016; DL; MD; FRCP, FRCPI, FRCPCH; Director, Liver Unit, Birmingham Children's Hospital, since 1989 (Medical Director, 2000–07); Hon. Professor of Paediatric Hepatology, University of Birmingham, since 2001; *b* 1 Feb. 1950; *d* of Frank Kelly and Kathleen Kelly (*née* Scannell); *m* 1st, 1973, Miles Parker (marr. diss. 1990); two *s*; 2nd, 1997, Sir Ian (Charles Rayner) Byatt, *qv*. *Educ:* Convent of Holy Child, Killiney, Dublin; TCD (MB BCh BAO 1973; MD 1979; Alumni Award, 2011). FRCPI 1990; FRCP 1995; FRCPCH 1997. Lectr in Medicine, TCD, 1980–82; Wellcome Res. Fellow, Royal Free Hosp., London, 1982–84; Lectr in Child Health, St Bartholomew's Hosp., 1987; Asst Prof. in Pediatrics, Univ. of Nebraska, 1987–89. Chm., Nat. Adv. Commn (formerly Panel) for Enquiry into Child Health, 2004–09; Board Member: Healthcare Commn, 2007–09; Care Quality Commn, 2008–13; Member: Adv. Cttee on Safety of Blood, Tissues and Organs, 2008–12; Adv. Gp on Hepatitis, 2010–15; Prog. Develt Gp, NICE, 2011–12; GMC, 2013–; Chm., NICE Guideline Cttee, 2019–. Associate non-exec. Dir, Royal Wolverhampton NHS Trust, 2013–15; non-exec. Dir, Health Res. Authy, 2015–18. President: Internat. Pediatric Transplant Assoc., 2002–05; British Soc. of Paediatric Gastroenterol., Hepatol. and Nutrition, 2004–07; Eur. Soc. of Paediatric Gastroenterol., Hepatol. and Nutrition, 2007–10; Eur. Fedn of Biliary Atresia Res., 2004–09. Chairman: Cttee of Hepatol., 2001–04, Public Affairs Cttee, 2017–, Eur. Soc. of Paediatric Gastroenterol., Hepatol. and Nutrition; Coll. Specialty Adv. Cttee, RCPCH, 2004–07; Lunar Soc., 2007–09; Clinicians Gp, New Congenital Heart Review, NHS England, 2012–18. Trustee: Breast Cancer UK, 2019–; Archdio. of Birmingham, 2019–. Gov., Health Foundn, 2008–16. Gov., St Martin's Sch., Solihull, 2004–05. DL W Midlands, 2008. Hosp. Dr of the Year, 1991; Lunar Soc. Medal, 2012; Dist. Service Award, Eur. Soc. of Paediatric Gastroenterol., Hepatol. and Nutrition, 2016; Recognition Award, Eur. Assoc. for Study of Liver Disease, 2019. *Publications:* Pediatric Gastroenterology and Hepatology, 1996; Diseases of the Liver and Biliary System in Children, 1999, 4th edn 2017; Paediatric Solid Organ Transplantation, 2000, 2nd edn 2007; Practical Approach to Paediatric Gastroenterology, Hepatology and Nutrition, 2014; Atlas of Pediatric Hepatology, 2018; contribs on clinical and basic sci. related to paediatric liver disease. *Recreations:* gardening, hill-walking, opera, entertaining friends and family. *Address:* Liver Unit, Birmingham Women's and Children's Hospital, Steelhouse Lane, Birmingham B4 6NH. *T:* (0121) 333 8253, *Fax:* (0121) 333 8251. *E:* deirdrekelly@nhs.net.

KELLY, Prof. Francis Patrick, (Frank), CBE 2013; FRS 1989; Professor of the Mathematics of Systems, University of Cambridge, 1990–2018, now Emeritus; Fellow, Christ's College, Cambridge, since 1976 (Master, 2006–16); *b* 28 Dec. 1950; *s* of Francis Kelly and Margaret Kelly (*née* McFadden); *m* 1972, Jacqueline Pullin; two *s*. *Educ:* Cardinal Vaughan Sch.; Van Mildert Coll., Durham (BSc 1971); Emmanuel Coll., Cambridge (Knight Prize 1975; PhD 1976; Hon. Fellow, 2007). Operational Research Analyst, Scicon, 1971–72; Cambridge University: Asst Lectr in Op. Res., Faculty of Engineering, 1976–78; Lectr in Statistical Lab., 1978–86; Reader in Faculty of Maths, 1986–90; Dir, Statistical Lab., 1991–93. Vis. Prof., Stanford Univ., 2001–02. For. Mem., NAE, 2012. Chm., Lindewede Research Ltd, 1987–2011. Non-exec. Dir, Autonomy Corp. plc, 2010–11. Chief Scientific Advr, DfT, 2003–06. Chairman: Council for Mathematical Scis, 2010–13; Adv. Cttee on Maths Educn, 2017–; Scientific Bd, Smith Inst. Mem., Bd of Trustees, RAND Europe, 2008–15. Trustee: Isaac Newton Trust; Applied Probability Trust; Glenfield Trust; Alan Turing Inst. Clifford Paterson Lectr, Royal Soc., 1995; Blackett Lectr, ORS, 1996. CompOR 2006. Foreign Mem. (formerly Associate), NAE, 2012. Hon. DSc: Heriot-Watt, 2001; Eindhoven Univ. of Technol., 2011; Imperial Coll. London, 2015. Rollo Davidson Prize, Cambridge Univ., 1979; Guy Medal in Silver, Royal Statistical Soc., 1989; Lanchester Prize, ORS of Amer., 1992; Naylor Prize, London Math. Soc., 1996; Koji Kobayashi Award, 2005, Alexander Graham Bell Medal, 2015, IEEE; John von Neumann Theory Prize, INFORMS, 2008; Sigmetrics Achievement Award, ACM, 2009; Gold Medal, Assoc. of Eur. Operational Res. Socs, 2009; Beale Medal, ORS, 2011; Saul Gass Expository Writing Award, INFORMS, 2013. *Publications:* Reversibility and Stochastic Networks, 1979, reissued 2011; (ed) Probability, Statistics and Optimization, 1994; (ed jtly) Stochastic Networks, 1995; Mathematical Models in Finance, 1995; Stochastic Networks: theory and application, 1996; (with E. Yudovina) Stochastic Networks, 2014; articles in math. and stat. jls. *Recreations:* golf, ski-ing. *Address:* Statistical Laboratory, Centre for Mathematical Sciences, Wilberforce Road, Cambridge CB3 0WB. *T:* (01223) 337963.

KELLY, Gerard Anthony; Partner, GK & Partners, since 2014; *b* Melton Mowbray, Leics, 10 Nov. 1960; *s* of Joseph Patrick Kelly and Ivy Kelly; *m* 2008, José Eduardo de Castro Oliveira. *Educ:* King Edward VII Upper Sch.; Univ. of Warwick (BA 1983). Times Higher Education Supplement: Journalist, 1991–2002; Dep. Ed., 2002–07; Ed., 2007–08; Ed., TES, 2008–13. Ed. of the Year, PPA, 2011. *Recreation:* food and drink. *Address:* (office) Henry Wood House, 2 Riding House Street, W1W 7FA. *Clubs:* h, Home House, Two Brydges.

KELLY, Graham; *see* Kelly, R. H. G.

KELLY, Iain Charles MacDonald; HM Diplomatic Service, retired; Foreign and Commonwealth Office, 2009–14; *b* 5 March 1949; *s* of Walter John Kelly and Doreen Sylvia Wilkins; *m* 1981, Linda Clare McGovern; two *s*. *Educ:* Cathays High Sch. for Boys; UCW, Aberystwyth (BSc Econ); Univ. of London (DipLib 1974); Army Sch. of Langs. Joined HM Diplomatic Service, 1974; Russian Wing, Army Sch. of Languages, 1975–76; Moscow, 1976–79; Kuala Lumpur, 1979–82; Istanbul, 1986–88; Los Angeles, 1990–92; Moscow, 1992–95; Amsterdam, 1995–98; Sen. Mem., Jesus Coll., Oxford, 1998–99; Ambassador and Consul General, Belarus, 1999–2003; FCO, 2003–07; Sen. Mem., St Antony's Coll., Oxford, 2007; Ambassador to Uzbekistan, 2007–09. FRGS 1999. *Recreations:* early music, privacy. *Clubs:* Highland Soc. of London; Phyllis Court (Henley-on-Thames).

KELLY, Ian Francis; screenwriter, historical biographer, playwright, actor; *b* Cambridge, 16 Jan. 1966; *s* of Prof. Donald Francis Kelly and Patricia Ann Kelly (*née* Holt); *m* 1998, Claire Janette Davies; one *s* one *d*. *Educ:* Backwell Sch., Avon; Calday Grange County Grammar Sch. for Boys, Wirral; Trinity Hall, Cambridge (BA Hist.; Open Exhibn Entrance Schol.); Film Sch., Univ. of Calif, Los Angeles (MA Film, Theater, TV; Schol.). Actor: *theatre* includes: The Changeling, LA, 1989; Pygmalion, Theatr Clywyd, 1991; Arsenic and Old Lace, Salisbury, 1992; A Busy Day, Bristol and King's Head, London, 1993–94, transf.

Bristol Old Vic and Lyric, 2000; Arcadia, Manchester, 2000; Relative Values, UK tour, 2002; Cooking for Kings (also writer), NY, 2004, 2006; Beau Brummell, NY, 2006; The Pitmen Painters, Newcastle, transf. NT, NY and West End, 2008–12 (Performance of the Year, NE Culture Awards, 2009); Mr Foote's Other Leg (also writer), Hampstead Th., transf. Th. Royal Haymarket, 2015; *films* include: Howards End, 1992; In Love and War, 1996; Voina, 2002; Admiral Kolchak, 2008; Creation, 2009; Harry Potter and the Deathly Hallows, Part 1, 2010, Part 2, 2011; The Children Act, 2018; Kingsman 3, 2019; *television* includes: Drop the Dead Donkey, 1998; In a Land of Plenty, 1999; Sensitive Skin, 2005; Beau Brummell, 2006; Downton Abbey, 2009. *Publications:* Cooking for Kings: the life of Antonin Carême, a biography with recipes, 2003; Beau Brummell, 2006 (filmed, 2006); Casanova (Sunday Times Biog. of the Year), 2008 (adapted for ballet with Kenneth Tindall, 2017); Mr Foote's Other Leg: comedy, tragedy and murder in Georgian London, 2012 (Theatre Book of the Year, Soc. for Theatre Res., 2013); (with Dame Vivienne Westwood) Vivienne Westwood, 2014; Mr Foote's Other Leg (playscript), 2015. *Recreations:* my children, art, cooking, gym. *Address:* (agent) Cathy King/Kate Buckley, 42 Management, First Floor, 8 Flitcroft Street, WC2H 8DL. *T:* (020) 7292 0554. *E:* cathyking@42mp.com. *Clubs:* Garrick, Last Tuesday Society.

**KELLY, James Anthony;** Member (Lab) Glasgow, Scottish Parliament, since 2016 (Glasgow Rutherglen, 2007–11); Rutherglen, 2011–16); *b* 23 Oct. 1963; *s* of Frank and Lilian Kelly; *m* 1992, Alexandra Mullan; two *d*. *Educ:* Trinity High Sch., Cambuslang; Glasgow Coll. of Technol. (BSc Computer Information Systems 1985). CIMA 1994. Analyst/programmer, Argyll and Clyde Health Bd, 1985–88; Scottish Power: Analyst/ Programmer, 1988–90; Computer Auditor, 1990–92; Analyst Programmer, 1992–93; Asset Mgt Proj., 1993–95; Finance Officer, 1995–99; Scottish Electricity Settlements, 1999–2004; Business Analyst, SAIC, 2004–07. *Recreations:* running, five-a-side football, golf. *Address:* Scottish Parliament, Edinburgh EH99 1SP. *E:* james.kelly.msp@parliament.scot.

**KELLY, Jane Maureen, (Mrs M. Blanckenhagen);** Founder Patron, Mulberry Centre, West Middlesex University Hospital, since 2000 (Chairman, 2005–08; Trustee, since 2005); *b* 20 Sept. 1948; *d* of late Captain Adrian Morgan Kelly and of Monica Dallas Kelly (*née* Edwards); *m* 1994, Michael Blanckenhagen; three step *d*. *Educ:* Notre Dame High Sch., Sheffield; Univ. of Birmingham (LLB). Admitted solicitor, 1971; solicitor in private practice, England, Hong Kong and Brunei, 1971–79; AMI Healthcare Group plc, 1979–90: legal advr, 1979–83; Co. Sec., 1983–88; Dir, Corporate Health Services, 1988–90; Dir, 1987–90; independent mgt consultant and exec. coach, 1990–. Chairman: W Middx Univ. Hosp. NHS Trust, 1992–2002; NW London Strategic HA, 2002–03; NHS Bd Leadership Prog., 2001–04; London Regl Comr, NHS Appts Commn, 2003–05. Mem. Adv. Cttee, Clinical Excellence Awards, DoH, subseq. DHSC, 2008–. Associate, Centre for Leadership and Mgt, Univ. of York, 1996–2006. Lay Mem., Gen. Council and Register of Osteopaths, 1990–95. Chm., Women in Mgt, 1987–89. Mem. Council, English Nature, 1992–2000. Mem. Council, Brunel Univ. London, 2006–17 (Dep. Chm., 2008–11; Chm., 2011–17; Pro-Chancellor, 2017–). Hon. LLD Brunel, 2018. *Recreations:* family life, wildlife holidays, walking in Italy, theatrical biographies. *Address:* Gable House, 18–24 Turnham Green Terrace, Chiswick, W4 1QP.

*See also Baroness Hollins.*

**KELLY, Prof. Janis Mary;** opera and concert singer (soprano); Professor of Vocal Performance, Royal College of Music, since 2017 (Voice Professor, 2007–17); *b* Glasgow, 30 Dec. 1954; *d* of Peter Crossan Kelly and Maureen Kelly (*née* McCann); *m* 1983, William Ward Veazey; three *d* (triplets). *Educ:* Royal Acad., Inverness; Royal Scottish Acad. of Music and Drama (DRSAMD 1976); Royal Coll. of Music (FRCM 2015). Début, ENO, 1980; Principal Guest Artist: ENO, 1980–; Opera North, 1990–; Grange Park Opera, 1990–; Scottish Opera, 1990–; début: Royal Opera House, 2009; Metropolitan Opera, NY, 2011; LA Opera, 2012. Roles include: Mrs Nixon, in Nixon in China; Violetta, in La Traviata; Magda, in La Rondine; Romilda, in Xerxes; Marschallin, in Der Rosenkavalier; Elizabeth, in Maria Stuarda; title role in Alcina; Countess, in Le Nozze di Figaro; Lady Billows, in Albert Herring; Musetta, Mimi, in La Bohème; Governess, Miss Jessel, in The Turn of the Screw; Sarah, in Clemency; Mrs Lovett, in Sweeney Todd; title role in Prima Donna (world premiere); Christine, in Intermezzo; Hazel, The Perfect American; Berta, in Il barbiere di Siviglia; Sister Helen Prejean, in Dead Man Walking. Director, Così fan tutte, 2001, and Iolanthe, 2003, Grange Park Opera. Volunteer, Wormwood Scrubs Pony Centre. *E:* janismkelly@aol.com.

**KELLY, John Philip,** CMG 2000; LVO 1994; MBE 1984; HM Diplomatic Service, retired; Vice-President, Victoria League for Commonwealth Friendship, since 2007 (Chairman, 2002–07); *b* 25 June 1941; *s* of William Kelly and Norah Kelly (*née* Roche); *m* 1964, Jennifer Anne Beuchert; one *s*. *Educ:* Oatlands Coll., Stillorgan, Dublin; Open Univ. (BA Hons 2013). Joined Foreign Office, 1959; Leopoldville, 1962–65; Cairo, 1965–68; Bonn, 1968–70; FCO, 1970–73; Canberra, 1973–77; Antwerp, 1977–78; FCO, 1978–81; seconded to Dept of Trade, 1981; Grenada, 1982–86; FCO, 1986–89; Dep. Gov., Bermuda, 1989–94; FCO, 1994–96; Gov., Turks and Caicos Islands, 1996–2000. *Recreations:* cruise lecturing, golf, walking, reading. *Address:* The Laurels, 56 Garden Lane, Royston, Herts SG8 9EH. *Club:* Royston Golf (Captain, 2003–04).

**KELLY, Joseph Anthony;** Managing (formerly Editorial) Director, Universe Media Group Ltd (formerly Gabriel Communications), since 1998; Editor, The Universe, since 1995; *b* 10 Aug. 1958; *s* of Terence Christopher Kelly and Catherine Ethel Kelly (*née* Walsh); *m* 1999, Catherine Jane, *d* of William and Margaret Brownlie; two *s*. *Educ:* Presentation Coll., Reading; Ruskin Coll., Oxford; Univ. of Manchester (MA Theol. 2004). Associate, Instn of Buyers, 1980. Sen. Buyer, Church & Co., Reading, 1979–81; Buyer, J. Sainsbury, Reading, 1981–82; freelance photo-journalist, 1984–91; Editor: Welsh Arts Council Lit. Rev., 1991–94; Deeside Midweek Leader, 1991–92; Dep. Editor, Wrexham Leader, 1992–93; Ed., Country Quest (mag. for Wales), 1993; Dep. Ed., The Universe, 1994; Editor: Catholic Life mag., 1995, 1998–2006; School Building mag., 2004–05; Urban Building mag., 2006; Church Building mag., 2006–. Chm., NW Region, Soc. of Editors, 1999; Vice Chm., Catholic Writers' Guild (North), 2002–03. Member: Historic Bldgs Adv. Council for Wales, 2008–10; Christian Assoc. of Business Execs, 2008–; MInstD 2009. Gov., RNLI, 1997–; Foundn Gov., St Richard Gwyn RC High Sch., Flint, 2002–10. Associate Mem., RIBA, 2008–. Photo-journalism Award, Irish Post, 1981. *Publications:* From Sulham Head, Collected Poems, 1980; The Pendulum, 1982. *Recreations:* hill-walking, ecclesiastical history, photography. *Address:* c/o Universe Media Group Ltd, 2nd Floor, Oakland House, 76 Talbot Road, Old Trafford, Manchester M16 0PQ. *T:* (office) (0161) 820 5722. *Club:* Frontline.

**KELLY, Judith Pamela, (Jude),** CBE 2015 (OBE 1997); Artistic Director, South Bank Centre, 2005–18; Chair, Metal, since 2005 (Artistic Director, 2002–05); *b* 24 March 1954; *d* of John Kelly and Ida Kelly; *m* 1993, Michael Bird (known professionally as Michael Birch); one *s* one *d*. *Educ:* Calder High Sch.; Birmingham Univ. (BA 2nd Cl. Hons). Freelance singer (folk and jazz), 1970–75; artistic director, 1975–76; Founder Dir, Solent People's Theatre, 1976–80; Artistic Dir, Battersea Arts Centre, 1980–85; Dir of Plays, Nat. Theatre of Brent, 1982–85; freelance dir, 1986–88; Festival Dir, York Fest. and Mystery Plays, 1986–88; Artistic Dir, 1988–2002, Chief Exec., 1993–2002, West Yorkshire Playhouse. Major productions include: West Yorkshire Playhouse: Merchant of Venice, 1994; Beatification of Area Boy, 1996 (also NY and Eur. tour); The Seagull, The Tempest, 1998; Singin' in the Rain, 1999, 2001 (also RNT, 2000; Olivier Award, 2001); Half a Sixpence, 2000; Sarcophagus, RSC, 1986; When We Are Married, Chichester Fest. Th., transf. Savoy, 1996; Othello, Shakespeare Th., Washington, 1997; English National Opera: The Elixir of Love, 1997; On the Town, 2005; The Wizard of Oz, RFH, 2008. British Rep. on culture for UNESCO, 1997–99. Visiting Professor of Drama: Leeds Univ.; Kingston Univ. Chair: Common Purpose Charitable Trust, 1997–2010; QCA, 2001–03. Chm., London 2012 Olympic Cttee for Culture, Educn and Ceremonies, 2004–09; Vice-Chm., Nat. Adv. Cttee on Creative and Cultural Educn, 1998–2000; Member: Council, RSA, 1998–2000; ITC, 1999–2004; Bd, British Council. Member Board: Liverpool Biennale, 2004–06; Cultural Olympiad; New Deal of the Mind; Mem., Dishaa Adv. Gp; Chair, World Book Night. Hon. Fellow, Dartington Coll. of Arts, 1999. Hon. Prof., York Univ., 2000. Hon. DLitt: Leeds Metropolitan, 1995; Bradford, 1996; Hon. LitD Leeds, 2000; DUniv Open, 2001; Hon. Dr: Birmingham, 2011; Loughborough, 2011; Goldsmiths, 2011. *Recreation:* wind-surfing.

**KELLY, Julian Thomas;** Chief Financial Officer, NHS Executive Group, since 2019; *b* London, 28 Dec. 1970; *s* of Justin and Valerie Kelly; *m* 1995, Katie Wilkins; four *d*. *Educ:* Lancaster Royal Grammar Sch.; Trinity Coll., Oxford (BA Hons Modern Langs). ACMA 2011. Policy Advr, HM Treasury, 1995–2000; on secondment, Treasury and Mkts Div., HSBC, 2000–02; Sen. Policy Advr, Prime Minister's Strategy Unit, Cabinet Office, 2002–03; Dep. Dir for Home Affairs, HM Treasury, 2003–07; Dir of Finance, UK Border Agency, Home Office, 2008–11; Finance Dir, 2011–12, Dir, Public Spending, 2012–14, HM Treasury; Dir Gen., Public Spending and Finance, HM Treasury, 2014–17; Dir Gen., Nuclear, MoD, 2017–19. *Recreations:* running, tennis, family.

**KELLY, Rt Hon. Dame Kathryn Mary;** *see* Thirlwall, Rt Hon. Dame K. M.

**KELLY, Laurence Charles Kevin,** FRSL; FRGS; non-executive Director, 1972–93, and Vice-Chairman, 1988–93, Helical Bar PLC (Deputy Chairman, 1981–84; Chairman, 1984–88); *b* 11 April 1933; *s* of late Sir David Kelly, GCMG, MC, and Lady Kelly (*née* Jourda de Vaux); *m* 1963, (Alison) Linda McNair Scott (*d* 2019); one *s* two *d*. *Educ:* Downside Sch.; New Coll., Oxford (Beresford Hope Schol.; MA Hons). Lieut, The Life Guards, 1949–52; served (temp.) Foreign Office, 1955–56; Guest, Keen and Nettlefolds, 1956–72; Director: GKN International Trading Ltd, 1972–77; Morganite International Ltd, 1984–91; KAE, subseq. Mintel, Ltd, 1980–2003; Chm., Queenborough Steel Co., 1980–89. Member: Northern Ireland Development Agency, 1972–78; Monopolies and Mergers Commn, 1982–89. Chairman, Opera da Camera Ltd (charity), 1981–87; Trustee: Apollo Foundn, 1984–2013; Choir of Carmelite Priory, Kensington (charity), 1997–2015. Vice-Chm., British Iron and Steel Consumers' Council, 1976–85. Sen. Associate Mem., St Antony's Coll., Oxford, 1985–91. FRGS 1972; FRSL 2003. Gen. Ed., Travellers' Companion series, 2004–. *Publications:* Lermontov, Tragedy in the Caucasus, 1978 (Cheltenham Literary Prize, 1979); (ed) St Petersburg, a Travellers' Anthology, 1981; (ed) Moscow, a Travellers' Anthology, 1983; Istanbul, a Travellers' Anthology, 1987; (with Linda Kelly) Proposals, 1989; Diplomacy and Murder in Teheran: Alexander Griboyedov and Imperial Russia's mission to the Shah of Persia, 2001; reviews, TLS, etc. *Recreation:* opera-going. *Address:* 44 Ladbroke Grove, W11 2PA. *T:* (020) 7727 4663. *Clubs:* Beefsteak, Brooks's, Turf; Kildare Street and University (Dublin).

**KELLY, Linda Mary;** Chief Executive, Lloyds TSB Foundation for England and Wales, 2006–12; *b* 2 Jan. 1955; *d* of John Nicholl Millar and Vicenta Amy Gibson Millar (*née* Smith); *m* 1987, Brian James Kelly; two *d*. *Educ:* Nottingham Univ. (BPharm Hons); Sch. of Oriental and African Studies, Univ. of London (Postgrad. Dip 2014; MA 2019). MRPharmS. Basic grade pharmacist, 1977–78; various appts in med. information, clin. trials, mkt res. and product mgt, Merck Sharpe & Dohme Ltd, 1978–87; New Product Planning Manager, 1987–88, Mktg Dir, 1988–91, Smith Kline Beecham; Man. Dir, Bristol Myers Squibb (UK and Ireland), 1991–95; Pres., Astra Pharmaceuticals Ltd (UK), 1995–99; Chief Exec., Parkinson's Disease Soc., 2001–05. FRSA 2003. *Recreations:* the arts, walking.

**KELLY, Dame Lorna (May) B.;** *see* Boreland-Kelly.

**KELLY, Mandi N.;** *see* Norwood, M.

**KELLY, Matthias John;** QC 1999; SC (Ire.) 2005; a Recorder, since 2002; *b* 21 April 1954; *s* of Ambrose and Annie Kelly; *m* 1979, Helen Holmes; one *s* one *d*. *Educ:* St Patrick's Secondary Modern; St Patrick's Acad., Dungannon; Trinity Coll., Dublin (BA Mod., LLB); Council of Legal Educn London. Called to the Bar, Gray's Inn, 1979, Bencher, 2002; in practice as Barrister, 1979–; called to Irish Bar, Belfast and Dublin, 1983; admitted Attorney: NY Bar, 1986; US Federal Bar, 1987; Consultant to EU Commn on UK Health and Safety Law, 1994–96. Examiner of the High Court, 2018–. Mem., Inter-Disciplinary Wkg Pty on Actuarial Tables (Ogden Tables), 1997–2003. Chairman: Personal Injuries Bar Assoc., 2001–02; Bar Council (England and Wales), 2003 (Mem., 1998–2003; Vice Chm., 2002; Chm., Public Affairs Gp, 2001; Chm., Policy Gp, 2000). Accredited mediator, 2008. Chairman: End the Vagrancy Act Campaign, 1989–93; Alcohol Recovery Project, 1993–96. FRSA 2003. *Publications:* (ed jtly) Personal Injury Manual, 1997, 2nd edn 2001, (contrib.) 3rd edn 2007; (contrib.) Munkman Employer's Liability, 13th edn 2001; (contrib.) Personal Injury and Wrongful Death Damages Calculations: a transatlantic dialogue, 2009; (contrib.) The Rights and Aspirations of the Magna Carta, 2016; articles in legal jls. *Recreations:* walking, reading, cycling, theatre, travel, life, family. *Address:* 39 Essex Chambers, 81 Chancery Lane, WC2A 1DD. *T:* (020) 7832 1111. *E:* clerks@39essex.com; Merchants Quay Chambers, 25–26 Merchants Quay, Dublin 8, Ireland. *T:* (1) 7079031, (87) 7746446.

**KELLY, Dr Michael,** CBE 1983; JP; DL; Managing Director, Michael Kelly Associates, since 1984; Chairman, ILI Group plc, since 2018; columnist, Scotsman, 1996–2001 and 2011–15; *b* 1 Nov. 1940; *s* of David and Marguerite Kelly; *m* 1965, Zita Harkins; one *s* two *d*. *Educ:* Univ. of Strathclyde (BScEcon, PhD). FCIM (FInstM 1988). Asst Lectr in Economics, Univ. of Aberdeen, 1965–67; Lectr in Economics, Univ. of Strathclyde, 1967–84. Councillor: Anderston Ward Corp. of Glasgow, 1971–75 (Convener, Schools and Sch. Welfare; Vice-Convener, Transport); Hillington Ward, Glasgow Dist, 1977–84 (Chairman: General Purposes Cttee; Buildings and Property Cttee); Lord Provost of Glasgow, 1980–84 (masterminded "Glasgow's Miles Better" Campaign); Campaign Dir, Edinburgh—Count Me In, 1987–89. Rector, Univ. of Glasgow, 1984–87. Director: Celtic Football Club, 1990–94; Intelligent Land Investments Ltd, 2009–18. Chm., Children 1st (formerly RSSPCC), 1987–96; Member: Scottish Cttee, NACF, 1990–93; ESRC External Relns Adv. Gp (formerly Media Relns Cttee), 2000–. Founding Editor, Jl Economic Studies, 1965. BBC Radio Scotland News Quiz Champion, 1986, 1987. Presenter, Clyde 2 Talk-In, 1997–2000; regular commentator: BBC Newsnight Scotland, 2010–; Scotland Tonight; Radio Scotland. Hon. Mem., Clan Donald, USA; Hon. Mayor, Tombstone, Ariz; Hon. Citizen: Illinois; San José; St Petersburg; Kansas City; Dallas; Fort Worth; Winnipeg. JP Glasgow 1973; DL Glasgow 1984. Hon. LLD Glasgow, 1984. Glasgow Herald Scot of the Year, 1983. OStJ 1983. Knight's Star, Order of Merit (Poland), 1998. *Publications:*

Studies in the British Coal Industry, 1970; Paradise Lost: the struggle for Celtic's soul, 1994; London Lines, 1996. *Recreations:* photography, ski-ing, golf (Mem. Cttee, Pollok Golf Club, 2009–12; Convenor, Marketing Cttee, 2012–; Winner, Senior Foursomes, 2017). *Address:* 6/5 Mains Avenue, Giffnock G46 6QY. *T:* (0141) 638 0811.

**KELLY, Prof. Michael Joseph,** FRS 1993; FREng; FInstP, FIET; Prince Philip Professor of Technology, University of Cambridge, 2002–16, now Emeritus; Fellow of Trinity Hall, Cambridge, 1974–81, 1989–92 and 2002–16, now Emeritus; *b* New Plymouth, NZ, 14 May 1949; *s* of late Steve and Mary Constance Kelly; *m* 1991, Ann Elizabeth Taylor, BA, *d* of late Dr Daniel Brumhall Cochrane Taylor; one *d*. *Educ:* Francis Douglas Meml Coll., New Plymouth, NZ; Victoria Univ. of Wellington (BSc Hons 1970; MSc 1971); Gonville and Caius Coll., Univ. of Cambridge (PhD 1974); Trinity Hall, Cambridge (MA 1975; ScD 1994). FInstP 1988; FIET (FIEE 1989); FREng (FEng 1998). IBM Res. Fellow, Univ. of Calif., Berkeley, 1975–76; SRC Advanced Fellow, Cavendish Lab., 1977–81; Mem., Research Staff, GEC Hirst Res. Centre, 1981–92, Co-ordinator, GEC Superlattice Res., 1984–92; University of Surrey: Prof. of Physics and Electronics, 1992–96; Hd of Dept of Electronic and Electrical Engrg, 1996; Hd of Sch. of Electronic Engrg, Inf. Technol. and Maths, then Sch. of Electronics, Computing and Maths, 1997–2001; Hd of Advanced Technol. Inst. and Dir, Centre for Solid State Electronics, 2001–02; Exec. Dir, Cambridge-MIT Inst., 2003–05; Chief Scientific Advr, DCLG, 2006–09. Vis. Scientist, Cavendish Lab., 1988–92; Royal Soc./SERC Industrial Fellow, 1989–91; Erskine Fellow, Univ. of Canterbury, NZ, 1999. Non-executive Director: Surrey Satellite Technol. Ltd, 1997–2002; Laird Gp, 2006–. Mem. Council, Royal Soc., 2001–02. Mem. Council, Univ. of Surrey, 1996–2002; Mem. Council, 1997–2001, Vice-Pres., 2001–05, Inst. of Physics. MAE 2009. Hon. FRSNZ 1999–2018. Hon. ScD Victoria Univ. of Wellington, 2002. Royal Soc. Rutherford Meml Lectr, NZ, 2000. Paterson Medal and Prize, Inst. of Physics, 1989; GEC Nelson Gold Medal, 1991; Silver Medal, Royal Acad. Engrg, 1999; Hughes Medal, Royal Soc., 2006. *Publications:* (ed jtly) The Physics and Fabrication of Microstructures and Microdevices, 1986; Low Dimensional Semiconductors, 1995; numerous papers and review articles on semiconductor physics-for-devices and nat. energy use and policies in scientific jls. *Recreations:* music, literature, travel. *Address:* Department of Engineering, University of Cambridge, Electronic Engineering Division, CAPE Building, 9 J. J. Thomson Avenue, Cambridge CB3 0FA. *T:* (01223) 748303, *Fax:* (01223) 748348. *E:* mjk1@cam.ac.uk.

**KELLY, Owen,** QPM 1987; Director, Webb Estate Ltd, since 2004; UK Director, Fairfax International Corporation, Virginia, USA, 1994–2001; *b* 10 April 1932; *s* of Owen Kelly and Anna Maria (*née* Hamill); *m* 1957, Sheila Ann (*née* McCarthy); five *s*. *Educ:* St Modan's High School, St Ninians, Stirlingshire. National Service, RAF, 1950–52; Metropolitan Police in all ranks from Police Constable to Commander, 1953–82; Asst and Dep. to Comr of Police for City of London, 1982–85; Comr of Police for City of London, 1985–93; created secure zone in City of London (Ring of Steel) for prevention of terrorist activity, July 1993, and scheme continues. 18th Senior Command Course, Nat. Police Coll., 1981; Graduate, 14th Session of Nat. Exec. Inst., FBI, USA, 1991. Mem., Police Disciplinary Appeals Bd, Home Office, 1994–2000. Mem. Panel, Ind. Enquiry into death of Christopher Edwards in HM Prison, Chelmsford, 1996; Special Advr to Ind. Enquiry into death of PC Nina MacKay, 1998. Hon. Sec., Chief Constables' Club, 1989–93. Chm., City of London Br., Leukaemia Res. Fund, 1985–93. Chm., Probus, Purley, 2013–14. Freeman, City of London, 1984. CStJ 1987 (OStJ 1986). Commendation, Order of Civil Merit, Spain, 1986; Ordre du Wissam Alouite Class III, Morocco, 1987; Ordre du Mérite, Senegal, 1988; Ordem do Merito, Class III (Portugal), 1993. *Publications:* contrib. Police Review and Policing. *Recreations:* enjoying the society of a large family, do-it-yourself house maintenance, reading, cycling, hill walking. *Address:* c/o City of London Police HQ, 37 Wood Street, EC2P 2NQ.

**KELLY, Philip Charles;** City Treasurer, then Director of Resources and Chief Finance Officer, Liverpool City Council, 1986–2000; *b* 23 Aug. 1948; *s* of late Charles and Irene May Kelly; *m* 1971, Pamela (*née* Fagan); one *s* two *d*. *Educ:* Inst. of Science and Technology, Univ. of Wales (BSc Econ). DipM; CIPFA. Market Research, British Steel Corp., 1970–72; Economist, Coventry City Council, 1972–74; Technical Officer, 1974–78, Asst Dir of Finance, 1978–82, Kirklees MDC; Dep. City Treasurer, Liverpool City Council, 1982–86; Treas., Merseyside Fire and Civil Defence Authy, 1986–2003. *Recreations:* family, National Observer with Institute of Advanced Motorists, Sefton Gp.

**KELLY, Philip John;** former journalist and political consultant; *b* 18 Sept. 1946; *s* of late William Kelly and Mary Winifred Kelly; *m* 1988, Dorothy Margaret Jones; two *s*. *Educ:* St Mary's Coll., Crosby; Leeds Univ. (BA Hons Politics). Freelance journalist and PR consultant, 1970–87; Editor, Tribune, 1987–91; Press Officer to Michael Meacher, MP, 1991–92. Director: Grandfield Public Affairs, 1995–98; Butler Kelly Ltd, 1998–2010. Co-Founder: Leveller, 1976; State Research, 1977; Chair, London Freelance Br., NUJ, 1983. Councillor (Lab) London Borough of Islington, 1984–86, 1990–98 (Chm., Educn Cttee, 1993–97; Dep. Leader, 1997–98), 2006–14 (Mayor of Islington, 2011–12). Contested (Lab) Surrey SW, 1992. *Recreations:* railways, model railways, Arsenal FC. *Address:* 56 Windsor Road, N7 6JL. *T:* (020) 7272 9093. *E:* philkelly46@gmail.com.

**KELLY, (Robert Henry) Graham;** freelance writer and broadcaster; Chief Executive/General Secretary of the Football Association, 1989–98; *b* 23 Dec. 1945; *s* of Thomas John Kelly and Emmie Kelly; *m* 1st, 1970, Elizabeth Anne Wilkinson (marr. diss. 1996); one *s* one *d*; 2nd, 1999, Romayne Armstrong (marr. diss. 2003); 3rd, 2004, Jeanette Bailey. *Educ:* Baines Grammar Sch., Poulton-le-Fylde. FCIS 1973. Barclays Bank, 1964–68; Football League, 1968–88, Sec., 1979–88. Trustee, Football Grounds Improvement Trust, 1985–88. Chm., Fylde and Wyre Older People's Strategic Partnership Bd, 2007–09.

**KELLY, Rt Hon. Ruth (Maria);** PC 2004; Pro Vice-Chancellor, Research and Enterprise, St Mary's University, Twickenham, since 2015; *b* 9 May 1968; *d* of late Bernard James Kelly and of Gertrude Anne Kelly (*née* Murphy); *m* 1996, Derek John Gadd; one *s* three *d*. *Educ:* Queen's Coll., Oxford (BA PPE); London School of Economics (MSc Econs). Economics Writer, The Guardian, 1990–94; Bank of England: Dep. Head, Inflation Report Div., 1994–96; Manager, Special Projects Div., 1997. MP (Lab) Bolton W, 1997–2010. PPS to Minister of Agric., Fisheries and Food, 1998–2001; Economic Sec., 2001–02, Financial Sec., 2002–04, HM Treasury; Minister of State, Cabinet Office, 2004; Secretary of State: for Educn and Skills, 2004–06; for Communities and Local Govt, 2006–07; Minister for Women, 2006–07; Sec. of State for Transport, 2007–08. Mem., Treasury Select Cttee, 1997–98. Sen. Manager, Strategy for Global Businesses, HSBC, 2010–11; various roles, 2011–12, Global Hd of Client Strategy, 2012–15, HSBC Global Asset Mgt. Non-executive Director: Nat. Grid, 2011–17; Financial Conduct Authy, 2016–19; Heathrow Airport Hldgs, 2019–. *Recreations:* walking, family.

**KELLY, Samuel Thomas, (Tom),** CB 2008; Director of Strategic Stakeholder Engagement, HS2, since 2018 (Strategic Communications Adviser, 2014–18); *b* Belfast, 8 July 1955; *s* of late Monty Kelly and of Mary Kelly; *m* 2003, Linda; two *s* two *d*. *Educ:* Royal Belfast Academical Instn; Univ. of Birmingham. Trainee journalist, Belfast Telegraph, 1979–81; Press Officer, NI Housing Exec., 1981–82; joined BBC, 1982: reporter, producer, asst ed., Radio and Current Affairs, NI, 1982–87; Producer, Newsnight, 1987–88; Political Ed., NI, 1988–91; Ed., NI News, 1992–95; Asst Ed., World at One, 1995–96; Actg Ed., Talkback prog., Radio Ulster, 1996–97; Dir of Communications, NI Office, 1998–2001; Prime Minister's Official Spokesman, 2001–07; Dir, Corporate Affairs, BAA Ltd, 2008–10; Director of Communications: FSA, 2010–11; Network Rail, 2011–14. Non-exec. Dir, DECC, 2014–16. *Recreations:* spending time with my family, gardening, beach walking, reading, music, watching Rugby when I can.

**KELLY, Stephen Paul;** Chief Executive Officer, Sage Group plc, 2014–18; 30 Dec. 1961; *m* 1987, Siobhan O'Sullivan; three *d*. *Educ:* Bath Univ. (BSc Hons 1984). Manager, ICL, 1984–88; Dir, Oracle, 1988–97; Chief Operating Officer, 1997–2001, Chief Exec. Officer, 2001–05, Chordiant Software Inc.; CEO, Microfocus Internat. Ltd, 2006–10; Chief Operating Officer for Govt and Hd, Efficiency and Reform Gp, Cabinet Office, 2012–14. UK Business Ambassador, 2015–. Hon. DBA Bath, 2016.

**KELLY, Susan;** *see* Hamilton, Her Honour S.

**KELLY, Tom;** *see* Kelly, S. T.

**KELMAN, James;** novelist, short story writer, occasional essayist and dramatist; *b* Glasgow, 9 June 1946. *Publications:* An Old Pub Near the Angel (short stories), 1973; (jtly) Three Glasgow Writers, 1975; Short Tales from the Nightshift, 1978; Not, Not While the Giro (short stories), 1983; The Busconductor Hines, 1984; A Chancer, 1985; (jtly) Lean Tales, 1985; Greyhound for Breakfast (Cheltenham Prize), 1987; A Disaffection (James Tait Black Meml Prize), 1989; The Burn (short stories), 1991; Hardie and Baird and Other Plays, 1991; Some Recent Attacks: essays cultural and political, 1992; How Late it Was, How Late (Booker Prize), 1994; The Good Times (short stories), 1998; Translated Accounts, 2001; Selected Stories, 2001; And the Judges Said… (essays), 2002; You have to be careful in the Land of the Free, 2004; Kieron Smith, Boy (Saltire Soc. Scottish Book of the Year Award), 2008; If It Is Your Life, 2010; Mo Said She Was Quirky (Saltire Soc. Scottish Book of the Year Award), 2012; Dirt Road, 2016. *Address:* c/o Rodgers, Coleridge and White, 20 Powis Mews, W11 1JN.

**KELNER, Simon;** Chief Executive Officer, Seven Dials Ltd, since 2013; *b* 9 Dec. 1957; *m* 1st, 1988, Karen Bowden (marr. diss. 2001); one *d*; 2nd, 2001, Sally Ann Lasson (marr. diss. 2015). *Educ:* Bury Grammar Sch.; Preston Poly. Trainee reporter, Neath Guardian, 1976–79; sports reporter, Extel, 1979–80; Sports Ed., Kent Evening Post, 1980–83; Asst Sports Ed., Observer, 1983–86; Dep. Sports Ed., Independent, 1986–89; Sports Editor: Sunday Correspondent, 1989–90; Observer, 1990–91; Ed., Observer Mag., 1991–93; Sports Ed., Independent on Sunday, 1993–95; Night Ed., 1995, Features Ed., 1995–96, Independent; Ed., Night & Day mag., Mail on Sunday, 1996–98; Ed.-in-Chief, The Independent and The Independent on Sunday, 1998–2008 and 2010–11; Man. Dir and Ed.-in-Chief, The Independent, 2008–10; CEO, Journalism Foundn, 2011–13. Vis. Fellow, Univ. of Gloucestershire, 2008–. Hon. Fellow, Univ. of Central Lancashire, 1999. Hon. DLitt: Bolton, 2008; Ulster, 2013. Ed. of the Year, What the Papers Say Awards, 1999 and 2003; Edgar Wallace Award, London Press Club, 2000; Ed. of the Year, GQ Awards, 2004, 2010; Media Achiever of the Year, Campaign Media Awards, 2004; Marketeer of the Year, Marketing Week Effectiveness Awards, 2004; Editorial Intelligence Comment Award, 2010. *Publications:* To Jerusalem and Back, 1996. *Clubs:* Groucho; Swinton Rugby League Supporters; Sunningdale Golf.

**KELSALL, John Arthur Brooks,** MA; Headmaster, Brentwood School, Essex, 1993–2004; *b* 18 June 1943; *o s* of late Joseph Brooks Kelsall and Dorothy Kelsall (*née* Bee); *m* 1965, Dianne Scott Woodward, *o d* of Rev. William James Vaughan Woodward and Jean Ewart Woodward; one *s* one *d*. *Educ:* Royal Grammar Sch., Lancaster; Emmanuel Coll., Cambridge (BA 1965; MA 1969). Head of Economics, King Edward VII Sch., Lytham St Annes, 1965–68; Head of Geography, Whitgift Sch., Croydon, 1968–78; Dep. Headmaster, 1978–81, Headmaster, 1981–87, Bournemouth Sch.; Headmaster, Arnold Sch., Blackpool, 1987–93. *Recreations:* golf, fell-walking, opera, ornithology. *Club:* Cretingham Golf.

**KELSEY, Linda;** journalist and author; *b* 15 April 1952; *d* of Samuel Cohen and Rhona (*née* Fox); *m* 1st, 1972 (marr. diss. 1980); 2nd, 1999, Christian Testorf (marr. diss 2013); one *s*. *Educ:* Woodhouse Grammar Sch., N12; Birkbeck, Univ. of London (BA Arts and Humanities 2015). Sub-editor, Good Housekeeping, 1970–72; Features Editor, Cosmopolitan, 1975–78; Deputy Editor: Company, 1978–81; Options, 1981–82; Cosmopolitan, 1983–85, Editor, 1985–89; Editor, She magazine, 1989–95; Editor at Large, Nat. Magazine Co., 1996–98; Consultant Ed., Parkhill Publishing, 1999–2000; Exec. Ed., In Style, 2000–02; freelance writer, 2002–; columnist, Daily Telegraph, 2008–, Daily Mail, 2009–. Editor of the Year Award: PPA, 1989, for Cosmopolitan; Brit. Soc. Mag. Editors, 1990, for She. *Publications:* Was it Good for You, Too?, 2003; Fifty is Not a Four-letter Word (novel), 2007; The Secret Lives of Sisters (novel), 2008; The Twenty Year Itch (novel), 2010. *Recreations:* reading, walking, theatre, film, family.

**KELSEY, Timothy Claude;** Chief Executive Officer, Australian Digital Health Agency, since 2016; *b* Welwyn Garden City, 7 May 1965; *s* of late Col Michael Kelsey, TD, ADC and of Dr Anthea Kelsey; four *s* with Alison Kelsey; two *s* with Hilary Rowell. *Educ:* Wellington Coll.; Magdalene Coll., Cambridge (BA Hons Hist. 1987; Exhibnr; MA). Foreign corresp., Turkey, Independent, 1988–90; reporter, Independent on Sunday, 1990–95; Sunday Times: Insight Team, 1995–97; Focus Ed., 1997–98; News Ed., 1998–2000; CEO, Dr Foster, 2000–06; Chm., Exec. Bd, Dr Foster Intelligence, 2006–10; Sen. Expert, McKinsey & Co., 2010–12; on secondment as UK Govt advr on transparency and open data policy, Efficiency and Reform Gp, 2011; Exec. Dir, Transparency and Open Data, Efficiency and Reform Gp, Cabinet Office, 2012; Nat. Dir for Patients and Information, NHS England (formerly NHS Commissioning Bd), 2012–15; Nat. Information Dir and Chair, Nat. Information Bd for Health and Care in England, 2014–15; Commercial Dir, Telstra Health, Melbourne, 2016. Prog. Dir, NHS Choices, 2006–08. Member: Nat. Quality Bd, 2009–12; 2020 Public Services Commn, 2009–11. Trustee, Nuffield Trust, 2008–14. *Publications:* Dervish: invention of modern Turkey, 1996; (with Roger Taylor) Transparency and the Open Society, 2016. *Recreations:* my family, jazz, sailing, writing. *W:* www.twitter.com/tkelsey1. *Club:* Bayview Yacht Racing (NSW).

**KELSON, Peter John;** QC 2001; His Honour Judge Kelson; a Circuit Judge, since 2010; *b* 7 March 1959; *s* of Gordon Charles and Patricia Sylvia Kelson; *m* 1982, Rosalind Margaret Clark; two *s*. *Educ:* Sheffield Univ. (LLB Hons). Called to the Bar, Middle Temple, 1981; Recorder, 1997–2010; Hd of Chambers, 2004–10. *Recreations:* golf, piano, chess, travel, music. *Address:* Sheffield Combined Court Centre, The Law Courts, 50 West Bar, Sheffield S3 8PH. *Club:* Sickleholme Golf (Derbys).

**KELTZ, Jennie, (Mrs James Keltz);** *see* Bond, J.

**KEMAKEZA, Allan;** Speaker, Solomon Islands Parliament, 2010–14; *b* 11 Oct. 1950; *m* Joycelyn; two *s* three *d*. *Educ:* Police Acad.; CID Course, W Yorks Metropolitan Police; VIP Protection Course, Fed. Police Coll., Canberra. Royal Solomon Is Police Force, 1972–88: Constable; Asst Superintendent of Police; ADC to Governor-Gen.; Hd of CID; Sen. SO to Comr of Police; Asst to Comr of Police Admin. MP (People's Alliance) Savo/Russel, Solomon Is, 1989–2010; Minister: for Police and Justice, 1989–90; for Housing and

Govt Services, 1991–93; for Forests, Envmt and Conservation, 1995–96; for Nat. Unity, Reconciliation and Peace, and Dep. Prime Minister, 2000–01; Prime Minister, 2001–06; Dep. Speaker of Parlt, 2006–07; Minister of Forestry, 2007–10. Dep. Leader of Opposition, 1993–94, Leader, 1997–99. *Recreations:* reading, fishing, farming.

**KEMBALL, Air Marshal Sir (Richard) John,** KCB 1990; CBE 1981; DL; FRAeS; Co-ordinator of British-American Community Relations, Ministry of Defence, 1994–2004; Chief Executive, Racing Welfare, 1995–2004; *b* 31 Jan. 1939; *s* of Richard and Margaret Kemball; *m* 1962, Valerie Geraldine Webster; two *d*. *Educ:* Uppingham; Open Univ. (BA 1990). Commissioned RAF, 1957; OC No 54 Squadron, 1977; OC RAF Laarbruch, 1979; Commandant, CFS, 1983–85; Comdr, British Forces, Falkland Islands, 1985–86; COS and Dep. C-in-C, Strike Command and UK Air Forces, 1989–93. ADC to HM The Queen, 1984–85. Chm., Essex Rivers Healthcare NHS Trust, 1993–95. Hon. Col, 77 Engr Regt (V), 1993–96. President: RAFA, 1995–98 (Vice-Pres., 1993–95; Life Vice-Pres., 1998); Corps of Commissionaires, 2002–08 (Gov., 1993–2008). Pres., Southend Br., RAeS, 1999–2009. Freeman, City of London, 1995. DL 1999, High Sheriff, 2007–08, Suffolk. FRAeS 2003. *Recreations:* country pursuits, tennis, cricket, gardening. *Address:* c/o HSBC, 46 Market Hill, Sudbury, Suffolk CO10 6ES. *Club:* Royal Air Force.

**KEMBER, William Percy,** FCA; FCT; Group Financial Controller, British Telecommunications, 1981–92; *b* 12 May 1932; *s* of late Percy Kember and Mrs Q. A. Kember, Purley, Surrey; *m* 1982, Lynn Kirkham. *Educ:* Uppingham. Chartered Accountant; Corporate Treasurer. Various posts with Royal Dutch/Shell Group in Venezuela, 1958–63; British Oxygen Co., 1963–67; Coopers & Lybrand, 1967–72; Post Office (Telecommunications), 1972–81. Director: Centel Financial Systems Inc., 1983–86; Marshalls Finance, 1991–98. Visitor, Royal Institution, 1977–79, Chm., 1979. *Recreation:* bridge. *Address:* 83 Hillway, N6 6AB. *Clubs:* Royal Automobile; Highgate Golf, Royal Dornoch Golf.

**KEMP,** family name of **Viscount Rochdale**.

**KEMP, Prof. Alexander George,** OBE 2006; FRSE; Professor of Petroleum Economics, University of Aberdeen, since 1983; *b* Aberdeenshire, 27 Oct. 1939; *s* of Alexander Rae Kemp and Emily Kemp. *Educ:* Skene Primary Sch.; Robert Gordon's Coll., Aberdeen; Univ. of Aberdeen (MA 1st Cl. Hons Econ. Sci.). Economist, Shell Internat. Petroleum Co., 1962–64; Lectr in Econs, Univ. of Strathclyde, 1964–65; University of Aberdeen: Lectr, 1966–77; Sen. Lectr, 1977–81; Reader, 1981–83. Member: Energy Adv. Panel to Minister of Energy, 1993–2003; Council of Econ. Advrs to First Minister of Scotland, 2007–11. FRSE 2001. *Publications:* Petroleum Rent Collection Around the World, 1988; Official History of North Sea Oil and Gas, 2 vols, 2011; over 200 articles on petroleum econs in acad. jls. *Recreations:* following football and cricket (passively), traditional Scottish music and songs, poems of Robert Burns, current affairs. *Address:* University of Aberdeen, Department of Economics, King's College, Aberdeen AB24 3QY. *T:* (01224) 272168, *Fax:* (01224) 272181. *E:* a.g.kemp@abdn.ac.uk.

**KEMP, Prof. Barry John,** CBE 2011; FBA 1992; Professor of Egyptology, 2005–07, now Emeritus, and Fellow, McDonald Institute of Archaeological Research, since 2008, University of Cambridge; Fellow of Wolfson College, Cambridge, 1990–2007, now Emeritus; *b* 14 May 1940. *Educ:* Liverpool Univ. (BA); MA Cantab 1965. Lectr, 1969–90, Reader in Egyptology, 1990–2005, Univ. of Cambridge. Project Dir, Amarna Project, 2006–; Chm., Amarna Trust, 2006–15. Corresponding Member: German Archaeological Inst., Berlin, 1982–; Archaeological Inst. of America, 2009–. *Publications:* Minoan Pottery in Second Millennium Egypt, 1980; Amarna Reports, Vols 1–6, 1984–95; Ancient Egypt: anatomy of a civilisation, 1989, 3rd edn 2018; (jtly) Survey of the Ancient City of El-Amarna, 1993; (jtly) The Ancient Textile Industry of Amarna, 2001; 100 Hieroglyphs, 2005; How to Read the Egyptian Book of the Dead, 2007; (jtly) Busy Lives at Amarna: excavations in the Main City, 2010; The City of Akhenaten and Nefertiti: Amarna and its people, 2012; Ancient Egypt: all that matters, 2015. *Address:* 4 Abu Hureiba Street, Darb el-Ahmar, Cairo, Egypt; (project office) No 1, Midan el-Tahrir, Flat 17, Floor 5, Downtown Cairo, Egypt. *E:* bjk2@cam.ac.uk.

**KEMP, Prof. Bruce Ernest,** AO 2019; PhD; FRS 2002; FAA; FAAAS; NHMRC Fellow, St Vincent's Institute of Medical Research, since 2008 (NHMRC Senior Principal Research Fellow and Deputy Director, 1989–2003; Hon. NHMRC Fellow, 2003–08); *b* 15 Dec. 1946; *s* of Norman Beck Kemp and Mary Frances Kemp (*née* Officer); *m* 1970, Alison Virginia Sanders; three *s*. *Educ:* Adelaide Univ. (BAgrSc Hons); Flinders Univ., SA (PhD 1975). Postdoctoral Fellow, Edwin G. Krebs Lab., Univ. of Calif, Davis, 1974–76; Nat. Heart Foundn Fellow, Flinders Med. Centre, 1977–78; Queen Elizabeth II Sen. Res. Fellow, Howard Florey Inst., Univ. of Melbourne, 1979–84; Sen. Res. Fellow, Dept of Medicine, Repatriation Gen. Hosp., Heidelberg, Vic, 1984–88; Fedn Fellow, CSIRO, 2003–08. FAA 2000; FAAAS 2006. Selwyn Smith Prize, Univ. of Melbourne, 1988; (jtly) Newman Award for Excellence in AIDS Res., 1989; AIDS Trust of Aust. Award, 1989; Pharmacia-LKB Medal and Travelling Fellowship Award, Aust. Soc. for Biochem. and Molecular Biol., 1990; Wellcome Rapid Diagnostics Award, 1991; Lemberg Medal, Aust. Soc. for Biochem. and Molecular Biol., 1996; Royal Soc. of Victoria Research Medal, 1996. *Publications:* (ed and contrib.) Peptides and Protein Phosphorylation, 1990; chapters in books; contrib. conf. procs and learned jls incl. Nature, Science. *Recreations:* tennis, walking, bicycle riding. *Address:* St Vincent's Institute of Medical Research, 41 Victoria Parade, Fitzroy, Vic 3065, Australia. *T:* (3) 92882480, *Fax:* (3) 94162676. *Club:* University House (Melbourne).

**KEMP, His Honour Charles James Bowring;** a Circuit Judge, 1998–2018; *b* 27 April 1951; *s* of late Michael John Barnett Kemp and of Brigid Ann (*née* Bowring; now Vernon-Smith); *m* 1974, Fenella Anne Herring; one *s* one *d*. *Educ:* Shrewsbury Sch.; University Coll. London (LLB). Called to the Bar, Gray's Inn, 1973; in practice at the Bar, 1974–98; Asst Recorder, 1987–91; a Recorder, 1991–98; South Eastern Circuit. Member: Sussex Probation Bd, 2001–07; Sussex Courts Bd, 2004–07; Surrey and Sussex Courts Bd, 2007–10. Vice Pres., E Sussex Magistrates' Assoc., 2013–. *Recreations:* music, tennis, swimming, golf, country pursuits. *E:* c.kemp2@me.com. *Clubs:* Piltdown Golf; Harbour (Portscatho).

**KEMP, Prof. David Thomas,** PhD; FRS 2004; Professor of Auditory Biophysics, University College London, 1990–2009, now Emeritus; Research Director and Chairman, Otodynamics Ltd, since 2010 (Founder and Director, 1989); *b* 24 Feb. 1945; *s* of Rev. Thomas Kemp and Alice Kemp (*née* Holliday); *m* 1970, Gillian Barbara Langford; one *s* one *d* (and one *s* one *d* decd). *Educ:* Southport Technical Coll.; KCL (BSc Hons (Physics) 1966; AKC; PhD (Radiophysics) 1970). Res. Scientist, CEGB, 1970; PSO, RNTNEH, London, 1971; Sen. Lectr, Inst. of Laryngol. and Otol., London, 1980–86; Reader in Auditory Biophysics, UCL, 1986–90. Discoverer of otoacoustic emissions; patented invention of otoacoustic emission hearing screening device, in widespread use (Queen's Award for Export Achievement, 1993, for Technol Achievement, 1998, Otodynamics Ltd; Queen's Award for Technol Achievement, Inst. of Laryngol. and Otol., UCL, 1998). Dr *hc* Claude-Bernard, Lyon, 2006. Award of Merit, Assoc. for Res. in Otol., 2003; Dist. Service Award, Amer. Speech and Hearing Assoc., 2003; Aram Glorig Award, Internat. Soc. of Audiology, 2012; von Bekesy Silver Medal, Acoustical Soc. of America, 2017; Internat. Award for Hearing, American Acad. of Audiology, 2018. *Publications:* articles in Jl of Acoustical Soc. of America and in jls concerned with hearing and geophysics; book chapters on otoacoustic emissions. *Recreations:* history of electronic technologies, astronomy, family history and genealogy, walking. *Address:* UCL Centre for Auditory Research, The Ear Institute, 332 Gray's Inn Road, WC1X 8EE; Otodynamics Ltd, 30–38 Beaconsfield Road, Hatfield, Herts AL10 8BB. *T:* (01707) 267540, *Fax:* (01707) 262327. *E:* d.kemp@ucl.ac.uk.

**KEMP, Edward Thomas;** freelance director, playwright, librettist, translator and dramaturg, since 1986; Director, Royal Academy of Dramatic Art, since 2008; Principal, Conservatoire for Dance and Drama, 2014–17; *b* Oxford, 9 Oct. 1965; *s* of late Rt Rev. Eric Waldram Kemp and of (Leslie) Patricia Kemp (*née* Kirk); partner, Jane Heather; one *s* one *d*. *Educ:* King's Sch., Worcester; New Coll., Oxford (BA). Staff Dir, NT, 1991–97; Dramaturg, Chichester Fest. Th., 2003–05; Guest Dramaturg, Bern Ballet, 2006–13; Artistic Dir, RADA, 2007–08. Vis. Prof., Bennington Coll., Vermont, 2000–01. *Stage plays* include: The Iron and the Oak, Chichester, 1983; A Proper Place, NYT, 1985; 5/11, Chichester, 2005; *plays directed* include: Wanted Man, 1999, Missing Reel, 2001, NT Studio; Wild Orchids, Chichester Fest., 2002; The Accrington Pals, 2002, Dr Faustus, 2004, Office Suite, 2007, Minerva, Chichester; Savages, Royal Court, 2006; Macbeth, Regent's Park, 2007; Penthesilea, 2008; Company, 2010, The Young Idea, 2011, King Lear, 2012, Six Pictures of Lee Miller, The Sea, 2013, Andromaque, 2015, A Little Night Music, Stuff Happens, 2017, RADA; Romeo and Juliet, 2019; *adaptations* include: Le Malade Imaginaire, W Yorks Playhouse, 1996; The Mysteries, RSC, 1997 (Radio 3, 1998); Molière's Don Juan, W Yorks Playhouse, 1998; Faulkner's As I Lay Dying, Young Vic, 1998, Baton Rouge, 1999; Sebald's The Emigrants, Radio 3, 2001; Lessing's Nathan the Wise, Chichester and Radio 3, 2003, Hampstead, 2005; Bulgakov's Master and Margarita, Chichester, 2004; Brecht's Turandot, Hampstead, 2008; Kleist's Penthesilea, RADA, 2008; Racine's Athalie (unperformed); The King James Bible, NT, 2011; Bulgakov's Master and Margarita, Complicite, 2012; Goldoni's Holiday Trilogy, RADA, 2014; Racine's Andromaque, RADA, 2015 (Radio 3, 2017); Lorca's House of Bernarda Alba, RADA, 2018; *lyric works* include: Ease, Donmar, 1993; Travels in the Arctic Circle, Royal Opera Hse at Riverside Studios, 1993; Ivan the Terrible, BBC Proms, 2003; Six Pictures of Lee Miller, Minerva, Chichester, 2005; Echo and Narcissus, Royal Opera Hse 2, 2007; The Ground Beneath Her Feet, Manchester Internat. Fest., 2007; The Yellow Sofa, Glyndebourne, 2009, 2012; How the Whale Became, Linbury Studio, ROH, 2013; *screenplays*: Chop Chop, 2015; The Ness, 2016; Augury, 2017; A Heart-shaped Stone, 2018; *ballet scenarios* include: Ghosts, Royal Opera Hse, 2005; Tale of Two Cities, Northern Ballet, 2008; Sturmhohe, 2009, Juliet and Romeo, Clara, 2010, Ein Winternachtstraum, 2011, Hexenhatz, 2013, Bern; Blood Wedding, Helsinki, 2010; Swan Maidens, Koblenz, 2015; Les Liaisons Dangereuses, Royal Danish Ballet, 2017; The Suit, Ballet Black, 2018; Lady Chatterley's Lover, Les Grands Ballets Canadiens, 2018. *Publications:* The Mysteries, 1997; Nathan the Wise, 2003; The Master and Margarita, 2004; 5/11, 2005. *Recreations:* music, art, reading, landscape, family, baking. *Address:* Royal Academy of Dramatic Art, 62–64 Gower Street, WC1E 6ED. *T:* (020) 7908 4713. *E:* edwardkemp@rada.ac.uk.

**KEMP, Fraser;** *b* 1 Sept. 1958; *s* of William and Mary Kemp; *m* 1989, Patricia Mary (marr. diss. 2002), *d* of Patrick and Patricia Byrne; two *s* one *d*. *Educ:* Washington Comp. Sch. Civil Servant (clerical asst/officer), 1975–81; Labour Party: Agent, Leicester, 1981–84; Asst Regl Organiser, E Midlands, 1984–86; Regl Sec., W Midlands, 1986–94; Nat. Gen. Election Co-ordinator, 1994–96. MP (Lab) Houghton and Washington E, 1997–2010. An Asst Govt Whip, 2001–05. Mem., Select Cttee on Public Admin, 1997–99. Chm., PLP Cabinet Office Cttee, 1997–2001; Vice-Chm., Labour Election Planning Gp, 2004–05. *Recreation:* people.

**KEMP, Prof. Martin John,** FBA 1991; Professor of the History of Art, 1995–2007, Research Professor of the History of Art, 2007–08, Emeritus Professor, 2008, University of Oxford; Fellow of Trinity College, Oxford, 1995–2008, now Emeritus; British Academy Wolfson Research Professor, 1993–98; *b* 5 March 1942; *s* of Frederick Maurice Kemp and Violet Anne Tull; *m* 1966, Jill Lightfoot (marr. diss. 2005), *d* of Dennis William Lightfoot and Joan Betteridge; one *s* one *d*. *Educ:* Windsor Grammar Sch.; Downing Coll., Cambridge (MA Nat. Scis and Art History; Hon. Fellow, 1999); Courtauld Inst. of Art, London Univ. (Academic Dip.). Lectr in History of Art, Dalhousie Univ., Halifax, NS, Canada, 1965–66; Lectr in History of Fine Art, Univ. of Glasgow, 1966–81; Fellow, Inst. for Advanced Study, Princeton, 1984–85; University of St Andrews: Prof. of Fine Arts, subseq. of Hist. and Theory of Art, 1981–95; Associate Dean of Graduate Studies, Faculty of Arts, 1983–87; Mem. Court, 1988–91; Provost of St Leonard's Coll., 1991–95. Prof. of History and Hon. Mem., Royal Scottish Acad., 1985–; Slade Prof. of Fine Art, Cambridge Univ., 1987–88; Visiting Professor: Benjamin Sonnenberg, Inst. of Fine Arts, New York Univ., 1988; Wiley, Univ. of N Carolina, Chapel Hill, 1993; Lila Wallace—Reader's Digest, Villa I Tatti, Harvard Univ., 2010; Louise Smith Brosse Prof., Univ. of Chicago, 2000; Vis. Scholar, Getty Res. Inst., LA, 2002; Mellon Sen. Res. Fellow, Canadian Centre for Architecture, Montreal, 2004. Page-Barbour Lectr, Univ. of Virginia, 2012; Robert Janson La Palme *60 Lectr, Princeton Univ., 2013. Co-Founder, Wallace Kemp/Artakt, 2001; Res. Dir, Universal Leonardo, 2001–07. Chair, Assoc. of Art Historians, 1989–92; Member: Board, Scottish Museums Council, 1990–95; Res. Awards Adv. Cttee, Leverhulme Trust, 1991–98; Board, Mus. Trng Inst., 1993–99; Board, Interalia, 1993–99; Council, Brit Soc. for History of Sci., 1994–97. Pres., Leonardo da Vinci Soc., 1987–96. Trustee: National Gall. of Scotland, 1982–87; V&A Museum, 1985–89; BM, 1995–2005. Broadcasts, Radio 3 and TV. For. Mem., American Acad. of Arts and Scis, 1996. FRSA 1983–98; FRSE 1992. Hon. FRIAS 1988. Hon. Fellow, Glyndŵr Univ., 2009. Hon. DLitt: Heriot-Watt, 1995; Uppsala, 2009. Mitchell Prize for best first book in English on Art History, 1981; Armand Hammer Prize for Leonardo Studies, 1992; President's Prize, Italian Assoc. of America, 1998. *Publications:* Leonardo da Vinci, The Marvellous Works of Nature and Man, 1981; (jtly) Leonardo da Vinci, 1989; (jtly) Leonardo on Painting, 1989; The Science of Art, 1990; Behind the Picture, 1997; (ed) The Oxford History of Western Art, 2000; Visualizations, 2000; (with Marina Wallace) Spectacular Bodies, 2000; Leonardo, 2004; Seen/Unseen, 2006; Leonardo da Vinci: experience, experiment, design, 2006; The Human Animal, 2007; (with Pascal Cotte) La Bella Principessa: the story of the new masterpiece by Leonardo da Vinci, 2010; (with T. Wells) Leonardo da Vinci's Madonna of the Yarnwinder, 2011; Christ to Coke: how image becomes icon, 2011; Continuity, Change and Progress: a message from the visual arts?, 2014; Leonardo da Vinci, Ritratto di Bianca Sforza: la bella Principessa, 2014; Art in History: 600 BC–2000 AD, 2014; The Chapel of Trinity College, Oxford, 2014; Structural Intuitions: seeing shapes in art and science, 2016; (with Giuseppe Pallanti) Mona Lisa, 2017; Living with Leonardo, 2018; (ed and trans.) Giorgio Vasari, The Life of Leonardo da Vinci, 2019; Leonardo da Vinci: the 100 milestones, 2019; Leonardo by Leonardo, 2019; (ed with D. Laurenza) Leonardo da Vinci's Codex Leicester: a new edition, 2019; articles in Jl of Warburg and Courtauld Insts, Burlington Magazine, Art History, Art Bull., Connoisseur, Procs of British Acad., Jl of RSA, L'Arte, Bibliothèque d'Humanisme et Renaissance, Med. History, TLS, London Rev. of Books, Guardian, Nature, Sunday Times, etc. *Recreations:* keeping fit, avoiding academics, music (especially early music).

**KEMP, Neil Reginald,** OBE 1990 (MBE 1980); PhD; international education consultant; Visiting Fellow, Institute of Education, University College London (formerly Institute of Education, University of London) (Senior Adviser (International), 2005); *b* 18 March 1945; *s* of Harry Reginald Kemp and Ada Mary Kemp (*née* Roberts); *m* 1982, Elizabeth Jacob; two *s*. *Educ*: University College of Wales, Swansea (BSc; PhD Analytical Chem. 1971). Laboratory technician, 1961–63; VSO as Lectr, Gordon Coll., Rawalpindi, Pakistan, 1967–68; joined British Council, 1971: Jakarta, 1971–74; Calcutta, 1976–79; Res. Associate, Univ. of London Inst. of Educn, 1979–80; Head, Sci. and Technol. Dept, London, 1981–85; New Delhi, 1985–89; Colombo, 1990–91; Develt and Trng Services, Manchester, 1991–95; Director: Indonesia, 1995–2001; Educn UK Div., 2001–05. Board Member: Assoc. of Ind. Higher Educn, 2005–; Open Univ. Worldwide Ltd, 2005–13; Council for Educn in Commonwealth. *Recreations*: athletics, cycling, cricket and basketball, travelling, jazz and blues. *Address*: 37 Houndean Rise, Lewes, E Sussex BN7 1EQ.

**KEMP, Prof. Peter Anthony,** DPhil; Vice Dean (formerly Associate Director), Blavatnik School of Government, since 2011, and Professor of Public Policy, since 2012, University of Oxford; *b* 25 Dec. 1955; *s* of Ronald Percy James Kemp and Emilie Kemp; two *d*. *Educ*: Univ. of Southampton (BSc 1977); Univ. of Glasgow (MPhil 1979); Univ. of Sussex (DPhil 1984). Researcher, SHAC, 1983–85; Res. Fellow, Univ. of Glasgow, 1985–87; Lectr, Univ. of Salford, 1987–90; Joseph Rowntree Prof. of Housing Policy and Founder Dir, Centre for Housing Policy, Univ. of York, 1990–95; Prof. of Housing and Social Policy, Univ. of Glasgow, 1996–2002; Prof. of Social Policy and Dir, Social Policy Research Unit, Univ. of York, 2002–06; Barnett Prof. of Social Policy, Univ. of Oxford, 2006–12; Fellow, St Cross Coll., Oxford, 2006–12. FAcSS (AcSS 2011). *Publications*: The Private Provision of Rented Housing, 1988; Housing and Social Policy, 1990; Tax Incentives and the Revival of Private Renting, 1991; A Comparative Study of Housing Allowances, 1997; Private Renting in Transition, 2004; Sick Societies?: trends in disability benefits in post-industrial welfare states, 2006; Cash and Care: challenges in the welfare state, 2006; Housing Allowances in Comparative Perspective, 2007; Transforming Landlords: housing, markets and public policy, 2011; Private Rental Housing: comparative perspectives, 2014. *Recreations*: cycling, going to the gym, reading. *Address*: Blavatnik School of Government, University of Oxford, Radcliffe Observatory Quarter, Walton Street, Oxford OX2 6GG.

**KEMP, Richard Geoffrey Horsford,** MA; Director, Langford Educational Ltd, since 2006; Head Master, Pate's Grammar School, Cheltenham, 2000–06; *b* 27 Oct. 1948; *s* of Athole Stephen Horsford Kemp and Alison Kemp (*née* Bostock); *m* 1st, 1970 (marr. diss. 1990); 2nd, 1996, Denise (*née* Fraser); one step *s* one step *d*. *Educ*: Westminster Sch.; Christ Church, Oxford (MA). Marketing and Advertising Manager, Unilever, 1970–73; Teacher: Eton Coll., 1973–74; Henry Box Sch., Witney, 1974–78; Lord Williams's Sch., Thame, 1978–84; res., Dept of Educn, Oxford Univ., 1984–85; Buckinghamshire LEA, 1985–92 (Sen. Educn Advr, 1989–92); Sen. Dep. Head, Actg Headmaster, Aylesbury Grammar Sch., 1992–99. *Publications*: various geography textbooks and atlases. *Recreations*: gardening, wine, travel, military history. *Address*: Kemp's Yard, Langford, Lechlade, Glos GL7 3LF. *T*: (01367) 860176.

**KEMP-GEE, Mark Norman;** non-executive Director: Murgitroyd Group plc, since 2001; Moncreiffe & Co. plc, since 1986; *b* 19 Dec. 1945; *s* of late Bernard Kemp-Gee and Ann Kemp-Gee (*née* Mackilligin); *m* 1980, Hon. Lucy Lyttelton, *d* of 10th Viscount Cobham, KG, GCMG, GCVO, TD, PC; three *s*. *Educ*: Marlborough Coll.; Pembroke Coll., Oxford (MA). Chm., Greig Middleton & Co. Ltd, 1978–99; Chief Exec., Exeter Investment Gp plc, 1999–2004. Director: King & Shaxson Hldgs plc, 1993–96; Gerrard Gp plc, 1996–99. Member (C): Lambeth BC, 1982–86; Hampshire CC, 2005–. Mem., S Downs Nat. Park Authy, 2011–13. Chm., E Hampshire Cons. Assoc., 2009–12 (Pres., 2012–). *Recreations*: point-to-pointing, French animalier bronzes. *Address*: Park House, Upper Wield, Alresford, Hants SO24 9RU. *Clubs*: City of London; Oxford Union.

**KEMP-WELCH, Sir John,** Kt 1999; Director, HSBC Holdings, 2000–06; Chairman, London Stock Exchange, 1994–2000 (Director, 1991–2000); *b* 31 March 1936; *s* of late Peter Wellesbourne Kemp-Welch, OBE and Peggy Penelope Kemp-Welch; *m* 1964, Diana Elisabeth Leishman (*d* 2013); one *s* three *d*. *Educ*: Abberley Hall, Worcs; Winchester Coll. Hoare & Co., 1954–58; Cazenove & Co., 1959–94 (Jt Sen. Partner, 1980–94). Chairman: Scottish Eastern Investment Trust, 1994–99 (Dir, 1993–99); Lowland Investment Co., 1993–97 (Dir, 1963–97); Claridge's Hotel, 1995–97; Martin Currie Portfolio Investment Trust plc, 1999–2000; Director: Savoy Hotel PLC, 1985–98; Royal & Sun Alliance Insurance Gp (formerly Sun Alliance Gp), 1994–99; British Invisibles, 1994–98; Pro Share, 1995–97. Dep. Chm., Financial Reporting Council, 1994–2000; Director: SFA, 1994–97; Accountancy Foundn, 2000–01. Member: City Capital Markets Cttee, 1989–94; Panel on Takeovers and Mergers, 1994–2000. Mem., Stock Exchange, 1959–86. Vice Pres., Fedn of European Stock Exchanges, 1996–98; Mem. Exec. Cttee, Federation Internationale des Bourses de Valeurs, 1994–98; President: Investor Relations Soc., 1994–2000; Securities Industry Mgt Assoc., 1994–2000. Member: (Lord Mayor of London's) City No 1 Consultancy, 1994–2000; Council, London First, 1994–96. Pres., Reed's Sch. Foundn Appeal, 2003–04; Vice-Pres., Reed's Sch., 2005–; Governor: Ditchley Foundn, 1980–2012; North Foreland Lodge Sch., 1980–92; Chm., King's Med. Res. Trust, 1991–2006 (Trustee, 1984–2006); Trustee: KCH Special Trustees, 1997–99; KCH Charitable Trust, 1998–99; Trustee and Mem. Council, Game Conservancy Trust, 1990–94 (Hon. Res. Fellow, 1998–); Mem. Adv. Council, PYBT, 1996–2000; Pres., Cazenove Assoc., 2005–; Trustee: Stock Exchange Benevolent Fund, 1980–2000; Sandford St Martin Trust, 1994–99; Dulverton Trust, 1994–2017 (Vice Chm., 2001–17); Farmington Trust, 2002–; St Paul's Knightsbridge Foundn, 2002–16; Chm., Lucy Kemp-Welch Meml Trust, 1965–. Fellow, Harris Manchester Coll., Oxford, 2015. Mem., Highland Soc. of London, 1992–. Mem., Guild of Internat. Bankers, 2004–. Hon. FCSI (MSI 1992; FSI 1996). CCMI (CBIM 1984); FRSA 1989. Hon. DBA London Guildhall Univ., 1998. Joseph Nickerson Heather Award, Joseph Nickerson Heather Improvement Foundn, 1988. *Recreations*: the hills of Perthshire, City of London history, cricket nostalgia, champagne and claret, Lucy Kemp-Welch paintings, heather moorland management. *Address*: 74 Melton Court, Onslow Crescent, SW7 3JH. *Clubs*: White's, City of London, Pilgrims, MCC; Essex.

**KEMPF, Frederick Albert, (Freddy);** concert pianist and conductor; *b* Croydon, 14 Oct. 1977; *s* of Fritz Kempf and Yoshimi Kempf; *m* 2007, Katja; two *s* one *d*. *Educ*: St Edmund's Sch., Canterbury; Royal Acad. of Music. First public appearance, 1981; first professional engagement, 1983; concerto debut with RPO, 1985, conducting debut, 2011; many performances and collaborations worldwide. BBC Young Musician of the Year, 1992; Bronze Medal, Internat. Tchaikovsky Competition, Moscow, 1998; Classical Brit Award, 2001. *Recreations*: sport, mountaineering, ski-ing, languages, food and wine. *Address*: Munich, Germany. *E*: (management) ekostova@imgartists.com.

**KEMPLE, Terence John,** FRCP, FRCGP; President, Royal College of General Practitioners, 2015–17 (Representative for Sustainability, Climate Change and Green Issues, since 2017); *b* Cheltenham, Glos, 14 July 1952; *s* of Laurence Jarlath Kemple and Katherine Marie Kemple; *m* 1977, Frederica Erna Newbery; one *s* one *d*. *Educ*: Whitefriars Sch., Cheltenham; Belmont Abbey Sch., Hereford; Univ. of Bristol (MB ChB 1975). DCH 1978; MRCP 1980, FRCP 2000; MRCGP 1981, FRCGP 1993. GP, Horfield Health Centre, Bristol, 1982–2015. *E*: tk@elpmek.demon.co.uk.

**KEMPSELL, Rosemary Ann,** CBE 2014; Worldwide President, Mothers' Union, 2007–12 (Trustee, 2001–06); *b* 29 Sept. 1943; *d* of Laurence and Ada Harriet Jackson; *m* 1967, John Baron Kempsell; two *d*. *Educ*: Collingwood Sch., Wallington; Willows Co. Sch., Morden; Open Univ. (BA 1992; DipEurHum 1993). Examr, Estate Duty Office, 1963–71. Mem., Mgt Bd, S London Industrial Mission, 1993–2002. Pres., Southwark Dio., Mothers' Union, 1998–2000. Trustee: Traidcraft Foundn, 2012–; USPG, 2012–18. *Recreations*: listening to opera, participating in choral singing, reading, swimming. *Address*: 3 All Saints Drive, South Croydon CR2 9ES. *Club*: Purley Downs Golf.

**KEMPSON, Prof. (Helen) Elaine,** CBE 2007; Associate Professor, Oslo Metropolitan University, since 2018; Consultant, World Bank, since 2010; Director, Personal Finance Research Centre, 1998–2010, and Professor of Personal Finance and Social Policy Research, 2001–10, now Emeritus, University of Bristol; *b* Bideford, 1947; *d* of Robert and Doreen Hersey; *m* 1982, Nick Moore. *Educ*: Univ. of Sussex (BSc Biol.); Coll. of Librarianship, Univ. of Wales (Postgrad. Dip.). Librarian, Lambeth BC, 1972–77; Dir, Community Information Project, Liby Assoc., 1977–82; Hd of Res., Social Services Dept, Somerset CC, 1982–84; Partner, Acumen Res. and Consultancy Ltd, 1984–; Principal Res. Fellow, Policy Studies Inst., 1988–98. Mem., Social Security Adv. Cttee, 2003–12. Non-executive Director: Banking Codes Standards Bd, 2006–08; Financial Ombudsman Service, 2008–12; Standard Life Foundn, 2017–; Lending Standards Board, 2018–; Money and Pension Service, 2018–. Member: Financial Inclusion Taskforce, HM Treasury, 2005–11; Bd, IFS Sch. of Finance, 2007–08; Sustainability Panel, Wessex Water, 2010–; Consumer Adv. Gp, Central Bank of Ireland, 2011–16; Universal Credit Evaluation Gp, 2012–. Ind. Reviewer of Banking Codes, 2002, 2004; Ind. Assessor of Financial Ombudsman, 2004–; Ind. Reviewer of Insolvency Practitioner Fees, 2013. *Publications*: (with R. Berthoud) Credit and Debt in Britain, 1992; (with K. Rowlingson) Gas Debt and Disconnection, 1993; Household Budgets and Housing Costs, 1993; (with N. Moore) Designing Public Documents: a review of research, 1994; (with K. Rowlingson) Paying with Plastic: a study of credit card debt, 1994; (jtly) Hard Times?: how poor families make ends meet, 1994; Outside the Banking System: a review of households without a current account, 1994; (with A. Herbert) Water Debt and Disconnection, 1995; Money Advice and Debt Counselling, 1995; (jtly) Mortgage Arrears and Possessions, 1995; (jtly) Paying for Rented Housing, 1995; (with A. Herbert) Credit Use and Ethnic Minorities, 1996; Life on a Low Income, 1996; (with C. Callender) Student Finances, 1996; (jtly) Money Matters, 1997; (jtly) Paying for Peace of Mind: access to home contents insurance for low-income households, 1998; Kept Out or Opted Out?: understanding and combating financial exclusion, 1999; Banking without Branches, 2000; (jtly) In or Out? financial exclusion: a literature and research review, 2000; Tackling Financial Exclusion, 2001; Over-indebtedness in Britain, 2002; (with S. McKay) Saving and Life Events, 2003; (with S. Collard) Affordable Credit: the way forward, 2005; (jtly) Levels of Financial Capability in the UK, 2006; (jtly) Easy come, easy go: borrowing over the life cycle, 2007; (jtly) Genworth Index: measuring consumer financial vulnerability in 10 European markets, 2008; (with A. Finney) Consumer purchasing outcomes survey, 2008; (with A. Atkinson) Investigating Debt, 2008; (jtly) Debt and older people, 2008; (jtly) Financial services provision and prevention of financial exclusion, 2008; (jtly) Towards a common operational definition of over-indebtedness, 2008; Looking beyond our shores: consumer protection regulation lessons from the UK, 2008; (jtly) Is a not-for-profit home credit business feasible?: building a business case, 2009; (with A. Finney) Saving in lower-income households, 2009; (with S. Collard) Money Guidance Pathfinder, 2010; (jtly) The Child Trust Fund, 2011; (with S. Collard) Developing a vision for financial inclusion, 2012; (jtly) Impact on business and consumers of a cap on the total cost of credit, 2013; (jtly) Measuring Financial Capability, 2013; (jtly) A Tool Kit for the Evaluation of Financial Capability Programs in Low- and Middle-income Countries, 2013; (contrib.) Consumer Debt and Social Exclusion in Europe, 2015; (contrib.) Comparative Perspectives of Consumer Over-Indebtedness: a view from the UK, Germany, Italy and Greece, 2016; (jtly) Banking Culture: a consumer perspective, 2016. *Recreations*: gardening, walking, cooking, travel, cinema. *Address*: School of Geographical Sciences, University of Bristol, University Road, Bristol BS8 1SS.

**KEMPSON, Martyn Rex;** Principal Advisor to John Lyon's Charity, since 2002; *b* 31 July 1947; *s* of Horace and Winifred May Kempson; *m* 1986, Carole J. Kendall; two *s*. *Educ*: Luton Grammar Sch.; North-Western Poly. MCLIP (ALA 1968). Librarian: Luton Public Libraries, 1963–68; Buckinghamshire CC Libraries, 1968–71; London Borough of Sutton Libraries, 1971–91: Borough Librarian, 1987–88; Asst Dir of Leisure, 1988–91; Barnet London Borough Council, 1991–2002: Controller: Libraries and Arts, 1991–94; Recreation, Leisure and Arts, and Dep. Dir, Educn Services, 1995–98; Dir, Educnl Services, 1998–99; Strategic Dir of Educn and Children, 1999–2002. Chairman: British Judo Council, British Judo Foundn, 2011–16; Wardown Develts Ltd, 2015–. Chair, Skinners' Debating Soc., 2018–. FRSA; FLS 2015. *Publications*: I-Spy Football, 1991; contrib. poetry, First Time mag. *Recreations*: supporting Luton Town FC, poetry, tennis.

**KEMPSON, Prof. Ruth Margaret, (Mrs M. J. Pinner),** FBA 1989; Professor of General Linguistics, King's College London, 1999–2009, now Emeritus; *b* 26 June 1944; *d* of Edwin Garnett Hone Kempson and late Margaret Cecilia Kempson; *m* 1973, Michael John Pinner; two *s*. *Educ*: Univ. of Birmingham (BA (2 ii) Music and English); Univ. of London (MA (with dist.) Mod. English Language 1969; PhD Linguistics 1972). Res. Asst to Survey of English Usage, UCL, 1969–70; School of Oriental and African Studies, University of London: Lectr in Linguistics, 1971–85; Reader in Gen. Linguistics, 1985–87; Prof. of Gen. Linguistics, 1987–99; Head of Linguistics Dept, 1992–96; Leverhulme Personal Res. Prof., KCL, 1999–2004. Vis. Prof. in Semantics, Univ. of Massachusetts, 1982–83. Pres., Linguistics Assoc. of GB, 1986–91. MAE 2000. *Publications*: Presupposition and the Delimitation of Semantics, 1975; Semantic Theory, 1977; Mental Representations: the interface between language and reality, 1988; (jtly) Dynamic Syntax: the flow of language understanding, 2001; The Dynamics of Language, 2005; Semantics: an introduction to meaning in language, 2009; (ed) The Handbook of Philosophy of Linguistics, 2012; articles in Linguistics and Philosophy, Jl of Linguistics, Dialogue and Discourse, Theoretical Linguistics and edited collections. *Address*: Philosophy Department, King's College London, Strand, WC2R 2LS.

**KEMPTON, (Barry) James;** Director, Kempton Consulting Ltd, since 2011; *b* London, 17 Sept. 1960; *s* of John Barry Kempton and Ivy Kempton (*née* Brookes); *m* 2010, Timothy Leonard Dean. *Educ*: Eltham Coll.; Univ. of York (BA Hons 1983); Inst. of Educn, Univ. of London (PGCE 1999). Exec. Officer, 1983–85, Exec. Sec., 1985–89, BMA; Hd, Secretariat, RCGP, 1989–96; Sec., RCPCH, 1996–98; history teacher, Plashet Sch., 1999–2002; Dir, Mgt Consulting, Mouchel plc, 2009–11; Dir, Educn and Social Policy, CentreForum, 2012–15. Mem., Islington Council, 1994–2010 (Lead Mem. for Children and Young People, 2000–06; Dep. Leader, 2000–06; Leader, 2006–09). Clerk to Bd, Chartered Coll. of Teaching (formerly Coll. of Teaching), 2015–16; non-exec. Dir. OFSTED, 2015–18 (Interim Chm., 2016–17); Chm., Oldham Opportunity Area Partnership Bd, 2017–. Trustee, Music First, 2010–; Trustee, Company Three, 2010– (Chm., 2012–16); Gov., Cripplegate Foundn, 2014–. *Recreations:* theatre, music, art history, golf. *Address:* 10 Halton Road, N1 2EU. *T:* (020) 7359 1018. *E:* james.kempton@me.com.

**KEMSLEY,** 3rd Viscount *cr* 1945, of Dropmore, co. Bucks; **Richard Gomer Berry;** Bt 1928; Baron Kemsley 1936; *b* 17 April 1951; *o s* of Hon. Denis Gomer Berry, 2nd *s* of 1st Viscount Kemsley, GBE and Pamela Berry (*née* Wellesley); *S* uncle, 1999; *m* 1994, Elizabeth Jane Barker; two *s. Educ:* Eton. *Heir: s* Hon. Luke Gomer Berry, *b* 2 Feb. 1998. *Address:* Church Hill Farm, Church Lane, Brockenhurst, Hants SO42 7UB.

**KENDAL, Felicity Ann,** CBE 1995; actress; *d* of late Geoffrey and Laura Kendal; *m* (marr. diss.); one *s*; *m* 1983, Michael Rudman, *qv* (marr. diss. 1994); one *s. Educ:* six convents in India. First appeared on stage at age of 9 months, when carried on as the Changeling boy in A Midsummer Night's Dream; grew up touring India and Far East with parents' theatre co., playing pageboys at age of eight and graduating through Puck, at nine, to parts such as Viola in Twelfth Night, Jessica in The Merchant of Venice, and Ophelia in Hamlet; returned to England, 1965; made London debut, Carla in Minor Murder, Savoy, 1967; Katherine in Henry V, and Lika in The Promise, Leicester, 1968; Amaryllis in Back to Methuselah, NT, 1969; Hermia in A Midsummer Night's Dream, and Hero in Much Ado About Nothing, Regent's Park, 1970; Anne Danby in Kean, Oxford, 1970, London, 1971; Romeo and Juliet, 'Tis Pity She's A Whore, and The Three Arrows, 1972; The Norman Conquests, Globe, 1974; Viktoska in Once Upon a Time, Bristol, 1976; Arms and The Man, Greenwich, 1978; Mara in Clouds, Duke of York's, 1978; Constanze Mozart in Amadeus, NT, 1979; Desdemona in Othello, NT, 1980; Christopher in On the Razzle, NT, 1981; Paula in The Second Mrs Tanqueray, NT, 1981; The Real Thing, Strand, 1982; Jumpers, Aldwych, 1985; Made in Bangkok, Aldwych, 1986; Hapgood, Aldwych, 1988; Ivanov, and Much Ado About Nothing, Strand, 1989 (Best Actress Award, Evening Standard); Hidden Laughter, Vaudeville, 1990; Tartuffe, Playhouse, 1991; Heartbreak House, Haymarket, 1992; Arcadia, NT, 1993; An Absolute Turkey, Globe, 1994; Indian Ink, Aldwych, 1995; Mind Millie for Me, Haymarket, 1996; Waste, and The Seagull, Old Vic, 1997; Alarms and Excursions, Gielgud, 1998; Fallen Angels, Apollo, 2000; Humble Boy, Gielgud, 2002; Happy Days, Arts Th., 2003; Amy's View, Garrick, 2006; The Vortex, Apollo, 2008; The Last Cigarette, Minerva, Chichester, 2009; Mrs Warren's Profession, Comedy, 2010; Relatively Speaking, Th. Royal, Newcastle, 2012, transf. Wyndham's, 2013; Chin-Chin, UK tour, 2013; Hay Fever, Th. Royal, Bath, 2014, Australia tour, 2014, transf. Duke of Yorks Th., 2015; A Room with a View, Th. Royal, Brighton, 2016; Lettice and Lovage, Menier Chocolate Factory, 2017; The Argument, Th. Royal, Bath, 2019. *Television:* four series of The Good Life, 1975–77; Viola in Twelfth Night, 1979; Solo, 1980, 2nd series 1982; The Mistress, 1985, 2nd series 1986; The Camomile Lawn, 1992; Honey for Tea, 1994; How Proust Can Save Your Life, 1999; Rosemary and Thyme, 3 series 2003–05; plays and serials. *Films:* Shakespeare Wallah, 1965; Valentino, 1976. Variety Club Most Promising Newcomer, 1974, Best Actress, 1979, 2001; Clarence Derwent Award, 1980; Variety Club Woman of the Year Best Actress Award, 1984. *Publications:* White Cargo (memoirs), 1998. *Recreations:* reading, working. *Address:* c/o Dallas Smith, United Agents, 12–26 Lexington Street, W1F 0LE. *T:* (020) 3214 0800.

**KENDALL, Bridget,** MBE 1994; Master, Peterhouse, Cambridge, since 2016; Presenter, The Forum, BBC World Service, since 2008; *b* 27 April 1956; *d* of Prof. David George Kendall, FRS. *Educ:* Lady Margaret Hall, Oxford (BA Hons; Hon. Fellow, 2015); Harvard Univ. (Harkness Fellow); Moscow State Univ.; St Antony's Coll., Oxford (Hon. Fellow, 2005); Voronezh State Univ. Joined BBC, 1983: trainee, World Service, 1983; presenter, Newsnight, 1983–84; producer/reporter, World Service, 1984–89; Moscow Corresp., 1989–93; Washington Corresp., 1994–98; Diplomatic Corresp., 1998–2016. Jubilee Lectr, St Antony's Coll., Oxford, 2000; Roskill Lectr, Churchill Coll., Cambridge, 2003; Darwin Coll. Lecture Series, Cambridge, 2013; Ramsay Murray Lectr, Selwyn Coll., Cambridge, 2015; Mountbatten Lectr, Edinburgh Univ., 2019. Vis. Prof., Univ. of Lincoln, 2005–16. Member, Advisory Boards: Russia and Eurasia Prog., Chatham House, 2000–06; RUSI Council, 2001–05; Mem. Adv. Council, Wilton Park, 2012–19. Trustee, Asia Hse, 2010–14. DUniv UCE, 1999; Hon. LLD: St Andrews, 2001; Exeter, 2002; York, 2018. *Publications:* (jtly) David the Invincible, 1980; (contrib.) The Day that Shook the World, 2001; (contrib.) The Battle for Iraq, 2003; (contrib.) From Our Own Correspondent: a celebration of fifty years, 2005; (contrib.) More From Our Own Correspondent, 2008; (contrib.) International News Reporting: frontlines and deadlines, 2008; The Cold War: a new oral history, 2016. *Recreations:* literature, cinema, tennis, hiking, gardening. *Address:* Master's Lodge, Peterhouse, Cambridge CB2 1RD.
See also W. S. Kendall.

**KENDALL, David William;** *b* 8 May 1935; *s* of William Jack Kendall and Alma May Kendall; *m* 1st, 1960, Delphine Hitchcock (marr. diss.); one *s* one *d;* 2nd, 1973, Elisabeth Rollison; one *s* one *d. Educ:* Enfield Grammar School; Southend High School. FCA. Elles Reeve, Shell-Mex & BP, Irish Shell & BP, 1955–70; British Petroleum Co.: Crude Oil Sales Manager, 1971–72; Manager, Bulk Trading Div., 1973–74; Organisation Planning Cttee, 1975; BP New Zealand: Gen. Manager, 1976–79; Man. Dir and Chief Exec., 1979–82; Chm., BP SW Pacific, 1979–82; BP Oil: Finance and Planning Dir, 1982–85; Man. Dir and Chief Exec., 1985–88; Director: BP Chemicals Internat., 1985–88; BP Oil Internat., 1985–88; Associated Octel Co., 1985–88. Chairman: Bunzl, 1990–93 (Dir, 1988–93); Ruberoid plc, 1993–2000; Whitecroft plc, 1993–2000; Blagden Industries plc, 1994–2000; Meyer Internat., 1994–95; Celtic Energy Ltd, 1994–2003; Wagon Industrial Hldgs, subseq. Wagon plc, 1997–2005; Danka Business Systems plc, 1998–2001 (Dir, 1993–2001); Dep. Chm., British Coal Corp., 1989–91; Director: STC plc, 1988–90; Gowrings plc, 1993–2005; South Wales Electricity plc, 1993–96; BSI, 2000–05. President: UK Petroleum Industries Assoc., 1987–88; Oil Industries Club, 1988. *Recreations:* golf, piano, France and its history. *Address:* Flat 1, Darling House, 35 Clevedon Road, Twickenham TW1 2TU. *Club:* Royal Mid Surrey Golf.

**KENDALL, Elizabeth Louise;** MP (Lab) Leicester West, since 2010; *b* 1971. *Educ:* Watford Grammar Sch. for Girls; Queens' Coll., Cambridge (BA 1st Cl. Hons Hist. 1993). Special Advr to Harriet Harman, MP, 1997–98; Res. Fellow, King's Fund; Associate Dir, Health, Social Care and Children's Early Years, IPPR; Dir, Maternity Alliance; Special Advr to Patricia Hewitt, MP, 2004–07; Dir, Ambulance Service Network, 2008–10. Shadow Minister for Care and Older People, 2011–15. Member: Educn Select Cttee, 2010; Communities and Local Govt Select Cttee, 2015–16; Sci. and Technol. Cttee, 2018–. *Address:* House of Commons, SW1A 0AA.

**KENDALL, Rev. Frank;** Non-stipendiary Priest, Diocese of Blackburn, since 2002 (Chairman, World Development Group, 2007–19); *b* 15 Dec. 1940; *s* of Norman and Violet Kendall; *m* 1965, Brenda Pickin; one *s* one *d. Educ:* Bradford Grammar School; Corpus Christi College, Cambridge (MA Classics); Southwark Ordination Course (London Univ. Dip. in Religious Studies). MPBW, 1962; DEA, 1967–68; MPBW, DoE and Dept of Transport, 1969–89; Under Secretary 1984; Chief Exec., St Helens MBC, 1989–91;

Venue Develt Manager, British Olympic Bid, 1992; Inspector of Schs, 1993–2000. Mem., Northern Rent Assessment Panel, later Residential Property Tribunal Service, 1997–2010. Ordained deacon, 1974, priest, 1975; Hon. Curate: Lingfield, Dio. of Southwark, 1974–75 and 1978–82; Sketty, Dio. of Swansea and Brecon, 1975–78; Limpsfield, Dio. of Southwark, 1982–84; Licensed Preacher, Dio. of Manchester, 1984–89; Non-stipendiary Priest, 1989–2001 and Chm., Bd for Social Responsibility, 1996–2001, Dio. of Liverpool. FRSA 1990–2004. *Recreations:* (i) writing for publication, (ii) decorating. *Address:* 52 Kingsway, Penwortham, Preston PR1 0ED. *T:* (01772) 748021.

**KENDALL, Prof. (John-) Michael,** PhD; FRS 2019; Professor of Geophysics, University of Oxford, since 2019; Fellow, St Cross College, Oxford, since 2019; *b* London, 21 Dec. 1962; *s* of John Kendall and Judi Kendall; one *s* one *d. Educ:* Queen's Univ., Kingston (BSc Hons Geol. with Phys 1984; PhD Geophys 1992). Geophysicist, Chevron Canada Resources Ltd, Calgary, 1984–86; Postdoctoral Res. Fellow, Inst. of Geophys and Planetary Phys, Scripps Inst. of Oceanography, Univ. of Calif, San Diego, 1992–93 (Green's Scholar, 1992); Asst Prof. of Phys, Univ. of Toronto, 1993–95; Prof. of Seismol., Univ. of Leeds, 1995–2005; BGS Prof. of Geophysics, Univ. of Bristol, 2005–19. Fellow, Amer. Geophysical Union, 2013. Bullerwell Lect., British Geophysical Assoc., 2003. Young Scientist Pubn Award, Eur. Geophysical Soc., 1993. *Publications:* over 200 articles in leading scientific jls. *Recreations:* running, ski-ing, hiking, cycling, music. *Address:* Department of Earth Sciences, University of Oxford, South Parks Road, Oxford OX1 3AN.

**KENDALL, Prof. Kevin,** FRS 1993; Professor of Formulation Engineering, University of Birmingham, 2000–11, now Honorary Professor; Director, since 1996, and Chief Executive Officer, since 2011, Adelan Ltd; *b* 2 Dec. 1943; *s* of Cyril Kendall and Margaret (*née* Swarbrick); *m* 1969, Patricia Jennifer Heyes; one *s* one *d. Educ:* London Univ. (BSc Physics External); PhD Cantab. Joseph Lucas, 1961–66; Cavendish Lab., 1966–69; British Rail Research, 1969–71; Monash Univ., 1972–74 (QEII fellowship); Akron Univ., 1974; ICI Runcorn, 1974–93; Prof. of Materials Science, Keele Univ., 1993–2000. *Publications:* Molecular Adhesion and its Applications, 2001; (with S. C. Singhal) High Temperature Solid Oxide Fuel Cells, 2003, 2nd edn (with M. Kendall), 2017; (jtly) Adhesion of cells, viruses and nanoparticles, 2012; papers in learned jls on adhesion, fracture, ceramics and materials. *Recreations:* walking, cycling. *Address:* Wycherley, Tower Road, Ashley Heath, Market Drayton, Shropshire TF9 4PY. *T:* (01630) 672665.

**KENDALL, Michael;** see Kendall, J. M.

**KENDALL, Sir Peter Ashley,** Kt 2015; Chairman, Agriculture and Horticulture Development Board, since 2014; *b* Bedford, 8 May 1960; *s* of John and Jasmine Kendall; *m* 1999, Emma McAlley; two *s* one *d. Educ:* Nottingham Univ. (BA Agricl Econs). Farmer, family business, farming and contracting. Chm., Cereals, 2003, Dep. Pres., 2004–06, Pres., 2006–14, NFU; Pres., World Farmers Orgn, 2014. Vice Pres., COPA, 2007–14. Mem., Policy Issues Council, IGD, 2006–. *Recreations:* countryside, shooting, ski-ing, cycling. *Address:* Eyeworth Lodge Farm, Ashwell, Baldock, Herts SG7 5JL. *T:* (01767) 631262.

**KENDALL, Raymond Edward,** QPM 1984; Secretary General, International Criminal Police Organization (Interpol), 1985–2000, now Hon. Secretary General; *b* 5 Oct. 1933; *m. Educ:* Simon Langton School, Canterbury; Exeter College, Oxford (MA Hons). RAF, 1951–53 (principally Malaya). Asst Supt of Police, Uganda Police, 1956–62; Metropolitan Police, New Scotland Yard, 1962–86 (principally Special Branch). Pres., Supervisory Cttee, EU Anti-Fraud Office, 2001–05. Exec. Chm., Brighterion. Mem., Forensic Sci. Soc. Editor-in-Chief: Counterfeits and Forgeries; Internat. Criminal Police Review. Chevalier de la Légion d'Honneur (France), 1997. *Recreations:* shooting, golf. *Address:* BP 202, 69657 Villefranche-Cedex, France. *Clubs:* Special Forces; Chief Constables.

**KENDALL, Prof. Tim,** DPhil; Professor of English Literature, since 2006, and Head of Department, since 2009, University of Exeter; *b* Plymouth, 11 Jan. 1970; *s* of Leslie and Susan Kendall; *m* 1995, Fiona Mathews; one *s* two *d. Educ:* Plymouth Coll.; Christ Church, Oxford (MA Hons 1991); Hertford Coll., Oxford (DPhil 1994). Lectr in English Lit., Christ Church, Oxford, 1994; Sir James Knott Res. Fellow, Univ. of Newcastle upon Tyne, 1995–97; Lectr, 1997–2001, Sen. Lectr, 2001–06, in English Lit., Univ. of Bristol. *Publications:* Paul Muldoon, 1996; Sylvia Plath: a critical study, 2001; Strange Land: poems, 2006; Modern English War Poetry, 2007; The Art of Robert Frost, 2012; (ed) Poetry of the First World War, 2013; (jtly) Norton Anthology of Poetry, 2018. *Recreations:* swimming, reading, writing poetry. *Address:* 2 Colybank, Rosemary Lane, Colyton, Devon EX24 6LR. *T:* (01297) 553222. *E:* t.kendall@exeter.ac.uk.

**KENDALL, Dr Timothy James Greaves,** FRCPsych; National Clinical Director for Mental Health, NHS England, since 2016, and NHS Improvement, since 2017; Director, National Collaborating Centre for Mental Health, Royal College of Psychiatrists, since 2002; *b* Sheffield, 23 Aug. 1957; *s* of William Nigel Kendall and Dinah Patricia Kendall; *m* 1997, Katriona Mary Malcolm; one *s* three *d. Educ:* Greensward Comp. Sch.; Newport Grammar Sch.; Univ. of Sheffield (BMedSci Physiol. and Neurochem.; MB ChB Medicine and Surgery). MRCPsych 1988, FRCPsych 2009. Consultant Psychiatrist (community and homelessness), Sheffield, 1992–; Dir, Centre for Psychotherapeutic Studies, Univ. of Sheffield, 1992–98; Dep. Dir, RCPsych res. unit, 1998–2002; Med. Dir, Sheffield Health and Social Care NHS Foundn Trust, 2003–16. Vis. Prof., Dept of Psychol., UCL, 2010–. Lancet Paper of the Year Award, 2004. *Publications:* papers in scientific jls. *Recreations:* walking, running, cooking, wine. *Address:* National Collaborating Centre for Mental Health, Royal College of Psychiatrists, 21 Prescott Street, E1 8BB. *T:* (020) 7235 2351. *E:* tim.kendall1@nhs.net.

**KENDALL, Prof. Wilfrid Stephen,** DPhil; Professor of Statistics, University of Warwick, since 1994; *b* 5 Nov. 1954; *s* of Prof. David George Kendall, FRS; *m* 1984, Catherine Mary Usher; two *s* two *d. Educ:* Perse Sch., Cambridge; Queen's Coll., Oxford (BA 1975; MA 1986); Linacre Coll., Oxford (MSc 1976; DPhil 1979); Univ. of Warwick (DSc 2013). Lectr, in Mathematical Stats, Univ. of Hull, 1978–84; Sen. Lectr in Stats, Univ. of Strathclyde, 1984–88; University of Warwick: Lectr in Stats, 1988–91; Reader, 1991–94; Chm., Dept of Stats, 1999–2002. Co-Dir, Acad. for PhD Trng in Statistics, 2006–16. Pres., Bernoulli Soc. for Mathematical Statistics and Probability, 2013–15 (Scientific Sec., 1996–2000). Member, Council: London Mathematical Soc., 2010–12; ISI, 2015–19. *Publications:* (jtly) Stochastic Geometry and its Applications, 1985, 2nd edn 1995; (jtly) New Directions in Dirichlet Forms, 1998; (ed jtly) Markov chain Monte Carlo: innovations and applications, 2005; (ed jtly) New Perspectives in Stochastic Geometry, 2009; contrib. numerous papers to learned jls. *Recreations:* family, hill-walking. *Address:* Department of Statistics, University of Warwick, Coventry CV4 7AL. *T:* (024) 7652 3082, *Fax:* (024) 7652 4532. *E:* w.s.kendall@warwick.ac.uk.
See also B. Kendall.

**KENDRICK, Prof. Anthony Robert,** MD; FRCGP; FRCPsych; FHEA; Professor of Primary Care, University of Southampton, since 2013; *b* Dover, 26 Sept. 1956; *s* of Anthony Ivor Kendrick and Robina Philp Smith Kendrick; *m* 2013, Dr Helen Mander; one *s* two *d. Educ:* Dover Grammar Sch.; St George's Hospital Med. Sch., Univ. of London (BSc 1978, MB BS 1981; DRCOG 1983; DCH 1984; MD 1996). FRCGP 1997; FRCPsych

2001; FHEA 2007. GP, 1985–2013; Mental Health Foundn Res. Fellow, 1990–94; Sen. Lectr, 1994–97, Reader, 1997–98, in Gen. Practice, St George's Hosp. Med. Sch., Univ. of London; Prof. of Primary Med. Care, Univ. of Southampton, 1998–2010; Dean, Hull York Med. Sch., 2010–13. Non-exec. Dir, Hull and E Yorks NHS Trust, 2010–13. President's Medal, RCGP, 2009. *Publications:* The Prevention of Mental Illness in Primary Care, 1996; Child Mental Health in Primary Care, 2001; (contrib.) Oxford Handbook of General Practice, 2005; Primary Care Mental Health, 2009; over 150 articles in jls on primary care mental health. *Recreations:* marathon running, ski-ing, long distance walking. *Address:* Aldermoor Health Centre, Southampton SO16 5ST. *T:* (023) 8024 1083, *Fax:* (023) 8070 1125. *E:* A.R.Kendrick@soton.ac.uk. *Club:* Totton Running.

**KENDRICK, Dominic John;** QC 1997; *b* 23 Feb. 1955; *s* of late Anthony Kendrick and Joan Kendrick; *m* 1984, Marice Chantal; one *s* two *d*. *Educ:* St Ambrose Coll.; Trinity Coll., Cambridge (BA Hons, MA); City Univ. (Dip. Law); Inns of Court Sch. of Law. Called to the Bar, Middle Temple, 1981, Bencher, 2013. *Recreations:* theatre, restoration of old houses, reading. *Address:* 7 King's Bench Walk, Temple, EC4Y 7DS. *T:* (020) 7583 0404.

**KENDRICK, Dame Fiona (Marie),** DBE 2015; Chairman, Nestlé UK and Ireland, since 2012 (Chief Executive Officer, 2012–17). Formerly teacher; joined Nestlé, 1980; Gen. Manager, Findus, 1991; Man. Dir, Nestlé UK, 2001–08; Sen. Vice-Pres. and Global Hd, Strategic Business Unit, Nestlé Coffee and Beverages, 2008–12. Mem. Bd, Inst. for Apprenticeships, then Inst. for Apprenticeships and Tech. Educn, 2017–. Pres., Food and Drink Fedn, 2015–16. *Address:* Nestlé UK, 1 City Place, Gatwick RH6 0PA.

**KENDRICK, Graham Andrew;** song and hymn writer; *b* 2 Aug. 1950; *s* of Maurice and Olive Kendrick; *m* 1976, Jill Gibson; four *d*. *Educ:* Avery Hill Coll. of Educn (Cert Ed 1972). Music Dir, British Youth for Christ, 1976–80; Kendrick & Stevenson (music and mime duo), 1981–84; Mem., Leadership Team, Ichthus Christian Fellowship, 1984–2004; Co-founder, March for Jesus, 1987. Songs and hymns sung in many languages worldwide; has recorded numerous albums, 1971–. Hon. DD Brunel, 2000. *Publications:* Worship, 1984; Ten Worshipping Churches, 1987; March for Jesus, 1992; Shine Jesus Shine, 1992; Awakening our Cities for God, 1993. *Recreations:* family, walking, music. *Address:* c/o Make Way Music, PO Box 320, Tunbridge Wells, Kent TN2 9DE. *E:* info@makewaymusic.com.

**KENEALLY, Thomas Michael,** AO 1983; FRSL; FAAAS; author; *b* 7 Oct. 1935; *s* of Edmond Thomas Keneally; *m* 1965, Judith Mary Martin; two *d*. Studied for NSW Bar. Schoolteacher until 1965; Commonwealth Literary Fellowship, 1966, 1968, 1972; Lectr in Drama, Univ. of New England, 1968–69. Vis. Prof., Dept of English, Univ. of California, Irvine, 1985; Berg Prof., Dept of English, New York Univ., 1988; Distinguished Prof., Dept of English and Comparative Lit., Univ. of Calif, Irvine, 1991–95. Chm., Australian Republican Movement, 1991–94. Member: (inaugural) Australia-China Council, 1978–83; Adv. Panel, Australian Constitutional Commn, 1985–88; Literary Arts Bd, Australia, 1985–88; Chm., Aust. Soc. Authors, 1987–90 (Mem. Council, 1985–); Pres., Nat. Book Council Australia, 1985–89. FRSL 1973. Silver City (screenplay, with Sophia Turkiewicz), 1985. Hon. DLitt: Queensland, 1993; NUI, 1994; Fairleigh Dickinson, NJ, 1994; Western Sydney, 1997. *Publications:* The Place at Whitton, 1964; The Fear, 1965, 2nd edn 1973; Bring Larks and Heroes, 1967, 2nd edn 1973; Three Cheers for the Paraclete, 1968; The Survivor, 1969; A Dutiful Daughter, 1971; The Chant of Jimmie Blacksmith, 1972 (filmed 1978); Blood Red, Sister Rose, 1974; Gossip from the Forest, 1975 (TV film, 1979); The Lawgiver, 1975; Season in Purgatory, 1976; A Victim of the Aurora, 1977; Ned Kelly and the City of the Bees, 1978; Passenger, 1979; Confederates, 1979; Schindler's Ark, 1982, reissued as Schindler's List, 1994 (Booker Prize; LA Times Fiction Prize; filmed as Schindler's List, 1994); Outback, 1983; The Cut-Rate Kingdom, 1984; A Family Madness, 1985; The Playmaker, 1987 (stage adaptation, perf. Royal Court, 1988); Towards Asmara, 1989; Flying Hero Class, 1991 (also screenplay); The Place where Souls are born, 1992; Now and in Time to be, 1992; Woman of the Inner Sea, 1992 (also screenplay); Memoirs from a Young Republic, 1993; Jacko, 1993; The Utility Player (biog.), 1994; A River Town, 1995; Homebush Boy: a memoir, 1995; The Great Shame, 1998; Bettany's Book, 2000; American Scoundrel: the life of the notorious Civil War General Dan Sickles, 2002; The Office of Innocence, 2002; The Tyrant's Novel, 2003; Lincoln, 2003; The Widow and Her Hero, 2007; Searching for Schindler (memoir), 2008; The People's Train, 2009; The Daughters of Mars, 2012; Shame and the Captives, 2014; Napoleon's Last Stand, 2016; Crimes of the Father, 2016; Two Old Men Dying, 2018; The Book of Science and Antiquities, 2018; (with Meg Keneally): The Soldier's Curse, 2016; The Unmourned, 2017; The Power Game, 2018; The Ink Stain, 2019; *non-fiction:* Australians: origins to eureka, 2009; Three Famines, 2010; Australians: eureka to the diggers, 2011; Australians: Flappers to Vietnam, 2013. *Recreations:* swimming, crosswords, hiking, cross-country ski-ing. *Address:* c/o Deborah Rogers, Rogers, Coleridge & White, 20 Powis Mews, W11 1JN.

**KENILWORTH,** 4th Baron *cr* 1937, of Kenilworth; **(John) Randle Siddeley;** Managing Director, Siddeley Landscapes, since 1976; Director, John Siddeley International Ltd; *b* 16 June 1954; *s* of John Tennant Davenport Siddeley (3rd Baron Kenilworth) and of Jacqueline Paulette, *d* of late Robert Gelpi; *S* father, 1981; *m* 1st, 1983, Kim (marr. diss. 1989), *o d* of Danie Serfontein, Newcastle upon Tyne; 2nd, 1991, Mrs Kiki McDonough (marr. diss. 2012); two *s*; 3rd, 2013, Catherine B. Bachand (marr. diss. 2016). *Educ:* Northeast Manor, near Lewes, Sussex; West Dean College (studied Restoration of Antique Furniture); London College of Furniture. Worked at John Siddeley International as interior designer/draughtsman, 1975; formed own company, Siddeley Landscapes, as landscape gardener, 1976; formed Randle Siddeley Associates, as landscape designer, 1994. *Recreation:* ski-ing. *Heir:* *s* Hon. William Randle John Siddeley, *b* 24 Jan. 1992. *Address:* Randle Siddeley Associates, Trafalgar House, Juniper Drive, SW18 1GY. *Clubs:* St James's, Annabel's, Hertford Street.

**KENNALLY, Katharine;** Chief Executive, Cornwall Council, since 2016; *b* Amersham, 22 Feb. 1971; *d* of David Brown and Elizabeth Bateman; *m* 2009, Rachael Rothero; one *s* one *d*. *Educ:* Univ. of Leeds (BA Hons Pols and Social Policy). Exec. Manager, Integrated Commissioning, Bucks CC, 2002–04; Area Prog. Lead, Hampshire and IoW Strategic HA, 2004–06; London Borough of Barnet: Asst Dir, 2006–08, Dep. Dir, 2008–10, Adult Social Services; Dir, Adult Social Care and Health, 2010–13; Strategic Dir of Communities (formerly Dir, People), 2013–16. *Recreations:* cinema, walking, local history, travel. *T:* (01872) 322100. *E:* Kate.Kennally@cornwall.gov.uk.

**KENNARD, Prof. Christopher,** PhD; FRCP, FMedSci; Professor of Clinical Neurology, and Head, Nuffield Department of Clinical Neurosciences (formerly Department of Clinical Neurology), 2008–16, now Professor Emeritus, and Senior Responsible Owner, Tinbergen Project, since 2017, University of Oxford (Head, Medical Sciences Division, 2017); Senior Kurti Fellow, Brasenose College, Oxford, since 2009; *b* 5 Jan. 1946; *s* of late Keith and Enid Kennard; *m* 1973, Cherry Fay Mortimer; two *d*. *Educ:* St Marylebone Grammar Sch., London; Charing Cross Hosp. Med. Sch., Univ. of London (MB BS Hons 1970; PhD 1978). FRCP 1988. Research Fellow: NIMR, 1973–76; Neuro-ophthalmology Unit, Univ. of Calif, San Francisco, 1980; Jun. hosp. appts, Charing Cross Hosp. and London Hosp., 1976–81; Consultant Neurologist, Royal London Hosp., 1981–91; Prof. of Clinical Neurology, Charing Cross and Westminster Med. Sch., 1991–97; Imperial College London: Prof. of Clinical Neurology, 1997–2008; Hd, Div. of Neurosci. and Psychol Medicine, 1997–2003; Dean, Charing Cross Campus, 2001–08; Dep. Principal, Faculty of Medicine, and Hd, Dept of Visual Neurosci., subseq. Dept of Clinical Neurosci., 2003–08; Chief of Service, 1995–98, Clinical Dir, 1998–2004, Neuroscis, Hammersmith Hosp. NHS Trust; Divl Dir, Neuroscis, Trauma and Specialist Surgery, Oxford Radcliffe Hosps NHS Trust, then Oxford Univ. Hosps NHS Trust, 2010–13. Non-exec. Mem., W London Mental Health NHS Trust, 2001–07. Chm., Cttee on Neurology, RCP, 1997–2005. Mem., MRC, 2006–08 (Mem., 2000–04, Chm., 2006–12, Neuroscience and Mental Health Bd). President: Assoc. of British Neurologists, 2003–05 (Asst Sec., 1990–92; Hon. Sec., 1992–95); European Neuro-ophthalmology Soc., 2011–15. Sec.-Gen., World Congress of Neurol., 2001 (Chair, Scientific Prog. Cttee, 2019–). Trustee: Migraine Trust, 1991–2008; Brain and Spine Foundn, 1993–2005. Deleg., OUP, 2010–. Chm., Pubn Cttee, World Fedn of Neurology, 2010–17. Ed., Jl Neurology, Neurosurgery and Psychiatry, 1997–2003. FMedSci 2001 (Mem. Council, 2004–07). Koetser Award, Betty and David Koetser Foundn for Brain Res., 2015; Assoc. of British Neurologists Medal, 2018. *Publications:* editor, several books on clinical neurology; papers on cognitive neuroscience and neuro-ophthalmology. *Recreation:* music. *Address:* Nuffield Department of Clinical Neurosciences, Level 6, West Wing, John Radcliffe Hospital, Oxford OX3 9DU. *Club:* Athenæum.

**KENNARD, Dr Olga, (Lady Burgen),** OBE 1988; ScD; FRS 1987; Director, Cambridge Crystallographic Data Centre, 1965–97; *b* 23 March 1924; *d* of Joir and Catherina Weisz; *m* 1st, 1948, David William Kennard (marr. diss. 1961); two *d*; 2nd, 1993, Sir Arnold Burgen, qv. *Educ:* Newnham Coll., Cambridge (BA 1945, MA 1948); Lucy Cavendish Coll., Cambridge (ScD 1973; Fellow). Res. Asst, Cavendish Laboratory, Cambridge, 1944–48; MRC Scientific Staff: Inst. of Ophthalmology, London, 1948–51; Nat. Inst. for Med. Res., London, 1951–61; seconded to University Chemical Laboratory, Cambridge, 1961–71; MRC special appt, 1974–89. Mem. Council, Royal Soc., 1995–97. Trustee, British Mus., 2004–12. Hon. LLD Cantab, 2003. *Publications:* about 800 pubns in field of X-ray structure determination of organic and bioactive molecules and correlation between structure, chemical properties and biological activity, and technical innovations in X-ray crystallography; ed 20 standard reference books. *Recreations:* reading, walking, architecture. *Address:* Keelson, 8A Hills Avenue, Cambridge CB1 7XA. *T:* (01223) 415381.

**KENNAWAY, Sir John-Michael,** 6th Bt *cr* 1791, of Hyderabad; *b* 17 Feb. 1962; *s* of Sir John Lawrence Kennaway, 5th Bt and of Christina Veronica Kennaway (née Urszenyi); *S* father, 2017; *m* 1988, Lucy Frances, *yr d* of Dr Jeremy Houlton Bradshaw-Smith; two *d*. *Educ:* Buckfast Abbey; Downside Abbey; King Edward's Sch., Bath. *Address:* Escot House, Escot Park, Ottery St Mary, Devon EX11 1LU.

**KENNEDY,** family name of **Marquess of Ailsa**.

**KENNEDY OF CRADLEY,** Baroness *cr* 2013 (Life Peer), of Cradley in the Metropolitan Borough of Dudley; **Alicia Pamela Kennedy;** *b* Birmingham, 22 March 1969; *d* of Frank and Mary Chater; *m* 2004, Roy Francis Kennedy (see Baron Kennedy of Southwark). *Educ:* Warwick Univ. (BSc Hons Psychol.). Labour Party: COS, 2001–03; Taskforce Leader, Field Ops, 2003–05 and 2009–10; Dep. Gen. Sec., 2006–11; Strategic Advr to Leader of Labour Party and of the Opposition, 2011–13; COS to Dep. Leader of Labour Party, 2015–. Member: Black Country Soc.; Child Poverty Action Gp; Amnesty Internat. Trustee, APT Action on Poverty, 2013–. MCIM. *Address:* House of Lords, SW1A 0PW. *T:* (020) 7219 6495. *E:* alicia.kennedy@parliament.uk.

**KENNEDY OF THE SHAWS,** Baroness *cr* 1997 (Life Peer), of Cathcart in the City of Glasgow; **Helena Ann Kennedy;** QC 1991; Director, International Bar Association Institute of Human Rights, since 2019 (Co-Chairman, 2012–17); *b* 12 May 1950; *d* of Joshua Patrick Kennedy and Mary Veronica (née Jones); partner, 1978–84, (Roger) Iain Mitchell; one *s*; *m* 1986, Dr Iain Louis Hutchison; one *s* one *d*. *Educ:* Holyrood Secondary Sch., Glasgow; Council of Legal Educn. Called to the Bar, Gray's Inn, 1972, Bencher, 1999; established chambers at: Garden Court, 1974; Tooks Court, 1984; Doughty St, 1990. Member: Bar Council, 1990–93; Cttee, Assoc. of Women Barristers, 1991–92; Nat. Bd, Women's Legal Defence Fund, 1989–91; Council, Howard League for Penal Reform, 1989– (Chm., commn of inquiry into violence in penal instns for children, report, 1995); CIBA Commn into Child Sexual Abuse, 1981–83; Exec. Cttee, NCCL, 1983–85; Bd, Minority Access to Legal Profession Project, Poly. of South Bank, 1984–85; British Council Law Adv. Cttee, 1995–98; Chairman: British Council, 1998–2004; Human Genetics Commn, 1998–2008; Pres., Council, Justice, 2011–. Principal, Mansfield Coll., Oxford, 2011–18. Founder, Bonavero Inst. of Human Rights, Oxford Univ., 2018 (Founding Fellow, 2019). Chancellor: Oxford Brookes Univ., 1994–2001; Sheffield Hallam Univ., 2018–. Chairman: Haldane Soc., 1983–86 (Vice-Pres., 1986–); Charter '88, 1992–97; Standing Cttee for Youth Justice, NACRO, 1993–; Cttee on widening participation of FEFC, 1995–97 (report, Learning Works); Leader of inquiry into health, envmtl and safety aspects of Atomic Weapons Establishment, Aldermaston (report, 1993). Member: Adv. Council, World Bank Inst.; Internat. Task Force On Terrorism, IBA, 2001–02; First Minister's Adv. Council on Women and Girls, 2017–. Commissioner: BAFTA inquiry into future of BBC, 1990; Hamlyn Nat. Commn on Educn, 1991–93. Chm., London Internat. Fest. of Theatre, 1993–2002. Member Board: City Limits Magazine, 1982–84; Counsel Magazine, 1990–92; Hampstead Theatre, 1989–98; Chm., Arts and Business, 2006–10. Broadcaster: first female moderator, Hypotheticals (Granada) on surrogate motherhood and artificial insemination; presenter: Heart of the Matter, BBC, 1987; Putting Women in the Picture, BBC2, 1987; The Trial of Lady Chatterley's Lover, Radio 4, 1990; Raw Deal, series of progs on med. negligence, BBC2, 1990; co-producer, Women Behind Bars, Channel 4, 1990; presenter, The Maguires: forensic evidence on trial, BBC2, 1991; creator, drama series, Blind Justice, BBC, 1988; host, After Dark, Channel 4, 1988; presenter, Time Gentlemen Please, BBC Scotland, 1994; presenter, Capital Justice, Radio 4, 2012. Trustee: BM, 2004–12; Booker Prize Foundn, 2008– (Chm., 2015–). FRSA; FCGI. Hon. Fellow, Inst. of Advanced Legal Studies, Univ. of London, 1997; Hon. FRCPath 2006; Hon. FRCPCH 2006; Hon. FRCPsych 2007; Hon. FBA 2013; Hon. FRSE 2014 (Royal Medal, 2011); Hon. FRSL 2018. Hon. Mem., Acad. Universelle des Cultures, Paris. Holds 40 hon. degrees. UK Woman of Europe Award, 1995. Cavaliere di Gran Croce, Order of Merit (Italy), 2004; Palme Académique (France), 2005. *Publications:* (jtly) The Bar on Trial, 1978; (jtly) Child Abuse Within the Family, 1984; (jtly) Balancing Acts, 1989; Eve was Framed, 1993; Just Law, 2004; Eve was Shamed, 2018; lectures; contribs on issues connected with law, civil liberties and women. *Recreations:* theatre, reading, spending time with family and friends. *Address:* House of Lords, SW1A 0PW. *T:* and *Fax:* (01708) 379482. *E:* hilary.hard@btinternet.com.

**KENNEDY OF SOUTHWARK,** Baron *cr* 2010 (Life Peer), of Newington in the London Borough of Southwark; **Roy Francis Kennedy;** Director of Finance, Labour Party, 2005–10; *b* Lambeth, 9 Nov. 1962; *s* of John Francis Kennedy and Frances Kennedy (née Hoban); *m* 2004, Alicia Chater (see Baroness Kennedy of Cradley). *Educ:* St Thomas the Apostle Sch., Peckham. Labour Party Official, 1990–2010: Organiser: London and SE, 1990–91; City of Coventry, 1991–93; Regl Officer, 1994–98, Regl Dir, 1998–2005, E Midlands. Election Agent to Harriet Harman, MP, 1985–87. Member (Lab): Southwark

LBC, 1986–94 (Dep. Leader, 1990–92); Lewisham LBC, 2014–18. An Opposition Whip, 2011–; opposition spokesperson: for communities and local govt, 2015–; on housing, 2015–; on home affairs, 2015–. Mem., Electoral Commn, 2010–14. Member: Nat. Exec. Cttee, Co-op. Party, 2016–; Exec. Cttee, Fabian Soc., 2017– (Vice Chair, 2019–). Chair, Council of People with Diabetes, Diabetes UK, 2012–16. Pres., Coll. of Podiatry, 2013–. Governor: Morley Coll., 2013–16; City of London Acad., Southwark, 2013–15. Trustee: Mayor of Southwark's Common Good Trust, 2013–; United St Saviour's Trust, 2014–. Dir, London Mutual Credit Union, 2014–. Hon. Alderman, Southwark LBC, 2007. *Recreations:* reading, walking, travelling, films, theatre. *Address:* House of Lords, SW1A 0PW. *T:* (020) 7219 1772. *E:* kennedyro@parliament.uk.

KENNEDY, Maj.-Gen. Alasdair Ian Gordon, CB 1996; CBE 1991 (OBE); LVO 2016; Secretary, Royal Automobile Club, 1998–2010 (Assistant General Secretary, 1997); *b* 6 Oct. 1945; *m* 1980, Meade Funsten; one *s* one *d*. *Educ:* RMCS; King's Coll., London (MA 2014). psc. Commnd Gordon Highlanders, 1966; Brig. 1988, Maj.-Gen. 1991. Comdr, HQ 24 Airmobile Bde, 1988–90; Dir Gen., Territorial Army, 1992–95; Sen. Army Mem., RCDS, 1995–96, retired 1997. Dir/Trustee, ABF: the Soldiers Charity. Hon. Col, Tayforth Univs OTC, 1991–97. Gentleman Usher to the Queen, 2005–15. *Address:* Tall Trees, Quarry Wood Road, Marlow, Bucks SL7 1RF.

KENNEDY, Alasdair John Samuel; Headmaster, Trinity School, Croydon, since 2016; *b* Edinburgh, 1973; *s* of David Kennedy and Olive Kennedy; *m* 1996, Ruth Caroe; three *s*. *Educ:* Fettes Coll., Edinburgh; St John's Coll., Cambridge (BA 1995; PGCE). Teacher of Physics: Rugby Sch., 1996–99; Sevenoaks Sch., 1999–2003; Hd of Physics, 2003–07, Dep. Master Academic, 2007–16, Dulwich Coll. *Recreations:* Rugby blue, sports fanatic, party busker, coffee lover, worship leader, under-gardener. *Address:* Trinity School, Shirley Park, Croydon CR9 7AT. *T:* (020) 8656 9541. *E:* ajk@trinity.croydon.sch.uk.

KENNEDY, (Alastair) James; Director, Global Engagement (formerly International Office), University of Warwick, 2008–17; *b* 6 May 1954; *s* of David Kennedy and Janet Farquahar Kennedy; *m* 1982, Kathryn Patricia Lawry; two *s* two *d*. *Educ:* Univ. of Exeter (BA Modern Langs); Inst. of Educn, Univ. of London (PGCE); Edinburgh Univ. (MSc Applied Linguistics). VSO, Laos, then Tanzania, 1978; British Council: Kuwait, 1982–84; Malaysia, 1984–86; London, 1986–90; Swaziland, 1990–94; Malawi, 1994–98; Manchester, 1998–2001; Kazakhstan, 2001–04; Regional Dir, Russia, 2004–08. Member (Green): Warwick DC, 2019–; Kenilworth Town Council, 2019–. Mem., Coventry Dio. Bd of Educn, 2010–17. Advr, Univ. of Yangon, Myanmar, 2018–. Trustee, UK Council for Internat. Student Affairs, 2011–17.

KENNEDY, Alison Louise; writer; *b* 22 Oct. 1965; *d* of Robert Alan Kennedy and Edwardene Mildred Kennedy. *Educ:* Warwick Univ. (BA Hons Theatre Studies and Dramatic Arts). Community arts worker, Clydebank and Dist, 1980–89; Writer-in-Residence: Hamilton and E Kilbride Social Work Dept, 1989–91; Project Ability, 1989–95; Copenhagen Univ., 1995; Lectr (pt-time), Creative Writing Prog., St Andrews Univ., 2003–07; Associate Prof., Creative Writing Prog., Warwick Univ., 2007–. *Publications:* Night Geometry and the Garscadden Trains, 1990; Looking for the Possible Dance, 1993; Now That You're Back, 1994; So I Am Glad, 1995; The Life and Death of Colonel Blimp, 1997; Original Bliss, 1997; On Bullfighting, 1999; Everything You Need, 1999; Indelible Acts, 2002; Paradise, 2004; Day, 2007; What Becomes, 2009; The Blue Book, 2011; On Writing, 2013; All the Rage, 2014; Dr Who and the Drosten's Curse, 2015; Serious Sweet, 2016; Uncle Shawn and Bill and the Almost Entirely Unplanned Adventure, 2016; Uncle Shawn and Bill and the Pajimminy Crimminy Unusual Adventure, 2018; The Little Snake, 2018; Uncle Shawn and Bill and the Not One Tiny Bit Lovey-Dovey Moon Adventure, 2019. *Recreations:* few. *Address:* c/o Antony Harwood, Antony Harwood Ltd, 103 Walton Street, Oxford OX2 6EB. *T:* (01865) 559615, *Fax:* (01865) 310660. *E:* ant@antonyharwood.com.

KENNEDY, Anthony McLeod; Associate Justice of the Supreme Court of the United States, 1988–2018; *b* 23 July 1936; *s* of Anthony J. Kennedy and Gladys Kennedy; *m* Mary Davis; two *s* one *d*. *Educ:* Stanford Univ. (AB 1958); LSE; Harvard Univ. (LLB 1961). Mem., Calif. Bar, 1962, US Tax Court Bar, 1971. Associate, Thelen Marrin Johnson & Bridges, San Francisco, 1961–63; sole practice, 1963–67; partner Evans, Jackson & Kennedy, 1967–75. Prof. of Constitutional Law, McGeorge Sch. of Law, Univ. of Pacific, 1965–88; Judge, US Court of Appeals, 9th Circuit, Sacramento, 1976–88. UN Commn on Legal Empowerment of the Poor, 2005–08. Hon. Fellow: Amer. Bar Assoc. (Medal for Dist. Service, 2007); Amer. Coll. of Trial Lawyers. Hon. Bencher, Inner Temple.

KENNEDY, Catherine Mary; see Law, C. M.

KENNEDY, Christopher Laurence Paul; QC 2010; a Recorder, since 2016; *b* Sheffield, 10 Aug. 1966; *s* of Rt Hon. Sir Paul (Joseph Morrow) Kennedy, *qv*; *m* 1992, Rebecca McCarthy; two *s* two *d*. *Educ:* Ampleforth Coll.; Gonville and Caius Coll., Cambridge (BA Law 1988). Called to the Bar, Gray's Inn, 1989. *Address:* 9 St John Street, Manchester M3 4DN. *T:* (0161) 955 9000. *E:* christopher.kennedy@9sjs.com.

KENNEDY, Danny; see Kennedy, T. D.

KENNEDY, David, CMG 1997; Director-General, Commonwealth War Graves Commission, 1993–2000; *b* 7 Nov. 1940; *s* of Lilian Alice Kennedy; *m* 1964, Peta Jennifer Hatton; two *d*. *Educ:* Ryhope Robert Richardson Grammar Sch., Co. Durham. City of London Coll. Exchequer and Audit Dept, 1959–69; Commonwealth War Graves Commission: Higher Exec. Officer, 1969–71; Sen. Exec. Officer, 1971–74; Principal: Dir of Management Services, 1975–79; Dir, Outer Area, 1979–84; Senior Principal: Dir, France Area, 1984–86; Dir of Personnel, 1986–87; Dep. Dir-Gen., Admin, 1987–92; rcds 1992. Mem., MENSA, 2002–; Licentiate, British Professional Photographers Assoc., 2004–. *Recreations:* golf, photography, hill-walking, travel. *Address:* March House, Blands Close, Burghfield Common, Berks RG7 3JY. *T:* (0118) 983 2941. *Club:* Reading Golf (Dir, 2005–11; Capt., 2018).

KENNEDY, David, CBE 2015; PhD; Director General for Food, Farming, Animal and Biosecurity (formerly Plant Health), Department for Environment, Food and Rural Affairs, since 2017; *b* Manchester, 29 Sept. 1969; *s* of Peter Kennedy and Anne Kennedy; *m* 2001, Philippa Stonebridge; two *s* one *d*. *Educ:* Sheffield Univ. (BA Economics/Econometrics); Univ. of Manchester (MA Econ); London Sch. of Economics (PhD Econs 1995). Res. Fellow, LSE, 1993–96; Consultant, Centre for Regulated Industries, 1996–97; Senior Economist: EBRD, 1997–2003; World Bank, 2003–06; Chief Exec., Cttee on Climate Change, 2008–14; Dir Gen. for Econ. Develt, DFID, 2014–16. *Publications:* Building a Low-carbon Economy (with Adair Turner), 2008; Meeting Carbon Budgets: the need for a step change, 2009; over 50 reports and articles on energy, infrastructure and climate change. *Recreations:* kids, classical clarinet, jazz saxophone, literature, Manchester City. *Address:* Department for Environment, Food and Rural Affairs, 2 Marsham Street, SW1P 4DF.

KENNEDY, David Patrick Leslie; Professional Photographer and Urbanist, Place Images, since 2017; *b* Cork, 21 Oct. 1959; *s* of Prof. Patrick Brendan Kennedy and Pamela Mary Kennedy; *m* 1998, Sarah Jacqueline Mela Sheehan. *Educ:* York Minster Song Sch.; Lord Wandsworth Coll.; Nunthorpe Grammar Sch., York; Newcastle Poly. (BA Hons Govt 1983); Univ. of Bristol (Masters Public Policy Studies 1987). Res. and Intelligence Asst, 1984–86, Res. and Analysis Officer, 1986–87, Arun DC; Performance Mgt Officer, 1987–89, Hd, Policy and Performance Services, 1989–90, City of York Council; Hd, Strategic Develt, Watford BC, 1990–96; Chief Exec., Gedling BC, 1996–2001; Dir, Envmt and Develt, 2001–03, Dir of Develt and Dep. Chief Exec., 2003–07, Barnsley MBC; Chief Exec., Northampton BC, 2007–17. Academician, Acad. of Urbanism. FRSA. *Recreations:* travel, photography, French wine, cricket and Rugby spectating, music, theatre. *E:* mail@placeimages.co.uk.

KENNEDY, Her Honour Denise Margaret; a County Court Judge, Northern Ireland, 2000–12; *b* 13 April 1942; *d* of late David L. R. Halliday and Doris Halliday (*née* Molyneaux); *m* 1966, John Andrew Dunn Kennedy; two *s* one *d*. *Educ:* Cheltenham Ladies' Coll.; Exeter Univ. (BA Hons); Queen's Univ. of Belfast. Called to the Bar: NI, 1977; Ireland, 1985; in practice at the Bar, 1977–90; Legal Sec. to Lord Chief Justice of NI, 1990–93; Master, High Court, Supreme Court of Judicature of NI, 1993–2000; Dep. County Court Judge, 1993–2000; Dep. Clerk of Crown for NI, 1993–2000. Part-time Chm., Industrial Tribunals, NI, 1985–90; Mem., Independent Commn for Police Complaints, NI, 1988–90. Mem., Civil Justice Reform Gp for NI, 1998–2000. *Recreations:* travel, gardening, cinema. *Address:* 2 Burnage Court, 6 Martello Park, Canford Cliffs, Poole, Dorset BH13 7BA. *Club:* Royal Over-Seas League.

KENNEDY, Sir George Matthew Rae, 9th Bt *cr* 1836, of Johnstown Kennedy, Co. Dublin; *b* 9 Dec. 1993; *s* of Sir Michael Edward Kennedy, 8th Bt and of Helen Christine Jennifer (*née* Rae), 2012, but his name does not appear on the Official Roll of the Baronetage.

KENNEDY, Heather Claire; see Lloyd, H. C.

KENNEDY, Prof. Hugh Nigel, PhD; FBA 2012; Professor of Arabic, School of Oriental and African Studies, University of London, since 2007; *b* Hythe, Kent, 22 Oct. 1947; *s* of David Kennedy and Janet Kennedy; *m* 1970, Hilary Wybar; one *s* two *d* (and one *d* decd). *Educ:* Pembroke Coll., Cambridge (BA 1969; PhD 1977). Lectr, 1972–97, Prof. of Middle Eastern Hist., 1997–2007, Dept of Mediaeval Hist., Univ. of St Andrews. *Publications:* The Early Abbasid Caliphate, 1981; The Prophet and the Age of the Caliphates, 600–1050, 1986 (trans. Hebrew), 2nd edn 2004; Al-Mansur and al-Mahdi: being an annotated translation of vol. xxix of the History of al-Tabari, 1990; Crusader Castles, 1994; Muslim Spain and Portugal, 1996 (trans. Portuguese); The Armies of the Caliphs, 2001; (ed) An Historical Atlas of Islam, 2nd edn 2002; Mongols, Huns and Vikings, 2003 (trans. French); The Court of the Caliphs, 2004 (trans. Arabic, Italian, Polish, Spanish); (ed jtly) Building Legitimacy, 2004; (ed) Muslim Military Architecture in Syria, 2006; The Great Arab Conquests, 2007 (trans. Arabic, Dutch, Italian, Spanish, Indonesian, Persian, Turkish); (ed) Al-Tabari, 2008. *Recreations:* visiting castles, hill walking, architectural history. *Address:* Faculty of Languages and Cultures, School of Oriental and African Studies, University of London, WC1H 0XG. *E:* hk1@soas.ac.uk.

KENNEDY, Sir Ian (Alexander), Kt 1986; Judge of the High Court of Justice, Queen's Bench Division, 1986–2000; *b* 7 Sept. 1930; *s* of late Gerald and Elizabeth Kennedy; *m* 1962, Susan Margaret, *d* of late Edward and Eileen Hatfield; three *s* one *d*. *Educ:* Wellington Coll., Berks; Pembroke Coll., Cambridge (BA). Called to the Bar, Middle Temple, 1953; Treas., 1999. Dep. Chm., IoW QS, 1971; a Recorder of the Crown Court, 1972; QC 1974. Judge, Employment Appeal Tribunal, 1990–2000. Mem., Parole Bd, 1991–94 (Vice-Chm., 1992–93). *Recreations:* theatre, walking, gardening. *Address:* c/o Messrs C. Hoare & Co., 37 Fleet Street, EC4P 4DQ.

KENNEDY, Sir Ian (McColl), Kt 2002; FBA 2002; Chairman, Independent Parliamentary Standards Authority, 2009–16; Professor of Health Law, Ethics and Policy, School of Public Policy, University College London, 1997–2001, now Emeritus; *b* 14 Sept. 1941; *s* of late Robert Charles Kennedy and Dorothy Elizabeth Kennedy; two *s*. *Educ:* King Edward VI Sch., Stourbridge; University Coll. London (1st Cl. Hons LLB; Fellow, 1999); Univ. of Calif, Berkeley (LLM); LLD London. Called to the Bar, Inner Temple, 1974 (Hon. Bencher, 1996). Fulbright Fellow, 1963–65; Lectr in Law, UCL, 1965–71; Ford Foundn Fellow, Yale Univ. and Univ. of Mexico, 1966–67; Vis. Prof., Univ. of Calif, LA, 1971–72; King's College, London: Lectr in Law, 1973–78; Reader in English Law 1978–83; British Acad. Res. Fellow, 1978; Dir, Centre of Law, Medicine and Ethics, subseq. Centre of Med. Law and Ethics, 1978–93; Prof. of Med. Law and Ethics, 1983–97; Hd, Dept of Laws, 1986–89; Hd and Dean of Sch. of Law, 1989–92 and 1993–96; Pres., Centre of Med. Law and Ethics, 1993–97. FKC 1988. Vis. Prof., LSE, 2003–. Vice-Pres., Coll. of Medicine, 2010–. Chairman: Sec. of State for Health's Adv. Gp on Ethics of Xenotransplantation, 1996–97; Minister of Agriculture's Adv. Gp on Quarantine, 1997–98; Public Inquiry into paediatric cardiac surgical services at Bristol Royal Infirmary, 1998–2001; Commn for Healthcare Audit and Inspection, 2004–09 (Shadow Chm., 2002–04); UK Panel for Res. Integrity in Health and Biomed. Sci., 2006–13; Inquiry into Innovation in Health Technologies, 2009; King's Fund Inquiry into quality of care in general practice, 2009–10; Internat. Panel for Designation of Academic Health Sci. Centres, DoH, 2009; Assessment Panel, Paediatric Cardiac Surgery, DoH, 2010–11; Breast Surgery Review, Heart of England NHS Foundn Trust, 2013; Nat. Adv. Gp on Mortality Outliers, DoH, 2013; Review of Response of HEFT to concerns about Mr Ian Paterson's Surgical Practice, 2013; Review of policy regarding stored organs, Birmingham Children's Hosp., 2014; Review of Paediatric Cardiac Surgery, Bristol Royal Infirmary, 2014–16; Member: Medicines Commn, 1984–91; GMC, 1984–93; Expert Adv. Gp on AIDS, DHSS, later Dept of Health, 1987–94; Gen. Adv. Council, BBC, 1987–91; Med. Ethics Cttee, BMA, 1990–98; Nuffield Council on Bioethics, 1991–2002 (Chm., 1998–2002); Archbishop of Canterbury's Adv. Gp on Med. Ethics, 1994–2003; Register of Ind. Mems, Defence Scientific Adv. Council, MoD, 1997–; Genetics Cttee, ABI, 1997–2001; Science in Society Cttee, Royal Soc., 2000–04; Adv. Gp on Human Remains, Natural Hist. Mus., 2006–; Adv. Cttee on Military Medicine, MoD, 2006–; Adv. Bd, NHS Staff Coll., 2011–; Expert Panel on PIP Breast Implants, DoH, 2011–12; Adv. Gp, Review of Cosmetic Surgery, DoH, 2012–13. Mem., Council, Open Section, RSM, 1978–88 (Vice-Pres., 1981–86; FRSocMed 1985); Regent, RCSE, 2006. Trustee, London Pathway - Healthcare for the Homeless, 2011–. Reith Lectr, 1980. Editor, Medical Law Review, 1993–98. Fellow, SLS, 2004. Hon. QC 2015. Hon. FRCGP 2002; Hon. FRCP 2003; Hon. FRCPCH 2004; Hon. FRCA 2004; Hon. FRCSE 2005; Hon. FIIA 2009; Hon. FRCS 2013. Hon. DSc Glasgow, 2003; Hon. DM Birmingham, 2006; DUniv York, 2016. McKeown Medal, RCSE, 2018. *Publications:* The Unmasking of Medicine, 1981, rev. edn 1983; Treat Me Right, 1988; (with A. Grubb) Medical Law: cases and materials, 1989, 2nd edn as Medical Law: text with materials, 1994, 3rd edn 2000; (with A. Grubb) Principles of Medical Law,

1998; Appraising the Value of Innovation and Other Benefits, 2009; Getting it Right for Children and Young Persons: review of children's services in the NHS, 2010; Cleaning Up the Mess: after the MPs' expenses scandal, 2019. *Recreations:* ballet, talking to my sons, gardening. *Club:* Garrick.

**KENNEDY, Cdre Inga Jane,** CBE 2017; Assistant Chief of Staff Medical, Head, Royal Naval Medical Service, and Medical Director General (Naval), Royal Navy, since 2017; *b* Aberdeen, 7 Sept. 1962; *d* of Richard and Rhoda Kennedy; *m* 2014, Mark Durkan. *Educ:* Queen Margaret Coll., Edinburgh (BA Nursing Studies); Univ. of Greenwich (Postgrad. DipHE). RN; RM; RN Lectr. SO, Healthcare Assce, Navy Comd HQ, 2010–11; Healthcare Assce, Jt Forces Comd, Afghanistan, 2011; DACOS Healthcare, Navy Comd HQ, 2012–15; Inspector Gen., HQ Surgeon Gen., 2015–17. QHNS 2012. Mem., Assoc. of RN Officers. *Recreations:* off-shore sailing, downhill ski-ing. *Address:* 21A Blackbrook Park Avenue, Fareham, Hants PO15 5JN. *T:* 07714 574328. *Club:* Royal Scots (Edinburgh).

**KENNEDY, James;** *see* Kennedy, A. J.

**KENNEDY, Rt Hon. Jane (Elizabeth);** PC 2003; Police and Crime Commissioner for Merseyside, 2012–May 2020 (Lab, 2012–19; Ind, 2019–May 2020); *b* 4 May 1958; *d* of Clifford and Barbara Hodgson; *m* 1977, Robert Malcolm Kennedy (marr. diss. 1998); two *s. Educ:* Haughton Comprehensive Sch., Darlington; Queen Elizabeth Sixth Form Coll.; Liverpool Univ. Child care residential worker 1979–84, Care Assistant 1984–88, Liverpool Social Services; Area Organiser, NUPE, 1988–92. MP (Lab) Liverpool Broadgreen, 1992–97, Liverpool, Wavertree, 1997–2010. An Asst Govt Whip, 1997–98; a Lord Comr of HM Treasury (Govt Whip), 1998–99; Parly Sec., LCD, 1999–2001; Minister of State: NI Office, 2001–04; DWP, 2004–05; DoH, 2005–06; Financial Sec., HM Treasury, 2007–08; Minister of State, DEFRA, 2008–09. Mem., Social Security Select Cttee, 1992–94. *Recreation:* dogs. *Address:* (office) Allerton Police Station, Rose Lane, Allerton, Liverpool L18 5ED.

**KENNEDY, Jane Hope, (Mrs J. Maddison),** RIBA; Partner, Purcell Architecture (formerly Purcell Miller Tritton (Architects)), since 1992 (Chairman, 2009–13); *b* 28 Feb. 1953; *d* of Thomas Brian Kennedy and Emily Hope Kennedy (*née* Bailey); *m* 1975, John Maddison; two *s. Educ:* Manchester Polytech. (DipArch). RIBA 1990; IHBC 1997; AABC 2000. Assistant: British Waterways Bd, 1978–80; David Jeffcoate, 1980–81; self-employed architect, 1981–86; Historic Bldgs Architect, Norwich CC, 1986–88; architect, 1988–90, Associate, 1990–92, Purcell Miller Tritton. Major projects include: repairs to North and South Fronts and re-presentation of interiors, Stowe House, Bucks, 1999–; repairs, 1997–2012, Processional Way, 2001, Ely Cathedral; restoration of Ballyfin, Central Eire, 2002–09; re-presentation of Kew Palace, 2004–. Surveyor to Fabric of Ely Cathedral, 1994–2017; Architect to Newcastle Cathedral, 2006–; refurbishment of Blue Boar Quad, Christ Church, Oxford, 2007–09; Architect to Foundn, Christ Church, Oxford, 2008–; repair and representation, Auckland Castle, 2012–. Comr, English Heritage, 2006–14. Mem. Heritage Adv. Panel, Canal and River Trust, 2012–. Trustee, Historic Royal Palaces, 2015–. Sec., Cathedral Architects' Assoc., 2000–06 (Chm., 2017–). FRSA 1994. Canterbury Cross for services to the Church of England, Archbishop of Canterbury, 2017. *Publications:* articles in conservation jls. *Recreations:* old buildings, walking, re-learning the violin, boating. *Address:* Purcell, 3 Colegate, Norwich NR3 1BN. *T:* (01603) 674444. *E:* jane.kennedy@purcelluk.com.

**KENNEDY, Joanna Alicia Gore,** OBE 1995; FREng, FICE; Director, 1996–2013, and Global Programme and Project Management Leader, 2010–13, Ove Arup and Partners; *b* 22 July 1950; *d* of late Captain G. A. G. Ormsby, DSO, DSC, RN and Susan Ormsby; *m* 1979, Richard Paul Kennedy, *qv*; two *s. Educ:* Queen Anne's School, Caversham; Lady Margaret Hall, Oxford (Scholar, 1969; BA 1st cl. Hons Eng. Sci. 1972; MA 1976). MICE 1979, FICE 1992; FREng (FEng 1997). Ove Arup and Partners, consulting engineers: Design Engineer, 1972; Sen. Engr, 1979; Arup Associates, 1987; Arup Project Management, 1990; Associate, 1992; Associate Dir, 1994; Leader, Arup Project Management Europe, 2006–10. Non-exec. Dir, Native Land Ltd, 2016–. Member: Engineering Council, 1984–86 and 1987–90; Council, ICE, 1984–87; Adv. Council, RNEC Manadon, 1988–94; Engrg, later Engrg and Technol. Bd, SERC, 1990–94; EPSRC, 2002–06 (Mem., Tech. Opportunities Panel, 1994–97); Dir, Engrg and Technol. Bd, 2002–05. Mem. Bd, PLA, 2000–09 (Vice-Chm., 2008–09); Dir, Port of London Properties Ltd, 2001–05. Comr, Royal Commn for Exhibn of 1851, 2003–12. Trustee: Nat. Mus. of Science and Industry, 1992–2002; Ove Arup Partnership, 1998–2005; Cumberland Lodge, 2001–11, 2013–18; Ove Arup Foundn, 2010–. Member, Board: ERA Foundn, 2014–; NPG, 2015–. Member, Council: Univ. of Southampton, 1996–99; RCA, 2001–16; Governor: Downe House Sch., 1985–89; Channing Sch., 1992–2002; Mem., Smeatonian Soc. of Civil Engineers, 2005–. Patron, Women into Sci. and Engrg, 2008–. Major, Engineer and Logistic Staff Corps, RE (V), 2004–14. Hon. DSc Salford, 1994. FRSA 1986. Hon. Fellow, RCA, 2017. Woman of the Year, Inspire Awards for Built Environment, 2007; RCUK Woman of Outstanding Achievement Award, 2008; CBI/ Real Business First Women Award for Engrg, 2013. *Address:* 9 Luscombe Road, Poole, Dorset BH14 8ST.

**KENNEDY, Rev. Joseph,** DPhil; Vicar of St Saviour's, Oxton, since 2011; Tutor and Lecturer in Theology, St Mellitus College, since 2015; *b* Edinburgh, 1 Jan. 1969; *s* of late Andrew Kennedy and of Margaret Anne Kennedy (*née* Lawson); *m* 2001, Emily Elizabeth Lyons Connell; one *s* one *d. Educ:* Edinburgh Univ. (BSc 1991; BD 1994); Moray House Inst. of Educn (PGCE 1997); St Stephen's House, Oxford; St Hugh's Coll., Oxford (MSt 2000); Keble Coll., Oxford (Gosden Scholar; DPhil 2006). Ordained deacon, 2002, priest, 2003; Assistant Curate: Mortimer, 2002–03; Abingdon, 2003–05; Dean of Chapel, Chaplain and Fellow, Selwyn Coll., Cambridge, 2005–08; Chaplain, Newnham Coll., Cambridge, 2005–08; Principal, Coll. of Resurrection, Mirfield, 2008–11. Hon. Canon, Wakefield Cathedral, 2010–11. *Recreations:* reading, travel, baking my own bread. *Address:* The Vicarage, 7 Willow Lea, Prenton, Wirral CH43 2GQ. *T:* (0151) 652 2402. *E:* Joe.Kennedy@oxtonstsaviour.co.uk.

**KENNEDY, Lulu,** MBE 2012; Founder and Director, Fashion East, since 2000; Creative Director, Lulu & Co., since 2010; *b* Newcastle upon Tyne, 28 Dec. 1969; *d* of John Paul Kennedy and Dr Ruth Kennedy. *Educ:* Middlesex Univ. (BA). Events Manager, Old Truman Brewery, 1996–2000. Ed.-at-Large, Love mag., 2012–. *Address:* Fashion East, Old Truman Brewery, 91 Brick Lane, E1 6QL. *T:* (020) 7770 6150. *E:* info@fashioneast.co.uk.

**KENNEDY, Dr Malcolm William,** CBE 2000; FRSE; FREng, FIET; Chairman, PB Power (incorporating Merz and McLellan), 1999–2002 (Executive Chairman, Merz and McLellan, 1995–98); *b* 13 March 1935; *s* of William and Lily Kennedy; *m* 1962, Patricia Ann Forster; (one *d* decd). *Educ:* Durham Univ. (BSc 1961); Univ. of Newcastle upon Tyne (PhD 1964). FIET (FIEE 1974); FREng (FEng 1985); FRSE 2002. Apprentice, C. A. Parsons, 1951–56; Merz and McLellan, 1964–2002: Power Systems Design Engr, 1964; Head, Electrical Div., 1976; Sen. Partner, 1988–91; Chm. and Man. Dir, 1991–95. Mem. Electricity Panel, 1993–98; Water and Telecommunications Panel, 1998–2001, Monopolies and Mergers Commn. Non-exec. Director: Port of Tyne Authority,

1994–2001; New and Renewable Energy Centre, 2003–12; Renewable Energy Generation Ltd, 2007–16. Advr, London Power Associates Ltd, 2011–14. Vice Pres., Nat. Energy Action, 2007–12 (Chm., 2001–07). Pres., IEE, 1999–2000 (Henry Nimmo Premium, 1961; Chm., Power Div., 1986–87; Vice-Pres., 1994–96; Dep. Pres., 1996–99). Methodist local preacher. *Publications:* papers on electricity industry, UK and overseas. *Recreations:* cricket, railways. *Address:* Apartment 5, St James Place, 7 Dacre Street, Morpeth, Northumberland NE61 1HW. *Club:* National.

**KENNEDY, His Honour Michael Denis;** QC 1979; a Circuit Judge, 1984–2006; *b* 29 April 1937; *s* of Denis George and Clementina Catherine (*née* MacGregor); *m* 1964, Elizabeth June Curtiss; two *s* two *d. Educ:* Downside School; Gonville and Caius College, Cambridge (open Schol., Mod. Langs; MA). 15/19 King's Royal Hussars, 1955–57. Called to the Bar, Inner Temple, 1961; a Recorder, 1979–84; Designated Civil Judge for Sussex, 1999–2004. *Address:* Iford Court, Iford, Lewes, E Sussex BN7 3EU. *T:* (01273) 476432.

**KENNEDY, Nigel Paul;** solo concert violinist; Artistic Director, Polish Chamber Orchestra, 2002–08; founder, Orchestra of Life, 2010; *b* 28 Dec. 1956; *s* of John Kennedy and Scylla Stoner; one *s; m* Agnieszka Chowaniec. *Educ:* Yehudi Menuhin School; Juilliard School of Performing Arts, NY. ARCM. Début at Festival Hall with Philharmonia Orch., 1977; regular appearances with London and major orchestras throughout the world, 1978–; Berlin début with Berlin Philharmonic, 1980; Henry Wood Promenade début, 1981; New York début with BBC SO, 1987; tour of Hong Kong and Australia, with Hallé Orch. 1981; foreign tours, 1978–: India, Japan, S Korea, Turkey, USA, Europe, Scandinavia; many appearances as jazz violinist with Stéphane Grappelli, incl. Edinburgh Fest., 1974 and Carnegie Hall, 1976; many TV and radio appearances, incl. Vivaldi's Four Seasons with ECO (Golden Rose of Montreux, 1990), and two documentaries. Pop, jazz and classical recordings, incl. Vivaldi's Four Seasons (best-selling album of a complete classical work; No 1 in UK Classical Chart for over one year (Guinness Book of Records, 1990)); Best Classical Record, British Record Industry Awards: for Elgar Violin Concerto, 1985; for Beethoven Violin Concerto, 1991; Best Recording, Gramophone mag., for Elgar Violin Concerto, 1985. Variety Club Showbusiness Personality of the Year, 1991. Hon. DLitt Bath, 1991. *Publications:* Always Playing, 1991. *Recreations:* football (watching and playing), cricket. *Address:* Terri Robson Associates, 63–64 Leinster Square, W2 4PS.

**KENNEDY, Rt Hon. Sir Paul (Joseph Morrow),** Kt 1983; PC 1992; a Lord Justice of Appeal, 1992–2005; Interception of Communications Commissioner, 2006–12; President, Court of Appeal of Gibraltar, 2011–15 (Member, 2006–15); *b* 12 June 1935; *o s* of late Dr J. M. Kennedy, Sheffield; *m* 1965, Virginia, twin *d* of Baron Devlin, FBA and of Madeleine, *yr d* of Sir Bernard Oppenheimer, 1st Bt; two *s* two *d. Educ:* Ampleforth Coll.; Gonville and Caius Coll., Cambridge (MA, LLB; Hon. Fellow, 1998). Called to Bar, Gray's Inn, 1960, Bencher, 1982 (Vice Treas., 2001; Treas., 2002); a Recorder, 1972–83; QC 1973; Judge, High Court of Justice, QBD, 1983–92; Presiding Judge, N Eastern Circuit, 1985–89; Vice-Pres., QBD, High Ct of Justice, 1997–2002. Mem., Judicial Studies Bd, 1993–96 (Chm., Criminal Cttee, 1993–96). Hon. LLD Sheffield, 2000.
*See also* C. L. P. Kennedy.

**KENNEDY, Prof. Peter Graham Edward,** CBE 2010; MD, PhD, DSc; FRCP, FRCPath, FMedSci; FRSE; Burton Professor of Neurology, 1987–2016, Honorary Senior Research Fellow, since 2016, University of Glasgow; Consultant Neurologist, Institute of Neurological Sciences, Southern General Hospital, Glasgow, since 1986; *b* 28 March 1951; *s* of Philip Kennedy and Trudy Sylvia Kennedy (*née* Summer); *m* 1983, Catherine Ann King; one *s* one *d. Educ:* University Coll. Sch.; University College London and UCH Med. Sch. (MB BS, MD, PhD, DSc); Univ. of Glasgow (MLitt, MPhil). FRCP 1988; FRCPath 1997. FRSE 1992. Med. Registrar, UCH and Whittington Hosps, 1977–78; Hon. Res. Asst, MRC Neuroimmunology Project, UCL, 1978–80; Registrar and Res. Fellow, Univ. of Glasgow, 1981; Registrar then Sen. Registrar, Nat. Hosp. for Nervous Diseases, 1982–84; Asst Prof. of Neurology, Johns Hopkins Univ. Hosp., USA, 1985; New Blood Sen. Lectr in Neurology and Virology, 1986–87, Hd, Div. of Clin. Neuroscis, 2004–10, Univ. of Glasgow. Chm., Scientist Panel on Infections incl. AIDS, European Fedn of Neurol Socs, 2000–07. Vis. Fellow in Medicine, Jesus Coll., Cambridge, 1992; Fogarty Internat. Scholar-in-Residence, NIH, 1993–94 (Fogarty Medal, 1994). Lectures: Fleming, 1990, Livingstone, 2004, RCPSG; Stevens, Univ. of Colorado, 1994; Brain Bursary, KCH, London, 1999; Richard T. Johnson Prize, Liverpool Univ., 2007; Dist. Lecture Series, Columbia Univ., NY, 2013. Guarantor of Brain, 1994–. Founder FMedSci 1998; FRAS 2004; Corresp. Fellow, Amer. Neurol Assoc., 1989 (Corresp. Mem., 1989). Member: Assoc. of British Neurologists, 1986; Assoc. of Physicians of GB and Ire., 1990. Pres., Internat. Soc. for Neurovirology, 2004–10 (Sec., 2000–03; Pres.-elect, 2003). Member Editorial Board: Jl of Neuroimmunology, 1988–; Jl of Neurovirology, 1994– (Sen. Associate Editor, 1996–); Jl of Neurological Scis, 1997–2013; Brain, 1998–2016; Neurocritical Care, 2004–; Scottish Med. Jl, 2004–. BUPA Med. Foundn Doctor of the Year Res. Award, 1990; Linacre Medal and Lectr, RCP, 1991; T. S. Srinivasan Gold Medal and Endowment Lectr, 1993; Dist. Service Award, 2010, Audrey Steinman Gilden Lectureship Award, 2012, Pioneer in Neurovirol. Award, 2018, Internat. Soc. for Neurovirol.; Sir James Black Medal (Sen. Prize in Life Scis), RSE, 2014. *Publications:* (with R. T. Johnson) Infections of the Nervous System, 1987; (with L. E. Davis) Infectious Diseases of the Nervous System, 2000; The Fatal Sleep, 2007; Reversal of David (novel), 2014; Brothers in Retribution (novel), 2015; Return of the Circle (novel), 2017; Catapult in Time (novel), 2018; numerous papers on neurology, neurobiology, neurovirology and sleeping sickness. *Recreations:* philosophy, tennis, music, astronomy, walking in the country, reading, writing. *Address:* Glasgow University Department of Neurology, Institute of Neurological Sciences, Southern General Hospital, Glasgow G51 4TF. *T:* (0141) 201 2500. *E:* peter.kennedy@glasgow.ac.uk.

**KENNEDY, Richard Paul,** MA; Head Master of Highgate School, 1989–2006; *b* 17 Feb. 1949; *e s* of David Clifton Kennedy and Evelyn Mary Hall (*née* Tindale); *m* 1979, Joanna Alicia Gore Ormsby (*see* J. A. G. Kennedy); two *s. Educ:* Charterhouse; New College, Oxford (BA Maths and Phil. 1970; MA 1977). Assistant Master, Shrewsbury Sch., 1971–77, Westminster Sch., 1977–84; Dep. Headmaster, Bishop's Stortford Coll., 1984–89 (Acting Headmaster 1989). Headmasters' Conference: Mem., Sports Cttee, 1992–95; Mem., Cttee, 1995–96; Chm., London Div., 1996; Mem., Finance Steering Gp, 2001–04. Mem. Council, ISCO, 1995–2000. Governor: The Hall Sch., Hampstead, 1989–2006; Wycombe Abbey Sch., 1992–2002. GB internat. athlete (sprints), 1973–76. Mem., Acad. of St Martin-in-the-Fields Chorus, 1977–2000. *Recreations:* choral music, family history, walking in Dorset. *Address:* Luscombe Hall, 9 Luscombe Road, Poole, Dorset BH14 8ST. *T:* (01202) 466810.

**KENNEDY, Rosemary;** *see* Foot, R. J.

**KENNEDY, Seema Louise Ghiassi,** OBE 2019; MP (C) South Ribble, since 2015; Parliamentary Under-Secretary of State, Home Office, since 2019; *b* Blackburn, 1974; *m* 2003, Paul Kennedy; three *s. Educ:* Westholme Sch., Blackburn; Pembroke Coll., Cambridge (BA Oriental Studies 1997); Université Sorbonne Nouvelle (Licence 1996).

**KENNEDY, Seema** (continued): Solicitor, Slaughter and May, 2000–03; Associate Solicitor, Bevan Brittan, 2003–06; Dir, Tustin Develts, 2006–15; PPS, DFE, 2016–17, to Prime Minister, 2017–19; Parly Under-Sec. of State, DHSC, 2019. *Recreations:* walking, opera, family. *Address:* House of Commons, SW1A 0AA. *T:* (020) 7219 4412. *E:* seema.kennedy.mp@parliament.uk.

**KENNEDY, Thomas Daniel, (Danny);** current affairs consultant and PR advisor; Member (UU) Newry and Armagh, Northern Ireland Assembly, 1998–2017; *b* 6 July 1959; *s* of John Trevor Kennedy and Mary Ida Kennedy (*née* Black); *m* 1988, Karen Susan McCrum; two *s* one *d*. *Educ:* Bessbrook Primary Sch.; Newry High Sch. With BTNI, 1978–98. Mem., UU Party, 1974–; Mem., Newry and Mourne DC, 1985–2010 (Chm., 1994–95). Northern Ireland Assembly: Minister for Employment and Learning, 2010–11; Minister for Regl Develt, 2011–15; Dep. Speaker, 2016–17; Chairman: Educn Cttee, 1999–2002; Cttee Office of First Minister and Dep. First Minister, 2007–10; Mem., Exec. Rev. Cttee, 2007–10; Dep. Leader, UU Assembly Party, 2005–10. Mem., NI Tourist Bd, 1996–98. Contested: (UU) Newry and Armagh, 1997, 2005, 2015; (UCUNF), 2010; (UU) Newry and Armagh, NI Assembly, 2017. Clerk of Kirk Session and Sabbath Sch. Superintendent, Bessbrook Presbyterian Church. *Recreations:* family, Church activities, sport (purely spectating), reading.

**KENNEDY, Thomas John,** LVO 2004; Foreign and Commonwealth Office, 2011–13; *b* 3 Feb. 1957; *m* 1985, Clare Marie Ritchie; one *s*. Entered FCO, 1992; Second Sec. (Aid/Information), Buenos Aires, 1994–97; First Sec., FCO, 1997–2002; Consul Gen., Bordeaux, 2002–06; Ambassador to Costa Rica and Nicaragua, 2006–11.

**KENNEDY, His Honour William Andrew;** a Circuit Judge, 2001–16; Deputy Resident Judge, Snaresbrook Crown Court, 2004–16; *b* 13 Feb. 1948; *s* of late Sidney Herbert and Kathleen Blanche Kennedy; *m* 1st, 1974, Alice Steen Wilkie (*d* 1987); 2nd, 1988, Lindsey Jane Sheridan; one *s* one *d*. *Educ:* Buckhurst Hill County High Sch.; College of Law, Lancaster Gate. Articled Clerk, Trotter Chapman & Whisker, Epping, Essex, 1966–72; admitted Solicitor, 1972; Partner 1972–75, Jt Sen. Partner 1975–91, Trotter Chapman & Whisker, later Whiskers; Notary Public, 1981; Metropolitan Stipendiary Magistrate, then Dist Judge (Magistrates' Courts), 1991–2001; Chm., Youth Courts, 1992–2001; an Asst Recorder, 1995–99; a Recorder, 1999–2001; part-time (Plate) Judge Advocate, 1995–2001. Judicial Mem., London Probation Bd, 2005–09; Judicial Dir, HM Court Service, 2010–12. Pres., W Essex Law Soc., 1983–84. *Recreations:* golf, gentle domestic pursuits. *Club:* Chigwell Golf.

**KENNERLEY, Prof. (James) Anthony (Machell),** CEng, CMath; Independent Commissioner, Stansted Airport, 2005–10, and Heathrow Airport, 2009–12, British Airports Authority; *b* 24 Oct. 1933; *s* of late William James Kennerley and Vida May (*née* Machell); *m* 1978, Dorothy Mary (*née* Simpson); one *s* one *d* (twins). *Educ:* Universities of Manchester (BSc; Silver Medallist, 1955) and London (MSc 1967; IMechE James Clayton Fellow). AFIMA, AFRAeS; MIMechE. Fourth Engr, Blue Funnel Line, Alfred Holt, 1954; Engineer, A. V. Roe, Manchester, 1955–58; Aerodynamicist, Pratt & Whitney, Montreal, Canada, 1958–59; Jet Pilot, RCAF, 1959–62; Asst Professor of Mathematics, Univ. of New Brunswick, Canada, 1962–67; Director of Graduate Studies, Manchester Business Sch., 1967–69; Associate Professor of Business Studies, Columbia Univ., New York, 1969–70; Director, Executive Programme, London Business Sch., 1970–73; Prof. of Business Admin, and Dir, Strathclyde Business Sch., 1973–83; Dir, InterMatrix Ltd, Management Consultants, 1984–92; Vis. Prof. of Management, City Univ., 1984–93; Prof. of Health Care Mgt, Univ. of Surrey, 1993–97. Complaints Comr, Channel Tunnel Rail Link, 1997–2007; Infrastructure Inf. Referee, Crossrail, 2002–09. Chm., London Region, Inland Waterways Assoc., 2010–11. Chm., Council for Professions Supplementary to Medicine, 1990–96. Tutor to sen. management courses in the public sector, Sunningdale, 1985–2000. Chairman: W Surrey and NE Hants, then NW Surrey, HA, 1986–95; W Surrey Health Commn, 1995–96. Chairman: Management Res. Gp, Scotland, 1981–82; Scottish Milk Marketing Scheme Arbitration Panel, 1981–83. Member: South of Scotland Electricity Bd, 1977–84; Management Studies Bd, CNAA, 1977–84; BIM Educn Cttee, 1982–92; Competition (formerly Monopolies and Mergers) Commn, 1992–2001; Adv. Bd, Meta Generics, Cambridge, 1992–95; Council, Inst. of Mgt, 1995–98. Chm., Conf. of Univ. Management Schs, 1981–83; Director: Business Graduates Assoc., 1983–86; First Step Housing Co., Waverley BC, 1990–94. Arbitrator, ACAS, 1976–2011. Mem., Trans-Turkey Highway World Bank Mission, 1982–83. Founder Mem., Bridgegate Trust, Glasgow, 1982–85. *Publications:* Guide to Business Schools, 1985; Arbitration: cases in industrial relations, 1994; Rebecca and the New Canadian Nation (novel), 2018; articles, papers on business studies, on Public Sector management, and on applied mathematics. *Recreations:* flying, travelling. *Address:* 15 Stone Lodge Lane, Ipswich, Suffolk IP2 9PF. *T:* (01473) 603127. *Clubs:* Reform, Caledonian.

**KENNET,** 3rd Baron *cr* 1935, of the Dene, co. Wilts; **William Aldus Thoby Young;** writer and entrepreneur; owner, Aldus Innovations, since 2014; *b* London, 24 May 1957; *o s* of 2nd Baron Kennet, (author, Wayland Young), and Elizabeth Ann Young (*née* Adams); *S* father, 2009; *m* 1987, Hon. Josephine Mary (marr. diss. 2018), *yr d* of 2nd Baron Keyes; two *s* one *d*. *Educ:* Marlborough Coll.; Dartington Hall Sch.; Sussex Univ. *Recreations:* music, art, travel. *Heir:* *s* Hon. Archibald Wayland Keyes Young, *b* 7 June 1992. *E:* thoby.kennet@gmail.com.

**KENNETT, Prof. Brian Leslie Norman,** AO 2019; PhD, ScD; FRS 2005; FAA; Professor of Seismology, Research School of Earth Sciences, Australian National University, 1984–2016, now Emeritus (Director, 2006–09); *b* 7 May 1948; *s* of Norman and Audrey Kennett; *m* 1971, Heather Margaret Duncan; one *s* one *d*. *Educ:* Dulwich Coll.; Emmanuel Coll., Cambridge (BA 1969; PhD 1973; ScD 1992). Fellow, Emmanuel Coll., Cambridge, 1972–84; Lectr, Univ. of Cambridge, 1976–84; Pro Vice Chancellor, 1994–97, Chm. Bd, Inst. of Advanced Studies, 1994–97 and 2001–03, ANU. Editor: Geophysical Jl Internat., 1979–99; Physics of the Earth and Planetary Interiors, 2003–06. Fellow, Amer. Geophysical Union, 1988; FAA 1994; Associate, RAS, 1996; Fellow, Geological Soc. of Australia, 2007. Humboldt Foundn Res. Award, 2004; Jaeger Medal, 2005, Flinders Medal (Physical Sci.), 2011, Australian Acad. of Sci.; Murchison Medal, Geol Soc., 2006; Gutenberg Medal, Eur. Geoscis Union, 2007; Gold Medal for Geophysics, Royal Astronomical Soc., 2008; Lehmann Medal, American Geophysical Union, 2017; IASPEI Medal, 2019. Centenary Medal (Australia), 2003. *Publications:* Seismic Wave Propagation in Stratified Media, 1983; IASPEI Seismological Tables, 1991; The Seismic Wavefield, Vol. I 2001, Vol. II 2002; (with H. P. Bunge) Geophysical Continua, 2008; Planning and Managing Scientific Research, 2014; numerous scientific contribs. *Recreations:* walking, photography, painting. *Address:* Research School of Earth Sciences, Australian National University, Canberra, ACT 2601, Australia. *T:* (2) 61254621, *Fax:* (2) 62572737. *E:* Brian.Kennett@anu.edu.au.

**KENNETT, Hon. Jeffrey (Gibb),** AC 2005; Chairman: Open Windows Australia Pty Ltd, since 2005; CT Management Group Pty Ltd, since 2011; The Torch, since 2015; Equity Trustees Ltd, since 2017; *b* 2 March 1948; *m* 1972, Felicity; three *s* one *d*. 2 Lt, Royal Australian Regt, 1968–70. Government of Victoria: MLA (L) Burwood, 1976–2000; Minister for Aboriginal Affairs, for Immigration and Ethnic Affairs, and for Housing, 1981–82; Leader of the Opposition, 1982–89, 1991–92; Premier of Victoria, 1992–99; Minister for Multicultural Affairs, 1992–99; Minister for the Arts, 1996–99. Dir, Equity Trustees Ltd, 2008–. Chairman: Beyondblue, the Nat. Depression Initiative, 2000–17; Australian Seniors Finance Ltd, 2004–08; Jumbuck Entertainment Ltd, subseq. Primary Opinion Ltd, 2004–15; Bd of Mgt, PFD Food Services Pty Ltd, 2006–14; Dir, Seven West Media Ltd, 2015–. Mem. Adv. Bd, Singapore Tourism, 2000–06. Pres., Hawthorn Football Club, 2005–11, 2017–. Chm., Enterprize Ship Trust, 2005–09.

**KENNEY, Anthony,** FRCS; FRCOG; Consultant Obstetrician and Gynaecologist: St Thomas' Hospital, 1980–2002; in independent sector, 1980–2007; *b* 17 Jan. 1942; *s* of late Eric Alfred Allen Kenney and Doris Winifred Kenney; *m* 1st, 1966, Elizabeth Dain Fielding (marr. diss.); two *s*; 2nd, 1973, Patricia Clare Newbery (*d* 2007); two *s* one *d*; 3rd, 2013, Jennifer Phillips. *Educ:* Brentwood School; Gonville and Caius College, Cambridge (MA 1967); London Hosp. Med. Coll. MB BChir 1966; FRCS 1970; MRCOG 1972, FRCOG 1987. House appts, London Hosp., Queen Charlotte's Hosp. and Chelsea Hosp. for Women, 1966–72; Registrar and Sen. Registrar, Westminster and Kingston Hosps, 1972–79. Teacher of Obstetric Life Saving Skills in Africa and Asia, 2008–12. Past Examiner: in Obstetrics and Gynaecology, RCOG; Univs of London, Liverpool and Cambridge. Mem., Higher Trng Cttee, RCOG, 1997–2000. Mus. Curator, RCOG, 2006–10. Co-founder and Trustee, Tommy's The Baby Charity (formerly Tommy's Campaign), 1989–2009; Trustee, Quit, 1995–2016. Chm. of Trustees, Med. Soc. of London, 2010–18 (Treas., 2002–07; Pres., 2007–08; Trans Ed., 2011–17). *Publications:* contribs to med. jls. *Recreations:* canal cruising, foreign travel. *Address:* Field End, Greenways, Ovingdean, Brighton, E Sussex BN2 7BA. *T:* (01273) 307360, 07703 162277. *Club:* Royal Society of Medicine.

**KENNEY, Prof. Edward John,** FBA 1968; Kennedy Professor of Latin, University of Cambridge, 1974–82; Fellow of Peterhouse, Cambridge, 1953–91; *b* 29 Feb. 1924; *s* of George Kenney and Emmie Carlina Elfrida Schwenke; *m* 1955, Gwyneth Anne, *d* of late Prof. Henry Albert Harris. *Educ:* Christ's Hospital; Trinity Coll., Cambridge. BA 1949, MA 1953. Served War of 1939–45: Royal Signals, UK and India, 1943–46; commissioned 1944, Lieut 1945. Porson Schol., 1948; Craven Schol., 1949; Craven Student, 1949; Chancellor's Medallist, 1950. Asst Lectr, Univ. of Leeds, 1951–52; University of Cambridge: Research Fellow, Trinity Coll., 1952–53; Asst Lectr, 1955–60, Lectr, 1960–70; Reader in Latin Literature and Textual Criticism, 1970–74; Peterhouse: Director of Studies in Classics, 1953–74; Librarian, 1953–82, Perne Librarian, 1987–91; Tutor, 1956–62; Senior Tutor, 1962–65; Domestic Bursar, 1987–88. James C. Loeb Fellow in Classical Philology, Harvard Univ., 1967–68; Sather Prof. of Classical Literature, Univ. of California, Berkeley, 1968; Carl Newell Jackson Lectr, Harvard Univ., 1980. President: Jt Assoc. of Classical Teachers, 1977–79; Classical Assoc., 1982–83; Horatian Soc., 2002–07. For. Mem., Royal Netherlands Acad. of Arts and Scis, 1976. Treasurer and Chm., Council of Almoners, Christ's Hosp., 1984–86. Jt Editor, Classical Qly, 1959–65; Jt Gen. Ed., Cambridge Greek and Latin Classics, 1966–. *Publications:* P. Ouidi Nasonis Amores etc (ed), 1961, 2nd edn 1995; (with Mrs P. E. Easterling) Ovidiana Graeca (ed), 1965; (with W. V. Clausen, F. R. D. Goodyear, J. A. Richmond) Appendix Vergiliana (ed), 1966; Lucretius, De Rerum Natura III (ed), 1971, 2nd edn 2014; The Classical Text, 1974 (trans. Italian 1995); (with W. V. Clausen) Latin Literature (ed and contrib.) (Cambridge History of Classical Literature II), 1982; The Ploughman's Lunch (*Moretum*), 1984; introd. and notes to Ovid, Metamorphoses, trans. A. D. Melville, 1986; Ovid, The Love Poems, 1990; Apuleius, Cupid & Psyche (ed), 1990; introd. and notes to Ovid, Sorrows of an Exile (*Tristia*), trans. A. D. Melville, 1992; Ovid, Heroides XVI-XXI (ed), 1996; (trans., with introd. and notes) Apuleius, The Golden Ass, 1998, 2nd edn 2004, Folio Soc. edn 2017; (ed) Ovidio, Metamorfosi, vol. IV (Libri VII–IX), 2011; articles and reviews in classical jls. *Recreations:* discursive reading, listening to the wireless. *Address:* 4 Belvoir Terrace, Trumpington Road, Cambridge CB2 7AA.

**KENNEY, Rt Rev. William,** CP; Auxiliary Bishop of Birmingham, (RC), since 2006; Titular Bishop of Midica, since 1987; *b* 7 May 1946; *s* of Leonard Kenney and Christine (*née* Farrell). *Educ:* Heythrop Coll., Oxon (STL 1969); Univ. of Gothenburg (Fil. Kand. 1973). Entered novitiate of Passionist Congregation, Broadway, Worcs, 1962; ordained priest, 1969; Researcher, Inst. for Sociology of Religion, Stockholm, 1973–77; Institute for Scientific Study of Religions, University of Gothenburg: Lectr, 1979–82; Dean of Studies, 1980–82; Lectr and Dean of Studies, 1984–87; Gen. Counsellor, Passionist Congregation, Rome, 1982–84; Superior, Passionists, Sweden, 1985–87; ordained bishop, 1987; Aux. Bishop of Stockholm, 1987–2006. Chair: Caritas Sweden, 1987–2006; Commn for Financing Religious Bodies, Swedish Govt, 1990–98 (Mem., 1988–98); Caritas Europe, 1991–99; Justice & Peace Commn, Stockholm, 1999–2006; Gothenburg Process, 2000–13 (Internat. Chair, 2007–13); Eur. Justice and Peace Network, 2011–14; Co-Pres., Internat. Lutheran-RC Commn on Unity, 2013–; Vice-Chair, Caritas Internationalis, 1991–99 (Mem., Legal Affairs Commn, 1999–2011); Member: Bd for Religious Affairs, Swedish Govt, 1998–2006; Commn of the Bishops' Confs of the EC, Brussels, 2000–16; Passionists Internat., NY, 2006–10; Internat. Adv. Bd, Life and Peace Inst., Uppsala, Sweden, 2011–17 (Mem. Governing Bd, 2008–11); Exec. Council of the European Council of Religious Leaders, 2014–. Spokesperson on European questions, 2006–16, Spokesperson on Sudan and S Sudan, 2012–19, Cath. Bishops' Conf. of England and Wales. Hon. PhD Gothenburg, 1988. KC*HS 2003. *Publications:* various articles on European, social and religious affairs. *Recreations:* listening to music, walking, reading (professionally but also history, biography and politics). *Address:* St Hugh's House, 27 Hensington Road, Woodstock, Oxon OX20 1JH. *T:* (01993) 812234. *E:* wk@sthughs.plus.com.

**KENNICUTT, Prof. Robert Charles, Jr,** PhD; FRS 2011; FRAS; Plumian Professor of Astronomy and Experimental Philosophy, University of Cambridge, 2005–17, now Emeritus (Director, Institute of Astronomy, 2008–11; Head, School of Physical Sciences, 2012–15); Fellow, Churchill College, Cambridge, 2006–17; Professor, University of Arizona, 1992–2012 and since 2018; Professor and Executive Director, Mitchell Institute, Texas A&M University, since 2018; *b* 4 Sept. 1951; *s* of Robert Charles Kennicutt and Joyce Ann Kennicutt; one *d*. *Educ:* Rensselaer Polytechnic Inst. (BS Phys 1973); Univ. of Washington (MS 1976, PhD Astronomy 1978). Carnegie Postdoctoral Fellow, Hale Observatories, 1978–80; Asst, then Associate Prof., Dept of Astronomy, Univ. of Minnesota, 1980–88; Associate, 1988–92, Astronomer, 1992–2012, 2018–, Steward Observatory, Univ. of Arizona. Beatrice M. Tinsley Centennial Prof., Univ. of Texas, 1994; Adriaan Blaauw Prof., Univ. of Groningen, 2001. Member: AAS, 1979– (Vice-Pres., 1998–2001); IAU, 1981–; NAS, 2006–. Fellow, American Acad. of Arts and Scis, 2001. FRAS 2006. Dannie Heineman Prize in Astrophysics, AIP/AAS, 2007; (jtly) Cosmology Prize, Gruber Foundn, 2009; Gold Medal, RAS, 2019. Editor-in-Chief, Astrophysical Jl, 1999–2006; Co-Editor, Annual Rev. of Astronomy and Astrophysics, 2019–. *Publications:* Galaxies: interactions and induced star formation, 1998; Hubble's Science Legacy in Future Optical/Ultraviolet Astronomy from Space, 2003; papers in astronomical jls. *Recreations:* rock and mineral collecting, lapidary arts. *Address:* Steward Observatory, University of Arizona, 933 North Cherry Avenue, Tucson, AZ 85721, USA. *T:* (520) 6213412. *E:* rck@email.arizona.edu.

**KENNON, Andrew Rowland**; Clerk of Committees, House of Commons, 2011–16; *b* 15 July 1955; *y s* of Vice-Adm. Sir James Edward Campbell Kennon, KCB, CBE and Anne Kennon; *m* 1983, Mary Gamblin; one *s* two *d*. *Educ*: Stowe Sch.; Jesus Coll., Cambridge (exhibitioner; BA Law 1977). Called to the Bar, Gray's Inn, 1979. House of Commons: Asst Clerk, 1977; various procedural, cttee and internat. posts, 1977–87; Clerk of Select Committees: on Trade and Ind., 1987–92; on Procedure, 1992–95; on Defence, 1995–97; on Home Affairs, 1999–2002; seconded to Cabinet Office to advise on parly and constitutional reform, 1997–99; Hd, Scrutiny Unit, 2002–04; Prin. Clerk of Select Cttees, 2004–06; Sec., H of C Commn, 2006–08; Clerk of Jls, 2008–09; Principal Clerk, Table Office, 2009–11. Lay Mem., Judicial Appointments Commn, 2017–. Associate, Global Partners Governance, 2017–; Mem., Ind. Monitoring Bd, HMP Exeter 2017–. Trustee, Constitution Soc., 2017–. Hon. Prof., KCL, 2017–. *Publications*: (with R. Blackburn) Griffith and Ryle, Parliament: functions, practice and procedures, 2nd edn 2002. *Recreation*: sailing.

**KENNY, Sir Anthony (John Patrick)**, Kt 1992; FBA 1974; Pro-Vice-Chancellor, Oxford University, 1984–2001 (Pro-Vice-Chancellor for Development, 1999–2001); Warden, Rhodes House, 1989–99; Professorial Fellow, St John's College, Oxford, 1989–99, now Emeritus Fellow; Master of Balliol College, Oxford, 1978–89; *b* Liverpool, 16 March 1931; *s* of John Kenny and Margaret Jones; *m* 1966, Nancy Caroline, *d* of Henry T. Gayley, Jr, Swarthmore, Pa; two *s*. *Educ*: Gregorian Univ., Rome (STL); St Benet's Hall, Oxford; DPhil 1961, DLitt 1980. Ordained priest, Rome, 1955; Curate in Liverpool, 1959–63; returned to lay state, 1963. Asst Lectr, Univ. of Liverpool, 1961–63; University of Oxford: Fellow, 1964–78, Sen. Tutor, 1971–72 and 1976–78, Balliol Coll.; Lectr in Philosophy, Exeter and Trinity Colls, 1963–64; University Lectr, 1965–78; Wilde Lectr in Natural and Comparative Religion, 1969–72; Speaker's Lectureship in Biblical Studies, 1980–83; Mem., Hebdomadal Council, 1981–93; Vice-Chm., Libraries Bd, 1985–88; Curator, Bodleian Library, 1985–88; Deleg., and Mem., Finance Cttee, OUP, 1986–93. Jt Gifford Lectr, Univ. of Edinburgh, 1972–73; Stanton Lectr, Univ. of Cambridge, 1980–83; Bampton Lectr, Columbia Univ., 1983. Visiting Professor: Univs of Chicago, Washington, Michigan, Minnesota and Cornell, Stanford and Rockefeller Univs. Chairman: British Liby Bd, 1993–96 (Mem., 1991–96); Soc. for Protection of Science and Learning, 1989–93; British Nat. Corpus Adv. Bd, 1990–95; British Irish Assoc., 1990–94; Bd, Warburg Inst., Univ. of London, 1996–2000. Pres., British Acad., 1989–93 (Mem. Council, 1985–88; Vice-Pres., 1986–88). MAE 1991; Member: Amer. Phil Soc., 1993; Norwegian Acad. of Scis, 1993; Amer. Acad. of Arts and Scis, 2003. Hon. Fellow, Harris Manchester Coll., Oxford, 1996. Hon. DLitt: Bristol, 1982; Liverpool, 1988; Glasgow, 1990; TCD, 1992; Hull, 1993; Sheffield, Warwick, 1995; Hon. DHumLitt: Denison Univ., Ohio, 1986; Lafayette Univ., Penn, 1990; Hon. DCL: Oxon, 1987; QUB, 1994; Hon. DLit London, 2002; Hon. DD Liverpool Hope, 2010. Hon. Bencher, Lincoln's Inn, 1999. Aquinas Medal, Amer. Catholic Philos. Assoc., 2006. Editor, The Oxford Magazine, 1972–73. *Publications*: Action, Emotion and Will, 1963, 2nd edn 2003; Responsa Alumnorum of English College, Rome, 2 vols, 1963; Descartes, 1968; The Five Ways, 1969; Wittgenstein, 1973, 2nd edn 2005; The Anatomy of the Soul, 1974; Will, Freedom and Power, 1975; The Aristotelian Ethics, 1978, 2nd edn 2016; Freewill and Responsibility, 1978; Aristotle's Theory of the Will, 1979; The God of the Philosophers, 1979; Aquinas, 1980; The Computation of Style, 1982; Faith and Reason, 1983; Thomas More, 1983; The Legacy of Wittgenstein, 1984; A Path from Rome (autobiog.), 1985; Wyclif, 1985; The Logic of Deterrence, 1985; The Ivory Tower, 1985; A Stylometric Study of the New Testament, 1986; The Road to Hillsborough, 1987; Reason and Religion, 1987; The Heritage of Wisdom, 1987; God and Two Poets, 1988; The Metaphysics of Mind, 1989; The Oxford Diaries of Arthur Hugh Clough, 1990; Mountains: an anthology, 1991; Aristotle on the Perfect Life, 1992; What is Faith?, 1992; Aquinas on Mind, 1993; (ed) Oxford Illustrated History of Western Philosophy, 1994; Frege, 1995; A Life in Oxford (autobiog.), 1997; A Brief History of Western Philosophy, 1998, 3rd illus. edn 2018; Essays on the Aristotelian Tradition, 2001; (ed) The History of the Rhodes Trust, 2001; Aquinas on Being, 2002; The Unknown God, 2004; A New History of Western Philosophy, vol. 1, 2004, vol. 2, 2005, vol. 3, 2006, vol. 4, 2007, single vol. edn 2010; Arthur Hugh Clough: the life of a poet, 2005; What I Believe, 2006; (with C. Kenny) Life, Liberty and the Pursuit of Utility, 2006; (with R. Kenny) Can Oxford be Improved?, 2007; From Empedocles to Wittgenstein, 2008; (with S. Perry) Balliol Poetry, 2011; (ed and trans.) Aristotle, the Eudemian Ethics, 2011; (ed and trans.) Aristotle, Poetics, 2013; (ed) Arthur Hugh Clough, Mari Magno, Dipsychus and other poems, 2014; (ed and trans. with Jonathan Barnes) Aristotle, the Ethical Works, 2014; Christianity in Review, 2015; Un Addio Affettuoso alla Chiesa, 2016; The Enlightenment: a short history, 2017; Brief Encounters, 2018; Immanuel Kant: a short history, 2019. *Address*: The Old Bakery, 1A Larkins Lane, Oxford OX3 9DW. *Club*: Athenæum.

**KENNY, Enda**; Member (FG) of the Dáil (TD) for Mayo, since 1975; Taoiseach (Prime Minister) of Ireland, 2011–17; Leader, Fine Gael, 2002–17; *b* Islandeady, Castlebar, Co. Mayo, 24 April 1951; *s* of Henry Kenny; *m* 1992, Fionnuala O'Kelly; two *s* one *d*. *Educ*: St Patrick's Coll. of Educn; University Coll., Galway. Primary sch. teacher. Mem., Mayo CC, 1975–95. Minister of State, Dept for Educn and Labour, 1986–87; Minister for Tourism and Trade, 1994–97; Leader of Opposition, 2002–11. *Address*: Dáil Éireann, Leinster House, Kildare Street, Dublin 2, D02 XR20, Ireland.

**KENNY, Dame Julie (Ann)**, DBE 2019 (CBE 2002); DL; Chairman and Chief Executive (formerly Managing Director), Pyronix Ltd, 1986–2016; Chief Executive and Chairman, Secure Holdings Ltd, 2011–16; *b* Sheffield, 19 Aug. 1957; *d* of Cyril Bower and Hendrika Bower; two *s* one *d*; *m* 2017, Iain Geoffrey Hall. FInstLEx. Litigation lawyer in private practice and with local authorities, 1982–89. Chm., Robson Handling Technol. Ltd, 2017–. Chairman: Regl Industrial Develt Bd, 1999–2002 (Mem., 1996–2002); Rotherham New Deal Employers' Coalition, 2000–02; S Yorks Steel Task Force, 2000–02; Business Link S Yorks, 2001–05; S Yorks New Deal Employers' Coalition, 2002–05; Rotherham Partnership, 2002–05; Small Business Council, 2005–07; Yorkshire Forward, 2010–12 (Mem., 2002–12); UK Commn for Employment and Skills, 2016–18 (Mem., 2007–18); Sheffield Cultural Compact, 2019–; Member, Board/Director: Rotherham TEC, 1995–2001; Rotherham Enterprise Agency, 2000–02; S Yorks Investment Fund, 2000–05; S Yorks Learning and Skills Council, 2001–02; Chamber Skills Solutions, 2001–03; S Yorks Partnership, 2004–07; Creative Sheffield, 2006–11; Panel for Regulatory Accountability, 2005–07; Socio-Economic Gp Skills Alliance, 2005–07; Small Business Service Strategy Bd, 2006–07; Administrative Burdens Adv. Bd, 2007–10; Small Business Forum, 2007–10; Better Regulation Stakeholder Gp, 2007–10; Sheffield City Reg. LEP, 2013–19; S Yorks Community Foundn, 2013–16. Intervention Commissioner: Doncaster MBC, 2010–14; Rotherham MBC 2015–19. Chm., British Security Industry Assoc., 2010–12 (Mem. Bd, 1992–2013; Chm., Security Equipment Manufrs' Section, 1998–2000, 2002–04); Mem., Regl Council, Engrg Employers Fedn, 2009–10. Mem. Bd and Pres., 1998–2002, Hon. Dir, 2004–10, Barnsley and Rotherham (formerly Rotherham) Chamber of Commerce. Chairman: Wentworth Woodhouse Preservation Trust, 2014– (Trustee, 2014–); Nat. Coal Mining Mus. Trading Co., 2016– (Trustee, 2016–); Trustee, Nat. Coal Mining Mus., 2014–. Dir and Trustee, Gallery Town Ltd, Rotherham, 2012–; Mem. Bd, Sheffield Theatres Trust, 2014–. Chm., Maltby Learning Trust (formerly Maltby Acad.), 2010–; Trustee, Rudston Prep. Sch., 2002–05; Gov., Mount St Mary's Coll., 2008–12. Mem., Adv. Bd, Univ. of Sheffield Mgt Sch., 2006–08. Ambassador, Whirlow Hall Farm Trust, 2008–16. Mem., Rotherham Hospice, 2010–. Pres., Sheffield and Hallamshire Br., NSPCC, 2012–14. Patron: Women in Business; In2Change; St Luke's Hospice, Sheffield; Lost Chord. South Yorkshire: DL 2005; High Sheriff 2012. Hon. Dr Sheffield Hallam, 2006. *Recreations*: theatre, ballet, music. *E*: juliek@juliekenny.com.

**KENNY, Mary Cecilia, (Mrs R. West)**; journalist and writer; *b* 4 April 1944; *d* of Patrick and Ita Kenny; *m* 1974, Richard West (*d* 2015); two *s*. *Educ*: Loreto Coll., Dublin; Birkbeck Coll., Univ. of London (BA Hons French Studies 1997). Journalist and broadcaster, 1966–: feature writer and European Corresp., London Evening Standard, 1966–69; Woman's Ed., Irish Press, Dublin, 1969–71; Features Ed. and writer, Evening Standard, 1971–73; freelance journalist, subseq. Columnist, Sunday Telegraph, 1976–96; TV Critic, Daily Mail, 1981–86; contributor: Daily Mail, The Tablet, Daily Telegraph, The Times, Guardian, Spectator, Listener, New Statesman, TLS, The Oldie (also columnist), Irish Independent (also columnist), Sunday Independent, Irish Times, Studies (Dublin), Catholic Herald, Irish Catholic, and others; *TV and radio* including: panellist, Late, Late Show, RTE; Question Time, BBC; Any Questions, Radio 4; The Panel, RTE; presenter, and contrib. to, various documentaries in UK and Ireland. Master of The Keys, Catholic Writers' Guild (formerly Guild of Catholic Writers), 2010–12. *Publications*: Abortion: the whole story, 1986; A Mood for Love (short stories), 1989; Goodbye to Catholic Ireland: a social history, 1997; Death by Heroin, Recovery by Hope, 2001; Germany Calling: a personal biography of William Joyce, Lord Haw-Haw, 2003; Allegiance: Michael Collins and Winston Churchill 1921–1922, 2005; Crown and Shamrock: love and hate between Ireland and the British monarchy, 2009; A State of Emergency: a drama set in neutral Eire 1940, 2010; Something of Myself… and others (memoir), 2013; Conversation before a Hanging: William Joyce's last days, 2016; A Day at a Time, 2016; Am I a Feminist? Are You?, 2017; Dearest Old Darling: a monologue drawn on the prison letters of Constance Markievicz, 2018. *Recreations*: cinema, theatre, reading in French, summer festivals in Ireland. *Address*: 84 West Street, Deal, Kent CT14 6AZ. *E*: mary@mary-kenny.com. *W*: www.mary-kenny.com, www.twitter.com/MaryKenny4; 56 Cranford Court, Stillorgan Road, Donnybrook, Dublin 4, Ireland. *Clubs*: Reform; United Arts (Dublin).

**KENNY, Prof. Neil Francis**, DPhil; FBA 2011; Professor of French, University of Oxford, since 2014; Senior Research Fellow, All Souls College, Oxford, since 2012; *b* Tolworth, 5 Nov. 1960; *s* of Alf and Maureen Kenny; *m* 2003, Dr Leslie Topp; one *s* one *d*. *Educ*: Gonville and Caius Coll., Cambridge (BA Modern and Medieval Langs 1981); St John's Coll., Oxford (DPhil French 1987). English Asst, Coll. Calvin, Geneva, 1981–82; Frances A. Yates Fellow, Warburg Inst., Univ. of London, 1985–87; Temp. Lectr in French, Birkbeck, Univ. of London, 1987; Stipendiary Lectr in French, New Coll., Oxford, 1987–89; Lectr in French, Queen Mary Coll., later Queen Mary and Westfield Coll., Univ. of London, 1989–94; University of Cambridge: Lectr in French, 1994–2000; Sen. Lectr in French, 2000–05; Reader in Early Modern French Literature and Thought, 2005–12; Fellow in French, Churchill Coll., Cambridge, 1994–2005. *Publications*: The Palace of Secrets: Béroalde de Verville and Renaissance conceptions of knowledge, 1991; Curiosity in Early Modern Europe: word histories, 1998; The Uses of Curiosity in Early Modern France and Germany, 2004; An Introduction to Sixteenth-Century French Literature and Thought: other times, other places, 2008; Death and Tenses: posthumous presence in early modern France, 2015. *Recreations*: family, music, sport. *Address*: All Souls College, Oxford OX1 4AL.

**KENNY, Siobhan Mary, (Mrs P. Pearson)**; Chief Executive Officer, RadioCentre, since 2014; *b* 15 Oct. 1959; *d* of late Patrick Kenny and Della Kenny (*née* Raftery); *m* 1996, Pat Pearson. *Educ*: St Michael's Convent Grammar Sch., Finchley, London; Univ. of Manchester (BA English, French, German 1982); Birkbeck Coll., London (MA French 1988). Press Officer: TV-am, 1986–89; Govt Inf. Service, 1989–93; Attachée de Presse, Council of Europe, Strasbourg, 1993–94; Press Officer, then Strategy Advr, No 10 Downing Street, 1994–99; Dir of Communications, National Magazine Co., 1999–2002; Dir of Strategic Communication, DCMS, 2002–05; Vice Pres., Communications, Europe, Middle E and Africa, Walt Disney TV, 2005–07; Gp Communications Dir, HarperCollins UK and Internat., 2007–13. *Recreations*: sailing, ski-ing, football, film. *T*: 07932 675133. *E*: siobhan.kenny@radiocentre.org, siobhanmarykenny@gmail.com.

**KENNY, Stephen Charles Wilfrid**; QC 2006; *b* 12 Aug. 1964; *s* of late Charles John Michael Kenny and Gillian Beatrice Maud Kenny (*née* Shelford); *m* 1998, Anna Aida, *d* of Dr the Rt Hon. Sir (John) Vincent Cable, *qv*; one *s*. *Educ*: Farleigh House Sch.; Ampleforth Coll. (scholar); Worcester Coll., Oxford (Exhibnr; MA; BCL 1st Cl. Hons). Called to the Bar, Inner Temple, 1987; in practice as a barrister, 1987–, specialising in commercial law. *Recreations*: family and friends, music, literature, early medieval history, ski-ing, cricket coaching, supporting doggedly Fulham FC. *Address*: 7 King's Bench Walk, Temple, EC4Y 7DS. *T*: (020) 7910 8300, *Fax*: (020) 7910 8400. *E*: skenny@7kbw.co.uk.

**KENNY, Yvonne Denise**, AM 1989; international opera singer; *b* Australia, 25 Nov. 1950; *d* of late Arthur Raymond Kenny and of Doris Jean (*née* Campbell). *Educ*: Sydney Univ. (BSc). Operatic début in Donizetti's Rosmonda d'Inghilterra, Queen Elizabeth Hall, 1975; joined Royal Opera House, Covent Garden as a principal soprano, 1976; roles include: Pamina in Die Zauberflöte; Ilia in Idomeneo; Marzelline in Fidelio; Susanna, and Countess, in Le Nozze di Figaro; Adina in L'Elisir d'Amore; Liu in Turandot; Aspasia in Mitridate; Alcina; Semele; Cleopatra in Giulio Cesare; Donna Anna in Don Giovanni; Fairy Queen; Countess in Capriccio; Die Feldmarschallin in Der Rosenkavalier; Alice Ford in Falstaff; international appearances include: ENO; Glyndebourne; Berlin Staatsoper; Vienna State Opera; La Scala, Milan; La Fenice, Venice; Paris; Munich; Zurich; Australian Opera, Sydney, etc; regular concert appearances with major orchs and conductors in Europe and USA. Prof. of Voice, GSMD, 2007–. Has made over 60 recordings. Hon. DMus Sydney, 2000. *Recreations*: swimming, walking, gardening.

**KENSINGTON**, 9th Baron *cr* 1776 (Ire.); **William Owen Alexander Edwardes**; Baron Kensington (UK) 1886; *b* 21 July 1964; *s* of 8th Baron Kensington and Juliet Elizabeth Massy Edwardes (*née* Anderson); *S* father, 2018; *m* 1991, Marie Hélène Anne Véronique, *d* of Jean-Alain Lalouette; one *s* two *d*. *Educ*: Michaelhouse, Kwazulu-Natal, S Africa. *Heir*: *s* Hon. William Francis Ivor Edwardes, *b* 23 March 1993. *Address*: Friar Tuck Farm, PO Box 549, Mooi River 3300, Republic of South Africa.

**KENSINGTON, Area Bishop of**, since 2015; **Rt Rev. Dr Graham Stuart Tomlin**; *b* Bristol, 1 Aug. 1958; *s* of Ivor Howard Tomlin and Anne Lilian Tomlin; *m* 1982, Janet Wynn; one *s* one *d*. *Educ*: Bristol Grammar Sch.; Lincoln Coll., Oxford (BA English 1980); Wycliffe Hall, Oxford (BA Theol. 1985); Exeter Univ. (PhD Theol. 1996). Ordained deacon, 1986, priest, 1987; Curate, St Leonard's, Exeter, 1986–89; part-time Chaplain, Jesus Coll., Oxford, 1989–94; Wycliffe Hall, Oxford: part-time, then full-time Tutor, 1989–98; Vice Principal, 1998–2005; Principal: St Paul's Theol Centre, 2005–15; St Mellitus Coll., 2007–15 (Pres., 2015–). *Publications*: The Power of the Cross, 1999; Walking in His Steps, 2001; The Provocative Church, 2002, 4th edn 2014; Luther and his World, 2002; The Responsive Church, 2006; Spiritual Fitness, 2007; The Seven Deadly Sins, 2007; The Prodigal Spirit, 2011; Philippians and Colossians: reformation commentary on scripture, 2013; Looking Through the Cross, 2013; The Widening Circle, 2014; Luther's Gospel: reimagining the world, 2017; Bound to be Free: the paradox of freedom, 2017. *Recreations*: football, cricket, Rugby, guitar. *Address*: Dial House, Riverside, Twickenham TW1 3DT. *T*: (020) 7932 1180. *E*: bishop.kensington@london.anglican.org. *Club*: MCC.

**KENSWOOD**, 3rd Baron *cr* 1951; **Michael Christopher Whitfield;** *b* 3 July 1955; *s* of 2nd Baron Kenswood and Deirdre Anna Louise Whitfield (*née* Methven); *S* father, 2016; *m* 1983, Catherine Noelle Michelle Pizzato; two *d*. *Heir*: *b* Hon. Anthony John Whitfield [*b* 1957; *m* 1st, 1978, Fiona Barter-Davies (marr. diss. 1986); one *s*; 2nd, 1987, Joanna English (marr. diss. 1994); two *s*; 3rd, 2001, Sara Annette Chadwick.

**KENT, Alan Peter;** QC 2009; *b* Billericay, 7 Aug. 1963; *s* of Peter Kent and late Linda Kent; *m* 1989, Barbara, *d* of John and Frances Mulhall; two *s* two *d*. *Educ*: Warden Park Comprehensive Sch., Cuckfield; Poly. of N London (LLB Hons). Called to the Bar, Inner Temple, 1986; in practice as barrister specialising in criminal law. Member: Criminal Bar Assoc.; Cttee, South Eastern Circuit, 2009–; Chm., Sussex Bar Mess, 2009–. *Recreations*: my family, football, doing the ironing, football hooliganism. *Address*: Westgate Chambers, 64 High Street, Lewes, E Sussex BN7 1XG.

**KENT, Brian Hamilton,** FREng, FIET, FIMechE; Chairman: Wellington Holdings plc, 1993–2005; Hallmark Industries Ltd, 2006–14; President, Institution of Mechanical Engineers, 1994–95; *b* 29 Sept. 1931; *s* of Clarence Kent and Edyth (*née* Mitchell); *m* 1954, Margery Foulds; one *s* two *d*. *Educ*: Hyde Grammar Sch.; Salford Coll. of Technology (BSc Eng). FREng (FEng 1995). Instructor Lieut, RN Short Service Commn, 1954–57. Mather & Platt Ltd: graduate apprentice, 1952–54; Asst Technical Manager, Electrical Gp, then Gen. Manager, Mather & Platt Contracting Ltd, 1957–65; Morgan Crucible Co. Ltd, London, 1965–69; Man. Dir and Chief Exec., Alfa-Laval Ltd, 1969–78; Dir, Staveley Industries Ltd, 1978–80; Staveley Industries plc: Chief Exec., 1980–87; Chm., 1987–93; non-exec. Chm., 1993–94. Chm., British Printing Co. Ltd, 1996–98; Dep. Chm., Industrial Acoustics Corp. Ltd, 2000–12. Senator, Engrg Council, 1996–99. Chm., Management Cttee, Industry and Parlt Trust, 1988–90. Gov., Kingston Univ., 1996–2003 (Chm., Finance Bd). FInstD. Hon. FIMechE 2006. Hon. DSc Salford, 1995. *Recreation*: sailing. *Club*: Royal Automobile.

**KENT, Bruce;** campaigner for peace and disarmament; Hon. Vice President, Campaign for Nuclear Disarmament, since 1985 (General Secretary, 1980–85; Vice-Chairman, 1985–87; Chairman, 1987–90); *b* 22 June 1929; *s* of Kenneth Kent and Rosemary Kent (*née* Marion); *m* 1988, Valerie Flessati. *Educ*: Lower Canada Coll., Montreal; Stonyhurst Coll.; Brasenose Coll., Univ. of Oxford (BCL 1956; Hon. Fellow 2013). Ordination, Westminster, 1958; Curate, Kensington, North and South, 1958–63; Sec., Archbishop's House, Westminster, 1963–64; Chm., Diocesan Schools Commn, 1964–66; Catholic Chaplain to Univ. of London, 1966–74; Chaplain, Pax Christi, 1974–77; Parish Priest, Somers Town, NW1, 1977–80; retired from active Ministry, Feb. 1987. President: Internat. Peace Bureau, 1985–92; Nat. Peace Council, 1999–2000; Vice President: Pax Christi, 1986–; CND, 1989–; Movement for the Abolition of War, 2002–. Mem., Nat. Exec., UNA, 1993–97. Contested (Lab) Oxford West and Abingdon, 1992. Hon. LLD Manchester, 1987; DUniv Middx, 2002. *Publications*: Undiscovered Ends (autobiog.), 1992; essays and pamphlets on disarmament, Christians and peace. *Recreations*: friends, walking, peace/war history. *Address*: 11 Venetia Road, N4 1EJ.

**KENT, Georgina; Her Honour Judge Georgina Kent;** a Circuit Judge, since 2009; *b* Malaysia, 25 June 1966; *d* of Derek Kent and Beatrice Kent; *m* 1st, 1992, Dominic Kern Chambers, *qv* (marr. diss. 2009); one *s* two *d*; 2nd, 2013, Martin Hale Scott; one step *d*. *Educ*: King's Coll. London (LLB Hons); Inns of Court Sch. of Law. Called to the Bar, Gray's Inn, 1989, Bencher, 2014; Recorder, 2002–09. Gov., Kingswood House Sch., 2012–. *Address*: Crown Court, 6–8 Penrhyn Road, Kingston-upon-Thames, Surrey KT1 2BB. *T*: (020) 8240 2500.

**KENT, Mark Andrew Geoffrey;** HM Diplomatic Service; Ambassador to the Argentine Republic, since 2016; *b* Spilsby, 14 Jan. 1966; *s* of Geoffrey Kent and Patricia June Kent; *m* 1991, Martine Delogne; one *s* one *d*. *Educ*: Horncastle Grammar Sch.; Lincoln Coll., Oxford (BA Law 1986); Univ. Libre de Bruxelles (Licence Spéciale en Droit Européen 1987); Open Univ. (Postgrad. Cert. in Business Admin 2007). Joined HM Diplomatic Service, 1987; Nr East and N Africa Dept, FCO, 1987–89; Third Sec., later Second Sec., Brasilia, 1989–93; Second, later First Sec., UK Perm. Repn to EU, 1993–98; First Sec., News Dept, FCO, 1998–2000; First Sec., later Counsellor (Commercial) and Consul-Gen., Mexico City, 2000–04; on secondment to SHAPE, 2004–05; Hd, Migration Gp, FCO, 2005–07; Ambassador to Socialist Republic of Vietnam, 2007–10; language and other trng, London and Thailand, 2010–12; Ambassador to Kingdom of Thailand, 2012–16. FInstLM 2011. *Recreations*: running, football (especially Arsenal), Michael Caine films, foreign languages. *Address*: c/o Foreign and Commonwealth Office, King Charles Street, SW1A 2AH. *E*: mark.kent@fco.gov.uk.

**KENT, Michael Harcourt;** QC 1996; a Recorder, since 2000; a Deputy High Court Judge, since 2010; *b* 5 March 1952; *s* of late Captain Barrie Harcourt Kent, RN and Margaret Harcourt Kent; *m* 1977, Sarah Ann Ling; two *s*. *Educ*: Nautical Coll., Pangbourne; Sussex Univ. (BA Hons). Called to the Bar, Middle Temple, 1975, Bencher, 2012; SE Circuit; Supplementary Panel, Junior Counsel to the Crown, Common Law, 1988–96; Asst Recorder, 1999–2000. Member: London Common Law and Commercial Bar Assoc. (Chm., 2011–13); Admin. Law Bar Assoc.; TecBar. *Recreation*: sailing. *Address*: Crown Office Chambers, 2 Crown Office Row, Temple, EC4Y 7HJ. *T*: (020) 7797 8100.

**KENT, Nicolas;** *see* Kent, R. N.

**KENT, Peter Humphreys,** CMG 2001; President, European Intelligent Building Group, 2002–09; private sector government trade adviser; Associate, Harvey's of Edinburgh, since 2010; *b* 21 April 1937; *s* of Cosmo Weatherly Kent and Beatrice Humphreys Tordoff; *m* 1964, Noel Mary Curwen; one *s*. *Educ*: Denehurst Prep. Sch.; Royal Grammar Sch., Guildford. Commnd Queen's Royal Regt, 1956; seconded RWAFF, 1956; served: 5 Bn Queen's Own Nigeria Regt, 1956–57; 1st Bn Queen's Royal Regt, TA, 1957–60. Union Internat. Co. Ltd, London and Nigeria, 1958–61; I. H. S. Lotinga Ltd, Nigeria, 1961–64; Newton Chambers & Co. Ltd, 1964–73 (Man. Dir, Izal Overseas Ltd, and Dir, Izal Ltd); Mktg Dir, Europe, Sterling Winthrop Ltd, 1973–76; Arthur Guinness & Sons, 1975–78 (Internat. Mktg Dir, Jackel Ltd); Man. Dir, Steinerco (UK) Ltd, 1978–83; Dir, More O'Ferrall Plc, 1983–97. Chairman: Starlite Media LLC, NY, 2000–02; Starlite Media Internat. Ltd, UK, 2000–02; non-exec. Dir, GruppeM Investments plc, 2007–09. Dir, Taiwan Trade Centre (TAITRA (formerly CETRA)) Ltd, 1993–2009; Chm., Taiwan Advrs Gp, 1997–2006; Vice-Chm., Taiwan Britain Business Council, 1998–; Mem., Singapore Britain Business Council, 2003–12. Asia Pacific Advr, DTI/BTI/UK Trade & Investment (formerly Trade Partners UK), 1985–2012. Mem., CBI Internat. Cttee, 1998–2000. Dir, 1993–2003, Mem. Council, 2005–, Internat. Shakespeare Globe Centre; Dir, Shakespeare's Globe Centre (USA) Ltd, 2007–14. Trustee, 1992–2005, Vice-Chm., 2004–05, Colchester and Dist Visual Arts Trust; Mem., Noel Coward Soc., 2009–. Freeman, City of London, 1980; Liveryman,

Co. of Launderers, 1980–. Member: RSAA, 2001; European-Atlantic Gp, 1993. FInstD 1968; Fellow, Inst. of Export, 1967. Friend of the Foreign Service Medal (Taiwan), 2000; Economic Medal (Taiwan), 2003. *Recreations*: film and theatre, travelling, socialising. *Address*: Cherry Ground, Holbrook, Suffolk IP9 2PS. *T*: and *Fax*: (01473) 328203; 202 Marlyn Lodge, Portsoken Street, E1 8RB. *E*: peterhkent1@btinternet.com. *Clubs*: Naval and Military; Jockey Club Rooms (Newmarket).

**KENT, (Robert) Nicolas;** director and producer, theatre, television and radio; Artistic Director, Tricycle Theatre, 1984–2012; *b* London, 26 Jan. 1945; *s* of Henry and Mary Kent. *Educ*: Stowe Sch.; St Catharine's Coll., Cambridge (BA Hons English 1967). ABC TV trainee dir, Liverpool Playhouse, 1967–68; Artistic Dir, Watermill Th., 1970; Associate Dir, Traverse Th., Edinburgh, 1970–72; Admin. Dir, Oxford Playhouse Co., 1976–82; freelance prodns at Royal Court Th., Young Vic, National Th., RSC and West End include: Ain't Misbehavin', Lyric, 1995; Colour of Justice, Victoria Palace, 1999; Guantanamo, New Ambassadors and NY, 2004; The Great Game: Afghanistan, USA nat. tour, incl. the Pentagon, 2010–11; The Nightmares of Carlos Fuentes, Arcola, 2014; Another World: losing our children to Islamic State, NT, 2016; Co-Dir, Drones, Baby, Drones, Arcola Th., 2016; All the President's Men, NT and NY, 2017; Co-Producer: Before the Party, Queens, 1979; The Price, Apollo, 2003; 39 Steps, Criterion, 2006–; director of plays for TV including: Playboy of the West Indies, 1984; Pentecost, 1990; Justifying War, 2003. Member: Council, AA, 1998–2000; Mayor of London's Cultural Strategy Gp, 1998–2000; Council, Arts Council, London, 2002–06. Dir, Soc. of London Theatres, 2000–07. Founding Trustee, Visitors' Art Foundn, 2016–. Hon. DLitt Westminster, 2007. Freedom, London Borough of Brent, 2012. Outstanding Individual Achievement Award, Theatre Managers' Assoc., 2009; Human Rights Arts Award, Liberty, 2010; Peter Brook Special Achievement Award, 2011. *Publications*: Srebrenica, 2005 (broadcast on BBC World Service); (contrib.) Verbatim Verbatim, 2008; (jtly) The Tricycle: collected Tribunal Plays 1994–2012, 2014; All the President's Men?, 2017. *Recreations*: country walks, tennis, African-American literature, art, architecture, politics, French films on winter afternoons, dead-heading roses in the sun. *Address*: Flat 3, 6 Castellain Road, W9 1EZ. *T*: (020) 7286 1436. *E*: nicolas@nicolaskent.com. *W*: www.nicolaskent.com.

**KENT, Roderick David;** Chairman, Caledonia Investments plc, 2011–17; *b* 14 Aug. 1947; *s* of Dr Basil Stanley Kent, MB, BS, FFARCS and Vivien Margaret Kent (*née* Baker); *m* 1972, Belinda Jane Mitchell; three *d*. *Educ*: King's Sch., Canterbury; Corpus Christi Coll., Oxford (MA); INSEAD (MBA 1972). MCSI. Investment Div., J. Henry Schroder Wagg, 1969–71; Triumph Investment Trust, 1972–74; Dir, 1974–2002, Chm., 1990–2002, Close Brothers Ltd; Man. Dir, 1975–2002, non-exec. Dir, 2002–06, Chm., 2006–08, Close Brothers Gp plc. Chairman: Grosvenor Ltd, 2000–09; Bradford & Bingley Gp plc, 2002–08; BT Pension Scheme, 2008–11. Non-executive Director: Wessex Water plc, 1988–98; English and Scottish Investors plc, 1988–98; M & G Gp plc, 1995–99 (non-exec. Chm., 1998–99); Grosvenor Group Ltd, 2000–12; Whitbread plc, 2002–08. Trustee, Esmée Fairbairn Foundn, 2001–08; Chm. Trustees, Calthorpe Estates, 2011–17. Gov., Wellcome Trust (formerly Wellcome Foundn), 2008–12. Liveryman, Pewterers' Co., 1976– (Master, 2016–17). *Recreations*: farming, antique furniture restoration, sports.

**KENT, Thomas George,** CBE 1979; CEng, MIMechE, FRAeS; aerospace and defence consultant; Director: Third Grosvenor Ltd, since 1987; Grosvenor General Partner, since 1995. *Educ*: Borden Grammar School; Medway College of Technology. Joined English Electric Co., 1951; Special Director, British Aircraft Corp., 1967; Dep. Man. Dir, 1974; Man. Dir, 1977; Director, Hatfield/Lostock Division and Stevenage/Bristol Div. of Dynamics Group, British Aerospace, 1977–79; Gp Dep. Chief Exec., BAe Dynamics Gp, 1980–85; Bd Mem., BAe, 1981–85; Director: BAe Australia Ltd, 1980–86 (Chm. 1984–86); Arab British Dynamics, 1980–85; BAJ Vickers Ltd, 1982–87 (non-exec.); Grosvenor Technol. Ltd, 1984–95; Grosvenor Develt Capital, 1993–95; Mercury Grosvenor Trust PLC, 1995–97.

**KENT-JONES, His Honour Trevor David,** TD; a Circuit Judge, 1991–2006; *b* 31 July 1940; *s* of late David Sandford Kent-Jones and Madeline Mary Kent-Jones (*née* Russell-Pavier); one *s* one *d*. *Educ*: Bedford Sch.; Liverpool Univ. (LLB; DIntLaw). Called to the Bar, Gray's Inn, 1962; Mem., NE Circuit, 1963–91, Junior, 1969; a Recorder, 1985–91. Commnd KOYLI TA, 1959; served 4th Bn KOYLI, 5th Bn Light Infantry, HQ NE Dist, 1959–85; Lt-Col 1977. Pres., Yorkshire RFU, 2011–12. *Recreations*: cricket, Rugby, travel, fell-walking. *Address*: Harrogate, N Yorks. *Club*: Naval and Military.

**KENTFIELD, Graham Edward Alfred;** Deputy Director, 1994–98, and Chief Cashier, 1991–98, Bank of England; *b* 3 Sept. 1940; *s* of late E. L. H. Kentfield and F. E. M. Kentfield (*née* Tucker); *m* 1965, Ann Dwelley Hewetson; two *d*. *Educ*: Bancroft's Sch., Woodford Green, Essex; St Edmund Hall, Oxford (BA 1st cl. Lit.Hum.). Entered Bank of England, 1963; seconded to Dept of Applied Econs, Cambridge, 1966–67; Editor, Bank of England Qly Bull., 1977–80; Adviser: Financial Stats Div., 1980–84; Banking Dept, 1984–85; Dep. Chief of Banking Dept and Dep. Chief Cashier, 1985–91; Chief of Banking Dept, 1991–94. Member: Bldg Socs Investment Protection Bd, 1991–2001; Financial Law Panel, 1994–98; Chm., Insolvency Practices Council, 2000–04. Trustee: CIB Pension Fund, 1994–2006 (Chm., 2000–06); Overseas Bishoprics Fund, 1999–2016 (Chm., 2005–12); Building Socs Trust Ltd, 2002– (Chm., 2002–16). Vice-Pres., CIB, 2000–. Hon. Treas., Soc. for Promotion of Roman Studies, 1991–2010. Mem. Council, Univ. of London, 2000–08 (Mem., 2000–14, Chm., 2005–08, Investment Cttee). *Recreations*: Roman history, genealogy, philately.

**KENTRIDGE, Sir Sydney (Woolf),** KCMG 1999; QC 1984; *b* Johannesburg, 5 Nov. 1922; *s* of Morris and May Kentridge; *m* 1952, Felicia Geffen (*d* 2015); two *s* two *d*. *Educ*: King Edward VII Sch., Johannesburg; Univ. of the Witwatersrand (BA); Exeter Coll., Oxford Univ. (MA; Hon. Fellow, 1986). War service with S African forces, 1942–46. Advocate 1949, Senior Counsel 1965, South Africa; called to the English Bar, Lincoln's Inn, 1977, Bencher, 1986. Mem., Ct of Appeal, Botswana, 1981–88; Judge, Cts of Appeal, Jersey and Guernsey, 1988–92; acting Justice, Constitutional Court of S Africa, 1995–96. Roberts Lectr, Univ. of Pennsylvania, 1979. Hon. Mem., Bar Assoc., NY, 2001. Hon. Fellow, American Coll. of Trial Lawyers, 1999. Hon. LLD: Seton Hall Univ., NJ, 1978; Leicester, 1985; Cape Town, 1987; Natal, 1989; London, 1995; Sussex, 1997; Witwatersrand, 2000; Buckingham, 2009. Granville Clark Prize, USA, 1978. *Publications*: Free Country, 2012. *Recreation*: opera-going. *Address*: Brick Court Chambers, 7–8 Essex Street, WC2R 3LD. *T*: (020) 7379 3550. *Club*: Athenæum.

**KENWARD, Michael Ronald John,** OBE 1990; science writer and editorial consultant; *b* 12 July 1945; *s* of late Ronald Kenward and Phyllis Kenward; *m* 1969, Elizabeth Rice. *Educ*: Woolverstone Hall; Sussex Univ. Res. scientist, UKAEA, Culham Laboratory, 1966–68; Technical editor, Scientific Instrument Res. Assoc., 1969; various editorial posts, New Scientist, 1969–79, Editor, 1979–90; Science Consultant, The Sunday Times, 1990. Member: Royal Soc. COPUS, 1986–90; Public Affairs Cttee, 1989–93, Sci. and Industry Cttee, 1994–99, BAAS; Bd, Assoc. of British Editors, 1986–90; Royal Instn Task Force, 1995–96; Centre Cttee, Wellcome Centre for Med. Sci., 1997–98; Medicine in Society Panel, Wellcome Trust, 1998–2000; Adv. Cttee, AlphaGalileo Foundn (formerly

AlphaGalileo electronic news service), 1999–2015. Writer in residence, OST Foresight Projects on Cognitive Systems, 2002–04, on Intelligent Infrastructure Systems, 2005. Internat. Rep., Assoc. of British Sci. Writers, 1993–97. Member: Editl Cttee, Science and Public Affairs, 1994–97; Editl Bd, Ingenia, Royal Acad. of Engrg, 2004– ; Ed.-at-Large, Science | Business, 2005–. Sustained Excellence Award, British Soc. of Mag. Editors, 1987. *Publications:* Potential Energy, 1976; articles on science, technology, and business. *Recreations:* walking, photography, listening to baroque opera, cleaning up the office. *Address:* Grange Cottage, Tanyard Lane, Staplefield, W Sussex RH17 6EL.

**KENWAY, Prof. Richard Donovan,** OBE 2008; DPhil; Tait Professor of Mathematical Physics, since 1994 and Vice-Principal, High Performance Computing, since 2005, University of Edinburgh; *b* Cardiff, 8 May 1954; *s* of Alfred Bertram Kenway and Sheila Ethel Kenway; *m* 1981, Anna Cass; one *s* two *d*. *Educ:* Stanwell Comp. Sch., Penarth; Univ. of Exeter (BSc Maths and Theoretical Phys 1975); Univ. of Oxford (DPhil Theoretical Phys 1978). CPhys 1985; FInstP 2001. Res. Associate, Materials Res. Lab., Brown Univ., Providence, 1978–80; Postdoctoral Fellow, Theoretical Div., Los Alamos Nat. Lab., Los Alamos, 1980–82; University of Edinburgh: SERC Postdoctoral Fellow, 1982–83; Lectr, 1983–90, Reader, 1990–94, in Phys; Dir, 1993–97, Chm., 1997–2016, Edinburgh Parallel Computing Centre; Particle Phys Theory Gp Leader, 1994–97, 2000–08, 2014–16; Hd, Sch. of Phys and Astronomy, 1997–2000, 2008–11; PPARC Sen. Res. Fellow, 2001–04; Chm., UK Nat. e-Sci. Centre, 2001–11; Asst Principal, High Performance Computing and e-Sci., 2002–05. Dir, UoE HPCX Ltd, 2002– . Vis. Scientist, Brookhaven Nat. Lab., Upton, 2003–05. Chairman: Technol. Watch Panel, High End Computing Strategy Cttee, Res. Councils UK, 2002–11; Scientific Steering Cttee, Partnership for Advanced Computing in Europe, 2010–12; Mem., STFC, 2016– . Actg CEO, 2010–11, Chm., Bd of Dirs, 2011–16, Scottish Univs' Phys Alliance. Trustee, Alan Turing Inst., 2015– ; Dir, Turing Innovations Ltd, 2016– (Chm., 2016–). FRSE 1997; FLSW 2015. *Publications:* (jtly) An Introduction to OCCAM 2 Programming, 1987, 2nd edn 1989; (ed jtly) Computational Physics: proceedings of 32nd Scottish Universities Summer School in Physics, 1987; (ed jtly) Lattice 97: proceedings of XVth International Symposium on Lattice Field Theory, 1998; over 135 papers on theoretical particle physics, condensed matter physics and high performance computing. *Recreations:* running, hill walking, gardening. *Address:* School of Physics and Astronomy, University of Edinburgh, James Clerk Maxwell Building, Peter Guthrie Tait Road, Edinburgh EH9 3FD. *T:* (0131) 650 5245. *E:* r.d.kenway@ed.ac.uk.

**KENWAY-SMITH, Wendy Alison,** FCA; Assistant Auditor General, National Audit Office, 2000–10; *b* 21 Feb. 1959; *d* of Derek Peter Kenway-Smith and Muriel Anne Kenway-Smith (*née* Stevens). *Educ:* Marist Sch., Ascot; Guildford Tech. Coll.; City of London Poly. (BA Hons Accountancy). ACA 1983, FCA 1993. Joined BDO Stoy Hayward, 1980, Partner, 1990–95; Dir, Nat. Audit Office, 1995–99. Freeman, City of London, 1993. *Recreations:* travel, gardening, good food, theatre, classical music.

**KENWOOD, Diane, (Mrs Cary Zitcer);** Editor, Woman's Weekly, 2007–17; *b* London, 25 Jan. 1960; *d* of 2nd Baron Morris of Kenwood and of Hon. Ruth, *d* of Baron Janner; *m* 1981, Cary Zitcer; two *d*. *Educ:* St Paul's Girls' Sch.; Central Sch. of Speech and Drama (Dip. Stage Mgt). TV and radio presenter, 1986–99, incl. Travelog, Channel 4, On the Road, BBC 2, children's progs, BBC 1, Woman's Hour, Radio 4, sports on Sky News, Spectrum Radio; Features Ed., Having a Baby mag., then Ed., Health Supplement, Good Housekeeping mag., 1999–2001; Ed., Marks & Spencer mag., 2001–07. Chair, British Soc. of Magazine Editors, 2013 (Mem. Cttee, 2011–15). Member: Council, Women of Year Lunch; Adv. Bd, Chai Cancer Care; Trustee, Internat. Longevity Centre, 2016– . JP Brent, 1997–2007. *Recreations:* sport, cinema, theatre, travel, DIY.

*See also Baron Morris of Kenwood.*

**KENWORTHY,** family name of **Baron Strabolgi.**

**KENWORTHY, Duncan Hamish,** OBE 1999; film producer; Managing Director, Toledo Productions Ltd, since 1995; *b* 9 Sept. 1949; *s* of Bernard Ian Kenworthy and Edna Muriel Kenworthy (*née* Calligan). *Educ:* Rydal Sch.; Christ's Coll., Cambridge (MA English 1975); Annenberg Sch., Univ. of Pennsylvania (MA Communications 1973). Children's Television Workshop, NY, 1973–76; Consulting Producer, Arabic Sesame Street, Kuwait, 1977–79; Prod. and Exec., Jim Henson Productions, London, 1979–95; Dir, DNA Films Ltd, 1997–2009. Associate Prod., The Dark Crystal (film), 1980; Producer: *television:* Fraggle Rock, 1982 (Outstanding Children's Programming, Internat. Emmy Award, 1983); The Storyteller, 1986–88 (Best Children's Prog. (Entertainment/Drama), BAFTA Children's Awards, 1988); Living with Dinosaurs, 1988 (Best Children's Prog., Internat. Emmy Award, 1990); Monster Maker, 1988; Greek Myths, 1990 (Best Children's Prog. (Fiction), BAFTA Children's Awards, 1991); Gulliver's Travels, 1996 (Outstanding Miniseries, Emmy Award, 1996); *films:* Four Weddings and a Funeral, 1994 (Best Film, and Lloyd's Bank Peoples' Choice Award, BAFTA, 1994; Best Comedy Film, British Comedy Awards, 1994; Best Foreign Film: Cesar Award, 1994; Australian Film Inst., 1994); Lawn Dogs, 1997; Notting Hill, 1999 (Orange Audience Award, BAFTA, 2000; Best Comedy Film, British Comedy Awards, 1999); The Parole Officer, 2001; Love Actually, 2003; The Eagle, 2011; The Pass, 2016; The Children Act, 2018. Vice-Pres., BAFTA, 2009–15 (Mem., Council of Mgt, 1996–2006); Chm., 2004–06; Chm., Film, 2002–04) Mem., Film Policy Review Gp, 1997–99; Dir, Film Council, 1999–2003; Chm., Film Adv. Cttee, British Council, 1999–2008; Mem., BAFTA Hong Kong Adv. Bd, 2013–16, Fellow, Nat. Film and TV Sch., 2015 (Gov., 2001–14). British Producer of the Year, London Film Critics, 1994. FRSA 2000. *Recreations:* working out, hiking, visual arts, gardening, beekeeping. *Address:* Toledo Productions, Suite 44, 10 Richmond Mews, W1D 3DD. *Club:* Garrick.

**KENWORTHY, (Frederick) John;** Adviser, University of Cambridge, 2008–10; Managing Director, Aktus (formerly Align) Consulting (UK) Ltd, 1997–2010; *b* 6 Dec. 1943; *s* of late Rev. Fred Kenworthy and of Mrs Ethel Kenworthy; *m* 1968, Diana Flintham; one *d*. *Educ:* William Hulme's Grammar Sch., Manchester; Manchester Univ. (BA Econ Hons, Politics). Entered Admin. Class, Home Civil Service, as Asst Principal, MoD (Navy), 1966; Treasury Centre for Admin. Studies, 1968–69; joined BSC, Sheffield, 1969; Principal, MoD, 1972; Royal Commn on the Press Secretariat, 1974; Asst Sec., Dir, Weapons Resources and Progs (Naval), MoD, 1979–83; Head of Resources and Progs (Navy) (formerly DS4), RN Size and Shape Policy, and Sec. to Navy Bd, MoD, 1983–86; Dir of Ops, Disablement Services Authy (formerly Div.), DHSS, 1986–88; Dir, IT Systems Directorate (Under Sec.), 1989–90, Chief Exec., IT Services Agency, 1990–93, Dept of Social Security; Management Consultant, ICL (Internat.), 1993–95; Prin. Consultant, Independent Management Consultants, 1996. Interim Dir of Mgt Inf. Services, 2001, Advr, Inf. Strategy, 2002–08, Univ. of Cambridge. Sen. Associate Mem., Hughes Hall, Cambridge, 2007– . MInstD. FBCS 2010. Freeman, Co. of Information Technologists, 1992. *Publications:* contribs on Hungarian revenue collection and pensions, and on social security in People's Republic of China. *Recreations:* music, American politics and history. *T:* 07831 580796. *E:* aktusconsulting@aol.com.

**KENWORTHY, Joan Margaret,** BLitt, MA; Principal, St Mary's College, University of Durham, 1977–99; *b* Oldham, Lancs, 10 Dec. 1933; *o d* of late Albert Kenworthy and Amy (*née* Cobbold). *Educ:* Girls Grammar Sch., Barrow-in-Furness; St Hilda's Coll., Oxford (BLitt, MA). Henry Oliver Beckit Prize, Oxford, 1955; Leverhulme Overseas Res. Scholar, Makerere Coll., Uganda, and E African Agriculture and Forestry Res. Org., Kenya, 1956–58; Actg Tutor, St Hugh's Coll., Oxford, 1958–59; Tutorial Res. Fellow, Bedford Coll., London, 1959–60; Univ. of Liverpool: Asst Lectr in Geography, 1960–63; Lectr, 1963–73; Sen. Lectr, 1973–77; Warden of Salisbury Hall, 1966–77 and of Morton House, 1974–77. Vis. Lectr, Univ. of Dar es Salaam, 1965; IUC short-term Vis. Lectr, Univ. of Sierra Leone, 1975; Vis. Lectr, Univ. of Fort Hare, Ciskei, 1983. Hon. Res. Associate, Dept of Geog., Univ. of Durham, 2009–15. Mem., NE England, Churches Regl Broadcasting Council, 1978–82; Bishop's Selector for ACCM, 1985–87. Member: Council, African Studies Assoc. of UK, 1969–71, 1994–97; Standing Cttee on Univ. Studies of Africa, 1994–98; Council, Inst. of Brit. Geographers, 1976–78; Cttee, Merseyside Conf. for Overseas Students Ltd, 1976–77; Council, RMetS, 1980–83 (Mem., Cttee, History Gp, 2001–12); Council, Friends of the Oriental Mus., 1995–98 and 2010–12; Treasurer, Assoc. of Brit. Climatologists, 1976–79. Northern Chm., Durham Univ. Soc., 1979–82. Gov., St Anne's Sch., Windermere, 1992–95. Member: Satley PCC, 2001–04 and 2009–12 (Treas., 2002–04); Stanhope Deanery Synod, 2001–04. A Dir (formerly Trustee), Wear Valley CAB, 2001–04. Hon. Fellow, Harris Manchester Coll., Oxford, 2009–. Jehuda Neumann Meml Prize, Royal Meteorol Soc., 2015. *Publications:* (contrib.) Geographers and the Tropics, ed R. W. Steel and R. M. Prothero, 1964; (contrib.) Oxford Regional Economic Atlas for Africa, 1965; (contrib.) Studies in East African Geography and Development, ed S. Ominde, 1971; (contrib.) An Advanced Geography of Africa, ed J. I. Clarke, 1975; (contrib.) Rangeland Management and Ecology in East Africa, ed D. J. Pratt and M. D. Gwynne, 1977; (contrib.) The Climatic Scene: essays in honour of Emeritus Prof. Gordon Manley, ed M. J. Tooley and G. Sheail, 1985; (ed with B. D. Giles) Observatories and Climatological Research, 1994; (ed with J. M. Walker) Colonial Observatories and Observations, 1997; articles in jls, encycs, reports of symposia and Occasional Papers on hist. of meteorology, RMetS. *Address:* 3 Satley Plough, Satley, Bishop Auckland, Co. Durham DL13 4JX. *T:* (01388) 730848. *Clubs:* Penn, Oxford and Cambridge.

**KENWORTHY, John;** *see* Kenworthy, F. J.

**KENWRIGHT, Prof. John,** MD; FRCS; FRCSE; Nuffield Professor of Orthopaedic Surgery, Oxford University, 1992–2001; Professorial Fellow, Worcester College, Oxford, 1992–2001, now Emeritus; *b* 2 May 1936; *s* of Cecil Kenwright and Norah (*née* Langley); *m* 1960, Vivien Mary Curtis; two *s*. *Educ:* University College Sch.; Nottingham High Sch.; St John's Coll., Oxford; University College Hosp. MA Oxon; BM, BCh; MD (by thesis) Karolinska Inst., Stockholm 1972. FRCS 1966; FRCSE (*ad hominem*) 1998. Nuffield Surgical Res. Fellow, Oxford, 1968; Res. Fellow, Karolinska Inst., Stockholm, 1971; Consultant Orthopaedic Surgeon, Nuffield Orthopaedic Centre and John Radcliffe Hosp., Oxford, 1973–2001. Royal College of Surgeons of England: Hunterian Prof., 1991–92; Robert Jones Lectr, 1998; Res. Dir, Wishbone Trust, British Orthopaedic Assoc., 2002–03. President: Girdlestone Orthopaedic Soc., 1993–2002; Oxford Medico-legal Soc., 1998–; British Limb Reconstruction Soc., 1998–2000; British Orthopaedic Res. Soc., 1999; Internat. Soc. for Fracture Repair, 2002–04. President's Medal for lifetime contribn to res., British Orthopaedic Res. Soc., 2017. *Publications:* articles in scientific jls on factors which control fracture and soft tissue healing; also on leg lengthening and correction of post traumatic deformity. *Recreations:* sailing, lawn tennis. *Address:* Nuffield Orthopaedic Centre, Headington, Oxford OX3 7LD. *T:* (01865) 862695. *E:* johnandvkenwright@gmail.com. *Club:* Oxford and Cambridge Sailing Society.

**KENWRIGHT, William, (Bill),** CBE 2001; theatre producer, since 1970; *b* 4 Sept. 1945; *s* of Albert Kenwright and Hope Kenwright (*née* Jones); partner, Jennifer Ann Seagrove, *qv*. *Educ:* Liverpool Inst. Actor, 1964–70; has produced more than 500 plays and musicals, including: Joseph and The Amazing Technicolor Dreamcoat; Evita; Cabaret; Jesus Christ Superstar; A Streetcar Named Desire; Stepping Out; Blood Brothers; Shirley Valentine; Travels with My Aunt; Piaf; Medea; A Doll's House; An Ideal Husband; Passion; Long Day's Journey into Night; Cat on a Hot Tin Roof, etc; *films:* Stepping Out; Don't Go Breaking My Heart; Die Mommie Die; The Purifiers; Cheri; Broken (Best British Ind. Film, BIFA, 2012); Another Mother's Son; My Pure Land. Chm., Everton FC, 2004– (Dir, 1989– ; Dep. Chm., 1998). Hon. Professor: Tameside Univ.; Liverpool Univ. Hon. Dr: Liverpool John Moores; West London; Hon. DLitt Nottingham Trent. Has won Tony, Olivier, Evening Standard, Variety Club and TMA Lifetime Achievement awards. *Address:* Bill Kenwright Ltd, BKL House, 1 Venice Walk, W2 1RR. *T:* (020) 7446 6200.

**KENYON,** family name of **Baron Kenyon.**

**KENYON, 7th Baron** *cr* 1788; **Lloyd Nicholas Tyrell-Kenyon;** Bt 1784; Baron of Gredington, 1788; *b* 9 April 1972; *s* of 6th Baron Kenyon and of Sally Carolyn, *e d* of J. F. P. Matthews; *S* father, 2019.

**KENYON, Eleanor Mary Henrietta;** *see* Hill, E. M. H.

**KENYON, Margaret;** DL; Headmistress, Withington Girls' School, Manchester, 1986–2000; *b* 19 June 1940; *d* of Hugh Richard Parry and Aileen Cole (*née* Morgan); *m* 1962, Christopher George Kenyon (CBE 2003); two *s*. *Educ:* Merchant Taylors' Sch. for Girls, Crosby; Somerville Coll., Oxford (MA; Hon. Fellow, 1999). Asst French Mistress, Cheadle Hulme Sch., 1962–63 and 1974–83; Hd of French, Withington Girls Sch., 1983–85. Girls' School Association: Chm., NW Region, 1989–91; Pres., 1993–94. Mem. Adv. Council, Granada Foundn, 1986–2012. Trustee, Mus. of Science and Industry, Manchester, 1998–2004. Mem. Court, Univ. of Manchester, 1991–2004 (Chair, Press Bd, 2001–10). Governor: Bolton Sch., 2001–12; Cheadle Hulme Sch., 2001–12; Haberdashers' Aske's Schs, Elstree, 2002–09. DL Greater Manchester, 1998. Medal of Honour, Manchester Univ., 2011. *Recreations:* reading, talking, family. *Address:* Alderley House, 33 Lemsford Road, St Albans, Herts AL1 3PP.

**KENYON, Sir Nicholas (Roger),** Kt 2008; CBE 2001; Managing Director, Barbican Centre, since 2007; *b* 23 Feb. 1951; *s* of late Thomas Kenyon and Kathleen Holmes; *m* 1976, Marie-Ghislaine Latham-Koenig; three *s* one *d*. *Educ:* Balliol College, Oxford (BA Hons 1972). Music critic: The New Yorker, 1979–82; The Times, 1982–85; The Observer, 1985–92; Music Editor, The Listener, 1982–87; Editor, Early Music, 1983–92; Controller, BBC Radio 3, 1992–98; Dir, BBC Promenade Concerts, 1996–2007; Controller, BBC Proms, Live Events and TV Classical Music, 2000–07. Member: AHRB, subseq. AHRC, 2004–08; Arts Council England, 2009–17. *Publications:* The BBC Symphony Orchestra 1930–80, 1981; Simon Rattle, 1987, 2nd edn 2001; The Faber Pocket Guide to Mozart, 2005; The Faber Pocket Guide to Bach, 2011; *edited:* Authenticity and Early Music, 1988; (jtly) The Viking Opera Guide, 1993; (jtly) The Penguin Opera Guide, 1995; Musical Lives, 2003; The City of London: a companion guide, 2012; BBC Proms Guide to: Great Symphonies, 2003; Great Concertos, 2003; Great Choral Works, 2004; Great Orchestral Works, 2004. *Recreation:* family. *Address:* Barbican Centre, Silk Street, EC2Y 8DS. *T:* (020) 7382 7005.

**KENYON-SLANEY, (William) Simon (Rodolph)**, OBE 2004; JP; Vice Lord-Lieutenant of Shropshire, 1996–2007; *b* 31 Jan. 1932; *s* of Major R. O. R. Kenyon-Slaney, Grenadier Guards, and Nesta, *d* of Sir George Ferdinand Forestier-Walker, 3rd Bt; *m* 1960, Mary Helena (*d* 2018), *e d* of Lt-Col Hon. H. G. O. Bridgeman, DSO, MC, RA, and Joan, *d* of Hon. Bernard Constable Maxwell; three *s*. *Educ*: Eton. FLAS 1964; FRICS 1970. Grenadier Guards, 1950–52; formerly: Chartered Land Agent and Surveyor; farmer. Non-exec. Dir, South Staffs Gp PLC, 1988–2002. Chm., Ludlow Cons. Assoc., 1989–91. Trustee, Ironbridge Gorge Museum, 1995–2012 (Dep. Chm., 2002–12; Vice Pres., 2012–). Former school governor. Shropshire: JP 1969 (Chairman: Probation Cttee, 1979–84; Staffs and Shropshire Magistrates' Assoc., 1982–87; Bridgnorth Bench, 1990–95; Magistrates' Courts Cttee, 1994–97); CC, 1977–85 (Chm., Planning and Transport Cttee, 1982–85); High Sheriff, 1979; DL 1986. Member: Council, Shropshire, SJAB, 1969–2012 (Chm., 1974–2002); Nat. Council, Magistrates' Assoc., 1982–92. KStJ 1993 (OStJ 1976; CStJ 1983; Mem., Chapter-General, 1990–99, Priory Chapter, 1999–2002). *Recreations*: gardening, travel, theatre, fishing. *Address*: Cedars House, 13 Victoria Road, Much Wenlock, Shropshire TF13 6AL. *T*: (01952) 726775.

**KEOGH, Prof. Sir Bruce (Edward)**, KBE 2003; MD; FRCS, FRCSE; Chair, Birmingham Women's and Children's Hospital NHS Foundation Trust, since 2018; *b* 24 Nov. 1954; *s* of Gerald Keogh and Marjorie Beatrice Keogh (*née* Craig); naturalised British citizen, 2004; *m* 1979, Ann Katherine (*née* Westmore); four *s*. *Educ*: St George's Coll., Zimbabwe; Charing Cross Hosp. Med. Sch., Univ. of London (BSc Hons 1977; MB BS 1980; MD 1989). MRCS 1980, FRCS *ad eundem* 2000; LRCP 1980; FRCSE 1985. Demonstrator in Anatomy, Charing Cross Hosp. Med. Sch., 1981–82; Registrar training: Northern Gen. Hosp., Sheffield, 1984–85; Hammersmith Hosp., 1985–89 (BHF Jun. Res. Fellow, 1987–88); Sen. Registrar in Cardiothoracic Surgery, St George's and Harefield Hosps, 1989–91; BHF Sen. Lectr in Cardiac Surgery, RPMS Hammersmith Hosp., 1991–95; Consultant in Cardiothoracic Surgery, 1995–2004, and Associate Med. Dir for Clinical Governance, 1998–2003, University Hosp. Birmingham NHS Trust; Prof. of Cardiac Surgery, 2004–07, Hon. Prof., 2008, UCL; Dir of Surgery, 2004–07, Consultant Cardiothoracic Surgeon, 2004–07, The Heart Hosp., UCL Hosps NHS Trust; NHS Medical Dir, DoH, 2007–13. Visiting Professor: Univ. of Tokyo, 2006; Chinese Univ. of HK, 2007; Univ. of Colorado, 2009; King James IV Prof., RCSE, 2005; RCS Tudor Edwards Lectr, 2007. Nat. Med. Dir, NHS England (formerly NHS Commng Bd), 2012–18. Member: Commn for Health Improvement, 2002–04; Commn for Healthcare Audit and Inspection, 2004–07 (Chm., Clinical Adv. Gp, 2004–06); Chairman: Jt Commn for Health Improvement and Audit Commn Nat. Service Framework Prog. Bd, 2002–04; Jt DoH, Healthcare Commn and Soc. for Cardio Thoracic Surgery Central Cardiac Audit Database Oversight Cttee, 2004–07; Co-Chm., Nat. Quality Bd, 2014–17. Member: NHS Nat. Taskforce for Coronary Heart Disease, 2000–06; NHS Standing Med. Adv. Cttee, 2002–04; Chairman: W Midlands NHS Regl Coronary Heart Disease and Tobacco Modernisation Gp, 2000–02; DoH Inf. Taskforce on Clinical Outcomes, 2006–07. Founder and Co-ordinator, Nat. Adult Cardiac Surgical Database, 1994–2007. Member: Intercollegiate Specialist Adv. Cttee on higher surgical trng in cardiothoracic surgery, 1999–2004; Intercollegiate Exam. Bd in Cardiothoracic Surgery, 1999–2004 (Examr, 1999–2004). Mem. Council, RCS, 2002–04, 2006–08; Cardiothoracic section, Royal Society of Medicine: Mem. Council, 1992–99; Hon. Sec., 1993–99; Pres., 2005–07; Society for Cardio Thoracic Surgery in GB and Ireland: Ronald Edwards Medal, 1991; Hon. Sec., 1999–2003; Pres., 2006–08; Sec.-Gen., European Assoc. for Cardio-Thoracic Surgery, 2004–08; Society of Thoracic Surgeons: Internat. Dir, 2005–11; Ferguson Lect., 2009; McKeown Medal Lect., RCSE, 2012; Hunterian Orator, RCS, 2013; Blalock Lect., Johns Hopkins Univ., 2017. Inaugural Judge, Hippocrates Prize for Poetry and Medicine, 2010. Fellow: European Soc. of Cardiology, 1992; European Bd of Thoracic and Cardiovascular Surgery, 1999. Member: Lunar Soc.; American Assoc. for Thoracic Surgery, 2007; Council, British Heart Foundn, 2008–13. Trustee, Healing Foundn, 2014–16; Chm., Scar Free Foundn, 2016–. Vice Patron, RBL Poppy Factory, 2011–16. Pres., Ex Fide Fiducia Trust, 2016–. Hon. FRCP 2005; Hon. FRCGP 2009; Hon. FACS 2009; Hon. FRCSI 2011; Hon. FRCA 2011; Hon. Fellow, Amer. Surgical Assoc., 2016. Hon. MD: Birmingham, 2009; Sheffield, 2009; Hon. DSc: Toledo, 2009; Coventry, 2010. Member, Editorial Board: Jl RSocMed, 1994–99; CTSNet, 1999–2007; Heart, 2000–06. *Publications*: Normal Surface Anatomy, 1984; (ed jtly) The Evidence for Cardiothoracic Surgery, 2004; National Adult Cardiac Surgical Database Report, 1999, 6th edn 2009; National Reports on: neonatal services, 2009; safety of breast implants, 2012; cosmetic interventions, 2013; trusts with high mortality, 2013; urgent and emergency care, 2013; articles in jls on cardiac surgery and measurement of health outcomes. *Recreations*: diving, photography. *Address*: Claremont House, 68 Oakfield Road, Selly Park, Birmingham B29 7EG.

**KEOHANE, Desmond John**, OBE 1991; consultant in education and training, retired; *b* 5 July 1928; *s* of William Patrick Keohane and Mabel Margaret Keohane; *m* 1960, Mary Kelliher; two *s* two *d*. *Educ*: Borden Grammar Sch., Sittingbourne; Univ. of Birmingham (BA and Baxter Prize in History, 1949); London Univ. (Postgrad. Cert in Educn). Postgrad. res., 1949–50; Nat. Service, Educn Officer, RAF, 1950–52; sch. teacher and coll. lectr, 1953–64; Head, Dept of Social and Academic Studies, 1964–68, and Vice-Principal, 1969–71, Havering Technical Coll.; Principal, Northampton Coll. of Further Educn, 1971–76; Principal, Oxford Coll. of Further Educn, 1976–90. Part-time Lectr in Educnl Management, Univ. of Leicester, 1990–93; Vis. Fellow (Educn), 1991–94, Hon. Fellow, 1991, Oxford Brookes Univ. (formerly Oxford Polytechnic). Member: Council, Southern Regional Council for Further Educn, 1977–90; Secondary Exams Council, 1983–86; Berks and Oxon Area Manpower Board, 1985–88; Special Employment Measures Adv. Gp, MSC, 1986–89; Northampton RC Diocesan Educn Commn, 1991–2002; E Midlands Panel, Nat. Lottery Charities Bd, 1995–98; Co-opted Mem. Educn Cttee, Northants CC, 1996–2002. Chm. Trustees, Stress at Work, 1987–2002. Formerly governor of various educnl instns; Chm. of Govs, Thomas Becket Sch., Northampton, 1983–98. Gen. Ed., series Managing Colleges Effectively, 1994–99. *Recreations*: enjoying family and friends, watching cricket. *Address*: 2 Neale Close, Weston Favell, Northampton NN3 3DB. *T*: (01604) 416474. *E*: desmond.keohane@btinternet.com.

**KEPPEL**, family name of **Earl of Albemarle**.

**KER**; *see* Innes-Ker, family name of Duke of Roxburghe.

**KERE, Dr Sir Nathan Kumamusa**, KCMG 2014; Medical Practitioner, since 1975; Infectious Disease Specialist and Malariologist, since 1994; *b* Sasamugga village, Choiseul Is., Solomon Is, 4 Aug. 1950; *s* of Nelson Kere and Nelly Zaoro; *m* 1984, Joy Finioa; three *s* four *d*. *Educ*: King George VI Sch.; Fiji Sch. of Medicine (DSM 1974); Otago Univ. (DPH 1978); Univ. of Liverpool (MCommH 1982); London Sch. of Hygiene and Tropical Medicine, Univ. of London (PhD Epidemiol. and Control of Infectious Diseases 1992). Solomon Islands: MO, then SMO, 1975–78; CMO (Communicable Diseases), 1979–83; Undersec. for Health Improvement, 1983–88; Dir, Solomon Is Medical Training and Res. Inst., and Govt Malariologist, 1988–93; Perm. Sec. for Health, 1993–94. Civil Aviation Authorised MO, 1994–, Maritime Authorised MO, 1994–, MO for Rotary, 1997–, Solomon Is. Hon. Consultant, Fiji Sch. of Medicine, 1993. Pres., Solomon Is Golf Fedn, 2010–. World Health Medal, 1988; Paul Harris Recognition, 2002; Service Above Self Medal, 2006, Sapphire Pin, 2011, Rotary Internat. *Publications*: articles in jls Health Policy and Planning, SE Asian Jl of Tropical Medicine and Public Health, Travel Medicine Internat. and Med. Veterinary Entomol. *Recreations*: golf, fishing, swimming, charity fund raising, cricket. *Address*: East Medical Centre Ltd, PO Box 1173, Honiara, Solomon Islands. *T*: 39220, 7475434, *Fax*: 39221. *E*: kere@solomon.com.sb. *Clubs*: Rotary (Honiara); Honiara Golf.

**KEREVAN, George**; *b* Glasgow, 28 Sept. 1949; *m* Angela. *Educ*: Univ. of Glasgow. Lectr in Econs, Napier Univ., Edinburgh; Associate Ed., Scotsman, 2000–09; Producer, What If Prodns (Television) Ltd, 2000–06; producer of documentary films for Discovery, Hist. Channel and PBS. Former Chm., Edinburgh Tourist Bd; Member, Board: Edinburgh Internat. Fest.; Edinburgh Internat. Film Fest.; Founder, Edinburgh Sci. Fest.; Co-organiser, Prestwick World Fest. of Flight. Mem. (Lab) Edinburgh CC, 1984–96. Contested (SNP) Edinburgh E, 2010. MP (SNP) E Lothian, 2015–17; contested (SNP) same seat, 2017.

**KERIN, Hon. John Charles**, AO 2018 (AM 2001); Chairman, Australian Meat and Livestock Corporation, 1994–97; Forestry Commissioner, New South Wales, 1998–2003; *b* 21 Nov. 1937; *s* of Joseph Sydney Kerin and Mary Louise Fuller; *m* 1st, Barbara Elizabeth Large (marr. diss.); one *d* and one step *s* two step *d*; 2nd, 1983, Dr June Raye Verrier. *Educ*: Univ. of New England (BA 1967); ANU (BEc 1977). Axeman and bricksetter, then farmer and businessman, 1952–71; Res. Economist, 1971–72, Principal Res. Economist, 1976–78, Bureau of Agricl Econs. MP (ALP) for Macarthur, NSW, 1972–75, for Werriwa, 1978–93; Minister: for Primary Industry, 1983–87; for Primary Industries and Energy, 1987–91; Treas., 1991; Minister: for Transport and Communications, 1991; for Trade and Overseas Develt, 1991–93. Statutory office holder and businessman, 1993–. Chairman: Corporate Investment Australia Funds Management Ltd, 1994–99; John Kerin and Associates, 1994; Spire Technologies, 1998–2001; Chm., Coal Mines Australia Ltd, subseq. Mem. Bd, Billiton, 1995–2001. Chairman: NSW Water Adv. Council, 1995–2003; Reef Fisheries Management Adv. Cttee, 1995–2003; Stored Grain Res. Lab., 2002–05; Co-operative Research Centres: Sustainable Plantation Forestry (formerly Temperate Hardwood Forests), 1994–2002; Tropical Savannas, 1995–2008; Australian Weed Mgt (formerly Weed Mgt Systems), 1995–2008; Sensor Signals and Information Processing, 1996–2005; Poultry, 2011–. Chm., Qld Fisheries Mgt Authy, 1999–2000; Bd Mem., Southern Rivers Catchment Mgt Authy, 2004–11. Chm. Adv. Cttee, Nat. Ovine Johne's Prog., 2000–06; Mem., Safe Food Prodn Adv. Cttee, NSW, 2000–03. Dep. Pres., UNICEF (Australia), 1994–2008; Mem., Birds Australia Council, 2002–05. Mem. Bd, CSIRO, 2008–11. Chm., Crawford Fund, 2010– (NSW Chm., 2000, ACT Chm., 2006). Mem. Bd of Trustees, Univ. of Western Sydney, 1996–2006; Trustee, Clunies Ross Foundn, 2004. Adjunct Prof., ANU, 2013–16. Fellow, Aust. Inst. of Agricl Sci., 1995; FTSE 2001. Hon. Dr Rural Sci., New England, 1993; Hon. DLitt Western Sydney, 1995; Hon. Dr Sci. Tasmania, 2001. *Recreations*: live arts, music, reading, walking. *Address*: 26 Harpur Place, Garran, ACT 2605, Australia. *T*: (2) 62852480.

**KERINS, Angela**; Chief Executive, Rehab Group, 2007–14; *b* Waterford City, 29 May 1958; *m* 1983, Sean Kerins; one *s* one *d*. *Educ*: Basildon and Thurrock Sch. of Nursing and Midwifery (SRN 1979; SCM 1981). Cert IoD. Clinical and healthcare mgt posts, 1980–92; Dir, Public Affairs and Gp Develt, Rehab Gp, 1992–2007; Chief Exec., RehabCare, 1995–2007. Chair: TBG Learning, 2006–14; Momentum Scotland, 2007–14; Rehab JobFit, 2011–14. Chair: Nat. Disability Authy, Ire., 1999–2009; Equality Authy, 2007–12; Co-Chair, Nat. Disability Strategy Stakeholders Monitoring Gp, 2005–11; Mem., Health Information and Quality Authy, 2007–12. Pres., European Platform for Rehabilitation, 2012–14. Mem., Nat. Council, Irish Business and Employers Confedn, 2004–14. Hon. LLD NUI, 2003. *Publications*: contribs to The Irish Times, Comment and Analysis. *Club*: Royal Irish Automobile.

**KERN, Karl-Heinz**; Head of Arms Control Department, Ministry of Foreign Affairs, German Democratic Republic, 1987–90; research in international affairs, since 1990; *b* 18 Feb. 1930; *m* 1952, Ursula Bennmann; one *s*. *Educ*: King George Gymnasium, Dresden; Techn. Coll., Dresden (chem. engrg); Acad. for Polit. Science and Law (Dipl. jur., post-grad. History). Leading posts in diff. regional authorities of GDR until 1959; foreign policy, GDR, 1959–62; Head of GDR Mission in Ghana, 1962–66; Head of African Dept, Min. of For. Affairs, 1966–71; Minister and Chargé d'Affaires, Gt Britain, 1973; Ambassador to UK, 1973–80; Dep. Head of Western European Dept, Min. of Foreign Affairs, 1980–82; Ambassador to N Korea, 1982–86. Holds Order of Merit of the Fatherland, etc. *Recreations*: sport, reading, music. *Address*: Karl-Marx-Allee 70a, 10243 Berlin, Germany.

**KERNAGHAN, Paul Robert**, CBE 2005; QPM 1998; Judicial Appointments and Conduct Ombudsman, since 2016; Commissioner for Standards, States of Jersey, since 2017; *b* Dec. 1955; *s* of Hugh Kernaghan and Diane Kernaghan (*née* Herdman); *m* 1983, Mary McCleery; one *d*. *Educ*: Methodist Coll., Belfast; Queen's Univ., Belfast (LLB Hons); Univ. of Ulster (DPM); Univ. of Leicester (MA Public Order). MIPD 1991. Served UDR (part-time), 1974–77; commnd 1976, Second Lieut; served RUC, 1978–91: grad. entrant, Constable, 1978; served Belfast, Londonderry, Strabane and Warrenpoint, operational and staff appts; Superintendent, 1991–92, Detective Superintendent, 1992–95, W Midlands Police; Asst Chief Constable, 1995; Asst Chief Constable (Designated), 1996–99, N Yorks Police; rcds 1997; Chief Constable, Hampshire Constabulary, 1999–2008. Internat. affairs portfolio holder, ACPO, 2000–08; Hd of Mission, EU Police Co-ordinating Office for Palestinian Police Support, 2009. Comr for Standards, H of L, 2010–16. Member: UN Internat. Policing Adv. Council, 2006–08; Armed Forces Pay Review Body, 2011–17; (non-exec.) Civil Nuclear Police Authy, 2013–20. *Recreations*: family, walking the dog, reading. *E*: p.kernaghan123@gmail.com.

**KERR**, family name of **Marquess of Lothian**, **Lady Herries of Terregles** and **Barons Kerr of Kinlochard**, **Kerr of Tonaghmore** and **Teviot**.

**KERR OF KINLOCHARD**, Baron *cr* 2004 (Life Peer), of Kinlochard in Perth and Kinross; **John Olav Kerr**, GCMG 2001 (KCMG 1991; CMG 1987); Deputy Chairman, Scottish Power, since 2012 (Director, since 2009); Member, Advisory Board, Edinburgh Partners, since 2012; *b* 22 Feb. 1942; *s* of late Dr J. D. O. Kerr; *m* 1965, Elizabeth, *d* of late W. G. Kalaugher; two *s* three *d*. *Educ*: Glasgow Academy; Pembroke Coll., Oxford (Hon. Fellow, 1991). HM Diplomatic Service, 1966–2002; HM Treasury, 1979–84: Principal Private Sec. to Chancellor of the Exchequer, 1981–84; Asst Under-Sec. of State, FCO, 1987–90; Ambassador and UK Perm. Rep. to the EU, 1990–95; Ambassador to USA, 1995–97; Perm. Under-Sec. of State, FCO, and Hd, Diplomatic Service, 1997–2002; Sec.-Gen., European Convention, 2002–03. Director: Shell Transport and Trading, 2002–05; Scottish American Investment Trust, 2002–19; Rio Tinto plc, 2003–15; Dep. Chm., Royal Dutch Shell plc, 2005–12. Indep. Mem., H of L, 2004–; Member: EU Select Cttee, H of L, 2006–10, 2014–15; Economic Affairs Select Cttee, H of L, 2015–. Mem. Council, Centre for Eur. Reform, 2004– (Chm., 2009–); Hon. Pres., UK/Korea Forum for the Future, 2007–13; Vice-Pres., Eur. Policy Centre, 2007–15. Trustee: Rhodes Trust, Oxford, 1997–2010; Nat. Gall., 2002–10; Fulbright Commn, 2004–09; Carnegie Trust for Univs of

Scotland, 2005–18; Refugee Council, 2016–. Chm., Ct and Council, 2005–11, Fellow, 2013, Imperial Coll. London. Hon. Pres., St Andrew's Clinics for Children, 2008–. Hon. FRSE 2006. Hon. LLD: St Andrews, 1996; Glasgow, 1999; Hon. DLitt Aston, 2010. *Address:* House of Lords, SW1A 0PW. *Clubs:* Garrick; Queen's Park Rangers Football.

**KERR OF TONAGHMORE,** Baron *cr* 2009 (Life Peer), of Tonaghmore in the County of Down; **Brian Francis Kerr,** Kt 1993; PC 2004; a Justice of the Supreme Court of the United Kingdom (formerly a Lord of Appeal in Ordinary), since 2009; *b* 22 Feb. 1948; *s* of late James William Kerr and Kathleen Rose Kerr; *m* 1970, Gillian Rosemary Owen Widdowson; two *s. Educ:* St Colman's College, Newry, Co. Down; Queen's Univ., Belfast (LLB 1969). Called to NI Bar, 1970, to the Bar of England and Wales, Gray's Inn, 1974 (Hon. Bencher, 1997); QC (NI) 1983; Bencher, Inn of Court of NI, 1990; Junior Crown Counsel (Common Law), 1978–83; Sen. Crown Counsel, 1988–93; Judge of the High Ct of Justice, NI, 1993–2004; Lord Chief Justice of NI, 2004–09. Chm., Mental Health Commn for NI, 1988. Member: Judicial Studies Bd, NI, 1995–2004; Franco British Judicial Co-operation Cttee, 1995–2001. Chm., Distinction and Meritorious Service Awards Cttee, NI, 1997–2001. Eisenhower Exchange Fellow, 1999. Hon. Bencher, King's Inns, 2004. Hon. Fellow, American Bd of Trial Advocates 2004. Hon. LLD: QUB, 2009; Ulster, 2014. *Recreation:* trying to be (and hoping to make my family) happy. *Address:* Supreme Court of the United Kingdom, Parliament Square, SW1P 3BD.

**KERR, Alan Grainger,** OBE 2000; FRCS, FRCSE; Consultant Otolaryngologist, Royal Victoria and Belfast City Hospitals, since 1968; *b* 15 April 1935; *s* of Joseph William and Eileen Kerr; *m* 1st, 1962, Patricia Margaret M'Neill (*d* 1999); two *s* one *d*; 2nd, 2015, Victoria Saunderson Glass. *Educ:* Methodist College, Belfast; Queen's Univ., Belfast (MB). DObst RCOG. Clinical and Res. Fellow, Harvard Med. Sch., 1967; Prof. of Otorhinolaryngology, QUB, 1979–81. Otolaryngology Mem. Council, RCS, 1987–92; President: Otorhinolaryngological Res. Soc., 1985–87; Internat. Otopathology Soc., 1985–88; Otology Sect., RSM, 1989–90; British Assoc. of Otorhinolaryngologists—Head and Neck Surgeons, 1993–96; Irish Otolaryngological Soc., 1997–99; Politzer Soc., 1998–2002. Master, British Academic Conf. in Otolaryngology, 2006. Lectures, UK, Europe and USA. Prizes: Jobson Horne, BMA; Harrison, RSocMed; Howells, Univ. of London. Gen. Editor, Scott-Brown's Otolaryngology, 1987–2008. *Publications:* papers on ear surgery. *Recreations:* tennis, hill walking, bowls and bridge. *Address:* 14 Mill Road, Drumbo, Lisburn BT27 5TT. *T:* (028) 9082 6854. *Club:* Royal Society of Medicine.

**KERR, Prof. Allen,** AO 1992; FRS 1986; FAA; Professor of Plant Pathology, University of Adelaide, 1980–91, Professor Emeritus, since 1992; *b* 21 May 1926; *s* of A. B. Kerr and J. T. Kerr (*née* White); *m* 1951, Rosemary Sheila Strachan (*d* 2010); two *s* one *d. Educ:* George Heriot's Sch., Edinburgh; Univ. of Edinburgh. North of Scotland Coll. of Agric., 1947–51; University of Adelaide: Lectr, 1951–59; Sen. Lectr, 1959–67 (seconded to Tea Research Inst., Ceylon, 1963–66); Reader, 1968–80. FAA 1978. For. Associate, Nat. Acad. of Scis, USA, 1991. *Recreation:* golf. *Address:* 419 Carrington Street, Adelaide, SA 5000, Australia. *T:* 0408 400332.

**KERR, Andrew Cameron;** Chief Executive, Edinburgh City Council, since 2015; *b* Falkirk, 17 March 1959; *s* of James Scott Kerr and Sheana Kerr; *m* 1994, Edda Hermannsdottir; one *s* two *d. Educ:* Falkirk High Sch.; London Univ. (BEd PE and Hist.); Cardiff Business Sch. (MBA 1996). Leisure Officer, Falkirk DC, 1983–87; Principal Leisure Officer, Cardiff CC, 1987–90; Hd, Participation, Sports Council for Wales, 1990–96; Hd, Lifelong Learning and Leisure, Caerphilly CBC, 1996–2000; Lead Inspector, Audit Commn, 2000–01; Birmingham City Council: Dir, Leisure and Culture, 2001–03; Dir, Performance Improvement, 2003–05; Chief Executive: North Tyneside Council, 2005–10; Wiltshire Council, 2010–11; Chief Operating Officer, Cardiff CC, 2012–13; Chief Exec., Cornwall Council, 2014–15. Owner, Kerr Strategic Consultancy Ltd, 2011–16. Mem., Govt Efficiency Task Force, 2010. Pres., Inst. of Leisure and Amenity Mgt, 2003. Trustee and Mem. Bd, NSPCC, 2018–. British athletics international, 1977–83; British Under-20 Indoor and Outdoor Champion, 400m, 1977; Bronze Medal, Eur. Jun. Championships, 1977; 17 Scottish Championship medals; 12 AAA Championship medals. *Recreations:* fitness, golf, reading political and sports biographies, science fiction, music. *Address:* 28 Montgomery Way, Musselburgh, East Lothian EH21 7BF. *T:* 07766 924803.

**KERR, Andrew Mark,** MBE 2017; Partner, Bell & Scott, WS, Edinburgh, 1969–99 (Senior Partner, 1987–96); Clerk to Society of Writers to HM Signet, 1983–2003; *b* Edinburgh, 17 Jan. 1940; *s* of William Mark Kerr and Katharine Marjorie Anne Stevenson; *m* 1967, Jane Susanna Robertson; one *d. Educ:* Edinburgh Acad.; Cambridge Univ. (BA); Edinburgh Univ. (LLB). Served RNR, 1961–76. British Petroleum, 1961–62; apprenticeship with Davidson & Syme, WS, Edinburgh, 1964–67; with Bell & Scott, Bruce & Kerr, WS, later Bell & Scott, WS, 1967–99. Vice-Chm., Edinburgh New Town Conservation Cttee, 1972–76; Chm., Edinburgh Solicitors' Property Centre, 1976–81. Chairman: Penicuik House Preservation Trust, 1985–2001; Arts Trust of Scotland, 1996–2015; Dunedin Concerts Trust, 1996–2009; Member: Council, Edinburgh Internat. Fest., 1978–82; Scottish Arts Council, 1988–94 (Chm., Drama Cttee, 1988–91, and 1993–94); Director: Edinburgh Fest. and King's Theatres, 1997–2003; Edinburgh World Heritage Trust, 1999–2010; Historic Scotland Foundn, 2001–06; Sec., Edinburgh Fest. Fringe Soc. Ltd, 1969–2002. Trustee: Thirlestane Castle Trust, 1984–91; Saltire Soc. Trust, 2014–. Mem. Council, St George's Sch. for Girls, Edinburgh, 1985–93; Gov., New Sch., Butterstone, 1995–2007. *Recreations:* architecture, hill walking, music, ships, ski-ing, theatre. *Address:* 16 Ann Street, Edinburgh EH4 1PJ. *T:* (home) (0131) 332 9857. *Club:* New (Edinburgh).

**KERR, Andrew Palmer;** Chief Executive Officer, Sense Scotland, since 2011; *b* 17 March 1962; *s* of William and May Kerr; *m* 1992, Susan Kealy; three *d* (incl. twins). *Educ:* Glasgow Coll. (BA Social Scis); Glasgow Caledonian Univ. (Postgrad. Cert. Mgt 2009; MBA 2010). Dep. Pres., Glasgow Coll. Students' Assoc., 1983–85; Convenor, Glasgow Area, NUS, 1985–86; Dep. Pres., NUS (Scotland), 1986–87; R&D Officer, Strathkelvin DC, 1987–90; Man. Dir, Achieving Quality, QA Consultancy, 1990–93; Strategy and Develt Manager, Cleansing Dept, Glasgow CC, 1993–99. Mem. (Lab) East Kilbride, Scottish Parlt, 1999–2011. Scottish Executive: Minister: for Finance and Public Services, 2001–04; for Health and Community Care, 2004–07; Shadow Cabinet Sec. for Finance and Sustainable Growth, 2007–11. Contested (Lab) East Kilbride, Scottish Parlt, 2011. Chm., Quality Scotland, 2016–. *Recreations:* family, half marathon and 10K running, football, reading. *Address:* 8 Threestanes Road, Strathaven ML10 6DX.

**KERR, Calum Robert;** *b* Galashiels, 5 April 1972; *m* Ros; three *c. Educ:* Peebles High Sch.; St Andrews Univ. (MA Hons Modern Hist. 1994). Account Manager, Philips Business Communications, 1995–98; Channel Account Manager, 1998–2003, High Touch Account Manager, 2004–09, Nortel Networks; Avaya: Named Account Manager, 2009–12; Practice Consultant – Sales Acceleration, 2012–13; Practice Leader – Sales Mgt Excellence, 2014–15. MP (SNP) Berwickshire, Roxburgh and Selkirk, 2015–17; contested (SNP) same seat, 2017.

**KERR, Caroline;** Media Consultant and Company Secretary, Millbank Media, since 2006; Independent Editorial Adviser, BBC Trust, 2007–12; *b* 27 May 1962; *d* of John and Maureen Kerr; one *s* one *d. Educ:* Newnham Coll., Cambridge (MA English). Joined ITN, 1984: trainee, 1984–91; gen. reporter, 1991–94; Asia Corresp., 1994–98; Consumer Affairs Corresp., 1998–99; Business and Economics Ed., 1999–2004. *Address:* Millbank Media, 4 Millbank, SW1P 3JA.

**KERR, David;** *see* Kerr, M. D.

**KERR, Prof. David James,** CBE 2002; MD; DSc; FRCP, FRCPE, FMedSci; Professor of Cancer Medicine, University of Oxford, since 2009; Fellow, Harris Manchester College, Oxford, since 2012; *b* 14 June 1956; *s* of Robert James Andrew Kerr and Sarah Pettigrew Kerr (*née* Hogg); *m* 1st, 1980, Anne Miller Young (marr. diss. 2012); one *s* two *d*; 2nd, 2013, Rachel Midgley; one *s* one *d. Educ:* Univ. of Glasgow (BSc 1st Cl. Hons 1977; MB ChB 1980; MSc 1985; MD 1987; PhD 1990; DSc 1997). FRCPGlas 1995; MRCP 1983, FRCP 1996; FRCPE 2009. Sen. Registrar (Med. Oncol.), Western Infirmary, Glasgow, 1985–89; Sen. Lectr, Glasgow Univ., 1989–92; Prof. of Clinical Oncol., and Clinical Dir, CRC Inst. For Cancer Studies, Univ. of Birmingham, 1992–2001; Rhodes Prof. of Therapeutics, Univ. of Oxford, 2001–09; Fellow, Corpus Christi Coll., Oxford, 2001–10. Visiting Professor: Univ. of Strathclyde, 1991–; Weill Cornell Med. Coll., NY, 2009–. FMedSci 2000. Hon. FRCGP 2007. *Publications:* (ed jtly) Regional Chemotherapy, 1999; Kerr Report on future of NHS in Scotland, 2005; Oxford Textbook of Oncology, 2014; contrib. numerous articles to peer reviewed med. and scientific jls. *Recreations:* football, busking. *Address:* Harris Manchester College, Mansfield Road, Oxford OX1 3TD; Nuffield Department of Clinical and Laboratory Sciences, Level 4, Academic Block, John Radcliffe Hospital, Oxford OX3 9DU. *Clubs:* Reform; Partick Thistle Supporters' (Glasgow).

**KERR, Frith Zelda;** graphic designer; Director, Studio Frith, since 2009; *b* 3 Oct. 1973; *d* of Peter and Jenny Kerr. *Educ:* Surbiton High Sch.; Kingston Poly.; Camberwell Coll. of Art (BA Hons); Royal Coll. of Art (MA). Vis. Lectr, Camberwell Coll. of Art, 1998–2003. Partner, Co-founder and Dir, Kerr/Noble, 1997–2008. Clients include Frieze Art Fairs, Guggenheim New York, Ilse Crawford, Roksanda, Philippe Parreno, Michael Clark and Co., Hotel Il Pellicano, Skye Gyngell and Spring. *Recreation:* reading in the bath. *Address:* Studio Frith, Pall Mall Deposit, 124–128 Barlby Road, W10 6BL. *E:* info@studiofrith.com.

**KERR, Hugh;** Press Officer, Solidarity, 2006–11; *b* 9 July 1944; *m*; one *s*. Former Sen. Lectr, Univ. of North London. Former Mem. (Lab) Harlow DC. MEP (Lab 1994–98, Ind. Lab 1998–99), Essex W and Herts E. Press officer for Scottish Socialist Party, 2000–04; Brussels corresp., The Scotsman, 2004.

**KERR, James,** QPM 1979; Chief Constable, Lincolnshire Police, 1977–83; *b* 19 Nov. 1928; *s* of William and Margaret Jane Kerr; *m* 1952, Jean Coupland (*d* 2009); one *d. Educ:* Carlisle Grammar School. Cadet and Navigating Officer, Merchant Navy, 1945–52 (Union Castle Line, 1949–52). Carlisle City Police and Cumbria Constabulary, 1952–74; Asst Director of Command Courses, Police Staff Coll., Bramshill, 1974; Asst Chief Constable (Operations), North Yorkshire Police, 1975; Deputy Chief Constable, Lincs, 1976. Officer Brother, OStJ, 1980. *Recreations:* music, squash. *Address:* 41/471 Maroondah Highway, Lilydale, Vic 3140, Australia. *Club:* Royal Automobile Club of Victoria (Victoria).

**KERR, Joanne Lesley;** *see* O'Hara, J. L.

**KERR, John,** MBE 1986; Vice Lord-Lieutenant of Suffolk, 2003–14; *b* 19 Nov. 1939; *s* of William Kerr and Mary Laurie Kerr; *m* 1967, Gillian Hayward; two *s* two *d. Educ:* Framlingham Coll.; Writtle Coll. Farmer and company dir. Director: Wm Kerr (Farms) Ltd, 1971–2012; Grosvenor Farms Ltd, 1992–2005; Easton Events Ltd, 1994–; Suffolk Top Attractions Gp, 1997–2014; Grosvenor Farms Hldgs Ltd, 1999–2005; Anglian Pea Growers, 1999–2009; Cogent Breeding Ltd, 2002–05; Forum for Sustainable Farming, 2004–10; Chm., Rural East, Clydesdale Bank, 2005–12. Dir, Suffolk Agricl Assoc. Ltd, 1983–2008 (Chm., 1999–2002; Pres., 2006; Hon. Dir, Suffolk Show, 1982–84). Director: Ipswich Town FC, 1983–2008 (Chm., 1991–95; Vice-Pres., 2007); Ipswich Town plc, 2004–15. Trustee, Farmers' Club Charitable Trust, 1995–2015 (Chm., 1995–2014). Governor: Seckford Foundn, 1986–2002 (Chm., Finance, 1993–2000); Framlingham Coll., 1987–2010. Liveryman, Farmers' Co., 1985. JP 1972–93, DL 1988, High Sheriff 1997, Suffolk. DUniv Essex, 2002. *Address:* Blaxhall, Suffolk. *Clubs:* Farmers (Chm., 1994); Ipswich and Suffolk.

**KERR, John Andrew Sinclair;** Director, Kerr Consulting, since 2005; *b* 29 May 1958; *s* of Andrew Kerr and Frances Kerr; *m* 1979, Beverly Johnston; one *s* one *d. Educ:* Hutcheson's' Grammar Sch., Glasgow; Univ. of Glasgow (LLB Hons). Contracts Lawyer, British Steel, 1979–83; film industry, 1983–88; Sen. Manager, Regulatory Affairs, Stock Exchange, 1988–98; Corporate Affairs Dir, 1998–2001, Chief Exec., 2001–05, Edexcel Ltd; Dir of Develt, Edge Foundn, 2005–10. Chm., AlphaPlus Ltd. FRSA. *Recreations:* gardening, running smallholding, film. *Address:* Holly Cottage, Water Lane, Cranbrook, Kent TN18 5AP.

**KERR, Adm. Sir John (Beverley),** GCB 1993 (KCB 1989); DL; FRIN; Commander-in-Chief, Naval Home Command, 1991–94; Flag Aide-de-Camp to the Queen, 1991–94; *b* 27 Oct. 1937; *s* of late Wilfred Kerr and Vera Kerr (*née* Sproule); *m* 1964, Elizabeth Anne, *d* of late Dr and Mrs C. R. G. Howard, Burley, Hants; three *s. Educ:* Moseley Hall County Grammar Sch., Cheadle; Britannia Royal Naval Coll., Dartmouth. Served in various ships, 1958–65 (specialised in navigation, 1964); Staff, BRNC, Dartmouth, 1965–67; HMS Cleopatra, 1967–69; Staff, US Naval Acad., Annapolis, 1969–71; NDC, Latimer, 1971–72; i/c HMS Achilles, 1972–74; Naval Plans, MoD, 1974–75; Defence Policy Staff, MoD, 1975–77; RCDS, 1978; i/c HMS Birmingham, 1979–81; Dir of Naval Plans, MoD, 1981–83; i/c HMS Illustrious, 1983–84; ACNS (Op. Requirements), 1984; ACDS (Op. Requirements) (Sea Systems), 1985–86; Flag Officer First Flotilla/Flotilla One, 1986–88; MoD, 1988–91. Member, Independent Review: of Armed Forces' Manpower, Career and Remuneration Structures, 1994–95; of Higher Educn Pay and Conditions, 1998–99. Mem., Museums and Galls Commn, 1994–2000. Mem., CWGC, 1994–2001 (Vice-Chm., 1998–2001). Cdre, RNSA, 1992–95; Member: Cttee of Management, RNLI, 1993–98; Cttee, Manchester Mus., 1994–2004 (Chm., 1996–2004); Central Council, Royal Over-Seas League, 2001–04. Member: Audit Cttee, 1994–98 (Chm., 1995–98), Council, 1995–98, Lancaster Univ.; Court and Council, Manchester Univ., 1998–2004; Court, UMIST, 2000–04; Pro-Chancellor, Univ. of Manchester, 2004–12. Mem., Lake District Nat. Park Authy, 2007–11 (Dep. Chm., 2008–11). CCMI (CIMgt 1993); FRIN 2008 (Associate FRIN 2006). DL Lancs 1995. Medal of Honour, Univ. of Manchester, 2012. *Recreations:* listening to music, sailing, hill walking, history.

**KERR, Liam;** *see* Kerr, M. L. P.

**KERR, Malcolm James;** Founder and Chief Executive Officer, DP9, planning consultants, since 2004; *b* Glasgow, 20 Oct. 1959; *s* of Michael and Evelyn Kerr; *m* 1st, 1989 (marr. diss. 2010); one *s* two *d*; 2nd, 2017, Caroline Hamilton. *Educ:* Jordanhill College Sch., Glasgow; Univ. of Strathclyde (LLB 1980; Dip. Legal Studies 1981). ARICS 1986. Trainee solicitor,

Shepherd and Wedderburn, WS, 1981–83; NP, 1983; Montagu Evans, Chartered Surveyors, 1983–2004. *Recreations:* countryside, walking, cycling, Roman history, architecture, Charlton Athletic. *Address:* DP9, 100 Pall Mall, SW1Y 5NQ. *T:* (020) 7004 1729. *E:* malcolm.kerr@dp9.co.uk. *Club:* Royal Automobile.

**KERR, Rear-Adm. Mark William Graham;** DL; freelance documentary photographer, 2010–16; *b* 18 Feb. 1949; *s* of Captain M. W. B. Kerr, DSC, RN and Pat Kerr; *m* 1978, Louisa Edwards; two *s* one *d*. *Educ:* Marlborough Coll.; New Coll., Oxford (BA). FCIPD 2002–09. Joined RN, 1967; i/c HMS Alert, 1976; Principal Warfare Officer, HMS Charybdis, 1978–79; Staff Navigation Officer, Captain MinecounterMeasures, 1979–81; i/c HMS Beachampton, 1982–84; Officer i/c RN Schs Presentation Team, 1984–85; First Lieut, HMS Ariadne, 1985–88; i/c HMS Broadsword, 1988–90; MoD, 1990–94; i/c HMS Cumberland, 1994–95; Captain, RN Presentation Team, 1995–96; Dep. Flag Officer, Sea Trng, 1996–99; Commodore, BRNC, Dartmouth, 1999–2002; Naval Sec., 2002–04. Hon. Col, Powys ACF, 2006–11. Chief Exec., Powys County Council, 2004–09. Vice Chm., Soc. of Local Authy Chief Execs (Wales), 2008–09. Trustee: Nat. Botanical Garden of Wales, 2011–15 (Interim Dir, 2009–10; Chm., Steering Cttee, Regency Restoration Project, 2014–15); Brecon Univ. Scholarship Fund, 2014–. President: Brecon Br., Royal Naval Assoc., 2010–11; Powys Br., SSAFA (formerly SSAFA Forces Help), 2012–; Vice-Pres., Friends of Gwent and Powys ACF, 2010–16. Gov. and Mem. Council, RNLI, 2012–. DL Powys, 2013. *Recreations:* walking, ski-ing, history, photography. *Address:* Ty Llyn, Llangorse, Powys LD3 7UD. *W:* markkerr.co.uk.

**KERR, (Matthew) Liam (Philip);** Member (C) North East Scotland, Scottish Parliament, since 2016; *b* Chester, 23 Jan. 1975; *s* of Brian and Diana Kerr; *m* 2010, Fiona Anne Muirhead; one *d*. *Educ:* George Watson's Coll., Edinburgh; Univ. of St Andrews; Univ. of Edinburgh (MA Sociol. 1997); Univ. of Law (CPE 2000; Legal Practice Cert. 2001); Open Univ. (Postgrad. Cert. Business Admin 2014; Postgrad. Dip. Business Admin 2018). Admitted as solicitor, England and Wales, 2003, Scotland, 2005; NP 2013; Coffin Mew & Clover, 2001–04, Solicitor, 2003–04; Employment Lawyer: McGrigors & Ledingham Chalmers LLP, 2004–11; CMS Cameron McKenna LLP, 2011–15; accredited by Law Soc. of Scotland as employment law specialist, 2015–; Man. Dir, Employment Lawyer and NP, Trinity Kerr Ltd, 2015–. Lectr/Tutor, Robert Gordon Univ., 2006–12. Non-executive Director: Family Mediation Grampian, 2004–07; Aberdeen Foyer, 2012–13. Mem., Soc. of Advocates, Aberdeen. Mem., Aberdeen 100 Round Table, 2006–. *Recreations:* sailing, squash, chess, piano recitals, studying for MBA (Open University). *Address:* Scottish Parliament, Edinburgh EH99 1SP. *T:* (0131) 348 6973. *E:* liam.kerr.msp@parliament.scot. *Club:* Aberdeen Squash and Racketball.

**KERR, (Michael) David;** Chief Executive Officer, Bird & Bird, since 1996; *b* Gosforth, 28 April 1960; *s* of Douglas Kerr and Patricia Kerr; *m* 1985, Rebecca Spiro; one *s* one *d*. *Educ:* Sevenoaks Sch.; Jesus Coll., Cambridge (BA 1982); Chester Coll. of Law. Admitted Solicitor, 1985. Clifford Turner, 1983–85; Bird & Bird: Asst, 1985–87; Partner, 1987–. *Address:* Bird & Bird, 12 New Fetter Lane, EC4A 1JP. *E:* david.kerr@twobirds.com.

**KERR, Sir Ronald (James),** Kt 2011; CBE 1998; Executive Vice Chairman, Guy's and St Thomas' NHS Foundation Trust, 2015–17 (Chief Executive, 2007–15; Special Adviser to the Board, since 2017); *b* 2 Feb. 1950; *s* of James Boe Kerr and Margaret Catherine Kerr (*née* Robson); *m* 2005, Nicola Jane Martin; one step *s* one step *d*; one *d* from a previous marriage. *Educ:* Sandbach Sch., Cheshire; Cambridgeshire Coll. of Arts and Technol.; London Univ. (BSc Hons Geog. with Econs); London Business Sch. (MSc Business Studies). Sec., S Manchester CHC, 1974–77; Asst Sec., NE Thames RHA, 1977–79; Dep. House Gov., Moorfields Eye Hosp., 1979–80; Hosp. Sec., London Hosp., 1980–85; Dist Gen. Manager, N Herts HA, 1985–88; Dep. Dir of Financial Mgt, NHS Exec., 1988–90; Dist Gen. Manager, Lewisham and N Southwark HA and Chief Exec., SE London Commng Agency, 1990–93; Regl Gen. Manager, NW Thames RHA, 1993–94; Regl Dir, N Thames Regl Office, NHS Exec., 1994–98; Dir of Ops, NHS Exec., DoH, 1998–2001; Chief Executive: Nat. Care Standards Commn, 2001–04; United Bristol Healthcare NHS Trust, 2004–07. Non-exec. Dir, DoH, subseq. DHSC, 2017–. Chm., Assoc. of UK University Hosps, 2007–14. Ind. Chair, Bristol, N Somerset and S Glos Sustainability and Transformation Partnership, 2017–. Trustee, Guy's and St Thomas' Charity, 2017–. Non-exec. Dir, Genomics England Ltd, 2017–. Mem. Council, Univ. of Bristol, 2010–18. Hon. FKC 2010. *Recreations:* travel, reading, restaurants, music, Manchester City FC. *Address:* 17 Julian Road, Sneyd Park, Bristol BS9 1JZ.

**KERR, Rose;** Deputy Keeper, Asian Department (formerly Curator, then Chief Curator, Far Eastern Collections, subseq. Far Eastern Department), Victoria and Albert Museum, 1990–2003; Consultant, East Asian Art and Archaeology, since 2003; Museums Specialist Adviser, Hong Kong, since 2014; *b* 23 Feb. 1953; *d* of William Antony Kerr and Elizabeth Rendell; *m* 1990. *Educ:* SOAS, Univ. of London (BA Hons 1st Cl., Art and Archaeology of China); Languages Inst., Beijing. Fellow, Percival David Foundn of Chinese Art, 1976–78; joined Far Eastern Dept, V&A, 1978, Keeper, 1987–90. Hon. Associate, Needham Res. Inst., Cambridge, 2003. Member: Council, Oriental Ceramic Soc., 1987–2000 (Pres., 2000–03); GB-China Educnl Trust, 1995– (Chm., 2005–). Trustee: Worcester Porcelain Mus., 2008–; Sir Percival David Foundn, 2012–. Hon. Fellow, Univ. of Glasgow, 2004. Hon. Citizen, Jingdezhen, China, 2015. *Publications:* (with P. Hughes-Stanton) Kiln Sites of Ancient China, 1980; (with John Larson) Guanyin: a masterpiece revealed, 1985; Chinese Ceramics: porcelain of the Qing Dynasty 1644–1911, 1986; Later Chinese Bronzes, 1990; (ed and contrib.) Chinese Art and Design: the T. T. Tsui Gallery of Chinese Art, 1991; (with Rosemary Scott) Ceramic Evolution in the Middle Ming Period, 1994; England's Victoria and Albert Museum: Chinese Qing Dynasty Ceramics (in Chinese), 1995; (with John Ayers *et al*) Blanc de Chine: porcelain from Dehua, 2002; Song Dynasty Ceramics, 2004; (with Nigel Wood) Science & Civilisation in China, vol. V, pt 12: Ceramic Technology, 2004; Song China through 21st Century Eyes, 2009; (with Luisa Mengoni) Chinese Export Ceramics, 2011; (jtly) East Asian Ceramics: the Laura collection, 2012; (with William R. Sargent) Treasures of Chinese Export Ceramics from the Peabody Essex Museum, 2012; (with John Johnston) Chinese Ceramics: the Leonora and Walter F. Brown Collection at the San Antonio Museum of Art, 2014; (contrib.) Asian Art, Rijksmuseum, 2014; Asian Ceramics in the Hallwyl Collection, 2015; (jtly) Chinese Ivory Carving: the Sir Victor Sassoon Collection, 2016; (with Maria Antonio Pinto de Matos) Tankards and Mugs: drinking from chinese export porcelain, 2016 articles in Oriental Art, Orientations, Apollo, Craft Magazine, V&A Album. *Recreations:* travel and research. *Address:* 14 St Joseph's Mews, Candlemas Lane, Beaconsfield HP9 1GA.

**KERR, Simon Douglas O.;** *see* Ofield-Kerr.

**KERR, Stephen;** MP (C) Stirling, since 2017; *b* Dundee, 1960; *m* 1983, Yvonne; four *c*. *Educ:* Forfar Acad.; Stirling Univ. (BA Hons Business 1986). Bank junior, Royal Bank of Scotland, 1977–79; missionary, Ch of Jesus Christ of Latter-day Saints, England London Mission, 1979–81; sales rep., Energis Kitchens, 1981–83; Kimberly-Clark Professional: UK: territory sales rep., 1986–88; Product Manager, 1988; Business Develt Manager, 1988–89; Distributor Account Manager, 1989–91; Regl Sales Manager, 1991–97; Sales Director: Unico Ltd, 1997–2004; Montague Lloyd Ltd, 2000–04; Man. Dir, Stephen Kerr Consultancy, 2004–06; Kimberly-Clark Professional: District Manager, 2006–08; Eur. Distributor Account Manager, 2008–10; Regl Sales Leader, EMEA, 2010–15; EMEA Sales Ops Leader, 2016–17. Mem., Business, Energy and Industrial Strategy Cttee, H of C, 2017–. Contested (C) Stirling, 2005, 2015. *Address:* House of Commons, SW1A 0AA.

**KERR, Hon. Sir Timothy Julian,** Kt 2015; **Hon. Mr Justice Kerr;** a Judge of the High Court, Queen's Bench Division, since 2015; *b* 15 Feb. 1958; *s* of Rt Hon. Sir Michael Robert Emanuel Kerr, PC and of Julia Kerr; one *s*; *m* 1990, Nicola Mary Croucher; two *s*. *Educ:* Westminster Sch.; Magdalen Coll., Oxford (BA 1st Cl. Hons Juris.). Called to the Bar, Gray's Inn, 1983, Bencher, 2015; in practice as barrister, specialising in public law, sport, education and employment law, 1983–2015; QC 2001; a Recorder, 2008–15; a Dep. High Court Judge (Chancery Div.), 2013–15. Pt-time Chm., Employment Tribunals, 2001–06. Member: Sport Resolutions UK Arbitrators' Panel, 2000–15; FA Premier League Arbitrators' Panel, 2007–15. Chairman: Anti-Doping Tribunal, ICC, 2011–15; Anti-Doping Tribunal, Bd of Control for Cricket in India, 2013–15. *Publications:* (jtly) Sports Law, 1999, 2nd edn 2012; contrib. various articles to learned jls. *Recreations:* music, travel, reading, friends, family, walking, supporting Chelsea Football Club, languages (French, German, Spanish). *Address:* Royal Courts of Justice, Strand, WC2A 2LL.

**KERR, William Andrew S.;** *see* Scott-Kerr.

**KERR-DINEEN, Peter Brodrick;** Chairman, P and M Consulting Services Ltd, since 2009 (Director, since 2010); *b* 26 Nov. 1953; *s* of late Canon F. G. Kerr-Dineen and Hermione Kerr-Dineen; *m* 1996, Dr Susan Dodd, FRCPath; one *s* one *d*. *Educ:* Marlborough Coll.; Gonville and Caius Coll., Cambridge (BA 1975, MA 1978). Mgt trainee, Ocean Transport and Trading, 1975–76; joined Howe Robinson, 1976; Jt Chm., 1994–2013, Chm., 2013–17, Howe Robinson and Co. Ltd; Jt Chm., 1996–2013, Chm., 2013–17, Howe Robinson Investments, later Howe Robinson Gp; Chm., Howe Robinson Partners Pte Ltd, 2015–16; Dir, Great Eastern Shipping Co. London Ltd, 1989–2016; Chm., Maritime Strategies Internat. Ltd, 2008–17; Chm., Shyvers Savoy Shipping Ltd, 2012–17. Chm., Baltic Exchange, 2003–05 (Mem., 1976–2016; Hon. Mem., 1998–2005, 2013). Mem., Singapore Adv. Cttee for Internat. Maritime Centre, 2016–17. Mem., Develt Campaign Bd, Gonville and Caius Coll., Cambridge, 2006–. FRAI 1975. Liveryman, Shipwrights' Co., 2007–. *Recreations:* riding, fishing, drama, anthropology, painting. *Address:* Uppington, Withypool, Somerset TA24 7RP. *E:* kerrdineen@hotmail.com. *Clubs:* Hurlingham, Oxford and Cambridge.

**KERR-DINEEN, Sarah Jane;** Head, Oundle School, since 2015; *b* Gosport, Hants, 7 Aug. 1963; *d* of John and Elizabeth Lyne; *m* 1987, Anthony Kerr-Dineen; two *s* two *d*. *Educ:* Steyning Grammar Sch.; Trinity Coll., Cambridge (BA 1985; MA); Christ Church, Oxford. Tutor, Open Univ., 1990–96; Teacher of English, Kelly Coll., Tavistock, 1991–92; Teacher of English, Housemistress of Corfe House, and Dir of Studies, St Edward's Sch., Oxford, 1994–97 and 1999–2009; Teacher of English and Dep. Hd of English, Oxford High Sch., 1997–99; Warden, Forest Sch., London, 2009–15. *Recreations:* family, reading, Cornwall. *Address:* The Great Hall, Oundle School, Oundle, Peterborough PE8 4GH. *T:* (01832) 277142. *E:* head@oundleschool.org.uk.

**KERR-WILSON, Most Rev. Gregory Keith;** *see* Calgary, Archbishop of.

**KERRIDGE, Thomas;** Chef Patron: The Hand and Flowers, Marlow, since 2005; The Coach, since 2014; Kerridge's Bar & Grill, since 2018; *b* Salisbury, Wilts, 27 July 1973; *s* of late Michael John Kerridge and Jackie Kerridge; *m* 2000, Beth Cullen. *Educ:* Saintbridge Comprehensive Sch., Glos. Commis chef: Calcot Manor, Tetbury, 1991–92; Painswick Hotel, Gloucester, 1992–94; chef de partie: Country Elephant, Gloucester, 1994–96; Capital Hotel, London, 1996; sous chef: Stephen Bull, St Martins, London, 1996–99; Rhodes in the Square, London, 1999; Odettes Restaurant, London, 1999–2001; head chef: Bellamy's Dining Room, London, 2001; Gt Fosters Hotel, Surrey, 2001; sen. sous chef, Monsieur Max Restaurant, Hampton, 2001–03; hd chef, Adlards, Norwich, 2003–05. Television presenter: Tom Kerridge's Proper Pub Food (series), 2013; Tom Kerridge Cooks Christmas, 2013; Spring Kitchen with Tom Kerridge, 2014; Tom Kerridge's Best Ever Dishes (series), 2014; Bake Off: crème de la crème, 2016; Lose Weight for Good, 2018; Top of the Shop with Tom Kerridge, 2018; Tom Kerridge's Fresh Start, 2019; Remarkable Places to Eat, 2019. MIH (MHCIMA 2007). Michelin Star, 2006, 2nd Michelin Star, 2012; 3 AA Rosettes, 2007, 2008. *Publications:* Tom Kerridge's Proper Pub Food, 2013; Tom Kerridge's Best Ever Dishes, 2014; Tom's Table: my favourite everyday recipes, 2015; Tom Kerridge's Dopamine Diet, 2017; Lose Weight for Good, 2017; Tom Kerridge's Fresh Start, 2018. *Address:* The Hand and Flowers, 126 West Street, Marlow, Bucks SL7 2BP. *T:* (01628) 482277. *E:* contact@thehandandflowers.co.uk.

**KERRIGAN, Greer Sandra,** CB 2006; former Director of Legal Services, Department for Work and Pensions; *b* Port of Spain, Trinidad, 7 Aug. 1948; *d* of Wilfred M. Robinson and Rosina Robinson (*née* Ali); *m* 1974, Donal Brian Mathew Kerrigan; one *s* one *d*. *Educ:* Bishop Anstey High Sch., Trinidad; Coll. of Law, Inns of Court. Called to the Bar, Middle Temple, 1971. Legal Advr, Public Utilities Commn, Trinidad, 1972–74; Department of Health and Social Security, subseq. Department of Social Security, then Department for Work and Pensions: Legal Assistant, 1974–77; Sen. Legal Assistant, 1977–85; Asst Solicitor, 1985–91; Principal Asst Solicitor, subseq. Legal Dir (Health), then Legal Director (Work and Pensions), later Dir of Legal Services (Work and Pensions), 1991; Principal Asst Solicitor, then Legal Dir (Health), DoH, 1991–2004. *Recreations:* reading, music, bridge.

**KERRIGAN, Herbert Aird;** QC (Scot.) 1992; *b* 2 Aug. 1945; *s* of Herbert Kerrigan and Mary Agnes Wallace Hamilton or Kerrigan; one adopted *s*. *Educ:* Whitehill, Glasgow; Univ. of Aberdeen (LLB Hons 1968); Hague Acad. of Internat. Law; Keele Univ. (MA 1970); Oxford Univ. (Postgrad. Dip. in Applied Theol. 2002). Admitted Faculty of Advocates, 1970; Lectr in Criminal Law and Criminology, 1969–73, in Scots Law, 1973–74, Edinburgh Univ.; called to the Bar, Middle Temple, 1990; in practice, 1991–. Vis. Prof., Univ. of Southern Calif., 1979–. Mem., Longford Commn, 1972. Church of Scotland: Elder, 1967– (now at Greyfriars Tolbooth and Highland Kirk, Edinburgh); Reader, 1969; Mem., Assembly Council, 1981–85; Sen. Chaplain to Moderator, Gen. Assembly of Church of Scotland, 1999–2000; Convener, Cttee on Chaplains to HM's Forces, 2001– (Vice Convener, 1998–2001). Pres., Edinburgh Royal Infirmary Samaritan Soc., 1992– (Vice-Pres., 1989–92). *Publications:* An Introduction to Criminal Procedure in Scotland, 1970; (contrib.) Ministers for the 1980s, 1979; (contributing ed.) The Law of Contempt, 1982; (contrib.) Sport and the Law, 2nd edn 1995. *Recreation:* travel. *Address:* c/o Advocates' Library, Parliament House, Edinburgh EH1 1RF. *T:* (0131) 226 5071; Foundry Chambers, Quality House, 5–9 Quality Court, Chancery Lane, WC2A 1HP. *T:* (020) 7400 1800, *Fax:* (020) 7400 1405; (home) 20 Edinburgh Road, Dalkeith, Midlothian EH22 1JY. *T:* (0131) 660 3007.

**KERRIGAN, Prof. John Francis,** FBA 2013; Professor of English 2000, University of Cambridge, since 2001; Fellow, St John's College, Cambridge, since 1982; *b* 16 June 1956; *s* of late Stephen Francis Kerrigan and of Patricia Kerrigan (*née* Baker); one *d*. *Educ:* St Edward's Coll., Liverpool (Christian Brothers); Keble Coll., Oxford (BA). Domus Sen. Schol., 1977–79, Jun. Res. Fellow, 1979–82, Merton Coll., Oxford; University of

Cambridge: Asst Lectr in English, 1982–86; Lectr in English, 1986–98; Reader in English Lit., 1998–2001; Dir of Studies in English, St John's Coll., 1987–97; Chm., English Faculty Bd, 2003–06. Visiting Professor: Meiji Univ., Tokyo, 1986; UCLA, 2009. Visiting Fellow: Jadavpur Univ., Calcutta, 2008; Univ. of Delhi, 2008; Univ. of Auckland, 2011; Princeton, 2017. Res. Reader, British Acad., 1998–2000; Leverhulme Res. Fellow, 2012–13. Lectures: Chatterton, British Acad., 1988; J. A. W. Bennett Meml, Perugia, 1998; Acad. for Irish Cultural Heritages, 2003; F. W. Bateson, Oxford, 2004; Nicholson and Poetics, Chicago, 2007; Shakespeare, British Acad., 2009; Andrew Lang, St Andrews, 2009; Alice Griffin, Auckland, 2011; Wells Shakespeare, Oxford, 2016. Foundn Fellow, English Assoc., 1999; Fellow, Wordsworth Trust, 2001. Trustee, Dove Cottage, Wordsworth Trust, 1984–2001. Charles Oldham Shakespeare Prize, 1976, Matthew Arnold Meml Prize, 1981, Oxford Univ.; Truman Capote Award for Literary Criticism, 1998. *Publications*: (ed) Love's Labour's Lost, 1982; (ed) Shakespeare's Sonnets and A Lover's Complaint, 1986, 2nd edn 1995; (ed with J. Wordsworth) Wordsworth and the Worth of Words, by Hugh Sykes Davies, 1987; Motives of Woe: Shakespeare and Female Complaint, 1991; (ed jtly) English Comedy, 1994; Revenge Tragedy: Aeschylus to Armageddon, 1996; (ed with P. Robinson) The Thing about Roy Fisher: critical studies, 2000; On Shakespeare and Early Modern Literature: essays, 2001; Archipelagic English: literature, history and politics 1603–1707, 2008; Shakespeare's Binding Language, 2016 (Roland H. Bainton Book Prize in Literature, Sixteenth Century Soc. and Conf., 2016); Shakespeare's Originality, 2018; contrib. London Rev. of Books, TLS and poetry mags. *Recreation*: music. *Address*: St John's College, Cambridge CB2 1TP. *T*: (01223) 338620. *E*: jk10023@cam.ac.uk.

**KERRY, Earl of; Simon Henry George Petty-Fitzmaurice;** *b* 24 Nov. 1970; *s* and *heir* of Marquess of Lansdowne, *qv*; *m* 2016, Nadine A. L. Mentior. *Educ*: Eton; Jesus Coll., Cambridge. *Publications*: Lansdowne: the last great Whig, 2017.

**KERRY, Knight of;** *see* FitzGerald, Sir A. J. A. D.

**KERRY, John Forbes,** JD; Secretary of State, United States of America, 2013–17; *b* 11 Dec. 1943; *s* of Richard John Kerry and Rosemary Kerry (*née* Forbes); *m* 1st, 1970, Julia S. Thorne (marr. diss. 1985); two *d*; 2nd, 1995, (Maria) Teresa (Thierstein) Heinz (*née* Simoes-Ferreira). *Educ*: Yale Univ. (BA 1966); Boston Coll. (MA; JD 1976). Served US Navy, 1966–70; Nat. Co-ordinator, Vietnam Veterans Against the War, 1969–71. Called to the Bar, Mass, 1976; Asst Dist Attorney, Middx Co., Mass, 1976–79; Partner, Kerry & Sragow, Boston, 1979–82; Lt Gov., Mass, 1982–84; US Senator from Mass, 1985–2013. Presidential cand. (Democrat), US elections, 2004. *Publications*: The New Soldier, 1971; The New War: the web of crime that threatens America's security, 1997; (memoir) Every Day is Extra, 2018.

**KERSE, Dr Christopher Stephen,** CB 2003; Second Counsel to Chairman of Committees and Legal Adviser to Select Committee on the European Union, House of Lords, 1995–2007; *b* 12 Dec. 1946; *s* of late William Harold Kerse and Maude Kerse; *m* 1st, 1971, Gillian Hanks (*d* 2007); one *s* one *d*; 2nd, 2008, Retha Coetzee. *Educ*: King George V Sch., Southport; Univ. of Hull (LLB; PhD 1995). Admitted Solicitor, 1972. Lecturer in Law: Univ. of Bristol, 1968–72; Univ. of Manchester, 1972–76; Asst Prof., Faculty of Law, Univ. of British Columbia, 1974–75; Sen. Legal Asst, OFT, 1976–81; Department of Trade and Industry: Sen. Legal Asst, 1981–82; Asst Solicitor, 1982–88; Head, Consumer Affairs Div., 1991–93; Under-Sec. (Legal), 1988–95; Prof. of Law, Univ. of Surrey, 2007–09. Vis. Prof., KCL, 1992–2010. *Publications*: The Law Relating to Noise, 1975; EC Antitrust Procedure, 1981, 5th edn 2005 (with N. Khan); (with J. C. Cook) EC Merger Control, 1991, 5th edn 2009; articles in various legal jls. *Recreations*: the double bass, orchestration, wood. *E*: kerse@btinternet.com.

**KERSFELT, Anita Ingegerd;** *see* Gradin, A. I.

**KERSHAW,** family name of **Baron Kershaw**.

**KERSHAW, 4th Baron** *cr* 1947; **Edward John Kershaw;** Chartered Accountant; business consultant; Partner, Bartlett Kershaw Trott, Chartered Accountants, 1996–2001; *b* 12 May 1936; *s* of 3rd Baron and Katharine Dorothea Kershaw (*née* Staines); *S* father, 1962; *m* 1963, Rosalind Lilian Rutherford; one *s* two *d*. *Educ*: Selhurst Grammar Sch., Surrey. Entered RAF Nov. 1955, demobilised Nov. 1957. Admitted to Inst. of Chartered Accountants in England and Wales, Oct. 1964. Mem., Acad. of Experts, 1995. Lay Governor, The King's Sch., Gloucester, 1986–95. JP Gloucester, 1982–95. *Heir*: *s* Hon. John Charles Edward Kershaw, *b* 23 Dec. 1971. *Address*: 1 Phillips Court, Baldock Street, Royston, Herts SG8 9DL.

**KERSHAW, Andrew;** broadcaster and journalist, since 1984; *b* 9 Nov. 1959; *s* of John (Jack) Kershaw and Eileen Kershaw (*née* Acton); one *s* one *d* by Juliette Banner. *Educ*: Hulme Grammar Sch., Oldham; Leeds Univ. Joined BBC, 1984: presenter: Whistle Test, 1984–87 (Live Aid, 1985); Andy Kershaw Prog., Radio 1, 1985–2000, Radio 3, 2001–07; Andy Kershaw's World of Music, World Service, 1987–2000; Music Planet (series), Radio 3, 2011; occasional foreign news reports for Radio 4, 1990 (incl. reports from Haiti, Angola, Rwanda, N Korea, Iraq); Travelog, Channel 4, 1991–97 (incl. first ever film made inside N Korea, 1995); freelance journalist, 1988–; Radio Critic, Independent, 1999; roving reporter, The One Show, BBC1, 2012–. One-man show for stage, The Adventures of Andy Kershaw, 2012–. Hon. MusD: UEA, 2003; Leeds, 2005. Sony Radio Awards, 1987, 1989 (two), 1996, 2002 (three). *Publications*: No Off Switch (autobiog.), 2011. *Recreations*: music, motorcycle racing, travels to extreme countries, boxing, fishing.

**KERSHAW, Dame Betty;** *see* Kershaw, Dame J. E. M.

**KERSHAW, David Andrew;** Chief Executive, M&C Saatchi plc, since 2004 (Founding Partner, 1995–2004); *b* 26 Feb. 1954; *s* of Lawrence Kershaw and Rona Kershaw (now Lucas); *m* 1993, Clare Whitley; one *s* one *d*. *Educ*: Bedales Sch.; Univ. of Durham (BA Hons Pols 1977); London Business Sch. (MBA 1982). Account Exec., Wasey Campbell-Ewald, 1977–80; Saatchi & Saatchi UK: Account Dir, 1982–90; Man. Dir, 1990–94; Chief Exec., 1994–95. Trustee, Creative and Cultural Skills, 2005–09; Chm., Cultural Leadership Prog., 2006–11; Mem., Strategic Adv. Cttee, Clore Leadership Prog., 2011–17 (Trustee, 2017–). Gov., Southbank Centre, 2009–18 (Dep. Chair, 2018–); Trustee, Grange Park Opera, 2017–. *Recreations*: Arsenal, golf, opera, clarinet. *Address*: M&C Saatchi plc, 36 Golden Square, W1F 9EE. *T*: (020) 7543 4300. *E*: davidk@mcsaatchi.com. *Clubs*: Groucho, Ivy; Coombe Hill Golf.

**KERSHAW, Dean Earl; His Honour Judge Kershaw;** a Circuit Judge, since 2018; *b* 19 Sept. 1971; *s* of Gabriel and Ann Kershaw. *Educ*: Archbishop Grimshaw Sch.; LLB Hons; Inns of Court Sch. of Law (Sir Thomas More Schol.). Called to the Bar, Lincoln's Inn, 1995; Crown Prosecutor, 1995–97; Sen. Lectr in Criminal Evidence, Nottingham Law Sch., 1997–2000; in practice as barrister, 2000–18; a Fee-paid Judge of First Tier Tribunal, Immigration and Asylum Chamber (formerly Fee-paid Immigration Judge), 2006–18; a Recorder, 2009–18. *Recreations*: theatre, cinema. *Address*: Wolverhampton Combined Court, Pipers Row, Wolverhampton WV1 3LQ.

**KERSHAW, Helen Elizabeth, (Mrs W. J. S. Kershaw);** *see* Paling, Her Honour H. E.

**KERSHAW, Sir Ian,** Kt 2002; DPhil; FBA 1991; Professor of Modern History, University of Sheffield, 1989–2008; *b* Oldham, 29 April 1943; *s* of late Joseph Kershaw and of Alice (*née* Robinson); *m* 1966, Janet Elizabeth Murray Gammie (*see* Dame J. E. M. Kershaw); two *s*. *Educ*: St Bede's Coll., Manchester; Univ. of Liverpool (BA 1965); Merton Coll., Oxford (DPhil 1969; Hon. Fellow, 2005). FR.HistS, 1972–74, 1991. University of Manchester: Asst Lectr in Medieval Hist., 1968–70, Lectr, 1970–74; Lectr in Modern Hist., 1974–79, Sen. Lectr, 1979–87, Reader elect, 1987; Prof. of Modern History, Univ. of Nottingham, 1987–89. Vis. Prof. of Contemporary Hist., Ruhr-Univ., Bochum, 1983–84. Fellow: Alexander von Humboldt-Stiftung, 1976; Wissenschaftskolleg zu Berlin, 1989–90. Bundesverdienstkreuz (Germany), 1994. Hon. DLitt: Manchester, 2004; QUB, 2007; Sheffield, 2009; Oxford, 2010; Leeds, 2012; DUniv: Stirling, 2006; Huddersfield, 2013. Meyer-Struckmann Prize, Univ. of Düsseldorf, 2013; Médaille Charlemagne pour les Médias Européens, 2018. *Publications*: (ed) Rentals and Ministers' Accounts of Bolton Priory 1473–1539, 1969; Bolton Priory: the economy of a northern monastery, 1973; Der Hitler-Mythos: Volksmeinung und Propaganda im Dritten Reich, 1980, Eng. trans. 1987; Popular Opinion and Political Dissent in the Third Reich: Bavaria 1933–1945, 1983; The Nazi Dictatorship: problems and perspectives of interpretation, 1985, 4th edn 2000; (ed) Weimar: why did German democracy fail?, 1990; Hitler: a profile in power, 1991, 2nd edn 2000; (ed with M. Lewin) Stalinism and Nazism, 1997; Hitler: vol. 1, 1889–1936: hubris, 1998, vol. 2, 1936–1945: nemesis, 2000 (Bruno Kreisky Prize (Austria), 2000; Wolfson Prize for History, 2000; British Acad. Prize, 2001); (ed with David M. Smith) The Bolton Priory Compotus 1286–1325, 2001; Making Friends with Hitler: Lord Londonderry and Britain's road to war, 2004 (Elizabeth Longford Historical Biog. Prize, 2005); Fateful Choices: ten decisions that changed the world 1940–1941, 2007; Hitler, the Germans and the Final Solution, 2008; Luck of the Devil: the story of Operation Valkyrie, 2009; The End: Hitler's Germany, 1944–45, 2011 (Leipzig Book Prize for European Understanding, 2012); To Hell and Back: Europe 1914–49, 2015; Roller-Coaster: Europe 1950–2017, 2018; articles in learned jls. *Recreations*: Rugby League, football, cricket, music, real ale, outings in the Yorkshire dales. *Address*: 13 Fairfax Avenue, Didsbury, Manchester M20 6AJ.

**KERSHAW, Dame Janet Elizabeth Murray, (Dame Betty),** DBE 1998; FRCN; Education Adviser, Royal College of Nursing, 2008–11; Professor and Dean, School of Nursing and Midwifery, University of Sheffield, 1999–2006, now Dean Emeritus; *b* 11 Dec. 1943; *d* of Ian U. Gammie and Janet Gammie; *m* 1966, Ian Kershaw (*see* Sir Ian Kershaw); two *s*. *Educ*: Crossley and Porter Grammar Sch., Halifax; United Manchester Hosps (SRN; OND); Manchester Univ. (MSc Nursing; RNT). Dir of Educn, Royal Marsden Hosp., 1984–87; Principal, Stockport, Tameside and Glossop Coll. of Nursing, 1987–94; Dir of Nurse Educn, Coll. of Midwifery and Nursing, Manchester, 1994–97; Dir, Centre for Professional Policy Develt, Sch. of Nursing, Midwifery and Health Visiting, Univ. of Manchester, 1997–98. Visiting Professor: Manchester Metropolitan Univ., 2006–12; Birmingham City Univ., 2007–14. Pres., RCN, 1994–98 (FRCN 2001). Trustee, GNC Trust, 2007–11. Chief Officer, Nursing and Social Care, St John Ambulance, 1998–2005. Hon. LLD Manchester, 1995. OStJ 1998. *Publications*: (with J. Salvage) Models For Nursing, 1986; (with J. Salvage) Models for Nursing 2, 1990; (with Bob Price) The Riehl Model of Care, 1993; (with J. Marr) Caring for Older People, 1998. *Recreations*: theatre, music, travel. *Address*: Royal College of Nursing, Cavendish Square, W1G 0RN.

**KERSHAW, Jann Peta Olwen;** *see* Parry, J. P. O.

**KERSHAW, (Philip) Michael;** QC 1980; DL; *b* 23 April 1941; *m* 1980, Anne (*née* Williams); one *s*. *Educ*: Ampleforth Coll.; St John's Coll., Oxford (MA). FCIArb 1991. Called to the Bar, Gray's Inn, 1963; in practice, 1963–90; a Recorder, 1980–90; Circuit Commercial Judge, 1990–91, Circuit Mercantile Judge, 1991–2006. Dir, Bar Mutual Insce Co. Ltd, 1988–90. Consulting Ed. and contrib., Atkin's Court Forms, 1997–2013. DL Lancs, 2007. *Publications*: Fraud and Misrepresentation, Injunctions, Bills of Sale, Bonds and Banking and Bills of Exchange, in Atkin's Court Forms; (contrib.) Interests in Goods, 1993. *Recreation*: choral singing.

**KERSHAW, Stephen Edward,** CBE 2016; Senior Director for Strategy, Transformation and Partnerships (formerly Senior Director for Strategy and Transformation), Immigration Enforcement, Home Office, since 2014; *b* 20 Sept. 1959; *s* of Barry Kershaw, railway signal engr, and Audrey Kathleen (*née* Breadmore). *Educ*: St Peter's C of E Primary Sch., Rickmansworth; William Penn Comprehensive Sch., Rickmansworth, Herts; Wadham Coll., Oxford (Open Schol.; BA 1st Cl. Hons Mod. Hist. 1981; MA; res., 1981–84). Lectr in Mod. Hist., Wadham Coll., Oxford, 1984–85; Cabinet Office, 1985–87 (Private Sec. to Second Perm. Sec., 1986–87); DES, 1987–89; Next Steps Team, Cabinet Office, 1989–92; DFE, later DfEE, 1992–99; on secondment as Hd, Strategic Planning, Manchester LEA, 1999–2000; Actg Dir, Pupil Support and Inclusion Gp, DfEE, 2000–01; Dir, Teachers' Gp, subseq. Sch. Workforce Unit, DfEE, later DfES, 2001–03; Finance Dir, DfES, 2003–06; Dir, Prime Minister's Delivery Unit, Cabinet Office, 2006–07; Home Office: Dir, Police Reform and Resources, 2007–10; Dir, Policing, 2010–12; Dir, Border Strategy, 2012–14. *Publications*: (contrib.) The Tudor Nobility, ed G. W. Bernard, 1992; (contrib.) Debrett's Peerage and Baronetage, ed C. Kidd, 2015; reviews in various jls. *Recreations*: family and peerage history, indulging my niece and nephews.

**KERSLAKE,** family name of **Baron Kerslake**.

**KERSLAKE, Baron** *cr* 2015 (Life Peer), of Endcliffe in the City of Sheffield; **Robert Walter Kerslake,** Kt 2005; Chair, King's College Hospital NHS Foundation, 2015–17; *b* 28 Feb. 1955; *m* Anne; one *s* one *d*. *Educ*: Univ. of Warwick (BSc Hons Maths). CPFA. Greater London Council, 1979–85: CIPFA trainee, 1979–82; Transport Finance, 1982–85; with ILEA, 1985–89; Dir of Finance, 1989–90, Chief Executive: London Borough of Hounslow, 1990–97; Sheffield CC, 1997–2008; Chief Exec., Homes and Communities Agency, 2008–10; Perm. Sec., DCLG, 2010–15; Hd of the Civil Service, 2012–14. Chairman: Peabody, 2015–; Centre for Public Scrutiny, 2015–. Chm., UK2070 Commn, 2018–Jan. 2020. Pres., LGA, 2015–. *Recreations*: music, walking.

**KERSLAKE, Deborah Ann;** Chief Executive, Cruse Bereavement Care, 2008–18; *b* Liverpool, 3 March 1958; *d* of Norman Thompson and Marjorie Thompson; *m* 1986, Michael Kerslake. *Educ*: Merchant Taylors' Sch. for Girls, Liverpool; Univ. of York (BA Hons Hist.); University Coll. Cardiff, Univ. of Wales (CQSW; DipSW); Univ. of Birmingham (Postgrad. Dip. Public Sector Mgt). Birmingham City Council: Social Worker, 1981–83; Sen. Social Worker Childcare, 1983–87; Sen. Social Worker Physical Disability, 1986–87; Actg Team Manager, 1988; Actg Principal Social Worker, 1988–89; Co-ordinator, 1989–93, Manager, 1993–99, Share Scheme; Cruse Bereavement Care: Proj. Manager, Quality in Bereavement Care, 1999–2002; Hd, Service Planning and Develt, 2002–08. Mem. Council, Cremation Soc. of Great Britain, 2019–. *Publications*: articles in Bereavement Care and Grief Matters: the Aust. Jl of Grief and Bereavement. *Recreations*: theatre, opera, tennis, reading, travel.

**KERSLAKE, Rosaleen Clare,** OBE 2016; Chief Executive, National Lottery Heritage Fund (formerly Heritage Lottery Fund) and National Heritage Memorial Fund, since 2016; *b* Bath, 8 March 1957; *d* of Robert James Kerslake and Maura Kerslake (*née* Moloney); partner, Stuart Sim; one *s* two *d*. *Educ*: Blue Sch., Wells, Som; Univ. of Keele (BA Law and Psychol.); Open Univ. Business Sch. (MBA). Admitted as solicitor, 1982; Chamberlins Solicitors, 1980–86, Partner, 1983–86; Legal Advr, Conoco Ltd, 1986–88; Dir, Gulf Oil, 1988–96; Internat. Hd, Gp Services, Booker plc, 1996–2000; Property Dir, Network Rail, 2000–03; Chief Executive: Regenco Urban Regeneration Co., 2003–06; Prince's Regeneration Trust, 2006–16. Chair, Regeneration Leaders' Network, 2008–16. Nonexec. Dir, Quintain plc, 2013–15; Non-exec. Dir, U+I Gp plc, 2017–. Trustee, Heritage Alliance, 2014–16. Mem., Community and Voluntary (formerly Community, Voluntary and Local) Services Honours Cttee, 2017–. DUniv: Staffordshire, 2016; Keele, 2017. Property Person of the Year, Univ. Coll. of Estate Management, 2016. *Recreations*: gardening, walking, fostering children and bringing up my own. *Address*: National Lottery Heritage Fund, International House, St Katherine Docks, E1W 1YL. *T*: (020) 7591 6196.

**KERSWELL, Prof. Richard Rodney,** PhD; FRS 2012; G. I. Taylor Professor of Fluid Mechanics, University of Cambridge, since 2017. *Educ*: Emmanuel Coll., Cambridge (BA Maths 1987); Univ. of Calif (MA Applied Maths 1988); Massachusetts Inst. of Technol. (PhD 1992). Prof. of Applied Maths, Univ. of Bristol, until 2017. *Publications*: articles in jls. *Address*: Department of Applied Mathematics and Theoretical Physics, Centre for Mathematical Sciences, Wilberforce Road, Cambridge CB3 0WA.

**KERVIN, Alison Cristine,** OBE 2017; author; Sports Editor, Mail on Sunday, since 2013; *b* Birmingham, 1969; *d* of Peter and Christine Kervin; one *s*. *Educ*: Kings Norton Girls' Sch.; Univ. of Sussex (BSc Hons). Chief Sports Writer, Slough Observer, 1989; PR Manager and Rugby Develt Officer, England Rugby Team, 1991–95; Ed., Rugby World mag., 1995–98; publisher of sports titles, IPC Mags, 1998–99; Rugby Ed., 1999–2002, Chief Sports Feature Writer, 2002–05, The Times; Chief Sports Interviewer, Daily Telegraph, 2005–13. *Publications: non-fiction*: Sports Writing: a guide to the profession, 1997; A Guide to the 1999 Rugby World Cup, 1999; (ed) Denise Lewis: personal best, 2001; (with J. Leonard) Jason Leonard: autobiography, 2001, 2nd edn 2004; Clive Woodward: the biography, 2005; Thirty Bullies: a history of the Rugby World Cup, 2007; Phil Vickery: raging bull, 2010; *fiction*: Wags Diary, 2007; A Wag Abroad, 2008; Celebrity Bride, 2009; Wags at the World Cup, 2010; A Wags Guide to Euro 2012, 2012; Mother & Son, 2014. *Recreations*: theatre, ballet, literature, sports. *E*: ak@alisonkervin.co.uk.

**KESCHNER, Catherine Mary;** see Muirden, C. M.

**KESSLER, Dinah Gwen Lison;** see Rose, D. G. L.

**KESSLER, Edward David,** MBE 2011; PhD; Founder Director, Woolf Institute (formerly Woolf Institute of Abrahamic Faiths), Cambridge, since 1998; Fellow, St Edmund's College, Cambridge, since 2002; *b* 3 May 1963; *s* of William and Joanna Kessler; *m* 1989, Patricia Josephine Oakley; one *s* two *d*. *Educ*: Univ. of Leeds (BA Jt Hons 1985); Harvard Univ. (MTS 1987); Univ. of Stirling (MBA 1989); Univ. of Cambridge (PhD 1999). W. H. Smith, 1987–89; Kesslers Internat. Ltd, 1989–95. Sternberg Interfaith Award, 2006. Co-Ed., Studies in Jewish-Christian Relns, 2005–07. *Publications*: An English Jew: the life and writings of Claude Montefiore, 1989, 2nd edn 2002; (ed with J. Pawlikowski) Jews and Christians in Conversation: crossing cultures and generations, 2002; Bound by the Bible: Jews, Christians and the Sacrifice of Isaac, 2004; The Founders of Liberal Judaism: Israel Abrahams, Claude Montefiore, Israel Mattuck and Lily Montagu, 2004; (ed with D. Goldberg) Aspects of Liberal Judaism: essays in honour of Rabbi John D. Rayner, 2004; (ed with M. Wright) Themes in Jewish-Christian Relations, 2005; (ed with N. Wenborn) A Dictionary of Jewish-Christian Relations, 2005; (ed with J. Aitken) Challenges in Jewish-Christian Relations, 2006; What do Jews Believe?, 2006; An Introduction to Jewish-Christian Relations, 2010; Jews, Christians and Muslims, 2013; Jesus, 2016. *Recreations*: family, supporting Arsenal, Mediterranean cycling. *Address*: Madingley Road, Cambridge CB3 0AA. *T*: (01223) 761984. *Club*: Athenæum.
See also J. R. Kessler.

**KESSLER, James Richard;** QC 2003; *b* 1959; *s* of William and Joanna Kessler; *m* 1983, Jane Marie Pinto; two *s* one *d*. *Educ*: Brasenose Coll., Oxford (MA). FTII 1990. Called to the Bar: Gray's Inn, 1984; Northern Ireland, 2003; in practice at Revenue Bar; Bencher, Lincoln's Inn, 2013; Head, Old Square Tax Chambers, 2015–. Founder, Trusts Discussion Forum, 1999. Trustee, Purbeck Film Charitable Trust, 2009–; Chm., Phoenix Cinema Trust, 2016–19. *Publications*: Tax Planning for the Foreign Domiciliary, 1987; Tax Planning and Fundraising for Charities, 1989, 12th edn as Taxation of Charities and Non-Profit Organisations, 2019; Drafting Trusts and Will Trusts, 1992, 14th edn 2019; Taxation of Foreign Domiciliaries, 2001, 18th edn as Taxation of Non-Residents and Foreign Domiciliaries, 2019; Drafting Trusts and Will Trusts in Canada, 2003, 4th edn 2016; Drafting Trusts and Will Trusts in Northern Ireland, 2004, 3rd edn 2012; Drafting Cayman Island Trusts, 2007; Drafting Trusts and Will Trusts in the Channel Islands, 2007, 3rd edn 2019; Drafting Trusts and Will Trusts in Singapore, 2007, 2nd edn 2015; Drafting Trusts and Will Trusts in Australia, 2008; Drafting Trusts and Will Trusts in New Zealand, 2010; Drafting Trusts and Will Trusts in Scotland, 2013, 2nd edn 2017; Drafting BVI Trusts, 2014; Drafting Trusts and Will Trusts in Hong Kong, 2016. *Recreations*: cinema, jogging. *Address*: Old Square Tax Chambers, 15 Old Square, Lincoln's Inn, WC2A 3UE. *T*: (020) 7242 2744. *E*: kessler@kessler.co.uk.
See also E. D. Kessler.

**KESTELMAN, Sara;** actor and writer; *d* of late Morris Kestelman, RA and Dorothy Mary (*née* Creagh). *Educ*: Hampstead Parochial Sch.; Camden Sch. for Girls; Cecchetti ballet trng; Central Sch. of Speech and Drama. Early rôles with Open Air Th., Regent's Park, Liverpool Playhouse, Manchester Liby Th., Castle Th., Farnham; Royal Shakespeare Co. includes: A Midsummer Night's Dream (dir. Peter Brook), 1970–72, Broadway, 1971; Macbeth, 1982–83; King Lear, 1983; Lear (by Edward Bond), 1983; The Custom of the Country, 1983; Moscow Gold, 1990–91; Misha's Party, 1994; National Theatre, subseq. Royal National Theatre, includes: As You Like It, 1979; Love for Love; 3D Opera; American Clock, 1986; Bedroom Farce; Square Rounds, 1992; Copenhagen, 1998, transf. Duchess, 1999; Hamlet, 2000; other productions: The Hollow Crown, RSC, Pleasure and Repentance US and Japan tour, 1974–75; Childe Byron, Young Vic, 1983; The Way of the World, Chichester Festival, 1984; Waste, Lyric, 1985; Three Sisters, Greenwich, transf. Albery, 1987; The Price, Watford Playhouse, 1987; Bussy D'Ambois, Old Vic, 1987; Lettice and Lovage, Globe, 1989; Another Time, Wyndham's, 1990; The Cabinet Minister, Albery, 1991; The Cherry Orchard, Gate, Dublin, 1992; Cabaret, Donmar, 1993–94 (Olivier and Clarence Derwent Awards, for best supporting performance in a musical); Fiddler on the Roof, London Palladium, 1994; Three Tall Women, Wyndham's, 1995; A Two Hander (songwriter, jt writer, performer), Hampstead, 1996; Nine, Donmar, 1996–97; one woman cabaret show, All About Me! (tour), 1998–2003; The Shape of Metal, Abbey Th., Dublin, 2003; Flower Drum Song (musical), Lilian Baylis Th., 2006; My Child, Royal Court, 2007; Girl with a Pearl Earring, Haymarket, 2008; Coco, Lilian Baylis, 2011; Making Noise Quietly, Donmar, 2012; Torch Song Trilogy, Menier Chocolate Factory, 2012; 4,000 Miles, Theatre Royal, Bath and Print Room, 2013; Ignis, Print Room, 2014; The Summer Book, Unicorn, 2014; The Girls (musical), tour, 2015–16; The Intelligent Homosexual's Guide to Capitalism and Socialism with a Key to the Scriptures, Hampstead, 2016; Filthy Business, Hampstead, 2017; The Lady in the Van, Th. Royal Bath, 2017; dir, Brass, Nat. Music Youth Th., 2014; Paradise, Hampstead, 2018; *films*: Zardoz, 1973; Lisztomania, 1975; Break of Day, 1976; Lady Jane, 1984; Ex Memoria, 2006; The Last Sparks of Sundown, 2015; *television* includes: Caucasian Chalk Circle, 1973; The Cafeteria, 1975; Crown Court; The Last Romantics, 1991; Casualty, 1996, 2003; Tom Jones, 1997; Kavanagh QC, 1997; Invasion Earth, 1998; Anna Karenina, 2000; Trial and Retribution, 2003, 2004; Midsomer Murders, 2004; Ultimate Force, 2004; Instinct, 2006; Rome, 2006; Holby City; From There to Here, 2014; In the Flesh, 2014; Maigret in Montmartre, 2017; narrations for documentaries; numerous radio plays, incl. Hitler in Therapy (Actress of the Year, World Air Awards, BBC World Service, 2005), Golda Meir in Payback, Life and Fate, 2011, A Small Person Far Away, 2012, and book readings; adapted Molly Keane's Full House for Book at Bedtime, 1991. Sen. Lectr, Central Sch. of Speech and Drama, 2007–10. Lead Reader, InterAct Stroke Support Reading Service, for sufferers of stroke in hosps, hospices and stroke gps. Life Coach certificates, 2006 and 2007; Master practitioner in Neuro-linguistic programming, 2007. *Publications*: (with Susan Penhalign) A Two Hander (poems), 1996. *Recreations*: writing - song writer and poet, tapestry, drawing, photography, dance. *Address*: c/o Shepherd Management Ltd, 3rd Floor, Joel House, 17–21 Garrick Street, WC2E 9BL.

**KESTENBAUM,** family name of **Baron Kestenbaum**.

**KESTENBAUM,** Baron *cr* 2011 (Life Peer), of Foxcote in the County of Somerset; **Jonathan Andrew Kestenbaum;** Chief Operating Officer, RIT Capital Partners plc, since 2010; *b* 5 Aug. 1959; *s* of late Ralph Kestenbaum and of Gaby Kestenbaum; *m* 1984, Deborah Zackon; three *s* one *d*. *Educ*: London Sch. of Econs (BA Hons 1982); Wolfson Coll., Cambridge; Hebrew Univ. (MA 1989); Cass Business Sch. (MBA 1994). Chief Executive: Office of Chief Rabbi, 1991–96; UJIA, 1996–2002; Portland Trust, 2002–06; COS to Sir Ronald Cohen, Chm. of Apax Partners, 2002–06; Chief Exec., NESTA, 2005–10; Chairman: Five Arrows Ltd, 2010–13; Capital Hldgs plc, 2014–18. Non-exec. Chm., Quest Ltd, 2002–06. Non-executive Board Member: Enterprise Insight, 2005–08; Design Council, 2006–10; Profero Ltd, 2006–14. Mem., Technology Strategy Bd, 2007–13. Tutor, Cass Business Sch., 1999–2006; Adjunct Prof., Imperial Coll. Business Sch., 2011–. Trustee, London Community Centre, 2003–10; Gov. and Mem. Bd, RSC, 2007–12. Chancellor, Plymouth Univ., 2013–. CCMI 2008. *Recreations*: tennis, ski-ing. *Address*: RIT Capital Partners plc, Spencer House, 27 St James's Place, SW1A 1NR. *T*: (020) 7647 8565. *Club*: MCC.

**KESTER, David Martin Albert;** Principal, David Kester and Associates, since 2014; Coach and Managing Partner, Design Thinkers Academy, since 2014; *b* 23 May 1964; *s* of Simon and Stephanie Kester; *m* 1992, Sophia Adamou; two *s*. *Educ*: Bristol Univ. (BA Hons). Friends of the Earth, 1990–93; Chartered Soc. of Designers, 1993–94; Chief Exec., British Design and Art Direction, 1994–2003; Chief Exec., Design Council, 2003–12. Chm., Caulder Moore Design, 2014–; Member: Bd, Design Business Assoc., 2003; Bd, Kingston Rose Th., 2007–13; Bd, Home Office Design and Technol. Alliance, 2007. Non-exec. Dir, Thames & Hudson, 2012–13.

**KESTING, Very Rev. Sheilagh Margaret;** Secretary, Committee on Ecumenical Relations, Church of Scotland, 1993–2007 and 2008–16; Moderator of the General Assembly of the Church of Scotland, 2007–08; *b* 10 June 1953; *d* of Douglas Norman Kesting and Joan Robertson Kesting (*née* Blair). *Educ*: Nicolson Inst., Stornoway; Edinburgh Univ. (BA 1974; BD Hons 1977). Ordained, C of S, 1980; Parish Minister: Overtown, Lanarkshire, 1980–86; St Andrew's High, Musselburgh, 1986–93. Hon DD Edinburgh, 2008. DSG 2016. *Recreations*: gardening, photography, embroidery.

**KESWICK, Hon. Annabel Thérèse, (Tessa), (Hon. Lady Keswick);** Deputy Chairman, Centre for Policy Studies, 2004–17 (Director, 1995–2004); *b* 15 Oct. 1942; *d* of 17th Baron Lovat, DSO, MC and of Rosamond, *o d* of Sir Delves, (Jock), Broughton, 11th Bt; *m* 1st, 1964, 14th Lord Reay (marr. diss. 1978; he *d* 2013); two *s* one *d*; 2nd, 1985, Henry Neville Lindley Keswick (see Sir H. N. L. Keswick). *Educ*: Convent of the Sacred Heart, Woldingham. Trainee, J. W. Thompson, 1960–62; Dir, Cluff Investments, 1980–95. Special Advr to Rt Hon. Kenneth Clarke, 1989–95. Non-exec. Dir, Daily Mail and Gen. Trust plc, 2013–. Member: Corporate Adv. Gp, Tate; Internat. Strategy Cttee, British Mus., 2012–16. Mem. (C), Kensington Council, 1982–86. Chancellor, Univ. of Buckingham, 2014–. Contested (C), Inverness, Nairn and Lochaber, 1987. Hon. FKC 2007. *Recreation*: travelling. *Address*: 6 Smith Square, SW1P 3HT.
See also Lord Reay.

**KESWICK, Sir Chippendale;** see Keswick, Sir J. C. L.

**KESWICK, Sir Henry (Neville Lindley),** Kt 2009; Director, Matheson & Co. Ltd, since 1975 (Chairman, 1975–2016); Chairman: Jardine, Matheson Holdings Ltd, Hong Kong, 1972–75 and 1989–2018, Chairman Emeritus, 2019 (Director, 1967–2018); Jardine Strategic Holdings, 1989–2018 (Director, 1988–2018); *b* 29 Sept. 1938; *e s* of Sir William Keswick and Mary, *d* of Rt Hon. Sir Francis Lindley, PC, GCMG; *m* 1985, Tessa, Lady Reay (*see* Hon. A. T. Keswick). *Educ*: Eton Coll.; Trinity Coll., Cambridge (BA Hons Econs and Law; MA). Commnd Scots Guards, Nat. Service, 1956–58. Director: Sun Alliance and London Insurance, 1975–96; Robert Fleming Holdings Ltd, 1975–2000; Rothmans Internat., 1988–94; Hongkong Land Co., 1988–2018; Mandarin Oriental Internat., 1988–2018; Dairy Farm Internat. Hldgs, 1988–2018; Royal & Sun Alliance (formerly Sun Alliance) Gp, 1989–2000; The Telegraph, 1990–2001; Mem., Adv. Bd, Telegraph Gp Ltd, 2002–04; Rothschilds Continuation Hldgs AG, 2006–11. Member: London Adv. Cttee, Hongkong and Shanghai Banking Corp., 1975–92; 21st Century Trust, 1987–97. Proprietor, The Spectator, 1975–81. Trustee: Nat. Portrait Gall., 1982–2001 (Chm., 1994–2001); Royal Botanic Gdns, Kew, 2008–17 (Mem., Foundn Council, 2017–). Pres., RHASS, 2003–04; Mem. Council, NT, 2005–07, 2009–10. Chm., Hong Kong Assoc., 1988–2001. *Recreation*: country pursuits. *Address*: Matheson & Co. Ltd, 3 Lombard Street, EC3V 9AQ. *Clubs*: White's, Turf; Third Guards.
See also Sir J. C. L. Keswick, S. L. Keswick.

**KESWICK, Sir (John) Chippendale (Lindley),** Kt 1993; Director, De Beers SA, 2001–10; Chairman, Arsenal Football Club, since 2013 (Director, since 2005); *b* 2 Feb. 1940; 2nd *s* of Sir William Keswick and Mary, *d* of Rt Hon. Sir Francis Lindley, PC, GCMG; *m* 1966, Lady Sarah Ramsay, *d* of 16th Earl of Dalhousie, KT, GCVO, GBE, MC; three *s*. *Educ*: Eton; Univ. of Aix/Marseilles. Glyn Mills & Co., 1961–65; Jt Vice Chm., 1986, Jt Dep. Chm., 1990–97, Gp Chief Exec., 1995–97, Chm., 1997–98, Hambros PLC; Chief Exec., 1985–95, Chm., 1986–98, Hambros Bank. A Dir, Bank of England, 1993–2001. Sen. Banking and Capital Mkts Advr, Société Générale, 1998–2000. Director: Persimmon Plc, 1984–2006; Edinburgh Investment Trust, 1992–2001; De Beers Consolidated Mines, 1993–2006; De Beers Centenary AG, 1994–2005; IMI plc, 1994–2003; Anglo Amer. plc, 1995–2001; Investec Bank (UK) Ltd, 2000–10; Investec plc, 2002–10; Arsenal Hldgs plc, 2005–. Mem., Queen's Body Guard for Scotland, Royal

Company of Archers, 1976. Chm., Test & Itchen Assoc., 1992–2009. *Recreations:* bridge, country pursuits. *Address:* c/o Oppenheimer Generations, 1 Charterhouse Street, EC1N 6SA. *T:* (020) 7421 9823. *Clubs:* White's, Portland.
*See also Sir H. N. L. Keswick, S. L. Keswick.*

**KESWICK, Simon Lindley;** Director, Jardine Matheson Holdings Ltd, since 1972 (Chairman, 1983–89); *b* 20 May 1942; *s* of Sir William Keswick and Mary, *d* of Rt Hon. Sir Francis Lindley, PC, GCMG; *m* 1971, Emma, *d* of Major David Chetwode; two *s* two *d*. *Educ:* Eton Coll. Director: Hong Kong and Shanghai Banking Corp., 1983–88; Matheson & Co. Ltd, 1982–; Jardine Strategic Hldgs Ltd, 1987– (Chm., 1987–89); Hanson plc, 1991–2005; Wellcome plc, 1995–96; Fleming Mercantile Investment Trust, 1988–2007 (Chm., 1990–2003); Jardine Lloyd Thompson Gp plc, 2001–13. Director: Hongkong Land Hldgs Ltd, 1983– (Chm., 1983–2013); Mandarin Oriental Internat. Ltd, 1984– (Chm., 1984–2013); Dairy Farm Internat. Hldgs Ltd, 1984– (Chm., 1984–2013). Trustee: British Museum, 1989–99; Henry Moore Foundn, 2003–13. Patron, RCS, 1998–. *Recreations:* country pursuits, bridge, soccer. *Address:* May Tower 1, 5–7 May Road, Hong Kong; 7 Ennismore Gardens, SW7 1NL. *Clubs:* White's, Portland; Shek O (Hong Kong).
*See also Sir H. N. L. Keswick, Sir J. C. L. Keswick.*

**KESWICK, Hon. Tessa;** *see* Keswick, Hon. A. T.

**KETT, Paul Michael;** Director General, Higher and Further Education, Department for Education, since 2019; *b* Norwich, 25 Feb. 1980; *s* of Rosemary Kett; partner, Jillian Gray Kay, *qv*. *Educ:* City of Norwich Sch.; Univ. of Leicester (BSc Hons Physics 2001); Univ. of Birmingham (MPhil Sci. and Engrg Materials 2002). DTI, 2002–04; Information Rights, DCA, 2005; Dep. Principal Private Sec. to Lord Chancellor and Sec. of State for Justice, 2006–08; Hd of Secretariat, Commn on Scottish Devolution, 2008–09; Prog. Dir, Implementation Prog., Ind. Parly Standards Authy, 2009–10; Dep. Dir, Strategy, 2010, Prog. Dir, 2010–11, Dir, Justice Reform, 2011–14, MoJ; Dir, Army Reform, British Army, 2014–16; Dir, Teachers and Teaching, 2016–17, Dir Gen., Educn Standards, 2017–18, DFE. *Recreations:* theatre, cooking, swimming, eating jamón, ski-ing. *Address:* Department for Education, Sanctuary Buildings, Great Smith Street, SW1P 3BT. *T:* (020) 7340 7726. *E:* Paul.Kett@education.gov.uk.

**KETTERLE, Prof. Wolfgang,** PhD; John D. MacArthur Professor of Physics, Massachusetts Institute of Technology, since 1998; *b* Heidelberg, 21 Oct. 1957; German and US citizen, 2014; *m*; three *d* two *s* from a former marriage. *Educ:* Univ. of Heidelberg (Vordiplom Physics 1978); Tech. Univ. Munich (Diplom Physics 1982); Ludwig Maximilians Univ. of Munich and Max-Planck Inst. for Quantum Optics (PhD 1986). Intern, Volkswagen Co., Puebla, Mexico, 1980; res. asst, 1982–85, staff scientist, 1985–88, Max-Planck Inst. for Quantum Optics, Germany; res. scientist, Dept of Physical Chem., Univ. of Heidelberg, 1989–90; Department of Physics, Massachusetts Institute of Technology: Res. Associate, 1990–93; Asst Prof. of Physics, 1993–97; Prof. of Physics, 1997–98. NATO/Deutscher Akademischer Austauschdienst Postdoctoral Fellow, 1990–91; David and Lucile Packard Fellow, 1996–2001; Dist. Traveling Lectr, Div. of Laser Sci., APS, 1998–99. Member: German Physical Soc.; Optical Soc. of America, 1997; Eur. Acad. of Scis and Arts, 2002; Acad. of Scis in Heidelberg, 2002; Eur. Acad. of Arts, Scis and Humanities, 2002; Bavarian Acad. of Scis, 2003; German Acad. of Natural Scientists Leopoldina, 2005; MNAS 2014 (For. Associate, 2002); Fellow: APS, 1997; Amer. Acad. Arts and Scis, 1999; FInstP 2002. Hon. DSc: Gustavus Adolphus Coll., St Peter, 2005; Connecticut, 2007; Ohio State, 2007. Michael and Philip Platzman Award, MIT, 1994; I. I. Rabi Prize, APS, 1997; Gustav-Hertz Prize, German Physical Soc., 1997; Award for Technological Innovation, Discover Mag., 1998; Fritz London Prize in Low Temp. Physics, 1999; Dannie-Heineman Prize, Acad. of Scis, Göttingen, 1999; Benjamin Franklin Medal in Physics, 2000; (jtly) Nobel Prize in Physics, 2001; Killian Award, MIT, 2004. Kt Comdr's Cross (Badge and Star), Order of Merit (Germany), 2002; Medal of Merit, State of Baden-Württemberg (Germany), 2002; Officer, Legion of Honour (France), 2002. *Address:* Massachusetts Institute of Technology, 77 Massachusetts Avenue, Cambridge, MA 02139, USA. *T:* (617) 2536815, *Fax:* (617) 2534876. *E:* ketterle@mit.edu; 80 Clifton Street, Belmont, MA 02478, USA.

**KEVERNE, Prof. Eric Barrington, (Barry),** DSc; FRS 1997; Professor of Behavioural Neuroscience, 1998–2009, now Emeritus, and Fellow of King's College, since 1985, University of Cambridge. *Educ:* London Univ. (BSc, PhD); MA 1975, DSc 1993, Cantab. University of Cambridge: Lectr, Dept of Anatomy, then of Zoology, until 1990; Reader in Behavioural Neurosci., 1990–98. Chm., Healthy Organism Strategy Panel, BBSRC, 2005–07; Member: Royal Soc. Res. Fellowships Cttee, 1998–2003; Animals Res. Cttee, Royal Soc., 2004–; MRC Cross Bds Cttee, 2000–03. FMedSci 2005. Foreign Hon. Fellow, American Acad. of Arts and Scis, 1998. *Address:* Sub-Department of Animal Behaviour, University of Cambridge, High Street, Madingley, Cambridge CB23 8AA. *T:* (01223) 741801; King's College, Cambridge CB2 1ST.

**KEVILL, Siân Louise;** Founder and Director: MAKE World Media Ltd, since 2011; MAKE Waves Ltd, since 2016; *b* Enfield, 29 Jan. 1961; *d* of David Courtney Kevill and Frances Morfydd Kevill; *m* 1987 (marr. diss. 1999); one *s* one *d*. *Educ:* Newnham Coll., Cambridge (BA 1st Cl. Hons Hist. 1982). Staff writer, Keesing's Contemp. Archives, Longman Publishing, 1983–84; BBC: Talks writer, BBC World Service, 1984–85; News Trainee, 1986–88; Asst Producer, 1988–90, Producer, 1990–92, Asst Ed., 1992–94, Newsnight; Dep. Ed., On the Record, 1994–95; Ed., Foreign Progs, BBC Radio, 1995–97; Dep. Hd, Political Progs, 1997–98; Ed., Newsnight, 1998–2003; Hd, Political Progs Rev. 2003–04; Editl Dir, 2004–08, Dir, 2008–10, BBC World News Ltd. Vis. Fellow, Reuters Inst. for Study of Journalism, Univ. of Oxford, 2012–14. *Publications:* Sino-Soviet Relations, 1984; Aquino and the Philippines, 1985. *Recreations:* sport, swimming, running, cinema, reading, socialising.

**KEY, Vice Adm. Benjamin John,** CBE 2016; Chief of Joint Operations, since 2019; *b* Rugby, 7 Nov. 1965; *s* of John and Loveday Key; *m* 1994, Eleanor Morton; two *s* one *d*. *Educ:* Bromsgrove Sch.; Royal Holloway Coll., Univ. of London (BSc Hons Physics 1988). Joined RN, 1984; Surface Fleet and Fleet Air appts, 1988–99; Commanding Officer: HMS Sandown, 1999–2000; HMS Iron Duke, 2000–01; HMS Lancaster, 2001–02; Aviation Desk Officer, Navy Resources and Plans, MoD, 2003–05; Advr, Iraqi Jt HQ, Baghdad, 2006; Dep. Asst COS, UK Perm. Jt HQ, 2006–08; CO, HMS Illustrious, 2009–10; Cdre, Jt Air Maritime Orgn, 2010; Hd, Navy Resources and Plans, MoD, 2011; Principal Staff Officer to CDS, 2011–13; Flag Officer Sea Trng, 2013–15; Fleet Comdr and Chief Naval Warfare Officer, 2016–19. Gov., Stover Sch., 2005–. Younger Brother, Trinity Hse, 2011–. Hon. DSc: Plymouth, 2015; RHUL, 2018. *Recreations:* talking about the many sports he can no longer play, jazz and classical music, outdoor activities, gardening. *Address:* c/o Naval Secretary, Navy Command Headquarters, Whale Island, Portsmouth PO2 8BY.

**KEY, Rt Hon. Sir John (Phillip),** GNZM 2017; AC 2017; Chairman, ANZ Bank New Zealand Ltd, since 2018 (non-executive Director, since 2017); *b* 9 Aug. 1961; *s* of George Key and Ruth (*née* Lazar); *m* 1984, Bronagh Dougan; one *s* one *d*. *Educ:* Canterbury Univ. (BCom Accounting 1981). Hd, Treasury, Bankers Trust of NZ, 1988–95; Merrill Lynch, 1995–2001: Asian Hd, Foreign Exchange, Singapore; Global Hd, Foreign Exchange, London; Eur. Hd, Bonds and Derivatives, London; Hd, Fixed Income, Australia. MP (Nat.) Helensville, NZ, 2002–17. Leader of the Opposition, NZ, 2006–08; Prime Minister of NZ, 2008–16. Leader, Nat. Party, 2006–16. Chm., Internat. Democratic Union, 2014–18. Non-executive Director: Air NZ, 2017–; ANZ Banking Gp Ltd, 2018–. *Recreations:* spending time with family, cooking, watching Rugby.

**KEY, Matthew David;** Chairman and Chief Executive Officer, Telefónica Digital, 2011–14; Member, Executive Committee, Telefónica SA, 2008–14; *b* 3 March 1963; *s* of Kenneth Charles Key and Christina Mary Key; *m* 1990, Karen Lorraine Cook; two *s* one *d*. *Educ:* Sir Joseph Williamson's Mathematical Sch., Rochester; Univ. of Birmingham (BSocSc 1st cl. Hons Econs; 2nd Yr Undergraduate Prize). ACA 1987. Arthur Young, 1984–89; Grand Metropolitan Foods Europe, 1989–91; Coca-Cola & Schweppes Beverages Ltd, 1991–95; Woolworths, Kingfisher plc, 1995–99; appts in retail and network divs, 1999–2001, Finance Dir, 2001–02, Vodafone UK; Chief Financial Officer, 2002–05, CEO, 2005–07, $O_2$ UK Ltd, subseq. Telefónica $O_2$ UK Ltd; Chm. and CEO, Telefónica Europe plc, 2008–11. Non-exec. Dir, Burberry Gp plc, 2013–. Chm., Dallaglio Foundn, 2013–.

**KEY, Dr Paul Anthony;** QC 2013; *b* Christchurch, NZ, 8 Sept. 1967; *s* of Jack and Erene Key. *Educ:* Univ. of Auckland (LLB Hons); Gonville and Caius Coll., Cambridge (PhD 1994). Called to the Bar, Inner Temple, 1997; in practice as barrister, 1997–. *Address:* Essex Court Chambers, 24 Lincoln's Inn Fields, WC2A 3EG. *T:* (020) 7813 8000.

**KEY, Very Rev. Robert Frederick;** Dean of Jersey, 2005–17; Anglican Communion Lead, Thy Kingdom Come, since 2017; permission to officiate, Diocese of Canterbury, since 2017; *b* 29 Aug. 1952; *s* of Frederick and Winifred Key; *m* 1974, Daphne Mary Manning; one *s* two *d*. *Educ:* Bristol Univ. (BA 1973); Oak Hill Coll. (DPS 1976). Ordained deacon, 1976, priest, 1977; Curate, St Ebbe's, Oxford, 1976–80; Minister, St Patrick's, Wallington, 1980–85; Vicar: Eynsham and Cassington, 1985–91; St Andrew's, Oxford, 1991–2001; Gen. Dir, CPAS, 2001–05; Priest-in-charge, 2005–08, Rector, 2008–17, St Helier's, Jersey. Canon Preacher, Dio. Rio Grande, 2004–. *Recreations:* civil aviation, detective fiction.

**KEY, (Simon) Robert;** *b* 22 April 1945; *s* of late Rt Rev. J. M. Key; *m* 1968, Susan Priscilla Bright Irvine, 2nd *d* of late Rev. T. T. Irvine; one *s* two *d* (and one *s* decd). *Educ:* Salisbury Cathedral Sch.; Forres Sch., Swanage; Sherborne Sch.; Clare Coll., Cambridge. MA; CertEd. Assistant Master: Loretto Sch., Edinburgh, 1967; Harrow Sch., 1969–83. Warden, Nanoose Field Studies Centre, Wool, Dorset, 1972–78; Governor: Sir William Collins Sch., NW1, 1976–81; Special Sch. at Gt Ormond Street Hosp. for Sick Children, 1976–81; Roxeth Sch., Harrow, 1979–83. Founder Chm., ALICE Trust for Autistic Children, 1977–82; Council Mem., GAP Activity Projects, 1975–84. Vice-Chm., Wembley Br., ASTMS, 1976–80. Contested (C) Camden, Holborn and St Pancras South, 1979. MP (C) Salisbury, 1983–2010. Political Sec. to Rt Hon. Edward Heath, 1984–85; PPS: to Minister of State for Energy, 1985–87; to Minister for Overseas Develt, 1987–89; to Sec. of State for the Envmt, 1989–90; Parly Under-Sec. of State, DoE, 1990–92, Dept of Nat. Heritage, 1992–93, Dept of Transport, 1993–94; Opposition front bench spokesman on defence, 1997–2001, on trade and industry, 2001–02, on internat. develt, 2002–03. Mem., Select Cttee on Educn, Science and the Arts, 1983–86, on Health, 1994–95, on Defence, 1995–97, on Science and Technology, 2003–05, on Defence, 2005–10; Chm., Select Cttee on Information, 2004–05; Sec., Cons. Parly Backbench Cttee on Arts and Heritage, 1983–84; Jt Parly Chm., Council for Educn in the Commonwealth, 1984–87; Vice-Chm., 1988–90, Chm., 1996–97, All-Party Gp on AIDS. Chm., Harrow Central Cons. Assoc., 1980–82; Vice-Chm., Central London Cons. Euro-Constit., 1980–82; Mem., Cons. Party Nat. Union Exec., 1981–83. Member: UK Nat. Commn for UNESCO, 1984–85; MRC, 1989–90 (Mem., AIDS Cttee, 1988–90). Director and Trustee: Wessex Archaeology, 2004–13 (Chm., 2011–13); Trussell Trust, 2014–17; Mem. Council, Winston Churchill Meml Trust, 2004–07; Trustee, Salisbury and S Wilts Mus., 2010–13. Mem., Gen. Synod, C of E, 2005–15; Lay Canon, Salisbury Cathedral, 2008–; Chm., Salisbury Cathedral Magna Carta 2015 Project, 2010–15. Chm., Salisbury Cathedral Sch., 2015–17. Vice-Pres., Haemophilia Soc., 1988–90. Hon. FCollP, 1989. FSA 2007. Freeman, City of Salisbury, 2017. *Recreations:* singing, cooking, country life.

**KEYES,** family name of **Baron Keyes**.

**KEYES, 3rd Baron** *cr* 1943, of Zeebrugge and of Dover, co. Kent; **Charles William Packe Keyes;** Bt 1919; *b* 8 Dec. 1951; *s* of 2nd Baron Keyes and Grizelda Mary Keyes (née Packe); *S* father, 2005, but does not use the title; *m* 1984, Sally Jackson; one *d*. *Educ:* Eton Coll.; Canterbury Coll. of Art; Thames Poly.; Camberwell Sch. of Arts and Crafts (OND Conservation of Paper). Retained Firefighter, Suffolk Fire and Rescue Service, 1990–2006. Operational Postal Grade, Royal Mail, 2000–08. Community bus driver. Queen's Golden Jubilee Medal, 2002. *Recreations:* bird watching, drawing, drinking coffee, Scotland, botany, gardening. *Heir: b* Hon. (Leopold Roger) John Keyes [*b* 8 June 1956; *m* 1988, Jane Owen (marr. diss. 1997); two *d*; *m* 2011, Lowri Elizabeth Cochlin; one *s* one *d*].

**KEYES, Timothy Harold,** MA; Headmaster, King's School, Worcester, 1998–2014; *b* 15 Dec. 1954; *s* of Alfred Edward Keyes and Mary Irene Keyes (née Mylchreest); *m* 1979, Mary Anne Lucas; two *s*. *Educ:* Christ's Hospital, Horsham; Wadham Coll., Oxford (BA 1st cl. Classics, MA, PGCE). Teacher: of classics and rowing, Tiffin Sch., Kingston upon Thames, 1979–83; of classics and hockey, Whitgift Sch., Croydon, 1983–88; Head of Classics, Perse Sch., Cambridge, 1988–93; Dep. Head, Royal Grammar Sch., Guildford, 1993–98. *Recreations:* choral singing, bell-ringing, walking, Yorkshire cricket. *Address:* 11 Bank Crescent, Ledbury, Herefordshire HR8 1AA.

**KEYNES, Prof. Simon Douglas,** PhD, LittD; FBA 2000; FSA, FRHistS; Elrington and Bosworth Professor of Anglo-Saxon, University of Cambridge, 1999–2019, now Emeritus; Fellow, Trinity College, Cambridge, since 1976; *b* Cambridge, 23 Sept. 1952; *y s* of Prof. Richard Darwin Keynes, CBE, FRS and of Anne Pinsent Keynes, *e d* of 1st Baron Adrian, OM, FRS, and Dame Hester Agnes Adrian, DBE. *Educ:* King's Coll. Choir Sch., Cambridge; Leys Sch., Cambridge; Trinity Coll., Cambridge (BA Hons 1973; MA 1977; PhD 1978; LittD 1992). FRHistS 1982; FSA 1985. University of Cambridge: Asst Lectr, Dept of Anglo-Saxon, Norse and Celtic, 1978–82; Lectr, 1982–92; Reader in Anglo-Saxon Hist., 1992–99; Head, Dept of Anglo-Saxon, Norse and Celtic, 1999–2006. British Acad. Res. Reader in Humanities, 1991–93. Member: British Acad./RHistS Jt Cttee on Anglo-Saxon Charters, 1982–2014 (Sec., 1983–2013; Chm., 2013–14); British Acad. Cttee for Sylloge of Coins of British Isles, 1995– (Chm., 2003–); Chm., Sect. H8 (Medieval Studies: Hist. and Lit.), British Acad., 2005–08. Member, Editorial Board: Anglo-Saxon England, 1979– (Exec. Ed., 1982–); Cambridge Studies in Anglo-Saxon England, 1986–2005; Early English MSS in Facsimile, 1996–2002; Associate Ed., Oxford DNB, 1993–2004. Liveryman, Goldsmiths' Co., 1991–. Hon. Fellow, Darwin Coll., Cambridge, 2019. *Publications:* The Diplomas of King Æthelred 'the Unready' 978–1016, 1980; (with M. Lapidge) Alfred the Great: Asser's Life of King Alfred and other contemporary sources, 1983; Anglo-Saxon History: a select bibliography, 1987, 8th edn, as Anglo Saxon England: a bibliographical handbook, 2010; Facsimiles of Anglo-Saxon Charters, 1991; The Liber

Vitae of the New Minster and Hyde Abbey, Winchester, 1996; (ed jtly and contrib.) The Blackwell Encyclopaedia of Anglo-Saxon England, 1999, 2nd edn 2014; Quentin Keynes: explorer, film-maker, lecturer and book collector 1921–2003, 2004; (ed and contrib.) Ethiopian Encounters: Sir William Cornwallis Harris and the British mission to the Kingdom of Shewa (1841–3), 2007; contrib. articles in books and learned jls, incl. Anglo-Saxon England, Anglo-Norman Studies, English Hist. Rev. and Early Medieval Europe. *Recreation:* 19th-century travel and exploration. *Address:* Trinity College, Cambridge CB2 1TQ. *T:* (01223) 338421; Primrose Farm, Wiveton, Norfolk NR25 7TQ. *T:* (01263) 740317. *Club:* Roxburghe.

**KEYS, Stuart Cameron;** Vice Lord-Lieutenant, City of Londonderry, since 2004; *b* Nottingham, 1946; *s* of Dr and Mrs Robin Keys; *m* 1969, Elizabeth Margaret Hosford; two *s* one *d. Educ:* Merchiston Castle Sch., Edinburgh; Stow Coll., Glasgow. Cert. Inst. Wood Sci. Works Dir, 1969–78, Man. Dir, 1978–91, Chm., 1991–99, Robert Keys Gp of Cos. Tutor, Sch. of Philosophy and Econ. Sci., St Columb's Park Hse Peace and Reconciliation Centre, 2004–. Port and Harbour Comr, Londonderry, 1986–92. Chairman: NI Builders Merchants Assoc., 1982–84; NI Timber Trade Assoc., 1989–91. Pres., NW Animal Welfare, 2009–. DL 1993, High Sheriff, 1997, Co. Bor. Londonderry. *Recreations:* practical philosophy, animal welfare, organic gardening, art. *Address:* Heronsway, 67 Balloughy Road, Molenan, Londonderry, Northern Ireland BT48 9XL. *T:* (028) 7126 0898. *E:* stuartckeys@gmail.com.

**KEYSER, Andrew John;** QC 2006; **His Honour Judge Keyser;** a Circuit Judge, since 2011; a Circuit Commercial Judge (formerly a Specialist Mercantile Circuit Judge), Wales Circuit, since 2012; *b* 19 Dec. 1963; *s* of late James William Keyser and of Elizabeth Jane Keyser (*née* Hall); *m* 1st, 1985 (marr. diss. 1998); two *s*; 2nd, 2011, Andrea Markham; one step *d. Educ:* Cardiff High Sch.; Balliol Coll., Oxford (BA 1st Cl. Hons 1985; MA 1989); Inns of Court Sch. of Law. Called to the Bar, Middle Temple, 1986, Bencher, 2017; Recorder, 2002–11; Dep. High Ct Judge, 2008–; Principal Technol. and Construction Court Judge for Leeds, 2011–12, for Wales, 2012–. An Asst Boundary Comr for Wales, 2003–11. Chancellor, Dio. of Llandaff, 2017– (Dep. Chancellor, 2007–11 and 2014–17); Church in Wales: Mem., Disciplinary Tribunal, 2007–11; Mem., Governing Body, 2013–; Chm., Legal sub-cttee of Standing Cttee, 2013–. *Recreations:* reading, music. *Address:* Cardiff Civil Justice Centre, 2 Park Street, Cardiff CF10 1ET.

**KEYWOOD, Richard David C.;** *see* Collier-Keywood.

**KHALIDI, Prof. Tarif,** PhD; Sheikh Zayed Professor of Islamic and Arabic Studies, Centre for Arab and Middle Eastern Studies, American University of Beirut, since 2002; *b* 24 Jan. 1938; *s* of Ahmad Samih Khalidi, MBE and Anbara Salam; *m* 1st, 1960, Amal Saidi (decd); one *s* one *d*; 2nd, 2001, Magda Moussallem. *Educ:* Haileybury Coll., Hertford; University Coll., Oxford (BA; MA); Univ. of Chicago (PhD). Prof. of History, American Univ. of Beirut, 1970–96; Sir Thomas Adams's Prof. of Arabic, and Fellow of King's Coll., Cambridge Univ., 1996–2002. *Publications:* Islamic Historiography, 1975; (ed) Land Tenure and Social Transformation in the Middle East, 1983; Classical Arab Islam, 1984; Arabic Historical Thought in the Classical Period, 1994; The Muslim Jesus: sayings and stories in Islamic literature, 2001; The Qu'ran: a new translation, 2008. *Recreations:* gliding, admiring trees. *Address:* American University of Beirut, PO Box 11–0236, Beirut, Lebanon.

**KHALIL, Prof. Asma,** MD; Consultant in Obstetric and Fetal Medicine, since 2012, and Professor of Obstetrics and Maternal-Fetal Medicine, since 2018, St George's Hospital, University of London; *b* Cairo, Egypt, 6 Oct. 1979; *d* of Ahmed Khalil Elboraey and Afaf Gabr; *m* 2003, Patrick O'Brien. *Educ:* Ain Shams Univ., Cairo (MB BCh 2002); Queen Mary, Univ. of London (MD Res. 2009); London Sch. of Hygiene and Tropical Medicine (MSc Epidemiol.). MRCOG 2008. Clinical Lectr and subspeciality trainee in Maternal Fetal Medicine, Inst. for Women's Health, UCL, 2009–12; Reader in Maternal Fetal Medicine, St George's, University of London, 2016–18. Expert Advr to NICE, 2016–. *Publications:* contribs to peer-reviewed scientific jls. *Recreations:* fashion, diving, opera, cinema, music, sports. *Address:* Apartment 64, 11 Sheldon Square, W2 6OQ. *T:* 07917 4000164. *E:* asmakhalil79@googlemail.com; Fetal Medicine Unit, 4th Floor, Lanesborough Wing, St George's Hospital, SW17 0QT. *E:* akhalil@sgul.ac.uk; Harley Street Centre for Women, 78 Harley Street, W1G 7HJ.

**KHALIL, Karim;** QC 2003; DL; a Recorder, since 2000; *b* 7 Jan. 1962; *s* of Dr Hassan and Anna Shakir-Khalil; *m* 1986, Sally Ann Boyle; two *s. Educ:* Cheadle Hulme Sch., Manchester; Queens' Coll., Cambridge (MA Hons Law). Called to the Bar, Lincoln's Inn, 1984, Bencher, 2013; in practice, specialising in criminal law, health and safety, and regulatory law; Asst Recorder, 1997–2000; Hd of Chambers, 2011–. Chairman: S Eastern Circuit Liaison Cttee, 2003–; Cambridge and Peterborough Bar Mess, 2003–; Member: SE Circuit Cttee, 2000–; Jt Advocate Selection Cttee, SE Circuit, 2011–. DL Cambs, 2019. Co-Ed., Drystone Newsletter, 2010–; Ed., The Circuiteer, 2015–. *Publications:* (contrib. chapter) Fraud: law, practice and procedure, 2005. *Recreations:* tennis, golf, alto sax in The Eye, ski-ing, lacrosse (Mem., Cambridge Univ. Lacrosse XVI), cycling (completed Tour of Cambridge and Prudential RideLondon-Surrey 100). *Address:* Drystone Chambers, 35 Bedford Row, WC1R 4JH. *T:* (020) 7404 1881, *Fax:* (020) 7404 1991. *E:* Karim.Khalil@drystone.com. *Clubs:* Hawks, Gog Magog Golf; Okeford Duck Golf, Quinta do Lago Golf.

**KHALIQUE, Nageena;** QC 2015; *b* Nottingham, 10 Dec. 1961; *d* of Abdul Khalique and Mumtaz Khalique; *m* 1992, Andrew Mark Sean Brown; one *s* one *d. Educ:* Nottingham High Sch. for Girls GPDST; University Coll. London (BDS 1987); Univ. of London (Dip. Vocational Trng 1989); City Univ. (DipLaw 1993); Inns of Court Sch. of Law (BVQ 1994). LDS 1987. Hosp. dentist, Birmingham Children's Hosp., 1987–90; Registrar in Oral and Maxillofacial Surgery, Selly Oak Hosp. and City Hosp., 1990–92; called to the Bar, Gray's Inn, 1994; in practice as a barrister, No5 Chambers, 1995–2007 and 2008–18, Serjeants' Inn, 2018–; Associate Barrister, Mills & Reeve LLP, 2007–08. Hon. Tutor in Med. Ethics, Univ. of Birmingham, 1992–2004; Postgrad. Lectr, Medico-Legal and Ethics, W Midlands Deanery, 2008–14. Chair, Court of Protection Practitioners Assoc. (Midlands), 2014–; Mem., Legal Panel, Assoc. of Child Psychotherapists, 2015–. *Publications:* contrib. to Lawtel, Law Reports, Kemp & Kemp, British Dental Jl, British Jl of Oral and Maxillofacial Surgery. *Recreations:* ballet, marathon runner and triathlete, opera, music, ski-ing. *Address:* Serjeants' Inn, 85 Fleet Street, EC4Y 1AE.

**KHAMENEI, Ayatollah Sayyed Ali;** religious and political leader of the Islamic Republic of Iran, since 1989; *b* Mashhad, Khorasan, 17 July 1939; *m* 1964; four *s* two *d. Educ:* Qom; studied under Imam Khomeini, 1956–64. Imprisoned six times, 1964–78; once exiled, 1978; Mem., Revolutionary Council, 1978 until its dissolution, 1979 (Rep. in Iranian Army and Assistant of Revolutionary Affairs in Min. of Defence); Rep. of First Islamic Consultative Assembly, and of Imam Khomeini in the Supreme Council of Defence, 1980; Comdr, Revolutionary Guards, 1980; Friday Prayer Leader, Teheran, 1980; Sec. Gen., and Pres. of Central Cttee, Islamic Republic Party, 1980–87; survived assassination attempt, June 1981; Pres., Islamic Republic of Iran, 1981–89. *Recreations:* reading, art, literature. *Address:* Office of Religious Leader, Tehran, Islamic Republic of Iran.

**KHAMISA, Mohammed Jaffer;** QC 2006; a Recorder, since 2003; Deemster, Isle of Man, since 2017; *b* 16 Feb. 1962; *s* of Isak Ismail and Sugra Khamisa; *m* 1992, Roumana; two *s* one *d. Educ:* City of London Poly. (BA Hons Law). Called to the Bar, Middle Temple, 1985, Bencher, 2010. Partner, Banking and Finance Litigation, Mishcon de Reya LLP, 2015–. Standing Counsel, DTI, 2005–10; Special Advocate, Special Immigration Appeals Commn, 2005–; Chair, Summary Disciplinary Panels, Bar Standards Bd, 2006–12. Chm., Bar Tribunals and Adjudication Service, 2017–. Legal Assessor, GMC, 2007–10; Chm., Phone Standards Authy (formerly Code Compliance Panel), PhonepayPlus, 2014–. *Recreations:* reading, cricket, Rugby, jazz and blues. *Address:* Mishcon de Reya LLP, Africa House, 70 Kingsway, WC2B 6AH.

**KHAN, Akram Hossain,** MBE 2005; dancer and choreographer; Artistic Director, Akram Khan Company, since 2000; *b* 29 July 1974; *s* of Mosharaf Hossain Khan and Anwara Khan. *Educ:* De Montfort Univ. (BA); Northern Sch. of Contemporary Dance (BPA Hons (Dance)). Performed in The Mahabharata, RSC, 1987–89; Associate Artist: RFH, 2003–05; Sadler's Wells Th., 2005–. Principal works include: Loose in Flight, Rush, 2000; Kaash, 2002; ma, 2004; Sacred Monsters, 2006; zero degrees, 2007; Confluence, 2009; Vertical Road, 2010; Gnosis, 2011; DESH, 2012 (Olivier Award for Best New Dance Prodn); iTMOi, 2013; Dust, 2014; (with Israel Galván) Torobaka, 2014; techné, 2015; Until the Lions, 2016, rev. 2019; Giselle, 2016; Chotto Desh, 2017; XENOS, 2018 (Olivier Award for Outstanding Achievement in Dance, 2019; film, XEN, 2019); Outwitting the Devil, Dragon Spring Phoenix Rise, 2019. Guest Artistic Dir, Nat. Youth Dance Co., 2013–. UK Critics' Circle Nat. Dance Award for Best Male Dancer, 2012. Hon. Fellow, Trinity Laban Conservatoire of Music and Dance, 2010. Hon. DArts De Montfort, 2004; Hon. DLitt Roehampton, 2010. *Recreations:* cinema, world music, Rugby. *Address:* Akram Khan Company, Somerset House, New Wing, Strand, WC2R 1LA. *T:* (020) 7354 4333, *Fax:* (020) 7354 5554. *E:* office@akramkhancompany.net.

**KHAN, Prof. Geoffrey Allan,** PhD; FBA 1998; Regius Professor of Hebrew, University of Cambridge, since 2012; *b* 1 Feb. 1958; *s* of Clive and Diana Khan; *m* 1984, Colette Alcock; one *s* one *d. Educ:* Acklam Sixth Form Coll.; SOAS, London Univ. (BA Semitic Langs 1980; PhD 1984). Res. Asst, 1983–87, Res. Associate, 1987–93, Taylor-Schechter Genizah Res. Unit, Cambridge Univ. Liby; Cambridge University: Lectr in Hebrew and Aramaic, 1993–99; Reader in Semitic Philology, 1999–2002; Prof. of Semitic Philology, 2002–12. Fellow, Inst. for Advanced Studies, Jerusalem, 1990–91. Lidzbarski Gold Medal for Semitic Philology, Deutsche Morgenländische Ges., 2004. *Publications:* Studies in Semitic Syntax, 1988; Karaite Bible manuscripts from the Cairo Genizah, 1990; Arabic Papyri: selected material from the Khalili collection, 1992; Arabic Legal and Administrative Documents in the Cambridge Genizah collections, 1993; Bills, Letters and Deeds: Arabic papyri of the 7th–11th centuries, 1993; A Grammar of Neo-Aramaic, 1999; The Early Karaite Tradition of Hebrew Grammatical Thought, 2000; Early Karaite Grammatical Texts, 2000; Exegesis and Grammar in Medieval Karaite Texts, 2001; The Neo-Aramaic Dialect of Qaraqosh, 2002; The Karaite Tradition of Hebrew Grammatical Thought in its Classical Form, 2003; The Jewish Neo-Aramaic Dialect of Sulemaniyya and Halabja, 2004; Arabic Documents from Early Islamic Khurasan, 2007; The Neo-Aramaic Dialect of Barwar, 2008; Neo-Aramaic Dialect Studies, 2008; The Jewish Neo-Aramaic Dialect of Urmi, 2008; The Jewish Neo-Aramaic Dialect of Sanandaj, 2009; A Short Introduction to the Masoretic Hebrew Bible and its Reading Tradition, 2012, 2nd edn 2013; The Neo-Aramaic Dialect of the Assyrian Christians of Urmi, 4 vols, 2016. *Recreations:* mountain-walking, miniature carpentry. *Address:* Faculty of Asian and Middle Eastern Studies, University of Cambridge, Sidgwick Avenue, Cambridge CB3 9DA. *T:* (01223) 335114.

**KHAN, Humayun;** Chairman, Institute of Rural Management, Pakistan; Director, Commonwealth Foundation, 1993–99; *b* 31 Aug. 1932; *s* of K. B. Safdar Khan and Mumtaz Safdar; *m* 1961, Munawar; three *d. Educ:* Bishop Cotton Sch., Simla; Trinity College, Cambridge (MA); Univ. of Southern California (MPA, Dr PA). Called to the Bar, Lincoln's Inn, 1954; joined Pakistan CS, 1955; Sec. to Govt of NWPP, 1970–73; Jt Sec., Pakistan Govt, 1973–74; Minister, Pakistan Embassy, Moscow, 1974–77; Dep. Perm. Rep., UNO, Geneva, 1977–79; Ambassador to Bangladesh, 1979–82; Additional Sec., Min. of Foreign Affairs, Pakistan, 1982–84; Ambassador to India, 1984–88; Foreign Sec. of Pakistan, 1988–89; High Comr in UK, 1990–92. Former Member: Nat. Finance Commn, Pakistan; Bd, Nat. Rural Support Prog., Pakistan. *Publications:* Cross-Border Talks: Diplomatic Divide, 2004. *Recreations:* golf, cricket, shooting, fishing. *Club:* Islamabad.

**KHAN, Idris Ali,** OBE 2017; visual artist, since 2004; *b* Birmingham, 2 Dec. 1978; *s* of Ali Khan and Cheryl Khan; *m* 2009, Annie Morris; one *s* one *d. Educ:* Walsall Coll. of Art and Technol. (BTEC Nat. Dip. Foundn Art and Design 1998); Univ. of Derby (BA 1st Cl. Photography 2000); Royal Coll. of Art, London (MFA with dist. for Res. 2004). Solo *exhibitions* include: City Gall., Leicester, 2000; Q Gall., Derby, 2001; Fraenkel Gall., San Francisco, 2006, 2012; inIVA, London, 2006; Victoria Miro Gall., London, 2006, 2010, 2013, 2015, 2017; Yvon Lambert Gall., Paris, 2006; Yvon Lambert Gall., NY, 2007, 2011; Thomas Schulte Gall., Berlin, 2007, 2012, 2016; K20, Dusseldorf, 2008; Elementa, Dubai, 2009; Kunsthaus Murz, Murzzuschlag, 2009; Espace Culturel Louis Vuitton, Paris, 2009; Göteborgs Konsthall, Gothenburg, 2011; Whitworth Art Gall., Univ. of Manchester, 2012, 2016; Gall. Isabelle van den Eynde, Dubai, 2013; Sean Kelly Gall., NY, 2015; New Art Gall., Walsall, 2017. Commissions include: permanent public art commn, Howick Place, London, 2008; wall drawing, Sadler's Wells Dance House, London, 2011; wall drawing, BM, 2012; stage design for Notations (ballet), Ballett Zürich, 2014; public monument, Abu Dhabi Meml Park, 2016. Work in collections incl.: Arts Council Collection, London; Art Gall. of NSW, Sydney; BM; Centre Pompidou, Paris; de Young Mus., San Francisco; Saatchi Gall., London; San Francisco Mus. of Mod. Art; Solomon R. Guggenheim Mus., NY; Whitworth Art Gall., Manchester. Vis. Lectr, Univ. of Derby, 2003. Hon. DLitt Worcester, 2017. *Publications:* Idris Khan, A World Within, 2017. *Recreations:* theatre, music, reading, running, playing soccer. *Address:* I&A Art Ltd, Unit 2–4, 133 Church Walk, N16 8QW. *E:* info@iandastudio.com. *Club:* Soho House (Founding Mem.).

**KHAN, Imran, (Imran Ahmad Khan Niazi);** Hilal-e-Imtiaz, Pakistan, 1993; Founder, 1997, and Chairman, Pakistan Teehreek-e-Insaf Party; MP (PTI) Mainwali, Pakistan, 2002–07 and since 2018 (Rawalpindi, 2013–18); Prime Minister of Pakistan, since 2018; *b* Lahore, 25 Oct. 1952; *m* 1995, Jemima (marr. diss. 2004), *d* of Sir James Goldsmith; two *s*; *m* 2015, Reham Khan (marr. diss. 2015); *m* 2018, Bushra Wattoo. *Educ:* Aitchison Coll.; Keble Coll., Oxford (BA Hons; cricket blue, 1973, 1974, 1975; Captain, Oxford XI, 1974; Hon. Fellow, 1988). Début for Lahore A, 1969; played first Test for Pakistan, 1970, Captain, 1982–84, 1985–87, 1988–89, 1992; with Worcs CCC, 1971–76 (capped, 1976); with Sussex CCC, 1977–88 (capped, 1978; Hon. Life Mem., 1988). Editor-in-Chief, Cricket Life Internat., 1989–90. Mem., Internat. Cricket Council, 1993. Chancellor, Bradford Univ., 2005–14. Special Sports Rep., UNICEF; Founder, Imran Khan Cancer Appeal (formerly Imran Khan Cancer Hosp. Appeal), 1991–; Chm., Bd of Govs, Shaukat Khanum Memorial Cancer Hosp. and Res. Centre. Pride of Performance Award, Pakistan. *Publications:* Imran, 1983; All-Round View (autobiog.), 1988; Indus Journey, 1990; Warrior Race, 1993; Pakistan: a personal history, 2011. *Recreations:* shooting, films, music.

**KHAN, Javed Akhtar;** Chief Executive, Barnardo's, since 2014; *b* Amersham, Bucks, 31 July 1963; *s of* Raja Jahan Dad Khan and Raj Begum Khan; *m* 1991, Aamirah Hussein; four *d. Educ:* Univ. of Salford (BSc Maths); Didsbury Sch. of Educn (PGCE). Teacher of Maths, Cadbury Sixth Form Coll., 1985–87; Lectr in Maths, 1988–95, Asst Principal, 1995–98, E Birmingham Coll.; Dir of Develt (Further Educn), City Coll., Birmingham, 1998–2000; Asst Dir of Educn, Birmingham CC, 2000–03; Harrow Council: Chief Educn Officer, 2003–06; Dir, Community and Cultural Services, 2006–09; Exec. Dir, London Serious Youth Violence Bd, 2009–10; Chief Exec., Victim Support, 2010–14. Mem., Sentencing Council for England and Wales, 2013–15; Comr, Voluntary Sector and Ageing Commn, 2013–15; Mem., Adv. Bd, Children's Comr for England, 2014–18. Mem., Hounslow CCG, 2013–19. Non-exec. Dir, Royal Brompton and Harefield Hospitals NHS Trust. Member: Exec. Bd, Children's Workforce Develt Council, 2010–13; Bd, Skills for Justice, 2010–14; Bd, Criminal Justice Council, 2010–14; Bd, Victim Support Europe, 2010–14; Public Sector Adv. Bd, Penna, 2015–19; Ind. Grenfell Recovery Task Force, 2016–. Hon. Dr: Birmingham City, 2015; Salford, 2018. Spirit of Britain Award, British Muslim Awards, 2016. *Publications:* (contrib.) Educational Leadership and the Community, 2003. *Recreations:* cricket, current affairs, voluntary work. *Address:* Barnardo's, Tanners Lane, Barkingside, Ilford, Essex IG6 1QG. *E:* javed.khan@barnardos.org.uk.

**KHAN, Karim Asad Ahmad;** QC 2011; barrister; a Recorder, since 2018; *b* Edinburgh, 30 March 1970; *s of* Dr Saeed Ahmad Khan and Selma Khan; three *s. Educ:* Silcoates Sch., Wakefield; King's Coll. London (LLB Hons; AKC); Univ. of Nice (Dip. Internat. Relns); Abo Akademi, Turku Law Sch. (Adv. Dip. Internat. Human Rights Law); Wolfson Coll., Oxford (DPhil candidate). Called to the Bar, Lincoln's Inn, 1992; in practice as a barrister, 1992–; Sen. Crown Prosecutor, CPS, 1992–96; Lawyer: Law Commn of England and Wales, 1996–97; Office of the Prosecutor, UN Internat. Criminal Tribunal for former Yugoslavia and for Rwanda, 1997–2000; defence counsel in numerous internat. criminal cases; Asst Sec. Gen., Special Advr and Hd, Investigative Team to promote Accountability for Da'esh/ISIL Crimes, UN, 2018–. Sen. Res. Fellow, KCL, 1999–2002; Hon. Lectr, Sch. of Law, Univ. of Utrecht, 2010–11, 2012–13; Vis. Prof., Internat. Law and Human Rights, Fourah Bay Coll., Univ. of Sierra Leone, 2017–. Founding Director: Peace and Justice Initiative, 2010–; Global Victims Initiative, 2011–. Member: wkg gp on ICC Act 2001, Criminal Bar Assoc., 2000; Attorney Gen.'s Panel of Prosecution Advocates, 2001–04; Pro Bono Human Rights Panel, FCO, 2002–. International Criminal Tribunal for former Yugoslavia: Chm. Amicus Cttee, 2007–08, Mem., Disciplinary Council, 2007–10, Mem., Exec. Cttee, 2010–11, Assoc. of Defence Counsel; Mem., Disciplinary Bd, 2009–10. Member: Internat. Legal Assistance Consortium, 2008; Disciplinary Appeals Bd, Internat. Criminal Court, The Hague, 2010–; Pres., Internat. Criminal Court Bar Assoc., 2017–. Dr hc Fama University Coll., Pristina, Kosovo, 2012. Co-Editor, Internat. Criminal Law Reports, 2006–. *Publications:* (contrib.) A Commentary to the Rome Statute on the ICC, 2000, 2nd edn 2008; (contrib.) Human Rights Practice, 2002–; (jtly) Archbold International Criminal Courts, 2003, 3rd edn 2009; (contrib.) Security Dimension to EU Enlargement, 2007; (ed jtly and contrib.) Principles of Evidence in International Criminal Justice, 2010. *Recreations:* tennis, driving, shooting, reading, travelling. *Address:* Temple Garden Chambers, 1 Harcourt Buildings, Temple, EC4Y 9DA. *T:* (020) 7583 1315, *Fax:* (020) 7353 3969. *E:* karimahmadkhan@hotmail.com. *Club:* Islamabad (Islamabad).

**KHAN, (Mohammed) Afzal,** CBE 2008; MP (Lab) Manchester Gorton, since 2017; *b* Jhelum, Pakistan, 5 April 1958; *m* Dr Shkeela Kayani; one *s* two *d. Educ:* Abraham Moss Coll.; Manchester Poly. (law degree). Admitted as Solicitor, 1996. Labourer; bus driver; police constable, Gtr Manchester Police, 1987; Sen. Partner, HSK Solicitors; Founder and Partner, Khan Solicitors, 2005–09; Partner, Mellor & Jackson Solicitors, Oldham, 2009–18. Mem. (Lab), Manchester CC, 2000–15; Lord Mayor of Manchester, 2005–06. MEP (Lab) NW Reg., 2014–17. Shadow Minister for Immigration, 2017–. *Address:* House of Commons, SW1A 0AA.

**KHAN, (Muhammad) Imran (Shah);** QC 2018; Partner, Imran Khan and Partners, Solicitors, since 2000; *b* 19 Nov. 1964; *s of* Habib Shah and Khursheed Shah. *Educ:* Univ. of East London (LLB Hons). Trainee Solicitor, Birnberg Pierce, 1989–91; Asst Solicitor, then Partner, J. R. Jones Solicitors, 1991–2000. Council Mem., Law Soc., 2002–03. Vis. Lectr, 2002, Vis. Prof., 2012–, London South Bank Univ. Vice Chm., Nat. Civil Rights Movement, 1999–2004. Trustee: Anne Frank Trust, 2002–06; British Inst. of Human Rights, 2013–. Patron, Law Clinic, UEL, 2013–. Hon. Dr: East London; Staffordshire; DUniv Oxford Brookes, 2000. Lawyer of the Year, Lawyer Mag., 1999. *Address:* Imran Khan and Partners, Lower Ground Floor, Elm Yard, 13–16 Elm Street, WC1X 0BL. *T:* (020) 7404 3004, *Fax:* (020) 7404 3005.

**KHAN, Nicholas Paul;** QC 2018; Legal Adviser, Legal Service, European Commission, since 2013; *b* Dartford, 3 Dec. 1959; *s of* Rafique Khan and Yvonne Khan; *m* 2003, Julia Hummel; two *s. Educ:* Sevenoaks Sch.; Univ. of Southampton (LLB 1982). Called to the Bar, Inner Temple, 1983; Legal Officer, DTI, 1986–88; Legal Service, EC, 1989–99; barrister in private practice, 1999–2003; Legal Service, EC, 2003–. *Publications:* EC and WTO Anti-Dumping Law (jtly), 1997, 2nd edn 2009; EU Anti-Trust Procedure, 5th edn (jtly) 2005, 6th edn 2012. *Recreations:* wine, jazz, avoiding loose paving stones on the streets of Brussels, motor sport. *Address:* Legal Service, European Commission, Berlaymont, 200 Rue de la Loi, 1049 Brussels, Belgium. *T:* (2) 2960420. *Clubs:* Athenæum, East India.

**KHAN, Rosena A.;** *see* Allin-Khan.

**KHAN, Rt Hon. Sadiq (Aman);** PC 2009; Mayor of London (Lab), since 2016; *b* 8 Oct. 1970; *s of* late Amanullah Ahmad Khan and Sehrun Nisa Khan; *m* 1994, Saadiya Ahmad; two *d. Educ:* Ernest Bevin Secondary Comprehensive Sch.; Univ. of N London (LLB Hons 1992); Coll. of Law, Guildford. Christian Fisher Solicitors: trainee solicitor, 1993–95; Solicitor, 1995–98; Partner, 1998–2000; Equity Partner: Christian Fisher Khan Solicitors, 2000–02; and Co-founder, Christian Khan Solicitors, 2002–04. Vis. Lectr, Univ. of N London and London Metropolitan Univ., 1998–2004. Mem. (Lab), Wandsworth BC, 1994–2006; Dep. Leader of Labour Gp, 1996–2001; Hon. Alderman, 2006. MP (Lab) Tooting, 2015–May 2016. PPS to Lord Privy Seal and Leader of H of C, 2007; Govt Whip, 2007–08; Parly Under-Sec. of State, DCLG, 2008–09; Minister of State, DfT, 2009–10; Shadow Sec. of State for Transport, 2010; Shadow Lord Chancellor and Sec. of State for Justice, 2010–15; Shadow Minister for London, 2013–15. Chm., All-Party Parly Gp for Citizens Advice, 2006–08. Chair, Liberty, 2001–04; Founding Mem., Human Rights Lawyers Assoc., 2003. Exec. Mem., Fabian Soc., 2006– (Vice Chair, 2007; Chair, 2008–10); Vice Chair, Legal Action Gp, 1999–2004; Patron, Progress, 2005. *Publications:* Challenging Racism, 2003; Police Misconduct: Legal Remedies, 2005; Fairness not Favours, 2008; Punishment and Reform: how our justice system can help cut crime, 2011. *Recreations:* playing and watching sport, cinema, family, friends, local community. *Address:* Greater London Assembly, City Hall, Queen's Walk, SE1 2AA.

**KHAN, Tahir Zaffar;** QC 2011; a Recorder, since 2004; *b* Bradford, 25 April 1964; *s of* Muzaffar Khan and Khadija Begum; *m* 1988, Samina Tahir; two *s* one *d. Educ:* Liverpool Poly. (LLB Hons Law); Inns of Court Sch. of Law. Called to the Bar, Lincoln's Inn, 1986. *Recreations:* playing tennis for Bingley Tennis Club, enjoy playing badminton, avid reader. *Address:* Broadway House Chambers, 9 Bank Street, Bradford, West Yorks BD1 1TW. *T:* (01274) 722560, *Fax:* (01274) 370708. *E:* clerks@broadwayhouse.co.uk.

**KHAN, Wajid;** Member (Lab) North West Region, European Parliament, 2017–19; *b* Burnley, 15 Oct. 1979. *Educ:* Univ. of Central Lancashire (LLB 2002; LLM Eur. Law 2004). MV Co-ordinator for E Lancs, 2005, Lectr in Volunteering and Community Action, 2006–, Univ. of Central Lancashire. Mem. (Lab) Burnley BC, 2007–. Contested (Lab) NW Reg., EP, 2019.

**KHANBHAI, Bashir Yusufali Simba;** Member (C) Eastern Region, England, European Parliament, 1999–2004; *b* 22 Sept. 1945; *s of* Yusufali Simba Khanbhai and Jenambai Khanbhai; *m* 1981, Maria Bashir Khanbhai (*née* Da Silva); one *s. Educ:* Sch. of Pharmacy, Univ. of London (BPharm Hons 1966); Balliol Coll., Oxford (MA Hons PPE 1969). Manufg industry, export and finance, 1970–97; Chief Executive Officer: Headlands Chemicals Ltd, 1970–76; Khanbhai Industries Ltd, 1977–84; Teqny Ltd, 1984–99. *Publications:* (ed) The Jowett Papers, 1970. *Recreations:* tennis, travel, theatre, music, food. *Address:* 20 Burntwood Road, Sevenoaks, Kent TN13 1PT. *E:* emailbashir@gmail.com.

**KHARAS, Dame Zarine,** DBE 2015; Joint Founder and Chief Executive Officer, JustGiving.com, since 1999; *b* Pakistan, 14 June 1951. *Educ:* Karachi Grammar Sch.; Girton Coll., Cambridge (BA Hons Law 1973). Articled clerk, Middleton Lewis; lawyer with Lawrence Graham, then Linklaters & Paines; Mem., Asia Pacific Team, Credit Suisse First Boston, 1984–91; lawyer, Simmons & Simmons, 1991–94; Exec. Dir, MC Securities, 1995–97; Man. Dir, Ceba Ltd, 1997–99. Albert Medal, RSA, 2019. *Address:* JustGiving, Blue Fin Building, 2nd Floor, 110 Southwark Street, SE1 0TA.

**KHARCHENKO, Ihor,** PhD; Ambassador of Ukraine to Japan, since 2013; *b* 15 May 1962; *s of* Yuri and Raiisa; *m* 1986, Maria Rozhytsina; two *d. Educ:* Taras Shevchenko Kyiv State Univ. (Internat. Relns; PhD History). Lectr, then Asst Prof., Taras Shevchenko Kyiv State Univ., 1988–92; Ministry of Foreign Affairs, Ukraine: Policy Planning Staff, 1992–93; Dir, Policy Planning Staff, 1993–97; Ambassador-at-Large, Hd of Secretariat of Pres. of UN Gen. Assembly and Dep. Perm. Rep. of Ukraine to the UN, NY, 1997–98; Ambassador of Ukraine to Romania, 1998–2000; Dep. Foreign Minister of Ukraine, 2000–03; Special Rep. of Pres. of Ukraine to the Balkans, 2001–03; Ambassador of Ukraine to Poland, 2003–05; Ambassador of Ukraine to the Court of St James's, 2005–10; Perm. Rep. of Ukraine to Internat. Maritime Orgn, 2006–11; Special Rep. of Ukraine on Transdniestrian Settlement, 2010–13. Order of Merit (Ukraine), 2002. *Recreations:* family, literature, music. *Address:* 3–5–31 Nishi-Azabu, Minato-ku, Tokyo 106–0031, Japan.

**KHARE, Prof. Chandrashekhar Bhalchandra,** PhD; FRS 2012; Professor of Mathematics, University of California, Los Angeles, since 2007; *b* Mumbai, 1967; *m* Rajanigandha; one *s* one *d. Educ:* Trinity Coll., Cambridge (BA Maths 1989); Calif Inst. of Technol. (PhD 1995). Vis. Fellow, 1995–96, Fellow, 1996–2001, Associate Prof., 2001–07, Tata Inst. of Fundamental Res., Mumbai; Associate Prof. of Maths, Univ. of Utah, 2005–07. Guggenheim Fellow, 2008. Fermat Prize, 2007; Infosys Prize in Math. Scis, 2010; (jtly) Frank Nelson Cole Prize in Number Theory, Amer. Math. Soc., 2011. *Address:* Mathematics Department, University of California, Los Angeles, PO Box 951555, Los Angeles, CA 90095–1555, USA.

**KHATAMI, Hojjatoleslam Seyed Mohammad;** President of the Islamic Republic of Iran, 1997–2005; *b* 29 Sept. 1943; *s of* Ayatollah Sayyid Ruhollah Khatami, religious scholar; *m* 1974, Zohreh Sadeghi; one *s* two *d. Educ:* High Sch.; Qom Theol. Sch.; Isfahan Univ. (BA Philosophy); Tehran Univ. (MA); Qom Seminary. Head, Hamburg Islamic Centre, Germany, 1979; Mem. for Ardakan and Maybod, first Islamic Consultative Assembly, 1980–82; Dep. Hd of Jt Comd of Armed Forces, and Chm., War Propaganda HQ, Iran-Iraq War, 1980–88; Dir, Keyhan Newspaper Inst., 1981; Minister of Culture and Islamic Guidance, 1982–92; Advr to Pres. Rafsanjani, 1992–96. Mem., High Council for Cultural Revolution, 1996. Chm., 8th Session, Islamic Summit Conf., 1997–2000. *Publications:* From the World of the City to the City of the World, 1994; Fear of Wave, 1997; Faith and Thought Trapped by Despotism; contrib. articles to Arabic mags and newspapers.

**KHAW, Prof. Kay-Tee, (Mrs Kay-Tee Fawcett),** CBE 2003; FRCP; Professor of Clinical Gerontology, University of Cambridge, 1989–2018, now Emeritus; Fellow, Gonville and Caius College, Cambridge, since 1991; *b* 14 Oct. 1950; *d of* Khaw Kai Boh and Tan Chwee Geok; *m* 1980, Prof. James William Fawcett, *qv*; one *s* one *d. Educ:* Girton Coll., Cambridge (BA, MA; MB BChir); St Mary's Hosp. Med. Sch., London; London Sch. of Hygiene and Tropical Med. (MSc). MRCP 1977, FRCP 1993; DCH 1978; MFPHM 1993. LTCL 1969. Wellcome Trust Research Fellow, LSHTM, St Mary's Hosp. and Univ. of California San Diego, 1979–84; Asst Adjunct Prof., Univ. of California Sch. of Med., San Diego, 1985; Sen. Registrar in Community Medicine, Univ. of Cambridge Sch. of Clinical Medicine, 1986–89. Member: NHS Central R&D Cttee, 1991–97; HEFCE, 1992–97; MRC Health Services and Public Health Res. Bd, 1999–2003; MRC Cross Bd Gp, 2001–05. Chair: Nutrition Forum, Food Standards Agency, 2002–09; World Heart Fedn Council on Epidemiology and Prevention, 2008–12 (Vice-Chair, 2002–07); Med. Protection Soc., 2012–. FMedSci 1999. Daland Fellow, Amer. Philosophical Soc., 1984. Trustee: Help the Aged, 1993–98; BHF, 2006–14. *Publications:* contribs to scientific jls on chronic disease epidemiology. *Address:* Clinical Gerontology Unit, Box 251, University of Cambridge School of Clinical Medicine, Addenbrooke's Hospital, Cambridge CB2 2QQ.

**KHAW, Prof. Sir Peng Tee,** Kt 2013; PhD; FRCS, FRCP, FRCOphth; FRCPath; FMedSci; CBiol, FRSB, FCOptom; Professor of Glaucoma and Ocular Healing, UCL Institute of Ophthalmology, since 1997; Consultant Ophthalmic Surgeon, Moorfields Eye Hospital, since 1993; Director: National Institute for Health Research Biomedical Research Centre in Ophthalmology, Moorfields Eye Hospital and UCL Institute of Ophthalmology, since 2007; Research and Development, Moorfields Eye Hospital, since 2008; Programme Director, Eyes and Vision, UCL Partners, Academic Health Science Centre, since 2009; *b* 1957; *m. Educ:* Southampton Univ. (BM 1980); Royal Coll. of Surgeons (DO 1985); Univ. of London (PhD Cell and Molecular Biol. Healing 1994). MRCP 1983, FRCP 1999; FRCSGlas 1985; FRCOphth 1989; FRCS 1996; CBiol 2000; FRSB (FIBiol 2000); FRCPath 2002; FCOptom 2011. SHO, then Registrar, Southampton Eye Hosp., 1981–85; Lectr in Ophthalmol., Southampton Eye Hosp. and Univ. of Southampton, 1985–87; Sen. Registrar, Moorfields Eye Hosp., 1987–89; Wellcome Trust Res. Fellow, 1989–92; Wellcome Trust Res. Fellow and Vis. Faculty, Inst. for Wound Res., Univ. of Florida, 1991–92; Wellcome Vision Res. Fellow, Inst. of Ophthalmol., UCL, 1992–93. FMedSci 2002; Fellow, ARVO, 2010 (Pres.), 2013; Gold Fellow 2014). Hon. DSc Anglia Ruskin, 2012. *Publications:* (jtly) ABC of Eyes, 1988, 4th edn 2003; (jtly) Ophthalmology Revision Aid, 1989, 2nd edn 1995; (ed with R. Pitts-Crick) Textbook of Clinical Ophthalmology, 1997, 2nd edn 2000; (jtly) Ophthalmology: clinical examination techniques, 1999; (jtly) Eye Disease in Clinical Practice: a concise clinical atlas, 2000; (with I. Russell-Eggitt) Glaucoma in Babies and Children: a guide for parents, 2004, 2nd edn 2008; The Moorfields Manual, 2007, 2nd edn 2014; some 450 pubns as papers, books, chapters and articles in jls. *Address:* UCL Institute of Ophthalmology and Moorfields Eye Hospital, 11–43 Bath Street, EC1V 9EL. *T:* and *Fax:* (020) 7608 6887. *E:* p.khaw@ucl.ac.uk.

**KHAYAT, His Honour Georges Mario;** QC 1992; a Circuit Judge, 2002–11; *b* 15 Aug. 1941; *s* of Fred Khayat and Julie Germain. *Educ:* Terra Sancta Coll., Nazareth; Prior Park Coll., Bath. Called to the Bar, Lincoln's Inn, 1967. A Recorder, 1987–2002. Head of Chambers, 1999–2002. Chm., Surrey and S London Bar Mess, 1995–98. *Recreations:* horse riding, reading, boating, music. *Address:* 2 Stephen Weiss, Haifa, Israel.

**KHEMKA, Dame Asha,** DBE 2014 (OBE 2009); DL; Principal and Chief Executive, West Nottinghamshire College Group, 2006–18; *b* Sitamarhi, India; *d* of late Mr and Mrs Agarwal; *m* 1967, Shankar Lal Khemka; two *s* one *d*. *Educ:* NE Wales Inst. of Higher Educn (BEd Hons, Cert Ed Cardiff Univ.). Lectr, Oswestry Coll., 1987–95; Dir of Quality and Dep. Hd of Faculty, Tamworth Coll., 1995–2001; Asst Principal, Stafford Coll., 2001–04; Dep. Principal, New Coll., Nottingham, 2004–06. Associate Inspector, Ofsted, 1996–2005. Member: Bd, Educn and Trng Foundn; Bd, D2N2 LEP; Educn Hons Cttee; Bd, Assoc. of Colls (Chair: Quality and Perf. Cttee; Assoc. of Colls India); Council, Univ. of Nottingham, 2009–; Bd. Inst. for Apprenticeships, 2017–19. Founder and Trustee, Inspire and Achieve Foundn, 2008–. DL Staffs, 2017. Dadabhai Naoroji Award for Educn, 2014; Asian Businesswoman of the Year, Asian Business Awards, 2017. *Recreations:* travel, cinema, music, entertaining.

**KHERAJ, Naguib;** Senior Adviser, Aga Khan Development Network, since 2010; *b* London, 15 July 1964; *m* Nina Hirji Kheraj; one *s*. *Educ:* Dulwich Coll.; Robinson Coll., Cambridge (MA Econs 1990). Dir, Investment Banking, then Man. Dir and Chief Financial Officer, Salomon Bros, London, 1986–96; with Robert Fleming, 1996–97; with Barclays plc, 1997–2007: Chief Operating Officer, Investment Banking Div.; Global Hd of Investment Banking; Dep. Chm., Asset Mgt; Chief Exec., Private Clients; Gp Finance Dir, 2004–07; Sen. Advr, 2007; Dir and Mem., Gp Exec. Cttee; CEO, JPMorgan Cazenove Ltd, 2008–10; Vice Chm., Barclays Bank plc, 2011–12. Non-exec. Dir, NHS Commng Bd, 2012–13; Independent Director: Standard Chartered PLC, 2014– (Sen. Ind. Dir, 2015–18; Dep. Chm., 2016–); Rothesay Life, 2014– (Chm., 2017–). Mem., Investment Cttee, Wellcome Trust, 2008–19; Mem., Finance Cttee, OUP, 2017–. Mem., Bd of Govs, Inst. of Ismaili Studies, 1995–; Trustee: Aga Khan Univ., 2008–; Univ. of Central Asia, 2017–.

**KHILNANI, Prof. Sunil,** PhD; Avantha Professor and Director, India Institute, King's College London, since 2011; *b* New Delhi, India, 28 Dec. 1960; *s* of Khemchand and Umadevi Khilnani; *m* 2004, Katherine Boo. *Educ:* British Sch., New Delhi; Edinburgh Acad.; Trinity Hall, Cambridge (MA Social and Pol Scis); King's Coll., Cambridge (PhD Social and Pol Scis 1989). Res. Fellow, Christ's Coll., Cambridge, 1987–89; Lectr, 1989–95, Sen. Lectr, 1995–98, Reader, 1998–2000, Prof., 2000–02, Birkbeck Coll., Univ. of London; Starr Foundn Prof., and Dir, S Asian Studies, Johns Hopkins Univ., Washington, 2002–11. Vis. Prof., Princeton Univ., 2017–. Fellow: Woodrow Wilson Center for Internat. Scholars, Washington, 2001–02; Inst. for Advanced Studies, Berlin, 2006–07; American Acad., Berlin, 2010–11. *Publications:* Arguing Revolution: the intellectual left in postwar France, 1993; The Idea of India, 1997, 20th Anniv. edn 2017; Incarnations: a history of India in fifty lives, 2016. *Recreations:* music (all kinds), idling, finding vegetables with real taste. *Address:* 37 Roupell Street, SE1 8TB; 1501 6th Street NW, Washington, DC 20001, USA; King's India Institute, King's College London, Strand, WC2R 2LS. *E:* sunilkhilnani@gmail.com. *Clubs:* Groucho, Brooks's.

**KHIYAMI, Dr Sami Madani;** Ambassador of the Syrian Arab Republic to the Court of St James's, 2004–12; independent consultant in technology and public diplomacy, since 2013; *b* Damascus, 28 Aug. 1948; *s* of Dr Madani and Jamila Khiyami; *m* 1978, Yamina Farhan; one *s* two *d*. *Educ:* American Univ. of Beirut (BE 1972); Univ. of Claude Bernard, Lyons, France (Dip. Electronics 1974; PhD 1979). Asst, Faculty of Mech. and Electrical Engrg, Damascus Univ., 1972–73; with Siemens-Karlsruhe, Germany, 1972–74; Asst Prof., Univ. of Damascus, and researcher and gp leader, Scientific Studies and Res. Centre, Damascus, 1979–85; Prof. of Computer Engrg and Electronic Measurements, Univ. of Damascus, 1985–94; Higher Institute of Applied Sciences and Technology, Damascus: Hd, Electronics Dept, Chief Researcher, then Dir of Res., 1986–95; Actg Dir, 1993; Vice-Dir for Res., 1993–95. Consultant, Systems Internat., Syria, 1993–94; Nat. Telecom and Technol. Consultant, 1999–2002. Board Member: Syrian Arab Airlines, 2004; Spacetel, 2004. Co-founder and Dir, Syrian Computer Soc., 1989. *Publications:* Electronic Measurements and Measuring Devices, 1982; Microprocessors and Microprocessor Based Systems, 1982; Algorithms and Data Structures, 1983; numerous contribs to scientific reviews on technol. and related econ. policies, IT and telecom strategies; articles, studies and initiatives towards a solution of the Syrian crisis. *Recreations:* philately, gardening, music.

**KHOKHAR, Mushtaq Ahmed; His Honour Judge Khokhar;** a Circuit Judge, since 2006; *b* 2 Feb. 1956; *s* of Yousaf and Sakina Khokhar; *m* 1991, Dr Ramla Mumtaz; two *s*. *Educ:* Leeds Poly. (BA Hons Law 1980); Queen Mary Coll., London (LLM 1981). Called to the Bar, Lincoln's Inn, 1982; Asst Recorder, 1998–2000; a Recorder, 2000–06. Standing Counsel to HM Customs and Excise, then HMRC, 2001–06. *Recreations:* watching cricket and football, sudoku, walking, theatre, eating out, reading biographies, playing snooker and squash. *Address:* Manchester Crown Court, Minshull Street, Manchester M1 3FS.

**KHUSH, Dr Gurdev Singh,** FRS 1995; consultant to Director General, International Rice Research Institute, Philippines, 2001–04 (Principal Plant Breeder, and Head, Division of Plant Breeding, Genetics and Biochemistry, 1989–2001); *b* 22 Aug. 1935; *s* of Kartar Singh and Pritam Kaur; *m* 1961, Harwant Kaur Grewal; one *s* three *d*. *Educ:* Punjab Univ., Chandigarh, India (BScAgri); Univ. of Calif, Davis (PhD Genetics 1960). University of California, Davis: Research Asst, 1957–60; Asst Geneticist, 1960–67; International Rice Research Institute, Philippines: Plant Breeder, 1967–72; Head, Dept of Plant Breeding, 1972–89. Adjunct Prof., Dept of Plant Scis (formerly Vegetable Crops), Univ. of Calif., Davis, 2003–. Hon. DSc: Punjab Agricl, 1987; Tamil Nadu Agricl, 1995; C. S. Azad Univ. of Agric. and Technol., 1995; G. B. Pant Univ. of Agric. and Technol., 1996; De Montfort, 1998; Cambridge, 2000; ND Univ. of Agric. and Technol., 2003. Borlaug Award in Plant Breeding, Coromandel Fertilizers Ltd, India, 1977; Japan Prize, Japan Sci. and Technol. Foundn, 1987; Fellows Award 1989, Internat. Agronomy Award 1990, Amer. Soc. of Agronomy; Emil M. Mrak Internat. Award, Univ. of California, Davis, 1990; World Food Prize, World Food Prize Foundn, 1996; Rank Prize, Rank Prize Funds, 1998; Wolf Prize, Wolf Foundn, Israel, 2000; UC Davis Medal, 2018. *Publications:* Cytogenetics of Aneuploids, 1973; Host Plant Resistance to Insects, 1995; *edited:* Rice Biotechnology, 1991; Nodulation and Nitrogen Fixation in Rice, 1992; Apomix: exploiting hybrid vigor in rice, 1994; Rice Genetics III, 1996; Rice Genetics IV, 2001; contrib. chapters in books; numerous papers in jls. *Recreation:* reading world history. *Address:* 39399 Blackhawk Place, Davis, CA 95616–7008, USA.

**KIBAKI, Mwai;** President (Nat. Rainbow Coalition, 2002–07, Party of National Unity, 2007–13), and Commander in Chief of the Armed Forces, Kenya, 2002–13; UNESCO Goodwill Ambassador of Water in Africa, since 2014; *b* Othaya, Kenya, 1931; *m* 1962, Lucy Muthoni (*d* 2016); three *s* one *d*. *Educ:* Makerere UC (BA); London Sch. of Econs (BSc Econs). Lectr in Econs, Makerere UC, 1959–60; Nat. Exec. Officer, Kenya African Nat. Union (KANU), 1960–64; Kenyan Rep. to E African Legislative Assembly of E African Common Services Orgn, 1962; Mem. (KANU) Nairobi Doonholm, House of Reps, 1963–74; Parly Sec. to Treasury, 1963–64; Asst Minister of Econ. Planning and Develt, 1964–66; Minister: for Commerce and Industry, 1966–69; of Finance, 1969–70; of Finance and Econ. Planning, 1970–78; of Finance, 1978–82; of Home Affairs, 1978–88; of Health, 1988–91; Vice Pres. of Kenya, 1978–88; Leader, Official Opposition, 1998–2002. Vice-Pres., KANU, 1978–91; Leader: Democratic Party, 1991–2002; Party of Nat. Unity, 2008. Chief of the Golden Heart (Kenya), 2002. *Recreations:* reading, golf.

**KIBASI, Thomas;** Director, Institute for Public Policy Research, since 2016; *b* London, 3 Feb. 1982; *s* of Kahtan Kibasi and Barbara Kibasi. *Educ:* Haberdashers' Aske's Sch.; Trinity Coll., Cambridge (MA Historical Studies). Policy Advr, DoH, 2006–08; McKinsey and Company, 2009–16, Partner, 2012–16. *Recreations:* church music, art, Georgian architecture, history. *Address:* Institute for Public Policy Research, 14 Buckingham Street, WC2N 6DF. *E:* tom.kibasi@ippr.org.

**KIDD, Charles William;** Consultant Editor, Debrett's Peerage and Baronetage, 2015–18 (Editor, 1980–2015); *b* 23 May 1952; *yr s* of late Charles Vincent Kidd and Marian Kidd, BEM (*née* Foster), Kirkbymoorside. *Educ:* St Peter's Sch., York; Bede Coll., Durham. Assistant Editor: Burke's Peerage, 1972–77; Debrett's Peerage and Baronetage, 1977–80. Mem., Friends of Margravine Cemetery. FSG 2000. *Publications:* Debrett's Book of Royal Children (jtly), 1982; Debrett Goes to Hollywood, 1986; articles in Genealogists' Mag. *Recreations:* cinema, researching film and theatre dynasties.

**KIDD, Prof. Colin Craig,** DPhil; FBA 2010; FRSE; Wardlaw Professor of Modern History, University of St Andrews, since 2012; *b* Ayr, 5 May 1964; *s* of George Kidd and Rine Kidd; *m* 1988, Lucy Isabelle Armstrong; one *s* one *d*. *Educ:* Glasgow Acad.; Gonville and Caius Coll., Cambridge (BA 1985); Univ. of Oxford (DPhil 1992). Vis. Choate Fellow, Harvard Univ., 1985–86; Fellow, All Souls Coll., Oxford, 1987–94; Lectr, then Reader, 1994–2003, Prof. of Modern Hist., 2003–10, Univ. of Glasgow; Prof. of Intellectual History and Political Thought, QUB, 2010–12. Fifty-pound Fellow, All Souls Coll., Oxford, 2005–19. Gov., Glasgow Acad., 2002–08. FRSE 2002. *Publications:* Subverting Scotland's Past, 1993; British Identities Before Nationalism, 1999; The Forging of Races, 2006; Union and Unionisms, 2008; The World of Mr Casaubon, 2016; (ed jtly) Literature and Union: Scottish texts, British contexts, 2018. *Recreations:* Watergate, Galloway. *Address:* School of History, University of St Andrews, St Katharine's Lodge, The Scores, St Andrews, Fife KY16 9BA.

**KIDD, Hon. Sir Douglas (Lorimer),** KNZM 2009 (DCNZM 2000); Member, Waitangi Tribunal, since 2004; Speaker, House of Representatives, New Zealand, 1996–99; District Licensing Commissioner, Wellington City Council, since 2013; *b* 12 Sept. 1941; *s* of Lorimer Edward Revington Kidd and Jessie Jean Kidd (*née* Mottershead); *m* 1964, Jane Stafford Richardson; one *s* two *d*. *Educ:* Ohau Primary Sch.; Horowhenua Coll.; Victoria Univ., Wellington (LLB 1964). Mil. service, Territorial Service, Royal Regt of NZ Artillery, 1960–64. Admitted Barrister and Solicitor, 1964; Partner, Wisheart Macnab & Partners, 1964–78. MP (N) Marlborough, 1978–96, Kaikoura, 1996–99; List MP (N), 1999–2002. Minister of Fisheries, 1990–93, and of State-Owned Enterprises, 1990–91; Associate Minister of Finance, 1990–94; Minister of Maori Affairs, 1991–94; Minister of Energy and Fisheries, 1993–96; Minister of Accident Rehabilitation and Compensation, 1994–96. Chairman: Cabinet Revenue and Expenditure Cttee; Regulations Rev. Select Cttee, 1999–2002; Ministerial Aquaculture Review Cttee, 2009; Joint Chm., Parly Appropriations Review Cttee, 2010; Mem., Privileges and Maori Affairs Select Cttee, 1999–2002. Mem., Commonwealth Observer Gp, Pakistan Federal and Provincial Elections, 2002; Chm., Commonwealth Election Monitoring Mission to Pakistan, 2013. Dir and Partner, plantation forestry, marine farming and wine co. ventures, Marlborough, 1968–94. Hon. Mem., Canterbury/Nelson/Marlborough/W Coast Regt, 1980–97 (Hon. Col, 1997–2003). CGS's Commendation for outstanding service to NZ Army, 1999. NZ Commemoration Medal, 1990; NZ Defence Service Medal (Territorial), 2011. *Recreations:* walking, fishing, reading, travel. *Club:* Marlborough (Blenheim).

**KIDD, (John Christopher William) Matthew,** CMG 2017; HM Diplomatic Service, retired; High Commissioner, Cyprus, 2010–14 and 2016–18; *b* Aberystwyth, 4 Feb. 1957; *s* of Captain John Franklin Kidd, RN and Gwenllian Anne Kidd (*née* Lewes); *m* 1995, Carine Celia Ann (*née* Coldwell), *widow of* Sir Richard John Maitland, 9th Bt; twin *d* and one step *s* one step *d*. *Educ:* Winchester Coll.; Jesus Coll., Oxford (BA). Entered FCO, 1978; Asst Desk Officer, S Asian Dept, 1978–79; Third, later Second Sec., Nicosia, 1980–83; UKMIS NY, 1983; Private Sec. to Ambassador to France, 1984–86; Head of Section: Western Eur. Dept, FCO, 1986–87; Security Policy Dept, FCO, 1987–90; Dep. Hd of Mission, Addis Ababa, 1990–93; Dep. Hd, Far Eastern and Pacific Dept, FCO, 1993–94; Dep. Hd, later Actg Hd, Policy Planning Staff, FCO, 1994–96; on secondment to Eur. Commn as Foreign Policy Advr, 1996–98; Head: Political and Public Affairs Section, Bonn, then Berlin, 1998–2001; Whitehall Liaison Dept, FCO, 2001–04; Dep. Perm. Rep., UK Delegn to NATO, 2004–08; Sec. Gen.'s Special Rep. for HQ Reform, NATO (on secondment), 2008–09; Dir, Mediterranean Migration, FCO, 2015.
*See also C. A. Maitland.*

**KIDD, Paul Ashley;** Head of Financial Services, Royal Borough of Kensington and Chelsea, 2008–11; *b* Gravesend, 6 Sept. 1951; *s* of Ronald William and Marion Kidd; *m* 1975, Jennifer Davies; one *s*. *Educ:* York Univ. (BA Hons Social Sci.). CPFA 1976. London Borough of Croydon: Finance trainee, 1973–75; Sen. Accountant, 1976–78; Royal Borough of Kensington and Chelsea: Sen. Accountant, 1978–81; Principal Accountant, 1981–82; Asst Chief Accountant, 1982–88; Chief Accountant, 1988–91; Hd, Accountancy Services, 1991–95; Hd, Financial Services, 1995–2008. *Recreations:* walking, gardening, DIY, digital photography, visiting France, sport (watching not playing), music (listening and playing badly), films, running local community cinema, reading.

**KIDDLE, Ven. John;** Archdeacon of Wandsworth, since 2015; *b* 28 June 1958. *Educ:* Monkton Combe Sch., Bath; Ridley Hall, Cambridge; Queens' Coll., Cambridge (MA 1983); Heythrop Coll., London (MTh 2002). Maths Teacher, Bacon's C of E Sch., Bermondsey, 1980–81; ordained deacon, 1982, priest, 1983; Curate, St Peter and St Paul, Ormskirk, 1982–86; Vicar: St Gabriel, Huyton Quarry, Liverpool, 1986–91; St Luke, Watford, 1991–2008; Rural Dean, Watford, 1999–2004; Hon. Canon, 2005–10, Canon Residentiary, 2010–15, St Albans Cathedral; Diocesan Officer for Mission and Develt, 2008–15, Dir of Mission, 2011–15, Diocese of St Albans. *Publications:* (contrib.) Ready Steady Slow: thoughts for advent, 2010; (contrib.) Reflections for Daily Prayer, 2011. *Address:* 620 Kingston Road, Raynes Park, SW20 8DN. *T:* (020) 8545 2440.

**KIDGELL, John Earle,** CB 2003; consultant in economic statistics; Director of Economic Statistics, Office for National Statistics (formerly Head of Economic Accounts Division, Central Statistical Office), 1994–2002 (Grade 3, 1988–2002); *b* 18 Nov. 1943; *s* of Gilbert James Kidgell and Cicely Alice (*née* Earle); *m* 1968, Penelope Jane Tarry; one *s* two *d*. *Educ*: Eton House Sch., Southend-on-Sea; Univ. of St Andrews (MA); London School of Economics and Political Science (MSc). NIESR, 1967–70; Gallup Poll, 1970–72; Statistician, CSO and Treasury, 1972–79; Chief Statistician, DoE, 1979–86; Hd of Finance Div., PSA, 1986–88; Head of Directorate D, Central Statistical Office, 1989–91. *Publications*: articles in Nat. Inst. Econ. Rev., Econ. Trends, etc. *Recreations*: hill walking, tennis, golf, reading.

**KIDMAN, Nicole Mary,** AC 2006; actress; *b* Hawaii, 20 June 1967; *d* of late Dr Antony David Kidman, AM and of Janelle Ann Kidman (*née* Glenny); *m* 1990, Tom Cruise (*see* T. Cruise Mapother) (marr. diss. 2001); one adopted *s* one adopted *d*; *m* 2006, Keith Urban; two *d*. *Educ*: N Sydney High Sch. Worked at Phillip Street Th., Sydney. *TV mini-series*: Vietnam, 1986; Bangkok Hilton, 1989; *TV series*: Big Little Lies, 2017 (Outstanding Lead Actress, Emmy Awards, 2017; Best Actress, Golden Globe Awards, 2018), 2019; Top of the Lake, 2017; *theatre*: The Blue Room, Donmar Warehouse, 1998, NY 1999; Photograph 51, Noël Coward Th., 2015; *films include*: Bush Christmas, 1983; Dead Calm, 1989; Days of Thunder, 1990; Billy Bathgate, 1991; Far and Away, Flirting, 1992; Malice, My Life, 1993; Batman Forever, To Die For, 1995; The Portrait of a Lady, 1996; The Peacemaker, 1997; Practical Magic, Eyes Wide Shut, 1999; Moulin Rouge, The Others, 2001; Birthday Girl, 2002; The Hours (Academy and BAFTA Awards for best actress, 2003), The Human Stain, Cold Mountain, 2003; Dogville, The Stepford Wives, Birth, 2004; The Interpreter, Bewitched, 2005; Fur: An Imaginary Portrait of Diane Arbus, The Invasion, The Golden Compass, 2007; Margot at the Wedding, Australia, 2008; Nine, 2009; Rabbit Hole, 2010; Hemingway & Gellhorn (TV film), 2012; The Paperboy, Stoker, 2013; The Railway Man, Grace of Monaco, Before I Go to Sleep, Paddington, 2014; Queen of the Desert, 2015; Genius, Secret in their Eyes, Lion, 2016; The Beguiled, The Killing of a Sacred Deer, 2017; How to Talk to Girls at Parties, Aquaman, 2018; The Upside, Destroyer, Boy Erased, The Goldfinch, 2019; prod., In the Cut, 2003. *Address*: c/o 42West, 1840 Century Park East, Suite 700, Los Angeles, CA 90067, USA.

**KIDNER, Rear-Adm. Peter Jonathan,** CEng, FRAeS; Chief Executive, Defence Medical Education and Training Agency (formerly Defence Medical Training Organisation), 2002–04; *b* 21 July 1949; *s* of Col Peter Kidner and Patricia (*née* Bunyard); *m* 1973, Jean Caley; one *s* one *d*. *Educ*: Sherborne Sch.; RNEC (BSc). CEng 1992; FRAeS 1995. Air Engineer Officer: 849 B Flight, HMS Ark Royal, 1975–76; 899 Sqn, 1981; Dir, Helicopter Support, 1997–2000; CO, HMS Sultan, 2000–02. Local Corresp., Open Spaces Soc., 2007–; Mem., Ramblers' Assoc. *Recreations*: walking, Dolomites.

**KIDNEY, David Neil;** Chief Executive, UK Public Health Register, since 2013; *b* 21 March 1955; *s* of Neil Bernard Kidney and Doris Kidney; *m* 1978, Elaine Dickinson; one *s* one *d*. *Educ*: Bristol Univ. (LLB). Solicitor in private practice, Kenneth Wainwright & Co., then Wainwrights, subseq. Jewels & Kidney, 1977–91, Partner, 1983–97. Mem. (Lab) Stafford BC, 1987–97. Contested (Lab) Stafford, 1992. MP (Lab) Stafford, 1997–2010; contested (Lab) same seat, 2010. Team PPS, DEFRA, 2002–03; Parly Under-Sec. of State, DECC, 2009–10. Hd of Policy, Chartered Inst. of Envmtl Health, 2010–13. *Recreations*: bridge, chess.

**KIDRON, Baroness** *cr* 2012 (Life Peer), of Angel in the London Borough of Islington; **Beeban Kidron,** OBE 2012; film director, since 1982; *b* 2 May 1961; *d* of late Michael Kidron and of Nina Kidron; one *s* one *d*; *m* 2003, Lee Hall, *qv*. *Educ*: Camden Sch. for Girls; Nat. Film and Television Sch. Maker of films, documentaries, TV drama and features, 1982–: director: *television* includes: Oranges are not the Only Fruit, 1989; Antonia and Jane, 1990; Itch, 1991; Great Moments in Aviation, 1993; Texarkana, 1998; Cinderella, 2000; Murder, 2002; *documentaries*: Carry Greenham Home, 1983; Hookers Hustlers Pimps and their Johns, 1993; Eve Arnold in Retrospect, 1996; Antony Gormley: Making Space, 2007; Storyville: Sex, Death and the Gods, 2011; In Real Life, 2013; *films*: Vroom, 1990; Used People, 1992; To Wong Foo Thanks for Everything, Julie Newmar, 1995; Swept from the Sea, 1997; Bridget Jones: The Edge of Reason, 2004; producer, film, Victoria and Abdul, 2017. Member: Directors Guild of America, 1990–; Directors UK; Acad. of Motion Picture Scis, 1992–; Council, ICA, 2011–16. Comr, UNESCO Broadband Commn for Sustainable Develt, 2016–; Member: Royal Foundn Taskforce for Prevention of Cyberbullying, 2016–; Children's Comr for England Taskforce on Growing Up Digital, 2016. Trustee: UK Film Council, 2008–10; Paul Hamlyn Foundn, 2011–15. Co-Founder, Into Film (formerly Film Club Educnl Charity), 2008 (Vice Chm., 2008), Gov., BFI, 2010–13. Vis. Fellow, LMH, Oxford, 2016–19. Hon. DEd Kingston, 2010; Hon. LittD UEA, 2015. *Recreations*: eating, reading, buying old crockery, shouting at the radio in exasperation. *Address*: House of Lords, SW1A 0PW. *E*: info@crossstreetfilms.com.

**KIDSTON, Catherine Isabel Audrey, (Cath Kidston),** MBE 2010; Founder and Creative Director, 1993–2014, and non-executive Director, 2014–16, Cath Kidston Ltd; Founder and Creative Director, Joy of Print Ltd, since 2017; *b* London, 6 Nov. 1958; *d* of Archibald Martin Glen Kidston and Susan Myrtle Kidston; *m* 2012, Hugh Padgham; one step *d*. *Educ*: boarding sch. Interior designer to Nicky Haslam, 1984–87; Jt Proprietor, Curtainalia and interior design store, 1987–92. Trustee, Fine Cell Work, 2016–. Ambassador, everywoman, 2011–. *Publications*: Vintage Style, 1999; Tips for Vintage Style, 2004; Cath Kidston in Print, 2005; Make!, 2008; Sew!, 2009; Stitch!, 2010; Patch!, 2011; Coming Up Roses: the story of growing a business, 2013. *Recreations*: family, art exhibitions, travel.

**KIEFEL, Hon. Susan Mary,** AC 2011; **Hon. Chief Justice Kiefel;** Chief Justice of Australia, since 2017; *b* Cairns, Qld, 17 Jan. 1954; *d* of Alf Abe Kiefel and Patricia Mary Kiefel (*née* Walsh); *m* 1987, Michael Philip Albrecht. *Educ*: Barristers Bd of Qld (Hons 1975); Wolfson Coll., Cambridge (LLM 1985; C. J. Hamson Prize for Comparative Law, Jennings Prize). Admitted Qld Bar, 1975; QC (Qld) 1987; a Justice, Supreme Court of Qld, 1993–94; a Justice, Federal Court, 1994–2007; a Justice, High Court, 2007–. *Address*: High Court of Australia, GPO Box 6309, Kingston, ACT 2604, Australia.

**KIERNAN, Prof. Kathleen Elizabeth,** OBE 2006; PhD; FBA 2012; Professor of Social Policy and Demography, University of York, 2004, now Emeritus; *b* Leeds, 11 Feb. 1948; *d* of Patrick Joseph Kiernan and Julia Anne Kiernan (*née* Hastings); *m* 1971, John Hobcraft; one *s* one *d*. *Educ*: Notre Dame Grammar Sch., Leeds; Univ. of Liverpool (BA Soc. Studies); London Sch. of Econs and Pol Sci. (MSc Demography); Univ. of London (PhD 1987). Res. Officer, 1972–75, SO, 1975–78, Nat. Survey of Health and Develt, MRC; Res. Fellow, 1978–83, Sen. Res. Fellow, 1983–86, Centre for Popn Studies, LSHTM; Dep. Dir, Social Statistics Res. Unit, City Univ., 1986–89; Res. Dir, Family Policy Studies Centre, 1989–93; London School of Economics and Political Science: Sen. Res. Fellow in Demography, 1993–95; Reader in Social Policy and Demography, 1995–2001; Prof. of Social Policy and Demography, 2001–04; Co-Dir, ESRC Centre for Analysis of Social Exclusion, 1997–2008. Vis. Res. Scholar, Center for Child Develt and Wellbeing, Office of Popn Res., Woodrow Wilson Sch. of Public and Internat. Affairs, Princeton Univ., 2004–16. *Publications*: (with M. Wicks) Family Change and Future Policy, 1990; (with V. Estaugh) Cohabitation, Extramarital Childbearing and Social Policy, 1993; (jtly) Lone Motherhood in the Twentieth Century: from footnote to front page, 1998; (ed jtly) Human Development across Lives and Generations: the potential for change, 2004; articles in demography, social policy, medical and social sci. jls. *Recreations*: family life, art and design, travel, photography, theatre. *Address*: Department of Social Policy and Social Work, University of York, Heslington, York YO10 5DD. *E*: kathleen.kiernan@york.ac.uk.

**KIERNAN, Peter Anthony;** Senior Adviser: OMERS Private Equity (Europe), since 2016; Egon Zehnder, since 2017; *b* Watford, 11 Sept. 1960; *s* of Joseph Kiernan and Mary, (Molly), Kiernan; *m* 1991, Felicity Pearce; one *d*. *Educ*: St Michael's Comp. Sch., Watford; Downing Coll., Cambridge (BA Natural Scis 1982; MA 1986). ACA 1986, FCA 2013. With Peat, Marwick Mitchell, 1982–86; Managing Director: S. G. Warburg, then Swiss Bank Corp., later UBS Warburg, 1986–2000; Goldman Sachs, 2000–04; Hd, UK Investment Banking, 2004–06, Man. Dir, 2004–11, Lazard; Vice Chm., 2012–13, Chm., 2013–15, European Investment Banking, Sen. Advr, 2015–16, Canaccord Genuity. Senior Adviser: Bell Pottinger (formerly Pelham Bell Pottinger), 2012–16; UK Bd of Practice, Hedrick and Struggles, 2015–16; non-executive Director: Tungsten Corporation plc, 2012–18; Listrac Hldgs Ltd, 2016– (Chm., 2018–); London First, 2016–. Mem. Adv. Bd, Masters Degree in Law and Finance, Oxford Univ., 2010–. Trustee, Ireland Fund of GB, until 2014. *Recreations*: family, friends, fitness, ski-ing, watching sports, supporting Watford FC.

**KILBRACKEN, 4th Baron** *cr* 1909, of Killegar, co. Leitrim; **Christopher John Godley;** *b* 1 Jan. 1945; *s* of 3rd Baron Kilbracken, DSC and Penelope Anne, *y d* of Rear-Adm. Sir Cecil Nugent Reyne, KBE; *S* father, 2006; *m* 1969, Gillian Christine, *yr d* of Lt-Comdr Stuart Wilson Birse, OBE, DSC, RN retd; one *s* one *d*. *Educ*: Rugby; Reading Univ. (BSc Agric. 1967). ICI: Agriculturalist, 1968–78; Gp Buyer, Hd Office, 1978–81; Countertrade Mgr, 1982–2000. Chm., London Countertrade Roundtable, 1997–2002. Patron, John Robert Godley Meml Trust, NZ; Vice Patron, Canterbury Assoc., NZ. *Recreations*: yachting, gardening. *Heir*: *s* Hon. James John Godley [*b* 3 Jan. 1972; *m* 2002, Anna Charlotte Weld-Forester; one *s* three *d*]. *Address*: Four Firs, Marley Lane, Haslemere, Surrey GU27 3PZ.

**KILBY, Prof. Mark David,** MD, DSc; FRCOG; Professor of Fetal Medicine, since 2002, and Dame Hilda Lloyd Professor of Fetal Medicine, since 2006, University of Birmingham; *b* London, 10 Feb. 1960; *s* of Edward William Kilby and Joyce Eleonor Kilby; *m* 1996, Julia Knight; one *s* one *d*. *Educ*: Guy's Hosp. Med. Sch., London (MB BS 1984); Univ. of Nottingham (MD 1990); Univ. of Birmingham (DSc 2011). FRCOG 2007. House physician and surgeon, London, 1984–85; training, W Midlands, 1990–93; Univ. of Toronto, 1993–94; subspecialty trainee, Birmingham, 1994–96; Hon. Consultant in Fetal Medicine, Birmingham Women's and Children's NHS Foundn Trust, 1996–. Hon. FRCPI 2015. *Publications*: (ed jtly) Fetal Therapy: scientific basis and clinical appraisal, 2012, 2nd edn 2019; over 280 original peer-reviewed articles. *Recreations*: cycling, gym, walking/ hiking. *Address*: Academic Department of Obstetrics and Gynaecology, Birmingham Women's Campus, Birmingham Women's and Children's NHS Foundation Trust, Birmingham B15 2TG. *E*: m.d.kilby@bham.ac.uk. *Clubs*: Priory Sports; Edgbaston Golf.

**KILCLOONEY, Baron** *cr* 2001 (Life Peer), of Armagh in the County of Armagh; **John David Taylor;** PC (NI) 1970; Member (UU) Strangford, Northern Ireland Assembly, 1998–2007; *b* 24 Dec. 1937; *er s* of George D. Taylor and Georgina Baird; *m* 1970, Mary Frances Todd; one *s* five *d*. *Educ*: Royal Sch., Armagh; Queen's Univ. of Belfast (BSc). AMInstHE, AMICEI. MP (UU) S Tyrone, NI Parlt, 1965–73; Mem. (UU), Fermanagh and S Tyrone, NI Assembly, 1973–75; Mem. (UU), North Down, NI Constitutional Convention, 1975–76; Parly Sec. to Min. of Home Affairs, 1969–70; Minister of State, Min. of Home Affairs, 1970–72; Mem. (UU), North Down, NI Assembly, 1982–86. Mem., Strangford, NI Forum, 1996–98. Mem. (UU) NI, Eur. Parlt, 1979–89. MP (UU) Strangford, 1983–2001 (resigned seat Dec. 1985 in protest against Anglo-Irish Agreement; re-elected Jan. 1986). Mem. Assembly, Council of Europe, 1997–2004. Resigned UU Party, 2007. Partner, G. D. Taylor and Associates, Architects and Civil Engineers, 1966–74; Director: West Ulster Estates Ltd, 1968–; Bramley Apple Restaurant Ltd, 1974–; West Ulster Hotels Co. Ltd, 1976–86; Gosford Housing Assoc. Ltd, 1977–2012; Tontine Rooms Ltd, 1978–; Ulster Gazette (Armagh) Ltd, 1983–; Cerdac (Belfast) Ltd, 1986–; Tyrone Printing Co. Ltd, 1986–; Tyrone Courier Ltd, 1986–; Sovereign Properties (NI) Ltd, 1989–; Tyrone Constitution Ltd, 1999–; Outlook Press Ltd, 1999–; Coleraine Chronicle Ltd, 2003–; Northern Constitution Ltd, 2003–; East Antrim Newspapers Ltd, 2003–; Northern Newspapers Ltd, 2003–; Midland Tribune Ltd, 2003–; Alpha Newspapers Ltd, 2003–; Northern Media Gp Ltd, 2003–14; BoL Pubs Ltd, 2006–; Newry Democrat Ltd, 2012–. *Publications*: (jtly) Ulster—the facts, 1982. *Recreation*: foreign travel. *Address*: Mullinure, 34 Portadown Road, Armagh, Northern Ireland BT61 9EL. *T*: (028) 3752 2409, (020) 7931 7211. *E*: johnkilclooney@hotmail.co.uk. *Clubs*: Farmers; Armagh County (Armagh).

**KILDUFF, Prof. Martin James,** PhD; Professor of Management, University College London, since 2012; *b* London, 16 July 1949; *s* of Michael Kilduff and Millicent Amy Kilduff (*née* Summerfield); *m* 1977, Constance Eleanor Johnson; one *s*. *Educ*: Quintin Grammar Sch., London; Washington State Univ. (BA, MBA); Cornell Univ. (MS; PhD 1988); MA Cantab 2009. Asst Prof., INSEAD, France, 1988–90; Penn State University: Asst Prof., 1990–94; Associate Prof., 1994–99; Prof., 1999–2006; King Ranch Centennial Prof. of Mgt, Univ. of Texas at Austin, 2006–08; Diageo Prof. of Mgt Studies, Judge Business Sch., Univ. of Cambridge, 2008–12; Fellow, Sidney Sussex Coll., Cambridge, 2008–12. *Publications*: Social Networks and Organizations, 2003; Interpersonal Networks in Organizations: cognition, personality, dynamics and culture, 2008; contribs to jls incl. Admin. Sci. Qly, Acad. of Mgt Jl. *Recreations*: running, walking, snorkelling. *Address*: UCL School of Management, University College London, 1 Canada Square, E14 5AB. *T*: (020) 3108 6021. *E*: mjkilduff@gmail.com.

**KILFOIL, His Honour Geoffrey Everard;** a Circuit Judge, 1987–2004; *b* 15 March 1939; *s* of Thomas Albert and Hilda Alice Kilfoil; *m* 1962, Llinos Mai Morris; one *s* one *d*. *Educ*: Acrefair Jun. Sch.; Ruabon Grammar Sch.; Jesus Coll., Oxford (BA Hons Jurisprudence; MA; Sankey Bar Schol., 1960). NCB underground worker, Gresford and Hafod Collieries, 1960–62; Lectr, English and Liberal Studies Dept, Denbs Tech. Coll. and Hd, English Dept, Gwersyllt Secondary Sch., 1962–66. Called to the Bar, Gray's Inn, 1966 (Holker Sen. Schol.); practised Wales & Chester Circuit; Dep. Circuit Judge, Asst Recorder then Recorder, 1974–87; pt-time *ad hoc* local Chm., Med. Appeals Tribunal (Wales) and Police Appeals Tribunals, 1976–87. Member (Lab), 1962–67: Cefn Mawr Parish Council (Chm., 1965–67); Wrexham RDC; Denbs CC; prospective parly cand. (Lab) Ludlow, 1965. Pres., Friends of Miners' Welfare Inst., Rhosllannerchrugog; Vice-Pres., Llangollen Internat. Musical Eisteddfod; Pres., Denbs Hist. Soc.

**KILFOYLE, Peter;** *b* 9 June 1946; *s* of Edward and Ellen Kilfoyle; *m* 1968, Bernadette (*née* Slater); two *s* three *d*. *Educ*: St Edward's Coll., Liverpool; Durham Univ.; Christ's Coll., Liverpool. Building labourer, 1965–70; student, 1970–73; building labourer, 1973–75; teacher/youth worker, 1975–85; Labour Party Organiser, 1985–91. MP (Lab) Liverpool,

Walton, July 1991–2010. Parly Sec., Cabinet Office, 1997–99 (OPS, 1997–98); Parly Under Sec. of State, MoD, 1999–2000. *Publications:* Left Behind: lessons from Labour's heartlands, 2000; Lies, Damned Lies and Iraq, 2007; Labour Pains: how the party I love lost its soul, 2010. *Recreations:* reading, music, spectator sport, bonsai.

**KILGALLON, William,** OBE 1992; independent consultant; National Director, Office for Professional Standards, Catholic Church in Aotearoa, New Zealand, 2013–18; *b* 29 Aug. 1946; *s* of William and Bridget Agnes Kilgallon (*née* Early); *m* 1978, Stephanie Martin (MBE 2012); two *s*, and one adopted *s*. *Educ:* Gregorian Univ., Rome (STL); London Sch. of Econs (Dip. Social Admin); Univ. of Warwick (MA); Univ. of Lancaster (MSc). RC Priest, Dio. Leeds, 1970–77; Asst Priest, St Anne's Cathedral, Leeds, 1970–74; Founder, and Chm., St Anne's Shelter & Housing Action, 1971–74; social work trng, 1974–76; Social Worker, Leeds Catholic Children's Soc., 1976–77; returned to lay state, 1977; Manager, St Anne's Centre, 1977–78; Chief Executive: St Anne's Shelter & Housing Action, 1978–2002; Social Care Inst. for Excellence, 2003–07; St Gemma's Hospice, Leeds, 2007–10. Leeds City Council: Mem. (Lab), 1979–92; Chairman: Housing Cttee, 1984–88; Social Services Cttee, 1988–90; Envmt Cttee, 1991–92; Lord Mayor, 1990–91. Member: Leeds FPC, 1978–80; Leeds AHA (T), 1980–82; Leeds E DHA, 1982–86; Yorks RHA, 1986–90 (non-exec. Dir and Vice Chm., 1990–92); Chairman: Leeds Community and Mental Health Services NHS Trust, 1992–98; Leeds Teaching Hosps NHS Trust, 1998–2002. Mem., W Yorks Police Authy, 2007–09. Member: Council, NHS Confedn, 1996–2002; CCETSW, 1998–2001. Leader: Ind. Inquiry into Abuse Allegations, Northumberland, 1994–95; Ext. Rev., Earls House Hosp., Durham, 1997–98; Ind. Rev. of Contracting for Neighbourhood Services, Leeds CC, 2010; Member: Cumberlege Commn reviewing protection of children and vulnerable adults in Catholic Ch in England and Wales, 2006–07; Joseph Rowntree Charitable Trust Commn of Inquiry into destitution among asylum seekers, 2006–07. Chair, Nat. Catholic Safeguarding Commn, 2008–10. Member: Ind. Ref. Gp on Mental Health, NSF, 1998–99; Nat. Task Force on Learning Disability, 2001–04; Pontifical Commn for Protection of Minors, 2014–17. Non-exec. Dir, Places for People Gp, 2004–05. Mem. Council, Univ. of Leeds, 1992–2000; Gov., Park Lane FE Coll., 2000–02. Mem., Leeds & Dist Rugby League Referees Soc., 1992–2009. Hon. LLD Leeds, 1997; DUniv Leeds Metropolitan, 2000. *Recreations:* reading, travel, cricket, Rugby League. *Address:* 119 Hinemoa Street, Birkenhead, Auckland 0626, New Zealand.

**KILGOUR, Rear Adm. Niall Stuart Roderick,** CB 2005; Secretary and Chief Executive, Hurlingham Club, 2005–15; *b* 4 March 1950; *s* of Leonard and Kathleen Kilgour; *m* 1974, Jane Birtwistle; one *s* two *d*. *Educ:* Nautical Coll., Pangbourne. Commanding Officer: HMS Porpoise, 1980–82; HMS Courageous, 1986–88; Captain, 6th Frigate Sqdn, 1994–96; Commanding Officer: HMS Norfolk, 1994–95; HMS Montrose, 1995–96; Asst COS Ops C-in-C Fleet, 1996–98; Comdr, Amphibious Task Gp, 1998–2001; Comdr Ops to C-in-C Fleet and Rear Adm. Submarines, 2001–04. Pres., Submariners' Assoc., 2016. Younger Brother, Trinity House. QCVS 2000. *Recreations:* shooting, walking, history, sport. *Address:* The Cottage, Beercrocombe, Taunton TA3 6AG. *T:* (01823) 480251. *Club:* Hurlingham.

**KILGOUR, Rev. Richard Eifl;** Rector of Holy Trinity, Motherwell, since 2018; *b* 26 Oct. 1957; *s* of Owen Frederick George Kilgour and Barbara Kilgour; *m* 1981, Janet Katharine Williams; three *d*. *Educ:* Eirias High Sch., Colwyn Bay; Hull Nautical Coll.; Edinburgh Univ. (BD Hons 1985); Univ. of Wales, Lampeter (MA Theol. 2010). Apprentice Navigation Officer, 1977–80, Serving Deck Officer, to 1981, Anchor Line, Glasgow; Jun. Officer, Trinity House Corp., 1981; 1st Officer, Fishery Protection Fleet, Dept of Agriculture and Fisheries, Scotland, 1981. Ordained deacon, 1985, priest, 1986, Church in Wales; Curate, Rectorial Benefice of Wrexham, 1985–88; Vicar, Whitford, and Industrial Chaplain, NE Wales, Industrial Mission for Council of Churches for Wales, 1988–97; Vicar/Rector, Newtown, Llanllwchaiarn, Aberhafesp, 1998–2003; Priest-in-charge, St Ninian, Aberdeen, 2003–06; Rector and Provost, Cathedral Church of St Andrew, Aberdeen, 2003–15; Gen. Sec., Internat. Christian Maritime Assoc., 2015–17. RD, Cedewain, Dio. of St Asaph, 2001–03. Hon. Canon, Christchurch Cathedral, Hartford, Conn, 2004–15. *Recreations:* sailing, foreign travel, dry-stone walling. *Address:* Holy Trinity Rectory, 14 Crawford Street, Motherwell ML1 3AD.

**KILLALEA, Stephen Joseph;** QC 2006; barrister; *b* 25 Jan. 1959; *s* of Edward James Killalea and (Isabelle) Marie-Louise Killalea (*née* Elliott); *m* 1991, Catherine Marie Stanley (*d* 2011); two *d*. *Educ:* Bishopshalt Sch., Hillingdon; Univ. of Sheffield (LLB Hons). Called to the Bar, Middle Temple, 1981, Bencher, 2012; barrister in private practice specialising in catastrophic brain and spinal injuries. Advanced Advocacy Trainer, Middle Temple, 2008–. *Publications:* (jtly) Health and Safety: the modern legal framework, 2nd edn 2001. *Recreations:* my girls, pubs, horse racing. *Address:* Devereux Chambers, Queen Elizabeth Building, Temple, EC4Y 9BS. *T:* (020) 7353 7534.

**KILLANIN,** 4th Baron *cr* 1900, of Galway, co. Galway; **George Redmond Fitzpatrick Morris;** Bt 1885; film producer; *b* 26 Jan. 1947; *e s* of 3rd Baron Killanin, MBE, TD and Mary Sheila Cathcart Morris (*née* Dunlop), MBE; *S* father, 1999; *m* 1st, 1972, Pauline Horton (marr. diss. 1999); one *s* one *d*; 2nd, 2000, Sheila Lynch; one *s* one *d*. *Educ:* Ampleforth Coll., York; Trinity Coll., Dublin. Films produced: The Miracle, 1991; Splitting Heirs, 1993; The Butcher Boy, 1998; co-producer: Interview with the Vampire, 1994; Michael Collins, 1996; In Dreams, 1999; The Reader, 2008. *Recreations:* film, theatre, music, Ireland. *Heir:* *s* Hon. Luke Michael Geoffrey Morris [*b* 22 July 1975; *m* 2010, Laura, 2nd *d* of Bernard Dewe Mathews]. *Address:* 9 Lower Mount Pleasant Avenue, Dublin 6, Ireland. *Club:* Groucho.

**KILLEARN,** 3rd Baron *cr* 1943, of Killearn, co. Stirling; **Victor Miles George Aldous Lampson;** Bt 1866; Director, AMP Ltd, 1999–2003; Chairman (non-executive), Henderson Global Investors (Holdings) Ltd, 2001–05; *b* 9 Sept. 1941; *s* of 1st Baron Killearn, GCMG, CB, MVO, PC and his 2nd wife, Jacqueline Aldine Leslie (*d* 2015), *o d* of Marchese Count Aldo Castellani; *S* half-brother, 1996; *m* 1st, 1971, Melita Amaryllis Pamela Astrid (*d* 2014), *d* of Rear-Adm. Sir Morgan Charles Morgan-Giles, DSO, OBE, GM; two *s* two *d*; 2nd, 2017, Hon. Victoria Isabella Warrender, *d* of 1st Baron Bruntisfield, MC and widow of 14th Lord Reay. *Educ:* Eton. Late Captain, Scots Guards. Partner, 1979–2001, Man. Dir, Corporate Finance, 2001–02, Cazenove & Co. Ltd. Non-executive Director: Maxis Communications Bhd, Malaysia, 2002–06; Shanghai Real Estate Ltd, 2002–07; Ton Poh Emerging Thailand Fund, 2005–17; Vietnam Dragon Fund, 2006–11. *Heir:* *s* Hon. Miles Henry Morgan Lampson [*b* 10 Dec. 1977; *m* 2008, Emily, *d* of Christopher Watkins; three *s* one *d*]. *Clubs:* White's; Hong Kong.

**KILLEN, Gerard;** MP (Lab Co-op) Rutherglen and Hamilton West, since 2017; *b* Glasgow, 15 May 1986. Mem. (Lab), S Lanarkshire Council, 2013–17. Mem., Scottish Affairs Cttee, H of C, 2017–. *Address:* House of Commons, SW1A 0AA.

**KILLEN, Prof. John Tyrrell,** PhD; FBA 1995; Professor of Mycenaean Greek, Cambridge University, 1997–99, now Emeritus; Fellow, Jesus College, Cambridge, since 1969; *b* 19 July 1937; *e s* of John Killen and Muriel Caroline Elliott Killen (*née* Bolton); *m* 1964, Elizabeth Ann Ross; one *s* two *d*. *Educ:* High Sch., Dublin; Trinity Coll., Dublin (1st Foundn Schol. in Classics 1957; 1st Vice-Chancellor's Latin Medallist 1959; BA 1st Cl. 1960); St John's Coll., Cambridge (Gardiner Meml Schol. 1959; PhD 1964). Cambridge University: Asst Lectr in Classics, 1967–70; Lectr, 1970–90; Reader in Mycenaean Greek, 1990–97; Chm., Faculty Bd of Classics, 1984–86; Churchill College: Gulbenkian Res. Fellow, 1961–62; Fellow and Librarian, 1962–69 (initiated Churchill Archives project, 1965); Jesus College: Lectr, 1965–97; acting Bursar, 1973; Sen. Bursar, 1979–89; Dir, Quincentenary Develt Appeal, 1987–90. *Publications:* (jtly) Corpus of Mycenaean Inscriptions from Knossos, 4 vols, 1986–98; (ed jtly) Studies in Mycenaean and Classical Greek, festschrift for John Chadwick, 1987; (with J.-P. Olivier) The Knossos Tablets, 1989; (ed with S. Voutsaki) Economy and Politics in the Mycenaean Palace States, 2001; Economy and Administration in Mycenaean Greece: collected papers on Linear B (ed M. Del Freo), 3 vols, 2015; articles in learned jls. *Recreations:* golf, watching sport on television, reading the FT, music. *Address:* Jesus College, Cambridge CB5 8BL.

**KILLEN, Patrick,** OBE 1991; Vice Lord-Lieutenant, County Tyrone, since 2013; independent business consultant, since 1995; *b* Co. Down, 25 Nov. 1945; *s* of James and Teresa Killen; *m* 1968, Gemma; two *s* three *d*. Salesman of agricl products, 1965–72; Chief. Exec., Tyrone Crystal Gp, 1972–95. Chm., NI Citizens' Charter Panel. Lay Mem., Industrial Tribunals; Panel Member: Criminal Injuries Appeal Panel for NI; Fair Employment Tribunals. Former Panel Mem., Wilson Cttee, examng and reporting on complaints procedure in UK Health Service. Formerly Member: Bd, Pigs Mktg Bd for NI; Bd, Health and Safety Agency for NI; NI Partnership Bd; Probation Bd for NI; Broadcasting Council, BBC NI. Gov., St Patrick's Coll., Dungannon. *Recreation:* walking. *T:* 07711 685997. *E:* patkillen@gmail.com.

**KILLICK, Angela Margaret;** Deputy Chairman, Children and Families Court Advisory and Support Service, 2001–03; *b* 18 May 1943; *o d* of late Tom Killick and Dora (*née* Jeffries); *m* 1983, Alec Grezo; one *s*. *Educ:* Watford Grammar Sch. for Girls. Various posts, incl. voluntary sector and abroad, until 1970; civil servant, incl. Hd, Res. Grants and Council Secretariat, SERC and AFRC; Hd, Radioactive Waste Policy Unit, DoE, 1970–91. Chairman: Hampstead HA, 1990–92; Enfield Community Care NHS Trust, 1992–98; Mt Vernon and Watford Hosps NHS Trust, 1998–2000. Member: Radioactive Waste Mgt Adv. Cttee, 1991–98; Lay Associate Mem., GMC, 2001–06. Lay Chm., NHS Ind. Review Panels, 2000–05; Lay Reviewer, Healthcare Commn, 2004–06. Member (C): Westminster CC, 1974–90; Three Rivers DC, 2015–19. Trustee: Tennant Housing Assoc., 1976–85; Westminster Children's Soc., 1988–95 (Chm., 1993–95). Lay Visitor, Postgrad. Med. Educn Trng Bd, 2005–10. Ind. Custody Visitor, 2008–15. Governor: St Clement Danes Sch., Covent Gdn, 1976–82; St Mary's Sch., Bryanston Sq., 1990–96; Russell Sch., Chorleywood, 1997– (Chm. of Govs, 1998–2002). Chm., Chorleywood Community Liby Volunteers, 2015–. Binney Award Certificate for Bravery, Binney Meml Trust, 1985. JP Camberwell, 1983–86. *Publications:* Council House Blues, 1976. *Recreations:* reading, gardening, family history, Private Pilot's licence, 1972.

**KILLICK, Anthony John, (Tony),** OBE 2007; consultant on economic development and aid policies, 1999–2011; Senior Research Associate, Overseas Development Institute, 1999–2015 (Director, 1982–87; Senior Research Fellow, 1987–99); *b* 25 June 1934; *s* of William and Edith Killick; *m* 1958, Ingeborg Nitzsche; two *d*. *Educ:* Ruskin and Wadham Colls, Oxford (BA Hons PPE). Lectr in Econs, Univ. of Ghana, 1961–65; Tutor in Econs, Ruskin Coll., Oxford, 1965–67; Sen. Econ. Adviser, Min. of Overseas Develt, 1967–69; Econ. Adviser to Govt of Ghana, 1969–72; Res. Fellow, Harvard Univ., 1972–73; Ford Foundn Vis. Prof., Econs Dept, Univ. of Nairobi, 1973–79; Res. Officer, Overseas Develt Inst., 1979–82. Vis. Fellow, Wolfson Coll., and Vis. Scholar, Dept of Applied Economics, Cambridge Univ., 1987–88. Vis. Prof., Dept of Economics, Univ. of Surrey, 1988–. Member: Commn of Inquiry into Fiscal System of Zimbabwe, 1984–86; Council, Royal Africa Soc. Chm. Bd of Dirs, African Econ. Res. Consortium, 1995–2001. Former consultant to various internat. orgns, and to Government of: Sierra Leone; Kenya; Republic of Dominica; Nepal; Ethiopia; Mozambique; Rwanda; Pakistan; Tanzania. Associate, Inst. of Develt Studies, Univ. of Sussex, 1986–94. Pres., Develt Studies Assoc., 1986–88. Hon. Res. Fellow, Dept of Political Economy, UCL, 1985–98. Editorial adviser: Journal of Economic Studies; Develt Policy Review; World Develt. *Publications:* The Economies of East Africa, 1976; Development Economics in Action: a study of economic policies in Ghana, 1978, 2nd edn 2010; Policy Economics: a textbook of applied economics on developing countries, 1981; (ed) Papers on the Kenyan Economy: structure, problems and policies, 1981; (ed) Adjustment and Financing in the Developing World: the role of the IMF, 1982; The Quest for Economic Stabilisation: the IMF and the Third World, 1984; The IMF and Stabilisation: developing country experiences, 1984; The Economies of East Africa: a bibliography 1974–80, 1984; A Reaction Too Far: the role of the state in developing countries, 1989; The Adaptive Economy: adjustment policies in low income countries, 1993; The Flexible Economy: causes and consequences of the adaptability of national economies, 1995; IMF Programmes in Developing Countries, 1995; Aid and the Political Economy of Policy Change, 1998; learned articles and contribs to books on Third World develt and economics. *Recreations:* gardening, music, Adviser at Citizens Advice Bureau 2011–16. *Address:* 35 Pauls Lane, Hoddesdon, Herts EN11 8TR. *T:* (01992) 275093. *E:* tonykillick@outlook.com.

**KILLICK, Sonia Natasha Clara;** *see* Solicari, S. N. C.

**KILLIK, Paul Geoffrey;** Senior Partner, Killik & Co., since 1989; *b* 24 Dec. 1947; *s* of Guy Frederick Killik and Rita Mildred (*née* Brewer); *m* 1981, Karen Virginia Mayhew; one *s* one *d*. *Educ:* Claysemore Sch., Dorset. MSI (Dip.) 1969; FCSI 2013. Hedderwick Borthwick, 1969–71; Killik Haley, 1971–74; Partner, Killik Cassel Haley, 1974–75; merged with Quilter Goodison, 1975: Partner, 1977–85, Dir, 1985–88; Head, Private Client Dept, 1983–88. Mem., Stock Exchange, 1973. Mem. Bd, Personal Investment Mgt and Financial Advice Assoc. (formerly Wealth Mgt Assoc.), 1997–. *Address:* (office) 46 Grosvenor Street, W1K 3HN. *T:* (020) 7337 0400.

**KILMAINE,** 8th Baron *cr* 1789 (Ire.); **John Francis Sandford Browne;** Bt 1636 (NS); *b* 4 April 1983; *o s* of 7th Baron Kilmaine and of Linda (*née* Robinson); *S* father, 2013.

**KILMARNOCK,** 8th Baron *cr* 1831; **Dr Robin Jordan Boyd;** Chief of Clan Boyd; *b* 6 June 1941; *s* of 6th Baron Kilmarnock, MBE, TD, and Hon. Rosemary Guest (*d* 1971), *er d* of 1st Viscount Wimborne; *S* brother, 2009; *m* 1st, 1977, Ruth Christine, *d* of Michael Fisher (marr. diss. 1986); two *s*; 2nd, 2000, Hilary Vivien, *d* of Peter Cox; one *s* by Catherine Hoddell. *Educ:* Eton; Keble Coll., Oxford (BA). MB BS (London) 1970; MRCS, LRCP, 1970; DCH 1973; AFOM, RCP, 1983. *Heir:* *s* Hon. Simon John Boyd [*b* 29 Oct. 1978; *m* 2004, Valeria Beatriz Matzkin; one *s* one *d*].

**KILMARTIN, Dr John Vincent,** FRS 2002; Staff Scientist, Medical Research Council Laboratory of Molecular Biology, Cambridge, 1969–2008, now Emeritus; *b* 22 July 1943; *s* of Vincent Kilmartin and Sadie (*née* Blake); *m* 1985, Margaret Scott Robinson, *qv*; one *d*. *Educ:* Mt St Mary's Coll., Spinkhill, Sheffield; St John's Coll., Cambridge (MA, PhD 1969).

Visitor, Yale Univ., 1976–77. Mem., EMBO, 1995. *Publications:* contrib. papers to scientific jls on hemoglobin and yeast mitosis. *Recreations:* reading, wine, cooking, opera, walking. *Address:* MRC Laboratory of Molecular Biology, Francis Crick Avenue, Cambridge Biomedical Campus, Cambridge CB2 0QH. *T:* (01223) 267000.

**KILMARTIN, Margaret Scott;** *see* Robinson, M. S.

**KILMISTER, (Claude Alaric) Anthony,** OBE 2005; Founder, 1994, and President, 2004–12, Prostate Action (formerly Prostate Research Campaign UK); Vice President, Prostate Cancer UK, since 2012; *b* 22 July 1931; *s* of late Dr Claude E. Kilmister; *m* 1st, 1958, Sheila Harwood (*d* 2006); 2nd, 2016, Christine Woodworth-Batho. *Educ:* Shrewsbury Sch. National Service (army officer), 1950–52. NCB, 1952–54; Conservative Party Org., 1954–60; Asst Sec. 1960–61, Gen. Sec. 1962–72, Cinema & Television Benevolent Fund; Sec., Royal Film Performance Exec. Cttee, 1961–72; Exec. Dir, Parkinson's Disease Soc. of UK, 1972–91. Founding Cttee Mem., Action for Neurological Diseases, 1987–91. Founding Mem. and Dep. Chm., Prayer Book Soc. (and its forerunner, BCP Action Gp), 1972–89, Chm., 1989–2001, Vice-Pres., 2001–; Mem. Council, 1975–, Pres., 2007–, Anglican Assoc.; Member: Internat. Council for Apostolic Faith, 1987–93; Steering Cttee, Assoc. for Apostolic Ministry, 1989–96; St Alban's Diocesan Synod, 2006–09. Freeman, City of London, 2002. MA Lambeth, 2002. *Publications:* The Good Church Guide, 1982; When Will Ye be Wise?, 1983; My Favourite Betjeman, 1985; The Prayer Book and Ordination: a Prayer Book view of women bishops, 2006; contribs to jls, etc. *Recreations:* walking, writing. *Address:* 11 Homewood Court, Cedars Village, Chorleywood, Herts WD3 5GB. *T:* (01923) 447367.

**KILMORE, ELPHIN AND ARDAGH, Bishop of,** since 2013; **Rt Rev. (Samuel) Ferran Glenfield;** *b* 1954; *m* 1979, Jean Glover; three *c.* *Educ:* Queen's Univ. Belfast (BA 1976); Trinity Coll. Dublin (MLitt 1990; MA 1994); Oxford Univ. (MTh 1999); Wycliffe Hall, Oxford. Teacher, Rainey Endowed Sch., 1978–88; ordained deacon, 1991, priest, 1992; Asst Curate, Douglas with Blackrock, Frankfield and Marmullane, 1991–94; Rector: Rathcooney Union of Parishes, 1994–96; Kill o'the Grange, Blackrock, 1996–2012; St Malachi, Hillsborough, 2012–13. *Address:* The See House, Kilmore, Cavan, Republic of Ireland.

**KILMOREY, 6th Earl of,** *cr* 1822; **Richard Francis Needham,** Kt 1997; PC 1994; Viscount Kilmorey 1625; Viscount Newry and Mourne 1822; independent company director; *b* 29 Jan. 1942; *e s* of 5th Earl of Kilmorey and Helen, *y d* of Sir Lionel Faudel-Phillips, 3rd Bt; *S* father, 1977; *m* 1965, Sigrid Juliane Thiessen-Gairdner; two *s* one *d.* *Educ:* Eton College. Chm., R. G. M. Print Holdings Ltd, 1967–85. CC Somerset, 1967–74. Contested (C): Pontefract and Castleford, Feb. 1974; Gravesend, Oct. 1974; MP (C): Chippenham, 1979–83; Wilts N, 1983–97. PPS to Sec. of State for NI, 1983–84, to Sec. of State for the Environment, 1984–85; Parly Under-Sec. of State, NI Office, 1985–92 (Minister for Health and Social Security, 1988–89, for Envmt and for Economy, 1989–92); Minister of State (Minister for Trade), DTI, 1992–95. Mem., Public Accts Cttee, 1982–83. Chairman: GPT Ltd, 1996–97; Quantum Imaging Ltd, 1999–2003; Biocompatibles plc, 2000–06; Newfield IT Ltd, 2003–08; Tetra Strategy Ltd, 2009–17; Rose Petroleum plc, 2010–15; Director: GEC plc, 1995–97; NEC Europe Ltd, 1998– (Vice Chm., 1997–2010); Avon Rubber plc, 2012–13 (Chm., 2007–11); Independent Director: Dyson Ltd, 1995–2011 (Dep. Chm., 2000–04); Mivan Ltd, 1995–99; Meggitt PLC, 1997–2002; Tough Glass Ltd, 1997–2001; MICE plc, 1998–2003; Hansard Gp plc, 2003–04; deltaDOT Ltd, 2006–07; non-executive Director: Lonrho plc, 2011–12; Rank Gp plc, 2012–18; Adaptive Modules Ltd, 2015–16; Halsbury Homes Ltd, 2016–; Advr, Amec plc, 1998–2009. Chm., Gleneagles (UK) Ltd (formerly Nat. Heart Hosp.), 1995–2001. Patron, Mencap (NI), 1996–2010. Pres., British Exporters Assoc., 1998–2017. Founder Member: Anglo-Japanese 21st Century (formerly 2000) Gp, 1984–2015; Anglo-Korean Forum for the Future, 1993–2000. Advr to Prime Minister Designate of Malaysia, 2018–. Governor, British Inst. of Florence, 1983–85. Hon. Life Mem., British-Singapore Business Council, 2002. Hon. LLD Ulster, 2010. Gold and Silver Star, Order of the Rising Sun (Japan), 2004; Order of San Carlos, Gran Cruz (Colombia), 2018. *Publications:* Honourable Member, 1983; Battling for Peace, 1999. *Heir: s* Viscount Newry and Morne, *qv. Clubs:* Pratt's, Brooks's.

**KILNER, Prof. John Anthony,** PhD; CPhys, FInstP; FIMMM; B. C. H. Steele Professor of Energy Materials, Imperial College London (formerly Imperial College of Science, Technology and Medicine, London University), since 2006; Principal Investigator, International Institute for Carbon-Neutral Energy Research, Kyushu University, Japan, since 2011; *b* 15 Dec. 1946; *s* of Arnold and Edith Kilner; *m* 1973, Ana Maria del Carmen Sánchez; one *s* one *d.* *Educ:* Univ. of Birmingham (BSc Hons 1968; MSc 1971; PhD 1975). MInstP, CPhys 1987; FIMMM (FIM 2000); FInstP 2002; CSci 2007; CEng 2007. Res. Fellow and SERC Postdoctoral Res. Fellow, Univ. of Leeds, 1975–79; Department of Materials, Imperial College: Wolfson Res. Fellow, 1979–83; SERC Advanced Res. Fellow, IT, 1983–87; Lectr, 1987–91; Reader in Materials, 1991–95; Prof. of Materials Sci., 1995–2006; Head of Dept, 2000–06; Dean, RSM, 1998–2000. Gp Leader, Ceramic Electrolytes Gp, CIC Energigune, Vitoria, Spain, 2011–. Co-Founder, Ceres Power Ltd, 2001, now Consultant. Member: Polar Solids Discussion Gp, RSC, 1981–; European Materials Res. Soc., 1991–. An Associate Ed., Materials Letters, 1992–; European Ed., Solid State Ionics, 2004–. FCGI 2007. Christian Frederick Schoenbein Gold Medal of Honour, European Solid Oxide Fuel Cell Forum, 2014; Verulam Prize and Medal, 2004; Platinum Medal, 2012, IMMM; Royal Soc. Armourers and Brasiers Award, 2005; Somiya Award, Internat. Union of Materials Res. Socs, 2012; Daiwa Adrian Award, Daiwa Adrian Foundn, 2016; Imperial Coll. Medal, 2017. *Publications:* contribs to sci. jls. *Recreations:* travel, walking, food, drink. *Address:* 34 Castle Avenue, Ewell, Surrey KT17 2PQ. *T:* (020) 8224 7959. *Club:* Athenæum.

**KILNER, Sarah-Jayne;** *see* Blakemore, S.-J.

**KILPATRICK, Francesca;** *see* Greenoak, F.

**KILPATRICK, Helen Marjorie,** CB 2010; HM Diplomatic Service, retired; Governor, Cayman Islands, 2013–18; *b* 9 Oct. 1958; *d* of Henry Ball and Nan Dixon Ball; one *s* one *d.* *Educ:* King's Coll., Cambridge (BA 1981). Mem. CIPFA 1986. Finance posts at GLC, London Bor. of Tower Hamlets and London Bor. of Southwark, 1982–89; Controller of Financial Services, London Bor. of Greenwich, 1989–95; Dir for Resources, Co. Treas. and Dep. Chief Exec., West Sussex CC, 1995–2005; Treas., Sussex Police Authy, 1995–2005; Dir Gen., Financial and Commercial, Home Office, 2005–13. *E:* helen.kilpatrick@btinternet.com.

**KILPATRICK, Reginald M.;** *see* Mitchell Kilpatrick.

**KILROY-SILK, Robert;** Chairman, The Kilroy Television Co., 1989; *b* 19 May 1942; *s* of William Silk (RN, killed in action, 1943) and Rose O'Rooke; *m* 1963, Jan Beech; one *s* one *d.* *Educ:* Saltley Grammar Sch., Birmingham; LSE (BScEcon). Lectr, Dept of Political Theory and Institutions, Liverpool Univ., 1966–74; television presenter: Day to Day, 1986–87; Kilroy, 1987–2004; Shafted, 2001. Contested (Lab) Ormskirk, 1970; MP (Lab): Ormskirk, Feb. 1974–1983; Knowsley N, 1983–86; PPS to Minister for the Arts, 1974–75; opposition frontbench spokesman on Home Office, 1984–85. Mem., Home Affairs Select Cttee, 1979–84; Vice-Chairman: Merseyside Gp of MPs, 1974–75; PLP Home Affairs Gp, 1976–86; Chairman: Parly All-Party Penal Affairs Gp, 1979–86; PLP Civil Liberties Gp, 1979–84; Parly Alcohol Policy and Services Group, 1982–83. Contested (Veritas) Erewash, 2005. MEP (UK Ind, then Veritas) E Midlands, 2004–09. Member: Council, Howard League for Penal Reform, 1979; Adv. Council, Inst. of Criminology, Cambridge Univ., 1984; Sponsor, Radical Alternatives to Prison, 1977–; Patron, APEX Trust; Chm., FARE, 1981–84. Governor, National Heart and Chest Hospital, 1974–77. Political columnist: Time Out, 1985–86; Police Review, 1983; columnist: The Times, 1987–90; Today, 1988–90; Daily Express, 1990–96; Sunday Express, 2001–04. *Publications:* Socialism since Marx, 1972; (contrib.) The Role of Commissions in Policy Making, 1973; The Ceremony of Innocence: a novel of 1984, 1984; Hard Labour: the political diary of Robert Kilroy-Silk, 1986; *novels:* Betrayal, 2011; Closure, 2011; Abduction, 2011; articles in Political Studies, Manchester School of Economic and Social Science, Political Quarterly, Industrial and Labor Relations Review, Parliamentary Affairs, etc. *Recreation:* gardening.

**KIMBER, Sir Rupert Edward Watkin,** 5th Bt *cr* 1904, of Lansdowne Lodge, co. London; Principal, Tiburon Partners LLP, since 2009; *b* 20 June 1962; *s* of Sir Timothy Roy Henry Kimber, 4th Bt and Antonia Kathleen Brenda, *d* of Sir Francis John Watkin Williams, 8th Bt, QC; *S* father, 2012; *m* 1997, Lisa Caroline Samantha Cave; three *d.* *Educ:* Univ. of York (BA Politics). With Cazenove, 1984–2003 (Partner, 1997–2003); KBC Financial Products, 2003–05; Polar Capital, 2005–07; Belvedere Investment Partners, 2007–09. *Heir: b* Hugo Charles Kimber [*b* 4 April 1964; *m* 1996, Alexandra Sabine Joanna Hoogeweegen; two *s* one *d*]. *Address:* The Old Hall, Blickling Road, Aylsham, Norfolk NR11 6ND.

**KIMBERLEY, 5th Earl of,** *cr* 1866; **John Armine Wodehouse,** CEng; Bt 1611; Baron Wodehouse 1797; internet and computer consultant, since 2012; *b* 15 Jan. 1951; *s* of 4th Earl of Kimberley and his 2nd wife, Carmel June (*née* Maguire); *S* father, 2002; *m* 1973, Hon. Carol Palmer, (Rev. Canon Countess of Kimberley), MA (Oxon), PGCE, *er d* of 3rd Baron Palmer, OBE; one *s* one *d.* *Educ:* Eton; Univ. of East Anglia (BSc (Chemistry) 1973; MSc (Physical Organic Chemistry) 1974). CEng 1993; MBCS 1988; CITP 2004. Glaxo, subseq. Glaxo Wellcome: Research Chemist, 1974–79; Systems Programmer, 1979–86, Prin. Systems Programmer, 1987–95; Advanced Informatics and Tech. Specialist, Glaxo Wellcome, subseq. GlaxoSmithKline, 1996–2003; Sen. Internet Analyst, GlaxoSmithKline, 2003–12. Chm., UK Info Users Gp, 1981–83. Fellow, British Interplanetary Soc., 1984 (Associate Fellow, 1981–83). Reader, C of E, 2008–. FRSA. *Recreations:* interest in spaceflight, photography, computing, cats, walking, spirituality. *Heir: s* Lord Wodehouse, *qv. Address:* Fieldfares, Ferry Lane, Medmenham, Marlow, Bucks SL7 2EZ.

**KIMBLIN, Richard Thomas;** QC 2016; *b* Oldham, 10 Dec. 1966; *s* of Thomas and Doris Kimblin; *m* 1994, Annette Jones; two *s.* *Educ:* Durham Univ. (BSc Hons; PhD 1991). Res. asst, 1988–92; Royal Soc. Western Eur. Fellow, Univ. de Paris XI, 1992; Consultant, CES, 1993–98; called to the Bar, Middle Temple, 1998; in practice as a barrister, 1999–. Mem. Council, UK Envmtl Law Assoc., 2005–15 (Chm., 2013–15). *Recreations:* upkeep of and keeping up with sons, good tastes and creating them. *Address:* No 5 Chambers, 4–7 Salisbury Court, EC4Y 8AA. *T:* (020) 7900 1582. *E:* rk@no5.com.

**KIMMINS, Charles Dominic;** QC 2010; *b* London, 1971; *s* of Malcolm Kimmins, CVO, DL and Jane Kimmins; *m* 2003, Talita De Brito e Cunha; one *s* two *d.* *Educ:* Eton Coll.; Trinity Coll., Cambridge (BA 1st Cl. Hons 1993). Called to the Bar, Inner Temple, 1994; in practice as barrister, specialising in commercial law. *Recreations:* horse racing, ski-ing, golf, theatre. *Address:* 20 Essex Street, WC2R 3AL. *T:* (020) 7842 1200, *Fax:* (020) 7842 1270. *E:* ckimmins@20essexst.com. *Clubs:* White's; Swinley Forest Golf; Derby.

**KIMMINS, Simon Edward Anthony,** VRD 1967; author; Lt-Comdr RNR; *b* 26 May 1930; *s* of late Captain Anthony Kimmins, OBE, RN, and Elizabeth Kimmins; two *s* three *d* (and one *s* decd); *m* 2007, Ingrid Jeanne Aleida Sickler. *Educ:* Horris Hill; Charterhouse. Man. Dir, London American Finance Corp. Ltd (originally BOECC Ltd), 1957–73; Dir, Balfour Williamson, 1971–74; Chief Exec., Thomas Cook Gp, 1973–75; Dir, Debenhams Ltd, 1972–85; Chief Exec., Delfinance SA Geneva, 1984–98; Chm., Associated Retail Develts Internat., 1980–85; Pres., Piguet Internat., 1986–91; Chief Exec., then Chm., Interoute Telecommunications (Switzerland) SA, 1996–99; Chief Exec., YoStream Holdings BV, Holland, 2000–05; Strategic Investment Dir, Ron Winter Gp, 2005–. Vice-Pres., British Export Houses Assoc., 1974–80 (Chm., 1970–72); Chm., Protelecom Carriers Cttee, 1998–2000. Governor, RSC, 1975–2007. *Recreations:* cricket (played for Kent), golf, writing. *Address:* 3 Westbourne House, Mount Park Road, Harrow on the Hill, Middx HA1 3JT. *Club:* Garrick.

**KIMMONS, Rear Adm. Michael,** CB 2008; Chief Executive, British Orthopaedic Association, 2010–17; *b* 24 Dec. 1953; *s* of Robert Edward Kimmons and Patricia Kimmons (*née* Wyn); *m* 1st, 1979, Christine Joy Spittle (marr. diss. 2015); one *s* one *d*; 2nd, 2015, Susan Kay Allen. *Educ:* Stamford Sch.; Heriot-Watt Univ. (BA Hons Modern Langs). Joined RN, 1972; served in HM Ships, Intrepid, Jupiter, Hermes, Active, Illustrious, Royal Yacht Britannia; Sec. to First Sea Lord, 1999–2001; rcds 2002; Director: Naval Personnel Corporate Programming, 2002–03; Naval Staff, 2003–05; COS to Second Sea Lord and COS (Support) to C-in-C Fleet, 2005–07; Chief Naval Logistics Officer, 2005–08; Sen. Directing Staff (Navy), RCDS, 2007–08. ADC to the Queen, 2004–05. Chief Exec., St Philips Chambers Ltd, Birmingham, 2008–09; Dir, Kimmons and Kimmons Ltd, 2009–12. NATO Medal 1995. *Publications:* (contrib.) Seaford House Papers, 2002. *Recreations:* golf, international relations. *Clubs:* Copthorne Golf (W Sussex); Victory Services (Chair, Council, 2016–).

**KINAHAN, Daniel de Burgh;** DL; Director, Upton Public Affairs, since 2017; *b* Belfast, 14 April 1958; *s* of Sir Robert George Caldwell Kinahan and of Coralie Kinahan (*née* de Burgh); *m* 1991, Anna Marguerite Bence-Trower; one *s* three *d.* *Educ:* Stowe Sch., Bucks; Royal Military Acad., Sandhurst; Edinburgh Univ. (BCom). Served Blues and Royals, 1977–84; Asst PR Manager, Short Bros, 1985–88; Rep. for Ireland and NI, Christie's, 1988–2003; estabd Danny Kinahan Fine Art and Castle Upton Gall., 2003–11. Mem. (UU) S Antrim BC, 2005–09. Mem. (UU) S Antrim, NI Assembly, 2009–June 2015. MP (UU) S Antrim, 2015–17; contested (UU) same seat, 2017. Sqdn Leader, N Irish Horse (TA), 1988–89 (Hon. Col, 2013–19). High Sheriff, Antrim, 1996. *Recreations:* tennis, football, walking, all sport, history, travel, reading, music. *Address:* Castle Upton, Templepatrick, Co. Antrim BT39 0AH. *T:* (028) 9443 3480. *E:* danny@dannykinahan.co.uk. *Club:* Reform (Belfast).

**KINCADE, James,** CBE 1988; MA, PhD; Headmaster, Methodist College, Belfast, 1974–88; *b* 4 Jan. 1925; *s* of George and Rebecca Jane Kincade; *m* 1952, Elizabeth Fay, 2nd *d* of J. Anderson Piggot, OBE, DL, JP; one *d* (and one *s* decd). *Educ:* Foyle Coll.; Magee University Coll.; Trinity Coll. Dublin (Schol. and Gold Medallist, MA, Stein Research Prize); Oriel Coll., Oxford (MA, BLitt); Edinburgh Univ. (PhD). Served RAF, India and Burma, 1944–47 (commnd, 1945). Senior English Master, Merchiston Castle Sch., 1952–61; Vis. Professor of Philosophy, Indiana Univ., 1959; Headmaster, Royal Sch., Dungannon, 1961–74. Dir, Design Council, NI, 1990–93; Mem., Design Council, UK, 1993–94 (Chm., NI Cttee, 1993–94); Chairman: Fashion Business Centre, NI, 1992–94; NI Fashion & Design Centre, 1992–94. Nat. Gov. for NI, BBC, 1985–91. President, Ulster

Headmasters' Assoc., 1975–77; Vice Pres., Assoc. for Art and Design Educn, 1991–; Mem., Council for Catholic Maintained Schools, 1987–90. Mem. of Senate, and Mem. Standing Cttee, QUB, 1982–98. Pres., Belfast Literary Soc., 2002–03. Trustee, Save the Homeless Fund, 1990–2007. Hon. LLD QUB, 2000. *Publications:* articles in Mind, Hermathena, Jl of Religion. *Recreation:* reading. *Address:* 10A Harry's Road, Hillsborough BT26 6HJ. *T:* (028) 9268 3865.

**KINCH, Carol Lesley;** *see* Atkinson, C. L.

**KINCH, Christopher Anthony;** QC 1999; **His Honour Judge Kinch;** a Circuit Judge, since 2012; a Senior Circuit Judge, Resident Judge for Woolwich, since 2013; Hon. Recorder of Greenwich, since 2014; *b* 27 May 1953; *s* of late Anthony Alec Kinch, CBE and Barbara Patricia Kinch; *m* 1994, Carol Lesley Atkinson, *qv*; one *s* two *d. Educ:* Bishop Challoner Sch., Shortlands, Bromley; Christ Church, Oxford (MA Modern Hist.). Called to the Bar, Lincoln's Inn, 1976, Bencher, 2007; Stagiare, EC Commn, 1976–77; in practice at the Bar, 1977–2012; Asst Recorder, 1994–98; Recorder, 1998–2012; Head of Chambers, 23 Essex Street, 2005–09. Mem., SE Circuit Cttee, 1992–95 and 1996–99. Dir of Educn, 2005–08, Vice-Chm., 2009–10, Chm., 2010–11, Criminal Bar Assoc. Chairman: Kent Bar Mess, 2001–04; Nat. Mock Trial for Schs Competition Working Party, 1999–2009. Trustee, Citizenship Foundn, 2006–15. *Recreations:* my family, Rugby, cricket. *Address:* Woolwich Crown Court, 2 Belmarsh Road, SE28 0EY. *Club:* Beckenham Rugby Football.

**KINCHEN, Richard,** MVO 1976; HM Diplomatic Service, retired; Ambassador to Belgium, 2003–07; *b* 12 Feb. 1948; *s* of Victor and Margaret Kinchen; *m* 1972, Cheryl Vivienne Abayasekera; one *s* two *d* (and one *d* decd). *Educ:* King Edward VI Sch., Southampton; Trinity Hall, Cambridge (BA). Entered FCO, 1970; attached British Commn on Rhodesian Opinion, 1972; MECAS, 1972; Kuwait, 1973; FCO, 1974; Luxembourg, 1975; Paris, 1977; FCO, 1980; Pvte Sec. to Parly Under-Sec. of State, 1982; Rabat, 1984; Counsellor, UK Mission to UN, 1988–93; Head: Regl Secretariat for British Dependent Territories in Caribbean, 1993–96; Resource Planning Dept, FCO, 1997–2000; Ambassador to Lebanon, 2000–03. Member: UN Adv. Cttee on Admin. and Budgetary Questions, 1991–93; UN Jt Staff Pension Bd, 1992–93. *Address:* 12 Windermere Way, Farnham, Surrey GU9 0DE.

**KINCLAVEN, Hon. Lord;** Alexander Featherstonhaugh Wylie, OBE 2017; a Senator of the College of Justice in Scotland, since 2005; *b* 2 June 1951; *s* of Ian Hamilton Wylie and Helen Jane Mearns or Wylie; *m* 1975, Gail Elizabeth Watson Duncan; two *d. Educ:* Edinburgh Univ. (LLB Hons). ACIArb 1977, FCIArb 1991. Qualified Solicitor in Scotland, 1976; called to the Scottish Bar, 1978; called to the Bar, Lincoln's Inn, 1990. Standing Junior Counsel in Scotland to Accountant of Court, 1986–89; Advocate Depute, 1989–92; QC (Scot.) 1991; part-time Sheriff, 2000–05. Chm. (part-time), Police Appeals Tribunal, 2001–05. Jt Chm., Discipline Cttee, Inst. of Chartered Accountants of Scotland, 1994–2005; Member: (part-time), Scottish Legal Aid Bd, 1994–2002; Scottish Council of Law Reporting, 2001–05; Scottish Criminal Cases Review Commn, 2004–05. *Address:* Supreme Courts, Parliament House, Parliament Square, Edinburgh EH1 1RQ.

**KINDER, David Stephen,** CBE 2018; UK Alternative Executive Director, Board of World Bank Group, since 2016; *b* Cardiff, 22 Aug. 1979; *s* of John and Pauline Kinder. *Educ:* Radyr Comprehensive Sch.; Leeds Univ. (BA French and German); Univ. de Marne-la-Vallée (MA Political Sci.). Branch Hd, Eur. Econ. Reform Team, 2005–08, Delivery Advr, Prime Minister's Delivery Unit, 2009, HM Treasury; Hd, Global Carbon Mkt Policy, DECC, 2009–11; Hd, MF Policy, 2011–12; Dep. Dir, Contingency Planning, Econ. and Domestic Affairs Secretariat, Cabinet Office, 2012; HM Treasury: Deputy Director: Tax Admin, Spending and Reform Team, Feb.–Aug. 2013; Financial Regulations and Mkt Services Gp, 2013–14; Workforce, Pay and Pensions, 2014–16. *Recreations:* sports - tennis, volleyball, soccer, pool, darts, travel, cooking, mental health and LGBT+ advocacy.

**KINDER, Ian David;** Chief Executive, UK Commission for Employment and Skills, 2016–17; *b* Ashton-Under-Lyne, 28 March 1958; *s* of James Edwin Kinder and Heather Margaret Kinder; *m* 1980, Jill Ashford; one *s* one *d. Educ:* Audenshaw Grammar Sch.; St John's Coll. of Further Educn, Manchester (ONC Business Studies). Customs Officer, HM Customs and Excise, 1976–81; MAFF, 1981–87; HEO, Manpower Services Commn, 1987–91; Regl Mgr, Management Charter Initiative, 1991–94; Business Manager, Go North West, 1994–2000; Nat. Policy Dir, Small Business Service, DTI, 2000–07; Partnership Dir, LSC, 2007–09; Dep. Dir, 2009–11, Exec. Dir, 2011–16, UK Commn for Employment and Skills. *Publications:* (contrib. and ed) 50 Activities for Developing Management Skills, vol. 6, 1991. *Recreations:* golf, gardening, classic cars, travel. *Address:* Manchester.

**KINDERSLEY,** family name of **Baron Kindersley.**

**KINDERSLEY, 4th Baron** *cr* 1941; **Rupert John Molesworth Kindersley;** Director, Investment Banking, Terastream Broadband Inc., Toronto, since 2014; Executive Director, Georgian Bay Association, since 2018; *b* London, England, 11 March 1955; *s* of 3rd Baron Kindersley and Venice Marigold Kindersley (*née* Hill), (Lady Rosie Kindersley) (*d* 2016); *S* father, 2013; *m* 1975, Sarah Anne (*née* Warde); one *s* one *d. Educ:* Eton Coll.; Trinity Coll. Univ. of Toronto (BA Econs). Asst Branch Manager, Toronto Dominion Bank, 1977–80; Project Finance Exec. and Mem., EEC Advr's team, Midland Bank International, 1989–85; Director and Company Secretary: Allied Entertainments Gp, 1985–86; Daniels Gp, 1986–93; Dir, Edgecombe Gp/Edgemark Capital Gp, 1993–98; Dir, Commercial Credit, Elliot Lake & North Shore Corpn for Business Develt, 1998–99; stockbroker, Brawley Cathers Ltd, 1999–2002; Dir and Treas., InnLand Hospitality Inc. 2002–; corporate finance, Cityspace Inc., 2002–; investment banker, Union Securities Ltd, 2006, team moved to MGI Securities Inc., 2009, merged with IA Securities Inc., 2014. *Recreations:* walking dogs, reading, swimming, cross-country ski-ing. *Heir: s* Hon. Frederick Hugh Molesworth Kindersley, *b* 9 Jan. 1987. *Address:* 15 Falcon Street, Toronto, ON M4S 2P4, Canada. *T:* (home) (416) 4855103, (office) (416) 4855103. *E:* rupert@kindersley.us.

**KINDERSLEY, Lydia Helena L. C.;** *see* Lopes Cardozo Kindersley.

**KINDERSLEY, Peter David;** Chairman, Dorling Kindersley, publishers, 1974–2000; *b* 13 July 1941; *s* of late David Kindersley, MBE and of Christine Kindersley; *m* 1965, Juliet Elizabeth Martyn; one *s* one *d. Educ:* King Edward VI School, Norwich; Camberwell School of Arts and Crafts. Founding Art Director, Mitchell Beazley, 1969–74. Owner, Sheepdrove Organic Farm. Chm., Neal's Yard Remedies, 2005–. Fellow, Univ. of the Arts London (formerly London Inst.), 2001; FRSA 2000. DUniv Open 2002. *Recreations:* environment, biodiversity, interesting work.

**KING,** family name of **Baron King of Bridgwater.**

**KING OF BOW,** Baroness *cr* 2011 (Life Peer), of Bow in the London Borough of Tower Hamlets; **Oona Tamsyn King;** broadcaster, campaigner and political diarist; Director of Diversity Strategy, Google, since 2018; *b* 22 Oct. 1967; *d* of Prof. Preston King and Hazel King; *m* 1994, Tiberio Santomarco; one *s* and one adopted *s* two adopted *d. Educ:* Haverstock Comprehensive Secondary Sch.; York Univ. (BA 1st cl. Hons Politics); Univ. of Calif, Berkeley (Scholar). Stagiare for Socialist Gp, EP, 1991; Political Asst to Glyn Ford, MEP, 1991–93; Mem., John Smith's Campaign Team for leadership of Labour Party, 1992; Political Asst to Glenys Kinnock, MEP, 1994–95; Trade Union Organiser, Equality Officer, GMB Southern Region, 1995–97. MP (Lab) Bethnal Green and Bow, 1997–2005; contested (Lab) same seat, 2005. PPS to Sec. of State for Trade and Industry, 2003–05. Member, Select Committee: on Internat. Develt, 1997–2001; on Urban Affairs, 2001–03; founding Chair, All-Party Gp on Genocide Prevention, 1998–2005. Freelance journalist and television presenter, 2005–07. Dep. Asst Pol Sec, 2007–08, Sen. Advr, 2008–09, to Prime Minister. Hd of Diversity, Channel 4, 2009–16; Dir of Diversity and Multicultural Marketing, YouTube, 2016–17. Vice-Chm., British Council, 1998–2001; founding Chair, Rich Mix Cultural Foundn, 1999–2009; Chair, Inst. of Community Cohesion, 2007–09. Gov., BFI, 2013–18. *Publications:* House Music, 2007. *Recreations:* cinema, music. *Address:* 129 Antill Road, E3 5BW.

**KING OF BRIDGWATER,** Baron *cr* 2001 (Life Peer), of Bridgwater in the County of Somerset; **Thomas Jeremy King,** CH 1992; PC 1979; *b* 13 June 1933; *s* of late J. H. King, JP; *m* 1960, Jane, *d* of late Brig. Robert Tilney, CBE, DSO, TD; one *s* one *d. Educ:* Rugby; Emmanuel Coll., Cambridge (MA). National service, 1951–53: commnd Somerset Light Inf., 1952; seconded to KAR; served Tanganyika and Kenya; Actg Captain 1953. Cambridge, 1953–56. Joined E. S. & A. Robinson Ltd, Bristol, 1956; various positions up to Divisional Gen. Man., 1964–69; Chairman: Sale, Tilney Co. Ltd, 1971–79 (Dir, 1965–79); London Internat. Exhibition Centre Ltd, 1994–2008 (Dir, 2008–); Dir, Electra Investment Trust, 1992–2008. MP (C) Bridgwater, March 1970–2001. PPS to: Minister for Posts and Telecommunications, 1970–72; Minister for Industrial Develt, 1972–74; Front Bench spokesman for: Industry, 1975–76; Energy, 1976–79; Minister for Local Govt and Environmental Services, DoE, 1979–83; Sec. of State for the Environment, Jan.–June 1983, for Transport, June–Oct. 1983, for Employment, 1983–85, for NI, 1985–89, for Defence, 1989–92. Chm., Parly Intelligence and Security Cttee, 1994–2001; Mem., Cttee on Standards in Public Life, 1994–97. *Recreations:* cricket, ski-ing. *Address:* House of Lords, SW1A 0PW.
*See also* S. R. Clarke.

**KING OF LOTHBURY,** Baron *cr* 2013 (Life Peer), of Lothbury in the City of London; **Mervyn Allister King,** KG 2014; GBE 2011; DL; FBA 1992; Professor of Economics and Law, since 2014 and Alan Greenspan Professor of Economics, New York University; School Professor of Economics, London School of Economics and Political Science, since 2015; Governor, Bank of England, 2003–13; *b* 30 March 1948; *s* of Eric Frank King and Kathleen Alice Passingham; *m* 2007, Barbara Melander. *Educ:* Wolverhampton Grammar School; King's College, Cambridge (BA 1st cl. hons 1969, MA 1973; Hon. Fellow, 2004). Research Officer, Dept of Applied Economics, Cambridge, 1969–76; Kennedy Schol., Harvard Univ., 1971–72; Fellow, St John's Coll., Cambridge, 1972–77 (Hon. Fellow, 1997); Lectr, Faculty of Economics, Cambridge, 1976–77; Esmée Fairbairn Prof. of Investment, Univ. of Birmingham, 1977–84; Prof. of Economics, LSE, 1984–95; Bank of England: non-exec. Dir, 1990–91; Chief Economist and Exec. Dir, 1991–98; Dep. Gov., 1998–2003; Founder Mem., Monetary Policy Cttee, 1997, Chm., 2003–13; Chm., Interim Financial Policy Cttee, 2011–13. Vice Chm., European Systematic Risk Bd, 2011–13. Visiting Professor of Economics: Harvard Univ., 1982–83, 1990; MIT, 1983–84; LSE, 1996–2013; Visiting Fellow: Nuffield Coll., Oxford, 2002–; Council on For. Relns, 2013–. Co-Dir, LSE Financial Markets Gp, 1987–91. Member: City Capital Markets Cttee, 1989–91; Group of Thirty, 1997–. President: Eur. Econ. Assoc., 1993; Inst. for Fiscal Studies, 1999–2003 (Hon. Life Mem., 2006). Member: Meade Cttee, 1975–78; Council and Exec., Royal Economic Soc., 1981–86, 1992–97; Bd, The Securities Assoc., 1987–89. Fellow, Econometric Soc., 1982. Managing Editor, Review of Economic Studies, 1978–83; Associate Editor: Jl of Public Economics, 1982–98; Amer. Economic Review, 1985–88. Trustee: Kennedy Meml Trust, 1990–2000; Nat. Gall., 2005–09, 2014–18. Mem., Adv. Council, LSO, 2001–. Patron, Worcs CCC, 2004– (Pres., 2015–17). Hon. Foreign Mem., Amer. Acad. of Arts and Scis, 2000. DL Kent, 2016. Hon. Dr: London Guildhall, 2001; City, Birmingham, 2002; Wolverhampton, LSE, 2003; Worcester, 2008; Hon. DCL Kent, 2012; Dr *hc* Edinburgh, 2005; Helsinki, 2006; Hon. LLD Cambridge, 2006. Helsinki Univ. Medal, 1982. *Publications:* Public Policy and the Corporation, 1977; (with J. A. Kay) The British Tax System, 1978, 5th edn 1990; (with D. Fullerton) The Taxation of Income from Capital, 1984; The End of Alchemy, 2016; (with J. Kay) Radical Uncertainty, 2020; numerous articles in economics jls. *Address:* House of Lords, SW1A 0PW. *Clubs:* Athenæum, Brooks's, Garrick; All England Lawn Tennis and Croquet.

**KING, Alison Sarah;** *see* Grief, A. S.

**KING, Andrew;** *b* 14 Sept. 1948; *s* of late Charles King and Mary King; *m* 1975, Semma Ahmet; one *d. Educ:* St John the Baptist Sch., Uddingston; Coatbridge Tech. Coll.; Missionary Inst., London; Hatfield Poly.; Stevenage Coll. (CQSW); Nene Coll., Northants (CMS). Labourer; Postal Officer; apprentice motor vehicle mechanic; Social Work Manager, Northants CC, 1989–97; social services, 2005–16. Member: Warwickshire CC, 1989–98 (Chm., Social Services, 1993–96); Rugby BC, 1995–98. MP (Lab) Rugby and Kenilworth, 1997–2005; contested: (Lab) same seat, 2005; (Lab) Rugby, 2010. Member: Social Security Select Cttee, 1999–2001; Deregulation Select Cttee, 1999–2005. Mem., Unison (formerly NALGO), 1978–. *Recreations:* golf, dominoes. *Clubs:* Hillmorton Ex-Servicemen's; Rugby Golf, Rugby Labour.

**KING, Prof. Andrew John,** PhD; FMedSci, FPhysiol; FRS 2018; Professor of Neurophysiology, since 2004, Director, Centre for Integrative Neuroscience, Department of Physiology, Anatomy and Genetics, since 2016, and Wellcome Trust Principal Research Fellow, since 2006, University of Oxford; Fellow, Merton College, Oxford, since 2002; *b* Greenford, Middx, 8 April 1959; *s* of Neville Douglas King and Audrey Kathleen King (*née* Manix); partner, Dr Scott Bryan. *Educ:* Eliot's Green Grammar Sch.; Northolt High Sch.; King's Coll. London (BSc Physiol.); King's Coll. London and Nat. Inst. for Med. Res. (PhD 1984). University of Oxford: Douglas McAlpine Jun. Res. Fellow in Neurol., Green Coll., 1983–86; SERC Postdoctoral Fellow, Lab. of Physiol., 1984–86; E. P. Abraham Cephalosporin Jun. Res. Fellow in Med. Scis, Lincoln Coll., 1986–89; Lister Inst. Res. Fellow, 1986–91, Wellcome Trust Sen. Res. Fellow in Basic Biomed. Sci., 1991–2006, Lab. of Physiology; Res. Lectr, 1996–2000; Reader in Auditory Physiol., 2000–04; Sen. Res. Fellow in Med. Scis, Merton Coll., 2002–07. Vis. Prof., Univ. of Salamanca, 2012; Vis. Asst Scientist, Eye Res. Inst., Retina Foundn, Boston, Mass, 1988. Chief Scientific Advr, Deafness Res. UK, 2011–13. FMedSci 2011; FPhysiol 2017. Layton Sci. Res. Award, KCL, 1980; Wellcome Prize Medal and Lect. in Physiol., 1990. *Publications:* (jtly) Auditory Neuroscience: making sense of sound, 2011; contrib. book chapters; contribs to scientific jls. *Recreations:* gardening, cooking, Renaissance and Baroque music. *Address:* Department of Physiology, Anatomy and Genetics, Sherrington Building, University of Oxford, Parks Road, Oxford OX1 3PT. *E:* andrew.king@dpag.ox.ac.uk.

**KING, Angela Audrey Mary;** Founder Director and Joint Director, Common Ground, 1982–2012; freelance campaigner; *b* 27 June 1944; *d* of Dr George John Graham King and Audrey Thora Dorothee King. *Educ:* Queensmount Sch.; St Christopher Sch., Letchworth; Millfield Sch., Som; Mayer Sch. of Fashion Design, NY. Fashion designer and buyer, NY,

1965–70; Friends of the Earth: wildlife campaigner, 1971–75; campaigned for ban on imports of leopard, cheetah and tiger skins, implemented 1972; (jtly) drafted Wild Creatures and Wild Plants Bill (enacted 1975), and Endangered Species (Import and Export) Act (enacted 1976); Initiator: Save the Whale Campaign, 1972 (campaigned for import ban on baleen whale products, introduced 1973, and Internat. Whaling Commn's 10 year ban on commercial whaling, introduced 1982); (jtly) Otter Project, 1976 (campaigned for ban on otter hunting in England and Wales, introduced 1978); Jt Co-ordinator, Otter Haven Project, 1977–80; Consultant, Earth Resources Res., 1979–80; author of NCC report on wildlife habitat loss, 1981; founded (with Sue Clifford and Roger Deakin) Common Ground, 1982; initiator with Sue Clifford of several projects, including: New Milestones, 1985; Trees, Woods and the Green Man, 1986; Parish Maps Project, 1987; Campaign for Local Distinctiveness, 1990; Confluence, 1998; Orgnr, exhibns which link the arts and the envmt. *Publications:* (ed jtly) Second Nature, 1984; (jtly) Holding Your Ground: an action guide to local conservation, 1987; (ed jtly) Trees Be Company (poetry anthology), 1989, 2nd edn 2001; (jtly) The Apple Source Book, 1991, enlarged edn 2007; (ed jtly) Local Distinctiveness: place particularity and identity, 1993; (jtly) Celebrating Local Distinctiveness, 1994; (ed jtly) from place to PLACE: maps and Parish Maps, 1996; (ed jtly) Field Days: an anthology of poetry, 1998; (ed jtly) The River's Voice: an anthology of poetry, 2000; (ed jtly) The Common Ground Book of Orchards, 2000; (with Sue Clifford) England in Particular: a celebration of the commonplace, the local, the vernacular and the distinctive, 2006; (with Sue Clifford) Community Orchards Handbook, 2008, 2nd edn 2011; conservation guides, and pamphlets, for Friends of the Earth, Common Ground, etc. *Recreations:* gardening, walking, watching wildlife, reading. *Address:* c/o Common Ground, Lower Dairy, Toller Fratrum, Dorchester, Dorset DT2 0EL. *T:* (01300) 321778.

**KING, Ann P.;** *see* Francke, A. P.

**KING, Annette, (Mrs Henry Stevens);** Chief Executive Officer, Publicis Groupe UK, since 2018; *b* Farnborough, 29 Sept. 1968; *d* of Frank and Linda King; *m* 2005, Henry Stevens; one *s*. *Educ:* Oxford Brookes Univ. (BA Hons Business Studies; DipM). Account Dir, Wunderman London, 1992–96; Vice Pres. Account Dir, Wunderman NY, 1996–2000; Man. Partner, 2000–06, Man. Dir, 2006–08, CEO, 2008–12, CEO EMEA, 2012–14, OgilvyOne UK; CEO, Ogilvy and Mather Gp UK, then Ogilvy Gp UK, 2014–17. Non-exec. Dir, London First, 2011–14. Advr, Strategic Adv. Council, Royal Mail, 2011–14. Mem. Council, IPA, 2010–16. *Recreations:* collecting art, theatre, entertaining. *Address:* Publicis UK, 82 Baker Street, W1U 6AE. *Clubs:* 30; Women in Advertising and Communications London, Marketing Group of GB.

**KING, Anthony James Langdale;** Isle of Man Pensions Ombudsman, 2007–18; Ombudsman, Financial Ombudsman Service, 2015–18; Lay Member, Office for Legal Complaints, 2015–18; *b* Birmingham, 20 Feb. 1953; *s* of late Norman Edward King and Florence Elizabeth King; *m* 2015, Alvine Elizabeth Baltzars (*d* 2018). *Educ:* St David's University Coll., Univ. of Wales (BA Hons 1976). Casework Dir for Pensions Ombudsman, 1994–2003; Financial Ombudsman Service: Ombudsman, 2003–05; Lead Ombudsman, Pensions and Securities, 2005–07; Pensions Ombudsman, 2007–15. Mem., Lord Chancellor's Adv. Cttee for the SW (formerly Dorset) and SW Regional Conduct Panel, 2017–. Chm., Ombudsman Assoc., 2012–14. *Recreations:* music (listening well and playing badly), gardening, walking, reading, beer.

**KING, His Honour Anthony William Poole;** a Circuit Judge, 1993–2012; *b* 18 Aug. 1942; *s* of late Edmund Poole King and Pamela Midelton King (*née* Baker); *m* 1971, Camilla Anne Alexandra Brandreth; two *s* one *d*. *Educ:* Winchester Coll.; Worcester Coll., Oxford (MA Jur.). Called to the Bar, Inner Temple, 1966; a Recorder, 1987–93; Midland and Oxford Circuit. *Recreations:* fishing, other people's gardens. *Address:* c/o Oxford Crown and County Court, St Aldate's, Oxford OX1 1TL.

**KING, (Austin) Michael (Henry);** charity mediator; Consultant Solicitor, Stone King LLP (formerly Stone King), 2014–18 (Partner, 1975–2014; Chairman, 1997–2014); *b* Bath, 9 Feb. 1949; *s* of Gerald and Pauline King; *m* 1975, Frances-Anne Sutherland; three *s*. *Educ:* Stonyhurst Coll. Admitted Solicitor, 1974. Chm., Charity Law Assoc., 1997–2000. Trustee, Holburne Mus. of Art, 1999–2007, 2010–. Chm. Govs, Prior Park Coll., 2014–. *Publications:* (with A. Phillips) Charities Act 2006: a guide to the new law, 2005. *Recreations:* sailing, shooting, tennis, watching Rugby, family. *Address:* 42 Flatwoods Road, Claverton Down, Bath BA2 7AQ. *T:* 07977 517304. *E:* michaelking1785@gmail.com. *Club:* Lansdowne.

**KING, Prof. Bernard,** Hon. CBE 2003; PhD; FIWSc; CBiol, FRSB; Vice-Chancellor, University of Abertay Dundee, 1994–2011 (Principal, Dundee Institute of Technology, 1992–94); *b* 4 May 1946; *s* of Bernard and Cathleen King; *m* 1970, Maura Antoinette Collinge; two *d*. *Educ:* Synge St Christian Brothers Sch., Dublin; Coll. of Technology, Dublin; Univ. of Aston in Birmingham (MSc 1972; PhD 1975). FIWSc 1975; CBiol, FRSB (FIBiol 1987). Research Fellow, Univ. of Aston in Birmingham, 1972–76; Dundee Institute of Technology: Lectr, 1976–79; Sen. Lectr, 1979–83; Head, Dept of Molecular Life Scis, 1983–91; Dean, Faculty of Sci., 1987–89; Asst Principal, Robert Gordon Inst. of Technol., 1991–92. Chairman: Scottish Crop Res. Inst., 2003–08; Mylnefield Res. Services Ltd, 2003–08. Board Member: ACU, 2003–06 (Mem. Audit Cttee, 2006–08); Scottish Leadership Foundn, 2004–08; Higher Educn Acad., 2005–10 (Chm., Audit Cttee, 2009–10); Mem., Council for Industry and Higher Educn, 2008–11; Convenor, Universities Scotland, 2010–11 (Vice Convenor, 2006–10); Vice Pres., Universities UK, 2010–11; Mem. Exec., Million +, 2007–11. Eur. Academic Advr, Mulloon Inst., NSW, 2013–. Dir, Plan-It-Cube Ltd, 2015–. Gov., Unicorn Preservation Soc., 1993–. CCMI (CIMgt 1999). *Publications:* numerous scientific and tech. papers on biodeterioration with particular ref. to biodeterioration and preservation of wood. *Recreations:* reading, music, sailing. *Address:* 11 Dalhousie Place, Arbroath, Angus DD11 2BT.

**KING, Billie Jean;** professional tennis player, 1968–83; Chief Executive Officer, Team Tennis, 1981–91; Founder, WTT Charities Inc., 1987; *b* 22 Nov. 1943; *d* of Willard J. Moffitt; *m* 1965, Larry King (marr. diss.). *Educ:* Los Cerritos Sch.; Long Beach High Sch.; Los Angeles State Coll. Played first tennis match at age of eleven; won first championship, Southern California, 1958; coached by Clyde Walker, Alice Marble, Frank Brennan and Mervyn Rose; won first All England Championship, 1966, and five times subseq., and in 1979 achieved record of 20 Wimbledon titles (six Singles, ten Doubles, four Mixed Doubles); has won all other major titles inc. US Singles and Doubles Championships on all four surfaces, and 24 US national titles in all. Pres., Women's Tennis Assoc., 1980–81. Presidential Medal of Freedom (USA), 2009; Lifetime Achievement Award, BBC, 2018. *Publications:* Tennis to Win, 1970; Billie Jean, 1974; (with Joe Hyams) Secrets of Winning Tennis, 1975; Tennis Love (illus. Charles Schulz), 1978; (with Frank Deford) Billie Jean King, 1982; (with Cynthia Starr) We Have Come a Long Way: the story of women's tennis, 1989; (with Christine Brennan) Pressure is a Privilege, 2008. *Address:* c/o World TeamTennis, 247 West 30th Street, 5th Floor, New York, NY 10001, USA.

**KING, Bradley Maurice;** President and Chief Executive Officer, America's Fleet Foundation, 2016–17; *b* 10 June 1955; *s* of Maurice Wilfrid King and June King (*née* Wright); *m* 1977, Linda Ann (*née* Baker); one *s*. *Educ:* Chigwell Sch.; Polytech. of North London (BA Hons 1988); Univ. of Greenwich (MA 1999). Imperial War Museum: joined as Clerical Officer, 1980; Public Services Officer, Film Archive, 1987–2000; on secondment as Mus. Project Officer, Bridport Mus., Dorset, 2000; Keeper, Photograph Archive, 2001–02; Dir, HMS Belfast, 2002–10; Exec. Dir, USS Mass Memorial Cttee Inc., and Battleship Cove Naval Heritage Mus., Battleship Cove, Fall River, 2010–16. Historic Naval Ships Association: Bd Mem., 2006–16; Internat. Co-ordinator, 2007–09; Vice Pres., 2009–11; Pres., 2011–13 (Internat. Leadership Award, 2006; William J. Diffley Award, 2010); Vice Pres., SE Mass Convention and Visitors Bureau, 2013–16. Freeman, City of London, 2007; Liveryman, Shipwrights' Co., 2007. Adviser: World Ship Trust, 2003–13; Bridport Mus. Trust, 2010–13 (Trustee, 2003–10); Member, Board: Sheppey Heritage Trust, 2003–09; London Bridge City Business Improvement District, 2006–10; Mem. Bd (ex Officio), Marine Mus. of Fall River, 2012–16. Volunteer and Ind. Mem. of Governance Cttee, Stow Maries Great War Aerodrome, 2019–. *Publications:* Royal Naval Air Service 1912–1918, 1997. *Recreations:* history, genealogy, woodworking, cooking, flying, motoring. *E:* bradking607@gmail.com.

**KING, Brenda;** First Legislative Counsel, Northern Ireland, since 2012; *b* Belfast, 13 June 1964; *d* of Thomas and Margaret King; *m* 1999, James Sullivan. *Educ:* Queen's Univ. Belfast (LLB Hons 1986; CPLS 1987); Wolfson Coll., Cambridge (LLM Internat. Law 1990); Univ. of S Carolina. Admitted as solicitor, 1989; in private practice, 1987–89; NI Office, 1990–91; Asst Legislative Counsel, NI, 1991–94; Sen. Asst Legislative Counsel, 1994–2001; Legislative Counsel, 2001–12. Mem. Council, Commonwealth Assoc. of Legislative Counsel, 2015– (Pres., 2017–19). *Publications:* (contrib. and ed jtly) Craies on Legislation, 10th edn 2012. *Recreations:* family, friends, theatre, art, travel, Turkey. *Address:* Office of the Legislative Counsel, Parliament Buildings, Stormont, Belfast BT4 3XX. *E:* Brenda.King@ofmdfmni.gov.uk.

**KING, Dr Brian Edmund;** owner manager, King Innovations, 1994–2000; *b* 25 May 1928; *s* of Albert Theodore King and Gladys Johnson; *m* 1952 (marr. diss.); two *s*; *m* 1972, Eunice Wolstenholme; one *d*. *Educ:* Pocklington Sch.; Leeds Univ. TMM (Research) Ltd, 1952–57; British Oxygen, 1957–67; Dir, 1967–87, and Chief Exec., 1977–87, Wira Technology Group Ltd (formerly Wool Industries Research Assoc.); Dir and Chief Exec., Barnsley Business and Innovation Centre, 1987–93. *Recreations:* bridge, swimming, travel, time with grandchildren (Bronte and Evan King and Lola, Cleo and Art Halsey).

**KING, Caradoc;** literary agent; Partner, United Agents LLP, since 2012; *b* 19 Dec. 1946; *s* of late Joan Bartlett (*née* Richardson); *m* 1st, 1975, Jane Grant Morris (marr. diss. 2001); one *s* one *d*; 2nd, 2013, Ingrid Boeck; one *d*. *Educ:* Belmont Abbey; Exeter Coll., Oxford (MA). With Associated Book Publishers, 1968–70; Senior Editor: Allen Lane, Penguin Press, 1970–72; Penguin Books, 1970–75; joined A. P. Watt, 1976: Associate, A. P. Watt & Son, 1976–81; Dir, A. P. Watt Ltd, 1981–2013; Man. Dir and Chm., 1992–96; Jt Man. Dir and Chm., 1996–2012. *Publications:* Problem Child (memoir), 2011. *Recreations:* ski-ing, lunch, collecting wine, motor-biking. *Address:* c/o United Agents LLP, 12–16 Lexington Street, W1F 0LE. *Clubs:* Soho House, Quo Vadis.

**KING, (Catherine) Mary;** mezzo soprano; Director of Voicelab, Southbank Centre, 2006–13. *Educ:* Univ. of Birmingham (BA English); St Anne's Coll., Oxford (PGCE); Guildhall Sch. of Music and Drama. Vocal career encompasses music theatre, opera and recital, with specialism in contemporary repertoire. Dir, The Knack, 1995–2006, Artistic Associate, Baylis Prog., 2004–06, ENO; Hd of Singing and Music, Millennium Performing Arts, Woolwich, 2006–15. Mem., Music Council, Royal Philharmonic Soc. Trustee, Orpheus Centre, 1999–2004. Hon. ARAM; Hon. Fellow, Rose Bruford Coll.; Hon. FRNCM 2011. *Publications:* (with A. Legge) The Singer's Handbook, 2007; Boosey Voice Coach, vol. 1: Singing in English, 2007, vol. 2: Singing in French, 2009, vol. 3: Singing in German, 2010. *Recreation:* gardening.

**KING, Prof. Christine Elizabeth,** CBE 2007; DL; PhD; FRHistS; Vice-Chancellor and Chief Executive, 1995–2011, now Vice-Chancellor Emeritus, and Professor of History, 1991–2011, now Emeritus, Staffordshire University (formerly Staffordshire Polytechnic); *b* 31 Aug. 1944; *d* of late William Edwin King and Elizabeth Violet May King (*née* Coates). *Educ:* Birmingham Univ. (BA Hons Hist. and Theol. 1966; MA Theol. 1973; PhD Religious Hist. 1980). FRHistS 1994. Teaching, research and management posts in sch., further and higher educn sectors; Head, Sch. of Histl and Critical Studies, 1985–87, Dean, Faculty of Arts, 1987–90, Lancs Poly.; Staffordshire Polytechnic, subseq. Staffordshire University: Dean of Business, Humanities and Social Scis, 1990–92; Pro Vice-Chancellor, 1992–95. Pres., NIACE, 2001–06. FRSA; CCMI (CIMgt 1995; FIMgt 1993). DL Staffs, 1999. Hon. Fellow, Univ. of Central Lancs, 2001; Hon. DLitt: Birmingham, 1998; Portsmouth, 2001; DUniv Derby, 2001; Dr *hc* Edinburgh, 2005. *Publications:* The Nazi State and the New Religions, 1983; (ed) Through the Glass Ceiling: effective management development for women, 1993; articles and chapters on history of religion in Nazi Germany, women in management, higher educn and on implicit religion. *E:* dr.c.e.king@gmail.com.

**KING, Christopher Peter Morgan;** Chief Executive, Independent Association of Preparatory Schools, since 2018; *b* Bristol, 3 Nov. 1955; *s* of Peter and Esme King; *m* 1982, Elizabeth; three *s*. *Educ:* Queen Elizabeth's Hosp., Bristol; Durham Univ. (BA, MA). Water Resource Planner, Wessex Water Authy, 1975–78; Teacher of Geog., Sutton Valence Sch., 1979–83; Hd of Geog. and Sen. Housemaster, Rendcomb Coll., 1983–95; Dep. Hd, Kimbolton Sch., 1995–2001; Headmaster, Leicester Grammar Sch. and Chief Exec., Leicester Grammar Sch. Trust, 2001–18. Chm., HMC, 2015–16, 2017–18 (Chm., Professional Develt Cttee, 2001–14). Governor: King's Sch., Macclesfield, 2014–; Uppingham Sch. Mem. Court, Univ. of Leicester. *Recreations:* golf, hill walking, theatre, Rugby. *Address:* Independent Association of Preparatory Schools, 11 Waterloo Place, Leamington Spa CV32 5LA.

**KING, Sir David (Anthony),** Kt 2003; FRS 1991; FRSC, FInstP; Director, Smith School of Enterprise and the Environment, University of Oxford, 2008–12; Fellow, University College, Oxford, 2009–12; Chief Scientific Adviser to the Government, and Head, Government Office for Science (formerly Office of Science and Technology, then of Science and Innovation), 2000–07; *b* 12 Aug. 1939; *s* of Arnold King and Patricia (*née* Vardy), Durban; *m* Jane Lichtenstein; one *s* one *d*, and two *s* by previous marriage. *Educ:* St John's Coll., Johannesburg; Univ. of the Witwatersrand, Johannesburg (BSc; PhD 1963); ScD E Anglia, 1974; ScD Cantab, 1999. Shell Scholar, Imperial Coll., 1963–66; Lectr in Chemical Physics, Univ. of E Anglia, Norwich, 1966–74; Brunner Prof. of Physical Chemistry, Univ. of Liverpool, 1974–88; Cambridge University: 1920 Prof. of Physical Chemistry, 1988–2005; Head, 1993–2000, Dir of Research, 2005–11, Dept of Chemistry; Fellow, St John's College, 1988–95; Master, Downing Coll., 1995–2000, Hon. Fellow, 2001; Fellow, Queens' Coll., 2001–08. Sen. Science Advr, UBS, 2008–13. Dir, Cambridge Kaspakas, 2011–; Chm., Future Cities Catapult, Clerkenwell, 2013–16; Partner, SystemiQ, 2017–. Foreign Secretary's Special Rep. on Climate Change, FCO, 2013–17. Sen. Strategy Advr to the Pres. of Rwanda, 2017–. Member: Comité de Direction of Centre de

Cinétique Physique et Chimique, Nancy, 1974–81; Nat. Exec., Assoc. of Univ. Teachers, 1970–78 (Nat. Pres., 1976–77); British Vacuum Council, 1978–87 (Chm., 1982–85); Internat. Union for Vacuum Science and Technology, 1978–86; Faraday Div., Council, Chem. Soc., 1979–82; Scientific Adv. Panel, Daresbury Lab., 1980–82; Res. Adv. Cttee, Leverhulme Trust, 1980–92 (Chm., 1995–2001); Beirat, Fritz Haber Inst., West Berlin, 1981–93. Pres., BAAS, 2007–08. Chairman: Gallery Cttee, Bluecoat Soc. of Arts, 1986–88; Kettle's Yard Gall., Cambridge, 1989–2000. Pres. Bd, Coll. Carlo Alberto, Turin, 2008–11. Chancellor, Univ. of Liverpool, 2010–13. Miller Vis. Res. Prof., Univ. of Calif, Berkeley, 1996. Chm. Jury, Prix Pictet, 2010–. Lectures: Tilden, Chem. Soc., 1989; Frontiers, Texas A & M Univ., 1993; Dupont Distinguished, Indianapolis Univ., 1993; Dow Chemical Canada, Univ. W Ont, 1994; Zuckerman, Foundn for Sci. and Technol., 2002; Plenary, AAAS, Seattle, 2003; Annual British Ecol Soc., 2004; Greenpeace Business, 2004; Pimentel, Berkeley, 2005; Magna Carta, Australian Parlt, 2005; ACU Centenary, Jamaica, Hong Kong, Brunei, Kuala Lumpur, 2013. Member Editorial Board: Jl of Physics C, 1977–80; Surface Science Reports, 1983–98; Surface Science, 2000–; Editor, Chemical Physics Letters, 1989–2001. Hon. FREng 2006; Hon. Fellow: Indian Acad. of Scis, 1998; Third World Acad. of Scis, 2000; Amer. Acad. of Arts and Scis, 2002; Hon. FRSSAf 2001; Hon. Life FRSA 2006. Hon. Fellow, Cardiff Univ., 2001. Hon. DSc: UEA, Liverpool, Cardiff, 2001; Leicester, Milan, Stockholm, 2002; Witwatersrand, York, St Andrews, 2003; La Trobe, QUB, 2005; Newcastle, Goldsmiths Coll. London, Turin, 2006; University Coll. London, 2009; Western Ontario, 2010; Warwick, 2012. Chem. Soc. Award for surface and colloid chemistry, 1978; British Vacuum Council medal and prize for research, 1991; Liversidge Lect. and Medal, 1997, Lewis Lect. and Medal, 2013, RSC; Rumford Medal and Prize, Royal Soc., 2002; WWF Awareness Award, 2004; Linnaeus Medal, Royal Swedish Acad. of Scis, 2007; Adamson Award for Surface Chem., Amer. Chem. Soc., 2009. Officier de la Légion d'Honneur (France), 2009. *Publications:* (with Gabrielle Walker) The Hot Topic, 2008; (with Oliver Inderwildi) Energy, Transport and the Environment, 2012; papers on the physics and chemistry of solid surfaces in Proc. Royal Soc., Surface Science, Science, Jl Chemical Physics, Physical Rev. Letters etc, and on science in govt, global warming etc in Nature and Science. *Recreations:* photography, art. *Address:* 20 Glisson Road, Cambridge CB1 2HD.

**KING, David E.,** FCCA; Chief Executive, DKI, 2009–12; *b* 18 Aug. 1945; *m* 1972, Jenny Hall; four s. *Educ:* Manchester Poly.; Cranfield Sch. of Mgt (MBA 1984). FCCA 1976. Qualified as Certified Accountant, 1976; sen. financial positions both overseas and in UK, 1976–; joined London Metal Exchange, 1987, Chief Exec., 1989–2001; Man. Dir, Supervision, later Acting CEO, Dubai Internat. Financial Centre, Dubai Financial Services Authy, 2003–05; Man. Dir, Business Develt, Global Banking, Middle East and N Africa, HSBC Middle East, and Sen. Exec. Officer, HSBC Middle East Leasing Partnership, 2005–09; Exec. Dir, Middle East Business Develt, China Construction Bank Internat., 2009–11; Chm., Gulf Region, FD Internat., 2009–11. Non-executive Director: IGI Co. (UK) Ltd, 2012– (Chm., Audit, Risk and Compliance Cttee, 2012–; Chm., 2017–); IGI Hldgs, 2014– (Chm., Risk and Audit Cttee, 2014–); FXCM, 2014– (Chm., Audit Cttee, 2014–; Chm., 2017–). Mem., Jersey Finance Gp, GCC, 2011–12. UAE Adv. Bd Mem., Chartered Inst. for Securities and Investment (formerly Securities and Investment Inst.), 2009–12; Mem., Middle E and N Africa Adv. Bd, Cass Business Sch., 2011–12. Judge, Platts Global Metals Awards, 2012–. *Recreations:* working and playing hard and, in the case of golf, playing badly; UK and international charitable and fundraising activities.

**KING, David John,** FCA; Chief Executive, JPIMedia, since 2018; *b* Bucks, 1959; *s* of James and Josephine King; *m* 2002, Debra Miller; two *d. Educ:* Lancing Coll.; Kingston Poly. (BA Hons Accounting and Finance). FCA 1984. Auditor, Neville Russell, 1980–86; Finance Mgr, Storecard, 1986–88; Mgt Consultant, Coopers & Lybrand, 1988–94; Hd, Corporate Finance, BBC, 1994–96; Finance Dir, 1996–98, Chief Financial Officer, 1998–2008, BBC Worldwide; CEO, Time Out Gp, 2008–12; Chief Financial Officer, Johnston Press, 2013–18. Non-executive Director: Reach to Teach, 2009–15; Regulatory Funding Co., 2015–18; News Media Assoc., 2018–. *Recreations:* golf, tennis, classic cars, Manchester United FC.

**KING, (Denys) Michael (Gwilym),** CVO 1989; FICE; Director, 1986–91, Assistant Chief Executive, 1991, BAA plc, retired (Member, British Airports Authority, 1980–86); *b* 29 May 1929; *s* of William James King, FCIS, and Hilda May King; *m* 1st, 1956, Monica Helen (marr. diss. 1973); three *d*; 2nd, 1985, Ann Elizabeth. *Educ:* St Edmund's Sch., Canterbury; Simon Langton Sch., Canterbury; Battersea Polytechnic, London (BScEng Hons London, 1949). MIMechE 1966; FICE 1977. Engr, J. Laing Construction Ltd, 1961–71, Dir, 1971–74; Engrg Dir, BAA, 1974–77; Dir, 1977–86, Man. Dir, 1986–88, Heathrow Airport; Man. Dir, Airports Div., BAA, 1988–91. *Recreations:* yachting, preserved railways.

**KING, Deryk Irving;** Chairman, iCON Infrastructure Management Ltd, since 2010; Managing Partner, iCON Infrastructure LLP, since 2011; *b* 20 Dec. 1947; *s* of Cyril Montford King and Irene Muriel King (née Irving); *m* 1971, Janet Lorraine Amos; one *d. Educ:* Arnold Sch., Blackpool; University Coll., Oxford (MA Chem.). Joined Air Products Ltd as sales engr, 1970; with Imperial Chemical Industries PLC, 1973–96: Product Manager, 1973–77; Asst Gen. Manager, Chemicals, ICI Japan Ltd, 1977–79; Sen. Product Manager, 1979–83; Export Sales Manager, Mond Div., 1983–84; Commercial Manager, ICI Soda Ash Products, and Dir, Magadi Soda Co., 1984–88; Dir, Ellis & Everard (Chemicals) Ltd, 1987–88; Commercial Manager, 1988–91, Gen. Manager, 1991–92, ICI Fertilizers; Chm., Scottish Agricl Industries and BritAg Industries, and Dir, Irish Fertilizer Industries, 1991–92; Man. Dir, ICI Polyester, 1992–96; Chm., ICI Far Eastern, 1995–96; Gp Man. Dir, PowerGen plc, 1996–98; Dir, Ellis & Everard plc, 1999–2001; Projects Dir, 1999–2000, Man. Dir, N America, 2000–09, Centrica plc; Chm. and CEO, Direct Energy Marketing Ltd, 2000–09; Chairman: Sutton and East Surrey Water plc, 2009–13; Firmus Energy Ltd, 2014–19. Chairman: Centrica Pension Plan Trustees Ltd, 2010–19; Centrica Trustees Ltd, 2010–19; Centrica Engineers' Trustees Ltd, 2010–19. Director: Kvaerner ASA, 1997–2001; Consumers' Waterheater Income Fund, 2002–09; Allstream (formerly AT&T Canada) Inc., 2003–04; Trustee, Coventry 2000, 1997–2000. Chm., W Midlands Regl Awards Cttee, and Mem., England Cttee, Nat. Lottery Charities Bd, 1998–2000. FCIM 1992; MInstD 2000. *Recreations:* travel, wine and food, watching sport. *Address:* iCON Infrastructure LLP, Pollen House, 10–12 Cork Street, W1S 3NP. *Club:* Oxford and Cambridge.

**KING, Prof. Desmond Stephen,** DLitt; FBA 2003; FRHistS; Andrew W. Mellon Professor of American Government, University of Oxford, and Fellow, Nuffield College, Oxford, since 2002; *b* Dublin, 23 Oct. 1957; *s* of late Desmond and of Margaret King; *m* 1995, Dr Carolyn Cowey; one *s. Educ:* The High Sch., Dublin; Trinity Coll., Dublin (BA 1st cl. 1979; Bastable Prize, 1979); Northwestern Univ., Illinois (MA 1981; David Minar Prize, 1981; PhD 1985); DLitt Oxon 2015. Lectr in Politics, Univ. of Edinburgh, 1984–88; Lectr in Govt, LSE, 1988–91; University of Oxford: Lectr in Politics, 1991–2002; titular Prof., 1996–; Official Fellow and Tutor in Politics, St John's Coll., 1991–2002, Emeritus Fellow, 2002–. Nuffield Foundn Social Sci. Fellow, 1997–98; Res. Reader, British Acad., 2000–02; Leverhulme Major Res. Fellow, 2005–08. Delegate and Mem., Finance Cttee, OUP, 1999–2010. FRSA 2000; FAcSS (AcSS 2013); FRHistS 2015; MAE 2016. FHMAAAS 2017. Hon. MRIA 2015. *Publications:* (jtly) the State and the City, 1987; The New Right: politics, markets and citizenship, 1987; (ed jtly and contrib.) Challenges to Local Government, 1990; Separate and Unequal: Black Americans and the US Federal Government, 1995, rev. edn. as Separate and Unequal: African Americans and the US Federal Government, 2007; Actively Seeking Work?: the politics of unemployment and welfare policy in the US and Britain, 1995; (ed jtly and contrib.) Preferences, Institutions and Rational Choice, 1995; (ed jtly and contrib.) Rethinking Local Democracy, 1996; In the Name of Liberalism: illiberal social policy in the USA and Britain, 1999; Making Americans: immigration, race and the origins of the diverse democracy, 2000; The Liberty of Strangers: making the American nation, 2005; (ed jtly and contrib.) The Polarized Presidency of George W. Bush, 2007; (ed jtly and contrib.) The Unsustainable American State, 2009; (ed jtly and contrib.) Democratization in America, 2009; (jtly) Still a House Divided: race and politics on Obama's America, 2011; (ed jtly and contrib.) Obama at the Crossroads, 2012; (jtly) Sterilized by the State, 2013; (ed jtly) Forging a Discipline, 2014; (jtly) Fed Power: how finance wins, 2016; articles in jls incl. Past and Present, World Politics, American Pol Sci. Rev. *Recreations:* walking, free jazz. *Address:* Nuffield College, Oxford OX1 1NF. *T:* (01865) 278500.

**KING, Douglas Alexander,** FREng; environmental engineer; Principal, Doug King Consulting Ltd, since 2008; *b* Stanton Drew, Avon, 10 April 1968; *s* of Ian King and Caroline King; *m* 2007, Alexandra Goloverova. *Educ:* Bideford Sch.; Imperial Coll. London (BSc ARCS Physics 1990). CPhys 1997; CEng 1997; CEnv 2009; FEI 2009; FCIBSE 2009; FInstP 2010; FREng 2012. Engr, Max Fordham and Partners, 1990–94; Partner, Max Fordham Associates, 1994–97; Associate Director: Capita Greatorex Ltd, 1997–98; Buro Happold Ltd, 1998–2002; Dir, King Shaw Associates, 2002–12. Building projects include: Sainsbury's, Greenwich, 2000 (Channel 4 Bldg of the Year; Design Council Millennium Product; RIBA Jl Sustainability Award); Genzyme Centre, Cambridge, Mass, 2002 (RIBA Worldwide Award); Rolls Royce Motor Cars, Goodwood, W Sussex, 2003 (Royal Fine Art Commn Bldg of the Year); RSC Courtyard Theatre, Stratford upon Avon, 2006 (RIBA Nat. Award; AIA Award); Innovate Green Office, Leeds, 2007 (British Construction Industry Envmtl Award; Construction News Green Bldg of the Year). Visiting Professor: Univ. of Bath, 2007–; Chongqing Univ., 2013–. Chief Sci. and Engrg Advr, BRE, 2012–13. Hon. FRIBA 2011. Edmund Hambley Medal, 2007; James Watt Medal, 2008, ICE; Silver Medal, RAEng, 2011. *Publications:* contrib. to jls incl. Sci. in Parliament and Energy; reports for RAEng. *Recreation:* experimenting with flavours. *T:* (01225) 839846. *E:* mail@dougking.co.uk.

**KING, Edmund Graham Ralph;** QC 2018; *b* London, Oct. 1975; *s* of John Michael King and Ruth King; *m* 2001, Louise Hutton; one *s* one *d. Educ:* Winchester Coll.; Balliol Coll., Oxford (BA Law); Harvard Law Sch. (LLM). Called to the Bar, Inner Temple, 1999; in practice as a barrister. *Address:* Essex Court Chambers, 24 Lincoln's Inn Fields, WC2A 3EG. *T:* (020) 7813 8000. *E:* eking@essexcourt.net.

**KING, Edmund Valerian,** OBE 2016; President, Automobile Association, since 2008; *b* Aldershot, 6 March 1958; *s* of Michael Dominic King and Mary Angela King; *m* 2000, Deirdre Elizabeth Lavelle; two *s* one *d. Educ:* St Hugh's Coll., Tollerton; Chipping Norton Sch.; Santa Monica Coll.; Newcastle upon Tyne Univ. (BA Hons Politics). Wine taster and PR, Bouchard Aîné et fils, Beaune, 1976–77; Cttee Sec., SSRC, 1981–82; grad. trainee, Dept of Employment, 1982–84; Job Centre Manager, Hackney, 1983–84; proprietor, English antiques business, Los Angeles, 1984–86; reporter, KRTH radio, LA, 1985–87; Dir, Marathon Rent a Car, LA, 1985–88; Campaign Dir, British Rd Fedn, 1988–92; Hd of Campaigns, RAC, 1992–99; Exec. Dir, RAC Foundn, 1999–2007. Vis. Prof. of Transport, Newcastle Univ., 2009–. *Recreations:* mountain biking, running, football (with sons), cooking, fine wines, antiques auctions, driving. *Address:* Automobile Association, Fanum House, Basing View, Basingstoke, Hants RG21 4EA. *T:* (01256) 491538, *Fax:* (01256) 492090. *E:* edmund.king@theAA.com. *Club:* 2 Brydges Place.

**KING, Rt Hon. Dame Eleanor (Warwick),** DBE 2008; PC 2014; **Rt Hon. Lady Justice King;** a Lady Justice of Appeal, since 2014; *b* 13 Sept. 1957; *d* of Selby William Guy Hamilton and Dr Margaret Hamilton; *m* 1981, (David) Thomas King; four *d. Educ:* Queen Margaret's Sch., Escrick; Hull Univ. (LLB). Called to the Bar, Inner Temple, 1979; QC 1999; Asst Recorder, 1996–2000; Recorder, 2000–08; a Dep. High Court Judge, 2000–08; a Judge of the High Court of Justice, Family Div., 2008–14. Chm. Governors, Queen Margaret's Sch., 1992–2011; Mem. Chapter, York Univ. Fellow, Internat. Acad. of Matrimonial Lawyers, 2004. Hon. DLaws Hull, 2011. *Recreations:* walking, cycling, running. *Address:* Royal Courts of Justice, Strand, WC2A 2LL.

**KING, Frances;** Lead Tutor, Master's of Education Course, National College of Education, since 2019; *b* 26 Sept. 1960; *d* of Sir Colin Henry Imray, *qv*; *m* 1982, Timothy King; one *s* one *d. Educ:* Ashford Sch., Kent; St Hilda's Coll., Oxford (MA Theology); Heythrop Coll., London Univ. (MA); Hull Univ. (MBA). Actg Hd of RE, Lady Eleanor Holles Sch., Hampton, 1984–85; Head of Religious Education: Francis Holland Sch., London, 1985–90; Guildford Co. Sch., 1990–93; Tormead Sch., Guildford, 1993–2000; Dep. Headmistress, 2000–03, Headmistress, 2003–07, St Mary's Sch., Ascot, later Heathfield, Ascot; Headmistress, Roedean Sch., 2008–13; Principal, Collège Alpin Beau Soleil, 2013–15; Hd, Mill Hill Sch. and Chief Exec., Mill Hill Sch. Foundn, 2016–18; on sabbatical focused on creative play in educn, 2018–19. *Recreation:* walking.

**KING, Graeme Crockatt;** Chairman, Hydro Hotel Eastbourne plc, since 2004; Chairman, Audit Committee and Board Consultant, Rank Foundation, since 2006; *b* 8 Sept. 1948; *s* of late William Ramsay Morrison King and Margaret Lowe Robertson (née Crockatt); *m* 1975, Dr Susan Margaret Hobbins; one *s* one *d. Educ:* High Sch. of Dundee; St Andrews Univ. (MA Science 1970). Member: ICAS, 1974; Inst. of Chartered Accts of Canada, 1976. Arthur Andersen, 1970–79; Finance Dir, Aurora Gp, 1979–81; Mintz and Partners, Toronto, 1982–84; Chief Acct, then Gen. Manager, Lloyd's of London, 1984–94; Principal, Binder Hamlyn/Arthur Andersen, 1994–96; Man. Dir, Insurance Captives, P & O, 1997–2000; Gen. Sec., SPCK, 2001–06. Chm., Rochester Dio. Bd of Finance, 2000–12; Trustee: All Saints Educnl Trust, 2001–06; NCVO, 2002–08; Hon. Treas., Farnborough Hosp. Special Care Baby Fund, 1985–2012. Master, Insurers' Co., 2009–10 (Hon. Treas., 2002–08). *Recreations:* golf, climbing (Mem., Munro Soc.), ski-ing, outdoors. *E:* hobbinsking@btinternet.com. *Clubs:* Nikaean, Caledonian; Grampian; Wildernesse Golf (Sevenoaks), Rye Golf; Royal Queensland Golf (Brisbane).

**KING, Harold Samuel;** Founder and Artistic Director, London City Ballet, 1978–96; choreographer and lecturer; special events consultant; *b* Durban, 13 May 1949. *Educ:* Sea Point Boys' High Sch.; University Ballet Sch., Cape Town; Univ. of Cape Town (Teacher Trng Course). Soloist, Cape Performing Arts Bd Ballet Co., 1968–70; joined Western Th. Ballet, in GB, as dancer and choreographer, 1970; with Opera Ballet, Covent Gdn, 1976–77, incl. seasons with Nat. Ballet of Zimbabwe, as Guest Artist with Cape Performing Arts Bd, and Guest Teacher, Royal Acad. of Dance Summer Sch.; Artistic Co-ordinator, Victor Hochhauser Gala Ballet Season, RFH, 1978; asst, Rudolf Nureyev seasons at London Coliseum, 1978; toured with, newly-formed London City Ballet, 1978–96; founder, and Artistic Dir, City Ballet of London, 1996–2001, produced Dances from Napoli and choreographed Prince Igor, Nutcracker Suite and Carmen; Artistic Dir, Ballet de Zaragoza, Spain, 2001; guest artist, Cape Town City Ballet (performed Madge, the witch, in La

Sylphide), Cape Town, 2003; Artistic Co-ordinator, Cape Town City Ballet, 2005–08; teacher, adult jazz and ballet, 2008–12, Guest Teacher and fundraising co-ordinator for Ikapa Dance Th., 2008–10, Cape Town; choreographed: The Little Princess, 1995 and created Flowers for Mrs Harris, 1998, for London Children's Ballet; The Lion, the Witch and the Wardrobe for London Studio Centre, 1996; Requiem de Fauré for Ballet de Zaragoza, 2001; Shostakovich Suites for Univ. of Cape Town Sch. of Ballet, 2004; Habanera for Dance for All, township dance co., S Africa, 2005. Chief Trustee, David Blair Meml Trust, 2000–05. Fundraising Consultant: Union Dance Co., 2003; Mavin Khoo Dance, 2003; The Army Biehl Foundn, 2011; Dance for All, outreach project, Cape Town, 2012–13. Jazz dance instructor and lectr, 5 world cruises, Queen Mary 2, 2010–. Patron, London Ballet, 2014–.

KING, Helen Mary, QPM 2011; Principal, St Anne's College, Oxford, since 2017; b Bishop's Stortford, Herts, 26 April 1965; d of late Robert Shirley King and Mary King; m (marr. diss.); two d. Educ: Herts and Essex High Sch., Bishop's Stortford; Perse Sch. for Girls, Cambridge; St Anne's Coll., Oxford (BA 1986; MA); Univ. of Manchester (MA 1994); Univ. of Cambridge (Postgrad. Dip. 2003). Police Officer (Constable to Chief Superintendent), Cheshire Constabulary, 1986–2005; Asst Chief Constable, Merseyside Police, 2005–12; Dep. Chief Constable, Cheshire Constabulary, 2012–14. ACPO lead for cash and valuables in transit attacks, 2007–12; Nat. Policing lead for Horizon Scanning, 2012–14; Asst Comr, Territorial Policing, Metropolitan Police Service, 2014–17. Trustee, PSS, 2007–14. Chair, Uniformed Policing Professional Community, Coll. of Policing, 2015–17. Hon. Fellow, Fitzwilliam Coll., Cambridge, 2017. Address: St Anne's College, Oxford OX2 6HS. T: (01865) 274820. E: helen.king@st-annes.ox.ac.uk.

KING, Henry George John; QC 2017; b London, 11 June 1969; s of John King and late Ruth King (née Lamyman); m 1996, Helen Outhwaite; one s two d (and one d decd). Educ: Winchester Coll.; Balliol Coll., Oxford (BA Lit. Hum. 1992); City Univ. (Dip. Law 1997). ACA 1996. Price Waterhouse, 1993–96; called to the Bar, Inner Temple, 1998; in practice as barrister, 1999–; Jun. Counsel to the Crown, 2010–17. Publications: (contrib.) Law of Privilege, 2006, 3rd edn 2018; (contrib.) Coppel, Information Rights, 4th edn 2014. Recreation: rural Lincolnshire. Address: Fountain Court, Temple, EC4Y 9DH. T: (020) 7583 3335.

KING, Ian David; Business Presenter, Sky News, since 2014; b Poole, Dorset, 23 March 1967; s of John and Sylvia King; m 2010, Angela Jameson; two s one d. Educ: Park Sch., Barnstaple, Devon; N Devon Coll.; Univ. of Manchester (BA Hons); City Univ. (Postgrad. Dip. Newspaper Journalism). Graduate trainee, 1989, Business Analyst, 1990–93, Midland Bank; City Reporter, Daily Telegraph, 1994–95; City Reporter, 1995–97, Stock Market corresp., 1998, Guardian; Sen. Financial Corresp., Mail on Sunday, 1998–2000; Business Ed., The Sun, 2000–08; Dep. Business Ed., 2008–11, Business Ed., 2011–14, columnist, 2014–, The Times. Mem. Adv. Bd, Alliance Manchester Business Sch., 2018–. Recreations: family, cricket, football. Address: Sky News, 14th Floor, The News Building, 1 London Bridge Street, SE1 9GF. Club: MCC.

KING, Isobel Wilson; see Buchanan, I. W.

KING, Sir James (Henry Rupert), 5th Bt cr 1888, of Campsie, Stirlingshire; schoolmaster, Aldro School, since 2002; b Westminster, 24 May 1961; s of Sir John Christopher King, 4th Bt and of Patricia Monica King (née Foster); S father, 2014; m 1995, Elizabeth Dora, d of late Richard Henry Ellingworth; two s one d. Educ: Sandroyd; Eton; Edinburgh Univ. (MA); Warwick Univ. (PGCE). Wine merchant, 1986–2002. Recreation: sailing. Heir: s John Alasdair Ellingworth King, b 4 June 1996. Address: 12 Great Stuart Street, Edinburgh EH3 7TN. Club: Royal Cruising.

KING, Jane; writer and lecturer; learning consultant; b 12 Dec. 1954; d of Tom and Mabel Scott; m 1st, 1978, Edward Isaacs (marr. diss. 2009); two d; 2nd, 2011, Reginald King. Educ: Edinburgh Univ. (MA); Wolverhampton Business Sch. (DMS, MBA); Open Univ. (Dip. Lit.). Associate Lectr, Open Univ. Business Sch., 1996–. Non-executive Director: Wolverhampton HA, 1994–98; Mid Staffordshire NHS Foundn Trust, 2011–15; Chm., Wolverhampton Healthcare NHS Trust, 1998–2001; Regl Appts Comr, W Midlands, NHS Appts Commn, 2001–05. Man. Partner, ATM Consulting, 2006–12. Member: Ethics, Transparency and Audit Panel, Staffordshire Police and Crime Comr, 2017–; Soroptimists Internat. Stafford, 2017–; Chm., Wolverhampton Voluntary Sector Council, 1992–95; non-exec. Dir, Wolverhampton TEC, 1993–95; Consultant, Internat. Develt Office, Open Univ., 2014–. Mem., Regl Panel, Nat. Lottery Charities Bd, 1995–97. Recreations: writing, food, keeping chickens. Address: 40 Rowley Bank, Stafford ST17 9BA.

KING, Jeremy Richard Bruce, OBE 2014; restaurateur; b 21 June 1954; s of late Charles Henry King and Molly King (née Chinn); m 1st, 1982, Debra Hauer (marr. diss. 2007); one s two d; 2nd, 2012, Lauren Gurvich. Educ: Christ's Hosp., Horsham. Co-founder (with Christopher Corbin) and Director: Caprice Hldgs Ltd, 1982–2003; Corbin and King, 2003–; restaurants: Le Caprice, 1981–2003; The Ivy, 1990–2003; J. Sheekey, 1998–2003; The Wolseley, 2003–; The Delaunay, 2011–; Brasserie Zédel, 2012–; Colbert, 2012–; Fischer's, 2014–; Beaumont Hotel, 2014–18; Bellanger, 2015–; Cafe Wolseley, 2018–. Dir, Tate Enterprises Ltd, 2006–14. Member, Council: Tate Gall. of Modern Art, 1999–2013; Tate Britain, 2014. Mem./Dir, Northbank BID, 2014–18. Trustee: Artangel Trust, 1994–2005; Soho Th., 2008–. Hon. MSc London Sch. of Hospitality and Tourism, 2014. Recreations: walking, cycling, solitude. Clubs: Garrick, Royal Automobile, Chelsea Arts (Trustee, 2014–), Groucho, MCC.

KING, John Arthur Charles; Chairman, Superscape plc (formerly Superscape VR), 1998–2003; b 7 April 1933; s of late Charles William King and Doris Frances King; m 1958, Ina Solavici; two s. Educ: Univ. of Bristol (BSc). IBM UK, 1956–70; Managing Director, Telex Computer Products UK Ltd, 1970–73; Dir, DP Div., Metra Consulting Gp, 1974–75; Marketing Dir, UK, later Europe (Brussels), ITT Business Systems, 1976–81; Commercial Dir, Business Communications Systems, Philips (Hilversum), 1981–83; Dir, Marketing and Corporate Strategy, subseq. Corporate Dir and Man. Dir, Overseas Div., BT plc, 1984–88; Man. Dir, Citicorp Information Business Internat., 1988–91; Chairman: Quotron Internat., 1988–91; Analysys Ltd, 1991–2001. Non-executive Director: olsy (formerly Olivetti) UK Ltd, 1991–98 (Chm., 1995–98); Leeds Permanent Building Society, 1991–95 (Vice-Chm., 1994–95); Knowledge Support Systems Ltd, 1997–2001 (non-exec. Chm., 1998–2001); TTP Capital Partners Ltd, 1999–2003. Non-exec. Dir, CSA, 1996–98 (Mem. Supervisory Bd, FUGRO NV, 1997–2003; Advr, Enterprise First (formerly Surrey Business Advice), 2004–08. Sec. Gen., Eur. Foundn for Quality Management, 1993–94. Mem., Restrictive Practices Ct, 1995–2000. Freeman, City of London, 1987; Liveryman, Co. of Information Technologists, 1992. FBCS 1968; CCMI (CBIM 1986); FInstD 1986; FRSA 1993. Recreations: golf, bridge, music. E: jacking33@btinternet.com. Club: Wisley.

KING, Jonathan Colin Harmsworth; anthropologist and museum curator; Von Hügel Fellow, Museum of Archaeology and Anthropology, since 2012, and Senior Fellow, McDonald Institute for Archaeological Research, since 2017, University of Cambridge; b 5 Jan. 1952; s of Michael King and Elizabeth King (née Hobhouse); m 1976, Fíonn O'Beirne (marr. diss. 2011); one s one d. Educ: Eton; St John's Coll., Cambridge (MA 1975). British Museum: Curator, Native N American Collections, Dept of Ethnography, 1975–2005; Keeper, Dept of Africa, Oceania and the Americas, 2005–10; Keeper of Anthropology, 2010–12. Gov. and Dir, Dr Johnson's House Trust, 1988– (Treas., 1990–2006). Publications: Artificial Curiosities from the Northwest Coast of America, 1981; (ed with H. Lidchi) Imaging the Arctic, 1998; First Peoples First Contacts, 1999; (ed jtly) Arctic Clothing, 2005; (with H. Waterfield) Provenance, 2006; (with C. Feest) Woodlands Art, 2007; (with G. Were) Extreme Collecting, 2012; (ed jtly) Turquoise in Mexico and North America, 2012; Blood and Land: the story of Native North America, 2016. Recreations: ephemera, reading, collecting, swimming. Address: Museum of Archaeology and Anthropology, Downing Street, Cambridge CB2 3DZ.

KING, Josanne Penelope Jeanne; see Rickard, J. P. J.

KING, Sir Julian Beresford, KCVO 2014 (CVO 2011); CMG 2006; Member, European Commission, 2016–19; b 22 Aug. 1964; s of Brian Harold King and Barbara Mary King (née Beresford); m 1992, Lotte Vindelov Knudsen. Educ: Bishop Vesey's Grammar Sch.; St Peter's Coll., Oxford (BA). FCO, 1985; Ecole Nat. d'Admin, Paris, 1987–88; Paris, 1988–90; Luxembourg and The Hague, 1991; Second, later First, Sec., FCO, 1992; Private Sec. to Perm. Under-Sec. of State, FCO, 1995–98; UK Perm. Repn to EU, Brussels, 1998–2003; Counsellor and Hd of Chancery, UK Mission to UN, NY, 2003–04; UK Rep. to EU Pol and Security Cttee and UK Perm. Rep. to WEU, Brussels, 2004–07; Chef de Cabinet to Mem., EC, 2008–09 (on loan); Ambassador to Ireland, FCO, 2009–11; Director General: NI Office, 2012–14; Econ. and Consular, FCO, 2014–16; Ambassador to France, 2016.

KING, Justin Matthew, CBE 2011; Vice Chairman, Terra Firma Capital Partners, since 2015; Senior Adviser, Atrato Capital, since 2019; b 17 May 1961; s of Alan and Elaine King; m 1990, Claire Andrea Simmons (marr. diss. 2010); one s one d. Educ: Tudor Grange Sch.; Solihull Sixth Form Coll.; Bath Univ. (BSc Business Admin). Nat. Account Manager, Mars Confectionery, 1983–89; Sales and Mktg Dir, Egypt, Pepsi Internat., 1989–90; Man. Dir, UK, Haagen-Dazs, 1990–93; Man. Dir, Hypermkts, Asda Stores, 1993–2000; Exec. Dir, Food, Marks and Spencer plc, 2000–04; Chief Exec., J. Sainsbury plc, 2004–14. Non-exec. Dir, Marks and Spencer plc, 2019–. Mem. Bd, LOCOG, 2009–13. Address: Terra Firma Capital Partners, 2 More London Riverside, SE1 2AP. Club: Hayling Island Sailing.

KING, Kanya, CBE 2018 (MBE 1999); Founder and Chief Executive Officer, MOBO Organisation, since 1996; b London; d of Christian Ocloo and Mary Folan; one s. Educ: Goldsmiths Coll., Univ. of London (BA English Lit.). TV researcher, Carlton TV. Patron, Horniman Mus., 2000–. Hon. Fellow, Goldsmith's Coll., Univ. of London, 2004. Hon. DBA London Metropolitan, 2006; Hon. DMus: Leeds Metropolitan, 2009; SOAS, 2017; Hon. Dr Univ. of Arts; Hon. DLaws Exeter. Natwest everywoman Ambassador Award, 2014; Media Pioneer Award, Music Week Women in Music Awards, 2016; Contribn to Music Award, Ghana Black Star Network; Lifetime Achievement Award, Inst. of Enterprise and Entrepreneurship. Recreations: walking, travelling, reading. Address: MOBO Organisation, 79 Tib Street, Manchester M4 1LS. Clubs: Library, h.

KING, Mary; see King, C. M.

KING, Mary Elizabeth, MBE 2013; DL; three-day event rider; b 8 June 1961; d of late Lt Comdr Michael Dillon Harding Thomson and of Patricia Gillian Thomson; m 1995, Alan David Henry King; one s one d. Educ: Manor House Sch., Honiton; King's Sch., Ottery St Mary; Evendine Court, Malvern (Distinction, Cordon Bleu, 1980). British Open Champion, 1990, 1991, 1997, 2007; Winner: Windsor Horse Trials, 1988, 1989, 1992; Badminton Horse Trials, 1992, 2000; Mem., Olympic Team, Barcelona, 1992, Atlanta, 1996, Sydney, 2000, Athens, 2004 (Team Silver Medal), Beijing, 2008 (Team Bronze Medal), London, 2012 (Team Silver Medal); European Championships: Team Gold Medal, 1991, 1994, 1997, 2007; World Equestrian Games: Team Gold Medal, 1995, 2010; Team Silver Medal, 2006. DL Devon, 2016. Publications: Mary Thomson's Eventing Year, 1993; All the King's Horses, 1997; William and Mary, 1998; Mary King: the autobiography, 2009; My Way, 2014. Recreations: tennis, snow and water ski-ing. Address: Thorn House, Salcombe Regis, Sidmouth, Devon EX10 0JH.

KING, Michael; see King, D. M. G.

KING, Michael; see King, A. M. H.

KING, Neil Gerald Alexander; QC 2000; b 14 Nov. 1956; s of late Joseph and of Leila King; m 1978, Matilda Magdalen Grenville (née Oppenheimer); four d. Educ: Harrow Sch.; New Coll., Oxford (MA). Called to the Bar, Inner Temple, 1980. Director: White Lodge Properties Ltd, 1985–; Scarista House Ltd, 2000–; Garsington Opera Ltd, 2002–; Harrison Housing Ltd, 2004–; Univ. of York Music Press Ltd, 2014–. Publications: (ed jtly) Ryde on Rating and the Council Tax, 1990–2004. Recreations: classical music and opera, golf, walking, spending time in Italy. Address: The White House, High Street, Whitchurch-on-Thames, Oxon RG8 7HA. T: (0118) 984 2915. Clubs: Army and Navy, Royal Automobile: Huntercombe Golf; Isle of Harris Golf; Royal St George's Golf.

KING, Dr Paul Frederick; Transport Consultant, KPMG Passenger Transport Group, 1997–2004; b 4 Jan. 1946; s of Cedric Marcus King and Theresa Mary King; m 1980, Bertha Ines Avila de King; two s. Educ: Charterhouse Sch.; Queens' Coll., Cambridge (MA); Univ. of London (MSc, PhD). Lectr, Management Studies, Cambridge Univ., 1970–75; Dir, Special Assignments, TI Group, 1975–79; Sales and Marketing Dir, TI Raleigh, 1979–87; Planning and Marketing Dir, British Shoe Corp., 1987–90; Regional Railways, BR: Planning and Marketing Dir, 1990–93; Man. Dir, 1993–94; Gp Man. Dir, North and West, BRB, 1994–97. Non-executive Director: British Waterways, 1998–2001; Connex Rail Ltd, 1999–2003. Recreation: boating. Address: 8 Steeple Close, SW6 3LE. T: (020) 7013 0818.

KING, Paul James; Managing Director, Sustainability and Social Impact (formerly External Affairs), Lend Lease Europe, since 2015; b Cheshunt, Herts, 17 June 1967; s of Gordon King and Joyce King; partner, Gail Murray; two s. Educ: Goffs Sch., Cheshunt; Univ. of Warwick (BA Hist. 1988); Univ. of Reading (MA 1999). Sales and mktg, Penguin Books, 1990–94; WWF-UK: Sponsorship Manager, 1994–98; Corporate Business Coordinator, 1998–99; Capacity Building secondment to WWF Bhutan, 1999–2000; Progs Sen. Manager and Campaigns Dir, WWF-UK, 2000–07; Chief Exec., UK Green Building Council, 2007–15. Chairman: Zero Carbon Hub, 2008–16; Bldgs Wkg Gp, Green Construction Bd, 2011–15; Sec., Bd, World Green Building Council, 2011–15. Mem., Footprint Adv. Bd, Igloo Regeneration, 2006–15. Trustee, Centre for London, 2017–. Publications: (with Pooran Desai) One Planet Living, 2006. Recreations: ocean and river rowing, a capella singing, writing, exotic travel, dog walking, exploring with my family. E: paul.king@lendlease.com.

KING, Paul William; Agent General for British Columbia in the United Kingdom and Europe, 1995–2002; b Srinagar, Kashmir, 6 Sept. 1943; s of late Rev. Canon Roderick King and of Kathleen King; m 1st, 1969, Susan Jane Glenny (d 2000); two s; 2nd, 2011, Mrs Jeni Sayer. Educ: Exeter Sch.; Univ. of Alberta (BA). With E. I. du Pont de Nemours, USA, 1964; Kodak Canada Ltd, 1965–77; Dir responsible for trade with Pacific Rim countries,

Govt of Alberta, 1977–81; Director: European Ops, Alberta House, London, 1982–90; Trade and Investment, BC House, London, 1990–95. MInstD. Freeman, City of London, 1996. *Publications:* Climbing Maslow's Pyramid, 2009. *Recreations:* gardening, travel, motor-racing. *Address:* 22 Saffrons Park, Eastbourne, E Sussex BN20 7UX. *Club:* East India.

**KING, Perry Allan**, RDI 2000; Co-Founder and Partner, King & Miranda Design, since 1976; *b* Lambeth, London, 1938; *s* of Allan King and Kathleen King; *m* 1967, Daniela Garrone; two *d. Educ:* Ackworth Sch.; Birmingham Coll. of Art (NDD 1959). Nat. Service, Army, 1959–60. Designer, Wilkes and Ashmore, 1962–64; Consultant, Olivetti, Italy, 1965–70 and 1972–76; travelling in Asia, 1970–71. Visiting Professor: RCA, 1996–97; Univ. of the Arts, London, 2004. Fellow, UCE, 1995. Hon. Fellow, Glasgow Sch. of Art, 1998. *Recreations:* walking, drawing, carving, family. *Address:* King & Miranda Design srl, Via Savona 97, 20144 Milan, Italy. *T:* (02) 48953851, 335202700. *E:* king@kingmiranda.com.

**KING, Peter Arthur**, CBE 2009; sports management consultant, since 2010; Chair, England Athletics, 2012–16; *b* Dorking, Surrey, 19 Oct. 1944; *s* of Arthur King and Alys King; *m* 1968, Judith Anne Lattimer; two *s* one *d. Educ:* Dorking Co. Grammar Sch. FCIS 1976; FCMA 1976; FCMI 2006; CGMA 2012. Chartered Sec. and Accountant, 1973–. Non-exec. Dir, Eur. Regions Airline Assoc., 1987. CEO, British Fencing, 2012–14; CEO, 1997–2008, Exec. Dir, 2009–14, non-exec. Dir, 2017–, British Cycling; CEO, Pentathlon GB, 2010–11. Director: Sport and Recreation Alliance, 2008–14; Sport and Recreation Ventures Ltd, 2008–14; Commonwealth Games England, 2009–12; Mem. Bd, Sport Wales, 2012–18. *Recreations:* cycling, walking, family activities, travelling. *Address:* (home) The Old Cottage, Lynwick Street, Rudgwick, Horsham, W Sussex RH12 3DN. *T:* (01403) 824073; (office) Jayes Park Courtyard, Ockley, Dorking, Surrey RH5 5RR. *T:* (01306) 621513, 07710 101801, *Fax:* (01403) 621514. *E:* peter@peteraking.co.uk. *Clubs:* Redhill Cycling, Dorking Cycling (Pres., 2013–).

**KING, Rev. Peter Duncan**, TD 1986; a Judge of the Upper Tribunal (Immigration and Asylum Chamber) (formerly a Vice President, Immigration Appeal Tribunal, later a Senior Immigration Judge, Asylum and Immigration Tribunal), 2004–19; *b* 13 Feb. 1948; *s* of Clifford Norman King and Margaret Fraser King; *m* 1982, Maureen Diane Williams; one *s* one *d. Educ:* King's Coll., London (LLB 1970; AKC; MA 2011); Fitzwilliam Coll., Cambridge (MA); Westcott House, Cambridge. ACIArb 2004. Called to the Bar, Gray's Inn, 1970; Legal Officer, Army Legal Services, 1972–77; barrister in private practice, specialising in common law and crime, in London and Cambridge, 1977–2000; Plate Judge Advocate, 1995–2010, then Deputy; Special Immigration Adjudicator, 1995; Acting Stipendiary Magistrate, 1998–2000; Legal Mem., Immigration Appeals Tribunal, 1999; Dep. Dist Judge (Magistrates' Courts), 2000–18; Immigration Adjudicator, 2000–04; Judge, Special Immigration Appeals Commn, 2013–19; Dep. Tribunal Judge, 2019–20. Pres., Council of Immigration Judges, 2007–09; Member: Internat. Assoc. of Refugee Law Judges, 2000–; Commonwealth Magistrates' and Judges' Assoc., 2005–. Ordained Minister in Secular Employment, C of E, 1980; Hon. Priest, Mortlake with E Sheen, 1982–; Dean for MSE, Kingston Episcopal Area, 1999–2016. Former Mem. Exec. and Moderator, CHRISM. Mem., Rotary Internat. (Dist Gov., 2002–03; Pres., RIBI, 2014–15. Liveryman, Co. of Arbitrators, 2004. RCT (TA) (Movt Control/Liaison), 1967–72 and 1977–97. *Recreations:* golf, bowls, Rotary International (Dist Gov., 2002–03). *Address:* Upper Tribunal (Immigration and Asylum Chamber), Field House, 15 Bream's Buildings, EC4A 1DZ.

**KING, Philip Henry Russell**; QC 2002; *b* 15 Feb. 1949; *s* of Percy Sydney King and Patricia Maude (*née* Ball); *m* 2005, Jacqueline Riley (*née* Green). *Educ:* Clifton Coll.; Univ. of East Anglia (BA Hons). Called to the Bar, Inner Temple, 1974; in practice as barrister, 1976. *Recreations:* history, food, the countryside, travel.

**KING, Phillip**, CBE 1975; RA 1991 (ARA 1977); sculptor; President, Royal Academy of Arts, 1999–2004; Professor of Sculpture: Royal College of Art, 1980–90, Emeritus since 1991; Royal Academy Schools, 1990–99; *b* 1 May 1934; *s* of Thomas John King and of Gabrielle (*née* Liautard); *m* 1st, 1957, Lilian Odelle (marr. diss. 1987); (one *s* decd); 2nd, 1988, Judith Corbalis. *Educ:* Mill Hill Sch.; Christ's Coll., Cambridge Univ. (languages; Hon. Fellow, 2002); St Martin's Sch. of Art (sculpture). Teacher at St Martin's Sch. of Art, 1959–78; Asst to Henry Moore, 1959–60. Trustee: Tate Gallery, 1967–69; NPG, 1999–2004; Mem. Art Panel, Arts Council, 1977–79. Vis. Prof., Berlin Sch. of Art, 1979–81. *One-man exhibitions include:* British Pavilion, Venice Biennale, 1968; European Mus. Tour, 1974–75 (Kröller-Müller Nat. Mus., Holland; Kunsthalle, Düsseldorf; Kunsthalle, Bern; Musée Galliera, Paris; Ulster Mus., Belfast); UK Touring Exhibn, 1975–76 (Sheffield, Cumbria, Aberdeen, Glasgow, Newcastle, Portsmouth); Hayward Gall. (retrospective), 1981; Forte di Belvedere, Florence, 1997; Bernard Jacobson Gall., London, 1998, 2001, 2006 and 2008; Flowers Gall., London, 2011, 2012; Thomas Dane Gall., London, 2014. Commissions include: Cross Bend, European Patent Office, Munich, 1978; Hiroshima Mus. of Art, 1989. Hon. LittD Cambridge, 2012. First Prize, Socha Piestanskych Parkov, Piestany, Czechoslovakia, 1969; Lifetime Achievement Award, Internat. Sculpture Center, 2010. *Address:* c/o Bernard Jacobson Gallery, 28 Duke Street, St James's, SW1Y 6AG.

**KING, Reyahn**; Chief Executive, York Museums Trust, since 2015; *b* Edinburgh, 2 May 1965; *d* of Robert Bruce King and Jamela King (*née* Abrams); *m* 2008, Garry Morris; one step *s* one step *d. Educ:* Balliol Coll., Oxford (BA Hons Modern Hist.); Boston Univ. (MA Hist. of Art). AMA 1997, FMA 2015. Archive Asst, NPG, 1990–91; Curatorial Asst, Boston Univ. Art Gall., Mass, 1991–93; Grad. Fellow, Photographic Resource Center, Boston (pt-time), 1992–93; Periodicals Librarian, National Gall., London, 1994–97; Guest Curator, Ignatius Sancho exhibn, NPG (pt-time), 1996–97; Curator, Prints and Drawings, Birmingham Mus and Art Gall., 1997–2001; Art Gall. and Mus. Develt Manager, Coventry Arts and Heritage, 2001–03; Hd, Interpretation and Exhibns, Birmingham Mus and Art Gall., 2003–07; Dir, Art Galleries, Nat. Museums Liverpool, 2007–12; Hd, Heritage Lottery Fund, W Midlands, 2012–15. Trustee, New Art Exchange, Nottingham, 2011– (Clore Fellow, 2010–11). FRSA. *Publications:* (ed) Ignatius Sancho: an African man of letters (1729–1780), 1997; Anwar Shenza, 1997; Varvara Shavrova: inscriptions, 2001; (ed) Aubrey Williams: Atlantic fire, 2010. *Recreations:* Tai Chi, seeing friends and family, enjoying food. *Address:* York Castle Museum, Eye of York, York YO1 9RY.

**KING, Robert John Stephen**; conductor; harpsichordist; Artistic Director, The King's Consort, since 1980; *b* 27 June 1960; *s* of Stephen King and Margaret Digby; *m* Viola Scheffel; one *s* one *d. Educ:* Radley Coll.; St John's Coll., Cambridge (MA). Writer; editor of much music *pre* 1750; broadcaster; conductor, orchestras and choirs, incl. New World SO, Houston SO, Minnesota SO, Atlanta SO, Seattle SO, Detroit SO, Nat. SO Washington, Stavanger SO, Aarhus SO, Norrköping SO, Danish Nat. Radio SO, Bergen Philharmonic, Malmö SO, Trondheim SO, Iceland SO, Zurich Chamber Orch., Netherlands Chamber Orch. and Chamber Choir, RAI Nat. SO, Orch. Verdi Milan, RTSI Orch., English Chamber Orch., Westdeutscher Rundfunk SO, Norddeutscher Rundfunk SO, Hamburg SO, Royal Seville SO, Orch. de Navarra, Granada SO, Swiss Radio Choir, BBC Singers, Danish Radio Choir, Buxton Fest. Opera. Work on Hollywood film scores incl. Da Vinci Code, Shrek 2, Pirates of the Caribbean, Chronicles of Narnia, Kingdom of Heaven. Artistic Director: Aldeburgh Easter Fest., 1998–2000; Nordic Baroque Music Fest., 2001–04; Internat. Organ Week Nuremberg, 2003–07. *Publications:* Henry Purcell, 1994; numerous musical edns incl. English Church Music, vol. 1, 2010, vol. 2, 2011. *Recreations:* ski-ing, cricket, breeding Hebridean Sheep, lupin growing. *E:* info@tkcworld.org.

**KING, Ven. Robin Lucas Colin**; Archdeacon of Stansted, since 2013; *b* Quebec, Canada, 15 Feb. 1959; *s* of Colin King and Alison King; *m* 1988, Katharine Mighall; two *s. Educ:* King's Sch., Canterbury; Dundee Univ. (MA Hons 1981); Ridley Hall Theol Coll. Ordained deacon, 1989, priest, 1990; Curate, St Augustine's, Ipswich, 1989–92; Vicar, St Mary's, Bures, 1992–2013; Rural Dean, Sudbury, 2006–13. Hon. Canon, St Edmundsbury Cath., 2009–13. Chair, Chelmsford Diocesan Bd of Educn, 2019–. *Recreations:* rowing, sailing, diving. *Address:* The House, The Street, Bradwell, Essex CM77 8EL. *T:* (01376) 563357. *E:* rlcking@hotmail.co.uk.

**KING, Roger Douglas**; Chief Executive, Road Haulage Association, 2000–09; *b* 26 Oct. 1943; *s* of Douglas and Cecilie King; *m* 1976, Jennifer Susan (*née* Sharpe); twin *s* one *d. Educ:* Solihull Sch. Served automobile engrg apprenticeship with British Motor Corp., 1960–66; sales rep., 1966–74; own manufg business, 1974–81; self-employed car product distributor, 1982–83; Dir of Public Affairs, 1992–99, Dep. Chief Exec., 1999–2000, SMMT. Director: Prince Michael Road Safety Awards Scheme, 1992–2009; Roadsafe, 2000–09. Non-executive Director: Nat. Express Hldgs, 1988–91; Coventry Bldg Soc., 1995–2007. Vice Chm., Internat. Road Transport Union Goods Transport Council, 2006–09. MP (C) Birmingham, Northfield, 1983–92. PPS to Minister for Local Govt, 1987–88, for Water and Planning, 1988, DoE, to Sec. of State for Employment, 1989–92. Mem., H of C Transport Select Cttee, 1984–87; Vice-Chm., All Party Motor Industry Gp, 1985–92; Jt Sec., Cons. Tourism Cttee, 1985–87. Volunteer, British Motor Mus. (formerly British Motor Industry Heritage Trust), 2012–. FIMI 1986–2009. Mem., Co. of Carmen, 2001–10. *Recreation:* classic car motoring. *Address:* 241 Tessall Lane, Northfield, Birmingham B31 5EQ. *T:* (0121) 476 6649.

**KING, Prof. Roger Patrick**; Vice-Chancellor, University of Lincolnshire and Humberside (formerly Humberside), 1992–2000; *b* 31 May 1945; *s* of late Timothy Francis King and Vera May King; *m* 1966, Susan Winifred Ashworth; one *d. Educ:* Wimbledon Coll.; Univ. of London (BSc Hons Econ.); Univ. of Birmingham (MSocSci). HM Civil Service, 1963; Sales Management Trainee, United Glass, 1964; Sales Manager, Marley Tiles, 1965; Lectr and Sen. Lectr in Social Scis, Manchester Polytechnic, 1970–75; Principal Lectr, later Head of Dept of Behavioural Scis, Huddersfield Poly., 1976–85; Dep. Dir, 1985–89, Dir and Chief Exec., 1989–92, Humberside Poly. Vis. Fellow, ACU, 2003–05; Visiting Professor: OU, 2003–11; Univ. of Bath, 2010–; Adjunct Prof., Univ. of Queensland, 2010–; Res. Associate, LSE, 2007–. Co-Chm., Higher Educn Commn's Inquiry, 2013 (Report, Regulating Higher Educn, 2013). Dir and Chair, Wells Advisory HE Consultancy Ltd. *Publications:* (with N. Nugent) The British Right, 1977; (with N. Nugent) Respectable Rebels, 1979; The Middle Class, 1981; Capital and Politics, 1983; The State in Modern Society, 1986; (with J. Simmie) The State in Action, 1990; (with G. Kendall) The State, Democracy and Globalization, 2004; The University in the Global Age, 2004; The Regulatory State in an Age of Governance, 2007; Governing Universities Globally, 2009; (jtly) Handbook of Globalization and Higher Education, 2011; (jtly) The Globalization of Higher Education, 2013; Handbook on the Politics of Higher Education, 2018. *Recreations:* reading, running, swimming. *Address:* Griffins, Hanging Birch Lane, Horam, Heathfield, E Sussex TN21 0BH. *T:* (01435) 813443.

**KING, Sarah Penelope**, RDI 2008; textile designer and consultant; designer, First Eleven Studio; designer and consultant, William Yeoward; *b* Welwyn Garden City, 1958; *d* of Hugh and Phoebe King. *Educ:* Goldsmith's Coll., London Univ. (BA Fine Art Textiles); Manchester Metropolitan Univ. (MA Textile Design). Textile design: for fashion, 1987–95; for furnishing fabrics, 1995–2009; exhibns with Crafts Council of GB, 1987–95. *Recreations:* walking, food, cinema. *Address:* 35 St Martins Road, SW9 0SP. *E:* sarah.king21@btinternet.com. *Club:* Two Brydges.

**KING, Stephen Edwin**; author; *b* Portland, Maine, 21 Sept. 1947; *s* of Donald King and Nellie Ruth King (*née* Pillsbury); *m* 1971, Tabitha Jane Spruce; two *s* one *d. Educ:* Lisbon Falls High Sch.; Univ. of Maine at Orono (BS 1970). Laundry worker, 1970; English Teacher, Hampden Acad., 1971–73; writer in residence, Univ. of Maine at Orono, 1978–79. Screenplay, Sleepwalkers, 1991; many of his stories have been filmed; writer, TV series, Kingdom Hospital, 2004; dir, Maximum Overdrive, 1986. *Publications:* Carrie, 1974; 'Salem's Lot, 1975; The Shining, 1976; The Stand, 1978; Night Shift (short stories), 1978; Firestarter, 1980; Danse Macabre, 1981; Cujo, 1981; Different Seasons, 1982; The Dark Tower: vol. 1, The Gunslinger, 1982, vol. 2, The Drawing of the Three, 1987, vol. 3, Waste Lands, 1991, vol. 4, Wizard and Glass, 1997, vol. 5, Wolves of the Calla, 2003, vol. 6, Song of Susannah, 2004, vol. 7, The Dark Tower, 2004; Christine, 1983; Pet Sematary, 1983 (filmed, 1989, 2019); (jtly) The Talisman, 1984; Cycle of the Werewolf, 1985; It, 1986 (filmed, 2017); Skeleton Crew (short stories), 1986; The Eyes of the Dragon, 1987; Misery, 1987; The Tommyknockers, 1987; The Dark Half, 1989; The Stand (unabridged edn), 1990; Four Past Midnight, 1990; (jtly) Dark Visions, 1990; Needful Things, 1991; Gerald's Game, 1992; Dolores Claiborne, 1992; Nightmares and Dreamscapes (short stories), 1993; Insomnia, 1994; Desperation, 1996; The Green Mile, 1996; Bag of Bones, 1998; The Girl Who Loved Tom Gordon, 1999; Hearts In Atlantis, 1999; On Writing: a memoir of the craft, 2000; Dreamcatcher, 2001; Everything's Eventual (short stories), 2002; From a Buick 8, 2002; (with Stewart O'Nan) Faithful: two diehard Boston Red Sox fans chronicle the historic 2004 season, 2004; Cell, 2006; Lisey's Story, 2006; Duma Key, 2008; Just After Sunset (short stories), 2008; Under the Dome, 2009; Full Dark, No Stars, 2010; 11.22.63, 2011; Joyland, 2013; Doctor Sleep, 2013 (filmed, 2019); Mr Mercedes, 2014; Revival, 2014; Finders Keepers, 2015; The Bazaar of Bad Dreams (short stories), 2015; End of Watch, 2016; (with Owen King) Sleeping Beauties, 2017; The Outsider, 2018; Elevation, 2018; The Institute, 2019; (as Richard Bachman): Rage, 1977; The Long Walk, 1979; Roadwork, 1981; The Running Man, 1982; Thinner, 1984; The Regulators, 1996; Blaze, 2007. *Address:* c/o Hodder & Stoughton, 338 Euston Road, NW1 3BH.

**KING, Timothy**; a District Judge (Magistrates' Courts), since 2016; *b* London, 1 Aug. 1978; *s* of Peter King and Elaine King; *m* 2010, Louise Campbell; one *s* one *d. Educ:* Brunel Univ. (LLB Hons 2000); London Metropolitan Univ. (Dip. Legal Practice 2003). Admitted solicitor, 2005; a Dep. District Judge (Magistrates' Courts), 2012–16. *Recreations:* football, old cars, Private Eye. *Address:* c/o Chelmsford Magistrates' Court, 10 New Street, Essex CM1 1NT.

**KING, Hon. Sir Timothy (Roger Alan)**, Kt 2007; a Judge of the High Court of Justice, Queen's Bench Division, 2007–19; *b* 5 April 1949; *s* of late Harold Bonsall King and Dorothy King; *m* 1986, Bernadette Goodman. *Educ:* Booker Avenue County Primary Sch., Liverpool; Liverpool Inst. High Sch.; Lincoln Coll., Oxford (MA, BCL). Called to the Bar, Lincoln's Inn, 1973 (Bencher, 2000); Mem., Northern Circuit, 1973; QC 1991; a Recorder, 1991–2007. *Recreations:* travel, Association football. *Club:* Travellers.

**KING, His Honour Timothy Russell;** a Circuit Judge, 1995–2012; *b* 4 June 1946; *s* of late Charles Albert King and Elizabeth Lily King (*née* Alexander); *m* 1st, 1973, Christine Morison (marr. diss. 1979); two *s*; 2nd, 1989, Rotraud Jane (*née* Oppermann). *Educ:* St Mary's Coll., Bitterne Park, Southampton; Inns of Court Sch. of Law. HM Diplomatic Service (Colonial Office), 1966–67; called to the Bar, Gray's Inn, 1970; in practice, SE Circuit, 1970–86; Dep. Judge Advocate, 1986; AJAG, 1990–95; Asst Recorder, 1989–93; Recorder, 1993–95. Mem. of UK Deleg., Soc. for Military Law and the Law of War, 1989–95; Legal Mem., Restricted Patients Panel, Mental Health Review Tribunal, 2002–16; Mem., Public Chairs Forum, 2010–17 (Mem., Mgt Cttee, 2011–13); Chm., Lord Chancellor's Adv. Cttee on Conscientious Objectors, 2008–13. Dir, Osborne Golf Club Ltd, 2013–. Chm., Friends of Osborne, 2015–. Pres., St Leonard's Soc., 1998–2006. Trustee, The Rehearsal Orchestra, 2019–. *Recreations:* sailing, ski-ing, classical music, reading, walking, cooking, golf. *Address:* c/o Judicial Office, Ministry of Justice, 102 Petty France, SW1H 9AJ. *Clubs:* Royal London Yacht, Osborne Golf (Cowes).

**KING, Prof. Ursula,** PhD; freelance lecturer and writer; Professor Emerita of Theology and Religious Studies, and Senior Research Fellow at Institute for Advanced Studies, University of Bristol, 2002–19; Professorial Research Associate, Department of the Study of Religions (formerly Centre for Gender and Religions Research), School of Oriental and African Studies, University of London, since 2002; Fellow Heythrop College, University of London, 2004–19; *b* 22 Sept. 1938; *d* of Hedwig and Adolf Brenke; *m* 1963, Prof. Anthony Douglas King; four *d*. *Educ:* Univs of Bonn, Munich, Paris (STL), Delhi (MA; Indian Philosophical Congress Gold Medal, 1969) and King's Coll. London (PhD). Lectr in Divinity, Coloma Coll. of Educn, 1963–65; Visiting Lecturer, 1965–70: Dept of Philosophy, Univ. of Delhi; Indian Inst. of Technology; Indian Social Inst.; Lectr and Sen. Lectr, Dept of Theology and Religious Studies, Univ. of Leeds, 1971–89; S. A. Cook Bye-Fellow, Newnham Coll. and Gonville and Caius Coll., Cambridge, 1976–77; Bristol University: Prof. of Theology and Religious Studies, 1989–2002; Head of Dept, 1989–97; Dir, Centre for Comparative Studies in Religion and Gender, 1996–2002. Pres., Catherine of Siena Virtual Coll., 2008–15. Visiting Professor: in Feminist Theology, Univ. of Oslo, 1999–2001; in Ecumenical Theology and Interreligious Dialogue, Xavier Univ., Cincinnati, 1999; Dist. Bingham Prof. of Humanities, Univ. of Louisville, Ky, 2005. Lectures include: Sri Aurobindo Meml, London, 1971; Cardinal Bea Meml, London, 1977; Sir Francis Younghusband Meml, London, 1978; Teilhard de Chardin Exhibn, London, 1983; Cardinal Heenan, London, 1984; Hibbert, London, 1984; Lambeth Interfaith, Lambeth Palace, 1985; Teape, Delhi, Calcutta, Santiniketan, 1986; Bampton, 1996, Whyte, 2000, Sir Alister Hardy, 2002, Oxford; Sir George Trevelyan, London, 2002; Anne Spencer, Bristol, 2002; Julian of Norwich, Norwich, 2007; Burke, UCSD, 2012; wide internat. lecturing in Europe, N America, Asia, Australasia, and S Africa. Past mem. of many editorial and adv. bds of jls; consultant to numerous internat. publishers. President: British Assoc. for the Study of Religions, 1991–94; European Soc. of Women in Theological Research, 1993–95; Vice-Pres., World Congress of Faiths, 1972–; Mem., Shap Working Party on World Religions in Educn, 1975–2019. Judge, Templeton Prize, 2014–17. Hon. Life Mem., Eur. Assoc. for Study of Religions, 2013–. Life FRSA. Hon. DD: Edinburgh, 1996; Dayton, 2003; Hon. Dr Theol Oslo, 2000. Student awards from Germany and France. *Publications:* Towards a New Mysticism, 1980; The Spirit of One Earth, 1989; Women and Spirituality, 1989; (ed) Turning Points in Religious Studies, 1990, repr. 2016; (ed) Feminist Theology from the Third World, 1994; (ed) Religion and Gender, 1995; Spirit of Fire: the life and vision of Teilhard de Chardin, 1996, rev. edn as Spirit of Fire: the life and vision of Pierre Teilhard de Chardin, 2016; Christ in All Things: exploring spirituality with Teilhard de Chardin, 1997, rev. edn, 2016; (ed) Pierre Teilhard de Chardin: writings selected with an introduction, 1999; (ed) Spirituality and Society in the New Millennium, 2001; Christian Mystics: their lives and legacies throughout the ages, 2001; (ed with Tina Beattie) Gender, Religion and Diversity: crosscultural approaches, 2004; The Search for Spirituality, 2008; Teilhard de Chardin and Eastern Religions, 2011; contribs to acad. jls. *Recreations:* walking, reading, travelling, meeting old friends.

**KING, Sir Wayne Alexander,** 8th Bt *cr* 1815; District Office Supervisor, The Canadian Hearing Society, Sault Ste Marie, since 2009; *b* 2 Feb. 1962; *s* of Sir Peter Alexander King, 7th Bt, and Jean Margaret (who *m* 2nd, 1978, Rev. Richard Graham Mackenzie), *d* of Christopher Thomas Cavell, Deal; *S* father, 1973; *m* 1984 (marr. diss. 1990); one *s*; *m* 2003, Deborah Lynn, *d* of Douglas Arthur and Marilyn MacDougall, Sydney, NS. *Educ:* Sir Roger Manwood's Sch., Sandwich, Kent; Algonquin Coll., Ottawa, Ont (majored in Accounting and Retail Management). Canadian Hearing Society: Devels Co-ordinator, Toronto, 2004–06; Manager of Admin, Kitchener and Waterloo, 2006–08. *Recreation:* all sports. *Heir: s* Peter Richard Donald King, *b* 4 May 1988. *Address:* 64 Fields Square, Sault Ste Marie, P6B 6H2, Canada.

**KING-HELE, Desmond George,** FRS 1966; author; Deputy Chief Scientific Officer, Space Department, Royal Aircraft Establishment, Farnborough, 1968–88, retired; *b* 3 Nov. 1927; *s* of late S. G. and of B. King-Hele, Seaford, Sussex; *m* 1954, Marie Thérèse Newman (separated 1992); two *d*. *Educ:* Epsom Coll.; Trinity Coll., Cambridge. BA (1st cl. hons Mathematics) 1948; MA 1952. At RAE, Farnborough, 1948–88, working on space research from 1955. Mem., International Academy of Astronautics, 1961. Chairman: Satellite Optical Tracking Cttee, Royal Soc., 1972–97; History of Science Grants Cttee, Royal Soc., 1990–93; British Nat. Cttee for History of Science, Medicine and Technol., 1985–89; Adv. Panel for Culture of Sci., Technol. and Medicine, BL, 1992–2002. Pres., Birmingham and Midland Inst., 2002. Lectures: Symons, RMetS, 1961; Duke of Edinburgh's, Royal Inst. of Navigation, 1964; Jeffreys, RAS, 1971; Halley, Oxford, 1974; Bakerian, Royal Soc., 1974; Sydenham, Soc. of Apothecaries, 1981; H. L. Welsh, Univ. of Toronto, 1982; Milne, Oxford, 1984; Wilkins, Royal Soc., 1997. FIMA; FRAS. Hon. DSc Aston, 1979; DUniv Surrey, 1986. Eddington Medal, RAS, 1971; Charles Chree Medal, Inst. of Physics, 1971; Lagrange Prize, Acad. Royale de Belgique, 1972; Nordberg Medal, Internat. Cttee on Space Res., 1990. Editor, Notes and Records of Royal Soc., 1989–96. *Publications:* Shelley: His Thought and Work, 1960, 3rd edn 1984; Satellites and Scientific Research, 1960; Erasmus Darwin, 1963; Theory of Satellite Orbits in an Atmosphere, 1964; (ed) Space Research V, 1965; Observing Earth Satellites, 1966, 2nd edn 1983; (ed) Essential Writings of Erasmus Darwin, 1968; The End of the Twentieth Century?, 1970; Poems and Trixies, 1972; Doctor of Revolution, 1977; (ed) The Letters of Erasmus Darwin, 1981; (ed) The RAE Table of Earth Satellites, 1981, 4th edn 1990; Animal Spirits, 1983; Erasmus Darwin and the Romantic Poets, 1986; Satellite Orbits in an Atmosphere: theory and applications, 1987; A Tapestry of Orbits, 1992; (ed) John Herschel, 1992; (ed) A Concordance to the Botanic Garden, 1994; Erasmus Darwin: a life of unequalled achievement (Society of Authors' Medical History Prize), 1999; Antic and Romantic (poems), 2000; (ed) Charles Darwin's The Life of Erasmus Darwin, 2002; (ed) The Collected Letters of Erasmus Darwin, 2007; (ed jtly) The Shorter Poems of Erasmus Darwin, 2012; Erasmus Darwin and Evolution, 2014; *radio drama scripts:* A Mind of Universal Sympathy, 1973; The Lunaticks, 1978; over 400 papers in Proc. Royal Society, Nature, Keats-Shelley Meml Bull., New Scientist, Planetary and Space Science, and other scientific and literary jls. *Recreations:* tennis, reading, writing verse.

**KING-TENISON,** family name of **Earl of Kingston**.

**KINGARTH, Rt Hon. Lord; Hon. Derek Robert Alexander Emslie;** PC 2006; a Senator of the College of Justice in Scotland, 1997–2010; *b* 21 June 1949; *s* of Baron Emslie, PC, MBE; *m* 1974, Elizabeth Jane Cameron Carstairs, *d* of Andrew McLaren Carstairs; one *s* two *d*. *Educ:* Edinburgh Acad.; Trinity Coll., Glenalmond; Gonville and Caius Coll., Cambridge (Hist. Schol.; BA); Edinburgh Univ. (LLB). Advocate 1977; Standing Jun. Counsel, DHSS, 1979–87; Advocate Depute, 1985–88; QC (Scot.) 1987; part time Chairman: Pension Appeal Tribunal (Scotland), 1988–95; Medical Appeal Tribunal (Scotland), 1990–95. Vice-Dean, Faculty of Advocates, 1995–97. *Recreations:* golf, cinema, football. *Address:* 35 Ann Street, Edinburgh EH4 1PL. *T:* (0131) 332 6648.
*See also Rt Hon. Lord Emslie.*

**KINGHAM, Teresa Jane, (Tess);** Romney Marsh Partnership Co-ordinator, 2013–15; *b* 4 May 1963; *d* of Roy Thomas Kingham and Patricia Ribian Kingham (*née* Murphy); *m* 1991, Mark Luetchford; one *s* two *d* (of whom one *s* one *d* are twins). *Educ:* Dartford Girls' Grammar Sch.; Royal Holloway Coll., Univ. of London (BA Hons German 1984); Univ. of East Anglia (PGCE Mod. Langs 1985); University Coll. London (MA Egyptian Archaeol. 2007). Appeals Dir, War on Want, 1986–90; Mktg and Communications Dir, Blue Cross (animal welfare), 1990–92; Editor, Youth Express, Daily Express, 1992–94; Communications Exec., Oxfam, 1994–96. Contested (Lab) Cotswolds, EP elecn, 1994. MP (Lab) Gloucester, 1997–2001. Chair, All Party Gp on Western Sahara, 1997–2001. Mem., Egypt Exploration Soc. *Publications:* (with Jim Coe) The Good Campaigns Guide, 2nd edn 2005. *Recreations:* international travel/affairs, archaeology, walking with family.

**KINGHAN, Neil,** CB 2005; PhD student of United States History, University College London; *b* 20 Aug. 1951; *s* of late Derek Kinghan and Esme Kinghan; *m* 1994, Dr Lilian Pusavat. *Educ:* Hertford Coll., Oxford (MA, MPhil); University Coll. London (MA US Hist. 2013). Department of the Environment: admin trainee, 1975; Private Sec. to Parly Under-Sec. of State, 1978–80; Principal, 1980; Private Sec. to Minister of State, 1984–87; Asst Sec., 1987; Head: Sport and Recreation Div., 1987–89; Homelessness Policy Div., 1989–92; Director: Housing Policy, 1992–94; DoE Mgt Review, 1994–96; Local Govt Finance, 1996–97; Local Government Association: Dir, Local Govt Finance, 1997–2002; Econ. and Envmtl Policy, 2002–03; Dir Gen., Local and Regl Govt, then Local Govt and Fire, ODPM, subseq. Local and Regl Governance, then Fire and Resilience, DCLG, 2003–07; Dir Gen., Equality and Human Rights Commn, 2009–10. Consultant, Essex CC, 2007–08; Advr, Assoc. of Chief Execs of Voluntary Orgns, 2011–13; Consultant, Executive Action, 2011–13; Independent Reviews: of Riot in Clapham Junction for Wandsworth BC, 2011; of Riot Damages Act 1886 for Home Sec., 2013. Chm., Policy Commn on Primary Sch. Orgn in Shropshire, 2008–09. Chm., Mgt Bd, Fire Service Coll., 2008–09. Trustee, Naomi House Children's Hospice, 2005–17. *Recreations:* ski-ing, cricket, watching ballet, cycling. *E:* neil.kinghan@btinternet.com. *Clubs:* Athenæum; Surrey County Cricket.

**KINGHORN, Dr George Robert,** OBE 2012; FRCP, FRCPGlas; Clinical Director, NIHR South Yorkshire Comprehensive Local Research Network, 2011–15; Consultant in Genitourinary Medicine, 1979–2015, and Clinical Director for Communicable Diseases, 1991–2010, Sheffield Teaching Hospitals NHS Foundation Trust; Hon. Professor of Genitourinary Medicine, University of Sheffield, 2006–15; *b* 17 Aug. 1949; *s* of Alan Douglas Kinghorn and Lilian Isabel Kinghorn; *m* 1973, Sheila Anne Littlewood; one *s* one *d*. *Educ:* Newburn Manor Sch.; Royal Grammar Sch., Newcastle upon Tyne; Univ. of Sheffield (MB ChB 1972; MD 1984). FRCP 1988; FRCPGlas 2003. Sen. Registrar, Royal Infirmary, Sheffield, 1976–79; Consultant Physician in Genitourinary Medicine, Leeds Gen. Infirmary, 1979. Hon. Sen. Clinical Lectr, Univ. of Sheffield, 1979–2006. Mem., Ind. Adv. Gp on Sexual Health and HIV, 2003–10. Mem., MRC Coll. of Experts, 2005–10. Fellow, BASHH (formerly Med. Soc. for Study of Venereal Diseases), 2001 (Mem., 1976; Pres., 1991–2001; Trustee, 2001–05; Lifetime Achievement Award, 2009; Hon. Life Fellow, 2011); Trustee, Med. Foundn for HIV and Sexual Health, 2003–16. FRSocMed 1998. Freeman: Soc. of Apothecaries, 2007; City of London, 2011. Platinum Nat. Clinical Excellence Award, 2006. *Publications:* scientific papers and book chapters on genital tract infections, sexual health and HIV. *Recreations:* gardening, travel, photography, antiques, coin collecting, philately. *Address:* 3 Serlby Drive, Harthill, Sheffield, S Yorks S26 7UJ. *T:* (01909) 772610. *E:* g.r.kinghorn@sheffield.ac.uk, george.r.kinghorn@gmail.com.
*See also M. A. Kinghorn.*

**KINGHORN, Myra Anne;** Chair, Scheme Management Committee, European Payments Council, 2007–15; *b* 24 Jan. 1951; *d* of Alan Douglas Kinghorn and Lilian Isabel Kinghorn; *m* 1986, Richard John Haycocks; two *s*. *Educ:* La Sagesse High Sch., Newcastle upon Tyne; Univ. of Wales, Aberystwyth (BLib Jt Hons (Hist. and Librarianship) 1973). FCA (ACA 1977); CDir 2000; FInstD 2015. Exec. Manager, Ernst & Young, 1984–88; Chief Exec., Dir and Company Sec., Investors Compensation Scheme, 1988–2001; non-exec. Dir, Serious Fraud Office, 2001–04; Chief Exec., Pension Protection Fund, 2004–06. Non-exec. Mem., OPRA, 2003–04. Mem., Architects Registration Bd, 2008–16. Gov., Morley Coll., 2007–15 (Vice Chair, 2012–15); Mem., Develt Adv. Bd, Aberystwyth Univ., 2010– (Chair, 2010–15). *Recreations:* theatre visits, history, French. *Address:* 10 Courtenay Drive, Beckenham, Kent BR3 6YE. *Club:* Institute of Directors.
*See also G. R. Kinghorn.*

**KINGMAN, Sir John (Frank Charles),** Kt 1985; FRS 1971; mathematician; Vice-Chancellor, University of Bristol, 1985–2001; *b* 28 Aug. 1939; *er s* of late Dr F. E. T. Kingman, FRSC and Maud (*née* Harley); *m* 1964, Valerie Cromwell, FSA, FRHistS (*d* 2018) (Dir, History of Parlt, 1991–2001; High Sheriff of Bristol, 2004–05), *d* of late F. Cromwell, OBE, ISO; one *s* one *d*. *Educ:* Christ's Coll., Finchley; Pembroke Coll., Cambridge (MA, ScD; Smith's Prize, 1962; Hon. Fellow, 1988). CStat 1993. Fellow of Pembroke Coll., 1961–65, and Asst Lectr in Mathematics, 1962–64; Lectr, 1964–65, Univ. of Cambridge; Reader in Maths and Stats, 1965–66; Prof. 1966–69, Univ. of Sussex; Prof. of Maths, Univ. of Oxford, 1969–85; Fellow, St Anne's Coll., Oxford, 1978–85, Hon. Fellow, 1985; N. M. Rothschild & Sons Prof. of Mathematical Scis, Dir of Isaac Newton Inst. for Mathematical Scis, and Fellow of Pembroke Coll., Univ. of Cambridge, 2001–06. Visiting appointments: Univ. of Western Australia, 1963, 1974; Stanford Univ., USA, 1968; ANU, 1978. Chairman: Science Bd, SRC, 1979–81; SERC, 1981–85; founding Chm., Statistics Commn, 2000–03; Vice-Pres., Parly and Scientific Cttee, 1986–89, 2002–05 (Vice-Chm., 1983–86); Mem. Bd, British Council, 1986–91. Chm., Cttee of Inquiry into the Teaching of English Language, 1987–88. Director: IBM UK Holdings Ltd, 1985–95; Beecham Group plc, 1986–89; SmithKline Beecham plc, 1989–90; Bristol United Press plc, 1989–2001 (Dep. Chm., 1998–2001); British Technology Group plc, 1992 (Mem. Council, British Technol. Gp, 1984–92); SW RHA, 1990–94; Avon HA, 1996–99. Chm., 1973–76, Vice-Pres., 1976–92, Inst. of Statisticians; President: Royal Statistical Soc., 1987–89 (Vice-Pres., 1977–79; Guy Medal in Silver, 1981, in Gold, 2013; Hon. Fellow, 1993); London Math. Soc., 1990–92; European Math. Soc., 2003–06. Mem., Brighton Co. Borough Council, 1968–71; Chm., Regency Soc. of Brighton and Hove, 1975–81. MAE 1995; AcSS 2000. For. Associate, US Nat. Acad. of Scis, 2007. Hon. Senator, Univ. of Hannover, 1991. Hon. DSc: Sussex, 1983; Southampton, 1985; West of England, 1993; Brunel, 2004; Hon. LLD: Bristol, 1989; Queen's Univ., Kingston, Ontario, 1999; Hon. DPhil Cheltenham and Gloucester, 1998; Dr *hc* St Petersburg Univ. of Humanities and

Social Scis, 1994. Royal Medal, Royal Soc., 1983. Officier des Palmes Académiques, 1989. Motoo Kimura Award, Kimura Fund, 2018. *Publications:* Introduction to Measure and Probability (with S. J. Taylor), 1966; The Algebra of Queues, 1966; Regenerative Phenomena, 1972; Mathematics of Genetic Diversity, 1980; Poisson Processes, 1993; papers in mathematical and statistical jls. *Address:* Harley Lodge, Clifton Down, Bristol BS8 3BP. *Clubs:* Lansdowne, Reform; Clifton (Bristol).
See also Sir J. O. F. Kingman.

**KINGMAN, Sir John (Oliver Frank),** KCB 2016; Chairman, Legal & General Group plc, since 2016; Chair, UK Research and Innovation, since 2016; *b* 24 April 1969; *s* of Sir John Frank Charles Kingman, *qv*; partner, Diana Judith Gerald, *qv*; one *d*. *Educ:* Dragon Sch., Oxford; Westminster Sch. (Queen's Schol.); St John's Coll., Oxford (Casberd Schol.; BA 1st Cl. Hons). HM Treasury, 1991–94, Private Sec. to Financial Sec., 1993–94; Prin. Private Sec. to Sec. of State, DNH, 1994–95; Lex Columnist, FT, 1995–97; Gp Chief Exec.'s Office, BP, 1997–98; Press Sec. to Chancellor of the Exchequer, 1999–2000; HM Treasury: Hd, Productivity and Structural Reform, 2000–02; Dir, Enterprise and Growth Unit, 2003–06; Man. Dir, Finance and Industry, 2006; Man. Dir, Public Services and Growth, 2006–08; Second Perm. Sec., 2007–08; Chief Exec., UK Financial Investments Ltd, 2008–09; Global Co-Hd, Financial Instns Gp, Rothschild, 2010–12; Second Perm. Sec., 2012–16. Dir, EIB, 2003–06; non-exec. Dir, Framestore CFC Ltd, 2004–06. Mem., Global Adv. Bd, Centre for Corporate Reputation, Univ. of Oxford, 2008–. Vis. Fellow, Inst. of Political and Econ. Governance, Univ. of Manchester, 2003–06; World Fellow, Yale Univ., 2004. Mem., Develt Trust Bd, St Martin-in-the-Fields, 2006–09; Trustee: Royal Opera Hse, 2014–; Nat. Gall., 2017– (Dep. Chair, 2018–). Chm. Judges, Wolfson Economics Prize, 2017. Liveryman, Goldsmiths' Co., 2018–. *Address:* Legal & General Group plc, One Coleman Street, EC2R 5AA.

**KINGS, Rt Rev. Dr Graham Ralph;** Assistant Curate, Holy Trinity with St Matthew, Southwark, since 2018 (Priest in Charge, 2017–18); an Honorary Assistant Bishop, since 2015, and World Mission Adviser, since 2019, Diocese of Southwark; *b* Barkingside, 10 Oct. 1953; *s* of Ralph Norman Kings and Kathleen Eugenia Kings (*née* Warren); *m* 1977, Alison Audrey Britton; three *d*. *Educ:* Buckhurst Hill County High Sch.; RMA Sandhurst; Hertford Coll., Oxford (MA Theology 1980); Ridley Hall Theol Coll., Cambridge; Selwyn Coll., Cambridge (DipTh 1980); Utrecht Univ. (PhD 2002). 2nd Lt, 5th Royal Inniskilling Dragoon Guards, 1973; Caretaker, All Souls', Langham Place, 1977; ordained deacon, 1980, priest, 1981; Asst Curate, St Mark, Harlesden, 1980–84; CMS Mission Partner, Kenya, 1985–91; Dir of Studies, 1985–88, Vice Principal, 1989–91, St Andrew's Coll., Kabare; Overseas Advr, Henry Martyn Trust, Cambridge, 1992–95; Lectr, Mission Studies, 1992–2000, Dir, Henry Martyn Centre for Mission Studies and World Christianity, 1995–2000, Cambridge Theol Fedn; Affiliated Lectr, Univ. of Cambridge, 1996–2000; Vicar, St Mary's, Islington, 2000–09; Bishop Suffragan of Sherborne, 2009–15; Mission Theologian in the Anglican Communion, 2015–17; Hon. Asst Bishop, Dio. of Durham, 2015–18. Theol Sec., Fulcrum, 2003–. Honorary Curate: Holy Trinity, Cambridge, 1992–96; St Andrew's, Chesterton, 1996–2000. Select Preacher (Ramsden), Univ. of Cambridge, 1996; Hon. Fellow, Dept of Theology and Religion, Durham Univ., 2015–18. Cross of St Augustine, 2019. *Publications:* (jtly) Offerings from Kenya to Anglicanism: liturgical texts and contexts, 2001; Christianity Connected: Hindus, Muslims and the world in the letters of Max Warren and Roger Hooker, 2002, 2017; Signs and Seasons: a guide for your Christian journey, 2008. *Recreations:* walking, swimming, tennis, poetry, art. *Address:* 483b Southwark Park Road, SE16 2JP. *E:* grahamrkings@gmail.com.

**KINGSALE,** 36th Baron *cr* 1223 (by some reckonings 31st Baron); **Nevinson Mark de Courcy;** Baron Courcy and Baron of Ringrone; Premier Baron of Ireland; *b* 11 May 1958; *s* of late Nevinson Russell de Courcy, and Nora Lydia de Courcy (*née* Plint); *S* cousin, 2005. *Educ:* Auckland Grammar Sch.; Univ. of Auckland; Emmanuel Coll., Cambridge. *Recreations:* reading, conservation, jigsaws. *Address:* 22 Armadale Road, Remuera, Auckland 1050, New Zealand. *T:* (9) 5248875. *E:* nmdecourcy@nmdec.co.nz.

**KINGSBOROUGH, Viscount; Charles Avery Edward King-Tenison;** *b* 18 Nov. 2000; *s* and *heir* of Earl of Kingston, *qv*.

**KINGSBURY, Derek John,** CBE 1988; FREng, FIET; Chairman: Fairey Group plc, 1987–96 (Group Chief Executive, 1982–91); David Brown Group plc, 1992–96; Goode Durrant plc, 1992–96; *b* 10 July 1926; *s* of late Major Arthur Kingsbury, BEM, Virginia Water and Gwendoline Mary Kingsbury; *m* 1st, 1959, Muriel June Drake; one *s* (and one *s* decd); 2nd, 1980, Sarah Muriel Morgan (*d* 2006); one *s*; 3rd, 2007, Wendy Christine Jacobs. *Educ:* Strode's Secondary Sch., City and Guilds Coll. BScEng Hons; DIC. FIET (FIEE 1968); FCGI 1977; FREng (FEng 1991). 2nd Lieut, REME, 1947–49. Apprentice, Metropolitan Vickers, 1949–51; Exch. Schol., Univ. of Pennsylvania, 1952–53; Associated Electrical Industries: Manager, E Canada, 1954–61; PA to Chm., 1961–63; Gen. Manager, AEI Distribution Transformers, 1963–66; Gen. Manager, Overseas Manufacturing Develt, 1966–69; Thorn Electrical Industries: Man. Dir, Foster Transformers, 1969–76; Man. Dir, Elect. & Hydr. Div., 1972–76, Exec. Dir, 1973–76; Dowty Group: Dep. Chief Exec., 1976–82. Chm., Ultra Electronics, 1977–82; industrial mission to China, 1978; non-executive Director: Vickers, 1981–91; ACAL plc, 1991–94. Institution of Electrical Engineers: Dir Peter Peregrinus, 1976–81; Mem., Finance Cttee, 1978–80; Confederation of British Industry: Mem. Council, 1980–86; Chm., Overseas Cttee, 1980–84; missions to Japan 1981, 1983, 1985; Defence Manufacturers Association: Mem. Council, 1985–92; Chm., 1987–90; Chm., F and GP Cttee, 1990–92; Vice-Pres., 1993–2002; Member: Review Bd for Govt Contracts, 1986–94; Engineering Council, 1990–93 (Chm., CET Pilot Scheme Steering Cttee, 1988–90); Council, BEAMA, 1973–75. Mem. Ct, Imperial Coll. London, 2012–16. Freeman, City of London, 1994; Liveryman, Scientific Instrument Makers' Co., 1994. CCMI; FRSA 1994. President: BHF Horse Show, 1977–98; Aircraft Golfing Soc., 1995–2005. *Recreations:* golf, swimming, walking. *Address:* Trecaven, Rock, Cornwall PL27 6LB. *T:* (01208) 863608. *Clubs:* Royal Automobile, MCC, St Enodoc Golf (Vice-Captain, 1997–99; Captain, 1999–2001); Rock Sailing.

**KINGSBURY, Sally Jane;** *see* O'Neill, Sally J.

**KINGSHOTT, (Albert) Leonard;** Director: International Banking Division, Lloyds Bank Plc, 1985–89; Mutual Management Services, since 1993; Member, Monopolies and Mergers Commission, 1990–96; *b* 16 Sept. 1930; *s* of A. L. Kingshott and Mrs K. Kingshott; *m* 1958, Valerie Simpson; two *s* one *d*. *Educ:* London Sch. of Economics (BSc); ACIS 1958, FCIS 1983. Flying Officer, RAF, 1952–55; Economist, British Petroleum, 1955–60; Economist, British Nylon Spinners, 1960–62; Financial Manager, Iraq Petroleum Co., 1963–65; Chief Economist, Ford of Britain, 1965; Treas., Ford of Britain, 1966–67; Treas., Ford of Europe, 1968–70; Finance Dir, Whitbread & Co., 1972; Man. Dir, Finance, BSC, 1972–77; Dir, Lloyds Bank International, responsible for Merchant Banking activities, 1977–80, for European Div., 1980–82, for Marketing and Planning Div., 1983–84; Dep. Chief Exec., Lloyds Bank International, 1985. Exec. Dir, The Private Bank & Trust Co., 1989–91; Director: Bank of London and South America Ltd, 1977–89; Lloyds Bank International, 1977–89; Lloyds Bank (France) Ltd, 1980–89; Lloyd's Bank California, 1985–88; Rosehaugh plc, 1991–92 (Chm.); Shandwick plc, 1993–2000; Newmarket Foods Ltd, 1994–97; Man. Dir, Cypher Science Ltd, 1996–. Mem. Bd, Crown Agents for Oversea Govts and Admin, and Crown Agents Hldg and Realisation Bd, 1989–92. Associate Mem. of Faculty, 1978, Governor, 1980–91, Ashridge Management Coll. Chm., Oakbridge Counselling, 1990–. FCIS. *Publications:* Investment Appraisal, 1967. *Recreations:* golf, chess. *Address:* 4 Delamas, Beggar Hill, Fryerning, Ingatestone, Essex CM4 0PW. *T:* (01277) 352077.

**KINGSLAND, Camilla Anne MacNeill;** *see* Campbell, C. A. M.

**KINGSLAND, Dr James Patrick,** OBE 2012; Senior Partner, General Practice, Wallasey, Merseyside, since 1989; National Lead for primary care home model programme, NHS England, since 2016; *b* Nottingham, 20 April 1960; *s* of late Richard Alan Kingsland and of Noreen Monica Kingsland; *m* 1986, Sarah Elizabeth Higham; two *d*. *Educ:* Mundella Grammar Sch., Nottingham; Univ. of Liverpool (MB ChB 1984; DRCOG 1988; DFFP 1998). Nat. Clinical Commng Network Lead, DoH, 2009–13. Pres., Nat. Assoc. of Primary Care, 2008– (Chm., 2004–08). Non-executive Director: Clatterbridge Centre for Oncology Foundn Trust, 2010–16; Royal Liverpool and Broadgreen Univ. Hosps NHS Trust, 2016–. GP Advr to DoH, 1998–2003, 2008–10. Chm., Jhoots Pharmacy Gp, 2014–17; Dir, Waring Health, 2013–; Sen. Med. Advr Assce Gp, 2013–16. Internat. Advr on Primary Care, Faculty of Disaster Medicine for India and Nepal, 2017–. Hon. Prof., Sch. of Medicine, Univ. of Central Lancs, 2018–. Resident Doctor, BBC Radio Merseyside. *Publications:* contrib. to numerous govt policy documents for NHS. *Recreations:* media, golf, football (Nottingham Forest supporter). *Address:* 7 Holm Hill, Wirral CH48 7JA. *T:* (0151) 625 5556. *E:* james.kingsland@nhs.net. *Club:* National Liberal (non-political Mem.).

**KINGSLEY, Sir Ben,** Kt 2002; actor; *b* 31 Dec. 1943; *s* of Rahimtulla Harji Bhanji and Anna Leina Mary Bhanji; surname changed to Kingsley by Deed Poll, 1982; *m* 2007, Daniela Lavender; three *s* one *d* from former marriages. *Educ:* Manchester Grammar Sch. Associate artist, Royal Shakespeare Co.; work with RSC includes, 1970–80; 1985–86: Peter Brook's Midsummer Night's Dream, Stratford, London, Broadway, NY; Gramsci in Occupations; Ariel in The Tempest; title role, Hamlet; Ford in Merry Wives of Windsor; title role, Baal; Squeers and Mr Wagstaff in Nicholas Nickleby; title role, Othello, Melons; National Theatre, 1977–78: Mosca in Volpone; Trofimov in The Cherry Orchard; Sparkish in The Country Wife; Vukhov in Judgement; additional theatre work includes: Johnny in Hello and Goodbye (Fugard), King's Head, 1973; Errol Philander in Statements After An Arrest (Fugard), Royal Court, 1974; Edmund Kean, Harrogate, 1981, Haymarket, 1983 (also televised); title role, Dr Faustus, Manchester Royal Exchange, 1981; Waiting for Godot, Old Vic, 1997; *television* 1974–, includes The Love School (series), 1974, Silas Marner (film), 1985, Murderers Amongst Us (mini-series), 1989, Anne Frank - the full story (Best Actor award, Screen Actors' Guild), 2001, and several plays; *films:* title role, Gandhi, 1980 (2 Hollywood Golden Globe awards, 1982; NY Film Critics' Award, 2 BAFTA awards, Oscar, LA Film Critics Award, 1983, Variety Club of GB Best Film Actor award, 1983); Betrayal, 1982; Turtle Diary, 1985; Harem, 1986; Testimony, Maurice, 1987; Pascali's Island, The Train, 1988; Without a Clue, 1989; Bugsy, Sneakers, Dave, 1992; Schindler's List, 1993; Innocent Moves, 1994; Death and the Maiden, Species, 1995; Twelfth Night, 1996; Photographing Fairies, 1997; The Assignment, Weapons of Mass Distraction, Sweeney Todd, Alice in Wonderland, Crime and Punishment, Spookey House, 1998; The Confession, Rules of Engagement, What Planet are you from?, 1999; Sexy Beast, 2001; Tuck Everlasting, 2002; Suspect Zero, Sound of Thunder, House of Sand and Fog, 2003; Thunderbirds, Triumph of Love, 2004; Oliver Twist, 2005; Lucky Number Slevin, 2006; The Last Legion, You Kill Me, 2007; War, Inc., Transsiberian, Elegy, The Wackness, The Love Guru, 2008; Fifty Dead Men Walking, 2009; Shutter Island, Prince of Persia, 2010; Hugo, 2011; The Dictator, 2012; Iron Man 3, 2012; Ender's Game, 2013; (short) Marvel One-Shot: All Hail the King, 2014; Exodus: Gods and Kings, 2014; Night at the Museum: Secret of the Tomb, 2014; Life, 2015; The Walk, 2015; The Jungle Book, 2016; Learning to Drive, 2016; War Machine, 2017; Operation Finale, 2018; Night Hunter, 2019. Best Film Actor, London Standard Award, 1983; Best Actor: European Film Acad., 2001; British Ind. Film Award, 2001; Screen Actors Guild, 2002; Broadcast Critics Award, 2002. Medici Soc. Award, 1989; Simon Wiesenthal Humanitarian Award, 1989; Berlin Golden Camera Award, 1990; Albert R. Broccoli Britannia Award for Worldwide Contribn to Entertainment, BAFTA, LA Britannia Awards, 2013; Nat. Leadership Award, US Holocaust Meml Mus., 2014. Hon. MA Salford, 1984; Hon. DLitt: Sussex, 2008; Hull, 2008. Padma Shri (India), 1984. *Address:* c/o Independent Talent Group Ltd, 40 Whitfield Street, W1T 2RH.

**KINGSLEY, Joy, (Mrs Michael Blackburn);** Senior Partner, JMW Solicitors LLP, since 2010; *b* Manchester, 16 Jan. 1956; *d* of late Roger James Kingsley, OBE and of Valerie Marguerite Mary Kingsley (*née* Hanna); *m* 1991, Michael Blackburn; two *s*. *Educ:* Manchester High Sch.; Nottingham Univ. (LLB). Admitted Solicitor, 1980. With Pannone LLP (formerly: Goldberg Blackburn, Goldberg Blackburn and Howards, Pannone and Partners, Pannone Marsh Pearson, Pannone Pritchard Englefield, Pannone and Partners), 1978–2010: Partner, 1983; Hd, Private Client Dept, 1989–95; Man. Partner, 1993–2008; Sen. Partner, 2008–10. Non-exec. Dir, I-COM, 2006–. Senator, Jun. Chamber Internat. Gov., Manchester GS, 1999–. *Recreations:* travel, reading, ski-ing, cinema and theatre, music. *Address:* JMW Solicitors LLP, 1 Byrom Place, Spinningfields, Manchester M3 3HG. *T:* (home) (0161) 941 1258, 07788 970020.

**KINGSLEY, Nicholas William,** FSA; Head, Archives Sector Development (formerly National Advisory Services), and Secretary, Historical Manuscripts Commission, National Archives, 2005–15; *b* 14 Sept. 1957; *s* of Philip Francis Kingsley and Joan Rosamond Kingsley (*née* Holliday); *m* 1980, (Susan) Mary Summerhayes. *Educ:* St Paul's Sch., London; Keble Coll., Oxford (BA 1978, MA 1982). Archive trainee, Bodleian Liby, Oxford, 1978–79; Asst Archivist, 1979–82, Modern Records Archivist, 1982–89, Glos Record Office; City Archivist, Birmingham City Archives, 1989–96; Central Liby Manager, Birmingham Central Liby, 1996–2000; Co. and Diocesan Archivist, Glos Record Office, 2000–05. Member: Nat. Council on Archives, 1991–2010 (Sec., 1993–99; Vice-Chm., 2000–01; Chm., 2001–05); Govt Archives Taskforce, 2002–04; MLA, 2004–06. Dir and Trustee, Media Archive of Central England, 1994–2004; Chairman: Nat. Cttee, Victoria County History, 2005–11; EU Document Lifecycle Mgt Forum, 2006; Adv. Cttee, Victoria History Trust, 2011–13; Archives Accreditation Bd, 2011–13. Member: Working Gp on Literary Heritage, 2006–13; Exec. Cttee, Friends of Nat. Libraries, 2006–15; Arts Adv. Panel, Nat. Trust, 2012–15; Archives Accreditation Panel, 2013–15. Volunteer Specialist Advr to Nat. Trust, 2016–. Trustee: Glos County History Trust, 2010–; Victoria Co. History Trust, 2013–. Gen. Ed., Phillimore & Co. English Country Houses series, 1994–2004. Author of blog, http://landedfamilies.blogspot.co.uk, 2013–. FSA 2003. Hon. DLitt Birmingham, 2006. *Publications:* Handlist of the Contents of the Gloucestershire Record Office, 1988, 4th edn 1998, Supplement, 2002; The Country Houses of Gloucestershire: 1500–1660, 1989, 2nd edn 2001, 1660–1830, 1992, 1830–2000 (with M. Hill), 2001; Archives Online, 1998; (jtly) Full Disclosure, 1999; Changing the Future of our Past, 2002; contribs and reviews for Country Life and professional jls. *Recreations:* architectural, historical and genealogical research, cooking, appreciation of food and wine. *Address:* Tor Bank, 38 Dial Hill Road, Clevedon, N Somerset BS21 7HN. *T:* (01275) 542263. *E:* nick.kingsley@blueyonder.co.uk.

**KINGSMILL,** family name of **Baroness Kingsmill**.

**KINGSMILL, Baroness** *cr* 2006 (Life Peer), of Holland Park, in the Royal Borough of Kensington and Chelsea; **Denise Patricia Byrne Kingsmill,** CBE 2000; a Deputy Chairman, Competition (formerly Monopolies and Mergers) Commission, 1997–2003; *b* 24 April 1947; *d* of Patrick Henry Byrne and Hester Jean Byrne; *m* 1st, 1970, David Gordon Kingsmill (marr. diss. 2002); one *s* one *d*; 2nd, 2006, Richard Wheatly (*d* 2015). *Educ*: Girton Coll., Cambridge. Admitted Solicitor, 1980. With ICI Fibres, then Internat. Wool Secretariat, 1968–75; Robin Thompson & Partners, 1979–82; Russell Jones and Walker, 1982–85; Denise Kingsmill & Co., 1985–90; Partner, D. J. Freeman, 1990–93; Consultant, Denton Hall, 1994–2000. Chm., Optimum Health Services NHS Trust, 1992–99. Non-executive Director: Rainbow UK, 1993–94; MFI Furniture Gp, 1997–2001 (Dep. Chm., 1999–2001); Norwich and Peterborough Bldg Soc., 1997–2001; Telewest Communications, 2001–03; Manpower UK, 2001–03; British Airways, 2004–11; Korn/Ferry Internat., 2009–12; Betfair, 2011–12; IAG Internat. Airlines Gp, 2011–17; E.ON AG, 2011–18; Telecom Italia, 2014– (Mem., Remuneration and Nomination Cttee, 2014–17); Sen. Ind. Dir, APR Energy plc, 2011–14 (Vice Chm., 2014–); Chm. Adv. Forum, Laing O'Rourke, 2003–04; Sen. Advr, RBS, 2005–08; Chm., Eur. Adv. Bd, (24)7, 2011–14; Mem., European Adv. Council, Microsoft, 2009–12; Dep. Chm., Adv. Bd, PwC, 2011–14; Chm., ASPEN Initiative UK, 2018–. Chairman: Women's Employment and Pay Review, 2001; Accounting for People Taskforce, DTI, 2003–; Model Health Inquiry, 2007; Kingsmill Review: Taking Care, 2014; Monzo Bank, 2016–18. Trustee, Design Mus., 2000–10. Chm., Sadler's Wells Foundn, 2003–04. Member: Develt Cttee, Judge Business Sch. (formerly Judge Inst.), Cambridge Univ., 2000–06; Internat. Adv. Bd, IESE Business Sch., Univ. of Navarra, 2011–; Bd, Inditex, 2016–; Pro-Chancellor, Brunel Univ., 2002–06. Gov., Coll. of Law, 1992–2001. Columnist, Mgt Today, 2008–. Hon. Fellow, Univ. of Wales, Cardiff, 2000. Hon. LLD: Brunel, 2001; Stirling, 2003; Hon. DSc Cranfield, 2007. *Recreations*: hiking, fly fishing. *Address*: House of Lords, SW1A 0PW.

**KINGSTON,** 12th Earl of, *cr* 1768 (Ire.); **Robert Charles Henry King-Tenison;** Bt 1682; Baron Kingston 1764; Viscount Kingston of Kingsborough 1766; Baron Erris 1800; Viscount Lorton 1806; *b* 20 March 1969; *o s* of 11th Earl of Kingston and his 1st wife, Patricia Mary (*née* Killip); *S* father, 2002; *m* 1994, Ruth Margaret Buckner (marr. diss. 2012); one *s* one *d*. *Heir*: *s* Viscount Kingsborough, *qv*.

**KINGSTON, (William) Martin;** QC 1992; a Recorder, 1991–99; *b* 9 July 1949; *s* of William Robin Kingston and Iris Edith Kingston; *m* 1972, Jill Mary Bache; one *s* two *d*. *Educ*: Middlewich Secondary Modern Sch.; Hartford Coll. of Further Educn; Liverpool Univ. (LLB). Called to the Bar, Middle Temple, 1972, Bencher, 2002; Asst Recorder, 1987. Dep. Chm., Agricl Lands Tribunal, 1985–. Asst Comr, Parly Boundary Commn for England, 1992–. *Recreations*: ski-ing, fishing, reading, going on holiday. *Address*: (chambers) Greenwood House, 4–7 Salisbury Court, EC4Y 8AA; Kemble House, Kemble, Cirencester, Glos GL7 6AD.

**KINGSTON-upon-THAMES, Area Bishop of,** since 2002; **Rt Rev. Dr Richard Ian Cheetham;** *b* 18 Aug. 1955; *s* of John Brian Margrave Cheetham and Mollie Louise Cheetham; *m* 1977, Felicity Mary Loving; one *s* one *d*. *Educ*: Kingston Grammar Sch.; Corpus Christi Coll., Oxford (MA, PGCE); Ripon Coll., Cuddesdon (Cert. Theol. 1987); King's Coll., London (PhD 1999). Science Teacher, Richmond Sch., N Yorks, 1978–80; Physics Master, Eton Coll., 1980–83; Investment Analyst, Legal & General, London, 1983–85; ordained deacon, 1987, priest 1988; Asst Curate, Holy Cross, Fenham, Newcastle upon Tyne, 1987–90; Vicar, St Augustine of Canterbury, Luton, 1990–99; RD of Luton, 1995–98; Archdeacon of St Albans, 1999–2002. Lead Bishop, Equipping Religious Leaders in an Age of Science, Durham Univ., 2015–18. Whitelands Professorial Fellow in Christian Theol. and Contemp. Issues, Univ. of Roehampton, 2013–; Hon. Res. Fellow, KCL, 2011–. Chairman: Southwark Diocesan Bd of Educn, 2002–15; Christian Muslim Forum, 2010–12 (Anglican Pres., 2012–15; Scholar Consultant, 2015–); British Regl Cttee, St George's Coll., Jerusalem, 2013–; Mem., C of E Envmt Working Gp, 2014–. Pres., YMCA London SW; Patron: Fircroft Trust; Kingston Bereavement Service. Mem. Council, Roehampton Univ., 2006–12. Pres., Old Kingstonians Hockey Club, 2009–15. *Publications*: Collective Worship: issues and opportunities, 2004. *Recreations*: hockey (England U19 hockey 1974; Oxford Hockey Blue, 1975; British Univs, 1975), squash, tennis, walking, theatre, cinema. *Address*: Kingston Episcopal Area Office, 620 Kingston Road, Raynes Park, SW20 8DN. *W:* www.bishoprichardcheetham.com.

**KINGWELL, Rear Adm. John Matthew Leonard,** CBE 2016; Deputy Commandant, Royal College of Defence Studies, 2016–19; *b* London, 26 Aug. 1966; *s* of John and Diane Kingwell; *m* 1990, Alison Hogg; two *d*. *Educ*: Streatham Modern Sch.; Southwark Coll.; Loughborough Univ. (BA Hons Hist. 1988); King's Coll. London (MA Defence Studies 2000). Joined RN as Warfare Officer, 1984; served: HMS Edinburgh, 1989–90; HMS Sheraton, 1990–92; CO, HMS Pursuer and O i/c Sussex Univ. Royal Naval Unit, 1993–94; HMS Monmouth, 1995–96; jscsc, 1999–2000; CO, HMS Argyll, 2001–02; Advr to Hd of Iraqi Navy, Baghdad, 2005; MA to VCDS/2nd Perm. Under Sec., MoD, 2006–08; CO, HMS Albion, 2009–10; Comdr, UK Task Gp, Libya, 2011; Hd, Navy Resources and Plans, MoD, 2011–13; Dir, Develt, Concepts and Doctrine Centre, MoD, 2013–16. President: Newhaven and Seaford Sea Cadets, 2005–; Hastings Sea Cadets, 2010–. Liveryman, Shipwrights' Co., 2003. Younger Brother, Trinity House, 2011–. QCVS 2012. *Recreations*: military history, jogging, family. *Club*: Army and Navy.

**KINLOCH, Prof. Anthony James,** PhD, DSc; FRS 2007; FREng, CEng; CChem, FRSC; FIMMM; FCGI; FIMechE; Professor of Adhesion, Imperial College London, since 1990; *b* 7 Oct. 1946; *s* of Nathan and Hilda May Kinloch; *m* 1969, Gillian Patricia Birch; two *s* one *d*. *Educ*: London Nautical Sch.; Queen Mary Coll., London (PhD 1972; DSc London 1989. CChem 1982; FRSC 1982; FIMMM (FIM 1982); FREng (FEng 1997); FIMechE 2009. RARDE, MoD, 1972–84; Reader, 1984–89, Chair, Mechanics of Materials Div., 2004–07, Imperial Coll., London. Visiting Professor: EPFL, Lausanne, 1986; Univ. of Utah, 1988; Univ. of Sydney, 2007; RMIT, Melbourne, 2014. Lectures: C&G Centenary, 1995; Thomas Hawksley, IMechE, 1996. Mem. Council, Inst. Materials, 1997–2002; Pres., 2002–04); FCGI 2001. Adhesion Soc. of Japan Award, 1994; Griffith Medal and Prize, 1996, Wake Meml Medal, 2002, Inst. of Materials; Thomas Hawksley Gold Medal, IMechE, 1997; Le Prix Dédale de la Société Française d'Adhesion, 2009; Armourers and Brasiers' Co. Prize for Excellence in Materials Sci. and Technol., Royal Soc., 2009. *Publications*: Adhesion and Adhesives: science and technology, 1987; (with R. J. Young) Fracture Behaviour of Polymers, 1983; (ed) Durability of Structural Adhesives, 1983; (ed jtly) Toughened Plastics: I 1993, II 1996; over 250 papers in learned jls. *Recreations*: opera, tennis, walking. *Address*: Imperial College London, Department of Mechanical Engineering, Exhibition Road, SW7 2AZ.

**KINLOCH, Sir David,** 13th Bt *cr* 1686, of Gilmerton; *b* 5 Aug. 1951; *s* of Sir Alexander Davenport Kinloch, 12th Bt and of Anna, *d* of late Thomas Walker, Edinburgh; *S* father, 1982; *m* 1st, 1976, Susan Middlewood (marr. diss. 1986); one *s* one *d*; 2nd, 1987, Maureen Carswell (marr. diss. 2009); two *s*; 3rd, 2018, Melanie Pumfrey. *Educ*: Gordonstoun. Career in research into, and recovery and replacement of, underground services. *Recreation*: treasure hunting. *Heir*: *s* Alexander Kinloch, *b* 31 May 1978. *Address*: Gilmerton House, North Berwick, East Lothian EH39 5LQ. *T*: (01620) 880207.

**KINLOCH, Sir David Oliphant,** 5th Bt *cr* 1873, of Kinloch, co. Perth; CA; Director, Caledonia Investments PLC, 1988–2004; *b* 15 Jan. 1942; *s* of Sir John Kinloch, 4th Bt and Doris Ellaline (*d* 1997), *e d* of C. J. Head; *S* father, 1992; *m* 1st, 1968, Susan Minette Urquhart (marr. diss. 1979), *y d* of Maj.-Gen. R. E. Urquhart, CB, DSO; three *d*; 2nd, 1983, Sabine Irene, *o d* of Philippe and Yolaine de Loës; one *s* one *d*. *Educ*: Charterhouse. *Heir*: *s* Alexander Peter Kinloch [*b* 30 June 1986; *m* 2016, Antonella Banszky von Ambroz]. *Address*: House of Aldie, Kinross KY13 0QH; 29 Walpole Street, SW3 4QS.

**KINLOCH, Henry, (Harry);** Chairman, Quartermaine & Co., since 1989; *b* 7 June 1937; *s* of William Shearer Kinloch and Alexina Alice Quartermaine Kinloch; *m* 1st, 1966, Gillian Anne Ashley (marr. diss. 1979); one *s* one *d*; 2nd, 1987, Catherine Elizabeth Hossack. *Educ*: Queen's Park Sch., Glasgow; Univs of Strathclyde, Birmingham and Glasgow. MSc, PhD, ARCST, CEng, FIMechE. Lecturer in Engineering: Univ. of Strathclyde, 1962–65; Univ. of Liverpool, 1966; Vis. Associate Prof. of Engrg, MIT, 1967; Sen. Design Engr, CEGB, 1968–70; PA Management Consultants, 1970–73; Chief Exec., Antony Gibbs (PFP) Ltd, 1973–74; Chm. and Chief Exec., Antony Gibbs Financial Services Ltd, 1975–77; Man. Dir, British Shipbuilders, 1978–80; Dep. Man. Dir and Chief Exec., Liberty Life Assce Co., 1980–83; Associate, Lazard Brothers, 1980–84; Chm. and Chief Exec., Ætna Internat. (UK), 1984–89. Chm., Helm Investments Ltd, 1995–98; Gp Man. Dir, Ultraseal Internat. Ltd, 1997–98. Associate, AA Advrs, 2014–. Director: Barfoots of Botley Ltd, 2005–; ACM Envmtl (formerly ACM Waste Mgt) plc, 2009–13; Strata Technology Ltd, 2011–; WES Ltd, 2014–16; Posbrook Hldgs Ltd, 2018–. Consultant, London Bridge Capital, 2010–13. Mem., Ct of Govs, Univ. of Westminster, 2013–. *Publications*: many publications on theoretical and applied mechanics, financial and business studies. *Recreations*: reading book reviews, opera, political biography, walking, sometimes with others! *Address*: AA Advisers LLP, Room 226, Linen Hall, 162–168 Regent Street, W1B 5TD. *Clubs*: Athenæum (Mem., Gen. and Exec. Cttees, 2003–08; Dep. Chm., 2005–08; Chm., 2009–12; Chm., Investment Cttee, 2013–19); Worplesdon Golf; Hunstanton Golf; Royal Dornoch Golf.

**KINLOSS,** Lady (13th in line, of the Lordship *cr* 1602); **Teresa Mary Nugent Freeman-Grenville;** *b* Tanga, Tanganyika, 20 July 1957; *er d* of Lady Kinloss (12th in line) and Dr Greville Stewart Parker Freeman-Grenville (*d* 2005); *S* mother, 2012. *Educ*: Rye St Antony Sch., Oxford; York Art Sch. (C&G Cert. in Women's Light Clothing); Cert. in Fashion, Yorkshire and Humberside Council. Milk Recorder for Nat. Milk Records, 1992–. *Recreations*: goat keeper, dogs, spinning, crochet, weaving, etc. *Heir*: sister Hon. Hester Josephine Anne Haworth, Mistress of Kinloss [*b* 9 May 1960; *m* 1984, Peter Haworth; three *s*]. *Address*: North View House, Main Street, Sheriff Hutton, N Yorks YO60 6ST. *T*: (01347) 878447.

**KINMONTH, Prof. Ann-Louise, (Mrs Ann-Louise Kinmonth-Davis),** CBE 2002; MD; FRCP, FRCPCH, FRCGP, FMedSci; Professor of General Practice, University of Cambridge, 1997–2011, now Emeritus; Fellow of St John's College, Cambridge, since 1997 (Director of Clinical Studies, 2002–17; Member of Council, 2013–16); *b* 8 Jan. 1951; *d* of late Maurice Henry Kinmonth and Gwendolyn Stella (*née* Phillipps); *m* 2004, Prof. John Allen Davis, *qv. Educ*: New Hall, Cambridge (MA); St Thomas' Hosp. Med. Sch. (MB, BChir, MSc, MD 1984); London Sch. of Hygiene and Tropical Medicine, Univ. of London (MPhil Epidemiology 1990). FRCGP 1992; FRCP 1994; FRCPCH 1997. House Officer, Lambeth and Salisbury Hosps, 1975–76; SHO, Oxford Hosps, 1976–78; Res. Fellow in Paediatrics, Oxford Univ., 1978–80; Oxfam MO, Somalia, 1981; general practice trng, Oxford, 1981–82; Principal, Aldermoor Health Centre, Southampton, 1983–96; University of Southampton: Lectr, 1983–84; Sen. Lectr, 1984–91; Reader, 1991–92; Prof., 1992–96. Advr in Primary Care to MRC/DoH, 2004–05; Associate Dir (Primary Care), UK Clinical Res. Network, 2005–07; Ext. Associate, Inst. of Medicine (USA), 2007. Chair of Govs, St John's Coll. Sch., 2019–. Founder FMedSci 1998 (Mem. Council, 1998–2001). *Publications*: (ed with J. D. Baum) Care of the Child with Diabetes Mellitus, 1986; (ed with R. Jones) Critical Reading for Primary Care, 1995; (ed jtly) Evidence Base for Diabetes Care, 2002, 2nd edn 2010; contrib. papers on diabetes care, prevention of cardio-vascular disease and inequalities in health in peer reviewed jls. *Address*: 1 Cambridge Road, Great Shelford, Cambridge CB22 5JE.

**KINNAIR, Dame Donna,** DBE 2008; Chief Executive and General Secretary, Royal College of Nursing, since 2019 (Director of Nursing, Policy and Practice, 2016–18; Acting Chief Executive and General Secretary, 2018–19); *b* London, 17 Feb. 1961; *d* of Victor and Dolores Nesbitt; *m* 1981, Stephen Kinnair; two *s* one *d*. *Educ*: Rushmore Prim. Sch.; Skinners' Company's Sch. for Girls; Princess Alexandra Sch. of Nursing; Univ. of E London (LLB 1996); King's Coll. London (Dip. Healthcare Ethics); Univ. of Greenwich (PGCE 1999); Univ. of Manchester (MA Ethics and Law 2006). Nurse: London Hosp., 1983–87; Antigua, WI, 1987; Health Visitor, London Boroughs of Newham, Tower Hamlets and Hackney, 1988–96; Child Protection Nurse Specialist, Optimum Health Services, Lewisham and Southwark, 1996–99; Strategic Comr, Children's Services, Lambeth, Southwark and Lewisham HA, 1999–2002; Dir of Nursing, 2002–11, Dir of Commissioning, 2008–11, Southwark PCT, later Southwark Health and Social Care; Dir of Nursing, NHS SE London, 2011–13; Dir of Governance and Special Projects, 2012–13 (on secondment), Clinical Dir for Emergency Medicine, 2014–15, Barking, Havering and Redbridge Univ. Hosps NHS Trust; Hd of Nursing, RCN, 2015–16. Nurse Advr, Victoria Climbié Inquiry, 2001. Vis. Prof. of Primary Care, London Southbank Univ., 2008–. Consultant Ed., Nursing Management, 2006–. *Recreations*: cycling, walking, theatre, cinema. *Address*: Royal College of Nursing, 20 Cavendish Square, W1G 0RN.

**KINNAIRD, Alison Margaret, (Mrs R. Morton),** MBE 1997; free-lance musician and artist, since 1970; *b* 30 April 1949; *d* of John and Margaret Kinnaird; *m* 1974, Robin Morton; one *s* one *d*. *Educ*: George Watson's Ladies' Coll.; Edinburgh Univ. (MA 1970). Artworks in public and private collections incl. V&A Mus., Scottish Nat. Portrait Gall., Corning Mus. of Glass, NY and Scottish Parlt; specialises in engraved glass. Has performed, playing Scottish harp, nationally and internationally; has made recordings. *Publications*: (with Keith Sanger) Tree of Strings: a history of the harp in Scotland, 1992; The Small Harp, 1989; The Lothian Collection, 1995. *Address*: Shillinghill, Temple, Midlothian EH23 4SH. *T*: (01875) 830328, *Fax*: (01875) 830392. *E*: alisonk@templerecords.co.uk. *W*: www.alisonkinnaird.com.

**KINNEAR, Jonathan Shea;** QC 2012; a Recorder, since 2009; *b* Ballymena, NI, 22 July 1971; *s* of John Brian Kinnear and Helga Louisa Kinnear; *m* 2006, Marlo Zoe Beaudet; two *s*. *Educ*: Methodist Coll., Belfast; Univ. of Newcastle upon Tyne (LLB Hons 1993). Called to the Bar: Gray's Inn, 1994; NI, 1996; a Dep. Dist Judge, 2004–09. Mem., Bar Standards

Professional Conduct Cttee, 2008–13. Disciplinary Tribunal Chair, ICAEW, 2018–. *Recreations:* playing and coaching Rugby, crossfit. *Address:* 2 Hare Court, Temple, EC4Y 7BH. *T:* (020) 7353 5324. *E:* jonathan.kinnearqc@2harecourt.com. *Clubs:* Wimbledon Rugby Football; Roehampton.

**KINNELL, Ian;** QC 1987; professional arbitrator; *b* 23 May 1943; *o s* of Brian Kinnell and Grace Madeline Kinnell; *m* 1970, Elizabeth Jane Ritchie; one *s* one *d*. *Educ:* Sevenoaks Sch., Kent. Called to the Bar, Gray's Inn, 1967. A Recorder, 1987–89; Immigration Appeal Adjudicator, 1990–91; part-time Chm., Immigration Appeal Tribunal, 1991–97. Mem., London Maritime Arbitrator's Assoc., 1991. *Recreation:* rural pursuits. *Address:* The Vineyard, Heyope, Knighton, Powys LD7 1RE. *T:* (01547) 520990.

**KINNIER, Andrew John;** QC 2018; *b* Wallasey, 31 March 1973; *s* of Robert Ian Kinnier and Agnes Eluned Kinnier (*née* Beattie); *m* 2008, Dr Andrea Jennifer Roberts; one *s* one *d*. *Educ:* Ruthin Sch.; Sidney Sussex Coll., Cambridge (BA 1st Cl. Hons 1995; MA 1997). Called to the Bar, Middle Temple, 1996 (Queen Mother-Fox Major Schol.); in practice as a barrister, specialising in mass tort claims, product liability law, public procurement law and public inquiries, 1997–; Jun. Counsel to the Crown, B Panel, 2008–11, A Panel, 2011–18; Jun. Counsel to Welsh Govt (Public Law), 2008–18; Counsel, Grenfell Tower Inquiry, 2017–. Gov., Chesham Prep. Sch., 2019–. Freeman, City of London, 2010. *Publications:* (contrib.) Halsbury's Laws of England, Vol. 37, 2001; (contrib.) Kluwer's International Product Liability Manual, 2011, 2nd edn 2012; (contrib.) Bullen & Leake & Jacob's Precedents and Pleadings, 18th edn 2019. *Recreations:* family, history, gardening. *Address:* Henderson Chambers, 2 Harcourt Buildings, Temple, EC4Y 9DB. *T:* (020) 7583 9020. *E:* clerks@hendersonchambers.co.uk. *Clubs:* Home House; Middlesex CC.

**KINNOCK,** family name of **Baron Kinnock** and **Baroness Kinnock of Holyhead.**

**KINNOCK,** Baron *cr* 2005 (Life Peer), of Bedwellty in the County of Gwent; **Neil Gordon Kinnock;** PC 1983; Chairman, British Council, 2004–09; *b* 28 March 1942; *s* of Gordon Kinnock, labourer, and Mary Kinnock (*née* Howells), nurse; *m* 1967, Glenys Elizabeth Parry (*see* Baroness Kinnock of Holyhead); one *s* one *d*. *Educ:* Lewis Sch., Pengam; University Coll., Cardiff. BA in Industrial Relations and History, UC, Cardiff (Chm. Socialist Soc., 1963–66; Pres. Students' Union, 1965–66; Hon. Fellow, 1982). Tutor Organiser in Industrial and Trade Union Studies, WEA, 1966–70; Mem., Welsh Hosp. Bd, 1969–71. MP (Lab) Bedwellty, 1970–83, Islwyn, 1983–95. PPS to Sec. of State for Employment, 1974–75; Chief Opposition spokesman on educn, 1979–83; Leader of the Labour Party, and Leader of the Opposition, 1983–92. Mem., 1995–2004, and a Vice Pres., 1999–2004, EC. Non-exec. Dir, Data & Research Services plc, 2005–12. Member: Nat. Exec. Cttee, Labour Party, 1978–94 (Chm., 1987–88); Parly Cttee of PLP, 1980–92. Chm. Internat. Cttee, Labour Party, 1993–94; Vice-Pres., Socialist Internat., 1984–. Chm., Adv. Bd, Hds of the Valleys Circuit Develt Co., 2011–. Trustee, IPPR, 2002–. Pres., Univ. of Cardiff, 1998–2009. Hon. FIHT 1997. Hon. LLD: Wales, 1992; Glamorgan, 1996; Robert Gordon, 2002; Queen Margaret, 2007; Glasgow Caledonian, 2009; Aston, 2013. Alexis de Tocqueville Prize, European Inst. of Public Admin, 2003; Danish Shipowners' Assoc. Maritime Award, 2004. *Publications:* Making Our Way, 1986; Thorns and Roses, 1992; contribs to various jls. *Recreations:* music esp. opera and male choral, Rugby and Association football, cricket, theatre, being with family. *Address:* House of Lords, SW1A 0PW.
*See also S. N. Kinnock.*

**KINNOCK OF HOLYHEAD,** Baroness *cr* 2009 (Life Peer), of Holyhead in the County of Ynys Môn; **Glenys Elizabeth Kinnock;** *b* 7 July 1944; *m* 1967, Neil Gordon Kinnock (*see* Baron Kinnock); one *s* one *d*. *Educ:* Holyhead Comprehensive Sch.; University College of Wales, Cardiff. Teacher in secondary and primary schools, and special sch., 1966–93. MEP (Lab) S Wales E, 1994–99, Wales, 1999–2009. Co-Pres., EU-Africa, Caribbean, Pacific Jt Parly Assembly, 2001–09. Minister of State, FCO, 2009–10. Vice-Pres., Univ. of Wales, Cardiff, 1988–95. Member: Bd, European Centre for Develt Policy, 2009–; Council, Overseas Develt Inst., 2009–; Bd, Burma Campaign UK. Patron: Saferworld; Drop the Debt Campaign; Med. Foundn for Victims of Torture; Nat. Deaf Children's Soc. Hon. Fellow: Univ. of Wales Coll., Newport, 1998; Univ. of Cardiff, 2013. Hon. LLD Thames Valley, 1994; Hon. Dr: Brunel, 1997; Kingston, 2001. *Publications:* Eritrea: images of war and peace, 1988; (ed) Voices for One World, 1988; Namibia: birth of a nation, 1990; By Faith and Daring, 1993; Zimbabwe on the Brink, 2003. *Address:* House of Lords, SW1A 0PW.
*See also S. N. Kinnock.*

**KINNOCK, Helle;** *see* Thorning-Schmidt, H.

**KINNOCK, Stephen Nathan;** MP (Lab) Aberavon, since 2015; *b* Tredegar, 1 Jan. 1970; *s* of Baron Kinnock, *qv* and Baroness Kinnock of Holyhead, *qv*; *m* 1996, Helle Thorning-Schmidt, *qv*; two *d*. *Educ:* Drayton Manor Comp. Sch.; Queens' Coll., Cambridge (BA Mod. Langs French and Spanish 1992); Coll. of Europe, Bruges. Policy Researcher for Gary Titley, MEP, 1993–94; Consultant, Lancashire Enterprises, 1994–96; British Council: Business Develt Manager, 1996–2001, Dep. Dir, 2001–03, Dir, Contract Mgt Change Prog., 2003–05, Brussels; Director: St Petersburg, 2005–08; Sierra Leone, 2008; Dir, Hd of Europe and Central Asia, WEF, 2009–12; Man. Dir, Global Leadership and Technol. Exchange, Xyntéo AS, 2012–15. *Recreations:* football, gym. *Address:* (office) Unit 2, Water Street Business Centre, Water Street, Port Talbot SA12 6LF. *T:* (01639) 897660. *E:* stephen.kinnock.mp@parliament.uk

**KINNOULL,** 16th Earl of, *cr* 1633 (Scot.); **Charles William Harley Hay;** Viscount Dupplin and Lord Hay of Kinfauns, 1627, 1633, 1697; Baron Hay (GB), 1711, DL; MA; barrister; *b* 20 Dec. 1962; *s* of 15th Earl of Kinnoull and Gay Ann, *er d* of Sir Denys Lowson, 1st Bt; *S* father, 2013; *m* 2002, Clare, *d* of His Honour William Hamilton Raymond Crawford, *qv*; one *s* three *d* (incl. twins). *Educ:* Summer Fields; Eton; Christ Church, Oxford (Scholar); City Univ. (Dip. in Law). Inns of Court Sch. of Law. Called to the Bar, Middle Temple, 1990. Associate, Credit Suisse First Boston Ltd, 1985–88; Underwriter, Roberts & Hiscox, then Hiscox Syndicates Ltd, 1990–95; Man. Dir (Europe), Hiscox Insce Co. Ltd, 1995–2000; Dir of Mergers and Acquisitions, Hiscox Ltd, 2000–14; Co. Sec., Hiscox Gp, 2009–12; CEO, Hiscox Insce Co. (Bermuda) Ltd, 2009–13. Non-executive Director: Construction & Gen. Guarantee Insce Co., 2001–15; Amorphous Sugar Ltd, 2001–; HIM Capital Ltd, 2007–09; non-exec. Chm., Heritage Group Ltd, 2001–05. Dir, Assoc. of Bermuda Insurers and Reinsurers, 2009–12; Member, Board: Reinsce Assoc. of America, 2009–12; Assoc. of Bermuda Internat. Cos, 2011–12. Member: H of L Select Cttee on Social Mobility, 2015–16, on Trade Union Bill, 2016; H of L EU Select Cttee, 2016–; EU Justice Sub-cttee, 2016–. Mem. Bd, Perth City Develt Bd, 2014–. Lieut, 1993–2008, Capt., 2008–15, Major, 2015–17, Lt-Col, 2017–, Atholl Highlanders. Mem., Queen's Bodyguard for Scotland (Royal Co. of Archers), 2000–. Pres., London Mems, NT for Scotland, 2007–12; Dir, Masterworks Mus. of Bermuda Art, 2012–17; Mem. Bd, Fine Art Fund, 2008–17. Pres., Royal Caledonian Charities Trust (formerly Royal Caledonian Ball), 2012– (Trustee, 1992–; Chm., 1996–2009; Vice-Pres., 2009–12); Chairman: Red Squirrel Survival Trust, 2013–; UK Squirrel Accord, 2014–; Culture Perth and Kinross, 2015–. Mem., Develt Cttee, Christ Ch, Oxford, 2004–09. Dir, Horsecross Arts Ltd, 2014–. Elected Mem., H of L, 2015. DL Perth and Kinross, 2018. FRPSL 2006 (Mem., 2000). *Publications:* contrib. Jl of Chem. Soc. *Recreations:* cricket, Cresta Run, Real tennis, ski-ing, philately. *Heir: s* Viscount Dupplin, *qv*. *Address:* 17 Cumberland Street, SW1V 4LS. *T:* (020) 7976 6973; Pitkindie, Abernyte, Perthshire PH14 9RE. *T:* (01828) 686342. *Clubs:* White's, Turf, Pratt's, MCC; Royal Perth (Perth); Jockey (Vienna).

**KINROSS,** 5th Baron *cr* 1902; **Christopher Patrick Balfour;** Partner in HBJ Gateley Wareing, 2005–09; *b* 1 Oct. 1949; *s* of 4th Baron Kinross, OBE, TD, and Helen Anne (*d* 1969), *d* of A. W. Hog; *S* father, 1985; *m* 1st, 1974, Susan Jane (marr. diss. 2004), *d* of I. R. Pitman, WS; two *s*; 2nd, 2004, Catherine Ierenka, *d* of Stanislav Ostrycharz. *Educ:* Belhaven Hill School, Dunbar; Eton College; Edinburgh Univ. (LLB). Mem., Law Soc. of Scotland, 1975; WS 1975. Partner: Shepherd & Wedderburn, WS, Solicitors, 1977–97; Taylor Kinross Legal Partnership, 1997–2005. Mem., James IV Assoc. of Surgeons, 1985–. Member, Queen's Body Guard for Scotland, Royal Company of Archers, 1980–. Member: Mil. Vehicle Trust; Scottish Land Rover Owners' Club. Golden Jubilee Medal, 2002; Diamond Jubilee Medal, 2012. Grand Baili, Grand Bailiwick of Scotland, Order of St Lazarus of Jerusalem, 2002–09. *Recreations:* shooting, motorsport. *Heir: s* Hon. Alan Ian Balfour [*b* 4 April 1978; *m* 2006, Lindsay Fiona Gourlay]. *Address:* 33/8 Orchard Brae Avenue, Edinburgh EH4 2UP.

**KINSELLA, (Jonathan) Neil;** Chief Executive Officer, Slater & Gordon Lawyers UK, 2012–13 (Chief Executive and Managing Partner, Russell Jones and Walker Solicitors, 2003–12); *b* Leigh, Lancs, 17 May 1958; *s* of Donald John and Irene Kinsella; *m* 1982, Susan Elizabeth Cotterell; one *s* one *d*. *Educ:* Manchester Univ. (LLB Hons Law); Coll. of Law, Chester. Admitted Solicitor, 1983; trained at Goldberg Blackburn, 1981–83; Partner, Pannone Napier, 1986–91, specialising in conduct of disaster litigation, incl. Manchester Air Crash, Chinook Helicopter Disaster, Piper Alpha Disaster; joined Russell Jones and Walker, 1991. Law Soc. apptd rep. on Lord Chancellor's Adv. Gp on awards of damages in serious injury cases. Founder Mem., Claims Standards Council. Mem., MoJ review panels and discussion forums on changes to personal injury litigation and fee structures. Trustee, Lancashire Mining Mus. (Red Rose Steam Soc. Ltd), 2018–. Medal for work on internat. transport, Assoc. of Young Internat. Lawyers, 1988. *Publications:* contrib. articles on legal issues with particular interest in access to justice and alternative business structures in legal profession. *Recreations:* painting, wild swimming, tennis.

**KINSELLA, Thomas;** poet; *b* 4 May 1928; *m* 1955, Eleanor Walsh; one *s* two *d*. Entered Irish Civil Service, 1946; resigned from Dept of Finance, 1965. Artist-in-residence, 1965–67, Prof. of English, 1967–70, Southern Illinois Univ.; Prof. of English, Temple Univ., Philadelphia, 1970–90. Elected to Irish Academy of Letters, 1965; Mem., Amer. Acad. of Arts and Scis, 2000. J. S. Guggenheim Meml Fellow, 1968–69, 1971–72; Hon. Sen. Fellow, Sch. of English, University Coll., Dublin, 2003–. Freeman, City of Dublin, 2007. Hon. PhD: NUI, 1984; Turin Univ., 2005. Ulysses Medal, Univ. Coll. Dublin, 2008. *Publications:* poetry: Poems, 1956; Another September, 1958; Downstream, 1962; Nightwalker and other poems, 1968; Notes from the Land of the Dead, 1972; Butcher's Dozen, 1972; A Selected Life, 1972; Finistère, 1972; New Poems, 1973; Selected Poems 1956 to 1968, 1973; Vertical Man and The Good Fight, 1973; One, 1974; A Technical Supplement, 1976; Song of the Night and Other Poems, 1978; The Messenger, 1978; Fifteen Dead, 1979; One and Other Poems, 1979; Poems 1956–73, 1980; Peppercanister Poems 1972–78, 1980; One Fond Embrace, 1981; Songs of the Psyche, 1985; Her Vertical Smile, 1985; St Catherine's Clock, 1987; Out of Ireland, 1987; Blood and Family, 1988; Personal Places, 1990; Poems from Centre City, 1990; Madonna, 1991; Open Court, 1991; From Centre City, 1994; Collected Poems 1956–1994, 1996; The Pen Shop, 1997; The Familiar, 1999; Godhead, 1999; Citizen of the World, 2000; Littlebody, 2000; Collected Poems 1956–2001, 2001; Marginal Economy, 2005; Man of War, 2007; Belief and Unbelief, 2007; Selected Poems, 2007; Fat Master, 2012; Love Joy Peace, 2012; Late Poems, 2013; La Pace della Pienezza: poesie scelte 1956–2006, 2016; *translations and general:* (trans.) The Táin, 1969; contrib. essay in Davis, Mangan, Ferguson, 1970; (ed) Selected Poems of Austin Clarke, 1976; An Duanaire—Poems of the Dispossessed (trans. Gaelic poetry, 1600–1900), 1981; (ed) Our Musical Heritage: lectures on Irish traditional music by Seán Ó Riada, 1982; (ed, with translations) The New Oxford Book of Irish Verse, 1986; The Dual Tradition: an essay on poetry and politics in Ireland, 1995; Readings in Poetry, 2005; A Dublin Documentary, 2006; Prose Occasions (1951–2006)—collected occasional prose, 2008.

**KINSEY, Thomas Richard Moseley,** FREng; Consultant, Delcam International (formerly Deltacam Systems), 2007 (Chairman, 1989–2007); *b* 13 Oct. 1929; *s* of late Richard Moseley Kinsey and Dorothy Elizabeth Kinsey; *m* 1953, Ruth (*née* Owen-Jones); two *s*. *Educ:* Newtown Sch.; Trinity Hall, Cambridge (MA). FIMechE; FREng (FEng 1982). ICI Ltd, 1952–57; Tube Investments, 1957–65; joined Delta plc, 1965: Director, 1973–77; Jt Man. Dir, 1977–82; Dir, 1980, Dep. Chief Exec., 1982–87, Mitchell Cotts plc, 1980–87. Chm., Birmingham Battery & Metal Co., 1984–89; Director: Gower Internat., 1984–89; Telcon, 1984–89; Unistrut Europe, 1989–92. CCMI. *Recreations:* golf, travel. *Address:* 6 Sutton Lodge, Blossomfield Road, Solihull, W Midlands B91 1NB. *T:* (0121) 704 2592. *Clubs:* Athenæum; Edgbaston Golf.

**KINSKY, Cyril Norman Francis;** QC 2010; designer and maker of marquetry furniture; *b* London, 4 Aug. 1954; *s* of Alfons and Monique Kinsky; *m* 1986, Natasha Farrant; two *s* two *d*. *Educ:* Ampleforth Coll.; Trinity Coll., Cambridge (BA 1975). Freelance theatre dir, 1976–86; called to the Bar, Middle Temple, 1988; in practice as barrister: Brick Court Chambers, 1988–2003; 3 Verulam Bldgs, 2003–16. Chm., Ecole Française de Londres Jacques Prévert, 2003–06. Trustee, Cardinal Hume Centre, 2010–13. Awarded Guild Mark, Furniture Makers' Co., 2004. *Address:* Chalcot Coach House, Short Street, Chapmanslade, Westbury BA13 4AA.

**KINSLER, Marie Louise;** QC 2017; *b* Scotland, 10 Dec. 1968; *d* of Dr Peter Kinsler and Doreen Kinsler; *m* 1993, Eoin O'Sullivan; two *s*. *Educ:* Gonville and Caius Coll., Cambridge (MA Hons Law); Coll. of Europe, Bruges (Dip. Advanced Eur. Studies (Law)); European Sch., Brussels. Called to the Bar, Inner Temple, 1992; in practice as barrister, specialising in private internat. law, 1992–. Supervisor, EU Law, Cambridge Univ. *Recreations:* walking and talking, cooking and baking. *Address:* 2 Temple Gardens, EC4Y 9AY. *T:* (020) 7822 1200. *E:* mlkinsler@2tg.co.uk.

**KINSMAN, Jeremy Kenneth Bell;** writer; director; international scholar, Institute of Governmental Studies, University of California, Berkeley, since 2011 (Regents' Lecturer, 2009–10); *b* Montreal, 28 Jan. 1942; *s* of Ronald Kinsman and Katharine Nixon Bell; *m* 1992, Hana Tallichova; two *d*. *Educ:* Princeton Univ.; Institut d'Etudes Politiques, Paris. Aluminium Co. of Canada, 1965–66; entered Foreign Service of Canada, 1966; Econ. Div., Ext. Affairs, 1966–68; Third, then Second, Sec. and Vice-Consul, Brussels/EEC, 1968–70; Central Secretariat, Ottawa, 1970–72; Commercial Div., 1972–73; First Sec., Algiers, 1973–75; Counsellor, then Minister and Dep. Perm. Rep., Perm. Mission of Canada to UN, NY, 1975–80; Chm., Policy Planning Secretariat, Ottawa, 1980–81; Minister, Pol Affairs, Washington, 1981–85; Assistant Deputy Minister: Cultural Affairs and Broadcasting, Ottawa, 1985–89; Pol and Internat. Security Affairs, and Pol Dir, Ext. Affairs, 1990–92; Ambassador: to Russia and several other Repubs, 1993–96; to Italy, 1996–2000 (concurrently Ambassador to Albania and High Comr to Malta); High Comr in UK,

2000–02; Ambassador to the EU, 2002–06. Mem., Canadian Prime Minister's Foreign Affairs Council, 2015–16. Project Dir, The Diplomat's Handbook for Democracy Development Support, Council of a Community of Democracies, 2007–; Diplomat in Residence, Woodrow Wilson Sch. of Public and Internat. Affairs, Princeton Univ., 2007–08; Distinguished Vis. Diplomat, Ryerson Univ., 2010–. Ind. Dir, Dundee Precious Metals Inc., 2007–; Mem. Bd, Byways, UK, 2004–. Commentator, Diplomatically Speaking, CBC News, 2006–; contributor, openCanada.org, 2012–. Gov., Victoria Conservatory of Music, 2007–. *Publications:* (jtly) A Diplomat's Handbook for Democracy Development Support, 3rd edn, 2013; (contrib.) Legacy: how French Canadians shaped North America, 2016; contrib. on foreign affairs in Policy Options; contrib. Globe, Mail, Internat. Herald Tribune. *Recreations:* tennis, running, ski-ing, hiking, books, theatre, music.

**KINSMAN, Prof. Rodney William,** RDI 1990; FCSD; Chairman and Design Director (formerly Managing Director), OMK Design Ltd, since 1966; *b* 9 April 1943; *s* of John Thomas Kinsman and Lilian Kinsman (*née* Bradshaw); *m* 1966, Lisa Sai Yuk; one *s* two *d*. *Educ:* Mellow Lane Grammar Sch.; Central Sch. of Art (NDD 1965). FCSD 1983. Founded: OMK Design Ltd, 1966; Kinsman Associates, 1981. Mem., British Furniture Council, 1995 (Exec. Mem., RDI Cttee). Numerous internat. exhibns; work in permanent collections incl. Omkstak Chair and other designs, in V&A, museums in USA, Spain, Germany. Broadcasts on TV and radio. Vis. Prof., 1985–86 and Ext. Examr, 1986–88, RCA; Vis. Prof., 1996–, Gov., 1996–2010, Univ. of the Arts (formerly London Inst.). Hon. FRCA 1988; FRSA 2012. Many internat. awards incl. Millennium Product, Design Council, 2000. *Recreations:* polo, ski-ing. *Address:* Kinsman Associates Ltd, Stephen Building, 30 Stephen Street, W1T 1QR. *T:* (020) 7631 1335. *Clubs:* Reform, Groucho, Chelsea Arts.

**KINTORE,** 14th Earl of, *cr* 1677 (Scot.); **James William Falconer Keith;** Lord Keith of Inverurie and Keith Hall, 1677 (Scot.); Bt 1897; Baron 1925; Viscount Stonehaven, 1938; *b* 15 April 1976; *s* of 13th Earl of Kintore and Mary Keith (*née* Plum); S father, 2004; *m* 2006, Carrie Fiona, *d* of Ian and Dr Fiona Paxton, Edinburgh; two *s*. *Heir: s* Lord Inverurie, *qv*.

**KIOUSSIS, Dimitris,** FRS 2009; FMedSci; Head, Division of Molecular Immunology, MRC National Institute for Medical Research, 1991–2010; *b* Athens, Greece, 3 Nov. 1949; *s* of Alexandros Kioussis and Maria Kioussis; partner, John W. Griffin. *Educ:* Athens University Medical Sch. (Med. Dr degree 1975); Temple Univ., Philadelphia (PhD Biochem. 1980). Mem., MRC Scientific Staff, Lab. of Gene Structure and Expression, NIMR, 1980–84; Lectr, Immunology Dept, Middlesex Hosp. Med. Sch., 1984–86; Mem., MRC Sen. Scientific Staff, Lab. of Gene Structure and Expression, NIMR, 1986–91. Mem., EMBO, 1997. FMedSci 2002. *Publications:* research articles in Nature, Science, Cell, EMBO Jl, Procs of NAS, Jl of Immunology. *Recreations:* theatre, music, dance, film, books, translation of contemporary British theatre plays into Greek. *E:* dkiouss@hotmail.com.

**KIRBY, Prof. Anthony John,** PhD; FRS 1987; CChem, FRSC; Professor of Bioorganic Chemistry, University of Cambridge, 1995–2002, now Emeritus; Fellow, Gonville and Caius College, Cambridge, since 1962; *b* 18 Aug. 1935; *s* of Samuel Arthur Kirby and Gladys Rosina Kirby (*née* Welch); *m* 1962, Sara Sophia Benjamina Niewęg; one *s* two *d*. *Educ:* Eton College; Gonville and Caius College, Cambridge (MA, PhD 1962). NATO postdoctoral Fellow: Cambridge, 1962–63; Brandeis Univ., 1963–64; Cambridge University: Demonstrator, 1964–68, Lectr, 1968–85, Reader, 1985–95, in Organic Chemistry; Gonville and Caius College: Dir of Studies in Natural Scis and Coll. Lectr, 1968–2002; Tutor, 1966–74. Visiting Professor/Scholar: Paris (Orsay), 1970; Groningen, 1973 (Backer Lectr, 2003); Cape Town, 1987; Paris VI, 1987; Haifa, 1991; Queen's, Kingston, Ont, 1996; Toronto, 1997; Western Ontario, 1997. Co-ordinator, European Network on Catalytic Antibodies, 1993–96, on Gemini Surfactants, 1997–2001, on Artificial Nucleases, 2000–04. Fellow, Japan Soc. for Promotion of Science, 1986; Royal Society of Chemistry: Fellow, 1980; Award in Organic Reaction Mechanisms, 1983; Tilden Lectr, 1987; Chm., Organic Reaction Mechanisms Gp, 1986–90; Ingold Lectr, 1996–97. Marin Drinov Medal, Bulgarian Acad. of Scis 2003. Hon. DPhil Univ. of Turku, 2006. *Publications:* (with S. G. Warren) The Organic Chemistry of Phosphorus, 1967; The Anomeric Effect and Related Stereoelectronic Effects at Oxygen, 1983; Stereoelectronic effects, 1996; (with F. Hollfelder) From Enzyme Models to Model Enzymes, 2009; papers in Jls of RSC and Amer. Chem. Soc. *Recreations:* chamber music, walking. *Address:* University Chemical Laboratory, Cambridge CB2 1EW. *T:* (01223) 336370; 87 Holbrook Road, Cambridge CB1 7SX. *T:* (01223) 210403.

**KIRBY, Carolyn,** OBE 2016; solicitor; President, Law Society of England and Wales, 2002–03; President, Mental Health Review Tribunal for Wales, since 1999; *b* 24 May 1953; *d* of Cyril Treharne-Jones and Elaine Margaret Sanders; *m* 1977, Anthony Robert Kirby. *Educ:* Cheltenham Ladies' Coll.; University Coll., Cardiff (LLB Hons). Admitted solicitor, 1979; Partner, Kirby & Partners, Solicitors, Swansea, 1985–97. Legal Registrar to Archdeacon of Gower, 1997–; Church in Wales: Mem., Disciplinary Tribunal, 2001–; Lay Judge, Provincial Court, 2014–. Trustee, Swansea and Brecon Diocesan Trust, 2009–. Chm., Cancer Information and Support Services, 1995–. Chm., Council of Govs, Cheltenham Ladies' Coll., 2004–12. Hon. Fellow: Univ. of Wales, Lampeter, 2002; Cardiff Univ., 2004. Hon. LLD UWE, 2003. *Recreations:* walking, dogs, gardening, interior design. *Address:* Admirals Wood, Vennaway Lane, Parkmill, Swansea SA3 2EA. *T:* (01792) 234494. *E:* carolynkirby.law@outlook.com.

**KIRBY, Dame Georgina (Kamiria),** DBE 1994; QSO 1989; JP; Executive Director, Maori Women's Development Inc. (formerly Maori Women's Development Fund), 1978–2011; *b* 31 Jan. 1936; *d* of William Tawhiri Matea Smith and Tuhe Nga Tukemata Christie (*née* Thompson); *m* 1961, Brian Ian Kirby (*d* 2014); two *s* one *d*. *Educ:* Horohoro Sch., Rotorua; Rotorua High Sch.; Auckland Univ. Cert. Book-keeping; Cert. Practical Accounting. Jun. Asst Teacher, Rotorua, 1953–55; NZ PO Trng Officer, 1955–63; managed and partnered husband in service businesses, 1966–70; Personnel Officer, Stock & Station, 1971–76. Estabd Te Taumata Art Gall., 1991; Foundn Trustee, Maori Arts NZ (Toi Maori Aotearoa). Mem., Maori Women's Welfare League Inc., 1976– (Nat. Pres., 1983–87); formed Matatau Maori In Business (Maori Business and Professional Assoc.), 2006. NZ Vice Pres., Commonwealth Countries League, London, 1988–. JP NZ, 1981. Commemoration Medal (NZ), 1988; Women's Suffrage Medal (NZ), 1993. *Publications:* Liberated Learning, 1993; Vision Aotearoa Kaupapa New Zealand, 1994; contrib. NZ Maori Artists and Writers Mag., Kowi. *Recreations:* reading, badminton, horse-riding. *Address:* 11A Northland Street, Grey Lynn, Auckland 1021, New Zealand. *T:* (9) 3767032, *T:* and *Fax:* (9) 3077014. *Club:* Zonta International (Auckland).

**KIRBY, Jill;** writer, broadcaster and policy analyst; *b* Bedford, 29 April 1957; *d* of Kenneth and Christine Fernie; *m* 1985, Richard Kirby; two *s* (and one *s* decd). *Educ:* Rugby High Sch.; Bristol Univ. (LLB). Admitted as solicitor, 1981; Solicitor: Speechly Bircham, 1979–84; Clifford Chance, 1984–86. Chairman: Full Time Mothers, 1998–2001; Family Policy Gp, Centre for Policy Studies, 2001–07; Dir, Centre for Policy Studies, 2007–11. Policy Advr, Renewing One Nation, 2001–03. Mem., Tax Reform Commn, 2005–06. *Publications:* Broken Hearts, 2002; Choosing to be Different, 2003; The Price of Parenthood, 2005; The Nationalisation of Childhood, 2006; Who Do They Think They Are?, 2008; The Reality Gap, 2009; contribs to newspapers and jls. *Recreations:* walking, gardening. *Address:* Yerdley House, Long Compton, Warwicks CV36 5LH.

**KIRBY, Hon. Michael Donald,** AC 1991; CMG 1983; jurist, arbitrator and mediator; Justice of the High Court of Australia, 1996–2009; Acting Chief Justice of Australia, 2007, 2008; Chair, UN Commission of Inquiry on Human Rights in North Korea, 2013–14; Co-Chair, Human Rights Institute, International Bar Association, since 2018; *b* 18 March 1939; *s* of late Donald Kirby and Jean Langmore Kirby; *m* 2019, Johan van Vloten. *Educ:* Fort Street Boys' High Sch.; Univ. of Sydney (BA, LLM, BEc). Admitted Solicitor, 1962; admitted to the Bar of NSW, 1967; Mem., NSW Bar Council, 1974; Judge, Federal Court of Australia, 1983–84; President, Court of Appeal: NSW, 1984–96; Solomon Is, 1995–96; Actg Chief Justice of NSW, 1988, 1990, 1993. Dep. Pres., Aust. Conciliation and Arbitration Commn, 1975–83; Chairman: Australian Law Reform Commn, 1975–84; OECD Inter-govtl Gp on Privacy and Internat. Data Flows, 1978–80; OECD Inter-govtl Gp on Security of Information Systems, 1991–92; Member: Admin. Review Council of Australia, 1976–84; Council of Aust. Acad. of Forensic Scis, 1978–89 (Pres., 1987–89); Aust. National Commn for Unesco, 1980–83, 1996–2007; Aust. Inst. of Multi-cultural Affairs, 1981–84; Exec., CSIRO, 1983–86; NSW Ministerial Adv. Cttee on AIDS, 1987; Trustee, AIDS Trust of Australia, 1987–93; Commissioner: Global Commn on AIDS, WHO, Geneva, 1989–91; UNAIDS/Lancet Commn on Sustainable Health, 2013–15; UNDP Global Commn on HIV and Law, 2010–12; Chm., UN AIDS expert gp on HIV testing of UN peacekeepers, 2001–02, on human rights and access to treatment, 2002. Deleg., Unesco Gen. Conf., Paris, 1983; Chm., Unesco Expert Gp on Rights of Peoples, 1989 (Rapporteur, Budapest, 1991); Special Rep. of UN Sec.-Gen., for Human Rights in Cambodia, 1993–96; Member: Unesco Expert Gps on Self-Determination and Rights of Peoples, 1984; Perm. Tribunal of Peoples, Rome, 1992; ILO Fact Finding and Conciliation Commn on S Africa, 1991–92; Ethics Cttee, Human Genome Orgn, 1995–2004; Internat. Bioethics Cttee, UNESCO, 1996–2005; Internat. Jury, UNESCO Prize for Teaching of Human Rights, 1994–96; UNODC Judicial Integrity Gp, 2002–; UN AIDS gp on AIDS and human rights, 2003–; Judicial Ref. Gp, UN High Comr for Human Rights, 2017–19; Eminent Persons Gp on future of Commonwealth of Nations, Commonwealth Secretariat, 2010–11; Adv. Council, Transparency Internat., 2011–; Global Fund to Fight Aids, Tuberculosis and Malaria, High Level Panel for Equitable Access to Healthcare, 2015–16; UN Sec. Gen.'s High Level Panel on Access to Essential Healthcare, 2015–16; Asia Pacific Leadership Network for Nuclear Non Proliferation, 2016–. Ind. Chm., Malawi Constit. Conf., 1994, Chm. Constit. Seminar, 1997; Hon. Advr on bioethics to UN High Comr for Human Rights, 2001–03. International Commission of Jurists: Comr, 1984–2001; Mem. Exec. Cttee, 1989–95, Chm., 1992–95; Pres., 1995–98; Pres., Aust. Section, 1989–96. Internat. Consultant, Commn for Transborder Data Flow Develt, Intergovtl Bureau of Informatics, Rome, 1985–86; Member, Board: Internat. Trustees, Internat. Inst. for Inf. and Communication, Montreal, 1986–2000; Aust. Centre for Internat. Commercial Arbitration, 2009–14; Mem. Council, Human Rights Inst., IBA, London, 2009– (Vice Chm., 2016–); Counselor, Amer. Soc. of Internat. Law, 2009–. President: Criminology Sect., ANZAAS, 1981–82; Law Sect., ANZAAS, 1984–85. Granada Guildhall Lectr, 1984; Acting Prof., Fac. of Salzburg Seminar, Salzburg, 1985, 2000, 2015; Hon. Prof., Nat. Law Sch. of India Univ., Bangalore, 1995–; Visiting Professor of Law: Univ. of NSW, ANU and Southern Cross Univ., 2009–; Univ. of Melbourne, Deakin and Univ. of Tasmania, 2010–; Victoria Univ., 2011–; Univ. of Hong Kong, 2013–; Chinese Univ. of Hong Kong, 2015–. Sen. Anzac Fellow, NZ Govt, 1981; Fellow, NZ Legal Res. Foundn, 1985. Pres., Nat. Book Council of Australia, 1980–83; Member: Library Council of NSW, 1976–85; Council, Australian Opera, 1983–89; Patron: RSPCA, Australia, 2000–09; Voiceless (Australia), 2013–. Fellow, Senate, Sydney Univ., 1964–69; Dep. Chancellor, Univ. of Newcastle, NSW, 1978–83; Chancellor, Macquarie Univ., Sydney, 1984–93, Chancellor Emeritus, 2019. Mem. Bd of Governors, Internat. Council for Computer Communications, Washington, 1984–2000; Bd Mem., Kinsey Inst. for Res. in Sex, Gender and Reprodn, Indiana Univ., 2001–13; Adv. Bd Mem., Internat. Human Rights Law Inst., De Paul Univ., Chicago, 2002–. Fellow, Inst. of Arbitrators and Mediators, Aust., 2009 (Pres., 2009–10). FRSN 2018. Hon. Member: Amer. Law Inst., 2000; Soc. of Legal Scholars, 2006; Hon. Life Member: Aust. Bar Assoc., 2008; NSW Bar Assoc., 2009; Law Council of Aust., 2009. Fellow, Australian Acad. Law, 2009. Hon. FASSA 1997; Hon. Fellow, Australian Acad. of Humanities, 2006; Hon. Bencher, Inner Temple, 2006. Hon. DLitt: Newcastle, NSW, 1987; Ulster, 1998; James Cook, 2003; Curtin, 2017; Hon. LLD: Macquarie, 1994; Sydney, 1996; Nat. Law Sch. of India Univ., Bangalore, 1997; Buckingham, 2000; ANU, 2004; NSW, 2008; Murdoch, Indiana, Melbourne, 2009; Bond, 2009; Univ. of Technol., Sydney, 2009; Colombo, 2010; Victoria, 2011; Deakin, 2012; Monash, 2015, Queen's, Ont, 2015; Wollongong, 2016; S Qld, 2017; Tasmania, 2017; Nat. Law Univ. Odisha, 2018; DUniv: S Australia, 2001; Southern Cross, 2007; Griffith, 2008; La Trobe, 2011; Central Queensland Univ., 2013; Adelaide, 2017. Australian Human Rights Medal, 1991; UNESCO Prize for Human Rights Educn, 1998; Gruber Justice Prize, 2010; Meritorious Service to Public Educn Award, Dept of Educn, NSW, 2012; Gold and Silver Star, Order of Rising Sun, Japan, 2017. *Publications:* Industrial Index to Australian Labour Law, 1978, 2nd edn 1983; Reform the Law, 1983; The Judges (Boyer Lectures), 1983; (ed jtly) A Touch of Healing, 1986; Through the World's Eye, 2000; Judicial Activism (Hamlyn Lectures), 2004; A Private Life, 2011; What Would Gandhi Do?, 2013; essays and articles in legal and other jls. *Recreation:* work. *Address:* Level 7, 195 Macquarie Street, Sydney, NSW 2000, Australia. *T:* (2) 92315800, *Fax:* (2) 92315811. *E:* mail@michaelkirby.com.au.

**KIRBY, Prof. Simon,** PhD; FBA 2019; FRSE; Professor of Language Evolution, since 2009, and Director, Centre for Language Evolution, since 2016, University of Edinburgh; *b* Nottingham, 29 April 1970; *s* of Gordon Kirby and Audrey Simpson; one *s* one *d*. *Educ:* Univ. of Edinburgh (MA Hons Linguistics and Artificial Intelligence 1992; PhD Linguistics 1996). University of Edinburgh: researcher, 1996–2003, Lectr, 2003–05, Dept of Linguistics; Reader, Linguistics and English Lang., 2005–09. Vis. Fellow, Inst. of Advanced Study, Budapest, 1997. MAE 2019. FRSE 2012. *Publications:* Function, Selection and Innateness, 1999; Language Evolution, 2003; over 200 articles. *Recreations:* playing modular synthesisers, building machines that make sound in art galleries, baking sourdough bread. *Address:* Centre for Language Evolution, University of Edinburgh, 3 Charles Street, Edinburgh EH8 9AD. *T:* (0131) 650 3494. *E:* simon.kirby@ed.ac.uk.

**KIRBY, Simon Gerard;** *b* Hastings, 22 Dec. 1964; *m* 1992, Elizabeth Radford; four *s* two *d*. *Educ:* Hastings Grammar Sch.; Open Univ. (BSc Hons). Man. Dir, C-Side Ltd, 1989–2001. Member (C): E Sussex CC, 1992–93, 2005–09; Brighton BC, 1995–97; Brighton and Hove CC, 1996–99; Mid Sussex DC, 1999–2001. MP (C) Brighton Kemptown, 2010–17. An Asst Govt Whip, 2015–16; Econ. Sec., HM Treasury, 2016–17.

**KIRBY-HARRIS, Robert,** PhD; Secretary General, International Union of Pure and Applied Physics, 2008–12; Founder Chair, Cornwall Area of Outstanding Natural Beauty Trust, since 2017 (Chairman, Cornwall Area of Outstanding Natural Beauty, 2013–18); *b* 12 June 1952; *s* of Lionel George Harris and Enid Josephine Harris; adopted surname

Kirby-Harris, adding family name, 1980; m 1979, Abigail Anne Mee; two s. *Educ:* Ashford Grammar Sch.; Univ. of Kent at Canterbury (BSc 1st Cl. Hons Theoretical Phys 1973); Clare Coll., Cambridge (MA (III) Applied Maths and Theoretical Phys 1974); Univ. of Sussex (PGCE Secondary Sci. 1975); Plymouth Poly. (DMS 1985); Lancaster Univ. (PhD Educnl Res. 2003). CPhys 1985, FInstP 2005; MIMA 1985, CMath 1999. Secondary Sci. Teacher, Wakeford Sch., Havant, 1975–77; RN Instructor Officer, Lt RN, 1977–82, Lt Comdr RN, 1982–85: Lectr in Electronics and Maths, RN Weapons Engrg Sch., Fareham, 1977–79; Sen. Instructor Officer, RN Supply and Secretariat Sch., Chatham, 1980–83; Sen. Lectr in Maths, RNEC Manadon, Plymouth, 1983–85; Exec. Dir, Poly Enterprise Plymouth, 1985–90; Dep. Vice-Chancellor (Resources), Middlesex Univ., 1991–95; Pro Vice-Chancellor (Admin and Finance), Univ. of Namibia, S Africa, 1996–2002; Corp. Dir, Ops and Finance, Royal Botanic Gardens, Kew, 2003–05; Chief Exec., Inst. of Physics, 2005–12. Mem. Bd, Science Council, 2008–12 (Vice Pres., 2006–08). Dir, Big Bang Fair Community Interest Co., 2010–13. Mem., SRHE, 1997–2007. *Publications:* contrib. Higher Educn jl. *Recreations:* hill walking, ski-ing, gardens, arts, family life. *Address:* Camel View House, St Breward, Bodmin, Cornwall PL30 4LU. *E:* r.kirby_harris@btinternet.com. *Club:* Naval.

**KIRCH, Sir David (Roderick),** KBE 2013; Senior Trustee, David Kirch Charitable Trust, since 1987; *b* Wimbledon, London, 23 July 1936; *s* of Leonard Kirch and Margaret Kirch. *Educ:* Tonbridge Sch. Property developments and property investments. Pres., Age Concern Jersey, 2007–. *Recreations:* golf when younger, now bridge. *Address:* The Octagon, Le Mont de Gouray, St Martin, Jersey JE3 6ET. *T:* (01534) 851339, *Fax:* (01534) 851120. *E:* admin@chapsjsy.net.

**KIRCHNER, Prof. Emil Joseph,** PhD; Professor of European Studies, Department of Government, University of Essex, since 1992; *b* 19 March 1942; *m* 1975, Joanna Bartlett; two *s. Educ:* Case Western Reserve Univ. (BA Econ 1970; MA 1971; PhD 1976, Pol Sci.). Essex University: Lectr and Sen. Lectr, Dept of Govt, 1974–92; Hon. Jean Monnet Prof. of European Integration, 1997–. Visiting Professor: Dept of Pol Sci., Univ. of Connecticut, 1986–87; Centre for Econ. Res. and Grad. Educn, Charles Univ., Prague, 1997–2000; Hon. Guest Prof., Renmin Univ. of China, 2001–; Dist. Vis. Scholar, Suffolk Univ., 2008; NATO Fellowship, 2001. Chm., Assoc. for Study of German Politics, 2002– (Mem., 1989–90). Gen. Series Editor, Europe in Change (Manchester Univ. Press), 1993; Exec. Ed., Jl of European Integration, 1997–2007. FAcSS (AcSS 2009). Lifetime Achievement Award in Contemp. Eur. Studies, University Assoc. of Contemp. Eur. Studies, 2012; Cross, Order of Merit (Germany), 2002. *Publications:* Decision Making in the European Community, 1992; (jtly) The Federal Republic of Germany and NATO: 40 years after, 1992; (jtly) The Future of European Security, 1994; (jtly) The Recasting of the European Order: security architectures and economic co-operation, 1996; (jtly) The New Europe: east, west, centre, 1997; Decentralization and Transition in the Visegrad, 1999; (jtly) Committee Governance in the EU, 2000; (jtly) Studies on Policies and Policy Processes of the European Union, 2003–; (ed with James Sperling) Global Security Governance, 2007; (with James Sperling) EU Security Governance, 2008; (ed with James Sperling) National Security Cultures, 2010; (ed with Roberto Dominguez) The Security Governance of Regional Organizations, 2011; (ed jtly) The Palgrave Handbook of EU Asia Relations, 2013; (ed jtly) EU-China Security Relations: from convergence to cooperation?, 2016; (jtly) The European Union and China, 2018; (ed jtly) EU-Japan Security Cooperation: trends and prospects, 2018. *Recreations:* music, sports, travel.

**KIRCHSCHLAGER, Angelika;** mezzo-soprano opera singer; *b* Salzburg, 24 Nov. 1965; *d* of Walter and Maria Kirchschlager; one *s. Educ:* Vienna Music Acad. (Singing Dip.). Opera début, Graz Opera, 1991; début, Vienna State Opera, 1993; major débuts include: NY Metropolitan Opera, 1997; Opéra Nat. de Paris, 1997; Teatro alla Scala, 1998; Bayerische Staatsoper Munich, 2001; Royal Opera Hse, Covent Gdn, 2002; Deutsche Oper Berlin, 2005. Guest Professor: Salzburg Mozarteum, 2007–11; Univ. of Graz, 2011–13. Kammersängerin, Vienna State Opera, 2007. Hon. Mem., Royal Acad. Music, 2009. ECHO Klassik Award, 2000, 2005, 2010; Grammy Award, 2004; BBC Music Mag. Award, 2013; Eur. Cultural Award, 2013. *Publications:* Was ich dir sagen möchte - Lass dir's gut gehen, 2005; Angelika Kirchschlager: liederreisebuch, 2012; Ich erfinde mich jeden Tag neu, 2013. *Address:* c/o Askonas Holt, 15 Fetter Lane, EC4A 1BW.

**KIRK, Anthony James Nigel;** QC 2001; *b* 3 May 1958; *s* of late James Brian Kirk and of Lavinia Mary Kirk (*née* Kellow). *Educ:* Ipswich Sch.; King Edward VII Sch., Lytham St Anne's; King's Coll., London (LLB Hons; AKC). Called to the Bar, Gray's Inn, 1981 (Stuart Cunningham Macaskie and Lord Justice Holker Schol.; Bencher, 2006); in practice as barrister, 1982–. Chm., Family Law Bar Assoc., 2006–08 (Vice-Chm., 2003–05; Nat. Sec., 1999–2002); Member: Bar Council, 1996–99 (Mem., Professional Conduct and Complaints Cttee, 1999–2002); Bd, Family Mediators' Assoc., 1999–2002; ADR Cttee, 2002–; Internat. Family Law Cttee, 2002–. Fellow, Internat. Acad. of Matrimonial Lawyers. FRSocMed. Mem., RCO. *Publications:* (contrib.) Jackson & Davies Matrimonial Finance and Taxation, 6th edn 1996; (contrib.) Rayden & Jackson on Divorce, 19th edn. *Recreation:* classical music. *Address:* (chambers) 1 King's Bench Walk, Temple, EC4Y 7DB. *T:* (020) 7936 1500.

**KIRK, Ven. Gavin John;** Archdeacon of Lincoln, since 2016; *b* 8 Dec. 1961. *Educ:* Univ. of Southampton (BTh); Heythrop Coll., Univ. of London (MA); Chichester Theol Coll. Ordained deacon, 1986, priest, 1987; Curate, St Leonard's, Seaford, 1986–89; Chaplain, Rochester Cathedral, 1989–91; Asst Chaplain and Hd of Classics, King's Sch., Rochester, 1991–98; Canon Res., Portsmouth Cathedral, 1998–2003; Canon Res. and Precentor, Lincoln Cathedral, 2003–16. *Address:* Edward King House, Minster Yard, Lincoln LN2 1PU.

**KIRK, Geoffrey Eric,** RDI 2001; FREng, FIMechE; FRAeS; FIED; Chief Design Engineer, Civil Aerospace, Rolls-Royce, 1994–2007; *b* 24 Feb. 1945; *s* of Eric and Lily Kirk (*née* Melbourne); *m* 1966, Linda Jean Butcher. *Educ:* Bramcote Hills Tech. Grammar Sch.; Loughborough Tech. Coll.; Loughborough Univ. (Associateship). CEng 1973, FREng 2005; FIMechE 1993; FRAeS 1993; FIED 2002. Drawing office student apprentice, 1961–66, Design Draughtsman, 1966–68, Brush Electrical Engrg Co.; design engr, Rolls-Royce, 1968–73; adult trainee, Rolls-Royce/Loughborough Univ., 1971–72; Chief Design Engr, Ariel Pressings, 1973–75; Rolls-Royce: Sen. Tech. Designer, 1975–82; Chief Design Engr, RB211-535E4, 1982–85; Chief Engineer: V2500, 1985–87; Res. and Mfg Technol., 1987–89; Chief Design Engineer, Civil Engineers, 1989–92; Head of Powerplant Engineering, 1992–94. Visiting Professor: Queen Mary, Univ. of London (formerly QMW), 1996–2011 (Hon. Fellow, 2005); Nottingham Univ., 2003–; Cambridge Univ., 2006–12. Mem., Design Council, 2005–10. FRSA 2002. Hon. EngD Nottingham, 2017. Hon. Pres., IED, 2006–10 (Gerald Frewer Meml Trophy, 2002; Founder's Prize, 2011). British Bronze Medal, RAeS, 1998; Prince Philip Designers' Prize, 2002; Sir Misha Black Medal, RCA, 2006. *Publications:* contribs to various confs and seminars, predominantly on design. *Recreations:* sport, photography, private flying.

**KIRK, Matthew John Lushington;** International Affairs Adviser, Squire Patton Boggs LLP, since 2018; *b* 10 Oct. 1960; *s* of Sir Peter Michael Kirk, MP and Elizabeth Mary Kirk (*née* Graham); *m* 1989, Anna Thérèse Macey, *d* of Rear-Adm. David Edward Macey, CB; two *d. Educ:* Vinehall Sch.; Coll. Joseph d'Arbaud; Felsted Sch.; St John's Coll., Oxford (MA Phil. and Theol.); Ecole Nat. d'Admin, Paris (Dip. Internat. d'Admin Public). Entered HM Diplomatic Service, 1982; UK Mission to UN, NY, 1982, Vienna, 1983; FCO, 1983–84; 3rd, later 2nd, Sec., Belgrade, 1984–87; FCO, 1987–88; Office of Governor of Gibraltar, 1988; FCO, 1989–92; 1st Secretary: Paris, 1993–97; FCO, 1997–98; Cabinet Secretariat (on secondment), 1998–99; FCO, 1999–2002; Ambassador to Finland, 2002–06. Dir, Ext. Relationships, Vodafone Gp Plc, 2006–09; Alternate Dir, Vodafone Essar Ltd (India), 2007–09; Gp Ext. Affairs Dir and Mem., Exec. Cttee, 2009–17, Advr, 2017–18, Vodafone Gp Plc. Dir, UK-India Business Council, 2010–12. Trustee, Vodafone Gp Foundn, 2009–17; Member: Adv. Council, World Wide Web Foundn, 2011–16; WEF Global Agenda Council, 2014–16; Adv. Bd, Royal Holloway Inst. for Cyber Security Innovation, 2016–; Adv. Bd, Bath Univ. Sch. of Mgt, 2016–. UK Chm., Aurora Forum. Mem., Koenigswinter Cttee, 2008–. Mem., BUPA Assoc., 2013–. Gov., Downe House Sch., 2009– (Chm., 2015–). FRGS 1989. *Recreations:* music, wine, walking, travel. *Address:* Squire Patton Boggs LLP, 7 Devonshire Square, EC2M 4YH. *E:* matthew.kirk@squirepb.com. *Clubs:* Brooks's, Beefsteak.

**KIRK, Prof. Raymond Maurice,** FRCS; Honorary Professor of Surgery, Division of Surgery and Interventional Sciences, University College London (formerly Royal Free Hospital School of Medicine, then Royal Free and University College Medical School), since 2004 (part time Lecturer in Anatomy, 1989–2011); Hon. Consulting Surgeon, Royal Free Hospital (Consulting Surgeon, 1989); *b* 31 Oct. 1923; *m* 1952, Margaret Schafran; one *s* two *d. Educ:* Mundella Sch., Nottingham; County Secondary Sch., West Bridgford; King's College London; Charing Cross Hosp. MB BS, MS, London; LRCP. RN 1942–46; Lieut RNVR. Charing Cross Hosp., 1952–53; Lectr in Anatomy, King's Coll. London, 1953–54; Hammersmith Hosp., 1954–56; Charing Cross Hosp., 1956–60; Senior Surgical Registrar, Royal Free Hosp., 1961; Consultant Surgeon: Willesden Gen. Hosp., 1962–74; Royal Free Hosp. Group, 1964–89. Dir, Overseas Doctors' Trng Scheme, RCS, 1990–95; formerly Mem. Court of Examrs, RCS; formerly Examr to RCPSG, Univs of London, Liverpool, Bristol, Khartoum, Colombo, Kuwait; Mem. Council, RCS, 1983–91; FRSocMed (Pres., Surgical Section, 1986–87). Member: British Soc. of Gastroenterol.; Soc. of Academic and Res. Surgery; Med. Soc. of London (Pres., 1988–89); Hunterian Soc. (Pres., 1995–96); Soc. of Authors. Hon. Fellow: Assoc. of Surgeons of Poland; Coll. of Surgeons of Sri Lanka. Hon. Editor, Annals of RCS, 1983–92. *Publications:* Manual of Abdominal Operations, 1967; Basic Surgical Techniques, 1973, 7th edn 2018; (jtly) Surgery, 1974; General Surgical Operations, 1978, 6th edn as Kirk's General Surgical Operations, 2013; Complications of Upper Gastrointestinal Tract Surgery, 1987; (jtly) Clinical Surgery in General, 1993, 4th edn 2004; A Career in Medicine, 1998; (jtly) Essential General Surgical Operations, 2001, 2nd edn 2007; papers in sci. jls and chapters in books on peptic ulcer, oesophageal, gastric and general abdominal surgery and surgical trng. *Recreations:* opera, theatre, surgical history. *Address:* 10 Southwood Lane, Highgate Village, N6 5EE. *T:* (020) 8340 8575. *E:* r.kirk@ucl.ac.uk, rm.kirk.kirk@gmail.com. *Club:* Royal Society of Medicine.

**KIRK, Richard Stanley,** CBE 2006; Chief Executive, Poundstretcher Ltd, 2012; *b* 16 Nov. 1945; *s* of Charles Kirk and Margaret (*née* Green); *m* 1st, 1969 (marr. diss. 1988); two *s*; 2nd, 1995, Barbara Mount (marr. diss. 2005). *Educ:* Chesterfield Grammar Sch. Store Manager, then Area Manager, F. W. Woolworth, 1966–77; Iceland Frozen Foods, subseq. Iceland Gp, PLC, 1977–96: Stores Dir, 1982–86; Man. Dir, 1986–96; Chief Exec., Peacock's Stores, 1996–2012. *Recreations:* ski-ing, shooting, travel.

**KIRKBRIDE, Julie;** Consultant: Tetra Strategy, since 2010; QuatroPR, since 2018; *b* 5 June 1960; *d* of late Henry Raymond Kirkbride and of Barbara (*née* Bancroft); *m* 1997, Andrew James MacKay, *qv*; one *s. Educ:* Highlands Sch., Halifax; Girton Coll., Cambridge. Researcher, Yorkshire TV, 1983–86; Producer: BBC news and current affairs, 1986–89; ITN, 1989–92; Political Correspondent: Daily Telegraph, 1992–96; also Social Affairs Ed., Sunday Telegraph, 1996. MP (C) Bromsgrove, 1997–2010. Shadow Sec. of State for Culture, Media and Sport, 2003–04. Mem. Bd, Ofsted, 2019–. Trustee, Volunteering Matters, 2016–. Rotary Foundn Scholar, Yorkshire Area, 1982–83. *Recreations:* walking, travelling, opera.

**KIRKBY, Dame (Carolyn) Emma,** DBE 2007 (OBE 2000); freelance classical concert singer; soprano; *b* 26 Feb. 1949; *d* of late Capt. Geoffrey Kirkby, CBE, DSC, RN and of Daphne Kirkby; one *s* by Anthony Rooley, *qv. Educ:* Hanford School; Sherborne School for Girls; Somerville College, Oxford (BA Classics). FGS (FGSM 1991). Private singing lessons with Jessica Cash. Regular appearances with Taverner Choir and Players, 1972–; Member: Consort of Musicke, 1973–; Academy of Ancient Music, 1975–; numerous radio broadcasts, gramophone recordings, appearances at the Proms, 1977–. Hon. DLitt Salford, 1985; Hon. DMus: Bath, 1994; Sheffield, 2000; Oxford, 2008; Newcastle, 2010; York, 2011. Queen's Medal for Music, 2010. *T:* (Consort of Musicke) (020) 8444 6565. *E:* consort@easynet.co.uk.

**KIRKHAM,** family name of **Baroness Berners** and **Baron Kirkham**.

**KIRKHAM,** Baron *cr* 1999 (Life Peer), of Old Cantley in the county of South Yorkshire; **Graham Kirkham,** Kt 1996; CVO 2001; Partner, Black Diamond Investments LP, since 2010; *b* 14 Dec. 1944; *m* 1965, Pauline Fisher; one *s* one *d.* Founder, 1969, Chm., 1983–2010, Northern Furnishing, subseq. DFS Furniture Co. Ltd. Sen. Party Treas., Conservative Party, 1997–98. Trustee, Duke of Edinburgh's Award Scheme (Chm., Bd of Trustees, 2010–); Dep. Patron, Outward Bound, 2006–. Dep. Pres., Animal Health Trust, 2003–. Hon. Liveryman, Furniture Makers' Co., 2007. Hon. Dr Bradford, 1997. *Address:* Black Diamond Investments, 8 Ebor Court, Redhouse Interchange, Adwick-le-Street, Doncaster DN6 7FE.

**KIRKHAM, Alison Jane;** Controller, Factual Commissioning, BBC, since 2016; *b* London, 14 March 1974; *d* of John Anthony Kirkham and Eleanor Hilary Kirkham; *m* 2003, Gideon Merton Joseph; two *s. Educ:* North London Collegiate Sch.; Wadham Coll., Oxford (BA Hons PPE 1995); City Univ. (MA Broadcast Journalism 1997). Legislative researcher, US Senate, 1996–97; broadcast asst, Today prog., Radio 4, 1997–98; asst producer, This Morning, ITV, 1998–2000; producer/dir, Tonight with Trevor McDonald, Granada TV, 2000–04; Associate Editor, Richard and Judy, Channel 4, 2004–05; BBC: Exec. Producer, Daytime, 2005–07; Commng Editor, 2007–10; Hd, Commng, Formats and Features, 2010–15. *Recreations:* my children, cinema and TV, travelling. *Address:* BBC, Zone D, 7th Floor, BBC New Broadcasting House, Portland Place, W1A 1AA. *E:* alison.kirkham@bbc.co.uk.

**KIRKHAM, Donald Herbert,** CBE 1996; FCIS; Group Chief Executive, Woolwich Building Society, 1991–95 (Chief Executive, 1986–90); *b* 1 Jan. 1936; *s* of Herbert and Hettie Kirkham; *m* 1960, Kathleen Mary Lond; one *s* one *d. Educ:* Grimsby Technical Sch. Woolwich Equitable Building Society, later Woolwich Building Society: Representative, 1959; Branch Manager, 1963; Gen. Manager's Asst, 1967; Business Planning Manager, 1970; Asst Gen. Manager, 1972; Gen. Manager, 1976; Mem. Local Board, 1979; Dep.

Chief Gen. Manager, 1981; Mem. Board, 1982; non-exec. Dir, 1996–97; Dir, Gresham Insurance Co. Ltd, 1995–96. President: Banque Woolwich SA, 1995–2001; Banca Woolwich SpA, 1995–2002. Director: Horniman Museum and Public Park Trust, 1989–2004 (Chm., 1996–2004); Building Socs Investor Protection Bd, 1995–97; Bexley and Greenwich HA, 1996–98 and 1999–2001; Oxleas NHS Foundn Trust, 2006–09. Chartered Building Societies Institute: Mem. Council, 1976; Dep. Pres., 1980; Pres., 1981; Vice-Pres., 1986–93, then Vice-Pres., CIB, 1993–98; Institute of Chartered Secretaries and Administrators: Mem. Council, 1979; Vice-Pres., 1985; Sen. Vice-Pres., 1990; Pres., 1991; Building Societies Association: Mem. Council, 1991–95; Dep. Chm., 1993–94; Chm., 1994–95. Trustee, Ranyard Meml Charitable Trust (formerly Ranyard Charitable Trust), 2001–10. Hon. DBA Thames Poly., 1991. *Address:* 2 Chaundrye Close, The Court Yard, Eltham, SE9 5QB. *T:* (020) 8859 4295.

**KIRKHAM, Elizabeth Anne, (Libby);** *see* Wiener, E. A.

**KIRKHAM, Her Honour Frances Margaret,** CBE 2011; FCIArb; a Senior Circuit Judge, Technology and Construction Court, Birmingham, 2000–11; Judge, Qatar International Court, since 2013; Chartered Arbitrator, adjudicator and mediator; trainer of advocacy and advanced litigation skills; *b* 29 Oct. 1947; *d* of Brian Llewellyn Morgan Davies and Natalie May Davies (*née* Stephens); *m* 1971, Barry Charles Kirkham. *Educ:* King's Coll. London (BA Hons 1969; AKC 1969). FCIArb 1991. Bank of England, 1969–73; Lloyds Bank Internat., 1973–74; admitted solicitor, 1978; Pinsent & Co., 1976–84; Bettinsons, 1984–87; Edge & Ellison, 1987–95; Dibb Lupton Alsop, 1995–2000. Parly Boundary Comr, 2000; Mem., Judicial Appts Commn, 2006–11. Member: Wkg Party on Civil Justice Reform, Law Soc. and Bar Council, 1992–93; Civil Litigation Cttee, 1988–92, Litigation Casework Cttee, 1990–92, Law Soc.; Civil Litigation Cttee, Birmingham Law Soc., 1992–93; Council, CIArb, 1992–97, 2000 (Chm., W Midlands Br., 1994–97). Non-exec. Dir, Royal Orthopaedic Hosp. NHS Foundn Trust, 2011–17. Founder Chm., W Midlands Assoc. Women Solicitors; Sec., UK Assoc. of Women Judges, 2003–06. Hon. Member: Arbrix, 2002–; Technol. and Construction Ct Solicitors' Assoc., 2005– (formerly Founder Cttee Mem.; Clare Edwards Award, 2008); Technol. and Construction Bar Assoc., 2011–; Member: Soc. of Construction Arbitrators, 2011–; Professional Conduct Cttee, CIArb, 2012– (Chm., 2017–). Mem., Adv. Bd, Centre for Advanced Litigation, Nottingham Law Sch., 1992–97. Consultant, Qatar Internat. Ct and Dispute Resolution Centre, 2012. Hon. Bencher, Inner Temple, 2008. Gov., Heathfield Sch., Harrow, 1981–91 (Chm., 1984–91). Hon. Life Mem., Soc. of Construction Law, 2014. Lifetime Achievement Award, Birmingham Law Soc., 2011. *Recreations:* time with friends, sailing, ski-ing, walking, music, theatre. *Address:* Atkin Chambers, Gray's Inn, WC1R 5AT. *Club:* University Women's.

**KIRKHAM, Rt Rev. John Dudley Galtrey;** Assistant Bishop, Diocese of Salisbury, since 2001; *b* 20 Sept. 1935; *s* of late Rev. Canon Charles Dudley Kirkham and Doreen Betty Galtrey; *m* 1986, Mrs Hester Gregory. *Educ:* Lancing Coll.; Trinity Coll., Cambridge (BA 1959, MA 1963). Commnd, Royal Hampshire Regt, seconded to 23 (K) Bn, King's African Rifles, 1954–56. Trinity Coll., Cambridge, 1956–59; Westcott House, 1960–62; Curate, St Mary-le-Tower, Ipswich, 1962–65; Chaplain to Bishop of Norwich, 1965–69; Priest in Charge, Rockland St Mary w. Hellington, 1967–69; Chaplain to Bishop of New Guinea, 1969; Asst Priest, St Martin-in-the-Fields and St Margaret's, Westminster, 1970–72; Domestic Chaplain to Archbishop of Canterbury, and Canterbury Diocesan Director of Ordinands, 1972–76; Bp Suffragan, later Area Bp, of Sherborne, 1976–2001; Canon and Preb., Salisbury Cath., 1977–2001, and 2002–10; Bp to the Forces, 1992–2001. Archbishop of Canterbury's Advr to HMC, 1990–92. Commissary to Bp of Polynesia and Archbp of PNG. Hon. Chaplain: Princess of Wales Royal Regt, 1992–; KAR and EAF Assoc., 2001–. Provost, Western Region, Woodard Schs, 2002–10. ChStJ 1991; Chaplain to the Guild of the Nineteen Lubricators. Croix d'Argent de Saint-Rombaut, 1973. *Recreations:* walking, bicycling, gardening, woodwork. *Address:* Flamston House, Flamstone Street, Bishopstone, Salisbury, Wilts SP5 4BZ. *Clubs:* Army and Navy, Kandahar.

**KIRKHAM, Keith Edwin,** OBE 1987; PhD; Administrative Director, Clinical Research Centre, Medical Research Council, 1988–94; *b* 20 Oct. 1929; *s* of Thomas Kirkham and Clara Prestwich Willacy; *m* 1953, Dorothea Mary Fisher; two *s*. *Educ:* Kirkham Grammar Sch.; Birmingham Univ. (BSc); Fitzwilliam House, Cambridge (DipAgrSci; T. H. Middleton Prize); MA, PhD Cantab. National Service, 2nd Lieut RA, 1955–57. Asst in Res., Cambridge, 1951–54; Univ. Demonstr, Cambridge, 1954–60; Sci. Staff, Clin. Endocrinology Res. Unit, MRC, 1960–73; Asst Dir (Admin), Clin. Res. Centre, MRC, 1973–88. Sec., Soc. for Endocrinology, 1975–79. Governor: Harrow Coll. of Higher Educn, 1983–90 (Chm. of Govs, 1986–90); Univ. of Westminster (formerly Poly. of Central London), 1990–2000. Hon. DSc Westminster, 1999. *Publications:* contribs to sci. jls on endocrinology. *Recreation:* sport (watching).

**KIRKHILL,** Baron *cr* 1975 (Life Peer), of Kirkhill, Aberdeen; **John Farquharson Smith;** *b* 7 May 1930; *s* of Alexander F. Smith and Ann T. Farquharson; *m* 1965, Frances Mary Walker Reid; one step *d*. Lord Provost of the City and Royal Burgh of Aberdeen, 1971–75. Mem., H of L, 1975–2018. Minister of State, Scottish Office, 1975–78. Chm., N of Scotland Hydro-Electric Bd, 1979–82. Deleg. to Parly Assembly of Council of Europe and WEU, 1987–2001 (Chm., Cttee on Legal Affairs and Human Rights, 1991–95). Hon. LLD Aberdeen, 1974. *Address:* 3 Rubislaw Den North, Aberdeen AB15 4AL. *T:* (01224) 314167.

**KIRKHOPE,** family name of **Baron Kirkhope of Harrogate**.

**KIRKHOPE OF HARROGATE,** Baron *cr* 2016 (Life Peer), of Harrogate in the City of North Yorkshire; **Timothy John Robert Kirkhope;** Member (C) Yorkshire and the Humber Region, European Parliament, 1999–2016; solicitor; *b* 29 April 1945; *s* of late John Thomas Kirkhope and Dorothy Buemann Kirkhope (*née* Bolt); *m* 1969, Caroline (*née* Maling); four *s*. *Educ:* Royal Grammar School, Newcastle upon Tyne; College of Law, Guildford. Conservative Party: joined 1961 (N Area Vice-Chm. of YC of Mem., Nat. Cttee); Hexham Treasurer, 1982–85; Exec., N Area, 1975–87; Mem., Nat. Exec., 1985–87; Mem. Bd, 2005–07 and 2008–10; Mem., Northern Bd and Yorks Bd, 2007–16. County Councillor, Northumberland, 1981–85. Mem., Newcastle Airport Bd, 1982–85; Mem., Northern RHA, 1982–86; Founder Lawyer Mem., Mental Health Act Commn, 1983–86. Contested (C): Durham, Feb. 1974; Darlington, 1979. MP (C) Leeds North East, 1987–97; contested (C) same seat, 1997. PPS to Minister of State for the Envmt and Countryside, 1989–90; an Asst Govt Whip, 1990–92; a Lord Comr of HM Treasury (Govt Whip), 1992–95; Vice Chamberlain, HM Household, 1995; Parly Under-Sec. of State, Home Office, 1995–97. Mem., Select Cttee on Statutory Instruments, 1987–90; Vice Chm., Backbench Legal Cttee, 1988–89; Jt Hon. Sec., Cons. Backbench Envmt Cttee, 1988–89. European Parliament: Chief Whip, 1999–2001, Leader, 2004–07 and 2008–10, UK Conservatives; Cons. spokesman: on justice and home affairs, 1999–2007, 2009–16; on transport and tourism, 2007–09; Mem., Culture, Media, Arts, Youth and Educn Cttee, 1999–2002 (Substitute Mem., 2009–16); Cons. Mem., Future of Europe Convention, 2002–04; Vice-Chm., EPP-ED, 2004–05; Vice-Pres., EP Const. Affairs Cttee, 2007–09; Dir, Movt for European Reform, 2007–09; Founder and First Chm., 2009, Dep. Chm., 2009–11, European Cons. and Reformist Gp; Chm., EP Delegn to Australia and NZ, 2008–09; Mem., EP Delegn to USA, 2009–16; substitute Mem., EP Transport Cttee, 2014–16; Mem., Special Justice Home Affairs and Civil Liberties Cttee of Inquiry into Electronic Mass Surveillance of EU Citizens, 2013–14. Member, All Party Parliamentary Group: British-American, 2017–; Historic Vehicles, 2017–; Gen. Aviation, 2018–; Mem., Sub-Cttee on Home Affairs, EU Select Cttee, H of L, 2018–; Chm., Special All Party Parly Gp Inquiry into UK Airspace, 2018–19. Vice-Chm., Special Cttee on Organised Crime, 2012–14. Mem., Adv. Panel, Europarl TV, 2009–16. Chm., Kirkhope Commn on Asylum, 2003, on Immigration, 2004, Cons Party. Dir, Bournemouth and W Hampshire Water Co., 1999–2011. Dep. Chm., GBA, 1990–98. Trustee, Biwater Retirement and Security Scheme, 2011–. Gov., Royal Grammar Sch., Newcastle upon Tyne, 1989–99. MInstD 1998. *Recreations:* flying (holds private pilot's licence), tennis, golf, swimming, watching TV quiz shows, collecting and appreciating classic cars. *Address:* Beechwood Farm, Scotton, Knaresborough, N Yorks HG5 9HY; House of Lords, SW1A 0PW. *Clubs:* Northern Counties (Newcastle upon Tyne); Dunstanburgh Castle Golf (Northumberland).

**KIRKMAN, (John) Paul;** Director, National Railway Museum, 2012–17; *b* Bolton, 8 Aug. 1967; *s* of John Kevan Kirkman and Susan Elizabeth Kirkman (*née* Fell); *m* 2013, Lilly Shahravesh. *Educ:* Univ. of Edinburgh (MA Philos. 1989); Goldsmiths Coll., Univ. of London (MA Art Hist. 1998). HM Treasury, 1991–95; Private Sec. to Dir Gen. of CBI, 1995–96; Hd, Policy and Planning, Natural Hist. Mus., 1999–2001; HM Treasury, 2001–05; Department for Culture, Media and Sport: Hd, Mus, Libraries and Cultural Property, 2005–06; Hd, Arts, 2006–08; Dep. Dir, Progs, 2008–11; Hd, Arts, 2011–12; Hd, Arts and Creative Industries, 2012. Trustee, Royal Armouries, 2018–. *Recreations:* cycling, cooking, museums.

**KIRKMAN, William Patrick,** MBE 1993; Secretary: University of Cambridge Careers Service, 1968–92; Cambridge Society, 1992–2003; Administrator, American Friends of Cambridge University, 2000–01; Fellow, Wolfson College, (formerly University College), Cambridge, 1968–2000, now Emeritus; *b* 23 Oct. 1932; *s* of late Geoffrey Charles Aylward Kirkman and Bertha Winifred Kirkman; *m* 1959, Anne Teasdale Fawcett; two *s* one *d*. *Educ:* Churcher's Coll., Petersfield, Hants; Oriel Coll., Oxford. 2nd cl. hons, mod. langs, 1955; MA 1959; MA (Cantab) by incorporation, 1968. National Service, 1950–52, RASC (L/Cpl); TA, 1952–59, Intell. Corps (Lieut). Editorial staff: Express & Star, Wolverhampton, 1955–57; The Times, 1957–64 (Commonwealth staff, 1960–64, Africa Correspondent, 1962–64). Asst Sec., Oxford Univ. Appointments Cttee, 1964–68. Chm., Standing Conf. of University Appointments Services, 1971–73; Member: Management Cttee, Central Services Unit for Univ. Careers and Appointments Services, 1971–74, 1985–87; British Cttee, Journalists in Europe, 1985–97; Cambridge Univ. PR Co-ordinating Cttee, 1987–96; Trng Bd, ESRC, 1990–93; Non-service Mem., Home Office Extended Interview Bds, 1993–2002. Member: BBC South and East Regl Adv. Council, 1990–92, Midlands and E Regl Adv. Council, 1992–93, E Regl Adv. Council, 1994–96; Chm., BBC Radio Cambridgeshire Adv. Council, 1992–96. Wolfson College: Vice-Pres., 1980–84; Mem. Council, 1969–73, 1976–80, 1988–92, 1994–95; Dir, Press Fellowship Programme, 1982–96. Churchwarden, St Mary and All Saints Willingham, 1978–85, 1996–97. Vice-Chm., Assoc. of Charitable Foundns, 1994–97; Mem. Regl Cttee, RSA, 1997–2003; Mem. Council, U3A, Cambridge, 2007–10. Trustee: Sir Halley Stewart Trust, 1969–2009, now Emeritus (Hon. Sec., 1978–82; Vice-Chm., 1998–2002); Willingham British Sch. Trust, 1974–91; Homerton Coll., 1980–89; Lucy Cavendish Coll., 1989–97; Chaplaincy to People at Work in Cambs, 1999–2014; Mem. Cttee, Cambridge Soc., 1979–83. Editor: Cambridge, 1992–2003; CRAC Newsletter, 1997–98; Chm., CAMREAD, 2004–12. *Publications:* Unscrambling an Empire, 1966; contrib.: Policing and Social Policy, 1984; Models of Police/Public Consultation in Europe, 1985; Managing Recruitment, 4th edn 1988; Graduate Recruitment: a 25-year retrospective, 1993; Reflections on Change, 2007; contributor to journals incl. The Hindu (Chennai), The Round Table, Africa Contemporary Record, Cambridge Rev. and to BBC. *Recreations:* local and international politics, church activities, writing. *Address:* 14 George Street, Willingham, Cambridge CB24 5LJ. *T:* (01954) 260393. *E:* wpk1000@cam.ac.uk.

**KIRKPATRICK, Sir Ivone Elliott,** 11th Bt *cr* 1685; *b* 1 Oct. 1942; *s* of Sir James Alexander Kirkpatrick, 10th Bt and Ellen Gertrude, *o d* of Captain R. P. Elliott, late RNR; *S* father, 1954. *Educ:* Wellington Coll., Berks; St Mark's Coll., University of Adelaide. *Heir: nephew* Glen Sydney Kirkpatrick, *b* 1 April 1973.

**KIRKPATRICK, Janice Mary,** OBE 2013; Designer and Creative Director, Graven (formerly Graven Images), since 1985; Chairman, Lighthouse Trust, 2004–07 (Director, 1999–2007); *b* 16 April 1962; *d* of James Burns Kirkpatrick and Jane Henry Coupland Kirkpatrick (*née* Borthwick); *m* 2008, Ross Buchanan Hunter. *Educ:* Glasgow Sch. of Art (BA 1st Cl Hons Graphic Design 1984; MA Design 1985). Vis. Prof., Glasgow Sch. of Art, 2000– (Gov., 1999–2010; Vice Chm., 2008–10). Trustee, NESTA, 1999–2005. Hon. DLitt Glasgow, 2014. *Recreations:* riding and driving Clydesdale horses, breeding British Saddleback pigs, trying to be a horseman, beekeeper and gardener. *Address:* Graven, 175 Albion Street, Glasgow G1 1RU. *T:* (0141) 522 6626, *Fax:* (0141) 552 0433. *E:* janice@graven.co.uk.

**KIRKSTALL, Bishop Suffragan of,** since 2018; **Rt Rev. Paul John Slater;** (Bishop Suffragan of Richmond, 2015–18); *b* 22 March 1958; *s* of Norman and Jean Slater; *m* 1981, Beverley Louise (*née* Knight); two *s* (and one *s* decd). *Educ:* Corpus Christi Coll., Oxford (MA (Natural Sci.) 1983); St John's Coll., Durham (BA (Theol.) 1983). Ordained deacon, 1984, priest, 1985; Asst Curate, St Andrew's, Keighley, 1984–88; Priest-in-charge, St John's, Cullingworth, 1988–93; Dir, Lay Trng Foundn Course, 1988–93; PA to Bishop of Bradford, 1993–95; Rector, St Michael's, Haworth, 1995–2001; Bishop's Officer for Ministry and Mission, Dio. of Bradford, 2001–14; Archdeacon of Craven, 2005–14; Archdeacon of Richmond and Craven, 2014–15. Mem., Gen. Synod, C of E, 2013–15. Mem., Brontë Soc., 1996–2005. Hon. Canon, Ripon Cathedral, 2015–. *Recreations:* playing and watching tennis, reading novels, learning Spanish. *Address:* 4 Borrowdale Court, 5 Clifford Drive, Menston, Ilkley LS29 6FZ. *T:* (01943) 870359. *E:* bishop.paul@leeds.anglican.org.

**KIRKUP, William,** CBE 2008; FRCP, FRCOG, FFPH; independent investigator; Lead Associate Investigator, Parliamentary and Health Service Ombudsman, since 2016; *b* 29 April 1949; *s* of late William Kirkup and Patience Kirkup (*née* Wilford); *m* 1972 (marr. diss. 1983); three *d*; *m* 2004, Denise Lambert; one *d*. *Educ:* Newcastle Royal Grammar Sch.; Worcester Coll., Oxford (MA, BM BCh 1974). MRCOG 1979, FRCOG 1993; MFPHM 1986, FFPH (FFPHM 1994); FRCP 2006. Obstetrics and gynaecology posts, Oxford, Sheffield and Newcastle, 1975–82; public health trng, 1982–86; Consultant, Newcastle, 1986–87; Sen. Lectr, Newcastle Univ., 1986–91; Dir of Public Health, N Tyneside, 1987–91; Dir posts, (Performance Review, Healthcare Develt, NHS Trusts Div.), Northern Reg. and NHS Exec., 1991–99; Department of Health: Regl Dir of Public Health and Healthcare, Northern and Yorks, NHS Exec., 1999–2002; Regl Dir of Public Health, NE, 2002–05; Associate Chief Med. Officer, 2005–08 (Dir Gen., Clinical Programmes, 2005–08; Associate NHS Med. Dir, 2008). Member: Hillsborough Ind. Panel; Gosport Ind. Panel. *Publications:* contribs to learned jls. *Recreations:* Newcastle United FC, music, playing with computers.

**KIRKWOOD,** family name of **Barons Kirkwood** and **Kirkwood of Kirkhope**.

**KIRKWOOD**, 3rd Baron cr 1951, of Bearsden; **David Harvie Kirkwood**; Hon. Senior Lecturer and Metallurgical Consultant, 1987–2002, Sheffield University (Senior Lecturer in Metallurgy, 1976–87); b 24 Nov. 1931; s of 2nd Baron Kirkwood and Eileen Grace (d 1999), d of Thomas Henry Boalch; S father, 1970; m 1965, Judith Rosalie, d of late John Hunt; three d. Educ: Rugby; Trinity Hall, Cambridge (MA, PhD); CEng. Lectr in Metallurgy, Sheffield Univ., 1962; Warden of Stephenson Hall, Sheffield Univ., 1974–80. Mem., Select Cttee on Sci. and Technology, H of L, 1987–92, 1996–99. Heir: b Hon. James Stuart Kirkwood [b 19 June 1937; m 1965, Alexandra Mary, d of late Alec Dyson; two d]. Address: 56 Endcliffe Hall Avenue, Sheffield S10 3EL. T: (0114) 266 3107.

**KIRKWOOD OF KIRKHOPE**, Baron cr 2005 (Life Peer), of Kirkhope in Scottish Borders; **Archibald Johnstone Kirkwood**, Kt 2003; b 22 April 1946; s of David Kirkwood and Jessie Barclay Kirkwood; m 1972, Rosemary Chester; one d one s. Educ: Cranhill School; Heriot-Watt Univ. (BSc Pharmacy). Solicitor. MP Roxburgh and Berwickshire, 1983–2005 (L/Alliance 1983–88, Lib Dem 1988–2005). Lib Dem convenor and spokesman on welfare, 1988–92, on social security, 1992–94 and 1997–2001, on community care, 1994–97; Chief Whip, 1992–97. Chairman: Social Security Select Cttee, 1997–2001; Work and Pensions Select Cttee, 2001–05. Trustee, Joseph Rowntree Reform Trust, 1985–2007 (Chm., 1999–2006). Address: House of Lords, SW1A 0PW.

**KIRKWOOD, Dr James Kerr**, OBE 2008; Chief Executive and Scientific Director: Universities Federation for Animal Welfare, 2000–14; Humane Slaughter Association, 2000–14; b 8 Nov. 1951; s of late Andrew Kerr Kirkwood and of Patricia Mary Kirkwood (née Brown); m 1983, Julia Mary Christine Brittain; two s one d. Educ: Bradfield Coll., Berks; Bristol Univ. (BVSc 1975; PhD 1982). CBiol, FRSB (FIBiol 1997). Research Associate, later Res. Fellow, Dept of Pathology, Bristol Univ., 1981–84; Sen. Vet. Officer, Zoological Soc. of London, and Head of Vet. Sci. Gp, Inst. of Zoology, 1984–96; specialist in zoo and wildlife medicine, RCVS, 1992–2000; Scientific Dir, UFAW, and Hon. Dir, Humane Slaughter Assoc., 1996–2000. Ed.-in-Chief, Animal Welfare, 1996–2014. Dir, Master's Course in Wild Animal Health, RVC/Inst. of Zoology, 1994–96; Vis. Prof., Dept of Pathology and Infectious Diseases, RVC, 1997–2014; Hon. Res. Fellow, Inst. of Zoology, 1997–2003. Chm., Zoos Forum, 2005–11 (Mem., 1999–2011); Dep. Chm., Companion Animal Welfare Council, 2003–12 (Mem., 2000–12); Chm., DEFRA Ind. Wkg Gp on Snares, 2004–05; Member: IUCN Vet. Specialist Gp, 1990–2012; Council, Zool Soc. of London, 2004–07; TB Adv. Gp, 2006–09, Wildlife Health and Welfare Strategy Bd, 2006–08, DEFRA; Head of UK Delegn at Internat. Whaling Commn Workshop on Welfare, St Kitts, 2006. Mem., Lead Ammunition Gp, 2010–16. Trustee, Zebra Foundn for Vet. Zool Educn, 1990–2012; Pres., British Vet. Zool Soc., 1994–96. Hon. FRCVS 2011. Publications: (with K. Stathatos) Biology, Rearing and Care of Young Primates, 1992; (ed jtly) Science in the Service of Animal Welfare, 2004; sundry publications in the scientific literature on aspects of the biology, diseases, conservation and welfare of animals. Recreations: music, cycling, literature, natural history. Address: c/o Universities Federation for Animal Welfare and Humane Slaughter Association, The Old School, Wheathampstead, Herts AL4 8AN. T: (01582) 831818.

**KIRKWOOD, Michael James**, CMG 2003; FCIB; Chairman, Ondra Partners LLP, 2009–12 and since 2016 (Senior Adviser, 2013–15); Senior Independent Director, Bushveld Minerals Ltd, since 2018; b Glasgow, 7 June 1947; s of James Kirkwood and June Alexandra Scott Kirkwood (née Peters); m 1969, Karen Marie Wolf; one s one d. Educ: Trinity Coll., Glenalmond; Stanford Univ., Calif. (BA Hons). FCIB 2001. Hongkong and Shanghai Banking Corp., 1965–68; Alt. Dir, Temenggong Securities Ltd, Singapore, 1973–76; Chief Exec., Temenggong Merchant Bankers Ltd, Singapore, 1974–76; Dir, Scotland, Ansbacher & Co. Ltd, 1976–77; Citigroup, 1977–2008: Country Senior Officer: Scotland, 1977–80; Denmark, 1981–83; CEO, Citicorp Investment Bank Switzerland SA, 1985–88; Gp COS, NY, 1988–91; Div. Hd, Continental Europe, 1991–92; Hd, UK Corporate Banking, 1993–2008; Chief Country Officer, Citigroup Inc., UK, 1999–2008. Mem. Bd, British American Business Inc. (Chm., 2001–03); non-executive Director: Kidde plc, 2001–05; UK Financial Investments Ltd, 2009–14; London Scottish International Ltd, 2009–; AngloGold Ashanti Ltd, 2012–19; AngloGold Ashanti Hldgs plc, 2019–; Verita Healthcare Gp Ltd, 2019–; Dep. Chm. Adv. Bd, PricewaterhouseCoopers, 2009–11; Sen. Advr, 2009–12, non-exec. Dir, 2012–14, Eros International plc; Chm., Health Investment Hldgs, then Circle Hldgs plc, 2011–17. Chairman: American Banks Assoc., 2000–02; Assoc. of Foreign Banks, 2004; Pres., Chartered Inst. of Bankers, 2003–04 (Dep. Pres., 2002–03); Vice Chm. (formerly Vice Pres.), British Bankers' Assoc., 2001–08; Mem. Adv. Bd, ACT. Chm., Habitat for Humanity GB, 2004–11; Dir and Trustee, Stone Foundn, 1996–2003. FRSA. Hon. FCT 2019. HM Lieut for the City of London, 2004. Freeman, City of London, 2002; Mem. Ct, Co. of Internat. Bankers, 2001–11, now Ct Emeritus (Master, 2005–06). Recreations: Mediterranean horticulture, golf, Rugby, shooting and travel. Address: 125 Old Broad Street, EC2N 1AR. Clubs: Pilgrims, Caledonian; Royal Mid-Surrey Golf; Country (Johannesburg).

**KIRKWOOD, Prof. Thomas Burton Loram**, CBE 2009; PhD; FRCPE; Professor of Medicine, 1999–2013, Distinguished Research Fellow, 2013–16, University of Newcastle upon Tyne, now Professor Emeritus (Associate Dean for Ageing, 2011–13; Scientific Director, NIHR Biomedical Research Centre on Ageing, 2007–13); Professor of Biogerontology (part-time), Centre for Healthy Ageing, Department of Molecular and Cellular Medicine, University of Copenhagen, since 2016; b 6 July 1951; s of late Kenneth Kirkwood; m 1973, Betty Rosamund Bartlett (marr. diss. 1995); one s one d; m 1995, Jane Louise Bottomley. Educ: Dragon Sch., Oxford; Magdalen Coll. Sch., Oxford; St Catharine's Coll., Cambridge (MA; PhD 1983); Worcester Coll., Oxford (MSc). FRCPE 2013. Scientist, Nat. Inst. for Biol Standards and Control, 1973–81; National Institute for Medical Research: Sen. Scientist, 1981–88; Head, Lab. of Mathematical Biol., 1988–93; Prof. of Biol Gerontology, Univ. of Manchester, 1993–99; University of Newcastle upon Tyne: Hd of Gerontology, 1999–2004; Co-Dir, 2004–06, Dir, 2006–11, Inst. for Ageing and Health; Dir, Centre for Integrated Systems Biol. of Ageing and Nutrition, 2005–11. Various distinguished lectures incl. Reith Lectures, 2001; Nathan Shock Award Lect., US Nat. Inst. on Aging, 2016; Paton Prize Lect., Physiological Soc., 2017. Chm., Brit. Soc. for Research on Ageing, 1992–99; Dir, Jt Centre on Ageing, Univs of Manchester and Newcastle upon Tyne, 1996–99; Gov., 1998–2001, and Chm., Res. Adv. Council, 1999–2000, Research into Ageing; Chm., Foresight Task Force on Health Care of Older People, 1999–2001; Member: WHO Expert Adv. Panel on Biol Standardization, 1985–2004; UK Human Genome Mapping Project Cttee, 1991–93; Basic Scis Interest Gp, Wellcome Trust, 1992–97; BBSRC, 2001–04; Science and Industry Council, NE England, 2007–09. Specialist Advr, Inquiry into Scientific Aspects of Ageing, H of Lords Select Cttee on Sci. and Technol., 2004–06. Trustee: Cumberland Lodge, 2007–17; Age Internat., 2017–; Dunhill Med. Trust, 2017–; Trustee Dir, Big Lottery Centre for Ageing Better, 2013–15. Co-Ed., Mechanisms of Ageing and Develt, 2000–06. President: Internat. Biometric Soc. (British Reg.), 1998–2000; (Biol.), Eur. Section, Internat. Assoc. of Gerontology, 2003–07; Scientific Bd, AXA Res. Fund, 2013–. Fellow, Inst. for Advanced Study, Budapest, 1997; Tower Fellow, NZ Inst. for Res. on Ageing, 2004. FMedSci 2001 (Mem. Council, 2002–06). Hon. FFA 2002. Hon. DSc Hull, 2003. Heinz Karger Prize, 1983; Fritz Verzár Medal, 1996; Dhole-Eddlestone Prize, British Geriatrics Soc., 2001; Henry Dale Prize, Royal Instn, 2002; Cohen Medal, British Soc. for Res. on Ageing, 2006; Longevity Prize, Ipsen Foundn, 2011. Publications: (jtly) Accuracy in Molecular Processes: its control and relevance to living systems, 1986; Time of Our Lives: the science of human ageing, 1999; (with C. E. Finch) Chance, Development and Aging, 2000; The End of Age, 2001; (jtly) Sex and Longevity: sexuality, gender, reproduction, parenthood, 2001; (jtly) Wellbeing in Later Life, 2014; many scientific articles. Recreations: travel, pottery, gardening. Address: Newcastle University Institute for Ageing, Newcastle University, Campus for Ageing and Vitality, Newcastle upon Tyne NE4 5PL. T: (0191) 208 1103, Fax: (0191) 208 1101. E: Tom.Kirkwood@newcastle.ac.uk.

**KIRSHBAUM, Ralph**; cellist; Gregor Piatgorsky Chair in Violoncello, University of Southern California, Los Angeles, since 2008; b Texas, 4 March 1946; m 1982, Antoinette Reynolds; one s. Founder and Artistic Dir, RNCM Manchester Internat. Cello Fest., 1988–2007. Has performed with major orchestras including: BBC Symphony; Boston Symphony; Cleveland Orch.; London Symphony; Orchestre de Paris; Pittsburgh Symphony; San Francisco Symphony; Chicago Symphony; Tonhalle; Berlin Radio Symphony; Royal Danish; Stockholm Philharmonic. Festival appearances at Aspen, Bath, Edinburgh, Lucerne, New York, Santa Fe, Ravinia and Verbier. Chamber music collaboration with Gyorgy Pauk, Peter Frankl, Shai Wosner and Pinchas Zukerman. Recordings include: concertos: Barber; Elgar; Haydn D major; Tippett Triple; Walton; Beethoven Triple; Brahms Double; Barber, Shostakovich and Prokofiev sonatas; Ravel, Shostakovich and Brahms Trios, complete Bach suites; complete Beethoven sonatas and variations.

**KIRTON, Muriel Elizabeth**; international consultant and teacher of Daoist philosophy and healing arts, management training and lifestyle, since 2002; b 4 July 1950; d of William Waddell Kirton and Belle Jane Kirton (née Barnett). Educ: Glasgow Univ. (MA Hons Eng. and French 1974); Kent Univ. (MA TEFL 1979); Edinburgh Univ. (DipEd 1975); Moray House Coll. of Educn (PGCE 1975). Teacher of French and English, Cornwall Coll., Montego Bay, Jamaica, 1975–77; teacher of French, Dane Court Tech. High Sch., Broadstairs, 1977–78; Lectr in ELT, Hilderstone Coll., Kent, 1978–79; Sen. Lectr in ELT, Nonington Coll., Kent, 1979–82; joined British Council, 1982: Project Manager, ELT, China, 1982–85; Projects Dir, Hong Kong, 1985–89; Educn Officer, Egypt, 1990–93; Director: Vietnam, 1993–96; Commonwealth Relations, 1996–2000; Cyprus, 2000–01; Yugoslavia, 2001–02. Recreations: scuba diving, alternative/complementary healing therapies, reading, cinema, theatre. Address: 15 Leven Terrace, Bruntsfield, Edinburgh EH3 9LW. E: murielkirton@gmail.com.

**KIRTON–DARLING, Judith**; Member (Lab) North East Region, European Parliament, since 2014; b Dar-es-Salaam, Tanzania, 2 June 1977; d of Hugh Fenwick Ridley Kirton-Darling and Janette Kirton Darling (née Kohn); m 2013, Benjamin Daune. Educ: Hall Garth Secondary Sch., Middlesbrough; Acklam 6th Form Coll., Middlesbrough; Univ. of Sheffield (BA Hons Social and Pol Studies); Univ. of Bath (MSc Eur. Social Policy Analysis). Prog. asst, Quaker Council for Eur. Affairs, 1999–2000; researcher, Eur. Trade Union Inst., 2001–03; Policy Advr, UNI Europa, 2003–06; Eur. Officer, Unite the Union, 2006–07; Industrial Policy Officer, Eur. Metalworkers' Fedn, 2007–11; Confederal Sec., ETUC, 2011–14. Address: Labour Party, Kings Manor, Newcastle upon Tyne NE1 6PA. E: jude.kirton-darling@europarl.europa.eu.

**KIRUI, Nancy Chepkemoi**; Permanent Secretary, Ministry of State for Defence, Kenya, 2008–13; b 4 June 1957; d of Isaiah Cheluget and Rael Cheluget; m 1993, Nicholas Kirui; two d, and three step s one step d. Educ: Alliance Girls' Sch., Kikuyu, Kenya; Univ. of Nairobi (LLB); Kenya Sch. of Law (Postgrad. Dip. Law). Legal Officer: Min. of Foreign Affairs, Nairobi, 1985–88; Perm. Mission of Kenya to UN, Geneva, 1988–91; Min. of Foreign Affairs, 1991–94; Kenya High Commn, London, 1994–98; Hd of Legal Div., then Hd, Americas Div., Min. of Foreign Affairs, 1998–2000; High Comr in London, 2000–03; Permanent Secretary: Min. of Gender, Sports, Culture and Social Services, Nairobi, 2003–04; Min. of Labour and Human Resource Develt, Nairobi, 2004–06; Office of the Vice-Pres. and Min. of Home Affairs, 2006–08. Recreations: sketching, painting, cooking. Address: c/o Ministry of State for Defence, Ulinzi House, Lenana Road, PO Box 40668–00100, Nairobi, Kenya.

**KIRWAN, Sir John (James Patrick)**, KNZM 2012 (ONZM 2007); MBE 1987; consultant; Head Coach, Blues Rugby, Auckland, 2013–15; b Auckland, 16 Dec. 1964; s of late Pat Kirwan and of Pat Kirwan; m Fiorella Tomasi; two s one d. Educ: De La Salle Coll., Auckland. Formerly butchers apprentice. Player: Rugby Union: Auckland and Marist team, 1983–94; NZ All Blacks, 1984–94 (35 tries in 63 Tests for NZ; Mem., winning team, Rugby World Cup, 1987); Benetton Treviso, 1986–90; NEC Green Rockets, Japan, 1997–99; Rugby League: Auckland Warriors, 1995–96. Coach, NEC Green Rockets, Japan, 1999–2001; asst coach, Auckland Blues, 2001; coach: Italian nat. Rugby team, 2002–05; Japanese nat. Rugby team, 2007–11; Barbarians, 2012. Ambassador for Auckland, 2017–. Spokesman and campaigner involved in mental health and depression awareness campaigns in NZ. Publications: Running on Instinct, 1992; Why I Am, 1999; All Blacks Don't Cry, 2010; Stand By Me, 2015. Recreation: surfing. Address: c/o 46 Autumn Avenue, Glen Eden, Auckland 0602, New Zealand.

**KIRYA, Prof. George Barnabas**; High Commissioner for Uganda in the United Kingdom, 1990–2003, and Ambassador to Ireland, 1995–2003 (Senior High Commissioner at the Court of St James's, 1997); Dean of the Diplomatic Corps, 1999–2003; b 9 Feb. 1939; m; five s one d. Educ: Univ. of E Africa (MB ChB 1966); Birmingham Univ. (MSc Gen. Virology 1971); Manchester Univ. (Dip. Bacteriology 1974). Med. House Officer, Mulago Hosp., Uganda, 1966–67; Sen. House Officer, Dept of Paediatrics and Child Health, Makerere Fac. of Medicine, 1967; East Africa Virus Res. Inst., Entebbe: Virologist, 1967; Sen. Med. Res. Officer, 1968; Principal Med. Res. Officer and Head, Dept of Arbovirology, 1969; Hon. Lectr, Dept of Med. Microbiol., Makerere Univ., 1970; Consultant on Yellow Fever Epidemics, WHO, 1970; Department of Microbiology, Faculty of Medicine, Makerere University: Sen. Lectr, 1973–75; Associate Prof. and Hd of Dept, 1975–78; Prof. and Hd of Dept, 1978; Makerere University: Mem. Senate, 1977–90; Mem. Univ. Council, 1981–90; Vice Chancellor, 1986–90. Chairman: Commonwealth Finance Cttee, 1993–2003; African Union (formerly OAU) Heads of Mission Gp, London, 1997–2003; Commonwealth Heads of Mission Gp, 1997–2003; Commonwealth Africa Gp, 1997–2003; Commonwealth People's Assoc. of Uganda, 2006–. Mem., WHO Scientific and Technical Adv. Gp, serving as WHO Temp. Advr, 1990–93. Dir, Central Public Health Labs in Uganda supported by WHO, UNICEF and Min. of Health, 1980–86; Chairman: Disease Surveillance Sub-Cttee, Min. of Health; Uganda Health Service Commn, 2007–11; Uganda Nat. Health Consumers' Orgn, 2010– (Chm. Bd, 2007–); Adv. Council, Amref Health Africa Uganda, 2011–; Mgt Bd, Butabika Nat. Referral Hosp., 2015–; Member: Nat. Cttee for Prevention of Blindness in Uganda; Adv. Cttee for Res. of Viruses in Uganda; E and Central African Physicians Assoc.; Founder Mem., Uganda Health Mktg Gp, 2006–; Uganda Medical Association: Treas., 1978–82; Pres., 1982–86; Chm., CPD, 2005–08. Chm., Advocates for Professionalism and Quality in Health, 2009–. Chancellor, Lugazi Univ., 2007–10; Mem. Gov. Council, Ernest Cook Ultrasound Research and Educn Inst., 2005–. Teaching and supervising undergrad. and post-grad. med. students, med. lab. technologists, nurses and midwives and health visitors. Internal examr and external examr for several univs incl. Univ. of Ibadan, Lagos Univ. and Univ. of Nairobi. Member, Editorial Bd: E African Jl for Med. Res.; Uganda Med. Jl. Hon. LLD Birmingham, 2001. *Address:* PO Box 5406, Kampala, Uganda. *Club:* Africa Cricket (Kampala).

KISIN, Prof. Mark, PhD; FRS 2008; Professor of Mathematics, Harvard University, since 2009; *b* Lithuania. *Educ:* Monash Univ. (BSc 1991); Princeton Univ. (MSc 1995; PhD 1998). Postdoctoral Fellow, Australian Res. Council, 1998–2001; res. at Westfälischen Wilhelms Univ., Germany, 1998–2003; Asst Prof., 2003–05, Prof., 2005–09, Univ. of Chicago. Editor: Inventiones Mathematicae; Cambridge Jl of Maths; Jl Number Theory, 2009–10; Mathematische Annalen, 2009–13; Algebra and Number Theory, 2013–15. *Publications:* contribs to jls incl. Jl Amer. Maths Soc., Invent. Maths, Current Develts in Maths, Annals of Maths. *Address:* Department of Mathematics, Harvard University, 1 Oxford Street, Cambridge, MA 02138, USA.

KISSACK, Paul; Deputy Chief Executive, Leadership and Organisational Development, Ministry for Vulnerable Children (Oranga Tamariki), New Zealand, since 2017; *b* Douglas, IOM, 3 April 1976; *s* of Frederick and Carole Kissack; *m* 2006, Emma Jane Lindsell; one *s* two *d*. *Educ:* Queen Elizabeth II High Sch., Peel, IOM; Univ. of Warwick (BA Hons Hist. 1997); Jesus Coll., Cambridge (MPhil Histl Studies 1998). HM Treasury: Hd of Communications and Press Spokesman for Chancellor of Exchequer, 2004–06; Hd of Productivity and Reform, 2006–08; Hd, Commng, Delivery and Service Improvement, Children's Services, Richmond upon Thames LBC, 2008–10; Principal Private Sec. to Cabinet Sec., 2010–11; Dir, DFE, 2011–14; Dir-Gen., Children's Services, Equalities and Communications, DFE, 2014–16; Dir-Gen., Cabinet Office, 2016–17. *Address:* Ministry for Vulnerable Children (Oranga Tamariki), Aurora Centre, 56 The Terrace, PO Box 1556, Wellington 6410, New Zealand.

KISSIN, Evgeny Igorevich; concert pianist; *b* 10 Oct. 1971; *s* of Igor Kissin and Emilia Kissina; *m* 2017, Karina Arzumanova. *Educ:* Gnessin Special Sch. of Music, Moscow; Gnessin Russian Acad. of Music, Moscow. Début, Moscow State Philharmonic Orch., conducted by Dmitry Kitaenko, Great Hall, Moscow Conservatoire, 1984; toured Japan, 1986; European début with Berlin Radio Orch., 1987; UK début with BBC Manchester Orch., Lichfield Fest., 1987; USA début with NY Philharmonic Orch., 1990. Has made numerous recordings. Hon. RAM 2005. Hon. DMus Manhattan Sch. of Music, 2001; Hon. DLitt Hong Kong, 2009; Hon. Dr Hebrew Univ., Jerusalem, 2010. Musician of the Year, Chigiana Music Acad., Italy, 1991; Instrumentalist of the Year, Musical America mag., 1994; Triumph Award for outstanding contrib. to Russian culture, Triumph Ind. Charity Foundn, 1997; various awards for recordings in UK, France, Holland, incl. Grammy Award, 2006. *Publications:* Evgeny Kissin: memoirs and reflections, 2017. *Recreations:* reading, long and fast walks, getting together with friends. *Address:* c/o Askonas Holt Ltd, 15 Fetter Lane, EC4A 1BW. *T:* (020) 7400 1700.

KISSINGER, Henry Alfred, Hon. KCMG 1995; Bronze Star (US); Chairman, Kissinger Associates Inc., since 1982; Counselor to Center for Strategic and International Studies, since 1977 and Trustee, since 1987; *b* Germany, 27 May 1923; *s* of late Louis Kissinger and Paula (*née* Stern); *m* 1st, 1949, Anne Fleischer (marr. diss. 1964); one *s* one *d*; 2nd, 1974, Nancy Maginnes. *Educ:* George Washington High Sch., NYC; Harvard Univ., Cambridge, Mass (BA 1950, MA 1952, PhD 1954). Emigrated to United States, 1938; naturalised, 1943. Served Army, 1943–46. Teaching Fellow, Harvard Univ., 1950–54; Study Director: Council on Foreign Relations, 1955–56: Rockefeller Bros Fund, 1956–58; Associate Professor of Govt, Harvard Univ., 1958–62, Prof. of Govt, 1962–71, and Faculty Mem., Center for Internat. Affairs, Harvard; Director: Harvard Internat. Seminar, 1951–69; Harvard Defense Studies Program, 1958–69; Asst to US President for Nat. Security Affairs, 1969–75; Secretary of State, USA, 1973–77. Chm., Nat. Bipartisan Commn on Central America, 1983–84; Member: President's Foreign Intelligence Adv. Bd, 1984–90; Commn on Integrated Long-Term Strategy of the National Security Council and Defense Dept, 1986–88; Dir, Internat. Rescue Cttee, 1987–; Hon. Gov., Foreign Policy Assoc., 1985–. Chm., Internat. Adv. Bd, American Internat. Group, Inc., 1988–; Counselor and Mem., Internat. Adv. Cttee, JP Morgan Chase & Co. (formerly Chase Manhattan Bank, then Chase Manhattan Corp.), 1977–; Advr to Bd of Dirs, American Express Co., 2005– (Dir, 1984–2005); Dir, ContiGroup Cos Inc., 1988–2014; Dir Emeritus, Freeport-McMoRan Copper and Gold Inc.; formerly Dir, Hollinger Internat. Inc. Trustee, Metropolitan Mus. of Art, 1977, now Emeritus. Syndicated writer, Los Angeles Times, 1984–. (Jtly) Nobel Peace Prize, 1973; Presidential Medal of Freedom, 1977; Medal of Liberty, 1986. *Publications:* A World Restored: Castlereagh, Metternich and the Restoration of Peace, 1957; Nuclear Weapons and Foreign Policy, 1957 (Woodrow Wilson Prize, 1958; citation, Overseas Press Club, 1958); The Necessity for Choice: Prospects of American Foreign Policy, 1961; The Troubled Partnership: a reappraisal of the Atlantic Alliance, 1965; Problems of National Strategy: A Book of Readings (ed), 1965; American Foreign Policy: three essays, 1969, 3rd edn 1977; White House Years (memoirs), 1979; For the Record: selected statements 1977–1980, 1981; Years of Upheaval (memoirs), 1982; Observations: selected speeches and essays 1982–1984, 1985; Diplomacy, 1994; Years of Renewal, 1999; Does America Need a Foreign Policy?, 2001; Ending the Vietnam War, 2003; Crisis, 2003; On China, 2011; World Order, 2014. *Address:* Suite 400, 1800 K Street NW, Washington, DC 20006, USA; 350 Park Avenue, New York, NY 10022, USA. *Clubs:* Century, River, Brook (New York); Metropolitan (Washington); Bohemian (San Francisco).

KISZELY, Lt-Gen. Sir John (Panton), KCB 2004; MC 1982; DL; defence and security consultant, since 2008; *b* 2 April 1948; *s* of Dr John Kiszely and Maude Kiszely; *m* 1984, Hon. Arabella Jane, *d* of 3rd Baron Herschell; three *s*. *Educ:* Marlborough Coll.; RMA Sandhurst. Commnd into Scots Guards, 1969; Co. Comdr, 2nd Bn Scots Guards, 1981–82; Bde Major, 7 Armd Bde, 1982–85; CO 1st Bn Scots Guards, 1986–88 (mentioned in dispatches); Comdr, 22 Armd Bde, 1991–92; Comdr, 7 Armd Bde, 1993; Dep. Comdt, Staff Coll., Camberley, 1993–96; GOC 1st (UK) Armd Div., 1996–98; ACDS (Resources and Plans), MOD, 1998–2001; Dep. Comdr, NATO Force, Bosnia, 2001–02; Comdr Regl Forces, Land Comd, 2002–04; Dep. Comdr, Multinat. Force, Iraq, 2004–05; Dir Gen., Defence Acad. of the UK, 2005–08. Regtl Lt-Col, Scots Guards, 1995–2001; Col Comdt, Intelligence Corps, 2000–08. Vis. Prof. in War Studies, King's Coll. London, 2008–13; Mem., Adv. Bd, Baltic Defence Coll., 2011–15. Trustee, Imperial War Mus., 2008–16 (Dep. Chm., 2011–16). Nat. Pres., RBL, 2009–12. Vice Patron, Disabled Sailors Assoc., 2010–17. CRAeS 2006. Hon. Col, Univ. of London OTC, 2003–09. Liveryman, Painter-Stainers' Co., 2008–. DL Glos, 2010. QCVS 1997. Officer, Legion of Merit (USA), 2005. *Publications:* (contrib.) The Science of War: back to first principles, 1993; Military Power: land warfare in theory and practice, 1997; The Falklands Conflict Twenty Years On, 2004; (contrib.) The Past as Prologue: history and the military profession, 2006; (contrib.) The Impenetrable Fog of War, 2008; Coalition Command in Contemporary Operations, 2008; (contrib.) British Generals in Blair's Wars, 2013; Anatomy of a Campaign: the British fiasco in Norway, 1940, 2017; numerous articles in military jls. *Recreations:* sailing, shooting, fishing, music. *Address:* c/o Headquarters Scots Guards, Wellington Barracks, Birdcage Walk, SW1E 6HQ. *Clubs:* Cavalry and Guards; Royal Solent Yacht.

KITAMURA, Hiroshi, Hon. KBE 2003; Corporate Advisor to Mitsubishi Corporation, 1994–99; President, Shumei University, 1998–2001; *b* 20 Jan. 1929; *s* of Teiji and Fusako Kitamura; *m* 1953, Sachiko Ito; two *d*. *Educ:* Univ. of Tokyo (LLB 1951); Fletcher School of Law and Diplomacy, Medford, USA, 1952. Joined Min. of Foreign Affairs, Tokyo, 1953; postings to Washington DC, New York, New Delhi, London; Dir, Policy Planning Div., Res. and Planning Dept, Tokyo, 1974; Private Sec. to Prime Minister, 1974–76; Dep. Dir-Gen., Amer. Affairs Bureau, 1977–79; Consul-Gen., San Francisco, 1979–82; Dir-Gen., American Affairs Bureau, 1982–84; Dep. Vice Minister for Foreign Affairs, 1984–87; Dep. Minister, 1987–88; Ambassador: to Canada, 1988–90; to UK, 1991–94. *Publications:* Psychological Dimensions of US-Japanese Relations, 1971. *Recreations:* traditional Japanese music, culinary arts, golf. *Address:* 1–15–6 Jingumae, Shibuya-ku, Tokyo 150–0001, Japan.

KITCHEN, Daniel John; Chairman: Workspace Group plc, since 2011; Hibernia REIT plc, since 2014; Applegreen plc, since 2015; *b* Belfast, 23 April 1952; *s* of Daniel and Thelma Kitchen; *m* 1974, Linda Barbour; one *s* one *d*. *Educ:* Grosvenor High Sch.; Queen's Univ. Belfast (BSc). FCCA 1977. Dir, Investment Bank of Ireland, 1985–94; Chief Finance Officer, Green Property plc, 1994–2002; Dep. Chief Exec., Heron International, 2003–08. Non-executive Director: LXB Retail Properties plc, 2009–; Irish Takeover Panel. Gov., St Patrick's Univ. Hosp., Dublin, 2012–. *Recreations:* football, golf, gardening. *Address:* Workspace Group plc, Canterbury Court, Kennington Park, 1–3 Brixton Road, SW9 6DE. *T:* (020) 7138 3300. *E:* daniel.kitchen@workspace.co.uk.

KITCHEN, Rev. Dr Martin; Priest-in-Charge, South Rodings, 2008–11; *b* 18 May 1947; *s* of Reginald Thomas Kitchen and Alice Kitchen (*née* Johnson); *m* 1971, Sheila Solveig Pettersen; one *s*. *Educ:* Sir Walter St John's Sch., Battersea; Poly. of N London (BA London Univ. 1971); King's Coll. London (BD 1976; AKC 1977); Univ. of Manchester (PhD 1988). Ordained deacon, 1979, priest, 1980; Lectr, Church Army Trng Coll., and Curate, St James, Kidbrooke, 1979–83; Chaplain, Manchester Poly., 1983–88; Team Vicar, 1983–86, Team Rector, 1986–88, Whitworth, Manchester; Diocese of Southwark: Advr, In-Service Trng, 1988–95; Co-ordinator of Trng, 1995–97; Residentiary Canon, Southwark Cathedral, 1988–97; Durham Cathedral: Residentiary Canon, 1997–2005; Sub-Dean, 1998–99; Vice Dean, 1999–2004; Dean of Derby, 2005–07. Permission to officiate: Dio. of Europe, 2011; Dio. of Newcastle, 2012. Theol Consultant, Ministry Div., Archbishop's Council, 2008–09. Sec., 1996–2001, Dir, 2001–, Archbishop's Exam. in Theol.; Sec., Anglo-Nordic-Baltic Theol Conf., 1997–2009; Consultant, C of E Doctrine Commn, 1999–2005. *Publications:* Ephesians, 1994; Guide to Durham Cathedral, 2000; A Talent for Living, 2003; editor and co-author: Word of Life, 1997; Word of Promise, 1998; Word of Truth, 1999; Word in Our Time, 2000; Word Among Us, 2001; various articles and translations in bks and jls. *Recreations:* music, poetry, good food and wine, needlepoint. *Address:* 4 Town Farm Close, Wall, Hexham NE46 4DH. *T:* (01434) 689696.

KITCHEN, Michael; actor; *b* 31 Oct. 1948; *s* of Arthur and Betty Kitchen; partner, Rowena Miller; two *s*. *Educ:* City of Leicester Boys' Grammar School. Entered acting profession, 1970; *stage includes:* seasons at Belgrade Theatre, Coventry, National Youth Theatre; Royal Court, 1971–73; Big Wolf, Magnificence, Skyvers; Young Vic, 1975: Othello, Macbeth, As You Like It, Charley's Aunt; National Theatre: Spring Awakening, 1974; Romeo and Juliet, 1974; State of Revolution, 1977; Bedroom Farce, 1977; No Man's Land, 1977; The Homecoming, 1978; Family Voices, 1981; On the Razzle, 1981; The Provok'd Wife, 1981; Rough Crossing, 1984; Royal Shakespeare Company: Romeo and Juliet, Richard II, 1986; The Art of Success, 1987; *films include:* The Bunker; Breaking Glass; Towards the Morning; Out of Africa; Home Run; The Russia House; Fools of Fortune; The Dive; Goldeneye; Mrs Dalloway; The Last Contract; The World is not Enough; My Week With Marilyn; *television series:* Steven Hind; Divorce; Freud, 1983; The Justice Game, 1989; The Guilty, 1992; To Play the King, 1993; Dandelion Dead, 1994; The Hanging Gale, 1995 (Best Actor Award, Internat. Fest. of Audiovisual Progs, Biarritz, 1996); Reckless, 1997; Oliver Twist (serial), 1999; Foyle's War, 2002–15 (9 series); Alibi, 2003; The Life of Rock, with Brian Pern, 2014; Brian Pern: A Life in Rock, 2014; Brian Pern: 45 Years of Prog and Roll, 2016; The Collection, 2016; Brian Pern: A Tribute, 2017; *television films and plays include:* Caught on a Train; Benefactors; Ball-Trap; Pied Piper; The Enchanted April; Hostage; Falling; Mobile, Hacks; numerous other TV and radio performances. *Recreations:* piano, guitar, sailing, writing, tennis. *Address:* c/o Independent Talent Group, 40 Whitfield Street, W1T 2RH.

KITCHENER-FELLOWES, family name of **Baron Fellowes of West Stafford**.

KITCHIN, Rt Hon. Lord; David James Tyson Kitchin, Kt 2005; PC 2011; a Justice of the Supreme Court, since 2018; *b* 30 April 1955; *s* of late Norman Tyson Kitchin and Shirley Boyd Kitchin (*née* Simpson); *m* 1989, Charlotte Anne Cadbury, *d* of Comdr David Jones; one *s* one *d*. *Educ:* Oundle Sch. (schol.); Fitzwilliam Coll., Cambridge (MA; Hon. Fellow, 2012). Called to the Bar, Gray's Inn, 1977, Bencher, 2003; pupilled to Robin Jacob, 1978; entered chambers of Thomas Blanco White, 1979; QC 1994; a Dep. High Ct Judge, 2001–05; apptd to hear Trade Mark Appeals, 2001–05; a Judge of the High Court, Chancery Div., 2005–11; Chancery Supervising Judge for Wales, Western and Midland Circuits, 2009–11; a Lord Justice of Appeal, 2011–18. Mem., Enlarged Bd of Appeal, European Patent Office, 2009–11. Chm., Vet. Code of Practice Cttee, Nat. Office of Animal Health, 1995–2001. Chm., Intellectual Property Bar Assoc., 2004–05; Mem., Bar Council, 2004–05 (Mem., European Cttee, 2004–05). Mem. Council, 2006–11, Chm., Adv. Council, Centre for Commercial Law Studies, 2015–, QMUL. Mem., Adv. Bd, Science Mus., 2019–. Hon. LLD QMUL, 2015. *Publications:* (ed jtly) Patent Law of Europe and the United Kingdom, 1979; (ed jtly) Kerly's Law of Trade Marks and Trade Names, Supplement to 12th edn 1994, 13th edn, 2001, 14th edn 2005; (jtly) The Trade Marks Act 1994 (text and commentary), 1995. *Recreations:* golf, tennis, theatre. *Address:* Supreme Court of the United Kingdom, Parliament Square, SW1P 3BD. *Clubs:* Hawks (Cambridge); Leander (Henley); Walton Heath Golf.

KITCHING, Alan, RDI 1994; Typographer and Proprietor, The Typography Workshop, since 1989; *b* 29 Dec. 1940; *s* of Walter Kitching and Kathleen (*née* Davies); *m* 1962, Rita Haylett (*d* 1984); two *s*; *m* 2007, Celia Stothard (*d* 2010). Apprentice compositor, 1955–61; Asst, Exptl Printing Workshop, Watford Coll. of Technol. Sch. of Art, 1963–68; Vis. Tutor in Typography, Central Sch. of Art and Design, 1968–72; Established freelance design practice, working in magazine, book and exhibition design, 1971; Partner, Omnific Studios (Graphic Design), 1977–88; established Typography Workshop, Printroom and Studio (with Celia Stothard), 2005; Vis. Tutor in Typography, RCA, 1988–2006; Vis. Prof., Univ. of the Arts London (formerly London Inst.), 2001–. Retrospective Exhibn, Alan Kitching and Celia Stothard: The Typography Workshop - twenty years of new letterpress prints, London, 2009; exhibited, RA, 2011, 2012; solo exhibn, Advanced Graphics, London, 2012, 2015; exhibited at The Discerning Eye, Mall Gall., London, 2013; solo exhibn, Alan Kitching and Monotype, London Coll. of Communication, 2014, Trent Univ., 2015, Bournemouth Coll. of Art, 2016; solo exhibn, Alan Kitching on Press at The Guardian, King's Place, 2015; retrospective exhibn, A Life in Letterpress, Somerset Hse, London, 2016, The Lighthouse, Glasgow, 2016–17, Manchester Univ., 2016, Lettering Arts Centre, Snape Maltings, 2016; retrospective exhibn, Letterpress Prints, North House Gall.,

2017–18. AGI 1994. Hon. FRCA 2006 (FRCA 1998). *Publications:* Typography Manual, 1970; Alan Kitching's A-Z of Letterpress, 2015; relevant publication: A Life in Letterpress, by John L. Walters, 2017. *Recreations:* reading, cooking. *Address:* 19 Cleaver Street, SE11 4DP. *Club:* Chelsea Arts.

**KITCHING, Christopher John,** CBE 2004; PhD; FSA, FRHistS; Secretary, Historical Manuscripts Commission, National Archives (formerly Royal Commission on Historical Manuscripts), 1992–2004; *b* 5 Aug. 1945; *s* of Donald Walton Kitching and Vera (*née* Mosley); *m* 1976, Hilary Mary Ruth Horwood; two *s*. *Educ:* Durham Univ. (BA Mod. Hist. 1967; PhD 1970). Registered Mem., Soc. of Archivists, 1987. Asst Keeper, PRO, 1970–82; Asst Sec., Royal Commn on Historical MSS, 1982–92. Asst Editor, Archivum, 1984–92. Hon. Treasurer, 1980–85, Vice-Pres., 2002–05, RHistS; Mem., Archives Task Force, MLA, 2002–04. Council Mem., Canterbury and York Soc., 1974–2004; Mem., Adv. Cttee, Durham Cath. Library, 2011–. Chm., Trustees, St Mary-the-Virgin, Primrose Hill, 1998–; Trustee: Miss E. M. Johnson's Charitable Trust, 1997–2005; Lambeth Palace Library, 2009–17. Mem. Editl Bd, Jl of Soc. of Archivists, 1992–2004. Hon. Sec., Essay Club, 2009–15. Alexander Prize, RHistS, 1973. *Publications:* The Royal Visitation of 1559, 1975; Survey of the Central Records of the Church of England, 1976; London and Middlesex Chantry Certificate 1548, 1980; Surveys of historical manuscripts in the United Kingdom: a select bibliography, 1989, 3rd edn 1997; The impact of computerisation on archival finding aids, 1990; Archive Buildings in the United Kingdom 1977–1992, 1993; Archives: the very essence of our heritage, 1996; Archive Buildings in the United Kingdom 1992–2005, 2007; A Passion for Records, Walter Rye (1843–1929), 2017; articles and reviews. *Recreations:* music, historical research, Freedom-pass exploration. *Address:* 11 Creighton Road, NW6 6EE. *T:* (020) 8969 6408.

**KITNEY, Prof. Richard Ian,** OBE 2001; PhD, DSc(Eng); FREng; FRSE; Professor of Biomedical Systems Engineering, Imperial College London (formerly Imperial College of Science, Technology and Medicine), since 1997; *b* 13 Feb. 1945; *s* of Leonard Walter Richard Kitney and Gladys Simpson Kitney; *m* 1977, Vera Baraniecka; two *s*. *Educ:* Enfield Grammar Sch.; Univ. of Surrey (MEng 1969); Imperial Coll., London Univ. (PhD, DIC 1972; DSc(Eng) 1993). FREng 1999. Electronics Engr, Thorn Electrical Industries, 1963–72; Lectr in Biophysics, Chelsea Coll., London Univ., 1972–78; Imperial College, London: Lectr, 1975–85; Reader, 1985–89; Dir, Centre for Biol and Med. Systems, 1991–97; Hd, Dept of Biol and Med. Systems, 1997–2001; Dean, 2003–06, Sen. Dean, 2007–11, Faculty of Engrg; Dir, Graduate Sch. of Engrg and Physical Scis, 2006–11; Chm., Inst. of Systems & Synthetic Biology, 2007–; Co-Dir, EPSRC Centre for Synthetic Biology and Innovation, 2010–; Co-Dir, UK Nat. Centre for Industrial Translation of Synthetic Biology, 2013–; Gov., 1995–98, 2006–; Gov., RPMS, 1995–98. Visiting Professor: Georgia Inst. of Technology, 1981–90; MIT, 1991–. Tech. Dir, Intravascular Res. Ltd, 1987–94; Dir, St Mary's Imaging plc, 1991–96; Dep. Chm. and Tech. Dir, comMedica Ltd, 1999–2006; Chm., Visbion Ltd, 2006–; Trustee, Smith and Nephew Foundn, 1996–2003. Mem., Adv. Cttee on Technology in Medicine, DTI, 1995; Chm., RAEng Inquiry on Synthetic Biology, 2008–09; Mem., Govt's Leadership Council for Synthetic Biology, 2012–. Fellow, Engrg Biol. Res. Consortium, USA, 2018. FIAMBE 2003; FAIMBE 2005. FRSocMed 1994; FRSA 2001; FCGI 2005; FRSE 2016. Hon. FRCS 2006; Hon. FRCP 2006; Hon. FRCPE. Freeman, City of London, 1996; Liveryman, Co. of Engineers, 1995. Regular contributor, BBC Radio. Nightingale Prize, Internat. Fedn of Biol Engrg Socs, 1975. *Publications:* (jtly) Recent Advances in the Study of Heart Rate Variability, 1980; (jtly) The Beat-by-Beat Investigation of Cardiac Function, 1987; (jtly) The Coming of the Global Healthcare Industry, 1998; (jtly) Synthetic Biology: a primer, 2012; conf. proceedings, papers in learned jls. *Recreations:* history, cooking, France. *Address:* Department of Bioengineering, Royal School of Mines, Imperial College London, South Kensington Campus, SW7 2AZ. *T:* (020) 7594 6226. *Club:* Athenæum.

**KITSON, Gen. Sir Frank (Edward),** GBE 1985; (CBE 1972; OBE 1968; MBE 1959); KCB 1980; MC 1955 and Bar 1958; DL; *b* 15 Dec. 1926; *s* of late Vice-Adm. Sir Henry Kitson, KBE, CB and Lady (Marjorie) Kitson (*née* de Pass); *m* 1962, Elizabeth Janet (OBE 2015; DL), *d* of late Col C. R. Spencer, OBE, DL; three *d*. *Educ:* Stowe. 2nd Lt Rifle Bde, 1946; served BAOR, 1946–53; Kenya, 1953–55; Malaya, 1957; Cyprus, 1962–64; CO 1st Bn, Royal Green Jackets, 1967–69; Defence Fellow, University Coll., Oxford, 1969–70; Comdr, 39 Inf. Bde, NI, 1970–72 (CBE for gallantry); Comdt, Sch. of Infantry, 1972–74; RCDS, 1975; GOC 2nd Division, later 2nd Armoured Division, 1976–78; Comdt, Staff College, 1978–80; Dep. C-in-C, UKLF, and Inspector-Gen., TA, 1980–82; C-in-C, UKLF, 1982–85. ADC Gen. to the Queen, 1983–85. 2nd Bn, The Royal Green Jackets: Col Comdt, 1979–87; Rep. Col Comdt, 1982–85; Hon. Col, Oxford Univ. OTC, 1982–87. DL 1989. *Publications:* Gangs and Counter Gangs, 1960; Low Intensity Operations, 1971; Bunch of Five, 1977; Warfare as a Whole, 1987; Directing Operations, 1989; Prince Rupert: portrait of a soldier, 1994; Prince Rupert: Admiral and General-at-sea, 1998; Old Ironsides: the military biography of Oliver Cromwell, 2004; When Britannia Ruled the Waves, 2007. *Address:* c/o Lloyds Bank, Farnham, Surrey GU9 7LT. *Club:* Boodle's.

**KITSON, Richard David;** a District Judge (Magistrates' Courts), since 2002; *b* 30 Dec. 1954; *s* of Stanley Kitson and Maisie Kitson; *m* 1980, Barbara Ann Kitching; one *s* one *d*. *Educ:* Doncaster Grammar Sch.; Newcastle upon Tyne Poly. (BA Hons 1976; Maxwell Prize). Admitted solicitor, 1979; Partner, Ward Bracewell & Co., then Taylor Bracewell, Solicitors, Doncaster, 1981–2002. Chairman: Doncaster FHSA, 1994–96 (non-exec. Mem., 1985–94); Doncaster Royal and Montagu Hosp. NHS Trust, 1996–2001; Doncaster Central Primary Care Trust, 2001–02. *Recreations:* hill walking, running, tennis, gardening, Rugby Union. *Address:* Leeds District Magistrates' Court, PO Box No 97, Westgate, Leeds LS1 3JP. *T:* (0113) 245 9653.

**KITSON, Richard David;** Deputy Chief Executive, Hachette UK, since 2018; *b* Newport, 6 June 1977; *s* of Patrick Kitson and Jennifer Ferris (*née* Harris); *m* 2006, Tamsin; two *d*. *Educ:* Bassaleg Comp. Sch., Newport; Univ. of Bristol (LLB Hons Law). Internat. Sales Dir, 2002–05, Dep. Chief Operating Officer, 2005–06, Little Brown & Co.; Gp Commercial Dir, Hachette UK, 2006–17; Chairman: Hachette India, 2007–; Hachette Ireland, 2010–; Hachette Australia and NZ, 2014–. *Recreations:* cycling, cricket, reading, travel, food and wine.

**KITTMER, John;** HM Diplomatic Service; Director, Overseas Territories, Foreign and Commonwealth Office, 2016–17; Commissioner: of the British Antarctic Territory, 2016–17; of the British Indian Ocean Territory, 2016–17; Chairman, Anglo-Hellenic League, since 2018; independent scholar; *b* Cuckfield, Sussex, 6 July 1967; *s* of Roy Kittmer and Jean Kittmer; *m* 2007, David Bates. *Educ:* Christ's Coll., Cambridge (BA 1988); King's Coll. London (MA 2007); Magdalen Coll., Oxford. Various posts, DFEE, 1993–98; First Sec., UK Perm. Repn to EU, Brussels, 1998–2002; Hd of Section, FCO, 2002–04; Hd of Section, DEFRA, 2005–06; Dep. Dir, Cabinet Office, 2006–07; Dep. Dir, Exotic Animal Diseases, DEFRA, 2008; Principal Private Sec. to Sec. of State, 2008–10; Dep. Dir, Inland Waterways, 2011–12, DEFRA; Ambassador to the Hellenic Republic, FCO, 2013–16. Non-exec. Dir, Okeanis Eco Tankers Corp. PhD student of Modern Greek, KCL, 2008–19. *Recreations:* walking, music, things Greek.

**KITZINGER, Uwe,** CBE 1980; Affiliate, Lowell House and Centre for European Studies, Harvard University, since 2003 (Visiting Scholar, 1993–2003); *b* 12 April 1928; *o s* of late Dr G. and Mrs L. Kitzinger, Abbots Langley, Herts; *m* 1952, Sheila Helena Elizabeth Webster, (Sheila Kitzinger, MBE) (*d* 2015); five *d*. *Educ:* Watford Grammar Sch.; Balliol Coll. and New Coll. (Foundn Schol.). Oxford (1st in Philosophy, Politics and Economics, MA, MLitt; Pres., Oxford Union; 1950; Ed., University—A Journal of Enquiry). Economic Section, Council of Europe, Strasbourg, 1951–58; Nuffield College, Oxford: Research Fellow, 1956–62, Official Fellow, 1962–76, Emeritus Fellow, 1976; Acting Investment Bursar, 1962–64; Investment Bursar, 1964–76; Mem., Investment Cttee, 1962–88; Assessor of Oxford University, 1967–68; leave of absence as Adviser to Sir Christopher (later Lord) Soames, Vice-Pres. of the Commn of the European Communities, Brussels, 1973–75; Dean, INSEAD (European Inst. of Business Admin), Fontainebleau, 1976–80 (Mem. Board, 1976–83); Dir, Oxford Centre for Management Studies, 1980–84; Founding Pres., Templeton Coll. (now Green Templeton Coll.), Oxford, 1984–91 (sabbatical, 1991–93; Hon. Fellow, 2001). Sen. Res. Fellow, Atlantic Council, 1993. Visiting Professor: of Internat. Relations, Univ. of the West Indies, 1964–65; of Government, Harvard, 1969–70; Univ. of Paris 1970–73. Member: ODM Cttee for University Secondment, 1966–68; British Universities Cttee of Encyclopædia Britannica, 1967–98; Nat. Council of European Movement, 1974–76; Council, RIIA, 1973–85; Court, Cranfield Inst. of Technology, 1984–85. Founding Chm., Cttee on Atlantic Studies, 1967–70. Co-Founder, Lentils for Dubrovnik, 1991–. Founding Pres., 1987–92, Pres., 1996–, Internat. Assoc. of Macro-Engrg Socs. Member: Oxfam Council, 1981–84; Major Projects Assoc., 1981–91 (Founding Chm., 1981–86); Adv. Bd, Pace Univ., NY, 1982–92; Berlin Science Centre, 1983–90; Acad. Adv. Bd, World Management Council, 1989–; Bd, Jean Monnet Foundn, Lausanne, 1990–; Tufts Inst. for Global Leadership, 2006–17. Chair, GARIWO Campaign for Civil Courage Sarajevo, 2001–12. Pres., Féd. Britannique des Alliances Françaises, 1999–2004. Trustee: European Foundn for Management Educn, Brussels, 1978–80; Oxford Trust for Music and the Arts, 1986–91. Patron, Asylum Welcome, 2005–. Chm., Oxford Radio Consortium, 1988. Founding Editor, Jl of Common Market Studies, 1962–. Hon. LLD Buena Vista, 1986. Dr Jean Mayer Award for Global Citizenship, Tufts Univ., 2016. Order of the Morning Star (Croatia), 1997. Documents, books and articles on Britain's relationship with emergent EU 1945–76 deposited Histl Archives of EU, Eur. Univ. Inst., Florence, 2012. *Publications:* German Electoral Politics, 1960 (German edn 1960); The Challenge of the Common Market, 1961 (Amer. edn, The Politics and Economics of European Integration, 1963, et al); Britain, Europe and Beyond, 1964; The Background to Jamaica's Foreign Policy, 1965; The European Common Market and Community, 1967; Commitment and Identity, 1968; The Second Try, 1968; Diplomacy and Persuasion, 1973 (French edn 1974); Europe's Wider Horizons, 1975; (with D. E. Butler) The 1975 Referendum, 1976, 2nd edn 1996; (ed with E. Frankel) Macro-Engineering and the Earth, 1998. *Recreations:* sailing, travel, old buildings. *Address:* Standlake Manor, 41 High Street, Standlake, Oxon OX29 7RH. *T:* (01865) 300266; La Rivière, 11100 Bages, France. *T:* (4) 68417013. *E:* uwe_kitzinger@yahoo.com. *Club:* Royal Thames Yacht.

**KIYOTAKI, Prof. Nobuhiro,** PhD; FBA 2003; Professor, Department of Economics, Princeton University, since 2006; *b* 24 June 1955. *Educ:* Univ. of Tokyo (BA 1978); Harvard Univ. (PhD 1985). Asst Prof., Dept of Econs, Univ. of Wisconsin-Madison, 1985–91; Lectr, Dept of Econs, LSE, 1989–91; Associate Prof., Dept of Econs, Univ. of Minnesota, 1991–97; Cassel Prof. of Econs, LSE, 1997–2006; Sen. Economist and Resident Schol., Fed. Reserve Bank of NY, 2005–06. Visiting Professor: LSE, 1995–96, 2010–11, 2015–16; Dept of Econs, MIT, 2000–01. Mem., Monetary Policy Panel, Federal Reserve Bank of NY, 2006–. *Address:* Department of Economics, Princeton University, Julis Romo Rabinowitz Building, Princeton, NJ 08544, USA.

**KLAUS, Prof. Václav;** President of Czech Republic, 2003–13; *b* 19 June 1941; *s* of Václav Klaus and Marie Klausová; *m* 1968, Livia Klausová; two *s*. *Educ:* Prague Sch. of Economics (Hon. Dr 1994); Cornell Univ. Researcher, Inst. of Econs, Czechoslovak Acad. of Scis, to 1970; Czechoslovak State Bank, 1971–86 (Head, Dept of Macroeconomic Policy); Inst. of Forecasting, Czechoslovak Acad. of Scis, 1987; founder, Civic Forum Movt (Chm., 1990–91); Minister of Finance, Czech Republic, 1989–92; Dep. Prime Minister, 1991–92; Prime Minister, 1992–97; Pres., Chamber of Deputies, 1998–2003. Chm., Civic Democratic Party, Czech Republic, 1991–2002. Vice-Chm., European Democratic Union, 1996–. Prof. of Finance, Prague Sch. of Economics, 1994. Hon. doctorates from Univs in USA, Canada, Guatemala, Mexico, Argentina, France, UK, Czech Republic, Germany; numerous awards from USA, Germany, France, Denmark, Austria, Switzerland, Czech Republic. *Publications:* A Road to Market Economy, 1991; Tomorrow's Challenge, 1991; Economic Theory and Economic Reform, 1991; Signale aus dem Herzen Europas, 1991; I Do Not Like Catastrophic Scenarios, 1991; Dismantling Socialism, 1992; Why Am I a Conservative?, 1992; The Year: how much is it in the history of the country?, 1993; The Czech Way, 1994; Rebirth of a Country, 1994; Summing Up to One, 1995; Tschechische Transformation & Europäische Integration, 1995; Economic Theory and Reality of Transformation Processes, 1995; Between the Past and the Future, 1996; Renaissance, 1997; The Defence of Forgotten Ideas, 1997; Thus Spoke Václav Klaus, 1998; Why I Am not a Social Democrat, 1998; The Country without Governing, 1999; The Way out of the Trap, 1999; From the Opposition Treaty to the Tolerance Patent, 2000; Europe from the Point of View of a Politician and an Economist, 2001; Conversations with Václav Klaus, 2001; The First Year, 2004; Europe of Václav Klaus, 2004; The Second Year, 2005; On the Road to Democracy, 2005. *Recreations:* tennis, ski-ing. *Address:* c/o Office of the President, Pražský hrad, 11908 Prague 1, Czech Republic.

**KLAUSNER, Laura Naomi J.;** *see* Janner-Klausner.

**KLEIN, Anita,** RE 1995 (ARE 1992); artist; President, Royal Society of Painter Printmakers, 2003–06; *b* Sydney, 14 Feb. 1960; *d* of Prof. Anthony George Klein and Mavis Klein; *m* 1984, Nigel Swift; two *d*. *Educ:* Chelsea Sch. of Art (Foundn Cert. 1979); Slade Sch. of Fine Art (Henrique Schol. 1982 and 1983; BA Hons Painting 1983; Higher Dip. Fine Art (Printmaking) 1985). Solo exhibitions include: paintings and prints: Creaser Gall., London, 1986; Printworks, Colchester, 1990; Wilson Hale, London, 1991; Royal Pavilion Contemp. Gall., Brighton, 1992; Woodlands Art Gall., 1993; Cambridge Contemp. Art, 1996, 1998, 2000, 2014; Advanced Graphics, London, 2010; Fine Art Partnership, London, 2010; Bankside Gall. and Menier Gall., London, 2010; Fine Art Partnership and Bankside Gall., 2011; RCM (and backdrop), 2012; Marine House, Beer, Devon, 2012; Galleri Bla, Linkoping, Sweden, 2013; Konst och Folk, Stockholm, 2013; Hayletts Contemp. Art, Essex, 2014; Eames Fine Art, London, 2014; Wetpaint Gall., Cirencester, 2015; prints: Leigh Gall., London, 1987; Tall House Gall., London, 1990; Victorian Artists Soc., Melbourne, 1992; Brighton Fest., Brighton Marina Arts Index, 1993; two person show (with Paula Rego), Gateway Arts Centre, Shrewsbury, 1995; CCA, Oxford, 1996; Leeds City Art Gall., 1997; New Ashgate Gall., Farnham, 1998; Old Town Gall., Tustin, Calif, 1999; Port Jackson Press, Melbourne, 1999, 2000; Pyramid Gall., York (and ceramics), 1999; Advanced Graphics, London, 2002 (retrospective exhibn, 20 Years of Printmaking), 2004; Oriel Wrecsam Gall., Wales, 2012, Printmaker in Focus, 2014; paintings: Royal Exchange Th., Manchester, 1994; Eur. Art Fair, Ghent, 1995; Beaux Arts, Bath, 1996,

1998; Helen Gory Gall., Melbourne, 2003; Boundary Gall., London, 2009; Bankside Gall., London, 2009; Story Mus., Oxford (and mural), 2012; Eames Fine Art, London, 2013, 2015, 2016, 2018, 2019; Marine House, Beer, Devon, 2015; paintings, drawings and watercolours: Boundary Gall., London, 2001 (and ceramics), 2002, 2004, 2006; Advanced Graphics, London, 2006, 2008; Bankside Gall., London, 2006; Royal Commonwealth Club, 2007; Chelsea and Westminster Hosp., 2008; linocuts: Fine Art Partnership, London, 2012; Birds Gall., Melbourne, 2013; Art Vault, Mildura, Australia, 2013; Eames Fine Art, London, 2017; *group exhibitions* include: Hayward Gall.; RA; ICA; Blond Fine Art; Contemp. Arts Soc.; Christies; Discerning Eye Exhibn, Mall Galls, London; Hunting Art Prizes, RCA; Cleveland Drawing Biennale; Glasgow Print Studio; London Art Fair; Barbican Concourse Gall.; *works in public collections* include: Collection of Prints and Drawings, BM; BL; Arts Council England. Trustee, Paintings in Hosps, 2007–. Joseph Webb Award, Royal Soc. of Painter Printmakers, 1984; John Purcell Award: for an outstanding print, Bankside Open, 1991; Nat. Print Exhibn, London, 1995; Univ. of Wales Purchase Prize, Nat. Print Exhibn, London, 2003; Print Block Prize, Masters Exhibn, Bankside Gall., 2018. Hon. RWS 2003. *Publications*: Anita Klein, Painter Printmaker, 2006; Anita Klein: Italian angels, 2009; Through the Looking Glass, 2011. *Recreations*: walking, cinema, visiting Italy, laughing, drinking red wine, playing with grandchildren. *T*: (020) 7407 5471, 07780 682841. *E*: anita@anitaklein.com, anitakleinart@gmail.com. *W*: www.anitaklein.com, www.twitter.com/anitakleinart, www.instagram.com/anitakleinart. *Club*: Chelsea Arts.

KLEIN, Calvin Richard; fashion designer; *b* 19 Nov. 1942; *s* of Leo Klein and Flore (*née* Stern); *m* 1st, 1964, Jayne Centre (marr. diss. 1974); one *d*; 2nd, 1986, Kelly Rector (marr. diss. 2006). *Educ*: Fashion Inst. of Technology, NY; High Sch. of Art and Design. Started own fashion business, 1968; Vice Chm., 1969, Consulting Creative Dir, 2003, Calvin Klein Inc. Dir, Fashion Inst. of Technology, 1975–. Numerous awards.

KLEIN, Deborah; Group Chief Marketing and Corporate Affairs Officer, Sky, since 2018; *b* Zimbabwe, 10 Aug. 1968; *d* of Len and Audrey Klein; *m* 2002, Max Cantor; one *s* one *d*. *Educ*: Brooklyn Primary Sch.; Pretoria High Sch. for Girls; Univ. of Cape Town (BBus Sci. (Econs and Mktg)). AC Nielson, 1990–92; strategic planner, Saatchi & Saatchi, 1993–97 (Dir, 1996–97); WCRS: Hd of Planning, 1997–2003; Chief Exec., 2004–08; Chm., 2008–14; Jt Chief Exec., Engine Gp, 2008–18; Chief Exec., Engine Europe and Asia, 2016–18. Member: WACL; Mktg Gp of GB. *Publications*: Women in Advertising, 2000. *Recreations*: yoga, cooking, walking, my children. *Address*: Sky plc, Grant Way, Isleworth TW7 5QD.

KLEIN, Prof. Jacob, PhD; FRSC; FInstP; Dr Lee's Professor of Physical Chemistry, University of Oxford, 2000–07, Professor Emeritus, since 2010; Professor, Weizmann Institute of Science, Israel, since 1987; *b* 20 Aug. 1949; *s* of Moshe Klein and Edna Klein (*née* Lipper); *m* 1974, Michele Castle; two *s* two *d*. *Educ*: in Israel; Whittingehame Coll., Brighton; St Catharine's Coll., Cambridge (BA 1st Cl. Hons Physics 1973; MA, PhD 1977). FRSC 2011. Mil. Service, Israel, 1967–70; Post-doctoral res., Weizmann Inst., Israel, 1977–80; Demonstrator, Cavendish Lab., and Fellow of St Catharine's Coll., Cambridge, 1980–84; Weizmann Institute, Israel: Sen. Scientist, 1980–84; Associate Prof., 1984–87; Chairman: Polymer Res. Dept, 1989–91; Scientific Council, 1998–2000; University of Oxford: Hd, Dept of Chemistry, 2000–05; Professorial Res. Fellow, 2008–10. MAE 2013; Mem., Israel Acad. of Scis and Humanities, 2016. FAPS 2003; FInstP 2004. Somach Sacks Prize, Weizmann Inst., 1983; Charles Vernon Boys Prize, Inst. Physics (GB), 1984; Jeanett and Samuel Lubel Prize, 1989; Internat. Kao Fellow (Japan), 1994; Ford Prize for Polymer Physics, APS, 1995; Kolthoff Prize, Technion Israel Inst. of Technology, 2007; Prize of Excellence, Israel Chem. Soc., 2010; Soft Matter and Biophysical Chem. Prize, RSC, 2011; Tribology Gold Medal, Tribology Trust/IMechE, 2012; David Turnbull Award, Materials Res. Soc., 2015; Triennial Liquid Matter Prize, Eur. Physical Soc., 2017. *Publications*: contrib. numerous papers to scientific jls, etc. *Recreations*: reading, family holidays, hiking. *Address*: 1 Ruppin Street, Rehovot 76353, Israel; Materials & Interfaces Department, Weizmann Institute of Science, Rehovot 76100, Israel; Physical and Theoretical Chemistry Laboratory, South Parks Road, Oxford OX1 3QZ.

KLEIN, Jonathan David; Co-Founder, since 1995 and Chairman, since 2015, Getty Images Inc. (Chief Executive Officer, 1995–2015); *b* 13 May 1960; *s* of Louis and Hilda Klein; *m* 1988, Deborah Ann Hunter; three *s*. *Educ*: Trinity Hall, Cambridge (MA). Hambros Bank Ltd, 1983–98: Dir, 1989–93; non-exec. Dir, 1993–98. *Recreations*: all sports, global health, adolescent education, theatre, press freedom, the Third World. *Address*: 760 Park Avenue, New York, NY 10021, USA.

KLEIN, Prof. Michael Lawrence, PhD; FRS 2003; Laura H. Carnell Professor of Science, and Director, Institute for Computational Molecular Science, Temple University, Philadelphia, since 2009; *b* 13 March 1940; *s* of Jack Klein and Bessie Klein (*née* Bloomberg); *m* 1962, Brenda Woodman (*d* 2018); two *d*. *Educ*: Bristol Univ. (BSc Hons 1961; PhD Chemistry 1964). Assoc. Res. Officer, 1968–74, Sen. Res. Officer, 1974–85, Prin. Res. Officer, 1985–87, Chemistry Div., NRCC, Ottawa; University of Pennsylvania, Philadelphia: Prof. of Chemistry, 1987–91; William Smith Prof. of Chemistry, 1991–93; Earle Hepburn Prof. of Physical Sci., and Dir, Lab. for Res. on the Structure of Matter, 1993–2009. Fellow Commoner, Trinity Coll., Cambridge, 1985–86; Louis Néel Prof., Ecole Normale Supérieure, Lyon, 1988; Guggenheim Fellow, 1989–90; Sen. Humboldt Fellow, Max Planck Inst., Stuttgart, 1995; Miller Prof., Univ. of Calif., Berkeley, 1997; Linnett Vis. Prof., Univ. of Cambridge, 1998; Schlumberger Prof., Oxford and Cambridge, 2003. Associate Fellow, Acad. of Scis for the Developing World, 2004–. FInstP 2003; FRSCan 1984; FCIC 1979; Fellow, American Acad. of Arts and Scis, 2003; Mem., NAS, 2009. Honorary Fellow: Indian Acad. of Scis, 2006; Trinity Coll., Cambridge, 2013. Computational Physics Prize, APS, 1999; CECAM Prize, 2004; Physical Chemistry Prize, ACS, 2008; Boys-Rahman Award, RSC, 2011. *Publications*: over 600 articles in scientific jls and books. *Address*: Institute for Computational Molecular Science, SERC Building 704E, Temple University, 1925 North 12th Street, Philadelphia, PA 19122, USA. *E*: mlklein@temple.edu.

KLEIN, Richard Henry; Head of Documentaries (UK and International), Plimsoll Productions, since 2018; *b* Burwash Common, Sussex, 12 Oct. 1958; *s* of Hans Joachim Klein and Bernadine Klein (*née* Thorne); one *d*. *Educ*: Prior Park Coll.; Aberdeen Univ. (MA Hons English 1983); City Univ. (Dip. Journalism 1985). Bank clerk, Lloyds Bank; researcher, reporter, then Dir, Weekend World, LWT, 1987–90; joined BBC TV as series producer, 1996; Commng Ed., Documentaries, 2005–07; Hd, Ind. Commng, Factual TV, 2007–08; Controller, BBC Four, 2008–13; Dir, Factual, ITV, 2013–16; Creative Dir, IWC Media, 2016–18. *Recreations*: cycling, reading, rock music, hill walking, theatre. *Address*: 83 Chesson Road, W14 9QS.

KLEIN, Prof. Rudolf Ewald, CBE 2001; FBA 2006; Professor of Social Policy, University of Bath, 1978–98, now Emeritus; *b* 26 Aug. 1930; *o s* of Robert and Martha Klein; *m* 1st, 1957, Josephine Parfitt (*d* 1996); one *d*; 2nd, 2012, Ans Ankone. *Educ*: Bristol Grammar Sch.; Merton Coll., Oxford (Postmaster) (Gibbs Schol. 1950; MA). Leader Writer, London Evening Standard, 1952–62; Editor, 'The Week', Leader Writer, Home Affairs Editor, The Observer, 1962–72; Research Associate, Organisation of Medical Care Unit, London Sch. of Hygiene and Tropical Medicine, 1972–73; Sen. Fellow, Centre for Studies in Social Policy, 1973–78; Professorial Fellow, then Sen. Associate, King's Fund, 1995–2001. Visiting Professor: LSE, 1996–2013; LSHTM, 2001–17. Member: Wiltshire AHA, 1980–82; Bath DHA, 1982–84. Jt Editor, Political Quarterly, 1981–87. Foreign Associate, Inst. of Medicine, NAS, USA, 2001. FMedSci 2006. Hon. DArts Oxford Brookes, 1998. Margaret E. Mahoney Award, Commonwealth Fund, NY, 1999. *Publications*: Complaints Against Doctors, 1973; (ed) Social Policy and Public Expenditure, 1974; (ed) Inflation and Priorities, 1975; (with Janet Lewis) The Politics of Consumer Representation, 1976; The Politics of the NHS, 1983; (ed with Michael O'Higgins) The Future of Welfare, 1985; (with Patricia Day) Accountabilities, 1987; (with Linda Challis et al) Joint Approaches to Social Policy, 1988; (with Patricia Day) Inspecting the Inspectorates, 1990; (with Neil Carter and Patricia Day) How organisations measure success, 1991; (with Patricia Day and David Henderson) Home Rules, 1993; The New Politics of the NHS, 1995, 7th edn 2013; (with Patricia Day and Sharon Redmayne) Managing Scarcity, 1996; papers on public policy, health policy and public expenditure in various jls. *Recreations*: opera, cooking, football. *Address*: 12A Laurier Road, NW5 1SG. *T*: (020) 7428 9767.

KLEIN, Suzy; broadcaster and writer; *b* London, 1 April 1975; *d* of Barry and Alison Klein; *m* 2005, James Fischelis; one *s* one *d*. *Educ*: S Hampstead High Sch., London; St Hugh's Coll., Oxford (BA 1st Cl. Hons Music); City Univ., London (Postgrad. Dip. Broadcast Journalism). Researcher, BBC Radio 4, 1997–98; BBC Television: Asst Producer, Arts, 1998–2000; Producer, Classical Music, 2001–08. Presenter: Proms, BBC TV; The Review Show, BBC2; Saturday Live, BBC Radio 4; Sky Arts TV; Leeds Piano Competition, BBC TV, In Tune, BBC Radio 3; Rule Britannia! (series), BBC TV, 2014; What a Performance!, BBC4, 2015; Musical Masters of the 19th Century, BBC4, 2016; Tunes for Tyrants, BBC Radio 4, 2017; Our Classical Century, BBC4, 2018. Feature writer and reviewer for The Guardian, New Statesman, BBC Music Mag. *Publications*: (jtly) What's That? Contemporary Arts for Children, 2011; (jtly) What is Contemporary Art? A Children's Guide, 2012. *Recreations*: walking, opera, concerts, wine, explaining complex existential matters to inquisitive 4 year-olds. *Address*: BBC Broadcasting House, W1A 1AA. *E*: suzy.klein@bbc.co.uk.

KLEINMAN, Mark Daniel; City Editor, Sky News, since 2009; *b* London, 25 April 1977; *s* of Louis Kleinman and Jacqueline Kleinman (*née* Cooper-Smith); partner, Barbara Serra. *Educ*: Eaglesfield Sch.; Univ. of York (BA Hons Eng. 1998). Reporter: Leisure Week, 1998–99; Precision Marketing, 1999–2000; Reporter, then Chief Reporter, Marketing, 2000–03; Business Correspondent: Sunday Express, 2004; Sunday Times, 2004–06; Asia Business Editor, Daily Telegraph and Sunday Telegraph, 2006–08; City Editor, Sunday Telegraph, 2008–09. Business Journalist of the Year, London Press Club, 2011. *Recreations*: football (supporter of Charlton Athletic), tennis, film, travel. *Address*: Sky News, 2nd Floor, 4 Millbank, SW1P 3JA. *T*: (020) 7032 2833. *E*: Mark.Kleinman@bskyb.com. *Club*: Soho House.

KLEINWORT, Sir Richard (Drake), 4th Bt *cr* 1909, of Bolnore, Cuckfield, Sussex; DL; Chairman, Richard Kleinwort Consultancy Group, since 2001; Member, Advisory Board, Kleinwort Hambros (formerly Kleinwort Benson), since 2011; *b* 4 Nov. 1960; *s* of Sir Kenneth Drake Kleinwort, 3rd Bt and his 1st wife, Lady Davina Pepys (*d* 1973), *d* of 7th Earl of Cottenham; *S* father, 1994; *m* 1989, Lucinda, *d* of William Shand Kydd; three *s* one *d*. *Educ*: Stowe; Exeter Univ. (BA). Kleinwort Benson, Geneva, 1979; Banco General de Negocios, Buenos Aires, 1983; Deutsche Bank AG, Hamburg and Frankfurt, 1985–88; Biss Lancaster plc, 1988–89; Grandfield Rork Collins Financial, 1989–91; Partner, 1991–94, Dir, 1994–2000, Cardew & Co.; Head of Financial PR, Ogilvy PR Worldwide, 2000–01. Non-exec. Dir, RDF Gp plc, 2008–10; non-exec. Chm., Hungry Hamsters Ltd, film prodn co., 2009–11; Vice Chm., Cubitt Consulting, 2010–18. President: Haywards Heath Hospital, 1991–97; The Little Black Bag Housing Assoc., 1991–. Dir, Steppes East Gp, 1998–. Life Mem., British Field Sports Soc., 1981; Member: WWF (1001) Club, 1979– (Mem., Council of Ambassadors, WWF, 2005–); S of England Agricl Soc., 1988–; RHS, 1991–; Sussex Club, 1996–; Countryside Alliance, 1997–; Compagnie Internat. de la Chasse, 1998–. Chm., Knepp Castle Polo Club, 1997–2006. Fellow, World Scout Foundn, Geneva, 1989. Mem., Instn of King Edward VII Hosp., Midhurst, 1992–2000; Trustee: Ernest Kleinwort Charitable Trust, 1988–; Patron: Cuckfield Soc., 1995–; Ackroyd Trust, 1995– (Trustee); Vice Patron, Sussex Young Cricketers Educn Trust, 2008–; Vice Pres., Chichester Cathedral Millennium Endowment Appeal, 1998–2005. Ambassador, The Prince's Trust, 1998–. Gov., Stowe Sch., 1999–2004 (Chairman: Foundn Appeal; Stowe Sch. Foundn, 1999–; Campaign for Stowe, 1999–2004). Pres., S of England Agricl Soc., 2019. DL 2005, High Sheriff 2008–09, W Sussex. *Recreations*: travel, my family, laughter, shooting, gardening, farming, watching England winning any sport. *Heir*: *s* Rufus Drake Kleinwort, *b* 16 Aug. 1994. *Clubs*: White's, MCC.

KLEISTERLEE, Gerard Johannes; Chairman, Vodafone Group plc, since 2011; *b* Ludwigsburg, 28 Sept. 1946; *m* 1971, Annemieke Janssen; one *s* two *d*. *Educ*: Eindhoven Tech. Univ. (Masters Electronic Engrg). Philips Electronics NV: various posts, 1974–96; Country Chm., Taiwan/China and Regl Pres., Philips Components Asia Pacific, 1996–99; CEO, Philips Components, 1999–2000; Exec. Vice Pres. and Chief Operating Officer, 2000–01; Chm. and CEO, 2001–11. Ind. Dir, Vivendi, 2002–05; non-executive Director: Dutch Central Bank, 2006–12; Daimler AG, 2009–14; Royal Dutch Shell, 2010–; Dell, 2011–13; IBEX Global Solutions, 2014–17; ASML Hldg NV, 2015–. Member: Asia Business Council, 2002–; World 50 Prog., 2011–19. Chm., Cancer Foundn Amsterdam, 2002–11. Hon. Dr Catholic Univ. of Leuven, 2005. Eur. Businessman of Year, Fortune mag., 2007. *Recreation*: opera. *Address*: Vodafone Group plc, Vodafone House, The Connection, Newbury, Berks RG14 2FN.

KLEMPERER, Prof. Paul David, PhD; FBA 1999; Edgeworth Professor of Economics, University of Oxford, since 1995; Fellow, Nuffield College, Oxford, since 1995; *b* 15 Aug. 1956; *s* of late Hugh G. Klemperer and Ruth M. M. Klemperer (*née* Jordan); *m* 1989, Margaret Meyer; two *s* one *d*. *Educ*: King Edward's Sch., Birmingham; Peterhouse, Cambridge (BA Engrg, 1st Cl. Hons with Dist., 1978); Stanford Univ. (MBA 1982 (Top Student Award); PhD Econs 1986). Consultant, Andersen Consulting, 1978–80; Harkness Fellow, Commonwealth Fund, 1980–82; Oxford University: Univ. Lectr in Operations Res. and Mathematical Econs, 1985–90; Reader in Econs, 1990–95; John Thomson Fellow and Tutor, St Catherine's Coll., 1985–95. Visiting positions: MIT, 1987; Berkeley, 1991, 1993; Stanford, 1991, 1993; Yale, 1994; Princeton, 1998. Mem., UK Competition Commn, 2001–05. Consultant: UK Radiocommunications Agency (principal auction theorist for UK 3G auction, 2000), 1997–2000; US Federal Trade Commn, 1999–2001; Bank of England, 2007–; US Treasury, 2008–09; Bank of Canada, 2009; Advr to EU, US, UK, and other govts and private firms. Mem., Council, Royal Econ. Soc., 2001–05. Foreign Hon. Mem., Amer. Acad. of Arts and Scis, 2005; Hon. Mem., Argentine Economic Assoc., 2006. Fellow: Econometric Soc., 1994 (Mem. Council, 2001–06); European Economic Assoc., 2004 (Mem. Council, 2002–07). Hon. Fellow, ESRC Centre for Econ. Learning and Social Evolution, 2001. Editor, RAND Jl of Econs, 1993–99; Associate Editor or Member, Editorial Board: Rev. of Econ. Studies, 1989–97; Jl of Industrial Econs, 1989–96; Oxford Econ. Papers, 1986–2000; Internat. Jl of Industrial Orgn, 1993–2000; Eur. Econ. Rev., 1997–2001; Rev. of Econ. Design, 1997–2000; Econ.

Policy, 1998–99; Econ. Jl, 2000–04; Frontiers in Econs, 2000–; BE Jl of Econ. Analysis and Policy, 2001–; Jl of Competition Law and Econs, 2004–. *Publications:* The Economic Theory of Auctions, 2000; Auctions: theory and practice, 2004; articles in econs jls on industrial organization, auction theory, and other econ. theory and policy. *Address:* Nuffield College, Oxford OX1 1NF. *T:* (01865) 278588. *E:* paul.klemperer@economics.ox.ac.uk.

**KLENERMAN, Sir David,** Kt 2019; PhD; FRS 2012; Professor of Biophysical Chemistry, University of Cambridge; Fellow, Christ's College, Cambridge, since 1994; *s* of late Leslie Klenerman and Naomi Klenerman. *Educ:* Christ's Coll., Cambridge (BA 1982); Churchill Coll., Cambridge (PhD 1986). Fulbright Schol., Stanford Univ.; Laser Spectroscopy Gp, BP Research; Univ. of Cambridge. Co-founded, Solexa, 1998. FMedSci 2015. *Publications:* contribs to learned jls incl. Proc. NAS, Biophysics Jl, Nature Methods, Jl Biol Chem., Nature Structural and Molecular Biol. *Address:* Department of Chemistry, University of Cambridge, Lensfield Road, Cambridge CB2 1EW.

**KLENERMAN, Prof. Paul,** DM, DPhil; FRCP, FRCPath; Sidney Truelove Professor of Gastroenterology, University of Oxford, since 2015; Fellow, Green Templeton College, Oxford, since 2015; *b* London, 26 March 1963; *s* of late Leslie Klenerman and Naomi Klenerman; *m* 1999, Sally Morse; one *s* one *d*. *Educ:* Clare Coll., Cambridge (BA 1985); Univ. of Oxford (BM BCh Clin. Medicine 1988; DPhil 1995; DM 2003). MRCP 1991; MRCPath 2001. Univ. of Oxford, 1992; Univ. Zurich; Wellcome Trust Sen. Res. Fellow, Nuffield Dept of Medicine, 2000–15, Prof. of Immunology, until 2015, Univ. of Oxford; Fellow, Brasenose Coll., Oxford, until 2015. Hon. Consultant Physician, Oxford, 2001–. FMedSci 2013. *Publications:* articles in gen. biosci., med. and immunol. jls. *Recreations:* fencing, triathlon, IMMposters (sax and fiddle). *Address:* Peter Medawar Building for Pathogen Research, University of Oxford, South Parks Road, Oxford OX1 3SY. *T:* (01865) 281885. *E:* paul.klenerman@ndm.ox.ac.uk.

**KLEOPAS, Myrna Y.;** Member, Committee against Torture, Office of the High Commissioner for Human Rights, 2008–11 (Rapporteur, 2008); *b* Nicosia, 23 Aug. 1944; *m* Yiangos P. Kleopas; one *s* one *d*. Called to the Bar, practised law in Cyprus, 1971–77; Legal Advr, Min. of Foreign Affairs, Cyprus, 1977–79; entered Cyprus Foreign Service, 1979; Pol Affairs Div., Min. of Foreign Affairs, 1979–80; Counsellor, 1980–86, Consul-Gen., 1981–86, London; Pol Affairs Div., 1986–90; Rep. of Min. of Foreign Affairs to Central Agency for Women's Rights, Cyprus, 1988; Rep. of Cyprus to UN Commn on Status of Women, 1989; Dir, Office of Perm. Sec., Min. of Foreign Affairs, 1990–93; Ambassador to China, and also to Japan, Pakistan, Mongolia and the Philippines, 1993–96; Dir, Pol Affairs Div. (Cyprus Question), Min. of Foreign Affairs, 1996–97; Ambassador to Italy, and also to Switzerland, Malta and San Marino, 1997–2000; High Comr in the UK, 2000–04. *Recreations:* reading, the arts, swimming, walking. *Address:* Office of the High Commissioner for Human Rights, Palais des Nations, 1211 Geneva 10, Switzerland.

**KLOOTWIJK, Jaap;** Managing Director, Shell UK Oil, and Joint Managing Director, Shell UK, 1983–88; *b* 16 Nov. 1932; *s* of J. L. Klootwijk and W. J. Boer. *Educ:* Rotterdam Grammar Sch.; Technological Univ., Delft (MSc Mech. Eng, 1956). Lieut Royal Netherlands Navy, 1956–58. Joined Royal Dutch/Shell Gp, 1958; worked in various capacities in Holland, UK, France, Switzerland, Sweden, Algeria, Kenya; Area Co-ordinator, SE Asia, 1976–79; Man. Dir, Shell Internat. Gas Ltd, 1979–82; Chm., UK Oil Pipelines, 1983–88. Pres., UK Petroleum Industry Assoc., 1985–87. Director: The Flyfishers' Co. Ltd, 1985–94; Grove Hldgs Ltd, 1991–2001. *Recreations:* shooting, fishing, reading. *Address:* 46 Oak Lodge, Chantry Square, W8 5UL. *T:* (020) 7937 6099. *Club:* Flyfishers' (Pres., 1985–87).

**KLOSE, Hans-Ulrich;** Member (SPD), Bundestag, Germany, 1983–2013; *b* 14 June 1937; *m* 1992, Dr Anne Steinbeck-Klose; two *s* two *d* by former marriages. *Educ:* Bielefeld; Clinton, Iowa; Freiburg Univ.; Hamburg Univ. (Law graduate 1965). Joined SPD 1964; Dep. Chm., Young Socialists, 1966; Dep. Chm., SPD, 1968; Mayor of Hamburg, 1974–81; Treasurer, SPD, 1987–91. Bundestag: Leader of the Opposition, 1991–94; Vice-Pres., 1994–98; Chm., 1998–2002, Vice-Chm., 2002–13, Cttee on Foreign Affairs; Chm., German-American Parly Gp, 2003–13. *Publications:* Altern der Gesellschaft, 1993; Altern hat Zukunft, 1993; poetry (3 vols), 1997, 1999, 2007. *Address:* Schloßstrasse 67A, 14059 Berlin, Germany.

**KLUG, Francesca Marilyn Simone,** OBE 2002; Professorial Research Fellow, London School of Economics, 2001–15 (Visiting Professor, since 2015); *b* 16 Dec. 1953; *d* of Isaac and Bertha Klug; *m* 1993, Michael Shew; one *d*. *Educ:* London Sch. of Econs (BSc Sociol.). Res. and Information Officer, Runnymede Trust, 1980–84; Policy Advr, Hackney Council, 1984–89; Dir, Civil Liberties Trust, 1989–92; Res. Fellow, Human Rights Centre, Essex Univ., 1992–96; Sen. Res. Fellow, Law Sch., KCL, 1996–2001. Vis. Prof., Sheffield Hallam Univ., 2018–. Mem., Commn for Equality and Human Rights, 2007–09. Chair, Freedom from Torture, 2016–17. *Publications:* (jtly) The Three Pillars of Liberty, Political Rights and Freedoms in the UK, 1996; Values for a Godless Age: the history of the Human Rights Act and its political and legal consequences, 2000; A Magna Carta for All Humanity: homing in on human rights, 2015; contribs to national press, various anthologies and jls incl. Public Law, Eur. Human Rights Law Rev., Policy and Politics. *Recreations:* reading, walking our dog Ruby with my daughter Tania, having fun with friends. *Address:* London School of Economics, Houghton Street, WC2A 2AE. *T:* (020) 7955 6429. *E:* f.m.klug@lse.ac.uk.

**KLYBERG, Rt Rev. Mgr Charles John;** *b* 29 July 1931; *s* of late Captain Charles Augustine Klyberg, MN and Ivy Lilian Waddington, LRAM; unmarried. *Educ:* Eastbourne College. Eaton Hall OCS, 1953; 2nd Lieut, 1st Bn The Buffs, Kenya Emergency, 1953–54; Lieut 1955. MRICS. Asst Estates Manager, Cluttons, 1954–57. Lincoln Theological Coll., 1957–60. Curate, S John's, East Dulwich, 1960–63; Rector of Fort Jameson, Zambia, 1963–67; Vicar, Christ Church and S Stephen, Battersea, 1967–77; Dean of Lusaka Cathedral, Zambia, and Rector of the parish, 1977–85, Dean Emeritus, 1985; Vicar General, 1978–85; Bishop Suffragan of Fulham, 1985–96; first Archdeacon of Charing Cross, 1989–96. Received into RC Ch and ordained priest, 1996; Prelate of Honour, 2000. UK Commissary for Anglican Church in Zambia, 1985–89. Chairman: Church Property Development Gp, 1978–85; Fulham Palace Museum Trust, 1991–96. Pres., Guild of All Souls, 1988–95. Guardian, Shrine of Our Lady of Walsingham, 1991–96. Warden, Quainton Hall Sch., Harrow, 1992–96. *Recreations:* reading, music, travel. *Club:* Athenæum.

**KNAPMAN, Dr Paul Anthony;** DL; FRCP, FRCS, FFFLM; HM Coroner for Westminster, 1980–2011 (Jurisdiction of Inner West London); *b* 5 Nov. 1944; *s* of Frederick Ethelbert and Myra Knapman; *m* 1970, Penelope Jane Cox; one *s* three *d*. *Educ:* Epsom Coll.; King's Coll., London; St George's Hosp. Med. Sch. (MB, BS 1968). MRCS, LRCP 1968; DMJ 1975; FRCP 1998; FRCS 1999; FFFLM 2003. Called to the Bar, Gray's Inn, 1972. Dep. Coroner for Inner W London, 1975–80. Hon. Lectr in Med. Jurisprudence, St George's Hosp. Med. Sch., 1978–2004; Hon. Clinical Teacher (Forensic Medicine), Royal Free and UC (formerly Middlesex and UCH) Med. Sch., 1981–2004; Hon. Clinical Sen. Lectr, ICSTM (formerly Westminster and Charing Cross Med. Sch.), 1987–2006. Langdon-Brown Lectr, RCP, 1998; Christmas Lectr, ICSTM, 1999. Legal Member: Mental Health Rev. Tribunal, 1978–88; Med. Appeal Tribunal, 1982–88; Disability Appeal Tribunal, 1988–89; Coroner Mem., Nat. Confidential Enquiry into Peri-Operative Deaths, 1995–2001. Chm., Mgt Cttee, Coroner's Ct Support Service, 2004–11 (Trustee, 2004–11). Member: Medicolegal Soc., 1971–; Chelsea Clin. Soc., 1977–; British Acad. of Forensic Scis, 1980– (Mem. Council, 1983–86); Soc. of Doctors of Law, 1989–; Exams Bd, Soc. of Apothecaries, 1994–2012. President: S Eastern England Coroners' Soc., 1980; Sect. of Clinical Forensic Medicine, RSocMed, 1995–97; Coroners' Soc. of England and Wales, 2008–09 (Mem., 1975–; Mem. Council, 1989–). Trustee: David Isaacs Fund, 1980–2011. Fellow, Med. Soc. of London, 2002–. Gov., London Nautical Sch., 1981–99 (Chm., 1995–99); Pres., Old Epsomian Club, 1999–2000. Liveryman, 1982–, and Mem., Ct of Assistants, 1993–, Soc. of Apothecaries (Master, 2006–07). DL Greater London, 2007; Rep. DL for City of Westminster (Commn of Gtr London), 2013–. Hon. Col, Westminster Dragoons (Comd and Support Sqdn), Royal Yeo., 2016–. Specialist Editor (Coroners Law), JP Reports, 1990–. *Publications:* (jtly) Coronership: the law and practice on coroners, 1985; Medicine and the Law, 1989; Casebook on Coroners, 1989; Sources of Coroners' Law, 1999; contributor to: Medical Negligence, 1990, 3rd edn 2000; Atkin's Court Forms, vol. 13, 1992, 3rd edn 2000; papers on medico-legal subjects. *Recreations:* boating, beagling, travel and family life. *Clubs:* Athenæum, Garrick; RNVR Yacht; Thurlestone Golf.

**KNAPMAN, Roger Maurice;** Leader, UK Independence Party, 2002–06 (Political Adviser, 2000–02); *b* 20 Feb. 1944; *m* 1967, Carolyn Trebell (*née* Eastman); one *s* one *d*. *Educ:* Royal Agricl Coll., Cirencester. FRICS 1967. MP (C) Stroud, 1987–97; contested (C) same seat, 1997; contested (UK Ind): N Devon, 2001; Totnes, 2005. PPS to Minister of State for Armed Forces, 1991–93; an Asst Govt Whip, 1995–96; a Lord Comr of HM Treasury (Govt Whip), 1996–97. Vice-Chm., Cons. backbench European Affairs Cttee, 1989–90; Mem., Select Cttee on Agric., 1994–95. MEP (UK Ind) SW Reg., 2004–09. Mem., AFRC, 1991–94. *Address:* Lower Crockers, Crockers Hele, Meeth, Okehampton, Devon EX20 3QN.

**KNAPP, Trevor Frederick William Beresford;** Director, KADE, since 1997; *b* 26 May 1937; *s* of Frederick William Knapp and Linda Knapp (*née* Poffley); *m* 1st, 1964, Margaret Fry; one *s* one *d*; 2nd, 2013, Eileen Poole. *Educ:* Christ's Hospital; King's College London (BSc 1958). MRSC (ARIC 1960), CChem. Ministry of Aviation, 1961; Sec., Downey Cttee, 1965–66; Sec., British Defence Research and Supply Staff, Canberra, 1968–72; Asst Sec., MoD, 1974; GEC Turbine Generators Ltd, 1976; Central Policy Review Staff, 1977–79; Ministry of Defence: Under-Sec., 1983; Dir Gen. (Marketing), 1983–88; Asst Under Sec. of State (Supply and Organisation) (Air), 1988–91; Asst Under-Sec. of State (Infrastructure and Logistics), 1992–96. Member Board: Waltham Abbey Royal Gunpowder Mills Co., 1997–2012 (Chm., 1998–2012); Waltham Abbey Trust, 1997–; Trustee: Bromley Voluntary Sector Trust, 1999–2014 (Chm., 2003–14); Bromley MIND, 2006–14. *Address:* c/o National Westminster Bank, Strand, WC2H 5JB.

**KNATCHBULL,** family name of **Earl Mountbatten of Burma.**

**KNATCHBULL, Hon. Philip Wyndham Ashley;** Chief Executive Officer, Curzon World Ltd (formerly Curzon Cinemas Ltd), since 2006; *b* London, 2 Dec. 1961; *s* of 7th Baron Brabourne, CBE and Countess Mountbatten of Burma, CBE, CD; *m* 1st, 1991 (marr. diss.); one *d*; 2nd, 2002, Wendy Wills; two *s*. *Educ:* Dragon Sch.; Gordonstoun Sch. CEO, Front Page Films, 1983–94; Chm., Showcase Cinemas, 1989; Dir, Silicon Media Gp (formerly Network Media Television), 1997–2001; CEO, Knatchbull Communications Gp, 1997–2006. *E:* info@knatchbull.com.
*See also* Earl Mountbatten of Burma, A. A. S. Zuckerman.

**KNEALE, (Robert) Bryan (Charles),** MBE 2019; RA 1974 (ARA 1970); sculptor; Professor of Drawing, Royal College of Art, 1990–95; *b* 19 June 1930; *m* 1956, Doreen Lister (*d* 1998); one *d* (one *s* decd). *Educ:* Douglas High Sch.; Douglas Sch. of Art, IOM; Royal Academy Schools: Rome prize, 1949–51; RA diploma. Tutor, RCA Sculpture Sch., 1964–; Head of Sculpture Sch., Hornsey, 1967; Assoc. Lectr, Chelsea Sch. of Art, 1970. Fellow RCA, 1972, Sen. Fellow, 1995; Head of Sculpture Dept, RCA, 1985–90 (Sen. Tutor, 1980–85); Royal Academy: Master of Sculpture, 1982–85; Prof. of Sculpture, 1985–90; Trustee, 1995–2007. Member: Fine Art Panels, NCAD, 1964–71, Arts Council, 1971–73, CNAA, 1974–82; Chm., Air and Space, 1972–73. *Organised:* Sculpture '72, RA, 1972; Battersea Park Silver Jubilee Sculpture, 1977 (also exhibited); Sade Exhibn, Cork, 1982. *Exhibitions:* Redfern Gallery, 1954, 1956, 1958, 1960, 1962, 1964, 1967, 1970, 1976, 1978, 1981; 1983; John Moores, 1961; Sixth Congress of Internat. Union of Architects, 1961; Art Aujourd'hui, Paris, 1963; Battersea Park Sculpture, 1963, 1966; Profile III Bochum, 1964; British Sculpture in the Sixties, Tate Gall., 1965; Whitechapel Gall. 1966 (retrospective), 1981; Structure, Cardiff Metamorphis Coventry, 1966; New British Painting and Sculpture, 1967–68; City of London Festival, 1968; Holland Park, Sculpture in the Cities, Southampton, and British Sculptors, RA, 1972; Holland Park, 1973, 2000; Royal Exchange Sculpture Exhibition, 1974; New Art, Hayward Gallery, 1975; Sculpture at Worksop, 1976; Taranman Gall., 1977, 1981; Serpentine Gall., 1978; Compass Gall., Glasgow, 1981; 51 Gall., Edinburgh, 1981; Bath Art Fair, 1981; Henry Moore Gall., RCA (retrospective), 1986; Fitzwilliam Mus., 1987; Sala Uno, Rome, 1988; Chichester Fest., 1988; New Art Centre, 1990; Nat. History Mus., 1991; Manx Mus., 1992; RWA (retrospective), 1995; Angela Flowers Gall., 1998; 70th Birthday Exhibn, Roche Court, 2000; Eye of the Storm, Turin, 2000; Hart Gall., 2002, 2004; Cass Sculpture Foundn, London, 2005; Royal British Sculptors Gall., 2010; Aspects of Drawing, RA, 2011; Phoenix Beaux Arts Gall., Cork St, 2011; Martini Arte Internazionale, Parco Culturale Le Serre, Turin, 2011; Crucible Exhibn, Gloucester Cathedral, 2012, 2014; Gall. Pangolin, 2015, 2016, 2017; *commissions:* LCC, Fenwick Place, 1961; Loughborough campus, 1962; Camberwell Beauty Liby, Old Kent Rd, 1964; Hall Caine Meml, Douglas, 1971; King Edward Sch., Totnes, 1972; Woodside Sculpture, Gloversville, NY, 1972–73; Monumental Sculpture for Manx Millennium, Ronaldsway, IOM, 1979; Wall Sculpture for Govt Bldgs, Douglas, IOM, 1996; Sculpture at Goodwood Sculpture Park, 1996; Bronze doors, Portsmouth Cathedral, 1997; Relief Sculpture for Westminster Cath., 1999; Sculpture for Villa Marina, Douglas, IOM, 2003; Sculpture for New Nobles Hosp., IOM, 2004; Trafalgar Meml Sculpture, Castletown, IOM, 2005; Meml to Illiam Dhone, Malew Ch, IOM, 2006; Sculpture for Rio Tinto Zinc HQ, Paddington, 2008. Arts Council Tours, 1966–71. *Collections:* Arts Council of GB; Contemp. Art Soc.; Manx Museum; Leics Educn Authority; Nat. Galls of Victoria, S Australia and New Zealand; City Art Galls, York, Nottingham, Manchester, Bradford and Leicester; Tate Gall.; Beaverbrook Foundn, Fredericton; Museum of Modern Art, São Paulo, Brazil; Bahia Museum, Brazil; Oriel Coll., Oxford; Museum of Modern Art, New York; City Galleries, Middlesbrough, Birmingham, Wakefield; Fitzwilliam Museum, Cambridge; W Riding Educn Authority; Unilever House Collection; Walker Art Gallery; Nat. History Mus., Taiwan; Nat. History Mus., London. Marsh Award for Public Sculpture, Public Monuments and Sculpture Assoc., 2007. *Address:* Pangolin London, Kings Place, 90 York Way, N1 9AG; Hart Gallery, 113 Upper Street, N1 1QN.

**KNEBWORTH, Viscount;** Philip Anthony Scawen Lytton; *b* 7 March 1989; *s* and heir of Earl of Lytton, *qv*.

**KNEEBONE, Prof. Roger Lister**, PhD; FRCS, FRCSE, FRCGP; Professor of Surgical Education and Engagement Science, Imperial College London, since 2011; Wellcome Trust Engagement Fellow, since 2012; Professor of Anatomy, Royal Academy of Arts, since 2019; *b* London, 1 Feb. 1954; *s* of Geoffrey Thomas Kneebone and Eileen Margaret Kneebone (*née* Lister); *m* 1979, Danuta Sarah McKay; two *d*. *Educ:* Westminster Sch.; St Andrews Univ. (BSc Med. Sci. 1974); Univ. of Manchester (MB ChB 1977); Univ. of Bath (PhD 2002). DRCOG 1981; FRCSE 1985; FRCS 1986; MRCGP 1987, FRCGP 2006. House Surgeon and Physician, Wrexham, 1977; Anatomy Demonstrator, Univ. of Manchester, 1978–79; SHO, in Orthopaedics and A&E, 1979–80, in Obstetrics and Gynaecol., 1980–81, Nottingham Univ. Hosp.; Surgical Registrar: Baragwanath Hosp., Johannesburg, 1981–84; Groote Schuur Hosp., Cape Town, 1984–86; Consultant Surgeon and Hd, Trauma Unit, Red Cross Children's Hosp., Cape Town, 1986; GP Trainee, St Chad Health Centre, Lichfield, 1986–87; GP Principal, Lovemead Gp Practice, Trowbridge, 1987–2003; Imperial College London: Clinical Sen. Lectr, 2003–08, Reader, 2008–11, in Surgical Educn. Hon. Lectr, 1997–2000, Hon. Sen. Lectr, 2000, Univ. of Bath; Visiting Professor: Univ. of Toronto, 1998; Lee Kong Chian Sch. of Medicine, Singapore, 2012; Gresham Coll., 2018–19; RCA; Affiliated Schol., Wilson Centre for Surgical Educn, Toronto, 2007. FHEA (ILTM 2000); FAcadMEd 2009. Mem., 2012, Brother, 2016, Art Workers' Guild. Hon. RCM 2016. Hon. Fellow, C&G Art Sch., 2017. Nat. Teaching Fellowship Award, Higher Educn Acad., 2011. *Publications:* (with J. Schofield) Skin Lesions, 1996; (with H. Fry) Surgical Education: theorising an emerging domain, 2011; 12 book chapters; 150 papers in scientific, social sci. and humanities jls. *Recreations:* playing the harpsichord, listening to jazz, walking in high and lonely places, exploring unexpected connections. *Address:* Centre for Engagement and Simulation Science, Imperial College London, Academic Surgery (3rd Floor), Chelsea and Westminster Hospital, 369 Fulham Road, SW10 9NH. *T:* (020) 3315 8470. *E:* r.kneebone@imperial.ac.uk.

**KNIBB, Prof. Michael Anthony,** PhD; FBA 1989; Samuel Davidson Professor of Old Testament Studies, 1997–2001, now Emeritus, and Head, School of Humanities, 2000–01, King's College London; *b* 14 Dec. 1938; third *s* of Leslie Charles Knibb and Christian Vera Knibb (*née* Hoggar); *m* 1972, Christine Mary Burrell. *Educ:* Wyggeston Sch., Leicester; King's Coll. London (BD, PhD; FKC 1991); Union Theol Seminary, NY (STM); Corpus Christi Coll., Oxford. King's College London: Lectr in OT Studies, 1964–82; Reader, 1982–86; Prof. of OT Studies, 1986–97; Head, Dept of Theology and Religious Studies, 1989–93, 1998–2000, Dep. Head, Sch. of Humanities, 1992–97. British Academy: Res. Reader, 1986–88; Mem. Council, 1992–95; Schweich Lectr, 1995; Mem., Humanities Res. Bd, 1995–98 (Chm., Postgrad. Cttee, 1996–98). Editor: Book List of SOTS, 1980–86; Guides to the Apocrypha and Pseudepigrapha, 1995–2004. Hon. Sec., Palestine Exploration Fund, 1969–76. Member, Governing Body: Watford GS for Girls, 1993–2002; SOAS, 2000–10 (Vice-Chm., 2006–10); Chm., Remuneration Cttee, Corpus Christi Coll., Oxford, 2008–14. FRAS 1993. Ullendorff Medal, British Acad., 2019. *Publications:* The Ethiopic Book of Enoch: a new edition in the light of the Aramaic Dead Sea Fragments, 2 vols, 1978; Het Boek Henoch, 1983; Cambridge Bible Commentary on 2 Esdras, 1979; (ed jtly) Israel's Prophetic Tradition: essays in honour of P. R. Ackroyd, 1982; The Qumran Community, 1987; (ed with P. W. van der Horst) Studies on the Testament of Job, 1989; Translating the Bible: the Ethiopic version of the Old Testament, 1999; (ed) The Septuagint and Messianism, 2006; Essays on the Book of Enoch and Other Early Jewish Texts and Traditions, 2009; The Ethiopic Text of the Book of Ezekiel: a critical edition, 2015; reviews and articles in books and learned jls. *Recreation:* hill walking. *Address:* 6 Shootersway Park, Berkhamsted, Herts HP4 3NX. *T:* (01442) 871459. *Club:* Athenæum.

**KNIBBS, Kevin;** Headmaster, Hampton School, since 2013; *b* Billericay, 18 Jan. 1972; *s* of Graham Arthur Knibbs and Jean Pamela Knibbs (*née* Robbins); *m* 2007, Jacqueline Francesca Taylor. *Educ:* King Edward VI Grammar Sch., Chelmsford; St Edmund Hall, Oxford (Exhibnr; Association Football Blue, 1992, 1993; BA Mod. Hist. 1993; MA); Univ. of Oxford (PGCE 1995). Bolton School: Hist. Master, 1995–98; Head: First Year, 1998–2003; Lower Sch., 2003–06; Sen. Master, 2006–07; Dep. Headmaster, Hampton Sch., 2007–13. *Recreations:* ski-ing, cycling, reading (especially history and politics), football coaching, theatre, film, following the fortunes of Arsenal FC. *Address:* Hampton School, Hanworth Road, Hampton, Middx TW12 3HD. *T:* (020) 8979 5526, *Fax:* (020) 8783 4035. *E:* headmaster@hamptonschool.org.uk.

**KNIFTON, David Alan;** QC 2018; a Recorder, since 2003; *b* Crosby, Liverpool, 4 Feb. 1964; *s* of Alan Knifton and Patricia Knifton; *m* 1991, Geraldine McGuire; four *s*. *Educ:* Merchant Taylors' Sch.; Univ. of Nottingham (LLB Hons 1985). Called to the Bar, Inner Temple, 1986; in practice as a barrister, specialising in catastrophic personal injury claims, Chavasse Court Chambers, 1986–98, 7 Harrington St Chambers, 1998–2006, Exchange Chambers, 2006–. *Recreations:* cycling, choral singing, walking. *Address:* Exchange Chambers, 1 Derby Square, Liverpool L2 9XX. *T:* (0151) 236 7747. *E:* kniftonqc@exchangechambers.co.uk.

**KNIGHT,** family name of **Baroness Knight of Collingtree** and **Baron Knight of Weymouth**.

**KNIGHT OF COLLINGTREE,** Baroness *cr* 1997 (Life Peer), of Collingtree in the co. of Northamptonshire; **Joan Christabel Jill Knight,** DBE 1985 (MBE 1964); *m* 1947, Montague Knight (*d* 1986); two *s*. *Educ:* Fairfield Sch., Bristol; King Edward Grammar Sch., Birmingham. Mem., Northampton County Borough Council, 1956–66. MP (C) Birmingham, Edgbaston, 1966–97. Member: Select Cttee on Race Relations and Immigration, 1969–72; Select Cttee for Home Affairs, 1980–83, 1992–97; Chairman: Lords and Commons All-Party Child and Family Protection Gp, 1978–97; Cons. Back Bench Health and Social Services Cttee, 1982–97; Member: Exec. Cttee, 1922 Cttee, 1979–97 (Sec., 1983–87; Vice-Chm., 1987–88, 1992–97); Council of Europe, 1977–88, 1999–2011; WEU, 1977–88, 1999–2011 (Chm., Cttee for Parly and Public Relations, 1984–88); Exec. Cttee, IPU, 1991–97 (Chm., 1994–97). Mem., Select Cttee on EU, 1999–2001. Mem., H of L, 1997–2016. Vice-Chm., Assoc. of Cons. Peers, 2002–05. Pres., West Midlands Conservative Political Centre, 1980–83. Vice-Pres., Townswomen's Guilds, 1986–95. Director: Computeach International plc, 1991–2006; Heckett Multiserv, 1999–2006. Pres., Sulgrave Manor Trust, 2012– (Chm., 2007–12). Hon. DSc Aston, 1999. Kentucky Colonel, USA, 1973; Nebraska Admiral, USA, 1980; Texas Ranger, 2014–. *Publications:* About the House, 1995. *Recreations:* music, reading, tapestry work, theatre-going, antique-hunting.

**KNIGHT OF WEYMOUTH,** Baron *cr* 2010 (Life Peer), of Weymouth in the County of Dorset; **James Philip Knight;** PC 2008; Chief Education and External Officer (formerly Managing Director, Online Learning, then Chief Education Adviser), TES Global (formerly TSL Education) Ltd, since 2014; *b* 6 March 1965; *s* of Philip Knight and Hilary Howlett; *m* 1989, Anna Wheatley; one *s* one *d*. *Educ:* Eltham Coll., London; Fitzwilliam Coll., Cambridge (BA Hons Geog. and Social and Pol Sci.). Worker, Works Theatre Co-operative Ltd, 1986–88; Manager, Central Studio Arts Centre, 1988–90; Dir, W Wilts Arts Centre Ltd, 1990–91; Dentons Directories Ltd: Sales Exec., 1991–96; Gen. Manager, 1997–98; Dir, 1998–2000; Prodn Manager, 2000–01. MP (Lab) S Dorset, 2001–10; contested (Lab) same seat, 2010. PPS to Minister of State, DoH, 2003–04; Parly Under-Sec. of State, DEFRA, 2005–06; Minister of State, DFES, later DCSF, 2006–09; Minister of State (Minister for Employment and Welfare Reform), DWP, and Minister for the SW, 2009–10. Dir, Egale Ltd. Vis. Prof., London Knowledge Lab., UCL Inst. of Educn (formerly Inst. of Educn, Univ. of London), 2013–. Trustee: Tinder Foundn Ltd, 2012–16; Centre for Accelerating Social Technol., 2016–. *Recreations:* Arsenal Football Club, English literature, tennis, walking. *Address:* House of Lords, SW1A 0PW. *E:* knightja@parliament.uk. *W:* www.twitter.com/jimpknight.

**KNIGHT, Dr Alan Paul,** OBE 1998; General Manager for Corporate Social Responsibility and Sustainable Development, Arcelor Mittal, since 2014; *b* London, 17 May 1964; *s* of Ernest Owen Knight and Anita Mavis Knight; civil partnership 2014, Tim Stainton. *Educ:* Univ. of Southampton (BSc Geol.); Royal Holloway and Bedford New Coll., Univ. of London (PhD Marine Biol.). Head of Sustainability: B&Q, 1990–2000; Kingfisher plc, 2000–03; SABMiller plc, 2003–06; Ind. Advr (formerly Special Advr), Virgin Gp on Sustainable Develt, 2007–12; Sustainability Dir, BITC, 2012–14. Non-executive Director: WRAP, 2012–15; Virgin Earth Challenge, 2012–. Vis. Fellow, Cambridge Prog. of Sustainability Leadership, 2006–. Chm., Adv. Cttee for Consumer Products and the Envmt, 1998–2004; Mem., Sustainable Develt Commn, 2000–09; Co-Chm., Roundtable of Sustainable Consumption, 2003–05; Chairman: Global Assoc. of Corp. Sustainability Officers, 2010–; Sustainable Growing Media Task Force, 2011–; Ebola Private Sector Mobilisation Gp, 2014–16. Dir, Forest Stewardship Council, 1991–93 and 2006–09. Founder, Single Planet Living, 2007–. Mem., Ind. Panel of UK Forestry. Chm., Cornwall and Isles of Scilly Local Nature Partnership, 2013–. Clinton Global Citizen Award, 2015. *Publications:* I Will If You Will, 2005; If the planet was a shop, 2013. *Recreations:* walking on Perranporth Beach, surfing, kayaks, taking photos, collecting fossils, masks, riding bicycles. *Address:* Silverstone, Northants. *T:* 07917 635161. *E:* Alan@DrAlanknight.com. *W:* www.dralanknight.com.

**KNIGHT, Prof. Alan Sydney,** DPhil; Professor of the History of Latin America, University of Oxford, 1992–2013, now Emeritus; Fellow of St Antony's College, Oxford, 1992–2013, now Emeritus; *b* 6 Nov. 1946; *s* of William Henry Knight and Eva Maud Crandon; *m* 1st, 1969, Carole Jones (marr. diss. 1979); one *d*; 2nd, 1985, Lidia Lozano; two *s*. *Educ:* Balliol Coll., Oxford (BA Modern Hist. 1968); Nuffield Coll., Oxford (DPhil 1974). Research Fellow, Nuffield Coll., Oxford, 1971–73; Lectr in Hist., Essex Univ., 1973–85; Worsham Centennial Prof. of History, Univ. of Texas at Austin, 1986–92. *Publications:* The Mexican Revolution (2 vols), 1986; US-Mexican Relations 1910–40, 1987; Mexico, vol. 1, From the Beginning to the Conquest, 2002, vol. 2, The Colonial Era, 2002; contrib. Jl of Latin American Studies, Bull. of Latin American Res., etc. Order of the Aztec Eagle (Mexico), 2010. *Recreation:* kayaking. *Address:* c/o St Antony's College, Oxford OX2 6JF.

**KNIGHT, Very Rev. Alexander Francis,** OBE 2006; Dean of Lincoln, 1998–2006, now Emeritus; *b* 24 July 1939; *s* of late Rev. Benjamin Edward Knight and of Dorothy Mary Knight; *m* 1962, Sheelagh Elizabeth (*née* Faris); one *s* three *d*. *Educ:* Taunton Sch.; St Catharine's Coll., Cambridge (MA). Curate, Hemel Hempstead, 1963–68; Chaplain, Taunton Sch., 1968–74; Dir, Bloxham Project, 1975–81; Dir of Studies, Aston Training Scheme, 1981–83; Priest-in-charge, Easton and Martyr Worthy, 1983–90; Archdeacon of Basingstoke and Canon Residentiary of Winchester Cathedral, 1990–98. Dean of the Priory of England and the Islands of Hosp. of St John of Jerusalem, 2007–. Hon. DLitt Lincoln, 2004. KStJ 2011 (CStJ 2009). *Publications:* contrib. SPCK Taleteller series. *Recreations:* hill walking, theatre, reading, gardening. *Address:* Shalom, Clay Street, Whiteparish, Salisbury SP5 2ST.

**KNIGHT, Andrew Stephen Bower;** company director and farmer in Warwickshire and Dannevirke; *b* 1 Nov. 1939; *s* of late M. W. B. Knight and S. E. F. Knight; *m* 1st, 1966, Victoria Catherine Brittain (marr. diss.); one *s*; 2nd, 1975, Sabiha Rumani Malik (marr. diss. 1991); two *d*; 3rd, 2006, Marita Georgina Phillips Crawley. *Educ:* Ampleforth Coll.; Balliol Coll., Oxford (MA). Editor, The Economist, 1974–86; Chief Exec., 1986–89, Editor-in-Chief, 1987–89, Daily Telegraph plc; Chairman: News Internat. plc, 1990–94; Times Newspapers Hldgs, 1990–94 and 2012– (Dir, 1990–). Dir, The News Corporation Ltd, 1991–2012; Dep. Chm., Home Counties Newspapers Hldgs, 1996–98; Dir, Rothschild Investment Trust CP, 1996–2008 (Mem. Adv. Bd, 2013–); Chm., 2008–11, Dir, 2011–13, J. Rothschild Capital Mgt. Member: Steering Cttee, Bilderberg Meetings, 1980–98; Adv. Bd, Center for Economic Policy Research, Stanford Univ., 1981–; Adv. Council, Inst. of Internat. Studies, Stanford Univ., 1990–. Chm., Harlech Scholars' Trust, 2001–10 (Trustee, 1986–2010). Governor and Mem. Council of Management, Ditchley Foundn, 1982–2014. Founder Chm., Shipston Home Nursing, 1997–2004; Founder Trustee, Spinal Muscular Atrophy Trust, 2003–14; Trustee: Mariinsky Theatre Trust, 1999–; Centre for Policy Studies, 2010–. *Address:* Compton Scorpion, Warwicks. *Clubs:* Beefsteak, Brooks's, Royal Automobile; Tadmarton Heath Golf.

**KNIGHT, Angela Ann,** CBE 2007; Chief Executive, Energy UK, 2012–14; *b* 31 Oct. 1950; *d* of late Andrew McTurk Cook and Barbara Jean (*née* Gale); *m* 1981, David George Knight (marr. diss.); two *s*. *Educ:* Penrhos Coll., N Wales; Sheffield Girls' High Sch.; Bristol Univ. (BSc Hons Chem. 1972). Management posts with Air Products Ltd, 1972–77; Man. Dir and Chm., Cook & Knight (Metallurgical Processors) Ltd, 1977–84; Chm., Cook & Knight (Process Plant), 1984–91. Chief Executive: Assoc. of Private Client Investment Managers and Stockbrokers, 1997–2006; BBA, 2007–12. Non-executive Director: PEP and ISA (formerly PEP) Managers Assoc., 1997–99; Scottish Widows, 1997–2006; Saur Water Services and South East Water plc (formerly Saur Water Services), 1997–2004; Mott MacDonald, 1998–2001; Logica, 1999–2003; Logica CMG plc, 2003–08; Lloyds TSB, 2003–06; Brewin Dolphin plc, 2008–17 (Chm., Tillman Brewin Dolphin, 2016–18); TP ICAP (formerly Tullett Prebon), 2011– (Sen. Ind. Dir, 2016–); Arbuthnot Latham & Co., 2016–; Provident Financial plc, 2018–; Ind. non-exec. Dir, Taylor Wimpey, 2016–. Member Board: PLA, 2002–08; Financial Services Skill Council, 2008–12; Chm., Office of Tax Simplification, 2016–19. MP (C) Erewash, 1992–97; contested (C) same seat, 1997. PPS to Minister for Industry, 1993–94, to Chancellor of the Exchequer, 1994–95; Econ. Sec. to HM Treasury, 1995–97. Governor: Gayhurst Sch., 2000–02; Bradfield Coll., 2001–07. *Recreations:* classic cars, ski-ing, renovating listed building, books. *Clubs:* Carlton, Goodwood Road Racing.

**KNIGHT, Prof. Bernard Henry,** CBE 1993; MD, FRCPath; novelist; consultant in forensic medicine; Consultant Pathologist to Home Office, 1965–96; Professor of Forensic Pathology, University of Wales College of Medicine, 1980–96, now Emeritus; *b* 3 May 1931; *s* of Harold Ivor Knight and Doris (*née* Lawes); *m* 1955, Jean Gwenllian Ogborne; one *s*. *Educ:* Univ. of Wales (BCh, MD); MRCPath 1964, FRCPath 1966; DMJ (Path) 1967; MRCP 1983. FHKCPath 1993. Called to the Bar, Gray's Inn, 1967. Captain RAMC, Malaya, 1956–59. Lecturer in Forensic Medicine: Univ. of London, 1959–61; Univ. of Wales, 1961–65; Sen. Lectr, Forensic Med., Univ. of Newcastle, 1965–68; Sen. Lectr, then Reader of Forensic Pathology, Univ. of Wales Coll. Med., 1968–80. Hon. Consultant Pathologist, Cardiff Royal Infirmary, 1968–96. Vis. Prof., Univs of Hong Kong, Kuwait, Malaya and Guangzhou (China). Mem., Home Office Policy Adv. Cttee in Forensic Pathology; Chm., Forensic Sub-Cttee and Bd Examnrs, RCPath, 1990–93; Mem.,

GMC, 1979–94. President: Brit. Assoc. Forensic Med., 1991–93; Forensic Science Soc., 1988–90; Vice-Pres., Internat. Acad. Legal Med., 1980–. Hon. FRSocMed 1994. Hon. Mem., German, Finnish and Hungarian Socs of Forensic Med. Hon. DSc Glamorgan, 1995; Hon. LLD Wales, 1998; Hon. MD Turku, Finland, 2000; Hon. PhD: Tokyo, 2000; Coimbra, 2009. GSM Malaya, 1956. *Publications: fiction*: The Lately Deceased, 1961; The Thread of Evidence, 1963; Russian Roulette, 1968; Policeman's Progress, 1969; Tiger at Bay, 1970; Deg y Dragwyddoldeb (Welsh), 1972; Edyfyn Brau (Welsh), 1973; Lion Rampant, 1973; The Expert, 1975; Prince of America, 1977; The Sanctuary Seeker, 1998; The Poisoned Chalice, 1998; Crowner's Quest, 1999; The Awful Secret, 2000; The Tinner's Corpse, 2000; The Grim Reaper, 2001; Fear in the Forest, 2003; Brennan, 2003; The Witch Hunter, 2004; Figure of Hate, 2005; The Tainted Relic, 2005; The Elixir of Death, 2006; The Sword of Shame, 2006; The Noble Outlaw, 2007; The House of Shadows, 2007; The Manor of Death, 2008; The Lost Prophesies, 2008; Crowner Royal, 2009; King Arthur's Bones, 2009; Where Death Delights, 2010; A Plague of Heretics, 2010; The Sacred Stone, 2010; According to Evidence, 2010; Hill of Bones, 2011; Grounds for Appeal, 2011; Dead in the Dog, 2012; The First Murder, 2012; Crowner's Crusade, 2012; The False Virgin, 2013; The Deadliest Sin, 2014; *biography*: Autopsy: the memoirs of Milton Helpern, 1977; *non-fiction*: Murder, Suicide or Accident, 1965; Discovering the Human Body, 1980; *medical textbooks*: Legal Aspects of Medical Practice, 1972, 5th edn 1992; Forensic Radiology, 1982; Sudden Infant Death, 1982; Post-mortem Technician's Handbook, 1983; Forensic Medicine for Lawyers, 1984, 2nd edn 1998; Forensic Medicine, 1985; (ed) Simpson's Forensic Medicine, 9th edn 1985, 11th edn 1996; Coroner's Autopsy, 1985; Forensic Pathology, 1991, 3rd edn 2004; Estimation of the Time of Death, 1995, 2nd edn 2002. *Recreation*: writing. *Address*: 26 Millwood, Llysfaen, Cardiff CF14 0TL. *T*: (029) 2075 2798.

**KNIGHT, His Honour Brian Joseph;** QC 1981; a Senior Circuit Judge, 1998–2011; Mercantile Judge, London Mercantile Court, and Judge in charge of the Technology and Construction Court List at Central London Civil Justice Centre (formerly Business List Judge, Central London County Court), 1998–2011; *b* 5 May 1941; *s* of Joseph Knight and Vera Lorraine Knight (*née* Docksey); *m* 1967, Cristina Karen Wang Noberga de Lima (*d* 2003); *m* 2010, Lyn Christine Thornton. *Educ*: Colbayns High Sch., Clacton; University Coll. London. LLB 1962, LLM 1963. FCIArb 1995–2015. Called to the Bar, Gray's Inn, 1964, *ad eundem* Lincoln's Inn, 1979; called to the Bar of Hong Kong, 1978, of Northern Ireland, 1979; a Recorder, 1991–98. Asst Parly Boundary Comr, 1992. *Club*: Garrick.

**KNIGHT, Brigid Agnes;** a District Judge (Magistrates' Courts), since 2002; *m*; one *s* two *d*. *Educ*: Liverpool Univ. (LLB Hons); Coll. of Law, Guildford. Solicitor in private practice, 1975–2002. *Recreations*: family, theatre, ballet, contemporary dance, drawing and sketching. *Address*: Cheshire Magistrates' Courts, Justices' Clerks' Office, Winmarleigh Street, Warrington WA1 1PB. *T*: (01925) 236250.

**KNIGHT, Rt Hon. Sir Gregory,** Kt 2013; PC 1995; MP (C) East Yorkshire, since 2001; writer, consultant solicitor; *b* 4 April 1949; *s* of late George Knight and Isabella Knight (*née* Bell). *Educ*: Alderman Newton's Grammar School, Leicester; College of Law, Guildford. Self employed solicitor, 1973–83. Member: Leicester City Council, 1976–79; Leicestershire County Council, 1977–83 (Chm., Public Protection Cttee). MP (C) Derby North, 1983–97; contested (C) same seat, 1997. PPS to the Minister of State: Home Office, 1987; Foreign Office, 1988–89; an Asst Govt Whip, 1989–90; a Lord Comr of HM Treasury, 1990–93; Dep. Govt Chief Whip and Treas. of HM Household, 1993–96; Minister of State, DTI, 1996–97; Shadow Dep. Leader, H of C, 2001–03; Opposition front bench spokesman: on transport and envmt, 2003–05; on transport, 2005–06; Vice-Chamberlain of HM Household (Govt Whip), 2012–13. Chm., H of C Procedure Select Cttee, 2005–12. Vice Chm., Cons. Candidates' Assoc., 1998–2001. Dir, Leicester Theatre Trust, 1979–85 (Chm., Finance Cttee, 1982–83). *Publications*: (jtly) Westminster Words, 1988; Honourable Insults: a century of political insult, 1990; Parliamentary Sauce: more political insults, 1992; Right Honourable Insults, 1998; Naughty Graffiti, 2005; Dishonourable Insults, 2011; pamphlets and articles for law, motoring and entertainment publications. *Recreations*: driving classic cars and making music. *Address*: House of Commons, SW1A 0AA. *Club*: Bridlington Conservative.

**KNIGHT, Henrietta Catherine, (Mrs T. W. Biddlecombe);** licensed racehorse trainer, 1989–2012; *b* 15 Dec. 1946; *d* of late Maj. Guy Knight, MC and Hester Knight; *m* 1995, Terence Walter Biddlecombe (*d* 2014). *Educ*: Didcot Girls' Grammar Sch.; Westminster Coll. of Educn, Oxford (BEd Oxon); Berkshire Coll. of Agric. (Advanced NCA). Schoolteacher, hist. and biol., St Mary's Sch., Wantage, 1970–74; ran private livery Point to Point yard, 1974–84 (trained over 100 Point to Point winners). Chm., Sen. Selection Cttee, British Horse Soc. (Three Day Eventing), 1984–88. National Hunt winners include: Stompin, Glenlivet Hurdle, Aintree, 1995; Karshi, Stayers Hurdle, Cheltenham, 1997; Edredon Bleu, Grand Annual Chase, Cheltenham, 1998; Lord Noelie, Sun Alliance Chase, Edredon Bleu, Queen Mother Champion Chase, Cheltenham, 2000; Best Mate, 2002, Edredon Bleu, 2003, King George VI Steeplechase, Kempton; Somersby, Victor Chandler Chase, Grade 1, Ascot, 2012; Best Mate, 3 Cheltenham Gold Cups, 2002, 2003, 2004. *Publications*: Best Mate: Chasing Gold, 2003; Best Mate: Triple Gold, 2004; Not Enough Time: my life with Terry Biddlecombe, 2015; The Jumping Game: how National Hunt trainers work and what makes them tick, 2018. *Recreations*: farming, breeding Connemara ponies, buying National Hunt horses, judging at major horse shows. *Address*: West Lockinge Farm, Wantage, Oxon OX12 8QF. *T*: (01235) 833535, 07860 110153, *Fax*: (01235) 820110. *E*: hen@westlockinge.co.uk. *W*: www.henknight.com.

**KNIGHT, Jeffrey Russell,** FCA; Chief Executive, The Stock Exchange, 1982–89; *b* 1 Oct. 1936; *s* of Thomas Edgar Knight and Ivy Cissie Knight (*née* Russell); *m* 1959, Judith Marion Delver Podger; three *d* (and one *d* decd). *Educ*: Bristol Cathedral Sch.; St Peter's Hall, Oxford (MA). Chartered Accountant, 1966; The Stock Exchange, London, 1967–90: Head of Quotations Dept, 1973; Dep. Chief Executive, 1975. Member: City Company Law Cttee, 1974–80; Dept of Trade Panel on Company Law Revision, 1980–84; Accounting Standards Cttee, 1982–89; Special Adviser to Dept of Trade, 1975–81; Adviser to Council for the Securities Industry, 1978–85; UK Delegate: to EEC Working Parties; to Internat. Fedn of Stock Exchanges, 1973–90 (Chm., Task Force on Transnational Settlement, 1987–91); to Fedn of Stock Exchanges in EEC, 1974–90 (Chm., Wking Cttee, 1980–90); to Internat. Orgn of Securities Commns, 1987–91 (Chm. Wkg Party on Capital Adequacy). *Recreations*: cricket, music. *Address*: Derryswood House, Wonersh, Surrey GU5 0QZ. *T*: (01483) 891978. *Clubs*: Brooks's, MCC; Woking Golf.

**KNIGHT, Julian Carlton;** MP (C) Solihull, since 2015; *b* Chester, 5 Jan. 1972; *s* of Carlton and Valerie Knight; *m* 2014, Philippa Harrison. *Educ*: Chester Catholic High Sch.; Hull Univ. (BA Hons). Field sales exec., News Internat., 1995–98; staff writer, Reader's Digest, 1998–2002; personal finance and consumer affairs reporter, BBC News, 2002–07; Money and Property Ed., Independent, 2007–15. PPS, MoJ, 2018, DWP, 2018–19, HM Treasury, 2019–. Prime Minister's Trade Envoy to Mongolia, 2018–. Member: Communities and Local Govt Select Cttee, 2015–17; Culture, Media and Sport, subseq. Digital, Culture, Media and Sport, Select Cttee, 2016–; Public Accounts Commn, 2017–; Member, All Party Parliamentary Group: on Credit Unions; on Infant Feeding and Inequality (Vice-Chm.);

Motor Gp (Vice-Chm.); Chairman, All Party Parliamentary Group: for Alternative Lending, 2016–; for Financial Educn for Young People, 2017–; for Fair Fuel, Motorists and Hauliers, 2017–18 (Vice-Chm., 2018–). Alternate Mem., OSCE Parly Assembly, 2017–. *Publications*: Wills, Probate and Inheritance Tax for Dummies, 2004, 2nd edn 2008; Retiring Wealthy, 2005; Cricket for Dummies, 2006, 2nd edn 2013; (with M. Pattison) British Politics for Dummies, 2010, 2nd edn 2015; Eurocrisis for Dummies, 2012. *Recreations*: tennis, cricket, golf, football, cycling, the arts. *Address*: House of Commons, SW1A 0AA. *T*: (020) 7219 3577. *E*: julian.knight.mp@parliament.uk.

**KNIGHT, Sir Kenneth John, (Sir Ken),** Kt 2006; CBE 2001; QFSM 1992; Chief Fire and Rescue Adviser, Department for Communities and Local Government, 2007–13; Lead Commissioner, London Borough of Tower Hamlets, 2014–17; *b* 3 Jan. 1947; *s* of Dennis and Nancy Knight; *m* 2016, Kelly. MIFireE 1970, FIFireE 2008. Westminster Bank, Reigate, 1964–66; joined Surrey Fire Bde, 1966; Home Office, 1985–87; Asst Chief Officer, London Fire Bde, 1987–92; Dep. Chief Officer, Devon Fire Bde, 1992–94; Chief Fire Officer: Dorset, 1994–98; W Midlands, 1998–2003; Comr for Fire and Emergency Planning, London Fire Bde, 2003–07. Efficiencies Review of Fire Service (reviews of N Iraq, Ireland, Bermuda, Gibraltar, England), 2013. Chair, Expert Panel, MHCLG, 2017–. Chm., Gresham (SMS) Ltd. Master, Worshipful Co. of Firefighters, 1998. DL Greater London, 2006 (Rep. DL London Borough of Richmond upon Thames, 2007–17). CCMI 2005. OStJ 2005. *Recreations*: theatre, walking. *Club*: East India.

**KNIGHT, Malcolm Donald;** Visiting Professor of Finance, London School of Economics and Political Science, since 2008; Distinguished Fellow, Centre for International Governance Innovation, Waterloo, Ontario, since 2014; *b* 11 April 1944; *s* of Gordon James Knight and Muriel Edith Knight (*née* McGregor); *m* 1972, Amy W. Crumpacker (marr. diss. 2015); three *d*. *Educ*: Amherstburg District High Sch. (Sen. Matric. 1963); Univ. of Toronto (BA Hons Pol Sci. and Econs 1967); London Sch. of Econs and Pol Sci. (MSc Econ. 1968; PhD 1972). Asst Prof. of Econs, Univ. of Toronto, 1971–72; Lectr in Econs, LSE, 1972–75; International Monetary Fund: economist, 1975–83, Chief, Ext. Adjustment Div., 1983–87, Res. Dept; Div. Chief, 1987–89, Asst Dir, 1989–91, ME Dept; Asst Dir, Res. Dept, 1991–93; Sen. Advr, 1993–95, and Dep. Dir, 1995–96, ME Dept; Dep. Dir, Monetary and Exchange Affairs Dept, 1996–98; Dep. Dir, European I Dept, 1998–99; Sen. Dep. Gov., Bank of Canada, 1999–2003; Gen. Manager and CEO, Bank for Internat. Settlements, 2003–08; Vice Chm., 2008–12, Advr, 2012–14, Deutsche Bank AG. Mem. Bd of Dirs, Swiss Reinsurance Inc., 2010–14. Adjunct Professor: Virginia Poly. and State Univ. Grad. Prog., Northern Virginia, 1978–85; Sch. of Advanced Internat. Studies, Johns Hopkins Univ., 1980–96; Vis. Prof. in Finance, LSE, 2008–. Trustee: Internat. Accounting Standards Cttee Foundn, 2003–07; Per Jacobsson Foundn, 2003–; Internat. Valuation Standards Council, 2010–16; Member: IMF Capital Markets Consultative Gp, 2003–08; Financial Stability Forum, 2005–08; Markets Monitoring Gp, Inst. of Internat. Finance, 2009–; Ext. Panel to Review IMF's Risk Mgt Framework, 2011; Bd of Dirs, Global Risk Inst. in Financial Services, Toronto, 2011–; Internat. Adv. Panel, Risk Mgt Inst., Univ. of Singapore, 2011–; Observer, IMF Internat. Monetary and Financial Cttee, 2003–08; Chm., Bd of Patrons, European Assoc. of Banking and Financial Hist., 2008–12 (Mem., Bd of Patrons, 2005–12); Dep. Chair, Bd of Dirs, Payments Canada (formerly Canadian Payments Assoc.), 2015–. Member: Soc. of Scholars, Johns Hopkins Univ., 2006–; N American Adv. Bd, LSE, 2008–; Bd of Dirs, New Jersey Center for Visual Arts, 2011–13. Mem., Hon. Senate, Lindau Nobel Prize Winners' Foundn, 2006–. Woodrow Wilson Nat. Fellow, 1967; Canada Council Doctoral Fellow, 1968–70. Hon. Dr Trinity Coll., Univ. of Toronto, 2006. *Publications*: (ed jtly) Transforming Financial Systems in the Baltics, Russia and Other Countries of the Former Soviet Union, 1999; The Canadian Economy, 1989, rev. edn 1996; (contrib.) Financial Crisis Management and Bank Resolution, 2009; contrib. numerous articles to learned jls on internat. finance, stabilization progs in developing countries, monetary policy, empirical aspects of growth theory and financial system structure and regulation. *Recreations*: tennis, ski-ing, bicycling, hiking, swimming, sailing, golf, watercolour. *Address*: 2 Crest Acre Court, Summit, NJ 07901, USA. *T*: (917) 3277266. *E*: malcolm.knight100@gmail.com.

**KNIGHT, Maureen R.;** *see* Rice-Knight.

**KNIGHT, Sir Michael (William Patrick),** KCB 1983 (CB 1980); AFC 1964; Life Vice-President, The Air League, since 2004 (Member of Council, 1990–2004; Chairman, 1992–98; President, 1998–2004; Founders' Medal, 2005); *b* 23 Nov. 1932; *s* of William and Dorothy Knight; *m* 1967, Patricia Ann (*née* Davies) (*d* 2008); one *s* two *d*. *Educ*: Leek High Sch.; Univ. of Liverpool (BA Hons 1954; Hon. LittD 1985). Univ. of Liverpool Air Sqn, RAFVR, 1951–54; commnd RAF, 1954; served in Transport and Bomber Comds, and in Middle and Near East Air Forces, 1956–63; Comd No 32 Sqn, RAF Akrotiri, 1961–63; RAF Staff Coll., 1964; Min. of Aviation, 1965–66; Comd Far East Strike Wing, RAF Tengah, 1966–68; Flying Wing, 1968–69; Head of Secretariat, HQ Strike Comd, 1969–70; Mil. Asst to Chm., NATO Mil. Cttee, 1970–73; Comd RAF Laarbruch, 1973–74; RCDS, 1975; Dir of Ops (Air Support), MoD, 1975–77; SASO, HQ Strike Command/DCS (Ops & Intelligence) HQ UK Air Forces, 1977–80; AOC No 1 Gp, 1980–82; Air Mem. for Supply and Organisation, 1983–86; UK Military Rep. to NATO, 1986–89; Air ADC to the Queen, 1986–89 (ADC, 1973–74); retd in rank of Air Chief Marshal, 1989; commnd Flying Officer, RAFVR (Trng Br.), 1989–2004. Adjunct Prof., Internat. Peace and Security, Carnegie Mellon Univ., Pittsburgh, 1989–95. Dep. Chm., 1994–95, Chm., 1995–2001, Cobham plc; Chairman: Page Gp Hldgs Ltd, 1996–2000; Cranfield Aerospace Ltd, 2000–03; Director: Craigwell Research, 1990–97; RAFC Co. Ltd, 1993–2003; SBAC (Farnborough) Ltd, 1996–98; non-executive Director: FR Group plc, 1990–94; Page Aerospace Gp, 1991–96; Smiths Industries Aerospace and Defence Systems Group, 1992–95; Associate, JGW Associates Ltd, 1989–2002; Chm., Northern Devon Healthcare NHS Trust, 1991–94. Mem., Internat. Adv. Bd, British/Amer. Business Council, 1995–2001. Mem., IISS, 1968–2002; Member Council: RUSI, 1984–87; SBAC, 1995–99; Exmoor Calvert Trust, 2000–09 (Chm., 2000–09; Hon. Vice-Pres., 2011); Pres., Council, NAAFI, 1984–86; Vice-Pres., Atlantic Council of UK, 1994–2008. Chm., N Devon Family Support Service, Leonard Cheshire Foundn, 1989–91; Devon County Rep., RAF Benev. Fund, 1990–; RAF Pres., 1991–97, Sen. Pres., 1999–2000, Officers' Assoc.; President: Aircrew Assoc., 1992–97; Buccaneer Aircrew Assoc., 1994–2014; No 32 (The Royal) Sqn Assoc., 1997–2016; Royal Internat. Air Tattoo, 2005–08 (Vice-Pres., 1991–2002); Vice-Patron, 2003–04; Hon. Vice-Patron, 2008–; Spirit of the Meet Award, 2008); Vice-Pres., The Youth Trust, 1994–98; Chm., 2004–07, Life Pres., 2007–, Vulcan to the Sky Trust (Patron, Vulcan Restoration Appeal, 2000–03); Chm., RAF Charitable Trust, 2005–08. Trustee: RAF Central Fund, 1983–86; RAF Mus., 1983–86. Pres., Mortehoe Mus. Trust (formerly Mortehoe Heritage Trust), 2009–. Patron, Guild of Aviation Artists, 2005–09 (Vice-Pres., 1997–2005); Vice-Patron, Yorks Air Mus., 1997–. Gov. and Council Mem., Taunton Sch., 1987–2000; Mem., Univ. of Liverpool Develt Team, 1986–. Rugby Football Union: Mem. Cttee, 1977–92; Mem. Exec. Cttee, 1989–92; Chm., Internat. Sub Cttee, 1987–90; Chm., Forward Planning Sub Cttee, 1990–92; Privilege Mem., 1992– (Chm., Privilege Members Assoc., 2011–17). President: RAF Rugby Union, 1985–89 (Chm., 1975–78); Combined Services RFC, 1987–89 (Chm., 1977–79); RAF Lawn Tennis Assoc., 1984–86; Vice-President: Leek RUFC, 1959–;

Crawshay's Welsh RFC, 1997–2016; Penguin Internat. RFC, 2001–14. Hon. Air Cdre, No 7630 (VR) Intelligence Sqn, RAuxAF, 2001–07. FRAeS 1985; FRGS 1994 (Mem. Council, 1995–97); FRSA 1994. Freeman, City of London, 1989; Liveryman, Hon. Co. of Air Pilots (formerly GAPAN), 1993– (Upper Freeman, 1990–93; Guild Award of Honour, 2007). *Publications:* (contrib.) War in the Third Dimension, 1986; Strategic Offensive Air Power and Technology, 1989; articles in prof. pubns, 1975–. *Recreations:* Rugby football, lesser sports, music, writing, travel, public speaking. *Address:* c/o National Westminster Bank, Leek, Staffs. *Clubs:* Royal Air Force (Vice-Pres., 1983–2003), Colonels (founder).

**KNIGHT, Nicholas David Gordon,** OBE 2010; photographer; Director: N. K. Image Ltd, since 1998; Showstudio Ltd, since 2000; *b* 24 Nov. 1958; *s* of Michael A. G. Knight and Beryl Rose Knight; *m* 1995, Charlotte Esme Wheeler; one *s* two *d*. *Educ:* Hinchingbrooke Comprehensive Sch., Huntingdon; Chelsea Coll., London Univ.; Bournemouth and Poole Coll. of Art (PQE Dip. in Art and Design (Distinction) 1982; Hon. Fellow, 1998). Commissioning Picture Editor, ID magazine, 1990; Photographer, Vogue, 1995–. Hon. MA Anglia Poly. Univ., 2000. *Publications:* Skinhead, 1982; Nicknight, 1994; Flora, 1997; Nick Knight, 2009. *Recreations:* architecture, natural history. *T:* (020) 8940 1086.

**KNIGHT, Dr Peter Clayton,** CBE 1995; DL; Vice-Chancellor, University of Central England in Birmingham, 1992–2006 (Director, Birmingham Polytechnic, 1985–92); *s* of Norman Clayton Knight and Vera Catherine Knight; *m* 1977, Catherine Mary (*née* Ward); one *s* one *d*. *Educ:* Univ. of York (BA 1st cl. Hons Physics; DPhil). SRC Studentship, 1968; Asst Teacher, Plymstock Comprehensive Sch., 1971; Plymouth Polytechnic: Lectr, 1972; Sen. Lectr, 1974; Head of Combined Studies, 1981; Dep. Dir, Lancashire Polytechnic, 1982–85. Nat. Pres., NATFHE, 1977; Chm., SRHE, 1987–89; Member: Burnham Cttee of Further Educn, 1976–81; Working Party on Management of Higher Educn, 1977; Nat. Adv. Body on Public Sector Higher Educn, 1982–85; PCFC, 1989–93; Polytechnic and Colleges Employers Forum, 1989–94; Teacher Training Agency, 1994–2000. Member: Armed Forces Pay Review Bd, 2004–10; Boundary Cttee for England, 2007–10; Local Govt Boundary Commn for England, 2010–17; Chair, Prison Service Pay Review Body, 2011–18. Mem., Focus Housing Assoc., 1991–; Chm., Prime Focus Regeneration Gp (formerly Focus Housing Gp), 1996–2006; Mem. Bd, Wolverhampton Homes, 2008–. DL W Midlands, 2008. DUniv: York, 1991; Middlesex, 2006; Birmingham City, 2007; Hon. DSc Aston, 1997. *Publications:* articles, chapters and reviews in learned jls on educnl policy, with particular ref. to higher educn. *Recreation:* flying and building light aircraft. *Address:* Sandy Lodge, Sandy Lane, Brewood, Staffs ST19 9ET.

**KNIGHT, Prof. Sir Peter Leonard,** Kt 2005; DPhil; FRS 1999; FInstP; Professor of Quantum Optics, 1988–2010, now Emeritus, Senior Principal, 2008–09, and Deputy Rector (Research), 2009–10, Imperial College of Science, Technology and Medicine; Senior Fellow in Residence (formerly Principal), Kavli Royal Society International Centre, Chicheley Hall, since 2010; *b* 12 Aug. 1947; *s* of Joseph and Eva Knight; *m* 1965, Christine Huckle; two *s* one *d*. *Educ:* Bedford Modern Sch.; Sussex Univ. (BSc, DPhil). FInstP 1991. Research Associate, Univ. of Rochester, NY, 1972–74; SRC Res. Fellow, Sussex Univ., 1974–76; Jubilee Res. Fellow, 1976–78, SERC Advanced Fellow, 1978–79, RHC; Imperial College, London: SERC Advanced Fellow, 1979–83; Lectr, 1983–87; Reader, 1987–88; Head, Laser Optics and Spectroscopy, then Quantum Optics and Laser Sci., Physics Dept, 1992–2001; Head, Physics Dept, 2001–05; Acting Principal of Physical Scis, 2004–05; Principal, Faculty of Natural Scis, 2006–08. Chief Scientific Advr, 2002–05, Chm., Quantum Metrology Inst. (formerly Quantum Measurement Inst.), 2014–, Mem., Sci. and Technol. Adv. Cttee, 2015–, NPL; Chm., Defence Scientific Adv. Council UK, MoD, 2007–10. Mem., SERC Atomic and Molecular Physics Sub Cttee, 1987–90; Co-ordinator, SERC Nonlinear Optics Initiative, 1989–92 (Chm., Prog. Adv. Gp, 1992–95). Member Council: Royal Soc., 2005–07; STFC, 2009–12 (Chm., Sci. Bd, 2007–08). Chm., Quantum Electronics Div., European Physical Soc., 1988–92; President: Physics Sect., BAAS, 1994–95; Optical Soc. of America, 2004 (Fellow 1996; Dir, 1999–2001); Inst. of Physics, 2011–13. Mem. Council, Sussex Univ., 2013–. Corresp. Mem., Mexican Acad. of Scis, 2000. Hon. DSc: Nat. Inst. for Astronomy, Optics and Electronics, Mexico, 1998; Slovak Acad. of Scis, 2000; Sussex, 2010; Heriot-Watt, 2010; Royal Holloway, 2013; Macquarie, 2014; Glasgow, 2015; Huddersfield, 2015; Birmingham, 2017. Parsons Meml Lectr, Royal Soc. and Inst. of Physics, 1991; Humboldt Res. Award, Alexander von Humboldt Foundn, 1993; Einstein Medal and Prize for Laser Science, Soc. of Optical and Quantum Electronics and Eastman Kodak Co., 1996; Thomas Young Medal and Prize, 1999, Glazebrook Medal, 2009, Inst. of Physics; Ives Medal, Optical Soc. of America, 2008; Royal Medal, Royal Soc., 2010; Herbert Walther Prize, Optical Soc. of America and German Phys. Soc., 2019. Ed., Contemporary Physics, 1993–. *Publications:* Concepts of Quantum Optics, 1983; (with Chris Gerry) Introductory Quantum Optics, 2004; papers in Phys. Rev., Phys. Rev. Letters and other jls. *Recreations:* traditional music, walking. *Address:* Blackett Laboratory, Imperial College London, Prince Consort Road, SW7 2AZ. *T:* (020) 7584 7727.

**KNIGHT, Roger David Verdon,** OBE 2007; Secretary & Chief Executive, Marylebone Cricket Club, 2000–06 (Secretary, 1994–2000); *b* 6 Sept. 1946; *s* of late David Verdon Knight and Thelma Patricia Knight; *m* 1971, Christine Ann McNab (*née* Miln); one *s* one *d*. *Educ:* Dulwich Coll.; St Catharine's Coll., Cambridge (BA Modern and Medieval Langs 1969; MA 1972; DipEd 1970). Assistant Master: Eastbourne Coll., 1970–78; Dulwich Coll., 1978–83; Housemaster, Cranleigh Sch., 1983–90; Headmaster, Worksop Coll., 1990–93. Professional cricketer (summers only): Gloucestershire, 1971–75; Sussex, 1976–77; Surrey, 1978–84 (Captain, 1978–83). Vice-Chm., SE Region, Sports Council, 1985–90; Chm. Management Cttee, SE Region, Centres of Excellence, 1987–90; Member: Cricket Cttee, Surrey CCC, 1987–90 (Pres., 2008–09); MCC Cttee, 1989–92; HMC Sports Sub-Cttee, 1991–93; ICC Develt Cttee, 1996–2006, 2007–10; Mgt Bd, ECB, 1997–2006; Council, London Playing Fields Soc., 1998–2002; European Cricket Council, 1998–2011 (Chm., 2006–11); Chm., ECB Assoc. of Cricket Officials, 2005–16; President: European Cricket Fedn, 1994–97; Cambridge Univ. CC, 2009–; MCC, 2015–16. Trustee, MCC Foundn, 2006–. Governor: TVS Trust, 1987–92; Rendcomb Coll., 1995–99; King's Coll., Taunton, 1998–2017 (Chm., Educn Cttee, 2005–10; Custos, King's Schs, 2010–17); Dulwich Coll., 2004–10; Millfield, 2008–09. *Recreations:* cricket, tennis, bridge, piano music, 17th Century French literature, walking, Real Tennis, travel.

**KNIGHT, Dr Roger John Beckett,** FRHistS; Professor of Naval History, University of Greenwich, 2006–09 (Visiting Professor, 2001–06 and 2009–14); Senior Research Fellow, Institute of Historical Research, University of London, since 2014; *b* 11 April 1944; *s* of John Beckett Knight and Alyson Knight (*née* Nunn); *m* 1st, 1968, Elizabeth Magowan (marr. diss. 1980); two *s*; 2nd, 1998, Jane Hamilton-Eddy. *Educ:* Tonbridge Sch.; Trinity Coll., Dublin (MA); Sussex Univ. (PGCE); University Coll. London (PhD). FRHistS 1988. Asst Master, Haberdashers' Aske's Sch., Elstree, 1972–73; National Maritime Museum: Dep. Custodian of Manuscripts, 1974–77, Custodian, 1977–80; Dep. Head, Printed Books and Manuscripts Dept, 1980–84; Head, Inf. Project Gp, 1984–86; Head, Documentation Div., 1986–88; Chief Curator, 1988–93; Dep. Dir, 1993–2000. Trustee, Nat. Maritime Mus., Cornwall, 1998–2002. Member Council: Soc. for Nautical Research, 1977–81 (Vice-Pres., 1993–2006); Navy Records Soc., 1974–2009 (Vice-Pres., 1980–84, 2003–07).

Caird Medal, Nat. Maritime Mus., Greenwich, 2014. *Publications:* Guide to the Manuscripts in the National Maritime Museum, vol. 1, 1977, vol. 2, 1980; (with Alan Frost) The Journal of Daniel Paine 1794–1797, 1983; Portsmouth Dockyard Papers 1774–1783: the American War, 1987; (ed jtly) British Naval Documents 1204–1960, 1993; The Pursuit of Victory: the life and achievement of Horatio Nelson, 2005 (Mountbatten Maritime Prize, British Maritime Charitable Foundn, 2005; Duke of Westminster's Medal, RUSI, 2006); (with Martin Wilcox) Sustaining the Fleet, 1793–1815: war, the British navy and the contractor state, 2010; Britain Against Napoleon: the organization of victory, 1793–1815, 2013; William IV: a king at sea, 2015; articles, reviews in jls. *Recreations:* walking, music. *Address:* Institute of Historical Research, University of London, Senate House, WC1E 7HU. *Club:* Athenæum.

**KNIGHT, Stephen John;** Operations Director, London Trading Standards, since 2018; *b* Roehampton, 15 May 1970; *s* of Dr David Knight and Ruth Knight (*née* Fry); partner, 2004, Jennifer Churchill; two *d*; one step *d* from previous marriage. *Educ:* Teddington Sch.; Richmond upon Thames Coll.; Univ. of Southampton (BSc Physics). Pres., Southampton Univ. Students Union, 1992–93; PR Officer, Jubilee Sailing Trust, 1994–95; Consultant, Argyll Public Relns, 1995–96; Political Advr to Lib Dem Gp, Assoc. of London Govt, subseq. London Councils, 1996–2008. Mem. (Lib Dem), Richmond upon Thames LBC, 1998–2018 (Dep. Leader, 2006–10; Leader of the Opposition, 2010–15). Mem. (Lib Dem) London Assembly, GLA, 2012–16. Mem., Standards Bd for England, 2009–12; Vice Chairman: Workforce Bd, LGA, 2011–13; Nat. Employers' Orgn for Sch. Teachers, 2011–13. Chm. Govs, St Mary's and St Peter's Primary Sch., 2002–12. FRSA. *Recreations:* family, cinema, sailing. *Address:* 73 Harrowdene Gardens, Teddington TW11 0DJ. *T:* (020) 8977 4541.

**KNIGHT, Steven;** writer, since 1989; *b* 5 Aug. 1959; *s* of George and Ida Knight. *Educ:* University Coll. London (BA Hons English). Writer, producer, Capital Radio, 1983–87; writer for television, 1990–: Detectives; Canned Carrott; Ruby Wax Show; Commercial Breakdown; All About Me; Peaky Blinders, 2013, 2014, 2016, 2017, 2019; Taboo, 2017; Co-creator, Who Wants To Be a Millionaire?, 1998; screenwriter: Gypsy Woman, 2000; Dirty Pretty Things, 2003 (awards include: Best British Screenwriter, London Film Critics' Circle Awards, 2003; Humanitas Award, 2004; Edgar Award for Best Motion Picture Screenplay, 2004); Amazing Grace, 2007 (Epiphany Prize, John Templeton Foundn, 2008); Eastern Promises, 2007 (Cadillac People's Choice Award, Tribeca Film Fest., 2007; Genie Award, Acad. of Canadian Cinema and TV, 2008); (also Dir) Hummingbird, 2013; Closed Circuit, 2013; The Hundred-Foot Journey, 2014; (also Dir) Locke, 2014; Seventh Son, 2015; Pawn Sacrifice, 2015; Burnt, 2015; Allied, 2016; November Criminals, 2017; Woman Walks Ahead, 2018; (co-writer) The Girl in the Spider's Web, 2018; Serenity, 2019; writer for theatre: The President of an Empty Room, NT, 2005. *Publications:* The Movie House, 1994; Alphabet City, 1998; Out of the Blue, 1999; The Last Words of Will Wolfkin, 2010. *Recreations:* writing, fishing, Birmingham City FC. *Address:* c/o Natasha Galloway, United Agents, 12–26 Lexington Street, W1F 0LE.

**KNIGHT, Terence Gordon,** FRICS; *b* 1 June 1944; *s* of Albert Henry and Eileen Doris Knight; *m* 1968, Gillian Susan West; two *s*. *Educ:* St Paul's Sch. FRICS 1976. Joined Weatherall Green & Smith, Chartered Surveyors, 1962; Partner, 1976–2001; Sen. Partner, 1992–98. Liveryman, Chartered Surveyors' Co., 1988 (Master, 2004–05). *Recreations:* golf, walking. *Clubs:* St Enodoc Golf, Worplesdon Golf.

**KNIGHT, Veronica Lesley;** *see* Hammerton, V. L.

**KNIGHT, William John Langford,** OBE 2012; Chairman, Financial Reporting Review Panel, 2004–12; Senior Partner, Simmons & Simmons, 1996–2001; portrait photographer; *b* 11 Sept. 1945; *s* of William Knight and Gertrude Alice Knight; *m* 1973, Stephanie Irina Williams; one *s* one *d*. *Educ:* Sir Roger Manwood's Sch., Sandwich; Bristol Univ. (LLB). Admitted solicitor, 1969; joined Simmons & Simmons, 1967; Partner, 1973; i/c Hong Kong Office, 1979–82; Head, Corporate Dept, 1994–96. Chairman: London Weighting Adv. Panel, GLA, 2002; Enforcement Cttee, Gen. Insce Standards Council, 2002–05; Member: Financial Reporting Council, 2004–07 (Dir, 2008–12); Gaming Bd for GB, 2004–05; Gambling Commn, 2005–12. Specialist Advr to Treasury Select Cttee in reln to report by FSA on failure of Royal Bank of Scotland, 2011–12. Trustee: Common Purpose Internat., 2008–10; National Life Stories, 2011–. Mem. Council, Lloyd's, 2000–08 (Dep. Chm., 2003–08). Liveryman, Solicitors' Co., 1983 (Master, 2007–08). FRSA. Photographic exhibitions: The Refugee's Gift, St Martin-in-the-Fields, 2014; Portrait of Elsbeth Juda, NPG, 2014; Where I Come From, Cumberland Lodge, Great Park, Windsor, 2017; Portrait of Gustav Born, NPG, 2018. *Publications:* The Acquisition of Private Companies and Business Assets, 1975, 7th edn 1997. *Recreations:* tennis, Arsenal FC. *W:* www.knightsight.co.uk. *Clubs:* Travellers; Hong Kong (Hong Kong).

**KNIGHT-SANDS, Catherine;** HM Diplomatic Service; Ambassador to Montenegro, 2009–13. British Council: Sen. Teaching Advr, Naples, 1984–87; Asst Dir of Studies, Jakarta, 1987–89; Dir of Studies, Milan, 1990–94; entered FCO, 1994; Desk Officer: France, Switzerland, Italy, Western Eur. Dept, FCO, 1994–96; Eur. Defence Section, Security Policy Dept, FCO, 1996–98; Hd, France/Italy Section, Western Eur. Dept, FCO, 1998–99; First Sec. Political (Balkans), UK Delegn to OSCE, Vienna, 1999–2003; Dep. Hd of Mission, Sarajevo, 2004–07; Political Counsellor, Baghdad, 2007–09.

**KNIGHT SMITH, Ian;** *see* Smith, Ian K.

**KNIGHTLEY;** *see* Finch-Knightley, family name of Earl of Aylesford.

**KNIGHTLEY, Sharman;** *see* Macdonald, S.

**KNIGHTON, Dr Tessa Wendy;** writer; ICREA Research Professor, Institució Milà i Fontanals (CSIC), Barcelona, since 2011; Fellow, Clare College, Cambridge, 1996–2011, now Emeritus; *b* 31 March 1957; *d* of Geoffrey Morris Knighton and (Margaret) Wendy Knighton; *m* 1984, Ivor Bolton, *qv*; one *s*. *Educ:* Felixstowe Coll., Suffolk; Clare Coll., Cambridge (MA 1980; PhD 1984). Jun. Res. Fellow, Lady Margaret Hall, Oxford, 1982–84; freelance writer and editor, 1984–; Asst Ed., 1988–91, Ed., 1992–2009, Early Music; Lectr, Faculty of Music, Cambridge Univ., 1991–93; Res. Associate, RHBNC, Univ. of London, 1993–99; Leverhulme Res. Asst, Faculty of Music, Univ. of Cambridge, 2000–03. Artistic Dir, Lufthansa Fest. of Baroque Music, 1986–97; Early Music Critic: Gramophone, 1988–; The Times, 1995–; radio broadcasts. Sec. to Editl Bd, Monumentos de la Música Española, 2013–; Series Ed., Studies in Medieval and Renaissance Music, 2004–. *Publications:* (ed jtly) Companion to Medieval and Renaissance Music, 1992; Música y Músicos en la Corte de Fernando de Aragón 1474–1516, 2000; (jtly) Felipe II y la Música, 2001; Early Music Printing and Publishing in the Iberian World, 2007; Devotional Music in the Iberian World, 1450–1800, 2008; Music and Urban Society in Colonial Latin America, 2011; Pure Gold: sacred music of the Iberian Renaissance, 2011; (ed) Companion to Music in the Age of the Catholic Monarchs, 2016; Hearing the City in Early Modern Europe, 2018; articles in Music and Letters, Early Music History, Early Music, Plainsong and Medieval Music, Revista de Musicología, Renaissance Studies, Artigrama, etc. *Recreations:* wine, walking, whippets, song. *Address:* Institució Milà i Fontanals (CSIC), Calle Egipcíaques 15, 08001 Barcelona, Spain.

**KNIGHTON, William Myles,** CB 1981; Principal Establishment and Finance Officer, Department of Trade and Industry, 1986–91; *b* 8 Sept. 1931; *s* of late George Harry Knighton, OBE, and Ella Knighton (*née* Stroud); *m* 1957, Brigid Helen Carrothers (*d* 2019); one *s* one *d*. *Educ*: Bedford School; Peterhouse, Cambridge (MA). Asst Principal, Min. of Supply, 1954; Principal, Min. of Aviation, 1959; Cabinet Office, 1962–64; Principal Private Sec. to Minister of Technology, 1966–68; Asst Sec., Min. of Technology, subseq. DTI and Dept of Trade, 1967–74; Under Sec., 1974–78, Dep. Sec., 1978–83, Dept of Trade; Dep. Sec., Dept of Transport, 1983–86. *Publications:* (with D. E. Rosenthal) National Laws and International Commerce, 1982. *Recreations:* gardening, hill-walking, music, painting, reading. *Address:* Court Green, St Anne's Hill, Midhurst, W Sussex GU29 9NN. *T:* (01730) 817860. *Club:* Oxford and Cambridge.

**KNIGHTS, Laurence James W.;** *see* West-Knights.

**KNIGHTS, Martin Christopher,** CEng, FREng, FICE; independent consulting engineer, since 2017; Senior Vice President, and Managing Director and Senior Fellow of Technology, Tunnelling and Earth Engineering Practice, CH2MHill, 2013–17; *b* Watford, 16 May 1948; *s* of Anthony and Rita Knights; *m* 1970, Jennifer Anne Gleeson; one *s* one *d*. *Educ*: St Gabriel's, Bury, Lancs; Bolton Inst. of Technol.; Univ. of Manchester Inst. of Sci. and Technol. (BSc Hons 1970). CEng 1974; FREng 2013. Site and Design Engr, Mott Hay and Anderson, 1970–76; Researcher, UMIST, 1972–73; Design Engr, Saudi Arabia, Yemen and UK, 1976–77; Project Design and Site Mgr, Sir Alexander Gibb and Partners, SA, 1977–81; Design Mgr, WS Atkins, 1981–89; Dir, KBR (UK), 1989–2005; Hd of Profession for Tunnelling, Jacobs Babtie (UK), 2005–10; Dir, Tunnelling and Earth Engrg, CH2MHill, 2010–13. Non-exec. Chm., London Bridge Associates Ltd, 2017–. Industrial Tutor, Univ. of Oxford, 1996–99. Pres., Internat. Tunnelling Assoc., 2007–10. Hon. Pres., Croatian Tunnelling Assoc., 2010–. Trustee, Brunel Mus., Rotherhithe, 2008–. Freeman, City of London, 2016; Liveryman, Engineers' Co., 2016. James Clarke Medal, ICE, 2010. *Publications:* The Story of Tunnels, 1989; contrib. tech. papers and guidelines on tunnel design; author and co-author of over 50 tech. papers and presentations to internat. gatherings. *Recreations:* family, music, travel, walking. *Address:* Hillview, Cliftonville, Dorking, Surrey RH4 2JF. *T:* 07956 029833. *E:* martinknightsconsulting@gmail.com.

**KNIGHTS, Peter David;** Co-Founder and Chief Executive Officer, WildAid, since 2000; *b* Birmingham, 9 Feb. 1964; *s* of James and Ruth Knights; *m* 2002, Corie Eva Henniger; two *d*. *Educ*: King Edward's Sch., Birmingham; London Sch. of Econs and Pol Sci. (BSc Econs 1987). Investigator and campaigner, Envmtl Investigation Agency, 1989–95; prog. dir of illegal wildlife trade, Global Survival Network, 1995–98; Dir, Barbara Delano Foundn, 1998–2000. *Address:* WildAid US, 333 Pine Street, Suite 300, San Francisco, CA 94104, USA. *T:* (415) 8343174. *E:* knights@wildaid.org. *Club:* Battery (San Francisco).

**KNIGHTS, Rosemary Margaret;** *see* Steven, R. M.

**KNIGHTS, Samantha Jane;** QC 2018; *b* Wimbledon, 24 Feb. 1971; *d* of Michael Timothy Knights and Sheila Judith Knights (*née* Warnes); *m* 2010, Bijan Omrani; one *s* one *d*. *Educ*: Somerville Coll., Oxford (BA Hons); London Sch. of Econs and Political Sci. (LLM 2004). Called to the Bar, Lincoln's Inn, 1996; in practice as a barrister, Matrix Chambers, 2005–. Adjunct Prof., Univ. of Miami, 2017–. Co-Dir, Shute Fest. (formerly Shute Fest. of Lit. and Landscape), 2016–. *Publications:* Freedom of Religion, Minorities, and the Law, 2007. *Recreations:* gardening and landscaping, swimming, ski-ing, singing, arts. *Address:* 1 Shute House, Shute EX13 7NY. *T:* (01297) 639748. *E:* samanthaknights@gmail.com.

**KNILL, Sir Thomas (John Pugin Bartholomew),** 5th Bt *cr* 1893, of The Grove, Blackheath, Kent; *b* 23 Aug. 1952; *er s* of Sir John Kenelm Stuart Knill, 4th Bt and Violette Maud Florence Martin (*née* Barnes; *d* 1983); *S* father, 1998; *m* 1977, Kathleen Muszynski (marr. diss. 1996, now partner); three *d*. *Gov.*, Lucton Sch., Herefordshire, 2010–. Member: Pugin Soc.; Old Luctonians Assoc. *Recreations:* reading, the arts, politics, current affairs, genealogy, thinking. *Heir: b* Jenkyn Martin Benedict Stuart Knill [*b* 19 Jan. 1954; *m* 1978, Helen Marguerite Gulliver; two *s* one *d*].

**KNIVETON, Patrick Edward,** CEng, FIMechE; Head, Engineering Skills and Knowledge Management, Rolls-Royce Marine Power, 2014–16; President, Institution of Mechanical Engineers, 2013–14; *b* Scarborough, 29 July 1954; *s* of Edward George Kniveton and Winifred Mary Kniveton (*née* Hopwood); *m* 1988, Melanie Lucas; one *s* two *d*. *Educ*: Scarborough High Sch. for Boys; Univ. of Leeds (BSc Hons Mech. Engrg 1976); Univ. of Newcastle upon Tyne (MBA Dist. 1999). CEng 1985; MIMechE 1985, FIMechE 1993. Tech. Asst, NEI Reyrolle, 1976–79; Asset Manager, Quality Control, Grubb Parsons, 1979–85; Sen. Applications Engr, SKF Engrg Products, 1985–87; Engrg Manager, Rotawing Fans, 1987–89; Sen. Design Engr, NEI Controls, 1989–92; Asst Chief Engr, RR Industrial Controls, 1992–98; Divl Engrg Manager, Rolls-Royce Materials Handling, 1998–99; Hd, Business Mgt, Rolls-Royce GT Ops Engrg, 1999–2007; Hd, Infrastructure, 2007–09; Hd, Engrg Improvement, 2009–14, Rolls-Royce Marine Power. Vis. Prof., Univ. of Derby, 2014–. Dir, Rolls-Royce (Pension Trustees) Ltd, 1998–2017. Institution of Mechanical Engineers: Mem. Council, 1992–2002; Mem., Trustee Bd, 2002–07; Vice Pres., 2004–07; Dep. Pres., 2011–13; Trustee, Sci. Council, 2017–. MCMI (MIMgt 1994), FCMI (FIMgt 2001); CMgr 2003; CCMI 2014. *Recreations:* theatre, Romano-British history, badminton, swimming, walking, ski-ing, cycling.

**KNOLLYS,** family name of **Viscount Knollys**.

**KNOLLYS,** 3rd Viscount *cr* 1911, of Caversham; **David Francis Dudley Knollys;** Baron *cr* 1902; *b* 12 June 1931; *s* of 2nd Viscount Knollys, GCMG, MBE, DFC, and Margaret (*d* 1987), *o d* of Sir Stuart Coats, 2nd Bt; *S* father, 1966; *m* 1959, Hon. Sheelin Virginia Maxwell (*see* Viscountess Knollys); three *s* one *d*. *Educ*: Eton. Lt, Scots Guards, 1951. *Heir: s* Hon. Patrick Nicholas Mark Knollys [*b* 11 March 1962; *m* 1998, Mrs Sarah Wright, *o d* of Michael Petch; one *s* one *d*]. *Address:* The Bailiff's House, Bramerton Hall Farm, Norwich, Norfolk NR14 7DN.

**KNOLLYS, Viscountess; Sheelin Virginia Knollys,** OBE 2005; Vice Lord-Lieutenant, Norfolk, 2005–12; *b* 5 Dec. 1937; *d* of late Hon. Somerset Maxwell, MP and Susan Maxwell (*née* Roberts); *m* 1959, Hon. David Francis Dudley Knollys (*see* Viscount Knollys); three *s* one *d*. *Educ*: Hatherop Castle Sch.; Sorbonne. Partner in dried flower business, 1975–97. Mem., E Anglian Tourist Bd, 1988–91; Chairman: Norwich Area Tourism Agency, 1993–2005; English Rural Housing Assoc., 1996–2009; Inland Waterways Amenity Adv. Council, 1997–2006; Norfolk and Suffolk Broads Authy, 1997–2003 (Mem., 1987–2003). Non-exec. Dir, E Norfolk HA, 1990–99; Dir, VisitNorwich Ltd, 2005–12. Vice Pres., Inland Waterways Assoc., 2004–09. Branch Pres., Arthritis Care, 1965–2005. Trustee: How Hill Trust, 2000–14 (Vice Chm., 2000–14); S Norfolk Buildings Preservation Trust, 2000–11 (Chm., 2000–08); Norfolk Partners Against Crime Taskforce, 2008–13. Mem. (C) S Norfolk DC, 1983–2003 (Chm., 1996–97). DL 1996, High Sheriff 2008–09, Norfolk. Gov., Wymondham Coll., 1989–97 (Visitor, 2014–16); Lay Mem., Council, UEA, 1997–2006. *Recreations:* gardening, golf. *Address:* The Bailiff's House, Bramerton Hall Farm, Norwich, Norfolk NR14 7DN.

*See also Baron Farnham.*

**KNOPF, His Honour Elliot Michael;** a Circuit Judge, 2002–15; a Deputy High Court Judge, 2008–15; *b* 23 Dec. 1950; *s* of Harry and Clara Knopf; *m* 1976, Elizabeth Carol Lieberman; one *s* one *d*. *Educ*: Bury Grammar Sch.; University Coll. London (LLB Hons); Coll. of Law, Chester. Admitted solicitor, 1976; Partner, Pannone and Partners, Manchester, 1979–91; a District Judge, 1991–2002; Asst Recorder, 1996–2000; a Recorder of the Crown Court, 2000–02. *Recreations:* foreign travel, reading, entertaining friends and being entertained by them, the family.

**KNOTT, David Mark;** Director, Office for Civil Society, Department for Digital, Culture, Media and Sport, since 2017 (Deputy Director, 2014–17); *b* Nottingham, 27 May 1981; *s* of Frederick Dieter Knott and Irene Knott (*née* Fairclough); *m* 2014, Thea Hutchinson; two *d*. *Educ*: Univ. of Sheffield (BA Econs 2002); Univ. of Nottingham (MA Econ. Analysis 2004); London Sch. of Econs and Pol Sci. (MA Public Policy (Dist.) 2017). Economist, Prime Minister's Strategy Unit, 2004–06; Economic Adviser: DFID, 2006; Prime Minister's Strategy Unit, 2006–08; on secondment as Sen. Policy Advr, Govt of Qld, Australia, 2008; Dep. Dir, and Hd, Social Mobility Commn, Cabinet Office, 2008–09; Dep. Hd, Govt Adv. Practice, 2009–14. FRSA 2011. *Recreations:* family, swimming, lido lounging, film, pharology, social history, tennis, architecture, travel. *Address:* Office for Civil Society, Department for Digital, Culture, Media and Sport, 100 Parliament Street, Westminster, SW1A 2BQ. *T:* (020) 7211 6000. *E:* david.knott@culture.gov.uk.

**KNOTT, (Graeme) Jonathan,** CMG 2019; HM Diplomatic Service; Ambassador to Republic of Poland, since 2016; *b* 2 Nov. 1966; *s* of Daniel Wilfred Knott and Anne Lesley Knott; *m* 2005, Angela Susan Jepson; two *s* one *d*. *Educ*: Portsmouth Grammar Sch.; Mansfield Coll., Oxford (MA Law); MSP. ACMA 2007. Entered FCO, 1988; Third, later Second Sec., Cuba, 1991–95; Dep. Eur. Corresp. to EU, 1995–96; Hd, Political/Econ. Section, Mexico City, 1996–2000; UK Trade and Finance negotiator, OECD, 2000–04; Prog. Dir, FCO Services Trading Fund, 2005–06; Hd, Financial Planning and Perf., FCO, 2006–08; Dep. Hd of Mission and Minister Counsellor, Seoul, S Korea, 2008–11; Ambassador to Hungary, 2012–15. *Recreations:* tennis, golf, travel. *Address:* c/o Foreign and Commonwealth Office, King Charles Street, SW1A 2AH.

**KNOWLES, Ben;** Innovation and Transformation Director, Hope and Homes for Children, since 2018 (Head of Innovation, 2015–18); *b* 29 Aug. 1973; *s* of John and Pat Knowles; *m* 2010, Charlotte Saxe; two *s*. *Educ*: Beverley Grammar Sch.; Hertford Coll., Oxford (BA Hons Hist.). Writer: Daily Mirror, 1994–95; Smash Hits, 1995–97; Melody Maker, 1998–2000; Ed., New Musical Express, 2000–02; Dep. Ed., Zoo mag., 2003–06; Jt Dep. Ed., Daily Star, 2006–08; Music and Entertainment Dir, 2008–11; Dir of Fundraising, 2011–14, Dir of Music, Marketing and Communications, 2014–15, War Child. Mem., Cultural Strategy Gp for London, GLA, 2000–04. Dir, War Child Music, 2004–15. *Recreations:* Fulham FC, pubs, rock 'n' roll, cooking, photography, spending time with my family.

**KNOWLES, Sir Charles (Francis),** 7th Bt *cr* 1765; architect in private practice, since 1984; *b* 20 Dec. 1951; *s* of Sir Francis Gerald William Knowles, 6th Bt, FRS, and of Ruth Jessie, *d* of late Rev. Arthur Brooke-Smith; *S* father, 1974; *m* 1979, Amanda Louise Margaret, *d* of late Lance Lee Bromley (marr. diss. 2003); two *s*. *Educ*: Marlborough Coll.; Oxford Sch. of Architecture (DipArch 1977; RIBA 1979). Director: Charles Knowles Design Ltd (architects); Richmond Knowles Architects; works include: new Battersea Dogs Home, London and Old Windsor; refurbishment of Bank of England, historic country houses and listed London properties. FRSA. *Recreations:* photography, shooting, travel, piloting light aircraft. *Heir: s* (Charles) William (Frederick Lance) Knowles [*b* 27 Aug. 1985; *m* 2011, Holly Koch]. *Address:* c/o Charles Knowles Design Ltd, 5 The Powerhouse, 70 Chiswick High Road, W4 1SY.

**KNOWLES, Colin George,** PhD; feudal title, Lord Knowles of Houghton and Burnett, 2006; Director of Development and Public Relations, University of Bophuthatswana, 1985–95; Secretary and Trustee, University of Bophuthatswana Foundation, 1985–95; *b* 11 April 1939; *s* of late George William Knowles, Tarleton, Lancs; three *d* by former marriages. *Educ*: King George V Grammar Sch., Southport; CEDEP, Fontainebleau, France; Trinity Coll., Delaware, USA (MA 1991; PhD 1994). MInstM 1966; MCIPR (MIPR 1970); Mem. BAIE 1972; FPRISA 1993 (MPRISA 1983); APR 1987; AAArb 1991; MSAAIE 1993. Appointed Comr of Oaths, 1991. Joined John Player & Sons, 1960; sales and marketing management appts; Head of Public Relations, 1971–73; joined Imperial Tobacco Ltd, 1973; Hd of Public Affairs, 1973–80; Company Sec., 1979–80. Chairman: Griffin Associates Ltd, 1980–83; Concept Communications (Pty) Ltd (S Africa), 1983–84; Dir, TWS Public Relations (Pty) Ltd (S Africa), 1984–85. Mem. Council, Tobacco Trade Benevolent Assoc., 1975–80; Chm., Bophuthatswana Reg., PRISA, 1988–91. Dir, Bophuthatswana Council for Consumer Affairs, 1991–94. Director: Nottingham Festival Assoc. Ltd, 1969–71; English Sinfonia Orchestra, 1972–80; Midland Sinfonia Concert Soc. Ltd, 1972–80; (also co-Founder) Assoc. for Business Sponsorship of The Arts Ltd, 1975–84 (Chm., 1975–80); Bristol Hippodrome Trust Ltd, 1977–81; Bath Archaeological Trust Ltd, 1978–81; The Palladian Trust Ltd, 1979–82; Mem., Chancellor of Duchy of Lancaster's Cttee of Honour on Business and the Arts, 1980–81. Arts sponsorship initiatives include responsibility for: Internat. Cello Competition (with Tortelier), Bristol, 1975 and 1977; Internat. Conductors Awards, 1978; Pompeii Exhibn, RA, 1976–77; new prodns at Royal Opera House, Covent Garden, at Glyndebourne, and at National Theatre. Governor: Manning Grammar Sch., Nottingham, 1972–73; Clayesmore Sch., Dorset, 1975–85. Chm., St John Ambulance Foundn in Bophuthatswana, 1989–94; Mem. Chapter, Priory of St John, S Africa, 1992–99. Liveryman, Worshipful Co. of Tobacco Pipe Makers and Tobacco Blenders, 1973; Freeman, City of London, 1974. FCMI (FBIM 1972); FRSA 1975; FRCSoc 1976. KStJ 1995 (CStJ 1991; OStJ 1977). *Recreations:* reading, travel, country pursuits. *E:* cgk@talktalk.net. *Clubs:* Carlton, MCC, XL.

**KNOWLES, Eric;** independent fine art valuer and broadcaster; *b* Nelson, Lancs, 19 Feb. 1953; *s* of James and June Knowles; *m* 1976, Anita Whiting; two *s*. *Educ*: Edge End Sch., Nelson; Nelson and Colne Coll. of Further Educn. Reservations Clerk, Lyons Tours, 1970–71; Cataloguer, Herbert Sutcliffe Antique Dealers, 1971–72; Quality Controller, Pioneer Weston Engrg, 1972–75; joined Bonham's Auctioneers, 1976; porter, then Hd, Ceramics Dept, 1981–2001; Dir, 1984–2005. Non-exec. Dir, W. Moorcroft Ltd, 2002–. Consultant: Dreweatt Neate Fine Art, 2013–15; Swan Fine Art Auctions, 2015–19. *Television* programmes include: expert: in ceramics, Antiques Roadshow, 1981–; Great Antiques Hunt, 1995–99; Antique Inspectors, 1997–98; (resident) Going for a Song, 1997–2000; The Really Useful Show, 1997; 20th Century Roadshow, 2004; (resident) Antique Master, 2010–11; presenter: Crimewatch UK, 1988–98; Noel's House Party, 1993–99; Good Morning with Anne and Nick, 1994–95; The Great House Game, 1998–99; Celebrity Ready Steady Cook, 1998, 2007; You Can't Take it with You, 1999; It's a Gift, 2000; Selling the Family Silver, 2000; Restoration Roadshow, 2010; Put Your Money Where Your Mouth Is, 2012–; Bargain Hunt, 2016–; presenter, Clash of the Collectables, Australian TV, 2016, 2017; panellist: Call My Bluff, 1994–2004; Going, Going Gone, 1995–96; various roles: Dictionary Corner, Countdown, 1998–2004; Pointless, 2014. Resident antiques expert, Jimmy Young Show, BBC Radio 2, 1993–2003; regular contrib., Homes and Antiques Mag., 1993–; resident antiques expert, Sunday

Times, 2005–. Ambassador, Prince's Trust, 2001–; Patron: Merchant's House, Marlborough; Rydale Folk Mus.; Cannon Hall Mus., Cawthorne; Haworth Art Gall., Accrington; De Morgan Foundn; Headway; FABLE; New Mozart Orch.; No 78 Derngate, Northampton; Hon. President: Pilkington Lancastrian Soc.; Friends of Ribchester Roman Mus.; Chm., The Hoard, 2019–; Vice-Chm., Assoc. of Lancastrians in London. Freeman, City of London, 2000. Hon. Fellow, Univ. of Central Lancs, 1999. Hon. MA Nottingham Trent, 1997. FRSA 1996. *Publications:* Victoriana, 1991, 2nd edn 2000; Art Deco, 1991, 2nd edn 2000; Art Nouveau, 1992, 2nd edn 2000; (contrib.) Treasures in your Home, 1993; Victoriana to Art Deco, 1993, repr. as 100 Years of Decorative Arts, 1994; Royal Memorabilia, 1994; Discovering Antiques, 1996; (contrib.) Miller's Understanding Antiques, 1997; Eric Knowles Antiques: a beginner's guide, 2006; (consultant ed.) English Furniture, 2010; Lalique, 2011; Art Deco, 2014. *Recreations:* country walking, jazz, soul and classical music, family, cinema, theatre, football, Roman Britain, visiting National Trust and English Heritage sites, historic buildings and museums. *T:* 07833 246453. *E:* eric@ericknowles.co.uk.

KNOWLES, Rt Rev. Graeme Paul, CVO 2012; Priest Vicar, Westminster Abbey, since 2014; an Honorary Assistant Bishop: Diocese of St Edmundsbury and Ipswich, since 2012; Diocese of Ely, since 2012; *b* 25 Sept. 1951; *s* of Grace and Stanley Knowles; *m* 1973, Susan Gail Marsden. *Educ:* Dunstable Grammar Sch., 1963–70; King's Coll. London, 1970–73 (AKC; FKC 2011). Ordained deacon, 1974, priest, 1975; Asst Curate, St Peter in Thanet, 1974–79; Precentor and Sen. Curate, Leeds Parish Church, 1979–81; Chaplain and Precentor, 1981–87, Chapter Clerk, 1985–87, Portsmouth Cathedral; Vicar of Leigh Park, 1987–93; Rural Dean of Havant, 1990–93; Archdeacon of Portsmouth, 1993–99; Dean of Carlisle, 1999–2003; Bishop of Sodor and Man, 2003–07; Dean of St Paul's, 2007–12; Acting Dean, St Edmundsbury Cathedral, 2017–18. Chm., Church Buildings Council (formerly Council for the Care of Churches), 2003–09 (Mem., 1991–2000); Mem., Gen. Synod of C of E, 2002–07. Registrar, Sons and Friends of the Clergy, 2012–15. Warden, Guild of Church Musicians, 2017–. Hon. Chaplain, RNR, 2008–13. *Recreations:* Victorian and Edwardian songs, the books of E. F. Benson, wine and food. *Address:* 102A Barons Road, Bury St Edmunds, Suffolk IP33 2LY.

KNOWLES, Graham Roy; QC 2009; His Honour Judge Knowles; a Circuit Judge, since 2010; *b* Manchester, 20 Feb. 1968; *s* of late Roy Knowles and of Margaret Knowles; *m* 1999. *Educ:* Queen Elizabeth II High Sch., Peel, IOM; King's Coll., Cambridge (BA 1989; MA 1993). Called to the Bar, Middle Temple, 1990 (Astbury Law Scholar); in practice as a barrister, 1990–2010; Junior, N Circuit, 1994; Recorder, 2005–10. Member: Gen. Council of the Bar, 1995–97; Professional Conduct Cttee of the Bar, 1997–99. *Recreations:* family life, Venice. *Address:* Law Courts, Openshaw Place, Ring Way, Preston, Lancs PR1 2LL. *T:* (01772) 844700.

KNOWLES, Rev. John Geoffrey; Warden of Readers, Diocese of Chester, 2005–16; Associate Minister, Handforth, 2013–19; *b* 12 June 1948; *s* of Geoffrey and Jean Knowles; *m* 1974, Roey Wills; three *d*. *Educ:* St Bees Sch.; Univ. of Manchester (BSc Physics); Worcester Coll., Oxford (CertEd); Univ. of London (MSc Nuclear Physics); W Midlands Ministerial Trng Course. Assistant Master: Mill Hill Sch., 1970–75; Wellington Coll., 1975–76; Head of Physics, Watford GS, 1976–84; Vice Master, Queen Elizabeth's GS, Blackburn, 1984–90; Headmaster, King Edward VI Five Ways Sch., Birmingham, 1990–99; Rector, Hutchesons' GS, 1999–2004. Ordained deacon 1998, priest 1999; Non-Stipendiary Curate, Holy Trinity, The Lickey, 1998–99; Vicar, Woodford, 2005–12. Chief Examr, A-Level Physics (Nuffield), 1990–99. Vice-Chm., 1996–98, Chm., 1998–99, Assoc. Heads of Grant Maintained Schools. Chm. Governors, Kingsmead Sch., 1986–92; Mem., Gen. Convocation, Univ. of Strathclyde, 2003–04. Elgar Society: Treas., 1976–84; Vice-Chm., 1991–95; Chm., NW Br., 2017–. *Publications:* Elgar's Interpreters on Record, 1978, 3rd edn 2015; (contrib.) Elgar Studies, 1988; (contrib.) This is the Best of Me, 1999. *Recreation:* music. *Address:* 15 Clare Avenue, Handforth, Wilmslow SK9 3EQ. *T:* (01625) 526531. *E:* john.knowles92@btinternet.com.

KNOWLES, Hon. Sir Julian (Bernard), Kt 2017; Hon. Mr Justice Knowles; a Judge of the High Court, Queen's Bench Division, since 2017; *b* Manchester, 26 Jan. 1969; *s* of Leo and Patricia Knowles; *m* 2011, Dr Nicola Levitt; one *s*. *Educ:* St John Plessington High Sch.; Xaverian Coll.; Balliol Coll., Oxford (BA 1990). Called to the Bar, Inner Temple, 1994; a Recorder, 2009–17; QC 2011; a Dep. High Ct Judge, 2017. *Publications:* The Law of Extradition and Mutual Assistance, 2002, 3rd edn 2013; The Abolition of the Death Penalty in the United Kingdom: how it happened and why it still matters, 2015. *Recreations:* electronic dance music, looking in bookshops, lager, making bread. *Address:* Royal Courts of Justice, Rolls Building, Fetter Lane, EC4A 1NL. *Clubs:* Oxford and Cambridge; Manchester City Football.

KNOWLES, Michael; governance consultant, 1992–2012; *b* 21 May 1942; *s* of Martin Christopher and Anne Knowles; *m* 1965, Margaret Isabel Thorburn; three *d*. *Educ:* Clapham Coll. RC Grammar Sch. Sales Manager, Export & Home Sales. Mem. (C), 1971–83, Leader, 1974–83, Kingston upon Thames Borough Council. MP (C) Nottingham East, 1983–92; PPS to Minister for Planning and Regional Affairs, 1986, to Minister for Housing and Planning, 1987–88, DoE; Member: Select Cttee on European Legislation, 1984; Select Cttee on Defence, 1990. Governance consultant in Africa, 1992–2003, and in Iraq, 2003–12. *Recreations:* walking, history. *Address:* 2 Ditton Reach, Portsmouth Road, Thames Ditton, Surrey KT7 0XB.

KNOWLES, Michael Ernest, PhD; CChem, FRSC; FIFST, FIAFoST; consultant in food science and regulatory affairs, Belgium, since 2013; *b* 6 May 1942; *s* of late Ernest Frederick Walter Knowles and Lesley (*née* Lambert); *m* 1st, 1965, Rosalind Mary Griffiths (marr. diss. 1975); two *s*; 2nd, 1994, Alexandra Knowles (*née* Hadjiyianni). *Educ:* Nottingham Univ. (BPharm 1st cl. Hons; PhD). CChem 1969; FRSC 1982; FIFST 1983; FIAFoST 2012. ICI Postdoctoral Fellow, Nottingham Univ., 1967–69; Ministry of Agriculture, Fisheries and Food: Food Sci. Unit, Norwich, 1969–74; Scientific Advr, Food Sci. Div., 1974–79; Head, Food Sci. Lab., 1979–85; Head, Food Sci. Div., 1985–89; Chief Scientist (Fisheries and Food), 1989–91; Dir, Scientific and Regulatory Affairs, EMEA, 1992–97; Gtr Europe, 1997–2008, Coca-Cola International; Vice Pres., Global Scientific and Regulatory Affairs, Coca-Cola Co., Brussels, 2009–13. Liveryman, Soc. of Apothecaries, 2011–; Freeman, City of London, 2011. FRSA. *Publications:* series of papers on chemical aspects of food safety in learned jls. *Recreations:* clay pigeon and practical pistol shooting, walking, gardening. *Address:* Kavakia, 59100 Veria, Greece. *T:* 2331071925. *E:* mek59100@gmail.com. *Club:* Royal Over-Seas League.

KNOWLES, Sir Nigel (Graham), Kt 2009; Global Ambassador, DLA Piper International LLP, since 2016 (Global Co-Chairman, 2015–16); *b* 1956; *m*; two *s* one *d*. *Educ:* Sheffield Univ.; Chester Coll. of Law. Broomhead & Neals, Yorkshire: articled clerk, 1978–80; Asst Solicitor, 1980–84; Partner, 1984–90; Dibb Lupton Broomhead, later Dibb Lupton Alsop, then DLA, subseq. DLA Piper Internat. LLP: Hd, Commercial Gp, 1990–95; Partner, 1993; Dep. Man. Partner, 1995–96; Man. Partner, 1996–2005; Jt CEO and Man. Partner for Europe and Asia, 2005–14. Non-executive Chairman: Blenheim Capital Services Ltd, 2010–; LawVest, 2011–; Zeus Capital, 2014–; DWF LLP, 2017–. Chairman: Managing Partners' Forum, 2004–13; Legal Sector Alliance, 2008–14. Member: Envmtl Leadership Team, Business in the Community; Steering Cttee, Prince of Wales Rainforest Initiative; Chm., Prince's Trust Internat., 2014–. Vis. Prof., Univ. of Sheffield, 2010. High Sheriff, Gtr London, 2016–17. Fellow, Harris Manchester Coll., Oxford. Hon. DCL Sheffield, 2011. *Address:* DLA Piper International LLP, 160 Aldersgate Street, EC1A 4HT.

KNOWLES, Peter Francis Arnold, CB 1996; Parliamentary Counsel, 1991–2008; *b* 10 July 1949; *s* of Sidney Francis Knowles and Patricia Anette Knowles; *m* 1972, Patricia Katharine Clifford; two *s*. *Educ:* Whitgift School, Croydon; University College, Oxford (MA). Called to the Bar, Gray's Inn, 1971. In practice at Chancery Bar, 1973–75; joined Parliamentary Counsel Office, 1975; with Law Commission, 1979–81, 1993–96; with Tax Law Rewrite Project, 2001–03. *Publications:* (contrib.) Halsbury's Laws of England; The Giulia Coupés 1963–1976, 1998. *Recreations:* music, walking, watercolours, bird watching, classic car restoration.

KNOWLES, Peter William; Controller, BBC Parliament, since 2006; Editor, Today in Parliament, since 2003; *b* Bolton, Lancs, 17 May 1961; *s* of Alan and Mary Knowles; *m* 1988, Kaye Barker; two *s*. *Educ:* Bolton Sch.; St Catherine's Coll., Oxford (BA Hons English Lang. and Lit. 1983); Univ. of Bradford (MBA 1997); Univ. of Chester (FdA Contextual Theol. 2013). Reporter, Carlisle News Agency, 1984; BBC: news trainee, 1984–86; journalist, BBC Manchester, 1986–87; sen. journalist, BBC Leeds, 1987–89; Prod., Nine O'Clock News, 1989–91; Asst Ed., BBC World Service TV News, 1991–96; News Ed., BBC World News, 1997–99; Man. Ed., BBC TV News, 2000–01; Channel Ed., BBC Parlt, 2001–06; Ed., Parliaments Online (formerly Democracy Live), 2010–18; Exec. Ed., Week in Westminster and radio specials. Dir, Parly Broadcasting Unit Ltd, 2003–11. Trustee: Hansard Soc., 2010–17; Pitzhanger Manor and Gall., 2013–15; Charles Dickens Mus., 2018–; Chm. Trustees, St Andrew's Ch Centre, Ealing, 2013–17. Lay Preacher, URC, 2013–. Convenor, Gen. Assembly Communications (formerly Communications and Editl) Cttee, URC, 2015–19. *Publications:* (ed) Flora of Laphroaig, 2017; (ed) God is With Us, 2018. *Recreations:* long distance walks, architectural conservation. *Address:* BBC Parliament, 4 Millbank, SW1P 3JQ. *E:* peter.knowles@bbc.co.uk. *Club:* Players.

KNOWLES, Hon. Sir Robin St John, Kt 2014; CBE 2006; Hon. Mr Justice Knowles; a Judge of the High Court, Queen's Bench Division, since 2014; *b* 7 April 1960; *s* of Norman Richard Knowles and Margaret Mary Knowles (*née* Robinson); *m* 1987, Gill Adams; one *d*. *Educ:* Sir Roger Manwood's Grammar Sch.; Trinity Coll., Cambridge (MA). Called to the Bar: Middle Temple, 1982, Bencher 2004; Gray's Inn (*ad eundem*); in practice at the Bar, 1983–; Asst Recorder, 1998–2000; QC 1999; a Recorder, 2000–14; a Deputy High Court Judge, 2006–14. Member: Exec., Commercial Bar Assoc., 1999– (Chm., 2005–07; Chm., N American Cttee, 2000–); various Bar Council and Commercial Bar Assoc. and Inn cttees and working parties; and Trustee, Mgt Cttee, Bar Pro Bono Unit, 1996– (Chm., 2005–); Trustee: Solicitors Pro Bono Gp, 2001–; Bar in the Community, 2001–; Advice Bureau, RCJ, 1999–. *Recreations:* the East End of London, and being with friends and family. *Address:* Royal Courts of Justice, Rolls Building, Fetter Lane, EC4A 1NL.

KNOWLES, Tanya; see Barron, T.

KNOWLES, Timothy; Director, Welsh Water, then Hyder, plc, 1989–99; *b* 17 May 1938; *s* of Cyril William Knowles and Winifred Alice Knowles (*née* Hood); *m* 1967, Gaynor Hallett (*d* 2016); one *d*. *Educ:* Bishop Gore Grammar Sch., Swansea. Chartered Accountant. Company Sec./Accountant, Louis Marx & Co. Ltd, 1960–68; Controller, Modco Valenite, 1968–69; HTV Ltd: Company Sec., 1969–78; Financial Dir, 1975–81; Asst Man. Dir, 1981–86; HTV Group plc: Financial Dir, 1976–86; Gp Man. Dir, 1986–88; Finance Dir, Insurance Services Gp, ECGD (for privatisation), 1990–91; Dir, Frost & Reed (Holdings) Ltd, 1985–88. Member: S Wales Electricity Bd, 1981–82; Welsh Water Authority, 1982–89; Disciplinary Cttee, 1993–2002 (Chm. Tribunals, 1996–2002), Appeal Cttee, 2002–09, ICAEW. Dir, University Hosp. of Wales Healthcare NHS Trust, 1995–99. Chm., CG90, 1994–97 (Treas., 2000–). Contested (C) Swansea East, 1966. Mem., Livery Co. of Wales (formerly Welsh Livery Guild), 1994– (Treas., 2001–05; Emeritus Treas., 2006–). *Recreations:* travel, watching cricket, golf, genealogy, challenging bureaucracy. *Address:* Cae Ffynnon, 12 Ger-y-Llan, St Nicholas, Cardiff CF5 6SY. *T:* (01446) 760726. *Clubs:* Cardiff and County (Cardiff); Glamorgan CC; Cottrell Park Golf.

KNOWSLEY AND SEFTON, Archdeacon of; see Spiers, Ven. P. H.

KNOX, family name of Earl of Ranfurly.

KNOX, Sir David (Laidlaw), Kt 1993; *b* 30 May 1933; *s* of late J. M. Knox, Lockerbie and Mrs C. H. C. Knox (*née* Laidlaw); *m* 1980, Mrs Margaret Eva Maxwell (*d* 2016), *d* of late A. McKenzie. *Educ:* Lockerbie Academy; Dumfries Academy; London Univ. (BSc (Econ) Hons). Management Trainee, 1953–56; Printing Executive, 1956–62; O&M Consultant, 1962–70. Contested (C): Stechford, Birmingham, 1964 and 1966; Nuneaton, March 1967. MP (C) Leek Div. of Staffs, 1970–83, Staffordshire Moorlands, 1983–97. PPS to Ian Gilmour, Minister of State for Defence, 1973, Sec. of State for Defence, 1974. Member: Select Cttee on European Legislation, 1976–97; House of Commons Chairmen's Panel, 1983–97; Secretary: Cons. Finance Cttee, 1972–73; Cons. Trade Cttee, 1974; Vice-Chm., Cons. Employment Cttee, 1979–80; Chairman: W Midlands Area Young Conservatives, 1963–64; W Midlands Area Cons. Political Centre, 1966–69; a Vice Chairman: Cons. Party Organisation, 1974–75; Cons. Gp for Europe, 1984–87. Editor, Young Conservatives National Policy Group, 1963–64. Chm., London Union of Youth Clubs, 1998–99; Dep. Chm., Fedn of London Youth Clubs, 1999–2008 (Vice Pres., 2011–). Vice President: Commercial Travellers' Benevolent Instn, 1998–2017; One World Trust, 2004–. Mem., Drama Panel, Buxton Opera House, 2007–15. *Recreations:* watching association football and cricket, reading, theatre, walking. *Address:* The Mount, Alstonefield, Ashbourne, Derbys DE6 2FS.

KNOX, James Peter Witherow; Partner, Bryan Cave Leighton Paisner (formerly Berwin Leighton Paisner) LLP, since 2010; *b* Redhill, 30 Sept. 1961; *s* of late Peter and of Georgina Knox; *m* 1988, Dee Pilgrim; three *s*. *Educ:* Reigate Grammar Sch.; Bristol Univ. (LLB Hons 1984). Articled clerk, Druces & Attlee, 1985–87; Solicitor, 1987–99, Partner, 1999–2010, Linklaters. *Recreations:* running, scuba diving, tennis, hill walking, clay pigeon shooting, cycling. *Address:* Bryan Cave Leighton Paisner LLP, Adelaide House, London Bridge, EC4R 9HA. *T:* (020) 3400 1000, *Fax:* (020) 3400 1111. *E:* james.knox@bclplaw.com. *Clubs:* Royal Automobile; Chilham Tennis.

KNOX, James Richard Dunsmuir, FSAScot; Director, Fleming-Wyfold Art Foundation, since 2015; *b* Kilwinning, Ayrshire, 18 Oct. 1952; *s* of Sir Bryce Muir Knox, KCVO, MC, TD and Patricia Mary Knox (*née* Dunsmuir); *m* 1983, Caroline Angela Owen; one *s* one *d*. *Educ:* Eton Coll.; Trinity Coll., Cambridge (BA 1974); INSEAD (MBA). FSAScot 1975. Writer, Antique Collector, 1975–77; Associate Publisher: Ebury Press, 1977–78; Illustrated London News Gp, 1980–82; Publisher, The Spectator, 1983–92; Founder, Art for Work Consultancy, 1992–2005; Man. Dir, The Art Newspaper, 2005–15. Curator, The Genius of Osbert Lancaster, Wallace Collection, 2008. Chm., Ayr Renaissance, 2014–. Trustee: Great Steward of Scotland's Dumfries House Trust, 2007–14; Nat. Galls of Scotland, 2007–13; NT for Scotland, 2011–15; Chm., Boswell (formerly Boswell Mus. and

Mausoleum) Trust, 2010–. *Publications:* The Trinity Foot Beagles, 1978; Robert Byron, 2003; Cartoons and Coronets: the genius of Osbert Lancaster, 2008; The Scottish Country House, 2012. *Recreations:* architecture, the visual arts. *Address:* Martnaham Lodge, by Ayr, Ayrshire KA6 6ES.

KNOX, (John) Robert, FSA; cultural consultant, since 2007; *b* Port Alberni, BC, Canada, 4 June 1946; *s* of John Arthur Knox and Rosalind Knox (*née* Kingscote); *m* 1981, Helen Elizabeth Irène Zarb; three *d*. *Educ:* Univ. of Victoria, BC (BA Hons); Emmanuel Coll., Cambridge (MA). Department of Oriental Antiquities, later Department of Asia, British Museum: Asst Keeper, 1978–92; Dep. Keeper, 1992–94; Keeper, 1994–2006. Museum strategic planning and educn work, Afghanistan, Indonesia and Timor Leste, 2007–. Mem. Council, Britain-Nepal Academic Council, 2000–06. Mem. Bd Dirs, UK Br., Global Heritage Fund, 2009–11. Trustee, Gurkha Mus., 2000–. FSA 1991 (Vice Pres., 1994–97). *Publications:* Ancient China, 1978; (jtly) India: past into present, 1982; (jtly) Explorations and Excavations in Bannu District, North-West Frontier Province, Pakistan 1985–88, 1991; Amaravati, Buddhist Sculpture from the Great Stupa, 1992; (jtly) Akra, the First Capital of Bannu (NWFP Pakistan), 2000; (jtly) Sheri Khan Tarakai and Early Village Life in the Borderlands of North-West Pakistan: Bannu archaeological project surveys and excavations 1985–2001, 2010; Practical Guide for Museum Revitalisation in Indonesia, 2011; articles in learned jls on archaeol. of India and Pakistan. *Recreations:* walking, music, theatre, classical 78s and vinyl. *E:* jrknox57@gmail.com.

KNOX, Lesley Mary; Chairman, V&A Dundee, since 2010; *b* South Africa, 19 Sept. 1953; *d* of Dr Eric Samuel and Vera Samuel; *m* 1991, Brian Knox; one *d*. *Educ:* Churchill Coll., Cambridge (BA Law 1975); MA Hist. of Art 2018. Admitted solicitor, 1979. With Slaughter and May, 1976–79; solicitor: Sherman & Sterling, 1979–80; Slaughter and May, 1980–81; Kleinwort Benson, 1981–96: Corp. Finance Dir, 1986; Hd, Instnl Asset Mgt, Kleinwort Benson Investment Mgt, 1991–96; Dir, 1996; Dep. Gov., 1997–98, Gov., 1999, British Linen Bank; Founder Dir, British Linen Advrs, 2000–03; Chm., Alliance Trust, 2004–12. Non-executive Director: Turcan Connell Asset Mgt, 2010–15; SAB Miller plc, 2011–16; Centrica plc, 2012–17; Thomas Cook Gp, 2016–19; Legal and General plc, 2016–. Chm., Design Dundee Ltd, 2010–. Chm., Grosvenor Gp Ltd, 2011–18. Trustee, Nat. Galls of Scotland, 2010–18. FRSE 2015. Hon. DLaws Abertay, 2012. *Recreations:* contemporary art, textile artist, opera. *Address:* 10A Circus Lane, Edinburgh EH3 6SU. *E:* lesley.knox@grosvenor.com. *Clubs:* Athenæum; New (Edinburgh).

KNOX, Peter; *see* Knox, S. C. P.

KNOX, Robert; *see* Knox, J. R.

KNOX, Prof. Selby Albert Richard, PhD, DSc; Pro-Vice-Chancellor, University of Bristol, 2004–08; *b* 24 Sept. 1944; *s* of George Henry Knox and Elsie (*née* Stobbart); *m* 1979, Julie Dawn Edwards; one *s* two *d*. *Educ:* Univ. of Bristol (BSc; PhD 1969; DSc 1985). University of Bristol: Prof. of Inorganic Chem., 1990–96, Alfred Capper Pass Prof. of Chem., 1996–2004; Hd, Sch. of Chem., 1992–2001; Hd of Inorganic and Materials Chem., 2001–04. Non-exec. Dir, Univ. Hosps Bristol NHS Foundn Trust, 2008–12. *Publications:* numerous contribs on organometallic chemistry to learned jls. *Recreations:* fly fishing, golf, ski-ing.

KNOX, (Simon Christopher) Peter; QC 2006; a Deputy High Court Judge, since 2018; *b* London, 21 Jan. 1957; *s* of Oliver Arbuthnot and Patricia Knox; *m* 1987, Teresa (separated 2003); one *s* two *d*. *Educ:* Westminster Sch., London; Wadham Coll., Oxford (BA Hons). Called to the Bar, Middle Temple, 1983. *Recreations:* music, wine. *Address:* 3 Hare Court, Temple, EC4Y 7BJ. *T:* (020) 7415 7800, *Fax:* (020) 7415 7811. *E:* peterknox@3harecourt.com.

KNOX, Timothy Aidan John, FSA; Director, Royal Collection, since 2018; *b* 9 Aug. 1962; *s* of Andrew Knox and Margaret Barbara Knox (*née* Allen); civil partnership 2006, Robert Todd Longstaffe-Gowan. *Educ:* Ratcliffe Coll., Leics; Courtauld Inst. of Art, Univ. of London (BA Hons). Liby Asst, King's Fund Inst. Liby, 1987–88; Photographic Librarian, Press Assoc., 1988–89; Res. Asst, 1989–91, Asst Curator, 1991–95, RIBA Drawings Collection; Architectural Historian, 1995–2002, Head Curator, 2002–05, NT; Dir, Sir John Soane's Mus., 2005–13; Dir, Fitzwilliam Mus., Cambridge, 2013–18; Fellow, Gonville and Caius Coll., Cambridge, 2013–18. Mem. Editl Bd, 2002–04, Mem. Consultative Cttee, 2005–, Sculpture Jl: Jl of Public Monuments and Sculpture Assoc. Historic Bldgs Advr to FCO, 2005–11. Member: Reviewing Cttee on Export of Works of Art, 2002–10; Conseil scientifique de l'Etablissement public du musée et du domaine nat. de Versailles, 2005–09; Adv. Cttee on Design of Coins, Medals, Seals and Decorations, Royal Mint, 2008–15; Council, Mus. of Archaeology and Anthropology, Cambridge, 2016–18. Chm., Acceptance in Lieu Panel, 2011–13. Chm. and Trustee, Mausolea and Monuments Trust, 1997–2004 (Patron, 2008–). Trustee: Monument 85 Trust, 1996–2005; Hall Bequest (Stowe Sch.), 1998–2009; Spitalfields Historic Bldgs Trust, 1999–2005; Pilgrim Trust, 2006–15; Stowe House Preservation Trust, 2006–09; Vice-Patron, Public Monuments and Sculpture Assoc., 2012–15; Historic Royal Palaces, 2018–. Member, Advisory Committee: Moggerhanger House Preservation Trust, 1998–2002; Strawberry Hill Trust, 2007–10; Nat. Heritage Meml Fund, 2014–; Grimsthorpe and Drummond Castles Trust, 2016–; Member: Council, Attingham Trust, 2006–14, 2018–; Soc. of Dilettanti, 2008–; Adv. Bd, Kettle Yard, 2013–18; Harley Gall. Adv. Cttee, Welbeck Abbey, 2013–18. Dir, Parham Park Ltd, 2017–. Curator of exhibn, The Return of the Gods: Neoclassical Sculpture in Britain, Tate Britain, 2008. Mem., Editl Bd, Georgian Gp Jl, 2009–. Hon. Fellow, Gonville and Caius Coll., Cambridge, 2018. FSA 2006. *Publications:* Sir John Soane's Museum, London, 2009, 3rd edn 2016; The British Ambassador's Residence, Paris, 2011; *contributor:* Artifici d'Acque e Giardini: la cultura delle grotte e dei ninfei in Italiae in Europa, 1999; Enlightenment: discovering the world in the eighteenth century, 2003; John Fowler: the invention of the country house style, 2005; Collecting Sculpture in Early Modern Europe, 2008; Follies of Europe: architectural extravaganzas, 2008; Scritti in onore di Mario Praz, 2013; Owners and their Art Collections: comparing experiences, 2014; Treasures of the Fitzwilliam, 2014; William Kent: designing Georgian Britain, 2014; Museums of the World, 2015; Ed Kulz: the lost house revisited, 2017; The Rebirth of an English Country House: St Giles House, 2018; numerous country house guidebooks; contribs to Apollo, Country Life, Sculpture Jl, Architectural Hist., Georgian Gp Jl, London Gardener. *Recreations:* art and architecture, collecting, smooth-haired miniature dachshunds. *Address:* Avenue House, 20 Church Street, Ampthill, Beds MK45 2PE.

KNOX-JOHNSTON, Sir William Robert Patrick, (Sir Robin), Kt 1995; CBE 1969; RD (and bar) 1983; Chairman, Clipper Ventures plc, since 1996; *b* 17 March 1939; *s* of late David Robert Knox-Johnston and Elizabeth Mary Knox-Johnston (*née* Cree); *m* 1962, Suzanne (*née* Singer) (*d* 2003); one *d*. *Educ:* Berkhamsted School. Master Mariner; FRIN. Merchant Navy, 1957–69. First person to sail single-handed non-stop Around the World, 14 June 1968 to 22 April 1969, in yacht Suhaili; won Sunday Times Golden Globe, 1969; won Round Britain Race, Ocean Spirit, 1970; won round Britain Race, British Oxygen, 1974; set British transatlantic sailing record, from NY to the Lizard, 11 days 7 hours 45 mins, 1981; established new record of 10 days 14 hours 9 mins, 1986; set world sailing record for around Ireland, 76 hours 5 mins 34 secs, May 1986; World Class II Multihull Champion, 1985; completed Guardian Columbus voyage, 1989; with Peter Blake, set non-stop around the world sailing record, 74 days, 22 hours, 17 mins 22 secs, 1994; Velux 5-Oceans Race, 2006–07; Route du Rhum Race, 2014. Marina consultant, 1974–96; Man. Dir, St Katharine's Yacht Haven Ltd, 1975–76; Director: Mercury Yacht Harbours Ltd, 1970–73; Rank Marine International, 1973–75; Troon Marina Ltd, 1976–83; National Yacht Racing Centre Ltd, 1979–86; Knox-Johnston Insurance Brokers Ltd, 1983–92; St Katherine's Dock, 1975–93 (Man. Dir, 1991–93); Caversham Lake Trust Ltd, 2001–03. Pres., British Olympic Yachting Appeal, 1972–77; Pres. (formerly Chm.), STA, 1993–2001; Pres., Cruising Assoc., 2008–10 (Patron, 2009–); Vice Pres., RNLI, 2009–. Member: Sports Council Lottery Panel, 1995–99; Sport England Council, 1999–2002. Trustee: Nat. Maritime Mus., Greenwich, 1993–2002; Nat. Maritime Mus., Cornwall, 1997–2006; Cutty Sark Trust, 2011–14. Younger Brother, Trinity House, 1973. Freeman: Borough of Bromley, Kent, 1969; City of London, 1992; Co. of Watermen and Lightermen, 2018. Liveryman, Co. of Master Mariners, 1975. Lt-Comdr RNR 1971, retired. Hon. Life Rear Cdre, RNSA; Hon. Captain, RNR, 2015. Fellow, Liverpool John Moores Univ., 2006. Hon. DSc Maine Maritime Acad., 1989; Hon. DTech Nottingham, 1993; Hon. Dr: Hull, 2012; Roehampton, 2012; Plymouth, 2014. Yachtsman of the Year, Yachting Journalists' Assoc., 1969, 1995, 2007, 2015; Silk Cut Seamanship Award, 1990; Seamanship Foundn Trophy, RYA, 1991; Gold Medal, RIN, 1992; ISAF Sailor of the Year, 1994; Blue Water Medal, Cruising Club of America, 2010. *Publications:* A World of my Own, 1969; Sailing, 1975; Twilight of Sail, 1978; Last but not Least, 1978; Bunkside Companion, 1982; Seamanship, 1986; The BOC Challenge 1986–1987, 1988; The Cape of Good Hope, 1989; History of Yachting, 1990; The Columbus Venture, 1991 (Book of the Sea Award); Sea, Ice and Rock, 1992; Cape Horn, 1994; Beyond Jules Verne, 1995; Force of Nature, 2007; Knox-Johnston on Sailing, 2009. *Recreations:* sailing, maritime history, shooting. *Address:* 1 Tower Street, Old Portsmouth, Hampshire PO1 2JR. *Clubs:* Royal Yacht Squadron (Hon. Mem.) (Cowes); Royal Harwich Yacht (Hon. Mem.); Royal Western Yacht (Hon. Mem.); Royal Southampton Yacht (Hon. Mem.); Royal Southern Yacht (Hon. Mem.); Benfleet Yacht (Hon. Mem.); Liverpool Yacht (Hon. Mem.); Royal Irish Yacht (Hon. Life Mem., 1969) (Dublin); Howth Yacht (Hon. Mem.) (Eire); Royal Bombay Yacht (Hon. Mem.); Nat. Yacht (Hon. Mem.) (Dublin); Royal North of Ireland Yacht (Hon. Mem.); Island Sailing Yacht (Hon. Mem.); Portsmouth Sailing; Erith Yacht (Hon. Mem.); Royal St George Yacht (Hon. Mem.) (Dublin); RNVR Yacht (Hon. Mem.); Cruising Assoc. (Hon. Mem. and Patron); Ocean Cruising (Hon. Mem.); Royal Cornwall Yacht (Hon. Mem.); Royal Ocean Racing.

KNUDSTORP, Jørgen Vig; Chairman: LEGO Group, since 2017; Lego Brand Group, since 2017; *b* Fredericia, Denmark, 21 Nov. 1968; *s* of Knud Lauesgaard Pedersen and Else Vig Olsen; *m* 1999, Vanessa Knudstorp; two *s* two *d*. *Educ:* Aarhus Univ. (BA Econs); Cranfield Univ. (MSc; MBA); Aarhus Univ. and Massachusetts Inst. of Technol. (PhD 1999). Mgt Consultant, McKinsey & Co., 1998–2001; LEGO Group: Dir, Strategic Develt, 2001–02; Sen. Dir, Global Strategic Develt and Alliance Mgt, 2002–03; Vice Pres., Strategic Develt, 2003; Sen. Vice Pres., Corporate Affairs, 2003–04; CEO and Pres., 2004–16. Mem., Foundn Bd, Internat. Inst. for Mgt Develt Sch. of Mgt, Lausanne, 2006–. Leader of Year, Denmark, 2006; Young Global Leader, WEF, Davos, 2006. *Address:* LEGO Brand Group, Koldingvej 2, 7190 Billund, Denmark. *T:* 75338833. *E:* corp.support@lego.com.

KNUTSFORD, 6th Viscount *cr* 1895; Michael Holland-Hibbert; Bt 1853; Baron 1888; *b* 27 Dec. 1926; *s* of Hon. Wilfrid Holland-Hibbert (*d* 1961) (2nd *s* of 3rd Viscount) and of Audrey, *d* of late Mark Fenwick; *S* cousin, 1986; *m* 1951, Hon. Sheila (*d* 2018), *d* of 5th Viscount Portman; two *s* one *d*. *Educ:* Eton College; Trinity Coll., Cambridge (BA). Welsh Guards, 1945–48. SW Regional Director, Barclays Bank, 1956–86. National Trust: Chm. Cttee for Devon and Cornwall, 1973–86; Mem. Exec. Cttee, 1973–86; Mem. Council, 1979–85; Mem. Finance Cttee, 1986–99. DL 1977, High Sheriff 1977–78, Devon. *Heir: er s* Hon. Henry Thurstan Holland-Hibbert [*b* 6 April 1959; *m* 1988, Katherine, *d* of Sir John Bruce Woollacott Ropner, 2nd Bt; two *s* two *d*]. *Address:* Munden, Watford, Herts WD25 8PZ. *Club:* Brooks's.

KOBAYASHI, Prof. Makoto, PhD; Professor, 1985–2003, Professor Emeritus, 2006, and Director, Institute of Particle and Nuclear Science, 2003–06, High Energy Accelerator Research Organisation, Tsukuba, Japan (formerly National Laboratory for High Energy Physics); *b* Nagoya, Japan, 7 April 1944; *s* of Hisashi Kobayashi and Ai Kobayashi (*née* Kaifu); *m* 1st, 1975, Sachiko Enomoto (decd); one *s*; 2nd, 1990, Emiko Nakayama; one *d*. *Educ:* Nagoya Univ. (BS 1967; PhD 1972). Res. Associate, Physics Dept, Kyoto Univ., 1972–79; Associate Prof., 1979–85, Hd of Physics Div. II, 1989–2003, Nat. Lab. for High Energy Physics, later High Energy Accelerator Res. Exec. Dir, Japan Soc. for the Promotion of Sci., 2007. Orgn. Nishina Meml Prize, Nishina Foundn, 1979; J. J. Sakurai Prize, Amer. Physical Soc., 1985; Japan Acad. Prize, 1985; Person of Cultural Merit, 2001, Order of Culture, 2008, Japan; High Energy Particle Physics Prize, Eur. Phys. Soc., 2007; (jtly) Nobel Prize in Physics, 2008. *Address:* c/o High Energy Accelerator Research Organisation (KEK), 1–1 Oho, Tsukuba, Ibaraki 305–0801, Japan.

KOBBORG, Johan; ballet dancer; Director, Romanian National Ballet, 2014–16; *b* Odense, Denmark; *s* of Martinus Vedel Kobborg and Käthe Kobborg. *Educ:* Royal Danish Ballet Sch. Joined Royal Danish Ballet, 1991, Principal, 1994–99; Principal, Royal Ballet, 1999–2013. Guest dancer with Mariinsky Ballet, Bolshoi Ballet, La Scala Ballet, Nat. Ballet of Canada, Stuttgart Ballet, Hamburg Ballet and Teatro San Carlo, Naples. Performances include main rôles in La Sylphide, Swan Lake, The Nutcracker, Coppélia, Romeo and Juliet, Giselle, Sleeping Beauty, Don Quixote, Onegin, Cinderella, Anastasia, The Dream, Masquerade and Manon.

KOBILKA, Prof. Brian Kent, MD; Professor of Medicine, Cardiology and Molecular and Cellular Physiology, since 1989, and Helene Irwin Fagan Chair in Cardiology, Stanford University School of Medicine; *b* Little Falls, Minnesota, 30 May 1955; *s* of Franklyn Kobilka and Elisabeth Kobilka; *m* 1978, Tong Sun Thian; one *s* one *d*. *Educ:* Univ. of Minnesota (BS Biol. and Chem. 1977); Yale Univ. (MD 1981). Clin. trng as Sen. Resident in Internal Medicine, Barnes Hosp., Washington Univ. Med. Center, St Louis, Missouri, 1981–84; Cardiol. Res. Fellow, 1984–89, Asst Prof., 1988–89, Dept of Medicine, Duke Univ. Med. Center; Investigator, Howard Hughes Med. Inst., 1987–2003. Co-Founder, ConfometRX. Mem., NAS, 2011. (jtly) Nobel Prize in Chemistry, 2012. *Publications:* contribs to learned jls incl. Nature. *Address:* School of Medicine, Stanford University, 157 Beckman Center, 279 Campus Drive, Stanford, CA 94305-5345, USA.

KOCIENSKI, Prof. Philip Joseph, PhD; FRS 1997; FRSE; FRSC; Professor and Head of Department of Organic Chemistry, University of Leeds, 2000–09, now Emeritus Professor; *b* 23 Dec. 1946; *s* of Philip Joseph Kocienski and Marian Edyth (*née* Peters); *m* 1st, 1967, Anna Petruso (marr. diss. 1987); one *s* one *d*; 2nd, 1987, Joanna Davie. *Educ:* Brown Univ., Providence, RI (PhD 1973). FRSC 1995; FRSE 1998. Lectr, Leeds Univ., 1979–85; Prof. of Chemistry, Southampton Univ., 1985–97. Regius Prof. of Chemistry, Glasgow Univ., 1997–2000. Mem., EPSRC, 1999. For. Mem., Polish Acad. of Sci., 2000.

Hon. Dr Univ. Paul Cézanne, Aix-Marseille, 2009. Marie Sklodowska Curie Medal, Polish Chem. Soc., 1997. *Publications:* Protecting Groups, 1994; numerous res. papers in learned jls. *Recreations:* Russian and Eastern European music, violin. *Address:* Department of Chemistry, Leeds University, Leeds LS2 9JT. *T:* (0113) 343 6555.

**KOFFMANN, Pierre;** chef, Koffmann's, 2010–16; *b* 21 Aug. 1948; *s* of Albert and Germaine Koffmann; *m* 1st, 1972, Annie Barrau (decd); one *d*; 2nd, 2014, Claire; one *s* one *d*; two step *s. Educ:* Ecole Jean Jacques Rousseau, Tarbes. Mil. Service, 1967–69. Commis: L'Aubette, Strasbourg, 1966; Grand Hôtel Palais, Juan les Pins, 1967; Le Provençal, La Ciotat, 1969–70; La Voile d'Or, Lausanne, 1970; Le Gavroche, 1970–71; Chef: Brasserie Benoist, London, 1971; Waterside Inn, Bray, 1971–77; Proprietor, La Tante Claire, 1977–2002; Jt Proprietor, Koffmann and Mr White's, Bath, 2018–. *Publications:* Memories of Gascony, 1990, 2012; La Tante Claire: recipes from a master chef, 1992; Classic Koffman, 2016.

**KÖHLER, Dr Horst;** President, Federal Republic of Germany, 2004–10; Personal Envoy of UN Secretary-General for Western Sahara, since 2017; *b* 22 Feb. 1943; *s* of Eduard and Elisa Köhler; *m* 1969, Eva Luise Bohnet; one *s* one *d. Educ:* Tübingen Univ. (PhD Econs and Pol Sci. 1977). Inst. for Applied Econ. Res., 1969–76; economist, German Federal Min. of Econs, 1976–80; Advr to Ministerpräsident, Chancellery, Schleswig-Holstein, 1981–82; German Federal Min. of Finance, 1982–93 (Permanent Under Sec., 1990–93); Pres., German Savings Banks Assoc., 1993–98; Pres., EBRD, 1998–2000; Man. Dir, IMF, 2000–04.

**KOHLHAUSSEN, Martin;** Chairman, Supervisory Board, Commerzbank AG, 2001–08; *b* 6 Nov. 1935; *m;* three *c. Educ:* Univs of Frankfurt (Main), Freiburg, Marburg (Law). Worked domestically in banking, Frankfurt and Hanau (Br. Manager), 1965–76; worked internationally in banking (Br. Manager), Tokyo and New York, 1976–81. Mem. 1982–2001, Chm., 1991–2001, Bd of Man. Dirs, Commerzbank AG.

**KOHLI, Jitinder;** Director, Deloitte Consulting, since 2012; *b* 2 Feb. 1973; *s* of Inder Pal and Swarn Kohli. *Educ:* Univ. of Oxford (BA Hons PPE 1995); Southampton Univ. (BSc Sociol. and Soc. Policy 1996). Co-ordinator, Oxford Access Scheme, 1992–93; DTI, 1996–98; Cabinet Office: Econ. and Domestic Secretariat, 1998–99; Prime Minister's Strategy Unit, 1999–2000; Productivity and Structural Reform Team, HM Treasury, 2000–02; Hd, Community Cohesion Unit, Home Office, 2002–03; Hd, Productivity and Structural Reform Team, HM Treasury, 2003–04; Dir, Active Communities, Home Office, 2004–05; Chief Exec., Better Regulation Exec., Cabinet Office, later at BERR, then BIS, 2005–09; Dir Gen., Strategy and Communications, BIS, 2009. Non-exec. Dir, Circle Anglia Housing Gp, 2003–09; Chm. of Trustees, EPIC Trust, 2005–09; Trustee, Adventure Capital Fund, 2008–09. Sen Fellow, Center for American Progress, 2009–12; Fellow: Young Foundn, 2009–; Nat. Acad. of Public Admin, 2012. *Address:* Deloitte Consulting, 1919 North Lynn Street, Arlington, VA 22209, USA.

**KOHN, David;** Director, David Kohn Architects, since 2007; *b* Cape Town, SA, 3 Oct. 1972; *s* of Richard and Gerda Kohn; *m* 2011, Margherita Laera; two *d. Educ:* Loughborough Grammar Sch.; Jesus Coll., Cambridge (BA 1994; DipArch). Associate, Caruso St John Associates, 2002–06. Projects include: Stable Acre, 2010; Thomas Dane Gall., 2011; The White Building, 2012; A Room for London, 2012; ICA, 2012–20; Sotheby's S|2 Gall., 2013; Apartment on Carrer Avinyó, 2013; new campus for New Coll., Oxford, 2015–; Photography Gall., V&A Mus., 2016–18. *Recreations:* contemporary art, travel. *Address:* David Kohn Architects, Bedford House, 125–133 Camden High Street, NW1 7JR. *T:* (020) 7424 8596.

**KOLADE, Christopher Olusola,** CON 2000; Pro-Chancellor, Pan-Atlantic (formerly Pan-African) University, 2009–15; *b* 28 Dec. 1932; *s* of Abraham and Lydia Kolade; *m* Beatrice; two *d. Educ:* Fourah Bay Coll., Sierra Leone (BA, DipEd). Educn Officer, 1955–60; Controller, 1960–72, Dir-Gen., 1972–78, Nigerian Broadcasting Corp.; Dir, 1978–89, CEO, 1989–93, Chm., 1993–2002, Cadbury Nigeria; High Comr for Nigeria in UK, 2002–07. Lectr, Lagos Business Sch., 1995. Hon. DCL 1976. *Recreations:* church music, lawn tennis, walking. *Address:* c/o Pan-Atlantic University, Km 22 Lekki-Epe Expressway, Ajah, Lagos, Nigeria.

**KOLANKIEWICZ, Prof. Jerzy, (George),** PhD; Professor of Sociology with special reference to Central Europe, 1999–2011, now Emeritus, and Director, 2001–06, School of Slavonic and East European Studies, University College London; Managing Director, ESRC/AHRC/HEFCE Centre for East European Language Based Area Studies, 2006–11; *b* 10 April 1946; *s* of late Józef and of Janina Kolankiewicz; *m* 1977, Danuta Elzbieta Manthey; one *s* one *d. Educ:* Salesian Coll., Farnborough; Univ. of Leeds (BA 1st cl. Hons 1968); Univ. of Essex (PhD 1984). Res. Officer, Univ. of Essex, 1969–71; Lecturer in Sociology: UC, Swansea, 1971–72; Univ. of Essex, 1972–99. Fellow, Woodrow Wilson Internat. Center for Scholars, Smithsonian Instn, Washington, DC, 1986–87. Dir, E-W Prog., ESRC, 1990–96; Member: Econ. and Social Cttee on Overseas Res., DFID, 1994–2000; HEFCE Chief Executive's Strategically Important Subjects Adv. Gp, 2005. Mem. Governing Body, British Assoc. for Central and Eastern Europe, 2002–08. Dep. Pres., Polish Educnl Soc., 2002–11. Member: Internat. Adv. Bd, Inst. of Global and Eur. Integration, Corvinus Univ., Budapest, 2010–; Excellence Initiative Review Panel, Humanities and Social Scis, German Res. Foundn, Bonn, 2012; Speaker, XXI Economic Forum, Krynica-Zdroj, Poland, 2011; Centenary MB Grabowski Meml Lect., Sch. of Slavonic and E Eur. Studies, UCL, 2015. Mem., Hon. Cttee, V Jubilee Edn, Internat. Fest. of Music, Music on the Peaks, Zakopane, Poland, 2013–. Mem., Polish Hearth (Ognisko Polskie), 2015–; Hon. Mem., Polish City Club, 2002–. Diploma of Polish Min. of Foreign Affairs, 2007. Comdr's Cross and Star, Order of Merit (Poland), 2004; Officer's Cross, Order of Merit (Hungary), 2006. *Publications:* (with D. Lane) Social Groups in Polish Society, 1973; (with P. Lewis) Poland: politics, economics and society, 1988; Towards a Sociology of the Transition: rights, resources and social integration in Poland, 2000; (ed with T. Zarycki) Regional Issues in Polish Politics, 2003; (contrib.) Oxford Companion to Comparative Politics, 2012; A Sociologist Abroad: understanding Polish society under Communism, 2015; contribs to British Jl Sociol., Internat. Affairs, Daedalus, E European Politics and Societies, Sociologia Ruralis. *Recreations:* walking (Lake District, Tatras), swimming, opera. *E:* george.kolankiewicz@btinternet.com.

**KOLBERT, His Honour Colin Francis;** Assistant Surveillance Commissioner, 2001–13; Deputy Chairman, Regulatory Decisions Committee, Financial Services Authority, 2001–06; *b* 3 June 1936; *s* of late Arthur Richard Alexander Kolbert and Dorothy Elizabeth Kolbert (*née* Fletcher); *m* 1959, Jean Fairgrieve Abson; two *d. Educ:* Queen Elizabeth's, Barnet; St Catharine's Coll., Cambridge (Harold Samuel Schol., 1959; BA 1959; PhD 1962; MA 1963). FCIArb 1997. RA, 1954–56. Called to the Bar, Lincoln's Inn, 1961, Bencher, 2005; a Recorder, SE Circuit, 1985–88; a Circuit Judge, 1988–95. Oxford University: Fellow and Tutor in Jurisprudence, St Peter's Coll., 1964–68 (MA, DPhil (Oxon) by incorp., 1964); CUF Lectr, Faculty of Law, 1965–68; Cambridge University: Fellow, Magdalene Coll., 1968– (Tutor, 1969–88); Univ. Lectr in Law, Dept of Land Economy, 1969–88; Sec., Faculty of Music, 1969–75; Coll. Rugby Administrator, CURUFC, 1982–88 (Trustee, 1989–2012); Mem. CUCC Cttee, 1996–. Vis. Prof. and Moderator,

Univs of Ife, Lagos, Enugu, and Ahmadu Bello, Nigeria, 1970–80. Ind. Bd Mem., 1995–2000, Chm., Disciplinary Tribunal, 1995–2001, SFA. Mem., Cambridge City Council, 1970–74. Member: Istituto di Diritto Agrario Internazionale e Comparato, Florence, 1964–; Secretariat, World Conf. on Agrarian Reform and Rural Develt, FAO Rome, 1978–79 (Customary Land Tenure Consultant, 1974–80). Freeman, City of London, 1998; Liveryman, Wax Chandlers' Co., 1999– (Master, 2009–10). Governor: Wellingborough Sch., 1970–80; Cranleigh Sch., 1970–88; Glenalmond Coll., 1978–89; Hurstpierpoint Coll., 1978–89; Wisbech GS, 2001–10; Feoffee, Chetham's Hosp. and Library, 1993–2010. Violin music critic, Records and Recording, 1972–78. *Publications:* (trans. and ed) The Digest of Justinian, 1979, 4th edn 1993; various legal and musical. *Recreations:* music (especially playing the violin), cricket, Rugby, military history, cooking, walking in London and Yorkshire. *Address:* Magdalene College, Cambridge CB3 0AG; Outer Temple Chambers, 222 Strand, Temple, WC2R 1BA. *Clubs:* MCC, Farmers; Hawks (Cambridge); Cambridge University Rugby Union Football; Colonsay Golf.

**KOLVIN, Philip Alan;** QC 2009; barrister; a Recorder, since 2018; *b* Edinburgh, 4 Aug. 1961; *s* of late Prof. Israel Kolvin and of Rona Kolvin; *m* 1991, Dr Laurie Ann Johnston; two *d. Educ:* Balliol Coll., Oxford (BA Juris. 1983; MA 2004). Called to the Bar, Inner Temple, 1985; Cornerstone Barristers (formerly Chambers of Mark Lowe, QC), 1994–, Hd of Chambers, 2014–; Associate Mem., Kings Chambers, Manchester, 2011–14. Co-opted expert, Commn for a Sustainable London, 2010–12. Chairman: Inst. of Licensing, 2004–11 (Patron, 2011–); Purple Flag, 2007–15. Chairman: Crystal Palace Campaign, 1998–2004; Civic Trust, 2007–09; Best Bar None, 2012–14; Adv. Bd, Nightworks, 2016–18; Mayor's Night Time Commn for London, 2017–18; Member: Bd, Sports Grounds Safety Authy, 2016–; Crystal Palace Park Trust, 2018– (Mem., Shadow Bd, 2016–18). Trustee: CPRE, 2004–07; KCH Charitable Trust, 2018–; Otherworld, 2018–. FRSA 2010. *Publications:* Saving Open Space, 2004; Licensed Premises: law, practice and policy, 2005, 2nd edn 2013; Gambling for Local Authorities: licensing, planning and regeneration, 2007, 2nd edn 2010; Sex Licensing, 2010; (ed) Atkins Court Forms (Licensing), 2011; (ed) Encyclopedia of Forms and Precedents (Licensing), 2014; (ed) Cornerstone on Councillors' Conduct, 2015; (ed) Cornerstone on Anti-social Behaviour, 2015. *Recreations:* Everton, the Blues, walking, cooking, the allotment, theatre. *Address:* Cornerstone Barristers, 2–3 Gray's Inn Square, WC1R 5JH. *T:* (020) 7242 4986, *Fax:* (020) 7405 1166. *E:* philipk@cornerstonebarristers.com.

**KOMISARENKO, Prof. Serhiy Vassiliovych,** MD; PhD; Director, Palladin Institute of Biochemistry, since 1998; Academician-Secretary, Ukrainian National Academy of Sciences, since 2004; *b* 9 July 1943; *s* of late Prof. Vassiliy Komisarenko and Lubov Drosovska-Komisarenko; *m* 1970, Natalia Ignatiuk; one *d. Educ:* Ukrainian-English Sch., Kiev; Kiev Med. Inst. (MD with dist. 1966); Kiev Univ.; Inst. of Biochem., Kiev (PhD 1970); Inst. of Molecular Biology, Kiev (DSc 1989). Palladin Institute of Biochemistry, Ukrainian Academy of Sciences, Kiev: Jun., then Sen. Scientific Researcher, 1969–75; Scientific Sec., 1972–74; Hd of Dept, 1975–92; Prof. of Biochem., 1989; Dir, 1989–92; Dep. Prime Minister, Ukraine, 1990–92; Ambassador of Ukraine to UK, 1992–98, and to Ireland, 1995–98. Visiting Scientist: Pasteur Inst., Paris, 1974–75; Sloan-Kettering Cancer Inst., NY, 1981. Chairman: Nat. Commn on Biosafety, 2007–; Bd, Internat. Foundn of the Ukrainian Nat. Heritage, 2007–; Mem., Bd of Dirs, British-Ukrainian Chamber of Commerce, 2010–. President: Ukrainian Biochem. Soc., 1999–; Ukrainian Inst. for Peace and Democracy, 1999–; Special Olympics, Ukraine, 2002–; Ukrainian Biosafety Assoc., 2013–. Hon. Prof., Odesa Nat. Univ., 2010. Member: Ukrainian Nat. Acad. of Scis, 1991; Ukrainian Acad. of Med. Scis, 1993. Hon. DSc: Kingston, 1997; N London, 1997. Ukrainian State Award, 1979; Ukrainian State Order of Merit (III degree), 1996, (II degree), 1998, (I degree), 2013; Ukrainian State Order of Yaroslav the Wise (V degree), 2005; Order of Friendship (China), 2012; Ukrainian State Order of Freedom, 2018. *Publications:* Radiation and Human Immunity, 1994; Structure and Biological Activity of Bacterial Biopolymers, 2003; Biochemistry and Biotechnology for Modern Medicine, 2013; Molecular Mechanisms of Foundation and Degradation of Fibrin, 2013; Nanosize Systems and Nanomaterials, 2014; numerous articles on biochem. and immunology; also articles on Ukrainian culture and politics. *Recreations:* music, alpine ski-ing, clay pigeon shooting, lawn tennis, swimming. *Address:* Palladin Institute of Biochemistry, 9 Leontovicha Street, Kyiv, 01030, Ukraine. *T:* (44) 2345974. *E:* svk@biochem.kiev.ua.

**KON, Stephen David;** Consultant, Macfarlanes LLP, since 2017; *b* London, 26 Sept. 1949; *s* of Teddy and Lillian Kon; *m* 1980, Sue Kamlish; three *d. Educ:* Harrow Co. Sch. for Boys; Univ. of Sussex (BA Law and Eur. Studies); Coll. of Europe, Brussels (Dip. Supérieur d'Hautes Études). Accredited Mediator, Centre for Effective Dispute Resolution. Admitted as solicitor, 1980, and as solicitor advocate, 2003; Lecturer in Law: Univ. of Reading, 1976–79; Univ. of Sussex, 1979–82; SJ Berwin, later King & Wood Mallesons LLP, 1982–2016: Partner and Hd of EU Competition and Regulatory Dept, 1984–2012; Sen. Partner, 2012–16; Co-Dep. Global Chm., 2013–16. Member, Editorial Board: Competition Law Insight; Jl Competition Law and Econs. *Publications:* (ed) The Competition Act 1998, 1998. *Recreations:* family, cinema, theatre, Watford FC, cricket, horseracing. *Address:* Macfarlanes LLP, 20 Cursitor Street, EC4A 1LT. *T:* (020) 7849 2797. *E:* Stephen.Kon@macfarlanes.com.

**KONG, Janis Carol,** OBE 2002; Chairman, Bristol Airport, since 2014. *Educ:* Univ. of Edinburgh (BSc Psychol.); Harvard Business Sch. Joined BAA, Edinburgh Airport, 1973; Mktg Manager, Scottish Airports; Gen. Manager, Terminal 4, Heathrow Airport; Ops Dir, 1994–97, Man. Dir, 1997–2001, Gatwick Airport Ltd; Chm., Heathrow Airport Ltd, 2001–06; Dir, BAA plc, 2002–06. Chm., Heathrow Express, 2006. Non-executive Director: Portmeirion Hldgs plc, 2000–; RBS plc, 2006–09; Kingfisher plc, 2006–16; Network Rail, 2010–16; TUI Travel plc, 2012–14; Copenhagen Airports, 2012–. Former Mem., SE England Develt Agency; Mem. Bd, VisitBritain, 2006–14. Chm. Trustees, Forum for the Future, 2007–12. DUniv Open.

**KONIGSBERG, Allen Stewart;** *see* Allen, Woody.

**KONSTA, Simon Nicholas;** Senior Partner, and Chairman of Global Management Board, Clyde & Co., since 2016; *b* Bristol, 19 Nov. 1964; *s* of Demetrios Konsta and Margaret Mary Konsta; *m* 1990, Katherine Amanda Procter; one *s* two *d. Educ:* Clifton Coll., Bristol; Univ. of Birmingham (LLB); Guildford Coll. of Law. Admitted solicitor, 1990; Litigator, 1993–2008, Sen. Partner, 2008–11, Barlow Lyde & Gilbert LLP; Clyde & Co. LLP: Principal Partner, 2011–13; Mem., Global Mgt Bd, 2011–16; Global Hd of Insce, 2013–16. *Recreations:* cycling, walking, golf, charitable trustee. *Address:* Clyde & Co. LLP, St Botolph Building, 138 Houndsditch, EC3A 7AR. *T:* (020) 7876 5000. *E:* simon.konsta@clydeco.com.

**KONZOTIS, Sotiroula Maria, (Roula);** voice and presentation coach, 2015; Director, Roula Konzotis Associates, 2011–14; *b* Eastbourne, 11 June 1953; *d* of Polychronis Konzotis and Evangelia Konzotis (*née* Michou); *m* 1988, Nicholas Jonathan Wood; two *s. Educ:* Burlington Grammar Sch. for Girls; Manchester Univ. (BEd 1st cl. Hons Drama 1976; Cert Ed (Dist.) 1976); City Univ. (Postgrad. Dip. Arts Admin 1983); Royal Central Sch. of Speech and Drama, Univ. of London (MA Voice Studies (Dist.) 2015). Hd of Drama and English, Cardinal Newman Sch., Sussex, 1976–79; English teacher, Kostea-Geitonas Sch.,

Athens, 1979–80; Press and PR Officer, Ballet Rambert, 1983–85; Touring Mktg Officer, Arts Council of GB, 1985–88; Dir of Mktg and Press, English Nat. Ballet, 1988–89; freelance contracts, 1989–94; Sen. Consultant, Bonnar Keenlyside, London, 1994–98; Dir of Communications, RIBA, 1999–2011. UK Trade & Investment: Member: Creative Industries Mktg Strategy Bd, 2006–11; Design Partners, adv. gp on design, 2008–11. Governor: English Nat. Ballet, 2005–11; Belmont Primary Sch., Chiswick, 2011–14. Trustee, Dancers' Career Develt, 2006–11. *Recreations:* the arts, architecture, attending major sporting events, swimming, collecting Rupert annuals. *Address:* 28 Linden Gardens, Chiswick, W4 2EQ. *T:* 07771 715332. *E:* roula@konzotis.com.

**KOOLHAAS, Prof. Remment;** Joint Founder and Partner, Office for Metropolitan Architecture, since 1975; Professor in Practice of Architecture and Urban Design, Graduate School of Design, Harvard University, since 1995; *b* Rotterdam, 17 Nov. 1944. *Educ:* Architectural Assoc. Sch. of Architecture (DipArch 1972). Journalist and script writer, 1962–72; taught at: Sch. of Architecture, UCLA, 1975; AA, 1976; Professor of Architecture: Technical Univ., Delft, 1988–89; Rice Univ., Houston, 1991–92; Arthur Rotch Adjunct Prof. of Architecture, Graduate Sch. of Design, Harvard Univ., 1990–95. Projects include: Netherlands Dance Theatre, The Hague, 1987; Nexus World Housing, Fukuoka, 1991; Kunsthal, Rotterdam, 1992; Grand Palais and city centre masterplan, Lille, 1994; Educatorium, Univ. of Utrecht, 1997; house in Bordeaux, 1998; Second Stage Theatre, NY, 1999; Prada stores, NY, 2001, LA, 2004; McCormick Tribune Campus, Illinois Inst. of Technol., Chicago, 2003; Seattle Central Library, 2004; Casa da Musica, Porto, 2005; Netherlands Embassy, Berlin, 2005 (Mies van der Rohe Award, EU, 2005); China Central Television, Beijing, 2008; Fondazione Prada Art Centre, Milan, 2015, 2018; Garage Mus. of Contemporary Art, Moscow, 2015; Qatar Nat. Liby and Qatar Foundn HQ, 2018. Dir, Venice Architecture Biennale, 2014. Pritzker Prize, 2000; Praemium Imperiale, Japan Art Assoc., 2003; Royal Gold Medal, RIBA, 2004; Golden Lion for Lifetime Achievement, Venice Biennale, 2010. Co-founder, Volume Magazine, 2005. *Publications:* Delirious New York: a retroactive manifesto for Manhattan, 1978; (jtly) S,M,L,XL, 1997; OMA Rem Koolhaas Living, Vivre, Leben, 1999; OMA 30: 30 Colours, 1999; Content, 2004; Lagos: how it works, 2007; (jtly) Project Japan: metabolism talks…, 2011. *Address:* Office for Metropolitan Architecture, Heer Bokelweg 149, 3032 AD Rotterdam, Netherlands; Department of Architecture, Harvard Design School, 48 Quincy Street, Cambridge, MA 02138, USA.

**KOONER, Prof. Jaspal Singh,** MD; FRCP, FMedSci; Professor of Clinical Cardiology, Imperial College London, since 2004; Consultant Cardiologist: Imperial College Healthcare Trust (formerly Royal Postgraduate Medical School and Hammersmith Hospital), since 1995; Ealing Hospital NHS Trust (formerly Ealing Hospital), since 1995; *b* Nairobi, 10 April 1956; *s* of Dhanna Singh Kooner and Bhagwant Kaur Kooner; *m* 1993, Ravinder Kaur; two *s* two *d*. *Educ:* Gillingham Grammar Sch.; St Thomas's Hosp. Med. Sch., Univ. of London (MB BS 1981; MD 1990). MRCP 1985, FRCP 1992. Sen. Lectr in Cardiovascular Medicine, RPMS, 1990–95; Consultant Cardiologist: Hammersmith Hosp., 1990–95; Ealing Hosp., 1990–95. Dir, Lolipop Res. Prog., 1995–. FMedSci 2012. *Publications:* over 30 papers in Nature and Nature Genetics on genetics of coronary artery disease, type-2 diabetes, obesity and other common diseases; papers on coronary heart disease and diabetes in Indian Asians. *Recreations:* research, keeping fit, Gurbani Kirtan, family. *Address:* 7 Alexandra Gardens, Hounslow, Middx TW3 4HT. *T:* (020) 3330 0030, *Fax:* (020) 8196 2273. *E:* j.kooner@imperial.ac.uk.

**KOONS, Jeff;** artist; *b* York, Penn, 21 Jan. 1955; *s* of Henry and Gloria Koons; one *d*; *m* 1991, Ilona Staller (marr. diss. 1994); one *s*; *m* 1995, Justine Wheeler; four *s*. *Educ:* Sch. of Art, Inst. of Chicago; Maryland Inst. Coll. of Art, Baltimore (BFA 1976). Wall St commodities broker, 1980; estabd studio to produce his work, 1980s; *solo exhibitions* include: New Mus. of Contemporary Art, NY, 1980; Equilibrium, NY and Chicago, 1985; Luxury and Degradation, NY and Daniel Weinberg Gall., LA, 1986; Banality, Chicago, Cologne and Sonnabend Gall., NY, 1988; Made in Heaven, Cologne and Sonnabend Gall., NY, 1991; Easyfun, Sonnabend Gall., NY, 1999; Puppy, Rockefeller Center, NY, 2000; Easyfun-Ethereal, Fruitmarket Gall., Edinburgh, 2001, Guggenheim Mus., NY and Sao Paulo Biennial, 2002; Popeye, Sonnabend Gall., NY, 2003; (retrospective) Astrup Fearnley MOMA, Oslo and Helsinki City Art Mus., 2004–05; Diamond, V&A Mus., 2006; Cracked Egg, 2006, Hulk Elvis, 2007, Gagosian Gall., London; Metropolitan Mus. of Art, NY, 2008; (retrospective) Château de Versailles, 2008; Gagosian Gall., LA, 2008–09, 2012–13, 2017; Popeye Series, Serpentine Gall., London, 2009; Nat. Galls Scotland, 2011; Brighton Mus. and Art Gall., 2013; Gagosian Gall., NY, 2013; Gagosian Gall., HK, 2014–15; Pompidou Centre, Paris (retrospective), 2015; Ashmolean Mus., Oxford, 2019; *group exhibitions* include: Whitney Mus., NY, 1985, 1987, 1989, 1990; ICA, Boston, 1988; Sonnabend Gall., NY, 1886; Saatchi Collection, London, 1987; Centre Georges Pompidou, 1987; MOMA, NY, 1990, 2001; Venice Biennale, 1990; Biennial, Sydney, 1990; Royal Acad., 1993, 2000, 2011; Hayward Gall., London, 1992; Mus. Contemp. Art, Sydney, 1995; Serpentine Gall. and V&A Mus., London, 2001; Guggenheim, Bilbao, 2007; Tate Gall., 2009–10; *work in collections* includes: MOMA, Whitney Mus. of American Art, Guggenheim Mus., NY; National Gall. and Hirshhorn Mus., Washington; MOMA, San Francisco; Tate Gall., London; Tokyo Metropolitan Mus.; *public works* include: Balloon Flower (Blue), Potsdamer Platz, Berlin, 1992; Puppy, 1992, Bad Arolsen, Germany, re-erected Mus. of Contemporary Art, Sydney, 1995, subseq. at Guggenheim Mus., Bilbao, 1997; Split-Rocker, Avignon, 2000; Balloon Flower (Red), 7 World Trade Center, NYC, 2006. Dir, Internat. Center for Missing and Exploited Children, 2002–. Fellow, Amer. Acad. Arts and Scis, 2005. Hon. RA 2010. Officier, Légion d'Honneur (France), 2007 (Chevalier, 2001). *Address:* Jeff Koons LLC, 601 W 29th Street, New York, NY 10001–1109, USA; c/o Gagosian Gallery, 17–19 Davies Street, W1K 3DE.

**KOOPMAN, Prof. Antonius Gerhardus Michael, (Ton);** harpsichordist, organist and conductor; Founder and Conductor, Amsterdam Baroque Orchestra, since 1978, and Choir, 1992–2013; Professor: of Harpsichord, Royal Conservatory, The Hague, since 1989; for Musicology, Leiden University, 2003, now Emeritus Professor of Historically Informed Performance of Early Music; *b* 10 Oct. 1944; *m* 1975, Tini Mathot; three *d*. *Educ:* Amsterdam Conservatory; Univ. of Amsterdam (degree in musicology 1968). Professor of: Harpsichord and Performance Practice, Early Music, Conservatory of Zwolle, 1968–73; of Harpsichord, Conservatory of Groningen, 1973–79; of Harpsichord, Conservatory of Amsterdam, 1979–89. Principal Conductor, Netherlands Radio Chamber Orch., 1994–2001; Principal Guest Conductor, Lausanne Chamber Orch., 1999–; guest conductor with orchestras in USA, Europe and Japan. Established: chamber ensemble, Musica da Camera, 1966; baroque orch., Musica Antiqua Amsterdam, 1968. Artist in Residence, Cleveland Orch., 2009–. Hon. Prof., Anton Bruckner Univ., Linz, 2010; Hon. Prof., Musik Hochschule, Lübeck, 2016. Lectures: Leiden Univ., 2006; Huizinga Lezing, Leiden Univ., 2016. Founder, Antoine Marchand, Challenge Classics, 2003–. Artistic Dir, Itinéraire Baroque Fest. Hon. RAM 1985. Hon. Dr Utrecht, 2000. Prix de l'Académie du Disque Lyrique, 1994; Prix Hector Berlioz, Paris, 1995; Deutsche Schallplattenpreis Echo Klassik, 1997; Silver Phonograph, NVPI, 2004; Klassieke Muziekprijs, VSCD, 2004; Silver Medal, KNAW, 2004; Bach Medal, Bach Fest., 2006; Edison Award, 2007; Choral Award, BBC Music Mag., 2008; ECHO Klassik Award, 2009; Buxtehude Preis Stad Lübeck, 2012; Bach Prize, RAM, 2014; RCO Medal, 2017; Edison Oeuvre Award, 2017. Companion, Order of Lion, 2003. *Publications:* Barokmuzick: theorie en praktijk, 1985; (contrib.) The World of the Bach Cantatas, ed Christopher Wolff, 1997; contrib. Early Music, Mens en Melodie, etc. *Address:* Meerweg 23, 1405 BC Bussum, The Netherlands. *T:* (35) 6926006, *Fax:* (35) 6926008. *E:* dagmar@tonkoopman.nl.

**KOOPMAN-BOYDEN, Dame Peggy Gwendoline,** DNZM 2017 (CNZM 1997); Professor of Social Gerontology, Dean, Faculty of Arts and Social Sciences, and Deputy Vice-Chancellor, University of Waikato, 1995–2015, Emeritus Professor, 2016; *b* Dannevirke, NZ, 16 Aug. 1943; *d* of Colin Boyden and Gwendoline Boyden; *m* 1968, Johannes (John), Koopman (marr. diss. 2002; he *d* 2016); one *s* one *d*. *Educ:* Dannevirke High Sch.; Palmerston North Teachers Coll. (Dip. Teaching 1964); Massey Univ. (BA 1968; MA 1972; DipEd 1973). Primary/intermediate teacher, 1964–69; Lectr, 1970–82, Sen. Lectr, 1983–92, Univ. of Canterbury; CEO, NZ Inst. of Res. and Develt, 1992–94. Founding Co-Dir (Academic), Southern Cross Lang. Inst., Christchurch, 1987–95. Member: Social Develt Council, 1978–84; NZ Planning Council, 1978–89 (Dep. Chair); Health Res. and Services Cttee, MRC, 1983–87; NZ Vice-Chancellor's Cttee on Univ. Acad. Progs, 2001–05; NZ Disability Strategy Revision Ref. Gp, 2014–16; NZ Positive Ageing Ind. Adv. Gp, 2016–; Chair: Nat. Council on HIV/AIDS, 1988–93; Expert Gp on Cervical Screening Prog., 1990–91; Ministerial Adv. Cttee on Complementary and Alternative Health, 2001–04; Rev. Panel, Sch. of Exercise and Health Scis, Univ. of Western Sydney, 2003; AgeWISE Adv. Gp, Waikato Dist Health Bd, 2010–. Professional Associate, East-West Center, Hawaii, 1985; Vis. Fellow, ANU, 1985; Vis. Prof., Internat. Relns Dept, Tokyo Univ., 1989–90. Hon. Lectr, Christchurch Med. Sch., 1989–97. Mem. and subcttee Chair, Bd, Wilson Carlisle Home for the Elderly, Hamilton, 1997–2002; Chair: Hamilton City Council Adv. Gp on Older People, 2013–15; Steering Gp, Age Friendly Hamilton proj., 2016–. Member: Royal Soc. of NZ; NZ IoD; Friends of Waikato Mus.; Friends of Te Papa Mus., Wellington; Cantando Choir. Hon. Life Member: Age Concern (Canterbury), 1996; NZ Assoc. of Gerontol., 2017. NZ 1990 Commemoration Medal, 1990; 75th Anniv. Medal, Massey Univ., 2002; Civic Award, City of Hamilton, NZ, 2015. *Publications:* (ed) Families in New Zealand Society, 1978; (with Claudia D. Scott) Family and Government Policy in New Zealand, 1984; (ed) New Zealand's Ageing Society, 1978; (ed jtly) Enhancing Wellbeing in an Ageing Society: 65–84 year old New Zealanders in 2007, 2009; (ed jtly) Making Active Ageing a Reality, 2014; over 120 articles in areas of social gerontology, public policy, retirement lifestyles, wellbeing, community care for older people, older people living alone, demography of an ageing population. *Recreations:* choral singing, opera, theatre, travel (international), walking, other cultures, voluntary work, membership of not-for-profit governance boards, family.

**KOOPS, Hon. Dame Mary Claire;** *see* Hogg, Hon. Dame M. C.

**KOPELMAN, Prof. Michael David,** PhD; FBPsS, FRCPsych, FMedSci, FRSB; Professor of Neuropsychiatry, Institute of Psychiatry, Psychology and Neuroscience (formerly Institute of Psychiatry), King's College London (formerly Guy's, King's and St Thomas's School of Medicine), 1998–2015, now Emeritus; *b* London, 8 Feb. 1950; *s* of late Dr Harry Kopelman and Joan Margaret Kopelman (*née* Knowlman); *m* 1985, Dr Sophie Janine Thomson; two *d*. *Educ:* Felsted Sch.; Univ. of Keele (BA Psychol. and Econs 1972); Middx Hosp. Med. Sch., UCL (MB BS 1978); Inst. of Psychiatry, Univ. of London (PhD 1988). FBPsS 1990; FRCPsych 1993; FRSB (FSB 2009). Sen. Lectr, 1988–93, Reader, 1994–97, UMDS, Guy's and St Thomas's Sch. of Medicine. Expert witness in criminal extradition, death row and civil liberties cases, Criminal Appeal Court. President: British Neuropsychol Soc., 2004–06; Internat. Neuropsychiatric Assoc., 2011–13; British Acad. of Forensic Scis, 2011–13; Internat. Neuropsychol Soc., 2017–18. FMedSci 2008. *Publications:* (jtly) Handbook of Memory Disorders, 2002; (jtly) Lishman's Organic Psychiatry, 4th edn 2009; (jtly) Forensic Neuropsychology in Practice, 2009; contribs to scientific jls. *Recreation:* enjoying a good book or a proper newspaper in print you can touch, feel and smell. *E:* michael.kopelman@kcl.ac.uk.
*See also* Prof. P. G. Kopelman.

**KOPELMAN, Prof. Peter Graham,** MD; FRCP, FFPH; FAcadMed; Vice-Chancellor, University of London, 2018–19; *b* London, 23 June 1951; *s* of late Dr Harry Kopelman and Joan Kopelman (*née* Knowlman); *m* 1981, Susan Mary Sarah Lewis; one *s* two *d*. *Educ:* Felsted Sch.; St George's Hosp. Med. Sch., London (MB BS 1974; MD 1982). FRCP 1992; FFPH 2005; FAcadMed 2015. Sen. Lectr in Medicine, 1986–97, Reader in Medicine, 1997–99, Prof. of Clinical Medicine, 1999–2006, London Hosp. Med. Coll., subseq. St Bartholomew's and Royal London Sch. of Medicine and Dentistry, then Barts and The London Sch. of Medicine and Dentistry, QMUL; Deputy Warden and Vice Principal, QMUL, 2001–06; Consultant Physician, Newham Gen. Hosp., 1986–95; Hon. Consultant Physician, Barts and The London NHS Trust, 1999–2006; Dean, Fac. of Health, UEA, 2006–08; Hon. Prof. of Medicine, Norfolk and Norwich Hosp., Norwich, 2006–08; Principal, St George's, Univ. of London, 2008–16, now Emeritus Prof.; Hon. Consultant Physician, St George's Hosp. NHS Trust, 2008–16. Adjunct Prof., Thomas Jefferson Univ., Philadelphia, 2016–. Non-executive Director: NE London Strategic HA, 2003–06; St George's Healthcare NHS Trust, 2012–. Member: Scientific Adv. Cttee on Nutrition, DoH/Food Standards Agency, 2001–10; HEFCE Res. Strategy Cttee, 2007–13; Bd, Med. Educn England, 2009–12; Exec. Cttee, Med. Schs Council, 2009–15; Bd, Centre for Workforce Intelligence, 2010–13; Steering Gp, Future Hosps Commn, 2011–13; Chairman: MRCP(UK) Clin. Examining Bd, RCP, 2004–08; NIHR Clin. Acad. Careers Panel, DoH, 2005–08; London Medicine Gp, London Higher, 2010–15; UCEA Clinical Academic Staff Adv. Gp, 2010–15; Faculty Bd, Royal Pharmaceutical Soc., 2013–; Med. Associate Professions Oversight Bd, Health Educn England, 2016–; Dep. Chm., Health Educn Res. Policy Gp, UUK, 2012–15. Pres., Eur. Assoc. for the Study of Obesity, 2003–06. Censor, RCP, 2010–14; Mem., Bd of Trustees, Univ. of London, 2011–13. Chair, Bd of Govs, Bancroft Sch., 2018–. Freeman, Drapers' Co., 2018; Freeman, City of London, 2018. FAcadMed 2015. Hon. DSc(Med) London, 2016; Hon. DSc Nicosia, 2016. *Publications:* (ed jtly) Clinical Obesity, 1998, 3rd edn 2009; (with J. Dacre) Handbook of Clinical Skills, 2002, 2nd edn 2019; scientific articles and book chapters on obesity, its causes, complications, treatment and prevention. *Recreations:* all sports, music, drawing, modern literature, political biographies. *Club:* Athenæum.
*See also* Prof. M. D. Kopelman.

**KOPELOWITZ, Dr Lionel,** MBE 2015; JP; General Medical Practitioner, 1953–2010; *b* 9 Dec. 1926; *s* of Maurice and Mabel Kopelowitz; *m* 1980, Sylvia Waksman (*née* Galler). *Educ:* Clifton Coll., Bristol; Trinity Coll., Cambridge (MA 1947); University Coll. Hosp. London. MRCS, LRCP 1951; MRCGP 1964. Resident MO, London Jewish Hosp., 1951–52; Flying Officer, RAF Med. Branch, 1952–53. Member: General Medical Council, 1984–94; General Optical Council, 1979–93; Standing Med. Adv. Cttee, DHSS, 1974–78; British Medical Association: Fellow, 1980; Mem. Council, 1982–94; Chm., Newcastle Div., 1968–69; Pres., Northern Regional Council, 1984–88; Mem., Gen. Med. Services Cttee, 1971–90 (Past Chm., Maternity Services Sub-Cttee); Chm., Central Adv. Cttee, Deputising Services, 1980–90; Dep. Chm., Private Practice Cttee, 1972–89; Chairman: St Marylebone and Bloomsbury Div., 1992–2016; London Regl Council, 2001–04; Pres., N London Central Div., 2017–. Chm., Newcastle upon Tyne FPC, 1979–85; Pres., Soc. of

FPCs of England and Wales, 1978–79; Mem. Council, RCGP, 1995–97. Vice-Pres., Trades Adv. Council, 1988–. President: Board of Deputies of British Jews, 1985–91; Nat. Council for Soviet Jewry, 1985–91; European Jewish Congress, 1986–91; Vice President: Conf. on Jewish Material Claims Against Germany, 1988–; Conf. on Jewish Material Claims Against Austria, 1988–; Council of Christians and Jews, 2009–. Member: Exec. Cttee, Meml Foundn for Jewish Culture, 1988–; United Synagogue, 1991–96. Vice-Pres., Assoc. of Baltic Jews, 1995–; Mem., Chm., Pres., numerous med. bodies and Jewish organisations, UK and overseas. Vice-Pres., British Council, Share Zedek Med. Centre, 1990–. Mem. Bd of Govs, Clifton Coll., Bristol, 1988–; Pres., Old Cliftonian Soc., 1991–93; Mem., Cambridge Union Soc. Liveryman, Apothecaries' Co., 1969. JP Northumberland, 1964. Grand Cross, Order of Merit (Germany), 1993. *Publications*: articles in med. jls; contrib. to Med. Annual. *Recreations*: foreign travel, contract bridge. *Address*: 10 Cumberland House, Clifton Gardens, W9 1DX. *T*: (020) 7289 6375. *Club*: Athenæum.

**KOPERNICKI, Jan Marceli,** CMG 2012; CBiol, FRSB; Director, 1994–95 and 1998–2011, and Shell Group Function Head for Shipping, 1998–2011, Shell International Trading and Shipping Co. Ltd (Member, Executive Committee, Shell Trading, 1998–2011); Director, Wangaratta Consulting Ltd, since 2011; *b* Overton, 15 Nov. 1948; *s* of Tadeusz Marceli Kopernicki and Irena Kopernicka; *m* 1976, Jennifer Gail Lack; one *s* one *d*. *Educ*: King Edward's Sch., Birmingham; Univ. of Leicester (BSc Hons Biol Scis 1971). CDipAF 1975; CBiol, FRSB (FSB 2009). Posts with Shell Internat. and Shell Oil Co. (USA), 1971–98. Director: Shell Tankers (UK) Ltd, 1996–2004; Shell Response Ltd, 1998–2011. Chamber of Shipping of UK: Dir, 1998–2014; Pres., 2010–11; Dir, Supervisory Bd, 2014–. Non-executive Director: Nordic Tankers Hldgs AB, 2012–16; J & J Denholm Ltd, 2012–; BMT Gp Ltd, 2014; Nordic Tankers A/S, 2016–19. Jt Chm., UK Shipping Defence Adv. Cttee, 2005–11; Mem., Internat. Business Adv. Bd, British Airways, 2007–12. Pres., Maritime UK, 2010–11; Chairman: Oil Cos Internat. Marine Forum, 2002–11; Nat. Cttee, Det Norske Veritas UK. Dir, Internat. Tank Owners' Pollution Fedn Ltd, 1998–2011. Mem. Bd, UK P&I Club. Chm., Exec. Bd, World Maritime Univ., 2010–11. Dir, UK Mutual Steam Ship Assce Assoc. (Bermuda) Ltd, 1998–2011. Vice Chm., RNLI, 2012–13; Dir, RNLI Heritage Trust, 2012–13. Pres., Shell Pensioners Assoc., 2012–18. Trustee: Royal Mus at Greenwich, 2003–11; Lloyd's Register Foundn, 2008–13. Hon. Captain, RNR, 2012. Freeman, City of London; Liveryman, Shipwrights' Co. Younger Brother of Trinity House. *Recreations*: photography, computing, science fiction, museums, travel.

**KOPIECZEK, Aloysius Michael, (Louis);** a Judge of the Upper Tribunal, Immigration and Asylum Chamber, since 2011; *b* Putney, 27 July 1959; *s* of Jozef Karol Kopieczek and Bernadette Marie Kopieczek (*née* Culhane); *m* 1990, Alison Patricia Hammond; two *s* one *d*. *Educ*: St Augustine's Coll., Westgate; Bristol Poly. (LLB Hons Law); Inns of Court Sch. of Law. Called to the Bar, Gray's Inn, 1983; in practice as a barrister, 1984–2002; Immigration Adjudicator: pt-time, 1999–2002; salaried, 2002–05; Immigration Judge, Asylum and Immigration Tribunal, 2005–08; Judge of First-tier Tribunal (Health, Educn and Social Care Chamber), 2008–10; Immigration Judge, First-tier Tribunal (Immigration and Asylum Chamber), 2010–11; Upper Tribunal Liaison Judge, Tribunal Procedure Cttee, 2017–. Legal Mem., Mental Health Rev. Tribunal, 1996–2008; Mem., First-tier Tribunal (Mental Health), 2008–. Judicial Observer, Justice Working Party report on Immigration and Asylum Appeals, 2018. Mem., Soc. of Old Augustinians. Mem., Traditional Internat. Shotokan Karate Assoc. *Recreations*: family, karate (3rd Dan Black Belt Shotokan Karate). *Address*: Upper Tribunal (Immigration and Asylum Chamber), Field House, 15 Breams Buildings, EC4A 1DZ.

**KORAB-KARPINSKI, Marek Romuald,** FRCS, FRCSE; Consultant Orthopaedic and Spinal Surgeon, Hull and East Yorkshire Hospitals NHS Trust, since 1987; *b* 29 Jan. 1950; *s* of Lt Col Marian Korab-Karpinski, MC, VM and Zofia Korab-Karpinska; *m* 1999, Dr Malgorzata Szymanska, orthopaedic surgeon; two *s* one *d* by previous marriage. *Educ*: Univ. of Nottingham (BMedSci 1977; BM BS); Univ. of Liverpool (MChOrth 1985). FRCS 1981; FRCSE 1981 (FRCSE (Orth) 1985). Higher surgical orthopaedic trng, Birmingham, 1981–83, Nottingham, 1983–87. Hon. Vis. Prof., Poznan Acad. of Orthopaedics, Poland, 1997. Fellow, Brit. Orthopaedic Assoc., 1985. Patron, PPA Internat., 1997. Hon. Fellow, Univ. of Hull, 1996. Computer Assisted Operative Surgery Prize, BCS, 1996. Designated co-inventor, Computer Assisted Robotic Surgery Technique, 1997. *Publications*: Posterior Lumbar Interbody Fusion and Cages, 1977; (contrib.) Current Concepts in Lumbar Spine Disorders, Vol. 2, 1997; various articles related to orthopaedics and computers, incl. robotic surgery; res. papers. *Recreations*: tennis, snow ski-ing, travel, charity work of a surgical nature. *Address*: 10 Harley Street, W1N 1AA. *T*: (020) 7436 5252. *Club*: Kandahar.

**KORALEK, Paul George,** CBE 1984; RA 1991 (ARA 1986); RIBA; consultant architect; Founding Partner, Ahrends Burton and Koralek, architects, 1961 (Consultant, until 2012); *b* 7 April 1933; *s* of late Ernest and Alice Koralek; *m* 1958, Jennifer Chadwick (*d* 2017); two *d* (one *s* decd). *Educ*: Aldenham School; Architectural Assoc. School of Architecture. RIBA 1957; AA Dip. Hons. Architect: with Powell & Moya, London, 1956–57; with Marcel Breuer, New York, 1959–60. Part-time teaching, Sch. of Arch., Leicester Polytechnic, 1982–84. *Major projects include: public buildings*: Maidenhead Libr., 1972; Roman Catholic Chaplaincy, Oxford, 1972; Nucleus Low Energy Hosp., IoW, 1982; winning entry, Nat. Gall. Extension Hampton Site Comp., 1982; Dover Heritage Centre, 1988–90 (Civic Trust Award, 1992); British Embassy, Moscow, 1993–99; Dublin Dental Hosp., Trinity Coll., 1994–98 (RIBA Arch. Award; RIAI Award); Techniquest Science Centre, Cardiff, 1995 (RIBA Arch. Award); Offaly County Council offices, 2002–; County Offices, Neneagh, Tipperary, 2004; *educational buildings*: Chichester Theol Coll., 1965; Berkeley Liby, TCD, 1967 (1st Prize, Internat. Comp., 1961); Templeton Coll., Oxford, 1967; Arts Faculty Bldg, TCD, 1975–79; Portsmouth Poly. Liby, 1979–75; Residential bldg, Keble Coll., Oxford, 1976 (RIBA Arch. Award, 1978); Selly Oak Colls Learning Resources Centre, 1997; Insts of Technol. at Tralee, Waterford and Blanchardstown, 1997–2002; Loughborough Univ. Business Sch., 1998; Innovation Centre, TCD, 2001; John Wheatley Coll., Glasgow, 2007–; *residential buildings*: houses, Dunstan Rd, Oxford, 1969; Nebenzahl House, Jerusalem, 1972; Chalvedon Housing, 1975–77; Whitmore Court Housing, Basildon, 1975 (RIBA Good Design in Housing Award, 1977); Felmore Housing, 1975–80; *commercial/industrial buildings*: Habitat Warehouse, Showroom and Offices, Wallingford, 1974 (Financial Times Indust. Arch. Award, and Structl Steel Design Award (Warehouse), 1976); factory bldgs and refurbishment, Cummins Engine Co., Shotts, Scotland, 1975–83 (Structl Steel Design Award, 1980); J. Sainsbury supermarket, Canterbury, 1984 (Structl Steel Design Award, 1985; FT Arch. at Work Award Commendation, 1986); W. H. Smith Offices, Greenbridge, 1985 and 1996 (FT Arch. at Work Award Commendation, 1987); John Lewis Dept Store, Kingston-upon-Thames, 1987 (Civic Trust Commendation, 1991). *Exhibitions of drawings and works*: RIBA Heinz Gall., 1980; Douglas Hyde Gall. Dublin, 1981; Technical Univ. of Braunschweig and Tech. Univ. of Hanover, Germany, Mus. of Finnish Arch., Helsinki, Univ. of Oulu, and Alvar Aalto Mus., Jvasklya, Finland, 1982; HQ of AA, Oslo, 1983. Chm., SE Regl Design Panel, 2002–. Member: Develt Adv. (formerly Design and Architectural Rev.) Panel, Cardiff Bay Develt Corp., 1988; ARCUK Bd of Architectural Educn, 1987–93; Trustee, Bldg Industry Youth Trust, 1981–95. External Examiner: Sch. of Arch., Univ. of Manchester, 1981–85; Plymouth Poly., 1988; Assessor: RIBA competitions, incl. Toyota UK HQ, 1997; Irish Dept of Educn Schs competition; Civic Trust Awards; Advr, Cardiff Bay Opera House, 1994–95. Papers and lectures, UK and abroad, 1964–. *Publications*: paper and articles in RIBA and other prof. jls. *Recreation*: drawing. *Address*: 3 Rochester Road, NW1 9JH.
*See also* C. L. Ricks.

**KORNBERG, Prof. Sir Hans (Leo),** Kt 1978; MA, DSc, ScD, PhD; FRS 1965; FRSB; University Professor and Professor of Biology, Boston University, since 1995 (Director, University Professors Program, 2002–05 and 2007–11); Sir William Dunn Professor of Biochemistry, University of Cambridge, 1975–95, and Fellow of Christ's College, Cambridge, since 1975 (Master, 1982–95); *b* 14 Jan. 1928; *o s* of Max Kornberg and Margarete Kornberg (*née* Silberbach); *m* 1st, 1956, Monica Mary King (*d* 1989); twin *s* two *d*; 2nd, 1991, Donna, *d* of William B. Haber and Ruth Haber. *Educ*: Queen Elizabeth Grammar Sch., Wakefield; Univ. of Sheffield (BSc, PhD); MA 1958, DSc 1961, Oxon; ScD Cantab 1975. FIBiol 1965, Hon. FRSB (Hon. FIBiol 2004). Commonwealth Fund Fellow of Harkness Foundation, at Yale University and Public Health Research Inst., New York, 1953–55; Mem. of scientific staff, MRC Cell Metabolism Res. Unit, University of Oxford, 1955–60; Lectr, Worcester Coll., Oxford, 1958–61 (Hon. Fellow 1980); Prof. of Biochemistry, Univ. of Leicester, 1960–75. Visiting Instructor, Marine Biological Lab., Woods Hole, Mass, 1964–66, 1981–85, Trustee, 1982–93. Dir, UK Nirex Ltd, 1986–95. Member: SRC, 1967–72 (Chm., Science Bd, 1969–72); UGC Biol. Sci. Cttee, 1967–77; NATO Adv. Study Inst. Panel, 1970–76 (Chm., 1974–75); Kuratorium, Max-Planck Inst., Dortmund, 1979–90 (Chm., Sci. Adv. Cttee); AFRC (formerly ARC), 1980–84; Priorities Bd for R & D in Agriculture, 1984–90; BP Venture Res. Council, 1981–91; ACARD, 1982–85; Adv. Council on Public Records, 1984–86; UK Cttee on Eur. Year of the Environment, 1986–88; Vice-Chm., EMBO, 1978–81; Chairman: Royal Commn on Environmental Pollution, 1976–81; Adv. Cttee on Genetic Modification, 1986–95; Co-ordinating Cttee on Environmental Res., Res. Councils, 1986–88; Sci. Adv. Cttee, Inst. for Mol. Biol. and Medicine, Monash Univ., 1987–; President: BAAS, 1984–85 (Hon. Mem., 2003); Biochemical Soc., 1990–95; IUBMB, 1991–94 (Dist. Service Award, 2003); Assoc. for Science Educn, 1991–92; Vice-Pres., Inst. of Biol., 1971–73. A Managing Trustee, Nuffield Foundn, 1973–93; Trustee, 1990–92, Gov., 1992–95, Wellcome Trust; Academic Governor, Hebrew Univ. of Jerusalem, 1976–97 (Hon. Gov., 1997–); Governor: Weizmann Inst., 1980–97 (Hon. Gov., 1997–); Lister Inst., 1990–95. Hon. Fellow: Brasenose Coll., Oxford, 1983; Wolfson Coll., Cambridge, 1990. FRSA 1972. Fellow, Amer. Acad. of Microbiol., 1992. For. Associate, Nat. Acad. of Sciences, USA, 1986; Foreign Member: Amer. Philosoph. Soc., 1993; Accademia Nazionale dei Lincei, 1997; Hon. For. Mem., Amer. Acad. of Arts & Scis, 1987; Member: Leopoldina German Acad. of Scis, 1982; Acad. Europaea, 1989; Hon. Member: Amer. Soc. Biol Chem., 1972; Biochem. Soc., FRG, 1973; Japanese Biochem. Soc., 1981; Biochem. Soc. (UK), 2001; Phi Beta Kappa, 1996; Hon. FRCP 1989. Hon. ScD Cincinnati, 1974; Hon. DSc: Warwick, 1975; Leicester, 1979; Sheffield, 1979; Bath, 1980; Strathclyde, 1985; South Bank, 1994; Leeds, 1995; La Trobe, 1997; DUniv Essex, 1979; Hon. Dr med Leipzig, 1984; Hon. LLD Dundee, 1999. Colworth Medal of Biochemical Soc., 1963; Otto Warburg Medal, Biochem. Soc. of Federal Republic of Germany, 1973. *Publications*: (with Sir Hans Krebs) Energy Transformations in Living Matter, 1957; articles in scientific jls. *Recreations*: cooking and conversation, playing the cello (badly). *Address*: Biology Department, Boston University, 5 Cummington Mall, Boston, MA 02215, USA; (home) 70 Carey Lane, Falmouth, MA 02540–1604, USA.

**KORNBERG, Prof. Roger David,** PhD; Mrs George A. Winzer Professor in Medicine, Stanford University School of Medicine, since 2003; *b* St Louis, Mo, 24 April 1947; *s* of late Prof. Arthur Kornberg (jtly, Nobel Prize in Physiology or Medicine, 1959) and Sylvy Ruth Kornberg (*née* Levy); *m* 1984, Yahli Lorch; two *s* one *d*. *Educ*: Harvard Univ. (BS 1967); Stanford Univ. (PhD 1972). Postdoctoral Fellow and Mem. of Scientific Staff, MRC Lab. of Molecular Biol., Cambridge, 1972–75; Asst Prof. in Biol Chem., Harvard Medical Sch., 1976–78; Prof. of Structural Biol., Stanford Univ. Sch. of Medicine, 1978– (Chair, Dept of Structural Biol., 1984–92). Foreign Mem., Royal Soc., 2009. Nobel Prize in Chemistry, 2006. *Publications*: articles in learned jls. *Address*: Department of Structural Biology, Stanford University School of Medicine, Fairchild Building, 299 Campus Drive, Stanford, CA 94305–5126, USA.

**KORNER, Joanna Christian Mary,** CMG 2004; QC 1993; **Her Honour Judge Korner**; a Circuit Judge, since 2012; *b* 1 July 1951; *d* of late John Hugh George Korner and Martha (*née* Tupay von Isertingen). *Educ*: Queensgate Sch.; Inns of Court Sch. of Law. Called to the Bar, Inner Temple, 1974, Bencher, 1996; Recorder, 1995–2012. Member: Bar Council, 1994–97; Crown Court Rules Cttee, 1994–2000; Hd, Internat. Section, Advocacy Trng Council, 2008–12. Sen. Prosecuting Counsel, Internat. Criminal Tribunal (formerly Internat. War Crimes Tribunal) for former Yugoslavia, 1999–2004, 2009–12. Chair, Adv. Cttee for Conscientious Objectors, 2013–. Dir, Internat. Course, Judicial Coll., 2014–17. *Recreations*: collecting books and porcelain, cinema, tennis. *Address*: Southwark Crown Court, 1 English Grounds, SE1 2HU.

**KORNICKI, Prof. Peter Francis,** DPhil, DLitt; FBA 2000; Professor of Japanese Studies and Head, Department of East Asian Studies, University of Cambridge, 2012–14, now Professor Emeritus; Fellow, Robinson College, Cambridge, since 1986 (Deputy Warden, 2008–16); *b* 1 May 1950; *er s* of late Sqn Leader Franciszek Kornicki, VM and Patience Ceridwen Kornicka (*née* Williams); *m* 1st, 1975, Catharine Olga Mikolaski (*d* 1995); one *s* one *d*; 2nd, 1998, Francesca Orsini. *Educ*: St George's Coll., Weybridge; Lincoln Coll., Oxford (BA 1972; MSc 1975; Hon. Fellow, 2004); St Antony's Coll., Oxford (DPhil 1979); DLitt Oxon 2011. Lectr, Univ. of Tasmania, 1978–82; Associate Prof., Kyoto Univ., 1982–84; Cambridge University: Lectr, 1985–95; Reader in Japanese History and Bibliography, 1995–2001; Prof. of Japanese History and Bibliography, 2001–07; Sandars Reader in Bibliography, 2007–08; Prof. of East Asian Studies, 2007–12; Chm., Faculty Bd of Oriental Studies, 1993–95, 2004–05. Chm., African and Oriental Studies sect., 2006–09, E Asia Panel, 2009–, British Acad. Pres., European Assoc. for Japanese Studies, 1997–2000. MAE 2012. Special Prize, Japan Foundn, 1992; Yamagata Banto Prize, Osaka Prefecture, 2013. Order of the Rising Sun, Gold Rays with Neck Ribbon (Japan), 2017. *Publications*: The Reform of Fiction in Meiji Japan, 1982; Early Japanese Books in Cambridge University Library, 1991; (jtly) Cambridge Encyclopedia of Japan, 1993; The Book in Japan: a cultural history, 1998; Early Japanese Books in the Russian State Library, 1999; The Iwakura Embassy, vol. 4, 2002; (jtly) The Female as Subject: reading and writing in early modern Japan, 2010; (jtly) Catalogue of the Japanese Coin Collection (pre-Meiji) at the British Museum, 2011; (jtly) F. V. Dickins' Letters to Ernest M. Satow, Kumagusu Minakata and others, 2011; (jtly) The History of the Book in East Asia, 2013; (jtly) Japanese studies in Britain: a survey and history, 2016; Languages, Scripts, and Chinese Texts in East Asia, 2018; numerous articles and reviews in jls. *Recreations*: travel, cooking, languages. *Address*: Robinson College, Cambridge CB3 9AN.

**KOSCIUSZKO, Stefan Henry;** Vice Chairman, Asia Pacific, CQS Ltd, 2013–16; *b* 2 June 1959; *s* of late Konstanty Kosciuszko and of Elisabeth Kerr Kosciuszko (*née* Havelock); *m* 1985, Takako Yamaguchi; two *d*. *Educ*: Gordonstoun Sch.; Divine Mercy Coll., Henley-on-Thames; Keele Univ. (Josiah Wedgwood Meml Award for Hist.; BA Hons (Internat.

Relns) 1980); Stanford Univ. (Sen. Leadership Prog., 2017). National Westminster Bank, 1980–82; Sumitomo Bank, London/Tokyo, 1985–88; Chemical Bank, London/Tokyo, 1985–88; Schroders: Gen. Manager, Tokyo, 1988–91; Asst Dir, Internat. Finance Dept, London, 1992–95; Director, 1995–98; Hd, Asia-Pacific Equity Capital Markets Regl Investment Banking Cttee and Asian Securities Mgt Cttee, 1995–97; Hd, Corporate Finance, Indonesia, 1997–98; Man. Dir, Gavin Anderson & Co., 1999–2000; Dir, Credit Suisse First Boston, 2000–02; Chief Exec., Asia House, 2002–07; Chief of Staff, Hinduja Group, 2007–09; Dir and Sen. Advr, Asia Pacific, Praetoria Ltd, 2010–13; Chm., TwoFoldTwenty, 2010–13; Dir of Marketing and Communications, fibre GarDen, 2010–14. Consultant, BTG Pactual, 2010–11. Executive Director: Pakistan Britain Trade and Investment Forum, 2003–07; Korea Forum for the Future, 2007–09; Sec., Indo-British Partnership Network, 2005–07. Mem. Cttee, 48 Gp Club, 2010–14 (Chief Exec., 2012–13). Gov., Gainsborough House Mus., 2002–06. Sec., Sudbury Soc., 2002–06; Pres., Sudbury Girls' Football Club, 2003–07. FRSA 2006. *Recreations:* sports, chess, fine wine, antiques, Asian culture, history, hard work and my two daughters—living life to fullest extent possible. *Address:* Swarthgill House, Garsdale, Sedbergh, Cumbria LA10 5PD. *Club:* Naval and Military.

KOSHIBA, Prof. Masatoshi, PhD; Professor, Department of Physics, 1970–87, now Emeritus, and Director, International Centre for Elementary Particle Physics, 1984–87, now Senior Counsellor, University of Tokyo; *b* 19 Sept. 1926; *m* 1959, Kyoko Kato. *Educ:* Univ. of Tokyo; Univ. of Rochester, NY (PhD 1955). Res. Associate, Dept of Physics, Univ. of Chicago, 1955–58; Associate Prof., Inst. of Nuclear Study, Univ. of Tokyo, 1958–63; Sen. Res. Associate, Dept of Physics, Univ. of Chicago, 1959–62 (on secondment); Associate Prof., Dept of Physics, Univ. of Tokyo, 1963–70. Founding Chm., Heisei Foundn for Basic Science, Tokyo, 2003. (Jtly) Nobel Prize in Physics, 2002. *Address:* International Centre for Elementary Particle Physics, University of Tokyo, 7–3–1 Hongo, Bunkyo-ku, Tokyo 113–0033, Japan.

KOSMINSKY, Peter; freelance film director and writer, since 1995; *b* London, 21 April 1956; *s* of Leon and Erika Kosminsky; two *d*; partner, Rose de Wend Fenton. *Educ:* Haberdashers' Aske's Sch., Herts; Worcester Coll., Oxford (BA Hons Chem. 1980; MA; Hon. Fellow 2016). Gen. trainee, 1980–82, Asst Producer, 1982–85, BBC; producer and dir, Documentaries Dept, Yorkshire TV, 1985–95; programmes include: The Falklands War: the untold story (UK Broadcast Press Guild Award, BFI Special Award, 1987); Cambodia: children of the killing fields (One World Broadcasting Trust Award, 1988); director: Shoot to Kill, 1990 (UK Broadcast Press and RTS Awards); (film) Wuthering Heights, 1992; dir and producer, The Dying of the Light, 1994; freelance, 1995–: *film:* White Oleander, 2002; *television:* producer and director: No Child of Mine, 1997 (BAFTA Award); Walking on the Moon, 1999; Innocents, 2000; director: Warriors, 1999 (BAFTA and RTS Awards); The Project, 2002; Wolf Hall, 2015 (Golden Globe for Best Limited Series, RTS Judges Award, BAFTA Award for Best Drama, Peabody Award); writer and director: The Government Inspector, 2005 (BAFTA and RTS Awards); Britz, 2007 (BAFTA and RTS Awards); The Promise, 2011 (Best Drama Prize, One World Media Awards); The State, 2017. Member: Council, BAFTA, 2003–07; Council, Liberty, 2008–13; Bd, Directors UK, 2008–11; Bd, First Light, 2011–12; Gov., BFI, 2012–16. Mem., Consultative Cttee, Worcester Coll., Oxford, 2009–15. FRSA 2005; FRTS 2006; Hon. Fellow, Univ. Coll. Falmouth, 2011. Hon. Mem., UN Internat. Criminal Tribunal for the former Yugoslavia Staff Union, 2009. Hon. DArt Bournemouth, 2009. Special Award for TV Achievement, BFI, 1989; Alan Clarke Award, BAFTA, 1999; EuroFipa d'Honneur, Biarritz, 2005. *Recreations:* photography, cinema, being a daddy. *Address:* c/o United Agents, 12–26 Lexington Street, W1F 0LE. *E:* ajones@unitedagents.co.uk. *Clubs:* Groucho, Century.

KOTCH, Laurie, (Mrs J. K. Kotch); *see* Purden, R. L.

KOUCHNER, Bernard Jean, Hon. KBE 2005; Minister of Foreign and European Affairs, France, 2007–10; *b* Avignon, 1 Nov. 1939; *s* of Georges Kouchner and Léone Mauric; *m* Evelyne Pisier (marr. diss.); three *c*, one *s* with Christine Ockrent. *Educ:* Faculté de Médicine de Paris (Cert. d'études spéciales in gastroenterology); Dip. digestive endoscopy. Co-founder, Evènement, 1965–69; Mem., Red Cross med. mission to Biafra, 1968–69; humanitarian missions to help victims in most of major natural and industrial disasters and political crises, 1968–; Co-founder, Actuel jl, 1970; Co-founder and Pres., Médecins Sans Frontières, 1971–79; Gastroenterologist, Cochin Hosp., Paris, 1975–87. Minister of State: with resp. for Social Integration, 1988; with resp. for Humanitarian Action, 1988–92; Minister: for Health and Humanitarian Action, 1992–93; MEP (Réunir/Socialiste), 1994–97; Pres., Commn for Develt and Co-operation, Eur. Parlt, 1994–96; Minister of State for Health, 1997–98, for Health and Social Action, 1998–99; UN Sec. Gen.'s Special Rep. for Kosovo, 1999–2001; Minister Delegate for Health, 2001–02. Mem., Socialist Party, 1997–2007. Prof. of Health and Develt, Conservatoire national des arts et métiers, 2002–07. Lectr, Harvard Sch. of Public Health, 2003. Founder Chm., BK Consultants. Mem., Bd of Dirs, PlaNet Finance. Founder, 1980, Pres., 1980–84, Hon. Pres., 1984–88, Médecins du Monde; Founder, Volontaires européens du développement, 1988. Chm., ESTHER public interest gp, 2001–07. Pres., then Hon. Pres., Réunir, 1993–2007. Member: Hon. Cttee, Children Action; Bd of Dirs, Internat. Women's Coalition. Founder Mem., La chaîne de l'espoir. Writer, TV series, under pseudonym Bernard Gridaine: Médecins de nuit, 1978; Hôtel de police, 1985. Prix Dag Hammarskjöld, 1979; Prix Athinai de la fondation Alexandre Onassis, 1981; Prix Europa, 1984; Prix européen des Droits de l'homme, 2005. *Publications:* (jtly) La France sauvage, 1970; (jtly) Les Voraces, 1974; L'Ile de lumière, 1979 (Prix Louise Weiss, Eur. Parlt); Charité business, 1986; (jtly) Le Devoir d'ingérence, 1988; Les Nouvelles solidarités, 1989; Le Malheur des autres, 1991; (jtly) Dieu et les hommes, 1993; Ce que je crois, 1995; Vingt idées pour l'an 2000, 1995; La Dictature médicale, 1996; Le Premier qui dit la vérité, 2002; Les Guerriers de la paix: du Kosovo à l'Irak, 2004; (jtly) Quand tu seras président, 2004; Deux ou trois choses que je sais de nous, 2006; articles.

KOUMI, Margaret, (Maggie); freelance editorial consultant, since 2001; *b* 15 July 1942; *d* of Yiasoumi Koumi and Melexidia Paraskeva; *m* 1980, Ramon Sola. *Educ:* Buckingham Gate Sch., London. Sec., Thomas Cook Travel, 1957–60; Sub-Editor and writer, Boyfriend and Trend magazines, 1960–66; Sub-Editor, TV World, 1967–68; Production Editor, 1968–70, Editor, 1970–86, 19 magazine; Man. Editor, Practical Parenting and Practical Health, 1986–87; Jt Ed., 1988–93, Ed., 1993–2001, Hello! mag. (the magazine has won several awards). *Publications:* Claridge's: within the image, 2004. *Recreations:* reading, travel.

KOURTZI, Prof. Zoe, PhD; Professor of Experimental Psychology, University of Cambridge, since 2013; *b* Athens, 12 Aug. 1971; *d* of Dimitrios Kourtzis and Maria Kourtzi; *m* 2004, Andrew Edward Welchman; two *s. Educ:* Univ. of Crete (BS Psychol. 1993); Rutgers Univ. (PhD Cognitive Psychol. 1998). Postdoctoral Fellow: Vision Sci. Lab., Harvard Univ., 1998–99; Dept of Brain and Cognitive Sci., MIT, 1998–2002; Vis. Scientist, 2000–02, Sen. Res. Scientist, 2002–05, Max Planck Inst. for Biol Cybernetics, Germany; Professor: of Brain Imaging, Birmingham Univ., 2005–13; Lab. for Neuro- and Psychophysiol., Catholic Univ. of Leuven, Belgium, 2011–13. *Publications:* contribs to learned jls. *Recreations:* dance, theatre. *Address:* Department of Psychology, University of Cambridge, Downing Street, Cambridge CB2 3EB. *T:* (01223) 766558. *E:* zk240@cam.ac.uk.

KOUZARIDES, Prof. Tony, FRS 2012; Professor of Cancer Biology, since 2002, Deputy Director, Wellcome Trust/Cancer Research UK Gurdon Institute, since 2004, and Director, Milner Therapeutics Institute, since 2016, University of Cambridge; *b* 17 Jan. 1958; *s* of Takis and Annie Kouzarides; *m* 1984, Penny Hall; one *s* one *d. Educ:* Univ. of Leeds (BSc Genetics 1981); Univ. of Cambridge (PhD Virology 1984). Postdoctoral Fellow: MRC Lab. of Molecular Biology, Cambridge, 1984–86; New York Univ. Med. Center, 1986–89; Res. Associate, Dept of Pathology, Univ. of Cambridge, 1989–91; Wellcome Trust/Cancer Research UK (formerly Cancer Research Campaign) Institute, University of Cambridge: Sen. Res. Associate, 1991–96; Reader, 1996–99; Prof. of Molecular Cancer Biology, 1999–2001; Hd of CRUK Labs, 2002–04. Gibb Fellow, CRUK, 2013–. Co-founder and Director: Abcom Ltd, 1998–; Chroma Therapeutics, 2001–; Founder, Storm Therapeutics, 2016–. FHMAAAS 2018. Novartis Medal and Prize, Biochem. Soc., 2012. *Publications:* various articles in many scientific jls. *Recreations:* films, music. *Address:* The Wellcome Trust/Cancer Research UK Gurdon Institute, Henry Wellcome Building of Cancer and Developmental Biology, University of Cambridge, Tennis Court Road, Cambridge CB2 1QN. *T:* (01223) 334112, *Fax:* (01223) 334089. *E:* tk106@cam.ac.uk.

KOVACEVICH, Stephen; pianist and conductor; *b* 17 Oct. 1940; *s* of Nicholas Kovacevich and Loreta (*née* Zuban, later Bishop). *Educ:* studied under Lev Shorr and Myra Hess. Solo and orchestral debut, San Francisco, USA 1951; London debut, Nov. 1961. First known professionally as Stephen Bishop, then as Stephen Bishop-Kovacevich, and since 1991 as Stephen Kovacevich. Concert tours: in England, Europe and USA, with many of the world's leading orchestras, incl. New York Philharmonic, Los Angeles Philharmonic, Israel Philharmonic, Amsterdam Concertgebouw, London Symphony, London Philharmonic, and BBC Symphony. Has appeared at Edinburgh, Bath, Berlin and San Sebastian Festivals. Gave 1st performance of Richard Rodney Bennett's Piano Concerto, 1969 (this work is dedicated to and has been recorded by him, under Alexander Gibson). Performed all Mozart Piano concertos, 1969–71; recorded all Beethoven sonatas, 2003. Principal Guest Conductor: Australian Chamber Orch., 1987–91; Zagreb Philharmonic Orch.; Music Dir, Irish Chamber Orch., 1990–93. Edison Award for his recording of Bartok's 2nd Piano Concerto and Stravinsky's Piano Concerto, with BBC Symphony Orch., under Colin Davis; Gramophone Award, 1993 and Stereo Review Record of the Year for Brahms' Piano Concerto No 1 with LPO, under Wolfgang Sawallisch. *Recreations:* snooker, chess, films, tennis. *Address:* c/o Wright Music Management, Suite 01–125, 12 Hammersmith Grove, W6 7AP.

KOVACH, Catherine Anne; *see* Duigan, C. A.

KOVÁCS, László; MP (MSzP) Hungary (formerly Republic of Hungary), 2010–14; *b* 3 July 1939; *m*; one *d. Educ:* Petrik Lajos Tech. Sch. for Chem. Industry, Budapest; Univ. of Econ. Scis, Budapest; Coll. of Politics. Chem. Technician, Medicolor, and Kóbánya Pharmaceutical Works, 1957–66; Consultant and Dep. Hd, Dept for Internat. Relns, Hungarian Socialist Workers' Party, 1975–86; Dep. Foreign Minister, Hungary, 1986–89; Sec. of State, Min. of Foreign Affairs, 1989–90; MP, 1990–2004; Minister for Foreign Affairs, 1994–98, 2002–04; Mem., Eur. Commn, 2004–10. Leader, Hungarian Socialist Party, 1998–2004.

KOVATS, Steven Laszlo; QC 2010; a Recorder, since 2010; a Deputy High Court Judge, since 2013; *b* London, 1 Feb. 1966; *s* of Laszlo Joseph Kovats and Joan Kovats; *m* 1999, Michelle Ewing; one *d. Educ:* Christ's Hosp.; Trinity Hall, Cambridge (BA Hons Law 1988). Called to the Bar, Middle Temple, 1989. Attorney Gen.'s Civil Litigation 'A' Panel, 2001–10. *Recreations:* running marathons, cooking. *Address:* 39 Essex Chambers, 81 Chancery Lane, WC2A 1DD. *T:* (020) 7832 1111, *Fax:* (020) 7353 3978. *E:* steven.kovats@39essex.com.

KOVOOR, Rev. George Iype; Rector, St Paul's Episcopal Church, Darien, Connecticut, since 2016; Chaplain to the Queen, since 2003; Chief Executive, Kairos Global, since 2002; *b* 6 June 1957. *Educ:* Delhi Univ. (BA 1977); Serampore Univ. (BD 1980); Christian Medical Assoc. of India (Dip. Counselling and Hosp. Chaplaincy 1985); Union Biblical Seminary, Yavatmal. Ordained deacon and priest, 1980, Ch of N India; Curate, Shanti Niwas Ch, Faridabad, 1980–82; Presbyter: Santokh Majra Ch, 1982–83; St Paul's Cathedral, Ambala, 1984–88; Nat. Youth Dir, Ch of N India, 1987–90; Principal Chaplain, St Stephen's Hosp., Delhi, 1988–90; Curate, St Augustine's, Derby, and Minister, Derby Asian Christian Ministry Project, 1990–94; Tutor, 1994–97, Principal, 1997–2004, Crowther Hall CMS Trng Coll.; Mission Educn Dir, CMS, 1997–2005; Principal, Trinity Coll., Bristol, 2005–13; Dir, Centre for Anglican Communion Studies, Selly Oak; Rector, St John's Episcopal Church, New Haven, CT, 2013–16. Canon Theologian, Province of Niger Delta North, 2010; Canon Missiologist, Dio. of Sabah, 2010. Hon. Canon, Worcester Cathedral, 2001–05.

KOWALSKI, Gregor; Parliamentary Counsel, 2005–09; consultant legislative drafter, since 2011; *b* 7 Oct. 1949; *s* of Mieczyslaw Kowalski and Jeanie Hutcheson Kowalski (*née* MacDonald); *m* 1974, Janet McFarlane Pillatt; two *s. Educ:* Airdrie Academy; Strathclyde Univ. (LLB 1971). Apprentice, then Asst Solicitor, Levy & McRae, Glasgow, 1971–74; Procurator Fiscal Depute, Glasgow, 1974–78; Asst, later Deputy Parly Draftsman for Scotland and Asst Legal Sec. to Lord Advocate, 1978–87; seconded to Govt of Seychelles as Legal Draftsman, 1982–83; Scottish Parly Counsel and Asst Legal Sec. to Lord Advocate, 1987–99; Scottish Parly Counsel to UK Govt, 1999–2000; Dep. Parly Counsel, 2000–05. Chm., Holywell Hook Heath Ltd, 2012–18. Vice-Chm., London Symphony Chorus, 2012–14. *Recreations:* singing, opera, travel. *Address:* 10 Holywell, Hook Heath Road, Woking, Surrey GU22 0LA.

KRAEMER, (Thomas Whilhelm) Nicholas; conductor; *b* 7 March 1945; *s* of William Paul Kraemer and Helen Bartrum; *m* 1984, Elizabeth Mary Anderson; two *s* two *d* (and one *s* decd). *Educ:* Edinburgh Acad.; Lancing Coll.; Dartington Coll. of Arts; Nottingham Univ. (BMus 1967); Guildhall Sch. of Music and Drama. ARCM. Harpsichordist with Acad. of St Martin in the Fields, 1972–80, with Monteverdi Choir and Orchestra, 1970–80; Musical Director: Unicorn Opera, Abingdon, 1971–75; West Eleven Children's Opera, 1971–88; Founder and Dir, Raglan Baroque Players, 1978–2003; Principal Conductor, Divertimenti, 1979–89; Permanent Guest Conductor: Manchester Camerata, 1995–2014 (Principal Conductor, 1992–95); Music of the Baroque, Chicago, 2002–; Conductor, Glyndebourne, 1980–82; Musical Dir, Opera 80, 1980–83; Associate Conductor, BBC Scottish SO, 1983–85; Artistic Director: London Bach Orch., 1985–93; Irish Chamber Orch., 1985–90; Guest Conductor: English Chamber Orch., Scottish Chamber Orch.; Northern Sinfonia; BBC Philharmonic; BBC Nat. Orch. of Wales; Hallé Orch.; St Paul Chamber Orch. (USA); Berlin Philharmonic; ENO; Bergen Philharmonic; Gothenburg SO; Chicago SO; Detroit SO; Colorado SO; Toronto SO; W Australian SO; Minnesota Orch.; Orch. ensemble Kanazawa; Musikkollegium Winterthur; Iceland SO; Aalborg SO; Auckland

Philharmonia; Lapland Chamber Orch.; Irish Chamber Orch.; Collegium Musicum Bergen; Scottish Opera; Opera Neo; Royal Scottish Nat. Orch.; Royal Liverpool Philharmonic Orch.; RTÉ Nat. SO; Principal Guest Conductor, Kristiansand SO; Conductor of Opera at Grange Park, 2012; Conductor of Opera at Buxton, 2013; Conductor, British Youth Opera; Associate Artist: Trinity Coll. of Music, 2012–17; Orquesta Metropolitana di Lisboa, 2014–; Civic Orch., Chicago, 2015–; Resident Conductor, Utah Univ. Prog. Dir, Bath Fest., 1994. Recordings include works by Vivaldi, Locatelli, Mozart, Handel, Thea Musgrave. *Recreation:* keeping fit. *Address:* c/o Caroline Phillips Management, 11 Pound Pill, Corsham, Wilts SN13 9HZ.

**KRAMER,** family name of **Baroness Kramer.**

**KRAMER,** Baroness *cr* 2010 (Life Peer), of Richmond Park in the London Borough of Richmond upon Thames; **Susan Veronica Kramer;** PC 2014; *b* 21 July 1950; *m* 1972, John Davis Kramer (*d* 2006); one *s* one *d*. *Educ:* St Hilda's Coll., Oxford (BA PPE, MA 1972); Illinois Univ. (MBA Business/Finance 1982). Staff Associate, Nat. Acad. of Engrg, 1972–73; Second Vice-Pres., Continental Bank, USA, 1982–88; Vice-Pres., Corporate Finance, Citibank/Citicorp, USA, 1988–92; Chief Operating Officer, Future Water Internat., 1992–95; Partner, Kramer & Associates, 1995–99. Board Mem., CAIB Infrastructure Project Advrs, 1997–99; Director: Infrastructure Capital Partners Ltd, 1999–2007; Speciality Scanners plc, 2001–11. Mem. Bd, Transport for London, 2000–05. London Mayoral candidate, 2000. MP (Lib Dem) Richmond Park, 2005–10; contested (Lib Dem) same seat, 2010. Minister of State, DfT, 2013–15. Lib Dem Spokesperson for economics, 2015–. *Publications:* (contrib.) Harnessing the Markets to Achieve Environmental Goals, 2004. *Recreations:* theatre, reading, kayaking. *Address:* House of Lords, SW1A 0PW. *Club:* National Liberal.

**KRAMER, Prof. Jeffrey,** PhD; FREng; Professor of Distributed Computing, Imperial College London (formerly Imperial College of Science, Technology and Medicine, London), since 1995; *b* 7 Jan. 1949; *s* of Dr Bobby Kramer and Joyce Kramer (*née* Feitelberg); *m* 1981, Nitza Omer; one *s* one *d*. *Educ:* Univ. of Natal (BSc Eng Electrical Engrg 1971); Imperial College, London (MSc Computing 1972; PhD Computing 1979). CEng 1986; FIET (FIEE 1992). Department of Computing, Imperial College, London: programmer, 1973–75; Res. Asst, 1975–76; Lectr, 1976–87; Sen. Lectr, 1987–90; Reader in Distributed Computing, 1990–95; Head of Dept, 1999–2004; Dean, Faculty of Engineering, 2006–09; Sen. Dean, 2009–12. Ernest Oppenheimer Meml Trust/W. D. Wilson Vis. Fellow, S Africa, 1995. Computing Expert, World Bank Project for Provincial Univs, Peoples Republic of China, 1991. Founding Mem., Wkg Gp on Requirements Engrg, IFIP, 1995; Chm., Steering Cttee, 2000–02, Gen. Chm., 2010, Internat. Conf. on Software Engrg. Ed.-in-Chief, IEEE Trans on Software Engrg, 2006–10. FACM 2000; FCGI 2007; FREng 2008. MAE 2015. (Jtly) Outstanding Res. Award, 2005, Distinguished Service Award, 2011, ACM Special Interest Gp on Software Engrg. *Publications:* (with M. S. Sloman) Distributed Systems and Computer Networks, 1986 (trans. Japanese and German); (ed jtly) Software Process Modelling and Technology, 1994; (with J. Magee) Concurrency: state models & Java programs, 1999, 2nd edn 2006; contrib. over 200 papers to learned internat. jls on software engrg, distributed computing, requirements engrg, software architectures, model checking and self-managed adaptive systems. *Recreations:* fanatical about films and music, travel, tennis, ski-ing, mountain walking, diving and surfing, whenever the opportunity arises. *Address:* Department of Computing, Imperial College London, SW7 2AZ. *T:* (020) 7594 8271, *Fax:* (020) 7594 8282.

**KRAMER, Prof. Matthew Henry,** JD, PhD, LLD; FBA 2014; Professor of Legal and Political Philosophy, University of Cambridge, since 2002; Fellow of Churchill College, Cambridge, since 1994; *b* Boston, Mass, 9 June 1959; *s* of Alton Marshall Kramer and Alma Eunice Kramer (*née* Bixon). *Educ:* Cornell Univ. (BA 1981); Harvard Law Sch. (JD 1985); Trinity Coll., Cambridge (PhD 1989; LLD 2004). Jun. Res. Fellow, Darwin Coll., Cambridge, 1989–91; Vis. Fellow, Inst. for Res. in Humanities, 1991–94; Lectr in Legal Philos., 1994–99, Reader in Legal and Pol Philos., 1999–2002, Univ. of Cambridge. *Publications:* Legal Theory, Political Theory, and Deconstruction, 1991; Critical Legal Theory and the Challenge of Feminism, 1995; Hobbes and the Paradoxes of Political Origins, 1997; John Locke and the Origins of Private Property, 1997; (jtly) A Debate over Rights, 1998; In Defense of Legal Positivism, 1999; In the Realm of Legal and Moral Philosophy, 1999; Rights, Wrongs, and Responsibilities, 2001; The Quality of Freedom, 2003; Where Law and Morality Meet, 2004; Objectivity and the Rule of Law, 2007; (ed jtly) Freedom: a philosophical anthology, 2007; (ed jtly) The Legacy of H. L. A. Hart, 2008; Moral Realism as a Moral Doctrine, 2009; (ed jtly) Hillel Steiner and the Anatomy of Justice, 2009; The Ethics of Capital Punishment, 2011; (ed jtly) Crime, Punishment and Responsibility, 2011; Torture and Moral Integrity, 2014; Liberalism with Excellence, 2017; H. L. A. Hart: the nature of law, 2018. *Recreations:* biblical commentary, Shakespearean drama, classical music, long-distance running. *Address:* Churchill College, Cambridge CB3 0DS. *T:* (01223) 336231, *Fax:* (01223) 336180. *E:* mhk1@cam.ac.uk.

**KRAMER, Philip Anthony; His Honour Judge Kramer;** Specialist Civil Circuit Judge, since 2017; *b* London, 26 July 1956; *s* of Michael Kramer and Yolande Kramer; *m* 1984, Fiona McElhatton; two *s*. *Educ:* Univ. of Newcastle upon Tyne (LLB Hons). Called to the Bar, Inner Temple, 1982; in practice on NE Circuit, 1983–2013; Dep. District Judge, 2000–13; Recorder, 2008–13; District Judge (Civil), 2013–17; Judge, Business and Property Courts, Newcastle upon Tyne, 2017–. Jun. Counsel to the Crown, 2000–13. Dir, Wansbeck Council for Vol. Service, 2006–14. Gov., Royal Grammar Sch., Newcastle upon Tyne, 2009–17. *Publications:* (ed jtly) Charlesworth and Percy on Negligence, 13th edn 2014, 14th edn 2018. *Recreations:* golf, cookery, chatting, history. *Address:* The Law Courts, Quayside, Newcastle upon Tyne NE1 3LA. *T:* (0191) 201 2000.

**KRAMER, His Honour Stephen Ernest;** QC 1995; a Senior Circuit Judge at the Central Criminal Court, 2005–17 (a Circuit Judge 2003–05); *b* 12 Sept. 1947; *s* of late Frederic Kramer and Lotte Karoline Kramer (*née* Wertheimer); *m* 1978, Miriam Leopold; one *s* one *d*. *Educ:* Hampton Grammar Sch.; Keble Coll., Oxford (BA 1969; MA 1987); Université de Nancy. Called to the Bar, Gray's Inn, 1970, Bencher, 2002; Standing Counsel to HM Customs and Excise (Crime), S Eastern Circuit, 1989–95; a Recorder, 1991–2003; Hd of Chambers, 2 Hare Court, 1996–2003. Chm., Liaison Cttee, Bar Council/Inst. of Barristers' Clerks, 1996–99; Criminal Bar Association: Chm., 2000–01; Vice-Chm., 1999–2000; acting Vice-Chm., 1998–99. Contested (L), Twickenham, Feb. and Oct. 1974. Master, Bakers' Co., 2017–18. Gov., Hampton Sch., 2005–15. *Recreations:* swimming, cycling, theatre, watching Rugby Union.

**KRAYE, Prof. Jill Adrian;** Professor of the History of Renaissance Philosophy, 2004–13, now Professor Emeritus, and Librarian, 2002–13, Warburg Institute, University of London (Hon. Fellow, 2014); *b* 27 Aug. 1947; *d* of Philip M. and Frances B. Kraye; *m* 1986, Martin Charles Davies. *Educ:* Univ. of Calif, Berkeley (BA Hist. 1969); Columbia Univ. (MA Hist. 1970; PhD 1991). Warburg Institute: Asst Librarian (Acad.), 1974–86; Lectr in Hist. of Philos., 1987–96; Sen. Lectr, 1996–98; Reader in Hist. of Renaissance Philos., 1999–2004. Vis. Prof., Seminar für Geistesgeschichte und Philosophie der Renaissance, Ludwig-Maximilians Univ., Munich, 2002. Vice-Pres., European Soc. for Early Modern Philosophy, 2007–10. Lectio Chair, Leuven Univ., 2018. Joint-Editor: Jl Warburg and Courtauld Insts, 1997–; Internat. Jl of Classical Tradition, 2012–; Member: Editl Bd (Renaissance and 16th Century), Stanford Encyclopedia of Philosophy, 2002–; Bd of Assoc. Editors, History of Humanities, 2014–; Coll. of Expert Reviewers, Eur. Sci. Foundn, 2016–; Editl Bd, History of Classical Scholarship, 2018–. *Publications:* (ed) The Cambridge Companion to Renaissance Humanism, 1996 (trans. Spanish 1998); (ed) Cambridge Translations of Renaissance Philosophical Texts, 2 vols, 1997; Classical Traditions in Renaissance Philosophy, 2002; (ed jtly) Conflicting Duties: science, medicine and religion in Rome, 1550–1750, 2009; (ed jtly) Fourteenth-Century Classicism: Petrarch and Bernat Metge, 2012; (ed jtly) Forms of Conflict and Rivalries in Renaissance Europe, 2015; (ed jtly) Palaeography, Manuscript Illumination and Humanism in Renaissance Italy: studies in memory of A. C. de la Mare, 2016; (ed jtly) Vernacular Aristotelianism in Italy from the Fourteenth to the Seventeenth Century, 2016; (ed jtly) The Afterlife of Aldus: posthumous fame, collectors and the book trade, 2018; contrib. articles to Jl Hist. of Philosophy, Renaissance Studies, Rinascimento, Common Knowledge and other jls. *Recreations:* reading, cinema, feeding squirrels, avoiding writing book reviews. *Address:* Warburg Institute, Woburn Square, WC1H 0AB. *T:* (020) 7862 8916, *Fax:* (020) 7862 8955. *E:* Jill.Kraye@sas.ac.uk.

**KREBS,** Baron *cr* 2007 (Life Peer), of Wytham in the county of Oxfordshire; **John Richard Krebs,** Kt 1999; DPhil; FRS 1984; Principal, Jesus College, Oxford, 2005–15; *b* 11 April 1945; *s* of Sir Hans Adolf Krebs, FRCP, FRS and Margaret Cicely Krebs; *m* 1st, 1968, Katharine Anne Fullerton (marr. diss. 2012); two *d*; 2nd, 2013, Sarah Margaret Phibbs. *Educ:* City of Oxford High School; Pembroke College, Oxford (BA 1966; MA 1970; DPhil 1970). Asst Prof., Univ. of British Columbia, 1970–73; Lectr in Zoology, UCNW, 1973–75; University of Oxford: Univ. Lectr in Zoology, 1976–88; Royal Soc. Res. Prof., Dept of Zoology, 1988–2005 (on leave of absence, 1994–99); Fellow, Pembroke Coll., 1981–2005 (E. P. Abraham Fellow, 1981–88; Hon. Fellow, 2005). Dir, AFRC Unit of Ecology and Behaviour, NERC Unit of Behavioural Ecology, 1989–94; Chief Exec., NERC, 1994–99; Chm., Food Standards Agency, 2000–05. Storer Lectr, Univ. of Calif, 1985; Croonian Lectr, Royal Soc., 2004. Mem., AFRC, 1988–94 (Animals Res. Cttee, 1990–94; sen. scientific consultant, 1991–94). Chair, Sci. and Technol. Select Cttee, H of L, 2011–15; Mem., Energy and Envmt Select Cttee, H of L, 2015–19. President: Internat. Soc. for Behavioral Ecology, 1988–90; Assoc. for the Study of Animal Behaviour, 1993–94; Campden BRI, 2011–12 (Hon. Fellow, 2015); British Sci. Assoc., 2012–13. Scientific Member: Max Planck Soc., 1985–; Council, Zoological Soc. of London, 1991–92; Academia Europæa, 1995; Leopoldina, German Nat. Acad. Scis, 2013. FMedSci 2004. Hon. Mem., British Ecol Soc., 1999; Internat. Mem. (formerly Foreign Mem.), Amer. Philosophical Soc., 2000; Hon. Foreign Mem., Amer. Acad. Arts and Scis, 2000; Hon. Fellow, German Ornithologists' Union, 2003; Foreign Associate, US Nat. Acad. of Scis, 2004. Hon. Fellow: Cardiff Univ., 1999; UWIC, 2006; Univ. of Wales, Bangor, 2006; Assoc. for Nutrition, 2012; Jesus Coll., Oxford, 2015; Hon. FZS 2006. Hon. DSc: Sheffield, 1993; Wales, Birmingham, 1997; Exeter, 1998; Warwick, 2000; Cranfield, Kent, Plymouth, 2001; QUB, Heriot-Watt, 2002; South Bank, 2003; Lancaster, 2005; Guelph, 2006; Aberdeen, 2010; Newcastle, 2012; Western, 2015; DUniv Stirling, 2000. Scientific Medal, Zool Soc., 1981; Bicentenary Medal, Linnaean Soc., 1983; Frink Medal, Zool Soc., 1997; Elliott Coues Award, Amer. Ornithol Union, 1999; Medal, Assoc. for Study of Animal Behaviour, 2000; Benjamin Ward Richardson Gold Medal, RSH, 2002; Wooldridge Medal, BVA, 2003; Lord Rayner Medal, RCP, 2005; Outstanding Achievement Award, Soc. for Food Hygiene Technology, 2005; Harben Gold Medal, RIPH, 2006. *Publications:* Behavioural Ecology, 1978, 4th edn 1997; Introduction to Behavioural Ecology, 1981, 4th edn 2012; Foraging Theory, 1986; Behavioural and Neural Aspects of Learning and Memory, 1991; Food: a very short introduction, 2013; articles in Animal Behaviour, Jl of Animal Ecology. *Recreations:* gardening, tennis, running, walking, cooking. *E:* john.krebs@zoo.ox.ac.uk.

**KREISBERGER, Ronit Charlotte;** QC 2019; *b* London, 19 May 1974; *d* of Marcel Kreisberger and Erica Kreisberger; partner, George Collings; two *d*. *Educ:* North London Collegiate Sch. for Girls; Wadham Coll., Oxford (BA Juris., BCL). Called to the Bar, Gray's Inn, 1999; admitted as solicitor, 2000; Solicitor, then Solicitor-Advocate, Herbert Smith, 1998–2005; in practice as a barrister, Monckton Chambers, 2006–. Mem., Attorney-Gen.'s C Panel, 2007–18, B Panel, 2011–18. Member: Bar Eur. Gp, 2007–; Competition Law Assoc., 2007–. *Publications:* (contrib. ed.) Bellamy and Child, 6th edn 2008 to 7th edn 2013. *Recreations:* running, pilates, theatre, ballet, family, restaurants. *Address:* Monckton Chambers, 1 & 2 Raymond Buildings, Gray's Inn, WC1R 5NR. *T:* (020) 7405 7211. *E:* rkreisberger@monckton.com.

**KREMER, Gidon;** violinist; founder and Artistic Director, Kremerata Baltica, since 1997; *b* 27 Feb. 1947. *Educ:* Riga Sch. of Music; Moscow Conservatory. First Prize, Internat. Tchaikovsky Competition, Moscow, 1970. Has played with most major internat. orchestras including: Berlin Philharmonic; Boston Symphony; Concertgebouw; London Philharmonic; LA Philharmonic; NY Philharmonic; Philadelphia; Royal Philharmonic; Vienna Philharmonic. Founded Lockenhaus Fest., Austria, 1981. *Address:* c/o Columbia Artists, 5 Columbus Circle, 1790 Broadway, New York, NY 10019–1412, USA.

**KREMER, Lorraine;** see Sutherland, L.

**KRESTOVNIKOFF, Miranda Jane;** television and radio broadcaster; author; President, Royal Society for the Protection of Birds, since 2014; *b* Taplow, Bucks, 29 Jan. 1973; *d* of F. D. and J. A. M. Harper-Jones; *m* 1998, Nicholas Krestovnikoff; one *s* one *d*. *Educ:* Abbey Sch., Reading; Univ. of Bristol (MSc Zool. 1994). Runner, then researcher, BBC Bristol, 1993–2001; television presenter: World Gone Wild, 1998–2000; Water Warriors, 2000; The Nature of Shopping, 2001; Smile, 2002; Hidden Treasure, 2003; Wreck Detectives, 2003–04; Time Trail, 2004; Coast, 2004–15; History Mysteries, How to Holiday Greener, Countrylives, Thames Wildlife Superhighway, Nature of Britain, 2007; One Show, 2008–; Big British Wildlife Revival, 2013; Inside Out, 2014–15; Animals After Dark, 2019; reporter, Costing the Earth, Living World, BBC Radio 4, 2012–14; presenter, Tweet of the Day, BBC Radio 4, 2013–14. Patron: Whale and Dolphin Conservation, 2008–; Alderney Wildlife Trust, 2008–. *Publications:* (with M. Halls) Scuba Diving, 2006; Best British Beaches, 2009; The Sea: exploring our blue planet, 2019. *Recreations:* walking the dog, scuba diving, singing, playing flute (flautist, New Bristol Sinfonia), charity, travel, cycling, keeping one step ahead of the children. *Address:* c/o Jo Sarsby Management, 154 Cheltenham Road, Bristol BS6 5RL. *T:* (0117) 927 9423. *E:* office@josarsby.com.

**KRETZMER, Herbert,** OBE 2011; journalist and lyricist; *b* Kroonstad, S Africa, 5 Oct. 1925; *s* of William and Tilly Kretzmer; *m* 1st, 1961, Elisabeth Margaret Wilson (marr. diss. 1973); one *s* one *d*; 2nd, 1988, Sybil Sever. *Educ:* Kroonstad High Sch.; Rhodes Univ., Grahamstown. Entered journalism, 1946, writing weekly cinema newsreel commentaries and documentary films for African Film Productions, Johannesburg. Reporter and entertainment columnist, Sunday Express, Johannesburg, 1951–54; feature writer and columnist, Daily Sketch, London, 1954–59; Columnist, Sunday Dispatch, London, 1959–61; feature writer and theatre critic, Daily Express, 1962–78; TV critic, Daily Mail, 1979–87. TV Critic of the Year, Philips Industries Award, 1980; commended in British Press Awards, 1981. As lyric writer, contributed weekly songs to: That Was The Week…,

Not So Much A Programme…, BBC 3, That's Life. Wrote lyrics of Goodness Gracious Me, 1960 (Ivor Novello Award) and Yesterday When I was Young, 1969 (ASCAP award); Gold record for She, 1974; Our Man Crichton, Shaftesbury Theatre, 1964 (book and lyrics); The Four Musketeers, Drury Lane, 1967 (lyrics); Les Misérables, RSC, 1985 (lyrics (Tony Award, 1987; Grammy Award, 1988)); Marguerite, Haymarket Th., 2008 (lyrics); Kristina, Carnegie Hall, NY, 2009, transf. Royal Albert Hall, 2010 (co-lyricist with Björn Ulvaeus); *film:* Can Heironymus Merkin Ever Forget Mercy Humppe And Find True Happiness?, 1969 (lyrics); Les Miserables, 2012 (lyrics and co-writer, screenplay) (Satellite Award for Best Original Song in Motion Picture for 'Suddenly', Internat. Press Acad., 2012); has also written lyrics for other films, and for TV programmes. Hon. Dr of Letters, Richmond Coll., Amer. Internat. Univ. in London, 1996; Hon. DLaws Rhodes, 2011. Jimmy Kennedy Award, British Acad. of Songwriters, Composers and Authors, 1989. Chevalier de l'Ordre des Arts et des Lettres, 1988. *Publications:* Our Man Crichton, 1965; (jointly) Every Home Should Have One, 1970; Snapshots: encounters with 20th century legends, 2014. *Address:* c/o Berlin Associates, 7 Tyers Gate, SE1 3HX. *Clubs:* Garrick, Royal Automobile, Mark's, 5 Hertford Street.

**KRIER, Léon;** architecture, urbanism and design consultant; *b* Luxembourg, 7 April 1946. *Educ:* Univ. of Stuttgart. Asst to James Stirling, London, 1968–70, 1973–74; Project Partner, J. P. Kleihues, Berlin, 1971–72; private architectl practice, London, 1974–97, Claviers, 1998–2002, Luxembourg, 2003–. Lecturer: Architectl Assoc. Sch., 1973–76; Princeton Univ., 1977; RCA, 1977; Jefferson Prof. of Architecture, Univ. of Virginia, 1982; Vis. Prof., 1990–2013, Inaugural Robert A. M. Stern Vis. Prof., 2015, Yale Sch. of Architecture. *Projects* include: Spitalfields Market, 1987; New Town of Poundbury develt (also masterplan), 1988–; Justice Palace, Luxembourg, 1995; Village Hall, Windsor, Fla, 1997; Krier House, Seaside, Fla, 1997 (extension, 2000); Archaeol Mus., Sintra, Portugal, 1999; Heulebrug Urban Develt, Knokke, Belgium (also masterplan), 1998; Citta Nuova Urban Centre Alessandria, Italy, 1999; tower block restyling, Alessandria, Italy, 2000; Sch. of Architecture Auditorium, Miami Univ., 2002; Brasserie Val d'Europe, Eurodisney, 2003; Tower and Markets, Seaside, Fla, 2003–; Oro Trend Factory restyling, Valenza, Italy, 2003; Cayala, Guatemala City (also masterplan), 2003–; Palazzo Saggini, Alessandria, Italy, 2005; Georgetown develt, Corbianca, Romania, 2008; Paralimni oceanside resort, Cyprus, 2009–; Town House, Uzés, France, 2009; Béguin House, Sanilhac, France, 2009; Queen Mother Monument, Dorset, 2009–16; Veterans Meml, Tannin Village, Alabama; New London Music Forum, London, 2016; *Masterplans* include: Area Fiat, Novoli, Italy, 1993; Hardelot, France, 2000; Noordwijk, Holland, 2002; Meriam Park, Chico, Calif, 2003; Newquay Growth Area, for Duchy of Cornwall, 2004–06; New Educnl Campus and Urban Centre, Osio Sotto, Bergamo, Italy, 2005–; New Urban Centre, Val d'Europe, France, 2006–11; Renovation Piazza Marconi EUR, Rome, 2008; Abu-Sidra, Qatar, 2009; Poundbury NE Quarter, 2009–11; Tor Bella Monaca, Rome, 2010; High Malton Village develt, Malton, Yorks, 2014; New Urban Quarter El Socorro, Guatemala City, 2015–; *Designs* include: Rita Wolff exhibn, Fondation de l'Architecture, Brussels, 1990; furniture for Giorgetti, Italy, 1991–; garden furniture for the Prince of Wales, Duchy Originals, 1995–2003; urban furniture for Poundbury, 1998–; urban furniture for Cayala, Guatemala City, 2011–. *Exhibitions* include: Triennale, Milan, 1973; Rational Architecture, London, Barcelona, 1975; Inst. for Architecture and Urban Studies, NY, 1976 and 1978; Roma Interrotta, Rome, 1978; Léon Krier La Ricostruzione Della Citta Europea, Museo di Castelvecchio, Verona, 1980; La Presenza del Passato, Venice Biennale of Architecture, 1980; Drawings, Max Protetch Gall., NY, 1981, 1984; Model Futures, ICA, 1983; (with R. Bofill) Architecture, Urbanism and History, MOMA, NY, 1985; Léon Krier and the Plan of Washington, Amer. Architectl Foundn Octagon, Washington DC, 1987; Atlantis Project, DAM, Frankfurt, 1987; Imago Luxemburgi, Amsterdam, 1991, Prague, 1993, Lisbon, 1995; Vision of Europe, Bologna, 1992; Biennale di Arte Sacra, Venice, 1992; Sensori del Futuro, Venice Biennale of Architecture, 1996; At the End of the Century, Mus. of Contemporary Art, LA, 2000; Furniture Designed by Léon Krier, Kunstgewerbemuseum, Berlin, 2000; Eisenman-Krier: two ideologies, Yale, 2003; Genialidad Krier, Univ. Francisco Marroquin, Guatemala City, 2010. City of Berlin Architecture Prize, 1977; Jefferson Meml Medal, 1985; Chicago AIA Award, 1987; Eur. Culture Prize, 1995; Silver Medal, Acad. Française, 1997; Richard Driehaus Prize, 2003; Lifetime Achievement Award, Congress of New Urbanism, 2006. *Publications* include: (ed) James Stirling: Buildings and Projects, 1974; (ed) Cities Within the City, 1977; (ed) Rational Architecture Rationelle, 1978; Houses, Palaces, Cities, 1984; Albert Speer: architecture 1932–42, 1985, rev. edn 2013; The Completion of Washington DC, 1986; Atlantis, 1987; (ed) New Classicism, 1990; Architecture and Urban Design 1967–1992, 1992; Architecture: choice or fate, 1997; Eisenman-Krier: two ideologies, 2005; (jtly) Get Your House Right, 2007; The Architectural Turning of Settlements, 2008; The Architecture of Community, 2009; Drawings for Architecture, 2009; articles in jls.

**KRIVANEK, Dr Ondrej Ladislav,** PhD; FRS 2010; President, Nion Co., since 1998; Affiliate Professor, Arizona State University, since 1998. *Educ:* Leeds Univ. (BSc 1971); Trinity Coll., Cambridge (PhD 1976). Postdoctoral res. at Kyoto Univ., Bell Labs and Univ. of Calif, Berkeley; Asst Prof., Arizona State Univ., 1980–85; Dir, Gatan R&D, 1985–95; Res. Visitor, Cavendish Lab., Cambridge, 1995–97; Res. Prof., Univ. of Washington, 1997–98. *Publications:* book chapters; contribs to Nature, Ultramicroscopy, Science, Phys. Rev. Letters. *Address:* Nion Co., 11511 NE 118th Street, Kirkland, WA 98034, USA.

**KROEMER, Prof. Herbert,** PhD; Professor of Electrical and Computer Engineering, University of California at Santa Barbara, 1976–2013, now Professor Emeritus; *b* Weimar, Germany, 25 Aug. 1928. *Educ:* Univ. of Göttingen (PhD 1952). Semiconductor research: Central Telecommunications Laboratory, Germany, 1952; RCA Labs, Princeton, NJ, 1954–57; Varian Associates, Palo Alto, Calif, 1959–66; Prof. of Physics, Univ. of Colorado, 1968–76. (Jtly) Nobel Prize for Physics, 2000. Grand Cross, Order of Merit (Germany), 2001. *Publications:* Quantum Mechanics: for engineering, materials science and applied physics; (jtly) Thermal Physics; articles in jls. *Address:* c/o Electrical and Computer Engineering Department, University of California, Santa Barbara, CA 93106–9560, USA.

**KROES, Neelie;** Member, 2004–14, and a Vice-President, 2010–14, European Commission; Special Envoy for Startups, Ministry of Economic Affairs, Netherlands, 2014–16; *b* 19 July 1941. *Educ:* Erasmus Univ., Rotterdam (MSc 1965). Asst Prof. of Transport Econs, Erasmus Univ., Rotterdam, 1965–71; Mem., Rotterdam Municipal Council, 1969–71; MP (VVD), Netherlands, 1971–77; Dep. Minister of Transport, Public Works and Telecommunications, 1977–81; Minister of Transport and Public Works, then of Transport and Waterways, 1982–89; Advr, European Transport Comr, Brussels, 1989–91; Pres., Nijenrode Univ., 1991–2000; Chm., Supervisory Bd, MeyerMonitor, until 2004. Non-executive Director: Ballast Nedam, 1990–2004; New Skies Satellites, 1999–2004; mmO$_2$, 2001–04; Volvo Gp, 2003–04; Royal P&O Nedlloyd, 2004; Open Data Inst., 2015–17; Salesforce, 2016–; Member: Global Adv. Bd, Uber, 2016–; Adv. Bd, CapitalT, 2019–; Adv. Bd, VCVolt, 2019–; Advr, Impraise BV, 2018–. Mem., Adv. Bd

Council, Amer. European Community Assoc., 2018–. Trustee, Prologis, 2002–04. Chair, Little Bitz Foundn, 2017–; Mem. Bd, Rijksmuseum Fund, 2015–; Mem., Recommendation Cttee, AMREF Flying Doctors, 2015–; Ambassador: Prinses Máxima Centrum, 2018–; Nat. Holocaust Mus., 2018–; Women's Heart, 2018–.

**KROLL, Prof. (John) Simon,** FRCP, FRCPCH; FMedSci; Professor of Paediatrics and Molecular Infectious Diseases, and Head, Molecular Infectious Diseases Group, Department of Paediatrics, Imperial College London, since 1993; Hon. Consultant in Paediatrics, Imperial College Healthcare NHS Trust, St Mary's Hospital (formerly St Mary's Hospital), since 1993; *b* London, 29 Nov. 1952; *s* of late Alexander Kroll and Maria Kroll (*née* Wolff); *m* 1978, Mary Eileen Soothill; one *s* one *d*. *Educ:* Bousfield Primary Sch.; St Paul's Sch., London; Balliol Coll., Oxford (BA 1st Cl. Natural Scis (Chem.) 1975; MA 1980; BM BCh 1980; Hon. Fellow 2009). FRCP 1995; FRCPCH 1997. University of Oxford: Clin. Lectr in Paediatrics, 1984–89; Lister Inst. Res. Fellow, 1986–89; Lectr in Paediatrics, 1989–93; Fellow, Corpus Christi Coll., Oxford, 1989–93; Hon. Consultant in Paediatrics, John Radcliffe Hosp., Oxford, 1989–93. Campus Dean and non-exec. Dir, St Mary's Hosp. NHS Trust, 2004–06. Mem., Lister Inst. of Preventive Medicine, 1991–. Hon. Med. Dir, Meningitis Trust, 2009–. FMedSci 2001. *Publications:* Meningitis: a guide for families, 1997; chapters on meningitis in med. textbooks; contribs to scientific jls on molecular basis of virulence of bacterial pathogens, especially Haemophilus influenzae and Neisseria meningitidis. *Recreation:* clarinet playing (jazz and classical). *Address:* Department of Paediatrics, Faculty of Medicine, Wright Fleming Institute, Imperial College London, St Mary's Campus, Norfolk Place, W2 1PG. *T:* (020) 7594 3695, *Fax:* (020) 7594 3984. *E:* s.kroll@imperial.ac.uk.
*See also* N. J. Kroll.

**KROLL, Nicholas James,** CB 2002; Director, BBC Trust, 2007–14; *b* 23 June 1954; *s* of late Alexander Kroll and Maria Kroll (*née* Wolff); *m* 1981, Catherine Askew; one *s* one *d* (and one *d* decd). *Educ:* St Paul's Sch.; Corpus Christi Coll., Oxford. Entered Civil Service, 1977: DoE/Dept of Transport, 1977–86; HM Treasury, 1986–93; Department of National Heritage, then Department for Culture, Media and Sport, 1993–2004: Dir, Creative Industries Media and Broadcasting Gp, 1996–2000; Corporate Services Dir, 2000–02 (acting Perm. Sec., 2001); Chief Operating Officer and Dep. to Perm. Sec., 2002–04; Dir of Governance, BBC, 2004–06. Member: Bd, NYO, 2005–11; Council, Hellenic Soc., 2010–11; Council, Univ. of Oxford, 2019–. *Recreation:* music.
*See also* J. S. Kroll.

**KROLL, Simon;** *see* Kroll, J. S.

**KROOK, (Elizabeth) Jane;** *see* Maher, E. J.

**KRUGMAN, Prof. Paul Robin,** PhD; Professor of Economics and International Affairs, Woodrow Wilson School of Public and International Affairs, Princeton University, 2000–15; now Emeritus; Distinguished Professor of Economics, Graduate Center, since 2015, and Senior Scholar, Stone (formerly Luxembourg Income Study) Center, since 2014, City University of New York; *b* New York, 28 Feb. 1953; *m* Robin Wells. *Educ:* Yale Univ. (BA 1974); Massachusetts Inst. of Technol. (PhD 1977). Asst Prof., Yale Univ., 1977–80; Associate Prof., 1980–83, Prof. of Econs, 1983–94 and 1996–2000, MIT; Prof. of Econs, Stanford Univ., 1994–96. Sen. Internat. Economist, US President's Council of Econ. Advrs, 1982–83. Consultant: Federal Reserve Bank of NY; World Bank; IMF; UN. Columnist, NY Times, 1999–. Res. Associate, Nat. Bureau of Econ. Res., 1979–. Centenary Prof., LSE. Fellow, Econometric Soc. John Bates Clark Medal, AEA, 1991; Asturias Award (Spain), 2004; Nobel Prize in Economics, 2008. *Publications:* Exchange Rate Instability, 1988; The Age of Diminished Expectations, 1990; Rethinking International Trade, 1990; Geography and Trade, 1991; Currencies and Crises, 1992; Peddling Prosperity, 1994; Development, Geography and Economic Theory, 1995; The Self-Organizing Economy, 1996; Pop Internationalism, 1996; The Accidental Theorist and Other Dispatches from the Dismal Science, 1998; Fuzzy Math: the essential guide to the Bush Tax Plan, 2001; The Great Unraveling, 2003; The Conscience of a Liberal, 2007; The Return of Depression Economics and the Crisis of 2008, 2009; End This Depression Now!, 2012; (with R. Wells) Microeconomics, 2004, 2nd edn, 2008; (with R. Wells) Macroeconomics, 2005, 2nd edn, 2009; International Economics, 2011; Essentials of Economics, 2011; articles in jls. *Address:* Graduate Center, City University of New York, 365 Fifth Avenue, New York, NY 10016, USA.

**KRZNARIC, Dr Roman Alexander;** cultural thinker and writer on the art of living; *b* Sydney, Australia, 21 Dec. 1970. *Educ:* Pembroke Coll., Oxford (BA Hons PPE 1992); Inst. of Latin American Studies, Univ. of London (MSc Latin American Politics 1996); Essex Univ. (PhD 2003). Lecturer and Tutor in Sociology and Politics: Essex Univ., 1996–99; Cambridge Univ., 1999–2001; City Univ., 2003; Policy Consultant for Oxfam, UNDP, Commonwealth Secretariat, 2002–08; Project Dir, Oxford Muse, 2003–07; Founding Faculty Mem., Sch. of Life, 2008–. *Publications:* (with T. Zeldin) Guide to an Unknown University, 2006; The First Beautiful Game: stories of obsession in Real Tennis, 2006; The Wonderbox: curious histories of how to live, 2011; How to Find Fulfilling Work, 2012; Empathy: a handbook for revolution, 2014; Carpe Diem Regained: the vanishing art of seizing the day, 2017. *Recreations:* fanatical Real Tennis player, obsessive symbolic gardener, greenwood furniture maker, struggling singer. *W:* www.romankrznaric.com.

**KUBEKOV, Susannah Kate;** *see* Simon, S. K.

**KUBIK, Heidi Marie;** QC 2018; **Her Honour Judge Kubik;** a Circuit Judge, since 2018; *b* Essex, 7 June 1969; *d* of James Joseph Kubik and Sandra Margaret Kubik; *m* 2000, Stephen; two *d*. *Educ:* St Maur's Convent; St George's Coll., Weybridge; Nottingham Univ. (BA Law 1991); Inns of Court Sch. of Law (BVC; Hardwicke Scholar). Lectr, Leicester Univ., 1991–92; called to the Bar, Lincoln's Inn, 1993; in practice as barrister, 1993–2018; a Recorder, 2016–18.

**KUBIŠ, Ján;** United Nations Special Coordinator for Lebanon, since 2019; *b* Bratislava, 12 Nov. 1952; *m*; one *d*. *Educ:* Jura Hronca High Sch., Bratislava; Moscow State Inst. for Internat. Affairs. Internat. Econ. Orgns Dept, Min. of Foreign Affairs, Prague, 1976–77; Office of the Minister, 1978–80; Attaché and Third Sec., Addis Ababa, 1980–85; Second Sec., 1985–87, Hd of Section, Security and Arms Control, 1987–88, Main Political Questions Dept, Min. of Foreign Affairs, Prague; First Sec. and Counsellor, Moscow, 1989–90; Dep. Hd of Embassy and Hd of Political Section, Moscow, 1990–91; Dir-Gen., Euro-Atlantic Section, Min. of Foreign Affairs, Prague, and Ambassador-at-large, 1991–92; Chm., Cttee of Sen. Officials, CSCE, 1992; Perm. Rep. of Czechoslovakia, 1992, of Slovak Republic, 1993–94, to UN and GATT, Geneva; Special Ministerial Envoy and Slovak Chief Negotiator on Pact for Stability in Europe, 1994; Dir, Conflict Prevention Centre, OSCE, 1994–98; Special Rep. of UN Sec.-Gen. for Tajikistan and Head, UN Mission of Observers to Tajikistan, 1998–99; Sec. Gen., OSCE, 1999–2005; EU Special Rep. for Central Asia, 2005–06; Minister of Foreign Affairs, Slovak Republic, 2006–09; Exec. Sec., UN Economic Commn for Europe, 2009–11; UN Special Rep. and Head, UN Assistance Mission: in Afghanistan, 2012–14, in Iraq, 2015–18. Mem., Adv. Bd, Geneva Centre for Security Policy. OSCE Medal, 1998. *Publications:* contrib. learned jls.

**KUCHMA, Leonid Danylovych;** President of Ukraine, 1994–2004; *b* 1938. *Educ:* Dnipropetrovsk State Univ. Constructor, Research-Production Union, Pirdenny Machine-Bldg Plant, 1960–75; Sec., Party Cttee, 1975–82; Dep. Dir Gen., 1982–86; Dir Gen., 1986–92; Chm., Ukrainian Union of Industrialists and Entrepreneurs, 1993–94. Deputy, Ukraine Parlt, 1991–94; Prime Minister, Ukraine, 1992–93. Mem., Central Cttee, Ukraine Communist Party, 1981–91; Mem., CPSU, 1960–91. *Publications:* Ukraina - ne Rossiia, 2003. *Address:* c/o Office of the President, Bankova Street 11, 01220 Kyiv, Ukraine.

**KUENSSBERG, Joanna Kate;** Vice-President, Government Relations, Russia and CIS, Royal Dutch Shell, since 2018; *b* Lima, Peru, 1973; *d* of Nicholas Christopher Kuenssberg, *qv*; *m* 1997; three *s*. *Educ:* New Coll., Oxford (BA Hons Modern Langs 1995). Desk Officer, DoE, 1995–96; Project Manager (EU enlargement), EC, 1996–97; entered FCO, 1997; Dep. Hd, Enlargement Section, EU Dept, FCO, 1997–99; on secondment: to Min. of Foreign Affairs, Hungary, 1999–2000; to Quai d'Orsay, EU Directorate, 2000–01; First Sec. (EU/Econ.), Paris, 2001–04; Business Team Leader, Global Business/Sustainable Develt and Business Gp, FCO, 2004–07; Project Manager, Consular Strategy Prog., FCO, 2008–09; Russian lang. trng, 2009–10; Policy Unit, FCO, 2010; Portuguese lang. trng, 2010; Dep. Hd of Mission, 2010–14, Chargé d'Affaires, 2011, Lisbon; High Comr to Mozambique, 2014–18. *Address:* Royal Dutch Shell, Carel van Bylandtlaan 16, 2596 HR The Hague, The Netherlands.

**KUENSSBERG, Nicholas Christopher,** OBE 2004; FRSE; Principal, Horizon Co-Invest, since 1995; *b* 28 Oct. 1942; *s* of late Ekkehard von Kuenssberg, CBE; *m* 1965, Sally Robertson (CBE 2000); one *s* two *d*. *Educ:* Edinburgh Acad.; Wadham Coll., Oxford (BA Hons), FCIS. Worked overseas, 1965–78; Dir, J. & P. Coats Ltd, 1978–91; Chm., Dynacast International Ltd, 1978–91; Director: Coats Patons Plc, 1985–91; Coats Viyella plc, 1986–91; Dawson International PLC, 1991–95. Chairman: David A. Hall Ltd, 1996–98; GAP Gp Ltd, 1996–2005; Stoddard Internat. PLC, 1997–2000; Canmore Partnership Ltd, 1999–2016; Iomart Gp Plc, 2000–08; Keronite PLC, 2005–07; eTourism Ltd, 2007–08; Scott and Fyfe Ltd, 2008–17; mLED Ltd, 2010–16; Social Investment Scotland, 2013–16; Klik2Learn Ltd, 2013–; Frog Systems Ltd, 2015–; Director: Scottish Power plc (formerly S of Scotland Electricity Bd), 1984–97; W of Scotland Bd, Bank of Scotland, 1984–88; Standard Life Assce Co., 1988–97; Baxi Partnership, 1996–99; Chamberlin & Hill plc, 1999–2006; Citizens Theatre Glasgow Ltd, 2000–03; RingProp plc, 2002–06; Amino Technols plc, 2004–07. Member: Scottish Legal Aid Bd, 1996–2004; SEPA, 1999–2007 (Dep. Chm., 2003–07); Scottish Cttee, British Council, 1999–2008; QAA Scotland, 2004–10 (Chm., 2007–10); Council, ICAS, 2008–11; Strategic Adv. Bd, Adam Smith Business Sch., 2008–; Dir, QAA, 2007–10. Chm., Assoc. of Mgt Educn & Trng in Scotland, 1996–98. Strathclyde Business School: Hon. Res. Fellow, 1986–88; Vis. Prof., 1988–91; Ext. Examr, Aberdeen Business Sch., 1998–2003; Hon. Prof., Univ. of Glasgow, 2008–17. Chairman: Scottish Networks Internat., 2001–08; ScotlandIS, 2001–03; Scotland the Brand, 2002–04; Glasgow Sch. of Art, 2003–10; Royal Conservatoire of Scotland, 2016–. Gov., Queen's Coll., Glasgow, 1989–91. Trustee: David Hume Inst., 1994–2008; Pitlochry Fest. Th., 2010–16. CCMI (FInstD (Chm., Scotland, 1997–99); FRSA; FRSE 2018. DUniv Glasgow, 2011. *Publications:* (ed) The First Decade: the first ten years of the David Hume Institute, 1996; (ed) Arguments Amongst Friends: twenty five years of sceptical enquiry, 2010; contrib. articles to business and policy jls. *Recreations:* sport, travel, opera, languages, employee ownership, social enterprise. *Address:* 9 Hillside Gardens Lane, Glasgow G11 5BX. *T:* (0141) 339 8345.
*See also J. K. Kuenssberg.*

**KUFUOR, John Agyekum,** Hon. GCB 2007; President, Republic of Ghana, 2001–09; Ambassador Against Hunger, United Nations World Food Programme, since 2009; Founder, The John A. Kufuor Foundation, 2011; *b* 8 Dec. 1938; *m* Theresa Mensah; five *c*. *Educ:* Prempeh Coll., Kumasi; Univ. of Oxford (BA 1964). Called to the Bar, Lincoln's Inn, 1961. Chief Legal Officer and Town Clerk of Kumasi, 1967; Mem., Constituent Assembly, Ghana, 1968–69, 1979; formerly MP and a Dep. Foreign Minister; imprisoned after mil. coup, 1972–73; returned to law practice; Sec. for Local Govt, 1982. Founding Member: Progress Party, 1969; Popular Front Party, 1979; New Patriotic Party, 1992 (Leader, 1996–2007). Member: High Level Commn on Modernization of World Bank Gp Governance, 2009; Internat. Adv. Bd, SNV Netherlands Develt Orgn, 2009–. Chairman: Governing Council, Interpeace, 2009–; Sanitation and Water for All, 2011–15. Hon. Fellow, Exeter Coll., Oxford, 2002. World Food Prize, 2011.

**KUH, Prof. Diana Jane Lewin,** PhD; FMedSci; Professor of Life Course Epidemiology, University College London, 2003–19, now Emeritus; Director, MRC National Survey of Health and Development, 2007–17; Director, MRC Unit for Lifelong Health and Ageing at UCL (formerly MRC Unit for Lifelong Health and Ageing), 2008–17; *b* Chichester, 23 Feb. 1953; *d* of Allan and Doris Lewin; *m* 1974, Peter Michael Kuh; one *s* one *d*. *Educ:* King Edward VI Camp Hill Sch. for Girls, Birmingham; New Hall Coll., Cambridge (BA Econs 1974); London Sch. of Econs (PhD 1993). Res. scientist, Inst. of Biometry and Community Medicine, 1975–81, Res. Fellow, Paediatric Res. Unit, 1982–87, Univ. of Exeter; Scientist, 1987–93, Sen. Scientist, 1994–2006, MRC Nat. Survey of Health and Develt, UCL. FFPH 2007; FMedSci 2015. *Publications:* (with Prof. Y. Ben-Shlomo) A Life Course Approach to Chronic Disease Epidemiology, 1997, 2nd edn 2004; (with Dr R. Hardy) A Life Course Approach to Women's Health, 2002; (jtly) A Life Course Approach to Healthy Ageing, 2014; contrib. over 450 articles to learned jls. *Recreations:* country walking, gardening, singing, relaxing and having fun with my grandchildren (Finn, Owen and Martha), family and friends, tennis. *Address:* MRC Unit for Lifelong Health and Ageing at UCL, 33 Bedford Place, WC1B 5JU. *T:* (020) 7670 5700, *Fax:* (020) 7580 1501. *E:* d.kuh@ucl.ac.uk.

**KUHN, Prof. Annette Frieda,** PhD; FBA 2004; Senior Professorial Fellow in Film Studies, Queen Mary University of London, since 2009 (Professor of Film Studies, 2006–09, Emeritus, 2014); *b* 29 Sept. 1945; *d* of Henry Philip Kuhn and Minnie Alice, (Betty), Cowley; *m* 1967, Peter Robert Brodnax Moore (marr. diss. 1982). *Educ:* Twickenham County Grammar Sch.; Univ. of Sheffield (BA (Econ.) 1969; MA 1975); Inst. of Educn, Univ. of London (PhD 1986). Adult Educn Tutor, Open Univ. and Univ. of London, 1971–88; pt-time Lectr in Film Studies, Polytech. of Central London, 1977–88; Lectr, 1989–91, Reader, 1991–98, in Film and TV Studies, Univ. of Glasgow; Reader in Cultural Res., 1998–2000, Prof. of Film Studies, 2000–06, Lancaster Univ. MAE 2016. *Publications:* (ed with AnnMarie Wolpe) Feminism and Materialism, 1978; (ed jtly) Ideology and Cultural Production, 1979; Women's Pictures: feminism and cinema, 1982, 2nd edn 1994; The Power of the Image, 1985; Cinema, Censorship and Sexuality 1909 to 1925, 1988; (ed) The Women's Companion to International Film, 1990; (ed) Alien Zone: cultural theory and contemporary science fiction cinema, 1990; Family Secrets, 1995, rev. edn 2002; (ed) Queen of the Bs: Ida Lupino behind the camera, 1995; (ed with Jackie Stacey) Screen Histories, 1998; (ed) Alien Zone II: the spaces of science fiction cinema, 1999; An Everyday Magic: cinema and cultural memory, 2002; (ed with Catherine Grant) Screening World Cinema, 2006; (ed with Kirsten Emiko McAllister) Locating Memory: photographic acts, 2006; Ratcatcher, 2008; (ed) Screen Theorizing Today, 2009; (with Guy Westwell) Oxford Dictionary of Film Studies, 2012; (ed) Little Madnesses: Winnicott, transitional phenomena and cultural experience, 2013. *Recreations:* vermiculture, housekeeping, rail travel. *Address:* School of Languages, Linguistics and Film, Queen Mary University of London, Mile End Road, E1 4NS.

**KUHN, Michael Ashton;** Chairman, Qwerty Films, since 1999; *b* 7 May 1949; *s* of George and Bea Kuhn; *m* 1995, Caroline Burton; two *s*. *Educ:* Dover Coll.; Clare Coll., Cambridge (BA 1971); Coll. of Law. Admitted Solicitor, 1974. Denton, Hall & Burgin, 1971–72; Legal Advr, Polygram UK, 1972–74; Asst Solicitor, Field, Fisher & Martineau, 1974–75; Sen. Legal Advr, Polygram Internat., 1975–98 (Gen. Counsel, 1975–77, Pres., Polygram Filmed Entertainment, 1990–98, Bd Mem., 1998). Chairman: Nat. Film and TV Sch., 2002–10 (Hon. Fellow, 2010); Ind. Cinema Office, 2004–15; AudioGo Ltd, 2011–13; Member, Board: Northern Ireland Screen, 2012–; UK Jewish Film. Mem. Council, BAFTA, 2006–09. Producer: The Duchess, 2008; Last Days on Mars, 2013; Suite Française, 2014; Florence Foster Jenkins, 2015. FRSA. Michael Balcon Award, BAFTA, 1998. *Publications:* 100 Films and a Funeral, 2001. *Recreation:* playwriting. *Address:* Qwerty Films, 2nd Floor, 29 Poland Street, W1F 8QR. *T:* (020) 7439 9524. *E:* info@qwertyfilms.com. *Club:* Groucho.

**KÜHNL, Karel;** Consul General of Czech Republic, St Petersburg, since 2015; *b* 12 Sept. 1954; *s* of Karel Kühnl and Marie Kühnlova (*née* Větrovcová); *m* 1983, Daniela Kusin; one *s* one *d*. *Educ:* Charles Univ., Prague (BA Law 1978); Univ. of Vienna (BA Econs 1983). Left Czechoslovakia in 1980 for political reasons; free-lance journalist, Vienna and Munich, 1983–87; editor and analyst, Radio Free Europe, Munich (Czech and Slovak broadcasting), 1987–91; returned to Czechoslovakia, 1991, after fall of communism in 1989; Sen. Lectr, Law Faculty, Charles Univ., Prague, 1991–93; Chief Advr to Prime Minister of Czech Republic, 1991–93; Ambassador to UK, 1993–97; Minister of Industry and Trade, 1997–98; Mem. (Civic Democratic Alliance, 1997–98, Freedom Union, 1998–2004), Chamber of Deputies, Czech Republic; Minister of Defence, 2004–06; Ambassador to Croatia, 2007–12; Agent for Expatriate Affairs, Ministry of Foreign Affairs, Czech Republic, 2013–15. Chm., Freedom Union Party, 1999–2001. Hd of Bd, Czech TV, 1992–93. *Publications:* numerous articles in Czech, German and Austrian newspapers and jls. *Recreations:* family, history, archaeology, architecture.

**KUHRT, Prof. Amélie Thekla Luise,** FBA 2001; Professor of Ancient Near Eastern History, University College London, 1997–2010, now Emeritus; *b* 23 Sept. 1944; *d* of Edith Woodger and Ernest Woodger (adoptive father); *m* 1965, David Alan Kuhrt (marr. diss. 1977); two *d*. *Educ:* King's Coll., London; University Coll. London; Sch. of Oriental and African Studies (BA Hons Ancient Hist.). Lectr in Near Eastern Hist., 1979–89, Reader, 1989–97, UCL. James Henry Breasted Prize, Amer. Historical Assoc., 1997. *Publications:* (with A. Cameron) Images of Women in Antiquity, 1983, 2nd edn 1993; (with H. Sancisi-Weerdenburg) Achaemenid History II–IV, 1987–90, VI, 1991, VIII, 1994; (with S. Sherwin-White) Hellenism in the East, 1987; From Samarkhand to Sardis, 1992; The Ancient Near East, 2 vols, 1995 (trans. Spanish, Persian, Hungarian, Turkish); The Persian Empire: a corpus of sources for the Achaemenid period, 2 vols, 2007 (World Prize Book of the Year, Iran, 2010). *Recreations:* music, literature. *Address:* Department of History, University College London, Gower Street, WC1E 6BT. *T:* (020) 7679 3634.

**KUHRT, Ven. Dr Gordon Wilfred;** Archdeacon Emeritus, Diocese of Southwark, since 1996; *b* 15 Feb. 1941; *s* of late Wilfred and Doris Kuhrt; *m* 1963, Olive Margaret Powell; three *s*. *Educ:* Colfe's Grammar School; London Univ. (BD Hons); Oak Hill Theol Coll.; Middx Univ. (Dr Professional Studies 2001). Religious Education teacher, 1963–65; Curate: Illogan, Cornwall, 1967–70; Wallington, Surrey, 1970–74; Vicar: Shenstone, Staffs, 1974–79; Emmanuel, South Croydon, Surrey, 1979–89; RD, Croydon Central, 1981–86; Hon. Canon, Southwark Cathedral, 1987–89; Archdeacon of Lewisham, 1989–96; Chief Sec., ABM, Gen. Synod of C of E, 1996–98; Dir of Ministry, Archbishops' Council, C of E, 1999–2006; Associate Minister, Tredington and Darlingscott with Ilmington with Stretton-on-Fosse, and Ditchford with Preston-on-Stour with Whitchurch and Atherstone-on-Stour, 2006–12. Permission to officiate, Dio. of Oxford, 2012–; Mem., Ministry Team, Wychert Vale Benefice. Member: C of E Gen. Synod, 1986–96 (Mem., Bd of Ministry, 1991–96); Steering Cttee for Draft Legislation on Women Priests, until 1992. Fellow, Coll. of Preachers (Mem. Council, 1992–97). Theological Lectr, London Univ. Extra-Mural Dept, 1984–89; Tutor, Wycliffe Hall, Oxford, 2006–07. Trustee, Church Pastoral-Aid Soc., 2008–13 (Vice-Chm., 2010–13). *Publications:* A Handbook for Council and Committee Members, 1985; Believing in Baptism, 1987; (contrib.) The Church and its Unity, 1992; (ed and contrib.) Doctrine Matters, 1993; (contrib.) Growing in Newness of Life: Christian initiation in Anglicanism today, 1993; (ed) To Proclaim Afresh, 1995; (contrib.) Church Leadership, 1997; Issues in Theological Education and Training, 1997; Clergy Security, 1998; An Introduction to Christian Ministry, 2000; Ministry Issues for the Church of England: mapping the trends, 2001; (ed) Bridging the Gap: Reader ministry today, 2002; Life's not always easy, 2011; contrib. reviews and articles to Anvil, Fulcrum. *Address:* 87 Churchway, Haddenham, Aylesbury, Bucks HP17 8DT. *T:* (01844) 698358.

**KULKARNI, Prof. Shrinivas Ramachandra,** PhD; FRS 2001; George Ellory Hale Professor of Astronomy and Planetary Science, California Institute of Technology, Pasadena, since 2017; Director, Caltech Optical Observatories, 2006–18; *b* 4 Oct. 1956; *s* of Dr Ramachandra H. Kulkarni and Vimala Kulkarni; *m* 1985, Dr Hiromi Komiya; two *d*. *Educ:* Indian Inst. of Technology, New Delhi (MS Physics 1978); Univ. of California at Berkeley (PhD Astronomy 1983). Post-doctoral Fellow, Radio Astronomy Lab., Univ. of California at Berkeley, 1983–85; California Institute of Technology: Robert A. Millikan Fellow in Radio Astronomy, 1985–87; Asst Prof. of Astronomy, 1987–90; Associate Prof. of Astronomy, 1990–92; Prof. of Astronomy, 1992–95; Prof. of Astronomy and Planetary Scis, 1996–2001; Exec. Officer, Astronomy, 1997–2000; McArthur Prof. of Astronomy and Planetary Sci., 2001–17; Sen. Fellow, Mount Wilson Inst., Pasadena, 1998–2001. A. D. White Prof.-at-Large, Cornell Univ., 2007–13. Mem., US Nat. Acad. of Scis, 2003. Helen B. Warner Prize, 1991, Alan T. Waterman Prize, 1992, NSF; Dan David Prize, 2017. *Publications:* (contrib.) Interstellar Processes, 1987; contrib. Nature in fields of pulsars, brown dwarfs and gamma-ray bursters. *Address:* Department of Astronomy, California Institute of Technology, 1200 East California Boulevard, Pasadena, CA 91125, USA. *T:* (626) 395 4010. *E:* srk@astro.caltech.edu.

**KULKARNI, Yash;** QC 2018; *b* Bombay, 18 Feb. 1975; *s* of Dr Dev Kulkarni and Dr Jaya Kulkarni; *m* 2002, Anagha; two *s*. *Educ:* Royal Grammar Sch., Newcastle upon Tyne; Selwyn Coll., Cambridge (BA Double 1st Cl. Law 1996). Called to the Bar, Lincoln's Inn, 1998; in practice as a barrister, 1998–. *Recreations:* music, tennis, whisky, gluttony. *Address:* Quadrant Chambers, 10 Fleet Street, EC4Y 1AV. *T:* (020) 7583 4444. *E:* yash.kulkarni@quadrantchambers.com.

**KULLMANN, Prof. Dimitri Michael,** DPhil; FRS 2018; FRCP; FMedSci; Professor of Neurology, UCL Institute of Neurology, University College London, since 2007; *b* London, 4 Oct. 1958; *s* of Michael Gustave Kullmann and Anna-Tatiana Prokosch (*née* Orlovsky); *m* 1988, Isabella Anne-Marie Vacca; three *s* one *d*. *Educ:* Lycée Français, London; Balliol Coll., Oxford (BA, MA; DPhil 1984); UMDS, London Univ. (MB BS). MRCP 1990, FRCP 2000. Prize Fellow, Magdalen Coll., Oxford, 1982; Post-doctoral

Res. Fellow, UCSF, 1990–92; MRC Clinician-Scientist Fellow, Inst. of Neurol., London, 1992–97; MRC Sen. Fellow, UCL Inst. of Neurol., 1997–2007. FMedSci 2001. Ed., Brain, 2014–. *Publications:* contribs on synaptic transmission and neurol. *Recreations:* ski touring, bee-keeping, tennis. *Address:* UCL Institute of Neurology, University College London, Queen Square, WC1N 3BG.

**KULUKUNDIS, Sir Eddie,** Kt 1993; OBE 1988; Chairman, Ambassadors Theatre Group, 1992–2010, now Life President; Director, Rethymnis & Kulukundis Ltd, since 1964; Member of Lloyd's, 1964–95 (Member Council, 1983–89); *b* 20 April 1932; *s* of late George Elias Kulukundis and Eugénie (*née* Diacakis); *m* 1981, Susan Hampshire, *qv. Educ:* Collegiate Sch., New York; Salisbury Sch., Connecticut; Yale Univ. Mem., Baltic Exchange, 1959–2001. Chairman: Sports Aid Foundn Ltd, 1988–93 (Gov., 1977–2006); London Coaching Foundn, 1990–2009; British Athletics Charitable Trust (formerly British Athletics Field Events Charitable Trust), 1996–2009; Vice-Pres., UK Athletics, 1998–2003. Governor: Royal Shakespeare Theatre, 1976–2003; The Raymond Mander and Joe Mitchenson Theatre Collection Ltd, 1981–2001; Vice-Pres., Traverse Theatre, 1988–; Director: Hampstead Theatre Ltd, 1969–2004; Hampstead Theatre Trust, 1980–2003. Mem., Richmond Theatre Trust, 2001–. Mem. Bd, SOLT, 1973–2003 (Hon. Vice-Pres., 2003). Trustee: Theatres Trust, 1976–95; Salisbury Sch., Connecticut, 1983–2007. FRSA. Theatrical Producer, 1969–96; London productions include (some jtly): Enemy, 1969; The Happy Apple, Poor Horace, The Friends, How the Other Half Loves, Tea Party and The Basement (double bill), The Wild Duck, 1970; After Haggerty, Hamlet, Charley's Aunt, Straight Up, 1971; London Assurance, Journey's End, 1972; Small Craft Warnings, A Private Matter, Dandy Dick, 1973; The Waltz of the Toreadors, Life Class, Pygmalion, Play Mas, The Gentle Hook, 1974; A Little Night Music, Entertaining Mr Sloane, The Gay Lord Quex, What the Butler Saw, Travesties, Lies, The Sea Gull, A Month in the Country, A Room With a View, Too True to Be Good, The Bed Before Yesterday, 1975; Dimetos, Banana Ridge, Wild Oats, 1976; Candida, Man and Superman, Once A Catholic, 1977; Privates on Parade, Gloo Joo, 1978; Bent, Outside Edge, Last of the Red Hot Lovers, 1979; Beecham, Born in the Gardens, 1980; Tonight At 8.30, Steaming, Arms and the Man, 1981; Steafel's Variations, 1982; Messiah, Pack of Lies, 1983; Of Mice and Men, The Secret Diary of Adrian Mole Aged 13¾, 1984; Camille, 1985; The Cocktail Party, 1986; Curtains, 1987; Separation, South Pacific, Married Love, 1988; Over My Dead Body, 1989; Never the Sinner, 1990; The King and I, Carmen Jones, 1991; Noël and Gertie, A Slip of the Tongue, Shades, Making it Better, 1992; The Prime of Miss Jean Brodie, 1994; New York productions (jtly): How the Other Half Loves, 1971; Sherlock Holmes, London Assurance, 1974; Travesties, 1975; The Merchant, 1977; Players, 1978; Once a Catholic, 1979. *Address:* c/o Ambassadors Theatre Group, 39–41 Charing Cross Road, WC2R 0AR. *T:* (020) 7534 6100. *Club:* Garrick.

**KUMAR, Sir Harpal Singh,** Kt 2016; Senior Vice-President and Head of Innovation, Johnson and Johnson, since 2018; *b* London, 13 Jan. 1965; *s* of Mohinder Singh and Prem Kaur Kumar; *m* 1998, Benita Sokhey; one *s* one *d. Educ:* St John's Coll., Cambridge (BA Chem. Engrg 1986; MEng 1987; Hon. Fellow, 2016); Harvard Grad. Sch. of Business Admin (MBA 1991). Associate Engagement Manager, McKinsey & Co. Inc., 1987–89, 1991–93; Chief Executive: Papworth Trust, 1993–97; Nexan Gp plc, 1997–2002; Cancer Research Technology, 2002–07. Mem. Bd, UK Res. and Innovation, 2017–; Sen. Ind. Mem., Innovate UK, 2017–. Hon. DSc: Manchester, 2011; Newcastle, 2015; Glasgow, 2018; London, 2018. *Recreations:* theatre, opera, football, tennis.

**KUMAR, Prof. Dame Parveen (June), (Mrs David Leaver),** DBE 2017 (CBE 2001); MD; FRCP, FRCPE; Professor of Medicine and Education, Barts and the London School of Medicine and Dentistry, Queen Mary University of London, since 2004 (Professor of Clinical Medical Education, 1999–2004); Hon. Consultant Physician and Gastroenterologist, Barts Health NHS Trust (formerly St Bartholomew's Hospital, then Barts and the London NHS Trust) and Homerton University Hospital Foundation NHS Trust (formerly Homerton Hospital), since 1983; Consultant Gastroenterologist: London Digestive Health, London Clinic, 2000–17; Princess Grace Hospital, since 2017; *b* 1 June 1942; *d* of Cyril Proshuno Fazal Kumar and Grace Nazira Kumar; *m* 1970, Dr David Leaver (*d* 2003); two *d. Educ:* Lawrence Sch., Sanawar, India; Maida Vale High Sch., London; St Bartholomew's Hosp. Med. Coll., London (BSc Hons 1963; MB BS; MD 1976). FRCP 1987; FRCPE 1998. Consultant Physician, 1982–, Sen. Lectr, 1985–94, Reader in Gastroenterology, 1994–99, Sub Dean for Undergrad. Educn, 1995–98, Barts and the London, Queen Mary Sch. of Medicine and Dentistry, Univ. of London; Dir of Postgrad. Med. Educn, Royal Hospital NHS Trust, 1994–96; Hd, Acad. Unit of Gastroenterology, Homerton Hosp., 1998–2002; Associate Med. Dir, 1998–2000, non-exec. Dir, 1999–2003, Barts and the London NHS Trust. Mem., 1994–2005, Chm., 2002–05, Medicines Commn; non-exec. Dir, NICE, 1999–2002. Mem., Internat. Adv. Bd, Southern African Consortium for Res. Excellence, 2010–. Mem., Access Rev. Cttee and Pubns Cttee, Genomics England/100,000 Genome Project. Royal College of Physicians: Dep. Regl Adv, Coll. and Clinical Tutor, 1989–96; Censor, 1996–98; Dir, Continual Professional Develt, 1998–2002; Sen. Vice-Pres. (Acad.), 2003–05; Chair: Develt Bd, 2016–18; Equality and Inclusion Cttee, 2016–17. President: BMA, 2006–07 (Acting Pres., 2007–08; Chair, Bd of Sci., 2016–); RSM, 2010–12 (Mem. Council, 2008–12); Royal Med. Benevolent Fund, 2013–; Vice Pres., 2013–14, Pres., 2016–18, Medical Women's Fedn; Mem. Council, British Soc. of Gastroenterology, 2001–04 (Trustee, 2009–13); Mem., Wesleyan Nat. Adv. Bd, 2008–19; Vice Chm., Galien Awards, 2008–19; Member: NI Medical Distinction Awards Cttee, 2000–10; Queen's Anniv. Awards Cttee, 2007–; Member, External Advisory Board: Fac. of Health and Med. Sci., Univ. of Surrey, 2008–12; Warwick Univ., 2013–17. Sen. examr for undergrad. and postgrad. med. degrees at home and abroad; lectured, examined and taught in over 40 countries (mainly low and middle income). Chm., e-learning Adv. Bd, BMJ Publishing, 2009–12. Erasmus Vis. Prof., Univ. Sapienza, Rome, 1992. Trustee: St Bartholomew's Hosp. Med. Coll. Trust, 2002–10; CancerBackup, 2003–08; Tropical Health and Educn Trust, 2009–14; British Youth Opera, 2013–; Gov., BUPA Foundn, 2007–13 (Chm., 2011–13). FCGI 2007; Fellow, Internat. Med. Acad., 2011; Hon. FAPI; Hon. FRCPath 2010; Hon. FRCPI 2018; FRCPSGlas 2019. Hon. Fellow, Mansfield Coll., Oxford, 2011. Hon. DM: Nottingham, 2006; Sussex, 2011; Plymouth, 2014; Hon. DSc: Hull, 2012; Glasgow, 2014; Hon. DEd Trinity Coll. Dublin, 2011. Gold Medal for Services to Med. Educn, BMA, 2008; British Assoc. for Physicians of Indian Origin Distinction Award, 2009; MDI Distinction Award, 2009; Lifetime Achievement Award, British Assoc. for Physicians of Indian Origin, 2017; Outstanding Contribution to Health Award, BMJ, 2019. *Publications:* Kumar and Clark's Clinical Medicine: a textbook for students and doctors (with Michael Clark), 1987, 9th edn 2017; Acute Clinical Medicine, 2000, 2nd edn 2006; Kumar and Clark's Handbook of Medical Management and Therapeutics, 2012; Kumar and Clark's Cases in Clinical Medicine, 2013 (BMA Prize, 2014); series co-editor, 6 pocket essentials; other books; res. articles mainly on coeliac disease and small bowel disorders in med. jls. *Recreations:* opera, ski-ing, walking, reading. *Address:* Wingate Institute, Barts and the London School of Medicine, 26 Ashfield Street, E1 2AJ. *T:* (020) 7882 7191. *E:* p.j.kumar@qmul.ac.uk. *Clubs:* Royal Automobile, Forum.

**KUMAR, Surendra,** FRCGP; general medical practitioner, since 1971; *b* 15 Sept. 1945; *m* 1971, Dr Santosh Kumar; two *d. Educ:* Univ. of Delhi (MB BS). Mem., 1999–2003, Assoc. Mem., and Chair, Fitness to Practise Panel, 2003–16, GMC; Mem., GPs' Cttee, BMA, 1993–2017; Pres., British Internat. (formerly Overseas) Doctors Assoc., 2003–09 (Nat. Chm., 1993–99). SBStJ 1991. *Recreation:* medical politics. *Address:* 11 Churchfields, Widnes WA8 9RP.

**KUMARATUNGA, Chandrika Bandaranaike;** President of Sri Lanka, 1994–2005; Chair, Office for National Unity and Reconciliation, Sri Lanka; Chairman: CBK Foundation for Democracy and Justice; South Asia Policy and Research Institute; *b* Colombo, 29 June 1945; *d* of late Solomon W. R. D. Bandaranaike, former Prime Minister of Ceylon, and Sirimavo R. D. Bandaranaike, former Prime Minister of Sri Lanka; *m* 1978, Wijaya Kumaratunga, film actor and political leader (*d* 1988); one *s* one *d. Educ:* St Bridget's Convent, Colombo; Inst. of Pol Studies, Paris; Ecole Pratique des Hautes Etudes, Paris. Chm. and Man. Dir, Dinakara Sinhala newspaper, 1975–85. Dir, Land Reform Commn, 1972–75; Chair, Janawasa Commn, 1975–77; Expert Consultant, FAO, 1978–81; Res. Fellow, Univ. of London, 1988–91. Guest Lecturer: Univ. of Bradford, 1989; Jawaharlal Nehru Univ., India, 1991; Virginia and Harvard Law Schs; Harvard Univ.; KCL; Oxford Univ. Debating Soc. Chief Minister and Minister for Law and Order, W Provincial Council, 1993–94; Prime Minister of Sri Lanka, Aug.–Nov. 1994; Minister of Finance and Planning, of Nat. Integration and Reconciliation, of Defence, of Educn and of Buddha Sasana, 1994–2005. Sen. Vice-Pres., 1993–2000, Pres., 2000–06, Sri Lanka Freedom Party; Pres., Sri Lanka Mahajana Party, 1988. Advr on poverty alleviation, Clinton Global Initiative, 2007–; Mem., Bd of Dirs, Club of Madrid, 2009–; Chm., Sri Lanka Chapter, S Asia Foundn, 2007–; Mem., Global Leadership Forum, 2012. *Publications:* research papers on land reform, food policies, poverty alleviation, democracy and good governance, political violence and conflict management. *Recreations:* swimming, Kandyan dance, music, reading, art and sculpture, drama, cinema. *Address:* (office) 27 Independence Avenue, Colombo 10, Sri Lanka. *T:* (1) 2694372. *E:* officecbk@gmail.com.

**KUNDERA, Milan;** writer; *b* Brno, 1 April 1929; *s* of Dr Ludvik Kundera and Milada Kunderova-Janosikova; *m* 1967, Věra Hrabánková. *Educ:* Film Faculty, Acad. of Music and Dramatic Arts, Prague, later Asst Prof. and Prof. there, 1958–69; Prof., Univ. of Rennes, 1975–80; Prof., Ecole des hautes études en sciences sociales, Paris, 1980. Mem., Union of Czechoslovak Writers, 1963–69. Member: Editl Bd, Literární noviny, 1963–67, 1968; Editl Bd, Listy, 1968–69. Czechoslovak Writers' Publishing House Prize, 1969; Commonwealth Award, 1981; Prix Europa-Littérature, 1982; Jerusalem Prize, 1985; Nelly Sachs Preis, 1987; Österreichische Staatspreis, 1988; London Independent Prize, 1991; State Prize for Literature (Czech Republic), 2007; Grand Prix de la Bibliothèque Nat. de France, 2012. *Publications:* The Joke, 1967; Laughable Loves (short stories), 1970; Jacques et son maître (drama), 1971–81; Life is Elsewhere, 1973 (Prix Médicis); The Farewell Waltz, 1976 (Prem. lett. Mondello); The Book of Laughter and Forgetting, 1979; The Unbearable Lightness of Being, 1984 (LA Times Prize); The Art of the Novel, 1987; Immortality, 1990; Les testaments trahis, 1993; Slowness, 1996; Francis Bacon, 1996; Identity, 1998; La Ignorancia, 2000; Le Rideau (essays), 2005 (English trans., The Curtain: an essay in seven parts, 2007); Une Rencontre (essays), 2009 (English trans., Encounter: essays, 2010); The Festival of Insignificance, 2014.

**KUNEVA, Meglena Shtilianova,** PhD; Head, European Union Delegation to Council of Europe, Strasbourg, since 2018; Deputy Prime Minister for European Policies Coordination and Institutional Affairs, 2014–17, and Minister of Education and Science, 2016–17, Bulgaria; *b* Sofia, 22 June 1957. *Educ:* Sofia Univ. St Kliment Ohridski (MA Law 1981; PhD Envmtl Law 1984); Georgetown Univ., Washington, DC (Postgrad. PEW Econ. Prog. 1995; Postgrad. Prog. Law Sch. 2000). Ed. and Radio Anchor, Bulgarian Nat. Radio, 1987–90; Asst Prof., Sofia Univ. St Kliment Ohridski, 1987–89; Prof., Bourgas Free Univ., 1992–94. Sen. Legal Advr, Council of Ministers, 1990–2001; legal consultant, 1992–98. Member: Supervisory Bd, Privatization Agency, 1994–95; Bulgarian Delegn, 4th Session Commn for Sustainable Develt, UN, 1995. Founder Mem. and Mem. Pol Council, Nat. Movement Simeon II. MP (Nat. Movement Simeon II), 2001, 2005. Dep. Minister of For. Affairs and Chief Negotiator with EU, 2001–02; Minister for Eur. Affairs, 2002–06, and Chief Negotiator with EU, 2002–05; Special Rep. of Bulgaria to Convention on Future of EU, 2002–03; Mem., Eur. Commn, 2007–10; Chm., Governing Body, Eur. Policy Centre, 2010; MP Bulgaria, 2014. Dir, BNP Paribas, 2010–13. Member: Bd Trustees, Berlin Conf. 'A Soul for Europe'; Internat. Council of Envmtl Law, UN; Access to Information Prog. Foundn; Adv. Bd and Steering Cttee, TIME Eco-projects Foundn; Atlantic Club, Bulgaria (Gold distinction, 2005); Union of Bulgarian Jurists. Writer of screenplay, Stories of Murders (documentary film), 1993. Order of Civil Merit (Spain), 2002; Legion d'Honneur (France), 2003; Order of Prince Enrique (Portugal), 2004; Order of Star of Italian Solidarity (Italy), 2005; Commandeur, Ordre Nat. du Mérite (France), 2019. *Publications:* articles in jls and newspapers.

**KÜNG, Prof. Dr Hans;** Ordinary Professor of Ecumenical Theology, 1980–96 and Director of Institute for Ecumenical Research, 1963–96, University of Tübingen, now Professor Emeritus; President, Global Ethic Foundation, Germany and Switzerland, 1995–2013 (Hon. President, since 2013); *b* Sursee, Lucerne, 19 March 1928. *Educ:* schools in Sursee and Lucerne; Papal Gregorian Univ., Rome (LPhil, LTh); Sorbonne; Inst. Catholique, Paris. DTheol 1957. Further studies in Amsterdam, Berlin, Madrid, London. Ordained priest, 1954. Pastoral work, Hofkirche, Lucerne, 1957–59; Asst for dogmatic theol., Univ. of Münster, 1959–60; Ord. Prof. of fundamental theol., 1960–63, Ord. Prof. of dogmatic and ecumenical theol., 1963–80, Univ. of Tübingen. Official theol. consultant (peritus) to 2nd Vatican Council, 1962–65; Guest Professor: Union Theol. Seminary, NYC, 1968; Univ. of Basle, 1969; Univ. of Chicago Divinity Sch., 1981; Univ. of Michigan, 1983; Toronto Univ., 1985; Rice Univ., Texas, 1987, 1989; guest lectures at univs in Europe, America, Asia and Australia; Hon. Pres., Edinburgh Univ. Theol Soc., 1982–83. Editor series, Theologische Meditationen; co-Editor series, Ökumenische Forschungen and Ökumenische Theologie; Associate Editor, Jl of Ecum. Studies. Mem., Amer. and German PEN Clubs. Holds hon. doctorates. *Publications:* (first publication in German) The Council and Reunion, 1961; That the World may Believe, 1963; The Living Church, 1963; The Changing Church, 1965; Justification: the doctrine of Karl Barth and a Catholic reflection, 1965; Structures of the Church, 1965; (contrib.) Theologische Meditationen, 1965 (Amer. edn as Freedom Today, 1966); The Church, 1967; (contrib.) Christian Revelation and World Religions, ed J. Neuner, 1967; Truthfulness: the future of the Church, 1968; Infallible? an inquiry, 1971 (paperback 1972); Why Priests?, 1972; 20 Thesen zum Christsein, 1975; On Being a Christian, 1977 (abridged as The Christian Challenge, 1979); Was ist Firmung?, 1976; Jesus im Widerstreit: ein jüdisch-christlicher Dialog (with Pinchas Lapide), 1976; Brother or Lord?, 1977; Signposts for the Future, 1978; Freud and the Problem of God, 1979; The Church—Maintained in Truth?, 1980; Does God Exist?, 1980; Art and the Question of Meaning, 1981; Eternal Life?, 1984; (jtly) Christianity and World Religions, 1986; The Incarnation of God, 1986; Church and Change: the Irish experience, 1986; Why I am still a Christian, 1987; (with Julia Ching) Christianity and Chinese Religions, 1989; Reforming the Church Today: keeping hope alive, 1990; Theology for the Third Millennium: an ecumenical view, 1991; Global

Responsibility: in search of a new world ethic, 1991; Judaism: the religious situation of our time, 1992; Mozart: traces of transcendence, 1992; Credo: the Apostles' Creed explained for today, 1993; Great Christian Thinkers, 1994; Christianity: essence and history, 1995; (jtly) A Dignified Dying: a plea for personal responsibility, 1995; Yes to a Global Ethic, 1996; A Global Ethic for Global Politics and Economics, 1997; (ed with Helmut Schmidt) A Global Ethic and Global Responsibilities: two declarations, 1998; The Catholic Church: a short history, 2001; (ed jtly) Crossing the Divide: dialogue among civilisations, 2001; Tracing the Way, 2002; Women in Christianity, 2002; My Struggle for Freedom (memoirs), 2003; Islam: History, Present, Future, 2007; The Beginning of All Things, 2007; Disputed Truth (memoirs, vol. 2), 2008; (with Rabbi Walter Homolka) How to do Good and Avoid Evil: a global ethic from the sources of Judaism, 2009; What I Believe, 2010; (ed jtly) Manifesto Global Economic Ethic: consequences and challenges for global businesses, 2010; Can We Save the Catholic Church? We Can Save the Catholic Church!, 2013. *Address:* Waldhäuserstrasse 23, 72076 Tübingen, Germany.

**KUNKEL, Edward Thomas;** Director, President and Chief Executive Officer, Foster's Group Ltd, 1992–2004; Chairman, Billabong International Ltd, 2005–12 (Director, 2002–12); *b* 22 May 1943; *s* of Francis James Kunkel and Doris Kunkel (*née* Baulcombe). *Educ:* Auckland Univ. (BSc Chem. and Zool.). Joined Carlton & United Breweries, Melbourne, 1968 as Asst Brewer; sen. positions throughout Group, 1968–84; Gen. Manager, NSW, 1985–87; Pres. and Chief Exec. Officer, Carling O'Keefe Breweries of Canada Ltd, 1987–89; Exec. Chm., Molson Breweries, N America, 1989–92; Chm., Molson Breweries, Canada, 1996–98. *Recreation:* golf. *Club:* Sanctuary Cove Country (Qld).

**KUPER, Prof. Adam Jonathan,** PhD; FBA 2000; Professor of Social Anthropology, Brunel University, 1985–2008; Centennial Professor of Anthropology, London School of Economics and Political Science, 2014–16; *b* 29 Dec. 1941; *s* of Simon Meyer Kuper and Gertrude (*née* Hesselson); *m* 1966, Jessica Sue Cohen (*d* 2013); two *s* one *d*. *Educ:* Univ. of Witwatersrand (BA 1961); King's Coll., Cambridge (PhD 1966). Lecturer: in Social Anthropol., Makerere Univ., Kampala, 1967–70; in Anthropol., UCL, 1970–76; Prof. of African Anthropol. and Sociol., Univ. of Leiden, 1976–85. Vice-Pres., British Acad., 2006–07. MAE 1993. Hon. DFil Gothenburg, 1978. Rivers Meml Medal, 2000, Huxley Medal, 2007, RAI. *Publications:* Kalahari Village Politics: an African democracy, 1970; (ed with A. Richards) Councils in Action, 1971; Anthropologists and Anthropology: the British School 1922–1972, 1973, 4th edn 2016; Changing Jamaica, 1976; (ed) The Social Anthropology of Radcliffe-Brown, 1977; Wives for Cattle: bridewealth and marriage in Southern Africa, 1982; (ed with J. Kuper) The Social Science Encyclopedia, 1985, 3rd edn 2004; South Africa and the Anthropologist, 1987; The Invention of Primitive Society: transformations of an illusion, 1988; (ed) Conceptualising Society, 1992; The Chosen Primate: human nature and cultural diversity, 1994; Culture: the anthropologists' account, 1999; Among the Anthropologists: history and context in anthropology, 1999; Incest and Influence: the private life of bourgeois England, 2009. *Address:* 16 Muswell Road, N10 2BG. *T:* (020) 8883 0400. *Club:* Hampstead Golf.

**KUREISHI, Hanif,** CBE 2008; writer; *b* 5 Dec. 1954; *s* of Rafiushan Kureishi and Audrey Buss. *Educ:* King's College London. PEN/Pinter Prize, 2010. *Filmscripts:* My Beautiful Laundrette, 1984 (adapted for stage, 2019); Sammy and Rosie Get Laid, 1987; (also dir.) London Kills Me, 1991; My Son the Fanatic, 1998; The Mother, 2003; Venus, 2007; Weddings and Beheadings, 2007; Le Week-End, 2013. *Publications:* plays: Outskirts, 1981; Borderline, 1981; Birds of Passage, 1983; Outskirts and Other Plays, 1992; Sleep With Me, 1999; When the Night Begins, 2004; The Black Album, 2009; *novels:* The Buddha of Suburbia, 1990 (televised 1993); The Black Album, 1995; Intimacy, 1998 (adapted as a film, 2000); Gabriel's Gift, 2001; Something to Tell You, 2008; The Last Word, 2014; The Nothing, 2017; *short stories:* Love in a Blue Time, 1997; Midnight All Day, 1999; Collected Stories, 2010; *novella and short stories:* The Body, 2002; *short stories and essays:* Love + Hate, 2015; What Happened?, 2019; *non-fiction:* (ed jtly) The Faber Book of Pop, 1995; Dreaming and Scheming: reflections on writing and politics, 2002; My Ear as his Heart (memoir), 2004; The Word and The Bomb (essays), 2005; Collected Essays, 2011. *Recreations:* pop music, cricket, sitting in pubs. *Address:* c/o Wylie Agency, 17 Bedford Square, WC1B 3JA.

**KURTEN, David Michael;** Member (UK Ind) London Assembly, Greater London Authority, since 2016; *b* Littlehampton, 22 March 1971; *s* of Reginald Kurten and Patricia Kurten. *Educ:* Univ. of St Andrews (BSc Hons Chem. 1993); Univ. of Bath (PGCE 1995); Univ. of Southampton (MRes Chem. 1998). Teacher of Chemistry: Burgate Sch., Fordingbridge, 1995–97; Selebi-Phikwe Sec. Sch., Botswana, 1999–2000; Royal Russell Sch., Croydon, 2001–03; Queenswood Sch., Hatfield, 2003–05; Channing Sch., Highgate, 2005–07; United World Coll., Bosnia-Herzegovina, 2008–10; EF Acad., NY, 2010–12; Saltus Grammar Sch., Bermuda, 2012–13; manager and performer, Einstein on the Road (Chemistry tour), 2014; Teacher of Chemistry, St George's Coll., Weybridge, 2015–16. UKIP spokesman on educn and apprenticeships, GLA, 2016–18. *Recreations:* theatre, cycling, walking, cinema, music. *Address:* Greater London Authority, City Hall, Queen's Walk, SE1 2AA. *T:* (020) 7983 4661. *E:* david.kurten@london.gov.uk.

**KURTH, Air Vice-Marshal Nicholas Julian Eugene,** CBE 2006 (OBE 1996; MBE 1990); Chairman of Trustees, Ulysses Trust, since 2013 (Vice Patron, 2013); Vice President, since 2015, and Acting President, 2017–18, British Mountaineering Council (Chairman, Access Management Group, 2013–15); *b* 13 Sept. 1955; *s* of Heinz Kurth and Renate Kurth; *m* 1984, Sandra Johnson; two *s* one *d*. *Educ:* Archbishop Tenison's Grammar Sch.; Open Univ. Business Sch. (MBA 1991); King's Coll. London (MA Internat. Studies 2001). CEng 1999. Joined RAF as apprentice, RAF Halton, 1972; commnd 1978; Jun. Engrg Officer 3(F) Sqdn, 1980–83; Sen. Engrg Officer XI(F) Sqdn, 1988–90; RAF advanced staff course, 1991; Support Mgt Develt, 1991–95; OC Engrg and Supply Wing, RAF Leuchars, 1995–97; Aircraft Logistics Policy, 1997–2000, Dep. Dir Support Mgt Airworthiness, 2000–01, HQ Logistics Comd; rcds, 2001; Ministry of Defence: Jt Warfare, 2002–03; Dir of Progs, Defence Estates, 2003–06; Dir Logistics (Strike) Plans/Future, Defence Logistics Orgn, 2006–07; COS Support Air Comd, 2007–10. Rail Business Dir, Amey, 2012. FRGS 1997; FRAeS 1999. *Recreations:* rock climbing, mountaineering (Pres., RAF Mountaineering Assoc., 2005–10 (Hon. Vice-Pres., 2011–); responsible for British Services Makalu Expedition, 2008; Vice-Patron, Himalayan Venture, 2018), fencing (President: RAF Fencing Union, 2002–10 (Hon. Vice-Pres., 2010–); Combined Services' Fencing Assoc., 2008–10), road cycling (Chm., Berkhamsted Cycling Club, 2014–16, now Chm. Emeritus), painting, playing the electric guitar (badly). *Clubs:* Royal Air Force, Geographical.

**KUSHNER, Her Honour Lindsey Joy;** QC 1992; a Circuit Judge, 2000–17; *b* 16 April 1952; *d* of Harry Kushner and Rita Kushner (*née* Alexander); *m* 1976, David Norman Kaye; one *s* one *d*. *Educ:* Manchester High Sch. for Girls; Liverpool Univ. (LLB). Called to the Bar, Middle Temple, 1974; part time Chm., Medical Appeal Tribunal, 1989–2000, Disablement Appeal Tribunal, 1992–99; Asst Recorder, 1989–93; a Recorder, 1993–2000. Mem., Ethnic Adv. Cttee, Lord Chancellor's Dept, 1994–99. *Recreations:* cooking, cinema.

**KUTNER, Kay Elizabeth;** *see* Burley, K. E.

**KVERNDAL, Simon Richard;** QC 2002; *b* 22 April 1958; *s* of late Ole Sigvard and of Brenda Kverndal; *m* 1997, Sophie Rowsell; two *s*. *Educ:* Haileybury; Sidney Sussex Coll., Cambridge (MA). Called to the Bar, Middle Temple, 1982, Bencher, 2015; barrister, specialising in maritime and commercial law, 1983–. Lloyd's Open Form Salvage Arbitrator, 2006–. Mem., Ct of Assts, Co. of Shipwrights, 1999– (Renter Warden, 2019). Comdr d'Honneur, Commanderie du Bontemps de Médoc et Graves, 1994. *Recreations:* Real tennis, rackets (Pres., Cambridge Univ. Rackets Club, 2015–), wine-tasting. *Address:* Quadrant Chambers, Quadrant House, 10 Fleet Street, EC4Y 1AU. *T:* (020) 7583 4444, *Fax:* (020) 7583 4455. *E:* info@quadrantchambers.com. *Clubs:* Garrick, Queen's, MCC, Jesters; Hawks (Cambridge); Mjolnirs Rackets.

**KWARTENG, Rt Hon. Dr Kwasi (Alfred Addo);** PC 2019; MP (C) Spelthorne, since 2010; Minister of State, Department for Business, Energy and Industrial Strategy, since 2019; *b* London, 26 May 1975; *s* of Alfred and Charlotte Kwarteng. *Educ:* Eton Coll. (King's Schol.; Newcastle Schol.); Trinity Coll., Cambridge (BA 1996; MA; PhD 2000); Harvard Univ. (Kennedy Schol.). FRHistS 2014. Financial Analyst: JP Morgan, then WestLB, 2000–04; Odey Asset Mgt, 2004–06; journalist and author, 2006–10. PPS to Leader of H of L and Lord Privy Seal, 2015–17, to Chancellor of Exchequer, 2017–18; Parly Under-Sec. of State, DExEU, 2018–19. Member: Transport Cttee, 2010–13; Work and Pensions Cttee, 2013–15; Finance Cttee, 2015–17; Public Accounts Cttee, 2016–17. Chm., Bow Gp, 2005–06. Trustee, History of Parliament Trust, 2011–. Contested (C): Brent E, 2005; London Assembly, GLA, 2008. *Publications:* Gridlock Nation (with J. Dupont), 2011; Ghosts of Empire, 2011; (jtly) After the Coalition, 2011; (jtly) Britannia Unchained, 2012; War and Gold, 2014; Thatcher's Trial, 2015; Masters of the World, 2020. *Recreations:* music, history. *Address:* House of Commons, SW1A 0AA.

**KWIATKOWSKA, Prof. Marta Zofia,** PhD; FRS 2019; FBCS; Professor of Computing Systems, University of Oxford, since 2007; Fellow, Trinity College, Oxford, since 2007; *b* Gorlice, Poland, 26 Feb. 1957; *d* of Jan Kwiatkowski and Teresa Kwiatkowska; *m* 1990, Paul Warren; one *d*. *Educ:* Univ. of Kraków (BSc Computer Sci. *summa cum laude*, MSc 1980); Univ. of Leicester (PhD Computer Sci. 1989). Asst Prof., Jagiellonian Univ., Kraków, 1980–88; University of Leicester: Res. Schol., 1984–86; Lectr in Computer Sci., 1986–94; University of Birmingham: Lectr in Computer Sci., 1994–98; Reader in Semantics for Concurrency, 1998–2001; Prof. of Computer Sci., 2001–07. Visiting Professor: Centrum voor Wiskunde en Informatica, Amsterdam, 1991; Lab. for Specification and Verification, Ecole Normale Supérieure de Cachan, Paris, 2002; Nuffield Sci. Foundn Res. Fellow, Imperial Coll., London, 1992–93. Associate Ed., IEEE Trans on Software Engrg, 2010–12; Mem., Editl Bd, Philosophical Trans Royal Soc. A, 2010–12. FBCS 2008. Professional Mem., ACM, 2009–. Milner Award, Royal Soc., 2018. *Publications:* (ed jtly) Semantics for Concurrency, 1990; contribs to Philosophical Trans Royal Soc. A and CRM Monograph Series. *Address:* Trinity College, Oxford OX1 3BH.

**KYD, Vice Adm. Jeremy Paul,** CBE 2019; Fleet Commander and Chief Naval Warfare Officer, since 2019; *b* Beaconsfield, 20 Aug. 1967; *s* of David Kyd and Janet Kyd; *m* 1996, Karen Leslie; four *s*. *Educ:* King's Sch., Macclesfield; Univ. of Southampton (BSc Hons 1989); Plymouth Univ. (PGDip 1999). Joined RN, 1985; Navigating Officer, HMS Ark Royal, 2001–02; CO, HMS Monmouth, 2004–06; Mil. Asst to CDS, 2006–09; Commanding Officer: HMS Ark Royal, 2011; HMS Illustrious, 2011–12; BRNC, 2012–14; Comdr, UK Task Gp, 2014–15; CO, HMS Queen Elizabeth, 2016–18; Comdr UK Maritime Forces, 2018–19. *Recreations:* shooting, ski-ing, lime mortar, family, wine. *Address:* c/o Naval Secretary, Fleet Headquarters, Whale Island, Portsmouth PO2 8BY. *Club:* Royal Yacht Squadron.

**KYDD, Ian Douglas;** HM Diplomatic Service, retired; *b* 1 Nov. 1947; *s* of late Alexander Henry John Kydd and Sheila Doreen Riley Kydd (*née* Kinnear); *m* 1968, Elizabeth Louise Pontius; one *s* one *d*. *Educ:* Melville Coll., Edinburgh. DSAO, later FCO, 1966; Attaché, New Delhi, 1970–74; Dep. Dir, later Dir, Radio and TV Div., British Inf. Services, NY, 1974–79; FCO, 1979; Press Officer to Prime Minister, 1981–83; First Sec., Lagos, 1984–88, Ottawa, 1988–92; Dep. Head, News Dept and Head of Newsroom, FCO, 1993–95; Consul-Gen. and Counsellor (Mgt), Moscow, 1995–98; Consul-Gen., Vancouver, 1998–2002; Counsellor (Mgt), New Delhi, 2003–06; Counsellor: Beirut, 2006; Kabul, 2006–07. Sen. Advr, Rainmaker Global Business Develt Ltd, Calgary, 2006–10. Trng Consultant, 2008–11. Trustee, UK Foundn, Univ. of British Columbia, 2009–16. Games Maker, London Olympics and Paralympics, 2012. Parish Councillor, Great Shelford, 2018– (Parish Clerk, 2014–15). *Recreations:* all sport, esp. golf, trekking. *E:* ian@kydd.com. *Clubs:* Gog Magog Golf (Cambridge); Tuesday Lunch (New Delhi).

**KYDLAND, Prof. Finn Erling,** PhD; Jeffrey Henley Professor, University of California, Santa Barbara, since 2004; Richard P. Simmons Distinguished Professor, Tepper School of Business, Carnegie Mellon University, since 2007; *b* 1943; *s* of Martin Kydland and Johanna Kydland; *m* 1968, Liv Kjellevold (marr. diss.); two *s* two *d*; *m* Tonya Schooler. *Educ:* Norwegian Sch. of Econs and Business Admin (BS 1968); Carnegie Mellon Univ. (PhD 1973). Norwegian Sch. of Econs and Business Admin, 1973–76; Associate Prof., then Prof. of Econs, Carnegie Mellon Univ., 1977–2004. (Jtly) Nobel Prize in Economics, 2004. *Publications:* contrib. learned jls. *Address:* Department of Economics, 2127 North Hall, University of California, Santa Barbara, CA 93106, USA.

**KYLE, Barry Albert;** freelance director, since 1991; Hon. Associate Director, Royal Shakespeare Company, since 1991 (Associate Director, 1978–91); *b* 25 March 1947; *s* of Albert Ernest Kyle and Edith Ivy Bessie Gaskin; *m* 1st, 1971, Christine Susan Iddon (marr. diss. 1988); two *s* one *d*; 2nd, 1990, Lucy Joy Maycock (marr. diss. 2015); one *d*. *Educ:* Birmingham Univ. (BA, MA). Associate Dir, Liverpool Playhouse, 1970–72; joined RSC as Asst Dir, 1973; first Artistic Dir, Swan Theatre, Stratford-upon-Avon, 1987; numerous RSC productions and directing abroad, incl. Australia, Israel, USA, Czechoslovakia, Japan, Italy and Asia; founding Artistic Dir, Swine Palace Productions, La, USA; Dir, Theatre for a New Audience, NYC, 1995–96; Shakespeare's Globe, London: Master of Play, 2001; Dir, Women's Co., 2003. Director: The Coventry Mysteries, 2006 (Daily Mail Dir of the Year); Cymru Theatr Clwyd, 2006 and 2008. Vis. Dir, Czechoslovak Nat. Theatre, Prague (first Briton to direct there). *Publications:* Sylvia Plath: a dramatic portrait, 1976; contribs to Literary Review. *Recreation:* foreign travel. *Address:* Flat 5, 20 Charing Cross Road, WC2H 0HU. *T:* (020) 7836 5911.

**KYLE, David William,** CBE 2006; Member, Criminal Cases Review Commission, 1997–2005; *b* 30 March 1951; *s* of William and Judy Kyle; *m* 1st, 1975, Rosemary Elizabeth Bazire (marr. diss. 2006); two *d*; 2nd, 2007, Glenys Jean Stacey (*see* Dame G. J. Stacey). *Educ:* Monkton Combe Sch.; Queens' Coll., Cambridge (BA). Called to the Bar, Inner Temple, 1973; Office of Director of Public Prosecutions: Legal Asst, 1975–79; Sen. Legal Asst, 1979–86; Crown Prosecution Service: Branch Crown Prosecutor, 1986–89; Head of Div., HQ Casework, 1989–93; Head of HQ Casework, then Chief Crown Prosecutor, Central Casework, 1993–97. Member: Fitness to Practise Panel, GMC, later MPTS, 2006–16; Conduct (formerly Disciplinary) Cttee, RICS, 2007–09; Professional Conduct Bd, BPsS, 2007–09; Conduct and Competence Cttee, 2008–16, Health Cttee, 2009–16, NMC; Appeal Cttee, HFEA, 2015–; Fitness to Practise Panel, Social Care Wales, 2017–. *Recreations:* music, walking, cycling, canal boating.

**KYLE, Francis Ferdinand**; Founder and Director, Francis Kyle Gallery, 1978–2014; *b* 20 Jan. 1944; *s of* Ferdinand and Dilys Kyle; *m* 1996, Christine Ann Caddick. *Educ*: Harrow; Jesus Coll., Oxford (Schol.; MA). Foreign Rights: George Rainbird Publishers, 1968–71; William Heinemann Publishers, 1972–73; Dir, Thumb Gall., 1974–78. *Publications*: (with R. Ingrams) The Ridgeway, Europe's Oldest Road: paintings from Francis Kyle Gallery, 1988; Lair of the Leopard: twenty artists go in search of Lampedusa's Sicily, 2006; (contrib.) I Was Sylvette: the story of Lydia Corbett, 2016; numerous exhibn catalogues. *Recreations*: reading, walking, theatre, museums. *E*: franciskylegallery@gmail.com. *Club*: Garrick.

**KYLE, James**, CBE 1989; FRCSE; FRCSI; FRCS; Chairman, Raigmore Hospital NHS Trust, 1993–97; *b* 26 March 1925; *s of* John Kyle and Dorothy Frances Kyle; *m* 1950, Dorothy Elizabeth Galbraith (*d* 2018); two *d*. *Educ*: Queen's Univ., Belfast. MB BCh BAO 1947 (Gold Medal in Surgery); MCh 1956 (Gold Medal); DSc 1972. FRCSI 1954; FRCS 1954; FRCSEd 1964. Mayo Clinic, USA, 1950; Tutor in Surgery, QUB, 1952; Lectr in Surgery, Univ. of Liverpool, 1957; Aberdeen University: Sen. Lectr, Surgery, 1959; Mem., Univ. Senatus, 1970; Consultant Surgeon, Aberdeen Royal Infirmary, 1959–89; Chm., Grampian Health Bd, 1989–93 (Mem., 1973). Mem., GMC, 1979–94; Chairman: Scottish Cttee for Hosp. Med. Services, 1977–81; Rep. Body, BMA, 1984–87; Scottish Jt Consultants' Cttee, 1984–89. British Council lectr, SE Asia, S America, 1963–74. Ext. Examr, Belfast, Dublin, Dundee, Edinburgh, Sydney, West Indies. Pres., Aberdeen Medico-Surgical Soc. Bicentenary, 1989–90; Member: Council, Surgical Res. Soc., 1972–74; Internat. Soc. of Surgery, 1971–84; Cons. Med. Soc., 1988–93. Regl Rep., War Memls Trust, 2004–. Patron, Royal Scottish Nat. Orch. FRPSL; FRAS. Burgess of Aberdeen, 1990. *Publications*: Peptic Ulceration, 1960; Pye's Surgical Handicraft, 21st edn, 1962; Scientific Foundations of Surgery, 4th edn, 1989; Crohn's Disease, 1973; papers on surgery, history, philately. *Recreations*: astronomy, amateur radio (callsign GM4 CHX), philately. *Address*: Grianan, 7 Fasaich, Gairloch, Ross-shire IV21 2DH. *T*: (01445) 712398.

**KYLE, (James) Terence**; General Counsel, Nomura International plc, 2004–07; *b* 9 May 1946; *s of* James Kyle and Elizabeth Kyle (*née* Cinnamond); *m* 1975, Diana Jackson; one *s* two *d*. *Educ*: Royal Belfast Academical Instn; Christ's Coll., Cambridge (MA). Linklaters & Paines, later Linklaters & Alliance, subseq. Linklaters: Articled Clerk, 1970–72; Solicitor, 1972–79; Partner, 1979–89; Head, Internat. Finance, 1989–95; Managing Partner, 1995–98; Chief Exec., 1998–2001; Managing Partner, Americas, 2001–03. *Recreations*: cricket, golf.

**KYLE, Dr Peter John**; MP (Lab) Hove, since 2015; *b* Rustington, 9 Sept. 1970; *s of* Leslie Kyle and Joanna Kyle (*née* Davies, later Murrell). *Educ*: Felpham Community Coll.; Sussex Univ. (BA Hons Geog., Envmtl Studies and Internat. Develt 1999; DPhil Community Econ. Develt 2003). Accounts Asst, The Body Shop International., 1989–92; Dir, Children on the Edge, 1992–96; Co-Founder, Fat Sand Films, 2003–06; Dep. CEO, ACEVO, 2007–13; Chief Exec., Working for Youth, 2013–15. Non-exec. Dir, CAF Bank, 2010–16. Mem., Business, Energy and Industrial Strategy (formerly Business, Innovation and Skills) Select Cttee, 2015–. *Address*: House of Commons, SW1A 0AA; (office) 99 Church Road, Hove BN3 2BA. *E*: peter.kyle.mp@parliament.uk.

**KYLE, Peter William**, OBE 2011; Director-General, English-Speaking Union of the Commonwealth, 2011–14; *b* 21 Nov. 1948; *s of* late Robert Kyle and Evelyn Kyle (*née* Palliser-Bosomworth); *m* Kathryn Anna Grundy; two *d*. *Educ*: Rambert Sch. of Ballet; Bretton Hall Coll., Yorks; Inst. für Bühnen Tanz, Cologne. Former ballet dancer; soloist: Northern Ballet Theatre, 1971–73; Royal New Zealand Ballet, 1973–75; Dance Advr, Leics Educn Authy, 1975–81; Dance Officer, Arts Council of GB, 1981–83; Artistic Dir, Queen's Hall Arts Centre, Hexham, 1983–88; Chief Exec., Scottish Ballet, 1988–95; arts consultant and choreographer, 1995–97; Dean, Arts Educational Sch., London, 1997–98; Gen. Dir, Internat. Shakespeare Globe Centre, later Chief Exec., The Shakespeare Globe Trust, 1998–2010. Chm., Shakespeare Birthplace Trust, 2011–; Trustee, John Ellerman Foundn, 2014–. CCMI 2002. Hon. Fellow, London South Bank Univ., 2005. DUniv Westminster.

**KYLE, Air Vice-Marshal Richard Henry**, CB 1997; LVO 2013; MBE 1977; an Extra Gentleman Usher to the Queen, since 2013 (a Gentleman Usher, 2002–13); *b* 4 Jan. 1943; *s of* Air Chief Marshal Sir Wallace Hart Kyle, GCB, KCVO, CBE, DSO, DFC and Lady (Molly) Kyle; *m* 1971, Anne Weatherup; two *s* two *d*. *Educ*: Cranbrook Sch., Kent; RAF Tech. College, Henlow; Southampton Univ. (BSc Eng 1964). CEng 1971. FRaeS 1993. Served RAF stations: Syerston, 1965–67; Acklington, 1967–68; Ternhill, 1968–69; Changi, 1969–71; MoD, 1971–73; No 1 (F) Sqn, RAF Wittering, 1973–76; MoD, 1976–78; RAF Staff Coll., 1978; RAF Gütersloh, 1979–81; MoD, 1982–84; RAF Halton, 1984–86; RCDS, 1987; MoD, 1988–89; RAF St Athan, 1990–92; Dir Gen. Support Services (RAF), 1992–93; AOC Maintenance Units, RAF Logistics Comd, 1993–97. *Recreations*: orienteering, golf, offshore sailing, hill walking. *Club*: Royal Air Force.

**KYLE, Terence**; *see* Kyle, J. T.

**KYLES, Raymond William**; HM Diplomatic Service; Deputy High Commissioner, Lagos, 2015–16; *b* 10 March 1956; *s of* William and Elizabeth Kyles; *m* 2007, Kate Short; two *s*. *Educ*: Glasgow Acad.; Univ. of Strathclyde (BA Business Admin 1980). Joined HM Diplomatic Service, 1980: FCO, 1980–82; UKMIS Geneva, 1982–85; UKREP Brussels, 1985–87; FCO, 1987–91; First Sec., Pretoria, 1991–95; Dep. Press Sec. to Sec. of State, 1996–98 and 2000–01; Dep. Perm. Rep. to OECD, 1998–2000; Pol Advr, Unilever UK, 2001–03 (on secondment); Deputy High Commissioner: Kenya, 2003–07; Islamabad, Pakistan, 2008–09; Kuala Lumpur, 2010–14. *Recreations*: indie music, football, golf, Rugby, films, travel. *Address*: c/o Foreign and Commonwealth Office, King Charles Street, SW1A 2AH. *E*: ray.kyles@fco.gov.uk.

**KYLIÁN, Jiří**; Resident Choreographer and Adviser, Nederlands Dans Theater, 1999–2009 (Artistic Director, 1975–99); *b* Prague, 21 March 1947; *s of* Vaclav Kylián and Marketá Pestová. *Educ*: Ballet Sch., Nat. Theatre, Prague; Prague Conservatory; Royal Ballet Sch., London. Stuttgarter Ballett, Germany; Guest Choreographer, Nederlands Dans Theater, 1973–75; *works choreographed* include: Viewers, 1973; Stoolgame, 1974; La cathédrale engloutie, 1975; Return to a Strange Land, 1975; Sinfonietta, 1978; Symphony of Psalms, 1978; Forgotten Land, 1981; Svadebka, 1982; Stamping Ground, 1983; L'Enfant et les Sortilèges, 1984; No More Play, 1988; Falling Angels, 1989; Sweet Dreams, 1990; Sarabande, 1990; Petite Mort, 1991; As If Never Been, 1992; No Sleep Till Dawn of Day, 1992; Whereabouts Unknown, 1993; Double You, 1994; Arcimboldo, 1995; Tears of Laughter, 1996; Wings of Wax, 1997; A Way a Lone, 1998; Indigo Rose, 1998; Half Past, 1999; Doux Mensonges, 1999; Study from Blackbird, 2002; Toss of a Dice, 2005; Vanishing Twin, 2008; Gods and Dogs, 2008, Last Touch First, Mémoires d'Oubliettes, 2009; East Shadow, 2013; Fortune Cookies, 2014. Has worked with numerous cos, incl. Royal Swedish Ballet, Royal Danish Ballet, Royal Ballet, London, Finnish Nat. Ballet, Aust. Ballet, Nat. Ballet of Canada, Amer. Ballet Theatre, Wiener Staatsoper, Tokyo Ballet, Opéra de Paris, Rambert Dance Co. Hon. Dr, Juilliard Sch., NY, 1997. Critics' Award for Dance, Edinburgh Fest., 1996, 1997; Joost van den Vondel Preis, 1997. Officier: Ordre des arts et des lettres (France); Order of Oranje Nassau (Netherlands), 1995; Golden Medal for Outstanding Merits (Czech Republic); Chevalier de la Légion d'Honneur (France), 2004; Golden Lion, Venice Biennale, 2008; Medal for Art and Sci. (Netherlands), 2008; Medal of Honour, Order of House of Orange (Netherlands), 2008. *Address*: Kylián Productions, Acaciastraat 14, 2565 KB The Hague, Netherlands.

**KYME, Rt Rev. Brian Robert**; Director, Institute of Anglican Studies at St George's Cathedral, Perth, WA, since 2006; *b* 22 June 1935; *s of* John Robert Kyme and Ida Eileen Benson; *m* 1961, Doreen Muriel Williams; one *s* one *d*. *Educ*: Melbourne High School; Ridley Theological Coll., Melbourne; Aust. Coll. of Theology (ThL 1956); Melbourne Coll. of Divinity (Dip RE 1958); WA Coll. of Advanced Educn (BA 1989); Edith Cowan Univ. (MA 2005). MACE 1991. Ordained deacon, 1958, priest, 1960; Curate: St John's, E Malvern, 1958–60; Glenroy and Broadmeadows, 1960–61; Morwell, 1961–63; Vicar, St Matthew's, Ashburton, 1963–69; Dean, Holy Cross Cathedral, Geraldton, WA, 1969–74; Rector, Christ Church, Claremont, Perth, 1974–82; Archdeacon of Stirling, 1977–82; Asst Bishop of Perth, 1982–93; Nat. Dir, Australian Bd of Missions, later Anglican Bd of Mission-Australia, 1993–2000; Episcopal Asst to Primate of Australia, 2000–05. ChLJ, WA, 1985–93; ChLJ, NSW, 1998–99. *Recreations*: reading, music. *Address*: 153 Carr Street, West Perth, WA 6005, Australia. *T*: (home) (8) 93286065, (office) (8) 9325 5766, *Fax*: (8) 93256741.

**KYNASTON, Dr David Thomas Anthony**; historian, since 1973; *b* Aldershot, 30 July 1951; *s of* Arthur Kynaston and Gisela Hunt (*née* Siedbürger); *m* 1985, Lucy Robbins; two *s* one *d*. *Educ*: New Coll., Oxford (BA Modern Hist. 1973); London Sch. of Econs and Pol Sci. (PhD 1983). *Publications*: King Labour, 1976; The Secretary of State, 1978; The Chancellor of the Exchequer, 1980; Bobby Abel: professional batsman, 1982; Archie's Last Stand, 1984; The Financial Times, 1988; WG's Birthday Party, 1990; Cazenove & Co., 1991; The City of London, vol. 1, 1994, vol. 2, 1995, vol. 3, 1999, vol. 4, 2001; (ed jtly) The Bank of England, 1995; LIFFE: a market and its makers, 1997; (with W. J. Reader) Phillips & Drew: professionals in the City, 1998; (with Richard Roberts) City State, 2001; Siegmund Warburg, 2002; Austerity Britain, 2007; Family Britain, 2009; Modernity Britain, Book One, 2013, Book Two, 2014; (with Richard Roberts) The Lion Wakes: a modern history of HSBC, 2015; Till Time's Last Sand: a history of the Bank of England 1694–2013, 2017; (with Stephen Fay) Arlott, Swanton and the Soul of English Cricket, 2018; (with Francis Green) Engines of Privilege: Britain's private school problem, 2019. *Recreations*: cricket, football (Aldershot Town), music (Dylan *et al*), reading. *Address*: c/o Rogers, Coleridge & White, 20 Powis Mews, W11 1JN. *Club*: MCC.

**KYNASTON, Nicolas**; freelance organist, since 1971; Professor of Organ, Royal Academy of Music, 2002–14; *b* 10 Dec. 1941; *s of* late Roger Tewkesbury Kynaston and Jessie Dearn Caecilia Kynaston (*née* Parkes); *m* 1st, 1961, Judith Felicity Heron (marr. diss. 1989); two *s* two *d*; 2nd, 1989, Susan Harwood Styles. *Educ*: Westminster Cathedral Choir Sch.; Downside; Accademia Musicale Chigiana, Siena; Conservatorio Santa Cecilia, Rome; Royal Coll. of Music. Organist of Westminster Cathedral, 1961–71; concert career, 1971–, travelling throughout Europe, North America, Asia and Africa; Organist, Athens Concert Hall, 1995–2010. Début recital, Royal Festival Hall, 1966; Recording début, 1968. Artistic Dir, Athens Organ Fest., 1997, 1999. Consultant, J. W. Walker & Sons Ltd, 1982–83 (Artistic Dir, 1978–82); Organ Consultant: Bristol Cathedral, 1986–91; St Chad's Cathedral, Birmingham, 1989–94; Bath Abbey, 1989–97; Tewkesbury Abbey, 1993–97; City of Halle, Germany, 1997–2000; Rugby Sch., 1998–2001. Mem., Westminster Abbey Fabric Commn, 2000–04. Jury member: Grand Prix de Chartres, 1971; St Albans Internat. Organ Festival, 1975. Pres., Incorp. Assoc. of Organists, 1983–85; Chm., Assoc. of Ind. Organ Advrs, 1997–2000. Chm., Nat. Organ Teachers' Encouragement Scheme, 1993–95. Hon. FRCO 1976. Hon. RAM 2010. Records incl. 6 nominated Critic's Choice; EMI/CFP Sales Award, 1974; MTA nomination Best Solo Instrumental Record of the Year, 1977; Deutscher Schallplattenpreis, 1978; Preis der Deutschen Schallplattenkritik, 1988; RCO Medal, 2018. *Publications*: Transcriptions for Organ, 1997. *Recreations*: reading, church architecture. *Address*: 28 High Park Road, Kew, Richmond-upon-Thames, Surrey TW9 4BH. *T*: (020) 8878 4455.

**KYNOCH, George Alexander Bryson**, OBE 2013; Drumduan Associates, since 1997; *b* 7 Oct. 1946; *s of* late Lt Col Gordon Bryson Kynoch, CBE and Nesta Alicia Janet Thora (*née* Lyon); *m* 1st, 1971, Dr Rosslyn Margaret McDevitt (*d* 2002); one *s* one *d*; 2nd, 2008, Dorothy Anne Stiven. *Educ*: Cargilfield Sch., Edinburgh; Glenalmond Coll., Perthshire; Univ. of Bristol (BSc Hons Mech. Engrg). Plant Engr Silicones Plant, ICI Ltd, Nobel Div., 1968–71; G. and G. Kynoch, subseq. Kynoch Group, 1971–92; Finance Dir, then Jt Man. Dir; Chief Exec., 1981–90; Gp Exec. Dir, 1990–92; non-exec. Dir, 1992–95. Non-executive Director: Aardvark Holdings Ltd, 1992–95; PSL Holdings, 1998; Premisys Technologies (formerly WML Gp, then Premisys Gp) plc, 1998–2001; Talent Gp plc, 2003–14; tecc-IS plc, 2003–04; non-executive Chairman: Silvertech Internat., 1997–2000; London Marine Gp, 1998–2004; Muir Matheson, 1998–2007; Benson Gp, 1998–2005; Jetcam Internat. Hldgs, 1999–2003; TEP Exchange Gp plc, 2001–13; RDF Gp plc (formerly Eurolink Managed Services plc), 2003–06; Toluna plc, 2005–11; OCZ Technology Inc., 2006–09; Madwaves (UK) Ltd, 2006–08; Mercury Group plc, 2007–08; ITWP Acquisitions Ltd, 2011–; Red Squirrel Wine Ltd, 2014–. Chm., Scottish Woollen Publicity Council, 1983–90; Pres., Scottish Woollen Industry, 1990–91; Mem., Aberdeen and Dist MMB, 1988–92; Dir, Moray Badenoch and Strathspey Local Enterprise Co. Ltd, 1991–92. MP (C) Kincardine and Deeside, 1992–97; contested (C) Aberdeenshire West and Kincardine, 1997. Parliamentary Private Secretary: to Minister of State, FCO, 1992–94; to Sec. of State for Educn, 1994–95; Parly Under Sec. of State, Scottish Office (Minister for Industry and Local Govt), 1995–97. Mem., Scottish Affairs Select Cttee, 1992–95. Dep. Chm., Scottish Cons. and Unionist Party, 2008–12. Chm., Moray and Banff Cons. and Unionist Assoc., 1990–92; Vice-Chm., Northern Area, Scottish Cons. and Unionist Assoc., 1991–92. *Recreations*: golf, travel. *Address*: Wallflowers, Queen Street, Bloxham, Oxon OX15 4QQ. *Club*: Carlton (Dep. Chm., 2012–18).

**KYPRIANOU, Markos**; Deputy Chairman, Democratic Party, since 2014; *b* 22 Jan. 1960. *Educ*: Univ. of Athens; Trinity Coll., Cambridge (LLM 1983); Harvard Law Sch. Associate, Antis Triantafyllides & Sons, law firm, 1985–91; Partner, Kyprianou & Boyiadjis, subseq. George L. Savvides & Co., 1991–2003. Mem., Nicosia Municipal Council, 1986–91. MP (Democratic) Nicosia, Cyprus, 1991–2003; Minister of Finance, 2003–04; Minister of Foreign Affairs, 2008–12. Mem., EC, 2004–08.

**KYRIAZIDES, Nikos Panayis**; Comdr, Order of George I of Greece; Deputy Minister, Ministry of Finance, Greece, 1994–96; *b* 3 Sept. 1927; *m* 1960, Ellie Kyrou; one *s* one *d*. *Educ*: Exeter Coll., Oxford Univ. (MA); Chicago Univ. Min. of Co-ordination, 1949; Head, Monetary Policy Div., 1950–51; Dir, External Payments and Trade, 1951–54; Alternate Economic Advr, Bank of Greece, 1956–60; Mem., Greek Delegn, negotiations for EFTA and assoc. of Greece to EEC, 1957–61; seconded to Min. of Co-ordination as Dir Gen., relations with EEC, 1962–64; Economic Advr, Nat. Bank of Greece, 1964–67; Sen. Economist, IMF, 1968–70; Advr to Cyprus Govt, negotiations for assoc. of Cyprus to EEC, 1971–72; Dep. Governor, Bank of Greece, 1974–77; Head of Greek delegn to Accession negotiations to the EEC, 1974–77; Advr to Cyprus Govt on relations with EEC,

1979–82; Ambassador to UK, and to Republic of Iceland, 1982–85; Alternate Exec. Dir, IMF, 1986–92. Knight Commander: Order of Merit (Italy); Order of Leopold II (Belgium); Comdr, Order of Merit (FRG). *Address:* 28 Loukianou Street, Athens 10675, Greece. *Club:* Athens (Athens).

**KYTE, Rear Adm. Andrew Jeffery;** Assistant Chief of Defence Staff (Logistic Operations) and Chief Naval Logistics Officer, since 2018; *b* Kettering, Northants, 31 Jan. 1966; *s* of Jeffery Sidney Kyte and Carol Patricia Kyte; *m* 1994, Alexandra Mary Cullen; two *d*. *Educ:* Kettering Boys' Sch.; Cambridge Coll. of Arts and Technol. (BA Hons Modern Hist.); Britannia Royal Naval Coll.; King's Coll. London (MA Defence Studies 2000). FCILT 2017. Joined RN, 1987; Dep. Comdr, UK Jt Force Support (Afghanistan), Operation Herrick, 2009–10; DACOS (Logistic Ops), Navy Comd HQ, 2010–12; HCSC 2011; Sec. to First Sea Lord, 2012–14; Hd, Defence Logistic Ops and Capability, 2014–17; Comdr, Standing Jt Force Logistic Component HQ, 2017–18. Pres., RN/RM Surfing Assoc., 2015–. *Recreation:* surfing. *T:* (home) (01752) 773718. *E:* Andrew.kyte66@gmail.com.

**KYTE, Peter Eric;** QC 1996; a Recorder, since 1991; *b* 8 May 1945; *s* of late Eric Frank Kyte and Cicely Evelyn Leslie Kyte; *m* 1969, Virginia Cameron Cornish-Bowden; one *s* one *d*; *m* 2014, Zoe Elisabeth Johnson, *qv*. *Educ:* Wellington Coll.; Trinity Hall, Cambridge (MA Law). Called to the Bar, Gray's Inn, 1970; in business, 1970–74; Asst Recorder, 1988. *Recreations:* tennis, motorcycling, scuba diving, watching England perform on the sports field. *Address:* QEB Hollis Whiteman Chambers, 1–2 Laurence Pountney Hill, EC4R 0EU. *Club:* Aula (Cambridge).

**KYUCHUKOV, Lyubomir Nedkov;** Chief Executive Officer, Economics and International Relations Institute, Sofia, since 2012; *b* Sofia, 14 June 1955; *s* of Nedko Georgiev Kyuchukov and Evgenia Pancheva Kyuchukova; *m* 1983, Rumyana Laleva Baeva; one *s* one *d*. *Educ:* English Lang. Secondary Sch., Varna; Moscow State Univ. (MA Internat. Relns 1981); Georgetown Univ., Washington, DC (Specialization 2002); Varna Free Univ. (PhD 2018). Mem., Embassy of Bulgaria, Bucharest, 1981; desk officer, Romania and Poland, E Europe Dept, Min. of Foreign Affairs, Bulgaria, 1981–84; Hd of Dept, Internat. Youth Movt, 1984–90; Researcher, Sofia Univ., 1991; political analyst, BBSS Gallup Internat., 1992–94; Chief Advr, Secretariat for Eur. Integration, Council of Ministers, 1996–97; Manager, Consultancy Co., 1997–2005; Mem., Council for Eur. and Euro-Atlantic Integration to Pres. of Bulgaria, 2001–05; Dep. Minister, 2005–09, Actg Minister, 2009, of Foreign Affairs; Mem., Nat. Security Council, 2005–09; Ambassador to the Court of St James's, 2009–12. Permanent Representative of Bulgaria to: Internat. Mobile Satellite Orgn, 2010–12; IMO, 2010–12. Participant in Nat. Round Table and Public Council on Nat. Issues, 1990; Vice-Chairman: Supreme Council, Bulgarian Socialist Party, 1990–91; Social Democratic Pol Movt, 2005–07. Founder Mem., Governing Council, Inst. of Econs and Internat. Relns, 2003–05; Mem. Bd, Diplomatic Inst. of Bulgaria, 2005–09. Mem., Nat. Council, UN Assoc. of Bulgaria, 1988–91. Founder, 1997, Mem. Bd, 2012–, Bulgarian Diplomatic Soc. Mem. Editl Bd, Internat. Relns mag., 2005–10. *Publications:* Regional Cooperation in Southeast Europe, 2009; New Regionalism in Southeast Europe, 2009; (ed.) Balkan Islam: a barrier or a bridge for radicalisation?, 2018; articles. *Recreations:* reading, walking, tourism. *E:* lyubomir@kyuchokov.com.

# L

**LAAJAVA, Jaakko;** Commander First Class, Order of the Lion of Finland, 2004; Hon. CMG 1995; Under-Secretary of State for Foreign and Security Policy, Ministry for Foreign Affairs, Finland, 2010–15; *b* Joensuu, Finland, 23 June 1947; *s* of Erkki Laajava and Aune Laajava; *m* 1971, Pirjoriitta, (Rita), Väyrynen; one *s* two *d*. *Educ*: Stockholm Univ. (BA 1972); Helsinki Univ. (MA 1972). Entered Finnish Foreign Service, 1972; assignments in Geneva, Paris, Warsaw, Belgrade, Madrid and Washington, DC, 1973–90; Dir-Gen. for Political Affairs, 1992; Ambassador to the US, 1996–2001; Under-Sec., 2001–05; Ambassador to the Court of St James's, 2005–10. Fellow, Harvard Univ., 1985. *Publications*: several articles on foreign and security policy. *Recreations*: music, golf. *Clubs*: Travellers, Royal Automobile; Harvard Club of Finland.

**LABANYI, Prof. Jo(sephine),** FBA 2005; Professor of Spanish, New York University, since 2006; *b* 28 March 1946; *d* of Cyril and Louisa Wood; *m* 1969, Peter Labanyi (marr. diss. 1975). *Educ*: Lady Margaret Hall, Oxford (BA Hons 1st cl. Spanish 1967). Birkbeck Coll., London, 1971–2000: Lectr, 1971–85, Sen. Lectr, 1985–92, Reader, 1992–95, in Spanish; Prof. in Spanish Cultural Studies, 1995–2000; Dir, Inst. of Romance Studies, Sch. of Advanced Study, London, 1997–2002; Prof. of Spanish and Cultural Studies, Univ. of Southampton, 2001–06. Vis. King Juan Carlos I Prof. of Spanish Culture and Civilization, NY Univ., 2002. Ed., Jl of Spanish Cultural Studies, 2000– (Founding Ed., 2000); Mem. Adv. Bd, Jl of Romance Studies, 2003– (Founding Ed., 2001). *Publications*: Ironía e historia en 'Tiempo de silencio', 1985; Myth and History in the Contemporary Spanish Novel, 1989; (ed) Galdós, 1992; (ed and trans) Benito Pérez Galdós, Nazarín, 1993; (ed jtly) Spanish Cultural Studies: an introduction, 1995; (ed jtly) Culture and Gender in Nineteenth-century Spain, 1995; Gender and Modernization in the Spanish Realist Novel, 2000; (ed) Constructing Identity in Contemporary Spain, 2002; Spanish Literature: a very short introduction, 2010; (ed jtly) Europe and Love in Cinema, 2012; (ed jtly) Companion to Spanish Cinema, 2012; Engaging the Emotions in Spanish Culture and History, 2017. *Recreations*: classical music, walking round cities. *Address*: Department of Spanish and Portuguese, New York University, 13–19 University Place, New York, NY 10003–4556, USA. *T*: (212) 9987570, *Fax*: (212) 9954149. *E*: jo.labanyi@nyu.edu.

**LABORDE, Prof. Cécile,** DPhil; FBA 2013; Nuffield Professor of Political Theory, University of Oxford, since 2017; *b* Dax, France, 16 April 1971; *d* of Jacques and Pierrette Laborde; partner, 1995, Mark Hewitson; two *d*. *Educ*: Inst. d'Études Politiques, Bordeaux; Hull Univ. (MA 1993); St Antony's Coll., Oxford (DPhil 1996). Lecturer in Political Theory: Univ. of Exeter, 1996–98; KCL, 1998–2003; University College London: Lectr in Pol Theory, 2003–05; Sen. Lectr, 2005–09; Reader, 2009; Prof. of Political Theory, 2009–17. Fellow, Inst. for Advanced Study, Princeton, 2010–11. *Publications*: Pluralist Thought and the State in Britain and France, 2000; (ed with J. Maynor) Republicanism and Political Theory, 2007; Critical Republicanism, 2008; Français encore un effort pour être républicains!, 2010; Liberalism's Religion, 2017. *E*: cecile.laborde@nuffield.ox.ac.uk.

**LACEY, Prof. (John) Hubert,** MD; FRCPsych; Professor of Psychiatry, St George's, University of London, 1991–2011, now Emeritus; Consultant, Nightingale Hospital (formerly Capio Nightingale Hospital), London, since 2006 (Clinical Director and Head of Eating Disorders, 2007); Research Director, Newbridge House Hospital, Birmingham, since 2013 (Medical Director, 2006–18); *b* 4 Nov. 1944; *s* of Percy Hubert Lacey and Sheila Margaret Lacey (*née* Neal); *m* 1976, Susan Millicent Liddiard; two *s* one *d*. *Educ*: Loughborough Grammar Sch.; Univ. of St Andrews (MB ChB 1969); Univ. of London (MPhil 1974); Univ. of Dundee (MD 1988); DRCOG 1972. MRCPsych 1974, FRCPsych 1985. Jun. hosp. appts, Dundee, St Thomas' and St George's Hosps, London, 1969–78; Sen. Lectr, Middlesex Hosp. Med. Sch., London, 1978–80; Sen. Lectr, 1980–87, Reader, 1987–91, Chm., 1991–2003, St George's, Univ. of London. Clinical Director and Consultant: St George's Eating Disorders Service, 1980–2011; Yorkshire Centre for Eating Disorders, Leeds, 2003–07; Peninsula Eating Disorder Service, Exeter, 2004–08; Medical Adviser: BUPA, 1994–99; Priory Hosp. Gp, 1990–2008; Surrey NHS Trust, 2004–09; Consultant, Eating Disorder Unit, Priory Hosp., 1989–2008; Hon. Consultant, SW London and St George's NHS Trust, 2015–. Non-exec. Dir, various NHS Trusts, 1991–99. Mem., Court of Electors, 1991–2006, Council, 2002–06, RCPsych. Chm., Eur. Council on Eating Disorders; Past Pres., Internat. Coll. of Psychosomatic Medicine. Advr, Groupe Sinoué, 2017–; Res. Dir and Med. Advr, Schoen UK, 2018–. Trustee, Beat, 2015–. Patron, Eating Disorders Assoc. Freeman, City of London, 1986; Liveryman, Co. of Plaisterers, 1986– (Master, 2010–11; Dep. Master, 2011–12; Chm., Charity Cttee, 2012–18). *Publications*: Psychological Management of the Physically Ill, 1989; Overcoming Anorexia Nervosa, 2007; Bulimia, Binge-Eating and Their Treatment, 2010; Managing Severe and Enduring Anorexia Nervosa, 2016; over 230 contribs in books and learned jls on anorexia nervosa, bulimia nervosa, obesity, psychosomatic illnesses. *Recreations*: art, jazz, hill walking, nine grandchildren. *Address*: 25 Belvedere Drive, Wimbledon, SW19 7BU. *E*: jhubertlacey@hotmail.com; Eating Disorders Service, Nightingale Hospital, 11–19 Lisson Grove, NW1 6SH. *T*: (020) 7535 7765. *E*: hlacey@sgul.ac.uk. *Club*: Athenæum.

**LACEY, Prof. Nicola Mary,** CBE 2017; FBA 2001; Professor of Law, Gender and Social Policy, London School of Economics and Political Science, since 2013; *b* 3 Feb. 1958; *d* of John McAndrew and Gillian Wroth; *m* 1991, David William Soskice, *qv*. *Educ*: University Coll. London (LLB 1979); University Coll., Oxford (BCL 1981; Hon. Fellow, 2010). Lectr in Law, UCL, 1981–84; Fellow in Law, New Coll., Oxford, and CUF Lectr, Univ. of Oxford, 1984–95; Prof. of Law, Birkbeck Coll., Univ. of London, 1995–97; Prof. of Criminal Law and Legal Theory, LSE, 1998–2010; Prof. of Criminal Law and Legal Theory, Univ. of Oxford, 2010–13; Sen. Res. Fellow, All Souls Coll., Oxford, 2010–13. Guest Prof., Humboldt Univ., 1995; Adjunct Prof., Res. Sch. of Social Scis, ANU, 1998–2007; Fellow, Wissenschaftskolleg zu Berlin, 1999–2000; Leverhulme Trust Major Res. Fellowship, 2006–09; Visiting Professor: Global Law Sch., New York Univ., 2001–; Center for Ethics, Politics and Economics, Yale Univ., 2004; Harvard Law Sch., 2013; Vis. Fellow, Center for European Studies, Harvard Univ., 2007; Dist. Global Fellow, Hauser Global Law Sch. Prog., NY Univ. Sch. of Law, 2014. Trustee, British Mus., 2015–. Hon. Fellow, New Coll., Oxford, 2007–. Hon. Bencher, Inner Temple, 2011. Hans Sigrist Prize, Univ. of Bern, 2011. *Publications*: State Punishment: political principles and community values, 1988; (with Celia Wells and Oliver Quick) Reconstructing Criminal Law, 1990, 3rd edn 2003; (with Elizabeth Frazer) The Politics of Community, 1993; Criminal Justice: a reader, 1994; Unspeakable Subjects: feminist essays in legal and social theory, 1998; A Life of H. L. A. Hart: the nightmare and the noble dream, 2004; The Prisoners' Dilemma: political economy and punishment in contemporary democracies, 2008; Women, Crime and Character: from Moll Flanders to Tess of the D'Urbervilles, 2008; In Search of Criminal Responsibility, 2016. *Address*: Department of Law, London School of Economics and Political Science, Houghton Street, WC2A 2AE. *E*: N.M.Lacey@lse.ac.uk.

**LACEY, Air Vice-Marshal Richard Howard,** CBE 2004; a Gentleman Usher to the Queen, since 2013; Consultant to Sodexo Defence Ltd, 2012–13 (Strategy Director, 2009–12); Commander British Forces and Administrator of the Sovereign Base Areas, Cyprus, 2006–08; *b* 11 Dec. 1953; *s* of Henry Howard Lacey and Mary Elliot Lacey; *m* 1980, Catherine Helen Brown; one *s* one *d*. *Educ*: John Ruskin Grammar Sch.; Peterhouse, Cambridge (BA 1975; MA 1980); RCDS. RAF Coll., Cranwell, 1975–77; Flying Instr, 1984–85; Flight Comdr, 72 Sqn, 1985–87; RAF Staff Coll., 1988; PSO to Dep. C-in-C, later C-in-C, HQ STC, 1989–91; OC 33 Sqn, 1992–94; Station Comdr, RAF Benson, 1997–99; Dir NATO Policy, MoD, 2000–03; Comdr British Forces Falkland Is, 2003–05; UK Nat. Mil. Rep. to SHAPE, 2005–06. *Recreations*: photography, model engineering, industrial archaeology. *E*: lacey.richardh@gmail.com. *Club*: Royal Air Force.

**LACEY, Robert (David Weston);** author and broadcaster; Royal and Historical Consultant, ITN, since 2018; *b* 3 Jan. 1944; *s* of late Leonard John Lacey and Vida Ivy Pamela (*née* Winch); *m* 1st, 1971, Alexandra Jane Avrach (marr. diss. 2010); two *s* one *d*; 2nd, 2012, Lady Jane Antonia Frances Rayne, *er d* of 8th Marquess of Londonderry and *widow* of Baron Rayne (Life Peer). *Educ*: Clifton Nat. Infants' Sch.; Bristol Grammar Sch.; Selwyn Coll., Cambridge (MA, DipEd). Reporter and columnist, Johannesburg Sunday Times, 1967; ed. and compiler, Jackdaw collections of historical documents for children, 1967–74; writer, Illustrated London News, 1968; writer and Asst Ed., Sunday Times mag., 1969–73; Ed., Look! pages, Sunday Times, 1973–74; Guest Ed., The Court Historian, 2003, 2004; book reviewer, Oxford Jl of Islamic Studies; royal commentator, ITN, CNN, Good Morning America, ABC; writer and presenter: Aristocrats, BBC2 series, 1983; BBC Radio 4 series: The Year 1000, 2000; The Year 1901, 2001; Crown and People, 2002; The Year 1953, 2003; 1914: The Diaries of King George V, 2004; Rehab for Terrorists (TV film), 2009; contrib., Sands of Time, BBC Radio 4 series, 2015; historical consultant, TV series, The Crown, 2015–. Mem., Cttee, Soc. for Court Studies, 2001–09. Chm. of Trustees, Kent Opera, 2018–. Pres., 2000–01, Sec., Careers Cttee, 2002–06, Old Bristolians' Soc. Pres., Selwyn Coll. Assoc., 2014–15. Al-Rawabi Holding Award for contribns to Saudi-British relations, Saudi-British Soc., 2011. *Publications*: Robert, Earl of Essex, 1971; The Life and Times of Henry VIII, 1972; The Queens of the North Atlantic, 1973; Sir Walter Ralegh, 1973; Majesty: Elizabeth II and the House of Windsor, 1977; The Kingdom: Arabia and the House of Saud, 1981; (with M. Rand) Princess, 1982; Aristocrats, 1983; Ford: the men and the machine, 1986; God Bless Her!, 1987; Little Man: Meyer Lansky and the gangster life, 1991; Grace, 1994; Sotheby's: bidding for class, 1998; (with D. Danziger) The Year 1000, 1999; (with M. Rand) The Queen Mother's Century, 1999; Royal: Her Majesty Queen Elizabeth II, 2002 (US edn as Monarch: the life and reign of Elizabeth II); series Great Tales from English History: vol. 1, Cheddar Man to the Peasants' Revolt, 2003; vol. 2, Chaucer to the Glorious Revolution, 2004; vol. 3, Battle of the Boyne to DNA, 2006; 3 vol. omnibus edn, Great Tales from English History, 2007, Folio Soc. edn 2008; Inside the Kingdom: kings, clerics, modernists, terrorists and the struggle for Saudi Arabia, 2009; A Brief Life of the Queen, 2012; (ed jtly) Gulf Charities and Islamic Philanthropy in the 'Age of Terror' and Beyond, 2014; Model Woman: Eileen Ford and the business of beauty, 2015; Meyer Lansky: the thinking man's gangster, 2016; The Crown: the official companion, 2017. *Recreations*: swimming, water ski-ing, yoga. *Address*: c/o Jonathan Pegg Literary Agency, 67 Wingate Square, SW4 0AF. *E*: robert@robertlacey.com. *Clubs*: Chelsea Arts, Savile; Italian (Jeddah).

**LACEY, Stephen Charles David Lloyd;** gardener, author, journalist and broadcaster; *b* 6 May 1957; *s* of late Charles Leslie Lacey and Myra Lloyd Lacey (*née* Lloyd Williams). *Educ*: Trearddur House Prep. Sch.; Shrewsbury Sch.; Trinity Coll., Oxford (MA Mod. Langs). Early career in property investment; gardening columnist and feature writer, Daily Telegraph, 1989–; a presenter, Gardeners' World, BBC TV, 1992–2002; freelance horticultural lectr in UK, USA and Canada; Pres., Welsh Historic Gardens Trust, 2018–. *Publications*: The Startling Jungle, 1986; Scent in Your Garden, 1991, rev. edn as RHS Companion to Scented Plants, 2014; Lawns and Ground Cover, 1991; Gardens of the National Trust, 1996, 4th edn 2016; Real Gardening, 2002. *Recreations*: adventurous travel, birdwatching (especially in tropics), collecting books, growing plants, skiing. *Address*: 37 Rosary Gardens, SW7 4NQ. *T*: (020) 7244 8111.

**LACHMANN, Sir Peter (Julius),** Kt 2002; FRCP, FRCPath; FRS 1982; FMedSci; Sheila Joan Smith Professor of Immunology (formerly Tumour Immunology), University of Cambridge, 1977–99, now Emeritus Professor; Fellow of Christ's College, Cambridge, 1962–71 and since 1976; Head, Microbial Immunology Group, Centre for Veterinary Science, Cambridge, 1997–2006; *b* 23 Dec. 1931; *s* of late Heinz Lachmann and Thea (*née* Heller); *m* 1962, Sylvia Mary, *d* of Alan Stephenson; two *s* one *d*. *Educ*: Christ's Coll., Finchley; Trinity Coll., Cambridge (Hon. Fellow, 2007); University College Hosp. MA, MB BChir, PhD, ScD (Cantab). FRCP 1973; FRCPath 1981. John Lucas Walker Student, Dept of Pathology, Cambridge, 1958–60; Vis. Investigator, Rockefeller Univ., New York, 1960–61; Empire Rheumatism Council Res. Fellow, Dept of Pathology, Cambridge, 1962–64; Asst Dir of Res. in Pathology, Univ. of Cambridge, 1964–71; Prof. of Immunology, Royal Postgraduate Med. Sch., 1971–75; Hd, 1976–77, Hon. Hd, 1977–80, MRC Gp on Mechanisms in Tumour Immunity; Hon. Dir, MRC Mechanisms in Tumour Immunity Unit, later MRC Molecular Immunopathology Unit, 1980–97; Hon. Clin. Immunologist, Cambridge HA, 1976–99. Member: Systems Bd, MRC, 1982–86; Med. Adv. Cttee, British Council, 1983–97; Council, RCPath, 1982–85, 1989–93 (Pres., 1990–93); Gene Therapy Adv. Cttee, 1993–96; UNESCO Internat.

Bioethics Cttee, 1993–98; Med. Educn Res. Co-ordinating Cttee, 1994–98; Scientific Adv. Bd, SmithKline Beecham, 1995–2000; Chm. Scientific Adv. Bd, Adprotech plc, 1997–2004; non-exec. Dir, Synovis plc, 2001–05; Dir, DioSynVax Ltd, 2018–. Chairman: Med. Res. Cttee, Muscular Dystrophy Gp, 1987–91; Sci. Cttee, Assoc. Medical Res. Charities, 1988–92; Res. Adv. Cttee, CORE, 2003–09. Trustee: Darwin Trust, 1991–2001; Arthritis Res. Campaign, 2000–06. President: Henry Kunkel Soc., 2003–05; European Fedn of Academies of Medicine, 2004–05. Vis. Investigator, Scripps Clinic and Research Foundn, La Jolla, 1966, 1975, 1980, 1986, 1989; Vis. Scientist, Basel Inst. of Immunology, 1971; RSM Vis. Prof. in USA (various centres), 1983; Smith Kline & French Vis. Prof. in Australia (various centres), 1987; Vis. Prof., Dept of Medicine, RPMS, London, 1986–89 (Fellow, 1995; FIC 2001). Meyerhoff Vis. Prof., Weizmann Inst., Rehovoth, 1989; Prof., Collège de France, 1993; RCS Sir Arthur Sims Travelling Prof., India, 1994; Lectures: Foundn, RCPath, 1983; Langdon-Brown, RCP, 1986; first R. R. Porter Meml, 1986; Heberden Oration, 1986; Prathap Meml, Malaysia, 1991; Charnock Bradley Meml, Royal (Dick) Vet. Sch., Edinburgh, 1994; Frank May Med. Scis, Univ. of Leicester, 1994; Vanguard Medica, Univ. of Surrey, 1998; Lloyd Roberts, Med. Soc. of London, 1999; first Jean Shanks, Acad. Med. Scis, 2001; Ver Heyden de Lancey, Faculty of Law, Univ. of Cambridge, 2011. Biological Sec., and a Vice-Pres., Royal Soc., 1993–98; Founder FMedSci 1998 (Pres., 1998–2002). Foreign Fellow, Indian Nat. Sci. Acad., 1997; Foreign Member: Norwegian Acad. of Science and Letters, 1991; Academia Europea, 1992. Hon. Fellow, Faculty of Pathology, RCPI, 1993; Hon. Member: Assoc. of Physicians, 1998; Czech Med. Acad., 2012. Hon. DSc Leicester, 2005. Gold Medal, Eur. Complement Network, 1997; Medicine and Europe Sen. Prize, Acad. des Scis de la Santé, 2013. Associate Editor, Clinical and Experimental Immunology, 1989–2001. *Publications:* co-ed, Clinical Aspects of Immunology, 3rd edn 1975, 4th edn 1982, 5th edn 1993; First Steps: a personal account of the formation of the Academy of Medical Sciences, 2010; papers in sci. jls on complement, microbial immunology, immunopathology, cultural evolution, religion and ethical aspects of biosci. *Recreations:* visiting mountains, keeping bees. *Address:* Conduit Tail, 38 Conduit Head Road, Cambridge CB3 0EY. *T:* (01223) 357842. *Club:* Athenæum.

**LACLOTTE, Michel René;** Commandeur de la Légion d'honneur; Commandeur de l'ordre national du Mérite; Hon. CBE 1994; Director, The Louvre Museum, Paris, 1987–94; b 27 Oct. 1929; s of Pierre Laclotte, advocate, and Huguette (née de Kermabon). *Educ:* Lycée Pasteur, Neuilly; Institut d'art et d'archéologie, l'Université de Paris; Ecole du Louvre. Inspector, Inspectorate General of provincial museums, 1955–66; Chief Conservator: Dept of Paintings, Louvre Mus., 1966–87; Collections of Musée d'Orsay, 1978–86. *Publications:* A Key to the Louvre: memoirs of a curator, 2004; works on history of art, catalogues, articles in art reviews, esp. on Italian paintings of 14th and 15th centuries and French primitives. *Address:* 10 bis rue du Pré-aux-Clercs, 75007 Paris, France.

**LACON, Sir (Edmund) Richard (Vere),** 9th Bt cr 1818, of Great Yarmouth, Norfolk; b 2 Oct. 1967; o s of Sir Edmund Vere Lacon, 8th Bt and of Gillian Lacon (née Middleditch); S father, 2014; m 1997, Natalie, o d of Joginder Shinh; one s. *Heir:* s Luke Edmund Lacon, b 28 May 2001.

**LACROIX, Christian Marie Marc;** Commandeur de l'Ordre des Arts et des Lettres, 1998; Chevalier de la Légion d'Honneur, 2002; designer; launched Christian Lacroix haute couture, 1987; b 16 May 1951; s of Maxime Lacroix and Jeannette Bergier; m 1989, Françoise Roesenstiehl. *Educ:* Paul Valéry Univ., Montpellier; Sorbonne. History of Art degree. Assistant at Hermès, 1978; Asst for Guy Paulin, 1980; designer for Patou, 1981–86; Creative Dir, Pucci, 2002–05. Artistic Advr, La Monnaie de Paris, 2010. Pres., Centre National du Costume de Scène, 2006–08, now Hon. Pres. Golden Thimble Award, 1986 and 1988; CFDA Award, NY, 1987; Prix Balzac, 1989; Goldene Spinnrad, Krefeld, Germany, 1990; Molière Theatre Award, 1996, 2007. *Publications:* Pieces of a Pattern (autobiog.), 1992; The Diary of a Collection, 1996; Qui est là?, 2004; illustrator of albums, Styles d'aujourd'hui, 1995; Christian Lacroix on Fashion, 2006.

**LACROIX, Prof. Robert,** OC 2018 (CM 2000); OQ; PhD; FRSC; Fellow, Centre for Interuniversity Research and Analysis of Organisations, Montreal; Rector, University of Montreal, 1998–2005, Emeritus Professor, 2006 and Emeritus Rector, 2010; b 15 April 1940; s of Léo Lacroix and Léonne Galarneau; m 1962, Ginette Teasdale; three d. *Educ:* Univ. of Montreal (BA, BSc, MA Econs); Univ. of Louvain, Belgium (PhD Econs 1970). University of Montreal: Asst Prof., 1970, Prof., 1979, Dept of Econs; Chm., Dept of Econs, 1977–83; Dir, Centre for R&D in Econs, 1985–87; Dean, Faculty of Arts and Scis, 1987–93; Pres. and CEO, Centre for Interuniv. Res. and Analysis of Orgns, 1994–98. Project Dir, Econ. Council of Canada, 1976–78. Member, Board of Directors: Assoc. of Univs and Colls of Canada, 1998–2004 (Pres., 2001–03); Conf. of Rectors and Principals of Quebec Univs, 1998–2000; Ecole Polytechnique de Montréal, 1998–2005; Ecole des Hautes Etudes Commerciales, 1998–2005; Bd of Trade, Metropolitan Montreal, 2001–04; CAE, 2006–13; Groupe Jean Coutu; Pomerleau. Mem., Academic Adv. Cttee, Inst. of Canadian Bankers, 1999–2003; Mem. Bd of Govs, Foundn for Educnl Exchange between Canada and USA, 2003–06. *Publications:* (with J. M. Cousineau) Wage Determination in Major Collective Agreements in the Private and Public Sectors, 1977; (with Y. Rabeau) Politiques nationales, Conjonctures régionales: la stabilisation économique, 1981; (with F. Martin) Les conséquences de la décentralisation régionale des activités de R&D, 1987; (with M. Huberman) Le partage de l'Emploi: solution au chômage ou frein à l'emploi, 1996; (with L. Maheu) Le CHUM, une tragédie québécoise, 2010; (with L. Maheu) Leading Research Universities in a Competitive World, 2015. *Address:* CIRANO, 1130 rue Sherbrooke Ouest, Suite 1400, Montreal, QC H3A 2M8, Canada.

**LACY, Very Rev. David William;** DL; Moderator of the General Assembly of the Church of Scotland, 2005–06; Minister, Kay Park (formerly Henderson) Church, Kilmarnock, 1989–2017; b 26 April 1952; s of Peter and Nan Lacy; m 1974, Joan Stewart Robertson; one s one d. *Educ:* Univ. of Strathclyde (BA 1972); Univ. of Glasgow (BD 1975). Asst Minister, St George's West Church, Edinburgh, 1975–77; Minister, St Margaret's, Knightswood, Glasgow, 1977–89. Convener: Bd of Practice and Procedure, 2000–04; Gen. Assembly Business Cttee, 2000–04. Hon. DLitt Strathclyde, 2006. DL Ayrshire and Arran, 2013. *Recreations:* sailing, choral singing, snooker. *Address:* 4 Cairns Terrace, Kilmarnock KA1 2JG. *T:* (01563) 523113. *E:* davidwlacy@outlook.com. *Clubs:* Kilmarnock; Troon Cruising.

**LACY, Sir Patrick Bryan Finucane,** 4th Bt cr 1921, of Ampton, co. Suffolk; b 18 April 1948; s of Sir Maurice John Pierce Lacy, 2nd Bt and his 2nd wife, Nansi Jean (née Evans); S brother, 1998; m 1971, Phyllis Victoria James (marr. diss. 1980); one s one d. *Educ:* Downside. *Heir:* s Finian James Pierce Lacy, b 24 Sept. 1972.

**LADDIE, James Matthew Lang;** QC 2012; b London, 25 Oct. 1972; s of Prof. Sir Hugh Ian Lang Laddie and Stecia Elizabeth Laddie; m 1999, Emma Louise Robinson; one s three d. *Educ:* St Paul's Sch.; Sidney Sussex Coll., Cambridge (BA 1994). Called to the Bar, Middle Temple, 1995. *Recreations:* bird watching, blues, cricket, crosswords, cycling. *Address:* Matrix Chambers, Gray's Inn, WC1R 5LN. *T:* (020) 7404 3447.

**LADDS, Rt Rev. Robert Sidney,** SSC; Bishop Suffragan of Whitby, 1999–2008; an Hon. Assistant Bishop, Diocese of London, since 2009; Honorary Curate, St Peter's, London Docks, since 2015; b 15 Nov. 1941; s of late Sidney Ladds and of Joan Dorothy Ladds (née Cant); m 1964, Roberta Harriet Sparkes; three s. *Educ:* Christ Church Coll., Canterbury (CertEd 1970, BEd Hons 1971, London Univ.); Canterbury Sch. of Ministry. LRSC 1972; FCS 1972. Industrial res. chemist, 1959–68; schoolmaster, 1971–80; ordained deacon, 1980, priest, 1981; Asst Curate, St Leonard, Hythe, 1980–83; Rector of Bretherton, 1983–91; Chaplain, Bishop Rawstorne Sch., 1983–86; Bishop of Blackburn's Chaplain for Ministry, 1986–90; Bishop's Audit Officer, 1990–91; Rector of Preston, 1991–97; Hon. Canon, Blackburn, 1993–97; Archdeacon of Lancaster, 1997–99; House-for-duty Priest, St Mary and Christ Church, Hendon, 2009–15. Fellow, 2010, and Provost (Eastern Region), 2014–, Woodard Corp. (Asst Provost, 2010–14). Commissary for Northern Province to Bp of Taejon, S Korea, 1997–99; Vice-Pres., Korea Mission Partnership, 1999–2016. Superior-General: Soc. of Mary, 2009–; Coll. of Chaplains of Mary Mother of the Ch, 2017–. *Recreations:* gardening, bonsai, church architecture. *Address:* St Peter's Mission House, Wapping Lane, E1W 2RW. *T:* (020) 7488 3864. *E:* episcopus70@gmail.com.

**LADE, Hilary Jane;** Director, Plymouth Culture Board, since 2014; b 11 June 1957; d of Herbert Alfred Lade and Margaret (née Clark); m 2002, Mark Wilson. *Educ:* Selwyn Coll., Cambridge (MA Oriental Studies (Chinese)); Harvard Univ. (MA E Asian Langs and Civilisations); Univ. of Calif, Berkeley (MA Internat. Relns). Oil trader, Shell Internat., 1984–87; Man. Dir, Shell Gas Ltd, Shell UK, 1987–91; Estate Manager, Fountains Abbey and Studley Royal, NT, 1991–93; Dir of Historic Properties, English Heritage, 1993–97; Hd of Business Improvement, Shell, 1997–99. Chm., Royal Parks Adv. Bd, 1999–2002. Director: Nat. Forest Co., 1998–2002; Southern Arts Bd, 1998–2002; YHA, 1999–2001; BTA, 2000–03; Oxford Inspires, 2003–09; Dir and Trustee, Heritage Lottery Fund, 2008–14. Trustee, Nat. Trust, 2001–06. Mem., Bd of Visitors, Ashmolean Mus., 2011–14. Gov., Plymouth Coll. of Art, 2014–18. Winston Churchill Travelling Fellow, 1978; Harkness Fellow, 1980. *Recreations:* music (violin player), travel, ski-ing, mountaineering. *E:* hilary.lade@live.co.uk.

**LADENIS, Nicholas Peter;** Chef Patron, Chez Nico Restaurants, 1973–2000; b 22 April 1934; s of Peter and Constandia Ladenis; m 1963, Dinah-Jane Zissu; two d. *Educ:* Prince of Wales Sch., Nairobi; Regent Street Poly.; LSE; Hull Univ. (BSc Econs 1958). Appts with various cos, incl. Caltex, Ford Motor Co., Sunday Times, up to 1970; entered catering trade, 1971; opened restaurants (with wife and business partner): Chez Nico, 1973; Simply Nico, 1986; Nico Central, 1989; Nico at Ninety, subseq. Chez Nico, 1992 (three Michelin stars, 1995); Consultant: Incognico, 2000–04; Deca, 2002–04. First restaurateur to achieve three Michelin stars and full marks in Good Food Guide at same time. Hon. DSc(Econ) Hull, 1997. Chef of Year, 1988, Lifetime Achievement Award, 2015, Catey Awards. *Publications:* My Gastronomy, 1987; Nico, 1996. *Recreations:* food, family, home, travel, expensive cars.

**LADER, Prof. Malcolm Harold,** OBE 1996; MD, PhD, DSc; FRCPsych, FMedSci; FLS; Professor of Clinical Psychopharmacology, Institute of Psychiatry, University of London, 1978–2001, now Emeritus; b 27 Feb. 1936; s of Abe and Minnie Lader; m 1961, Susan Ruth Packer; three d. *Educ:* Univ. of Liverpool (BSc 1956; MB ChB 1959; MD 1964); University Coll. London (PhD 1963; DSc 1976); DPM 1966; Open Univ. (LLB 2006); Inst. of Historical Res., Univ. of London (MA Hons Hist. 2017). FRCPsych 1976. Res. Asst, UCL, 1960–63; Registrar in Psychiatry, 1963–66, Hon. Consultant, 1970–2001, Maudsley Hosp.; Mem., MRC External Staff, 1966–2001. Trustee, Psychiatry Res. Trust, 2002–. FRSocMed 1963; FMedSci 1999; FLS 2016. Hon. Fellow: Amer. Coll. of Psychiatrists, 1993; Soc. for Study of Addiction, 1998; British Assoc. for Psychopharmacology, 1994. *Publications:* Psychiatry on Trial, 1978; (ed jtly) Psychiatry and General Practice, 1982; (jtly) Role of Neurotransmitter Systems in Anxiety Modulation, 1984; (contrib.) Patterns of Improvement in Depressed In-patients, 1987; (ed) Psychopharmacology of Addiction, 1988; Biological Treatments in Psychiatry, 1990, 2nd edn 1996; (ed jtly) Nature of Alcohol and Drug-related Problems, 1992; (jtly) Anxiety, Panic and Phobias, 1997; 670 articles in scientific jls. *Recreations:* antiques, eating too much. *Address:* 16 Kelsey Park Mansion, 78 Wickham Road, Beckenham, Kent BR3 6QH. *T:* (020) 8650 0366.

**LADER, Philip,** JD; Chairman, WPP Group, 2001–15; Senior Adviser, Morgan Stanley International, since 2001; b 17 March 1946; s of Phil and Mary Tripoli Lader; m 1980, Linda LeSourd; two d. *Educ:* Duke Univ. (BA 1966); Univ. of Michigan (MA History 1967); Pembroke Coll., Oxford (Hon. Fellow, 1994); Harvard Law Sch. (JD). Admitted to Bar: Florida, 1972; District of Columbia, 1973; S Carolina, 1979; Associate, Sullivan & Cromwell, 1972; Law Clerk to US Circuit Judge, 1973; President: Sea Pines Co., 1979–83; Winthrop Univ., 1983–86; GOSL Land Assets Mgt, 1986–88; Business Execs for Nat. Security, 1990; Exec. Vice-Pres., Sir James Goldsmith's US Hldgs, 1986–89; Pres. and Vice Chancellor, Bond Univ., Australia, 1991–92; Dep. Dir for Mgt, Office of Mgt and Budget, US Govt, 1993; White House Dep. Chief of Staff and Asst to the Pres., 1993–94; Adminr, Small Business Admin, and Mem., President's Cabinet, 1994–97; Ambassador of the USA to the UK, 1997–2001. West Prof. of Internat. Studies, The Citadel, 2001–07. Partner, Nelson Mullins Law Firm, 2001–; Director: American Red Cross, 1995–96; AES Corp., 2001–; Marathon Oil, 2001–; Songbird Estates, 2006–10; UC RUSAL, 2007–. Mem. Council, Lloyd's, 2004–10. Trustee: British Museum, 2001–06; RAND Corp., 2001–11, 2013–; St Paul's Cathedral Trust, 2002–07; Windsor Leadership Trust, 2002–06; Salzburg Global Seminar, 2004–; Smithsonian Mus. of American Hist., 2006–16. Chm., Amer. Assoc., Royal Acad. of Arts Trust, 2001–04; Founder, Renaissance Inst., 1981. Mem., Council on Foreign Relns, Chief Execs' Orgn; Advisory Board: British-American Business Council, 2000–; The Prince's Trust, 2001–06. John C. Whitehead Lecture, RIIA, 1998. Hon. Bencher, Middle Temple, 1998. Hon. Fellow: Liverpool John Moores Univ., 1998; London Business Sch., 2000. Fourteen hon. doctorates. Benjamin Franklin Medal, RSA, 2001; Global Service to Humanity Award, Rotary Internat. Foundn, 2007. *Recreations:* walking, tennis. *Address:* (office) 20 Bank Street, Canary Wharf, E14 4AD. *Clubs:* Harvard (New York); Metropolitan (Washington); Lost Tree (Florida).

**LADYMAN, Dr Stephen John;** Chairman, Somerset Partnership NHS Foundation Trust, since 2013; b 6 Nov. 1952; s of Frank Ladyman and Winifred Ladyman; m 1st, 1975 (marr. diss. 1994); 2nd, 1995, Janet Ann Baker; one d, and one step s one step d (and one step s decd). *Educ:* Liverpool Poly. (BSc Hons Applied Biol. 1975); Strathclyde Univ. (PhD 1982). Res. scientist, MRC Radiobiol. Unit, 1979–84; Head: of Computing, Mathilda and Terence Kennedy Inst. of Rheumatology, 1984–90; of Computer-User Support, Pfizer Central Res., 1990–97. Mem. (Lab) Thanet DC, 1995–99 (Chm., Finance and Monitoring, 1995–97). Contested (Lab) Wantage, 1987. MP (Lab) S Thanet, 1997–2010; contested (Lab) same seat, 2010. PPS to Minister for the Armed Forces, 2001–03; Parly Under-Sec. of State, DoH, 2003–05; Minister of State, DfT, 2005–07. Mem., Select Cttee on Envmt, Transport and the Regs, 1999–2001 (Mem., Transport Sub-Cttee, 1999–2001); Chm., SE Reg. Select Cttee, 2009–10. Chairman: All Party Parly Gp on Autism, 2000–03; All-Party British-Netherlands Parly Gp, 2001–03; All Party Major Infrastructure Projs Gp, 2009–10. Vice Chm. with responsibility for SE England, Labour Party, 2007–10. Chief Exec., Retirement Security Ltd, 2010–12; Founder and Dir, Oak Retirement Ltd, 2012–; Chair, Retirement Housing Gp, 2013–; Chair, Somerset Sustainability and Transformation

Partnership, 2018–. Strategic Advr, Clearview Traffic Gp, 2012–17. *Publications:* Natural Isotopic Abundances in Soil Studies, 1982; various learned articles. *Recreations:* occasional golf, walking the dog, watching soccer, house renovations. *Address:* Manzano, St Mary's Lane, Pilton, Somerset BA4 4BD. *T:* (01749) 890224.

**LAFFERTY, Austin Joseph Aloysius;** President, Law Society of Scotland, 2012–13 (Vice-President, 2011–12); *b* Cambuslang, 3 June 1959; *s* of Austin Lafferty and Ada Lafferty (*née* Paterson); *m* 1983, Yvonne McCabe; one *s* one *d*. *Educ:* St Aloysius Coll., Glasgow; Univ. of Glasgow (LLB). Admitted solicitor, 1981; NP 1981; solicitor in private practice, 1981–. Broadcaster on TV and radio incl. BBC and STV; journalist with various newspapers and mags; web blogger. *Publications:* It's the Law, 2004. *Recreations:* karate (2nd dan black belt), drawing, painting. *Address:* 213 Fenwick Road, Glasgow G46 6JD. *T:* (0141) 621 2212, *Fax:* (0141) 621 1342. *E:* alafferty@laffertylaw.com. *Clubs:* Glasgow Art; Bushido Karate.

**LAFFERTY, John; His Honour Judge Lafferty;** a Circuit Judge, since 2007; *b* Baillieston, 26 Dec. 1949; *s* of James and Susannah Lafferty. *Educ:* Univ. of Strathclyde (BA Hons English and Hist.); Nottingham Trent Univ. (LLM); Univ. of Glasgow (MPhil); Jordan Hill Coll. of Educn (Cert Ed) Leeds Poly. (CPE and Solicitors' Finals). Adminr/ instructor, W Africa, 1974–76; English teacher, Our Lady's High Sch., Motherwell, 1976–80; Edward Fail, Bradshaw and Waterson: Articled clerk, 1983–85; Solicitor, 1985–87; Partner, 1987–90; Man. Partner, 1990–2005; Consultant, 2005–07; Recorder, 2000–07. Trustee: Disability Law Service, 2004–12; Sightsavers Internat., 2005–15. *Recreations:* walking, reading history, literature, theatre, music, travel. *Address:* Snaresbrook Crown Court, 75 Hollybush Hill, E11 1QW.

**LAFFIN, Simon Timothy;** Chairman, Flybe Group plc, 2013–19; *b* Croydon; *s* of Trevor and Patricia Laffin; *m* 1982, Diana Carola Wilson; two *s* one *d*. *Educ:* Trinity Hall, Cambridge (BA 1981; MA 1983). Trainee Accountant, BP Oil, 1981–82; Financial Analyst, Rank Xerox, 1982–85; Finance Manager, Mars Confectionery, 1985–90; Dir of Finance, Argyll Gp, subseq. Safeway plc, 1990–95; Chief Financial Officer and Property Dir, Safeway plc, 1995–2004; Advr, CVC Capital Partners, 2004–13. Chairman: Hozelock Gp, 2009–13; Assura plc, 2011–18. Non-executive Director: Northern Rock, 2007–08; Mitchells & Butlers, 2009–10; Aegis Gp plc, 2009–12; Watkin Jones, 2016–. Chm., Audit Cttee, Dentsu Aegis Network, 2013–. FCMA 2010. *Recreations:* tennis, flying light aircraft, baking bread, playing guitar. *W:* www.simonlaffin.com.

**LAFONTAINE, Oskar;** Member of Bundestag, 1990–94, 1998–99 and 2005–10; Minister of Finance, Germany, 1998–99; *b* 16 Sept. 1943; *m* 1993, Christa Müller (marr. diss. 2013); one *s*; *m* 2014, Sahra Wagenknecht; and one *s* from a former marriage. *Educ:* Bonn Univ.; Saarbrücken Univ. Social Democratic Party (SPD), Germany: joined, 1966; officer, Saarland, 1970–75; Chm., Saarland Reg., 1977–96; Mem., Nat. Exec., 1994–2005; Chm., SPD, 1995–99; Left Party (Die Linke): Parly Leader, 2005–09; Chm., 2007–10. Mem., 1970–75 and 1985–98, Premier, 1985–98, Saarland Regl Parlt; Mayor, 1974–76, Lord Mayor, 1976–85, Saarbrücken; Pres., Bundesrat, 1995–96; Chm., Jt Cttee of Bundesrat and Bundestag, 1995–96. *Publications:* Angst vor den Freunden: die Atomwaffen-Strategie der Supermächte Zerstört die Bündnisse, 1983; Der andere Fortschritt: Verantwortung statt Verweigerung, 1985; Die Gesellschaft der Zukunft, 1988; Das Lied vom Teilen, 1989; Deutsche Wahrheiten, 1990; Das Herz schlägt links (autobiog.), 1999; Die Wut wächst, 2002.

**LA FRENAIS, Ian,** OBE 2007; writer, screenwriter and producer; *b* 7 Jan. 1937; *s* of Cyril and Gladys La Frenais; *m* 1984, Doris Vartan; one step *s*. *Educ:* Dame Allan's School, Northumberland. *Television:* writer or co-writer (with Dick Clement): The Likely Lads, 1965–68; The Adventures of Lucky Jim, 1968; Whatever Happened to the Likely Lads, 1971–73; Thick as Thieves, 1974; Porridge, 1974–77 (one-off revival, 2016); Going Straight, 1978; Further Adventures of Lucky Jim, 1983; Auf Wiedersehen Pet, 1983–84, 2002–04; Mog, 1985; Lovejoy, 1986; Spender, 1990; Freddie and Max, 1990; Old Boy Network, 1991; Full Stretch, 1993; Over the Rainbow, 1993; The Rotters' Club (adaptation), 2005; Archangel (adaptation), 2005; Spies of Warsaw (adaptation), 2013; Henry IX, 2017; Porridge, 2017; *US television:* On The Rocks, 1976–77; Billy, 1979; Sunset Limousine, 1983; Tracy Ullman Special, 1993; Tracy Takes On, 1995–99; *films:* writer or co-writer (with Dick Clement): The Jokers, 1967; The Touchables, 1968; Otley, 1968; Hannibal Brooks, 1969; The Virgin Soldiers, 1969; Villain, 1970; Catch Me a Spy, 1971; The Likely Lads, 1975; Porridge, 1979; To Russia with Elton, 1979; Prisoner of Zenda, 1981; Water, 1984; writer-producer, Vice Versa, 1987; co-writer (with Dick Clement): The Commitments, 1991; Excess Baggage, 1997; Still Crazy, 1998 (also Exec. Prod.); Honest, 2000; Goal!, 2005; Flushed Away, 2006; Across the Universe, 2007; The Bank Job, 2008; Killing Bono, 2011; My Generation, 2018; *stage:* writer, Billy, 1974; co-producer, Anyone for Denis?, 1982; writer: Gwen, 2001; The Likely Lads, 2008; Porridge, 2009; Chasing Bono, 2018; Jukebox Hero, 2019. Partner (with Dick Clement and Allan McKeown), Witzend Productions; producer, co-producer, director, numerous productions. Hon. DCL Northumbria, 2006. Awards from BAFTA, Broadcasting Guild, Screen Writers' Guild, Soc. of TV Critics, Writers' Guild of America, London Film Critics' Circle, Acad. of Television Arts and Scis, Nat. Television Awards, British Comedy Awards, Royal Television Soc. *Publications:* (with Dick Clement) More than Likely: a memoir, 2019.

**LAGARDE, Christine Madeleine Odette;** Chevalier de la Légion d'Honneur (France), 2000; Commandeur du Mérite agricole (France); *b* 1 Jan. 1956; *d* of Robert Lallouette and Nicole Lallouette (*née* Carre); *m* (marr. diss.); two *s*. *Educ:* Université Paris X (BA Eng.; BA Law; MPhil Law; JD); Institut d'Études Politiques Aix-en-Provence (MA Pol Sci.). Lawyer, Baker & McKenzie, 1981–2005: Partner, 1987–95; Hd of Western Europe, 1995–99; Chm., 1999–2005; Pres., Global Strategic Cttee, 2004–05; Minister of Commerce and Industry, 2005–07, of Agric. and Fisheries, 2007, of Economy, Finance and Industry, 2007–11, France; Man. Dir, Internat. Monetary Fund, 2011–19. Hon. Fellow, Robinson Coll., Cambridge, 2019. Hon. Dr: KU Leuven, 2012; Montréal, 2014; Hon. LLD Washington Coll., 2017. *Recreations:* swimming, scuba diving, opera, ballet.

**LAGARDÈRE, Arnaud Georges André;** General and Managing Partner, Lagardère SCA, since 2003 (Co-Managing Director, 1998–2003); Chairman and Chief Executive Officer: Lagardère Media (formerly Hachette SA), since 1999; Arjil Commanditée-Arco, since 2004; Chairman, Europel, since 2017; *b* Boulogne-Billancourt, 18 March 1961; *s* of late Jean-Luc Lagardère. *Educ:* Univ. of Paris-Dauphine (DEA Econs). Dir, 1986, then CEO, 1989–92, Multi Média Beaujon; Vice-Chm., Supervisory Bd, Arjil & Cie, 1987–2005; Mem. Bd, 1988–2003, CEO, 1988–, Chm., 2003–, Lagardère Capital and Mgt (formerly Arjil &p); manager of emerging activities and media, Mem. Mgt and Strategic Cttee, Lagardère Gp, 1989–92; Dep. Chm. and Chief Operating Officer, Arjil Commanditée Arco, 1992–2004; Chairman: Grolier Inc., USA, 1994–98; Lagardère Active Broadband (formerly Grolier Interactive Europe), 1994–2008; Chm., Europe 1 Communication, subseq. Lagardère Active Broadcast, 1999–2007; Chm. and CEO, 1999–2001, Man. Dir, 2001–03, Europe Régies, subseq. Lagardère Publicité; Chairman, Supervisory Board: Lagardère Active (Chm., 2001–06); Lagardère Travel Retail (formerly Lagardère Services); Chm., Exec. Cttee, Lagardère Sports and Entertainment (formerly Lagardère Unlimited). Man. Dir, Nouvelles Messageries de la Presse Parisienne, 1999–2003; Member Board: Société d'Agences et de Diffusion, 2000–03; CanalSatellite, 2001–03; Lagardère-Sociétés, 2002–03; France Telecom, 2003–08; Moët Hennessy Louis Vuitton, 2003–09; Eur. Aeronautic Defence and Space Co. (EADS NV), 2003–13 (Chm., 2012–13); Fimalac, 2003–06; Hachette Livre; Lagardère Ressources; Member Supervisory Board: Aérospatiale Matra, 1999–2000; Daimler (formerly DaimlerChrysler) AG, 2005–10; Le Monde, 2005–08; Virgin Stores, 2005–08. Member: France Galop Cttee, 2003–06; Conseil Stratégie des Technologies de l'Information, 2004–. Chm., Jean-Luc Lagardère (formerly Hachette) Foundn, 2003– (Pres.). Chairman: Club des Entreprises Paris 2012, 2004–06; Assoc. des Amis de Paris Jean-Bouin, 2004–10; Nouvel Elan Croix Catelan Assoc., 2006–; Lagardère Paris Racing Assoc. *Address:* Lagardère SCA, 4 rue de Presbourg, 75116 Paris, France. *T:* (1) 40691640. *E:* secretariatal@lagardere.fr.

**LAGDAMEO, Antonio Manuel Revilla;** Ambassador of the Philippines to the Court of St James's, and concurrently to Republic of Ireland, 2009–10 and since 2017, and concurrently Permanent Representative to the International Maritime Organisation, 2009–10 and since 2018; *b* Manila, Philippines, 13 June 1942; *s* of Ernesto V. Lagdameo, KSMOM, KSS and Pilar Revilla de Lagdameo, DSMOM, DHS; *m* 1967, Maria Linda Floirendo, DHS; three *s* four *d*. *Educ:* De La Salle Coll.; Univ. of Philippines (Associate in Arts (Medicine)); Univ. of E Manila, Philippines (BBA (Accounting) 1964); Ateneo Univ., Manila (MBA). Vice Pres. and Dir, Combined Mgt Corp., Rebar Building Inc., Milvaney, McMillan, Inc., Concrete Piles and Poles Corp., 1962–65; Vice Pres. and Sales Manager, General Paint Corp. (Philippines), Inc., 1965–67; Vice Pres., Davao Motor Sales, Mindanao Motors Corp., United Motors Corp., 1968–75; Exec. Vice Pres., Fortune Cement Corp., 1976–83; Vice Pres., Revere Sugar Corp. (NY), 1983–91; Vice Chm., House of Travel, Inc., 1993–; Chm. Bd, Carrije Hldgs, Inc., 1995–. Ambassador: to Mexico, and concurrently to Belize, Costa Rica, Guatemala, Honduras, Panama and Nicaragua, 2006–08; to Spain, 2008–09. Member: Philippine Italian Assoc.; Philippine Thoroughbred Owners and Breeders Orgn. Kt, Equestrian Order of Holy Sepulchre of Jerusalem, 2005. *Recreations:* theatre, ballet, opera with family. *Address:* Embassy of the Philippines, 6–11 Suffolk Street, SW1Y 4HG. *T:* (020) 7451 1801, *Fax:* (020) 7930 9787. *E:* ambassador@philemb.co.uk. *Clubs:* Travellers; Manila House, Manila Polo, Manila; Rotary (Makati West).

**LAGNADO, Prof. Leon,** PhD; FMedSci; Professor of Neuroscience, University of Sussex, since 2013; *b* London, 26 Sept. 1963; *s* of Maurice Lagnado and Fortunée Lagnado (*née* Yaluz); *m* 1990, Dr Ruth Murrell; three *d*. *Educ:* Whitefield Comprehensive Sch.; University Coll. London (BSc 1985); Gonville and Caius Coll., Cambridge (PhD 1988). Human Frontier Sci. Prog. Long-term Fellow, Stanford Univ., 1990–93; MRC Prog. Leader (tenure track), 1993–99, MRC Prog. Leader, 1999–2013, MRC Lab. of Molecular Biol., Cambridge. FMedSci 2014. Wellcome Prize in Physiol., 1998. *Publications:* contribs to scientific jls, esp. dealing with neurosci. of vision. *Recreations:* reading, football, building microscopes, hoping for the best. *Address:* School of Life Sciences, University of Sussex, Falmer, Brighton BN1 9QG. *T:* (01273) 877431. *E:* l.lagnado@sussex.ac.uk. *Club:* Fulbourn Institute Sports and Social.

**LAGOS ESCOBAR, Ricardo,** PhD; Professor at Large, Watson Institute for International Studies, Brown University, USA, since 2007; President of Chile, 2000–06; *b* 2 March 1938; *s* of Froilán Lagos and Emma Escobar; *m* 1971, Luisa Durán; five *c*. *Educ:* Sch. of Law, Univ. of Chile; Duke Univ., N Carolina (PhD 1962). University of Chile, 1963–72: Prof., and Hd, Sch. of Pol and Admin. Scis; Dir, Inst. of Econs; Sec. Gen., 1969–72; Sec. Gen., Latin American Faculty of Social Scis (UNESCO initiative), 1972–74; Vis. Prof., Univ. of N Carolina, 1974–75; Econ. Hd, Regl Prog. for Latin America and the Caribbean, UN, 1978–84. Chairman: Alianza Democrática, 1983–84; Partido por la Democracia, 1987–90; Minister of Educn, 1990–92, of Public Works, 1994–98. UN Special Envoy on Climate Change, 2007–10. Founder and Pres., Foundn for Democracy and Develt, 2006–. *Publications:* Población, Pobreza y Mercado de Trabajo en América Latina, 1997; books and articles on econs and politics. *Address:* c/o Palacio de la Moneda, Santiago, Chile.

**LA GRENADE, Dame Cécile (Ellen Fleurette),** GCMG 2013; OBE 2005; PhD; Governor General of Grenada, since 2013; *b* Grenada, 30 Dec. 1952; *d* of Alan La Grenade and Sibyl La Grenade (*née* Sylvester). *Educ:* St Joseph's Convent, St George's, Grenada; Univ. of West Indies, Trinidad (BSc 1978); Univ. of Maryland (MSc 1986; PhD 1990). Teacher, Holy Faith Convent, Couva, Trinidad, 1978–79; Produce Chemist, Min. of Agric., 1979–82; res. asst (pt-time), US Dept of Agric., 1987–90; res. biologist, US Food and Drug Admin, 1990–91; Man. Dir, De La Grenade Industries, 1991–2013. Member: Grenada Orchid Soc., 1998–; Horticulture Soc. of Grenada, 2005–13. *Recreations:* gardening, orchid cultivation. *Address:* Office of the Governor General, PO Box 369, St George's, Grenada, West Indies. *T:* 4402401, *Fax:* 4406688. *E:* patogg@spiceisle.com.

**LAHIRI, Prof. Aditi,** DPhil; FBA 2010; Professor of Linguistics, University of Oxford, since 2007; Fellow, Somerville College, Oxford, since 2007; *b* Calcutta, 14 July 1952; *d* of Haranath and Arundhati Roy; *m* 2003, Prof. Henning Reetz. *Educ:* Univ. of Calcutta (BA Maths and Econs 1971; MA Comparative Philol. 1973; DPhil Comparative Philol. and Linguistics 1979); Brown Univ. (PhD 1982). Postdoctoral Res. Asst, Dept of Linguistics, Brown Univ., 1982–83; Vis. Asst Prof., Dept of Linguistics, UCLA, 1983–84; Adjunct Asst Prof., Bd of Studies in Linguistics, Univ. of Calif, Santa Cruz, 1984–85; Sen. Res. Scientist, Max Planck Inst. for Psycholinguistics, Nijmegen, 1985–92; Prof. of Gen. Linguistics, Univ. of Konstanz, 1992–2007. Hon. Life Mem., Linguistic Soc. of America, 2013. Max Planck Forschungspreis für internationale kooperation, 1994; Leibniz Prize, Deutsche Forschungsgemeinschaft, 2000; Prof. Sukumar Sen Gold Medal for Excellence in Res., 2009. *Publications:* contrib. to Jl Acoustical Soc. of America, Cognitive Brain Res., Jl Cognitive Neurosci., Trans Philological Soc., Jl Phonetics. *Recreations:* visiting the Cotswolds, reading crime fiction. *Address:* Centre for Linguistics and Philology, University of Oxford, Walton Street, Oxford OX1 2HG. *T:* (01865) 280400. *E:* aditi.lahiri@ling-phil.ox.ac.uk.

**LAÏDI, Ahmed;** Algerian Ambassador to Mexico, 1988–89; *b* 20 April 1934; *m* 1964, Aicha Chabbi-Lemsine; one *s* one *d* (and one *s* decd). *Educ:* Algiers Univ. (BA); Oran Univ. (LLB). Counsellor to Presidency of Council of Algerian Republic, 1963; Head of Cabinet of Presidency, 1963–64; Dir Gen. of Political and Economic Affairs, Min. of Foreign Affairs, 1964–66; Chm., Prep. Cttee, second Afro-Asian Conf., 1964–65; Special Envoy to Heads of States, Senegal, Mali, Ivory Coast and Nigeria, 1966; Ambassador to Spain, 1966–70; Head, Delegn to Geneva Conf. of non-nuclear countries, 1968; Wali (Governor): province Médéa, 1970–74; province Tlemcen, 1975–78; Ambassador to Jordan, 1978–84; Special Envoy to Heads of States and govts, Zambia, Malawi, Botswana, Zimbabwe, 1985; Ambassador to UK, 1984–88, and to Ireland, 1985–88. Member: Algerian Football Fedn, 1964–66; Algerian Nat. Olympic Cttee, 1965–72. Foreign Orders: Liberia, 1963; Bulgaria, 1964; Yugoslavia, 1964; Spain, 1970; Jordan, 1984. *Recreations:* theatre, cinema, football.

**LAIDLAW,** Baron *cr* 2004 (Life Peer), of Rothiemay in Banffshire; **Irvine Alan Stewart Laidlaw;** founder Chairman, IIR Holdings Ltd, 1974–2005; *b* 22 Dec. 1942; *s* of Roy Alan and Margaret Laidlaw; *m* 1987, (Marie) Christine Laidlaw. *Educ:* Merchiston Castle Sch.; Univ. of Leeds (BA Hons); Columbia Univ. (MBA). Chm., Abbey Business Centres Ltd, 1998–2010. Chairman: Veja Mate Offshore Hldgs; British Wind Energy, 2014–19; SPLK,

Rwanda, 2018–; L2FR, Netherlands, 2018–. Chairman: Laidlaw Youth Trust, 2003–09; Laidlaw Foundn, 2018–. Sponsor, Excelsior Acad., Newcastle upon Tyne, 2004–; founder and sponsor, Laidlaw Schs Trust, 2011–. Mem., H of L, 2004–10. Chm., Laidlaw Estates. Patron, Diva Opera. Hon. LLD St Andrews, 2003; Hon. DHC Aberdeen, 2007. *Recreations:* cars, sailing, travel, opera. *Address:* 11 Avenue President J F Kennedy, MC 98000, Monaco. *E:* irvine.laidlaw@rothiemay.net. *Clubs:* Royal Thames Yacht; Monaco Yacht; Costa Smeralda Yacht; Royal Cape Yacht.

**LAIDLAW, (Henry) Renton**; golf correspondent, Evening Standard, 1973–98; *b* 6 July 1939; *s* of late Henry Renton Laidlaw and Margaret McBeath Laidlaw (*née* Raiker). *Educ:* James Gillespie's Boys' School, Edinburgh; Daniel Stewart's College, Edinburgh. Golf corresp., Edinburgh Evening News, 1957–67; news presenter and reporter, Grampian Television, Aberdeen, 1968–69; BBC news presenter, Edinburgh, 1970–72; BBC Radio golf reporter, 1976–90; presenter: BBC Radio Sport on 2, 1986, 1987; ITV Eurosport, 1988; golf presenter: BSB, 1989–91; Golf Channel, US, 1995–2016; Chief Commentator, PGA European Tour Prodns, 1988–2013. Pres., Assoc. of Golf Writers, 2004–15. Jack Nicklaus Meml Journalism Award, 2000; PGA of America Lifetime Achievement Award in Journalism, 2003; PGA Lifetime Achievement Award, 2012; Augusta Masters Achievement Award, 2013; PGAs of Europe Achievement Award, 2019. *Publications:* Play Golf (with Peter Alliss), 1977; Jacklin—the first 40 years, 1984; (ed) Johnnie Walker Ryder Cup '85, 1985; Play Better Golf, 1986; (ed) Johnnie Walker Ryder Cup '87, 1987; Ten Years—the history of the European Open, 1988; Golf Heroes, 1989; (ed) Johnnie Walker Ryder Cup '89, 1989; (with Bernard Gallacher) Captain at Kiawah, 1991; Wentworth: a host of happy memories, 1993; (ed) The Royal and Ancient Golfer's Handbook, 1998–2014; (ed) The Golfers' Guide to Scotland, 2000–01. *Recreations:* theatre, golf. *T:* (c/o Mrs Kay Clarkson) (01707) 275639, 07768 746605. *Clubs:* Caledonian; Royal & Ancient (St Andrews); Sunningdale Golf, Wentworth, Royal Burgess Golf, Ballybunion Golf.

**LAIDLAW, Prof. James Alexander**, PhD; William Wyse Professor of Social Anthropology, University of Cambridge, since 2016; Fellow, King's College, Cambridge, since 1989; *b* Renfrewshire, Scotland, 12 Sept. 1963; *s* of James and Florence Laidlaw; *m* 2014, Peter David Allen. *Educ:* Park Mains High Sch., Erskine; King's Coll., Cambridge (BA 1984; MA 1989; PhD 1990). Jun. Res. Fellow, 1989–93, Sen. Res. Fellow, 1993–97, Sen. Tutor, 2002–05, King's Coll., Cambridge; Asst Lectr, 1995–2000, Lectr, 2000–15, Univ. of Cambridge. *Publications:* The Archetypal Actions of Ritual, 1994; Riches and Renunciation, 1995; The Essential Edmund Leach, 2000; Ritual and Memory, 2004; Religion, Anthropology, and Cognitive Science, 2007; The Subject of Virtue, 2014. *Recreations:* hill walking, theatre, cinema, opera. *Address:* King's College, Cambridge CB2 1ST. *T:* (01223) 331227. *E:* JAL6@cam.ac.uk.

**LAIDLAW, Jonathan James**; QC 2008; a Recorder, since 1998; *b* 28 Feb. 1960. *Educ:* Univ. of Hull (LLB). Called to the Bar, Inner Temple, 1982. Jun. Treasury Counsel, 1995–2001; Sen. Treasury Counsel, 2001–08; First Sen. Treasury Counsel, Central Criminal Court, 2008–10. Hd of Chambers, 2 Hare Court, 2013–. *Address:* 2 Hare Court, Temple, EC4Y 7BH.

**LAIDLAW, Renton**; see Laidlaw, H. R.

**LAIDLAW, William Samuel Hugh, (Sam)**; Chairman: Neptune Oil and Gas, since 2015; Neptune Energy, since 2018; *b* 3 Jan. 1956; *s* of Sir Christophor Charles Fraser Laidlaw and Nina May (*née* Prichard); *m* 1989, Deborah Margaret Morris-Adams; three *s* one *d*. *Educ:* Eton College; Gonville and Caius College, Cambridge (MA); MBA. Admitted Solicitor, 1980; Insead, Fontainebleau, 1981. Soc. Françaises Pétroles BP, 1980; Amerada Hess: Manager, corporate planning, NY, 1981–83; Vice-Pres., London, 1983–85, Sen. Vice-Pres., 1986–90, Man. Dir, 1986–95, London; Exec. Vice-Pres., NY, 1990–95; Pres. and CEO, NY, 1995–2001; Chm., London, 1995–2001; Chief Exec., Enterprise Oil plc, 2001–02; Exec. Vice-Pres., ChevronTexaco Corp., 2003–06; Chief Exec., Centrica plc, 2006–14. Leader, Govt Inquiry into Rail Franchising (Laidlaw Enquiry), 2013. Non-executive Director: Premier Oil, 1995; Yes Television plc, 2000–03; Hanson plc, 2003–07; HSBC Hldgs plc, 2008–17; Rio Tinto plc, 2017–; Lead non-exec. Dir, DfT, 2010–14; Chm., Sponsorship Consulting Ltd, 2002–07. Dir, Business Council of Internat. Understanding, 1998–2014. Member: Govt Energy Adv. Panel, 1994–98; Prime Minister's Business Adv. Gp, 2010–12. Chairman: Petroleum Sci. and Tech. Inst., 1993–94; NEL, 1993–95; Nat. Centre for Univs and Business, 2014–. Mem., Adv. Bd, British Olympic Assoc., 2008–12. Pres., UKOOA, 1991. Chm., CBI Higher Educn Task Force, 2008–09. Member: Council, Radley Coll., 2008–; Bd, Said Business Sch., 2015–. FInstPet (Vice-Pres., 1994–95); FRSA 1990. *Clubs:* Royal Thames Yacht, Royal Yacht Squadron.

**LAIN-PRIESTLEY, Ven. Rosemary**; Adviser on Policy and Strategy to Bishop of London, since 2019; *b* 1967. *Educ:* Univ. of Kent (BA English Lit. and Theol. 1989); King's College London (MA 2002); Carlisle Diocese Trng Course. Immigration Advr; ordained deacon, 1996, priest, 1997; Curate: St Paul, Scotforth, Lancaster, 1996–98; St Martin-in-the-Fields, Trafalgar Square, 1998–2006; Dean of Women's Ministry, Two Cities Area, Dio. of London, 2006–15; Archdeacon for the Two Cities, 2016–19. *Address:* c/o The Old Deanery, Dean's Court, EC4V 5AA.

**LAINE, Dame Clementine Dinah, (Dame Cleo), (Lady Dankworth)**, DBE 1997 (OBE 1979); vocalist, actress; *b* 28 Oct. 1927; British; *m* 1st, 1947, George Langridge (marr. diss. 1957); one *s*; 2nd, 1958, Sir John Philip William Dankworth, CBE (*d* 2010); one *s* one *d*. Joined Dankworth Orchestra, 1953; with John Dankworth estabd Performing Arts Centre, Wavendon Stables, 1969. Melody Maker and New Musical Express Top Girl Singer Award, 1956; Moscow Arts Theatre Award for acting role in Flesh to a Tiger, 1958; Top place in Internat. Critics Poll by Amer. Jazz magazine, Downbeat, 1965. Lead, in Seven Deadly Sins, Edinburgh Festival and Sadler's Wells, 1961; acting roles in Edin. Fest., 1966, 1967, Cindy-Ella, Garrick, 1968; film, Last of the Blonde Bombshells, 2000. Many appearances with symphony orchestras performing Façade (Walton), Pierrot Lunaire and other compositions; played Julie in Show Boat, Adelphi, 1971; title role in Colette, Comedy, 1980; Hedda Gabler; Valmouth; A Time to Laugh; The Women of Troy; The Mystery of Edwin Drood, 1986; Into the Woods (US nat. tour), 1989; Noyes Fludde (Proms), 1990. Frequent TV appearances. Ambassador, SOS Children's Villages UK. Hon. Freeman, Musicians' Co., 2002. Freedom of Bor. of Milton Keynes, 2011. Hon. Fellow, Hughes Hall, Cambridge. Hon. MA Open, 1975; Hon. DMus: Berklee Sch. of Music, 1982; York, 1993; Cambridge, 2004; Brunel, 2007; Hon. Dr Luton. Woman of the Year, 9th annual Golden Feather Awards, 1973; Edison Award, 1974; Variety Club of GB Show Business Personality Award (with John Dankworth), 1977; TV Times Viewers Award for Most Exciting Female Singer on TV, 1978; Grammy Award for Best Female Jazz Vocalist, 1985; Theatre World Award, 1986; NARM Presidential Lifetime Achievement Award, 1990; British Jazz Awards Vocalist of the Year, 1990; Distinguished Artists Award, Internat. Soc. for the Performing Arts, 1999; Bob Harrington Lifetime Achievement Award (with John Dankworth), Back Stage, 2001; Lifetime Achievement Award: BBC Radio Jazz Awards (with John Dankworth), 2002; Musicians' Co., 2002; Jazz FM Awards, 2018; Gold Medal, BBC Jazz Awards, 2008. Gold Discs: Feel the Warm; I'm a Song; Live at Melbourne; Platinum Discs: Best Friends; Sometimes When We Touch. *Publications:* Cleo (autobiog.), 1994; You Can Sing If You Want To, 1997. *Recreation:* painting. *Fax:* (01908) 584414.

**LAING, Alastair David**, FSA; Curator of (formerly Adviser on) Pictures and Sculpture, National Trust, 1986–2013; *b* 5 Aug. 1944; *s* of late Malcolm Strickland Laing and Margaret Clare Laing (*née* Briscoe); *m* 1979, Hana Novotná; one *s*. *Educ:* Chafyn Grove Sch.; Bradfield Coll.; Corpus Christi Coll., Oxford (BA Hons 1966; Dip. Hist. Art 1967); Courtauld Inst. of Art, Univ. of London. FCO, 1967–68; translator, 1969–76; Night Operator, Internat. Telephone Exchange, 1973–76; Researcher, Heim Gall., 1976–83; Researcher and Jt Curator, François Boucher exhibn, NY, Detroit and Paris, 1983–85; Area Editor, Macmillan Dictionary of Art, 1985–86. Member: Adv. Council, Hamilton Kerr Inst., 1986–; Paintings Panel, Council for the Care of Churches, 1993–2006; Academic Cttee, Waddesdon Manor, 1994–; Acceptance in Lieu Panel, 1994–2005; Export Reviewing Cttee, 1996–2002; Old Master Paintings Vetting Cttee, The European Fine Art Fair, Maastricht, 1996–; Sci. Cttee for restoration of The Apotheosis of Hercules, Versailles, 1999–2001; Sci. Cttee, Arthéna, 1999–; Adv. Panel, Apsley House, 2005–09; Conservation Cttee, Chatsworth House, 2008–; Adv. Bd, A. G. Leventis Gall., Nicosia, 2013–. Trustee: Holburne Mus., Bath, 1998–2007; Mausolea and Monuments Trust, 2008–10; Art Fund, 2012–; Heritage Conservation Trust, 2012–; Hall Bequest Trust, Stowe Sch., 2016–; Trustee and Dir, Burlington Mag., 2001–. Mus. Scholar, Getty Res. Inst., LA, 2017. Thaw Sen. Fellow, Morgan Library, NY, 2015. Co-Curator, Une des provinces du Rococo, Musée des Beaux-Arts, Besançon, 2019. Chevalier, l'Ordre des Arts et des Lettres (France), 1988. *Publications:* (with Anthony Blunt) Baroque & Rococo, 1978; Lighting, 1982; (with Richard Walker) Portrait Miniatures in National Trust Houses: vol. 1, Northern Ireland, 2003; vol. II, Cornwall, Devon and Somerset, 2005; (jtly) The James A. de Rothschild Bequest at Waddesdon Manor: drawings for architecture, design and ornament, 2006; exhibition catalogues include: François Boucher, 1986; In Trust for the Nation, 1995; The Drawings of François Boucher, 2003; Oil Paintings in National Trust Properties, 6 vols, 2013; Boucher's Drawings: who and what were they for?, 2016; articles in Country Life, Apollo, Burlington Mag., Umění, etc. *Recreation:* church- and tomb-crawling. *Address:* 24 Aberdeen Road, N5 2UH. *Club:* Travellers.

**LAING, Andrew**; HM Inspector of Constabulary for Scotland, 2010–13; Director, Optimise Design and Build Ltd, since 2013; *b* Edinburgh, 9 Aug. 1963; *s* of John Harvey Laing and Agnes Stirling Laing (*née* Wightman); partner, June Kennedy Russell; two *s*. *Educ:* Leith Acad. Primary Sch., Edinburgh; Portobello High Sch., Edinburgh; Napier Univ., Edinburgh (BA Hons Business Studies 1996). Dip. IoD. Lothian and Borders Police, 1982–2004 (Superintendent, 2002–04); Fife Constabulary: Chief Superintendent, 2004–09; Dep. Chief Constable, 2009–10. Dir, Scottish Business Resilience Centre (formerly Scottish Business Crime Centre), 2011–15. FRSA. *Recreations:* squash, badminton, golf, cooking.

**LAING, Prof. Angus Wallace**, PhD; Dean, Lancaster University Management School, since 2015; *b* Glasgow, 24 May 1965; *s* of John and Mari Laing; *m* 1994, Moira Young; one *s* one *d*. *Educ:* Univ. of Witwatersrand (BA Hons 1988); Rhodes Univ. (MA 1990); Univ. of Aberdeen (PhD 1998). Lectr, Univ. of Aberdeen, 1993–2002; Professor: of Mktg, Open Univ., 2002–05; of Mgt, Univ. of Glasgow, 2005–10; Dean, Sch. of Business Econs, Loughborough Univ., 2010–15. Chm., Chartered Assoc. of Business Schs, 2010–15. Co-Founder, Nurture HE Gp. FRSA 2014. *Publications:* Managing and Marketing Health Services, 2002; contribs to jls incl. British Jl Mgt, Eur. Jl Mktg, Industrial Mktg Mgt. *Recreations:* walking, theatre, riding. *Address:* Lancaster University Management School, Bailrigg, Lancaster LA1 4YX. *T:* (01524) 510741. *E:* a.w.laing@lancaster.ac.uk.

**LAING, Catriona Wendy Campbell**, CB 2012; HM Diplomatic Service; High Commissioner to Nigeria, since 2018; *b* Cardiff; *m* 2014, Clive David Nicholas Bates, *qv*, one adopted *d*. *Educ:* London Sch. of Econs and Pol Sci. (MSc Econs 1986); Cranfield Sch. of Mgt, Cranfield Univ. (MBA 1996). ODI Fellow Planning Officer, Min. of Works, Transport and Communications, Botswana, 1986–89; Overseas Development Administration: Asst Economist, W Africa Dept, 1989–90; Asst Economist, British Develt Div. (E Africa), Kenya, 1990–91; Econ. Advr, Aid Policy Dept, 1992–93; Hd, UN Develt Office, UN Mission in Somalia, 1993–94; Overseas Development Administration, then Department for International Development: Econ. Advr, Latin America, Caribbean and Atlantic Dept, 1994–95; Team Leader, EU and Internat. Econs Policy Dept, 1996–98; Hd, Eastern Europe, Western Hemisphere Policy Dept, 1999–2000; Mem., Globalisation White Paper Team, 2000; Dep. Dir, Prime Minister's Strategy Unit, Cabinet Office, 2001–05; Hd, Internat. Div. Adv. Dept, DFID, 2005–06; Hd, Sudan, DFID, 2006–09; Dir, Human Rights and Internat., MoJ, 2009–12; Hd, Helmand Provincial Reconstruction Team and NATO and UK Sen. Civilian Rep., Southern Afghanistan, FCO (on loan), 2012–13; entered FCO, 2013; Alternate Crisis Leader, Ukraine Crisis and Additional Dep. Amb., Moscow, 2013–14; Ambassador to Zimbabwe, 2014–18. *Recreations:* yoga, dance, tennis, hiking. *Address:* c/o Foreign and Commonwealth Office, King Charles Street, SW1A 2AH.

**LAING, Christine Katherine**; QC 2006; **Her Honour Judge Laing**; a Circuit Judge, since 2014; *b* 4 Nov. 1961; *d* of late Ludovic Baillie Laing and Christina (*née* Easton). *Educ:* St Thomas of Aquinas RC High Sch., Edinburgh; Univ. of Newcastle-upon-Tyne (LLB Hons 1983). Called to the Bar, Lincoln's Inn, 1984; criminal practitioner, 1984–2014; a Recorder, 2004–14. *Recreations:* travel, music, arts, rich friends, inexpensive wine. *Address:* Lewes Combined Court Centre, High Street, Lewes BN7 1YB. *T:* (01273) 480400. *E:* c.laing957@btinternet.com.

**LAING, David Eric**, RIBA; FZS; Lord-Lieutenant of Northamptonshire, since 2014; *b* Budleigh Salterton, Devon, 28 March 1945; *s* of Sir (William) Kirby Laing and Joan Laing; *m* 1968, Frances Mary Underwood; four *s* one *d*. *Educ:* St Lawrence Coll., Ramsgate; Bartlett Sch. of Architecture, University Coll. London (BA Arch. 1967; MA Hons Arch. 1969). RIBA 1971. With Spence, Bonnington and Collins, Architects, 1969–72; Partner: Bryant Laing Partnership, 1972–2001; G. H. M. Rock Townsend Architects, 1985–98. Chm., Country and Metropolitan Homes plc, 1996–2005; Dir, Eskmuir Properties, 2003–. Chairman: Rural Develt Commn, Herts and Beds, 1988–96; Northants Community Foundn, 2005–14; Vice Chm., Northants Enterprise Partnership, 2008–13. Chm., St John Ambulance, Herts, 1998–2005, Northants, 2010–14. Chairman: David Laing Foundn, 1979–; Sir Kirby Laing Foundn, 2007–; Adrenaline Alley, 2010–. Trustee: Grove Hse Hospice, St Albans, 1988–95; St Andrew's Hosp., 2010– (Chm., Pension Fund, 2011–); Youth Sports Trust, 1998–2010; Nat. Hockey Foundn, 2002–; Northants Assoc. Youth Clubs, 2006– (Pres., 2005–); Church Schs Trust, 2009–12; Educn Fellowship Foundn, 2012–14; Northants Historic Churches Trust, 2015–. Pro-Chancellor, Univ. of Northampton, 2014–. FZS 1995. Mem. Court, Paviors' Co., 1993– (Master, 2006). *Recreations:* motor racing, rallying, hockey, ski-ing, sailing, music. *Address:* The Manor House, Grafton Underwood, Northants NN14 3AA. *T:* (01536) 330404. *E:* david@david-laing.co.uk, david.laing@mhqu.org. *Clubs:* Farmers; Aston Martin Owners, Vintage Sports Car, Lawn Tennis Association.

*See also* Sir J. M. K. Laing.

**LAING, Rt Hon. Dame Eleanor (Fulton)**, DBE 2018; PC 2017; MP (C) Epping Forest, since 1997; First Deputy Chairman of Ways and Means, and a Deputy Speaker, House of Commons, since 2013; *b* 1 Feb. 1958; *d* of late Matthew and Betty Pritchard; *m* 1983, Alan Laing (marr. diss. 2003); one *s*. *Educ:* St Columba's Sch., Kilmacolm; Edinburgh Univ. (Pres., Union, 1980–81; BA, LLB 1982). Solicitor, Edinburgh and London, 1983–89; Special Advr to Rt Hon. John MacGregor, MP, 1989–94. Contested (C) Paisley N, 1987. An Opposition Whip, 1999–2000; frontbench opposition spokesman on constitutional affairs, 2000–01, on educn, 2001–03, on women and equality, 2004–07; Shadow Sec. of State for Scotland, 2005; Shadow Minister for Justice, 2007–10. *Recreations:* theatre, music, golf, Agatha Christie Society. *Address:* House of Commons, SW1A 0AA.

**LAING, Hon. Dame Elisabeth Mary Caroline**, DBE 2014; **Hon. Mrs Justice Laing**; a Judge of the High Court, Queen's Bench Division, since 2014; *b* 19 Nov. 1956. Called to the Bar, Middle Temple, 1980, Bencher, 2013; a Recorder, 1999–2014; QC 2008; a Dep. High Court Judge, 2010–14. *Publications:* (contrib.) Halsbury's Laws; contribs to Judicial Rev. *Address:* Royal Courts of Justice, Strand, WC2A 2LL.

**LAING, Ian Michael**, CBE 2004; DL; Chairman, MEPC Milton Park Ltd, 1993–2006; *b* 24 Dec. 1946; *s* of Anthony and Ruth Laing; *m* 1973, Caroline Pender Cudlip; two *s* one *d*. *Educ:* Bedford Sch.; St Edmund Hall, Oxford (MA); London Business Sch. (MSc). Dir, English Property Corp. plc, 1972–85; Man. Dir, Lansdown Estates Gp Ltd, subseq. MEPC Milton Park Ltd, 1984–93. Non-executive Director: Oxford Radcliffe NHS Trust, 1992–99; Stanhope plc, 2006–12; Adaptimmune Therapeutics plc, 2008–16; Immunocore Ltd, 2008–. Nuffield Medical Trustee, 2004–. Governor: London Business Sch., 1996–2005; Royal Shakespeare Co., 1998–2005 and 2006–. Hon. Bencher, Inner Temple, 2004; Fellow, Green Templeton Coll., Oxford, 2013–. DL 1998, High Sheriff, 2005–06, Oxon. *Recreations:* sailing, ski-ing, opera, theatre, farming. *T:* (01865) 516826. *E:* ian@laingox.uk. *Clubs:* Boodle's; Royal Yacht Squadron; New York Yacht; Royal Norwegian Yacht; Kandahar Ski.

**LAING, James Findlay**; Under Secretary, Scottish Office Environment Department (formerly Scottish Development Department), 1988–93; *b* 7 Nov. 1933; *s* of Alexander Findlay Laing and Jessie Ross; *m* 1969, Christine Joy Canaway; one *s*. *Educ:* Nairn Academy; Edinburgh Univ. MA (Hons History). Nat. Service, Seaforth Highlanders, 1955–57. Asst Principal and Principal, Scottish Office, 1957–68; Principal, HM Treasury, 1968–71; Asst Sec., Scottish Office, 1972–79; Under Sec., Scottish Econ. Planning Dept, later Industry Dept for Scotland, 1979–88. *Recreations:* squash, chess. *Address:* 6 Barnton Park Place, Edinburgh EH4 6ET. *T:* (0131) 336 5951. *Club:* Edinburgh Sports.

**LAING, Jennifer Charlina Ellsworth**; Associate Dean, External Relations, London Business School, 2002–07; Chairman and Chief Executive Officer, North American Operations, Saatchi & Saatchi, 1997–2000; *b* 1947; *d* of late James Ellsworth Laing, FRCS, and Mary McKane (*née* Taylor); *m* John Henderson (marr. diss.). Joined Garland-Compton, 1969; Dir, Saatchi & Saatchi Garland-Compton, 1977; Dep. Chm., 1983, Jt Chm., 1987, Saatchi & Saatchi Advertising UK; Chm. and CEO, Aspect Hill Holliday (later Laing Henry Ltd), 1988, which was acquired by Saatchi & Saatchi Advertising UK, 1995; Chm., Saatchi & Saatchi Advertising UK, 1995–97. Non-executive Director: Hudson Highland Gp Inc., 2003–14 (Chm., Compensation Cttee, 2011–14); InterContinental Hotels Gp, 2005–16 (Chm., Corporate Responsibility Cttee, 2009–16); Premier Foods plc, 2012–. Former non-executive Director: Remploy; Great Ormond Street Hosp. for Children NHS Trust.

**LAING, Sir (John) Martin (Kirby)**, Kt 1997; CBE 1991; DL; Chairman, 1985–2001, non-executive Director, 2001–04, Hon. President, 2004–06, John Laing plc; non-executive Chairman, NHP plc, 1999–2005; *b* 18 Jan. 1942; *s* of Sir (William) Kirby Laing; *m* 1965, Stephanie Stearn Worsdell; one *s* one *d*. *Educ:* St Lawrence College, Ramsgate; Emmanuel College, Cambridge (MA). FRICS. Joined Laing Group 1966; Dir, John Laing, 1980. Chairman: BOTB, 1995–99; Construction Industry Employers Council, 1995–2000; Vice-Chm., British Trade Internat., 1999; Member: Major Contractors Gp, 1985 (Chm., 1991–92); CBI Council, 1986–2002; CBI Overseas Cttee, 1983–96 (Chm., 1989–96); CBI Task Force on Business and Urban Regeneration, 1987–88; Cttee for Middle East Trade, 1982–86; SE Asia Trade Adv. Group, 1985–89; UK Adv. Cttee, British American Chamber of Commerce, 1985–2002; Council, World Economic Forum, 1986–2002; NEDO Construction Industry Sector Gp, 1988–93; Business in the Community, 1986–2002 (Mem. Bd, 1995–2000); World Business Council for Sustainable Develt, 1991–2002; UK-Japan 2000 Gp, 1988–2002; British Council, 1997–; Council, BESO, 1999–2003; Corporate Finance Adv. Bd, PricewaterhouseCoopers, 2003–05; Chm., British Urban Develt, 1988–90; Dep. Chm., Building Experience Trust, 1992–95. Chairman: Americas Advrs, Trade Partners UK, 2000–03; Ecologic Malta, 2007–11; BioRem Internat., Malta, 2007–14. Member: Council, London First, 1992–2002; Valletta Alive Foundn, 2007–. Non-executive Director: Parsons Brinckerhoff Inc., USA, 2003–06; Eskmuir Properties Ltd, 2003–; Lam Investments Internat., Malta, 2010–. Member: Home Office Parole Review Cttee, 1987–88; Archbishop's Council, Church Urban Fund, 1987–94; Trilateral Commn, 1993–99. President: Construction Confedn, 1997–2000; Inst. of Export, 2001–08. Dir, City of London Sinfonia, 1988–95. Dir, Herts Groundwork Trust, 1986–91; Trustee: Nat. Energy Foundn, 1988–99; WWF Internat., 1991–97; Marine Stewardship Council, 1998–2006; Trustee Emeritus, WWF (UK), 1998– (Trustee, 1988–97; Chm., 1990–97). Adv., RP&C Internat. Ltd, 2006–07. Crown Mem., Court of Univ. of London, 1987–95; Member: Council, United World Coll. of the Atlantic, 1996–; Board of Governors, Papplewick School, Ascot, 1983–93; Governor: St Lawrence Coll., Ramsgate, 1988–95; NIESR, 1999–. Trustee, RICS Foundn, 2001–04. Jt Chm., St Paul's Cathedral Malta Restoration Appeal, 2017–. Master, Paviors' Co., 1995–96. CIEx 1987; FICE 1993; FCIOB 1995. DL Hertford, 1987. Hon. DSc: City, 1996; Birmingham, 2002; Kingston, 2004. Hon. DEng UWE, 1997. *Recreations:* gardening, music, travel.
*See also* D. E. *Laing*.

**LAING, (John) Stuart**; Master, Corpus Christi College, Cambridge, 2008–18; *b* 22 July 1948; *s* of late Dr Denys Laing and Dr Judy Laing (*née* Dods); *m* 1972, Sibella Dorman, *d* of Sir Maurice Dorman, GCMG, GCVO; one *s* two *d*. *Educ:* Rugby Sch.; Corpus Christi Coll., Cambridge (MA, MPhil). Joined HM Diplomatic Service, 1970; FCO, 1970–71; MECAS, Lebanon, 1971–72; 2nd Sec., Jedda, 1973–75; First Secretary: UK Perm. Rep. to EC, 1975–78; FCO, 1978–83; Cairo, 1983–87; FCO, 1987–89; Counsellor, Prague, 1989–92; Dep. Hd of Mission, British Embassy, Riyadh, 1992–95; Hd, Know How Fund for Central Europe, FCO, later DFID, 1995–98; High Comr to Brunei, 1998–2002; Ambassador: to Oman, 2002–05; to Kuwait, 2005–08. Pres., British Soc. for Middle Eastern Studies, 2018–; Chm., Anglo-Oman Soc., 2018. *Publications:* (with Robert Alston) Unshook Till the End of Time: a history of relations between Britain and Oman, 2012; Tippu Tip: ivory, slavery and discovery in the scramble for Africa, 2017. *Recreations:* playing music, hill-walking, desert travel.

**LAING, Sir Martin**; *see* Laing, Sir J. M. K.

**LAING, Richard George**, FCA; Chair: Miro Forestry, since 2014 (non-executive Director, since 2012); 3i Infrastructure plc, since 2016; Perpetual Income and Growth Investment Trust plc, since 2017 (non-executive Director, since 2012); *b* 24 Feb. 1954; *s* of George Denys Laing, MB BChir and Julian (Judy) Ursula Laing (*née* Dods), MB ChB; *m* 1979, Susan Pamela Mills, MA, MSc, PhD; four *s*. *Educ:* Rugby Sch.; Corpus Christi Coll., Cambridge (BA 1975; MA). FCA 1980. Asst Manager, Marks & Spencer, 1975–76; Manager, Price Waterhouse, 1976–81; Analyst, Booker Agric. Internat., 1981–84; Analyst, De la Rue Plc, 1984–86; De la Rue Brazil: Finance Dir, 1986–89; Gp Financial Controller, 1989–96; Gp Finance Dir, 1996–99; Finance Dir, 2000–04, Chief Exec., 2004–11, Advr, 2011–12, Commonwealth Develt Corp., then CDC Gp plc. Non-executive Director: Camelot, 1997–99; Pacific Rim Palm Oil, 2001–06; Aureos Capital, 2005–10; London Metal Exchange, 2011–12; Madagascar Oil plc, 2013–15; JP Morgan Emerging Markets Investment Trust plc, 2015–; Tritax Big Box, 2018–. Trustee: ODI, 2004–16; Plan Internat. UK, 2010–19; Leeds Castle Foundn, 2012–. *Recreations:* classical music, gardening, Munro bagging, and much else that involves being outside.

**LAING, Sophie Henrietta T.**; *see* Turner Laing.

**LAING, Stuart**; *see* Laing, J. S.

**LAIRD, David Logan**, OBE 2000; JP, DL; WS; FRICS; solicitor; Partner, Thorntons WS, 1985–2002; chartered surveyor; *b* 13 April 1937; *s* of William Twaddle Laird and Janet Nicolson (*née* MacDonald); *m*; two *s* one *d*. *Educ:* Bell Baxter Sch., Cupar; Edinburgh and East of Scotland Coll. of Agriculture. Chartered surveyor and land agent, 1963; Partner, Clark Oliver Dewar & Webster, SSC, 1971–85. Mem., and Chm. NE Region, NCC Scotland, now Scottish Natural Heritage, 1990– (Chm., E Area Bd, 1997–2000); Chm. Bd, Cairngorms Partnership, 1994–97. JP 1968, DL 1989, Angus. *Recreations:* stalking, gardening, shooting, fishing. *Address:* West Memus, Forfar, Angus DD8 3TY. *T:* (01307) 860251. *Club:* New (Edinburgh).

**LAIRD, Francis Joseph**; QC 2011; **His Honour Judge Laird**; a Circuit Judge, since 2015; *b* Middlesbrough, 18 March 1964; *s* of Christopher Laird and Carmel Laird (*née* Murtha); *m* 2004, (marr. diss. 2013); two *d*. *Educ:* St George's Catholic Secondary Sch., Middlesbrough; Acklam Coll., Middlesbrough; University of Newcastle upon Tyne (LLB Hons 1985); Inns of Court Sch. of Law (Bar Finals 1986). Called to the Bar, Gray's Inn, 1986; 3 Fountain Court Chambers, 1989–2006; St Philips Chambers, 2006–15; a Recorder, 2009–15. Vis. Fellow, Aston Univ. Law Sch., 2018–. *E:* HHJ.Francis.Laird.QC@eJudiciary.net.

**LAIRD, Lesley**; MP (Lab) Kirkcaldy and Cowdenbeath, since 2017; *b* Greenock, Nov. 1958; *d* of late John Langan; *m*; one *s*. *Educ:* James Watt Coll.; Caledonian Univ.; Napier Univ. (BA Business Mgt and Human Resources 2002); Inst. of Leadership and Mgt (Exec. Coaching and Leadership Mentoring 2011). Sen. Talent Manager, Royal Bank of Scotland, 2009–12; Man. Dir, Lesley Laird & Associates Ltd, 2012–14. Mem. (Lab), Fife Council, 2012–18. Contested (Lab) Kirkcaldy and Cowdenbeath, 2015. Shadow Sec. of State for Scotland, 2017–. Dep. Leader, Scottish Labour Party, 2018–. *Address:* House of Commons, SW1A 0AA.

**LAIT, Jacqui**; *b* 16 Dec. 1947; *d* of Graham Harkness Lait and Margaret Stewart (*née* Knight); *m* 1974, Peter Jones, CBE. *Educ:* Paisley Grammar Sch.; Univ. of Strathclyde. Public relations posts: jute trade, Dundee; Visnews, internat. TV news agency; with Govt Inf. Service, in Scottish Office, Privy Council Office and Dept of Employment, 1974–80; Parly Advr, Chemical Inds Assoc., 1980–84; Parly Consultancy, 1984–92. Contested (C): Strathclyde W, Euro-election, 1984; Tyne Bridge, Dec. 1985. MP (C) Hastings and Rye, 1992–97; contested (C) same seat, 1997; MP (C) Beckenham, Nov. 1997–2010. An Asst Govt Whip, 1996–97; Opposition Whip, 1999–2000; Opposition spokesman on pensions, 2000–01; Shadow Scottish Sec., 2001–03; Shadow Minister for Home, Constitutional and Legal Affairs, 2003–05, for London, 2005–07, for Planning, 2007–10. Chm., City and E London FHSA, 1988–91. Chm., British Section, European Union of Women, 1990–92; Vice-Chm., Cons. Women's Nat. Cttee, 1990–92. Chairman: of Patrons, Rye Studio Sch., 2012–; Rye Academy Trust, 2015–16; Mem. Bd, Five Villages Housing Assoc., 2012–. *Recreations:* walking, theatre, food and wine.

**LAITHWAITE, Anthony Hugh Gordon**, CBE 2019; Founder, Bordeaux Direct, subsequently Laithwaite's Wine, 1969; Chairman, Direct Wines Ltd, since 1972; *b* 22 Dec. 1945; *s* of late Eric and Winneth Laithwaite; *m* 1975, Barbara Anne Hynds; three *s*. *Educ:* Windsor Boys' Grammar Sch.; Bishop Vesey's Grammar Sch., Sutton Coldfield; Univ. of Durham (BA Hons (Geog.) 1968). Founded first shop, Windsor, 1969; Co-founder, Sunday Times Wine Club, 1973. FRGS 1999. Freeman, City of London, 2017; Liveryman, Distillers' Co., 2017. Hon. DCL Durham, 2014. Chevalier, Ordre Nat. du Mérite Agricole (France), 2011. *Publications:* Laithwaite's Great Wine Trek, 1984. *Recreation:* wine. *Address:* The Old Brewery House, 86 New Street, Henley-on-Thames, Oxon RG9 2BT. *T:* (01491) 844780. *E:* tony.laithwaite@directwines.com. *Clubs:* Royal Automobile; Phyllis Court (Henley-on-Thames).

**LAITTAN, James S.**; *see* Smith-Laittan.

**LAITY, Mark Franklyn**; Director Communications, Supreme Headquarters Allied Powers Europe, since 2017; *b* 18 Dec. 1955; *s* of Frank and Pamela Laity. *Educ:* Redruth Co. Grammar Sch.; Univ. of York (BA Hons Hist./Politics; MA Southern African Studies). Reporter, Western Mail, 1978–81; BBC Radio: Producer: Radio Wales, 1981–82; Today prog., 1982–86; Sen. Producer, Analysis prog., 1986–88; Dep. Ed., The World This Weekend, 1988–89; Defence Corresp., BBC, 1989–2000; Dep. Spokesman and Personal Advr, subseq. Special Advr to NATO Sec.-Gen., 2000–03; Special Advr, later Chief of Public Inf., SACEUR, 2004–06; NATO spokesman in Kabul, Afghanistan, 2006–07, 2008; Advr to NATO Sen. Civilian Rep., 2010; Chief Strategic Communications, SHAPE, 2007–17. Vis. Fellow, King's Centre for Strategic Comms, KCL, 2016–. Hon. Fellow, Strategy and Security Inst., Univ. of Exeter, 2015. Meritorious Service Medal, NATO, 2007. *Publications:* Preventing War in Macedonia: pre-emptive diplomacy for the 21st century, 2008; (contrib.) Strategy in NATO: preparing for an imperfect world, 2014. *Recreation:* sailing. *Address:* Rue Fetis 17, Bte C1, Mons 7000, Belgium. *Clubs:* Royal Air Force; Thames Sailing.

**LAKE, Ben Morgan**; MP (Plaid Cymru) Ceredigion, since 2017; *b* Glangwili, 22 Jan. 1993; *s* of Emyr Wyn Morgan Lake and Elizabeth Joy Lake. *Educ:* Ysgol Gyfun Llambed; Trinity Coll., Oxford (BA Hist. and Politics 2014; MSt Mod. British and Eur. Hist. 2015). Mem., Welsh Affairs Cttee, H of C, 2017–. *Recreations:* football, Rugby, cricket. *Address:* (office) Bryndulais, 67 Bridge Street, Lampeter, Ceredigion SA48 7AB. *E:* ben.lake.mp@parliament.uk.

**LAKE, (Charles) Michael**, CBE 1996; Director, Royal Commonwealth Society, 2014–18 (Interim Director, 2013–14); Special Adviser, City of London, since 2018; *b* 17 May 1944; *s* of Stanley Giddy and late Beryl Giddy (*née* Heath); step *s* of late Percival Redvers Lake; *m* 1970, Christine Warner; three *d*. *Educ:* Humphry Davy Grammar Sch., Penzance; RMA, Sandhurst. FILog 1995. SCLI 1963; commnd RCT, 1965; Regtl appts, Germany, Hong Kong, NI, Oman; attached Commandant-Gen., RM, 1977–78; Directing Staff, Staff Coll., 1982–83; Comd, 1st Div. Transport Regt, 1983–86; Comdr Transport, HQ British Forces Riyadh, Gulf War, 1990–91; Regtl Col, RLC, 1992–96; retired 1997. Dir Gen., Help the

Aged, 1996–2009; Dir-Gen., English-Speaking Union of the Commonwealth, 2009–11 (Sec. Gen., Internat. Council, 2009–11); Chm., Morley Coll., 2011–12. Member: Bd, HelpAge Internat., 1996–2004; Benevolent and Strategy Cttee, RBL, 1997–2000 (External Advr, RBL, 1999); Council, Occupational Pensions Adv. Service, 1997–2001; Bd, Network Housing Assoc., 1999–2001; Bd, Cornwall Care, 2000–17; Council, Oxford Inst. of Ageing, 2001–05; Bd, CAF, 2006–09; Bd, Charity Bank, 2007–10; Bd, Orchard Care Homes, 2012–16; Lay Mem., Lord Chancellor's Adv. Cttee on Conscientious Objectors, 2002–12; Special Advr, Charities Benevolent Fund, 2010–13. Mem. Bd, Golden Charter Ltd, 2009–14. Vice-Chm., Air Ambulance Foundn, 2003–04; Chm., Internat. Longevity Centre UK, 2009–13; Trustee: Disasters Emergency Cttee, 1999–2009; Pensions Policy Inst., 2001–09; Chm., British Gas Energy Trust, 2005–10. Chm. Bd, Chelsea Arts Club Ltd, 1997–2011. Chm., Help for Heroes, 2017–. Freeman: City of London, 1995; Carmen's Co., 1995. *Recreations:* sports, avid golfer, cricketer, Rugby; Post Impressionism, Penzance and Newlyn school. *Address:* c/o Holt's Bank, Royal Bank of Scotland, Farnborough, Hants GU14 7NR. *Clubs:* MCC, Sloane (Hon. Life Mem.), Chelsea Arts (Life Mem.); Penguin International Rugby; W Cornwall Golf, North Hants Golf.

**LAKE, Sir Edward Geoffrey,** 11th Bt *cr* 1711, of Edmonton, Middlesex; *b* 17 July 1928; *y s* of Captain Sir Atwell Henry Lake, 9th Bt, CB, OBE, RN and Kathleen Marion Lake (*née* Turner); *S* brother, 2013; *m* 1965, Judith Ann, *d* of John Fox; one *s* one *d*. *Educ:* Eton. *Heir: s* Mark Winter Lake, *b* 26 Oct. 1968.

**LAKE, Maria;** *see* Fitzgerald, M.

**LAKE, Michael;** *see* Lake, C. M.

**LAKE, Robert Andrew;** health and social care consultant; Independent Chairman, Walsall Safeguarding Children Board, since 2012; *b* 14 April 1948; *s* of Rev. William Henry Lake and Ruth Lake (*née* Hammond); *m* 1975, Celia Helen Probert; one *s* two *d*. *Educ:* Hull Grammar Sch.; Univ. of Coventry (CQSW). Welfare Asst, Bolton Welfare Dept, 1968–70; various posts, Coventry Social Services Dept, 1972–80; Area Manager, 1980–82, Principal Asst, 1982–84, Newcastle upon Tyne Social Services; Asst Dir, 1984–91, Dir, 1991–96, Humberside Social Services Dept; Dir of Social Services, Staffs CC, 1996–2005; Chm., Staffordshire Ambulance Service, 2005–07; Dir of Social Care, NHS Information Centre, 2007–11. Non-exec. Dir (Care and Support), Midland Heart Housing Assoc., 2008–. FRSocMed 2006. Vis. Fellow, Keele Univ., 1997. *Recreations:* music, D-I-Y, the family. *E:* ralake1@btinternet.com.

**LAKE, Very Rev. Stephen David;** Dean of Gloucester, since 2011; *b* 17 Dec. 1963; *s* of David Lake and late Heather Lake; *m* 1986, Carol Waltham; two *s* one *d*. *Educ:* Chichester Theol Coll. (BTh Southampton Univ.); King's Coll. London (MA 2013). Ordained deacon, 1988, priest, 1989; Asst Curate, Sherborne Abbey, 1988–92; Priest-in-charge, 1992–96, Vicar, 1996–2001, St Aldhelm, Branksome; Rural Dean, Poole, 2000–01; Canon Res. and Sub-Dean, St Albans Cathedral, 2001–11; Chaplain to Lord Lieut of Glos, 2012–. Proctor in Convocation, 2003–10. A Church Comr, 2016–. Chm., Gloucester City Regeneration Adv. Bd, 2013–; Member: Glos Dio. Academies Trust, 2014–16; Nat. Safeguarding Steering Gp, 2016–. Trustee, Scout Assoc., 2010–15; Chm., Glos Co. Scout Exec., 2015–. Hon. Fellow, Univ. of Glos, 2015. Queen's Scout, 1982; Scout Silver Acorn Award, 2019. *Publications:* Using Common Worship: marriage, 2000; Confirmation Prayer Book, 2002; Let the Children Come to Communion, 2006; Prayer Book for Lay People, 2008; Welcoming Marriage, 2009; Rethinking Confirmation, 2011. *Recreations:* hill-walking, Tottenham Hotspur FC. *Address:* The Deanery, 1 Miller's Green, Gloucester GL1 2BP. *T:* (01452) 524167.

**LAKE-TACK, Dame Louise (Agnetha),** GCMG 2007; Governor-General, Antigua and Barbuda, 2007–14; *b* Long Lane Estate, Antigua, 26 July 1944; *m* (decd); two *c*. *Educ:* Antigua Girls' High Sch. Nurse, Charing Cross Hosp., Nat. Heart Hosp. and Harley Street Clinic, London. JP 1995. *Address:* c/o Governor-General's Residence, St John's, Antigua, West Indies.

**LAKHA, (Gulam) Abbas;** QC 2003; *b* 2 Oct. 1962; *s* of Hassan Lakha and Leila (*née* Alibhai); *m* 1992, Shamira Fazal; one *s* two *d*. *Educ:* Stowe Sch.; Leeds Poly. (BA Hons Law). Called to the Bar, Inner Temple, 1984, Bencher, 2007; *ad eundem* Mem., Gray's Inn, 2002; in practice as barrister, specialising in all areas of serious and complex litigation, 1984–. Inspector, DTI, 1997–99. Mem., N London Bar Mess Cttee, 1998–. *Recreations:* travel, fast cars, modern architecture, work. *Address:* 9 Bedford Row, WC1R 4AZ. *T:* (020) 7489 2727, *Fax:* (020) 7489 2828. *E:* abbaslakha@9bedfordrow.co.uk.

**LAKHANI, Kamlesh, (Mrs N. Lakhani);** *see* Bahl, K.

**LAKHANI, Mayur Keshavji,** CBE 2007; FRCP, FRCPE, FRCGP, SFFMLM; Principal in General Practice, Highgate Medical Centre, Sileby, Loughborough, since 1991; President, Royal College of General Practitioners, 2017–19; *b* 20 April 1960; *s* of Keshavji Vithaldas. Lakhani and Shantaben Keshavji Lakhani; *m* 1988, Mayuri Jobanputra; one *s* two *d*. *Educ:* Univ. of Dundee (MB ChB 1983). DFFP 1997; FRCGP 1998; FRCPE 2002; FRCP 2006; SFFMLM. Vis. Prof., Dept of Health Scis, Leicester Univ. Sch. of Medicine, 2006–. Chm., W Leics CCG. Chairman: RCGP, 2004–07; Nat. Council for Palliative Care, 2008–15; Dying Matters Coalition. *Publications:* (ed jtly) Evidence Based Audit in General Practice, 1998; (ed) A Celebration of General Practice, 2003; (ed jtly) Recent Advances in Primary Care, 2005; various articles on quality in health care and health policy. *Recreation:* tennis (Mem., Rothley Ivanhoe Tennis Club). *Address:* Highgate Medical Centre, 5 Storer Close, Sileby LE12 7UD. *E:* mklakhani@aol.com.

**LAKIN, His Honour Peter Maurice;** a Circuit Judge, 1995–2014; Resident Judge, Manchester Crown Court, 2006–14; *b* 21 Oct. 1949; *s* of late Ronald Maurice Lakin and of Dorothy Kathleen Lakin (*née* Cowlishaw); *m* 1971, Jacqueline Jubb; one *s* one *d*. *Educ:* King Henry VIII Sch., Coventry; Manchester Univ. (LLB). Articled Clerk, Conn Goldberg, solicitors, Manchester, 1971–74; Goldberg Blackburn, solicitors, Manchester (later Pannone & Partners): Asst Solicitor, 1974–76; Partner i/c of Corporate Defence and Forensic Unit, 1976–95; Asst Recorder, 1989–93; Recorder, 1993–95. Hon. Sec., Manchester and Dist Medico-Legal Soc., 1989–95. *Recreations:* fell-walking, opera, gardening, local history, grandchildren.

**LAKIN, Sir Richard Anthony,** 5th Bt *cr* 1909, of The Cliff, Borough of Warwick; *b* 26 Nov. 1968; *s* of Sir Michael Lakin, 4th Bt and of Felicity Ann Lakin (*née* Murphy); *S* father, 2014; *m* 1997, Lara Maryanne Rose (marr. diss. 2009); one *s* one *d*. *Educ:* Treverton Coll., Natal, SA. *Heir: s* Henry Anthony Lakin, *b* 22 June 1999. *Address:* c/o Lowesmoor Farm, Cherington, Tetbury, Glos GL8 8SP.

**LALANNE, Bernard Michel L.;** *see* Loustau-Lalanne.

**LALL, Vikram,** CBE 2005; Director, Heriot Services, since 1996; *b* 5 Dec. 1946; *s* of late Jag Mohan Lall and Dr Shuki Lall; *m* 1981, Carol Anne Ask; one *s* one *d*. *Educ:* Doon Sch., Dehra Dun; St Stephen's Coll., Delhi (BA Hons Econs 1966). CA 1972. Executive Director: Noble Grossart Ltd, 1975–77; Vikram Lall & Co. Ltd, 1977–82; McNeill Pearson Ltd, 1982–85; Heriot & Co. Ltd, 1985–87; Bell Lawrie White & Co., 1987–2003; Brewin Dolphin Hldgs plc, 1989–2003 (non-exec. Dir, 2003–08). Non-executive Director: Isis Property Trust, 2003–13; Crown Place VCT, 2006–12; Ramco Hldgs Ltd, 2005–13; Corsie Gp plc, 2006–08; Elephant Capital plc, 2010– (Chm., 2011–16); F&C Real Estate Investments Ltd, 2013– (Chm., 2015–); non-exec. Chm., Ryden LLP, 2005–09. Chm., Scottish Industrial Devel Adv. Bd, 2002–07 (Mem., 2000–07). Member: Bd, Royal Lyceum Th. Co., 2002–07; Governing Body, Queen Margaret UC, Edinburgh, 2003–09; Finance and Develt (formerly Finance and Investments) Cttee, RCSE, 2005–18. *Recreations:* golf, travel, mind exercise. *Address:* Newmains House, Drem, East Lothian EH39 5BL. *T:* 07739 800223. *E:* vikramlall@macace.net. *Club:* Luffness New Golf.

**LALLA-MAHARAJH, Julia,** OBE 2016; Founder and Chief Executive Officer, Orchid Project, since 2010; *b* London, 25 Feb. 1970. *Educ:* James Allen's Girls' Sch.; Thames Valley Univ. (BA Hons). Dir of Transport, London First, 1995–99 and 2001–06; Communications Manager, Bass plc, 2000–01; Volunteer: VSO Cambodia, 2007; VSO Ethiopia, 2008. Winner, Davos Debates, 2010. *Address:* Orchid Project, The Foundry, 17–19 Oval Way, SE11 5RR. *E:* julia@orchidproject.org.

**LALONDE, Hon. Marc;** PC (Can.) 1972; OC 1989; QC 1971; international commercial and investment arbitrator, since 1986; *b* 26 July 1929; *s* of late J. Albert Lalonde and Nora (*née* St Aubin); *m* 1955, Claire Tétreau; two *s* two *d*. *Educ:* St Laurent Coll., Montreal (BA 1950); Univ. of Montreal (LLL 1954; MA Law 1955); Oxford Univ. (Econ. and Pol Science; MA 1957); Ottawa Univ. (Dip. of Superior Studies in Law, 1960). Prof. of Commercial Law and Econs, Univ. of Montreal, 1957–59; Special Asst to Minister of Justice, Ottawa, 1959–60; Partner, Gelinas, Bourque Lalonde & Benoit, Montreal, 1960–68; Lectr in Admin. Law for Doctorate Students, Univ. of Ottawa and Univ. of Montreal, 1961–62; Policy Advisor to Prime Minister, 1967; Principal Sec. to Prime Minister, 1968–72; MP (L) Montreal-Outremont, 1972–84; Minister of National Health and Welfare, 1972–77; Minister of State for Federal-Provincial Relations, 1977–78; Minister resp. for Status of Women, 1975–78; Minister of Justice and Attorney-Gen., 1978–79; Minister of Energy, Mines and Resources, 1980–82; Minister of Finance, 1982–84. Law Partner, 1984–2003, Sen. Counsel, 2003–06, Stikeman Elliott, Montreal. *Ad hoc* Judge, Internat. Court of Justice, 1985–. Counsel before several Royal Commns inc. Royal Commn on Great Lakes Shipping and Royal Commn on Pilotage. Mem., Cttee on Broadcasting, 1964; Dir, Canadian Citizenship Council, 1960–65; Member, Bd of Directors: Inst. of Public Law, Univ. of Montréal, 1960–64; Citibank Canada, 1985–2011; O&Y Properties, 1993–2005; Sherritt Power, subseq. Sherritt International, Inc., 1998–2013; Oxbow Equities Corp., 2000–07. Dr *hc:* Limburg, Maastricht, 1992; Western Ontario, 1996. Dana Award, Amer. Public Health Assoc., 1978. *Publications:* The Changing Role of the Prime Minister's Office, 1971; New Perspectives on the Health of Canadians (working document), 1974; contrib. articles on internat. arbitration to professional pubns. *Recreations:* ski-ing, jogging, sailing, reading.

**LALUMIÈRE, Catherine;** French politician; President: Maison de l'Europe, Paris, since 2003 (President, Fédération Français des Maisons de l'Europe, 2008–17); European Association of Schools of Political Studies, Council of Europe, since 2008; *b* Rennes, 3 Aug. 1935. Dr in Public Law; degree in Pol Scis and History of Law. Asst, Univ. of Bordeaux I, and Bordeaux Inst. of Pol Studies, 1960–71; Sen. Lectr, Univ. of Paris I, 1971–81. Mem., National Assembly for Gironde, 1981, and 1986–89: Vice-Pres., Cttee of For. Affairs; Vice-Pres., Delegn to EC. Sec. of State i/c Public Service, 1981; Minister of Consumer Affairs, 1981–84; Sec. of State, resp. for Eur. Affairs, Min. of For. Affairs, 1984–86; Mem., Parly Assembly, Council of Europe, 1987–89; Sec. Gen., Council of Europe, 1989–94; Mem., 1994–2004, a Vice-Pres., 2001–04, Eur. Parlt; Pres., Eur. Radical Alliance Gp, 1994–2004. Mem., Parti Radical de Gauche (Vice Pres., 1994); Vice-President: Eur. Movement, France; Eur. Movement Internat.; Pres., Relais-Culture Europe. Regl Councillor, Ile de France, 1998–2004. *Recreation:* walking. *Address:* Maison de l'Europe de Paris, 29 avenue de Villiers, 75017 Paris, France.

**LALVANI, Prof. Ajit,** DM; FRCP, FMedSci; Professor of Infectious Diseases and Director, Tuberculosis Research Centre, National Heart and Lung Institute, since 2007, and Director, NIHR Health Protection Research Unit in Respiratory Infections, since 2014, Imperial College London; Hon. Consultant Physician, St Mary's Hospital, Imperial College Healthcare NHS Trust, since 2007; *b* New Delhi, 1 Dec. 1963; *s* of Dr Kartar Lalvani and Dr Mira Lalvani; *m* 2002, Maria-Jesus Ordoñana San Vicente. *Educ:* University Coll. Sch., London; St Peter's Coll., Oxford (BA Physiol Scis 1986; MA 1991); Royal Free Hosp. Sch. of Medicine, Univ. of London (MB BS Dist. 1989); Balliol Coll., Oxford (DM 1999). FRCP 2006; FRSB (FSB 2011); FMedSci 2012. SHO, Royal Brompton Hosp., London and Addenbrooke's Hosp., Cambridge, 1990–91; Specialist Registrar, Universitaetsspital, Basel and Churchill Hosp., Oxford, 1992–93; University of Oxford: MRC Clin. Res. Fellow, Weatherall Inst. Molecular Medicine and Sen. Res. Associate, Balliol Coll., 1993–96; Clin. Lectr in Gen. Medicine and Infectious Diseases, Nuffield Dept of Clin. Medicine, John Radcliffe Hosp., 1997–2001; Sherrington Lectr in Medicine, Magdalen Coll., 1999–2005; Wellcome Trust Sen. Res. Fellow in Clin. Sci. and Hon. Consultant Physician in Infectious Diseases and Gen. Medicine, Nuffield Dept of Clin. Medicine, John Radcliffe Hosp., 2001–06; Wellcome Trust Sen. Res. Fellow in Clin. Sci., Imperial Coll. London, 2007–13. Vis. Prof. of Medicine, Nuffield Dept of Medicine, Univ. of Oxford, 2012–. Sen. Investigator, NIHR, 2009–. Snell Meml Lectr, British Thoracic Soc., 2008. Trustee, Sci. Mus. Gp, 2019–. Mem., Academic Medicine Cttee, RCP, 2012–. Mem., Assoc. of Physicians, 2000. FRSocMed 2010. Chair, Bromley-by-Bow Centre, 2014–. Gov., Internat. Students House, 2017–. Scientific Prize, Internat. Union against Tuberculosis and Lung Disease, 2005; Weber-Parkes Medal, RCP, 2008. *Publications:* contrib. res. articles, reviews, editls and book chapters on infectious diseases (tuberculosis, HIV, malaria, influenza), immunol., epidemiol. and public health. *Recreations:* gardening, philosophy, walking, cycling, cinema, architecture. *Address:* Tuberculosis Research Centre, National Heart and Lung Institute, Imperial College London, St Mary's Campus, Norfolk Place, W2 1PG. *E:* a.lalvani@imperial.ac.uk.

**LAM, Martin Philip;** *b* 10 March 1920; *m* 1953, Lisa Lorenz (*d* 2008); one *s* one *d*. *Educ:* University College Sch.; Gonville and Caius Coll., Cambridge (Scholar). Served War of 1939–45, Royal Signals and Special Ops Mediterranean. Asst Principal, Board of Trade, 1947; Nuffield Fellowship (Latin America), 1952–53; Asst Sec., 1960; Counsellor, UK Delegn to OECD, 1963–65, Advr, Commercial Policy, 1970–74, Leader UNCTAD Delegn, 1972; Under-Sec. (Computer Systems and Electronics), DoI, 1974–78; Associate of BIS Mackintosh, and of General Technology Systems, 1979–90; on contract to Directorate-Gen. XIII, European Commn, 1986–88; consultant: Scaneurope, 1989–90; KCL, 1991–92. *Publications:* (with Shimizu Kaoru) Kanji from the Start, 1995; contrib. Jl of World Trade, Knowledge Engrg Review. *Address:* 44 York Lodge, Pegasus Court, Park Lane, Tilehurst, Reading RG31 5DB.

**LAMB,** family name of **Baron Rochester**.

**LAMB, Sir Albert Thomas, (Sir Archie),** KBE 1979 (MBE 1953); CMG 1974; DFC 1945; HM Diplomatic Service, retired; *b* 23 Oct. 1921; *s* of R. S. Lamb and Violet Lamb (*née* Haynes); *m* 1944, Christina Betty Wilkinson; one *s* two *d*. *Educ:* Swansea Grammar Sch. Served RAF 1941–46. FO 1938–41; Embassy, Rome, 1947–50; Consulate-General,

Genoa, 1950; Embassy, Bucharest, 1950–53; FO 1953–55; Middle East Centre for Arabic Studies, 1955–57; Political Residency, Bahrain, 1957–61; FO 1961–65; Embassy, Kuwait, 1965; Political Agent in Abu Dhabi, 1965–68; Inspector, 1968–70, Sen. Inspector, 1970–73, Asst Under-Sec. of State and Chief Inspector, FCO, 1973–74; Ambassador to Kuwait, 1974–77; Ambassador to Norway, 1978–80. Mem., BNOC, 1981–82; Dir, Britoil plc, 1982–88; Member Board: British Shipbuilders, 1985–87; Nat. Bank of Kuwait (Internat.), 1994–2008; Sen. Associate, Conant and Associates Ltd, Washington DC, 1985–93; Adviser, Michael Montagu and Co. Ltd, 1986–88. Clerk to Parish Councils of Zeals and Stourton with Gasper, 1991–97. Hon. Fellow: Swansea Inst. of Higher Educn, 2004; Univ. of Wales Swansea, 2005. *Publications*: A Long Way from Swansea, 2003; Abu Dhabi 1965–1968, 2003; The Last Voyage of SS Oronsay, 2004; The World Moves On, 2015. *Club*: Royal Air Force.
See also R. D. Lamb.

**LAMB, (Emma) Harriet**, CBE 2006; Chief Executive Officer, Ashden, since 2019; *b* 3 June 1961; *d* of late Gilbert and Sarah Lamb; partner, Steve Percy; one *s* one *d*. *Educ*: Trinity Hall, Cambridge (BA Social and Pol Sci. 1982); Inst. of Develt Studies Univ. of Sussex (MPhil Develt Studies 1986). Volunteer, village co-operatives, India, 1982–84; researcher, Northern Reg. Low Pay Unit, 1987–90; Co-ordinator, NE Refugee Service, 1990–92; Campaigns Co-ordinator, World Develt Movt, 1992–99; Interim Dir/Banana Co-ordinator, Fairtrade Labelling Orgns Internat., Germany, 1999–2001; Exec. Dir, Fairtrade Foundn, 2001–12; Chief Executive Officer: Fairtrade Internat., 2012–15; Internat. Alert, 2015–19. *Publications*: Working for Big Mac, 1987; Fighting the Banana Wars and Other Fairtrade Battles: how we took on the corporate giants to change the world, 2008; (contrib.) The Fair Trade Revolution, 2011. *Recreations*: cycling slowly, gardening badly, chatting loudly, playing with my kids, walking Northumbrian hills, swimming. *Address*: Ashden, The Peak, 5 Wilton Road, SW1V 1AP.

**LAMB, Air Vice-Marshal George Colin**, CB 1977; CBE 1966; AFC 1947; Chairman, Yonex (UK) Ltd, 1995–97 (Managing Director, 1990–95); *b* 23 July 1923; *s* of late George and Bessie Lamb, Hornby, Lancaster; *m* 1st, 1945, Nancy Mary Godsmark; two *s*; 2nd, 1981, Mrs Maureen Margaret Mepham (*d* 2015). *Educ*: Lancaster Royal Grammar School. War of 1939–45: commissioned, RAF, 1942; flying duties, 1942–53; Staff Coll., 1953; Air Ministry, special duties, 1954–58; OC No 87 Sqdn, 1958–61; Dir Admin. Plans, MoD, 1961–64; Asst Comdt, RAF Coll., 1964–65; Dep. Comdr, Air Forces Borneo, 1965–66; Fighter Command, 1966; MoD (Dep. Command Structure Project Officer), 1967; HQ, Strike Command, 1967–69; OC, RAF Lyneham, 1969–71; RCDS, 1971–72; Dir of Control (Operations), NATS, 1972–74; Comdr, Southern Maritime Air Region, RAF Mount Batten, 1974–75; C of S, No 18 Gp Strike Comd, RAF, 1975–78. RAF Vice-Pres., Combined Cadet Forces Assoc., 1978–94. Chief Exec., Badminton Assoc. of England, 1978–89; Gen. Sec., London Inst. of Sports Medicine, 1989–90. Consultant, Television, Sport and Leisure Ltd, 1989–90. Chairman: Lilleshall Nat. Sports Centre, 1984–2005; British Internat. Sports Develt Aid Trust, 1995–2005; Member: Sports Council, 1983–88 (Mem., Drug Abuse Adv. Gp, 1988–92); Sports Cttee, Prince's Trust, 1985–88; British Internat. Sports Cttee, 1989–2005; Privilege Mem. of RFU, 1985– (Mem., RFU Cttee, 1973–85). Dir (non-exec.), Castle Care-Tech. Security, 1993–2005. President: St George's Day Club, 1994–2012; Assoc. of Lancastrians in London, 1999. Vice-Pres., British Berlin Airlift Assoc., 1998–2009. Internat. Rugby referee, 1966–71. FCMI. *Publications*: Touchdown (autobiog.), 2015. *Recreations*: Rugby football, cricket (former Pres., Adastrian Cricket Club), gardening, walking. *Address*: Hambledon, 17 Meadway, Berkhamsted HP4 2PN. *T*: (01442) 862583. *Club*: Royal Air Force.

**LAMB, Lt-Gen. Sir Graeme (Cameron Maxwell)**, KBE 2009 (OBE 1991; MBE 1988); CMG 2003; DSO 2004; Commander, Field Army, 2007–09; *b* 21 Oct. 1953. *Educ*: Rannoch Sch.; Royal Mil. Acad. Sandhurst. Commnd Queen's Own Highlanders, 1973; Comdr, 81 Army Youth Team, Inverness, 1975–77; Northern Ireland (despatches, 1981); Staff Coll., Camberley, 1985; Comdr, B Co., 1st Bn, 1988–90; jsdc, 1989–90; Comdr, 1st Bn, 1991–93; Mil. Ops, MoD, 1993–94; HCSC, 1996; Comdr, 5th Airborne Bde, 1996–97; rcds, 1998; Asst Comdt (Land), JSCSC, 1999–2001; MoD, 2001–03; GOC 3rd (UK) Div., 2003–05; Dir Gen., Trng Support, MoD, 2005–06; Dep. Comdg Gen., Multinat. Force, Iraq, 2006–07. Special Advr to Gen. McChrystal, Comdr ISAF, 2009–10; consultant in defence and security, 2009–10. Strategic Partner, C5 Capital, 2013–. Chm., Army Snowboarding Assoc., 2001–09. QCVS 1994. Officer, Legion of Merit (USA), 2009.

**LAMB, Harriet;** see Lamb, E. H.

**LAMB, Juliet;** see Warkentin, J.

**LAMB, Maria-Jane Carmel;** Her Honour Judge Lamb; a Circuit Judge, since 2016; *b* London, 27 Nov. 1960; *d* of Dr Stephen Lamb and Laura Teresa Lamb; *m* 1991, William Tudhope; two *d* (one *s* decd). *Educ*: Lady Eleanor Holles Sch., Hampton; Robinson Coll., Cambridge (MA Hons Law). Called to the Bar, Gray's Inn, 1984; in practice as a barrister, specialising in criminal law, Western Circuit, 1984–2016; a Recorder, 2005–16. *Address*: c/o Oxford Crown Court, St Aldate's, Oxford OX1 1TL. *T*: (01865) 264200. *E*: HHJ.Maria.Lamb@ejudiciary.net.

**LAMB, Martin James;** Chairman: Evoqua Water Technologies, since 2014; Rotork plc, since 2015; *b* 7 Jan. 1960; *s* of Dr Trevor Lamb and Shirley Lamb; *m* 1983, Jayne Louise Bodenham; four *d*. *Educ*: Bradford Grammar Sch.; Solihull Sixth Form Coll.; Imperial Coll., London (BSc Mech. Eng. 1982); Cranfield Business Sch. (MBA 1990). Grad. Trainee, IMI Cornelius Inc., USA, 1982–83; Project Engr, IMI Air Conditioning, UK, 1983–85; R&D Manager, Coldflow Ltd, 1985–87; Mktg Dir, 1987–91, Man. Dir, 1991–96, IMI Cornelius (UK) Ltd; Exec. Dir, 1996–2000, Chief Exec., 2001–13, IMI plc. Non-executive Director: Spectris plc, 1999–2006; Mercia Technologies plc, 2014–17; Sen. Ind. Dir, Severn Trent plc, 2008–16. Trustee, City Technol. Coll., Birmingham, 1997–2008. *Recreations*: tennis, golf.

**LAMB, Prof. Michael Ernest**, PhD; Professor of Psychology, University of Cambridge, 2004–19, now Emeritus; Fellow, Sidney Sussex College, Cambridge, 2009–19, now Emeritus; *b* Lusaka, N Rhodesia, 22 Oct. 1953; *s* of Frank Lamb and Michelle Lamb (née de Lestang); *m* 2005, Hilary S. Clark; four step *d*, and three *s* one *d* from previous marriage. *Educ*: Univ. of Natal, S Africa (BA Psychol. and Econs); Johns Hopkins Univ. (MA Psychol.); Yale Univ. (MS, MPhil; PhD 1976). Assistant Professor of Psychology: Univ. of Wisconsin, 1976–78; Univ. of Michigan, 1978–80; Prof. of Psychol., Psychiatry and Pediatrics, Univ. of Utah, 1980–87 (Dist. Res. Award, 1986); Sen. Scientist and Section Chief, Nat. Inst. of Child Health and Human Develt, USA, 1987–2004. Ed., Psychol. Public Policy and Law, 2013–. Mem. Panel, Child Abuse Inquiry, Scotland, 2015–16. Mem., ESRC, 2006–11. Mem., REF 2014 sub-panel 4, 2011–15. Pres., Div. 7 (Develtl Psychol.), Amer. Psychol Assoc., 2017–18. Hon. PhD Goteborg, 1995; Hon. DCL UEA, 2006; Hon. DSc: Abertay, 2015; Montreal, 2019. Cattell Award for Lifetime Contribn to Psychol., Assoc. for Psychol. Sci., 2004; Dist. Contribns Award, American Psychology-Law Soc., 2013; Tom Williamson Award, Internat. Investigative Interviewing Res. Gp, 2013; Stanley Hall Award, 2014, Dist. Scientific Award for Applications of Psychol. and Award for Dist. Contribns to Sci. in the Public Interest, 2015, Amer. Psychol Assoc. *Publications*: (ed) The Role of the Father in Child Development, 1976, trans. Japanese 1981, 5th edn 2010; (ed) Social and Personality Development, 1978; (ed jtly) Social Interaction Analysis, 1979; (ed jtly) Developmental Science: an advanced textbook, 1981, 7th edn 2015; (jtly) Child Psychology Today, 1982, 2nd edn 1986; (ed jtly) Advances in Developmental Psychology, vol. 1, 1981, vol. 2, 1982, vol. 3, 1984, vol. 4, 1986; (ed jtly) Infant Social Cognition, 1982; (jtly) Development in Infancy: an introduction, 1982, 4th edn 2002; (jtly) Socialization and Personality Development, 1982; (ed) Nontraditional Families, 1982, trans. Japanese 1998; (jtly) Infant-Mother Attachment, 1985; (ed) The Father's Role: applied perspectives, 1986; (ed jtly) Adolescent Fatherhood, 1986; (ed) The Father's Role: cross-cultural perspectives, 1987; (ed jtly) Adolescent Problem Behaviours, 1994; (ed jtly) Images of Childhood, 1996; (jtly) Investigative Interviews of Children, 1998; (ed) Parenting and Child Development in Nontraditional Families, 1999; (ed jtly) Hunter-gatherer Childhoods, 2005; (ed jtly) Child Sexual Abuse, 2007; (jtly) Tell Me What Happened: structured investigative interviews of child victims and witnesses, 2008, 2nd edn 2018; (ed jtly) Children's Testimony, 2011; (ed jtly) Children and Cross-Examination: time to change the rules?, 2012; (ed jtly) Fathers in Cultural Context, 2013; (ed jtly) Handbook of Child Psychology and Development Science, 7th edn, vol. 3: social, emotional, and personality development, 2015. *Recreations*: travel, family, performing arts, literature. *Address*: Department of Psychology, Free School Lane, University of Cambridge, Cambridge CB2 3RQ. *E*: mel37@cam.ac.uk.

**LAMB, Rt Hon. Sir Norman (Peter)**, Kt 2019; PC 2014; MP (Lib Dem) North Norfolk, since 2001; *b* 16 Sept. 1957; *s* of late Hubert Horace Lamb and of Beatrice Moira Lamb; *m* 1984, Mary Elizabeth Green; two *s*. *Educ*: Wymondham Coll., Norfolk; Leicester Univ. (LLB). Sen. Asst Solicitor, Norwich CC, 1984–86; Solicitor, 1986–87, Partner, 1987–2001, Steele & Co. Lib Dem spokesman for health, 2007–10; an Asst Govt Whip, and Chief Parly and Political Advr to the Dep. Prime Minister, 2010–12; Parly Under-Sec. of State (Minister for Employment Relns, Consumer and Postal Affairs), BIS, 2012; Minister of State, DoH, 2012–15. Chm., Select Cttee on Sci. and Technol., 2017–. Vis. Fellow, Nuffield Coll., Oxford, 2015–. *Publications*: Remedies in the Employment Tribunal, 1998. *Recreations*: football, walking. *Address*: House of Commons, SW1A 0AA. *T*: (020) 7219 0542; (office) Unit 4, The Garden Centre, Nursery Drive, Norwich Road, North Walsham, Norfolk NR28 0DR.

**LAMB, Robin David;** HM Diplomatic Service, retired; Director General, Libyan British Business Council, since 2009; Executive Director, Egyptian British Business Council, since 2009; *b* 25 Nov. 1948; *s* of Sir Albert Thomas Lamb, *qv*; *m* 1977, Susan Jane Moxon; two *s* one *d*. *Educ*: St John's, Leatherhead; Brasenose Coll., Oxford (MA Oriental Studies). Mgt asst, Abu Dhabi Cement Mktg Assoc., 1966–67; Mgt Develt Prog., Barclays Bank, 1970–71; joined FCO, 1971: lang. trng, MECAS, 1974–75; Res. Officer, FCO, 1975–79; Second Sec., Jedda, 1979–82; Principal Res. Officer, FCO, 1982–85; First Secretary: Riyadh, 1985–87; FCO, 1988–93; Hd, Pol Section, Cairo, 1993–96; FCO, 1996–99; British Trade Internat., 1999–2001; Counsellor and Dep. Hd of Mission, Kuwait, 2001–03; Ambassador, Bahrain, 2003–06; Consul-Gen., Basra, April–Aug. 2006. Hd, Business Develt, Arab British Chamber of Commerce, 2007–09. Dir, Egyptian British Chamber of Commerce, 2016–. Mem., Ahtisaari Leadership Fund Wkg Gp, 2013–. Dir, BESO, 1999–2001. Mem. Council, RSAA, 2017–. Non-exec. Dir, Middle East Assoc., 2018–. Trustee, British Univ. in Egypt, 2014–. Fellow, British Soc. for ME Studies, 1992. Bahrain Medal (1st cl.) (Bahrain), 2006; Iraq Reconstruction Service Medal, 2007. *Recreations*: family, reading. *E*: robinebbc@gmail.com.

**LAMB, Shona Hunter;** see Dunn, S. H.

**LAMB, Sophie Jane;** QC 2018; Partner, and Co-Chair, International Arbitration, Latham & Watkins LLP, since 2016; *b* London, 14 Aug. 1974; *m* 2004, Douglas McAllister; one *d*. *Educ*: Cranford Community Sch., Hounslow; Univ. of Manchester and Université de Bourgogne (LLB 1st Cl. Hons English Law and French Law 1996); London Sch. of Econs and Pol Sci. (LLM Banking and Internat. Finance Law 1997); Inns of Court Sch. of Law (BVC 1998). Prince of Wales' Schol., Gray's Inn. Called to Bar, Gray's Inn, 1998; in practice as barrister, One Essex Court and Wilmer Hale LLP, 1998–2006; admitted solicitor, 2006; Partner: Bird & Bird LLP, 2006–08; Debevoise & Plimpton LLP, 2008–16. UK Mem., Internat. Court of Arbitration, ICC, 2015–. *Address*: Latham & Watkins LLP, 99 Bishopsgate, EC2M 3XF. *T*: (020) 7710 1000. *E*: sophie.lamb.qc@lw.com.

**LAMB, Hon. Timothy Michael;** Chief Executive: England and Wales Cricket Board (formerly Test and County Cricket Board), 1996–2004; Sport and Recreation Alliance (formerly Central Council of Physical Recreation), 2005–14; *b* 24 March 1953; *s* of 2nd Baron Rochester; *m* 1978, Denise Ann Buckley; one *s* one *d*. *Educ*: Shrewsbury Sch.; Queen's Coll., Oxford (MA Modern Hist.). Professional cricketer: with Middx CCC, 1974–77 (Hon. Life Mem.); with Northants CCC, 1978–83 (Hon. Life Mem.); Sec. and Gen. Manager, Middx CCC, 1984–88; Cricket Sec., 1988–96, Dep. Chief Exec., May–Oct. 1996, TCCB. Director: TML Sports Connections Ltd, 2014–; Sports Mktg Intelligence Gp, 2015–; Sport Support CIC, 2018–. Chair, Sports Betting Gp, 2010–14. Mem., Sport Hons Cttee, Cabinet Office, 2011–17. Hon. Life Mem., Cricket Writers' Club. *Recreations*: golf, travel, walking, photography. *Clubs*: MCC (Hon. Life Mem.); Durham County Cricket (Hon. Life Mem.).

**LAMB, Timothy Robert;** QC 1995; His Honour Judge Lamb; a Circuit Judge, since 2008; *b* 27 Nov. 1951; *s* of Stephen Falcon Lamb and Pamela Elizabeth Lamb (née Coombes); *m* 1978, Judith Anne Ryan; one *s* one *d*. *Educ*: Brentwood Sch.; Lincoln Coll., Oxford (MA Jurisp.). Called to the Bar, Gray's Inn, 1974, Bencher, 2003. Asst Recorder, 1998–2000; Recorder, 2000–08. Jt Head of Chambers, 3 Paper Buildings, Temple, 2004–08. Bar Council: Western Circuit Rep., 2005–08; Circuits Rep., Law Reform Cttee, 2005–08. Legal Assessor, GDC, 2002–08; Legal Adviser: Royal Pharmaceutical Soc., 2006–08; General Optical Council, 2006–08. Member: Restricted Patients Panel, Mental Health Review Tribunal, 2009–12; Lord Chancellor's N and E London Magistrates' Adv. Cttee, 2012–. Accredited mediator and adjudicator. FCIArb. *Recreations*: family, travel, water sports. *Address*: Kingston-upon-Thames Crown Court, 6–8 Penrhyn Road, Kingston-upon-Thames, Surrey KT1 2BB.

**LAMB, Prof. Trevor David**, FRS 1993; FAA; Distinguished Professor, 2008–11, now Emeritus Professor, and Research Director, ARC Centre of Excellence in Vision Science, 2006–10, John Curtin School of Medical Research, Australian National University (ARC Federation Fellow, 2003–07); *b* 20 Sept. 1948; *s* of Arthur and Margaret Lamb; *m* 1979, (Janet) Clare Conway; two *s* one *d*. *Educ*: Melbourne Grammar Sch.; Univ. of Melbourne (BE 1st Cl. Hons 1969); Univ. of Cambridge (PhD 1975; ScD 1988). University of Cambridge: Wellcome Sen. Res. Fellow, 1978–80, Royal Soc. Locke Res. Fellow, 1980–84, Physiological Lab.; Univ. Lectr in Physiol., 1984–91; Reader in Neuroscience, 1991–94; Prof. of Neurosci., 1994–2002; Fellow, Darwin Coll., 1985–2002. FAA 2005. *Publications*: articles on photoreceptors, sensory transduction and eye evolution in Jl Physiol. and other learned jls. *Address*: Eccles Institute of Neuroscience, John Curtin School of Medical Research, Australian National University, Canberra, ACT 2601, Australia. *T*: (2) 61258929. *E*: trevor.lamb@anu.edu.au.

**LAMBART**, family name of **Earl of Cavan**.

**LAMBECK, Prof. Kurt**, AO 2009; DPhil, DSc; FRS 1994; FAA; Professor of Geophysics, Australian National University, since 1977; *b* 20 Sept. 1941; *s* of Jacob and Johanna Lambeck; *m* 1967, Bridget Marguerite Nicholls; one *s* one *d*. *Educ:* Univ. of NSW (BSurv. Hons); Hertford Coll., Oxford (DPhil, DSc). Geodesist, Smithsonian Astrophysical Observatory and Harvard Coll. Observatory, Cambridge, Mass, 1967–70; Directeur Scientifique, Observatoire de Paris, 1970–73; Prof. of Geophysics, Univ. of Paris, 1973–77; Dir, Res. Sch. of Earth Scis, ANU, 1984–93. Tage Erlander Prof., Swedish Res. Council, 2001–02; Blaise Pascal Chair, 2011–12, Vis. Prof., 2013–, École Normale Supérieure, Paris; Johannes Geiss Fellow, Internat. Space Sci. Inst., Berne, Switzerland, 2016–17; Vis. Prof., Istituto Nazionale di Geofisica e Vulcanologia, Rome, 2018–19. Pres., Aust. Acad. Sci., 2006–10 (Vice Pres., 1998–2000; Foreign Sec., 2000–04). Fellow, Amer. Geophysical Union, 1976; FAA 1984. Foreign Member: Royal Netherlands Acad. of Arts and Scis, 1993; Norwegian Acad. of Science and Letters, 1994; Foreign MAE, 1999; Associé étranger, Institut de France, Académie des Sciences, 2005; For. Associate, NAS, 2009; For. Hon. Mem., Amer. Acad. of Arts and Scis, 2011; Hon. Mem., European Geophysical Soc., 1987. Hon. DEng Nat. Tech. Univ., Athens, 1994; Hon. DSc: NSW, 1999; Wollongong, 2015. Macelwane Medal, 1976, Whitten Medal, 1993, Amer. Geophysical Union; Jaeger Medal, Aust. Acad. of Sci., 1995; Alfred Wegener Medal, Eur. Union of Geoscis, 1997; Georges Lemaître Prize, Catholic Univ. of Louvain, 2001; Federation Medal, 2003; Balzan Prize, Internat. Balzan Foundn, 2012; Wollaston Medal, Royal Geol Soc., 2013; Matthew Flinders Medal, Australian Acad. of Sci., 2015; Prime Minister's Prize for Sci. (Australia), 2018. Chevalier, Légion d'Honneur (France), 2011; Cavaliere, Ordine al Merito della Repubblica Italiana, 2013. *Publications:* The Earth's Variable Rotation, 1980; Geophysical Geodesy: the slow deformations of the earth, 1988; numerous articles in fields of geodesy, geophysics and geology. *Address:* Research School of Earth Sciences, Australian National University, Canberra, ACT 0200, Australia; 31 Brand Street, Hughes, ACT 2605, Australia.

**LAMBERT, Anne;** *see* Lambert, G. M. A.

**LAMBERT, David Arthur Charles;** General President, National Union of Knitwear, Footwear and Apparel Trades, 1991–94 (General Secretary, 1975–82, General President, 1982–90, National Union of Hosiery and Knitwear Workers); President, International Textile, Garment and Leather Workers' Federation, Brussels, 1992–96 (Vice-President, 1984–92); *b* 2 Sept. 1933; *m* Beryl Ann (*née* Smith); two *s* one *d*. *Educ:* Hitchin Boys' Grammar Sch., Herts. Employed as production worker for major hosiery manufr; active as lay official within NUHKW; full-time official, NUHKW, 1964–90. Member: Employment Appeal Tribunal, 1978–2004; TUC Gen. Council, 1984–94; CRE, 1987–93. Gov., Welbeck Coll., 2001–09.

**LAMBERT, David Austen;** Director, The Parks Agency, since 2002; *b* Farnborough, Kent, 28 March 1959; *s* of Brian Austen Lambert and Angela Vera Margaret Lambert; *m* 1st (marr. diss.); two *s* one *d*; 2nd, 2015, Juliet Elisabeth Richardson. *Educ:* Dulwich Coll.; Exeter Coll., Oxford (MA 1st Cl. Eng. Lang. and Lit.); Bristol Poly. (Cert. Planning Law 1989). Teacher, Clifton Coll., 1984–88; Conservation Officer, Garden History Soc., 1989–2002. Research Fellow: Univ. of York, 1990–92; De Montfort Univ., 1994–98. Advr to Select Cttee Inq., Town and Country Parks, 1999–2000, Cemeteries, 2001, Sport, Recreation and Open Space, 2001–02, H of C. Member: Parks Adv. Bd, 1995–98, Historic Bldgs and Land Panel, 1998–2002, HLF (monitor and mentor, HLF, then NLHF, 2001–); Wkg Gp on Historic Envmt, DCMS, 2000; Urban Green Spaces Taskforce, DTLR, 2001; Gardens Panel, NT, 2001–15; Strategic Enabling Panel, CABE Space, 2003–11; Gardens Strategy Gp, Historic Royal Palaces, 2006–; Architl Adv. Panel, World Monuments Fund, 2006–; Bd, Welsh Historic Gardens Trust, 2010–; Adv. Cttee, 2013–19, Adv. Gp, 2019–, Historic England; Bd, Gardens Trust, 2015–. Ext. examr, MA Garden Hist., Univ. of Bristol, 2004–09; ext. examr and moderator, MA Conservation of Historic Parks and Gardens, Univ. of Bath, 2010–15. IHBC 1997. Columnist, Perambulator column, London Gardener, 1995–. *Publications:* The English Garden Tour (with Mavis Batey), 1990; (with Stewart Harding) Historic Parks and Gardens of Avon, 1994; (jtly) Arcadian Thames, 1995; Historic Public Parks of Weston-super-Mare, 1998; Four Purbeck Arcadias, 1998; Historic Public Parks of Bristol, 2000; (jtly) Indignation: the campaign for conservation, 2000; Parks and Gardens: a researcher's guide to sources for designed landscapes, 2006; *contributions to:* The Regeneration of Public Parks, 2000; Bourgeois and Aristocratic Cultural Encounters in Garden Art, 1550–1850, 2002; Architectural Conservation: issues and developments, 2006; Sculpture and the Garden, 2006; Performance and Appropriation: profane rituals in gardens and landscapes, 2007; Wentworth Castle and Georgian Political Gardening, 2012; A Cultural History of Gardens in the Age of Enlightenment, 2013; Gardens and Landscapes in Historic Building Conservation, 2014; articles in jls. *Recreations:* Irish music, walking, dancing, mountaineering, rock-climbing, birdwatching, travel in British Isles, gardening, cinema, opera, sailing, visiting parks and gardens. *Address:* Walcourt House, 12 Nelson Street, Stroud, Glos GL5 2HN. *T:* (01453) 790660.

**LAMBERT, (Gillian Mary) Anne,** CMG 2006; Panel Chair and Board Member, Competition and Markets Authority, 2016–18 (Inquiry Chair, 2014–19); *b* 11 July 1956; *d* of late Roy and Joyce Lambert. *Educ:* St Anne's Coll., Oxford (BA Hons Exptl Psychol. 1977). Joined Department of Trade and Industry, 1977: Telecommunications Div., 1982–84; Industrial Policy Div. (Grade 7), 1984–86; Insce Div., 1986–88; Personnel Div. (Grade 6), 1989–90; Insce Div. (Grade 5), 1990–93; on secondment to FCO as Counsellor (Industry), UK Perm. Repn to EU, Brussels, 1994–98; Dep. Dir Gen., Oftel, 1998–2002; Hd of Nuclear Liabilities, DTI, 2002–03; UK Dep. Perm. Rep. to EU, Brussels, 2003–08; Dir, Govt and Eur. Affairs, NATS, 2008–14. Non-exec. Dir, CAA, 2019–. Trustee, Woodland Trust, 2009–18. Gov., Portsmouth Univ., 2012–. *Recreations:* theatre, tennis, horse racing, walking. *E:* gmalambert@gmail.com.

**LAMBERT, Jean Denise;** Member (Green) London Region, European Parliament, 1999–2019; *b* 1 June 1950; *d* of Frederick John and Margaret Archer; *m* 1977, Stephen Lambert; one *s* one *d*. *Educ:* Palmers Grammar Sch. for Girls, Grays, Essex; University Coll., Cardiff (BA Modern Langs); St Paul's Coll., Cheltenham (PGCE). ADB(Ed). Secondary sch. teacher, Waltham Forest, 1972–89 (examr in spoken and written English, 1983–88). Green Party: joined 1977 (then Ecology Party); London Area Co-ordinator, 1977–81; Co-Chm. Council, 1982–85, 1986–87; Rep. to European Green Parties, 1985–86, 1988–89; UK rep. to Green Gp in European Parlt, 1989–94; Green Party Speaker, 1988–, Jt Principal Speaker, 1992–93; Chair of Executive, 1993–94. Vice-Pres., Green/EFA Gp, 2002–19. Chair, EP's Delegn for Relns with Countries of S Asia, 2009–19. Contested (Green Party): GLC, 1981; local Council, 1986; London NE, European Parlt, 1984, 1989, 1994; Walthamstow, Gen. Elecn, 1992. Founder Member: Ecology Building Soc., 1981 (Bd, 1981–84; Chm., 1982–83); Play for Life, 1984; Member: Council, Charter 88, 1990; Cttee, Voting Reform Gp, 1995. Trustee, London Ecology Centre, 1995–97. Radio and TV broadcaster. *Publications:* (contrib.) Into the 21st Century, 1988; No Change? No Chance!, 1996; Refugees and the Environment, 2002; (contrib.) Greens for a Better Europe, 2019; articles to magazines. *Recreations:* reading (esp. detective fiction), cooking, dance.

**LAMBERT, Jenni Cecily;** *see* Russell, J. C.

**LAMBERT, John Sinclair;** *b* 8 April 1948; *s* of late Norman and Doris Lambert; *m* 1971, Ann Dowzell (*d* 2011); two *s*. *Educ:* Denstone Coll.; Selwyn Coll., Cambridge (MA); Sheffield Hallam Univ. (MSc 2005). Department of Employment, subseq. Department for Education and Employment, 1970–2000: Private Sec. to Perm. Sec., 1973–74; on secondment to Marconi Space and Defence Systems, 1977–78; Dep. Chief Conciliation Officer, ACAS, 1982–83; Head of European Communities Branch, 1983–85; Dir of Field Ops, MSC, 1987–90; Dir of Ops (N and W), 1990–92; Dir, Adult Learning Div., 1992–93; Dir, Sheffield First Partnership, 1993–97 (on secondment); Regl Dir, Govt Office for Eastern Reg., 1997–98; Dir, Learning Ops, Univ. for Industry, 1998–99. Partner, John Lambert Associates, 2000–13. Chm., Friends of the Peak District (CPRE S Yorks), 2014–17. Dep. Chm., Govs, 2007–09, Trustee, Students' Union, 2010–14, Sheffield Hallam Univ. Chm., Save Longstone Edge, 2008–13. *Recreations:* birdwatching, music, mountain walking. *Address:* 1 Calver Mill, Calver, Hope Valley, Derbys S32 3YU.

**LAMBERT, Rear Adm. Nicholas Richard;** Director: Nick Lambert Associates Ltd, since 2012; NLA International Ltd, since 2017; *b* Isleworth, Middx, 27 April 1958; *s* of Michael and Anne Lambert; *m* 1989, Beverly Slim; one *s* one *d*. *Educ:* Devizes Sch.; Durham Univ. (BA Hons Geog.); BRNC Dartmouth; Henley Business Sch., Univ. of Reading (Cert. Coaching). Entered RN, 1977; in command: HMS Brazen, 1996; HMS Newcastle, 1996–98; Dep. Asst Dir, Above Water Warfare, MoD, 1998–99; Chief Maritime and Amphibious Ops, NATO Regl HQ, Brunssum, 1999–2002; COS, UK Maritime Battlestaff, 2002–05; i/c HMS Endurance, 2005–07; Comdr, Task Force 158, 2007; Talent Mgt Study Team Leader, Staff of Naval Sec., 2007–08; Dep. FOST, 2008–09; ACOS (Ops and Capability Integration), 2009–10. Nat. Hydrographer and Dep. CEO, UK Hydrographic Office, 2010–12. Non-exec. Dir, ECDIS Ltd, 2013–. Younger Brother, Corp. of Trinity House, 2010–. Friend and Cttee Mem., Friends of Scott Polar Res. Inst., 2010– (Chm., 2010–18); Chm., James Caird Soc., 2017–. Chm., 2004–13, Pres., 2014–18, RN Gliding and Soaring Assoc.; Life Mem., Portsmouth Naval Gliding Centre, 2003–. Freeman, Master Mariners' Co., 2000. FRGS 2011; FInstD. Legionnaire, Legion of Merit (USA), 2004. *Recreations:* family, unfulfilled ambition to manage the construction of a house, passionate glider pilot, cookery, gardening, sailing.

**LAMBERT, Nigel Robert Woolf;** QC 1999; a Recorder, since 1996; *b* 5 Aug. 1949; *s* of Dr E. Vivian Lambert, MB BS, MRCS, LRCP, and Sadie Lambert (*née* Woolf); *m* 1975, Roamie Elisabeth Sado; one *s* one *d*. *Educ:* Cokethorpe Sch., Oxford; Coll. of Law, London. Called to the Bar, Gray's Inn, 1974, Bencher, 2004; *ad eundem* Mem., Inner Temple, 1986. In practice, SE Circuit, 1974–; Asst Recorder, 1992–96; Dep. Hd of Chambers, 2004–09; Hd of Chambers, 2009–14. Member: Bar Council, 1993–2000 (Member: Professional Standards Cttee, 1993–95, 1997–99; Public Affairs Cttee, 1994; Finance Cttee, 1994; Legal Aid and Fees Cttee, 1996); S Eastern Circuit Cttee, 1992–2007 (Mem. Exec. Cttee, 2001–07; Chm., S Eastern Circuit/Inst. of Barristers' Clerks Cttee, 2001–07); Inner Temple Bar Liaison Cttee, 2002–03; Inner Temple Circuit Cttee, 2002–03. Member: Criminal Bar Assoc. (Mem., Cttee, 1993–2000); Justice; Fraud Lawyers Assoc., 2017–. Chm., N London Bar Mess, 2001–07. Gov., Cokethorpe Sch., 1971–78 (Life Vice Pres., Cokethorpe Old Boys' Assoc., later Cokethorpe Soc.). *Recreations:* supervising, organising, gossiping. *Address:* (chambers) Carmelite Chambers, 9 Carmelite Street, EC4Y 0DR. *T:* (020) 7936 6300. *E:* nlambertqc@carmelitechambers.co.uk. *Clubs:* Garrick, MCC.

**LAMBERT, Vice Adm. Sir Paul,** KCB 2012 (CB 2008); Secretary-General, Order of St John, since 2012; *b* 17 Nov. 1954; *s* of Ernest Harry Lambert and late Lillian Lambert (*née* Rutten); *m* 2012, Enid Wynn Pugh (*née* Rogers); one step *s*, and three *s* one *d* from a previous marriage. *Educ:* City Univ., London (BSc 1978); Darwin Coll., Cambridge (MPhil 1989); DipFM, ACCA 2002. Joined RN, 1974; Commanding Officer: HMS Onyx, 1989–91; HMS Tireless, 1991–92; submarine comd course, 1992–94; CO, HMS Coventry, 1996–98; Capt. Submarine Sea Trng, 1998–99; rcds 2000; hcsc 2001; Dir, Equipment Capability (Underwater Battlespace), MoD, 2001–04; Comdr Ops to C-in-C Fleet, Comdr Submarines and Allied Naval Force N and Rear Adm. Submarines, 2004–06; Capability Manager (Precision Attack), 2006–09; Controller of the Navy, 2007–09; DCDS (Equipment Capability), 2009–12. Pres., Merseyside Submarine Assoc., 2008–. Mem. Council, Bangor Univ., 2016–. KStJ 2018. *Recreations:* walking, modern history, politics, learning Welsh. *Address:* St John House, 3 Charterhouse Mews, EC1M 6BB. *Club:* Royal Navy of 1765 and 1785.

**LAMBERT, Paul Julian Lay; His Honour Judge Lambert;** a Circuit Judge, since 2004; a Deputy High Court Judge, since 2010; *b* 24 Aug. 1961; *s* of late Arnold Michael Lay Lambert and Rowena Lambert; *m* 2003, Sharon Dawn Curzon; two *s*. *Educ:* LSE (LLB). Called to the Bar, Middle Temple, 1983; in practice as barrister, 1983–2004, specialising in fraud and corporate crime. Mem., Professional Conduct Cttee, Bar Council, 1998–2001. *Recreation:* urbane pursuits. *Address:* Bristol Crown Court, Small Street, Bristol BS1 1DA.

**LAMBERT, Sir Peter John Biddulph,** 10th Bt *cr* 1711, of London; teacher; *b* 5 April 1952; *s* of John Hugh Lambert (*d* 1977) (*g s* of 5th Bt) and of Edith May, *d* of late James Bance; *S* kinsman, Sir Greville Foley Lambert, 9th Bt, 1988, but his name does not appear on the Official Roll of the Baronetage; *m* 1989, Leslie Anne, *d* of R. W. Lyne; one *s* one *d*. *Educ:* Upper Canada Coll., Toronto; Trent Univ. (BSc 1975); Univ. of Manitoba (MA 1980); Univ. of Toronto (BEd). *Heir: s* Thomas Hugh John Lambert, *b* 14 March 1999.

**LAMBERT, Sir Richard (Peter),** Kt 2011; Director General, Confederation of British Industry, 2006–11; *b* 23 Sept. 1944; *s* of late Peter and Mary Lambert; *m* 1973, Harriet Murray-Browne; one *s* one *d*. *Educ:* Fettes Coll.; Balliol Coll., Oxford (BA). Staff of Financial Times, 1966–2001: Lex Column, 1972; Financial Editor, 1978; New York Correspondent, 1982; Dep. Editor, 1983; Editor, 1991–2001. Mem., Monetary Policy Cttee, Bank of England, 2003–06; Lead Ind. Dir, FCO, 2011–16. Chm., Bloomsbury Publishing plc, 2017–; Ind. non-exec. Dir, EY (formerly Ernst & Young), 2011–17; Mem. Adv. Panel, EDF Energy, 2011–17. UK Business Ambassador, 2011–15. Chairman: Big Society Trust, 2011–15; Fair Educn Alliance, 2015–19. Chancellor, Univ. of Warwick, 2008–16. Trustee, BM, 2003–11 (Chm., Bd of Trustees, 2014–). Hon. Fellow, Liverpool John Moores Univ., 2011. Hon. DLitt: City, 2000; Herts, 2010; Hon. LLD: Warwick, 2004; Brighton, 2005; DUniv York, 2007; Hon. DSc: Cranfield, 2008; (Econs) QUB, 2008; Aston, 2011; Hon. DLaws Exeter, 2010.

**LAMBERT, Sarah Katrina;** QC 2018; a Recorder, since 2012; *b* Brighton, 24 Feb. 1971; *d* of Stuart and Patricia Lambert; *m* 2011, Amos Christie; three *s*. *Educ:* Brighton and Hove High Sch., GPDST; Magdalen Coll., Oxford (BA Hons). Called to the Bar, Gray's Inn, 1994; in practice as barrister, specialising in clinical negligence and costs; Dep. Costs Judge (Taxing Master), Sen. Courts Costs Office, 2013–. Granted Serious Sex Offence Ticket, 2016, Civil Ticket, 2017; Accredited Arbitrator, 2017. Contributor, Westlaw online law encyclopaedia, 2012. *Publications:* (contrib.) An Introduction to Human Rights and the Common Law, 2000; (contrib.) Sweet & Maxwell Personal Injury Handbook, 2001, 2007; (contrib.) Ethics for Advocates Manual, 2008; (contrib.) Jowitt's Dictionary of Law, 2010. *Recreations:* family, travel, yoga. *Address:* 1 Crown Office Row, Temple, EC4Y 7HH. *T:* (020) 7797 7500.

**LAMBERT, Sophia Jane,** CB 2004; *b* 15 May 1943; *d* of Michael Lambert and Florence Lambert (*née* Macaskie). *Educ:* Univ. of Paris; LSE (BSc). Entered FCO, 1966; Second Secretary: Bonn, 1968–72; FCO, 1972–76; First Secretary: Pretoria, 1976–80; FCO, 1980–82; Counsellor, Cabinet Office, 1982–85; Department of Transport: Head: Internat. Div., 1985–87; Public Transport (Metropolitan) Div., 1987–91; Channel Port Link Div., 1991–92; Director: Road and Vehicle Safety, 1992–98; Wildlife and Countryside, DETR, then DEFRA, 1998–2003 (also Dir, Flood Mgt, 2001–03). Chair, Standards Cttee, RBKC, 2006–12. Lay Mem., Gen. Council of the Inns of Court, 2005–12. Mem. Bd, London TravelWatch, 2009–12. Chm., Ladbroke Assoc., 2015–. Trustee: NOVA New Opportunities, 2012–17; Kensington Soc., 2014–. *E:* s@sophialambert.com.

**LAMBERT, Stephen;** Chief Executive, Studio Lambert Ltd, since 2008; Chairman: Seven Stories Ltd, since 2015; Parable Ventures Ltd, since 2017; Unstoppable Film and Television Ltd, since 2018; *b* 22 March 1959; *s* of Roger Lambert and Monika Lambert (*née* Wagner); *m* 1988, Jenni Cecily Russell, *qv*; one *s* one *d. Educ:* Univ. of East Anglia; Nuffield Coll., Oxford. Joined BBC Television, 1983; Producer and Dir, BBC Documentary Features Dept, 1986–94, prog. series incl. 40 Minutes (East Side Story, Dolebusters, Greenfinches, Who'll win Jeanette?, Crack Doctors, Hilary's in Hiding, Malika's Hotel), Inside Story (Children of God, The Missing, Suicide Killers, Dogs of War), and True Brits; Exec. Producer, BBC Documentaries Dept, 1994–99, progs incl. The System (Best Factual Series, RTS, 1996), 42 Up (Best Documentary, BAFTA, 1998), The Mayfair Set (Best Factual Series, BAFTA, 1999), Mersey Blues, The Clampers, Lakesiders, Premier Passions, The Day the Guns Fell Silent; Editor: Modern Times, BBC TV, 1994–98; Real Life, ITV, 1998–2001; RDF Television, later RDF Media: Dir of Progs, 1998–2005; Exec. Producer, 1999–2007; Chief Creative Officer, RDF Media Gp, 2005–07; progs incl. Faking It (Best Popular Arts Prog., Internat. Emmy Awards, 2002; Best Features Prog., BAFTA, 2002 and 2003; Best Primetime Features Prog., RTS, 2002; Golden Rose, Montreux, 2003), Perfect Match (Silver Rose, Montreux, 2002), The Century of the Self (Best Documentary Series, Broadcast Awards, 2003), Wife Swap (Best Features Prog., BAFTA, 2004; Golden Rose, Lucerne, 2004; Golden Nymph, Monte Carlo, 2004), The Power of Nightmares (Best Factual Series, BAFTA, 2005; Best Documentary Series, RTS, 2005), The Secret Millionaire (Best Reality Prog., Golden Rose, Lucerne, 2007), The Hip Hop Years, Shipwrecked, Going Native; Studio Lambert progs incl. Undercover Boss (Best Reality Prog., Primetime Emmy Awards, 2012, 2013), Gogglebox (Best Reality and Constructed Factual Prog., BAFTA, 2014; Best Popular Factual and Features Prog., RTS, 2014; Best Factual Entertainment Prog., Nat. TV Awards, 2015, 2016, 2017, 2018), Gogglesprogs, Three Girls (Best Drama Mini-Series, RTS, 2018), Four in a Bed, Tattoo Fixers, Top of the Shop with Tom Kerridge, Buy It Now, How to Get a Council House, The Great Interior Design Challenge, The Flaw, In Real Life, Doctor in the House, The Fairy Jobmother, Seven Days, The Pitch, Supermarket Superstars, Outlaw Empires. Chm., All3Media America LLC, 2013–16. Trustee: RSA, 2009–11; Impetus Trust, 2009–12. Mem. Exec. Cttee, Edinburgh Internat. TV Fest., 2002–07; Dir, Sheffield Internat. Documentary Fest., 2003–05. Mem. Council, BAFTA, 1996–98. FRTS 2016; FRSA. Best Commissioning Editor, Broadcast Awards, 1996. *Publications:* Channel Four: television with a difference?, 1982. *Recreations:* sailing, ski-ing, walking, cinema. *Address:* Studio Lambert Ltd, 1 Denmark Street, WC2H 8LP. *T:* (020) 3040 6800. *E:* stephen.lambert@studiolambert.com. *Clubs:* Royal Thames Yacht; Real Nautico de Palma (Majorca).

**LAMBERT, Prof. Susan Barbara,** (Mrs J. T. Rees); Professor, since 2014, and Head, Museum of Design in Plastics, since 2007, Arts University Bournemouth (formerly Arts Institute Bournemouth, then Arts University College Bournemouth); *b* 24 Jan. 1944; *d* of Alan Percival Lambert and Barbara May Lambert (*née* Herbert); *m* 1st, 1990, John Derek Walter Murdoch, *qv* (marr. diss. 2007); 2nd, 2017, James T. Rees. *Educ:* Downe House; Courtauld Inst. of Art, London Univ. (BA). Victoria and Albert Museum: Department of Prints and Drawings, subseq. Prints, Drawings and Paintings: Res. Asst, 1968–75; Asst Keeper, 1975–79; Dep. Keeper, 1979–89; Chief Curator, 1989–2002; Keeper, Word & Image Dept, 2002–05. *Publications:* Printmaking, 1983; Drawing, Technique and Purpose, 1984; The Image Multiplied, 1987; Form Follows Function?, 1993; Prints, Art and Technique, 2001. *Address:* Brick Hill, Burghclere, Berks RG20 9HJ. *T:* (01635) 278295.

**LAMBERTS, Prof. Koen,** PhD; Vice-Chancellor, University of Sheffield, since 2018; *b* Hasselt, Belgium. *Educ:* Univ. of Leuven (BA Philosophy 1985; BSc Exptl Psychol. 1987; PhD Exptl Psychol. 1992). Res. Associate, Univ. of Chicago, 1991–92; Lectr, Sen. Lectr, then Reader, Univ. of Birmingham, 1992–98; University of Warwick: Reader, 1998–2000; Prof. of Cognitive Sci., 2000–13; Hd, Dept of Psychol., 2000–08; Dir, Centre for Cognitive and Neural Systems, 2006–14; Chair, Sci. Faculty, 2007; Pro-Vice-Chancellor for Res. (Sci. and Medicine), 2010–12; Dep. Vice-Chancellor and Provost, 2012–13; Vice-Chancellor, Univ. of York, 2014–18. Non-exec. Dir, Warwick Ventures Ltd, 2010–13. Cognitive Award, British Psychol. Soc., 1996; Exptl Soc. Prize, 1997. *Address:* University of Sheffield, Firth Court, Western Bank, Sheffield S10 2TN.

**LAMBETH, Archdeacon of;** *see* Gates, Ven. S. P.

**LAMBIE, David;** *b* 13 July 1925; *m* 1954, Netta May Merrie; one *s* four *d. Educ:* Kyleshill Primary Sch.; Ardrossan Academy; Glasgow University; Geneva University. BSc, DipEd. Teacher, Glasgow Corp., 1950–70. Chm., Glasgow Local Assoc., Educnl Inst. for Scotland, 1958–59; Chm., Scottish Labour Party, 1964; Chief Negotiator on behalf of Scottish Teachers in STSC, 1969–70; Sec., Westminster Branch, Educnl Inst. of Scotland, 1985–88, 1991–92. MP (Lab) Ayrshire Central, 1970–83, Cunninghame South, 1983–92. Chm., Select Cttee on Scottish Affairs, 1981–87; Sec., Parly All-Party Cttee for Energy Studies, 1980–92; Chm., PLP Aviation Cttee, 1990–92. Chm., Saltcoats Labour Party, 1993–95, 2000–03; Member: Cunninghame N Constituency Labour Party, 1993–2004; N Ayrshire and Arran Constituency Labour Party, 2004. Chm. Develt Cttee, Cunninghame Housing Assoc., 1992. Dir, Galloway Training Ltd, 1997–2011. Member: Council of Europe, 1987–92; WEU, 1987–92. FEIS 1970. *Recreation:* watching football. *Address:* 11 Ivanhoe Drive, Saltcoats, Ayrshire KA21 6LS. *T:* (01294) 464843. *Club:* North Ayrshire and Arran Constituency Labour Social (Saltcoats).

**LAMBIE-NAIRN, Martin John,** RDI 1987; FCSD; consultant creative director, since 2011; *b* 5 Aug. 1945; *s* of Stephen John and Joan Lois Lambie-Nairn; *m* 1970, Cordelia Margot Summers; one *s* two *d. Educ:* King Ethelbert Sch., Birchington, Kent; Canterbury Coll. of Art. NDD. Asst Designer, Graphic Design Dept, BBC, 1965; Designer, Rediffusion, 1966; freelance graphic designer, 1967; Art Dir, Conran Associates, 1968; Dep. to Sen. Designer, ITN, overseeing changeover from black and white to colour TV, 1968; Designer, LWT, working on light entertainment, drama and current affairs progs, 1970; Founder and Creative Director, Robinson Lambie-Nairn Ltd, later Lambie-Nairn, design consultancy producing film and TV graphics, corporate identity, packaging and financial lit., 1976–2008 (Chm., 1976–97); work included Channel 4 TV corporate identity, 1982, develt of original idea for Spitting Image, 1984, Anglia TV corporate identity, 1988, TFI (France) corporate identity, 1989, BBC1 and BBC2 channel identities, 1991, Carlton Television corporate identity, 1993, Orange (Sky NZ) channel identity, and ARTE corporate identity, 1995, BBC corporate identity, 1997–, New Millennium Experience corporate identity, 1998, BAE SYSTEMS corporate identity, 1999; Founder and Partner, ML-N Branding Consultancy, 2008–09, 2011–. Non-exec. Chm., Red & White, 2015–. Creative Director: NTL, 2001–03; Heavenly, 2010–11. Mem. Cttee, D & AD, 1985– (Pres., 1990–91); Chm., Corporate Identity Jury, 2000); Chm., Graphics Jury, BBC Design Awards, 1987. Visiting Prof., Lincoln Univ., 2006–10. FCSD (FSIAD 1982); FRTS 2004. Hon. Fellow, Kent Inst. of Art and Design, 1994. Hon. DArts: Lincoln, 2004; Northampton, 2010. Jt winner, BAFTA Craft Awards (for excellence in craft of graphics), 1991; RTS Judges' Award, 1996; President's Award, D&AD, 1997; Prince Philip Designers' Prize, 1998; Lifetime Achievement Award, Eyes and Ears of Europe, 2000; Lifetime Achievement Award, Promax UK, 2008, Promax Europe, 2018; Lion d'Or, Cannes (for brand identity), 2009. *Publications:* Brand Identity for Television with Knobs On, 1997. *Recreations:* opera, family, France.

**LAMBIRTH, Mark Nicholas;** Director of Corporate Strategy, Department for Transport, 2008–09; *b* 30 May 1953; *s* of late Peter Mabson Lambirth and of Jean Margaret Lambirth; *m* 1986, Anne Catherine Wood. *Educ:* St Albans Sch.; Queens' Coll., Cambridge. Price Commn, 1975; entered Civil Service, 1977; Department of Transport, 1983–95: Ministerial speechwriter and Dep. Head, Inf. Div., 1988–89; Asst Sec., 1989; Head, Public Transport in London Div., 1989–92; Head, Central Finance Div., 1992–95; Under-Sec., 1995; Dir of Planning and Transport, Govt Office for London, 1995–98; Dir of Local Govt Finance Policy, DETR, then of Local Govt Finance, DTLR, 1998–2002; Dir of Railways, then of Rail Strategy and Resources, DTLR, then DfT, 2002–05; Dir of Rail Strategy and Finance, subseq. of Rail Strategy, 2005–07; Dir of Planning and Perf., 2007–08; DfT. *Recreations:* transport history, food, wine. *Address:* 13, 28 Oktovriou Street, Mesa Chorio, Paphos 8290, Cyprus. *Club:* MCC.

**LAMBTON,** family name of **Earl of Durham**.

**LAMBTON, Viscount; Frederick Lambton;** *b* 23 Feb. 1985; *s* and *heir* of Earl of Durham, *qv. Educ:* Bedales; Stowe.

**LAMBTON, Lucinda;** photographer and writer, since 1960; broadcaster, since 1983; *b* 10 May 1943; *e d* of Viscount Lambton (disclaimed Earldom, 1970; *d* 2006), *s* of 5th Earl of Durham, and Belinda, *d* of Major D. H. Blew-Jones; *m* 1st, 1965, Henry Mark Harrod (marr. diss. 1973); two *s*; 2nd, 1986, Sir Edmund Fairfax-Lucy, *qv* (marr. diss. 1989); 3rd, 1991, Sir Peregrine Worsthorne, *qv. Educ:* Queensgate Sch., London. Television series include: Hurray for Today, 1989; Hurray for Today, USA, 1990; Lucinda Lambton's Alphabet of Britain (3 series), 1990; Old New World, 2001; Lucinda Lambton's Jamaican Adventure, 2004. Monthly columnist, The Oldie, 2014–. Gives talks throughout Britain. Hon. FRIBA 1997. *Publications:* Vanishing Victoriana, 1976; Temples of Convenience, 1978, Chambers of Delight, 1983, combined 3rd edn, 2007; Beastly Buildings, 1985; An Album of Curious Houses, 1988; (ed) Magnificent Menagerie (anthology), 1992; Lucinda Lambton's Alphabet of Britain, 1996; Old New World, 2000; The Queen's Doll House, 2010; Palaces for Pigs, 2011. *Recreations:* looking at buildings, talking to dogs and taking them for walks. *Address:* The Old Rectory, Hedgerley, Bucks SL2 3UY. *T:* (01753) 646167. *Clubs:* Chelsea Arts, City University.

**LAMDIN, Rev. Canon Keith Hamilton;** Principal, Sarum College, Salisbury, 2008–15, now Principal Emeritus; Non-residentiary Canon, Salisbury Cathedral, 2009–15; *b* Eastbourne, 4 Feb. 1947; *s* of Ronald Lamdin and Joan Lamdin; *m* 1970, Ruth Mary Turpin; three *s. Educ:* Monkton Combe Sch., Bath; Bristol Univ. (BA 1969). Chaplain, Bristol Univ., 1969–73; Minister, Devizes Baptist Church, 1973–80; Trng Officer, Guisborough Deanery, 1980–83; ordained deacon, 1986, priest, 1987; Diocese of Oxford: Adult Educn Officer, 1983–86; Dir of Trng, 1986–90; Dir, Dept of Stewardship Trng, Evangelism and Ministry, 1990–2008. Honorary Canon: Christ Church, Oxford, 1997–2008, now Emeritus; St Cyprians, Kimberley, SA, 2008–. *Publications:* Ready for Action, 1988; Monday Matters, 1995; Supporting New Ministers in the Local Church, 2007; Finding Your Leadership Style, 2012. *Recreations:* walking, gardening. *Address:* 2 Forge Close, West Overton, Marlborough, Wilts SN8 4PG. *T:* (01672) 861550. *E:* khlamdin@gmail.com.

**LAMEY, Steven;** Chief Executive Officer, Student Loans Company, 2016–17; *b* 26 Dec. 1955; *s* of Kenneth Gordon Lamey and Sylvia Patricia Lamey; *m* 1981, Ann Williams; one *s* one *d. Educ:* UC Cardiff (BSc Mining and Mineral 1978). BOC Group, 1978–99: Proj. Manager; Sen. Ops Manager; European Infrastructure Manager; Inf. Mgt Dir, Global User Service; British Gas Gp, 1999–2004: Vice Pres., Inf. Mgt; Chief Inf. Officer; HM Revenue and Customs: Chief Inf. Officer and Dir Gen., 2004–07; Chief Operating Officer and Dir Gen., 2007–08; Dir Gen., Benefits and Credits, 2008–12; Comr, 2008–12; Chief Operating Officer, Kelway, 2012; Man. Dir, Chessdale Ltd, 2014–16. *Recreations:* music—Bruce Springsteen/Marillion through to classical/opera, Rugby.

**LAMING,** Baron *cr* 1998 (Life Peer), of Tewin in the co. of Hertfordshire; **William Herbert Laming,** Kt 1996; CBE 1985; PC 2014; DL; Chief Inspector, Social Services Inspectorate, Department of Health, 1991–98; *b* 19 July 1936; *s* of William Angus Laming and Lillian Laming (*née* Robson); *m* 1962, Aileen Margaret Pollard (*d* 2010). *Educ:* Univ. of Durham (Applied Social Scis); Rainer House (Home Office Probation Trng, 1960–61); LSE (Mental Health Course, 1965–66). Notts Probation Service: Probation Officer, 1961–66; Sen. Probation Officer, 1966–68; Asst Chief Probation Officer, Nottingham City and Co. Probation Service, 1968–71; Dep. Dir, 1971–75, Dir, 1975–91, Social Services, Herts CC. Pres., Assoc. of Dirs Social Services, 1982–83. Chairman: Ind. Inquiry into care and treatment of Ms Justine Cummings, 2000; Modernising the Management of the Prison Service, 2000; Victoria Climbié Inquiry, 2001–03; Progress Report on the Protection of Children, 2009. Convenor, Crossbench Peers, 2011–15; Chm. of Cttees, 2015–16, Chm. of Services Cttee, 2016–, H of L. DL Herts, 1999. *Publications:* Lessons from America: the balance of services on social care, 1985; In Care, Out of Trouble: life choices of children in care, 2016. *Address:* House of Lords, SW1A 0PW.

**LAMMER, Dr Peter;** non-executive Director, Sophos Ltd, 2006–15 (Joint Chief Executive Officer, 2000–05); Special Adviser, Sophos plc, since 2015; *b* 18 Dec. 1958; *s* of Alfred Ritter von Lammer and Benedicta (*née* Gräfin von Wengersky); one *d. Educ:* Alleyn's Sch.; Univ. of Warwick (BSc (Eng) 1981); St John's Coll., Oxford (DPhil 1986). Co-founder, 1985, Man. Dir, 1985–2000, Sophos Ltd. KM 2004. *Recreations:* music, bridge, forestry, old sports cars. *Address:* c/o Sophos plc, The Pentagon, Abingdon Science Park, Abingdon, Oxon OX14 3YP. *T:* (01235) 559933. *Club:* Travellers'.

**LAMMY, Rt Hon. David (Lindon);** PC 2008; MP (Lab) Tottenham, since June 2000; *b* 19 July 1972; *s* of David and Rosalind Lammy; *m* 2005, Nicola Green; two *s* one *d. Educ:* King's Sch., Peterborough; SOAS, London Univ. (LLB Hons 1993); Harvard Law Sch. (LLM 1997). Called to the Bar, Lincoln's Inn; Attorney, Howard Rice, Calif, 1997–98; with D. J. Freeman, 1998–2000. Mem. (Lab), London Assembly, GLA, May–June 2000. PPS to Sec. of State for Educn and Skills, 2001–02; Parliamentary Under-Secretary of State: DoH, 2002–03; DCA, 2003–05; DCMS, 2005–07; DIUS, 2007–08; Minister of State, DIUS, then BIS, 2008–10. Member: Procedure Cttee, 2001; Public Admin Cttee, 2001; Chair: All Party Parly Gp on Fatherhood, 2013–, on Crossrail2, 2013–, on Race and Equality, on Wellbeing Economics, on London-Stansted-Cambridge Corridor. Chair,

Govt Review into BAME Disproportionality in Criminal Justice System, 2016–. Member: Gen. Synod, C of E, 1999–2002; Archbishops' Council, 1999–2002. Pres., British Foreign Schs Soc., 2009–. Trustee, ActionAid, 2001–06. *Publications:* Out of the Ashes: Britain after the riots, 2011. *Recreations:* film, theatre, live music, Spurs FC. *Address:* c/o House of Commons, SW1A 0AA. *T:* (020) 7219 0767.

**LAMOND, Prof. Angus Iain**, PhD; FRS 2010; FRSE; FMedSci; Wellcome Principal Research Fellow and Professor of Biochemistry, Centre for Gene Regulation and Expression, University of Dundee, since 1995; Co-founder, Dundee Cell Products, since 2006. *Educ:* Univ. of Glasgow (BSc Molecular Biol. 1981); Christ's Coll. and St John's Coll., Cambridge (PhD 1984). Postdoctoral trng, MIT, 1984–87; Gp Leader, Eur. Molecular Biol. Lab., Heidelberg, 1987–95. Molecular and Proteomics Prize Lect. in Proteomics, 2012. FRSE 1996; FMedSci 2014. Novartis Medal and Prize, Biochem. Soc., 2011. *Publications:* contribs to jls incl. Current Biol., Jl Cell Biol., EMBO Reports, Molecular & Cellular Proteomics, Molecular Biol. of the Cell, Molecular Cell, Proteomics. *Address:* School of Life Sciences, University of Dundee, Dundee DD1 5EH.

**LAMOND, Jilly;** *see* Forster, J.

**LAMONT,** family name of **Baron Lamont of Lerwick**.

**LAMONT OF LERWICK**, Baron *cr* 1998 (Life Peer), of Lerwick in the Shetland Islands; **Norman Stewart Hughson Lamont**; PC 1986; politician, writer and company director; *b* Lerwick, Shetland, 8 May 1942; *s* of late Daniel Lamont and of Helen Irene; *m* 1971, Alice Rosemary White (marr. diss. 1998); one *s* one *d*. *Educ:* Loretto Sch. (scholar); Fitzwilliam Coll., Cambridge (BA; Hon. Fellow 2014). Chm., Cambridge Univ. Conservative Assoc., 1963; Pres., Cambridge Union, 1964. PA to Rt Hon. Duncan Sandys, MP, 1965; Conservative Research Dept, 1966–68; Merchant Banker, N. M. Rothschild & Sons, 1968–79; Dir, Rothschild Asset Mgt, 1978. Non-exec. Dir, N. M. Rothschild & Sons, 1993–95; Director: Balli Gp Plc, 1995–2012; RAB Capital, 2004–11; Jupiter Second Split Trust, 2005–15; Small Companies Dividend Trust, 2008–. Pres., British-Romanian Chamber of Commerce, 2003–08; Chm., British-Iranian Chamber of Commerce, 2004–; Adviser to: Monsanto Corp., 2006–07; Western Union Corp., 2007–08; Stanhope Capital, 2013–. Prime Minister's Trade Envoy to Iran, 2015–. Contested (C) East Hull, Gen. Election, 1970. MP (C) Kingston-upon-Thames, May 1972–97; contested (C) Harrogate and Knaresborough, 1997. PPS to Norman St John-Stevas, MP, Minister for the Arts, 1974; an Opposition Spokesman on: Prices and Consumer Affairs, 1975–76; Industry, 1976–79; Parly Under Sec. of State, Dept of Energy, 1979–81; Minister of State, DTI (formerly DoI), 1981–85; Minister of State for Defence Procurement, 1985–86; Financial Sec. to HM Treasury, 1986–89; Chief Sec. to HM Treasury, 1989–90; Chancellor of the Exchequer, 1990–93. Chairman: G7 Gp of Finance Ministers, 1991; EU Finance Ministers, 1992; Mem., H of L Select Cttee on EU, 1999–2003, EU Sub-Cttee on Economic Affairs, 2005–08, EU Sub-Cttee on External Affairs, 2010–15. Chairman: Coningsby Club, 1970–71; Bow Group, 1971–72; Vice Pres., Bruges Gp; Pres., Economic Res. Council, 2008–. Mem. Adv. Bd, Iran Heritage Foundn, 2011–; Pres., British Inst. for Study of Iraq, 2011–. Pres., Clan Lamont Soc., 2006–08. Commander, Order of Faithful Service (Romania), 2010. *Publications:* Sovereign Britain, 1995; In Office, 1999. *Recreations:* books, ornithology, theatre. *Address:* House of Lords, SW1A 0PW. *T:* (020) 7219 3000. *Clubs:* Garrick, Beefsteak, White's.

**LAMONT, Donald Alexander;** HM Diplomatic Service, retired; *b* 13 Jan. 1947; *s* of Alexander Lamont and Alexa Lee Lamont (née Will); *m* 1981, Lynda Margaret Campbell; one *s* one *d*. *Educ:* Aberdeen Grammar Sch.; Aberdeen Univ. (MA). British Leyland Motor Corp., 1970; Second Sec., subseq. First Sec., FCO, 1974; First Sec., UNIDO/IAEA, Vienna, 1977; First Sec. (Commercial), Moscow, 1980; First Sec., FCO, 1982; Counsellor on secondment to IISS, 1988; Political Advr and Head of Chancery, British Mil. Govt, Berlin, 1988–91; Ambassador to Uruguay, 1991–94; Hd of Republic of Ireland Dept, FCO, 1994–97; COS and Dep. High Rep., Sarajevo, 1997–99; Gov., Falkland Is, and Comr for S Georgia and S Sandwich Is, 1999–2002; Ambassador to Venezuela, 2003–06. Chief Exec., Wilton Park, 2007–09. Mem. Bd, Sistema Scotland, 2007–. Dep. Chm., British Venezuelan Soc., 2011–13; Chm., British Uruguayan Soc., 2014–19. Chairman: UK Antarctic Heritage Trust, 2013–17 (Trustee, 2008–17); Friends of Falkland Is Mus. and Jane Cameron Nat. Archives, 2013–19; Falklands Maritime Heritage Trust, 2014–. Gov., Steyning Grammar Sch., 2010–16. FRGS 2017. Hon. LLD Aberdeen, 2017. *Address:* 3 Southdown Terrace, Steyning, W Sussex BN44 3YJ. *Club:* Caledonian.

**LAMONT, Douglas Ross;** Chief Executive Officer, innocent drinks, since 2013; *b* Haslemere, 7 Sept. 1973; *s* of Angus and Cordelia Lamont; *m* 2008, Francesca Wightman; one *s* three *d*. *Educ:* Sherborne Sch., Dorset; Univ. of Edinburgh (MA Hons Politics and Geog. 1996); Harvard Business Sch. (Gen. Mgt Prog. 2006). Associate, KPMG Corporate Finance, 1996–99; Corporate Develt Dir, Freeserve plc, 1999–2006; innocent drinks: New Ventures Innovation Dir, 2006–12; Mktg and Innovation Dir, 2012–13. Trustee, innocent Charity Foundn, 2013–. *Recreations:* family, sport, cooking, wine. *Address:* innocent drinks, 342 Ladbroke Grove, W10 5BU.

**LAMONT, Graham William;** Chief Executive, Lamont Pridmore, since 1979; *b* Workington, Cumbria, 7 May 1952; *s* of Gordon and Marjorie Lamont; *m* 1986, Maggie Rudd; one *s*. *Educ:* Workington Tech. Sch.; W Cumbria Coll. Chartered Sec. 1973; FCA 1978; FCCA (ACCA 1985). Home Sec.'s Rep., Selection Panel for Ind. Mems, Cumbria Police Authy, 1998–2004. Mem., Cumbria Foot and Mouth Task Force, 2001. Vice Chm., Cumbria Sub-Regl Assembly, 1999–2002; Business Mem., Cumbria Strategic Partnership, 2002–07; Vice Chm., W Cumbria Strategic Partnership, 2007–10; Chair, Cumbria Employment and Skills Bd, 2008–11. Non-executive Member: W Cumbria Healthcare Trust, 1993–2001 (Chm., Audit Cttee); Govt Taskforce to merge Business Link Cumbria, 1996–97 (non-exec. Dir, Activ8: Business Link Cumbria, 2001–05); Enterprise Cumbria, 1998–2001; Cumbria LSC, 2001–08 (Chm., 2006–08); NW LSC, 2006–09. Mem., Cumbria Panel, Rural Develt Commn, 1995–97; Private Sector Mem. Bd, Cumbria LEP, 2013–15. Ind. Mem., Cumbria Vision, 2004–05. Founding Pres., Cumbria Chamber of Commerce, 1998–2008. Institute of Chartered Accountants of England and Wales: Member: Financial Services Authorisation Cttee, 1997–98; nat. taskforce on How to Create the Modern Gen. Accountancy Practice, 2001–03; Practice Cttee, 2015–18; Ed., Adding Value newsletter, 2000–05; Mem. Cttee, 1987–94, Courses Chm., 1990–93, Chm., 1992–93, Cumberland Soc. Chartered Accountants; Mem. Cttee, 1991–93, Mem., Tech. Adv. Cttee, 1993–94, Northern Soc. of Chartered Accountants. Jt Chair, Theatre by the Lake, Keswick, 1984–. Governor: St Bees Sch., 1997–2002; Lakes Coll., W Cumbria, 2001–04; Carlisle Coll., 2002–04. MCMI 1990; MIMC 2002. FRSA 2007. High Sheriff Cumbria, 2008–09. *Publications:* 57 Ways to Grow Your Business, 2013. *Recreations:* theatre, art, reading, jogging, golf. *Address:* Bank Farm, Lorton, Cockermouth, Cumbria CA13 0RQ. *T:* (01900) 85617. *E:* graham@bank-farm.com.

**LAMONT, Johann MacDougall;** Member (Lab) Glasgow, Scottish Parliament, since 2016 (Glasgow Pollok, 1999–2016); *b* 11 July 1957; *y d* of Archie Lamont and Effie Lamont (née Macleod); *m* Archie Graham; one *s* one *d*. *Educ:* Univ. of Glasgow (MA Hons); Jordanhill Coll. of Educn (postgrad. secondary teaching qualification). Secondary School teacher, 1979–99. Dep. Minister for Communities, 2004–06, for Justice, 2006–07, Scottish Exec. Dep. Leader, 2008–11, Leader, 2011–14, Labour Party, Scottish Parlt. Mem., EIS, 1979–. *Recreations:* running, watching football, doing crosswords, enjoying time with my children. *Address:* Scottish Parliament, Edinburgh EH99 1SP.

**LAMONT, John;** MP (C) Berwickshire, Roxburgh and Selkirk, since 2017; *b* 15 April 1976; *s* of Robert Lamont and Elizabeth Lamont. *Educ:* Kilwinning Acad.; Univ. of Glasgow. Solicitor: Freshfields, 2000–04; Bristows, 2004–05; Brodies, 2005–07. Mem. (C) Roxburgh and Berwickshire, 2007–11, Ettrick, Roxburgh and Berwickshire, 2011–17, Scottish Parlt. Mem., Scottish Affairs Cttee, H of C, 2017–. Contested (C) Berwickshire, Roxburgh and Selkirk, 2005, 2010, 2015. *Recreations:* travel, running, swimming, cycling. *Address:* House of Commons, SW1A 0AA. *E:* john.lamont.mp@parliament.uk; (office) 25 High Street, Hawick, Roxburghshire TD9 9BU.

**LAMONTE, Air Vice Marshal Dr Jonathan;** Chief Executive, Sydney Metro, since 2018; *b* London, 30 Dec. 1959; *s* of late Jack Lamonte and of Sheila Lamonte. *Educ:* Southgate Sch., Cockfosters, Herts; Keele Univ. (BSc Maths and Geol.); King's Coll. London (MA Defence Studies); Birmingham Univ. (PhD History 2011). CMath, FIMA 1993; CDipAF 2001; FRIN 2002; FRICS 2013; FCILT 2013. Hercules navigator, No 24 Sqdn, 1984–86; Instructor, No 6 Flying Trng Sch., RAF Finningley, 1986–87; Gen. Duties, Aerosystems Course, 1987–88; Flt Comdr, No 115 (Andover) Sqdn, RAF Benson, 1988–92; SO, MoD, 1993–96; OC No 30 (Hercules) Sqdn, RAF Lyneham, 1996–98; Strategic Defence Rev. Implementation, MoD, 1998–99; Dep. Dir, Resources and Plans Centre, MoD, 1999–2001; Detachment Comdr, Ali-Al-Salem Air Base, Kuwait, 2001; OC, RAF Brize Norton, 2002–04; Dir, Resources and Prog. Mgt, Defence Logistics Orgn, 2005–07; Dir, Material Progs, 2007–08, Dir Gen. Finance, 2008, Defence Equipment and Support Orgn; COS for Strategy, Policy and Plans, RAF, 2009–10; Chief Executive: Tube Lines Ltd, 2011–12; Transport for Gtr Manchester, 2013–18. Chair, Urban Transport Gp (formerly Passenger Transport Exec. Gp), 2015–17. President: European Metropolitan Transport Authorities, 2017–18; Polis, 2017–18. Vice-Pres., CILT, 2016–18. Slessor Fellow, Univ. of Birmingham, 2008. CCMI 2012 (FCMI 2005); Fellow and Chartered Dir, IoD, 2007. FRSA 2013. President: Southgate and Wood Green RAFA, 1998–2014; No 2267 Sqdn ATC, 2002–14; No 2473 Sqdn ATC, 2009–14; Deptherapy, 2015–. Freeman, City of London, 1996. Liveryman, Hon. Co. of Air Pilots (formerly GAPAN), 2002–. DL Gtr Manchester, 2014–18. *Address:* Sydney Metro, Level 43, 680 George Street, Sydney, NSW 2000, Australia.

**LAMPARD, Helen Jayne S.;** *see* Stokes-Lampard, H. J.

**LAMPARD, Kathryn Felice, (Kate), (Mrs John Leigh-Pemberton),** CBE 2015; DL; independent consultant, since 2012; Chair, GambleAware, since 2016; *b* London, 20 April 1960; *d* of Martin Robert Lampard and Felice Lampard; *m* 1986, Hon. John Leigh-Pemberton; two *s* one *d*. *Educ:* Exeter Univ. (BA Hons); City Univ. (Dip. Law); Inns of Court Sch. of Law. Called to the Bar, Lincoln's Inn, 1984; in practice as barrister, 1984–97; non-exec. Dir, W Kent HA, 1997–2000; Chairman: Invicta Community Care NHS Trust, 2000–02; Kent and Medway Strategic HA, 2002–06; Consultant to NHS and other public bodies, 2006–09; Chm., SE Coast Strategic HA, 2009–11; Vice Chm., NHS South of England, 2011–13. Overseer, DoH and NHS investigations into activities of Jimmy Savile, 2012–15; leader, ind. investigation into Yarl Wood Immigration Removal Centre for Serco plc, 2015–16; interim Chair, Adv. Panel on Deaths in Custody, 2015–16; leader, ind. investigation into Gatwick Immigration Removal Centre for G4S, 2017–. Non-executive Director: Ind. Housing Ombudsman, 1997–2000 (Chm., 2000–02); Financial Ombudsman Service Ltd, 2002–12; DoH, subseq. DHSC, 2017–. Non-exec. Dir, RHS Enterprises Ltd, 2008–11; Mem. Council, RHS, 2017–. Chair, Gamble Aware, 2016–. Trustee, Esmée Fairbairn Foundn, 2000–. DL Kent, 2002. *Recreations:* gardens and gardening, family life, sea bathing. *Address:* Yokes Court, Frinsted, Sittingbourne, Kent ME9 0ST.

**LAMPERT, Catherine Emily;** independent curator; Director, Whitechapel Art Gallery, 1988–2001; *b* 15 Oct. 1946; *d* of Emily F. Schubach and Chester G. Lampert; *m* 1st, 1971, Robert Keith Mason (marr. diss. 1994); one adopted *d*; 2nd, 2006, (James) Andrew Dempsey, *qv*. *Educ:* Brown Univ. (BA); Temple Univ. (MFA). UCL, 1966–67; Asst Curator, RI Sch. of Design, Mus. of Art, 1968–69; Studio Internat., 1971–72; Sen. Exhibn Organiser, Hayward Gall., 1973–88. Vis. Prof., Univ. of the Arts, 2007–. Curator: Frank Auerbach: painting and drawing 1954–2001, RA, 2001–02; Nan Goldin, Centre Pompidou and tour, 2001; Lucian Freud, Dublin, Humlebaek, The Hague, 2007–08; Miquel Barceló, CaixaForum, Madrid, CaixaForum Barcelona, 2010; Francis Alÿs, Dublin 2010; Daumier, RA, 2013; Co-curator: Rodin, RA, 2006; Bare Life: London artists working from life 1950–80, LWL-Mus. für Kunst und Kultur, Münster, 2014; Frank Auerbach, Kunstmus. Bonn, Tate Britain, 2015–16; Anish Kapoor, Archaeol. and Biol., Mus. Univ. Arte Contemporáneo, Mexico, 2016. *Publications:* Rodin: sculpture and drawings, 1986; Lucian Freud: recent work, 1993; The Prophet and the Fly: Francis Alÿs, 2003; Euan Uglow: the complete paintings, 2007. Peter Doig, 2011; The Mystery of Appearance: conversations between ten post-war British painters, 2011; Frank Auerbach: speaking and painting, 2015; numerous catalogue essays on Frank Auerbach, Barry Flanagan, Tony Cragg, Francisco Toledo, Georg Baselitz, Miquel Barceló, Peter Doig and other subjects of Twentieth Century art. *Address:* 92 Lenthall Road, E8 3JN. *T:* (020) 7249 7650.

**LAMPL, Sir Peter,** Kt 2003; OBE 2000; Chairman: Sutton Trust, since 1997; Education Endowment Foundation, since 2011; *s* of Frederick and Margaret Lampl; *m* 1st, 1976, Janet Clowes (marr. diss. 1980); 2nd, 1994, Karen Gordon (marr. diss. 2010; she *d* 2013); one *s* two *d*; 3rd, 2012, Susan Hollo. *Educ:* Reigate Grammar Sch.; Cheltenham Grammar Sch.; Corpus Christi Coll., Oxford (BA, MA; Hon. Fellow, 1998); London Business Sch. (MBA). Mktg Exec., Beecham Gp, London, 1970–71; Mgt Consultant, Boston Consulting Gp, Boston, Paris, Munich, 1973–77; Dir, Planning and Business Develt, Internat. Paper, NY, then Pres., Internat. Paper Realty, 1977–83; Founder, Pres., then Chm., Sutton Co. (leveraged buyout firm), NY, London, Munich, 1983–97; Founder, Sutton Trust, 1997 (increases social mobility through education and employment). Hon. Fellow: Birkbeck Coll., London, 2007; City Univ., London, 2007; LSE, 2008; London Business Sch., 2009. Hon. DSc: Nottingham, 1999; Imperial Coll. London, 2004; City, 2007; St Andrews, 2011; Hon. Dr jur Bristol, 2001; DUniv: Birmingham, 2003; Brunel, 2004; Open, 2015; Hon. LLD Exeter, 2010; Hon. DLaws Coll. of Law, 2010; Hon. DCL Durham, 2013. *Recreations:* golf, swimming, theatre. *Address:* The Sutton Trust, 9th Floor, Millbank Tower, 21–24 Millbank, SW1P 4QP. *T:* (020) 7802 1660. *Clubs:* 5 Hertford Street, Athenæum, Queen's; Queenwood (Surrey); Florida Country (Palm Beach).

**LAMPORT, Sir Stephen (Mark Jeffrey),** GCVO 2018 (KCVO 2002; CVO 1999); DL; Chapter Clerk and Receiver General, Westminster Abbey, 2008–18; *b* 27 Nov. 1951; *s* of late Eric and Jeanne Lamport; *m* 1979, Angela Vivien Paula Hervey; two *s* one *d*. *Educ:* Dorking Co. Grammar Sch.; Corpus Christi Coll., Cambridge (Schol., MA); Sussex Univ. (MA). HM Diplomatic Service, 1974–2002: UK Mission to UN, 1974; Tehran, 1975–79; FCO, 1979–84; Private Secretary to Minister of State, 1981–84; First Sec., Rome, 1984–88; FCO, 1988–93; Dep. Private Sec. to the Prince of Wales, 1993–96; Private Sec. and Treas. to Prince of Wales, 1996–2002; Gp Dir, RBS, 2002–07. Non-exec. Dir, Brewin Dolphin Holdings plc, 2007–15. Sen. Advr, Sanctuary Counsel, 2019–. Ind. Person,

Westminster CC, 2015–18. Member: Exec. Cttee, British Red Cross Queen Mother Meml Fund, 2003–06; Court, Royal Foundn of St Katharine, 2004–; Council of Mgt, Arvon Foundn, 2004–08; Council, Guildford Cathedral, 2006–10; Adv. Council, Inst. of Business Ethics, 2015–; Chairman: British Red Cross Flood Relief Adv. Panel, 2007–08; British Red Cross UK Solidarity Fund, 2017–. Trustee, Community Foundn for Surrey (formerly Surrey Community Foundn), 2006–10 (Vice-Pres., 2010–). DL Surrey, 2006. *Publications:* (with D. Hurd) The Palace of Enchantments, 1985. *Address:* Elm Tree Cottage, Downside, nr Cobham, Surrey KT11 3NQ. *Clubs:* Royal Automobile (Mem., Bd of Dirs, 2012–18), Grillion's, Nobody's Friends.

**LAMPSON**, family name of **Baron Killearn**.

**LAMY, Pascal Lucien Fernand**; Director General, World Trade Organisation, 2005–13; *b* 8 April 1947; *s* of Jacques Lamy and Denise (*née* Dujardin); *m* 1972, Geneviève Luchaire; three *s*. *Educ:* Ecole des Hautes Etudes Commerciales; Inst d'Etudes Politiques, Paris; Ecole Nat. d'Admin. Inspector-Gen. of Finances, 1975–79; French Treasury, 1979–81; Advr to Minister for Econ. Affairs and Finance, 1981–83; Dep. Hd, Prime Minister's Pvte Office, 1983–84; Head, Pvte Office of Pres. of EC, 1985–94; with Crédit Lyonnais, 1994–99, Dir Gen., 1997; Mem., European Commn, 1999–2004. Mem. Steering Cttee, Socialist Party of France, 1985–94. Chair, Eur. Gp of Experts in Charge of Evaluating Impact of EU Res. Funding; Member: Global Ocean Commn, 2013–16; UNAIDS; Lancet Commn; Bd of Dirs, Fondation nat. des Scis politiques; Bd, Centre on Eur. Regulation; Global Foundn Rome Roundtable; Bd, Pierre Mendès France Inst.; Bd, Mo Ibrahim Foundn; Member, Advisory Board: Transparency Internat.; Oxford Martin Sch.; UNITAID; Friedland Inst.; Special Advisor: TradeMarkEastAfrica; World Trade Bd. Trustee Dir, Thomson Reuters, 2009–. President: World Cttee of Tourism Ethics; Conseil d'Admin des Musiciens du Louvre-Grenoble, 2009–; French Cttee, Pacific Econ. Cooperation Council, 2016–; Vice-Pres., Foundn for European Progressive Studies; Hon. Pres., Notre Europe, Jacques Delors Inst. Dr *hc*: Geneva, 2009; Warwick, 2009; Montréal, 2010; Dhaka, 2012; Edinburgh, 2012. Grosses Verdienstkreuz (Germany), 1991; Commandeur: de l'Ordre Nat. du Mérite (Luxembourg), 1995; Légion d'Honneur (France), 2012; Officer: Order of Merit (Gabon), 2000; Nat. Order (Burkina Faso), 2012; Order of Aztec Eagle (Mexico), 2003; Order of Merit (Chili), 2003; Médaille de la Fraternité (Vietnam), 2007; Medal of Merit (Vanuatu), 2011; Great Cross: Royal Order Sahametrey (Cambodia), 2012; Royal Order (Orange-Nassau); Great Officer, Order of Merit (Italy), 2013; Medal of Nat. Order (Tadjikistan), 2013; Friendship Medal (Laos), 2013. *Publications:* L'Europe de nos Volontes, 2000; L'Europe en Première Ligne, 2002; La Démocratie-monde, 2004; The Geneva Consensus, 2013; Quand la France s'éveillera, 2014; Où va le monde, 2017. *Address:* Jacques Delors Institute, 19 rue de Milan, 75009 Paris, France.

**LAN, David Mark**, CBE 2014; PhD; writer, producer, director and social anthropologist; Artistic Director, Young Vic Theatre, 2000–18; *b* 1 June 1952; *s* of Joseph Lan and Lois Lan (*née* Carklin). *Educ:* Univ. of Cape Town (BA 1972); London Sch. of Econs (BSc; PhD 1984). Writer in Residence, Royal Court Th., 1995–97; Consulting Artistic Dir, Performing Arts Center, World Trade Center, NY, 2013–15. *Plays:* Painting a Wall, Almost Free Th., 1974; Bird Child, 1974, Homage to Been Soup, Paradise, The Winter Dancers, 1975, Royal Ct Th. Upstairs; Red Earth, ICA, 1976; Not in Norwich, Royal Ct Young People's Th. Scheme, 1977; Sergeant Ola and His Followers, Royal Ct, 1979; (with C. Churchill) A Mouthful of Birds, Jt Stock Th. Gp, 1986; Flight, RSC, 1986; Ghetto (English trans. of play by Joshua Sobol), NT, 1989; Desire, 1990; Hippolytos (version of Euripides' play), 1991, Almeida; Ion (version of Euripides' play), RSC, 1994; The Ends of the Earth, NT, 1996; Uncle Vanya (new version), RSC at Young Vic, 1998; La Lupa (English version of play by Giovanni Verga), RSC, 2000; Cherry Orchard (new version), NT, 2000; *television:* BBC 2: The Sunday Judge, 1985; The Crossing, 1988; Welcome Home Comrades, Dark City, 1989; *film:* (jtly) Streets of Yesterday, 1988; *radio:* Charley Tango, Radio 4 and World Service, 1995; *libretti:* Tobias and the Angel, 1999, Ion, 2000, The Magic Flute (trans.), 2008, Almeida Opera; *director:* Artist Unknown, 1995, Royal Court Diaries, 1996, BBC 1; The Glass Menagerie, Palace Th., Watford, 1998; for Young Vic: Tis Pity She's a Whore, 1999; Julius Caesar, 2000; A Raisin in the Sun, 2001, tour 2005; Dr Faustus, The Daughter-in-Law, 2002; The Skin of Our Teeth, 2004; As You Like It, Wyndham's, 2005; The Soldier's Fortune, 2007; Joe Turner's Come and Gone, 2010; Blackta, 2012; Why It's Kicking Off Everywhere, 2017. Member, Board: Motley Theatre Design Sch., 2013–; Good Chance Th., 2016–; Belarus Free Th., 2017– (Chm., 2012–17); Sadlers Wells; Co-Chair, Internat. Council Isango Ensemble, 2015–. Hon. DLitt London South Bank, 2009. John Whiting Award, Arts Council, 1975; George Orwell Award, 1980; Zurich Internat. TV Award, 1989; Laurence Olivier Award, 2004; Critics Circle Special Award, 2018; Olivier Special Award, 2018; Marsh Award for Anthropology in the World, RAI, 2018. *Publications:* Guns and Rain: guerillas and spirit mediums in Zimbabwe, 1985; all plays published. *Address:* c/o Judy Daish Associates, 2 St Charles Place, W10 6EG. *T:* (020) 8964 8811.

**LANCASHIRE, Sarah Jane Abigail, (Mrs P. Salmon)**, OBE 2017; actress; *b* 10 Oct. 1964; *d* of late Geoffrey Lancashire and of Hilda Lancashire (*née* McCormack); *m* 1st, 1987, Gary Hargreaves (marr. diss. 1997); two *s*; 2nd, 2001, Peter Salmon, *qv*; one *s*. *Educ:* Werneth Private Prep. Sch., Oldham; Hulme Grammar Sch. for Girls, Oldham; Oldham Coll. of Technol.; Guildhall Sch. of Music and Drama. Lectr (pt-time), Salford Univ. Coll., 1987–90. *Theatre:* professional début, The Beauty Game and Pacific Overtures, Manchester Liby Th., 1986; Educating Rita, Hornchurch, 1991; The Little Shop of Horrors, Oldham, 1993; West End début, Blood Brothers, Albery, 1990; Betty Blue Eyes, Novello, 2011; *television:* Coronation Street, 1991–96 (Best Actress Award, RTS (NW), 1996); Where the Heart Is, 1996–99; Blooming Marvellous, 1997; Clocking Off, 1999; Seeing Red, 1999 (Best Actress, Nat. TV Awards, 2000; Drama TV Performer of Year, TV and Radio Industry Awards, 2001); Chambers, 2000; Gentleman's Relish, 2000; My Fragile Heart, 2000; The Cry, 2000 (Best Actress, Monte Carlo TV Fest., 2002); The Glass, 2000; The Birthday Girl, 2001; Sons and Lovers, 2002; Rose & Maloney, 2002–05; Rotters' Club, 2004; Cherished, 2004; All the Small Things, 2009; Wuthering Heights, 2009; Five Daughters, 2010; The Paradise, 2012, 2013; Last Tango in Halifax, 2012–17; Happy Valley, 2014, 2016 (Best Leading Actress Award, BAFTA, 2017); The Dresser, 2015; Kiri, 2018; MotherFatherSon, 2019; The Light, 2019; *film:* Dad's Army, 2016; Dir, Viva las Blackpool, 2003 (Best New Talent, RTS (Midlands), 2004). Hon. MA Salford, 2002. *Recreations:* gardening, family, cinema. *Address:* c/o Independent Talent Group Ltd, 40 Whitfield Street, W1T 2RH.

**LANCASTER, Bishop Suffragan of,** since 2018; **Rt Rev. Dr Jillian Louise Calland Duff;** *b* Bolton, 25 July 1972; *d* of Graham and Sylvia Worsley; *m* 1994, Rev. Prof. Jeremy Nicholas Duff; two *s*. *Educ:* Bolton Sch. Girls' Div.; Christ's Coll., Cambridge (BA Natural Scis 1993); Worcester Coll., Oxford (DPhil Chemistry 1996); Wycliffe Hall, Oxford (BA Theology 1st cl. 2002). Res., Marketing and Logistics, Esso Petroleum Co., 1997–2000; ordained deacon, 2003, priest, 2004; Curate, St Philip's Litherland, Liverpool, 2003–06; Pioneer Minister, Liverpool City Centre, 2006–11; Project Leader, St Aidan's/St Mellitus, 2011–13; Dir, St Mellitus Coll., NW, 2013–18. Chaplain, Liverpool Coll., 2009–16. *Publications:* contrib. Bible Reading Fellowship Bible Reading Notes; over 10 scientific and fuel quality papers. *Recreations:* walking, wild camping, holidays in fresh air with big vistas, running, piano for relaxation, writing fun lyrics to well-known songs. *Address:* Diocesan Offices, Clayton House, Walker Office Park, Blackburn BB1 2QE. *T:* (01254) 503099. *E:* bishop.lancaster@blackburn.anglican.org.

**LANCASTER, Bishop of, (RC),** since 2018; **Rt Rev. Paul Swarbrick;** *b* 2 July 1958; *s* of George Vincent Swarbrick and Alice Swarbrick (*née* Horn). *Educ:* Lancaster Royal Grammar Sch.; Ushaw Coll., Co. Durham. Ordained priest, 1982; Assistant Priest: St Mary, Kells, Whitehaven, 1982–83; St Maria Goretti, Preston, 1983–84; St Cuthbert, Blackpool, and Chaplain, St Mary's Catholic High Sch., 1984–90; missionary work in Monze Dio., Zambia, 1990–2005; Asst Priest, English Martyrs, Preston, 2005–06; Parish Priest: Sacred Heart, Preston and St Walburge, Preston, 2007–10; Our Lady and St Michael, Workington, 2010–18. Hon. Canon, Lancaster Cathedral, 2015–. *Address:* Bishop's Office, Pastoral Centre, Balmoral Road, Lancaster LA1 3BT.

**LANCASTER, Archdeacon of;** *no new appointment at time of going to press.*

**LANCASTER, His Honour Anthony Trevor;** a Circuit Judge, 2001–18; Designated Diversity and Community Relations Judge for Cumbria, 2011–18; *b* 26 June 1948; *s* of late Thomas William Lancaster and of Jean Margaret Lancaster (*née* Grainger); *m* 2012, Louise Askins; four *s* two *d* by previous marriage. *Educ:* Austin Friars Sch., Carlisle; Univ. of Leeds (LLB Hons 1970). Admitted solicitor, 1973; in private practice, 1973–88; County Court Registrar, 1988–91; a Dist Judge, 1991–2001; Asst Recorder, 1995–99; a Recorder, 1999–2001. Pt-time Chm., Social Security Appeals Tribunal, 1985–88. Judicial Mem., Parole Bd, 2018–. Pres., Assoc. of Dist Judges, 2000–01. *Recreations:* cooking, music.

**LANCASTER, (Charles) Roy**, CBE 2014 (OBE 1999); freelance author, lecturer, plant explorer and dendrologist, since 1980; *b* 5 Dec. 1937; *s* of Charles and Norah Lancaster; *m* 1977, Susan Lloyd; one *s* one *d*. *Educ:* Castle Hill Co. Secondary Sch., Bolton; Cambridge Univ. Botanic Garden. Curator, Hillier Arboretum, 1970–80. Member: Mgt Cttee, Sir Harold Hillier Gardens and Arboretum, 1990–2007 (Patron, 2007–); Arboreta Adv. Cttee, Nat. Arboreta (formerly Consultative Cttee, Westonbirt Nat. Arboretum), 1990–2017; Gardens Panel, NT, 2000–09; Vice Chm., Woody Plant Cttee (formerly Floral Cttee B), RHS, 1998–2010 (Hon. Mem., 2010). Vice Pres., RHS, 2005–; Pres., The Hardy Plant Soc., 2007–. Trustee, Tree Register of Britain and Ireland, 2001–; Patron: Soc. of Floral Painters, 2008–16; Garden Media Guild, 2015–. Hon. DSc: Bolton, 2010; Winchester, 2016. Veitch Meml Medal, RHS, 1972; VMH 1989; Inst. of Horticulture Award, 1996; TV Gardening Presenter of the Year, 1993, Lifetime Achievement Award, 2002, Garden Writers' Guild; Journalist of the Year, Garden Media Guild, 2008; Lifetime Achievement Award, RHS, 2017. *Publications:* Trees for your Garden, 1974; (with Vicomte Noailles) Mediterranean Gardens and Plants, 1977; A Plantsman in Nepal, 1981; In Search of the Wild Asparagus, 1983; Garden Plants for Connoisseurs, 1987; Travels in China: a plantsman's paradise, 1989; Garden Shrubs Through the Seasons, 1991; What Plant Where, 1995; What Perennial Where, 1997; (with Matthew Biggs) What House Plant Where, 1998; Perfect Plant Perfect Place, 2001; My Life With Plants, 2017; contribs to Gdn Jl of RHS. *Recreations:* bird watching, walking, travel, gardening, music. *Address:* 58 Brownhill Road, Chandlers Ford, Hants SO53 2EG. *Club:* Farmers.

**LANCASTER, Rt Hon. (John) Mark,** TD 2002; PC 2018; DSc; MP (C) Milton Keynes North, since 2010 (Milton Keynes North East, 2005–10); Minister of State (Minister for the Armed Forces), Ministry of Defence, since 2017; *b* 12 May 1970; *s* of Rev. Ronald Lancaster, *qv*; *m* (marr. diss.); one *d*; *m* 2014, Caroline Dinenage, *qv*; two step *s*. *Educ:* Kimbolton Sch., Cambs; Buckingham Univ. (BSc 1992; DSc 2007); Exeter Univ. (MBA 1993). Served Army, RE, 1988–90; Officer, TA, RE, 1990–. Dir, Kimbolton Fireworks Ltd, 1993–2005. PPS to Sec. of State for Internat. Develt, 2010–12; a Lord Comr of HM Treasury (Govt Whip), 2012–15; Parly Under-Sec. of State, MoD, 2015–17. Mem. (C) Huntingdon DC, 1995–99. Consultant, Palmer Capital Partners, 2010–12. *Publications:* (contrib.) Fireworks Principles and Practice, 3rd edn 1998. *Recreations:* collector and restorer of classic British motorcycles, avid football supporter. *Address:* House of Commons, SW1A 0AA. *E:* lancasterm@parliament.uk.

**LANCASTER, Rev. Ronald,** MBE 1993; Founder, 1964, Managing Director, 1986–2006, Director and Chairman, since 2007, Kimbolton Fireworks Limited; *b* 9 March 1931; *s* of Jack and Kathleen Lancaster; *m* 1966, Kathleen Smith; one *s* one *d*. *Educ:* Durham Univ. (BA 1953; MA 1956); Cuddesdon Coll., Oxford. Ordained deacon, 1957, priest, 1958; Curate: St Peter, Morley, Yorks, 1957–60; St Peter, Harrogate, 1960–63; Chaplain, Kimbolton Sch., Huntingdon, 1963–88. Hon. CChem, FRSC 1983. Hon. MSc Durham, 2009. *Publications:* Fireworks Principles and Practice, 1972, 4th edn 2006. *Recreations:* gardening, organist. *Address:* 7 High Street, Kimbolton, Huntingdon, Cambs PE28 0HB. *T:* (01480) 860498, *Fax:* (01480) 861217. *E:* ron@kimboltonfireworks.co.uk.
*See also Rt Hon. J. M. Lancaster.*

**LANCASTER, Roy;** *see* Lancaster, C. R.

**LANCE, Seán Patrick;** Chairman, African Leadership Institute, since 2003; *b* 4 Aug. 1947; *s* of James Lance and Kathleen (*née* Carmody); *m* 1st, 1969, Pamela Joan Gray (marr. diss. 1990); two *s* two *d*; 2nd, 1990, Patricia Anne (*née* Bungay). *Educ:* Christian Brothers Coll., Pretoria. Noristan Gp, S Africa, 1967–82; Chm., Boots Co., S Africa, 1982–85; Man. Dir, Glaxo, S Africa, 1985–87; Regl Dir (London), Glaxo Hldgs plc, 1987–89; Man. Dir, Glaxo Pharms UK Ltd, 1989–93; Dir, Glaxo Hldgs plc, 1993–97; Chief Operating Officer, Glaxo Wellcome plc, 1997; Chief Exec. and Pres., 1998–2003, Chm., Bd of Dirs, 1998–2004, Chiron Corp. Mem., Supervisory Bd, Crucell, 2004–10. President: Proprietary Assoc. of S Africa, 1983–84; Pharmaceutical Manufacturers Assoc. of S Africa, 1987–88; Internat. Fedn of Pharmaceut. Manufacturers Assoc., 1996–2000; Vice-Pres., Assoc. of British Pharmaceutical Industry, 1993–94. Special Forces, S Africa, 1965–75. *Recreations:* hockey, golf, football, cricket, Kyukoshin karate (2nd Dan). *Clubs:* Special Forces; Harlequins, Pretoria Country (Pretoria); Richmond Hockey.

**LANCELOT, James Bennett,** FRCO; Master of the Choristers and Organist, Durham Cathedral, 1985–2017, now Canon Organist Emeritus; Interim Organist and Director of Music, Worcester Cathedral, 2018–19; *b* 2 Dec. 1952; *s* of late Rev. Roland Lancelot; *m* 1982, Sylvia Jane (*née* Hoare); two *d*. *Educ:* St Paul's Cathedral Choir Sch.; Ardingly Coll.; Royal College of Music (ARCM); King's Coll., Cambridge (Dr Mann Organ Student; MA; BMus). Asst Organist, St Clement Danes and Hampstead Parish Ch., 1974–75; Sub-Organist, Winchester Cath., 1975–85; Asst Conductor, Winchester Music Club, 1983–85; Conductor, Durham Univ. Choral Soc., 1987–2013; Organist, Durham Univ., 2002–17. Member: Council, RCO, 1988–99, 2002–06; Cathedrals Liturgy Gp, 1993–2003. President: Cathedral Organists' Assoc., 2001–03; Darlington and Dist Organists' and Choirmasters' Assoc., 2004–05; IAO, 2013–15; Newcastle and District Soc. of Organists, 2016–17. Lay Canon, Durham Cathedral, 2002–17. Hon. FGCM 2007; Hon. FRSCM 2008; Hon. Fellow, St Chad's Coll., Durham, 2006; Hon. Fellow, Hatfield Coll., Durham, 2017. Hon. DMus Durham, 2014. Cranmer Award, Archbishop of Canterbury, 2016. Has played or conducted premières, incl. Mathias' Berceuse, Tavener's Ikon of St Cuthbert, Josephs' Mass for St Cuthbert, MacMillan's Missa Dunelmi, Casken Magnificat and Nunc dimittis. Organ recitals and broadcasts in UK; concerts in Germany, Denmark, France,

Norway, Sweden, Poland, Belgium, Russia, Brazil, Canada, USA, NZ. Recordings with choirs of King's Coll., Cambridge, Winchester Cath., Durham Cath., and as soloist. *Publications:* (with R. Hird) Durham Cathedral Organs, 1991; (contrib.) The Sense of the Sacramental, 1993. *Recreations:* railways, the works of John Buchan. *Address:* 18 Cotteswold Road, Tewkesbury, Glos GL20 5DL.

**LANCHESTER, John Henry,** FRSL; writer; *b* Hamburg, 25 Feb. 1962; *s* of G. W., (Bill), Lanchester and Julie Lanchester; *m* 1994, Miranda Carter; two *s*. *Educ:* Gresham's Sch., Holt; St John's Coll., Oxford (BA 1st cl. Hons; Violet Vaughan Morgan Award, Charles Oldham Shakespeare Prize). Asst Ed., London Review of Books, 1987–91; Ed., Penguin Books, 1991–92; Dep. Ed., London Review of Books, 1993–96. FRSL 2003. *Publications:* The Debt to Pleasure, 1996 (Whitbread First Novel Award, Betty Trask Prize, 1996; Hawthornden Prize, Julia Child Award, 1997); Mr Phillips, 2000; Fragrant Harbour, 2002 (Premi Llibreter, 2005); Family Romance, 2007 (E. M. Forster Award, AAAL, 2008); Whoops!: why everyone owes everyone and no one can pay, 2010; Capital, 2012; How to Speak Money, 2014; The Wall, 2019. *Recreation:* watching television. *Address:* c/o A. P. Watt Ltd, United Agents, 12–26 Lexington Street, W1F 0LE. *T:* (020) 3214 0800, *Fax:* (020) 3214 0801. *E:* apw@apwatt.co.uk.

**LAND, Alastair;** *see* Land, W. M. A.

**LAND, Prof. Michael Francis,** FRS 1982; PhD; Professor of Neurobiology, University of Sussex, 1984–2005, now Emeritus; *b* 12 April 1942; *s* of late Prof. Frank William Land and of Nora Beatrice Channon; *m* 1980, Rosemary (*née* Clarke); one *s* one *d* (and one *d* decd). *Educ:* Birkenhead Sch., Cheshire; Jesus Coll., Cambridge (MA); University Coll. London (PhD). Asst Lectr in Physiology, UCL, 1966–67; Miller Fellow, 1967–79, and Asst Prof. of Physiology-Anatomy, 1979–81, Univ. of Calif, Berkeley; Lectr in Biol Sciences, 1971–77, Reader, 1977–84, Univ. of Sussex. Vis. Prof., Univ. of Oregon, 1980; Sen. Res. Fellow, ANU, 1982–84. Frink Medal, Zool Soc. of London, 1994; Rank Prize for Optoelectronics, 1998. *Publications:* (with D. E. Nilsson) Animal Eyes, 2002, 2nd edn 2012; (with B. W. Tatler) Looking and Acting, 2009; A Very Short Introduction to the Eye, 2014; numerous papers on animal and human vision in learned jls. *Recreations:* photography, music. *Address:* Dart Cottage, 1 The Elms, Ringmer, East Sussex BN8 5EZ. *T:* (01273) 813911.

**LAND, Nicholas Charles Edward,** FCA; Chairman, Ernst & Young, 1995–2006; *b* 6 Feb. 1948; *s* of Charles and Norma Land; *m* 1975, Sonia Tan; one *s*. *Educ:* Steyning Grammar Sch. FCA 1971. Articled Spain Brothers Dalling & Co., 1967–71; joined Turquand Young, later Ernst & Young, 1971: Partner, 1978–2006; Managing Partner, London Office, 1986–92; Managing Partner, 1992–95; Mem., Global Exec. Bd, 1992–2006; Chm., Northern Europe, Middle East, India and Africa Area, 2001–06. Non-executive Director: Royal Dutch Shell plc, 2006–10; BBA Aviation plc (formerly BBA Gp plc), 2006–16; Ashmore Gp plc, 2006–16; Vodafone Gp plc, 2006–17; Alliance Boots GmbH, 2008–15; Financial Reporting Council, 2011– (Chm., Codes and Standards Cttee, 2015–); Thames Water Utilities Ltd, 2017; Astro Hldgs Ltd, 2017; Advisory Board Member: Three Delta LLP, 2006–11; Aecus Ltd (formerly Alsbridge plc), 2010–14. Chairman: Practice Adv. Bd, ICAEW, 2006–10; Audit and Assurance Council (formerly Auditing Practices Bd), 2012–15; Private Equity Reporting Gp (formerly Guidelines Monitoring Gp), BVCA, 2013–; Advr to Bd, Dentons UKEMEA (formerly Denton Wilde Sapte, later SNR Denton), 2008–; Advr, Silicon Valley Bank, London, 2013–16. Member: Adv. Bd, Cambridge Judge Business Sch., 2005–07; Finance and Audit Cttees, Nat. Gall., 2005–13. Chairman, Board of Trustees: Farnham Castle, 2007–14; Vodafone Gp Foundn, 2009– (Trustee, 2007–). CCMI 1992; FRSA 1995. Hon. Chartered Dir, IoD, 2009. *Recreations:* carpentry, ballet. *Address:* (office) Sheil Land Associates Ltd, 52 Doughty Street, WC1N 2LS.

**LAND, (William Martin) Alastair;** Headmaster, Harrow School, since 2019; *b* Manchester, 24 Sept. 1971; *s* of Martin Land and Elaine Land; *m* 2010, Madeleine Copin; two *s* one *d*. *Educ:* Manchester Grammar Sch.; Trinity Coll., Cambridge (BA Nat. Scis 1st Cl. 1993; PGCE 1994). Asst Master, Eton Coll., 1994–2003; Master in Coll., Winchester Coll., 2003–12; Dep. Head Master, Harrow Sch., 2012–16; Headmaster, Repton Sch., 2016–19. FLS 2003; FRSB (FSB 2014). *Recreations:* CCF officer, family cycle touring, antiquarian natural history books. *Address:* Harrow School, 5 High Street, Harrow on the Hill HA1 3HP. *E:* alastairland@gmail.com. *Clubs:* East India, Lansdowne.

**LANDALE, Tina Jeanette; Her Honour Judge Landale;** a Circuit Judge, since 2015; *b* Hebden Bridge, 25 Nov. 1965; *d* of John Barry Landale and Marjorie Landale; *m* 2002, Christopher Rainham; one *s* one *d*. *Educ:* Calder High Sch., Mytholmroyd; Wolverhampton Poly. (LLB Hons). Called to the Bar, Middle Temple, 1988; a Recorder, 2009–15. *Recreations:* theatre, art, family, travel, music. *Address:* Minshull Street Crown Court, Manchester M1 3FS.

**LANDAU, Dr David,** Hon. CBE 2007; Chairman, Saffron Hill Investors (Guernsey), since 2000; *b* 22 April 1950; *s* of Aharon Landau and Evelyne Conti; *m* 2001, Marie-Rose Kahane; one *s* one *d* (twins). *Educ:* Univ. of Pavia, Italy (MD 1978); Wolfson Coll., Oxford (MA 1979). Print Curator, The Genius of Venice, RA, 1983; Chm., Steering Cttee, Andrea Mantegna exhibn, RA and Metropolitan Mus. of Art, NY, 1992. Founder and Jt Man. Dir, Loot, 1985–95; Chm., Loot Gp of Cos, 1995–2000. Founder and Editor, Print Qly, 1984–2010 (Trustee, 2010–); Founder, FAPIA (Free-ad Papers Internat. Assoc.), 1986, Chm., 1990–91; Dir, Nat. Gall. Co. (formerly Nat. Gall. Pubns), 1995–2003 (Chm., 1998–2003); Dir, Getty Images, 2003–06. Director: Yad Hanadiv (Rothschild Foundn), 2012–19; Yad Hanadiv Israel, 2012–; Trustee: British Friends of Art Museums of Israel, 1995–2007; Nat. Gall. Trust, 1995–; NACF (The Art Fund), 1996–2010; Nat. Gall., 1996–2003; Venice in Peril Fund, 1996–2012 (Treas., 1997–2010); NGT Foundn, 1997–; Rothschild Foundn (Hanadiv) Europe (formerly Rothschild Foundn Europe), 2001–; Warburg Charitable Trust, 2001–09; Borletti-Buitoni Charitable Trust, 2002–; Courtauld Inst., 2002–12; Fondazione dei Musei Civici di Venezia, 2010. Supernumerary Fellow, Worcester Coll., Oxford, 1980–2009. Commendatore dell'Ordine al Merito della Repubblica Italiana, 2007. *Publications:* Georg Pencz, 1978; Federica Galli, 1982; (with Prof. P. Parshall) The Renaissance Print, 1994; articles in Print Qly, Master Drawings, Burlington Mag., etc. *Recreations:* looking at and collecting art, opera, Venice. *Address:* Chesa Carla, 7505 Celerina, Switzerland. *T:* (81) 8321550.

**LANDAU, Toby Thomas;** QC 2008; FCIArb; *b* London, 9 Oct. 1967; *s* of late Dr Thomas L. Landau and of Marianne Landau; *m* 1988, Nudrat B. Majeed; one *d*. *Educ:* University Coll. Sch., Hampstead; Merton Coll., Oxford (BA 1st Cl. Hons Juris; BCL 1st Cl.); Harvard Law Sch. (LLM); Inns of Court Sch. of Law. FCIArb 2000; Chartered Arbitrator, 2000. Called to the Bar, Middle Temple, 1993; Member: NY State Bar, 1994; NI Bar, 2000; BVI Bar, 2011; called to the Bar, Singapore, 2017; in private practice as barrister and arbitrator, 1993–. Vis. Prof., KCL, 2009– (Vis. Sen. Lectr, 2005–09). Mem., Panel of Advrs, Attorney Gen. of Singapore, 2012–. Dir, London Court of Internat. Arbitration, 2000–15 (Mem. Court, 2014–); Mem. Bd, Arbitration Inst., Stockholm Chamber of Commerce, 2012–; Court Mem., Singapore Internat. Arbitration Centre, 2014–; Mem., Singapore Bar, 2017–. Trustee, CIArb, 2004–08. Advr and Asst on drafting of English Arbitration Act, 1996. Member, Editorial Board: Global Arbitration Rev., 2005–; Jl Internat. Arbitration, 2007–. *Publications:* contrib. articles to ICCA Congress series and other law jls. *Address:* c/o Essex Court Chambers, 24 Lincoln's Inn Fields, WC2A 3EG.

**LANDE, Prof. Russell Scott,** PhD; FRS 2012; Royal Society Research Professor in Natural Sciences, Imperial College London, 2007–16, now Emeritus; International Chair Professor, Norwegian University of Science and Technology, since 2017; *b* Mississippi, USA, 1951. *Educ:* Univ. of Calif, Irvine (BS 1972); Univ. of Chicago; Harvard Univ. (PhD 1976). Post-doctoral work, Univ. of Wisconsin, 1976–78; Asst Prof., Dept of Biophys and Theoretical Biol., 1978–82, Associate Prof. of Ecol. and Evolution, 1982–89, Louis Block Prof., Dept of Ecol. and Evolution, 1989–90, Univ. of Chicago; Professor of Biology: Univ. of Oregon, 1990–99; UCSD, 1999–2007. Adjunct Prof., Centre for Conservation Biol., Norwegian Univ. of Sci. and Technol. Guggenheim Meml Fellow, 1996; MacArthur Foundn Fellow, 1997–2002. Pres., Soc. for Study of Evolution, 1997. Fellow, Amer. Acad. Arts and Scis, 1997. Sewall Wright Award, Amer. Soc. Naturalists, 1992; Weldon Meml Prize and Medal, Univ. of Oxford, 2010; Balzan Prize, Balzan Prize Foundn, 2011. *Publications:* (jtly) Stochastic Population Dynamics in Ecology and Conservation, 2003; articles in jls. *Address:* Department of Biology, Norwegian University of Science and Technology, 7491 Trondheim, Norway.

**LANDEG, Frederick John,** CBE 2008; Deputy Chief Veterinary Officer, 2004–07; Interim Chief Veterinary Officer, 2007–08, Department for Environment, Food and Rural Affairs; *b* 16 Jan. 1948; *s* of Frederick Henry Landeg and Ivy May Landeg; *m* 1973, Sandra Stagg; three *s*. *Educ:* Sir Walter St John's Sch., Battersea; Royal Veterinary Coll., London (BVetMed; MSc). MRCVS. Gen. veterinary practice, 1971–75; Ministry of Agriculture, Fisheries and Food: Vet. Officer, 1975–83; Sen. Vet. Officer, 1983–87; Div. Vet. Officer, Preston, 1987–90; Dep. Regl Vet. Officer, Reading, 1990–93; Hd, Vet. Resources Div., 1993–2000; Hd, Vet. Exotic Diseases Div., 2000–04, MAFF, subseq. DEFRA. *Recreations:* reading, walking. *Address:* 6 Oak Tree Copse, Tilehurst, Reading RG31 6PX.

**LANDELS, William, (Willie);** painter, typographer; *b* Venice, 14 June 1928; *s* of late Reynold Landels and Carla Manfredi; *m* 1st, 1958, Angela Ogden (marr. diss. 1986); two *d*; 2nd, 2002, Josephine Grever. *Educ:* privately. Apprentice stage designer at La Scala, Milan, 1947; Art Director: J. Walter Thompson, 1950; Queen Magazine, 1965; Editor, Harpers & Queen, 1970–86; Editor, Departures, 1989–90. One-man Exhibitions: Hamburg, 1992; Rebecca Hossack Gall., London, 1993, 1995, 1998, 2013; Olsen-Carr Gall., Sydney, 1994; Gallery 482, Brisbane, 1997; Pasricha Fine Arts, London, 2002. Designer, carpets, furniture and books. *Publications:* (with Alistair Burnet) The Best Years of Our Lives, 1981. *Address:* 292 South Lambeth Road, SW8 1UJ.

**LANDER, Nicholas Laurence;** Restaurant Correspondent, The Financial Times, since 1989; foodservice consultant; *b* 8 April 1952; *s* of Israel Lennard and Pauline Lander; *m* 1981, Jancis Mary Robinson, *qv*; one *s* two *d*. *Educ:* Manchester Grammar Sch.; Jesus Coll., Cambridge (MA); Manchester Business Sch. (DipBA). Restaurateur, 1980–88; Foodservice Consultant: South Bank Centre, 1993–; Royal Opera House, Covent Garden, 1999–; St Pancras, 2007–; Ashmolean, Oxford, 2007; Barbican, 2008–; Chiswick House Trust, 2009. *Publications:* Dinner for a Fiver, 1994; Harry's Bar London, 2005; The Art of the Restaurateur, 2012. *Recreations:* cooking, reading, sitting round a table with friends. *E:* nick@jancisrobinson.com. *Club:* Manchester United.

**LANDER, Sir Stephen (James),** KCB 2000 (CB 1995); Lay Member, Special Immigration Appeals Commission, 2011–17; Member, Solicitors Regulation Authority (formerly Regulation Board, Law Society), 2006–09 (Independent Commissioner, 2002–05); Chairman, Serious Organised Crime Agency, 2004–09; *b* 1947; *s* of John N. B. Lander and (Eleanor) Tessa Lander (*née* Heanley); *m* 1972, Felicity Mary Brayley; one *d* (one *s* decd). *Educ:* Bishop's Stortford Coll.; Queens' Coll., Cambridge (BA, MA, PhD). Inst. of Historical Research, Univ. of London, 1972–75; Security Service, 1975–2002, Dir Gen., 1996–2002; non-exec. Dir, HM Customs and Excise, 2002–05. Non-executive Director: Northgate Information Solutions, 2004–08; Streamshield Networks, 2004–07. Panel Chair, Judicial Appts Commn, 2008–12. Trustee, Dawes Trust, 2012–. Gov., Bishop's Stortford Coll., 2002–. Hon. LLD Hertfordshire, 2005; Hon. DSc Cranfield, 2007. *Address:* PO Box 12378, SW1P 1XU.

**LANDERER, John,** CBE 1997; AM 1990; lawyer; Senior Partner, Landerer & Co., since 1979; *b* 3 May 1947; *s* of William and Felicia Landerer; *m* 1986, Michelle H. Sugar; one *s* one *d*. *Educ:* Sydney Univ. (LLB 1969). Chairman: FAI Insurances Ltd, 1989–99 (Actg Chm., 1988); Tiger Investment Co. Ltd, 1994–99; Goldsearch Ltd, 1995–; Nat. Hire Gp Ltd, 1997–2004; Terrace Tower Gp, 1997–2007; Director: TNT Ltd, 1985–93; Internat. Distillers Hldgs Ltd, 1986–99; Advance Bank Aust. Ltd, 1989–97; Goodman Fielder Ltd, 1989–94; Aust. Nat. Industries Ltd, 1989–96; Bridge Oil Ltd, 1991–94; Gandel Gp Pty Ltd, 1995–98; D. W. Gp of Cos, 1996–. Chm., NSW Govt Home Purchase Assistance Authy, 1994–2001. University of Sydney: Hon. Fellow, 1990; Hon. Gov., Law Sch. Foundn, 1990–; Mem. Bd, Asia Pacific Law Centre, 1994; Chm., Endocrinol. and Diabetes Res. Foundn, 2008– (Councillor, 2006–); Macquarie University: Chm., Adv. Bd, Business Law Dept, 1994–; Vis. Prof., 1998–. Trustee, WWF Australia, 1992–99. Councillor, Sydney Conservatorium of Music Foundn, 1994–96. Vice Pres., Temora Aviation Mus., 1998–; Board Member: Sydney Jewish Mus., 2004 (Pres., 2005–10); Life Educn Aust., 2004–; JewishCare Foundn, 2004–; Garvan Res. Foundn, 2007–. Dir, Royal Inst. of Deaf and Blind Children, 2005–. Member: Fundraising Cttee, 1989–93, Victor Chang Cardiac Centre Appeal Cttee, 1993–96, St Vincent's Hosp.; Red Shield Appeal Cttee, Salvation Army, 1991–98. Vice Chm., Bd of Govs, Tel Aviv Univ., 2000– (Hon. Fellow, 2008). Hon. LLD Macquarie, 1999. B'nai B'rith Internat. Award, 2001. Commendatore dell'Ordine della Stella della Solidarietà Italiana, 2008. *Recreations:* reading, walking, swimming. *Address:* (office) Level 31, 133 Castlereagh Street, Sydney, NSW 2000, Australia. *T:* (612) 92614242, *Fax:* (612) 92618523. *Clubs:* Carlton; American, Tattersalls (Sydney).

**LANDERS, Brian James,** OBE 2018; author; Chairman, Companies House, 2012–17; *b* 21 April 1949; *s* of James Jocelyn Landers, OBE and Beatrice Edith Landers (*née* Western); *m* 1st, 1975, Elsa Louise Dawson (marr. diss.); 2nd, 1986, Thérèse Doumit (marr. diss.); one *s*; 3rd, 1993, Sarah Catherine Cuthbert (marr. diss.); two *d*; 4th, 2015, Elizabeth Camille Best (*née* Maguire-Denlegh-Maxwell). *Educ:* Univ. of Exeter (BA); London Business Sch. (MSc). With Commercial Union, 1973–79; Internat. Planned Parenthood Fedn, 1979–82; Tenneco Automotive, 1982–83; Chief Internal Auditor, then Retail Financial Controller, J. Sainsbury plc, 1985–88; Price Waterhouse, 1988–90; UK Finance Dir, then Gp Finance Dir, Habitat, 1990–93; Finance Director: HM Prison Service, 1993–96; W. H. Smith Retail, 1996–97; with Waterstone's Ltd, 1997–98; Gp Finance Dir, 2000, Chief Operating Officer, 2000–03, Pearson Education; Finance and Ops Dir, Penguin Gp, 2003–09. Dep. Chm., Financial Ombudsman Service, 1999–2005; Member: Audit Commn, 2010–15; Competition Appeal Tribunal, 2011–18; non-exec. Ind. Dir, Ombudsman Services, 2017–. Trustee: Royal Armouries, 1999–2002; Refugee and Migrant Justice, 2009–10. Treas., Amnesty Internat. UK, 2010–13. *Publications:* Empires Apart, 2009; Families of Spies, 2019. *Address:* 63 Elm Quay Court, Nine Elms Lane, SW8 5DF.

**LANDERS, Dr John Maxwell;** Principal, 2005–11, Senior Research Fellow, 2011–16, Hon. Fellow, 2016, Hertford College, Oxford; *b* 25 Jan. 1952; *s* of William Maxwell Landers and Muriel Landers; *m* 1991, Diana Clare Parker, *qv*. *Educ:* Southgate Tech. Coll.; Hertford Coll., Oxford (MA; LittD 2006); Churchill Coll., Cambridge (PhD 1984). Oil demand analyst, Shell UK Ltd, 1979–80; Lectr in Biol Anthropol., UCL, 1980–90; Lectr in Histl Demography, and Fellow, All Souls Coll., Oxford, 1991–2005. Chair, Animals in Science Cttee, 2013–19. *Publications:* Death and the Metropolis: studies in the historical demography of London 1670–1830, 1993; The Field and the Forge: population, production and power in the pre-industrial West, 2003. *Address:* Hertford College, Oxford OX1 3BW. *Clubs:* Athenæum, Oxford and Cambridge.

**LANDON, Prof. David Neil;** Professor of Neurocytology, University of London, 1991–2001, now Emeritus Professor; Dean, and Member Committee of Management, Institute of Neurology, London, 1987–95; *b* 15 May 1936; *er s* of late Christopher Guy Landon and Isabella Catherine (*née* Campbell); *m* 1960, Karen Elizabeth, LRCP, MRCS, *yr d* of late John Copeland and Else Margrethe Poole, Bolney, Sussex; two *s* one *d*. *Educ:* Lancing Coll.; Guy's Hospital Med. Sch. (BSc Hons Anat. 1957; MB BS 1960). LRCP, MRCS 1959. Ho. Officer, Guy's Hosp., 1959–60; Lectr in Anatomy, Guy's Hosp. Med. Sch., 1961–64; Lectr, later Sen. Lectr, in Neurobiology, MRC Res. Gp in Applied Neurobiology, 1964–77; Reader in Neurocytology, Inst. of Neurology, 1977–91. Hon. Cons. in Morbid Anatomy, National Hosps, Queen Square, 1974–2001. University of London: Member: Senate and Academic Council, 1992–94; Univ. Council, 1996–2001; Mem., Med. Cttee, 1996–98; Convenor, Subject Panel in Anatomy, 1996–2001. Vis. Prof., Coll. of Medicine, Lagos, 1975. Gov., National Hosps for Nervous Diseases SHA, 1988–95; Appointed Mem., GMC, 1988–94. Member: Res. Cttee, World Fedn of Neurology, 1987–2001; Cttees of Management, Inst. of Child Health, 1987–96, Inst. of Dental Surgery, 1993–95; Chm., Med. Res. Ethics Cttee, 1987–93, Chm., Med. Cttee, 1998–2000, Nat. Hosp. for Neurology and Neurosurgery. Mem. Grants Council, 1999–2001, Mem. Adv. Council, 2001–05, Charities Aid Foundn; Trustee, Brain Res. Trust, 2004–10. FLS 2013; FAS 2010; FRMS. Hon. Fellow, Inst. of Child Health, London Univ., 1996. Freeman, 2001, Liveryman, 2009, Pewterers' Co.; Freeman, City of London, 2009. Editorial Cttee, Jl of Anatomy, 1981–94; Associated Editor: Jl of Neurocytol., 1980–83; Neuromuscular Disorders, 1990–94; Muscle and Nerve, 1997–2001. *Publications:* The Peripheral Nerve, 1976; contribs to learned jls on the fine structure, develt and pathology of nerve and muscle. *Recreations:* gardening, travel. *Address:* Woodmans, Wallcrouch, Wadhurst, East Sussex TN5 7JG.

**LANDSHOFF, Prof. Peter Vincent,** PhD; Professor of Mathematical Physics, University of Cambridge, 1994–2004; Fellow, Christ's College, Cambridge, since 1963 (Vice-Master, 1999–2002); Consultant, Cambridge-MIT Institute, 2004–07; *b* 22 March 1937; *m* 1962, Pamela Carmichael; three *s*. *Educ:* City of London Sch.; St John's Coll., Cambridge (MA, PhD). FInstP 1999. Cambridge University: Fellow, St John's Coll., 1961–63; Reader in Mathematical Physics, 1974–94. Instructor, Princeton Univ., 1961–62; Scientific Associate, CERN, Geneva, 1975–76, 1984–85, 1991–92. Chairman, Management Committee: Isaac Newton Inst. for Mathematical Scis, 1990–94 and 2001–06; Cambridge eScience Centre, 2001–04; Nat. Inst. for Envmtl eScience, 2002–04; Cambridge Computational Biol. Inst., 2003–04; Council, Sch. of Physical Scis, Cambridge Univ., 2004. Trustee, Cambridge Past, Present and Future (formerly Cambridge Preservation Soc.), 2007–14; Chairman: E of England Assoc. of Civic Trust Socs, 2008–15; E of England RSA, 2010–12 (Vice-Chm., 2009–10); Cam Catchment Partnership, 2013–; Leader, E of England Transport Information project, 2009–; Mem. Bd, Natural Cambridgeshire, 2018–. Hon. Vice-Chm., Cambridge Ahead, 2013–. Editor, Physics Letters B (Elsevier Science), 1982–2005. *Publications:* (jtly) The Analytic S-Matrix, 1966; (jtly) Simple Quantum Physics, 1979, 2nd edn 1997; Pomeron Physics and QCD, 2002; research papers on theoretical high-energy physics. *Address:* Department of Applied Mathematics and Theoretical Physics, Centre for Mathematical Sciences, Wilberforce Road, Cambridge CB3 0WA. *T:* (01223) 337880. *E:* pvl@damtp.cam.ac.uk. *W:* www.damtp.cam.ac.uk/user/pvl.

**LANDSMAN, David Maurice,** OBE 2000; PhD; Co-Founder, Agora Envisioning Ltd, 2019; writer and speaker; *b* 23 Aug. 1963; *s* of Sidney Landsman and Miriam Landsman (*née* Cober); *m* 1990, Catherine Louise Holden; one *s*. *Educ:* Chigwell Sch.; Oriel Coll., Oxford (BA Lit. Hum. 1985; MA 1988); Clare Coll., Cambridge (MPhil 1986; PhD 1989). Univ. of Cambridge Local Exams Syndicate, 1988–89; entered FCO, 1989; Second Secretary: (Econ.) Athens, 1991–94; FCO, 1994–97; Dep. Hd of Mission, Belgrade, 1997–99; FCO 1999; Hd of Office, Banja Luka, and concurrently First Sec., Budapest, 1999–2000; Hd, British Interests Section, Embassy of Brazil, and subseq. Chargé d'Affaires, British Embassy Belgrade, 2000–01; Ambassador to Albania, 2001–03; Hd, Counter-Proliferation Dept, FCO, 2003–06; on secondment as Internat. Affairs Advr, De La Rue Identity Systems, 2006–08; Balkans Dir, FCO, 2008; Ambassador to Greece, 2009–13; Exec. Dir, Tata Ltd, 2013–18. Non-exec. Dir, DocuChain Ltd, 2019–; Mem., Adv. Bd, D Gp, 2019–. Dir, UK-India Business Council, 2013–. Mem., London Council, CBI, 2015–17; Chair, Confedn of Indian Industry India-UK Business Forum, 2017–18. Vis. Fellow, Judge Business Sch., Univ. of Cambridge, 2018–. MInstD 2013, FInstD 2016; Dip. Inst. of Dirs, 2015; CDir 2016. *Publications:* contrib. occasional articles on the Greek lang. and other langs, leadership, communications and other subjects. *Recreations:* travel, languages, music, food, visiting zoos. *Club:* Athenæum.

**LANDY, John Michael,** AC 2001; CVO 2005; MBE 1955; Governor of Victoria, Australia, 2001–06; *b* 12 April 1930; *s* of Clarence Gordon Landy and Elva Katherine Ashton; *m* 1971, Lynne (*née* Fisher); one *s* one *d*. *Educ:* Malvern Grammar Sch.; Geelong Grammar; Univ. of Melbourne (BAgrSc). Holder: 1500m World Record, 1954–55; one mile World Record, 1954–57; Olympic and Commonwealth Games medals; second man to run the mile in under 4 mins. ICI Australia, 1962–82, R&D Manager, Biological Gp, 1971–82. Comr Gen., Australian Pavilion Expo 86, Vancouver, 1986. Chairman: Wool R&D Corp., 1989–94; Clean-up Australia, 1990–94; Australia Day Cttee (Victoria), 1990–93; Coode Is. (major chemical spill) Review Panel, 1991–92; Athletics Task Force, 1992–93; Meat Res. Corp., 1995–98; Dir, Australian Sports Drug Agency, 1998–2000. Chairman: Bd Governors, Australian Nat. Insect Collection, 1995–2000; Aust. Wool Testing Authy Ltd Wool Educn Trust, 1997–2000; Athletics Internat. Trust, 1997–2000; Pres., Greening Australia (Victoria), 1998–2000; Member: Land Conservation Council of Victoria, 1971–79; Reference Areas Cttee, Victoria's system of Scientific Reference Areas, 1979–86; Bd Dirs, Australian Inst. of Sport, 1985–87; External Earnings Review Working Party, Aust. Sci. and Technol. Council, 1993–94. Chm., Adv. Panel, Victorian Bushfire Appeal Fund, 2009. Hon. LLD: Victoria, BC, 1994; Melbourne, 2003; Deakin, 2004; Hon. D Rural Sci. New England, 1997. *Publications:* Close to Nature, 1985 (C. J. Dennis Award); A Coastal Diary, 1993.

**LANDY, Michael Anthony Andrew,** RA 2008; artist; Associate Artist in Residence, National Gallery, 2010–12; *b* London, 13 May 1963; *s* of John and Ethel Landy; partner, Gillian Wearing, *qv*. *Educ:* Goldsmiths' Coll., Univ. of London (BA 1st Cl. Hons Fine Art 1988). Solo exhibitions include: Market, 1990; Nourishment, 2002; Saints Alive, 2013; Breaking News, 2015; Out of Order, 2016; works include, Break Down, 2001; Semi-Detached, 2004; Art Bin, 2010; Acts of Kindness, 2010–11. Sir Roland Penrose Meml Lect., Tate Modern, 2013. *Publications:* Michael Landy: everything must go, 2008. *Recreation:* running. *Club:* Ivy.

**LANE, Anthony John,** CB 1990; Deputy Secretary, Department of Trade and Industry, 1987–96; *b* 30 May 1939; *e s* of late Eric Marshall Lane and Phyllis Mary Lane; *m* 1967, Judith Sheila (*née* Dodson); two *s* one *d*. *Educ:* Caterham Sch.; Balliol Coll., Oxford (BA PPE, MA). Investment Analyst, Joseph Sebag & Co., 1964–65; joined Civil Service as Asst Principal, 1965; various appts in DTI, Dept of Transport, DoE and OFT; Prin. Pvte Sec. to several Ministers; Asst Sec., 1975; Under Sec., 1980; Head of Internat. Trade Policy, DTI, 1984–87; Dep. Dir Gen., OFT, 1987–90; Dir Gen. for Industry, DTI, 1990–94; Chief Exec., PSA, 1994–96. Associate Dir, Maxwell Stamp plc, econ. consultants, 1997–2009. Brighton University: Mem., Bd of Govs, 1997–2006 (Dep. Chm., 1999–2002); Chm., Univ. Property Cttee, 1998–99. *Recreations:* music, gardens, travel. *Address:* Fountain House, Dulcote, Wells, Som BA5 3NU.

**LANE, Maj.-Gen. Barry Michael,** CB 1984; OBE 1974 (MBE 1965); Chief Executive, Cardiff Bay Development Corporation, 1987–92; *b* 10 Aug. 1932; *m* 1st, 1956, Eveline Jean (*d* 1986), *d* of Vice-Adm. Sir Harry Koelle, KCB and Enid (*née* Corbould-Ellis); one *s* one *d*; 2nd, 1987, Shirley Ann, *d* of E. V. Hawtin. *Educ:* Dover Coll. Commissioned, 1954; served Somerset LI, 1954–59, Somerset and Cornwall LI, 1959–68, LI, 1968–75; Instructor, Staff Coll. Camberley, 1970–72; CO, 1st Bn, LI, 1972–75; Comd, 11 Armoured Bde, 1977–78; RCDS, 1979; Dep. Dir, Army Staff Duties, MoD, 1980–81; Dir, Army Quartering, 1981–82; VQMG, 1982–83; GOC SW Dist, 1984–87. Col, The LI, 1982–87. Hon. Colonel: 6th Bn, LI, 1987–97; Bristol Univ., OTC, 1988–99. Pres. of Council, and Chm. of Govs, Taunton Sch., 1997–2001; Vice Pres., St Margaret's Somerset Hospice, 2003–. *Club:* Army and Navy.

**LANE, Prof. Christine Susanna,** DPhil; Professor of Geography, University of Cambridge, since 2016; *b* Harlow, 9 Sept. 1980; *d* of Cdre Christopher Lane and Elizabeth Ann Lane. *Educ:* Univ. of Wales, Cardiff (BSc Geol. 2003); Royal Holloway, Univ. of London (MSc Geog. 2004); Linacre Coll., Oxford (DPhil Archaeol. 2008). Postdoctoral Res. Asst, 2009–12, Postdoctoral Fellow, 2012–14, Univ. of Oxford; Lectr in Quaternary Envmtl Change, Univ. of Manchester, 2014–16. Leverhulme Trust Early Career Fellow, 2012–15. *Address:* Department of Geography, University of Cambridge, Downing Place, Cambridge CB2 3EN. *T:* (01223) 330242. *E:* csl44@cam.ac.uk.

**LANE, Clive Nicholas;** a Judge of the Upper Tribunal (Immigration and Asylum Chamber), since 2009; *b* Worcester, 16 Nov. 1957; *s* of late Frank Henry Lane and June Maureen Lane (*née* Moore); *m* 1985, Heather Elizabeth Owen; one *d*. *Educ:* St Stephen's Primary Sch., Worcester; Royal Grammar Sch., Worcester; New Coll., Oxford (BA Hons Mod. Hist. 1979); City of Birmingham Poly. (Law Soc. Final Exam. 1983). Admitted solicitor, 1985; Partner, Ginn & Co. solicitors, Cambridge, 1986–2001, Sen. Partner, 2000–01; Dep. Dist Chm., Social Security Tribunal (Appeals Service), 1999–2007; a Dep. District Judge, 2001–; Immigration Judge (formerly Adjudicator), Asylum and Immigration Tribunal (formerly Immigration Appellate Authy), 2001–09; Legal Mem., Special Immigration Appeals Commn, 2014–. Mem., Friends of Ilkley Lido. Trustee, Prestiegne Festival of Music and the Arts, 2018– (Chm., 2018–). *Publications:* contribs to legal jls incl. Family Law. *Recreations:* hill walking, ornithology, 'cello, theatre, opera, Worcestershire County Cricket Club, urban vinyl, seeking out doom paintings in English churches. *Address:* Upper Tribunal (Immigration and Asylum Chamber), Phoenix House, Rushton Avenue, Bradford BD7 3BH. *T:* (01274) 267063. *E:* uppertribunaljudge.lane@ejudiciary.net. *Club:* Oxford and Cambridge.
See also Hon. Sir P. R. Lane.

**LANE, David Goodwin;** QC 1991; a Recorder of the Crown Court, since 1987; *b* 8 Oct. 1945; *s* of James Cooper Lane and Joyce Lilian Lane; *m* 1991, Jacqueline Elizabeth Cocks. *Educ:* Crypt Sch., Gloucester; King's College London (LLB, AKC). Lord Justice Holker Junior Exhibnr; Lee Essay Prizeman, H. C. Richard Ecclesiastical Law Prizeman; Albion Richardson Scholar. Called to the Bar, Gray's Inn, 1968; Asst Recorder, 1982. Freeman, City of London.

**LANE, David Ian, (David Ian);** theatre producer, since 1991; Chairman: Global Theatre, Live Nation, 2005–07; David Ian Productions Ltd, since 2006; *b* 15 Feb. 1961; *s* of Reg and Jean Lane; *m* 1994, Tracy Carter; one *s* one *d*. *Educ:* Ilford County High Grammar Sch. Joined Live Nation (formerly Clear Channel Entertainment), 2000. Actor: title rôle, Joseph and the Amazing Technicolor Dreamcoat; Pirates of Penzance, London Palladium; Time, Dominion. Producer, 1991–: Ain't Misbehavin', Lyric, 1995; Saturday Night Fever, London Palladium, 1998; Defending the Caveman, Apollo, 1999; The King and I, London Palladium, 2000; Grease (revival), Dominion, 2001, transf. Cambridge Th. and Victoria Palace; Daisy Pulls It Off, Lyric, 2002; Anything Goes, 2003, The Producers, 2004, Drury Lane Th. Royal; Guys and Dolls, Piccadilly, 2005; The Sound of Music, London Palladium, 2006; Grease, Piccadilly, 2007; La Cage aux Folles, Playhouse; Shawshank Redemption, Wyndhams; Sweet Charity, Haymarket; Flashdance, Shaftesbury; The Bodyguard, Adelphi; Gypsy, Savoy; Cats, Palladium; Show Boat, New London; also many UK tours and productions in USA and Australia. *Recreations:* running, football, fishing, boating. *Address:* (office) David Ian Productions Ltd, 45 Monmouth Street, 2nd Floor, WC2H 9DG.

**LANE, David Neil,** CMG 1983; HM Diplomatic Service, retired; *b* 16 April 1928; *er s* of late Clive and Hilda Lane, Bath; *m* 1968, Sara, *d* of late Cecil Nurcombe, MC; two *d*. *Educ:* Abbotsholme Sch.; Merton Coll., Oxford. Army, 1946–48; Foreign (later Foreign and Commonwealth) Office: 1951–53, 1955–58, 1963–68, 1972–74; British Embassy, Oslo, 1953–55; Ankara, 1959–61, 1975–78; Conakry, 1961–63; UK Mission to the United Nations, New York, 1968–72, 1979; NI Office, 1978–79; High Comr in Trinidad and Tobago, 1980–85; Ambassador to the Holy See, 1985–88. Pres., UN Trusteeship Council, 1971–72; UK Delegate, Internat. Exhibns Bureau, 1973–74. Asst Sec.-Gen., 1989–92, Sec., 1990–92, Order of St John; OStJ 1990. Chm., Anglo-Turkish Soc., 1995–2001. Composer, Three Carols for chorus and orchestra, 1949. *Address:* 6 Montagu Square, W1H 2LB. *T:* (020) 7486 1673.

**LANE, Sir David (Philip),** Kt 2000; PhD; FRCPath, FMedSci; FRS 1996; FRSE; Chief Scientist, Agency for Science, Technology and Research, Singapore, since 2009 (Executive Director, Institute of Molecular and Cell Biology, 2004–07 (on sabbatical); Chairman, Biomedical Research Council, 2007–09); *b* 1 July 1952; *s* of John Wallace Lane and Cecelia Frances Evelyn Lane (*née* Wright); *m* 1975, Ellen Birgitte Muldal; one *s* one *d*. *Educ:* John Fisher Sch., Purley; University College London (BSc 1973, PhD 1976; Fellow). FRCPath 1996. FRSE 1992. Res. Fellow, ICRF, 1976–77; Lectr, Imperial Coll., 1977–85; Staff Scientist, ICRF, 1985–90; Prof. of Molecular Oncology, Univ. of Dundee, 1990–2009; CEO, Experimental Therapeutic Centre, Singapore, 2007–09; Chief Scientist, CRUK, 2007–10; Scientific Dir, Ludwig Inst., 2013–16. Prof., Karolinska Inst., Sweden, 2016–. Vis. Fellow, Cold Spring Harbor Labs, NY, 1998–87; Gibb Fellow, Cancer Res. UK (formerly CRC), 1990–. Founder, Dir and Chief Scientific Officer, Cyclacel Pharmaceuticals Inc., 1996–2004; Chm., Chugai Pharmabody Res., 2013–. Mem., EMBO, 1990. Founder FMedSci 1998; FAACR 2016. Hon. DSc: Abertay Dundee, 1999; Stirling,

2000; Aberdeen, 2002; Birmingham, 2002; Hon. MD Nottingham, 2006; Dr *hc* Univ. Paul Sabatier, Toulouse, 2007. Prize, Charles Rodolphe Brupbacher Foundn, 1993; Prize, Joseph Steiner Foundn, 1993; Howard Hughes Internat. Scholar, Howard Hughes Med. Inst., 1993; Yvette Mayent Prize, Inst. Curie, 1994; Medal, Swedish Soc. of Oncology, 1994; Prize, Meyenburg Foundn, 1995; Black Prize, Jefferson Hosp., 1995; Silvanus Thompson Medal, British Inst. of Radiol., 1996; Henry Dryerre Prize, 1996; Paul Ehrlich Prize, 1998; Tom Connors Prize, 1998; Bruce-Preller Prize, 1998; SCI Medal, 2003; Anthony Dipple Carcinogenesis Award, 2004; Buchanan Medal, Royal Soc., 2004; Biochem. Soc. Award, 2004; Internat. Agency for Res. on Cancer Medal, 2005; Sergio Lombroso Award for Cancer Research Work, 2005; INSERM Medal d'Etranger, 2006; Gregor Mendel Medal, Masaryk Cancer Inst., Czech Republic, 2006; Colin Thomson Medal, Beatson Inst., Glasgow, 2007; David Hungerford Medal, Bangalore, 2007; Royal Medal, RSE, 2008; CRUK Lifetime Achievement Award, 2013; President's Sci. and Technol. Medal, Singapore, 2017; Debrecen Award for Molecular Medicine, Univ. of Debrecen, 2018. *Publications:* Antibodies: a laboratory manual, 1988; over 400 papers in learned jls. *Recreations:* tennis, motorcycles, old cars, walking. *Address:* Agency for Science, Technology and Research, 8A Biomedical Grove, #06–06 Immunos, Singapore 138648, Republic of Singapore.

**LANE, David Stuart,** PhD, DPhil; FAcSS; Reader in Sociology, 1992–2000, now Reader Emeritus, and Fellow of Emmanuel College, 1974–80 and 1990–2000, now Emeritus Fellow, Senior Research Associate, 2001–07, University of Cambridge; *b* Monmouthshire (now Gwent), 24 April 1933; *s* of Reginald and Mary Lane; *m* 1962, Christel Noritzsch; one *s* one *d*. *Educ:* Univ. of Birmingham (BSocSc); Univ. of Oxford (DPhil); PhD Cantab. Graduate student, Nuffield Coll., Oxford, 1961–62, 1964–65. Formerly engrg trainee, local authority employee, sch. teacher; univ. teacher, Birmingham, Essex (Reader in Sociology) and Cambridge Univs; Prof. of Sociology, Univ. of Birmingham, 1981–90; Lectr in Sociology, Cambridge Univ., 1990–92. Visiting Professor: Lund Univ., 1985; Cornell Univ., 1987; Univ. of Graz, 1991, 1996; Harvard Univ., 1993, 2001; Kennan Inst., Washington, 1986, 1996; Sabanci Univ., 2000–02; Peking Univ., 2018–. Member: Exec. Cttee, British Sociol Assoc., 1987–92; Exec. Cttee, European Social Assoc., 1999–2001; Cttee, Free Economic Soc. of Russia; Vice Pres., Soc. for Co-operation in Russian and Soviet Studies, 2013–; Co-Chair, first European Conf. of Sociology, 1992. Vice-Chm., Birmingham Rathbone, 1986–90; Vice-Chm., Down's Children's Assoc., 1981–82; Chm., W Midlands Council for Disabled People, 1983–86. ESRC res. award to study Soviet and Russian political elites, 1991–95, econ. elites, 1996–98, and financial business elite, 1999–2002; Leverhulme Trust res. award to study transformation of state socialism, 2004–07; British Acad. network award for study of strategic elites and European enlargement, 2004–08, award to study coloured revolutions, 2009–10, res. award to study unemployment in Ukraine and China, 2012; Mem., EU Inter-Univs Consortium to study new modes of governance within the EU, 2004–08. FAcSS (AcSS 2011). Participates in meetings of Valdai Discussion Club (Russian Fedn) (contrib. website), Moscow Econ. Forum, and Assoc. for Slavic, E Eur. and Eurasian Studies. Member, Editorial Boards: Sociology, 1985–88; Disability, Handicap and Society, 1987–90; Eur. Politics and Society (formerly Perspectives on European Politics and Society), 1990–; Mir Rossii, 2006–. *Publications:* Roots of Russian Communism, 1969, 2nd edn 1975; Politics and Society in the USSR, 1970, 2nd edn 1978; The End of Inequality?, 1971; (with G. Kolankiewicz) Social Groups in Polish Society, 1973; The Socialist Industrial State, 1976; (with F. O'Dell) The Soviet Industrial Worker, 1978; The Work Needs of Mentally Handicapped Adults, 1980; Leninism: a sociological interpretation, 1981; The End of Social Inequality?: class status and power under state socialism, 1982; State and Politics in the USSR, 1985; Soviet Economy and Society, 1985; (ed jtly and contrib.) Current Approaches to Down's Syndrome, 1985; (ed) Employment and Labour in the USSR, 1986; Soviet Labour and the Ethic of Communism, 1987; (ed and contrib.) Political Power and Elites in the USSR, 1988; Soviet Society under Perestroika, 1990, 2nd edn 1992; (ed and contrib.) Russia in Flux, 1992; (ed and contrib.) Russia in Transition, 1995; The Rise and Fall of State Socialism, 1996, trans. Russian, 2006, Japanese, 2007; (with C. Ross) The Transition from Communism to Capitalism: ruling elites from Gorbachev to Eltsin, 1998; (ed and contrib.) Political Economy of Russian Oil, 1999; (ed and contrib.) The Legacy of State Socialism and the Future of Transformation, 2002; (ed and contrib.) Russian Banking: evolution, problems and prospects, 2002; (ed with M. Myant and contrib.) Varieties of Capitalism in Post-Communist Countries, 2007; (ed and contrib.) The Transformation of State Socialism: system change, capitalism or something else?, 2007; (ed jtly and contrib.) Revolution in the Making of the Modern World, 2007; (ed jtly) Restructuring of Economic Elites after State Socialism: recruitment, institutions and attitudes, 2007; (ed with A. Gamble and contrib.) European Union and World Politics, 2009; (ed jtly) Migration and Mobility in Europe, 2009; (ed with S. White and contrib.) Rethinking the 'Coloured Revolutions', 2010; (ed and contrib.) Elites and Identities in Post-Soviet Space, 2011; Elites and Classes in the Transformation of State Socialism, 2011; The Capitalist Transformation of State Socialism, 2013; The Capitalist Transformation of State Socialism: the making and breaking of state socialist society and what followed, 2014; (contrib.) Political Elites in the Transatlantic Crisis, 2014; (ed with V. Samokhvalov and contrib.) The Eurasian Project and Europe: regional discontinuities and geopolitics, 2015; (ed and contrib.) The Eurasian Project in Global Perspective, 2018; contribs to jls incl. Perspectives on European Politics and Society, Pol Studies, Europe-Asia Studies, Sociology, Jl of Communist Studies and Transition Politics, Political Qly, Studies in Comparative Econ. Develt, British Jl of Pols and of Internat. Relns, New Pol Economy, Comparative Econ. Studies, Eur. Politics and Society, Eur. Societies, Mir Rossii, Sotsiologicheski Zhurnal, Sotsiologicheskie Issledovaniya, Revue Française de Sci. Politique, POLIS (Moscow), Mir Peremen (Moscow), Russian Analytical Digest (Zurich), Alternativy (Moscow), Voprosy politicheskoy ekonomikii (Moscow), Internat. Critical Thought. *Recreations:* soccer, squash, films, TV, theatre, watching Arsenal FC. *Address:* Emmanuel College, Cambridge CB2 3AP. *T:* (01223) 359113, *Fax:* (01223) 334426. *E:* dsl10@cam.ac.uk.

**LANE, Rt Rev. Elizabeth Jane Holden;** *see* Derby, Bishop of.

**LANE, Ian Francis,** DM; FRCS, FRCSE; vascular surgeon; Consultant Surgeon: University Hospital of Wales, 1988–2012; Spire Hospital, 1988–2016; Medical Director, Cardiff and Vale NHS Trust, 1999–2009; *b* 14 May 1952; *s* of Frank Ernest Lane and Teresa Ellen Lane (*née* Wallace); *m* 1980, Carol Myhill Morris; one *s* one *d*. *Educ:* Downside Sch.; Lincoln Coll., Oxford (BA (Physiol.) 1973; BM BCh 1976; MA 1979; DM 1987; MCh 1988); St Thomas' Hosp. Med. Sch. MRCS 1976, FRCS 1981; FRCSE 1981. Lectr in Surgery, Charing Cross and Westminster Med. Sch., 1981–88; Hon. Teacher in Vascular Surgery, Univ. of Wales Coll. of Medicine, 1988–. Dir, Ethics Cttee, Dr Foster Research, 2006–. Mem. Council, Vascular Surgical Soc. of GB and Ireland, 1999–2002; Sec., Venous Forum, RSocMed, 2000–03. Non-exec. Dir, Time for Medicine, 2010–16. Mem., Ct of Examrs, RCS, 1995–2001. *Publications:* res. and teaching articles in peer-reviewed jls on aspects of arterial and venous disease. *Recreations:* fine arts, travel to remote areas, exotic cars, wine.

**LANE, Jane;** *see* Tewson, J.

**LANE, John Bristowe;** Partner, Linklaters, since 2000; *b* Johannesburg, 18 May 1965; *s* of William and Elizabeth Lane; *m* 1990, Karen Ann Maher; three *s*. *Educ:* St John's Coll., Johannesburg; Univ. of Cape Town (BA 1985; LLB 1987); Trinity Hall, Cambridge (LLM 1991). Qualified as Attorney, Webber Wentzel, Johannesburg, 1989; Linklaters: trainee, 1991–93; admitted Solicitor, 1993; Asst Solicitor, Corporate Dept, London, 1993–99. *Recreations:* walking, cycling, tennis, the Listing Rules. *Address:* Linklaters LLP, One Silk Street, EC2V 8HQ. *T:* (020) 7456 3542, *Fax:* (020) 7456 2222. *E:* john.lane@linklaters.com.

**LANE, Rev. John Ernest,** OBE 1994; charity consultant; Associate: Craigmyle & Co., 2001–05; Bill Bruty Associates, 2001–14; Fundraising Training Co., 2001–14; Director, Corporate Affairs, St Mungo Community Housing Association Ltd, 1996–2001; *b* 16 June 1939; *s* of Ernest William Lane and Winifred (*née* Lloyd); *m* 1st, 1962, Eileen Williams (marr. diss. 1988); three *d*; 2nd, 2001, Ishbel Margaret, *d* of late William Curr and of Jean Curr (*née* Payne). *Educ:* Burnley Grammar Sch.; Handsworth Coll., Birmingham; City of London Polytechnic (DMS); Cranfield Inst. of Technol. (MSc). Methodist Minister: Llanharan, 1962–64; Great Harwood, 1964–67; Lewisham and Peckham, 1967–72; Dir, Peckham Settlement, 1972–77; Nat. Public Relns Officer, YWCA of GB, 1977–80; Dir and Sec., St Mungo Community Housing Assoc. Ltd, 1980–96; Sec., 1980–96, Dir, 1994–96, St Mungo Assoc. Charitable Trust. Ordained deacon and priest, 1980; Hon. Curate, St John and St Andrew, Peckham, 1980–95; permission to officiate: dio. of Southwark, 1995–98; Lichfield Cathedral, 2002–; NSM, St Alfege with St Peter, Greenwich, 1998–2000. Administrateur, European Fedn of Nat. Orgns Working with the Homeless, 1991–95. Dir, Nat. Sleep Out Week, 1990–94. Trustee: Newton's Trust, 2006–16; Dr Milley's Hosp., 2008–12. *Publications:* (ed) Homelessness in Industrialised Countries, 1987. *Recreations:* politics, social affairs, cooking, washing up, cricket, travel, arts. *Address:* 2 Tregony Rise, Lichfield, Staffs WS14 9SN. *T:* (01543) 415078.

**LANE, Jonathan Stewart,** OBE 2015; FRICS; Chairman, Shaftesbury PLC UK, 2013–16 (Deputy Chairman, 2011–13); *b* Camborne, Cornwall, 10 Nov. 1945; *s* of Thurstan Tregoning Lane and Mary Lane (*née* Marriott); *m* 1969, Kerry Grant; two *d*. *Educ:* Clifton Coll., Bristol; Oriel Coll., Oxford (MA Modern Hist. 1967; Hon. Fellow 2016). FRICS 1971. Cadet valuer, Valuation Office, Inland Revenue, 1968–71; Stock Conversion plc: Exec., 1971–78; Dir, 1978–82; Gen. Manager, 1982–84; Man. Dir, 1984–86; Chief Exec., Shaftesbury PLC UK, 1986–2011. Non-executive Director and Chairman: Porthminster Hotel Ltd, 1979–2008; Tregarthen's Hotel (Scilly) Ltd, 1980–2015; non-exec. Chm., EasyHotel plc, 2015– (non-exec. Dir, 2014–15); non-exec. Dir, Capital and Counties plc, 2019–. Member: Property Cttee, Art Fund (formerly NACF), 2006–10; Property Panel, 2010– (Chm.), Investment Adv. Cttee, 2015–, Oriel Coll., Oxford; Capital Develt Cttee (formerly 2020 Strategy Gp, then Estates 2025 Cttee), Royal Botanic Gdns, Kew, 2014–; Commercial Adv. Gp, Nat. Trust, 2016–. Trustee and Deputy Chairman: Crafts Council, 1988–98; Theatres Trust, 1994–2003 (Special Advr, 2003–); Trustee: Royal Shakespeare Trust, later Royal Th. Support Trust, 2008–; Oppenheim-John Downes Meml Trust, 2013–. Gov., RSC, 1997–2009. Councillor, LTA, 1997–2015; Chm., 2007–16, Vice Pres. 2016–19, Tennis Foundn. *Recreations:* family, theatre, music, walking, fishing. *Address:* 35 Hillcroft Crescent, Ealing, W5 2SG.

**LANE, Kenneth Frederick;** former mining consultant; Director, RTZ Consultants, 1988–97; *b* 22 March 1928; British; *m* 1950, Kathleen Richards; one *s* two *d*. *Educ:* Emmanuel Coll., Cambridge. Degree in Maths. Steel Industry in Sheffield, 1951–59; North America, 1959–61; Rio Tinto-Zinc Corp., 1961–65; Man. Dir, RTZ Consultants Ltd, 1965–70; Dir, RTZ Corp., 1970–75. Vis. Prof., RSM, 1979–85. *Publications:* The Economic Definition of Ore, 1988. *Recreations:* bridge, boat building, sailing. *Address:* 4 Towerdene, 16 Tower Road, Poole, Dorset BH13 6HZ. *T:* (01202) 751958.

**LANE, Lindsay Ruth Busfield;** QC 2019; *b* Colchester, 1972; *d* of Michael Lane and Joan Busfield; partner, Mark John Summers, *qv*; one *s* one *d*. *Educ:* Colchester Co. High Sch. for Girls; Newnham Coll., Cambridge (BA 1994); European University Inst., Florence (LLM). Called to the Bar, Middle Temple, 1996; in practice as a barrister, 1996–. *Publications:* (jtly) The Modern Law of Copyright and Designs, 2000, 5th edn as The Modern Law of Copyright, 2018. *Recreation:* cooking. *Address:* 8 New Square, Lincoln's Inn, WC2A 3QP. *T:* (020) 7405 4321.

**LANE, Dr Nancy Jane,** OBE 1994; CBiol, FRSB; FZS; Senior Research Associate, Zoology Department, University of Cambridge, since 1990; Lecturer, since 1970, Fellow, 1970–2006, now Life Fellow, Girton College, Cambridge; *d* of Temple Haviland Lane and Frances de Forest Gilbert Lane; *m* 1969, Prof. Richard Nelson Perham, FRS (*d* 2015); one *s* one *d*. *Educ:* Dalhousie Univ., Nova Scotia (BSc, MSc); Lady Margaret Hall, Oxford (DPhil 1963); Girton Coll., Cambridge (PhD 1968; ScD 1981). CBiol 1991, FRSB (FIBiol 1991); FZS 1986. Res. Asst Prof., Albert Einstein Coll. of Medicine, NY, 1964–65; Res. Staff Biologist, Yale Univ., 1965–68; University of Cambridge: SSO, 1968–73, PSO, 1973–82, SPSO, 1982–90, AFRC Unit, Zoology Dept; Tutor, Girton Coll., 1975–98; Project Dir, Women in Science, Engrg and Technology Initiative, 1999–2006. Editor-in-Chief, Cell Biol. Internat., 1995–98; Chm., Editl Cttee, People and Science (formerly Science and Public Affairs), 2001–13. Vis. Lectr, British Council, 1999–2004. Non-executive Director: Smith & Nephew plc, 1991–2000; Peptide Therapeutics plc, 1995–98. Mem., PM's Adv. Panel for Citizen's Charter, 1991–93; Chairman: BTEC's Adv. Bd for Sci. and Caring, 1991–94; Wkg Party for Women in Sci. and Engrg (OST), Cabinet Office, 1993–94. Member: Forum UK, 1994–2008; All Souls Gp, Oxford, 1994–2005; CVCP's Commn on Univ. Career Opportunities (CUCO), 1996–2000; UNESCO's Sci. Cttee for Women, Sci. and Technol., 1997–; Scientific, Engrg and Envmt Adv. Cttee, British Council, 2003–07; UNESCO Cttee for Natural Scis, 2005–10. Founder, Athena Project, 1998; Dep. Chm., Steering Cttee for CUCO/OST/HEFCE Athena Project, 1998–2003; Chm., Athena Project, 2003–07. Dir, 1997–2004, Mem. Council, 2005–, Women of the Year Lunch and Assembly; Partner, UK Resource Centre for Women in Sci., DTI, 2004–08; Chm., UK Resource Centre Experts Database, 2005–07; Gender Equality Champion, Zoology Dept, Cambridge Univ., 2013–. Pres., Inst. of Biology, 2002–04; Member: Council, Zool Soc. of London, 1998–2001 (Vice-Pres., 1999–2001); Brit. Soc. Cell Biol., 1980– (Sec., 1982–90); Exec. Council, Biosciences Fedn, 2002–06. Co-author, SET Fair, Greenfield Report, 2002. Mem., Selection Bd, Vanier/Banting Canada Grad. Scholarships Prog., 2009–11. FRSA 1992; MInstD 1991. Hon. Fellow, BAAS, 2005. Hon. LLD Dalhousie, 1985; Hon. ScD: Salford, 1994; Sheffield Hallam, 2002; Oxford Brookes, 2003; Surrey, 2005; Heriot-Watt, 2015. Elected to Nova Scotia Hall of Fame for Sci. and Technology, 2006. *Publications:* contrib. numerous scientific papers and chapters on cell-cell junctions, cellular structures and interactions, in field of cell biology, and on women in science, in a range of learned scientific jls. *Recreations:* theatre, ballet and opera, 20th century art, travelling. *Address:* Department of Zoology, University of Cambridge, Downing Street, Cambridge CB2 3EJ. *T:* (01223) 336600/363710. *E:* njl1@cam.ac.uk.

**LANE, Peter Alfred;** artist potter, photographer and author; *b* 26 April 1932; *s* of late Alfred John Lane and Freda Margaret Lane; *m* 1958, Margaret Jean Edwards (*d* 2009); two *d*. *Educ:* Bath Acad. of Art (Art Teacher's Cert.); Cert Ed Bristol 1956. Art teacher: Botley Co. (All-Age) Sch., Berks, 1956–58; Head, Art Department: Matthew Arnold Secondary Sch.,

Cumnor, Berks, 1958–60; Andover GS, 1961–64; Lectr/Organiser, Somerset Coll. of Art, Taunton, 1964–66; Keswick Hall College of Education, Norwich: Lectr in Art Educn and Ceramics, 1966–70; Sen. Lectr, 1970–80; Hd, Art Dept, 1980–81; University of E Anglia: Sen. Lectr and Hd, Dept of Art Educn and Ceramics, 1981–84; Sen. Fellow in Art Educn, 1984–87. Examr/Assessor at various art colls, 1980–88. Judge, ceramics exhibns in UK, 1964–; Judge, international ceramics exhibitions: 2nd Biennale Canadian Ceramics, 1986; Fletcher Challenge Ceramics Award, NZ, 1989; 1st Taiwan Ceramics Biennale, 2004; Zelli Porcelain Award, 2005. Has exhibited, lectured and demonstrated ceramics widely throughout the world; individual ceramics in many public collections in UK, Australia, Canada, Europe, Korea, USA; retrospective exhibn, Peter Lane: 60 years in ceramics, Devon Guild of Craftsmen, Bovey Tracey, Devon, 2018. Co-founder, Norfolk Contemporary Crafts Soc., 1971. Fellow: Craft Potters' Assoc. of GB, 1962 (Hon. Fellow 2004); Soc. of Designer Craftsmen, 1976 (Hon. Fellow, 2015). Member: Devon Guild of Craftsmen, 2013 (Mem., Selection Cttee, 2014–17). Mem., Internat. Acad. Ceramics, Geneva, 1997. Chairman: New Alresford Probus Club, Hants, 2009–; Tavistock Probus Club, Devon, 2017–. Centennial Silver Medal, Soc. Designer Craftsmen, 1981. *Publications:* Studio Porcelain, 1980; Studio Ceramics, 1983; Ceramic Form, 1988, new enlarged edn 1998; (consultant ed and contrib.) Ceramics Manual, 1990; Contemporary Porcelain, 1995; Contemporary Studio Porcelain, 2003; contrib. numerous mag. articles on ceramics; book and exhibn reviews, 1970–. *Recreations:* fell-walking, painting, foreign travel, theatre, landscape and nature photography. *Address:* Tavistock, Devon.

**LANE, Hon. Sir Peter (Richard)**, Kt 2017; **Hon. Mr Justice Lane;** a Judge of the High Court, Queen's Bench Division, since 2017; President, Upper Tribunal (Immigration and Asylum Chamber), since 2017; *b* 26 April 1953; *s* of late Frank Henry Lane and of June Maureen Lane (*née* Moore); *m* 1980, Shelley Ilene Munjack (*see* S. I. M. Lane); one *s* one *d*. *Educ:* St Stephen's Primary Sch., Worcester; Worcester Royal Grammar Sch.; Hertford Coll., Oxford (BA 1st cl. (Jurisprudence) 1974); Univ. of Calif, Berkeley (LLM 1975). Called to the Bar, Middle Temple, 1976, Bencher, 2018; re-qualified as Solicitor, 1985. In practice at Bar, 1977–80; Lectr in Laws, QMC, 1978–80; Asst Parly Counsel, 1980–85; Solicitor and Parly Agent, 1985–2001, Partner, 1987–2001, Rees & Freres; Immigration Adjudicator, pt-time, 1996–2001, full-time, 2001–03; Vice Pres., Immigration Appeal Tribunal, then Sen. Immigration Judge, Asylum and Immigration Tribunal, later a Judge of the Upper Tribunal (Immigration and Asylum Chamber), 2003–17; Legal Mem., Special Immigration Appeals Commn, 2005–17; Pres., Gen. Regulatory Chamber of the First-tier Tribunal, 2014–17; a Dep. High Court Judge, 2016–17. *Publications:* (jtly) Blackstone's Guide to the Transport and Works Act 1992, 1992; (jtly) Blackstone's Guide to the Environment Act 1995, 1995; (contrib.) Douglas & Geen on the Law of Harbours, Coasts and Pilotage, 5th edn 1997. *Recreations:* hill-walking, opera, American and British film music 1930–1975. *Address:* Royal Courts of Justice, Strand, WC2A 2LL.
*See also* C. N. Lane.

**LANE, Philip Anthony**, OBE 2009; Strategic Head of Sport Development, Greenwich Leisure Ltd, since 2011; *b* Ruardean, Glos, 2 Sept. 1953; *s* of Ronald Lane and Vanda Lane; *m* 1999, Emma; three *s* one *d*. *Educ:* Royal Forest of Dean Grammar Sch.; Shoreditch Coll., London (MSc, BEd 1st Cl., CertEd). Headteacher, 1990–2001. Hd Coach, England Under 18 Rugby Team, 1999–2001; Chef de Mission, GB Paralympic Team, 2002, 2004, 2006, 2008, 2010. Director: Paralympic World Cup, 2005–11; Team 2012, 2009–11; Chm., Pro-Active E London, 2006–08; CEO, British Paralympic Assoc., 2001–11. Visiting Lecturer: Hull Univ., 2002–05; Reading Univ., 2005–07; Vis. Prof., UEL, 2007–. Hon. DBA London Metropolitan, 2007; Hon. PhD Middlesex. *Recreations:* sport, music (playing and listening), literature.

**LANE, Dr Richard Paul**, OBE 2011; Director of Science, Natural History Museum, 2003–11; *b* 16 May 1951; *s* of Alfred George Lane and Patricia Ann Lane (*née* Trotter); *m* 1972, Maureen Anne Grogan; two *s* one *d*. *Educ:* Imperial Coll., Univ. of London (BSc, ARCS, DIC, PhD). Dept of Entomology, British Museum (Natural History), 1974–85, Head of Med. Insects Sect., 1983–85; Sen. Lectr, LSHTM, Univ. of London, 1985–92, Head of Vector Biology and Transmission Dynamics Unit, 1989–92; Keeper of Entomology, Natural History Mus., 1992–97; Internat. Prog. Dir, Wellcome Trust, 1997–2004. Vis. Prof., Imperial Coll., London, 2005–11. Member: Council, RSTM&H, 1985–89, 1999–2003; Biological Council, 1985–89; Wellcome Trust Panels, 1986–97; Expert Adv. Panel on Parasitic Diseases, WHO, 1988–; Steering Cttee on Leishmaniasis, WHO, 1988–93; Bd of Trustees, Biosis, Philadelphia, 1993–98; Steering Cttee on research ethics related to healthcare in developing countries, Nuffield Council on Bioethics, 2001–08; Exec. Cttee and Founding Mem., Consortium for DNA Barcode of Life, 2005–09; Institutional Council and Governance Bd, Encyclopaedia of Life, 2007–11; Chairman: Sci. Collections Internat., OECD Global Sci. Forum, 2005–08. Member, External Scientific Advisory Board: Leibniz-Institut für Evolutions und Biodiversitätsforschung, Berlin, 2007–10; Netherlands Centre for Biodiversity Naturalis, Leiden, 2010–; Natural History Museum of Denmark, 2010–13. Royal Entomological Society: Mem. Council, 1980–83, 1989–92; Vice-Pres., 1991–92; Pres., 1994–96. Mem. Council, Internat. Congress of Entomology, 1992–2008. Trustee, Against Malaria Foundn, 2004–. Hon. DSc Kingston, 2010. *Publications:* (ed jtly) Medical Insects and Arachnids, 1993; (jtly) Biology of Parasites, 2017; papers on insects of medical importance in sci. jls, esp. on sandflies and transmission of leishmaniasis. *Recreations:* natural history, gardening.

**LANE, Robert Charles**, CBE 2001; Partner, since 1990, and Head of Regulated Industries, since 2000, CMS Cameron McKenna Nabarro Olswang LLP (formerly McKenna & Co., then CMS Cameron McKenna LLP); *b* London, 29 Aug. 1958; *s* of Sidney Lane and Eileen Lane (*née* Cleave); *m* 1986, Margaret Stubbs; two *s* one *d*. *Educ:* Buckhurst Hill Sch.; University Coll. London (LLB Hons 1979). Admitted as solicitor, 1982; Solicitor: Slaughter and May, 1982–88; McKenna & Co., 1988–90. Chm., Govt Power Sector Adv. Gp, 2004–13; Executive Member: British Energy Assoc./Energy Inst., 2003–; Parly Gp for Energy Studies, 2004–. Mem. Bd, Energy Industries Club, 2004–. Chm., Energy Cttee, City of London Solicitors' Co., 2010–. Chm. Trustees, Orchid Cancer Charity, 2014– (Trustee, 2008–). FEI 2016. *Recreations:* theatre, opera, music, Rugby, cricket, family. *Address:* CMS Cameron McKenna Nabarro Olswang LLP, Cannon Place, 78 Cannon Street, EC4N 6AF. *T:* (020) 7367 3000, *Fax:* (020) 7367 2000. *E:* robert.lane@cms-cmno.com. *Clubs:* Garrick, Royal Automobile, City of London.

**LANE, Maj.-Gen. Roger Guy Tyson**, CBE 2003 (OBE 1994); Managing Director, Roger Lane Consulting Ltd, since 2007; *b* 23 Feb. 1954; *s* of Capt. and Mrs M. E. Lane; *m* 1981, Nichola J. Redrobe; one *s* one *d*. *Educ:* Christ's Hospital, Horsham. Joined RM, 1972; OC, HMS Zulu, 1977–79; Intelligence Security Gp, NI, 1979–80 (despatches 1981); Adjutant, 1982–84; Canadian Comd and Staff Coll., 1985–86; Co. Comdr 42 Commando, 1988–90 (despatches 1990); Staff Officer (Grade 2), Mil. Ops 2 Br., resp. for NI Ops Policy, MoD, 1991–94; RM Rep., US Marine Corps Combat and Develt Comd, USA, 1994–96; CO 42 Commando, 1996–98; CSO Ops HQ RM, 1998–99; rcds, 2000; HCSC, 2001; Comdr 3 Commando Bde, 2001–02; Dir, HCSC, 2002–03; Dep. Comdr, HQ NATO Rapid Deployable Corps, Italy, 2003–06; Dep. Comdr Ops, HQ ISAF, Kabul, 2005–06. NATO Sen. Mentor, 2008–14; Sen. OPFOR/EXCON Advr, NATO Jt Warfare Centre, 2014–. FCMI. Bronze Star, USA, 2002; Commendatore, Order of Merit (Italy), 2006; Baryal Medal, 1st Grade (Afghanistan), 2007. *Publications:* articles on NATO, leadership, empowerment and stabilisation. *Recreations:* sailing, gardening, fly fishing, genealogy, writing.

**LANE, Shelley Ilene Munjack;** an Upper Tribunal Judge (Administrative Appeals Chamber) (formerly a Social Security and Child Support Commissioner), since 2008; *b* Brooklyn, New York; *d* of late Morris Munjack and Helen Munjack; *m* 1980, Peter Richard Lane, *qv*; one *s* one *d*. *Educ:* Case Western Reserve Univ., Cleveland (BA magna cum laude, phi beta kappa); Queen Mary Coll., Univ. of London (LLB Hons). Called to the Bar, Gray's Inn, 1977; Lectr, then Sen. Lectr in Laws, QMUL, 1978–99; immigration adjudicator (pt-time), 1997–99; Dist Chm., Social Security and Child Support Appeals Tribunals, 1999–2008; Mem. (pt-time), Gender Recognition Panel, 2004. *Publications:* The Status of Licensing Common Law Marks, 1991; (jtly) Video Law, 1992; Intellectual Property (study guides), 1994, 2nd edn 1997; (jtly) Readings in Intellectual Property, 1998; (contrib.) Yearbook of Copyright and Media Law, 1999; numerous pubns in field of intellectual property. *Recreations:* opera, theatre, gardening. *Address:* Upper Tribunal, Administrative Appeals Chamber, 5th Floor, Rolls Building, 7 Rolls Buildings, Fetter Lane, EC4A 1NL.

**LANE, Shirley Christine;** *see* Price, S. C.

**LANE-FOX OF SOHO**, Baroness *cr* 2013 (Life Peer), of Soho in the City of Westminster; **Martha Lane Fox**, CBE 2013; *b* Oxford, 10 Feb. 1973; *d* of Robin James Lane Fox, *qv*; partner, Chris Gorell Barnes; twin *s*. *Educ:* Westminster Sch.; Magdalen Coll., Oxford (BA). Former Consultant, Spectrum Strategy; Co-Founder, Man. Dir, 1997–2003, non-exec. Dir, 2003–05, lastminute.com; Founder and Chairman: Lucky Voice Gp Ltd, 2005–; Go On UK, 2012–; Chm., MakieLab, 2012–; Founder and Exec. Chair, Doteveryone, 2015–. Non-executive Director: Channel 4, 2006–12; mydeco.com, 2007–; Marks & Spencer plc, 2007–15; Women's Prize for Fiction, 2011–; Twitter, 2016–. UK Digital Champion, 2009–13. Mem., Jt Cttee on Nat. Security Strategy, H of L, 2017–. Chancellor, Open Univ., 2014–. Mem. Bd, Founders Forum for Good; Founder and Chm., Antigone Foundn, 2007–; Patron: Reprieve (Founding Trustee, 2000–10). *Address:* House of Lords, SW1A 0PW.

**LANE FOX, Robin James**, FRSL; Tutorial Fellow, 1977–2014, now Emeritus Fellow, and Garden Master, since 1981, New College, Oxford (Lecturer in Classical Languages and Literature, 2016–17); Reader in Ancient History, Oxford, 1990–2014; *b* 5 Oct. 1946; *s* of James Henry Lane Fox and Anne (*née* Loyd); *m* 1970, Louisa Caroline Mary (marr. diss. 1993), *d* of Charles and Lady Katherine Farrell; one *s* one *d*. *Educ:* Eton; Magdalen Coll., Oxford (Craven and de Paravicini scholarships, 1966; Passmore Edwards and Chancellors' Latin Verse Prize, 1968). FRSL 1974. Fellow by examination, Magdalen Coll., Oxford, 1970–73; Lectr in Classical Lang. and Lit., 1973–76, Res. Fellow, Classical and Islamic Studies, 1976–77, Worcester Coll., Oxford; Lectr in Ancient Hist., Oxford Univ., 1977–90. Writer and presenter, Greek Myths and Tales of Travelling Heroes, BBC4, 2010. Weekly gardening correspondent, Financial Times, 1970–. *Publications:* Alexander the Great, 1973, 3rd edn 1978 (James Tait Black, Duff Cooper, W. H. Heinemann Awards, 1973–74); Variations on a Garden, 1974, rev. edn 1986; Search for Alexander, 1980; Better Gardening, 1982; Pagans and Christians, 1986; The Unauthorized Version, 1991; The Making of 'Alexander', 2004; (ed and contrib.) The Long March: Xenophon and the Ten Thousand, 2004; The Classical World: an epic history from Homer to Hadrian, 2005 (Runciman prize, 2006); Travelling Heroes: Greeks and their myths in the epic age of Homer, 2008; Thoughtful Gardening, 2010; (ed and contrib.) Brill's Companion to Ancient Macedon, 2011; Augustine: conversions and confessions, 2015 (Wolfson History Prize, 2016). *Recreations:* gardening, remembering fox-hunting. *Address:* New College, Oxford OX1 3BN. *Club:* Beefsteak.
*See also* Baroness Lane-Fox of Soho.

**LANE-FOX-PITT-RIVERS, Valerie;** *see* Pitt-Rivers, V.

**LANE-NOTT, Rear Adm. Roger Charles**, CB 1996; FCMI; Director General and Chief Executive Officer, Agricultural Engineers Association, Milking Equipment Association, and National Sprayer Testing Scheme, 2007–15; *b* 3 June 1945; *s* of John Henry Lane-Nott, MBE and Kathleen Mary Lane-Nott; *m* 1968, Róisin MacQuillan; one *s* two *d*. *Educ:* Pangbourne Coll.; BRNC, Dartmouth. Joined RN, 1963: qualified submarines, 1966; served in HM Submarines: Andrew, Opossum, Otus, Revenge (Starboard), Conqueror, Aeneas, 1966–74; commanded HM Submarines: Walrus, 1974–76; Swiftsure, 1979; Splendid, 1979–82 (mentioned in despatches, Falklands, 1982); US Naval War Coll., 1983; Captain SM, Third Submarine Sqdn, 1985–86; Asst Dir, Defence Concepts, MoD, 1986–89; RCDS 1989; Captain First Frigate Sqdn and in comd HMS Coventry, 1990–91; Sen. Naval Officer, ME, 1991; Chief of Staff to Flag Officer Submarines, 1992–93; Flag Officer Submarines, and Comdr Submarines (NATO), Eastern Atlantic and Northwest, 1993–96; COS (Ops) to C-in-C Fleet, 1994–96; RN retd, 1996. Formula One Race Dir and Safety Delegate, Fédn Internat. de l'Automobile, 1996–97; Chief Exec., Centre for Marine and Petroleum Technol., 1997–99; Sec., British Racing Drivers' Club, 1999–2007; Dir Gen. and CEO, Assoc. of Manufacturers of Power Generating Systems, 2007–14. Chm. of Trustees, RN Submarine Mus., 2005–10; Bd Dir, Nat. Mus. of RN, 2008–10. Chm. Govs, Pangbourne Coll., 2010–. Dir, Veterans for Britain. MRIN 1976; MNI 1991; FCMI (FIMgt 1983); FIAgrE 2008–14; MInstPet 1997; Associate RASE 2014. *Recreations:* watching sport (Rugby, cricket, motor racing), unusual stationery, lighthouses. *Address:* The Hawthorns, 5 Dudley Hill, Shenley Church End, Bucks MK5 6LL. *Club:* British Racing Drivers'.

**LANE-SMITH, Roger;** Senior Partner, DLA (formerly Dibb Lupton Alsop), Solicitors, 1998–2005; Senior Consultant, DLA Piper, since 2005; Chairman, Lomond Capital Partners, 2009; *b* 19 Oct. 1945; *s* of Harry Lane-Smith and Dorothy Lane-Smith; *m* 1969, Pamela; one *s* one *d*. *Educ:* Stockport Grammar Sch.; Guildford Coll. of Law. Admitted Solicitor, 1969; founded Lee Lane-Smith, 1977; Lee Lane-Smith merged with Alsop Stevens, 1983; Alsop Stevens merged with Wilkinson Kimbers to form Alsop Wilkinson, 1988; Chm. and Sen. Partner, Alsop Wilkinson, 1993–96; Alsop Wilkinson merged with Dibb Lupton to form Dibb Lupton Alsop, 1996; Dep. Sen. Partner, Dibb Lupton Alsop, 1996–98. Non-executive Director: JJB Sports, 1998–2009 (Chm., 2005–09); MS Internat., 1983–; Timpson, 1984–; Dolphin Capital Investors, 2006–; WH Ireland, 2007–14. *Publications:* A Fork in the Road: from single partner to largest legal practice in the world, 2014. *Recreations:* golf, wine. *Club:* Mark's.

**LANG**, family name of **Baron Lang of Monkton**.

**LANG OF MONKTON**, Baron *cr* 1997 (Life Peer), of Merrick and the Rhinns of Kells in Dumfries and Galloway; **Ian Bruce Lang;** PC 1990; DL; Chairman: Marsh & McLennan Companies Inc., 2011–16 (Director, 1997–2016); Lovat Parks Ltd, since 2019; *b* 27 June 1940; *y s* of late James Fulton Lang, DSC, and Maude Margaret (*née* Stewart); *m* 1971, Sandra Caroline, *e d* of late John Alastair Montgomerie, DSC; two *d*. *Educ:* Lathallan Sch., Kincardineshire; Rugby Sch.; Sidney Sussex Coll., Cambridge (BA 1962). Insurance Broker, 1962–79. Director: CGU (formerly General Accident) plc, 1997–2000; Lithgows

Ltd, 1997–2008; Automobile Assoc., 1998–99; Charlemagne Capital Ltd, 2006–17. Trustee: Savings Bank of Glasgow, 1969–74; West of Scotland Trustee Savings Bank, 1974–83. Member, Queen's Body Guard for Scotland (Royal Company of Archers), 1974–. Contested (C): Central Ayrshire, 1970; Glasgow Pollok, Feb. 1974; MP (C) Galloway, 1979–83, Galloway and Upper Nithsdale, 1983–97; contested (C) Galloway and Upper Nithsdale, 1997. An Asst Govt Whip, 1981–83; a Lord Comr of HM Treasury, 1983–86; Parliamentary Under Secretary of State: Dept of Employment, 1986; Scottish Office, 1986–87; Minister of State, Scottish Office, 1987–90; Sec. of State for Scotland and Lord Keeper of the Great Seal of Scotland, 1990–95; Pres., Board of Trade, and Sec. of State for Trade and Industry, 1995–97. Member: Constitution Cttee, H of L, 2001–05 and 2012–17 (Chm., 2014–17); Special Cttee on the Barnett Formula, H of L, 2008–09; Liaison Cttee, H of L, 2017–; Chm., Prime Minister's Adv. Cttee on Business Appts, 2009–14. Chm., Patrons of Nat. Galls of Scotland, 1999–2007. Gov., Rugby Sch., 1997–2007. DL Ayrshire and Arran, 1998. OStJ 1974. *Publications:* Blue Remembered Years, 2002. *Address:* House of Lords, SW1A 0PW. *Clubs:* Pratt's; Prestwick Golf.

**LANG, Alistair Laurie,** MBE 1970; Chief Executive, Drugs Abuse Resistance Education (DARE) UK Ltd, 2002–05; *b* 9 Sept. 1943; *s* of late Comdr John Robert Lang, RN (retd) and Jennifer Douglas Lang; *m* 1979, Ilona Augusta Avery; one *s* one *d. Educ:* Hurstpierpoint Coll.; BRNC; University Coll., Oxford (BA 1979); Internat. Management Inst., Geneva (MBA 1989). Served Royal Navy, 1962–75: in HM Ships Wizard, Salisbury, Devonshire, Malcolm, Plymouth and Kent; loan service to: Kenya Navy (Kenya Navy Ship Chui), 1966; Royal Malaysian Navy (i/c Kapel di-Raja Sri Sarawak and Fleet Ops Officer), 1968–70; Imperial Iranian Navy, 1974. Hong Kong Civil Service, 1979–90: Asst Sec. for Security, 1980–82; City Dist Officer, Kowloon City, 1982–83; support to Governor during negotiation with China on future of Hong Kong, 1983–85; Clerk of Councils (Sec. to Exec. and Legislative Councils), 1985–88; attached British Embassy, Beijing (on secondment), 1989; UK Rep., Hong Kong Exec. and Legislative Councils, 1990–92. Clerk to Drapers' Co., 1993–2000; Chief Exec., Canine Partners for Independence, 2000–02. *Recreations:* swimming, walking, reading, theatre. *Address:* Little Mead, Home Lane, Sparsholt, Winchester, Hants SO21 2NN. *T:* (01962) 776204.

*See also Rear-Adm. J. S. Lang.*

**LANG, Dame Beverley Ann Macnaughton,** DBE 2011; **Hon. Mrs Justice Lang;** a Judge of the High Court, Queen's Bench Division, since 2011; *b* 13 Oct. 1955; *d* of William Macnaughton Lang and Joan Margaret Mantua Lang (*née* Utting); one *d. Educ:* Wycombe Abbey Sch., Bucks; Lady Margaret Hall, Oxford (BA Hons Jurisprudence 1977; Hon. Fellow, 2011). Called to the Bar, Inner Temple, 1978, Bencher, 2006; Lectr, UEA, 1978–81; in practice at the Bar, 1981–2011; QC 2000; a Recorder, 2006–11. Chm. (part-time), Employment Tribunals, 1995–2001; Chm. (part-time), later Judge (part-time), Special Educnl Needs and Disability Tribunal, 2004–09. *Address:* Royal Courts of Justice, Strand, WC2A 2LL.

**LANG, Dr Brian Andrew,** CBE 2016; Principal and Vice-Chancellor, University of St Andrews, 2001–08, now Principal Emeritus; *b* 2 Dec. 1945; *s* of Andrew Ballantyne Lang and Mary Bain Lang (*née* Smith); *m* 1st, 1975 (marr. diss. 1982); one *s;* 2nd, 1983 (marr. diss. 2000); one *s* one *d;* 3rd, 2002, Tari Hibbitt (*see* Tari Lang). *Educ:* Royal High Sch., Edinburgh; Univ. of Edinburgh (MA, PhD). Social anthropological field research, Kenya, 1969–70; Lectr in social anthropology, Aarhus Univ., 1971–75; Scientific Staff, SSRC, 1976–79; Scottish Office (Sec., Historic Buildings Council for Scotland), 1979–80; Sec., Nat. Heritage Meml Fund, 1980–87; Dir of Public Affairs, Nat. Trust, 1987–91; Chief Exec. and Dep. Chm., British Library, 1991–2000; Chairman: Eur. Nat. Libraries Forum, 1993–2000; Heritage Image Partnership (formerly Nat. Heritage Image Liby), 2000–02; Internat. Adv. Council, Internat. Leadership Sch. (Glasgow), 2011–15. Member: Bd, Scottish Enterprise, Fife, 2003–08; Scottish Exec. Cultural Commn, 2004–05; Cttee for Scotland, Heritage Lottery Fund, 2004–11 (Chair, 2005–11). Member: Liby and Inf. Services Council (England), 1991–94; Liby and Inf. Commn, 1995–2000. Vis. Prof., Edinburgh Napier (formerly Napier) Univ., 1999–; Vis. Scholar, Getty Inst., Calif, 2000. Pforzheimer Lecture, Univ. of Texas, 1998. Trustee: 21st Century Learning Initiative, 1995–99; Hopetoun House Preservation Trust, 2001–05; Nat. Heritage Meml Fund, 2005–11; Nat. Museums of Scot., 2014–. Chm., Royal Scottish Nat. Orch., 2008–15. Chm. Trustees, Newbattle Abbey Coll., 2004–08; Chm., Edinburgh World Heritage Trust, 2015–; Chair, Dovecot Gall. and Dovecot Tapestry Studio, Edinburgh, 2017–; Member, Council: Nat. Trust for Scotland, 2001–04; St Leonard's Sch., 2001–08. Pres., Inst. of Information Scientists, 1993–94 (Hon. Fellow, 1994). FRSE 2006. Hon. FCLIP (Hon. FLA 1997). Dr *hc* Edinburgh, 2008; Hon. LLD St Andrews, 2008. *Publications:* numerous articles, contribs etc to professional jls. *Recreations:* music, museums and galleries, pottering. *Address:* 4 Manor Place, Edinburgh EH3 7DD. *Club:* New (Edinburgh).

**LANG, David Geoffrey,** CMG 2007; CBE 1992; QC (Turks and Caicos) 1985; Attorney General, Falkland Islands, 1987–2006; *b* Scarborough, 4 Nov. 1941; *s* of Alexander and Nora Lang; *m* 1975, Theresa Margaret Hurt; one *s* three *d. Educ:* St Edmund's Sch., Canterbury; College of Law, London. Admitted solicitor, 1965; Asst Solicitor, Bognor Regis UDC, 1965–68; Partner, Wintle & Co. Solicitors, Bognor Regis, 1968–69; Asst Solicitor, 1969–71, Partner, 1971–76, Hedges & Mercer Solicitors, Oxon; Sec. for Justice, Rep. of Nauru, 1977–82; Attorney General, Turks and Caicos Is, 1982–87. *Recreations:* bridge, computer strategy games, science fiction, amateur dramatics. *Address:* 28 Goss Road, Stanley, Falkland Islands FIQQ 1ZZ.

**LANG, Rt Rev. Declan;** *see* Clifton, Bishop of, (RC).

**LANG, Hugh Montgomerie,** CBE 1978; Chairman, Acertec Holdings Ltd, 1999–2006; *b* Glasgow, 7 Nov. 1932; *s* of John Montgomerie Lang and Janet Allan (*née* Smillie); *m* 1st, 1959, Marjorie Jean Armour (marr. diss. 1981); one *s* one *d;* 2nd, 1981, Susan Lynn Hartley (*née* Russell). *Educ:* Shawlands Acad., Glasgow; Glasgow Univ. (BSc). ARCST 1953; CEng 1967; FIET (FIProdE 1976); FIMC 1970. Officer, REME, 1953–55 (National Service). Colvilles Ltd, 1955–56; Glacier Metal Co. Ltd, 1956–60; L. Sterne & Co. Ltd, 1960–61; P-E Consulting Group, 1961–92: Manager for ME, 1965–68; Scottish Reg. Manager, 1968–72; Man. Dir, 1974–77; Chm., P-E Internat., 1980–92 (Dir, 1972–92; Chief Exec., 1977–92). Chairman: Brammer plc, 1990–98; Manganese Bronze Hldgs, 1992–2000; Victaulic, 1995; Albion Automotive, 1997–98; Director: Redman Heenan Internat., 1981–86 (Chm., 1982–86); Fairey Holdings Ltd, 1978–82; UKO International, 1985–86; B. Elliott, 1986–88; Siebe, 1987–91; Strong & Fisher (Hldgs), 1988–90; Co-ordinated Land and Estates, 1988–93; OGC International, 1993–94; Ericsson Ltd, 1993–99. Chairman: Food, Drink and Packaging Machinery Sector Working Party, 1976–81; Technology Transfer Services Adv. Cttee, 1982–85 (Mem., 1978–85); Member: Business Educn Council, 1980–81; CBI Industrial Policy Cttee, 1980–83; Design Council, 1983–90 (Dep. Chm., 1986–90); Engrg Council, 1984–86. *Recreations:* fishing, gardening, golf, reading, walking. *Address:* Welders Wood, Chalfont St Peter, Bucks SL9 8TT. *Club:* Denham Golf.

**LANG, Jack Mathieu Emile,** Chevalier de la Légion d'Honneur; Hon. GCVO 1992; Deputy (Soc.) for Pas de Calais, National Assembly, France, 2002–12; President, Institut du Monde Arabe, since 2013; *b* 2 Sept. 1939; *s* of Roger Lang and Marie-Luce Lang (*née* Bouchet); *m* 1961, Monique Buczynski; one *d* (and one *d* decd). *Educ:* Inst. d'Etudes Politiques; Dr of Public Law. Founder and Producer, World Fest. Univ. Theatre, Nancy, 1963–72; Dir, Nancy Univ. Theatre, 1963–72; Dir, Palais de Chaillot Théâtre, 1972–74; Prof. of Internat. Law, 1971–81; Dir, teaching and research unit in legal and econ. scis, Nancy, 1977–80; Prof., Univ. of Paris X, 1986–88. Paris councillor, 1977–89; nat. deleg. for cultural affairs, Socialist Party, 1979–81; Minister of Culture, 1981–83 and 1984–86; Deputy, Loir-et-Cher, 1986–88 and 1997–2000; Minister of Culture and Communication, 1988–92; Govt Spokesman, 1991–92; Minister of State, and Minister of Nat. Educn and Culture, 1992–93; Minister for Educn, 2000–02. Pres., Foreign Affairs Cttee, French Nat. Assembly, 1997–2000. Mayor of Blois, 1989–2001; Conseiller Général de Blois, 1992–93. Order of Orange Nassau (Netherlands), 1991; Order of the Crown of Belgium, 1992. *Publications:* L'Etat et le Théâtre, 1968; Le plâteau continental de la mer du nord, 1970; Les politiques culturelles comparée en Europe; La jonction au fond des exceptions préliminaires devant la cour, 1971; (with J.-D. Bredin) Éclats, 1978; Demain les femmes, 1995; Lettre à Malraux, 1996; François 1$^{er}$ ou le rêve italien, 1997; (jtly) La politique, d'où ça vient?, 2000; Laurent le Magnifique, 2002; (with C. Lang) Anna au Muséum, 2002; (with C. Brétécher) Qu'apprend-on au collège?, 2002; Une école élitaire pour tous, 2003; Un nouveau régime politique pour la France, 2004; Nelson Mandela: leçon de vie pour l'avenir, 2005; Changer, 2005; (with H. Le Bras) Immigration Positive, 2006; Faire la révolution fiscale, 2006; L'école abandonnée: lettre à Xavier Darcos, 2008; (with J.-M. Helvig) Demain comme hier, 2009; Le Choix de Versailles, 2009; contribs to newspapers. *T:* (Sec.) 668545488. *E:* j.lang@wanadoo.fr.

**LANG, Jacqueline Shelagh;** Headmistress, Walthamstow Hall, Sevenoaks, 1984–2002; *b* 17 June 1944; *d* of James Wicks and Mary Mills Wicks (*née* Green); *m* 1965, Andrew Lang; two *d. Educ:* Walthamstow Hall; St Anne's Coll., Oxford (Schol.; MA). Res., mediaeval French literature, KCL, 1964–66; Ursuline Convent School, Wimbledon: Asst Mistress, 1970–76; Head of Langs, 1976–83; Foundn Gov., 1984–93. Chairman: London and SE Region, ISIS, 1991–95; Assisted Places Cttee, ISC, 1998–2002; Pres., GSA, 1997. *Recreations:* history of architecture, gardens, visiting archaeological sites. *Address:* 82 Richmond Road, SW20 0PD.

**LANG, Rear-Adm. John Stewart;** Royal Navy, retired; Chief Inspector of Marine Accidents, Marine Accident Investigation Branch, Department for Transport, Local Government and the Regions (formerly Department of Transport, then Department of the Environment, Transport and the Regions), 1997–2002; *b* 18 July 1941; *s* of late Comdr John Robert Lang, RN and Jennifer Douglas Lang; *m* 1971, Joanna Judith Pegler; two *d. Educ:* Cheltenham Coll. Jun. Sch.; Nautical Coll., Pangbourne. FNI 1986; FRIN 1997. Navigating Officer Apprentice, P&OSN Co., 1959–62; RN 1962; served HM Ships Chilcompton, Totem, Auriga, Oberon, Revenge, Opossum, 1964–71; qualified Submarine Command, 1971; commanded: HMS Walrus, 1971–72; HMS Renown, 1976–78; HMS Beaver, 1983–85; Captain, Royal Naval Presentation Team, 1986–87; ACOS (Ops) to C-in-C Fleet, 1987–89; Dir, Naval Ops and Trade, 1989–91; Dep. Chief of Defence Intelligence, 1992–95. Chm., EC Marine Accident Investigation Wkg Gp, 2004–06. President: Inst. of Seamanship, 2001–; Assoc. of Sail (formerly Sea) Trng Orgns, 2003–; Winchester Sea Cadets TS Itchen, 2003–. Mem., Yachtmaster Qualification Panel, RYA, 2008–; Vice Pres., RNLI, 2012– (Mem. Council, 2006–12). Patron, Sea Safety Gp, 2002–04; Trustee: Shipwrecked Mariners Soc., 2003–11 (Chm., 2008–11); Royal Nat. Mission to Deep Sea Fishermen, 2003– (Dep. Chm., 2009–16); Chm., Nautical Inst. Fellowship Cttee, 2002–13; Trustee Dir, Nautilus Internat. (formerly NUMAST, then Nautilus UK), 2003–18 (Mem., Nautilus Internat. Welfare Cttee, 2009–18; Chm., Trustees, 2011–18). Younger Brother, Trinity House, 1982–. Gov., Southampton Solent Univ. (formerly Southampton Inst.), 2004–10. DL Hants, 2008. Hon. DTech Nottingham Trent, 2002. *Publications:* Titanic: a fresh look at the evidence by a former Chief Inspector of Marine Accidents, 2012. *Recreations:* sailing, photography, oil painting, writing, lecturing. *Address:* 2 The Mulberries, Alresford, Hants SO24 9FL.

*See also A. L. Lang.*

**LANG, Kirsty;** broadcaster; presenter, Front Row, BBC Radio 4, since 2004; *b* Guildford, 3 July 1962; *d* of Jeremy John Lang and Patricia Anne Lang; *m* 2006, Misha Glenny, *qv;* one *s. Educ:* Nishimachi Internat. Sch., Tokyo; Lauriston Sch., Melbourne; Dartington Hall; Cranborne Chase, Tisbury; Internat. Sch., Geneva; London Sch. of Econs and Political Sci. (BSc, MSc (Econ) Internat. Relns). BBC: graduate trainee, 1986–88; Central Europe Corresp., 1989–91; reporter, Newsnight, 1992–95; Paris Corresp., Sunday Times, 1995–99; presenter, Channel 4 News, 1999–2002; BBC World TV, 2002–13. Trustee, British Council, 2014–; Chair, Baltic Centre for Contemp. Art, Gateshead, 2018–. *Recreations:* theatre, film, reading, cooking.

**LANG, Tari;** advisor and non-executive director; Partner, Lang Consultancy, since 2009; *b* Prague, 18 June 1951; *d* of late Suwondo Budiardjo and of Carmel Budiardjo; *m* 1st, 1971, Roger Hibbitt (marr. diss. 1996); one *s* one *d;* 2nd, 2002, Dr Brian Andrew Lang, *qv.* Founder and Dir, Clasma Software, 1980–86; Man. Dir, Rowland Co., 1988–95; UK CEO, Edelman PR, 1995–2002; Founding Partner, Reputation Inc., 2002–09. Member, Board: National Th. of Scotland, 2008–16; Edinburgh Internat. Fest., 2012–18; Nat. Galls of Scotland, 2014–; Edinburgh Fest. Fringe Soc., 2018–; Vice Chair, Royal Conservatoire of Scotland, 2016–. Mem., Nominating Council, Women of Year, 2002–16. *Recreations:* theatre, cinema. *E:* tari@lang-uk.com.

**LANG, Prof. Timothy Mark,** PhD; FFPH; Professor of Food Policy, City, University of London (formerly City University London), since 2002 (Director, Centre for Food Policy, 2002–16); *b* Lincoln, 7 Jan. 1948; *s* of Robert Antony Lang and Katharine Margaret Lang (*née* Alcock); *m* 2004, Valerie Elizabeth Castledine; one step *s* one step *d. Educ:* Leeds Univ. (BA Hons Psychol. and Sociol. 1970; PhD Psychol. 1974). Lectr, Trinity and All Saints Coll., Horsforth, Leeds, 1973–74; Partner, Simfield & Ramsclough Farms, Slaidburn, Clitheroe, Lancs, 1973–80; Sen. Lectr, Preston Poly., 1975–82; Sen. Lectr, and Dir, Food Policy Unit, Manchester Poly., 1982–84; Director: London Food Commn, 1984–90; Parents for Safe Food, 1990–94; Prof. of Food Policy, Thames Valley Univ., 1994–2002. Chair, Scottish Diet Action Plan Rev., Scottish NHS Exec., 2005–06; Member: Expert Adv. Gp for Healthy Weight Healthy Lives prog., DoH, 2008–10; Council of Food Policy Advrs to Sec. of State for Envmt, Food and Rural Affairs, 2008–10; Adviser to Parliamentary Select Committee inquiries: Agric. (Globalisation), 2000; Health and Agric. (Food Standards), 2000; Health (Obesity), 2003–04. Tech. Advr, Food and Nutrition Initiative, French Presidency of EC, 1999–2000; Advr, Prime Minister's Strategy Unit Review of Food and Food Policy, 2007–08; Mem., Mayor of London's Food Bd, 2010–16. Natural Resources and Land Use Comr, Sustainable Develt Commn, 2006–11. Consultant, WHO, Geneva and Copenhagen, 1996–2002. Mem., EAT-Lancet Commn on Healthy Diets from Sustainable Food Systems, 2016–18. Mem. Council, Public Health Alliance, 1987–99 (Sec., 1987–88). Chair: Sustain, 1999–2005; Food Res. Collaboration, 2014–16. Vice-Pres., Chartered Inst. of Envmtl Health, 1999–. Trustee: Friends of the Earth, 1994–2001; Borough Market, 2007–17; President: Caroline Walker Trust, 2005–; Garden Organic, 2008–. FFPH 2001 (Mem. 1999); FRSA 1998. Hon. Fellow, UWIC, 2018. Freeman, Cooks' Co., 2016. Hon. DSc Lincoln, 2009. Derek Cooper Award, Food and Farming Awards, BBC Radio 4, 2004. *Publications:* (with C. Clutterbuck) More Than We Can Chew, 1982; (with A. Webb) Food Irradiation, 1987, 2nd edn 1990 (trans. 5 langs);

Food Adulteration and How to Beat It, 1988; (with C. Clutterbuck) P is for Pesticides, 1991; (with C. Hines) The New Protectionism, 1993 (trans. 7 langs); (with Y. Gabriel) The Unmanageable Consumer, 1995, 3rd edn 2015; (with E. Millstone) The Atlas of Food, 2003 (André Simon Food Book of Year, 2003), 2nd edn 2008; (with M. Heasman) Food Wars, 2004, 2nd edn 2015; (jtly) Food Policy, 2009; (with G. Rayner) Ecological Public Health, 2012; (with Pamela Mason) Sustainable Diets, 2017. *Recreations:* trying to grow fruit and vegetables in my London garden, thinking, reading the papers, riding my bike around London, talking with family and friends, eating home-cooking in our summerhouse at the end of the garden, collecting family pottery. *Address:* Centre for Food Policy, City, University of London, Northampton Square, EC1V 0HB. *T:* (020) 7040 8798. *E:* t.lang@city.ac.uk.

**LANG LANG;** concert pianist; *b* Shenyang, China, 14 June 1982. *Educ:* Central Music Conservatory, Beijing; Curtis Inst. of Music, Philadelphia. Began piano lessons, aged 3; winner, Shenyang Piano Comp. and first recital, aged 5; winner, Internat. Tchaikovsky Comp. for Young Musicians, 1995. Has performed with major orchestras in USA and worldwide, incl. Vienna Philharmonic, Berlin Philharmonic and Shanghai SO; work with conductors incl. Zubin Mehta, Sir Simon Rattle, Daniel Barenboim and Seiji Ozawa; world tour, 2009, with Herbie Hancock. Has held masterclasses at instns incl. Curtis Inst. of Music, Juilliard Sch., Manhattan Sch. of Music, Hanover Conservatory and conservatories in China. Founder, Lang Lang Internat. Music Foundn, NY, 2008. Chm., Montblanc de la Culture Arts Patronage Award Project; Member: Adv. Cttee, Weill Music Inst., 2004–; Bd of Trustees, Carnegie Hall, 2007–. Goodwill Ambassador, UNICEF, 2004–. Hon. DMus RAM, 2011; Hon. Dr Musical Arts Manhattan Sch. of Music, 2012. Presidential Merit Award, 2007, Cultural Ambassador to China, 2008, Recording Acad. Order of Merit (Germany), 2012. *Publications:* Journey of a Thousand Miles (autobiog.), 2008; Playing with Flying Keys (autobiog. for young readers), 2008. *Address:* Columbia Artists Music LLC, 1500 Broadway, 19th Floor, New York, NY 10036, USA. *T:* (212) 8419564, *Fax:* (212) 8419719. *E:* jcesbron@camimusic.com.

**LANGAN, His Honour Peter St John Hevey;** QC 1983; a Circuit Judge, 1991–2013; Specialist Mercantile Circuit Judge, North Eastern Circuit, 2004–13; acting Puisne Judge, Gibraltar, since 2013; practising mediator and arbitrator, since 2014; *b* 1 May 1942; *s* of late Frederick Hevey Langan and Myrrha Langan (*née* Jephson), Mount Hevey, Hill of Down, Co. Meath; *m* 1st, 1976, Oonagh May Winifred McCarthy (marr. diss.); 2nd, 2003, Alison Felicity Tuffnell; one step *d. Educ:* Downside School; Trinity College, Dublin (MA, LLB); Christ's College, Cambridge (PhD). Lectr in Law, Durham Univ., 1966–69. In practice at the Bar, 1970–91; a Recorder, 1989–91; Designated Civil Judge, Norwich and Cambridge, 1998–2001; Mercantile and Chancery Judge, NE Circuit, 2001–04. Legal Assessor: GMC, 1990–91; GDC, 1990–91. Mem., Legal Commn, Caritas Internationalis, Rome, 1991–93; Trustee, CAFOD, 1993–99 (Mem., Management Cttee, 1984–91). *Publications:* Maxwell on Interpretation of Statutes, 12th edn 1969; Civil Procedure and Evidence, 1st edn 1970, 3rd edn (with L. D. J. Henderson) as Civil Procedure, 1983; (with P. V. Baker) Snell's Principles of Equity, 28th edn 1982, 29th edn 1990. *Address:* 6 Catley Grove, Long Ashton, Bristol BS41 9NH. *T:* (01275) 394235; Enterprise Chambers, 9 Old Square, Lincoln's Inn, WC2A 3SR. *T:* (020) 7405 9471.

**LANGDALE, Prof. Jane Alison,** CBE 2018; PhD; FRS 2015; Professor of Plant Development, University of Oxford, since 2006; Professorial Fellow, Queen's College, Oxford, since 2016 (Senior Research Fellow, 2006–16); *b* Coventry, 25 Aug. 1960; *d* of Edwin S. and Jean M. Langdale. *Educ:* Barr's Hill Grammar Sch., Coventry; Univ. of Bath (BSc Applied Biol. 1982); Univ. of London (PhD Human Genetics 1985). Postdoctoral Res. Associate, Biol. Dept, Yale Univ., 1985–90; University of Oxford: Department of Plant Sciences: SERC Res. Fellow, 1990–93; Royal Soc. Res. Fellow, 1993–94; Lectr, 1994–2007; Hd of Dept, 2007–12; Founding Dir, Plants for 21st Century Inst., 2008–13; Associate Hd, Maths, Physical and Life Scis Div., 2009–13; Tutorial Fellow, Queen's Coll., Oxford, 1994–2006. *Publications:* (jtly) How to Succeed as a Scientist: from postdoc to professor, 2007; contribs to learned jls incl. Nature, Sci., Current Biol., Develt, EMBO Jl, Genes & Develt, Plant Cell, Plant Jl. *Recreations:* gardening, cooking, Airedale Terriers. *Address:* Department of Plant Sciences, University of Oxford, South Parks Road, Oxford OX1 3RB. *T:* (01865) 275099. *E:* jane.langdale@plants.ox.ac.uk.

**LANGDALE, Rachel;** QC 2009; *b* Coventry, 1965; *d* of Edwin and Jean Langdale; *m* 1999, Simeon Andrew Maskrey, QC; one *s* one *d. Educ:* Bristol Poly. (LLB Hons); Darwin Coll., Cambridge (MPhil Criminol.). Called to the Bar, Middle Temple, 1990, Bencher, 2011; in practice as barrister specialising in public and regulatory law, and child and family law. *Recreation:* family life. *Address:* 7 Bedford Row, WC1R 4BU. *T:* (020) 7242 3555.

**LANGDALE, Simon John Bartholomew;** Director of Grants and Special Projects (formerly Educational and General Grants), The Rank Foundation, 1988–2002; Chairman, Arthur Rank Training, 2001–08; *b* 26 Jan. 1937; *s* of late Geoffrey Ronald Langdale and Hilda Joan Langdale (*née* Bartholomew); *m* 1962, Diana Marjory Hall; two *s* one *d. Educ:* Tonbridge Sch.; St Catharine's Coll., Cambridge. Taught at Radley Coll., 1959–73 (Housemaster, 1968–73); Headmaster: Eastbourne Coll., 1973–80; Shrewsbury Sch., 1981–88. *Recreations:* reading, gardening, golf. *Address:* Park House, Culworth, Banbury, Oxon OX17 2AP. *T:* (01295) 760222. *Clubs:* Hawks (Cambridge); Free Foresters, Jesters.
*See also T. J. Langdale.*

**LANGDALE, Timothy James;** QC 1992; a Recorder, 1996–99; *b* 3 Jan. 1940; *m* twice; two *d*; *m* 3rd, 2001, Susan Smith (*née* Hare). *Educ:* Sevenoaks Sch.; St Andrews Univ. (MA). Called to the Bar, Lincoln's Inn, 1966. Res. Assistant, Community Justice Center, Watts, Los Angeles, 1969–70; Jun. Prosecuting Counsel to the Crown, 1979–87, Sen. Prosecuting Counsel, 1987–92, CCC. Appeal Steward, BBB of C, 2002– (Chm., 2012–). *Recreations:* reading, the arts. *Address:* Cloth Fair Chambers, 39–40 Cloth Fair, EC1A 7NT. *T:* (020) 7710 6444.
*See also S. J. B. Langdale.*

**LANGDON, Andrew Dominic;** QC 2006; a Recorder, since 2002; *b* 23 July 1963; *s* of Michael and Phillipa Langdon; *m* 1989, Caroline; one *s* three *d. Educ:* Bristol Univ. (LLB). Called to the Bar, Middle Temple, 1986. Chm., Bar Council of England and Wales, 2017. *Recreations:* music, tennis, swimming, fishing. *Address:* Guildhall Chambers, 23 Broad Street, Bristol BS1 2HG. *T:* (0117) 927 3366. *E:* andrew.langdon@guildhallchambers.co.uk.

**LANGDON, Anthony James;** Deputy Under Secretary of State, Home Office, 1989–95; *b* 5 June 1935; *s* of Dr James Norman Langdon and Maud Winifred Langdon; *m* 1969, Helen Josephine Drabble, *y d* of His Honour J. F. Drabble, QC; one *s* one *d. Educ:* Kingswood Sch., Bath; Christ's Coll., Cambridge. Entered Home Office, 1958; Office of Minister for Science, 1961–63; Treasury, 1967–69; Under Sec., Cabinet Office, 1985–89. *Publications:* Tough Justice (with Ian Dunbar), 1998; A Guide to Baroque Rome: the palaces, 2015.

**LANGDON, Janet Mary;** Director and Secretary, Water Services Association of England and Wales, 1992–98; *b* 5 March 1940; *d* of late Geoffrey Harry Langdon and Iris Sarah Langdon. *Educ:* St Hilda's Coll., Oxford (BSc, MA). Asst Lectr, Wellesley Coll., Mass, 1962–63; Distillers' Co. Ltd, 1963–68; NEDO, 1968–71; Shell Chemicals UK Ltd and Shell Internat. Chemical Co. Ltd, 1971–82; Projects and Export Policy Div., DTI, 1982–85; Director: Asia, Gp Exports, GEC PLC, 1985–89; Export Div., GEC ALSTHOM Ltd, 1989–92. Member: Sch. Teachers' Rev. Body, 1996–2002; POUNC, 1998–2000. *Recreations:* walking, tennis, travel, theatre. *Address:* 43 Fairfax Place, NW6 4EJ. *T:* (020) 7624 3857.

**LANGDON, Prof. John Dudley,** FDSRCS, FRCSE, FMedSci; Professor of Oral and Maxillofacial Surgery, King's College London, 1992–2004; *b* 24 March 1942; *s* of Jack Langdon and Daphne Irene Heloise Liebsch. *Educ:* London Hosp. Med. Coll., Univ. of London (BDS, MB BS, MDS). LDSRCS 1965, FDSRCS 1971; FRCSE 1985. Sen. Lectr in Oral and Maxillofacial Surgery, KCL, 1983–92; Consultant Oral and Maxillofacial Surgeon, Queen Mary's Hosp., Roehampton and Ashford Gen. Hosp., Middx, 1977–83; Hon. Consultant: St George's Hosp., 1984–2000; Royal Surrey Co. Hosp., Guildford, 1993–2003; Epsom Gen. Hosp., 1994–2004. Dean of Dental Scis, Baqai Medical Univ., Karachi, 2006–08. FMedSci 1998; FKC 2002. *Publications:* Malignant Tumours of the Mouth, Jaws and Salivary Glands, 1985, 2nd edn 1995; Surgical Pathology of the Mouth and Jaws, 1996; Operative Maxillofacial Surgery, 1998; The Infratemporal Fossa, 2002; Operative Oral and Maxillofacial Surgery, 2010, 3rd edn 2017. *Recreations:* opera, ballet, gardening, antiques. *Address:* The Old Rectory, Limington, Somerset BA22 8EQ.

**LANGDON-DAVIES, Mary Eleanor;** see Quicke, M. E.

**LANGER, Bernhard,** Hon. OBE 2006; golfer; *b* Germany, 27 Aug. 1957; *m* 1984, Vikki Lopez; two *s* two *d*. Major championships include: US Masters, 1985, 1993; German Open 5 times; US Senior Open, 2010; Senior British Open, 2010, 2014, 2017; 10 Ryder Cup appearances for Europe, 1981–97, and 2002, Europe Captain, 2004. Founder, Bernhard Langer Foundn, 2003. Order of Merit (Bavaria), 2012. *Publications:* (with Bill Elliott) While the Iron is Hot (autobiog.), 1988; (with Stuart Weir) Bernhard Langer: the autobiography, 2002. *Address:* Hausener Str. 29, 86420 Diedorf, Germany.

**LANGFORD, 10th Baron** *cr* 1800; **Owain Grenville Rowley-Conwy;** *b* 27 Dec. 1958; *s* of 9th Baron Langford, OBE and Grete (*née* von Freiesleben); *S* father, 2017; *m* 1st, 1986, Joanna (marr. diss. 1993), *d* of Jack Featherstone; one *s* one *d*; 2nd, 2008, Lorraine Hennequin. *Educ:* Marlborough Coll.; Royal Agricl Coll., Cirencester. *Heir: s* Thomas Alexander Rowley-Conwy, *b* 20 March 1987.

**LANGFORD, Anthony John,** CB 1996; FRICS; Chief Executive, Valuation Office Agency, 1994–96; *b* 25 June 1936; *s* of Freeman and Ethel Langford; *m* 1958, Joan Winifred Barber; one *s* one *d. Educ:* Soham Grammar School. FRICS 1978. Joined Valuation Office, Inland Revenue, 1957; District Valuer, Camden, 1976; Superintending Valuer, Northern Region, 1981; Asst Chief Valuer, 1983; Dep. Chief Valuer, then Dep. Chief Exec., Valuation Office Agency, 1988–94. *Recreations:* walking, gardening, bowls.

**LANGFORD, Carole Willis;** see Tonkinson, C. W.

**LANGHAM, Sir John (Stephen),** 16th Bt *cr* 1660, of Cottesbrooke, Northampton; *b* 14 Dec. 1960; *s* of Sir James Michael Langham, 15th Bt, TD and of Marion Audrey Eleanor Langham (*née* Barratt); *S* father, 2002; *m* 1991, Sarah Jane Verschoyle-Greene (marr. diss. 2017); one *s* two *d*. Farmer and landowner. Web media and internet consultant. *Heir: s* Tyrone Denis James Langham, *b* 13 Aug. 1994. *Address:* Tempo Manor, Demesne, Tempo, Co. Fermanagh BT94 3PA. *T:* (028) 8954 1953.

**LANGHAM, Patricia Anne,** CBE 2009; Principal, Wakefield Grammar School Foundation, 2000–09; Headmistress, Wakefield Girls' High School, 1987–2009; Chairman, Independent and State Schools Partnership Forum, 2011–14 (Co-Chairman, 2008–11); *b* Carlisle, 1 Jan. 1951; *d* of Andrew and Mary Lowrie; *m* 2008, Nev Hanley; one step *s* two step *d. Educ:* Carlisle and County High Sch. for Girls; Univ. of Leeds (BA English and Russian; MEd). Ilkley Grammar Sch., 1973–78; Brigshaw Comp. Sch., 1978–82; Dep. Head, Woodkirk High Sch., 1982–87. Pres., GSA, 2007. Trustee: Royal Armouries, 2004–13 (now Emeritus); Th. Royal Wakefield. Chm., Friends of Wakefield Cathedral. *Recreations:* literature, gardening, travel, dog walking, collecting flying ducks. *E:* patlangham@aol.com.

**LANGHORNE, Prof. Richard Tristan Bailey,** FRHistS; Professorial Fellow, Division of Global Affairs, Rutgers University, since 2010; *b* 6 May 1940; *s* of late Eadward John Bailey Langhorne and Rosemary Scott-Foster; *m* 1971, Helen Logue (*d* 2005), *o d* of William Donaldson, CB and Mary Donaldson; one *s* one *d. Educ:* St Edward's Sch., Oxford; St John's Coll., Cambridge (Exhibnr). BA Hist. Tripos, 1962; Certif. in Hist. Studies, 1963; MA 1965. Tutor in History, Univ. of Exeter, 1963–64; Research Student, St John's Coll., Cambridge, 1964–66; Lectr in History, 1966–74 and Master of Rutherford Coll., 1971–74, Univ. of Kent at Canterbury; St John's College, Cambridge: Steward, 1974–79; Junior Bursar, 1974–87; Fellow, 1974–93; Dir, Centre of Internat. Studies, Univ. of Cambridge, 1987–93; Dir and Chief Exec., Wilton Park, FCO, 1993–96; Prof. of Political Sci., 1996–2010, Dir, 1996–2008, Center for Global Change and Governance, later Division of Global Affairs, Rutgers Univ., NJ; Prof. of Global Politics, and Dir, Centre for Global Studies, Univ. of Buckingham, 2010–14, now Hon. Prof. Vis. Prof., Univ. of Southern Calif, 1986; Hon. Prof. of Internat. Relns, Univ. of Kent at Canterbury, 1994–97; Vis. Prof., Canterbury Christchurch Univ., 2006; Hon. Prof. of Global Pols, Univ. of Buckingham, 2007–10. Freeland K. Abbott Meml Lectr, Tufts Univ., 1990; Queen Beatrix Lectr, Royal Foundn, Amsterdam, 1998. *Publications:* The Collapse of the Concert of Europe, 1890–1914, 1980; (ed) Diplomacy and Intelligence during the Second World War, 1985; (with K. Hamilton) The Practice of Diplomacy, 1994, 2nd edn 2010; The Coming of Globalization, 2000; (ed) Guide to International Relations and Diplomacy, 2002; (with C. Jönsson) Diplomacy (3 vols), 2004; The Essentials of Global Politics, 2006; reviews and articles in Historical Jl, History, Review of International Studies, and Diplomacy and Statecraft. *Recreations:* music, railways. *Address:* May Cottage, South Street, Castle Cary, Somerset BA7 7EW. *Club:* Athenæum.

**LANGLANDS, Sir Alan;** see Langlands, Sir R. A.

**LANGLANDS, Allister Gordon;** Chairman, John Wood Group PLC, 2012–14 (Chief Executive, 2007–12); *b* 31 March 1958; *s* of John and Diana Langlands; *m* 1993, Helen Shoreman; four *s* one *d. Educ:* Forfar Acad.; Univ. of Edinburgh (MA Hons Econs 1980); Harvard Univ. (AMP 1999). CA. Deloitte Haskins & Sells: Trainee Chartered Accountant, 1980–83; Manager Corporate Finance/Audit, 1984–89; Partner, 1989–91; John Wood Group PLC: Gp Finance Dir, 1991–99; Dep. Chief Exec., 1999–2006. Non-exec. Dir, Atkins, 2013–. *Recreations:* family, golf, racquet sports, gardening.

**LANGLANDS, Sir (Robert) Alan,** Kt 1998; Vice-Chancellor, University of Leeds, since 2013; *b* 29 May 1952; *s* of James Langlands and May Langlands (*née* Rankin); *m* 1977, Elizabeth McDonald; one *s* one *d. Educ:* Allan Glen's Sch.; Univ. of Glasgow (BSc Pure Sci). Grad. Trainee, NHS Scotland, 1974–76; Argyll and Clyde Health Bd, 1976–78; Simpson Meml Maternity Pavilion, Elsie Inglis Hosp., 1978–81; Unit Administrator, Middx and University Coll. Hosps and Hosp. for Women, Soho, 1982–85; Dist Gen. Manager, Harrow HA, 1985–89; Practice Leader, Health Care, Towers Perrin, 1989–90; Gen.

Manager, NW Thames RHA, 1990–92; Dep. Chief Exec., 1993–94, Chief Exec., 1994–2000, NHS Executive; Principal and Vice-Chancellor, Dundee Univ., 2000–09; Chief Exec., HEFCE, 2009–13. Member: Central R&D Cttee, NHS, 1990–93; Nat. Forum R&D, 1994–99; Health Sector Gp, BOTB, 1998–2000. Chairman: UK Biobank, 2004–12; Commn on Good Governance, 2004–05; Health Foundn, 2009–17. Non-executive Director: Office for Strategic Coordination of Health Research, 2013–17; UK Statistics Authy, 2008–09; Medicines and Healthcare Products Regulatory Agency, 2012–13. Trustee, Nuffield Trust, 2007–09. Hon. Prof., 1996–2016, and Mem. Bd, Univ. of Warwick Business Sch., 1995–2000; Member: Council and Court, Univ. of York, 1998–2000; Adv. Bd, INSEAD, 1999–2004; US Nat. Adv. Bd, Johns Hopkins Univ. Bioethics Inst., 2000–05. Fellow, Birkbeck, Univ. of London, 2014. FRSE 2002. Hon. FFPH (Hon. FFPHM 1994); FIA 1999; FCGI 2000; CCMI (CIMgt 2000); Hon. FRCP 2001; Hon. FRCGP 2001; Hon. FRCSE 2001; Hon. FRCPSGlas 2002; Hon. FMedSci 2009; Hon. FRCPE 2014. DUniv Glasgow, 2001; LLD Dundee, 2010; Dr *hc* Edinburgh, 2010; DUniv Sheffield Hallam, 2016. *Recreation:* living and walking in Scotland and Yorkshire. *Address:* Vice-Chancellor's Office, University of Leeds, Leeds LS2 9JT.

**LANGLANDS, Prof. Robert Phelan,** FRS 1981; Professor of Mathematics, Institute for Advanced Study, Princeton, New Jersey, 1972–2007, now Emeritus; *b* 6 Oct. 1936; *s* of Robert Langlands and Kathleen Johanna (*née* Phelan); *m* 1956, Charlotte Lorraine Cheverie; two *s* two *d. Educ:* Univ. of British Columbia (BA 1957, MA 1958); Yale Univ. (PhD 1960). FRSC 1972. Princeton University: Instructor, 1960–61; Lectr, 1961–62; Asst Prof., 1962–64; Associate Prof., 1964–67; Prof., Yale Univ., 1967–72. Associate Prof., Ortadoğu Teknik Universitesi, 1967–68; Gast Prof., Universität Bonn, 1980–81. Mem., Nat. Acad. of Scis, USA, 1993; Foreign Member: Russian Acad. of Scis, 2012; Turkish Bilim Akademesi, 2013. Hon. DSc: British Columbia, 1985; McMaster, 1985; CUNY, 1985; Paris VII, 1989; McGill, 1991; Toronto, 1993; Montreal, 1997; Laval, 2002; Madras, 2005; Chicago, 2011; Hon. DMath Waterloo, 1988. Wilbur L. Cross Medal, Yale Univ., 1975; Cole Prize, 1982, Steele Prize, 2005, Amer. Math. Soc.; Common Wealth Award, Sigma Xi, 1984; Maths Award, Nat. Acad. of Scis, 1988; Wolf Prize in Maths, Wolf Foundn of Israel, 1996; Grande Médaille d'Or, Acad. des Scis, Paris, 2000; Frederic Esser Nemmers Prize, Northwestern Univ., 2006; Shaw Prize, Shaw Foundn, Hong Kong, 2007; Abel Prize, 2018. *Publications:* Automorphic Forms on GL(2) (with H. Jacquet), 1970; Euler Products, 1971; On the Functional Equations satisfied by Eisenstein Series, 1976; Base Change for GL(2), 1980; Les débuts d'une formule des traces stable, 1983; contrib. Canadian Jl Maths, Proc. Amer. Math. Soc. Symposia, Springer Lecture Notes. *Address:* Institute for Advanced Study, School of Mathematics, 1 Einstein Drive, Princeton, NJ 08540, USA. *T:* (609) 7348106.

**LANGLEY, Sir (Julian Hugh) Gordon,** Kt 1995; Chairman, Panel on Takeovers and Mergers, 2010–16 (a Deputy Chairman, 2009–10); *b* 11 May 1943; *s* of late Gordon Thompson Langley and of Marjorie Langley; *m* 1968, Beatrice Jayanthi Langley; two *d. Educ:* Westminster School; Balliol College, Oxford (MA, BCL). Called to the Bar, Inner Temple, 1966, Bencher, 1996; QC 1983; a Recorder, 1986–95; a Judge of the High Ct of Justice, QBD, 1995–2007. *Recreations:* music, sport. *Address:* c/o Fountain Court Chambers, Temple, EC4Y 9DH.

**LANGLEY, Ven. Robert;** Archdeacon of Lindisfarne, 2001–07, now Archdeacon Emeritus; *b* 25 Oct. 1937; *s* of Maurice and Kathleen Langley; *m* 1961, Elisabeth Hart; one *s* two *d. Educ:* Worksop Coll.; St Catherine's Coll., Oxford (BA Maths 1961). Ordained deacon, 1963, priest, 1964; Asst Curate, Aston cum Aughton, Sheffield, 1963–68; Midlands and HQ Sec., Christian Educn Movt, 1968–74; Principal: Ian Ramsay Coll., Brasted, 1974–77; St Albans Dio. Ministerial Trng Scheme, 1977–85; Canon Missioner, Newcastle Dio., 1985–98; Dir, Ministry and Trng, Newcastle Dio., 1998–2001. Chm., Northumberland Strategic Partnership, 2008–11. Chairman: William Temple Foundn, 1994–2006; Community Action Northumberland, 2005–08; Vice Chm., SE Northumberland and N Tyneside Regeneration Initiative, 2006–09. *Recreations:* cycling, walking, music, furniture restoration. *Address:* 1 Castle Farm Mews, Newcastle upon Tyne NE2 3RG.

**LANGLEY, Prof. Robin Stewart,** PhD; FREng, FRAeS; Professor of Mechanical Engineering, since 1998, and Head, Division of Mechanics, Materials and Design, Department of Engineering, since 2008, Cambridge University; Fellow of Fitzwilliam College, Cambridge, since 1998; *b* 5 April 1957; *s* of Robert Langley and Marie Langley (*née* Lewins); *m* 1st, 1982, Pamela Heath (marr. diss. 1997); 2nd, 2007, Elizabeth Nachapkina. *Educ:* Univ. of Leicester (BSc 1978); Cranfield Univ. (MSc 1981; PhD 1983). CMath, FIMA 1989; CEng, MRAeS 1990; FREng 2018. Accountant, Armitage and Norton, 1978–79; Teaching Associate, 1983–84, Lectr in Structural Dynamics, 1984–91, Cranfield Univ.; Sen. Lectr in Aerospace Structures, 1991–95, Prof. of Structural Dynamics, 1995–98, Southampton Univ.; Dep. Hd (Grad. Studies), Dept of Engrg, Cambridge Univ., 1999–2002. Fellow: Acoustical Soc. of Amer., 2000; Internat. Inst. of Acoustics and Vibration, 2005; Royal Aeronautical Soc., 2011. *Publications:* articles in academic jls, mainly on random vibration, structural dynamics, and acoustics. *Recreations:* walking, literature, family and friends. *Address:* Department of Engineering, University of Cambridge, Trumpington Street, Cambridge CB2 1PZ. *T:* (01223) 748242.

**LANGLEY, Susan Carol,** OBE 2015; Chairman, Arthur J Gallagher Holdings (UK) Ltd, since 2015; *b* London, 2 July 1963; *d* of James Robert Walford and Shirley Walford; *m* 2003, Gary Phillip Langley. *Educ:* Univ. of Southampton (BSc Geography 1985). Travelling (sabbatical), 1985–87; Prog. Manager, Thomson Tour Ops, 1987–96; Principal Consultant, Price Waterhouse, then PricewaterhouseCoopers, 1996–98; Chief Operating Officer, Hiscox plc, 1998–2007; Dir, N America and Mkt Develt, Lloyds of London, 2007–12; CEO, Financial and Professional Services, DIT, 2013–15. Sen. Ind. Dir, UK Asset Resolution, 2010–. Lead non-exec. Dir, Home Office, 2013–. Trustee, Macmillan Cancer, 2017–. Alderman, City of London, 2018–. *Recreations:* travelling, music, desert islands. *Address:* AJ Gallagher Holdings (UK) Ltd, 25 Walbrook, EC4N 8AF. *T:* (020) 3425 3265. *E:* suelangley01@gmail.com.

**LANGRIDGE, Stephen Maitland;** stage director; Artistic Director, Glyndebourne, since 2019; *b* London, 28 May 1963; *s* of Philip Langridge, CBE and Hilary Holloway (*née* Davidson); *m* 1996, Denise L. Mellion; two *d. Educ:* John Lyon Sch., Harrow; Exeter Univ. (BA Hons Drama). Asst Dir, Opera Factory, 1985–90; freelance opera dir, 1990–, incl. prodns for Glyndebourne, Lyric Opera Chicago, Opera di Roma, Salzburg Festspiele, Bregenzer Festspiele, Royal Opera Hse, Covent Gdn, Kunlinga Operan Stockholm, Den Norske Opera, Malmö Opera, Gothenburg Opera; Artistic Dir, Gothenburg Opera, 2013–19. Occasional lectr in opera and music th., 1985–2013. A dir, Share Music (has devised music theatre with integrated gps of people with and without disabilities), 1989–. Leader: creative music projects with professional and non-professional gps in schs, prisons, hosps and in wider community; trng courses for teachers, singers, instrumentalists, composers and librettists. Mem., Gothenburg Beekeeping Gp. *Recreation:* running. *Address:* c/o Rayfield Allied, Studio 26 China Works, 100 Black Prince Road, SE1 7SJ. *W:* www.stephenlangridge.com.

**LANGRISH, Rt Rev. Michael Laurence;** Bishop of Exeter, 2000–13; an Honorary Assistant Bishop: Diocese of Chichester, since 2014; Diocese of Europe, since 2018; *b* 1 July 1946; *s* of Douglas Frank and Brenda Florence Langrish; *m* 1968, Esther Vivien (*née* Rudd); one *s* two *d. Educ:* King Edward Sch., Southampton; Birmingham Univ. (BSocSc 1967; PGCE 1968); Fitzwilliam Coll., Cambridge (BA 1973; MA 1978); Ridley Hall, Cambridge. Lectr in Educn, Mid-West State Coll. of Educn, Nigeria, 1969–71. Ordained deacon, 1973, priest, 1974; Asst Curate, Stratford-upon-Avon with Bishopston, 1973–76; Chaplain, Rugby Sch., 1976–81; Vicar, Offchurch and Diocesan Dir of Ordinands, 1981–87; Team Rector, Rugby Team Ministry, 1987–93; Bishop Suffragan of Birkenhead, 1993–2000. Chm., Rural Strategy Gp (formerly Rural Affairs Cttee), C of E Bd of Mission, 2001–09. Chairman: Devon Strategic Partnership, 2002–07; Melanesian Mission (UK), 2003–09; Churches' Legislation Advisory Service, 2009–13; Chichester Theological Coll. Trust, 2017–; Mem. Bd, Christian Aid, 2003–11. Mem. Council, Univ. of Exeter, 2001–10. Entered House of Lords, 2005. ARAgs 2009. Hon. DD: Birmingham, 2006; Exeter, 2007. *Recreations:* gardening, local history, theatre, railways, music. *Address:* 39 The Meadows, Walberton, Arundel, W Sussex BN18 0PB.

**LANGRISHE, Sir James Hercules,** 8th Bt *cr* 1777, of Knocktopher Abbey, Kilkenny; *b* 3 March 1957; *o s* of Sir Hercules Ralph Hume Langrishe, 7th Bt and of Hon. Grania Sybil Enid Wingfield, *o d* of 9th Viscount Powerscourt; *S* father, 1998; *m* 1985, Gemma Mary Philomena (marr. diss. 2010), *e d* of Patrick O'Daly; one *s* one *d. Heir: s* Richard James Hercules Langrishe, *b* 8 April 1988. *Address:* Bellingham Stables, Castlebellingham, Co. Louth, Ireland.

**LANGSHAW, George Henry;** Managing Director, UK Regions, British Gas, 1992; *b* 6 Dec. 1939; *s* of George Henry and Florence Evelyn Langshaw; *m* 1962, Maureen Cosgrove; one *s* two *d. Educ:* Liverpool Inst. High Sch. FCMA; ACIS. Various accountancy appts, Wm Crawford & Sons, 1957–63, Littlewoods Orgn, 1963–67; British Gas: Accountant, NW, 1967–70; Develt Accountant, Southern, 1970–73; Prin. Financial Analyst, HQ, 1973–76; Chief Accountant, Wales, 1976–78; Dir of Finance, Southern, 1978–82; Dep. Chm., NW, 1982–87; Regional Chm., British Gas (Wales), 1987–89; Gp Dir of Personnel, 1989–90; Man. Dir, Global Gas, 1990–92. Chm., BG Corporate Ventures, 1990. Director: British Gas Deutschland GmbH, 1991; British Gas Holdings (Canada), 1992; BG Holdings Inc., 1992. Dir, Bd of Gas Consumers, Canada, 1990. CIGEM (CIGasE 1988); CCMI (CBIM 1991). *Recreations:* soccer, reading, golf.

**LANGSLOW, Prof. David Richard,** DPhil; FBA 2019; Professor of Classics, since 1999, and Hulme Professor of Latin, since 2018, University of Manchester; *b* Ealing, 25 June 1960; *s* of Brian Langslow and Angela Langslow (*née* Fry); *m* 1992, Anne Karin Woermer (*d* 2012); two *s* two *d. Educ:* Whitgift Sch.; University Coll., Oxford (BA 1982; MPhil 1984); Wolfson Coll., Oxford (DPhil 1991). Lectr in Latin Philology and Linguistics, Univ. of Oxford, 1984–99; Fellow, Wolfson Coll., Oxford, 1984–99, now Emeritus. A Dir, JACT Greek Summer Sch., 2002–. Founding Chair, Manchester Classics for All, 2015–; Trustee, Classics for All, 2016–. *Publications:* Medical Latin in the Roman Empire, 2000; The Latin Alexander Trallianus, 2006; Jacob Wackernagel, Lectures on Syntax, 2009; (ed with B. Maire) Body, Disease and Treatment in a Changing World: Latin texts and contexts in ancient and medieval medicine, 2010; Alexander of Tralles on Fevers, 2020. *Recreations:* family, sport, music, theatre, travel, the outdoors. *Address:* Department of Classics, Ancient History, Archaeology, and Egyptology, University of Manchester, Manchester M13 9PL. *T:* (0161) 275 3028. *E:* david.langslow@manchester.ac.uk.

**LANGSLOW, Derek Robert,** CBE 2000; PhD; Acting Chairman, Marine Management Organisation, 2010–11; *b* 7 Feb. 1945; *s* of Alexander Frederick Langslow and Beatrice Bibby Langslow (*née* Wright); *m* 1969, Helen Katherine (*née* Addison); one *s* one *d. Educ:* Ashville College, Harrogate; Queens' College, Cambridge (MA, PhD). Post-Doctoral Fellow, Cambridge and Univ. of Kansas; Lectr, Univ. of Edinburgh, 1972–78; Nature Conservancy Council: Senior Ornithologist, 1978–84; Asst Chief Scientist, 1984–87; Dir, Policy and Planning, 1987–90; Chief Scientist, 1990; Chief Exec., English Nature, 1990–2000; Chm., Rail Passenger Cttee for Eastern England, 2000–05; Chm., East of England Tourism, 2006–10. Director: British Waterways, 2000–06; Harwich Haven Authy, 2001–09 (Dep. Chm., 2007–09); Marine Mgt Orgn, 2010–. Member: Agriculture and Envmt Biotechnol. Commn, 2000–05; Passenger Focus, 2005–11. Trustee: Heritage Lottery Fund, 2002–08; Natural History Mus., 2008–16; Beds, Cambs, Northants and Peterborough Wildlife Trust, 2009– (Chm., 2013–16). *Publications:* numerous papers in learned jls. *Recreations:* badminton, hill-walking, sheep, bird watching, music. *Address:* 4 Engaine, Orton Longueville, Peterborough PE2 7QA. *T:* (01733) 232153.

**LANGSTAFF, Hon. Sir Brian (Frederick James),** Kt 2005; a Judge of the High Court, Queen's Bench Division, 2005–18; Liaison Judge (with responsibility for the Administrative Court) for the North of England, 2009–11; President, Employment Appeal Tribunal, 2012–15 (Judge, 2000–03); Chair, Infected Blood Inquiry, since 2018; *b* 30 April 1948; *s* of Frederick Sidney Langstaff and Muriel Amy Maude Langstaff (*née* Griffin); *m* 1975, Deborah Elizabeth Weatherup; one *s* one *d. Educ:* George Heriot's Sch.; St Catharine's Coll., Cambridge (BA); Inns of Court Sch. of Law. VSO, Sri Lanka, 1966–67. Called to the Bar, Middle Temple, 1971 (Harmsworth Schol., 1975), Bencher, 2001. Called to the Bar of NI, 1999. Lectr and Sen. Lectr in Law, Mid-Essex Technical Coll. and Sch. of Art, Chelmsford, 1971–75; Asst Recorder, SE Circuit, 1991–95; QC 1994; a Recorder, 1995–2005. Hd of Cloisters Chambers, 2002–05. Leading Counsel, Bristol Royal Infirmary Inquiry, 1998–2000. Chairman: Personal Injury Bar Assoc., 1999–2001 (Hon. Pres., 2011–17); Exec. Cttee, Industrial Law Soc., 1997–2005 (Hon. Vice-Pres., 2005–); Law Reform Cttee, Bar Council, 2001–03 (Vice-Chm., 1999–2001); Master of Rolls' working party on structured settlements, 2001–02; Serious Injury and Clinical Negligence Cttee, Civil Justice Council, 2003–06; Tribunals Procedure Cttee, 2012–; Exec. Mem., Judicial Studies Bd, 2008–11 (Chm., Tribunals Cttee, 2008–11). Gov., 1986–2010, Associate Gov., 2010–, local primary sch. (Chm. Govs, 1991–98). Adv. Editor, Occupational Health, Safety & Environment, 1997–2000. *Publications:* Concise College Casenotes: equity and trusts, 1975; Health and Safety at Work: Halsbury's Laws vol. 20, 4th edn 1994; (ed and contrib.) Personal Injury Handbook, 2000, 3rd edn 2007; Bullen, Leake and Jacobs, Precedents of Pleading, (adv. ed.) 14th edn 2001 to (gen. ed.) 19th edn 2019; (contrib.) Munkman's Employers' Liability, 13th edn 2001 to 16th edn 2013; Personal Injury Schedules: calculating damages, 2001, (Adv. Ed.) 4th edn 2017; (contrib.) Butterworths Personal Injury Litigation Service, part 1, 2004–; (contrib.) Occupational Illness Litigation, 2010; (Chm. Editl Bd) Guidelines for Assessment of Damages in Personal Injury Cases, 13th edn, 2015, 14th edn, 2017; legal articles. *Recreations:* sport, current affairs, mowing the lawn, bell-ringing, solving sudoku, cooking and eating, travel. *Address:* Infected Blood Inquiry, Fleetbank House, 1st Floor, 2–6 Salisbury Square, EC4Y 8AE.

**LANGSTAFF, Rt Rev. James Henry;** *see* Rochester, Bishop of.

**LANGSTON, Ven. Clinton Matthew,** QHC 2017; Archdeacon to the Army, since 2017, and Chaplain-General, since 2018; *b* Birmingham, 1962; *m* 1987, Debbie. *Educ:* Sir Wilfrid Martineau Sch., Birmingham; Derbys Coll. of Higher Educn (BCS); Queen's Coll., Birmingham (Cert. Theol. Studies). Ordained deacon, 1990, priest, 1991; Asst Curate, St James the Great, Solihull, 1990–94; Chaplain, Royal Army Chaplains' Dept, 1994–. Hon.

Canon, Salisbury Cathedral, 2018–. *Recreations:* walking, dancing, golf, coaching, cooking. *Address:* Ministry of Defence Chaplains (Army), Army Headquarters, IDL 3, Blenheim Buildings, Marlborough Lines, Andover, Hants SP11 8HT. *E:* clinton.langston1945@mod.gov.uk. *Club:* Royal Air Force.

**LANGSTON**, Group Captain John Antony S.; *see* Steff-Langston.

**LANGTON**; *see* Temple-Gore-Langton, family name of Earl Temple of Stowe.

**LANGTON, Bryan David**, CBE 1988; Director, Bass plc, 1985–96; Chairman and Chief Executive Officer, Holiday Inn Worldwide, 1990–96; *b* 6 Dec. 1936; *s* of Thomas Langton and Doris (*née* Brown); *m* 1960, Sylva Degenhardt; two *d. Educ:* Accrington Grammar Sch.; Westminster Tech. Coll. (Hotel Operation Dip.); Ecole Hôtelière de la SSA, Lausanne (Operations Dip.). Dep. Manager, Russell Hotel, London, 1959–63; General Manager: Victoria Hotel, Nottingham, 1964–66; Grand Hotel, Manchester, 1966–71; Crest Hotels: Divl Manager, 1971–73; Ops Dir UK, 1973–75; Ops Dir Europe, 1975–77; Divl Managing Dir, Europe, 1977–81; Managing Dir, Ops, 1981–82; Man. Dir, 1982–88; Chairman, 1985–90. Chairman: Holiday Inns International, 1988–90; Toby Restaurants, 1988–90; Fairfield Communities Inc., 1999–2002 (non-exec. Dir, 1996–99); Dir, Caribiner Internat. Inc., 1996–2001; Vice Chm., E Suites LLC, 2007–; Member: Adv. Bd, Mote Marine Sarasota, 1997–2001; Bd, Florida West Coast Symphony, 1997–2008 (Pres., 2005–06). Vice Pres., Internat. Hotel Assoc., 1990. Trustee, Educnl Inst., Amer. Hotel and Motel Assoc., 1990–97. Member, Board of Trustees: Woodruff Arts Center, Atlanta, 1990–97; Northside Hosp. Foundn Bd, 1990–97; YMCA, Sarasota, Fla, 1999–2002. Trustee, Bd of Visitors, Emory Univ., 1990–97. Hon. Fellow, Manchester Poly., later Manchester Metropolitan Univ., 1990–99. Corporate Hotelier of the World Award, 1995. *Recreations:* golf, cricket, reading, theatre, soccer.

**LANGTON, Prof. Rae Helen**, PhD; FBA 2014; Knightbridge Professor of Philosophy, University of Cambridge, since 2017 (Professor of Philosophy, 2013–17); Fellow, Newnham College, Cambridge, since 2013; *b* Ludhiana, India, 14 Feb. 1961; *m* Richard Holton. *Educ:* Hebron Sch., Coonoor and Ootacamund, India; Univ. of New England, NSW; Univ. of Sydney (BA 1st Cl. Hons 1986); Princeton Univ. (PhD 1995). Lectr, then Sen. Lectr, Monash Univ., 1990–98; Fellow in Philosophy, Res. Sch. of Social Scis, ANU (on secondment), 1997–98; Lectr, Sheffield Univ., 1998–99; Professor: of Moral Philosophy, Univ. of Edinburgh, 1999–2004; Dept of Linguistics and Philosophy, MIT, 2004–13. Visiting Professor: Dartmouth Coll., NH, 2001; Yale Univ., 2009; Cambridge Univ., 2012; Visiting Fellow: Res. Sch. of Social Scis, ANU, 2003; All Souls Coll., Oxford, 2015. *Publications:* Kantian Humility: our ignorance of things in themselves, 1998; Sexual Solipsism: philosophical essays on pornography and objectification, 2009; contribs to jls incl. Philosophy, Philosophy and Public Affairs, Canadian Jl Law and Jurisprudence, Australasian Jl Philosophy, Kantian Rev., Philosophical Rev. *Address:* Faculty of Philosophy, University of Cambridge, Sidgwick Avenue, Cambridge CB3 9DA.

**LANGTRY, (James) Ian**; Education Officer, Association of County Councils, 1988–96; *b* 2 Jan. 1939; *s* of late Rev. H. J. Langtry and I. M. Langtry (*née* Eagleson); *m* 1st, 1959, Eileen Roberta Beatrice (*née* Nesbitt) (*d* 1999); one *s* one *d*; 2nd, 2007, Alison Mitchell Burgoyne (*née* Mann). *Educ:* Coleraine Academical Instn; Queen's Univ., Belfast (Sullivan Schol.; BSc 1st Cl., Physics). Asst Master, Bangor Grammar Sch., 1960–61; Lectr, Belfast College of Technology, 1961–66; Asst Director of Examinations/Recruitment, Civil Service Commission, 1966–70; Principal, Dept of Educn and Science, 1970–76, Asst Sec., 1976–82, Under Sec., 1982–87; Under Sec., DHSS, 1987–88. *Address:* 7 Bucklerburn Drive, Peterculter, Aberdeen AB14 0XJ.

**LANIGAN, Audrey Cecelia**; *see* Slaughter, A. C.

**LANKESTER, Patricia**; consultant in the arts, heritage, social justice and learning; *b* 28 July 1946; *d* of Leo Cockcroft and Jennie Cockcroft; *m* 1968, Sir Timothy Patrick Lankester, *qv*; three *d. Educ:* King's Coll., London (BA 1967); Inst. of Educn, London (PGCE 1976). Hd of Hist., Barnsbury Sch., Islington, 1980–83; Hd of Humanities, Islington VI Form Centre, 1983–85; Hd of Educn, Nat. Trust, 1988–96; Dir, Paul Hamlyn Foundn, 1998–2004. Member: Learning Panel, RSC, 2009–; Council, Tate Britain, 2013–17. Trustee: Heritage Lottery Fund, 1998–2003 (Mem., Expert Panel, 2008–11); Tate, 2005–13; Nat. Gall. 2007–13. Trustee: Open Coll. of the Arts, 1988–96; Farms for City Children, 1996–99; Villiers Park Educnl Trust, 2000–07; Eureka!, Halifax, 2004–09; Foundling Mus., 2005–14; The Hanover Foundn, 2006–10; Sage Music Centre, Gateshead, 2007–15; Chelsea Physic Gdn, 2009–; Clore Social Leadership Prog., 2010–17; Bristol Museums Develt Trust, 2010–11; Holburne Mus., Bath, 2014–. Adviser to: Clore Duffield Foundn, 2005–; Heritage Lottery Fund, 2008–; Freelands Foundn, 2015–18. Founder Mem., Cultural Learning Alliance, 2015–. *Recreations:* art, theatre, historic buildings, fiction, walking. *E:* patricia.lankester@btinternet.com. *Club:* Academy.

**LANKESTER, Sir Timothy Patrick, (Sir Tim)**, KCB 1994; President, Corpus Christi College, Oxford, 2001–09, Honorary Fellow, 2010; *b* 15 April 1942; *s* of late Preb. Robin Prior Archibald Lankester and Jean Dorothy (*née* Gilliat); *m* 1968, Patricia Cockcroft (*see* P. Lankester); three *d. Educ:* Monkton Combe Sch.; St John's Coll., Cambridge (BA; Hon. Fellow 1995); Jonathan Edwards Coll., Yale (Henry Fellow, MA). Teacher (VSO), St Michael's Coll., Belize, 1960–61; Fereday Fellow, St John's Coll., Oxford, 1965–66; Economist, World Bank, Washington DC, 1966–69; New Delhi, 1970–73; Principal 1973, Asst Sec. 1977, HM Treasury; Private Secretary to Rt Hon. James Callaghan, 1978–79; to Rt Hon. Margaret Thatcher, 1979–81; seconded to S. G. Warburg and Co. Ltd, 1981–83; Under Sec., HM Treasury, 1983–85; Economic Minister, Washington and Exec. Dir, IMF and World Bank, 1985–88; Dep. Sec., HM Treasury, 1988–89; Perm. Sec., ODA, FCO, 1989–94; Perm. Sec., Dept for Educn, 1994–95; Dir, SOAS, London Univ., 1996–2000. Dep. Chm., British Council, 1997–2003. Non-executive Director: CGU plc, 1997–2002; London Metal Exchange, 1997–2002; Smith and Nephew plc, 1997–2003; Mitchells and Butler plc, 2003–10; Actis Capital LLP, 2004–09. Vice-Chm., Worldwide Support for Develt, Tokyo, 2002–; SE Asia Advr, Oxford Analytica, 2005–. Chm., Council, LSHTM, 2006–15. Gov., Asia-Europe Foundn, 1997–2011; Mem., UK-India Round Table, 1997–2014. Mem., Jt Adv. Bd, Georgetown Univ., Qatar, 2005–. Chm., Contemporary Dance Trust, 2007–13; Chm., Wells Maltings Trust, 2018–. *E:* tim.lankester@ccc.ox.ac.uk.

**LANNON, Dame Frances**, DBE 2016; DPhil; FRHistS; Principal, Lady Margaret Hall, University of Oxford, 2002–15; *b* 22 Dec. 1945; *d* of Martin Lannon and Margaret (*née* O'Hare). *Educ:* Sacred Heart Grammar Sch., Newcastle upon Tyne; Lady Margaret Hall, Oxford (BA 1st Cl. Hons Mod. Hist., MA 1972); St Antony's Coll., Oxford (DPhil Mod. Spanish Hist. 1976). FRHistS 1986. Lectr in Hist., QMC, London, 1975–77; Fellow and Tutor in Mod. Hist., LMH, Oxford, 1977–2002. Vis. Prof., Univ. of South Carolina, 1986. Mem., Commonwealth Scholarship Commn, 1982–91; Fellow, Woodrow Wilson Center, Washington, 1992. *Publications:* Privilege, Persecution and Prophecy: the Catholic Church in Spain 1875–1975, 1987; (ed with Paul Preston) Elites and Power in Twentieth-Century Spain, 1990; The Spanish Civil War, 2002; contrib. Oxford DNB, TLS, Jl of Contemporary Hist., other learned jls. *Recreations:* Spain, visual arts, contemporary fiction. *E:* frances.lannon@lmh.ox.ac.uk.

**LANSBURY, Dame Angela (Brigid)**, DBE 2014 (CBE 1994); actress; *b* London, England, 16 Oct. 1925; *d* of Edgar Lansbury and late Moyna Macgill (who *m* 1st, Reginald Denham); *m* 1st, Richard Cromwell; 2nd, 1949, Peter Shaw (*d* 2003); one *s* one *d* and one step *s. Educ:* South Hampstead High Sch. for Girls; Webber Douglas Sch. of Singing and Dramatic Art, Kensington; Feagin Sch. of Drama and Radio, New York. With Metro-Goldwyn-Mayer, 1943–50; *films:* Gaslight, 1944; National Velvet, 1944; The Picture of Dorian Gray, 1945; The Harvey Girls, 1946; The Hoodlum Saint, 1946; Till the Clouds Roll By, 1946; The Private Affairs of Bel-Ami, 1947; If Winter Comes, 1948; Tenth Avenue Angel, 1948; State of the Union, 1948; The Three Musketeers, 1948; The Red Danube, or Storm over Vienna, or Vespers in Vienna, 1949; Samson and Delilah, 1949; Kind Lady, 1951; Mutiny, 1952; Remains to be Seen, 1953; A Life at Stake, or Key Man, 1955; The Purple Mask, 1956; The Court Jester, 1956; A Lawless Street, 1956; Please Murder Me, 1956; The Long Hot Summer, 1958; The Reluctant Debutante, 1958; Breath of Scandal, 1960; The Dark at the Top of the Stairs, 1960; Season of Passion, 1961; Blue Hawaii, 1961; All Fall Down, 1962; The Manchurian Candidate, 1962; In the Cool of the Day, 1963; The World of Henry Orient, 1964; Dear Heart, 1964; The Greatest Story Ever Told, 1965; Harlow, 1965; The Amorous Adventures of Moll Flanders, 1965; Mister Buddwing, or Woman Without a Face, 1966; Something for Everyone, or Black Flowers for the Bride, 1970; Bedknobs and Broomsticks, 1971; Death on the Nile, or Murder on the Nile, 1978; The Lady Vanishes, 1980; The Mirror Crack'd, 1980; The Pirates of Penzance, 1982; The Company of Wolves, 1983; Beauty and the Beast, 1991; Nanny McPhee, 2005; Mr Popper's Penguins, 2011; Mary Poppins Returns, 2018; *plays:* appearances include: Hotel Paradiso (Broadway debut), 1957; Helen, in A Taste of Honey, Lyceum Theatre, New York, 1960; Anyone Can Whistle (Broadway musical), 1964; Mame (Tony Award for best actress in a Broadway musical), Winter Garden, NYC, 1966–68; Dear World (Broadway), 1969 (Tony Award); Pretty Belle, 1971; All Over, RSC, 1971; Gypsy (Broadway Musical), Piccadilly, 1973, US tour, 1974 (Tony Award; Chicago, Sarah Siddons Award, 1974); Gertrude, in Hamlet, Nat. Theatre, 1975; Anna, in The King and I (Broadway), 1978; Mrs Lovett, in Sweeney Todd (Broadway), 1979 (Tony Award); A Little Family Business, 1983; Deuce, NY, 2007; Blithe Spirit (Broadway), 2009 (Tony Award); Gielgud Th., 2014 (Best Supporting Actress, Olivier Awards, 2015); A Little Night Music (Broadway), 2009; The Best Man (Broadway), 2012; Driving Miss Daisy (Australia tour), 2013; *television includes:* series, Murder She Wrote, 1984–95 (Golden Globe Award, 1984, 1986, 1991, 1992); Little Gloria, Happy At Last, 1982; The Gift of Love: a Christmas Story, 1983; A Talent for Murder (with Laurence Olivier), 1984; Lace, 1984; The First Olympico-Athens 1896, 1984; Rage of Angels II, 1986; Shootdown, 1988; The Shell Seekers, 1989; The Love She Sought, 1990; Mrs Arris Goes to Paris, 1992; Mrs Santa Claus, 1996; South by Southwest, 1997; The Unexpected Mrs Pollifax, 1998; A Story to Die for, 2000; Little Women, 2017. NY Drama Desk Award, 1979; Sarah Siddons Award, 1980 and 1983; inducted Theatre Hall of Fame, 1982; Silver Mask for Lifetime Achievement, BAFTA, 1991; Lifetime Achievement Award, Screen Actors' Guild, 1997; Nat. Medal of the Arts, USA, 1997; Hon. Acad. Award, 2013; Rose d'Or, 2017.

**LANSDOWN, Gillian Elizabeth, (Mrs Richard Lansdown)**; *see* Tindall, G. E.

**LANSDOWNE**, 9th Marquess of, *cr* 1784 (GB); **Charles Maurice Petty-Fitzmaurice**, LVO 2002; 30th Baron of Kerry and Lixnaw, 1181; Viscount Clanmaurice and Earl of Kerry, 1722; Baron Dunkeron and Viscount Fitzmaurice, 1751; Earl of Shelburne, 1753; Baron Wycombe (GB), 1760; Viscount Calne and Calston and Earl of Wycombe (GB), 1784; Vice Lord-Lieutenant, Wiltshire, 2012–16; *b* 21 Feb. 1941; *s* of 8th Marquess of Lansdowne, PC and Barbara, *d* of Harold Stuart Chase; *S* father, 1999; *m* 1st, 1965, Lady Frances Eliot, *o d* of 9th Earl of St Germans; two *s* two *d*; 2nd, 1987, Fiona Merritt, *d* of Lady Davies and Donald Merritt. *Educ:* Eton. Page of Honour to The Queen, 1956–57. Served with Kenya Regt, 1960–61; with Wiltshire Yeomanry (TA), amalgamated with Royal Yeomanry Regt, 1963–73. Pres., Wiltshire Playing Fields Assoc., 1965–74; Wiltshire County Councillor, 1970–85; Mem., South West Economic Planning Council, 1972–77; Chairman: Working Committee Population & Settlement Pattern (SWEPC), 1972–77; North Wiltshire DC, 1973–76; Mem., Calne and Chippenham RDC, 1964–73. Mem., Historic Bldgs and Monuments Commn, 1983–89; President: HHA, 1988–93 (Dep. Pres., 1986–88); South West Tourism, 1989–2006; Wiltshire Historic Bldgs Trust, 1994–; Wilts & Berks Canal Partnership, 2001–. Mem., Prince's Council, Duchy of Cornwall, 1990–2001; President: Wiltshire Assocs Boys Clubs and Youth Clubs, 1976–2003; North-West Wiltshire District Scout Council, 1977–88; N Wilts Cons. Assoc., 1986–89. Contested (C) Coventry North East, 1979. DL Wilts, 1990. *Heir: s* Earl of Kerry, *qv. Address:* Bowood House, Calne, Wiltshire SN11 0LZ. *T:* (01249) 813343. *Clubs:* Turf, White's.

**LANSLEY**, family name of **Baron Lansley**.

**LANSLEY, Baron** *cr* 2015 (Life Peer), of Orwell in the County of Cambridgeshire; **Andrew David Lansley**, CBE 1996; PC 2010; DL; *b* 11 Dec. 1956; *s* of late Thomas Lansley and Irene Lansley; *m* 1st, 1985, Marilyn Jane Biggs (marr. diss. 2001); three *d*; 2nd, 2001, Sally Anne Low; one *s* one *d. Educ:* Univ. of Exeter (BA). Administration trainee, Dept of Industry, 1979; Private Sec. to Sec. of State for Trade and Industry, 1984–85; Principal Private Sec. to Chancellor of Duchy of Lancaster, 1985–87; Dir, Policy, 1987–89, Dep. Dir-Gen., 1989–90, ABCC; Director: Cons. Res. Dept, 1990–95; Public Policy Unit, 1995–97. MP (C) S Cambridgeshire, 1997–2015. Shadow Minister for the Cabinet and Shadow Chancellor of the Duchy of Lancaster, 1999–2001; Shadow Sec. of State for Health, 2003–10; Sec. of State for Health, 2010–12; Lord Privy Seal and Leader of H of C, 2012–14. Member: Select Cttee on Health, 1997–98; Trade and Industry Select Cttee, 2001–04. A Vice-Chm., Cons. Party, 1998–99. UK Co-Chm., UK-Japan 21st Century Gp, 2015–. DL Cambs, 2016. *Publications:* A Private Route?, 1988; Conservatives and the Constitution, 1997. *Recreations:* travel, cricket, films, history. *Address:* House of Lords, SW1A 0PW.

**LANSMAN, Jonathan**; Co-Founder and Chair, Momentum, since 2016; *b* London, 9 July 1957; *s* of Bernard Lansman and Pauline Pearl Lansman (*née* Rothstein); *m* 1st, Bethany Wagstaff (*d* 1999); two *s* one *d*; 2nd, 2011, Kyla Harris (separated 2015). *Educ:* Clare Coll., Cambridge (BA Econs 1979); London Business Sch. (MBA). Circulation Manager, Tribune Publications Ltd, 1982–83; Coordinator, Capital Transport Campaign, 1984–88; Political Coordinator, Campaign Gp of MPs, 1988–89; Sen. Consultant, Union Communications Ltd, 1989–91; freelance transport consultant, 1990–2007; Political Advr to Michael Meacher, MP, 2008–15. Mem., Labour Party NEC, 2018–. Trustee, Breast Cancer Care, 1999–2008. *Publications:* (ed) Beyond Thatcher: the real alternative, 1983. *E:* jonlansman@me.com.

**LANTOS, Prof. Peter Laszlo**, PhD, DSc; FRCPath, FMedSci; Professor of Neuropathology, Institute of Psychiatry, King's College, London, 1979–2001, now Professor Emeritus; *b* 22 Oct. 1939; *s* of late Sandor Leipniker and Ilona Leipniker (*née* Somlo); name changed by deed poll to Lantos, 1961. *Educ:* Medical Univ. Szeged,

Hungary (MD 1964); Middlesex Hosp. Sch. of Medicine, Univ. of London (PhD 1973, DSc 1992). FRCPath. Wellcome Res. Fellow, 1968–69; Lectr, 1969–75, Sen. Lectr and Hon. Consultant, 1976–79, in Neuropathol., Middx Hosp. Sch. of Medicine; Hon. Consultant in Neuropathology: Bethlem Royal and Maudsley Hosp., 1979–2001; KCH, 1984–2002; St Thomas' Hosp., 1992–2002; Dir, Neuropathol. Service, King's Neurosci. Centre, 1995–2001. Advr, German Fed. Ministry for Educn and Res., 2000–02. Chairman: Bd of Examrs in Neuropathol., RCPath, 1983–89; Scientific Adv. Panel, Brain Res. Trust, 1985–91; Samantha Dickson Res. Trust, 2003–; Trustee: Psychiatry Res. Trust, 1996–; Alzheimer Res. UK (formerly Alzheimer Res. Trust), 2001–14. FMedSci 2001. *Publications:* (ed) Greenfield's Neuropathology, 6th edn 1997, 7th edn 2002; Parallel Lines (autobiog.), 2006; Closed Horizon (novel), 2012; The Visitor (play), 2013; Distorting Mirrors (play), 2014; Stolen Years (play), 2016; Light and Shadow (play), Stolen Lives (play), 2018; contrib. numerous book chapters and scientific and med. papers and rev. articles to jls incl. Lancet and Nature. *Recreations:* travel, languages, theatres, fine arts. *T:* (020) 7487 5275. *E:* peter.lantos@btinternet.com. *Club:* Athenæum.

**LANYON, (Harry) Mark;** Regional Director, Government Office for East Midlands, 1994–98; *b* 15 July 1939; *s* of late Henry Lanyon and Heather Gordon (*née* Tyrrell); *m* 1970, Elizabeth Mary Morton; one *s* one *d*. *Educ:* Ardingly Coll.; St Andrews Univ. (BSc Hons 1962). CEng 1965; MIMechE 1965. Ministry of Aviation: Engr Cadet, 1963–65; Aeronautical Inspectorate, 1965–68; Concorde Div., Min. of Technol., 1968–75; Department of Trade and Industry: Shipbuilding Policy Div., 1975–77; Dep. Dir, SW Region, 1977–82; Regl Dir, W Midlands, 1982–85; Hd of Br., Mechanical and Electrical Engrg Div., 1985–90; Asst Dir, Consumer Affairs, OFT, 1990–93; Regl Dir, Yorks and Humberside, 1993–94.
*See also L. E. Lanyon.*

**LANYON, Prof. Lance Edward,** CBE 2001; Principal, Royal Veterinary College, 1989–2004; Pro-Vice-Chancellor, University of London, 1997–99; *b* 4 Jan. 1944; *s* of late Henry Lanyon and Heather Gordon (*née* Tyrrell); *m* 1st, 1972, Mary Kear (marr. diss. 1997); one *s* one *d*; 2nd, 2003, Joanna Price. *Educ:* Christ's Hospital; Univ. of Bristol (BVSC, PhD, DSc). MRCVS. Lectr, 1967, Reader in Vet. Anatomy, 1967–79, Univ. of Bristol; Associate Prof., 1980–83, Prof., 1983–84, Tufts Sch. of Vet. Medicine, Boston, Mass; Prof. of Vet. Anatomy, Royal Vet. Coll., Univ. of London, 1984–89, personal title, 1989–2004, now Prof. Emeritus (Head, Dept of Vet. Anatomy, 1984–87, of Vet. Basic Scis, 1987–88). Vis. Prof., Univ. of Bristol, 2010. Almoner, Christ's Hosp., 1998–2009. Chm., Governing Body, Christ's Hosp. Sch., 2007–09. Founder FMedSci 1998; FRVC 2005. Hon. FRCVS 2012. Hon. DSc Bristol, 2004. *Publications:* chapters in books on orthopaedics, osteoporosis, and athletic training; articles in professional jls. *Recreations:* building, home improvements, sailing.
*See also H. M. Lanyon.*

**LANYON, Mark;** *see* Lanyon, H. M.

**LAPIDGE, Prof. Michael,** PhD, LittD; FBA 1994; Fellow of Clare College, Cambridge, since 1990; *b* 8 Feb. 1942; *s* of Rae H. Lapidge and Catherine Mary Lapidge (*née* Carruthers). *Educ:* Univ. of Calgary (BA 1962); Univ. of Alberta (MA 1965); Univ. of Toronto (PhD 1971); LittD Cantab 1988. Cambridge University: Lectr, 1974–88; Reader in Insular Latin Literature, 1988–91; Elrington and Bosworth Prof. of Anglo-Saxon, 1991–98; Notre Dame Prof. of English, Univ. of Notre Dame, Indiana, 1999–2004. Corresponding Fellow: Bayerische Akademie der Wissenschaften, 1997; Accad. dei Lincei, 2001. Hon. DLitt Toronto, 2011. *Publications:* Aldhelm: the prose works, 1979; Alfred the Great, 1983; Aldhelm: the poetic works, 1985; A Bibliography of Celtic Latin Literature 400–1200, 1985; Wulfstan of Winchester: the life of St Ethelwold, 1991; Anglo-Saxon Litanies of the Saints, 1991; Anglo-Latin Literature 900–1066, 1993; Biblical Commentaries from the Canterbury School of Theodore and Hadrian, 1994; Archbishop Theodore, 1995; Byrhtferth's Enchiridion, 1995; Anglo-Latin Literature 600–899, 1996; The Cult of St Swithun, 2003; The Anglo-Saxon Library, 2006; Beda: storia degli Inglesi, vol. 1, 2008, vol. 2, 2010; Byrhtferth of Ramsey: the lives of St Oswald and St Ecgwine, 2009; (with M. Winterbottom) The Early Lives of St Dunstan, 2012; (with H. Gneuss) Anglo-Saxon Manuscripts, 2014; Hilduin of Saint-Denis: the Passio S. Dionysii in prose and verse, 2017; The Roman Martyrs, 2018; Bede's Latin Poetry, 2019; articles in learned jls. *Recreation:* hill-walking. *Address:* 143 Sturton Street, Cambridge CB1 2QH. *T:* (01223) 363768.

**LA PLANTE, Lynda,** CBE 2008; writer and producer; Founder and Chairman: La Plante Productions, since 1994; La Plante Global, since 2014; *m* Richard La Plante (marr. diss.). *Educ:* RADA (schol.). Former actress. Writer: *television: series:* Widows, 1983; Prime Suspect, 1991, series 3, 1993; Civvies, 1992; Seekers, 1993; The Lifeboat, 1994; The Governor, 1995, series 2, 1996; The Prosecutors (US); Supply and Demand, 1996, series 2, 1998; Trial and Retribution, annual series, 1997–2009; Killer Net, 1998; Mind Games, 2000; The Commander, 2003, 2005; Above Suspicion, 2009; The Red Dahlia, 2010; *play:* Seconds Out. Hon. Fellow, Forensic Sci. Soc., 2013. *Publications:* The Legacy, 1988; The Talisman, 1989; Bella Mafia, 1991 (televised, US); Entwined, 1992; Framed, 1993; Seekers, 1993; Widows, 1994; Cold Shoulder, 1994; Prime Suspect, 1995; Prime Suspect 3, 1995; She's Out, 1995; The Governor, 1995; Cold Blood, 1986; Cold Heart, 1998; Trial and Retribution no 1, 1997, no 2, 1998, no 3, 1999, no 4, 2000; Sleeping Cruelty, 2000; Royal Flush, 2002; Above Suspicion, 2004; The Red Dahlia, 2006; Clean Cut, 2007; Deadly Intent, 2008; Silent Scream, 2009; Blind Fury, 2010; Blood Line, 2011; The Little One, 2012; Backlash, 2012; Wrongful Death, 2013; Twisted, 2014; Tennison, 2015; Hidden Killers, 2017; Good Friday, 2017; Murder Mile, 2018; The Dirty Dozen, 2019. *Address:* c/o Simon & Schuster, 222 Gray's Inn Road, WC1X 8HB.

**LAPLI, Sir John Ini,** GCMG 1999; Governor General, Solomon Islands, 1999–2004; baptized 24 June 1955; *s* of Christian Mekope and Ellen Lauai; *m* 1985, Helen; three *s* one *d*. *Educ:* Nabakanga Jun. Primary Sch., Solomon Is; Lueslemba Sen. Primary Sch., Solomon Is; Selwyn Coll., Guadalcanal; Bp Patterson Theol Coll., Guadalcanal (Cert. Theol.); St John's Theol Coll., Auckland (LTh, Dip. and Licentiate in Theol.). Tutor, Theol Coll., 1982–83; teacher, Catechist Sch., Rural Trng Centre, 1985; parish priest, 1986; Bible translator, 1987–88; Premier, Temotu Province, Solomon Is, 1988–99. *Recreations:* gardening, before taking up public office. *Address:* c/o Government House, PO Box 252, Honiara, Solomon Islands.

**LAPOTAIRE, Jane Elizabeth Marie;** actress; *b* 26 Dec. 1944; *d* of unknown father and Louise Elise Lapotaire; *m* 1st, 1965, Oliver Wood (marr. diss. 1967); 2nd, 1974, Roland Joffé (marr. diss. 1982); one *s*. *Educ:* Northgate Grammar Sch., Ipswich; Old Vic Theatre Sch., Bristol. Bristol Old Vic Co., 1965–67; Nat. Theatre Co., 1967–71, incl. Measure for Measure, Flea in Her Ear, Dance of Death, Way of the World, Merchant of Venice, Oedipus, The Taming of the Shrew; freelance films and TV, 1971–74; RSC, 1974–75 (roles included Viola in Twelfth Night, and Sonya in Uncle Vanya); Prospect Theatre Co., West End, 1975–76 (Vera in A Month in the Country, Lucy Honeychurch in A Room with a View); freelance films and TV, 1976–78; Rosalind in As You Like It, Edin. Fest., 1977; RSC, 1978–81: Rosaline in Love's Labours Lost, 1978–79; title role in Piaf, The Other Place 1978, Aldwych 1979, Wyndhams 1980, Broadway 1981 (SWET Award 1979, London Critics Award and Variety Club Award 1980, and Broadway Tony Award 1981); National Theatre: Eileen, Kick for Touch, 1983; Belvidera, Venice Preserv'd, Antigone, 1984; Saint Joan (title rôle), Compass Co., 1985; Double Double, Fortune Theatre, 1986; RSC, 1986–87: Misalliance, 1986; Archbishop's Ceiling, 1986; Greenland, Royal Court, 1988; Shadowlands, Queen's, 1989–90 (Variety Club Best Actress Award); RSC, 1992–94: Gertrude in Hamlet, 1992; Mrs Alving in Ghosts, 1993; Katharine of Aragon in Henry VIII, RSC, UK and USA tour, 1996–98 (Helen Hayes Award, USA, 1998); one-woman show, Shakespeare as I knew her, Bristol, 1996, Stratford and UK, 1997; Duchess of Gloucester in Richard II, RSC, 2013–14; Richard II, Henry V, RSC, 2015–16; *television:* Marie Curie (serial), 1977; Antony and Cleopatra, 1981; Macbeth, 1983; Seal Morning (series), 1985; Napoleon and Josephine, 1987; Blind Justice (serial), 1988 (British Press Guild Best Actress Award); The Dark Angel, 1989; Love Hurts (series), 1992, 1993; The Big Battalions (series), 1992; Johnny and the Dead (series), 1994; He Knew He Was Right, 2004; Trial and Retribution, 2008; Lucan, 2013; The Crown, 2019; *films* include: Eureka, 1983; Lady Jane, 1986; Surviving Picasso, 1996; There's Only One Jimmy Grimble, 2000. Vis. Fellow, Sussex Univ., 1986–2002. Mem., Marie Curie Meml Foundn Appeals Cttee, 1986–88. Pres., Bristol Old Vic Theatre Club, 1985–2009; Hon. Pres., Friends of Shakespeare's Globe, 1986–2002. Hon. Associate Artist, RSC, 1992. Hon. Fellow, Exeter Univ., 2007. Hon. DLitt: Bristol, 1997; East Anglia, 1998; Warwick, 2000; Exeter, 2005. Pragnell Prize Award, 2018. *Publications:* Grace and Favour (autobiog.), 1989 (repubd as Everybody's Daughter, Nobody's Child, 2007); Out of Order: a haphazard journey through one woman's year, 1999; Time Out of Mind: recovering from a brain haemorrhage, 2003. *Recreation:* walking. *Address:* c/o Gardner Herrity, 24 Conway Street, W1T 6BG. *T:* (020) 7388 0088.

**LAPPIN, Prof. Shalom,** PhD; FBA 2010; Professor of Computational Linguistics, King's College London, 2005, now Emeritus; Professor of Computational Linguistics and Director, Centre for Linguistic Theory and Studies in Probability, University of Gothenburg, since 2015. *Educ:* York Univ., Toronto (BA Philosophy 1970); Brandeis Univ. (MA 1973; PhD 1976). Lectr in Philosophy, Ben Gurion Univ., 1974–80; Lecturer in Linguistics: Univ. of Ottawa, 1980–84 (Chair, Linguistics Dept, 1981–84); Univ. of Haifa, 1984–88; Tel Aviv Univ., 1988–89; Res. Staff Mem., Natural Lang. Gp, Computer Sci. Dept, IBM T. J. Watson Res. Center, 1989–93; Linguistics Dept, SOAS, Univ. of London, 1993–99; Philosophy, then Computer Sci. Dept, KCL, 1999–2005 (Hd, Natural Lang. Processing Gp, 2000–05). Member, Linguistics Panel: RAE 2001, 1999–2001; RAE 2008, 2005–08. *Publications:* Linguistic Nativism and the Poverty of the Stimulus, 2010; (ed jtly and contrib.) Handbook of Computational Linguistics and Natural Language Processing, 2010; contribs to jls incl. Linguistic Analysis, Computational Linguistics, Jl Linguistics, Computational Modelling. *Address:* Department of Philosophy, King's College London, Strand, WC2R 2LS.

**LAPPING, Anne Shirley Lucas,** CBE 2005; independent television producer; Founder Director, Brook Lapping Productions (formerly Brook Associates), 1982–2008; *b* 10 June 1941; *d* of late Frederick Stone and of Dr Freda Lucas Stone; *m* 1963, Brian Michael Lapping, *qv;* three *d*. *Educ:* City of London Sch. for Girls; London Sch. of Econs. New Society, 1964–68; London Weekend TV, 1970–73; writer on The Economist, 1974–82. Other writing and broadcasting. Director: Channel Four, 1989–94; NW London Mental Health NHS Trust, 1992–99; Scott Trust, 1994–2004; Interights, 2006–12; Vice-Chm., Central and NW London Mental Health Trust, 1999–2004. Member: SSRC, 1977–79; Nat. Gas Consumers' Council, 1978–79; Bd, IPSO, 2014– (Dep. Chm., 2015–17). Trustee, openDemocracy, 2006–. Gov., LSE, 1994, now Emeritus Gov. (Mem. Council, 2004–14; Vice Chm., 2008–14; Hon. Fellow). *Recreations:* reading, cooking, arguing. *Address:* 61 Eton Avenue, NW3 3ET. *T:* (020) 7586 1047.

**LAPPING, Brian Michael,** CBE 2005; television producer; Chairman, Brook Lapping Productions Ltd; *b* 13 Sept. 1937; *s* of Max and Doris Lapping; *m* 1963, Anne Shirley Lucas Stone (*see* A. S. L. Lapping); three *d*. *Educ:* Pembroke Coll., Cambridge (BA). Reporter, Daily Mirror, 1959–61; reporter and Dep. Commonwealth Corresp., The Guardian, 1961–67; Ed., Venture (Fabian Soc. monthly jl), 1963–68; feature writer, Financial Times, 1967–68; Dep. Ed., New Society, 1968–70; Granada TV, 1970–88: Producer: What the Papers Say; Party confs; This is Your Right; Executive Producer: World in Action; Hypotheticals; End of Empire; Apartheid; Breakthrough at Reykjavik, etc; Dir, Brian Lapping Associates, subseq. Brook Lapping Productions, 1988–: executive producer: Countdown to War, 1989; The Second Russian Revolution, 1991; Question Time, 1991–94; Watergate, 1993; The Death of Yugoslavia, 1995; Fall of the Wall, Death of Apartheid, 1996; The 50 Years' War—Israel and the Arabs, 1998; Hostage, Playing the China Card, Finest Hour, 1999; Endgame in Ireland, 2001; Tackling Terror, 2002; The Fall of Milosevic, 2003; Elusive Peace, Israel and the Arabs, 2005; Iran and the West, 2009; The Day that Changed the World, 2011; Putin's Russia and the West, 2012; The Iraq War, 2013; Inside Obama's White House, 2016. Awards include: RTS Awards, 1978, 1991, 1995, 2006, 2010; Emmy Award, 1994; BPG Awards, 1986, 1991, 1995, 2003; Gold Medal, NY Internat. Film and TV Fest., 1986, 1990, 1995; Silver/Gold Batons, du Pont/Columbia Awards, 1994, 1996 and 2007; History-Makers, 2010; The Indie, Producers Alliance for Cinema and Television, 1996; BAFTA Lifetime Achievement Award, 2003. *Publications:* (with G. Radice) More Power to the People, 1962; The Labour Government 1964–70, 1970; End of Empire, 1985; Apartheid: a history, 1987. *Recreation:* tending vines. *Address:* 61 Eton Avenue, NW3 3ET. *T:* (020) 7586 1047.

**LAPPING, Peter Herbert;** Headmaster of Sherborne, 1988–2000; *b* 8 Aug. 1941; *s* of late Dr Douglas James Lapping, MBE and Dorothy Lapping (*née* Horrocks) of Nhlangano, Swaziland; *m* 1967, Diana Dillworth, *d* of late Lt-Col E. S. G. Howard, MC, RA; one *s* one *d*. *Educ:* St John's College, Johannesburg; Univ. of Natal, Pietermaritzburg (BA Hons *cum laude*); Lincoln College, Oxford (MA). Asst Master, Reed's Sch., Cobham, 1966–67; Head of History, Loretto Sch., 1967–79 (Housemaster, Pinkie House, 1972–79); Headmaster, Shiplake Coll., Oxon, 1979–88. *Recreations:* cricket and other games, golf, basking in the beauty of the Cotswolds. *Address:* Lower Bubblewell, Minchinhampton, Glos GL6 9DL. *Clubs:* MCC, Victory Services; Vincent's (Oxford); Glos County Cricket (Vice Pres.).

**LAPSLEY, Angus Charles William,** CMG 2019; HM Diplomatic Service; Director General, Strategy and International, Ministry of Defence (on loan), since 2018; *b* Cheltenham, 16 March 1970; *s* of Howard and Susan Lapsley; *m* 1999, Georgina Power; two *s*. *Educ:* Warwick Sch.; Corpus Christi Coll., Oxford (BA Hons English Lit. and Lang. 1991). HEO, DoH, 1991–94; Second Sec., UK Representation to EU, 1994–95; Private Sec. (Home Affairs) to Prime Minister, 1996–99; entered FCO, 1999; Hd, EU Institutions Unit, FCO, 1999–2001; First Sec., Paris, 2001–05; Dep. Hd, Western Balkans Gp, FCO, 2005–06; Counsellor, UK Representation to EU, 2006–10; Dir, The Americas, FCO, 2010–12; Dir, Eur. and Global Issues Secretariat, Cabinet Office, 2012–15; Ambassador (Political and Security), UK Perm. Repn to EU, Brussels, 2015–17; Dir, Defence, Internat. Security and SE Europe, 2017–18. *Recreations:* touch Rugby, motorsport, French food and wine. *Address:* Foreign and Commonwealth Office, King Charles Street, SW1A 2AH. *E:* angus.lapsley@fco.gov.uk; Ministry of Defence, Main Building, Whitehall, SW1A 2HB. *Club:* Royal Automobile.

**LAPTHORNE, Sir Richard (Douglas)**, Kt 2010; CBE 1997; Chairman, CPP Group plc, since 2016; *b* 25 April 1943; *s* of Eric Joseph Lapthorne and Irene Ethel Lapthorne; *m* 1967, Valerie Waring; two *s* two *d*. *Educ*: Calday Grange GS, West Kirby; Liverpool Univ. (BCom). FCMA, FCCA, FCT. Unilever plc: Audit, 1965–67; Lever Brothers, Zambia, 1967–69; Central Pensions Dept, 1969–71; Food Industries, 1971–75; Synthetic Resins, 1975–77; Sheby, Paris, 1978–80; Crosfield Chemicals, 1980–83; Gp Financial Controller, 1983–86, Gp Finance Dir, 1986–92, Courtaulds plc; Gp Finance Dir, 1992–98, Vice Chm., 1998–99, British Aerospace plc; Chm., 1996–97, 1999–2003, Dep. Chm., 1997–99, Nycomed Amersham, subseq. Amersham plc; Chairman: Morse Hldgs plc, 1998–2008; Avecia Ltd, 1999–2005; Tunstall Ltd, 2000–04; TI Automotive Systems plc, 2001–03; Cable and Wireless plc, then Cable and Wireless Communications plc, 2003–16; Arlington Securities Ltd, 2005; New Look Retailers Ltd, 2005–07; McLaren Gp, 2009–10; Vice-Chm., JP Morgan Investment Bank, 2001–05. Non-executive Director: Orange plc, 1992–99; Oasis Internat. Leasing (Abu Dhabi), 1998–2006; Robert Fleming, 2001; Sherritt Internat. (Toronto), 2011–. Mem., Public Interest Body, PricewaterhouseCoopers, 2010–16 (Chm., 2011–16). Dir, Working Age Project, HM Treasury, 2000; Ext. Advr, Navy Bd, 2000–03; Chm., Lead Expert Gp, Govt Foresight Study on Future of UK Manufacturing, 2012–13. Trustee: Royal Botanic Gdns, Kew, 1998–2009 (Chm., Foundn and Friends, 1997–2004; HM the Queen's Trustee, 2004–09); Calibre, 1999–2008; Tommy's Campaign, 2003–14. CCMI. Hon. CRAeS 1997. *Recreations*: gardening, opera, travel.

**LARA, Brian Charles**, TC 1994; OCC 2008; cricketer; Ambassador for Sport, Trinidad and Tobago; *b* Trinidad, 2 May 1969; *s* of late Bunty and Pearl Lara; two *d* with Leasal Rovedas. *Educ*: San Juan Secondary Sch.; Fatima Coll., Port of Spain. Started playing cricket aged 6; left-handed batsman; played for: WI Under-19s (Captain, WI Youth XI against India); Trinidad and Tobago, 1987–2008 (Captain, 1993); Warwickshire, 1994, 1998 (Captain) (world record 1st cl. score of 501 not out, *v* Durham at Edgbaston, 1994); West Indies, 1990–2007 (played in 131 Test Matches, scoring 11,953 runs; Captain, 1997, 1998–99, 2000, 2003–04, 2007; world record score of 400 in a Test Match, St John's, Antigua, 2004); 34 Test, 65 1st class, centuries. Founded charity, Pearl and Bunty Lara Foundn. Ambassador, Chittagong Kings, Bangladesh Premier League, 2013–. Hon. Dr Sheffield, 2007; Hon. LLD UWI, 2011. Hon. AM 2009. *Publications*: Beating the Field (autobiog.), 1995. *Recreations*: golf, horse-racing.

**LARCOMBE, Brian Paul**; Chief Executive, 3i Group plc, 1997–2004; *b* 27 Aug. 1953; *s* of John George Larcombe and Joyce Lucille Larcombe (*née* Westwood); *m* 1983, Dr Catherine Bullen (*d* 2015). *Educ*: Bromley Grammar Sch.; Univ. of Birmingham (BCom); Harvard Business Sch. (AMP). Joined 3i Gp, 1974: Local Dir, 1982; Regl Dir, 1988; Finance Dir, 1992–97. Non-executive Director: Smith and Nephew plc, 2002–17 (Sen. Ind. Dir, 2014–17); F&C Asset Management, 2005–10; Party Gaming plc, 2005–06; Gallaher Gp plc, 2006–07; gategroup Hldg AG (formerly Gate Gourmet Gp Hldg LLC), 2008–; Incisive Media Hldgs Ltd, 2010–14; Kodak Alaris Hldgs, 2014–; Cape plc, 2016–17. Chm., Bramdean Alternatives Ltd, 2007–09. Member: Council, British Venture Capital Assoc., 1989–96 (Chm., 1994–95); UK Council, INSEAD, 1997–2006; Singapore British Business Council, 1997–2004; Exchange Markets Gp, London Stock Exchange, 2001–03. *Recreations*: golf, biographies, modern paintings, breeding dressage horses.

**LARGE, Sir Andrew (McLeod Brooks)**, Kt 1996; Deputy Governor, Bank of England, 2002–06; Founding Partner, Systemic Policy Partnership, since 2012; adviser on systemic policy issues, since 2008; *b* 7 Aug. 1942; *s* of late Maj.-Gen. Stanley Eyre Large, MBE and Janet Mary Large (*née* Brooks); *m* 1967, Susan Mary Melville; two *s* one *d*. *Educ*: Winchester Coll.; Corpus Christi Coll., Cambridge (BA Hons Econ; MA); INSEAD, Fontainebleau (MBA). BP, 1964–71; Man. Dir, Orion Bank, 1971–79; Exec. Bd Mem., Swiss Bank Corp., 1980–89; Large, Smith & Walter, 1990–92; Chairman: SIB, 1992–97; IOSCO, 1992; a Dep. Chm., Barclays Bank, 1998–2002. Chm., Euroclear, 1998–2000; non-executive Director: Nuclear Electric, 1990–94; Rank Hovis McDougall, 1990–92; Phoenix Securities, 1990–92; Dowty Gp, 1991–92; English China Clays, 1991–96; London Fox, 1991–92 (Chm.); Luthy Baillie Dowsett Pethick, 1990–92 (Chm.); Axis Capital, Bermuda, 2006–16; MW Tops Ltd, 2006–09 (Chm.); Oliver Wyman, 2006– (Chairman: Sen. Adv. Bd; Oliver Wyman—SPP, 2017–); Marshall Wace, 2009–12 (Chm., Adv. Cttee). Chm., Securities Assoc., 1986–87; Vice Chm., Bermuda Financial Policy Council, 2015–; Member: Council, Stock Exchange, 1986–87; Panel on Takeovers and Mergers, 1987–88; Lloyds Council, 1992–93; Bd of Banking Supervision, 1996–97; Sen. Advr, Standards Bd for Alternative Investments (formerly Hedge Fund Standards Bd), 2008– (Chm., Wkg Gp, 2007–08). Member Board: Inst. of Internat. Finance, Washington, 1998–2001; INSEAD, 1998–2010 (Chm. UK Council, 1997–2002; Chm., Adv. Council, 2011–). Pres. and Trustee, Marcher Apple Network, 2012–. Governor: Abingdon Sch., 1991–98; Winchester Coll., 1998–2008 (Warden, 2003–08); Christ Coll., Brecon, 1998–2010. *Recreations*: old apple trees, ski-ing, walking, photography, music. *Clubs*: Brooks's, Mark's.

**LARIZADEH, Cyrus Raïs**; QC 2016; *b* Tehran, Iran, 2 Feb. 1968; *s* of Mehdi Larizadeh and Golnar Larizadeh; *m* 1996, Joanne Stuart; one *d*. *Educ*: Harrow Sch. (Rothschild Leaving Schol.); Kent Univ. (BA Hons; Hallet Prize for Law); Univ. de Bordeaux (Dip. de Droit); Inns of Court Sch. of Law. Called to the Bar, Inner Temple, 1992, Bencher, 2018; in practice as barrister, specialising in family law, 1993–. Advocacy Trainer, Inner Temple, 2016–. Mem., Nat. Cttee, Family Law Bar Assoc., 2015– (Vice-Chair, 2018–). Mem., Magic Circle. *Publications*: (jtly) Rayden and Jackson on Children Law, 2016; contribs to Family Law Week. *Recreations*: conjuring, cycling. *Address*: 4 Paper Buildings, Temple, EC4Y 7EX. *T*: (020) 7427 5200. *E*: cl@4pb.com.

**LARKCOM, Joy Kerr, (Mrs D. A. Pollard)**; garden writer, since 1973; *b* Farnborough, Hants, 16 Nov. 1935; *d* of Eric Herbert Jacobs-Larkcom and Dorothy Primrose Kerr Jacobs-Larkcom (*née* Tasker); *m* 1967, Donald Aloysius Pollard (*d* 2017); one *s* one *d*. *Educ*: Ancaster House Sch.; Wye Coll., Univ. of London (BSc Hort.). Teacher at sch. for American children, Thailand, 1958–59; Library Asst, Sci. and Med. Div., Toronto Univ. Library, 1959–61; Journalist, Discovery and Personnel mags, 1961–64; Ed., Personnel Mag., 1964–67; careers columnist, Observer newspaper, 1967–68, then freelance journalist. Mem., Garden Media Gp. Veitch Meml Medal, RHS, 1993; Lifetime Achievement Award, Garden Writers' Guild, 2003. *Publications*: Vegetables from Small Gardens, 1977, 3rd edn 1995; Salads the Year Round, 1980; RHS Vegetable Garden Displayed, 1982, rev. edn 1992; Sainsbury's Homebase Guide to Vegetable Gardening, 1983; The Salad Garden, 1984, rev. edn 2017; Oriental Vegetables, 1991, 2nd edn 2007; Salads for Small Gardens, 1995; Creative Vegetable Gardening, 1997, 4th edn 2008; The Organic Salad Garden, 2001; Grow Your Own Vegetables, 2002; Just Vegetating, 2012; contribs to RHS Jl. *Recreations*: photography, music, omnivorous reading, gardening by outwitting West Cork's wind, languages, swimming, fighting off Old Father Time, letter writing, mildly malicious gossip. *Address*: c/o Quarto Publishing plc, 74–77 White Lion Street, Islington, N1 9PF. *T*: (020) 7284 9300. *E*: info@quarto.com. *Club*: Wye College Agricola.

**LARKEN, Comdt Anthea**, CBE 1991; Director and Company Secretary, Operational Command Training Organisation Ltd, 1991–96; *b* 23 Aug. 1938; *d* of Frederick William Savill and Nance (*née* Williams); *m* 1987 (marr. diss. 1997). *Educ*: Stafford Girls' High Sch. Joined WRNS as Range Assessor, 1956; commnd, 1960; qualified: as Photographic Interpreter, 1961; as WRNS Secretarial Officer, 1967; Staff Officer in Singapore, 1964–66; i/c WRNS Officers' Training, BRNC Dartmouth, 1976–78; NATO Military Agency for Standardisation, Brussels, 1981–84; CSO (Admin) to Flag Officer Plymouth, 1985–86; RCDS, 1987; Dir, WRNS, 1988–91. ADC to the Queen, 1988–91. Lady Pres., Not Forgotten Assoc., 1995–; Pres., Assoc. of Wrens, 1999–2019. Hon. LLD Greenwich, 2000. *Recreations*: theatre, music, reading, home, family and friends. *Club*: Army and Navy.

**LARKEN, Rear Adm. (Edmund Shackleton) Jeremy**, DSO 1982; Managing Director, OCTO, since 1991; advisory consultant in corporate crisis and emergency management and leadership; *b* 14 Jan. 1939; *s* of Rear Adm. Edmund Thomas Larken, CB, OBE and Eileen Margaret (*née* Shackleton); *m* 1st, 1963, Wendy Nigella Hallett (marr. diss. 1987); two *d*; 2nd, 1987, Comdt Anthea Savill (*see* Comdt Anthea Larken) (marr. diss. 1997); 3rd, 1997, Helen Shannon; one *s* one *d*. *Educ*: Bryanston Sch.; BRNC, Dartmouth. Joined RN as Cadet, 1957; qualified: in Submarines, 1960; in Navigation, 1965; in Submarine Comd, 1960; served HMS Tenby, Finwhale, Tudor, Ambush and Narwhal; Navigation Officer, HMS Valiant; First Lieut, HMS Otus; commanded HMS Osiris, Glamorgan and Valiant, Third Submarine Sqn, and HMS Fearless (including Falklands Campaign, 1982); exchange with USN (Submarines), 1971–73; Naval Plans; Dir, Naval Staff Duties, 1985; Cdre Amphibious Warfare, 1985–87; ACDS (Overseas), 1988–90. Mem., RUSI, 1970–2006. Governor, Bryanston Sch., 1988–99. FInstD 2003 (MInstD 1996). *Publications*: papers and articles in professional books and periodicals. *Recreations*: defence, maritime and aviation interests, strategy, travel, sailing, theatre, reading, home, family and friends. *Address*: OCTO, Caerlleon House, 142 Boughton, Chester CH3 5BP. *E*: Jeremy.Larken@octo.uk.com.

**LARKIN, Sean**; QC 2010; *b* London, 29 April 1963; *s* of James Larkin and Joan Larkin; *m* 1998, Ann Walsh; two *s*. *Educ*: Salesian Coll.; Queen Mary Coll., London (LLB). Called to the Bar, Inner Temple, 1987. *Publications*: (contrib.) Fraud: law, practice and procedure. *Recreations*: sport, music (listening and performing). *Address*: QEB Hollis Whiteman, 1–2 Laurence Pountney Hill, EC4R 0EU. *T*: (020) 7933 8855, *Fax*: (020) 7929 3732. *E*: sean.larkin@qebholliswhiteman.co.uk.

**LARKINS, Prof. Richard Graeme**, AC 2019 (AO 2002); MD, PhD; FTSE, FAAHMS; Vice-Chancellor and President, Monash University, 2003–09; Chair, Universities Australia, 2008–09; *b* 17 May 1943; *s* of Graeme Larkins and Margaret Larkins (*née* Rosanove, now Lusink); *m* 1966, Caroline Cust; three *d*. *Educ*: Univ. of Melbourne (MB BS 1966; MD 1972); RPMS London (PhD 1974). FRACP 1975; FRCP 1990; FRCPI 2000. Resident, Sen. Resident, then Med. Registrar, 1967–69, Asst Endocrinologist, 1970–72, Royal Melbourne Hosp.; Res. Fellow (Churchill Fellow and MRC Fellow), Endocrine Unit, RPMS, Hammersmith Hosp., London, 1972–74; Physician to Endocrine Lab., and to Outpatients, Royal Melbourne Hosp., 1974–77; University of Melbourne: First Asst, 1978–83, Reader in Medicine, 1983, Dept of Medicine, and Dir, Endocrine and Metabolic Unit, 1979–83, Repatriation Gen. Hosp., Heidelberg, Vic; James Stewart Prof. of Medicine, and Hd, Dept of Medicine, Royal Melbourne Hosp./Western Hosp., 1984–97; Associate Dean, Planning, 1996–97, Dean, 1998–2003, Fac. of Medicine, Dentistry and Health Scis; Royal Melbourne Hospital: Endocrinologist, 1984; Dir, Dept of Diabetes and Endocrinology, 1989–93; Chm., Div. of Medicine, 1991–94; Med. Dir, Clinical Business Unit, Internal Medicine, 1994–96. Chairman: Accreditation Cttee, Australian Med. Council, 1991–95; NH&MRC, Australia, 1997–2000; EMBL Australia Council, 2009–15; Chair, Victorian Comprehensive Cancer Centre, 2009–16; Member: Prime Minister's Sci., Engrg and Innovation Council, 1997–2000; Nat. Aboriginal and Torres Strait Islander Health Council, 1997–2000. President: Endocrine Soc. of Aust., 1982–84; RACP, 2000–02; Nat. Stroke Foundn, 2009–15; Australian Univ. Sport, 2009–13. Chair, Council, Melbourne Grammar Sch., 2010–15; Mem., Council, LaTrobe Univ., 2014–19 (Chancellor, 2017–19). Chair: Life Scis Expert Cttee, Nat. Res. Foundn, Singapore, 2016–; Life Scis Res. Bd, Austin Health, 2019–. Mem., Bd of Govs, Ian Potter Foundn, 2013–. FTSE 2008; FAAHMS 2015; Fellow: Academy of Medicine: Malaysia; Singapore. Honorary Fellow: Royal Coll. of Physicians of Thailand; Ceylon Coll. of Physicians; Hon. FACP. Hon. LLD: Melbourne; Monash. Eric Susman Prize for Med. Res., RACP, 1982; Sir William Upjohn Medal, Univ. of Melbourne, 2002; Centenary of Federation Medal, 2003. *Publications*: (jtly) A Textbook of Clinical Medicine: an approach to patients' major problems, 1983; A Practical Approach to Endocrine Disorders, 1985; (jtly) Problems in Clinical Medicine, 1989; (ed jtly) Diabetes 1988, 1989; (with R. A. Smallwood) Clinical Skills, 1993; New Tricks, 2014; many scientific articles. *Recreations*: golf, reading, rowing. *Address*: PO Box 33061, Melbourne, Vic 3004, Australia. *T*: (3) 99038002, (0) 413433000. *Clubs*: Melbourne; Royal Melbourne Golf; Barwon Heads Golf; 13th Beach Golf; Melbourne Univ. Boat.

**LaROCQUE, Judith Anne**, CVO 1992; Ambassador and Permanent Representative of Canada to the Organisation for Economic Co-operation and Development, 2011–15; *b* Hawkesbury, Ontario, 27 Sept. 1956; *d* of Olier LaRocque and Elizabeth (*née* Murray); *m* 1991, André Roland Lavoie. *Educ*: Carleton Univ. (BA Pol Sci. 1979; MA Public Admin 1992). Admin. Asst, Internal Audit Directorate, Public Service Commn, 1979; writer/researcher, Prime Minister's Office, 1979; Special Asst, Office of Leader of Opposition, 1980–82; Cttee Clerk, Cttees and Private Legislation Br., H of C, 1982–84; Legislative Asst to Govt House Leader, 1984–85; Head of House Business, Office of Govt House Leader, Pres. Queen's Privy Council for Canada and Minister Responsible for Regulatory Affairs, 1985–86; Exec. Asst to Minister of Justice and Attorney Gen. of Canada, 1986–89; COS to Govt Leader in Senate and Minister of State for Federal-Provincial Relns, 1989–90; Sec. to Gov. Gen. of Canada, 1990–2000; Sec. Gen., Order of Canada and Order of Military Merit, and Herald Chancellor of Canada, 1990–2000; Associate Dep. Minister, 2000–02, Dep. Minister, 2002–10, of Canadian Heritage. Member: Bd of Govs, Banff Centre for Arts and Creativity, 2015–; Bd of Dirs, Hawkesbury and District Gen. Hosp., 2016–; Lay Mem., Ontario Judicial Council, 2016–. Chair, Bd of Govs, Canadian Mus. of Nature. OStJ 1990. 125th Anniv. of Confedn Medal (Canada), 1992; Queen Elizabeth II Golden Jubilee Medal, 2002; Queen Elizabeth II Diamond Jubilee Medal, 2012. *Recreations*: gardening, cross-country ski-ing. *Address*: 3715 Front Road, Hawkesbury, ON K6A 2W5, Canada.

**LAROSIÈRE de CHAMPFEU, Jacques Martin Henri Marie de**; *see* de Larosière de Champfeu.

**LARPENT, Andrew Lionel Dudley de H.**; *see* de Hochepied Larpent.

**LARSON, Gary**; cartoonist; *b* 14 Aug. 1950; *s* of Vern and Doris Larson; *m* 1988, Toni Carmichael. *Educ*: Washington State Univ. (BA Communications). Cartoonist: The Far Side syndicated panel (1900 newspapers worldwide), 1980–95 (Best Syndicated Panel Award, 1985); The Far Side syndicated panel (syndicated internationally in 40 countries), 1995–2009. *Films*: Gary Larson's Tales From The Far Side, 1994; Gary Larson's Tales From The Far Side II, 1998. Reuben Award for Outstanding Cartoonist of Year, 1991 and 1994; Max and Moritz Prize, Best Internat. Cartoon, 1993; Grand Prix, Annecy Film Fest., 1995; Internat. Comics Fest. Award, for French lang. edn of Hound of The Far Side, 1997. *Publications*: The Far Side, 1982; Beyond The Far Side, 1983; In Search of The Far Side, 1984; Valley of The Far Side, 1985; Bride of The Far Side, 1985; It Came From The Far Side, 1986; Hound of The Far Side, 1987; The Far Side Observer, 1987; Night of The

Crash-Test Dummies, 1988; Wildlife Preserves, 1989; Wiener Dog Art, 1990 (Wheatley Medals Award, Liby Assoc., 1991); Unnatural Selections, 1991; Cows of Our Planet, 1992; The Chickens are Restless, 1993; The Curse of Madame C, 1994; Last Chapter and Worse, 1996; There's a Hair in My Dirt! A Worm's Story, 1998; *anthologies:* The Far Side Gallery, 1, 2, 3, 4, 5; The PreHistory of The Far Side, 1989; The Complete Far Side, 2 vols, 2003. *Recreations:* jazz guitar, pick-up basketball. *Address:* c/o Andrews McMeel Publishers, 1130 Walnut Street, Kansas City, MO 64106-2109, USA. *T:* (816) 5817500.

**LARSSON, Gen. John;** General of The Salvation Army, 2002–06; *b* 2 April 1938; *s* of Sture and Flora Larsson; *m* 1969, Freda Turner; two *s*. *Educ:* London Univ. (BD). Commnd as Salvation Army Officer, 1957, in corps, youth and trng work; Chief Sec., S America West, 1980–84; Principal, William Booth Meml Trng Coll., 1984–88; Admin. Planning, 1988–90; Territorial Commander: UK and Republic of Ireland, 1990–93; NZ and Fiji, 1993–96; Sweden and Latvia, 1996–99; COS, Salvation Army Internat. HQ, 1999–2002. *Publications:* Doctrine Without Tears, 1974; Spiritual Breakthrough, 1983; The Man Perfectly Filled with the Spirit, 1986; How Your Corps can Grow, 1988; Saying Yes to Life (autobiog.), 2007; 1929—A Crisis That Shaped The Salvation Army's Future, 2009; Inside a High Council, 2013; Those Incredible Booths, 2015. *Recreations:* music, walking, reading. *Address:* 3 Oakbrook, 8 Court Downs Road, Beckenham, Kent BR3 6LR.

**LARTER, Prof. Stephen Richard,** PhD; FRS 2009; FRSC; FGS; J. B. Simpson Professor of Geology, University of Newcastle upon Tyne, 1989–2015, now Emeritus; Canada Research Chair in Petroleum Geology, University of Calgary, since 2004; Co-Director, Alberta Ingenuity Center for In situ Energy, Calgary, 2004–10; *b* Christchurch, Cambs, 31 Jan. 1953; *s* of Jack and Jean Larter; *m* 1982, Karen Cullen; three *s*. *Educ:* Peterhouse, Cambridge (BA Natural Scis 1974); Univ. of Newcastle upon Tyne (MSc 1975; PhD 1978). Res. Geochemist, Sen. Res. Geochemist, then Res. Associate, Unocal Corp., USA, 1979–86; Nordisk Ministeraad Prof. of Geochem., Univ. of Oslo, 1987–89; University of Newcastle upon Tyne: Founder and Hd, Fossil Fuels and Envmtl Geochem., Postgrad. Inst., 1989–94 and 1997–99; Dean of Res., Faculty of Sci., Agric. and Engrg, 2002–04; Mem., Univ. Res. Cttee, 1997–2003 (Chm., 2000–02). CEO and Chief Scientific Officer, Gushor Inc., 2008–13; Scientific Dir, Carbon Mgt Canada, 2010–14. Dist. Lectr, Amer. Assoc. Petroleum Geologists, 2005–06. Chm., Gordon Conf. in Organic Geochem., 2006. Foreign Mem., Norwegian Acad. Sci. and Letters, 2004. William Smith Medal, Geol Soc., 1998. FRSC 2012. Friendship Medal (China), 2000; Medal of Merit, Canadian Soc. of Petroleum Geologists, 2012 and 2014; Treibs Medal, Geochemical Soc., 2014. *Recreations:* walking, playing the bagpipes and yoga… not simultaneously! *Address:* Department of Geosciences, University of Calgary, 2500 University Drive NW, Calgary AB T2N 1N4, Canada. *E:* slarter@ucalgary.ca. *Club:* Cowtown Yeast Wranglers (Calgary).

**LASCELLES,** family name of **Earl of Harewood.**

**LASCELLES, Viscount; Alexander Edgar Lascelles;** *b* 13 May 1980; *s* and *heir* of Earl of Harewood, *qv*.

**LASH, Prof. Nicholas Langrishe Alleyne,** DD; Norris-Hulse Professor of Divinity, University of Cambridge, 1978–99, now Emeritus; Fellow, Clare Hall, Cambridge, since 1988; *b* 6 April 1934; *s* of late Henry Alleyne Lash and Joan Mary Lash (*née* Moore); *m* 1976, Janet Angela Chalmers; one *s*. *Educ:* Downside Sch.; Oscott Coll.; St Edmund's House, Cambridge. MA, PhD, BD, DD. Served RE, 1952–57. Oscott Coll., 1957–63; Asst Priest, Slough, 1963–68; Fellow, 1969–85, Dean, 1971–75, St Edmund's House, Cambridge; Univ. Asst Lectr, Cambridge, 1974–78. Hon. DD: London, 2002; Durham, 2011; Sacred Heart, Fairfield, Conn, 2012. KSG 2017. *Publications:* His Presence in the World, 1968; Change in Focus, 1973; Newman on Development, 1975; Voices of Authority, 1976; Theology on Dover Beach, 1979; A Matter of Hope, 1982; Theology on the Way to Emmaus, 1986; Easter in Ordinary, 1988; Believing three ways in one God, 1992; The Beginning and the End of 'Religion', 1996; Holiness, Speech and Silence, 2004; Seeing in the Dark: university sermons, 2005; Theology for Pilgrims, 2008. *Address:* 4 Hertford Street, Cambridge CB4 3AG.

**LASKEY, Prof. Ronald Alfred,** CBE 2011; FRS 1984; FMedSci; FLSW; Charles Darwin Professor, University of Cambridge, 1983–2011, now Emeritus; Fellow of Darwin College, Cambridge, 1982, now Emeritus Fellow; Hon. Director, 1999–2006, Joint Hon. Director, 2006–10, MRC Cancer Cell Unit; *b* 26 Jan. 1945; *s* of Thomas Leslie and Bessie Laskey; *m* 1971, Margaret Ann Page; one *s* one *d*. *Educ:* High Wycombe Royal Grammar Sch.; Queen's Coll., Oxford (MA, DPhil 1970; Hon. Fellow, 2011). Scientific Staff: Imperial Cancer Research Fund, 1970–73; MRC Lab. of Molecular Biology, 1973–83; Co-Dir, Molecular Embryology Group, Cancer Research Campaign, 1983–91; CRC Dir, Wellcome Cancer Res. UK (formerly CRC) Inst., 1991–2001. Mem. Bd, UK Panel for Res. Integrity, 2005–11. Member, Scientific Advisory Committee: EMBL, 1999–2004; Max-Planck Inst. for Biochem., 2000–11 (Chm., 2002–10); CRUK London Res. Inst., 2006–13; Louis Jeantet Foundn, 2008–16 (Vice-Pres., 2010–16). Pres., British Soc. of Cell Biology, 1996–99. Vice-Pres., Acad. of Med. Scis, 2007–12; Pres., Biochemical Soc., 2012–14. Mem., Academia Europaea, 1989; Founder FMedSci 1998. Trustee: Strangeways Res. Lab., 1993–2010; ICRF, 2000–02; Inst. of Cancer Res., 2007–12. Croonian Lect., Royal Soc., 2001; Werner Heisenberg Lect., Bavarian Acad., 2010. FLSW 2013. Hon. LLD Dundee, 2014; Hon. DMedSci London, 2014. Colworth Medal, Biochem. Soc., 1979; CIBA Medal, Biochem. Soc., 1997; Feldberg Foundn Prize, 1998; Louis Jeantet Prize for Medicine, Jeantet Foundn, Geneva, 1998; Medical Futures Health Innovation Award, 2007; Royal Medal, Royal Soc., 2009; Lifetime Achievement in Cancer Res. Prize, Cancer Res. UK, 2014. *Publications:* articles on cell biology in scientific jls; Songs for Cynical Scientists and Selected Songs for Cynical Scientists. *Recreations:* music, mountains, walking. *Address:* Department of Zoology, University of Cambridge, Downing Street, Cambridge CB2 3EJ. *T:* (01223) 334106, 334107.

**LASOK, (Karol) Paul (Edward);** QC 1994; PhD; a Recorder, 2000–12; *b* 16 July 1953; *s* of Prof. Dominik Lasok, QC; *m* 1991, Karen Bridget Morgan Griffith; two *d*. *Educ:* St Mary's Sch., Clyst St Mary; Jesus Coll., Cambridge (MA); Exeter Univ. (LLM, PhD). Called to the Bar, Middle Temple, 1977, Bencher, 2002; Legal Sec., Court of Justice of the EC, 1980–84 and (*locum tenens*) 1985; private practice, 1985–2016. Chairman: Bar European Gp, 2007–09; VAT Practitioners' Gp, 2009–11. FIIT. Consultant Editor, Butterworths European Court Practice; Jt Editor, Common Market Law Reports, 1996–2010. *Publications:* The European Court of Justice: practice and procedure, 1984, 3rd edn as Lasok's European Court Practice and Procedure, 2017; (jtly) Judicial Control in the EU, 2004; contribs to: Halsbury's Laws of England, 4th edn, vols 51 and 52, 5th edn, vol. 47A, 2014; Law of European Communities (ed D. Vaughan); Law and Institutions of the European Union, 7th edn 2001; Atkin's Court Forms, vol. 10, 2009, 2016, vol. 17, 2011, vol. 16, 2016; (contrib. and Gen. Ed.) Value Added Tax: commentary and analysis, 2009; Weinberg and Blank on Takeovers and Mergers; legal periodicals. *Recreation:* amusing daughters. *Address:* 57 Ellington Street, N7 8PN. *T:* (020) 7607 5874.

**LASSALLE, Tashi;** Director of Communications, Church of England, since 2017; *b* London, 1 May 1978; *d* of Rex and Patricia Lassalle. *Educ:* Camden Sch. for Girls; Corpus Christi Coll., Cambridge (MA English). Dir, 2007–09, Chief Mktg Officer, 2009, Heidrick & Struggles, NY; Dir of Communications, Actis, 2009–14; Dir of Mktg, Lloyd's of London, 2014–16. *Recreations:* cinema, family, art, school governor (primary). *Address:* Church House, Great Smith Street, SW1P 3NZ. *T:* (020) 7898 1295. *E:* Tashi.Lassalle@ churchofengland.org.

**LAST, Maj.-Gen. Christopher Neville,** CB 1990; OBE 1976; health management consultant, 1998–2000; *b* 2 Sept. 1935; *s* of late Jack Neville Last, MPS, FSMC, FBOA and Lorna (*née* Goodman), MPS; *m* 1961, Pauline Mary Lawton, BA; two *d*. *Educ:* Culford Sch.; Brighton Tech. Coll. psc†, ndc. Commnd Royal Signals, 1956; Germany, Parachute Bde, Borneo, Singapore, 1956–67; OC 216 Para. Signal Sqdn, 1967; RMCS and Staff Coll., Logistics Staff 1 (BR) Corps, 1968–71; NDC, 1972; Lt-Col, Signal Staff HQ, BAOR, 1973; CO Royal Signals NI, 1974; Staff, MoD Combat Develt, 1976, Mil. Ops, 1977; Col, Project Manager MoD (PE) for Army ADP Comd and Control, 1977; CO (Col) 8 Signal Regt Trng, Royal Signals, 1980; Brig., Comd 1 Signal Bde 1 (BR) Corps, 1981; Dir, Mil. Comd and Control Projects, MoD (PE), 1984; Head of Defence Procurement Policy (Studies Team), on Chief of Defence Procurement Personal Staff, MoD (PE), 1985; Maj.-Gen. 1986; Vice Master Gen. of the Ordnance, 1986–88; Mil. Dep. to Head of Defence Export Services, 1988–90; Chief Exec., Clwyd FHSA, 1990–96; Dir of Business Management, Clwyd and Oswestry Tissue Bank, 1996–97; Advr and Chm. (designate), 2002–05, UK Human Tissue Bank. Col Comdt, RCS, 1990–96. Chairman: Royal Signals Instn, 1994–98; Bd of Trustees, Royal Signals Mus., 1994–2004. Mem., RFCA for Wales, 1996–2015. President: BRCS N Wales, 1996–2004, 2007–13 (Chm., 2004–07); Airborne Signals Assoc., 2013–; Vice-Pres., BRCS Wales, 2000–04. Chm., Kigezi Foundn, 2001–02; Trustee, The Community Foundn in Wales, 2002–09. Liveryman, Co. of Information Technologists, 1988 (Chm., Med. and Health Panel, 1998–2002); Freeman, City of London, 1988. *Recreations:* formerly travel, theatre, ballet, sailing, ski-ing, shooting and country pursuits. *Address:* Regimental HQ Royal Signals, Griffin House, Blandford Camp, Blandford Forum, Dorset DT11 8RH. *Clubs:* Special Forces, Fadeaways.

**LAST, John;** see Last, R. J.

**LAST, John William,** CBE 1989; Director, Public Affairs, United Utilities plc (formerly North West Water Group), 1993–98; Chairman, Museums Training Institute, 1990–97; *b* 22 Jan. 1940; *s* of late Jack Last (sometime Dir of Finance, Metrop. Police) and Freda Last (*née* Evans); *m* 1967, Susan Josephine, *er d* of late John and Josephine Farmer; three *s*. *Educ:* Sutton Grammar Sch., Surrey; Trinity Coll., Oxford (MA 1965). Littlewoods Organisation, Liverpool, 1969–93. Chairman: Dernier Properties Ltd, 1996–2009; Bute Communications Ltd, 2004–08; Director: Boom, 1990–93; Inward, investment agency for NW, 1992–96; sparesFinder.com Ltd, 1999–2002. Mem., Merseyside CC, 1973–86 (Chm., Arts Cttee, 1977–81). Prospective Parly Cand. (L), Ilkeston, 1963; contested (C) Liverpool, West Derby, Feb. and Oct. 1974, Stockport N, 1979. Hon. Treas., 2002–03, Chm., 2008–13, Pres. 2013–, Welsh Lib Dem Party; UK Lib Dem Party: Dep. Treas., 2003–05; Welsh Mem., UK Exec., 2007–09; Federal Vice Pres., 2009–. Vis. Prof., 1987–98, Prof. of Museum Studies, 1998–2006, City Univ., London. Bd Mem., Royal Liverpool Philharmonic Soc., 1973–93 (Chm., 1977–81, 1986–92); Founder Chairman: Merseyside Maritime Museum, 1977; Empire Theatre (Merseyside) Trust, 1979–81 (Bd Mem., 19862017); Chairman: Walker Art Gall., Liverpool, 1977–81; Library Assoc./Arts Council Wkg Party on Art in Libraries, 1982–84; Wkg Party to form Merseyside TEC, 1989–90; Enquiry into Local Authorities and Museums, 1989–91; Develt Bd, Nat. Mus. of Wales, 2006–; Nat. Chm., Area Museums Councils of GB, 1979–82; Vice-Pres., NW Museum and Art Gall. Service, 1992– (Chm., 1977–82, 1987–92); Vice-Chm., Merseyside Arts, 1985–88; Member: Museums Assoc. Council, 1978–86 (Vice-Pres., 1983); Arts Council of GB, 1980–84 (Chm., Housing the Arts Cttee, 1981–84; Chm., Regional Cttee, 1981–84); Museums and Galleries Commn, 1983–95 (Mem., Scottish Wkg Pty, 1984–85); Enquiry into Tyne and Wear Service, 1988–89; Bd, Northern Ballet Theatre, 1986–98 (Vice Chm., 1986–88); Merseyside Tourism Bd, 1986–92; NW Industrial Council, 1985–98; Calcutt Cttee on Privacy and Intrusion by the Press, 1989–90; Video Appeals Cttee, BBFC, 2002–11; Lay Member: Press Council, 1980–86; Bar Standards Bd, 2008–14. Advr on Local Govt to Arts Council, 1984–91; Chm., Arts, Initiative and Money Cttee, Gulbenkian Foundn, 1980–83. Mem. Bd, Charities Trust, 1990–94; Trustee: Norton Priory Museum, 1983–87; V&A Museum, 1984–86 (Mem., Adv. Council, 1978–84; Mem., Theatre Museum Cttee, 1983–86); Nat. Museums and Galls on Merseyside, 1986–99; Community Foundn in Wales, 2004–06; Governor: NYO, 1985–93; Nat. Mus. of Wales, 1994–97 and 2003–12. Member Court: Liverpool Univ., 1973–96 (Mem., Council, 1977–81, 1986–96); Univ. of Wales, 2005–08; Vice-Chm. Council, NE Wales Inst., 2002–08 (Mem., 1999–2008). Mem., Peel Gp, 2002–. Vice Pres., N Wales Music Festival, subseq. N Wales Internat. Music Festival, 2000– (Patron, 1994–). Chm., Centenary Develt Trust, Sutton Grammar Sch., 1998–2005. FRSA 1988. Hon. FMA, 1987. Hon. Fellow, Liverpool John Moores Univ. (formerly Liverpool Polytechnic), 1989; Hon. Fellow, Glyndŵr Univ., 2009. Freedom of City of London, 1985; Barber Surgeons' Co.: Freeman, 1985; Liveryman, 1987–; Mem., Ct of Assts, 1999–; Master, 2005–06; Freeman, Guild of Educators, 2006–08. Hon. DLitt City, 1995. Merseyside Gold Medal for Achievement, 1991. Order of St Asaph, 2016. *Publications:* A Brief History of Museums and Galleries, 1986; The Last Report on Local Authorities and Museums, 1991; reports: (jtly) Arts: the way forward, 1978; (jtly) A Future for the Arts, 1987. *Recreations:* swimming, music, memorabilia of Edward VIII. *Address:* Llannerch Hall, near St Asaph, Denbighshire LL17 0BD. *Club:* Garrick.

**LAST, Prof. (Richard) John,** OBE 2018; Vice-Chancellor, Norwich University of the Arts (formerly Norwich University College of the Arts), since 2009; *b* Peterborough, 23 Dec. 1953; *s* of Frederick and Vera Last; one *d*. *Educ:* Abbey Grammar Sch., Ramsey; Univ. of Sussex (BA Hons 1975; MA (Ed) 1984); Univ. of Leeds (PGCE 1977). Croydon College: Lectr, 1976–79; Principal Lectr, 1979–94; Asst Principal and Hd, Croydon Sch. of Art, 1994–98; Dep. Principal, Arts UC Bournemouth, 1998–2008. Member, Board: Higher Educn Stats Agency, 2009–18; GuildHE, 2011–18 (Vice Chm., 2013–18); Dir, Higher Educn Acad., 2015–18. Member, Board: Forum Trust, 2010–; East Anglia Art Fund, 2016–; Britten Sinfonia, 2018–. Chair, UK Arts and Design Instns Assoc., 2016–. Trustee: Norwich Sch., 2014–; Sapienta Trust, 2018–. FRSA. *Recreations:* visual arts, opera, jazz, watching cricket. *Address:* Norwich University of the Arts, Francis House, 3–7 Redwell Street, Norwich NR2 4SN. *T:* (01603) 756224, *Fax:* (01603) 615728. *E:* j.last@nua.ac.uk. *Clubs:* Athenæum, MCC.

**LATASI, Rt Hon. Sir Kamuta,** KCMG 2007; OBE 1982; PC 1996; MP for Funafuti, Tuvalu, since 2000; Speaker of Parliament of Tuvalu, 2006–14; *b* 4 Sept. 1936; *s* of Latasi and Malili; *m* 1966, Naama (*d* 2012); two *s* two *d* (and one *d* decd). *Educ:* South Devon Tech. Coll., Torquay (Dip. Public and Soc. Admin). Gilbert and Ellice Islands Colony: Admin. Officer (Cadet), 1960–64; Lands Officer, 1965–66; Secretary: Min. of Natural Resources, 1967; Min. of Works and Utilities, 1968–70; Dist Officer, Funafuti, Ellice Is, 1972; Dist Comr, Ocean Is., 1972–75; Magistrate, Criminal and Civil Courts, 1965–75; Tuvalu Government: Asst Sec. to Chief Minister's Office, 1975; Sec., Min. of Natural Resources, 1976–77; First High Comr of Tuvalu to Fiji, also accredited to PNG and Perm. Rep. to S Pacific Commn, Noumea, New Caledonia and S Pacific Forum, Suva, 1978–83; Dean, Diplomatic Corps, Fiji, 1981–83; Manager, SW Pacific, British Petroleum Co.,

Tuvalu, 1983–93. MP, Tuvalu, 1983–97; Prime Minister of Tuvalu, 1993–96. *Recreations:* fishing, gardening. *Address:* Parliament of Tuvalu, Vaiaku, Funafuti, Tuvalu. *T:* 20252, 20254.

**LATCHMAN, Prof. David Seymour,** CBE 2010; Professor of Genetics, and Master of Birkbeck College, University of London, since 2003; Professor of Human Genetics, University College London, since 1999; *b* 22 Jan. 1956; *s* of Emanuel Latchman and Ella Latchman (*née* Wohl); *m* 2002, Hannah Garson; one *s*. *Educ:* Haberdashers' Aske's Sch.; Queens' Coll., Cambridge (BA 1978; MA 1981; PhD 1981); DSc London 1994. FRCPath 1999; FRCSEd 2017. Lectr in Molecular Genetics, Dept of Biology, UCL, 1984–88; Dir, Med. Molecular Biology Unit and Reader in Molecular Biology, Dept of Biochemistry, UCL and Middlesex Sch. of Medicine, 1988–91; University College London: Prof. of Molecular Pathology, 1991–99; Head, Div. of Pathol., 1995–99; Dir, Windeyer Inst. of Med. Scis, 1996–99; Dep. Hd, UCL Graduate Sch., 1998–99; Dean, Inst. of Child Health, UCL and Great Ormond Street Hosp. for Children, 1999–2002. Chm., Sci. Expert Adv. Cttee, Univ. of London, 1988–97. External Examiner: Brunel Univ., 1993–97; Nottingham Univ., 1999–2002; Mem., Examng Panel in Genetics, RCPath, 1999–. Member: Med. Adv. Panel, Parkinson's Disease Soc., 1995–2008 (Dep. Chm., 1997–2008); MRC Adv. Bd, 1997–2004; Project Grants Cttee, BHF, 1998–2002; Sci. Policy Adv. Cttee, 1998–2009 (Chm., 2003–09), Nat. Biol Standards Bd, 2002–09, Nat. Inst. for Biol Standards and Control; Home Office Nat. DNA Database Ethics Gp, 2011–18; DoH Genetics and Insurance Cttee, 2002–09; Health Protection Agency Bd, 2003–07; HEFCE Res. Strategy Cttee, 2003–06; MRC Coll. of Experts, 2004–; UUK Res. Strategy Cttee, 2004–; Bd, UUK, 2013–16 (Mem., England and NI Council, 2007–11; Mem., Membership Cttee, 2015–); Lifelong Learning Commn, Labour, 2019–. Non-exec. Dir, Gt Ormond St Hosp. for Children NHS Trust, 2001–02; Chairman: London 'Ideas' Genetic Knowledge Park, 2002–09; London Higher, 2006–10. Member, Council: Lifelong Learning UK, 2005–11; CBI London, 2009–13; Promote London, 2009–10; Member, Board: London Skills and Employment Bd, 2009–10; London First, 2009–18; Bd Observer, LDA, 2006–12; Governor: SOAS, 2004–09; LSHTM, 2004–09 (Mem. Bd of Mgt, 2004–09); Mem., Bd of Trustees, Univ. of London, 2011–. Pres., The Maccabaeans, 2007–. FRSA 2003; FKC 2014. Haldane Lectr, 1994, Crabtree Orator, 1997 (Pres., 2008), Sainer Lectr, 2007, Roth Lectr, 2011, UCL. Dep. Chm., Editl Bd, Biochemical Jl, 1995–97. *Publications:* Gene Regulation, 1990, 5th edn 2005; Eukaryotic Transcription Factors, 1991, 5th edn 2008; (ed) Transcription Factors: a practical approach, 1993, 2nd edn 1999; (ed) From Genetics to Gene Therapy, 1994; (ed) PCR applications in Pathology, 1995; (ed) Genetic Manipulation of the Nervous System, 1995; (ed) Basic Molecular and Cell Biology, 1997; (ed) Landmarks in Gene Regulation, 1997; (ed) Stress Proteins, 1999; (ed) Viral Vectors for Treating Diseases of the Nervous System, 2003; Gene Control, 2010, 2nd edn 2015. *Recreations:* book collecting, opera. *Address:* Birkbeck College, Malet Street, WC1E 7HX. *Club:* Athenæum.

**LATHAM,** family name of **Baron Latham**.

**LATHAM,** 2nd Baron *cr* 1942, of Hendon; **Dominic Charles Latham;** Senior Telecommunications Engineer, Aurecon Australia Pty Ltd, since 1994; *b* 20 Sept. 1954; *s* of Hon. Francis Charles Allman Latham (*d* 1959) and Gabrielle Monica (*d* 1987), *d* of Dr S. M. O'Riordan; *S* grandfather, 1970. *Educ:* Univ. of New South Wales, Australia (BEng (civil), 1977, Hons I; MEngSc 1981). Civil Engr, Electricity Commn, NSW, 1979–88; Structl Engr, Rankine & Hill, Consulting Engrs, 1988–91; Sen. Structl Engr, Gerard Barry Associates, 1992; Teacher, Rock around the Clock Dancing, 1993–94. *Recreations:* rock-'n'-roll/ballroom dancing, electronics, personal computing, sailboarding. *Heir:* yr twin *b* Anthony Michael Latham [*b* 20 Sept. 1954; *m* Margot].

**LATHAM, Alison Mary;** editor and writer; *b* 13 July 1948; *d* of John Llewellyn Goodall and Patricia Anne Goodall (*née* Tapper); *m* 1972, Richard Brunton Latham, *qv*; three *s*. *Educ:* Univ. of Birmingham (BMus Hons). Associate Editor, The Musical Times, 1977–88; Publications Editor, Royal Opera House, Covent Garden, 1989–2000; Commng Ed., Edinburgh Internat. Fest. progs, 2003–. FRSA 1999. *Publications:* (ed with S. Sadie) The Cambridge Music Guide, 1985; (ed with R. Parker) Verdi in Performance, 2001; The Oxford Companion to Music, 2002; (ed) Sing, Ariel: essays and thoughts for Alexander Goehr's seventieth birthday, 2003. *Address:* c/o The Oxford Companion to Music, Oxford University Press, Great Clarendon Street, Oxford OX2 6DP. *E:* Alison.Latham@btinternet.com.

**LATHAM, Christopher George Arnot;** Chairman, James Latham PLC, 1988–95; *b* 4 June 1933; *s* of late Edward Bryan Latham and Anne Arnot Duncan; *m* 1963, Jacqueline Cabourdin; three *s*. *Educ:* Stowe Sch.; Clare Coll., Cambridge (MA). FCA. Articled Fitzpatrick Graham, chartered accountants, 1955; joined James Latham Ltd, timber importers, 1959, Dir 1963. A Forestry Comr, 1973–78. Dir, CILNTEC, 1991–97. Pres., Inst. of Wood Sci., 1977–79; Chairman: Timber Res. and Develt Assoc., 1972–74; Commonwealth Forestry Assoc., 1975–77; Psychiatric Rehabilitation Assoc., 1983–91. Mem., Co. of Builders Merchants, 1985– (Master, 1999–2000; Almoner, 2002–07; Trustee, 2008–11). Mem. Cttee, Millennium Masters Assoc. *Recreations:* forestry, classic cars. *Address:* Marlow.

**LATHAM, David John;** President, Employment Tribunals (England and Wales), 2009–14; *b* 21 April 1946; *s* of William and Edna Latham; *m* 1969, Cherill Disley; one *s* one *d*. *Educ:* Quarry Bank Sch., Liverpool; Hull Univ. (LLB Hons). Admitted solicitor, 1971; Partner, Chambers Thomas, Solicitors, Hull, 1972–85; Principal, D. J. Latham & Co., Solicitors, Hull, 1986–87; Partner, Sandersons, Solicitors, Hull, 1988–96. Chm., Employment Tribunals, (pt-time), 1992–96, (full-time), 1996–2001; Regl Chm., Employment Tribunals, later Regl Employment Judge, London Central Reg., 2001–08; Dir, Nat. Trng Employment Tribunals, Judiciary, 1998. Chm., Hull FC, 1993–95. *Recreations:* sport, particularly basketball and Rugby, walking, gardening, theatre, opera, Rotary member. *E:* djl.froburn@yahoo.co.uk.

**LATHAM, Rt Hon. Sir David (Nicholas Ramsay),** Kt 1992; PC 2000; Chairman, Parole Board of England and Wales, 2009–12; a Lord Justice of Appeal, 2000–09; Vice-President, Court of Appeal (Criminal Division), 2006–09; *b* 18 Sept. 1942; *s* of late Robert Clifford Latham, CBE, FBA and Eileen (*née* Ramsay); *m* 1967, Margaret Elizabeth (*née* Forrest); three *d*. *Educ:* Bryanston; Queens' Coll., Cambridge (MA). Called to the Bar, Middle Temple, 1964, Bencher, 1989; QC 1985; one of the Junior Counsel to the Crown, Common Law, 1979–85; Junior Counsel to Dept of Trade in export credit matters, 1981–85; a Recorder, 1983–92; a Judge of the High Court, QBD, 1992–2000; Presiding Judge, Midland and Oxford Circuit, 1995–99. Vice-Chm., Council of Legal Educn, 1992–97 (Mem., 1988–97); Member: Gen. Council of the Bar, 1987–92; Judicial Studies Bd, 1988–91. Trustee, Slynn Foundn, 2013–. Gov., Warminster Sch., 2009–. Chm., Justice Working Party on Mental Health and Fair Trial report, 2017. *Recreations:* reading, music, travel. *Address:* 3 Manor Farm Close, Pimperne, Blandford Forum, Dorset DT11 8XL. *Clubs:* Travellers, Beefsteak, Pilgrims; Leander.

**LATHAM, Derek James,** RIBA; Chairman, Derek Latham & Co., (Lathams), 1989–2015 (Managing Director, 1989–2010); *b* 12 July 1946; *s* of late James Horace Latham and Mary Pauline Latham (*née* Turner); *m* 1968, Pauline Elizabeth Tuxworth (see P. E. Latham); two *s* one *d*. *Educ:* King Edward VI Grammar Sch., Retford; Leicester Sch. of Architecture (DipArch 1970); Nottingham Trent Poly. (DipTP 1974, DipLD 1977). RIBA 1972; MRTPI 1975; AABC 2003. Clifford Wearden & Associates (architects and planners), London, 1968–70; Housing Architect and Planner, Derby CC, 1970–73; Design and Conservation Officer, Derbys CC, 1974–78; Principal, Derek Latham and Associates, 1980–89; Man. Dir, Michael Saint Develts Ltd, 1984–96; Dir, Acanthus Associated Architectural Practices Ltd, 1984–98 (Chm., 1987–89). RIBA Client Design Advr, 2005–. Chairman: Church Converts Ltd, 1996–; Opun (Architecture and Built Envmt Centre for E Midlands), 2002–04, 2009–10 (Mem. Cttee, 2010–); Urban Partnership Gp, 2008–; Dir, Regeneration E Midlands, 2004– (Chm., 2006–10). Chair, Derbys Historic Bldgs Trust, 2017– (Tech. Advr, 1978–2017); Member: Exec. Cttee, Council for Care of Churches, 1985–91; Cttee, SPAB, 1993–2001. Regl Ambassador, 2001–11, Educn Enabler, 2002–11, CABE. Vis. Prof., Univ. of Derby, 2014–. Chm., RSA at Dean Clough, 1995–98. Member: Regl Cttee, Heritage Lottery Fund, 2001–06; Urban Panel, English Heritage, 2011–17. Chair, Derwent Valley Trust, 2017–. Dir, Great Northern Classics, 2018–. MLI 1979–2016; IHBC 1999–2016; Member: AHI, 1976–2006; IEMA, 1991–2006. Founder Academician, Acad. of Urbanism, 2002–. FRSA. Hon. PrD Derby, 2008. *Publications:* Creative Re-use of Buildings, 2000; various tech. articles on urban design and conservation. *Recreations:* racquet ball, sailing, ski-ing, rambling, cycling, swimming, painting, horse riding. *Clubs:* Duffield Squash and Lawn Tennis, Little Eaton Lawn Tennis (Pres., 1991–2003).

**LATHAM, Ian;** Founder and Publishing Editor, Architecture Today, since 1989; Director, Rightangle Publishing, since 1998; *b* Dover, Kent, 20 March 1956; *s* of Michael and Brenda Latham; *m* 1985, Christine Watson; one *s* one *d*. *Educ:* St Olave's Grammar Sch., Orpington; Oxford Poly. (BA; DipArch). Tech. Ed., Architectural Design, 1979–83; Dep. Ed., Building Design, 1983–89. Hon. FRIBA 2015. *Publications:* Joseph Maria Olbrich, 1980; (ed) Dixon Jones, 2002; (ed) Feilden Clegg Bradley, 2007; (ed) van Heyningen and Haward, 2010; (ed) MacCormac Jamieson Prichard, 2010; (ed) Allies and Morrison, 2011; Peter Ahrends, 2015; Richard Burton, 2015. *Recreation:* Hellenic studies. *Address:* Architecture Today, 34 Pentonville Road, N1 9HF. *T:* (020) 8883 4207. *E:* watson.latham@virgin.net.

**LATHAM, John,** CBE 2019; Vice-Chancellor and Chief Executive Officer, Coventry University, since 2014; *b* St Asaph, Denbighshire, 22 Feb. 1960; *s* of John and Barbara Latham; one *d*. *Educ:* Coventry Univ. (BSc Hons Computer Sci. 1983; MBA 1998). Software engr, Plessey Telecoms Ltd, Liverpool, 1981–84; Coventry Polytechnic, later Coventry University: Lectr, then Sen. Lectr, Dept of Computer Sci., 1984–92 (on secondment: researcher, GEC Electrical Projects Ltd, 1986; Res. Fellow, British Telecom, Martlesham, 1989); Principal Lectr and Hd of Trng Consultancy, 1992–95, Business Develt Manager, 1995–97, Commercial Develt Unit (on secondment: Business Develt Dir, JHP Gp Ltd, Coventry, 1994–95; Fire Service Coll., Moreton-in-Marsh, Home Office, 1995–97; Competitiveness Unit, Govt Office for W Midlands, 1997–2000; Competitiveness Team, Advantage W Midlands RDA, 1999–2001); Asst Dir, 1997–99, Dir/Man. Dir, 1999–2006, Commercial Affairs Dept/Coventry Univ. Enterprises Ltd; Pro-Vice-Chancellor, then Dep. Vice-Chancellor (Business Develt), 2005–13. Extraordinary Prof., Stellenbosch Univ., SA, 2014–. Mem., UK Govt Measurement Bd, 2002–14; Mem., Ministerial Brexit Forum, 2017–. Dir, UK Nat. Animation and Dissemination Unit, EC EUROTECNET Prog., 1993–94; IT Advr, Coventry HA, 1993–2000; Project Advr, Heart of England Tourist Bd, 1998–99; Evaluator and Prog. Advr, FP7/Horizon 2020, 2010–. Director: Midlands Assoc. for Skills and Trng using Educnl Resources, Univ. Enterprise Trng Partnership, 1997–99; SW Innovation Relay Centre, 1997–2000; Multi Academy Trust, 2017–; W Midlands Growth Co., 2017–. Non-executive Director: Membrasense Ltd, 2004–06; Coventry UC Ltd, 2005–15; Coventry Univ. London Campus Ltd, 2005–15; CUE Ltd, 2005–15; CU Social Enterprise CIC, 2005–15; CU Services Ltd, 2005–15; UK Plugged Ltd, 2008–10; ACUA Ltd, 2010–13; ACUA Solutions Ltd, 2010–13; Serious Games Internat. Ltd, 2012–16; Serious Games (Singapore) Ltd, 2012–. Board Member: EBN SA, 2003–10; UKBi Ltd, 2004–13; Business Link W Midlands, 2007–10; Coventry and Warwickshire LEP, 2010–; Innovate UK, 2015– (Mem., Strategic Adv. Bd, Enterprise Europe Network scale up pilot, 2017–); Growth Prog. Bd, 2015–; Univs UK, 2016–17; UKRI Implementation Prog. Audit and Assurance Bd, 2017–. Member: Adv. Bd, Centre for Carbon Measurement, 2012–; Adv. Bd, Design Council, 2013–; Advr Network, Connected Digital Econ. Catapult, 2014–16; Res. and Knowledge Exchange Cttee, HEFCE, 2014–18; RIS3 Expert Gp, European Univ. Assoc., 2016–. Chair, Eur. Structural and Investment Funds Cttee, Coventry and Warwickshire, 2016–. Chm., Univ. Alliance, 2016–; Mem., Innovation and Growth Policy Network, Univs UK, 2014–; Mem., Leadership Council, Nat. Centre for Univs and Business, 2014–. Mem., Stratford-upon-Avon Coll. Corp., 2001–10 (Chm., 2004–09); Mem., Tanku Abdul Rahman Univ. Coll., 2017–. Gov., Chipping Camden Acad. Sch., 2009–14. MInstD 2016. Hon. FBCS 2016. *Recreations:* travel and exploring new parts of the world, widening my skills knowledge and competence through new challenges; with a background in engineering, looking to keep abreast of the latest technological developments; a keen interest in company, financial markets and current affairs, keeping fit through swimming and walking. *Address:* Vice-Chancellor's Office, Coventry University, Priory Street, Coventry CV1 5FB. *T:* (024) 7765 8212. *E:* j.latham@coventry.ac.uk.

**LATHAM, Paul Robert;** President, Live Nation UK, 2002–18 and Chief Operating Officer, Live Nation Entertainment (International) (formerly Live Nation Europe), 2009–18; *b* Crewe, 24 Sept. 1960; *s* of Norman and Iris Latham; marr. diss.; two *s*. *Educ:* Brierley St Sch., Crewe. Joined Apollo Leisure as Manager, 1984. Chm., Nat. Skills Acad. for Creative and Cultural Skills, 2008–18. Mem. Bd, UK Music, 2011– (Chm., UK Music (Live), 2011–). *Recreations:* vice in Miami, Arsenal FC, NFL and Chicago Bears in particular (visited all 32 NFL teams at home, now for 119 1A colleges), the adoration of Alan Ball, punting ponies, Hooters and Tilted Kilts, going from juvenile to senile without anyone noticing the difference.

**LATHAM, Pauline Elizabeth,** OBE 1992; MP (C) Mid Derbyshire, since 2010; *b* Lincs, 4 Feb. 1948; *m* 1968, Derek James Latham, *qv*; two *s* one *d*. *Educ:* Bramcote Hills Tech. Grammar Sch. Proprietor, Humble Pie, 1976–87; Dir, Michael St Develt, 1982–2000. Member (C): Derbys CC, 1987–93; Derby CC, 1992–96 and 1998–2010 (Mayor, 2007–08). Contested (C): Broxtowe, 2001; E Midlands, EP, 1999, 2004. Mem., Internat. Develt Select Cttee, 2010–. Member, Board: WE (formerly Free the Children), 2013–; Furthest from the Sea, 2017–. *Address:* House of Commons, SW1A 0AA.

**LATHAM, His Honour Peter Heaton;** a Circuit Judge, 1997–2008; *b* 3 June 1938; *s* of Tom Heaton Latham and Dorothy Latham (*née* Williams). *Educ:* The Grammar Sch., Ashton-in-Makerfield, Lancs; Pembroke Coll., Oxford (BA Juris 1962). Nat. Service, 2nd Lieut, RA, 1957–59. Instructor, Univ. of Pennsylvania Law Sch., 1962–64; called to the Bar Gray's Inn, 1965 (James Mould Schol., 1965; Lee Essay Prize, 1965); in practice, 1965–97.

**LATHAM, Richard Brunton;** QC 1991; a Recorder, 1987–2010; *b* 16 March 1947; *s* of Frederick and Joan Catherine Latham; *m* 1972, Alison Mary Goodall (*see* A. M. Latham); three *s*. *Educ:* Farnborough Grammar School; Univ. of Birmingham (LLB 1969). Called to the Bar, Gray's Inn, 1971; Bencher, 2000; formerly in practice in London and on Midland Circuit. *Recreations:* sailing, opera. *Address:* 7 Bedford Row, WC1R 4BS. *T:* (020) 7242 3555.

**LATHAM, Sir Richard Thomas Paul,** 3rd Bt *cr* 1919, of Crow Clump; *b* 15 April 1934; *s* of Sir (Herbert) Paul Latham, 2nd Bt, and Lady Patricia Doreen Moore (*d* 1947), *o d* of 10th Earl of Drogheda; *S* father, 1955; *m* 1958, Marie-Louise Patricia, *d* of Frederick H. Russell, Vancouver, BC; two *d*. *Educ:* Eton; Trinity Coll., Cambridge. *Address:* 2125 Birnam Wood Drive, Santa Barbara, CA 93108, USA.

**LATHAM, Roger Alan;** Chief Executive, Nottinghamshire County Council, 2002–08; *b* 3 May 1950; *s* of Edward and Florrie Latham; *m* 1973, Angela Judith Warwick (*née* Pearce); one *s*. *Educ:* Bristol Univ. (BSc Econs with Stats); Birmingham Univ. (MSocSc); Liverpool Polytechnic. CPFA; CStat. Economic Assistant, National Westminster Bank, 1972–76; Economist, 1976–85, Asst Chief Finance Officer, 1985–90, Dudley MBC; Dep. County Treasurer, 1990–91, County Treasurer, 1991–2002, Notts CC. Visiting Fellow: Nottingham Trent Univ., 2008–; Univ. of Gloucestershire, 2017–. Pres., CIPFA, 2009–10 (Vice Pres., 2008–09). Methodist Local Preacher. *Recreations:* photography, gardening, computers, reading, dinosaurs, Japanese films, t'ai chi. *Address:* 25 Potters Lane, East Leake, Loughborough, Leics LE12 6NQ. *T:* (01509) 856562.

**LA THANGUE, Prof. Nicholas Barrie,** PhD; FRSE; FMedSci; Professor of Cancer Biology, University of Oxford, since 2005; Fellow, Linacre College, Oxford, since 2005; *b* Manchester, 29 Nov. 1957; *s* of David. L. Easty and Patricia A. La Thangue (*née* Mayhew). *Educ:* Cheadle Hulme Sch.; Birmingham Univ. (BSc); Reading Univ. (MSc); University Coll. London (PhD 1983); Oxford Univ. (MA). Jenner Fellow, Lister Inst., MRC NIMR, London, 1987–95; Cathcart Prof. of Biochem., Univ. of Glasgow, 1995–2005. Chief Scientific Officer: Prolifix Ltd, 1993–2001; Topo Target A/S, 2001–06. Mem., EMBO, 2003. FRSE 2004; FMedSci 2008. *Publications:* (ed) Seminars in Cancer Biology: cell cycle regulation and cancer, 1995; Targets for Cancer Chemotherapy, 2002; contribs to learned scientific and med. jls. *Recreations:* fishing, music, wine. *Address:* Department of Oncology, University of Oxford, Old Road Campus Research Building, off Roosevelt Drive, Oxford OX3 7DQ. *T:* (01865) 617090. *E:* nick.lathangue@oncology.ox.ac.uk.

**LATHE, Dr Richard Frank;** Professor and Honorary Fellow, University of Edinburgh Medical School, since 2015; Director, Pieta Research, since 2002; Associate Professor, Institute of Bio-Organic Chemistry, State University of Pushchino, Russia, since 2011; *b* 23 April 1952; *s* of late Prof. Grant Henry Lathe; one *s* four *d*. *Educ:* Univ. of Edinburgh (BSc Molecular Biol. 1973); Free Univ. of Brussels (DSc 1976). Research Scientist: Univ. of Heidelberg, 1977–79; Univ. of Cambridge, 1979–81; Asst Sci. Dir, Transgene SA, Strasbourg, 1981–84; Principal Sci. Officer, Animal Breeding Res. Orgn, 1984–85; Prof. of Genetics and Genetic Engrg, Lab. of Eukaryotic Molecular Genetics, and Co-Dir, Ecole Supérieure de Biotechnologie, Univ. of Strasbourg, 1985–89; University of Edinburgh: Dir, Centre for Genome Res., 1989–95; Res. Prof., 1989–2002. *Publications:* Autism, Brain, and Environment, 2006. *Address:* Division of Infection and Pathway Medicine, University of Edinburgh Medical School, Chancellor's Building, 49 Little France Crescent, Edinburgh EH16 4SB.

**LATIMER-SAYER, William Laurence;** QC 2016; *b* London, 6 March 1973; *s* of Edward and Annette Latimer-Sayer; *m* 2002, Sarah; one *s* one *d*. *Educ:* Highcliffe Sch., Dorset; King Edward VI Sch., Southampton; Leicester Univ. (BA Law 1994); Inns of Court Sch. of Law; King's Coll. London (MA Med. Law and Ethics 1996). Called to the Bar, Gray's Inn, 1995; in practice as barrister, 1996–. Mem., Ogden Wkg Party, 2011. Chambers and Partners Personal Injury Jun. of Year, 2008 and 2010. *Publications:* (Gen. Ed.) Schedules of Loss: calculating damages, 2001, 3rd edn 2010; (ed jtly) The ABC of Medical law, 2009; (contrib.) PIBA Personal Injuries Handbook, 3rd edn 2007; (contrib.) Clinical Negligence: a practical guide, 7th edn 2012; contrib. articles to practitioner jls incl. Personal Injury Law, Clin. Risk, Medico-Legal Soc. Jl. *Recreation:* tennis. *Address:* Cloisters, 1 Pump Court, Temple, EC4Y 7AA. *T:* (020) 7827 4000, *Fax:* (020) 7827 4100. *E:* wls@cloisters.com.

**LATNER, Stephen;** Managing Director, Warburg Dillon Read, 1998–99; *b* 23 July 1946; *s* of late Julius Latner and Anita Latner; *m* 1971, Jennifer Keidan; three *s*. *Educ:* Grocers' Sch.; Queen Mary Coll., London (BSc); Manchester Business Sch. (MBA). With ICL, 1968–71; joined S. G. Warburg, 1973: Dir, 1983–96; Dep. Chm., 1993–96; UK Country Hd, SBC Warburg, then Warburg Dillon Read, 1996–98. Chm. Council, Bobath Centre for Children with Cerebral Palsy, 2002–18 (Mem. Council, 1999–2018). *Recreations:* music, cinema, theatre, reading, sport.

**LA TROBE-BATEMAN, Richard George Saumarez;** structures designer/maker; *b* 17 Oct. 1938; *s* of late John La Trobe-Bateman and of Margaret (*née* Schmid); *m* 1969, Mary Elizabeth Jolly (OBE 2000); one *s* two *d*. *Educ:* Westminster Sch.; St Martin's Sch. of Art; Royal Coll. of Art (MDesRCA). Set up workshop, 1968. Member: Council of Management, British Crafts Centre, 1975–86; Council, Contemporary Applied Arts, 1987–94; Crafts Council: Mem., 1984–86; Index Selector, 1972–73; Chm., Index Selection Cttee, 1980–82. Work in: V&A Collection, 1979; Crafts Council Collection, 1981 and 1984; Keble Coll., Oxon, 1981; Temple Newsam Collection, 1983; Southern Arts Collection, 1983; Pembroke Coll., Oxon, 1984; Crafts Study Centre Collection, Bath, 1985; Northern Arts Collection, 1988; Royal Soc. of Arts, 1994; work presented by Crafts Council to the Prince of Wales, 1982; Longlands footbridge, Cumbria, 1995; Nat. Pinetum footbridge, Kent, 1999; swing-lift opening bridge, Glos (Wood Award), 2003; Langport footbridge, Somerset, 2005–06; Tassajara footbridge, Calif, 2005–06; Rolling drawbridge, Buscot, Oxon, 2010–11; series of truss bridges, Napa Valley, Calif, 2011–12; Conference footbridge, Madison, Wisconsin, 2017. Vis. Prof., San Diego State Univ., 1986–87. *Publications:* Making Triangles, 2012; articles in Crafts, American Crafts. *Recreations:* listening to music, hill-walking. *Address:* 3 Avondale Buildings, Bath BA1 6RD. *T:* (01225) 330895. *Club:* Contemporary Applied Arts.

**LATTER, (Henry) James (Edward);** a Judge of the Upper Tribunal (Immigration and Asylum Chamber) (formerly a Vice President, Immigration Appeal Tribunal, later Senior Immigration Judge, Asylum and Immigration Tribunal), 2001–15; Principal Resident Judge, 2014–15; *b* 19 April 1950; *s* of Henry Edward Latter and Hilda Bessie Latter; *m* 1978, Penelope Jane Morris; one *s* one *d*. *Educ:* Reigate Grammar Sch.; Trinity Hall, Cambridge (BA 1971; MA 1974). Called to the Bar, Middle Temple, 1972; in practice as Barrister, 1972–95; full-time Immigration Adjudicator, 1995–96; Regl Adjudicator, Hatton Cross, 1996–98; Dep. Chief Adjudicator, 1998–2001.

**LATTO, Prof. Jennifer Elizabeth,** MBE 2016; Provost, Liverpool John Moores University, 1994–2002; *b* 3 Aug. 1944; *d* of Prof. Sir Henry Clifford Darby, CBE, FBA, and Eva Constance Darby (*née* Thomson); *m* 1967, Richard Matheson Latto; one *s*. *Educ:* Berkhamsted Sch. for Girls; Newnham Coll., Cambridge (BA Exptl Psychol. 1966); Homerton Coll., Cambridge (PGCE 1967); University Coll. London (Dip. Educnl Psychol. 1969). Educnl Psychologist, Essex CC, 1968–72; Lectr in Educnl Psychol., Homerton Coll., Cambridge, 1970–73; SSRC Studentship, Dept of Education, Univ. of Cambridge, 1972–75; Educnl Psychologist, Cheshire CC, 1978–79; Sen. Lectr, then Hd, Educn Dept, Liverpool Poly., 1979–92; Prof. of Educnl Psychol., 1992–2002, Dir, Sch. of Educn and Community Studies, 1992–94, Liverpool John Moores Univ.; Adviser: on Higher Educn, Govt Office NW, 2002–05; on Higher Educn Strategy, NW Develt Agency, 2003–07. Chm., NW Heritage Lottery Fund, 2005–11. Dir, Liverpool City of Learning, 2000–02. Chm., Univs Council for Educn of Teachers, 1993–95. Trustee, Tate, and Chm. Council, Tate Liverpool, 1998–2007. Mem., Adv. Cttee, 2004–11, Trustee, 2011–, Granada Foundn. *Publications:* (with Richard Latto) Study Skills for Psychology Students, 2009. *Recreations:* modern design, opera. *Address:* Monksferry House, Grassendale Park, Liverpool L19 0LS.

**LATYMER,** 9th Baron *cr* 1431; **Crispin James Alan Nevill Money-Coutts;** *b* 8 March 1955; *s* of 8th Baron Latymer and Hon. Penelope Ann Clare (*née* Emmet); *S* father, 2003; *m* 1st, 1978, Hon. Lucy Rose (marr. diss. 1995), *y d* of Baron Deedes, KBE, MC, PC; one *s* two *d*; 2nd, 1995, Mrs Shaunagh Heneage. *Educ:* Eton Coll.; Keble Coll., Oxford. E. F. Hutton & Co., 1977–81; Bankers Trust, 1981–84; European Banking Co., 1984–86; Coutts & Co., 1986–99; Cazenove & Co., 2000–08. Director: Manek Investment Mgt, 1994–2018; Throgmorton Trust, 2007–17 (Chm., 2012–17). Trustee: Astor Foundn, 1993–; UCLH Charity (formerly Charities), 2005–15 (Chm., 2008–15). *Publications:* Where the Ocean Meets the Sky, 2009. *Recreations:* travelling, sailing. *Heir:* s Hon. Drummond William Thomas Money-Coutts, *b* 11 May 1986. *Address:* 8 Turner House, Erasmus Street, SW1P 4DZ. *E:* crispin@latymer.org. *Clubs:* House of Lords Yacht, Ocean Cruising; Velo Rocacorba.

**LAU, Dame Sandra Geok Mei,** DBE 2019 (MBE 2012); owner and Managing Director, Tropicana Ltd, Papua New Guinea, since 1971; *b* Klang, Selangor, Malaysia, 8 Nov. 1948; *d* of Tan Jit Kee and Chew Ger Tan; *m* John Yak Hon Lau; one *s* three *d*. *Educ:* Kwang Hwa Secondary Sch., Klang, Selangor; Univ. of Cambridge (Gen. Cert. Educn). Member, Board: PNG Univ. of Natural Resources and Envmt, Vudal; Divine Word Univ., Kabaleo; East New Britain Tourism Authy, 2019–; Nonga Gen. (formerly Nonga Base) Hosp., Rabaul; Mem., Cttee, Vunabosco Benefactors Assoc. *Recreations:* reading, swimming, tennis, walking, jogging. *Address:* Tropicana Ltd Compound, Williams Road, Kokopo, East New Britain Province, Papua New Guinea. *T:* 9829188, *Fax:* 9829166. *E:* sandra@tropicana.com.pg; 55 Belvedere Crescent, Sunny Bank Hills, Qld, Australia. *T:* (418) 183898.

**LAU-WALKER, Anthony Stanley,** CBE 2013; Chief Executive Officer, Eastleigh College, 2002–14; Member, UK Commission for Employment and Skills, since 2011; *b* Shipley, W Yorks, 3 May 1951; *s* of Benjamin Meek and Vera Meek (*née* Killip, later Walker); *m* 1987, Margaret Lau; one *s* one *d*. *Educ:* Hanson's Boys' Grammar Sch., Bradford; University Coll. of Swansea (BA Politics); University Coll. of Wales, Aberystwyth (MSc Strategic Studies); Thames Valley Coll. of HE (Dip. Mgt); Surrey Univ. (Dip. Counselling). Hd, Teacher Trng and Staff Develt, 1977–87, Hd of Div., 1987–97, Guildford Coll. of Further and Higher Educn; Curriculum Dir, Eastleigh Coll., 1997–2002. Chm., Windsor Gp of Colls, 2009–14. Trustee: Awarding Body, Vocational Trng Charitable Trust, 2007–; Vocational Trng Charitable Trust Foundn, 2015–; Director: Good Shepherd Trust, 2013–; South Downs Educn Trust, 2018–; Gov., Onslow First Sch., 2017–. *Recreations:* theatre, cinema, art, walking, foreign travel, family.

**LAUDER, Desmond Michael Frank Scott;** Programme Manager, International Network Development: Cambridge International Examinations, 2013–15; Cambridge Assessment, 2016; *b* 28 July 1947; *s* of late Col Philip Lauder and Frances Lauder; *m* 1975, Xanthe Aristidou Theodosiadou; one *s* one *d*. *Educ:* Magdalene Coll., Cambridge (BA, MA); Inst. of Education, Univ. of London (PGCE). Teacher: Royal Grammar School, Guildford, 1970–72; Saint Ignatius Coll., Enfield, 1972–73; British Council: Asst Dir, Salonika, Greece, 1973–76; Asst Dir, Rio de Janeiro, Brazil, 1976–79; Asst Sec., CNAA, 1979–83; British Council: service in Czechoslovakia and Singapore, 1983–87; Corporate Planning Dept, 1987–91; Dir, Ecuador, 1991–93; Regl Dir, Asia Pacific, 1994–97; Director: Hong Kong, 1997–2003; Greece, 2003–07; Acting Dir, Marketing and Customer Services, 2007–08; Hd, Contracts and Projects Delivery, 2008–10; Asst Chief Exec., VSO, 2010–11. *Recreations:* walking, reading. *Address:* 44 Lings Coppice, Dulwich, SE21 8SX.

**LAUDER, Prof. Ian,** FRCPath; FMedSci; Dean of Medicine, 2000–08, and Dean, Faculty of Medicine and Biological Sciences, 2003–08, University of Leicester; *b* 17 June 1946; *s* of late Thomas William Lauder and of Joan Lauder; *m* 1969, Patricia Christine Purvis; one *s* one *d*. *Educ:* King James 1st Grammar Sch., Bishop Auckland; Univ. of Newcastle upon Tyne (MB BS 1969). FRCPath 1985. Lectr in Pathol., Univ. of Newcastle upon Tyne, 1970–78; Sen. Lectr, Pathol., Univ. of Leeds, 1978–84; Prof. of Pathol., Univ. of Leicester, 1984–2000, Prof. Emeritus, 2008; Dean: Leicester Warwick Med. Schs, 2000–07; Faculty of Medicine, Univ. of Warwick, 2002–04. Hon. Prof. of Pathology, Univs of Leicester and Warwick, 2008–. Chairman: Adv. Cttee on Assessment of Lab. Standards, DoH, 1990–95; Armed Services Consultants Appts Bd Pathology, 2003–08. Non-exec. Dir, Univ. Hosps of Leicester NHS Trust, 2000–08; Mem., GMC, 2002–03. Treas., Council of Hds of Med. Schs, 2000–05. Chm. Council, Internat. Jl Exptl Pathol., 2015–. Mem. (Liberal), Gateshead MDC, 1976–78. Sec., British Lymphoma Pathol. Gp, 1980–90; Royal College of Pathologists: Chm., Speciality Adv. Cttee, 1990–93; Vice-Pres., 1996–99. Pres., 1942 Club, 2008–10. Vice-Chm., Hope Against Cancer, 2006–. Mem., Illston Parish Council, 2015– (Vice-Chm., 2017–); Treas., Illston Village Hall, 2014–. FMedSci 1998 (Treas., 2005–10). Chancellor's Medal, Univ. of Warwick, 2007. *Publications:* Lymphomas other than Hodgkin's Disease, 1981; Malignant Lymphomas, 1988; contrib. numerous papers on malignant lymphomas, cancer pathol. and quality assurance in pathol. *Recreations:* fly-fishing, hill-walking, running, ballroom dancing, bridge. *Address:* Paddock House, Illston on the Hill, Leicester LE7 9EG. *T:* (0116) 259 6511. *E:* prof_lauder@hotmail.com.

**LAUDER, Sir Piers Robert Dick-,** 13th Bt *cr* 1688; *S* father, 1981.

**LAUDERDALE,** 18th Earl of, *cr* 1624; **Ian Maitland;** Baron Maitland, 1590; Viscount Lauderdale, 1616; Viscount Maitland, Baron Thirlestane and Boltoun, 1624; Bt (NS), 1680; Hereditary Bearer of the National Flag of Scotland, 1790 and 1952; Chief of the Clan Maitland; Marketing Adviser, London School of Economics and Political Science, 1995–2001; *b* 4 Nov. 1937; *er s* of 17th Earl of Lauderdale and Stanka (*née* Lozanic); *S* father, 2008; *m* 1963, Ann Paule, *d* of Geoffrey Clark; one *s* one *d*. *Educ:* Radley Coll., Abingdon; Brasenose Coll., Oxford (MA Modern History). Various appointments since 1960; with Hedderwick Borthwick & Co., 1970–74; National Westminster Bank, 1974–95: Regl Manager, Maghreb, 1986, ME and N Africa, 1989–91; Sen. Regl Manager, Africa and ME, 1991–95. Dir, Maitland Consultancy Services Ltd, 1995–2009. Lecturer: NY Inst. of Finance, 1997–2000; Euromoney Instnl Investor (formerly Euromoney Publications) PLC, 1998–2006; LSE Gurukul Scholarship Course, 1999. Royal Naval Reserve (Lieutenant), 1963–73; Mem., Queen's Body Guard for Scotland, Royal Co. of Archers, 1986–. Freeman, City of London, 1998; Liveryman, Fanmakers' Co., 1998–2004. *Recreations:* photography, sailing. *Heir:* s The Master of Lauderdale, Viscount Maitland, *qv*. *Address:* 150

Tachbrook Street, SW1V 2NE; Newlands Barn, By Thornhill, Dumfriesshire DG3 5EE. *Clubs:* Royal Ocean Racing; New, Puffin's (Edinburgh).
*See also Lady H. O. Maitland.*

**LAUDERDALE, Master of;** *see* Maitland, Viscount.

**LAUENER, Peter Rene,** CB 2004; Interim Chief Executive, Student Loans Company, 2017–18; *b* 29 Sept. 1954; *s* of Rene George Lauener and Anne McLean Lauener (*née* Ross); *m* 1976, Angela Margaret Mulliner; one *s* two *d. Educ:* George Watson's Coll., Edinburgh; Univ. of Durham (BA Hons Econs 1975). Economic Assistant, Scottish Office, 1975–82; Manpower Services Commission: Economic Advr, 1982–85; Hd of Strategy, Evaluation and Res., 1986–87; Area Manager, Manchester, 1987–89; Dept of Employment, 1989–92, 1995–96; Dir, Skills & Enterprise, Govt Office for E Midlands, 1992–95; Head of Resources & Budget Mgt, DfEE, 1996–2000; Dir, Learning, Delivery and Standards Gp, DfEE, subseq. DfES, 2000–04; Dir, Qualifications and Young People's Gp, 2004–05, Acting Dir Gen. for Lifelong Learning, 2005, DfES; Dir of Local Transformation, DfES, later DCSF, 2006–09; Chief Exec., Young People's Learning Agency, 2009–12; Chief Executive: Educn Funding Agency, 2012–17; Skills Funding Agency, 2014–17; Educn and Skills Funding Agency, 2017; Interim Chief Exec., Inst. for Apprenticeships, 2017. Mem. Bd, DFE, 2012–17. Non-exec. Dir, Sheffield Children's Hosp., 2016–. Chair: Newcastle Coll. Gp, 2018–; CITB, 2018–. Trustee: Educators Internat., 2012–; Orchard Hill Coll. and Acad. Trust, 2019–. *Recreations:* being enchanted by granddaughter since 2013 and grandson since 2017, reading, walking, wine. *Address:* 82 Pingle Road, Sheffield S7 2LL. *T:* (0114) 236 2188.

**LAUGHARNE, Albert,** CBE 1983; QPM 1978; Deputy Commissioner, Metropolitan Police, 1983–85; *b* 20 Oct. 1931; *s* of Reginald Stanley Laugharne and Jessica Simpson Laugharne; *m* 1st, 1954, Barbara Thirlwall (*d* 1994); two *d*; 2nd, 1999, Margaret Ann Blackmore; four step *s. Educ:* Baines' Grammar Sch., Poulton-le-Fylde; Manchester Univ. Detective Inspector, Manchester City Police, 1952–66; Supt, Cumbria Constab., 1966–70; Chief Supt, W Yorks Constab., 1970–73; Asst Chief Constable, Cheshire Constab., 1973–76; Chief Constable: Warwicks, 1977–78; Lancashire, 1978–83. RCDS, 1975. *Publications:* Seaford House Papers, 1975. *Recreations:* gardening, painting.

**LAUGHLIN, Prof. Robert Betts,** PhD; Anne T. and Robert M. Bass Professor of Physics, School of Humanities and Sciences, Stanford University, since 1992; *b* 1 Nov. 1950; *s* of David H. and Margaret B. Laughlin; *m* 1979, Anita R. Perry; two *s. Educ:* Univ. of Calif, Berkeley (AB Maths 1972); Massachusetts Inst. of Technol. (PhD Physics 1979). Postdoctoral res., Bell Telephone Labs, 1979–81; post-doctoral res., then Res. Physicist, Lawrence Livermore Nat. Lab., 1981–84; Associate Prof. of Physics, 1984–89, Prof., 1989–, Stanford Univ. Member: Amer. Acad. Arts and Scis, 1990–; NAS, 1994–. E. O. Lawrence Award for Physics, US Dept of Energy, 1985; Oliver E. Buckley Prize, APS, 1986; Franklin Medal for Physics, 1998; (jtly) Nobel Prize for Physics, 1998. *Publications:* A Different Universe: remaking physics from the bottom down, 2005; The Crime of Reason: and the closing of the scientific mind, 2008; contrib. numerous articles in Physical Rev. Letters, Physical Rev., Advances in Physics, etc. *Recreations:* hiking, ski-ing, computers, music. *Address:* Department of Physics, Stanford University, Stanford, CA 94305, USA. *T:* (650) 7234563, *Fax:* (650) 72565411. *E:* rbl@large.stanford.edu.

**LAUGHLIN, Prof. Simon Barry,** PhD; FRS 2000; Professor of Neurobiology, Department of Zoology, University of Cambridge, 2004–15, now Emeritus; Fellow, Churchill College, Cambridge, since 1991; *b* 19 Dec. 1947; *s* of Peter and Margaret Laughlin; *m* 1980, Barbara Frances Howard; two *s* one *d. Educ:* Clare Coll., Cambridge (BA, MA); Australian Nat. Univ. (PhD Neurobiol. 1974). Fellow, Res. Sch. of Biol Scis, ANU, 1976–84; Cambridge University: Lectr in Zool., 1984–96; Reader in Sensory Neuroscience, 1996–99; Rank Res. Prof. in Opto-electronics, 1999–2004. *Publications:* Principles of Neural Design, 2015; contribs on vision, neural processing and energy efficiency to learned jls. *Recreation:* classical bassoon. *Address:* Department of Zoology, Downing Street, Cambridge CB2 3EJ. *T:* (01223) 336608.

**LAUGHTON, Sir Anthony Seymour,** Kt 1987; FRS 1980; oceanographic consultant; Director, Institute of Oceanographic Sciences, 1978–88; *b* 29 April 1927; *s* of Sydney Thomas Laughton and Dorothy Laughton (*née* Chamberlain); *m* 1st, 1957, Juliet Ann Chapman (marr. diss. 1962); one *s*; 2nd, 1973, Barbara Clare Bosanquet; two *d. Educ:* Marlborough Coll.; King's Coll., Cambridge (MA, PhD). RNVR, 1945–48. John Murray Student, Columbia Univ., NY, 1954–55; Nat. Inst. of Oceanography, later Inst. of Oceanographic Sciences, 1955–88: research in marine geophysics in Atlantic and Indian Oceans, esp. in underwater photography, submarine morphology, ocean basin evolution, midocean ridge tectonics; Principal Scientist of deep sea expedns. Member: Co-ordinating Cttee for Marine Sci. and Technol., 1987–91; nat. and internat. cttees on oceanography and geophysics. President: Challenger Soc. for Marine Sci., 1988–90; Soc. for Underwater Technol., 1995–97 (Mem. Council, 1986–92; President's Award, 1998); Hydrographic Soc., 1997–99. Member Council: Royal Soc., 1986–87; Marine Biology Assoc., 1980–83, 1988–92. Mem. Cttee, 1966–2003, Chm., 1987–2003, Gen. Bathymetric Chart of the Oceans. Member: Governing Body, Charterhouse Sch., 1981–2000 (Chm., 1995–2000); Council, University Coll. London, 1983–93; Adv. Council, Ocean Policy Inst., Hawaii, 1991–93. Trustee, Natural Hist. Mus., 1990–94. Pres., Haslemere Musical Soc., 1997–. Silver Medal, RSA, 1958; Cuthbert Peek grant, RGS, 1967; Prince Albert 1er Monaco Gold Medal for Oceanography, 1980; Founders Medal, RGS, 1987; Murchison Medal, Geol. Soc., 1989. *Publications:* (ed jtly) Of Seas and Ships and Scientists, 2010; papers on marine geophysics and oceanography. *Recreations:* music, gardening, sailing. *Address:* Okelands, Pickhurst Road, Chiddingfold, Surrey GU8 4TS. *T:* (01428) 683941.

**LAUGHTON, Prof. Michael Arthur,** PhD, DSc(Eng); FREng, FIET, FIEEE; Professor of Electrical Engineering, Queen Mary and Westfield (formerly Queen Mary) College, University of London, 1977–2000, now Emeritus; *b* 18 Dec. 1934; *s* of William Arthur Laughton and Laura (*née* Heap); *m* 1960, Margaret Mary Coleman (marr. diss. 1994); two *s* two *d. Educ:* King Edward's Five Ways Sch., Birmingham; Etobicoke Collegiate Inst., Toronto; Toronto Univ. (BASc 1957); Univ. of London (PhD 1965; DSc(Eng) 1976). FREng (FEng 1989); FIET (FIEE 1977); FIEEE 2010; CEng 1965. GEC, Witton, 1957–61; Queen Mary, later Queen Mary and Westfield, College, London University: Res. Student, Dept of Elect. Engrg, 1961–64; Lectr, 1964–72; Reader, 1972–77; Dean, Faculty of Engrg, 1983–85; Pro-Principal, 1985–89; Dean of Engrg, London Univ., 1990–94. Visiting Professor: Purdue Univ., USA, 1966; Tokyo Univ., 1977; ICSTM, 2002–. Sec. and Dir, Unicom Ltd, 1971–74; Dir, QMC Industrial Res. Ltd, 1979–91 (Chm., 1988–91); Chm., Tower Shakespeare Co. Ltd, 1985–93. Organising Sec., 1963–81, Chm., Exec. Cttee, 1981–2014, Pres. of Council, 2014–18, Power Systems Computation Confs; Science and Engineering Research Council: Chm., Machines and Power Educn and Trng Cttee, 1983–86; Member: Elect. Engrg Cttee, 1982–84; Wind Energy Panel, 1985–86; Institution of Electrical Engineers: Chm., Wkg Gp on New Electronic Technol. in Publishing, 1983–87; Member: Council, 1990–94; Governing Cttee, Benevolent Fund, 1990–93; Mem. Exec., Watt Cttee on Energy, 1986– (Chm., Wkg Gp on Renewable Energy Sources, 1986–88); Mem., Inf. Cttee, 1988–92, Mem, Energy Policy Adv. Gp, 2001–, Royal Soc.; Mem., Internat. Cttee, Royal Acad. of Engrg, 2002–06. Specialist Adviser: Sub-Cttee B (Energy, Transport and Technol.), H of L Select Cttee on Eur. Communities, 1987–89; H of C Select Cttee on Welsh Affairs, 1993–94. Member: Fulbright Commn Scholarships Cttee, 1991–; Council, Cranfield Inst. of Technol., 1991–96. Freeman: City of London, 1990; Liveryman: Barbers' Co., 1995; Engineers' Co., 2009. Founder and Jt Ed., Internat. Jl of Electrical Power and Energy Systems, 1978–; Ed., Procs of Power System Computation Confs 5–8, 1975–84. Career Achievement Medal, IEE, 2002. *Publications:* edited: Energy Policy Planning, 1979; Electrical Engineers Reference Book, 14th edn 1985, 15th edn 1993, 16th edn 2002; Renewable Energy Sources, 1990; Expert System Applications in Power Systems, 1990; numerous papers and contribs in the fields of control systems, electrical power systems, energy economics, electrical machines, computational techniques and modelling theory. *Recreations:* science, music, cricket, Rugby. *Address:* 28 Langford Green, Champion Hill, SE5 8BX. *T:* (020) 7326 0081. *E:* michael.laughton1@btinternet.com. *Club:* Athenæum.

**LAUGHTON, Roger Froome,** CBE 2000; Chairman, Arts University Bournemouth, 2012–16; *b* 19 May 1942; *s* of late Eric Laughton and Elizabeth Laughton (*née* Gibbons); *m* 1967, Suzanne Elizabeth Taylor; one *d. Educ:* King Edward VII Sch., Sheffield; Merton Coll., Oxford (Postmaster; BA 1st Cl. Hons Modern Hist.); Inst. of Educn, Oxford Univ. (DipEd (Dist)). Royal Insce Co. Fellow, Stanford Univ., USA, 1964–65; BBC, 1965–90: Producer, 1965–77; Editor, Features, Manchester, 1977–80; Head: Network Features, 1980–85 (Jt Series Producer, River Journeys (BAFTA Award for best documentary series), 1984); Daytime Programmes, 1985–87; Dir, Co-prodns and BBC Enterprises, 1987–90; Man. Dir, MAI Media, 1990–96; Chief Executive: Meridian Broadcasting, 1991–96; United Broadcasting and Entertainment, 1996–99; Hd, Media Sch., Bournemouth Univ., 1999–2005. Chm., ITV Broadcast Bd, 1995–97; Director: ITV, 1992–99; United News and Media, 1996–2000; ITN, 1997–99. Laughton Media Associates, 2003–11; Chm., South West Screen, 2004–10; Member, Board: Metfilm, 2006–10; Services Sound and Vision Corp., 2007–14. Chm., DCMS/Skillset Audio-Visual Industries Trng Gp, 1999–2001. Chm., Screen Heritage Prog. Bd, 2008–11. Visiting Professor: Bournemouth Univ., 2005–; Univ. of Lincoln, 2010–. Governor: BFI, 2002–08 (Dep. Chair, 2006–08); Arts Univ. Coll. of Bournemouth (formerly Arts Inst. at Bournemouth), 2006–12. Mem., Internat. TV Acad., 1994; FRTS 1994 (Gold Award, 1999). Hon. DA Lincoln, 2009. *Recreations:* walking, cricket, reading, allotment. *Address:* 6 Lawn Crescent, Richmond, Surrey TW9 3NR. *T:* (020) 8948 0231. *Club:* Royal Automobile.

**LAUNDER, Prof. Brian Edward,** FRS 1994; FREng, FIMechE, FRAeS; Research Professor, School of Mechanical, Aerospace and Civil Engineering, University of Manchester (formerly Department of Mechanical, Aerospace and Manufacturing Engineering, UMIST), since 1998 (part-time, since 2004); *b* 20 July 1939; *s* of Harry Edward Launder and Elizabeth Ann Launder (*née* Ayers); *m* 1967, Dagny Simonsen; one *s* one *d. Educ:* Enfield Grammar Sch.; Imperial Coll., London (BScEng Mech Engrg 1961); MIT (SM 1963; ScD 1965 Mech Engrg). Res. Asst, MIT, 1961–64; Lectr, 1964–71, Reader in Fluid Mechanics, 1971–76, Imperial Coll.; Prof. of Mech. Engrg, Univ. of California, Davis, 1976–80; University of Manchester Institute of Science and Technology: Prof. of Mech. Engrg, 1980–98; Head, Thermo-Fluids Div., 1980–90; Head, Dept of Mech. Engrg, 1983–85 and 1993–95; Regl Dir (North), Tyndall Centre for Climate Change Res., 2000–06; Dir, Mason Centre for Envmtl Flows, 2003–06. Hon. Prof., Nanjing Aeronautics Inst., 1993. FREng (FEng 1994); FASME. Dr *hc:* Inst Nat. Polytechnique de Toulouse, 1999; Thessaloniki, 2005; Univ. Paul Cézanne, Aix-en-Provence, 2008; Hon. Dip. Russian Acad. of Sci., 2013. Nusselt-Reynolds Prize in Fluid Mechanics, Assembly of World Confs on Experimental Heat, Transfer, Fluid Mechanics, and Thermodynamics, 2013; Energy Systems Award, AIAA, 2018. Editor-in-Chief, Internat. Jl of Heat and Fluid Flow, 1987–2012. *Publications:* (with D. B. Spalding) Mathematical Models of Turbulence, 1972; (with A. D. Gosman and G. J. Reece) Computer-aided Engineering: heat transfer and fluid flow, 1985; (with B. S. Petukov and A. F. Polyakov) Heat Transfer in Turbulent Mixed Convection, 1988; (ed) Turbulent Shear Flows, vol. 1, 1978–vol. 9, 1994; (ed with N. D. Sandham) Closure Strategies for Turbulent and Transitional Flows, 2002; (ed with J. M. T. Thompson) Geo-engineering Climate Change: environmental necessity or Pandora's Box?, 2010; (with K. Hanjalic) Modelling Turbulence in Engineering and the Environment: second-moment routes to closure, 2011; numerous articles on turbulent flow in learned jls. *Recreations:* vacationing in France, photography, country walking, writing biographies of deceased leaders in fluid mechanics. *Address:* School of Mechanical, Aerospace and Civil Engineering, University of Manchester, George Begg Building, Sackville Street, Manchester M13 9PL. *T:* (0161) 306 3801.

**LAURANCE, Anthony John,** CBE 2005; Chief Executive Officer, Medical Aid for Palestinians, 2013–16; *b* 11 Nov. 1950; *s* of Dr Bernard Laurance and Margaret Audrey Laurance (*née* Kidner); *m* 1981, Judith Allen; two *d. Educ:* Bryanston Sch.; Clare Coll., Cambridge (MA). Drum Publications, Zambia, 1973–74; News Training Scheme, BBC, 1975; joined DHSS, 1975; Admin. Trainee, subseq. HEO(D), 1975–80; Mgt Services, 1980–81; Policy Strategy Unit, 1981–83; Finance Div., 1983–85; Prin. Private Sec. to Sec. of State for Social Services, 1985–87; Newcastle Central Office, 1987–90; Territorial Dir, Benefits Agency, 1990–95; Regl Gen. Manager/Regl Dir, South and West RHA, 1995; Regl Dir, SW, NHS Exec., DoH, 1995–2002; Prog. Dir, NHSU, DoH, 2002–04; Iraq: Health Team Leader, Coalition Provisional Authy, 2004; Sen. Advr to Minister of Health, 2004–05; Adviser to Centre of Govt, 2005–06; Advr, Public Admin Develt Prog., Libya, 2006–07; Technical Officer, WHO, Geneva, 2007–08; Hd, WHO, West Bank and Gaza, 2008–13. *Recreations:* modern fiction, tennis, walking. *Address:* Old Musgraves Farm, West Monkton TA2 8NW.

**LAUREN, Ralph,** Hon. KBE 2017; fashion designer; Chairman and Chief Creative Officer, Ralph Lauren Corporation (formerly Polo Ralph Lauren Corporation) (Chief Executive, until 2015); *b* 14 Oct. 1939; *s* of Frank and Frieda Lifschitz; changed name to Lauren, 1955; *m* 1964, Ricky Beer; three *s.* Salesman, New York: Bloomingdale's; Brooks Bros; Asst Buyer, Allied Stores; Rep., Rivetz Necktie Manufrs; Neckwear Designer, Polo Div., Beau Brummel, 1967–69; creator of designer and ready-to-wear clothing, accessories, fragrances, home furnishings, etc; Founder: Polo Menswear Co., 1968; Ralph Lauren's Women's Wear, 1971; Polo Leathergoods, 1978; Polo Ralph Lauren Luggage, 1982; Ralph Lauren Home Collection, 1983. Numerous fashion awards. *Address:* Ralph Lauren Corporation, 625 Madison Avenue, New York, NY 10022, USA.

**LAURENCE, Ven. Christopher;** *see* Laurence, Ven. J. H. C.

**LAURENCE, George Frederick;** QC 1991; *b* 15 Jan. 1947; *s* of Dr George Bester Laurence and Anna Margaretha Laurence; *m* 1st, 1976, (Ann) Jessica Chenevix Trench (*d* 1999); one *s* one *d*, and one step *s*; 2nd, 2000, (Anne) Jacqueline Baker; one *s* one *d. Educ:* Pretoria High Sch. for Boys; Univ. of Cape Town (Smuts Meml Scholarship; BA); University College, Oxford (Rhodes Scholar; MA). Called to the Bar, Middle Temple, 1972 (Harmsworth Law Scholar; Bencher, 1999); Asst Recorder, 1993–2000; Dep. High Court Judge, 1997–2004; a Recorder, 2000–04. Mem. Council, S African Inst. of Race Relns, 1998–2008. Fellow, Soc. for Advanced Legal Studies, 1998. Patron, Sir John Soane's

Mus., 2007–14. *Publications:* articles in Jl of Planning and Envmt Law and Rights of Way Law Review. *Recreations:* theatre, access to the countryside, cricket, tennis. *Address:* 12 New Square, Lincoln's Inn, WC2A 3SW. *T:* (020) 7419 8000.

**LAURENCE, Ven. (John Harvard) Christopher;** Archdeacon of Lindsey, Diocese of Lincoln, 1985–94, now Archdeacon Emeritus; *b* 15 April 1929; *s* of Canon H. P. Laurence and Mrs E. Laurence; *m* 1952, E. Margaret E. Chappell (*d* 2014); one *s* one *d*. *Educ:* Christ's Hospital; Trinity Hall, Cambridge (MA); Westcott House, Cambridge. Nat. service commn, Royal Lincolnshire Regt, 1948–50. Asst Curate, St Nicholas, Lincoln, 1955–59; Vicar, Crosby St George, Scunthorpe, 1959–73; St Hugh's Missioner, Lincoln Diocese, 1974–79; Bishops' Director of Clergy Training, London Diocese, 1979–85. *Recreation:* sculpture. *Address:* 5 Haffenden Road, Lincoln LN2 1RP. *T:* (01522) 531444.

**LAURENCE, Vice Adm. Sir Timothy (James Hamilton),** KCVO 2011 (MVO 1989); CB 2007; ADC(P) 2004; company director and adviser, since 2010; *b* 1 March 1955; *s* of late Guy Stewart Laurence and Barbara Alison Laurence (*née* Symons); *m* 1992, HRH The Princess Royal. *Educ:* Sevenoaks Sch.; Durham Univ. (BSc Geog.). Joined RN, 1973; in command: HMS Cygnet, 1979–80; HMS Boxer, 1989–91; MoD, 1992–95; in command: HMS Cumberland, 1995–96; HMS Montrose and 6th Frigate Sqdn, 1996–97; MoD, 1997–98; Hudson Vis. Fellow, St Antony's Coll., Oxford, 1999; Asst Comdt (Maritime), JSCSC, Shrivenham, 1999–2001; Dir, Navy Resources & Plans, MoD, 2001–04; ACDS (Resources and Plans), MoD, 2004–07; Chief Exec., Defence Estates, 2007–10; RN retd, 2010. Dir, Saturn Land, 2011–14; non-exec. Dir, Capita (P&I) (formerly Capita Symonds), 2011–14; Chairman: Dorchester Regeneration, 2011–; Major Projects Assoc., 2013–; Purfleet Centre Regeneration Ltd, 2014–; Sen. Advr, PA Consulting, 2011–15. Commissioner: CWGC, 2011–19 (Vice-Chm., 2016–19); English Heritage, 2011–15; Chm., English Heritage Trust, 2015–; Dir, HMS Victory Preservation Co., 2011–; Chm., Ops Commn, 2013–. Mem. Council, 2004–, Trustee, 2011–, RNLI; Pres., Craft Club, 2012–. Hon. Fellow, Nautical Inst., 2008–; Younger Brother, Trinity House, 2008–; Hon. MRICS 2009. Master, Coachmakers' and Coach Harness Makers' Co., 2010–11. *Recreation:* most sporting and outdoor activities. *Address:* c/o Buckingham Palace, SW1A 1AA.
*See also under Royal Family.*

**LAURENCE SMYTH, Liam Cledwyn;** Clerk of Legislation, House of Commons, since 2015; *b* 2 Sept. 1955; *s* of Wing Comdr William Laurence Smyth, MBE, RAF, retired, and late Joan Laurence Smyth (*née* Davies); *m* 1st, 1983, Helen Susan Elizabeth Kingham (marr. diss. 1988); one step *d*; 2nd, 1990, Sally Anne de Ste Croix (*née* Coussins); one *s*, and one step *s* one step *d*. *Educ:* Plymouth Coll.; New Coll., Oxford (Scholar; MA PPE). A Clerk, House of Commons, 1977–: Clerk: Social Security Cttee, 1994–99; Educn and Employment Cttee, 1999–2001; Educn and Skills Cttee, 2001–02; Delegated Legislation, 2003–05; Overseas Office, 2005–08; of Bills, 2008–09; of Journals, 2009–14; Acting Clerk of Legislation, 2014–15; Acting Clerk Asst, 2019. *Recreation:* Gascony in August. *Address:* Public Bill Office, House of Commons, SW1A 0AA. *T:* (020) 7219 3255.

**LAURENS, André Antoine;** Editor-in-Chief of Le Monde, 1982–84; *b* 7 Dec. 1934; married. Journalist: L'Eclaireur méridional, Montpellier, 1953–55; l'Agence centrale de la presse, Paris, 1958–62; joined Le Monde, 1963; Home Affairs reporter, 1969; Associate Editor, Home Affairs, 1979; Dir, 1982–85; Médiateur, 1992–96; Vice-Pres. Dir Gen. L'Indépendant du Midi, 2000–07; Vice-Pres., Directoire des Journaux du Midi (Midi-Libre, L'Indépendant, Centre Presse), 2004–07. Vice-Pres., Société des Rédacteurs. *Publications:* Les nouveaux communistes, 1972; D'une France à l'autre, 1974; Le métier politique, 1980.

**LAURENSON, James Tait;** Managing Director, Adam & Company Group, 1984–93 (founder Director and Deputy Chairman, 1983); Chairman, Adam & Company plc, 1985–93; *b* 15 March 1941; *s* of James Tait Laurenson, FRCS and Vera Dorothy Kidd; *m* 1969, Hilary Josephine Thompson (*d* 2009); one *s* three *d*. *Educ:* Eton; Magdalene College, Cambridge (MA). FCA. Ivory & Sime, investment managers, 1968–83, Partner 1970, Dir 1975; Tayburn Design Group: Man. Dir, 1983–84; Chm., 1984–89; Man. Dir, Hillhouse Investments Ltd, 1993–2005. Director: Alvis, 1971–95; ISIS (formerly I & S UK) Smaller Companies Trust, 1983–2005; The Life Association of Scotland, 1991–93; Fidelity Special Values, 1994–2005. Chairman: Hopetoun House Preservation Trust, 1999–2004; Hohepa Auckland Regl Bd, 2009–16; Helensville Birthing Trust, 2009–14; Governing Council, Erskine Stewart's Melville, 1994–99. *Recreations:* family, golf, gardening, New Zealand history. *Address:* Woodhill House, 38 Kaipara View Road, RD2, Helensville 0875, New Zealand. *T:* (9) 4207195. *Club:* Hon. Company of Edinburgh Golfers.

**LAURIE, Sir Andrew (Ronald Emilius),** 8th Bt *cr* 1834; *b* 20 Oct. 1944; *s* of Ronald Edward Laurie and Rosemary Lilian, *d* of John Gauld Fullerton; *S* cousin, 2017; *m* 1970, Sarah Anne, *e d* of Christopher Drew Patterson; two *s*. *Educ:* Repton; Trinity Coll., Oxford (MA). Engrg Manager, Grubb Parsons Ltd, 1968–76, 1982–85; Gen. Manager, Submarine Products Ltd, 1976–82; New Product Officer, Tyne and Wear Enterprise Trust, 1985–87; Chief Prodn Engr, Sevcon Ltd, 1987–2001; Project Engr, Darchem Aerospace Fabrications, 2001–02; Project Manager, The Engineering Business Ltd, 2002–09. *Heir:* *s* John Christopher Emilius Laurie [*b* 12 June 1971; *m* 1993, Lucie Françoise Géraldine, *y d* of Jean Wackermann; three *d*]. *Address:* 7 St Oswald's Road, Hexham, Northumberland NE46 2HF.

**LAURIE, (James) Hugh (Calum),** CBE 2018 (OBE 2007); actor, comedian, writer; *b* 11 June 1959; *s* of late Dr (William George) Ranald (Mundell) Laurie; *m* 1989, Jo Green; two *s* one *d*. *Educ:* Dragon Sch., Oxford; Eton Coll.; Selwyn Coll., Cambridge (Rowing Blue; Pres., Footlights). *Television series:* Alfresco, 1982–84; Blackadder II, 1985; Blackadder the Third, 1987; Blackadder Goes Forth, 1989; A Bit of Fry and Laurie, 1989–95; Jeeves and Wooster, 1990–92; All or Nothing at All; Fortysomething, 2003; House, 2005–12 (Best Actor, Golden Globes, 2006, 2007); Veep, 2015–17; Chance, 2016–17; *serial:* The Night Manager, 2016; Catch-22, 2019; *television film:* The Young Visiters, 2003; *films:* Plenty, 1985; Peter's Friends, 1992; Sense and Sensibility, 1996; 101 Dalmatians, 1996; Cousin Bette, 1998; Maybe Baby, 2000; Stuart Little, 2000; That Girl from Rio, 2001; Stuart Little 2, 2002; Flight of the Phoenix, 2003; Street Kings, 2008; The Oranges, 2012; *theatre:* Gasping, Theatre Royal, Haymarket, 1990. Blues albums: Let Them Talk, 2011; Didn't It Rain, 2013. *Publications:* The Gun Seller, 1996; Paper Soldiers, 2009. *Address:* Hamilton Hodell Ltd, 20 Golden Square, W1F 9JL. *T:* (020) 7636 1221.

**LAURIE, His Honour Robin;** a Circuit Judge, 1986–2003; a Deputy Circuit Judge, 2003–10; *b* 26 Jan. 1938; *s* of J. R. Laurie and Dr W. Metzner; *m* 1965, Susan Jane (*née* Snelling); two *d*. *Educ:* Fettes Coll.; Geneva Univ.; Jesus Coll., Oxford (MA). Called to the Bar, Inner Temple, 1961; practice at the Bar (South Eastern Circuit), 1961–86. Pres., later Tribunal Judge, Mental Health Rev. Tribunals (restricted patients panel), 1994–2010. *Recreations:* mountaineering, mycology. *Club:* Alpine.

**LAURITZEN, Prof. Steffen Lilholt;** Knight, Order of Dannebrog (Denmark), 1999; FRS 2011; Professor of Statistics, University of Oxford, 2004–14, now Emeritus; Fellow of Jesus College, Oxford, 2004–14, now Emeritus; Professor of Statistics, University of Copenhagen, since 2014; *b* Frederiksberg, Denmark, 22 April 1947; *m* 1967, Kirsten Bodil Larsen; three *d*. *Educ:* Univ. of Copenhagen (candidatus statisticae 1972; licentiatus statisticae 1975; dr scientiarum 1982); Univ. of Oxford (MA 2004). Lectr, Univ. of Copenhagen, 1972–81; Prof., 1981–2004, Adjunct Prof. of Statistics, 2015–, Univ. of Aalborg. *Publications:* Graphical Models, 1996; Thiele: pioneer in statistics, 2001; articles in learned jls. *Address:* Department of Mathematical Sciences, University of Copenhagen, Universitetsparken 5, 2100 Copenhagen, Denmark. *E:* lauritzen@math.ku.dk.

**LAUTENBERG, Alexis Peter;** Senior Advisor: Covington & Burling LLP, since 2018; Board, Swiss Finance Council, since 2018 (Chairman, 2014–18); *b* Zürich, 28 Oct. 1945; *s* of Anatole Lautenberg and Nelly Schnapper-Lautenberg; *m* 1972, Gabrielle Feik; one *s* two *d*. *Educ:* Univ. of Lausanne (BA Pol Sci.). Entered Swiss Diplomatic Service, 1974; Attaché, CSCE, Geneva and Stockholm, 1974–75; Dep. Hd of Mission, Warsaw, 1976; Mem., Swiss Delegn to EFTA and GATT, Geneva, 1977–81; Econ. Counsellor, Bonn, 1981–85; Dep. Dir of Internat. Orgns, Berne, 1985–86; Hd, Econ. and Finance Div., Fed. Dept of Foreign Affairs, Berne, 1986–93; Ambassador and Hd, Mission to EC, Brussels, 1993–99; Ambassador to Italy and Malta, in Rome, 1999–2004; Ambassador to the Court of St James's, 2004–10. Sen. Policy Advr, Steptoe & Johnson LLP, Brussels, 2010–16. Mem. Bd, Sisal SpA, Milano, 2011. Pres., British Swiss Chamber of Commerce, 2010–16. Chairman: Gp for negotiations on financial services during Uruguay Round, GATT, 1990–91; Financial Action Task Force on Money Laundering, OECD, 1991–92. Mem. Bd, Foundn for Res. in Internat. Banking and Finance, at Calif Univ., Riverside, 1987–94. Member, Board: Coll. of Europe, Bruges, 1994–99; Internat. Yehudi Menuhin Foundn, Brussels. *Recreations:* golf, ski-ing. *Club:* Athenæum.

**LAVELLE, Roger Garnett,** CB 1989; financial executive; Hon. Vice-President, European Investment Bank, since 1993 (Vice-President, 1989–93); *b* 23 Aug. 1932; *s* of Henry Allman Lavelle and Evelyn Alice Garnett; *m* 1956, Elsa Gunilla Odeberg; three *s* one *d*. *Educ:* Leighton Park; Trinity Hall, Cambridge (BA, LLB). Asst Principal, Min. of Health, 1955; Principal, HM Treasury, 1961; Special Assistant (Common Market) to Lord Privy Seal, 1961–63; Private Sec. to Chancellor of the Exchequer, 1965–68; Asst Secretary, 1968, Under Sec., 1975, Dep. Sec., 1985, HM Treasury; Dep. Sec., Cabinet Office, 1987. Dir, EBRD, 1993–2000. *Recreations:* music, gardening. *Address:* 36 Cholmeley Crescent, Highgate, N6 5HA. *T:* (020) 8340 4845.

**LAVENDER, Anuja Ravindra;** *see* Dhir, A. R.

**LAVENDER, Hon. Sir Nicholas,** Kt 2016; **Hon. Mr Justice Lavender;** a Judge of the High Court of Justice, Queen's Bench Division, since 2016; Presiding Judge, North Eastern Circuit, since 2019; *b* Barnsley, 7 Aug. 1964; *s* of Brian and Betty Lavender; *m* 2002, Anuja Ravindra Dhir, *qv*; two *s* one *d*. *Educ:* Queen Elizabeth Grammar Sch., Wakefield; Corpus Christi Coll., Cambridge (BA 1987); Oriel Coll., Oxford (BCL). Called to the Bar, Inner Temple, 1989; QC 2008; a Recorder, 2010–16; a Dep. High Court Judge, 2013–16. Chm., Bar Council, 2014 (Vice Chm., 2013). *Publications:* (ed jtly) Barristers, Vol. 3(1) of Halsbury's Laws of England, 2005. *Address:* Royal Courts of Justice, Strand, WC2A 2LL. *Clubs:* Garrick, MCC; Yorkshire County Cricket.

**LAVENDER, Dame Tina,** DBE 2012; PhD; Professor of Midwifery, since 2007, and Director, Centre for Global Women's Health, since 2013, University of Manchester; *m* Steve; one *s* one *d*. *Educ:* Roby Comp. Sch. RGN 1987; RM 1990; MSc 1995; PhD 1999. Clinical midwife, Oxford Street and Mill Lane Maternity Hosps; Prof. of Midwifery and Women's Health, Univ. of Central Lancashire; Hon. Consultant Midwife: Liverpool Women's Hosp.; St Mary's Hosp., Manchester. Vis. Prof., Univ. of Nairobi. Advr, WHO. Co-ed. in Chief, Brit. Jl of Midwifery; Associate Ed., African Jl of Midwifery and Women's Health. Hon. Fellow, Royal Coll. of Midwives. *Publications:* articles in jls. *Address:* School of Nursing, Midwifery and Social Work, University of Manchester, Jean McFarlane Building, University Place, Oxford Road, Manchester M13 9PL.

**LAVER, Gillian Margaret;** *b* 10 Jan. 1949; *d* of Alfred Robert Mansbridge and Doris Edna Mansbridge; *m* 1999, Barry Charles Laver. *Educ:* Horsham High Sch. for Girls; Univ. of Keele (BA Hons 1971). CA 1977. Sen. Consultant, Strategy Div., PA Management Consultants, 1986–89; Finance Dir, Wedgwood Div., Waterford Wedgwood plc, 1989–94; Gp Finance and IT Dir, GEC Avery Ltd, 1994–98; Nat. Dir of Finance, Eversheds, 1998–2000; Cogenza Consulting Ltd, 2001–05; Dir of Finance and Central Services, Archbishops' Council, 2005–06. Non-executive Director and Chairman, Audit Committee: W Midlands Strategic HA, 2006–10; Nat. Treatment Agency for Substance Misuse, 2009–13. Chm., Adv. Cttee on Clinical Excellence Awards, W Midlands Region, 2008–. Member: Auditing Practices Bd, 2001–06; Audit Cttee, Arts Council England, 2004–10; Council, Univ. of Keele, 2009–10; Ind. Mem., Audit and Governance Cttee, Human Fertilisation and Embryology Authy, 2013–18. Trustee and Hon. Treas., Diabetes UK, 2001–05. *Recreations:* tennis, golf, bridge, gardening, music.

**LAVER, Prof. John David Michael Henry,** CBE 1999; FBA 1990; FRSE; Emeritus Professor of Speech Sciences, Queen Margaret University (formerly Queen Margaret University College) (Research Professor, 2001–04, Vice-Principal, 2002–03, Deputy Principal, 2003–04); *b* 20 Jan. 1938; *s* of Harry Frank Laver and Mary Laver; *m* 1st, 1961, Avril Morna Anel Macqueen Gibson; two *s* one *d*; 2nd, 1974, Sandra Traill; one *s*. *Educ:* Churcher's Coll., Petersfield; RAF Coll., Cranwell; Univ. of Edinburgh (MA Hons Postgrad. Dip. in Phonetics; PhD; DLitt). Asst Lectr and Lectr in Phonetics, Univ. of Ibadan, 1963–66; University of Edinburgh: Lectr, Sen. Lectr, Reader in Phonetics, 1966–85; Prof. of Phonetics, 1985–2000; Dir, 1984–89, Chm., 1989–94, Centre for Speech Technology Research; Associate Dean, Faculty of Arts, 1989–92; Vice-Principal, 1994–97. Pres., Internat. Phonetic Assoc., 1991–95 (Mem. Council, 1986–); Member: Board, European Speech Communication Assoc., 1988–92; Council, Philological Soc., 1994–97; Council, British Acad., 1998–2001 (Chm., Humanities Res. Bd, 1994–98); Board of Governors: Edinburgh Univ. Press, 1999–2000; Caledonian Res. Foundn, 1999–2006; Chm., Bd of Governance, Trinity Long Room Hub, Trinity Coll. Dublin, 2008–10. FRSE 1994 (Vice-Pres., 1996–99; Fellowship Sec., 1999–2002; Bicentenary Medal, 2004; Royal Medal, 2007); Fellow, Inst. of Acoustics, 1988–2001. Hon. FRCSLT 2003. Hon. DLitt: Sheffield, 1999; De Montfort, 1999; Queen Margaret UC, 2006; Hon. LittD Trinity Coll. Dublin, 2013. *Publications:* Communication in Face to Face Interaction, 1972; Phonetics in Linguistics, 1973; The Phonetic Description of Voice Quality, 1980; The Cognitive Representation of Speech, 1981; Aspects of Speech Technology, 1988; The Gift of Speech, 1991; Principles of Phonetics, 1994; The Handbook of Phonetic Sciences, 1997, 2nd edn 2010. *Recreations:* reading, birdwatching, lexicography.

**LAVERCOMBE, Dr Brian James;** Honorary Member, British Council, since 1997 (Regional Director for the Americas, 1994–96); *b* 17 Dec. 1938; *s* of Ralph Lavercombe and Doris (*née* Hawkins); *m* 1966, Margaret Jane Chambers; one *s* one *d*. *Educ:* Barnstaple Grammar Sch.; Imperial Coll., London (BSc Hons Physics, ARCS, MSc, DIC, PhD 1966); Reading Univ. (MA Medieval Studies 2001). Post-doctoral Fellow and Asst Prof. in Residence, UCLA, 1966–68; British Council: Science Officer: Chile, 1968–72; Spain, 1972–77; Israel, 1977–80; Projects Officer, Science and Technol. Div., 1980–81; Dir, Science Dept, 1981–84; Rep., Colombia, 1984–87; Dep. Controller, Sci., Technol. and Educn Div., 1987–90; Dir, Mexico, 1990–94. Advr, Earthwatch, 1997–2002. *Publications:*

papers on scientific co-operation and technology transfer; research papers in Nature and Accoustica; articles on ornithology. *Recreations:* cricket, ornithology, painting, mediaeval history. *Address:* 37 Playfield Road, Kennington, Oxford OX1 5RS. *T:* (01865) 739659. *Club:* Isis Probus (Oxford).

**LAVERICK, David John;** Principal Judge, First-tier Tribunal, Local Government Standards in England, 2010–17; *b* 3 Aug. 1945; *s* of Wilfred Henry Laverick and I. M. Doreen Laverick (*née* Lockhart); *m* 1968, Margaret Elizabeth Myatt; three *s*. *Educ:* Sir William Turner's Sch., Redcar; King's Coll. London (LLB Hons 1967); Coll. of Law. Admitted solicitor, 1970; Asst Solicitor, Beds and Lincs CC, 1970–73; Dir of Admin, E Lindsey DC, 1973–75; Dir, Local Govt Ombudsman Service, 1975–95; Chief Exec., Family Health Services Appeal Authy, 1995–2001; Pensions Ombudsman, 2001–07; Pres., Adjudication Panel for England, 2001–10. Legal Mem., Mental Health Rev. Tribunals, 1999–2002. *Recreations:* Scottish country dancing, guide dogs.

**LAVERS, Richard Douglas;** HM Diplomatic Service, retired; Ambassador to Guatemala, 2001–06, and concurrently non-resident Ambassador to El Salvador, 2003–06 and to Honduras, 2004–06; *b* Nairobi, 10 May 1947; *s* of Douglas Arthur Lavers and Edyth Agnes (*née* Williams); *m* 1986, Brigitte Anne Julia Maria Moers, *e d* of late Robert Moers, Turnhout, Belgium; two *s*. *Educ:* Hurstpierpoint Coll.; Exeter Coll., Oxford (MA). Joined HM Diplomatic Service, 1969; Third Sec., Buenos Aires, 1970–72; second, later First Sec., Wellington, 1973–76; FCO, 1976–81; First Sec., Pol and Econ., Brussels, 1981–85; on secondment to Guinness Mahon, 1985–87; FCO, 1987–89; NATO Defence Coll., Rome, 1989; Dep. Hd of Mission and HM Consul General, Santiago, 1990–93; Ambassador to Ecuador, 1993–97; FCO, 1997–99; Hd of Research Analysts, FCO, 1999–2001. Non-exec. Dir, PetroLatina, 2006–07; Dir, FORO Consulting, 2011–14. Chairman: Anglo-Ecuadorian Soc., 2007–12; Anglo-Central American Soc., 2008–12. Vis. Res. Fellow, Inst. of Latin American Studies, 2001. *Recreations:* books, pictures, travel, fishing, golf. *Club:* Oxford and Cambridge.

**LAVERTY, Ashley;** *see* Page, Ashley.

**LAVERY, Gerald,** CBE 2016; Senior Finance Director, Department of Agriculture and Rural Development, Northern Ireland, 2013–15; *b* 9 April 1952; *s* of David and Mary Lavery; *m* 2002, Kathy McClurg; one *s* two *d*. *Educ:* Christian Brothers' Grammar Sch., Belfast; Queen's Univ., Belfast (BA Hons Italian Lang. and Lit. 1974). Joined NI Civil Service, 1974; Dept of Manpower Services, 1974–81; Dept of Econ. Develt, 1982–89; Trng and Employment Agency, 1990; NI Office, 1991–94; Sen. Civil Service, 1995; Department of Agriculture and Rural Development, 1995–: Fisheries Sec., 1996–2000; Finance Dir, 2000–03; Sen. Finance Dir, 2003–10; Permanent Sec., 2010–13. Mem., CAP Conciliation Body, 2016–19. *Recreations:* prayer and Christian life, choral singing, keeping fit, enjoyment of all arts. *Address:* 26 Ravara Dale, Ballygowan, Newtownards BT23 6HP.

**LAVERY, Ian;** MP (Lab) Wansbeck, since 2010; *b* Newcastle upon Tyne, 6 Jan. 1963; *s* of John Robert Lavery and Patricia Lavery; *m* 1986, Hilary Baird; two *s*. *Educ:* New Coll., Durham (HNC Mining Engrg). Miner, National Coal Board: Lynemouth Colliery, 1980; Ellington Colliery, 1981–92; National Union of Mineworkers: Mem., Nat. Exec. Cttee, 1992–2010; Gen. Sec., Northumberland Area, 1992–2002; Pres., 2002. Mem. (Lab) Wansbeck DC, 1995–2002. Shadow Minister for Cabinet Office, 2015–17; Co-Nat. Campaign Co-ordinator and Chair, Labour Party, 2017–. Member, Select Committee: on NI Affairs, 2010–11; on Regulatory Reform, 2010–15; on Energy and Climate Change, 2010–15. *Address:* House of Commons, SW1A 0AA.

**LAVERY, Dr Kevin Gregory;** Chief Executive, Wellington City Council, New Zealand, since 2013; *b* Newcastle upon Tyne, 9 May 1960; *s* of Matthew and Kathleen Lavery; *m* 1986, Catherine Wilkey; two *s*. *Educ:* Manchester Univ. (BA Hons); Kent Univ. (PhD 1987); Univ. of Southern Calif (Harkness Fellow). Graduate trainee, Assoc. of Dist Councils, 1984–86; Gen. Asst to Chief Exec., London Bor. of Bexley, 1986–87; Corporate Policy Manager, Kent CC, 1987–91; Hd of Corporate Team, City of Westminster, 1991–93; Sen. Manager, Price Waterhouse, 1993–97; Chief Executive Officer: City of Newcastle upon Tyne, 1997–2001; Agilisys, 2001–03; Man. Dir, Enterprise plc, 2004–05; Dir, BT Local and Regl Govt, 2005–06; CEO, Serco Solutions, 2006–08; Chief Exec., Cornwall Council (formerly Cornwall CC), 2008–13. *Publications:* Smart Contracting for Local Government, 1999. *Recreations:* running, watching Newcastle United. *Address:* Wellington City Council, 101 Wakefield Street, PO Box 2199, Wellington 6140, New Zealand. *T:* (4) 8013462. *E:* Kevin.Lavery@wcc.govt.nz. *Club:* Lansdowne.

**LAVIE, Prof. Nilli,** PhD; FBA 2016; Professor of Psychology and Brain Sciences, Institute of Cognitive Neuroscience, University College London, since 2004; *b* Tel Aviv; *d* of Samuel Lavie and Ilana Lavie; *m* 1995, Prof. Jonathon Stevens Driver, FBA (*d* 2011); two *s*. *Educ:* Tel Aviv Univ. (BA Psychol. 1987; BA Philos. 1987; PhD Cognitive Psychol. 1993). Res. Fellow, Miller Inst., Univ. of Calif, Berkeley, 1993–94; Res. Scientist, MRC Applied Psychol. Unit, Cambridge, 1994–96; Lectr, 1996–2001, Reader, 2001–03, Psychol. Dept, UCL. *Publications:* over 100 articles in learned jls incl. Science, Nature Neurosci., Philosophical Trans. of Royal Soc., Psychol Sci., Jl of Neurosci., Current Biology, Neuropsychologia. *Recreations:* keeping fit, fine dining, spending time with my boys, following advanced technology news, sunny breaks. *Address:* Institute of Cognitive Neuroscience, University College London, 17 Queen Square, WC1N 3AR. *E:* n.lavie@ucl.ac.uk.

**LAVIGNE, Marc T.;** *see* Tessier-Lavigne.

**LAVIN, Deborah Margaret;** Principal, Trevelyan College, 1980–95 (Hon. Fellow, 1997), Principal-elect of new college, 1995–97, and President, Howlands Trust, 1993–97, University of Durham; *b* 22 Sept. 1939. *Educ:* Roedean Sch., Johannesburg, SA; Rhodes Univ., Grahamstown, SA; Lady Margaret Hall, Oxford (MA, DipEd). Asst Lectr, Dept of History, Univ. of the Witwatersrand, 1962–64; Lectr, 1965–78, Sen. Lectr, 1978–80, Dept of Mod. Hist., The Queen's Univ. of Belfast. Sen. Associate, St Antony's Coll., Oxford, 2001–. Trustee: Westlakes Research Ltd, 1995–2001; UK Friends of South African Peace Quartet Trust, 2013–; Quartet of Peace Trust (UK), 2013–. Chm., East Hendred Heritage Trust, 2005–. Member: Council, Benenden Sch., 1998–2009; Ct of Govs, Truro Coll., 2005–09. Hon. Life Mem., Nat. Maritime Mus. Cornwall, 2003–. Assoc. Fellow, RIIA, 1997–2000. *Publications:* South African Memories, 1979; The Making of the Sudanese State, 1990; The Transformation of the Old Order in the Sudan, 1993; From Empire to International Commonwealth: a biography of Lionel Curtis, 1995; Friendship and Union: the South African correspondence of Patrick Duncan and Lady Maud Selborne, 1907–1943, 2010; articles in learned jls. *Recreations:* the arts, gardening, tennis. *Address:* 20 Penstones Court, Marlborough Lane, Stanford in the Vale, Faringdon, Oxon SN7 8SW. *T:* (01367) 718264. *Club:* Reform.

**LAVOIE, Judith Anne, (Mrs A. R. Lavoie);** *see* LaRocque, J. A.

**LAW,** family name of **Barons Coleraine** and **Ellenborough**.

**LAW, Andrew Jonathan Parker;** Executive Chairman, SuperCommunications, 2014–15; Director, Parity Group plc, 2014–15; *b* Bromley, 25 May 1956; *s* of Peter Leslie Law and Audrey Iris Law; *m* 2015, Alessandra Lemma; one *s* two *d*, and one step *s*. *Educ:* Portsmouth Grammar Sch.; Univ. of Bristol (BA Jt Hons Classics 1978). Dir, Collett Dickenson Pearce, 1982–89; CEO/Business Develt Dir, Chiat/Day, London, 1990–95; Founder and Chairman: St Luke's, 1995–2003; The Law Firm, 2003–12; Chm., Fearlessly Frank, 2012–14. Entrepreneur of the Year, Ernst & Young, 2003. *Publications:* Open Minds, 1998; Experiment at Work, 2003; Implosion, 2013; Upgraded: how the Internet has modernised the human race, 2016. *Recreations:* Latin, Greek, ancient history, Italy.

**LAW, Prof. Catherine Mary,** CBE 2014 (OBE 1999); MD; FRCP, FRCPCH; FMedSci; Professor of Public Health and Epidemiology, UCL Great Ormond Street Institute of Child Health (formerly Institute of Child Health), since 2007, and Vice Dean Research, Faculty of Population Health Sciences, since 2018, University College London; *b* Northampton, 26 Oct. 1954; *d* of Thomas and Margaret Law; *m* 1983, Colin Kennedy; two *s*. *Educ:* Eggars Grammar Sch., Alton, Hants; London Hosp. Med. Coll., Univ. of London (MB BS 1979; MD 1989). MRCP 1981, FRCP 1996; MFPHM 1991, FFPH 2001; FRCPCH 1997. Jun. doctor, various London hosps, 1979–82; Lectr, Inst. of Child Health, 1983–85; Res. Fellow, Johns Hopkins Sch. of Hygiene and Public Health, Baltimore, 1985–87; Sen. Res. Fellow, 1987–92, Sen. Lectr, 1992–2003, Univ. of Southampton Med. Sch.; Consultant in Public Health Medicine, Wessex RHA, 1992–97; Reader in Children's Health, Inst. of Child Health, subseq. Inst. of Child Health, University Coll. London, 2003–07. Hon. Consultant, Gt Ormond St Hosp. for Children NHS Foundn Trust, 2003–. Prog. Dir, NIHR Public Health Res. Prog., 2008–14. Chair, Public Health Adv. Cttee, NICE, 2005–15. FMedSci 2015. *Publications:* contrib. scientific papers on epidemiol. and public health to peer-reviewed jls. *Recreations:* gardening, watching Southampton Football Club, sailing, reading, feeling guilty. *Address:* UCL Great Ormond Street Institute of Child Health, 30 Guilford Street, WC1N 1EH. *T:* (020) 7905 2304. *E:* catherine.law@ucl.ac.uk.

**LAW, Christopher Murray Alexander;** MP (SNP) Dundee West, since 2015; *b* Edinburgh, 21 Oct. 1969; *s* of John and Jean Law. *Educ:* Madras Coll., St Andrews; Dundee Coll. of Further Educn (C&G Catering); Univ. of St Andrews (MA 1st Cl. Hons Social Anthropol.; postgrad. dip. in IT). Raleigh Internat., Namibia; organiser, motorbike expeditions in Himalayas; proprietor, Freewheeling Tours; businessman in financial sector. SNP spokesperson on Internat. Develt, 2017–, on Climate Justice, 2017–. Member: Scottish Affairs Cttee, 2015–17; Internat. Develt Cttee, 2017–; Vice Chm., All Party Parly Gp on Canada, 2015–, on Wine and Spirits, 2015–, on Whisky, 2015–, on Tibet, on Motorcycles, on Digital Economy. *Recreations:* reading, travel, motorcycles. *Address:* (office) 2 Marshall Street, Lochee, Dundee DD2 3BR. *T:* (01382) 848906. *E:* chris.law.mp@parliament.uk.

**LAW, Prof. Colin Nigel,** PhD; Head of Laboratory, Cambridge Laboratory, Institute of Plant Science Research, John Innes Centre, Norwich, 1989–92; *b* 18 Nov. 1932; *s* of Joseph and Dorothy Mildred Law; *m* 1964, Angela Patricia Williams; three *d*. *Educ:* Queen Elizabeth's Grammar Sch., Blackburn; Univ. of Birmingham (BSc Hons Genetics); UCW, Aberystwyth (PhD). Nat. Service, RA, 1955–57. Res. worker, Plant Breeding Inst., Cambridge, 1960–87, Head of Cytogenetics Dept, 1972–87; Divl Head, Plant Genetics and Breeding, Inst. of Plant Sci. Res., 1987–89. Sen. Foreign Res. Fellow, Nat. Sci. Foundn, N Dakota State Univ., 1969. Hon. Prof., Univ. of East Anglia, 1990–. Prix Assinsel, Assoc. Internationale des Sélectionneurs, 1982. *Publications:* papers and articles on chromosome manipulation techniques to identify genes of agric. importance in crop plants, esp. wheat; genetic control of cereal plant responses to envmtl stress, particularly salinity. *Recreations:* fishing, painting. *Address:* 41 Thornton Close, Girton, Cambridge CB3 0NF. *T:* (01223) 276554.

**LAW, (David) Jude;** actor; *b* 29 Dec. 1972; *s* of Peter Law and Maggie Law; *m* 1997, Sadie Frost (marr. diss. 2003); two *s* one *d*; *m* 2019, Phillipa Coan. *Educ:* Alleyn's Sch., Dulwich. Co-founder and Dir, Natural Nylon, prodn co., 2000–03. *Theatre includes:* Les Parents Terribles, NT, 1994; Death of a Salesman, W Yorks Playhouse; Ion, Royal Court, 1995; 'Tis a Pity She's a Whore, 1999, Doctor Faustus, 2002, Young Vic; Hamlet, Wyndham's Th., transf. NY, 2009; Anna Christie, Donmar Warehouse, 2011; Henry V, Noël Coward, 2013; Obsession, Barbican, 2017. *Films include:* Shopping, 1994; Gattaca, Wilde, Midnight in the Garden of Good and Evil, Bent, 1997; Music From Another Room, Final Cut, The Wisdom of Crocodiles, 1998; eXistenZ, The Talented Mr Ripley (Best Supporting Actor, BAFTA, 2000), 1999; Love, Honour and Obey, 2000; Enemy at the Gates, A. I. Artificial Intelligence, 2001; Road to Perdition, 2002; Cold Mountain, 2003; I Heart Huckabees, (also prod.) Sky Captain and the World of Tomorrow, Alfie, 2004; Closer, The Aviator, 2005; All The King's Men, Breaking and Entering, The Holiday, 2006; Sleuth, 2007; My Blueberry Nights, 2008; The Imaginarium of Dr Parnassus, Sherlock Holmes, 2009; Repo Men, 2010; Contagion, Sherlock Holmes: A Game of Shadows, 2011; 360, 2012; Anna Karenina, 2012; Side Effects, Dom Hemingway, 2013; The Grand Budapest Hotel, Black Sea, 2014; Genius, 2016; King Arthur: legend of the sword, 2017; Fantastic Beasts: the crimes of Grindelwald, 2018; Captain Marvel, Vox Lux, 2019. *TV series:* The Young Pope, 2016. Chevalier des Arts et des Lettres (France), 2007; Variety Award, BIFA, 2012. *Address:* c/o Julian Belfrage Associates, 3rd Floor, 9 Argyll Street, W1F 7TG.

**LAW, Prof. Malcolm Ross,** FRCP, FFPH, FMedSci; Professor of Epidemiology and Preventive Medicine, Wolfson Institute of Preventive Medicine, Barts and The London, Queen Mary's School of Medicine and Dentistry, since 2001; *b* 9 May 1946; *s* of Harold Palmer Law and Jessie Maud Law; *m* 1976, Amelia Anne McRedmond; one *s*. *Educ:* Adelaide High Sch.; Univ. of Adelaide (MB BS 1970; MSc 1984). MRCP, FRCP 1995; FFPH 2002. Jun. med. posts, Adelaide, London and Cardiff, 1971–78; Lectr and Sen. Registrar, Royal Brompton Hosp., London, 1979–83; Lectr, 1984–87, Sen. Lectr, 1987–94, Reader, 1994–2001, in Epidemiology and Preventive Medicine, Wolfson Inst. of Preventive Medicine, Barts and The London, Queen Mary's Sch. of Medicine and Dentistry. FMedSci 2006. *Publications:* contrib. to learned jls on prevention of cardiovascular disease by drugs and diet. *Address:* Wolfson Institute of Preventive Medicine, Barts and The London, Queen Mary's School of Medicine and Dentistry, Charterhouse Square, EC1M 6BQ. *T:* (020) 7882 6268.

**LAW, Patricia;** Member (Ind) Blaenau Gwent, National Assembly for Wales, June 2006–2011; *m* 1976, Peter John Law, MP (*d* 2006); two *s* three *d*. *Educ:* Glanyravon Secondary Modern Sch.; Ebbw Vale Coll. Former Nursing Asst, Gwent Healthcare NHS Trust.

**LAW, Prof. Robin Christopher Charles,** PhD; FBA 2000; FRSE; FRHistS; Professor of African History, Stirling University, 1993–2009, now Emeritus; *b* 7 Aug. 1944. *Educ:* Balliol Coll., Oxford (BA 1st cl. Hons Lit.Hum. 1966); PhD (Hist. and African Studies) Birmingham 1971. Res. Asst to Dir of African Studies, Lagos Univ., 1966–69; Res. Fellow, Centre of W African Studies, Birmingham Univ., 1970–72; Stirling University: Lectr in Hist., 1972–78; Sen. Lectr, 1978–83; Reader, 1983–93. Visiting posts: Ilorin Univ., Nigeria, 1978; Leiden Univ., Netherlands, 1993–94; York Univ., Canada, 1996–97; Hebrew Univ. of Jerusalem, 2000–01; Vis. Prof., Sch. of History, Univ. of Liverpool, 2008, now Hon. Sen. Res. Fellow. FRHistS 1997; FRSE 2002. UK Distinguished Africanist

Award, African Studies Assoc. of UK, 2010. *Publications:* The Oyo Empire c1600–c1836, 1977; The Horse in West African History, 1980; The Slave Coast of West Africa 1550–1750, 1991; (ed) From Slave Trade to Legitimate Commerce: the commercial transition in 19th century West Africa, 1995; (with Paul Lovejoy) The Biography of Mahommah Gardo Baquaqua, 2001; Ouidah: the social history of a West African slaving 'port' 1727–1892, 2004. *Address:* History and Politics Division, Stirling University, Stirling FK9 4LA.

**LAW, Roger,** RDI 2000; artist and caricaturist; *b* 6 Sept. 1941; *m* 1960, Deirdre Amsden; one *s* one *d. Educ:* Littleport Secondary Mod. Sch.; Cambridge Sch. of Art (expelled 1960). Cartoonist and illustrator, The Observer, 1962–65; illustrator, Sunday Times, 1965–67; Artist in Residence, Reed Coll., Oregon, and first puppet film, 1967; freelance illustrator, Pushpin Studios, NY, 1968–69; caricaturist and features editor, Sunday Times, 1971–75; with Peter Fluck: formed Luck & Flaw, 1976; founder, Spitting Image, 1982 (first series televised, 1984, 18th series, 1996); Creative Dir, Spitting Image Productions Ltd, 1983–97; first American show for NBC TV, 1986; TV series, The Winjin' Pom, 1991; presenter of radio programmes including: Nasty, Brutish and Short: the History of Mr Punch, 1997; Spitting Images, Art Made in China, 2008; Whatever Happened to the Teapots?, 2009; Spitting in Russian, The Secrets of the Art and the Artist Caravaggio, Archive on 4: Satire the Great British Tradition, I'm a Celebrity Get Me Into Here, 2010; The New Silk Road, Roger's Rabbits, 2011; Roger Law and the Chinese Curiosities, 2012; South Africa Spits Back, 2013; Wow! How Did They Do That?, 2013; Art & Seoul, BBC Radio 4, 2015; Roger Law and the Giant Pot, BBC Radio 4, 2017. Artist in residence, Nat. Art Sch., Sydney, 1998; film, Potshots, 1999; TV film, Arena: whatever happened to Spitting Image, 2014. Major installation for Barbican art gall., 1992; ceramic exhibitions with Janice Tchalenko: V&A, 1993; Richard Dennis Gall., 1996; puppet installation, RA, 1997; gp exhibn, Porcelain City: Jingdezhen, V&A, 2011; Her Maj - 60 Years of Unofficial Portraits of the Queen, Cartoon Mus., 2012; Spitting Image, From Start to Finish, Cartoon Mus., 2014; Internat. Art Fair for Contemp. Objects, Saatchi Gall., 2018; Laughing Matters: The State of a Nation, V&A, 2018; one-man exhibitions: Aussie Stuff, Hossack Gall., 2000; The Land of Oz, Fine Art Soc., 2005; Travelling Light, Mary Place Gall., Sydney, 2012; Roger Law - Porcelain, Sladmore Contemporary Gall., 2014; retrospective exhibn, Still Spitting at Sixty, Newsroom Archive and Visitor Centre, 2005; exhibn with Stephen Bird, Transported, Scottish Gall., 2016; Roger Law: from satire to ceramics, Sainsbury Centre for Visual Arts, 2017; Roger Law: drawings and ceramics, Sladmore Contemp. Gall., 2017; work in collections: V&A Mus., British Council, 1993; Norwich Castle Mus., 1995; Print Collection of Nat. Gall. of Australia, 2008. Spitting Image Archive on loan, Cambridge Univ. Liby, 2018. Mem., AGI, 1993; Fellow, Internat. Specialised Skills, Melbourne, 1997. Hon. FRCA 2004. Hon. DLitt Loughborough, 1999. DAAD Award, 1967; Assoc. of Illustrators Award (to Luck & Flaw), 1984; BPG TV Award for Best Light Entertainment Prog., 1984; DAAD Award (to Luck and Flaw), 1984; Internat. Emmy Award (for Spitting Image), 1986; Grammy Award, 1987; Emmy Award (for Peter and the Wolf), 1994; Lifetime Achievement Award, Cartoon Art Trust, 1998. *Publications:* The Appallingly Disrespectful Spitting Image Book, 1985; Spitting Images, 1987; The Spitting Image Giant Komic Book, 1988; (with L. Chester) A Nasty Piece of Work, 1992; Goodbye, 1992; Thatcha: the real Maggie memoirs, 1993; Still Spitting at Sixty (autobiog.), 2005; illustrator with Peter Fluck: A Christmas Carol, 1979; Treasure Island, 1986. *Recreation:* making mischief.

**LAWES, Glenville Richard;** Director, Robert Jones and Agnes Hunt Orthopaedic Hospital Foundation Trust, 2009–13; *b* 28 May 1945; *s* of Eric Lawes and Phyllis (née Witchalls); *m* 1969, Isobel Prescott Thomas; one *s* two *d. Educ:* Univ. of Birmingham (BSc Eng). Technol. Editor, New Scientist, 1967–70; HM Diplomatic Service, 1970–80: served Moscow, Geneva and Paris; First Sec., FCO, 1976; with British Petroleum Co. plc, 1980–91; Sen. Analyst, BP Internat., 1980–86; Gen. Manager, BP Middle East, 1986–90; Regl Manager, BP Oil Internat., 1990–91. Chief Exec., Ironbridge Gorge Mus. Trust, 1991–2006; Mem. Bd, MLA, 2009–12 (Chm, W Midlands MLA, 2006–09). FRSA 1999. *Recreations:* music, reading, theatre, renovating old houses. *Address:* 10 Church Street, Bathford, Bath BA1 7TU. *E:* glenlawes@btopenworld.com.

**LAWES, William Patrick Lagan;** Managing Director, Lazard & Co. Ltd, since 2017; *b* Swanage, Dorset, 2 Jan. 1964; *s* of Colin Lawes and Paddy Lawes (née Lagan); *m* 1995, Rebecca Yongman; three *s* one *d. Educ:* Victoria Univ., Wellington (LLB Hons); Gonville and Caius Coll., Cambridge (LLM 1986). Law Clerk, NZ Court of Appeal and the High Court, Wellington, 1984–85; Freshfields, later Freshfields Bruckhaus Deringer, 1986–2017: Partner, 1994–2017; Sen. Partner, 2011–15. Vis. Fellow, Centre for Corporate Reputation, Univ. of Oxford, 2008–. Mem., Soc. of Merchants Trading to the Continent, 2007–. *Recreations:* golf, sailing, ski-ing, Real tennis. *Clubs:* Hurlingham; Brancaster Golf, Berkshire Golf, Royal Worlington Golf, Royal North Devon Golf.

**LAWLER, Geoffrey John;** Managing Director, The Public Affairs Company (GB) Ltd (formerly Lawler Associates), since 1987; Vice-President, International Access Inc., 1987–94; *b* 30 Oct. 1954; *s* of late Major Ernest Lawler, RAEC and Enid Lawler; *m* 1989, Christine (marr. diss. 1998), *d* of Carl Roth, Cheyenne, Wyoming. *Educ:* Richmond Sch., N Yorks; Hull Univ. (BSc (Econ); Pres., Students' Union, 1976–77). Trainee chartered accountant, 1977–78. Community Affairs Dept, 1978–80, Research Dept, 1980–82, Cons. Central Office; Public Relations Exec., 1982–83; Dir, publicity co., 1983. Contested (C) Bradford N, 1987. MP (C) Bradford N, 1983–87. EC Observer for Russian elections, 1993, 1995, 1996, for Liberian election, 1997; UN Observer for S African elections, 1994; OSCE Observer, Ukraine, 2014, Bosnia, 2018. Dir, Democracy Internat. Ltd, 1995–2006. Mem. Council, UKIAS, 1987–93. Hon. Pres., British Youth Council, 1983–87; Pres., W Yorks Youth Assoc., 1995–2004 (Vice-Pres., 1986–95). *Recreations:* cricket, music, travel. *Address:* Public Affairs Company (GB) Ltd, Castlehill House, 21 Otley Road, Leeds LS6 3AA.

**LAWLER, His Honour Simon William;** QC 1993; a Circuit Judge, 2002–16; *b* 26 March 1949; *s* of Maurice Rupert Lawler and Daphne Lawler (née Elkins); *m* 1985, Josephine Sallie Day; two *s. Educ:* Winchester County Secondary Sch.; Peter Symonds, Winchester; Univ. of Hull (LLB Hons). Called to the Bar, Inner Temple, 1971; in practice at the Bar, 1972–2002; Asst Recorder, 1983–89; a Recorder, 1989–2002. A Pres., Mental Health Rev. Tribunal, 2002–07. *Recreations:* cricket, gardening, opera, wine.

**LAWLEY, Susan, (Sue),** OBE 2001; broadcaster, since 1970; *b* 14 July 1946; *d* of late Thomas Clifford and Margaret Jane Lawley; *m* 1st, 1975, David Ashby (marr. diss. 1985); one *s* one *d*; 2nd, 1987, Hugh Williams. *Educ:* Dudley Girls' High Sch., Worcs; Bristol Univ. (BA Hons Modern Languages). Thomson Newspapers' graduate trainee, Western Mail and South Wales Echo, Cardiff, 1967–70; BBC Plymouth: sub-editor/reporter/presenter, 1970–72; presenter, BBC Television: Nationwide, 1972–75; Tonight, 1975–76; Nationwide, 1977–83; Nine O'Clock News, 1983–84; Six O'Clock News, 1984–88; Here and Now, 1995–97; Presenter, Desert Island Discs, BBC Radio Four, 1988–2006; Chair, Reith Lectures, BBC, annually, 2001–18. Board Member: English Tourism Council, 2000–03; ENO, 2001–05. Hon. LLD Bristol 1989; Hon. MA Birmingham, 1989; Hon. DLitt CNAA, 1991. *Publications:* Desert Island Discussions, 1989. *Recreations:* family, walking, golf, bridge. *Address:* c/o BBC, Broadcasting House, W1A 1AA.

**LAWRANCE, Cynthia;** *see* Lawrance, J. C.

**LAWRANCE, Prof. Jeremy Norcliffe Haslehurst,** DPhil; FBA 2011; Professor of Spanish Golden Age Studies, University of Nottingham, since 2006; *b* Jinja, Uganda, 12 Dec. 1952; *s* of Jeremy Charles Dalton Lawrance and Elizabeth Ann Lawrance; *m* 1975, Martha María de las Mercedes Camargo Álvarez; one *d. Educ:* King's Sch., Canterbury; Balliol Coll., Oxford (MA 1978; DPhil 1983). Fellow, Magdalen Coll., Oxford, 1978–85; University of Manchester: Lectr in Spanish, 1985–93; Prof. of Spanish, 1993–2006. Pres., Assoc. of Hispanists of GB and Ire., 2004–06. *Publications:* (ed and trans. with Anthony Pagden) Francisco de Vitoria: political writings, 1991; (ed and trans. with Brian Tate) Alfonso de Palencia: Gesta Hispaniensia, vol. 1, 1998, vol. 2, 1999; Spanish Conquest, Protestant Prejudice: Las Casas and the Black Legend, 2009; approx. 60 articles in learned jls. *Recreations:* searching for stone circles with daughter, entertaining friends, evading capture by elephants, loud music, geriatric football, Bologna. *Address:* School of Cultures, Languages and Area Studies, University of Nottingham, Nottingham NG7 2RD. *E:* jeremy.lawrance@nottingham.ac.uk.

**LAWRANCE, John Ernest;** Under Secretary, Director, Technical Division 1, Inland Revenue, 1982–88, retired; *b* 25 Jan. 1928; *s* of Ernest William and Emily Lewa Lawrance; *m* 1956, Margaret Elsie Ann Dodwell; two *s* one *d. Educ:* High School for Boys, Worthing; Southampton Univ. (BA Hons Modern History). Entered Inland Revenue as Inspector of Taxes, 1951; Principal Inspector, 1968; Senior Principal Inspector on specialist technical duties, 1974. *Address:* 71A Alderton Hill, Loughton, Essex IG10 3JD. *T:* (020) 8508 7562.

**LAWRANCE, Mrs (June) Cynthia;** Headmistress of Harrogate Ladies' College, 1974–93; *b* 3 June 1933; *d* of late Albert Isherwood and Ida Emmett; *m* 1957, Rev. David Lawrance, MA, BD (*d* 1999); three *d. Educ:* St Anne's Coll., Oxford (MA). Teaching appts: Univ. of Paris, 1954–57; Cyprus, 1957–58; Jordan, 1958–61; Oldham, Lancs, 1962–70; Headmistress, Broughton High Sch., Salford, 1971–73. *Recreations:* music, French literature. *Address:* Kinver House, The Green, Kirklington, Bedale DL8 2NQ.

**LAWRANCE, Keith Cantwell;** Deputy Chairman, Civil Service Appeal Board, 1981–89 (Member 1980–89); Vice-President, Civil Service Retirement Fellowship, since 1988 (Chairman, 1982–88); *b* 1 Feb. 1923; *s* of P. J. Lawrance; *m* 1952, Margaret Joan (née Scott) (*d* 2018); no *c. Educ:* Latymer Sch., N9. Clerical Officer, Admiralty, 1939. Served War, RNVR, 1942–46; Sub-Lt (A), 1945. Exec. Officer, Treasury, 1947; Asst Principal, Post Office, 1954; Principal, Post Office, 1959; Asst Sec., Dept of Economic Affairs, Dec. 1966; Under-Sec., Civil Service Dept, 1971–79. Vice-Chm., Inst. of Cancer Research, 1989–95. *Recreations:* model engineering, music. *Address:* White Gables, 35 Fairmile Avenue, Cobham, Surrey KT11 2JA. *T:* (01932) 863689.

**LAWRENCE,** family name of **Barons Lawrence** and **Trevethin and Oaksey,** and **Baroness Lawrence of Clarendon.**

**LAWRENCE,** 5th Baron *cr* 1869; **David John Downer Lawrence;** Bt 1858; *b* 4 Sept. 1937; *s* of 4th Baron Lawrence and Margaret Jean (*d* 1977), *d* of Arthur Downer, Kirdford, Sussex; *S* father, 1968. *Educ:* Bradfield College. *Address:* c/o Bird & Bird, 15 Fetter Lane, EC4A 1JP.

**LAWRENCE OF CLARENDON,** Baroness *cr* 2013 (Life Peer), of Clarendon in the Commonwealth Realm of Jamaica; **Doreen Delceita Lawrence,** OBE 2003; rights campaigner; Founder, Stephen Lawrence Charitable Trust, 1998; *b* Jamaica, 24 Oct. 1952; *d* of Ruby Howe and Blandford Graham; *m* 1972, Neville Lawrence (marr. diss. 1999); one *s* one *d* (and one *s* decd). *Educ:* Univ. of Greenwich (BA Hons Humanities 1995; Postgrad. prog. in Counselling Skills 1997; Dip. Therapeutic Counselling 1999). Emigrated to UK, 1961. Bank worker; Student Financial Advr, Univ. of Greenwich, 1996–2002. Mem. Exec. Cttee, Liberty, 2005– (Mem. Council, 2012–14). Chancellor, De Montfort Univ., 2015–. Patron, Stop Hate UK. Hon. Dr Greenwich, 2006; Hon. DEd E London, 2012. Lifetime Achievement Award, Pride of Britain Awards, 2012. *Publications:* And Still I Rise: seeking justice for Stephen, 2006. *Address:* c/o Stephen Lawrence Charitable Trust, The Stephen Lawrence Centre, 39 Brookmill Road, Deptford, SE8 4HU.

**LAWRENCE, Prof. Andrew,** PhD; FRAS; Regius Professor of Astronomy, University of Edinburgh, since 1994 (Head, Institute for Astronomy, 1994–2004; Head, School of Physics, 2003–08); *b* 23 April 1954; *s* of Jack Lawrence and Louisa Minnie (née Sandison); partner, Debbie Ann Capel; three *s* one *d. Educ:* Chatham House Grammar Sch., Ramsgate; Univ. of Edinburgh (BSc Hons 1976); Univ. of Leicester (PhD 1980). FRAS 1983. Exchange scientist, MIT, 1980–81; Sen. Res. Fellow, Royal Greenwich Observatory, 1981–84; PDRA, QMC, 1984–87; Queen Mary and Westfield College, London: SERC Advanced Fellow, 1987–89; Lectr, 1989–94. Vis. Scientist, SLAC, 2008–09. Mem., various res. councils and internat. cttees, panels, etc, 1983–99; Mem., PPARC, 2000–03. FRSE 1997. *Publications:* (ed) Comets to Cosmology, 1987; Astronomical Measurement: a concise guide, 2014; numerous contribs to professional astronomy jls. *Recreations:* acting, painting electrons, teasing publishers. *Address:* Edinburgh Institute for Astronomy, University of Edinburgh, Royal Observatory Edinburgh, Blackford Hill, Edinburgh EH9 3HJ. *T:* (0131) 668 8346.

**LAWRENCE, Andrew Steven;** Director of Corporate Affairs and Communications, Hutchison Whampoa Europe Ltd, since 2012; *b* Epsom, 26 Jan. 1973; *s* of Keith Lawrence and Val Long; *m* 2001, Nicolette Sanders; three *d. Educ:* Corpus Christi Coll., Cambridge (BA Modern Langs 1995; MA); Imperial Coll. Bus. Sch. (MBA 2002). Ministry of Agriculture, Fisheries and Food, subseq. Department for Environment, Food and Rural Affairs: EU Policy Team, Veterinary Medicines Directorate, 1995–96; Envmt, Fisheries and Internat. Sci. Div., 1996–97; Stagiaire DG XIV (Fisheries), EC, Brussels, 1997–98 (on secondment); Pvte Sec. to Perm. Sec., 1998–99; Hd, EU Enlargement Unit, 1999–2001; Manager, Waste Implementation Prog., 2002–03; Dep. Dir, CAP Reform and EU Strategy, 2003–07; Dir, Delivery Transformation (formerly Customer Focus and Regulation), 2007–08; Dir, Transition, DECC, 2008–09; Dir, Green Economy and Strategy (formerly Strategy and Sustainability), DEFRA, 2009–12. *Recreations:* spending time with family, enjoying the great outdoors, armchair sports expert - cricket and Rugby in particular, admiring others' gardens and beautiful buildings, travelling, very amateur ornithology. *Address:* Hutchison Whampoa Europe Ltd, Hutchison House, 5 Hester Road, SW11 4AN.

**LAWRENCE, Sir Aubrey Lyttelton Simon,** 6th Bt *cr* 1867, of Ealing Park, Middlesex; *b* 22 Sept. 1942; *s* of Peter Stafford Hayden Lawrence and Helena Francis Lawrence (née Lyttelton); *S* cousin, 2015, but his name does not appear on the Official Roll of the Baronetage; *m* 1984, Danielle de Froidment; one *s*. *Heir: s* Thomas Lyttelton de Froidment Lawrence, *b* 12 April 1985.

**LAWRENCE, (Barbara) Jane;** *see* Elliott, B. J.

**LAWRENCE, Most Rev. Caleb James;** Archbishop of Moosonee, and Metropolitan of Ontario, 2004–09; Interim Incumbent (part-time), St Mary's Parish, Nanoose Bay, 2013, 2014–15, St Mark's Parish, Qualicum Beach, 2018, Diocese of British Columbia; *b* 26 May 1941; *s* of James Otis Lawrence and Mildred Viola Burton; *m* 1966, Maureen Patricia Cuddy; one *s* two *d. Educ:* Univ. of King's College; BA Dalhousie Univ. 1962; BST 1964.

Deacon 1963, priest 1965; Missionary at Anglican Mission, Great Whale River, Quebec, 1965–75; Rector of St Edmund's Parish, Great Whale River, 1975–79; Canon of St Jude's Cathedral, Frobisher Bay, Diocese of The Arctic, 1974; Archdeacon of Arctic Quebec, 1975–79; Bishop Coadjutor, Jan.–Nov. 1980, Bishop, 1980–2010, Diocese of Moosonee; Asst Bishop and Diocesan Administrator, Diocese of British Columbia, 2013–14. Hon. DD: Univ. of King's Coll., Halifax, NS, 1980; Huron University Coll., 2010. *Recreations:* reading, photography, gardening.

**LAWRENCE, Hon. Carmen (Mary)**, PhD; Professorial Fellow, Institute of Advanced Studies, University of Western Australia, since 2008; *b* 2 March 1948; *d* of Ern and Mary Lawrence; *m* (marr. diss.); one *s. Educ:* Univ. of Western Australia (BPsych 1st cl. Hons 1968; PhD 1983). Univ. lectr, tutor, researcher, consultant, 1968–83; Research Psychologist, Psychiatric Services Unit, Health Dept, 1983–86. MLA (ALP): Subiaco, WA, 1986–89; Glendalough, WA, 1989–94; Fremantle, WA, 1994–2007; Minister for Education, 1988–90; Premier of WA, 1990–93; Leader of the Opposition, WA, 1993–94; Minister for Human Services and Health, and Minister assisting the Prime Minister for the Status of Women, Australia, 1994–96; Shadow Minister: for the Envmt, for the Arts, and assisting the Leader of the Opposition on the Status of Women, Australia, 1996–97; for Industry, Innovation and Technol., 2000–01; for the Arts and Status of Women, 2000–02; for Reconciliation, Aboriginal and Torres Strait Islander Affairs, 2001–02. *Publications:* psychological papers. *Recreations:* literature, theatre, music. *Address:* School of Psychology, Mail Bag M304, University of Western Australia, 35 Stirling Highway, Crawley, WA 6009, Australia.

**LAWRENCE, Christopher Nigel**, NDD, FTC; FIPG; goldsmith, silversmith; modeller, medallist, industrial and graphic designer; *b* 23 Dec. 1936; *s* of late Rev. William W. Lawrence and Millicent Lawrence; *m* 1958, Valerie Betty Bergman; two *s* two *d. Educ:* Westborough High Sch.; Central School of Arts and Crafts. Apprenticed, C. J. Vander Ltd; started own workshops, 1968. *One man exhibitions:* Galerie Jean Renet, 1970, 1971; Hamburg, 1972; Goldsmiths' Hall, 1973; Ghent, 1975; Hasselt, 1977. Major commissions from Royalty, British Govt, City Livery cos, banks, manufacturing cos; official silversmith to Bank of England. Judge and external assessor for leading art colleges; specialist in symbolic presentation pieces and limited edns of decorative pieces, e.g. silver mushrooms; large commissions for Middle East palaces. Chm., Goldsmiths, Craft and Design Council, 1976–77; Liveryman, Goldsmiths' Co., 1978–; television and radio broadcaster. Jacques Cartier Meml award for Craftsman of the Year, 1960, 1963, 1967 (unique achievement); Lifetime Achievement Award, Goldsmiths' Craft and Design Council, 2013. *Recreations:* badminton, tennis, bowls, carpentry, painting. *Address:* 44 St Johns Road, Westcliff-on-Sea, Essex SS0 7JZ. *T:* (01702) 338443.

**LAWRENCE, Claire Louise**; HM Diplomatic Service; Ambassador to Lithuania, 2015–19; *b* Poole, 1978; *d* of Angela Finch; *m* 2006, Mark Gee; one *s. Educ:* Sch. of St Helen and St Katharine; Christ's Coll., Cambridge (BA Hist.); Peking Univ. (Mandarin Chinese). Joined FCO, 2000; Consul (Pol/Econ), Guangzhou, 2004–06; Sen. Mgt Officer, Freetown, 2006–08; First Sec., UK Repn to EU, Brussels, 2008–11; Dep. Dir, Western Balkans, 2011–14. *Recreations:* reading, art, classical music, ballet, travel. *Address:* c/o Foreign and Commonwealth Office, King Charles Street, SW1A 2AH.

**LAWRENCE, Sir Clive Wyndham**, 4th Bt *cr* 1906, of Sloane Gardens, Chelsea; *b* 6 Oct. 1939; *yr s* of Sir Roland Lawrence, 2nd Bt, MC and Susan, 3rd *d* of Sir Charles Addis, KCMG; *S* brother, 2002; *m* 1st, 1966, Sophia Annabel Stuart (marr. diss. 2003), *d* of late (Ian) Hervey Stuart Black, TD; three *s*; 2nd, 2007, Susan Jane St Pierre, *d* of late Denis John Neal Smith. *Heir: s* James Wyndham Stuart Lawrence, *b* 25 Dec. 1970.

**LAWRENCE, Craig;** see Lawrence, J. C.

**LAWRENCE, David Kenneth**, DPhil; Head, Research, 2000–03, Research and Development, 2003–09, non-executive Director, 2009–17, Syngenta AG (Chairman, Science and Technology Advisory Board, 2009–17; Member, Audit Committee, 2013–17); *b* 9 March 1949; *s* of Ken and Dorothy Lawrence; *m* 1971, Elizabeth Ann Robertson; two *d. Educ:* Highbury Avenue Jun. Sch., Salisbury; Bishop Wordsworth Grammar Sch., Salisbury; Keble Coll., Oxford (BA Hons Chem. 1971; DPhil 1974). ICI: Scientist, 1974–86; Manager, Biochemistry, 1986–90; Proj. Leader, 1990–95; Hd, Plant Sci, Zeneca, 1995–2000; Hd, Projects, Syngenta, 2000–02. Member: Council, BBSRC, 2008–14 (Mem., Biomolecular Scis Panel, 1991–94; Chm., Industrial Biotechnol. Strategy Adv. Panel, 2012–15); UK Industrial Biotechnol. Leadership Forum, 2009–19; Agri-tech Strategy Leadership Council, 2013–15; Nuffield Council for Bioethics, 2014–; Agri-Food Technol. Council, 2016–; Dir, Bioscis Knowledge Transfer Network, 2010–13; Chair, Industrial Biotechnol. Sector Gp, 2010–14. Chairman: Plastid AS, 2012–14 (non-exec. Dir, 2009–12); Knowledge Transfer Network Ltd, 2016– (Dir, 2014–16); Agrimetrics Ltd, 2016–; Dir, Spectrum (Gen. Partner) Ltd, 2015–; Mem. Bd, Tropic Bioscis, 2017–; Ind. Dir, UK Innovation and Sci. Seed Fund (formerly Rainbow Seed Fund), 2015–; non-exec. Dir, MOA Ltd, 2018–. Mem. Adv. Bd, Krebs Inst., 1990–95; Dep. Chm., Adv. Bd, Nottingham Synthetic Biol. Res. Centre, 2016–. Dir and Trustee, Rothamsted Research Ltd, 2007–15; Trustee, John Innes Foundn, 2016–. Mem., Biotechnol. Council, WEF, 2012–14. *Recreations:* trying to understand how things work, photography, music including choral singing as a tenor, travel, gadgets, anything else which stimulates the mind and avoids boredom but is suitable for an introvert. *Email:* davelaw2@btinternet.com.

**LAWRENCE, Sir Edmund (Wickham)**, GCMG 2013 (KCMG 2010); OBE 1998; CSM 2009; JP; Managing Director, St Kitts-Nevis-Anguilla National Bank Ltd Group of Companies, since 1972; Governor General, St Christopher and Nevis, 2013–15 (Deputy Governor General, 1997–2013); *m* Hulda; one *s* six *d. Educ:* Basseterre Boys' Sch., St Kitts; Univ. of London (BSc Econ). Teacher, elementary schs, St Kitts, 1951–54; Lectr, Walbrook Coll., London, 1967–69; estabd St Kitts-Nevis-Anguilla Nat. Bank Ltd, 1970, Man. Dir, 1971–72; Gp Man. Dir, 1972–80, Chm. and Gp Man. Dir, 1980–82, Nat. Bank Gp of Cos. Director: Cable Bay Hotel Develt Co. Ltd; Digicel (St Kitts-Nevis) Ltd; Develt and Finance Corp., St Kitts; Nat. Agricl Corp., St Kitts; Central Housing Authy, St Kitts; Caribbean Credit Card Corp.; Republic Bank (Grenada) Ltd; E Caribbean Financial Hldgs Ltd; Eastern Caribbean Currency Union Bankers Assoc. Mem., Electoral Commn, St Kitts-Nevis. Consultant for establishment of: Nat. Commercial Bank of Dominica Ltd, 1977; Nat. Commercial Bank of St Vincent Ltd, 1978; Nat. Bank of Anguilla Ltd, 1985 (Advr, 1985–90); Nat. Investment Co. of Anguilla Ltd and Anguilla Nat. Insce Co. Ltd, 1990; Anguilla Mortgage Co. Ltd, 1991; Gen. Business Services Ltd, St Kitts, 1992; Ind. Consultant on Banking and Finance, Caribbean Develt Bank, to Govts of Antigua, 1977, St Kitts-Nevis, 1979 and Montserrat, 1980. *Recreations:* football, cricket, chess, bridge, table tennis.

**LAWRENCE, Felicity;** journalist, The Guardian, since 1995 (Special Correspondent, since 2006); *b* London, 15 Aug. 1958; *d* of late Prof. Hugh Lawrence and Helen Lawrence (*née* Curran); *m* 1989, Matthew Bullard; three *d. Educ:* St Anne's Coll., Oxford (BA Hons Lit. Hum. 1980). Trainee, then Editor, Haymarket Publishing, 1981–86; Ed., Sunday Telegraph mag., 1986–88; aid work, North West Frontier Province, Pakistan, 1989–91. Orwell Prize for Exposing Britain's Social Evils, Orwell Foundn, 2017. *Publications:* Not on the Label, 2004; Eat Your Heart Out, 2008. *Address:* c/o The Guardian, King's Place, 90 York Way, N1 9GU.

**LAWRENCE, Sir Henry (Peter)**, 7th Bt *cr* 1858, of Lucknow; Deputy Head, Radiotherapy Physics, Ipswich Hospital, 2012–14; *b* 2 April 1952; *s* of late George Alexander Waldemar Lawrence and Olga Lawrence (*née* Schilovsky); *S* uncle, 1999; *m* 1st, 1979, Penny Maureen Nunan (marr. diss. 1993); one *s* one *d*; 2nd, 2001, Elena Jennie Norman, theatre designer. *Educ:* Eton Coll.; Hackney Coll. BSc Physics with Astronomy, MSc Radiation Physics, London Univ. Builder and scaffolder, 1970–79; Physicist, Royal London Hosp., 1981–86; Sen. Physicist, Cheltenham Gen. Hosp., 1986–90; Head, Radiation Metrology (formerly Dosimetry), Bristol Haematology and Oncology Centre (formerly Bristol Oncology Centre), 1991–2012. Author of Europlan radiotherapy treatment planning system. Mem., Inst. of Physics and Engineering in Medicine. Hon. Mem., Romanian Assoc. of Medical Physics. *Publications:* Physics in Medicine and Biology, 1990. *Recreations:* songwriter, musician, juggler. *Heir: s* Christopher Cosmo Lawrence, *b* 10 Dec. 1979.

**LAWRENCE, (Henry) Richard (George)**; Music Director, Arts Council of Great Britain, 1983–88; *b* 16 April 1946; *s* of late George Napier Lawrence, OBE, and Peggy Neave (*née* Breay). *Educ:* Westminster Abbey Choir Sch.; Haileybury (music schol.); Worcester Coll., Oxford (Hadow Schol.); BA 1967. Overseas Dept, Ginn & Co., educational publishers, 1968–73; Music Officer, Arts Council of GB, 1973–83; Chief Exec., RSCM, 1990–94; Acting Ed., 1994–95, Ed., 1995–96, Early Music News; Ed., Leading Notes, 1997–99. Tutor at various adult educn colls and for WEA, 1997–; lectr abroad on opera, 2000–. Qualif. London Registered Blue Badge Guide, 2001. Occasional broadcaster, 1989–. Mem., Critics' Circle, 2016–. Chm., Arts Council Staff Assoc., 1974–76. Voluntary work, Friends of the Earth Trust, 1989–90. *Publications:* (contrib.) Collins Classical Music Encyclopedia, 2000; revs and articles in TLS, Church Times, Opera Now, BBC Music Mag, Jl of RAS, Early Music Today, The Gramophone, Amadeus (Milan). *Recreations:* travelling in Asia, pre-1914 Baedekers. *Address:* 1 Claverton Street, SW1V 3AY. *T:* (020) 7834 9846.

**LAWRENCE, Sir Ivan (John)**, Kt 1992; QC 1981; barrister-at-law; broadcaster, author, law and politics lecturer and after-dinner speaker; *b* 24 Dec. 1936; *o s* of late Leslie Lawrence and Sadie Lawrence, Brighton; *m* 1966, Gloria Hélène *d* 2016); (one *d* decd). *Educ:* Brighton, Hove and Sussex Grammar Sch. (State Schol.); Christ Church, Oxford (MA). Nat. Service with RAF, 1955–57. Called to Bar, Inner Temple, 1962 (Yarborough-Anderson Schol.; Bencher, 1991); S Eastern Circuit; Asst Recorder, 1983–87; a Recorder, 1987–2006; Hd of Chambers, 1 Essex Ct, 1997–2000. Contested (C) Peckham (Camberwell), 1966 and 1970. MP (C) Burton, Feb. 1974–1997; contested (C) same seat, 1997. Mem., Select Cttee on Foreign Affairs, 1983–92; Chm., Select Cttee on Home Affairs, 1992–97; Chairman: Cons. Parly Legal Cttee, 1987–97; Cons. Parly Home Affairs Cttee, 1988–97; All-Party Parly Anti-Fluoridation Cttee; All-Party Parly Barristers Gp, 1987–97; Member: Parly Expenditure Select Sub-Cttee, 1974–79; Jt Parly Cttee on Consolidation of Statutes, 1974–87. Mem. Exec., 1922 Cttee, 1988–89, 1992–97. Chm., Exec. Cttee, UK CPA, 1994–97 (Mem., 1989–97). Member: Council of Justice, 1989–95; Council, Statute Law Soc., 1985–95; Exec., Soc. of Conservative Lawyers, 1989–97 and 1999–2012 (Chm., Criminal Justice Cttee, 1997–); Bar Council, 2004–10. Fellow, Soc. of Advanced Legal Studies, 2002–. Visiting Professor of Law: Univ. of Buckingham, 2004–; BPP Univ., 2015–. Vice-Pres., Fed. of Cons. Students, 1980–82; Mem., W Midlands Cons. Council, 1985–97; Pres., Spelthorne Cons. Assoc., 2013–; Vice-Pres., Soc. of Cons. Lawyers, 2015–. Vice Chm. (and intermittently Chm.), Cons. Friends of Israel, 1979–97; Mem. Bd of Deputies of British Jews, 1979–. Chm., Burton Breweries Charitable Trust, 1979–97; Trustee, Holocaust Educnl Trust, 2002–18. Pres., Past and Present Assoc., Brighton, Hove and Sussex Grammar Sch., 1999–. Freeman, City of London, 1993. Hon. LLD Buckingham, 2013. *Publications:* My Life of Crime (memoir), 2010, 2nd edn 2012; pamphlets (jointly): Access to Justice; Correcting the Scales; The Conviction of the Guilty; Towards a New Nationality; Financing Strikes; Trial by Jury under attack; nat. newspaper and magazine articles on law and order and foreign affairs. *Recreations:* piano, travel, friends. *Address:* 5 Pump Court Chambers, Temple, EC4Y 7AP. *Clubs:* Carlton; Burton (Burton-on-Trent).

**LAWRENCE, Jacqueline Rita, (Jackie)**; *b* 9 Aug. 1948; *d* of Sidney and Rita Beale; *m* 1968, David Lawrence; two *s* one *d. Educ:* Upperthorpe Sch., Darlington, Co. Durham; Upperthorpe Coll.; Open Univ. With TSB Bank plc, until 1992. Member (Lab): Dyfed CC, 1993–96; Pembs CC, 1995–97 (Leader, Lab Gp). MP (Lab) Preseli Pembrokeshire, 1997–2005. PPS to Dep. Minister for Women and Equality, DTI, 2003–05. Member, Select Committee: on Welsh Affairs, 1997–99; on Trade and Industry, 2001–03; Chm., All Pty Parly Gp on Nat. Parks, 2001–05. Hon. Sec., Welsh Gp of Labour MPs, 2000–05.

**LAWRENCE, Maj. Gen. (John) Craig**, CBE 2013 (MBE 1997); Chief of Staff Joint Warfare Development, 2014–16; *b* Wakefield, Yorks, 18 Oct. 1963; *s* of Michael Edmund Lawrence and Vera Veronica Lawrence; *m* 2001, Laura-Jo Newton; two *d*, and three step *s. Educ:* St Peter's Sch., York; Durham Univ. (BSc Engrg Sci.); Cranfield Univ. (MSc Inf. Systems Design); King's Coll. London (MA Conflict, Security and Develt). Commnd 2nd King Edward VII's Own Gurkha Rifles, 1987; Command: 1st Bn, Royal Gurkha Rifles, 2003; 52 Inf. Bde, 2008; COS Force Develt and Trng Comd, 2009. Col, Royal Gurkha Rifles, 1999–2016. QCVS 2005. *Publications:* The Gurkhas: 200 years of service to the Crown, 2015; The Legacy (novel), 2015. *Recreations:* scuba-diving, running, writing, climbing. *Club:* Army and Navy.

**LAWRENCE, Air Vice-Marshal John Thornton**, CB 1975; CBE (mil.) 1967 (OBE (mil.) 1961); AFC 1945; *b* 16 April 1920; *s* of late T. L. Lawrence, JP, and Mrs B. M. Lawrence; *m* 1951, Hilary Jean (*née* Owen); three *s* one *d. Educ:* The Crypt School, Gloucester. RAFVR 1938. Served War of 1939–45 in Coastal Command (235, 202 and 86 Squadrons); Directing staff, RAF Flying Coll., 1949–53; CO 14 Squadron, 1953–55; Group Captain Operations, HQ AFME, 1962–64; CO RAF Wittering, 1964–66; AOC, 3 Group, Bomber Command, 1967; Student, IDC, 1968; Dir of Organisation and Admin. Plans (RAF), 1969–71; Dir-Gen. Personnel Management (RAF), 1971–73; Comdr N Maritime Air Region and AOC Scotland and NI, 1973–75, retired 1975. Vice-Pres., Glos County SSAFA, 1990– (Chm., 1980–90); Mem., Nat. Council, SSAFA, 1987–90. Order of Leopold II, Belgium, 1945; Croix de Guerre, Belgium, 1945. *Recreation:* reading. *Address:* The Coach House, Wightfield Manor, Apperley, Glos GL19 4DP. *Club:* Royal Air Force.

**LAWRENCE, John Wilfred**, RE 1987; book illustrator and wood engraver; *b* 15 Sept. 1933; *s* of Wilfred James Lawrence and Audrey Constance (*née* Thomas); *m* 1957, Myra Gillian Bell; two *d. Educ:* Salesian Coll., Cowley, Oxford; Hastings Sch. of Art; Central Sch. of Art. Visiting Lecturer in Illustration: Brighton Polytech., 1960–68; Camberwell Sch. of Art, 1960–94; Visiting Professor in Illustration: London Inst., 1994–2000; Cambridge Sch. of Art, Anglia Ruskin Univ., 2006–15; External Assessor in Illustration: Bristol Polytech., 1978–81; Brighton Polytech., 1982–85; Duncan of Jordanstone Coll. of Art, 1986–89; Exeter Coll. of Art, 1986–89; Kingston Polytechnic, 1989–93; Edinburgh Coll. of Art, 1991–94. Member: Art Workers Guild, 1972 (Master, 1990); Soc. of Wood Engravers,

1984; Wynken de Worde Soc., 2013–. Work represented in Ashmolean Mus., V&A Mus., Nat. Mus. of Wales, Manchester Metropolitan Univ. Special Collections, and collections abroad. *Publications:* The Giant of Grabbist, 1968; Pope Leo's Elephant, 1969; Rabbit and Pork Rhyming Talk, 1975 (Francis Williams Book Illustration Award, 1977); Tongue Twisters, 1976; George, His Elephant and Castle, 1983; A Selection of Wood Engravings, 1986; Good Babies, Bad Babies, 1987; *illustrated:* more than 250 books, incl.: Colonel Jack, 1967 (Francis Williams Book Illustration Award, 1971); Diary of a Nobody, 1969; The Blue Fairy Book, 1975; The Illustrated Watership Down, 1976; Everyman's Book of English Folk Tales, 1981; The Magic Apple Tree, 1982; The Cranks Recipe Book, 1982; Mabel's Story, 1984; Entertaining with Cranks, 1985; Emily's Own Elephant, 1987; Christmas in Exeter Street, 1989; A New Treasury of Poetry, 1990; The Sword of Honour trilogy, 1990; Treasure Island, 1990, 2009; Shades of Green, 1991 (Signal Prize for Poetry); Poems for the Young, 1992; King of King's, 1993; The Twelve Days of Christmas, 1994; The Christmas Collection, 1994; Memoirs of a Georgian Rake, 1995; Robin Hood, 1995; Poems for Christmas, 1995; Collected Poems for Children by Charles Causley, 1996; (with Allan Ahlberg) The Mysteries of Zigomar, 1997; A Year and a Day, 1999; This Little Chick, 2002 (NY Times Cert. of Excellence); The Once and Future King, 2003; Lyra's Oxford, by Philip Pullman, 2003; Tiny's Big Adventure, 2004; Sea Horse: the shyest fish in the sea, 2006; Once Upon a Time in the North, by Philip Pullman, 2008; The Arthur Trilogy, by Kevin Crossley-Holland, 2010; Wayland The Smith, by Tony Mitton, 2013; Shakespeare's Songs, 2017. *Address:* 6 Worts Causeway, Cambridge CB1 8RL. *Club:* Double Crown (Pres., 2005).

**LAWRENCE, Josie;** actress; *b* 6 June 1959; *d* of late Bert and Kathleen Lawrence. *Educ:* Dartington Coll. of Arts (BA Hons Theatre). Professional acting début, 1983; joined Comedy Store Players, 1986; *theatre* includes: Painting Churches, 1988; Tatyana, 1992, Eliza in Pygmalion, 1994, Nottingham Playhouse; Moll Flanders, Lyric Hammersmith, 1993; The Cherry Orchard, Faust and Kate in The Taming of the Shrew, RSC, 1995; The Alchemist, NT, 1996; Alarms and Excursions, Gielgud, 1998; Anna in The King and I, Palladium, 2001; Frozen, NT, 2002; Much Ado About Nothing, Globe, 2004; Acorn Antiques - The Musical, Th. Royal, Haymarket, 2005; Hapgood, 2008, The Cherry Orchard, 2010, Edmond de Bergerac, 2019, Birmingham Rep.; Mother Courage and Her Children, Southwark, 2017; Love-Lies-Bleeding, Print Room at the Coronet, 2018; Oklahoma!, Chichester Fest., 2019; *films* include: Enchanted April, 1992; The Sin Eater, 1999; Bonobo, 2014; *television* includes: Friday Night Live, 1988; Whose Line Is It Anyway?, 1988–97; Not With a Bang, 1990; Josie, 1991; Downwardly Mobile, 1994; Maggie in Outside Edge, 3 series, 1994–96; A Many Splintered Thing, 2000; Fat Friends, 2000; Easy Peasy, 2006; Robin Hood, 2007; The Old Curiosity Shop, 2007; Minder, 2008; Eastenders, 2009–10; Beat the Brain, 2015; Good Omens, 2019. Hon. Dr Plymouth; Hon. DLitt Wolverhampton; Hon. DA Aston. Best Actress Award, Manchester Evening News; Globe Award for Best Actress; Dame Peggy Ashcroft Prize, Shakespeare Golden Globe Awards, 1997. Charity walks for breast cancer research in Cuba, Peru, Africa and China; climbed Kilimanjaro for Sunfield Sch., 2005 (Patron, 1995–). *Recreations:* painting, walking.

**LAWRENCE, Michael John,** PhD; Chief Executive, London Stock Exchange, 1994–96; *b* 25 Oct. 1943; *s* of Geoffrey Frederick Lawrence and Kathleen (*née* Bridge); *m* 1967, Maureen Joy Blennerhassett; two *s* one *d. Educ:* Exeter Univ. (BSc 1st Cl. Hons Physics); Bristol Univ. (PhD Mathematical Physics). FCA 1972. With Price Waterhouse, 1969–87, Partner 1978; Finance Dir, Prudential Corp., 1988–93. Non-executive Director: PLA, 1983–89; London Transport, 1994–99; Yattendon Investment Trust, 1998–. Chm., 100 Gp of Finance Dirs, 1991–93. Mem. (C), Royal Borough of Windsor and Maidenhead Unitary Council, 1996–2004 (Leader, 2000–04). Freeman, City of London, 1974; Liveryman, Tin Plate Workers' Co., 1974– (Master, 2000–01). *Recreations:* sailing, bridge, tennis, opera. *Address:* Springmead, Bradcutts Lane, Cookham Dean, Berks SL6 9AA.

**LAWRENCE, Murray;** see Lawrence, W. N. M.

**LAWRENCE, Nigel Stuart;** QC 2014; *b* Heswall, Wirral, 4 Nov. 1965; *s* of Dr T. L. J. Lawrence and E. R. D. Lawrence; *m* 1994, Jane C. E.; two *s* three *d. Educ:* Kingsmead Sch., Wirral; Rydal Sch., Colwyn Bay; Univ. of Leicester (LLB Hons); Inns of Court Sch. of Law. Called to the Bar, Lincoln's Inn, 1988; in practice as barrister, specialising in regulatory crime and enforcement, particularly health and safety, manslaughter, personal injury and criminal negligence, 1988–; Standing Counsel: to HSE, 2004–; to Office of Rail and Road (formerly Rail Regulation), 2007–. *Recreations:* sport, wine, travel. *Address:* 7 Harrington Street Chambers, 7 Harrington Street, Liverpool L2 9YH. *T:* (0151) 242 0707. *E:* n.lawrence4@ntlworld.com.

**LAWRENCE, Peter Anthony,** PhD; FRS 1983; Staff Scientist, Medical Research Council Laboratory of Molecular Biology, Cambridge, 1969–2006, now emeritus researcher, Department of Zoology, University of Cambridge, supported by Wellcome Trust; *b* 23 June 1941; *s* of Ivor Douglas Lawrence and Joy Lawrence (*née* Liebert); *m* 1971, Birgitta Haraldson. *Educ:* Wennington Sch., Wetherby, Yorks; Cambridge Univ. (MA, PhD). Harkness Fellowship, 1965–67; Dept of Genetics, Univ. of Cambridge, 1967–69. *Publications:* Insect Development (ed), 1976; The Making of a Fly, 1992; (jtly) Principles of Development, 1998, 5th edn 2015; scientific papers. *Recreations:* Ascalaphidae, fungi, gardening, golf, theatre, trees. *Address:* Department of Zoology, University of Cambridge, Cambridge CB2 3EJ; MRC Laboratory of Molecular Biology, Hills Road, Cambridge CB2 0QH.

**LAWRENCE, Richard;** see Lawrence, H. R. G.

**LAWRENCE, Vanessa Vivienne,** CB 2008; FRICS; Global Advisor for Geospatial Information, World Bank Group, since 2015; Director, Location International Ltd, since 2015; *b* 14 July 1962; *d* of Leonard Walter Sydney Lawrence and Margaret Elizabeth Lawrence. *Educ:* St Helen's Sch., Northwood, Middx; Sheffield Univ. (BA (Soc. Sci.) Hons Geography); Dundee Univ. (MSc Remote Sensing, Image Processing and Applications). CGeog 2002; FRICS 2003. Longman Group UK Ltd: Publisher, 1985–89; Sen. Publisher, 1989–91; Publishing Manager, 1991–92; Tech. Dir, GeoInformation Internat. (Pearson Gp), 1993–96; Regl Business Develt Manager, UK, ME, Africa, GIS Solutions Div., Autodesk Ltd, 1996–2000; Global Manager, Strategic Mktg and Communications, GIS Solutions Div., Autodesk Inc., 2000; Dir Gen. and Chief Exec., Ordnance Survey, 2000–14. Co-Chair, UN Cttee of Experts on Global Geospatial Inf. Mgt, 2011–15. Non-executive Director: DCLG (formerly ODPM), 2002–06; Satellite Applications Catapult Ltd, 2015–. Hon. Res. Associate, Manchester Univ., 1990–2000; Vis. Prof., 2000–15, Adjunct Prof., 2015–, Southampton Univ.; Vis. Prof., Kingston Univ., 2003–. Mem. Court, Southampton Univ., 2001–12 (Mem. Council, 2002–09); Mem. Council, Univ. of Cambridge, 2009–12. Member: RGS, 1987– (Mem. Council, 2002–); Assoc. for Geographic Inf., 1992– (Mem. Council, 1995–2000; Chm., 1999); Bd, Open Geospatial Consortium, 2005–15; Adv. Bd, Urban Big Data Centre, 2016–; Spatial Data Adv. Cttee, HKSAR, 2019–; Spatial Finance Adv. Bd, 2019–; European Investment Bank Space Finance Lab, 2019–; Hon. Vice-Pres., Geographical Assoc., 2006–. Trustee, Winchester Sci. Centre, 2008–17. Chm., ACE, 2003–08; Patron: MapAction, 2006–; Cure Parkinson's Trust, 2007–. Freedom, City of London, 2008; Freeman, 2008, Liveryman, 2009, Goldsmiths' Co. CCMI 2003. FRSGS 2014; Hon. FInstCES 2001; Hon. FREng 2008. Hon. Fellow, UCL, 2003. Hon. Col, 135 Geographic Sqdn, Royal Engineers (formerly 135 Ind. Geographic Sqdn, RE (Volunteers)), 2009–. Hon. DSc: Sheffield, 2001; Southampton Inst., 2002; Kingston, 2002; Glasgow, 2005; Southampton, 2014; DUniv: Oxford Brookes, 2001; RHUL, 2014; Hon. LLD Dundee, 2003. Scottish Geographical Medal, RSGS, 2006; SE Dir of the Year, IoD, 2008; Geospatial Person of the Decade Award 2000–10, Geospatial World Forum, 2011. *Publications:* contrib. many books and jls on Geographical Inf. Systems. *Recreations:* scuba diving, sailing, tennis, collecting antique maps. *Clubs:* Rickmansworth Sailing; Horsley Sports.

**LAWRENCE, Vernon John;** freelance television producer; *b* 30 April 1940; *m* 1960, Jennifer Mary Drewe; two *s* one *d. Educ:* Dulwich Coll.; Kelham Coll. BBC Studio Manager, 1958; BBC Radio Producer, 1964; BBC TV Producer and Dir, 1967; Yorkshire Television: Exec. Producer, 1973; Controller, Entertainment, 1985; Controller, Network Drama and Entertainment, ITV, 1993–95; Man. Dir, 1995–97, Chm., 1997–2000, MAI Prodns, subseq. United Film & TV Prodns, then United Prodns. *Productions* include: Rising Damp, 1978 (also dir); Duty Free, 1984–86 (also dir, 1984); The Darling Buds of May, 1991–93; A Touch of Frost, 1992; Hornblower, 1998–99; New Statesman, 1987–92; dir, Song by Song, 1978–80. FRTS 1995. *Recreations:* oil painting, fishing, walking, gardening.

**LAWRENCE, (Walter Nicholas) Murray;** Chairman of Lloyd's, 1988–90 (a Deputy Chairman 1982, 1984–87; Member: Committee of Lloyd's, 1979–82; Council of Lloyd's, 1984–91); Chairman, Murray Lawrence Holdings Ltd, 1988–94; *b* 8 Feb. 1935; *s* of Henry Walter Neville Lawrence and Sarah Schuyler Lawrence (*née* Butler); *m* 1961, Sally Louise O'Dwyer (*d* 2008); two *d. Educ:* Winchester Coll.; Trinity Coll., Oxford (BA, MA). C. T. Bowring & Co. (Ins.) Ltd, 1957–62; Asst Underwriter, H. Bowring & Others, 1962–70, Underwriter, 1970–84; Director: C. T. Bowring (Underwriting Agencies) Ltd, 1973–84; C. T. Bowring & Co. Ltd, 1976–84; Murray Lawrence Members Agency Ltd, 1988–94 (Chm., 1988–93); Murray Lawrence & Partners Ltd, 1989–95 (Sen. Partner, 1985–89; Chm., 1989–92); Chm., Fairway (Underwriting Agencies) Ltd, 1979–85. Mem., Lloyd's Underwriters Non-Marine Assoc., 1970–84 (Dep. Chm., 1977; Chm., 1978). *Recreations:* golf, opera, travelling. *Clubs:* Boodle's, MCC; Royal & Ancient (St Andrews), Royal St George's (Sandwich), Rye, Pine Valley Golf, Merion Golf.

**LAWRENCE-JONES, Sir Christopher,** 6th Bt *cr* 1831; *S* uncle, 1969; *m* 1967, Gail Pittar, Auckland, NZ; two *s. Educ:* Sherborne; Gonville and Caius Coll., Cambridge; St Thomas' Hospital. MA Cantab 1964; MB, BChir Cantab 1964; DIH Eng. 1968. MFOM 1979, FFOM 1987; FRCP 1991. Medical adviser to various orgns, 1967–94; CMO, Imperial Chemical Industries PLC, 1985–93; Chm., Medichem, 1986–92. Pres., Section of Occupational Medicine, RSM, 1990–91. *Heir: s* Mark Christopher Lawrence-Jones, *b* 28 Dec. 1968. *Club:* Royal Cruising.

**LAWRENSON, Mark Thomas;** football pundit, BBC Television, 1997; *b* Preston, 2 June 1957; *s* of Thomas and Theresa Lawrenson; *m* 2001, Suzanne; one *s* one *d. Educ:* Preston Catholic Coll. Professional footballer: Preston N End, 1974–77; Brighton & Hove Albion, 1977–81; Republic of Ireland, 1977–87 (39 Caps); Liverpool, 1981–88; Barnet, 1988–89; Tampa Bay Rowdies, 1989; Corby Town, 1990–91; Manager: Oxford United, 1988; Peterborough United, 1989–90. Hon. Citizen of Preston, 2002. *Recreations:* cricket, golf.

**LAWREY, Keith;** JP; Learned Societies' Liaison Officer, Foundation for Science and Technology, since 1997; *b* 21 Aug. 1940; *s* of George William Bishop Lawrey and Edna Muriel (*née* Gass); *m* 1969, Helen Jane Marriott, BA; two *s* two *d. Educ:* Colfe's Sch.; Birkbeck Coll., Univ. of London (MSc Econ; LLB); Heythrop Coll., Univ. of London (MA). Barrister-at-Law; called to Bar, Gray's Inn, 1972 (Sec. to Seniors-in-Hall, 1997–2017; Hon. Bencher, 2016). Education Officer, Plastics and Rubber Inst., 1960–68; Lectr and Sen. Lectr, Bucks Coll. of Higher Educn, 1968–74; Head of Dept of Business Studies, Mid-Kent Coll. of Higher and Further Educn, 1974–78; Sec.-Gen., Library Assoc., 1978–84; Dean, Faculty of Business and Management, Harrow Coll. of Higher Educn, subseq. Head, Sch. of Business and Management, Polytechnic of Central London/Harrow Coll., 1984–90; Sec. and Registrar, RCVS, 1990–91; Headmaster, Cannock Sch., 1992–95; Clerk (pt-time) to Corp. of S Kent Coll., 1996–99. Member: Social Security Appeal Tribunal, 1996–99; Registration Authy, Sci. Council, 2004–10; Privy Council and Governance Panel (formerly Privy Council Panel, subseq. Privy Council and Regulations Panel), Engrg Council, 2004–; Exec. Cttee, Fellowship of Clerks, 2010–15; Dep. Chm., Chartered Security Professionals Registration Authy, 2012–. FCollT (FCollP 1982), Hon. FCollT 2012 (Hon. Treas., Coll. of Preceptors, then Coll. of Teachers, 1987–2010); FCIS; Companion, Security Inst., 2016. Associate, Engrg Council, 2010. Gov., Cannock Sch., 1976–92; Mem. Court, City Univ., 2004–. Mem., Orpington Rotary Club, 1993–2007 (Pres., 1999–2000); Trustee, Carers Bromley (formerly Carers Support and Information Service), 2001–05; Sec., Alice Shepherd Foundn, 2002–05; Trustee: and Hon. Treas., Trust for Educn and Care of Child Workers in Ecuador, 2003–06; Hosp. Saturday Fund, 2007–10 (Mem., Grant-Making Cttee, 2006–); Mus. of Timekeeping, 2018–; Co. Sec., Premier Christian Radio, 2018–; Trust Sec., Premier Christian Media Trust, 2018–. Hon. Mem., RPS, 2004 (Fenton Medallist, 2004); Hon. MCIL 2005; Hon. FRIN 2007; Hon. FCIPHE 2009; Hon. FAcadMed 2010; Hon. Fellow: Security Inst., 2011; Chartered Assoc. of Building Engrs, 2013; Soc. for Envmt, 2019; Hon. Affiliate MRSB, 2016 (Pres.'s Medal, 2016). Liveryman, Chartered Secretaries and Administrators' Co., 1976; Hon. Liveryman: Hackney Carriage Drivers' Co., 2014; Livery Co. of Wales, 2014; Educators' Co., 2015 (Hon. Clerk, Guild of Educators, subseq. Co. of Educators, 2001–15); Hon. Freeman: Master Mariners' Co., 2014; Guild of Nurses, 2017 (Hon. Foundn Clerk, 2016–17). JP Inner London, 1974–2009 (Supplemental List, 2009–). Medal of Appreciation, IED, 2012; Root and Branch Award, City Livery Club, 2017. Mem. Editl Bd, Graya, 1976– (Sec., 1992–); Ed., Foundn Sci. Technol. Newsletter (bi-monthly), 1997–. *Publications:* papers in Law Soc. Gazette, Educn Today, Jl Assoc. of Law Teachers, Trans and Jl of Plastics Inst., Graya, Graya News. *Recreations:* preaching, sailing, swimming, theatre, gardening. *Clubs:* Old Colfeians; Dell Quay Sailing; City Livery.

**LAWS, Rt Hon. David (Anthony);** PC 2010; Executive Chairman: Education Policy Institute, since 2015; Education Partnerships Group of Ark Schools, since 2015; *b* 30 Nov. 1965; *s* of David Anthony, (Tony), Laws and Maureen Teresa Laws. *Educ:* St George's Coll., Weybridge (Observer Mace Schs Debating Champion 1984); King's Coll., Cambridge (schol.; Double 1st Cl. Hons Econs 1987). Vice Pres., Treasury Dept, J. P. Morgan and Co., 1987–92; Man. Dir, Hd of Sterling and US Dollar Treasury, Barclays de Zoete Wedd, 1992–94; Econs Advr, Lib Dem Parly Party, 1994–97; Dir of Policy and Res., Lib Dems, 1997–99; drafted first Partnership Agreement for Lib Dem-Lab Coalition in Scottish Parlt, 1999. Contested (Lib Dem) Folkestone and Hythe, 1997. MP (Lib Dem) Yeovil, 2001–15; contested (Lib Dem) same seat, 2015. Lib Dem Treasury spokesman, 2002–05; Lib Dem spokesman for work and pensions, 2005–07, for children, schools and families, 2007–10; Chief Sec. to the Treasury, 2010; Minister of State, DfE and Cabinet Office, 2012–15. Mem., Treasury Select Cttee, 2001–03. Strategic Advr to GK Strategy. *Publications:* 22 Days in May: the birth of the Lib Dem-Conservative Coalition, 2010; Coalition, 2016; Coalition Diaries, 2017. *Recreations:* running, watching Rugby, visiting desert regions.

**LAWS, Eleanor Jane, (Mrs C. L. D. Nelson);** QC 2011; a Recorder, since 2016; b Manchester, 10 Nov. 1966; d of David Laws and Barbara Laws; m 1998, Cairns Louis David Nelson, qv; two s two d. Educ: North London Collegiate Sch.; Univ. of Birmingham (BA Hons Hist. 1988; DipLaw 1989). Called to the Bar, Inner Temple, 1990; in practice as a barrister, specialising in crime, 5 King's Bench Walk, 1991–2001, 6 Pump Court, 2001–15, QEB Hollis Whiteman, 2015–. *Publications:* The Sexual Offences Referencer, 2007. *Recreations:* reading, tennis, ballet. *Address:* QEB Hollis Whiteman, 1–2 Laurence Pountney Hill, EC4R 0EU. *T:* (020) 7933 8855, *Fax:* (020) 7929 3732. *E:* barristers@qebhw.co.uk.

**LAWS, Rt Hon. Sir John (Grant McKenzie),** Kt 1992; PC 1999; a Lord Justice of Appeal, 1999–2016; b 10 May 1945; s of late Dr Frederic Laws and Dr Margaret Ross Laws, d of Prof. John Grant McKenzie; m 1973, Sophie Susan Sydenham Cole Marshall, MLitt, MA (d 2017); one d. Educ: Durham Cathedral Choir Sch.; Durham Sch. (King's Scholar); Exeter Coll., Oxford (Sen. Open Classical Scholar; BA 1967, Hon. Sch. of Lit. Hum. 1st Cl.; MA 1976; Hon. Fellow, 2000). Called to the Bar, Inner Temple, 1970, Bencher, 1985, Reader, 2009, Treas., 2010; practice at Common Law Bar, 1971–92; First Junior Treasury Counsel, Common Law, 1984–92; Asst Recorder, 1983–85; Recorder, 1985–92; a Judge of the High Court of Justice, QBD, 1992–98; admitted to Bar: New South Wales, 1987; Gibraltar, 1988. President: Bar European Gp, 1994–; Proceeds of Crime Law Assoc., 2010–; Constitutional and Admin. Law Bar Assoc., 2012–. An Hon. Vice-Pres., Administrative Law Bar Assoc., 1992. Vis. Prof., Northumbria Univ., 2011–14; Arthur Goodhart Vis. Prof. in Legal Sci., Univ. of Cambridge, 2016–17. Judicial Visitor, UCL, 1997–; Visitor, Cumberland Lodge, 2004–. Hon. Fellow, Robinson Coll., Cambridge, 1992. *Publications:* contributor to: Dict. of Medical Ethics, 1977; Supperstone and Goudie, Judicial Review, 1992, 2nd edn 1997; Importing the First Amendment, 1998; The Golden Metwand and the Crooked Cord, 1998; Cicero the Advocate, 2004; The Common Law Constitution, 2014; Le huitième centenaire de la Magna Carta, 2016; reviews for Theology, Law & Justice, Ecclesiastical Law Jl, Public Law; contribs to legal jls. *Recreations:* Greece, living in London, philosophy. *Club:* Garrick.

**LAWS, Simon Reginald;** QC 2011; b 16 May 1966; s of Alfred Reginald Laws and Mary Margaret Laws (née Jones); m 1994, Sarah Anne Conlon; two d. Educ: Univ. of York (BA English and Related Lit.); City Univ. (DipLaw); Inns of Court Sch. of Law. Called to the Bar, Inner Temple, 1991; in practice as barrister, London, 1991–98, Exeter, 1999–; Trial Attorney, Office of Prosecutor, Internat. Criminal Tribunal for Former Yugoslavia, 2008–10. Consultant: TWL Legal Consulting Ltd, 2014–; to govt depts and NGOs overseas. Hon. Fellow, Exeter Centre for Ethno-Political Studies, Univ. of Exeter, 2010–. *Recreations:* hiking, running, books. *Address:* Walnut House, 63 St David's Hill, Exeter EX4 4DW. *Club:* Devon and Exeter Institution.

**LAWS, Sir Stephen (Charles),** KCB 2011 (CB 1996); First Parliamentary Counsel, 2006–12; Senior Research Fellow, Judicial Power Project, Policy Exchange; b 28 Jan. 1950; s of late Dennis Arthur Laws, MC and Beryl Elizabeth Laws (née Roe); m 1st, 1972, Angela Mary Deardon (d 1998); two s three d; 2nd, 2001, Elizabeth Ann Owen (née Williams). Educ: St Dunstan's College, Catford; Bristol Univ. (LLB Hons 1972). Called to the Bar, Middle Temple, 1973, Bencher, 2008. Asst Lectr, Univ. of Bristol, 1972; Legal Asst, Home Office, 1975; Asst, Sen. Asst, then Dep. Parly Counsel, 1976–91; Parly Counsel, 1991–2006. Chm., Civil Service Benevolent Fund, 2009–12. Member: Exec. Cttee, Commonwealth Assoc. of Legislative Counsel, 2009–11; Exec. Council, Statute Law Soc., 2012–16; McKay Commn on consequences of devolution for H of C, 2012–13; Adv. Panel, Strathclyde Rev. on Secondary Legislation and the Primacy of the H of C, 2015; Strategic Bd, Navigating Brexit publishing project, Intersentia, 2017–; Chm., Adv. Bd, Big Data for Law Project, 2014–16. Sen. Associate Res. Fellow, Inst. of Advanced Legal Studies, Univ. of London, 2012–; Hon. Sen. Res. Associate, UCL, 2013–. Mem., Adv. Bd, Univ. of Bristol Law Sch., 2013–18. Member: Thomas More Soc., 1976–; Soc. of Legal Scholars, 2012–. Study of Parlt Gp, 2013–. Mem., Westbere Parish Council, 2016– (Vice Chair, 2017–). Hon. QC 2011. Hon. Fellow, Univ. of Kent Law Sch., 2015–. Hon. LLD: Bristol, 2012; London, 2014. *Publications:* (with Peter Knowles) Statutes title in Halsbury's Laws of England, 4th edn, 1983; (contrib.) Drafting Legislation: a modern approach, 2008; (contrib.) Statute Law Review, 2011; (contrib.) Law in Politics, Politics and Law, 2013; (contrib.) Parliament: legislation and accountability, 2016; contrib. to Eur. Jl Law Reform, and Policy Exchange papers on judicial power and Brexit-related matters. *Recreations:* Italy, medieval and constitutional history, gadgets, cricket watching, golf. *Club:* Canterbury Golf.

**LAWSON,** family name of **Barons Burnham** and **Lawson of Blaby**.

**LAWSON OF BLABY,** Baron cr 1992 (Life Peer), of Newnham in the County of Northamptonshire; **Nigel Lawson;** PC 1981; b 11 March 1932; o s of Ralph Lawson and Joan Elisabeth Lawson (née Davis); m 1st, 1955, Vanessa Salmon (marr. diss. 1980; she d 1985); one s two d (and one d decd); 2nd, 1980, Thérèse Mary Maclear (marr. diss. 2012); one s one d. Educ: Westminster; Christ Church, Oxford (Scholar; 1st class hons PPE, 1954). Served with Royal Navy (Sub-Lt RNVR, CO HMMTB Gay Charger), 1954–56. Mem. Editorial Staff, Financial Times, 1956–60; City Editor, Sunday Telegraph, 1961–63; Special Assistant to Prime Minister (Sir Alec Douglas-Home), 1963–64; Financial Times columnist and BBC broadcaster, 1965; Editor of the Spectator, 1966–70; regular contributor to: Sunday Times and Evening Standard, 1970–71; The Times, 1971–72; Fellow, Nuffield Coll., Oxford, 1972–73; Special Pol Advr, Cons. Party HQ, 1973–74. Contested (C) Eton and Slough, 1970; MP (C) Blaby, Leics, Feb. 1974–1992. An Opposition Whip, 1976–77; an Opposition Spokesman on Treasury and Economic Affairs, 1977–79; Financial Sec. to the Treasury, 1979–81; Sec. of State for Energy, 1981–83; Chancellor of the Exchequer, 1983–89. Member: Econ. Affairs Cttee, H of L, 2004–08, 2010–15; Barnett Formula Cttee, H of L, 2008–09; Parly Commn on Banking Standards (Jt Cttee), 2012–13; EU Financial Affairs Sub-Cttee, H of L, 2015–16. Chairman: Central Europe Trust Co. Ltd, 1990–2012; Oxford Investment Partners (OXIP), 2006–13; Dir, Barclays Bank, 1990–98. Founding Chm., 2009–19, Dir, 2009–, Hon. Pres., 2019–, Global Warming Policy Foundn. Chm., Vote Leave, 2016; Pres., Conservatives for Britain, 2015–16. Pres., British Inst. of Energy Econs, 1995–2003. Mem., Governing Body, Westminster Sch., 1999–2005. Hon. Student, Christ Church, Oxford, 1996. Hon. DSc Buckingham, 2011. IEA Nat. Free Enterprise Award, 2008. Mousquetaire d'Armagnac, 2010. *Publications:* (with Jock Bruce-Gardyne) The Power Game, 1976; The View from No 11, 1992, rev. edn as Memoirs of a Tory Radical, 2010; (with Thérèse Lawson) The Nigel Lawson Diet Book, 1996; An Appeal to Reason: a cool look at global warming, 2008. *Address:* House of Lords, SW1A 0PW. *Clubs:* Garrick, Pratt's.
*See also Hon. D. R. C. Lawson, N. L. Lawson.*

**LAWSON, Sir Charles (John Patrick),** 4th Bt cr 1900, of Weetwood Grange, West Riding of Yorks; b 19 May 1959; o s of Sir John Charles Arthur Digby Lawson, 3rd Bt, DSO, MC and Tresilla Anne Elinor (née Buller-Leyborne-Popham); S father, 2001; m 1987, Lady Caroline Lowther, d of 7th Earl of Lonsdale; three s one d. Educ: Harrow; Univ. of Leeds; RAC Cirencester. MRICS. Director: Jackson-Stops & Staff, Exeter, 1992– (Mem., Exec. Cttee, 2011–); JSS Development Land and New Homes Co. Ltd, 2010–. Heir: s Jack William Tremayne Lawson, b 6 Dec. 1989. *Address:* Hayton Holme, Great Asby, Appleby in Westmorland CA16 6TH. *T:* (office) (01392) 214222. *E:* charlielawson@outlook.com.

**LAWSON, Christopher John;** Chief Executive, Meat Hygiene Service, Food Standards Agency, 2001–07; b 16 March 1947; s of late John Hedley Lawson and of Joyce Patricia Lawson (née Robson); m 1969, Janice Ray Langley; two s one d (and one d decd). Educ: Ascham House Sch.; Rossall Sch.; Univ. of Newcastle upon Tyne (BSc Hons Agric.). Livestock Husbandry Advr, NAAS, 1970–72, ADAS, 1972–73; MAFF, 1973–2000: Dir of Policy, Vet. Medicines Directorate, 1991–96; Hd, Meat Hygiene Div., 1996–2000; Food Standards Agency, 2000–07. Member: NE Rly Assoc. (Trustee, 2017–); NE Locomotive Preservation Gp (Sec., 2012–18; Chm., 2018–); N Yorks Moors Rly; Vintage Carriages Trust. *Recreations:* steam railway preservation, fell walking, photography, DIY, industrial archaeology, supporting Newcastle United, sport generally, the North East. *Address:* 67 The Mount, York YO24 1AX.

**LAWSON, Prof. Colin James,** CBE 2016; PhD, DMus; FRCM, FLCM, FRNCM; international clarinet soloist; Director, Royal College of Music, since 2005; b 24 July 1949; s of Eric William and Edith Mary Lawson; m 1982, Aileen Hilary Birch; one s. Educ: Keble Coll., Oxford (MA); Univ. of Birmingham (MA); Univ. of Aberdeen (PhD 1976); Univ. of London (DMus 2000). ARCM 1967, FRCM 2005; FLCM 2005; FRNCM 2009. Lectr in Music, Aberdeen Univ., 1973–77; Sheffield University: Lectr, 1978–90; Sen. Lectr, 1991–96; Reader, 1996–97; Prof. of Performance Studies, Goldsmiths Coll., Univ. of London, 1998–2001; Pro-Vice Chancellor, Thames Valley Univ., 2001–05. Concert appearances as clarinet soloist include: Carnegie Hall; Lincoln Center, NY; Principal Clarinet: Hanover Band, 1987–2006; English Concert, 1991–2006. Recordings incl. Mozart Clarinet Quintet and fragments (with the Revolutionary Drawing Room), 2012, Mozart Basset Horn Trios (with M. Harris and T. Lines), 2015. Hon. RAM, 2015; Hon. DMus Sheffield, 2015. *Publications:* The Chalumeau in Eighteenth-Century Music, 1981; (ed) Cambridge Companion to the Clarinet, 1995; Mozart Clarinet Concerto, 1996; Brahms' Clarinet Quintet, 1998; (with R. Stowell) The Historical Performance of Music, 1999; The Early Clarinet, 2000; (ed) Cambridge Companion to the Orchestra, 2003; (ed with R. Stowell) Cambridge History of Musical Performance, 2012; (ed with R. Stowell) The Cambridge Encyclopaedia of Historical Performance in Music, 2018. *Recreations:* travel, acquisition of early clarinets. *Address:* Royal College of Music, Prince Consort Road, SW7 2BS. *T:* (020) 7591 4363, *Fax:* (020) 7591 4356. *Club:* Athenæum.

**LAWSON, Prof. David Hamilton,** CBE 1993; Hon. Consultant Physician, Glasgow Royal Infirmary, since 2003 (Consultant Physician, 1973–2003); b 27 May 1939; s of David Lawson and Margaret Harvey Lawson (née White), m 1st, 1963, Alison Diamond (d 1996); three s; 2nd, 2010, Avril Eleanor Yarrow Meighan (née Scott). Educ: High Sch. of Glasgow; Univ. of Glasgow. MB, ChB 1962; MD 1973. FRCPE 1975; FRCPGlas 1986; FFPM 1989; FRCP 2001; FFPH (FFPHM 2001). Junior medical posts in Royal Infirmary and Western Infirmary, Glasgow; Boston Collaborative Drug Surveillance Prog., Boston, Mass, 1970–72; Attending Physician, Lemuel Shattuck Hosp., Boston, 1971; Adviser on Adverse Drug Reactions, Wellcome Foundn, 1975–87; Vis. Prof., Faculty of Sci., Univ. of Strathclyde, 1976–2005; Hon. Prof. of Medicine, Univ. of Glasgow, 1993–. Chairman: Medicines Commn, 1994–2001; Scottish Medicines Consortium, 2000–04; Bd Trustees, Drug Safety Research Unit, Univ. of Southampton, 2010–; Member: Health Services Res. Cttee of Chief Scientist Office, SHHD, 1984–88; Cttee on Safety of Medicines, Dept of Health (formerly DHSS), 1987–93; Mem., 1979–91, Chm., 1987–91, Cttee on Review of Medicines, Dept of Health (formerly DHSS). Mem. Council, RCPE, 1992–99 (Vice-Pres., 1997–99; Trustee, 2005–). Examiner, Final MB, Univs of Glasgow, Dundee, Birmingham, London, Kota Bharu, Malaysia. Pres., Antonine Probus Club, Bearsden and Milngavie, 2008–09. Hon. DSc: Hertfordshire, 2000; Strathclyde, 2001. *Publications:* Clinical Pharmacy and Hospital Drug Management (ed with R. M. E. Richards), 1982; Current Medicine 2, 1990; (ed jtly) Risk Factors for Adverse Drug Reactions: epidemiological approaches, 1990; Current Medicine 3, 1991; Current Medicine 4, 1994; papers on clinical pharmacol, haematol and renal topics. *Recreations:* hill-walking, photography, bird-watching. *Address:* 5 Tannoch House, 138 Mugdock Road, Milngavie, Glasgow G62 8NP. *T:* (0141) 956 2766.

**LAWSON, Denis;** actor and director; b 27 Sept. 1947; s of Laurence and Phyllis Lawson; m 1st, 2004, Sheila Gish (d 2005); one s, and two step d; 2nd, 2017, Karen Prentice. Educ: Crieff Primary Sch.; Morrison's Acad., Crieff; Royal Scottish Acad. of Music and Drama, Glasgow. *Productions:* as actor. theatre includes: Pal Joey, Albery, 1980 (Most Promising New Actor, Drama Critics' Award); Mr Cinders, Fortune, 1983; (Best Actor in a Musical Award, SWET, 1984); Lend Me a Tenor, Globe, 1986; The Importance of Being Earnest, Royalty, 1987; Volpone, Almeida, 1990; Lust, Haymarket, 1993; La Cage aux Folles, Playhouse, 2008; Acid Test, Royal Court, 2011; films include: Providence, The Man in the Iron Mask, 1977; Local Hero, 1983; The Chain, 1984; Perfect Sense, 2011; Broken, The Machine, 2013; television includes: The Kit Curran Radio Show, 1984; That Uncertain Feeling, Dead Head, 1986; The Justice Game, 1989; Natural Lies, 1992; Hornblower, The Ambassador, 1998; Bob Martin, Other People's Children, 2000; The Fabulous Bagel Boys, 2001; Holby City, 2002–04; Sensitive Skin, Bleak House, 2005; Jekyll, 2006; Criminal Justice, 2009; Marchlands, 2011; New Tricks, 2012–15; as director. theatre: Little Malcolm and His Struggle Against the Eunuchs, Comedy, 1998; The Anniversary, Garrick, 2004; films: The Bass Player, 1998; Solid Geometry, 2002. *Recreations:* vodka martinis, jazz. *Address:* c/o Claire Maroussas, Independent Talent Group Ltd, 40 Whitfield Street, W1T 2RH. *T:* (020) 7636 6565, *Fax:* (020) 7323 0101.

**LAWSON, Hon. Dominic Ralph Campden;** journalist and broadcaster; b 17 Dec. 1956; s of Baron Lawson of Blaby, qv and late Vanessa Mary Addison Lawson (née Salmon); m 1st, 1982, Jane Whytehead (marr. diss.); 2nd, 1991, Hon. Rosamond Mary Monckton, qv; two d. Educ: Westminster Sch.; Christ Church, Oxford (exhibnr; Hons PPE). Researcher, BBC TV and radio, 1979–81; Financial Times: joined 1981; energy corresp., 1983–86; columnist (Lex), 1986–87; The Spectator: Dep. Editor, 1987–90; Editor, 1990–95; Editor, Sunday Telegraph, 1995–2005; columnist: Sunday Correspondent, 1990; Financial Times, 1991–94; Daily Telegraph, 1994–95; Independent, 2006–13; Sunday Times, 2008–; Standpoint, 2008–17; Daily Mail, 2013–. Presenter, BBC Radio series: Across the Board, 2013–; Why I Changed My Mind, 2015–. Mem., Press Complaints Commn, 1998–2002. Vis. Schol., Green Templeton (formerly Green) Coll., Oxford, 2007–08. Pres., English Chess Fedn, 2014–. FRSA 1993. Harold Wincott Prize for financial journalism, 1987; Columnist of the Year, British Press Awards, 2014, 2016. *Publications:* (with Raymond Keene) Kasparov-Korchnoi, the London Contest, 1983; (jtly) Britain in the Eighties, 1989; The Inner Game, 1993; (ed) Snake Oil and Other Preoccupations, 2001. *Recreation:* chess. *Address:* Cox's Mill, Dallington, Heathfield, East Sussex TN21 9JG. *Club:* MCC.
*See also N. L. Lawson.*

**LAWSON, Elizabeth Ann;** QC 1989; a Recorder, 1998–2007; b 29 April 1947; d of Alexander Edward Lawson, FCA, and Helen Jane Lawson (née Currie). Educ: Croydon High School for Girls (GPDST); Nottingham Univ. (LLB). Called to Bar, Gray's Inn, 1969,

Bencher, 1999. Chm., Family Law Bar Assoc., 1995–97. Chm., Leeways Enquiry for London Borough of Lewisham, 1985; Chm., Liam Johnson Review for Islington Area Child Protection Cttee, 1989. *Recreations:* knitting, reading, cake decoration.

**LAWSON, Sir John Philip H**; *see* Howard-Lawson.

**LAWSON, Dame Lesley, (Dame Twiggy)**, DBE 2019; actress, singer and model; *b* 19 Sept. 1949; *y d* of late (William) Norman Hornby and of Nell (Helen) Hornby (*née* Reeman); *m* 1st, 1977, Michael Whitney Armstrong (*d* 1983); one *d*; 2nd, 1988, Leigh Lawson. Started modelling in London, 1966; toured USA and Canada, 1967; world's most famous model, 1966–71. *Films:* The Boy Friend, 1971 (most promising newcomer and best actress in a musical or comedy, Golden Globe Awards); W, 1973; There Goes the Bride, 1979; Blues Brothers, 1981; The Doctor and the Devils, 1986; Club Paradise, 1986; Madame Sousatzka, 1989; Harem Hotel, Istanbul, 1989; Woundings, 1998; *stage:* Cinderella, 1976; Captain Beaky, 1982; My One and Only, 1983, 1984; Blithe Spirit, Chichester, 1997; Noel and Gertie, NY, 1998; If Love Were All, NY, 1999; Blithe Spirit, NY, 2002; Mrs Warren's Profession (UK tour), 2003; *television:* numerous appearances and series, UK and USA, incl. The Taming of the Shrew, 2005; judge on America's Next Top Model, 2005–08; Twiggy's Frock Exchange, 2008; numerous recordings, incl. Romantically Yours, 2011. Exhibn, Twiggy: a life in photographs, NPG, 2009–10. Launched own 'Twiggy' label clothing range, 2012–; beauty products, 2016–, for Marks and Spencer. Many awards and honours. *Publications:* Twiggy, 1975; An Open Look, 1985; Twiggy in Black and White (autobiog.), 1997; Twiggy: a guide to looking and feeling fabulous over forty, 2008; (contrib.) Twiggy: a life in photographs, 2009. *Recreations:* music, dressmaking. *Address:* c/o Peters, Fraser & Dunlop, 55 New Oxford Street, WC1A 1BS. *T:* (020) 7344 1010, *Fax:* (020) 7836 9544.

**LAWSON, Mark Gerard**; journalist, broadcaster and author; *b* 11 April 1962; *s* of late Francis Lawson and Teresa Lawson (*née* Kane); *m* 1990, Sarah Bull; two *s* one *d*. *Educ:* St Columba's Coll., St Albans; University College London (BA Hons English). Junior reporter and TV critic, The Universe, 1984–85; TV previewer, Sunday Times, 1985–86; TV critic and parly sketchwriter, The Independent, 1986–89; feature writer, Independent Magazine, 1988–95; columnist, critic and feature writer, The Guardian, 1995–; theatre critic, The Tablet, 2006–; presenter for radio and TV, 1990–, including: Late Review, later Review, subseq. Newsnight Review (BBC2), 1994–2005; Front Row (Radio 4), 1998–2014; Mark Lawson Talks To… (BBC4), 2006–; Never Ending Stories (BBC2); Defoe: The Facts and the Fictions (Radio 4), 2016; Setting the Past Free (Radio 4), 2016; plays for radio and TV, including: The Vision Thing (BBC2), 1993; Absolute Power (BBC2), 2003–05; The Number of the Dead (Radio 3), 2009; for Radio 4: The Man Who Had 10,000 Women, 2002; St Graham and St Evelyn, Pray for Us, 2003; The Third Soldier Holds His Thighs, 2005; London, this is Washington, 2006; Expand This, Sex After Death, 2007; Reading Between the Lines, 2009; Suspicion for 10 Voices, 2013; Foreign Bodies, 2013–14; The Szacki Trilogy (from Zygmunt Milosewski), 2015–19; The Unseen Government, The Moon That Night, 2018; Baselines, 2019. British Press Award, 1987; TV critic of the Year, 1989, 1990. *Publications:* Bloody Margaret, 1991; The Battle for Room Service, 1993; Idlewild, 1995; John Keane, 1995; Going Out Live, 2001; Enough Is Enough, 2005; The Deaths, 2013; Troubles My Sight: the art of John Keane, 2015; The Allegations, 2016. *Recreations:* theatre, football, cricket, wine, reading. *Address:* c/o Cat Ledger Literary Agency, 20–21 Newman Street, W1T 1PG. *E:* mglawson@dircon.co.uk.

**LAWSON, Matthew Richard Ambrose**; HM Diplomatic Service; Ambassador to Tajikistan, since 2019; *b* Colchester, Essex, 22 Oct. 1975; *s* of Colin and Elizabeth Lawson; *m* (marr. diss.); one *s* one *d*. *Educ:* Philip Morant Comprehensive Sch., Colchester; Colchester Sixth Form Coll.; Univ. of York (BA 1st Cl. Hons PPE 1997); Simon Fraser Univ., BC (MA Pol Sci. 2000); Univ. of British Columbia (MFA Creative Writing 2019). Policy Analyst, HM Treasury, 2002–03; Dep. Prog. Manager, Afghanistan, DFID, 2003–04; entered FCO, 2004; Desk Officer, Afghanistan, FCO, 2004–05; Hd, British Embassy Office, Banja Luka, Bosnia and Herzogovina, 2005–07; Political Advr to UN High Rep./EU Special Rep., Bosnia and Herzogovina, 2008–09; Hd, Pakistan Team, FCO, 2009–11; Jt Hd, Policy Planners, FCO, 2011–13; Hd, Global Issues Gp, Ottawa, 2013–15; Dep. Hd of Mission, Sarajevo, 2015–18. *Publications:* Beetle (poetry), 2014. *Recreations:* fiction and poetry, music, travel, being outdoors. *Address:* British Embassy Dushanbe, 65 Mirzo Tursunzade Street, Dushanbe 734002, Tajikistan. *T:* 372242221. *E:* Matthew.lawson@fco.gov.uk.

**LAWSON, Ven. Michael Charles**; film maker and composer; Archdeacon of Hampstead, 1999–2010; Rector, St Saviour's, Guildford, 2010–12; *b* 23 May 1952; *s* of Gerald Simon Lawson and Myrtle Helena Lawson; *m* 1978, Claire Mary MacClelland; three *d*. *Educ:* Hove Grammar Sch.; Guildhall Sch. of Music; Ecoles d'Art Américaines, Fontainebleau; Univ. of Sussex (BA); Trinity Coll., Bristol (BCTS). Composer and pianist, 1970–75. Deacon 1978, priest 1979; Curate, St Mary the Virgin, Horsham, 1978–81; Dir of Pastoring, All Souls, Langham Place, W1, 1981–86; Vicar, Christ Church, Bromley, 1987–99. Permission to officiate, Dio. of Ely, 2013–. Chaplain and Counsellor, HMP Littlehey, 2013–. Maker of documentaries: Aids Orphans, Mozambique, 2002; India's Broken People, 2005; India's Hidden Slavery, 2007; India's New Beginnings, 2009; India's Forgotten Women, 2010; India's Forgotten Children, 2013. Member and Fellow, Inst. of Videography. *Publications:* Sex and That, 1985, 2nd edn 1992; Facing Anxiety and Stress, 1986, 2nd edn 1995; The Unfolding Kingdom, 1987; Facing Depression, 1989, 2nd edn 1997; Facing Conflict, 1990; The Better Marriage Guide, 1998; Conflict, 1999; Living by God's Master Plan, 2000; D is for Depression, 2006; Three Pieces for Saxophone and Piano, 2018. *Recreations:* my wife and children, friends, music, writing, video production, photography, computers, theatre, cookery, lots of things.

**LAWSON, His Honour Michael Henry**; QC 1991; a Circuit Judge, 2004–16; *b* 3 Feb. 1946; *s* of late Dr Richard Pike Lawson, MC and Margaret Haines (*née* Knight); *m* 1969, Ann Pleasance Symons Brisker; two *d*. *Educ:* Monkton Combe School, Bath; London Univ. (LLB). Called to the Bar, Inner Temple, 1969, Bencher, 1993; a Recorder, 1987–2004. Leader, SE Circuit, 1997–2000. Mem., Parole Bd, 2017–. Mem., Bar Council, 1997–2003. Ct Asst, Curriers' Co., 2011– (Master, 2007–08). *Publications:* (jtly) Professional Conduct (Inns of Court School of Law Manual), annually, 1989–2000; (contrib.) Refocus on Child Abuse, 1994. *Recreations:* opera, music, wine, walking, cycling. *T:* 07831 315590.

**LAWSON, Nigella Lucy**; freelance journalist and broadcaster, since 1982; *b* 6 Jan. 1960; *d* of Baron Lawson of Blaby, *qv* and late Vanessa Mary Addison Lawson (*née* Salmon); *m* 1st, 1992, John Diamond (*d* 2001); one *s* one *d*; 2nd, 2003, Charles Saatchi, *qv* (marr. diss. 2013). *Educ:* Lady Margaret Hall, Oxford (BA (Hons) Medieval and Mod. Langs). Presenter, television series: Nigella Bites, 2000; Nigella Bites II, 2001; Forever Summer with Nigella, 2002; Nigella's Christmas Kitchen, 2006, 2008; Nigella Express, 2007; Nigella Kitchen, 2010; Nigellissima, 2012; Simply Nigella, 2015; At My Table, 2017; mentor, The Taste, 2013–15. *Publications:* How to Eat, 1998; How to be a Domestic Goddess, 2000; Nigella Bites, 2001; Forever Summer, 2002; (contrib.) Oxford Companion to Italian Literature, 2002; Feast, 2004; Nigella Express, 2007; Nigella Christmas, 2008; Kitchen: recipes from the heart of the home, 2010; Nigellissima: instant Italian inspiration, 2012; Simply Nigella: feel good food, 2015; At My Table, 2017. *Address:* c/o Curtis Brown, Haymarket House, 28–29 Haymarket, SW1Y 4SP. *T:* (020) 7393 4400.
*See also* Hon. D. R. C. Lawson.

**LAWSON, Gen. Sir Richard (George)**, KCB 1980; DSO 1962; OBE 1968; Commander-in-Chief, Allied Forces Northern Europe, 1982–86; *b* 24 Nov. 1927; *s* of John Lawson and Florence Rebecca Lawson; *m* 1956, Ingrid Lawson (*d* 2006); one *s*. *Educ:* St Albans Sch.; Birmingham Univ. CO, Independent Squadron, RTR (Berlin), 1963–64; GSO2 MoD, 1965–66; C of S, South Arabian Army, 1967; CO, 5th RTR, 1968–69; Comdr, 20th Armoured Bde, 1972–73; Asst Military Deputy to Head of Defence Sales, 1975–77; GOC 1st Armoured Div., 1977–79; GOC Northern Ireland, 1980–82. Col Comdt, RTR, 1980–82. Leopold Cross (Belgium), 1963; Knight Commander, Order of St Sylvester (Vatican), 1964. *Publications:* Strange Soldiering, 1963; All the Queen's Men, 1967; Strictly Personal, 1972. *Address:* c/o Drummonds, 49 Charing Cross, SW1A 2DX.

**LAWSON, Robert John**; QC 2009; Partner, since 2017, and Chairman, Aviation Global Practice Group, since 2018, Clyde & Co. LLP; *b* Burnham, 7 Nov. 1964; *s* of Alan and Katherine Lawson; *m* 1992, Rachel Claire Stanton; two *s* two *d*. *Educ:* Sheredes Comprehensive Sch.; Queen's Coll., Oxford (BA Hons PPE; MA); City Univ., London (DipLaw). Called to the Bar, Inner Temple, 1989; in private practice, 1989–2017, specialising in aviation, travel and professional discipline. Fellow, Internat. Acad. of Trial Lawyers, 2006. MRAeS 1998, FRAeS 2010; MCIArb 2005. *Publications:* contrib. on aviation, Halsbury's Laws of England, Vol. 2 (3), 4th edn reissue, 2003; (contrib.) The Aviation Law Review, 4th edn, 2016, 5th edn, 2018; contrib. articles on issues of aviation law. *Recreations:* sport, classical music. *Address:* Clyde & Co. LLP, St Botolph Building, 138 Houndsditch, EC3A 7AR. *E:* rob.lawson@clydeco.com. *Club:* Corkscrew (Herts).

**LAWSON, Roger Hardman**; Director, 3i plc, 1993–2001; *b* 3 Sept. 1945; *s* of Harold Hardman Lawson and Mary Doreen Lawson; *m* 1974, Jenniferjane Grey; three *d*. *Educ:* Bedford School. ACA 1967; FCA. Articled Wilson de Zouche & Mackenzie, 1963–67; joined ICFC, subseq. 3i, 1968; Manager, UK Regions, 1968–84; Dir, 3i International (USA, Asia and Pacific), 1984–92. Dir, Zotefoams plc, 2002–12. Mem., Takeover Panel, 1994–95. Chm., London Soc. of Chartered Accountants, 1985–86; Pres., ICAEW, 1994–95. Trustee: Thalidomide Trust, 2001–14; St Paul's Cathedral Staff Pension Fund, 2003–14. *Recreations:* food, family, fun. *Clubs:* Royal Wimbledon Golf; Rye Golf.

**LAWSON, Hon. Rosa(mond) Mary**; *see* Monckton, Hon. R. M.

**LAWSON, Sara Lucy Jane**; QC 2017; General Counsel, Serious Fraud Office, since 2019; *b* Kent, 1968; *er d* of Douglas Lawson and late Brenda Lawson. *Educ:* W Preston Manor Sch.; Rosemead Sch.; Gads Hill Place Sch.; Gravesend Grammar Sch. for Girls; Huddersfield Poly. (LLB Hons Business Law); Inns of Court Sch. of Law. Consultant researcher, Law Commn, 1989; called to the Bar, Inner Temple, 1990, Bencher, 2015; in practice as barrister, specialising in financial crime, 1990–2019; Standing Counsel to BIS, subseq. BEIS, 2012–17. *Recreations:* fast cars, France, reeling, Radio 4, music. *Address:* Serious Fraud Office, 2–4 Cockspur Street, SW1Y 5BS.

**LAWSON, Sonia**, RA 1991 (ARA 1982); RWS 1988 (ARWS 1985); artist; Visiting Lecturer, Royal Academy Schools, 1985–2003; *b* 2 June 1934; *d* of Frederick Lawson and Muriel (*née* Metcalfe), artists; *m* 1969, C. W. Congo; one *d*. *Educ:* Leyburn; Southwick Girls' Sch.; Doncaster Sch. of Art; Royal Coll. of Art (ARCA 1st cl. 1959). Postgraduate year, RCA; Travelling Scholarship, France, 1960. Annual exhibitions: RA, 1961–; RWS, 1983–. Solo exhibitions: Zwemmer, London, 1960; New Arts Centre, London, 1963; Queen's Sq. Gall., Leeds, 1964; Trafford Gall., London, 1967; Bradford New Liby, 1972; Middlesbrough and Billingham, 1977; Open Univ., Darlington and Harrogate Art Galls, 1979; Harrogate Northern Artists, 1980; Manchester City Art Gall., 1987; Wakefield City Art Gall., 1988, 2008; Cartwright Hall, Bradford, 1989; Boundary Gall., London, 1989, 1995, 1998, 2000, 2003, 2005; Univ. of Birmingham, 1994, 2006; Shire Hall, Stafford, 1999; RWA, Bristol, 2000; Carlow Arts Fest., Ireland, 2001; Vertigo Gall., London, 2002; *retrospectives:* Shrines of Life, toured 1982–83, Sheffield (Mappin), Hull (Ferens), Bradford (Cartwright), Leicester Poly., Milton Keynes (Exhibn Gall.); Dean Clough Gall., Halifax, 1996; Aylesbury Art Gall. and Mus., 2006; Mercer Gall., Harrogate, 2015–16; *mixed exhibitions:* Arts Council of GB Touring Exhibns (Fragments against Ruin, The Subjective Eye); Tolly Cobbold National Exhibns; Moira Kelly Fine Art; Hayward Annual; Soho, New York (8 in the 80s); Fruitmarket Gall., Edinburgh; London Gp; RCA (Exhibition Road, to celebrate 150 years of RCA), 1988; Smith Gall., London, 1988, 1989; Faces of Britain, China (British Council Touring Exhibn), 1989–90; Glasgow Royal Inst. of Fine Art, 1990; Galerie zur alten deutschen Schule, Thun, Switzerland, 1990; Royal Academy (The Infernal Method, etchings by Academicians), 1991; John Moores, Liverpool, 1991; Bonnington Gall., Nottingham Trent Univ. (Representing Lives), 1999. Works in public collections: Arts Council of GB; Graves Art Gall., Sheffield; Huddersfield, Bolton, Carlisle, Belfast, Middlesbrough, Bradford, Dewsbury, Rochdale, Hepworth Wakefield, and Harrogate Art Galls; Imperial War Mus.; Min. of Educn; Min. of Works; Leeds Univ.; Open Univ.; Cranfield Univ.; RCA; St Peter's Coll., Oxford; Nuffield Foundn; Royal Acad.; Univ. of Qld; Augustine (commissioned), presented by Archbishop of Canterbury to Pope John Paul II, Vatican Collection, Rome, 1989; private collections in UK, Germany, Australia, USA. BBC TV, Monitor, 1960, John Schlesinger's doc. "Private View". Visual records of Exercise Lionheart, BAOR, Germany, 1984 (Imperial War Mus. commn). Hon. RWA 2005. Rowney Prize, Royal Acad., 1984; Gainsborough House Drawing Prize, Eastern Arts, 1984; Lorne Scholarship, Slade Sch. of Fine Art, 1986; Lady Evershed Drawing Prize, Eastern Arts Open, 1990. *Publications:* (illustrator) Look At It This Way: poems for young people, by James Kirkup, 1994; (illustrator) New Year's Eve, by Fay Weldon, 1995; Passions & Alarms, 2014. *Address:* c/o Royal Academy of Arts, Burlington House, Piccadilly, W1J 0BD. *T:* (020) 7300 5680. *E:* art@sonialawson.co.uk. *W:* www.sonialawson.co.uk. *Club:* Arts.

**LAWSON JOHNSTON**, family name of **Baron Luke**.

**LAWSON-ROGERS, (George) Stuart**; QC 1994; a Recorder, 1990–2019; *b* 23 March 1946; *s* of late George Henry Roland Rogers, CBE, sometime MP and Mary Lawson; *m* 1969, Rosalind Denise Leach; one *s* one *d*. *Educ:* LSE (LLB Hons). Called to the Bar, Gray's Inn, 1969; Asst Recorder, 1987–89. Asst Comr, Parly and Local Govt Boundary Commns, 1981, 1983; Chm., Structure Plan Exams in Public, DoE, 1984; Legal Assessor, GMC and GDC, 1988–2005; Standing Counsel (Crime, SE Circuit) to HM Customs and Excise, 1989–94; DTI Inspector, Insider Dealing, 1989; Dept of Transport Inspector, Merchant Shipping Act 1988, 1989–90. Dir, Watford AFC Ltd, 1990–96. *Recreations:* theatre, music, opera, reading, gardening.

**LAWSON-TANCRED, Sir Andrew (Peter)**, 11th Bt *cr* 1662, of Boroughbridge, Yorks; Chairman, Northern Aldborough Festival, since 2010; *b* Wetherby, Yorks, 18 Feb. 1952; *e s* of Sir Henry Lawson-Tancred, 10th Bt and Jean Veronica (*d* 1970), 4th and *y d* of late G. R. Foster; *S* father, 2010; *m* 2003, Julia Francesca, *d* of John Murray; one *s* one *d*. *Educ:* Eton Coll.; Univ. of Leeds; Inns of Court Sch. of Law. Called to the Bar, Middle Temple, 1977; in practice as a barrister, 1977–84. Director: Legal and Business Affairs, WH Smith

TV, 1990–94; TV Corp. Plc, 1995–99. Chair: Ripon Cathedral Music Trust; Friends of Roman Aldborough. *Recreations:* flying, music. *Heir: s* Thomas Alexander Claude Lawson-Tancred, *b* 17 June 2006. *Address:* Aldborough Manor, Boroughbridge, York YO51 9EP. *E:* andrew@aldborough.com.

LAWTIE, Andrew McNab; Vice Lord-Lieutenant of City of Aberdeen, since 2015; *b* Aberdeen, 29 July 1949; *s* of George Lawtie and Catherine Lawtie (*née* Archibald); *m* 1979, Sheila Donald; one *d* (and one *s* decd). *Educ:* Kaimhill Secondary Sch. Aberdeen City Council, 1971–99; Analyst/programmer, 1971–81; computer auditor, 1981–84; Project Team Leader, 1984–86; Systems Manager, 1986–89; Dir, IT, 1989–99; Support Worker, 2000; Aberdeen Foyer, 2000, 2001–06; General Register of Scot., 2000–01; Census Area Manager, 2000–01, 2010–11; Hd, Educn and Trng, 2001–06; self-employed, 2006–10; Fundraising and Resources Officer, North East Sensory Services, 2011–16. Chm., Grampian Soc. for the Blind, 2010–11. Burgess of Guild, City of Aberdeen, 1994. DL City of Aberdeen, 2003. OStJ 2006 (SBStJ 1981). *Recreations:* photography, listening to music, watching sports, holidays. *Address:* 51 Queens Den, Aberdeen AB15 8BN. *T:* (01244) 208236. *E:* alawtie@sky.com.

LAWTON, Prof. Denis; Professor of Education, University of London Institute of Education, 1974–2003, now Emeritus; *b* 5 April 1931; *s* of William Benedict Lawton and Ruby (*née* Evans); *m* 1953, Joan Weston; two *s*. *Educ:* St Ignatius Coll.; Univ. of London Goldsmiths' Coll. (BA); Univ. of London Inst. of Education (PhD). Asst Master, Erith Grammar Sch., 1958–61; Head of English/Housemaster, Bacon's Sch., SE1, 1961–63; University of London Institute of Education: Research Officer, 1963–64; Lectr in Sociology, 1964–67; Sen. Lectr in Curriculum Studies, 1967–72; Reader in Education, 1972–74; Dep. Dir, 1978–83; Dir, 1983–89. Chairman: Univ. of London Sch. Exams Bd, subseq. Sch. Exams and Assessment Council, 1984–96; Consortium for Assessment and Testing in Schools, 1989–91; Jt Council for GCSE, 1996–99; Acad. Sec., UCET, 2000–02. Hon. Fellow, College of Preceptors, 1983. *Publications:* Social Class, Language and Education, 1968; Social Change, Education Theory and Curriculum Planning, 1973; Class, Culture and the Curriculum, 1975; Social Justice and Education, 1977; The Politics of the School Curriculum, 1980; An Introduction to Teaching and Learning, 1981; Curriculum Studies and Educational Planning, 1983; (with P. Gordon) HMI, 1987; Education, Culture and the National Curriculum, 1989; Education and Politics in the 1990s, 1992; The Tory Mind on Education, 1994; Beyond the National Curriculum, 1996; Royal Education Past, Present and Future, 1999; (with P. Gordon) A History of Western Educational Ideas, 2002; Education and Labour Party Ideologies 1900–2001 and Beyond, 2004. *Recreations:* walking German Shepherd dogs, photographing bench-ends, sampling real ale, music. *Address:* Laun House, Laundry Lane, Nazeing, Essex EN9 2DY.

LAWTON, Sir John (Hartley), Kt 2005; CBE 1997; FRS 1989; Chairman, Royal Commission on Environmental Pollution, 2005–11 (Member, 1989–96); Chief Executive, Natural Environment Research Council, 1999–2005; *b* 24 Sept. 1943; *s* of Frank Hartley Lawton and Mary Lawton; *m* 1966, Dorothy (*née* Grimshaw); one *s* one *d*. *Educ:* Balshaw's Grammar Sch., Leyland, Lancs; University Coll. and Dept of Zoology, Univ. of Durham (BSc, PhD). Res. Student, Univ. of Durham, 1965–68; Deptl Demonstrator in Animal Ecology, Oxford Univ., 1968–71; College Lectr in Zoology, St Anne's and Lincoln Colls, Oxford, 1970–71; University of York: Lectr, 1971–78; Sen. Lectr, 1978–82; Reader, 1982–85; Personal Chair, 1985–89; Dir, NERC Centre for Population Biology, ICSTM, 1989–99. Mem., NERC, 1995–99. Hon. Vis. Res. Fellow, Nat. Hist. Mus., 1990–2005; Adjunct Scientist, Inst. of Ecosystem Studies, NY Botanic Garden, 1991–2000. President: Yorks Wildlife Trust, 2014–; Instn of Envmtl Scis, 2015–; Vice-President: RSPB, 1999– (Chm. Council, 1993–98); British Trust for Ornithology, 1999–2008; Chm., York Museums Trust, 2012–18; Patron: Chartered Inst. of Ecology and Envmtl Mgt, 2011–; Nat. Biodiversity Network, 2019. Foreign Member: US NAS, 2008; Amer. Assoc. of Arts and Scis, 2008. FIC 2006. Hon. DSc: Lancaster, 1993; Birmingham, York, 2005; East Anglia, Aberdeen, 2006. *Publications:* Insects on Plants: community patterns and mechanisms (with D. R. Strong and T. R. E. Southwood), 1984; (ed jtly) The Evolutionary Interactions of Animals and Plants, 1991; (ed jtly) Extinction Rates, 1996; (ed jtly) Linking Species and Ecosystems, 1996; Community Ecology in a Changing World, 2000; over 300 sci. papers in specialist jls. *Recreations:* bird watching, natural history photography, travel, gardening, walking, cooking. *Address:* The Hayloft, Holburns Croft, Heslington, York YO10 5DP.

LAWTON, Julie Grace; Headmistress, Wolverhampton Girls' High School, 2004–12; *b* 2 April 1958; *d* of Arthur and Audrey Barber; *m* 1979, Mark Lawton. *Educ:* Univ. of Hull (BA; PGCE); Univ. of Birmingham (MEd); NPQH 2002. Teacher: of French and German, Newland High Sch. for Girls, Hull, 1980–83; i/c German, Parkfield Sch., Wolverhampton, 1983–86; Hd, Modern Langs, Kingswinford Sch., Dudley, 1987–94; Vice Principal and Dir, Sixth Form Studies, St Peter's Collegiate Sch., Wolverhampton, 1995–2003. *Recreations:* walking, travelling abroad, foreign languages.

LAWTON, Paul Anthony; His Honour Judge Lawton; a Circuit Judge, since 2014; *b* Stoke on Trent, 12 July 1964; *s* of George Lawton and Joan Lawton; *m* 1991, Andrea Walker; three *d*. *Educ:* Alsager Sch.; Manchester Poly. (LLB Hons 1986). Called to the Bar, Lincoln's Inn, 1987; a Recorder, 2005–14. Mem., Bar Disciplinary Tribunal, 2012–14; Visitor, Inns of Court, 2013. *Recreations:* kitchen gardening, fly fishing, walking.

LAXTON, Robert; *b* 7 Sept. 1944; *s* of Alan and Elsie Laxton; *m*; one *s*. *Educ:* Woodlands Secondary Sch.; Derby Coll. of Art and Technology. Branch Officer, CWU, 1974–97; Telecommunications Engr, BT plc, 1961–97. Mem., Derby CC, 1979–97 (Leader, 1986–88, 1994–97). MP (Lab) Derby North, 1997–2010. PPS to Minister of State: DTI, 2001–03; DFES, 2003–04; PPS to Secretary of State: DWP, 2004–05; DTI, 2005. Mem., Trade and Industry Select Cttee, 1997–2001. Vice Chairman: Trade Union Gp of Lab. MPs; PLP DTI Deptl Cttee. Chm., E Midlands Local Govt Assoc., 1995–97; Vice Pres., LGA.

LAY, Richard Neville, CBE 2001; Chairman of Trustees, Portman Estate, 1999–2015; Chairman, DTZ (formerly Debenham Tewson & Chinnocks) Holdings plc, 1987–2000; President, Royal Institution of Chartered Surveyors, 1998–99; *b* 18 Oct. 1938; *s* of late Edward John Lay and Nell Lay; *m* 1st, 1964; one *s* one *d*; 2nd, 1991; 3rd, 2003, Veronica Anne Jones (*née* Hamilton-Russell). *Educ:* Whitgift School. FRICS. Partner, Debenham Tewson & Chinnocks, 1965–87. Vice Chm., 1992–2001, Chm., 2001–18, Central London Board, RSA (formerly Sun Alliance and London, then Royal and Sun Alliance) Insurance Group. Dir, Nat. House Building Council, 2001–07. Chairman: cttee advising RICS on market requirements of the profession, 1991; Commercial Property Panel, RICS, 1992–95; Member: Council, British Property Fedn, 1992–99; General Council, RICS, 1994–2000; Bank of England Property Forum, 1994–99; Chm., Commercial Property Gp, DCLG (formerly Wkg Party on Commercial Property Issues, ODPM), 2004–10; Mem., Adv. Panel on Standards in Planning Inspectorate, 1993–2000. Co-Chm., Corby Regeneration Co. Ltd, 2003–06; Chm., N Northants Develt Co. Ltd, 2006–08. Chm., London Underwriting Centre, 2005–. Trustee, Tate Gall. Foundn, 1989–94. Master, Armourers' and Brasiers' Co., 2003–04 (Surveyor, 1983–98; Mem., Ct of Assts, 1998–2019). Governor, Belmont Sch., Surrey, 1983–88; Mem. Bd, Coll. of Estate Mgt, 2000–05. Property Person of the Year, Property Week, 1999. *Recreations:* gardening, walking the dogs. *Address:* Meadow Cottage, Winderton, Banbury OX15 5JF. *T:* (01608) 685458.

LAYARD, Baron *cr* 2000 (Life Peer), of Highgate in the London Borough of Haringey; **Peter Richard Grenville Layard**, FBA 2003; Director, Well-Being Programme, Centre for Economic Performance, London School of Economics, since 2003 (Professor of Economics, 1980–99, now Emeritus); *b* 15 March 1934; *s* of Dr John Layard and Doris Layard; *m* 1991, Molly Meacher (*see* Baroness Meacher). *Educ:* Eton Coll.; King's Coll., Cambridge (BA); London School of Economics (MScEcon; Hon. Fellow, 2004). History Master: Woodberry Down Sch., 1959–60; Forest Hill Sch., 1960–61; Senior Research Officer, Robbins Cttee on Higher Educn, 1961–63; London School of Economics: Dep. Director, Higher Educn Research Unit, 1964–74 (part-time from 1968); Lectr in Economics, 1968–75; Reader in the Economics of Labour, 1975–80; Hd, Centre for Labour Econs, 1974–90; Dir, Centre for Econ. Performance, 1990–2003. Chm., Employment Inst., 1987–92. Mem., UGC, 1985–89. Econ. Consultant to Russian Govt, 1991–97; Consultant: DfEE, 1997–2001; Cabinet Office, 2001; DoH, 2006–15. Co-founder, Action for Happiness, 2011. Chair, Global Agenda Council on Wellbeing and Mental Health, WEF, 2012. Fellow: Econometric Soc., 1986; Eur. Econ. Assoc., 2004; Soc. of Labor Economists, 2008. Leontief Medal, Russian Acad. of Natural Scis, 2005; President's Medal, RCPsych, 2010; (jtly) IZA Prize in Labor Econs, 2008. *Publications:* (jtly) The Causes of Graduate Unemployment in India, 1969; (jtly) The Impact of Robbins: Expansion in Higher Education, 1969; (jtly) Qualified Manpower and Economic Performance: An Inter-Plant Study in the Electrical Engineering Industry, 1971; (ed) Cost-Benefit Analysis, 1973, 2nd edn 1994; (jtly) Microeconomic Theory, 1978; (jtly) The Causes of Poverty, 1978; More Jobs, Less Inflation, 1982; How to Beat Unemployment, 1986; (jtly) Handbook of Labour Economics, 1986; (jtly) The Performance of the British Economy, 1988; (jtly) Unemployment: Macroeconomic Performance and the Labour Market, 1991; (jtly) Reform in Eastern Europe, 1991; (jtly) East-West Migration: the alternatives, 1992; (jtly) Post-Communist Reform: pain and progress, 1993; Macroeconomics: a text for Russia, 1994; (jtly) The Coming Russian Boom, 1996; What Labour Can Do, 1997; Tackling Unemployment, 1999; Tackling Inequality, 1999; (ed) What the Future Holds, 2002; Happiness: lessons from a new science, 2005, 2nd edn, 2011; (jtly) A Good Childhood: searching for values in a competitive age, 2009; (ed jtly) World Happiness Report, annually, 2012–; (jtly) Thrive: the power of evidence-based psychological therapies, 2014; (jtly) The Origins of Happiness, 2018. *Recreation:* tennis. *Address:* London School of Economics, Houghton Street, WC2A 2AE. *T:* (020) 7955 7048.

LAYARD, Adm. Sir Michael (Henry Gordon), KCB 1993; CBE 1982; Second Sea Lord, and Chief of Naval Personnel (Member of Admiralty Board, Defence Council), 1993–95; Commander-in-Chief Naval Home Command, 1994–95; Flag Aide-de-Camp to the Queen, 1994–95; *b* Sri Lanka, 3 Jan. 1936; *s* of late Edwin Henry Frederick and Doris Christian Gordon (*née* Spence); *m* 1966, Elspeth Horsley Fisher; two *s*. *Educ:* Pangbourne Coll.; RN Coll., Dartmouth. Joined RN, 1954; specialised in aviation, 1958; Fighter Pilot, 1960–72; Air Warfare Instructor, 1964; Commanded: 899 Naval Air Sqn, in HMS Eagle, 1970–71; HMS Lincoln, 1971–72; ndc, 1974–75; Directorate, Naval Air Warfare, MoD, 1975–77; Comdr (Air), HMS Ark Royal, 1977–78; CSO (Air), FONAC, 1979–82; Sen. Naval Officer, SS Atlantic Conveyor, Falklands conflict, 1982 (CBE); Commanded: RNAS Culdrose, 1982–84; HMS Cardiff, 1984–85; Task Gp Comdr, Persian Gulf, 1984; Dep. Dir, Naval Warfare (Air), MoD, 1985–88; Flag Officer Naval Aviation (formerly Air Comd), 1988–90; Dir Gen., Naval Manpower and Trng, 1990–92; Leader of RN Officers Study Gp, MoD, 1992–93; Adm. Pres., RNC, Greenwich, 1993–94. Gentleman Usher to the Sword of State, 1997–2005. Non-exec. Dir, Taunton & Somerset NHS Trust, 1996–2000. Trustee, FAA Mus., 1995–2006 (Life Vice Pres., 2010–). Mem., FAA Officers' Assoc., 1964–; Member Council: White Ensign Assoc., 1996–2006 (Chm., 1996–99); Royal Patriotic Fund, 1995–2010. Governor: Pangbourne Coll., 1995–2014; King's Coll., Taunton, 1997–2005; King's Hall, Taunton, 1997–2005. Chevalier Bretvin, 1984. Freeman, City of London, 1994. *Recreations:* painting, sailing, music, history, collecting experiences. *Address:* Harwood House, Aller, Somerset TA10 0QN. *Clubs:* Royal Navy of 1765 and 1785; Royal Naval Sailing Association; Royal Navy Golfing Society (Pres., 1988–94).

LAYDEN, Anthony Michael, CMG 2009; HM Diplomatic Service, retired; *b* 27 July 1946; *s* of Sheriff Michael Layden, SSC, TD and Eileen Mary Layden; *m* 1969, Josephine Mary McGhee; three *s* one *d*. *Educ:* Holy Cross Academy, Edinburgh; Edinburgh Univ. (LLB Hons Law and Econ. 1968). Lieut, 15th (Scottish Volunteer) Bn, Parachute Regt, 1966–69. Foreign Office, 1968; MECAS, Lebanon, 1969; Jedda, 1971; Rome, 1973; FCO, Middle East, Rhodesia, Personnel Ops Depts, 1977–82; Head of Chancery, Jedda, 1982–85; Hong Kong Dept, FCO, 1985–87; Counsellor and Head of Chancery, Muscat, 1987–91; Counsellor (Economic and Commercial), 1991–95, and Dep. Hd of Mission, 1994–95, Copenhagen; Head of Western European Dept, FCO, 1995–98; Ambassador to Morocco and Mauritania (non-resident) to Mauritania, 1999–2002; Ambassador to Libya, 2002–06. Special Rep. for Deportation with Assurances, FCO, 2006–13. *Recreations:* sailing, walking, music, bridge. *Club:* Travellers (Chm., 2010–14).
See also P. J. Layden.

LAYDEN, Patrick John, TD 1981; QC (Scot.) 2000; Commissioner, Scottish Law Commission, 2008–14; *b* 27 June 1949; *s* of Sheriff Michael Layden, SSC, TD and Eileen Mary Layden; *m* 1984, Patricia Mary Bonnar; three *s* one *d*. *Educ:* Holy Cross Acad., Edinburgh; Edinburgh Univ. (LLB Hons). Called to the Scottish Bar, 1973; Lord Advocate's Department: Dep. Scottish Parly Counsel and Asst Legal Sec., 1977–87; Scottish Parly Counsel and Sen. Asst Legal Sec., 1987–99; Legal Sec. to Lord Advocate, 1999–2003; Dep. Solicitor, Office of the Solicitor to the Scottish Exec., later Govt, 2003–08. Univ. of Edinburgh OTC, 1967–71; 2/52 Lowland Vol., TA, 1971–77; 1/51 Highland Vol., 1977–81 (OC London Scottish, 1978–81); OC 73 Ord. Co. (V), 1981–84. *Recreations:* reading, walking, woodworking.
See also A. M. Layden.

LAYER, Prof. Geoffrey Mark, OBE 2003; DL; Professor and Vice Chancellor, University of Wolverhampton, since 2011; *b* Corbridge, 31 Oct. 1955; *s* of John Layer and Winifred Layer; two *s* one *d*. *Educ:* Newcastle Royal Grammar Sch.; Soham Grammar Sch.; City of Ely Sixth Form Coll.; Newcastle Poly. (LLB Hons). Sheffield City Polytechnic, later Sheffield Hallam University: Lectr, Sheffield Business Sch., 1983–89; Hd of Access, 1989–99; Prof. of Lifelong Learning, 1996–99; University of Bradford: Dean, 1999–2004; Pro Vice Chancellor, 2004–08; Dep. Vice Chancellor, 2008–11. Dir, Action on Access, 2000–05. DL W Midlands, 2014. *Publications:* (ed) Closing the Equity Gap, 2005; (ed jtly) Widening Participation: which way forward for English higher education, 2005. *Recreations:* playing cricket for Sheffield Collegiate, watching Sunderland Football Club, cinema, friends. *Address:* Vice Chancellor's Office, University of Wolverhampton, Wulfruna Street, Wolverhampton WV1 1LY. *T:* (01902) 322102. *E:* geoff.layer@wlv.ac.uk.

**LAYER, Prof. Graham Tansley,** DM; FRCS, FRCSEd; FACS; Consultant Surgeon, since 2002, and Director, Professional Standards, since 2008, Royal Surrey County Hospital; Vice President, Royal College of Surgeons of Edinburgh, 2015–18 (Hon. Secretary, 2012–15); *b* Brentwood, Essex, 9 Dec. 1952; *s* of Henry William Tansley Layer and Irene May Layer; *m* 1989, Dr Jennifer Mabel Sillick. *Educ:* Royal Liberty Sch., Gidea Park, Essex; Pembroke Coll., Oxford (BM BCh 1977; MA 1978; DM MCh 1991); St Thomas's Hosp. Med. Sch. FRCS 1981; FRCSEd 2002; FACS 2002. Sen. Registrar (Gen. Surgery), St Thomas's Hosp. and St George's Hosp.; Consultant Surgeon: St Peter's Hosp., Chertsey, 1993–2001; Charing Cross and Hammersmith Hosps, 2001–02; Jt Med. Dir and Mem. Bd, 2007–08, Vis. Prof. of Surgical Scis, 2008–, Univ. of Surrey. Associate Ed., The Surgeon, 2010–. Columnist, Surgeons' News, 2009–. Member: Steering Gp, Nat. Confidential Enquiry into Perioperative Deaths, 1997–2016 (Hon. Treas., 2004–10); Specialist Adv. Cttee in Gen. Surgery, 2007–12; Foundn Mem., Clin. Reference Gp, Monitor, 2009–15. Hon. Sec., Assoc. of Surgeons of GB and Ireland, 2000–06; Mem., Intercollegiate Specialist Exams Bd in Gen. Surgery, 2004–17 (Mem. Panel of Examrs, 2002–17; Hon. Sec., 2005–10). Pres., Section of Surgery, RSocMed, 2009–10. Chm., Dirs of Continuing Professional Develt, Acad. of Med. Royal Colls, 2010–15. UK Gov., Amer. Coll. of Surgeons, 2008–14. External Examiner: Coll. of Surgeons, Hong Kong, 2005, 2013–; Univ. of Brighton, 2009–13; Univ. of Sussex, 2009–13; Univ. of Southampton, 2011–13; Univ. of Edinburgh, 2011–16; NUS, 2016. Hon. Fellow, Indian Assoc. of Surgeons, 2016. *Publications:* book chapters; contrib. peer-reviewed papers to surgical jls. *Recreations:* long haul travel, photography, opera, food (restaurant critic). *Address:* Royal College of Surgeons of Edinburgh, Nicolson Street, Edinburgh EH8 9DW. *T:* (0131) 527 1600, *Fax:* (0131) 557 6406. *E:* gtlayer@rcsed.ac.uk. *Clubs:* Athenæum, Royal Society of Medicine; Wentworth Golf.

**LAYMAN, Rear-Adm. Christopher Hope,** CB 1991; DSO 1982; LVO 1977; Commander, British Forces, Falkland Islands, 1986–87; *b* 9 March 1938; *s* of late Captain H. F. H. Layman, DSO, RN and Elizabeth Hughes; *m* 1964, Katharine Romer Ascherson (*d* 2008); one *s* one *d*. *Educ:* Winchester. Joined Royal Navy, 1956; specialised Communications and Electronic Warfare, 1966; commanded HM Ships: Hubberston, 1968–70; Lynx, 1972–74; Exec. Officer, HM Yacht Britannia, 1976–78; Captain, 7th Frigate Sqn, 1981–83; commanded HM Ships: Argonaut, 1981–82; Cleopatra, 1982–83; Invincible, 1984–86; Asst Dir (Communications and Information Systems), IMS, NATO HQ, Brussels, 1988–91, retd. Consultant in communications and inf. systems and maritime affairs, 1991–2001. Gentleman Usher of the Green Rod, Order of the Thistle, 1997–. *Publications:* Man of Letters, 1990; The Falklands and the Dwarf, 1995; The Wager Disaster, 2015. *Recreations:* fishing, archaeology. *Club:* New (Edinburgh).

**LAYTON,** family name of **Baron Layton**.

**LAYTON, 4th Baron** *cr* 1947, of Danehill; **Jonathan Francis Layton**; *b* 16 Feb. 1942; *s* of late Hon. David Layton, MBE and Elizabeth Layton (*née* Gray); *S* cousin, 2018; *m* 1971, Julia Goodwin; two *s* one *d*. *Heir:* *s* Jeremy Stephen Layton, *b* 1978.

**LAYTON, Alexander William;** QC 1995; barrister; a Recorder, since 2000; a Deputy High Court Judge, since 2007; *b* 23 Feb. 1952; *s* of Paul Henry Layton and Frances Evelyn Layton (*née* Weekes); *m* 1988, Sandy Forshaw (*née* Matheson); two *d*. *Educ:* Marlborough Coll.; Brasenose Coll., Oxford (MA); Ludwig-Maximilian Univ., Munich. Called to the Bar, Middle Temple, 1976 (Astbury Law Scholar), Bencher, 2004; Asst Recorder, 1998–2000. Chairman: British-German Jurists Assoc., 1988–93; Bar European Gp, 2005–07; Bd of Trustees, Brit. Inst. of Internat. and Comparative Law, 2005–11. Trustee: Allachy Trust, 1979–2008; Rivendell Trust, 1979–2004; Lincoln Clinic and Centre for Psychotherapy, 2003–06; Frensham Heights Sch., 2008–11; Acad. of Eur. Law, 2012–. Member: Adv. Bd, Bingham Centre for Rule of Law, 2011–; Adv. Council, Inst. of European and Comparative Law, Oxford Univ., 2014–. Vis. Fellow, NYU, 2011, 2018; Vis. Prof., KCL, 2015–. FCIArb 2000. *Publications:* (contrib.) The Bar on Trial, 1977; (jtly) European Civil Practice, 1989, 2nd edn 2004; (contrib.) Practitioners' Handbook of EC Law, 1998; (contrib.) Forum Shopping in the European Judicial Area, 2007; (contrib.) The Brussels I Review Proposal Uncovered, 2012; (contrib.) Extraterritoriality and Collective Redress, 2012; (contrib.) Forum Shopping in the International Arbitration Context, 2013; (contrib.) Encyclopedia of Private International Law, 2017. *Recreations:* family, contemporary art. *Address:* 20 Essex Street, WC2R 3AL. *T:* (020) 7842 1200, *Fax:* (020) 7842 1270. *E:* alayton@20essexst.com.

**LAYTON, Hon. Christopher Walter;** Trustee (formerly Director), Action for a Global Climate Community, since 2008 (Chairman, 2003–08); *b* 31 Dec. 1929; *s* of 1st Baron Layton, CH, CBE; *m* 1st, 1961, Anneliese Margaret, *d* of Joachim von Thadden, Hanover (marr. diss. 1957); one *s* one *d*; 2nd, 1961, Margaret Ann, *d* of Leslie Moon, Molesey, Surrey (marr. diss. 1995); two *d* (and one *d* decd); 3rd, 1995, Wendy Daniels (*d* 2009), *d* of Kenneth Bartlett, Hemel Hempstead; one *d*. *Educ:* Oundle; King's Coll., Cambridge. Intelligence Corps, 1948–49; ICI Ltd, 1952; The Economist Intelligence Unit, 1953–54; Editorial writer, European affairs, The Economist, 1954–62; Economic Adviser to Liberal Party, 1962–69; Dir, Centre for European Industrial Studies, Bath Univ., 1968–71; Commission of European Communities: Chef de Cabinet to Commissioner Spinelli, 1971–73; Dir, Computer Electronics, Telecomms and Air Transp. Equipment Manufg, Directorate-Gen. of Internal Market and Industrial Affairs, 1973–81, now Hon. Dir-Gen.; Editor, Alliance, 1982–83, Associate Editor, New Democrat, 1983–85. Dir, World Order Project, Federal Trust, 1987–90; Fellow, Findhorn Foundn, 1987–; Trustee: One World Trust, 1986–2007 (Vice Pres., 2018–); Peace Building UK, 2006–11 (Chm., 2006–08); Founder Mem., Grimstone Community, 1990–2007; Jt Founder and Vice Chm., Moor Trees, 1996–2006. Contested: (L) Chippenham, Nov. 1962, 1964, 1966; (SDP) London W, European Parly Elecn, 1984. *Publications:* Transatlantic Investment, 1966; European Advanced Technology, 1968; Cross-frontier Mergers in Europe 1970; (jtly) Industry and Europe, 1971; (jtly) Ten Innovations: International Study on Development Technology and the Use of Qualified Scientists and Engineers in Ten Industries, 1972; Europe and the Global Crisis, 1987; A Step Beyond Fear, 1989; The Healing of Europe, 1990; A Climate Community: a European initiative with the South, 2001, 3rd edn 2006. *Recreations:* painting, sculpture, writing. *Address:* Wrey Cottage, Madge Lane, Tavistock, Devon PL19 0DY.

**LAYTON, Matthew Robert;** Managing Partner, Clifford Chance LLP, since 2014; *b* Leeds, 27 Feb. 1961; *s* of Prof. D. Layton; *m* 2002, Emma-Marie Brown; two *s* two *d*. *Educ:* Leeds Grammar Sch.; Univ. of Leeds (LLB). Admitted as Solicitor, 1986. With Clifford Chance LLP, 1983–: Partner, 1991–; Global Hd, Corporate Practice, 2008–14. *Recreations:* theatre, Cornish artists, music. *Address:* Clifford Chance LLP, 10 Upper Bank Street, E14 5JJ. *T:* (020) 7006 1000, *Fax:* (020) 7006 5555. *E:* matthew.layton@cliffordchance.com.

**LAYTON, Peter Stephen;** Founder and Managing Director: London Glassblowing, since 1976; Peter Layton & Associates Ltd, since 1992; *b* 21 June 1937; *s* of Freddie Layton (né Löwe) and Edith Beatrice Layton (*née* Hecht); *m* 1st, 1966, Tessa Schneideman (marr. diss. 1982; she *d* 2001); one *s*; 2nd, 1984, Ann Ashmore; one *s* one *d*. *Educ:* Belle Vue Grammar Sch. for Boys, Bradford; Bradford Coll. of Art (Hon. Fellow); Central Sch. of Art and Design (Dip.). Various lectureships and professorships including: Univ. of Iowa, Sacramento State Univ., Univ. of Calif, Davis and Art Inst. of Chicago, 1966–68; Stoke on Trent Coll. of Art, Hornsey Coll. of Art, Camberwell Coll. of Art, Croydon Coll. of Art and Sir John Cass Coll. of Art, 1968–78. Chairman: British Artists in Glass, 1983–85; Contemp. Glass Soc., 1997–99 (Hon. Life Mem.); Member: Glass Circle; Glass Assoc.; Glass Art Soc.; Bd, Internat. Glass Art Soc.; Hon. Fellow, Soc. of Designer Craftsmen. With Ann Layton, created Emerging Talent Award for British Glass Biennale, 2015. Residency, Mus. of Glass, Tacoma, Wash, USA, 2017. Freeman: City of London; Glass Sellers' Co. Hon. DLitt Bradford, 2003. *Publications:* Glass Art, 1996; Neues Glas, 2003; Peter Layton and Friends, 2006; Past and Present: Peter Layton and London Glassblowing, 2012. *Recreations:* art, travel, beachcombing, theatre, film, food, country living. *Address:* London Glassblowing, 62–66 Bermondsey Street, SE1 3UD. *T:* (020) 7403 2800, *Fax:* (020) 7403 7778. *E:* peter@londonglassblowing.co.uk.

**LAYTON, Prof. Robert Hugh,** DPhil; FBA 2012; Professor of Anthropology, Durham University, 1991, now Emeritus; *b* Welwyn Garden City, 1 Dec. 1944. *Educ:* University Coll. London (BSc Anthropol. 1966; MPhil (Dist.) 1968); Univ. of Sussex (DPhil 1971). Lectr in Anthropol., UCL, 1970–74; res. consultant in social anthropol., Australian Inst. of Aboriginal and Torres Strait Islander Studies, Canberra, 1974–79; anthropologist resp. for land claims, Northern (Aboriginal) Land Council, Darwin, 1979–81; Reader in Anthropol., Durham Univ., 1982–91. High-End For. Expert, Chinese Nat. Acad. Arts, 2013–. Rivers Medal, RAI, 2003. *Publications:* The Anthropology of Art, 1981, 2nd edn 1991; Uluru: an aboriginal history of Ayers Rock, 1986, re-issued 2001; (ed) Conflict in the Archaeology of Living Traditions, 1989; Australian Rock Art: a new synthesis, 1992; An Introduction to Theory in Anthropology, 1997; (ed with P. Ucko) The Archaeology and Anthropology of Landscape, 1999; (ed jtly) Destruction and Conservation of Cultural Property, 2000; Anthropology and History in Franche Compté: a critique of social theory, 2000; (ed jtly) Hunter-gatherers: an interdisciplinary perspective, 2001; Order and Anarchy: civil society, social disorder and war, 2006; articles in jls. *Address:* c/o Department of Anthropology, Durham University, Dawson Building, South Road, Durham DH1 3LE.

**LAYTON, Stephen David,** FRCO; conductor; Fellow and Director of Music, Trinity College, Cambridge, since 2006; *b* 23 Dec. 1966; *s* of David Layton and Hazel Layton (*née* Bestwick); *m* 2005, Christine Counsell (*née* Watts). *Educ:* Pilgrim's Sch., Winchester; Eton Coll. (Music Schol.); King's Coll., Cambridge (A. H. Mann Organ Schol.; BA 1988; MA 1991). FRCO 1985. Asst Organist, Southwark Cathedral, 1988–97; Dir. of Music, 1997–2006, Organist, 1997–2004, Temple Church, London; Founder and Music Dir, Polyphony, 1986–; Music Dir, Holst Singers, 1993–; Artistic Dir and Principal Conductor, City of London Sinfonia, 2010. Conductor, BBC Promenade Concerts, 1995–; Chief Guest Conductor, Danish Nat. Choir, 1999–2012; Chief Conductor, Netherlands Kammerchor, 2001–05 (Guest Conductor, 1998–2001); Guest Conductor: Orch. of the Age of Enlightenment, 1999–; ENO, 2000, 2002; Australian Chamber Orch., 2000, 2001; Irish Chamber Orch., 2001, 2008; Britten Sinfonia, 2001–; Acad. of Ancient Music, 2002–; Scottish Chamber Orch., 2002, 2004; English Chamber Orch., 2003, 2004, 2009–; London Sinfonietta, 2004; Odense SO, 2004, 2007, 2010; LPO, 2005; Philadelphia Orch., 2005; Minnesota Orch., 2007; Aalborg SO, 2007, 2011, 2013; Melbourne SO, Qld Orch., 2009; Opera North, 2013; tours as conductor include: USA, 1989, 1994, 1996, 2004, 2005, 2007, 2009, 2012; Brazil, 1995, 1998; Estonia, 1993, 1995, 2009; Australia, 2000, 2001, 2009, 2010, 2012, 2014; Poland, 2005, 2006, 2008, 2013; Latvia, 2007, 2013; Korea, 2009; Hong Kong, 2012; New Zealand, 2012, 2014. Recordings incl. premières of Pärt, Tavener, Adès, Macmillan, Jackson, Lukaszewski, Whitacre, Lauridsen, Esenvalds, Tormis, Briggs and Praulins. Hon. Bencher, Middle Temple, 2007. Gramophone Award, 2001, 2012. *Recreations:* food, cyberspace, kite flying, gadgets. *Address:* Trinity College, Cambridge CB2 1TQ. *Club:* Athenaeum.

**LAYZELL, Prof. Paul John;** DL; PhD; CEng; FBCS; Principal, Royal Holloway, University of London, since 2010; *b* London, 23 July 1957; *s* of Andrew and Celia Layzell; *m* 1982, Pamela Margaret Seymour. *Educ:* Univ. of Manchester (BA Econ. 1978); Univ. of Manchester Inst. of Technol. (MSc Computation 1979; PhD Computation 1982). CEng 1990; FBCS 1990. University of Manchester Institute of Science and Technology: Lectr, 1982–92; Sen. Lectr, 1992–95; Prof. of Computer Sci., 1995–2004; Pro-Vice-Chancellor, 2000–04; Vice-Pres. (Univ. Develt), Univ. of Manchester, 2004–06; Dep. Vice-Chancellor, Univ. of Sussex, 2006–10. Chair: Eduserv, 2008–13; Assessment and Qualifications Alliance, later AQA, 2009–. DL Surrey, 2017. FHEA 2007. *Publications:* COBOL 85 Reference Summary, 1986; (with P. Loucopoulos) Systems Analysis and Development, 1986; (ed with K. Spurr) CASE on Trial, 1990; (ed with K. Spurr) CASE: current practice, future prospects, 1992; (with C. G. Davies) The Jackson Approach to System Development: an introduction, 1993; (ed jtly) Software Assistance for Business Process Re-Engineering, 1993; (ed jtly) Computer Support for Co-operative Work, 1994; (ed jtly) Business Objects: software solutions, 1994; contribs to learned business, computing and IT jls and articles in conf. proceedings. *Recreations:* walking, gardening, travel. *Address:* Royal Holloway, University of London, Egham, Surrey TW20 0EX. *T:* (01784) 443033. *E:* principal@royalholloway.ac.uk.

**LAZARE, Philippe Henri;** Chief Executive Officer, 2007–18, and Chairman, 2010–18, Ingenico Group (Board Member, 2005–18); *b* Neuilly-sur-Seine, 30 Oct. 1956; *s* of Robert Lazare and Suzanne (*née* Legallo); *m* 2010, Mrs Nathalie Rouvet; four *s* from previous marriages. *Educ:* Lycée Marcel Roby, Saint-Germain-en-Laye; École Supérieure d'architecture, Paris-la-Défense (Architect Govt Dip.). Industrial buyer, 1983–87; Project Manager for 605 Peugeot, 1987–89; Peugeot Planning Manager, Soc. Gén. d'achats PSA gp, 1989–90; Groupe Sextant Avionique: Industrial sub-contracting Manager, 1990–91; Site Industrial Manager, 1991–93; Site Dir at Châtellerault, 1993–94; Dir, Peat Marwick Consultants, 1994–95; Air France: Dir, Maintenance Result Centre, 1995–96; Man. Dir, Industries Profit Centre, and Dep. Manager i/c industrial logistics, 1996; Chm. and CEO, Servair Gp and Cie de réparation de moteurs d'avion (CRMA), 1997–98; Man. Dir, Lucien Barrière Gp, 1998–2000; Man. Dir, 2000–01, CEO, 2001–02, Eurotunnel; Dir of Buying, Property and Cost-Reduction, Groupe La Poste, 2003–06; Chm. and CEO, Poste Immo, 2004–07; Dep. Dir, Territorial Develt, Groupe La Poste.

**LAZAREV, Alexander Nikolaevich;** Principal Conductor, Japan Philharmonic Orchestra, 2008–16, now Conductor Laureate; *b* 5 July 1945; *m* Tamara Lazareva; one *d*. *Educ:* St Petersburg Conservatory; Moscow Conservatory. Bolshoi Theatre: Founder, Ensemble of Soloists, 1978; Chief Conductor and Artistic Dir, 1987–95; UK début with Royal Liverpool Philharmonic Orch., 1987; Principal Guest Conductor: BBC SO, 1992–95; Royal Scottish Nat. Orch., 1994–97; Principal Conductor, Royal Scottish Nat. Orch., 1997–2005. Hon. Prof., Univ. of Glasgow, 2005–. 1st Prize and Gold Medal, Karajan Comp., Berlin, 1972; People's Artist of Russia, 1982; Glinka Prize, 1986. Commendatore dell'Ordine al Merito della Repubblica Italiana, 2004; Order of Merit for the Fatherland (Russia), 2010. *Address:* c/o Tennant Artists, Unit 2, 39 Tadema Road, SW10 0PZ.

**LAZARIDIS, Mihal, (Mike),** OC 2005; OOnt 2005; FRS 2014; Managing Partner and Joint Founder, Quantum Valley Investments Fund, since 2013; philanthropist; *b* Istanbul, 14 March 1961; *s* of Nick and Dorothy Lazaridis; *m* Ophelia Tong; one *s* one *d*. *Educ:* Univ. of Waterloo, Ont. Research in Motion, later BlackBerry: Jt-Founder, 1984; Co-Chm. and

Co-CEO, 1984–2012; invented BlackBerry smartphone device, launched 1999; Vice-Chm. Bd, 2012–13; Chm., Innovation Cttee, 2012–13. Founder and Chm. Bd, Perimeter Inst. for Res. in Theoretical Physics, 2000–; Founder, Inst. for Quantum Computing, 2002, Quantum-Nano Centre, 2012, Univ. of Waterloo. Chancellor, Univ. of Waterloo, Ont, 2003–09. Hon. DEng Waterloo, 2000; Hon. LLD: McMaster, 2005; Laval; Windsor. Emmy Award, 1994, Academy Award, 1999, for tech. achievements in film and TV; (jtly) Ernest C. Manning Principal Award, 2002. *Address*: Quantum Valley Investments Fund, 560 Westmount Road North, Waterloo, ON N2L 0A9, Canada.

**LAZAROWICZ, Marek Jerzy, (Mark)**; advocate, since 1996; *b* 8 Aug. 1953; *m* 1992, Caroline Elizabeth Johnston; three *s* one *d*. *Educ*: Univ. of St Andrews (MA); Univ. of Edinburgh (LLB; Dip. Legal Practice). Member (Lab): City of Edinburgh DC, 1980–96; City of Edinburgh Council, 1999–2001. MP (Lab) Edinburgh N and Leith, 2001–15; contested (Lab) same seat, 2015. Special Rep. of the Prime Minister on carbon trading, 2008–10; Shadow Minister for Internat. Develt, 2010–11. Member: Modernisation of H of C Select Cttee, 2005–10; Envmtl Audit Select Cttee, 2007–15. *Publications*: (jtly) The Scottish Parliament: an introduction, 1999, 4th edn 2010; (jtly) The Scottish Parliament: law and practice, 2018; various articles and papers on legal and political matters.

**LAZARUS, Mary Helen; Her Honour Judge Lazarus**; a Circuit Judge, since 2015; *b* Bristol, 27 Sept. 1966; *d* of Peter Lazarus and Joanna Brown (*née* Smijth-Windham); *m* 2001, Nicholas Cooper (separated 2017); one *s* two *d*. *Educ*: Downs Sch., Wraxall; Malvern Girls' Coll.; Marlborough Coll.; Newnham Coll., Cambridge (BA 1988; MA 1992). Called to the Bar, Middle Temple, 1991; in practice as barrister, 1991–2015; Fee-paid Judge of First-tier Tribunal (Health, Educn and Social Care Chamber (Mental Health)), 2002–; a Recorder, 2012–15. *Recreations*: loves reading, drawing, art, music, architecture, nature, walking, clouds (Member of Cloud Appreciation Society). *Address*: Bromley County Court, College Road, Bromley BR1 3PX. *E*: enquiries@bromley.countycourt.gsi.gov.uk.

**LAZARUS, Prof. Neil,** PhD; FBA 2014; Professor of English and Comparative Literary Studies, University of Warwick; *b* S Africa. *Educ*: Univ. of Witwatersrand (BA Hons); Univ. of Essex (MA); Univ. of Keele (PhD Sociol.). Postdoctoral Fellow, Centre for Humanities, then Lectr, English Dept, Yale Univ.; Wesleyan Univ.; Louisiana State Univ.; Brown Univ. *Publications*: Resistance in Postcolonial African Fiction, 1990; Nationalism and Cultural Practice in the Postcolonial World, 1999; Marxism, Modernity and Postcolonial Studies, 2002; (ed) The Cambridge Companion to Postcolonial Literary Studies, 2004; The Postcolonial Unconscious, 2011; (contrib.) Global Modernisms, 2012; (contrib.) Oxford Handbook to Postcolonial Studies, 2013; (contrib.) Combined and Uneven Development: towards a new theory of world-literature, 2015; contribs to jls incl. Cultural Critique, Diaspora, differences, Mediations, New Formations, Race & Class, Res. in African Literatures, S Atlantic Qly, Textual Practice, Jl Postcolonial Writing, Jl Commonwealth Lit. *Address*: Department of English and Comparative Literary Studies, Humanities Building, University Road, University of Warwick, Coventry CV4 7AL.

**LAZARUS, Sandra Lynne**; *see* Boss, S. L.

**LAZENBY, Prof. Alec,** AO 1988; FTSE, FRSB, FAIAST; consultant on agricultural research and development and higher education, 1991–2011; *b* 4 March 1927; *s* of G. and E. Lazenby; *m* 1957, Ann Jennifer, *d* of R. A. Hayward; one *s* two *d*. *Educ*: Wath on Dearne Grammar Sch.; University Coll. of Wales, Aberystwyth. BSc 1949, MSc 1952, Wales; MA 1954, PhD 1959, ScD 1985, Cantab. Scientific Officer, Welsh Plant Breeding Station, 1949–53; Demonstr in Agricultural Botany, 1953–58, Lectr in Agricultural Botany, 1958–65, Univ. of Cambridge; Fellow and Asst Tutor, Fitzwilliam Coll., Cambridge, 1962–65; Foundation Prof. of Agronomy, Univ. of New England, NSW, 1965–70, now Professor Emeritus; Vice-Chancellor, Univ. of New England, Armidale, NSW, 1970–77; Dir, Grassland Res. Inst., 1977–82; Vice-Chancellor, Univ. of Tasmania, 1982–91. Principal Consultant, Internat. Develt Prog., Aust. Univs, 1985–99. Vis. Prof., Reading Univ., 1978. Hon. Professorial Fellow, Univ. of Wales, 1979; Hon. Prof., Victoria Univ. of Technol., 1992–97. Hon. DRurSci New England, NSW, 1981; Hon. LLD Tasmania, 1992. Centenary Medal, Australia, 2003. *Publications*: (ed jtly) Intensive Pasture Production, 1972; (ed jtly) Australian Field Crops, vol. I, 1975, vol. II, 1979; Australia's Plant Breeding Needs, 1986; (ed jtly) The Grass Crop, 1988; (jtly) The Story of IDP, 1999; (ed jtly) Competition and Succession in Pastures, 2001; papers on: pasture plant breeding; agronomy; weed ecology, in various scientific jls. *Recreations*: golf, gardening, public affairs, reading. *Address*: 16/99 Groom Street, Hughes, ACT 2605, Australia.

**LAZENBY, Andrew Neil;** Chief Executive Officer: Royal Agricultural Society of England, since 2018; Innovation for Agriculture, since 2018; *b* Yorks, 11 Aug. 1974; *s* of Barry Lazenby and Pauline Lazenby; one *d*. *Educ*: South Axholme Sch.; Harper Adams Coll. (BSc Hons); Univ. of Lincoln (DipM). MCIM. Hd of Commercial, Leckford Estate, 2011–15; Dir of Ops, Farmcare, Wellcome Trust, 2015–17. *Recreations*: field sports, ski-ing, sailing. *Address*: Fullwood Holmes, Edale Road, Hope, Hope Valley S33 6RF. *E*: Laz80@me.com.

**LEA OF CRONDALL, Baron** *cr* 1999 (Life Peer), of Crondall in the county of Hampshire; **David Edward Lea,** OBE 1978; Assistant General Secretary of the Trades Union Congress, 1977–94; *b* Tyldesley, Lancs, 2 Nov. 1937; *s* of Edward Cunliffe Lea and Lilian May Lea. *Educ*: Farnham Grammar Sch.; Christ's Coll., Cambridge (MA). Pres., CU Liberal Club, 1960; Nat. Pres., Union of Liberal Students, 1961; Inaugural Chair, Cambridge Univ. Students' Representative Council, 1961. Nat. Service, RHA, 1955–57. Economist Intelligence Unit, 1961; Economic Dept, TUC, 1964, Asst Sec., 1967, Sec. 1970. Jt Sec., TUC-Labour Party Liaison Cttee, 1972–86; Secretary: TUC Cttee on European Strategy, 1989–99; Envmt Action Gp, 1989–99; Task Force on Representation at Work, 1994–99; Chm., Econ. Cttee, 1980–91, Mem. Steering Cttee, 1991–99, Vice Pres., 1997–98, ETUC; Member: Royal Commn on the Distribution of Income and Wealth, 1974–79; Adv. Gp on Channel Tunnel and Cross-Channel Services, 1974–75; Cttee of Inquiry on Industrial Democracy, 1975–77; Energy Commn, 1977–79; Retail Prices Index Adv. Cttee, 1977–99; Delors Cttee on Economic and Social Concepts in the Community, 1977–79; NEDC Cttee on Finance for Investment, 1978–92; Kreisky Commn on Unemployment in Europe, 1986–89; Franco-British Council, 1982–99; EU Steering Cttee on Social Dialogue, 1992–99; Central Arbitration Cttee, 2000–; UK Round Table on Sustainable Develt, 1995–99; Chm., Round Table Gp on Greening Business, 1997–98; Expert Adviser, UN Commn on Transnational Corporations, 1977–81; Hon. Mem., UK Delegn, Earth Summit on Envmt and Develt, Rio, 1992. Mem., Sub Cttee A, EU Cttee, 1999–, Sub Cttee C, Foreign Affairs, Defence and Develt, 2003–, h of L; Chairman: All Party Parly Gp on Bolivia, 2005–09; All Party Parly Gp on Madagascar, 2006–; Vice-Chairman: All Party Gp on Africa, 2003–; PLP Gp on Transport, 2003–; Anglo-Swiss Parly Gp, 2003–; Franco-British Parly Gp, 2004–; Vice-Pres., All Party Gp on Arts and Heritage, 2003–; Secretary: All Party Parly Gp on Algeria, 2007–; All Party Gp on Faroe Is, 2010–; Treas., All Party Parly Gps on Serbia and Macedonia, 2003–. Governor, NIESR, 1981–; Trustee, Employment Policy Inst., 1992–99. Chairman: Farnham Roads Action, 1986–; Hammarskjold Inquiry Trust, 2012–14; Mem. Cttee, Tilford Bach Soc., 1995–99; Patron, Third Age Trust, 1991–97. Joined Labour Party, 1963. FRSA 1993. Mem. Editl Bd, New Economy (IPPR review), 1993–2000. *Publications*: Trade Unionism, 1966; (contrib.) The Multinational Enterprise, 1971; Industrial Democracy (TUC), 1974; Keynes Plus: a participatory economy (ETUC), 1979; (jtly) Europe and Your Rights at Work, 2006; The Labour Social Democracy Project, 2010. *Address*: South Court, Crondall, Hants GU10 5QF. *T*: (01252) 850711; 17 Ormonde Mansions, 106 Southampton Row, WC1B 4BP. *T*: (020) 7405 6237. *Club*: Bourne (Farnham).

**LEA, Jeremy Hugh Chaloner; His Honour Judge Lea;** a Circuit Judge, since 2005; Judge of Family Court (Mental Health), since 2018; *b* 29 March 1954; *s* of Henry Hugh Edgar Lea and Teresa Lea (*née* Baker); *m* 1992, Jane Elizabeth Turrill; one *s* one *d*. *Educ*: John Fisher Sch., Purley; Univ. of Sussex (BA 1976; LLB 1977); Univ. de Strasbourg. Called to the Bar, Middle Temple, 1978; a barrister, Midland Circuit, 1979–2005; a Recorder, 2001–05; Designated Family Judge: Leicester County Court, 2008–12; Nottingham County Court, 2013–17. Trustee, Nat. Youth Advocacy Service, 2016–. *Recreations*: coarse ski-ing, real ale, watching cricket. *Address*: c/o Nottingham County Court, 60 Canal Street, Nottingham NG1 7EJ. *T*: (0115) 910 3500.

**LEA, Dame Judith Elizabeth;** *see* Hackitt, Dame J. E.

**LEA, Lyndon;** Co-founder and Partner, Lion Capital, since 2004; *b* Morecambe, 13 Jan. 1969; *s* of David and Sylvia Lea; one *s* one *d*; *m* 2015, Sophie Dickens; one *d*. *Educ*: Univ. of Western Ontario (BA Business Admin 1990). Investment banker: Goldman Sachs, 1990–92; Schroders, 1992–94; Glenisla, 1994–98; Partner, Hicks Muse Tate & Furst, 1998–2004. Mem. Bd, Not For Sale charity. *Recreations*: jiujitsu, golf, family time.

**LEA, Ruth Jane,** CBE 2015; Economic Adviser, Arbuthnot Banking Group, since 2007 (non-executive Director, 2005–15); *b* 22 Sept. 1947; *d* of late Thomas Lea and Jane (*née* Brown). *Educ*: Lymm Grammar Sch.; York Univ. (BA); Bristol Univ. (MSc). Asst Statistician, later Sen. Economic Assistant, HM Treasury, 1970–73; Lectr in Econs, Thames Poly., 1973–74; Statistician: CS Coll., 1974–77; HM Treasury, 1977–78; CSO, 1978–84; Statistician, 1984–87, Dep. Dir, Invest in Britain Bureau, 1987–88, DTI; Sen. Economist, 1988–90, Chief Economist, 1990–93, Mitsubishi Bank; Chief UK Economist, Lehman Bros, 1993–94; Econs Ed., ITN, 1994–95; Hd of Policy Unit, Inst. of Dirs, 1995–2003; Director: Centre for Policy Studies, 2004–07; Global Vision, 2007–10. Member: Retail Prices Adv. Cttee, 1992–94; NCC, 1993–96; Nurses' Pay Rev. Body, 1994–98; Bd, ESRC Res. Priorities (formerly ESRC Res. Centres), 1996–97; ONS Stats Adv. Cttee, 1996–97; Cttee of Experts, DIT, 2017–. Member Council: REconS, 1995–2000; Univ. of London, 2001–06. Gov., LSE, 2003–08. Trustee, Global Warming Policy Foundn, 2019–. Freeman, City of London, 2014; Liveryman: Curriers' Co., 2014; World Traders' Co., 2015. Hon. DBA: Greenwich, 1997; BPP Univ. Coll., 2010; Chester, 2015. *Publications*: numerous research papers and articles on economic issues. *Recreations*: music, natural history and countryside, heritage, philately. *Address*: 25 Redbourne Avenue, N3 2BP. *T*: (020) 8346 3482. *Club*: Reform.

**LEA, Prof. Susan Mary,** DPhil; Professor of Microbiology, Sir William Dunn School of Pathology, University of Oxford, since 2016; Fellow, Wadham College, Oxford, since 2016; *b* 10 Feb. 1969; *d* of William and Deborah Lea. *Educ*: Oxford High Sch., GDST; New Coll., Oxford (BA Physiol Scis 1990; DPhil Structural Biol. 1993). Royal Soc. Dorothy Hodgkin Fellow, Dept of Biochem., Univ. of Oxford, 1995–99; Lectr in Biochem., St Hilda's Coll., Oxford, 1999–2006; Lectr, Brasenose Coll. and Sir William Dunn Sch. of Pathol., Univ. of Oxford, 2006–16. *Recreation*: early music. *Address*: Sir William Dunn School of Pathology, South Parks Road, Oxford OX1 3RE. *E*: susan.lea@path.ox.ac.uk.

**LEA, Sir Thomas (William),** 5th Bt *cr* 1892, of The Larches, Kidderminster and Sea Grove, Dawlish; *b* 6 Sept. 1973; *s* of Sir Julian Lea, 4th Bt and of Gerry Valerie, *d* of late Captain Gibson C. Fahnestock; *S* father, 1990; *m* 2017, Laura Ng. *Educ*: Uppingham Sch. *Heir*: *b* Alexander Julian Lea, *b* 28 Oct. 1978.

**LEABEATER, James Ferguson;** QC 2019; *b* Reading, 26 Aug. 1975; *s* of Bruce Leabeater and Elizabeth Leabeater; *m* 2015, Melissa Lessi; one *s*. *Educ*: Oundle Sch.; Corpus Christi Coll., Oxford (BA Hons Mod. Hist. 1996). Called to the Bar, Lincoln's Inn, 1999; in practice as a barrister, specialising in commercial law, 1999–. *Address*: 4 Pump Court, Temple, EC4Y 7AN. *T*: (020) 7842 5555. *E*: jleabeater@4pumpcourt.com.

**LEACH OF FAIRFORD, Lady;** *see* Douglas-Home, J. V.

**LEACH, Clive William,** CBE 2000; Chairman: YFM (formerly Yorkshire Enterprise) Group Ltd, 1995–2008; Universe Media Group Ltd (formerly Gabriel Communications Ltd), since 1997; *b* 4 Dec. 1934; *s* of Stanley and Laura Leach; *m* 1st, 1958, Audrey (*née* Parker) (*d* 1978); three *s*; 2nd, 1980, Stephanie (*née* McGinn); one *s*. *Educ*: Sir John Leman Grammar Sch., Beccles, Suffolk. Professional cricketer, Warwickshire CCC, 1955–58. Gen. Sales Manager, Tyne Tees Television, 1968–74; Sales Dir, 1974–79, Dir of Sales and Marketing, 1979–82, Trident Television; Man. Dir, Link Television, 1982–85; Dir of Sales and Marketing, 1985–88, Man. Dir, 1988–93, Yorkshire Television; Man. Dir, 1985–88, Chm., 1988–93, Yorkshire Television Enterprises. Chairman: Yorkshire Television Internat., 1988–93; Yorkshire-Tyne Tees Television Holdings, 1993 (Gp Chief Exec., 1992–93); Dir, ITN, 1988–93. Chairman: Yorkshire Fund Managers Ltd, 1996–2008; Serene Pavilions (Sri Lanka) Ltd; Dir, British Small Cos Venture Capital Trust plc, 1996–2004. Dep. Chm., Regl Chamber, subseq. Regl Assembly, for Yorks and Humber, 2001–05. Chairman: Leeds TEC, 1991–2000; Leeds HA, 1996–2000; W Yorks Learning and Skills Council, 2000–09; Yorks Cultural Consortium, 2001; Dir, Opera North Ltd, 1992–2003; Chm., Durham CCC (Hldgs) Ltd, 2004–16. FRSA; MCIM 1994. *Recreations*: golf, cricket, travel. *Address*: The White House, Barkston Ash, Tadcaster, N Yorks LS24 9TT. *Clubs*: Reform, MCC; Alwoodley Golf.

**LEACH, Jennifer Irene,** CBE 2006; Vice President, Girlguiding UK (Guide Association), since 2008 (Chief Guide, 2001–06); Chief Commissioner, Commonwealth Girl Guides Associations, 2001–06; *b* 11 Oct. 1944; *d* of Arthur and Beatrice Garner; *m* 1966, Arthur John Leach; one *s* one *d*. Guide Association: Unit Guider, 1974–87; Dist Comr, 1980–86; Co. Comr, W Yorks, 1987–92; Chief Comr, NE England, 1994–99 (Vice Pres., 2000). FRSA 2002. *Recreations*: four grandsons, cooking, France. *Address*: Laithe Croft, Rastrick, Brighouse, W Yorks HD6 3HL. *T*: (01484) 714950.

**LEACH, Joanne;** *see* Wade, J.

**LEACH, Katherine Jane;** HM Diplomatic Service; Ambassador to Armenia, 2014–15 (Joint Ambassador, 2012–14); *m* Jonathan James Aves, *qv*; one *s* two *d*. Joined FCO, 2000; Desk Officer, EU Trade and Develt Policy, FCO, 2000–01; Hd, External Pol Section, 2002–03, First Sec. (Internal Pol), 2003–04, Moscow; Dep. Hd, Passports and Documentary Services, Consular Directorate, FCO, 2005; Japanese lang. trng, FCO, 2005–07; Hd, Energy and Envmt Team, Tokyo, 2007–11. *Address*: c/o Foreign and Commonwealth Office, King Charles Street, SW1A 2AH.

**LEACH, Prof. Melissa Anne,** CBE 2017; PhD; FBA 2017; Professor, since 2004, and Director, Institute of Development Studies, since 2014, University of Sussex; *b* London, 5 Jan. 1965; *d* of late Gerald Leach and of Penelope Leach, *qv*; *m* 1993, James Fairhead; one *s* three *d*. *Educ*: South Hampstead High Sch.; Newnham Coll., Cambridge (BA Hons 1st Cl.

Geog. 1985; MA); Sch. of Oriental and African Studies, Univ. of London (PhD Anthropol. 1990). Fellow, Inst. of Develt Studies, Univ. of Sussex, 1990–. *Publications:* Rainforest Relations, 1994; Misreading the African Landscape, 1996; The Lie of the Land, 1996; Reframing Deforestation, 1998; Science, Society and Power, 2003; Science and Citizens, 2005; Vaccine Anxieties, 2007; Dynamic Sustainabilities, 2010; Epidemics, 2010; Green Grabbing, 2012; Gender Equality and Sustainable Development, 2015; Carbon Conflicts, 2015; The Politics of Green Transformations, 2015. *Recreations:* riding, travel, family. *Address:* Flints, Rotten Row, Lewes, E Sussex BN7 1TN. *T:* (01273) 471543. *E:* m.leach@ids.ac.uk.

**LEACH, Penelope,** PhD; psychologist and writer on childcare; *b* 19 Nov. 1937; 2nd *d* of late Nigel Marlin Balchin and Elisabeth Balchin; *m* 1963, Gerald Leach (*d* 2004); one *s* one *d*. *Educ:* Newnham Coll., Cambridge (BA Hons 1959); LSE (Dip. in Soc. Sci. Admin 1960; MA Psychol. 1962; PhD Psychol. 1964). Home Office, 1960–61; Lectr in Psychol., LSE, 1965–67; Res. Officer and Res. Fellow, MRC, 1967–76; Ext Med. Ed., Penguin Books, 1970–78; Founder and Dir, Lifetime Productions (childcare videos), 1985–87; Res. Consultant, Internat. Centre for Child Studies, 1984–90. Dir, Families, Children and Child Care Project, 1997–2005, and Hon. Sen. Res. Fellow, 1997–2002, Royal Free and UCL Med. Sch., Univ. of London. Hon. Senior Research Fellow: Tavistock Centre, 2000–; Inst. for the Study of Children, Families and Social Issues, Birkbeck Coll., Univ. of London, 2002–; Hon. Prof., Dept of Educn, Univ. of Winchester, 2014–. Member: Voluntary Licensing Authy on IVF, 1985–89; Commn on Social Justice, 1993–95; Commn on Children and Violence, 1993–95; Mental Health Rev., Social Justice Commn, 2010–. Founder and Parent-Educn Co-ordinator, End Physical Punishment for Children, 1989–; Chm., Child Develt Soc., 1993–95 (Pres., 1992–93); Adv. Assoc. for Infant Mental Health, 2000– (Mem., Founding Cttee, 2005–); non-exec. Dir, Mindful Policy Gp, 2010–. Pres., Nat. Child Minders' Assoc., 1999–; Vice-President: Pre-School Playgroups Assoc., 1977; Health Visitors Assoc., 1982–99. Mem. Adv. Council, Amer. Inst. for Child, Adolescent and Family Studies, 1993–. Mem., professional socs and assocs; FBPsS 1989; Hon. Fellow, Dept of Mental Health, Bristol Univ., 1988. Hon. DEd Kingston, 1996. *Publications:* Babyhood, 1974; Baby and Child, 1977, 2nd edn 1989; Who Cares?, 1979; The Parents' A–Z, 1984; The First Six Months, 1987; The Babypack, 1990; Children First, 1994; Your Baby and Child, 1997, 4th edn 2010; Child Care: what we know and what we need to know, 2009; The Essential First Year, 2010; Family Breakdown: helping children hang on to both their parents, 2014; (ed) Transforming Infant Wellbeing, 2017; Putting the Children First When You Divorce, 2018. *Recreations:* cooking, family and friends, gardening, travel. *Address:* 2 Bull Lane, Lewes, E Sussex BN7 1UA. *T:* (01273) 474702.
*See also* M. A. Leach.

**LEACH, Philippa Mary;** *see* McAtasney, P. M.

**LEACH, Dr Renny Philip;** Chairman, Snowdon Trust, since 2010; *b* Brighton, 9 April 1956; *s* of Robert and Marie-Hélène Leach; *m* 1975, Karin Eneberg; one *s* one *d* (and one *d* decd). *Educ:* Univ. of Sussex (BSc Hons Biochem. 1982; DPhil 1986). Sen. Scientist, MRC, 1989–90; Dir of Res., Action Res., 1990–94; Dir, R&D, Gt Ormond St Hosp. and Inst. of Child Health, 1994–98; Chief Executive: Intercern, 1998–2003; iResearch, 2003–09; SW Academic Health Sci. Network, 2013–15; Eastern Academic Health Sci. Network, 2015–16. Mem., Clin. Medicine Sub-Panel, REF 2014, 2012–. Sen. Ind. Dir, Queen Victoria Hosp. NHS Foundn Trust, 2008–13. Hon. Med. Dir, Sparks, 2007–13. Non-exec. Dir, Isogenica Ltd, 2008–. *Recreations:* cycling, family. *Address:* Forest Row, East Sussex. *E:* rleach@iresearch-ltd.com. *Club:* Royal Society of Medicine.

**LEACH, Stephen James,** CB 2007; Director of Criminal Justice, Northern Ireland Office, and Chairman, Criminal Justice Board, 2000–09; Commissioner, Criminal Cases Review Commission, 2014–19; *b* 12 Feb. 1951; *s* of late Edward Stephen Leach and Mollie Leach (*née* O'Hara); *m* 1982, Jane Williams; one *s* two *d*. *Educ:* De La Salle Coll., Jersey; Peterhouse, Cambridge (1st cl. Hons English Tripos). NI Office, 1975–84; Dept of Energy, 1984–87; Prin. Private Sec. to Sec. of State for NI, 1988–90; Humphrey Fulbright Fellow, Univ. of Minnesota, 1990–91; Northern Ireland Office: responsibilities in policing, security and personnel policy and political development, 1991–96; Associate Political Dir, then Associate Policing and Security Dir, 1996–2000. Lay Mem., Nat. Security Certificate Appeals Tribunal, 2012–. A Parole Comr for NI, 2009–15. Non-exec. Dir, Health and Social Care Bd, NI, 2009–. *Recreations:* reading, tennis, watching Rugby.

**LEADBEATER, Charles Richard;** independent writer, since 1996; *b* Preston, Lancs, 9 Jan. 1959; *s* of William Leadbeater and Olive Leadbeater; *m* 1997, Geraldine Claire Bedell; two *s*, and one step *s* one step *d*. *Educ:* Vyne Comp. Sch., Basingstoke; Queen Mary's Sixth Form Coll., Basingstoke; Balliol Coll., Oxford (BA PPE 1st Cl. 1981). Researcher, Weekend World, LWT, 1983–85; Financial Times: journalist, 1985–89; Labour Ed., 1989–91; Industrial Ed., 1991–92; Tokyo Bureau Chief, 1992; Asst Ed., 1992–95; Asst Ed., Independent, 1995–96. Co-Founder, Participle, 2007. Associate, Demos, 1996; Mem., Policy Adv. Council, IPPR, 2010. Trustee: Apps for Good, 2010; Nominet Trust, 2011. Mem., Tate. *Publications:* In Search of Work (with John Lloyd), 1987; The Rise of the Social Entrepreneur, 1997; Living on Thin Air, 1998; The Independents, 1998; Up the Down Escalator, 2000; The Pro-Am Revolution, 2004; We-Think, 2008; Innovation in Education, 2012; The Frugal Innovator: creating change on a shoestring budget, 2014. *Recreations:* reading, cooking, walking. *W:* www.charlesleadbeater.net.

**LEADER-WILLIAMS, Prof. Nigel,** PhD, ScD; Director, Conservation Leadership, University of Cambridge, since 2009; Fellow, Churchill College, Cambridge, since 2009; *b* Hatton, Ceylon, 24 Nov. 1949; *s* of Geoffrey and Honor Leader-Williams (*née* Tindall); *m* 1982, Alison Mary Rosser; two *s*. *Educ:* Blundell's Sch., Tiverton; Liverpool Univ. (BVSc; MRCVS 1972); Corpus Christi Coll., Cambridge (PhD 1981; ScD 2011). Practising veterinary surgeon, 1972; research: S Georgia with British Antarctic Survey, Cambridge, 1973–80; Zambia, with Dept of Zool., Univ. of Cambridge, 1980–90; Chief Tech. Advr to Dept of Wildlife, Tanzania, 1991–95; University of Kent: Prof. of Biodiversity Mgt, 1995–2009 (Hon. Prof., 2010–); Dir, Durrell Inst. of Conservation and Ecol., 1999–2009. Leverhulme Res. Fellow, 1987; Research Fellow: Wildlife Conservation Soc., NY, 1993–95; Inst. of Zool., London, 1995 (Hon. Res. Fellow, 1996–99). Prog. Fellow, Envmtl Planning Gp, Internat. Inst. for Envmt and Develt, London, 1996–99. Mem., Organising Cttee, Student Conf. on Conservation Sci., 1999–. Member: Council, Fauna and Flora Internat., 1998–2006 and 2008– (Vice-Chm., 2012–); Council, Zool Soc. of London, 2001–04. Sec., Durrell Trust for Conservation Biol., 2001–09; Mem., Bd of Trustees, Resource Africa, 2001–. Mem., Darwin Expert Cttee (formerly Darwin Adv. Cttee), 2006–12. Mem. Council, Churchill Coll., Cambridge, 2012–16. *Publications:* Reindeer on South Georgia: the ecology of an introduced population, 1988; The World Trade in Rhino Horn: a review, 1992; (ed jtly) The Live Bird Trade in Tanzania, 1996; (ed jtly) Tourist Hunting in Tanzania, 1996; (ed jtly) Community-based Conservation in Tanzania, 1996; (ed jtly) Mining in Protected Areas in Tanzania, 1996; (jtly) Take Only Photographs, Leave Only Footprints: the environmental impacts of wildlife tourism, 1997; (ed jtly) Wildlife and People: conflict and conservation in Masai Mara, Kenya, 2003; (ed jtly) Trade-offs in Conservation: deciding what to save, 2010; contrib. book chapters and papers to learned jls, incl. Nature and Science. *Recreations:* snow and mountains, sights, smells and sounds of Africa, young minds, Liverpool FC. *Address:* Department of Geography, University of Cambridge, David Attenborough Building, Cambridge CB2 3QZ. *T:* (01223) 333397, *Fax:* (01223) 333392. *E:* nigel.leader-williams@geog.cam.ac.uk.

**LEADLAY, Prof. Peter Francis,** DPhil, PhD; FRS 2000; FRSC; Herchel Smith Professor of Biochemistry, University of Cambridge, 2006–17, now Emeritus; Fellow of Clare College, Cambridge, since 1979; Co-Founder and Director, BIOTICA Technology Ltd, 1996–2013; *b* 13 Dec. 1949; *s* of late Kenneth Rupert Simpson Leadlay, RN and Ellen Theresa Leadlay (*née* Coleman); *m* 1974, Christina Maria Peake; three *d*. *Educ:* St Joseph's Coll., London; New Coll., Oxford (Gibbs Schol.; BA 1971); Corpus Christi Coll., Oxford (Sen. Schol.; DPhil 1974; MA 1974); Clare Coll., Cambridge (PhD 1979). FRSC 2006. Royal Soc. European Res. Fellow, ETH, Zürich, 1974–76; Demonstr, Dept of Biochemistry, and Jun. Res. Fellow, Wolfson Coll., Univ. of Oxford, 1976–79; University of Cambridge: Demonstr in Biochemistry, 1979–84; Lectr, 1984–95; Reader, 1995–99; Prof. of Molecular Enzymology, 1999–2006; Sen. Res. Fellow, BBSRC, 1999–2004. Blaise Pascal Res. Prof., Institut Pasteur, Paris, 2002–03; Smets Prof., Univs of Leuven and Louvain-la-Neuve, 2009; Hon. Prof., Univ. of Wuhan, 2011. Remsen Award, Amer. Chem. Soc., 2007; Humboldt Res. Prize, Alexander von Humboldt Foundn, 2011; Inhoffen Medal, Helmholtz Centre for Infection Res. and Tech. Univ. Braunschweig, 2012; Wolfson Merit Award, Royal Soc., 2014. *Publications:* Enzyme Chemistry, 1969; articles in scientific jls, particularly on enzymes and antibiotic biosynthesis. *Recreations:* reading, walking, sailing, identifying plants. *Address:* Department of Biochemistry, University of Cambridge, 80 Tennis Court Road, Cambridge CB2 1GA. *T:* (01223) 766041.

**LEADSOM, Rt Hon. Andrea (Jacqueline);** PC 2016; MP (C) South Northamptonshire, since 2010; Secretary of State for Business, Energy and Industrial Strategy, since 2019; *b* Aylesbury, 13 May 1963; *d* of Richard Salmon and Judy Crompton (*née* Kitchin); *m* 1993, Ben Leadsom; two *s* one *d*. *Educ:* Tonbridge Girls' Grammar Sch.; Warwick Univ. (BA Hons). Fixed Interest and Treasury, BZW, 1987–91; Financial Instns Dir, Barclays Bank, 1993–97; Man. Dir, DPFM Ltd, 1997–99; Sen. Investment Officer, Invesco Perpetual, 1999–2009. Mem. (C) S Oxfordshire DC, 2003–07. Econ. Sec., HM Treasury, 2014–15; Minister of State, DECC, 2015–16; Sec. of State for Envmt, Food and Rural Affairs, 2016–17; Leader of the H of C and Lord Pres. of the Council, 2017–19. Contested (C) Knowsley S, 2005. *Address:* House of Commons, SW1A 0AA. *T:* (020) 7219 7149. *E:* andrea.leadsom.mp@parliament.uk.

**LEAFE, Richard Neil,** FRGS; Chief Executive, Lake District National Park Authority, since 2007; *b* Nottingham, 26 Jan. 1965; *s* of Leonard and Kathleen Leafe. *Educ:* Fernwood Comprehensive Sch., Nottingham; Bilborough Coll., Nottingham; Univ. of Sheffield (BSc Hons Geog. 1987; MPhil 1990). FRGS 1991. Res. asst, Dept of Geog., Univ. of Sheffield, 1987–90; tour leader, Explore Worldwide, 1990; coastal geomorphologist, NCC/English Nature, 1990–94; English Nature: Hd, Coastal Initiative and coastal geomorphologist, Maritime Team, 1994–96; Eur. and Internat. Relns Manager, 1996–99; Team Manager, Ext. Relns Team, 1999–2003; Gen. Manager and Regl Dir, E Midlands, 2003–06; Dir, NW Reg., Natural England, 2006–07. Winston Churchill Meml Trust Travelling Fellow, 1992. Member: Res. Tech. Adv. Gp on policy issues, Flood and Coastal Defence Div., DEFRA, 2000–03; Panel, Making Space for Nature rev. of England's wildlife sites, 2009–10; Bd, Envmt Agency, 2012–15. Chair, Scientific Council, Eur. Centre for Nature Conservation, Netherlands, 2000–05. Mem., NW Regl Cttee, RGS, 2011–16. Hon. DLitt Sheffield, 2016. *Publications:* contrib. papers on marine and coastal mgt. *Recreations:* ski-ing, ski mountaineering, fell walking and running, cycling, wild swimming, climbing, performing arts and film. *Address:* Lake District National Park Authority, Murley Moss, Oxenholme Road, Kendal LA9 7RL.

**LEAFE, Susannah Mary;** Director of Operations, Gafcon UK, since 2018; *b* King's Lynn, 28 Dec. 1971; *d* of David Henderson Cowie and Alison Margaret Graham Cowie; *m* 1997, Daniel John Leafe. *Educ:* Wimbledon High Sch.; Univ. of Bristol (BSc Geog.); Univ. of Nottingham (PGCE). Hd of Geography, Clifton High Sch., 1997–2008; Women's Worker, Fowey Parish Church, 2008–13; Dir, Reform, 2013–18. Family Life and Marriage Educn Co-ord., Dio. of Truro, 2008–09. *Recreations:* tennis, sailing. *Address:* 6 Troy Court, Daglands Road, Fowey PL23 1JX. *E:* ds.leafe@gmail.com.

**LEAHY, Helen Blodwen R.;** *see* Rees Leahy.

**LEAHY, Michael James,** OBE 2004; General Secretary, Community (formerly Iron and Steel Trades Confederation), 1999–2014; *b* 7 Jan. 1949; *s* of Michael James Cyril Leahy, ISM, and Iris Jarrett Leahy; *m* 1974, Irene Powell; two *s*. *Educ:* Twmpath Secondary Modern Sch., Pontypool. Chargehand, Cold Rolling Dept, Panteg Works, Richard Thompson & Baldwins Ltd, 1965–77; Iron and Steel Trades Confederation, later Community: Mem., 1965–; Organiser, 1977–86; Sen. Organiser, 1986–92; Asst Gen. Sec. Elect, 1992–93; Asst Gen. Sec., 1993–98; Gen. Sec. Elect, 1998–99. Various posts, British Steel/Corus Gp plc, 1995– (Employees' Sec., Eur. Works Council, 1998–). Chm., Communitas (formerly Steel Partnership Trng Ltd, later Knowledge Skills Partnership), 2000–; Member Board: Unions Today Ltd, 1999–2002; UK Steel Enterprise Ltd, 2003–. Mem., 1992–, Chm., 1998–, Steel Co-ordinating Cttee, Nat. Trades Union; Mem. Exec. Council, CSEU, 1994–99; Mem., 1995–2002, Mem., Sub-cttee for Mkts and Forward Studies, 1995–2002, Consultative Cttee, ECSC; General Federation of Trade Unions: Mem., Exec. Council, 1996–2003; Mem., Educnl Trust, 1996–2003 (Trustee, 1999–); Vice Pres., 1999–2001; Pres., 2001–03; Trades Union Congress: Mem. Gen. Council, 1999–; Mem., Exec. Cttee, 2000–; Pres., 2010–11; Mem., Consultative Commn on Industrial Change, Eur. Econ. and Social Cttee, 2002–. Hon. Sec., British Section, 1999–, Pres., Iron, Steel and Non-Ferrous Metals Dept, 1999–, Internat. Metalworkers Fedn; European Metalworkers' Federation: Member: Exec. Cttee, 1999– (Steering Gp, 2003–); Industrial Policy Cttee, 1999–; Steel Cttee, 1999–. Mem., Central Arbitration Cttee, 2002–. Labour Party: Mem., 1966–; Member: NEC, 1996; Nat. Policy Forum, 1996–99; Auditor, 2002–13. Chairman: Bevan Foundn, 2000–02 (Mem., Bd of Dirs, 2002–; Chm. Trustees, 2002–; Hon. Vice-Pres., 2009); Trade Union Friends of Israel, 2014–. Pres., Welsh Trust for Prevention of Abuse, 2005–. FRSA. *Recreations:* golf, Rugby.

**LEAHY, Sir Terence Patrick, (Sir Terry),** Kt 2002; Chief Executive, Tesco plc, 1997–2011; *s* of Terence and Elizabeth Leahy; *m* Alison; two *s* one *d*. *Educ:* St Edward's Coll., Liverpool; UMIST (BSc Hons Mgt Scis). Joined Tesco, 1979, as Mktg Exec.; Marketing Dir, 1984–86; Dir, 1992–2011; Dep. Man. Dir, 1995–97. Sen. Advr, Clayton Dubilier & Rice LLP, 2011–; Chairman: B&M Retail (formerly Bargains), 2012–17; BUT France, 2016–; Dir, Motor Fuel Gp, 2015–. *Publications:* Management in 10 Words, 2012. *Recreations:* sport, reading, theatre, architecture.

**LEAKE, Prof. Bernard Elgey,** PhD, DSc, FRSE, FGS; Hon. Research Fellow, School of Earth and Ocean Sciences (formerly School of Earth, then Earth, Ocean and Planetary Sciences), Cardiff University, since 1998; Leverhulme Emeritus Fellow, 2000–02; Professor of Geology, Department of Geology and Applied Geology (formerly Department of Geology), and Keeper of Geological Collections in Hunterian Museum, University of Glasgow, 1974–97, now Professor Emeritus (Head, Department of Geology and Applied

Geology (formerly Department of Geology), 1974–92); *b* 29 July 1932; *s* of late Norman Sidney Leake and Clare Evelyn (*née* Walgate); *m* 1955, Gillian Dorothy (*d* 2018), *d* of Prof. Charles Henry Dobinson, CMG; five *s*. *Educ:* Wirral Grammar Sch., Bebington, Cheshire; Liverpool Univ. (1st Cl. Hons BSc, PhD); Bristol Univ. (DSc 1974); Glasgow Univ. (DSc 1998). Leverhulme post-doctoral Res. Fellow, Liverpool Univ., 1955–57; Asst Lectr, subseq. Lectr in Geology, Bristol Univ., 1957–68, Reader in Geol., 1968–74. Res. Associate, Berkeley, Calif, 1966; Gledden Sen. Vis. Fellow, Univ. of W Australia, 1986; Erskine Vis. Res. Fellow, Univ. of Canterbury, NZ, 1999. Chm., Cttee on amphibole nomenclature, Internat. Mineral Assoc., 1982–2006 (Sec., 1968–79); Member: NERC, 1978–84 (Chm., Vis. Gp to Brit. Geol Survey, formerly Inst. of Geological Sciences, 1982–84; Chm., Isotope Facilities Prog. Cttee, 1981–85, 1987–91); Council, Mineral Soc., 1965–68, 1978–80, 1996–99 (Vice-Pres., 1979–80, 1996–97; Pres., 1998–99; Managing Trustee, 1997–98, 2000–04; Hon. Life Mem., 2004); Council, Geol Soc., 1979–85, 1986–96, 2002–05 (Vice-Pres., 1980; Treasurer, 1981–85, 1989–96; Pres., 1986–88; Lyell Medal, 1977); Council, RSE, 1988–90; publication cttees, Mineral Soc., 1970–85, Geol Soc., 1970–85, and 1986–96; Geol Soc. Publication Bd, 1987–2005 (Chm., 1987–96); Geologists' Association: (Treas., 1997–2009; Hon. Life Mem., 2009; Foulerton Award, 2010). Mem. Ct, Cardiff Univ., 2001–14. FRSE 1978. Hon. Life Mem., Liverpool Geol Soc., 2007. Sodic amphibole mineral, leakeite, named by Internat. Mineral Assoc., 1992. Editor: Mineralogical Magazine, 1970–83; Jl of Geol Soc., 1973 and 1974. *Publications:* A Catalogue of analysed calciferous and sub-calciferous amphiboles, 1968; The Geology of South Mayo, 1989; The Geology of the Dalradian and associated rocks of Connemara, W Ireland, 1994; The Life of Frank Coles Phillips (1902–82) and the Structural Geology of the Moine Petrofabric Controversy, 2002; The Life and Work of Professor J. W. Gregory FRS (1864–1932): geologist, writer and explorer, 2011; over 160 papers in geol, mineral and geochem. jls on geol. of Connemara, study of amphiboles, X-ray fluorescence anal. of rocks and use of geochem. in identifying origins of highly metamorphosed rocks; geological maps: Connemara, 1982; South Mayo, 1985; Slyne Head, 1985; Errismore, 1990; Clifden, 1997; Central Galway granite and its northern margin, Oughterard, 2006; The Western Galway Granite, 2011; Camus, Co. Galway, 2012; Joyces Country, Co. Galway, 2014. *Recreations:* reading, theatre, museums, genealogy, study of railway and agricultural development. *Address:* School of Earth and Ocean Sciences, Cardiff University, Main Building, Park Place, Cardiff CF10 3AT. *T:* (029) 2087 6421; The Chippings, Bridge Road, Llanblethian, Cowbridge, Vale of Glamorgan CF71 7JG.

**LEAKE, Rt Rev. David,** CBE 2003; Bishop of Argentina, 1990–2002; an Hon. Assistant Bishop, Diocese of Norwich, since 2002; *b* 26 June 1935; *s* of Rev. Canon William Alfred Leake and Dorothy Violet Leake; *m* 1961, Rachel Yarham; two *s* one *d*. *Educ:* St Alban's Coll., Buenos Aires; London Coll. of Divinity. ALCD 1959 (LTh). Deacon 1959, priest 1960; Assistant Bishop: Paraguay and N Argentina, 1969–73; N Argentina, 1973–79; Bishop of Northern Argentina, 1979–89; Presiding Bishop, Province of Anglican Ch of Southern Cone of America, 1982–89. *Publications:* Under an Algarrobo Tree, 2012. *Recreation:* observing people's behaviour at airports, railway stations and bus terminals. *Address:* The Anchorage, Lower Common, East Runton, Cromer, Norfolk NR27 9PG. *T:* (01263) 513536.

**LEAKE, Nicholas Howard;** HM Diplomatic Service; Head of Policy Division, Office of the Secretary of State for Scotland (on secondment), since 2018; *b* Wordsley, 15 Jan. 1972; *s* of late John Howard Leake and of Karen Leake; *m* 2013, Oana Maria Bucsa; one *s*. *Educ:* Univ. of Warwick (LLB); Univs of Warwick, Lille and Saarbrücken (Integrated Common Prog. Eur. Law); Open Univ. (MBA). Entered FCO, 1994; Second Sec., Budapest, 1996–2000; First Sec., UK Perm. Repn to EU, 2000–02; Hd of Public Sector Preparations and Consumer Protection, Eur. Preparations Unit, HM Treasury (on secondment), 2002–04; Economy Theme Manager, Commn for Africa, 2004; Private Sec. to Minister for Europe, and Minister for Trade, 2005; Dep. Hd of Mission, Sofia, 2006–10; Chargé d'Affaires, Madagascar, 2010–12; High Comr to Mauritius and Ambassador to The Comoros, 2010–14; Counsellor, EU/Economic, and Dep. Hd of Mission, Berlin, 2014–18. *Recreations:* cricket, cycling, travel, food and wine. *Address:* Office of the Secretary of State for Scotland, 1 Melville Crescent, Edinburgh EH3 7HW; c/o Foreign and Commonwealth Office, King Charles Street, SW1A 2AH. *E:* nick.leake@fco.gov.uk.

**LEAKEY, Lt Gen. (Arundell) David,** CMG 2006; CVO 2018; CBE 1997; consultant and adviser in industrial, chemicals and IT sector, since 2018; Gentleman Usher of the Black Rod and Serjeant-at-Arms, House of Lords, and Secretary to the Lord Great Chamberlain, 2011–17; *b* 18 May 1952; *s* of Maj.-Gen. (Arundell) Rea Leakey, CB, DSO, MC and Muriel Irene Le Poer Trench; *m* 1983, Shelagh Jane Lawson; two *s*. *Educ:* Sherborne Sch.; Fitzwilliam Coll., Cambridge (MA Law); RMA Sandhurst. CO 2nd RTR, 1991; Comdr 20 Armoured Bde, 1996; Dir Mil. Ops, MoD, 1997–99; COS HQ NI, 1999–2001; Dir Gen., Army Trng and Recruiting, and Chief Exec., Army Trng and Recruiting Agency, 2001–04; Comdr, EU Force in Bosnia and Herzegovina, 2004–05; MoD, 2006–07; Dir Gen., EU Mil. Staff, 2007–10. Col Comdt, RTR, 2006–10 (Dep. Col Comdt, 1999–2006); Col, Dorset Yeomanry, 2008–. Hon. Col, ACF Music, 2004–11; Col, Dorset ACF, 2018–. Chm., Wyke Hall (Management) Ltd, 1996–2010 (Dir, 1993–2010). Mem. Adv. Bd, Security Defence Agenda, 2008–. Trustee, Nat. Children's Orch., 2001–14 (Vice Chm., 2012–13; Chm., 2013–14). President: Army Squash Rackets Assoc., 1997–2010; Tank Memorial Ypres Salient, 2008–; Sherborne Pilgrims, 2012–. Gov., Sherborne Sch., 2018–. *Recreations:* music, field sports, squash, tennis, sailing, ski-ing, golf, chain-sawing. *E:* davidleakey@aol.com. *Clubs:* Hawks (Cambridge); Jesters; Escorts; GB Veterans Squash.

**LEAKEY, Richard Erskine Frere,** FRS 2007; Professor of Anthropology, since 2002 and Chairman, Turkana Basin Institute, since 2005, Stony Book University; Permanent Secretary, Secretary to the Cabinet and Head of the Public Service, Kenya, 1999–2001; *b* 19 Dec. 1944; *s* of late Louis Seymour Bazett Leakey, FBA, and Mary Douglas Leakey, FBA; *m* 1970, Dr Meave (*née* Epps); three *d*. *Educ:* Nairobi Primary Sch.; Lenana (formerly Duke of York) Sch., Nairobi. Self employed tour guide and animal trapper, 1961–65; Dir, Photographic Safaris in E Africa, 1965–68; Administrative Dir, 1968–74, Dir, 1974–89, Nat. Museums of Kenya; Dir, Wildlife and Conservation Management Service, Kenya, 1989–90; Chm., 1989–93, Dir, 1993–94 and 1998–99, Kenya Wildlife Service; Man. Dir, Richard Leakey and Associates, wildlife consultancy, 1994–98; Sec. Gen. SAFINA, 1995–98. MP Kenya, 1998. Co-leader, palaeontol expedn to Lake Natron, Tanzania, 1963–64; expedn to Lake Baringo, Kenya, in search of early man, 1966; Co-leader, Internation Omo River Expedn, Ethiopia, in search of early man, 1967; Leader: E Turkana (formerly E Rudolf) Res. Proj. (multi-nat., interdisciplinary sci. consortium investigation of Plio/Pleistocene, Kenya's northern Rift Valley), 1968; Koobi Fora Res. Proj., 1979–81; W Turkana Res. Proj., 1981–82, 1984–89; Buluk - Early Miocene Proj., 1982. Chairman: Foundn for Res. into Origin of Man (FROM), 1974–81; E African Wild Life Soc., 1984–89 (Vice-Chm., 1978–84); Kenya Cttee, United World Colls, 1987; Bd of Governors and Council, Regent's Coll., London, 1985–90; Nat. Museums of Kenya, 1989–94; Kenya Wildlife Service, 2015–; Trustee: Nat. Fund for the Disabled, 1980–95; Wildlife Clubs of Kenya, 1980–94; Rockford Coll., Illinois, 1983–85. Presenter: The Making of Mankind, BBC TV series, 1981; Earth Journal, US TV series, 1991. Mem., Selection Cttee, Beyond War Award, 1985–; Juror: Kalinga Prize, Unesco, 1986–88; Rolex Awards, 1990. Hon. Mem., Bd of Dirs, Thunderbird Res. Corp., USA, 1988–. Hon. DSc: Wooster Coll., 1978; Rockford Coll., 1983; Aberdeen, 1994; Washington, 1994; Bristol, 1996; Bradley, 1997; SUNY, 1998; Alma Coll., 2005; Cambridge, 2007; Rutgers, 2014; New Jersey, 2014; Hon. DLit Kent, 1987; Hon. DHLitt Ohio, 1990; Hon. Dr Agricl and Envmtl Scis Wageningen, 2003; Hon. DSc Conservation Biol. Jomo Kenyatta Univ. of Agric. and Technol., 2014. Golden Ark Medal for Conservation, 1989. *Publications:* (contrib.) General History of Africa, vol. 1, 1976; (with R. Lewin) Origins, 1978; (with R. Lewin) People of the Lake, 1979; (with M. G. Leakey) Koobi Fora Research Project, vol. I, 1979; The Making of Mankind, 1981; Human Origins, 1982; One Life, 1984; (with R. Lewin) Origins Reconsidered, 1992; (with R. Lewin) The Origins of Humankind, 1995; (with R. Lewin) The Sixth Extinction: biodiversity and its survival, 1996; articles on palaeontol. in Nature, Jl of World Hist., Science, Amer. Jl of Phys. and Anthropol. *Address:* PO Box 24926, Nairobi 00502, Kenya.

**LEAMAN, Rear Adm. Richard Derek,** CB 2010; OBE 1993; Chief Executive Officer, Tall Ships Youth Trust, since 2017; *b* Lynton, Devon, 26 July 1956; *s* of late Derek Alan Leaman of Jean Rita Leaman. *Educ:* Britannia Royal Naval Coll.; Manchester Business Sch. (Advanced Mgt Achievement Course 2010). Joined RN, 1975; navigation and gunnery duties in ships deployed worldwide, 1976–90; in command: HMS Dumbarton Castle, 1991–92; HMS Cardiff, 1993–94; ops and trng appts, 1995–98; HMS Cumberland, 1999–2000; HCSC, 2000; Dir, RN Communications, 2000–01; Comdr, UK Maritime Task Gp, 2002–03; Defence Strategic Leadership Course, 2004; Dir, HCSC, 2003–05; COS, Maritime HQ, Naples, 2005–07; Dep. COS, NATO Strategic Comd, Norfolk, Va, 2007–09. CEO, Guide Dogs for the Blind, 2010–16. Trustee: Vision 2020 UK, 2010–13; NCVO, 2012–18. Chm., Assoc. of RN Officers, 2013–16. *Recreations:* swimming, listening to music, theatre, dog walking, fly fishing. *Address:* Tall Ships Youth Trust, 2A The Hard, Portsmouth, Hants PO1 3PT. *T:* (023) 9283 2055. *E:* richard.leaman@tallships.org.

**LEAN, Very Rev. (David) Jonathan Rees;** Dean and Precentor, St Davids Cathedral, 2009–17; *b* Fishguard, 29 May 1952; *s* of late David Samuel Lean and of Sylvia Patricia Lean. *Educ:* St David's Univ. Coll., Lampeter (DipTh 1974); Coll. of the Resurrection, Mirfield. Ordained deacon, 1975, priest, 1976; Asst Curate, Rectorial Benefice of Tenby, 1975–81; Vicar: Llanrhian, Llanhowell and Llanrheithan, 1981–88; St Martin's, Haverfordwest with Lambston, 1988–2000; Area Dean of Rhoose, 1999–2000; Canon Residentiary, St Davids Cathedral, 2000–09. *Recreations:* music, gardening.

**LEAN, Geoffrey;** journalist, author and consultant; Contributing Editor, Environment, Daily Telegraph, 2009–15; *b* 21 April 1947; *s* of late Garth Dickinson Lean and Margaret Mary Lean (*née* Appleyard); *m* 1972, Judith Eveline Wolfe; one *s* one *d*. *Educ:* Sherborne Sch.; St Edmund Hall, Oxford (BA (Hons) Mod. Hist). Grad. Trainee, Yorkshire Post Newspapers, 1969–72; reporter, Goole Times, 1969; Yorkshire Post: reporter, 1969–72; Feature Writer, 1972–77; Envmt Correspondent, 1973–77; Reporter, 1977–79, Envmt Correspondent, 1979–93, The Observer; Dir, Central Observer, 1990–93; Envmt Correspondent, 1993–2000, Envmt Editor, 2000–09, Independent on Sunday; Columnist, Grist.org, 2009–10. Contrib. Editor, Fairness Radio, USA, 2010–13. Editor, Our Planet, 1994–, Tunza, 2003–11, UNEP; Mem., Exec. Cttee, Stakeholder Forum for Our Common Future (formerly UNED Forum), 1989–95. Trustee, European Sect., Internat. Inst. of Energy Conservation, 1995–98; UK rep. to Commn IV, Gen. Conf. of UNESCO, 1997; Mem. Bd, Leadership in Envmt and Develt Internat., 1998–2003; Trustee, LEAD UK, 2000–06. Consultant: Global Envmt Facility, 2016–; Inst. for Governance and Sustainable Develt, 2016–. Consultancies for UNEP, UNDP, UNICEF, World Bank, FAO and WMO. Clerk, Yorkshire Post and Yorkshire Evening Post jt chapels, NUJ, 1975–77; Vice Chm., Leeds Branch, NUJ, 1977. Chair of Judges, Andrew Lees Meml Award, 1994–2009; Juror, Goldman Envmtl Prize, 1996–2019; Judge, British Journalism Awards, 2016–. Yorkshire Council for Social Services Press Award, 1972; Glaxo Science Fellowship, 1972; World Envmt Fest. Rose Award, 1986; Communication Arts Award of Excellence, 1986; UN Global 500, 1987; Awareness Award, 1991, Journalist of the Year, 1993, 2002, British Envmt and Media Awards; Schumacher Award, 1994; Foundn Award to launch IUCN/Reuters press awards, 1998; Scoop of the Year, London Press Club Awards, 2000, British Press Awards, 2001; Martha Gellhorn Prize, Martha Gellhorn Trust Cttee, 2002; Journalist of the Year, Green Ribbon Political Awards, 2016; Lifetime Achievement Award, Internat. Media Awards, Internat. Press Council, 2017. *Publications:* Rich World, Poor World, 1978; (jtly) The Worst Accident in the World, 1986; (jtly) Chernobyl: the end of the nuclear dream, 1987; (gen. ed.) Atlas of the Environment, 1990, revd edn 1994; (ed) Radiation: doses, effects, risks, 1985; (ed) Action on Ozone, 1988, revd edn 1990; (contrib. ed.) Dimensions of Need: a world atlas of food and agriculture, 1995; (ed) Down to Earth, 1995; (ed) Human Development Report, 1998; (ed) Progress of Nations Report, 1999; (ed) A Sea of Troubles, 2001; (ed) Protecting the Oceans from Land-Based Activities, 2001. *Recreations:* family, garden, West Cork, bad puns. *E:* Geoffrey.Lean@outlook.com.

**LEAN, Very Rev. Jonathan;** *see* Lean, Very Rev. D. J. R.

**LEAR, Joyce, (Mrs W. J. Lear);** *see* Hopkirk, Joyce.

**LEAR, Michael John;** consultant curator and landscape architect; Co-Director, Lear Associates Ltd, since 2003; *b* Bristol, 1958; *s* of Francis and Margery Lear; *m* 1983, Beverley Woods. *Educ:* Clarks Grammar Sch., Clifton; evening art tuition with Jack Chalker, RWA, 1969–76; Univ. of Aberdeen (BSc Forestry Sci. 1979); Univ. of Aberdeen and Royal Botanic Gdns, Kew (MSc 1984). Horticultural taxonomist, NT and Royal Botanic Gdns, Kew, 1980–84; Botanical Consultant, NT, 1985–97; Curator, Castlewellan Nat. Arboretum Forest Service, NI, 1997–2005; estabd own practice, with Beverley Lear, Lear Associates, 1990–; Planner, Heritage Services, Oxford CC, 2005–07. Consultant Landscape Architect to Keeper of the Groves, St John's Coll., Oxford, 2017–. Vis. Prof., Univ. of Genoa, 1985; Winston Churchill Fellow, NZ, 1990. Founder Dir, Plant Network UK (formerly PlantNet), 1993–2002. Member: UK Dependent Territories Conservation Forum, 1985–98; NI Heritage Gdns Trust, 1997–; National Trust: Mem., Gdns and Parks Panel, 2007–14; Associate Member: Historic Envmt Panel, 2016–; Specialist Advice Network, 2016–. Trustee: Marks Hall, 2008–; Royal Botanic Gdns, Kew, 2017–. Mem., Editl Bd, Arboricultural Jl, incorporating Internat. Jl Urban Forestry, 2017–. *Works* with Beverley Lear, research and design include: Marks Hall Masterplan; Salisbury Cathedral and Harnham Water Meadows Landscape Study; Oare Hse Gdn and Arboretum (Georgian Gp Award, 2005); Peace Maze, NI; Truro East Dist Centre/Tregurra Park; Coed Darcy masterplan and town code; City of Bath heritage study; Waddesdon Estate Millennium landscape; *restorations:* Heligan; Biddulph Grange; Fulham Palace; Castlewellan Arboretum; Wrest Park; Chiswick Hse; Nymans Pinetum; *botanical/curation:* Woody Plant Catalogue, NT/Kew, 1980–97; La Mortola/Giardini Botanici Hanbury plant catalogue, 1985; Great Storm propagation scheme; Rhododendron surveys incl. Exbury and Westonbirt; dendroarchaeological surveys, incl. Hestercombe, Wanstead; plant conservation projects for ODA and WWF in Fiji and Mauritius; discovery of Davidia forest on Yunnan/Burma border; expedition to Dulong for Kumming Inst. of Botany, Kew. *Publications:* The Threatened Temperate Tree List, 1990; (with M. Wickenden) Exploring the Upper Dulong River: the KWL expedition to North-West Yunnan, 2008; (with B. Lear) Oare

**LEAR, Peter;** see Lovesey, P. H.

**LEARMONT, Gen. Sir John (Hartley),** KCB 1989; CBE 1980 (OBE 1975); Quarter Master General, Ministry of Defence, 1991–94, retired; *b* 10 March 1934; *s* of Captain Percy Hewitt Learmont, CIE, RIN and Doris Orynthia Learmont; *m* 1957, Susan (*née* Thornborrow); three *s. Educ:* Fettes College; RMA Sandhurst. Commissioned RA, 1954; Instructor, RMA, 1960–63; student, Staff Coll., 1964; served 14 Field Regt, Staff Coll. and 3 RHA, 1965–70; MA to C-in-C BAOR, 1971–73; CO 1 RHA, 1974–75 (despatches 1974); HQ BAOR, 1976–78; Comdr, 8 Field Force, 1979–81; Dep. Comdr, Commonwealth Monitoring Force, Rhodesia, Nov. 1979–March 1980; student RCDS, 1981; Chief of Mission, British Cs-in-C Mission to Soviet Forces in Germany, 1982–84; Comdr Artillery, 1 (British) Corps, 1985–87; COS, HQ UKLF, 1987–88; Comdt, Staff Coll. Camberley, 1988–89; Mil. Sec., MoD, 1989–91. Conducted review (Learmont Inquiry) of Prison Service security in Eng. and Wales, 1995. Colonel Commandant: Army Air Corps, 1988–94; RA, 1989–99; RHA, 1990–99; Hon. Colonel: 2nd Bn Wessex Regt (Vols), 1990–95; 2nd (Vol.) Bn, Royal Gloucestershire, Berkshire and Wiltshire Regt, 1995–97. Patron: Glider Pilot Regtl Assoc., 1996–2016; Air OP Officers' Assoc., 2000–. *Recreations:* fell walking, golf, theatre.

**LEARY, Brian Leonard;** QC 1978; FCIArb; *b* 1 Jan. 1929; *o s* of late A. T. Leary; *m* 1965, Myriam Ann Bannister, *d* of Kenneth Bannister, CBE, Mexico City. *Educ:* King's Sch., Canterbury; Wadham Coll., Oxford (MA). Called to the Bar, Middle Temple, 1953; Harmsworth Scholar; Bencher, 1986. Senior Prosecuting Counsel to the Crown at Central Criminal Court, 1971–78. Chm., British-Mexican Soc., 1989–92. *Recreations:* travel, sailing, growing herbs. *Address:* Calle Reforma, No. 13, San Angel, Mexico DF 01000, Mexico. *T:* (55) 55508270.

**LEASK, Maj.-Gen. Anthony de Camborne Lowther,** CB 1996; CBE 1990 (OBE 1984; MBE 1979); *b* 4 Jan. 1943; *s* of Lt-Gen. Sir Henry Leask, KCB, DSO, OBE, and Zoë Leask (*née* Paynter); *m* 1974, Heather Catherine Moir; one *s* two *d. Educ:* Wellington Coll.; RMA, Sandhurst. Commnd Scots Guards, 1963; mentioned in despatches, 1974; CO Bn, 1981–83; attached US Army, 1983–85; Col Mil. Ops 2, MoD, 1986–89; in Comd, 15 Inf. Bde, 1989–91; rcds 1992; Dir, Defence Commitments, Far East and Western Hemisphere, 1993–94; Maj.-Gen. 1994; Comdr Land Forces NI, 1994–95; retd 1996. Director: Nat. Assoc. of Almshouses, 1996–2004; Corps of Commissionaires Mgt Ltd, 1999–2010 (Chm., 2001–10). Mem., Queen's Bodyguard for Scotland, Royal Co. of Archers, 1976–. *Publications:* Sword of Scotland, 2006; Putty: biography of Lieutenant General Sir William Pulteney 1861–1941, 2015. *Recreations:* wildlife, country pursuits. *Address:* c/o Bank of Scotland, Aberfoyle, by Stirling. *Club:* Cavalry and Guards.

*See also Earl of Clarendon.*

**LEASK, Derek William;** High Commissioner for New Zealand in the United Kingdom, 2008–12; *b* Wellington, NZ, 29 Feb. 1948; *s* of Lloyd Samuel Leask and Judith Leask (*née* Poynter); *m* 1972, Annabel E. Murray (marr. diss.); one *s* one *d*; partner, Patricia D. Stevenson. *Educ:* Victoria Univ. of Wellington (BCA); Univ. of Canterbury, NZ (MComm Hons). Entered NZ Diplomatic Service, 1969; Counsellor, London, 1985–89; Ambassador to EC, 1995–99; Dep. Sec., NZ Ministry of Foreign Affairs and Trade, 2005–08. *Recreations:* golf, NZ history (19th century wars in NZ). *Clubs:* Wellington; Royal Wellington Golf.

**LEASK, Prof. Nigel James,** PhD; FBA 2012; FRSE; FEA; Regius Professor of English Language and Literature, since 2004, and Head, School of Critical Studies, 2010–13, University of Glasgow; *b* Glasgow, 29 Sept. 1958; *s* of F. Reay Mackay Leask and M. Anne Leask (*née* Boyd); *m* 1994, Evelyn Arizpe; two *d. Educ:* Edinburgh Acad.; University Coll., Oxford (BA 1980); Trinity Coll., Cambridge (PhD 1987). FEA 2006; FRSE 2008. Jun. Res. Fellow, 1986–89, Fellow and Dir of Studies in English, 1989–2004, Queens' Coll. Cambridge; Lectr, Faculty of English, 1989–2004, Lectr, then Reader in Romantic Lit., 2004, Univ. of Cambridge. *Publications:* British Romantic Writers and the East: anxieties of Empire, 1992 (Indian imprint 1994); Curiosity and the Aesthetics of Travel Writing, 1770–1840: from an antique land, 2002; (ed jtly) Land, Nation and Culture, 1740–1840: thinking the republic of taste, 2004; (ed with Dr P. Connell) Romanticism and Popular Culture in Britain and Ireland, 2009; Robert Burns and Pastoral: poetry and improvement in late 18th century Scotland, 2010 (jtly) Saltire/Nat. Liby of Scotland Prize for Best Res. Book of Year). *Recreations:* hill-walking, fiddle-playing, Gaelic, pre-Hispanic Mexico. *Address:* 2 Hamilton Drive, Glasgow G12 8DR; School of Critical Studies, 4 University Gardens, University of Glasgow, Glasgow G12 8QQ. *E:* nigel.leask@glasgow.ac.uk.

**LEATES, Margaret;** freelance parliamentary draftsman, since 1990; *b* 30 March 1951; *d* of Henry Arthur Sargent Rayner and Alice (*née* Baker); *m* 1973, Timothy Philip Leates; one *s* one *d. Educ:* Lilley and Stone Girls' High Sch., Newark; King's Coll., London (LLB 1st cl. hons, LLM distinction; undergrad. and postgrad. schol.; AKC); MA (Theol) distinction, Univ. of Kent. Admitted Solicitor, 1975; joined Office of Parliamentary Counsel, 1976; with Law Commn, 1981–83 and 1987–89; Dep. Parly Counsel, 1987–90; drafting for Tax Law Rewrite, 1997–2010. *Publications:* When I'm 64: a guide to pensions law; Review of Planning Law of States of Guernsey. *Recreations:* hermeneutics, junk, other people's gardens, walking, reading. *Address:* Crofton Farm, 161 Crofton Lane, Petts Wood, Orpington, Kent BR6 0BP. *T:* (01689) 820192; Nyanza, 87 Bennell's Avenue, Whitstable, Kent CT5 2HR. *T:* (01227) 272335. *E:* ml@leates.org.uk.

**LEATHAM, Dorian;** Chief Executive, Arhag Housing Association, 2011–16; freelance consultant, 2015–17; *b* 2 Aug. 1949; *s* of Robert Clement Leatham and Anna Ismay Leatham; partner, Janet Patrick; one *s* one *d. Educ:* High Wycombe Coll. of Technol. (BSc Sociol. (ext.) London); Brunel Univ. (MA Public and Social Admin). Various posts, 1970–75; Allocations Manager, Lambeth, 1975–77; District Housing Manager: City of Westminster, 1977–83; Camden, 1983–87; Dep. Dir of Housing, Brent, 1987–92; Dir, Housing Mgt, Circle 33 Housing Trust, 1992–93; Asst Dir of Housing, Hounslow, 1993–95; Dir of Housing, Croydon, 1995–98; Chief Exec., London Bor. of Hillingdon, 1998–2006; Chair, Nottingham Housing Strategic Partnership, 2007–09; Interim Exec. Dir, Housing and Develt, London Bor. of Lambeth, 2009–11. Special Advr, Homes and Communities Agency, 2008–13. *Recreations:* watching cricket, going to cinema and theatre, cooking, reading, supporting voluntary groups.

**LEATHER, Dame Susan Catherine, (Dame Suzi),** DBE 2006 (MBE 1994); DL; Chair: Office of the Independent Adjudicator for Higher Education, since 2016; Sustainability and Transformation Partnership, Devon, since 2018; *b* 5 April 1956; *d* of late Dr Hugh Moffat Leather and of Dr Catherine Margaret Leather (*née* Stephen); *m* 1986, Prof. Iain Hampsher-Monk; one *s* two *d. Educ:* Exeter Univ. (BA Hons Politics 1977; BPhil Dist. Social Work 1986); Leicester Univ. (MA Eur. Politics 1978). CQSW 1986. Lectr, Politics Dept, Trent Poly. and Tutor, Leicester Univ., 1977–78; Mkt res. exec., AMR, 1978–79; Res. Officer, then Sen. Res. Officer, Consumers in Europe Gp, 1979–84; trainee Probation Officer, 1984–86; freelance consumer consultant, 1988–97; Chair: Exeter and Dist Community NHS Trust, 1997–2001; Human Fertilisation and Embryology Authy, 2002–06; Charity Commn for England and Wales, 2006–12. Chair: Sch. Meals Rev. Panel, 2005; Sch. Food Trust, 2005–06; Council of Food Policy Advrs, 2008–10; Ethics Cttee, RCOG, 2011–; Lankelly Chase Foundn, 2012–16; Plymouth Fairness Commn, 2013–16; Dep. Chair, Food Standards Agency, 2000–02. Board Member: Human Tissue Authy, 2004–06; UK Accreditation Service, 2006–15; Consumer Focus, 2008–13; Mem., GMC, 2013–. Member: Council, Exeter Univ., 2004–13; State Hons Cttee, 2008–14; Bd, SW Min. Trng Course, 2014–17. Vice Pres., Hospicare, 2012–. Trustee, StepChange, 2015–18. Pres., Devonshire Assoc., 2018–19. DL Devon, 2009. FRCOG *ad eund* 2004. Hon. FRSPH (Hon. FRSH 2006). Hon. DLitt Exeter, 2003; Hon. DCL Huddersfield, 2005; DLaws Leicester, 2007; DUniv Aberdeen, 2007. *Publications:* The Making of Modern Malnutrition, 1996; contrib. articles on consumer, food and health policy. *Recreations:* walking, trekking, triathlon, cinema, gardening, family discussions.

**LEATHERBARROW, Prof. Robin John,** DPhil, DSc; CChem, FRSC, FRSB; Pro-Vice-Chancellor (Scholarship, Research and Knowledge Transfer), Liverpool John Moores University, since 2013; *b* Farnworth, 14 Jan. 1959; *s* of John and Dorothy Leatherbarrow; *m* 1988, Marcella Mary Beale; two *d. Educ:* St John's C of E Primary Sch., Mosley Common; Leigh Grammar Sch.; Eccles Sixth Form Coll.; Liverpool Univ. (BSc Hons Biochem.); Exeter Coll., Oxford (DPhil 1983); Imperial Coll. London (DSc 2014). CChem 2004, FRSC 2004; FRSB (FSB 2010). Res. Lectr, Christ Church, Oxford, 1982–84; Imperial College London: MRC Postdoctoral Fellow, 1984; Royal Soc. Pickering Res. Fellow, 1984; Lectr, 1984–99; Reader, 1999–2002; Prof. and Hd of Biol and Biophysical Chem., then Chemical Biol., Dept of Chem., 2002–13; Dir, 2001–13, Co-Chm., 2010–13, Chemical Biol. Centre, then Inst. of Chemical Biol.; Dean, Faculty of Natural Scis, 2010–13. Man. Dir, Erithacus Software Ltd, 1989–. Hon. Treas., British Biophysical Soc., 1993–99; Chm., Peptide and Protein Sci. Gp, RSC, 2009–. *Publications:* scientific contribs to learned jls; computer progs. *Recreations:* playing cricket and squash, watching Manchester United on TV, programming computers, refurbishing old houses. *Address:* Liverpool John Moores University, Egerton Court, 2 Rodney Street, Liverpool L1 2UA.

**LEATHERBARROW, Prof. William John;** Professor of Russian, University of Sheffield, 1994–2007, now Emeritus; *b* 18 Oct. 1947; *s* of William and Lily Leatherbarrow; *m* 1968, Vivien Jean Burton; one *s* one *d. Educ:* Univ. of Exeter (BA Hons 1969; MA 1972). University of Sheffield: Lectr, 1970–90; Sen. Lectr, 1990–92; Reader in Russian, 1992–94; Dean, Faculty of Arts, 1997–99; Chm., Sch. of Modern Langs, 2001–04, 2005–06. British Astronomical Association: Mem. Council and Dir, Lunar Section, 2009–; Pres., 2011–13; Vice Pres., 2013–15; Mem., Bd of Trustees, 2015–16. Regular columnist, Astronomy Now mag., 2016–. Minor planet 2003 FT127 officially designated 95852 Leatherbarrow by IAU, 2016. Hon. DSc Sheffield, 2016. *Publications:* Fedor Dostoevsky, 1981; (with D. C. Offord) A Documentary History of Russian Thought, 1987; Fedor Dostoevsky: a reference guide, 1990; Dostoyevsky: The Brothers Karamazov, 1992; Dostoevsky and Britain, 1995; Dostoevsky's "The Devils", 1999; The Cambridge Companion to Dostoevskii, 2002; A Devil's Vaudeville: the demonic in Dostoevsky's major fiction, 2005; (with D. C. Offord) A History of Russian Thought, 2010; The Moon, 2018; many edns and articles in scholarly jls, and papers and articles on astronomy. *Recreations:* wine, hiking, cricket, astronomy. *Address:* Russian and Slavonic Studies, School of Languages and Cultures, University of Sheffield, Jessop West, 1 Upper Hanover Street, Sheffield S3 7RA. *E:* w.leatherbarrow@sheffield.ac.uk.

*See also C. J. S. Robertson.*

**LEATHERS,** family name of **Viscount Leathers**.

**LEATHERS,** 3rd Viscount *cr* 1954, of Purfleet, Co. Essex; **Christopher Graeme Leathers;** Baron Leathers, 1941; *b* 31 Aug. 1941; *er s* of 2nd Viscount Leathers and his 1st wife, Elspeth Graeme Stewart (*d* 1985); *S* father, 1996; *m* 1964, Maria Philomena, *yr d* of late Michael Merriman, Charlestown, Co. Mayo; one *s* one *d. Educ:* Rugby Sch.; Open Univ. (BA Hons). New Zealand Shipping Co. Ltd, 1961–63; Wm Cory & Son Ltd, 1963–84; Mostyn Docks Ltd, 1984–88; with Dept of Transport, then DETR, subseq. DTLR, then DfT, 1988–2003. MICS 1965; MCMI (MIMgt 1987). Liveryman, Shipwrights' Co., 1969–. JP Clwyd, 1993. *Heir: s* Hon. James Frederick Leathers, *b* 27 May 1969. *Address:* 53 Daisy Avenue, Bury St Edmunds, Suffolk IP32 7PG.

**LEATHWOOD, Barry,** OBE 1998; National Secretary, Rural, Agricultural and Allied Workers National Trade Group, Transport and General Workers' Union, 1987–2002; *b* 11 April 1941; *s* of Charles and Dorothy Leathwood; *m* 1963, Veronica Ann Clarke; one *d*. Apprentice Toolmaker, 1956–62; Toolmaker/Fitter, 1962–73; District Organiser, Nat. Union of Agric. and Allied Workers, 1973–83; Regional Officer, TGWU Agric. Group, 1983–87. Member: British Potato Council, 2002–; Nat. Access Forum, 1999–. UK Delegate/Expert to ISO Wkg Gp on Social Responsibility, 2005. Patron, Community Council for Somerset, 2001–; CAB Voluntary Advr, 2004–; Trustee and Mem. Bd, Sedgemoor CAB, 2018. Mem., Otterhampton Parish Council, 2006–19. FRSA 1996. *Recreations:* socialist politics, reading, walking, photography. *Address:* 32 Nursery Close, Combwich, Bridgwater, Som TA5 2JB.

**LEATT, Allen Frederick,** FREng, CEng, FICE; Chief Executive Officer, International Marine Constructors Association, since 2015; *b* Cullompton, 13 April 1954; *s* of Leslie and Dorothy Leatt; *m* 1981, Carol Ann Shillabeer; one *s. Educ:* Aston Univ. (BSc Hons); Cranfield Univ. (MBA). CEng 1981; FICE 2010; FREng 2012. Civil engr, John Laing Construction, 1977–81; offshore engr, Subsea Offshore, 1982–87; Commercial Manager, Stena Offshore, 1988–89; Gen. Manager, Stena Drilling, 1990–93; Strategy Director: Stena Offshore, 1994–95; Coflexip Stena Offshore, 1995–96; CEO, Perry Tritech, 1997–2000; Chm. and CEO, Perry Slingsby Systems, 2000–02; Exec. Vice Pres., Technip, 2002–03; Chief Technol. Officer, Acergy, 2003–11; Sen. Vice Pres., Subsea 7, 2011–15. Mem., Smeatonian Soc., 2015–. Hon. DSc Aston, 2016. *Recreations:* modern art, technology, golf. *Address:* International Marine Constructors Association, 52 Grosvenor Gardens, SW1W 0AU. *T:* (020) 7824 5520. *E:* allen.leatt@gmail.com.

**LEAVER, Sir Christopher,** GBE 1981; JP; director of private and public companies; Vice Chairman, Thames Water Plc, 1994–2000 (Deputy Chairman, 1989–93; Chairman, 1993–94); *b* 3 Nov. 1937; *s* of Dr Robert Leaver and Mrs Audrey Kerpen; *m* 1975, Helen Mireille Molyneux Benton; one *s* two *d. Educ:* Eastbourne Coll. Commissioned (Army), RAOC, 1956–58. Member, Retail Foods Trades Wages Council, 1963–64. JP Inner London, 1970–83, City, 1974–92; Member: Council, Royal Borough of Kensington and Chelsea, 1970–73; Court of Common Council (Ward of Dowgate), City of London, 1973; Alderman (Ward of Dowgate), City of London, 1974–2002; Sheriff of the City of London, 1979–80; Lord Mayor of London, 1981–82; one of HM Lieutenants, City of London, 1982–2002. Chm., London Tourist Bd, 1983–89; Dep. Chm., Thames Water Authority, 1983–89; Chm., Thames Line Plc, 1987–89; Director: Bath & Portland Gp, 1983–85; Thermal Scientific plc, 1986–88; Unionamerica Holdings Plc, 1994–97. Advr on Royal Parks to Sec. of State for Nat. Heritage, 1993–96. Member: Bd of Brixton Prison, 1975–78; Court, City Univ., 1978–2002 (Chancellor, 1981–82); Council of the Missions to Seamen,

1983–95; Council, Wine and Spirit Benevolent Soc., 1983–88; Finance Cttee, London Diocesan Fund, 1983–86; Transitional Council, St Paul's Cathedral, 1999; Trustee: Chichester Festival Theatre, 1982–97; LSO, 1983–91; Vice-President: Bridewell Royal Hosp., 1982–89; NPFA, 1983–99; Governor: Christ's Hospital Sch., 1975–2002; City of London Girls' Sch., 1975–78; City of London Freemen's Sch., 1980–81; Chm., Council, Eastbourne Coll., 1989–2005 (Mem., 1988–2005); Almoner Trustee, St Paul's Cathedral Choir Sch. Foundn, 1986–90. Trustee, Music Therapy Trust, 1981–89; Chairman, Young Musicians' Symphony Orch. Trust, 1979–81; Hon. Mem., Guildhall Sch. of Music and Drama, 1982–. Church Warden, St Olave's, Hart Street, 1975–90 (Patronage Trust, 1990–96); Church Comr, 1982–93, 1996–99. Mem., Ct of Assistants, Carmen's Co., 1973 (Master, 1987–88); Hon. Liveryman: Farmers' Company, 1980; Water Conservators' Co., 2000 (Hon. Freeman, 1995); Freeman, Co. of Watermen and Lightermen, 1988; Hon. Freeman, Co. of Environmental Cleaners, 1983; Hon. Col, 151 (Greater London) Tpt Regt RCT (V), 1983–88; Hon. Col Comdt, RCT, 1988–91. Hon. DMus City, 1981. KStJ 1982. Order of Oman Class II. *Recreations:* gardening, music.

**LEAVER, Prof. Christopher John,** CBE 2000; FRS 1986; FRSE; Sibthorpian Professor of Plant Sciences, 1990–2007, now Professor Emeritus, and Head, Department of Plant Sciences, 1991–2007, University of Oxford; Fellow, St John's College, Oxford, 1989–2007, now Emeritus; *b* 31 May 1942; *s* of Douglas Percy Leaver and Elizabeth Constance Leaver; *m* 1971, Anne (*née* Huggins); one *s* one *d*. *Educ:* Lyme Regis Grammar Sch. (State Scholarship); Imperial College, University of London (BSc 1st Cl. Hons, ARCS, DIC 1963, PhD 1966); MA (Oxon) 1990. Botanist, Imperial Coll., London: Hornsund Expedition, Spitzbergen, 1962; Beerenberg Expedition, Jan Mayen, 1963; Fulbright Scholar, Purdue Univ., 1966–68; Scientific Officer, ARC Plant Physiology Unit, Imperial Coll., 1968–69; University of Edinburgh: Lectr, Dept of Botany, 1969–80; Reader, 1980–86; SERC Sen. Res. Fellow, 1985–89; Prof. of Plant Molecular Biol., 1986–89. EMBO Sen. Fellow, Biozentrum Basel, 1980; Royal Soc./Academie des Scis Vis. Lectr to France, 1994; Raine Med. Res. Foundn Vis. Prof., 2001, Vis. Prof., 2002–15, Univ. of WA, Perth. Founder Mem., Bd of Dirs, Internat. Soc. of Plant Molecular Biol., 1982–87; Member: AFRC, 1990–94; Priorities Bd for R&D to advise MAFF, 1990–94 (Chm., Arable Crops Adv. Sectoral Gp, 1990–94); Council, EMBO, 1991–97 (Chm., 1996–97); ACOST for HM Govt, 1992–93; Adv. Council on Sci. and Technol., NIAB Japan, 1992–94; Council, Royal Soc., 1992–94 (Member: Finance and Gen. Purposes Cttee, 1995–2000; Educn Cttee, 1995–2000; Scientific Unions Cttee, 2005–10; Internat. Networks Cttee, 2005–15; Africa Exchange Cttee, 2015–18); BBSRC, 2000–03 (Chair, Individual Merit Promotion Panel, 1996–2005; Mem., Scientific CS Personal Merit Promotion Panel, 2005–10); Instituto de Tecnologica Química e Biológica António Xavier Adv. Commn, Lisbon, 2000–06; Govt GM Sci. Review Panel, 2002–04; Scientific Adv. Bd, Australian Res. Council Centre of Excellence in Plant Energy Biol., Perth, 2005–13; Internat. Adv. Panel, Nat. Univ. of Singapore Graduate Sch., 2006– (Chm., 2009–); Cttee of Scientific Planning and Rev., ICSU, Paris, 2006–12; Chairman: Sci. Adv. Bd, IACR, Rothamsted, 1995–2000; Ext. Scientific Adv. Bd, Inst. of Molecular and Cell Biol., Univ. of Porto, 1999–. Advr in Biol Scis, Carnegie Trust for Univs of Scotland, 2000–14; Sen. Scientific Advr in Bioscis, Farming in Africa, 2011–17. Biochemical Society: Mem. Council, 1995–99; Chm., Nucleic Acids and Molecular Biol. Gp, 1995–2000; Vice Chm., 2002–04, Chm., 2005–07, Exec. Cttee; Trustee, 2005–07; Mem., Educn Cttee, 2005–12. Curator, Oxford Botanic Garden, 1991–98. Mem. Gov. Council, John Innes, 1984–2012; Trustee: John Innes Foundn, 1987–2017; Nat. History Mus., 1997–2006 (Mem., Audit Commn); Founding Trustee, Sense About Sci., 2001–13. Deleg., OUP, 2002–07. Corresp. Mem., Amer. Soc. of Plant Biologists, 2003, Fellow, 2007. Mem., EMBO, 1982. FRSE 1987; MAE 1988. Hon. FRI 2002. T. H. Huxley Gold Medal, Imperial Coll., 1970; Tate & Lyle Award, Phytochem. Soc. of Europe, 1984; Humboldt Prize, Alexander von Humboldt Foundn, Bonn, 1997; Sibthorp Medal, Univ. of Oxford, 2007. *Publications:* over 160 scientific papers in internat. sci. jls based on res. interests incl. molecular, biochem. and cellular basis of plant develt, regulation of mitochondrial biogenesis and function and programmed cell death in plants, GM crops and food security and sustainability. *Recreation:* walking and talking in Upper Coquetdale. *Address:* St John's College, Oxford OX1 3JP. *E:* chris.leaver@plants.ox.ac.uk.

**LEAVER, David;** *see* Leaver, J. D.

**LEAVER, Elaine Kildare;** *see* Murray, E. K.

**LEAVER, Prof. (John) David,** PhD; FRSB; FRAgS, FIAgrE, FRASE; Principal, Royal Agricultural College, Cirencester, 2002–07, now Professor Emeritus; *b* 5 Jan. 1942; *s* of John and Elsie Leaver; *m* 1969, Sally Ann Posgate; two *s* one *d*. *Educ:* Univ. of Durham (BSc Agric.); Wye Coll., Univ. of London (PhD 1967). FRSB (FIBiol 1988); FRAgS 1986; FIAgrE 2003; FRASE 2009. PSO, Nat. Inst. for Res. in Dairying, 1967–76; Hd, Dept of Animal Prodn and Farm Dir, Crichton Royal W of Scotland Agricl Coll., 1976–87; Prof. of Agriculture and Vice Principal, Wye Coll., Univ. of London, 1987–2000; Vice Provost, Wye, Imperial Coll., 2000–02. Dir, UCAS, 2006–07. Dir, NMR plc, 1994–97. Member: Adv. Cttee, BSE, the Cost of a Crisis, Nat. Audit Office, 1997; Prog. Mgt Cttee, DEFRA Sustainable Livestock Prog., 2002–12 (Chm., 2007–12); Council of Food Policy Advrs, 2008–10; Chief Scientific Advr's Food Res. Partnership, 2009–15. Chm., Practice with Sci. Adv. Gp, RASE, 2009–13. Mem., Wilson Cttee, Nat. Cattle Genetic Database, 1989–90; Scientific Advr, Internat. Foundn for Science, 1994–2014. President: British Soc. of Animal Sci., 1995–96; British Grassland Soc., 2000–01; British Inst. of Agricl Consultants, 2009–; Wye Coll. Agricola Club, 2009–; Royal Assoc. of British Dairy Farmers, 2012–16. Trustee: Frank Parkinson Agricl Trust, 1994– (Chm., 1999–2011); Frank Parkinson Yorks Trust, 1999– (Chm., 2008–11); Sir Emrys Jones Meml Trust, 2005–; Stapledon Meml Trust, 2010–; Wye Coll. Meml Trust, 2011–. *Publications:* Herbage Intake Handbook, 1982; Milk Production, Science and Practice, 1983; over 250 articles in peer-reviewed jls and conf. papers on dairy systems res. *Recreations:* sport, music, poetry, countryside. *Address:* Sole Street Farm, Crundale, Canterbury, Kent CT4 7ET. *E:* jdleaver@gmail.com. *Club:* Farmers.

**LEAVER, Marcus Edward;** Executive Director, Welbeck Publishing Group, since 2019; Chairman, Trigger Publishing, since 2018; *b* 1 April 1970; *s* of Peter Lawrence Oppenheim Leaver, *qv*; *m* 1997, Anna Gwendoline Morgan; one *s* three *d*. *Educ:* Eton Coll.; UEA (BA Hons (Hist. of Art and Architecture) 1992); London Business Sch. (MBA 1999). Corporate Develt Dir, Chrysalis Gp plc, 2001–03; Chief Exec., Chrysalis Books Gp plc, 2003–05; Exec. Vice-Pres. and Chief Operating Officer, 2005–08, Pres., 2008–12, Sterling Publishing Co. Inc.; Chief Operating Officer, 2012, CEO, 2012–18, Quarto Gp Inc. *Recreations:* Tottenham Hotspur, New York Yankees, cricket. *Address:* Welbeck Publishing Group, 20–22 Mortimer Street, W1T 3JW. *Clubs:* MCC, Soho House.

**LEAVER, Dame Parveen June;** *see* Kumar, Dame P. J.

**LEAVER, Peter Lawrence Oppenheim;** QC 1987; a Recorder, 1994–2017; a Deputy High Court Judge, 1994–2017; *b* 28 Nov. 1941; *er s* of Marcus Isaac Leaver and Lena Leaver (*née* Oppenheim); *m* 1969, Jane Rachel, *o d* of Leonard and Rivka Pearl; three *s* one *d*. *Educ:* Aldenham Sch., Elstree; Trinity Coll., Dublin. Called to the Bar, Lincoln's Inn, 1967, Bencher, 1995. Chairman: Bar Cttee, 1989; Internat. Practice Cttee, 1990; Member: Gen. Council of the Bar, 1987–90; Cttee on the Future of the Legal Profession, 1986–88; Council of Legal Educn, 1986–91. Chief Exec., FA Premier League, 1997–99. Dir, IMRO Ltd, 1994–2000. Chm., London Court of Internat. Arbitration, 2008–12. Pres., UK Nat. Anti-Doping Panel, 2008–15. *Recreations:* sport, theatre, wine. *Address:* 1 Essex Court, Temple, EC4Y 9AR. *T:* (020) 7583 2000. *Clubs:* Garrick, MCC.

*See also* M. E. Leaver.

**LEAVEY, Thomas Edward,** PhD; Director General, International Bureau of Universal Postal Union, 1995–2005; *b* Kansas City, 10 Nov. 1934; *s* of Leonard J. Leavey and Mary (*née* Horgan); *m* 1968, Anne Roland. *Educ:* Josephinium Coll., Columbus, Ohio (BA 1957); Institut Catholique, Paris; Princeton Univ. (MA 1967; PhD 1968). Sch. administrator and teacher, Kansas City, Mo, 1957–63; Prof., Fairleigh Dickinson Univ., NJ and George Washington Univ., Washington, 1968–70; United States Postal Service: Prof., Trng and Develt Inst., Bethesda, Md, 1970–72; Dir, Postal Service Trng and Develt Mgt Trng Center, LA, 1973–75; Gen. Manager, Employment and Placement Div., HQ, 1976–78; Dir, Postal Career Exec. Service, HQ, 1979; Postmaster/Sectional Manager, Charlottesville, Va, 1980; Regl Dir of Human Resources, Central Reg., Chicago, 1981; Controller, HQ, 1982; Gen. Manager, Internat. Mail Processing Div., HQ, 1982–87; Asst PMG and Sen. Dir, Internat. Postal Affairs, HQ, 1987–94. Universal Postal Union: Chairman: Customs Co-operation Council Contact Cttee, 1987–89; Private Operators Contact Cttee, 1991–94; Postal Develt Action Gp, 1991–94; Provident Scheme Mgt Bd, Internat. Bureau, 1989–94; Exec. Council, 1989–94. USPS Special Achievement Awards for Distinguished Service, 1970–90; John Wanamaker Award, USPS, 1991. Chevalier de la Légion d'Honneur (France), 2001. *Publications:* numerous articles on business and postal matters in postal and trade jls. *Recreations:* golf, tennis, ski-ing. *Address:* 13978 Siena Loop, Lakewood Ranch, FL 34202–2443, USA.

**LEBOW, Prof. (Richard) Ned,** PhD; FBA 2017; Professor of International Political Theory, King's College London, since 2012; Bye-Fellow in International Relations, Pembroke College, Cambridge, since 2012; *b* Paris, 1941; *s* of Joseph Lebow and Ruth Lebow (*née* Newman); *m* 1975, Carol Bohmer; two *s* one *d*. *Educ:* Univ. of Chicago (BA Pol Sci. 1963); Yale Univ. (MA Internat. Relns 1964); City Univ. of NY (PhD Pol Sci. 1968). Instructor, Brooklyn Coll., CUNY, 1966–68; Asst and Associate Prof. of Pol Sci., City Coll. and Grad. Center, CUNY, 1968–78; Prof. of Strategy, Nat. War Coll., 1978–80; Schol.-in-Residence, CIA, 1980–81; Prof. of Pol Sci., Bologna Center, Johns Hopkins Univ., 1981–83; Prof. of Pol Sci. and Dir, Peace Studies Prog., Cornell Univ., 1983–92; Prof. of Public Affairs and Pol Sci., Grad. Sch. of Public and Internat. Affairs and Dept of Pol Sci., Univ. of Pittsburgh, 1992–96; Prof. of Pol Sci., Hist. and Psychol., Ohio State Univ., 1996–2002; James O. Freedman Presidential Prof. of Govt, Dartmouth Coll., 2002–12, now Prof. Emeritus. Visiting Professor: Univ. of Munich, 1995–96; Univ. of Milan, 1998; LSE, 2004; Austrian Diplomatic Acad., Vienna, 2010, 2011; Dept of Politics and Internat. Studies, Univ. of Cambridge, 2010; Olof Palme Prof., Sweden, 2011–12; Vis. Dist. Res. Prof., ANU, 2007; Centennial Prof., LSE, 2008–11; Vis. Fellow, Wolfson Coll., Cambridge, 2006–07; Fellow, Centre of Internat. Studies, Univ. of Cambridge, 2006–11; Overseas Fellow, St John's Coll., Cambridge, 2008; Vis. Schol., Pembroke Coll., Cambridge, 2009–10. *Publications:* (ed jtly) Divided Nations in a Divided World, 1974; White Britain and Black Ireland: social stereotypes and colonial policy, 1976; (ed) John Stuart Mill on Ireland, 1979; (ed) Richard Cobden, England, Ireland and America, 1980; Between Peace and War: the nature of international crisis, 1981; (ed jtly) The Fallacy of Star Wars, 1984; (jtly) Psychology and Deterrence, 1985; Nuclear Crisis Management: a dangerous illusion, 1987; (with J. Gross-Stein) When Does Deterrence Succeed and How Do We Know?, 1990 (trans. French 1990); (ed with Barry R. Strauss) Hegemonic Rivalry: from Thucydides to the nuclear age, 1991; (with J. Gross-Stein) We All Lost the Cold War, 1994; (ed with T. Risse-Kapper) International Relations Theory and the End of the Cold War, 1995; The Art of Bargaining, 1996; The Tragic Vision of Politics: ethics, interests and orders, 2003; (ed with R. K. Herrmann) Ending the Cold War, 2003; (ed jtly) The Politics of Memory in Postwar Europe, 2006; A Cultural Theory of International Relations, 2008 (trans. Chinese 2012, Japanese 2017) (Susan Strange Award, British Internat. Studies Assoc., 2009; Jervis-Schroeder Award, Amer. Pol Sci. Assoc., 2009); (ed jtly) Unmaking the West: 'What If' scenarios that rewrite world history, 2006; (ed with I. Lichbach) Theory and Evidence in Comparative Politics and International Relations, 2007; Forbidden Fruit: counterfactuals and international relations, 2010; Why Nations Fight: past and future motives for war, 2010 (trans. Chinese, 2013, Arabic 2017); (ed with T. Erskine) Tragedy and International Relations, 2011; The Politics and Ethics of Identity: in search of ourselves, 2012 (Alexander L. George Award, Internat. Soc. of Pol Psychol., 2013); Constructing Cause in International Relations, 2014; (with S. Reich) Good-Bye Hegemony! Power and Influence in the Global System, 2014 (trans. Chinese, 2016); Archduke Franz Ferdinand Lives! A World without World War 1, 2014; National Identifications and International Relations, 2016; (ed jtly) Return of the Theorists: encounters with the great thinkers of the past, 2016; (ed) Max Weber and International Relations, 2017; Avoiding War, Making Peace, 2017 (trans. Chinese as Strategies of Peace, 2017); Self Interest in Politics and Business from Tocqueville to Trump, 2017; The Rise and Fall of Political Orders, 2018; contribs to learned jls. *Address:* Hampden House, 2 Weymouth Street, W1W 5BT; 81 Ruddsboro Road, Etna, NH 03750, USA. *E:* nedlebow@gmail.com. *Club:* Athenæum.

**LEBRECHT, Andrew John,** CB 2006; Deputy Permanent Representative, UK Permanent Representation to the European Union, 2008–12; *b* 13 Dec. 1951; *s* of late Heinz Martin Lebrecht and Margaret Lebrecht (*née* Cardis); *m* 1978, Judit Catan; two *d*. *Educ:* De La Salle Coll., Hove; Leeds Univ. (BA Econs); Reading Univ. (MSc Agricl Econs). Ministry of Agriculture, Fisheries and Food, 1977–2001: Private Sec. to Parly Sec., 1980–82; on secondment to HM Diplomatic Service as First Sec. (Fisheries and Food), UK Rep. Brussels, 1985–89; Principal Private Sec. to Minister of Agriculture, 1989–91; Head: Sheep and Livestock Subsidies Div., 1991–93; Review of Animal Health and Veterinary Gp, 1993–94; EU Div., 1994–98; EU and Internat. Policy, 1998–2001; Dir Gen., Food, Farming and Fisheries, then Sustainable Farming, Food and Fisheries, then Sustainable Farming and Food, subseq. Food and Farming, DEFRA, 2001–07. Mem., Sen. European Experts Gp, 2012. Hon. Sen. Res. Associate, UCL, 2015–18. Gov., Garth Hill Coll., Bracknell, 2015–. Trainer, 2016–, Associate Dir, 2018–, Centre for Political and Diplomatic Studies, London. *Recreations:* family life, the countryside, reading.

**LEBRECHT, Norman;** writer and broadcaster; *b* 11 July 1948; *s* of late Solomon and Marguerite Lebrecht; *m* 1977, Elbie Spivack; three *d*. *Educ:* Hasmonean Grammar Sch. Radio and TV producer, 1970–79; specialist contributor: Sunday Times, 1982–91; Independent mag., 1991–92; Music Columnist, Daily Telegraph, 1993–2002; Asst Ed. and Arts Columnist, Evening Standard, 2002–09. Owner and publisher, Slipped Disc, 2008–. Contributor: Bloomberg, 2010–14; Wall St Jl, 2010–; Standpoint mag., 2011–17; Spectator, 2017–. Contributor, The Late Show, BBC TV, 1994–95; Presenter, Lebrecht Live, BBC Radio 3, 2000–15. *Publications:* Discord, 1982; Hush, Handel's in a Passion, 1985; The Book of Musical Anecdotes, 1985; Mahler Remembered, 1987; The Book of Musical Days, 1987; The Maestro Myth, 1991; The Companion to 20th Century Music, 1992; When the Music Stops, 1996; The Complete Companion to 20th Century Music, 2000; Covent Garden: the untold story, 2000; Maestros, Masterpieces and Madness, 2007;

Why Mahler?, 2010; Genius and Anxiety, 2019; *novels:* The Song of Names (Whitbread First Novel Award), 2002; The Game of Opposites, 2009. *Recreations:* reading, prayer, listening to music, watching cricket, vigorous disputation, deltiology. *Address:* 3 Bolton Road, NW8 0RJ. *E:* norman@normanlebrecht.com.

**LE BRETON, David Francis Battye,** CBE 1978; HM Diplomatic Service, retired; Head of Nationality and Treaty Department, Foreign and Commonwealth Office, 1986–87; *b* 2 March 1931; *e s* of late Lt-Col F. H. Le Breton, MC, and Elisabeth, (Peter), Le Breton (*née* Trevor-Battye), Endebess, Kenya; *m* 1961, Patricia June Byrne; one *s* two *d*. *Educ:* Winchester; New Coll., Oxford. Colonial Administrative Service, Tanganyika, 1954; Private Sec. to Governor, 1959–60; Magistrate, 1962; Principal, CRO, 1963; HM Diplomatic Service, 1965; First Sec., Zanzibar, 1964; Lusaka, 1964–68; FCO, 1968–71; Head of Chancery, Budapest, 1971–74; HM Comr in Anguilla, 1974–78; Counsellor and Head of Chancery, Nairobi, 1978–81; High Comr in The Gambia, 1981–84; Head of Commonwealth Co-ordination Dept, FCO, 1984–86. Financial Advr/Sales Associate, Allied Dunbar Assurance, 1987–91; Sec., Overseas Service Pensioners' Assoc. and Benevolent Soc., 1992–2017. *Publications:* (ed) I Remember It Well: Colonial Service reminiscences, 2010. *Recreations:* country living, African and colonial affairs. *Address:* Brackenwood, French Street, near Westerham, Kent TN16 1PN.

**LE BRUN, Christopher Mark,** RA 1997; RI 2015; artist; President, Royal Academy, since 2011 (Professor of Drawing, 2000–02); *b* 20 Dec. 1951; *s* of late John Le Brun, BEM and Eileen Betty (*née* Miles); *m* 1979, Charlotte Eleanor Verity; two *s* one *d*. *Educ:* Portsmouth Southern Grammar Sch.; Slade Sch. of Fine Art (DFA); Chelsea Sch. of Art (MA). Lecturer: Brighton Coll. of Art, 1975–82; Wimbledon Coll. of Art, 1982–84; Vis. Lectr, Slade Sch. of Fine Art, 1984–90. Deutscher Akademischer Austauschdienst Fellowship, Berlin, 1987–88. Designer, Ballet Imperial, Royal Opera Hse, Covent Gdn, 1984. Designed stained glass window, LSE, 2014. One man exhibitions include: Nigel Greenwood Gall., London, 1980, 1982, 1985, 1989; Gillespie-Laage-Salomon, Paris, 1981; Sperone Westwater, NY, 1983, 1986, 1988; Fruitmarket Gall., Edinburgh, 1985; Arnolfini Gall., Bristol, 1985; Kunsthalle, Basel, 1986; Daadgalerie, Berlin, 1988; Galerie Rudolf Zwirner, Cologne, 1988; Art Center, Pasadena, Calif, 1992; LA Louver Gall., Venice, Calif, 1992; Marlborough Fine Art, 1994, 1998, 2001, 2003; Galerie Fortlaan 17, Ghent, 1994, 2002; Astrup Fearnley Mus. of Modern Art, Oslo, 1995; Fitzwilliam Mus., Cambridge, 1995; Marlborough Chelsea, NY, 2004; New Art Gall., Walsall, 2008; Hohenthal und Bergen, Berlin, 2009; New Art Centre, E Winterslow, Salisbury, 2010; Friedman Benda, NY, 2014; Colnaghi, London, 2015; Arndt, Singapore, 2016; Windsor, Fla, 2017; Albertz Benda, NY, 2017; Arndt, Berlin, 2017; Lisson Gall., 2018; group exhibitions include: Milan, 1980; Berlin, 1982; Tate Gall., 1983; Mus. Modern Art, NY, 1984, 2005; The British Show, toured Australia and NZ, 1985; Oxford, Budapest, Prague, Warsaw, 1987; LA County Mus., 1987; Cincinnati Mus. and American tour, 1988–89; Setagaya Art Mus. and Japanese tour, 1990–91; Scottish Nat. Gall. Modern Art, 1995; Yale Center for British Art, New Haven, 1995; Nat. Gall., 2000; Tate Britain, 2011; Chatsworth, 2015; work in public collections includes: Arts Council England, British Council, BM, NY Mus. Modern Art, NY Metropolitan Mus., Scottish Nat. Gall. Modern Art, Tate Gall., Walker Art Gall., Liverpool, Whitworth Art Gall., Manchester and Fitzwilliam Mus., Cambridge. Trustee: Tate Gall., 1990–95; Nat. Gall., 1996–2003; Dulwich Picture Gall., 2000–05; NPG, 2012–; Member: Slade Cttee, 1992–95; Develt Cttee, Tate Gall. of British Art, 1995–97. Chm., Royal Acad. Masterplan Briefing Gp, 2005–11. Advr, Prince of Wales's Drawing Sch., 2000–03; Trustee and Chm., Academic Bd, Royal Drawing Sch. (formerly Prince of Wales's Drawing Sch.), 2004–16. President: Artists' Gen. Benevolent Inst., 2012–; Gainsborough's House, Suffolk, 2012–; Vice Pres., Turner Soc., 2018–; Patron, Turner's House Trust, 2012–. Hon. Fellow, Univ. of the Arts, London, 2010; Hon. RBSA, 2013; Hon. RWS, 2016; Hon. RE 2017. Prizewinner, John Moores Liverpool Exhibns, 1978 and 1980; Gulbenkian Foundn Printmakers Award, 1983. *Relevant publications:* Christopher Le Brun, by Charles Saumarez Smith and Bryan Robertson, 2001; Christopher Le Brun, by David Anfam and Edmund de Waal, 2014; Christopher Le Brun: composer, by Barbara Rose, 2017. *Address:* c/o Royal Academy of Arts, Piccadilly, W1J 0BD.

**LE CARRÉ, John;** *see* Cornwell, David John Moore.

**LECHLER, Sir Robert (Ian),** PhD; Kt 2012; FRCP, FRCPE, FRCPath; FMedSci; Professor of Immunology, since 2004, Vice-Principal for Health, since 2005 and Dean, School of Medicine and Dental Institute, Guy's, King's College and St Thomas' Hospitals (formerly Guy's, King's and St Thomas' Schools of Medicine and Dentistry), since 2005, King's College London; Executive Director, King's Health Partners Academic Health Science Centre, since 2009; Hon. Consultant, Department of Renal Medicine and Transplantation, Guy's Hospital, since 2004; President, Academy of Medical Sciences, since 2015; *b* 24 Dec. 1951; *s* of Ian Lechler and Audrey Lechler (*née* Wilson); *m* 1st, 1975, Valerie Susan Johnston (separated 1990; marr. diss. 2007); two *s* one *d*; 2nd, 2008, Giovanna Lombardi; one *s* one *d*. *Educ:* Monkton Combe Sch.; Victoria Univ. of Manchester (MB ChB 1975); Royal Postgrad. Med. Sch., Univ. of London (PhD 1983). FRCP 1990; FRCPath 1996; FRCPE 2012. Postgrad. med. trng in internal medicine and renal medicine, Manchester Royal Infirmary, Wythenshawe Hosp. and St Bartholomew's Hosp., London, 1975–79; Med. Res. Trng Fellow, Dept of Immunol., RPMS, 1979–82; Renal Registrar, 1982–83, Sen. Renal Registrar, 1983–84, Professorial Med. Unit, Hammersmith Hosp.; Wellcome Trust Travelling Fellow, Lab. of Immunol., NIH, Bethesda, USA, 1984–86; Royal Postgraduate Medical School: Sen. Lectr in Immunol., 1986–98; Reader in Immunol., 1989–92; Prof. of Molecular Immunol., 1992–94; Hon. Consultant in Medicine, 1986–94; Consultant Transplant Physician, Hammersmith Hosps NHS Trust, 1986–2004; Imperial College, University of London: Prof. of Immunol., 1994–2004; Dean of Hammersmith Campus, 2001–04; Hd, Div. of Medicine, 2003–04; Dean, GKT Sch. of Medicine, KCL, 2004–05. Internat. Advr to NIH Immune Tolerance Network, 2000–. Chairman: Scientific Adv. Bd, Embryonic Stem Cell Internat., 2003–; Expert Adv. Gp, Cttee for Safety of Medicines, 2007–. Councillor, Internat. Xenotransplantation Assoc., 2001–05; Mem. Exec., Council of Hds of Med. Schs, 2006–. Mem., Scientific Cttee, Inst de transplantation et de recherche en transplantation, Nantes, 2000–06; Dir, Ruggero Ceppellini Sch. of Immunol., Naples, 2001–. Chm., Chairs and Prog. Grants Cttee, 2003–07, Trustee and Mem. Council, 2010–16, BHF. Member, Board: London and Partners, 2014–; HCA Healthcare UK, 2018–; Founder and Mem. Mgt Bd, MedCity, 2014–. Mem. Bd, Francis Crick Inst., 2016–. Pres., Patrons, Imperial Sinfonietta, 2017–. FMedSci 2000. *Publications:* HLA in Health and Disease, 1994, 2nd edn 2000; numerous contribs to leading jls on transplantation and immune tolerance. *Recreations:* theatre, music, sketching. *Address:* (home) 78 Woodstock Road, W4 1EQ; King's Health Partners Academic Health Sciences Centre Headquarters, Ground Floor, Counting House, Guy's Hospital Campus, St Thomas' Street, SE1 9RT. *E:* robert.lechler@kcl.ac.uk.

**LECHMERE, Sir Nicholas Anthony Hungerford,** 8th Bt *cr* 1818, of The Rhydd, Worcs; *b* 24 April 1960; *e s* of Sir Reginald Lechmere, 7th Bt and Anne Jennifer (*née* Dind); *S* father, 2010; *m* 1991, Caroline Gahan; three *s* one *d*. High Sheriff, Worcs, 2016–17. *Heir: s* Frederick Patrick Hungerford, *b* 9 Dec. 1992.

**LECKEY, Mark;** artist; *b* Birkenhead, 25 June 1964; *s* of Bruce and Carole Leckey; *m* 2012, Lizzie Carey-Thomas; one *d*. *Educ:* Whitby Comprehensive Sch., Ellesmere Port; Newcastle Poly. (BA Fine Art 1990). Prof. of Film Studies, Städelschule, Frankfurt, 2005–09. Solo exhibitions include: Gavin Brown's enterprise, NY, 2000, 2002, 2004, 2006, 2010; Migros Mus., Zurich, 2003; Tate Britain, 2003, 2008, 2019; Portikus, Frankfurt, 2005; Industrial Light and Magic, Consortium, Dijon, 2007; Guggenheim Mus., NY, Kölnischer Kunstverein, Cologne, 2008; ICA, London 2009; Milton Keynes Gall., 2010; Serpentine Gall., 2011; Walter Phillips Gall., Banff Centre, Alberta, Canada, Galerie Buchholz, Berlin, 2012; The Bluecoat, Liverpool, Nottingham Contemp., De La Warr Pavilion, Bexhill-on-Sea, 2013; MOMA, NY, 2016; Cubitt Gall., London, 2017; *group exhibitions* include: ICA, London, 1990, 2000, 2001; Tate Modern, 2001, 2011; Tate Liverpool, 2002; Manifesta 5, Eur. Biennial of Contemp. Art, San Sebastian, Spain, 2004; 9th Istanbul Biennial, 2005; Mus. of Contemp. Art, Chicago, 2007; Contemp. Art Gall., Vancouver, 2009; 8th Gwangju Biennale, S Korea, 2010; Venice Biennale, 2013; *work in public collections* including: Centre Georges Pompidou, Paris; Mus. of Contemp. Art, LA; MOMA, NY; Tate Gall., London; Trussardi Foundn, Milan; Walker Art Center, Minneapolis. Winner, Turner Prize, 2008; Central Art Award, Kölnischer Kunstverein, 2008. *Recreation:* walking. *Address:* 32 Wallace House, Caledonian Road, N7 8TL. *T:* 07894 711830. *E:* mark.leckey@hotmail.com.

**LECKIE, Carolyn;** NP; solicitor, Bruce Short Solicitors, since 2017; *b* 5 March 1965. *Educ:* Univ. of Strathclyde (LLB 2014). Midwife. Contested (Scot Socialist), Springburn, 2001. Mem. (Scot Socialist) Scotland Central, Scottish Parlt, 2003–07. Scot Socialist spokesperson for Health and Community Care, Scottish Parlt, 2003–07. Columnist, The National, 2014–.

**LE CLÉZIO, Jean-Marie Gustave;** writer; *b* Nice, 13 April 1940; *s* of Raoul Le Clézio; *m* 1975, Jémia Jean; one *d*; one *d* from a previous marriage. *Educ:* Bristol Univ.; Institut d'Études Littéraires, Nice; Univ. of Aix-en-Provence (MA 1964); Univ. of Perpignan (PhD 1983). Prix Théophraste Renaudot, 1963; Nobel Prize for Literature, 2008. *Publications:* Le procès-verbal, 1963 (The Interrogation, 1964); Le jour où Beaumont fit connaissance avec sa douleur, 1964; La fièvre, 1965 (Fever, 1966); Le déluge, 1966 (The Flood, 1967); L'extase matérielle, 1967; Terra Amata, 1967 (Terra Amata, 1969); Le livre des fuites, 1969 (The Book of Flights, 1971); La guerre, 1970 (War, 1973); Haï, 1971; Mydriase, 1973; Les géants, 1973 (The Giants, 1975); Voyages de l'autre côté, 1975; L'inconnu sur la terre, 1978; Vers les icebergs, 1978; Voyage au pays des arbres, 1978; Mondo et autres histoires, 1978; Désert, 1980; Trois villes saintes, 1980; Lullaby, 1980; La ronde et autres faits divers, 1982 (The Round & Other Cold Hard Facts, 2002); Celui qui n'avait jamais vu la mer, La montagne du dieu vivant, 1982; Balaabilou, 1985; Le chercheur d'or, 1985 (The Prospector, 1993); Villa Aurore, Orlamonde, 1985; Voyage à Rodrigues, 1986; Le rêve mexicain ou la pensée interrompue, 1988 (The Mexican Dream or The Interrupted Thought of Amerindian Civilizations, 1993); Printemps et autres saisons, 1989; La grande vie, Peuple du ciel, 1990; Onitsha, 1991 (Onitsha, 1997); Étoile errante, 1992 (Wandering Star, 2004); Pawana, 1992; Diego et Frida, 1993; La quarantaine, 1995; Poisson d'or, 1996; La fête chantée, 1997; Hasard, Angoli Mala, 1999; Coeur brûlé et autres romances, 2000; Révolutions, 2003; L'Africain, 2004; Ourania, 2005; Raga: approche du continent invisible, 2006; Ballaciner, 2007; Ritournelle de la faim, 2008; Histoire du pied et autres fantaisies, 2011; Les musées sont des mondes, 2011. *Address:* c/o Éditions Gallimard, 5 rue Gaston-Gallimard, 75328 Paris cedex 07, France.

**LE COCQ, Timothy John;** QC (Jersey) 2008; Bailiff of Jersey, since 2019 (Deputy Bailiff, 2015–19); *b* Jersey, 9 Dec. 1956; *s* of Bernard Reginald Le Cocq and Janet Le Cocq (*née* Gibbs); *m* 1st, 1988, Elizabeth Case (marr. diss. 1994); one *s*; 2nd, 1994, Ruth Iona Leighton (marr. diss. 2018); two *s* one *d*. *Educ:* De La Salle Coll., Jersey; Univ. of Keele (BA Hons Law and Psychol. 1980). Called to the Bar, Inner Temple, 1981, Overseas Bencher, 2016; called to Jersey Bar, 1985; in practice as Jersey Advocate, 1985–2008; Crown Advocate, Jersey, 1996–2008; HM Solicitor Gen. for Jersey, 2008–09; HM Attorney Gen. for Jersey, 2009–15. *Address:* c/o Bailiff's Chambers, Royal Court House, St Helier, Jersey JE1 1BA. *T:* (01534) 441103, *Fax:* (01534) 441137. *E:* Bailiffof Jersey@gov.je. *Clubs:* Oriental; United (Jersey).

**LECONFIELD,** Baron; *see* Egremont.

**LEDERER, Peter Julian,** CBE 2005 (OBE 1994); Chairman: Royal Edinburgh Military Tattoo, since 2017 (Director, since 2011; Vice Chairman, 2015–17); Gleneagles Hotels Ltd, 2007–14 (Managing Director, 1984–2007); non-executive Chairman: Taste Communications, since 2011; Hamilton & Inches Ltd, since 2012 (Director, since 2008); Applecrate, since 2012; *b* 30 Nov. 1950; *s* of Thomas F. Lederer and Phoebe J. Lederer; *m* 1981, Marilyn R. MacPhail; two *s*. *Educ:* City of London Sch.; Middlesex Poly. (Nat. Dip. Hotelkeeping and Catering); INSEAD (AMP 1994). Manager, Four Seasons Hotels, 1972–79; Partner and Vice Pres., Wood Wilkings Ltd, 1979–81; Gen. Manager, Plaza Hotels Ltd, 1981–83. Non-executive Director: Leading Hotels of the World, 1998–2012; Diageo Scotland, 2008–14; Pod Global Solutions, 2013–; Baxters Food Gp, 2014–; Hotel Management Co., 2016–. Chairman: Scottish Tourist Bd, later VisitScotland, 2001–10; Saltire Foundn, 2009–14; Internat. Leadership Sch., 2010–14. Patron: Hospitality Industry Trust Scotland, 2004– (Chm., 1992–2003); Queen Margaret UC Foundn, 1998. FIH (FHCIMA 1987; Pres., Inst. of Hospitality, 2007–12); CCMI 2002. Liveryman, Co. of Innholders, 1999–. Hon. Prof., Univ. of Dundee, 1994. Hon. DBA Queen Margaret UC, 1997; DUniv Stirling, 2009. Master Innholder, 1988. *Recreations:* motor racing, current affairs, travel. *Address:* 18 Great Stuart Street, Edinburgh EH3 7TN. *T:* 07803 855421. *E:* pjlederer@icloud.com.

**LEDERMAN, David;** QC 1990; a Recorder, 1987–2014; *b* 8 Feb. 1942; *s* of late Eric Kurt Lederman and Marjorie Alice Lederman; *m* 2003, Jennifer Oldland; one *s* two *d* from a previous marriage. *Educ:* Clayesmore School, Dorset; Gonville and Caius College, Cambridge. Called to the Bar, Inner Temple, 1966; criminal practice, fraud, murder, etc. *Recreations:* tennis, horses, France, family, cookery, passionate interest in the Renaissance.

**LEDGER, Frank,** CBE 1992 (OBE 1985); FREng; Deputy Chairman, Nuclear Electric plc, 1990–92, retired; *b* 16 June 1929; *s* of Harry and Doris Ledger; *m* 1953, Alma Moverley; two *s*. *Educ:* Leeds College of Technology (BSc Eng). FREng (FEng 1990); FIMechE; FIET. Student Apprentice, Leeds Corp. Elect. Dept, 1947; appts in power station construction and generation operation in CEA then CEGB, 1955–65; Station Manager, Cottam Power Station, 1965; Central Electricity Generating Board: Group Manager, Midlands Region, 1968; System Operation Engineer, 1971; Dir, Resource Planning, Midlands Region, 1975; Dir of Computing, 1980; Dir of Operations, 1981; Exec. Bd Mem. for Prodn, 1986. Sen. Associate, Nichols Associates Ltd, 1992–98. Member: Council, IEE, 1987–92; British Nat. Cttee, UNIPEDE, 1981–90; Council, British Energy Assoc., 1990–92; Vice-Pres., Energy Industries Club, 1988–92. *Publications:* (jtly) Crisis Management in the Power Industry: an inside story, 1994. *Recreations:* music, photography, gardening, walking. *Address:* 3 Barns Dene, Harpenden, Herts AL5 2HH. *T:* (01582) 762188.

**LEDGEWAY, Prof. Adam Noel,** PhD; FBA 2017; Professor of Italian and Romance Linguistics, since 2013, and Chair, Faculty of Modern and Medieval Languages, 2015–19, University of Cambridge; Fellow, Downing College, Cambridge, since 1996; *b* Swindon, 29 Dec. 1970; *s* of Alfred Ledgeway and Brenda Margaret Ledgeway (*née* Harwood); *m* 2011, Dr Alessandra Lombardi; two *s* one *d*. *Educ*: Caldicot Comp. Sch.; Croesyceiliog Comp. Sch.; Univ. of Salford (BA Hons 1st Cl. French and Italian 1992); Univ. of Manchester (MA Gen. Linguistics (Distinction) 1993; PhD Linguistics 1996). Res. Fellow, Downing Coll., Cambridge, 1995–96; University of Cambridge: temp. asst lectureship, 1997–98, Asst Lectr, 1998–2001, Lectr, 2001–04, Sen. Lectr, 2004–13, in Romance Philology; Hd, Italian Dept, 2007–11. Visiting Professor: Univ. of Zurich, 2009; in Romance Linguistics, Univ. of Venice, 2013–14. Co-Editor: The Italianist, 2003–16; Oxford Studies in Diachronic and Historical Linguistics, series, 2010–; The Oxford Guides to the World's Languages, series, 2012–. Hon. Mem., Institutul de Lingvistică, Bucharest, 2012. Hon. Dr Bucharest, 2016. *Publications:* A Comparative Syntax of the Dialects of Southern Italy: a minimalist approach, 2000; (ed jtly) Didattica della lingua italiana: Testo e contesto, 2008; Grammatica diacronica del napoletano, 2009; (ed jtly) Syntactic Variation: the dialects of Italy, 2010; (ed jtly) In and Out of Italy: Lingua e cultura della migrazione italiana, 2010; (ed jtly) The Cambridge History of the Romance Languages, Vol. 1, Structures, 2011, Vol. 2, Contexts, 2013; From Latin to Romance: morphosyntactic typology and change, 2012, 2nd edn 2015 (trans. Romanian 2017); (ed jtly) Le comunità immigranti nel Regno Unito: il caso di Bedford, 2012; (ed jtly) Diachrony and Dialects: grammatical change in the dialects of Italy, 2014; (ed jtly) The Oxford Guide to the Romance Languages, 2016; De la latină la limbile romanice: schimbare morfosintactică si tipologică, 2017; (ed jtly) The Cambridge Handbook of Historical Syntax, 2017; (ed jtly) Italian Dialectology at the Interfaces, 2018; (ed jtly) The Cambridge Handbook of Romance Linguistics, 2020; contrib. articles in learned jls. *Recreations:* reading, travelling, piano, cooking, family. *Address:* Downing College, Regent Street, Cambridge CB2 1DQ. *T:* (01223) 334800, *Fax:* (01223) 363852. *E:* anl21@cam.ac.uk.

**LEDINGHAM, Prof. John Gerard Garvin,** DM; FRCP; May Reader in Medicine, 1974–95, Professor of Clinical Medicine, 1989–95, and Director of Clinical Studies, 1977–82 and 1991–95, University of Oxford; Fellow of New College, Oxford, 1974–95, Emeritus, 1995–2000, Hon. Fellow, since 2000; Hon. Clinical Director, Biochemical and Clinical NMR Unit, Medical Research Council, Oxford, 1988–95; *b* 19 Oct. 1929; *s* of late John Ledingham, MB BCh, DPH, and late Una Ledingham, MD, FRCP, *d* of J. L. Garvin, CH, Editor of The Observer; *m* 1962, Elaine Mary, *d* of late R. G. Maliphant, MD, FRCOG, and of Dilys Maliphant, Cardiff; four *d*. *Educ:* Rugby Sch.; New Coll., Oxford; Middlesex Hosp. Med. Sch. (1st Cl. Physiol. 1954; BM BCh 1957; DM 1966). FRCP 1971 (MRCP 1959). Junior appts, Middlesex, London Chest, Whittington, and Westminster Hospitals, London, 1957–64; Travelling Fellow, British Postgraduate Med. Fedn, Columbia Univ., New York, 1965–66; Consultant Physician, Oxford AHA(T), 1966–82, Hon. Consultant Physician, Oxfordshire HA, 1982–. Chm., Medical Staff Council, United Oxford Hosps, 1970–72. Chm., Medical Res. Soc., 1988–92; Hon. Sec., Assoc. of Physicians of Gt Britain and Ireland 1977–82, Hon. Treas., 1982–88; Pro-Censor, RCP, 1983–84, Censor, 1984–85. Member: Commonwealth Scholarship Commn, ACU, 1993–98; Nuffield Council on Bioethics, 2000–03. Governing Trustee, Nuffield Trust (formerly Nuffield Provincial Hosps Trust), 1978–2002; Trustee, Beit Trust, 1989–2008. Osler Meml Medal, Oxford Univ., 2000. Distinguished Friend of Univ. of Oxford, 2011. *Publications:* (ed jtly) Oxford Textbook of Medicine, 1982, 3rd edn 1995; (ed with Mark Pottle) We Hope to Get Word Tomorrow: the Garvin family letters 1914–16, 2009; contribs to med. books and scientific jls in the field of hypertension and renal diseases. *Recreations:* music, golf. *Address:* 124 Oxford Road, Cumnor, Oxford OX2 9PQ. *T:* (01865) 865806. *E:* jeled@btinternet.com. *Club:* Vincent's (Oxford).

**LEDLIE, John Kenneth,** CB 1994; OBE 1977; Director, Peter Harrison Foundation, 2002–11; *b* 19 March 1942; *s* of late Reginald Cyril Bell Ledlie and Elspeth Mary Kaye; *m* 1st, 1965, Rosemary Julia Allan (marr. diss. 2006); three *d*; 2nd, 2011, Elisabeth Leader. *Educ:* Westminster School (Hon. Schol.); Brasenose Coll., Oxford (Triplett Exhibnr; MA Lit Hum); Open Univ. (BA Hons 2011). Solicitor of the High Court; articles with Coward Chance, 1964–67; Min. of Defence, 1967; Asst Private Sec. to Minister of State for Equipment and Sec. of State for Defence, 1969–70; First Sec., UK Delegn to NATO, Brussels, 1973–76; Dep. Chief, Public Relations, 1977–79; NI Office and Cabinet Office, 1979–81; Procurement Exec., MoD, 1981–83; Head, Defence Secretariat 19, MoD, 1983; Regional Marketing Dir, Defence Sales Orgn, 1983–85; Chief of PR, MoD, 1985–87; Fellow, Center for Internat. Affairs, Harvard Univ., 1987–88; Asst Under-Sec. of State, MoD, 1988–90; Dep. Sec., NI Office, 1990–93; Dep. Under Sec. of State (Personnel and Logistics), MoD, 1993–95; Partnership Sec., Linklaters & Paines, subseq. Linklaters, 1995–2002. *Recreations:* ornithology, cricket, tennis, theatre, opera. *Address:* 1030 Mission Ridge Road, Santa Barbara, CA 93103, USA.

**Le DRIAN, Jean-Yves;** Minister for Europe and Foreign Affairs, France, since 2017; *b* Lorient, 30 June 1947. *Educ:* Univ. of Rennes. Mem., Lorient Town Council, 1977–2004 (Mayor, 1981–98). Mem. (Soc.) for Morbihan, Nat. Assembly, 1978–91 and 1992–2007; Sec. of State for Sea, Min. of Works, Housing and Transport and Space, 1991–92. Pres., Regl Council, Brittany, 2004–12. Nat. Sec. i/c defence matters, Socialist Party, 2004–12. Minister of Defence, 2012–17. Hon. Inspector Gen., Nat. Educn Dept, 1993–. *Address:* Ministry for Europe and Foreign Affairs, 37 Quai d'Orsay, 75351, Paris, France.

**LEDSOME, Neville Frank,** CB 1988; Deputy Chairman, Civil Service Appeal Board, 1994–99; Under Secretary, Personnel Management Division, Department of Trade and Industry, 1983–89, retired; *b* 29 Nov. 1929; *s* of late Charles Percy Ledsome and Florence Ledsome; *m* 1953, Isabel Mary Lindsay; three *s*. *Educ:* Birkenhead Sch. Exec. Officer, BoT, 1948; Monopolies Commn, 1957; Higher Exec. Officer, BoT, 1961; Principal, 1964; DEA, 1967; HM Treasury, 1969; DTI, 1970; Asst Sec., 1973; Under Sec., 1980. *Recreations:* gardening, theatre.

**LEE,** family name of **Baron Lee of Trafford**.

**LEE OF TRAFFORD, Baron** *cr* 2006 (Life Peer), of Bowdon in the County of Cheshire; **John Robert Louis Lee;** DL; FCA; company director, investor and financial journalist; *b* 21 June 1942; *s* of late Basil and Miriam Lee; *m* 1975, Anne Monique Bakirgian; two *d*. *Educ:* William Hulme's Grammar Sch., Manchester. Accountancy Articles, 1959–64; Henry Cooke, Lumsden & Co., Manchester, Stockbrokers, 1964–66; Founding Dir, Chancery Consolidated Ltd, Investment Bankers; non-executive Director: Paterson Zochonis (UK) Ltd, 1974–75; Paterson Zochonis PLC, 1990–99; Emerson Developments (Hldgs), 2000–. Contested (C) Manchester, Moss Side, Oct. 1974; MP (C) Nelson and Colne, 1979–83, Pendle, 1983–92; contested (C) Pendle, 1992. PPS to Minister of State for Industry, 1981–83, to Sec. of State for Trade and Industry, 1983; Parly Under Sec. of State, MoD, 1983–86, Dept of Employment, 1986–89 (Minister for Tourism, 1987–89). Chm., All-Party Tourism Cttee, 1991–92. Jt Sec., Conservative Back Benchers' Industry Cttee, 1979–80. Lib Dem spokesman on Defence, H of L, 2007–12. Mem., Jt Cttee on Nat. Security Strategy, 2010–. Trustee, Armed Forces Parly Trust, 2014–. Chm., Christie Hosp. NHS Trust, 1992–98. Chairman: ALVA, 1990–; Mus. of Sci. and Industry in Manchester, 1990–2001; Mem., English Tourist Bd, 1992–99; Trustee and Dep. Chm., Mus. of Richmond, 2017–. Vice-Chm., NW Conciliation Cttee, Race Relations Bd, 1976–77; Chm. Council, Nat. Youth Bureau, 1980–83. DL 1995, High Sheriff 1998, Greater Manchester. *Publications:* How to Make a Million - Slowly, 2014. *Recreations:* golf, fly fishing, collecting. *Address:* House of Lords, SW1A 0PW.

**LEE, Alan John;** book illustrator, since 1972; film conceptual designer, since 1983; *b* 20 Aug. 1947; *s* of George James Lee and Margaret Lee (*née* Cook); *m* 1979, Marja Kruyt (marr. diss.); one *s* one *d*. *Educ:* Manor Secondary Modern Sch., Ruislip; Ealing Sch. of Art. Conceptual designer of films: Legend, 1985; Erik the Viking, 1989; The Hobbit: An Unexpected Journey, 2012; The Desolation of Smaug, 2013; The Battle of the Five Armies, 2014; conceptual designer and set decorator of films: The Fellowship of the Ring, 2001; The Two Towers, 2002; The Return of the King, 2003 (Academy Award for Art Direction, 2004). *Publications: illustrator:* The Importance of Being Ernest, 1972; Faeries, 1978, 2nd edn 2003; The Mabinogion, 1982, 2nd edn 2002; Castles, 1984; Michael Palin, The Mirrorstone, 1986; Joan Aiken, The Moon's Revenge, 1987; Peter Dickinson, Merlin Dreams, 1988; J. R. R. Tolkien, The Lord of the Rings, 1992; Rosemary Sutcliff, Black Ships Before Troy (Kate Greenaway Medal), 1993; Rosemary Sutcliff, The Wanderings of Odysseus, 1995; J. R. R. Tolkien, The Hobbit, 1997; J. R. R. Tolkien, The Children of Hurin, 2007; J. R. R. Tolkien, Tales from the Perilous Realm, 2008; Adrian Mitchell, Shapeshifters, 2009; (ed by Stephen Jones) Fearie Tales, 2013; J. R. R. Tolkien, Beren and Luthien, 2017; (trans. by Michael Alexander) The Wanderer and other Old English Poems, 2018; J. R. R. Tolkien, The Fall of Gondolin, 2018; *written and illustrated:* The Lord of the Rings Sketchbook, 2005; The Hobbit Sketchbook, 2019. *Recreation:* tango dancing. *E:* alanlee@dircon.co.uk. *Club:* Pudding (Chagford).

**LEE, Allen;** *see* Lee Peng-Fei, A.

**LEE, Dr Anne Mary Linda;** independent academic consultant, since 2010; *b* 14 Oct. 1953; *d* of Cecil and Eugenie Covell; *m* 1973, Anthony Mervyn Lee, *qv*; one *s* one *d*. *Educ:* Shenfield High Sch.; Open Univ. (BA); Univ. of Surrey (PhD). FCIPD; GMBPS; FHEA 2007; FSEDA 2009, SFSEDA 2011. Inf. Officer, Unilever, 1972–74; Trng Officer, G. D. Searle & Co., 1974–76; Management and Trng Advr, Industrial Soc., 1976–78; Head of Trng, Morgan Guaranty Trust Co., 1978–81; Dir, Anne M. Lee (Training) Ltd, 1983–94; Headmistress, Malvern Girls' Coll., 1994–96. Dir, Next Chapter Ltd, 1998–2006. Mem., Huhne Commn on Future of Public Services, 2001–02. Mem. (Lib Dem), Guildford BC, 1997–2001. Contested (Lib Dem): Norfolk S, 2001; Woking, 2005. Sen. Academic Develt Advr, Univ. of Surrey, 2005–10. Sen. Res. Fellow, Roehampton Univ., 2013–18; Res. Fellow, Univ. of Bristol, 2014–; Associate Prof., Univ. of Stavanger, 2015–19. Member Board/Trustee: Guildford CAB, 1998–2001; Merrow Sunset Homes, 1998–2001; Guildford and Waverly PCT, 1999–2001; Lay Chm., Guildford Deanery Synod, 2012–16. Gov., Queenswood Sch., 1996–2005. *Publications:* Supervision Teams: making them work, 2008; Helping New Postgraduates: a guide for academics, 2009; (with M. Pettigrove) Preparing to Teach in Higher Education, 2010; Successful Research Supervision, 2012, 2nd edn 2019; Successful Research Projects, 2019; contribs to educnl, personnel and management jls and The Times. *Recreations:* singing, walking, friendship, words and music, comedy playwriting. *W:* www.drannelee.wordpress.com, https://feestandlee.home.blog.

**LEE, Anthony Mervyn;** Chief Executive (formerly Director), Age Concern Surrey, 2001–10; *b* 21 Feb. 1949; *s* of Sydney Ernest Lee and Evelyn May Lee; *m* 1973, Anne Mary Linda Lee, *qv*; one *s* one *d*. *Educ:* Romford Sch.; Cranfield Sch. of Mgt (MBA). FCCA 1971; FCMA 1975. Financial trng, Eastern Electricity Bd, 1971–72; Finance Manager, ITT SemiConductors, 1972–74; Financial Controller, Mars Confectionery, 1974–77; Managing Director: Am Bruning Ltd, 1978–82; Citibank Trust, 1982–86; Chief Exec., Access (JCCC Ltd), 1987–91; Ops Dir, Natwest Card Services, 1991–97; Exec. Dir, Muscular Dystrophy Campaign, 1998–2001. *Recreations:* keep fit, gardening, politics. *Address:* 1 St David Mews, Bristol BS1 5QP. *T:* (0117) 316 9313.

**LEE, Christopher Robin James,** RD 1981 (Bar 1991); historian, writer and broadcaster; *b* 13 Oct. 1941; *s* of James Thomas Lee and Winifred Lee (*née* Robertson); *m* 1st, 1969, Christine Elizabeth Adams (marr. diss. 2010); two *d*; 2nd, 2011, Fiona Margaret Graham-Mackay (*née* Bain). *Educ:* Dartford Tech. Sch.; Wilmington Grammar Sch.; Goldsmiths' Coll., London; Birkbeck Coll., London (MA History of Ideas). Deck apprentice, 1958–59; freelance writer, 1962–67; journalist, Daily Express, 1967–76 (Asst Ed., 1975–76); Defence and Foreign Affairs Corresp., BBC radio, 1976–86; Quatercentenary Fellow in Contemporary Hist., Emmanuel Coll., Cambridge, 1986–91; lecturer, author and scriptwriter, 1991–; various BBC radio drama and comedy series incl. The Archers, The House, Colvil and Soames, The Trial of Walter Ralegh, Our Brave Boys, A Pattern in Shrouds, 1987–2009; Kicking the Habit, 2007–08; Air Force One, 2013; The King's Matter, 2016; This Sceptred Isle, hist. of Britain, 1995–96, This Sceptred Isle, 90-pt hist. series, 2005–06, Radio 4. Dir, Sceptred Isle Publishing Ltd, 2006–; Editl Advr Bd, BBC History Mag., 2001–; Historical Advr to NT production of Saint Joan, 2007. Sen. Tutor, Creative Writing, Bayford Studios, 2008–16; global politics analyst, Limehouse Gp of Commentators, 2001–; defence and foreign affairs advr, British Forces Broadcasting Services, 2010–; internat. politics analyst on climate change, Fort Foundn, 2014–15. Vis. Lectr, Univ. of Utah, 1986; Gomes Lectr, Emmanuel Coll., Cambridge, 2001. FRSA 2008. Royal Naval Reserve: Services Intelligence Wing, 1966–82; OC Public Affairs Br., 1982–86; CO, HMS Wildfire, 1988–90. Trustee, Sail Trng Assoc., 1994–2001. Younger Brother, Trinity House, 2002–. *Publications:* Seychelles: political castaways, 1976; Final Decade, 1981; (with Bhupendra Jasani) Countdown to Space War, 1984; War in Space, 1987; (ed) Nicely Nurdled Sir, 1988; From the Sea End, 1989; The Madrigal, 1993; The House, 1994; The Bath Detective, 1995; (ed) Through the Covers, 1996; Killing of Sally Keemer, 1997; This Sceptred Isle 55 BC–1901, 1997; (ed) History of the English-speaking Peoples, 1998; The Killing of Cinderella, 1998; The 20th Century, 1999; Eight Bells and Topmasts, 2001; Dynasties, 2002; 1603: a turning point in English history, 2003; This Sceptred Isle: Empire, 2005; Nelson & Napoleon: the long haul to Trafalgar, 2005; This Sceptred Isle: the making of the British, 2012; Monarchy: past, present… future?, 2013; Royal Ceremonial, 2015; Viceroys, 2018; Carrington: an honourable man, 2018. *Recreations:* opera, sailing. *Address:* Woodside, Beckley, E Sussex TN31 6UE. *E:* christopherleesays@gmail.com. *Clubs:* Athenæum, Eccentrics, MCC; Royal Naval Sailing Association.

**LEE, Colin Geoffrey;** Clerk of Bills, Public Bill Office, House of Commons, since 2016; *b* Petts Wood, 18 Sept. 1965; *s* of Geoffrey and Susan Lee; *m* 2006, Brenda Barker. *Educ:* Trinity Sch., Croydon; Pembroke Coll., Cambridge (BA 1988). House of Commons: procedural, cttee and internat. posts, 1988–97; Clerk: Culture, Media and Sport Cttee, 1997–2001; Public Bill Office, 2001–05; Treasury Cttee, 2005–08; Dir, Departmental Services, 2008–10; Clerk, Table Office, 2010–11; on secondment to Cabinet Office as Parly Advr, 2011–12; Clerk, Parly Commn on Banking Standards, 2012–13; Principal Clerk, Cttee Office, 2013–16. *Recreations:* theatre, watching Chelsea FC. *Address:* House of Commons, SW1A 0AA. *T:* (020) 7219 3000.

**LEE, Ven. David John**, PhD; Archdeacon of Bradford, 2004–15; Archdeacon for Mission Resources, 2015–16, now Archdeacon Emeritus; *b* 31 Jan. 1946; *s* of John and Sheila Lee; *m* 1989, Janet Mary Strong; two *s*. *Educ:* Bristol Univ. (BSc Mech. Eng 1967); London Univ. (DipTh 1973); Fitzwilliam Coll., Cambridge (BA (Theol.) 1976, MA 1979); Birmingham Univ. (PhD (NT Studies) 1996). Schoolmaster: Lesotho, Southern Africa, 1967; Walsall, 1968. Ordained deacon, 1977, priest, 1978; Curate, St Margaret's, Putney, 1977–80; Lecturer: in Theol., Bp Tucker Coll., Mukono, Uganda, 1980–86; in Missiology, Selly Oak Colls, Birmingham, 1986–91; Rector, Middleton and Wishaw, Birmingham 1991–96; Dir of Mission, Dio. Birmingham, and Canon Residentiary, Birmingham Cathedral, 1996–2004. Non-exec. Dir, Bradford Churches for Dialogue and Diversity, 2005–15; Director and Chairman: Wellsprings Together Bradford, 2011–16; Bradford Diocese Acads Trust, 2012–16; Chm., Bradford Diocesan Adv. Cttee, 2012–15; Interim Diocesan Dir of Ordinands, C of E, Birmingham, 2017–18. Mem., IAM. *Publications:* Discovering Science (jtly), 1970; Jesus in the Stories of Luke, 1999; (ed) Ministry and Mission in a Multifaith Context, 2001. *Recreations:* conversation, music, walking, motoring, multi-media, DIY in its better manifestations, redeeming the vocation of property landlords. *Address:* 16 Tudor Hill, Sutton Coldfield B73 6BH. *T:* (0121) 681 4347, 07711 671351. *E:* davidjlee@blueyonder.co.uk.

**LEE, Prof. David Morris**, FInstP; James Gilbert White Distinguished Professor of Physical Sciences, Cornell University, 1997–2009, now Emeritus; Professor of Physics, Texas A&M University, since 2009; *b* 20 Jan. 1931; *s* of Marvin and Annette Lee; *m* 1960, Dana Thorangkul; two *s*. *Educ:* Harvard Univ. (AB 1952); Connecticut Univ. (MS 1955); Yale Univ. (PhD Physics 1959). FInstP 1998. US Army, 1952–54. Cornell University: Instructor in Physics, 1959–60; Asst Prof., 1960–63; Associate Prof., 1963–68; Prof. of Physics, 1968–. Guggenheim Fellow, 1966, 1974; Fellow, Japan Soc. for Promotion of Sci., 1977. Member: Amer. Acad. Arts and Scis, 1987; Nat. Acad. of Scis, 1991. Sir Francis Simon Meml Prize, British Inst. of Physics, 1976; Oliver Buckley Prize, APS, 1981; (jtly) Nobel Prize for Physics, 1996. *Publications:* articles in learned jls. *Recreations:* hiking in the mountains, fishing, boating, running. *Address:* Department of Physics and Astronomy, Texas A&M University, 4242 TAMU, College Station, TX 77843–4242, USA.

**LEE, Derek William**, FCIB; Chairman, Friendly Societies Commission, 1992–98; *b* 11 April 1935; *s* of Richard William Lee and Ivy Elizabeth Lee; *m* 1960, Dorothy Joan Preece; one *d*. *Educ:* St Dunstan's Coll.; London Univ. (LLB Hons external). FCIB 1973. Nat. Service, REME, Malaya, 1953–55. Lloyds Bank, 1955–73, Manager, Threadneedle St Br., 1970–73; Asst Gen. Manager, 1973–77, Gen. Manager, 1977–87, Mercantile Credit Co. Ltd; Man. Dir, H & H Factors, 1988–89; Registrar, Friendly Societies, 1989–95. Gov., Guy's and St Thomas' Hosp. Foundn Trust, 2004–07; Mem. Cttee, Samaritan Fund, Hosp. Authy Charitable Foundn, 2007–08. Freeman, City of London, 1999. *Recreations:* art, golf, bowls. *Clubs:* Bromley Town Bowling; Duke of Kent Bowls.

**LEE, Francis Henry**, CBE 2016; former professional footballer; Founder and Chairman, F. H. Lee Ltd, 1970–2000; *b* Westhoughton, Lancs; *s* of Colin Lee and Millie Lee; *m* 1986, Gillian May Wilson; three *s* one *d*. *Educ:* Horwich Tech. Coll., Bolton. Professional footballer: Bolton Wanderers, 1959–67; Manchester City, 1967–74; Derby County, 1974–76; internat. appearances for England, 1968–72. Chm., Manchester City FC, 1994–98. Dir, Hazlewood Foods plc, 1987–2000. Racehorse trainer, 1985–93. President: Bolton Boys Fedn, 1981; Almancil Internat. Boys Club, Algarve, Portugal; Vice Pres., Bolton Lads and Girls Club, 1984. Nat. Racehorse Trainers Fedn. *Publications:* Soccer Round the World, 1970. *Recreations:* football, cricket, golf, horse racing. *Address:* Little Stanneylands, Stanneylands Road, Wilmslow, Cheshire SK9 4ER. *Club:* Quinta do Lago Golf (Algarve).

**LEE, Prof. Dame Hermione**, DBE 2013 (CBE 2003); FRSL; FBA 2001; President, Wolfson College, Oxford, 2008–17 (Hon. Fellow, 2017); Pro-Vice-Chancellor, University of Oxford, 2014–15; *b* 29 Feb. 1948; *d* of Dr Benjamin Lee and Josephine Lee (*née* Anderson); *m* 1991, Prof. John Michael Barnard, *qv*. *Educ:* St Hilda's Coll., Oxford (MA, Hon. Fellow, 1998); St Cross Coll., Oxford (MPhil; Hon. Fellow, 1998). Instructor, Coll. of William and Mary, Williamsburg, Va, 1970–71; Lectr, Dept of English, Univ. of Liverpool, 1971–77; Department of English and Related Literature, University of York: Lectr, 1977–87; Sen. Lectr, 1987–90; Reader, 1990–93; Prof., 1993–98; Goldsmiths' Prof. of English Literature, Univ. of Oxford, 1998–2008; Fellow, New Coll., Oxford, 1998–2008 (Hon. Fellow, 2009). Presenter, Book Four, Channel 4, 1982–86. Chair of Judges, Man Booker Prize, 2006. FRSL 1992. For. Hon. Mem., Amer. Acad. of Arts and Scis, 2003. Hon. DLitt: Liverpool, 2002; York, 2007; KCL, 2013. *Publications:* The Novels of Virginia Woolf, 1977; Elizabeth Bowen, 1981, 2nd edn 1999; Philip Roth, 1982; (ed) The Mulberry Tree: writings of Elizabeth Bowen 1986; Willa Cather: a life saved up, 1989, US edn as Willa Cather: double lives, 1991, 2nd edn 2017; (ed) The Selected Stories of Willa Cather, 1989; Virginia Woolf, 1996; Body Parts: essays on life-writing, 2005; Edith Wharton, 2007; Biography: a very short introduction, 2009; Penelope Fitzgerald: a life, 2013. *Recreations:* reading, music, countryside. *Club:* Athenæum.

**LEE, James Giles**; Principal, Lee & Company, since 1992; *b* 23 Dec. 1942; *s* of John Lee, CBE and Muriel Giles; *m* 1966, Linn Macdonald; one *s* two *d*. *Educ:* Trinity Coll., Glenalmond; Glasgow Univ.; Harvard Univ., USA. Consultant, McKinsey & Co., 1969–80; Mem., Central Policy Review Staff, 1972. Dep. Chm. and Chief Exec., Pearson Longman, 1980–83; Chairman: Penguin Publishing Co., 1980–84; Direct Broadcasting by Satellite Consortium, 1986–87; Deputy Chairman: Westminster Press, 1980–84; Financial Times, 1980–84; Yorkshire TV, 1982–85; Dir, S. Pearson & Son, 1981–84; Chm., 1981–85, Chief Exec., 1983–85, Goldcrest Films and Television; Dir, Boston Consulting Gp, 1987–92. Non-executive Director: Pearson Television, 1993–2001; Phoenix Pictures Inc., 1996–2004; Nation Media Gp, Kenya, 2001–10. Chairman: Performing Arts Labs Trust, 1989–99; Scottish Screen, 1998–2002; Bureau of Investigative Journalism, 2010–; Dir, Film Council, 1999–2004. Chm., Maidstone and Tunbridge Wells NHS Trust, 2003–07. *Publications:* Planning for the Social Services, 1978; The Investment Challenge, 1979. *Recreations:* photography, travelling, sailing. *Address:* Meadow Wood, Penshurst, Kent TN11 8AD. *T:* (01892) 870309. *Clubs:* Reform; Harvard (New York).

**LEE, Hon. James Matthew**; PC (Can.) 1982; Chairman, PEI Workers Compensation Board, 1998–2007; Leader, Progressive Conservative Party, Prince Edward Island, 1981–96; *b* Charlottetown, 26 March 1937; *s* of late James Matthew Lee and of Catherine Blanchard Lee; *m* 1960, Patricia, *d* of late Ivan Laurie; one *s* two *d*. *Educ:* Queen's Square Sch.; St Dunstan's Univ. Architectural draftsman. Elected MLA (PC) for 5th Queens Riding, by-election, 1975; former Minister: of Health and Social Services; of Tourism, Parks and Conservation; Premier and Pres. Exec. Council, PEI, 1981–86. Comr, Canadian Pension Commn, 1986–97. Jaycee Internat. Senator, 1983. Hon. LLD, 2005. *Address:* 516 North River Road, Charlottetown, PE C1E 3H4, Canada. *T:* (902) 5664899.

**LEE, Maj.-Gen. (James) Stuart**, CB 1990; MBE 1970; Director of Army Education, 1987–90; *b* 26 Dec. 1934; *s* of George Lee and Elizabeth (*née* Hawkins); *m* 1960, Alice Lorna (*d* 2007); one *s*. *Educ:* Normanton Grammar Sch.; Leeds Univ. (BA Hons); King's Coll., London (MA War Studies, 1976). Pres., Leeds Univ. Union, 1958–59. Educn Officer in UK Trng Units, Catterick, Taunton, Bovington, 1959–64; Mil. Trng Officer, Beaconsfield, 1964; RMCS and Staff Coll., 1964–65; DAQMG HQ Cyprus Dist, 1966 and HQ NEARELF, 1967; SO2 MoD (Army Educn 1), 1968–70; DAA&QMG HQ FARELF, 1970 and GSO2 HQ FARELF, 1970–71; OC Officer Wing, Beaconsfield, 1971–74; Gp Educn Officer, 34 AEC, Rheindahlen, 1974–75; Chief Educn Officer, HQ NE Dist, 1976–78; Hd, Officer Educn Br., 1978–79; SO1 Trng HQ UKLF, 1979; Chief Inspector of Army Educn and Col Res., 1980–82; Res. Associate, IISS, 1982–83; Comdr Educn, HQ BAOR, 1983–87. Dep. Col Comdt, AGC, 1993–97. Pres., RAEC Assoc., 1993–97. Dep. Comr, British Scouts Western Europe, 1983–87; Mem., Management Bd, NFER, 1987–90. Non-exec. Dir, Exhibition Consultants Ltd, 1990–99. Dir and Trustee, Assessment and Qualifications Alliance, 1998–2002; Member: Nat. Adv. Bd, Duke of Edinburgh Award Scheme, 1987–90; Council, Scout Assoc., 1988–98. City and Guilds of London Institute: Mem. Council, 1989–2007; Jt Hon. Sec., 1993–2004; Chm., Sen. Awards Cttee, 1990–99; Chm., Inst. Affairs and Awards Cttee, 1999–2002; Chm., Strategy and Advancement Cttee, 2002–04. Trustee and Sec., Gallipoli Meml Lecture Trust, 1987–90. Gov., 1991–99, Mem. Court, 1999, Imperial Coll.; Mem. Court, Univ. of Leeds, 1994–2004. FRSA 1987; FIPD (FITD 1991); Hon. FCGI 1996. *Publications:* contrib. Arms Transfers in Third World Development, 1984; Old Wine in a New Bottle, 2010; Magic Aces, 2011; Out Of The Box, 2012; All Together Now, 2012. *Recreations:* theatre, boats, card magic, horse racing.

**LEE, Jeremy**; Chef Proprietor, Quo Vadis, since 2012; *b* Dundee, 21 Oct. 1963; *s* of Norman Lee and Eileen Lee. *Educ:* High Sch. of Dundee. Head Chef: Alastair Little, 1990–94; Euphorium, 1994–95; Blueprint Café, 1994–2011. *Publications:* articles for The Guardian, Times, Telegraph, Independent, etc. *Recreations:* cooking and eating. *Address:* Flat 214, 5 King Edward's Road, E9 7SG. *E:* jeremy@qvsoho.co.uk. *Clubs:* Quo Vadis, Groucho, Union, Ivy.

**LEE, Jessica Katherine**; *b* Nottingham, 7 April 1976; *d* of John Anthony and Rosemary Lee. *Educ:* Loughborough High Sch.; Royal Holloway, Univ. of London (BA Hons); Coll. of Law, London (CPE, BVC). Called to the Bar, Middle Temple, 2000, Bencher, 2018; in practice as barrister specialising in family law, London, 2001–08, 2010–, Nottingham, 2008–10. MP (C) Erewash, 2010–15. PPS to Attorney-General, 2010–15. Mem., Justice Select Cttee, 2010–15. *Recreations:* food and drink, theatre, parties, travel. *Club:* Carlton.

**LEE, John Michael Hubert**; Barrister-at-Law; *b* 13 Aug. 1927; *s* of late Victor Lee, Wentworth, Surrey, and late Renee Lee; *m* 1960, Margaret Ann, *d* of late James Russell, ICS, retired, and late Kathleen Russell; one *s* one *d*. *Educ:* Reading Sch.; Christ's Coll., Cambridge (Open Exhibnr Modern Hist.; 2nd Cl. Hons Pts I and II of Hist. Tripos; MA). Colonial Service: Administrative Officer, Ghana, 1951–58; Principal Assistant Secretary, Min. of Communications, Ghana, 1958. On staff of BBC, 1959–65. Called to the Bar, Middle Temple, 1960; practising, Midland and Oxford Circuit, 1966–; Dep. Circuit Judge, 1978–81; Assistant Recorder, 1981–87. MP (Lab) Reading, 1966–70; MP (Lab) Birmingham, Handsworth, Feb. 1974–1979; Chm., W Midland Gp of Labour MPs, 1974–75. *Recreations:* watching tennis, watching cricket, walking, studying philosophy, studying green issues. *Club:* Royal Over-Seas League.

**LEE, Karen**; MP (Lab) Lincoln, since 2017; four *c*. *Educ:* St Hugh's RC Sch.; South Park Sch.; Lincoln Coll. RN. Nurse, 2003–, latterly at Lincoln Co. Hosp. Mem. (Lab), City of Lincoln Council, 2003–; Mayor of Lincoln, 2012–13. Shadow Fire Minister, 2018–. *Address:* House of Commons, SW1A 0AA.

**LEE, Dame Laura (Elizabeth)**, DBE 2019; Chief Executive, Maggie Keswick Jencks Cancer Caring Centres Trust, since 1996 (Programme Director, 1996–98); *b* Whitbank, 15 Oct. 1966; *d* of David and Elizabeth Lee; two *s* one *d*. *Educ:* Peterhead Acad.; RGN 1987; St Bartholomew's Hosp., London (Oncol. Course 237 1990); Univ. of Abertay (Dip. Nursing 1994); Birmingham Univ. (MSc Clin. Oncol. 1997); Inst. of Dirs (Dip. Co. Direction 2006). Nursing trng, N Edinburgh Sch. of Nursing, 1984–87; Radiotherapy Unit, Western Gen. Hosp., Edinburgh, 1987–88; Staff Nurse: Bone Marrow Transplant Unit, Royal Infirmary Hosp., Edinburgh, 1989–90; Longmore Ward, Longmore Hosp., Edinburgh, 1990–91; Clin. Nurse Specialist, Breast Unit, Western Gen. Hosp., Edinburgh, 1991–96. Hon. Fellow, RIBA, 2009. DUniv Queen Margaret, 2016. *Recreations:* running, swimming. *Address:* Maggie's, 20 St James Street, W6 9RE. *T:* (020) 7386 3551. *E:* pam.richardson@maggiescentres.org.

**LEE, Linda Karen Hadfield**; Solicitor, specialising in regulatory law, Radcliffes Le Brasseur, London, since 2012; President, Law Society of England and Wales, 2010–11; *b* Sheffield, 28 Nov. 1962; *d* of George Alan Hadfield and late Barbara June Hadfield; *m* Michael Alfred Lee (marr. diss.); three *d*. *Educ:* Univ. of Sheffield (BA Law). Admitted as solicitor, 1994; with Hopkins, Solicitors, Mansfield, 1992–99; Shoosmiths, Northampton, 1999–2006. Law Society of England and Wales: Mem. Council, 2003–; Chair: Legal Affairs Policy Bd, 2008–11; Regulatory Affairs Bd, 2013–; Dep. Vice Pres., 2008–09; Vice Pres., 2009–10. Mem., Queen's Counsel Selection Panel, 2011–15. Asst Comr, Boundary Commn for England, 2011–13; Comr, Criminal Cases Review Commn, 2017–; Legal Chairman: Code Compliance Panel, Phone Paid Services Authy (formerly PhonePay Plus), 2013–; Taxation Disciplinary Bd, 2014–; Legal Chair: Primary Care Appeals (formerly Family Health Services Appeal Unit), 2014–; Med. Practitioners Tribunal Service, 2017–; Chair: Voice (Victims and Witness Service, Northants), 2014–16; Solicitors' Assistance Scheme, 2015–; Dir, Incorporated Council of Law Reporting, 2016–; Panel Mem., HS2 Need to Sell Panel, 2017–. Consultant to Action Against Medical Accidents, 2006–10, 2013–16. Member: Council, Medico-Legal Soc., 2008– (Pres., 2014–16); Cttee, Northants Law Soc., 2003– (Pres., 2013–15). *Publications:* (contrib. ed.) Cordery on Legal Services, 2014–. *Address:* 91 Buttmead, Blisworth NN7 3DQ. *T:* (01604) 949223. *E:* lindakhlee@aol.com.

**LEE, Martin**; *see* Lee Chu-Ming, M.

**LEE, Dr Melanie Georgina**, CBE 2009; FMedSci; Chief Executive Officer, LifeArc, since 2018; *d* of William and Pamela Brown; *m* 1981 (*d* 2012); two *s*. *Educ:* York Univ. (BSc Hons 1979); NIMR (PhD 1982). Postdoctoral Research Fellow: CRC, London, at Imperial Coll., 1982–85; ICRF, London, at Lincoln's Inn Fields, 1985–88; R&D, Glaxo Gp Res. and Glaxo Wellcome, 1988–98; Bd Dir, Celltech Gp plc, 1998–2004; Exec. Vice-Pres., R&D, 2004–09, Mem. Scientific Adv. Bd, 2009–10, UCB Gp; Chief Executive Officer: Syntaxin Ltd, 2010–13; NightstaRx Ltd, 2014; Chief Scientific Officer, BTG plc, 2015–18 (non-exec. Dir, 2010–14). Non-executive Director: H. Lundbeck, 2012–15; Bd, Sanofi, 2017–. Chairman: Applied Genomics Link Scheme, 2000–05; Cancer Res. Technol., 2003–10. Trustee: CRUK, 2010–14 (Dep. Chm., Council, 2007–10); UK Dementia Res. Inst., 2018–. FMedSci 2003. Lifetime Achievement Award, UK Bioindustry Assoc., 2019. *Recreations:* gym, keeping fit, gardening in containers, flowers. *Address:* LifeArc, Accelerator Building, SBC Open Innovation Campus, Stevenage SG1 2FX.

**LEE, Michael Charles M.**; *see* Malone-Lee.

**LEE, Maj.-Gen. Patrick Herbert,** CB 1982; MBE 1964; CEng, FIMechE; Director: Road Haulage Association, 1988–98 (Chairman, 1994–96; Vice-Chairman, 1990–94); Wincanton Ltd (formerly Wincanton Transport, subseq. Wincanton Distribution Services, Ltd), 1983–98; *b* 15 March 1929; *s* of Percy Herbert and Mary Dorothea Lee; *m* 1952, Peggy Eveline Chapman; one *s* one *d*. *Educ:* King's Sch., Canterbury; London Univ. (BSc (Gen.), BSc (Special Physics)). Commnd RMA Sandhurst, 1948; Staff Coll., 1960; WO Staff Duties, 1961–63; CO, Parachute Workshop, 1964–65; JSSC, 1966; Military Asst to Master General of Ordnance, 1966–67; Directing Staff, Staff Coll., 1968–69; Commander, REME 2nd Div., 1970–71; Col AQ 1 British Corps, 1972–75; Dep. Comdt, Sch. of Electrical and Mechanical Engrg, 1975–77; Comdt, REME Trng Centre, 1977–79; Dir Gen., Electrical and Mechanical Engrg (Army), 1979–83. Col Comdt, REME, 1983–89. Mem., Wessex Water Authy, 1983–88. Confederation of British Industry: Mem. Council, 1991–98; Vice-Chm., 1992–94, Chm., 1994–96, SW Region. Gov., Wellington Sch., Som, 1992–2002 (Chm., 2000–02). FCMI; MIEMA. *Recreations:* gardening, railways, Roman history, industrial archaeology. *Club:* Army and Navy.

**LEE, Paul Anthony;** DL; Chairman: Horserace Betting Levy Board, since 2009; Opera North, since 2014; *b* Manchester, 26 Jan. 1946; *s* of Wilfred Lee and Ann Molyneux-Lee; *m* 1977, Elisabeth Lindsay Taylor; two *s* one *d*. *Educ:* Manchester Central Grammar Sch.; Clare Coll., Cambridge (MA, LLM); Coll. of Law. Admitted solicitor, 1970; Addleshaw Sons & Latham, subseq. Addleshaw Booth & Co., then Addleshaw Goddard LLP: Partner, 1973–2013; Man. Partner, 1991–97; Sen. Partner, 1997–2010. Chm., Leaf Properties Ltd, 1985–; non-executive Director: Yorkshire Building Soc., 1998–2007 (Vice Chm., 2005–06); Dewhurst Torevell Ltd, then Torevell & Partners, 2012–. Mem. Bd, CBI, 2004–12; Dir, North West Business Leadership Team, 2007–13 (Dep. Chm., 2007–09; Chm., 2009–12). Dir, Royal Exchange Th., 1985–2015 (Chm., 1998–2015); non-exec. Dir, Northern Ballet Th., 1997–2004. Chm., Feoffees, Chetham's Sch. of Music, 2005– (Gov., 1989–2013; Chm. of Govs, 1991–2005); Mem., Bd of Govs, Univ. of Manchester, 2010–. DL 1998, High Sheriff 2014, Gtr Manchester. *Recreations:* horseracing, arts, wine, France. *Address:* c/o Opera North, Grand Theatre, 46 New Briggate, Leeds LS1 6NU. *E:* paul.lee@leafassociates.co.uk. *Clubs:* Garrick, Savile, Turf.

**LEE, Sir Paul (Joseph) S.;** *see* Scott-Lee.

**LEE, Paul Winston Michael B.;** *see* Boyd-Lee.

**LEE, Peter Gavin;** DL; Senior Partner, Strutt & Parker, 1979–96; *b* 4 July 1934; *s* of late Mr and Mrs J. G. Lee; *m* 1963, Caroline Green; two *s* one *d*. *Educ:* Midhurst Grammar School; College of Estate Management; Wye College. FRICS 1966. Joined Strutt & Parker, 1957. Chm., Prince's Trust for Essex, 1998–2005. Gov., Felsted Sch., 1986–2019. High Sheriff, 1990, DL 1991, Essex. *Recreations:* the restoration and enjoyment of vintage cars, country pursuits. *Address:* Fanners, Great Waltham, Chelmsford, Essex CM3 1EA. *T:* (01245) 360470.

**LEE, Peter Wilton,** CBE 1994; Vice Lord-Lieutenant of South Yorkshire, 1997–2010; Director, 1987–2009, Chairman, 1994–2005, Edward Pryor & Son Ltd; *b* 15 May 1935; *s* of Sir (George) Wilton Lee, TD and late Bettina Stanley Lee (*née* Haywood); *m* 1962, Gillian Wendy Oates; three *s* one *d*. *Educ:* Uppingham Sch.; Queens' Coll., Cambridge (MA). Lieut, RE, 1956. Grad. Engr, Davy & United Engrg Co. Ltd, 1958–62; Arthur Lee & Sons plc: Engr, Works Manager, 1962–67; Works Dir, 1967–70; Jt Man. Dir, 1970–72; Man. Dir, 1972–79; Chm. and Man. Dir, 1979–92; Chm., 1992–93; Dep. Chm., 1993–95, Dir, 1995–2003, Carclo Engrg Gp PLC. Dir, Sanderson Gp (formerly Sanderson Electronics) PLC, 1994–2000. Dir, Sheffield Enterprise Agency Ltd, 1987–2002. President: Brit. Independent Steel Producers' Assoc., 1981–83; Engrg Employers' Sheffield Assoc., 1994–96. Confederation of British Industry: Member: Nat. Council, 1992–95; Nat. Mfg Council, 1992–94; Chm., Yorks and Humberside Regl Council, 1993–95. University of Sheffield: Mem. Council, 1965–2005 (Chm., 1996–2005); Pro Chancellor, 1987–2005. Trustee: Sheffield Church Burgesses Trust, 1977–; S Yorks Community Foundn, 1986–99 (Vice-Pres., 1999–2017); Dir, Sheffield Royal Soc. for Blind, 1997– (Chm., 1998–2015). Chm. Council, Sheffield & Dist YMCA, 1972–81 (Pres., 2009–11); Pres., YMCA White Rose, 2011–. CCMI (CIMgt 1976). Chm. Govs, Monkton Combe Sch., 1996–2001 (Gov., 1982–2001). Master, Co. of Cutlers in Hallamshire, 1985–86. DL 1978, High Sheriff, 1995–96, S Yorks. Hon. DEng Sheffield, 2005. *Recreations:* family, music and the arts, walking. *Address:* Willow Cottage, Old Fulwood Road, Sheffield S10 3TG. *T:* (0114) 230 5555.

**LEE, Philippa Jane;** *see* Cross, P. J.

**LEE, Phillip James;** MP for Bracknell, since 2010 (C, 2010–19; Lib Dem, since 2019); *b* Taplow, Bucks, 28 Sept. 1970; *s* of Antony and Marilyn Lee. *Educ:* Sir William Borlase Sch., Marlow, Bucks; King's Coll. London (BSc Hons Human Biol. 1993); Keble Coll., Oxford (MSc Human Biol. 1994); St Mary's Hosp. Med. Sch., London (MB BS 1999). House Officer: Wexham Park Hosp., Slough, 1999–2000; St Mary's Hosp., London, 2000; Sen. House Officer, Stoke Mandeville Hosp., Aylesbury, 2000–02; GP, Thames Valley, 2002–. Parly Under-Sec. of State, MoJ, 2016–18. Mem., Energy and Climate Change Select Cttee, 2010–15; Vice Chm., Parly Space Cttee, 2010–16; Vice Chm., Cons. Middle East Council, 2010–. *Recreations:* cricket, water ski-ing, football, ski-ing. *Address:* House of Commons, SW1A 0AA. *T:* (020) 7219 1270. *E:* phillip@phillip-lee.com.

**LEE, Prof. Robert Gregory,** LLD; Professor of Environmental Law, since 2014, and Head, Birmingham Law School, since 2015, University of Birmingham; *b* Preston, Lancs, 27 Nov. 1952; *s* of Bernard and Violet Lee; *m* 1976, Anne Claire Birkett; one *s* one *d*. *Educ:* Preston Catholic Coll.; Brunel Univ. (LLB 1977); Cardiff Univ. (LLD 2009). Lectr, 1977–79, Sen. Lectr, 1979, Lancashire Poly.; Lectr and Sen. Tutor, Lancaster Univ., 1979–88; Dir of Res., Denton Wilde Sapte, 1988–94; Develt Dir, Hammonds, 1994–95; Prof. of Law, Cardiff Law Sch., 1995–2013, Co-Dir, ESRC Res. Centre for Business Relationships, Accountability, Sustainability and Society, 2001–12, Cardiff Univ.; Prof. of Law, Univ. of Exeter, 2013–14. FRSocMed 2008. Life Mem., UK Envmtl Law Assoc., 2009. *Publications:* (with C. Douglas) The Estate Agents Act 1979, 1979; Constitutional and Administrative Law, 1985, 4th edn 1995; Statutes on Public Law and Human Rights, 1988, 28th edn 2018; (with G. Bennett) A Practical Guide to Private Residential Lettings, 1989; (with D. Morgan) Guide to the Human Fertilisation and Embryology Act 1990, 1991; (with D. Morgan) Human Fertilisation and Embryology: regulating the reproductive revolution, 2001; (with B. Filgueira) Environmental Law, Vol. 14 of Encyclopaedia of Forms and Precedents, 2008, 2017; (jtly) The New Regulation and Governance of Food, 2009; edited collections and res. reports; contrib. papers to jls. *Recreations:* theatre, walking, running, church music group, Preston North End. *Address:* Centre for Professional Legal Education and Research, Birmingham Law School, University of Birmingham, Edgbaston, Birmingham B15 2TT. *E:* r.g.lee@bham.ac.uk.

**LEE, Robert William;** Co-Founder, and Senior and Managing Partner, Lee & Thompson, 1983–2011, Consultant, since 2011; Consultant: Queen Productions; IE Music Ltd; *b* Bromley, 18 Oct. 1945; *s* of Jack William Lee; *m* 1976, Caroline Boucher; one *s* one *d*. *Educ:* King's Sch., Rochester; Bristol Univ. (LLB). Admitted as solicitor, 1970; Solicitor and Partner, Harbottle & Lewis, 1971–83. Trustee, Noel Coward Foundn, 2000–. *Recreations:* theatre, music, reading, sailing, cricket. *Address:* c/o Lee & Thompson, 4 Gee's Court, St Christopher Place, W1U 1JD. *E:* robertlee@leeandthompson.com. *Clubs:* Groucho, Little Ship; MCC.

**LEE, Sarah Joanne;** QC 2016; *b* Walsall, 28 Aug. 1966; *d* of David Edward Lee and Mavis Patricia Lee; *m* 1995, Timothy Armitage; two *d*. *Educ:* King Edward VI High Sch. for Girls, Birmingham; Wadham Coll., Oxford (BA Juris.; BCL). Called to the Bar, Middle Temple, 1990; in practice as barrister, specialising in EU, regulatory and competition law, 1990–. *Recreations:* tennis, outdoors, cooking, reading, painting, arts. *Address:* Brick Court Chambers, 7–8 Essex Street, WC2R 3LD. *E:* sarah.lee@brickcourt.co.uk.

**LEE, Sarah Tien Mee;** Partner, Slaughter and May, since 1999; *b* Manchester, 21 Dec. 1964; *d* of Loret Lee and Patricia Lee; *m* 2000, Michael Hills; one *s* one *d*. *Educ:* Fallowfield C of E High Sch.; Univ. of Birmingham (LLB 1986). Admitted solicitor, 1990; Slaughter and May: joined, 1993; Hd, Dispute Resolution Gp, 2017–. Mem., Judicial Appts Commn, 2018–. *Address:* Slaughter and May, One Bunhill Row, EC1Y 8YY. *T:* (020) 7090 4311. *E:* sarah.lee@slaughterandmay.com.

**LEE, Seng Tee;** Director: Singapore Investments (Pte) Ltd, since 1951; Lee Rubber Co. (Pte) Ltd, since 1951; Lee Pineapple Co. (Pte) Ltd, since 1951; Lee Foundation, since 1952; *b* April 1923; *s* of Lee Kong Chian and Alice Lee; *m* 1950, Betty Wu; two *s* one *d*. *Educ:* Anglo-Chinese Sch., Singapore; Wharton Business Sch., Univ. of Pennsylvania. Member: Singapore Preservation of Monuments Bd, 1971–88; Bd, Singapore Art Mus., 1995– (Mem., Adv. Cttee, 1992–94). Member Council: Univ. of Malaya in Singapore, 1959–61; Univ. of Singapore, 1962–63; Hon. Advr, Xiamen Univ., China, 1993–; Member: Bd of Advrs, Nat. Univ. of Singapore Endowment Fund, 1997–; Adv. Cttee, E Asia Inst., Cambridge Univ., 1998–. Mem., Chancellor's Court of Benefactors, Oxford, 1996–. Hon. Trustee, Royal Botanic Gardens, Kew, 1996. Hon. Foreign Mem., American Acad. of Arts and Scis, 2001. Hon. FBA 1998; Hon. Fellow: Wolfson Coll., Cambridge, 1986; Needham Res. Inst., Cambridge, 1992; Oriel Coll., Oxford, 1992; SOAS, London Univ., 2001. Hon. DTech Asian Inst. of Technol., Thailand, 1998; Hon. LitD Victoria Univ. of Wellington, NZ, 2006. Distinguished Service Award, Wharton Sch., Univ. of Penn., 1995. *Recreations:* reading, natural history. *Address:* Robinson Road PO Box 1892, Singapore 903742, Republic of Singapore. *Club:* Executive (Singapore).

**LEE, Prof. Simon Francis;** Chairman, Level Partnerships Ltd, 2009–15; *b* 29 March 1957; *s* of Norman John Lee and Mary Teresa Lee (*née* Moran); *m* 1982, Patricia Mary, *d* of Bernard Anthony McNulty and Maud Catherine McNulty (*née* Kenny); one *s* two *d*. *Educ:* Balliol Coll., Oxford (Scholar, BA 1st Cl. Jurisp); Yale Law Sch. (Harkness Fellow, LLM). Lecturer in Law: Trinity Coll., Oxford, 1981–82; KCL, 1982–88; Queen's University, Belfast: Prof. of Jurisprudence, 1989–95; Dean, Faculty of Law, 1992–94; Prof. Emeritus, 1995; Rector and Chief Exec., Liverpool Hope UC, 1995–2003; Vice-Chancellor, Leeds Metropolitan Univ., 2003–09. Gresham Prof. of Law, 1995–98; Hon. Prof., Univ. of Liverpool, 1995–2003. Mem., Standing Adv. Commn on Human Rights, 1992–96. Mem., Nat. Standards Task Force, DFEE, 1997–2001. Non-exec. Dir, S & E Belfast Health and Social Services NHS Trust, 1994–95. Chairman: Merseyside Rapid Transit Project Bd, 1997–99; Netherley-Valley Partnership, 1998–2002; Liverpool & Merseyside Theatres Trust (Everyman & Playhouse), 1998–2002; Ind. Monitoring Bd, Liverpool Educn Authy, 1999–2001; Leeds Carnegie Rugby Union FC, 2007–09; John Paul II Foundn for Sport, 2010–14. Co-founder, Initiative '92, 1992. Mem. Bd, The Tablet, 2002–. *Publications:* Law and Morals, 1986; Judging Judges, 1988; (with Peter Stanford) Believing Bishops, 1990; The Cost of Free Speech, 1990; (with Marie Fox) Learning Legal Skills, 1991; (ed) Freedom from Fear, 1992; Uneasy Ethics, 2003. *Recreations:* family, sport.

**LEE, Simon Philip Guy;** International Advisor: Fairfax Financial, since 2014; Global Advisory Board, Afiniti, since 2014; Chairman: Osirium Technologies plc, since 2015; IDefigo Ltd, since 2018; Senior Consultant, GLG Consulting, since 2014; *b* Reading, 4 March 1961; *s* of late Philip Michael Lee, CBE and of Janet Betty Lee; *m* 1987, Fiona Jean Andrews; three *d*. *Educ:* Tonbridge Sch.; Univ. of Leeds (BA Jt Hons English and French). National Westminster Bank Group, 1983–2002, various posts including: CEO, Mortgage Corp., US, 1992–93; Man. Dir, US Retail Banking, 1993–96; CEO, NatWest Offshore, 1996–98; Dir, Wholesale Mkts, 1998–2002; Royal & Sun Alliance, later RSA Group: CEO, Internat. Business, 2003–11; Dir, 2007–13; Gp CEO, RSA Insurance, 2011–13. Non-executive Director: TIA Technology, 2014–; DGS Ltd, 2015–17; Advent Underwriting, 2015–19; Brit Syndicates Ltd, 2015–. Chm., Hospice in the Weald, 2014–. *Recreations:* cricket, golf, travel, ski-ing. *Club:* Royal Ashdown Forest Golf.

**LEE, Prof. Stephen;** Professor of Voluntary Sector Management (formerly Professor of Management), Cass Business School, since 2010; Chief Executive, CentreForum, 2012–15; Chairman, Cilex Law School, since 2018; *b* London, 26 Dec. 1957; *s* of Robert Lee and Elizabeth Lee; *m* 2003, Vivienne Hibbitt (marr. diss. 2017); one *d*. *Educ:* Huddersfield Poly. (BA (Hons) Pols and Geog. 1979); London Sch. of Econs and Political Sci. (MSc (Econ) Internat. Relns 1980). Tutor in Politics, Lancaster Univ., 1980–83; Dep. Dir, Charities Adv. Trust, 1983–85; Man. Dir, Family Welfare Assoc. Ltd, 1985–89; Chief Exec., Inst. of Fundraising, 1989–2000; Consultant, Kingston Smith, 2000–03; Henley Management College, subseq. Henley Management School: Lectr, 2003–08; Coll. Sec., 2008–09; Faculty Dir, Strategy, 2009–10. Vis. Prof. of Mgt, Bath Spa Univ., 2010–12. Trustee, Amy Winehouse Foundn, 2018–. FRSA 1987. *Recreations:* Brighton FC, Sussex cricket, wet camping, cooking, family.

**LEE, Maj.-Gen. Stuart;** *see* Lee, Maj.-Gen. J. S.

**LEE, Prof. Tak Hong,** CBE 2012; MD, ScD; FHKCP, FRCP, FRCPath, FMedSci; Director, Allergy Centre and Specialist in Immunology and Allergy, Hong Kong Sanatorium and Hospital, since 2012; *b* 26 Jan. 1951; *s* of Ming and Maria Lee; *m* (marr. diss.); one *s* one *d*. *Educ:* Clare Coll., Cambridge (BA 1972; MB BChir 1976; MD 1985; ScD 1996). FHKCP 1987; FRCP 1989; FRCPath 1997. House Physician, House Surgeon, then Jun. Registrar, Guy's Hosp., 1975–77; SHO, Brompton Hosp., 1977–78, Nat. Hosp., Queen Square, 1978; Registrar, Guy's Hosp., 1978–89; Clin. Lectr, Cardiothoracic Inst., Brompton Hosp., 1980–82; Res., Fellow, Harvard Univ., USA, 1982–84; Lectr, 1984–85, Sen. Lectr, 1985–88, Guy's Hosp.; Asthma UK Prof. of Allergy and Respiratory Medicine, KCL, 1988–2011; Dir, MRC and Asthma UK Centre in Allergic Mechanisms of Asthma at KCL and Imperial Coll. London, 2005–11. Pres., Hong Kong Inst. of Allergy, 2014–. Hon. Consultant Physician, Guy's and St Thomas' NHS Foundn Trust, 1988–2011. Hon. Clinical Prof., 2012–, Mem. Panel of Consultants, Univ. Health Service, 2014–, Univ. of Hong Kong. Mem., Jt Scientific Cttee, phase 1 clinical trials, Consortium on Harmonization of Instnl Requirements for Clinical Res., Chinese Univ. Hong Kong and Hong Kong Univ. and Hosp. Authy, 2014–17. Fellow, Amer. Acad. of Allergy, Asthma and Immunology, 1989; FMedSci 2000; FKC 2007; FAAAAI. *Recreations:* golf, wining and dining, travelling to exotic places. *Address:* Hong Kong Sanatorium and Hospital, Allergy Centre, 9th Floor, Li Shu Pui Building, 2 Village Road, Happy Valley, Hong Kong. *E:* takhong.lee@hksh.com. *Clubs:* Royal Automobile; China, Chariot, Hong Kong Jockey, Shek O Golf and Country (Hong Kong).

**LEE, Taryn Jane**; QC 2012; a Recorder, since 2008; *b* Cleethorpes, 4 March 1968; *d* of Thomas Edwin Lee, BEM, and Joan Gylettie Lee (*née* Meadows); *m* 1994, Andrew Skudder; one *s* one *d*. *Educ:* Bursar Street Primary Sch., Cleethorpes; Lindsey Comp. Sch., Cleethorpes; Huddersfield Poly. (LLB Hons Business Law); Inns of Court Sch. of Law (BVC). Called to the Bar, Inner Temple, 1992, Bencher, 2012; Jt Hd of Chambers, Spire Barristers (formerly 37 Park Square), Leeds, 2010–18; Public Access trained, 2011–; Mediator, 2012–. Bar Council: Mem., 2004–15; Chairman: Annual Bar Conf., 2011; Social Mobility Cttee, 2012–15. *Recreations:* family, music, theatre, fitness, literature, good food, wine and company; and I love shoes. *Address:* Spire Barristers, 3 St Davids Court, St Davids Street, Leeds LS11 5QA. *T:* (0113) 200 2400. *E:* TLee@spirebarristers.co.uk.

**LEE, Tiina Le-Seong**; Head, Equities and Fixed Income and Currencies UK (formerly Global Markets UK), and Chief Executive Officer, UK and Ireland, Deutsche Bank, since 2018; *b* London, 1 Jan. 1968; *d* of Johnson G. H. Lee and Olivia Lee; one *d*; partner, David Abraham, *qv*. *Educ:* S Hampstead High Sch.; King's Coll. London (BSc Food Sci. with specialisation in Mgt Studies 1990). Treasury Div., Hill Samuel Bank, 1990–94; Hd, Euro-Medium Term and Commercial Paper Trading, Lehman Bros, 1994–97; Deutsche Bank: Head: Euro Medium Term Note Trading, 1997–2001; Financial Instns, N Europe, 2001–10; UK Strategy, 2010–14; Chief Operating Officer, UK and Ireland, 2014–15; Dep. CEO, UK and Ireland, 2015–18. Non-exec. Dir, CAF Bank, 2015–18 (Chm., Risk and Compliance Cttee, 2015–18). Trustee, CAF, 2013–. *Recreations:* travel, contemporary art, good food, Arsenal Football Club. *Address:* Deutsche Bank, Winchester House, 1 Great Winchester Street, EC2N 2DB. *T:* (020) 7545 8480. *E:* tiina.lee@db.com. *Clubs:* Soho House; Carnegie (Dornoch).

**LEE, Sir Timothy John B.**; *see* Berners-Lee.

**LEE, Tsung-Dao**; Enrico Fermi Professor of Physics, 1964–2012, and University Professor, 1984–2012, now Emeritus, Columbia University, USA; *b* 25 Nov. 1926; 3rd *s* of C. K. and M. C. Lee; *m* 1950, Jeannette H. C. Chin; two *s*. *Educ:* National Chekiang Univ., Kweichow, China; National Southwest Associated Univ., Kunming, China; University of Chicago, USA. Research Associate: University of Chicago, 1950; University of California, 1950–51; Member, Inst. for Advanced Study, Princeton, 1951–53. Columbia University: Asst Professor, 1953–55; Associate Professor, 1955–56; Professor, 1956–60; Member, Institute for Advanced Study, Princeton, 1960–63; Columbia University: Adjunct Professor, 1960–62; Visiting Professor, 1962–63; Professor, 1963–2012. Hon. Professor: Univ. of Sci and Technol. of China, 1981; Jinan Univ., China, 1982; Fudan Univ., China, 1982; Qinghua Univ., 1984; Peking Univ., 1985; Nanjing Univ., 1985; Nankai Univ., 1986; Shanghai Jiao Tong and Suzhou Univs, 1987; Zhejiang Univ., 1988; Northwest Univ., Xian, 1993. Member: Acad. Sinica, 1957; Amer. Acad. of Arts and Scis, 1959; Nat. Acad. of Scis, 1964; Amer. Philosophical Soc., 1972; Acad. Nazionale dei Lincei, Rome, 1982; Chinese Acad. of Scis, Beijing, 1994. Hon. DSc: Princeton, 1958; City Coll., City Univ. of NY, 1978; Bard Coll., 1984; Peking, 1985; Bologna, 1988; Columbia, 1990; Adelphi, 1991; Tsukuba, 1992; Rockefeller, 1994; Hon. LLD Chinese Univ. of Hong Kong, 1969; Hon. LittD Drexel Univ., 1986; Dip. di Perfezionamento in Physics, Scuola Normale Superiore, Pisa, 1982. Nobel Prize for the non-conservation of parity (with C. N. Yang), 1957; Albert Einstein Award in Science, 1957; Ettore Majorana-Erice Sci. for Peace Prize, 1990. Grand'Ufficiale, Order of Merit (Italy), 1986. *Publications:* Particle Physics: an introduction to field theory, 1981; papers mostly in Physical Review, and Nuclear Physics. *Address:* Department of Physics, Columbia University, New York, NY 10027, USA.

**LEE, Most Rev. William**, DCL; Bishop of Waterford and Lismore, (RC), 1993–2013, now Bishop Emeritus; *b* 2 Dec. 1941; *s* of John Lee and Bridget Ryan. *Educ:* Newport Boys' Nat. Sch.; Rockwell Coll.; Maynooth Coll. (BA, BD, LPh, DCL); Gregorian Univ. Rome. Ordained priest, 1966; Catholic Curate, Finglas, West Dublin, 1969–71; Bursar, 1971–87, President, 1987–93, St Patrick's Coll., Thurles. Sec., Irish Episcopal Conf., 1998. *Recreations:* reading, walking, golf.

**LEE, Prof. William Edward**, DPhil; FREng, FIMMM; Professor of Ceramic Engineering, since 2006, and Co-Director, Institute for Security Science and Technology, since 2017, Imperial College London; *b* Gosport, Hants, England, 7 Feb. 1958; *s* of Arthur Edward Lee and Sylvia Lee (*née* Male); *m* 1987, Jacqueline Tonie Tregellis; one *d*. *Educ:* Price's Sch., Fareham; Aston Univ. (BSc Hons 1980); Linacre Coll., Oxford (DPhil 1983). Case Western Reserve Univ., 1983–86; Asst Prof., Ohio State Univ., 1986–89; Lectr, 1989–94, Sen. Lectr, 1994–96, Reader, 1996–98, Prof., 1998–2005, Univ. of Sheffield; Imperial College London: Hd, Dept of Materials, 2006–10; Co-Dir, 2011–12, Dir, 2013–16, Centre for Nuclear Engrg. William Penney Fellow, Atomic Weapons Establishment, Aldermaston, 2013–16. Dep. Chm., Cttee on Radioactive Waste Mgt, 2007–13. Member: Scientific and Envmtl Adv. Bd, Tokamak Energy plc, 2009–; Nuclear Innovation and Res. Adv. Bd, 2014–17; Nat. Nuclear Lab. Technical Adv. Panel, 2014–; Fellow, Amer. Ceramic Soc., 1999 (Pres., 2016–17). FIMMM 1989; FCGI 2009; FREng 2012. Freeman, City of London, 2017; Freeman, Armourers and Brasiers' Co., 2016. *Publications:* (with W. M. Rainforth) Ceramic Microstructures: property control by processing, 1994; (with M. I. Ojovan) An Introduction to Nuclear Waste Immobilisation, 2005, 2nd edn 2014; (jtly) Ceramics for Actinide Immobilisation, 2011; (ed jtly) Radioactive Waste Management and Contaminated Site Clean-up, 2014; (with D. W. Richerson) Modern Ceramic Engineering: properties processing and use in design, 4th edn 2018. *Recreations:* watching Pompey, running, swimming, building walls, walking, family tree. *Address:* Department of Materials, Imperial College London, South Kensington Campus, SW7 2AZ. *E:* w.e.lee@imperial.ac.uk.

**LEE, William Ernest**; Chief Executive, Renishaw plc, since 2018; *b* Bristol, 21 March 1975; *s* of Martin and Betty Lee; *m* 2008, Lucy Britten; two *s*. *Educ:* Pembroke Coll., Oxford (BA Physics 1996; MA); Bath Univ. (MBA 2009). Joined Renishaw plc, 1997; Gen. Manager, laser and calibration products line, 2007–14; Dir and Gen. Manager, machine tool products line, 2014–15; Dir, Gp Sales and Mktg, and Mem., Exec. Bd, 2015–18; Mem., Bd of Dirs, 2016. *Address:* Renishaw plc, New Mills, Wotton-under-Edge, Glos GL12 8JR.

**LEE YONG LENG, Dr**; Professor of Geography, National University of Singapore, 1977–90, retired; *b* 26 March 1930; *m* Wong Loon Meng; one *d*. *Educ:* Univs of Oxford, Malaya and Singapore. BLitt (Oxon), MA (Malaya), PhD (Singapore). Research Asst, Univ. of Malaya, 1954–56; University Lectr/Sen. Lectr, Univ. of Singapore, 1956–70; Associate Prof., Univ. of Singapore, 1970–71; High Comr for Singapore in London, 1971–75; Ambassador to Denmark, 1974–75, and Ireland, 1975; Min. of Foreign Affairs, Singapore, 1975–76. Mem., Govt Parly Cttee on Defence and For. Affairs, 1987–90. Chm., Singapore Nat. Library Bd, 1978–80. Dir, Centre for Advanced Studies, National Univ. of Singapore, 1983–85. *Publications:* North Borneo, 1965; Sarawak, 1970; Southeast Asia and the Law of the Sea, 1978; The Razor's Edge: boundaries and boundary disputes in Southeast Asia, 1980; Southeast Asia: essays in political geography, 1982; articles in: Population Studies; Geog. Jl; Erdkunde; Jl Trop. Geog., etc. *Recreations:* swimming, tennis, travelling, reading.

**LEE, Prof. Yuan Tseh**; President, Academia Sinica, Taiwan, 1994–2006; Distinguished Research Fellow, Institute of Atomic and Molecular Sciences, Taiwan, since 1994; *b* 29 Nov. 1936; *s* of Tse Fan Lee and Pei Tsai; *m* 1963, Bernice Chinli Wu; two *s* one *d*. *Educ:* Nat. Taiwan Univ. (BSc 1959); Nat. Tsinghua Univ., Taiwan (MSc 1961); Univ. of California (PhD 1965). Military service, 1961–62. University of California, Berkeley: Postdoctoral Fellow, 1965–67; Research Fellow, 1967–68; James Franck Inst. and Dept of Chemistry, Univ. of Chicago: Asst Prof. of Chemistry, 1968–71; Associate Prof. of Chemistry, 1971–72; Prof. of Chemistry, 1973–74; University of California, Berkeley: Prof. of Chemistry, 1974–91; Univ. Prof. of Chemistry, 1991–94; Principal Investigator, Materials and Molecular Research Div., Lawrence Berkeley Lab., 1974–94. Vis. Lectr, US and overseas univs. Mem., edit boards, chem. and sci. jls. Mem., Nat. Acad. of Scis, 1979, and other learned bodies; Pres., Internat. Council for Sci., 2011–16. Nobel Prize in Chemistry (jtly), 1986; numerous awards from US and foreign instns. *Publications:* papers on molecular chemistry and related subjects. *Recreations:* sports (baseball, ping pong, tennis), classical music. *Address:* Academia Sinica, Nankang, Taipei 11529, Taiwan.

**LEE CHU-MING, Martin, (Martin Lee)**; QC (Hong Kong) 1979; JP; Chairman, Democratic Party, Hong Kong, 1994–2002; Member, Hong Kong Legislative Council, 1985–97 and 1998–2008; *b* 8 June 1938; *m* 1969, Amelia Lee; one *s*. *Educ:* Wah Yan College, Kowloon; Univ. of Hong Kong (BA 1960). Called to the Bar, Lincoln's Inn, 1966. Member: Hong Kong Law Reform Commn, 1985–91; Hong Kong Fight Crime Cttee, 1986–92; Basic Law Drafting Cttee, 1985–89; numerous groups and cttees advising on Govt, law, nationality and community matters. Chm., United Democrats of Hong Kong, 1990–94. JP Hong Kong, 1980. *Publications:* The Basic Law: some basic flaws (with Szeto Wah), 1988. *Address:* Admiralty Centre, Room 704A, Tower I, 18 Harcourt Road, Hong Kong. *T:* 25290864. *Clubs:* Hong Kong; Hong Kong Golf, Hong Kong Jockey.

**LEE-EMERY, Louise Wendy**; *see* Tulett, L. W.

**LEE-JONES, Christine**; JP; DL; MA; Head Mistress, Manchester High School for Girls, 1998–2008; non-executive Director, Walton Centre NHS Foundation Trust Liverpool, 2008–14; *b* 13 June 1948; *d* of George and Marion Pickup; *m* 1972, Denys Lee-Jones; one *d*. *Educ:* Lawnswood High Sch. for Girls, Leeds; St Mary's Coll., Bangor; University Coll. of N Wales (BEd Biblical Studies and Far Eastern Religions); Univ. of London Inst. of Educn (MA 1982); Open Univ. (Advanced Dip. Educnl Mgt 1990). Primary teacher, Bethnal Green, 1970–71; Head, Religious Education: Archbp Temple Sch., London, 1971–74; Archbp Michael Ramsey Sch., London, 1974–82; Sen. Lectr, Woolwich Coll. of Further Educn, 1983–86; Vice-Principal, Leyton Sixth Form Coll., 1986–91; Principal, Eccles Sixth Form Coll., Salford, 1991–98. Teacher/Tutor, Univ. of London Inst. of Educn, 1978–79. University of Manchester: Member: Gen. Assembly, 2005–; Gov. Body, 2010–16; Audit Cttee, 2010–16; Nominations and Awards Cttee, 2012–16. Jt Chair, Professional Develt Cttee, HMC/GSA, 2005–. Trustee: Greater Manchester Police High Sheriff Trust, 2011–; Prevent Breast Cancer (formerly Genesis Breast Cancer Prevention Charity), 2012–; Henshaw Soc. for Blind People, 2013–14; volunteer, Breast Cancer Care, 2013–. Mem., Network Club, 1998–. Mem., RSC, 2003–. FRSA 1999. DL 2007, High Sheriff, 2011–12, Greater Manchester; JP Trafford, 2008. *Recreations:* literature, theatre, the arts, travel, tennis, fine wines. *E:* cleejones01@gmail.com.

**LEE PENG-FEI, Allen, (Allen Lee)**, CBE 1988 (OBE 1982); JP; Chairman, Pacific Dimensions Consultants Ltd, since 1998; *b* 24 April 1940; *m* Maria Lee; two *s* one *d*. *Educ:* Univ. of Michigan (BSc Engineering Maths). Test Engineer Supervisor, Lockheed Aircraft International, 1966–67; Engineering Ops Manager, Fabri-teck, 1967; Test Engineer Manager, Lockheed Aircraft International, 1968–70; Test Manager, Ampex Ferrotec, 1970–72; Gen. Manager, Dataproducts HK, 1972–74; Managing Dir, Ampex Ferrotec, 1974–79; Gen. Manager, Ampex World Operations, 1979–83; Managing Dir, Ampex Far East Operations, 1983–84; Pres., Meadville, 1984–95. Appointed Mem., Hong Kong Legislative Council, 1978–98; MEC, Hong Kong, 1985–92; Dep. for HKSAR, 9th Nat. People's Congress, China, 1997–2004; Chm., HK Liberal Party, 1993. Mem., Commn on Strategic Develt, HKSAR, 1998. Chm., Bd of Overseers, Hong Kong Inst. of Biotechnol., 1990–. JP Hong Kong, 1980. FHKIE, 1985. Hon. DEng Hong Kong Poly., 1990; Hon. LLD Chinese Univ. of Hong Kong, 1990. Nat. Award, Asian Productivity Organization, 1986; Outstanding Young Persons Award, Hong Kong, 1977. *Recreations:* swimming, tennis. *Clubs:* Hong Kong Jockey, Hong Kong Country, Dynasty (Hong Kong).

**LEE-POTTER, Jeremy Patrick**, FRCPath; Consultant Haematologist, Poole General Hospital, 1969–95; *b* 30 Aug. 1934; *s* of Air Marshal Sir Patrick Lee Potter, KBE, MD, QHS and Audrey Mary (*née* Pollock); *m* 1957, Lynda Higginson (OBE 1998) (*d* 2004); one *s* two *d*. *Educ:* Epsom Coll.; Guy's Hosp. Med. Sch. (MB BS 1958). MRCS, LRCP 1958; DTM&H 1963; DCP 1965; FRCPath 1979. Specialist in Pathology, 1960, Sen. Specialist, 1965, RAF (Sqn Ldr); in charge of Haematology Dept, RAF Inst. of Pathology and Tropical Medicine; Lectr in Haematology, St George's Hosp. Med. Sch., 1968–69. British Medical Association: Chm. Council, 1990–93 (Mem. Council, 1988–95); Dep. Chm., Central Consultants and Specialists Cttee, 1988–90 (Chm., Negotiating Cttee); Vice Pres., 1998–; Chm., Audit Cttee, 1999–2002. Member: Standing Med. Adv. Cttee, 1990–93; GMC, 1994–99 (Dep. Chm., Professional Conduct Cttee, 1996–99); Clinical Disputes Forum, 1999. Consultant Surveyor, King's Fund Orgnl Audit, 1993–95. Engineering Council: Mem. Senate, 2000–02; Mem., Bd for Engrs' Regulation, 2001–02. Pres., Old Epsomian Club, 2004–05. *Publications:* A Damn Bad Business: the NHS deformed, 1997. *Recreations:* art, birdwatching, natural history, photography. *Address:* Icen House, Stoborough, Wareham, Dorset BH20 5AN. *T:* (01929) 556307. *Clubs:* Athenæum; Parkstone Golf.

**LEE-STEERE, Gordon Ernest**; Vice Lord-Lieutenant of Surrey, 1996–2014; *b* 26 Dec. 1939; *s* of Charles Augustus Lee-Steere and Patience Hargreaves Lee-Steere; *m* 1966, Mary Katharine Stuart; one *s* three *d*. *Educ:* Eton; Trinity Coll., Cambridge (MA). Computer consultant, 1966–74; self-employed farmer, 1960–. Pres., CLA, 1987–89. *Recreations:* shooting, walking. *Address:* Hale House, Oakwoodhill, Surrey RH5 5NA. *T:* (01306) 627112. *Club:* Boodle's.

**LEE-THORP, Prof. Julia Anne**, PhD; FBA 2013; Professor of Archaeological Science, since 2010, and Head, School of Archaeology, since 2016, University of Oxford; Fellow, St Cross College, Oxford; *b* Cape Town, 20 April 1951. *Educ:* Univ. of Cape Town (BA; BSc; PhD 1989). Archaeology and Faculty of Science, University of Cape Town: Sen. Res. Officer, Archaeometry Res. Unit, 1991–97; Sen. Lectr, 1998–2000; Associate Prof., 2001–04; Prof. of Archaeol., 2005–06; Res. Dir, Archaeol, Geographical and Envmtl Scis, Univ. of Bradford, 2006–10. Founding Mem. and Dir, Quarternary Res. Centre, Western Cape, 2000–04. Vis. Prof., Dept of Geog., Stockholm Univ. and Fachbereich Geowissenschaften, Univ. of Bremen 2000. *Publications:* (contrib.) The First Humans: origin and early evolution of the genus homo, 2009; (ed jtly) African Genesis: perspectives on hominin evolution, 2012; (ed jtly and contrib.) Early Hominin Ecology, 2013; contribs to learned jls. *Address:* Research Laboratory for Archaeology and the History of Art, Dyson Perrins Building, South Parks Road, Oxford OX1 3QY.

**LEECH, John**; Member (Lib Dem), Manchester City Council, since 2016; *b* 11 April 1971; *s* of Rev. John Leech and Jean Leech; partner, Catherine Kilday. *Educ:* Manchester Grammar Sch.; Loreto Coll.; Brunel Univ. (BA Hons Pols and Hist.). Mem. (Lib Dem), Manchester CC, 1998–2008 (Dep. Leader, Lib Dem Gp, 2003–05). MP (Lib Dem)

Manchester Withington, 2005–15; contested (Lib Dem) same seat, 2015, 2017. Member: Transport Select Cttee, 2005–12; Culture, Media and Sport Cttee, 2012–15. *Recreations*: sport, amateur dramatics, season ticket holder Manchester City. *Address*: 53b Manley Road, Whalley Range, Manchester M16 8HP.

LEECH, John, (Hans-Joachim Freiherr von Reitzenstein), MBE 2014; Head of External Relations and Member of Management Board, Commonwealth Development Corporation, 1981–85; Chairman, Farm Services Co. BV, 1988–2000; Deputy Chairman, Rural Investment Overseas Ltd, 1990–2000 (Chairman, 1985–90); *b* 21 April 1925; *s* of Hans-Joachim and Josefine von Reitzenstein; *m* 1st, 1949, Mair Eiluned Davies (marr. diss. 1958); one *d*; 2nd, 1963, Noretta Conci (MBE 2014), concert pianist. *Educ*: Bismarck Gymnasium, Berlin; Whitgift, Croydon. L. G. Mouchel & Partners, Consulting Civil Engineers, 1942–52; Bird & Co. Ltd, Calcutta, 1953–57; Dir, Europe House, London, and Exec. Mem. Council, Britain in Europe Ltd, 1958–63; Pres., Internat. Fedn of Europe Houses, 1961–65; Dir, Joint Industrial Exports Ltd, 1963–65; with Commonwealth Develt Corp., London and overseas, 1965–85; Co-ordinator, Interact Gp of European develt finance instns, 1973–85; Eur. Co-ordinator, West-West Agenda, 1987–2010. Asst Dir, NATO Parliamentarians' Conf., 1959–60. Vice-Chm., Indian Concrete Soc., 1953–57; Member: Council, Federal Trust for Educn and Research, 1985–; Adv. Council (formerly Exec. Cttee), London Symphony Orch., 1979–96; Council, Royal Commonwealth Soc. for the Blind, 1983–99; Internat. Council, Duke of Edinburgh's Award Internat. Assoc., 1993–98. Chm., Keyboard Charitable Trust for Young Professional Performers, 1991–2013. Liveryman, Worshipful Co. of Paviors, 1968– (Mem. Court of Assts, 1992–2002, now Emeritus). FRSA. *Publications*: The NATO Parliamentarians' Conference 1955–59, 1960; Europe and the Commonwealth, 1961; Aid and the Community, 1972; Halt! Who Goes Where?: the future of NATO in the new Europe, 1991; Asymmetries of Conflict: war without death, 2002; (ed) Whole and Free: EU enlargement and transatlantic relations, 2002; Too Many Lives, 2019; contrib. to jls on aspects of overseas devlt, European matters and arts subjects. *Recreations*: music, travel, Italy. *Address*: 8 Chester Square Mews, SW1W 9DS. *T*: (020) 7730 2307. *Club*: Travellers.

LEECH, Kevin Ronald; Founder and Chairman, ML Laboratories plc, 1987–2000; Chairman, Accura Animal Health, 2007–08; *b* 18 Aug. 1943; two *s* one *d* from former marriage. *Educ*: St Bede's Coll., Manchester. Accountancy, until 1964; built up family business, R. T. Leech & Sons Ltd, into UK's largest private funeral dir, 1964–82; entrepreneur, business manager, and venture capitalist, 1982–; non-executive Chairman: Queensborough Holdings plc, 1994–2000; Top Jobs on the Net, 1999; CI4Net.Com Ltd, 1999; non-exec. Dir, Devilfish Gaming plc, 2007–10. FCMI (FIMgt 1983); FInstD 1984; FRSA 1997. Hon. LLD Manchester, 1998. *Recreations*: Manchester United, football generally, ski-ing, sailing, fishing. *Address*: La Vignette, Rue de la Vignette, St Saviour, Jersey JE2 7HY.

LEECH, Melanie Jane, CBE 2015; Chief Executive, British Property Federation, since 2015; *b* 28 May 1962; *d* of Michael and Margaret Leech; two *s*. *Educ*: Brighton and Hove High Sch. for Girls GDST; St Hugh's Coll., Oxford (BA Hons Maths). Principal Private Sec. to Cabinet Sec. and Hd of Home Civil Service, 1992–95; Hd of Arts Policy, 1995–98, Hd of Broadcasting Policy, 1998–99, DCMS; Dir, Office of the Rail Regulator, 1999–2001; Exec. Dir, Assoc. of Police Authorities, 2001–04; Dir of Communications, Cabinet Office, 2004–05; Dir Gen., FDF, 2005–15. Trustee: Carnegie UK Trust, 2005–15; Land Aid, 2018–. Mem. Council, Univ. of Essex, 2019–. MInstD. FRSA. *Address*: British Property Federation, St Albans House, 57–59 Haymarket, SW1Y 4QX.

LEECH, Stewart; QC 2011; *b* Willenhall, 23 May 1963; *s* of late William Brian Leech and of Barbara Leech; *m* 2006, Olivier Riche. *Educ*: Wolverhampton Grammar Sch.; Christ Church, Oxford (Open Exhibnr; BA Hons; MA); City Univ.; Inns of Court Sch. of Law. Teacher of French and German: Shrewsbury Sch., 1986–88; Eton Coll., 1988–90; called to the Bar, Lincoln's Inn, 1992; in practice as barrister, 1992–. *Recreations*: gardening, reading, painting. *Address*: 3rd Floor, Queen Elizabeth Building, Temple, EC4Y 9BS.

LEECH, Thomas Alexander Crispin; QC 2010; *b* London, 16 Feb. 1964; *s* of Prof. Geoffrey Neil Leech, FBA; *m* 1990, Jane Elizabeth McKendrick; four *d*. *Educ*: Lancaster Royal Grammar Sch.; Wadham Coll., Oxford (Major Schol.; BA 1st Cl. Juris.; BCL). Called to the Bar, Middle Temple, 1988; in practice as barrister, 1989–. *Publications*: Flenley and Leech on Solicitors' Negligence and Liability, 1999, 4th edn 2019; (ed jtly) Spencer Bower: Estoppelby Representation, 4th edn 2004, 5th edn as Spencer Bower: Reliance-based Estoppel, 2017; (ed jtly) Snell's Equity, 30th edn 2005. *Recreations*: walking (especially in the Lake District), sport (especially Rugby and cricket). *Address*: Herbert Smith Freehills LLP, Exchange House, Primrose Street, EC2A 2EG.

LEEDER, Prof. Michael Robert, PhD; Professor of Environmental Sciences, University of East Anglia, 1999, then Hon. Research Professor, now Professor Emeritus; *b* 22 Nov. 1947; *s* of Norman George Leeder and Evelyn (*née* Patterson). *Educ*: Univ. of Durham (BSc 1st Cl. Hons Geology); Univ. of Reading (PhD 1972). University of Leeds: Lectr in Earth Scis, 1972–85; Reader, 1985–91; Prof., 1991–99. Lyell Medal, Geol Soc., 1992; Phillips Medal, Geol Soc. of Yorks, 1990. *Publications*: Dynamic Stratigraphy of the British Isles, 1979; Sedimentology, 1982; Sedimentology and Sedimentary Basins, 1999, 2nd edn 2011; Fire Over East Anglia, 1999; Physical Processes in the Earth and Environmental Sciences, 2006; contrib. various scientific papers. *Recreation*: living generally. *Address*: School of Environmental Sciences, University of East Anglia, Norwich NR4 7TJ.

LEEDHAM, Carol Jean; *see* Mountford, C. J.

LEEDS, Bishop of, since 2014; Rt Rev. Nicholas Baines; *b* 13 Nov. 1957; *s* of Frank Baines and Beryl Amy Baines; *m* 1980, Linda Margaret Higgins; two *s* one *d*. *Educ*: Holt Comprehensive Sch., Liverpool; Univ. of Bradford (BA (Hons) Mod. Langs); Trinity Coll., Bristol (BA (Hons) Theol Studies). Linguist specialist, GCHQ, Cheltenham, 1980–84; ordained deacon, 1987, priest, 1988; Asst Curate, St Thomas, Kendal, 1987–91; Asst Priest, Holy Trinity with St John, Leicester, 1991–92; Vicar, St Mary and St John, Rothley, Leicester, 1992–2000; Archdeacon of Lambeth, 2000–03; Area Bishop of Croydon, 2003–11; Bishop of Bradford, 2011–14. Non-exec. Dir, Ecclesiastical Insce Gp, 2002–10. English Co-Chair, Meissen Commn, 2007–17. Mem., Gen. Synod of C of E, 1995–2005. Took seat in H of L, 2014. Chair, Sandford St Martin Trust, 2008–18. Regular broadcaster, BBC Radio. Hon. Fellow, Bradford Coll., 2014–. DUniv Bradford, 2013; Hon. DTh Friedrich-Schiller-Univ., Jena, 2014. *Publications*: Hungry for Hope, 1991, reissued as Hungry for Hope?, 2007; Speedbumps and Potholes, 2003; Jesus and People Like Us, 2004, reissued as Scandal of Grace: the danger of following Jesus, 2008; Marking Time: 47 reflections on Mark's Gospel for Lent, Holy Week and Easter, 2005; Finding Faith: stories of music and life, 2008; Why Wish You a Merry Christmas?: what matters (and what doesn't) in the festive season, 2019; Freedom is Coming, 2019; chapters in German and English academic books. *Recreations*: music, reading, sport, travelling. *Address*: Hollin House, Weetwood Avenue, Leeds LS16 5NG. *T*: (0113) 284 4300. *E*: bishop.nick@leeds.anglican.org. *W*: nickbaines.wordpress.com.

LEEDS, Bishop of, (Catholic), since 2014; Rt Rev. Marcus Nigel Ralph Peter Stock; *b* London, 27 Aug. 1961. *Educ*: Highdown Sch., Caversham; Keble Coll., Oxford (MA Theol.); Pontifical Gregorian Univ. (STL Dogmatic Theol.). Ordained priest, 1988; Asst Priest, Our Lady and St Brigid's Parish, Northfield, 1988–91; Parish Priest: St Birinus, Dorchester-on-Thames, 1991–94; St Peter's, Bloxwich, Walsall, 1994–99; Sacred Heart and St Theresa, Coleshill, 1999–2009; Asst Dir of Schs, 1995–99, Dir of Schs, 1999–2009, Archdiocese of Birmingham; Gen. Sec., Catholic Bishops' Conf. of Eng. and Wales, 2009–14. Apptd Prelate of Honour by Pope Benedict XVI, 2012. *Publications*: Christ at the Centre, 2005, 2nd edn 2013. *Address*: Bishop's House, 13 North Grange Road, Leeds LS6 2BR. *T*: (0113) 230 4533, *Fax*: (0113) 278 9890. *E*: bishop@dioceseofleeds.org.uk.

LEEDS, Archdeacon of; *see* Ayers, Ven. P. N.

LEEDS, Sir John (Charles Hildyard), 9th Bt *cr* 1812, of Croxton Park, Cambridgeshire; *b* 25 Dec. 1941; *e s* of late Charles Hildyard Denham Leeds and Merran Elizabeth, *d* of John Hilary Drew; *S* cousin, 2009; *m* 1965, Eileen Rose, *d* of Joseph Francis Shalka; one *s* two *d*. *Educ*: Univ. of Alberta (BSc Civil Engrg 1965). Mem., Assoc. of Professional Engrs and Geoscientists of Alberta (formerly Assoc. of Professional Engrs, Geologists and Geophysicists of Alberta). *Heir*: *s* Michael John Hildyard Leeds, *b* 16 May 1975.

LEEMING, Dame Cheryl Elise Kendall; *see* Gillan, Rt Hon. Dame C. E. K.

LEEMING, Geraldine Margaret; *see* Coleridge, G. M.

LEEMING, His Honour Ian; QC 1988; a Circuit Judge, 2006–18; *b* Preston, Lancs, 10 April 1948; *s* of late Thomas Leeming (Bombing Leader, RAF), and of Lilian (*née* Male); *m* 1973, Linda Barbara Cook; one *s* two *d*. *Educ*: The Catholic Coll., Preston; Manchester Univ. (LLB 1970). Called to the Bar: Gray's Inn, 1970; Lincoln's Inn (*ad eundem*), 1981; in practice at Chancery and Commercial Bars, 1971–2006; a Recorder, 1989–2006. Dep. Deemster, Manx High Court, 1998; Mem., Court of Appeal, IOM, 1998. Legal Assessor: GMC, 2002–06; GDC, 2003–06. Lectr in Law (part-time), Manchester Univ., 1971–75. Formerly Counsel to Attorneys, Malcolm A. Hoffmann & Co., NY. Dir of limited cos. Vice-Chm., Northern Soc. of Cons. Lawyers, 1985–88. Fellow, Soc. for Advanced Legal Studies, 1998. Member: Chancery Bar Assoc.; Professional Negligence Bar Assoc.; Technol. and Construction Court Bar Assoc. FCIArb, Chartered Arbitrator, 2005–18. *Publications*: (with James Bonney) Observations upon the Insolvency Bill, 1985; (ed) Equity and Trusts sect., Butterworth's Law of Limitation, 2000; articles, notes and reviews in legal jls and specialist periodicals. *Recreations*: the family, reading, walking, wine.

LEEMING, Michael Peter George; His Honour Judge Michael Leeming; a Circuit Judge, since 2012; *b* Salford, 16 April 1961; *s* of George Leeming and Eileen Leeming (*née* Stanford); *m* 1995, Clare Rees; one *s* one *d*. *Educ*: Thornleigh Salesian Coll., Bolton; Leeds Univ. (LLB Hons). Called to the Bar, Inner Temple, 1983; in practice as barrister, Manchester, 1983–2012; Asst Recorder, 1999–2000; Recorder, 2000–12. *Recreations*: family, ski-ing, football (Manchester City FC). *Address*: Manchester Crown Court, Courts of Justice, Crown Square, Manchester M3 3FL. *T*: (0161) 954 1800. *E*: HHJ.Michael.Leeming@ejudiciary.net.

LEES, Andrew James; His Honour Judge Andrew Lees; a Circuit Judge, since 2010; *b* Chester, 15 April 1961; *s* of Alan James Lees and Violet Mary Lees (*née* Buckingham); *m* 1986, Clare Milne; two *s* two *d*. *Educ*: Rydal Sch., Colwyn Bay; Queen's Park High Sch., Chester; Liverpool Univ. (LLB Hons). Called to the Bar, Gray's Inn, 1984; a Recorder, 2001–10. *Recreations*: horn playing, walking, wildlife, food and wine, cooking, arts, vintage shops. *Address*: Woolwich Crown Court, 2 Belmarsh Road, SE28 0EY.

LEES, Prof. Andrew John, MD; FRCP, FMedSci; Professor of Neurology, Institute of Neurology, since 1998 and Director, Reta Lila Weston Institute of Neurological Studies, 1998–2012, now Emeritus Director, University College London; Consultant Neurologist, National Hospital for Neurology and Neurosurgery (now part of University College London Hospitals NHS Trust), since 1982; *b* 27 Sept. 1947; *s* of Lewis Lees and Muriel Lees (*née* Wadsworth); *m* 1973, Juana Luisa Pulin Perez Lopez; one *s* one *d*. *Educ*: Roundhay Sch., Leeds; Royal London Hosp. Med. Sch., Univ. of London (MD 1978). FRCP 1982. Co-Ed.-in-Chief, Movement Disorders Jl, 1994–2004. Dir, Sara Koe PSP Res. Centre, Inst. of Neurol., 2002–12. Chm., Med. Adv. Panel, Progressive Supranuclear Palsy (PSP Europe) Assoc., 1995–. Pres., Movt Disorder Soc., 2005–06 (Pres., Eur. Sect., 1998–2000). Appeal Steward, BBB of C, 1998–. Visiting Professor: Univ. of Liverpool, 2002–; São Rafael Hosp., Salvador, Brazil, 2000–; Univ. Fed. de Minas Gerais, Belo Horizonte, Brazil, 2007–. Mem. Council, Acad. of Med. Scis, 2012–. FMedSci 2009. Corresp. Mem., Academia Nacional de Medicina, Brazil. Mem., London Liby. *Publications*: Parkinson's Disease, The Facts, 1980; Tics and Related Disorders, 1984; Ray of Hope: authorised biography of Ray Kennedy, 1992; The Hurricane Port: a social history of Liverpool, 2010; Exploring the Victorian Brain: a biography of Sir William Gowers, 2012; Alzheimer's: the silent plague, 2012; Mentored by a Madman: the William Burroughs experiment, 2016. *Recreations*: writer, Brazilian studies, Liverpool FC supporter, St Helens Rugby League supporter. *Address*: Reta Lila Weston Institute for Neurological Studies, Institute of Neurology, 1 Wakefield Street, WC1N 1PG. *T*: (020) 7679 4246. *E*: andrew.lees@ucl.ac.uk. *Club*: Groucho.

LEES, Sir Antony; *see* Lees, Sir W. A. C.

LEES, Sir Christopher (James), 5th Bt *cr* 1897, of South Lytchett Manor; TD 1992; *b* Lytchett Minster, Dorset, 4 Nov. 1952; *s* of Sir Thomas Edward Lees, 4th Bt and Faith Justin Lees (*née* Jessiman) (*d* 1996); *S* father, 2016; *m* 1989, Helen Clare Young; two *s* three *d*. *Educ*: Eton Coll.; Edinburgh Univ. (BSc Hons Agricl Sci.); Bournemouth and Poole Coll. of Art and Design (BTEC Foundn Art and Design). Farmer and landowner, 1976–. Mem., Dorset CC, 1984–88. TA Officer, Royal Wessex Yeomanry (Major, 1974–94). Trustee, Talbot Village Trust, 1992– (Chm., 2005–). *Recreations*: sailing, ski-ing, fishing. *Heir*: *s* John Austen Lees, *b* 15 Feb. 1992. *Address*: Post Green, Lytchett Minster, Poole, Dorset BH16 6AP. *T*: (01202) 622505. *E*: christopher.lees@postgreen.co.uk. *Clubs*: Royal Cruising; Poole Yacht.

LEES, Sir David (Bryan), Kt 1991; DL; FCA; Chairman, Court of Directors, Bank of England, 2009–14 (a Director, 1991–99); *b* 23 Nov. 1936; *s* of late Rear-Adm. D. M. Lees, CB, DSO, and C. D. M. Lees; *m* 1961, Edith Mary Bernard; two *s* one *d*. *Educ*: Charterhouse. 2nd Lieut, RA, 1955–57. Qualified as a chartered accountant, 1962. Chief Accountant, Handley Page Ltd, 1964–68; GKN Sankey Ltd: Chief Accountant, 1970–72; Dep. Controller, 1972–73; Director, Secretary and Controller, 1973–76; Guest Keen and Nettlefolds, later GKN plc: Group Finance Executive, 1976–77; General Manager Finance, 1977–82; Dir, 1982–2004; Finance Dir, 1982–87; Man. Dir, 1987–88; Chief Exec., 1988–96; Chm., 1988–2004. Chairman: Courtaulds plc, 1996–98 (Dir, 1991–98); Tate & Lyle plc, 1998–2009; Deputy Chairman: Brambles Industries Ltd, and Brambles Industries plc, 2001–06; QinetiQ Gp plc, 2005–12. Mem. Council, CBI, 1988–96 (Chm., Economic Affairs (formerly Economic and Financial Policy) Cttee, 1988–94); Pres., EEF, 1990–92; Member: Audit Commission, 1983–90; Listed Cos Adv. Cttee, 1990–97; European Round Table, 1995–2001; Nat. Defence Industries Council, 1995–2004; Panel on Takeovers and

Mergers, 2001–16. Dir, Inst. for Manufacturing, 1998–2001. Pres., Soc. of Business Economists, 1994–99. Director: Royal Opera House, 1998–2008; Royal Opera House Enterprises (formerly Opus Arte) Ltd, 2007–16; Trustee, Royal Opera House Endowment Fund, 2001–. Mem. Governing Body, Shrewsbury Sch., 1986–2007 (Chm., 2004–07); Governor: Suttons Hosp., Charterhouse, 1995–2005; Shrewsbury Internat. Sch., Bangkok (Riverside), 2005– (Chm., 2016–); Royal Ballet Sch., 2008–13; Chairman of Governors: Shrewsbury Internat. Sch. Hong Kong, 2017–; Shrewsbury Internat. Sch., Bangkok (City Campus), 2018–; Chm., Adv. Bd, University Centre Shrewsbury, 2015–. Hon. Patron, Shrewsbury Town FC, 2010–. DL Shropshire, 2007. Hon. Fellow, Wolverhampton Poly., 1990. Hon. DBA Chester, 2016. ICAEW Award for outstanding achievement, 1999. Officer's Cross, Order of Merit (Germany), 1996. *Recreations:* walking, golf, opera, music. *Clubs:* Carlton, MCC.
*See also* Rear-Adm. R. B. Lees.

**LEES, Diane Elizabeth,** CBE 2015; Director-General, Imperial War Museum, since 2008; *b* 28 March 1964; *d* of late William Lees and of Brenda Lees (*née* Gilman); *m* 2007, Michael Hague. *Educ:* Oriel Bank High Sch.; Stockport Coll. of Technol.; Open Univ. (BA History). Exhibns Asst, Mary Rose Project, 1982–84; Registrar, Royal Naval Mus., 1984–89; Nottingham City Museums, 1989–91; Nat. Outreach Manager, Museums Documentation Assoc., 1991–94; Chief Exec., Galls of Justice, 1994–2000; Dir, Mus. of Childhood, 2000–08. Vice Chair, Assoc. of Ind. Museums, 2005–08 (Sec., 1998–2002); Instnl Vice Pres., Museums Assoc., 2002–04; Chm., Nat. Mus. Dirs Council, 2013–. Mem., Adv. Bd, Nat. World War One Mus., Kansas City, 2014–18. Gov., Univ. of Lincoln, 2014–. Liveryman, Goldsmiths' Co., 2018. FMA 1996; FRSA 2004; CCMI 2011. Hon. DLitt Reading, 2015; Hon. DArts Nottingham Trent, 2017. *Publications:* (ed) Museums and Interactive Multimedia, 1993; Computers in Museums, 1994, 3rd edn 1996; contribs to Museums Jl, IBBY Procs, Library and Inf. Scis. *Recreations:* walking, tennis, cooking, collecting ceramics. *Address:* Imperial War Museum, Lambeth Road, SE1 6HZ. *T:* (020) 7416 5207, *Fax:* (020) 7416 5374. *E:* dlees@iwm.org.uk.

**LEES, Michael Anthony M.;** *see* Mather-Lees, M. A.

**LEES, Captain Nicholas Ernest Samuel;** Chairman, Leicester Racecourse, since 2006 (Assistant Manager, 1970–71; Clerk of the Course, 1972–2004; Managing Director, 1972–2005); Chairman, Stratford-on-Avon Racecourse Co. Ltd, since 2001 (Director, since 1990); *b* 3 May 1939; *s* of Ernest William Lees and Marjorie May Lees; *m* 1st, 1969, Elizabeth Helen Spink (marr. diss. 1985); one *d*; 2nd, 1985, Jocelyn Kosina; one *d*. *Educ:* Abbotsholme Sch., Rocester, Staffs. Shell Oil, 1956–59; commnd 17/21 Lancers, 1959; retd from Army, 1967; studied for Chartered Surveyors exams, 1967–69 (passed final exams but never practised); auctioneer, Warner, Sheppard & Wade Ltd, Leicester, 1969–73; Clerk of the Course: Teesside Park, 1972–73; Great Yarmouth, 1977–91; Chief Exec., 1974–97, Clerk of the Course, 1974–2000, and Dir of Racing, 1998–2000, Newmarket. Dir, Racecourse Assoc. Ltd, 1988–93, 2004–05. *Recreations:* horse racing, antique furniture, silver, sporting art. *Address:* Capers End, Bradfield St George, Bury St Edmunds, Suffolk IP30 0AY. *T:* (01284) 386651.

**LEES, Peter Derick,** FRCP, FRCS, SFFMLM; Chief Executive and Medical Director, Faculty of Medical Leadership and Management, since 2011; *b* Newcastle under Lyme, 19 April 1953; *s* of George Lees and Doreen Lees; *m* 1987, Ha Yen Chan; one *d*. *Educ:* Manchester Univ. (MB ChB 1975); Univ. of Southampton (MS 1990). FRCS 1981; FRCP 2012; SFFMLM 2017. Sen. Lectr in Neurosurgery, Univ. of Southampton, 1989–2012; Dir, R&D, 1995–99, Med. Dir, 1999–2002, University Hosp. Southampton; Med. Dir, NHS Leadership Centre, 2002–05; NHS South Central Strategic Health Authority: Med. Dir, 2009–12; Dir, Leadership, 2009–12; Dir, Workforce and Educn, 2011–12. Mem. Bd, West Hants CCG, 2012–15. Mem., Strategy Cttee, Guy's and St Thomas' Charity, 2015–17. Hon. Vis. Prof., Cass Business Sch., City, Univ. of London, 2017–. *Publications:* Navigating the NHS, 1996; res. papers on pituitary blood flow and pituitary tumours; articles on medical leadership (medical). *Address:* Faculty of Medical Leadership and Management, 34 Red Lion Square, WC1R 4SG. *T:* (020) 8051 2060. *E:* peter.lees@fmlm.ac.uk.

**LEES, Robert Ferguson,** CBE 1999; Regional Procurator Fiscal for Lothian and Borders, 1991–98; *b* 15 Sept. 1938; *s* of William Lees and Martha Lees (*née* McAlpine); *m* 1966, Elizabeth (Elsie) Loughridge. *Educ:* Bellshill Acad.; Strathclyde Univ. (LLB). Joined Procurator Fiscal Service, 1972; Legal Asst, Paisley, 1972–75; Legal Asst, 1975–76, Sen. Legal Asst, 1976–78, and Sen. Depute Fiscal, 1978–81, Glasgow; Asst Procurator Fiscal, Dundee, 1982–88; Regl Procurator Fiscal for N Strathclyde, 1989–91. Vis. Scholar, Valdosta State Univ., Ga, 1999–2000. *Publications:* (jtly) Criminal Procedure, 1990. *Recreations:* music, travel, languages, photography.

**LEES, Rear-Adm. Rodney Burnett,** CVO 2001; Defence Services Secretary to the Queen, and Director General of Reserve Forces and Cadets, 1998–2001; Chief Naval Supply Officer, 1998–2000; *b* 31 Dec. 1944; *s* of Rear-Adm. Dennis Maresceaux Lees, CB, DSO and Daphne Lees; *m* 1st, 1969, Rosemary Elizabeth Blake (marr. diss. 1978); two *s*; 2nd, 1982, Molly McEwen. *Educ:* Charterhouse. Called to Bar, Gray's Inn, 1976. Joined RN 1962; HMS Devonshire, 1966–68; Captain SM10, 1968–70; HMS Apollo, 1972–74; legal training, 1974–77; Staff Legal Adviser to FO Portsmouth and Command Legal Adviser to C-in-C Naval Home Comd, 1977–79; Dep. Supply Officer, HM Yacht Britannia, 1980; DCSO (Pay), MoD 1980–82; Supply Officer, HMS Illustrious, 1982–83; Fleet Legal and Admin. Officer, 1984–86; Sec. to Chief of Fleet Support, 1986–88; Dep. Comd Sec. to C-in-C Fleet, 1988–90; Sec. to First Sea Lord, 1990–92; Dir, Defence Personnel, 1992–95; Dir Gen., Naval Personnel Strategy and Plans, COS to Second Sea Lord and C-in-C Naval Home Comd, 1995–98. *Recreations:* horse racing, soccer, country and folk music. *Address:* Langham House, Langham, Norfolk NR25 7BX. *Club:* Victory Services.
*See also* Sir D. B. Lees.

**LEES, Sir Thomas Harcourt Ivor,** 8th Bt *cr* 1804 (UK), of Black Rock, County Dublin; *b* 6 Nov. 1941; *s* of Sir Charles Archibald Edward Ivor Lees, 7th Bt, and Lily, *d* of Arthur Williams, Manchester; *S* father, 1963. *Heir:* (presumptive) kinsman Trevor John Cathcart d'Olier-Lees [*b* 7 Jan. 1961; *m* 1990, Susan Ciambriello; two *d*].

**LEES, Sir (William) Antony Clare,** 3rd Bt *cr* 1937; *b* 14 June 1935; *s* of Sir (William) Hereward Clare Lees, 2nd Bt, and of Lady (Dorothy Gertrude) Lees, *d* of F. A. Lauder; *S* father, 1976; *m* 1986, Joanna Olive Crane. *Educ:* Eton; Magdalene Coll., Cambridge (MA). *Heir:* none.

**LEESE, Sir Richard Charles,** Kt 2006; CBE 2001; Member (Lab), since 1984, and Leader, since 1996, Manchester City Council; *b* 21 April 1951; *s* of Samuel and Hilda Leese; *m* 1st, 1982, Michal Evans (marr. diss. 2000); one *s* one *d*; 2nd, 2003, Joanne Green (marr. diss. 2013). *Educ:* Warwick Univ. (BSc Maths). Teacher of Maths, Sidney Stringer Sch. and Community Coll., Coventry, 1974–78, with one year at Washington Jun. High School, Duluth, Minn; youth worker, 1979–82; researcher, 1983–84; community worker, 1984–88. Manchester City Council: Chair: Educn Cttee, 1986–90; Finance Cttee, 1990–95; Dep. Leader, 1990–96. *Recreations:* running, football (Manchester City), cricket, political campaigning, the Labour Party, travel, friends, family, music. *Address:* Manchester City Council, Town Hall, Albert Square, Manchester M60 2LA. *T:* (0161) 234 3004.

**LEESE, Dr Robert Anthony;** Chief Technical Officer, Smith Institute for Industrial Mathematics and System Engineering, Guildford, since 2017 (Director, then Chief Executive, 1999–2017); Fellow, St Catherine's College, Oxford, since 1993; *b* Warrington, 3 July 1965; *s* of John Malcolm and Alison Marjorie Leese; *m* 1991, Kathleen Erin Patrick; two *s* two *d*. *Educ:* Manchester Grammar Sch.; St John's Coll., Cambridge (BA 1986; Cert. Advanced Study 1987; MA 1990; MMath 2011); Durham Univ. (PhD 1990). Jun. Res. Fellow, St John's Coll., Cambridge, 1990–93. Vis. researcher, Brown Univ., 1990–91. FIMA 2003. President's Medal, ORS, 2018. *Publications:* (ed jtly) Methods and Algorithms for Radio Channel Assignment, 2002; contrib. articles on maths and physics to learned jls. *Recreations:* family, fell-walking, swimming, fountain pens. *Address:* St Catherine's College, Oxford OX1 3UJ. *T:* (01865) 271700. *E:* robert.leese@smithinst.co.uk.

**LEESON, Sir Kevin (James),** KCB 2012; CBE 2003; FREng; CEng, FIET; aerospace consultant, since 2012; Director, Military Affairs, Airbus UK, since 2016; Senior Advisor: Newton Europe Ltd, since 2017; Airtanker, since 2019; MCF Corporate Finance, since 2019; *b* 11 June 1956; *s* of Albert V. Leeson and Joan Leeson (*née* Teale). *Educ:* Univ. of Manchester Inst. of Sci. and Technol. (BSc). CEng 1983; FIET (FIEE 1997); FREng 2012. MoD PE, 1988–93; OC Engrg and Supply Wing, RAF Marham, 1994–96; Gp Capt. Logistics 3, HQ Strike Comd, 1996–99; rcds 1999; Dir, Air Resources and Plans, MoD, 2000–04; ACDS (Logistics Ops), 2005–07; ACDS (Resources and Plans), 2007–09; Chief of Materiel (Air), Defence Equipment and Support and RAF Chief Engr, 2009–12; retired in rank of Air Marshal, 2012. Sen. Advr, Atkins Defence and Aerospace 2013–19. Mem., Main Bd, Safety Rev. Cttee, British Airways, 2013–16. Vice Pres., Royal Internat. Air Tattoo, 2005–11. Mem. Council, IET, 2011–13. Pres., Combined Services Winter Sports Assoc., 2006–12 (Vice Patron, 2012–17); Chm., RAF Charitable Trust, 2013– (Vice Patron, 2011–13). Liveryman, Coachmakers' and Coach Harness Makers' Co., 2016. *Recreation:* snow ski-ing. *Club:* Royal Air Force.

**LE FANU, Mark,** OBE 1994; General Secretary, The Society of Authors, 1982–2011; *b* 14 Nov. 1946; *s* of Admiral of the Fleet Sir Michael Le Fanu, GCB, DSC and Prudence, *d* of Admiral Sir Vaughan Morgan, KBE, CB, MVO, DSC; *m* 1976, Lucy Cowen; three *s* one *d*. *Educ:* Winchester; Univ. of Sussex. Admitted Solicitor, 1976. Served RN, 1964–73; McKenna & Co., 1973–78; The Society of Authors, 1979–2011. Vice Chm., British Copyright Council, 1992–98. Chm., W11 Opera, 1997–2000. Trustee: Royal Literary Fund, 2011–; Authors' Foundn, 2011–; Harrison Housing, 2012–18. *Recreations:* sailing, singing. *Address:* 27 Sterndale Road, W14 0HT. *T:* (020) 7603 4119. *E:* marklefanu@gmail.com. *Club:* Chelsea Arts.

**LeFANU, Prof. Nicola Frances;** composer; Professor of Music, University of York, 1994–2008, now Emeritus (Head of Department of Music, 1994–2001); *b* 28 April 1947; *d* of late William Richard LeFanu and Dame Elizabeth Violet Maconchy, DBE; *m* 1979, David Newton Lumsdaine; one *s*. *Educ:* St Mary's Sch., Calne; St Hilda's Coll., Oxford (BA Hons 1968, MA 1972; Hon. Fellow, 1993); Royal Coll. of Music; DMus London, 1988. Cobbett Prize for chamber music, 1968; BBC Composers' Competition, 1st Prize, 1971; Mendelssohn Scholarship, 1972; Harkness Fellowship for composition study, Harvard, 1973–74. Dir of Music, St Paul's Girls' Sch., 1975–77; Composer in Residence (jtly with David Lumsdaine), NSW Conservatorium of Music, Sydney, 1979; Sen Lectr in Music, 1977–93, Prof. of Musical Composition, KCL, 1993–94. Deleg. to Moscow Internat. New Music Festival, 1984. Leverhulme Res. Award, 1989; Royal Philharmonic Soc. Elgar Bursary, 2014. FRCM 1995. FTCL 2002. Hon. DMus Durham, 1995; DUniv: Open, 2004; Aberdeen, 2006. *Publications:* numerous compositions, incl. opera, orchestral works, chamber music with and without voice, choral music and solo pieces; *major works include:* The Same Day Dawns (for soprano and ensemble), 1974; Columbia Falls (for symphony orch.), 1975; Dawnpath (chamber opera), 1977; The Old Woman of Beare (for soprano and ensemble), 1981; The Story of Mary O'Neill (radio opera), 1986; The Green Children (children's opera), 1990; Blood Wedding (opera), 1992; The Wildman (opera), 1995; Duo Concertante (for violin, viola and orch.), 1999; Amores (for solo horn and strings), 2004; Light Passing (chamber opera), 2004; Dream Hunter (chamber opera), 2010; String Quartet No 3, 2011; Harlequin Memories (quintet), 2012; Tokaido Road, a Journey after Hiroshige (chamber opera), 2014; Threnody (for orch.), 2015; The Crimson Bird (for soprano and orch.), 2017. *Recreations:* natural history, and therefore conservation; peace movement, women's movement. *Address:* 5 Holly Terrace, York YO10 4DS. *T:* (01904) 651759. *W:* www.nicolalefanu.com. *Club:* Athenæum.

**LEFF, Prof. Gordon;** Professor of History, University of York, 1969–88, now Emeritus; *b* 9 May 1926; *m* 1953, Rosemary Kathleen (*née* Fox) (marr. diss 1980); one *s*. *Educ:* Summerhill Sch.; King's Coll., Cambridge. BA 1st Cl. Hons, PhD, LittD. Fellow, King's Coll., Cambridge, 1955–59; Asst Lectr, Lectr, Sen. Lectr, in History, Manchester Univ., 1956–65; Reader in History, Univ. of York, 1965–69. Carlyle Vis. Lectr, Univ. of Oxford, 1983. *Publications:* Bradwardine and the Pelagians, 1957; Medieval Thought, 1958; Gregory of Rimini, 1961; The Tyranny of Concepts, 1961; Richard Fitzralph, 1963; Heresy in the Later Middle Ages, 2 vols, 1967; Paris and Oxford Universities in 13th and 14th Centuries, 1968; History and Social Theory, 1969; William of Ockham: the metamorphosis of scholastic discourse, 1975; The Dissolution of the Medieval Outlook, 1976; Heresy, Philosophy and Religion in the Medieval West, 2002; Plato: the supremacy of reason, 2012; St Augustine: fallen man, 2012; Man and the Universe: from Plotinus to Cusa, 2012; The Medieval Concept of Man: twelfth to fourteenth centuries and the end of the Middle Ages, 2012. *Recreations:* walking, gardening, watching cricket, listening to music. *Address:* The Sycamores, 12 The Village, Strensall, York YO32 5XS. *T:* (01904) 490358.

**LEFF, Prof. Julian Paul,** MD; FRCPsych; Director, Team for Assessment of Psychiatric Services, 1985–2005; *b* 4 July 1938; *s* of Samuel Leff and Vera Miriam (*née* Levy); *m* 1975, Joan Lilian Raphael; three *s* one *d*. *Educ:* University Coll. London (BSc, MB BS); MD London 1972. FRCPsych 1979, Hon. FRCPsych 2015; MRCP. House Officer: University Coll. Hosp., 1961–62; Whittington Hosp., 1962–63; career scientist, MRC, 1972–2002; Prof. of Social and Cultural Psychiatry, Inst. of Psychiatry, Univ. of London, 1987–2002, now Emeritus; Dir, MRC Social and Community Psychiatry Unit, 1989–95. Hon. Prof., Univ. of Cape Town, 2009–. Inventor of Avatar Therapy for people who hear voices, 2010. FMedSci 2000. Starkey Prize, Royal Coll. of Health, 1976; Burghölzli Award, Univ. of Zürich, 1999; Marsh Award for Mental Health Work, Marsh Christian Trust, 2010; Pelicier Lifetime Achievement Award, World Assoc. of Social Psychiatry, 2017. *Publications:* Psychiatric Examination in Clinical Practice, 1978, 3rd edn 1990; Expressed Emotion in Families, 1985; Psychiatry around the Globe, 1981, 2nd edn 1988; Family Work for Schizophrenia, 1992, 2nd edn 2002; Principles of Social Psychiatry, 1993; Care in the Community: illusion or reality?, 1997; The Unbalanced Mind, 2001, 2nd edn 2012; Advanced Family Work for Schizophrenia, 2005; Social Inclusion of People with Mental Illness, 2006. *Recreations:* piano, swimming, silversmithing.

**LEFKOWITZ, Prof. Robert Joseph,** MD; James B. Duke Professor of Medicine and of Biochemistry, Duke University Medical Center, since 1982; Investigator, Howard Hughes Medical Institute, since 1976; *b* New York, 15 April 1943; *s* of Max and Rose Lefkowitz; *m* 1963, Arna Gornstein; three *s* two *d*; *m* 1991, Lynn Tilley. *Educ:* Bronx High Sch. of Science; Columbia Univ. (BA 1962; MD 1966). Hse staff trng in internal medicine, Columbia Presbyterian Med. Center, 1966–68; Clin. and Res. Associate, NIH, Bethesda, Maryland, 1968–70; Sen. Resident and Cardiol. Fellow, Massachusetts Gen. Hosp., Boston, 1970–73; Associate Prof. of Medicine, and Asst Prof. of Biochem., 1973–77, Prof. of Medicine, 1977–82, Duke Univ. Estabd Investigator, Amer. Heart Assoc., 1973–76. Nine hon. degrees. Gairdner Foundn Internat. Award, 1988; Bristol-Myers Squibb Award for Dist. Achievement in Cardiovascular Res., 1992; Fred Conrad Koch Award, Endocrine Soc., 2001; Jessie Stevenson Kovalenko Medal, NAS, USA, 2001; Grand Prix for Sci., Inst. de France, Fondn Lefoulon-Delalande, 2003; Nat. Medal of Sci., USA, 2007; Shaw Prize in Life Sci. and Medicine, 2007; Albany Med. Center Prize in Medicine and Biomed. Res., 2007; Res. Achievement Award, Amer. Heart Assoc., 2009; BBVA Foundn Frontiers of Knowledge Award, 2010; (jtly) Nobel Prize in Chemistry, 2012. *Publications:* contrib. papers to Jl Biol Chem., Proc. NAS, Molecular Pharmacol., Nature, Science. *Address:* Duke University Medical Center, PO Box 3821, Durham, NC 27710, USA.

**le FLEMING, Sir David (Kelland),** 13th Bt *cr* 1705, of Rydal, Westmorland; freelance designer-artist; *b* 12 Jan. 1976; *s* of Sir Quentin John le Fleming, 12th Bt and of Judith Ann le Fleming (*née* Peck); *S* father, 1995. *Educ:* Queen Elizabeth Coll., Palmerston North; Wairarapa Polytech. Coll.; Wellington Polytech. Coll. (BA Visual Communications Design 1997). *Heir: b* Andrew John le Fleming, *b* 4 Oct. 1979. *Address:* 250 Colyton Road, RD5, Feilding, Manawatu, New Zealand. *T:* (6) 3287719.

**le FLEMING, Morris John;** DL; Chief Executive, Hertfordshire County Council, and Clerk to the Lieutenancy, Hertfordshire, 1979–90; *b* 19 Aug. 1932; *s* of late Morris Ralph le Fleming and Mabel le Fleming; *m* 1960, Jenny Rose Weeks (*d* 2013); one *s* three *d*. *Educ:* Tonbridge Sch.; Magdalene Coll., Cambridge (BA). Admitted Solicitor, 1958. Junior Solicitor, Worcester CC, 1958–59; Asst Solicitor: Middlesex CC, 1959; Nottinghamshire CC, 1959–63; Asst Clerk, Lindsey (Lincolnshire) CC, 1963–69; Hertfordshire CC: Second Dep. Clerk, 1969–74; County Secretary, 1974–79; Clerk, Magistrates' Courts Cttee, 1979–90; Sec., Probation Care Cttee, 1979–90. Dir, Herts TEC, 1989–90. Chm., Stansted Airport Consultative Cttee, 1991–2007; Mem., N Wales Child Abuse Tribunal of Enquiry, 1996–99. Dir, Herts Groundwork Trust, 1990–98; Trustee, Herts Community Trust, 1991–96. Pres., Herts Scouts, 1997–2002 (Chm., 1991–97). DL Herts, 1991. Hon. LLD Hertfordshire, 1994. *Address:* Holt, Wilts BA14 6TB. *T:* and *Fax:* (01225) 783514. *Club:* Royal Over-Seas League.

**LEFROY, Jeremy John Elton;** MP (C) Stafford, since 2010; *b* London, 30 May 1959; *s* of Rev. Christopher John Elton Lefroy and Sarah Ursula Lefroy (*née* Blacking); *m* 1985, Dr Janet Elizabeth MacKay; one *s* one *d*. *Educ:* Highgate Sch.; King's Coll., Cambridge (BA 1980; MA 1984). ACA 1985. Gen. Manager, 1989–91, Man. Dir, 1991–2000, African Coffee Co. Ltd, Moshi, Tanzania; Dir, African Speciality Products Ltd, Keele, 2000–. Dir, Tanzania Coffee Bd, 1997–99. Mem. (C) Newcastle-under-Lyme BC, 2003–07. Member: Internat. Develt Cttee, 2010–17; Cttee on Exiting the EU, 2016–. Trustee, Liverpool Sch. of Tropical Medicine, 2016–. *Recreations:* music (playing, singing, listening), walking, cricket, tennis, badminton. *Address:* House of Commons, SW1A 0AA. *T:* (020) 7219 7154. *E:* jeremy.lefroy.mp@parliament.uk.

**LEFROY, Timothy Patterson,** OBE 2017; Chairman, Leonardo Advisory, since 2018; *b* Bristol, 3 March 1948; *s* of C. B. H., (Ben), Lefroy and Leonora Lefroy (*née* Vicary); *m* 1978, Susan Russell-Jones; three *d*. *Educ:* All Saints Clifton; Colston's Sch. Marketing: Cadbury, 1966–77; Gillette (Paper:Mate), 1977–78; Dir, McCann Erickson, 1978–85; Dep. Chm., Young & Rubicam, 1985–88; CEO, Yellowhammer, 1988–90; CEO, Young & Rubicam, 1990–91; Chm. and CEO, Alliance Advertising, 1991–94; Founder, Radical, 1994–2009; CEO Advertising Assoc., 2009–16. Mem., Pensions Reform Gp, 2005–. Director: Assoc. for Television on Demand, 2006–10; Advertising Standards Bd of Finance, 2009–16; Broadcast Advertising Standards Bd of Finance, 2009–16; Cttee of Advertising Practice, 2009–16; Broadcast Cttee of Advertising Practice, 2009–16. Trustee, Riverside Studios, 2013–. *Recreations:* ski-ing, sailing, golf, opera. *T:* 07836 294631. *E:* tim@thelefroys.co.uk, Tim.Lefroy@Leonardo-Advisory.com. *Clubs:* Ivy, Roehampton, Marketing Group of GB, Solus, Thirty Club of London (Sec., 2009–12).

**LEGARD, Sir Charles Thomas,** 15th Bt *cr* 1660; *S* father, 1984. *Heir: s* Christopher John Charles Legard [*b* 19 April 1964; *m* 1986, Miranda, *d* of Maj. Fane Gaffney; one *s* one *d*].

**LÉGER, Most Rev. Ernest Raymond;** Archbishop of Moncton, (RC), 1996–2002, now Emeritus; *b* 27 Feb. 1944; *s* of Sifroid Léger and Imelda Johnson. *Educ:* Univ. du Sacré Coeur, Bathurst, NB (BA); Univ. de Moncton (BEd); Univ. Laval, Quebec (MTh); Univ. St Paul, Ottawa (LCL). Ordained, 1968; Parish priest, 1968–96: Moncton, 1968–70, 1972–73; St Louis de Kent, 1970–72, 1974–75; St Charles de Kent, 1975–80; Rogersville, 1980–83; Irishtown, 1985–87; St Paul de Kent, 1988–92, 1995–96; Sackville and Dorchester, 1993–95; Judicial Vicar of Marriage Tribunal, Halifax Region, 1985–96; Vicar General, 1992–94, Administrator, 1995–96, Archdio. of Moncton. *Address: c/o* Paroisse Saint-Paul, 460 rue Main, CP 160, Plantagenet, ON K0B 1L0, Canada.

**LEGG, Barry Charles,** FCCA; investor and company director; *b* 30 May 1949; *s* of Henry and Elfreda Legg; *m* 1974, Margaret Rose; one *s* two *d*. *Educ:* Sir Thomas Rich's Grammar Sch., Gloucester; Manchester Univ. (BA Hons Hist.). ATII. Courtaulds Ltd, 1971–76; Coopers & Lybrand, 1976–78; Hillsdown Holdings plc, 1978–92. MP (C) Milton Keynes South West, 1992–97; contested (C) same seat, 1997. Member: Treasury and Civil Service Select Cttee, 1992–96; Treasury Select Cttee, 1996–97 (Chm.). Chief Exec., Conservative Party, 2003. Chm., Bruges Gp, 2010– (Co-Chm., 2005–10). *Publications:* Maintaining Momentum: a radical tax agenda for the 1990s, 1992; Who Benefits?—Reinventing Social Security, 1993; Civil Service Reform, a Case for More Radicalism, 1994. *Recreation:* watching cricket. *Club:* Gloucestershire CC.

**LEGG, Prof. Brian James,** FRSB; FREng; Director, NIAB (formerly National Institute of Agricultural Botany), 1999–2005; *b* 20 July 1945; *s* of Walter and Mary Legg; *m* 1972, Philippa Whitehead; one *s* one *d*. *Educ:* Balliol Coll., Oxford (BA Physics 1966); Imperial Coll. London (PhD 1972). FRSB (FIBiol 1994); FREng (FEng 1994). Voluntary Service Overseas, The Gambia, 1966–67; Res. Scientist, Rothamsted Exptl Station, 1967–83; Head, Res. Divs, Silsoe Res. Inst., 1983–90; Dir, Silsoe Res. Inst., BBSRC (formerly AFRC), 1990–99. Vis. Scientist, CSIRO Div. of Envmtl Mechanics, Canberra, 1980–82; Vis. Prof., Silsoe Coll., Cranfield Univ. (formerly Inst. of Technology), 1990–2005. *Publications:* Heartwood Arboretum: a living guide to all the trees and shrubs native to the British Isles, 2017; contribs to learned jls. *Recreations:* supporting African farmers through 'Send a Cow', volunteering for Woodland Trust, sailing, playing bassoon, golf.

**LEGG, Cyrus Julian Edmund;** Blue Arrow Personnel Services, 1997–2001; *b* 5 Sept. 1946; *s* of Cyrus and Eileen Legg; *m* 1967, Maureen Jean (*née* Lodge); two *s*. *Educ:* Tiffin School. Agricultural and Food Research Council, 1967–83; HM Treasury, 1983–87; Sec., BM (Natural Hist.) subseq. Natural History Mus., 1987–97. *Recreation:* gardening. *Address:* 34 Colchester Way, Bedford MK41 8BG. *T:* (01234) 364198.

**LEGG, Sir Thomas (Stuart),** KCB 1993 (CB 1985); QC 1990; Permanent Secretary, Lord Chancellor's Department, and Clerk of the Crown in Chancery, 1989–98; *b* 13 Aug. 1935; *e s* of late Stuart Legg and Margaret Legg (*née* Amos); *m* 2009, Mrs Margaret Wakelin-Saint (*d* 2013); two *d* by a previous marriage. *Educ:* Horace Mann-Lincoln Sch., New York; Frensham Heights Sch., Surrey; St John's Coll., Cambridge (MA, LLM). 2nd Lieut, Royal Marines (45 Commando), 1953–55. Called to the Bar, Inner Temple, 1960, Bencher, 1984; joined Lord Chancellor's Dept, 1962; Private Secretary to Lord Chancellor, 1965–68; Asst Solicitor, 1975; Under Sec., 1977–82; SE Circuit Administrator, 1980–82; Dep. Sec., 1982–89; Dep. Clerk of the Crown in Chancery, 1986–89; Sec. of Commns, 1989–98. Conducted Sierra Leone Arms Investigation, 1998. Consultant, Clifford Chance, 1998–2010. Ext. Mem., Audit Cttee, H of C, 2000–09; Mem., Audit Commn, 2005–11. Conducted Additional Costs Allowance Rev. of MPs' Expenses, 2009–10. Chm., Hammersmith Hosps NHS Trust, 2000–07; Dir, Imperial Coll. Healthcare Trust, 2007–14. Trustee, Civil Service Benevolent Fund, 1998–2000 (Chm., 1993–98). Chm., London Library, 2004–09 (Trustee, 2001–09). Visitor, Brunel Univ., 2001–06 (Mem. Council, 1993–2000). Hon. FRCP 2010; FRSocMed 2014. Hon. LLD Brunel, 2006. *Address:* Flat 54 Greenhill, Prince Arthur Road, Hampstead, NW3 5UA. *Club:* Garrick.

**LEGGATT, Rt Hon. Sir Andrew (Peter),** Kt 1982; PC 1990; Chief Surveillance Commissioner, 1998–2006; a Lord Justice of Appeal, 1990–97; *b* 8 Nov. 1930; *er s* of late Captain William Ronald Christopher Leggatt, DSO, RN and Dorothea Joy Leggatt (*née* Dreyer); *m* 1953, Gillian Barbara Newton; one *s* one *d*. *Educ:* Eton; King's Coll., Cambridge (Exhibnr). MA 1957. Commn in Rifle Bde, 1949–50; TA, 1950–59. Called to the Bar, Inner Temple, 1954, Bencher, 1976. QC 1972; a Recorder of the Crown Court, 1974–82; Judge, High Court of Justice, QBD, 1982–90. Mem., Top Salaries Review Body, 1979–82; conducted review, Tribunals for Users, 2000–01; Chm. Appeals Cttee, Takeover Panel, 2001–06. Mem., Judges' Council, 1988–97. Pres., Council of Inns of Court, 1995–97; Member: Bar Council, 1971–82; Senate, 1974–83; Chm. of the Bar, 1981–82. Hon. Member: American Bar Assoc.; Canadian Bar Assoc.; non-resident mem., American Law Inst.; Hon. Fellow, Amer. Coll. of Trial Lawyers, 1996. *Recreations:* listening to music, personal computers. *Club:* MCC.
See also Rt Hon. Sir G. A. M. Leggatt.

**LEGGATT, Rt Hon. Sir George Andrew Midsomer,** Kt 2012; PC 2018; **Rt Hon. Lord Justice Leggatt;** a Lord Justice of Appeal, 2018–April 2020; a Justice of the Supreme Court of the United Kingdom, from April 2020; *b* 12 Nov. 1957; *s* of Rt Hon. Sir Andrew Peter Leggatt, *qv* and Gillian Barbara Leggatt (*née* Newton); *m* 1987, Dr Stavia Brigitte Blunt; one *s* one *d*. *Educ:* Eton (King's Schol.); King's Coll., Cambridge (MA); Harvard (Harkness Fellow); City Univ. (Dip. Law). Bigelow Teaching Fellow, Univ. of Chicago Law Sch., 1982–83; called to the Bar, Middle Temple, 1983, Bencher, 2004; Associate, Sullivan & Cromwell, New York, 1983–84; QC 1997; a Recorder, 2002–12; a Dep. High Court Judge, 2008–12; a Judge of the High Court of Justice, QBD, 2012–18. Sec., Commercial Bar Assoc., 2004–07. Vice-Chm., Bar Standards Bd, 2006–08. *Recreations:* visiting Greece, cooking, wine, philosophy. *Address:* (until April 2020) Royal Courts of Justice, Strand, WC2A 2LL; (from April 2020) Supreme Court of the United Kingdom, Parliament Square, SW1P 3BD.

**LEGGE,** family name of **Earl of Dartmouth**.

**LEGGE, Anthony;** international opera coach and conductor; Sir Arthur Sullivan Professor of Opera, Royal Academy of Music, since 2009; *b* 12 March 1948; *s* of Harry and Nancy, (Judy), Legge; *m* 1980, Christine Elizabeth Anderson Tyrer; one *d*. *Educ:* Dean Close Sch., Cheltenham; Queen's Coll., Oxford (MA). Member, Music Staff: London Opera Centre, 1971–72; Scottish Opera, 1972–77; Visiting Guest Coach: Australian Opera, 1978–88; Bayreuth, 1988–93; Nederlandsche Oper, 1995–; Hd of Music, ENO, 1989–2003; Dir of Opera, RAM, 2003–08; Music Dir, Clonter Opera, 2004–09; Music Advr, Grange Park Opera, 2006–10; Associate Music Dir, Opera Australia, 2009–17. Chm., The Rehearsal Orch., 2004–09. Reader for the Queen's Anniversary Prize, 1999–. Judge, Operatunity, Channel 4, 2003. Has made numerous recordings. Hon. RAM 2007. *Publications:* The Art of Auditioning, 1988, 2nd edn 1993, updated and re-issued 2017; The Singer's Handbook, 2007. *Recreation:* walking the dog. *Club:* Garrick.

**LEGGE, Cressida Mary;** *see* Hogg, C. M.

**LEGGE, Hon. Henry;** QC 2012; *b* London, 28 Dec. 1968; *y s* of 9th Earl of Dartmouth and Countess of Dartmouth (later Raine, Countess Spencer); *m* 1995, Cressida Mary Hogg, *qv*; three *d*. *Educ:* Eton Coll.; Worcester Coll., Oxford (BA); City Univ. (Dip. Law). Called to the Bar, Middle Temple, 1993; in practice as a barrister, specialising in trusts, pensions and art law, 1993–. *Publications:* (contrib.) Subrogation, 2007; (contrib.) Company Directors, 2009. *Recreations:* riding, fencing, fishing. *Address:* 5 Stone Buildings, Lincoln's Inn, WC2A 3XT. *T:* (020) 7242 6201.

**LEGGE, (John) Michael,** CB 2001; CMG 1994; Chairman, Civil Service Healthcare, 2001–11; *b* 14 March 1944; *s* of late Alfred John Legge and Marion Frances Legge (*née* James); *m* 1971, Linda (*née* Bagley); two *s*. *Educ:* Royal Grammar Sch., Guildford; Christ Church Oxford (BA, MA). Ministry of Defence: Asst Principal, 1966; Asst Private Sec. to Sec. of State for Defence, 1970; Principal, 1971; 1st Sec., UK Delegn to NATO, 1974–77; Asst Sec., MoD, 1979–87; Rand Corp., Santa Monica, California, 1982; Asst Under Sec. of State (Policy), MoD, 1987–88; Asst Sec. Gen. for Defence Planning and Policy, NATO, 1988–93; Deputy Under-Secretary of State: NI Office, 1993–96; MoD, 1996–2001. Sec. and Dir of Admin, Royal Hosp. Chelsea, 2001–07. *Publications:* Theatre Nuclear Weapons and the NATO Strategy of Flexible Response, 1983. *Recreations:* golf, gardening, travel. *Address:* 53 St Mary's Road, Leatherhead, Surrey KT22 8HB.

**LEGGE-BOURKE, Hon. Dame (Elizabeth) Shân (Josephine),** DCVO 2015 (LVO 1988); Lord-Lieutenant of Powys, 1998–2018; *b* 10 Sept. 1943; *o c* of 3rd Baron Glanusk, DSO and Margaret (*née* Shoubridge, later Dowager Viscountess De L'Isle); *m* 1964, William Legge-Bourke, DL (*d* 2009); one *s* two *d*. Lady-in-waiting to HRH Princess Anne, now HRH Princess Royal, 1978–. President: Royal Welsh Agricl Soc., 1997; Nat. Fedn of Young Farmers Clubs of England and Wales, 1998–2000; Save the Children Fund (Wales), 1989–2017. High Sheriff of Powys, 1991–92. *Address:* Gliffaes-Fach, Crickhowell, Powys NP8 1RL.

**LEGGETT, Sir Anthony (James),** KBE 2004; DPhil; FRS 1980; John D. and Catherine T. MacArthur Professor of Physics, and Center for Advanced Study Professor of Physics, University of Illinois, since 1983; Mike and Ophelia Lazaridis Distinguished Research Professor, Institute for Quantum Computing, University of Waterloo, since 2007; *b* 26 March 1938. *Educ:* Balliol Coll., Oxford (BA 1959; Hon. Fellow 1994); Merton Coll., Oxford (BA 1961; Hon. Fellow 2004); Magdalen Coll., Oxford (DPhil 1964). Res.

Associate, Univ. of Illinois, 1964–65; Fellow, Magdalen Coll., Oxford, 1963–67; Lectr, 1967–71, Reader, 1971–78, Prof. of Physics, 1978–83, Univ. of Sussex. Hon. FInstP 1999. (Jtly) Nobel Prize for Physics, 2003. *Publications:* The Problems of Physics, 1987; (jtly) Quantum Tunnelling in Condensed Media, 1992; (jtly) Quantum Computing and Quantum Bits in Mesoscopic Systems, 2003; articles in learned jls. *Address:* Department of Physics, University of Illinois at Urbana-Champaign, 1110 West Green Street, Urbana, IL 61801–3080, USA; 607 West Pennsylvania Avenue, Urbana, IL 61801–4818, USA.

**LEGGETT, Dr Jeremy Kendal;** Founder and Chairman, Solarcentury, 1997–2015; Founder and Chairman, SolarAid, since 2006; Chairman, Carbon Tracker Initiative, 2011–17; *b* 16 March 1954; *s* of Dennis and Audrey Leggett; *m* 1st (marr. diss.); one *d*; 2nd (marr. diss); 3rd, Aki Maruyama. *Educ:* Univ. of Wales, Aberystwyth (BSc Hons 1975); Wolfson Coll., Oxford (DPhil (Earth Scis) 1978). Lectr in Earth Scis, 1978–87, Reader, 1987–89, Royal Sch. of Mines, ICSTM; Founder and Dir, Verification Technol. Inf. Centre (VERTIC), 1985–89; Scientific Dir, Climate Campaign, Greenpeace Internat., 1989–96. Vis. Fellow, Centre for Envmtl Policy and Understanding, Oxford Univ., 1996. Blog columnist, Guardian website, 2007–. Award for advancing understanding, US Climate Inst., 1996; Sustainable Leadership Award, Sustainable Asset Mgt, 2006; CNN Principal Voice, 2007; Entrepreneur of Year Award, New Energy Awards, 2009; Hillary Laureate, Hillary Inst. for Internat. Leadership, NZ, 2009; Gothenburg Award, City of Gothenburg, 2015. *Publications:* Global Warming: the Greenpeace report, 1990 (ed and contrib.); The Carbon War, 1999; Half Gone, 2005; The Solar Century, 2009; The Energy of Nations: risk blindness and the road to renaissance, 2013; The Winning of the Carbon War, 2016. *Recreations:* salsa dancing, golf. *Address:* Solarcentury, 90 Union Street, SE1 0NW. *E:* jeremy.leggett@solarcentury.com. *W:* www.jeremyleggett.net.

**LEGH;** see Cornwall-Legh, family name of Baron Grey of Codnor.

**LEGH,** family name of **Baron Newton.**

**LEGH-JONES, (Piers) Nicholas;** QC 1987; *b* 2 Feb. 1943; *s* of late John Herbert Legh-Jones and Elizabeth Anne (*née* Halford). *Educ:* Winchester College; New College, Oxford (MA Hist. 1964, Jurisp. 1966). Legal Instructor, Univ. of Pennsylvania, 1966–67; Lectr in Law, New College, Oxford, 1967–71; Eldon Law Scholar, Univ. of Oxford, 1968. Called to the Bar, Lincoln's Inn, 1968; in practice as a barrister, 1969–2012. Vis. Prof., King's Coll., London, 1998–2005. *Publications:* (ed) MacGillivray and Parkington on Insurance Law, 6th edn, to 8th edn 1988; (gen. ed.) MacGillivray on Insurance Law, 9th edn 1997 to 11th edn 2008; contribs to Modern Law Review and Cambridge Law Jl. *Recreations:* vintage motorcars, modern history.

**LEGON, Prof. Anthony Charles,** PhD, DSc; FRS 2000; Professor of Physical Chemistry, 2005–08, now Emeritus, and University Senior Research Fellow, since 2008, University of Bristol; *b* 28 Sept. 1941; *s* of late George Charles Legon and Emily Louisa Florence Legon (*née* Conner); *m* 1963, Deirdre Anne Rivers; two *s* one *d*. *Educ:* Coopers' Co. Sch., London (Gibson Exhibnr); UCL (BSc 1963; PhD 1967; DSc 1981). FRSC 1978. Turner & Newall Fellow, Univ. of London, 1968–70; University College London: Lectr, 1970–83, Reader, 1983–84, in Chemistry; Thomas Graham Prof. of Chemistry, 1989–90; Prof. of Physical Chemistry, 1984–89 and 1990–2005, and EPSRC Sen. Fellow, 1997–2002, Univ. of Exeter. Vis. Res. Associate Prof., Univ. of Illinois, 1980; Visiting Professor: Chem. Dept, Texas A&M Univ., 2010; Univ. of Newcastle, 2013–. Leverhulme Emeritus Fellow, 2009–10. Hassel Lectr, Univ. of Oslo, 1997; Moscowitz Lectr, Dept of Chemistry, Univ. of Minnesota, 2012–13. Mem., Physical Chemistry Sub Cttee, 1984–87, NATO Postdoctoral Fellowships (Chemistry) Cttee, 1987, 1988, 1991–93, Advanced Fellowships (Chemistry) Cttee, 1991–92 (Chm., 1991), SERC; Royal Society of Chemistry: Chairman: Peninsula Section, 1988–89, 2002–03; High Resolution Spectroscopy Gp, 1998–2000; Tilden Lectr and Medallist, 1990; Mem. Council, 1996–99, Vice-Pres., 2001–04, Faraday Div.; Associate Ed., Chem. Communications, 1996–98; Spectroscopy Award, 1999; Liversidge Award, 2012. Springer Award for Outstanding Achievements in Halogen Bonding, Springer-Verlag, 2009. Member Editorial Board: Chemical Physics Letters, 1988–2008; Spectrochimica Acta, 1989–97; Jl of Molecular Structure, 1990–2005; Jl Chem. Soc. Faraday Trans, 1994–98. *Publications:* Principles of Molecular Recognition, 1993; numerous res. papers in learned jls. *Recreations:* watching soccer, reading. *Address:* School of Chemistry, University of Bristol, Bristol BS8 1TS. *E:* a.c.legon@bristol.ac.uk.

**LEGRAND, Janet, (Mrs Neil Tidmarsh);** Consultant, DLA Piper International LLP, since 2019 (Chair of Board and Senior Partner, 2008–12; Senior Elected Board Member, 2012–19; Senior Partner and Global Co-Chair, 2017–18); *b* London, 2 Oct. 1958; *d* of Charles and Gladys Legrand; *m* 1989, Neil Tidmarsh; two *d*. *Educ:* Green Sch. for Girls; Trinity Hall, Cambridge (BA Law 1980; MA 1983); Coll. of Law. Trainee and Solicitor, Lovell, White & King, 1981–91; admitted Solicitor, 1983; Partner: Alsop Wilkinson, 1991–96; Dibb Lupton Alsop, 1996–99; DLA Piper International LLP: Mem. Bd, 1999–2019; Chm., Remuneration Cttee, 1999–2009; Hd, Specialist Litigation, 2008–09. Mem., Adv. Bd, New Perimeter (DLA Piper's internat. pro bono affiliate), 2009–19. Chm., Western Riverside Envmtl Fund, 1999–2016; Mem., Develt Bd, Trinity Hall, Cambridge, 2005–10; a Comr, Marshall Aid Commemoration Commn, 2013– (Dep. Chair, 2016–). Director and Trustee: PRIME, 2012–19; Leadership Foundn for Higher Educn, 2013–18. Chair, Children's Soc., 2016– (Vice Chm., Trustee Bd, 2013–16). Mem., Audit Cttee, Univ. of Cambridge, 2013–; Mem., 2015–18, Dep. Chair, 2018–, Council, City, Univ. of London (formerly City Univ.); Adv. Panel, INTOUniversity, 2019–. Freeman, City of London, 2011. Hon. QC 2018. *Recreations:* family, walking, reading, cinema. *Address:* DLA Piper UK LLP, 3 Noble Street, EC2V 7EE. *T:* (020) 7796 6827. *E:* janet.legrand@dlapiper.com.

**LE GRAND, Sir Julian (Ernest Michael),** Kt 2015; PhD; FBA 2012; FAcSS; Professor, Marshall Institute, London School of Economics, since 2015 (Richard Titmuss Professor of Social Policy, 1993–2015; on secondment as Senior Policy Advisor to Prime Minister's Office, 2003–05); *b* 29 May 1945; *s* of late Roland John Le Grand and Eileen Joan Le Grand; *m* 1971, Damaris May Robertson-Glasgow; two *d*. *Educ:* Eton; Univ. of Sussex (BA 1967); Univ. of Pennsylvania (PhD 1972). Lectr in Econs, Univ. of Sussex, 1971–78; Lectr in Econs, 1978–85, Sen. Res. Fellow, 1985–87, LSE; Prof. of Public Policy, Univ. of Bristol, 1987–93. Mem., ESRC Bds, 1982–86 and 1988–92. Mem., Commn for Health Improvement, 1999–2003; Chairman: Social Care Practices Wkg Gp, DFES, 2006–07; Health England, DoH, 2007–10; Mutuals Taskforce, Cabinet Office, 2011–13; Panels on Doncaster's and Birmingham's Children's Services, DfE, 2013–14. Sen. Associate, 2005–07, Trustee, 2007–15, King's Fund. Non-executive Director: Avon FHSA, 1990–94; Avon HA, 1994–95; Vice-Chm., Frenchay NHS Trust, 1996–99. Gov., LSE, 1999–2003. FAcSS (Founding AcSS 1999). Hon. FPH (Hon. FPHM 1997). Hon. DLitt Sussex, 2006; DUniv Birmingham, 2018. Eupolis Prize, Eupolis Inst., Milan, 2012. *Publications:* (with R. Robinson) The Economics of Social Problems, 1976, 4th edn 2008; The Strategy of Equality, 1982; (ed with R. Robinson) Privatisation and the Welfare State, 1984; (with R. Goodin) Not Only the Poor, 1987; (ed with S. Estrin) Market Socialism, 1989; Equity and Choice, 1991; (ed with W. Bartlett) Quasi-markets and Social Policy, 1993; (with R. Robinson) Evaluating the NHS Reforms, 1994; (with B. New) Rationing in the NHS, 1996; (ed jtly) A Revolution in Social Policy, 1998; (ed jtly) Learning from the NHS Internal Market, 1998; (ed with E. Mossialos) Health Care and Cost Containment in the European Union, 1999; (ed jtly) Understanding Social Exclusion, 2002; Motivation, Agency and Public Policy: of knights and knaves, pawns and queens, 2004, 2nd edn 2006; The Other Invisible Hand, 2007; (with Bill New) Government Paternalism, 2015; contrib. articles to Econ. Jl, Jl Public Econs, Economica, Jl Social Policy, Jl Human Resources, Eur. Econ. Review, British Jl Pol Sci., Jl Health Econs, BMJ, Health Affairs, Social Sci. and Medicine, The Lancet, Jl Royal Statistical Soc., Public Admin Rev., Rev. of Behavioral Econs, Econs and Philosophy. *Recreations:* reading, drawing. *Address:* 7 Victoria Square, Bristol BS8 4EU. *T:* (0117) 973 0975, 07771 985294. *E:* J.Legrand@lse.ac.uk.

**LE GREW, Daryl John,** AO 2019; Director, Le Grew Design Pty Ltd, since 2010; Vice-Chancellor and President, University of Tasmania, 2003–10; *b* Melbourne, 17 Sept. 1945; *s* of A. J. and N. M. R. Le Grew; *m* 1971, Josephine de Tarczynska; one *s* two *d*. *Educ:* Trinity Grammar Sch., Kew; Univ. of Melbourne (BArch, MArch). University of Melbourne: Lectr, Dept of Town and Regl Planning, 1969–73; Lectr, then Sen. Lectr, Dept of Architecture and Bldg, 1973–85; Deakin University: Prof. of Architecture, 1986–98; Dean, Faculty of Design and Technol., 1992–93; Chm., Academic Bd, 1992–98; Pro-Vice-Chancellor (Academic), 1993–94; Dep. Vice-Chancellor and Vice-Pres. (Academic), 1994–98; Vice-Chancellor, Univ. of Canterbury, NZ, 1998–2002. Vice Chancellor Fellow: Monash Univ., 2011–15; Univ. of Melbourne, 2011–18 (Interim Dean, Faculty of Architecture, Bldg and Planning, 2015–16; Hon. Professorial Fellow, 2017–); Bond Univ. Council, 2017–. Sen. Consultant, Gehl Architects, Copenhagen, 2010–. Pres. of Senate, Australian Acad. of Design, 2011–; Pres., Creative Futures Ltd, 2017–. Life Fellow, Mus. of Victoria, 1997. FAIM. Hon. DLitt Tasmania, 2010; Hon. DArch Melbourne, 2019. *Recreations:* swimming, music, poetry, philosophy.

**LEHEC, Stephen Robert;** Head, Kingston Grammar School, since 2014; *b* Fulham, 17 Oct. 1970; *s* of Stephen Joseph Lehec and Valerie Frances Seaton Lehec (*née* Reid); *m* 1999, Penelope Anne Vaughn; two *d*. *Educ:* Archbishop Tenison's C of E Sch.; King Alfred's Coll., Winchester (BA Hons Hist. and English 1993); St Anne's Coll., Oxford (PGCE Hist. 1994); NPQH 2006. Maidstone GS (Boys), 1994–2006 (Asst Headteacher, 2001–06); Dep. Headmaster, 2006–08, Headmaster, 2008–14, Aylesbury GS. *Address:* Kingston Grammar School, 70 London Road, Kingston upon Thames, Surrey KT2 6PY. *Club:* Lansdowne.

**LEHMANN, Prof. Alan Robert,** PhD; FRS 2010; FMedSci; FRSB; Professor of Molecular Genetics, University of Sussex, 2001–11, Research Professor of Molecular Genetics, since 2011; *b* Rochdale, Lancs, 30 Aug. 1946; *s* of late Henry Louis Lehmann and Lore Ruth Lehmann; *m* 1967, Judith Selbourne; one *s* one *d*. *Educ:* Littleborough Central Primary Sch.; Manchester Grammar Sch. (Foundn Schol.); Pembroke Coll., Cambridge (Open Schol. Natural Scis); BA 1st Cl. Biochem. 1967). Inst. of Cancer Res., Univ. of London (PhD 1970). Postdoctoral Investigator, Oak Ridge Nat. Labs, Tenn, 1970–71; University of Sussex: Beit Meml Fellow, Dept of Biochem., 1971–73; Scientific Staff, MRC Cell Mutation Unit, 1973–2001; Professorial Fellow, 1987–2001; Chm., Genome Damage and Stability Centre, 2001–11. FMedSci 2004. *Publications:* contribs to scientific jls and books. *Recreations:* walking, travel, opera, birdwatching. *Address:* 25 Montacute Road, Lewes, E Sussex BN7 1EW.

**LEHMANN, Rt Rev. David Thomas James;** see Caledonia, Bishop of.

**LEHN, Prof. Jean-Marie,** Chevalier, Ordre des Palmes Académiques, 1989; Officier, Ordre National du Mérite, 1993 (Chevalier, 1976); Grand Officier, Légion d'Honneur, 2014 (Chevalier, 1983; Officier, 1988; Commandeur, 1996); Professor of Chemistry, Collège de France, Paris, 1979–2010, now Honorary Professor; Emeritus Professor, University of Strasbourg, since 2010; Professor, and Chair, Chemistry of Complex Systems, Institute for Advanced Study, University of Strasbourg, since 2012; *b* Rosheim, Bas-Rhin, 30 Sept. 1939; *s* of Pierre Lehn and Marie Lehn (*née* Salomon); *m* 1965, Sylvie Lederer; two *s*. *Educ:* Univ. of Strasbourg (PhD); Research Fellow, Harvard, 1964. Mem., CNRS, 1960–66; Asst Prof., Univ. of Strasbourg, 1966–69; University Louis Pasteur, Strasbourg: Associate Prof., 1970; Prof. of Chemistry, 1970–79. Visiting Professor: Harvard Univ., 1972, 1974, 1980; ETH, Zürich, 1977; Univ. of Barcelona, 1985; Alexander Todd Vis. Prof. of Chem., Univ. of Cambridge, 1984; Rolf-Sammet Vis. Prof., Univ. of Frankfurt, 1985–86; Heinrich-Hertz Vis. Prof., Univ. of Karlsruhe, 1989; Robert Burns Woodward Vis. Prof., Harvard Univ., 1997, 2000; Newton Abraham Prof., Lincoln Coll., Oxford, 1999–2000; Adjunct Prof., Asian Inst. of Technol., Bangkok, 2005; Prof.-at-Large, City Univ. of Hong Kong, 2008. Hon. Dir, Lehn Inst. of Functional Materials, Guangzhou. Mem. or Associate, and hon. degrees from professional bodies in Europe, Asia and USA; Hon. FRSC 1987; For. Mem., Royal Soc., 1993. Nobel Prize for Chemistry (jtly), 1987, and numerous awards from sci. instns. Orden pour le mérite für Wissenschaften und Künste (FRG), 1990; Österreichisches Ehrenkreuz für Wissenschaft und Kunst, 1st cl. (Austria), 2001; Grand Officer, Order of Cultural Merit (Romania), 2004; Grosses Verdienstkreuz mit Stern (Germany), 2009; Officier de l'Ordre du Mérite de la République de Pologne (Poland), 2015. *Publications:* 971 publications; chapters in books and contribs to learned jls on supramolecular chemistry, physical organic chemistry and photochemistry. *Recreation:* music. *Address:* Institut de Science d'Ingénierie Supramoléculaires, Université de Strasbourg, 8 allée Gaspard Monge, 67000 Strasbourg, France. *T:* (3) 68855145, *Fax:* (3) 68855140. *E:* lehn@unistra.fr.

**LEHRER, Thomas Andrew;** writer of songs, since 1943; *b* 9 April 1928; *s* of James Lehrer and Anna Lehrer (*née* Waller). *Educ:* Harvard Univ. (AB 1946, MA 1947); Columbia Univ.; Harvard Univ. Student (mathematics, especially probability and statistics) till 1953. Part-time teaching at Harvard, 1946–53. Theoretical physicist at Baird-Atomic, Inc., Cambridge, Massachusetts, 1953–54. Entertainer, 1953–55, 1957–60. US Army, 1955–57. Lecturer in Business Administration, Harvard Business Sch., 1961; Lecturer: in Education, Harvard Univ., 1963–66; in Psychology, Wellesley Coll., 1966; in Political Science, MIT, 1962–71; Lectr, Univ. of Calif, Santa Cruz, 1972–2008. *Publications:* Tom Lehrer Song Book, 1954; Tom Lehrer's Second Song Book, 1968; Too Many Songs by Tom Lehrer, 1981; contrib. to Annals of Mathematical Statistics, Journal of Soc. of Industrial and Applied Maths. *Recreation:* piano. *Address:* 11 Sparks Street, Cambridge, MA 02138–4711, USA. *T:* (617) 3547708.

**LEICESTER, 8th Earl of,** *cr* 1837; **Thomas Edward Coke;** Viscount Coke 1837; *b* 6 July 1965; *er s* of 7th Earl of Leicester, CBE and Valeria Phyllis Coke (*née* Potter); *S* father, 2015; *m* 1996, Polly, *y d* of David Whately, MC; one *s* three *d*. *Educ:* Eton; Univ. of Manchester (BA). Scots Guards, 1987–93. Pres., Caravan and Motorhome (formerly Caravan) Club, 2006–. *Heir: s* Viscount Coke, *qv*. *Address:* Holkham Hall, Wells-next-the-Sea, Norfolk NR23 1AB. *Clubs:* White's; Norfolk (Norwich); Newmarket and Suffolk Real Tennis.

**LEICESTER, Bishop of,** since 2016; **Rt Rev. Martyn James Snow;** *b* 1968. *Educ:* Sheffield Univ. (BSc 1989); Wycliffe Hall, Oxford (BTh 1995); Durham Univ. (MA 2012). Ordained deacon 1995, priest 1996; Asst Curate, St Andrew's, Brinsworth with Catcliffe and Treeton, 1995–97; with CMS, Guinea, 1998–2001; Vicar, Christ Ch, Pitsmoor, Sheffield, 2001–10; Priest-in-charge, St Mathias', Stockbridge, 2007–08; Area Dean, Ecclesfield, 2007–10; Archdeacon of Sheffield and Rotherham, 2010–13; Bishop Suffragan of Tewkesbury, 2013–16. Chm., Central Readers' Council, 2016–. Chair of Trustees: Redcliffe Coll., Glos, 2014–; Church Pastoral Aid Soc., 2016–. Chair, Council, Coll. of Evangelists. *Address:* 12 Springfield Road, Leicester LE2 3BD.

**LEICESTER, Dean of;** *see* Monteith, Very Rev. D. R. M.

**LEICESTER, Archdeacon of;** *see* Worsfold, Ven. R. V.

**LEIGH,** family name of **Barons Leigh** and **Leigh of Hurley**.

**LEIGH,** 6th Baron *cr* 1839, of Stoneleigh, co. Warwick; **Christopher Dudley Piers Leigh;** *b* 20 Oct. 1960; *s* of 5th Baron Leigh and his 1st wife, Cecilia Poppy, *y d* of Robert Cecil Jackson; *S* father, 2003; *m* 1990, Sophy-Ann (marr. diss. 2008), *d* of Richard Burrows, MBE; one *s* one *d*. *Educ:* Eton; RAC Cirencester. *Heir: s* Hon. Rupert Dudley Leigh, *b* 21 Feb. 1994.

**LEIGH OF HURLEY,** Baron *cr* 2013 (Life Peer), of Hurley in the Royal County of Berkshire; **Howard Darryl Leigh;** Founder, 1988, and Senior Partner, since 2010, Cavendish Corporate Finance LLP; Deputy Chairman, finnCap Group plc, since 2018; *b* London, 3 April 1959; *s* of late Philip Mark Leigh and of Jacqueline Leigh (*née* Freeman); *m* 1998, Jennifer Peach; two *d*. *Educ:* Clifton Coll., Bristol; Univ. of Southampton (BSc (SocSci) Econs). FCA; Mem., Chartered Inst. of Taxation. With Deloitte Haskin & Sells, 1980–88. Mem. Bd, Bolton Building Soc., 1986–92; Mem. Adv. Bd, Metro Bank plc, 2017–. Member: DTI Deregulation Task Force Tax Cttee, 1994–97; Etherington Report on Aggressive Fundraising by Charities, 2015. Sen. Treasurer, Cons. Party, 2005– (Treas., 2000–); Pres., Westminster N Cons. Assoc., 2010–18 (Patron, 2018–). Mem. Council, ICAEW, 1998–2004 (Chm., Corporate Finance Faculty, 1998–2004; Alt. to Pres. on Takeover Panel Appeal Cttee, 1998–2004). President: Westminster Synagogue, 2010– (Chm., 2002–10); Inst. for Jewish Policy Res., 2015–. Chm., Jewish Care Business Gp, 2000–; Mem. Exec. Bd, Cons. Friends of Israel, 2008–; Vice Pres., Jewish Leadership Council, 2010–. Trustee: The Jerusalem Foundn, 1992– (Chm., 2016–); Jewish Care, 2009–12. Mem., Deliver Life Bd, WaterAid, 2015–16. *Recreations:* running, The Thames. *Address:* Cavendish Corporate Finance LLP, 40 Portland Place, W1B 1NB. *T:* (020) 7908 6000, *Fax:* (020) 7908 6006. *E:* hleigh@cavendish.com. *Club:* Carlton.

**LEIGH, Bertie;** *see* Leigh, M. A. M. S.

**LEIGH, His Honour Christopher Humphrey de Verd;** QC 1989; a Circuit Judge, 2001–08; *b* 12 July 1943; *s* of late Wing Commander Humphrey de Verd Leigh and of Johanna Leigh; *m* 1970, Frances Powell. *Educ:* Harrow. Called to the Bar, Lincoln's Inn, 1967, Bencher, 1999. A Recorder, 1985–2001. *Recreations:* ski-ing, photography. *Address:* Drystone Chambers, 35 Bedford Row, WC1R 4JH.

**LEIGH, David,** PhD; Secretary-General, International Institute for Conservation, 2006–10; *b* 11 Jan. 1943; *s* of Jacques Leigh and Gwendoline (*née* Bright); *m* 1969, Judith Mary Latham; one *s* two *d*. *Educ:* Univ. of Durham (BSc Physics 1966); Inst. of Archaeology, Univ. of London (Dip. Archaeol Conservation 1968); UC, Cardiff (PhD 1980). Experimental Officer (Conservation), Dept of Archaeology, Univ. of Southampton, 1968–74; Lectr in Archaeol Conservation, UC, Cardiff, 1975–87; Head of Conservation Unit, Museums and Galls Commn, 1987–93; Dir, Mus. Training Inst., 1993–95; Principal, West Dean Coll., 1995–2000; Exec. Dir, 2001–05, Sen. Policy Advr and Communications Manager, 2005–07, UK Inst. for Conservation, subseq. Inst. of Conservation. Member: Internat. Inst. for Conservation, 1970– (Fellow, 1975; Mem. Council, 1990–94; Treas., 2001–06); Sci. and Conservation Panel, 1984–94, Ancient Monuments Adv. Cttee, 1988–90, English Heritage; Arts Panel, 2004–15, Council, 2007–16 (Nominee, 2007–16, Observer, 2016–18, Inst. of Conservation; Volunteer Specialist, 2016–) NT; Cttee B/560: Conservation of Tangible Cultural Heritage, BSI, 2008– (Chm., 2008–11); Bd, Inst. of Conservation, 2011–14; Rescue, 1972– (Trustee, 1972–78). Trustee: Conf. on Trng in Architectural Conservation, 2000–08; Anna Plowden Trust, 2007–. FSA; ACR. Plowden Medal, Royal Warrant Holders' Assoc., 2002. *Publications:* (contrib.) Marine Archaeology, 1973; (contrib.) Rescue Archaeology, 1974; (ed) First Aid for Finds, 1976; articles on Anglo-Saxon artefacts, especially early Anglo-Saxon jewellery, conservation and restoration, training and educn. *Recreations:* family, music, travel, walking, gardening, amateur dramatics.

**LEIGH, Prof. David Alan,** PhD; FRS 2009; Royal Society Research Professor, since 2016, and Sir Samuel Hall Professor of Chemistry, since 2014, University of Manchester; *b* Birmingham, 31 May 1963; *s* of Peter Leigh and Hylda Leigh; *m* 1998, Sau Yin Sek; one *d*. *Educ:* Codsall High Sch.; Sheffield Univ. (BSc Hons Chem. 1984; MSc Organic Chem. 1985; PhD Organic Chem. 1987). Res. Associate, Nat. Res. Council of Canada, Ottawa, 1987–89; Lectr, then Reader, UMIST, 1989–98; Prof. of Synthetic Chem., Univ. of Warwick, 1998–2001; Forbes Prof. of Organic Chem., Univ. of Edinburgh, 2001–12; Prof. of Organic Chem., Univ. of Manchester, 2012–13. EPSRC Sen. Res. Fellow, 2005–10. FRSC 2005; FRSE 2005. *Recreations:* contract bridge, magic, popular music. *Address:* Meadow Barn, Sugar Lane, Adlington, Cheshire SK10 5SN. *T:* (0161) 275 1926; School of Chemistry, University of Manchester, Oxford Road, Manchester M13 9PL. *E:* David.Leigh@manchester.ac.uk.

**LEIGH, Rt Hon. Sir Edward (Julian Egerton),** Kt 2013; PC 2019; MP (C) Gainsborough, since 1997 (Gainsborough and Horncastle, 1983–97); *b* 20 July 1950; *s* of Sir Neville Egerton Leigh, KCVO; *m* 1984, Mary Goodman; three *s* three *d*. *Educ:* St Philip's Sch., Kensington; Oratory Sch., Berks; French Lycée, London; UC, Durham Univ. (BA Hons). Called to the Bar, Inner Temple, 1977. Mem., Cons. Res. Dept, seconded to office of Leader of Opposition, GLC, 1973–75; Prin. Correspondence Sec. to Rt Hon. Margaret Thatcher, MP, 1975–76. Member (C): Richmond Borough Council, 1974–78; GLC, 1977–81. Contested (C) Teesside, Middlesbrough, Oct. 1974. PPS to Minister of State, Home Office, 1990; Parly Under-Sec. of State, DTI, 1990–93. Chairman: Public Accounts Cttee, H of C, 2001–10; Public Accounts Commn, H of C, 2011–; Backbench Cttee on Foreign Affairs, Defence, Internat. Devplt, 2011–15; All-Party Parly Gp on France, 2010– (Mem., 1983–); All-Party Parly Gp on the Holy See, 2010–; All-Party Parly Gp on Italy, 2015–; All-Party Parly Gp on Russia, 2015–17; Secretary: Conservative backbench Cttees on agric., defence and employment, 1983–90; All-Party Parly Gp on Insurance, 2010– (Mem., 1993–); Vice Chm., Conservative Back bench Cttees on foreign affairs and social security, 1997–2001; Financial Advr to HM Treasury, 2010–11. Delegate, Parly Assembly, Council of Europe, 2011–15, 2017–. Non-exec. Dir, Europe Arab Bank, 2012–. Pres., Catholic Union of GB, 2015–. Chm., Nat. Council for Civil Defence, 1980–82; Dir, Coalition for Peace Through Security, 1982–83. Kt of Honour and Devotion, SMO Malta, 1994; Officier, Légion d'Honneur (France), 2015; Comdr, Star of Italy, 2017. *Publications:* Right Thinking, 1979; Responsible Individualism, 1994; Monastery of the Mind, 2012; The Nation That Forgot God, 2016. *Recreations:* walking, reading. *Address:* House of Commons, SW1A 0AA.

**LEIGH, Sir Geoffrey (Norman),** Kt 1990; Chairman, Leigh Academies Trust, since 2009; Chairman, Allied London Properties, 1987–98 (Managing Director, 1970–87); Director, Arrow Property Investments Ltd, 2000–06; *b* 23 March 1933; *s* of Rose Leigh and Morris Leigh; *m* 1st, 1955, Valerie Lennard (marr. diss. 1975; she *d* 1976); one *s* two *d*; 2nd, 1976, Sylvia Pell; one *s* one *d*. *Educ:* Haberdashers' Aske's Hampstead Sch.; Univ. of Michigan. Man. Dir, 1965, Chm., 1980–98, Sterling Homes. Founder and First Pres., Westminster Junior Chamber of Commerce, 1959–63; Underwriting Mem., Lloyd's, 1973–97. Special Advisor, Land Agency Bd, Commn for the New Towns, 1994–96; Member: Cttee, Good Design in Housing for Disabled, 1977; Cttee, Good Design in Housing, 1978–79; British ORT Council, 1979–80; Internat. Adv. Bd, American Univ., Washington, 1983–97; Adv. Council, Prince's Youth Business Trust, 1985–2005; Main Finance Bd, NSPCC, 1985–2003 (Hon. Mem. Council, 1995–); Governing Council, Business in the Community, 1987–; Somerville Coll. Appeal, 1987–2010; Royal Fine Art Commn Art and Arch. Educn Trust, 1988–99; Per Cent Club, 1988–2000; Council, City Technology Colls Trust, 1988–2005; City Appeal Cttee, Royal Marsden Hosp., 1990–93; Review Body on Doctors' and Dentists' Remuneration, 1990–93; Wellbeing Council, 1994–2009; Chancellor's Ct of Benefactors, Oxford Univ., 1991–; Emmanuel Coll., Cambridge, Revell Campaign, 1994–96; Chm., St Mary's Hosp. 150th Anniversary Appeal, 1995–2009. Comr and Trustee, Fulbright Commn, 1991–99 (Chm., Fulbright US-UK Adv. Bd, 1995–2009); Mem., Duke of Edinburgh's Award World Fellowship, 1992–; Sponsor, Leigh City Technology Coll., subseq. Leigh Technology Acad., Dartford (Chm. of Govs and Trustees, 1988–2006; Chm., Leigh Acad. Trust, 2006–); Founder/Sponsor, Friends of British Liby, 1987– (Vice-Pres., 2000–); Founder, Margaret Thatcher Centre, Somerville Coll., Oxford, 1991; Treasurer: Commonwealth Jewish Council, 1983–89; Commonwealth Jewish Trust, 1983–89; a Treas., Cons. Party, 1995–97; Vice President: Hampstead and Highgate Cons. Assoc., 1997–2005 (Patron, 1991–94; Pres., 1994–97); Conservatives Abroad, 1995–; Republicans Abroad, 1995–2005; Treas. and Trustee, Action on Addiction, 1991–2003; Trustee: Margaret Thatcher Foundn, 1991–; Industry in Educn, 1993–98; Philharmonia, 1992–99. Governor: Royal Sch., Hampstead, 1991–2003; City Lit. Inst., 1991–98. Hon. Mem., Emmanuel Coll., Cambridge, 1995; Foundn Fellow, Somerville Coll., Oxford, 1998; Univ. of Greenwich Assembly, 2003. Hon. Life Mem., Cons. Med. Soc., 1998. Freeman, City of London, 1976; Liveryman: Haberdashers' Co., 1992–; Furniture Makers' Co., 1987– (Chm., Premises Cttee, 2003–06; Asst *hc*, 2006; Liveryman *hc* 2018). Mem., Soc. of the Four Arts, 2007–; Dir, Palm Beach Civic Assoc., 2013–; Trustee, Palm Beach United Way, 2014–. FRSA. Hon. FICPD. Presidential Citation, The American Univ., 1987. *Recreations:* photography, reading, golf. *Address:* 42 Berkeley Square, W1J 5AW. *T:* (020) 7409 5054. *Clubs:* Carlton (Hon. Mem., Political Cttee, 2004–), United and Cecil, Pilgrims, Royal Automobile; Pilgrims of the US; St George's Society of New York; Palm Beach Country, Palm Beach Yacht, Palm Beach Ocean.

**LEIGH, Prof. Irene May,** CBE 2012 (OBE 2006); MD; DSc; FRCP, FMedSci; FRSE; Professor of Cellular and Molecular Medicine, Barts and the London School of Medicine and Dentistry, since 2018, and Dean for Global Engagement for Medicine and Dentistry, since 2019, Queen Mary University of London; *b* 25 April 1947; *d* of Archibald and May Lilian Allen; *m* 1st, 1969, (Peter) Nigel Leigh, *qv* (marr. diss. 1999); one *s* three *d*; 2nd, 2000, John E. Kernthaler. *Educ:* London Hosp. Med. Coll. (BSc 1968; MB BS 1971; MD 1992; DSc 1999). FRCP 1987. Consultant Dermatologist and Sen. Lectr, 1983–92, Prof. of Dermatol., 1992–97, Royal London Hosp. and London Hosp. Med. Coll.; St Bartholomew's and Royal London School of Medicine and Dentistry, QMW, then Barts and the London, Queen Mary's School of Medicine and Dentistry, London University: Prof. of Cellular and Molecular Medicine, 1999–2006, Hon. Prof., 2006–18; Research Dean, 1997–2002; Jt Res. Dir, 2002–05; University of Dundee: Prof. of Cellular and Molecular Medicine, 2006–17, now Emeritus; Vice Principal, and Hd, Coll. of Medicine, Dentistry and Nursing 2006–11. Dir, CRUK Skin Tumour Lab., 1989–2017; Res. Dir, Internat. Prevention Res. Inst., Lyon, 2012–. FMedSci 1999; FRSE 2009. *Publications:* contrib. numerous articles on keratinocyte biol., genodermatoses and skin carcinogenesis to peer-reviewed jls. *Recreations:* music, film, opera, theatre. *Address:* 14 Oakeshott Avenue, N6 6NS.

**LEIGH, Jonathan;** Master, Marlborough College, 2012–18; *b* 17 June 1952; *s* of Rupert M. Leigh and Isabel A. Leigh (*née* Villiers); *m* 1976, Emma Mary, *d* of Rear-Adm. Michael Donald Kyrle Pope, CB, MBE; one *s* one *d*. *Educ:* Eton Coll.; Corpus Christi Coll., Cambridge (MA History). Cranleigh School: Asst Master, 1976–82; Housemaster, 1982–88; Head of History, 1987; Second Master, 1988–92; Head Master, Blundell's Sch., 1992–2004; Headmaster, Ridley Coll., Ontario, 2005–12. Mem., Devon County Residential Care Standards Adv. Cttee, 1993–2002 (Chm., 1994–98); Vice Pres., Devon Playing Fields Assoc., 1998–2004. Member: Council, ISIS South-West, 1995–2001; Cttee, Belgian Sect., Assoc. Européene des Enseignants, 1994–2004; Admiralty Interview Bd, 1994–2004; Interviewing Panel, ESU, 1996–2018; Sec., SW Div., HMC, 2000 (Chm., 2001). Member: Adv. Bd, Vimy Foundn, 2005–18; Bd, Canadian Accredited Ind. Schs (formerly Canadian Educnl Standards Inst.), 2009–18 (Mem. Evaluation Gp, 2008–12); Internat. Confedn of Principals, 2009–18; World Leading Schs Assoc., 2011–18; G30 Schs Gp, 2012–18. Trustee: Tiverton Adventure Playground Assoc., 1992–2004; Inner Cities Young People's Project, 1996–2004; Sarum St Michael Trust, 2018–. FRSA 1994. Governor: St Petroc's Sch., Bude, 1993–2004; Wolborough Hill Sch., Newton Abbot, 1998–2000; Abbey Sch., Tewkesbury, 2000–03 (Chm., 2002); Marlborough Coll., Malaysia, 2012–18; Director: Highfield Sch., Liphook, 2000–; Cheam Sch., 2013–18; Educnl Advr to Pembroke House Sch., Kenya, 2014–18. Dir, 2000–04, Vice Chm., 2002–04, Devon and Exeter Steeplechases. *Recreations:* singing, horse racing, opera, labradors, late 19th century African history, the Charente. *Clubs:* East India, Lansdowne.

**LEIGH, Prof. Leonard Herschel;** freelance author and lecturer; Professor of Criminal Law in the University of London, at the London School of Economics and Political Science, 1982–97; *b* 19 Sept. 1935; *s* of Leonard William and Lillian Mavis Leigh; *m* 1960, Jill Diane Gale (*d* 2015); one *s* one *d*. *Educ:* Univ. of Alberta (BA, LLB); Univ. of London (PhD 1966). Admitted to Bar: Alberta, 1959; NW Territories, 1961; Inner Temple, 1993. Private practice, Province of Alberta, 1958–60; Dept of Justice, Canada, 1960–62; London School of Economics: Asst Lectr in Law, 1964–65; Lectr, 1965–71; Reader, 1971–82. Vis. Prof., Queen's Univ., Kingston, Ont, 1973–74; Bowker Vis. Prof., Univ. of Alberta, 1999. British Council Lecturer: Univ. of Strasbourg, 1978; National Univ. of Mexico, 1980; UN Asia and Far East Inst., Tokyo, 1986; South India, 1989, 1991. Mem., Canadian Govt Securities Regulation Task Force, 1974–78. Bd Mem., Criminal Cases Review Commn, 1997–2005. UK Convenor, Université de l'Europe Steering Cttee, 1987–90; Chm., English Nat. Section, 1988–, Mem., Conseil de Direction, 1989–, Internat. Assoc. of Penal Law. Mem., Exec. Cttee, Canada-UK Colloquia, 1993–. Member, Council of Europe Training Missions: Hungary, 1990; Poland, 1991; Albania, 1992; Mem., Council of Europe Wkg Party on Reform of Russian Penal Law, 1994–95. UK Rep., Internat. Penal and Penitentiary Foundn, 1994–2005. Chm., Awards Cttee, Canada Meml Fellowships, 2002–14. Hon. Fellow, Faculty of Law, Birmingham Univ., 1997–2010. Mem., Bloxham Parish Council, 2017–. *Publications:* The Criminal Liability of Corporations in English Law, 1969; (jtly) Northey and Leigh's Introduction to Company Law, 1970, 4th edn 1987; Police Powers in England and Wales, 1975, 2nd edn 1986; Economic Crime in Europe, 1980; (jtly) The Companies Act 1981, 1981; (jtly) The Management of the Prosecution Process in Denmark, Sweden and the Netherlands, 1981; The Control of Commercial Fraud, 1982; Strict and Vicarious Liability, 1982; (jtly) A Guide to the Financial Services Act, 1986;

(contrib.) Blackstone's Criminal Practice, 1991–2007; (ed) Criminal Procedure in English Public Law, 2005, 2nd edn 2009; articles in British, European, Amer., S Amer. and Canadian jls. *Recreations:* music, walking.

**LEIGH, Lucy Claire;** *see* Frazer, L. C.

**LEIGH, Mark Andrew Michael Stephen, (Bertie);** Partner, 1977–2015, Senior Partner, 1998–2015, and Consultant, since 2015, Hempsons; Solicitor Advocate of the High Court, since 2005; *b* Cheshire, 30 Aug. 1946; *s* of Robert Arthur Leigh and Shelagh Elizabeth Leigh (*née* Ruddin); *m* 1976, Helen Mary; one *s* one *d*. *Educ:* St Christopher Sch., Letchworth; Univ. of E Anglia (BA 1969). Joined Hempsons, 1973; admitted as solicitor, 1976. Chair: Clin. Disputes Forum, 2009–; Nat. Confidential Enquiry into Patient Outcome and Death, 2010–15 (Trustee, 2009–15). President: Medico-Legal Soc., 2006–08; Soc. for Ethics in Law and Medicine, 2014–. Trustee: CORE (Gastroenterol.), 2007–11; Charm UK, 2008–. Chair of Govs, St Christopher Sch., 2014–; Gov., City Lit Adult Educn Coll., 2004–12. Hon. FRCPCH 1997; FRCOG *ad eundem* 2003; Hon. FRCA 2016. *Recreations:* theatre, opera, concerts, reading. *Address:* 51 Larkhall Rise, SW4 6HT. *T:* (020) 7622 4243, 07725 938510. *E:* b.leigh@hempsons.co.uk. *Clubs:* Reform, Royal Society of Medicine.

**LEIGH, Sir Michael,** KCMG 2012; PhD; Senior Adviser, German Marshall Fund of the United States, since 2011; *b* London, 25 Feb. 1948; *s* of Victor Leigh and Esther Leigh; *m* 2010, Ventura Mancilla; two *s* by a previous marriage. *Educ:* Orange Hill County Grammar Sch.; St Catherine's Coll., Oxford (BA PPE); Massachusetts Inst. of Technol. (PhD Pol Sci. 1974). Asst Prof. in Pol Sci., Wellesley Coll., Mass, 1973–74; Lectr in Internat. Relns, Univ. of Sussex, 1974–76; Asst Prof. in Internat. Relns, Johns Hopkins Univ., Sch. for Advanced Internat. Studies, Bologna, 1976–77; Official, Secretariat-Gen., Council of Eur. Communities, 1977–80; European Commission: Directorate-General: for Fisheries, 1980–82; for Information, Press and Information, 1982–85; for External Relns, 1985–88; Member of Cabinet: of Lord Cockfield, Vice-Pres., 1988–89; of Frans Andriessen, Vice-Pres., 1989–92; of Comr Hans van den Broek, 1993–98; Dir, 1998–2000; Dir, Directorate-Gen. Enlargement, Turkey, Cyprus, Bulgaria, Malta, Romania, 2000–03; Dep. Dir-Gen., Directorate-Gen. External Relns, 2003–05; Dir-Gen. for Enlargement, 2006–11. Member, Advisory Board: Salzburg Global Seminar, 2010–12; Wilton Park, 2012–; Foundn for Effective Governance, Kiev, 2012–13. *Publications:* Mobilizing Consent: public opinion and American foreign policy, 1937–1947, 1976; European Integration and the Common Fisheries Policy, 1983; articles on foreign policy. *Recreations:* tango, pilates, travel. *E:* leigh.michael@gmail.com.

**LEIGH, Mike,** OBE 1993; dramatist; theatre and film director; *b* 20 Feb. 1943; *s* of late Alfred Abraham Leigh, MRCS, LRCP and Phyllis Pauline Leigh (*née* Cousin); *m* 1973, Alison Steadman, *qv* (marr. diss. 2001); two *s*. *Educ:* North Grecian Street County Primary Sch.; Salford Grammar Sch.; RADA; Camberwell Sch. of Arts and Crafts; Central Sch. of Art and Design (Theatre Design Dept); London Film Sch. Assoc. Dir, Midlands Arts Centre for Young People, 1965–66; Asst Dir, RSC, 1967–68; Drama Lectr, Sedgley Park and De La Salle Colls, Manchester, 1968–69; Lectr, London Film Sch., 1968–74. Arts Council of GB: Member: Drama Panel, 1975–77; Dirs' Working Party and Specialist Allocations Bd, 1976–84; Member: Accreditation Panel, Nat. Council for Drama Trng, 1978–91; Gen. Adv. Council, IBA, 1980–82; Council, RADA, 2009–. Chm., Bd of Govs, London Film Sch., 2001–18. NFT Retrospectives, 1979, 2005; BBC TV Retrospective (incl. Arena: Mike Leigh Making Plays), 1982. Fellow, BFI, 2005; BAFTA Fellowship, 2015. Hon. Fellow, Univ. of the Arts, 2006. Hon. MA: Salford, 1991; Northampton, 2000; Hon. DLitt: Staffordshire, 2000; Exeter, 2014; DU Essex, 2002; Hon. Dr London Metropolitan, 2005; Hon. DA Manchester Metropolitan, 2012. George Devine Award, 1973; Michael Balcon Award, 1995; Alexander Korda Award, 1996. Ordre des Arts et des Lettres (France), 1998. Productions of own plays and films; *stage plays:* The Box Play, 1965, My Parents Have Gone To Carlisle, The Last Crusade Of The Five Little Nuns, 1966, Midlands Arts Centre; Nenaa, RSC Studio, Stratford-upon-Avon, 1967; Individual Fruit Pies, E15 Acting Sch., 1968; Down Here And Up There, Royal Ct Th. Upstairs, 1968; Big Basil, 1968, Glum Victoria And The Lad With Specs, Manchester Youth Theatre, 1969; Epilogue, Manchester, 1969; Bleak Moments, Open Space, 1970; A Rancid Pong, Basement Th., 1971; Wholesome Glory, Dick Whittington and his Cat, Royal Ct Th. Upstairs, 1973; The Jaws of Death, Traverse, Edinburgh Fest., 1973; Babies Grow Old, Other Place, 1974, ICA, 1975; The Silent Majority, Bush, 1974; Abigail's Party, Hampstead, 1977; Ecstasy, Hampstead, 1979, 2011; Goose-Pimples, Hampstead, Garrick, 1981 (Standard Best Comedy Award); Smelling a Rat, Hampstead, 1988; Greek Tragedy, Sydney, 1989, Edinburgh Fest. and Theatre Royal, Stratford East, 1990; It's A Great Big Shame!, Theatre Royal, Stratford East, 1993; Two Thousand Years, NT, 2005; Grief, NT, 2011 (Critics' Circle and Evening Standard Awards for Best Dir); *opera:* The Pirates of Penzance, ENO, 2015, 2017. *BBC radio play:* Too Much Of A Good Thing, 1979; *feature films:* Bleak Moments, 1971 (Golden Hugo, Chicago Film Fest., 1972; Golden Leopard, Locarno Film Fest., 1972); High Hopes, 1989 (Critics' Award, Venice Film Fest., 1988; Evening Standard Peter Sellers Comedy Award, 1989); Life is Sweet, 1991; Naked, 1993 (Best Dir, Cannes Film Fest., 1993); Secrets and Lies, 1996 (Palme d'Or, Cannes Film Fest., 1996; BAFTA Award for Orig. Screenplay, 1997); Career Girls, 1997; Topsy-Turvy, 1999 (Evening Standard Best Film Award, 2001); All or Nothing, 2002; Vera Drake, 2004 (Golden Lion, Venice Film Fest., 2004); BAFTA Award for Best Dir, 2005); Happy-Go-Lucky, 2008; Another Year, 2010; A Running Jump, 2012; Mr Turner, 2014; Peterloo, 2018; *BBC TV plays and films:* A Mug's Game, 1972; Hard Labour, 1973; The Permissive Society, Afternoon, A Light Snack, Probation, Old Chums, The Birth Of The 2001 FA Cup Final Goalie, 1975; Nuts in May, Knock For Knock, 1976; The Kiss Of Death, Abigail's Party, 1977; Who's Who, 1978; Grown-Ups, 1980; Home Sweet Home, 1982; Four Days In July, 1984; *Channel Four films:* Meantime, 1983 (People's Prize, Berlin Film Fest., 1984); The Short and Curlies, 1987. *Relevant publications:* The Improvised Play: the work of Mike Leigh, by Paul Clements, 1983; Mike Leigh, by Gilles Laprevotte, 1991; The World According to Mike Leigh, by Michael Coveney, 1996; The Films of Mike Leigh: embracing the world, by Ray Carney and Leonard Quart, 2000; All or Nothing: the cinema of Mike Leigh, by Edward Trostle-Jones, 2004; The Cinema of Mike Leigh: a sense of the real, by Garry Watson, 2004; Mike Leigh, by Tony Whitehead, 2007; Mike Leigh on Mike Leigh, ed by Amy Raphael, 2008; Mike Leigh, by Stefano Boni and Massimo Quaglia, 2009; Mike Leigh, by Sean O'Sullivan, 2011. *Address:* c/o United Agents, 12–26 Lexington Street, W1F 0LE.

**LEIGH, Prof. (Peter) Nigel;** Professor of Neurology, Brighton and Sussex Medical School, since 2011; Hon. Consultant Neurologist, Brighton and Sussex University Hospitals NHS Trust, since 2011; Emeritus Professor of Neurology, King's College London, 2010; *b* 26 Sept. 1946; *s* of Dr A. Denis Leigh and Pamela Leigh (*née* Parish); *m* 1st, 1969, Irene May Allen (*see* Irene May Leigh) (marr. diss. 1999); one *s* three *d*; 2nd, 2000, Catherine Margaret Lloyd; one *d*. *Educ:* Sevenoaks Sch., Kent; London Hosp. Med. Sch., Univ. of London (BSc 1st Cl. Hons; MB BS Dist.); PhD London 1986. FRCP 1988. House Physician and House Surgeon, 1970–71, SHO, 1971–72, The London Hosp.; SHO, Hammersmith Hosp., 1972–73; Registrar, UCH, 1974, Hammersmith Hosp., 1974–75; Specialist in Neurology, Muhimbili Hosp., and Lectr in Neurology, Univ. of Dar es Salaam, 1975–77; Sen. Registrar, St George's Hosp., 1977–82; Wellcome Trust Res. Fellow, Inst. of Psychiatry, 1980–81; Consultant Neurologist, Wessex Neurol Centre, Southampton, 1982–86, and Sen. Lectr in Neurology, Southampton Univ., 1984–86; Sen. Lectr in Neurology and Hon. Cons. Neurologist, St George's Hosp. Med. Sch., 1986–89; Prof. of Clinical Neurology, Inst. of Psychiatry and KCL Sch. of Medicine, 1989–2010, Hd, Dept of Clinical Neurosci., 1989–2007, King's Coll. London. FMedSci 2003; FAAN. Forbes Norris Award, Internat. Alliance of ALS/MND Assocs, 1997; Erb-Duchenne Prize, German Neuro-Muscular Soc., 2003; Sheila Essey Prize, Amer. Acad. of Neurology, 2004. *Publications:* (ed with M. Swash) Motor Neurone Disease: biology and management, 1995; articles on motor neurone disease, Parkinson's disease and related disorders and other medical topics. *Recreations:* neurological research, fly-fishing, birdwatching, walking, reading. *Address:* Brighton and Sussex Medical School, Trafford Centre for Biomedical Research, University of Sussex, Falmer, East Sussex BN1 9RY. *T:* (01273) 877357, *Fax:* (01273) 872941. *E:* P.Leigh@bsms.ac.uk.

**LEIGH, Sir Richard (Henry),** 3rd Bt *cr* 1918, of Altrincham, Cheshire; *b* 11 Nov. 1936; *s* of Eric Leigh (*d* 1982), 2nd *s* of Sir John Leigh, 1st Bt, and his 1st wife, Joan Lane Fitzgerald (*d* 1973), *e d* of M. C. L. Freer, South Africa; *S* uncle, 1992; *m* 1st, 1962, Barbro Anna Elizabeth (marr. diss. 1977), *e d* of late Stig Carl Sebastian Tham, Sweden; 2nd, 1977, Cherie Rosalind, *e d* D. D. Dale, Cherval, France and *widow* of Alan Reece, RMS. *Educ:* England and Switzerland. *Recreations:* fishing, gardening. *Heir:* half *b* Christopher John Leigh [*b* 6 April 1941; *m* 1963, Gillian Ismay, *o d* of W. K. Lowe; one *s* one *d*]. *Address:* PO Box 984, Canterbury CT1 9EB.

**LEIGH, Richard Rowland, (Rowley);** Chef Proprietor, Le Café Anglais, 2007–14; Chef-Consultant, The Continental, Hong Kong, 2013–16; *b* Manchester, 23 April 1950; *s* of Robert Arthur Leigh and Shelagh Elizabeth Leigh (*née* Ruddin); *m* 1st, 1982, Sara George; two *d*; 2nd, 2001, Katharine Chancellor; one *s*. *Educ:* Clifton Coll.; Christ's Coll., Cambridge. Chef, Roux Restaurants, 1978–87; Chef and Partner, Kensington Place, 1987–2006. Cookery Corresp., Financial Times. *Publications:* No Place Like Home, 2001; A Long and Messy Business, 2018. *Recreations:* golf, epicureanism. *Club:* Groucho.

**LEIGH, Prof. Roger Allen,** PhD; Professor, School of Agriculture, Food and Wine, University of Adelaide, 2006–14, now Emeritus (Head, School of Agriculture, Food and Wine, 2006–11); *b* 7 Feb. 1949; *s* of Harry Leigh and Catherine Leigh (*née* O'Neill); *m* 1st, 1974, Beatrice Katherine Halton (marr. diss. 1999); 2nd, 2008, Janet Ann Dibb-Smith. *Educ:* Ellesmere Port Boys' GS; UCNW, Bangor (BSc 1970; PhD 1974). FIBiol 1991. Maria Moors Cabot Fellow in Botanical Res., Harvard Univ., 1974–76; Royal Society Pickering Res. Fellow, Botany Sch., Univ. of Cambridge, 1976–79; Scientist, Rothamsted Experimental Station, Harpenden, 1979–98; Head of Crop Production Dept, 1987–89; Head of Biochemistry and Physiology Dept, 1989–98; Head of Soils and Crop Scis Div., 1989–94; Dep. Dir, 1994–98; Prof. of Botany, Univ. of Cambridge, 1998–2006; Professorial Fellow, Girton Coll., Cambridge, 1998–2006; Dir, Waite Res. Inst., Univ. of Adelaide, 2010–12. President: Soc. for Experimental Biology, 2005–07 (Vice-Pres., 2003–05); Australian Council, Deans of Agriculture, 2008–10. *Publications:* (jtly) Long-Term Experiments in Agricultural and Ecological Sciences, 1994; (jtly) Membrane Transport in Plants and Fungi: molecular mechanisms and control, 1994; scientific papers in learned jls, incl. Plant Physiology, Planta, Jl of Exptl Botany. *Recreations:* sports of all kinds, bird watching, photography. *Address:* 162 Molesworth Street, North Adelaide, SA 5006, Australia. *T:* (8) 82672487. *E:* roger.leigh@adelaide.edu.au.

**LEIGH, Rowley;** *see* Leigh, R. R.

**LEIGH, Samantha Ceri; Her Honour Judge Leigh;** a Circuit Judge, since 2015; *b* Essex, 1970; *d* of Michael Leigh and Maureen Leigh; *m* 2004, Alan Pearce. *Educ:* Univ. of Essex (BA Hons Public Policy and Admin); Guildford Coll. of Law (CPE). Called to the Bar, Inner Temple, 1995; in practice as a barrister specialising in criminal law; a Dep. District Judge (Magistrates' Courts), 2005–15; a Recorder, 2009–15. *Recreations:* scuba diving, travel. *Address:* Basildon Crown Court, The Gore, Basildon, Essex SS14 2BU. *T:* (01268) 458000.

**LEIGH-HUNT, Barbara;** actress; *b* 14 Dec. 1935; *d* of Chandos A. Leigh-Hunt and Elizabeth Leigh-Hunt; *m* 1967, Richard Edward Pasco, CBE (*d* 2014). *Educ:* Bath, Som; Kensington High Sch.; Bristol Old Vic Theatre Sch. (Most Promising Student, Bristol Evening Post Award, 1953). Began broadcasting for BBC at age 12 in Children's Hour, and has continued to do so regularly on Radios 3 and 4. *Theatre:* début in Midsummer Night's Dream, London Old Vic tour to USA and Canada, 1954–55; subseq. also Twelfth Night and Merchant of Venice, Old Vic and tours, 1957–60; seasons at Nottingham and Guildford, 1960–62; Bristol Old Vic and tours to Europe, Middle East, US and Canada, 1961–68; The Seagull, Hedda Gabler, She Stoops to Conquer, Much Ado About Nothing, Blithe Spirit, Love's Labour's Lost, Hamlet, and Macbeth; A Severed Head, Criterion, 1963; Mrs Mouse, are you within?, Duke of York's, 1968; Venice Preserv'd, Prospect Th. Co. tour, 1970; Royal Shakespeare Company: Sherlock Holmes, Travesties, 1974; A Winter's Tale, Richard III, 1975; King Lear, Troilus and Cressida, 1976; That Good Between Us, Every Good Boy Deserves Favour, 1977; Richard III, Hamlet, 1980; The Forest, La Ronde, 1981; Pack of Lies, Lyric 1983; Barnaby and the Old Boys, Theatr Clwyd, 1987; Royal National Theatre: Cat on a Hot Tin Roof, 1988; Bartholomew Fair, The Voysey Inheritance, 1989; Racing Demon, 1990 and Los Angeles, 1995; An Inspector Calls, 1992 (Best Supporting Actress, Olivier Award, 1993); Absence of War, 1993; A Woman of No Importance, RSC, and Haymarket, 1992; The Importance of Being Earnest, Old Vic, 1995; frequent appearances in poetry and prose anthology progs in UK and abroad; works as speaker with Medici String Quartet. *Films:* Frenzy, 1972, Henry VIII and his Six Wives, 1972; A Bequest to the Nation, 1973; Oh, Heavenly Dog, 1978; Paper Mask, 1990; Keep the Aspidistra Flying, 1997; Billy Elliott, 2000; The Martins, 2000; Iris, 2001; Vanity Fair, 2003. *Television* includes: Search for the Nile, 1971; Loves Lies Bleeding; The Voysey Inheritance; Macbeth; Wagner, 1984; The Siegfried Idyll; All for Love; Tumbledown, 1988; A Perfect Hero; Cold Feet; Pride and Prejudice, 1995; The Echo, 1998; Sunburn, Wives and Daughters, 1999; Longitude, 2000; Kavanagh QC, 1998, 2000; Midsummer Murders, 2001; George Eliot, 2002. Gov. and Associate Actor, RSC; Pres., Friends of the Other Place, 1993–97; Vice-President: Theatrical Guild of Charity (formerly Theatrical Ladies Guild of Charity), 1983–; Royal Theatrical Fund, 1995; J. B. Priestley Soc., 1997–; Patron: Soc. of Teachers of Speech and Drama, 1995; Orch. of The Swan, 1997. Tutor, Samling Foundn, 2002–. *Recreation:* book collecting. *Address:* c/o Conway Van Gelder Grant Ltd, 8–12 Broadwick Street, W1F 8HW. *T:* (020) 7287 0077, *Fax:* (020) 7287 1940.

**LEIGH-PEMBERTON, Kathryn Felice;** *see* Lampard, K. F.

**LEIGH-SMITH, Alfred Nicholas Hardstaff;** a District Judge (Magistrates' Courts), since 2004; *b* 21 Dec. 1953; *s* of late Dr Alfred Leigh Hardstaff Leigh-Smith, TD, DL and Marguerite Calvert Leigh-Smith; *m* 1996, Samantha Sian Morgan; two *s*. *Educ:* Epsom Coll.; Leeds Univ. (LLB 1975). Called to the Bar, Lincoln's Inn, 1976; in practice as barrister, Lincoln's Inn, 1976–80; Court Clerk, then Sen. Court Clerk, then Princ. Asst, Willesden Magistrates' Court, 1980–85; Deputy Clerk: to Bromley Justices, 1985–89; to Brent Justices, 1989–94; Clerk to Justices, Cambridge and E Cambs, 1995–2001; in practice as barrister, Leicester, 2001–04. Asst Stipendiary Magistrate, then Dep. Dist Judge (Magistrates' Courts), 1999–2004. *Recreations:* walking, clay-pigeon shooting, church bell ringing, Rugby Union (watching now), reading history and biographies, vegetable gardening. *Address:* Luton Magistrates' Court, Stuart Street, Luton LU1 5BL. *T:* (01582) 524244, *Fax:* (01582) 524259. *E:* a.leighsmith@btinternet.com.

**LEIGHFIELD, John Percival**, CBE 1998; FBCS; Chairman, RM plc, 1993–2011; *b* 5 April 1938; *s* of Henry Tom Dainton Leighfield and Patricia Zilpha Maud Leighfield (*née* Baker); *m* 1963, Margaret Ann Mealin; one *s* one *d. Educ:* Magdalen Coll. Sch., Oxford (State Scholarship); Exeter Coll., Oxford (MA Lit.Hum.; Hon. Fellow 2018). FIDPM 1990; FBCS 1991. Mgt trainee, Ford Motor Co., 1962–65; Systems Manager, EDP Exec., Plessey Telecomms, 1965–69; Systems Planning, EDP Exec., Plessey Co. Ltd, 1969–72; British Leyland: Systems Planning Manager, 1972–75; Systems Dir, 1975–79; Man. Dir, BL Systems Ltd, 1979–84; Man. Dir and Chm. ISTEL Ltd, 1984–89; AT&T ISTEL: Chm., 1989–93; Dir, 1993–97; Officer and Sen. Vice-Pres., AT&T, 1989–93; Chairman: Infinity SDC, 2005–11; Synstar plc, 1998–2004; Minerva Computer Systems, 2001–03; Director: Birmingham Midshires Bldg Soc., 1993–99 (Chm., 1996–99); ICom Solutions Ltd, 1997–98; Halifax plc, 1999–2001; KnowledgePool Ltd, 2000–01; Getmapping, 2005–16. Dir, Central England TEC, 1991–97. Mem., Alvey Prog. Steering Cttee, 1983–87. President: BCS, 1993–94; Computing Services and Software Assoc., 1995–96; Inst. Data Processing Mgt, 2000–06. Hon. Prof., 1992, Chm., Adv. Bd, 1997–2002, Warwick Business Sch.; Vis. Prof., Warwick Manufg Gp, 2011–; Mem. Council, Warwick Univ., 1991–96, 1997– (Pro-Chancellor and Chm., 2002–11); Governor: Magdalen Coll. Sch., Oxford, 1993–2001 (Chm. 1996–2001); WMG Acad. for Young Engrs, 2014–16 (Chm. 2014–16). Mem., Bodleian Library Develt Bd, 2008–16. Liveryman: Co. of Information Technologists, 1992– (Master, 2005–06); Educators' Co., 2015– (Master, 2015–16). FInstD 1989; FRSA 1996; FRGS 2012. DUniv Central England, 1993; Hon. DTech: De Montfort, 1994; Wolverhampton, 2001; Hon. DLaws Warwick, 2011. *Publications:* various papers on information technology. *Recreations:* historical cartography, music, walking, computing, historical cartography. *Address:* 91 Victoria Road, Oxford OX2 7QG. *T:* (01865) 559055. *Clubs:* Royal Automobile; Royal Fowey Yacht.

**LEIGHTON OF ST MELLONS**, 3rd Baron *cr* 1962, of St Mellons, co. Monmouth; **Robert William Henry Leighton Seager;** Bt 1952; *b* 28 Sept. 1955; *er s* of 2nd Baron Leighton of St Mellons and Elizabeth Rosita (*née* Hopgood; *d* 1979); *S* father, 1998; *m* 1978, Wendy Elizabeth Hopwood; one *d. Heir: b* Hon. Simon John Leighton Seager [*b* 25 Jan. 1957; *m* 1982, Gillian Rawlinson; three *d*].

**LEIGHTON, Prof. Angela**, FBA 2000; Senior Research Fellow, Trinity College, Cambridge, since 2006; *b* 23 Feb. 1954; *d* of Kenneth Leighton and Lydia Leighton (*née* Vignapiano). *Educ:* St Hugh's Coll., Oxford (BA Hons 1976; MLitt 1981). University of Hull: Lectr in English, 1979–93; Sen. Lectr, 1993–95; Reader, 1995–97; Prof. of English, 1997–2006. *Publications:* Shelley and the Sublime, 1984; Elizabeth Barrett Browning, 1986; Victorian Women Poets: writing against the heart, 1992; Victorian Women Poets: a critical anthology, 1995; Victorian Women Poets: a critical reader, 1996; A Cold Spell, 2000; On Form: poetry, aestheticism and the legacy of a word, 2007; Sea Level, 2007; (ed) Voyages over Voices: critical essays on Anne Stevenson, 2010; The Messages, 2012; Spills, 2016; (ed with Adrian Poole) Trinity Poets, 2017; Hearing Things: the work of sound in literature, 2018; Clutag Five Poems Series, No 21, 2018. *Address:* Trinity College, Cambridge CB2 1TQ.

**LEIGHTON, Sir John (Mark Nicholas)**, Kt 2013; FRSE; Director-General, National Galleries of Scotland, since 2006; *b* Belfast, 22 Feb. 1959; *s* of Edwin Leighton and Norah Leighton (*née* Winternheim, later Schwab); *m* 1987, Gillian Helen Keay; one *s* one *d. Educ:* Portora Royal Sch., Enniskillen; Univ. of Edinburgh (MA Fine Art); Courtauld Inst. of Art, Univ. of London (MA Hist. of Art). Curator, 19th-Century Paintings, Nat. Gall., London, 1986–97; Dir, Van Gogh Mus., Amsterdam, 1997–2006. FRSE 2008. Dr *hc* Edinburgh, 2009. *Publications:* The Van Gogh Museum: a portrait, 2003; 100 Masterpieces from the National Galleries of Scotland, 2015; exhibn catalogues. *Recreations:* oil painting, hill walking. *Address:* National Galleries of Scotland, 73 Belford Road, Edinburgh EH4 3DS. *E:* jleighton@nationalgalleries.org.

**LEIGHTON, Sir Michael (John Bryan)**, 11th Bt *cr* 1693; *b* 8 March 1935; *o s* of Colonel Sir Richard Tihel Leighton, 10th Bt, and Kathleen Irene Linda (*d* 1993), *o d* of Major A. E. Lees, Rowton Castle, Shrewsbury; *S* father, 1957; *m* 1st, 1974 (marr. diss. 1980); 2nd, 1988 (marr. diss. 1990); 3rd, 1991, Diana Mary Gamble (marr. diss. 1998; remarried 2009); one *d. Educ:* Stowe; Tabley House Agricultural Sch.; Cirencester Coll. *Address:* Loton Park, Shrewsbury, Salop SY5 9AJ.

**LEIGHTON, Prof. Timothy Grant**, PhD; FRS 2014; FREng; CPhys, CEng; FInstP, FIOA; FMedSci; Professor of Ultrasonics and Underwater Acoustics, Institute of Sound and Vibration Research, Faculty of Engineering and the Environment, University of Southampton, since 1999; Founding Chairman: Network for Anti-Microbial Resistance and Infection Prevention, since 2014; Health Effects of Ultrasound in Air, since 2014; *b* Blackburn, Lancs, 16 Oct. 1963; *s* of John Owen Leighton and Christine Leighton (*née* Coulthwaite); *m* 1995, Sian Lloyd Jones; one *s* one *d. Educ:* Heversham Grammar Sch., Cumbria; Magdalene Coll., Cambridge (BA Hons Nat. Scis Double 1st Cl. Hons Phys and Theoretical Phys 1985); Cavendish Lab., Univ. of Cambridge (PhD 1989). FIOA 1999; CPhys 2000; FInstP 2000; CEng 2004; FREng 2012. Sen. and Advanced Res. Fellow, Magdalene Coll., Cambridge and EPSRC, 1988–92; University of Southampton: Lectr in Underwater Acoustics, 1992–97; Reader, 1997–99; Associate Dean (Res.), Faculty of Engrg and the Envmt, 2011–15; Founder, Centre for Ultrasonics and Underwater Acoustics, 1992; Chm., Fluid Dynamics and Acoustics Res. Gp, Inst. of Sound and Vibration Res., 2010–; Founder and Chair: Health Effects of Ultrasound on Air (HEFUA), 2015–; Network for AntiMicrobial Resistance and Infection Prevention (NAMRIP), 2015–; Global-NAMRIP, 2016–. Fellow, Acoustical Soc. of Amer., 1998; FMedSci 2018. Clifford Paterson Medal and Lect., Royal Soc., 2018. A. B. Wood Medal, 1994, Tyndall Medal, 2002, R. W. B. Stephens Medal, 2009, Rayleigh Medal, 2014, Inst. of Acoustics; Internat. Medwin Prize for Acoustical Oceanog., 2001, Helmholtz-Rayleigh Interdisciplinary Silver Medal, 2013, Acoustical Soc. of Amer.; Early Career Medal and Award, Internat. Commn of Acoustics, 2004; Paterson Medal and Prize, Inst. of Physics, 2006; Brian Mercer Award for Innovation, 2011, Translation Award, 2018, Royal Soc.; Water Management and Supply Award, Inst. of Chem. Engrg, 2012. *Publications:* The Acoustic Bubble, 1994; over 400 articles incl. res. in Procs of Royal Soc. A, Nature Climate Change, Jl Fluid Mechanics, Jl Acoustical Soc. of Amer., Earth Moon and Planets, Icarus, Bulletin of Amer. Meteorol Soc., Physics Letters A, Ultrasound in Medicine and Biol. *Recreations:* lives in New Forest where enjoys activities with family including walking, spotting wildlife, painting and stargazing, sailing yacht moored nearby, plays oboe and cor anglais with Marchwood Orchestra (Chm., 2011–). *Address:* Institute of Sound and Vibration Research, Faculty of Engineering and the Environment, University of Southampton, Highfield, Southampton SO17 1BJ.

**LEIGHTON, Trevor;** photographer and director; *b* Carlisle, 20 June 1957; *s* of Ronald and Isabella Leighton; *m* 2007, Suzanna; two *s* two *d* and one step *s* one step *d. Educ:* Carlisle Coll. of Art and Design. Fashion and portrait photographer; has photographed many of world's most interesting and influential personalities, incl. Sean Connery, Kate Bush, Norman Parkinson, Quentin Crisp, Katherine Jenkins, Tom Jones, Helen Mirren, John Cleese; editorial credits include portraits for Vogue, Elle, Marie Claire, Tatler, Arena, Sunday Times, Daily Telegraph, Observer and Evening Standard and many internat. pubns. One of the largest collections of archive photographs at NPG. *Publications:* The Jokers, 2000. *Recreations:* private pilot, fanatical Liverpool supporter. *E:* trevor@trevorleighton.com. *W:* www.trevorleighton.com. *Club:* Groucho.

**LEIGHTON WILLIAMS, John;** *see* Williams, John Leighton.

**LEINSTER**, 9th Duke of, *cr* 1766; **Maurice FitzGerald;** Baron of Offaly, 1205; Earl of Kildare, 1316; Viscount Leinster (GB), 1747; Marquess of Kildare, 1761; Earl of Offaly, 1761; Baron Kildare, 1870; Premier Duke, Marquess, and Earl, of Ireland; landscape and contract gardener; *b* 7 April 1948; *s* of 8th Duke of Leinster, and Anne, *d* of Lt-Col Philip Eustace Smith, MC; *S* father, 2004; *m* 1972, Fiona Mary Francesca, *d* of Harry Hollick; two *d* (only *s* Thomas FitzGerald (Earl of Offaly) *d* 1997). *Educ:* Millfield School. Pres., Oxfordshire Dyslexia Assoc., 1978–2014. Chm., Thomas Offaly Meml Fund, 1999–2016. *Address:* Courtyard House, Oakley Park, Frilford Heath, Oxon OX13 6QW.

**LEINSTER, Prof. Paul**, CBE 2008; PhD; Professor of Environmental Assessment, Cranfield University, since 2015; *b* 20 Feb. 1953; *s* of Victor and Eva Leinster; *m* 1976, Felicity Lawrence; two *s* one *d. Educ:* Imperial Coll., London (BSc Chemistry 1974; PhD Envmtl Engrg 1977); Cranfield Sch. of Management (MBA 1991). CChem, FRSC 1998; FIEMA 2004; CEnv 2005. BP International plc: Analytical Support and Res. Div., Res. Centre, 1977–79; Health, Safety and Envmt Directorate, 1979–85; Schering Agrochemicals, 1985–88; Thomson-MTS Ltd: Head of Res. and Consultancy, 1988–90; Man. Dir, 1990–94; Dir, Envmtl Services, SmithKline Beecham, 1994–98; Dir of Envmtl Protection, 1998–2004, Dir of Ops, 2004–08, Chief Exec., 2008–15, Envmt Agency. Hon. DSc: Cranfield, 2012; UWE, 2012. *Recreations:* golf, local church, reading, walking. *See also* S. J. Leinster.

**LEINSTER, Prof. Samuel John**, MD; FRCS, FRCSE, SFHEA, FAcadMed; Professor of Medical Education, University of East Anglia, 2001–11, now Emeritus (Inaugural Dean, School of Medicine, Health Policy and Practice, 2001–10); *b* 29 Oct. 1946; *s* of Victor and Eva Leinster; *m* 1971, Jennifer Woodward; three *s* one *d. Educ:* Univ. of Edinburgh (BSc 1968; MB ChB 1971); Univ. of Liverpool (MD 1990). FRCSE 1976; FRCS 1998. MO, RAF, 1971–77; Lectr in Surgery, Welsh Nat. Sch. of Medicine, 1978–81; University of Liverpool: Sen. Lectr in Surgery, 1982–92; Reader in Surgery, 1992–95; Prof. of Surgery, 1995–2000. FHEA 2007, SFHEA 2008; FAcadMed 2009. *Publications:* Systemic Diseases for Dental Students, 1984; Shared Care in Breast Cancer, 1999; The Changing Face of Medical Education, 2011; The Changing Role of Doctors, 2013; articles on breast cancer care, psychological impact of cancer and med. educn in learned jls. *Recreations:* family, gardening, DIY, wood turning, active committed Christian. *Address:* Vassars, Common Road, East Tuddenham, Dereham, Norfolk NR20 3AH. *E:* s.leinster@uea.ac.uk. *Clubs:* Royal Air Force; Royal Society of Medicine.
*See also* P. Leinster.

**LEIPER, Quentin John**, CBE 2009; FREng; FICE; civil engineer, geotechnical engineer and sustainability expert; President, Institution of Civil Engineers, 2006–07; Group Chief Engineer, Carillion plc, 2006–14; *b* 7 Oct. 1951; *s* of John W. G. Leiper and Betty Leiper; *m* 1980, Dorothy Ellen East; two *s* one *d. Educ:* King's Sch., Ely; Univ. of Glasgow (BSc 1975); Univ. of Surrey (MSc 1984). CCE 1985; CEng 1985; MICE 1985, FICE 1994; CEnv 2005; FREng 2011. Nuttall Geotechnical Services, 1975–77; Geotechnical Engr, Soil Mechanics, 1977–78; Manager: Nuttall Geotechnical Services, 1978–80; Terresearch, 1982–86; Contracts Manager, GKN Keller Foundns, 1986–89; Chief Engr, Westpile, 1989–91; Piling Ops Manager, Lilley Construction, 1990–91; Chief Geotech. Engr, Tarmac plc, 1991–96; Co. Chief Engr, 1996–2000, Dir for Engrg and the Envmt, 2000–06, Carillion plc. Initiated and developed the Carillion sustainability strategy model and "sun" impacts diagram, 2001. Vis. Prof., Sch. of Civil Engrg, Univ. of Edinburgh, 1998–. Mem., Vice-Chm., 1997–99, Chm., 1999–2001, British Geotechnical Assoc. (formerly British Geotechnical Soc.); Institution of Civil Engineers: Founding Chm. and Hon. Ed., Engineering Sustainability, 2002–04; Vice Pres., 2003–06; Chm., Queen's Jubilee Scholarship Trust, 2007–16. Trustee, BRE Trust, 2013–16. Gov., Royal Sch. Wolverhampton, 2015–17. *Publications:* over 50 jl articles and conf. papers. *Recreations:* hockey, kites (including fighting and traction), sailing, saxophone and clarinet. *E:* qleiper@gmail.com. *Club:* Bridgnorth Cricket and Hockey.

**LEISER, Helen Kinty;** JP; Policy Director, Generation IV International Forum (intergovernmental nuclear energy research collaboration), 2005–07; *b* 3 July 1947; *d* of George and Audrey Leiser; acquired German dual nationality, 2016. *Educ:* Twickenham County Grammar Sch.; LSE (BScEcon 1968); Birkbeck, Univ. of London (MA Eur. Hist. 2012). Economic Dept, TUC, 1968–73; HM Customs and Excise, 1973–74; Employment Dept, 1974–83; Cabinet Office, Machinery of Govt Div., 1983–85; Asst Sec., gen. policy, then resources and planning, later offshore safety reforms, HSE, 1986–93; Dir, Business Develt, Employment Service, 1993; Head, Industrial Relations Div., Dept of Employment, 1994; Dir, Employment Relns Policy, DTI, 1995–98; Dir, Nuclear Industries, DTI, and nonexec. Dir, UKAEA, 1998–2003; seconded to US Dept of Energy, 2003–05; consultant for Nuclear Decommissioning Authy on Nat. Nuclear Archive, 2005–06. Mem. Council, Hampstead Garden Suburb Residents' Assoc., 2019–. JP NW London (formerly Barnet and Hendon), 2006–17. *Recreations:* travel, listening to music, study of German history and literature, spending time with relatives. *Address:* 11 Asmuns Place, NW11 7XE. *E:* helen.leiser@btinternet.com. *Club:* Lansdowne.

**LEITCH**, family name of **Baron Leitch**.

**LEITCH**, Baron *cr* 2004 (Life Peer), of Oakley in Fife; **Alexander Park Leitch;** Chairman, BUPA, 2005–18; Chief Executive, Zurich Financial Services (UKISA Asia Pacific) Ltd, 1998–2004; *b* 20 Oct. 1947; *s* of late Donald Leitch, Blairhall, Dunfermline, and Agnes Smith (*née* Park); *m* 1st (marr. diss.); three *d*; 2nd, 2003, Noelle Dowd, Dallas, Texas; one *d. Educ:* Dunfermline High Sch. MBCS 1966. Chief Systems Designer, Nat. Mutual Life, then Hambro Life, 1969–88; Allied Dunbar Plc, 1988–96 (Dep. Chm. 1990; Chief Exec., 1993–96); Chm., Allied Dunbar Asscce Plc, 1996–2001; Chief Exec., British American Financial Services (UK and Internat.) Ltd, 1996–98; Chairman: Dunbar Bank, 1994–2001; Eagle Star Hldgs Plc, 1996–2004; Threadneedle Asset Mgt, 1996–2004; Intrinsic Financial Services Ltd, 2005–17; Dir, BAT Industries Plc, 1997–98; non-executive Director: United Business Media plc, 2005–08; Lloyds Banking (formerly Lloyds TSB) Gp plc, 2005–12 (Dep. Chm. 2009–12); Paternoster, 2006–10; Scottish Widows, 2007–12 (Chm., 2007–12); Falcon Energy, 2013–14; Old Mutual Wealth, 2014–17. Chairman: Pensions Protection and Investment Accreditation Bd, 2001–02; Balance Charitable Foundn for Unclaimed Assets, 2004–05; Leitch Rev. of UK Skills, 2005; FNZ, 2014–. Mem. Bd, 1996–98, Dep. Chm., 1997–98, Chm., 1998–2000, ABI. Dep. Chm., BITC, 1996–2004;

Chm., Nat. Employment Panel, 2001–07; Dep. Chair, Commonwealth Educn Fund, 2003–. Chairman: SANE, 1999–2000; Medical Aid Films, 2010–13; Vice-Pres., UK Cares, 2004. Trustee: Nat. Galls Scotland, 1999–2003; Philharmonia Orch., 2000–04. Chancellor, Carnegie Coll., Dunfermline, 2012–14 (Fellow). Freeman, City of London, 2002; Mem., Co. of Insurers, 2002. FCGI 2014. Hon. DBA Sunderland, 2012. Prince of Wales Ambassador's Award for charitable work, 2001. *Recreations:* football, antiques, poetry, antiquarian books. *Address:* House of Lords, SW1A 0PW.

**LEITCH, David Alexander;** Under Secretary, Social Work Services Group, Scottish Education Department, 1983–89; *b* 4 April 1931; *s* of Alexander and Eileen Leitch; *m* 1954, Marie (*née* Tain); two *s* one *d*. *Educ:* St Mungo's Acad., Glasgow. Min. of Supply, 1948–58; Department of Agriculture and Fisheries for Scotland: Asst Principal, 1959; Principal, 1963; Asst Sec., 1971; Asst Sec., Local Govt Finance, Scottish Office (Central Services), 1976–81, Under Sec., 1981–83. Part-time Mem., Scottish Legal Aid Bd, 1989–97. *Recreation:* hill-walking.

**LEITCH, Dr John Gaston,** FREng; Upstream Engineering Authority for BP, VP and OR Engineering, since 2018; Engineering Authority for Global Projects, since 2013; *b* Coleraine, NI, 9 April 1959; *s* of Cecil and Mildred Leitch; *m* 1993, Cornelia Aletta Geldenhuys; one *s* one *d*. *Educ:* Coleraine Academical Instn; Queen's Univ., Belfast (BSc 1st Cl. Civil Engrg 1980; PhD Civil Engrg 1986); Manchester Univ. (Cert. Engrg Mgt 2009). CEng 1989; Eur Ing 1989; MRINA 1991; FICE 2012; FREng 2014. Industrial Associate, Harland & Wolff, 1986–88; Naval Architect and Project Engr, John Brown E & C Ltd, 1988–89; Brown and Root Vickers, then Brown and Root, later Halliburton Brown and Root, subseq. Brown and Root Energy Services, then Kellogg Brown and Root: Naval Architect, North Sea platforms, 1989–93, Qatar Gas develt, 1993; Lead Naval Architect, Lufeng field develt, Ampolex (on secondment), 1993–95; Structural Engr, BHP Liverpool Bay Field, 1996; Project Engr, then Engrg Manager, Terra Nova Floating Prodn Storage and Offloading, S Korea, 1996–2000; short-term projects, incl. assignments in Houston and Bohai Bay, 2000–03; Deptl Manager, Marine, Subsea and Pipelines, 2003–05; Prodn and Engrg Manager, Carrier Vessel Future Project, 2005–06; BP: Team Manager, Subsea and Floating Systems, 2006–09; Dir of Engrg, BP Upstream Engrg Centre, 2009–13. *Recreation:* family. *Address:* BP International Ltd, Chertsey Road, Sunbury on Thames, Middx TW16 7LN. *T:* 07810 056606. *E:* John.leitch@uk.bp.com.

**LEITH,** family name of **Baron Burgh.**

**LEITH, Sir George Ian David F.;** *see* Forbes-Leith.

**LEITH, Prudence Margaret, (Mrs John Playfair),** CBE 2010 (OBE 1989); DL; Chairman, Leith's Ltd, 1992–96; Deputy Chairman, Royal Society of Arts, since 1998 (Council Member, since 1992; Chairman, 1995–97); *b* 18 Feb. 1940; *d* of late Sam Leith and Margaret Inglis; *m* 1st, Rayne Kruger (*d* 2002); one *s* one *d*; 2nd, 2016, John Playfair. *Educ:* Cape Town Univ.; Sorbonne, Paris; Cordon Bleu, London. French studies at Sorbonne, and preliminary cooking apprenticeship with French families; Cordon Bleu sch. course; small outside catering service from bedsitter in London, 1960–65; started Leith's Good Food (commercial catering co.), 1965, and Leith's (restaurant), 1969 (Michelin star, 1994); Man. Dir, Prudence Leith Ltd, 1972; Cookery Corresp., Daily Mail, 1969–73; opened Leith's Sch. of Food and Wine, 1975; added Leith's Farm, 1976; Cookery Corresp., Sunday Express, 1976–80; Cookery Editor, 1980–85, Columnist, 1986–90, The Guardian. Board Member: British Transport Hotels, 1977–83; Halifax plc (formerly Leeds Permanent, then Halifax, Bldg Soc.), 1992–99; Whitbread plc, 1995–2005; Triven VCT, 1999–2003; Woolworths plc, 2002–09; Omega Internat. plc, 2004–09; Nations Healthcare, 2006–07; Belmond (formerly Orient Express Hotels) Ltd, 2006–15; pt-time Mem., BRB, 1980–85. Member: Food from Britain Council, 1983–86; Leisure Industries EDC, NEDO, 1986–90; Nat. Trng Task Force, 1989–90; NCVQ, 1992–96; Chm., 3E's Enterprises, 1997–2007. Chm., Restaurateurs' Assoc. of GB, 1990–94; Mem. Council, Museum of Modern Art, Oxford, 1984–90. Governor, City Technology Coll., 1994–2007; Chairman of Governors: King's Coll., Guildford, 1999–2007; Ashridge Mgt Coll., 2002–07 (Gov., 1992–2007); Chancellor, Queen Margaret Univ., Edinburgh, 2016–. Chairman: British Food Trust, 1997–2006; Forum for the Future, 2000–03; School Food Trust, 2007–10. Television: judge: Great British Menu, 2006–16; My Kitchen Rules UK, 2016; Great British Bake Off, 2017–. FRSA 1984–90; FCGI 1992. DL Greater London, 1998. Business Woman of the Year, 1990. *Publications:* Leith's All-Party Cook Book, 1969; Parkinson's Pie (in aid of World Wild Life Fund), 1972; Cooking For Friends, 1978; The Best of Prue Leith, 1979; (with J. B. Reynaud) Leith's Cookery Course (3-part paperback), 1979–80, (comp. hardback with C. Waldegrave), 1980; The Cook's Handbook, 1981; Prue Leith's Pocket Book of Dinner Parties, 1983; Dinner Parties, 1984; (with Polly Tyrer) Entertaining with Style, 1986; Confident Cooking (52 issue part-work), 1989–90; (with Caroline Waldegrave): Leith's Cookery School, 1985; Leith's Cookery Bible, 1991; Leith's Complete Christmas, 1992; Leith's Book of Baking, 1993; Leith's Vegetarian Cookery, 1993; Relish: my life on a plate (autobiog.), 2012; Pru: my all-time favourite recipes, 2018; *novels:* Leaving Patrick, 1999; Sisters, 2001; A Lovesome Thing, 2004; The Gardener, 2007; Choral Society, 2009; A Serving of Scandal, 2010; The Food of Love, 2015, reissued as The House at Chorlton, 2018; The Prodigal Daughter, 2016; The Lost Son, 2019. *Recreations:* walking, grandchildren. *Address:* (office) Chastleton Glebe, Chastleton, Moreton-in-Marsh, Glos GL56 0SZ. *T:* (01608) 674908. *E:* pmleith@prue-leith.com. *W:* www.prue-leith.com, www.twitter.com/PrueLeith.

**LEITH-BUCHANAN, Sir Gordon Kelly McNicol,** 8th Bt *cr* 1775, of Burgh St Peter, Norfolk; *b* 18 Oct. 1974; *s* of Sir Charles Alexander James Leith-Buchanan, 7th Bt and of Marianne (*née* Kelly); *S* father, 1998, but his name does not appear on the Official Roll of the Baronetage.

**le JEUNE d'ALLEGEERSHECQUE, Susan Jane,** CMG 2010; HM Diplomatic Service; High Commissioner to Canada, since 2017; *b* 29 April 1963; *d* of Gerald Miller, FCA, and Judith Anne Miller (*née* Rolfe); *m* 1991, Stéphane Hervé Marie le Jeune d'Allegeershecque; two *s*. *Educ:* Ipswich High Sch. for Girls, GPDST; Univ. of Bristol (BA Hons 1985); London Sch. of Econs and Pol Sci. (MSc 2012). Licentiate, CIPD 1999. Joined HM Diplomatic Service, 1985; FCO, 1985–87; Third, later Second Sec., UK Perm. Representation to EC, 1987–90; FCO, 1990–92; Second Sec. (Press/Econ.), Singapore, 1992–95; FCO, 1995–99; Dep. Hd of Mission, Caracas, 1999–2002; Dep. Hd of Mission, Colombia, 2002–05; Consul Gen. and Counsellor (Change Mgt), Washington, 2005–07; Dir, HR, FCO, 2007–12; Ambassador to Austria, and UK Perm. Rep. to the UN, Vienna, 2012–16; Minister Counsellor, Paris, 2016–17. *Recreations:* art, music, France. *Address:* c/o Foreign and Commonwealth Office, King Charles Street, SW1A 2AH.

**LELLIOTT, David Patrick,** OBE 2006; HM Diplomatic Service; Ambassador to the Republic of El Salvador, since 2019; *b* London, 13 Sept. 1966; *s* of Patrick Arthur Lelliott and Margaret Rose Lelliott; *m* 2009, Lizeth de la Cruz Herrera Cocoletzi; two *d*. *Educ:* Ewell High Sch.; Univ. of Bristol (BSc Maths 1988; MA Philos. 1989). Asst Desk Officer, Chem. and Biol Weapons Conventions, FCO, 1993–95; Special Asst to Dir, Baghdad Monitoring and Verification Centre, UN Special Commn, 1995; Third Sec. (Political), Doha, 1996–99; Second Sec. (Commercial), Mexico City, 2000–03; UK Political Officer, US Embassy, Monrovia, 2003–06; Hd, Conflict Prevention Team, FCO, 2006–08; Hd, British Embassy Office, Juba, 2008–09; Asst Dep. Gov., Gibraltar, 2009–13; Dep. High Comr, Chandigarh, 2013–17; Dep. Hd of Mission and Consul Gen., Khartoum, 2017–19. *Recreations:* travel, drama, music, family. *Address:* British Embassy, Edificio Torre Futura, 14th Floor, San Salvador, El Salvador. *T:* 25115703. *E:* david.lelliott@fco.gov.uk.

**LELLIOTT, John George,** OBE 2016; Finance Director, Crown Estate, 1985–2016; *b* Lewes, 16 Aug. 1952; *s* of John Harry Lelliott and Dulcie Mollie Lelliott; *m* 1980, Wendy Bull; one *s* one *d*. *Educ:* Lewes Co. Sec. Mod. Sch. FCCA 1993. HM Revenue and Customs, 1968–85. Chm., Natural Capital Coalition, 2016–. Non-executive Director: Royal Bournemouth and Christchurch NHS Foundn Trust, 2016–; Covent Garden Mkt Authy, 2016–; Envmt Agency, 2018–. Mem., Adv. Council, Accounting for Sustainability, Prince of Wales's Charitable Foundn, 2016–. Chm., Global Forum on Sustainability, Assoc. of Chartered Certified Accountants, 2017–. Trustee, Asthma UK, 2008–17. *Recreations:* golf, cricket, music. *T:* 07785 731901. *E:* j.lelliott@btinternet.com.

**LE MAIRE, Bruno;** Minister of Economy and Finance, France, since 2017; *b* Neuilly sur Seine, 15 April 1969; four *s*. *Educ:* Ecole Normale Supérieure (Higher degree in French Lang. and Lit. 1992); Sciences Po, Paris; Ecole Nat. d'Admin. Foreign Affairs Advr, Min. of Foreign Affairs; Strategic Affairs Advr to Minister of Foreign Affairs, 2002–04; Special Adviser: to Minister of Interior, 2004–05; to Prime Minister, 2005–06; COS, Prime Minister's Private Office, 2006–07; Mem. for Eure, Nat. Assembly, 2007–09, 2012–; Minister of Agric., Food, Fisheries, Rural Affairs and Spatial Planning, 2009–12. Regl Councillor, Haute-Normandie, 2010–16. *Publications:* Le Ministre, 2004; Des hommes d'Etat, 2007; Sans mémoire, le présent se vide, 2010; Musique absolue, une répétition avec Carlos Kleiber, 2012; Jours de pouvoir, 2013; A nos enfants, 2014; Ne vous résignez pas!, 2016; Paul, 2019; Le Nouvel Empire, 2019. *Address:* Ministry of the Economy, 139 rue de Bercy, 75012 Paris, France. *T:* (1) 53184200. *E:* sp.mineco@cabinets.finances.gouv.fr.

**LE MARCHANT, Sir Piers (Alfred),** 7th Bt *cr* 1841, of Chobham Place, Surrey; Global Chief Compliance Officer, JP Morgan Chase Corporate and Investment Bank, since 2014; *b* London, 11 April 1964; *s* of Michael Le Marchant and of Philippa Nancy Le Marchant (*née* Denby, later Fullerton); *S* cousin, 2016; *m* 1995, Hon. Silvia Maria Francesca Pearson, *e d* of Baron Pearson of Rannoch, *qv*; two *s* two *d*. *Educ:* Canford Sch.; Queen Mary Coll., Univ. of London (LLB). Compliance dir and lawyer, Nomura Internat. plc, 1987–90; capital markets lawyer, 1990–98, Eur. Legal Dir, 1998–2008 Lehman Bros; Hd, Legal Compliance, EMEA, Nomura, 2008–13; Gen. Counsel, EMEA, JP Morgan Chase, 2013–14. FRGS. *Recreations:* charity work, sailing, fishing. *Heir: s* Edward Le Marchant, *b* 16 Jan. 1998. *Address:* 5 Queen Anne's Gate, SW1H 9BU. *E:* piers@lemarchant.com. *Club:* Houghton (Stockbridge).

**LE MARECHAL, Robert Norford,** CB 1994; Deputy Comptroller and Auditor General, National Audit Office, 1989–2000; *b* 29 May 1939; *s* of late Reginald Le Marechal and of Margaret Le Marechal; *m* 1963, Linda Mary (*née* Williams); two *d*. *Educ:* Taunton's School, Southampton. CIPFA 1983. Joined Exchequer and Audit Dept, 1957; Nat. Service, RAEC, 1958–60; Senior Auditor, Exchequer and Audit Dept, 1971; Chief Auditor, 1976; Dep. Dir of Audit, 1980; Dir of Audit, 1983; Dir of Policy and Planning, 1984–86, Asst Auditor General, 1986–89, Nat. Audit Office. FRSA 1997. *Recreations:* reading, gardening. *Address:* 62 Woodcote Hurst, Epsom, Surrey KT18 7DT. *T:* (01372) 721291.

**LEMLEY, Jack Kenneth,** Hon. CBE 1996; Principal, Lemley International, Inc. (formerly Lemley & Associates), Boise, Idaho, 1988; *b* 2 Jan. 1935; *s* of Kenneth Clyde Lemley and Dorothy Whitsitte; *m* 1st, 1961, Georgia Marshall (marr. diss. 1978); two *s* one *d*; 2nd, 1983, Pamela (*née* Hroza). *Educ:* Coeur d'Alene High Sch., Idaho; Univ. of Idaho (BA Architecture 1960). Asst Project Engineer, Guy F. Atkinson Co., 1960–69; Pres., Healthcare, 1969–70; Manager, Indust. and Power Construction Div., Guy F. Atkinson Co., 1971–77; Sen. Vice-Pres., Constr. Div., Morrison-Knusden Co., 1977–87; Pres. and Chief Exec., Blount Construction Gp, 1987–88; Management Consultant, Lemley & Associates, 1988–89; Chief Exec. Officer, Transmanche-Link, Channel tunnel contractors, 1989–93; Chm. and CEO, American Ecology Corp., 1995–2001. Chm., Olympic Delivery Authy, London, 2006. Hon. DSc: Idaho, 1998; Albertson's Coll. of Idaho, 2006. *Publications:* numerous papers on underground construction projects and international tunnelling. *Recreations:* snow ski-ing, sailing, white water rafting, reading. *Club:* Arid (Boise, Idaho).

**LE MOIGNAN, Rev. Christina;** Chair, Birmingham Methodist District, 1996–2004; President, Methodist Conference, 2001–02; *b* 12 Oct. 1942; *d* of Edward Frank Le Moignan and (Winifred) Muriel Le Moignan. *Educ:* Somerville Coll., Oxford (MA; Dip. Public and Social Admin); Univ. of Ibadan, Nigeria (PhD 1970); Wesley House, Cambridge (MA). Ordained, 1976; Methodist minister, Huntingdon, Southampton, Portchester, 1976–89; Tutor, Queen's Coll., Birmingham, 1989–94; Principal, W Midlands Ministerial Trng Course (Queen's Coll., Birmingham), 1994–96. Hon. DD Birmingham, 2002. *Publications:* Following the Lamb: a reading of Revelation for the new millennium, 2000. *Recreation:* music. *Address:* 29 Hound Street, Sherborne, Dorset DT9 3AB.

**LEMOINE, Prof. Nicholas Robert,** MD, PhD; FRCPath, FMedSci; Professor of Molecular Oncology, and Director, Barts Cancer Institute (formerly Institute of Cancer), Queen Mary University of London, since 2003; Director, Cancer Research UK Centre, Barts Health NHS Trust (formerly Barts and the London NHS Trust), since 2003; National Medical Director, National Institute of Health Research Clinical Research Network, since 2014; *b* 11 Dec. 1957; *s* of Robert and Janet Lemoine; *m* 1st, 1980, Louise Nunley (marr. diss. 2008); one *s* one *d*; 2nd, 2010, Christine Rajah. *Educ:* Abingdon Sch.; St Bartholomew's Med. Coll., Univ. of London (BSc 1980; MB BS 1983; MD 1992); PhD Wales 1989. FRCPath 1992. Lectr, University Hosp. of Wales, 1985–88; Lectr, 1989–92, Sen. Lectr, 1992–96, Prof., 1996–2003, RPMS, London; Dir, Cancer Res. Molecular Oncol. Unit, Imperial Coll., London, 1997–2003. Dean, Acad. of Med. Scis, Zhengzhou Univ., China, 2015–. FMedSci 2006. Academician, Chinese Acad. of Engrs, 2017. Ed. in Chief, Gene Therapy (Nature Specialist Jls), 1997–2018; Commissioning Ed., British Medical Bulletin, 2008–. *Publications:* Understanding Gene Therapy, 1999; Progress in Pathology, 2001; numerous scientific articles on molecular pathology of cancer and gene therapy. *Recreations:* motorcycles, Rugby football, family and the fruit of serendipity. *Address:* Barts Cancer Institute, Queen Mary University of London, Ground Floor, Old Anatomy Building, Charterhouse Square, EC1M 6BQ. *T:* (020) 7882 3503, *Fax:* (020) 7882 3888.

**LEMON, Prof. Roger Nicholas,** PhD; FMedSci; Sobell Professor of Neurophysiology, Institute of Neurology, University College London, 1994–2017, now Emeritus (Director, 2002–08); *b* 6 March 1946; *s* of late Charles Lemon, MBE and Rosaleen Lemon (*née* Morrissey); *m* 1971, Judith Christine (*née* Kirby); two *s* one *d*. *Educ:* Sheffield Univ. (BSc, PhD 1971); MA Cantab. Lectr, Dept of Physiol., Univ. of Sheffield, 1971–77; Res. Fellow, Dept of Physiol., Monash Univ., Australia, 1974–75; Sen. Lectr, Dept of Anatomy, 1977–84, Reader, 1984–85, Erasmus Univ., Rotterdam; Lectr, Dept of Anatomy, 1985–94, and Fellow, New Hall, 1987–94, Univ. of Cambridge; Hd, Sobell Dept, Inst. of Neurol., UCL, 1994–2002 and 2010–11. Guarantor, Brain, 2007–. Mem. Council, Understanding

Animal Res., 2009–12. FMedSci 2002 (Mem. Council, 2012–). Fyssen Internat. Prize, 2015. *Publications:* (with R. Porter) Corticospinal Function and Voluntary Movement, 1993; contrib. papers and articles in general area of motor neurosci. *Recreations:* walking, naval history, Samuel Pepys. *Address:* Institute of Neurology, University College London, Sobell Department of Motor Neuroscience and Movement Disorders (Box 28), Queen Square, WC1N 3BG.

**LEMOS, Gerard Anthony,** CMG 2001; writer, social researcher; Partner, Lemos & Crane, since 1990; *b* 26 Feb. 1958; *s* of late Ronald Lemos and Cynthia (*née* Mitchell). *Educ:* Dulwich Coll.; Univ. of York. Dir, ASRA Housing Assoc., 1982–85; Area Manager and Dir of Develt, Circle 33 Housing Trust, 1985–90; Dir of Studies, Sch. for Social Entrepreneurs, 1997–99. Director: Mortgage Code Compliance Bd, 2000–01; Banking Code Standards Bd, 2000–10 (Dep. Chm., 2001–05, Chm., 2005–10); Chairman: Notting Hill Housing Gp, 2004–06; Money Advice Service, 2010–13. Mem., Audit Commn, 2000–04; Civil Service Comr, 2001–06. Non-exec. Dir, CPS, 2006–10; Ind. Dir, Payments Council, 2012–14 (Chm., 2014–15); Chm., Payments UK, 2015–18. Vis. Prof., Chongqing Business and Technology Univ., 2006–10. Vice-Pres., BBFC, 2008–18. Member of Board: London Internat. Fest. of Theatre, 1993–2001; British Council, 1999–2010 (Dep. Chm., 2003–09; Acting Chm., 2008–10); The Place Theatre, 2002–03; Chairman: Bd of Dirs, Akram Khan Dance Co., 2003–08; Council, Univ. of York, 2016–; Hofesh Shechter Dance Co., 2017–; Trustee, Dartington Hall Trust, 2008–09, 2010–16. *Publications:* Interviewing Perpetrators of Racial Harassment, 1994; Fair Recruitment and Selection, 1995; Safe as Houses: supporting people experiencing racial harassment, 1996; (jtly) The Communities We Have Lost and Can Regain, 1997; Urban Village, Global City: the regeneration of Colville, 1998; Steadying the Ladder: social and emotional aspirations of homeless and vulnerable people, 2006; reports: A Future Foretold: new approaches to meeting the long-term needs of single homeless people, 1999; Racial Harassment: action on the ground, 2000; (jtly) Dreams Deferred: the families and friends of homeless and vulnerable people, 2002; The Search for Tolerance: challenging and changing racist attitudes and behaviour among young people, 2005; Military History: the experiences of people who become homeless after military service, 2005; (jtly) Different World: how young people can work together on human rights and citizenship, 2007; Freedom's Consequences: reducing teenage pregnancies and their negative effects in the UK, 2009; The Meaning of Money: why homeless and vulnerable people see money as a route to security, respect and freedom, 2010; The End of the Chinese Dream: why Chinese people fear the future, 2012; The Good Prison: conscience, crime and punishment, 2015. *Recreations:* literature, cricket. *Address:* (office) The Music Base, Kings Place, York Way, N1 9AG. *T:* (020) 8348 8263.

**LENAERTS, Prof. Koen,** PhD; Baron; Professor of European Law, University of Leuven, since 1983; Judge, since 2003, and President, since 2015, Court of Justice of the European Union; *b* Mortsel, Belgium, 20 Dec. 1954; *m* Kris Grimonprez; six *d. Educ:* Univ. of Namur (Candidat en droit *summa cum laude* 1974); Univ. of Leuven (Licentiaat in de Rechten summa cum laude 1977; PhD Law 1982); Harvard Univ. (LLM 1978; MPA 1979). Prof., Coll. of Europe, Bruges, 1984–89; Dir, Inst. of Eur. Law, Univ. of Leuven, 1990–2009; law clerk to Judge René Joliet, Court of Justice of EC, 1984–85; Mem., Brussels Bar, actg as attorney in Eur. Court of Justice, *inter alia* on behalf of Belgian state, 1986–89; Judge, Court of First Instance of Eur. Communities, 1989–2003; Vice-Pres., Court of Justice of EU, 2012–15. *Publications:* Le juge et la constitution aux Etats-Unis d'Amérique et dans l'ordre juridique européen, 1988; (with P. Van Nuffel) European Union Law, 3rd edn 2011; (jtly) EU Procedural Law, 2014. *Address:* Court of Justice of the European Union, Rue du Fort Niedergrünewald, 2925 Luxembourg.

**LENDRUM, Christopher John,** CBE 2005; Group Vice Chairman, 2004, and Executive Director, 1998–2004, Barclays plc; *b* 15 Jan. 1947; *s* of late Herbert Colin Lendrum and of Anne Margaret (*née* Macdonell); *m* 1970, Margaret Patricia Parker; one *s* one *d. Educ:* Felsted Sch., Essex; Durham Univ. (BA Econs 1968). FCIB 1992. Joined Barclays Bank plc, 1969: Regl Dir, 1991–93; Dep. Man. Dir of Banking Div., 1993–95; Man. Dir of UK Business Banking, 1995–98; Chief Exec., Corporate Banking, 1998–2003. Chm., Barclays Pension Fund Trustees Ltd, 2005–11. Non-executive Director: Co. Durham Community Foundn, 2008–14; North East Finance Ltd, 2009–18; Motability Ops plc, 2009–18. Trustee, CAB, 2005–06 (Mem. Adv. Bd, 2001–04); Gov., Motability, 2005–09. Freeman, City of London, 1999; Liveryman, Woolmen's Co., 1999–. CCMI 2002. Gov., Kent Coll., Pembury, 2000–08. Chm., Aston Martin Heritage Trust, 2006–09 (Trustee, 2003–10); Trustee: City of London Trust for St Paul's Cathedral, 2007–16; Alnwick Garden, 2012–15; Tyne, Wear and Northumberland Community Foundn, 2015–17. Churchwarden, St James, Shilbottle, 2013–. Hon. DLitt Durham, 2008. *Recreations:* gardening, travel, restoring neglected motor cars. *Address:* Hazon House, Guyzance, Northumberland NE65 9AT. *E:* lendrumsofhazon@btinternet.com. *Club:* Royal Automobile.

**LENG, Gillian Catherine,** CBE 2011; MD; Deputy Chief Executive, National Institute for Health and Care Excellence (formerly for Health and Clinical Excellence), since 2007 (Executive Director, since 2004); *b* Newport, 16 Sept. 1960; *d* of Mark Sanderson and Mary Sanderson; *m* 2006, Paul Anthony Cosford, *qv*; two *d* by a previous marriage. *Educ:* Harrogate Grammar Sch.; Univ. of Leeds (BSc Hons 1st Cl. 1982; MB ChB 1987; MD 1994). FFPH 2006; FRCP 2007; FRCPE 2012. HO, St James' Univ. Hosp., Leeds, 1987–88; SHO, Western Gen. Hosp., Edinburgh, 1988–89; Trainee in Gen. Practice, 1989–90; Clin. Res. Fellow, Univ. of Edinburgh, 1990–97; Registrar in Public Health Medicine, W of Scotland and N Thames, 1997–2000; Consultant in Public Health, Beds, 2000–01; Guidelines Prog. Dir, NICE, 2001–04. Hon. Sen. Lectr, LSHTM, 2007–12; Vis. Prof., KCL, 2012–. Trustee: RSM, 2013–; Centre for Ageing Better, 2014–15; Guidelines Internat. Network, 2016–. Assoc. Mem., BUPA, 2014–. FRSocMed 2002. FRSA 2008. Ed., Cochrane Gp on Effective Practice and Orgnl Change, 2015–. *Publications:* Achieving High Quality Care: practical advice from NICE, 2014; contrib. articles to jls relating to evidence-based care, epidemiology and guideline methodology. *Recreations:* walking, painting, keeping the garden free of ubiquitous sycamore saplings. *Address:* National Institute for Health and Care Excellence, 10 Spring Gardens, SW1A 2BU. *T:* 07811 209586. *E:* gcleng@doctors.org.uk.

**LENG, James William;** European Chairman, AEA Investors (UK) LLP, 2007–15 (Member, Board, since 2007); Deputy Chairman and Senior Independent Director, RHI Magnesita NV, since 2017; Chairman, Nomura International plc, 2015–17; *b* 19 Nov. 1945; *m* 1974, Carole Ann Guyll. John Waddington plc, 1967–84; Low & Bonar plc: Man. Dir, Bonar & Flotex, 1984–86; Chief Exec., Plastics Div., 1986–88; Chief Exec., European Ops, 1988–92; Dir, 1989–95; Group Chief Exec., 1992–95; Chief Exec., Laporte plc, 1995–2001; Dep. Chm., 2001–03, Chm., 2003–09, Corus Gp plc, later Corus Gp Ltd (non-exec. Dir, 2001–07); Dep. Chm., Tata Steel of India, 2007–09; Chm., Doncasters Gp Ltd, 2001–03 and 2006–09. Lead non-exec. Dir, Ministry of Justice, 2010–12. Chm., HSBC Bank plc, 2011–13 (non-exec. Dir, 2010–13); non-executive Director: Pilkington plc, 1998–2006; IMI plc, 2002–05 (Chm., 2015); Alstom SA, 2003–15; Hanson plc, 2004–07; J O Hambro Investment Mgt Ltd, 2010–12; Genel Energy (formerly Vallares), 2011–16; Aon Corp., 2014–; Ind. Dir, TNK-BP, 2009–11; Chm. Designate, Rio Tinto plc, 2009. Chm., Guyll-Leng Charitable Trust, 2010–. Vice-Pres., CIA, 1999–2001. Governor: NIESR, 1999–; Univ. of Newcastle-upon-Tyne, 2005–09; Ashridge Coll., 2008–11. FRSA 2005. *Recreations:* sport, music. *Club:* Royal Automobile.

**LENG, Virginia Helen Antoinette;** *see* Elliot, V. H. A.

**LENNAN, David John;** business and organisational development consultant; Chief Executive, Timber Trade Federation, 2014–16; *b* 15 Dec. 1948; *s* of John D. Lennan and Mair E. Lennan; *m* 1975, Diane Griffiths (marr. diss. 2013); partner, Mary Rudd. *Educ:* Northampton Town and Co. Grammar Sch. ACIB 1971. Joined District Bank, 1966; NatWest Group PLC: Dep. Regl Dir, SE Reg., 1992–93; Hd, UK Develt, Human Resources, 1993–95; Dir, Retail Insce Services, 1995–98; Dir, Corporate Develt, Surrey CC, 1998–2001; Dir Gen., British Chambers of Commerce, 2001–02; CEO, Agricultural Industries Confedn, 2003–04; Man. Dir, Business HR Solutions Ltd, 2004–10. Non-exec. Chm., Workwise UK, 2006–; Chm., Loftzone Ltd. Tuck Exec. Prog., Dartmouth Univ., USA, 1996. *Recreations:* sailing, theatre, flying. *Address:* Hove Creek, 82 Coast Road, West Mersea, Colchester CO5 8LS.

**LENNARD, Sir Peter John B.;** *see* Barrett-Lennard.

**LENNIE,** family name of **Baron Lennie.**

**LENNIE,** Baron *cr* 2014 (Life Peer), of Longsands Tynemouth in the County of Tyne and Wear; **Christopher John Lennie;** *b* Perth, Australia, 1953; *s* of Magnus and Elizabeth Lennie; *m* 1978, Anne Doffegnies; one *s* one *d. Educ:* Newcastle Poly. (BA Hist. and Eng. Lit. 1976). Unison official, until 2000; Lab Party official, 2000, Dep. Sec. Gen., 2001–12. *Recreations:* Newcastle Utd supporter, running, cycling, golf. *Address:* c/o House of Lords, SW1A 0PW. *Club:* Tynemouth Social Club Institute and Union.

**LENNON, Francis Patrick,** OBE 2002; Head Teacher, Dunblane High School, 2010–16; *b* Glasgow, 18 June 1952; *s* of William and Margaret Lennon; *m* 1974, Marie Connolly; one *s* four *d. Educ:* Salesian Coll., Shrigley, Cheshire; Holy Cross High Sch., Hamilton; Univ. of Glasgow (MA Hons English and Hist.); Open Univ. (MPhil). Teacher of English, St Gerard's Secondary Sch., Glasgow, 1975–78; Asst Principal Teacher of English, St Columba of Iona Secondary Sch., Glasgow, 1978–81; Asst Principal Teacher of English, Holyrood Secondary Sch., Glasgow, 1981–84; Principal teacher of English, Holy Cross High Sch., 1984–90; Asst Head Teacher, St Patrick's High Sch., 1990–93; Depute Head Teacher, St Andrew's Secondary Sch., Glasgow, 1993–96; Head Teacher, St Modan's High Sch., Stirling, 1996–2010. Tutor, Tapestry Partnership, 2016–. FRSA. *Recreations:* football, American football, music, opera, theatre. *Address:* 6 Richmond Grove, Rutherglen, Glasgow G73 3LD. *T:* (0141) 647 3754. *E:* fpl@sky.com.

**LENNON, Prof. (Justin) John,** PhD; Director, Moffat Centre, since 1998, Moffat Professor of Travel and Tourism Business Development, since 1999, and Dean, since 2018, Glasgow Caledonian University; *b* Birmingham, 19 June 1961; *s* of John and Mary Lennon; *m* 1985, Joanne Wolstenholme; two *s* one *d. Educ:* Oxford Poly. (BSc Hons Hotel and Tourism Mgt); Strathclyde Univ. (MPhil Mgt 1990); Glasgow Caledonian Univ. (PhD Mgt 2010). Mgt trainee, Penta Hotels, Germany, 1980–81; Asst Food and Beverage Manager, Poste Hotels Ltd, 1983–85; Personnel and Trng Manager, Food and Beverage Manager, and Dep. Gen. Manager, Midland Hotels, 1985–88; Gen. Manager, Midland Hotel, Sheffield, 1988–90; Consultant, Hospitality Consultants Ltd, 1990–95; Lectr and Industrial Liaison Tutor, Strathclyde Univ., 1993–95; Sen. Lectr, then Reader in Mgt, 1996–99, Vice Dean, 2012–18, Glasgow Caledonian Univ. Principal Advr, All Party Tourism Inquiry, Scottish Govt, 2007–09; Specialist Policy Advr, VisitScotland, 2004–09. Director: Scottish Tourism Forum, 2004–08; Canadian Tourism Commn (Eur. Mktg Bd), 2005–08; non-exec. Dir, Historic Scotland, 2006–. *Publications:* (with M. Peet) Hospitality Management: a case study approach, 1990, instructor's manual, 1990; Guide to Catering Practice, 1996; (with V. Russell) Guide to Events Management, 1997; (ed jtly) Hospitality, Tourism and Leisure Management: issues in strategy and culture, 1997; (with M. Foley) Dark Tourism: the attraction of death and disaster, 2000, 4th edn 2009; (ed) Tourism Statistics: international perspectives and current issues, 2001; (jtly) Benchmarking National Tourism Organisation: lessons from best practice internationally, 2006; contrib. chapters in textbooks; contrib. articles in jls incl. Internat. Jl Hospitality Mgt, Internat. Jl Contemporary Hospitality Mgt, Internat. Jl heritage Studies, Tourism Mgt. *Address:* Shirgarton House, Kippen, Stirlingshire FK8 3EA.

**LENNON, Linda Susan,** CBE 2009; Director, Crown Estate Paving Commission, since 2018; *b* Sutton, Surrey, 13 March 1963; *d* of Anthony Harry Smith and Rita Joan Smith. *Educ:* Wallington High Sch. for Girls; Civil Service Coll. (IPD Trng and Develt). Appts with LCD, MoJ and HM Courts, 1981–2009, incl. Area Dir for London, Civil and Family Courts, until 2009; Chief Executive Officer: Parole Bd (England and Wales), 2009–12; Royal Parks, 2012–15; London Stadium 185, 2015–17. *Recreations:* swimming, walking my dog, bird watching, reading, theatre and musical performances. *Address:* Crown Estate Paving Commission, 12 Park Square East, Regent's Park, NW1 4LH.

**LENNON, Hon. Paul Anthony,** AO 2015; Chairman: Common Ground Tasmania, since 2012; Australian Bauxite Ltd, since 2014; Premier of Tasmania, Australia, 2004–08; *b* 8 Oct. 1955; *s* of Charles and Marg Lennon; *m* 1978, Margaret Gaff; two *d.* Storeman/clerk, 1974–78; Tasmanian Branch, Storemen and Packers Union: Organiser, 1978–80; Sec., 1980–84; Sen. Vice-Pres., Federated Storemen and Packers Union of Australia, 1982–84; Sec., Tasmanian Trades and Labor Council, 1984–89; Asst Gen. Manager, Develt, Tasmanian Develt Authy, 1989–90. MHA (ALP) Franklin, Tasmania, 1990–2008; Opposition Whip and Shadow Minister for Police and Emergency Services, 1992; Shadow Minister for: Racing and Gaming, 1992–98; Industrial Relns, 1993–98; Employment and Trng, 1993–95; Forestry, 1995–96; Opposition Leader of Business in the House, 1995–96; Dep. Leader of Opposition, 1996–98; Minister for Workplace Standards and Workers' Compensation, Forests and Mines, 1997–98; Dep. Premier, 1998–2004; Minister for Infrastructure, Energy and Resources and for Racing and Gaming, 1998–2002; Minister for Econ. Develt, Energy and Resources, and for Racing and Sport and Recreation, 2002–04; Treas., 2004–06; Minister for Local Govt, 2004–08, for Econ. Develt and Resources, 2006–08. Mem., Parly Public Accounts Cttee, 1990–96.

**LENNOX, Annie,** OBE 2011; singer and songwriter; humanitarian aid campaigner; *b* 25 Dec. 1954; *d* of late Thomas A. Lennox and Dorothy Lennox (*née* Ferguson); *m* 1st, 1984, Radha Raman (marr. diss.); 2nd, 1988, Uri Fruchtmann; two *d* (and one *s* decd) (marr. diss.); 3rd, 2012, Dr Mitch Besser. *Educ:* Aberdeen High Sch. for Girls; Royal Acad. of Music. Singer with: The Catch, subseq. The Tourists, 1977–81; Eurythmics, 1981–89, 1999; solo singer, 1988–. Albums include: with The Tourists: The Tourists, 1979; Reality Affect, 1980; Luminous Basement, 1980; with Eurythmics: In the Garden, 1981; Sweet Dreams (Are Made of This), 1983; Touch, 1984; 1984 (For the Love of Big Brother), 1984; Be Yourself Tonight, 1985; Revenge, 1986; Savage, 1987; We Too Are One, 1989; Peace, 1999; solo: Diva, 1992; Medusa, 1995; Train in Vain, 1995; Bare, 2003; Songs of Mass Destruction, 2007; The Annie Lennox Collection, 2009; A Christmas Cornucopia, 2010;

Nostalgia, 2014. Mayor of London's HIV Ambassador, 2011–. Chancellor, Glasgow Caledonian Univ., 2017–. *Address*: c/o XIX Entertainment Ltd, Unit 5B, The Albion Riverside, SW11 4AX.

**LENNOX, Lionel Patrick Madill**; Registrar: of the Diocese of York, and Legal Secretary to the Archbishop of York, 1987–2014; of the Province of York, 1987–2015; of the Convocation of York, 1987–2016; of Tribunals, Province of York, 2006–17; of the Diocese of Sodor and Man, 2014–17; Deputy Registrar of the Diocese of York, 2014–17; Consultant, Lupton Fawcett, since 2017 (Partner, Denison Till, solicitors, 1987–2013; Director, Lupton Fawcett Denison Till, subseq. Lupton Fawcett LLP, 2013–17); *b* 5 April 1949; *s* of late Rev. James Lennox and May Lennox; *m* 1979, Barbara Helen Firth; two *s* one *d*. *Educ*: St John's Sch., Leatherhead; Univ. of Birmingham (LLB). Admitted Solicitor, 1973; Ecclesiastical Notary, 1987; Notary Public in practice, 1992–. Solicitor in private practice, 1973–81; Asst Legal Advr to Gen. Synod, 1981–87. Secretary: Archbishop of Canterbury's Gp on Affinity, 1982–84; Legal Adv. Commn, Gen. Synod of C of E, 1986–2015. Pres., Yorks Law Soc., 2007–08. Sec., Yorks Mus. of Farming, 1991–94. Trustee: Yorks Historic Churches Trust, 1988–2010; St Leonard's Hospice, York, 2000–09; York Centre for Voluntary Service, 2012–18. Under Sheriff, City of York, 2006–07. Canon Provincial of York, 2015–. *Address*: Stamford House, Piccadilly, York YO1 9PP. *T*: (01904) 623487.

**LENNOX-BOYD**, family name of **Viscount Boyd of Merton**.

**LENNOX-BOYD, Arabella, (Lady Lennox-Boyd)**; landscape designer; Principal, Arabella Lennox-Boyd Landscape Design, since 1984; *b* 15 Jan. 1938; *d* of Piero Parisi and Irene Diaz della Vittoria; *m* 1974, Hon. Sir Mark Alexander Lennox-Boyd, *qv*; one *d*, and one *d* from former marriage. *Educ*: privately in Italy. Commissioned designs in UK, Europe and worldwide incl. Russia, USA and Caribbean, range from small town gdns to country landscapes; major projects incl. roof gdn at No 1 Poultry, gdns at Ascott House and Eaton Hall. Trustee: Kew Gdns, 1989–98; Castle Howard Arboretum Trust, 1997–; Chelsea Physic Gdn, 2014–; former Mem., Historic Parks and Gdns Cttee, English Heritage. Hon. DDes Greenwich, 2003. Gold Medals, RHS Chelsea Flower Show, 1990, 1993, 1995, 1998, 2000, 2008. Premio Firenze Donna, 2005; Veitch Meml Medal, RHS, 2008. *Publications*: Traditional English Gardens, 1987; Private Gardens of London, 1990; (jtly) Designing Gardens, 2002. *Recreations*: collecting rare trees and propagating, gardening, listening to music. *Address*: 45 Moreton Street, SW1V 2NY. *T*: (020) 7931 9995, *Fax*: (020) 7821 6585. *E*: office@arabellalennoxboyd.com.

**LENNOX-BOYD, Hon. Sir Mark (Alexander)**, Kt 1994; *b* 4 May 1943; 3rd *s* of 1st Viscount Boyd of Merton, CH, PC and of Lady Patricia Guinness, 2nd *d* of 2nd Earl of Iveagh, KG, CB, CMG, FRS; *m* 1974, Arabella Lacloche (*see* A. Lennox-Boyd); one *d*. *Educ*: Eton Coll.; Christ Church, Oxford. Called to the Bar, Inner Temple, 1968. MP (C) Morecambe and Lonsdale, 1979–83, Morecambe and Lunesdale, 1983–97; contested (C) Morecambe and Lunesdale, 1997. Parliamentary Private Secretary: to Sec. of State for Energy, 1981–83; to the Chancellor of the Exchequer, 1983–84; Asst Govt Whip, 1984–86; a Lord Comr of HM Treasury (Govt Whip), 1986–88; PPS to Prime Minister, 1988–90; Parly Under-Sec. of State, FCO, 1990–94. Chm., Georgian Gp, 2014–. *Recreation*: travel. *Address*: Gresgarth Hall, Caton, Lancashire LA2 9NB. *Clubs*: Brooks's, Pratt's, Beefsteak.

**LENON, Andrew Ralph Fitzmaurice**; QC 2006; *b* 7 April 1957; *s* of late Rev. Philip John Fitzmaurice Lenon and of Jane Alethea Lenon (*née* Brooke); *m* 1987, Sheila Cook; one *s* three *d*. *Educ*: St John's Sch., Leatherhead; Lincoln Coll., Oxford (BA); City Univ. (Dip. Law). Called to the Bar, Lincoln's Inn, 1981; in practice specialising in commercial law; a Chm., Competition Appeal Tribunal, 2012–. *Publications*: contribs to legal jls. *Recreations*: music, languages. *Address*: Chambers of Lord Grabiner, QC, One Essex Court, Temple, EC4Y 9AR. *T*: (020) 7583 2000.
*See also* B. J. Lenon.

**LENON, Barnaby John**, CBE 2019; MA; Chairman, Independent Schools' Council, since 2011; Dean, School of Education, University of Buckingham, since 2019; *b* 10 May 1954; *s* of late Rev. Philip John Fitzmaurice Lenon and of Jane Alethea Lenon (*née* Brooke); *m* 1983, Penelope Anne Thain, BA; two *d*. *Educ*: Eltham Coll.; Keble Coll., Oxford (schol.; BA 1st Cl. Hons 1976; MA); St John's, Cambridge (PGCE; Univ. Prize for Educn 1978). Assistant Master: Eton Coll., 1977; Sherborne Sch., 1978–79; Eton Coll., 1979–90; Teacher, Holland Park Sch., 1988; Dep. Head Master, Highgate Sch., 1990–95; Headmaster: Trinity Sch. of John Whitgift, 1995–99; Harrow School, 1999–2011. Mem. Bd, Ofqual, 2012–18. Governor: John Lyon Sch., 1999–2011; Swanbourne Sch., 1999–2005; Orley Farm Sch., 1999–2011; Wellesley House Sch., 1999–2011; Beacon Sch., 2000–05; Papplewick Sch., 2001–11; Francis Holland Schs, 2002–11; Aysgarth Sch., 2006–11; Chelsea Acad., 2009–18; London Acad. of Excellence, 2011– (Chm., 2012–). Trustee: Vocal Futures, 2011–19; Yellow Submarine Charity, Oxford, 2012–; King Edward Sixth Foundn, Birmingham, 2018–; Dir, New Schs Network, 2014–19. FRGS 1987 (Mem. Council, 1987–90 and 1998–2000; Chm., Educn Sub-Cttee, 1996–99; Vice-Pres., 2009–12). CGeog 2000. *Publications*: Techniques and Fieldwork in Geography, 1983; London, 1988; London in the 1990s, 1993; Fieldwork Techniques and Projects in Geography, 1994; The United Kingdom: geographical case studies, 1995; (ed jtly) Directory of University Geography Courses, 1995, 2nd edn 1997; Fieldwork and Skills, 2015; Cambridge AS and A Level Geography, 2016; Much Promise: successful schools in England, 2017; Other People's Children: what happens to the 50% least successful academically?, 2018; contribs to geographical jls. *Recreations*: oil painting, athletics, deserts. *Address*: 55 St John Street, Oxford OX1 2LQ.
*See also* A. R. F. Lenon.

**LEON, Sir John (Ronald)**, 4th Bt *cr* 1911; actor (stage name, **John Standing**); *b* 16 Aug. 1934; *er s* of 3rd Bt and late (Dorothy) Katharine (stage name Kay Hammond), *d* of Sir Guy Standing, KBE; *S* father, 1964; *m* 1961, Jill (marr. diss. 1972), *d* of Jack Melford; one *s*; *m* 1984, Sarah, *d* of Bryan Forbes, CBE; one *s* two *d*. *Educ*: Eton. Late 2nd Lt, KRRC. Plays include: Darling Buds of May, Saville, 1959; leading man, season, Bristol Old Vic, 1960; The Irregular Verb to Love, Criterion, 1961; Norman, Duchess, 1963; So Much to Remember, Vaudeville, 1963; The Three Sisters, Oxford Playhouse, 1964; See How They Run, Vaudeville, 1964; Seasons at Chichester Theatre, 1966, 1967; The Importance of Being Earnest, Ring Round the Moon, Haymarket, 1968; The Alchemist, and Arms and the Man, Chichester, 1970; Popkiss, Globe, 1972; A Sense of Detachment, Royal Court, 1972; Private Lives, Queen's and Globe, 1973, NY and tour of USA, 1974; Jingo, RSC, 1975; Plunder, The Philanderer, NT, 1978; Close of Play, NT, 1979; Tonight at 8.30, Lyric, 1981; The Biko Inquest, Riverside, 1984; Rough Crossing, National, 1984; Hay Fever, Albery, 1992; A Month in the Country, Albery, 1994; Son of Man, RSC, 1995; A Delicate Balance, Haymarket, 1997; Shadowlands, Wyndham's, 2007. *Films*: The Wild and the Willing, 1962; Iron Maiden, 1962; King Rat, 1964; Walk, Don't Run, 1965; Zee and Co., 1973; The Eagle has Landed, 1976; The Class of Miss MacMichael, 1977; The Legacy, 1977; The Elephant Man, 1979; The Sea Wolves, 1980; (TV film) The Young Visiters, 1984; Nightflyers; 8½ Women, Rogue Trader, 1999; The Good Woman, 2003; V for Vendetta, 2005; I Want Candy, Shooter, Before the Rains, 2007. *Television* appearances incl.: for British TV: Arms and the Man; The First Churchills; Charley's Aunt; Rogue Male; The Sinking of HMS Victoria; Home and Beauty; Tinker, Tailor, Soldier, Spy; The Other 'Arf; Old Boy Network; Tonight at 8.30; Count of Solar; Gulliver's Travels; Shadow in the North; for American TV: Lime Street; Hotel; Flap Jack Floozie; Visitors; Murphy's Law; The Endless Game; Murder She Wrote; LA Law; Windmills of the Gods; Drovers' Gold; A Dance to The Music of Time; Longitude; King Solomon's Mines. *Cabaret*: John Standing Sings Coward, 2009; John Standing Swings Cole Porter, 2011. *Recreation*: painting. *Heir*: *s* Alexander John Leon [*b* 3 May 1965; *m* 1996, Susan Janice Paul; two *s*]. *Address*: c/o United Agents, 12–26 Lexington Street, W1F 0LE.

**LEONARD, Anthony James**; QC 1999; **His Honour Judge Leonard**; a Circuit Judge, since 2009; a Senior Circuit Judge, Central Criminal Court, since 2017; *b* 21 April 1956; *s* of late Sir (Hamilton) John Leonard and Doreen Enid Leonard (*née* Parker); *m* 1983, Shara Jane Cormack; two *d*. *Educ*: Hurstpierpoint Coll., Sussex; Council of Legal Educn. Short Service Limited Commn, Queen's Regt, 1975–76; Major, 6/7 Queen's (TA), 1976–85. Called to the Bar, Inner Temple, 1978, Bencher, 2002; Standing Counsel to Inland Revenue, S Eastern Circuit, 1993–99; Recorder, 2000–09. Vice-Chm., Professional Conduct Cttee, 2001–04, 2006–08. Adjunct Prof. of Law, Loyola Univ., Chicago, 2019–. Dep. Chancellor, Dio. of St Edmundsbury and Ipswich, 2009–; Chancellor, Dio. of Ely, 2012–; Commissary to the Archbishop of Canterbury, 2012–. Liveryman, Plaisterers' Co. *Recreations*: opera, wine, reading. *Club*: Garrick.

**LEONARD, Brian Henry**, CBE 2008; Chief Executive, The Sports and Recreation Trusts Association Ltd (Sporta), 2010–18; *b* 6 Jan. 1948; *s* of William Henry Leonard and Bertha Florence Leonard; *m* 1975, Margaret Meade-King; two *s*. *Educ*: Dr Challoner's Grammar Sch., Amersham; LSE (BSc Econ 1969). Heal & Son, 1969–73; Price Commn, 1973–74; joined DoE, 1974; Circle 33 Housing Trust, 1982–83; Fellow, Hubert H. Humphrey Inst., Minneapolis, 1987–88; Regl Dir, N Eng., DoE and Dept of Transport, 1993–94; Regl Dir, Govt Office for SW, 1994–97; Dir, Envmt Protection Strategy, DETR, 1997–98; Dir, Regions, Tourism, Millennium and Internat., then Tourism, Lottery and Regions, subseq. Tourism, Libraries and Communities, DCMS, 1998–2005; Dir, Industry, DCMS, 2005–08. Chairman: Storylines Ltd, 2008–14; Push Once Ltd, 2008–16; Director: Business in Sport and Leisure, 2008–12; South West Screen, 2008–12. Chm., video games wkg gp, UK Council for Child Internet Safety, 2009–10. *Recreations*: friends, games, pottering about. *Address*: 2 Five House, North Street, Winchelsea TN36 4HN. *Club*: MCC.

**LEONARD, Colum Charles**; a Master of the Senior Courts Taxing Office, since 2010; *b* Belfast, 23 Nov. 1956; *s* of Philip and Rose Leonard; *m* 1990, Carole Collins; one *d*. *Educ*: Abbey Primary and Grammar Schs, Newry, Co. Down; Univ. of Southampton (LLB Hons 1979); Guildford Coll. of Law. Admitted Solicitor, 1984; Articled Clerk, 1982–84, Solicitor, 1984–86, Wilde Sapte; Solicitor, Clarke Willmott and Clarke, 1986–89; Partner, Stewarts Law LLP, 1990–2010; a Dep. Dist Judge, 2002–; a Tribunal Judge, First-tier (Property Chamber), 2006–; Dep. Costs Judge, 2006–10. *Recreations*: running slowly, swimming badly, occasional sub-aqua, reading almost anything, grandchild wrangling, theatre and cinema. *Address*: Senior Courts Costs Office, Royal Courts of Justice, Thomas More Building, Strand, WC2A 2LL.

**LEONARD, David Charles**; Chairman, Kingfieldheath Ltd, 2001–04; Group Chief Executive, BPB plc, 1999–2000; *b* 26 June 1938; *s* of Charles and Audrey Leonard; *m* 1961, Jennifer Capes; two *s* one *d*. *Educ*: Hellesdon Secondary Sch., Norwich. FCMA, ACIS. Managing Dir, food and other manufacturing industries; BPB plc: Man. Dir, British Gypsum, 1990–94; Dir, New Business Develt, 1993–97; Mem. Main Bd, 1995; Dep. Chm., Gypsum, 1996; Chm., British Gypsum, 1996; Chief Operating Officer, all building products, 1997; Dir, BMP, 1999. Dir, Lincoln City FC Ltd, 2010–11. FRSA. *Recreations*: reading, music, opera, an interest in most sports, tennis, walking, golf.

**LEONARD, David John**, TD 1974; Judge, Court of Appeal, Brunei Darussalam, 2010–18; *b* 18 Sept. 1937; *s* of Jeremiah Leonard and Rosaleen Oonagh Leonard (*née* Mellett); *m* 1966, Frances Helen Good; two *s*. *Educ*: Hendon Grammar Sch.; Magdalene Coll., Cambridge (MA); Bath Spa Univ. Coll. (MA 2005). Admitted solicitor, 1967; admitted solicitor and barrister, Victoria, Australia, 1982. Solicitors' Dept, New Scotland Yard, 1966–71; Batten & Co., Solicitors, Yeovil, 1971–77; Hong Kong: Permanent Magistrate, 1977–81; Dist Judge, 1981–91; Judge, Supreme Ct, 1991–97; Judicial Comr, High Court, Brunei Darussalam, 2001–07. Chm., Judicial Studies Bd, Hong Kong, 1994–97. Served in TA: HAC, RA, Intelligence Corps, 1960–77, Maj. (retd) Intelligence Corps; Royal Hong Kong Regt (Volunteers), 1977–91, Maj. (retd). Part-time Immigration and Asylum Adjudicator, 1997–98. Member: Acad. of Experts, 1995–98 (Vice-Chm., 1997–98); Arbitration Panel: Hong Kong Internat. Arbitration Centre, 1996–98; China Internat. Economic and Trade Arbitration Commn, 1997–2007; Professional Conduct Cttee, Chartered Inst. of Arbitrators, 2000–06; Qingdao Arbitration Commn, 2003–07; Internat. Commn for Holocaust Era Insce Claims, 2002–06; Beijing Arbitration Commn, 2003–. Chm., Bath Br., ESU, 2010–13; Mem. Cttee, Britain Australia Soc., W Country Br., 2009–. Mem. Cttee, Wilts RFCA (formerly TAVRA), 1997–2007. FCIArb 1995–2009. Fellow, Hong Kong Inst. of Arbitrators, 1997–2007. Freeman and Liveryman, Painter-Stainers' Co., 1996–. Member: RBL; Corsham Civic Soc. *Recreations*: travel, reading, walking. *E*: dleo1937@aol.com. *Clubs*: Victory Services, HAC Mess; Bath & County (Bath); Corsham (Corsham); Hong Kong (Hong Kong); Royal Brunei Yacht.

**LEONARD, Dick**; *see* Leonard, Richard L.

**LEONARD, (Fergus) Miles**; Chief Executive Officer, Viva La Music, since 2018; *b* 17 June 1967; *s* of Eric and Yvonne Leonard; *m* 2005, Luca Smit; two *s* one *d*. *Educ*: Great Marlow Sch. A&R Scout, Virgin Records, 1991–93; A&R Manager, Roadrunner Records, 1993–95; Parlophone Records: A&R Manager, 1995–96; Sen. A&R Manager, 1996–99; Dir of A&R, 1999–2003; Man. Dir, 2003–08; Pres., then Chm., 2008–18; Pres., Virgin A&R, 2011–13; Co-Chm., 2013–14, Chm., 2014–18, Warner Bros Records. *Recreations*: Glastonbury, Secrets, Ring O' Bells public house (owner), Christmas. *Address*: Warner Bros, 27 Wrights Lane, Kensington, W8 5SW. *Clubs*: Soho House; Mendip Shooting Ground; Bowls (Marrakech); DC10 (Ibiza).

**LEONARD, Prof. James Vivian**, PhD; FRCP; Professor of Paediatric Metabolic Disease, Institute of Child Health, University of London, 1992–2004; *b* 1944; *s* of Rt Rev. Mgr and Rt Hon. Graham Douglas Leonard, KCVO, PC; *m* 1966, Dr Halcyon Sheila Deriba (*née* Disney); one *s* one *d*. *Educ*: Pembroke Coll., Cambridge (MB BChir 1970); St Thomas's Hosp. Med. Sch.; Inst. of Child Health, London (PhD 1979). FRCP 1983. Sen. Lectr, 1979–85, Reader, 1985–92, Inst. of Child Health; Consultant Paediatrician, Gt Ormond St Children's Hosp., 1979–2004. *Publications*: contribs on paediatric metabolic medicine. *Recreations*: gardening, travel, woodwork.

**LEONARD, Miles**; *see* Leonard, F. M.

**LEONARD, Ven. Peter Philip**; Archdeacon of Isle of Wight, since 2019; *b* Slough, 6 Feb. 1970; *s* of Brian and Jennifer Hiller; *m* 2017, Mark Pittaway; one *s* one *d*. *Educ*: Chartered Inst. of Marketing (Cert. Marketing 1990); Trinity Coll., Bristol Univ. (BA Hons Theol. 1997); St Mary's Coll., Twickenham (PGCE 2006); Counselling Cert., Bridge Pastoral Foundn. Heathrow Airport Ltd, 1988–89; Corporate Sales Manager, Woods Car Rental,

1992–93; Market Researcher, Cornhill Insurance, 1993–94; ordained deacon, 1997, priest, 1998; Curate, Parish Church, Haslemere, 1997–2001; Priest-in-charge, St Michael's Church, Sheerwater, 2001–06; Class Teacher, PE Manager, IT Manager and Mem., Sen. Mgt Team, Pirbright Village Primary Sch., 2007–10; Dep. Headteacher, 2010–12, Hd of Sch., 2012–14, Mill Hill Primary Sch., Waterlooville; Canon Chancellor, 2014–19, Acting Dean, 2018–19, Portsmouth Cathedral. *Publications:* Our Witness, 2017. *Recreations:* kayaking, baking, fitness. *Address:* 5 The Boltons, Kite Hill, Wootton, Isle of Wight PO33 4PB. *T:* (01983) 884432. *E:* peter.leonard@portsmouth.anglican.org.

**LEONARD, Richard Lawrence, (Dick Leonard);** writer and journalist; *b* 12 Dec. 1930; *s* of late Cyril Leonard, and Kate Leonard (*née* Whyte), Pinner, Middx; *m* 1963, Irène, *d* of late Dr Ernst Heidelberger and Dr Gertrud Heidelberger, Bad Godesberg, Germany; one *s* one *d. Educ:* Ealing Grammar Sch.; Inst. of Education, London Univ.; Essex Univ. (MA). School teacher, 1953–55; Dep. Gen. Sec., Fabian Society, 1955–60; journalist and broadcaster, 1960–68; Sen. Research Fellow (Social Science Research Council), Essex Univ., 1968–70. Mem., Exec. Cttee, Fabian Soc., 1972–80 (Chm., 1977–78); Chm., Library Adv. Council, 1978–81. Trustee, Assoc. of London Housing Estates, 1973–78. Vis. Prof., Free Univ. of Brussels, 1988–96. European Advr, Publishers Assoc., 1987–94; Sen. Advr, Centre for European Policy Studies, 1994–99; Sen. Res. Associate, Foreign Policy Centre, London, 2003–. Contested (Lab) Harrow W, 1955; MP (Lab) Romford, 1970–Feb. 1974; PPS to Rt Hon. Anthony Crosland, 1970–74; Mem., Speaker's Conf. on Electoral Law, 1972–74. Introduced Council Housing Bill, 1971; Life Peers Bill, 1973. Asst Editor, The Economist, 1974–85; Brussels and EU correspondent, The Observer, 1989–97; Brussels correspondent, Europe magazine, 1992–2003. *Publications:* Guide to the General Election, 1964; Elections in Britain, 1968, 5th edn 2005; (ed jtly) The Backbencher and Parliament, 1972; Paying for Party Politics, 1975; BBC Guide to Parliament, 1979; (ed jtly) The Socialist Agenda, 1981; (jtly) World Atlas of Elections, 1986; Pocket Guide to the EEC, 1988; Elections in Britain Today, 1991; The Economist Guide to the European Community, 1992, 4th edn as The Economist Guide to the European Union, 1997, 10th edn 2010 (French, German, Polish, Bulgarian, Georgian, Hungarian, Romanian, Serbian, Spanish, Portuguese, Russian and Korean edns); Replacing the Lords, 1995; (jtly) Eminent Europeans, 1996; (ed) Crosland and New Labour, 1999; (ed jtly) The Pro-European Reader, 2001; A Century of Premiers: Salisbury to Blair, 2004; (ed) The Future of Socialism by Anthony Crosland, 50th anniv. edn, 2006; 19th Century Premiers: Pitt to Rosebery, 2008; 18th Century Premiers: Walpole to the Younger Pitt, 2010; The Great Rivalry: Gladstone and Disraeli - a dual biography, 2013; A History of British Prime Ministers: Walpole to Cameron, 2014, 2nd edn 2015; (jtly) The Routledge Guide to the European Union, 2015; (jtly) Titans: Fox vs Pitt, 2019; contribs to Guardian, Financial Times, TLS, European Voice, The Bulletin, Prospect, and leading newspapers in USA, Canada, Japan, India, Australia and New Zealand. *Recreations:* walking, book-reviewing, family pursuits. *Address:* 16 Albert Street, NW1 7NZ.

**LEONG, Dr Louise,** FRSB; Director, Partnerships and Industry, Medical Research Council, since 2018; *d* of Joseph Hong-Chiew Leong and Cecilia Leong. *Educ:* National Univ. of Singapore (BSc Hons); St Catharine's Coll., Cambridge (PhD 1992); Birkbeck Coll., Univ. of London (Postgrad. Dip. Mgt 2002). Res. Scientist, Babraham Inst., 1992–98; Adjunct Fellow, Inst. of Molecular Agrobiol., Singapore, 1995–98; Fellow, Churchill Coll., Cambridge, 1996–98; Res. Fellow, Inst. for Molecular Medicine, Univ. of Auckland; Sci. Funding and Private Office Dir, Wellcome Trust, 2000–06; R&D Policy Manager, 2006–09, Hd, R&D, 2010–13, Dir, R&D, 2014, ABPI; Dir, Sci. Relations, AstraZeneca, 2014–17. Sci. Dir, Stem Cells for Safer Medicine, 2007–09. Mem. Council, Royal Soc. of Biol., 2017–. FRSB 2012. *Address:* Medical Research Council, One Kemble Street, WC2B 4AN.

**LÉOTARD, François Gérard Marie;** European Union Special Envoy to Macedonia, 2001; *b* Cannes, 26 March 1942; *s* of André Léotard and Antoinette (*née* Tomasi); *m* 1992, Ysabel Duret; one *s* one *d. Educ:* Paris Law Univ.; Institut d'Etudes Politiques de Paris; Ecole Nationale d'Administration. Various appts in French admin, 1968–76; Mem., Nat. Assembly, 1978–86, 1988–92, 1995–2002; Minister of Culture and Communication, 1986–88; Minister of Defence, 1993–95. Mayor of Fréjus, 1977–92, 1993–97; Member: General Council, Var, 1980–88; Regl Council, Provence. Republican Party (Parti Républicain): Gen. Sec., 1982–88; Pres., 1988–90 and 1995–97; Hon. Pres., 1990–95; Pres., UDF, 1996–98. *Publications:* A Mots Découverts, 1987; Culture: les chemins de printemps, 1988; La Ville Aimée: mes chemins de Fréjus, 1989; Pendant la Crise, le Spectacle Continue, 1989; Adresse au Président des Républiques Françaises, 1991; Place de la République, 1992; Ma Liberté, 1995; Pour l'honneur, 1997; Je vous hais tous avec douceur, 2000; Paroles d'immortels, 2001; La Couleur des femmes, 2002; A mon frère qui n'est pas mort, 2003; Ça va mal finir, 2008; Habitare Secum, 2011.

**LEPAGE, Robert,** CC 2009 (OC 1995); OQ 1999; Director and President, RLI, since 1988; Founder, President and Artistic Director, Ex Machina Theatre Company, since 1994; *b* 12 Dec. 1957; *s* of Fernand and Germaine Lepage. *Educ:* Ecole Joseph-François Perreault, Quebec City; Conservatoire d'Art Dramatique de Québec. Joined Théâtre Repère, as actor, 1980, also Jt Artistic Dir and writer, 1986–89; Artistic Dir, Théâtre Français, Ottawa Nat. Arts Theatre, 1989–93; Artistic Dir, La Caserne, 1997–. *Stage* includes: joint writer, director and actor: Théâtre Repère: Circulations, 1984; The Dragons' Trilogy, 1985; Vinci (one-man show), 1986; Polygraph, 1987; Tectonic Plates, 1988; Needles and Opium (one-man show), 1991, 2nd adaption 2013; The Far Side of the Moon (one-man show), 2000; The Andersen Project (one-man show), 2006; 887 (one-man show), 2015, 2017; *director:* Carmen, Théâtre d'Bon'Humeur, 1983; Le songe d'une nuit d'été, Théâtre du Nouveau Monde, Montreal, 1988; A Midsummer Night's Dream, RNT, London, 1992; Le Cycle William Shakespeare, Quebec City, Maubeuge, Frankfurt and Paris, 1992; Macbeth and The Tempest, Tokyo Globe Theatre, Tokyo, 1993; Secret World Tour (Peter Gabriel), 1993; Les Sept branches de la rivière Ota (also jt writer), 1994, 2nd adaption 2019; Elseneur (one-man show, also adapter and actor), 1995; La géométrie des miracles (world tour; also jt writer), 1998; Zulu Time, 1999; La Damnation de Faust, 1999; Growing Up Tour (Peter Gabriel), 2002; KÀ (Cirque du Soleil show), LA, 2004; 1984, Royal Opera, Covent Garden, 2005; The Rake's Progress, 2007; Lipsynch, 2007; The Blue Dragon, 2008; Eonnagata, Sadler's Wells, 2009; The Nightingale and Other Short Fables, COC Toronto, 2009; Totem (Cirque du Soleil show), 2010; Shakespeare's La Tempête, Quebec City, 2011; Wagner's Ring Cycle, NY Met. Opera; Das Rheingold, 2010, 2019; Die Walküre, Siegfried, 2011, 2019; Götterdämmerung, 2012, 2019; Thomas Adès' The Tempest, Quebec City and NY Met. Opera, 2012; Playing Cards 1: SPADES and HEARTS, Roundhouse, 2012–13; L'Amour de loin, Quebec City and NY Met Opera, 2015; Quills, 2016; Frame by Frame, Nat. Ballet of Canada, 2018; Coriolanus, Toronto, 2018, Quebec, 2019; SLAV, Montreal Jazz Fest., 2018; Magic Flute, Quebec Opera, 2018; KANATA, Théâtre du Soleil, Paris, 2018; TV advertisements; *films include: writer and director:* Le Confessionnal, 1995; Le Polygraphe, 1996; Nô, 1997; Possible Worlds, 2000; Triptych, 2013; Marie, 2014; Michelle, 2014; Thomas, 2014; orig. concept of architectural projection, The Image Mill, 2009; Dir, exhibn, The Library at Night, 2015. Chevalier de l'Ordre des Arts et des Lettres (France), 1990. Europe Th. Prize, EC, 2007; Governor General's Performing Arts Award, 2009; Eugene McDermott Award in the Arts, MIT, 2012; Glenn Gould Prize, 2013. *Address:* 966 Saint-Jean Street, Quebec City, QC G1R 1R5, Canada.

**LEPINE, Very Rev. Jeremy John;** Dean of Bradford, since 2013; *b* 24 April 1956; *s* of John and Patricia Lepine; *m* 1980, Christine Harvey; one *s* one *d. Educ:* Council for Nat. Academic Awards (BA Business); St John's Coll., Nottingham. Ordained deacon, 1984, priest, 1985; Curate, Trinity St Michael, Harrow, 1984–88; Team Vicar, Horley, 1988–95; Evangelism Advr, Croydon Area Mission Team, 1995–2002; Evangelism Advr, Dio. of Southwark, and Hon. Chaplain, Southwark Cath., 1997–2002; Rector, St Leonard, Wollaton, 2002–13; Area Dean, Nottingham N, 2008–13. Hon. Canon, Southwell Minster, 2009–13. *Recreations:* film, theatre, gardening, music. *Address:* The Deanery, 1 Cathedral Close, Bradford BD1 4EG. *T:* (01274) 777722, *Fax:* (01274) 777730.

**LE POER TRENCH,** family name of **Earl of Clancarty.**

**LE POIDEVIN, Nicholas Peter;** QC 2010; a Deputy High Court Judge, since 2013; *b* Ashbourne, Derbys, 12 Oct. 1950; *s* of Roy Le Poidevin and Barbara Le Poidevin; *m* 1st, 1979, Saundra Susan Hicks (*d* 1988); one *d*; 2nd, 2016, Janet Mary Atkinson. *Educ:* Repton Sch.; Trinity Hall, Cambridge (BA 1972; LLB 1973; MA 1975). Called to the Bar, Middle Temple, 1975; Bencher, Lincoln's Inn, 2005; a Recorder, 2009–19. Commons Comr, 2000–10. *Publications:* (ed) Lewin on Trusts, 17th edn 2000 to 19th edn 2015; (contrib.) A Portrait of Lincoln's Inn, 2007; (contrib.) Sham Transactions, 2013. *Recreations:* legal history, concert-going, things other people find boring. *Address:* 12 New Square, Lincoln's Inn, WC2A 3SW. *T:* (020) 7419 8000, *Fax:* (020) 7419 8050. *E:* nicholas.lepoidevin@newsquarechambers.co.uk.

**LEPPARD, Adrian Allen,** CBE 2016; QPM 2012; Commissioner, City of London Police, 2011–15; *b* Redhill, Surrey, 11 Feb. 1962; *s* of Norman and Constance Leppard. *Educ:* City Univ. London (MBA 1998). Joined Surrey Police, 1984; various posts up to Divl Comr, 1984–2005; Asst Chief Constable, then Dep. Chief Constable, Kent Police, 2005–10. *Recreations:* paragliding, sailing.

**LEPPARD, Raymond John,** CBE 1983; conductor, harpsichordist, composer; Music Director, Indianapolis Symphony Orchestra, 1987–2001; *b* 11 Aug. 1927; *s* of A. V. Leppard. *Educ:* Trinity Coll., Cambridge. Fellow of Trinity Coll., Cambridge, and Univ. Lecturer in Music, 1958–68. Hon. Keeper of the Music, Fitzwilliam Museum, 1963–82. Conductor: Covent Garden, Sadler's Wells, Glyndebourne, and abroad; Principal Conductor, BBC Northern Symphony Orchestra, 1972–80; Prin. Guest Conductor, St Louis SO, 1984–93. Hon. RAM 1972; Hon. GSM 1983; Hon. FRCM 1984. Hon. DLitt Univ. of Bath, 1972. Commendatore al Merito della Repubblica Italiana, 1974. *Publications:* realisations of Monteverdi: Il Ballo delle Ingrate, 1958; L'Incoronazione di Poppea, 1962; L'Orfeo, 1965; Il Ritorno d'Ulisse, 1972; realisations of Francesco Cavalli: Messa Concertata, 1966; L'Ormindo, 1967; La Calisto, 1969; Magnificat, 1970; L'Egisto, 1974; L'Orione, 1983; realisation of Rameau's Dardanus, 1980; Authenticity in Music, 1988; Raymond Leppard on Music, 1993; Music Made Me (memoir), 2011; British Academy Italian Lecture, 1969, Procs Royal Musical Assoc. *Recreations:* music, theatre, books, friends. *Address:* 5040 Buttonwood Crescent, Indianapolis, IN 46228–2323, USA. *T:* (317) 259 9020, *Fax:* (317) 259 0916.

**LEPPER, David;** *b* 15 Sept. 1945; *s* of late Henry George Lepper and Maggie Lepper (*née* Osborne); *m* 1966, Jeane Stroud; one *s* one *d. Educ:* St John's C of E Primary Sch., Richmond; Gainsborough Secondary Sch., Richmond; Wimbledon Co. Secondary Sch.; Univ. of Kent (BA Hons); Univ. of Sussex (PGCE); PCL (Dip. Film); Univ. of Sussex (Dip. Media). Teacher: Westlain GS, Brighton, 1968–73; Falmer Sch., Brighton, 1973–96. Mem. (Lab), Brighton BC, 1980–97 (Leader, 1986–87; Mayor, 1993–94). MP (Lab and Co-op) Brighton Pavilion, 1997–2010. Trustee: ARDIS (Alzheimer's and Related Diseases), 1993–2018 (Chm., 2015–18); Sussex Beacon, 2010–13; Brighton and Hove Carers' Centre, 2010–15 (Chm., 2012–15). Life Member: Assoc. of Town and City Mgt; English UK. *Publications:* John Wayne, 1986; various articles in film and media jls. *Recreations:* cinema, music, books, watching professional cycling.

**LEPSCHY, Prof. Giulio Ciro,** FBA 1987; Emeritus Professor of Italian, University of Reading, since 2000 (Professor, 1975–97; part-time Professor, 1997–2000); Visiting Professor, University of Cambridge, since 2000; *b* 14 Jan. 1935; *s* of Emilio Lepschy and Sara Castelfranchi; *m* 1962, Anna Laura Momigliano. *Educ:* Univ. of Pisa (Dott. Lett.); Scuola Normale Superiore, Pisa (Dip. Lic. and Perf.). Lib. Doc., Italy. Research, 1957–64, at Univs of Zurich, Oxford, Paris, London, Reading; Lectr 1964, Reader 1967, Univ. of Reading. Mem. Council, Philological Soc., 1984–89, 1992–96; Pres., MHRA, 2001. Corresp. Mem., 1991, Mem., 2011, Accademia della Crusca. Hon. Prof., UCL, 1998; Goggio Vis. Prof., 2000, Adjunct Prof., 2010–, Univ. of Toronto. Hon. Dr, Univ. of Turin, 1998. Serena Medal, British Acad., 2000. Commendatore of the Italian Republic, 2003. *Publications:* A Survey of Structural Linguistics, 1970, new edn 1982; (jtly) The Italian Language Today, 1977, 2nd edn 1988; Saggi di linguistica italiana, 1978; Intorno a Saussure, 1979; Mutamenti di prospettiva nella linguistica, 1981; Nuovi saggi di linguistica italiana, 1989; Sulla linguistica moderna, 1989; Storia della linguistica, 1990; La linguistica del Novecento, 1992; History of Linguistics, 1994; (jtly) L'amanuense analfabeta e altri saggi, 1999; Mother Tongues and Other Reflections on the Italian Language, 2002; Parole, parole, parole e altri saggi di linguistica, 2007; Tradurre e traducibilità, 2009; contribs to learned jls. *Address:* 335 Latymer Court, Hammersmith Road, W6 7LH. *T:* and *Fax:* (020) 8748 7780.

**LE QUESNE, Caroline;** *see* Lucas, Caroline.

**LERCHE-THOMSEN, Kim Stuart,** FIA; Founder and Chief Executive, Primetime Retirement (formerly Living Time), 2004–19; *b* 2 Sept. 1952; *s* of Paul Lerche-Thomsen and Patricia Lerche-Thomsen (*née* Williams); *m* 1991, Emma Jane Grace Brook; one *s* one *d. Educ:* Sevenoaks; Brunel Univ. (BTech). FIA 1984. Dir, Pensions, Prudential, 1991–96; Man. Dir, Prudential Annuities, 1997–2001; Dir, Prudential Assurance Co. Ltd, 1999–2002; Chief Exec., Scottish Amicable, 2001–02; Chm., AssetCo (formerly Asset Investment Gp), 2003–04. FRMetS 1975. *Recreations:* walking, travelling, ski-ing, meteorology. *E:* kim.lt@offermoreoptions.co.uk. *Clubs:* Leander, Phyllis Court (Henley-on-Thames).

**LEREGO, Prof. Michael John;** QC 1995; a Recorder, 2002–15; *b* 6 May 1949; *s* of late Leslie Ivor Lerego and Gwendolen Frances Lerego; *m* 1972, Susan Northover; three *d* (one *s* decd). *Educ:* Manchester Grammar Sch.; Haberdashers' Aske's Sch., Elstree; Keble Coll., Oxford (Open Schol.; Dist. Law Mods 1968; Gibbs Prize in Law 1969; BA Jurisp. 1st Cl. 1970; BCL 1st Cl. 1971; MA Oxon 1978). Called to the Bar, Inner Temple, 1972, Bencher, 2006; in practice, 1972–2012; Jt Hd of Chambers, Fountain Ct, 2003–07. Weekender, Queen's Coll., Oxford, 1972–78. Member: Jt Working Party of Law Soc. and Bar on Banking Law, 1987–91; Law Soc.'s Sub-Cttee on Banking Law, 1991–96; an Arbitrator: Lloyd's Modified Arbitration Scheme, 1988–92; Lloyd's Arbitration Scheme, 1993–2007. Vis. Lectr, 2006–07, Lectr, 2007–08, Sen. Lectr, 2008–09, Prof., 2009–13, Univ. of Law (formerly Coll. of Law). Governor: Wroxham Sch., Potters Bar, 1995–2004. FCIArb

1997–2015; FHEA 2009. *Publications:* (ed jtly) Commercial Court Procedure, 2000; (contrib.) The Law of Bank Payments, 3rd edn 2004, 4th edn 2010; (regulatory editor) Encyclopaedia of Insurance Law, 2007–09; (contrib.) Blackstone's Criminal Practice, 2008–. *Recreation:* watching sport.

**LERENIUS, Bo Åke,** Hon. CBE 2005; non-executive Chairman: Koole Group (formerly Koole Tanktransport), since 2011; Hector Rail and GB Railfreight, since 2014; Board Director: Contanda (formerly Westway Group), since 2012; ARR, since 2013; *b* 11 Dec. 1946; *s* of Åke Lerenius and Elisabeth Lerenius; *m* 1st (marr. diss.); one *s* one *d*; 2nd, 2002, Gunilla Jöhncke. *Educ:* St Petri, Malmö, Sweden; Westchester High Sch., LA; Univ. of Lund, Sweden (BA Business Admin). Div. Dir, Tarkett (part of Swedish Match Gp), 1983–85; Gp Pres. and CEO, Ernstromgruppen, 1985–92; Gp Chief Exec., Stena Line, 1992–98; Vice Chm., Stena Line and Dir, New Business Investments, Stena AB, 1998–99; Gp Chief Exec., ABP Hldgs plc, 1999–2007 (non-exec. Dir, 2007). Non-executive Director: G4S plc (formerly Securicor plc, then Group 4 Securicor), 2004–13; Land Securities Gp plc, 2004–12; Thomas Cook Gp plc, 2007–13; non-executive Chairman: Mouchel plc, 2009–11; Brunswick Rail, 2011–12. Hon. Vice Pres., Swedish Chamber of Commerce for the UK, 2010 (Chm., 2007–10). Hon. DBA London Metropolitan, 2006. *Recreations:* golf, shooting. *Address:* Strandvägen 7B, 11456 Stockholm, Sweden. *Clubs:* Royal Bachelors (Gothenburg); Nya Sällskapet (Stockholm); Falsterbo Golf, Halmstad Golf (Sweden).

**LE ROY LADURIE, Prof. Emmanuel Bernard;** Commandeur de la Légion d'Honneur, 1996; Commandeur de l'Ordre des Arts et des Lettres; Grand Croix, l'Ordre national du Mérite, 2018; Professor of History of Modern Civilisation, Collège de France, 1973–99, now Honorary Professor; *b* 19 July 1929; *s* of Jacques Le Roy Ladurie and Léontine (*née* Dauger); *m* 1955, Madeleine Pupponi; one *s* one *d*. *Educ:* Univ. of Sorbonne (agrégé d'histoire); DèsL 1952. Teacher, Lycée de Montpellier, 1955–57; Res. Assistant, CNRS, 1957–60; Assistant, Faculté des Lettres de Montpellier, 1960–63; Asst Lectr, 1963, Dir of Studies, 1965–, Ecole Pratique des Hautes Etudes; Lectr, Faculté des Lettres de Paris, 1969; Prof., Sorbonne, 1970; UER Prof. of Geography and Social Sci., Univ. de Paris VII, 1971–. General Administrator, Bibliothèque Nationale, 1987–94 (Pres., Conseil scientifique, 1994–99). Mem. de l'Institut, Acad. des Scis morales et politiques, 1993–. Internat. Mem. (formerly Foreign Mem.), Amer. Philosophical Soc., 2000; Foreign Mem., Polish Acad. of Scis, 2000; For. Hon. Mem., American Acad. of Scis, 1984; Hon. FBA 1985. Hon. doctorates incl. Geneva, 1978; Michigan, 1981; Leeds, 1982; East Anglia, 1985; Leicester, York, 1986; Carnegie Mellon, Pittsburgh, 1987; Durham, 1987; Hull, 1990; Dublin, 1992; Albany, Haifa, Montréal, Oxford, 1993; Pennsylvania, 1995; HEC, Paris, 1999. *Publications:* Histoire du Languedoc, 1963; Les Paysans du Languedoc, 1966; Histoire du climat depuis l'an mil, 1967, 2nd edn 1983; Le Territoire de l'historien, vol. 1 1973, vol. 2 1978; Montaillou: village occitan 1294–1324, 1975; (jtly) Histoire économique et sociale de la France, vol. 1 1450–1660, vol. 2 Histoire de la France rurale, 1976; (with B. Bray) Montaillou: Cathars and Catholics in a French village 1294–1324, 1978; (with B. Bray) Montaillou: the promised land of error, 1978, 2008; Le Carnaval de Romans 1579–1580 (Prix Pierre Lafue), 1980; L'Argent, l'Amour et la Mort en pays d'Oc, 1980; (jtly) Inventaire des campagnes, 1980; (jtly) L'Histoire urbaine de la France, vol. 3, 1981; (with J. Goy) Tithe and Agrarian History from the Fourteenth to the Nineteenth Century, 1982, repr. 2008; Paris—Montpellier, 1982; La Sorcière de Jasmin, 1982; Parmi les historiens, 1983; Pierre Prion: scribe, 1987; L'Histoire de France: l'état royal 1460–1610, 1987; (ed) Monarchies, 1987; L'Ancien Régime, 1991; Le siècle des Platter 1499–1628, vol. 1 Le mendiant et le professeur, 1995, vol. 2 Le voyage de Thomas Platter 1595–1599, 2000; vol. 3 L'Europe de Thomas Platter, 2006; (ed jtly) Mémoires de Jacques Le Roy Ladurie, 1997; Saint-Simon et le système de la cour, 1997; L'Historien, le chiffre et le texte, 1997; Histoire de la France des Régions, 2001; Histoire des paysans français de la peste noire à la Révolution, 2002; Histoire humaine et comparée du climat, vol. 1, 2004, vol. 2, 2006, vol. 3, 2009; Personnages et caractères, 2005; Ouverture, société, pouvoir, 2005; Trente-trois questions sur l'histoire du climat: du Moyen Age à nos jours, 2010; Naissance de l'histoire du climat, 2012; Une vie avec l'Histoire, 2014; Les paysans français d'Ancien Régime du 14e au 18e siècle, 2015; (ed) Huit leçons d'histoire, 2016; Brève Histoire de l'Ancien Régime, 2017; De la BN à la BNF, 2018. *Address:* Collège de France, 11 place Marcelin Berthelot, 75231 Paris cedex 05, France; (home) 88 rue d'Alleray, 75015 Paris, France.

**LERWILL, Robert Earl,** FCA; Chief Executive Officer, Aegis Group plc, 2005–08 (non-executive Director, 2000–05); *b* 21 Jan. 1952; *s* of Colin and Patricia Lerwill; *m* 1994, Nicola Keddie; two *s* three *d*. *Educ:* Nottingham Univ. (BA Hons Industrial Econs 1973); Harvard Univ. (AMP 1996). FCA 1977. Articled clerk to Sen. Manager, Arthur Andersen & Co., 1973–86; Gp Finance Dir, WPP Gp plc, 1986–96; Cable & Wireless plc: Exec. Dir, Finance, 1997–2002; CEO, Cable & Wireless Regl, 2000–03; Dep. Gp CEO, 2002–03. Non-executive Director: Healthcare plc, subseq. Synergy Health plc, 2005–12 (Chm., 2010–12); British American Tobacco plc, 2005–13; Transcom Worldwide SA, 2010–12; ITC Ltd (India), 2013–16; DJI Hldgs plc, 2014–16; Spire Healthcare plc, 2014–16; Reynolds America Inc., 2015–16; First Utility plc, 2015–16. Ind. Dir, Payments Council, 2014–15. Dir/Trustee, Anthony Nolan Trust, 2002–07. Vice Chm., Runwell Parish Council, Essex, 2014–16. *Recreations:* travel, motoring, motor cruising, shooting. *Clubs:* Old Blues Rugby (Motspur Park); Twickenham Yacht, Royal Burnham Yacht.

**LESCHLY, Jan;** founding Chairman and Partner, Care Capital LLC, since 2000; *b* 11 Sept. 1940; *m* 1963, Dr Lotte Engelbredt; four *s*. *Educ:* Copenhagen Coll. of Pharmacy (MSc Pharmacy); Copenhagen Sch. of Econs and Business Admin (BS Business Admin). Pharmaceutical industry, 1972–2000: Exec. Vice Pres. and Pres., Pharmaceutical Div., Novo Industries A/S, Denmark, 1972–79; Squibb Corporation: joined 1979; Vice-Pres., Commercial Develt, 1979–81; US Pres., 1981–84; Gp Vice-Pres. and Dir, 1984–86; Exec. Vice-Pres., 1986–88; Pres. and Chief Operating Officer, 1988–90; Chm., SmithKline Beecham Pharmaceuticals, 1990–94; Chief Exec., SmithKline Beecham, 1994–2000. Member, Board of Directors: Amer. Express Co.; Viacom Corp.; Ventro Corp.; APM-Maersk Gp; Mem. Internat. Adv. Bd, DaimlerChrysler. Member: British Pharma Group; Bd of Dirs, Pharmaceutical Res. and Manufrs of America; Pharmaceutical Res. and Manufrs Foundn; Bd of Trustees, Nat. Foundn for Infectious Diseases; Dean's Adv. Council, Emory Univ. Business Sch. *Address:* Care Capital LLC, PO Box 276, Avon by the Sea, NJ 07717, USA.

**LESCOEUR, Bruno Jean;** Chairman, Corda-International SAS, since 2017; *b* 19 Nov. 1953; *m* 1976, Janick Dreyer; two *s* one *d*. *Educ:* Ecole Polytechnique, Paris; Institut d'études politiques, Paris. Electricité de France (EDF): responsible for pricing, 1978–87, for distribn of gas and electricity, Mulhouse, France, 1987–89; Rep., as Founder Mem., Electricity Pool in London, 1990; Head, Distribution Unit, EDF and GDF, South of France, 1991–93; Dep. Chief Financial Officer, 1994–98; Chm. and Chief Exec., London Electricity Gp plc, 1999–2002; Exec. Vice-Pres., Head of Generation and Trading, 2002–04; Mem. Exec. Cttee and Sen. Exec. Vice-Pres., 2004–15; Head of Internat. and Gas, 2005–10; CEO, Edison Spa, Italy, 2011–18. Ind. Mem., Supervisory Bd, NAFTOGAZ, Ukraine, 2017–. Chevalier: Ordre National du Mérite (France), 2001; Légion d'honneur (France), 2012. *Recreation:* sailing. *Address:* 6 rue Masseran, 75007 Paris, France.

**LESIRGE, Ruth;** independent third sector consultant, since 2003; Head of Governance Practice, 2006–12, and Senior Visiting Fellow, 2010–15, Cass Business School, City University (Visiting Fellow, 2006–10); Chief Executive, Mental Health Foundation, 2000–02; *b* 9 Aug. 1945; *d* of Alfred Brandler and Mirjam Brandler; *m* 1969, John Lesirge; two *s*. *Educ:* Manchester Univ. (Cert Ed 1967; Cert Children with Learning Difficulties 1972); Univ. of London Inst. of Educn (Dip. Adult and Contg Educn, 1984); Office of Public Management/Sheffield Hallam Univ. (Post-grad. Cert. in Mgt 2000). Secondary sch. teacher of Eng. and literacy, Haringey, 1967–72; Adult Literacy Develt Worker, Islington and Haringey, 1973–83; Islington Adult Education Institute: Hd, Women's Educn, 1983–85; Hd, Soc. and Cultural Studies Dept, 1985–87; Hd of Area, Camden Adult Educn Inst., 1987–89; Principal, Adult Educn Service, London Bor. Waltham Forest, 1989–92; Chief Exec., Retail Trust charity, 1992–99. Member: Appraisal Cttee, NHS NICE, 2001–04; Private Inquiry, DoH, 2002–05. Vice-Chm., ACENVO, subseq. ACEVO, 1998–2002 (Trustee, 1995–2002); Trustee: Centre for Policy on Ageing, 1997–2002; Nat. Foundn for Entrepreneurship, 2000–; London Internat. Film Sch.; Governance Advr, Bishopsgate Inst., 2016. Founding Trustee and Dir, Assoc. of Chairs, 2013– (Chair, Bd, 2015–19). Hon. Lectr Medical Educn, Univ. of London, 1996. Churchill Fellow, 1981–82; Commonwealth Trust Bursary, 1988. *Publications:* (jtly) On Site, 1976; (jtly) Working Together: an approach to functional literacy, 1977; (jtly) Write Away, 1979; Images and Understandings: sequences for writing and discussion, 1984; (jtly) Appraising the Chief Executive, 2002; (jtly) Tools for Success, 2004, 2nd edn 2009; (jtly) Trustee Recruitment Toolkit, 2006; (jtly) Getting Ready for Enterprise, 2007; (jtly) A Chair's Compass: a guide for chairs, 2014; (jtly) A Question of Balance: the chair-CEO relationship, 2015; articles on not-for-profit boards and governance for third sector pubns, 2012–14. *Recreations:* theatre, gardening. *Address:* 5 Strathmore Gardens, N3 2HL. *T:* 07971 109248.

**LESITER, Ven. Malcolm Leslie;** Archdeacon of Bedford, 1993–2003, now Emeritus; *b* 31 Jan. 1937; *m*; four *d*. *Educ:* Cranleigh Sch.; Selwyn Coll., Cambridge (BA 1961; MA 1965); Cuddesdon Coll., Oxford. Ordained deacon, 1963, priest, 1964; Curate, Eastney, 1963–66; Curate, 1966–71, Team Vicar, 1971–73, St Paul, Hemel Hempstead; Vicar: All Saints, Leavesden, 1973–88; Radlett, 1988–93. RD, Watford, 1981–88. Mem., Gen. Synod, 1985–2000. Chm., St Albans Ministerial Trng Scheme, 1980–82. *Address:* 349 Ipswich Road, Colchester, Essex CO4 0HN.

**LESLIE,** family name of **Earl of Rothes**.

**LESLIE, Dame (Alison) Mariot,** DCMG 2012 (CMG 2005); HM Diplomatic Service, retired; UK Permanent Representative, UK Delegation to NATO, 2010–14; *b* Edinburgh, 25 June 1954; *d* of Stewart Forson Sanderson and Alison Mary Sanderson; *m* 1978, Andrew David Leslie; two *d*. *Educ:* George Watson's Ladies' Coll., Edinburgh; Leeds Girls' High Sch.; St Hilda's Coll., Oxford (BA 1975). Scottish Office, 1975; joined HM Diplomatic Service, 1977: Singapore, 1978–81; Bonn, 1982–86; Paris (on secondment to Quai d'Orsay), 1990–92; Head, Envmt, Sci. and Energy Dept, FCO, 1992–93; Scottish Office Industry Dept, 1993–95; Head, Policy Planning Staff, FCO, 1996–98; Minister and Dep. Head of Mission, Rome, 1998–2001; Ambassador to Norway, 2002–06; Dir, Defence and Strategic Threats, 2007, Dir Gen., Defence and Intelligence, 2007–10, FCO; Mem., Jt Intelligence Cttee, 2007–10. Mem., Scottish First Minister's Standing Council on Europe, 2016–. Dir, Scottish American Investment Co., 2019–. Mem. Exec. Council, RUSI, 2006–10. Associate Fellow, Chatham House, 2017–. DUniv Heriot-Watt, 2013. *Recreations:* food, travel, argument.

**LESLIE, Dr Andrew Greig William,** FRS 2001; Senior Staff Scientist, MRC Laboratory of Molecular Biology, Cambridge, 1991–2018, now Emeritus (Staff Scientist, 1988–91); *b* 26 Oct. 1949; *s* of John and Margaret Leslie; *m* 1977, Catherine Alice Fuchs; two *s* one *d* (and one *d* decd). *Educ:* Jesus Coll., Cambridge (BA, MA); Univ. of Manchester (PhD 1974). Res. Asst, Purdue Univ., Indiana, 1974–79; Res. Asst, 1979–83, MRC Sen. Fellow, 1983–88, ICSTM. *Publications:* numerous contribs to scientific jls incl. Nature, Science, Cell, Molecular Cell. *Recreations:* walking, cycling, swimming, films, music. *Address:* MRC Laboratory of Molecular Biology, Francis Crick Avenue, Cambridge CB2 0QH. *T:* (01223) 267072.

**LESLIE, Dame Ann (Elizabeth Mary),** DBE 2007; journalist and broadcaster; *b* Pakistan, 28 Jan. 1941; *d* of Norman Leslie and Theodora (*née* McDonald); *m* 1969, Michael Fletcher; one *d*. *Educ:* Presentation Convent, Matlock, Derbyshire; Convent of the Holy Child, Mayfield, Sussex; Lady Margaret Hall, Oxford (BA). Daily Express, 1962–67; freelance, 1967–: regular contributor to Daily Mail. Variety Club Women of the Year Award for journalism and broadcasting, 1981; British Press Awards Feature Writer of the Year, 1981, 1989; British Press Awards Commendation, 1980, 1983, 1985, 1987, 1991, 1996, 1999; Feature Writer of the Year Award, What the Papers Say, Granada Television, 1991; Lifetime Achievement Award, Media Soc., 1997; James Cameron Meml Award for internat. reporting, James Cameron Meml Trust, 1999; Gerald Barry Lifetime Achievement Award, BBC2/Granada/What the Papers Say, 2001; Edgar Wallace Award for outstanding reporting, London Press Club, 2002; Foreign Corresp. of the Year, BBC/Granada/What the Papers Say, 2004; Outstanding Contribution to Journalism Award, Next Century Foundn, 2012. *Publications:* Killing My Own Snakes (memoir), 2008. *Recreation:* family life. *Address:* c/o Daily Mail, Northcliffe House, 2 Derry Street, W8 5TT. *T:* (020) 7938 6120, *Fax:* (020) 7267 9914. *E:* aemleslie@aol.com.

**LESLIE, Charlotte Ann;** Director, Conservative Middle East Council, since 2017 (Vice-Chairman, 2015–17); *b* Liverpool, Aug. 1978; *d* of Ian and Jane Leslie. *Educ:* Badminton Sch.; Millfield Sch.; Balliol Coll., Oxford (BA Lit. Hum.). Special Advr to Shadow Sec. of State for Educn and Skills, 2006; Educn Associate, Young Foundn, 2008. MP (C) Bristol NW, 2010–17. Member: Educn Select Cttee, 2010–13; Health Select Cttee, 2013–15; Chair, All Party Parly Gp on Saudi Arabia, 2016–17. Hon. Steward, British Boxing Bd of Control, 2012–; Trustee, Football Foundn, 2017–. Back Bencher of the Year, Spectator, 2013.

**LESLIE, Christopher Michael;** MP for Nottingham East, since 2010 (Lab, 2010–19; Ind Gp for Change (formerly Change UK), since 2019); *b* 28 June 1972; *s* of Michael N. Leslie and Dania K. Leslie; *m* 2005, Nicola Murphy; one *d*. *Educ:* Bingley Grammar Sch.; Univ. of Leeds (BA Hons Pol. and Parly Studies 1994; MA Indust. and Labour Studies 1996). Research Assistant: Rep. Bernie Sanders, US Congress, 1992; Gordon Brown, MP, 1993; Adminr, Bradford Labour Party, 1995–97; Researcher, Barry Seal, MEP, 1997. Dir, New Local Govt Network, 2005–10. MP (Lab) Shipley, 1997–2005; contested (Lab) same seat, 2005. PPS to Minister of State, Cabinet Office, 1998–2001; Parly Sec., Cabinet Office, 2001–02; Parly Under-Sec., ODPM, 2002–03; Parly Under-Sec. of State, DCA, 2003–05; Shadow Financial Sec. to HM Treasury, 2010–13; Shadow Chief Sec. to HM Treasury, 2013–15; Shadow Chancellor of the Exchequer, 2015. Mem. (Lab), Bradford MDC, 1994–98. *Recreations:* music, tennis, travel. *Address:* House of Commons, SW1A 0AA.

**LESLIE, Prof. Esther Rose Irene Tiley,** PhD; FBA 2019; Professor of Political Aesthetics, Birkbeck, University of London, since 2006 (Lecturer in English and Humanities, 2000–06); *b* Barnet, 12 July 1964; *d* of George Tiley Leslie and Sheila Leslie (*née* Lahr); partner, 1995, Benedick Harold Guy Watson; one *s* one *d*. *Educ:* E Barnet Sch.; Univ. of

Sussex (BA German and Eur. Studies; MA Critical Theory; PhD German Studies 1995). Lectr in Art and Design (contextual studies) (pt-time), Middx Univ. (pt-time), 1995–97; Lectr in Communication Studies (pt-time), London Guildhall Univ., 1995–97; Lectr in Cultural Studies, Univ. of E London, 1995–97 (pt-time) and 1997–99 (full time). *Publications:* Walter Benjamin: overpowering conformism, 2000; Hollywood Flatlands: animation, critical theory and the avant-garde, 2002; Synthetic Worlds: nature, art and the chemical industry, 2005; Walter Benjamin: critical lives, 2007, repr. 2018; Derelicts: thought worms from the wreckage, 2014; (ed and trans.) Walter Benjamin: on photography, 2015; Liquid Crystals: the science and art of a fluid form, 2016; (with M. Jackson) Deeper in the Pyramid, 2018. *Recreations:* if the suspicion is true that, as Adorno notes, free time is tending toward its opposite, I should answer as did he: I have no hobbies. *Address:* 21 Crowndale Court, Crowndale Road, NW1 1TY. *T:* (020) 7388 8679, (office) (020) 3073 8401. *E:* e.leslie@bbk.ac.uk. *Club:* Somers Town History.

LESLIE, (Harman) John; Master, Queen's Bench Division, High Court of Justice, 1996–2016 (Deputy Senior Master, then Acting Senior Master and Queen's Remembrancer, 2013–14); *b* 8 April 1946; *s* of Percy Leslie and Sheila Mary Leslie (née Harris); *m* 1st, 1971, Alix Helen Cohen (marr. diss. 1980); two *s*; 2nd, 1986, Valerie Gibson. *Educ:* Dover Coll.; Clare Coll., Cambridge (BA 1968). Called to the Bar, Middle Temple, 1969, Bencher, 2001; in practice at the Bar, 1969–96. Member: Civil Procedure Rule Cttee, 1997–2002; Vice-Chancellor's Wkg Party on Civil Procedure Practice Directions, 1997–2000. Gov., Dover Coll., 1974–2016 (Mem. Council, 1975–84). *Publications:* (contrib.) Halsbury's Laws of England, 4th edn, 1999, reissued 2001; (ed jtly) Civil Court Practice, 1999–; Civil Court Manual, 1999; (contrib.) Atkin's Court Forms, 2001–. *Recreations:* France, bridge, woodworking. *Clubs:* Royal Automobile; Slinfold Cricket (Hon. Life Mem.).

LESLIE, Prof. Ian Malcolm, PhD; FREng 2010; Robert Sansom Professor of Computer Science, 1998–2019 and Head of Department, 1999–2004, University of Cambridge Computer Laboratory; Pro-Vice-Chancellor, University of Cambridge, 2004–09; Fellow, Christ's College, Cambridge, since 1985 (President, 2014–19); *b* 11 Feb. 1955; *s* of Douglas Alexander Leslie and Phyllis Margaret Leslie; *m* 1st, 1986, Patricia Valerie Vyoral (marr. diss. 2000); one *s* one *d*; 2nd, 2001, Celia Mary Denton (marr. diss. 2004); one *d*; 3rd, 2013, Anne Elizabeth Willenbrock. *Educ:* Univ. of Toronto (BASc 1977; MASc 1979); Darwin Coll., Cambridge (PhD 1983). University of Cambridge: Asst Lectr, 1983–86, Lectr, 1986–98, Computer Lab.; Sen. Advr to Vice-Chancellor on Inf. Strategy and Envmtl Sustainability, 2017–; Interim Dir of Inf. Services, 2017–18. Dir, Cambridge Innovation Capital, 2013–. FREng 2010. *Address:* Christ's College, Cambridge CB2 3BU.

LESLIE, John; see Leslie, H. J.

LESLIE, Keith John; Chairman, Mental Health Foundation, since 2014; *b* Kirkcaldy, 1 May 1958; *s* of David S. Leslie and Charlotte Leslie; *m* 1st (marr. diss.); two *s*; 2nd, 2017, Senna Cook. *Educ:* Kirkcaldy High Sch.; Univ. of Edinburgh (LLB 1st Cl. Hons); Wharton Sch., Univ. of Pennsylvania (MBA *summa cum laude*). Royal Dutch Shell: Analyst, Shell Internat., 1982–84; Sales Manager, Shell NZ, 1984–87; Gen. Manager, Shell Lubricants Sweden, 1987–89; Chief Exec., Shell Cyprus, 1989–92; Planning Manager, Shell Internat., 1992–93; Partner, McKinsey and Co., 1993–2006; Partner, Deloitte LLP, 2006–17. Dir, The Tablet Publishing Co., 2006–14. Chm. Bd, Build Africa, 2010–15. Fellow, Windsor Leadership, 2008–. *Publications:* contrib. to Eur. Mgt Jl, The Times, Wall St Jl. *Recreations:* opera, walking, writing. *Address:* 403 Cedar Court, 1 Royal Oak Yard, SE1 3GA. *T:* 07768 773995. *E:* kleslie10@hotmail.com.

LESLIE, Dame Mariot; see Leslie, Dame A. M.

LESLIE, Sir Shaun Rudolph Christopher, 5th Bt *cr* 1876, of Glaslough, Co. Monaghan; *b* 4 June 1947; *s* of Desmond Peter Arthur Leslie and Agnes Leslie (née Bernauer); *S* uncle, 2016, but his name does not appear on the Official Roll of the Baronetage; *m* 1987, Charlotte Victoria Byng (marr. diss. 1989). *Educ:* Ampleforth; King's Coll., Cambridge; Univ. of York. *Heir:* *b* Christopher Mark Leslie [*b* 7 Dec. 1952; *m* 1982, Cliona Manahan (marr. diss.) one *s* one *d*].

LESLIE, Stephen Windsor; QC 1993; Leader, South Eastern Circuit, 2009–10; Advocate, Public Defender Service, since 2014; *b* 21 April 1947; *s* of Leslie Leonard, (Lou), Leslie and Celia Leslie (née Schulsinger); *m* 2017, Melissa Louise Barbara Coutinho; one *s* two *d* by previous marriages. *Educ:* Brighton Coll.; King's Coll. London (LLB). Called to the Bar, Lincoln's Inn, 1971, Bencher, 2001. Chm., Commonwealth in England Barristers' Assoc., 2011–14 (Vice Chm., 2014–). Liveryman, Feltmakers' Co., 1998–. *Publications:* articles in The Times and New Law Jl. *Recreations:* globe trotting with Melissa, haggling for a bargain. *Address:* 102 Petty France, SW1H 9AJ. *Clubs:* Carlton, MCC (Associate Mem.); Thunderers'.

LESLIE MELVILLE, family name of **Earl of Leven and Melville**.

LESOURNE, Jacques François; Commandeur de la Légion d'Honneur, 2010; Commandeur de l'ordre National du Mérite, 1981; Officier des Palmes Académiques, 1995; Directeur-gérant, Le Monde, 1991–94; Professor of Economics, Conservatoire National des Arts et Métiers, since 1974; *b* 26 Dec. 1928; *s* of André Lesourne and Simone Guille; *m* 1961, Odile Melini; one *s* two *d* (and one *s* decd). *Educ:* Ecole Polytechnique; Ecole Nationale Supérieure des Mines, Paris. Head, Econ. Dept, French Coal Mines, 1954–57; Directeur général, later Pres., SEMA, 1958–75; Dir, Interfutures Project, OECD, 1976–79. Pres., Internat. Fedn of OR Socs, 1986–88; Vice-President: Internat. Inst. for Applied Systems Analysis, 1973–79; Centre for European Policy Studies, 1987–93; Member Council: Inst. of Mgt Science, 1976–79; Eur. Econ. Assoc., 1984–89. Pres., Futuribles International, 1993–. Mem., Acad. des Technologies, 2000–. Harold Lander Prize, Canadian OR Soc., 1991. *Publications:* Technique économique et gestion industrielle, 1958 (Economic Technique and Industrial Management, 1962); Le Calcul économique, 1964; Du bon usage de l'étude économique dans l'entreprise, 1966; (jtly) Matière grise année O, 1970 (The Management Revolution, 1971); Le Calcul économique, théorie et applications, 1972 (Cost-Benefit Analysis and Economic Theory, 1975); Modèles économiques de croissance de l'entreprise, 1972; (jtly) Une Nouvelle industrie: la matière grise, 1973; Les Systèmes de destin, 1976; A Theory of the Individual for Economic Analysis, 1977; (jtly) L'Analyse des décisions d'aménagement regional, 1979; Demain la France dans le monde, 1980; Les Mille Sentiers de l'avenir, 1982 (World Perspectives—a European Assessment, 1982); (jtly) Facilitating Development in a Changing Third World, 1983; Soirs et lendemains de fête: journal d'un homme tranquille, 1981–84 (autobiog.), 1984; (jtly) La gestion des villes, analyse des décisions d'économie urbaine, 1985; (jtly) La Fin des habitudes, 1985; L'Entreprise et ses futurs, 1985; L'après-Communisme, de l'Atlantique à l'Oural, 1990 (After-communism, from the Atlantic to the Urals, 1991); L'économie de l'ordre et du désordre, 1991 (The Economics of Order and Disorder, 1992); Vérités et mensonges sur le chômage, 1995; Le modèle français, grandeur et décadence, 1998; Un homme de notre siècle, 2000; (jtly) Leçons de microéconomie evolutionniste, 2003; Démocratie, marché et gouvernance, 2004; (jtly) Evolutionary Microeconomics, 2006; (jtly) FutuRIS, la recherche et l'innovation en France (annually), 2006–; Les crises et le vingt et unième siècle, 2009; Les temps de la prospective, 2012; L'Europe à l'heure de son crépuscule?, 2014; Les Chemins de l'avenir, une approche pragmatique - Les humains, les États, le monde, 2017. *Recreation:* piano. *Address:* 52 rue de Vaugirard, 75006 Paris, France.

LESSELS, Norman, CBE 1993; Chairman, Cairn Energy PLC, 1991–2002 (Director, 1988–2002); *b* 2 Sept. 1938; *s* of John Clark Lessels and Gertrude Margaret Ellen Lessels (née Jack); *m* 1st, 1960, Gillian Durward Lessels (née Clark) (*d* 1979); one *s* (and one *s* one *d* decd); 2nd, 1981, Christine Stevenson Lessels (née Hitchman). *Educ:* Melville Coll.; Edinburgh Acad. CA (Scotland) 1961. CA apprentice with Graham Smart & Annan, Edinburgh, 1955–60; with Thomson McLintock & Co., London, 1960–61; Partner, Wallace & Somerville, Edinburgh, merged with Whinney Murray & Co., 1969, latterly Ernst & Whinney, 1962–80; Partner, 1980–93, Sen. Partner, 1993–98, Chiene & Tait, CA. Director: Standard Life Assurance Co., 1978–2002 (Dep. Chm., 1982–88; Chm., 1988–98); Scottish Eastern Investment Trust, 1980–99; Bank of Scotland, 1988–97; Havelock Europa, 1989–98 (Chm., 1993–98); Robert Wiseman Dairies, 1994–2003; Martin Currie Portfolio Investment Trust, 1999–2001. Pres., Inst. of Chartered Accountants of Scotland, 1987–88. *Recreations:* golf, bridge, music. *Address:* 15 India Street, Edinburgh EH3 6HA. *T:* (0131) 225 5596. *Clubs:* New (Edinburgh); Hon. Company of Edinburgh Golfers, Royal & Ancient Golf.

LESSOF, Leila, OBE 2000; FRCP, FFPH; Chairman, Moorfields Eye Hospital NHS Trust, 1998–2001; *b* 4 June 1932; *d* of Lionel Liebster and Renée (née Segalov); *m* 1960, Maurice Hart Lessof, *qv*; one *s* two *d*. *Educ:* Queen's Coll., Harley St; Royal Free Hosp. Sch. of Medicine (MB BS; DMRD). FFPH (FFPHM 1986); FRCP 2000. Jun. posts, Royal Free Hosp., London Hosp. and UCH; Consultant Radiologist and Clinical Tutor, Hackney Hosp., 1964–78; Registrar in Public Health Medicine, KCH and Guy's Hosp., 1978–82; Director of Public Health: Islington HA, 1982–90; Kensington, Chelsea and Westminster HA, 1990–95; Chm., Westminster Assoc. for Mental Health, 1995–98. *Recreations:* opera, theatre, travel. *Address:* 8 John Spencer Square, N1 2LZ. *T:* (020) 7226 0919.

LESSOF, Prof. Maurice Hart, FRCP; Professor of Medicine, University of London at United Medical and Dental Schools (Guy's Hospital), 1971–89, now Emeritus; *b* 4 June 1924; *s* of Noah and Fanny Lessof; *m* 1960, Leila Liebster (see L. Lessof); one *s* two *d*. *Educ:* City of London Sch.; King's Coll., Cambridge (MA 1945; MD 1956). Appts on junior staff of Guy's Hosp., Canadian Red Cross Memorial Hosp., Johns Hopkins Hosp., etc; Clinical Immunologist and Physician, Guy's Hosp., 1967. Chairman: SE Thames Regl Med. Audit Cttee, 1990–91; Lewisham NHS Trust, 1993–97 (Dep. Chm., Guy's and Lewisham NHS Trust, 1991–93); Royal Hospitals NHS Trust, 1998–99. Adviser on Allergy, DHSS, 1982–91. Vice-Pres. and Sen. Censor, RCP, 1987–88; Past Pres., British Soc. for Allergy. Mem. Senate, London Univ., 1981–85. Mem., Johns Hopkins Soc. of Scholars, 1991. FKC 2005. *Publications:* (ed) Immunological Aspects of Cardiovascular Diseases, 1981; (ed) Immunological and Clinical Aspects of Allergy, 1984 (Spanish and Portuguese edns, 1987); (ed) Clinical Reactions to Food, 1983; (ed) Allergy: an international textbook, 1987; Food Intolerance, 1992 (Spanish edn 1996); Food Allergy: issues for the food industry, 1997. *Recreations:* sculpting, painting. *Address:* 8 John Spencer Square, Canonbury, N1 2LZ. *T:* (020) 7226 0919. *Club:* Athenæum.

LESSORE, John Viviand; artist; *b* 16 June 1939; *s* of Frederick and Helen Lessore; *m* 1962, Paule Marie Reveille; four *s*. *Educ:* Merchant Taylors' Sch.; Slade Sch. of Fine Art. *Principal exhibitions:* London: Beaux Arts Gall., 1965; New Art Centre, 1971; Theo Waddington, 1981; Stoppenbach & Delestre, 1983, 1985; Nigel Greenwood, 1990; Theo Waddington and Robert Stoppenbach, 1994; Theo Waddington Fine Art, 1997; Berkeley Sq. Gall., 2002; Annely Juda Fine Art, 2004; Kings Place, Thomas Williams Fine Art, 2013; Solomon Gall., Dublin, 1995; Miriam Shiell Fine Art, Toronto, 1997; Wolsey Art Gall., Christchurch Mansion, Ipswich, 1999; Ranger's House, Blackheath, 2000; Annandale Gall., Sydney, 2005; Univ. Gall., Newcastle, 2013; Norwich Castle, Norwich Univ. of the Arts, 2014; *works in public collections* include: Leicester Educn Cttee; Arts Council; Royal Acad.; Tate Gall.; Contemporary Arts Soc.; Norwich Castle; British Council; Accenture; NPG; BM. Co-founder, Prince's Drawing Sch., 2000. Trustee, Nat. Gall., 2003–11. 1st Prize, Korn/Ferry Internat. Public Award, 1991; Lynn Painter-Stainers' 1st Prize and Gold Medal, 2006. *Address:* c/o Jonathan Clark Fine Art, 18 Park Walk, SW10 0AQ. *T:* (020) 7351 3555. *E:* john.lessore@gmail.com.

LESTER, family name of **Baron Lester of Herne Hill**.

LESTER OF HERNE HILL, Baron *cr* 1993 (Life Peer), of Herne Hill in the London Borough of Southwark; **Anthony Paul Lester**; QC 1975; QC (NI); a Recorder, 1987–93; *b* 3 July 1936; *e s* of Harry and Kate Lester; *m* 1971, Catherine Elizabeth Debora Wassey; one *s* one *d*. *Educ:* City of London Sch.; Trinity Coll., Cambridge (Exhibnr) (BA); Harvard Law Sch. (Harkness Commonwealth Fund Fellowship) (LLM). Served RA, 1955–57, 2nd Lieut. Called to Bar, Lincoln's Inn, 1963 (Mansfield scholar), Bencher, 1985; called to Bar of N Ireland, 1984; Irish Bar, 1983. Special Adviser to: Home Secretary, 1974–76; Standing Adv. Commn on Human Rights, 1975–77; UK Legal Expert, Network Cttee on Equal Pay and Sex Discrimination, EEC, 1983–93. Mem., H of L, 1993–2018. Member: H of L Sub-Cttee on Inter-Govtl Conf., 1996; H of L EU Sub-Cttee on European Law and Instns, 1999–2003, 2003–08; Parly Jt Human Rights Cttee, 2001–15; Constitution Cttee, H of L, 2013–16. Mem., Commn on Bill of Rights, 2011–12. Ind. Advr to Sec. of State for Justice on aspects of constitutional reform, 2007–08. Hon. Vis. Prof., UCL, 1983–; Hon. Adjunct Prof. of Law, Univ. Coll. Cork, 2007–. Lectures: Owen J. Roberts, Univ. of Pennsylvania Law Sch., 1976; F. A. Mann, London, 1983; Rubin, Columbia Law Sch., 1988; Street, Manchester, 1993; Lionel Cohen, Hebrew Univ. of Jerusalem, 1994; Stephen Lawrence, London, 2000; Thomas More, and Denning Soc., Lincoln's Inn, 2000. Mem., Bd of Overseers, Univ. of Pennsylvania Law Sch., 1978–89. Pres., Interights, 1991–2014; Chm., Runnymede Trust, 1991–93; Member: Council, Justice, 1977–; Amer. Law Inst., 1985–; Bd of Dirs, Salzburg Seminar, 1996–2000; Internat. Adv. Bd, Open Soc. Inst., 2000–15; Co-Chm., Exec. Bd, European Roma Rights Center, Budapest, 1999–2001. Gov., British Inst. of Human Rights. Member: Adv. Bd, Inst. of European Public Law, Hull Univ. Adv. Cttee, Centre for Public Law, Univ. of Cambridge, 1999–. Mem., Amer. Philos. Soc., 2003; Hon. Mem., Amer. Acad. of Arts and Scis, 2002. Mem., Bd of Govs, James Allen's Girls' Sch., 1984–94 (Chm., 1987–91); Gov., Westminster Sch., 1998–2001. Mem. Editl Bd, Public Law. Chevalier de la Légion d'Honneur (France), 2009. *Publications:* Justice in the American South, 1964 (Amnesty Internat.); (co-ed.) Shawcross and Beaumont on Air Law, 3rd edn, 1964; (co-author) Race and Law, 1972; (ed) Constitutional Law and Human Rights, 1996; (co-ed) Human Rights Law and Practice, 1999, 3rd edn, 2009; contributor to: British Nationality, Immigration and Race Relations, in Halsbury's Laws of England, 4th edn, 1973, repr. 1992; The Changing Constitution (ed Jowell and Oliver), 1985, 6th edn 2007; (contrib.) Freedom of Expression: essays in honour of Nicolas Bratza, 2012; Five Ideas to Fight For, 2016. *Address:* Blackstone Chambers, Blackstone House, Temple, EC4Y 9BW. *T:* (020) 7583 1770.

See also M. E. J. Lester.

LESTER, Guy Anthony, TD 2000; FCA; Finance Director, Cabinet Office, since 2015; *b* London, 1963; *s* of Albert Lester and Dr Barbara Lester; *m* 2006, Victoria Bain; one *s*. *Educ:* Dulwich Coll.; Sidney Sussex Coll., Cambridge (BA Chemical Engrg 1984; Dip. Advanced

Study 1985; MEng 1993). ACA 1989, FCA 2017. KPMG, 1985–88; Ministry of Defence, 1989–2015: Asst Private Sec. to Defence Sec., 1992–93; Defence and Overseas Secretariat, Cabinet Office (on secondment), 1998; PS/Permanent Sec., 1999–2001; Director: Defence Resources and Plans, 2001–04; Capability Resources and Scrutiny, 2004–08; Dir Gen. Equipment, subseq. Dir, Equipment Resources, 2008–11; Comd Sec., subseq. Dir, Resources, Air Comd, 2011–15. Officer, Royal Signals, TA, 1986–97. *Address*: Cabinet Office, 70 Whitehall, SW1A 2AS.

**LESTER, Sir James Theodore, (Sir Jim),** Kt 1996; adviser on parliamentary and government affairs; *b* 23 May 1932; *s* of Arthur Ernest and Marjorie Lester; *m* (marr. diss. 1989); two *s*; *m* 1989. *Educ*: Nottingham High School. Mem. Notts CC, 1967–74. MP (C) Beeston, Feb. 1974–1983, Broxtowe, 1983–97; contested (C) Broxtowe, 1997. An Opposition Whip, 1976–79; Parly Under-Sec. of State, Dept of Employment, 1979–81. Mem., Select Cttee on Foreign affairs, 1982–97; Vice-Chm., All Party Gp on overseas develt, 1983–97. Deleg. to Council of Europe and WEU, 1975–76. *Recreations*: reading, music, motor racing, travelling. *Address*: 47 St John Drive, Westham, E Sussex BN24 5HX.

**LESTER, (Mary) Tamara;** *see* Box, M. T.

**LESTER, Maya Elizabeth Jane;** QC 2016; *b* Dulwich, 22 Aug. 1974; *d* of Baron Lester of Herne Hill, *qv*; one *s* two *d*. *Educ*: James Allen's Girls' Sch., Dulwich; Clare Coll., Cambridge (BA 1st Cl. Hons Hist. 1996); Yale Law Sch. (Paul Mellon Fellow; MSL 1998); City Univ. (CPE (Dist.) 1999). Called to the Bar, Lincoln's Inn, 2000; in practice as barrister, specialising in public and European law, Brick Court Chambers, 2000–. Visiting Scholar: Yale Law Sch., 1996–98; Columbia Law Sch., NY, 2011–12. *Recreation*: chamber music (viola and guitar). *Address*: 4 Whittlesey Street, SE1 8SZ. *T*: 07971 603754. *E*: maya.lester@brickcourt.co.uk.

**LESTER, Paul John,** CBE 2007; CEng, FIMechE; non-executive Chairman: Knight Square (formerly Peverel), since 2012; Essentra plc, since 2016; McCarthy & Stone plc, since 2017; Algeco, since 2017; Signia Wealth, since 2017; *b* 20 Sept. 1949; *s* of late John Trevor Lester and Joyce Ethel Lester; *m* 1st, 1973, Valerie Osbourn (marr. diss.); one *s* one *d*; 2nd, Karen White; one *d*. *Educ*: Trent Poly. (BSc (Hons) Mech. Engrg); Univ. of Gloucestershire (Dip Mgt Studies (Distinction)). CEng 2011; FIMechE 2011. Sen. Management, Dowty Group, 1968–80; Gen. Management, Schlumberger, UK, France, USA, 1980–87; Man. Dir, Defense & Air Systems, Dowty Gp, 1987–90; Chief Exec., Graseby plc, 1990–97; Gp Man. Dir, Balfour Beatty plc, 1997–2002; Chief Exec., VT Gp plc (formerly Vosper Thornycroft Hldgs), 2002–10; Chm., Marine Current Turbines Ltd, 2010–12. Dir, Vosper Thornycroft Hldgs plc, 1998–2002. Chairman: A & P Gp, 1993–99; High Integrity Solutions Ltd, 2003–08; Solent Synergy Ltd, 2006–10; John Laing Infrastructure Fund, 2010–17; Greenergy, 2010–17; Norland Managed Services, 2011–14; Survitec, 2011–15; Parabis, 2012–15; Signia, 2014–; Forterra plc, 2016–19; non-executive Director: Civica plc, 2004–08; Chloride plc, 2007–13; Invensys plc, 2010–14. Mem., Adv. Bd, Alchemy Partners Ltd, 1997–2008. Pres., EEF, 2000–03 (Sen. Dep. Pres., 1999–2000; Chm., Economic Policy Cttee, 1993–2000). Vis. Prof., Nottingham Trent Univ., 2003–11. Member: SE England Sci., Engrg and Technol. Adv. Council, 2003–07; Govt Manufg Forum, 2004–07; Major Projects Rev. Gp, HM Treasury, 2009–; Chairman: SE Regl Adv. Gp, Nat. Skills Acad. for Manufg, 2007–09; SkillENG, 2007–11; Chm., Solent Leadership Team, 2007–11, Mem., SE Leadership Team, 2007–10, BITC. President: Business Services Assoc., 2004–07; Soc. of Maritime Industries, 2005–10. Gov., Barnet Coll. of Further Educn, 1993–2002; Mem. Council, Southampton Univ., 2007–11. Hon. LLD Portsmouth, 2008. *Recreations*: tennis, weight training, running, football; life-long West Bromwich Albion supporter. *E*: paullester@essentra.com.

**LESTER, Richard;** film director; *b* 19 Jan. 1932; *s* of Elliott and Ella Young Lester; *m* 1956, Deirdre Vivian Smith; one *s* one *d*. *Educ*: Wm Penn Charter Sch.; University of Pennsylvania (BSc). Television Director: CBS (USA), 1951–54; AR (Dir TV Goon Shows), 1956. Directed The Running, Jumping and Standing Still Film (Acad. Award nomination; 1st prize San Francisco Festival, 1960). Feature Films directed: It's Trad, Dad, 1962; Mouse on the Moon, 1963; A Hard Day's Night, 1964; The Knack, 1964 (Grand Prix, Cannes Film Festival); Help, 1965 (Best Film Award and Best Dir Award, Rio de Janeiro Festival); A Funny Thing Happened on the Way to the Forum, 1966; How I won the War, 1967; Petulia, 1968; The Bed Sitting Room, 1969 (Gandhi Peace Prize, Berlin Film Festival); The Three Musketeers, 1973; Juggernaut, 1974 (Best Dir award, Teheran Film Fest.); The Four Musketeers, 1974; Royal Flash, 1975; Robin and Marian, 1976; The Ritz, 1976; Butch and Sundance: the early days, 1979; Cuba, 1979; Superman II, 1981; Superman III, 1983; Finders Keepers, 1984; The Return of the Musketeers, 1989; Get Back, 1991. *Recreations*: music, tennis.

**LESTER, Sheila Mary;** *see* Corrall, S. M.

**LESTER-DAVIS, Nicholas;** Director, Nick Lester-Davis Consulting, since 2017; *b* 20 March 1953; *s* of Frank and Eve Lester; *m* 2014, Tom Lester-Davis. *Educ*: Manchester Grammar Sch.; University Coll. London (BSc 1976; DipArch 1978). FCILT 1986. Architect Asst, Sutton LBC, 1977–78; Asst Dir, 1978–80, Dir, 1980–84, Transport 2000; Greater London Council: Industry and Employment Officer, 1984–85; Public Transport Officer, 1985–86; Planning and Transport Officer, ALA, 1986–91; London Parking Dir, 1992–98; Chief Exec., Transport Cttee for London, 1998–2001; Dir, Transport, Envmt and Planning, 2008–16, Corporate Dir, Services, 2008–16, Assoc. of London Govt, subseq. London Councils. Founder and Chm., London Cycling Campaign, 1978–80. Dir, Friends of the Earth Ltd, 1986–88. Chairman: London Transport Passengers' Cttee, 1983–85; Nat. Consumer Congress, 1985; President: British Parking Assoc., 1997–2000; European Parking Assoc., 2009–15 (Vice Pres., 2004–07); Vice Chm., Eur. Road Traffic Res. Adv. Council, 2014–17. Mem., Chilham Parish Council, 2017–. *Publications*: (contrib.) Travel Sickness, 1992. *Recreations*: food and drink, travel (especially by train and bicycle), dogs and cats (especially otterhounds), entertaining and being entertained. *Address*: Nick Lester-Davis Consulting, Vine Cottage, Cobbs Hill, Old Wives Lees, Kent CT4 8AL. *T*: 07802 725258. *E*: nick@nicklesterdavis.com.

**L'ESTRANGE, Michael Gerard,** AO 2007; Founding Executive Director, National Security College, 2009–14 and Professor of National Security, until 2015, Australian National University; *b* 12 Oct. 1952; *m* 1983, Jane Allen; five *s*. *Educ*: St Aloysius Coll., Sydney; Univ. of Sydney (BA Hons) Oxford Univ. (NSW Rhodes Schol., 1976–79; BA 1st Cl. Hons, MA). Dept of Prime Minister and Cabinet, Canberra, 1981–89; Harkness Fellow, Georgetown Univ. and Univ. of Calif, Berkeley, 1987–89; Sen. Advr, Office of Leader of Opposition, 1989–95; Exec. Dir, Menzies Res. Centre, Canberra, 1995–96; Sec. to Cabinet, and Hd, Cabinet Policy Unit, 1996–2000; High Comr for Australia in UK, 2000–05; Sec., Dept of Foreign Affairs and Trade, 2005–09. Non-executive Director: Rio Tinto, 2014–; Qantas, 2016–. Dep. Chancellor, Univ. of Notre Dame, Australia, 2017– (Dir, 2014–). *Recreations*: cricket, Rugby, golf.

**LE SUEUR, Prof. Andrew Philip;** Professor of Constitutional Justice, since 2013, and Executive Dean, Faculty of Humanities, since 2018, University of Essex; *b* 7 April 1964; *s* of George and Elaine Le Sueur. *Educ*: Hautlieu Sch., Jersey; London Sch. of Econs (LLB 1986). Called to the Bar, Middle Temple, 1987, Bencher, 2010; University College London: Lectr in Laws, 1988–98, Reader in Laws, 1998–2000, Faculty of Laws; Hon. Sen. Res. Fellow, Constitution Unit, 2001–05; Barber Prof. of Jurisprudence, Univ. of Birmingham, 2001–06; Prof. of Public Law, QMUL, 2006–13; Dir of Studies, Inst. of Law, Jersey, 2009–11. Law Comr, Jersey, 2013–18. Specialist Adviser: H of C Constitutional Affairs Cttee, 2003–05; H of L Select Cttee on Constitutional Reform Bill, 2005; H of C Justice Cttee, 2010; H of L Constitution Cttee, 2011–12 (Legal Advr, 2006–09). Co-Convenor, UK Constitutional Law Gp, 2010–13; Pres., UK Constitutional Assoc., 2013–15; Mem., Exec. Cttee, Internat. Assoc. of Constitutional Law, 2010–18. Editor, Public Law, 2002–11. *Publications*: (with M. Sunkin) Public Law, 1997; (ed) Building the UK's New Supreme Court: national and comparative perspectives, 2004; (with Lord Woolf and J. Jowell) de Smith's Judicial Review, 5th edn 1995 to 7th edn 2013; (with M. Sunkin and J. Murkens) Public Law: text, cases, and materials, 2010, 4th edn 2019; (ed with A. Horne) Parliament: legislation and accountability, 2016; articles on constitutional and administrative law. *Recreation*: pottering about. *Address*: School of Law, University of Essex, Wivenhoe Park, Colchester CO4 3SQ. *E*: alesueur@essex.ac.uk.

**LETHBRIDGE, Prof. Robert David,** PhD; Master of Fitzwilliam College, Cambridge, 2005–13; Hon. Professor of Nineteenth-Century French Literature, University of Cambridge, 2006–14, now Emeritus Hon. Professor; *b* 24 Feb. 1947; *s* of Albert Lethbridge and Muriel Alice (née de Saram); *m* 1970, Vera Lenore Laycock; one *s* one *d*. *Educ*: Mill Hill Sch.; Univ. of Kent at Canterbury (BA 1st cl. Hons 1969); McMaster Univ. (MA 1970); St John's Coll., Cambridge (MA 1973; PhD 1975). Fitzwilliam College, Cambridge: Fellow, 1973–94 (Life Fellow, 1994; Hon. Fellow, 2013); Leathersellers' Fellow, 1973–78; Tutor, 1975–92, Sen. Tutor, 1982–92; Coll. Lectr (jtly with Trinity Hall), 1978–80; Asst Lectr in French, 1980–85, Lectr, 1985–94, Univ. of Cambridge; University of London: Prof. of French Lang. and Lit., 1994–2005, now Emeritus; Hd, Dept of French, 1995–97, Dean, Grad. Sch., 1997–98, Vice-Principal (Acad.), 1997–2002, Vis. Prof., 2003–05, Royal Holloway; Dir, British Inst. in Paris, later Univ. of London Inst. in Paris, 2003–05. Provost, Gates Cambridge Trust, 2010–13. Visiting Professor: UCSB, 1986; Univ. of Melbourne, 2003; Honorary Professor: Queen Mary, Univ. of London, 2003–05; Univ. of St Andrews, 2015–. Commandeur des Palmes Académiques (France), 2012. *Publications*: Maupassant: Pierre et Jean, 1984; (ed with T. Keefe) Zola and the Craft of Fiction, 1990; (ed) Germinal, 1993; (ed with P. Collier) Artistic Relations, Literature and the Visual Arts in Nineteenth-Century France, 1994; (ed with C. Lloyd) Maupassant: conteur et romancier, 1994; (ed) L'Assommoir, 1995; (ed) Pot-Bouille, 2000; (ed) La Débâcle, 2000; (ed) Bel-Ami, 2001; (ed) Pierre et Jean, 2001; (ed) Selected Works, 2016; contribs to learned jls and collective works. *Recreations*: watching Rugby, contemplating the sea. *Address*: The Old Manse, Kirk Wynd, Markinch, Fife KY7 6DT. *Club*: Oxford and Cambridge.

**LETT, Hugh Brian Gordon;** QC 2008; a Recorder of the Crown Court, 1993–2014; author of military history; *b* Belfast, 9 Aug. 1949; *s* of Maj. Gordon Lett, DSO and Sheila Buckston Lett; *m* 1979, Angela Susan Jaques (marr. diss. 2014); three *s* one *d*. *Educ*: Marlborough Coll.; Council of Legal Educn. Called to the Bar, Inner Temple, 1971; in practice as barrister specialising in fraud, money laundering and serious crime. Asst Recorder, 1990–93; Hd of Chambers, South Western Chambers, Taunton, 1993–2002. Chm., Monte San Martino Trust, 1997–2005. Facilitator and Lectr, judicial confs of E Caribbean High Court, and judiciary of N Cyprus, Albania, Kosovo and Montenegro. Commendatore, Ordine al Merito della Repubblica Italiana, 2007. *Publications*: SAS in Tuscany, 2011; Ian Fleming and SOE's Operation Postmaster, 2012; The Small Scale Raiding Force, 2013; An Extraordinary Italian Imprisonment, 2014; SOE's Mastermind: an authorised biography of Major General Sir Colin Gubbins, KCVO, DSO, MC, 2016. *Recreations*: mountain walking in Italy, re-creating POW escape routes, history of Italian War of Liberation, watching cricket and Rugby. *Address*: 4 King's Bench Walk, 2nd Floor, Temple, EC4Y 7DL. *T*: (020) 7822 7000, *Fax*: (020) 7822 7022. *E*: bl@4kbw.co.uk, brian@brianlettauthor.com.

**LETTE, Kathryn Marie;** author; *b* Sydney, 11 Nov. 1958; *d* of Mervyn and Val Lette; *m* 1990, Geoffrey Ronald Robertson, *qv* (marr. diss. 2018); one *s* one *d*. Author, playwright, satirical columnist; TV presenter; Writer-in-Residence, Savoy Hotel, London, 2003–04. Ambassador: Plan International, 2009–; Nat. Autistic Soc., 2010–; Ambitious About Autism, 2012–. Hon. DA Southampton Solent, 2009. *Publications*: novels: Puberty Blues, 1979 (jtly); Hits and Ms, 1984; Girls' Night Out, 1988; The Llama Parlour, 1991; Foetal Attraction, 1993; Mad Cows, 1996; Altar Ego, 1998; Nip 'n' Tuck, 2000; Dead Sexy, 2002; How to Kill your Husband (and other handy household hints), 2006; To Love, Honour and Betray—Till Divorce Us Do Part, 2008; Men: a user's guide, 2010; The Boy Who Fell to Earth, 2012; Love is Blind, 2013; Courting Trouble, 2014; Best Laid Plans, 2017; plays: Wet Dreams, 1985; Perfect Mismatch, 1985; Grommitts, 1986; I'm So Happy for You, I Really Am, 1991. *Address*: c/o Curtis Brown, Haymarket House, 28–29 Haymarket, SW1Y 4SP. *T*: (020) 7393 4400.

**LETTS, Anthony Ashworth;** President, Charles Letts Group, 1994–96 (Chairman, Charles Letts Holdings Ltd, 1977–94); *b* 3 July 1935; *s* of Leslie Charles Letts and Elizabeth Mary (née Gibson); *m* 1962, Rosa Maria Ciarrapico; one *s* one *d*. *Educ*: Marlborough Coll.; Cambridge Univ. (MAEcon); Yale Univ. (Industrial Admin). National Service, RE, 2 Lieut, 1954–56. Joined Charles Letts & Co. Ltd, 1960; Man. Dir, 1965 (Charles Letts family business founded by John Letts (g g g grandfather), 1796). Director: Cambridge Market Intelligence, 1994–2002; Accademia Club Ltd, 1996–2002; Gov., Westminster Kingsway (formerly Westminster) Coll., London, 1993–2002. *Recreations*: tennis, sailing, hill walking, theatre. *Address*: The Dell, Pound Lane, Wood Street Village, Guildford GU3 3DT. *T*: 07720 812183. *Club*: Hurlingham.

**LETTS, Dr Melinda Jane Frances,** OBE 2003; Tutor in Greek and Latin Languages: Jesus College, Oxford, since 2013; Harris Manchester College, Oxford, since 2017; *b* 6 April 1956; *d* of late Richard Letts and of Jocelyn (née Adami); *m* 1991, Neil Scott Wishart McIntosh, *qv*; one *s* one *d*. *Educ*: Wycombe Abbey; Cheltenham Coll.; St Anne's Coll., Oxford (BA Hons, Lit Hum Cl. I); Christ Church, Oxford (MSt Classical Langs and Lit.; DPhil). Theatre Jobs, 1978–80; Res. Asst, Brunel Univ., 1980–81; Head of Admin, CND, 1982–84, VSO, 1985–87; Prog. Funding Manager, 1987, Regl Prog. Manager, ME and S Asia, 1987–89, VSO; Staffing Manager, McKinsey & Co., 1989–91; Dep. Dir, 1991–92, Dir, later Chief Exec., 1992–98, Nat. Asthma Campaign. Chm., Long Term Medical Conditions Alliance, 1998–2004 (Trustee, 1996–2004); Member: Commn for Health Improvement, 1999–2004; NHS Modernisation Bd, 2000–03; Commn for Healthcare Audit and Inspection, 2003–04; Chair, Cttee on Safety of Medicines Working Gp on Patient Information, 2003–05; Dir, Ask About Medicines, 2003–09. Chair, Nat. Strategic Partnership Forum, 2005–07. Sen. Associate, Compass Partnership, 2004–15; executive coach and mentor, 2004–. Trustee: NCVO, 1997–2002; Comic Relief, 1998–2002; General Practice Airways Gp, 2001–08; Parkinson's UK (formerly Parkinson's Disease Soc.), 2007– (Vice-Chm., 2008–09; Chair, 2009–11); Patron, Men's Health Forum, 2004; Member: Exec. Cttee, Tobacco Control Alliance, 1997–98; Bd, New Opportunities Fund, 1998–2001. Mem. Council, Cheltenham Coll., 1990–93; Governor, Oakley Hall Sch.,

Cirencester, 1993–94. Mem., ACENVO, 1992–98. MCMI (MIMgt 1992). FRSA 1996. *Recreations:* reading, yoga, music, gardening, crosswords. *E:* melindajletts@gmail.com.

*See also* Q. R. S. Letts.

**LETTS, Quentin Richard Stephen;** freelance journalist; Parliamentary Sketchwriter, The Times, since 2019; *b* 6 Feb. 1963; *s* of late Richard Francis Bonner Letts, schoolmaster, and of Jocelyn Elizabeth Letts (*née* Adami); *m* 1996, Lois Henrietta, *d* of Patrick and Marion Rathbone; one *s* two *d*. *Educ:* Haileybury; Bellarmine Coll., Kentucky; Trinity Coll., Dublin (BA); Jesus Coll., Cambridge (Dip. Classical Archaeol.). Writer, specialist pubns, Cardiff, 1987; Daily Telegraph, 1988–95: City Diarist, 1989–90; NY Corresp., 1991; Ed., Peterborough Column, 1991–95; NY Bureau Chief, The Times, 1995–97; Parly Sketchwriter, Daily Telegraph, 1997–2000; Parly Sketchwriter, 2000–18, theatre critic, 2004–18, Daily Mail. Creator, 'Clement Crabbe', Daily Mail, 2006–09. Presenter, What's the Point of…?, BBC Radio 4, 2008–16; contrib., This Morning, ITV, 2013–15. Judge: Stagestruck, 2012; Nation's Best Am-Dram, 2012, Sky Arts. Gov., Hereford Cathedral Perpetual Trust, 2015–; Dep. Churchwarden, How Caple Ch, 2014–. Edgar Wallace Award, London Press Club, 2003; Feature Writer of Year, What the Papers Say Awards, 2007; Political Journalist of the Year, 2009, Critic of the Year, 2010, Columnist of the Year, 2014, British Press Awards; Westminster Villager, Comment Awards, 2010. *Publications:* 50 People Who Buggered Up Britain, 2008; Bog Standard Britain, 2009; Letts Rip!, 2010; The Speaker's Wife (novel), 2015 (Beryl Bainbridge Award, People's Book Prize, 2016); Patronising Bastards, 2017. *Recreations:* watching cricket, singing hymns. *Address:* The Old Mill, How Caple, Herefordshire HR1 4SR. *T:* (01989) 740688. *Clubs:* Savile, MCC.

*See also* M. J. F. Letts.

**LETWIN, Isabel Grace, (Lady Letwin),** CBE 2013; Director of Legal Services, Ministry of Defence, since 2016; *b* 7 Aug. 1956; *d* of Prof. John Frank Davidson, *qv*; *m* 1984, Oliver Letwin (*see* Rt Hon. Sir Oliver Letwin); one *s* one *d* (twins). *Educ:* Perse Sch. for Girls; Girton Coll., Cambridge (BA Law Tripos, MA). Admitted solicitor, 1981; Asst Solicitor, Private Client Dept, Macfarlanes, 1981–84; Treasury Solicitor's Department: Litigation Div., 1984–88; on secondment to HSE, 1988–91; Treasury Div., 1991–93; Central Adv. Div., 1994–99; Legal Advr to DCMS, 1999–2006; on secondment to FCO, 2006–09; Director of Legal Services: DWP, 2009–11; DoH, 2011–16. Lector (pt-time) in Family Law, Trinity Coll., Cambridge, 1981–86. *Recreations:* gardening, tennis, alpine walking, cooking.

**LETWIN, Rt Hon. Sir Oliver,** Kt 2016; PC 2002; PhD; MP for West Dorset, since 1997 (C, 1997–2019; Ind, since 2019); *b* 19 May 1956; *s* of late Prof. William Letwin; *m* 1984, Isabel Grace Davidson (*see* I. G. Letwin); one *s* one *d* (twins). *Educ:* Eton Coll.; Trinity Coll., Cambridge (BA, MA, PhD 1982). Vis. Fellow, Princeton Univ., 1981; Research Fellow, Darwin Coll., Cambridge, 1982–83; Special Advr, DES, 1982–83; Mem., Prime Minister's Policy Unit, 1983–86; with N. M. Rothschild & Sons Ltd, 1986–2003 (Dir, 1991–2003; non-exec. Dir, 2005–09). Opposition front-bench spokesman on constitutional affairs, 1998–99, on Treasury affairs, 1999–2000; Shadow Chief Sec. to HM Treasury, 2000–01; Shadow Home Sec., 2001–03; Shadow Chancellor, 2003–05; Shadow Sec. of State for Envmt, Food and Rural Affairs, 2005; Chairman: Conservative Policy Review, 2005–10; Conservative Res. Dept, 2005–10; Conservative Policy Forum, 2010–16; Minister for Govt Policy, Cabinet Office, 2010–14; Chancellor of the Duchy of Lancaster, 2014–16. FRSA 1991. *Publications:* Ethics, Emotion and the Unity of the Self, 1984; Aims of Schooling, 1985; Privatising the World, 1987; Drift to Union, 1990; The Purpose of Politics, 1999; Hearts and Minds, 2017; numerous articles in learned and popular jls. *Recreations:* ski-ing, tennis, walking. *Address:* House of Commons, SW1A 0AA. *T:* (020) 7219 3000.

**LEUNG Chun-Ying;** Vice-Chairman, National Committee, Chinese People's Political Consultative Conference, since 2017. *Educ:* King's Coll., Hong Kong; Hong Kong Poly.; Bristol Poly. Land and housing reforms, China; preparatory work for estabt of HKSAR, 1984–97; Mem., Exec. Council, 1997–2011; Convenor, non-official mems, 1999–2011; Chief Exec., HKSAR, 2012–17. Formerly Asia Pacific Chm., DTZ. Formerly: Chm., RICS Hong Kong; Pres., Inst. of Surveyors in Hong Kong.

**LEUNG Kin Pong, Andrew,** SBS 2005; Founder, Andrew Leung International Consultants Ltd, Hong Kong, since 2010 (UK, 2005–10); Director-General, Government Office of Hong Kong Special Administrative Region in United Kingdom, 2000–04; *b* 13 Nov. 1945; *m* 1974, Peggy Fung Lin Tong; one *s* one *d*. *Educ:* BA (ext.) London; Wolfson Coll., Cambridge (postgrad. Dip. in Develt Studies); Harvard Univ. (PMD); Solicitor's qualifying certs, England and Hong Kong. Hong Kong Civil Service: Exec. Officer, then Sen. Exec. Officer, 1967–73; Asst Sec. for Security, 1973–75; Council Office, 1976–77; Asst Financial Sec., 1979–82; on secondment to Standard Chartered Bank, 1982–83; Counsellor (Hong Kong Affairs), Brussels, 1983–87; Dep. Dir-Gen. of Industry, 1987–91; Dep. Sec. for Transport, 1991–92; Police Admin Officer, 1994–96; Dir-Gen. of Social Welfare, 1996–2000. Sen. Consultant, MEC Internat., 2005–. Distinguished Contrib., Asymmetric Threats Contingency Alliance, 2005–; Founding Chm., China Interest Gp, Inst. of Dirs City Br., 2005–10; Global Commercial Agent, Changsha City, China, 2006–; Mem. Cttee, London Reg., RSA, 2007–10; Member: Royal Soc. for Asian Affairs, 2007–; Brain Trust, Evian Gp, Lausanne, 2007–; Expert, Community of Experts, Reuters Insight, 2007–; Council, Gerson Lehrman Gp, 2008–; Exec. Cttee, Harvard Business Sch. Assoc. of Hong Kong, 2010–13; China Futures Fellow, Berkshire Publishing Gp LLC, MA, 2011–13; Member, Board of Advisers: Executive Global Network, Hong Kong, 2011–; The Global Analyst, India, 2012–; Sen. Analyst, Wikistrat, Washington DC, 2013–; Mem., Adv. Bd, Eur. Centre for e-Commerce and Internet Law, Vienna, 2014–. Member: Governing Council, KCL, 2004–10; Adv. Bd, China Policy Inst., Nottingham Univ., 2005–10. Visiting Professor: Internat. MBA Prog., Sun Yat-sen Univ., China, 2005–10; Internat. MBA Prog., Lingnan Univ., China, 2006–07; NIMBAS Graduate Sch. of Mgt, Netherlands, 2006–07; London Metropolitan Univ. Business Sch., 2009–; Think-Tank Res. Fellow, Beijing Normal Univ., Zhuchai Campus, 2017–; Prof. of Practice, Hong Kong Inst. of Educn for Sustainable Develt, 2018–20. Certified Sustainable Develt Planner, 2018–. Mem., Exec. Cttee, 48 Gp Club, 2004–10 (Vice Chm., 2008–10); Network Member: Cambridge Soc., 1978–; Harvard Club UK, 2000–10; Mem., China-Britain Business Council, 2005–10. Mem. Bd, Multitude Foundn, 2012–14. Hon. Advr, Internat. Inst. of Mgt, Hong Kong, 2016–; Hon. Pres., China Hong Kong Econ. and Trade Internat. Assoc., 2016–. FRSA 2002. JP Hong Kong, 1989. SBS (Hong Kong), 2005. *Recreations:* tennis, swimming, jogging, travelling, singing, reading, Chinese calligraphy, art appreciation. *Address:* 1E Block A, The Beachside, 82 Repulse Bay Road, Hong Kong. *E:* andrewkpleung@hotmail.com. *Club:* Hong Kong Jockey.

**LEUNIG, Dr Timothy,** FRHistS, FSS, FAcSS; Associate Professor (formerly Reader) in Economic History, London School of Economics and Political Science, since 2008; *b* London, 1971; *s* of (Patrick) Ray and Judith Leunig; *m* 1996, Julia Cerutti; one *d*. *Educ:* Sir Joseph Williamson's Math. Sch., Rochester; Queen's Coll., Oxford (BA 1st Cl. Modern Hist. and Econs 1992); St Antony's Coll. and Nuffield Coll., Oxford (MPhil Econs 1994; DPhil Econs 1996). FRHistS 2007; FSS 2014. Prize Fellow, Nuffield Coll., Oxford, 1995–97; Lectr in Econs, Royal Holloway, Univ. of London, 1997–98; Lectr in Econ.

Hist., LSE, 1998–2008; Ed., Explorations in Econ. Hist., 2009–12; Chief Economist, CentreForum think tank, 2011–12; Sen. Ministerial Policy Advr, 2012–14, Chief Analyst and Chief Scientific Advr, 2014–17, DFE. Econ. Advr on Housing Supply to Sec. of State, DCLG, then MHCLG, 2015–18; Sen. Policy Advr to Sec. of State, DEFRA, 2017–; Expert Advr, DFE, 2018–. Gov., NIESR, 2015–. Vis. Internat. Fellow, Univ. of Lund, 2010–12. FRSA 2013. *Publications:* In My Back Yard: unlocking the planning system, 2007; Cities Unlimited, 2008; Mastering Postgraduate Funding, 2011; Bigger and Quieter, 2012; contribs to jls incl. Econ. Hist. Rev., Explorations in Econ. Hist., Jl Econ. Hist. *Recreations:* thinking, cycling, gardening. *Address:* London School of Economics and Political Science, Houghton Street, WC2A 2AE. *E:* t.leunig@lse.ac.uk. *W:* www.twitter.com/timleunig.

**LEVEN,** 15th Earl of, *cr* 1641, **AND MELVILLE,** 14th Earl of, *cr* 1690; **Alexander Ian Leslie Melville;** Baron Melville 1616; Baron Balgonie 1641; Viscount Kirkcaldie 1690; *b* London, 29 Nov. 1984; *s* of Lord Balgonie (*d* 2007) and of Lady Balgonie, Julia Clare, *yr d* of Col Ian Ranald Critchley, OBE; *S* grandfather, 2012. *Educ:* Gordonstoun Sch. *Recreations:* photography, extensive overland travel in Europe, Asia, Middle East, Caucasus, Balkans, Pacific Is, Australia and Africa. *Heir:* uncle Hon. Archibald Ronald Melville [*b* 15 Sept. 1957; *m* 1987, Julia Mary Greville Fox; three *d*]. *Address:* Glenferness House, Nairn IV12 5UP. *T:* (01309) 651202.

**LEVENE,** family name of **Baron Levene of Portsoken.**

**LEVENE OF PORTSOKEN,** Baron *cr* 1997 (Life Peer), of Portsoken, in the City of London; **Peter Keith Levene,** KBE 1989; JP; Chairman: Lloyd's, 2002–11; Starr Underwriting Agents Ltd, since 2012; *b* 8 Dec. 1941; *s* of late Maurice Levene and Rose Levene; *m* 1966, Wendy Ann (*née* Fraiman); two *s* one *d*. *Educ:* City of London School; Univ. of Manchester (BA Econ). Joined United Scientific Holdings, 1963; Man. Dir, 1968–85; Chm., 1982–85; Chief of Defence Procurement, MoD, 1985–91; UK Nat. Armaments Dir, 1988–91; Chm., European Nat. Armaments Dirs, 1989–90. Member: SE Asia Trade Adv. Group, 1979–83; Council, Defence Manufacturers' Assoc., 1982–85 (Vice-Chm., 1983–84; Chm., 1984–85; Pres., 2006–); Citizen's Charter Adv. Panel, 1992–93; Personal Adviser to: Sec. of State for Defence, 1984; Sec. of State for the Envmt, 1991–92; Chancellor of the Exchequer on Competition and Purchasing, 1992; Pres. of BoT, 1992–95; Prime Minister on Efficiency and Effectiveness, 1992–97. Member: Select Cttee on Econ. Affairs, H of L, 2009–12; Select Cttee on Artificial Intelligence, H of L, 2017–19. Chm., Defence Reform Gp, MoD, 2010–16. Chairman: Docklands Light Railway Ltd, 1991–94; Bankers Trust Internat. plc, 1998–99; IFSL (formerly British Invisibles), 2000–10; General Dynamics UK Ltd, 2001–; NBNK Investments plc, 2011–12; Tikehau Investment Ltd, 2014–; Chm., Investment Banking Europe, 1999–2001, Vice-Chm., 2001–02, Deutsche Bank; Dep. Chm., Wasserstein Perella & Co. Ltd, 1991–94; Chm. and Chief Exec., Canary Wharf Ltd, 1993–96; Director: Haymarket Gp Ltd, 1997–; J. Sainsbury plc, 2001–04; China Construction Bank, 2005–12; China Construction Bank (Asia) Hong Kong, 2013–; Getlink (formerly Eurotunnel) SA, 2012–. Sen. Advr, Morgan Stanley & Co. Ltd, 1996–98; Member: Supervisory Bd, Deutsche Börse, 2004–05; Bd, Total SA, 2005–11. Chm., World Trade Centre Disaster Fund (UK), 2001–06. Member: Bd of Management, London Homes for the Elderly, 1984–93 (Chm., 1990–93); Internat. Adv. Bd, Singapore Govt Nat. Labs, 1998–99; Chairman's Council, Alcatel, 2000–03. Governor: City of London Sch. for Girls, 1984–85; City of London Sch., 1986–; Sir John Cass Primary Sch., 1985–93 (Dep. Chm., 1990–93). Mem. Court, HAC, 1984–2012; Mem., Court of Common Council, City of London, 1983–84 (Ward of Candlewick); Alderman, Ward of Portsoken, 1984–2005, Ward of Aldgate, 2005–12; Sheriff, City of London, 1995–96; Lord Mayor of London, 1998–99; Liveryman: Carmen's Co., 1984– (Master, 1992–93); Information Technologists' Co., 1993–; Hon. Liveryman, Mgt Consultants' Co. Hon. Col Comdt, RCT, 1991–93, RLC, 1993–2006. JP City of London, 1984. Fellow, QMW, 1995. CCMI; FCIPS. Hon. FCII. Hon. DSc: City, 1998; London, 2005. Insurance Leader of the Year Award, St John's Univ. Sch. of Risk Mgt, USA, 2010. KStJ 1998. Commandeur, Ordre National du Mérite (France), 1996; Kt Comdr, Order of Merit (Germany), 1998; Middle Cross, Order of Merit (Hungary), 1999. *Recreations:* ski-ing, watching association football, travel. *Address:* 4th Floor, 30 Fenchurch Avenue, EC3M 5AD. *T:* (020) 7398 5087. *E:* peter.levene@starrcompanies.com. *Clubs:* Guildhall, Walbrook, Royal Automobile.

**LEVENE, Jacqueline Anne;** *see* Perry, J. A.

**LEVENE, Prof. Malcolm Irvin,** MD; FRCP; FRCPCH, FMedSci; Professor of Paediatrics and Child Health, 1989–2010, now Emeritus, Chairman, Division of Paediatrics, 1992–98, University of Leeds; *b* 2 Jan. 1951; *s* of Maurice Levene and Helen Levene (*née* Kutner); *m* 1st, 1972, Miriam Bentley (marr. diss. 1990); three *d*; 2nd, 1991, Susan Anne Cave; one *s* one *d*. *Educ:* Varndean Grammar Sch., Brighton; Guy's Hosp. Med. Sch., London Univ. (MB BS 1972); MD 1981. MRCS, LRCP, 1972; MRCP 1978, FRCP 1988; FRCPCH 1996. Junior posts at Royal Sussex, Northampton General and Charing Cross Hosps, 1974–77; Registrar, Derby Children's and Charing Cross Hosps, 1977–79; Res. Lectr, RPMS, Hammersmith Hosp., 1979–82; Sen. Lectr and Reader, Dept of Paediatrics, Univ. of Leicester, 1982–88; Med. Dir, Women's and Children's Subsidiary, 1998–2010, Chm., Child Health Cttee, 2005–10, Leeds Teaching Hosp. NHS Trust. Mem., DoH Nat. Adv. Body, Confidential Enquiry into Stillbirths and Deaths in Infancy, 1991. Chm., Scientific Adv. Cttee, Action Res., 1994–97. Ed.-in-Chief, MRCPCH Master Course, 2007–10. FMedSci 1999; Fellow, Acad. Perinatal Medicine, 2005. Hancock Prize, RCS, 1974; British Paediatric Association: Donald Paterson Prize, 1982; Michael Blecklow Meml Prize, 1982; Guthrie Medal, 1987; Ronnie MacKeith Prize, British Paed. Neurology Assoc., 1984; BUPA Res. Prize, 1988; William Liley Medal, Internat. Soc. of Fetus as a Patient, 2009; Sir James Spence Medal, RCPCH, 2010. *Publications:* (with H. Nutbeam) A Handbook for Examinations in Paediatrics, 1981; (jtly) Ultrasound of the Infant Brain, 1985; (jtly) Essentials of Neonatal Medicine, 1987, 3rd edn 2000; (ed jtly) Fetal and Neonatal Neurology and Neurosurgery, 1988, 4th edn 2009; Diseases of Children, 6th edn, 1990; Paediatrics and Child Health, 1999, 2nd edn 2006; chapters in books and articles in learned jls on paed. topics, esp. neurology of new-born. *Recreations:* music, occasional gentle golf and gardening. *Address:* Acacia House, Acacia Park Drive, Apperley Bridge, W Yorks BD10 0PH. *T:* (0113) 250 9959.

**LEVENSON, Howard;** an Upper Tribunal Judge, Administrative Appeals Chamber, since 2009 (Social Security Commissioner and Child Support Commissioner, 1997–2009, and Pensions Appeal Commissioner, 2005–09); *b* 4 Dec. 1949; *s* of Albert and Marlene Levenson; *m* 1971, Ros Botsman; one *s* one *d*. *Educ:* Tottenham Grammar Sch.; Univ. of Sheffield (BJur Hons 1970; LLM 1972); Coll. of Law, London; Birkbeck, Univ. of London (MA 2007); London Sch. of Econs and Pol Sci. (Cert. in Internat. Human Rights Law 2009). Admitted solicitor, 1974; Legal Officer, NCCL, 1974–77; Law Lectr, Poly., then Univ., of E London, 1977–92; Consultant, Nash and Dowell (Solicitors), 1981–91; part-time Chm., Tribunals, 1986–92; Chm., Independent Tribunal Service, 1993–97. Mem., Internat. Adv. Gp, Centre on Human Rights in Conflict, 2010–15. Chm., Haldane Soc., 1980–83. Hon. LLD UEL, 2009. *Publications:* The Price of Justice, 1981; (jtly) Social Welfare Law: Legal Aid and Advice, 1985; (jtly) Police Powers, 1985, 3rd edn 1996; (contrib. ed.) Jowitt's Dictionary of English Law, 3rd edn 2010; contrib. vols of Atkin's

Court Forms on Child Support, Judicial Review, Personal Rights, Social Security, Tribunals, War Pensions; contrib. to Modern Law Rev., Criminal Law Rev., New Law Jl, etc. *Address*: Upper Tribunal, Administrative Appeals Chamber, 5th Floor, Rolls Building, 7 Rolls Buildings, Fetter Lane, EC4A 1NL. *Club*: Leyton Orient Football.

**LEVENTHAL, Colin David**; Director, HAL Films Ltd, 2000–12; Partner, HAL Film Services; *b* 2 Nov. 1946; *s* of Morris and Olga Leventhal; *m* 1995, Petrea, *d* of late Thomas Hoving; three *d*. *Educ*: Carmel Coll., Wallingford, Berks; King's Coll., Univ. of London (BA Philosophy). Solicitor of Supreme Court of England and Wales. Admitted Solicitor, 1971; BBC, 1974–81, Head of Copyright, 1978; Head of Prog. Acquisition, Channel Four TV, 1981–87; Dir of Acquisition and Sales, Channel Four TV Co., 1987–92 (Dir, 1988–92); Dir of Acquisition, Channel Four TV Corp., 1993–97; Man. Dir, Channel Four Internat. Ltd, 1993–97; Jt Chief Exec., Miramax HAL Films Ltd, 1998–2000. Mem., Film Council, 1999–2002. *Recreations*: theatre, film. *Address*: 10 Well Walk, Hampstead, NW3 1LD. *T*: (020) 7435 3038.

**LEVER, Hon. Bernard Lewis; His Honour Judge Lever**; a Circuit Judge, since 2001; *b* 1 Feb. 1951; *s* of Baron Lever and of Ray Rosalia, Lady Lever; *m* 1985, Anne Helen Ballingall, only *d* of Patrick Chandler Gordon Ballingall, MBE; two *d*. *Educ*: Clifton; Queen's Coll., Oxford (Neale Exhibnr; MA). Called to the Bar, Middle Temple, 1975; in practice, Northern Circuit, 1975–2001; Standing Counsel to Inland Revenue, 1997–2001. Co-founder, SDP in NW, 1981. Contested (SDP) Manchester Withington, 1983. *Recreations*: walking, music, picking up litter. *Address*: Manchester Crown Court, Minshull Street, Manchester M1 3FS. *T*: (0161) 954 7500. *Club*: Vincent's (Oxford).

**LEVER, Sir Christopher**; *see* Lever, Sir T. C. A. L.

**LEVER, Giles**; HM Diplomatic Service; Deputy Ambassador to Afghanistan, since 2018; *s* of His Honour (John) Michael Lever and Elizabeth Lever (née Marr); *m* Gill; one *s* one *d*. *Educ*: Bolton Sch.; Bristol Univ. Entered FCO, 1990; Desk Officer, SE Asia Dept, FCO, 1991–92; Second Sec. (Pol), Vietnam, 1993–97; Hd, Export Control Policy Section, Non-Proliferation Dept, FCO, 1997–2000; Japanese lang. trng, 2000–02; First Sec. (Pol), then Hd, Political Section, Tokyo, 2002–06; Dep. Hd, Iraq Gp, FCO, 2006–09; Actg Consul Gen., Erbil, 2009; Strategy Develt, Counter-Terrorism Dept, FCO, 2009; Hd, ME and N Africa Dept, DFID (on secondment), 2009–11; Dep. High Comr, Abuja, 2011–14; Ambassador to Vietnam, 2014–18. *Address*: c/o Foreign and Commonwealth Office, King Charles Street, SW1A 2AH.

**LEVER, Sir Jeremy (Frederick)**, KCMG 2002; QC 1972; QC (NI) 1988; *b* 23 June 1933; *s* of late A. Lever; civil partnership 2006, Brian Collie. *Educ*: Bradfield Coll.; University Coll., Oxford; Nuffield Coll., Oxford. Served RA, 1951–53. 1st cl. Jurisprudence, 1956, MA Oxon; Pres., Oxford Union Soc., 1957, Trustee, 1972–77 and 1988–2014. Fellow, All Souls Coll., Oxford, 1957–2017, Hon. Fellow, 2017 (Sub-Warden, 1982–84; Sen. Dean, 1988–2011). Called to Bar, Gray's Inn, 1957, Bencher, 1985. Chairman: Oftel Adv. Body on Fair Trading in Telecommunications, 1996–2000; Appeals Panel, PRS, 1997–2002. Mem. Council, British Inst. of Internat. and Comparative Law, 1987–2004. Director (non-exec.): Dunlop Holdings Ltd, 1973–80; Wellcome plc, 1983–94. Mem., Arbitral Tribunal, US/UK Arbitration concerning Heathrow Airport User Charges, 1989–94. Vis. Prof., Wissenschaftszentrum, Berlin, für Sozialforschung, 1999. Lectures: Hamlyn, Hamlyn Trust, 1991; Lord Fletcher Meml, Law Soc., 1997; Grotius, British Inst. of Internat. and Comparative Law, 1998. Governor, Berkhamsted Schs, 1985–95. FRSA. *Publications*: The Law of Restrictive Practices, 1964; other legal works. *Recreations*: ceramics, music. *Address*: Monckton Chambers, 1 Raymond Buildings, Gray's Inn, WC1R 5NR. *T*: (020) 7405 7211, *Fax*: (020) 7405 2084; All Souls College, Oxford OX1 4AL. *T*: (01865) 279379, *Fax*: (01865) 279299, (01304) 750015. *E*: chambers@monckton.com. *Club*: Garrick.

**LEVER, John Darcy**, MA; Headmaster, Canford School, 1992–2013; *b* 14 Jan. 1952; *s* of late Prof. Jeffrey Darcy Lever; *m* 1981, Alisoun Margaret Yule; one *s* two *d*. *Educ*: Westminster Sch.; Trinity Coll., Cambridge (MA); Christ Church, Oxford (Cert Ed). St Edward's Sch., Oxford, 1974–76; Winchester Coll., 1976–92. *Recreations*: walking, clocks, maps. *Address*: Shores Farm, Frog Street, Lopen, South Petherton, Somerset TA13 5JR.

**LEVER, (Keith) Mark**; Chief Executive, Helpforce, since 2019; *b* 20 Sept. 1960; *s* of Keith Lever and Rosemary Anne Lever (née Wakeley); *m* 1989, Amanda Jane Sackville Davison; four *s*. *Educ*: Wakeman Grammar Sch., Shrewsbury; Royal Holloway Coll., London (BSc Hons Physics and Mgt Sci. 1982); Cranfield Univ. Sch. of Mgt (MBA 1999). DipChA; DipM. FCA 2009 (ACA 1986). Partner and Nat. Dir, Mkt Res. and Trng, Kidsons Impey, 1994; Women's Royal Voluntary Service: Dir, Trng, 1995–99; Dir, Strategic Develt, 1999–2002; Chief Exec. Officer, 2002–07; Chief Exec., Nat. Autistic Soc., 2008–19. MCIPD 1992; ACIM 2000. *Recreations*: drinking wine with my wife, negotiating peace settlements and behaviour related pay with my four sons, regularly losing at tennis and golf, long distance cycling. *E*: marklever@aol.com. *Clubs*: Harrow Golf Society, Wanborough Amateur Golf Society.

**LEVER, Sir Paul**, KCMG 1998 (CMG 1991); HM Diplomatic Service, retired; Chairman, Royal United Services Institute, 2004–09; *b* 31 March 1944; *s* of John Morrison Lever and Doris Grace (née Battey); *m* 1990, Patricia Anne, *d* of John and Anne Ramsey. *Educ*: St Paul's Sch.; The Queen's Coll., Oxford (MA; Hon. Fellow, 2006). 3rd Secretary, Foreign and Commonwealth Office, 1966–67; 3rd, later 2nd Secretary, Helsinki, 1967–71; 2nd, later 1st Secretary, UK Delegn to NATO, 1971–73; FCO, 1973–81; Asst Private Sec. to Sec. of State for Foreign and Commonwealth Affairs, 1978–81; Chef de Cabinet to Christopher Tugendhat, Vice-Pres. of EEC, 1981–85; Head of UN Dept, FCO, 1985–86; Head of Defence Dept, 1986–87; Head of Security Policy Dept, FCO, 1987–90; Ambassador and Hd, UK Delegn to Conventional Arms Control Negotiations, Vienna, 1990–92; Asst Under-Sec. of State, FCO, 1992–94; Dep. Sec., Cabinet Office, and Chm., Jt Intelligence Cttee, 1994–96; Dep. Under-Sec. of State (Dir for EU and Economic Affairs), FCO, 1996–97; Ambassador to Germany, 1997–2003. Global Develt Dir, RWE Thames Water, 2003–06; non-exec. Dir, Sellafield Ltd, 2007–11. Pres., Anglo-Finnish Soc., 2015–. Hon. LLD Birmingham, 2001. *Publications*: (contrib.) Oxford Handbook of War, 2012; Berlin Rules: Europe and the German way, 2017. *Recreations*: walking, art deco pottery. *Address*: 48 Jubilee Place, SW3 3TQ.

**LEVER, Sir (Tresham) Christopher (Arthur Lindsay)**, 3rd Bt *cr* 1911; PhD; *b* 9 Jan. 1932; *s* of Sir Tresham Joseph Philip Lever, FRSL, 2nd Bt, and Frances Yowart (*d* 1959), *d* of Lindsay Hamilton Goodwin; step *s* of Pamela Lady Lever (*d* 2003), *d* of late Lt-Col Hon. Malcolm Bowes Lyon; *S* father, 1975; *m* 1st, 1970, 2nd, 1975, Linda Weightman McDowell, *d* of late James Jepson Goulden, Tennessee, USA. *Educ*: Eton; Trinity Coll., Cambridge (BA Hist. and English 1954; MA 1957; PhD Biol. 2011). FLS; FRGS. Commissioned, 17th/21st Lancers, 1950. Peat, Marwick, Mitchell & Co., 1954–55; Kitcat & Aitken, 1955–56; Dir, John Barran & Sons Ltd, 1956–64. Consultant: Zoo Check Charitable Trust, 1984–91; Born Free Foundn, 1991–2003; Chairman: African Fund for Endangered Wildlife (UK), 1987–90; UK Elephant Gp, 1991–92; UK Rhino Gp, 1992–93; Member: IUCN Species Survival Commn, 1988–; IUCN UK Cttee, 1989–2011; Scientific Advr, Galapagos Conservation Trust, 2012–; Trustee: Internat. Trust for Nature Conservation, 1980–92 (Vice-Pres. 1986–91; Pres., 1991–92); Rhino Rescue Trust, 1986–91 (Patron 1985–2003); Chm., 1990–2004, Hon. Life Pres., 2004, Tusk Trust; Chm., Ruaha Trust, 1990–95; Member Council: Soc. for Protection of Animals in N Africa, 1986–88; British Trust for Ornithology, 1988–91 (Chm., Nat. Centre Appeal, 1987–92); SOS Sahel Internat. (UK), 1995–2010; Director: WSPA, 1998–2003; Earthwatch Inst., Europe, 2003–04; Mem., Council of Ambassadors, WWF-UK, 1999–2005 (Fellow, 2005); Patron: Lynx Educnl Trust for Animal Welfare, 1991–2010; Respect for Animals, 1995–2011; Vice-Patron, Conservation Foundn, 2005–06. MBOU. Hon. Life Member: Butterfly Conservation, 2014; Soc. for Protection of Animals Abroad; FFI. Mem., Editl Bd, Jl of Applied Herpetology, 2005–09. H. H. Bloomer Award, Linnean Soc., 2014. *Publications*: Goldsmiths and Silversmiths of England, 1975; The Naturalized Animals of the British Isles, 1977; (contrib.) Wildlife '80: the world conservation yearbook, 1980; (contrib.) Evolution of Domesticated Animals, 1984; Naturalized Mammals of the World, 1985; Naturalized Birds of the World, 1987; (contrib.) Beyond the Bars: the zoo dilemma, 1987; The Mandarin Duck, 1990; They Dined on Eland: the story of the acclimatisation societies, 1992; (contrib.) The New Atlas of Breeding Birds in Britain and Ireland: 1988–1991, 1993; Naturalized Animals: the ecology of successfully introduced species, 1994; (contrib.) The Introduction and Naturalisation of Birds, 1996; Naturalized Fishes of the World, 1996; (contrib.) Stocking & Introduction of Fish, 1997; (contrib.) The EBCC Atlas of European Breeding Birds: their distribution and abundance, 1997; The Cane Toad: the history and ecology of a successful colonist, 2001; (contrib.) The Migration Atlas: movements of the birds of Britain and Ireland, 2002; Naturalized Reptiles and Amphibians of the World, 2003; (contrib.) Biological Invasions: from ecology to control, 2005; Naturalised Birds of the World, 2005; The Naturalized Animals of Britain and Ireland, 2009; (contrib.) Silent Summer: the state of wildlife in Britain and Ireland, 2010; (contrib.) Encyclopedia of Biological Invasions, 2011; The Mandarin Duck, 2013. *Heir*: none. *Address*: Newell House, Winkfield, Berks SL4 4SE. *T*: (01344) 882604, *Fax*: (01344) 891744. *Clubs*: Boodle's; Swinley Forest Golf.

**LEVERTON, Colin Allen H.**; *see* Hart-Leverton.

**LEVERTON, Roger Frank**, FCA; Chairman, Renold plc, 1998–2006; *b* 22 April 1939; *s* of Frank Arthur Leverton and Lucia Jean Leverton (née Harden); *m* 1st, 1962, Patricia Jones (marr. diss.); one *s* one *d* (and one *d* decd); 2nd, 1992, Marilyn Williams. *Educ*: Haberdashers' Aske's Sch. FCA 1962. Black & Decker Manufacturing Co., 1968–84: European Dir and Gen. Manager, France, 1978–81; Gp Vice-Pres., Southern Europe, 1981–84; Chief Exec., MK Electric Gp, subseq. Pillar Electrical plc, 1984–89; Pres. and Chief Exec., Indal Ltd (RTZ Corp. plc), 1989–92; Chief Exec., Pilkington plc, 1992–97. Chairman: Infast Gp plc, 1997–2002; Betts Gp Hldgs Ltd, 1998–2005. *Recreations*: tennis, golf, theatre.

**LEVESON, Lord**; George James Leveson Gower; *b* 22 July 1999; *s* and *heir* of Earl Granville, *qv*.

**LEVESON, Rt Hon. Sir Brian (Henry)**, Kt 2000; PC 2006; President, Queen's Bench Division, 2013–19; Head of Criminal Justice, 2017–19; *b* 22 June 1949; *er s* of late Dr Ivan Leveson and Elaine Leveson, Liverpool; *m* 1981, Lynne Rose (née Fishel); two *s* one *d*. *Educ*: Liverpool College, Liverpool; Merton College, Oxford (MA; Hon. Fellow, 2001). Called to the Bar, Middle Temple, 1970, Bencher, 1995 (Dep. Treas., 2019); Harmsworth Scholar, 1970; practised Northern Circuit, 1971; University of Liverpool: Lectr in Law, 1971–81; Mem. Council, 1983–92; Asst Recorder, 1984–88; QC 1986; a Recorder, 1988–2000; a Dep. High Court Judge, 1998–2000; a Judge of the High Court, QBD, 2000–06; a Lord Justice of Appeal, 2006–13; Presiding Judge, Northern Circuit, 2002–05; Sen. Presiding Judge for England and Wales, 2007–09 (Dep. Sen. Presiding Judge, 2006). Investigatory Powers Comr, 2019–. Chm., Inquiry into Culture, Practices and Ethics of the Press, 2011–12. Mem., Parole Bd, 1992–95. Chairman: Criminal Justice Council, 2008–11; Sentencing Council for England and Wales, 2010–13. Mem. Council, UCS, Hampstead, 1998–2015 (Chm., 2009–15); Foundn Mem., Liverpool Coll., 2001–; Chancellor, Liverpool John Moores Univ., 2013–. Pres., Merton Soc., 2010–16. Ambassador, Young Citizens (formerly Citizenship Foundn), 2018–. Hon. Fellow, Liverpool John Moores Univ., 2012. Hon. LLD Liverpool, 2007; DUniv Kingston, 2019. *Recreations*: walking, travel.

**LEVESON GOWER**, family name of **Earl Granville**.

**LEVETE, Amanda**, CBE 2017; RIBA 1984; Principal, Amanda Levete Architects, since 2009; *b* Bridgend, Wales, 1955; one *s*; *m* 2008, Ben Evans. *Educ*: Architectural Assoc. In practice as architect: Alsop & Lyall, 1980–81; YRM Architects, 1982–84; Richard Rogers & Partners, 1984–89; Partner, Future Systems, 1989–2009: projects include: Stonehenge Visitor Centre, 1993 (Bovis Royal Acad. Award); Hauer/King House, 1994; West India Quay Bridge, 1998 (British Construction Ind. Award, Civic Trust Award, RIBA Award); Natwest Media Centre at Lord's cricket ground, 1999 (British Construction Ind. Award, Stirling Prize, RIBA, Civic Trust Award, World Architectural Award); Selfridges dept store in Birmingham, 2004 (Civic Trust Award; RIBA Award for Architecture); Amanda Levete Architects projects include: 10 Hills Place, 2009; Spencer Dock Bridge, 2009; Globe Acad., 2010; Tincan, 2014; MPavilion, 2015; Sky, 2016; Central Embassy, 2016; Museum of Art, Architecture and Technol., Lisbon, 2016; Exhibition Road, V&A, 2017; individual furniture pieces for Established & Sons. Vis. Lectr, 1995–, Ext. Assessor, 2004–06, Vis. Prof., 2008–, RCA; Ext. Examiner, Architectural Assoc., 2013–. Trustee: Architecture Foundn, 1997–2008; Artangel, 2000–14; Young Foundn, 2009–16; Arts Foundn, 2011–14. *Address*: 14a Brewery Road, N7 9NH. *T*: (020) 7243 7670, *Fax*: (020) 7243 7690. *E*: info@ala.uk.com.

**LEVETT, Martyn Neale; His Honour Judge Levett;** a Circuit Judge, since 2015; *b* 7 April 1954; *s* of late Frank Arthur Levett and Dorothy Joyce Levett. *Educ*: Univ. of Leeds (BSc Hons Chem. Engrg). Called to the Bar, Middle Temple, 1978; a Recorder, 2000–15. *Address*: Ipswich Crown Court, The Courthouse, 1 Russell Road, Ipswich IP1 2AG.

**LEVI, Andrew Peter Robert**; HM Diplomatic Service; Director, Foreign and Commonwealth Office, since 2018; *b* 4 March 1963; *s* of Paul George Carl Levi and Paula Levi; *m* 2002, Dr Roswitha Elisabeth von Studnitz. *Educ*: Reading Blue Coat Sch. (Aldworth's Hosp.); Univ. of Manchester (BSc Hons 1985); Univ. of Freiburg im Breisgau. Entered FCO, 1987; Bonn, 1990–93; First Secretary: FCO, 1993–96; on secondment to EC (EU enlargement), 1996–98, and to OECD Secretariat, 1998; Bonn, 1998–99; on secondment to: German FO, Bonn, 1999; DCS, Stability Pact for S Eastern Europe, 1999–2001; Dep. Hd, Eastern Adriatic Dept, FCO, 2001–03; Hd, Aviation, Maritime and Energy Dept, FCO, 2003–04; Asst Dir (EU), FCO, 2004–05; Counsellor (Econ.), Moscow, 2005–07; Border Review Team, Cabinet Office, 2007; Dir for Investment, 2008–10, Man. Dir, Business Gp, 2010–12, UK Trade & Investment; Vice Pres., EMEA and Russia, Cisco Systems, 2012–14.

**LEVI, Malcolm Sydney**; Group Chief Executive, Home Group, 1998–2008; housing adviser and non-executive director; *b* 3 March 1948; *s* of David and Fanny Levi; *m* 1972, Joy Poloway; two *s*. *Educ*: King Edward's Five Ways Grammar Sch., Birmingham;

Mansfield Coll., Oxford (MA (Modern Hist.)). FCA 1978; MCIH 2001. Dir of Finance, Merseyside Improved Houses, 1977–82; Asst Dir of Housing, London Borough of Hammersmith and Fulham, 1983–85; Chief Executive: Paddington Churches Housing Assoc., 1985–94; Warden Housing Assoc., 1994–97; Gp Dep. Chief Exec., Home Gp, 1997–98. Member: Bd, Newcastle Gateshead Housing Mkt Renewal Pathfinder, 2003–08; Bd, Richmond Housing Partnership, 2010–16; Adv. Panel, Tenant Services Authy, subseq. Homes and Communities Agency, then Regulator for Social Housing, 2011–18; Adviser: Savills, 2009–; Coactiva Aspiren, 2011–13; Statutory appointee, Novas Scarman Gp, 2009–10; Chm., Fit for Living, 2010–12. Mem. Bd, Richmond Synagogue, 2002–10, 2013–. Gov. (non-exec. Dir), Peabody, 2009–17 (Vice Chair, 2014; Actg Chair, 2015). Mentor, 2018–. *Recreations:* family and friends, films, theatre, travel, walking in Northumberland. *Address:* 23 Martingales Close, Richmond upon Thames, Surrey TW10 7JJ. *T:* (020) 8948 1683.

**LEVICK, William Russell,** FRS 1982; FAA; Professor, John Curtin School of Medical Research, Australian National University, 1983–96, now Emeritus Professor; *b* 5 Dec. 1931; *s* of Russell L. S. Levick and Elsie E. I. (*née* Nance); *m* 1961, Patricia Jane Lathwell; two *s* one *d*. *Educ:* Univ. of Sydney (BSc 1st Cl. Hons, MSc, MB, BS 1st Cl. Hons). Registered Medical Practitioner, State of ACT. RMO, Royal Prince Alfred Hosp., Sydney, 1957–58; National Health and Med. Res. Council Fellow, Univ. of Sydney, 1959–62; C. J. Martin Travelling Fellow, Cambridge Univ. and Univ. of Calif, Berkeley, 1963–64; Associate Res. Physiologist, Univ. of Calif, Berkeley, 1965–66; Sen. Lectr in Physiol., Univ. of Sydney, 1967; Professorial Fellow of Physiology, John Curtin Sch. of Medicine, ANU, 1967–83. FAA 1973; Fellow, Optical Soc. of America, 1977. *Publications:* articles on neurophysiology of the visual system in internat. scientific jls. *Address:* John Curtin School of Medical Research, Australian National University, Canberra, ACT 0200, Australia. *T:* (2) 62950336.

**LEVIEN, Robin Hugh,** RDI 1995; owner, since 1999, Partner, since 2006, Studio Levien; *b* 5 May 1952; *s* of John Blomefield Levien and Louis Beryl Levien; *m* 1978, Patricia Anne Stainton. *Educ:* Bearwood Coll., Wokingham; Central Sch. of Art and Design (BA Hons 1973); Royal Coll. of Art (MA 1976). MCSD. Joined Queensberry Hunt, 1977; Partner, Queensberry Hunt, later Queensberry Hunt Levien, 1982–99. Designer of mass market products for manufrs and retailers, incl. Thomas China, Wedgwood, Ideal Standard, American Standard, Habitat, Dartington Crystal; *major products designed:* Trend (for Thomas China), 1981 (Die Gute Industrieform, Hanover, 1982; Golden Flame Award, Valencia, 1983); Studio bathroom range (for Ideal Standard), 1986; Domi bathroom taps, 1989; Symphony range of bathtubs (for American Standard), 1990 (Winner, Interior Design Product Award, Amer. Soc. of Interior Designers, 1991); Kyomi bathroom range (for Ideal Standard), 1996 (Winner, Design Week Awards, 1997); Space bathroom range (for Ideal Standard) (D&AD Silver Award; Winner, FX Internat. Interior Design Award), 1999; Home Elements range (for Villeroy & Boch), 2002; Concept bathroom range (for Ideal Standard), 2008; New Cottage tableware (for Villeroy & Boch), 2009; Concept Air bathroom range (for Ideal Standard), 2016. Vis. Prof., London Inst., 1997–. Mem. Council, RCA, 2001–12 (Sen. Fellow, 2013). Master, Faculty of RDI, 2009–11. FRSA 1991 (Chm., Product Design, Student Design Awards, 1991–98; Paul Reilly Meml Lectr, 1998). DUniv Staffs, 2006. *Publications:* articles in Design mag. *Recreations:* Fulham farmer on 1952 Ferguson tractor, films, cooking. *Address:* Cooks Farm, North Brewham, Som BA10 0JQ. *T:* (01749) 850610.

**LEVIN, David Roger;** Managing Director, Independent Schools, United Learning, 2014–15; *b* 2 Oct. 1949; *s* of Jack Levin, Cape Town and Isobel Elizabeth Levin (*née* Robinson), Norfolk, England; *m* 1977, Jean Isobel, *d* of Major J. A. P. Hall. *Educ:* Kearsney Coll., Natal; Univ. of Natal (BEcon); Univ. of Sussex (MA). Gen. Manager, Cutty Sark Hotel, Scottburgh, S Africa (family business), 1972–73; Asst Master, Whitgift Sch., Croydon, 1974–75; Articled Clerk, Radcliffes & Co., Solicitors, 1976–78; Asst Master, Portsmouth Grammar Sch., 1978–80; Head of Economics, 1980–93 and Second Master, 1987–93, Cheltenham Coll.; Headmaster: Royal Grammar Sch., High Wycombe, 1993–99; City of London Sch., 1999–2013. Advr to Minister for London Challenge, 2002–05. Chm., HMC, 2010–11; Dir, Assoc. of Governing Bodies in Ind. Schs, 2017–. Gov., Canford Sch., 1995– (Chm. of Govs, 2017–); Corporate Educn Fellow, Woodard Gp of Schs, 2017. *Recreations:* long distance swimming, hill walking, opera, military history. *Address:* Malden Court, Cheltenham, Glos GL52 2BL. *T:* (01242) 321633.

**LEVIN, David Saul;** Chief Executive, McGraw-Hill Education, New York, 2014–17; *b* 28 Jan. 1962; *s* of late Archie Z. Levin and of Leah S. Levin, OBE; *m* 1992, Lindsay Caroline White; three *s*. *Educ:* Wadham Coll., Oxford (MA 1983); Stanford Grad. Sch. of Business (MBA 1987). Served Army, SSLC, 2nd Lieut, 1st Bn RRF, 1980. Manager, Bain & Co., 1983–89; Associate Dir, Apax Partners & Co., 1990–94; Man. Dir, Unicorn Abrasives Ltd, 1992–94; Chief Operating Officer, Euromoney Pubns plc, 1994–99; CEO, Psion plc, 1999–2002; CEO, Symbian, 2002–05; Chief Exec., United Business Media plc, 2005–14. Non-executive Director: COFRA Hldg AG, 2017–; Crumpton Gp LLC, 2018–.

**LEVIN, Gerald Manuel;** Chief Executive Officer, AOL Time Warner Inc., 2001–02; Chairman, Elation Media, Inc., since 2013; Presiding Director, Moonview Sanctuary, Santa Monica, since 2003; *b* 6 May 1939; *m* Barbara J. Riley (marr. diss.); *m* Laurie Ann Perlman. *Educ:* Haverford Coll. (BA 1960); Univ. of Pennsylvania Law Sch. (LLB 1963). Attorney, Simpson Thacher & Bartlett, NYC, 1963–67; Develt and Resources Corp., 1967–71 (Gen. Manager and Chief Operating Officer, 1969–71); Rep., Internat. Basic Economy Corp., Tehran, 1971–72; joined Time Inc., 1972: Vice-Pres., Programming, 1972–73; Pres. and CEO, 1973–76, Chm., 1976–79, Home Box Office; Gp Vice-Pres., Video, 1979–84; Exec. Vice-Pres., 1984–88; Vice-Chm. and Dir, 1988–90; merger with Warner Communications Inc. to form Time Warner, 1990: Chief Operating Officer, Vice-Chm. and Dir, 1991–92; Pres. and Co-CEO, Feb.–Dec. 1992; CEO, 1992–2001; Chm., 1993–2001; merger with AOL to form AOL Time Warner, 2001. Dir, NY Stock Exchange Inc. Member: Council on Foreign Relns; Trilateral Commn. Member, Board: NY City Partnership; Nat. Cable TV Center and Mus., now Hon. Dir; Aspen Inst.; Mus. of Jewish Heritage. Dir and Treas., NY Philharmonic. Hon. LLD: Texas Coll., 1985; Middlebury Coll., 1994; Haverford Coll.; Hon. LHD Denver, 1995.

**LEVIN, Prof. Richard Charles,** PhD; Frederick William Beinecke Professor of Economics, 1992, now Emeritus, and President, 1993–2013, Yale University; Senior Advisor, Coursera, since 2017 (Chief Executive, 2014–17); Senior Fellow, Yale Jackson Institute for Global Affairs; *b* San Francisco, 7 April 1947; *s* of D. Derek Levin and Phylys (*née* Goldstein); *m* 1968, Jane Ellen Aries; two *s* two *d*. *Educ:* Stanford Univ. (BA 1968); Merton Coll., Oxford (LittB 1971; Hon. Fellow, 1996); Yale Univ. (PhD 1974). Yale University, 1974–2013: Chm., Econs Dept, 1987–92; Dean, Grad. Sch., 1992–93; Res. Associate, Nat. Bureau of Econ. Res., Cambridge, Mass, 1985–90; Program Dir, Internat. Inst. Applied System Analysis, Vienna, 1990–92. Dir, Yale-New Haven Health Services Corp. Inc., 1993. Consultant, numerous law and business firms. Trustee: Yale-New Haven Hosp., 1993; Tanner Lectures on Human Values, 1993. Member: Univs Res. Assoc., 1994; Nat. Res. Council Bd on Sci., Technol. and Econ. Policy, 1998. Member: Amer. Econ. Assoc.; Econometric Soc. Hon. LLD: Princeton, 1993; Harvard, 1994; Hon. DCL Oxford, 1998. *Publications:* The Work of the University, 2003; The Worth of the University, 2013. *Recreations:* hiking, basket-ball.

**LEVINE, Gemma;** *see* Levine, J. A.

**LEVINE, James;** American conductor and pianist; Music Director: Metropolitan Opera, New York, 1976–2016, Emeritus, 2016–18 (Principal Conductor, 1973–2011; Artistic Director, 1986–2004); Boston Symphony Orchestra, 2004–11; *b* 23 June 1943; *s* of Lawrence Levine and Helen Levine (*née* Goldstein). *Educ:* Walnut Hills High Sch.; Juilliard Sch. of Music. Asst Conductor, Cleveland Orch., 1964–70; Music Director: Ravinia Fest., 1973–93; Cincinnati May Fest., 1974–78; UBS Verbier Fest. Youth Orch., 2000–04; Conductor: Salzburg Fest., 1975–93; Bayreuth Fest., 1982–98; Chief Conductor, Munich Philharmonic, 1999–2004. Piano début with Cincinnati SO, 1953; conducting début, Aspen Music Fest., 1961; has conducted many major orchestras throughout US and Europe, incl. Vienna Philharmonic, Berlin Philharmonic, Chicago Symphony, NY Philharmonic, Dresden Staatskapelle, Israel Philharmonic, Philharmonia, London Symphony, Boston Symphony, Philadelphia, etc. Has made numerous recordings. Smetana Medal (Czechoslovakia), 1987; nine Grammy awards; Nat. Medal of Arts, 1997; Kennedy Center Honors, 2002.

**LEVINE, Jennifer Ann, (Gemma);** photographer; *b* 10 Jan. 1939; *d* of Ellis and Mae Mathilda Josephs; *m* 1961, Eric A. Levine (marr. diss. 1986); two *s*. *Educ:* Hasmonean Grammar Sch., London. Antique print designer, 1961; interior designer, 1970–75; professional photographer, 1975–; author, 1978–. FRSA 1990. *Exhibitions:* Personalities, 1977; Four Seasons, 1977; With Henry Moore, 1978, 1984; My Jerusalem (photographs, poetry and watercolours), 1982; Jerusalem, 1983; Henry Moore, 1982; Henry Moore, Wood Sculpture, 1983, 1984, 1985; My Jerusalem (photographs and poetry), 1983; Tel-Aviv Faces and Places, 1984; Ethiopian Jews, 1985; Faces of the 80's, 1987; Faces of British Theatre, 1990–91; Gemma Levine: 20 Years of Photography, 1995; People of the 90's, 1995, 1996; Henry Moore, 1995; Memories, 1998; Retrospective to celebrate 25 years of photography, NPG, 2001; Claridge's—Within the Image, 2004; Israel Retrospective, 2005; Mayfair, Sotheby's, 2008; Henry Moore (photographic archive), Tate Gall., 2010; Go with the Flow, 2012. *Publications:* Israel: faces and places, 1978; Living with the Bible (painter in watercolour and photographer), 1978; With Henry Moore (author and photographer), 1978; We Live in Israel, 1981; Living in Jerusalem, 1982; The Young Inheritors, 1982; Henry Moore, Wood Sculpture (author and photographer), 1983; Henry Moore: an illustrated biography, 1985; Faces of the 80's, 1987; Faces of British Theatre, 1990; People of the 90's, 1995; Memories, 1998; My Favourite Hymn, 1999; Claridge's Within the Image, 2004; Mayfair, 2008; Go with the Flow, 2012; Just One More: a photographer's memoir, 2014; (with Prof. Peter Mortimer) Let's Talk Lymphoedema, 2017. *Recreations:* swimming, music, design. *Address:* 35–37 Grosvenor Square, W1K 2HN. *T:* (020) 7491 4494. *E:* gemmalevine@aol.com.

**LEVINE, Simon Robert;** Global Co-Chief Executive Officer and Managing Partner, DLA Piper UK LLP, since 2015; *b* Hull, 2 Dec. 1965; *s* of Mark and Patricia Levine; *m* 1992, Jane Golding; one *s* two *d*. *Educ:* Hymers Coll., Hull; Emmanuel Coll., Cambridge (BA 1987; MA 1990; Sen. Exhibnr). Admitted Solicitor, 1990; Solicitor and Partner, Frere Cholmeley, 1990–98; Partner, Denton Wilde Sapte, 1998–2005; DLA Piper UK LLP: Partner and Hd, IP and Technol. Gp, 2005–12; Mem., Exec. and Global Bd, 2012–14. Vis. Lectr, 2013–15, Vis. Prof., Innovation and Entrepreneurship Dept, 2015–, Imperial Coll. Business Sch., Imperial Coll. London. Mem. Bd, Office for Students, 2018–. Mem., Editl Bd, PLC Mag., 2005–. *Recreations:* music, cinema, travel, sport, family. *Address:* DLA Piper UK LLP, 3 Noble Street, EC2V 7EE. *T:* (020) 7796 6020, *Fax:* (020) 7796 6586. *E:* simon.levine@dlapiper.com.

**LEVINE, Sydney;** a Recorder, North-Eastern Circuit, 1975–95; *b* 4 Sept. 1923; *s* of Rev. Isaac Levine and Mrs Miriam Levine; three *s* one *d*. *Educ:* Bradford Grammar Sch.; Univ. of Leeds (LLB). Called to the Bar, Inner Temple, 1952; Chambers in Bradford, 1953–98. *Recreations:* music, gardening, painting, learning to use a computer. *Address:* 82A Walsingham Road, Hove, E Sussex BN3 4FF. *T:* (01273) 323590.

**LEVINGE, Sir Richard (George Robin),** 12th Bt *cr* 1704; farming since 1968; *b* 18 Dec. 1946; *s* of Sir Richard Vere Henry Levinge, 11th Bt, MBE, TD, and Barbara Mary (*d* 1997), *d* of late George Jardine Kidston, CMG; *S* father, 1984; *m* 1st, 1969, Hilary (marr. diss. 1978), *d* of Dr Derek Mark; one *s*; 2nd, 1978, Donna Maria d'Ardia Caracciolo; one *s* one *d*. *Educ:* Brook House, Bray, Co. Wicklow; Hawkhurst Court, West Sussex; Mahwah High School, New York; Craibstone Agricultural Coll. *Heir: s* Richard Mark Levinge, *b* 15 May 1970.

**LEVINSON, Prof. Stephen Curtis,** PhD; FBA 1988; Director, Max Planck Institute for Psycholinguistics, 1994–2017, Emeritus, 2018 (Managing Director, 1998–2001, 2007–08); Professor, Radboud University (formerly Catholic University), Nijmegen, 1995, now Emeritus; *b* 6 Dec. 1947; *s* of Dr Gordon A. Levinson and Dr Mary C. Levinson; *m* 1976, Dr Penelope Brown; one *s*. *Educ:* Bedales Sch.; King's Coll., Cambridge (Sen. Schol.; 1st Cl. Hons. Archaeology and Anthropology Tripos 1970); PhD Linguistics Anthropology, Calif., 1977. Asst Lectr, 1975–78, Lectr, 1978–91, Reader, 1991–94, Linguistics Dept, Cambridge; Hd, Res. Gp for Cognitive Anthropol., Max Planck Inst. for Psycholinguistics, 1991–97. Vis. Res. Fellow, ANU, 1980–82; Vis. Associate Prof., Stanford Univ., 1987–88. MAE, 2003–. *Publications:* Pragmatics, 1983; (with Dr P. Brown) Politeness, 1987; (with J. Gumperz) Rethinking Linguistic Relativity, 1996; Presumptive Meanings: the theory of generalized conversational implicature, 2000; (ed with M. Bowerman) Language Acquisition and Conceptual Development, 2001; (ed with P. Jaisson) Evolution and Culture, 2006; (ed with D. Wilkins) Grammars of Space, 2006; (ed with N. Enfield) Roots of Human Sociality, 2006; articles in books and jls. *Recreations:* Sunday painting, hiking. *Address:* Max Planck Institute for Psycholinguistics, PO Box 310, 6500 AH Nijmegen, The Netherlands.

**LEVISON, Jeremy Ian;** Founding Partner, Levison Meltzer Pigott, since 1998; *b* Ryde, IoW, 3 Feb. 1952; *s* of Eric Levison and Sally Levison; partner, Kathryn Jackson. *Educ:* Charterhouse Sch.; Univ. of Kent, Canterbury (BA Hons 1973). Admitted solicitor, 1976; Solicitor: Theodore Goddard, 1976–80; Collyer Bristow, 1980–98 (Partner, 1988). Founder, Collyer Bristow Art Gall., 1993; owner, Bermondsey Project Space. Chm., Old Carthusian Art Soc., 2014–. *Publications:* articles for legal and motoring mags. *Recreations:* cricket, modern and contemporary art, classic cars, classical music/opera/violin. *Address:* Levison Meltzer Pigott, 45 Ludgate Hill, EC4M 7JU. *T:* (020) 7556 2400. *E:* jlevison@lmplaw.co.uk. *Club:* Groucho.

**LEVITT, Alison Frances Josephine, (Lady Carlile of Berriew);** QC 2008; a Recorder, since 2007; *b* London, 27 May 1963; *d* of Frederick David Andrew Levitt, OBE and Her Honour Christian Veronica Bevington, *qv*; *m* 1st, 1993, Matthew Miller (marr. diss.); two *d*; 2nd, 2007, Baron Carlile of Berriew, *qv*. *Educ:* City of London Sch. for Girls; Univ. of St Andrews (MA Hons 1986). Called to the Bar, Inner Temple, 1988, Bencher, 2009. Chm., Young Barristers Cttee, Bar Council, 1995; Sec., Criminal Bar Assoc., 2006–07;

Principal Legal Advr to Dir of Public Prosecutions, 2009–14 Partner and Hd of Business Crime, Mishcon de Reya LLP, 2014–18. *Recreations:* crime fiction, film. *Address:* 2 Hare Court, Temple, EC4Y 7BH.

**LEVITT, Prof. Malcolm Harris,** DPhil; FRS 2007; Professor of Physical Chemistry, University of Southampton, since 2001; *b* 10 Jan. 1957; *s* of Max and Stella Levitt; *m* 1990, Latha Kadalayil; one *d*. *Educ:* Keble Coll., Oxford (BA; DPhil 1981). Res. Scientist, MIT, 1986–92; Lectr, 1992–97, Prof. of Chemical Spectroscopy, 1997–2001, Stockholm Univ. *Publications:* Spin Dynamics: basics of nuclear magnetic resonance, 2001, 2nd edn 2007; contribs to jls. *Recreations:* electric guitar, classical guitar, politics, jazz, sketching, walking, gardening. *Address:* School of Chemistry, University of Southampton, Southampton SO17 1BJ. *T:* (023) 8059 6753, *Fax:* (023) 8059 3781. *E:* mhl@soton.ac.uk.

**LEVITT, Prof. Michael,** PhD; FRS 2001; Robert W. and Vivian K. Cahill Professor of Cancer Research, School of Medicine, Stanford University, California, since 2010 (Professor of Structural Biology, 1987–2010); *b* 9 May 1947; *s* of Nathan and Gertrude Levitt; *m* 1968, Rina Harel; three *s*. *Educ:* King's Coll., London (BSc Physics 1967); Gonville and Caius Coll., Cambridge (PhD Computational Biol. 1972). Royal Soc. Exchange Fellow, Weizmann Inst., Israel, 1967–68; Staff Scientist, MRC Lab. of Molecular Biol., Cambridge, 1973–80; Prof. of Chemical Physics, Weizmann Inst., 1980–87; Chair, 1993–2003, Associate Chair, 2005–10, Dept of Structural Biol., Stanford Univ. Mem., American Acad. of Arts and Scis, 2010. (Jtly) Nobel Prize in Chemistry, 2013. *Publications:* contrib. articles on computational biol. with an emphasis on structure, particularly of protein molecules. *Recreations:* cycling, ski-ing, travel. *Address:* Stanford School of Medicine, Stanford, CA 94305, USA. *T:* (650) 2760500, *Fax:* (650) 7238464. *E:* michael.levitt@stanford.edu.

**LEVITT, Tom;** freelance writer and consultant on responsible business, since 2010; *b* 10 April 1954; *s* of John and Joan Levitt; *m* 1983, Teresa Sledziewska; one *d*. *Educ:* Lancaster Univ. (BSc Hons 1975); New Coll., Oxford (PGCE 1976). Biology teacher: Wootton Bassett Sch., 1976–79; Cirencester Sch., 1980–81; Brockworth Sch., Glos, 1981–91; supply Teacher, Staffs, 1991–95; freelance res. consultant, 1993–97. Member (Lab): Cirencester Town Council, 1983–87; Stroud DC, 1990–92; Derbys CC, 1993–97. Contested (Lab): Stroud, 1987; Cotswold, EP elecn, 1989; High Peak, 1992. MP (Lab) High Peak, 1997–2010. PPS to Minister of State, Home Office, 1999–2001, Cabinet Office, 2001, ODPM, 2001–03; PPS to Sec. of State for Internat. Develt, 2003–07; Asst Regl Minister, E Midlands, 2008–10. Member: Standards and Privileges Select Cttee, 1997–2003; Jt Cttee on Draft Disability Bill, 2004; DWP Select Cttee, 2007–10. Chm., Community Develt Foundn, 2004–10. Trustee: RNID, 1998–2003; Coalition for Efficiency, 2011–; Work Foundn Alliance, 2012–18; Chm., Trustees, Concern Worldwide (UK), 2011–14; Founder and Chm., Trustees, Fair for You, 2015–; non-exec. Dir, Fair for You Enterprise CIC, 2015–. Non-exec. Dir, Outreach Solutions Ltd (formerly Digital Outreach and Convey), 2014–. Patron, READ Internat., 2007–. DUniv Derby 2011. *Publications:* Sound Practice, 1995; Clear Access, 1997; Partners for Good: business, government and the third sector, 2012; Welcome to GoodCo: using the tools of business to create public benefit, 2014; The Company Citizen: good for business, plant, nation and community, 2018. *Recreations:* cricket, theatre, walking, travel.

**LEVVY, (Clinton) George;** management consultant, since 2004; *b* 30 Nov. 1953; *s* of late Guildford Albert Levvy and Averil Clinton Levvy (*née* Chance); *m* 1st, 1984, Irené M. Young (marr. diss. 1989); 2nd, 1991, Bethe R. Alpert; one *s* one *d*. *Educ:* Robert Gordon's Coll., Aberdeen; Univ. of Edinburgh (MB ChB). Jun. hosp. doctor, 1977–84; Med. Dir and Consultant, Excerpta Medica, Tokyo, 1984–88; Commercial Manager, Countrywide Communications Gp Ltd, 1988–91; Hd, Mktg and Communications, BRCS, 1991–94; Chief Exec., Motor Neurone Disease Assoc., 1995–2004. Member: Appraisal Cttee, NICE, 2000–06; Adv. Cttee, New and Emerging Applications of Technol., DoH, 2000–03. Chair: Oxford Low Carbon Hub, 2018–; Rewilding Britain, 2019–. Trustee: Haemophilia Soc., 1999–2002; Self Help Africa, 2008–13. *Publications:* contribs to jls and ed vols. *Recreations:* walking, singing, tennis, travel. *Address:* GLCE Ltd, Units 4 and 5, Swinford Farm, Eynsham OX29 4BL. *T:* (01865) 865800.

**LEVY,** family name of **Baron Levy**.

**LEVY,** Baron *cr* 1997 (Life Peer), of Mill Hill in the London Borough of Barnet; **Michael Abraham Levy;** International Consultant, Global Consultancy Services, since 2008; Chairman, Chase Mill Hill Ltd, since 2013; *b* 11 July 1944; *s* of Samuel and Annie Levy; *m* 1967, Gilda (*née* Altbach); one *s* one *d*. *Educ:* Fleetwood Primary Sch. (Head Boy); Hackney Downs Grammar Sch. FCA 1966. Lubbock Fine (Chartered Accountants), 1961–66; Principal, M. Levy & Co., 1966–69; Partner, Wagner Prager Levy & Partners, 1969–73; Chairman: Magnet Group of Cos, 1973–88; D & J Securities Ltd, 1988–92; M & G Records, 1992–97; Wireart Ltd, 1992–2002; Chase Music (formerly M & G Music) Ltd, 1992–2002; Internat. Standard Asset Mgt, 2008–11; Vice Chairman: Phonographic Performance Ltd, 1979–84; British Phonographic Industry Ltd, 1984–87. Mem., Develt Bd, BL, 2008–11. Nat. Campaign Chm., United Jt Israel Appeal, 1982–85 (Hon. Vice Pres., 1994–2000; Hon. Pres., 2000–); Chairman: Jewish Care, 1992–97 (Pres., 1998–); Jewish Care Community Foundn, 1995–2010; Vice Chm., Central Council for Jewish Community Services (formerly Central Council for Jewish Social Services), 1994–99. Chairman: Chief Rabbinate Awards for Excellence, 1992–2007; Foundn for Educn, 1993–2006; Member: Jewish Agency World Bd of Governors, 1990–95 (World Chm., Youth Aliyah Cttee, 1991–95); Keren Hayesod World Bd of Governors, 1991–95; World Commn on Israel-Diaspora Relns, 1995–; Internat. Bd of Governors, Peres Center for Peace, 1997–2009; Adv. Council, Foreign Policy Centre, 1997–2006; NCVO Adv. Cttee, 1998–2011; Community Legal Service Champions Panel, 1999–2005; Hon. Cttee, Israel, Britain and the Commonwealth Assoc., 2000–11; World Bd of Dirs, Internat. Peace Inst., 2014–19. Personal Envoy for Prime Minister and Advr on Middle East, 1999–2007. President: Volunteering Matters (formerly Community Service Volunteers), 1998–; Specialist Schs and Acads Trust, 2005–08; Trustee: Holocaust Educnl Trust, 1998–2007; Policy Network Foundn, subseq. New Policy Network Foundn, 2000–07; Jewish Leadership Council, 2006–10; Mem. Exec. Cttee, Chai-Lifeline, 2001–02; Mem. Adv. Council, Step Up to Serve Campaign, 2013–; Patron: British Music Industry Awards, 1995– (Chm., Awards Cttee, 1992–95); Prostate Cancer Charitable Trust, 1997–2011; Friends of Israel Educnl Trust, 1998–2011; Save a Child's Heart Foundn, 2000–; Simon Marks Jewish Primary Sch. Trust, 2002–; Etz Chaim Jewish Primary Sch., 2011–; Mathilda Marks-Kennedy Jewish Primary Sch., 2011–. Governor, Jews' Free Sch., subseq. JFS, 1990–95 (Hon. Pres., 1995–2001; Pres., 2001–). Pres., Barnet and Southgate Coll., 2017–. Hon. Patron, Cambridge Univ. Jewish Soc., 2002–; Pres., Jewish Lads' and Girls' Brigade, 2006–. Hon. Dr Middlesex Univ., 1999. B'nai B'rith First Lodge Award, 1994; Scopus Award, Hebrew Univ. of Jerusalem, 1998; Special Recognition Award, Israel Policy Forum (USA), 2003; Jewish Chronicle 175th Anniv. Award, 2016. *Publications:* A Question of Honour (memoirs), 2008. *Recreations:* tennis, swimming. *Address:* House of Lords, SW1A 0PW.

**LEVY, Rabbi Dr Abraham,** OBE 2004; Spiritual Head, Spanish and Portuguese Jews' Congregation in UK, 1983–2012, now Emeritus Spiritual Head; *b* 16 July 1939; *s* of Isaac Levy and Rachel (*née* Hassan); *m* 1963, Estelle Nahum; one *s*. *Educ:* Carmel Coll.; Jews' Coll.; UCL (PhD 1978). Minister, Spanish and Portuguese Jews' Congregation, 1962–80; Communal Rabbi and Spiritual Head, 1980–2012. Chaplain to Lord Mayor of London, 1998–99 and 2010–11. (With Chief Rabbi) Ecclesiastical Authy, Bd of Deputies of British Jews, 1980–2012. Founder and Dir, Young Jewish Leadership Inst., 1970–86; Founder and Principal, Naima Jewish Prep. Sch., 1983–; Dep. Pres., London Sch. of Jewish Studies (formerly Jews' Coll.), 1985–2012 (Hon. Dep. Pres., 2015); Founder, Sephardi Centre, 1993; Hon. Principal, Judith Lady Montefiore Coll., 2005–. Mem., Standing Cttee, Conf. of Eur. Rabbis. Rabbinical Authy, London Bd of Shechitah, 2006–13; Vice Chm., Commn for the Licensing of Shochtim, 2006–13. Jewish Faith Advr, MoD, 2010–. President: Union Anglo-Jewish Preachers, 1973–75; Council of Christians and Jews, 2009–13; Vice President: Anglo-Jewish Assoc., 1984–; Jewish Historical Soc. of England, 2006–. Patron, Jewish Med. Assoc. (UK), 2007–13; Hon. Patron, Cambridge Univ. Jewish Soc. Hon. Fellow, QMUL, 2012. Kt Comdr (Encomienda), Order of Merit (Spain), 1993. *Publications:* The Sephardim: a problem of survival, 1972; (jtly) Ages of Man, 1985; (jtly) The Sephardim, 1992; A Rocky Road, 2017. *Recreation:* collecting antique Judaica. *Address:* 2 Ashworth Road, W9 1JY. *T:* (020) 3637 5531.

**LEVY, David Anthony Lipton,** DPhil; Director, Reuters Institute for the Study of Journalism, University of Oxford, 2008–18, now Senior Research Associate; Fellow of Green Templeton College, Oxford, 2008–18, now Emeritus Fellow; *b* London, 12 Aug. 1953; *s* of Robert Levy and Rita Levy; *m* 1990, Joanna Moffett; one *s* one *d*. *Educ:* Haberdashers' Aske's Sch., Elstree; Univ. of York (BA Hons Mod. Hist. 1976); London Sch. of Econs and Pol Sci. (MA Area Studies Europe 1977); Nuffield Coll., Oxford (DPhil Mod. Hist. 1982). BBC: talks writer and producer, World Service and Radio 4, 1982–85; News and Current Affairs, 1985–94, Reporter: File on 4, Newsnight, Editor, Analysis, Public Policy, 1995–2007, Controller Public Policy, 2000–07. Lectr in French Politics and Contemp. Hist., Univ. of Salford, 1985–87; Associate Mem., Nuffield Coll., Oxford, 2009–. Vis. Prof., Sciences Po, Paris, 2012. Member: Content Bd, Ofcom, 2011–17; Bd, UK Statistics Authy, 2012–19. Member: Commn pour une nouvelle télévision publique, France, 2008; Bd, France 24, 2009–12. Jt Ed., Reuters Inst. Digital News Report, 2012–18. *Publications:* Europe's Digital Revolution: broadcasting regulation, the EU and the nation state, 1999; (ed with Tim Gardam) The Price of Plurality: choice, diversity and broadcasting institutions in the digital age, 2008; (ed with R. K. Nielsen) The Changing Business of Journalism and its Implications for Democracy, 2010; (ed with Robert G. Picard) Is There a Better Structure for News Providers?: the potential for charitable and trust ownership, 2011; (ed jtly) Transparency and Accountability in Media and Government, 2013. *Recreations:* reading politics and history, rural France. *Address:* c/o Reuters Institute for the Study of Journalism, University of Oxford, 13 Norham Gardens, Oxford OX2 6PS. *Club:* Frontline.

**LEVY, Deborah;** novelist, playwright and poet; *b* Johannesburg, SA, 1959; *d* of Norman Levy and Philippa Beatrice Levy (*née* Murrell); *m* 1997, David Gale (marr. diss.); two *d*. *Educ:* St Saviour's and St Olave's Sch., London; Hampstead Sch., London; Dartington Coll. of Arts (BA Hons Theatre Lang. 1981). Playwright, incl. for RSC, 1981–. Fellow Commoner, Creative Arts, Trinity Coll., Cambridge, 1989–91; Lannan Lit. Fellow for Fiction, 2001; AHRB Fellow in Creative and Performing Arts, RCA, 2006–09; Vis. Prof., Falmouth Sch. of Art, Falmouth Univ., 2013–15; Fellow, Columbia Univ. Inst. for Ideas and Imagination, 2018–19. *Plays:* Pax, 1984; Heresies, 1985; Clam, 1985; The B-File; Call Blue Jane, 1993; Honey Baby, 1995; Macbeth - False Memories, 2000; The Inner Voice - I am Big, 2005. *Libretti include:* Blood Wedding (with composer Nicola LeFanu; adapted from Lorca), 1993; Shiny Nylon, 1994 and Walk Into Me, 2010 (with composer Emily Cowie). *Radio:* dramatisations incl. In a German Pension (Katherine Mansfield short stories), 2006; Freud: The Case Histories (2 episodes), 2012; The Glass Piano - Tormented Objects (drama documentary), 2019. Joseph Beuys Lect., Ruskin Sch. of Art, 2001. Co-Judge, Folio Prize, 2015. FRSL 2017. *Publications: short stories:* Ophelia and The Great Idea, 1985; Black Vodka, 2013; *novels:* Beautiful Mutants, 1987; Swallowing Geography, 1991; The Unloved, 1994; Billy and Girl, 1996; Swimming Home, 2011 (UK Author of Year, Specsavers Nat. Book Awards, 2012; Wingate Prize, Jewish Qly, 2013); Hot Milk, 2016; The Man who Saw Everything, 2019; *other works:* An Amorous Discourse in the Suburbs of Hell (poetry), 1990; Diary of a Steak, 1997; Levy: Plays 1, 2000; Things I Don't Want to Know: a response to Orwell's essay 'Why I Write' (writing memoir), 2013; The Cost of Living (writing memoir part 2), 2018; introductory essays to books. *Recreations:* wild swimming in rivers, lakes and oceans. *Address:* c/o Wylie Agency, 17 Bedford Square, WC1B 3JA. *Club:* Blacks.

**LEVY, His Honour Dennis Martyn;** QC 1982; a Circuit Judge, 1991–2007; a Deputy Circuit Judge, 2007–11; *b* 20 Feb. 1936; *s* of late Conrad Levy and Tillie (*née* Swift); *m* 1967, Rachel Jonah; one *s* one *d*. *Educ:* Clifton Coll.; Gonville and Caius Coll., Cambridge (MA). Called to the Bar, Gray's Inn, 1960, Hong Kong, 1985, Turks and Caicos Is, 1987. Granada Group Ltd, 1960–63; Time Products Ltd, 1963–67; in practice at the Bar, 1967–91; a Recorder, 1989–91. Member: Employment Appeal Tribunal, 1994–2006; Lands Tribunal, 1998. Hon. Vice Pres., UK Assoc. of Jewish Lawyers and Jurists (Vice Pres., 2011–12). Trustee, Fair Trials Internat. (formerly Fair Trials Abroad), 2002–11. *Recreation:* living in London and travelling abroad. *Address:* 25 Harley House, Marylebone Road, NW1 5HE. *T:* 07773 429372, *Fax:* (020) 7487 3231. *E:* dennis.levy.uk@gmail.com.

**LEVY, Jacob;** QC 2014; *b* Bombay, 1962; *s* of Japheth and Iris Levy; *m* 1989, Sarah Jane; one *s* one *d*. *Educ:* Beal Grammar Sch. for Boys; London Sch. of Econs and Pol Sci. (LLB Hons). Called to the Bar, Inner Temple, 1986; in practice as barrister, specialising in personal injury and clinical negligence. *Recreations:* film, music, writing unproduced screenplays, watching rock bands. *Address:* 9 Gough Square, EC4A 3DG. *T:* (020) 7832 0538. *E:* jlevy@9goughsq.co.uk.

**LEVY, Paul,** PhD; FRSL; author, journalist and broadcaster; freelance writer, since 2015; Senior Contributor, Europe Leisure and Arts, Wall Street Journal, 1993–2015; *b* 26 Feb. 1941; *er s* of late H. S. Levy and Mrs Shirley Meyers, Lexington, Ky, USA; adopted dual citizenship, 1996; *m* 1977, Penelope, *oc* of late Clifford and Ruby Marcus; two *d*. *Educ:* Univ. of Chicago (AB 1963); University Coll. London; Harvard Univ. (PhD 1979); Nuffield Coll., Oxford. FRSL 1980. Teaching Fellow, Harvard, 1966–68; lapsed academic, 1971–; freelance journalist, 1974–80; Food Correspondent, 1980–82, Food and Wine Ed., 1982–92, The Observer; writer, London Letter, Gourmet Mag., 1992–2004; Wine and Food Writer, You Mag., Mail on Sunday, 1993–2013; Sen. Contrib., Europe Leisure and Arts, Wall Street Jl, 1993–2015; Restaurant Critic, Travel + Leisure Mag., 1995–2014; frequent radio and television broadcasting; writer and presenter, TV series, The Feast of Christmas, 1992–93. Dir, Isishome Ltd, 1980–2017. Member: Soc. of Authors; PEN; Critics' Circle (Music, Drama, Books and Art and Arch. Sections); Mem. Court, Oxford Brookes Univ., 2003–10. Co-literary executor, Lytton and James Strachey, 1972–; Trustee: Strachey Trust, 1972–; Jane Grigson Trust, 1990–2014; Oxford Symposium on Food and Cooking, subseq. Oxford Food Symposium, 2002–09, 2010–15 (co-Chair, 2005–15; Chair of Trustees, 2011–15; Chair Emeritus, 2019). Blog: Plain

English, www.artsjournal.com, 2008–; Podcast, www.talkingoffood.com, 2015–. Susan Potter Prize for Comparative Lit., Harvard, 1968; Corning Award for food writing, 1980, 1981; Glenfiddich Food Writer of the Year, 1980, 1983; Glenfiddich Restaurant Critic of the Year, 1983; Specialist Writer Commendation, British Press Awards, 1985, 1987; Wine Journalist of the Year, Wine Guild of the UK, 1986. Confrérie des Mousquetaires, 1981; Chevalier du Tastevin, 1987; Chevalier de l'Ordre des Dames du Vin et de la Table, 1989; Chevalier de l'Ordre de la Dinde de Licques, 1991. *Publications:* (ed) Lytton Strachey: the really interesting question, 1972; The Bloomsbury Group, in Essays on John Maynard Keynes, ed Milo Keynes, 1975; G. E. Moore and the Cambridge Apostles, 1979, 3rd edn 1989; (ed with Michael Holroyd) The Shorter Strachey, 1980, 2nd edn 1989; (with Ann Barr) The Official Foodie Handbook, 1984; Out to Lunch, 1986 (Seagrams/Internat. Assoc. of Cookery Professionals Award, USA, 1988), 2nd edn 2003; Finger-Lickin' Good: a Kentucky childhood (autobiog.), 1990; The Feast of Christmas, 1992 (also TV series); (ed) The Penguin Book of Food and Drink, 1996; (contrib.) Consuming Passions, 2001; (ed) Eminent Victorians: the definitive edition, 2002; Frances Partridge: a memoir, 2004; (ed) The Letters of Lytton Strachey, 2005; Bloomsbury Reassessed, in Irrepressible Adventures with Britannia, ed Wm Roger Louis, 2013; contribs to TLS, 1974–; (as obituarist) Independent, 1990–, Guardian, 2009–; Daily and Sunday Telegraph, 2012–; Spectator, 2016–; Literary Rev., 2016–; New York Rev. of Books, 2017–; blog, London Rev. of Books, 2019; contrib. Oxford DNB, 2000–. *Recreations:* being cooked for, drinking better wine, trying hard to remember, being my own best diagnostician. *Address:* Millwood Farmhouse, Millwood End, Long Hanborough, Witney, Oxon OX29 8BP. *T:* (01993) 881312, 07812 382066. *Clubs:* Groucho, Quo Vadis.

**LEVY, Prof. Raymond,** FRCPE, FRCPsych; Professor of Old Age Psychiatry, University of London at Institute of Psychiatry, 1984–96, now Emeritus Professor, King's College London; Hon. Consultant, Bethlem Royal and Maudsley Hospitals, since 1984; *b* 23 June 1933; *o s* of late Gaston Levy and Esther Levy (*née* Bigio); *m* 1st, 1956, Katherine Margaret Logie (marr. diss. 1982); two *d*; 2nd, 2012, Aykan Pulular̦. *Educ:* Victoria Coll., Cairo; Edinburgh Univ. (MB, ChB 1957; PhD 1961); Univ. of London (DPM 1964). Jun. hosp. appts, Royal Infirmary, Northern Gen., Leith, Bethlem Royal and Maudsley Hosps, to 1966; Sen. Lectr and Hon. Consultant Psychiatrist, Middx Hosp. Med. Sch., 1966–71; Consultant Psychiatrist, Bethlem Royal and Maudsley Hosps, 1971–84. Mem., Med. Adv. Commn on Res. into Ageing. Pres., Internat. Psychogeriatric Assoc., 1995–98 (Mem., Bd of Dirs, 1998–2000); Vice-Pres., Eur. Assoc. Geriatric Psych.; Foundn Mem., RCPsych, 1971. Asst Editor, Internat. Jl Geriatric Psych. *Publications:* (all jtly) The Psychiatry of Late Life, 1982; Diagnostic and Therapeutic Assessment in Alzheimer's Disease, 1991; Delusions and Hallucinations in Old Age, 1992; Clinical diversity in late onset of Alzheimer's Disease, 1992; Treatment and Care in Old Age Psychiatry, 1993; Dementia, 1993; The Complex of Beyazid II in Edirne, 2008; The Strange Life and Death of Dr de Clérambault, 2009; Mamnou': a return to Cairo, 2012; contribs to learned jls. *Recreations:* looking at pictures, drinking good wine, travelling, playing tennis. *Address:* Institute of Psychiatry, Psychology and Neuroscience, King's College London, 16 De Crespigny Park, SE5 8AF. *T:* (020) 7467 0512; 4 Hillsleigh Road, W8 7LE. *Clubs:* Campden Hill Lawn Tennis, Holland Park Lawn Tennis.

**LEVY, Robert Stuart;** QC 2010; *b* London, 18 Jan. 1964; *s* of Dr Ralph Levy and Elizabeth Levy; *m* 1990, Karen Frances Prooth; one *s* one *d*. *Educ:* City of London Sch.; Hatfield Poly.; Magdalene Coll., Cambridge (LLB; LLM 1987). Called to the Bar: Middle Temple, 1988; British Virgin Is; Anguilla; St Vincent; admitted to: DIFC; (ad hoc) Cayman Bar; in practice as barrister, specialising in internat. commercial litigation. *Recreations:* ukelele, piano, banjo, accordion, ski-ing. *Address:* XXIV Old Buildings, Lincoln's Inn, WC2A 3UP. *T:* (020) 7691 2323. *E:* robert.levy@xxiv.co.uk.

**LEVY-LANG, André;** Légion d'Honneur; Chairman: Compagnie Financière de Paribas, 1990–99; Banque Paribas, 1991–99; *b* 26 Nov. 1937. *Educ:* Ecole Polytechnique; Stanford Univ. (PhD Business Admin; Harkness Fellow, 1963–65). Res. physicist, French Atomic Energy Commn, 1960–62; Schlumberger Gp, 1962–74; Compagnie Bancaire: joined 1974; Mem. Bd, 1979; Chm., 1982; Chm., Adv. Bd, 1993. Director: Schlumberger, 1993; AGF, 1994; Dexia, 2000; Mem. Exec. Cttee, Pargesa Holding; Chm., Supervisory Bd, Les Echos. Bd mem., banking and employers' assocs. Associate Prof. of Finance, Univ. Paris-Dauphine, 2001, now Emeritus. *Publications:* L'Argent, la Finance et le Risque, 2006. *Address:* 48 boulevard Emile Augier, 75116 Paris, France.

**LEW, Julian David Mathew;** QC 2002; barrister and international arbitrator; *b* 3 Feb. 1948; *s* of Rabbi Maurice Abram Lew and Rachel Lew (*née* Segalov); *m* 1978, Margot (*née* Perk); two *d*. *Educ:* Carmel Coll.; Univ. of London (LLB Hons ext. 1969); Catholic Univ. of Louvain (PhD 1977). Barrister at Law, 1970; Solicitor, 1981; Attorney-at-Law, NY, 1985; Partner: S. J. Berwin & Co., 1986–92; Coudert Brothers, 1992–95; Herbert Smith, 1995–2005. Dir, 1983–88, Mem. Court, 2002–07, London Court of Internat. Arbitration; UK Mem., Internat. Court of Arbitration, ICC, 2005–18; Mem. Court, Singapore Internat. Arbitration Centre, 2013–15; Mem., Adv. Council, Hong Kong Internat. Arbitration Centre, 2014–. Mem. Council, ICC Inst. of World Business Law, 2000–. Chm., Taskforce on Intellectual Property and Internat. Arbitration, 1992–97, Co-Chm., Taskforce on Costs in Internat. Arbitration, 2011–17, ICC Commn on Internat. Arbitration; Mem., Taskforce on Third-Party Funding in Internat. Arbitration, ICCA-QMUL, 2013–18. Prof. and Head, Sch. of Internat. Arbitration, Centre for Commercial Law Studies, QMUL (formerly QMC, then QMW), 1986–; Visiting Professor: Faculty of Law, Tel Aviv Univ., 2002; Bar Ilan Univ., Israel, 2005; Hebrew Univ., Jerusalem, 2010. Hon. Fellow, QMUL, 2009. Ed., Internat. Arbitration Law Liby Series, Kluwer Publishers, 1992–. *Publications:* Applicable Law on International Commercial Arbitration, 1978; (ed jtly) International Trade: law and practice, 1983, 2nd edn 1990; (ed) Contemporary Problems in International Commercial Arbitration, 1986; (ed) Immunity of Arbitrators, 1990; (ed jtly) Recognition of Foreign Judgments, 1994–; (jtly) Comparative International Commercial Arbitration, 2003; (jtly) Parallel State and Arbitral Procedures in International Arbitration, 2005; (ed jtly) Pervasive Problems in International Arbitration, 2006; (ed jtly) Arbitration Insights: twenty years of the annual lecture of the School of International Arbitration, 2007; (ed jtly) Arbitration in England (with chapters on Scotland and Ireland), 2013. *Address:* (chambers) 20 Essex Street, WC2R 3AL. *T:* (020) 7842 1200, *Fax:* (020) 7842 1270. *E:* jlew@20essexst.com.

**LEWELL-BUCK, Emma Louise;** MP (Lab) South Shields, since May 2013; *b* South Shields, 8 Nov. 1978; *d* of David and Linda Lewell; *m* 2010, Simon John Paul Buck. *Educ:* Northumbria Univ. (BA Hons Politics and Media Studies 2002); Durham Univ. (MSW 2008). Sales asst, Fenwick Ltd, 1998–2002; sessional playworker, N Tyneside Council, 2001–02; customer services, Traidcraft plc, 2002–05; Child Protection Social Worker: Sunderland CC, 2007–10; Newcastle CC, 2010–13. Mem. (Lab) S Tyneside Council, 2004–13 (Lead Mem., Adult Social Care and Support Services, 2009–13). PPS to Shadow Sec. of State for NI, 2013–15; to Shadow Home Sec., 2015–16; Shadow Minister for Communities and Local Govt, 2016, for Educn, Children and Families, 2016–19. *Recreations:* walking, spending time with friends and family, travelling, foreign languages, reading. *Address:* House of Commons, SW1A 0AA. *T:* (020) 7219 4468, *Fax:* (020) 7219 0264; (office) Ede House, 143 Westoe Road, South Shields, Tyne and Wear NE33 3PD. *T:* (0191) 427 1240, *Fax:* (0191) 427 6418. *E:* emma.lewell-buck.mp@parliament.uk.

**LEWER, Andrew Iain,** MBE 2014; MP (C) Northampton South, since 2017; *b* Burnley, Lancs, 18 July 1971; *s* of Clifford and Sandra Lewer; *m* 2005, Maria Gabriela Ciacia Lobo; one *s*. *Educ:* Queen Elizabeth Grammar Sch., Ashbourne, Derbys; Univ. of Newcastle upon Tyne (BA Hist. 1992). Former Sales and Mktg Manager, Landmark Publishing Ltd. Member (C): Derbys Dales DC, 2003–15; Derbys CC, 2005–15 (Leader, 2009–13). Dep. Chm., 2011–14, Vice-Pres., 2014–, LGA. MEP (C) E Midlands Reg., 2014–17. Mem., Communities and Local Govt Cttee, H of C, 2017–. Vice Pres., New Direction - Foundn for Eur. Reform, 2015–. Dir, Derbys Historic Bldgs Trust, 2003–17. Gov., Univ. of Derby, 2009–. *Publications:* (contrib.) The Oxford Companion to British History, 1997. *Recreations:* collecting books, history and conservation, swimming, family, cinema, opera. *Address:* House of Commons, SW1A 0AA.

**LEWER, Michael Edward,** CBE 2002; QC 1983; a Recorder of the Crown Court, 1983–98; a Deputy High Court Judge, 1989–98; *b* 1 Dec. 1933; *s* of late Stanley Gordon Lewer and Jeanie Mary Lewer; *m* 1965, Bridget Mary Gill; two *s* two *d*. *Educ:* Tonbridge Sch.; Oriel Coll., Oxford (MA). Called to Bar, Gray's Inn, 1958, Bencher, 1982. Territorial Army: Captain, 300 LAA Regt, RA, 1955–64; APIS, Intelligence Corps, 1964–67. Chm., Home Secretary's Adv. Cttee on Local Govt Electoral Arrangements for England, 1971–73; Comr, Parly Boundary Commn for England, 1997–2008 (Asst Comr, 1965–69, 1976–88, 1992–96). Member: Criminal Injuries Compensation Appeals Panel, 1994–2008 (Chm., 1994–2002); Criminal Injuries Compensation Bd, 1986–2000; Consultant, Criminal Injuries Compensation Authy, 2008–09. Mem., European Parly Constituency Cttee for England, 1993–94. Member: Bar Council, 1978–81; Bar Council Professional Conduct Cttee, 1993–95 (Vice Chm., 1995).

**LEWERS, Rt Rev. Richard Alexander;** *see* Armidale, Bishop of.

**LEWES, Bishop Suffragan of,** since 2014; **Rt Rev. Richard Charles Jackson;** *b* Hillingdon, 22 Jan. 1961; *s* of Donald and Mary Jackson; *m* 1985, Deborah Lee; two *s* one *d*. *Educ:* Latymer Upper Sch.; Christ Church, Oxford (MA); Cranfield Univ. (MSc 1985); Trinity Coll., Bristol (DipHE). Sen. Agronomist, Cleanacres Ltd, 1985–92; ordained deacon, 1994, priest, 1995; Curate, Lindfield, 1994–98; Vicar, Rudgwick, 1998–2009; Rural Dean of Horsham, 2005–09; Diocesan Mission and Renewal Advr, 2009–14. *Recreations:* walking, woodwork, motorcycling. *Address:* Church House, 211 New Church Road, Hove BN3 4ED. *T:* (01273) 421021. *E:* bishop.lewes@chichester.anglican.org.

**LEWIN SMITH, Jane;** Vice Lord-Lieutenant for Cambridgeshire, 2006–17; *b* 18 Feb. 1950; *d* of late Brian Frederick Bartholomew and Thelma Evelyn Bartholomew; *m* 1972, John Mann Lewin Smith; one *s* one *d*. *Educ:* Perse Sch. for Girls, Cambridge; Univ. of Bristol (BSc Soc. Sci.); Homerton Coll., Cambridge (Cert Ed). Chm., W Suffolk Co. Riding for the Disabled Assoc., 1988–96. Chm., British American Community Relns Cttee, RAF Mildenhall, 2003–09. Patron, Isle of Ely Arts Fest., 2014–19; Trustee, Ely Cathedral, 2014–. JP E Cambs, 1994–2008; High Sheriff, 2002–03, DL 2003, Cambs. *Recreations:* horseracing, fishing, gardening. *Club:* Royal Worlington and Newmarket Golf.

**LEWINGTON, Charles;** *see* Lewington, T. C.

**LEWINGTON, Richard George;** HM Diplomatic Service, retired; Chief Technical Adviser, EU Border Management in Central Asia Programme, Dushanbe, Tajikistan, 2007–09; *b* 13 April 1948; *s* of late Jack and Ann Lewington; *m* 1972, Sylviane Paulette Marie Cholet; one *s* one *d*. *Educ:* Orchard Secondary Modern Sch., Slough; Slough Grammar Sch.; Bristol Coll. of Commerce. Joined HM Diplomatic Service, 1967; full-time Russian lang. trng, RAEC Beaconsfield, 1971–72; Ulaan Baatar, 1972–75; Lima, 1976–80; FCO, 1980–82; Moscow, 1982–83; First Sec. (Commercial), Tel Aviv, 1986–90; FCO, 1991–95; Dep. High Comr, Malta, 1995–99; Ambassador: to Kazakhstan and Kyrgyzstan, 1999–2002; to Ecuador, 2003–06. Monitor, Field Office Gori, EU Monitoring Mission, Georgia, 2011–12. Mem. Council, Royal Soc. for Asian Affairs, 2007–16. Trustee, Dorset Expeditionary Soc., 2007–; Mem., Soc. of Dorset Men, 2006–. *Recreations:* country walks, classical music, old maps and books on Dorset.

**LEWINGTON, Richard John;** wildlife and scientific illustrator, since 1971; *b* Taplow, Bucks, 8 Oct. 1951; *s* of Jack and Beryl Lewington; *m* 1987, Georgina Lever; one *d*. *Educ:* Berkshire Coll. of Art and Design. Designer: Royal Mail Butterflies stamps, 2013; Royal Mail Bees stamps, 2015. Life Mem., Butterfly Conservation. Stamford Raffles Award, Zool Soc. London, 2010. *Publications: illustrator:* Insects, 1979; Butterfly Watching, 1980; The Mitchell Beazley Pocket Guide to Butterflies, 1981; The Moths and Butterflies of Great Britain and Ireland, 5 vols, 1989–2002; The Butterflies of Britain and Ireland, 1991, 2nd edn 2010; The Pocket Guide to Insects of the Northern Hemisphere, 1992; The Natural History of the Oak Tree, 1993; The Butterflies of the West Indies and South Florida, 1994; Collins Field Guide to Butterflies of Britain and Europe, 1997; Field Guide to the Dragonflies and Damselflies of Great Britain and Ireland, 1997, 5th edn 2014; How to Identify Butterflies, 1999; Essential Entomology, 1999; Pocket Guide to the Butterflies of Great Britain and Ireland, 2003, 2nd edn 2015; Field Guide to the Moths of Great Britain and Ireland, 2003, 3rd edn 2017; Field Guide to the Dragonflies and Damselflies of Britain and Europe, 2006; Concise Guide to the Moths of Great Britain and Ireland, 2007; Guide to Garden Wildlife, 2008; Field Guide to the Micro Moths of Great Britain and Ireland, 2012; The Bees of Great Britain and Ireland, 2015; The Ladybirds of Great Britain and Ireland, 2018. *Recreations:* natural history, photography, cycling, walking. *Address:* 22 Chambrai Close, Appleford on Thames, Oxon OX14 4NT. *T:* (01235) 848451. *E:* rlewington@btopenworld.com.

**LEWINGTON, (Thomas) Charles,** OBE 1997; Chief Executive (formerly Managing Director), Hanover Communications International (formerly Media Strategy Ltd), since 1998; *b* 6 April 1959; *s* of late Maurice Lewington and Sheila Lewington; *m* 1995, Philippa Jane Kelly; one *d*. *Educ:* Sherborne Sch., Dorset; Univ. of Bath (BSc Econs). Reporter, Bath Evening Chronicle, 1981–86; Western Daily Press: Asst News Editor, 1986–88; Political Corresp., 1988–90; Political Corresp., Daily Express, 1990–92; Political Editor, Sunday Express, 1992–95; Dir of Communications, Cons. Party, 1995–97. Non-exec. Dir, Cobra Beers Ltd, 2008–09; Director: We are Multiple Ltd, 2016–; Playbook Consulting Ltd, 2017–. Comr, Royal Hosp. Chelsea, 2014–. *Recreations:* reading, playing the piano. *Address:* (office) 70 Gray's Inn Road, WC1X 8BT. *T:* (020) 7400 4480; 62 Wandle Road, SW17 7DW. *T:* (020) 8672 3944. *Clubs:* Garrick, Soho House, Ivy, Ned.

**LEWINTON, Sir Christopher,** Kt 1993; CEng; FIMechE, FREng; FRAeS; Chairman: CL Partners, since 2000; Camper & Nicholsons Marina Investments Ltd, 2008, now Chairman Emeritus; *b* 6 Jan. 1932; *s* of Joseph and Elizabeth Lewinton; *m* 1st, Jennifer Alcock (marr. diss.); two *s*; 2nd, 1979, Louise Head; two step *s*. *Educ:* Acton Technical College. CEng 1965; FIMechE 1992. Army Service, Lieut REME. Pres., Wilkinson Sword, N America, 1960–71; Chief Exec., Wilkinson Sword Group, 1970–85; Pres., Internat. Gp, Allegheny International, 1978–85 (Mem. Board, 1976–85); TI Gp plc: Chief Exec., 1986–99; Chm., 1989–2000; Chm., Dowty Gp PLC, 1992–2000. Mem., Exec. Bd, J. F. Lehman & Co., 2000–; non-executive Director: Reed Elsevier, 1993–99; Mannesmann AG, 1995–99; Messier-Dowty, 1994–98; Young & Rubicam, NY, 1996–2001; WPP, 2001–03; Advr, Booz Allen Hamilton, 2001–07; Mem. Adv. Bd,

Morgan Stanley/Metalmark Capital, 2001–. FRAeS 1993; FREng (FEng 1994). Hon. DTech Brunel, 1997. *Recreations:* golf, tennis, shooting, reading. *Address:* CL Partners, Fifth Floor, Cording House, 34–35 St James's Street, SW1A 1HD. *T:* (020) 7201 5490. *Clubs:* Boodle's; Royal Thames Yacht; Sunningdale Golf; University (New York); Everglades, Four Arts (Palm Beach).

LEWIS; *see* Day-Lewis.

LEWIS, family name of **Baron Merthyr**.

LEWIS, **Adam Anthony Murless**, CVO 2006; FRCS, FRCSE; Serjeant Surgeon to the Queen, 2001–06; Consultant Surgeon, Royal Free Hospital, 1975–2006; Surgeon: St John and Elizabeth Hospital, London, 1975–2006; King Edward VII Hospital for Officers, London, 1991–2006; *s* of late Bernard S. Lewis, CBE, DSC and Mary Lewis (*née* Murless); *m* 1964, Margaret Catherine Ann Surgey; two *s* two *d*. *Educ:* St Bartholomew's Hosp. Med. Coll. (MB, BS London 1963); FRCSE 1968; FRCS 1969. Formerly: Sen. Registrar (Surg.), Royal Free Hosp.; Post Doctoral Fellow, Stanford Univ.; Sen. Lectr (Surg.), Univ. of Benin. Surgeon to Royal Household, 1991–2001. *Publications:* papers on general and gastro-intestinal surgery.

LEWIS, **Adam Valentine Shervey**, QC 2009; *b* Oxford, 20 Feb. 1963; *s* of Peter and Gillian Lewis; *m* 1996, Beate Mjaaland; one *s* one *d*. *Educ:* Trinity Hall, Cambridge (BA 1984). Called to the Bar, Gray's Inn, 1985; in practice as barrister, specialising in public law, EU and competition law, sport. *Publications:* Sport: law and practice, 2003, 3rd edn 2014. *Recreations:* cycling, cross country ski-ing, open water swimming, mountaineering. *Address:* Blackstone Chambers, Blackstone House, Temple, EC4Y 9BW.

LEWIS, **Prof. Alastair Charles**, PhD; FRSC; Professor of Atmospheric Chemistry, University of York, since 2006; Research Director, National Centre for Atmospheric Science, since 2006; *b* Chatham, 6 Aug. 1971; *s* of Raymond Ernest Lewis and Dulcie Margaret Lewis (*née* Woods); *m* 1999, Prof. Lucy Jane Carpenter, *qv*; one *s* one *d*. *Educ:* Sir Joseph Williamson's Mathematical Sch., Rochester; Univ. of Leeds (BSc Hons Chem. 1992; PhD Chem. 1995). Lectr, Univ. of Leeds, 1997–2003; Reader, Univ. of York, 2003–06. Lectr, RMIT Univ., Melbourne, 1999. Advr (pt-time), NERC, 2007–13; Member: Air Quality Expert Gp, DEFRA, 2011–; Sci. Adv. Panel, UNEP, 2015–19. FRSC 2012. Desty Meml Prize for Innovation in Separation Sci., 2001; Philip Leverhulme Award, 2004; SAC Silver Medal, 2006, John Jeyes Award, 2012, RSC. *Publications:* Multidimensional Chromatography, 2002; over 250 articles in jls on atmospheric sci., analytical chemistry and envmtl policy. *Recreations:* distance running, cycling, mountain biking, ski-ing. *Address:* Wolfson Atmospheric Chemistry Laboratories, Innovation Way, University of York, Heslington, York YO10 5DD. *T:* (01904) 322522, *Fax:* (01904) 322516. *E:* ally.lewis@york.ac.uk, ally.lewis@ncas.ac.uk.

LEWIS, **Andrew James**; Chief Executive, Cheshire West and Chester Council, since 2018; *b* St Andrews, Fife, 20 Nov. 1969; *s* of Christopher and Patricia Lewis; *m* 1994, Rose Dawn Hale; one *s* two *d*. *Educ:* Burscough Priory High Sch., Lancs; Winstanley Sixth Form Coll., Wigan; Robinson Coll., Cambridge (BA Econs 1991); Wolfson Coll., Oxford (MPhil Econs). HM Treasury, 1991–2004; Dep. Dir, 2004–07, Dir, Northern Way, 2007–10, Govt Office NE; Asst Chief Exec., Newcastle CC, 2010–16; Man. Dir, Tees Valley Combined Authy, 2016–18. *Address:* Cheshire West and Chester Council, Civic Way, Ellesmere Port, Cheshire CH65 0BE. *E:* andrew.lewis@cheshirewestandchester.gov.uk.

LEWIS, **Andrew William**; QC 2009; a Recorder, since 2001; a Deputy High Court Judge, since 2010; *b* London, 23 Oct. 1962; *s* of Norman John Lewis and Sylvia Lillian Lewis (*née* Allen); *m* 1990, Ruth Alison Hobson; four *s*. *Educ:* Beechen Cliff Comprehensive Sch., Bath; Coventry Poly. (BA Hons Business Law). Called to the Bar, Lincoln's Inn, 1985; in practice as barrister, specialising in personal injury and clinical negligence; Hd, Park Square Barristers. Co-Ed., Butterworths Personal Injury Litigation Service, 2012–. *Recreations:* watching four sons play sport, veterans football with HOTH FC, ski-ing, photography. *Address:* Park Square Barristers, 6 Park Square, Leeds LS1 2LW. *E:* lewisqc@psqb.co.uk.

LEWIS, **Ann Walford**, CMG 2000; HM Diplomatic Service, retired; *b* 2 May 1940; *d* of Dr Gwyn Walford Lewis and Winifred Marguerite Emma Lewis; one *s*. *Educ:* Allerton High Sch., Leeds; Leeds Univ. (BA). Teacher, translator and journalist, Finland, 1962–66; HM Diplomatic Service, 1966–2000: Research Dept, FCO, 1966–70; Second Secretary: Moscow, 1970–71; Res. Dept, FCO, 1971–72; Helsinki, 1972–74; Res. Dept, FCO, 1974–79; on secondment as Mem., Assessments Staff, Cabinet Office, 1979–82; Head of Chancery, E Berlin, 1982–85; Eastern Eur. Dept, FCO, 1985–91 (Dep. Head, 1988–91); Dep. Head, 1991–96, Head, 1996–2000, Cultural Relns Dept, FCO. Founder Dir, 1992, Dep. Chm., 1998–, English Coll. Foundn; Governor: English Coll., Prague, 1995– (Chm. of Govs, 2017–); St Clare's, Oxford, 2000– (Dep. Chm., 2006–). Trustee, BEARR Trust, 1999–. *Publications:* (ed) The EU and Ukraine: neighbours, friends, partners?, 2002; (ed) The EU and Belarus: between Moscow and Brussels, 2002; (ed) The EU and Moldova: on a fault-line of Europe, 2003; (ed) Old Roots, New Shoots: the story of the English College in Prague, 2004; (ed) Leaves and Branches: the first 20 years of the English College in Prague, 2014. *Recreations:* theatre, gardening, travel. *Address:* 16 Townley Road, SE22 8SR. *T:* (020) 8693 6418.

LEWIS, **Anthony Meredith**; Senior Partner, 1986–89, Joint Senior Partner, 1989–94, Taylor Joynson Garrett; *b* 15 Nov. 1940; *s* of Col Glyndwr Vivian Lancelot Lewis and Gillian Lewis (*née* Fraser); *m* 1970, Mrs Ewa Maria Anna Strawinska, former Social Editor of Tatler; one *s* one *d*. *Educ:* Rugby School; St Edmund Hall, Oxford (MA Law). Freshfields, 1964–70; Partner, Joynson-Hicks, 1970–86. Panel Mem., The Prince's Trust, 1996–2005. *Recreations:* opera, tennis, ski-ing, golf, piano.

LEWIS, **(Anthony) Rhydian**, OBE 2017; Founder and Chief Executive Officer, RateSetter, since 2010; *b* Wallingford, 18 May 1977; *s* of John Henry Peter Sebastian Beale Lewis and Mary Virginia Lewis (*née* Hutchinson); *m* 2017, Sophie Joanna Scholes; one *s* one *d*. *Educ:* Sunningdale Sch.; Eton Coll.; Bristol Univ. (BA 1st Cl. Modern Langs (French and Spanish) and Arabic 2000). Associate, Lazard, 2003–09. *Recreations:* horse racing, running, reading, ski-ing. *Address:* RateSetter, 55 Bishopsgate, EC2N 3AS. *T:* (020) 3142 6225. *E:* rhydian.lewis@ratesetter.com.

LEWIS, **Anthony Robert, (Tony Lewis)**, CBE 2002; writer, broadcaster; *b* 6 July 1938; *s* of Wilfrid Llewellyn Lewis and Florence Marjorie Lewis (*née* Flower); *m* 1962, Joan (*née* Pritchard); two *d*. *Educ:* Neath Grammar Sch.; Christ's Coll., Cambridge (MA). Double Blue, Rugby football, 1959, cricket, 1960–62, Captain of cricket, 1962, Cambridge Univ. Glamorgan CCC: cricketer, 1955–74; Captain, 1967–72; Chm., 1988–93; Trustee, 1992–97; Pres., 1999–2005; 9 Tests for England, 1972–73 (Captain of 8); Captained MCC to India, Ceylon and Pakistan, 1972–73. MCC: Mem. sub-cttees, 1967–, incl. five years framing 1980 Code of Cricket Laws; Trustee, 2002–03; Chm. of Cricket, 2003–07; Chm., World Cricket Cttee, 2006–11. Presenter: sports and arts magazine programmes, HTV, 1971–82; Sport on Four, BBC Radio, 1977–86; BBC TV presenter of cricket and commentator, 1974–98; Cricket Correspondent, Sunday Telegraph, 1974–93; freelance sports contributor, Sunday Telegraph, 1993–99. Chm., World Snooker Ltd, 2003. Dir,

Bulldog Publications, 2000–11; Marketing Consultant, Long Reach Internat. Insurance, 2003–11. Consultant, Univ. of Wales, Newport, 2004–07. Chm. Cttee, Assoc. of Business Sponsorship of the Arts (Wales), 1988–90; Member: Bd, Sports Council for Wales, 1967–69; Welsh Economic Council, 1994–96; Tourism Action Gp, CBI, 1994–2000; Bd, BTA, 1992–2000; Chm., Wales Tourist Bd, 1992–2000. Chm., Wales Ryder Cup bid, 2000–01. Chm., Bd, WNO, 2003–06. Trustee, Wales Millennium Centre, 2003–07. Pres., Lord's Taverners Wales, 2012–. DL, 1994, High Sheriff, 1998–99, Mid Glam. Hon. Fellow: St David's Univ. Coll., Lampeter, 1993; Univ. of S Wales (formerly Glamorgan Univ.), 1995; Univ. of Wales, Swansea, 1996; Cardiff Univ., 1999; Univ. of Wales, Newport, 2008. *Publications:* A Summer of Cricket, 1976; Playing Days, 1985; Double Century, 1987; Cricket in Many Lands, 1991; MCC Masterclass, 1994; Taking Fresh Guard, 2003; contrib. articles in Media Wales mag. *Recreations:* classical music, golf. *Clubs:* East India (Hon. Mem., 2013), MCC (Pres., 1998–2000; Hon. Life Vice Pres., 2011); Royal Porthcawl Golf (Capt., 2012–13), Royal & Ancient Golf.

LEWIS, **Prof. Barry**, MD, PhD; FRCP; FRCPath; Professor Emeritus, University of London; *b* 16 March 1929; *s* of George Lewis and Pearl Lewis; *m* 1972, Eve Simone Rothschild; two *s* one *d*, and one *s* two *d* by a previous marriage. *Educ:* Rondebosch School, Cape Town; University of Cape Town (MB ChB 1952; PhD 1956; MD 1958). MRCPE 1959; MRCP 1964, FRCP 1975; FRCPath 1980. Training posts, Groote Schuur Hosp., Cape Town, 1953; lectureship and fellowships, St George's Hosp., 1959; Consultant Pathologist, St Mark's Hosp., 1967; opened lipid clinic, 1968, Sen. Lectr in Chemical Pathology, and Hon. Consultant Physician, 1969–76, Hammersmith Hosp.; Chm., Dept of Chem. Path. and Metabolic Disorders, Hon. Consultant Physician, and Dir of Lipid Clinic, St Thomas' Hosp., 1976–88; Consultant Physician, specialising in lipid disorders: St Thomas' Hosp., 1989–95; 14 Wimpole St, 1995–2002; London Medical, 2002–06. Principal Investigator, St Thomas' Atherosclerosis Regression Trial, 1984–92. Recent research and clinical interests: hyperlipidaemia, causes, prevention and regression of atherosclerosis, prevention of cardiovascular disease. Founder Chm., Internat. Taskforce for Prevention of Coronary Heart Disease, 1987–94. Life FRSocMed, 1989. Heinrich Wieland Prize, 1980. *Publications:* The Hyperlipidaemias: clinical and laboratory practice, 1976; (with Eve Lewis) The Heart Book, 1980; (with N. Miller) Lipoproteins, Atherosclerosis and Coronary Heart Disease, 1981; (jtly) Metabolic and Molecular Bases of Acquired Disease, 1990; Handbook on Prevention of Coronary Heart Disease, 1990; (with G. Assmann) Social and Economic Contexts of Coronary Disease Prevention, 1990; (jtly) Prevention of Coronary Heart Disease in the Elderly, 1991; (jtly) Prevention of Coronary Heart Disease: scientific background and clinical guidelines, 1993; (jtly) Low Blood Cholesterol: health implications, 1993; Paradise Regained: insights into coronary heart disease prevention, 1997; (contrib.) Nutrition, Metabolism and Cardiovascular Disease, 2009; (jtly) On reducing cardiovascular disease to a rarity, 2010; (jtly) The Classification of Dyslipidaemia and its implications for Clinical Management, 2011; (contrib.) Evolution of the Lipid Clinic 1968–2008, 2014; Thought for food: clinical evidence for the dietary prevention strategy in cardiovascular disease, 2013; (contrib.) Lipoproteins in Diabetes Mellitus, 2014; 300 papers on heart disease, nutrition and lipoproteins in med. and sci. jls. *Recreations:* music, travel, reading, French language. *Address:* 48 Landing Drive, Dobbs Ferry, NY 10522, USA.

LEWIS, **Rt Hon. Brandon**, CBE 2019; PC 2016; MP (C) Great Yarmouth, since 2010; Minister of State, Home Office, since 2019; *b* 20 June 1971; *m* 1999, Justine Yolande Rappolt; one *s* one *d*. *Educ:* Forest Sch.; Univ. of Buckingham (BSc Hons Econs; LLB); King's Coll. London (LLM Commercial Law). Called to the Bar, Inner Temple. Dir, Woodlands Schs Ltd, 2001–12. Mem. (C) Brentwood BC, 1998–2009 (Leader, 2004–09). Parly Under-Sec. of State, 2012–14, Minister of State, 2014–16, DCLG; Minister of State, Home Office, 2016–18; Minister without Portfolio, Cabinet Office, 2018–19; Chm., Cons. Party, 2018–19. Mem. Council, Univ. of Buckingham, 2014–. *Recreations:* running, cycling, cinema, triathlon. *Address:* House of Commons, SW1A 0AA. *T:* (020) 7219 7231, *Fax:* (020) 7219 6558. *E:* brandon.lewis.mp@parliament.uk. *Club:* Carlton.

LEWIS, **His Honour Brian William**; a Circuit Judge, 1997–2015; *b* 23 July 1949; *o s* of Gilbert Pryce Lewis and Mary Williamson Lewis; *m* 1981, Maureen O'Hare; one *s*. *Educ:* Sale Co. GS for Boys; Univ. of Hull (LLB Hons). Called to the Bar, Inner Temple, 1973; Lectr, Barnet Coll., 1973–74; in practice at the Bar, Cardiff, 1974–75, Liverpool, 1976–97; Asst Recorder, 1989–93; a Recorder, 1993–97. *Recreations:* family life, sport, reading, military history.

LEWIS, **Byron**; *see* Lewis, D. B.

LEWIS, **Carl**; *see* Lewis, F. C.

LEWIS, **Very Rev. Christopher Andrew**, PhD; Dean of Christ Church, Oxford, 2003–14 (Honorary Student, 2014); Pro-Vice-Chancellor, University of Oxford, 2010–14 (Member of Council, 2008–13); *b* 4 Feb. 1944; *s* of Adm. Sir Andrew Lewis, KCB and late Rachel Elizabeth (*née* Leatham); *m* 1970, Rhona Jane Martindale; two *s* one *d*. *Educ:* Marlborough Coll.; Bristol Univ. (BA 1969); Episcopal Divinity Sch., Cambridge, Mass; Corpus Christi Coll., Cambridge (PhD 1974); Westcott House, Cambridge. Served RN, 1961–66; ordained deacon, 1973, priest, 1974; Asst Curate, Barnard Castle, 1973–76; Tutor, Ripon Coll., Cuddesdon, 1976–81; Dir, Oxford Inst. for Church and Soc., 1976–79; Priest-in-charge, Aston Rowant and Crowell, 1978–81; Vice Principal, Ripon Coll., Cuddesdon, 1981–82; Vicar of Spalding, 1982–87; Canon Residentiary, Canterbury Cathedral, 1987–94; Dir of Ministerial Trng, dio. of Canterbury, 1989–94; Dean of St Albans, 1994–2003. Chm., Assoc. of English Cathedrals, 2000–09. Hon. DLitt Hertfordshire, 1999. *Recreations:* guinea fowl, bicycles. *Address:* The Old Brewery, 16 Victoria Road, Aldeburgh, Suffolk IP15 5ED. *E:* christopher.lewis@chch.ox.ac.uk.

LEWIS, **Clive Anthony**; MP (Lab) Norwich South, since 2015; *b* London, 11 Sept. 1971; *m* 2017, Katy Steel. *Educ:* Univ. of Bradford (BSc Econs). Pres., Univ. of Bradford Students' Union; Vice Pres., NUS. BBC: News trainee, 1999–2000; journalist, 2000–11, incl. Chief Political Reporter, Eastern Reg.; technician, 2011–15. Joined TA, 2003 (Infantry Officer, 7 Rifles; in Afghanistan, 2009). Shadow Sec. of State for Defence, 2016, for Business, Energy and Industrial Strategy, 2016–17; Shadow Treasury Minister, 2018–. Member: Public Accounts Select Cttee, 2015; Sci. and Technol. Select Cttee, 2017–18. *Address:* House of Commons, SW1A 0AA.

LEWIS, **Hon. Sir Clive (Buckland)**, Kt 2013; **Hon. Mr Justice Lewis**; a Judge of the High Court, Queen's Bench Division, since 2013; *b* 13 June 1960; *s* of John Buckland Lewis and late Vera May Lewis (*née* Prosser). *Educ:* Cwmtawe Comp. Sch.; Churchill Coll., Cambridge (BA 1981); Dalhousie Univ. (LLM 1983). Lectr, UEA, 1983–86; Fellow, Selwyn Coll., Cambridge, 1986–93; Univ. Lectr, Univ. of Cambridge, 1989–93. Called to the Bar, Middle Temple, 1987, Bencher, 2011; in practice at the Bar, 1992–2013; QC 2006; a Recorder, 2003–13; a Dep. High Court Judge, 2010–13; Presiding Judge, Wales Circuit, 2016–19. First Counsel to Nat. Assembly for Wales, later Welsh Assembly Govt, then Welsh Govt, 2000–13. Asst Boundary Comr for England, 2011–13; Asst Boundary Comr for Wales, 2011–16; Dep. Chair, Boundary Commn for Wales, 2016–. Mem. Editl Bd, Public Law, 2006–. *Publications:* Judicial Remedies in Public Law, 1992, 5th edn 2014; (ed) Civil Procedure (annually); Remedies and the Enforcement of European Community

Law, 1996; (gen. ed.) Halsbury's Laws of England, Judicial Rev. *Recreations:* travel, walking, reading, golf, bridge. *Address:* Royal Courts of Justice, Strand, WC2A 2LL. *Clubs:* Athenæum, Royal Automobile.

**LEWIS, Clive Hewitt,** FRICS; President, Royal Institution of Chartered Surveyors, 1993–94; *b* 29 March 1936; *s* of Thomas Jonathan Lewis, OBE and Marguerite Eileen Lewis; *m* 1961, Jane Penelope White; two *s* one *d. Educ:* St Peter's Sch., York (Head Boy). FRICS 1963; FSVA 1979. With Goddard & Smith, 1957–62; Founder and Sen. Partner, Clive Lewis & Partners, 1963–92, when merged with Edward Erdman; Jt Chm., Colliers Erdman Lewis, 1993–95. Non-executive Director: St Modwen Properties, 1983–2002; Town Centre Securities, 1994–2009; Freeport Leisure, 1997–2004. Dep. Chm., Merseyside Develt Corp., 1989–98. Chm., Bank of England Property Forum, 1994–2002. Mem. Council, Internat. Year of Shelter for the Homeless, 1985–88. Mem., Gen. Council, RICS, 1987–95 (Pres., Gen. Practice Div., 1989–90); President: Eur. Council of Real Estate Professionals, 1990; UK, 1976–77, World, 1984–85, Internat. Real Estate Fedn (Mem. Exec. Cttee, 1977–92). Pres., Land Aid Charitable Trust, 1986–2003. Chm., Copthall Sports Cttee, 2015–. Dir, Club Cricket Conference, 2017– (Chm., Club Cricket Conference Charity, 2017–). Freeman, City of London, 1983; Liveryman, Chartered Surveyors' Co., 1983–2002. Hon. DLitt S Bank, 1993. *Recreations:* bridge, dogs, golf, cricket. *Address:* 8 The Pastures, Totteridge, N20 8AN. *T:* (020) 8445 5109. *Clubs:* MCC; S Herts Golf; Totteridge Millmillians Cricket (Pres., 2005–07).

**LEWIS, Damian Watcyn,** OBE 2014; actor; *b* 11 Feb. 1971; *s* of Watcyn Lewis and Charlotte Lewis; *m* 2007, Helen McCrory (OBE 2017); one *s* one *d. Educ:* Ashdown House Prep. Sch.; Eton Coll.; Guildhall Sch. of Music and Drama (Fellow 2006). Actor: *theatre* includes: Hamlet, Open Air Th., Regent's Park, 1994; School for Wives, Almeida, 1994; on Broadway, 1995; RSC, 1996–98; Into the Woods, Donmar, 1999; Pillars of the Community, NT, 2005; The Misanthrope, Comedy, 2009; American Buffalo, Wyndham's Th., 2015; The Goat, or Who is Sylvia?, Th. Royal Haymarket, 2017; *television* includes: Warriors, 1999; Band of Brothers, 2000; Soames Forsyte in The Forsyte Saga, 2001; Life, 2007; Stolen, 2011; Homeland (3 series), 2012, 2013 (Emmy Award, Best Actor, 2012; Golden Globe Award, Best Actor in TV Drama, 2012); Romeo and Juliet, 2013; Wolf Hall, 2015; Billions, 2016, 2017; *films* include: Dreamcatcher, 2002; An Unfinished Life, 2003; Keane, 2004; The Baker (also producer), 2008; Queen of the Desert, Bill, 2015; Our Kind of Traitor, The Silent Storm, 2016; Once Upon a Time in Hollywood, 2019. Partner, Picture Farm Ltd, prodn co., 2004–. Ambassador for: Prince's Trust, 2002–; Christian Aid, 2005– (made report on privatization in Bolivia, 2005); Patron, Scene and Heard, 2004–. Mem., Stage Golfing Soc. *Recreations:* football, tennis, golf, gardening, bicycling, watching film, theatre, reading, travelling, day dreaming, playing piano badly. *Address:* c/o Markham, Froggatt & Irwin, 4 Windmill Street, W1T 2HZ. *Clubs:* Groucho, Queen's.

**LEWIS, (David) Byron,** CVO 2019; FCA; Lord-Lieutenant of West Glamorgan, since 2008; *b* Swansea, 14 Feb. 1945; *s* of late William Edward Lewis and Eiddwen Lewis; *m* 1969, Hilary Ann Morgan; two *d. Educ:* Gowerton Grammar Sch., Swansea. FCA 1968. Dir, various private companies, 1969–75; Div. Man. Dir, 1975–85, Asst Gp Man. Dir, 1985–91, Christie-Tyler Gp plc; Man. Dir, subsidiaries of Hillsdown Hldgs plc, 1991–93; non-exec. Chm., Blackwood Ltd, Birdel Ltd and various private companies, 1993–2008. Chairman: S Wales Magistrates' Adv. Cttee; W Glam Jt Archives Service. President: W Glam Council of St John; W Glam SSAFA; W Glam Area Scouts; W Glam ABF; RFCA Wales. Co. Patron, RBL. Freeman, City of London, 1989. High Sheriff, W Glamorgan, 2004–05. Hon. Fellow UWTSD. KStJ 2016 (CStJ 2008). *Recreations:* sport, music, gardening. *Address:* Bryn Newydd House, 1 Derwen Fawr Road, Sketty Green, Swansea SA2 8AA. *T:* (01792) 203012. *E:* byron.lewis@btinternet.com. *Clubs:* Army and Navy; Langland Bay Golf.

**LEWIS, David John;** Chairman, Molyneux Management Services Ltd, since 1974; *b* London, 17 May 1939; *s* of Reuben Lewis and Jean Lewis; *m* 1961, Hannah Schorr; one *s* two *d* (and one *d* decd). *Educ:* Hackney Downs Grammar Sch.; Coll. of Estate Mgt, Univ. of London (BSc 1959). FRICS 1969. Sen. Partner, David Lewis & Partners, 1964–94; Chief Executive Officer: Cavendish Land Co., 1972–73; Hampton Trust plc, 1983–87; Chm., Molyneux Estates plc, 1989–95. Non-executive Director: Mount Martin Gold Mines, 1983–94; TBI plc, 1995–2001. Chairman: Jewish Blind Soc., 1979–90; Jewish Care, 1991–92. Pres., Eur. Council of Jewish Communities, 1992–99; Co-Founder and Co-Chairman, Commn for Looted Art in Europe, 1998–. Chm., Oxford Centre Muller Liby, 1974–2011; Founder Gov., Harris City Technol. Coll., 1990–2009; Gov., Oxford Centre for Hebrew and Jewish Studies, 1992–; Trustee: Leuka, 1998–2018; Weiner Liby, 2012–17; Birmingham Mus Trust, 2012–18; Dep. Chm., London Jewish Cultural Centre, 2006–15. *Recreations:* art, music, grandchildren. *Address:* Catherine House, 76 Gloucester Place, W1U 6HJ. *T:* (020) 7487 3401. *E:* david.lewis@catherinehouse.com. *Club:* Savile.

**LEWIS, David Nicholas;** QC 2019; *b* Liverpool, 8 Aug. 1975; *s* of Arnold Joseph Lewis and Patricia Anne Lewis; one *s* one *d. Educ:* King David High Sch.; Univ. of Sheffield (LLB). Called to the Bar, Lincoln's Inn, 1997; in practice as a barrister, specialising in commercial law, 1997–. *Address:* Hardwicke Building, New Square, Lincoln's Inn, WC2A 3SB. *T:* (020) 7242 2523. *E:* david.lewis@hardwicke.co.uk.

**LEWIS, David Patrick;** QC 2014; *b* Salisbury, 23 April 1977; *s* of Roger and Deirdre Lewis; *m* 2009, Patricia O'Driscoll; one *s* two *d* (of which one *s* one *d* are twins). *Educ:* Warwick Sch., Warwick; St Edmund Hall, Oxford (BA 1st Cl. Juris. 1998). Called to the Bar, Middle Temple, 1999; in practice as barrister, specialising in commercial law, 2000–. CEDR Accredited Mediator, 2005. *Recreations:* sport, music, tickling the kids. *Address:* 20 Essex Street, WC2R 3AL. *T:* (020) 7842 1200. *E:* dlewis@20essexst.com.

**LEWIS, Sir David (Thomas Rowell),** Kt 2009; JP; DL; Senior Partner, Norton Rose, 1997–2003 (Consultant, 2003–13); Lord Mayor of London, 2007–08; *b* 1 Nov. 1947; *s* of Thomas Price Merfyn Lewis; *m* 1970, Theresa Susan Poole; one *s* one *d. Educ:* Dragon Sch., Oxford; St Edward's Sch., Oxford; Jesus Coll., Oxford (MA 1969; Hon. Fellow 1998; Queen Elizabeth I Fellow 2012). Admitted solicitor, 1972, Hong Kong, 1977; joined Norton Rose, 1969: articled, 1969–72; Asst Solicitor, 1972–76; Partner, 1977; Managing Partner, Hong Kong Office, 1979–82; Head: Corporate Finance, 1989–94; Professional Resources, 1994–99. Non-exec. Dir, Standard Life Assurance Co., 2003–04. Comr, I of M Financial Supervision Commn, 2012–16. Trustee: Oxford Univ. Law Foundn, 1997–2007; Oxford Inst. of Legal Practice, 2001–03; Member: Oxford Univ. Law Develt Council, 1997–2006 (Chm., 2003–06); Oxford Univ. Chancellor's Ct of Benefactors, 1997–2009. Member: Royal Soc. of St George, 2004–13; City Pickwick Club, 2007–13. Governor: Dragon Sch., Oxford, 1987–2017 (Chm., 2003–08); Oxford Brookes Univ., 1995–2003; Blackbird Acad., 2013–14; Swansea Univ., 2014–16; Gov. and Almoner, Christ's Hosp., 2004–10; Chancellor, City Univ., 2007–08. Mem., Law Soc. Legal Practice Course Bd, 1995–2000. President: St Edward's Sch. Soc., 1995–96; Broad Street Ward Club, 2001–13; City of London Law Soc., 2009–10. Gov., Hon. Irish Soc., 2009–12. Trustee: Wellbeing of Women, 2009–12; Awen Cymru, 2010–12; ORBIS UK, 2011–12. An Ambassador for Wales, 2008–. Churchwarden, St Margaret Lothbury, 2001–13. Alderman, Broad Street Ward, 2001–13; Sheriff, City of London, 2006–07; Liveryman: Solicitors' Co. (Master, 2009–10); Fletchers' Co.; Livery Co. of Wales (formerly Welsh Livery Guild); Hon. Liveryman, Security Professionals Co. JP: City of London, 2002–09; Dinefwr, 2009–; DL Dyfed, 2009. Hon. Fellow: Hunan, 2008; Xiamen, 2008; GSMD, 2008; Cardiff, 2009; Trinity Coll., Carmarthen, 2009. Hon. DCL: City, 2007; Wales, 2008. KStJ 2008. *Publications:* Cynwyl Gaeo The Land of My Fathers, 2009; Family Histories and Community Life in North Carmarthenshire, 2012; Dolaucothi and Brunant: a tale of two families, 2016; A History of the Edwinsford and Clovelly Communities, 2017; The Vaughan (Earls of Carbery) and Campbell (Earls and Thanes of Cawdor) Families of Golden Grove Carmarthenshire, 2018; contrib. articles to jls. *Recreations:* charity, spoiling my dogs, collecting maps, travel, supporting Welsh Rugby. *Address:* Erwhen, Cwrt-y-Cadno, Pumsaint, Cynwyl Gaeo, Carms SA19 8YP. *E:* lewis.erwhen@icloud.com. *Clubs:* Achilles, Pilgrims; Hong Kong (Hong Kong).

**LEWIS, Denise,** OBE 2001 (MBE 1999); athlete; *b* 27 Aug. 1972; *d* of Joan Lewis; one *d* by Patrick Stevens; *m* 2006, Stephen Joseph Finan O'Connor; three *s.* Mem., Birchfield Harriers. Heptathlon wins include: Commonwealth Games: Gold Medal, 1994, 1998; European Cup: Gold Medal, 1995, Silver Medal, 2003; Olympic Games: Bronze Medal, 1996, Gold Medal, 2000; World Championships: Silver Medal, 1997, 1999; European Championships: Gold Medal, 1998. *Publications:* Personal Best (autobiog.), 2001; The Flat Tummy Book, 2008.

**LEWIS, Denise, (Mrs Mark Poulton);** Co-Founder and Managing Director, Blodwen Ltd, since 2010; a Trustee, Wallace Collection, 2009–14; *b* Adpar, Newcastle Emlyn, Cardiganshire; *d* of William David Lewis and Valmai Jones; *m* 1998, Mark Poulton; one *s* one *d. Educ:* Llandysul Grammar Sch.; King's Coll., London (BD 1987; AKC). Dir, Corporate Communications, Encom, later Bell Cablemedia, 1993–97; Gp Vice Pres., Corporate Affairs, Orange plc, 1997–2003. Vice Pres., Hay Literary Fest., 1998–; Trustee: Wessex Youth Trust, 1999–; Cadwgan Building Preservation Trust, 2010–14; non-exec. Dir, WNO, 2003–12. FRSA. Hon. Mem., BAFTA, 2002. *Recreation:* Welsh affairs. *E:* Denise@Blodwen.com.

**LEWIS, Dr Dennis Aubrey,** MBE 2014; Director, Aslib, the Association for Information Management, 1981–89; *b* 1 Oct. 1928; *s* of Joseph and Minnie Lewis; *m* 1956, Gillian Mary Bratby; two *s. Educ:* Latymer Upper Sch.; Univ. of London (BSc 1st Cl. Hons Chemistry, 1953; PhD 1956). FCLIP (FIInfSc 1984). Res. Chemist, 1956–68, Intelligence Manager, 1968–81, ICI Plastics Div. Member: Adv. Council, British Library, 1976–81; Library Adv. Cttee, British Council, 1981–. Member: Welwyn Garden UDC, 1968–74; Welwyn Hatfield DC, 1974–2007 (Chm., 1976–77); Chm., Welwyn Hatfield Alliance, 2004–08. Hon. LLM Herts, 2005. Welwyn Hatfield Civic Award, 2013. *Publications:* Index of Reviews in Organic Chemistry, annually 1963–; (ed jtly) Great Information Disasters, 1991; pubns on information management in Aslib Procs and other journals. *Recreations:* music, old churches, 'futurology'.

**LEWIS, Derek (Compton);** Chairman of Trustees, Royal Mencap Society, since 2014; *b* 9 July 1946; *s* of late Kenneth Compton Lewis and Marjorie Lewis; *m* 1969, Louise (*née* Wharton); two *d. Educ:* Wrekin Coll., Telford; Queens' Coll., Cambridge (MA); London Business Sch. (MSc). Ford Motor Co., 1968–82, Dir of Finance, Ford of Europe, 1978–82; Dir of Corporate Develt and Gp Planning Man., Imperial Gp, 1982–84; Granada Group: Finance Dir, 1984–87; Man. Dir, 1988–89; Gp Chief Exec., 1990–91; Dir, Courtaulds Textiles, 1990–93; Chief Exec. and Dir Gen., HM Prison Service, 1993–95. Chairman: UK Gold Television Ltd, 1992–97; Sunsail International, 1997–99; Patientline plc, 1998–2006 (Chief Exec., 1998–2001; Pres., 2006–07); Director: Protocol Associates, 2002– (Chm., 2002–09); JHP Gp Ltd, 2008–12 (Chm., 2010–12); learndirect, 2012–14; Ncn'ean Distillery, 2014–; Chairman: Drinkaware Trust, 2008–14; Community Alcohol Partnerships, 2014–; Trustee: Patients Assoc., 1999–2002; RVS (formerly WRVS), 2007–13. Mem. Council, Univ. of Essex, 1999–2009 (Treas., 2001–07; Pro-Chancellor, 2007–09). *Publications:* Hidden Agendas, 1997. *Club:* Caledonian.

**LEWIS, (Derek) Trevor;** Chairman, Bradford & Bingley Pensions Ltd, 1995–2012; Vice-Chairman, Bradford & Bingley plc (formerly Bradford & Bingley Building Society), 1995–2003 (Director, 1990–2003); *b* 21 Oct. 1936; *s* of Lionel Lewis and Mabel (*née* Clare); *m* 1961, Pamela Jean Ratcliffe; one *s* one *d. Educ:* Bradford Grammar Sch.; Leeds Univ. (LLB); 2nd Cl. Hons Solicitors' Final Exam., 1960. With A. V. Hammond & Co., subseq. Hammond Suddards: articled to Sir Richard Denby, 1955–60; Asst Solicitor, 1960–63; Partner 1964–87; Jt Sen. Partner, 1987–95. Dir, W Yorks Independent Hosp., 1979–85 (Chm., 1985–88); Chairman: Little Germany Urban Village Co. Ltd, 1999–2003; Arts and Business Yorkshire Ltd, 2000–10; Bradford Breakthrough Ltd, 2005–10; Dep. Chm., Bradford City Centre Urban Regeneration Co. Ltd, 2003–10. *Address:* 5 Royal Gardens, Harrogate, N Yorks HG2 0NR. *T:* (01423) 523996.

**LEWIS, Dr Dewi Meirion,** FInstP; Head of Physics, GE Healthcare (formerly Nycomed Amersham, then Amersham plc), 1999–2010; *b* Chester, 4 Sept. 1948; *s* of Hugh and Mair Lewis; *m* 1972, Elizabeth Mary Williams; two *s* one *d. Educ:* Ysgol Ardudwy Harlech, Gwynedd; UCW, Swansea (BSc 1969; PhD 1972). FInstP 1995; FRAS 2004. Res. Fellow, CERN, Geneva, 1973–74; Engr i/c, CERN ISR collider, 1974–79; Cyclotron Ops Manager, TRC Ltd, 1979–83; Amersham International plc: Hd, Cyclotron Dept, 1983–88; Business Manager, Cyclotron and Reactor Pharmaceuticals, 1988–91; Mfg Strategy Manager, 1991–94; R&D Strategy Manager, 1994–99. Visiting Professor of Physics: Liverpool Univ., 1997–2001; Cockcroft Inst., 2008–10 (Mem., Industrial Adv. Bd, 2009–10); Vis. Lectr of Physics, Oxford Univ., 2008–10. Non-exec. Dir, Reviss Services Ltd, 1992–95. Member: OECD/NEA Expert Panel on Isotopes, 1997–99; PPARC, 2000–06 (Mem., 2000–07, Chm., 2001–04, Audit Cttee); EPSRC Coll., 2000–10; CCLRC, 2006–07; Adv. Bd, All-Wales PET Imaging Centre, 2008–10; CLASP grant panel, STFC, 2008–10; Case Studentship Panel, MRC, 2009. Vice-Pres., Assoc. of Imaging Producers and Equipment Suppliers (Chm., Cttee on Isotopes and Reactors, 1992–2007); Scientific Advr, EC DG XII, 1994–97; Mem., EMIR Network, Brussels, 2001– (Chm., Isotopes Cttee, 2001–). Member: British Astronomical Soc., 2001; UK Res. Council. Member: Amer. Assoc. Physicists in Medicine, 2001; Eur. Assoc. Nuclear Medicine, 2001–10; Soc. of Nuclear Medicine, 2003–10. Mem., Mgt Cttee, Amersham Pension Scheme, 2005–07; Dir and Trustee, Bd, GE Pension Plan, 2010. *Publications:* contrib. articles to res. jls. *Recreations:* ski-ing, Alpine walking, golf, choral music, astronomy. *Club:* Harewood Downs (Bucks).

**LEWIS, Rev. Edward John;** JP, Vicar, St Mary the Virgin, Kenton, since 2011; Chaplain to the Queen, since 2008; *b* Swansea, 4 Aug. 1958; *s* of Donald Lewis and Adeline Lewis; *m* 2000, Katherine; two *s. Educ:* Univ. of Wales (BEd 1980; BA Theol. 1982); Theol Coll., Chichester (DipTh 1983); Univ. of Surrey (MA Bioethics 2007). Ordained deacon, 1983, priest, 1984; Curate, Parish of Llangiwg, Pontardawe, 1983–85; Sen. Curate, Parish of Morriston, and Asst Chaplain, Morriston Hosp., Swansea, 1985–87; Vicar Tregaron, Strata Florida, Ystrad Meurig, and Chaplain, Tregaron Hosp., 1987–89; Sen. Chaplain, Walsall Hosps NHS Trust, 1989–2000; Asst, later Acting Rural Dean, Walsall, 1995–2000; CEO, Hosp. Chaplaincies Council, C of E, 2000–10; Priest-in-charge, St John's, Watford, 2010–11. Priest Associate, Shrine of our Lady of Walsingham, 2000; Priest Vicar, Westminster Abbey, 2006–10; Surrogate, Dio. of London, 2016. Chaplain: RBL, 1987–89; Nat. Band of Church Lads & Church Girls, 1995–2000. Trustee: St Luke's Hospice, Kenton

Grange, 2011–14; Harrow Bereavement Gp, 2011–. JP Walsall, 1993–2000, City of Westminster, 2000–12. Freedom, City of London, 2006. MInstD 2000–15. FRSA 1997. *Recreations:* entertaining friends, theatres, travel in Italy. *Address:* St Mary's Vicarage, 3 St Leonard's Avenue, Kenton, Middx HA3 8EJ. *T:* 07500 557953. *E:* fredward58@icloud.com. *Club:* Royal Over-Seas League.

LEWIS, Frederick Carlton, (Carl); athlete; *b* 1 July 1961; *s* of Bill and Evelyn Lewis. *Educ:* Univ. of Houston. Winner, 100m, 200m, and long jump, US National Athletics Championships, 1983; *Olympic Games:* Gold medals, 100m and 200m, long jump and 4×100m, 1984; Gold medals, 100m and long jump, Silver medal, 200m, 1988; Gold medals, long jump and 4×100m, 1992; Gold medal, long jump, 1996; *World Championships:* Gold medals, 100m, long jump, 4×100m, 1983; Gold medals, long jump, 4×100m, 1987; Gold medals, 100m, 4×100m, 1991. World Record: long jump (8.79m), 1983; 100m (9.86 seconds), 1991. James E. Sullivan Meml Award, Amateur Athletic Union of US, 1981; Athlete of the Century, IAAF, 1999. UN Goodwill Ambassador, FAO, 2009.

LEWIS, Gillian Marjorie, FMA, FIIC; heritage consultant, since 1994; *b* 10 Oct. 1945; *d* of late William Lewis and of Marjorie Lewis (*née* Pargeter). *Educ:* Tiffin Sch., Kingston upon Thames; Univ. of Newcastle upon Tyne (BA 1967); DCP, Gateshead Tech. Coll., 1969; Birkbeck Coll., London (Cert. Ecology 1991). FIIC 1977; FMA 1988. Shipley Art Gallery, Co. Durham, 1967–69; free-lance conservator, 1969–73; Nat. Maritime Mus., 1973–94; Keeper of Conservation, 1978; Hd, Div. of Conservation and Technical Services, 1978–88; Asst Dep. Dir, 1982–86; Hd of Conservation and Registration, 1988–91; Head of Collection Projects, 1991–92; Head of External Affairs, 1992–94. Vice-Chm., UK Inst. for Conservation, 1983–84 (Mem. Cttee, 1978–80). Member: Technical Cttee, City and Guilds of London Sch. of Art, 1981–2012; Cttee, Dulwich Picture Gall., 1983–92; Wallpaintings Conservation Panel, Council for Care of Churches, 1985–88; Volunteer Steering Cttee, Office of Arts and Libraries, 1988–90; Adv. Cttee, Museums and Galleries Commn, 1988–96; Trng Standards Panel, Museums Trng Inst., 1990–93; Council, Leather Conservation Centre, 1991–92; Fabric Adv. Cttee, Southwark Cathedral, 1997–; Preservation Advr to Dean and Chapter, Peterborough Cathedral, 1994–2013; Adviser: Heather Trust for the Arts, 1997–2000; Royal Warrant Holders' Assoc., 1999–2003. Examiner, London Inst., Camberwell Sch. of Art, 1991–93; Assessor: Clore Small Grants Prog., 1998–2003; Attingham Trust, 2002. Trustee: Whatmore Trust, 1988–; Southwark Cathedral Millennium Trust, 1998–2011; Cathedral Camps, 1998–2001; Edward James Foundn, 1999–2013. UN50 UK Ambassador, 1995. FRSA 1987.

LEWIS, Prof. Glyn Hywel, PhD; FRCPsych; Professor of Psychiatric Epidemiology, since 2013, and Director, Division of Psychiatry, since 2014, University College London; *b* 6 Dec. 1956; *s* of Jeffrey and Marion Lewis; *m* 1982, Priscilla Hall; one *s. Educ:* University Coll., Oxford (MSc 1980; MA 1983); University Coll. London (MB BS 1982); London Sch. of Hygiene and Tropical Medicine (MSc 1989); Inst. of Psychiatry, London Univ. (PhD 1991). FRCPsych 1998. Registrar, Bethlem and Maudsley Hosp., 1983–86; Res. Fellow, 1986–91, Sen. Lectr, 1991–95, Inst. of Psychiatry, London Univ.; on secondment to DoH, 1991–94; Res. Fellow, LSHTM, 1993–95; Prof. of Community and Epidemiological Psychiatry, Univ. of Wales Coll. of Medicine, 1996–2001; Prof. of Psychiatric Epidemiology, Univ. of Bristol, 2001–13. *Address:* UCL Division of Psychiatry, University College London, Maple House, 149 Tottenham Court Road, W1T 7NF.

LEWIS, Dr Gwyneth; writer; *b* Cardiff, 4 Nov. 1959; *d* of Gwilym and Eryl Lewis; *m* 1993, Leighton Denver Davies. *Educ:* Ysgol Gyfun Rhydfelen; Girton Coll., Cambridge (MA 1982); Harvard Univ.; Columbia Univ., NY; Balliol Coll., Oxford (DPhil 1991). Researcher, Agenda Television, 1989–92; Asst Producer, 1992–93, Producer, 1993–98, BBC; Chief Asst to Controller, BBC Wales, 1998–2000. Nat. Poet of Wales, 2005–06. Mildred Londa Weisman Fellow, Radcliffe Inst. of Advanced Study, Harvard Univ., 2008–09; SiCa Fellow, Stanford Humanities Center, Stanford Univ., 2009–10; Mary Amelia Cummins Vis. Commoner, Girton Coll., Cambridge, 2010–11; Bain-Swigget Vis. Lectr in English and Poetry, Princeton Univ., 2014; Robert Frost Prof. of Poetry and Literature, Bread Loaf Sch. of English, Middlebury Coll., 2016. *Publications:* Sonedau Redsa, 1990; Parables and Faxes, 1995; Cyfrif Un ac Un yn Dri, 1996; Zero Gravity, 1998; Y Llofrudd Iaith, 1999; Sunbathing in the Rain: a cheerful book on depression, 2002; Tair mewn Un, 2005; Two in a Boat: a marital voyage, 2005; Chaotic Angels, 2005; A Hospital Odyssey, 2010; The Meat Tree, 2010; Arthur's Talk with the Eagle, 2011; Sparrow Tree, 2011; Clytemnestra, 2012; Y Storm, 2012; Advantages of the Older Man, 2014; Quantum Poetics, 2015; Medeia, 2016; Treiglo, 2017; *translation:* (with Rowan Williams) The Book of Taliesin, 2019. *E:* gl@gwynethlewis.com.

LEWIS, Helen Alexandra; staff writer, The Atlantic, since 2019; *b* Worcester, 1983; *d* of Reginald Lewis and Jonathan Paul Haynes. *Educ:* St Mary's Convent Sch., Worcester; St Peter's Coll., Oxford (BA 1st Cl. Hons Eng. Lang. and Lit. 2004; MA); City Univ., London (Postgrad. Dip. Newspaper Journalism 2005); Open Univ. (MA (Dist.) Eng. Lit. 2011). Graduate trainee, 2005, a sub-editor, 2006–10, a jun. commng editor, Features Desk, 2009–10, Daily Mail; Asst Editor, 2010–12, Dep. Editor, 2012–19, New Statesman. Chair, Nia—Ending Violence Against Women, 2014–17. Women in the Humanities Hon. Writing Fellow, Univ. of Oxford, 2018–19. *Recreation:* more work. *E:* helenlewisbook@gmail.com.

LEWIS, Huw George; Member (Lab) Merthyr Tydfil and Rhymney, National Assembly for Wales, 1999–2016; *b* 17 Jan. 1964; *m* 1996, Lynne Neagle, *qv*; two *s. Educ:* Edinburgh Univ. (BSc Hons Chemistry). Teacher, N Berwick High Sch., and Bathgate Acad., 1987–90; House of Commons Researcher, 1990–91; Teacher, Afon Taf High Sch., 1991–94; Asst Gen. Sec., Wales Labour Party, 1994–99. National Assembly for Wales: Dep. Minister for Social Justice and Regeneration, 2003–07, for Regeneration, 2007, for Children, 2009–11; Minister for Housing, Regeneration and Heritage, 2011–13, for Communities and Tackling Poverty, 2013, for Educn and Skills, 2013–16. *Publications:* To Hear the Skylark's Song: a memoir of Aberfan, 2017.

LEWIS, Ivan; MP for Bury South, since 1997 (Lab, 1997–2018; Ind, since 2018); *b* 4 March 1967; *s* of Joel and Gloria Lewis; *m* (marr. diss.); two *s. Educ:* William Hulme's Grammar Sch.; Stand Coll.; Bury Coll. of FE. Co-ordinator, Contact Community Care Gp, 1986–89; Jewish Social Services: Community Worker, 1989–91; Community Care Manager, 1991–92; Chief Exec., 1992–97. Mem., Bury MBC, 1990–98. PPS to Sec. of State for Trade and Industry, 1999–2001; Parly Under-Sec. of State, DfES, 2001–05; Econ. Sec., HM Treasury, 2005–06; Parliamentary Under-Secretary of State: for Care Services, DoH, 2006–08; DFID, 2008–09; Minister of State, FCO, 2009–10; Shadow Sec. of State for Culture, Media and Sport, 2010–11, for Internat. Develt, 2011–13, for NI, 2013–15. Member: H of C Deregulation Select Cttee, 1997–99; Health Select Cttee, 1999; Internat. Develt Cttee, 2017–; Sec., All Party Parly Gp on Parenting, 1998–2001; Vice Chm., Inter-Parly Council Against Anti-Semitism, 1998–2001. Trustee, Holocaust Educnl Trust. *Recreation:* supporter of Manchester City FC. *Address:* House of Commons, SW1A 0AA; 11 Deansgate, Radcliffe, Manchester M26 2SH. *E:* ivan.lewis.mp@parliament.uk. *W:* www.ivanlewis.org.uk.

LEWIS, Hon. James Thomas; QC 2002; a Recorder, since 2000; a Deputy High Court Judge, since 2013; Chief Justice of the Falkland Islands and the British Indian Ocean Territory, since 2018; a Judge of the Supreme Court of South Georgia and the South Sandwich Islands, and of the British Antarctic Territory, since 2018; *b* 8 Feb. 1958; *s* of Benjamin Ivor and Katherine Lewis; *m* 1985, Kathleen Mary Gallacher; one *s* two *d. Educ:* St John Fisher Sch., Purley; Kingston Poly. (BSc Hons); City Univ., London (DipLaw). Univ. of London OTC, 1977–80; Commnd 2nd Lieut, 1979; Royal Yeo., 1980–82; RARO, 1982–86, 1993–; HAC, 1986–93. Called to the Bar, Gray's Inn, 1987, Bencher, 2007; Attorney General's List, 2000. An Election Comr, 2016–; Internat. Observer, Kazakhstan Elections, 2016. Mem., Criminal Cttee, Judicial Studies Bd, 2008–12. Kt Comdr, Order of St Maurice and St Lazarus (Italy), 2009. *Recreations:* ski-ing, clay pigeon shooting, tennis. *Address:* 3 Raymond Buildings, Gray's Inn, WC1R 5BH. *T:* (020) 7400 6400. *Clubs:* Honourable Artillery Company, Garrick.

LEWIS, Prof. Jane Elizabeth, PhD; FBA 2004; FRSC; Professor of Social Policy, London School of Economics, 2004–16, now Emeritus; *b* 14 April 1950; *d* of Hedley Lewis and Dorothy Lewis (*née* Beck); *m* 1971, Mark Shrimpton. *Educ:* Reading Univ. (BA Hons 1971); Univ. of Western Ontario (PhD 1979). Department of Social Policy and Administration, London School of Economics: Lectr, 1979–87; Reader, 1987–91; Prof., 1991–96; Fellow of All Souls Coll., and Dir, Wellcome Unit for the Hist. of Medicine, Oxford, 1996–98; Prof. of Social Policy, Nottingham Univ., 1998–2000; Barnett Prof. of Social Policy and Fellow, St Cross Coll., Oxford, 2000–04. FRSC 1995. *Publications:* The Politics of Motherhood: child and maternal welfare in England 1900–1939, 1980; (ed) Women's Welfare/Women's Rights, 1983; Women in England, 1870–1950: sexual divisions and social change, 1984; (ed) Labour and Love: women's experience of home and family 1850–1950, 1986; (ed jtly) Women and Offshore Oil in Britain, Canada and Norway, 1987; (ed) Before the Vote was Won, 1987; (jtly) Daughters Who Care: daughters looking after mothers at home, 1988; (ed jtly) The Goals of Social Policy, 1989; Women and Social Action in Victorian and Edwardian England, 1991; Women in Britain since 1945: women, family and work in the post-war years, 1992; (jtly) Whom God Hath Joined: marriage and the marital agencies 1930–1990, 1992; (ed) Women and Social Policies in Europe, 1993; The Voluntary Sector, the State and Social Work in Britain, 1995; (ed jtly) Comparing Social Welfare Systems in Europe, vol. I, 1995; (ed jtly) Protecting Women: labor legislation in Europe, the United States and Australia 1880–1920, 1995; (jtly) Implementing the New Community Care, 1996; (ed) Lone Mothers in European Welfare Regimes, 1998; (jtly) Lone Motherhood in Twentieth-Century Britain, 1998; The End of Marriage?, 2001; Work-family Balance, Gender and Policy, 2009; articles in jls. *Address:* Flat 2, 16 Barnsbury Square, N1 1JL.

LEWIS, His Honour Jeffrey Allan; a Circuit Judge, 2002–17; *b* 25 May 1949; *s* of late David Meyer Lewis and Esther (*née* Kirson); *m* 1985, Elizabeth Ann Swarbrick; one *s* one *d. Educ:* Univ. of the Witwatersrand (BA); Univ. of Leeds (LLB). Teacher, 1973–75; called to the Bar, Middle Temple, 1978; in practice, N Eastern Circuit, 1978–2002; Asst Recorder, 1993–97; Recorder, 1997–2002. Chm. (pt-time), Industrial Tribunals, Leeds Reg., 1991–95. *Recreations:* music, reading, gardening.

LEWIS, Sir John (Anthony), Kt 2004; OBE 1996; Principal, 1989–2006, Academy Adviser and School Improvement Partner, 2006–11, Dixons City Academy (formerly Technology College), Bradford; *b* 9 May 1946; *s* of John D. C. Lewis and Dorothy Lewis (*née* Roberts); *m* 1969, Penny Ward; three *s. Educ:* Queens' Coll., Cambridge (BA (Hist.) 1968; MA 1971); CNAA (MSc Educnl Mgt 1982). History Teacher: Northgate GS, Ipswich, 1969–73; Appleton Hall GS, Warrington, 1973–75; Culcheth High Sch., Warrington, 1975–79; Dep. Hd, Bishop Heber High Sch., Malpas, 1979–84; Head Teacher, Birchwood Community High Sch., Warrington, 1984–89. Hon. DEd Bradford, 2009. *Recreations:* sport (Cambridge soccer Blue, 1968), cricket, tennis. *E:* ja.lewis@dsl.pipex.com.

LEWIS, Ven. John Arthur; Archdeacon of Cheltenham, 1988–98, now Archdeacon Emeritus; *b* 4 Oct. 1934; *s* of Lt-Col Harry Arthur Lewis and Evaline Helen Ross Lewis; *m* 1959, Hazel Helen Jane Morris; one *s* one *d. Educ:* Jesus College, Oxford (MA); Cuddesdon College. Assistant Curate: St Mary, Prestbury, Glos 1960–63; Wimborne Minster, 1963–66; Rector, Eastington with Frocester, 1966–70; Vicar of Nailsworth, 1970–78; Vicar of Cirencester, 1978–88; RD of Cirencester, 1984–88. Hon. Canon, 1985–88, Canon, 1988–98, Canon Emeritus, 1998–, Gloucester Cathedral. Hon. Chaplain, Glos Constabulary, 1988–98. Chairman: Diocesan Stewardship Cttee, 1988–96; Diocesan Redundant Church Uses Cttee, 1988–98; Diocesan Bd of Educn, 1990–98. Mem. Council, Cheltenham Ladies' Coll., 1992–97. *Recreations:* travel, music, walking, gardening. *Address:* 5 Vilverie Mead, Bishops Cleeve, Cheltenham, Glos GL52 7YY. *T:* (01242) 678425.

LEWIS, John Elliott, MA; Head Master, Eton College, 1994–2002; *b* 23 Feb. 1942; *s* of John Derek Lewis and Margaret Helen (*née* Shaw); *m* 1968, Vibeke Lewis (*née* Johansson). *Educ:* King's College, Auckland, NZ; Corpus Christi Coll., Cambridge (Girdlers' Company Schol.; MA Classics). Assistant Master, King's Coll., Auckland, 1964, 1966–70; Jun. Lecturer in Classics, Auckland Univ., 1965; Asst Master, 1971–80, Master in College, 1975–80, Eton College; Head Master, Geelong Grammar Sch., Australia, 1980–94.

LEWIS, Sir John (Henry James), Kt 2019; OBE 2004; Consultant, Eversheds, since 1995; Chairman, Photo-Me International Plc, since 2010; *b* Reigate, 12 July 1940; *s* of Leonard Lewis, QC and Rita Jeanette Lewis (*née* Stone); *m* 1984, Susan Frances Merton; two *s* two *d. Educ:* Shrewsbury Sch.; University Coll., London (LLB Hons). Admitted as solicitor, 1966. Chm., Cliveden Plc, 1984–2002; non-exec. Dir, Prime People Plc, 2001–. Mem. Bd, British Tourist Authy, 1990–96. Chm., Public Monuments and Sculpture Assoc., 2013–. Chairman of Trustees: Attingham Trust for Study of Historic Houses and Collections, 1990–; Wallace Collection, 1997–2004; Hertford Hse Trust, 2004–14; Trustee: Burlington Mag., until 2008; Henry Moore Foundn, until 2008; Watts Gall., until 2008; Historic Houses Assoc., until 2008; London Trust for Overseas Graduates, until 2008. *Recreations:* architecture, sculpture, tennis. *Address:* Shute House, Donhead St Mary, Shaftesbury, Dorset SP7 9DG. *T:* (01747) 828866, (020) 7730 5420. *E:* mail@jhjlewis.com. *Clubs:* Garrick, Brooks's.

LEWIS, Rt Rev. (John Hubert) Richard; Bishop of St Edmundsbury and Ipswich, 1997–2007; *b* 10 Dec. 1943; *s* of John Wilfred and Winifred Mary Lewis; *m* 1968, Sara Patricia Hamilton; two *s* (and one *s* decd). *Educ:* Radley; King's Coll., London (AKC). Curate of Hexham, 1967–70; Industrial Chaplain, Diocese of Newcastle, 1970–77; Communications Officer, Diocese of Durham, 1977–82; Agricultural Chaplain, Diocese of Hereford, 1982–87; Archdeacon of Ludlow, 1987–92; Bishop Suffragan of Taunton, 1992–97. Prebendary, Wells Cathedral, 1992–97. Nat. Chm., Small Farmers' Assoc., 1984–88. Mem., Gen. Synod of C of E, 1987–92. *Publications:* (ed jtly) The People, the Land and the Church, 1987; Sampans and Saffron Cake, 2012. *Recreations:* bricklaying, bumble bees, kit car building.

LEWIS, John Simon Carl, FSA; General Secretary and Chief Executive, Society of Antiquaries of London, since 2010; *b* Three Crosses, Swansea, 19 March 1962; *s* of late Ivor Lewis and of Mary Lewis (*née* Grinter); *m* 1991, Catherine Rogers; two *s* one *d. Educ:*

Gowerton Comprehensive Sch.; Univ. of London Inst. of Archaeol. (BSc Hons). FSA 2005. Museum of London: Sites and Monuments Record Officer, 1984–86; Sen. Archaeologist, 1986–96; Project Manager, 1996; Wessex Archaeology: Project Manager, 1996–2000; Hd, Framework Archaeol. Jt Venture, 2000–10. *Publications:* contrib. articles to learned jls and monographs. *Recreations:* playing hockey, watching Association Football (Swansea and Arsenal), reading, walking, cooking. *Address:* Society of Antiquaries of London, Burlington House, Piccadilly, W1J 0BE. *T:* (020) 7479 7093, *Fax:* (020) 7287 6967. *E:* jlewis@sal.org.uk. *Clubs:* Salisbury Hockey, Ashford (Middx) Hockey.

**LEWIS, Rt Hon. Dr Julian (Murray);** PC 2015; MP (C) New Forest East, since 1997; *b* 26 Sept. 1951; *s* of late Samuel Lewis, tailor and designer, and Hilda Lewis. *Educ:* Dynevor Grammar Sch., Swansea; Balliol Coll., Oxford (MA 1977); St Antony's Coll., Oxford (DPhil 1981). Sec., Oxford Union, 1972. Seaman, RNR, 1979–82. Res. in defence studies, 1975–77, 1978–81; Sec., Campaign for Representative Democracy, 1977–78; Res. Dir and Dir, Coalition for Peace Through Security, 1981–85; Dir, Policy Res. Associates, 1985–; Dep. Dir, Cons. Res. Dept, 1990–96. Contested (C) Swansea W, 1983. Opposition Whip, 2001–02; Shadow Defence Minister, 2002–04, 2005–10; Shadow Minister for the Cabinet Office, 2004–05. Member: Select Cttee on Welsh Affairs, 1998–2001; Select Cttee on Defence, 2000–01 and 2014– (Chm., 2015–); Exec., 1922 Cttee, 2001; Intelligence and Security Cttee, 2010–15; Sec., Cons. Parly Defence Cttee, 1997–2001; Vice-Chairman: Cons. Parly Foreign Affairs Cttee, 2000–01; Cons. Parly European Affairs Cttee, 2000–01. Parly Chm., First Defence, 2004–09. Mem., Armed Forces Parly Scheme (RAF), 1998, 2000, (RN), 2004, (RCDS), 2006, (Jt Services), 2008. Vis. Sen. Res. Fellow, Centre for Defence Studies, Dept of War Studies, KCL, 2010–. Trustee, 1998–2001, Vice-Pres., 2001–07, Pres., 2007–09, British Military Powerboat Trust; Pres., Calshot Assoc., 2017–. Jt Patron, Pilgrim Bandits Charity, 2016–. Trench Gascoigne Essay Prize, RUSI, 2005 and 2007; Dissertation Prize, RCDS, 2006. *Publications:* Changing Direction: British military planning for post-war strategic defence 1942–47, 1988, 2nd edn 2003; Who's Left?: an index of Labour MPs and left-wing causes 1985–1992, 1992; Labour's CND Cover-up, 1992; Racing Ace: the fights and flights of 'Kink' Kinkead, DSO, DSC★, DFC★, 2011; political pamphlets. *Recreations:* history, fiction, films, music, photography. *Address:* House of Commons, SW1A 0AA. *T:* (020) 7219 4179. *Clubs:* Athenæum; Totton Conservative.

**LEWIS, Katherine Harriet;** *see* Thorne, K. H.

**LEWIS, Sir Leigh (Warren),** KCB 2007 (CB 2000); Permanent Secretary, Department for Work and Pensions, 2005–10; *b* 17 March 1951; *s* of Harold and Ray Rene Lewis; *m* 1973, Susan Evelyn Gold; two *s*. *Educ:* Harrow County Grammar Sch. for Boys; Liverpool Univ. (BA Hons 1973). MIPD. Dept of Employment, 1973; Private Sec. to Parly Under Sec. of State, 1975–76; Incomes and Indust. Relations Divs, 1978–84; Principal Private Sec. to Minister without Portfolio and Sec. of State for Employment, 1984–86; Asst Sec., EC Br., 1986–87; Dir of Ops, Unemployment Benefit Service, 1987–88; Group Dir of Personnel, Cable and Wireless plc, 1988–91 (on secondment); Dir, Internat. Div., 1991–94; Dir, Finance and Resource Mgt Div., 1994–95; Dir, Finance, DfEE, 1995–96; Chief Executive: Employment Service, DfEE, then DWP, 1997–2002; Jobcentre Plus, DWP, 2002–03; Perm. Sec., Crime, Policing, Counter-Terrorism and Delivery, Home Office, 2003–05. Chm., UK Bill of Rights Commn, 2011–12. Non-exec. Dir, Ombudsman Service Ltd, 2016–. Chairman, Board of Trustees: Broadway, 2011–14; DrinkAware, 2014–; Vice Chm., Bd of Trustees, St Mungo's (formerly St Mungo's Broadway), 2014–18 (Hon. Vice Pres., 2018); Trustee, Holocaust Meml Day Trust, 2017– (Vice Chm., 2018–). Vis. Fellow, Univ. of Greenwich, 2012–. *Publications:* (with John Hutton) How to be a Minister: a 21st-century guide, 2014. *Recreation:* Watford Football Club. *E:* leighwlewis@yahoo.com.

**LEWIS, Lennox Claudius,** CM 1988; CBE 2002 (MBE 1998); professional boxer, 1989–2004; *b* 2 Sept. 1965; *s* of Violet Blake; *m* 2005, Violet Chang; one *s* two *d*. World jun. heavyweight champion, 1983; Olympic heavyweight champion (rep. Canada), 1988; European heavyweight champion, 1990; British heavyweight champion, 1991; WBC world heavyweight champion, 1993, 1997, 2002–04; undisputed world heavyweight champion, 1999, 2001–02; world heavyweight champion, 2000. Boxing commentator, HBO, 2006–10. Founder: Lennox Lewis Coll., Hackney, London, 1994; Lennox Lewis Family Foundn. DUniv N London, 1999. Inducted into Internat. Boxing Hall of Fame, NY, 2009. *Publications:* Lennox Lewis (autobiog.), 1993, 2nd edn 1997; (jtly) Lennox (autobiog.), 2002. *Recreations:* chess, golf, reading, listening to music.

**LEWIS, Lucy Jane;** *see* Carpenter, L. J.

**LEWIS, Marilyn;** Director, Cadw, 2005–14; *b* 29 Aug. 1954; *d* of Thomas and Jacqueline Clements; *m* 1979, David Lewis. *Educ:* Univ. of Manchester (BA Hons Medieval Studies 1975); Univ. of Bangor (DAA 1976); Liverpool John Moores Univ. (MBA 1995); Aberystwyth Univ. (MA (Dist.) Medieval Welsh Lit. 2017). Asst Archivist, Suffolk CC, 1976–78; Bor. Archivist, Walsall, 1978–87; City Archivist, Chester CC, 1987–97; Shropshire County Council: Hd, Heritage, 1997–2000; Asst Dir, Cultural Services, 2000–05. *Publications:* The Book of Walsall, 1986. *Recreations:* castles, wildlife, Aston Villa Football Club, Madagascar.

**LEWIS, Mark;** Partner, Patron Law, since 2019; *b* Radcliffe, 10 Dec. 1964; *s* of Brian Ellis Aaron Lewis and Elaine Lewis. *Educ:* William Hulme Grammar Sch.; Middlesex Poly. (LLB Hons Law); Chester Law Sch.; Manchester Metropolitan Univ. (Dip. Commercial Litigation). Admitted as solicitor, 1990; Partner: George Davies, 2001–09; Stripes Solicitors, 2009–10; Consultant, 2010–11, Partner, 2011–15, Taylor Hampton; Partner, Seddons Solicitors, 2015–18. Dir, UK Lawyers For Israel, 2014–. Member: Lawyers for Media Standards, 2010–; Law Soc., 1990–. Hon. Dr Middlesex, 2018. *Recreations:* veteran and vintage cars, fashion, music, theatre, Middle Eastern politics. *Address:* Patron Law, 2A Norland Place, Holland Park, W11 4QG.

**LEWIS, Martin John;** Director of Library Services and University Librarian, University of Sheffield, 2003–15; *b* Cardiff, 9 April 1955; *s* of John and Betty Lewis; *m* 1986, Susan Elizabeth Smith; one *d*. *Educ:* Duffryn High Sch., Newport, Wales; Fitzwilliam Coll., Cambridge (BA Natural Scis 1976); Univ. of Wales, Aberystwyth (Postgrad. DipLib). MCLIP 1981. Asst Librarian, Univ. of Leeds, 1978–86; Health Scis Librarian, 1986–94, Dep. Librarian, 1994–2002, Univ. of Sheffield. Vis. Librarian, MIT, 1984–85. Member: Bd, Res. Libraries UK, 2004–10; Adv. Council, BL, 2005–12. Mem. Council, Univ. of Sheffield, 2008–14. *Publications:* contrib. papers to librarianship and information sci. jls, and conf. proceedings. *Recreations:* hill walking, travel, modern architecture.

**LEWIS, Martin Steven,** OBE 2014; broadcaster and newspaper columnist, since 2000; Money Saving Expert, MoneySavingExpert.com, since 2003; *b* Manchester, 9 May 1972; *s* of Stuart Lewis and late Susan Lewis; *m* 2009, Lara Lewington; one *d*. *Educ:* London Sch. of Econs (BSc Econ 1994); Cardiff Sch. of Journalism (Postgrad. Dip. Broadcast Journalism 1998). Gen. Sec., LSE Students' Union, 1994–95; Account Exec., Brunswick PR, 1995–97; Reporter/Producer, BBC Business Unit, 1998–99; Business Corresp., then Money Saving Expert, Simply Money TV, 2000–01; columnist: Sunday Express, 2001–05; Guardian, 2005–06; Sunday Times, 2006–07; Sunday Post, 2007–14; News of the World, 2008–11; Daily Telegraph, 2009–17; Sunday Mirror, 2014–; Financial Times, 2017–; television: Money Saving Expert: This Morning, 2003–05, 2012–; GMTV, 2006–10; Daybreak, 2010–14; Good Morning Britain, 2014–; presenter: Make Me Rich, 2005; It Pays to Watch, 2008; The Martin Lewis Money Show, 2012–; reporter, Tonight, 2006; contributor: Jeremy Vine Show, BBC Radio 2, 2005–; Radio 5 Lunch Money Martin (formerly Consumer Panel), 2010–. Chm., Ind. Taskforce on Student Finance Communication, 2011–13; Member: Ind. Panel, Money Advice Service, 2015–16; Financial Inclusion Policy Forum, 2018–. Chm., MSE charity, 2008–; Founder and Chm. Trustees, Money and Mental Health Policy Inst., 2016–; works with John Schofield Trust's Young Journalist Mentee Scheme, 2017–; Patron: Grief Encounter, 2015–; Personal Support Unit, 2017–; Social Mobility Business Partnership, 2018–. Gov., LSE, 2009–. Hon. DBA Chester, 2013; DUniv Open, 2016; Hon. DArts Leeds Beckett, 2016. *Publications:* The Money Diet, 2004, 2nd edn 2005; Thrifty Ways for Modern Days, 2006; The Three Most Important Lessons, 2008. *Recreations:* trying to get my average Scrabble score above 410 (currently 407) and to run over 2,000km per year, reading historic novels, very poor golf, anything with lists. *W:* www.moneysavingexpert.com.

**LEWIS, Sir Martyn (John Dudley),** Kt 2016; CBE 1997; journalist, broadcaster and businessman; Director, PL Education Ltd (formerly TS Elite Group Ltd), since 2014; Executive Chairman, YourBigDay Ltd, since 2016; *b* 7 April 1945; *s* of late Thomas John Dudley Lewis and Doris (*née* Jones); *m* 1st, 1970, Elizabeth Anne Carse (*d* 2012); two *d*; 2nd, 2012, Patsy St Clair Baker. *Educ:* Dalriada Sch., Ballymoney, NI; Trinity Coll., Dublin (BA 1967). Reporter: BBC, Belfast, 1967–68; HTV, Cardiff, 1968–70; Independent Television News: reporter, 1970–86; Head, Northern Bureau, 1971–78; presenter, News at Ten, 1981–86; Presenter: BBC One O'Clock News, 1986–87; BBC Nine O'Clock News, 1987–94; BBC TV Six O'Clock News, 1994–99; Today's the Day, BBC2, 1993–99; Crimebeat, 1996–98; Agenda, The Wireless (Age UK radio), 2012–18. Documentaries include: Battle for the Falklands; The Secret Hunters; Fight Cancer; Living with Dying; Great Ormond Street—a Fighting Chance; Health UK; A Century to Remember; series for ITV: Bethlehem—Year Zero, 1999; Dateline Jerusalem, 2000; News 40, 2000; Ultimate Questions, 2000–02. Mem. Bd, IPSO, 2014–18. Dir, Drive for Youth, 1986–99 (Chm., 1990–99); Chm. and Founder, YouthNet UK, 1995–2014, Founder at Large, 2014–16; Co-Founder and Chairman: Global Intercasting Ltd, 1999–2007; Teliris Ltd, 2001–12; Chm., NICE TV Ltd, 2005–12; EU Chm., Teliris Inc., 2007–12. Chm., Beacon Fellowship, 2005–07. Advr, Ogden Educnl Trust, 2000–11. Member: Policy Adv. Cttee, Tidy Britain Gp, 1988–98; Volunteer Partnership (govt cttee), 1995–97; Internat. Adv. Cttee, RADA, 2007–11; Ext. Adv. Bd, Long Room Hub, TCD, 2009–11; Team London Adv. Bd, 2013–15; Bd Advr, Fountain Partnership Ltd, 2013–. Director: Hospice Arts, 1989–97; CLIC UK, 1990–96; Adopt-A-Student, 1988–96; Inst. for Citizenship Studies, 1993–97; Friends of Nelson Mandela Children's Fund, 1997–2002; President: United Response, 1989–; George Thomas Centre for Hospice Care, 1996–2005; Fixers, 2016–; Vice-President: Macmillan Cancer Support (formerly Cancer Relief Macmillan Fund, then Macmillan Cancer Relief), 1988– (Dir, 1990–96); Marie Curie Cancer Care, 1990–; Hospice UK (formerly Help the Hospices), 1990–; British Soviet Hospice Soc., 1990–96; Demelza House Children's Hospice, 1996–; Voices for Hospices, 1996–2011; East Anglia Children's Hospices, 1999–; Barrett's Oesophagus Campaign, 2000–; Chairman: Families of the Fallen, 2010–15; NCVO, 2010–16; Commn on Donor Experience, 2016–17; Civil Soc. Implementation Gp, DCMS, 2017–18; Trustee: Windsor Leadership Trust, 2001–10; Edutrust, 2008–10; Patron: London Lighthouse, 1990–99; SW Children's Hospice, 1991–2007; Internat. Sch. for Cancer Care, 1991–99; Hope House Children's Hospice, 1992–2007; Cities in Schools, 1995–97 (Dir, 1989–95); Tomorrow Project, 1996–2007; Dementia UK (formerly Dementia Relief Trust, then For Dementia), 1998–; James Powell (UK) Trust, 1998–2007; Mildmay Mission Hosp., 1998–2010; Volunteering England (formerly Nat. Centre for Volunteering), 1998–2012; Patchwork Foundn, 2013–; Positive News, 2013–; Ambassador, Pennies, 2015–. Chair, Award Cttee, Queen's Award for Voluntary Service, 2009–; Dep. Chair, Lord Mayor of London's Dragon Awards, 2010–18. Mem., BAFTA, 1980–. Freeman, City of London, 1989; Liveryman, Pattenmakers' Co., 1989–. FRSA 1990. Hon. DLitt Ulster, 1994. *Publications:* And Finally, 1983; Tears and Smiles—the Hospice Handbook, 1989; Cats in the News, 1991 (trans. Japanese 1994); Dogs in the News, 1992 (trans. Japanese 1996); Go For It: Martyn Lewis's essential guide to opportunities for young people (annual), 1993–97, as Book of the Site, 1998–99; Reflections on Success, 1997; Seasons of our Lives, 1999. *Recreations:* photography, good food, keeping fit. *T:* 07836 570405. *E:* martyn@martynlewis.tv, martyn.lewis@yourbigday.tv. *Club:* Garrick.

**LEWIS, Mary Elizabeth, (Mrs N. Woolley);** Director General, International Federation of Purchasing and Supply Management, 2012–13; *b* 29 Dec. 1952; *d* of Kenneth Richard Lewis and Joan Lewis; *m* 1988, Nicholas Woolley. *Educ:* St Angela's Convent, Harringay; University Coll. of Wales, Aberystwyth (BA Hons English 1975). CDipAF 1991. FCIHT (FIHT 2006). Asst Sec., 1987–94, Dir, Finance and Personnel, 1994–98, CIB; Exec. Sec., Physiol Soc., 1999–2001; Chief Exec., Chartered Instn of Highways and Transportation (formerly Instn of Highways and Transportation), 2001–11. Trustee, Rees Jeffreys Road Fund, 2013–. *Recreations:* embroidery, gardening, music, travel, running a smallholding. *Address:* Manor Farm, East Ilkerton, Barbrook, Lynton, Devon EX35 6PH. *T:* (01598) 752113.

**LEWIS, Most Rev. Michael Augustine Owen;** *see* Cyprus and the Gulf, Bishop in.

**LEWIS, Michael David;** Director, Avenue53 Consulting (strategy, communications and broadcasting consultancy), since 2009; *b* 5 June 1947; *s* of late David Lloyd Lewis and Gwendoline Lewis; *m* 1992, Hilary Anne East; two *d*. *Educ:* Erith Grammar Sch., Kent. Dartford Reporter newspaper, 1966–70; Brighton Evening Argus, 1970–73; LBC/Independent Radio News, 1973–82; BBC Radio Sport: Duty Editor, 1982–83; Dep. Editor, 1983–84; Editor, 1984–91; Head of Sport and Outside Broadcasts, 1991–93; Dep. Controller, BBC Radio 5 Live, 1994–2000; Controller, Radio Sports Rights, BBC Sport, 1996–2007; broadcasting consultant, 2007–14; AELTC: Dep. Broadcast Manager, 2010–14; Broadcast Ops Manager, 2015–17; Broadcast Liaison Manager, 2018–19. *Recreations:* watching Arsenal through gritted teeth, helping two daughters make their way in the world, enjoying live theatre and dance, helping the Lord's Taverners raise money. *Address:* 53 Wallingford Avenue, W10 6PZ. *T:* 07850 762259.

**LEWIS, Pamela;** *see* Cameron, Pamela.

**LEWIS, Paul Arthur;** freelance financial journalist, broadcaster, author and speaker; *b* 22 April 1948; *s* of late William Denis Lewis and Betty Blanche Lewis; *m* 1st, 1969, Eileen Margaret Tame (marr. diss. 2002); two *s* one *d*; 2nd, 2014, Emma Sheila Lynch. *Educ:* Univ. of Stirling (BA Psychology, MSc Res. Psychology 1972). Dep. Dir, Nat. Council for One Parent Families, 1976–83; Dir, Youthaid, 1983–86; Money Corresp., Saga Magazine, 1984–; Presenter, BBC: Wake Up To Money, Radio Five Live, 1998–2000; Money Box, Radio 4, 2000–; contrib., BBC Breakfast, 2008–. Chm., Nat. Right to Fuel Campaign, 1975–81; Gov., Pensions Policy Inst., 2002–. Sec., Wilkie Collins Soc., 1996–. Mem., Maidstone BC, 1974–84. DUniv Essex, 2013. *Publications:* Saga Rights Guide, 1988; Saga Money Guide, 1988; Your Taxes and Savings, 2002, 4th edn 2005; The Complete Money Plan, 2004; Money Magic, 2005; (ed jtly) The Public Face of

Wilkie Collins, 2005; Live Long and Prosper, 2006; Understanding Taxes and Savings, 2006; Pay Less Tax (annually), 2007–09; Beat the Banks, 2008; Making Your Money Work, 2008; Can You Claim It? (annually), 2010–; contrib. to The Dickensian, Reader's Digest, Daily Telegraph, Radio Times, TES, Community Care, Good Homes, PensionDCisions, The Oldie, Heathrow Express, Money Marketing, Financial Times. *Recreations:* annoying financial companies, making bad jokes, Wilkie Collins. *E:* paul@paullewis.co.uk. *T:* 07836 217311. *W:* www.paullewis.co.uk, www.paullewismoney.blogspot.com, www.twitter.com/paullewismoney.

**LEWIS, Paul Keith;** QC 2001; a Recorder, since 2000; *b* 26 May 1957; *s* of late John Keith Lewis and of Susan Patricia Lewis (*née* Cronin); *m* 1983, Siân Price; one *s* one *d*. *Educ:* Pontypridd Grammar Sch. for Boys; Univ. of Leicester (LLB Hons); Inns of Court Sch. of Law. Called to the Bar, Gray's Inn, 1981, Bencher, 2014; in practice, Cardiff and London, 1981–; an Asst Recorder, 1998–2000; Leader, Wales and Chester Circuit, 2014–16. *Recreations:* sport, travel, music. *Address:* Farrar's Building, Temple, EC4Y 7BD. *T:* (020) 7583 9241, *Fax:* (020) 7583 0090. *E:* chambers@farrarsbuilding.co.uk. *Club:* Monmouthshire Golf (Abergavenny).

**LEWIS, Prof. Penney Jaye,** JD; Professor of Law, since 2007, and Co-Director, Centre of Medical Law and Ethics, since 2013, King's College London; *b* London, 3 Nov. 1967; *d* of Alan Michael Lewis and Frumie Lewis (*née* Davson). *Educ:* Havergal Coll., Toronto; Massachusetts Inst. of Technol. (SB Maths 1989); Univ. of Toronto (JD 1992); King's Coll. London (MA Med. Ethics and Law 1994); Columbia Univ. (LLM 1995). Law Clerk, Supreme Court of Canada, 1992–93; Lectr, 1995–2005, Reader, 2005–07, in Law, KCL. Barrister and solicitor, Law Soc. of Upper Canada, 2000–. Member: UK Donation Ethics Cttee, 2010–16; Human Tissue Authy, 2016–; Nat. Res. and Ethics Advrs' Panel, Health Res. Authy, 2017–; Genomics England Ethics Adv. Cttee, 2018–; Law Comr for Criminal Law, Law Commn, 2020–. *Publications:* Delayed Prosecution for Childhood Sexual Abuse, 2006; Assisted Dying and Legal Change, 2007. *Recreations:* travel, languages, theatre, art, music. *Address:* Dickson Poon School of Law, King's College London, Strand, WC2R 2LS. *T:* (020) 7848 1103. *E:* penney.lewis@kcl.ac.uk.

**LEWIS, Peter;** Director, Policy Co-ordination Unit, 1994–96, and the Tax Simplification Project, 1995–96, Inland Revenue; *b* 24 June 1937; *s* of Reginald George and Edith Lewis; *m* 1962, Ursula Brigitte Kilian; one *s* one *d*. *Educ:* Ealing Grammar School; St Peter's Hall, Oxford. Royal Navy, 1955–57. Inland Revenue Inspector of Taxes, 1960–69; Inland Revenue Policy and Central Divs, 1969–85; Director: Personal Tax Div., 1986–91; Company Tax Div., 1991–95. *Address:* Glyndavas, 9 Waterloo Close, St Mawes, Cornwall TR2 5BD.

**LEWIS, Peter Adrian;** Director, StubbsStorey Ltd, 2012–16; *b* 9 Feb. 1954; *s* of Mrs Beryl Williams; *m* 1976, Lynn Cook. *Educ:* Madeley Coll., Keele (Cert Ed); Bristol Poly. (BEd). Teacher, Eastwood Middle Sch., Stoke on Trent, 1975–77; social worker, Staffs, Avon and Hants, 1977–88; Educn Officer, Hants CC, 1988–96; Asst Dir, Educn and Leisure Services, Southampton CC, 1996–2004; Dir, Educn, Children's Services and Leisure, 2004–09, Dep. Chief Exec., 2008–09, Enfield LBC; Dir, Children's Services, Haringey LBC, 2009–11; Interim Dir, Children's Services, Somerset CC, 2013–14. *Recreations:* opera, reading, walking, travel.

**LEWIS, Peter Tyndale;** Chairman, John Lewis Partnership, 1972–93; *b* 26 Sept. 1929; *s* of Oswald Lewis and Frances Merriman Lewis (*née* Cooper); *m* 1st, 1961, Deborah Anne (*d* 2014), *d* of late Sir William (Alexander Roy) Collins, CBE and Priscilla Marian, *d* of late S. J. Lloyd; one *s* one *d*; 2nd, 2017, Mary Angela Philippa Anderson (*née* Wellesley-Colley), *widow* of David Anderson. *Educ:* Eton; Christ Church, Oxford (MA 1953). National service, Coldstream Guards, 1948–49; called to Bar (Middle Temple) 1956; joined John Lewis Partnership, 1959. Member: Council, Industrial Soc., 1968–79; Design Council, 1971–74; Chm., Retail Distributors' Assoc., 1972. Member: Southampton Univ. Develt Trust, 1994–2003; Council, Queen's Coll., Harley St, 1994–99. Trustee, Jt Educnl Trust, 1985–87. Governor: NIESR, 1983; Windlesham Hse Sch., 1979–95; The Bell Educnl Trust, 1987–97. *Address:* 145 Rivermead Court, SW6 3SE.

**LEWIS, Rhodri Price;** QC 2001; a Recorder, since 1998; a Deputy High Court Judge, since 2013; *b* 7 June 1952; *s* of George Lewis and Nansi Lewis (*née* Price); *m* 1983, Barbara Sinden; two *d*. *Educ:* Ysgol Gymraeg Ynyswen; Cowbridge Grammar Sch.; Pembroke Coll., Oxford (MA); Sidney Sussex Coll., Cambridge (Dip. Criminol.). Called to the Bar, Middle Temple, 1975, Bencher, 2016. An Asst Parly Boundary Comr, 2003–; an Election Comr, 2016–. A legal chm., police misconduct inquiries in Wales, 2016–. *Publications:* Environmental Law, 2000; contrib. to Jl Planning and Envmt Law. *Recreations:* Rugby, playing the guitar, enjoying the company, coast and country of Pembrokeshire. *Address:* Landmark Chambers, 180 Fleet Street, EC4A 2HG. *Clubs:* Garrick, London Welsh Rugby Football; St David's Rugby Football.

**LEWIS, Rhydian;** *see* Lewis, A. R.

**LEWIS, Rt Rev. Richard;** *see* Lewis, Rt Rev. J. H. R.

**LEWIS, Very Rev. Richard;** Dean of Wells, 1990–2003, now Emeritus; *b* 24 Dec. 1935; *m* 1959, Jill Diane Wilford; two *s*. *Educ:* Royal Masonic Sch.; Fitzwilliam House, Cambridge (BA 1958; MA 1961); Ripon Hall, Oxford. Asst Curate, Hinckley, Leicester, 1960–63; Priest-in-Charge, St Edmund, Riddlesdown, 1964–66; Vicar: All Saints, South Merstham, 1966–72; Holy Trinity and St Peter, Wimbledon, 1972–79; St Barnabas, Dulwich and Foundation Chaplain of Alleyn's College of God's Gift at Dulwich, 1979–90. *Publications:* (contrib.) Cathedrals Now, 1996; (contrib.) Wells Cathedral, 2005. *Recreations:* music of all sorts, gardening, reading, tapestry. *Address:* 1 Monmouth Court, Union Street, Wells, Som BA5 2PX. *T:* (01749) 672677. *E:* Dean.Richard@wellshouse.co.uk.

**LEWIS, Richard Alan,** CBE 2013; Chief Executive, All England Lawn Tennis Club (Championships) Ltd (formerly All England Lawn Tennis and Croquet Club), since 2012; *b* Winchmore Hill, London, 6 Dec. 1954; *s* of Wilfred and Marian Lewis; *m* 2005, Jan; two *s*. *Educ:* Goffs Grammar Sch. Professional tennis player and coach, 1969–87. Dir, Nat. Trng, 1987–96, Dir of Tennis, 1997–2000, LTA; Merryck & Co., 2000–02; Chm., Rugby Football League, 2002–12. Chm., Sport England, 2009–13. Chm., Major Spectator Sports Div., CCPR, 2007–09. Chm., Rugby League Eur. Fedn, 2003–12; Dep. Chm., Rugby League Internat. Fedn, 2003–12. Chm., Rev. of Young Player Develt in Professional Football, 2006–07. *Recreations:* cycling, walking, tennis, gardening. *Address:* Shepley, W Yorks. *Club:* All England Lawn Tennis.

**LEWIS, Hon. Robin William,** CVO 2015; OBE 1988; Lord-Lieutenant of Dyfed, 2006–16; *b* 7 Feb. 1941; *s* of 3rd Baron Merthyr, KBE, TD, PC, and Violet (*née* Meyrick); *m* 1967, Judith Ann Giardelli; one *s* one *d*. *Educ:* Eton; Magdalen Coll., Oxford (MA; Dip. Econ. Develt). Commonwealth Develt Corp., 1964–66; Alcan Aluminium Ltd, 1967–68; Westminster Bank Ltd, 1968–72; Develt Corp. for Wales, 1972–83; Man. Dir, Novametrix Med. Systems Ltd, 1983–90; Chairman: The Magstim Co. Ltd, 1990–2013; J. P. Morgan US Discovery Investment Trust, 2003–08. Chm., Gen. Adv. Council, IBA, 1988–90.

Chairman: NT Cttee for Wales, 1994–97; Trustees, Nat. Botanic Garden of Wales, 2006–08. High Sheriff, 1987–88, DL 2002, Dyfed. CStJ 2008. *Address:* The Cottage, Cresswell Quay, Kilgetty, Pembs SA68 0TE. *Club:* Leander (Henley-on-Thames).

**LEWIS, Roger Charles;** President, National Museum Wales, since 2019; Chairman, Racecourse Media Group, since 2019 (Director, since 2012); Group Chief Executive, Welsh Rugby Union, 2006–15; *b* 24 Aug. 1954; *s* of late Griffith Charles Job Lewis and Dorothy Lewis (*née* Russ); *m* 1980, Dr Christine Trollope; two *s*. *Educ:* Cynffig Comprehensive Sch., Bridgend; Univ. of Nottingham (BMus Hons 1976). Musician, 1976–80: Avon Touring Th. Co., 1977–79; Birmingham Rep. Th. Studio, 1978; Ludus Dance in Educn Co., 1979; Scottish Ballet Workshop Co., 1979; Music Officer, Darlington Arts Centre, 1980–82; Presenter, Radio Tees, 1981–84; Producer: Capital Radio, 1984–85; BBC Radio 1, 1985–87; Hd of Music, Radio 1, 1987–90; Dir, 1990–95, Man. Dir, 1995, Classical Div., EMI Records; Man. Dir, EMI Premier, 1995–97; Pres., Decca Record Co., 1997–98; Man. Dir and Prog. Controller, Classic FM, 1998–2004; Man. Dir, ITV Wales, 2004–06. Chm., Cardiff Internat. Airport Ltd, 2015–19; Director: GWR plc, 1998–2004; European Rugby Cup Ltd, 2007–14; Celtic Rugby Ltd, 2007–15; British and Irish Lions, 2014–15; non-exec. Dep. Chm., Boosey & Hawkes, 2004–06; non-exec. Dir, Barchester Gp, 2001–06. Chairman: Classical Cttee, British Phonographic Industry Ltd, 1996–98 (Mem., 1990–96); Music and Dance Scheme Adv. Gp, DFES (formerly DFEE), 2000–04; Arts and Business Wales, 2006; Internat. Adv. Bd, Cardiff Univ. Business Sch., 2008–18; Yes for Wales, Referendum Campaign, 2010–11; Cardiff Capital Region, 2013–15. Member: Bd, Liverpool European Capital of Culture, 2003–06; Bd, Wales Millennium Centre, 2004–06; Welsh Arts Review Panel, 2006; Adv. Bd, D Gp, 2011–18; Six Nations Rugby Council, 2012–15. Chm., Royal Liverpool Philharmonic, 2003–06; Vice-President: London Welsh Male Voice Choir, 2004–; Welsh Music Guild, 2005. Trustee: Masterprize (Internat. Composers' Competition), 1995–2010; Masterclass Charitable Trust, 2000–04; Chairman: Trustees, Ogmore Centre, 1996–2008; Classic FM Charitable Trust, 2000–04; Churchill Lines Foundn (formerly Charitable Fund), 2014–; Trustee, Inst. of Welsh Affairs, 2014–17. President: Bromley Youth Music Trust, 2000–06 (Vice-Pres., 2006–); Cefn Cribwr RFC, 2007–; Mem., Founder Partners Bd, Beacon Fellowship Awards, 2003–06. Patron, Sam Warburton Testimonial Year, 2018–19. FRSA 2000. Hon. FRWCMD 2004; Hon. RCM 2005; Hon. Fellow, Cardiff Univ., 2007. Hon. DLitt Nottingham, 2010; Hon. Dr Glamorgan, 2011. Sony Radio Award, 1987, 1988, 1989; Grand Award Winner and Gold Medal, NY Radio Fest., 1987; One World Broadcasting Trust Award, 1989; NTL Commercial Radio Programmer of the Year, 2002; Alumni Laureate Lifetime Achievement Award, Univ. of Nottingham, 2009. MStJ 2015 (Mem., St John Cymru/Wales Centenary Cttee, 2015–18). *Recreations:* music, Rugby, ski-ing, horse-riding, cycling, member of Wine Soc. *Club:* Cardiff and County.

**LEWIS, Dr Roger Clifford;** homemaker; former writer; *b* 26 Feb. 1960; *e s* of late Wyndham Gardner Lewis and Barbara Mary Lewis (*née* George), Bedwas, Monmouthshire; *m* 1982, Anna Margaret Jane Dickens, *d* of late Eric John Dickens and Iris Grace (*née* Taylor); three *s*. *Educ:* Bassaleg Comp. Sch., Newport; Univ. of St Andrews (Lawson Meml Prize, Gray Prize, Coll. Bursary, Walker Trust Award; MA 1st cl. Hons 1982); Magdalen Coll., Oxford (Charles Oldham Shakespeare Prize, Matthew Arnold Meml Prize, Chancellor's English Essay Prize; MA status 1985); Univ. of Hertfordshire (PhD 2009). University of Oxford: Jun. Res. Fellow, Wolfson Coll., 1985–89, Mem. Common Room, 1989–; Tutor, Univ. of Massachusetts Summer Sch., Trinity Coll., 1985; Lecturer and Tutor: Boston Univ. Mod. British Studies prog., St Catherine's Coll., 1986–90; Stanford Univ. and Smithsonian Instn English Lit. courses, Oxford, 1987; Lectr, Magdalen Coll., 1988. Vis. Prof., Faculty of Law, Humanities, Develt and Society, Birmingham City Univ. (formerly UCE, Birmingham), 2006–09. Arts journalism: American Scholar, American Spectator, Amorist, Areté: the arts tri-quarterly; Encounter, Erotic Review, Financial Times, GQ Magazine, Independent, The Lady, Listener, Mail on Sunday, New Statesman, Observer, Opera Now, Punch, Spectator, Sunday Times, Telegraph Mag., *etc*; lead book reviewer: Express Newspapers, 2001–09; Daily Mail, 2009–; television critic, The Oldie, 2014–. Frequent interviewee on nat. and local radio and television arts and culture progs; consultant on documentaries: Larry and Viv: the Oliviers in love, C4, 2001; The Paranormal Peter Sellers, C4, 2002; Profondo Rosa: la vera storia della Pantera Rosa, Sky Italia, 2004; Les Couples Mythiques du Cinéma, Adamis Prodns Paris, 2014. Mem., Welsh Acad., 2010–. FRAS; FRGS; FZS; FRSA. Hon. DLitt Herts, 2010. Commnd Col by Gov. of Kentucky, 2007 (Medal of Dist., 2007–09); Admiral, Gt Navy of State of Nebraska, 2007 (Scholarship Donor Medal, 2009). Observer/Anthony Burgess Prize for Arts Journalism, 2013. *Publications:* (contrib.) The New Compleat Imbiber, 1986; (ed) Rewards and Fairies, by Rudyard Kipling (Penguin Classics), 1987; Stage People, 1989; (ed) The Memoirs and Confessions of a Justified Sinner, by James Hogg (Everyman's Liby), 1992; The Life and Death of Peter Sellers, 1994, reissued 2004 (filmed 2004 (Primetime Emmy Award 2005)); The Real Life of Laurence Olivier, 1996, reissued 2007; The Man Who Was Private Widdle: Charles Hawtrey, 2001; Anthony Burgess, 2002; Seasonal Suicide Notes: my life as it is lived, 2009; What am I Still Doing Here?, 2011. *Recreation:* filling boxes with books. *Address:* 66 rue Kennedy, Barenton 50720, France. *E:* annajlewis@aol.com. *Clubs:* Groucho, English-Speaking Union; Players (NY).

**LEWIS, Roger St John Hulton;** Chairman, Berkeley Group plc, 1999–2007; *b* 26 June 1947; *m* 1973, Vanessa England; three *s*. *Educ:* Eton Coll. ACA 1969. KPMG, 1966–72; Finance Dir, 1972–75, Man. Dir, 1975–83, Crest Homes; Gp Chief Exec., Crest Nicholson, 1983–91; Finance Dir, 1992–98, Exec. Dir, 1998–99, Berkeley Gp. Ind. Dir, Camper & Nicholsons Marinas International Ltd, 2007–; Ind. Dir, Picton Property Income Ltd, 2010–. *Recreations:* cricket, travel, ski-ing, food.

**LEWIS, Sarah,** OBE 2018; Secretary General, International Ski Federation, since 2000; *b* London, 29 Nov. 1964; *d* of John Lewis and late Pamela Lewis (*née* Hart); partner, 1991, Jorn Kasine. *Educ:* City of London Sch. for Girls; École de Ski Études, Moutiers, France. Trainee, Kent Imports Ltd (Ski Equipment Importers), 1981–83; Mem., British Alpine ski team, 1982–88 (competed Olympic Winter Games, Calgary, 1988); Mktg and Promotions, Kent Schuss, 1983–88; consultant, Consultanski PR and Consulting, 1989–91; Alpine Dir, British Ski Fedn, 1990–94; Co-ordinator, Continental Cups, 1994–98, Dir, 1998–2000, Internat. Ski Fedn. *Recreations:* sport for own fitness, football, golf, technology. *Address:* International Ski Federation, Blochstrasse 2, 3653 Oberhofen/Thunersee, Switzerland. *T:* 332446121. *E:* lewis@fisski.com.

**LEWIS, Sean Michael,** PhD; Director, British Council, Canada, 1997–2000, retired; *b* 23 Oct. 1943; *s* of Leonard Leon Lewis and Margaret Lewis (*née* Moore); *m* 1971, Jennifer M. Williams; one *s*. *Educ:* Univ. of Liverpool (BSc 1967; PhD 1971). British Council: London, 1970, 1973–75, 1978–89, 1992–97; Nigeria, 1971–73; Sri Lanka, 1975–78; Sweden, 1989–92. *Documentary films:* (co-prod.) There We Are John, 1993; (prod.) Lucky Man, 1995. *Recreations:* challenging ill health, family, moving image, real ale, country pubs. *Address:* 38 Ninehams Road, Caterham on the Hill, Surrey CR3 5LD. *T:* (020) 8763 1644.

**LEWIS, Prof. Shôn William,** MD; Professor of Adult Psychiatry, since 1994 and Director, Institute of Brain, Behaviour and Mental Health, since 2012, University of Manchester; *b* Stafford, 21 Sept. 1954; *s* of Evelyn Lewis and Gwyn Lewis; *m* 1987, Amanda Poynton; two *d. Educ*: Dulwich Coll.; Guy's Hosp. Med. Sch., Univ. of London (BSc 1st Cl. Hons Psychol. 1976; MB BS 1980; MPhil 1986; MD 1993). Registrar and Res. Fellow, Maudsley Hosp. and Inst. of Psychiatry, 1981–89; Sen. Lectr in Psychiatry, Charing Cross and Westminster Med. Sch., 1989–94; Hon. Consultant Psychiatrist, Manchester Mental Health and Social Care Trust, 1994–; Hd, Sch. of Community Based Medicine, Univ. of Manchester, 2008–12. Vis. Prof., Univ. of Melbourne, 2001. Associate Dir, NIHR Mental Health Res. Network, 2004–15; NIHR Sen. Investigator, 2008–. Trustee, Rethink, charity, 2009–12. FMedSci 2007. *Publications*: (with J. N. Higgins) Brain Imaging in Psychiatry, 1996; (with R. W. Buchanan) Schizophrenia, 1998, 3rd edn 2007; (with E. Guthrie) Psychiatry: a core clinical text, 2002; 200 articles in learned jls on psychosis and schizophrenia. *Recreations*: theatre, cinema, visual arts, hill walking, ski-ing, family, 1970s jazz fusion, good food and wine. *Address*: Institute of Brain, Behaviour and Mental Health, University Place, University of Manchester, Oxford Road, Manchester M13 9PL. *T*: (0161) 306 7944, *Fax*: (0161) 306 7945. *E*: shon.lewis@manchester.ac.uk.

**LEWIS, Simon David**, OBE 2014; Chief Executive, Association for Financial Markets in Europe, since 2010; *b* 8 May 1959; *s* of David Lewis and Sally Lewis (*née* Valentine); *m* 1985, Claire Elizabeth Anne Pendry; two *s* one *d*. *Educ*: Whitefield Comprehensive, London; Brasenose Coll., Oxford (MA); Univ. of Calif, Berkeley (Fulbright Scholar; MA). FCIPR (FIPR 1998). PR Consultant, Shandwick Consultants, 1983–86; Head: of Communications, SDP, 1986–87; of PR, S. G. Warburg Gp plc, 1987–92; Director, Corporate Affairs: NatWest Gp, 1992–96; Centrica plc, 1996–98; on secondment as first Communications Sec., Buckingham Palace, 1998–2000; Man. Dir, Europe, Centrica plc, 2000–04; Gp Dir, Corporate Affairs, Vodafone plc, 2004–09; Dir of Communications and Prime Minister's Official Spokesman, Prime Minister's Office, 2009–10; Strategic Commns Advr, UK Trade & Investment, 2010. Mem. Bd, TheCityUK, 2017–. Vis. Fellow, Centre for Corporate Reputation, Oxford Univ., 2007–16. Chm., Fulbright Commn, 2008–13 (Patron, 2013–). Member: Governing Council, UCS, 2005– (Chm., 2015–); N American Adv. Council, 2013–; Academic Adv. Bd, Chatham House, 2013–; Hon. Treas., Eur. Policy Forum, 2019–. Pres., IPR, 1997. Hon. Prof., Cardiff Sch. of Journalism, 2000–. Hon. Fellow, CIPR, 2016. *Recreations*: family, sport, current affairs, cinema. *Address*: Association for Financial Markets in Europe, Level 39, 25 Canada Square, E14 5LQ. *Clubs*: Reform, Arsenal, Conduit.

**LEWIS, Simon Jeremy Quentin W.**; *see* Wren-Lewis.

**LEWIS, Stephen John B.**; *see* Brimson-Lewis.

**LEWIS, Stephen Michael**; a Law Commissioner, since 2015; *b* London, 23 Aug. 1949; *s* of Harry Lewis and Celia Lewis; *m* 1974, Erica Pesate; one *s* two *d*. *Educ*: Orange Hill Co. Grammar Sch. for Boys; St Catherine's Coll., Oxford (BA PPE 1970); Univ. of London ext. (LLB). Admitted solicitor, 1974; Solicitor; Partner, Clifford Chance, 1985–2004; Consultant, Clyde & Co. LLP, 2004–14. *Publications*: articles on English insurance law. *Recreations*: history, opera, travel, football. *Address*: 37A Stormont Road, N6 4NR. *T*: (020) 8348 4139, 07739 696798. *E*: stephenmichaellewis@gmail.com, stephen.lewis@lawcommission.gov.uk.

**LEWIS, Susan**, CBE 2008; HM Chief Inspector of Education and Training in Wales (formerly HM Chief Inspector of Schools in Wales), 1997–2008; *b* 7 Nov. 1947; *d* of late Kenneth A. L. Lewis and Elsie Stonehouse (*née* Woods). *Educ*: Billingham South Infants' and Jun. Sch.; Lakefield Rd Primary Sch., Llanelli; Henry Smith Sch., Hartlepool; Univ. of Newcastle upon Tyne (BSc Hons); Univ. of Sheffield (DipEd); Sch. of Psychotherapy and Counselling, Regent's Coll., London (certified mediator, 2005, coach, 2006). Asst teacher, Bradfield Sch., WR Yorks, 1970–74; Hd of Dept and Asst Hd of Sixth Form, Shelley High Sch., Kirklees, 1974–80; Dep. Head, later Actg Head, Wisewood Sch., Sheffield, 1980–86; HM Inspector of Schools, 1986–95; Staff Inspector, Office of HM Chief Inspector, 1995–97. Life FRSA. *Publications*: Home on the Range: growing up on Teeside in the 50s and 60s, 2011; Diagonal Ties: a family history in Wales and the North East of England, 2013. *Recreations*: gardening, writing, walking, genealogy, drawing, painting. *E*: hoosehoo08@tiscali.co.uk

**LEWIS, Terence;** *b* 29 Dec. 1935; *s* of Andrew Lewis; *m* 1958, Audrey, *d* of William Clarke; one *s* (and one *s* decd). *Educ*: Mt Carmel Sch., Salford. Nat. service, RAMC, 1954–56. Personnel Officer. Member: Kearsley UDC, 1971–74; Bolton BC, 1976–84 (Chm., Educn Cttee, 1982–83). MP (Lab) Worsley, 1983–2005; Mem., Standards and Privileges Select Cttee, 1997–2001. *Address*: 54 Greenmount Park, Kearsley, Bolton, Lancs BL4 8NS.

**LEWIS, Tony;** *see* Lewis, A. R.

**LEWIS, Trevor;** *see* Lewis, D. T.

**LEWIS, Dr Trevor**, CBE 1992; Director, AFRC Institute of Arable Crops Research, 1989–93; Head, 1987–93, Lawes Trust Senior Fellow, 1993–2003, Rothamsted Experimental Station; Visiting Professor in Invertebrate Zoology, University of Nottingham, 1977–98; *b* 8 July 1933; *s* of Harold and Maggie Lewis; *m* 1959, Margaret Edith Wells; one *s* one *d*. *Educ*: Univ. of Nottingham (DSc 1986); Imperial Coll. of Science and Technol., Univ. of London (PhD, DIC 1958); MA Cambridge, 1960. University Demonstr in Agricl Zoology, Sch. of Agriculture, Cambridge, 1958–61; scientific staff, Rothamsted Experimental Station, 1961–2003; seconded to ODA as Sen. Res. Fellow, Univ. of WI, Trinidad, 1970–73; Head, Entomology Dept, 1976–83; Dep. Dir, 1983–87; Hd of Crop and Envmt Protection Div., 1983–89. Special Lectr in Invertebrate Zool., Univ. of Nottingham, 1968–69 and 1973–75. AFRC Assessor to MAFF Adv. Cttee on Pesticides, 1984–89; Member: Management Bd, British Crop Protection Council, 1985–94; Bd, British Crop Protection Enterprises, 1994–2008; R&D Cttee, Potato Marketing Bd, 1985–89. Mem. Council, British Ecological Soc., 1982–84; Pres., Royal Entomol Soc. of London, 1985–87; Pres., Agric. and Forestry Sect., BAAS, 1997. Huxley Gold Medal, Imperial Coll. of Science and Technol., Univ. of London, 1977; British Crop Protection Council Medal, 2002. *Publications*: (with L. R. Taylor) Introduction to Experimental Ecology, 1967; Thrips—their biology, ecology and economic importance, 1973; (ed) Insect Communication, 1984; Thrips as Crop Pests, 1997; contribs to scientific jls on topics in entomology. *Recreations*: music, gardening.

**LEWIS, Dame Vera Margaret;** *see* Lynn, Dame Vera.

**LEWIS-BOWEN, Thomas Edward Ifor;** a Circuit Judge, 1980–98; *b* 20 June 1933; *s* of late Lt-Col J. W. Lewis-Bowen and K. M. Lewis-Bowen (*née* Rice); *m* 1965, Gillian, *d* of late Reginald Brett, Puckington, Som; one *s* two *d*. *Educ*: Ampleforth; St Edmund Hall, Oxford. Called to Bar, Middle Temple, 1958. A Recorder of the Crown Court, 1974–80.

**LEWISHAM AND GREENWICH, Archdeacon of;** *see* Cutting, Ven. A. M.

**LEWISOHN, His Honour Anthony Clive Leopold;** a Circuit Judge, 1974–90; *b* 1 Aug. 1925; *s* of John Lewisohn and Gladys (*née* Solomon); *m* 1957, Lone Ruthwen Jurgensen; two *s*. *Educ*: Stowe; Trinity Coll., Oxford (MA). Royal Marines, 1944–45; Lieut, Oxf. and Bucks LI, 1946–47. Called to Bar, Middle Temple, 1951; S Eastern Circuit.

**LEWISON, Jeremy Rodney Pines;** freelance curator and art consultant; Director of Collections, Tate Gallery, 1998–2002; *b* 13 Jan. 1955; *s* of late Anthony Frederick Lewison and Dinora Pines; *m* 1993, Caroline Maria Aviva Schuck; one step *s* one step *d*. *Educ*: Westminster Sch.; Magdalen Coll., Oxford (MA; Dip Hist. of Art). Curator, Kettle's Yard, Univ. of Cambridge, 1977–83; Tate Gallery: Asst Keeper, Print Collection, 1983–86; Asst Keeper, 1986–90, Dep. Keeper, 1990–97, Modern Collection. Associate Mem., British Psychoanalytical Soc. Trustee: Kiln (formerly Tricycle) Th., London, 2010–19; Arnolfini Gall., Bristol, 2012–19. *Publications*: Anish Kapoor Drawings, 1990; Ben Nicholson, 1991; David Smith Medals for Dishonour, 1991; Brice Marden Prints 1961–91, 1992; Ben Nicholson, 1993; Shirazeh Houshiary, 1995; Karl Weschke, 1998; Interpreting Pollock, 1999; Looking at Barnett Newman, 2002; Ben Nicholson, 2002; Alice Neel, 2004; Anish Kapoor Drawings, 2005; Ra'anan Levy, 2006; Henry Moore, 2007; Ben Nicholson Prints 1928–1968: the Rentsch collection, 2007; Brice Marden: a retrospective of prints, 2008; Alice Neel: painted truths, 2010; Turner, Monet, Twombly: later paintings, 2011; Looking at Pistoletto: looking at myself, 2011; The 'Grim' and 'Tragic' Art of Henry Moore, 2012; (contrib.) Late Style and its Discontents, 2016; articles and essays in exhibn catalogues. *Recreations*: tennis, ski-ing, mountain walking, running, cycling. *Address*: 2 Fellows Road, NW3 3LP.
*See also* Rt Hon. Sir K. M. J. Lewison.

**LEWISON, Rt Hon. Sir Kim (Martin Jordan)**, Kt 2003; PC 2011; **Rt Hon. Lord Justice Lewison;** a Lord Justice of Appeal, since 2011; *b* 1 May 1952; *s* of late Anthony Frederick Lewison and Dinora Lewison (*née* Pines); *m* 1979, Helen Mary Janecek (marr. diss. 1998); one *s* one *d*; *m* 2002, Sharon Moross. *Educ*: St Paul's Sch., London; Downing Coll., Cambridge (MA 1973); Council of Legal Education. Called to the Bar, Lincoln's Inn, 1975, Bencher, 1998; QC 1991. Asst Recorder, 1994–97, Recorder, 1997–2003; a Dep. High Ct Judge, 2000–03; a Judge of the High Court of Justice, Chancery Div., 2003–11. Mem. Council, Liberal Jewish Synagogue, 1990–96. Mem. Council, Leo Baeck Coll., 1997–2002; Gov., Anglo-American Real Property Inst., 1996–2000 (Chm., 2002). *Publications*: Development Land Tax, 1978; Drafting Business Leases, 1979, 6th edn 2000; Lease or Licence, 1985; The Interpretation of Contracts, 1989, 5th edn 2011; (Gen. Editor) Woodfall on Landlord and Tenant, 1990–. *Recreations*: visiting France, avoiding tsores. *Address*: Royal Courts of Justice, Strand, WC2A 2LL.
*See also* J. R. P. Lewison.

**LEWSLEY-MOONEY, Patricia**, CBE 2015; Northern Ireland Commissioner for Children and Young People, 2007–15; *b* 3 March 1957; *d* of Patrick and Mary Killen; *m* 1st, 1976, Hugh Lewsley (marr. diss. 1998); three *s* two *d*; 2nd, 2011, William Mooney. *Educ*: St Dominic's High Sch.; Univ. of Ulster. Mem. (SDLP) Lagan Valley, NI Assembly, 1998–2007. Contested (SDLP) Lagan Valley, 2001, 2005. *Recreations*: reading, travel.

**LEWTY, (David) Ian;** HM Diplomatic Service, retired; *b* 27 July 1943; *s* of late Harry Lewty and Ruby Lewty (*née* Buck); *m* 1968, Mary Law; two *d*. *Educ*: Lancing Coll.; Magdalen Coll., Oxford (MA). Third Sec., FO, 1965; MECAS, Lebanon, 1966; Third, later Second Sec., Ottawa, 1967–71; Hd, British Interests Section, Baghdad, 1971–72; First Sec., FCO, 1972–76; Hd of Chancery, Jedda, 1976–79; (on secondment) L'Ecole Nationale d'Administration, Paris, 1979–81; UK Delegn to OECD, Paris, 1981–84; FCO, 1984–87; Counsellor and Dep. Hd of Mission, Khartoum, 1987–89; Diplomatic Service Inspector, 1989–92; Hd, Migration and Visa Dept, FCO, 1992–95; Ambassador to Bahrain, 1996–99. *Address*: 38 Burlington Avenue, Richmond, Surrey TW9 4DH.

**LEXDEN, Baron** *cr* 2010 (Life Peer), of Lexden in the County of Essex and of Strangford in the County of Down; **Alistair Basil Cooke**, OBE 1988; PhD; Consultant and Editor in Chief, Conservative Research Department, 2004–10; official historian, Conservative Party, since 2009; official historian and archivist, Carlton Club, since 2007; *b* 20 April 1945; 2nd *s* of Dr Basil Cooke and Nancy Irene Cooke (*née* Neal). *Educ*: Framlingham Coll., Suffolk; Peterhouse, Cambridge (MA 1970); Queen's Univ., Belfast (PhD 1979). Lectr and Tutor in Modern History, Queen's Univ., Belfast, 1971–77; Conservative Research Department: Desk Officer, 1977–83; Political Advr to Shadow Minister for NI, 1977–79; Asst Dir, 1983–85; Dep. Dir, 1985–97. Dir, Conservative Political Centre, 1988–97. Gen. Sec., ISC, 1997–2004. Chm. of Trustees, Friends of the Union, 1995–2003; Founder, 1997, Mem., 2005–, Cons. Party Archive Trust; Sen. Trustee, T. E. Utley Meml Fund, 2000–12; Trustee, Hansard Soc., 2013–. Chm., Conservative History Gp, 2012–. Member: H of L Select Cttee on the Constitution, 2012–15; Jt Cttee on Statutory Instruments, 2015–; Ecclesiastical Jt Cttee, 2017–; British-Irish Parly Assembly, 2017–; Dep. Speaker, H of L, 2017–. Gov., John Lyon Sch., Harrow, 1999–2005. Patron, NI Schs Debating Comp., 2001–16. Vice Pres., Council of British Internat. Schs, 2011–; President: Ind. Schs Assoc., 2013–; Council for Ind. Educn, 2013–. *Publications*: (ed jtly) Lord Carlingford's Journal, 1971; (jtly) The Governing Passion; cabinet government and party politics in Britain 1885–86, 1974; (ed) The Ashbourne Papers 1869–1913, 1974; (ed) The Conservative Party's Campaign Guides, 7 vols, 1987–2005; (ed) The Conservative Party: seven historical studies, 1997; (ed) The Conservative Research Department 1929–2004, 2004; (jtly) The Carlton Club 1832–2007, 2007; Tory Heroine: Dorothy Brant and the rise of Conservative women, 2008; A Party of Change: a brief history of the Conservatives, 2008, 3rd edn 2014; (contrib.) Between the Thin Blue Lines, 2008; (jtly) Tory Policy-Making: the Conservative Research Department 1929–2009, 2009; A Gift from the Churchills: the Primrose League 1883–2004, 2010; (contrib.) Enoch at 100: a re-evaluation of the life, politics and philosophy of Enoch Powell, 2012; Neville Chamberlain: redressing the balance, 2018; (ed) Stanley Baldwin: a statesman in bronze, 2018; contrib. DNB; pamphlets on Northern Ireland and constitutional issues; articles in historical jls and educnl pubns. *Recreations*: writing letters to the press (and getting them published), collecting royal and political memorabilia, music, walking as briskly as age allows, book reviewing, adding to my website. *Address*: Flat 1, 68 St George's Square, SW1V 3QT. *T*: (020) 7821 9520. *W*: www.alistairlexden.org.uk. *Club*: Carlton.

**LEY, Sir Christopher Ian**, 6th Bt *cr* 1905, of Epperstone, Nottingham; Executive Divisional Director, Besso Ltd, since 1996; *b* 2 Dec. 1962; *s* of Sir Ian Francis Ley, 5th Bt and of Caroline Margaret Ley; *S* father, 2017; *m* 1999, Henrietta, *yr d* of David Nicholls; one *d*. *Educ*: Eton Coll.; Bransons Coll. Short Service Commn, HM Forces, 1982–90; Claims Broker, Blackwall Green, 1990–93; Claims Manager, Lowndes Lambert, 1993–96.

**LEY, Prof. Steven Victor**, CBE 2002; FRS 1990; FMedSci; Professor of Organic Chemistry, Department of Chemistry, University of Cambridge, since 2013 (BP (1702) Professor of Organic Chemistry, 1992–2013); Fellow of Trinity College, Cambridge, since 1993. *Educ*: Loughborough Univ. of Technology (BSc 1st cl. Hons 1969; DIS 1969; PhD 1972); DSc London 1983; MA 1997; ScD 1999, Cantab. CChem, FRSC 1980; FIC 2000; CBiol, FRSB (FIBiol 2003). Res. Fellow, Ohio State Univ., 1972–74; Imperial College, London: Res. Asst, 1974–75; Lectr, 1975–83; Prof. of Organic Chemistry, 1983–92; Head of Chemistry Dept, 1989–92. Royal Soc. Bakerian Lectr, 1997. Chm. Exec. Cttee, Novartis (formerly Ciba) Foundn, 1993–. Pres., Royal Soc. of Chem., 2000–02. FMedSci 2005. Hon. Fellow, Cardiff Univ., 2005. Hon. DSc: Loughborough, 1994; Salamanca, 2000; Huddersfield, 2003. Royal Society of Chemistry: Hickinbottom Res. Fellow, 1981–83 (1st recipient); Corday Morgan Medal and Prize, 1980; Tilden Lectr and Medal,

1988; Award for Synthetic Chem., 1989; Pedlar Lectr and Medal, 1992; Simonsen Lectr and Medal, 1993; Award for Natural Products Chemistry, 1994; Flintoff Medal, 1996; Rhône-Poulenc Lectureship Medal and Prize, 1998; Haworth Meml Lectr, Medal and Prize, 2001; Award in Carbohydrate Chemistry, 2003; Robert Robinson Award and Medal, 2006; High Throughput Drug Discovery Methodologies Award, 2008; Perkin Prize for Organic Chemistry, 2009; Longstaff Prize, 2013; German Chemical Society: Adolf Windaus Medal, 1994; August Wilhelm von Hofmann Medal, 2001; Dr Paul Janssen Prize for Creativity in Organic Synthesis, European Chem. Soc., 1996; Davy Medal, 2000, Royal Medal, 2011, Royal Soc.; Pfizer Central Research: Pfizer Res. Award, 1983 (1st recipient); Pfizer Award for Innovative Science, 2001; Ernst Guenther Award, 2003, Award for Creative Work in Synthetic Organic Chem., 2007, Arthur C. Cope Award, 2018, ACS; Innovation of the Year Award, CIA, 2003; iAc Award (for Innovation in Applied Catalysis), IChemE, 2004; Alexander von Humboldt Award, 2005; Yamada-Koga Prize, Japan Res. Foundn for Organocatalysis, 2006; Paul Karrer Medal, Univ. of Zurich, 2007; Innovation Award, Soc. of Chem. Ind. (1st recipient), 2007; Inhoffen Medal, Helmholtz Zentrum für Infektionsforschung, 2008; Paracelsus Prize, Swiss Chem. Soc., 2010; Franco-Britannique Prize, French Chemical Soc., 2013; IUPAC-Thales Prize in Flow Chemistry, 2014. *Publications:* over 880 papers in internat. jls of chemistry. *Address:* Department of Chemistry, Lensfield Road, Cambridge CB2 1EW. *W:* http://leygroup.ch.cam.ac.uk.

**LEYDECKER, (Veronica) Sonya;** consultant and business coach, since 2017; Joint Chief Executive Officer, Herbert Smith Freehills LLP, 2014–17; *b* Scarborough, 18 July 1954; *d* of George Michael Leydecker and Sabina Leydecker (*née* Murtagh); *m* 1997, Steven Roderick Larcombe. *Educ:* Convent of the Ladies of Mary, Scarborough; Univ. of Manchester (BA Hons Hist.); Coll. of Law. Grad., Meyler Campbell Mastered Prog., 2017. Admitted solicitor, 1984; Herbert Smith, later Herbert Smith Freehills: Partner, 1991–2017, specialising in dispute resolution; Global Head of Dispute Resolution, 2005–14. Trustee: Friends of Gunnersbury Park and Mus., 2004–; RESTART, 2018–; Ambassador, Women Supporting Women Gp, Prince's Trust, 2012–. Mem. Council, Nottingham Univ., 2019–. FRSA. *Recreations:* the arts (especially music and theatre), swimming, cycling. *Address:* 69 Onslow Square, SW7 3LS. *T:* 07785 254973.

**LEYLAND, Sir Philip Vyvian N.;** *see* Naylor-Leyland.

**LEYLAND, Ronald Arthur;** Chief Executive, North Yorkshire County Council, 1990–94; *b* 23 Aug. 1940; *s* of Arthur and Lucy Leyland; *m* 1962, Joan Virginia Sinclair; three *s*. *Educ:* Merchant Taylors' Sch., Crosby; Liverpool Univ. (LLB Hons 1961). Solicitor (Hons 1964). Assistant Solicitor: Bootle CBC, 1964–65; Nottingham City Council, 1965–68; Sen. Asst Solicitor, then Dir of Admin, Leeds MDC, 1968–75; County Sec., Hampshire CC, 1975–90. Dir, N Yorks TEC, 1990–94. Chm., Soc. of County Secretaries, 1986–87. Mem., U3A. *Recreations:* family history, boating. *Address:* 6 Swan Close, Walton on Thames, Surrey KT12 2FH.

**LEYSER, Dame (Henrietta Miriam) Ottoline,** DBE 2017 (CBE 2009); PhD; FRS 2007; Professor of Plant Development, since 2011, and Director, since 2013, Sainsbury Laboratory, University of Cambridge; *b* 7 March 1965; *d* of Prof. Karl Joseph Leyser, TD, FBA and Henrietta Louise Valerie Leyser (*née* Bateman); *m* 1986, Stephen John Day (*d* 2014); one *s* one *d*. *Educ:* Newnham Coll., Cambridge (BA Genetics 1986; PhD Genetics 1990). Post-doctoral Research Fellow: Indiana Univ., Bloomington, 1990–93; Cambridge Univ., 1993–94; Lectr, 1994–99, Reader, 1999–2002, Prof. of Plant Develtl Genetics, 2002–10, Univ. of York. Editor: The Plant Jl, 2001–08; Current Opinion in Plant Biol., 2009–18 (Co-Editor in Chief); Development, 2011–17. Biotechnology and Biological Sciences Research Council: Chm., Biosci. Skills and Careers Strategy Panel, 2008–12; Member: Strategy Bd, 2003–04 and 2007–11; Data Policy wkg gp, 2005–06; Bioinformatics and Biol Resources Initiative Panel, 2007. Member: MRC/BBSRC/Wellcome Trust Eur. Bioinformatics Inst. Rev. Panel, 2004; Life Sci. Interface Doctoral Trng Centres Rev. Panel, EPSRC, 2007; Nuffield Council on Bioethics, 2009–15 (Dep. Chair, 2012–15); Council for Sci. and Technol., 2017–; UKRI-BBSRC, 2018–; Bd, Francis Crick Inst., 2018–. Chair., British Soc. for Develtl Biol., 2014–19 (Treas., 1999–2004); Mem. Council, Internat. Plant Molecular Biol. (formerly Internat. Soc. for Plant Molecular Biol.), 2003– (Pres., 2011–15). Chair, Athena Forum, 2013–16; Trustee, Sci. Media Centre, 2015–18. For. Associate, US Nat. Acad. of Sci., 2012; Mem., Leopoldina, 2014. Hon. Dr Aberdeen, 2019. K. M. Stott Res. Fellow Prize, Newnham Coll., Cambridge, 1993; President's Medal, Soc. for Exptl Biol., 2000; Rosalind Franklin Award, Royal Soc., 2007; Silver Medal, Internat. Plant Growth Substance Assoc., 2010; Genetics Soc. Medal, 2016; FEBS/EMBO Women in Sci. Award, 2017. *Publications:* (with S. Day) Mechanisms in Plant Development, 2002; chapters in: Plant Gene Isolation, 1996; Plant Cell Proliferation and its Regulation in Growth and Development, 1997; Plant Hormone Protocols, 2000; Grafting, 2005; contribs to learned jls incl. Nature, Cell, Current Biol., Development, Plant Physiol., Plant Jl. *Recreations:* singing, walking, swimming. *Address:* Sainsbury Laboratory, Bateman Street, University of Cambridge, Cambridge CB2 1LR. *T:* (01223) 761103. *E:* ol235@cam.ac.uk.

**LEZALA, Andrew Peter,** CEng, FIMechE; Managing Director, Metro Trains Australia, since 2016; *b* 8 Dec. 1955; *s* of Jozef and Constance Lezala; *m* 1980, Helen Addison; one *s* two *d*. *Educ:* Derby Grammar Sch.; Univ. of Leicester (BSc Hons Eng). CEng, FIMechE 1989. British Rail: Engrg Grad. Trainee, 1977–79; bogie and suspension design engr, 1979–81; Asst Brakes Engr, 1981–84; Project Engr, 1984–86, Chief Engr, New Vehicles, 1986–87, BREL Ltd; Gp Operating and Engrg Dir, RFS Hldgs Ltd, 1987–93; Vice Pres., Business Area Metro's and Multiple Units, ABB Transportation Ltd, 1993–94; Hd of Metro's, ABB China Ltd, 1994–98; Man. Dir, Australia Ltd, 1998–99, Pres., Worldwide Metro Div., 1999–2001, Daimler Chrysler Rail Systems; Pres., Worldwide Services Div., Bombardier, 2001–04; Chief Operating Officer, Jarvis plc, 2004–05; CEO, Metronet Rail BCV Hldgs Ltd and Metronet Rail SSL Hldgs Ltd, 2005–07; Man. Dir, Air Rail Transit Ltd, 2008; CEO, Metro Trains Melbourne, 2009–16. Institution of Mechanical Engineers: Mem. Bd, 2000–08, Chm., 2006–07, Railway Div.; Mem., Trustee Bd, 2008–10. Mem. Council, Railway Ind. Assoc., 2004–07. FIEAust 2012. FRSA. *Recreations:* family gatherings, motor sport, swimming, cycling, playing guitar.

**LI, Sir David Kwok Po,** GBM 2007 (GBS 2001); Kt 2005; OBE 1991; FCIB; FCA; Chairman, since 1997, and Chief Executive, since 1981, Bank of East Asia Ltd; *b* 13 March 1939; *s* of Li Fook Shu and Woo Tze Ha; *m* 1971, Penny Poon; two *s*. *Educ:* Selwyn Coll., Cambridge (BA 1964; MA; LLD 1993). FCPA 1973; FCA 1977; FCIB 1988. Bank of East Asia Ltd: Chief Accountant, 1969–72; Asst Chief Manager, 1973–76; Dep. Chief Manager, 1977–81; Dir, 1977–; Dep. Chm., 1995–97. Hon. Fellow: Robinson Coll., Cambridge, 1989; Selwyn Coll., Cambridge, 1992. Hon. LLD: Warwick, 1994; Hong Kong, 1996; Hon. DSc Imperial Coll. London, 2007; Hon. DLitt Macquarie, 2011. Commandeur de la Légion d'Honneur (France), 2012. *Recreations:* tennis, art, antiques, reading. *Address:* Bank of East Asia Ltd, 21st Floor, 10 Des Voeux Road Central, Hong Kong. *T:* 36080808. *Clubs:* Hong Kong Country, Hong Kong Golf, Hong Kong Yacht (Hong Kong).

**LI Ka-shing, Sir,** KBE 2000 (CBE 1989); Senior Advisor: CK Hutchison Holdings Ltd, since 2018 (former Chairman); CK Asset (formerly Cheung Kong Property) Holdings Ltd, since 2018 (former Chairman); *b* Chaozhou, 1928; *m* Chong Yuet-Ming (decd); two *s*. Moved from mainland China to Hong Kong, 1940; took first job, 1942; promoted to gen. manager, 1947; founded Cheung Kong Industries (later Cheung Kong (Holdings) Ltd), 1950, listed 1972; acquired Hutchison Whampoa Ltd, 1979; acquired Hongkong Electric Hldgs Ltd, 1985; founded: CK Infrastructure (formerly Cheung Kong Infrastructure) Hldgs Ltd, listed 1996; Tom.com (later TOM Group), listed 2000; CK Life Sciences Internat. (Hldgs) Inc., listed 2002; business interests in over 50 countries incl. mainland China, UK, Canada, Hong Kong and many other parts of the world. HK Affairs Adviser, 1992–97; Member: Drafting Cttee for Basic Law, HKSAR, 1985–90; Preparatory Cttee for the HKSAR, 1995–97; Selection Cttee for the govt of the HKSAR, 1996–; Internat. Business Adv. Council of the UK, 2006. Established Li Ka Shing Foundn, 1980; founded Shantou Univ., 1981. Hon. Citizen: Shantou, Guangzhou, Shenzhen, Nanhai, Foshan, Zhuhai, Chaozhou, Beijing (China) and Winnipeg (Canada). JP 1981. Hon. LLD: Hong Kong, 1986; Calgary, 1989; Chinese Univ. of Hong Kong, 1997; Cambridge, 1999; Hon. Dr Peking, 1992; Hon. DScoSc: Hong Kong Univ. of Sci. and Technology, 1995; City Univ. of Hong Kong, 1998; Open Univ. of Hong Kong, 1999. Entrepreneur of the Millennium Award, Times/Ernst & Young, 1999; Internat. Dist. Entrepreneur Award, Univ. of Manitoba, 2000; Malcolm S. Forbes Lifetime Achievement Award, Forbes, 2006; Lifetime Award for Philanthropy, Chinese Min. of Civil Affairs, 2007; Presidential Award, TESOL Inc., 2007; Robert H. Alway Lifetime Achievement Award, Stanford Univ., 2010; Special Hon. Award for Econ. Contribn, China Central TV, 2007; Lifetime Achievement Award, Hong Kong Business Awards, DHL/South China Morning Post, 2010; Carnegie Medal of Philanthropy, Carnegie Corp., 2011; Berkeley Medal, Univ. of Calif, Berkeley, 2011. Grand Bauhinia Medal, HKSAR, 2001. Grand Officer, Order Vasco Núñez de Balboa (Panama), 1982; Commander: Order of the Crown (Belgium), 1986; Order of Leopold (Belgium), 2000; Commandeur de la Légion d'honneur (France), 2005. *Recreations:* golf, boating. *Address:* CK Asset Holdings Ltd, 7–12/F Cheung Kong Center, 2 Queen's Road Central, Hong Kong. *Club:* Hong Kong Golf.

**LI Kwok Nang, Andrew,** GBM 2008; CBE 1993; JP; Chief Justice, and President of the Court of Final Appeal, Hong Kong, 1997–2010; *b* 12 Dec. 1948; *s* of Li Fook Kow, CMG; *m* 1973, Judy M. Y. Woo; two *d*. *Educ:* St Paul's Primary Sch., Hong Kong; St Paul's Co-Educnl Coll., Hong Kong; Repton Sch.; Fitzwilliam Coll., Cambridge (MA, LLM; Hon. Fellow, 1999). Called to the Bar: Middle Temple, 1970 (Hon. Bencher, 1997); Hong Kong, 1973; QC (Hong Kong) 1988. Guest Prof., Tsinghua Univ., Beijing, 1997–; Hon. Professor of Law: Univ. of Hong Kong, 2010–; Chinese Univ. of Hong Kong, 2010–; City Univ. of Hong Kong, 2010–; Shue Yan Univ., Hong Kong, 2010–. Patron, Bingham Centre for the Rule of Law, 2010–. JP Hong Kong, 1985. Hon. Life Member: Hong Kong Bar Assoc., 2011; Law Soc. of Hong Kong, 2011. Hon. Fellow, St Hugh's Coll., Oxford, 2016. Hon. DLitt Hong Kong Univ. of Sci. and Technol., 1993; Hon. LLD: Baptist Univ., Hong Kong, 1994; Open Univ., Hong Kong, 1997; Univ. of Hong Kong, 2001; Griffith, 2001; NSW, 2002; Univ. of Technol., Sydney, 2005; Chinese Univ. of Hong Kong, 2006; Shue Yan Univ., Hong Kong, 2009; Lingnan Univ., Hong Kong, 2010; City Univ. of Hong Kong, 2010; Tsinghua, 2013; Hon. DCL Oxford, 2013. Woodrow Wilson Award for Public Service, Woodrow Wilson Internat. Centre for Scholars, 2010; Sing Tao Leader of the Year Award, 2010. *Recreations:* hiking, reading, tennis, the turf. *Address:* 2213 Bank of America Tower, 12 Harcourt Road, Hong Kong. *T:* 25213018. *Clubs:* Athenæum; Hong Kong Jockey (Hon. Steward), Hong Kong, Hong Kong Country, Shek O Country (Hong Kong).

**LI, Prof. Lin,** PhD; CEng, FREng, FIET; Professor of Laser Engineering, and Director, Laser Processing Research Centre, University of Manchester (formerly University of Manchester Institute of Science and Technology), since 2000; *b* Shenyang, China, 24 June 1959; *s* of Dr Honglian Li and Dr Shuchun Guo; *m* 1986, Dr Zhu Liu; one *d*. *Educ:* Dalian Univ. of Technol. (BSc 1982); Imperial Coll. London (PhD 1989). CEng 2005; FIET 2005; FREng 2013. Res. Associate, Res. Fellow, Laser Gp, Dept of Mech. Engrg, Univ. of Liverpool, 1988–94; University of Manchester Institute of Science and Technology, subseq. University of Manchester: Lectr, then Reader, Dept of Mech. Engrg, 1994–2000; Hd of Manufg Res. Gp, 2006–14; Dir of Res., Dep. Hd, Sch. of Mech., Aerospace and Civil Engrg, 2009–13. Chm., Process and Product Innovation Gp, Assoc. of Laser Users, 2008–14; Pres., Internat. Acad. of Photonics and Laser Engrg, 2013–14. Fellow: Laser Inst. of America, 2007 (a Dir, 2009–14); Internat. Acad. of Prodn Engrg, 2008. Sir Frank Whittle Award, RAEng, 2013; Wolfson Res. Merit Award, Royal Soc., 2014; Researcher of the Yr, Univ. of Manchester, 2014. *Publications:* over 550 articles and 47 patents in lasers, photonics and manufg. *Recreation:* member of Oriental Breeze (Chinese music performance group, Manchester). *Address:* School of Mechanical, Aerospace and Civil Engineering, University of Manchester, Manchester M13 9PL. *T:* (0161) 306 3816, *Fax:* (0161) 306 3803. *E:* lin.li@manchester.ac.uk.

**LIANG, Prof. Wei Yao,** PhD; Professor of Superconductivity, University of Cambridge, 1994–2007, now Emeritus; Fellow and Lecturer, Gonville and Caius College, Cambridge, since 1971 (President, 2005–13; Life Fellow, 2007); *b* 23 Sept. 1940; *s* of late Tien Fu Liang and of Po Seng Nio Lie; *m* 1968, Lian Choo (*née* Choong) (*d* 2014); three *d*. *Educ:* Pah Chung Chinese High Sch., Jakarta; Portsmouth Coll. of Technology; Imperial Coll., London (BSc, ARCS 1st Class Hons Theoretical Physics); Univ. of Cambridge (PhD). Gonville and Caius College, Cambridge: Comyns Berkeley Unofficial Fellow, 1969–71; Dir of Studies in Natural Scis, 1975–89; University of Cambridge: Demonstrator, 1971–75; Lectr in Physics, 1975–92; Reader in high temperature superconductivity, 1992–93; Co-Dir, 1988–89, Dir, 1989–98, Interdisciplinary Res. Centre in Superconductivity. Vis. Scientist, Xerox Palo Alto Res. Centre, 1975, 1976; Visiting Professor: EPF Lausanne, 1978; Inst. of Semiconductors, Beijing, 1983; Sci. Univ. of Tokyo, 2000; Univ. of Tokyo, 2001; Xiamen Univ., 2002; Hon. Fellow and Vis. Prof. of Materials Sci., S Univ. Coll., Univ. of Hong Kong, 2009–. *Publications:* (ed with A. S. Alexandrov and E. K. H. Salje) Polarons and Bipolarons in High Tc Superconductors and Related Materials, 1995; (ed with W. Zong) Fundamental Research in High Tc Superconductivity, 1999; (ed with D. Shi and W. Zong) Research in High Temperature Superconductivity Applications, 2008. *Recreations:* music, photography. *Address:* Gonville and Caius College, Cambridge CB2 1TA. *T:* (01223) 332425.

**LIANOS, Prof. Ioannis,** PhD; Professor of Global Competition Law and Public Policy, University College London, since 2014; *b* Athens, 9 March 1975; *s* of Kostantinos Lianos and Pigie Lianou. *Educ:* Univ. of Strasbourg (LLB 1996; LLM Eur. Law 1997; PhD Law 2004); New York Univ. Sch. of Law (LLM Trade Regulation 2003); Ecole Nat. du Barreau. Lecturer: Univ. of Strasbourg, 1997–2002, 2003–04; Univ. of Southampton, 2004–05; Mem., Paris Bar Assoc., 2004; admitted as solicitor, Athens Bar Assoc., 2005; Lectr, then Reader, Faculty of Laws, UCL, 2005–14; Chief Researcher, Higher Sch. of Econs, Nat. Res. Univ., Moscow, 2014–. Visiting Professor: Centre d'Etudes Internat. de la Propriété Intellectuelle, Univ. of Strasbourg, 2004–; Univ. of Chile, Santiago, 2011–; Univ. of Hong Kong Law Sch., 2014; Emile Noel Fellow, NY Univ. Law Sch., 2008–09; Gutenberg Res. Chair, Ecole Nat. d'Admin, 2012–14; Alexander von Humboldt Fellow,

2014–15. Emile Girardeau Prize, Acad. des Scis Morales et Politiques, 2005; Philip Leverhulme Prize, 2012. *Publications:* La Transformation du droit de la concurrence par le recours à l'analyse économique, 2007; The Reform of EC Competition Law, 2010; The EU after the Treaty of Lisbon, 2012; The Global Limits of Competition Law, 2012; Regulating Trade in Services in the EU and the WTO: trust, distrust and economic integration, 2012; Handbook in EU Competition Law: enforcement and procedure, 2013; Handbook in EU Competition Law: substantive aspects, 2013; Competition Law and Development, 2013; Competition and the State, 2014; Damages Claims for the Infringement of Competition Law, 2015; contribs to Common Market Law Rev., Eur. Law Rev., Jl Competition Law and Econs, Antitrust Law Jl, Columbia Business Law Rev., Cambridge Jl Eur. Legal Studies, Eur. Business Law Rev., Revue Française d'Admin Publique, Foreign Affairs, Rev. Trimestrielle de Droit européen, Tulane Jl Internat. and Comparative Law, Current Legal Problems. *Recreations:* sailing, theatre, opera, cinema, archaeology, modern art, politics. *Address:* UCL Laws, Bentham House, Endsleigh Gardens, WC1H 0EG. *T:* (020) 7679 1028, (020) 7679 1407. *E:* i.lianos@ucl.ac.uk.

**LIAO Poon-Huai, Donald,** CBE 1983 (OBE 1972); company director; *b* 29 Oct. 1929; *s* of late Liao Huk-Koon and Yeo Tsai-Hoon; *m* 1963, Christine Yuen Ching-Me; two *s* one *d. Educ:* Univ. of Hong Kong (BArch Hons); Univ. of Durham (Dip. Landscape Design). Architect, Hong Kong Housing Authority, 1960, Housing Architect, 1966; Commissioner for Housing and Member, Town Planning Board, 1968; Director of Housing and Vice-Chm., Hong Kong Housing Authority, 1973; Sec. for Housing and Chm., Hong Kong Housing Authority, 1980; Sec. for Dist Admin, Hong Kong, 1985. Chm., HSBC China Fund, 1992–2004. MLC, Hong Kong, 1980; MEC, 1985. Mem., Sino-British Jt Liaison Gp, 1987–89. Fellow, Hong Kong Inst. of Architects. Hon. FIH. Hon. DSc Durham, 2011. *Recreations:* golf, ski-ing, riding. *Address:* (residence) 55 Kadoorie Avenue, Kowloon, Hong Kong. *T:* 27155822. *Clubs:* Athenæum; Hong Kong Golf, Hong Kong Jockey (Hong Kong).

**LIARDET, Rear-Adm. Guy Francis,** CB 1990; CBE 1985; *b* 6 Dec. 1934; *s* of Maj.-Gen. Henry Maughan Liardet, CB, CBE, DSO; *m* 1962, Jennifer Anne O'Hagan; one *s* two *d. Educ:* Royal Naval Coll., Dartmouth; Southampton Univ. (BA Hons 1999). Trng Comdr, BRNC, Dartmouth, 1969–70; comd HMS Aurora, 1970–72; Exec. Officer, HMS Bristol, 1974–76; Defence Policy Staff, MoD, 1978–79; RCDS, 1980; CSO (Trng), C-in-C Naval Home Comd, 1981–82; comd HMS Cleopatra and Seventh Frigate Sqn, 1983–84; Dir of Public Relations (Navy), MoD, 1984–86; Flag Officer Second Flotilla, 1986–88; Comdt, JSDC, 1988–90, retd. Dir of Public Affairs, CIA, 1990–93. Mem., RNSA, 1970–. *Publications:* contrib. Naval Review. *Address:* The Downs Cottage, New Road, Meonstoke, Southampton SO32 3NN.

**LIBBY, Donald Gerald,** PhD; Under Secretary, Office of Science and Technology, Cabinet Office, and Secretary, Advisory Board for the Research Councils, 1991–94; *b* 2 July 1934; *s* of late Herbert Lionel Libby and Minnie Libby; *m* 1st, 1961, Margaret Elizabeth Dunlop McLatchie (*d* 1979); one *d*; 2nd, 1982, June Belcher. *Educ:* RMA, Sandhurst; London Univ. (BSc, PhD Physics). CEng, FIET (FIEE 1993). Department of Education and Science: Principal Scientific Officer, 1967–72; Principal, 1972–74; Asst Sec., 1974–80; Under Sec., 1980–91 (Planning and Internat. Relations Br., 1980–82, Architects, Bldg and Schs Br., 1982–86, Further and Higher Educn Br. 2, 1986–91). Adviser, Logica UK Ltd, 1995–96. *Recreations:* music, rowing, golf. *Address:* 7 Coach House Mews, Whiteley Village, Walton-on-Thames KT12 4BT.

**LIBESKIND, Daniel,** Hon. RA 2003; Architect, Studio Daniel Libeskind, New York (formerly Architectural Studio Libeskind, Berlin), since 1989; *b* Łódź, Poland, 12 May 1946; *s* of Nachman Libeskind and Dora Libeskind (*née* Blaustein); *m* 1969, Nina Lewis; two *s* one *d. Educ:* in Poland and Israel; Bronx High Sch. of Sci., NYC; Cooper Union Sch. of Architecture, NYC (BArch 1970); Sch. of Comparative Studies, Univ. of Essex (MA Hist. and Theory of Architecture 1971). Architectural trng in The Hague, NYC and Helsinki; Inst. for Architecture and Urban Studies, NY, 1971–72; Irving Grossman Associates, Toronto, 1972–73; Project Planners Associates, Toronto, 1973; Asst Prof. of Architecture, Univ. of Kentucky, 1973–75; Unit Master, AA, London, 1975–77; Sen. Lectr, Poly. of Central London, and Critic in Architecture, Centre of Advanced Studies in Architecture, 1975–77; Associate Prof. of Architecture, Univ. of Toronto, 1977–78; Hd, Sch. of Architecture, and Architect-in-Residence, Cranbrook Acad. of Art, Bloomfield Hills, Mich, 1978–85; Founder and Dir, *Architecture Intermundium*, Milan, 1986–89; Architect, Berlin, 1989–94, LA, 1994–95. Vis. Critic in Architecture, Houston, Lund, London, Harvard and Helsinki, 1981–84; Visiting Professor, Europe, US and Canada, 1985–, including: Bannister Fletcher Architecture Prof., Univ. of London, 1990–91; Hochschule Weissensee, Berlin, 1993–95; Sch. of Architecture and Urban Planning, UCLA, 1994–98; Hochschule für Gestaltung, Karlsruhe; First Louis Kahn Prof., Yale Univ. Sch. of Architecture; Univ. of Pennsylvania. Ext. Examr, Bartlett Sch. of Architecture, Univ. of London, 1993. Major works include: Uozu Mt Pavilion, Japan, 1997; Polderland Gdn, Netherlands, 1997; Felix Nussbaum Haus, Osnabrück, 1998, extension, 2011; Jewish Mus., Berlin, 1999 (German Architecture Award, 1999); Imperial War Mus. North, Manchester, 2002 (RIBA Award, 2004); London Metropolitan Univ. Graduate Centre (RIBA Award, 2004); Denver Art Mus., 2006; Grand Canal Th., Dublin, 2010; Creative Media Center, Hong Kong, 2011; Mil. History Mus. Dresden, 2011; Haeundae Udong Hyundai I'Park, Busan, 2012; Reflections at Keppel Bay, Singapore, 2012; Acad. of Jewish Mus., Berlin, 2012; Kö-Bogen, Dusseldorf, 2013; Magnet, Tirana, 2014; Centre des Congrès, Mons, 2015; Vitra Tower, Sao Paulo, 2015; L Tower, Toronto, 2016; Sapphire, Berlin, 2016; Corals at Keppel Bay, Singapore, 2016; Ogden Centre, Durham University, Durham, 2017; Zlota 44, Warsaw, 2017; Forum, Leuphana Univ., Luneburg, 2017; Nat. Holocaust Monument, Ottawa, 2017; Zhang Zhidong Mus., Wuhan, 2017; MO Mus., Vilnius, 2018. Ongoing projects include: FieraMilano, Milan; World Trade Centre master plan, NY City; Archipelago 21, Seoul; Harmony Tower, Seoul; Kurdistan Mus., Erbil; Tampere Central Deck and Arena, Tampere; Century Spire, Manila; Sen. Housing, Brooklyn; Occitanie Tower, Toulouse; Iconic, Nice; Downtown Tower, Vilnius; Verve, Frankfurt; Maggie's Centre, London. Mem., European Acad. of Arts and Letters, 1990. Hon. Dr: Humboldt Univ., 1997; Coll. of Arts and Humanities, Essex Univ.; Edinburgh, 2002; DePaul, Chicago, 2002; Toronto, 2004. Academician, IAA, 2012; Fellow, AIA, 2017. Numerous awards, including: 1st prize, Biennale de Vinezia, 1985; Award for Architecture, AAAL, 1996; Berlin Cultural Prize, 1996; Goethe Medallion, 2000; Hiroshima Art Prize, 2001; Lifetime Achievement Award, Emirates Glass LEAF Awards, 2012; AIA Nat. Service Medal, 2012. *Publications:* Breaking Ground: adventures in life and architecture (memoir), 2004; Edge of Order (memoir), 2018; numerous monographs. *Address:* Studio Libeskind, 150 Broadway, 18th Floor, New York, NY 10038, USA.

**LIBSON, James;** Partner, since 1991, and Executive Partner and Head of Mishcon Private, since 2010, Mishcon de Reya; *b* London, 20 May 1966; *s* of John and Maxine Libson; *m* 1993, Anne Joseph; two *s. Educ:* St Paul's Sch.; Univ. of Leeds (BA Hons English and Arabic 1987); Coll. of Law. Northern field worker, RSY Netzer, 1987–88; Mgt trainee, Unilever, 1988–89. Admitted solicitor, 1993. Chm., World Jewish Relief, 2012–16; Trustee, Jewish Leadership Council, 2010–17. Chm., Prism - the Gift Fund, 2017–. Gov., Muswell Hill Primary Sch.. Hon. Dr of Laws Univ. of Law, 2018. Hist. Makers Award, Univ. of Law, 2018. *Recreations:* cinema, cooking, family, walking. *Address:* Mishcon de Reya LLP, 70 Kingsway, WC2B 6AH. *T:* (020) 3321 7000, *Fax:* (020) 3761 1846. *E:* james.libson@mishcon.com.

**LICHFIELD, 6th Earl of,** *cr* 1831; **Thomas William Robert Hugh Anson;** Viscount Anson and Baron Soberton, 1806; *b* 19 July 1978; *s* of 5th Earl of Lichfield and of Lady Leonora Grosvenor (LVO 1997), *d* of 5th Duke of Westminster, TD; *S* father, 2005; *m* 2009, Lady Henrietta Conyngham, *er d* of Marquess of Conyngham, *qv*; two *s* one *d*. *Heir: s* Viscount Anson, *qv*.

**LICHFIELD, Bishop of,** since 2016; **Rt Rev. Michael Geoffrey Ipgrave,** OBE 2011; PhD; *b* 18 April 1958; *s* of Geoffrey William Ipgrave and Ellen Ruth Ipgrave; *m* 1981, Julia Dawn Bailey; three *s. Educ:* Magdalen College Sch., Brackley; Oriel Coll., Oxford (BA 1978, MA 1994); Ripon Coll., Cuddesdon; St Chad's Coll., Durham (PhD 1999); SOAS, Univ. of London (MA 2005). Ordained deacon, 1982, priest, 1983; Asst Curate, All Saints, Oakham, 1982–85; Asst Priest, Ch of the Resurrection, Chiba, Japan, 1985–87; Team Vicar, The Ascension, Leicester, 1987–90; Team Vicar, 1990–95, Team Rector, 1995–99, The Holy Spirit, Leicester; Inter Faith Relns Advr, Archbishops' Council, and Sec., Chs' Commn on Inter Faith Relns, 1999–2004; Priest-in-charge, St John with St Andrew, Peckham, 2009–10; Archdeacon of Southwark, 2004–12, and Canon Missioner, Southwark Cathedral, 2010–12; Area Bishop of Woolwich, 2012–16. Hon. DLitt De Montfort, 2015. *Publications:* Christ in Ten Thousand Places, 1994; Trinity and Inter Faith Dialogue, 2003; The Road Ahead: Christian-Muslim dialogue, 2003; (ed) Scriptures in Dialogue, 2004; (ed) Bearing the Word, 2005; (ed) Building a Better Bridge, 2008; (ed) Justice and Rights: Christian and Muslim perspectives, 2010; (ed) Humanity: texts and contexts, 2011. *Recreations:* walking, all things Japanese. *Address:* Bishop's House, 22 The Close, Lichfield WS13 7LG. *T:* (01543) 306000. *E:* bishop.michael@lichfield.anglican.org.

**LICHFIELD, Dean of;** *see* Dorber, Very Rev. A. J.

**LICHFIELD, Archdeacon of;** *see* Weller, Ven. S. K.

**LICKISS, Sir Michael (Gillam),** Kt 1993; DL; Chairman: VisitBritain (formerly British Tourist Authority), 2003–05; Theatre Royal Plymouth Group, 2008–16; *b* 18 Feb. 1934; *s* of Frank Gillam and Elaine Rheta Lickiss; *m* 1st, 1959, Anita (marr. diss. 1979); two *s* two *d*; 2nd, 1987, Anne; one *s. Educ:* Bournemouth Grammar Sch.; London Sch. of Economics (BSc Econ 1955; Hon. Fellow 2006). FCA. Articled, Bournemouth, 1955–58; commissioned, Army, 1959–62; practised Bournemouth, 1962–68; Partner, Thornton Baker, Bournemouth, 1968–73, London, 1973–94: Exec. Partner, 1975; Managing Partner, 1985–89; firm's name changed to Grant Thornton, 1986; Sen. Partner, 1989–94. Chm., BTEC, subseq. Edexcel Foundn, 1994–2000 (former Mem., Council; Chm., Finance Cttee, 1985–93). DTI Inspector, jtly with Hugh Carlisle, QC, 1986–88; Lectr, UK and overseas. Chairman: Accountancy Television Ltd, 1992–94; Somerset Economic Partnership, 1994–99; West of England Develt Agency, 1994–97; South West of England RDA, 1998–2002; Director: MAI plc, 1994–96; United News and Media plc, 1996–97, and other cos. Institute of Chartered Accountants: Mem. Council, 1971–81, 1983–95; Vice-Pres., 1988–89; Dep. Pres., 1989–90; Pres., 1990–91; Past Chairman: Educn and Training, Tech. Cttee and Ethics Cttee; Professional Conduct Directorate; Chm., Somerset Rural Youth Project, 1997–99; Dir, British Trng Internat., 1998–2000. Chm., CCAB, 1990–91; Dep. Chm., Financial Reporting Council, 1990–91; Member: FEFCE, 1992–96; Copyright Tribunal, 1994–99; Senate, Engrg Council, 1996–99; Learning and Skills Nat. Council, 2000–02; Industrial Develt Adv. Bd, DTI, 2000–03. Founder President, Assoc. of Accounting Technicians, 1980–82. Chm., Genesis Project, Somerset, 2004–07. Trustee: Parnham Trust, 1992–96; RNAS Mus., 2001–03; World Heritage Coast, 2004–. Mem., Court of Govs, LSE, 1992–2009 (Gov. Emeritus, 2009–); Vice Chm., Court of Govs, Plymouth Univ., 1995–98; Mem. Council, London Univ., 1997–2003. Pres., Royal Cornwall Polytechnic Soc., 2006–08. DL Somerset, 2003. Hon. DBA: Bournemouth, 1994; UWE, 2002; Hon. DEd Plymouth, 2005. *Publications:* articles in learned jls. *Recreations:* walking, gardening. *E:* Lickissm@aol.com. *Club:* Royal Automobile.

**LICKLEY, Gavin Alexander Fraser,** CA; *b* 14 Aug. 1946; *s* of Alexander Thompson Lickley and Gladys Ann Fraser (*née* Smith); *m* 1973, Anne Muir Forrester; two *d. Educ:* Univ. of Edinburgh (LLB Hons 1967). CA 1970. Corporate Finance Exec., GKN plc, 1971–72; with Morgan Grenfell & Co. Ltd, 1972–95: Head of Banking, 1991–95; Chm., 1996–98; Bd Mem., Global Corporates and Instns Div., Deutsche Morgan Grenfell, then Deutsche Bank AG, 1995–99. Non-exec. Dir, Paragon Gp of Cos plc, 2003. *Recreations:* golf, ski-ing. *Address:* 6 Westmoreland Road, SW13 9RY. *T:* (020) 8748 7618. *Clubs:* City of London, Roehampton; Royal Wimbledon Golf.

**LICKLEY, Nigel James Dominic;** QC 2006; **His Honour Judge Lickley;** a Circuit Judge, since 2018; a Deputy High Court Judge, since 2018; *b* 27 Aug. 1960; *s* of James Edwin and Veronica Mabel Lickley; *m* 2000, Melanie De Freitas; two *d. Educ:* Queen Mary's Coll., Basingstoke; University Coll. London (LLB 1982). Called to the Bar, Gray's Inn, 1983, Bencher, 2011; Asst Recorder, 1998–2000; a Recorder, 2000–18; Leader, Western Circuit, 2010–13; Hd of Chambers, 3PB Barristers, 2015–18. Mem. (Lab) Winchester CC, 1994–98. Contested (Lab): Christchurch, July 1993; Basingstoke, 1997. *Recreations:* fly fishing, beekeeping. *Address:* Central Criminal Court, Old Bailey, EC4M 7EH. *Clubs:* Athenæum; Queen's Park Cricket (Trinidad).

**LICKORISH, Prof. William Bernard Raymond,** ScD; Professor of Geometric Topology, University of Cambridge, 1996–2004, now Emeritus; Fellow, Pembroke College, Cambridge, 1964–2004, now Emeritus; *b* 19 Feb. 1938; *s* of William Percy Lickorish and Florence Lickorish; *m* 1962, Margaret Ann Russell; one *s* two *d. Educ:* Merchant Taylors' Sch.; Pembroke Coll., Cambridge (ScD 1991). Asst Lectr in Maths, Univ. of Sussex, 1963–64; University of Cambridge: Asst Lectr, 1964–69; Lectr, 1969–90; Reader, 1990–96; Hd, Dept of Pure Maths and Mathematical Stats, 1997–2002; Asst Dir, then Dir of Studies in Maths, Pembroke Coll., 1964–91. Visiting Professor: Univ. of Wisconsin, 1967–68; Univ. of Calif, Berkeley, 1974, Santa Barbara, 1979–80 and 1996–97; Univ. of Texas, 1989; UCLA, 1990; Univ. of Melbourne, 2002–03. Sen. Whitehead Prize, London Mathematical Soc., 1991. *Publications:* An Introduction to Knot Theory, 1997; contrib. many articles on topology. *Recreations:* gardening, to walk, to bathe. *Address:* Pembroke College, Cambridge CB2 1RF.

**LIDDELL,** family name of **Baroness Liddell of Coatdyke** and **Baron Ravensworth.**

**LIDDELL OF COATDYKE,** Baroness *cr* 2010 (Life Peer), of Airdrie in Lanarkshire; **Helen Lawrie Liddell;** PC 1998; High Commissioner to Australia, 2005–09; Chairman, Annington Ltd, since 2017; *b* 6 Dec. 1950; *d* of late Hugh Reilly and Bridget Lawrie Reilly; *m* 1972, Dr Alistair Henderson Liddell; one *s* one *d. Educ:* St Patrick's High Sch., Coatbridge; Strathclyde Univ. Head, Econ. Dept, 1971–75, and Asst Sec., 1975–76, Scottish TUC; Econ. Correspondent, BBC Scotland, 1976–77; Scottish Sec., Labour Party, 1977–88; Dir, Personnel and Public Affairs, Scottish Daily Record and Sunday Mail (1986) Ltd, 1988–92; Chief Exec., Business Venture Prog., 1993–94. Contested (Lab) Fife E, Oct. 1974; MP (Lab): Monklands E, July 1994–1997; Airdrie and Shotts, 1997–2005. Opposition spokeswoman on Scotland, 1995–97; Economic Sec., HM Treasury, 1997–98;

Minister of State, Scottish Office, 1998–99; Minister of Transport, 1999; Minister of State for energy and competitiveness in Europe, DTI, 1999–2001; Sec. of State for Scotland, 2001–03. Mem., Adv. Cttee on Business Appts, 2014–. Non-exec. Dir, Visit Britain, 2010–14. Chm., G3 Gp, 2014–18 (Sen. Advr, 2012–14); Mem. Adv. Bd, PwC, 2015–. Trustee: Britain Australia Soc. Educn Trust, 2010–; Northcote Educnl Trust, 2011–. Dir, Aust. Chamber Orch., 2018–. *Publications:* Elite, 1990. *Recreations:* cooking, hill-walking, music, writing.

**LIDDELL, Dame Jennifer Gita;** *see* Abramsky, Dame J. G.

**LIDDELL, Air Vice-Marshal Peter,** CB 2002; CEng, FIET, FRAeS; Managing Director, Select Solutions Ltd, 2003–15; *b* 9 Oct. 1948; *s* of late Stanley Liddell and Mary Elizabeth Liddell (*née* Underwood); *m* 1979, Jennifer Marion, *d* of late Lt-Col Jack Prichard, DSO, MC and Eileen Patricia Prichard; two *s* one *d*. *Educ:* Keswick Sch.; Manchester Univ. (BSc). FIET (FIEE 1996); FRAeS 1996. Commnd (Univ. Cadet), 1966; served No 20 Sqn, Wildenrath, 1970–73; St Mawgan, 1973–75; Swanton Morley, 1975–77; MoD, 1978–80; Marham, 1981–82; sc 1983; OC Engrg Wing, Brize Norton, 1984–85; Cranwell, 1986–88; HQ Support Comd, 1989–90; Stn Comdr, Sealand, 1991–92; rcds 1993; HQ Logistics Comd, 1994–96; HQ Strike Comd, 1997–98; AO Communications Inf. Systems and Support Services, 1999–2000; Dir Gen., Equipment Support (Air), Defence Logistics Orgn, 2000–03. *Recreations:* golf, hill walking, theatre. *Club:* Royal Air Force.

**LIDDELL-GRAINGER, Ian Richard Peregrine;** MP (C) Bridgwater and West Somerset, since 2010 (Bridgwater, 2001–10); *b* 23 Feb. 1959; *s* of late David Ian Liddell-Grainger of Ayton and of Anne Mary Sibylla Liddell-Grainger (*née* Smith); *m* Jill Nesbit; one *s* two *d*. *Educ:* Wellesley House Sch., Kent; Millfield Sch., Somerset; S of Scotland Agricl Coll., Edinburgh (NCA). Farmer, Berwicks, 1980–85; Man. Dir, property mgt and develt co., 1985–. Mem., Tynedale DC, 1989–95. Contested (C) Torridge and Devon West, 1997. Major, Queen's Div., TA (formerly with 6th (Vol.) Bn), RRF. *Address:* (office) 16 Northgate, Bridgwater, Somerset TA6 3EU; c/o House of Commons, SW1A 0AA.

**LIDDIMENT, David;** media consultant, since 2015; Chairman, FremantleMedia UK, since 2015. *Educ:* Liverpool Univ. Benton and Bowles, Advertising Agency, 1974–75; Granada TV: Promotions Scriptwriter, 1975; researcher, dir, prod. and journalist; Exec. Prod., Children's Progs, 1986–88; Head of Entertainment, 1988–92; Dir of Progs, 1992–93; Head of Entertainment Gp, BBC TV, 1993–95; Dep. Man. Dir and Dir of Progs, 1995–96, Dep. Chm., 1997, LWT; Man. Dir, Granada UK Broadcasting, 1996–97; Dir of Progs, ITV Network Ltd, 1997–2002; Producer, The Old Vic Th. Co., 2003–07; Creative Dir, All3Media, 2003–14. Trustee, BBC Trust, 2007–14. Chm., The Hepworth Wakefield Trust, 2010–18.

**LIDDINGTON, Sir Bruce,** Kt 2000; freelance consultant; Managing Director, Transtatus Associates Ltd, since 2013; *b* 4 Sept. 1949; *s* of Gordon Philip Liddington and Joan Liddington; *m* 1978, Carol Jane Tuttle; two *s* one *d*. *Educ:* Queen Mary Coll., London Univ. (BA 1st Cl. Eng. Lit. 1971); King's Coll., Cambridge (PGCE 1972); Washington State Univ., USA (MA Eng. Lit. 1977). Teacher: Northcliffe Sch., Conisbrough, 1972–75; Westfield Sch., Wellingborough, 1975–76; Head of English, Westwood High Sch., Leek, 1977–81; Dep. Head, Ousedale Sch., Newport Pagnell, 1981–86; Headteacher, Northampton Sch. for Boys, 1986–2000. Advr, Quality Assce Unit, DfEE, 1999–2001; Professional Advr, Academies Div., DfES, 2000–06; Schs Comr for England, DfES, later DCSF, 2006–09; Dir Gen., E-ACT, 2009–13. *Recreations:* opera, reading, music, films, travel, food, six grandchildren.

**LIDDLE,** family name of **Baron Liddle**.

**LIDDLE,** Baron *cr* 2010 (Life Peer), of Carlisle in the County of Cumbria; **Roger John Liddle;** *b* 14 June 1947; *s* of John Thwaites Liddle and Elizabeth Liddle; *m* 1983, Caroline Thomson, *qv*; one *s*. *Educ:* Robert Ferguson Primary Sch., Carlisle; Denton Holme Jun. Sch., Carlisle; Carlisle Grammar Sch.; Queen's Coll., Oxford (BA (Modern Hist.) 1968; MPhil (Mgt Studies) 1970). Oxford Sch. of Social and Administrative Studies, 1970–74; Ind. Relns Officer, Electricity Council, 1974–76; Special Advr to Rt Hon. William Rodgers, MP, 1976–81; Dir, Public Policy Centre, 1982–87; Man. Dir, Prima Europe Ltd, 1987–97; Special Advr on European Affairs to Prime Minister, 1997–2004; Mem., cabinet of Peter Mandelson, EC, 2004–06; Principal Advr to the Pres. of the EC, 2006–07. Chm., Adv. Panel on New Industry, New Jobs to Sec. of State for Business, Innovation and Skills, 2009–10. Opposition front bench spokesman on Europe, H of L, 2011–14. Vice-Chm., 2007–09, Chm., 2009–17, Policy Network. Member: (Lab) Oxford CC, 1971–76; Lambeth BC, (SDP) 1982–86, (Lib Dem) 1994–95; (Lab) Cumbria CC, 2013–. Chm., Cumbria Vision, 2007–10. Pro-Chancellor, Lancaster Univ., 2013–. *Publications:* (with Peter Mandelson) The Blair Revolution, 1996; The New Case for Europe, 2005; (ed jtly) Global Europe, Social Europe, 2006; (with P. Diamond) Beyond New Labour, 2009; Lectr The Europe Dilemma: Britain and the drama of EU integration, 2014; The Risk of Brexit, 2015. *Recreations:* history, politics, entertaining, holidays in Italy. *Address:* House of Lords, SW1A 0PW. *Club:* Reform.

**LIDDLE, Caroline;** *see* Thomson, C.

**LIDINGTON, Rt Hon. Sir David (Roy),** KCB 2019; CBE 2016; PhD; PC 2010; MP (C) Aylesbury, since 1992; *b* 30 June 1956; *s* of Roy N. and Rosa Lidington; *m* 1989, Helen Mary Farquhar Parry; four *s* (incl. twins). *Educ:* Haberdashers' Aske's Sch., Elstree; Sidney Sussex Coll., Cambridge (MA, PhD). British Petroleum plc, 1983–86; RTZ plc, 1986–87; Special Adviser to: Home Sec., 1987–89; Foreign Sec., 1989–90; Consultant, PPU Ltd, 1991–92. PPS to Leader of the Opposition, 1997–99; Opposition front-bench spokesman on: home affairs, 1999–2001; HM Treasury affairs, 2001–02; environment, food and rural affairs, 2002–03; NI, 2003–07; foreign affairs, 2007–10; Minister of State, FCO, 2010–16; Leader of the H of C and Lord President of the Council, 2016–17; Lord Chancellor and Sec. of State for Justice, 2017–18; Minister for the Cabinet Office and Chancellor of the Duchy of Lancaster, 2018–19. Trustee, NPG, 2016–17. *Publications:* articles on Tudor history. *Recreations:* history, choral singing. *Address:* House of Commons, SW1A 0AA. *T:* (020) 7219 3000; 100 Walton Street, Aylesbury, Bucks HP21 7QP. *T:* (01296) 482102.

**LIDSTONE, Russ;** Group Chief Executive Officer, The Creative Engagement Group, since 2016; *b* Brixham, S Devon, 16 March 1970; *s* of Derek Lidstone and Rita Lidstone; *m* 1999, Amanda Rees; one *s* one *d*. *Educ:* Churston Grammar Sch.; Univ. of Keele (BA Jt Hons Hist. and Sociol.). Ethnographic Researcher, Coca-Cola, 1992–93; Planner, McCann Erickson Advertising, 1993–96; Senior Planner: Butterfield Day Devito Hockney, 1996–99; HHCL & Partners, 1999–2001; Head of Planning: Lowe, 2001–05; JWT, 2005–06; Chief Strategy Officer, 2006–09, CEO, 2009–15, Euro RSCG London, subseq. Havas Worldwide London. Non-exec. Dir, Basketball England, 2015–18. Mentor, Marketing Acad., 2012–; Mem., Marketing Gp of GB, 2014–. Entrepreneurial projects evaluator, Saïd Business Sch., 2011–; Vis. Lectr, Univ. of W London, 2011–. FRSA 2015. *Recreations:* gym, spinning, music, basketball, family. *Address:* The Creative Engagement Group, 36 Great Titchfield Street, W1W 8BQ.

**LIEBERMAN, Joseph I.;** Member for Connecticut, US Senate, 1989–2012 (Democrat 1989–2006, Ind Democrat, 2006–12); *b* 24 Feb. 1942; *s* of Henry Lieberman and Marcia Lieberman; *m* 1983, Hadassah Freilich; one *d*; one step *s*, and one *s* one *d* from a previous marriage. *Educ:* Yale Univ. (BA 1964; JD 1967). Called to the Bar, Conn, 1967; Partner, Lieberman, Segaloff & Wolfson, New Haven, 1972–83. Mem. (Democrat), State Senate of Connecticut, 1971–81 (Majority Leader, 1975–81); Attorney-Gen., Conn, 1983–89. Democratic candidate for US Vice-President, 2000. *Publications:* The Power Broker, 1966; The Scorpion and the Tarantula, 1970; The Legacy, 1981; Child Support in America, 1986; In Praise of Public Life, 2000.

**LIEBESCHUETZ, Prof. (John Hugo) Wolfgang (Gideon),** PhD; FSA; FBA 1991; Professor of Classical and Archaeological Studies, and Head, Department of Classics and Archaeology, Nottingham University, 1979–92, now Professor Emeritus; *b* Hamburg, 22 June 1927; *s* of Prof. H. Liebeschuetz and Dr E. A. R. Liebeschuetz (*née* Plaut); *m* 1955, Margaret Rosa Taylor; one *s* three *d*. *Educ:* UCL (BA 1951; Fellow 1997); PhD London 1957. Schoolteacher, 1957–63; Leicester University: Lectr in Classics, 1963–74; Sen. Lectr, 1974–78; Reader, 1978–79. FSA 1999. Mem., Princeton Inst. for Advanced Study, 1993. Corresp. Mem., German Archaeol Inst., 1994. *Publications:* Antioch: city and imperial administration in the later Roman Empire, 1972; Continuity and Change in Roman Religion, 1979; Barbarians and Bishops: army, church and state in the age of Arcadius and Chrysostom, 1990; From Diocletian to the Arab Conquest: change in the late Roman Empire, 1990; The Decline and Fall of the Roman City, 2001; Ambrose of Milan: political letters and speeches, 2005; Decline and Change in Late Antiquity: religion, barbarians and their historiography, 2006; Ambrose and John Chrysostom: clerics between desert and empire, 2011; East and West in Late Antiquity, 2015; contribs to learned jls. *Address:* 1 Clare Valley, The Park, Nottingham NG7 1BU.

**LIEBLING, Prof. Alison,** PhD; Director, Prisons Research Centre, since 2000, and Professor of Criminology and Criminal Justice, since 2006, University of Cambridge; *b* Birmingham, 26 July 1963; *d* of Leonard Irving Liebling and Angela Joan Liebling (*née* Griffiths). *Educ:* John Willmott Sch.; Univ. of York (BA Politics 1984); Univ. of Hull (MA Criminol. (Dist.) 1986); Trinity Hall, Cambridge (PhD Criminol. 1991). Res. Asst, Univ. of Hull, 1986–87; University of Cambridge: Res. Associate, 1990–92; Jun. Res. Fellow, Trinity Hall, 1991–94; Sen. Res. Associate, 1992–2001; Lectr, 2001–03; Reader, 2003–06; ESRC Post-doctoral Res. Fellow, 1994–98; Leverhulme Special Res. Fellow, 1998–2000. Adjunct Prof., Key Centre for Ethics, Law, Justice and Governance, Griffith Univ., Qld, 2013–16. Hon. Dr Örebro, 2012. *Publications:* Suicides in Prison, 1992; (jtly) The Prison Officer, 2001, 2nd edn 2010; (with H. Arnold) Prisons and Their Moral Performance: a study of values, quality and prison life, 2004; (with S. Maruna) The Effects of Imprisonment, 2005; (with J. Tankebe) Legitimacy and Criminal Justice: international explorations, 2013; contrib. articles to jls incl. Punishment and Society, British Jl Criminol., Theoretical Criminol., British Jl Sociol., Howard Jl Criminal Justice, Australian and NZ Jl Criminol., Qualitative Inquiry, Criminol. and Criminal Justice. *Address:* Institute of Criminology, University of Cambridge, Sidgwick Site, Sidgwick Avenue, Cambridge CB3 9DA. *T:* (01223) 335364, 335371. *E:* al115@cam.ac.uk.

**LIESNER, Hans Hubertus,** CB 1980; Member, 1989–97, Deputy Chairman, 1989–95, Monopolies and Mergers Commission; *b* 30 March 1929; *e s* of Curt Liesner, lawyer, and Edith L. (*née* Neumann); *m* 1st, 1957, Jane Boland (marr. diss. 1964); one *s* one *d*; 2nd, 1968, Thelma Seward. *Educ:* German grammar schs; Bristol Univ. (BA); Nuffield Coll., Oxford; MA Cantab. Asst Lectr, later Lectr, in Economics, London Sch. of Economics, 1955–59; Lectr in Economics, Univ. of Cambridge; Fellow, Dir of Studies in Economics and some time Asst Bursar, Emmanuel Coll., Cambridge, 1959–70; Under-Sec. (Economics), HM Treasury, 1970–76; Dep. Sec., and Chief Econ. Advr, DTI (formerly Industry, Trade and Prices and Consumer Protection), 1976–89. Standing Mem., Adv. Bd on Fair Trading in Telecoms, 1997–2000; Gov., 1989–, Mem. Council of Mgt, 1989–2011, NIESR; Chm. Adv. Gp, ESRC Centre for Economic Learning and Social Evolution, 1996–2010. *Publications:* The Import Dependence of Britain and Western Germany, 1957; Case Studies in European Economic Union: the mechanics of integration (with J. E. Meade and S. J. Wells), 1962; Atlantic Harmonisation: making free trade work, 1968; Britain and the Common Market: the effect of entry on the pattern of manufacturing production (with S. S. Han), 1971; articles in jls, etc. *Recreations:* walking, gardening. *Address:* 32 The Grove, Brookmans Park, Herts AL9 7RN. *T:* (01707) 653269. *Club:* Reform.

**LIEU, Prof. Judith Margaret,** PhD; FBA 2014; Lady Margaret's Professor of Divinity, University of Cambridge, 2007–18, now Emerita (Chair, Faculty Board of Divinity, 2010–14; University Gender Champion, Arts, Humanities, Social Sciences, 2015–17); Fellow, Robinson College, Cambridge, 2008–18, now Emerita; *b* 25 May 1951; *d* of John and Zoe Bending; *m* 1976, Samuel N. C. Lieu; one *d*. *Educ:* Bromley High Sch. for Girls; Univ. of Durham (BA Hons Theol. 1972, MA Theol. 1973); Univ. of Oxford (PGCE 1974); Univ. of Birmingham (PhD 1980). Hd of RE, Abbey Sch., Reading, 1974–76; Lectr in Biblical Studies, Queen's Coll., Birmingham, 1981–84; Lectr in Christian Origins and Early Judaism, 1985–95, Reader in New Testament, 1995, KCL; Sen. Lectr in Hist., 1996–98, Associate Prof., 1998, Macquarie Univ., Sydney; Prof. of New Testament Studies, KCL, 1999–2007. President: Studiorum Novi Testamenti Societas, 2015–16; Colloquium Biblicum Lovaniense, 2019. Internat. Hon. Mem., Amer. Acad. of Arts and Scis, 2019. Editor, New Testament Studies, 2003–09. *Publications:* The Second and Third Epistles of John: history and background, 1986; The Theology of the Johannine Epistles, 1991; (ed jtly) The Jews between Pagans and Greeks, 1994; Image and Reality: the Jews in the world of the Christians in the second century, 1996; The Gospel According to Luke, 1997; Neither Jew nor Greek: constructing early Christianity, 2002, 2nd edn 2015; Christian Identity in the Jewish and Graeco-Roman World, 2004; (ed jtly) The Oxford Handbook of Biblical Studies, 2006; (ed jtly) Biblical Traditions in Transmission, 2006; I, II, III John, 2008; Marcion and the Making of a Heretic, 2015; (ed jtly) Christianity in the Second Century, 2017; (ed jtly) The Oxford Handbook of Johannine Studies, 2018. *Recreations:* reading, walking, theatre. *Address:* Robinson College, Grange Road, Cambridge CB3 9AN.

**LIEVEN, Prof. Dominic Christophe Bogdan,** PhD; FBA 2001; Senior Research Fellow, Trinity College, Cambridge, 2011–19; *b* 19 Jan. 1952; *s* of Prince Alexander Lieven and Veronica Lieven (*née* Monahan); *m* 1985, Mikiko Fujiwara; one *s* one *d*. *Educ:* Downside Sch.; Christ's Coll., Cambridge (BA); SSEES, London Univ. (PhD 1978). Kennedy Schol., Harvard Univ., 1973–74; FCO, 1974–75; London School of Economics and Political Science: Lectr, 1978–93; Prof. of Russian Govt and History, 1993–2011; Hd, Dept of Govt, 2001–04; Hd, Dept of Internat. Hist., 2009–11; Mem., Govg Council, 2005–10. Humboldt Fellow, 1986; Visiting Professor: Univ. of Tokyo, 1992–94; Harvard Univ., 1993. Member, Editorial Board: Jl Contemporary Hist., 1994–2004; Slavonic Rev., 2000–. Order of Friendship (Russia), 2014. *Publications:* Russia and the Origins of the First World War, 1983; Russia's Rulers under the Old Regime, 1989; The Aristocracy in Europe 1815–1914, 1992; Nicholas II, 1993; Empire: the Russian Empire and its rivals, 2000; Russia against Napoleon: the struggle for Europe, 1807–1814, 2009 (Wolfson History Prize, 2009; Prix de la Fondation Napoleon, 2010); Towards the Flame: empire, war and the end of Tsarist Russia, 2015 (Pushkin House (London) Prize, 2016); books trans.

German, Japanese, Italian, Dutch, Russian, French, Spanish, Portuguese and Chinese. *Recreation:* collecting Russian regimental models. *Club:* Travellers.
*See also E. V. M. Lieven, N. M. D. Lieven.*

**LIEVEN, Prof. Elena Veronica Maria,** PhD; FBA 2018; Professor of Psychology, University of Manchester, since 2000; Director, ESRC International Centre for Language and Communicative Development, Universities of Manchester, Liverpool and Lancaster, since 2014; *b* London, 18 Aug. 1947; *d* of Alexander Lieven and Veronica Lieven (*née* Monahan); partner, 1981, Patrick John Devine. *Educ:* More Hse Sch.; City of Westminster Coll.; New Hall, Cambridge (BA 1969; PhD 1980). Asst Lectr, Univ. of Cambridge, 1974–79; University of Manchester: Lectr, 1979–95; Sen. Lectr, 1995–97; Reader, 1997–2000; Dir, Max Planck Child Study Centre, 1998–2014; Sen. Res. Scientist, Max Planck Inst. for Evolutionary Anthropol., Leipzig, 1998–2012. Ed., Jl Child Lang., 1996–2005. Hon. Prof. of Child Lang. Develt, Univ. of Leipzig, 1999–2012. Nijmegen Lectr, Max Planck Inst. for Psycholinguistics, 2018. Pres., Internat. Assoc. for Study of Child Lang., 2008–11. Vice Chm., CND, 1986–88. Jun. Vice Pres., 1989–90, Pres., 1990–91, Sen. Vice Pres., 1991–92, Manchester Univ. Br., Assoc. of Univ. Teachers, 1989–92. MAE 2018. Fellow, Cognitive Sci. Soc., 2017. *Publications:* (ed jtly) Women in Society, 1981; (ed jtly) Crosslinguistic Approaches to the Psychology of Language: research in the tradition of Don Isaac Slobin, 2009; (with B. Ambridge) Child Language Acquisition: contrasting theoretical approaches, 2011; contribs to learned jls incl. Develtl Psychol., Cognition, Cognitive Sci., Cognitive Linguistics, Jl Child Lang., Lang. and Cognition, Jl Exptl Child Psychol., Infancy, Proc. NAS, Lang. *Recreations:* classical music, opera and playing the piano, living up to my reputation in the Papua New Guinea village of Imbiyip as a 'tripela meri', operating within and against the establishment, cooking, gardening, walking in the great outdoors, travelling, spending time with the young of my various families. *Address:* Child Study Centre, Coupland 1 Building, University of Manchester, Oxford Road, Manchester M13 9PL. *T:* (0161) 275 2580, (0161) 275 2444, *Fax:* (0161) 275 8587. *E:* elena.lieven@manchester.ac.uk.
*See also D. C. B. Lieven, N. M. D. Lieven.*

**LIEVEN, Hon. Dame Nathalie Marie Daniella,** DBE 2019; **Hon. Mrs Justice Lieven;** a Judge of the High Court, Family Division, since 2019; *b* 20 May 1964; *d* of Alexander Lieven and Veronica Lieven; *m* 1995, Stewart Wright; one *s* two *d*. *Educ:* Godolphin and Latymer Sch.; Poly. of Central London (Dip. Law); Trinity Hall, Cambridge (BA 1986). Called to the Bar, Gray's Inn, 1989, Hon. Bencher, 2010; QC 2006; a Dep. High Court Judge, 2016–19. *Recreation:* books. *Address:* Royal Courts of Justice, Strand, WC2A 2LL.

**LIEW Foo Yew,** OBE 2018; PhD, DSc; FRCPath; FRS 2012; FRSE; Gardiner Professor and Head of Department of Immunology, University of Glasgow, 1991, now Distinguished Professor in Immunology; *b* 22 May 1943; *s* of Liew Soon and Chai Man Ngon; *m* 1973, Dr Woon Ling Chan; one *s*. *Educ:* Monash Univ., Australia (BSc 1st cl. Hons); ANU (PhD; DSc). MRCPath 1990, FRCPath 1996. FRSE 1995. Lectr, Univ. of Malaya, 1972–77; Sen. Scientist, 1977–84, Head, Dept of Immunology, 1984–91, Wellcome Res. Lab., Beckenham. Life Mem., Nat. Biol Standards Bd, 1996. FMedSci 1999. *Publications:* Vaccination Strategies of Tropical Diseases, 1989; Immunology of intracellular parasitism, 1998; more than 250 papers in learned jls. *Recreations:* reading classical Chinese, gardening. *Address:* Centre for Immunology, Institute of Infection, Immunity and Inflammation, University of Glasgow, Sir Graeme Davies Building, 120 University Place, Glasgow G12 8TA; 37 Elwill Way, Beckenham, Kent BR3 3AB.

**LIFE, Vivien Frances;** Director, Asia and Australasia Negotiations, Department for International Trade; *b* 30 May 1957; *m* 1989, Timothy Michael Dowse, CMG; two *d*. *Educ:* St Hilda's Coll., Oxford (BA). Civil Service Fast Stream, 1979–81; HM Treasury, 1981–88; entered FCO, 1988; EU Ext. Dept, FCO, 1988–91; First Sec., Washington, 1992–96; Deputy Head: EU Dept Ext., FCO, 1996–97; Latin America and Caribbean Dept, FCO, 1997–99; Head: Consultancy Gp, FCO Services, 1999–2003; Strategy Gp, FCO, 2003–06; Ext. Relns Gp, Europe Directorate, FCO, 2006–08; Enlargement SE and Wider Europe Gp, FCO, 2008–10; Climate Change and Energy Dept, FCO, 2010–12; Ambassador to Denmark, 2012–16; Dir, Free Trade Agreements, DIT, 2016. *Address:* Department for International Trade, King Charles Street, SW1A 2AH.

**LIFFORD,** 9th Viscount *cr* 1781 (Ire.); **Edward James Wingfield Hewitt;** DL; *b* 27 Jan. 1949; *s* of 8th Viscount Lifford and Alison Mary Patricia, *d* of T. W. Ashton; *S* father, 1987; *m* 1976, Alison Mary, *d* of Robert Law; one *s* two *d*. *Educ:* The Old Malthouse, Dorset; Aiglon College, Switzerland. DL Hants, 2004. *Recreation:* country sports. *Heir: s* Hon. James Thomas Wingfield Hewitt [*b* 29 Sept. 1979; *m* 2008, Lady Iona Douglas-Home, *er d* of Earl of Home, *qv;* one *s*]. *Address:* Field House, Hursley, Hants SO21 2LE. *T:* (01962) 775203. *Clubs:* Boodle's, Pratt's.

**LIFSCHUTZ, Alexander Joseph;** Director, Lifschutz Davidson Sandilands (formerly Lifschutz Davidson), architects, since 1986; *b* 11 Feb. 1952; *s* of late Simon Lifschutz and of Hanna Lifschutz; *m* 1978, Monique Charlesworth; one *s* one *d*. *Educ:* St Paul's Sch.; Univ. of Bristol (BSc Jt Hons Sociology and Psychology 1974); Architectural Assoc. Foster Associates, 1981–86. *Projects* include: Broadwall Community Housing, 1994 (Royal Fine Arts Commn/Sunday Times Building of the Year, 1995; RIBA Award, 1995; Nat. Housing Design Award, DoE, 1996; Civic Trust Housing Award, 1996); mixed use develt, Oxo Tower Wharf, 1996 (Urban Regeneration Award, Royal Fine Art Commn, 1997; RIBA Award, 1997; Civic Trust Award, 1997); Oxo 8th Floor Restaurant, 1997 (RIBA Award, 1998); Royal Victoria Dock Bridge, 1999 (AJ/Bovis/Royal Acad. Award, 1997; ICE Merit Award, 1998; RIBA Award, 1999; Civic Trust Award, 2000); Hungerford Bridge, 2002 (Royal Fine Art Commn Award, 2003; Civic Trust Award, 2003); Davidson Bldg, 2003 (RIBA Award, 2004; BCO Award, 2005); Bonhams Auction House, 2013 (AIA Award 2014); JW3, 2013 (RIBA Award, 2014); *current projects* include: Doon St Leisure Centre, London's South Bank. Mem. Council, Architectural Assoc., 2002– (Pres., 2009–11). Chm., Trustees, Body and Soul, 2008–. *Recreation:* family. *Address:* Lifschutz Davidson Sandilands Ltd, Island Studios, 22 St Peter's Square, W6 9NW.

**LIGHT, Johanne Erica;** *see* Delahunty, J. E.

**LIGHT, Prof. Paul Henry,** PhD; CPsychol, FBPsS; Vice Chancellor, University of Winchester (formerly Principal and Chief Executive, King Alfred's College, then University College Winchester), 2000–06; *b* 26 Aug. 1947; *s* of Ronald and Gladys Light; *m* 1970, Vivienne Mary Baker; one *s* two *d*. *Educ:* St John's Coll., Cambridge (Schol.; BA 1st cl. Natural Scis 1969; PhD Develtl Psychol. 1975); Univ. of Nottingham (MA Educnl Psychol. 1970). FBPsS 1987; CPsychol 1988. Demonstrator in Exptl Psychol., Univ. of Cambridge, 1972–74; Lectr, then Sen. Lectr, Dept of Psychol., Univ. of Southampton, 1978–87; Prof. of Educn, and Dir, Centre for Human Develt and Learning, Open Univ., 1987–92; Prof. of Psychol., Univ. of Southampton, 1992–97; Pro Vice Chancellor (Acad.), Bournemouth Univ., 1997–2000. Vis. lectureships and professorships at Univ. of NC and Univ. of Provence. FRSA 1995. DUniv Winchester, 2008. *Publications:* The Development of Social Sensitivity, 1979; (with G. Butterworth) Social Cognition, 1982; (with M. Richards) Children of Social Worlds, 1986; (jtly) Learning to Think, 1991; (jtly) Becoming a Person, 1991; (jtly) Growing up in a Changing Society, 1991; (with G. Butterworth) Context and Cognition, 1993; (with K. Littleton) Learning with Computers, 1999; (jtly) Learning Sites, 1999; contrib. numerous articles to ed collections and refereed jls. *Recreations:* gardening, walking, sailing. *Address:* Yawl Cliff, Yawl Hill Lane, Lyme Regis DT7 3XF. *T:* (01297) 442252. *E:* paul.light@hotmail.co.uk.

**LIGHT, Sally Elizabeth;** Chief Executive, Motor Neurone Disease Association, since 2012; *b* Groby, Leics, 9 Dec. 1959; *d* of Herbert Royston Light and Peggy Light. *Educ:* Chelsea Coll., Univ. of London (BSc Nursing Studies 1983); NHS Gen. Mgt Trng Scheme 1995; Univ. of Manchester (MA Health Services Mgt 1998). Acute hospital staff nurse: Salford Royal 1983–84; Manchester Royal Infirmary, 1984–85; health visitor, N Manchester HA, 1985–91; Primary Care Facilitator, Manchester FHSA, 1991–93; Service and Rehab Manager, Central Manchester Healthcare Trust, 1995–98; Associate Dir, Manchester HA, 1998–2000; Service Improvement Mgt, NHS Modernisation Agency, 2000–02; Exec. Dir, Barnsley Hosp. NHS Foundn Trust, 2002–06; Dir, Vancouver HA, Canada, 2006–10; Dir of Rehabilitation, Royal Hosp. for Neuro-Disability, 2010–12. *Recreations:* adventure, travelling, wildlife spotting (home and abroad), cycling, daily yoga and good food (sourcing, cooking and eating). *Address:* Motor Neurone Disease Association, 10–15 Notre Dame Mews, Northampton NN1 2BG. *T:* (01604) 250505, *Fax:* (01604) 611858. *E:* sally.light@mndassociation.org.

**LIGHTBOWN, Ronald William,** MA; FSA, FRAS; art historian and author; Keeper of the Department of Metalwork, Victoria and Albert Museum, 1985–89; *b* Darwen, Lancs, 2 June 1932; *s* of late Vincent Lightbown and Helen Anderson Lightbown (*née* Burness); *m* 1962, Mary Dorothy Webster; one *s*. *Educ:* St Catharine's Coll., Cambridge (MA). FSA, FRAS. Victoria and Albert Museum: Asst Keeper, Library, 1958–64; Asst Keeper, Dept of Metalwork, 1964–73; Dep. Keeper, 1973–76, Keeper, 1976–85, Library. Fellow, Inst. for Res. in the Humanities, Wisconsin Univ., 1974. Pres., Jewellery History Soc., 1990–93; a Vice-Pres., Soc. of Antiquaries, 1986–90 (Sec., 1979–86); Associate Trustee, Soane Mus., 1981–98. Socio dell' Ateneo Veneto, for contrib. to study of culture of Venice and the Veneto, 1987; Socio dell' Accademia Clementina, Bologna, for contribns to study of Italian art, 1988; Serena Medal for Italian Studies, British Acad., 2005. *Publications:* Secular Goldsmiths' in Medieval France: a history, 1978; Sandro Botticelli, 1978, 2nd edn, 1989 (Prix Vasari, 1990); (with M. Corbett) The Comely Frontispiece, 1978; (ed and trans. with A. Caiger-Smith) Piccolpasso: the art of the potter, 1980, 2nd edn 2007; Donatello and Michelozzo, 1980; Andrea Mantegna, 1986; Piero della Francesca, 1992 (Prix de Mai des Libraires de France, 1992); Viaggio in un capolavoro di Piero della Francesca, 1992; (with J. Delumeau) Histoire de l'art: la Renaissance, 1995; Carlo Crivelli, 2004; An Architect Earl: Edward Augustus Stratford, 2nd Earl of Aldborough (1736–1801), 2008; (ed and introd) History of Art in 18th Century England (series of source-books on 18th century British art), 14 vols, 1970–71; V&A Museum catalogues and publications: (pt author) Italian Sculpture, 1964; Tudor Domestic Silver, 1970; Scandinavian and Baltic Silver, 1975; French Silver, 1979; (with M. Archer) India Observed, 1982; Medieval European Jewellery, 1992; contrib. to books, and many articles in learned jls, incl. Burlington Magazine, Warburg Jl and Art Bulletin. *Recreations:* reading, travel, music, conversation. *Address:* Barrowmount House, Goresbridge, Co. Kilkenny, Ireland.

**LIGHTFOOT, His Honour George Michael;** a Circuit Judge, 1986–2001; *b* 9 March 1936; *s* of Charles Herbert Lightfoot and Mary Lightfoot (*née* Potter); *m* 1963, Dorothy (*née* Miller); two *s* two *d*. *Educ:* St Michael's Catholic College, Leeds; Exeter College, Oxford (MA). National Service, 1955–57: York and Lancaster Regt; interpreter and interrogator, Intelligence Corps, Cyprus, 1956–57. Schoolmaster, 1962–66. Called to the Bar, Inner Temple, 1966; practised on NE circuit. Recorder, 1985–86; Dep. Circuit Judge, 2001–06. Mem., Home Farm Trust, 1980–; President: Leeds Friends of Home Farm Trust, 1987–2015; Mencap, Leeds, 1987–2003. Vice-Pres., Hunslet Hawks Rugby League Football Club, 1999–2009. Mem., Catholic Union of GB. *Recreations:* cricket and sport in general, gardening (labourer), learning to listen to music, reading. *E:* gmlightfoot@hotmail.com. *Clubs:* Yorkshire County Cricket; Northern Cricket Society.

**LIGHTFOOT, Prof. Jane Lucy,** DPhil; FBA 2018; Professor of Greek Literature, University of Oxford, since 2014; Charlton Fellow and Tutor in Classics, New College, Oxford, since 2003; *b* Liverpool, 25 Oct. 1969; *d* of Thomas Henry Lightfoot and Audrey Lightfoot (*née* Croall). *Educ:* Belvedere Sch. GPDST; St John's Coll., Oxford (BA 1st Cl. 1992; MA 1994; DPhil 1995; Conington Prize for Thesis 1999). Jubilee Scholar, St Hugh's Coll., Oxford, 1993–94; Prize Fellow, 1994–2000, Post-doctoral Fellow, 2000–03, All Souls Coll., Oxford. *Publications:* (ed) Parthenius of Nicaea, 1999; (ed) Lucian, On the Syrian Goddess, 2003; The Sibylline Oracles, 2003; Hellenistic Collection, 2009; Dionysius Periegetes, 2014; articles in learned jls. *Recreations:* Schubert, necrology, literary pilgrimages. *Address:* New College, Holywell Street, Oxford OX1 3BN. *T:* (01865) 279547. *E:* jane.lightfoot@new.ox.ac.uk.

**LIGHTFOOT, Nigel Francis,** CBE 2009; FRCPath, FFPH; Managing Director and Head, Chemical, Biological, Radiological and Nuclear strategies and crisis management, Nigel Lightfoot Associates Ltd, since 2010; Executive Director, Connecting Organizations for Regional Disease Surveillance, 2012–16; Chief Advisor, and Head, Pandemic Influenza Programme, Health Protection Agency, 2007–10; *b* 19 March 1945; *s* of Leslie and Joyce Lightfoot; *m* 1967, Antonia Calascione; two *s* one *d*. *Educ:* Brunts Sch.; St Mary's Hospital Med. Sch., London (MB BS 1968); London Sch. of Hygiene and Tropical Medicine (MSc 1976). FRCPath 1979. MO, RN, 1966–82, served in nuclear submarines, Malta and NI, and became consultant med. microbiologist, 1979; Public Health Laboratory Service, 1982–2002: Dir, Taunton Public Health Lab.; Dir, Newcastle Public Health Lab.; Dir, PHLS North; developed chemical, biol, and radionuclear trng and exercises strategy, DoH, 2002; Dir, Emergency Response, HPA, 2003–07. Hon. Consultant to RN, 1982–2010. Mem., Adv. Gp on Medical Countermeasures, MoD, 1995–2010; Special Advr, Global Health Security, DoH, 2002–13; ind. consultant advr on Chem., Biol, Radiol and Nuclear to EC Directorate-Gen. for Internat. Cooperation and Develt and to ISTC Kazakhstan, 2016–. Mem., Kangaroo Gp, EP, 2012–. Trustee, Global Action Fund for Fungal Diseases, 2015– (Chm., 2017–); Chm., Amref Health Africa UK, 2018–. Visiting Professor: Cranfield Univ., 2007–14; Keio Univ., Tokyo, 2008–16. Sen. Consulting Fellow (formerly Associate Fellow), RIIA, 2012–. FFPH 2010. *Publications:* Microbiological Analysis of Food and Water: guidelines for quality assurance, 1998; over 100 learned papers on microbiology and bioterrorism. *Recreations:* horses, riding to hounds, shooting, photography, cooking. *Address:* 53 Fern Avenue, Jesmond, Newcastle upon Tyne NE2 2QU. *E:* Nigel.Lightfoot@mac.com.

**LIGHTING, Jane;** non-executive Director, Countrywide plc, since 2014; *b* 22 Dec. 1956. Founder, and Man. Dir, Minotaur International, 1995–99; Man. Dir, Broadcast and Television, 1999–2002, CEO, 2002–03, Flextech; CEO, Five (formerly Channel Five Broadcasting Ltd), 2003–08. Non-executive Director: Trinity Mirror plc, 2008–15; Paddy Power, 2009–13. Chairman: British Television Distributors Assoc., 1995–96; RTS, 2006–16 (Trustee, 2008–16). Gov., Nat. Film and Television Sch., 2001–07. FRSA 2006; FRTS 2006. *Recreations:* gardening, escaping to the country. *Club:* Groucho.

**LIGHTMAN, Brian Peter Leon**; Director, Lightman Consulting Ltd, since 2016; General Secretary, Association of School and College Leaders, 2010–16; *b* London, 15 June 1955; *s* of Ivor Harry Lightman, CB; *m* 1981, Eva Maria Ursula; four *d*. *Educ*: Westminster City Sch.; Univ. of Southampton (BA (Hons) German 1978; PGCE Mod. Langs 1979); Open Univ. (MA Educn 1993). Teacher of German and French, Hazelwick Sch., Crawley, 1979–84; Hd, Mod. Langs, 1984–89, Hd, 6th Form, 1986–89, Sondes Place Sch., Dorking, Sen. Teacher and Curriculum Develt Manager, 1989–91, Dep. Hd, 1991–95, St Martin's Sch., Hutton, Brentwood; Headteacher: Llantwit Major Sch., Vale of Glamorgan, 1995–99; St Cyres Sch., Vale of Glamorgan, 1999–2010. O Level Examnr, Oxford Delegacy, 1982–87; ESTYN Ind. Inspector, 1999–2010; Member: Bd of Dirs, Cardiff and the Vale, Careers Wales, 2002–06; 14–19 Specialist Panel, Ministerial Adv. Gp, Welsh Govt, 2006–10. Secondary Heads Association, subseq. Association of School and College Leaders: Welsh rep., Nat. Council, 1998–2010; Pres., Wales, 2002–03; Hon. Treas., 2002–05; Pres., 2007–08. Member, Board of Directors: St Donat's Arts Centre, 1996–99; Careers and Enterprise Co., 2015–; Mem., Bd of Trustees, E-ACT Acad. Trust (Chair, Educn Cttee); Trustee, PiXL Edge, 2015–18; Patron, Nat. Citizen Service, 2014–17. *Publications*: Lesson Learned, 2018; articles in jls, newspapers, etc. *Recreations*: family, walking, caravanning, music. *T*: 07977 541868. *E*: brian@lightmanconsulting.co.uk. *W*: www.twitter.com/brianlightman.

**LIGHTMAN, Daniel**; QC 2016; *b* London, 14 Oct. 1970; *s* of Hon. Sir Gavin (Anthony) Lightman, *qv*; *m* 2000, Felicia Epstein; one *s* one *d*. *Educ*: University Coll. Sch.; Magdalen Coll., Oxford (BA Lit.Hum. 1st Cl. Hons 1993); City Univ., London (DipLaw Dist.); Inns of Court Sch. of Law. Called to the Bar, Lincoln's Inn, 1995 (Hardwicke, Mansfield and Denning Schol.); in practice as barrister, specialising in company and chancery/commercial law, 1996–. *Publications*: (contrib.) Lightman and Moss, The Law of Receivers and Administrators of Companies, 1986, 6th edn 2017; (contrib.) Joffe: Minority Shareholders: law, practice and procedure, 2000, 6th edn 2018; (with Z. Cooper) Cricket Grounds from the Air, 2009, 2nd edn 2010; contribs to legal jls esp. on company law and civil procedure. *Recreations*: cricket, jazz, sitting in coffee shops. *Address*: Serle Court, 6 New Square, Lincoln's Inn, WC2A 3QS. *T*: (020) 7242 6105, *Fax*: (020) 7405 4004. *E*: dlightman@serlecourt.co.uk. *Clubs*: MCC, Lord's Taverners; Cricket Writers'.

**LIGHTMAN, Hon. Sir Gavin (Anthony)**, Kt 1994; a Judge of the High Court of Justice, Chancery Division, 1994–2008; arbitrator, mediator and consultant, since 2008; Consultant with Assersons; *b* 20 Dec. 1939; *s* of Harold Lightman, QC and of Gwendoline Joan (*née* Ostrer); *m* 1965, Naomi Ann Claff; one *s* two *d*. *Educ*: University College London (LLB 1st cl. Hons 1961; Fellow, 2002); Univ. of Michigan (LLM). Called to the Bar, Lincoln's Inn, 1963, Bencher 1987, Treas., 2008–09; QC 1980. Chm., Investment Cttee, Harbour Litigation Funding Ltd, 2010–14. Pres., GEMME (European Assoc. of Judges for Mediation), 2009–12; Chm., UK Assoc. of Jewish Lawyers and Jurists, 2011. Vice Pres., Anglo Jewish Assoc., 1995 (Dep. Pres., 1986–92); Chairman: Educn Cttee, Anglo Jewish Assoc., 1986–94; Educn Cttee, Hillel House, 1992–96 (Vice-Pres., 1996–); Legal Friends, Haifa Univ., 1990–2001 (Gov., 1994); Leonard Sainer Legal Educn Foundn, 2000–. Patron: Jewish Commonwealth Council, 1994–2000; Hammerson Home, 1996–: British Fulbright Schol. Assoc., 2009–. *Publications*: (with G. Battersby) Cases and Statutes on Real Property, 1965; (with G. Moss) The Law of Administrators and Receivers of Companies, 1986, 5th edn 2011; A Report on the National Union of Miners, 1990. *Recreations*: reading, grandchildren, walking, travel. *Address*: Serle Court, 6 New Square, Lincoln's Inn, WC2A 3QS. *Club*: Royal Automobile.
*See also* D. Lightman, S. L. Lightman.

**LIGHTMAN, Lionel**; Lay Observer attached to Lord Chancellor's Department, 1986–90; *b* 26 July 1928; *s* of late Abner Lightman and late Gitli Lightman (*née* Szmul); *m* 1952, Helen, *y d* of late Rev. A. Shechter and late Mrs Shechter; two *d*. *Educ*: City of London Sch.; Wadham Coll., Oxford (MA). Nat. Service, RAEC, 1951–53 (Temp. Captain). Asst Principal, BoT, 1953; Private Sec. to Perm. Sec., 1957; Principal 1958; Trade Comr, Ottawa, 1960–64; Asst Sec. 1967; Asst Dir, Office of Fair Trading, 1973–75; Under Sec., Dept of Trade, 1975–78, DoI, 1978–81; Dir of Competition Policy, OFT, 1981–84.

**LIGHTMAN, Prof. Stafford Louis**, PhD; FRS 2017; FRCP, FMedSci; Professor of Medicine, University of Bristol, since 1993; *b* 7 Sept. 1948; *s* of Harold Lightman, QC and of Gwendoline Joan (*née* Ostrer); *m* 1st, 1977, Susan Louise Stubbs (*see* Susan Lightman) (marr. diss. 1995); three *s* one *d*; 2nd, 2010, Rhona Isabel Macpherson. *Educ*: Repton Sch.; Gonville and Caius Coll., Cambridge (MA, MB BChir, PhD); Middlesex Hosp. Med. Sch. Vis. Sen. Scientist, MRC Neuro. Pharm. Unit, Cambridge, 1980–81; Wellcome Trust Sen. Lectr, St Mary's Hosp. Med. Sch. and Hon. Consultant Physician and Endocrinologist, St Mary's Hosp., 1981–82; Charing Cross and Westminster Medical School: Reader in Medicine, 1982–88; Prof. of Clinical Neuroendocrinology, 1988–92; Consultant Physician and Endocrinologist to Charing Cross and Westminster Hosps, 1988–92; Hon. Sen. Res. Fellow, Inst. of Neurology and Consultant Endocrinologist to Nat. Hosp. for Neurology and Neurosurgery, 1988–. Chm., Pituitary Foundn, 1995–2004. Pres., British Neurosci. Assoc., 2017–. Founder FMedSci 1998. Editor-in-Chief, Jl of Neuroendocrinology, 1989–96. *Publications*: (ed with B. J. Everitt) Neuroendocrinology, 1986; (with Michael Powell) Pituitary Tumours: a handbook on management, 1996, 2nd edn 2003; (ed) Horizons in Medicine Vol. 7, 1996; (with A. Levy) Core Endocrinology, 1997; (with Graham Rook) Steroid Hormones and the T cell Cytokine Profile, 1997. *Recreations*: squash, ski-ing, hill walking, scuba diving, music, theatre, anthropology. *Address*: Henry Wellcome Laboratories, Dorothy Hodgkin Building, Whitson Street, Bristol BS1 3NY. *T*: (0117) 331 3167.
*See also* Hon. Sir G. A. Lightman.

**LIGHTMAN, Prof. Susan Louise**, PhD; FRCP, FRCPE, FRCOphth, FMedSci; Professor of Clinical Ophthalmology, Institute of Ophthalmology and Moorfields Eye Hospital, 1993; *b* 2 Sept. 1952; *d* of John and Valerie Stubbs; *m* 1st, 1977, Prof. Stafford Louis Lightman, FRCP (marr. diss. 1995); three *s* one *d*; 2nd, 1995, Hamish Towler; one *s*. *Educ*: St Paul's Girls' Sch.; Middlesex Hosp., Univ. of London (MB BS Hons 1975); PhD London 1987. MRCP 1978, FRCP 1992; FRCOphth 1988; FRCPE 1998. Wellcome Training Fellowship: in Ophthalmology, Inst. of Ophthalmol. and Moorfields Eye Hosp., 1979–83; in Immunology, NIMR, 1983–85; MRC Travelling Fellowship and Vis. Scientist, NIH, 1985–87; MRC Sen. Clinical Fellow, 1988–90; Duke Elder Prof. of Ophthalmology, BPMF, 1990–93. FMedSci 2000. *Publications*: Immunology of Eye Diseases, 1989; Diagnosis and Management of Uveitis, 1998; HIV and the Eye, 1999; over 200 papers in peer reviewed jls. *Recreations*: walking, music, sewing, reading.

**LIGHTON, Sir Thomas (Hamilton)**, 9th Bt *cr* 1791 (Ire.), of Merville, Dublin; Chairman, Society of London Art Dealers, 1993–95 and 1998–2000; Director, Merville Galleries Ltd, since 2012; *b* 4 Nov. 1954; *o s* of Sir Christopher Robert Lighton, 8th Bt, MBE and his 2nd wife, Horatia Edith (*d* 1981), *d* of A. T. Powlett; *S* father, 1993; *m* 1990, Belinda, *d* of John Fergusson; twin *s* one *d* (and one *s* decd). *Educ*: Eton. *Heir*: *s* James Christopher Hamilton Lighton, *b* 20 Oct. 1992.

**LIGHTWOOD, Louise Naima Rachell**; *see* Kamill, L. N. R.

**LIGRANI, Prof. Phillip Meredith**, PhD; Eminent Scholar in Propulsion, Professor of Mechanical and Aerospace Engineering, Propulsion Research Center, since 2014, and Member, President's Council, since 2017, University of Alabama in Huntsville; Distinguished Advisory Professor, Inje University, Gimhae, South Korea, since 2010; *b* 2 Feb. 1952; *s* of Alfred Joseph Ligrani and Marilyn Virginia Ligrani (*née* Whittaker); one *d*. *Educ*: Univ. of Texas at Austin (BS 1974); Stanford Univ. (MS 1975; PhD 1980). Asst Prof., Turbomachinery Dept, von Karman Inst. for Fluid Dynamics, Rhode-St-Genese, Belgium, 1979–82; Vis. Sen. Res. Fellow, Dept of Aeronautics, Imperial Coll., London, 1982–84; Associate Prof., Dept of Mechanical Engrg, US Naval Postgrad. Sch., 1984–92; Prof. and Associate Chm., Dept of Mechanical Engrg, Univ. of Utah, 1992–2006; Donald Schultz Prof. of Turbomachinery, and Dir of Rolls-Royce Univ. Technol. Centre in Heat Transfer and Aerodynamics, Oxford Univ., 2006–09; Fellow, St Catherine's Coll., Oxford, 2006–09; Oliver L. Parks Endowed Chair and Prof. of Aerospace and Mech. Engrg, Parks Coll. of Engrg, Aviation and Technol., St Louis Univ., 2010–14. Guest Prof., Univ. of Karlsruhe, 2000. Mem., K-14 Gas Turbine Heat Transfer Cttee, ASME, 1986– (Vice Chm., 2014–16; Chm., 2016–18); Mem. and Vice Chm., Academic Cttee, Inst. for Turbomachinery, Tsinghua Univ., Beijing, 2012–. Co-inventor on three US and internat. patents. Lectures include: 5th Internat. Symposium on Turbulence, Heat and Mass Transfer, Dubrovnik, 2006; Aerospace 2030, Oxford Univ., 2007; 15th Internat. Symposium on Field- and Flow-based Separations, Internat. Separation Sci. Soc., San Francisco, 2011; Sixth Internat. Conf., Heat and Mass Transfer and Hydrodynamics in Swirling Flows, Nat. Cttee, Russian Acad. of Scis, Novosibirsk, 2017; Forum of Future of Aerospace Engrg, 2018, Internat. Conf. in Aerospace for Young Scientists, 2018, Beihang Univ., Beijing. Mem., Scientific Cttee, Seventh Internat. Conf., Heat and Mass Transfer and Hydrodynamics in Swirling Flows, Nat. Cttee, Russian Acad. of Scis, Novosibirsk, 2019; Invited Expert, Aerospace Center of Multiscale Mechanics and Thermodynamics, Sch. of Aeronautic Sci. and Engrg, Beihang Univ., Beijing, 2018–. Mem., EU Acad. of Scis 2019. FASME 2000; Associate FAIAA 2016. Associate Editor: ASME Transactions: Jl Heat Transfer, 2003–07, 2010–13; ASME Transactions: Jl Fluids Engrg, 2005–08; ASME Transactions: Jl Engrg for Gas Turbines and Power, 2018–; Mem., Editl Rev. Bd, Advances in Transport Phenomena, book series, 2006–; Member, Editorial Board: Power and Thermal Engrg Processes and Equipment Jl, 2015–; Internat. Jl of Innovative Works in Engrg and Technol., 2015–; Jl of Propulsion Technol., 2015–; Advances in Aerodynamics Jl, 2018–; Energies Jl, 2018–; Mem., Internat. Editl Bd, Industrial Thermal Engrg Jl, 2018–. Carl E. and Jessie W. Menneken Faculty Award for Excellence in Scientific Res., 1990; NASA Space Act Tech. Brief Award, 1991; Silver winner, HE Marketing, Educnl Advertising Awards, 2011; Dist. Lecture Award, Coll. of Engrg, Univ. of Wisconsin-Milwaukee, 2011; Outstanding Mechanical Engr of Year Award, N Alabama Section, ASME, 2016; Dist. Res. Award for Excellence, 2019, Outstanding Sen. Faculty Mem., Coll. of Engrg, 2019, Univ. of Alabama, Huntsville. *Publications*: book chapters and contribs to learned jls incl. Internat. Jl Heat and Mass Transfer, ASME Trans: Jl Turbomachinery, ASME Trans: Jl Heat Transfer, ASME Trans: Jl Fluids Engrg, Jl Fluid Mechanics, AIAA Jl, Expts in Fluids, Physics of Fluids, AIAA Jl Heat Transfer and Thermophysics, Internat. Jl Rotating Machinery, Separation Sci. and Technol., Sensors and Acutors A: Physical, Jl Microcolumn Separations, Scientific Reports. *Address*: Propulsion Research Center, Department of Mechanical and Aerospace Engineering, University of Alabama in Huntsville, Huntsville, AL 35811, USA. *T*: (256) 8245173, *Fax*: (256) 8247205. *E*: p_ligrani@msn.com.

**LIIKANEN, Erkki Antero**; Governor, Bank of Finland, 2004–18; *b* 19 Sept. 1950; *m* 1971, Hanna-Liisa Issakainen; two *d*. *Educ*: Helsinki Univ. MP (SDP), Finland 1972–90; Minister of Finance, 1987–90; Ambassador to EU, 1990–95; Mem., EC, 1995–2004. Gen. Sec., SDP, 1981–87. Chair, IFRS Foundn, 2018–.

**LIKIERMAN, Prof. Sir (John) Andrew**, Kt 2001; Professor of Management Practice, London Business School, since 2001 (Dean, 2009–17); *b* 30 Dec. 1943; *s* of Dolek and Olga Likierman; *m* 1987, Dr Meira, *d* of Joshua and Miriam Gruenspan (*d* 2019); one step *s* one step *d*. *Educ*: Stowe Sch.; Univ. of Vienna; Balliol Coll., Oxford (MA). FCMA, FCCA. Divl Management Accountant, Tootal Ltd, 1965–68; Asst Lectr, 1968–69, Lectr, 1972–74, Dept of Management Studies, Leeds Univ.; Qualitex Ltd, 1969–72 (Man. Dir, Overseas Div., 1971–72); Vis. Fellow, Oxford Centre for Management Studies, 1972–74; Chm., Ex Libris Ltd, 1973–74; London Business Sch., 1974–76 and 1979–: Dir, Part-time Masters Programme, 1981–85; Dir, Inst. of Public Sector Management, 1983–88; Prof. of Accounting and Financial Control, 1987–97; Vis. Prof., 1997–2001; Dean of External Affairs, 1989–92; Dep. Principal, 1990–93; Elected Governor, 1986–89, *ex officio* Governor, 1990–93; Acting Dean, 2007. Dir, Bank of England, 2004–08. Asst Sec., Cabinet Office (Mem., Central Policy Review Staff), 1976–79, Advr, 1979–82; Advisor, H of C Select Committees: Treasury and CS, 1981–90; Employment, 1985–89; Transport, 1981, 1987–90; Social Services, 1988; Social Security, 1991; Head, Govt Accountancy Service and Chief Accountancy Advr, HM Treasury, 1993–2003; Principal Finance Officer, 1995–2000, Dir, subseq. Man. Dir, Financial Mgt, Reporting and Audit, 1995–2003, HM Treasury; Chm., Nat. Audit Office, 2009–15; Mem., various govt inquiries including: North Sea Oil Costs, 1975; Power Plant Industry, 1976; Post Office Internat. Comparisons, 1981; Accounting for Econ. Costs (Byatt Cttee), 1986; Professional Liability (Chm.), 1989. Member: Finance Cttee, Oxfam, 1974–84; Audit Commn, 1988–91; Financial Reporting Council, 1990–2003 (Observer, 1993–2003); Cttee on Financial Aspects of Corporate Governance (Cadbury Cttee), 1991–95; Council: RIPA, 1982–88; Consumers' Assoc., 1983–85; Chartered Inst. of Management Accountants, 1985–94 (Pres., 1991–92); Civil Service Coll., 1989–94; Scientific Council, Eur. Inst. of Public Admin, 1990–93; Defence Operational Analysis Centre, 1992–93; Bd, Tavistock and Portman NHS Trust, 2000–08. Non-executive Director: Barclays plc, 2004–13; Market & Opinion Res. Internat. Ltd, 2004–05 (Chm., 2005); Beazley plc, 2015–; non-exec. Chm., Applied Intellectual Capital plc, 2006–08; Nat. Ind. Dir (non-exec.), Times Newspapers Ltd, 2015–. Non-exec. Dir, Economists' Bookshop, 1981–91 (non-exec. Chm., 1987–91). Mem., Steering Cttee, Governance of the UN, 2006. Trustee, Inst. for Govt, 2008–17. Freeman, City of London, 2014. Hon. DBA: Southampton Business Sch., 1997; Oxford Brookes, 2006; Hon. DPhil London Metropolitan, 1999; Hon. DSc (Econs) London Business Sch., 2017. Gold Medal, CIMA, 2002; Financial Mgt Award, 2004; Public Sector non-exec. Dir of the Year, Sunday Times, 2009. *Publications*: The Reports and Accounts of Nationalised Industries, 1979; Cash Limits and External Financing Limits, 1981; (jtly) Public Sector Accounting and Financial Control, 1983, 4th edn 1992; (with P. Vass) Structure and Form of Government Expenditure Reports, 1984; Public Expenditure, 1988; (jtly) Accounting for Brands, 1989; contribs to academic and professional jls. *Recreations*: cycling, music, architecture, measuring judgement. *Address*: London Business School, Sussex Place, Regents Park, NW1 4SA. *T*: (020) 7000 7012. *Club*: Reform.

**LILANI, Nusrat Mehboob, (Pinky)**, CBE 2015 (OBE 2007); DL; Chief Executive Officer, Spice Magic Ltd, since 2001; *b* Calcutta, 25 March 1954; *d* of Salim and Sherbanoo Nathani; *m* 1977, Mehboob Lilani; two *s*. *Educ*: Loreto House Sch.; Loreto Coll. (BA Hons); Sophia Coll. (Postgrad. Dip. Media); Croydon Coll. (DMS). Chairman: Asian Women of Achievement Awards, 1999–; Women of the Future Awards, 2006–; Global Empowerment Awards, 2008–. Patron, Westminster Educnl Soc., 2008–. DL Gtr London,

2014. *Publications:* Soul Magic, 1998; Spice Magic, 2001; Coriander Makes the Difference, 2009. *Recreations:* walking, cinema, travelling, cooking, talking to people I don't know, eating out. *Address:* Majon, 1A Furze Lane, Purley, Surrey CR8 3EJ. *T:* (020) 8668 8404, *Fax:* (020) 8668 2558. *E:* pinky@spicemagic.com.

**LILEY, Ven. Christopher Frank;** Archdeacon of Lichfield, 2001–13, now Archdeacon Emeritus; Treasurer and Canon Residentiary of Lichfield Cathedral, 2001–13; *b* 1947. *Educ:* Nottingham Univ. (BEd 1970); Lincoln Theol Coll. Ordained deacon, 1974, priest, 1975; Curate, Holy Trinity, Kingswinford, 1974–79; Team Vicar, Stafford, 1979–84; Vicar, Norton, 1984–96; RD Hitchin, 1989–94; Vicar, St Chad and St Mary, and Priest i/c St Alkmund, Shrewsbury, 1996–2001. Chm., Lichfield Diocesan Bd of Ministry, 2001–03; Jt Dean of Retired Clergy, Dio. of Worcester, 2016–. *Address:* 15 Holloway Drive, Pershore, Worcs WR10 1JL. *E:* lileyc@aol.com.

**LILFORD, 8th Baron** *cr* 1797; **Mark Vernon Powys;** *b* 16 Nov. 1975; *s* of 7th Baron Lilford and Margaret, *d* of A. Penman; *S* father, 2005; *m* 2015, Tracey Mahon. *Educ:* Winchester Coll.; University Coll. London. *Heir: kinsman* Michael John Powys [*b* 1934; *m* 1957, Lynette Bernice Hodges; one *s* one *d* (and two *s* decd).

**LILFORD, Prof. Richard James,** CBE 2018; PhD; FRCP, FRCOG, FFPH; Professor of Public Health, University of Warwick, since 2014; Director: Warwick Centre for Applied Health Research and Delivery, since 2014; NIHR Collaboration for Leadership in Applied Health Research and Care West Midlands, since 2014; *b* Cape Town, 22 April 1950; *m* 1982, Victoria Lomax; one *s* two *d. Educ:* St John's Coll., Johannesburg; Univ. of Witwatersrand (MB BCh 1973); PhD London 1984. MRCOG 1979, FRCOG 1996; MRCP 1981, FRCP 1998; MFPHM 1995. House officer in Medicine, Johannesburg Gen. Hosp., 1974; house officer in Surgery, Tygerberg Hosp., Cape Town, 1974–75; GP in S African Army, 1975; Groote Schuur Hospital, Cape Town: SHO in Obstetrics and Gynaecol., 1976; Registrar, 1977–78; Lecturer and Senior Registrar: Royal Free Hosp., London, 1979–80; St Bartholomew's Hosp. and Med. Coll., 1980–83; Sen. Lectr and Consultant in Obstetrics and Gynaecol., Queen Charlotte's Hosp. for Women and Inst. of Obstetrics and Gynaecol., 1983–85; University of Leeds: Prof. of Obstetrics and Gynaecol., 1985–95; Chm., Inst. of Epidemiology and Health Services Res., 1991–95; Dir of Res., United Leeds Teaching Hosps NHS Trust, 1993–95; Dir of R&D, W Midlands Regl Office, NHS Exec., DoH, 1996; Prof. of Health Services Res., 1996, Prof. of Clinical Epidemiology, 2001–14, Univ. of Birmingham; Dir, Birmingham Clinical Res. Acad., 2007. Mem., Internat. Editl Adv. Bd, Jl RSocMed, 1974–. Mem., Leeds E HA, 1989–90. Advr, NHS Nat. Clinical Trials, 1996–2003; Director: NHS Methodology Res. Prog.; NHS Patient Safety Res. Prog. Chm. and Mem., numerous cttees incl. DoH adv. cttees and working parties. Royal College of Obstetricians and Gynaecologists: Mem. Council, 1989–92 and 1992–95; Chm., Audit Cttee, 1992–95; Member: Scientific Adv. Cttee, 1992–95; Educn Bd, 1992–94. *Publications:* (with T. Chard) Basic Sciences for Obstetricians and Gynaecologists, 1983, 4th edn 1995; (with M. Setchell) Multiple Choice Questions in Gynaecology and Obstetrics: with answers and explanatory comments, 1985, 2nd edn 1991; Prenatal Diagnosis and Prognosis, 1990; Computing and Decision Support in Obstetrics and Gynaecology, 1990; (with T. Chard) Multiple Choice Questions in Obstetrics and Gynaecology, 1993; (with M. Levine) Fetal and Neonatal Neurology and Neurosurgery, 1994; contrib. chapters in books and numerous articles to medical and professional jls. *Address:* Warwick Medical School, University of Warwick, Coventry CV4 7AL.

**LILL, John Richard,** CBE 2005 (OBE 1978); concert pianist; Visiting Professor of Piano, Royal College of Music; *b* 17 March 1944; *s* of George and Margery Lill; *m* Jacqueline Clifton Smith. *Educ:* Leyton County High Sch.; Royal College of Music. FRCM; Hon. FTCL; FLCM; Hon. RAM 1988. Gulbenkian Fellowship, 1967. First concert at age of 9; Royal Festival Hall debut, 1963; Promenade Concert debut, 1969. Numerous broadcasts on radio and TV; has appeared as soloist with all leading British orchestras. Recitals and concertos throughout Great Britain, Europe, USA, Canada, Scandinavia, USSR, Japan and Far East, Australia, New Zealand, etc. Overseas tours as soloist with many orchestras including London Symphony Orchestra and London Philharmonic Orchestra. Complete recordings of Beethoven sonatas and concertos, Prokofiev sonatas, Brahms concertos and Rachmaninov piano music; complete Beethoven cycle, London, 1982, 1986, and Tokyo, 1988. Chappell Gold Medal; Pauer Prize; 1st Prize, Royal Over-Seas League Music Competition, 1963; Dinu Lipatti Medal in Harriet Cohen Internat. Awards; 1st Prize, Internat. Tchaikovsky Competition, Moscow, 1970. Hon. DSc Aston, 1978; Hon. DMus Exeter, 1979. *Recreations:* amateur radio, chess, walking. *Address:* c/o Askonas Holt Ltd, 15 Fetter Lane, EC4A 1BW. *T:* (020) 7400 1700.

**LILLEY, Baron** *cr* 2018 (Life Peer), of Offa in the County of Hertfordshire; **Peter Bruce Lilley;** PC 1990; *b* 23 Aug. 1943; *s* of Arnold Francis Lilley and Lilian (*née* Elliott); *m* 1979, Gail Ansell. *Educ:* Dulwich Coll.; Clare Coll., Cambridge. MA; FInstPet 1978. Economic consultant in underdeveloped countries, 1966–72; investment advisor on energy industries, 1972–84. Chm., London Oil Analysts Gp, 1979–80; Partner, 1980–86, Dir, 1986–87, W. Greenwell & Co., later Greenwell Montagu. Consultant Dir, Cons. Res. Dept, 1979–83. Chm., Bow Group, 1972–75. Contested (C) Tottenham, Oct. 1974. MP (C) St Albans, 1983–97, Hitchin and Harpenden, 1997–2017. PPS to Ministers for Local Govt, Jan.–Oct. 1984, to Chancellor of the Exchequer, 1984–87; Economic Sec. to HM Treasury, 1987–89, Financial Sec., 1989–90; Secretary of State for Trade and Industry, 1990–92; for Social Security, 1992–97; front bench Opposition spokesman on HM Treasury, 1997–98. Co-Chair, All Party Parly Gp, Trade Out of Poverty, 2010–17; Chair, Jt Cttee of Financial Services Bill, 2011–12; Member: Energy and Climate Change Select Cttee, 2012–15; Envmtl Audit Cttee, 2015–17; DExEU Cttee, 2016–17. Dep. Leader, Cons. Party, 1998–99. *Publications:* (with S. Brittan) Delusion of Incomes Policy, 1977; (contrib.) Skidelsky: End of the Keynesian Era, 1980; various pamphlets. *Clubs:* Carlton, Beefsteak.

**LILLEY, Anthony William,** OBE 2008; Director: Magic Lantern Productions Ltd, since 1997; Lilley Associates Ltd, since 2013; Scenario Two Ltd, since 2016; Executive Chairman, Myra Ventures Ltd (formerly Myra Media Ltd), since 2015; *b* Bolton, 8 June 1970; *s* of Bernard Charles Lilley and Brenda Lilley; *m* 2000, Ruth Joanne Harris; one *s* one *d. Educ:* Bolton Sch. (Boys' Div.); Magdalen Coll., Oxford (BA Juris. 1991; MA 2012). Member: Content Bd, Ofcom, 2006–13; Gambling Commn, 2012–15 (Mem., Nat. Lottery Cttee, 2013–15); AHRC, 2013–. Chm., UK Digital Content Forum, 2002; Vice Chm., Producers Alliance for Cinema and TV Ltd, 2006. News International Vis. Prof. of Broadcast Media, Univ. of Oxford, 2007; Vis. Prof., Centre of Excellence in Media Practice, Bournemouth Univ., 2009; Prof. of Creative Industries, Univ. of Ulster, 2013–. Trustee: ENO, 2007–13; Crafts Council, 2017–; NESTA, 2018–; Chairman, Trustees: Lighthouse Arts and Trng, 2009–15; Blast Theory, 2017–. Coach, Ringmer Rovers Jun. FC, 2016–. Mem., BAFTA. FRSA 2004. *Recreations:* family, theatre and opera, singing, reading, gaming, gardening, football, football coaching, travel, learning new things. *Address:* The Long Barn, Lewes Road, Laughton, E Sussex BN8 6BQ. *E:* anthony.lilley@magiclantern.co.uk. *Club:* h.

**LILLEY, Prof. David Malcolm James,** PhD; FRS 2002; FRSE; FRSC; Professor of Molecular Biology, since 1989, and Director, Cancer Research UK Nucleic Acid Structure Research Group, since 1993, University of Dundee; *b* 28 May 1948; *s* of Gerald Albert Thomas Lilley and Betty Pamela Lilley; *m* 1981, Patricia Mary Biddle; two *d. Educ:* Univ. of Durham (BSc 1st Cl. Hons Chemistry 1969; PhD Physical Chemistry 1973); Imperial Coll., London (MSc Biochem. 1973). FRSC 2002. Lectr, 1981–84, Reader, 1984–89, in Biochem., Univ. of Dundee. Vis. Prof., Xiamen Univ., China, 2013–. Mem., EMBO, 1984. FRSE 1988. Colworth Medal, British Biochemical Soc., 1982; Gold Medal of G. J. Mendel, Czech Acad. Scis, Prague, 1994; Prelog Gold Medal in Stereochemistry, ETH, Zürich, 1996; Award in RNA and Ribozyme Chemistry, 2001, Interdisciplinary Award, 2006, Khorana Prize, 2016, RSC. *Publications:* ed. numerous books, incl. DNA-proteins: structural interactions, 1995; (ed with Dr F. Eckstein, and contrib.) Ribozymes and RNA Catalysis, 2007; (with Dr F. Eckstein) Nucleic Acids and Molecular Biology series, 1987–98; contrib. numerous scientific papers. *Recreations:* foreign languages, running, skiing. *Address:* MSI/WTB Complex, University of Dundee, Dundee DD1 5EH. *T:* (01382) 384243. *E:* d.m.j.lilley@dundee.ac.uk.

**LILLEYMAN, Sir John (Stuart),** Kt 2002; DSc; FRCP, FRCPE, FRCPath, FRCPCH, FMedSci; Professor of Paediatric Oncology, St Bartholomew's Hospital Medical College, subseq. Bart's and The London School of Medicine and Dentistry, Queen Mary, University of London, 1995–2006, now Emeritus; *b* 9 July 1945; *s* of Ernest Lilleyman and Frances Lilleyman (*née* Johnson); *m* 1st, 1970, Patricia Ann Traylen (marr. diss. 1996); one *s*; 2nd, 1998, Elizabeth Anne Lawrence. *Educ:* Oundle Sch.; St Bartholomew's Hosp. Med. Coll. (MB BS 1968; DSc Med. 1996). FRCP 1983; FRCPath 1984; FRCPCH 1997; FRCPE 2000. Jun. Posts at St Bartholomew's Hosp. and United Sheffield Hosps, 1968–72; Res. Fellow, Welsh Nat. Sch. of Medicine, 1972–74; Consultant Haematologist, Sheffield Children's Hosp., 1975–95; Prof. of Paediatric Haematology, Univ. of Sheffield Med. Sch., 1993–95. Med. Dir, NHS Nat. Patient Safety Agency, 2004–07; Strategic Advr, Nat. Res. Ethics Service, 2007–09; Dir, Appointing Authy for Phase 1 Ethics cttees, 2007–12. Non-exec. Dir, Medicines and Healthcare Products Regulatory Agency, 2009–12. President: UK Assoc. of Clinical Pathologists, 1998–99; RCPath, 1999–2002; RSocMed, 2004–06. Vice Chairman: Acad. of Med. Royal Colls, 2000–02; Jt Consultants Cttee, 2001–02; Mem., Health Professions Council, 2002–04. FMedSci 2007. Hon. Fellow: Inst. Biomed. Sci., 1996; Faculty of Path., RCPI, 2003; RSocMed, 2007. Hon. MD Sheffield, 2003. *Publications:* (Chief Ed.) Pediatric Hematology, 1992, 2nd edn 2000; Childhood Leukaemia: the facts, 1994, 2nd edn 2000; contrib. articles on childhood leukaemia and blood diseases. *Recreations:* reading, walking. *Address:* 7 Village Meadows, Lowick, Berwick upon Tweed, Northumberland TD15 2TX.

**LILLFORD, Prof. Peter John,** CBE 1998; PhD; FRSC; FIFST, FIAFoST; consultant, food science and technology, since 2005; *b* 16 Nov. 1944; *s* of John Leslie Lillford and Ethel Ruth Lillford (*née* Wimlett); *m* 1969, Elisabeth Rosemary Avery; two *s. Educ:* King's Coll., London (BSc Hons Chemistry; PhD 1968); Cornell Univ. FRSC 2009. Res. Fellow, Cardio Vascular Res. Inst., San Francisco, 1970–71; Res. Scientist, 1971–87, Principal Scientist, 1987–99, Unilever; Chief Scientist (Foods), Unilever Research, 1999–2001; Pres., Inst. of Food Sci. and Technol., 2001–03; Dir, Nat. Centre for Non Food Crops, 2003–09. Chm., Inst. of Food Res. UK, 2007–13. Special Prof. of Biophysics, Nottingham Univ., 1988–2007; Hon. Prof., Stirling Univ., 1989–2000; Visiting Professor: York Univ., 2000–13; Univ. of Birmingham, 2007–. Chairman: Foresight Food and Drink Panel, OST, 1993–97; Agri-Food Cttee, BBSRC, 1997–2000. FIFST 1992; FIAoFST 2003; McMaster Fellow, Food Sci. Australia, 2004–05; Flagship Fellow, CSIRO, 2005–08. FRSA 1996. Hon. DEng Birmingham 1999. Sen. Medal, RSC, 1991; Outstanding Achievement Award, Eur. Fedn of Food Sci. and Technol., 2004. *Publications:* Foods Structure and Behaviour, 1987; Feeding and the Texture of Food, 1991; Glassy States in Foods, 1993; (ed) Technology Foresight, Food and Drink, 1995; Food Materials Science, 2008. *Recreations:* old houses, old cars, old whisky. *Address:* The Firs, 20 Pavenham Road, Carlton, Beds MK43 7LS. *T:* (01234) 720869.

**LILLIE, Stephen,** CMG 2017; HM Diplomatic Service; High Commissioner to Cyprus, since 2018; *b* 4 Feb. 1966; *s* of Christopher Stanley Lillie and Maureen Lillie; *m* 1991, Denise Chit Lo; two *s. Educ:* S Wolds Comprehensive Sch., Nottingham; Queen's Coll., Oxford (MA Modern Langs 1988); Sch. of Oriental and African Studies, London and Chinese Univ. of Hong Kong (FCO Chinese lang. trng, 1989–91). HM Diplomatic Service: FCO, 1988–90; Hong Kong, 1990–91; Second, later First Sec., Beijing, 1992–95; First Sec., FCO, 1996–98; Dep. Hd, China Hong Kong Dept, FCO, 1998–99; Consul-Gen., Guangzhou, 1999–2003; Counsellor (Econ. and Commercial), New Delhi, 2003–06; Hd, Far Eastern Dept, FCO, 2006–09; Ambassador to the Philippines, and non-resident Ambassador to Micronesia, the Marshall Is and Palau, 2009–13; Dir, Asia Pacific, FCO, 2013–17. *Recreations:* reading, travel, walking. *Address:* c/o Foreign and Commonwealth Office, King Charles Street, SW1A 2AH. *E:* stephen.lillie@fco.gov.uk.

**LILLIS, Patrick;** General Secretary, Union of Shop, Distributive and Allied Workers, since 2018; *b* Belfast, 27 April 1958; *s* of Archie Lillis and Gretta Lillis; *m* 1980, Jacqueline Johnston; four *s. Educ:* Stella Maris Secondary Sch., Newtownabbey, NI. Heavy goods driver, Abbey Meat Packers, Newtownabbey, 1979–89; Union of Shop, Distributive and Allied Workers: full-time organiser and regl official, 1989–2004; Dep. Gen. Sec., 2004–18. Mem., Labour NEC, 2004–. *Recreation:* family: 4 sons and 10 grandchildren. *Address:* USDAW, 188 Wilmslow Road, Manchester M14 6LJ. *E:* paddy.lillis@usdaw.org.uk.

**LILLY, Prof. Simon John,** PhD; FRS 2014; Professor, since 2002, and Head, since 2015, Department of Physics, Institute for Astronomy, ETH Zürich. *Educ:* Sidney Sussex Coll., Cambridge (BA 1st Cl. Hons Natural Sci 1980); Univ. of Edinburgh (PhD Astronomy 1984). SERC/NATO Res. Fellow, Princeton Univ., 1984–85; Asst, then Associate Prof., Univ. of Hawaii, 1985–90; Dir Gen., Herzberg Inst. of Astrophysics, Canada, 2000–02. Interdisciplinary Scientist and Mem., Flight Sci. Wkg Gp, NASA/ESA James Webb Space Telescope, 2002–. R & B Sackler Dist. Vis. Astronomer, Univ. of Cambridge, 1996; Vis. Fellow, Clare Hall, Cambridge, 1996–97; Fellow, Canadian Inst. for Advanced Res., 1997–2002; R & B Sackler Lectr, Leiden Univ., 2000. European Space Agency: Member: Astronomy Wkg Gp, 2004–07; Euclid Sci. Study Team, 2008–11; Space Sci. Adv. Cttee, 2009–11. Member: Advanced Grants Panel, ERC, 2008–; Swiss Nat. Res. Council, 2009–. Mem., Hubble Space Telescope Users' Cttee, NASA, 1991–94. Pres., IAU Commn #47 Cosmology, 2003–06. *Publications:* contribs to learned jls incl. Astrophysical Jl, Jl Cosmol. and Astroparticle Physics, Astron. Astrophysics, Advances in Space Res., Proc. IAU, Nature, Jl Plasma Physics. *Address:* ETH Zürich, Institut für Astronomie, Wolfgang-Pauli-Strasse 27, 8093 Zürich, Switzerland.

**LILLYWHITE, Lt-Gen. Louis Patrick,** CB 2009; MBE 1985; FRCPGlas, FRCGP; Senior Research Consultant, Centre for Global Health Security, Royal Institute of International Affairs (Chatham House), since 2010; Master General Army Medical Services, since 2017; *b* 23 Feb. 1948; *s* of Dr William Henry Lillywhite and Annie Kate (*née* Vesey); *m* 1975, Jean Mary Daly, *d* of Bernard Daly and Margaret Mary (*née* Cooke); one *s* two *d. Educ:* King Edward VI Grammar Sch., Lichfield; University Coll. Cardiff and Welsh Nat. Sch. of Medicine (MB BCh 1971); London Sch. of Hygiene and Tropical Medicine (MSc Occupational Medicine 1989, top student prize). MFOM 1990, FFOM 2019; FRCPGlas 2008; FRCGP 2009. Regtl MO, 3rd Bn Parachute Regt, 1973–77; O i/c Technical Div., RAMC Trng Centre, 1977–81; RMCS and Army Staff Coll. (psc), 1982; SO, Med. Policy,

Equipment and Intelligence, 1983–85; CO 23 Parachute Field Ambulance, 1985–89; Comdr Med., HQ 1 UK Armoured Div., incl. Gulf War (despatches 1991), 1990–92; Hd of Personnel, AMS, 1992–93; Mem., MoD Defence Cost Studies, 1993–95; DCS Med., HQ Land Comd, 1995–96; Med. Advr, HQ Allied Forces NW Europe, 1998–99; Dir Med. Personnel, Training and Clinical Policy, MoD, 1999–2001; Dir (CE), BF Germany Health Service, 2001–03; Dir Gen., Army Med. Services, 2003–05; Dir Gen., Med. Operational Capability, 2005–06; Surgeon Gen., MoD, 2006–09; Chief Med. Officer, St John Ambulance, 2010–16. QHS 2002–10. Medical Mem., Tribunal Appeal Service, Social Entitlement Chamber (Wales and S West), 2011–; Mem., Bevan Commn, Welsh Govt, 2012–; Chair, R&D Div. External Strategy Gp, Welsh Govt. Mem., WHO Rev. Cttee on Role of Internat. Health Regulations (2005) in the Ebola Outbreak and Response, 2015–16. Comr, Royal Hosp. Chelsea, 2003–05; Gov., Royal Star and Garter Home, 2003–05; Pres., Bratton Br., RBL, 2011–. Mem. Adv. Bd, RBL Centre for Blast Injuries, Imperial Coll. London. Patron: TREAT Wales, 2011–; Orders of St John Care Trust, 2014–; Trustee, Airborne Forces Security Fund, 2016–. Member: BMA; SOM; Fellow, Medical Soc. of London, 1985 (Pres., 2009–10; Trustee, 2012–); FRSocMed 1999. Mem., Catenian Assoc., 1971– (Pres., Bath Circle, 2018–19). Member: British Army Orienteering Club; British Army Mountaineering Assoc.; Fell Runners Assoc. Hon. FRCGP 2010. Hon. Member: Assoc. of Military Surgeons of the USA, 2009; Assoc. of Med. Consultants to Armed Forces of the United States, 2009. CStJ 2016 (OStJ 2007). Medal for Exceptional Public Service, Office of Secretary of Defense, USA, 2009. *Publications*: (contrib.) Gulf Logistics: Blackadder's War, 1995; occasional contrib. to prof. jls incl. Philos. Trans. Royal Soc., BMJ, New England Jl of Medicine, Lancet. *Recreations*: cross country, long distance running, genealogy, hashing, computers, mountaineering. *Address*: 4 Cassways Orchard, Bratton, Westbury, Wilts BA13 4TY. *E*: louis@lillywhi.demon.co.uk, llillywhite@chathamhouse.org.

**LIM, Prof. C. J.;** Founder and Director, Studio 8 Architects, since 1994; Director of International Development, since 2005, and Professor of Architecture and Urbanism, since 2007, The Bartlett, Faculty of the Built Environment, University College London (Vice-Dean, International, 2011–13; Pro-Provost, 2008–11); *b* Malaysia, 1964. *Educ*: Architectural Assoc. (DipArch 1987). Assistant Architect: Eva Jiricna Architects, 1987–88; Rock Townsend Architects, 1988–89; Sidell Gibson Architects, 1989–91; Sen. Lectr, Univ. of East London, 1990–93, Univ. of North London, 1991–99; University College London: Dir, Bartlett Architecture Res. Lab., 1997–2007; Pro-Provost for Canada, Mexico and USA, 2008–11. RIBA External Examiner and Visiting Professor: Curtin Univ., Perth, Australia, 1996; Stadelschule, Frankfurt, 1997, 2000; Mackintosh Sch. of Architecture, Glasgow, 2001–11; Lund Univ., Sweden, 2001, 2003, 2005–12; Aarhus Sch. of Architecture, Denmark, 2002, 2009, 2012–; Waseda Univ., Tokyo, 2002; Chiba Inst. of Technol., Japan, 2004; Oslo Sch. of Architecture, 2005; Royal Danish Acad. Fine Arts, Copenhagen, 2006; Univ. of Girona, Spain, 2008; Seoul Nat. Univ., 2012; RMIT, 2012. Principal investigator for res. projects on eco-cities, sustainable urban planning, landscape and architecture; sustainable masterplanning and infrastructure commns from Chinese and Korean Govts. Solo and group international exhibitions: Chicago, LA, NY, York, Copenhagen, Frankfurt, Lisbon, Istanbul, Beijing, Singapore, Brisbane, Melbourne, Sydney, Orleans; V&A Mus.; Royal Acad. Arts; Dulwich Picture Gall.; RIBA; ICE; Future Cities, Barbican Arts Centre; Venice Architecture Biennale; Hong Kong Shenzhen Urbanism Biennale; Mackintosh Mus., Glasgow; Chicago Architecture Foundn; Storefront Gall., NY; Portland Mus., Oregon; Cincinnati Art Mus.; Acad. de France, Rome; Canadian Inst. Architecture, Montreal; Nara World Architecture Triennale, Union of Internat. Architects 2011; Tokyo Convention, Mori Art Mus., Tokyo; World Art Mus., Beijing; State Liby of Qld, Brisbane; Nat. Gall. Mus., Athens; Museo Nazionale, Rome. Represented UK: Venice Architecture Biennale, 2004; New Trend of Architecture in Europe and Asia Pacific, Japan, 2008–10. FRSA. President's Medal (Internat.), Contribution to Educn Awards, RIBA, 1997, 1998, 1999; Best Work, First-time Exhibitor, 2005, Grand Architecture Prize, 2006, RA Summer Exhibn. *Publications*: 441/10… We'll Reconfigure the Space When You're Ready, 1996; Sins and Other Spatial Relatives, 2000; (ed with Ed Liu) Realms of Impossibility: Vol. 1, Air, 2002, Vol. 2, Ground, Vol. 3, Water, 2002; (with Ed Liu) How Green is Your Garden?, 2003; (ed with Ed Liu) Devices, 2005; Neo Architecture, 2005; Virtually Venice, 2006; (with Ed Liu) Smartcities and Eco-warriors, 2010; (with Ed Liu) Short Stories: London in two-and-a-half dimensions, 2011; Food City, 2014; Inhabitable Infrastructures: science fiction or urban future?, 2017; contribs to books, jls and newspapers on cities, urban planning and urbanism. *Address*: The Bartlett, UCL Faculty of the Built Environment, 22 Gordon Street, WC1H 0QB. *T*: (020) 3108 9681. *E*: c.j.lim@ucl.ac.uk.

**LIM PIN, Professor,** MD; FRCP, FRCPE, FRACP, FACP; University Professor and Professor of Medicine, National University of Singapore, since 2000; Senior Consultant in Endocrinology, National University Hospital, since 2000; *b* 12 Jan. 1936; *s* of late Lim Lu Yeh and of Choo Siew Kooi; *m* 1964, Shirley Loo; two *s* one *d*. *Educ*: Queens' Coll., Cambridge (Queen's Schol., 1957; MA; MD 1970). FRCP 1976; FRCPE 1981; FRACP 1978; FACP 1981. MO, Min. of Health, Singapore, 1965–66; Univ. of Singapore: Lectr in Medicine, 1966–70; Sen. Lectr in Medicine, 1971–73; Associate Prof. of Medicine, 1974–77; Prof. and Head, Dept of Medicine, 1978–81; Dep. Vice-Chancellor, 1979–81; Vice-Chancellor, Nat. Univ. of Singapore, 1981–2000. Mem., Lee Kuan Yew Sch. of Public Policy, 2011–. Eisenhower Fellow, USA, 1982. Founder Pres., Endocrine and Metabolic Soc. of Singapore. Chairman: Nat. Wages Council, 2001–15; Bio-ethics Adv. Cttee, 2001–10; Nat. Longevity Insce Cttee, 2007–08. Chm., Mgt Bd, Tropical Marine Sci. Inst., 2001–; Dep. Chm., Lee Kuan Yew Water Prize Council, 2009–11. Mem. Bd of Dirs, Raffles Medical Gp, 2001–. Chairman: Special Needs Trust Co., 2008–; Singapore Millennium Foundn Ltd, 2008; Nat. Univ. Health System Fund Ltd, 2016–; Nat. Univ. Health System Res. Endowment Fund, 2016–; CREATE Governing Council, 2017–; Adv. Council, Temasek Foundn Innovates, 2017–; Co-Chairman: Singapore-MIT Alliance for Res. and Technol., 2007; ETH Singapore SEC Ltd, 2010; TUM CREATE Centre, 2011; Governing Bd, Berkeley Educn Alliance for Res. in Singapore Ltd, 2012; Governing Bd, Cambridge Centre for Advanced Res. and Educn in Singapore Ltd, 2013. Hon. Fellow: Coll. of Gen. Practitioners of Singapore, 1982; Internat. Coll. of Dentists, USA, 1999; (Dental Surgery), RCSE, 1999; Hon. FRACOG 1992; FRCPSGlas 1997; Hon. FRCSE 1997. Hon. DSc Hull, 1999. Public Administration Medal (Gold), Singapore, 1984; Meritorious Service Medal, Singapore, 1990; Friend of Labour Award, NTUC, 1995; Outstanding Service Award, NUS, 2003; Distinguished Service Award, NTUC, 2015; Outstanding Volunteer Award, Min. of Social and Family Develt. Distinguished Service Order (Singapore), 2000; Officier, Ordre des Palmes Académiques (France), 1988. *Publications*: articles in New England Jl of Medicine, Med. Jl of Australia, BMJ, Qly Jl of Medicine, and Tissue Antigens. *Recreation*: swimming. *Address*: Department of Medicine, National University of Singapore, 1E Kent Ridge Road, Singapore 119228, Republic of Singapore. *Club*: Singapore Island Country.

**LIMB, Ann Geraldine,** CBE 2015 (OBE 2011); DL; Chair, Scout Association, since 2015; *b* Moss Side, Manchester, 13 Feb. 1953; *d* of Norman Limb and Elsie Geraldine Limb (*née* Bromley); civil partnership 2006, *m* 2019, Margaret Ann Cook, PhD. *Educ*: Marple Hall Girls Grammar Sch.; Univ. of Liverpool (BA Hons French 1975; MA 1976). Lecturer: Univ. de Nancy, 1976–77; St John's Coll., Manchester, 1977–78; Abraham Moss Centre, Manchester, 1978–80; Hd of Langs, High Peak Coll., Buxton, 1980–84; Hd of Business Studies and Mgt, NE Derbyshire Coll., 1984–86; Vice Principal, 1986–87, Principal, 1987–96, Milton Keynes Coll.; Principal, Cambridge Regional Coll., 1996–2001; Gp Chief Exec., Univ. for Industry, 2001–04. Vis. Prof. of Mgt, Univ. of W London (formerly Thames Valley Univ.), 2005–. Chair, Milton Keynes Partnership, 2008–11 (Ind. Mem., 2004–08), Mem. Bd, 2011–17, Homes England (formerly Homes and Communities Agency). Non-executive Director: Electricity Consumer's Council, 1989–92; Trng Standards Council, 1997–2001; Addenbrooke's NHS Trust, 1997–2001 (Chm., Audit Cttee; Vice Chm., Clin. Governance Cttee); DRS plc, 2004–11 (Chm., Remuneration and Ethics Cttees); HM Govt Communications Centre, 2008–13; Milton Keynes Hosp. NHS Foundn Trust, 2009–12; Member: Bd, Council for Ind. and Higher Educn, 1996–2004; Bd, Further Educn, NTO, 1996–2001; Bd, Adult Learning Inspectorate, 2001–03; Cambs, Learning and Skills Council, 2001–03; Ministerial Task Force on Feminising IT, 2001–03; Prime Minister's Digital Inclusion Panel, 2001–07; Council, C&G, 2014– (Trustee, 2015–); SE Council, Arts Council England, 2015–; Chair: Knowledge and Inf. Adv. Bd, British Council, 2002–06; Legal Deposit Adv. Cttee, DCMS, 2005–10; Milton Keynes Higher Educn Bd, 2008–18; Destination Milton Keynes, 2009–18; SE Midlands LEP, 2012–19; E-ACT, 2012–15; Women in Labour, 2013–15; Adv. Bd, Univ. Campus Milton Keynes, Univ. of Bedfordshire, 2014–17; Further Educn Funding Reform and Localism Steering Gp, Skills Funding Agency, 2015–17; Milton Keynes Bid for 2023 European Capital of Culture, 2016–18; London-Cambridge Innovation Corridor, 2017–; Milton Keynes Educn Trust, 2017–; Mem. Bd, Wavendon All Music Plan, Stables Th., Milton Keynes, 2009– (Chm., Milton Keynes Internat. Fest., 2012–). Chair, Board of Trustees: Helena Kennedy Foundn, 1998–; Nat. Extension Coll., 1998–2011; Student Volunteering England, 2005–07; Anne Frank Trust UK, 2006–12; Milton Keynes Arts for Health, 2007–13; Chm., Cambridge Fundraising Bd, Maggie's Cancer Care Centres, 1999–2001; Member, Board of Trustees: Milton Keynes Counselling Foundn, 1992–96; Willen Hospice, Milton Keynes, 1994–96; Trustee and Dir, Centre for Excellence in Leadership, 2006–08; Trustee, Volunteering England, 2006–08; Mem. Bd, ENTRUST, 2012–14 (Chair, 2014–). Member, Council: Open Univ., 2002–08; Univ. of Surrey, 2003–06; Univ. of Buckingham, 2018–. Gov., Milton Keynes Acad., 2008–11. Non-exec. Dir, Nat. Council, IoD, 2006–12. First Vis. Scholar, Lucy Cavendish Coll. Centre for Women Leaders, 1997–. FRSA 1997. FCGI 2002. Hon. Fellow, Milton Keynes Coll., 2014. DL Bucks, 2011. Hon. PhD Anglia Ruskin, 2003; Hon. DBA: Manchester Metropolitan, 2011; Bedfordshire, 2014; DUniv Open, 2016; Hon. Dr W London. Mary Lou Carrington Award, Educators' Co., 2012. *Publications*: Introducing PET: the Cambridge Preliminary English Test, 1982; Objectifs: assignments in practical language skills, 1985; Managing Colleges in the 21st Century, 1991; Preparing for Incorporation, 1993; Changing Organisational Cultures, 1994; Further Education Under New Labour, 1999; Taking Education Really Seriously, 2001; Leading, Learning, 2005; Women in Leadership, 2009. *Recreations*: theatre, opera, ski-ing, trekking, bird watching, spending time with my niece, nephew and many godchildren, active member of Quakers. *Address*: Trinity House, 3 Willow Lane, Stony Stratford, Bucks MK11 1FG. *T*: (01908) 307171, 07775 817980. *E*: agl@annlimb.co.uk. *W*: www.annlimb.co.uk. *Club*: Athenæum (Mem., 2016–, Chm., 2017–, Exec. Cttee; Dep. Chm., Gen. Cttee, 2017–).

**LIMB, Patrick Francis;** QC 2006; *b* 23 June 1965; *s* of late Anthony Patrick Limb and of Yvonne Thérèse Léoncie Limb; *m* 1st, 1992, Anne Elizabeth Fentem (marr. diss. 2010); one *s* one *d*; 2nd, 2012, Allison Garner; one step *d*. *Educ*: Edinburgh Acad.; Pembroke Coll., Cambridge (Open Exhibnr; BA Hons 1986). Called to the Bar, Middle Temple, 1987; Jun. Counsel to the Crown, Provincial Panel, 2002–06. Trustee, Nottingham City of Literature, 2017–. *Recreations*: running down dunes, being walked by Alfie and Daisy, random acts of dancing. *Address*: c/o Ropewalk Chambers, 24 The Ropewalk, Nottingham NG1 5EF. *T*: (0115) 947 2581, *Fax*: (0115) 947 6532. *E*: patricklimbqc@ropewalk.co.uk.

**LIMBU;** *see* Rambahadur Limbu.

**LIMEBEER, Prof. David John Noel,** PhD, DSc; FREng, FIEEE, FIET; Professor of Control Engineering, University of Oxford, 2009–18, now Emeritus; Fellow, New College, Oxford, 2009–18, now Emeritus; Distinguished Professor, University of Johannesburg, since 2018; *b* Johannesburg, 31 July 1952; *s* of Gerald J. N. Limebeer and Joan C. Limebeer; *m* 2017, Veronica Irene (*née* Sham). *Educ*: Michaelhouse; Witwatersrand Univ. (BSc Engrg 1974); Natal Univ. (MSc Engrg 1976; PhD 1980); Univ. of London (DSc 1992). Res. Associate, Selwyn Coll., Cambridge, 1980–84; Imperial College London: Lectr, 1984–89; Reader, 1989–93; Prof., 1993–2009; Hd, Dept of Electrical and Electronic Engrg, 1999–2009. FIEEE 1992; FREng 1997; FCGI. *Publications*: Linear Robust Control (with M. Green), 1995; (with M. Massaro) Dynamics and Optimal Control of Road Vehicles, 2018. *Recreations*: cinema, weight training, reading, antique lamps and furniture, building restoration. *E*: david.limebeer@eng.ox.ac.uk.

**LIMERICK, 7th Earl of,** *cr* 1803 (Ire.); **Edmund Christopher Pery;** Baron Glentworth, 1790 (Ire.); Viscount Limerick, 1800 (Ire.); Viscount Pery, 1800 (Ire.); Baron Foxford, 1815; Partner, Altima Partners LLP, 2005–09; *b* 10 Feb. 1963; *s* of 6th Earl of Limerick, KBE, AM and of Sylvia Rosalind Lush (*see* Sylvia, Countess of Limerick); *S* father, 2003; *m* 1st, 1990, Emily Kate (marr. diss. 2000), *o d* of Michael Thomas; two *s*; 2nd, 2002, Lydia Ann (marr. diss. 2010), 4th *d* of Richard Johnson; 3rd, 2012, Kate Mary, *e d* of Peter Inglis Hall; one *s* one *d*. *Educ*: Eton; New Coll., Oxford (MA); Pushkin Inst., Moscow; City Univ. (Dip. Law). Called to the Bar, Middle Temple, 1987. HM Diplomatic Service, 1987–92: FCO, 1987–88; Ecole Nationale d'Administration, Paris, 1988–89; attachment to Ministère des Affaires Etrangères, Paris, 1990; Second Sec., Senegal, 1990–91, Amman, 1991–92; lawyer: with Clifford Chance, 1992–93; with Freshfields, 1993–94; solicitor with Milbank Tweed, 1994–96; Chief Rep., Morgan Grenfell (Deutsche Bank), Moscow, 1996–98; Dir, Deutsche Bank AG London, 1996–2004; Middle East Regl Manager, Man Gp, Dubai, 2004; Sen. Vice-Pres., Dubai Internat. Capital, 2005. Director: Saddleback Ltd, 2007–16; GRDC 1 Ltd, 2007–13; Chagala Gp Ltd, 2009–13; Caspian Sunrise plc (formerly Roxi Petroleum plc), 2010–; Prestige Security Mgt Ltd, 2014–15; Chairman: ESL (UK) Ltd, 2010–13; Thermotec South East Ltd, 2012–14; Eagle iii Ltd, 2015–. Gov., Ardingly Coll., 2007–18. *Recreations*: ski-ing, kitesurfing, tennis. *Heir*: *s* Viscount Pery, *qv*. *Address*: Chiddinglye, West Hoathly, East Grinstead, W Sussex RH19 4QT. *T*: (01342) 810987. *E*: eclimerick@hotmail.com. *Clubs*: Garrick; Sussex; Royal Ashdown Forest Golf.

**LIMERICK, Sylvia Countess of; Sylvia Rosalind Pery,** CBE 1991; Hon. Vice-President, British Red Cross Society, since 1999; Vice-President, Lullaby Trust (formerly Foundation for the Study of Infant Deaths), since 2012 (Vice-Chairman, 1971–2012); *b* 7 Dec. 1935; *e d* of Maurice Stanley Lush, CB, CBE, MC; *m* 1961, Viscount Glentworth (later 6th Earl of Limerick, KBE, AM; *d* 2003); two *s* one *d*. *Educ*: St Swithun's, Winchester; Lady Margaret Hall, Oxford (MA). Research Asst, Foreign Office, 1959–62. British Red Cross Society: Nat. HQ Staff, 1962–66; Pres., Kensington and Chelsea Div., 1966–72; a Vice-Pres., London Br., 1972–85; Vice-Chm., Council, 1984–85; Chm., 1985–95 (Chm. Emeritus, 1995–97); a Vice-Pres., Internat. Fedn of Red Cross Red Crescent Socs, 1993–97. Mem., Bd of Governors, St Bartholomew's Hosp., 1970–74; Vice-Chm., CHC,

S District of Kensington, Chelsea, Westminster Area, 1974–77; Chairman: Eastman Dental Inst., 1996–99; Eastman Foundn for Oral Res. and Trng, 1996–2002; Member: Kensington, Chelsea and Westminster AHA, 1977–82; St Mary's Med. Sch. Council and District Ethics Cttee, 1977–83; Eastman Dental Hosp. SHA, 1990–96. Non-exec. Dir, UCL Hosps NHS Trust, 1996–97. A Vice-Pres., 1978–84, Pres., 1984–2002, Health Visitors' Assoc., subseq. Community Practitioners' and Health Visitors' Assoc.; President: UK Cttee for UN Children's Fund, 1972–79 (Vice Pres., 1979–99); Nat. Assoc. for Maternal and Child Welfare, 1973–84 (Vice Pres., 1985–90); St Catherine's Hospice, 2010–15. Member: Cttee of Management, Inst. of Child Health, 1976–96; Council, King Edward's Hospital Fund, 1977–2008 (Mem., Cttee of Management, 1977–81, 1985–89); Maternity Services Adv. Cttee, DHSS, 1981–84; CS Occupational Health Service Adv. Bd, 1989–92; Vice-Chm., Jt Res. Ethics Cttee, Nat. Hosp. for Neurology and Neurosurgery/Inst. of Neurology, 1993–2004; Chm., CMO's Expert Gp to investigate Cot Death Theories, 1994–98. Trustee: Child Accident Prevention Trust, 1979–87; Voluntary Hosp. of St Bartholomew, 1991–2004; Child Health Res. Appeal Trust, 1996–2006. Patron: Childhealth Advocacy Internat., 1998–2009; Lodge Hill Trust, W Sussex, 2006–. Reviewed National Association of Citizens Advice Bureaux, 1983. FRSocMed 1977. Hon. FRCP 1994 (Hon. MRCP 1990); Hon. FRCPCH 1996 (Hon. Mem., BPA, 1986); Hon. Fellow, Inst. of Child Health, London, 1996. Hon. DLitt CNAA, 1990; Hon. LLD Bristol, 1998. Hon. Freeman: Salters' Co., 1992; World Traders' Co., 2003. Humanitarian Award, European Women of Achievement, 1995. Order of Croatian Star, 2003. *Publications:* (jtly) Sudden Infant Death: patterns, puzzles and problems, 1985. *Recreations:* music, mountaineering, ski-ing. *Address:* Chiddinglye, West Hoathly, East Grinstead, W Sussex RH19 4QT. *T:* (01342) 810214.

**LIMERICK AND KILLALOE, Bishop of,** since 2015; **Rt Rev. Kenneth Arthur Kearon;** *b* 4 Oct. 1953; *s* of Hubert Kenneth Maurice Kearon and Ethel Maria Kearon (*née* Shattock); *m* 1978, Jennifer Poyntz; three *d*. *Educ:* Trinity Coll., Dublin (BA Mod. 1976, MA 1979); Irish Sch. of Ecumenics (MPhil Ecum. 1991); Jesus Coll., Cambridge. Ordained deacon, 1981, priest, 1982; Curate, All Saints Raheny and St John's Coolock, Dublin, 1981–84; pt-time Lectr, 1981–99, Dean of Residence, 1984–91, Trinity Coll., Dublin; Rector, Tullow Parish, Dublin, 1991–99; Dir, Irish Sch. of Ecumenics, Trinity Coll., Dublin, 1999–2004; Sec. Gen., Anglican Communion, 2005–15. Canon, 1996–2015, Chancellor, 2002–04, Christ Church Cathedral, Dublin. Hon. Canon: St Paul's Cathedral, London, 2005–15; St George's Cathedral, Jerusalem, 2005–15; Christ Church Cathedral, Canterbury, 2005–15; Christ Church Cathedral, Cape Coast, W Africa, 2013–15. Hon. DD: General Theological Seminary, NY, 2006; Berkeley Divinity Sch., Yale, 2015. *Publications:* Medical Ethics: an introduction, 1995, 2nd edn 1999; (ed with F. O'Ferrall) Medical Ethics and the Future of Healthcare, 2000; *contributions to:* A Parish Adult Education Handbook, 1987; Ethics and the Christian, 1991; Family: fading embers, kindling flames, 1994; Minorities—the right to be different, 1995; Relationships and Sexuality Education in Primary Schools, 1996; Bioethics Research: policy methods and strategy, 1997; A Time to Build, 1999; A New Dictionary of Christian Spirituality, 2006; The Irish School of Ecumenics (1970–2007), 2008; jls, inc. Search, Medico-Legal Jl of Ireland. *Address:* Kilbane House, Golf Links Road, Limerick, Republic of Ireland. *E:* bishop@limerick.anglican.org. *Clubs:* Blainroe Golf (Wicklow); Adare Manor Golf.

**LINACRE, Christina Margaret;** see McComb, C. M.

**LINAKER, Lawrence Edward, (Paddy);** Deputy Chairman and Chief Executive, M&G Group, 1987–94; *b* 22 July 1934; *s* of late Lawrence Wignall and Rose Linaker; *m* 1963, Elizabeth Susan Elam; one *s*. *Educ:* Malvern College. FCA. Esso Petroleum, 1957–63; joined M&G Group, 1963; Man. Dir, 1972, Chm., 1987–94, M&G Investment Management. Chairman: Fisons, 1994–95; Marling Industries, 1996–97; Fleming Technol. Investment Trust plc, 1997–2001; Director: Fleming Mercantile Investment Trust, 1994–2005; TSB Gp, 1994–95; Lloyds TSB Gp, 1995–2001; Wolverhampton & Dudley Breweries plc, 1996–2002. Chm., Institutional Fund Managers' Assoc., 1992–94; Dir, Securities Inst., 1992–94. Trustee, Lloyds TSB Foundn for Eng. and Wales, 1995–2001; Life Trustee, Carnegie UK Trust, 1995–2005. Chm., YMCA Nat. Coll., 1992–2000; Treas., Childline, 1994–2000; Member: Council, RPMS, 1977–88; Governing Body, SPCK, 1976–95; Council, Malvern College, 1988–2003 (Treas., 1993–2002); Governing Body, Canterbury Christ Church Coll., 1993–98; Court, ICSTM, 1999–2005. *Recreations:* music, wine, gardening. *Clubs:* Athenæum, Brooks's.

**LINCOLN,** 19th Earl of, *cr* 1572; **Robert Edward Fiennes-Clinton;** *b* 19 June 1972; *s* of Hon. Edward Gordon Fiennes-Clinton and Julia (*née* Howson); *S* grandfather, 2001. *Educ:* Pinjarra High Sch., WA. FZS 2010. *Heir:* b William James Howson (name assumed in 1996 in lieu of William Roy Fiennes-Clinton) [*b* 6 March 1980; *m* 1999, Rebecca Danielle Hazell; one *s*].

**LINCOLN, Bishop of,** since 2011; **Rt Rev. Christopher Lowson;** *b* 3 Feb. 1953; *s* of George Frederick Lowson, CEng, FIMarE and Isabella Annie Lowson (*née* Spence); *m* 1976, Susan Mary Osborne, RGN, RSCN, MSc; one *s* one *d*. *Educ:* Newcastle Cathedral Sch.; Consett Grammar Sch.; King's Coll. London (AKC 1975); St Augustine's Coll., Canterbury; Pacific Sch. of Religion, Berkeley, Calif (STM 1978); Heythrop Coll., Univ. of London (MTh 1996); Cardiff Law Sch. (LLM 2003). Deacon 1977, priest 1978; Asst Curate, Richmond, Surrey, 1977–82; Priest in charge, 1982–83, Vicar 1983–91, Holy Trinity, Eltham; Chaplain: Avery Hill Coll., 1982–85; Thames Poly., 1985–91; Vicar of Petersfield and Rector of Buriton, Hants, 1991–99; RD of Petersfield, 1995–99; Archdeacon of Portsmouth, 1999; Archdeacon of Portsdown, 1999–2006, Archdeacon Emeritus, 2006–11; Dir, Ministry Div., Archbishops' Council, 2006–11; Priest Vicar, Westminster Abbey, 2006–11. Member: Clergy Discipline Commn, 2012–; Legal Adv. Commn, C of E, 2012–. A Church Comr, 2015–. Mem., H of L, 2017–; Mem., Regenerating Seaside Towns and Communities Cttee, H of L, 2018–19. Chm., Portsmouth Diocesan Bd of Ministry, 1999–2006; Bp of Portsmouth's Liaison Officer for Prisons, 1999–2003; Bp of Portsmouth's Advr to Hosp. Chaplaincy, 2003–06. Vis. Lectr, Portsmouth Univ., 1998–2004; Dir, Portsmouth Educn Business Partnership, 2000–03. Foundn Trustee, Gallipoli Meml Lecture Trust, 1985–91. *Recreations:* watching cricket, the theatre. *Address:* Bishop's Office, Edward King House, Minster Yard, Lincoln LN2 1PU. *Clubs:* MCC, Garrick, Savile; Castle Hill (Lincoln).

**LINCOLN, Dean of;** see Wilson, Very Rev. C. L.

**LINCOLN, Archdeacon of;** see Kirk, Ven. G. J.

**LINCOLN, Paul Arthur;** education consultant, since 2013; Chief Operating and Education Officer, USA, EdisonLearning Inc., 2011–13 (Managing Director UK and Senior Vice President International, 2010); *b* 11 April 1946. *Educ:* Clare Coll., Cambridge (BA (Hons) History; PGCE 1969; MA 1971). Various teaching posts in secondary schools in Sussex and Essex, 1969–82; Sen. Dep. Head, William de Ferrers Sch., Essex, 1982–88; Essex County Council Education Department: Sen. Inspector, 1988–89; Principal Inspector, 1989–91; Head of Strategic Planning, 1991–92; Principal Educn Officer, Quality, 1992–93; Dep. County Educn Officer, 1994–95; Dir of Educn, 1995–97; Dir of Learning Services, Essex CC, 1997–2002; Chief Exec., Eastern Leadership Centre, Cambridge, 2003–04; Dir of Educn, EdisonLearning UK and Internat. (formerly Edison Schs UK Ltd), 2003–10. Chm., Collaborative Academies Trust, 2013–15. *Publications:* The Learning School, 1987; Supporting Improving Primary Schools, 1999. *Recreations:* reading, walking, gardening.

**LINCOLN, Paul Michael,** OBE 2008; Director General, Border Force, Home Office, since 2017; *b* Cambridge; *s* of Prof. Andrew T. Lincoln and Francesca Paula Nicholson; *m* 2008, Jo Tribble. *Educ:* Nottingham High Sch.; Trinity Coll., Cambridge (BA 1995; MEng 1996); Imperial Coll. London (MBA Dist. 2004). Policy and Pol Advr to Sen. UK Military Comdr in Iraq, 2006–07; Hd, Defence and Security Policy, Cabinet Office, 2007–09; Hd, Defence Resources, MoD, 2009–11; Comd Sec., PJHQ, 2011–12, Dir, Resources and Policy, Jt Forces Comd, 2011–14, MoD; Dir, Nat. Security, 2014–15, Actg Dir, Gen. Office for Security and Counter-Terrorism, 2015–16, Dir Gen., Crime, Policing and Fire Gp, 2016–17, Home Office. *Recreations:* walking, foreign travel, pets. *Address:* Home Office, Marsham Street, SW1P 4DF. *T:* (020) 7035 4848.

**LINDAHL, Göran;** company director; *b* Umeå, Sweden, 28 April 1945; *s* of Sven Lindahl and Frida (*née* Johansson); *m* 1971, Kristina Gunnarsdotter; one *s* one *d*. *Educ:* Chalmers Univ. of Technology, Gothenburg (MSc Electrical Eng 1971); Univ. of Gothenburg (Astronomy). ASEA Ludvika, Sweden: various positions in Engrg Res., Mktg and Sales, 1971–83; Pres., ASEA Transformers, 1983–85; Pres., ASEA Transmission, 1985–86, Exec. Vice-Pres. and Mem. ASEA Gp Mgt, ASEA AB, 1986–87; Vice-Chm.: ABB Ltd, Zurich: Exec. Vice-Pres. and Mem. Gp Mgt Cttee, responsible for Power Transmission and Distribution Segment, 1988–93, responsible for Asia, 1993–96; Pres. and CEO, 1996–2001; Mem. Bd, ABB Ltd, 1999–2001. Chm., Alliance for Global Sustainability, 2001–02; Under-Sec.-Gen. of UN and Special Advr on Global Compact to Kofi Annan, UN Sec.-Gen., 2001–02. Member Board: Saab AB, Sweden, 1991–97; Atlas Copco AB, Sweden, 1994–97; Ericsson AB, Sweden, 1999–2002; DuPont, USA, 1999–2004; INGKA Holding BV (IKEA), Holland, 2001–; Sony Corp., Japan, 2001–07 (Mem. Internat. Adv. Bd, 2007–11); Nanomix Inc., USA, 2001–06; Sony Ericsson AB, Sweden, 2003–07; iGate Corp., 2006–15; Patni Computer Systems Ltd, India, 2011–12; Vice-Chm. Bd, Anglo American plc, 2001–05; Chairman, Board: Sony Group Europe, UK, 2003–04; LivSafe Gp, Sweden and USA, 2005–; West Coast Locators Inc., USA, 2005–13; IKEA GreenTech AB, Sweden, 2006–; Cuptronic Technology AB, Sweden, 2008–; Avinode Holding AB, Sweden, 2009–14; Evry ASA, Norway, 2015–; West & Bergh IT Consulting AB, Sweden, 2016–; Mem. Internat. Adv. Bd, Citigroup USA, 1999–2006; Chm. Internat. Adv. Bd, IIT, USA, 2003–12. Chm., World Childhood Foundn, USA, 2001–02 (Mem. Bd, World Childhood Foundn, Sweden, USA, Germany, 2001–02); Vice Chairman Board: Prince of Wales Business Leaders Forum, 1998–2001; John F. Kennedy Center Corporate Fund, 1999–2001; Mem. Bd, Schwab Foundn for Social Entrepreneurship, Switzerland, 2001–02. Mem. Bd Trustees, Illinois Inst. of Technol., 2006–12. Chm., EU-Hong Kong Business Co-operation Cttee, 1999–2000; Co-Chm., ASEAN-EU Industrialists Round Table, 1998–2000; Member: EU-Russia Industrialists Round Table, 1999–2000; US-EU-Poland Action Commn, 1999–2000; Member: EU-Japan Industrialists Round Table, 1999–2000; European Round Table of Industrialists, 2000–01. Mem. Royal Swedish Acad. of Engrg Scis, 1999. Hon. DSc Eng Chalmers Univ. of Technol., Gothenburg, 1993; Hon. PhD Umeå, 2001. Paul Harris Fellow, Rotary Club Internat., 1997. *Recreations:* astronomy, golf. *Address:* Ginstvägen 14, 23642 Höllviken, Sweden. *E:* nstargl@aol.com.

**LINDAHL, Tomas Robert,** MD; FRS 1988; Principal Scientist, Cancer Research UK London Research Institute (formerly Imperial Cancer Research Fund), 1981–2010, now Emeritus; *b* 28 Jan. 1938; *s* of Robert and Ethel Lindahl; *m* 1967, Alice Adams (marr. diss. 1979); one *s* one *d*. *Educ:* Karolinska Inst., Stockholm (MD). Research Fellow, Princeton Univ., 1964–67; Helen Hay Whitney Fellow, 1967–69, Asst Prof., 1968–69, Rockefeller Univ.; Asst Prof., 1969–75, Associate Prof., 1975–77, Karolinska Inst.; Prof. of Medical Biochemistry, Univ. of Gothenburg, 1978–81; Imperial Cancer Research Fund: Staff Scientist, 1981–83; Dir, Clare Hall Labs, 1983–2005; Asst Dir of Research, 1985–89; Associate Dir of Research, 1989–91; Dep. Dir, Res., 1991–96; Dir, Res., 1996–98; Dep. Dir, Res., 1998–2005. Croonian Lecture, Royal Soc., 1996. Member: EMBO; Royal Swedish Acad. of Scis; Norwegian Acad. of Sci. and Letters; Academia Europaea; Foreign Associate, US NAS, 2018. Founder FMedSci 1998. Royal Medal, 2007, Copley Medal, 2010, Royal Soc.; Prix Étranger, INSERM, France, 2008; (jtly) Nobel Prize in Chemistry, 2015; HM King's Medal (Sweden), 2016. *Publications:* res. papers in biochem. and molecular biol. *Recreations:* piano, wine, modern art. *Address:* Francis Crick Institute, 1 Midland Road, Kings Cross, NW1 1AT.

**LINDBLOM, Rt Hon. Sir Keith John,** Kt 2010; PC 2016; **Rt Hon. Lord Justice Lindblom;** a Lord Justice of Appeal, since 2015; *b* 20 Sept. 1956; *s* of John Eric Lindblom and June Elizabeth Lindblom (*née* Balloch); *m* 1991, Fiona Margaret Jackson; one *s* three *d*. *Educ:* Whitgift Sch.; St John's Coll., Oxford (MA). Called to the Bar: Gray's Inn, 1980, Bencher, 2003; NI, 2002; admitted to: Hong Kong Bar, 2000 and 2008; Bar of Turks and Caicos Is, 2006; in practice as barrister, 1981–2010; QC 1996; Recorder, 2001–10; Deputy High Court Judge, 2009–10; a Judge of the High Court of Justice, QBD, 2010–15; Pres., Upper Tribunal (Lands Chamber), 2013–15; Planning Liaison Judge, 2014–15; Vice-Pres. of Tribunals, 2018–; Pres., Upper Tribunal (Admin. Appeals Chamber), 2018–19. An Asst Parly Boundary Comm., 2000. *Recreations:* music, reading, walking. *Address:* Royal Courts of Justice, Strand, WC2A 2LL. *Club:* Caledonian.

**LINDEN, Anya, (Lady Sainsbury of Preston Candover),** CBE 2003; Ballerina, Royal Ballet, 1958–65, retired; *b* 3 Jan. 1933; English; *d* of George Charles and Ada Dorothea Eltenton; *m* 1963, John Davan Sainsbury (see Baron Sainsbury of Preston Candover); two *s* one *d*. *Educ:* Berkeley, Calif; Sadler's Wells Sch., 1947. Entered Royal Ballet (formerly Sadler's Wells) Co. at Covent Garden, 1951; promoted Soloist, 1952; Ballerina, 1958. Principal rôles in the ballets: Coppelia; Sylvia; Prince of Pagodas; Sleeping Beauty; Swan Lake; Giselle; Cinderella; Agon; Solitaire; Noctambules; Fête Etrange; Symphonic Variations; Hamlet; The Invitation; Firebird; Lady and the Fool; Antigone; Ondine; Seven Deadly Sins. Ballet coach: Royal Ballet Sch., 1989–; Rambert Sch., 1989–. Member: Nat. Council for One-Parent Families, 1978–90 (Hon. Vice-Pres., 1985–90); Mem. Appeal Cttee, 1966–87); Adv. Council, British Theatre Museum, 1975–83; Drama and Dance Adv. Cttee, British Council, 1981–83; Theatre Museum Assoc., 1984–86. Dep.-Chm. and Dir, Rambert Dance Co. (formerly Ballet Rambert), 1975–89. Trustee: Royal Opera Hse, 2003–07 (Mem., Bd of Hon. Dirs, 2016–); Rambert Sch. of Ballet and Contemp. Dance, 2003–06 (Mem. Adv. Cttee, 1985–2003). Gov., Royal Ballet Sch., 1977–2004; Dep. Chm. and Mem. Council of Management, Benesh Inst. of Choreology (formerly Benesh Inst. of Movement Notation), 1986–97. Founder and Chm., Linbury Prize for Stage Design, 1987–2010. Dir, Anvil Trust, 1992–98; Trustee, Galitzine Library—St Petersburg, 1993–2004. Patron: Landfile, 1993–; Heatherley Sch. of Fine Art, 2007–. FRWCMD 2008. DUniv Brunel, 1995. *Recreations:* gardening, painting, photography.

**LINDEN, David;** MP (SNP) Glasgow East, since 2017; *b* Glasgow, 14 May 1990; *m* Roslyn; one *s*. *Educ:* Bannerman High Sch., Baillieston. Mem., underwriting team, Access Loans and Mortgages; with Glasgow Credit Union; caseworker, Glasgow E constituency office,

2008; Manager, office of Alison Thewliss, MP, 2015–17. SNP Whip, 2017–. Mem., Procedure Cttee, 2017–, Standing Orders Cttee, 2017–, H of C. *Address:* House of Commons, SW1A 0AA.

**LINDEN, Ian,** CMG 2000; PhD; Associate Professor, Department for the Study of Religion, School of Oriental and African Studies, University of London, since 2002; Executive Director, Catholic Institute for International Relations, 1986–2001; *b* 18 Aug. 1941; *s* of Henry Thomas William Linden and Edna Jessie Linden; *m* 1963, Jane Winder; two *s* two *d. Educ:* Southend High Sch. for Boys; St Catharine's Coll., Cambridge (MA 1966); PhD London Univ. (Middx Hosp. Med. Sch., 1966, SOAS 1975). Asst Lectr in Zoology, Nat. Univ. of Ireland, 1965–66; Res. Associate, Rockefeller Univ., NY, 1966–68; Lectr in Biology, Univ. of Malawi, 1968–71; Lectr, subseq. Sen. Lectr, in History, Ahmadu Bello Univ., 1973–76; Researcher, Arbeitskreis Entwicklung und Frieden, 1977–79; Prof. of African History, Univ. of Hamburg, 1979–80; Southern Africa Desk Officer and Co-ordinator of Policy Dept, Catholic Inst. for Internat. Relns, 1980–86. Vis. Prof., St Mary's Univ., Twickenham, 2016–. Hon. PhD Southampton, 1998. *Publications:* Catholics, Peasants and Chewa Resistance in Nyasaland, 1974; Church and Revolution in Rwanda, 1977; The Catholic Church and the Struggle for Zimbabwe, 1980; (jtly) Islam in Modern Nigeria, 1984; Christianisme et pouvoirs au Rwanda 1900–1990, 1999; A New Map of the World, 2004; Global Catholicism, 2009. *Recreations:* swimming, theology, walking. *Address:* 31 Royal Close, Manor Road, N16 5SE.
See also S. K. Linden, T. D. Linden.

**LINDEN, Prof. Paul Frederick,** PhD; FRS 2007; G. I. Taylor Professor of Fluid Mechanics, Department of Applied Mathematics and Theoretical Physics, 2010–14, now Emeritus, and Director of Research, since 2014, University of Cambridge; Fellow, Downing College, Cambridge, 2010–14, now Emeritus; *b* 29 Jan. 1947; *s* of Frederick Henry Victor Linden and Muriel Constance Linden; *m* 1979, Diana Readman; two *d. Educ:* Univ. of Adelaide (BSc Hons 1967); Flinders Univ. of South Australia (MSc 1968); Emmanuel Coll., Cambridge (PhD 1972). University of Cambridge: Asst Dir of Res., 1976–91; Reader in Geophysical Fluid Dynamics, 1991–98; Dir, Fluid Dynamics Lab., 1976–98; Fellow, Downing Coll., 1977–98; University of California, San Diego: Blasker Distinguished Prof. of Envmtl Sci. and Engrg, 1998–2010, now Emeritus; Chm., Dept of Mechanical and Aerospace Engrg, 2004–10; Director: Envmt and Sustainability Initiative, 2007–08; Sustainability Solutions Inst., 2009–10. Dep. Ed., Jl Fluid Mechanics, 2010– (Associate Ed., 2005–10); Editor: JFM Rapids, 2013–15; JFM Perspectives, 2015–. *Publications:* over 150 articles in refereed jls. *Recreations:* running, swimming, clarinet. *Address:* Department of Applied Mathematics and Theoretical Physics, Centre for Mathematical Sciences, Wilberforce Road, Cambridge CB3 0WA. *E:* p.f.linden@damtp.cam.ac.uk.

**LINDEN, Sophia Kizito, (Sophie);** Deputy Mayor of London for Policing and Crime, since 2016; *b* Blantyre, Malawi, 27 Feb. 1970; *d* of Ian Linden, *qv; m* 1994, John-Paul Morrison; three *s* one *d. Educ:* St Gregory's Comp. Sch., Bath; Our Lady Convent High Sch., Hackney; Emmanuel Coll., Cambridge (BA Hons 1992). Researcher, H of C, 1992–97; Special Adviser: DFEE, 1997–2001; Home Office, 2001–04; Dir, Policy and Campaigns, End Child Poverty Campaign, 2005–06; Dir, Bell Pottinger Public Affairs (pt-time), 2006–08. Mem. (Lab), Hackney LBC, 2006–16 (Dep. Mayor). *Address:* Greater London Authority, City Hall, The Queen's Walk, SE1 2AA.
See also T. D. Linden.

**LINDEN, Thomas Dominic;** QC 2006; a Recorder, since 2005; *b* London, 26 Nov. 1964; *s* of Ian Linden, *qv; m* 1991, Brigit Connolly; four *d. Educ:* Beechen Cliff Comp. Sch., Bath; St Brendan's Sixth Form Coll., Bristol; Keble Coll., Oxford (BA Juris. 1st Cl. 1987; BCL 1988). Called to the Bar, Gray's Inn, 1989. *Recreations:* cycling, playing with our children. *Address:* Matrix Chambers, Griffin House, Gray's Inn, WC1R 5LN. *T:* (020) 7404 3447. *E:* tomlinden@matrixlaw.co.uk.

**LINDESAY-BETHUNE,** family name of **Earl of Lindsay**.

**LINDHURST, Gordon John;** Member (C) Lothian, Scottish Parliament, since 2016; *b* 2 July 1967. *Educ:* Univ. of Edinburgh (LLB Hons 1989); Univ. of Glasgow (DipLP 1990); Heidelberg Univ. (LLM 1994). Admitted as solicitor, Law Soc. of Scotland, 1992; Advocate, Faculty of Advocates, 1995; Curator, Advocates' Liby, 2000–07 (Clerk to Curators, 2000–02); called to the Bar, Middle Temple, 2008; barrister-at-law, 2008–. Reporter, Session Cases, 2000–. Mem. Council, Faculty of Advocates, 2013–16. Vis. Lectr, British Court Practice, Univ. of Bonn, 2014–. Scottish Parliament: Convener, Economy, Jobs and Fair Work Cttee, 2016–; Mem., Social Security Cttee, 2016–. Mem., Merchant Co. of City of Edinburgh, 2006. *Publications:* (contrib.) The Blue Book: Scottish Conservatism in the 21st century, 2006; contrib. articles to Scots Law Times, Criminal Law and Justice Weekly, Scottish Legal Rev., The Firm. *Recreations:* music, sailing, hill walking, cycling. *Address:* Scottish Parliament, Edinburgh EH99 1SP.

**LINDISFARNE, Archdeacon of;** *see* Robinson, Ven. P. J. A.

**LINDLEY, Bryan Charles,** CBE 1982; Chairman and Chief Executive, Lord Lindley Associates, since 1990; Director, J & B Imaging, since 1998; *b* 30 Aug. 1932; *m* 1987; one *s* by former *m. Educ:* Reading Sch.; University Coll. London (Fellow 1979). BSc (Eng) 1954; PhD 1960. FIMechE 1968; FIET (FIEE 1968); FInstP 1968; FInstD 1968; FPRI 1984. National Gas Turbine Establishment, Pyestock, 1954–57; Hawker Siddeley Nuclear Power Co. Ltd, 1957–59; C. A. Parsons & Co. Ltd, Nuclear Research Centre, Newcastle upon Tyne, 1959–61; International Research and Development Co. Ltd, Newcastle upon Tyne, 1962–65; Man., R&D Div., C. A. Parsons & Co. Ltd, Newcastle upon Tyne, 1965–68; Electrical Research Assoc.: Dir, 1968–73; Chief Exec. and Man. Dir, ERA Technology Ltd, 1973–79; Dir, ERA Patents Ltd, 1968–79; Chm., ERA Autotrack Systems Ltd, 1971–79. Director: Dunlop Ltd, 1982–85; Soil-Less Cultivation Systems, 1980–85; Chm. and Dir, Thermal Conversions (UK), 1982–85; Dir of Technology, Dunlop Holdings plc, 1979–85; Director: BICC Cables Ltd, 1985–88; BICC Research and Engineering Ltd, 1985–88; Thomas Bolton & Johnson Ltd, 1986–88; Settle-Carlisle Railway Devlt Co., 1992–94; Chairman: Optical Fibres, 1985–87; Linktronic Systems Ltd, 1990–92; Wetheriggs Pottery Ltd, 1992–94; SKAND Systems Ltd, 1995–97; Chief Exec., Nat. Advanced Robotics Res. Centre, 1989–90. Chm, N Lakeland Healthcare NHS Trust, 1993–97. Vis. Prof., Univ. of Liverpool, 1989–. Chairman: Materials, Chemicals and Vehicles Requirements Bd, DTI, 1982–85; RAPRA Council, 1984–85; Dir, RAPRA Technology Ltd, 1985–97; Member: Nat. Electronics Council, 1969–79; Res. and Technol. Cttee, CBI, 1974–80; Design Council, 1980–86 (Mem., Design Adv. Cttee, 1980–86); Cttee of Inquiry into Engineering Profession, 1977–80; Adv. Council for Applied Research and Develt, 1980–86; Adv. Cttee for Safety of Nuclear Installations, 1987–90; Chm., Sci. Educn and Management Div., IEE, 1974–75; Dep. Chm., Watt Cttee on Energy Ltd, 1976–80. Mem., SAE, 1984. Trustee, John Allen Foundn, 2016–. *Publications:* NOMAD: a life story (autobiog.), 2012; articles on direct generation of electricity, plasma physics, electrical and mechanical engineering, technological innovation, etc, in learned jls. *Recreations:* music, photography, ski-ing, fell-walking, sailing, cycling. *Address:* Lindenthwaite, Beacon Edge, Penrith, Cumbria CA11 8BN.

**LINDLEY, Jonathan Mark;** Public Service Mutuals Programme Director, Department for Digital, Culture, Media and Sport (formerly Department for Culture, Media and Sport), 2016–18 (on loan from Department for Work and Pensions); *b* Huddersfield, 9 July 1962; *s* of late Rev. Harold Lindley and Betty Lindley; *m* 1987; three *d. Educ:* Repton Sch. Civil Servant with DWP, 1981–2003, Legal Services Commn, 2003–07; Strategic Dir, Enforcement, Border and Immigration Agency, 2007–08; Regl Dir, Govt Office for the E Midlands, 2008–09; Integration Dir, Change Prog., 2009–11, Transformation Dir, 2011–16, DWP. Trustee and Treas., Bamford Community Arts and Crafts, 2016–. *Recreations:* cycling, ski-ing, walking, reading, singing.

**LINDLEY, Simon Geoffrey;** Master of the Music, Leeds Minster (formerly Leeds Parish Church), 1975–2016, now Organist Emeritus; Leeds City Organist, 1976–2017, now Emeritus; General Secretary, Guild of Church Musicians, since 2013; *b* 10 Oct. 1948; *s* of Rev. Geoffrey Lindley and Jeanne Lindley (*née* Cammaerts); *m;* three *s* one *d. Educ:* Magdalen Coll. Sch., Oxford; Royal Coll. of Music. FRCO(CHM), FTCL, GRSM (Lond), ARCM, LRAM. Studies with Richard Silk, David Carver, Dr Bernard Rose, Vincent Packford, Dr Philip Wilkinson and, principally, Dr John Birch. Dir of Music, St Anne & St Agnes and St Olave, London, 1968–70; Asst Master of Music, St Alban's Abbey, 1970–75; Dir of Music, St Alban's Sch., 1971–75; Sen. Lectr, Leeds Poly., 1976–88. Sen. Asst Music Officer, Leeds City Council, 1988–2011. Chorus Master: Leeds Phil. Soc., 1975–83 (Vice-Pres., 2005–); Halifax Choral Soc., 1975–87 (Vice-Pres., 1988–); Conductor: St Peter's Singers and Chamber Orch., 1977–; Univ. of Huddersfield Chamber Choir, 1997–98; Leeds Coll. of Music Choral Soc., 1999–; Chief Guest Conductor, Yorkshire Evening Post Band, 1998– (Resident Conductor, 1995–98); Music Dir, Overgate Hospice Choir, Halifax, 1997–; Conductor: Sheffield Bach Soc., 2009–; Doncaster Choral Soc., 2010–. Grand Organist, Utd Grand Lodge of England, 2010–12; Provincial Grand Organist, Masonic Province of Yorks West Riding, 2010–. Special Comr, RSCM, 1975–; Centre Chm., ISM, 1976–82; Mem. Council, RCO, 1977–98, 2012– (Pres., 2000–02; Vice-Pres., 2003); Sec., Church Music Soc., 1991–; Pres., IAO, 2003–05. Dir, English Hymnal Co. Ltd, 1996. Advr, Yorks TV Religious and Educnl Progs, 1981; Artistic Advr, Leeds Summer Heritage Festivals, biennially, 1989–97. Hon. Life Patron, Doncaster Choral Soc., 2006. Pres., Campaign for the Traditional Cathedral Choir, 2008–18. Chm., Friends of Musicians' Chapel, St Sepulchre-without-Newgate, 2004–14; Trustee: Sir George Thalben-Ball Meml Trust, 1989–; Ecclesiastical Music Trust, 1998– (Chm., 2004–); Pilling Trust, 1999–. Governor: Whinmoor St Paul C of E Primary Sch., 2003–10 (Vice Chm., 2005–10); Yorkshire Coll. of Music and Drama, 2005–13 (Chm., 2006–13). Churchwarden, St Sepulchre-without-Newgate, 2006–14. Liveryman, Co. of Musicians, 2006. Concert Organist début, Westminster Cathedral, 1969; tours of USA, France, Germany, Far East, Russia. Numerous recordings as organist and as conductor. FRSCM 2002. Hon. FGMS 1996; Hon. FGCM 2000; Hon. Fellow, Leeds Coll. of Music, 2000. DUniv: Leeds Metropolitan, 2001; Huddersfield, 2012. Spirit of Leeds Award, Leeds Civic Trust, 2006; Leeds Award, Leeds CC, 2016. *Compositions:* Anthems for Unison and 2 part singing, vol. 2, 1979; Ave Maria, 1980, 2003; Matthew, Mark, Luke and John, 1986; Lord, I have loved the habitation of Thy house, 2002; Confitemini Domino, 2011; Confortare, 2012; *carols:* Come, sing and dance, 1977; How far is it to Bethlehem?, Jacob's Ladder, Now the green blade riseth, On Easter morn, 1995; The Bellman's Song, Here is joy for every age, 2004. *Publications:* (ed jtly) New English Praise, 2006; (ed jtly) Revised English Hymnal, 2018; contribs to Musical Times, Choir and Organ, Organists' Review, The Dalesman, The Organ. *Recreations:* churches, cathedrals, Victorian architecture, food. *Address:* 17 Fulneck, Pudsey LS28 8NT. *T:* and *Fax:* (0113) 255 6143. *E:* lindleysimon@gmail.com. *Clubs:* Leeds (Leeds) (Hon. Mem., 2004), Leeds Rotary (Hon. Mem. 2009).

**LINDO, Samuel;** Winemaker, Camel Valley, since 2002; *b* 12 Sept. 1976; *s* of Robert and Anne Lindo; *m* 2009, Kathryn Richards; one *s* two *d. Educ:* Univ. of Bath (BSc Mathematical Scis). Lectr in Maths, Ngee Ann Poly., Singapore. Chm., UK Vineyards Assoc., 2015–. UK Winemaker of Year, UK Vineyards Assoc., 2007, 2010, 2011. *Recreations:* cycling, swimming. *E:* info@camelvalley.com.

**LINDSAY,** family name of **Earl of Crawford** and **Baron Lindsay of Birker**.

**LINDSAY, 16th Earl of,** *cr* 1633 (Scot.); **James Randolph Lindsay-Bethune;** DL; Lord Lindsay of The Byres, 1445; Lord Parbroath, 1633; Viscount of Garnock, Lord Kilburnie, Kingsburn and Drumry, 1703; *b* 19 Nov. 1955; *s* of 15th Earl of Lindsay and Hon. Mary Clare Douglas-Scott-Montagu, *y d* of 2nd Baron Montagu of Beaulieu; *S* father, 1989; *m* 1982, Diana, *er d* of Major Nigel Chamberlayne-Macdonald, Cranbury Park, Winchester; two *s* three *d* (of whom one *s* one *d* are twins). *Educ:* Eton; Univ. of Edinburgh (MA Hons); Univ. of Calif. Davis. A Lord in Waiting (Govt Whip), 1995; Parly Under-Sec. of State, Scottish Office, 1995–97; elected Mem., H of L, 1999. Chairman: Assured British Meat, 1997–2001; Aquaculture Scotland, 1998–2000; Scottish Quality Salmon, 1998–2006; Genesis Quality Assurance Ltd, 2001–02; UK Accreditation Service, 2002–; SRUC (formerly Scottish Agricultural College Ltd), 2007–15 (Dir, 2005–; Vice-Chm., 2006–07); British Polythene Pension Scheme, 2009–; Greenfield Hldgs, 2009–11; Director: UA Group plc (formerly United Auctions (Scotland) Ltd), 1998–2005; Scottish Resources Gp (formerly Mining (Scotland) Ltd), 2001–13; British Polythene Industries plc, 2006–15 (Advr, 2015–); Hargreaves Energy Projects Ltd, 2015–17; Brockwell Energy Ltd, 2017–; Bd Mem., Cairngorms Partnership, 1998–2003; 4Front Farming Co. Ltd, 2016–; Adviser: IndigoVision Ltd, 2006–07; Hargreaves (UK) Services Ltd, 2015–17; 3R Energy, 2016–. Chm., Grant Implementation Steering Cttee, ClearBank Tide Business Banking, 2019–. Member: UK Round Table on Sustainable Develt, 1998–2000; Better Regulation Commn, 2006–07 (Vice Chm., 2007); Commn on Scottish Devolution, 2008–09; Risk and Regulation Adv. Council, 2008–10; Better Regulation Strategy Gp, 2013–15; Vice Pres., Trading Standards Inst., 2011–. Dir, Leven Valley Develt Trust, 2009–19. Trustee: Gardens for the Disabled Trust, 1984–98; Common Good Foundn, 2014–; Prince's Countryside Fund, 2018–. Chairman: Landscape Foundn, 1991–95; Moorland Forum, 2007–18; President: Internat. Tree Foundn, 1995–2005 (Vice-Pres., 1994–95, 2005–); RHASS, 2005–06; RSGS, 2005–12 (Vice-Pres., 2004–05, 2012–); Nat. Trust for Scotland, 2012–17. Mem., Adv. Council, World Resource Foundn, 1994–98. Chm., RSPB Scotland, 1998–2003 (Mem., UK Council, 1998–2003); Vice-Pres., RSPB, 2004–. Chm., Elmwood Coll., 2001–09. Vice-Pres., Royal Smithfield Club, 1999–. ARAgS 2000. DL Fife, 2007. *Publications:* (jtly) Garden Ornament, 1989; Trellis, 1991. *Heir: s* Viscount Garnock, *qv. Address:* Lahill, Upper Largo, Fife KY8 6JE.
See also Sir G. R. B. Wrey, Bt.

**LINDSAY, Master of; Alexander Thomas Lindsay;** *b* 5 Aug. 1991; *s* and *heir* of Lord Balniel, *qv.*

**LINDSAY OF BIRKER, 3rd Baron** *cr* 1945, of Low Ground, Co. Cumberland; **James Francis Lindsay;** Co-founder and Chief Technical Officer, Sun Fire Cooking, since 2003; *b* 29 Jan. 1945; *s* of 2nd Baron Lindsay of Birker and Li Hsiao-li, *d* of Col Li Wen-chi; *S* father, 1994; *m* 1st, 1969, Mary Rose (marr. diss. 1985), *d* of W. G. Thomas, Cwmbran, Mon; no *c;* 2nd, 2000, Pamela Collett, *d* of late Lon Hutchison, Kansas City, Mo. *Educ:* Univ. of Keele (BSc 1966); Univ. of Liverpool (Post-grad. Dip. in transport design). Lectr in physics, Tunghai Univ., Taichung, Taiwan, 1967–68; exploration geophysicist, Darwin,

Australia, 1969–70; Australian Foreign Service, 1972–2000; served in Chile, 1973–76; Laos, 1980–81; Bangladesh, 1982–84; Venezuela, 1987–90; Deputy High Commissioner: Pakistan, 1993–96; Kenya, 1996–2000; Dep. Perm. Rep. for Australia to UN Envmt Prog., 1996–2000. Consultant: Horn Relief (formerly Horn of Africa Relief and Develt), 2000–; Uganda Rural Develt and Trng, 2002–03. *Recreation:* hiking. *Heir:* cousin Alexander Sebastian Lindsay, *b* 27 May 1940. *Address:* 21 Carnegie Crescent, Narrabundah, Canberra, ACT 2604, Australia. *E:* mukindu@yahoo.com.

**LINDSAY, Caroline;** Executive Director, Education and Children's Services, Fife Council, since 2017; *b* Newport on Tay, Fife, Scotland, 27 Feb. 1963; *d* of Angus and Betty Lindsay; one *s*. *Educ:* Bell Baxter High Sch., Fife; Kirkcaldy Coll. of Technol. (Nat. Nursery Exam Bd 1979); Moray Hse Coll., Edinburgh (Primary DipEd 1984); Stirling Univ. (BEd 1985). Teacher, Dombustle Primary Sch., 1985–97; Headteacher, Cowdenbeath Primary Sch., 1997–2000; Advr, Angus Council, 2000–03; Fife Council: Educn Officer, 2003–11; Area Educn Officer, 2011–15; Hd, Educn and Children's Services, 2015–17. *Recreations:* gardening, walking, family, charity (Board). *Address:* Fife Council, Fife House, North Street, Glenrothes, Fife KY7 5LT. *E:* carrie.lindsay@fife.gov.uk.

**LINDSAY, His Honour Crawford Callum Douglas;** QC 1987; a Circuit Judge, 1998–2008; *b* 5 Feb. 1939; *s* of Douglas Marshall Lindsay, FRCOG and Eileen Mary Lindsay; *m* 1963, Rosemary Gough; one *s* one *d*. *Educ:* Whitgift Sch., Croydon; St John's Coll., Oxford. Called to the Bar, Lincoln's Inn, 1961, Bencher, 1994. A Recorder, 1982–98. Mem., Criminal Injuries Compensation Bd, 1988. *Clubs:* Garrick, MCC.

**LINDSAY, David Christopher;** Lord-Lieutenant of Co. Down, since 2009; *b* Belfast, 25 Sept. 1946; *s* of Christopher and Lesley Lindsay; *m* 1970, Judy Sinclair; one *s* three *d*. *Educ:* Ludgrove Sch., Wokingham; Eton; Royal Military Acad., Sandhurst. Served Inniskilling Dragoon Guards (Lieut), 1967–69. With Lindsay Cars Ltd, 1969–2008, Man. Dir, 1972–2008; IT Consultant (pt-time), 2008–11. Chm., UK Ford Dealers, 2007–08. *Recreations:* sailing, ski-ing, vintage tractors, bee-keeping. *Address:* Clerk to the Lieutenancy, Crawford & Lockhart, 7/11 Linenhall Street, Belfast BT2 8AH. *Club:* Strangford Lough Yacht.

**LINDSAY, Dr Hilary Frances,** FCA; President, Institute of Chartered Accountants of England and Wales, 2016–17; Chair, Consultative Committee of Accountancy Bodies, 2016–17; *b* Birkenhead, 23 Dec. 1948; *d* of Rev. Dr Bernard Jones and Marjorie Jones; *m* 1995, Colin Lindsay; one *s* one *d*. *Educ:* Withington Girls' Sch.; University Coll. London (BSc Hons Stats 1970); Open Univ. (MBA 2001; MSc Internat. Finance Mgt 2007; EdD 2013). FCA 1974. Partner, Davies & Crane, Preston, 1979–86; Dir, ICAEW, 1986–99; Lectr and researcher, Open Univ., 2000–. Pres., Assoc. of Accounting Technicians, 2011–12. Trustee, Chartered Accountants' Benevolent Assoc., 2007–16. Mem., Court of Assts, Chartered Accountants' Co., 2014– (Sen. Warden, 2018–). *Publications:* Adaptability: the secret to lifelong learning, 2014; contrib. articles to Accounting Educn, Studies in Higher Educn, Studies in Graduate and Postdoctoral Educn. *Address:* 23 Stourhead Drive, Northampton NN4 0UH. *E:* hl@hilarylindsay.co.uk.

**LINDSAY, Iain Ferrier,** OBE 2002; HM Diplomatic Service; Ambassador to Hungary, since 2016; *b* Falkirk, 9 March 1959; *s* of James and Margaret Lindsay; *m* 1983, Bridget O'Riordan; one *s*. *Educ:* John Lyon Sch.; Edinburgh Acad.; Glasgow Univ. Entered FCO, 1980; Japanese lang. trng, SOAS, 1981–82; Warsaw, 1982–83; Doha, 1983; Asst Mgt Officer, Tokyo, 1983–86; Third, later Second Sec. (Political), Canberra, 1986–89; Australia Desk Officer, FCO, 1989–91; Hd, Baltic Unit, FCO, 1991–94; First Sec. (Political), Tokyo, 1994–99; Dep. Hd, S Asian Dept, FCO, 1999–2002; Romanian lang. trng, 2003; Advr to Romanian Foreign Minister, 2003; Dep. Hd and Political Counsellor, Bucharest, 2003–07; Dep. Hd and Dir, Trade and Investment, Hong Kong, 2007–11; Ambassador to Bahrain, 2011–15; Hungarian lang. trng, 2015–16. *Recreations:* cinema, history, travel, cricket, golf, ski-ing, scuba diving, watching Rugby and football (Stenhousemuir FC). *Address:* c/o Foreign and Commonwealth Office, King Charles Street, SW1A 2AH. *Club:* Caledonian.

**LINDSAY of Dowhill, Sir James Martin Evelyn,** 3rd Bt *cr* 1962, of Dowhill, co. Kinross; 24th Representer of Baronial House of Dowhill; *b* 11 Oct. 1968; *s* of Sir Ronald Alexander Lindsay of Dowhill, 2nd Bt and of Nicoletta Lindsay; *S* father, 2004; *m* 2000, Annabel Julia, *yr d* of Dr Peter Knight; one *s* one *d*. *Educ:* Shiplake Coll.; RMA Sandhurst; UMIST (BSc). Lieut, Grenadier Guards, 1988–93. Cheshire Yeomanry, 1994– (Major). *Heir: s* Archibald Ronald Frederick Lindsay, *b* 26 Oct. 2004.

**LINDSAY, Hon. Sir John (Edmund Fredric),** Kt 1992; a Judge of the High Court of Justice, Chancery Division, 1992–2008; *b* 16 Oct. 1935; *s* of late George Fredric Lindsay and Constance Mary Lindsay (*née* Wright); *m* 1967, Patricia Anne Bolton; three *d*. *Educ:* Ellesmere Coll.; Sidney Sussex Coll., Cambridge (BA 1959; MA). Fleet Air Arm, 1954–56; Sub-Lt, RNVR. Called to the Bar, Middle Temple, 1961, Bencher, 1987; joined Lincoln's Inn (*ad eundem*); Junior Treasury Counsel, *bona vacantia*, 1979–81; QC 1981; a Judge of the Employment Appeals Tribunal, 1996–99; Pres., Employment Appeal Tribunal, 1999–2002; a Judge of the Administrative Court, 2002–08. Member: Senate of Inns of Court and Bar, 1979–82; Legal Panel, Insolvency Law Review Cttee (Cork Report), 1980–82; Insolvency Rules Adv. Cttee, 1985–92. *Recreations:* works of A. A. Scott, L. van Beethoven, H. R. Godfrey and Henry Royce, as he then was. *Club:* Athenæum.

**LINDSAY, Mark Stanley Hunter;** QC (Scot.) 2011; *b* Irvine, Ayrshire, 17 May 1969; *s* of Martin and Sandra Lindsay; *m* 1993, Rosemary; two *s* one *d*. *Educ:* Carrick Acad., Maybole, Ayrshire; Univ. of Glasgow (LLB Hons; DipLP). Trainee solicitor, Tods Murray, 1991–93; Solicitor, Scottish Office, 1993–95; admitted to Faculty of Advocates, 1996. *Recreations:* squash, ski-ing, golf, Lotus sports cars. *Address:* Advocates Library, Parliament House, Parliament Square, Edinburgh EH1 1RF. *T:* (0131) 226 5071. *E:* mark.lindsay@axiomadvocates.com.

**LINDSAY, Most Rev. and Hon. Orland Ugham,** OJ 1997; OD (Antigua) 1996; Archbishop of the West Indies, 1986–98; Bishop of the North-Eastern Caribbean and Aruba (formerly Antigua), 1970–98; *b* 24 March 1928; *s* of Hubert and Ida Lindsay; *m* 1959, Olga Daphne (*née* Wright); three *s*. *Educ:* Culham Coll., Oxon (Teachers' Cert.); St Peter's Coll., Jamaica; McGill Univ. BD (London) 1957. RAF, 1944–47. Teacher, Franklyn Town Govt School, Jamaica, 1949–52; Asst Master, Kingston College, 1952–53. Deacon 1956, priest 1957; Asst Curate, St Peter's Vere, Jamaica, 1956–57; Asst Master, Kingston Coll., 1958–67, Chaplain 1962–63; Priest-in-Charge, Manchioneal Cure, Jamaica, 1960; Chaplain, Jamaica Defence Force, 1963–67; Principal, Church Teachers' Coll., Mandeville, 1967–70. Sec. to Jamaica Synod, 1962–70. Hon. DD: Berkeley Divinity School at Yale, 1978; St Paul's Coll., Va, 1998; Hon. STD, Montreal Diocesan Theol Coll., 1997. *Recreations:* jazz music, photography. *Address:* Flagstaff, Crosbies, PO Box 3456, St John's, Antigua.

**LINDSAY, Richard Stephen;** HM Diplomatic Service; High Commissioner to Brunei Darussalam, since 2017; *b* Salisbury, Wilts, 18 Feb. 1969; *s* of Lt Col Stephen James Lindsay and Margaret Ann Lindsay; *m* 1997, Xanthe Clare, *d* of Sir Ian George Lorraine Critchett, 3rd Bt; two *s* one *d*. *Educ:* Eton Coll.; St Catherine's Coll., Oxford (BA Hons Mod. Hist. 1992). Mktg Exec., W. H. Smith plc, 1993–96; joined FCO, 1996; Second Sec., Harare, 1998–2001; First Sec., Canberra, 2006–10; Counsellor, Brasília, 2013–14; Hd, Security Policy Dept, FCO, 2014–16. *Recreations:* long distance running, gardening, history, current affairs. *Address:* British High Commission, Jalan Pretty, Bandar Seri Begawan, Brunei Darussalam. *T:* (2) 222231. *E:* richard.lindsay@fco.gov.uk.

**LINDSAY, Robert;** see Stevenson, R. L.

**LINDSAY, Shuna Taylor, (Mrs D. R. Waggott),** CBE 2001; Deputy Director, Strategy and Projects, Defence Academy College of Management and Technology, Ministry of Defence, 2008–09; *b* 24 Nov. 1954; *d* of late John Lindsay and Jessie Simpson Lindsay (*née* Taylor); *m* 1979, David Reginald Waggott. *Educ:* Greenock Acad.; Univ. of Geneva (Cert. d'Etudes Françaises 1975); Univ. of Aberdeen (MA Hons French Studies 1977). Entered MoD as admin trainee, 1977; policy appts, 1977–81; Private Sec. to Air Mem. for Supply and Orgn, 1981–82; First Sec., Defence Procurement, Paris, 1989–93; Project Dir, Mil. Aircraft Projects, 1998–99; Integrated Project Team Leader for Airlift and Future Tanker Progs, 2000–01; on secondment to Rand, Calif, 2001–02; Minister, Defence Materiel, Washington, 2002–04; Dir Gen., Acquisition People, MoD, 2005–06; Dir, Defence Mgt Consultancy Services, MoD, 2007–08. *Publications:* (jtly) Re-examining Military Acquisition Reform: are we there yet?, 2005. *Recreations:* music, family research, learning Spanish, building wooden replica model warships, collecting dolphins, walking the dog, playing golf badly. *T:* (01670) 783059. *E:* shuna.lindsay@gmail.com.

**LINDSAY, Simon John;** Director General, Panel on Takeovers and Mergers, since 2018; *b* Littlehampton, 9 June 1967; *s* of John and Christine Lindsay; *m* 1993, Natalie Norminton; three *s* one *d*. *Educ:* Lancing Coll.; New Coll., Oxford (BA Lit. Hum.). Eur. Mergers and Acquisitions, Credit Suisse First Boston, 1990–97; UK Investment Banking, J Henry Schroder, 1997–2000; Hd, UK Mergers and Acquisitions, Citigroup, 2000–18. *Recreations:* wildlife photography, mountains, travel, family. *Address:* The Takeover Panel, One Angel Court, EC2R 7HJ.

**LINDSAY, Vaughan Emerson;** Executive Director, LeapFrog Labs, since 2015; *b* Canterbury, 24 Sept. 1962; *s* of John and Audrey Lindsay; *m* 1994, Rachel Carter; one *d*. *Educ:* Simon Langton Grammar Sch.; Hertford Coll., Oxford (BA); London Sch. of Econs (MSc); London Business Sch. (MBA). Mktg post, Proctor & Gamble, 1986–87; Manager, King's Fund, 1987–89; Dep. Dir, Shelter, 1989–95; Dir, NCVO, 1995–98; Consultant, McKinsey & Co., 1998–2004; CEO, Dartington Hall Trust, 2004–15. *Recreations:* running, triathlons, cycling. *Address:* LeapFrog Labs, 6 Broad Street Place, EC2M 7JH.

**LINDSAY-HOGG, Sir Michael Edward,** 5th Bt *cr* 1905, of Rotherfield Hall, Rotherfield, Sussex; film and theatre director; *b* 5 May 1940; *o s* of Sir Edward William Lindsay-Hogg, 4th Bt and Geraldine Mary, *d* of E. M. Fitzgerald; *S* father, 1999, but his name does not appear on the Official Roll of the Baronetage; *m* 1st, 1967, Lucy Mary (marr. diss. 1971), *o d* of Donald Davies; 2nd, 2002, Lisa, *e d* of Benjamin Holt Ticknor III. *Films* include: Let It Be, 1970; Nasty Habits, 1977; Dr Fischer of Geneva, 1983; The Object of Beauty, 1992; Frankie Starlight, 1996; Waiting for Godot, 2001; *theatre* includes: Whose Life Is It Anyway?, Mermaid, 1978, transf. NY, 1979; *television* includes: Electra, 1962; Professional Foul, 1977; (co-dir) Brideshead Revisited, 1981. *Publications:* Luck and Circumstance (memoir), 2011. *Heir:* none.

**LINDSAY-SMITH, Iain-Mór;** Deputy Managing Director, 1987–90, Chief Executive and Managing Director, 1991–97, and Executive Deputy Chairman, 1997–98, Lloyd's of London Press Ltd, later LLP Group Ltd; Chairman, Lloyds List, 1990–98 (Publisher, 1984–98); *b* 18 Sept. 1934; *s* of Edward Duncanson Lindsay-Smith and Margaret Wilson Anderson; *m* 1st, 1960, Carol Sara Paxman (marr. diss. 1997); one *s*; 2nd, 2014, Jane Elizabeth Cramp. *Educ:* High Sch. of Glasgow; London Univ. (diploma course on Internat. Affairs). Scottish Daily Record, 1951–57; Commissioned 1st Bn Cameronians (Scottish Rifles), 1953–55; Daily Mirror, 1957–60; Foreign Editor, subseq. Features Editor, Daily Mail, 1960–71; Dep. Editor, Yorkshire Post, 1971–74; Editor, Glasgow Herald, 1974–77; Exec. Editor, The Observer, 1977–84. Lloyd's of London Press, subseq. LLP Ltd: Exec. Dir, 1984–87; Chm. and Chief Exec., Lloyd's, then LLP, Information Services Ltd, 1990–98 (Chm., LLP Business Publishing Ltd, 1990–98; Director: LLP Incorporated, USA, 1985–97 (Chm., 1992–97); LLP Asia, 1989–98; LLP GmbH, Germany, 1989–96; Lloyd's Maritime Information Services Inc., USA, 1990–97 (Chm., 1993–97); Lutine Publications Ltd, 1984–97 (Chm., 1992–97); Internat. Art & Antique Loss Register Ltd, 1990–97; PPA, 1992–98; DYP Gp Ltd, 1995–98; IBJ Associates Ltd, 1995–98; Cotton Investments Ltd, 1995–98. Dir, Mercury Th., Colchester, 1990–95. Member: Little Horkesley Parish Council, 1987–91; PCC, 1985–92. Chm., Glasgow Newspaper Press Fund, 1974–77. Founding Fellow, Inst. of Contemp. Scotland, 2001–. FRSA 1992. *Publications:* article in Electronics and Power. *Recreations:* shooting (game and clay), playing Highland bagpipes, the outdoors.

**LINDSELL, David Clive,** FCA; Partner, Ernst & Young, 1978–2007; *b* 9 May 1947; *s* of late Alfred and Florence Lindsell; *m* 2008, Felicity Daphne Hother; two *d*. *Educ:* Haberdashers' Aske's, Hampstead; Elstree Sch.; Christ's Coll., Cambridge (BA 1968). FCA 1972. Joined Ernst & Young, 1969; Ernst & Young International: Dir, Planning and Mktg, 1985–88; Chm., Accounting and Auditing Standards Cttee, 1989–95; Chm., Multinat. Client Gp, 1995–99; Global Dir, Internat. Financial Reporting Standards, 2003–07; Mem. Council, Ernst & Young UK, 1991–2007. Mem. Adv. Bd, Gartmore Investment Ltd, 2007–09; non-executive Director: Gartmore Gp Ltd, 2009–11; Hellermann Tyton Gp plc, 2013–15; Premier Oil plc, 2008–17; Drax Gp plc, 2008–19. Institute of Chartered Accountants in England and Wales: Member: Business Law Cttee, 1989–94; Turnbull Cttee, 1999; Chm., Co. Law Sub-Cttee, 1989–94. Dep. Chm., Financial Reporting Review Panel, 2008–12; Member: Oil Industry Accounting Cttee, 1982–85; Auditing Practices Bd for UK and Ireland, 1994–2002 (Mem., Ethics Gp, 2003–04); Bd, Eur. Financial Reporting Adv. Gp, 2004–09; Standards Adv. Council, Internat. Accounting Standards Bd, 2005–08. Trustee, 1999–2008, Mem., Audit Cttee, 2006–14, BM; Dir, British Mus. Co. Ltd, 2005–12; Trustee, Cancer Res. UK, 2014– (Chm., Audit Cttee, 2014–). University of the Arts London: Mem., Audit Cttee, 2009–15 (Chm., 2011–15); Gov., 2011– (Dep. Chm. Govs, 2015–). Governor: Cranleigh Sch., 1979–85; St Albans Sch., 1995–2010. *Recreations:* playing and listening to jazz, museums and galleries, theatre, opera. *Club:* Oxford and Cambridge.

**LINDSEY,** 14th Earl of, *cr* 1626, **AND ABINGDON,** 9th Earl of, *cr* 1682; **Richard Henry Rupert Bertie;** Baron Norreys, of Rycote, 1572; *b* 28 June 1931; *o s* of Lt-Col Hon. Arthur Michael Bertie, DSO, MC (*d* 1957) and Aline Rose (*d* 1948), *er d* of George Arbuthnot-Leslie, Warthill, Co. Aberdeen, and *widow* of Hon. Charles Fox Maule Ramsay, MC; *S* cousin, 1963; *m* 1957, Norah Elizabeth Farquhar-Oliver, *yr d* of late Mark Oliver, OBE; two *s* one *d*. *Educ:* Ampleforth. Late Lieut, Royal Norfolk Regt. Insurance broker and underwriting agent at Lloyd's, 1958–92. Chm., Dawes and Henderson (Agencies) Ltd, 1988–92. Chm., Anglo-Ivory-Coast Soc., 1974–77. High Steward of Abingdon, 1963–. *Heir: s* Lord Norreys, *qv*. *Address:* The Old Farmhouse, Blairston Mains, Ayr KA7 4EF. *Club:* Turf.

**LINDSEY, Prof. Keith,** PhD; FRSB, FLS; Professor of Plant Molecular Biology, since 1996, and Head, Department of Biosciences (formerly School of Biological and Biomedical Sciences), 1997–2000 and since 2013, Durham University; *b* London, 22 Aug. 1957; *s* of Brian and Sylvia Lindsey; *m* 1989, Jennifer Topping; one *s* one *d*. *Educ:* Skinners' Sch., Tunbridge Wells; St Catherine's Coll., Oxford (BA 1978); Edinburgh Univ. (PhD 1982). FRSB (FIBiol) 2004. Res. Fellow, Edinburgh Univ., 1981–86; Higher Scientific Officer, Rothamsted Exptl Station, 1986–88; Lectr, 1989–95, Sen. Lectr, 1995, Leicester Univ. Member: Adv. Cttee on Releases to the Envmt, 2003–13; BBSRC, 2010–14. Vis. Prof., Huazhong Agricl Univ., Wuhan, China, 2015–. Pres., Soc. for Exptl Biol., 2011–13. Chm., New Phytologist Trust, 2012–. FLS 2014. *Publications:* Plant Biotechnology in Agriculture, 1989, 2nd edn 1992; Plant Tissue Culture Manual, 1991, 9th edn 1997; Transgenic Plant Research, 1998; Polarity in Plants, 2004. *Recreations:* playing guitar, photography, cinema, art history, the gym. *Address:* Department of Biosciences, Durham University, South Road, Durham DH1 3LE. *T:* (0191) 334 1309, *Fax:* (0191) 334 1202. *E:* keith.lindsey@durham.ac.uk.

**LINE, Frances Mary, (Mrs James Lloyd),** OBE 1996; Controller, BBC Radio 2, 1990–96; *b* 22 Feb. 1940; *d* of Charles Edward Line and Leoni Lucy Line (*née* Hendriks); *m* 1972, James Richard Beilby Lloyd. *Educ:* James Allen's Girls' Sch., Dulwich. Joined BBC as clerk/typist, 1957; Sec. in TV and Radio, 1959–67; Radio 2 producer, 1967–73; senior producer, 1973–79; Chief Assistant: Radio 2, 1979–83; Radio 4, 1983–85; Head, Radio 2 Music Dept, 1985–89. Vice-Pres., Eastbourne Soc., 1998–. Hon. Fellow, Radio Acad., 1996. *Recreations:* visual arts, theatre. *Address:* 24 Marlborough Court, Eastbourne, E Sussex BN21 1BT.

**LINE, Matthew John Bardsley;** Director, Rivington Bye Ltd (formerly Craft London Ltd), since 2010; *b* 22 April 1958; *s* of John Line and Jill Line (*née* Rowland); *m* 1987, Elinor Jane Fairhurst; two *d*. *Educ:* Chiswick Sch.; Exeter Univ. (BA Hons Drama). Actor, 1982; Asst Publisher, Shepheard-Walwyn Publishers, 1984–87; Production Dir, Concertina Publications, 1988; freelance journalist, 1987–92; Editor: Up Country, 1992–93; Dialogue, 1993–95; Launch Editor, Colour, 1995; Gp Editor, home interest titles, Redwood Publishing, 1996–97; Ed., Homes & Gardens, 1997–2002; Chief Exec., The Prince's Foundn, 2002–04; Ed. in Chief, relaunched She, 2004–06; Editl Consultant, Rich, 2006; Editl Dir, Craft Publishing, 2007–10. Launched annual Homes & Gardens V&A Mus. Classic Design Awards, 1999–. *Publications:* Homes & Gardens Book of Design, 2000. *Recreations:* family, gardening, philosophy. *Address:* Rivington Bye Ltd, 3 Albemarle Way, EC1V 4JB.

**LINEHAN, Anthony John;** President, Construction Health & Safety Group, 1993–2003; *b* 27 June 1931; *s* of Daniel and Ada Linehan; *m* 1955, Oonagh Patricia FitzPatrick; two *s* two *d*. *Educ:* Bristol Univ. (BA Hons 1952). Short Service Commission, RN, 1953–57. HM Factory Inspectorate: joined 1958; HM District Inspector, 1969; Labour Adviser, Hong Kong Govt, 1973–76; Health and Safety Executive: HQ, 1976–79; Area Dir, Wales, 1979–84; HM Dep. Chief Inspector of Factories, 1984–88; Chief Inspector of Factories, 1988–92; Dir of Field Ops, 1990–92. *Recreations:* walking, reading, watching Rugby. *Address:* 2 Brookside Manor, Leigh Road, Wimborne, Dorset BH21 2BZ. *T:* (01202) 848597.

**LINEHAN, Fergus;** Festival Director, Edinburgh International Festival, since 2014; *b* Dublin, 14 May 1969; *s* of late Fergus Linehan and of Rosaleen Linehan; two *s*; *m* 2014, Sophie Hodges; one *s* one *d*. *Educ:* Gormanston Coll., Co. Meath, Ireland; University Coll. Dublin (BA English and Greek and Roman Civilization). Dir and Founder, Pigsback Th. Co., Dublin, 1991; Gen. Manager, Tivoli Th., Dublin, 1992; Dublin Theatre Festival: Gen. Manager, 1993–96; Dep. Dir, 1996–99; Fest. Dir, 2000–04; Fest. Dir, Sydney Fest., 2005–09; Dir, Warehouse Arts Ltd, 2010–14; Hd of Contemp. Music, Sydney Opera Hse, 2011–13. *Address:* Edinburgh International Festival, The Hub, Castlehill, Edinburgh EH1 2NE. *T:* (0131) 473 2032. *E:* director@eif.co.uk.

**LINEHAN, Dr Peter Anthony,** FBA 2002; FRHistS; Fellow, St John's College, Cambridge, since 1966; *b* 11 July 1943; *er s* of John James Linehan and Kathleen Margaret Linehan (*née* Farrell); *m* 1971, Christine Ann Callaghan; one *s* two *d*. *Educ:* St Benedict's Sch., Ealing; St John's Coll., Cambridge (Mullinger Schol.); BA 1st Cl. 1964, MA 1968 (Thirlwall Prizeman and Seeley Medallist), PhD 1968). FRHistS 1971. St John's College, Cambridge: Res. Fellow, 1966–69; Lectr, 1969–2010; Tutor, 1977–97; Tutor for Grad. Affairs, 1983–97; Dean, 1999–2010; University of Cambridge: Sen. Proctor, 1976–77; affiliated lectr, Faculty of Hist., 1986–92. Woodward Lectr, Yale Univ., 1999; Birkbeck Lectr in Ecclesiastical Hist., Trinity Coll., Cambridge, 1999. Co-Ed., Jl Ecclesiastical Hist., 1979–91. Member: Accad. Senese degli Intronati, 1988; IAS, Princeton, NJ, 1988; Séminaire Interdisciplinaire de Recherches sur l'Espagne Médiévale, CNRS, Univ. of Paris 13, 2000. Corresp. Mem., Real Acad. de la Historia, Madrid, 1996. Gov., Gigglewsick Sch., 1983–96. Antiquary Prizeman, Univ. of Edinburgh, 1985. Hon. Dr Universidad Autonoma, Madrid, 2018. *Publications:* The Spanish Church and the Papacy in the Thirteenth Century, 1971 (trans. Spanish 1975); (ed with B. Tierney) Authority and Power, 1980; Spanish Church and Society 1150–1300, 1983; (ed) Proceedings of the Seventh International Congress of Medieval Canon Law 1984, 1988; Past and Present in Medieval Spain, 1992; History and the Historians of Medieval Spain, 1993 (trans. Spanish 2012); The Ladies of Zamora, 1997 (trans. French 1998, Spanish 2000, Portuguese 2008); (ed) Life, Law and Letters, 1998; (ed with J. L. Nelson) The Medieval World, 2001; The Processes of Politics and the Rule of Law, 2002; (with J. C. de Lera Maíllo) Las postrimerías de un obispo alfonsino, 2003; (with F. J. Hernández) The Mozarabic Cardinal, 2004; Spain, 1157–1300: a partible inheritance, 2008 (trans. Spanish 2009); (ed with S. Barton) Cross, Crescent and Conversion, 2008; (ed) St John's College Cambridge: a history, 2011; Historical Memory and Clerical Activity in Medieval Spain and Portugal, 2012; Portugalia Pontificia, 2013; At the Edge of Reformation: Iberia before the Black Death, 2019; contribs to learned jls. *Recreation:* reading obituaries. *Address:* Brookside, 20 Glebe Way, Impington, Cambs CB24 9HJ. *T:* (01223) 233934; St John's College, Cambridge CB2 1TP. *T:* (01223) 338720. *E:* pal35@cam.ac.uk. *Club:* Hawks (Cambridge).

**LINEHAN, Stephen;** QC 1993; a Recorder, since 1990; *b* 12 March 1947; *s* of Maurice Gerald Linehan and Mary Joyce (*née* Norrish); one *s*; *m* 2012, Naomi Gilchrist. *Educ:* Mount St Mary's Coll., Spinkhill, Derbys; King's Coll., London (LLB Hons). Called to the Bar, Lincoln's Inn, 1970, Bencher, 1999. *Address:* St Philips Chambers, 55 Temple Row, Birmingham B2 5LS. *T:* (0121) 246 7000.

**LINEKER, Gary Winston,** OBE 1992; journalist and broadcaster; professional footballer, 1976–94; *b* 30 Nov. 1960; *s* of late Barry and Margaret Lineker; *m* 1st, 1986, Michelle Cockayne (marr. diss. 2006); four *s*; 2nd, 2009, Danielle Bux (marr. diss. 2016). Football Clubs played for: Leicester City, 1976–85; Everton, 1985–86; Barcelona, 1986–89; Tottenham Hotspur, 1989–92; Nagoya Grampus 8, 1993–94; England team, 1984–92. Captain, 1990–92; 80 appearances, 48 goals. Presenter, Match of the Day, BBC TV, 1995–. Freeman, City of Leicester, 1995. Hon. MA: Loughborough, 1992; Leicester, 1992. *Publications:* (with D. Baker) Behind Closed Doors: life, laughs and football, 2019. *Recreations:* cricket, theatre, food and wine. *Address:* c/o Jon Holmes Media Ltd, West Waylands Farm, Esher Road, Walton-on-Thames KT12 4LJ. *T:* 07802 461706. *Clubs:* Groucho, MCC.

**LING, Norman Arthur;** HM Diplomatic Service, retired; Ambassador to the Federal Democratic Republic of Ethiopia, Djibouti and the African Union, 2008–11; *b* 12 Aug. 1952; *s* of late William Arthur Ling and of Helma Ling (*née* Blum); *m* 1979, Selma Osman. *Educ:* Sheffield Univ. (BA Hons German and Econ. Hist.). British Commercial Transport, 1975–76; Ocean Transport and Trading, 1976–78; joined Diplomatic Service, 1978; FCO, 1978–80; Second Sec., Tripoli, 1980–81; Second, later First, Sec., British Interests Section, Tehran, 1981–84; FCO, 1984–88; Dep. Consul Gen., Johannesburg, 1988–92; Dep. Head of Mission, Ankara, 1993–97; Head, Aviation, Maritime, Sci. and Energy Dept, FCO, 1997–2001; High Comr, Malawi, 2001–04; Change Dir, FCO, 2005–07. Non-executive Director: Nyota Minerals, 2012–14; Kefi Minerals, 2014–. *Recreations:* travel, walking, gardening. *Address:* Uplands, Evershot, Dorchester, Dorset DT2 0PQ.

**LING, Prof. Roger John,** PhD; FSA; Professor of Classical Art and Archaeology, University of Manchester, 1992–2010, now Emeritus; *b* 13 Nov. 1942; *s* of Leslie James Ling and Kathleen Clara Ling (*née* Childs); *m* 1967, Lesley Ann Steer. *Educ:* Watford Grammar Sch.; St John's Coll., Cambridge (BA 1964; MA 1969; PhD 1970). FSA 1979. Lectr in Classics, UC of Swansea, 1967–71; University of Manchester: Lectr in History of Art, 1971–75; Sen. Lectr, 1975–83; Reader, 1983–92; Head of Dept of Hist. of Art, 1988–91. British Acad. Res. Reader, 1991–93; Balsdon Sen. Res. Fellow, British Sch. at Rome, 1994–95. *Publications:* The Greek World, 1976, 2nd edn as Classical Greece, 1988; (jtly) Wall Painting in Roman Britain, 1982; (ed) Cambridge Ancient History, Plates to vol. VII.1, 1984; Romano-British Wall Painting, 1985; Roman Painting, 1991; The Insula of the Menander at Pompeii I: the structures, 1997; Ancient Mosaics, 1998; Stuccowork and Painting in Roman Italy, 1999; (ed) Making Classical Art: process and practice, 2000; (with L. A. Ling) The Insula of the Menander at Pompeii II: the decorations, 2005; Pompeii: history, life and afterlife, 2005; numerous articles in learned jls. *Recreations:* fresh air and exercise, watching football. *Address:* School of Arts, Languages and Cultures, University of Manchester, Manchester M13 9PL. *T:* (0161) 275 3020.

**LINGARD, Joan Amelia,** MBE 1998; author, since 1963; *b* 1932; *d* of Henry James Lingard and Elizabeth Lingard; *m* Martin Birkhans; three *d*. *Educ:* Bloomfield Collegiate Sch., Belfast; Moray House Coll. of Educn. Mem. Bd and Mem., Literature Cttee, Scottish Arts Council, 1980–84. Chair, Soc. of Authors in Scotland, 1980–84. Hon. Pres., Scottish Pen, 2013. Hon. Fellow, Assoc. for Scottish Literary Studies, 2013. *Publications:* novels: Liam's Daughter, 1963; The Prevailing Wind, 1964; The Tide Comes In, 1966; The Headmaster, 1967; A Sort of Freedom, 1968; The Lord on Our Side, 1970; The Second Flowering of Emily Mountjoy; Greenyards; Reasonable Doubts, 1979; The Women's House, 1981; Sisters by Rite, 1984; After Colette, 1993 (Scottish Arts Council Award); Dreams of Love and Modest Glory, 1995; The Kiss, 2002; Encarnita's Journey, 2005; After You've Gone, 2007; *children's novels:* The Twelfth Day of July, 1970; Frying as Usual, 1971; Across the Barricades, 1972 (Buxtehude Bülle, 1986); Into Exile, 1973; The Clearance, 1973; A Proper Place; The Resettling; Hostages to Fortune; The Pilgrimage, 1975; The Reunion, 1977; Snake among the Sunflowers, 1977; The Gooseberry, 1978; The File on Fraulein Berg, 1980; Strangers in the House, 1981; The Winter Visitor, 1983; The Freedom Machine, 1986; The Guilty Party, 1987; Rags and Riches, 1988; Tug of War, 1989; Glad Rags, 1990; Between Two Worlds, 1991; Secrets and Surprises, 1991; Hands off Our School, 1992; Night Fires, 1993; Clever Clive and Loopy Lucy, 1993; Slo Flo and Boomerang Bill, 1994; Sulky Suzy and Jittery Jack, 1995; Lizzie's Leaving, 1996; Morag and the Lamb, 1996; Dark Shadows, 1998; A Secret Place, 1998; Tom and the Tree House, 1998 (Scottish Arts Council Award); Can You Find Sammy the Hamster?, 1998; The Egg Thieves, 1999; River Eyes, 2000; Natasha's Will, 2000; The Same Only Different, 2000; Me and My Shadow, 2001; Tortoise Trouble, 2002; Tell the Moon to Come Out, 2003; Tilly and the Wild Goats, 2005; The Sign of the Black Dagger, 2005; The Eleventh Orphan, 2008; What to do about Holly, 2009; The Chancery Lane Conspiracy, 2010; The Stolen Sister, 2011; What Holly Did, 2012; What To Do About Holly, 2013. *Recreations:* reading, walking, travelling. *Address:* c/o David Higham Associates, 7th Floor, Waverley House, 7–12 Noel Street, W1F 8GQ. *Club:* Lansdowne.

**LINGARD, Robin Anthony;** owner/manager, Kinnairdie Consulting, 1997–2009; *b* 19 July 1941; *s* of late Cecil Lingard and Lucy Lingard; *m* 1968, Margaret Lucy Virginia Elsden; two *d*. *Educ:* Felsted School; Emmanuel College, Cambridge (Exhibnr, MA). Min. of Aviation, 1963–66; Min. of Technology, 1966–70 (Private Sec. to Jt Parly Sec., 1966–68); DTI, 1971–74; DoI, 1974–83, Asst Sec., 1976; Under Sec., DTI, 1984, Cabinet Office (Enterprise Unit), 1984–85; Hd, Small Firms and Tourism Div., Dept of Employment, 1985–87; Mem. Bd, Highlands and Islands Develt Bd, 1988–91; Dir of Trng and Social Develt, 1991–93, Dir of Highlands and Is Univ. Project, 1993–97, Highlands and Islands Enterprise. Member: NEDC Sector Gp for Tourism and Leisure Industries, 1987–92; Scottish Tourist Bd, 1988–92; Management Bd, Prince's Trust and Royal Jubilee Trusts, 1989–95; Chairman: Highlands, Orkney and Western Isles Cttee, Prince's Trust, 1992–98; YouthLink Scotland, 1997–2000; BBC Scotland Appeals Adv. Cttee, 1998–2004; Fusion Scotland, 2000–05; Sustainable Develt Res. Centre, 2005–09; Highland Community Care Forum, 2007–09. FTS 1988. *Recreations:* reading, walking, watching birds, aviation history. *Address:* Kinnairdie House, Dingwall, Ross-shire IV15 9LL. *T:* (01349) 861044.

**LINGFIELD, Baron** *cr* 2010 (Life Peer), of Lingfield in the County of Surrey; **Robert George Alexander Balchin,** Kt 1993; DL; Knight President, Imperial Society of Knights Bachelor, since 2012; *b* 31 July 1942; *s* of late Leonard George Balchin and Elizabeth Balchin (*née* Skelton); *m* 1970, Jennifer, OStJ, *d* of late Bernard Kevin Kinlay, Cape Town; twin *s* (of whom one decd). *Educ:* Bec Sch.; Univ. of London; Univ. of Hull. Teacher, 1964–69; Res., Univ. of Hull Inst. of Educn, 1969–71; Chairman: HSW Ltd, 1972–2000; Blacker Publishing Ltd, 2003–09; Grant-Maintained Schs Foundn and Centre, 1989–99; Centre for Educn Mgt, 1994–2002; CEFM (formerly Centre for Education Finance) Ltd, 2002–; Cadet Vocational Qualification Orgn, 2012–. Chairman: Educn Commn, 2003–10; Commn on Special Educn Needs, 2006–10; Govt Review of Professionalism in Further Educn, 2012–13; Chartered Instn for Further Educn, 2013–. St John Ambulance: Asst Dir-Gen., 1982–84; Dir-Gen., 1984–88; Mem. Chapter-Gen., Order of St John, 1984–99. Imperial Society of Knights Bachelor: Mem. Council, 1995–; Registrar, 1998–2006; Knight Principal, 2006–12. Mem., FAS, 1994–97 (Chairman: New Schs Cttee, 1994–97; Schs Improvement Cttee, 1996–97); President: English Schs Orch., 1998–; League of Mercy, 1999–; Chm., ARNI Trust, 2008–. Chairman: Balchin Family Soc., 1993–; Maritime Heritage Foundn, 2011–. Mem., Surrey CC, 1981–85. Member: Court, Univ. of Leeds, 1995–2000; Council, Goldsmiths' Coll., London, 1997–2009 (Dep. Chm. Council, 1999–2005); Pro-Chancellor, Brunel Univ., 2006–13. Freeman, 1980, Liveryman, 1987, Goldsmiths' Co.; Liveryman, Soc. of Apothecaries of London, 2013. Hon. Colonel: Humberside & S Yorks ACF, 2004–12; ACF Bands, 2018–. DL Greater London, 2001. FCP 1971 (Hon. FCP 1987); Hon. FHS 1987; Hon. FCGI 1998. Hon. DLitt Hull, 2006; Hon. EdD Brunel, 2013. KStJ 1984. Grand Cross of Merit, SMO Malta, 2017 (Comdr 1st Cl., 1987); Grand Cross, Order of the Eagle of Georgia, 2014. *Publications:* Emergency Aid in Schools, 1984; New Money, 1985, 2nd edn 1989; (jtly) Choosing a State School, 1989; numerous articles on educn/politics. *Address:* New Place, Lingfield, Surrey RH7 6EF; House of Lords, SW1A 0PW. *T:* (020) 7219 3000. *Club:* Athenæum.

**LINGWOOD, James,** MBE 2012; Co-Director: Artangel, since 1991; Artangel Media Ltd, since 2000; *b* 28 May 1959; *s* of Robert Lingwood and Patricia Brown; partner, Jane Sarah Hamlyn, *qv*; one *s* two *d*. *Educ:* Corpus Christi Coll., Oxford (BA Hons Mod. Hist. 1979; MPhil dist. Art Hist. 1980). Curator: Inst. of Contemporary Arts, 1986–90; TSWA Sculpture Projects, 1987–90; independent curator, internat. museums, 1992–. Trustee: Paul Hamlyn Foundn, 2003–; Art Fund, 2008–18. Hon. Fellow, Goldsmiths, Univ. of London, 2012. *Publications:* (jtly) Une Autre Objective, 1989; (ed) Rachel Whiteread, House, 1993; Robert Smithson: the entropic landscape, 1993; The Epic and the Everyday: contemporary photographic art, 1994; Juan Muñoz: monologues and dialogues, 1996; (ed) Vija Celmins: works 1963–1996, 1997; Juan Muñoz: Double Bind, 2001; (ed) Field Trips: Robert Smithson, Bernd and Hilla Becher, 2002; (jtly) Off Limits: 40 Artangel projects, 2002; Susan Hiller: Recall, 2004; (ed and contrib.) Francis Alÿs: Seven Walks, 2005; (ed) Gregor Schneider: Die Familie Schneider, 2006; (contrib.) Thomas Schütte: Political Work, 2007; (ed jtly) Thomas Struth Photographs 1978–2010, 2010; (ed jtly) Yael Bartana, And Europe will be Stunned, 2012; (ed and contrib.) Julião Sarmento, White Nights, 2012; (ed) Susan Philipsz, You Are Not Alone, 2014; (ed and contrib.) Cristina Iglesias, Tres Aguas, 2015; (ed and contrib.) Inside: artists and writers in Reading Prison, 2017; Richard Hamilton, Serial Obsessions, 2017; Luigi Ghirri, The Map and the Territory: photographs from the 1970s, 2018. *Address:* Artangel, 31 Eyre Street Hill, EC1R 5EW. *T:* (020) 7713 1400, *Fax:* (020) 7713 1401. *E:* jl@artangel.org.uk.

**LINK, Joan Irene,** LVO 1992; HM Diplomatic Service, retired; independent consultant in human resources and business coaching, 2007–16; *b* 3 March 1953; *d* of William and Kathleen Mary Wilmot; *m* (marr. diss.); two *s*. *Educ:* Pear Tree Infant and Jun. Schs, Derby; Homelands Grammar Sch. for Girls, Derby; Lady Margaret Hall, Oxford (BA Mod. Langs); Open Univ. (Dip. Internat. Relns). FCIPD. Entered FCO, 1974; UK Delegn to the Cttee on Disarmament, 1980–83; Hd, Press and Inf., British Embassy, FRG, 1990–94; Hd, Resource Mgt Gp, 1996–2001, Hd, Conflict Prevention Unit, 2002–04, Hd, Conflict Issues Gp, 2004–07, FCO. Mem., Adv. Bd (formerly Trustee), Gender Action for Peace and Security, 2008–; Trustee, Peace Direct, 2008–15. Tour Guide (volunteer), Arkwright Mills, Cromford, 2010–. Parish Safeguarding Officer, St Giles Ch, Matlock, 2016–; Lay Chaplain, Matlock Police and Fire Stations, 2019–. *Recreations:* talking and walking, textile art (exhibited in Bookmark project, UWE, 2016; art for heritage projects, 2017), singing, writing. *Address:* c/o FCO Association, Foreign and Commonwealth Office, King Charles Street, SW1A 2AH.

**LINKLATER,** family name of **Baroness Linklater of Butterstone**.

**LINKLATER OF BUTTERSTONE,** Baroness *cr* 1997 (Life Peer), of Riemore in Perth and Kinross; **Veronica Linklater;** Founder, 1991, Executive Chairman, 1991–2004, President, since 2004, The New School, Butterstone; *b* 15 April 1943; *d* of late Lt-Col A. M. Lyle, OBE, and Hon. Elizabeth Lyle, *y d* of 1st Viscount Thurso, KT, CMG, PC; *m* 1967, Magnus Duncan Linklater, *qv*; two *s* one *d*. *Educ:* Cranborne Chase Sch.; Univ. of Sussex; Univ. of London (DipSoc Admin). Child Care Officer, 1967–68; Co-Founder, Visitors' Centre, Pentonville Prison, 1971–77; Winchester prison project, Prison Reform Trust, 1981–82; Founder, Administrator, then Consultant, The Butler Trust, 1983–87 (Trustee, 1987–2001; Vice Pres., 2001–); Trustee, Esmée Fairbairn Foundn, 1991–; Dir, Maggie Keswick Jencks Cancer Caring Centres Trust, 1997–2004. Mem., H of L, 1997–2016; Chm., H of L All-Party Gp on Offender Learning and Skills, 2005–06. Chm., Rethinking Crime and Punishment, 2001–08; Pres., Crime Reduction Initiative, 2007–11; Member: Children's Panel, Edinburgh S, 1989–97; Scottish Assoc. for the Study of Offending, 2005–. Member: Scottish Cttee, Barnardo's, 2001–04; Adv. Bd, Beacon Fellowship Charitable Trust, 2003–; Council, Winston Churchill Meml Trust, 2005–. Co-ordinator, Trustee and Vice Chm., Pushkin Prizes (Scotland), 1989–; Trustee: Lyle Charitable Trust, 2001–; Riemore Trust, 2007–; Adviser, Koestler Award Trust, 2004–. President: Soc. of Friends of Dunkeld Cathedral, 1989–; SOVA, 2009–. Patron: Airborne Initiative, 1998–2004; Nat. Schizophrenia Fellowship Scotland, 2000–; Nat. Family & Parenting Inst., 2002–; Research Autism (formerly Autism Intervention Res. Trust), 2004–; The Calyx—Scotland's Garden Trust, 2004–08; Probation Bds Assoc., 2005–; Action for Prisoners' Families, 2005–; Univ. of St Andrews Medical Campaign Cttee, 2007–; PUSH, 2007–; Home Start, 2007–; Epilepsy Scotland, 2009–; TACADE, 2009–; Contact a Family, 2011–. Foundn Patron, Queen Margaret Univ. Coll., Edinburgh, 1998–. Contested (Lib Dem) Perth and Kinross, May 1995. JP Inner London, 1985–88. *Recreations:* music, theatre, gardening. *Address:* Flat 1f2, 71 Cumberland Street, Edinburgh EH3 6RD. *T:* (0131) 558 9616. *E:* veronica.linklater@gmail.com.

**LINKLATER, Prof. Andrew,** PhD; FBA 2005; FLSW; Woodrow Wilson Professor of International Politics, Aberystwyth University (formerly University of Wales, Aberystwyth), since 2000; *b* 3 Aug. 1949; *s* of Andrew Linklater and Isabella (*née* Forsyth); *m* 1971, Jane Adam. *Educ:* Univ. of Aberdeen (MA 1971); Balliol Coll., Oxford (BPhil 1973); London Sch. of Econs (PhD 1978). Lectr, Univ. of Tasmania, 1976–81; Lectr, 1982–84, Sen. Lectr, 1985–91, Associate Prof., 1992, Monash Univ.; Prof., Keele Univ., 1993–99. Founding FLSW 2010. *Publications:* Men and Citizens in the Theory of International Relations, 1982, 2nd edn 1990; Beyond Realism and Marxism, 1990; The Transformation of Political Community, 1998; (with H. Suganami) The English School of International Relations, 2006; Critical Theory and World Politics: citizenship, sovereignty and humanity, 2007; The Problem of Harm in World Politics: theoretical investigations, 2011; Violence and Civilisation in the Western States-Systems, 2016. *Recreations:* the Turf, Australian aboriginal art, Wedgwood ware, ECM recordings. *Address:* Department of International Politics, Aberystwyth University, Aberystwyth SY23 3FE. *T:* (01970) 621596. *E:* adl@aber.ac.uk.

**LINKLATER, Magnus Duncan,** CBE 2013; FRSE; Scotland Editor, The Times, 2007–12; *b* 21 Feb. 1942; *s* of late Eric Robert Linklater, CBE, TD, and Marjorie MacIntyre; *m* 1967, Veronica Lyle (*see* Baroness Linklater of Butterstone); two *s* one *d*. *Educ:* Eton Coll.; Freiburg Univ.; Sorbonne; Trinity Hall, Cambridge (BA 2nd Cl. Hons (Mod. Lang.)). Reporter, Daily Express, Manchester, 1965–66; Diary Reporter, London Evening Standard, 1966–67; Editor: Londoner's Diary, Evening Standard, 1967–69; 'Spectrum', Sunday Times, 1969–72; Sunday Times Colour Magazine, 1972–75; Assistant Editor: News, Sunday Times, 1975–79; Features, Sunday Times, 1979–81; Exec. Editor (Features), Sunday Times, 1981–83; Man. Editor (News), The Observer, 1983–86; Editor: London Daily News, 1987; The Scotsman, 1988–94; columnist: The Times, 1994–; Scotland on Sunday, 1998–2007; broadcaster, Radio Scotland, 1994–97. Chairman: Edinburgh Book Fest., 1995–96; Scottish Arts Council, 1996–2001; Horsecross Arts (Perth Concert Hall and Th.), 2013–. Member: judging panel, 2008 City of Culture, 2002–03; WWI Commemoration Panel, Scotland, 2014–. Chm., Little Sparta Trust, 2001–. Pres., Saltire Soc., 2011–17. FRSE 2002. Hon. DArts Napier, 1994; Hon. LLD Aberdeen, 2007; Hon. DLitt: Glasgow, 2001; Queen Margaret Univ., 2007; Hon. Dr Edinburgh, 2017. Lifetime Achievement Award, Scottish Daily Newspaper Soc., 2005. *Publications:* (with Stephen Fay and Lewis Chester) Hoax—The Inside Story of the Howard Hughes/Clifford Irving Affair, 1972; (with Lewis Chester and David May) Jeremy Thorpe: a secret life, 1979; Massacre: the story of Glencoe, 1982; (with the Sunday Times Insight Team) The Falklands War, 1982; (with Isabel Hilton and Neal Ascherson) The Fourth Reich—Klaus Barbie and the Neo-Fascist Connection, 1984; (with Douglas Corrance) Scotland, 1984; (contrib.) A Scottish Childhood, 1985; (with David Leigh) Not With Honour: inside story of the Westland Scandal, 1986; (with Christian Hesketh) For King and Conscience: the life of John Graham of Claverhouse, Viscount Dundee, 1989; (ed jtly) Anatomy of Scotland, 1992; (with Colin Prior) Highland Wilderness, 1993; People in a Landscape, 1997; (ed) Great Scottish Lives, 2017. *Recreations:* fishing, alpine walking, theatre, opera. *Address:* Flat 1f2, 71 Cumberland Street, Edinburgh EH3 6RD. *T:* (0131) 558 9616. *E:* magnus.linklater1@gmail.com. *Club:* MCC.

**LINLEY, Viscount; Charles Patrick Inigo Armstrong-Jones;** *b* 1 July 1999; *s* and heir of 2nd Earl of Snowdon, *qv*. Page of Honour to the Queen, 2012.

**LINLITHGOW, 4th Marquess of,** *cr* 1902; **Adrian John Charles Hope;** Bt (NS) 1698; Baron Hope, Viscount Aithrie, Earl of Hopetoun 1703 (Scot.); Baron Hopetoun 1809 (UK); Baron Niddry 1814 (UK); Stockbroker; *b* 1 July 1946; *s* of 3rd Marquess of Linlithgow, MC, TD, and Vivienne (*d* 1963), *d* of Capt. R. O. R. Kenyon-Slaney and of Lady Mary Gilmour; *S* father, 1987; *m* 1st, 1968, Anne (marr. diss. 1978), *e d* of A. Leveson, Hall Place, Hants; two *s*; 2nd, 1980, Peta C. Binding (marr. diss. 1997; she *d* 2009); one *s* one *d*; 3rd, 1997, Auriol Mackeson-Sandbach (marr. diss. 2005), former wife of Sir John Bruce Woollacott Ropner, 2nd Bt. *Educ:* Eton. Joined HM Navy, 1965. *Heir: s* Earl of Hopetoun, *qv*. *Address:* Philpstoun House, Linlithgow, West Lothian EH49 7NB. *T:* (01506) 834685.

**LINNARD, Robert Wynne;** Director of Rail Strategy, Department for Transport, 2007–10; Specialist Adviser, House of Commons Transport Committee, 2011–15; *b* 18 June 1953; *s* of late John Adrian Linnard and Gwenita Linnard (*née* Jenns); *m* 1974, Sally Judith Gadsden; three *s* three *d*. *Educ:* Dulwich Coll. Entered Civil Service, DoE, 1973; Principal, Dept of Transport, 1984–91; Asst Sec., 1991–99; Dir of Railways, DETR, subseq. DTLR, 1999–2002; Dir, Local Govt Finance, DTLR, then ODPM, 2002–04; Dir of Integrated and Local Transport, subseq. Regl and Local Transport Policy, DfT, 2004–07. Mem. Bd, Transport Focus (formerly Passenger Focus), 2013–18. *Recreations:* family, labradors, walking. *Address:* Field House, Downe Road, Keston, Kent BR2 6AD. *T:* (01689) 852367. *E:* rlinnard@hotmail.co.uk.

**LINNELL, Andrew John,** CGeog, FRGS; Head of Geography, Prospect School, 2012–16; part-time teacher, Bulmershe School, since 2017; *b* 28 June 1956; *s* of late Cyril Barrie Linnell and Maureen Linnell (*née* Goodyear); *m* 1989, Juliet, *d* of late Prof. Oswald Hanfling and of Helga Hanfling; one *s* one *d*. *Educ:* Wolstanton Grammar Sch., Staffs; Univ. of Salford (BSc); Univ. of Keele (PGCE). FRGS 1983, Hon. FRGS 2018; CGeog 2002; ACP 1988, MCollP 1988, FCollP 2005. Teacher, Howard Sch., Gillingham, Kent, 1979–86; Educn Officer, Kent CC, 1986–92; Dep. Headteacher, Sir Joseph Williamson's Mathematical Sch., Rochester, 1992–97; Head Master, Reading Sch., 1997–2005; Head Teacher, Desborough Sch., 2005–12. Pt-time teacher, Abbey Sch., Reading, 2016. Mem. Council, RGS, 2005–09, 2013–15 (Vice-Pres., 2006–09, 2013–15); Chm., Final and Initial Assessors' Cttees for CGeog, RGS, 2006–; Sec., Council of British Geog., 2016–19. *Recreations:* jogging, swimming, cycling, travelling. *Address:* Bulmershe School, Woodlands Avenue, Woodley, Berks RG5 3EU. *T:* (0118) 935 3353. *E:* alinnell@bulmershe.wokingham.sch.uk.

**LINNETT, Simon John Lawrence;** Vice Chairman, Rothschild & Co. (formerly N. M. Rothschild & Sons Ltd), since 2017 (Executive Vice Chairman, 2014–17); *b* Oxford, 14 Feb. 1954; *s* of John Wilfrid Linnett and Rae Ellen Fanny Linnett; *m* 1987, Penelope Jane, *d* of Sir Charles Willink, 2nd Bt; two *s*. *Educ:* Leys Sch.; Balliol Coll., Oxford (MA Maths 1975). With Rothschild & Co. (formerly N. M. Rothschild & Sons Ltd), 1975–; Banking Div., 1975–78; Dir, 1987–98, Man. Dir, 1998–2004, Corporate Finance, then Investment Banking, then Global Financial Advisory, later Rothschild Global Advisory. Chm., Ind. Transport Commn, 2010–16 (Mem., 2000–; Patron, 2016–). Chm., Adv. Bd, Nat. Railway Mus., 2015–19 (Mem., 2000–; Dep. Chair, 2013–14). Chm., Luton and Dunstable Univ. Hosp. NHS Foundn Trust, 2014–. Treas., QMUL, 2010–17 (Hon. Fellow 2018). Trustee: Queen's Nursing Inst., 2000–10; Science Mus. Gp (formerly Nat. Mus. of Sci. and Industry), 2011–; Exbury Gardens Trust, 2012–; NESTA, 2014–. *Recreations:* walking, heavy gardening, reading, community action. *Address:* Rothschild & Co., New Court, St Swithin's Lane, EC4N 8AL. *E:* simon.linnett@rothschildandco.com. *Clubs:* Athenæum; Bosham Sailing.

*See also* Sir E. D. Willink, Bt.

**LINNEY, (Jonathan) Piers (Daniel);** Chairman, Soulmatefood, since 2017; Founder and Trustee, workinsight.org, since 2014; *b* Stoke-on-Trent, 15 Feb. 1971; *s* of Derek and Norma Linney; *m* 2003, Tara Bishop (*d* 2018); two *d*. *Educ:* Univ. of Manchester (BA Jt Hons Accounting and Law). Trainee solicitor, SJ Berwin, 1995–97; admitted solicitor, 1997; Exec., Investment Banking, Barclays de Zoete Wedd, 1997; Sen. Associate, M&A, Credit Suisse, 1997–2000; investor, 2000–; corporate finance and fund mgt, 2003–08; Jt Chief Exec., Genesis Communications td, 2008–11; Co-Founder and Jt CEO, Outsourcery plc, 2011–16. Non-exec. Dir, British Business Bank, 2017–. Trustee: Powerlist Foundn, 2010–; Nesta, 2014–; Plotr, 2014–16. Appeared as investor, Dragons' Den, BBC TV series, 2013–15. *Recreations:* family, downhill mountain biking and cycling, personal fitness, motor boating, field target shooting, cinema. *W:* www.pierslinney.com.

**LINSTEAD, Stephen Guy;** Director, Department of Trade and Industry, West Midlands Region, 1990–94; *b* 23 June 1941; *s* of late George Frederick Linstead and May Dorothy Linstead (*née* Griffiths); *m* 1st, 1971 (marr. diss.); two *s*; 2nd, 1982, Rachael Marian Feldman; two *d*. *Educ:* King Edward VII Sch., Sheffield; Corpus Christi Coll., Oxford (MA Mod. Hist.; Dip. Public and Social Admin.); Carleton Univ., Ottawa (MA Political Sci.); Huddersfield Univ. (Dip. Law). Board of Trade, 1964–76 (Private Sec. to Minister of State, 1967–69); Principal, 1969; Asst Sec., Dept of Prices and Consumer Protection, 1976–79; Dept of Trade, 1979–82; Office of Fair Trading, 1982–90; Under-Sec., DTI, 1990–94. Mem. Steering Gp, Industry '96, 1994–96. Vice-Chm., Assoc. of First Div. Civil Servants, 1982–84. Member: Exec. Cttee, Solihull Chamber of Commerce and Industry, 1996–2002 (Vice-Pres., 2000–02); Oversight Cttee, United Coll. of the Ascension, Selly Oak, 1996–2002. Reader, dio. of Birmingham, 1991–. Sec., St Alpheage Millennium Co-ordinating Cttee, 2010–12. Chair, English Spelling Soc., 2013–17. *Publications:* Hymns of Hope for a New Millennium, 2008; contrib. Ottawa Law Review. *Recreations:* hymn writing (various hymns in Worship Live), swimming, travel, entertainment. *Address:* 20 Silhill Hall Road, Solihull B91 1JU. *T:* and *Fax:* (0121) 705 1376. *Club:* Royal Over-Seas League.

**LINTON, Martin;** Director, Travel2Palestine, since 2011; *b* 11 Aug. 1944; *s* of Sydney and Karin Linton; *m* 1st, 1975, Kathleen Stanley (*d* 1995); two *d*; 2nd, 2008, Sara Apps. *Educ:* Christ's Hosp.; Pembroke Coll., Oxford (MA). Journalist: Daily Mail, 1966–71; Labour Weekly, 1971–79; Daily Star, 1979–81; The Guardian, 1981–97. Mem. (Lab), Wandsworth

LBC, 1971–82. MP (Lab) Battersea, 1997–2010; contested (Lab) same seat, 2010. PPS to Minister for the Arts, 2001–03, to Leader of Commons, 2003–05, to Lord Chancellor, 2005–07. Member: Home Affairs Select Cttee, 1997–2001; Admin Cttee, 2001–05; Modernisation Cttee, 2003–05. Chm., Make Votes Count, 2011–16. Dir, Labour Friends of Palestine and the Middle East, 2010–12 (Chm., 2009–10). *Publications:* The Swedish Road to Socialism, 1974; Guardian Guide to the House of Commons, 1992; Money and Votes, 1994; Was It the Sun Wot Won It?, 1995; Guardian Election Guide, 1997; Making Votes Count, 1998; Beyond 2002: long-term policies for Labour, 1999. *Recreations:* playing music, watching football. *T:* (020) 7228 4897. *E:* martin@martinlinton.org.

**LINTON, Prof. Oliver Bruce**, PhD; FBA 2008; Professor of Political Economy, University of Cambridge, since 2011; Fellow of Trinity College, Cambridge, since 2011; *b* Gloucester, 20 Dec. 1960; *s* of Geoffrey and Margaret Linton; *m* 1st, 1990, Elisabetta Zancan (marr. diss. 2010); one *s* one *d*; 2nd, 2011, Jianghong Song; one *s*. *Educ:* Hereford Cathedral Sch.; London Sch. of Econs (BSc 1st cl. Hons Maths 1983; MSc Econometrics and Math. Econs 1986); Univ. of Calif, Berkeley (PhD Econs 1991). Jun. Res. Fellow, Nuffield Coll., Oxford, 1991–93; Yale University: Asst Prof., 1993–97; Associate Prof., 1997–98; Prof. of Economics, 1998–2000; Prof. of Econometrics, LSE, 1998–2011. Fellow, Econometric Soc., 2007; FIMS 2007. *Publications:* Probability, Statistics and Econometrics, 2017. *Address:* Department of Economics, University of Cambridge, Austin Robinson Building, Sidgwick Avenue, Cambridge CB3 9DD. *T:* (01223) 335299. *E:* obl20@cam.ac.uk.

**LIP, Prof. Gregory Yoke Hong**, MD; FRCP, FRCPE, FRCPGlas; David A. Price-Evans Professor of Cardiovascular Medicine, University of Liverpool, since 2019; Director, Liverpool Centre for Cardiovascular Science, University of Liverpool and Liverpool Heart and Chest Hospital NHS Foundation Trust, since 2019; *b* Ipoh, 6 June 1964; *s* of Stephen Lip and Philomena Lip; *m* 1993, Peck Lin; one *s* one *d*. *Educ:* Univ. of Glasgow (MB ChB (with commendation) 1988; Brunton Meml Prize; Robert Fullerton Prize; MD 1994); DFM 1993. MRCP 1991, FRCP 2001; FACC 1996; FESC 1997; FRCPE 1998; FRCPGlas 1999. Consultant Cardiologist, Sandwell and West Birmingham Hosps NHS Trust, 1996–2019; University of Birmingham: Hon. Sen. Lectr, 1996–99; Hon. Reader, 1999–2001; Hon. Prof., 2001–09; Prof. of Cardiovascular Medicine, Inst. of Cardiovascular Scis, 2009–19. Hon. Consultant Cardiologist, Liverpool Heart and Chest Hosp. NHS Foundn Trust, 2019–. Visiting Professor: of Haemostasis Thrombosis and Vascular Scis, Aston Univ., Birmingham, 2009–; of Cardiol., Univ. of Belgrade, 2013–; of Cardiol., Univ. of Leeds, 2016–; of Cardiol., Nat. Yang-Ming Univ., Taipei, Taiwan; Adjunct Prof. of Cardiovascular Scis, Thrombosis Res. Unit, Aalborg Univ., 2011–; Hon. Prof., Chinese PLA Med. Sch., Beijing, 2013–; Wu Chung Vis. Prof., Univ. of Hong Kong, 2014; Adjunct Prof., Yonsei Univ., Seoul. Razavi Lectr, Cleveland Clinic Med. Sch., Cleveland, 2014. Member, Board: Eur. Heart Rhythm Assoc., 2013– (Chm., Scientific Documents Cttee, 2013–; Acute Cardiac Care Assoc., Eur. Soc. of Cardiol., 2014–16. Bradshaw Lect., RCP, 2013. Fellow, Eur. Heart Rhythm Assoc., 2016. Hon. Dr Medicinae Aalborg, 2013; Hon. Dr: Carol Davila Univ. of Medicine and Pharmacy, Bucharest, 2016; Belgrade, 2016; Tours, 2017. *Publications:* articles in cardiovascular medicine, specifically in atrial fibrillation, stroke, hypertension, heart failure, thrombosis and antithrombotic therapy. *Recreations:* travelling, good food, cinema, family. *Address:* Faculty of Health and Life Sciences, University of Liverpool, Brownlow Hill, Liverpool L69 3BX.

**LIPMAN, Maureen Diane, (Mrs J. M. Rosenthal)**, CBE 1999; actress; *b* 10 May 1946; *d* of late Maurice and Zelma Lipman; *m* 1973, Jack Morris Rosenthal, CBE (*d* 2004); one *s* one *d*. *Educ:* Newland High Sch. for Girls, Hull; London Acad. of Music and Dramatic Art. Professional début in The Knack, Watford, 1969; Stables Theatre, Manchester, 1970; National Theatre (Old Vic), 1971–73: The Front Page; Long Day's Journey into Night; The Good Natur'd Man; *West End:* Candida, 1976; Outside Edge, 1978; Meg and Mog, 1982; Messiah, 1983; Miss Skillen, in See How They Run, 1984 (Laurence Olivier Award; Variety Club of GB Award); Wonderful Town, Queen's, 1986; Re: Joyce!, Fortune, 1988, Vaudeville, 1989 and 1991, Long Wharf, Conn, USA, 1990; The Cabinet Minister, Albery, 1991; Lost in Yonkers, Strand, 1992 (Variety Club Best Stage Actress, 1993); The Sisters Rosenweig, Old Vic, 1994; Live and Kidding, Duchess, 1997; Oklahoma!, RNT, 1998, transf. Lyceum, 1999; Peggy For You, Comedy, 2000; Thoroughly Modern Millie, Shaftesbury, 2003; Aladdin, Old Vic, 2004; Glorious!, Duchess, 2005–06; When We Are Married, Garrick, 2010; The Best Man, Playhouse Th., 2018; other plays include: Celia, in As You Like It, RSC, 1974; Jenny, in Chapter Two, Hammersmith, 1981; Kitty McShane, in On Your Way, Riley, Stratford East, 1983; The Rivals, Manchester Royal Exchange, 1996; Sitting Pretty, Th. Royal, Bath, 2001; Martha Josie & the Chinese Elvis, touring, 2007; The Cherry Orchard, Chichester, 2008; A Little Night Music, Menier Chocolate Factory, 2008, transf. Garrick, 2009; Barefoot in the Park (also co-dir), touring, 2012; Old Money, Hampstead Th., 2012; Daytona, Park Th., London, 2013, Th. Royal, 2014; Harvey, Birmingham Repertory Th., transf. Th. Royal, 2015; My Mother Said I Never Should, St James Th., 2016; Sleeping Beauty, Richmond Th., 2016; Lettice and Lovage, Menier Chocolate Factory, 2017; dir, The Sunshine Boys, Royal Lyceum, Edinburgh, 1993; dir, The Knowledge, Charing Cross Th., 2017; *television:* plays, series and serials include: The Evacuees; Smiley's People; The Knowledge; Rolling Home; Outside Edge; Princess of France, in Love's Labour's Lost; Absurd Person Singular; Shift Work; Absent Friends; Jane Lucas, in 4 series of Agony; All at No 20 (TV Times Award, 1989); About Face, 1989 and 1990; Re: Joyce; Enid Blyton, in Sunny Stories, 1992; Eskimo Day, 1996; Cold Enough for Snow, 1997; The Fugitives, 2004; In Search of Style, 2005; Sensitive Skin, Dr Who, Casualty, 2007; He Kills Coppers, 2008; Minder, Ladies of Letters (2 series), 2009–10; Midsomer Murders, 2013; Bull, The Job Lot, 2015; Plebs, 2016; presenter, If Memory Serves Me Right (documentary), 2013; *films include:* Up the Junction, 1969; Educating Rita, 1983; Captain Jack, 1998; Solomon and Gaenor, 1999; Oklahoma! (video), 1999; Discovery of Heaven, 2001; The Pianist, 2002; Caught in the Act, 2008; *radio:* The Lipman Test (2 series), 1996, 1997; Choice Grenfell, 1998; dir, Jack Rosenthal's Last Act, 2006. BAFTA Award, for BT Commercials, 1992. Magazine columnist: Options, 1983–88; She, 1988–91 (PPA Columnist of the Year, 1991); Good Housekeeping, 1993–2003. Hon. DLitt: Hull, 1994; Sheffield, 1999; Hon. MA Salford, 1995; Hon. PhD Tel Aviv, 2012. *Publications:* How Was it for You?, 1985; Something to Fall Back On, 1987; You Got an 'Ology?, 1989; Thank You for Having Me, 1990; When's It Coming Out?, 1992; You Can Read Me Like a Book, 1995; Lip Reading, 1999; The Gibbon's in Decline, but the Horse is Stable, 2006; Past-it Notes, 2008; I Must Collect Myself, 2011; It's a Jungle Out There, 2016.

**LIPNER, Prof. Julius Joseph**, PhD; FBA 2008; Professor of Hinduism and the Comparative Study of Religion, University of Cambridge, 2003–13, now Emeritus; Fellow, Clare Hall, Cambridge, 1990–2013, now Emeritus (Vice-President, 2007–09); *b* Patna, India, 11 Aug. 1946; *s* of Vojtech Lipner and Sylvia Teresa Lipner (*née* Coutts); *m* 1971, Anindita Neogy; one *s* one *d*. *Educ:* Pontifical Athenæum (Jnana Deepa Vidyapeeth), Pune, India (Licentiate in Philosophy *summa cum laude* 1969); King's Coll., London (PhD 1974); MA Cantab 1975. Lectr in Indian Religions, Dept of Theol., Univ. of Birmingham, 1973–74; University of Cambridge: Lectr in Indian Religion and Comparative Study of Religion, 1975–99, Reader in Hinduism and Comparative Study of Religion, 1999–2003, Dir of Research, 2013, Divinity Faculty; Fellow, St Edmund's Coll., 1976–89; Chm., Faculty Bd of Divinity, 2003–06. Visiting Professor: Univ. of Calgary, 1987, 1989, 1996; Vanderbilt Univ., Nashville, 1992; Liverpool Hope Univ., 2003–04; Hon. Prof., Kurukshetra Univ., India, 1995–97; Vis. Fellow, Vishwabharati Univ., India, 1984; Sen. Fellow, Oxford Centre for Hindu Studies, 2014–; Dist. Vis. Fellow, 2015, Vis. Prof., 2015–19, S. Rajaratnam Sch. of Internat. Studies, Nanyang Technol Univ., Singapore. Named Lectures. Member, Editorial Advisory Board: Jl Hindu-Christian Studies; Internat. Jl Hindu Studies; (Jl) Religions of S Asia; Jl of Hindu Studies, 2008–. Trustee: Spalding Trusts, 1992–; Woolf Inst. (formerly Centre for Study of Jewish Christian Relations), 2001–; Teape Trust, 2008–; Ancient India and Iran Trust, 2012–. *Publications:* The Face of Truth: a study of meaning and metaphysics in the Vedantic theology of Ramanuja, 1986; (ed jtly) A Net Cast Wide: investigations into Indian thought in memory of David Friedman, 1986; (jtly) Hindu Ethics: purity, abortion and euthanasia, 1989; (ed jtly) The Writings of Brahmabandhab Upadhyay, vol 1, 1991, vol 2, 2002; Hindus: their religious beliefs and practices, 1994, 2nd edn 2010; (ed) The Fruits of our Desiring: an enquiry into the ethics of the Bhagavadgita, 1997; Brahmabandhab Upadhyay: the life and thought of a revolutionary, 1999 (Best Book in Hindu-Christian Studies, Soc. for Hindu-Christian Studies, 1999); Bankimchandra Chatterji's Anandamath or the Sacred Brotherhood (introd., trans. and critical apparatus), 2005 (A. K. Ramanujan Prize for trans., Assoc. for Asian Studies, 2008); (ed) Truth, Religious Dialogue and Dynamic Orthodoxy: essays in honour of Brian Hebblethwaite, 2005; Bankimchandra Chatterji's Debi Chaudhurani or The Wife Who Came Home (introd., trans. and critical apparatus), 2009; Hindu Images and Their Worship with Special Reference to Vaisnavism: a philosophical-theological inquiry, 2017; contrib. articles to learned jls and edited collections. *Recreations:* following Test Cricket (especially England and India), enjoying good food, listening to Indian and Western music, reading, travel, enjoying my six grandchildren growing up. *Address:* Divinity Faculty, University of Cambridge, West Road, Cambridge CB3 9BS.

**LIPPIETT, Rear-Adm. Richard John**, CB 2004; CBE 2014 (MBE 1979); DL; Chief Executive Officer, Mary Rose Trust, 2003–15; *b* 7 July 1949; *s* of late Rev. Canon Vernon Kingsbury Lippiett and Katharine F. I. S. Lippiett (*née* Langston-Jones); *m* 1976, Jennifer Rosemary Wratislaw Walker; two *s* one *d*. *Educ:* Brighton, Hove and Sussex Grammar Sch.; BRNC, Dartmouth. Joined RN 1967; served HM Ships Appleton, Eagle, Yarmouth, Achilles, Fife, Ambuscade and ashore at HMS Raleigh and Fleet HQ; Flag Lieut to C-in-C Fleet, 1973–74; Comd, HMS Shavington, 1975–77 and HMS Amazon, 1986–87; jsdc 1987; Naval Asst to First Sea Lord, 1988–90; Comd, HMS Norfolk and 9th Frigate Sqdn, 1991–92; rcds, 1993; COS Surface Flotilla, 1993–95; Comd, HMS Dryad and Sch. of Maritime Ops, 1995–97; Flag Officer Sea Trng, 1997–99; COS to Comdr Allied Naval Forces Southern Europe, and Sen. British Officer Southern Region, 1999–2002; Comdt, JSCSC, 2002–03. Trustee: Naval Review, 2001–14; Royal Mint Mus., 2011–; Chichester Fest. Th., 2016–. Naval Vice Pres., CCF, 2004–16; Pres., Ton Class Assoc., 2007–. Patron, Nautical Trng Corps, 2007–. Gov., Bedales Sch., 2011–. Younger Brother of Trinity House, 1993. DL W Sussex, 2014. Hon. Dr Maritime Southampton Solent, 2011; Hon. DLaws Portsmouth, 2012. *Publications:* The Type 21 Frigate, 1990; War and Peas: intimate letters from the Falklands War 1982, 2007. *Recreations:* family, classical music, gardening, travelling, maritime history, theatre and opera. *Address:* c/o Mary Rose Trust, College Road, HM Naval Base, Portsmouth PO1 3LX.

**LIPPINCOTT, Dr Kristen Clarke**; Director, The Saxl Project, since 2018; *b* 18 Nov. 1954; *d* of Lt-Col Clifford Ellwood Lippincott and Maureen Virginia Lippincott (*née* O'Brien); *m* 1992, Gordon Stephen Barrass, *qv*. *Educ:* Bennington Coll., Vermont, USA (BA); Univ. of Chicago (MA, PhD). Fellowships in Italy and at Warburg Inst., 1982–90; National Maritime Museum: Curator of Astronomy, 1990 and Head of Navigational Scis, 1991–94, Old Royal Observatory; Mus. Planner and Strategist, 1994–95; Director: Display Div., 1995–96; Millennium Project, Old Royal Observatory, Greenwich, 1996–2000; Royal Observatory Greenwich, 1998–2001; Dep. Dir, Nat. Maritime Mus., 2000–06. Dir, The Exhibitions Team, 2007–19. Vis. Prof., Harvard Univ., Villa I Tatti, Florence, 2004. Council Mem., Scientific Instruments Soc., 1994–96; Trustee: Bennington Coll., Vt, 1976–81; Cubitt Gall., 1996–2003. Freeman, Clockmakers' Co., 2000. FRAS 2004; FRSA 1997. *Publications:* Eyewitness Science: Astronomy, 1994; The Story of Time, 1999; (ed) Symbols of Time in the History of Art, 2002; A Guide to the Royal Observatory, Greenwich, 2007; The Stained Glass Windows of King's College Chapel, 2012; An Introduction to King's College Chapel, 2013; numerous articles on Italian Renaissance and on history of art, of science, of scientific instruments, in learned jls. *Recreations:* travelling, photography. *E:* kl@thesaxlproject.com.

**LIPPONEN, Paavo Tapio**; MP (SDP) Helsinki, Finland, 1983–87 and 1991–2006; Prime Minister of Finland, 1995–2003; Proprietor, Cosmopolis Oy, since 2007; Chairman, Protagon Consulting Oy, since 2014; *b* 23 April 1941; *s* of Orvo and Hilkka Lipponen; *m* 1998, Paivi Hertzberg; two *d*, and one *d* from former marriage. *Educ:* Kuopio; Univ. of Helsinki (MScSoc 1971); Dartmouth Coll., USA. Journalist, 1963–67; SDP Res. and Internat. Affairs Sec. and Head, political section, 1967–79; Prime Minister's Sec. (Special Political Advr), 1979–92; Head, Finnish Inst. Internat. Affairs, 1989–91; Mem., Helsinki City Council, 1985–95; Speaker of Parliament, 1995 and 2003–07. Social Democratic Party: Chm., Helsinki Dist, 1985–92; Member: Exec. Cttee, 1987–92; Party Council, 1990–93; Chm., 1993–2005. Man. Dir, Viestinta Teema Oy, 1988–95; Chm., Supervisory Bd, Outokumpu Oy, 1999–90. Member: Exec. Cttee, Internat. Commn on Employment, 1987–89; Adv. Bd, Notre Europe Jacques Delors Inst., 2005–; Adv. Bd, Oslo Center, 2010–. Chm., Assoc. Alvar Aalto en France, 2008–. Hon. LLD: Dartmouth Coll., USA, 1997; Finlandia Univ., USA, 2000; Hon. Dr: Tampere Univ. of Tech., Finland, 2002; Åbo Akademi Univ., Finland, 2002; Univ. of Art and Design, Finland, 2007; Univ. of Joensuu. Grand Cross, Order of White Rose (Finland). Holds several foreign decorations and several Finnish and internat. prizes. *Publications:* Muutoksen Suunta, 1986; Kohti Eurooppaa, 2001; Järki voittaa, 2006; Memoirs, I, 2010, II, 2014; Die Vernunft siegt, 2015; articles in Finnish, Swedish, English and German in domestic and foreign books, newspapers and periodicals. *Recreations:* swimming, architecture, collecting medals (sculpted). *Address:* Dagmarinkatu 5B8, 00100 Helsinki, Finland. *Clubs:* Finnish (Helsinki); Kuopio (Kuopio).

**LIPSCOMB, Rachel Elizabeth**, OBE 2006; JP; a Vice President, Magistrates' Association, since 2005 (Deputy Chairman, 1999–2002, Chairman, 2002–05, of Council); *b* 24 Aug. 1948; *d* of George Edwards and Joan (*née* Button); *m* 1969, Peter W. Lipscomb, OBE; two *s* one *d*. *Educ:* St Felix Sch., Southwold; Middlesex Hosp., London (SRN). Magistrates' Association: Mem. Council, 1994–; Chm., Sentencing Guidelines Working Party, 2002–05; Chm., Criminal Justice Cttee, 2000–02; Mem., Street Crime Action Gp, 2002–05. Member: Adv. Gp on Prison Popn, 2002–04; Audit Commn Victims and Witnesses Adv. Gp, 2002–04. Member: Unified Admin Judicial Cttee, 2002–04; Judges Council, 2003–05. Chm., Local Crime Community Sentence, 2008–13; Mem. Adv. Bd, Rethinking Crime and Punishment - Implementing the Findings, Esmée Fairbairn Foundn, 2005–08. Chairman: MID Mediation and Counselling, 2005–17; Mediation, Support and Counselling for Separating Partners and Families, 2009–. Pres., Ham and Petersham Assoc., 2016–. Governor, Kingston Grammar Sch., 1996–2002. JP Kingston upon Thames, 1981.

*Publications:* articles for The Magistrate and other criminal and civil justice pubns. *Recreations:* gardening, outdoor sports, family life. *Address:* c/o Magistrates' Association, 10A Flagstaff House, St George Wharf, SW8 2LE. *T:* (020) 7387 2353, *Fax:* (020) 7383 4020.

**LIPSEY**, family name of **Baron Lipsey**.

**LIPSEY**, Baron *cr* 1999 (Life Peer), of Tooting Bec in the London Borough of Wandsworth; **David Lawrence Lipsey;** *b* 21 April 1948; *s* of Lawrence and Penelope Lipsey; *m* 1982, Margaret Robson; one *d*, and two step *s*. *Educ:* Bryanston Sch.; Magdalen Coll., Oxford (1st Cl. Hons PPE). Research Asst, General and Municipal Workers' Union, 1970–72; Special Adviser to Anthony Crosland, MP, 1972–77 (Dept of the Environment, 1974–76; FCO, 1976–77); Prime Minister's Staff, 10 Downing Street, 1977–79; Journalist, New Society, 1979–80; Sunday Times: Political Staff, 1980–82; Economics Editor, 1982–86; Editor, New Society, 1986–88; Co-founder and Dep. Editor, The Sunday Correspondent, 1988–90; Associate Ed., The Times, 1990–92; journalist, The Economist, 1992–99 (Political Ed., 1994–98); Chm., Impower plc, 2001–03. Vis. Prof. in Public Policy, Univ. of Ulster, 1993–98; Vis. Fellow, Health and Social Care, LSE, 2002–04; Vis. Prof., Salford Univ., 2008–12. Member: Royal Commn on Long Term Care of the Elderly, 1997–99; Ind. Commn on the Voting System, 1997–98; Licence Fee Rev. Panel (Davies Inquiry), 1999; Council, ASA, 1999–2005; Bd, Starting Price Regulatory Commn; Chairman: Make Votes Count, 1999–2008; Social Market Foundn, 2001–10; Shadow Racing Trust, 2002–07; British Greyhound Racing Bd, 2004–08; Financial Services Consumer Panel, 2008; Campaign for Straight Statistics, 2009–12. Chairman: All Party Statistics Gp; All Party Classical Music Gp; Vice-Chairman: All Party Media Gp; All Party Betting and Gaming Gp, 2009–14; All Party Channel 4 Gp; Council, Constitution Unit; Editl Bd, Study on Decumulation, Assoc. of Ind. Financial Advrs, 2009. Secretary, Streatham Labour Party, 1970–72; Chm., Fabian Soc., 1981–82; Mem., Exec. Cttee, Charter for Jobs, 1984–86. A public interest Dir, PIA, 1994–2000; non-executive Director: Horserace Totalisator Bd, 1998–2002; LWT, 2002–03; London ITV, 2003–05; Consultant, Greyhound Bd of Great Britain, 2009–. Trustee: Retired Greyhound Trust, 2003–11; Cambrian Music Trust, 2009–; Sidney Nolan Trust (Chm., 2013–); President: British Harness Racing Club, 2004–; Soc. of Later Life Advisers, 2009–; Patron, Glasbury Festival; Chm., Trinity Laban Conservatoire of Music and Dance, 2012–. FAcSS 2015. *Publications:* Labour and Land, 1972; (ed, with Dick Leonard) The Socialist Agenda: Crosland's Legacy, 1981; Making Government Work, 1982; The Name of the Rose, 1992; The Secret Treasury: how Britain's economy is really run, 2000; In the Corridors of Power (autobiog.), 2012; Counter Coup, 2014. *Recreations:* golf, greyhound racing, harness racing, horse racing, music, opera. *Address:* House of Lords, SW1A 0PW. *T:* (020) 7219 8509.

**LIPSEY**, Prof. Richard George, OC 1991; FRSC; Professor of Economics, Simon Fraser University, Burnaby, BC, 1989–97, now Emeritus; Fellow, Canadian Institute for Advanced Research, 1989–2002; *b* 28 Aug. 1928; *s* of R. A. Lipsey and F. T. Lipsey (*née* Ledingham); *m* 1961, Diana Louise Smart; one *s* two *d*. *Educ:* Univ. of British Columbia (BA 1st Cl. Hons 1951); Univ. of Toronto (MA 1953); LSE (PhD 1957). Dept of Trade and Industry, British Columbia Provincial Govt, 1950–53; LSE: Asst Lectr, 1955–58; Lectr, 1958–60; Reader, 1960–61; Prof. 1961–63; Univ. of Essex: Prof. of Economics, 1963–70; Dean of School of Social Studies, 1963–67; Sir Edward Peacock Prof. of Econs, Queen's Univ., Kingston, Ont, 1970–86. Vis. Prof., Univ. of California at Berkeley, 1963–64; Simeon Vis. Prof., Univ. of Manchester, 1973; Irving Fisher Vis. Prof., Yale Univ., 1979–80. Economic Consultant, NEDC, 1961–63; Sen. Econ. Advr, C. D. Howe Inst., Toronto, 1983–89. Mem., Canada's Ecofiscal Commn, 2014–19. Member of Council: SSRC, 1966–69; Royal Economic Soc., 1968–71. President: Canadian Economics Assoc., 1980–81 (Life Fellow, 2010); Atlantic Economic Assoc., 1986–87. Editor, Review of Economic Studies, 1960–64. Fellow, Econometric Soc., 1972. FRSC 1980. Hon. LLD: McMaster, 1984; Victoria, 1985; Carleton, 1987; Queen's Univ. at Kingston, 1990; Guelph, 1993; Western Ontario, 1994; Essex, 1996; British Columbia, 1999; Simon Fraser Univ., 2007; Hon. DSc Toronto, 1992. Gold Medal, Social Scis and Humanities Res. Council, 2005. *Publications:* An Introduction to Positive Economics, 1963, 14th edn (with A. Chrystal) as Economics, 2019; (with P. O. Steiner) Economics, 1966, 12th edn 1999; (with G. C. Archibald) An Introduction to a Mathematical Treatment of Economics, 1967, 3rd edn 1977; The Theory of Customs Unions: a general equilibrium analysis, 1971; (with G. C. Archibald) An Introduction to Mathematical Economics, 1975; (with C. Harbury) An Introduction to the UK Economy, 1983, 5th edn 1993; (with F. Flatters) Common Ground for the Canadian Common Market, 1984; (with M. Smith): Canada's Trade Options in a Turbulent World, 1985; Global Imbalance and US Policy Response, 1987; (with R. York) A Guided Tour through the Canada-US Free Trade Agreement, 1988; (with C. Harbury) First Principles of Economics, 1988, 2nd edn 1992; (jtly) The NAFTA: what's in, what's out, what's next, 1994; (with K. Carlaw) A Structuralist Assessment of Innovation Policies, 1998; (jtly) Economic Transformations: general purpose technologies and long-term economic growth, 2005 (Schumpeter Prize for best writing in evolutionary econs (jtly), 2006); A Reconsideration of the Theory of Non-Linear Scale Effects, 2018; articles in learned jls on many branches of theoretical and applied economics. *Recreations:* travel, sailing, rambling. *Address:* 1125 West 26th Street, North Vancouver, BC V7R 1A4, Canada. *E:* rlipsey@sfu.ca.

**LIPSON**, Julian David; Partner, since 2003, and Head of Family Law, since 2008, Withers LLP; *b* Liverpool, 5 July 1969; *s* of Gerald Lipson and Marion Lipson (*née* Elman). *Educ:* King David High Sch., Liverpool; St Edmund Hall, Oxford (MA Juris. 1990). Admitted Solicitor, 1996; trainee solicitor, then Solicitor, Macfarlanes, 1994–97; Solicitor, Withers LLP, 1997–. Fellow, Internat. Acad. of Matrimonial Lawyers, 2009. *Recreations:* travel, cinema, theatre. *Address:* Withers LLP, 20 Old Bailey, EC4M 7EG. *T:* (020) 7597 6098, *Fax:* (020) 7597 6543. *E:* julian.lipson@withersworldwide.com.

**LIPTON**, Elliot; Managing Director, First Base Ltd, since 2002; *b* London, 17 March 1969; *s* of Sir Stuart (Anthony) Lipton, *qv; m* 1999, Alex Miller; one *s* two *d*. *Educ:* Mill Hill Sch.; Imperial Coll. London (BSc Hons Estate Mgt; MBA). FRICS 2014. Gov., Mill Hill Sch. FRSA. *Recreation:* ski-ing. *Address:* First Base Ltd, 91 Wimpole Street, W1G 0EF. *T:* (020) 7851 5555. *E:* info@firstbase.com.

**LIPTON**, Prof. Michael, CMG 2003; FBA 2006; Research Professor, Poverty Research Unit, 1997–2015, now Emeritus Professor of Economics, and Emeritus Fellow, Institute of Development Studies, 2015, Sussex University; *b* 13 Feb. 1937; *s* of Leslie and Helen Lipton; *m* 1966, Merle Babrow; one *s*. *Educ:* Haberdashers' Aske's Sch., London; Balliol Coll., Oxford (BA 1st Cl. Hons PPE 1960, MA 1963); Massachusetts Inst. of Technol.; DLitt Sussex 1982. Fellow, All Souls Coll., Oxford, 1961–68 and 1983–84; University of Sussex: Fellow, Inst. of Develt Studies, and Professorial Fellow, 1970–94; Founding Dir, Poverty Res. Unit, 1994–97; 50th Anniversary Fellow, 2012. Dir, Consumption and Nutrition Prog., Internat. Food Policy Res. Inst., 1987–89. Employment Advr, Govt of Botswana, 1977–79; Sen. Advr, World Bank, 1981–82; Advr, Dept of Rural Develt and Land Reform, Govt of S Africa, 2015–. Sen. Advr and topic leader, Quality of Life, ADB study of Emerging Asia, 1995–97; Lead Schol., Rural Poverty Report, IFAD, 1994–2001. Member: Wkg Party on GM crops, Bioethics Council, Nuffield Foundn, 1998–99 and 2002–03; Prog. Adv. Cttee, HarvestPlus (Biofortification) Prog. (formerly Biofortification Challenge Grant), Consultative Gp for Internat. Agricl Res., 2002–; UK and Internat. Bds, Internat. Develt Enterprises, 2004–; Bd, Centre for Chinese Agricl Policy, Chinese Acad. Scis, 2005–. Mem., Council, 2000–05, Bd, 2005–, ODI. Fellow, Stellenbosch Inst. for Advanced Studies, 2011. Leontief Prize for Advancing Frontiers of Econ. Thought, Global Develt and Envmt Inst., Tufts Univ., 2012. *Publications:* Chess Problems: introduction to an art, 1963; (jtly) The Two-move Chess Problem: tradition and development, 1966; Assessing Economic Performance, 1968; Why Poor People Stay Poor: urban bias and world development, 1977, 2nd edn 1988; (with R. Longhurst) New Seeds and Poor People, 1989; (with J. Toye) Does Aid Work in India?, 1991; (ed jtly and contrib.) Including the Poor, 1993; Successes in Anti-poverty, 1998, 2nd edn 2002; Land Reform in Developing Countries: property rights and property wrongs, 2009; Malthus in Africa, 2019; contrib. learned jls. *Recreations:* chess problems (Pres., British Chess Problem Soc., 1999–2001; Internat. Master of Chess Problem Composition, 1975–), classical music, poetry, theatre. *Address:* 15 Eaton Place, Brighton, Sussex BN2 1EH. *Club:* Lansdowne.

**LIPTON**, Sir Stuart (Anthony), Kt 2000; Director, Lipton Rogers Developments LLP, since 2013; *b* 9 Nov. 1942; *s* of late Bertram Green and Jeanette Lipton; *m* 1966, Ruth Kathryn Marks; two *s* one *d*. *Educ:* Berkhamsted Sch. Director: Sterling Land Co., 1971–73; First Palace Securities Ltd, 1973–76; Man. Dir, Greycoat PLC, 1976–83; Chief Exec., Stanhope Properties PLC, 1983–2003; Chm., Stanhope PLC, 2003–06; Dep. Chm., Chelsfield LLP, 2006–16. Advr to Hampton Site Co. for Sainsbury Bldg, Nat. Gall., 1985–91; Advr, new Glyndebourne Opera House, 1988–94; Member: Adv. Bd, Dept of Construction Management, Reading Univ., 1983–91; Property Adv. Gp, DoE, 1986–96; Mil. Bldgs Cttee, MoD, 1987–98; Barbican Centre Adv. Council, 1997–2007. Mem. Council, British Property Fedn, 1987–99. Mem., Royal Fine Art Commn, 1988–99; Chm., CABE, 1999–2004. Dir, Nat. Gall. Trust Foundn, 1998–2018. Trustee: Whitechapel Art Gall., 1987–94; Architecture Foundn, 1992–99 (Dep. Chm., 1992–99); Urban Land Inst., Washington, 1996–; Millennium Bridge Trust, 1998–2002; King Edward VII Hosp., 2014–; Member: English Partnerships Millennium Housing Trust Jury, 1998–99; Jury, RIBA Gold Medal Award, 1998–99. Member of Board: Royal Nat. Theatre, 1988–98; Royal Opera House, 1998–2006. Edward Bass Vis. Architectural Fellow, Yale Sch. of Architecture, 2006. Member, Governing Body: Imperial Coll., 1987–2002 (FIC 1998); LSE, 2000–06. Liveryman, Goldsmiths' Co., 1997–. Hon. Bencher, Inner Temple, 2002. Hon. RIBA 1986. Hon. LLD Bath, 2005; Hon. DSc(Eng) UCL, 2009. Bicentenary Medal, RSA, 1999. *Recreations:* architecture, art and technology, opera. *Address:* (office) 33 Cavendish Square, W1G 0PW.
*See also* E. Lipton.

**LIPWORTH**, Sir (Maurice) Sydney, Kt 1991; Trustee, International Accounting Standards Committee Foundation, 2000–06; Chairman, Financial Reporting Council, 1993–2001; *b* 13 May 1931; *s* of Isidore and Rae Lipworth; *m* 1957, Rosa Liwarek (CBE 2010); two *s*. *Educ:* King Edward VII Sch., Johannesburg; Univ. of the Witwatersrand, Johannesburg (BCom, LLB). Admitted Solicitor, Johannesburg, 1955; called to the South African Bar, 1956; called to Bar, Inner Temple, 1991; in practice at the Bar, 2002–. Barrister, Johannesburg, 1956–64; non-exec. Dir, Liberty Life Assoc. of Africa Ltd, 1956–64; Director: private trading/financial gps, 1965–67; Abbey Life Assurance Gp, 1968–70; Allied Dunbar Assurance plc (formerly Hambro Life Assurance), 1971–88 (Jt Man. Dir, 1980–84; Dep. Chm., 1984–87); Chairman: Dunbar Bank, 1983–88; Allied Dunbar Unit Trusts, 1985–88 (Man. Dir, 1983–85); ZENECA Group, 1995–99 (Dir, 1994–99); Dep. Chm., Nat. Westminster Bank, 1993–2000; Director: J. Rothschild Holdings plc, 1984–87; BAT Industries plc, 1985–88; Carlton Communications plc, 1993–2004; Centrica plc, 1999–2002; Goldfish Bank Ltd, 2001–04; Cazenove Gp Ltd, 2005–. Mem., 1981–93, Chm., 1988–93, Monopolies and Mergers Commn; Member: Sen. Salaries Review Body, 1994–2002; Cttee on Financial Aspects of Corporate Governance, 1994–95. Mem. Adv. Panel, BreakThrough Breast Cancer Res. Trust, 1990; Trustee: Allied Dunbar Charitable Trust, 1971–94; Philharmonia Orchestra, 1982– (Dep. Chm., 1986–93, Chm., 1993, of Trustees); Royal Acad. Trust, 1988–2003; South Bank Foundn Ltd, 1996–2003; Chairman: NatWest Gp Charitable Trust, 1994–2001; Marie Curie Cancer Care 50th Anniversary Appeal, 1997–2002; Governor: Contemp. Dance Trust, 1981–87; Sadler's Wells Foundn, 1987–90. Chm., Bar Assoc. for Commerce, Finance and Industry, 1991–92. Mem., Gen. Council of the Bar, 1992–94. Hon. Bencher, Inner Temple, 1989; Hon. QC 1993. Hon. LLD Witwatersrand, 2003. *Publications:* chapters and articles on investment, life insurance, pensions and competition law. *Recreations:* tennis, music, theatre. *Address:* International Accounting Standards Board, 30 Cannon Street, EC4M 6XH. *Clubs:* Reform, Queen's.

**LISBURNE**, 9th Earl of, *cr* 1776 (Ire.); **David John Francis Malet Vaughan;** Baron Fethard, 1695; Viscount Lisburne and Lord Vaughan, 1695; artist; *b* 15 June 1945; *e s* of 8th Earl of Lisburne and Shelagh Vaughan (*née* Macauley); *S* father, 2014; *m* 1973, Jennifer Jane Sheila Fraser Campbell, artist, *d* of James and Dorothy Campbell, Invergarry; one *s* one *d*. *Educ:* Ampleforth Coll. *Heir: b* Hon. Michael John Wilmot Malet Vaughan [*b* 26 June 1948; *m* 1978, Hon. Lucinda Mary Louis Baring, *d* of 7th Baron Ashburton, *qv*; one *s* two *d*].

**LISHMAN**, Alwyn; see Lishman, W. A.

**LISHMAN**, (Arthur) Gordon, CBE 2006 (OBE 1993); Director General, Age Concern, and Chief Executive, Age Concern Group, 2000–09; *b* 29 Nov. 1947; *s* of Dr Arthur Birkett Lishman and Florence May Lishman; *m* 1st, 1968, Beverley Ann Witham (marr. diss. 1972); 2nd, 1973, Stephanie Margaret Allison-Beer (marr. diss. 1984); one *s* one *d*; 3rd, 1988, Margaret Ann Brodie-Browne (*née* Long); one step *d*. *Educ:* Univ. of Manchester (BA Econ 1968). Age Concern England, 1974–2009: Field Officer, 1974–77; Head of Fieldwork, 1977–87; Ops Dir, 1987–2000; Dir, Age Concern Hldgs Ltd, 1995–2009. Member: Steering Gp for Commn on Equalities and Human Rights, 2004–06; Nat. Stakeholder Forum, DoH, 2006–09; Chairman: Nutrition Action Plan Delivery Bd, DoH, 2008–10; Audit Cttee, Older People's Comr in Wales, 2009–19. Vice-Pres., Internat. Fedn on Ageing, 2004–12 (Dir, 2001–12); Sec.-Gen., Eurolink Age, 2001–; Sec., AGE—the Eur. Older People's Platform, 2001–07 (Council Mem., 2001–08). Campaigner on age equality, 1971–; involvement in Campaign for Homosexual Law Reform/Campaign for Homosexual Equality and Stop the Seventy Tour; former Mem., Race Equality Councils in Manchester, Northants and E Lancs; Member: Liberty; Fawcett Soc.; Humanists UK (formerly British Humanist Assoc.); Friends of Ruskin's Brantwood. Gov., Pensions Policy Inst., 2002–. Mem., Liberal, later Liberal Democrat, Party, 1963– (Mem., Federal Bd, 1969–); Chm., Human Rights Cttee, Liberal Internat., 2009–11; Pres., NW Liberal Democrats, 2010–14 (Treas., 2017–19); Chm., Burnley Liberal Democrats, 2011–13, 2016–. Founder, Africa Liberal Network, 2001–; Treas., Social Liberal Forum, 2019–. Chair: Burnley and Pendle CAB, 2011–18; Gas Safe Charity, 2012–. Trustee: John Stuart Mill Inst., 2009–; Safer Tourism Foundn, 2017–. Mem. (Lib Dem), Burnley BC, 2018–. Hon. Fellow, Univ. of Central Lancs, 2002. MCMI. FRSA. MMLJ 2006. *Address:* 42 Halifax Road, Briercliffe, Burnley BB10 3QN. *T:* (01282) 421865. *E:* gordon@lishman.co.uk. *Club:* National Liberal (Dir, 2018–).

**LISHMAN, Suzannah Claire**, CBE 2018; FRCPath, FRCPEd; Consultant Histopathologist, North West Anglia NHS Foundation Trust (formerly Peterborough and Stamford Hospitals NHS Foundation Trust), since 2006; President, Royal College of Pathologists, 2014–17; *b* Beverley, 16 Dec. 1967; *d* of Dr John Derek Lishman and Bridgette Lishman (*née* McLaughlin); *m* 2011, Douglas Mackay Pattisson. *Educ*: Neale Wade Community Coll., March; Girton Coll., Cambridge (BA 1989; BChir 1992, MB 1993); London Hosp. Med. Sch. MRCPath 1999, FRCPath 2007; FRCPEd 2015. Hse Surgeon, Harold Wood Hosp., 1992–93; Hse Physician, Newham Gen. Hosp., 1993; Histopathol. Trainee, UCH, 1993–99; Consultant Histopathologist, Hinchingbrooke Healthcare NHS Trust, 1999–2006. Royal College of Pathologists: Asst Registrar, 2005–09; Registrar, 2009–11; Vice-Pres., 2011–14. Hon. FRCPI 2016. Hon. DSc Swansea, 2016. *Publications*: A History of Pathology in 50 Objects, 2012. *Recreations*: scuba diving, Italian Renaissance art. *E*: suzylishman@doctors.org.uk.

**LISHMAN, Prof. (William) Alwyn**, MD, DSc; FRCP, FRCPsych; Professor of Neuropsychiatry, Institute of Psychiatry, University of London, 1979–93, now Professor Emeritus; Consultant Psychiatrist, Bethlem Royal and Maudsley Hospitals, 1967–93; *b* 16 May 1931; *s* of George Hackworth Lishman and Madge Scott (*née* Young); *m* 1966, Marjorie Loud (*d* 2000); one *s* one *d*. *Educ*: Houghton-le-Spring Grammar Sch.; Univ. of Birmingham (BSc Hons Anatomy and Physiology, 1953; MB, ChB Hons 1956; MD 1965). DPM London, 1963; DSc London, 1985. MRCP 1958, FRCP 1972; FRCPsych 1972. House Phys. and House Surg., Queen Elizabeth Hosp., Birmingham, 1956–57; MO Wheatley Mil. Hosp., 1957–59 (Major, RAMC); Registrar, United Oxford Hosps, 1959–60; Registrar, later Sen. Registrar, Maudsley Hosp., London, 1960–66; Consultant in Psychol Medicine, Nat. Hosp. and Maida Vale Hosp., London, 1966–67; Sen. Lectr in Psychol Medicine, Hammersmith Hosp. and RPMS, 1967–69; Consultant Psychiatrist, Bethlem Royal and Maudsley Hosps, 1967–74; Reader in Neuropsychiatry, Inst. of Psychiatry, 1974–79. Vis. Fellow, Green Coll., Oxford, 1983. Advisor to Bermuda Hosps Bd, 1971; Scientific Advisor, DHSS, 1979–82; Civilian Consultant, RAF, 1987–93. Member: Neurosciences Bd, MRC, 1976–78 (Dep. Chm., 1976–77); Scientific Adv. Panel, Brain Res. Trust, 1986–93; Adv. Cttee, Mason Med. Res. Trust, 1986–93. Examiner: Univ. of Oxford (also Mem. Bd of Examrs), 1975–79; Univ. of Birmingham, 1984–87; Nat. Univ. of Malaysia, 1989. Chm., British Neuropsychiatry Assoc., 1987–93; (Hon. Life Pres., 1993); Member: Experimental Psychology Soc., 1975–95; Assoc. of British Neurologists, 1979–95; Court of Electors, and Exams Subcttee, RCPsych, 1991–96. Trustee, Psychiatry Res. Trust, 1999–2007. Gaskell Gold Medal, Royal Medico-Psychol Assoc., 1965. Member, Editorial Boards: Psychological Medicine, 1970–93; Neuropsychiatry, Neuropsychology and Behavioral Neurology, 1988–95; Cognitive Neuropsychiatry, 1996–. Guarantor of Brain, 1984–99. *Publications*: Organic Psychiatry: the psychological consequences of cerebral disorder, 1978, 3rd edn 1998; physiol and psychol papers on brain maturation, cerebral dominance, organisation of memory; clinical papers on head injury, dementia, epilepsy, neuroimaging, and alcoholic brain damage. *Recreations*: organ, piano, harpsichord, travelling.

**LISLE, 9th Baron** *cr* 1758 (Ire.), of Mount North, co. Cork; **John Nicholas Geoffrey Lysaght**; *b* 20 May 1960; *s* of 8th Baron Lisle and Mary Louise Lysaght (*née* Shaw, now Blackwell); *S* father, 2003. *Educ*: Lingfield. Gardener, specialising in exotic climbers; beekeeper; charity shop volunteer. *Recreations*: collecting early 20th-century Christmas tree decorations, gardening, writing rhymes and poems. *Heir*: *b* Hon. David James Lysaght [*b* 10 Aug. 1963; *m* 1989, Rebecca Tamsin, *d* of Russell Charles Abbott; one *s* two *d*]. *Address*: 50 The Fairstead, Scottow, Norwich, Norfolk NR10 5AQ.

**LISLE, Paul David O.**; *see* Orchard-Lisle.

**LISS, Prof. Peter Simon**, CBE 2008; PhD; FRS 2008; Professor, School of Environmental Sciences, University of East Anglia, 1985–2008, now Emeritus; *b* 27 Oct. 1942; *s* of Michael and Gertrude Liss; *m* 1967, Ruth Adler; three *s*. *Educ*: University College, Durham (BSc); Marine Science Labs, Univ. of Wales (PhD). NERC Post-doctoral Res. Fellow, Dept of Oceanography, Southampton Univ., 1967–69; Lectr, 1969–77, Reader, 1977–85, Sch. of Envmtl Scis, UEA. Vis. Prof., Univ. of Washington, Seattle, 1977; Visiting Scientist: Ocean Chem. Lab., Canada, 1975; Grad. Sch. of Oceanography, Univ. of Rhode Island, 1989, 1990; Guest Prof., Ocean Univ., Qingdao, China, 1997–; Adjunct Prof., Texas A&M Univ., 2016–. Envmtl Chemistry Dist. Lectr, 2002, John Jeyes Lect. Award, 2003, RSC; Eminent Schol., Texas Inst. for Advanced Study, Texas A&M Univ., 2013–14. Scientific Advisor, CEGB, London, 1979–82. Exec. Dir, ICSU, 2014–15 (Mem., Task Team for Future Earth, 2011–12). Member: NERC, 1990–95; Royal Commn on Envmtl Pollution, 2005–11; Science Adv. Council, DEFRA, 2011–16; Cttee for Life, Envmt and Geo-Scis, Science Europe, 2012–15; Marine Sci. Coordination Cttee (Chair: Marine Envmtl Data and Info. Network; Underwater Sound Forum); Wolfson Fellowships Cttee, Royal Soc. (Vice-Chm., 1998–2007, Chm., 2007–09, Global Envmtl Res. Cttee). Treasurer, 1990–93, Chm., 1993–97, Sci. Cttee for Internat. Geosphere-Biosphere Prog.; Chairman: Scientific Steering Cttee, Surface Ocean - Lower Atmosphere Study (SOLAS), 2001–07; Nat. Oceanography Centre Assoc., 2011–; Adv. Bd, Marine Alliance for Sci. and Technol. Scotland, 2011–; Ind. Mem., Inter-Agency Cttee for Marine Sci. and Technol., 2000–08. Chm., Earth System Sci. Advanced Grants Panel, 2008–12, Mem., Consolidator Grants Panel, 2014–, European Res. Council. President: Challenger Soc. for Marine Sci., 2006–08 (Challenger Medal, 2000); Sir Alister Hardy Foundn for Ocean Sci., 2011–18. MAE 2012. *Publications*: Estuarine Chemistry, 1976; Environmental Chemistry, 1980; Man-Made Carbon Dioxide and Climatic Change, 1983; Quimica Ambiental, 1983; Air-Sea Exchange of Gases and Particles, 1983; Power Generation and the Environment, 1990; An Introduction to Environmental Chemistry, 1996, 2nd edn 2004; The Sea Surface and Global Change, 1997; Ocean-Atmosphere Interactions of Gases and Particles, 2014. *Recreations*: reading, music, house renovation. *Address*: 5 Chester Place, Norwich, Norfolk NR2 3DG. *T*: (01603) 623815. *E*: p.liss@uea.ac.uk.

**LISSACK, Richard Antony**; QC 1994; a Recorder, since 1999; a Deputy High Court Judge, since 2010; *b* 7 June 1956; *s* of late Victor Jack Lissack and Antoinette Rosalind Lissack; *m* 1st, 1986, Carolyn Dare Arscott (marr. diss. 2014); three *d* (incl. twins); 2nd, 2014, Susan Jane Stille (*née* Stone). *Educ*: UCS, Hampstead. Called to the Bar, Inner Temple, 1978, Bencher, 2007; an Asst Recorder, 1993–99; QC: Eastern Caribbean, 2002; New York, 2007; NI, 2007; admitted DIFC, Dubai, 2008; Head of Strategic Develt, Outer Temple Chambers, 2008–11; Head of Internat. Law, Riverview Law, 2012–16. Chairman: S & W Wilts Hunt, 1996–2002 (Pres., 2002–19); Disciplinary Cttee, British Horse Trials, 2000–05. Ambassador for ActionAid, 2008–. Mem., Develt Bd, RADA, 2009–. *Recreations*: sailing, climbing, theatre, occasionally falling off thoroughbred horses. *Address*: Fountain Court Chambers, Temple, EC4Y 9DH. *T*: (020) 7583 3335. *Clubs*: Soho House; Rock Sailing.

**LIST, Prof. Christian**, DPhil; FBA 2014; Professor of Philosophy and Political Science, Department of Philosophy, Logic and Scientific Method, London School of Economics and Political Science, since 2018 (Professor of Political Science and Philosophy, Departments of Government and of Philosophy, 2007–18). *Educ*: St Peter's Coll., Oxford (BA Maths and Philosophy 1996; MPhil Politics 1998); Nuffield Coll., Oxford (DPhil Politics 2001). Postdoctoral Res. Fellow, Nuffield Coll., Oxford, 2001–03; Postdoctoral Fellow, ANU, 2003; Lectr, 2002–05, Reader, 2005–07, in Political Sci., LSE. Vis. Prof. of Law, Harvard Law Sch., 2015; Harsanyi Fellow, ANU, 2014; Fellow, Swedish Collegium for Advanced Study, 2011; Visiting Fellow: Univ. of Konstanz, 2005; ANU, 2006, 2007, 2011; Center for Human Values, Princeton Univ., 2009–10; Vis. Schol., MIT, 2000–01. Philip Leverhulme Prize in Philosophy, 2007; (jtly) Social Choice and Welfare Prize, Soc. for Social Choice and Welfare, 2010. *Publications*: (with P. Pettit) Group Agency: the possibility, design and status of corporate agents, 2011; contribs to jls incl. Philosophical Rev., Jl Econ. Theory, Philosophical Perspectives, Episteme, Erkenntnis, Econs and Philosophy, Jl Political Philosophy, Jl Politics, Ethics, Rationality and Society.

**LISTER**; *see* Cunliffe-Lister, family name of Earl of Swinton.

**LISTER OF BURTERSETT**, Baroness *cr* 2011 (Life Peer), of Nottingham in the County of Nottinghamshire; **(Margot) Ruth (Aline) Lister**, CBE 1999; FBA 2009; Professor of Social Policy, Loughborough University, 1994–2010, now Emeritus; *b* 3 May 1949; *d* of Dr Werner Bernard Lister and Daphne (*née* Carter). *Educ*: Univ. of Essex (BA Hons Sociology); Univ. of Sussex (MA Multi-Racial Studies). Child Poverty Action Group: Legal Res. Officer, 1971–75; Asst Dir, 1975–77; Dep. Dir, 1977–79; Dir, 1979–87; Prof. of Applied Social Studies, Univ. of Bradford, 1987–93. Donald Dewar Vis. Prof. of Social Justice, Univ. of Glasgow, 2005–06. Vice-Chair, NCVO, 1991–93. Member: Opsahl Commn, 1992–93; Commn for Social Justice, 1992–94; Commn on Poverty, Participation and Power, 1999–2000; Fabian Commn on Life Chances and Child Poverty, 2004–06; Nat. Equality Panel, 2008–10; Jt Cttee on Human Rights, 2012–15; Bishop of Leicester Commn on Poverty, 2014. Hon. President: CPAG, 2011–; Social Policy Assoc., 2016–. Eleanor Rathbone Meml Lect., Univ. of Leeds, 1989; British Acad. Annual Lect., 2015. Founding Academician, Acad. of Social Scis, 1999. Hon. LLD: Manchester, 1987; Brighton, 2012; Hon. DLitt: Glasgow Caledonian, 2011; Loughborough, 2015; DUniv Essex, 2012; Hon. DSc Lincoln, 2013; Hon. LLD Bath, 2014. Lifetime Achievement Award, Social Policy Assoc., 2010. *Publications*: Supplementary Benefit Rights, 1974; Welfare Benefits, 1981; The Exclusive Society, 1990; Women's Economic Dependency and Social Security, 1992; Citizenship: feminist perspectives, 1997, 2nd edn 2003; Poverty, 2004; (jtly) Gendering Citizenship in Western Europe, 2007; (co-ed) Why Money Matters, 2008; Understanding Theories and Concepts in Social Policy, 2010; pamphlets, articles, and contrib. to many books on poverty, social security and women's citizenship. *Recreations*: walking, music, films, Tai Chi, watching tennis, meditation, pilates. *Address*: House of Lords, SW1A 0PW; 45 Quayside Close, Nottingham NG2 3BP.

**LISTER, Andrew**; *see* Lister, T. A.

**LISTER, Sir Edward Julian Udny-**, Kt 2011; Chief Strategic Advisor to the Prime Minister, since 2019; *b* London, 25 Oct. 1949; *s* of George and Margot Udny-Lister; *m* 1979, Eileen Elizabeth McHugh; one *s* one *d* (and one *s* decd). *Educ*: London Nautical Sch. Trainee, Mather and Platt Ltd, Manchester, 1969–79; Commercial Dir, Mather and Platt Alarms, London, 1979–87; Sales Manager, Britannia Security plc, 1987–90; Major Projects Dir, ADT Security Ltd, 1990–98; Gen. Manager, London ADT Fire and Security plc, 1998–2007; Dir, Govt Relns, Tyco Fire and Security, 2007–11; Chief of Staff and Dep. Mayor Policy and Planning, GLA, 2011–16; Chm., Homes England (formerly Homes and Communities Agency), 2016–19. Director: Localis, 2010–; GLA Hldgs Ltd, 2011–16; GLA Property, 2011–16; London Legacy Develt Corp., 2012–15; London and Partners Ltd, 2015–16 (Chm., 2015–16); Covent Garden Market Authy, 2016–; Ecoworld Mgt and Adv. Services (UK) Ltd, 2016–; Edward Lister Consultants Ltd, 2016–; Chm. and Dir, Old Oak and Park Royal Develt Corp., 2015–17. Non-exec. Dir, FCO, 2017–. Senior Advisor: Regeneration and Investment Orgn, UKTI, 2016; Capital Investment, DIT, 2016–. Mem. Bd, Euralarm, 2009–12. Gov., Mus. of London, 2016–. Mem. (C) Wandsworth LBC, 1976–2011 (Leader, 1992–2011). *Publications*: Local Limits, 1995; LEA's Old and New, 1997. *Recreations*: gardening, walking, travel. *Address*: 10 Downing Street, SW1A 2AA; 51 Seymour Road, SW18 5JB. *E*: edwardlister@btconnect.com.

**LISTER, Geoffrey Richard**, CBE 1994; FCA; FCIB; Joint Vice Chairman, 1996–97, Director, 1988–97, Bradford & Bingley Building Society; *b* 14 May 1937; *s* of Walter and Margaret Lister; *m* 1962, Myrtle Margaret (*née* Cooper); one *s* two *d*. *Educ*: St Bede's Grammar Sch., Bradford. Articled clerk, J. Pearson & Son, 1955–60, qual. chartered accountant, 1960; Computer and Systems Sales, Burroughs Machines Ltd, 1961–63; Audit Man., Thos Gardner & Co., 1963–65; Bradford & Bingley Building Society: Asst Accountant, 1965–67; Computer Man., 1967–70; Chief Accountant, 1970–73; Asst Gen. Man., 1973–75; Dep. Gen. Man., 1975–80; Gen. Man., 1980–84; Dep. Chief Exec., 1984–85; Chief Exec., 1985–95. Director: NHBC, 1992–97; PIA, 1994–95; Anchor Trust, 1997–99. Building Societies' Association: Mem. Council, 1984–97; Dep. Chm., 1992–93; Chm., 1993–94. CCMI. *Recreations*: walking, gardening. *Address*: Harbeck House, Harbeck Drive, Harden, Bingley, W Yorks BD16 1JG. *T*: (01535) 272350. *Clubs*: Carlton; Bradford and Bingley Sports (Bingley, W Yorks).

**LISTER, Jane Sara Anne**; Senior Partner, Foot Anstey Solicitors, 2008–12; *b* Plymouth; *d* of Roger and Maureen Morris; *m* 1982, Paul Lister; two *d*. *Educ*: Bath High Sch.; Plymouth High Sch.; Coll. of Law. Solicitor and NP, 1976–2012; Man. Partner, Foot Anstey Solicitors, 1997–2008. Mem., S Western RHA, 1986–90; Vice-Chm., Plymouth Hosps Trust, 1990–92. Dir, Theatre Royal (Plymouth) Ltd, 1995–2003. Pres., Plymouth Law Soc., 1993–94. Gov., Univ. of Plymouth, 1992–94. *Recreation*: my family. *Address*: c/o Foot Anstey Solicitors, Salt Quay House, 4 North East Quay, Sutton Harbour, Plymouth PL4 0BN. *T*: (01752) 675000, *Fax*: (01752) 675500.

**LISTER, Monica**; *see* Burch, M.

**LISTER, Prof. (Thomas) Andrew**, MD; FRCP, FRCPath, FMedSci, FRCR; Professor of Medical Oncology, 1995–2010, now Emeritus, and Director of Cancer Research UK (formerly Imperial Cancer Research Fund) Medical Oncology Unit, 1995–2010, Barts and The London School of Medicine and Dentistry, Queen Mary (formerly St Bartholomew's and the Royal London School of Medicine and Dentistry, Queen Mary and Westfield College), University of London, at St Bartholomew's Hospital; *b* 15 Dec. 1944; *s* of late John and Eileen Lister; *m* 1969, Sarah Leigh Martin; two *s*. *Educ*: Shrewsbury; St John's Coll., Cambridge (BA Hons 1966; MB BChir 1969); St Bartholomew's Hosp. Med. Sch. FRCP 1982; FRCPath 1994; FRCR 2001. St Bartholomew's Hospital Medical Coll., later St Bartholomew's and the Royal London Sch. of Med. and Dentistry, QMW Coll., Univ. of London: Sen. Lectr and Hon. Consultant Physician, Dept of Med. Oncology, 1977–83; Reader in Clinical Oncology, 1983–87; Prof. of Clinical Oncology, 1987–95; Postgrad. Asst Dean, and Clinical Tutor, Med. Coll. of St Bartholomew's, 1987–93; Dir of Cancer Services and Clinical Haematol., St Bartholomew's Hosp. and Bart's and the London NHS Trust, 1994–2004. Hon. Consultant Physician, Broomfield Hosp., Chelmsford, 1979–2010. FMedSci 2002. Associate Ed., Jl of Clinical Oncology, 2008–. *Publications*: (ed jtly) Leukemia, 6th edn 1996, 7th edn 2002; (ed jtly) The Lymphomas, 1997, 2nd edn 2006; contrib. Jl of Clinical Oncology, Blood, British Jl of Cancer, British Jl of Haematology, Annals of Oncology. *Recreations*: golf, bird watching. *Clubs*: New (Edinburgh); Honourable Company of Edinburgh Golfers.

**LISTER-KAYE, Sir John (Phillip Lister)**, 8th Bt cr 1812, of Grange, Yorks; OBE 2003; naturalist, writer, lecturer; Director of the Aigas Trust, since 1979; b 8 May 1946; s of Sir John Christopher Lister Lister-Kaye, 7th Bt and Audrey Helen (d 1979), d of E. J. Carter; S father, 1982; direct linear descendant of Kaye Btcy cr 1641, of Woodsome (ext 1809); m 1st, 1972, Lady Sorrel Deirdre Bentinck (marr. diss. 1987), d of 11th Earl of Portland; one s two d; 2nd, 1989, Lucinda Anne (formerly Hon. Mrs Evan Baillie), d of Robin Law, Withersfield; one d. Educ: Allhallows School. Naturalist, author, lecturer. Created first field studies centre in Highlands of Scotland, 1970; Founder Director of Scottish conservation charity, the Aigas Trust, 1979; Dir, Aigas Quest Ltd, 1997–. Mem., Internat. Cttee, World Wilderness Foundn, 1983–; Chairman: Scottish Adv. Cttee, RSPB, 1986–92; Cttee for Scotland, NCC, 1989–91; NW Region, NCC for Scotland, 1991–92; NW Region, Scottish Natural Heritage, 1992–96. Pres., Scottish Wildlife Trust, 1996–2001 (Hon. Mem., 2003); Vice-Pres., Council for Protection of Rural Scotland, 1998–; Hon. Vice-Pres., RSPB, 2006–. Hon. FRSGS 2016. DUniv Stirling, 1995; Hon. LLD St Andrews, 2005. Geddes Medal, RSGS, 2016. Publications: The White Island, 1972; Seal Cull, 1979; The Seeing Eye, 1980; One for Sorrow, 1994; Ill Fares The Land, 1995; Song of the Rolling Earth, 2003; Nature's Child, 2004; At the Water's Edge: a personal quest for wildness, 2010; Gods of the Morning, 2014 (Richard Jefferies Prize for Nature Writing, 2015); The Dun Cow Rib, 2017. Recreations: beach-combing, driving hydraulic diggers. Heir: s John Warwick Noel Lister-Kaye, b 10 Dec. 1974. Address: House of Aigas, Beauly, Inverness-shire IV4 7AD. T: (01463) 782729, Fax: (01463) 782097. Club: Caledonian.

**LISTON, Gerald John**, CMG 2002; Regional Director, Central and South Asia, British Council, 2008–10; b 21 April 1949; s of Sidney George Liston and Ivy Mary Liston (née Matthews). Educ: Cheltenham Grammar Sch.; St Catherine's Coll., Oxford (BA Physics, MA); London Sch. of Econs (MSc Econs). Volunteer, VSO, Malaysia, 1970–71; joined British Council, 1972: Secretariat, 1972–73; Asst Regl Dir, Kumasi, Ghana, 1973–75; Asst Rep., Malaysia, 1975–80; Staff Insp., Mgt Services, 1980–84; Director: Office Systems, 1985–88; Corporate IT, 1988–96; UK Ops, 1996–98; Resources, 1999–2003; Dir, Malaysia, 2003–08. Recreations: music, reading, walking, travel, modern prints, growing tropical palms in Malaysia. Address: 19 The Hall, Foxes Dale, SE3 9BE. E: gerry_liston@yahoo.co.uk.

**LISTON, Stephanie Way**; Senior Counsel, Coffey Graham Ltd, 2015; Chief Legal Advisor, Telecommunications Regulatory Commission, Virgin Islands, 2015–17; b Galesburg, Ill, USA, 15 March 1958; d of Thomas S. Liston and Susan Liston (née Way); partner, Genevieve Liston-Oakden; one d. Educ: Colorado Coll. (BA 1980); Univ. of San Diego (JD 1983); Trinity Hall, Cambridge (LLM 1984). Mem., Corp., Banking and Business and Internat Law Sections, 1984–89, Participating Associate, 1989, Fulbright and Jaworski, London, Houston and Washington; admitted: to State Bar of Texas, 1985; to DC Bar, 1988; Sen. Attorney, MCI Communications Corp., 1990–92; Manager, Freshfields, London, 1992–95; admitted as solicitor, England and Wales, 1994; Partner: Baker & McKenzie, London, 1995–99; McDermott, Will & Emery, London, 1999–2003; Partner, 2003–05, Sen. Counsel, 2005–06, WilmerHale LLP, London; Sen. Counsel, Charles Russell Speechlys (formerly Charles Russell LLP), 2011–15. Non-exec. Dir, Ofcom, 2005–08. Business Develt Dir, Fentiman Consultants, 2014–17. Member, Advisory Board: Orga Systems GmbH, 2010–14; Push Technology Ltd, 2015–17. Mem., Equality of Access Bd, BT, 2013–18. Co-founder and Dir, Women in Telecoms and Technol. Member: Law Soc.; Internat Bar Assoc. (Co-Chair, Communications Cttee, 2004–06). MInstC. Freeman, Information Technologists' Co. Publications: Planning your Information Super Highway: Telecommunications Users' Association official reference book, 1995; contribs to jls incl. Global Telecoms Business, IoD Mag., Global Counsel Jl, Legal Week, Computer and Telecommunications Law Rev., The Voice. Address: The Hall, Peasenhall, Suffolk IP17 2HL. T: 07713 786666.

**LISTOWEL, 6th Earl of**, cr 1822 (Ire.); **Francis Michael Hare**; Baron Ennismore (Ire.), 1800; Viscount Ennismore and Listowel (Ire.), 1816; Baron Hare (UK), 1869; b 28 June 1964; s of 5th Earl of Listowel, GCMG, PC and of his 3rd wife, Pamela Reid (née Day); S father, 1997. Educ: Westminster Sch.; Queen Mary and Westfield Coll., London Univ. (BA 1992). Elected Mem., H of L, 1999; Mem., Sub-Cttee F (Home Affairs), Select Cttee on EU, H of L, 2003–07; Treas., All-Party Parly Gp for Children; Vice-Chm., Associate Parly Gp for Children in Care. Trustee, Michael Sieff Foundn. Heir: b Hon. Timothy Patrick Hare, b 23 Feb. 1966.

**LISVANE, Baron** cr 2014 (Life Peer), of Blakemere in the County of Herefordshire and of Lisvane in the City and County of Cardiff; **Robert James Rogers**, KCB 2013; DL; Clerk of the House of Commons, and Chief Executive of the House of Commons Service, 2011–14; b 5 Feb. 1950; o s of late Francis Barry Day Rogers and Jeanne Turner Prichard Rogers (née Prichard-Williams); m 1st, 1973, Sarah Elizabeth Anne Howard (marr. diss. 1978); 2nd, 1981, Rev. Constance Jane Perkins; two d. Educ: Tonbridge Sch. (Scholar); Lincoln Coll., Oxford (Scholar and Judd Exhibitioner; BA Hons 1971; Rhodes Res. Scholar 1971; MA 1978; Hon. Fellow 2012). MoD, 1971–72; House of Commons: an Asst Clerk, 1972; a Sen. Clerk, 1977; a Dep. Principal Clerk, 1985; Clerk: of Select Cttee on Defence, 1983–89; of Private Members' Bills, 1989–92; of Select Cttee on European Legislation, 1993–98; Parly Counsellor to the Pres., Parly Assembly of Council of Europe, 1992–95; Principal Clerk: of Delegated Legislation, 1998–99; of Select Cttees, 1999–2001; of Domestic Cttees, and Sec., H of C Commn, 2001–04; Clerk of the Journals, 2004–05; Principal Clerk of the Table Office, 2005–06; Clerk of Legislation, 2006–09; Clerk Asst and Dir Gen., Chamber and Cttee Services, 2009–11. Member: Select Cttee on Delegated Powers and Regulatory Reform, H of L, 2015–19; Ecclesiastical Jt Cttee, 2015–; Secondary Legislation Scrutiny Cttee, H of L, 2019–; Ind. Mem., Parly and Political Service Honours Cttee, 2014–. Ind. Chm., Standards Cttee, Herefords CC, 2002–11; Ind. Chm., 2002–06, Mem., 2006–12, Standards Cttee, Herefords and Worcs Fire Authy; Ind. Mem., 2002–04, Chm., 2004–08, Selection Panel, Ind. Mem., Standards Cttee, 2007–11, W Mercia Police Authy. Chm., Fabric Adv. Cttee, Hereford Cathedral, 2018– (Acting Chm., 2016–18). Ind. Vice-Pres., LGA, 2016–17. Gov., Skinners' Co. Sch. for Girls, 2005–10. Chm., Hereford Cathedral Perpetual Trust, 2007–09. Fellow, Industry and Parliament Trust, 1981 (Trustee, 2009–11); FLSW 2018. Trustee: History of Parliament, 2009–11, 2017–; Voces 8 Foundn 2017–. Associate: Nat. Sch. of Govt, 2007–12; Global Partners Governance, 2016–. Hon. Bencher, Middle Temple, 2013. Liveryman, Skinners' Co., 2004 (Extra Mem. Court, 2005–07; Master, 2018). DL Herefordshire, 2015. Chief Steward, City of Hereford, 2016. Churchwarden, St Leonard's, Blakemere. Patron, Herefordshire Headway. Parliamentarian of Year, Spectator, 2014. Publications: How Parliament Works (with Rhodri Walters), 5th edn 2004 to 7th edn 2015; Order! Order!: a parliamentary miscellany, 2009; Who Goes Home?: a parliamentary miscellany, 2012; contribs to various books and jls on European and Parly affairs. Recreations: music (church organist), cricket, Real tennis, sailing, shooting, the natural world. Address: Blakemere House, Blakemere, Herefordshire HR2 9JZ. E: lisvane@parliament.uk. Clubs: Travellers, Reform.

**LIT, Avtar**; Chairman and Chief Executive: Litt Corporation, 1989–2014; London Media Company, 2003–14; b 7 April 1950; s of Gurbax Kaur Lit and late Sarwan Singh Lit; m 1995, Anita Loomba; three s two d. Educ: Temple Secondary Sch., Rochester; Collingwood Naval Coll., Chatham. Man. Dir, Cable Vision, 1982–; Chm. and Chief Exec., Sunrise Radio Ltd, 1989–2014; Director: Sunrise TV, 2003–14; Kismat Radio, 2004–14; Punjabi Radio; Time 106.6 FM, 2004–09; Time 107.5 FM, 2004–14; Palm FM; Exeter FM, 2009–11; Sunrise Mobile Ltd, 2015–; Moby Mobile Ltd, 2015–. Former Dir, West London TEC. Hon. PhD Thames Valley, 2003. Recreations: new projects, travelling, fundraising, para-sailing, ski-ing. Club: Reform.

**LITHERLAND, Prof. Albert Edward, (Ted)**, FRS 1974; FRSC 1968; University Professor, 1979–93, now Emeritus, and Professor of Physics, 1966–93, University of Toronto; b 12 March 1928; e s of Albert Litherland and Ethel Clement; m 1956, (Elizabeth) Anne Allin (d 2016); two d. Educ: Wallasey Grammar Sch.; Univ. of Liverpool (BSc, PhD). State Scholar to Liverpool Univ., 1946; Rutherford Memorial Scholar to Atomic Energy of Canada, Chalk River, Canada, 1953; Scientific Officer at Atomic Energy of Canada, 1955–66. Dir, Isotrace Lab., 1982–2009, Guggenheim Fellow, 1986–87, Univ. of Toronto. Hon. DSc Toronto, 1998. Canadian Assoc. of Physicists Gold Medal for Achievement in Physics, 1971; Rutherford Medal and Prize of Inst. of Physics (London), 1974; JARI Silver Medal, Pergamon Press, 1981; Henry Marshall Tory Medal, RSC, 1993. Izaac Walton Killam Memorial Scholarship, 1980. Publications: numerous, in scientific jls. Address: 14 Nicholson Crescent, Minesing, ON L9X 3G8, Canada. T: (647) 5549770. E: ted.litherland@utoronto.ca.

**LITHGOW, Sir William (James)**, 2nd Bt cr 1925, of Ormsary; DL; CEng; General Partner, Ormsary Farmers and Inver Farmers, since 1995; Director, Lithgows Ltd, 1956–2006 (Chairman, 1959–84 and 1988–99); b 10 May 1934; o s of Colonel Sir James Lithgow, 1st Bt of Ormsary, GBE, CB, MC, TD, DL, JP, LLD, and Gwendolyn Amy, d of late John Robinson Harrison of Scalesceugh, Cumberland; S father, 1952; m 1964, Valerie Helen (d 1964), 2nd d of late Denis Scott, CBE and Mrs Laura Scott; m 1967, Mary Claire, (DL Argyll and Bute), d of late Colonel F. M. Hill, CBE and Mrs Hill; two s one d. Educ: Winchester Coll. CEng; FRINA; CCMI (FBIM 1969; CBIM 1980). Chm., Scott Lithgow Drydocks Ltd, 1967–78; Vice-Chm., Scott Lithgow Ltd, 1968–78; Chairman: Western Ferries (Argyll) Ltd, 1972–85; Hunterston Develt Co. Ltd, 1987–2008 (Dir, 1971–2008); Director: Bank of Scotland, 1962–86; Campbeltown Shipyard Ltd, 1970–96; Lithgows Pty Ltd, 1972–2008; Landcatch, 1981–96. Member: Council, Shipbuilding Employers Fedn, 1961–62; British Cttee, Det Norske Veritas, 1966–92; Exec. Cttee, Scottish Council Develt and Industry, 1969–85; Scottish Regional Council of CBI, 1969–76; Clyde Port Authority, 1969–71; Bd, National Ports Council, 1971–78; West Central Scotland Plan Steering Cttee, 1970–74; General Board (Royal Soc. nominee), Nat. Physical Lab., 1963–66; Greenock Dist Hosp. Bd, 1961–66; Scottish Milk Marketing Bd, 1979–83. Chm., Iona Cathedral Trustees Management Bd, 1979–83; Mem. Council, Winston Churchill Meml Trust, 1979–83. Hon. President: Mid Argyll Agricl Soc., 1976–99; Inverclyde and Dist Bn, Boys' Brigade, 1998–2000 (Vice Hon. Pres., 2000–); former Hon. Pres., W Renfrewshire Bn Boys' Brigade. Hon. Pres., Students Assoc., and Mem. Court, Univ. of Strathclyde, 1964–69 (Fellow, 2018). Petitioner in case of Lithgow and others v UK, at Eur. Court of Human Rights, 1986. Member, Queen's Body Guard for Scotland (Royal Company of Archers), 1964. Fellow: Scottish Council, 1988; Bishop Mus., Hawaii, 1969. FRSA 1990. DL Renfrewshire, 1970. Hon. LLD Strathclyde, 1979. Publications: lectures and papers. Recreations: rural life, invention, photography. Heir: s James Frank Lithgow [b 13 June 1970; m 1997, Claire, yr d of Nicholas du Cane Wilkinson; two s one d]. Address: Ormsary House, by Lochgilphead, Argyllshire PA31 8PE. T: (01880) 770252; Drums, Langbank, Renfrewshire PA14 6YH. T: (01475) 540606; (office) Ormsary Estate Office, Ormsary, Lochgilphead, Argyllshire PA31 8PE. T: (01880) 770715. Clubs: Oriental; Western (Glasgow).

**LITHMAN, Nigel Mordecai Lloyd**; QC 1997; **His Honour Judge Nigel Lithman**; a Circuit Judge, since 2017; b 9 March 1952; s of Dr Leslie Henry Lithman, FFARCS, and Ethel Imber Lithman; m Debbie; three step s. Educ: Bancroft's Sch., Woodford Green; Mid Essex Coll., Chelmsford (LLB Hons). Called to the Bar, Inner Temple, 1976, Bencher, 2009; in practice at the Bar, 1976–2017; Asst Recorder, 1996–2000; Recorder, 2000–17. Chm., Criminal Bar Assoc., 2013–14 (Vice Chm., 2012–13). Chm., Essex Bar Mess. Chm., Highgate Synagogue, 2008–. Recreations: fresh air, the arts, public speaking. Club: Garrick.

**LITTLE, Alastair**; see Little, R. A.

**LITTLE, Allan**; see Little, J. A. S.

**LITTLE, Anthony Richard Morrell**; President, World Leading Schools Association Academy, Shanghai, since 2018; b 7 April 1954; s of Edward Little and Rosemary Margaret Little (née Morrell); m 1978, Jennifer Anne Greenwood; one d. Educ: Eton Coll.; Corpus Christi Coll., Cambridge (MA English); Homerton Coll., Cambridge (PGCE). FCollP 1990. Asst Master, Tonbridge Sch., 1977–82; Hd of English and Boarding Housemaster, Brentwood Sch., 1982–89; Headmaster: Chigwell Sch., 1989–96; Oakham Sch., 1996–2002; Eton Coll., 2002–15; Gp Chief Educn Officer, GEMS Educn, 2015–18. Mem. Council, Brunel Univ., 2013–16. Pres., Internat. Boys' Schs Coalition, 2012–15 (Vice Pres., 2010–12); Hon. Pres., Boarding Schs Assoc., 2015–16. Governor: Northwood Coll., 1990–98; St Albans Sch., 1994–2014; Windsor Boys' Sch., 2002–15; Oakham Sch., 2009–; Sevenoaks Sch., 2011–16; London Acad. of Excellence, 2012–15; Holyport Coll., 2013–15; Westminster Sch., 2015–18; Norwich Sch., 2016–. Chairman: Mvumi Sch. Trust, 2008–15; World Leading Schs Assoc., 2011–18; Laurus Trust, 2016–. Mem., Adv. Bd, Royal Prime, 2018–. FRSA 1991. Publications: An Intelligent Person's Guide to Education, 2015; Adolescence: how to survive it, 2019. Recreations: films, theatre, music, Norfolk. Club: Garrick.

**LITTLE, Catherine Joanna**; Director General, Finance, Ministry of Defence, since 2017; b Amersham, 19 May 1980; d of Peter Anthony Little and Percila Alberto Little; m 2014, Ruth Anne Nolan. Educ: Beaconsfield High Sch.; Univ. of Birmingham (BA 2002). Roles from Associate to Sen. Manager, PricewaterhouseCoopers, 2002–13; Dep. Dir and Financial Controller, MoJ, 2013–14; Actg Dir, then Dir, Finance and Performance, Legal Aid Agency, 2014–16; Dir, Finance and Planning, MoJ, 2016–17. Address: Ministry of Defence, Main Building, Whitehall, SW1A 2HB.

**LITTLE, Ian**; see Little, J. MacC.

**LITTLE, (James) Allan (Stuart)**; Special Correspondent, BBC News, 2008–14 and since 2016; Chairman, Edinburgh International Book Festival, since 2015; b Dunragit, Wigtownshire, 11 Oct. 1959; s of Francis Robert Little and Elizabeth Margaret Little (née Clare); m 2006, Sheena Elizabeth McDonald. Educ: Univ. of Edinburgh (MA 1982). BBC: researcher, BBC Scotland, 1983; reporter: BBC Radio, 1984; Today prog., Radio Four, 1988; reporter and correspondent, BBC Foreign News, 1990–95, Iraq, 1990–91, former Yugoslavia, 1991–95; BBC Africa Corresp., Johannesburg, 1995–97 and 2000–01; Moscow Corresp., 1997–99; Presenter, Today prog., Radio Four, 1999–2003; Paris Corresp., 2003–05; World Affairs Corresp., 2005–08, BBC News. Sen. Fellow, Inst. of European Studies, Univ. of Calif, Berkeley. Hon. Fellow in History, Univ. of Edinburgh. Mem., Scotch Malt Whisky Soc., Edinburgh. Publications: (with Laura Silber) Death of Yugoslavia, 1995. Recreations: books, countryside, walking. Address: c/o BBC News World Affairs Unit, 3rd Floor Bridge, New Broadcasting House, W1A 1AA. Club: Frontline.

**LITTLE, John MacCalman, (Ian),** CMG 2003; CBE 1983; Deputy Chairman and Chief Executive, Anderson Strathclyde plc, 1980–88; *b* 23 Feb. 1936; *s* of John Little and Margaret Haddow Little (*née* King); *m* 1962, Irene Pirrie Frame; one *s* one *d*. *Educ*: Marr Coll., Troon. CA 1958; ACMA 1962. Financial positions: Stewarts & Lloyds Ltd, 1961–63; Pressed Steel Fisher Ltd, 1963–69; Anderson Strathclyde plc: Gp Accountant, 1969–70; Divl Financial Dir, 1971–73; Financial Dir, 1973–77; Asst Man. Dir, 1977–80. Dir, Scottish Exhibition Centre Ltd, 1989–96. Member: Council, CBI Scotland, 1980–89 (Chm., 1985–87); Scottish Industrial Adv. Bd, 1981–93; Accounts Commn for Scotland, 1989–97; Eur. Econ. and Social Cttee, 1990–2002 (Chm., Employers' Gp, 2000–02). Treas., Strathaven Rankin Parish Church, 1974–2007. *Recreations*: golf, gardening, bridge. *Address*: 8 Wateryett Loan, Strathaven, Lanarkshire ML10 6EJ. *T*: (01357) 520762. *E*: j.little211@btinternet.com. *Clubs*: Strathaven Golf (Chm., 2000–04); Strathaven Bridge (Capt., 2013–16).

**LITTLE, Maria Milagros;** *see* Delgado, M. M.

**LITTLE, Prof. Richard,** PhD; FBA 2010; Professor of International Politics, Bristol University, 1993–2009, now Emeritus; *b* Shotley Bridge, 26 Oct. 1944; *s* of late Thomas Lowden Little and Marjorie Annie Little; *m* 1981, Christine Stratford. *Educ*: Dame Allan's Boys' Sch., Newcastle upon Tyne; University Coll. London (BSc (Econ)); Lehigh Univ., Penn (MA); Lancaster Univ. (PhD 1973). Lecturer: Lancaster Univ., 1969–76; Open Univ., 1976–80; Lectr, 1980–82, Sen. Lectr, 1982–93, Lancaster Univ. *Publications*: Intervention: external involvement in civil wars, 1975; (ed with M. Smith) Perspectives on World Politics, 1981; (with R. D. McKinlay) Global Problems and World Order, 1986; (jtly) The Logic of Anarchy, 1991; (with B. Buzan) International Systems in World History, 2000; The Balance of Power, 2007. *Address*: 11 Canynge Square, Bristol BS8 3LA. *E*: r.little@bris.ac.uk.
*See also* T. W. A. Little.

**LITTLE, (Robert) Alastair;** chef and delicatessen proprietor; *b* 25 June 1950; *s* of Robert Geoffrey Little and Marion Irving Little; one *s* one *d*; *m* 2000, Sharon Jacob; one *s*. *Educ*: Kirkham Grammar Sch., Lancs; Downing Coll., Cambridge (MA). Chef proprietor: Le Routier, Suffolk, 1976; Simpson's, Putney, 1979; L'Escargot, Soho, 1981; 192, London, 1983; Alastair Little, Soho, 1985–2002; Alastair Little, Lancaster Road, 1995–2002; proprietor: La Cacciata, Orvieto, Italy, 1994; Tavola delicatessen, Westbourne Grove, 2003–17. *Publications*: (with Richard Whittington) Keep it Simple, 1993; (with Richard Whittington) Food of the Sun, 1995; Alastair Little's Italian Kitchen, 1996; Soho Cooking, 1999. *Recreations*: reading, mycology. *Club*: Groucho.

**LITTLE, Tasmin,** OBE 2012; violinist; *b* 13 May 1965; *d* of George Villiers Little and Gillian (*née* Morris); one *s* one *d*. *Educ*: Yehudi Menuhin Sch.; Guildhall Sch. of Music (DipGSM 1986). ARCM 1984. Has performed as soloist in UK, Europe, USA, Scandinavia, S America, Hong Kong, Oman, Zimbabwe and SA. Concerto performances with leading orchestras including: Leipzig Gewandhaus; Berlin Symphony; LSO; Philharmonia; Royal Philharmonic; Hallé; Bournemouth; Royal Liverpool Philharmonic; EC Chamber Orch.; Royal Danish; Stavanger Symphony; NY Philharmonic; Cleveland; Sir Simon Rattle and Berlin Philharmonic; acknowledged interpreter of music of Delius. TV appearances, radio broadcasts; 28 commercial recordings released (incl. Classic BRIT Award for Elgar violin concerto, 2011). Ambassador: Prince's Foundn for Children and the Arts; for Youth Music. Pres., Yehudi Menuhin Sch. 50th Anniv. Appeal, 2013–16. Former Pres., Eur. String Teachers' Assoc. FGS; Hon. RAM 2016. Hon. DLitt Bradford, 1996; Hon. DMus Leicester, 2002; Hon. Dr: Herts; City London. Gold Badge Award for services to music, BASCA, 2009. *Publications*: contrib. Delius Soc. Jl. *Recreations*: theatre, cinema, swimming, cooking, languages. *Address*: c/o Kantor Concert Management & PR, 67 Teignmouth Road, NW2 4EA. *T*: (020) 8208 2480. *W*: www.tasminlittle.org.uk.

**LITTLE, Dr Thomas William Anthony,** CBE 2001; FRSB; Director and Chief Executive, Veterinary Laboratories Agency (formerly Central Veterinary Laboratory), Ministry of Agriculture, Fisheries and Food, 1990–2000; *b* 27 June 1940; *s* of late Thomas Lowden Little and Marjorie Annie Little; *m* 1st, 1963 (marr. diss.); one *s* one *d*; 2nd, 1985, Sally Anne Headlam; two *s*. *Educ*: Dame Allan's Sch., Newcastle upon Tyne; Edinburgh Univ. (BVMS); London Univ. (Dip. Bact., PhD). MRCVS 1963. General veterinary practice, March, Cambs, 1963–66; joined MAFF, 1966; Central Vet. Lab., Weybridge, 1966–82, Sen. Res. Officer 1973–82; Dep. Regl Vet. Officer, 1982–85, Vet. Head of Section, 1985–86, Tolworth; Dep. Dir, Central Vet. Lab., 1986–90. Vice-Pres., BVA, 2000–02. Chair of Govs, Fullbrook Sch., 2006–14. FRSA. *Publications*: contribs to veterinary jls and text books. *Recreation*: outdoor activities. *Address*: 10 Fox Close, Pyrford, Woking, Surrey GU22 8LP.
*See also* R. Little.

**LITTLE-PENGELLY, Emma;** MP (DemU) Belfast South, since 2017; *b* Dungannon, NI; *d* of John Noel Little and Maureen Elizabeth Little (*née* Irwin); *m* 2014, Richard James Pengelly; three step *s*. *Educ*: Markethill High Sch.; Portadown Coll.; Queen's Univ., Belfast (LLB). Called to the Bar, NI, 2003; in practice as barrister, 2003–07; Special Advr to First Minister of NI, 2007–15. Mem. (DemU) NI Assembly, 2015–17; contested (DemU) same seat, 2017. Jun. Minister, Office of First Minister, NI, 2015–16. DUP spokesperson on Equality, Justice, and Internat. Trade, 2017–. Mem., Internat. Trade Cttee, H of C, 2017–. *Recreations*: literature, poetry, politics and history, long walks and occasional runs! *Address*: House of Commons, SW1A 0AA. *E*: emma.littlepengelly.mp@parliament.uk.

**LITTLECHILD, Prof. Stephen Charles;** international consultant on privatisation, competition and regulation, since 1999; Fellow (formerly Senior Research Associate), Judge Business School (formerly Judge Institute of Management Studies), University of Cambridge, since 2004 (Principal Research Fellow, 2000–04); *b* 27 Aug. 1943; *s* of Sidney F. Littlechild and Joyce M. Littlechild (*née* Sharpe); *m* 1974, Kate Crombie (*d* 1982); two *s* one *d*. *Educ*: Wisbech Grammar Sch.; Univ. of Birmingham (BCom); Univ. of Texas (PhD). Temp. Asst Lectr in Ind. Econs, Univ. of Birmingham, 1964–65; Harkness Fellow, Stanford Univ., 1965–66; Northwestern Univ., 1966–68; Univ. of Texas at Austin, 1968–69; ATT Post-doctoral Fellow, UCLA and Northwestern Univ., 1969; Sen. Res. Lectr in Econs, Graduate Centre for Management Studies, Birmingham, 1970–72; Prof. of Applied Econs and Head of Econs, Econometrics, Statistics and Marketing Subject Gp, Aston Management Centre, 1972–75; Prof. of Commerce and Hd of Dept of Industrial Econs and Business Studies, Univ. of Birmingham, 1975–89; Dir Gen., Electricity Supply, 1989–98. Vis. Scholar, Dept of Econs, UCLA, 1975; Vis. Prof., New York, Stanford and Chicago Univs, and Virginia Polytechnic, 1979–80; Hon. Prof., Sch. of Business, Univ. of Birmingham, 1994–2004, now Emeritus Prof. Member: Monopolies and Mergers Commn, 1983–89; Sec. of State for Energy's Adv. Council on R&D, 1987–89; Postal Services Commn, 2006–11. Dist. Fellow, Regulatory Policy Inst., Univ. of Oxford, 2009. Hon. DSc Birmingham, 2001; Hon. DCL UEA, 2004. Zale Award, Stanford Univ., 1999; Pace Catalyst Award, UMS Gp, 2000. *Publications*: Operational Research for Managers, 1977, 2nd edn (with M. F. Shutler) as Operations Research in Management, 1991; The Fallacy of the Mixed Economy, 1978, 2nd edn 1986; Elements of Telecommunications Economics, 1979; Energy Strategies for the UK, 1982; Regulation of British Telecommunications' Profitability, 1983; Economic Regulation of Privatised Water Authorities, 1986; Privatization, Competition and Regulation in the British Electricity Industry, with Implications for Developing Countries, 2000; 200 articles in books and jls. *Recreations*: football, genealogy. *Address*: White House, The Green, Tanworth-in-Arden B94 5AL. *E*: sclittlechild@tanworth.mercianet.co.uk.

**LITTLEJOHN, Bel;** *see* Brown, C. E. M.

**LITTLEJOHN, Doris,** CBE 1998; President, Industrial Tribunals (Scotland), 1991–2000; *b* 19 March 1935; *m* 1958, Robert White Littlejohn (decd); three *d*. *Educ*: Univ. of Glasgow (BL). Chm., Forth Valley Primary Care NHS Trust, until 2004. Mem., Govt Human Genetics Adv. Commn, until 1999. Non-executive Director: Law at Work (Holdings) Ltd, 2002–14; Saga Radio (Glasgow) Ltd, 2004–06. Chm. Ct, Univ. of Stirling, 1999–2007. JP Stirlingshire, 1970–2010. DUniv Stirling, 1993. *Address*: 125 Henderson Street, Bridge of Allan, Stirlingshire FK9 4RQ. *T*: (01786) 832032.

**LITTLER, Richard Mark;** QC 2019; *b* Preston, 13 Aug. 1970; *s* of Gordon Littler and Barbara Littler; *m* 1999, Tessa; one *s* two *d*. *Educ*: Manchester Metropolitan Univ. (LLB 1992). BVC 1993. Called to the Bar, Gray's Inn, 1994; in practice as a barrister, 1994–. *Recreation*: music production and performance (guitarist). *Address*: 6 Park Road, Hale, Altrincham WA15 9NJ. *T*: (0161) 941 5361. *E*: littlerqc@exchangechambers.co.uk.

**LITTLER, Rosalyn Elaine;** *see* Moore, R. E.

**LITTLETON,** family name of **Baron Hatherton**.

**LITTLEWOOD, Dr (David) Timothy (Jan);** Merit Researcher, since 2005, and Head of Life Sciences, since 2013, Natural History Museum; *b* Kumasi, Ghana, 9 June 1961; *s* of David Stuart Littlewood and Adriana Littlewood (*née* van de Poll); *m* 1985, Sita Elaine Dickson; one *s* one *d*. *Educ*: Ernest Bailey Grammar Sch., Matlock; Univ. of Manchester (BSc Zool. 1982; DSc 2004); Univ. of West Indies (PhD Zool. 1988). Res. Associate in Biol Scis, 1988–91; NERC Postdoctoral Res. Asst, Natural Hist. Mus., 1991–94; Res. Fellow, KCL, 1995; Wellcome Sen. Res. Fellow, Natural Hist. Mus., 1996–2005. FLS 1992. C. A. Wright Medal, British Soc. Parasitol., 2009. *Publications*: contrib. articles and book chapters. *Recreations*: music, art, travel, nature. *Address*: Department of Life Sciences, Natural History Museum, Cromwell Road, SW7 5BD. *T*: (020) 7942 5742. *E*: t.littlewood@nhm.ac.uk.

**LITTLEWOOD, Mark James;** Director General, and Ralph Harris Fellow, Institute of Economic Affairs, since 2009; *b* Reading, 28 April 1972; *s* of Kenneth Littlewood and Elizabeth Sheila Littlewood; partner, Angela Harbutt. *Educ*: Forest Sch., Winnersh; Henley Coll., Henley-upon-Thames; Balliol Coll., Oxford (BA Hons 1993); City Univ., London. Hd, Regl Campaigning, European Movement, 1996–99; Campaign Director: Pro-Euro Conservative Party, 1999–2001; Liberty, 2001–04; Hd of Media, Liberal Democrats, 2004–07; Communications Dir, Progressive Vision, 2007–09. Chm., NO2ID, 2005–09. Mem., Bd of Dirs, Big Brother Watch, 2017–. *Recreations*: long suffering season ticket holder of Southampton Football Club, enthusiastic - and acceptably competent - player of Texas hold'em poker, British cult television - especially Doctor Who. *Address*: 2 Lord North Street, SW1P 3LB. *T*: (office) (020) 7799 8900. *E*: mlittlewood@iea.org.uk. *Club*: Reform.

**LITTLEWOOD, Prof. Peter Brent,** PhD; FRS 2007; FInstP; Professor of Physics, James Franck Institute, University of Chicago, since 2011; *b* 18 May 1955; *s* of Horace Victor Littlewood and Edna May Littlewood; *m* 1978, Elizabeth Lamb; one *s* one *d*. *Educ*: St Olave's Sch., Orpington; Trinity Coll., Cambridge (BA 1976); Massachusetts Inst. of Technol. (Kennedy Schol.); Clare Coll., Cambridge (Denman Baynes Student; PhD 1980). FInstP 2007. Bell Laboratories, Murray Hill, New Jersey: Mem., Technical Staff, 1980–97; Hd, Theoretical Physics Res. Dept, 1992–97; Prof. of Physics, 1997–2012, Hd, Dept of Physics, 2005–11, Cavendish Lab., Univ. of Cambridge; Fellow, Trinity Coll., Cambridge, 1997–2012; Associate Lab. Dir for Phys. Scis and Engrg, 2011–14, Dir, 2014–16, Argonne Nat. Lab. Mem., TWAS, 2009. Fellow, APS, 1988. *Publications*: numerous contribs to learned jls on theoretical condensed matter physics. *Recreations*: squash, music. *Address*: James Franck Institute, Gordon Center for Integrative Study, University of Chicago, 929 E 57th Street, Chicago, IL 60637, USA; Cavendish Laboratory, Cambridge University, J. J. Thomson Avenue, Cambridge CB3 0HE.

**LITTLEWOOD, Timothy;** *see* Littlewood, D. T. J.

**LITTON, Andrew;** conductor and pianist; Music Director, New York City Ballet, since 2016; *b* New York, 16 May 1959; *m*; one *c*. *Educ*: Fieldston Sch., NYC; Juilliard Sch. of Music, NYC (piano with Nadia Reisenberg; Bruno Walter Meml Conducting Scholar). Rehearsal pianist, La Scala, Milan, 1980–81; Staff Conductor, 1983–85, Associate Conductor, 1985–86, National SO, Washington; sometime Principal Conductor, Virginia Chamber Orch.; Principal Guest Conductor, 1986–88, Principal Conductor and Artistic Advr, 1988–94, Bournemouth SO, now Conductor Laureate; Music Director: Dallas SO, 1994–2006, now Music Dir Emeritus; Bergen Philharmonic Orch., 2005–15, now Music Dir Laureate; Colorado SO, 2013–16 (Principal Guest Conductor, 2016–); Principal Guest Conductor, Singapore SO, 2017–. Début piano recital, Carnegie Hall, NY, 1979; conducting débuts include: Henry Wood Promenade Concert, 1983; RPO, 1983; Royal Opera House, Covent Garden, 1992. Winner: William Kappell Piano Comp., 1978; BBC/Rupert Foundn Internat. Conductors Comp., 1982. *Address*: c/o MusicVine, 2576 Broadway #239, New York, NY 10025, USA.

**LITTON, John Letablere;** QC 2010; *b* Hong Kong, 20 May 1966; *s* of Henry and Jennifer Litton; *m* 1997, Christine Lowthian; two *s* one *d*. *Educ*: Sedbergh Sch.; Southampton Univ. (LLB). Called to the Bar, Middle Temple, 1989; in practice as barrister, specialising in town and country planning and envmtl and public law; Treasury Counsel, A Panel, 2004–09. *Recreations*: ski-ing, running, food and wine. *Address*: Landmark Chambers, 180 Fleet Street, EC4A 2HG. *T*: (020) 7430 1221, *Fax*: (020) 7421 6060. *E*: Jlitton@landmarkchambers.co.uk.

**LIVELY, Dame Penelope (Margaret),** DBE 2012 (CBE 2002; OBE 1989); writer; *b* 17 March 1933; *d* of Roger Low and Vera Greer; *m* 1957, Jack Lively (*d* 1998); one *s* one *d*. *Educ*: St Anne's Coll., Oxford (BA Mod. History; Hon. Fellow, 2007). Member: Soc. of Authors, 1973–; PEN, 1985–; British Library Bd, 1993–99; Bd, British Council, 1998–2002. FRSL 1985. Hon. Fellow, Swansea Univ., 2002. Hon. DLitt: Tufts, 1992; Warwick, 1998. *Publications*: *children's books*: Astercote, 1970; The Whispering Knights, 1971; The Wild Hunt of Hagworthy, 1971; The Driftway, 1972; The Ghost of Thomas Kempe, 1973 (Carnegie Medal); The House in Norham Gardens, 1974; Going Back, 1975; Boy Without a Name, 1975; A Stitch in Time, 1976 (Whitbread Award); The Stained Glass Window, 1976; Fanny's Sister, 1976; The Voyage of QV66, 1978; Fanny and the Monsters, 1979; Fanny and the Battle of Potter's Piece, 1980; The Revenge of Samuel Stokes, 1981; Fanny and the Monsters (three stories), 1983; Uninvited Ghosts and other stories, 1984; Dragon Trouble, 1984; Debbie and the Little Devil, 1987; A House Inside Out, 1987; The Cat, the Crow and the Banyan Tree, 1994; Staying with Grandpa, 1997; In Search of a Homeland: the story of the Aeneid, 2001; *non-fiction*: The Presence of the Past: an introduction to landscape history, 1976; Oleander, Jacaranda: a childhood perceived, 1994; A House Unlocked (memoir), 2001; Ammonites & Leaping Fish: a life in time, 2013; Life in the Garden, 2017; *fiction*: The Road to Lichfield, 1976; Nothing Missing but the Samovar and other stories, 1978 (Southern Arts Literature Prize); Treasures of Time, 1979 (National Book Award); Judgement Day, 1980; Next to Nature, Art, 1982; Perfect Happiness, 1983; Corruption and other stories, 1984; According to Mark, 1984; Pack of Cards, collected short stories 1978–86, 1986; Moon Tiger, 1987 (Booker Prize); Passing On, 1989; City of the Mind, 1991; Cleopatra's Sister, 1993; Heat Wave, 1996; Beyond the Blue Mountains, 1997; Spiderweb, 1998; (ed with George Szirtes) New Writing 10, 2001; The Photograph, 2003; Making It Up, 2005; Consequences, 2007; Family Album, 2009; How It All Began, 2011; The Purple Swamp Hen and Other Stories, 2016; television and radio scripts. *Recreations*: gardening, landscape history, talking and listening. *Address*: c/o David Higham Associates, 7th Floor, Waverley House, 7–12 Noel Street, W1F 8GQ. *T*: (020) 7434 5900.

**LIVERMAN, Prof. Diana Margaret,** PhD; Regents Professor, School of Geography and Development, University of Arizona, since 2009; *d* of late John Gordon Liverman, CB, OBE, and Peggy Liverman. *Educ*: University Coll. London (BA Geog. 1976); Univ. of Toronto (MA Geog. 1980); Univ. of Calif, LA (PhD Geog. 1984). Asst Prof. of Geog., Univ. of Wisconsin, Madison, 1984–89; Associate Prof. of Geog. and Associate Dir, Earth System Science Center, Penn State Univ., 1990–96; University of Arizona: Prof. of Geog. and Dir, Center for Latin American Studies, 1997–2003; Dean, Coll. of Social and Behavioral Science, 2002; University of Oxford: Prof. of Envmtl Science, 2003–09; Dir, Envmtl Change Inst., 2003–09 (Sen. Res. Fellow, 2009–); Vis. Prof. of Envmtl Policy and Develt, 2009–. Founder's Gold Medal, RGS, 2010; Dist. Scholarship Hons, Assoc. American Geographers, 2011. *Publications*: People and Pixels: linking remote sensing and social science, 1988; (jtly) World Regions in Global Context, 2002, 5th edn 2013; (ed jtly) A Companion to Environmental Geography, 2009; (ed jtly) Global Environmental Change and Food Security, 2010; (jtly) Climate Change: global risks, challenges and decisions, 2011. *Address*: School of Geography and Development, University of Arizona, Tucson, AZ 85721, USA.

**LIVERMORE,** Baron *cr* 2015 (Life Peer), of Rotherhithe in the London Borough of Southwark; **Spencer Elliot Livermore;** partner, Sebastian Dance, *qv*. *Educ*: London Sch. of Econs and Pol Sci. (BSc Econs 1996). Sen. Advr, 1998–2003, Chief Strategic Advr to Chancellor of the Exchequer, 2003–07, HM Treasury; Dir of Strategy to Prime Minister, 2007–08; Sen. Strategist, Saatchi & Saatchi, 2008–09; Dir of Strategy, Blue Rubicon, 2009–14; Founder and Dir, Thirty Six Strategy, 2012–15; Partner and Dir, BritainThinks, 2016–18; Sen. Advr, Teneo Strategy, 2016–. Labour Party: Chief Strategic Advr, Gen. Elections, 2001, 2005; Gen. Election Campaign Dir, 2013–15; Sen. Campaign Strategist, 2015. Mem., Econ. Affairs Cttee, H of L, 2016–. Vis. Sen. Fellow in media and communications, LSE, 2016–; Vis. Res. Fellow, QMUL, 2016–18. *Address*: House of Lords, SW1A 0PW.

**LIVERPOOL, 5th Earl of,** *cr* 1905 (2nd creation); **Edward Peter Bertram Savile Foljambe;** Baron Hawkesbury, 1893; Viscount Hawkesbury, 1905; Joint Chairman, Melbourns Brewery Ltd, since 1975 (Managing Director, 1970–87); Chairman and Managing Director, Rutland Properties Ltd, since 1987 (Director, since 1986); Chairman, Rutland Group, since 1996; *b* (posthumously) 14 Nov. 1944; *s* of Captain Peter George William Savile Foljambe (killed in action, 1944) and of Elizabeth Joan (who *m* 1947, Major Andrew Antony Gibbs, MBE, TD), *d* of late Major Eric Charles Montagu Flint, DSO; *S* great uncle, 1969; *m* 1st, 1970, Lady Juliana Noel (marr. diss. 1994), *e d* of 5th Earl of Gainsborough; two *s*; 2nd, 1995, Marie-Ange (marr. diss. 2001), *e d* of Comte Géraud Michel de Pierredon; 3rd, 2002, Georgina, *yr d* of late Stanley and of Hilda Rubin. *Educ*: Shrewsbury School; Univ. for Foreigners, Perugia. Director: Rutland Properties Ltd, 1985–; Hart Hambleton Plc, 1986–92; J. W. Cameron & Co., 1987–90; Hilstone Developments Ltd, 1987–91; Rutland Management Ltd, 1989–. Elected Mem., H of L, 1999. *Heir*: *s* Viscount Hawkesbury, *qv*. *Address*: House of Lords, SW1A 0PW. *Clubs*: Turf, Pratt's, Royal Air Squadron.

**LIVERPOOL, Archbishop of, (RC),** and Metropolitan of the Northern Province with Suffragan Sees, Hallam, Hexham, Lancaster, Leeds, Middlesbrough and Salford; since 2014; **Most Rev. Malcolm Patrick McMahon,** OP; *b* 14 June 1949; *s* of Patrick McMahon and Sarah McMahon (*née* Watson). *Educ*: St Aloysius Coll., Highgate; Univ. of Manchester Inst. of Sci. and Technol. (BSc); Blackfriars, Oxford; Heythrop Coll., London Univ. (BD; MTh). Pres., Students' Union, UMIST, 1970–71; contracts engr, London Transport, 1971–76; joined Dominican Order, 1976; ordained priest, 1982; Student Chaplain, Leicester Univ., 1984–85; Asst Priest, 1985–89, Prior and Parish Priest, 1989–92, St Dominic's Priory, NW5; Prior Provincial, English Province of Order of Preachers (Dominican Order), 1992–2000; Prior of Blackfriars, Oxford, 2000; Bishop of Nottingham, (RC), 2000–14. John Hopton Fellow, Blackfriars Hall, Oxford, 2001. Chairman: Catholic Educn Service of England and Wales, 2010–; Bishop's Dept of Educn and Formation, 2010–; Catholic Trust for England and Wales, 2010–. *Publications*: contrib. articles and reviews in New Blackfriars, Dominican Ashram and Signum. *Recreations*: walking, golf, reading thrillers. *Address*: Archbishop's House, 19 Salisbury Road, Cressington Park, Liverpool L19 0PH.

**LIVERPOOL, Bishop of,** since 2014; **Rt Rev. Paul Bayes;** *b* Bradford, 2 Nov. 1953; *m* 1976, Katharine Soley; one *s* two *d*. *Educ*: Birmingham Univ. (BA 1975); Queen's Coll., Birmingham. Ordained deacon, 1979, priest, 1980; Asst Curate, St Paul, Cullercoats, 1979–82; Chaplain: Queen Elizabeth Coll., 1982–87; Chelsea Coll. of Art and Design, 1985–87; Team Vicar, High Wycombe Team Ministry, 1987–90; Team Rector, All Saints, High Wycombe, 1990–94; Team Rector, Totton, 1995–2004; Area Dean, Lyndhurst, 2000–04; Nat. Mission and Evangelism Advr, Archbishop's Council, 2004–10; Bishop Suffragan of Hertford, 2010–14. Hon. Canon, Worcester Cathedral, 2007–10. *Publications*: The Table: Knowing Jesus: prayer, friendship, justice, 2019. *Recreations*: walking, reading, conversation and laughter. *Address*: Bishop's Lodge, Woolton Park, Woolton, Liverpool L25 6DT. *T*: (0151) 421 0831.

**LIVERPOOL, Auxiliary Bishop of, (RC);** *see* Williams, Rt Rev. T. A.

**LIVERPOOL, Dean of;** *see* Jones, Very Rev. S. H.

**LIVERPOOL, Archdeacon of;** *see* McGurk, Ven. M. J. P.

**LIVERSIDGE, Pamela Edwards,** OBE 1999; DL; DSc; FREng, FIMechE; Managing Director, Quest Investments Ltd, since 1997; President, Institution of Mechanical Engineers, 1997–98; *b* 23 Dec. 1949; *d* of William H. Humphries and Dorothy Humphries; *m* 1st, 1971, Dr Dale S. Edwards (marr. diss. 1980); 2nd, 1991, Douglas B. Liversidge; two step *s* one step *d*. *Educ*: Aston Univ. (BSc Hons 1971; DSc 1998). CEng 1980; FIMechE 1988; FCGI 1997; FREng 1999. Graduate trainee and project engr, GKN plc, 1971–73; Thornton Precision Forgings: Asst Technical Manager, 1973–78; Prodn Control Manager, 1978–81; Aerofoils Product Manager, 1981–86; Sales and Mkting Dir, 1986–89; Strategic Planning Manager, E Midlands Electricity plc, 1989–93; Man. Dir, Scientific Metal Powders Ltd, 1993–97. Dir, Tool and Steel Products Ltd, 1993–2017; non-executive Director: Rainbow Seed Fund, Spectrum Ltd, 2006–13; Source BioScience plc, 2014–16. Dir, Sheffield TEC, 1997–98; Chm., Sheffield Business Link, 1998–2001; non-exec. Dir, Chesterfield Royal Foundn Trust Hosp., 2006–12. Vis. Prof., Sheffield Univ., 1996–99. Gov., Sheffield Hallam Univ., 1994–2006. Mem. Chapter, Sheffield Cath., 2013–. Trustee and Mem., Exec. Cttee and Council, City and Guilds of London Inst., 2006–11. FRSA 1996. DL, 1999, High Sheriff, 2004–05, S Yorks. Liveryman, Engineers' Co., 1997– (Mem., Ct of Assts, 2000–06); Master, Co. of Cutlers in Hallamshire, 2011–12. A Guardian, Sheffield Assay Office, 2005–. DUniv: UCE, 1998; Sheffield Hallam, 2006; Hon. DEng: Bradford, 2000; Sheffield, 2005; Hon. DSc: Aston, 1998; Huddersfield, 2001. *Recreations*: golf, public speaking at specialist events. *Address*: Nicholas Hall, Thornhill, Bamford, Hope Valley S33 0BR. *T*: (01433) 651475. *E*: liversidge1@btconnect.com.

**LIVESEY, Bernard Joseph Edward;** QC 1990; *b* 21 Feb. 1944; *s* of late Joseph Augustine Livesey and Marie Gabrielle Livesey (*née* Caulfield); *m* 1971, Penelope Jean Harper; two *d*. *Educ*: Cardinal Vaughan Sch., London; Peterhouse, Cambridge (MA, LLB). Called to the Bar, Lincoln's Inn, 1969, Bencher, 1999; a Recorder, 1987–2011; a Dep. High Court Judge, 1998–2012. Fellow, Internat. Acad. of Trial Lawyers, 1993. Mem. Adv. Bd, City Univ., 2001–08. Chm. Council, Friends of Peterhouse, 2002–10. *Address*: Hailsham Chambers, 4 Paper Buildings, Temple, EC4Y 7EX. *T*: (020) 7643 5000.

**LIVESEY, David Anthony,** PhD; Secretary-General, League of European Research Universities, 2005–09; Fellow, Emmanuel College, Cambridge, since 1974; *b* 30 May 1944; *s* of Vincent Livesey and Marie Livesey (*née* Parr); *m* 1967, Sally Anne Vanston; one *s* two *d*. *Educ*: Derby Sch.; Imperial Coll., Univ. of London (ACGI; BSc Eng); Christ's Coll., Cambridge (PhD 1971). University of Cambridge: Res. Officer in Applied Econs, 1969–75; Lectr in Engrg, 1975–91; Sec. Gen. of Faculties, 1992–2003; Cambridge Dir, Cambridge-MIT Inst., 1999–2000; Res. Fellow, Peterhouse, 1971–74; Tutor, 1975–83, Bursar, 1983–91, Vice-Master, 2006–11, Emmanuel Coll. Mem., HM Treasury Cttee on Policy Optimisation, 1976–78. Dir, Cambridge Econometrics Ltd, 1981–84 (Chm., 1982–84). Non-exec. Dir, Addenbrooke's NHS Trust, 1993–99. Trustee: Bedford Charity (Harpur Trust), 2004–09; Citizens Advice, 2005–11; Cambridge and Dist CAB, 2004– (Chm. Trustees, 2004–10); Cambridge City Foodbank, 2011– (Chm. Trustees, 2014–). Chm., Vital Spark Forum, 2005–11. Chm., Friends of Fulbourn Hosp. and the Community, 2009–; Vice-Chair, Walsingham Trust, 2019–. Governor: St Albans RC Primary Sch., 1977–92, 2001–05 (Chm., 1984–92, 2001–05); Henley Mgt Coll., 2005–07; St Mary's Univ. (formerly St Mary's Coll.), Twickenham, 2013–16. DUniv Derby, 2011. *Recreations*: books, swimming, trying to learn Welsh. *Address*: Emmanuel College, Cambridge CB2 3AP. *T*: (01223) 334243.

**LIVESEY, Timothy Peter Nicholas;** Chief Executive, Embrace the Middle East, since 2017; *b* 29 June 1959; *s* of Kevin and Mary Livesey; *m* 1986, Catherine Joan Eaglestone; two *s* three *d*. *Educ*: Stonyhurst Coll.; New Coll., Oxford (Open Schol.; BA 1st Cl. Hons Modern Hist. 1981). 2nd Lieut, Royal Irish Rangers, 1977–78. Asst Registrar and Dep. Sec., UMDS, Guy's and St Thomas' Hosps, 1984–87; Foreign and Commonwealth Office, 1987–2006: First Sec. (Aid), Lagos, 1989–93; Hd, Press and Public Affairs, Paris, 1996–2000; Asst Press Sec., 10 Downing St, 2000–02; on secondment as Principal Advr for Public Affairs to Cardinal Archbp of Westminster, 2002–04; Asst Dir, Information and Strategy, FCO, 2004–06; Archbishop of Canterbury's Sec. for Public Affairs, 2006–10, for Internat. Affairs, 2010–11; Chief of Staff to Leader of the Opposition, 2011–15; Dir, Good Faith Partnership, 2015–16; Hd of Policy and Govt Relns, Oxfam, 2016–17. Pres., Stonyhurst Assoc., 2019. Chair, Internat. Community of the Holy Sepulchre. *Recreations*: family, reading, writing, volunteering.

**LIVESLEY, Prof. Brian,** MD; FRCP; medical historian, since 1973; Professor in the Care of the Elderly, University of London at Imperial College School of Medicine (formerly Charing Cross and Westminster Medical School), 1988–2001, Emeritus Professor, 2003; Consultant Forensic Physician, 2001–11; Member, Harris Manchester College, Oxford, since 2012; *b* 31 Aug. 1936; *s* of late Thomas Clement Livesley and Stella Livesley; *m* 1st, 1963, Beryl Hulme (*d* 1966); one *s*; 2nd, 1969, Valerie Anne Nuttall; two *d*. *Educ*: King George V Grammar Sch., Southport; Leeds Univ. Med. Sch. (MB, ChB 1960); Univ. of London (MD 1979). MRCP 1971, FRCP 1989. DHMSA 1973. Hospital appointments: Leeds Gen. Infirmary, 1961–62; Dist and Univ. Hosps, Leeds, Manchester and Liverpool, 1963–68; Harvey Res. Fellow, KCH, 1969–72; Cons. Physician in Geriatric Medicine, Lambeth, Southwark and Lewisham HA, 1973–87. Asst Dir-Gen., 1993–94, Dir-Gen., 1994–96, St John Ambulance. Clinical Examr in Medicine, Univ. of London, 1980–94 (Sen. Examr, 1990–94); External Examr, Royal Free and UC Med. Sch., 1998–2001; Examiner: for Dip. in Geriatric Medicine, RCP, 1987–93; in Medicine, Soc. of Apothecaries, 1987–93; Mem., United Examng Bd for England and Scotland, 1993–96. NW Thames Regl Advr on Medicine for the Elderly, 1990–2001; Chm., N Thames Regl Trng Commn, 1993–96. Mem., Med. Commn on Accident Prevention, 1984–89 (Chm., Home and Family Safety Commn, 1988–89). NHS Exec. Assessor for NHS R&D Nat. Primary Care Awards, 2002–03. Member: British Acad. Forensic Sci., 2002–08; Assoc. of Forensic Physicians, 2004–06. Lectures: Osler, 1975, Gideon de Laune, 2001 and 2016, Faculty of Hist. of Medicine and Pharmacy, Soc. of Apothecaries; Hunterian, 2003; Med. Soc. of London and Osler Club (jt meeting), 2006; John Keats Meml, Guy's Hosp., 2009. Liveryman, Soc. of Apothecaries, 1980– (Yeoman, 1975; Mem. Ct of Assts, 1990–2016; Master, 2005–06; Immediate Past Master, 2006–07; Past Master Emeritus, 2016; Chm., Futures Cttee, 1999–2004; Chm., Acad. Cttee, 2000–03). JP SE London, 1983–96. KStJ 1994. Master's Medal, Soc. of Apothecaries, 2017. *Publications*: The Dying Keats: a case for euthanasia?, 2009; Quid est veritas, 2017; monographs and investigations on clinical, scientific, historical, educnl and forensic problems of medicine in our ageing soc. *Recreations*: family, Christian culture study at the time of St Paul, encouraging people to think. *Address*: Wolfson House, Yarnells Hill, Oxford OX2 9BG.

**LIVINGSTON,** family name of **Baron Livingston of Parkhead**.

**LIVINGSTON OF PARKHEAD,** Baron *cr* 2013 (Life Peer), of Parkhead in the City of Glasgow; **Ian Paul Livingston;** *b* Glasgow, 1964; *m* Debbie; one *s* one *d*. *Educ*: Univ. of Manchester (BA Econ). ACA 1987. With Arthur Andersen, 1984–87; with Bank of America, 1987–88; with 3i Gp plc, 1988–91; sen. mgt roles, 1991–96, Chief Finance Officer, 1996–2002, Dixons Gp plc; Chief Finance Officer, BT Gp plc, 2002–05; CEO, BT Retail, 2005–08; Chief Exec., BT Gp plc, 2008–13. Non-executive Director: Freeserve plc, 1999–2001; Hilton Gp plc, 2003–06; Celtic plc, 2007–17; Man Gp plc, 2016–Jan. 2020 (Chm., 2016–Jan. 2020); Chm., Dixons Carphone plc, 2017–. Minister of State (Minister for Trade and Investment), BIS and FCO, 2013–15. *Recreation*: football.

**LIVINGSTON, Prof. Andrew Guy,** PhD; FREng; Professor of Chemical Engineering, since 1999, and Director, Barrer Centre, since 2016, Imperial College London; *b* 4 Nov. 1962; *s* of Derek Heathcoat Livingston and Muriel Livingston; *m* 1996, Luisa Freitas dos Santos; one *s* one *d*. *Educ*: Univ. of Canterbury, NZ (BEng Hons Chem. 1984); PhD Cantab 1990; London Sch. of Econs (MSc Econs 1994). Company Chem. Engr, Canterbury Frozen Meat Co., NZ, 1984–86; Cambridge Commonwealth Trust Scholar, Trinity Coll., Cambridge, 1986–89; Imperial College London: Lectr, 1990–96; Reader, 1996–99; Head, Dept of Chem. Engrg, 2008–16. Founder, and Man. Dir, Membrane Extraction Technology Ltd, 1996–. FREng 2006. Cremer and Warner Medal, IChemE,

1997. *Publications:* over 150 articles in learned jls and monographs. *Recreations:* fruit trees, windsurfing. *Address:* c/o Department of Chemical Engineering, Imperial College London, SW7 2AZ. *T:* (020) 7594 5382, *Fax:* (020) 7584 5629. *E:* a.livingston@imperial.ac.uk.

**LIVINGSTON, Dorothy Kirby**; Consultant, Herbert Smith Freehills LLP (formerly Herbert Smith LLP), since 2008; *b* Gosforth, Northumberland, 6 Jan. 1948; *d* of Albert Paulus Livingston and Margaret Alice Livingston (*née* Kirby); *m* 1971, Julian Millar (marr. diss. 2001); two *d*. *Educ:* Central Newcastle High Sch. GDST; St Hugh's Coll., Oxford (BA Juris. 1969; MA); Coll. of Law. Admitted Solicitor, 1982; solicitor advocate, higher courts civil, 2002; Herbert Smith LLP: trainee, 1970; Asst Solicitor, 1972–80; Partner, 1980–2008. Chm., Financial Law Cttee, 1997–; Member: Competition Law Cttee, City of London Law Soc., 2001–; Financial Mkts Law Cttee, 2002–05; Banking Liaison Panel, 2009–. Chm., Cttee on Banking Reforms, 2011–15, Mem., Brexit Taskforce, 2016–, Law Soc. of England and Wales. Dist. Friend, St Hugh's Coll., Oxford, 2019. City of London Law Soc. Lifetime Achievement Award, British Legal Awards, 2013. *Publications:* Competition Law and Practice, 1995; The Competition Act 1998: a practical guide, 2001; contributor: Leasing and Asset Finance, 3rd edn 1997, 4th edn 2003; Business Innovation and the Law: perspectives from intellectual property, labour, competition and corporate law, 2013; Complexity's Embrace: international law implications of Brexit, 2018. *Recreations:* photography, history, art, gardening in Cornwall, family and friends. *Address:* Herbert Smith Freehills LLP, Exchange House, Primrose Street, EC2A 2EG. *T:* (020) 7374 8000, *Fax:* (020) 7374 0888. *E:* dorothy.livingston@hsf.com.

**LIVINGSTON, Prof. David Noel**, CBE 2019 (OBE 2002); PhD; FBA 1995; Professor of Geography and Intellectual History, Queen's University of Belfast, since 1997 (Professor of Geography, 1993–97); *b* 15 March 1953; *s* of Robert Livingston and Winifred (*née* Turkington); *m* 1977, Frances Allyson Haugh; one *s* one *d*. *Educ:* Queen's Univ. of Belfast (BA; PhD; DipEd). Queen's University, Belfast: Curator of Maps, 1984–89; Lectr, 1989–91; Reader, 1991–93; British Acad. Res. Reader, 1999–2001. Visiting Professor: Calvin Coll., Michigan, 1989–90; Univ. of Notre Dame, Indiana, 1995; Regent Coll., Vancouver, 1997, 2000, 2003; Dist. Vis. Prof., Baylor Univ., Texas, 2004–05; Vis. Noted Scholar, Univ. of BC, 1999; Leverhulme Maj. Res. Fellow, 2011–12 and 2013–15. Lectures: Charles Lyell, BAAS, 1994–95; Hettner, Univ. of Heidelberg, 2001; Murrin, Univ. of BC, 2002; Progress in Human Geography, RGS, 2005; Appleton, Univ. of Hull, 2007; Humboldt, UCLA, 2007; Manley, Royal Holloway, Univ. of London, 2007; Gunning, Univ. of Edinburgh, 2009; Gregory, Univ. of Southampton, 2010; Gifford, Univ. of Aberdeen, 2014; Dudleian, Harvard Univ., 2015; Walton, Christians in Science Ireland, 2015. Writer and presenter, The Empire of Climate, BBC Radio 4, 2010. Mem., RAE 2001 Geog. Panel, RAE 2008 Geog. and Envmtl Studies sub-panel, HEFCE. Mem. Ct, Univ. of Ulster, 1996–2000, 2001–04. Pres., Geog. Sect., BAAS, 2005; Vice-Pres., Research, RGS, 2007–10; Mem. Council, British Soc. for History of Sci., 2009–11. MRIA 1998 (Member: Nat. Cttee for Hist. and Philosophy of Sci., 1988–96, for Geography, 1996–2000; Council, 2001–02; Brexit Task Force, 2017–18; Adv. Cttee on Membership, 2018–); FRSA 2001; MAE 2002; FAcSS (AcSS 2002). Corresp. Mem., Internat. Acad. of Hist. of Sci., 2011. Hon. DLitt Aberdeen, 2013. Adm. Back Award, RGS, 1997; Centenary Medal, RSGS, 1998; Templeton Foundn Lect. Award, 1999; Gold Medal in Soc. Scis, RIA, 2008; Founder's Medal, RGS, 2011. *Publications:* Nathaniel Southgate Shaler and the Culture of American Science, 1987; Darwin's Forgotten Defenders, 1987; The Preadamite Theory, 1992; The Geographical Tradition, 1992; (ed jtly) The Behavioural Environment, 1989; (ed jtly) Charles Hodge, What is Darwinism, 1994; (ed jtly) Human Geography: an essential anthology, 1996; (jtly) Them and Us, 1997; (jtly) Ulster-American Religion, 1999; (ed jtly) Evangelicals and Science in Historical Perspective, 1999; (ed jtly) Geography and Enlightenment, 1999; Science, Space and Hermeneutics, 2002; Putting Science in its Place, 2003; (ed jtly) Geography and Revolution, 2005; Adam's Ancestors: race, religion and the politics of human origins, 2008; (ed jtly) Geographies of Science, 2010; (ed jtly) Geographies of Nineteenth Century Science, 2011; (ed jtly) The Sage Handbook of Geographical Knowledge, 2011; Dealing with Darwin: place, politics and rhetoric in religious encounters with evolution, 2014; articles in learned jls. *Recreations:* music, photography. *Address:* Geography, School of Natural and Built Environment, Queen's University of Belfast, Belfast BT7 1NN. *T:* (028) 9097 5145.

**LIVINGSTON, Dawn Lesley**; *see* Warwick, D. L.

**LIVINGSTON, Iain Thomas**, QPM 2015; Chief Constable, Police Service of Scotland, since 2018; *b* Dunfermline, 6 Oct. 1966; *s* of William Livingston and Jean Livingstone (*née* Roy); *m* 1990, Jane Cairney; three *d*. *Educ:* Aberdeen Univ. (LLB Hons 1988); Strathclyde Univ. (DipLP 1989); John Jay Coll., City Univ. of New York (MA Criminal Justice 1998). Solicitor, Maclay Murray and Spens, 1989–92; Police Officer, Lothian and Borders Police, 1992–2013; Dep. Chief Constable, Police Service of Scotland, 2013–18. *Recreations:* sport, running, dog walking, family. *Address:* Police Scotland Headquarters, Tulliallan Castle, Kincardine, Fife FK10 4BE. *T:* (01259) 733111. *E:* ccoffice@scotland.pnn.police.uk.

**LIVINGSTONE, Ian**, CBE 2013 (OBE 2006); Founder and Chairman, The Livingstone Foundation, since 2013; Co-founder and Chairman, The Livingstone Foundation Academies Trust, 2013–15; *b* 29 Dec. 1949; *s* of Neville and Anna Livingstone; *m* 1997, Frances Patricia Fletcher; two *s* two *d*. *Educ:* Stockport Coll. of Technology (HND 1970); Garnett Coll. (Cert Ed 1977). MCIM 1970. Co-founder and Jt Man. Dir, 1975–85, non-exec. Dir, 1985–91, Games Workshop Ltd (launched Dungeons and Dragons game in Europe); writing children's books and designing board games, 1982–93; Dep. Chm., Domark Ltd, 1993–95; Eidos plc, later Eidos Interactive Ltd: Exec. Chm., 1995–2002; Creative Dir, 2002–06; Product Acquisition Dir, 2006–09; Life Pres., 2009–13; Vice Pres., SpecialEffect, 2015–. Non-executive Chair: Bright Things plc, 2004–10; Playdemic Ltd, 2012–17; Playmob Ltd, 2012–; Midoki Ltd, 2013–; Sumo Digital Ltd, 2015–17; Sumo Gp plc, 2017–; The Secret Police, 2015–; Antstream Ltd, 2015–; Flavourworks Ltd, 2015–; non-executive Director: SocialGO plc, 2010–13; Tangentix Ltd, 2011–18; Mediatonic Ltd, 2012–14; Creative England, 2014–; Young Rewired State, 2014–; Creative Industries Fedn, 2015–17; Fusebox Games Ltd, 2018–. Creative Industries advr, British Council, 2003–18; Chair: Skillset Computer Games Skills Council, 2005–12; Video Games Skills Council, 2012–14; Co-Chair, Next Gen Skills Cttee, 2011–15; Mem., Creative Industries Council, 2012–19. Non-executive Director: Entertainment and Leisure Software Publishers Assoc., 2009–10; UK Interactive Entertainment Assoc., 2012–. Creative Industries Champion, BIS, 2014–15. Mem., BAFTA, 2005–. Mem., Raspberry Pi Foundn, 2015–; non-exec. Dir, Aspirations Acads Trust, 2016–; Mem. Bd, Nat. Citizen Service Trust, 2018–. Patron: Creative Skillset, 2014– (non-exec. Dir, 2016–18); Nat. Videogames Foundn, 2016–; GamesAid, 2016– (Trustee, 2010–16). Hon. DTech: Abertay Dundee, 2000; Greenwich, 2014; Hon. DArt Bournemouth, 2011. Special Award, BAFTA, 2002. *Publications:* (with Steve Jackson) Warlock of Firetop Mountain, 1982; Dicing with Dragons, 1982; The Forest of Doom, 1983; City of Thieves, 1983; Deathtrap Dungeon, 1984; Island of the Lizard King, 1984; Caverns of the Snow Witch, 1984; Freeway Fighter, 1985; Temple of Terror, 1985; Trial of Champions, 1986; Crypt of the Sorcerer, 1987; Casket of Souls, 1987; Armies of Death, 1988; Return to Firetop Mountain, 1992; Legend of Zagor, 1993; Darkmoon's Curse, 1995; The Demon Spider, 1995; Mudworm Swamp, 1995; Ghost Road, 1995; Eye of the Dragon, 2005; (with Jamie Thomson) How Big is Your Brain?, 2007; Blood of the Zombies, 2012; The Port of Peril, 2017; (with Shahneila Saaed) Hacking the Curriculum, 2017. *Recreations:* golf, photography, games design, writing, sailing. *E:* ian.livingstone@gmail.com. *W:* www.twitter.com/ian_livingstone. *Clubs:* Roehampton; Wimbledon Park Golf; Barnes Bowling.

**LIVINGSTONE, Ian Lang**, CBE 1998 (OBE 1993); Chairman: Lanarkshire Health Board, 1993–2002 (Member, 1989–2002); Scottish Enterprise Lanarkshire (formerly Lanarkshire Development Agency), 1991–2000; *b* 23 Feb. 1938; *s* of John Lang Livingstone and Margaret Steele Livingstone (*née* Barbour); *m* 1967, Diane Hales; two *s*. *Educ:* Hamilton Acad.; Glasgow Univ. (BL). NP 1960. Qualified as solicitor, 1960; apprentice, Alex L. Wright & Co., Solicitors, 1957–60, legal asst, 1960–62; Ballantyne & Copland, Solicitors: Partner, 1962–70; Sen. Partner, 1970–86; Consultant, 1986–2013; Chm. and Dir, Bowmere Properties Ltd, 1967–; Chairman: House Sales (Motherwell) Ltd, 1978–; New Lanarkshire Ltd, 1993–2014; Kingdom FM Radio Ltd, 2008–18; David Livingstone Centre, Blantyre, 2008–14; NL2017 Ltd, 2013–15. Chm., Scottish Local Authorities Remuneration Cttee, 2005–13; Hon. Pres., Lanarkshire Chamber of Commerce, 2006–13. Chm., Motherwell Coll. Bd, 1991–98. Chm., Motherwell FC, 1975–88. DL Lanarkshire, 2008. Hon. Dr West of Scotland, 2008. *Recreations:* football, walking, travelling, music. *Address:* Roath Park, 223 Manse Road, Motherwell, Strathclyde ML1 2PY. *T:* (01698) 253750.

**LIVINGSTONE, Kenneth Robert, (Ken)**; writer and commentator; Mayor of London, 2000–08 (Ind 2000–04, Lab 2004–08); *b* 17 June 1945; *s* of late Robert Moffat Livingstone and Ethel Ada Livingstone. *Educ:* Tulse Hill Comprehensive Sch.; Philippa Fawcett Coll. of Educn (Teacher's Cert.). Technician, Chester Beatty Cancer Res. Inst., 1962–70. Joined Labour Party, 1969; Reg. Exec., Greater London Lab. Party, 1974–86; Lambeth Borough Council: Councillor, 1971–78; Vice-Chm., Housing Cttee, 1971–73; Camden Borough Council: Councillor, 1978–82; Chm., Housing Cttee, 1978–80; Greater London Council: Mem. for Norwood, 1973–77, for Hackney N, 1977–81, for Paddington, 1981–86; Lab. Transport spokesman, 1980–81; Leader of Council and of Lab. Gp, 1981–86. Mem., NEC, Labour Party, 1987–89, 1997–98, 2010–16. Contested (Lab) Hampstead, 1979. MP (Lab) Brent East, 1987–2001. Mem., NI Select Cttee, 1997–99. London Mayoral Candidate, 2012. Mem. Council, Zoological Soc. of London, 1994–2000 (Vice-Pres., 1996–98). FZS. *Publications:* If voting changed anything they'd abolish it, 1987; Livingstone's Labour, 1989; You Can't Say That, 2011; Being Red, 2016; Livingstone's London, 2019. *Recreations:* cinema, science fiction, thinking while gardening, natural history. *E:* emmabeal@btinternet.com.

**LIVINGSTONE, Marilyn**, MBE 2018; Chief Executive, Adam Smith Global Foundation; *b* 30 Sept. 1952; *m* Peter W. Livingstone; two *d*. *Educ:* Viewforth Secondary Sch.; Fife Coll. Fife College of Further and Higher Education: Youth Trng Manager; Hd, Admin and Consumer Studies; Hd, Business Sch., until 1999. Mem. (Lab Co-op) Kirkcaldy, Scottish Parlt, 1999–2011; contested (Lab) same seat, 2011. Former Member: Kirkcaldy DC; Fife Council. Chm., Scottish PLP, 1999–2003; Ministerial Parly Aid to the First Minister, 2003–07.

**LIVINGSTONE, Michael William**; Strategic Director of Children's Services, Manchester City Council, 2011–14; *b* Hazel Grove, Stockport, 23 Oct. 1961; *s* of Richard and Mary Livingstone; *m* 1996, Linda Ann Smith. *Educ:* Hazel Grove High Sch.; Manchester Univ. (BA Dist.); Manchester Metropolitan Univ. (CQSW 1985; Postgrad. DipSW; MA Dist.). Social Worker: Sefton MBC, 1985–86; Trafford MBC, 1986–91; Principal Manager, Social Services, Oldham MBC, 1991–99; Asst Dir, Children's Services, Wirral MBC, 1999–2001; Social Services Inspectorate, 2001–07; Asst Dir, Children's Services, 2007–10, Dep. Dir, Children's Services, 2011–14, Manchester CC. Non-exec. Dir, Pennine Care NHS Foundn Trust, 2015–. *Recreations:* philately, very keen Manchester United fan.

**LIVINGSTONE, Prof. Sonia Mary**, OBE 2014; DPhil; FBA 2018; Professor of Social Psychology, Department of Media and Communications, London School of Economics and Political Science, since 2003; *b* Adelaide, Australia, 30 April 1960; *d* of Prof. Rodney Simon Livingstone and Prof. Angela Mary Livingstone; partner, Prof. Peter Lunt; one *s* one *d*. *Educ:* University Coll. London (BSc Hons Psychol.); Wolfson Coll., Oxford (DPhil 1987). Lectr, Dept of Human Scis, Brunel Univ., 1987–88; Open Prize Res. Fellow, Nuffield Coll., Oxford, 1988–89; Lectr, Inst. of Social and Applied Psychol., Univ. of Kent, 1990; Lectr, 1990–97, Sen. Lectr, 1997–99, Prof., 1999–2003, Dept of Social Psychol., LSE. Guest Prof., Media, Film and Television, Copenhagen Univ., 1996; Bonnier Prof. of Journalism, Media and Communication, Stockholm Univ., 1998; Visiting Professor: Speech Communication/Inst. of Communication Res., Univ. of Illinois-Urbana-Champaign, 2000; Dept of Communication, Univ. of Bergen, 2002; Libera Univ. di Lingue e Communicazione, Milan, 2004; Univ. Panthéon Assas, Paris II, 2009; Guest Prof., InterMedia, Univ. of Oslo, 2008; Vis. Researcher, Microsoft Res. New England, Cambridge, Mass, 2013; Faculty Fellow, Berkman Center for Internet and Society, Harvard Univ., 2013–14. Member: Res. Priorities Bd, ESRC, 1996–98; Bd, Internet Watch Foundn, 2001–07 (Vice Chm., 2004–06); Bd of Dirs, Voice of the Listener and Viewer, 2006–09; Exec. Bd, UK Council for Child Internet Safety, 2008–. Hon. Dr: Erasmus, Rotterdam, 2008; Montreal, 2014; Panthéon Assas (Paris II), 2016. FRSA. *Publications:* Making Sense of Television: the psychology of audience interpretation, 1990, 2nd edn 1998 (trans. Chinese 2006); (with P. Lunt) Mass Consumption and Personal Identity: everyday economic experience, 1992; (with P. Lunt) Talk on Television: audience participation and public debate, 1994; (ed with M. Bovill) Children and their Changing Media Environment: a European comparative study, 2001; Young People and New Media: childhood and the changing media environment, 2002; (ed with L. Lievrouw) Handbook of New Media: social shaping and social consequences, 2002, rev. and updated student edn 2006 (trans. Italian 2007, Chinese 2008); (ed) Audiences and Publics: when cultural engagement matters for the public sphere, 2005; (jtly) Harm and Offence in Media Content: a review of the empirical literature, 2006, 2nd edn 2009; Lo Spettatore Intraprendente: analisi del pubblico televisivo, trans. D. Cardini, 2006; (jtly) Media Consumption and Public Engagement: beyond the presumption of attention, 2007, 2nd edn 2010; (with K. Drotner) The International Handbook of Children, Media and Culture, 2008; Children and the Internet: great expectations, challenging realities, 2009 (trans. Italian 2010, Chinese 2013); (ed with L. Lievrouw) New Media: Sage benchmarks in communication, vols 1–4, 2009; (ed with L. Haddon) Kids Online: opportunities and risks for children, 2009; (with P. Lunt) Media Regulation: governance and the interests of citizens and consumers, 2012; (ed jtly) Children, Risk and Safety Online: research and policy challenges in comparative perspective, 2012; (ed with R. Butsch) Meanings of Audiences: comparative discourses, 2013; (ed jtly) Digital Technologies in the Lives of Young People, 2014; (with J. Sefton-Green) The Class: living and learning in the digital age, 2016; contrib. articles to peer-reviewed acad. jls. *Recreations:* walking, baking, gardening, listening to music, yoga. *Address:* London School of Economics and Political Science, Houghton Street, WC2A 2AE. *E:* s.livingstone@lse.ac.uk. *W:* www.sonialivingstone.net.

**LIZIERI, Prof. Colin Martyn**, PhD; Grosvenor Professor of Real Estate Finance, since 2009, and Head, Department of Land Economy, since 2016, University of Cambridge; Fellow of Pembroke College, Cambridge, since 2009; *b* Beverley, Yorks, 27 July 1955; *s* of

Ronald Lizieri and Marjorie Lizieri (*née* Maher); one *s*. *Educ:* Magdalen College Sch., Oxford; St Edmund Hall, Oxford (BA Hons Geog. 1976); London Sch. of Econs (PhD 1982). Res./Proj. Officer, London Bor. of Hammersmith and Fulham, 1979–82; Computer Liaison Officer, Royal Bor. of Kensington and Chelsea, 1982–85; Lectr, Sch. of Built Envmt, South Bank Poly., 1985–88; Reader in Internat. Real Estate Mkts, City Univ. Business Sch., 1988–95; Sen. Lectr, 1996–99, Prof. of Real Estate Finance, 1999–2009, Univ. of Reading. Vis. Prof., Univ. of Toronto, 1995. Weimer Fellow, Homer Hoyt Inst., 2012. Chm., Industry Council on Future of Real Estate and Urbanisation, WEF, 2014–. Consultant, GHK Internat., 1996–2012; Manager, Estate Mgt Develt Fund, 2016–. Dir, Cambridge Land Economy Adv. Bd, 2014–. Mem., Academic Adv. Panel, Acadametrics, 2009–14; non-exec. Dir, Howard Day Associates, 2007–13. FRGS 1995. Hon. FRICS 2004. David Ricardo Medal, American Real Estate Soc., 2014. *Publications:* The Economics of Commercial Property Markets, 1998; Towers of Capital, 2009; over 100 book chapters and articles in leading academic jls. *Recreations:* cycling (Nat. Veterans 30m Team Champion with Cambridge Cycling Club, 2017, 2018), music, football, hurricanes. *Address:* c/o Pembroke College, Cambridge CB2 1RF.

**LLANDAFF, Bishop of,** since 2017; **Rt Rev. June Osborne;** *b* 10 June 1953; *d* of Wilfred and Enid Osborne; *m* 1984, Paul Anthony Goulding, *qv*; one *s* one *d*. *Educ:* Manchester Univ. (BA Hons (Econ.) 1974); St John's Coll., Nottingham; Wycliffe Hall, Oxford; Birmingham Univ. (MPhil 1993). Lay Asst, St Aldates, Oxford, 1975–77; ordained dss, 1980, deacon, 1987, priest, 1994; Curate, St Martin in the Bull Ring, and Chaplain, Birmingham Children's Hosp., 1980–84; Minister-in-charge, St Paul with St Mark, Old Ford, 1984–95; Canon Treas., Salisbury Cathedral, 1995–2004; Dean of Salisbury, 2004–17. Mem., Dean Selection Panel, 2009–17. DL Wilts, 2006–17. *Recreations:* supporting Manchester City FC and Cardiff City, friendships. *Address:* Llys Esgob, The Cathedral Green, Llandaff, Cardiff CF5 2YE. *T:* (029) 2056 2400. *E:* bishop.llandaff@churchinwales.org.uk.

**LLANDAFF, Assistant Bishop of;** *no new appointment at time of going to press.*

**LLANDAFF, Dean of;** *see* Capon, Very Rev. G. H.

**LLANDAFF, Archdeacon of;** *see* Jackson, Ven. F. A.

**LLANWARNE, Trevor John,** CB 2013; Government Actuary, 2008–14; consultant on strategic risk, since 2014; *b* Farnborough, Hants, 31 Dec. 1952; *s* of Douglas and Margaret Llanwarne; *m* 1984, Margaret Kirstine Hansen (*d* 2017); two *s* one *d*. *Educ:* Forest Fields Grammar Sch., Nottingham; Christ Church, Oxford (MA). FIA 1979; FSS 2016. Actuarial trainee and actuary, Sun Life, 1974–84; Hd, SSAS, Pointon York Ltd, 1984–88; with Price Waterhouse, later PricewaterhouseCoopers, 1988–2008: Partner, 1992–2008, latterly Chief Actuary, Pensions and Leader, Pensions Practice. Member: Govt heads of analysis, 2011–14; Govt steering gps on demography, 2013–14, on quality assurance on modelling, 2013, on risk improvement, 2016. Mem. Council, Inst. of Actuaries, subseq. Inst. and Faculty of Actuaries, 2009–13; Life Mem., Inst. of Risk Mgt. Gov., PPI, 2009–. FIRM 2014. Trustee, Internat. Longevity Centre UK, 2015–; Chm. and Trustee, Rye Art Gall., 2017–. Treas., Royal Statistical Soc., 2016–. *Publications:* 2005 Quinquennial Review of the National Insurance Fund, 2010; 2010 Quinquennial Review of the National Insurance Fund, 2014; Strategic Risk for Public Sector Bodies, 2015; Greater Savings for Retirement, 2015. *Recreations:* family history, bridge, renovated important Tudor house in Rye, researching the house history on possibility of visitation by King Henry VII. *Address:* 19 Kippington Road, Sevenoaks, Kent TN13 2LJ. *T:* (01732) 460709. *E:* trevor@llanwarne.com.

**LLEWELLIN, Rt Rev. (John) Richard (Allan);** Head of the Archbishop of Canterbury's staff (with title of Bishop at Lambeth), 1999–2003; an Hon. Assistant Bishop, Diocese of Canterbury, since 2008; *b* 30 Sept. 1938; *s* of John Clarence Llewellin and Margaret Gwenllian Llewellin; *m* 1965, Jennifer Sally (*née* Hussey); one *s* two *d*. *Educ:* Clifton College, Bristol; Westcott House and Fitzwilliam Coll., Cambridge (MA). Solicitor, 1960. Ordained deacon, 1964; priest, 1965; Curate at Radlett, Herts, 1964–68; Curate at Johannesburg Cathedral, 1968–71; Vicar of Waltham Cross, 1971–79; Rector of Harpenden, 1979–85; Suffragan Bishop: of St Germans, 1985–92; of Dover, 1992–99. Chm., USPG, 1994–97. *Recreations:* sailing, DIY. *Address:* 15a The Precincts, Canterbury, Kent CT1 2EL. *T:* (01227) 764645. *E:* rllewellin@clara.co.uk.

**LLEWELLIN, Magnus Clenyg Crush;** Editor, Scotland, The Times, since 2016; *b* Oswestry, Shropshire, 6 Aug. 1965; *s* of Phil Llewellin and Beth Llewellin; *m* 2004, Katie McAuley; two *d*. *Educ:* Oswestry Boys' High Sch.; St David's University Coll., Lampeter, Univ. of Wales (BA Hons Hist. 1986); Watford Coll. (Post Grad. Dip. Advertising 1987). Jun. account exec., Gannaway, 1987; Reporter, Ellesmere Port Pioneer, 1988–89; Dep. News Editor, Chester Chronicle, 1989–90; Newsdesk, Edinburgh Evening News, 1990–95; Asst News Editor, Daily Record, 1995–98; News Editor, The Scotsman, 1998–2000; Asst Editor, Business AM, 2000–02; The Herald: News Editor, 2002–06; Sen. Asst Editor, 2006–11; Dep. Editor, Glasgow, 2011–12; Editor, 2012–16; Ed.-in-Chief, Herald and Times Gp, 2015–16. *Recreations:* family, friends, travel, cinema, walking. *Address:* The Times, The News Building, 1 London Bridge Street, SE1 9GF.

**LLEWELLYN,** family name of **Baron Llewellyn of Steep.**

**LLEWELLYN OF STEEP,** Baron *cr* 2016 (Life Peer), of Steep in the County of Hampshire; **Edward David Gerard Llewellyn,** OBE 2006 (MBE 1997); PC 2015; Ambassador to France, since 2016; *b* 23 Sept. 1965; *s* of Comdr David Llewellyn, RN (Retd) and Margaret Llewellyn (*née* Chapman); *m* 2010, Dr Anne Charbord; one *s* two *d*. *Educ:* Eton Coll.; New Coll., Oxford (BA Hons Modern Langs). Cons. Res. Dept, 1988–92 (on secondment as Private Sec. to Margaret Thatcher, 1990–91); Personal Advr to Gov. of Hong Kong, 1992–97; Office of High Rep. for Bosnia and Herzegovina, 1997–99; Cabinet of Eur. Comr for Ext. Relns, 1999–2002; Chief of Staff: to High Rep. for Bosnia and Herzegovina, 2002–05; to Leader of Opposition, 2005–10; COS to the Prime Minister, 2010–16. *Recreation:* ski-ing. *Address:* British Embassy, 35 Rue du Faubourg St Honore, 75008 Paris, France.

**LLEWELLYN, Anthony John S.;** *see* Seys Llewellyn.

**LLEWELLYN, Bryan Henry;** Director, Granada Travel PLC, 1989–92; *s* of Nora and Charles Llewellyn; *m* 1983, Joanna (*née* Campbell) (marr. diss. 2012); two *s*. *Educ:* Charterhouse; Clare Coll., Cambridge (BA). Commissioned, The Queen's, 1946. Research Asst, Dept of Estate Management, Cambridge, 1954; joined Fisons Ltd, 1955; Marketing Manager, Greaves & Thomas Ltd, 1960; Regional Marketing Controller, Thomson Regional Newspapers Ltd, 1962; Marketing Dir, TRN Ltd, 1966; Managing Director: Thomson Holidays Ltd, 1969; Thomson Travel Ltd, 1972 (Chm., 1977–78); Exec. Dir, Thomson Organisation Ltd, 1972–80; Man. Dir and Chief Exec., Thomson Publications Ltd, 1977–80; Dir, Burlington Magazine, 1983–2013; Man. Dir, The Kitchenware Merchants Ltd, 1985–88. Non-exec. Dir, Orion Insurance Ltd, 1976–92.

**LLEWELLYN, Dr David George,** FIAgrE, FRAgS; Vice-Chancellor, Harper Adams University (formerly Principal, Harper Adams University College), since 2009; *b* Cardiff, 14 Dec. 1960; *s* of George Llewellyn and Heather Llewellyn (now Fountain); *m* 1984, Noelle Winterburn; one *d*. *Educ:* University Coll. London (BSc); Birkbeck Coll., Univ. of London (MSc); Univ. of Bath (DBA). FIAgrE 2009; FRAgS 2018. Admin. Asst and Asst Sec., 1983–88, Asst Registrar, 1988–90, Queen Mary Coll., Univ. of London; Sch. Admin. Officer, KCL, 1990–94; Sec., Inst. of Psychiatry, 1994–98; Dir, Corporate Affairs, Harper Adams Agricl Coll., later UC, 1998–2009. Mem., RASE, 2009–. Mem. Bd, The Marches LEP, 2014–. Chm., GuildHE, 2018–. Chm. Govs, Newport Girls High Sch., 2008–16. *Recreations:* Antarctic book collecting, family, music, coastal and mountain walking. *Address:* Harper Adams University, Newport, Shropshire TF10 8NB. *T:* (01952) 815240, *Fax:* (01952) 814783. *E:* dllewellyn@harper-adams.ac.uk. *Club:* Farmers'.

**LLEWELLYN, Prof. David Thomas;** Professor of Money and Banking, Loughborough University, 1976, now Emeritus; *b* 3 March 1943; *s* of Alfred George Llewellyn and Elsie Alexandria Frith; *m* 1970, Wendy Elizabeth James; two *s*. *Educ:* William Ellis Grammar Sch., London; London Sch. of Econs and Pol Science (BSc Econ). FCIB. Economist: Unilever NV, Rotterdam, 1964; HM Treasury, London, 1965–67; Lectr in Econs, Nottingham Univ., 1967–73; Economist, IMF, Washington, 1973–76; Chm., Banking Centre, Loughborough Univ., 1976–2004. Public Interest Dir, PIA, 1994–2001; Dir, PIA Ombudsman Bureau Ltd, 1994–2001. Visiting Professor: City Univ. Business Sch., 2001–; Cass Business Sch., London, 2003–; Swiss Finance Inst. (formerly Swiss Banking Sch.), Zurich, 2003, 2006–09; IESE Business Sch., Madrid, 2006–07; Vienna Univ. of Econs and Admin, 2007–; Res. Assoc., Centre for European Policy Studies, Brussels, 2009–; Associate Mem., Kellogg Coll., Oxford, 2010–. Consultant Economist to: Harlow Butler Ueda, 1981–99; Garban Intercapital plc; ICAP plc, 2004–; Member: London Bd of Dirs, Halifax Building Soc., 1988–93; Expert Panel on Banking, Bank Indonesia, 2004–; Credit Risk Consortium, Harland Financial Solutions, 2009–; at various times Consultant to World Bank, Building Societies Assoc., bldg socs, banks, central banks and regulatory authorities in UK and overseas. Member: Bank of England Panel of Academic Consultants; Banking Competition Task Gp, S Africa, 2003–04; Internat. Adv. Bd, Italian Bankers' Assoc., 1994–; Exec. Bd, European Financial Management Assoc., 1994–; Internat. Adv. Bd, NCR Financial Solutions (formerly NCR Financial Systems) Gp, 1997–2001; Financial Services Panel, DTI Technology Foresight Prog., 1997–2000; Consultative Gp, IMF, 2004–; Academic Bd, Internat. Centre for Financial Regulation, 2010–12; Scientific Cttee, Eur. Assoc. of Cooperative Banks, 2010–; Banking Stakeholder Gp, Eur. Banking Authy, 2011– (Vice Chm., 2011–13; Chm., 2013–). Special Advr, H of C and H of L Jt Cttee on Financial Services and Markets, 1999–. Pres., Société Universitaire Européenne Recherches Financières, 2000–08 (Mem., Council of Mgt, 1998–; Hon. Mem., 2019). TV and radio broadcasts on financial issues. Regular presentations at internat. conferences on finance and regulation incl. London, Frankfurt, Madrid, Paris, Vienna, Brussels and Oxford, and at in-house conferences at financial instns and regulatory agencies in various countries. Member of Editorial Board: Jl of Financial Regulation and Compliance, 2002–; Bombay Technology, 2004–; Jl of Bank Regulating, 2005–; Guest Ed., Special Issue, Jl Financial Regulation and Compliance, 2017. FRSA. DUniv Loughborough, 2017. *Publications:* International Financial Integration, 1980; Framework of UK Monetary Policy, 1984; The Evolution of the British Financial System, 1985; Prudential Regulation and Supervision of Financial Institutions, 1986; Reflections on Money, 1989; (ed) Recent Developments in International Monetary Economics, 1991; (ed) Surveys in Monetary Economics, vols 1 and 2, 1991; Competition or Credit Controls?, 1991; (jtly) Financial Regulations: why, how and where now?, 1998; Economic Rationale of Financial Regulation, 1998; The New Economics of Banking, 1999; Competitive Strategy in the New Economics of Retail Financial Services, 2002; (ed jtly) Financial Innovation in Retail and Corporate Banking, 2009; (jtly) Investigating Diversity in the Banking Sector in Europe, 2010; The Global Banking Crisis and the Post-Crisis Banking and Regulatory Scenario, 2011; New Paradigms in Banking, Financial Markets and Regulation, 2012; (contrib.) Stability of the Financial System, 2013; Fifty Years of Bank Business Models, 2013; (jtly) Business Models in European Banking: a pre- and post-crisis screening, 2015; (contrib.) Europe's New Supervisory Toolkit, 2015; (contrib.) Oxford Handbook of Mutual, Co-operative and Co-Owned Business, 2017; (contrib.) Oxford Handbook of Central Banks, 2019; articles in academic and professional jls, incl. Financial World, and books on monetary policy and instns, on internat. finance, and regulation of the financial system. *Recreations:* DIY, culinary arts, travel, boating. *Address:* 8 Landmere Lane, Ruddington, Notts NG11 6ND. *T:* (0115) 921 6071; School of Business and Economics, Loughborough University, Loughborough, Leics LE11 3TU. *T:* (01509) 222700. *E:* D.T.Llewellyn@lboro.ac.uk; Hameau des Pins, Les Hauts du Golf, Villa 10, 8760 chemin de la Tire, 06250 Mougins, France.

**LLEWELLYN, John,** DPhil; Partner, Llewellyn Consulting, since 2009; *b* 1944; *s* of Sir (Frederick) John Llewellyn and Joyce Llewellyn; *m* 1990, Ruth Mariette; three *s* two *d*. *Educ:* Christchurch Boys' High Sch.; Scots Coll., Wellington; Victoria Univ. of Wellington (BA Hons 1st Cl. Econs 1966); Trinity Coll., Oxford (DPhil Econs 1970). Res. Officer, Dept of Applied Econs, 1970–74, Asst Dir of Res., Fac. of Econs, 1974–77, Univ. of Cambridge; Fellow, St John's Coll., Cambridge, 1972–77; OECD: Hd, Econ. Prospects Div., 1978–86; Dep. Dir for Social Affairs, Manpower and Educn, 1986–89; Hd, Private Office of Sec.-Gen., 1989–94; Lehman Brothers: Chief Economist Europe, 1995–96; Global Chief Economist, 1996–2006; Sen. Economic Policy Advr, Lehman Brothers, 2006–08. Dir, Genesis Emerging Markets Fund, 2009–; Member, Advisory Board: Ondra Partners LLP, 2009–; Osmosis Hldgs Ltd, 2013–. Mem., President of EC's Gp of Econ. Analysis, 2000–04; Advr, HM Treasury, 2009–12; Mem., Adv. Panel, Office for Budget Responsibility, 2011–. Member of Council: Chatham House, 2007–13; UK Soc. of Business Economists, 2006–09; Nat. Inst. of Economic and Social Res., 2010–. Member, Editorial Board: OECD Economic Studies, 1983–89; Economic Modelling, 1983–93. *Publications:* (jtly) Economic Forecasting and Policy: the international dimension, 1985; (ed jtly) Economic Policies for the 1990s, 1991; reports, and articles in learned jls. *Recreations:* motorsport, writing, photography, music. *E:* john.llewellyn@llewellyn-consulting.com. *Clubs:* Athenæum, Royal Automobile.

**LLEWELLYN, Rev. Richard Morgan,** CB 1992; OBE 1979 (MBE 1976); DL; Director, Christ College, Brecon Foundation, 2001–05; *b* 22 Aug. 1937; *s* of Griffith Robert Poyntz Llewellyn and Bridget Margaret Lester Llewellyn (*née* Karslake); *m* 1964, Elizabeth Lamond (Polly) Sobey; three *s* one *d* (and one *d* decd). *Educ:* Haileybury; Imperial Service College; rcds, psc; Salisbury and Wells Theol Coll. (Dip. Theol. and Christian Ministry); Open Univ. (BA 2012). Enlisted Royal Welch Fusiliers (Nat. Service), 1956; active service, Malaya and Cyprus, 1957–59; Instructor, Army Outward Bound Sch., 1962–63; Staff Coll., 1970; MA to CGS, 1971–72; Brigade Major, 1974–76; CO, 1st Bn RWF, 1976–79; Directing Staff, RCDS, 1979–81; Comdr, Gurkha Field Force, 1981–84; Dir, Army Staff Duties, 1985–87; GOC Wales, 1987–90; C of S, HQ UKLF, 1990–91; retired in rank of Maj.-Gen. Ordained deacon, 1993, priest, 1994; Minor Canon, Brecon Cathedral and Asst Curate, Brecon with Battle and Llanddew, 1993–95; Chaplain, Christ Coll., Brecon, 1995–2001. Regtl Col, Gurkha Transport Regt, subseq. Queen's Own Gurkha Transport Regt, 1984–94; Col, RWF, 1990–97. Chairman: Army Mountaineering Assoc., 1988–91; Gurkha Welfare Trust in Wales, 1995–2010; Powys Br., Army Benevolent Fund, 2001–12; Armed Forces Art Soc., 2007–11; Vice-Pres., Soldiers' and Airmen's Scripture Readers Assoc., 1996–. Hon. Chaplain, Univ. of Wales OTC, 2002. Welsh Vice-Patron, War Memls Trust (formerly

Friends of War Memls), 1999–2010. DL Powys, 2006. FCMI. OStJ 2011. *Recreations:* most outdoor pursuits, gardening, painting, reading. *Address:* Field House, The Legar, Llangattock, Crickhowell, Powys NP8 1HL. *Club:* Army and Navy.

**LLEWELLYN, Sir Roderic Victor,** 5th Bt *cr* 1922, of Bwllfa, Aberdare, co. Glamorgan; landscape architect, author, lecturer and presenter; *b* Crickhowell, 9 Oct. 1947; *yr s* of Sir Harry Llewellyn, 3rd Bt, CBE and Hon. Christine Saumarez, 2nd *d* of 5th Baron de Saumarez; *S* brother, 2009; *m* 1981, Tatiana Manora Caroline, *d* of late Paul Soskin; three *d*. *Educ:* Shrewsbury; Aix-en-Provence. Designed gardens worldwide, 1977–. Consultant Gardens Director, Sudeley Castle gardens, 2010–15. Gardening Presenter: TV AM, 1983–84; The Home Show, 1990; The Gardening Roadshow, 1992–93; Grass Roots, 1993–2003 (guest presenter); Famous Welsh Gardens, 2001; This Morning, 1996–2000; Roddy Llewellyn's Garden Guide, 1997–99; Grand Gardens, 2001–02; Turf Wars, 2003; Best of Britain, 2003; Gardeners' World, 2008; guest panellist, Gardeners' Question Time, Radio 4, 1995. Gardening corresp., The Star, 1981–85; Garden writer, Oracle, 1982–83; Gardening corresp., Mail on Sunday, 1987–99. Regular contribs to magazines incl. Country Illustrated, 2001–05, Country Life, Cotswold Life and Saga Mag. Lectr in UK, USA and Australia; lecture series, Sotheby's Inst. of Art, 2001–02. Patron: Southport Flower Show, 1996–2015; Gardening Disabled Trust, 2011–. Silver Gilt Medal, Chelsea Flower Show and Hampton Court Palace Flower Show, 1998. *Publications:* Town Gardens, 1981; Beautiful Backyards, 1985; Water Gardens: the connoisseur's choice, 1987; Elegance & Eccentricity, 1989; Growing Gifts, 1992; Grow It Yourself: gardening with a physical disability, 1993; Roddy Llewellyn's Gardening Year, 1997. *Recreations:* walking, talking, philately. *E:* roddy.llewellyn@virgin.net. *Club:* Chelsea Arts.

**LLEWELLYN, Susan Pauline;** *see* Holdham, S. P.

**LLEWELLYN, Timothy David,** OBE 2007; Chairman: The Burlington Magazine Publications Ltd and supporting foundations, 2008–16 (Director, 2006–16; Trustee, Burlington Magazine Foundation, since 2006); British School at Rome, 2013–17 (Member, Council, 2000–17); *b* 30 May 1947; *s* of late Graham David Llewellyn and Dorothy Mary Driver; *m* 1st, 1970, Irene Sigrid Mercy Henriksen (marr. diss.; she *d* 2017); one *s*; 2nd, 1978, Elizabeth Hammond. *Educ:* St Dunstan's College; Magdalene College, Cambridge. Sotheby's: Old Master Painting Dept, 1969; Director, 1974; Man. Dir, 1984–91; Chief Exec., 1991–92; Dep. Chm., Europe, 1992–94; Dir, Henry Moore Foundn, 1994–2007 (Mem., Adv. Bd, 2007). Chm., Friends of the Courtauld Inst. of Art, 1986–2002. Mem. Council, Harvard Univ. Center for Italian Renaissance Studies, Villa I Tatti, 1996–2005 (Mem., Internat. Council, 1990–96). Co-Chm., Elgar Birthplace Appeal, 1992–99; Trustee: Elgar Foundn, 1992–99; Bd, Courtauld Inst. of Art, 1992–2001; Gilbert Collection Trust, 1998–2001; Kettles Yard, Univ. of Cambridge, 2000–18; Metropole Arts Trust, 2004–15, and Creative Foundn 2008–; Samuel Courtauld Trust, 2007–15; Chm., Henry Moore Sculpture Trust, 1994–99; Member: Council, Walpole Soc., 1994–99; Visual Arts Adv. Cttee, British Council, 1995–2007. Fellow, Ateneo Veneto, 1992. Hon. DLitt Southampton Inst., 1998. Order of Cultural Merit, Min. of Culture and Fine Arts, Poland, 1986. *Publications:* Owen McSwiny's Letters, 1720–1744, 2010. *Recreations:* music, travel. *Address:* 3 Cranley Mansion, 160 Gloucester Road, SW7 4QF. *T:* (020) 7373 2333, *Fax:* (020) 7244 0126. *E:* tdllewellyn@btinternet.com. *Club:* Brooks's.

**LLEWELLYN-JONES, Benedict,** OBE 2009; HM Diplomatic Service; Deputy High Commissioner to South Africa, since 2017; *b* Cardiff, 29 Nov. 1976; *s* of Christopher and Christine Llewellyn-Jones; *m* 2007, Laura Harries; one *s* one *d*. *Educ:* Jesus Coll., Oxford (BA). Joined CS, 2000; Desk Officer, EU and Internat. Affairs, 2000–01; Press Officer for Internat. Affairs, 2002, Home Office; Second Sec., Policing and Drugs, 2002–04; First Sec., Policing and Organised Crime, 2005–06, UK Perm. Repn to EU, Brussels; Head: Third Country Relns Team, Home Office, 2006; Zimbabwe Team, FCO, 2007–08; Dep. Hd, Climate Change and Energy Gp, FCO, 2009–11; High Comr to Rwanda and non-resident Ambassador to Burundi, 2011–14; Head of Chancery, Abuja, 2014–17. *Address:* c/o Foreign and Commonwealth Office, King Charles Street, SW1A 2AH.

**LLEWELLYN SMITH, Prof. Sir Christopher Hubert, (Sir Chris),** Kt 2001; FRS 1984; Visiting Professor, Department of Physics, University of Oxford, 2004–19, now Emeritus (Director of Energy Research, 2011–17); Director, Culham Division, United Kingdom Atomic Energy Authority, and Head of Euratom/UKAEA Fusion Association, 2003–08; *b* 19 Nov. 1942; *s* of late J. C. and M. E. F. Llewellyn Smith; *m* 1966, Virginia Grey; one *s* one *d*. *Educ:* Wellington College; New College, Oxford (Scholar; BA 1964; DPhil 1967; Hon. Fellow, 2002; full Blue for cross-country running, 1961–63, Captain 1963; full Blue for Athletics, 1963). Royal Society Exchange Fellow, Lebedev Inst., Moscow, 1967; Fellow, CERN, Geneva, 1968; Research Associate, SLAC, Stanford, Calif, 1970; Staff Mem., CERN, 1972; Oxford University: Lectr, 1974; Reader in Theoretical Physics, 1980; Prof. of Theoretical Physics, 1987–98 (on leave of absence, 1994–98); Chm. of Physics, 1987–92; Fellow, St John's Coll., 1974–98 (Hon. Fellow, 2000); Dir-Gen., CERN, 1994–98; Provost and Pres., UCL, 1999–2002. Chm., Adv. Cttee on Maths Educn, 2002–04. Mem. of various policy and programme cttees for CERN (Chm., Scientific Policy Cttee, 1990–92), SLAC, Deutsches Elektronen-Synchrotron Hamburg and SERC, 1972–92; Mem., ACOST, 1989–92; Chairman: Consultative Cttee on Fusion, Euratom, 2004–09; Council, Internat. Tokamak Experimental Reactor, 2007–09; Pres., Council, Synchrotron Light for Experimental Sci. and Applications in the ME, 2008–17. Vice-Pres., Royal Society, 2008–10. MAE 1989; Fellow, APS, 1994; For. Fellow, INSA, 1998. Hon. Fellow, Cardiff Univ., 1998. Hon. FIMA 2003. Hon. DSc: Bristol, 1997; Shandong, 1997; York, 2014; Guelph; Hon. DCien Granada, 1997. Maxwell Prize and Medal, Inst. of Physics, 1979; Medal, Japanese Assoc. of Med. Scis, 1997; Gold Medal, Slovak Acad. of Scis, 1997; Glazebrook Medal, Inst. of Physics, 1999; Distinguished Associate Award, US Dept of Energy, 1998; Distinguished Service Award, US Nat. Sci. Foundn, 1998; Royal Medal, Royal Soc., 2015; Award for Science Diplomacy, AAAS, 2019. *Publications:* numerous articles in Nuclear Physics, Physics Letters, Phys. Rev., etc. *Recreations:* books, travel, opera. *Address:* Rudolf Peierls Centre for Theoretical Physics, Clarendon Laboratory, University of Oxford, Parks Road OX1 3PU. *E:* c.llewellynsmith@physics.ox.ac.uk.

*See also* E. M. Llewellyn-Smith, Sir M. J. Llewellyn-Smith.

**LLEWELLYN-SMITH, Elizabeth Marion,** CB 1985; Principal, St Hilda's College Oxford, 1990–2001; *b* 17 Aug. 1934; *d* of late John Clare Llewellyn Smith and Margaret Emily Frances (*née* Crawford). *Educ:* Christ's Hospital, Hertford; Girton Coll., Cambridge (MA; Hon. Fellow, 1992). Joined Board of Trade, 1956; various appointments in Board of Trade, Cabinet Office, Dept of Trade and Industry, Dept of Prices and Consumer Protection, 1956–76; Royal Coll. of Defence Studies, 1977; Under Sec., Companies Div., Dept of Trade, later DTI, 1978–82; Dep. Dir Gen., OFT, 1982–87; Dep. Sec., DTI, 1987–90. UK Dir, EIB, 1987–90. Member: Hebdomadal Council, Oxford Univ., 1993–2000; Res. Ethics Cttee, HSE, 1993–2004; Business Appointments Panel, DTI, 1996–2002; Investigation and Discipline Bd, Accountancy Foundn, later Accountancy Investigation and Discipline Bd, then Accountancy and Actuarial Investigation and Discipline Bd, Financial Reporting Council, 2001–09; Council, Consumers' Assoc., 2002–08. Ind. Public Appts Assessor, 2008–12. Trustee: Jacqueline du Pré Meml Fund, 1991–2001; Auditory Verbal UK Ltd, 2004–11. Mem., Governing Body, Rugby Sch., 1991–2004. Chm., Charlotte M. Yonge Fellowship, 1995–2011. Hon. Fellow: St Mary's Coll., Univ. of Durham, 1999; St Hilda's Coll., Oxford, 2001. *Recreations:* travel, books, especially Trollope and C. M. Yonge, entertaining, Burmese cats, Border Terriers. *Address:* Brook Cottage, Taston, near Charlbury, Oxon OX7 3JL. *T:* (01608) 811874. *Club:* University Women's.

*See also* Sir C. H. Llewellyn Smith, Sir M. J. Llewellyn-Smith.

**LLEWELLYN-SMITH, Sir Michael (John),** KCVO 1996; CMG 1989; HM Diplomatic Service, retired; Ambassador to Greece, 1996–99; *b* 25 April 1939; *s* of late J. C. Llewellyn Smith and M. E. F. Crawford; *m* 1967, Colette Gaulier; one *s* one *d*. *Educ:* Wellington Coll.; New Coll., Oxford; St Antony's Coll., Oxford (MA, DPhil; Hon. Fellow, 2007). FCO, 1970; Cultural Attaché, Moscow, 1973; Paris, 1976; Royal Coll. of Defence Studies, 1979; Counsellor and Consul Gen., Athens, 1980–83; Hd of Western European Dept, FCO, 1984–85; Hd of Soviet Dept, FCO, 1985–87; Minister, Paris, 1988–91; Ambassador to Poland, 1991–96. Non-exec. Dir, Coca-Cola HBC SA, 2000–16. Vice-Chm., Cathedrals Fabric Commn for England, 1999–2006. Vice-Pres., British Sch. at Athens, 2000–. *Publications:* The Great Island: a study of Crete, 1965, 2nd edn 1973; Ionian Vision: Greece in Asia Minor 1919–22, 1973, 2nd edn 1998; The British Embassy Athens, 1998; Olympics in Athens 1896: the invention of the modern Olympic Games, 2004; Athens: a cultural and literary history, 2004. *Recreations:* music, walking. *Address:* 4 Frouds Close, Childrey, Wantage OX12 9NT. *Club:* Oxford and Cambridge.

*See also* Sir C. H. Llewellyn Smith, E. M. Llewellyn-Smith.

**LLEWELYN, Sir John Michael Dillwyn-V.;** *see* Venables-Llewelyn.

**LLOYD OF BERWICK, Baron** *cr* 1993 (Life Peer), of Ludlay in the County of East Sussex; **Anthony John Leslie Lloyd,** Kt 1978; PC 1984; DL; a Lord of Appeal in Ordinary, 1993–99; Chairman, Security Commission, 1992–99 (Vice-Chairman, 1985–92); *b* 9 May 1929; *o s* of late Edward John Boydell Lloyd and Leslie Johnston Fleming; *m* 1960, Jane Helen Violet, MBE, DL, *er d* of C. W. Shelford, Chailey Place, Lewes, Sussex. *Educ:* Eton (Schol.); Trinity Coll., Cambridge (Maj. Schol.). 1st cl. Classical Tripos Pt I; 1st cl. with distinction Law Tripos Pt II. National Service, 1st Bn Coldstream Guards, 1948. Montague Butler Prize, 1950; Sir William Browne Medal, 1951. Choate Fellow, Harvard, 1952; Fellow of Peterhouse, 1953 (Hon. Fellow, 1981); Fellow of Eton, 1974–86. Called to Bar, Inner Temple, 1955 (Bencher, 1976; Treasurer, 1999); QC 1967; Attorney-General to HRH The Prince of Wales, 1969–77; Judge of the High Court of Justice, Queen's Bench Div., 1978–84; a Lord Justice of Appeal, 1984–93; Mem., H of L, 1993–2015. Vice-Chm., Parole Bd, 1984–85; Mem., Criminal Law Revision Cttee, 1981. Chairman: Inquiry into Legislation against Terrorism (reported 1996); Inquiry into Gulf War Illnesses (reported 2004). Chm., Sussex Assoc. for Rehabilitation of Offenders, 1985–91; Pres., Sussex Downsmen, 1995–2004; Vice-Pres., British Maritime Law Assoc., 1983–. Mem., Top Salaries Review Body, 1971–77. Chm., H of L Select Cttee on the Speakership, 2003–05. Chairman: Ct of Ecclesiastical Causes Reserved, 1987; Jt Ecclesiastical Cttee, 2003–15. Trustee: Smiths Charity, 1971–94; Glyndebourne Arts Trust, 1973–94 (Chm., 1975–94); Dir, RAM, 1979– (Hon. FRAM 1985). Chm., Chichester Diocesan Bd of Finance, and Mem., Bishop's Council, 1972–76; Vice-Pres., Corp. of the Sons of the Clergy, 1997–2004. Hon. Mem., Salters' Co., 1988 (Master, 2000–01). DL E Sussex, 1983. Hon. LLD: QUB, 2005; Sussex, 2006. *Recreations:* music, carpentry; formerly running (ran for Cambridge in Mile, White City, 1950). *Address:* 2 Mitre Court, Temple, EC4Y 7BX. *T:* (020) 7583 9335; Ludlay, Berwick, East Sussex BN26 6TE. *T:* (01323) 870204. *Club:* Brooks's.

**LLOYD, Andrew,** CMG 2011; MBE 1995; Vice President, Communication, Global Strategy and Business Development, 2012–18, and Global Politics and Public Affairs, 2014, Statoil (UK) Ltd; *b* 22 Oct. 1964; *s* of Roderick Allen Lloyd and Jacqueline Lloyd (*née* Quinn); *m* 1997, Tania Mechlenborg; one *s* one *d*, and one *s* from previous marriage. *Educ:* Birkbeck Coll., London (BSc Hons Financial Econs); London Business Sch. (MBA); Columbia Univ., NY (MBA). Joined HM Diplomatic Service, 1982; FCO, 1982–84; Washington, 1984–87; Nigeria, 1987–90; FCO, 1990–92; Second Sec. (Econ.), Korea, 1992–95; Spokesman, UK Mission to UN, NY, 1995–2000; Hd of Post, Kosovo, 2000–02; rcds 2003; Hd, Africa Dept (Southern), 2003–06, Dir (Africa), 2006–08, Dir, Corporate Services, 2008–10, FCO; High Comr to Nigeria, 2011–12. *Recreations:* fly-fishing, long distance running, travel, design, cooking.

**LLOYD, Ann Judith,** CBE 2008; independent advisor and coach, since 2012; Chair, Aneurin Bevan University Health Board, since 2018; *b* 22 April 1948; *d* of Joseph Barnard and Beryl Greer; *m* 1998, Dr Geert Jan Koning. *Educ:* St Asaph Grammar Sch.; University Coll. of Wales, Aberystwyth (BSc (Hons)); University Coll. of Wales, Cardiff (MSc Econ); Bristol Poly. (DMS); Univ. of Aberdeen (DipHEcon); Univ. of Strathclyde (Dip. Mentoring). Area Planning Dir, Dyfed HA, 1974–82; Unit Gen. Manager, Llanelli-Dinefwr, 1982–88; Dist Gen. Manager, Frenchay HA, 1988–92; Chief Executive: Frenchay Healthcare NHS Trust, 1992–99; N Bristol NHS Trust, 1999–2001; Dir Gen. Health and Social Services, Welsh Assembly Govt and Chief Exec., NHS Wales, 2001–09; Health and Social Care Comr for London, Appts Commn, 2009–11. Chm., Welsh Health Specialised Services Cttee, 2015–18; Mem., Bevan Commn, 2014–. Associate Fellow, Office of Public Mgt, 2012–. Sen. Associate, Good Governance Inst., 2012–17. Chair: Caxton Foundn, 2013–15; Mind Cymru, 2016–18; Trustee: Shaw Trust, 2009–16; Patients' Assoc., 2009–12. *Publications: contributions to:* Managing Service Quality, 1992; The Health Care Management Handbook, 2nd edn 1997; NHS Handbook: 1996–1997, 1997–1998, 1998–1999; Clinical Governance: the sequel, 2000; contrib. articles in Health Service Jl, BMJ, Health Services Mgt, Croner's Health Service Manager, Health Mgt. *Recreations:* horse riding, dancing, playing the piano. *Address:* Belvoir, 4 Woodcroft Close, Woodcroft, Glos NP16 7HX. *T:* (01291) 627008. *E:* ann.lloyd.koning@gmail.com.

**LLOYD, Anthony Joseph;** MP (Lab) Rochdale, since 2017; *b* 25 Feb. 1950; *s* of late Sydney and Ciceley Beaumont Lloyd; *m* 1974, Judith Ann Tear; one *s* three *d*. *Educ:* Stretford Grammar Sch.; Nottingham Univ. (BSc Hons); Manchester Business Sch. (DipBA). Lectr, Dept of Business and Administration, Salford Univ., 1979–83. MP (Lab): Stretford, 1983–97; Manchester Central, 1997–Oct. 2012. Opposition spokesman: on transport, 1988–89; on employment, 1988–92, 1993–94; on education, 1992–94; on the environment, 1994–95; on foreign and commonwealth affairs, 1995–97; Minister of State, FCO, 1997–99; Shadow Minister for Housing, 2017–18; Shadow Sec. for NI, 2018–. Chm., PLP, 2006–12. Leader, British delegn to parly assembly of Council of Europe and of WEU, 2002–07, and of OSCE, 2005–12. Police and Crime Comr (Lab) for Gtr Manchester, 2012–17; Interim Mayor of Gtr Manchester, 2015–17. *Address:* House of Commons, SW1A 0AA.

**LLOYD, Ven. (Bertram) Trevor;** Archdeacon of Barnstaple, 1989–2002; *b* 15 Feb. 1938; *s* of Bertram and Gladys Lloyd; *m* 1962, Margaret Eldey; two *s* one *d* (and one *s* decd). *Educ:* Highgate School; Hertford Coll., Oxford (schol.; BA History 1960, Theology 1962; MA 1962); Clifton Theol Coll., Bristol. Curate, Christ Church, Barnet, 1964–69; Vicar, Holy Trinity, Wealdstone, 1970–84; Priest-in-charge, St Michael and All Angels, Harrow Weald, 1980–84; Vicar, Trinity St Michael, Harrow, 1984–89; Area Dean of Harrow, 1977–82;

Prebendary of Exeter Cathedral, 1991–2002. Member: C of E Liturgical Commn, 1981–2002; Gen. Synod of C of E, 1990–2002 (Mem., Standing Cttee, 1996–98); Central Bd of Finance, C of E, 1990–98; Council for the Care of Churches, 1992–2001; Churches' Main Cttee, 1996–2001. Chairman: Children's Hospice South West, 1991–2017; Living Stones Trust, 2002–08. *Publications:* Informal Liturgy, 1972; Institutions and Inductions, 1973; The Agape, 1973; Liturgy and Death, 1974; Ministry and Death, 1974; Lay Presidency at the Eucharist?, 1977; Evangelicals, Obedience and Change, 1977; (ed) Anglican Worship Today, 1980; Ceremonial in Worship, 1981; Introducing Liturgical Change, 1984; Celebrating Lent, Holy Week and Easter, 1985; Celebrating the Agape today, 1986; The Future of Anglican Worship, 1987; A Service of the Word, 1999; Dying and Death Step by Step, 2000; (consultant ed.) Common Worship Today, 2001; Thanksgiving for the Gift of a Child, 2001; Celebrating Forgiveness, 2004; Pocket Prayers for Healing and Wholeness, 2004; Introducing Times and Seasons 1, 2006; (ed) Connecting with Baptism, 2007; How to Share the Leadership of Worship, 2009; How to Plan Seasonal Events, 2010; Children at Communion, 2010; (with J. Steven and P. Tovey) Social Science Research Methods in Contemporary Liturgical Research: an introduction, 2010; Rites Surrounding Death, 2012; How to Distribute Communion, 2014; (ed) Reimagining Worship, 2017; (with C. Buchanan) The Church of England Eucharist 1958–2012, 2019. *Recreations:* hill and beach walking, photography, gardening, making things from wood. *Address:* 8 Pebbleridge Road, Westward Ho!, Bideford, N Devon EX39 1HN. *T:* (01237) 424701.

LLOYD, Christopher Hamilton, CVO 2002 (LVO 1996); Surveyor of The Queen's Pictures, 1988–2005; *b* 30 June 1945; *s* of Rev. Hamilton Lloyd and Suzanne Lloyd (*née* Moon); *m* 1967, Christine Joan Frances Newth; four *s*. *Educ:* Marlborough Coll.; Christ Church, Oxford (BA 1967; MA 1971; MLitt 1972). Asst Curator of Pictures, Christ Church, Oxford, 1967–68; Dept of Western Art, Ashmolean Museum, 1968–88. Fellow of Villa I Tatti, Florence (Harvard Univ.), 1972–73; Vis. Res. Curator of Early Italian Painting, Art Inst., Chicago, 1980–81. Mem., Exhibitions Cttee, RA, 2008–15. Pres., NADFAS, 2007–14. Trustee, Art Fund, 2005–15; Patron, Living Paintings Trust, 2009– (Trustee, 2005–09). Gov., Gainsborough's House, 2005–13. *Publications:* (ed) Studies on Camille Pissarro, 1986; The Royal Collection: a thematic exploration of the paintings in the collection of HM the Queen, 1992; (with John Berger and Michael Hofmann) Arturo di Stefano, 2001; Philip Morsberger: a passion for painting, 2007; In Search of a Masterpiece: an art lover's guide to Great Britain and Ireland, 2011; Edgar Degas Drawings and Pastels, 2014; Cézanne: drawings and watercolours, 2015; Picasso and the Art of Drawing, 2018; Impressionist & Post-Impressionist Drawings, 2019; *catalogues of permanent collections:* Catalogue of Earlier Italian Paintings in the Ashmolean Museum, 1977; (with Richard Brettell) Catalogue of Drawings by Camille Pissarro in the Ashmolean Museum, 1980; (introd. and ed) Catalogue of Old Master Drawings at Holkham Hall, by A. E. Popham, 1986; Early Italian paintings in the Art Institute of Chicago, 1993; *exhibition catalogues:* Art and its Images, 1975; Camille Pissarro, 1980; (with Richard Thomson) Impressionist Drawings from British Collections, 1986; (with Simon Thurley) Henry VIII—images of a Tudor King, 1990; The Queen's Pictures: Royal collectors through the centuries, 1991; (contrib.) Alfred Sisley, ed M. A. Stevens, 1992; Gainsborough and Reynolds: contrasts in Royal patronage, 1994; (with Vanessa Remington) Masterpieces in Little: portrait miniatures from the collection of Her Majesty Queen Elizabeth II, 1996; The Quest for Albion: monarchy and the patronage of British painting, 1998; (contrib.) Royal Treasures: a Golden Jubilee celebration, 2002; Ceremony & Celebration: Coronation Day 1953, 2003; (contrib.) George III and Queen Charlotte: patronage, collecting and Court taste, 2004; Enchanting the Eye: Dutch paintings of the Golden Age, 2004; Impressionism: pastel, watercolour, drawings, 2011; (with Daniel Charles and Phillip Dennis Cate) Impressionists on the Water, 2013; (contrib.) American Adversaries: West and Copley in a Transatlantic World, 2013; (contrib.) Toulouse-Lautrec and La Vie Moderne: Paris 1880–1910, 2013; reviews and contribs to learned jls. *Recreations:* books, theatre, cinema, music, Real tennis. *Address:* Hubbards, Queens Street, Stradbroke, Eye, Suffolk IP21 5HG. *T:* (01379) 384189.

LLOYD, Clive Hubert, AO 1985; CBE 1992; OJ 1985; OB 1986; International Match Referee, 2002–06, Chairman, Cricket Committee, 2008–12, International Cricket Council; Chairman of Selectors, 2014–16, Special Ambassador, 2016, West Indies Cricket Board; *b* Georgetown, Guyana, 31 Aug. 1944; *er s* of late Arthur Christopher Lloyd and of Sylvia Thelma Lloyd; *m* 1971, Waveney Benjamin; one *s* two *d*. *Educ:* Chatham High Sch., Georgetown (schol.). Clerk, Georgetown Hosp., 1960–66. Began cricket career, Demerara CC, Georgetown, 1959; début for Guyana, 1963; first Test Match, 1966; played for Haslingden, Lancs League, 1967; Lancashire County Cricket Club: Mem., 1968–86, capped 1969; Captain, 1981–84 and 1986; Captain, WI cricket team, 1974–78 and 1979–85; World Series Cricket in Australia, 1977–79. Made first 1st class century, 1966; passed total of 25,000 runs (incl. 69 centuries), 1981; captained WI teams which won World Cup, 1975, 1979; Manager, WI cricket tour in Australia, 1988–89; WI Team Manager, 1996–99, 2007–08. First Pres., WI Players' Assoc., 1973. West Indies Cricket Board: Mem., Bd of Dirs; Chm., Cricket Cttee. Exec. Promotion Officer, Project Fullemploy, 1987. Former Dir, Red Rose Radio. Mem. (part-time), Commn for Racial Equality, 1987–90. Hon. Fellow: Manchester Polytechnic, 1986; Lancashire Polytechnic, 1986. Hon. MA: Manchester; Hull; Hon. Dr of Letters, Univ. of West Indies, Mona. Golden Arrow of Achievement (Guyana), 1975; Cacique Crown of Honours, Order of Rorima (Guyana), 1985. *Publications:* (with Tony Cozier) Living for Cricket, 1980; *relevant publications:* Clive Lloyd, by Trevor McDonald, 1985; Supercat: the authorised biography of Clive Lloyd, by Simon Lister, 2007.

LLOYD, David Alan; Chairman, David Lloyd Associates, since 1980; *b* 3 Jan. 1948; *s* of Dennis and Doris Lloyd; *m* 1972, Veronica Jardine; one *s* two *d*. *Educ:* Southend High Sch. Tennis player; mem., British Davis Cup team, 1973–82; ranked in Britain's top ten, 1970–81; semi-finalist, Wimbledon Championship doubles, 1973; British Wightman Cup coach, 1981; non-playing Captain, British Davis Cup team, 1995–2000. Chm., David Lloyd Leisure, 1981–96; Chm. and owner, Hull City AFC, 1997–2002; Man. Dir, Next Generation Clubs, 1998–2006; Chm., David Lloyd Signature Homes, 2007–13. Freeman, City of London, 1985. Entrepreneur of the Year, PLC Awards, 1994. *Publications:* Improve Your Tennis Skills, 1989; Successful Tennis, 1989; Winning Tennis Fitness, 1991; How to Succeed in Business by Really Trying, 1995. *Recreations:* golf, swimming, tennis, football. *Clubs:* All England Lawn Tennis; Queenwood and Loch Lomond Cricket.

LLOYD, David Andrew, OBE 1993; HM Diplomatic Service, retired; Senior Consultant, Pathfinder Trade and Invest, since 2017; *b* 24 Dec. 1940; *s* of John Owen Lloyd and Ellen Marjorie Howard Lloyd; *m* 1st, 1965, Janet Elizabeth Rawcliffe (*d* 2011); one *s* one *d*; 2nd, 1979, Patricia Villa (marr. diss.); 3rd, 1987, Katharine Jane Smith; three *d*. *Educ:* Lancing Coll.; Clare Coll., Cambridge (BA Hons Arabic). Entered Foreign Office, 1964; served Kuwait, Bogotá, FCO and Madrid; First Sec., FCO, 1983–88; Head, British Trade Office, Al Khobar, Saudi Arabia, 1988–93; FCO, 1994–96; Ambassador to Slovenia, 1997–2000. Dir, Inf. Services, 2001–06, Sen. Consultant, 2007–17, Middle East Assoc. Trustee and Patron, British-Slovene Soc., 2003– (Chm., 2013–); Trustee and Cttee Mem., Saudi British Soc., 2007–. *Recreations:* indoor rowing, tennis, theatre, concerts. *Address:* 19 Brewhouse Lane, Hertford SG14 1TZ. *T:* (01992) 583795. *E:* davidalloyd@btinternet.com.

LLOYD, David Bernard; Secretary, Royal College of Physicians, 1986–98; *b* 14 Jan. 1938; *s* of George Edwards and Lilian Catherine Lloyd; *m* 1968, Christine Vass; three *d*. *Educ:* Presteigne Grammar Sch.; Hereford High Sch. FCCA. Early posts in local govt, UCL, UCH Med. Sch.; Royal College of Obstetricians and Gynaecologists: Accountant, 1971–76; Secretary, 1976–82; Secretary, Nat. Inst. of Agricultural Engineering, 1982–86. Chm., Management Cttee, St Albans CAB, 1990–94 (Mem., 1985–94); Dir, Harpenden Day Centre Assoc., 2000–14 (Co. Sec., 2000–11). Member (C): Harpenden Town Council, 1992–99, 2001–03; Herts CC, 1997–2013 (Chm., Protection Cttee, 1999–2000; Cabinet, 2001–03; Chm., Health Scrutiny Cttee, 2006–09; Chm., 2009–11). Hon. Vice Pres., Hitchin and Harpenden Cons. Assoc., 2014–17. Trustee and Dir, Herts Healthwatch, 2013–15. Chm., Harpenden Trust, 1995–96. Governor: Sir John Lawes Sen. Sch., 1986–87 (also Chm.); Roundwood Jun. Sch., 1980–89 (Chm., 1985–88). Hon. FRCP 1998; Hon. FFPM 1998. *Recreations:* local charity, walking, volunteer with Rennie Grove Hospice and Chiltern Dog Rescue Society. *Address:* 8 Graces Maltings, Tring, Herts HP23 6DL. *T:* (01442) 890822.

LLOYD, David Emanuel Joseph Julian; Headmaster, Solihull School, since 2010; *b* Mtarfa, Malta, 13 Dec. 1967; *s* of Kenneth and Elvira Lloyd; *m* 1996, Debbie Jane Wale; two *d*. *Educ:* St Edmund Arrowsmith Catholic Sch.; Lancaster Univ. (BSc Econ 1989); Nottingham Trent Univ. (PGCE 1991). Grad. recruit, Advanced Develt Prog., Midland Montagu Internat. Investment Bank, 1989–90; Teacher of Econs and Business and Asst Boarding Housemaster, Trent Coll., 1991–94; Hd of Econs and Sen. Master, Warwick Sch., 1994–2005; Dep. Headmaster, Ryde Sch., 2005–10. *Recreations:* British studio pottery, 20th century glass, horology. *Address:* Solihull School, Warwick Road, Solihull, W Midlands B91 3DG. *T:* (0121) 705 0958. *E:* lloydd@solsch.org.uk. *Club:* Old Silhillians.

LLOYD, David Mark; Head of News, Current Affairs and Business, Channel Four Television, 1997–2004; *b* 3 Feb. 1945; *s* of late Maurice Edward and Roma Doreen Lloyd; *m* 1982, Jana Tomas; one *s* one *d*, and one step *s*. *Educ:* Felsted Sch.; Brentwood Sch.; Brasenose Coll., Oxford (MA 1967). Joined BBC as Gen. Trainee, 1967: Dep. Ed., Nationwide, 1978; Editor: Money Prog., 1980; Newsnight, 1982; Sixty Minutes, 1983; Breakfast Time, 1984; Sen. Commng Editor, News and Current Affairs, Channel 4, 1988–97. Vis. Prof. of TV Journalism, City, Univ. of London (formerly City Univ.), 2005–. Shell Film and TV Award, 1982; Judges Award, RTS, 2003. *Recreations:* cricket, golf, music, travel. *Address:* 9 Richmond Crescent, Islington, N1 0LZ.

LLOYD, David Rees, FRCGP; Member (Plaid Cymru) South Wales West, National Assembly for Wales, 1999–2011 and since 2016; *b* 2 Dec. 1956; *s* of Aneurin Rees Lloyd and Dorothy Grace Lloyd; *m* 1982, Dr Catherine Jones; two *s* one *d*. *Educ:* Lampeter Comprehensive Sch.; Welsh Nat. Sch. of Medicine, Cardiff (MB BCh 1980; Dip. in Therapeutics, 1995). MRCGP 1989, FRCGP 2001. Jun. hosp. med. posts, 1980–84; GP, 1984–99 and 2011–. National Assembly for Wales: Shadow Health Sec., 1999–2003; Shadow Finance Minister, 2003–07. Contested (Plaid Cymru) S Wales W, Nat. Assembly for Wales, 2011. *Recreation:* lay preacher. *Address:* National Assembly for Wales, Cardiff Bay, Cardiff CF99 1NA. *E:* dai.lloyd@cynulliad.cymru.

LLOYD, Rev. David Richard, (Rev. Denys Lloyd); Parish Priest, Our Lady and St Joseph, Sheringham and Cromer, since 2008; *b* 28 June 1939; *s* of Richard Norman Lloyd and Grace Enid Lloyd. *Educ:* Brighton College (George Long Scholar); Trinity Hall, Cambridge (Exhibitioner; BA 1961, MA 1965); Leeds Univ. (MA 1969). Asst Curate, St Martin's, Rough Hills, Wolverhampton, 1963–67; professed as Mem. of Community of Resurrection, 1969 (taking name Denys); Tutor, Coll. of Resurrection, 1970–75, Vice-Principal, 1975–84; Principal, 1984–90; Associate Lecturer, Dept of Theology and Religious Studies, Univ. of Leeds, 1972–90. Received into Roman Catholic Church at Quarr Abbey, 1990; Missionary Inst., London, 1993–94; ordained priest, 1994; Asst Priest, St Mark's, Ipswich, and RC Chaplain, Ipswich Hosp., 1994–96; Parish Priest, Our Lady's, Stowmarket, 1996–2008. Rural Dean: Bury St Edmunds, 2001–08; North Norfolk Deanery, 2014–15; Norwich Deanery, 2015–. *Publications:* Pieta (Stations of the Cross), 1986; The Sheringham Stations of the Cross, 2010; contribs to theol. jls. *Address:* The Presbytery, 58 Cromer Road, Sheringham, Norfolk NR26 8RT. *T:* (01263) 822036.

LLOYD, Eve, (Lady Lloyd); *see* Pollard, E.

LLOYD, Frances Mary, (Mrs James Lloyd); *see* Line, F. M.

LLOYD, Gaynor Elizabeth; Her Honour Judge Gaynor Lloyd; a Circuit Judge, since 2015; *b* Aberystwyth, 15 June 1970; *d* of Lyndon and Lorraine Lloyd; *m* 2000, Steven Philip Moore; two *d*. *Educ:* Ysgol Penweddig; Univ. of Nottingham (LLB Hons 1991); Inns of Court Sch. of Law. Called to the Bar, Lincoln's Inn, 1992; in practice as barrister, 1992–2015; a Recorder, 2012–15. *Recreations:* reading, collecting 70s vinyl, family ski-ing holidays. *Address:* Caernarfon County Court and Family Court Hearing Centre, Llanberis Road, Caernarfon, Gwynedd LL55 2DF. *T:* (01286) 684600. *E:* family@caernarfon.countycourt.gsi.gov.uk.

LLOYD, Sir Geoffrey (Ernest Richard), Kt 1997; PhD; FBA 1983; Professor of Ancient Philosophy and Science, University of Cambridge, 1983–2000, now Emeritus; Master of Darwin College, Cambridge, 1989–2000 (Hon. Fellow, 2000); *b* 25 Jan. 1933; *s* of William Ernest Lloyd and Olive Irene Neville Lloyd; *m* 1956, Janet Elizabeth Lloyd; three *s*. *Educ:* Charterhouse; King's Coll., Cambridge (BA 1954; MA 1958; PhD 1958). Cambridge University: Asst Lectr in Classics, 1965–67; Lectr, 1967–74; Reader in Ancient Philosophy and Science, 1974–83; Fellow, 1957–89 (Hon. Fellow, 1990), and Sen. Tutor, 1969–73, King's Coll. Bonsall Prof., Stanford Univ., 1981; Sather Prof., Berkeley, 1983–84; A. D. White Prof.-at-large, Cornell Univ., 1990–97. Chm., E Asian Hist. of Sci. Trust, 1992–2002. Fellow, Japan Soc. for the Promotion of Science, 1981. For. Mem., Accademia Nazionale dei Lincei, 2016; Hon. For. Mem., Amer. Acad. of Arts and Scis, 1995. FLSW 2015. Hon. LittD: Athens, 2003; Oxford, 2012; St Andrews, 2016. Sarton Medal, History of Science Soc., USA, 1987; Kenyon Medal, British Acad., 2007; Dan David Prize, Dan David Foundn, 2013; Internat. Prize, Fyssen Foundn, 2014. *Publications:* Polarity and Analogy, 1966; Aristotle: the growth and structure of his thought, 1968; Early Greek Science: Thales to Aristotle, 1970; Greek Science after Aristotle, 1973; (ed) Hippocratic Writings, 1978; (ed) Aristotle on Mind and the Senses, 1978; Magic, Reason and Experience, 1979; Science, Folklore and Ideology, 1983; Science and Morality in Greco-Roman Antiquity, 1985; The Revolutions of Wisdom, 1987; Demystifying Mentalities, 1990; Methods and Problems in Greek Science, 1991; Adversaries and Authorities, 1996; Aristotelian Explorations, 1996; (ed) Le Savoir grec, 1996 (English edn, Greek Thought, 2000); (with N. Sivin) The Way and the Word, 2002; The Ambitions of Curiosity, 2002; In the Grip of Disease: studies in the Greek imagination, 2003; Ancient Worlds, Modern Reflections: philosophical perspectives on Greek and Chinese science and culture, 2004; The Delusions of Invulnerability: wisdom and morality in ancient Greece, China and today, 2005; Principles and Practices in Ancient Greek and Chinese Science, 2006; Cognitive Variations: reflections on the unity and diversity of the human mind, 2007; Disciplines in the Making, 2009; Being, Humanity and Understanding: studies in ancient and modern societies, 2012; The Ideals of Inquiry, 2014; Analogical Investigations: historical and cross-cultural perspectives on human reasoning, 2015; The Ambivalences of Rationality: ancient and modern cross-cultural explorations, 2018; (ed) Ancient Greece and China Compared, 2018; (ed jtly) Regimes of Comparatism, 2018; contribs to classical and philosophical jls. *Recreation:* travel. *Address:* 2 Prospect Row, Cambridge CB1 1DU; Needham Research Institute, Sylvester Road, Cambridge CB3 9AF.

**LLOYD, Graham;** *see* Lloyd, J. G.

**LLOYD, Heather Claire, (Mrs P. N. D. Kennedy); Her Honour Judge Heather Lloyd;** a Circuit Judge, since 2007; *b* Bebington, Wirral, 16 May 1957; *d* of late John Howson Lloyd and Nancy Beatrice Lloyd (née Barlow); *m* 1982, (Peter) Nicholas (Dodgson) Kennedy, barrister; two *s*. *Educ:* St Edmund's Coll., Liverpool; Univ. of Liverpool (LLB Hons 1978). Called to the Bar, Gray's Inn, 1979; in practice at Peel House Chambers, Liverpool, 1979–99, Chavasse Court Chambers, Liverpool, 1999–2007; Asst Recorder, 1998–2000; Recorder, 2000–07. *Address:* Preston Combined Court Centre, The Law Courts, Ringway, Preston PR1 2LL.

See also W. J. Lloyd.

**LLOYD, His Honour Humphrey John;** QC 1979; arbitrator; a Judge of the Technology and Construction Court (formerly an Official Referee) of the High Court, 1993–2005; *b* 16 Nov. 1939; *s* of Rees Lewis Lloyd of the Inner Temple, barrister-at-law, and Dorothy Margaret Ferry (née Gibson); *m* 1969, Ann Findlay; one *s* one *d*. *Educ:* Westminster; Trinity Coll., Dublin (BA (Mod), LLB; MA). Called to the Bar, Inner Temple, 1963, Bencher, 1985. A Recorder, 1990–93. Chm., Architects' Registration Bd, 2002–07. Pres., Soc. of Construction Law, 1985–88. Vis. Prof., Leeds Beckett (formerly Leeds Metropolitan) Univ., 2002–17. Hon. Sen. Vis. Fellow, QMC, 1987; Professorial Fellow, 2005–11, Hon. Prof., 2011–, Queen Mary, London Univ. Pres., Electricity Arbitration Assoc., 2009–17. Hon. Fellow: Amer. Coll. of Construction Law, 1997; Canadian Coll. of Construction Lawyers, 2002. Editor-in-chief: Building Law Reports, 1977–93 (Consultant Editor, 1993–98); The Internat. Construction Law Rev., 1983–2015; Consultant Editor: Emden's Construction Law, 1993–; Technology and Construction Law Reports, 1999–. Fellow Emeritus, Internat. Acad. of Construction Lawyers, 2016. Hon LLD Leeds Metropolitan, 2009. *Publications:* (ed) The Liability of Contractors, 1986; (contrib.) Halsbury's Laws of England, 4th edn, 1992. *Address:* Atkin Chambers, 1 Atkin Building, Gray's Inn, WC1R 5AT. *Club:* Reform.

**LLOYD, Illtyd Rhys;** HM Chief Inspector of Schools (Wales), 1982–90, retired; *b* 13 Aug. 1929; *s* of John and Melvina Lloyd; *m* 1955, Julia Lewis; one *s* one *d*. *Educ:* Port Talbot (Glan-Afan) County Grammar Sch.; Swansea UC (Hon. Fellow, Univ. of Wales, 1987). BSc, MSc; DipStat, DipEd. Commnd Educn Br., RAF, 1951–54 (Flt Lieut). Second Maths Master, Howardian High Sch. for Boys, Cardiff, 1954–57; Hd of Maths Dept, Pembroke Grammar Sch., 1957–59; Dep. Headmaster, Howardian High Sch., 1959–63; Welsh Office: HM Inspector of Schs, 1964–70; Staff Inspector (Secondary Educn), 1971–82. Chm., Educn Resources Centre, Aberystwyth Univ., 1991–2001; Vice-Chm., S Glam FHSA, 1993–96 (Mem., 1990–96); Member: Ind. Schs Tribunal Educn Panel, 1990–2004; Exec. Cttee, Council for Educn in World Citizenship-Cymru, 1990–2003 (Treas., 1962–63; Chm., 1997–2003). Churches Together in Wales: Mem. Council, 1991–2003; Treas., 1999–2003; Mem., Finance Cttee, 1990–2003 (Vice Chm., 1995–98; Chm., 1999–2003); Baptist Union of Wales: Mem. Council, 1990–; Treas., 1992–2003; Vice-Pres., 1995–96; Pres., 1996–97; Member: Educn Cttee, Free Churches Council, 1993–2001; Finance Cttee, CTBI, 1994–2003. Cardiff Theological College: Trustee, 1973–2010; Mem. Council, 1990–2003 (Chm., 1995–2003); Univ. of Wales, Lampeter, 1999–2004; Gov., Swansea Inst. of Higher Educn, 1990–95. Chairman: Mgt Cttee, Glyn Nest Christian Home, 1992–2003; Bryn Llifon Baptist Home, 1999–2003; Sec., Capel Gomer Church, Swansea, 1969–83; Treas., Tabernacl Welsh Baptist Church, Cardiff, 1992–2012. Trustee: Churches Counselling Service, 1994–2000; Churches Tourism Network Wales, 2001–05. Hon. Mem., Gorsedd of Bards, 1990. *Publications:* Geirfa Mathemateg, 1956; Secondary Education in Wales 1965–85, 1991; Gwyr y Gair, 1993; Yr Hyn a Ymddiriedwyd i'n Gofal, 1996. *Recreation:* walking. *Address:* 134 Lake Road East, Roath Park, Cardiff CF23 5NQ. *T:* (029) 2075 5296.

**LLOYD, Janet Frances;** *see* Gough, J. F.

**LLOYD, (John) Graham;** consultant, 1994–96; Director of Property Services, Commission for the New Towns, 1992–94; *b* Watford, 18 Feb. 1938; *s* of late Richard and Edith Lloyd; *m* 1st, 1960, Ann (née Plater) (marr. diss. 1989); three *s*; 2nd, 1989, Monica (née Barlow). *Educ:* City of London Sch.; College of Estate Management, London Univ. (BSc Estate Management). FRICS. In private practice, London and Leamington Spa, 1959–75. Commission for the New Towns: Commercial and Industrial Manager, 1975–78, Manager, 1978–81, Hemel Hempstead; Exec. Officer/Commercial Surveyor, Corby, 1981–91; Head of Estate Management Services, 1991–92. *Recreations:* soccer, motor racing, jazz and popular music, gardening, steam railways. *Address:* 4 Fairway, Kibworth Beauchamp, Leics LE8 0LB.

**LLOYD, John Nicol Fortune;** journalist; Contributing Editor, Financial Times, since 2006; Senior Research Fellow, Reuters Institute for the Study of Journalism, University of Oxford, since 2016 (Director of Journalism, 2006–15); Associate Fellow, Nuffield College, Oxford, since 2009; *b* 15 April 1946; *s* of Joan Adam Fortune and Christopher Lloyd; *m* 1983, Marcia Levy (marr. diss. 1997); one *s*; *m* 2000, Ilaria Poggiolini. *Educ:* Waid Acad. Comprehensive School; Edinburgh Univ. (MA Hons). Editor, Time Out, 1972–73; Reporter, London Programme, 1974–76; Producer, Weekend World, 1976–77; industrial reporter, labour correspondent, industrial and labour editor, Financial Times, 1977–86; Editor, New Statesman, 1986–87; re-joined Financial Times, 1987; E European Editor, 1987–90; Moscow Correspondent, 1991–95; Associate Ed., New Statesman & Soc., subseq. New Statesman, 1996–2003; columnist, The Times, 1997–98; founding Editor, FT Magazine, 2003–05. Director: East-West Inst., NY, 1997–2004; Foreign Policy Centre, 1999–2004. Sen. Associate Fellow, Kennedy Sch., Harvard Univ., 1995; Sen. Associate Mem., St Antony's Coll., Oxford, 1996–99. Chm., Bd of Dirs, Sch. (formerly Moscow Sch.) of Civic Educn, 2016–. Journalist of the Year, Granada Awards, 1984; Specialist Writer of the Year, IPC Awards, 1985; Rio Tinto David Watt Meml Prize, 1997; Biagio Agnes Premio Internazionale, Fondazione Biagio Agnes, Rome, 2013. *Publications:* (with Ian Benson) The Politics of Industrial Change, 1982; (with Martin Adeney) The Miners' Strike: loss without limit, 1986; (with Charles Leadbeater) In Search of Work, 1987; (contrib.) Counterblasts, 1989; Rebirth of a Nation: an anatomy of Russia, 1998; Re-engaging Russia, 2000; The Protest Ethic, 2001; What the Media have done to our Politics, 2004; (with F. Giugliano) Eserciti di Carta, 2013; (with C. Marconi) Reporting the EU, 2014; (with L. Toogood) Journalism and PR, 2015; The Power and the Story, 2017; (jtly) Journalism in an Age of Terror, 2017. *Recreations:* opera, theatre. *Address:* c/o Reuters Institute, University of Oxford, 13 Norham Gardens, Oxford OX2 6PS.

**LLOYD, John Wilson,** CB 1992; JP; Clerk and Head of the Office of the Presiding Officer, National Assembly for Wales, 1999–2001; *b* 24 Dec. 1940; *s* of late Dr Ellis Lloyd and Mrs Dorothy Lloyd; *m* 1967, Buddug Roberts (*d* 1996); two *s* one *d*. *Educ:* Swansea Grammar Sch.; Clifton Coll., Bristol; Christ's Coll., Cambridge (MA). Asst Principal, HM Treasury, 1962–67 (Private Sec. to Financial Sec., 1965–67); Principal, successively HM Treasury, CSD and Welsh Office, 1967–75 (Private Sec. to Sec. of State for Wales, 1974–75); Welsh Office: Asst Sec., 1975–82; Under Sec., 1982–88; Principal Establishment Officer, 1982–86; Hd, Housing, Health and Social Servs Policy Gp, 1986–88; Dep. Sec., 1988; Dir, Social Policy and Local Govt Affairs, 1988–98. Mem., Royal Commn on Ancient and Historical Monuments of Wales, 2002–11. JP Cardiff, 2001–10. *Recreations:* walking, swimming. *Address:* c/o National Assembly for Wales, Cardiff Bay, Cardiff CF99 1NA. *T:* (029) 2082 5111. *Club:* Oxford and Cambridge.

**LLOYD, Jonathan Bruce;** composer; writer; *b* 30 Sept. 1948; *s* of Geoffrey and Nancy Lloyd; *m* 1st, 1970, Poppy Holden (marr. diss. 1975); one *s*; 2nd, 1981, Katherine Bones; two *s*. *Educ:* Royal Coll. of Music. Mendelssohn Scholar, 1969; Fellow, Berkshire Music Centre, Tanglewood, USA, 1973 (Koussevitzky Composition Prize); Composer-in-residence, Dartington Coll., 1978–79. Paul Hamlyn Foundn Composers' Award, 2007; Elgar Bursary Award, Royal Philharmonic Soc., 2011. *Principal works:* Cantique, 1968; Till the Wind Blows, 1969; Scattered Ruins, 1973; Everything Returns, 1977; Viola Concerto, 1979; Toward the Whitening Dawn, 1980; Waiting for Gozo, 1981; Three Dances, 1982; Mass, 1983; 5 Symphonies, 1983–89; The Shorelines of Certainty, 1984; The Adjudicator, 1985; Almeida Dances, 1986; Revelation, 1990; Wa Wa Mozart, 1991; Ballad for the Evening of a Man, 1992; Blackmail, 1993; Tolerance, 1994; Violin Concerto, 1995; And Beyond, 1996; A Dream of a Pass, 1997; Shadows of our Future Selves, 1998; The Beggar's Opera (musical adaptation), 1999; Inventing Bach, Summon the Spirit, 2000; Music to Maze, Songs, 2001; Between us a River before us the Sea, 2002; What 'ave we got 'ere? (music'all opera in 3 acts), 2008–10; There's Only You (play in 3 acts), 2009; Old Racket, 2012; New Balls, 2013. *Recreations:* tennis, walking, cycling. *Address:* 18 Emmanuel Court, Guthrie Road, Bristol BS8 3EP.

**LLOYD, Jonathan Salusbury;** Chairman, Curtis Brown Group Ltd, since 2012 (Director, 1994–2012); Group Managing Director, 1995–2012); *b* 1 Dec. 1946; *s* of late Reginald Lloyd and Maureen Lloyd; *m* 1977, Marion Dickens; two *s* one *d*. *Educ:* Shrewsbury Sch.; Alliance Française, Paris. Joined Collins publishers as mgt trainee, 1967; export sales in Europe and Middle E, incl. Afghanistan; UK Sales Manager, 1976; Sales and Mktg Dir, 1980; Gp Rights and Contracts Dir, 1983; Managing Director: Grafton Books, 1986–91; HarperCollins, 1991–94. Vice-Pres., 1997–2000, Pres., 2000–02, Assoc. of Authors' Agents. Chm., Soc. of Bookmen, 2011–12 (Dep. Chm., 2010–11). *Recreations:* reading, sailing, theatre, opera, film, squash, running for one hour (except in the 2006 London Marathon which took longer). *Address:* c/o Curtis Brown, Haymarket House, 28–29 Haymarket, SW1Y 4SP. *T:* (020) 7393 4408, *Fax:* (020) 7393 4399. *E:* jlloyd@curtisbrown.co.uk. *Clubs:* Garrick, Royal Automobile, MCC.

**LLOYD, Marie-Pierre;** High Commissioner for the Republic of the Seychelles in the United Kingdom, 2012–17; *b* Victoria, Seychelles, 15 June 1952; *d* of François Sinon and Monique Woodcock; *m* 1978, Alan Lloyd (marr. diss.); two *d*. *Educ:* St Teresa Primary Sch.; Regina Mundi Convent Grammar Sch.; Seychelles Coll.; Liverpool Univ. (BA Hons Sociol. 1976); Loughborough Univ. of Technol. (MSc Negotiating Studies 1991). Special Advr to Minister for Social Affairs, 2000–03; owner/Manager: Holistic Living, 2003–12; MPower (Seychelles), 2003–12; CEO, MP Consulting Services, 2011–. Minister for Health and Social Develt, 2007–10; Ambassador for Women and Children, 2010–12. *Recreations:* reading, dancing, listening to music. *E:* lloydmpe@gmail.com. *Club:* Rotary (Victoria, Seychelles) (Pres., 2004–05).

**LLOYD, Mark;** Chief Executive, Local Government Association, since 2015; *b* 4 July 1967; *s* of late David Lloyd and Joan Lloyd (née Bowyer); *m* 2007, Shân Warren; one *s* one *d*. *Educ:* Rhyn Park Comp. Sch., St Martins, Shropshire; Oswestry Coll.; Durham Univ. (MBA Distn 2002). Civil Service, 1985–93: actg Chief Exec., Powys TEC, 1992–93; served on Lord Justice Scott's Inquiry into defence related exports to Iraq, 1993; Dir, Educn and Trng, Central England TEC, 1994–96; Dep. Chief Exec., Bolton and Bury Chamber of Commerce, Trng and Enterprise, 1996–99; Chief Exec., Co. Durham TEC and Business Link, 1999–2000; Durham County Council: Dir, Econ. Develt and Planning, 2000–03; Man. Dir, Co. Durham Develt Company, 2000–05; Dep. Chief Exec. (Policy and Strategy), 2003–05; Chief Exec., 2005–08; Chief Exec., Cambs CC, 2008–15. *Recreations:* travel, running, Rugby. *Address:* c/o Local Government Association, Local Government House, Smith Square, SW1P 3HZ. *T:* (020) 7664 3000. *E:* mark.lloyd@local.gov.uk.

**LLOYD, Rev. Dr Michael Francis;** Principal, Wycliffe Hall, Oxford, since 2013; *b* Bishop's Waltham, Hants, 1 Nov. 1957; *s* of Major David P. J. Lloyd and Beryl M. D. Lloyd; *m* 2008, Abigail. *Educ:* Highfield Sch., Liphook; Radley Coll., Abingdon; Downing Coll., Cambridge (BA 1979); St John's Coll., Durham (BA Theol. 1983); Worcester Coll., Oxford (DPhil Theol. 1997). Ordained deacon, 1984, priest, 1985; Asst Curate, St John's, Locks Heath, 1984–87; Chaplain: Christ's Coll., Cambridge, 1990–94; Fitzwilliam Coll., Cambridge, 1995–96; Hon. Curate, St James the Less, Pimlico, 1990–2003; Tutor in Doctrine, St Stephen's House, Oxford, 2003–05; Tutor, St Mellitus' Coll., London, 2006–13; Associate Vicar, St Andrew, Holborn, 2006–10; Chaplain, Queen's Coll., Oxford, 2010–13. *Publications:* Café Theology: exploring love, the universe and everything, 2005, 3rd edn 2012; (ed jtly) Finding Ourselves After Darwin: conversations on the image of God, original sin, and the problem of evil, 2018; academic articles, chapters and reviews on theol. *Recreations:* walking, theatre (especially puppetry), music (especially Handel). *Address:* Wycliffe Hall, 54 Banbury Road, Oxford OX2 6PW. *T:* (01865) 274209. *E:* principal@wycliffe.ox.ac.uk.

**LLOYD, Air Vice-Marshal Michael Guy,** CB 2013; International Programme Director and General Manager in Abu Dhabi, since 2015; *b* Shifnal, Shropshire, 7 Dec. 1959; *s* of Air Vice-Marshal Darrell Clive Arthur Lloyd, CB and of Pamela Lloyd (née Woodside); one *s* one *d*; *m* 2014, Ghislaine Fluck. *Educ:* Kent Coll., Canterbury; qualified as helicopter and tactics instructor and display pilot, 1989; RAF Staff Coll. Commnd RAF, 1979; operational helicopter pilot, 1981–92; Personnel Desk Officer, RAF Innsworth, 1992–93; Advanced Staff Coll., Bracknell, 1994; Operational Requirements (RAF), MoD, 1995–97; in command: No 72 Sqdn, RAF Aldergrove, 1997–99; RAF Benson, 2001–02; rcds 2003; HCSC 2004; Director: PR, 2004–06; Reserve Forces and Cadets, 2007–09; COS Personnel and Air Sec., 2009–11; AOC No 22 Gp and COS Trng, HQ Air Comd, 2011–14. *Recreations:* golf, ski-ing, walking, Rugby Union, history of the First World War. *Club:* Royal Air Force.

**LLOYD, Sir Nicholas (Markley),** Kt 1990; MA; Chairman, BLJ London (formerly Brown Lloyd James), since 1997; *b* 9 June 1942; *s* of Walter and Sybil Lloyd; *m* 1st, 1968, Patricia Sholliker (marr. diss. 1978); two *s* one *d*; 2nd, 1979, Eve Pollard, qv; one *s*. *Educ:* Bedford Modern Sch.; St Edmund Hall, Oxford (MA Hons History); Harvard Univ., USA. Reporter, Daily Mail, 1964; Educn Correspondent, Sunday Times, 1966; Dep. News Editor, Sunday Times, 1968; News Editor, The Sun, 1970; Asst Editor, News of the World, 1972; Asst Editor, The Sun, 1976; Dep. Editor, Sunday Mirror, 1980; Editor: Sunday People, 1982–83; News of the World, 1984–85; Daily Express, 1986–95. Presenter, LBC, 1997–99. *Recreations:* Arsenal, golf (Pres., Press Golfing Soc., 2010–), books, theatre. *Address:* 15 and 17 Grosvenor Gardens, SW1W 0BD.

**LLOYD, Prof. Noel Glynne**, CBE 2010; PhD; FLSW; Vice-Chancellor and Principal, 2004–11, Professor of Mathematics, 1988–2011, and Distinguished Research Professor, 2011–16, Aberystwyth University (formerly University of Wales, Aberystwyth), now Professor Emeritus; *b* 26 Dec. 1946; *s* of Joseph John Lloyd and Gwenllian Lloyd; *m* 1970, Dilys June Edwards; one *s* one *d*. *Educ*: Llanelli Grammar Sch.; Queens' Coll., Cambridge (BA 1968, MA 1972; PhD 1972). FTCL 1965. Res. Fellow, St John's Coll., Cambridge, 1972–74; University College of Wales, then University of Wales, Aberystwyth: Lectr, 1974–77; Sen. Lectr, 1977–81; Reader, 1981–88; Hd, Mathematics Dept, 1991–97; Dean of Sci., 1994–97; Pro Vice-Chancellor, 1997–99; Registrar and Sec., 1999–2004. Chairman: Higher Educn Wales, 2008–11; High Performance Computing Wales, 2011–13; Fair Trade Wales, 2011–17. Mem., Maths Cttee, 1989–93, Educn and Trng Cttee, 1993–95, SERC/EPSRC. Member: Selection Cttee, Royal Soc. Exchange Fellowship Prog., 1991–94; Bd, Mid-Wales TEC, 1999–2001; Mid-Wales Regl Cttee, Educn and Learning Wales, 2001–04; Bd, Inst. of Grassland and Envmtl Res., 2004–08; Bd, UCEA, 2005–11 (Chm., Health and Safety Cttee, 2007–11); Bd, QAA, 2005–11 (Chm., Access Regulation and Licensing Cttee, 2006–11); Shadow Bd, 2011–12, Bd, 2012–14, JISC; Commn on Devolution in Wales, 2011–14; Judicial Appts Commn, 2012–19; Hub Cymru Africa, 2015–17. Vice-Pres., UUK, 2008–11. Sec., Capel y Morfa, Aberystwyth, 1989–2004; Chm., Ch and Soc Dept, Presbyterian Ch of Wales, 2014–. Member: Bd, Aberystwyth Challenge Fund, 1999–2011; Bd, Aberystwyth Musicfest, 2016–17; Pres., Aberystwyth Music club, 2011–. Ed., Jl of London Math. Soc., 1983–88. Hon. Mem., Gorsedd of Bards, 2012. FLSW 2012. *Publications*: Degree Theory, 1978; numerous jl articles on Nonlinear Differential Equations. *Recreation*: music (piano, organ). *Address*: 44 Erw Goch, Waunfawr, Aberystwyth, Ceredigion SY23 3AZ. *E*: ngl@aber.ac.uk. *Club*: Oxford and Cambridge.

**LLOYD, Rt Hon. Sir Peter (Robert Cable)**, Kt 1995; PC 1994; President, National Council of Independent Monitoring Boards for Prisons, 2003–07; *b* 12 Nov. 1937; *s* of late David and Stella Lloyd; *m* 1967, Hilary Creighton (*d* 2008); one *s* one *d*. *Educ*: Tonbridge Sch.; Pembroke Coll., Cambridge (MA). Formerly Marketing Manager, United Biscuits plc; Chm., London English Sch. Ltd, 2007–13. MP (C) Fareham, 1979–2001. Sec., Cons. Parly Employment Cttee, 1979–81; Vice-Chm., Cons. European Affairs Cttee, 1980–81; PPS to Minister of State, NI Office, 1981–82, to Sec. of State for Educn and Sci., Sir Keith Joseph, 1983–84; Asst Govt Whip, 1984–86; a Lord Comr of HM Treasury (Govt Whip), 1986–88; Parly Under-Sec. of State, Dept of Social Security, 1988–89, Home Office, 1989–92; Minister of State, Home Office, 1992–94. Member: Select Cttee on Public Affairs, 1996–97; Treasury Select Cttee, 1997–99; Chm., All Party Penal Affairs Cttee, 1997–2001; Vice-Chm., All Party Human Rights Gp, 1997–2001; Mem., H of C Commn, 1998–2000; Chm., Home Office Prisons Bds of Visitors Review Cttee, 2000–01. Vice-Chm., British Section, IPU, 1994–99; Parly Advr, Police Fedn, 1997–2001. Chairman, Bow Group, 1972–73; Editor of Crossbow, 1974–76. Jt Chm., CAABU, 1997–2001; Chm., Arab British Centre, 2001–03. Chm., New Bridge, 1994–2008. *Recreations*: theatre, gardening. *Address*: 32 Burgh Street, N1 8HG. *T*: (020) 7359 2871. *Club*: Players' Theatre.

**LLOYD, Dr Philip Michael**; Director, Adults, Community, Health and Wellbeing, Cheshire East Council, 2010–11; *b* Stockport, 3 Nov. 1952; *s* of James and Dorothy Lloyd; *m* 2010, Ceri Harrison; four *d* from previous marriages. *Educ*: Moseley Hall Grammar Sch.; Univ. of York (BA Hons Hist. and Politics 1974; PhD Railway Studies 2018); Univ. of Manchester (MA Econ) Social Admin 1978). Probation Officer, Gtr Manchester, 1978–98; Principal Social Care Manager, Manchester CC, 1998–99; Youth Offending Team Manager, Manchester and Cheshire, 1999–2006; County Manager, Cheshire CC, 2006–09; Hd, Adult Services, Cheshire E Council, 2009–10. Mem., Neston Town Council, 2014–16. Sec., Railway and Canal Histl Soc. *Recreations*: walking the Welsh coastal path, reading and writing history, supporting Stockport County and Wales Rugby; voluntary work with Neston Town Council.

**LLOYD, Phyllida Christian**, CBE 2010; freelance theatre director; *b* 17 June 1957; *d* of late Patrick Lloyd and Margaret (*née* Douglas-Pennant). *Educ*: Birmingham Univ. (BA English and Drama 1979). Arts Council trainee dir, Wolsey Theatre, Ipswich, 1985. Cameron Mackintosh Vis. Prof. of Contemporary Th., Oxford Univ., 2006; Fellow Emeritus, St Catherine's Coll., Oxford, 2007. Productions include: The Comedy of Errors, A Streetcar Named Desire, Dona Rosita the Spinster, Oliver Twist, Bristol Old Vic, 1989; The Winter's Tale, The School for Scandal, Death and the King's Horseman, Medea, Manchester Royal Exchange, 1990–91; The Virtuoso, Artists and Admirers, RSC, 1991–92; L'Etoile, La Bohème, Gloriana, Medea, Opera North, 1991–96; Six Degrees of Separation, Hysteria, Royal Court, 1992, 1993; Pericles, What the Butler Saw, The Way of the World, RNT, 1994–95; Threepenny Opera, Donmar Warehouse, 1994; Doña Rosita, Almeida, 1997; The Prime of Miss Jean Brodie, RNT, 1998; Carmen, Opera North, 1998; Macbeth, Paris Opera, 1999, Royal Opera, 2002; The Carmelites, 1999, Verdi's Requiem, 2000, ENO; Mamma Mia!, Prince Edward, 1999, and worldwide; The Handmaid's Tale, Royal Danish Opera, 2000, ENO, 2003; Gloriana (BBC TV film), 2000 (Internat. Emmy, Royal Philharmonic Soc. award, FIPA d'or); Boston Marriage, Donmar Warehouse, transf. New Ambassadors, 2001; Albert Herring, Opera North, 2002; The Duchess of Malfi, NT, The Taming of the Shrew, Globe, 2003; The Ring Cycle, ENO, and Macbeth, Liceu Th., Barcelona, 2004; Wild East, Royal Court, 2005; Mary Stuart, Donmar Warehouse, transf. Apollo, 2005 (South Bank Award, 2005); Twilight of the Gods, ENO, 2005; The Fall of the House of Usher, Bregenz, Peter Grimes (South Bank Award, 2006), Opera North, 2006, 2013; Mamma Mia! (film), 2008; The Iron Lady (film), 2012; Julius Caesar, Donmar, 2012, trans. NY, 2013; Josephine and I, Bush Th., 2013; Henry IV, Donmar, 2014; The Taming of the Shrew, Central Park, NY, 2016; Julius Caesar, Henry IV, The Tempest, Donmar, King's Cross, 2016; Macbeth, Royal Opera, 2017; Tina - The Tina Turner Musical, Aldwych, 2018. Hon. DLitt: Bristol, 2006; Birmingham, 2009. *Address*: c/o Annette Stone, Arthouse, B7–3, 1 York Way, N1C 1AT. *T*: (020) 3725 6893.

**LLOYD, Sir Richard (Ernest Butler)**, 2nd Bt *cr* 1960, of Rhu, Co. Dunbarton; Chairman: Vickers plc, 1992–97 (Director, 1978–97; Deputy Chairman, 1989–92); Argos plc, 1995–98; *b* 6 Dec. 1928; *s* of Major Sir (Ernest) Guy Richard Lloyd, 1st Bt, DSO, and Helen Kynaston (*d* 1984), *yr d* of Col E. W. Greg, CB; *S* father, 1987; *m* 1955, Jennifer Susan Margaret, *e d* of Brigadier Ereld Cardiff, CB, CBE; three *s*. *Educ*: Wellington Coll.; Hertford Coll., Oxford (MA). Nat. Service (Captain, Black Watch), 1947–49. Joined Glyn, Mills & Co., 1952; Exec. Dir, 1964–70; Chief Executive, Williams & Glyn's Bank Ltd, 1970–78; Hill Samuel & Co. Ltd: Dep. Chm., 1978–87, 1991–95; Chief Exec., 1980–87; Chm., 1987–91. Member: CBI Council, 1978–96; Industrial Develt Adv. Bd, 1972–77; Nat. Econ. Develt Council, 1973–77; Cttee to Review the Functioning of Financial Institutions, 1977–80; Overseas Projects Bd, 1981–85; Advisory Bd, Royal Coll. of Defence Studies, 1987–95; Chm., Business and Industry Adv. Cttee, OECD, Paris, 1998–99. Hon. Treas., 1989–94, Pres., 1995–2004, British Heart Foundn; Gov., Ditchley Foundn, 1975–2004 (Chm., Finance Cttee, 1985–93). *Recreations*: walking, fly-fishing, gardening. *Heir*: *s* Richard Timothy Butler Lloyd [*b* 12 April 1956; *m* 1989, Wilhelmina, *d* of Henri Schut]. *Address*: Easton Court, Little Hereford, Ludlow SY8 4LN. *T*: (01584) 810475. *Club*: Boodle's.

**LLOYD, Richard Hey**; *b* 25 June 1933; *s* of Charles Yates Lloyd and Ann Lloyd (*née* Hey); *m* 1962, Teresa Morwenna Willmott; four *d*. *Educ*: Lichfield Cathedral Choir Sch.; Rugby Sch. (Music Scholar); Jesus Coll., Cambridge (Organ Scholar; MA). FRCO; ARCM; FRSCM 2010. Asst Organist, Salisbury Cath., 1957–66; Organist and Master of the Choristers, Hereford Cath., 1966–74; Conductor, Three Choirs Festival, 1966–74 (Chief Conductor 1967, 1970, 1973); Organist and Master of the Choristers, Durham Cathedral, 1974–85; Dep. Headmaster, Salisbury Cathedral Choir Sch., 1985–88. Examiner, Associated Bd of Royal Schs of Music, 1967–2011. Mem. Council, RCO, 1974–93. FRSA. Hon. FGCM 2006. *Publications*: church and organ music. *Recreations*: cricket, theatre, travel, reading. *Address*: Duneaves, Lucton, Herefordshire HR6 9PH. *T*: (01568) 780735.

**LLOYD, Robert Andrew**, CBE 1991; freelance opera singer, broadcaster, writer and teacher; *b* 2 March 1940; *s* of William Edward Lloyd and May (*née* Waples); *m* 1st, 1964, Sandra Dorothy Watkins (marr. diss. 1990); one *s* three *d*; 2nd, 1992, Lynda Anne Hazell (*née* Powell). *Educ*: Southend-on-Sea High Sch.; Keble Coll., Oxford (MA Hons Mod. History; Hon. Fellow, 1990). Instructor Lieut RN (HMS Collingwood), 1963–66; Civilian Tutor, Police Staff Coll., Bramshill, 1966–68; studied at London Opera Centre, 1968–69; début in Leonore, Collegiate Theatre, 1969; Principal Bass, Sadler's Wells Opera, Coliseum, 1969–72; Principal Bass, 1972–82, Sen. Artist, 2004–10, Royal Opera House; Parsifal, Covent Garden, 1988; Flying Dutchman, La Scala, 1988; début at Metropolitan Opera, NY, in Barber of Seville, 1988; début at Vienna State Opera in La Forza del Destino; début at Bolshoi Opera, Moscow in Billy Budd, 2016. Guest appearances in Amsterdam, Berlin, Hamburg, Aix-en-Provence, Milan (La Scala), San Francisco, Florence, Paris, Munich, Nice, Boston, Toronto, Salzburg, Tokyo; soloist with major orchestras; over 90 recordings; associated with rôles of King Philip, Boris Godunov (first British bass to sing this rôle at Kirov Opera), Gurnemanz (opened 1991 season, La Scala), Fiesco, Banquo, King Henry; created rôle of Tyrone in Tower (opera by Hoddinott), 1999; film, Parsifal; TV productions: Six Foot Cinderella, 1988; Bluebeard's Castle (opera), 1988; Bob the Bass, 2002; 20 progs for BBC Radio 3, incl. presenter, Opera in Action, 2000–01. Vis. Prof., RCM, 1996. President: British Youth Opera, 1989–94; Southend Choral Soc., 1996–; ISM, 2005–06; Founding Pres., Highgate Opera Circle, 2013–. Member: Exec. Cttee, Musicians Benevolent Fund, 1988–94; Conservatoires Adv. Gp, HEFCE, 1993–97; Mgt Cttee, Highgate Scientific and Literary Instn, 2013–. Patron, Carl Rosa Trust, 1993–. Hon. RAM 1999. FRWCMD 2005. Sir Charles Santley Award, Musicians' Co., 1997; Foreign Artist of the Year Medal, Buenos Aires, 1997; Chaliapin Commem. Medal, St Petersburg, 1998. *Publications*: contrib. miscellaneous jls. *Recreations*: sailing, straight theatre. *Address*: c/o Askonas Holt Ltd, 15 Fetter Lane, EC4A 1BW.

**LLOYD, Prof. Robert Glanville**, DPhil; FRS 2000; Professor of Genetics, 1990, now Professor Emeritus, and Research Professor, School of Physics and Astronomy, University of Nottingham; *b* 25 June 1946; *m* Priscilla Barbara Vaughton; two *d*. *Educ*: Univ. of Bristol (BSc); Univ. of Sussex (DPhil). University of Nottingham: Lectr, 1974–85; Reader in Genetics, 1985–90; Head of Dept of Genetics, 1993–96. *Address*: Centre for Genetics and Genomics, School of Life Science, University of Nottingham, Queen's Medical Centre, Nottingham NG7 2UH; 199 Attenborough Lane, Attenborough, Nottingham NG9 6AB.

**LLOYD, Stephen**; MP for Eastbourne, since 2017 (Lib Dem, 2017–18; Ind, since 2018); *b* Mombasa, Kenya, 15 June 1957; *s* of John Lloyd and Nuala Lloyd; partner, Cherine Maskill. *Educ*: St George's Coll., Weybridge. Commodity broker, Cominco (UK) Ltd, 1977–80; actor, 1980–82; proprietor, Tamarind Sound, radio prodn co., 1982–88; charity consultant, 1988–98; Business Develt Dir, Grass Roots Gp plc, 1998–2005; consultant, 2005–06; Business Develt Consultant, FSB, 2006–10; Business Innovations Dir, 2015–16, Associate Business Innovations Dir, 2016–17, West End Studios Ltd, Eastbourne. Lib Dem frontbench spokesman, DWP, 2017–18. Contested (Lib Dem): Beaconsfield, 2001; Eastbourne, 2005. MP (Lib Dem) Eastbourne, 2010–15; contested (Lib Dem) same seat, 2015. *Recreations*: film, current affairs, motor racing, theatre, history. *Address*: House of Commons, SW1A 0AA.

**LLOYD, His Honour Stephen Harris**; a Circuit Judge, 1995–2007; a Deputy Circuit Judge, since 2007; *b* 16 Sept. 1938; *s* of Thomas Richard Lloyd and Amy Irene Lloyd; *m* 1972, Joyce Eileen Baxter; two step *d*. *Educ*: Ashville Coll., Harrogate; Leeds Univ. (LLB). Dale & Newbery, solicitors: articled, 1961; admitted solicitor, 1965; Partner, 1968–85; Sen. Partner, 1985–95; Asst Recorder, 1989–93; Recorder, 1993–95. Chairman: Nat. Council for One Parent Families, 1975–83; Mediation in Divorce, 1986–90. Vice-Chm., St Peter's NHS Trust, Chertsey, 1991–95. Chm., Bd of Govs, Manor House Sch., 1987–95. Member: Ashvillian Soc., 1958–; 750 (Brooklands) Motor Club, 1986–; Alvis Owners Club, 2001–. *Recreations*: 1936 motor car, 1971 Triumph 2000 Webasto Roof Saloon, organising annual private classic car rallies for friends, charity and committee work, walking, arts. *Address*: Brighton County Court, Family Centre, 1 Edward Street, Brighton BN2 0JD. *T*: (01273) 811333, *Fax*: (01273) 607638.

**LLOYD, Thomas Owen Saunders**, OBE 2004; DL; FSA; heritage consultant; Wales Herald of Arms Extraordinary (Herodr Arbennig Cymru), since 2010; *b* 26 Feb. 1955; *s* of John Audley Lloyd, MC and Mary Ivy Anna Lloyd (*née* Owen); *m* 1987, Christabel Juliet Anne Harrison-Allen (*d* 1996); *m* 2017, Willa, Lady Elphinstone. *Educ*: Radley; Downing Coll., Cambridge (MA Law). FSA 1992. Solicitor, in private practice, London, 1978–87; Dir and Co. Sec., Golden Grove Book Co., Carmarthen, 1987–89; non-executive Director: Dyfed FHSA, 1990–95 (also Chm., Patients' Complaints Cttees); Wales Tourist Bd, 1995–99. Consultant (Wales), Sotheby's, 1999–2012. Chairman: Historic Buildings Council for Wales, 1992–2004; Cathedrals and Churches Commn (Ch in Wales), 2012–; Mem., Royal Commn on the Ancient and Historical Monuments of Wales, 2010–. Chairman: Pembrokeshire Historical Soc., 1991–94; Buildings at Risk Trust, 1992–2008; Carmarthenshire Antiquarian Soc., 1999–2002 and 2009–12; Picton Castle Trust, 2006–10; Bookplate Soc., 2019–; Pres. Cambrian Archaeological Assoc., 2007–08. Trustee, Architectural Heritage Fund, 2006–12; Vice Patron for Wales, War Memls Trust, 2014–. DL 2001, High Sheriff, 2011–12, Dyfed. Hon. Fellow: Soc. of Architects in Wales, 1993; Univ. of Wales Trinity St David, 2011. *Publications*: The Lost Houses of Wales, 1986, 2nd edn 1989; Pevsner Buildings of Wales series: (jtly) Pembrokeshire, 2004, 2nd edn 2010; (jtly) Carmarthenshire & Ceredigion, 2006; contribs to jls of various Welsh historical socs. *Recreation*: old books and bookplates. *Address*: Court Henry, Dryslwyn, Carmarthen SA32 8RU. *T*: (01558) 668252.

**LLOYD, Rt Hon. Sir Timothy (Andrew Wigram)**, Kt 1996; PC 2005; a Lord Justice of Appeal, 2005–13; *b* 30 Nov. 1946; *s* of late Thomas Wigram Lloyd and Margo Adela Lloyd (*née* Beasley); *m* 1978, Theresa Sybil Margaret Holloway. *Educ*: Winchester College; Lincoln College, Oxford (Hon. Fellow, 2006). MA. Called to the Bar, Middle Temple, 1970, Bencher, 1994; QC 1986; Mem., Middle Temple and Lincoln's Inn; a Judge of the High Ct of Justice, Chancery Div., 1996–2005. Attorney Gen., Duchy of Lancaster, 1993–96; Vice-Chancellor, County Palatine of Lancaster, 2002–05. *Publications*: (ed) Wurtzburg & Mills, Building Society Law, 15th edn 1989. *Recreation*: music.

**LLOYD, Tom**, RDI 2008; Founding Partner and Director, PearsonLloyd, since 1997; *b* London, 18 Sept. 1966; *s* of Sam and Jane Lloyd; *m* 1998, Polly Richards; two *d*. *Educ*: Trent Poly. (BA 1st Cl. Hons 1991); Royal Coll. of Art (MA Dist. 1993). Sen. Designer,

Pentagram, 1993–97. *Recreations:* family, food, Cornwall. *Address:* PearsonLloyd, 117 Drysdale Street, N1 6ND. *T:* (020) 7033 4440, *Fax:* (020) 7033 4441. *E:* tom.lloyd@pearsonlloyd.com.

**LLOYD, Ven. Trevor;** *see* Lloyd, Ven. B. T.

**LLOYD, Valerie;** Member (Lab) Swansea East, National Assembly for Wales, Sept. 2001–2011; *b* 16 Nov. 1943; *m* 1964, Robert John Lloyd; two *d. Educ:* Llwyn-y-Bryn High Sch. for Girls; Univ. of Wales, Swansea (BEd 1986; MEd 1992). SRN 1966; RNT 1980. Staff nurse, Swansea, 1966–69, 1971–73; nursing sister, Zambia, 1969–71; teacher: Cwmrhydyceirw Primary Sch., Swansea, 1976–77; St Christopher's Sch., Bahrain, 1977–80; Nurse Tutor, 1980–86, Sen. Nurse Tutor, 1986–92, W Glamorgan Sch. of Nursing; Sen. Lectr in Nursing, Sch. of Health Sci., Univ. of Wales, Swansea, 1992–2001. Mem. (Lab) Swansea City and County Councils, 1999–2003.

**LLOYD, Vanessa;** a District Judge (Magistrates' Courts), since 2013; *b* Hammersmith, 17 Feb. 1966; *d* of Alan Lloyd and late Leonora Lloyd; *m* 2003, Mark Martynski; one *s* two *d. Educ:* Lady Margaret Sch., London; Trent Poly. (LLB Hons); Coll. of Law. Admitted as solicitor, 1991; Hudson Freeman Berg, 1990–2000; Lewis Nedas & Co., 2000–13. Dep. District Judge, Magistrates' Cts, 2005–13. Mental Health Tribunal Judge, 2002–. *Recreations:* reading, running, knitting, badminton, theatre. *Address:* Bromley Magistrates' Court, 1 London Road, Bromley, Kent BR1 1RA. *T:* (020) 8437 3585. *E:* DJMC.Vanessa.Lloyd@ejudiciary.net.

**LLOYD, Wendy Jane, (Mrs M. Sellars);** a District Judge (Magistrates' Courts), Merseyside; *b* 31 Oct. 1960; *d* of John Howson Lloyd and Nancy Beatrice Lloyd (*née* Barlow); *m* 1987, Michael Sellars; one *s* two *d. Educ:* Liverpool Univ. (LLB Hons). Called to the Bar, Middle Temple, 1983; in practice as barrister, Liverpool, 1984–2005; Dep. Dist Judge (Crime), 2003–05; a Dist Judge (Magistrates' Courts), Gtr Manchester, 2005–14. *Recreation:* amateur operatics and theatre (mainly Gilbert and Sullivan).
*See also* H. C. Lloyd.

**LLOYD-CLARKE, Tracey Norma Beatrice; Her Honour Judge Lloyd-Clarke;** a Circuit Judge, since 2016; *b* Abercynon, 18 Sept. 1964; *d* of Victor D. Lloyd-Nesling, JP, and Dr Norma V. Lloyd-Nesling; *m* 2013, Richard Stephen Clarke, FCA. *Educ:* Univ. of Buckingham (LLB Hons); Inns of Court Sch. of Law. Called to the Bar, Middle Temple, 1988; in practice as barrister: Mitre Court Chambers, London, 1989–95; CPS, 1995–99; St Phillips Chambers, Birmingham, 1999–2005; 30 Park Place Chambers, Cardiff, 2005–16; a Recorder, 2009–16. *Recreations:* reading, dancing, cooking, supporting Welsh Rugby.

**LLOYD-DAVIES, Andrew;** an Upper Tribunal Judge (Administrative Appeals Chamber) (formerly Social Security and Child Support Commissioner), since 1998; Deputy Social Security and Child Support Commissioner for Northern Ireland, since 2011; *b* 18 June 1948; *s* of late Martyn Howard Lloyd-Davies and Penelope Catherine (*née* Vevers); *m* 1989, Lucy Laetitia Anne, *d* of late Christopher William Trelawny Morshead, MC, and Hope (*née* Rodd); one *s* one *d. Educ:* Haileybury; St John's Coll., Oxford (BA Lit. Hum.). Called to the Bar, Lincoln's Inn, 1973; in practice at Chancery Bar, 1975–98; Dep. Social Security Comr, 1996–98. *Address:* Upper Tribunal, Administrative Appeals Chamber, 5th Floor, Rolls Building, 7 Rolls Buildings, Fetter Lane, EC4A 1NL. *Club:* MCC.

**LLOYD-EDWARDS, Captain Sir Norman,** KCVO 2008; RD 1971 and Bar 1980, RNR; JP; Lord-Lieutenant of South Glamorgan, 1990–2008 (Vice Lord-Lieutenant, 1986–90); *b* 13 June 1933; *s* of Evan Stanley Edwards and Mary Leah Edwards. *Educ:* Monmouth School for Boys; Quaker's Yard Grammar School; Univ. of Bristol (LLB). Joined RNVR 1952, RN 1958–60; RNR 1960–86; CO S Wales Div., RNR, 1981–84; Naval ADC to the Queen, 1984. Partner, Cartwrights, later Cartwrights, Adams & Black, Solicitors, Cardiff, 1960–93, Consultant, 1993–98. Cardiff City Councillor, 1963–87; Dep. Lord Mayor, 1973–74; Lord Mayor, 1985–86. Member: Welsh Arts Council, 1983–89; BBC Adv. Council (Wales), 1987–90. Chapter Clerk, Llandaff Cathedral, 1975–90. Chm. of Wales, 1981–96, Pres., 1996–, Duke of Edinburgh's Award; Nat. Rescue Training Council, 1983–95. Chm., Glamorgan TAVRA, 1987–90; President: Utd Services Mess, Cardiff, 1986–; S Glam Scouts, 1989–2008; Cardiff Assoc., National Trust, 1990–2013; Seafarers UK (formerly King George's Fund for Sailors), 1990–2016; Friends of Llandaff Cath., 1990–; Friends of St John's Ch, Cardiff, 1990–; Christian Aid (Cardiff and Dist), 1992–2003; Wales Community Foundn (formerly SE Wales Community Foundn), 1993–; Masonic Samaritan Fund, 1998–2007; RFCA Wales, 1999–2005; Cowbridge Charter Trust, 2004–18; City (formerly George Thomas) Hospice, 2006–; Cardiff and Vale of Glamorgan Br., SSAFA, 2011–18 (Patron, 1997–2012). Vice-Pres., RWCMD (formerly WCMD), 1995–; Chm., NYO of Wales, 2009–18. Chm., Insole Court Trust, 2011–19 (Pres., 2019–). Founder Master, Welsh Livery Guild, 1992–95. Patron: British Red Cross (S Glam), 1991–2008; Welsh Music Guild, 2008–. Hon. Colonel: 2 Bn (TA), Royal Regt of Wales, 1996–99; Royal Welsh Regt, 1999–2003; 160 (Wales) Bde, 2007–11; 53 (Wales and Western) Signal Sqdn, 2017–19. DL S Glamorgan 1978; JP 1990. Provincial Grand Master, S Wales Freemasons, 2008–13. Hon. LLD Wales, 2008; Hon. Dr Glamorgan, 2008. Paul Harris Fellow, Rotary, 2009. GCStJ 1996 (KStJ 1988, Prior of Wales, 1989–2005; Dep. Lord Prior, 2005–11). Gold Medal, RNLI, 2015. *Recreations:* music, gardening, table talk. *Address:* Hafan Wen, Llantrisant Road, Llandaff CF5 2PU. *Clubs:* Army and Navy; Cardiff and County, United Services Mess (Cardiff).

**LLOYD GEORGE,** family name of **Earl Lloyd-George of Dwyfor.**

**LLOYD-GEORGE,** family name of **Viscount Tenby.**

**LLOYD-GEORGE OF DWYFOR,** 4th Earl *cr* 1945; **David Richard Owen Lloyd George;** Viscount Gwynedd, 1945; *b* 22 Jan. 1951; *er s* of 3rd Earl Lloyd George of Dwyfor and Ruth Margaret (*née* Coit); *S* father, 2010; *m* 1985, Pamela, *d* of late Alexander Kleyff; two *s. Educ:* Eton. *Heir: s* Viscount Gwynedd, *qv.*
*See also* S. E. Prior-Palmer.

**LLOYD-JONES, Rt Hon. Lord; David Lloyd Jones,** Kt 2005; PC 2012; a Justice of the Supreme Court of the United Kingdom, since 2017; *b* 13 Jan. 1952; *s* of William Elwyn Jones and Annie Blodwen Jones (*née* Lloyd-Jones); *m* 1983, Annmarie Harris; one *s* one *d. Educ:* Pontypridd Boys' Grammar Sch.; Downing Coll., Cambridge (MA, LLB, Whewell Scholar; Hon. Fellow, 2012). Called to the Bar, Middle Temple, 1975, Bencher, 2005; Fellow, Downing Coll., Cambridge, 1975–91; Asst Recorder, 1989–94; a Recorder, 1994–2005; Junior Crown Counsel (Common Law), 1997–99; QC 1999; a Dep. High Court Judge, 2001–05; a Judge of the High Court, QBD, 2005–12; Presiding Judge of Wales, 2008–11; a Lord Justice of Appeal, 2012–17. Asst Comr, 1996–2005, Dep. Chm., 2006–12, Parly Boundary Commn for Wales; Mem., Lord Chancellor's Adv. Cttee on Private Internat. Law, 1997–; Chairman: Lord Chancellor's Standing Cttee on the Welsh Lang., 2008–11; Law Commn, 2012–15. Mem., Council of Legal Educn, 1991–96; Gov., Inns of Court Sch. of Law, 1996–2002; Trustee, British Inst. of Internat. and Comparative Law, 2015–; Pres., Lord Edmund-Davies Legal Educnl Trust, 2019–. Chm., Bar European Gp, 2004–05 (Pres., 2018–); Vice Pres., Admin. Law Bar Assoc., 2012–. Vis. Prof., City Univ., 1999–2005. President: Holdsworth Club, Univ. of Birmingham, 2016; Downing Coll. Alumni Assoc., 2016–17. FLSW 2016. Hon. Fellow: Aberystwyth Univ., 2012; Bangor Univ., 2018. Hon. LLD: Glamorgan, 2010; Swansea, 2014. *Publications:* articles in legal jls. *Recreations:* music, hill walking. *Address:* Supreme Court of the United Kingdom, Parliament Square, SW1P 3BD.

**LLOYD-JONES, David Mathias;** freelance conductor; *b* 19 Nov. 1934; *s* of late Sir Vincent Lloyd-Jones, and Margaret Alwena, *d* of late G. H. Mathias; *m* 1964, Anne Carolyn Whitehead (*d* 2016); two *s* one *d. Educ:* Westminster Sch.; Magdalen Coll., Oxford (BA). Repetiteur, Royal Opera House, Covent Garden, 1959–60; Chorus Master, New Opera Co., 1961–64; conducted at: Bath Fest., 1966; City of London Fest., 1966; Wexford Fest., 1967–70; Scottish Opera, 1968; WNO, 1968; Royal Opera House, 1971; ENO (formerly Sadler's Wells Opera), 1969 (Asst Music Dir, 1972–78); Founder and Artistic Dir, Opera North, 1978–90; Cheltenham, Leeds and Edinburgh Fests; also conductor of BBC broadcasts, TV operas (Eugene Onegin, The Flying Dutchman, Hansel and Gretel), and operas and concerts in France, Holland, Russia, Germany, Italy, Switzerland, Bulgaria, Poland, Chile, America, Canada, Argentina, Ireland, Norway, Sweden, Israel, Japan and Australia; has appeared with most British symph. orchs. Numerous recordings with LPO, RSNO, Bournemouth SO and Sinfonietta, BBC SO, Royal Liverpool Philharmonic Orch., Nash Ensemble and English Northern Philharmonia (Founder Conductor). Chairman: Delius Trust, 1997–2017; Berners Trust, 2016–. Gen. Ed., William Walton Edition, 1996–2014. Hon. Mem., Royal Philharmonic Soc., 2007. FGS (FGSM 1992). Hon. DMus Leeds, 1986. *Publications:* (trans.) Boris Godunov (vocal score), 1968; (trans.) Eugene Onegin (vocal score), 1971; Boris Godunov (critical edn of original full score), 1975; The Gondoliers, 1986; contrib. 6th edn Grove's Dictionary of Music and Musicians, 1981; contrib. Musik in klassischen und Gegenwart, Music and Letters, and The Listener. *Recreations:* theatre, old shrub roses, travel. *Address:* 94 Whitelands House, Cheltenham Terrace, SW3 4RA. *T:* (020) 7730 8695.

**LLOYD-JONES, Prof. Guy Charles,** DPhil; FRS 2013; FRSC; FRSE; Forbes Chair of Organic Chemistry, University of Edinburgh, since 2013; *b* London, 17 May 1966; *s* of Peter George and Jennifer Mary Lloyd-Jones; *m* 2004, Kathryn Anne Stockley. *Educ:* Huddersfield Poly. (BSc Chem. 1989); Linacre Coll., Oxford (DPhil Chem. 1992). FRSC 2003. Res. Associate, Basel Univ., 1993–95; University of Bristol: Lectr, 1996–2000; Reader, 2000–03; Prof., 2003–13. FRSE 2015. DUniv. Huddersfield, 2014. *Recreations:* fly fishing, salmon and trout, Scottish single malt whiskies. *Address:* School of Chemistry, University of Edinburgh, Joseph Black Building, West Mains Road, Edinburgh EH9 3JJ. *T:* (0131) 650 4795. *E:* guy.lloyd-jones@ed.ac.uk.

**LLOYD-JONES, Isabel Anne; Her Honour Judge Lloyd-Jones;** a Circuit Judge, since 2019; *b* Bedford, 2 Jan. 1957; *d* of Thomas Lloyd-Jones and Joan Margaret Lloyd-Jones; *m* 1981, Stephen Richard Hughes; one *s* one *d. Educ:* Herts and Essex High Sch. for Girls; St Albans Girls' Grammar Sch.; St Hugh's Coll., Oxford (MA Jt Hons Mod. Langs). Admitted solicitor, 1983; Solicitor: Rutherfords Solicitors, 1983–84; Handsworth Law Centre, Birmingham, 1984–86; Howells Solicitors, Sheffield, 1987–2011; a District Judge, Midlands Circuit, 2011–19. *Recreations:* sail cruising, choral singing. *Address:* Oxford Combined Court Centre, St Aldate's, Oxford OX1 1TL.

**LLOYD JONES, John;** *see* Jones, John Lloyd.

**LLOYD-JONES, John Benedict;** QC 2013; *b* Liverpool, 4 June 1965; *s* of Elwyn and Anne Lloyd-Jones; *m* 1997, Gaile; one *s* one *d. Educ:* Eton Coll.; Univ. of Durham (BA Hons Anthropol.); Poly. of Central London (CPE); Inns of Court Sch. of Law. Served as Officer, Coldstream Guards, 1988–91. Called to the Bar, Inner Temple, 1993; Hd, Criminal Team, 36 Bedford Row, 2011. *Recreation:* collecting 2000 AD and Judge Dredd comics. *Address:* 36 Group, 4 Field Court, Gray's Inn, WC1R 5EF. *T:* (020) 7421 8000. *E:* jlloyd-jones@36crime.co.uk.

**LLOYD JONES, Sir Richard (Anthony),** KCB 1988 (CB 1981); Permanent Secretary, Welsh Office, 1985–93; Chairman, Arts Council of Wales, 1994–99; *b* 1 Aug. 1933; *s* of Robert and Anne Lloyd Jones; *m* 1st, 1955, Patricia Avril Mary Richmond (*d* 2002); two *d;* 2nd, 2005, Helen Margaret Yewlett (*née* Lewis). *Educ:* Long Dene Sch., Edenbridge; Nottingham High Sch.; Balliol Coll., Oxford (MA). Entered Admiralty, 1957; Asst Private Sec. to First Lord of the Admiralty, 1959–62; Private Sec. to Secretary of the Cabinet, 1969–70; Asst Sec., Min. of Defence, 1970–74; Under Sec., 1974–78, Dep. Sec. 1978–85, Welsh Office. Chairman: Civil Service Benevolent Fund, 1987–93 (Trustee, 1993–2000); Adv. Cttee on local govt staff transfers (Wales), 1993–94; Local Govt Staff Commn for Wales, 1994–97. Member: BBC Gen. Adv. Council, 1994–96; Commn for Local Democracy, 1994–95. President: Welsh Council, Ramblers' Assoc., 1993–2011; Groundwork Merthyr and Rhondda Cynon Taff, 1996–2013; Chm., Age Concern Cymru, 1999–2005 (Pres., 1996–99); Vice-Chairman: Prince of Wales' Cttee, 1993–96; Prince's Trust Bro, 1996–99; Age Concern England, 2005–09. Vice Pres., Univ. of Wales, Cardiff, 1993–2004; Member: Ct, Univ. of Wales, 1995–2000; Ct, Nat. Mus. of Wales, 1996–99; Ct and Council, Cardiff Univ., 2004–10. Chm., Fishguard Internat. Music Fest., 1999–2005. Hon. Fellow: UCW Aberystwyth, 1990; Trinity Coll., Carmarthen, 1996. Hon. Dr Glamorgan, 1996; Hon. LLD Wales, 2004. *Recreations:* music, railways. *Address:* Radyr, Cardiff. *Clubs:* Oxford and Cambridge; Cardiff and County.

**LLOYD MOSTYN,** family name of **Baron Mostyn.**

**LLOYD WEBBER,** family name of **Baron Lloyd-Webber.**

**LLOYD-WEBBER,** Baron *cr* 1997 (Life Peer), of Sydmonton in the co. of Hampshire; **Andrew Lloyd Webber,** Kt 1992; composer; *b* 22 March 1948; *s* of late William Southcombe Lloyd Webber, CBE, DMus, FRCM, FRCO, and Jean Hermione Johnstone; *m* 1st, 1971, Sarah Jane Tudor (*née* Hugill) (marr. diss. 1983); one *s* one *d;* 2nd, 1984, Sarah Brightman (marr. diss. 1990); 3rd, 1991, Madeleine Astrid Gurdon; two *s* one *d. Educ:* Westminster Sch.; Magdalen Coll., Oxford; Royal Coll. of Music (FRCM 1988). Composer: (with lyrics by Timothy Rice): The Likes of Us, 1965; Joseph and the Amazing Technicolor Dreamcoat, 1968, rev. 1973, 1991, 2003 and 2007; Jesus Christ Superstar, 1970, rev. 1996 (Emmy Award, 2018); Evita, 1976 (stage version, 1978, rev. 2006, 2019); (with lyrics by Alan Ayckbourn) Jeeves, 1975, revived as By Jeeves, 1996; (with lyrics by Don Black) Tell Me on a Sunday, 1980, rev. 2003; Cats, 1981, rev. 2014 (based on poems by T. S. Eliot); (with lyrics by Don Black) Song & Dance, 1982; (with lyrics by Richard Stilgoe) Starlight Express, 1984; (with lyrics by Richard Stilgoe and Charles Hart) The Phantom of the Opera, 1986; (with lyrics by Don Black and Charles Hart) Aspects of Love, 1989, rev. 2018; (with lyrics by Christopher Hampton and Don Black) Sunset Boulevard, 1993; (with lyrics by Jim Steinman) Whistle Down the Wind, 1996; (with lyrics by Ben Elton) The Beautiful Game, 2000; (with lyrics by David Zippel) The Woman in White, 2004; (with lyrics by Glenn Slater) Love Never Dies, 2010; Stephen Ward (with lyrics by Christopher Hampton and Don Black), 2013; (with lyrics by Glenn Slater) School of Rock (also prod.), 2015. Producer: *theatre:* Joseph and the Amazing Technicolor Dreamcoat, 1973, 1974, 1978, 1980, 1991; Jeeves Takes Charge, 1975; Cats, 1981; Song and Dance, 1982; Daisy Pulls It Off, 1983; The Hired Man, 1984; Starlight Express, 1984; On Your Toes, 1984; The Phantom of the Opera, 1986; Café Puccini, 1986; The Resistible Rise of

Arturo Ui, 1987; Lend Me a Tenor, 1988; Aspects of Love, 1989; Shirley Valentine, 1989 (Broadway); La Bête, 1992; Sunset Boulevard, 1993; By Jeeves, 1996; Jesus Christ Superstar, 1996, 1998; Whistle Down the Wind, 1996, 1998; Bombay Dreams, 2002; The Sound of Music, 2006; The Wizard of Oz, 2011, and others; *film:* Phantom of the Opera, 2004. Film scores: Gumshoe, 1971; The Odessa File, 1974. Composed "Variations" (based on A minor Caprice No 24 by Paganini), 1977, symphonic version, 1986; Requiem Mass, 1985. Mem., H of L, 1997–2017. Awards include Acad. Award (Oscar), Golden Globe, Tony, Drama Desk, Grammy, and Kennedy Center Honor. *Publications:* (with Timothy Rice) Evita, 1978; Cats: the book of the musical, 1981; (with Timothy Rice) Joseph and the Amazing Technicolor Dreamcoat, 1982; The Complete Phantom of the Opera, 1987; The Complete Aspects of Love, 1989; Sunset Boulevard: from movie to musical, 1993; Unmasked: a memoir, 2018. *Recreations:* architecture, art. *Address:* The Really Useful Group, 6 Catherine Street, WC2B 5JY.
*See also* J. Lloyd Webber.

**LLOYD WEBBER, Prof. Julian,** FRCM; 'cellist, conductor; Founder, In Harmony, 2008; Chairman, Sistema England, since 2012; Principal, Royal Birmingham Conservatoire, since 2015; *b* 14 April 1951; *s* of late William Southcombe Lloyd Webber, CBE, DMus, FRCM, FRCO, and Jean Hermione Johnstone; *m* 1st, 1974, Celia Mary Ballantyne (marr. diss. 1989); 2nd, 1989, Princess Zohra Mahmoud Ghazi (marr. diss. 1999); one *s*; 3rd, 2001, Kheira Bourahla (marr. diss. 2007); 4th, 2009, Jiaxin Cheng; one *d*. *Educ:* University College Sch., London; Royal College of Music. ARCM 1967, FRCM 1994. Studied 'cello with: Douglas Cameron, 1965–68; Pierre Fournier, Geneva, 1972. Début, Queen Elizabeth Hall, 1972; USA début, Lincoln Center, NY, 1980. Has performed with the world's major orchestras; toured: USA, Germany, Holland, Africa, Bulgaria, S America, Spain, Belgium, France, Scandinavia, Portugal, Denmark, Australasia, Singapore, Japan, Korea, Czechoslovakia, Austria, Canada, Hong Kong, Taiwan, Vietnam, Turkey, Lebanon and China. Has made first recordings of works by Benjamin Britten, Frank Bridge, Gavin Bryars, Michael Nyman, Delius, Rodrigo, Holst, Vaughan Williams, Haydn, Philip Glass, Sullivan, John McCabe, Malcolm Arnold, John Ireland, Eric Whitacre; recorded: Elgar Cello Concerto (cond. Menuhin), 1985 (British Phonographic Industry Award for Best Classical Recording, 1986); Dvořák Cello Concerto with Czech Philharmonic Orchestra, 1988; Evening Songs; also concertos by Britten, Delius, Glass, Haydn, Honegger, Lalo, Miaskovsky, Rodrigo, Saint-Saëns, Walton, Vivaldi and Tchaikovsky Rococo Variations; Unexpected Songs. Pres., Elgar Soc., 2009–. Crystal Award, World Economic Forum, Switzerland, 1998; Classic FM Red Award, 2004; Dist. Musician Award, ISM, 2014; Musician of Year, Churchill Awards, 2017. *Publications:* Travels with My Cello, 1984; Song of the Birds, 1985; *edited:* series, The Romantic 'Cello, 1978, The Classical 'Cello, 1980, The French 'Cello, 1981; Frank Bridge 'Cello Music, 1981; Young Cellist's Repertoire, Books 1, 2, 3, 1984; Holst, Invocation, 1984; Vaughan Williams, Fantasia on Sussex Folk Tunes, 1984; Recital Repertoire for Cellists, 1987; Short, Sharp Shocks, 1990; The Great 'Cello Solos, 1992; Cello Moods, 1999; Made in England, 2004; A Tale of Two 'Cellos, 2014; Vivaldi: Six Concertos for Two 'Cellos, 2015; contribs to music jls and national Press in UK, US, Canada and Australia. *Recreations:* countryside (especially British), Leyton Orient FC. *E:* julian@julianlloydwebber.com, julian.lloydwebber@bcu.ac.uk.
*See also* Baron Lloyd-Webber.

**LLOYD WILLIAMS, Ven. Martin Clifford;** Archdeacon of Brighton and Lewes, since 2015; Priest-in-charge, Ovingdean, since 2019; *b* Watford, 12 May 1965; *s* of Peter and Angela Lloyd Williams; *m* 1989, Jacqueline Beaumont; one *s* two *d*. *Educ:* Westminster Coll. (BEd 1987); Trinity Coll., Bristol (BA 1993). Ordained deacon, 1993, priest, 1994; Curate, St Swithun's, Walcot, 1993–97; Rector, St Michael's Without, Bath, 1997–2014; Rural Dean, Bath, 2010–15. *Publications:* Beauty and Brokenness, 2007. *Recreations:* supporting Bath RFC, working with people with learning disabilities, walking, cooking and eating, supporting Sussex CCC. *Address:* 12 Walsingham Road, Hove, E Sussex BN3 4FF. *T:* (01273) 725479. *E:* archbandl@chichester.anglican.org.

**LLWYD, Rt Hon. Elfyn;** PC 2011; barrister-at-law; *b* 26 Sept. 1951; *s* of late Huw Meirion Hughes and Hefina (*née* Roberts); surname Hughes abandoned by deed poll, 1970; *m* 1974, Eleri Llwyd; one *s* one *d*. *Educ:* Ysgol Dyffryn Conwy Llanrwst; Univ. of Wales, Aberystwyth (LLB Hons); Coll. of Law, Chester. Admitted solicitor, 1977; called to the Bar, 1997. MP (Plaid Cymru) Meirionnydd Nant Conwy, 1992–2010, Dwyfor Meirionnydd, 2010–15. Plaid Cymru Parly Whip, 1995–2002; Plaid Cymru Parly Leader, 1998–2015. Parly Ambassador to NSPCC. Pres., Gwynedd Law Soc., 1990–91. Member, Court: Univ. of Wales, Aberystwyth, 1993–; of Govs, Nat. Liby of Wales, 1994–2001; of Govs, Nat. Eisteddfod, 1995–; Vice-Pres., Llangollen Internat. Eisteddfod, 2000–. President: Clwb Rygbi y Bala, 1985–; Betws-y-Coed FC, 1998–; Clwb Peldroed Llanuwchllyn, 2005–; Three Peaks Yacht Race, Barmouth, 2013–; Vice-Pres., Dolgellau Rugby Club. Pres., Estimaner Angling Soc., 1989–. Fellow: Inst. of Welsh Affairs; UWTSD 2019. Mem., Gorsedd of Bards. *Recreations:* pigeon breeding, Rugby, choral singing, fishing. *Address:* Glandwr, Llanuwchllyn, Y Bala, Gwynedd LL23 7TW.

**LLWYD MORGAN, Derec;** *see* Morgan, Derec L.

**LO, Anna Manwah,** MBE 2000; Member (Alliance) Belfast South, Northern Ireland Assembly, 2007–16; *b* 17 June 1950; *m* (marr. diss.); two *s*. *Educ:* Univ. of Ulster (Dip. Soc. Work; MSc). Social Worker: N Down and Ards HSS Trust, 1993; Barnardo's, 1995; Chief Exec., Chinese Welfare Assoc., 1997–2007. Vice Chair (first), NI Council for Ethnic Minorities, 1995; founding Comr, Equality Commn for NI, 1999. Chair (first), S Belfast Partnership Bd, 1998–2007. Contested (Alliance) Belfast S, 2010. Chair, Cttee for Envmt, NI Assembly, 2011–16. DUniv Open. *Publications:* The Place I Call Home (autobiog.), 2016.

**LO, Prof. Yuk Ming Dennis,** SBS 2011; DM, DPhil; FRCP, FRCPE, FRCPath; FRS 2011; Professor of Chemical Pathology, since 2003, Li Ka Shing Professor of Medicine, since 2005 and Director, Li Ka Shing Institute of Health Sciences, since 2007, Chinese University of Hong Kong; *b* Hong Kong, 1963; *s* of Wai Hoi Lo and Chiu Man Ku; *m* 1994, Siu Ling Alice Wong. *Educ:* St Joseph's Coll., Hong Kong; Emmanuel Coll., Cambridge (BA 1986); Christ Church, Oxford (BM BCh 1989); Hertford Coll., Oxford (DPhil 1994). MRCP 1995; DM 2001; FRCPE 2004; FRCPath 2005; FRCP 2006. University of Oxford: Wellcome Med. Graduate Fellow, 1990–93; Wellcome Career Develt Fellow, 1993–94; Lectr in Clin. Biol., 1994–97; Fellow, Green Coll., Oxford, 1994–97; Chinese University of Hong Kong: Sen. Lectr, 1997–2000; Reader, 2000–03. Foreign Associate, US NAS, 2013. Hon. FHKCPath 2010. King Faisal Prize for Medicine, 2014; Future Sci. Prize in Life Sci., 2016. *Publications:* over 400 articles in learned jls incl. Lancet, BMJ and Science Translational Medicine. *Recreations:* cinema, travel, photography, golf. *Address:* Department of Chemical Pathology, Prince of Wales Hospital, Shatin, New Territories, Hong Kong. *T:* 37636001, *Fax:* 26365090. *E:* loym@cuhk.edu.hk. *Clubs:* Hong Kong Jockey; Kowloon Cricket; Mission Hills Golf (China).

**LOACH, Kenneth;** television and film director; *b* 17 June 1936; *s* of late John Loach and Vivien Loach (*née* Hamlin); *m* 1962, Lesley Ashton; two *s* two *d* (and one *s* decd). *Educ:* King Edward VI School, Nuneaton; St Peter's Hall, Oxford (Hon. Fellow, St Peter's Coll., 1993). BBC Trainee, Drama Dept, 1963. *Television:* Diary of a Young Man, 1964; 3 Clear Sundays, 1965; The End of Arthur's Marriage, 1965; Up The Junction, 1965; Coming Out Party, 1965; Cathy Come Home, 1966; In Two Minds, 1966; The Golden Vision, 1969; The Big Flame, 1969; After A Lifetime, 1971; The Rank and File, 1972; Days of Hope, 1975; The Price of Coal, 1977; The Gamekeeper, 1979; Auditions, 1980; A Question of Leadership, 1981; Questions of Leadership, 1983 (banned from TV); The Red and the Blue, 1983; Which Side Are You On?, 1985; The View from the Woodpile, 1988; Dispatches, 1991; Flickering Flame, 1996; Another City, 1998. *Films:* Poor Cow, 1967; Kes, 1969; In Black and White, 1970; Family Life, 1972; Black Jack, 1979; Looks and Smiles, 1981; Fatherland, 1987; Hidden Agenda, 1990 (Jury Prize, Cannes Film Fest., 1990); Riff-Raff, 1991; Raining Stones, 1993; Ladybird, Ladybird, 1994; Land and Freedom, 1995; Carla's Song, 1996; My Name is Joe, 1998; Bread and Roses, 2000; The Navigators, 2001; Sweet Sixteen, 2002; Ae Fond Kiss, 2004; Tickets, 2005; The Wind that Shakes the Barley, 2006 (Palme d'Or, Cannes Film Fest.); It's a Free World, 2007; Looking for Eric, 2009; Route Irish, 2010; The Angels' Share, 2012 (Jury Prize, Cannes Film Fest.); The Spirit of '45, 2013; Jimmy's Hall, 2014; I, Daniel Blake, 2016 (Palme d'Or, Cannes Film Fest., 2016; BAFTA Award, 2017); Sorry We Missed You, 2019. BAFTA Fellow, 2006. *Address:* Sixteen Films, 2nd Floor, 187 Wardour Street, W1F 8ZB.

**LOACH, Phil,** QFSM 2018; Chief Fire Officer, West Midlands Fire Service, since 2013; *b* 1 Dec. 1966; *m* Samantha; one *s* one *d*. *Educ:* Univ. of Worcester (Dip. Mgt Studies 2005); Univ. of Coventry (Leadership capability prog. 2010; Postgrad. Cert. Mgt and Leadership 2011; MA Leadership 2014); Fire Service Coll. (Gold Comdr 2011). West Midlands Fire Service: fire fighter, 1994–97; Leading Fire Fighter, 1997–99; Sub Officer, 1999–2001; Sub Officer, Trng Centre, 2001–03; Stn Officer Project Manager, 2003–05; Stn Comdr, B Sutton, 2005–07; Group Commander: A Sheldon, 2007; B Birmingham Central, 2007–09; B Birmingham N, 2009–10; Area Comdr, B Hd of Emergency Response, 2010–11; Asst Chief Fire Officer, Dir of Ops, 2011–13; Actg Dep. Chief Fire Officer, 2013. Gov., W Midland Ambulance. Patron, Burn Aid. *Recreation:* fishing. *Address:* West Midlands Fire Service, 99 Vauxhall Road, Birmingham B7 4HW. *T:* (0121) 380 6909. *E:* phil.loach@wmfs.net.

**LOADER, Air Chief Marshal Sir Clive (Robert),** KCB 2006; OBE 1996; FRAeS; Police and Crime Commissioner (C) for Leicestershire, 2012–16; *b* 24 Sept. 1953; *s* of Ralph George Loader and Vera May Harrington; *m* 1976, Alison Anna Louise Leith. *Educ:* Judd Sch., Tonbridge; Southampton Univ. Officer/Flying Trng, 1973–76; Harrier Pilot and Weapons Instructor, 1977–87; RAF Staff Coll., 1988; Sqn Ldr, Air Offensive, MoD, 1989; Wing Comdr, Air Offensive, HQ RAF Germany, 1990–91; PSO to C-in-C Strike Command, 1991–93; Comdg Harrier Sqn and Stn, 1993–99; Air Cdre, Harrier, HQ 3 Gp (Strike Comd), 1999–2001; ACDS (Ops), MoD, 2002–04; Dep. C-in-C, RAF Strike Comd, 2004–07; C-in-C, HQ Air Comd, 2007–09; Air ADC to the Queen, 2007–09. FRAeS 2004. *Recreations:* golf, cricket, military history, rowing. *Club:* Royal Air Force.

**LOADER, Prof. Ian Spencer,** PhD; FBA 2018; Professor of Criminology, University of Oxford, since 2005 (Director, Centre for Criminology, 2005–12); Fellow, All Souls College, Oxford, since 2005; *b* Harrow, 2 April 1965; *s* of Tony and Pamela Loader; three *d*. *Educ:* Park High Sch., Harrow; Lowlands Sixth Form Coll., Harrow; Univ. of Sheffield (LLB 1986); Univ. of Edinburgh (MSc 1988; PhD 1993). Lectr in Law, Liverpool Poly., 1986–87; Lectr in Criminol. and Jurisprudence, Univ. of Edinburgh, 1990–92; Keele University: Lectr, 1992–99, Sen. Lectr, 1999–2002, Reader, 2002–04, in Criminol.; Prof. of Criminol., 2004–05. Jean Monnet Fellow, European University Inst., Florence, 2004. Res. Associate, IPPR, 2009–. Trustee, Police Foundn, 2007–11; Member: Commn on English Prisons Today, 2007–09; Ind. Commn on Future of Police in England and Wales, 2011–13. Mem. Council, Liberty, 2008–12. FRSA. *Publications:* (jtly) Cautionary Tales, 1994; Youth, Policing and Democracy, 1996; (jtly) Crime and Social Change in Middle England, 2000; (with Aogan Mulcahy) Policing and the Condition of England, 2003; (with Neil Walker) Civilizing Security, 2007; (with Richard Sparks) Public Criminology?, 2010; (ed jtly) Emotions, Crime and Justice, 2011; (ed with Anita Dockley) The Penal Landscape, 2013; (ed with Sarah Percy) Reordering Security, 2014; (ed jtly) Justice and Penal Reform, 2016; (ed jtly) The SAGE Handbook of Global Policing, 2016; (ed jtly) Democratic Theory and Mass Incarceration, 2016. *Recreations:* road cycling, Arsenal FC. *Address:* Centre for Criminology, St Cross Building, St Cross Road, Oxford OX1 3UL. *T:* (01985) 279288. *E:* ian.loader@crim.ox.ac.uk.

**LOADES, Prof. Ann Lomas,** CBE 2001; PhD; Professor of Divinity, Durham University, 1995–2003, now Emeritus; *b* 21 Sept. 1938; *d* of Gerard Joseph Glover and Amy Lomas. *Educ:* Durham Univ. (BA Theol. 1960; PhD 1975); McMaster Univ. (MA 1965). Durham University: Lectr in Theology, 1975–81; Sen. Lectr, 1981–90; Reader, 1990–95; Chm., Bd of Studies in Theol., 1989–91. Arts and Humanities Research Board: Convenor, assessment panel for postgrad. awards in philosophy, law and religious studies, 1999–2003; Mem., Postgrad. Cttee, 1999–2003; Mem., Res. Centres Scheme Cttee, 1999–2003. Pres., Soc. for the Study of Theol., 2005 and 2006. Mem., Council of Archbishop's Examination in Theology, 2006–. Res. Assessor for Res. Council for Culture and Soc., Acad. of Finland, 2007, 2010, 2011, 2013. Lay Mem., Chapter, 2001–07, Lay Canon Emeritus, 2008, Chm., Choir Assoc., 2003–11, Durham Cathedral. Hon. Prof., Sch. of Divinity, Univ. of St Andrews, 2009–. Editor, Theology, 1991–97. *Publications:* (ed) W. A. Whitehouse, The Authority of Grace, 1981; (ed with J. C. Eaton) For God and Clarity, 1983; Kant and Job's Comforters, 1985; Searching for Lost Coins (Scott Holland Lectures), 1987; (ed) Feminist Theology: a reader, 1990; (ed with M. McLain) Hermeneutics, the Bible and Literary Criticism, 1992; (ed with L. Rue) Contemporary Classics in Philosophy of Religion, 1991; (ed) Dorothy L. Sayers, Spiritual Writings, 1993; (ed with D. W. Brown) The Sense of the Sacramental, 1995; (ed) Spiritual Classics from the late Twentieth Century, 1995; (ed with D. W. Brown) Christ: the sacramental word, 1996; Evelyn Underhill, 1997; Feminist Theology: voices from the past, 2001; (ed with J. Astley and D. W. Brown) Problems in Theology series: Creation, 2003; Evil, 2003; War and Peace, 2003; Science and Religion, 2003; God in Action, 2004; (ed with R. C. MacSwain) The Truth-Seeking Heart: Austin Farrer and his writings, 2006; Christology, 2009; (contrib.) From the Margins 2, 2009; (contrib.) New Perspectives on the Nativity, 2009; (contrib.) The Cambridge Companion to C. S. Lewis, 2010; (contrib.) C. S. Lewis and Friends: faith and the power of imagination, 2011; (contrib.) The Oxford Handbook of the Reception History of the Bible, 2011; (contrib.) The Sacred Plays of Dorothy Sayers, 2011; (contrib.) Theology, Aesthetics and Culture, 2012; (contrib.) The Routledge Companion to Modern Christian Thought, 2013; (contrib.) Exploring Lost Dimensions of Christian Mysticism, 2013; (contrib.) The Oxford Handbook of Anglican Studies, 2015; (contrib.) Music, Theology and Justice, 2017; (contrib.) Christian Theology and the Transformation of Natural Religion, 2018; (contrib.) La Bibbia, le donne, la profezia, 2018. *Recreations:* going to the theatre, cooking.

**LOADES, David Henry,** CB 1996; FIA; Directing Actuary, Government Actuary's Department, 1983–97; *b* 16 Oct. 1937; *s* of John Henry Loades and Evelyn Clara Ralph; *m* 1962, Jennifer Glenys Stevens (*d* 2008); one *s* two *d*. *Educ:* Beckenham and Penge County Grammar Sch. for Boys. BA. FIA 1961. Govt Actuary's Dept, 1956–97. Medal of Merit for services to the Scout Assoc., 1986. *Publications:* papers in actuarial jls. *Recreations:* painting, visiting art galleries.

**LOASBY, Prof. Brian John**, FBA 1994; FRSE; Professor of Management Economics, University of Stirling, 1971–84, Emeritus and Hon. Professor of Economics, since 1984; *b* 2 Aug. 1930; *s* of Frederick Thomas Loasby and Mabel Phyllis Loasby; *m* 1957, Judith Ann Robinson; two *d. Educ:* Kettering GS; Emmanuel Coll., Cambridge (BA 1952; MLitt 1958; MA 1998). Assistant in Pol Economy, Aberdeen Univ., 1955–58; Bournville Res. Fellow, Birmingham Univ., 1958–61; Tutor in Management Studies, Bristol Univ., 1961–67; Stirling University: Lectr in Econs, 1967–68; Sen. Lectr, 1968–71. Management Fellow, Arthur D. Little Inc., Cambridge, Mass, 1965–66; Vis. Fellow, Oxford Centre for Management Studies, 1974. Shackle Meml Lect., Univ. of Cambridge, 2010. Pres., Scottish Economic Soc., 1987–90; Vice-Pres., Internat. Schumpeter Soc., 2000–04. FRSE 2007. DUniv Stirling, 1998. (Jtly) Schumpeter Prize, 2000. *Publications:* The Swindon Project, 1973; Choice, Complexity and Ignorance, 1976; The Mind and Method of the Economist, 1989; Equilibrium and Evolution, 1991; (ed with N. J. Foss) Economic Organization, Capabilities and Co-ordination: essays in honour of G. B. Richardson, 1998; Knowledge, Institutions and Evolution in Economics, 1999; contrib. books, and econs and management jls. *Recreation:* gardening. *Address:* Division of Economics, University of Stirling, Stirling FK9 4LA. *T:* (01786) 467470; 8 Melfort Drive, Stirling FK7 0BD. *T:* (01786) 472124.

**LOBBAN, Sir Iain (Robert)**, KCMG 2013; CB 2006; Director, Government Communications Headquarters, 2008–14; *b* 1960; *s* of late Tony and Judy Lobban; *m* 1993, Jane Elizabeth Gully; one *d. Educ:* Merchant Taylors' Sch., Crosby; Univ. of Leeds (BA Hons French with German). Joined GCHQ, 1983; Dir Gen. Ops, 2004–08; HCSC (Jt) 2001. Sen. Expert Advr, Standard Chartered Bank, 2015–; Strategic Partner, C5, 2015–; Chm., Cyber London Adv. Bd, 2015–18; Member, Advisory Board: Global Strategy Forum, 2015–; Lloyd's Register, 2018–; Mem., Internat. Adv. Bd, Hakluyt, 2015–. Vis. Prof., KCL, 2015–. Fellow, Judge Business Sch., Univ. of Cambridge, 2015–. *Recreations:* travel, photography, cricket, football (Everton FC), birdwatching.

**LOBBAN, Prof. Michael John Warrender**, PhD; FBA 2015; Professor of Legal History, London School of Economics and Political Science, since 2013; *b* Cape Town, 22 Oct. 1962; *s* of late John Lobban and Faith Lobban (*née* Cassy, later McDonald). *Educ:* Dulwich Coll.; Corpus Christi Coll., Cambridge (BA 1984; MA 1987; PhD 1988). Jun. Lectr, Dept of Hist., Univ. of Witwatersrand, Johannesburg, 1988; Jun. Res. Fellow, St John's Coll., Oxford, 1988–91; Lectr, 1991–95, Reader in Law, 1995–97, Univ. of Durham; Reader in Law, Brunel Univ., 1997–2000; Reader, 2001–03, Prof. of Legal Hist., 2003–13, Queen Mary, Univ. of London. *Publications:* The Common Law and English Jurisprudence, 1760–1850, 1991; White Man's Justice: South African political trials in the black consciousness era, 1996; A History of the Philosophy of Law in the Common Law World, 1600–1900, 2007; (jtly) The Oxford History of the Laws of England, vols XI–XIII, 2010. *Recreations:* art, travel, music. *Address:* Department of Law, London School of Economics and Political Science, Houghton Street, WC2A 2AE. *E:* m.j.lobban@lse.ac.uk.

**LOBBENBERG, Nicholas;** QC 2014; *b* Shrewsbury, 19 April 1964; *s* of George and Margaret Lobbenberg; *m* 2001, Anna; two *s* one *d. Educ:* Shrewsbury Sch.; Magdalen Coll., Oxford (BA Law); Inns of Court Sch. of Law. Called to the Bar, Gray's Inn, 1987; in practice as barrister, specialising in crime, 1987–. *Recreations:* Rugby, fine wine, travel, toy soldiers, jazz, obscure history. *Address:* 4 Breams Buildings, Chancery Lane, EC4A 1HP. *T:* (020) 7092 1900. *E:* niclobb@aol.com.

**LOBO ANTUNES, Manuel**, Grand Cross, Order of Infante D. Henrique, 2013 (Comdr, 1986); Comdr, OM Portugal, 1990; Hon. LVO 1986; Ambassador of Portugal to the Court of St James's, since 2016; *b* Lisbon, 27 June 1958; *s* of João Alfredo Figueiredo Lobo Antunes and Maria Margarida Machado de Almeida Lima Lobo Antunes; *m* 1984, Maria Plantier Santos; three *s* two *d. Educ:* Catholic Univ. of Lisbon (BA Law; Postgrad. Eur. Studies). Joined Portuguese Diplomatic Service, 1983; Diplomatic Advr to Pres. of Portugal, 1984–88; Second Secretary: The Hague, 1988–94; Harare, 1994–96; Hd, Services for Sub-Saharan Africa, 1996–2001; Diplomatic Advr to Prime Minister, 2001; Dep. Dir Gen. for Eur. Affairs, 2002; Alt. Mem., Convention on Future of Europe, 2002–04; Dir Gen. for Eur. Affairs, 2004; Secretary of State: for Nat. Defence and the Sea, 2005; for Eur. Affairs, 2006–08; Perm. Rep. of Portugal to EU, 2008–12; Ambassador to Italy, 2012–16. Officer, Order of Orange Nassau (Netherlands), 1991; Grand Officer, Order of Bernardo O'Higgins (Chile), 2001; Grand Cross, Order of Merit: Italy, 2002; Luxembourg, 2004; Norway, 2009; Chile, 2012; Lithuania, 2012. *Recreations:* classical music, gardening. *Address:* Embassy of Portugal, 11 Belgrave Square, SW1X 8PP. *T:* (020) 7235 5331, *Fax:* (020) 7235 0739. *E:* Londres@mne.pt.

**LOCATELLI, Giorgio;** Chef Proprietor, Locanda Locatelli, London, since 2002; Consultant, Ronda Locatelli, Atlantis Hotel, Dubai, since 2008; *b* 7 April 1963; *s* of Ferrucio Locatelli and Giuseppina Caletti; *m* 1995, Plaxy Exton; one *s* one *d.* Worked in local restaurants, N Italy and Switzerland; came to England and joined kitchens of Anton Edelmann at The Savoy, London, 1986; worked at Restaurant Laurent and La Tour D'Argent, Paris, 1990; returned to London as Hd Chef, Olivo, 1991; opened restaurants: Zafferano, 1995 (Michelin Star, 1999); Spighetta, 1997; Spiga, 1999; Locanda Locatelli, 2002 (Michelin Star, 2003–). Television series: (with Tony Allan) Tony and Giorgio, 2000; Pure Italian, 2002; (with Andrew Graham-Dixon): Sicily Unpacked, 2012; Italy Unpacked, 2013–15; Rome Unpacked, 2018; judge, The Big Family Cooking Showdown, 2017. *Publications:* Tony & Giorgio (with Tony Allan), 2003; Made in Italy, 2006; Made in Sicily, 2011; Made at Home, 2017. *Recreations:* motorbikes, swimming. *Address:* Locanda Locatelli, 8 Seymour Street, W1H 7JZ. *T:* (020) 7486 9271. *E:* info@locandalocatelli.com. *Clubs:* Home House, Soho House, Shoreditch House.

**LOCH, Prof. Christoph Hubert**, PhD; Director, Cambridge Judge Business School, University of Cambridge, since 2011; *b* Saarbrücken, Germany, 20 June 1960; *s* of August Loch and Irmgard Loch; *m* 1991, Ingela Björk; one *s. Educ:* Technical Univ. of Darmstadt (Diplom-Wirtschafts-Ingenieur 1985); Univ. of Tennessee, Knoxville (MBA 1986); Stanford Graduate Sch. of Business (PhD 1991); INSEAD (Dip. Clin. Organizational Psychol. 2009). Strategic analyst, Siemens AG, 1986–89; Associate, McKinsey & Co., 1991–93; INSEAD, Fontainebleau: Asst Prof., 1994–97, Associate Prof., 1997–2001, of Technol. Mgt; Prof. of Technol. and Operations Mgt, 2001–11; GlaxoSmithKline Prof. of Corporate Innovation, 2006–11; Dean, PhD prog., 2006–09. Visiting Professor: Information Dynamics Lab., Hewlett Packard Labs, Palo Alto, 2002–03; Stockholm Sch. of Econs, 2009. *Publications:* Industrial Excellence, 2003; Managing the Unknown, 2006; Handbook of New Product Development Management, 2007; Management Quality and Competitiveness, 2008. *Recreations:* soccer, family, golf, caricatures. *Address:* Cambridge Judge Business School, Trumpington Street, Cambridge CB2 1AG. *T:* (01223) 339592, *Fax:* (01223) 339701. *E:* c.loch@jbs.cam.ac.uk.

**LOCHHEAD, Richard Neilson;** Member (SNP) Moray, Scottish Parliament, since April 2006; Minister for Further Education, Higher Education and Science, since 2018; *b* 24 May 1969; *s* of Robert William Lochhead and Agnes Robertson Cloughley; *m*; two *s. Educ:* Williamwood High Sch., Clarkston, Glasgow; Central Coll. of Commerce; Univ. of Stirling (BA Hons Political Studies, 1994). SSEB, 1987–89; Office Manager for Alex Salmond, MP, 1994–98; Develt Officer, Dundee CC, 1998–99. Contested (SNP) Gordon, 1997; MSP (SNP) NE Scotland, 1999–2006; Cabinet Sec. for Rural Affairs and the Envmt, 2007–14, for Rural Affairs, Food and the Envmt, 2014–16, Scottish Parlt. *Recreations:* travel, reading novels and history books, cinema, cycling, listening to mainly pop and rock music, attending gigs, Aberdeen Football Club and occasionally Elgin City Football Club, learning to play the drums and golf! *Address:* (office) 80 South Street, Elgin IV30 1JG. *W:* www.richardlochhead.org, www.twitter.com/RichardLochhead, www.facebook.com/RichardLochheadMSP.

**LOCHRANE, Damien Horatio Ross; His Honour Judge Lochrane;** a Circuit Judge, since 2009; *b* London, 6 Feb. 1958; *s* of Charles Leo Horatio Ross Lochrane and Emmeline Jeanne Effie Lochrane (*née* Lomont); civil partnership 2006, Steven William Mertz. *Educ:* Ampleforth Coll., Yorks; Royal Grammar Sch., Worcester; Christ Church, Oxford (BA Hist. 1980; MA); City Univ., London (DipLaw). Called to the Bar, Gray's Inn, 1983; a Recorder, 2002–09. Treasurer: Bar Lesbian and Gay Gp, 1998–2009; Wessex Family Law Bar Assoc., 2000–09. *Recreations:* cooking, the Vienne (France). *Address:* Chelmsford County Court, Priory Place, New London Road, Chelmsford CM2 0PP. *T:* (01245) 264670, *Fax:* (01245) 295395. *Clubs:* Boodle's, Garrick.

**LOCK, Prof. Andrew Raymond**, PhD; CITP, FSS, FCIM; Professor of Marketing and Business Administration, and Dean, Leeds University Business School, University of Leeds, 2000–08, now Emeritus Professor; *b* 23 Sept. 1947; partner, Sally Cooper; one *s* one *d. Educ:* Manchester Grammar Sch.; Solihull Sch.; Univ. of Leeds (BA French 1970); London Business Sch. (MSc Econ 1972; PhD 1979). Kingston Polytechnic: Lectr, then Sen. Lectr, 1972–85; Principal Lectr, 1978; Hd, Sch. of Mktg and Corp. Strategy, 1985–87; Manchester Polytechnic, subseq. Manchester Metropolitan University: Dean, Faculty of Mgt and Business, and Asst Dir, 1988–92; Dean and Pro-Vice-Chancellor, 1993–2000. Vis. Asst Prof. in Mktg, Univ. of British Columbia, 1979–80; Vis. Prof., Zhejiang Univ., China, 2016–. Chm., Assoc. of Business Schs, 1998–2000; Assessor, Business Sch. Accreditation Scheme, Eur. Quality Improvement System, 1998–; Mem., 2002–, Chm., 2014–, Internat. Academic Adv. Bd, Assoc. of MBAs. Liveryman, Co. of Marketors, 1999–. CCMI; Companion, Assoc. of Business Schs; FRSA. Hon. FIDM. *Publications:* contrib. Jl of Mktg Mgt, European Jl of Mktg, Jl of Advertising Research, Jl of OR Soc. and Mgt Learning. *Recreations:* ski-ing, classic motorcycles, watching Rugby and cricket. *Address:* Biscay House, 153 Craig Walk, Bowness on Windermere, Cumbria LA23 3AX. *E:* arl@lubs.leeds.ac.uk.

**LOCK, David;** *see* Lock, G. D.

**LOCK, David Anthony;** QC 2011; barrister; with Landmark Chambers, since 2014; *b* 2 May 1960; *s* of late John Kirby Lock and of Jeannette Mary Lock (*née* Bridgewater); *m* 1985, Dr Bernadette Clare Gregory; one *s* two *d. Educ:* Jesus Coll., Cambridge (MA 1982); Central London Poly. (Dip. Law 1984). Mgt Trainee, GEC Telecommunications, 1982–83; called to the Bar, Gray's Inn, 1985 (Wilson Schol.); started practice at the Bar, 1987; Head of Healthcare Law, Mills & Reeve, 2003–07; with No5 Chambers, Birmingham, London and Bristol, 2008–14. Mem. (Lab), Wychavon DC, 1995–97 (Chairman: Amenities and Economic Develt Cttee, 1995; Community and Leisure Cttee, 1995–97). MP (Lab) Wyre Forest, 1997–2001; contested (Lab) same seat, 2001. PPS, Lord Chancellor's Dept, 1997–98, to Lord Chancellor and Minister of State, Lord Chancellor's Dept, 1998–99; Parly Sec., Lord Chancellor's Dept, 1999–2001. Secretary: All-Party Occupational Pensions Gp, 1997–99; All Party Cycling Gp, 1998–99; Vice Chm., Textiles, Carpets and Footwear Industry Gp, 1998–99. Chm., Labour W Mids Finance & Industry Gp, 2006–. Chm., Service Authorities, Nat. Crime Squad and Nat. Criminal Intelligence Service, 2002–03. Director: Conveyancing Channel Ltd, 2002–06; Insolvency Management Ltd, later IM Litigation Funding Ltd, 2002–07; Lawbook Consulting Ltd, 2002–; MDA Searchflow, 2006–. Non-exec. Dir, Heart of England NHS Foundn Trust, 2013–. Chm., Child Advocacy Internat., 2003–07. *Recreations:* cycling, family, wine and friends, paragliding.

**LOCK, David Peter**, CBE 2007; Chief Planning Adviser, Department of the Environment, 1994–97; Strategic Planning Adviser, David Lock Associates Ltd, since 2013 (Chairman, 1988–2013); *b* 12 March 1948; *s* of Arthur Lovering Lock and late Kathleen Barbara (*née* Nash); *m* 1970, Jeanette Anita Jones; three *d. Educ:* Sir Roger Manwood's Grammar Sch., Sandwich, Kent; Nottingham Coll. of Art and Design/Trent Poly. (DipT&CP). MRTPI 1975. Area Planning Officer, Leicester CC, 1970–73; Planning Aid Officer, TCPA, 1973–78; Planning Manager, Milton Keynes Develt Corp., 1978–81; Associate Dir, Conran Roche Ltd, 1981–88. Chairman: DLA Architects Ltd, 1998–; David Lock Associates (Australia) Pty Ltd, 1999–2015; DLA Architects Practice Ltd, 2001–; Director: City Discovery Centre Ltd, 1987–2010; City Discovery Centre (Trading) Ltd, 1997–; non-exec. Dir, Rapid Transport Technol. Ltd (formerly Rapid Transport Internat. plc), 1997–2004; Dir, Integrated Transport Planning Ltd, 2000–09; Mem. Bd, Ebbsfleet UDC, 2015–18. Visiting Professor: Univ. of Central England in Birmingham, 1988–98; Univ. of Reading, 2002–10. Chm., 2001–08, Vice Pres., 2008–, TCPA. Milton Keynes Business Lifetime Achievement Award, 2019. *Publications:* (contrib.) People and their Settlements, 1976; (contrib.) Growth and Change in the Future City Region, 1976; (contrib.) New Towns in National Development, 1980; Riding the Tiger: planning the South of England, 1989; (jtly) Alternative Development Patterns: new settlements, 1993; (contrib.) Best Practice in Urban Extensions and New Settlements, 2007. *Recreations:* history, geography, reading, research. *Address:* David Lock Associates Ltd, 50 North Thirteenth Street, Central Milton Keynes, Bucks MK9 3BP. *T:* (01908) 666276.

**LOCK, (George) David;** Managing Director, Private Patients Plan Ltd, 1975–85; *b* 24 Sept. 1929; *s* of George Wilfred Lock and Phyllis Nita (*née* Hollingworth); *m* 1965, Ann Elizabeth Biggs; four *s* one *d. Educ:* Haileybury and ISC; Queens' Coll., Cambridge (MA). British Tabulating Machine Co. Ltd (now ICL), 1954–59; Save & Prosper Group Ltd, 1959–69; American Express, 1969–74; Dir, Plan for Active Retirement, Frizzell Insce and Financial Services Ltd (formerly New Business Ventures, Frizzell Consumer Services Ltd), 1986–89. Director: Priplan Investments Ltd, 1979–85; Priplan Services Ltd, 1979–85; PPP Medical Centre Ltd (incorp. Cavendish Medical Centre), 1981–85. Director: Home Concern for the Elderly, 1985–87, 1989–96; The Hosp. Management Trust, 1985–92; Bd of Management, St Anthony's Hosp., Cheam, 1986–2009; HMT Hospitals Ltd, 1993–2005 (Vice-Pres., 2006–); Gainsborough Clinic Ltd, 2000–03; Sec., Frizzell Foundn, 1989–93. Sec., Friends of Children of Great Ormond Street, 1986. Trustee, Eynsham Trust, 1975–83; Gov., PPP Medical Trust Ltd (Dir, 1983–89). Member: Nuffield Nursing Homes Trust, 1979–; Exec. Cttee, Assoc. of Independent Hosps, 1981–87. Mem., RSocMed, 1979–92. Freeman, Barbers' Co., 1982–. *Recreations:* bridge, golf, music, family activities, entertaining. *Address:* Bell House, Bonfire Lane, Horsted Keynes, Sussex RH17 7AJ. *T:* (01825) 790599.

**LOCK, Graham;** *see* Lock, T. G.

**LOCK, Ven. Peter Harcourt D'Arcy;** Archdeacon of Rochester and Residentiary Canon of Rochester Cathedral, 2000–09; *b* 2 Aug. 1944; *s* of Edward and Ruth Lock; *m* 1968, Susan Reed; one *s* one *d. Educ:* King's College, London (AKC 1967). Ordained deacon, 1968, priest, 1969; Curate: Meopham, 1968–72; Wigmore with Hempstead, 1972; S Gillingham, 1972–77; Rector: Hartley, 1977–83; Fawkham and Hartley, 1983–84; Vicar:

Holy Trinity, Dartford, 1984–93; St Peter and St Paul, Bromley, 1993–2000; RD, Bromley, 1996–2000. Mem., Gen. Synod, 1980–2000. *Recreations:* cricket, football, calligraphy, walking. *E:* peter.lock123@btinternet.com.

**LOCK, Air Vice-Marshal Raymond**, CBE 2004 (OBE 2002); FRAeS; Chief Executive, Forces in Mind Trust, since 2012; *b* Worcester Park, Surrey, 2 Nov. 1958; *s* of Frank Deccan Lock and Margaret Lock (*née* Youdale); *m* 1988, Sarah Elizabeth Jones; two *s* one *d*. *Educ:* Glyn Grammar Sch., Ewell; Bristol Univ. (BSc Hons Mech. Engrg). FRAeS 2010. Flying trng completed 1983; qualified Flying Instructor, RAF Cranwell, 1983–84; served 16 Sqdn, RAF Laarbruch, Germany, 1987–90; Sqdn Ldr, 1990; Flt Comdr, IX Sqdn, RAF Bruggen, 1990–93; Fast Jet Staff Officer, HQ Strike Comd, 1993–95; acsc 1995; OC, Flying Wing, RAF Valley, 1996–99; Directing Staff, JSCSC, 1999–2000; OC, RAF Lyneham, 2002–03; ADC to the Queen, 2002–03; DACOS J3 Perm. Jt HQ, 2004–05; Director: Advanced Comd and Staff Course, JSCSC, 2007–09; Doctrine Air and Space, Develt Concepts and Doctrine Centre, 2009–10; Comdt, JSCSC, 2010–12. Chair of Trustees, Stoll, 2018–. FCMI 2012; FRSA 2017. *Recreations:* cycling and camping, and sometimes the two combined; refereeing, for the Gloucester and District Referees Society, teams well versed in the art of coarse Rugby. *Club:* Royal Air Force.

**LOCK, Sheila Mary;** Managing Director, LMC Ltd, since 2012; *b* 7 Dec. 1959; *d* of Thomas and Kate Donaghy. *Educ:* Our Lady's Grammar Sch., Newry; Manchester Univ. (BSc Hons; DipSW 1989; CQSW 1989); London Sch. of Econs and Pol Sci. (MBA 1984). Social worker, 1987–89, Prin. Social Worker, Child Protection, 1989–91, Tameside; Prin. Officer, 1992–96, Asst Dir, 1996–98, Children's Services, Barnsley; Hd, Children's Services, Sheffield CC, 1998–2002; Hd of Student and Community Services, Calderdale MBC, 2002–06; Corporate Dir, Children & Young People's Services, 2006–08, Interim Chief Exec., 2008, Chief Exec., 2008–11, Leicester CC. Chair, Safeguarding Board: Ealing, 2016–; Kirklees, 2017–. Dir, GR8 AS U R, 2017–. Dir, Nat. Space Centre, Sch. Standards and Develt Agency, 2006. Mem., Nat. Migration Impact Forum, 2010–. Trustee, Sports Partnership Trust. *Recreations:* walking, sport, music, cooking.

**LOCK, Stephen Penford,** CBE 1991; MA, MD; FRCP; Research Associate in History, Wellcome Trust (formerly Wellcome Institute for the History of Medicine), 1992–2000; Editor, British Medical Journal, 1975–91; Volunteer assistant, Britten-Pears Library, Aldeburgh, since 2006; *b* 8 April 1929; *er s* of Wallace Henry Lock, Romford, Essex; *m* 1955, Shirley Gillian Walker (*d* 2016), *d* of E. W. Walker, Bridlington, Yorks; one *d* (one *s* decd). *Educ:* City of London Sch.; Queens' Coll., Cambridge; St Bartholomew's Hosp., London. MA 1953; MB 1954; MD 1987; MRCP 1963; FRCP 1974; FACP 1989; FRCPE 1989. Jun. hosp. appts, 1954–63; Asst Editor, British Med. Jl, 1964–69, Sen. Asst Editor, 1969–74, Dep. Editor, 1974–75. Consulting Editor: Encyclopaedia Britannica Year Book of Medicine, 1992–99; Med. Jl of Australia, 1994–96; an Associate Ed., DNB, 1995–. Organiser and/or participant in numerous Postgrad. Courses in Med. Writing and confs in scientific editing worldwide, 1971–2010. Mem., Res. Ethics Cttee, KCH Medical Sch., 1992–96. Mem. Council, Harveian Soc., 1992–96 (Pres., 1994); Founder Pres., 1982–85, Mem. Council, 1985–91, European Assoc. of Sci. Editors. Vis. Prof. in Medicine, McGill Univ., 1978; Visitor, Acad. Dept of Medicine, Monash Univ., 1982; Rockefeller Scholar, Villa Serbelloni, Bellagio, 1985; Foundn Vis. Prof. in Medicine, RCSI, 1986; Vis. Prof. in Epidemiology and Biostatistics, McGill Univ., 1992; Vis. Lectr, Erasmus Summer Sch., Rotterdam, 1993–2006; Vis. Prof., Norwegian Tech. Univ., Trondheim, 2003–10. Lectures: Wade, Keele Univ., 1980; Morgan, Royal Cornwall Hosp., 1984; Rock Carling, Nuffield Provincial Hosps Trust, 1985; Maurice Bloch, Glasgow Univ., 1986; Wolfson, Wolfson Coll., Oxford, 1986; Estelle Brodman, Washington Univ., St Louis, 1989; Sarah Davies, TCD, 1990; William Hey, Leeds Univ., 1990; George McGovern, Med. Library Assoc. of America, San Francisco, 1991; College, RCP, 1996; Carmichael, RCSI, 1999. Chairman: Friends of Dulwich Picture Gall., 1993–96; Aldeburgh Soc., 1998–2001 (Mem., Cttee, 1997–; Acting Sec., 2001–02); Vice-Pres., 2002–05; Pres., 2005–08); Aldeburgh Fest. Club, 2003–05 (Vice-Chm., 2001–03; Pres., 2008–12). Hon. FRCPI 1987; Hon. Fellow, Amer. Med. Writers Assoc., 1994; Hon. Founder Fellow, RCPCH, 1997 (Hon. Mem., BPA, 1991). Hon. MSc Manchester, 1985. Donders Medal, Ned. Tijdsch. Geneesk, 1981; Internat. Medal, Finnish Med. Soc. Duodecim, 1981; Medal of Honour, Finnish Med. Jl, 1987; Fothergillian Medal, Med. Soc., London, 1992; Meritorious Award, Council of Biol. Eds, 1993. Officer, first cl., White Rose of Finland, 1982. *Publications:* An Introduction to Clinical Pathology, 1965; Health Centres and Group Practices, 1966; The Enemies of Man, 1968; Better Medical Writing, 1970; Family Health Guide, 1972; (ed) Personal View, 1975; Medical Risks of Life, 1976; Thorne's Better Medical Writing, 2nd edn 1977; (ed) Adverse Drug Reactions, 1977; (ed) Remembering Henry, 1977; (contrib.) Oxford Companion to Medicine, 1983; (ed) As You Were, 1984; A Difficult Balance: editorial peer review in medicine, 1985; (ed) The Future of Medical Journals, 1991; Medical Journals and Medical Progress, 1992; (ed) Fraud and Misconduct in Medical Research, 1993, 3rd edn 2001; (ed) Eighty-five Not Out: essays to honour Sir George Godber, 1993; (ed jtly) The Oxford Medical Companion, 1995; (contrib.) Oxford Illustrated History of Medicine, 1996; (ed) Ashes to Ashes, 1998; (contrib.) Our NHS, 1998; (ed) Oxford Illustrated Companion to Medicine, 2001; (contrib.) Leoš Janáček: years of a life, vol. 1, 2006, vol. 2, 2008; (contrib.) World Dictionary of Medical Biography, 2007; (contrib.) Medisinsk publisering og fagformidling, 2008; (contrib.) Great Discoveries in Medicine, 2011; What Went Wrong with Britten's Health?, 2016; contrib. DNB and Oxford DNB. *Recreations:* reading reviews of operas I can't afford to see, avoiding operas whose producers know better than the composer. *Address:* 3 Alde House, Alde House Drive, Aldeburgh, Suffolk IP15 5EE. *T:* (01728) 452411. *E:* splock@globalnet.co.uk.

**LOCK, (Thomas) Graham;** Chief Executive, Amalgamated Metal Corporation plc, 1983–91; *b* 19 Oct. 1931; *s* of Robert Henry Lock and Morfydd Lock (*née* Thomas); *m* 1st, 1954, Janice Olive Baker Lock (*née* Jones) (marr. diss. 1992; she *d* 1995); two *d*; 2nd, 2005, Judith Elizabeth Lucy (*née* Butterworth) (marr. diss. 2010). *Educ:* Whitchurch Grammar School; University College of South Wales and Monmouthshire (BSc Metall); College of Advanced Technology, Aston; Harvard Business School. CEng, FIMMM. Instructor Lieut, RN, 1953–56; Lucas Industries and Lucas Electrical, 1956–61; Dir, Girling Bremsen GmbH, 1961–66; Gen. Man. and Overseas Ops Dir, Girling Ltd, 1966–73; Gen. Man. and Dir, Lucas Service Overseas Ltd, 1973–79; Man. Dir, Industrial Div., Amalgamated Metal Corp., 1979–83; non-exec. Director: Marshall's Universal plc, 1983–86; Evode Gp plc, 1985–91. CCMI. Liveryman, Co. of Gold and Silver Wyre Drawers, 1988–. Freeman, City of London, 1987. *Recreations:* sailing, music, ski-ing. *Address:* Parolas Villa, 4520 Parekklisia, near Limassol, Cyprus. *Club:* Army and Navy.

**LOCKE, John Christopher,** FRICS; Chief Executive, Property Advisers to the Civil Estate, 1997–2000; *b* 4 March 1947; *s* of late Comdr Cyril Frederick Locke, RN, CEng, FIEE and Marjorie Alice Batt Locke (*née* Collins); *m* 1st, 1969 (marr. diss. 1989); two *s*; 2nd, 1990, Maria Patricia, *d* of late Eileen Rogers (*née* Mahony). *Educ:* Pangbourne Coll.; Regent Street Poly.; Brixton Sch. of Building; Northern Poly. ARICS 1971 (Wainwright Prizewinner), FRICS 1981. Prudential Assurance Co. Ltd, 1964–88 (Dir, Estate Management, 1987–88); Divl Dir, Estate Management, Prudential Portfolio Managers Ltd, 1989–91; Director: Southbank Technopark Ltd, 1985–91 (Chm., 1989–90); City Aviation Insurance Tenancies Ltd, 1989–90; Chm., Briggait Co. Ltd, 1987–90; Surveyor, Watling Street Properties, 1989–90; Chief Exec., NHS Estate Mgt and Health Bldg Agency, 1991–97. Member: Commercial Property Cttee, RICS, 1983–89; Central Govt Support Panel, RICS, 1997–2000 (Chm., 1999–2000); Mgt Consultancy Practice Panel, RICS, 1997–2000; Govt Construction Client Panel, HM Treasury, 1997–2000 (Chm. of Strategy, Dialogue with Industry Gp, 1998–2000); Bd of Mgt, British Council for Offices, 1997–2000 (Mgt Exec., 1999–2000). Mem. Editl Adv. Bd, Property Week, 2000. Hon. FIHEEM (Hon. FIHospE 1992). *Recreations:* opera, theatre, music, film, reading, travel, family, home. *Address:* 11 Shrewsbury Road, Beckenham, Kent BR3 4DB.

**LOCKERBIE, Catherine;** Director, Edinburgh International Book Festival, 2000–09; *b* 4 Sept. 1958; *d* of Prof. Samuel Ian Johnstone Lockerbie and Rowena May Lockerbie (*née* Berry); one *s*. *Educ:* Univ. of Edinburgh (MA 1st Cl. double Hons French and Philosophy). Literary Ed., 1990–2000, Chief Leader Writer, 1995–97, The Scotsman. Founding Trustee, Edinburgh UNESCO City of Literature, 2004. Hon. LLD Dundee, 2005; Hon. DLitt: Queen Margaret UC, 2006; Edinburgh, 2007; Napier Univ., 2008; DUniv Open, 2007. *Publications:* (ed) Looking for the Spark: Scottish short stories, 1994. *Recreations:* reading, reading, and learning to understand my fellow humans (through reading).

**LOCKETT, David Jeffery;** farmer and estate manager, since 1971; Vice Lord-Lieutenant for Ross and Cromarty, since 2019; *b* Lima, Peru, 20 April 1948; *s* of Richard Jeffery Lockett, CBE and Mary Edna Lockett; *m* 1973, Denise Blackwood; two *s*. *Educ:* Harrow Sch.; Royal Agricl Coll., Cirencester (HND Agric.). Mem., Dingwall Community Council, 2007–. Gov., Blairmore Sch., 1985–93. DL Ross, Cromarty and Skye, 1990. Mem., Light Aviation Soc. *Recreations:* vintage aviation, gardening, travel, music. *Address:* Knockbain House, Dingwall, Ross-shire IV15 9TJ. *T:* (01349) 862476. *E:* knockbainhouse@gmail.com.

**LOCKETT, Sir Michael (Vernon),** KCVO 2012 (CVO 2002); Chairman, Audley Ltd, since 2008; *b* Bury St Edmunds, Suffolk, 8 April 1948; *s* of Francis and Vera Lockett; *m* 1975, Margaret Dietzold; one *s* two *d*. *Educ:* Woolverstone Hall, Suffolk. Account Dir, Grey Advertising, 1970–75; Chairman: WCT Live, 1975–97; CCO Conferences, 1993–2009; Booth, Lockett Makin, 1993–94; Carabiner, 1998–99; Live Communication, 2000–08; Aura Events, 2005–12; Unspun, 2009–15; Leadership Agency, 2009–; Chief Exec., Thames Diamond Jubilee Foundn, 2011–13; non-executive Director: Populus, 2001–; Grace Blue, 2009–; CTN, 2010–; Grace Blue USA, 2012–. Director: Oracle Cancer Trust, 2010–: GEMS Educn, 2016–18. Trustee: Varkey Foundn, 2015–; 5% Club, 2016–; Internat. Rescue Cttee, 2017–. *Recreations:* sport (past player at Leicester Tigers), travel. *Address:* Audley House, 13 Palace Street, SW1E 5HX. *T:* (020) 7592 0898, *Fax:* (020) 7963 0989. *E:* mlockett@audley.uk.com. *Clubs:* Arts, Oswald's, Royal Automobile, 5 Hertford Street, Ivy, Annabel's; Guards Polo; Thorpeness Golf.

**LOCKETT, Rev. Preb. Paul;** Chaplain to the Queen, 2011–18; Priest-in-charge, All Saints with St Michael, Shrewsbury, since 2016; *b* Wolverhampton, 13 Feb. 1948; *s* of Peter and Freda Joyce Lockett. *Educ:* Regis Comp. Sch., Tettenhall; Wulfrun Coll. of Further Educn (HNC Business Studies); Salisbury and Wells Theol Coll.; Southampton Univ. (CTh). Ordained deacon, 1976, priest, 1977; Curate: Horninglow, Burton-on-Trent, 1976–78; Tewkesbury Abbey, 1978–81; Priest-in-charge, St Peter, W Bromwich, 1981–90; Rector, Norton Canes, 1990–95; Vicar, St Mary and Chad, Longton, 1995–2012; Priest-in-Charge, Hempton with Pudding Norton, 2012–16; Chantry Priest, Guild of All Souls and Pastoral Asst, Shrine of Our Lady of Walsingham, 2012–16. Dean's Vicar, 1991–2012, Preb., 2004–12, Lichfield Cath. Chaplain, Heath Lane Hosp., W Bromwich, 1985–90; Staffs Wing Chaplain, ATC, 1985–2000. Mem., British Pottery Manufacturers Fedn, 1996–2012. *Recreations:* France, music, antiques. *Address:* The Vicarage, 5 Lingen Close, Shrewsbury SY1 2UN. *Club:* Royal Over-Seas League.

**LOCKEY, John Charlton Gerard;** QC 2006; barrister; *b* 8 April 1963; *s* of Bryan Lockey and Anne Lockey (*née* Conroy, now Day); *m* 1992, Louise O'Sullivan; two *d*. *Educ:* Haberdashers' Aske's Sch., Elstree; Downing Coll., Cambridge (BA 1985); Harvard Law Sch. (LLM 1986). Called to the Bar, Middle Temple, 1987; in practice, specialising in insurance and commercial law, 1988–. Chm., British Insce Law Assoc., 2004–06. *Address:* Essex Court Chambers, 24 Lincoln's Inn Fields, WC2A 3EG. *T:* (020) 7813 8000, *Fax:* (020) 7813 8080.

**LOCKHART, Andrew William Jardine;** QC 2010; **His Honour Judge Lockhart;** a Circuit Judge, since 2014; *b* Northampton, 15 March 1963; *s* of Alec Lockhart and Jean Lockhart; *m* 1990, Joanna Freeman; two *s* one *d*. *Educ:* Rugby Sch.; King's Coll., London (LLB Hons 1985). Army Officer, 7th Parachute Regt RHA, 1985–90. Called to the Bar, Lincoln's Inn, 1991; in practice as a barrister, St Philips Chambers, 1991–2014; a Recorder, 2005–14. Mem., RFU Disciplinary Panel, 2007–. *Recreations:* sailing, military history, gardening, hill-walking, running. *Address:* Warwickshire Justice Centre, Newbold Terrace, Leamington Spa, Warwickshire CV32 4EL.

**LOCKHART, Brian Alexander;** Sheriff Principal of South Strathclyde, Dumfries and Galloway, 2005–15; Temporary High Court Judge, 2008–15; Appeal Sheriff, Sheriff Appeal Court, 2015–17; *b* 1 Oct. 1942; *s* of John Arthur Hay Lockhart and Norah Lockhart; *m* 1967, Christine Ross Clark; two *s* two *d*. *Educ:* Glasgow Academy; Glasgow Univ. (BL). Qualified as solicitor, 1964; Partner in Robertson Chalmers & Auld, Solicitors, Glasgow, 1966–79; Sheriff in North Strathclyde, 1979–81, in Glasgow and Strathkelvin, 1981–2005. Mem., Parole Bd for Scotland, 1997–2003. Pres., Sheriffs' Assoc., 2004–05 (Sec., 1997–2002; Vice-Pres., 2002–04). Comr, Northern Lighthouse Bd, 2005–14. *Recreations:* fishing, family. *Address:* 18 Hamilton Avenue, Glasgow G41 4JF. *T:* (0141) 427 1921.

**LOCKHART, Brian Robert Watson;** Headmaster, Robert Gordon's College, Aberdeen, 1996–2004; *b* 19 July 1944; *s* of late George Watson Lockhart and Helen Lockhart (*née* Rattray); *m* 1970, Fiona Anne Sheddon, MA; one *s* two *d*. *Educ:* Leith Acad.; George Heriot's Sch.; Aberdeen Univ. (MA); Edinburgh Univ. (DipEd); Moray House Coll. (Cert Ed). History Teacher, 1968–72, Principal History Teacher, 1972–81, George Heriot's Sch.; Dep. Rector, High Sch. of Glasgow, 1981–96. Council Mem., 1988–2004, Asst Sec. and Exec. Mem., 1989–94, Headteachers' Assoc. of Scotland; Mem., Higher Still Implementation Gp, 1997–2000; Chm., UCAS Scottish Standing Cttee, 2001–02 (Mem., 1994–2003; Co-Chm., 1998–99); Mem., HMC Univs Working Party, 1999–2003; Sec., 2003, Chm., 2004, Scottish Div., HMC. University of Aberdeen: Member: Business Cttee, 2001–12 (Vice Convener, 2006–10); Audit Cttee, 2007–13; Teaching and Learning Cttee, 2009–12; Remuneration Cttee, 2010–12; Staff Promotion Cttee, 2012; Gen. Council Assessor to Court, 2008–12; Chm., Student Affairs Cttee, 2010–12. Mem. Bd, Voluntary Service Aberdeen, 2004–11. Member: Council, St Margaret's Sch. for Girls, Aberdeen, 2004–13; Bd, Hutchesons' GS, Glasgow, 2005–12 (Educn Cttee Convener, 2011–12); Bd, Lathallan Sch., 2013–17; Friends of Aberdeen Univ. Liby Exec., 2013–17. Trustee, Robert Nicol Trust, 2006–14 (Convener, 2015–). *Publications:* History of the Architecture of George Heriot's Hospital and School 1628–1978, 1978; Jinglin' Geordie's Legacy, 2003, 350th anniv. edn 2009; Robert Gordon's Legacy, 2007; The Town School: a history of the High School of Glasgow, 2010; Bon Record: a history of Aberdeen Grammar School, 2012;

A Great Educational Tradition: a history of Hutchesons' Grammar School, 2015. *Recreations:* architecture, reading biographies, sport, films, politics, educational history research. *Address:* 80 Gray Street, Aberdeen AB10 6JE. *T:* (01224) 315776.

**LOCKHART, Carla Rebecca;** Member (DemU) Upper Bann, Northern Ireland Assembly, since 2016; *b* 28 Feb. 1985; *d* of Kenneth and Valerie Lockhart; *m* 2011, Rodney Condell. *Educ:* Univ. of Ulster (BA Hons Business). Political researcher for Stephen Moutray, Mem., NI Assembly; work in Lurgan DUP Advice Centre. Mem. (DemU), Craigavon BC, 2007–16 (Mayor of Craigavon, 2012–13). Pres., LGA NI, 2015–16. Governor: Lurgan Jun. High Sch.; Magheralin Primary Sch. *Address:* 31 High Street, Lurgan BT66 8AH. *T:* (028) 3831 0088. *E:* Carlalockhart@outlook.com.

**LOCKHART, Dean;** Member (C) Mid Scotland and Fife, Scottish Parliament, since 2016; *b* Scotland, 24 Dec. 1968; *s* of Robert and Iris Lockhart; *m* 1999, Jacqueline Isobel Leitch; one *s* one *d*. *Educ:* Univ. of Glasgow (LLB 1st Cl. 1990); Harvard Law Sch. (Leadership Prog.). Admitted as solicitor: England and Wales, 1994; High Court of HKSAR, 2003. Journalist, Euromoney Pubns, London, 1991; Solicitor, Linklaters, London, Tokyo, Singapore and Hong Kong, 1992–2015 (Partner, 2001–15); Sen. Diplomat, First Sec. (Privatisation), Manila (on secondment), 1999. Shadow Cabinet Sec. for Economy, Jobs and Fair Work, Scottish Parlt, 2016–. *Recreations:* family time, travel, tennis, cycling, comedy. *Address:* Scottish Parliament, Edinburgh EH99 1SP. *T:* (0131) 348 5994, *Fax:* (0131) 348 5000. *E:* Dean.Lockhart.msp@parliament.scot.

**LOCKHART, Harry Eugene, (Gene),** CPA; Chairman and Managing Partner, MissionOG; *b* 4 Nov. 1949; *s* of Harry Eugene Lockhart, Sen., Austin, Texas, and Gladys Cummings Lockhart; *m* 1974, Terry Lockhart; one *s* three *d*. *Educ:* Univ. of Virginia (MechEng degree); Darden Graduate Bus. Sch. (MBA). CPA 1976. Sen. Cons., Arthur Anderson & Co., 1974–77; Man. Principal, Europe, Nolan Norton & Co., 1977–82; Gp Dir, Management Services, C. T. Bowring & Co., 1982–85; Vice Pres., First Manhattan Consulting Gp, 1985–87; Chief Exec., IT, 1987–88, Gp Ops, 1988–92, UK Banking, 1990–92, Midland Bank; Pres., First Manhattan Consulting Internat., 1992–94; Pres. and CEO, Mastercard International, 1994–97; Pres. and CEO, The New Power Co., 2000–03. Chm., Financial Instns, Diamond Castle Hldgs LLC, 2005. Dir, Qsent Inc., 2003. *Recreations:* tennis, golf, running, ski-ing, photography, riding, classical music, ballet. *Address:* MissionOG, 1760 Market Street, Suite 902, Philadelphia, PA 19103, USA. *Clubs:* Blind Brook; Indian Harbor Yacht; Mill Reef.

**LOCKHART, James Lawrence,** FRCM, FRCO(CHM); Director of Opera, London Royal Schools' Vocal Faculty, 1992–96 (Opera Consultant, 1996–98); *b* 16 Oct. 1930; *s* of Archibald Campbell Lockhart and Mary Black Lawrence; *m* 1954, Sheila Margaret Grogan; two *s* one *d*. *Educ:* George Watson's Boys' College; Edinburgh Univ. (BMus); Royal College of Music (ARCM, FRCM). Yorkshire Symphony Orchestra, 1954–55; Münster City Opera, 1955–56; Bavarian State Opera, 1956–57; Glyndebourne Festival Opera, 1957, 1958, 1959; Opera Workshop, Univ. of Texas, 1957–59; Royal Opera House, Covent Garden, 1959–60; BBC Scottish Orchestra, 1960–61; Scottish Opera, 1960–61; Conductor, Sadler's Wells Opera, 1961–62; Conductor and Repetiteur, Royal Opera House, Covent Garden, 1962–68; Music Dir, Welsh National Opera, 1968–73; Generalmusikdirektor: Staatstheater, Kassel, 1972–80; Koblenz Opera, 1981–88; Rheinische Philharmonie, 1981–91 (Ehrendirigent, 1991); Dir of Opera, RCM, 1986–96. Guest Conductor, Sydney Conservatorium of Music, 2005. Guest Prof. of Conducting, Tokyo Nat. Univ. of Fine Arts and Music (Tokyo Geidai), 1998–2001, now Prof. Emeritus. Hon. RAM 1993. *Recreations:* swimming, hill-walking, travel, languages. *Address:* 5 The Coach House, Mill Street, Fontmell Magna, Shaftesbury, Dorset SP7 0NU. *T:* (01747) 811980.

**LOCKHART, Logie B.;** see Bruce Lockhart.

**LOCKHART, Sir Simon John Edward Francis S.;** see Sinclair-Lockhart.

**LOCKHART-MUMMERY, Christopher John;** QC 1986; a Recorder, 1994–2004; a Deputy High Court Judge, 1995–2004; *b* 7 Aug. 1947; *s* of Sir Hugh Lockhart-Mummery, KCVO, MD, MChir, FRCS and late Elizabeth Jean Crerar, *d* of Sir James Crerar, KCSI, CIE; *m* 1st, 1971, Elizabeth Rosamund (marr. diss. 1992), *d* of late N. P. M. Elles and Baroness Elles; one *s* two *d*; 2nd, 1993, Mary Lou Hopley (MBE 2015). *Educ:* Stowe; Trinity College, Cambridge (BA). Called to the Bar, Inner Temple, 1971 (Bencher, 1991). Specialist Editor, Hill and Redman's Law of Landlord and Tenant, 1974–89; Gen. Ed., Planning Encyclopedia, 2010–. *Recreations:* fishing, listening to music, opera, walking the dog. *Address:* Landmark Chambers, 180 Fleet Street, EC4A 2HG. *T:* (020) 7430 1221; 83 Abbotsbury Road, W14 8EP. *T:* (020) 7603 7200; Hookeswood House, Farnham, Blandford Forum, Dorset DT11 8DQ. *T:* (01725) 516259. *Club:* Garrick.

**LOCKHEAD, Sir Moir,** Kt 2008; OBE 1996; Chairman, National Trust for Scotland, 2015–19; Deputy Chairman and Chief Executive, FirstGroup plc, 1995–2010; *b* 25 April 1945; *s* of Len and Ethel Lockhead; *m* 1966, Audrey Johnson; three *s* one *d*. Chief Engr, Strathclyde Passenger Transport Exec., 1979–85; Gen. Manager, Grampian Transport, 1985–89; led employee/mgt buyout, 1989; Exec. Chm., Grampian Transport, subseq. GRT Bus plc, FirstBus plc, then FirstGroup plc, 1989–94. Chm., Scottish Rugby Union, 2011–16. Sen. Gov., Univ. of Aberdeen, 2009–16. Patron, Soc. of Ops Engrs, 2013–16. *Recreations:* amateur farming, breeding Highland cattle.

**LOCKLEY, Andrew John Harold;** Judge of the Health, Education and Social Care Chamber, First-tier Tribunal (formerly Chairman, Special Educational Needs Tribunal, later Special Educational Needs and Disability Tribunal), since 1996; Judge of the Social Entitlement Chamber, First-tier Tribunal, 2010–16; *b* 10 May 1951; *s* of late Ven. Harold Lockley and Ursula Margarethe Lockley, JP; *m* 1st, 1974, Ruth Mary Vigor (marr. diss.); two *s* one *d*; 2nd, 2005, Caryl Jane Berry (*née* Seymour). *Educ:* Marlborough Coll.; Oriel Coll., Oxford (BA Lit. Hum. 1973; MA 1982). Admitted a Solicitor, 1979. Res. Fellow, World Council of Churches, 1973–75; Solicitor in private practice, 1979–82; Law Society Asst Sec., 1982–85, Sec., 1985–87, Contentious Business Dept; Dir, Legal Practice, 1987–95, Dir, Corporate and Regl Affairs, 1995–96; Hd of Public Law (formerly Professional Services and Public Law), Irwin Mitchell, Solicitors, 1996–2013. Legally Qualified Chair, Medical Practitioners Tribunal Service (formerly Fitness to Practise Panels), GMC, 2016–17 (Legal Assessor, 2007–15); Legal Advr, Professional Conduct Cttees, Gen. Teaching Council, 2009–12, Teaching Agency, 2012–13. Chairman: Ind. Policing Ethics Panel for S Yorks, 2014–; Adv. Panel on Policing Protests (S Yorks), 2016–. Mem., Editl Adv. Bd, Educn, Public Law and the Individual, 2005–12. Non-exec. Chm., Solicitors Property Centres Ltd, 1998–2000 (Dir, 1997–98); non-exec. Dir, Legal Aid Agency, 2013–19. Member: Commn on Efficiency in the Criminal Courts, 1986–93; Working Party, Delivering Justice in an Age of Austerity, 2014–15; Working Party, School Exclusions, Justice, 2019–. Mem., IT and Courts Cttee, 1990–95. Gov., William Austin Sch., Luton, 1989–94. Hon. Fellow, Univ. of Sheffield, 1999. *Publications:* Christian Communes, 1976; (ed) The Pursuit of Quality: a guide for lawyers, 1993; contribs to legal periodicals. *Recreations:* growing fruit and vegetables, choral singing, swimming, walking, cooking. *E:* alockley1@yahoo.co.uk. *Club:* Royal Over-Seas League.

**LOCKLEY, Stephen Randolph,** FCILT; transport consultant; *b* 19 June 1943; *s* of Randolph and Edith Lockley; *m* 1968, Angela; two *d*. *Educ:* Manchester Univ. (BScCivEng, 1st Cl. Hons). MICE; MCIHT; FCILT (FCIT 1987, FILT). Lancashire County Council: North West Road Construction Unit, Highway Engrg and Planning, 1964–72; Highway/Transportation Planning, 1972–75; Lanarkshire CC, Strathclyde Regional Council: Prin. Engr (Transportation), 1975–77; Depute Dir of Policy Planning, 1977–80; Prin. Exec. Officer, 1980–86; Dir Gen., Strathclyde PTE, 1986–97. *Address:* 64 Townhead Street, Strathaven ML10 6DJ. *T:* (01357) 521774.

**LOCKWOOD, David Charles,** OBE 2011; FCA; Chief Executive, Cobham plc, since 2016; *b* Ilford, 23 March 1962; *s* of Kenneth Lockwood and Irene Lockwood; *m* 1987, Sarah Willis; one *s* two *d*. *Educ:* Saffron Walden County High Sch.; Univ. of York (BA Maths). ACA 1988, FCA 2014. Various roles, GPT Ltd, 1989–95; Managing Director: Defence Control Systems, Marconi, 1995–97; Sensor Systems, BAE Systems, 1998–2000; CEO, Intense Ltd, 2001–06; Thales UK: Man. Dir, Thales Optronics Ltd, 2007–10; Vice Pres., Defence and Security C4I Systems and Air Ops, 2010–11; Vice Pres., Global Defence and Security, BT Global Services, BT plc, 2011–12; Chief Exec., Laird plc, 2012–16. Non-exec. Chm., Knowledge Transfer Network Ltd, 2014–16; non-exec. Dir, Samsung Thales Corp. (Korea), 2008–11. Chm., Technol. Adv. Gp, Scottish Govt, 2006–11. Vis. Prof., Univ. of Glasgow, 2005–11. FRSA. *Recreations:* sailing, running, bridge. *Address:* Cobham plc, Brook Road, Wimborne, Dorset BH21 2BJ. *Club:* Royal Air Force.

**LOCKWOOD, Prof. Michael,** PhD; FRS 2006; Professor of Space Environment Physics, University of Reading, since 2009; *b* 1954; *s* of Fred T. Lockwood, CBE and Stephanie Lockwood; *m* 1976, Celia; one *s* one *d*. *Educ:* Skinners' Sch., Tunbridge Wells; Univ. of Exeter (BSc 1st Cl. Hons Physics 1975; PhD Physics 1978). FRAS 1985; CPhys, FInstP 2003. Res. Fellow, Auckland Univ., 1978–79; Higher SO, RAE, Farnborough, 1979–80; Prof. of Physics and Astronomy, Southampton Univ., 2000–09. Scientist, Space Sci. and Technol. Dept, Rutherford Appleton Lab., 1980 (Chief Scientist, 2001). Res. Associate, NASA/Marshall Space Flight Center, Huntsville, 1984–85. Vis. Hon. Lectr, 1987–2004, Vis. Hon. Prof., 2004–, Imperial Coll., London; Guest Lectr, Univ. Centre in Svalbard, Longyearbyen, Svalbard, 1994–. Mem., NERC, 2007–14. Vice Pres. (Geophysics), RAS, 1995–97; President: Div. III, Internat. Assoc. of Geomagnetism and Aeronomy, 1999–2003; Solar-Terrestrial Physics Sect., Eur. Geophysical Soc., 2000–03; Chm. Council, Internat. EISCAT Scientific Assoc., 2001–03; Mem., Astronomy Cttee, 1997–2000, Sci. Cttee, 2002–05, PPARC. Mem., American Geophysical Union, 1981. Issac Koga Gold Medal, URSI, 1990; Zel'dovich Award for Commn C (Ionospheric Phys), COSPAR, 1990; Chapman Medal, RAS, 1998; Charles Chree Medal and Prize, Inst. of Physics, 2003; Gold Medal, RAS, 2015. *Publications:* (jtly) The Sun, Solar Analogs and the Climate, 2004; over 330 articles in jls on solar influences on the Earth. *Recreations:* playing music, watching cricket, Rugby and soccer. *Address:* Department of Meteorology, University of Reading, Earley Gate, PO Box 243, Reading RG6 6BB.

**LOCKWOOD, Rear Adm. Roger Graham,** CB 2005; Chief Executive, Northern Lighthouse Board, 2006–14; *b* 26 June 1950; *s* of Eric Garnett Lockwood and Nunda Lockwood (*née* Doak); *m* 1984, Susan Jane Cant; three *s* two *d*. *Educ:* Kimbolton Sch., Cambs; Univ. of Warwick (BA Maths). BRNC Dartmouth, 1971; Sub Lieut, HMS Fearless, 1972; Lieut, HMS Soberton, 1973; Supply Officer (Cash), HMS Tiger, 1974–76; Captain's Sec., 2nd Submarine Sqn, 1976–78; Supply Officer, HMS Naiad, 1979–81; Lt Comdr, 1980; Flag Lieut to CDS, 1981–82; Captain's Sec., RNAS Culdrose, 1982–84; jsdc 1985; Comdr, 1985; Base Supply Officer, HMS Dolphin, 1985–87; Comdr, RN Supply Sch., 1987–89; Supply Officer, HMS Ark Royal, 1989–91; Captain, 1991; Dep. Dir, Naval Service Conditions (Pay), 1991–93; rcds 1994; Secretary to: Second Sea Lord, 1995–96; First Sea Lord, 1996–98; Cdre, 1998; Cdre, HMS Raleigh, 1998–2000; Rear Adm., 2000; COS to Second Sea Lord, and C-in-C Naval Home Comd, 2000–02; Sen. Naval Directing Staff, RCDS, and Chief Naval Supply, subseq. Chief Naval Logistics, Officer, 2002–05. Chairman: Forth Pilots Disciplinary Cttee, 2006–; Perth Sea Cadet Unit, 2006–10. Mem. Council, RNLI, 2015– (Chair: Scottish Council, 2017–; Ops Cttee, 2020–; Trustee, 2018–). Mem., Hon. Co. of Master Mariners, 2007–15. Co. Sec., Dunblane Develt Trust, 2005–07; Dir, Scottish Shipping Benevolent Assoc., 2009–12 (Pres., 2011–12). Area Vice Patron (Scotland), War Memorials Trust, 2007–; Trustee: Merchant Navy Memorial Trust (Scotland), 2009–16; Bell's Nautical Trust, 2015–. Gov., Kimbolton Sch., 2001–05; Comr, Queen Victoria Sch., Dunblane, 2006–18. High Constable of Port of Leith, 2008–19. *Recreations:* family, studying the history of the SOE in France and history more generally. *Address:* Springbank, 2 Bellenden Grove, Dunblane, Perthshire FK15 0FD.

**LOCKWOOD, Venetia;** see Butterfield, V.

**LOCKYER, Rear-Adm. (Alfred) Austin,** LVO 1973; Chief Staff Officer (Engineering) to Commander-in-Chief Fleet, 1982–84, retired; Director General, Timber Trade Federation, 1985–92; *b* 4 March 1929; *s* of late Austin Edmund Lockyer and Jane Russell (*née* Goldman); *m* 1965, Jennifer Ann Simmons; one *s*. *Educ:* Frome County School; Taunton School; Royal Naval Engineering College. Entered RN 1947; Comdr 1965; Staff of Commander Far East Fleet, 1965–67; jssc, 1968–69; Ship Dept, 1969–71; HMY Britannia, 1971–73; Captain 1973; sowc, 1973–74; Naval Ship Production Overseer, Scotland and NI, 1974–76; Dep. Dir, Fleet Maintenance, 1976–78; Dir, Naval Officers Appointments (Engrg), 1978–80; HMS Sultan in Comd, 1980–82; ADC to the Queen, 1981; Rear-Adm. 1982. Governor: Forres Sch., Swanage, 1980–92 (Chm., 1983–92); Sherborne Sch., 1981–97. *Recreations:* golf, listening to good music. *Address:* 25 Kingfisher Court, Avonpark, Limpley Stoke, Bath BA2 7JS. *Club:* Army and Navy.

**LOCKYER, Lynda Dorothy;** on secondment to Civil Contingencies Secretariat, Cabinet Office, 2002; *b* 17 Aug. 1946; *d* of Donald Lockyer and Gwendoline Lockyer (*née* Fulcher); *m* 1984, John Anthony Thompson; one *s*. *Educ:* Bromley High Sch.; Newnham Coll., Cambridge (MA Classics); Warburg Inst., Univ. of London (MA 2005; PhD 2013); University Coll. London (MA 2008). Press Officer: Shell-Mex, BP Ltd, 1968–73; Sperry Univac, 1974; DHSS, later DoH, 1974–96; Home Office, 1996–2002; Head of Police Resources Unit, 1996–99; Dir, Corporate Resources, 1999–2000; Dir, Corporate Develt and Services, 2000–02. *Recreations:* films, theatre, opera, Europe.

**LODDER, Peter Norman;** QC 2001; **His Honour Judge Lodder;** a Senior Circuit Judge and Resident Judge, Kingston-upon-Thames Crown Court, since 2015; *b* 3 Feb. 1958; *s* of Lt Comdr Norman George Lodder, RN and Ann Lodder; *m* 1992, Elizabeth Gummer (marr. diss. 2007); two *c*. *Educ:* King's Sch., Gloucester; Portsmouth Grammar Sch.; Univ. of Birmingham (LLB). Called to the Bar, Middle Temple, 1981 (Blackstone Exhibnr 1980; Jules Thorn Major Schol. 1982), Bencher, 2010; specialist in fraud and criminal law; Asst Recorder, 1998–2000; Recorder, 2000–15. Hon. Recorder of Richmond upon Thames, 2015–. Mem., Gen. Council of the Bar, 1994–2013 (Vice Chm., 2010; Chm., 2011); Chm., Criminal Bar Assoc., 2008–09. Trustee: Spark Inside, 2012–; Council, Inns of Court, 2013–; Leadership Through Sport, 2017–. Vis. Prof., St Mary's Univ., Twickenham, 2019–. Gov. Portsmouth GS, 2013–. *Address:* Kingston-upon-Thames Crown Court, 6–8 Penrhyn Road, Kingston-upon-Thames, Surrey KT1 2BB.

**LODER,** family name of **Baron Wakehurst.**

**LODER, Sir Edmund Jeune,** 4th Bt cr 1887, of Whittlebury, Northamptonshire, and of High Beeches, Slaugham, Sussex; b 26 June 1941; er s of Sir Giles Rolls Loder, 3rd Bt and Marie Violet Pamela Loder (née Symons-Jeune); S father, 1999; m 1st, 1966, Penelope Jane Forde (marr. diss. 1971); one d; 2nd, 1992, Susan Warren Pearl. Heir: b Robert Reginald, (Robin), Loder [b 12 Nov. 1943; m 1967, Quenelda Jane, d of Sir John Royden, 4th Bt; two s two d (of whom one s one d are twins)]. Address: Eyrefield Lodge, The Curragh, Co. Kildare, Ireland.

**LODGE, Anton James Corduff;** QC 1989; a Recorder, since 1985; b 17 April 1944; s of Sir Thomas Lodge and Aileen (née Corduff). Educ: Ampleforth College; Gonville and Caius College, Cambridge (MA). Called to the Bar, Gray's Inn, 1966, Bencher, 1998. Recreations: cricket, tennis, ski-ing, music, theatre. Club: Yorkshire (York).

**LODGE, Prof. David John,** CBE 1998; MA, PhD; FRSL; writer; Emeritus Professor of English Literature, University of Birmingham, since 2001 (Professor of Modern English Literature, 1976–87, Hon. Professor, 1987–2000); b 28 Jan. 1935; s of William Frederick Lodge and Rosalie Marie Lodge (née Murphy); m 1959, Mary Frances Jacob; two s one d. Educ: St Joseph's Acad., Blackheath; University College, London (Hon. Fellow, 1982). BA hons, MA (London); PhD (Birm). FRSL 1976. National Service, RAC, 1955–57. British Council, London, 1959–60. Univ. of Birmingham: Asst Lectr in English, 1960–62; Lectr, 1963–71; Sen. Lectr, 1971–73; Reader in English, 1973–76. Harkness Commonwealth Fellow, 1964–65; Visiting Associate Prof., Univ. of California, Berkeley, 1969; Henfield Writing Fellow, Univ. of E Anglia, 1977. Hon. Fellow, Goldsmiths' Coll., London, 1992. Hon. DLitt: Warwick, 1997; Birmingham, 2001. Yorkshire Post Fiction Prize, 1975; Hawthornden Prize, 1976; Whitbread Book of the Year Award, 1980; Sunday Express Book of the Year Award, 1988. Chevalier, l'Ordre des Arts et des Lettres (France), 1997. Stage plays: The Writing Game, Birmingham Rep., 1990 (adapted for television, 1996); Home Truths, Birmingham Rep., 1998; Secret Thoughts, Bolton Octagon Th., 2011 (Best New Play, Manchester Th. Awards, 2011). Adaptation of Dickens, Martin Chuzzlewit, for television, 1994. Publications: novels: The Picturegoers, 1960; Ginger, You're Barmy, 1962; The British Museum is Falling Down, 1965; Out of the Shelter, 1970, rev. edn 1985; Changing Places, 1975; How Far Can You Go?, 1980; Small World, 1984 (televised 1988); Nice Work, 1988 (adapted for television, 1989); Paradise News, 1991; Therapy, 1995; Home Truths: a novella, 1999; Thinks..., 2001; Author, Author, 2004; Deaf Sentence, 2008; A Man of Parts, 2011; short stories: The Man Who Wouldn't Get Up, 2016; plays: The Writing Game, 1991; Home Truths, 1998; Secret Thoughts, 2011; criticism: Language of Fiction, 1966; The Novelist at the Crossroads, 1971; The Modes of Modern Writing, 1977; Working with Structuralism, 1981; Write On, 1986; After Bakhtin (essays), 1990; The Art of Fiction, 1992; The Practice of Writing, 1996; Consciousness and the Novel (essays), 2002; The Year of Henry James (essays), 2006; Lives in Writing (essays), 2014; edited: Jane Austen's Emma: a casebook, 1968; Twentieth Century Literary Criticism, 1972; Modern Criticism and Theory, 1988, 3rd edn 2008; non-fiction: Quite a Good Time to be Born: a memoir 1935–1975, 2015; Writer's Luck: a memoir 1976–1991, 2018. Recreations: television, cinema, theatre, Pilates. Address: c/o Curtis Brown, 28–29 Haymarket, SW1Y 4SP.

**LODGE, Dr Denise Valerie;** educational consultant, since 2015; Headmistress, Putney High School, GDST, 2002–15; m (decd); one s one d. Educ: Bury Grammar Sch. (Girls); Royal Holloway Coll., London Univ. (BSc Botany and Zool.; PhD Zool. 1979); Chelsea Coll., London Univ. (MSc Applied Hydrobiol.); Reading Univ. (PGCE). Teacher, later Hd of Chem., Hd of Sixth Form, and Sen. Teacher, Curriculum, Sir Roger Manwood's Sch., Sandwich, 1987–96; Dep. Hd, Sheffield High Sch., GDST, 1996–99; Headmistress, Sydenham High Sch., GDST, 1999–2002. Treas., GSA, 2004–07 (Fellow, 2015). Mem. Ct, Imperial Coll. London, 2007–15. Governor: Kent Coll., Pembury, 2016–; Kensington Wade Prep. Sch., 2017–. Recreations: jazz, cooking, the gym, theatre, art. E: contact@deniselodge.co.uk.

**LODGE, Prof. Geoffrey Arthur,** BSc, PhD; FRSB; FRSE 1986; Professor of Animal Science, Sultan Qaboos University, Muscat, 1986–90, retired; b 18 Feb. 1930; m 1956, Thelma (née Calder); one s two d. Educ: Durham University (BSc). PhD Aberdeen. Formerly Reader in Animal Production, Univ. of Nottingham School of Agriculture, and Principal Research Scientist, Animal Research Inst., Ottawa; Strathcona-Fordyce Prof. of Agriculture, Univ. of Aberdeen, and Principal, North of Scotland Coll. of Agriculture, 1978–86. Publications: (ed jointly) Growth and Development of Mammals, 1968; contribs to journals and books. Recreations: food, malt whisky, travelling. Address: 18 Queen Victoria Park, Inchmarlo, Banchory, Kincardineshire AB31 4AL.

**LODGE, John Robert; His Honour Judge Lodge;** a Circuit Judge, since 2008; Resident Judge, Basildon Combined Court Centre, 2011–19; b Alvanley, Cheshire, 6 Oct. 1958; s of Anthony William Rayner Lodge and Monica Lodge (née Beddow); m 1986, Sally Nicole Cummings, (Rev. Canon Sally Lodge); two s one d. Educ: Ripon Grammar Sch.; Wadham Coll., Oxford (BA Juris. 1979). Called to the Bar, Middle Temple, 1980; in practice as barrister, Leeds, 1982–2008. Recreations: ski-ing, Rugby Union, modern military history, following West Ham United. Address: c/o Basildon Combined Court Centre, The Gore, Basildon, Essex SS14 2EW. E: HHJ.John.Lodge@ejudiciary.net.

**LODGE, Prof. Juliet,** DLitt; PhD; Professor of European Integration and Politics and Director, Jean Monnet Centre of Excellence, University of Leeds, 1996–2012, now Professor Emerita; Senior Research Analyst, Saher UK, since 2016; b London; d of Arthur and Lenore; two s one d. Educ: Univ. of Reading (MA; DLitt); Univ. of Hull (PhD). Fellow in Internat. Relns, LSE, 1977; Lectr in Euro Politics, Univ. of Auckland, 1978; Prof. of EU Politics, Univ. of Hull, 1978–95; Prof. of Internat. Politics, Vrije Universiteit Brussel, 1994; Prof. of EU Politics, Institut für Höhere Studien, Vienna, 1995. Vis. Prof. of EU Politics, Université Libre de Bruxelles, 1993; Vis. Lectr and Hon. Cormorant, JSDC. Expert Mem., Privacy Cttee, Biometrics Inst., 2011–; Mem., Patients Reference Gp, Coll. of Optometrists, 2011–. Sen. Res. Analyst, Saher Ltd, 2016–. Freelance broadcaster and journalist on EU policies and instns; res. evaluator for EU. Convenor, UK Ethics Cttee on judicial co-operation in EU, 2004. Member: European Movement, 1994–; New Europeans, 2016–17. Carer Ambassador, Carers UK, 2010–14. Woman of Europe Award, 1992. Publications: The European Policy of the SPD, 1977; (jtly) European Parliament and the European Community, 1978; (ed) Terrorism: a challenge to the state, 1981; (jtly) Direct Elections to the European Parliament: community perspective, 1982; The European Community and New Zealand, 1982; Direct Elections to the European Parliament 1984, 1986; (ed) European Union: the European Community in search of a future, 1986; Threat of Terrorism, 1987; The 1989 Election of the European Parliament, 1990; (ed) The European Community and the Challenge of the Future, 1993; (ed) The 1994 Elections to the European Parliament, 1995; (ed) The 1999 Elections to the European Parliament, 2001; The European Union, 2003; The 2004 Elections to the European Parliament, 2005; (ed) Are You Who You Say You Are: the EU and biometric borders, 2007; The 2009 Elections to the European Parliament, 2010; Communication, Mediation and Culture in the Making of Europe, 2013; chapters on EU, borders, biometrics, transparency and democratic accountability, constitutional reform, e-citizenship, ethical impact assessments of privacy and data linkage, ethics and e-governance in smart environments; reports on biometrics, interoperability, ICT ethics and liberty for the EP and nat. parlts, research on e-security, e-identity, interoperability, robotics and ICTs, biometrics and border controls, cybercrime, e-gov and e-society, internet of us and the ethics of artificial intelligence. Recreations: art, laughing, satire, ceramics, ethics, writing occasional blogs on EU. E: Juliet@saher-uk.com. Club: Women of Europe.

**LODGE, Matthew James;** HM Diplomatic Service; Minister, Paris, and Ambassador and Permanent Delegate to UNESCO, since 2017; b Crosby, Lancs, 3 June 1968; s of David James Lodge and Helen Mary Lodge; m 2001, Alexia Ipirotis; two s. Educ: Abingdon Sch.; Birmingham Univ. (BA Hons French and Russian). Officer, RM, 1986–96; joined FCO, 1996; Desk Officer, Bosnia Sect., E Adriatic Dept, FCO, 1996–97; Entry Clearance Officer, Tbilisi and Yerevan, 1997; Second Sec. (Pol/EU/Press and Public Affairs), Athens, 1998–2000; Desk Officer, Czech Republic and Slovakia, Central NW Europe Dept, FCO, 2000; Second Secretary: (Press and Public Affairs), Paris, 2001; (Pol/Mil.), UKREP, Brussels, 2001–03; Hd, Cyprus and Greece Sect., Europe Directorate, 2003–04, Private Sec., Perm. Under Sec.'s Office, 2004–07, FCO; Dep. Hd of Mission, Baghdad, 2007; HCSC, UK Defence Acad., 2008; Hd, Afghanistan Gp, S Asia and Afghanistan Directorate, FCO, 2008–10; Ambassador to Finland, 2010–13; FCO, 2014; Ambassador to Kuwait, 2014–17. Recreations: family, swimming, music, outdoors. Address: c/o Foreign and Commonwealth Office, King Charles Street, SW1A 2AH. E: matthew.lodge@fco.gov.uk.

**LODGE, Ven. Michael John;** Archdeacon of Southend, since 2017; b Bishops Cleeve, Tewkesbury, 1 Aug. 1953; s of John Lodge and Barbara Lodge; m 1979, Linda Cook; one s one d. Educ: Cleeve Sch.; North Glos Coll. of Technol. (Mech. Engrg C&G; HNC Mech. Engrg; HNC Stress Analysis); Wycliffe Hall, Oxford (Gen. Ministerial Examination). Design Draughtsman, Res. and Design Engr, Sen. Product Engr, Walker Crosweller, later Caradon Mira, 1969–87; ordained deacon, 1989, priest, 1990; Asst Curate, Highworth, 1989–93; Priest-in-charge, St Luke and St John, Cheltenham, 1993–2005; Team Rector, Rayleigh, Essex, 2005–17; Hon. Canon, Chelmsford Cathedral, 2012–. Chaplain: Cheltenham Town FC, 2005; Southend Utd FC, 2013–. Fellow, 1993–2015, Mem. Council, 1994–2003, Cheltenham and Glos Coll. of HE, later Univ. of Glos. Gov., FitzWimarc Sch., Rayleigh, 2006–19. Recreations: travelling, gardening, reading, DIY projects, family. Address: The Archdeacon's Lodge, 459 Rayleigh Road, Benfleet, Essex SS7 3TH. T: (01268) 779345. E: a.southend@chelmsford.anglican.org.

**LODGE, Nicholas John;** Programme Director, Bank of England, since 2018; b Ipswich, 7 Oct. 1961; s of John and Pauline Lodge; m 1988, Angela Garnham; one s one d. Educ: Northgate Grammar Sch., Ipswich. With Inland Revenue, 1990–93, then HM Treasury and Cabinet Office, 1993–95; Inland Revenue, later HM Revenue and Customs: Ops Manager, 1995–98; Prog. Dir for tax credits and child benefit, 1998–2005; Dir, Customer Contact, 2005–07; work on data security, 2007–08; Dir for Debt Mgt and Banking, 2008–11; Personal Tax Change Dir and Dir, Customer Contact, 2011–12; Change Dir for Personal Tax, 2012; a Comr, 2012–18; Dir Gen., Benefits and Credits, 2012–16; Dir Gen., Transformation, 2015–18. Address: Bank of England, Threadneedle Street, EC2R 8AH.

**LOEHNIS, Anthony David,** CMG 1988; Chairman, Alpha Bank London, 2005–15 (Director, 1994–2016); b 12 March 1936; s of Sir Clive Loehnis, KCMG; m 1965, Jennifer Forsyth Anderson; three s. Educ: Eton; New Coll., Oxford (MA); Harvard Sch. of Public Administration. HM Diplomatic Service, 1960–66; J. Henry Schroder Wagg & Co. Ltd, 1967–80 (on secondment to Bank of England, 1977–79); Bank of England: Associate Dir (Overseas), 1980–81; Exec. Dir, 1981–89; Dir, S. G. Warburg Group plc, 1989–92; a Vice-Chm., S. G. Warburg & Co., 1989–92. Director: St James's Place Capital plc, 1993–2005; Mitsubishi UFJ Securities Internat., 1996–2007 (formerly Tokyo-Mitsubishi Internat., then Mitsubishi Securities Internat.); AGCO Corp. (US), 1997–2005; VTB Capital (formerly VTB Bank Europe) plc, 2007–13. A Public Works Loan Comr, 1994–2005 (Chm., 1997–2005). Exec. Dir, UK-Japan 21st Century (formerly UK-Japan 2000) Gp, 1999–2002 (Dir, 1990–2005). Member: Council: Ditchley Foundn, 1992–2012 (Chm., F & G P Cttee, 1993–2009); Baring Foundn, 1994–2005; Japan Soc., 1998–2005. Chm., Villiers Park Educnl Trust, 2000–09. Gov., British Assoc. for Central and Eastern Europe, 1994–2003. Address: 55 Bainton Road, Oxford OX2 7AG. Clubs: Garrick, Beefsteak.

**LOEWE, Very Rev. Andreas,** FRHistS; Dean of Melbourne, since 2012; b Munich; m Dr Katherine Firth. Educ: St Peter's Coll., Oxford (BA Hons 1st cl. Theol. 1995; MPhil Ecclesiastical Hist. 1997; MA 1999); Selwyn Coll., Cambridge (PhD 2001). FRHistS 2011. Ordained deacon, 2001, priest, 2002; Asst Curate, Upton-cum-Chalvey Team, Dio. of Oxford, 2001–04; Sen. Mem., Faculty of Divinity, Cambridge Univ., 2004–09; Assoc. Vicar, Gt St Mary's, Cambridge, 2004–09; Chaplain of Michaelhouse, Dio. of Ely, 2004–09; University of Melbourne: Coll. Chaplain, Trinity Coll., 2009–12; Anglican Chaplain, 2010–12; Gavan Sen. Lectr in Theology, Trinity Coll. Theol Sch., MCD Univ. of Divinity, 2010–12. Rex J. Lipman Fellow, St Peter's Coll., Adelaide, 2012–; Fellow and Lectr in Music, Melbourne Conservatorium of Music, 2012–. Member: Council, Dio. of Melbourne, 2012–; Chapter, St Paul's Cathedral, Melbourne, 2012–; Trustee, Melbourne Anglican Trust Corp., 2012–. Member, Synod: Dio. of Ely, 2006–09; Dio. of Melbourne, 2009–. Theol Sec., Ecumenical Forum for Young Theologians, 2001–09; Comr, Nat. Council of Churches in Australia Faith and Unity Commn, 2010–12. Member, Council: Trinity Coll., Melbourne, 2009–12; MCD Univ. of Divinity, Melbourne, 2010–18; Melbourne Girls' Grammar Sch., 2012–19. Chair, Art Beyond Belief, 2004–09; Mem. Bd, Michaelhouse Centre, Cambridge, 2004–. OStJ. Publications: (contrib.) Die Zürcher Reformation, 2000; (contrib.) Peter Martyr Vermigli: humanism, republicanism, reformation, 2002; Richard Smyth and the Language of Orthodoxy: re-imagining Tudor Catholic polemicism, 2003; Johann Sebastian Bach's St John Passion: a theological commentary, 2014. Recreations: classical music, jazz, opera, gardening. Address: St Paul's Cathedral, 209 Flinders Lane, Melbourne, Vic 3000, Australia. E: dean@stpaulscathedral.org.au.

**LOFTHOUSE, Simon Timothy,** QC 2006; a Recorder, since 2003; b 25 Aug. 1966; s of Adam Robert Lofthouse and Angela Anne Lofthouse (née Manning); m 1994, Sophia Ann Gawlik. Educ: Fernwood Comp. Sch., Nottingham; Becket Upper Sch., Nottingham; University Coll. London (LLB Hons 1987). Called to the Bar, Gray's Inn, 1988, Bencher, 2009; in practice specialising in international arbitration, construction, energy and professional negligence. Mem., Professional Conduct Cttee, Bar Council, 2001–04. Bar Standards Board: Prosecutor, 2005–07; Vice-Chm., 2008–11, Chm., 2011–15, Complaints Cttee; Mem. Bd, 2011–15. Recreations: opera, sculpture, travel. Address: Atkin Chambers, 1 Atkin Building, Gray's Inn, WC1R 5AT. T: (020) 7404 0102, Fax: (020) 7405 7456. E: slofthouse@atkinchambers.com. Club: Reform.

**LOFTUS, Simon Pierse Dominic,** OBE 2007; Chairman, 1996–2006, non-executive Director, 2006–14, Adnams plc; b 5 Aug. 1946; s of late Nicholas Alastair Ayton Loftus and Prudence Loftus (née Wootten); m 1980, Irène Yamato; one d. Educ: Ampleforth; Trinity Coll., Cambridge (MA). Joined Adnams, 1968, Dir, 1973. Founding Chm., E Anglian Arts Trust, 1975–79; Dir, Aldeburgh Music (formerly Aldeburgh Productions), 1998–2010; non-executive Director: 1st East, 2005–10; Norwich & Peterborough Bldg Soc., 2007–11; St George's Theatre Trust Ltd, 2010–13. Pres., Southwold Mus. and Archaeol Soc., 2011–17. Chm., Suffolk Foundn, 2003–06; Trustee, Adnams Charity, 1990– (Chm.,

1992–2006). Hon. DCL Suffolk Coll., UEA, 2010. *Publications:* Anatomy of the Wine Trade, 1985; A Pike in the Basement, 1987; Puligny Montrachet, 1992; (ed) Guides to the Wines of France series, 1988–90; An Illustrated History of Southwold, 2012; The Invention of Memory, 2013; numerous articles in jls. *Recreations:* cooking, Anglo-Irish history, writing, being a grandfather. *Address:* Bulcamp House, Halesworth, Suffolk IP19 9LG. *T:* (01502) 478409. *Club:* Groucho.

LOGAN, Andrew David; sculptor, since 1968; b 11 Oct. 1945; s of William Harold Logan and Irene May Logan. *Educ:* Oxford Sch. of Architecture (DipArch Oxon 1970). Founded Alternative Miss World (performance event), London, 1972; opened Andrew Logan Mus. of Sculpture, Berriew, Wales, 1991. Work in public collections: Australian Gall. of Nat. Art; NPG; Arts Council of GB; Warner Bros, UK; Costume Inst., Metropolitan Mus., NY; Curzon Tussaud, London; Cleveland Jewellery Collection, Middlesbrough; Nat. Museums and Galls on Merseyside. Member: Contemporary Glass Soc.; RSA. *Recreations:* yoga, travel, theatre. *E:* andrewdl@andrewlogan.com.

LOGAN, Sir David (Brian Carleton), KCMG 2000 (CMG 1991); HM Diplomatic Service, retired; Director, Centre for Studies in Security and Diplomacy, and Hon. Professor, School of Social Sciences, University of Birmingham, 2002–06; b 11 Aug. 1943; s of late Captain Brian Ewen Weldon Logan, RN (Retd) and Mary Logan (née Fass); m 1967, Judith Margaret Walton Cole; one s one d (and one s decd). *Educ:* Charterhouse; University College, Oxford (MA). Foreign Office, 1965; served Istanbul, Ankara and FCO, 1965–70; Private Sec. to Parly Under Sec. of State for Foreign and Commonwealth Affairs, 1970–73; First Sec., 1972; UK Mission to UN, 1973–77; FCO, 1977–82; Counsellor, Hd of Chancery and Consul-Gen., Oslo, 1982–86; Hd of Personnel Ops Dept, FCO, 1986–88; Sen. Associate Mem., St Antony's Coll., Oxford, 1988–89; Minister and Dep. Head of Mission, Moscow, 1989–92; Asst Under Sec. of State (Central and Eastern Europe), 1992–94, (Defence Policy), 1994–95, FCO; Minister, Washington, 1995–97; Ambassador to Turkey, 1997–2001. Advr, HSBC, 2016–18. Chairman: GAP Activity Projects, 2002–07; British Inst. of Archaeology, Ankara, 2006–16 (Vice Pres., 2016–); Member: Internat. Advisory Bd, Thames Water, 2002–07; Supervisory Bd, Efes Pilsen Internat., 2004–10; Director: European Nickel plc, 2004–10; Magnitogorsk Iron and Steel Co., 2007–14. Sen. Fellow, Inst. for Strategic Dialogue, 2013–15. Trustee, St Andrew's Ecumenical Trust, 2006–13. DUniv Birmingham, 2014. *Recreations:* music, reading, sailing. *Club:* Royal Ocean Racing.

LOGAN, Prof. David Edwin, PhD; Coulson Professor of Theoretical Chemistry, University of Oxford, and Fellow, University College, Oxford, since 2005; b 27 Aug. 1956; s of late James Henry Logan and Mona Elizabeth Logan; m 1981, Philippa Mary Walmsley; two s two d. *Educ:* Gilnahirk Primary Sch., E Belfast; Sullivan Upper Sch., Holywood; Trinity Coll., Cambridge (BA 1978; PhD Theoretical Chem. 1982). Jun. Res. Fellow, Christ's Coll., Cambridge, 1982–86; Postdoctoral Res. Associate, Univ. of Illinois, Urbana-Champaign, 1982–83; University of Oxford: Univ. Lectr in Phys. Chem., 1986–96; Prof. of Chem., 1996–2005; Official Fellow, Waters Fellow and Tutor in Phys. and Theoretical Chem., Balliol Coll., 1986–2005, Emeritus Fellow, 2005. Staff Mem., Theory Div., Institut Laue-Langevin, Grenoble, 1996; Infosys Vis. Chair Prof. in Physics, Indian Inst. of Sci., Bangalore, 2019–. Foreign Fellow, NAS, India, 2012. Royal Society of Chemistry: Marlow Medal and Prize, Faraday Div., 1990; Corday-Morgan Medal and Prize, 1994; Tilden Lecture and Medal, 2007. *Publications:* numerous res. articles on theoretical condensed matter chem. and phys. *Recreations:* music, poetry, weeding, liberal baiting. *Address:* Physical and Theoretical Chemistry Laboratory, South Parks Road, Oxford OX1 3QZ. *T:* (01865) 275418. *E:* david.logan@chem.ox.ac.uk.

LOGAN, Elaine; Warden, Glenalmond College, 2015–19; b Perth, 10 Nov. 1961; d of James Logan and Janette Logan; m 2011, Richard Selley; two s one d. *Educ:* Ross High Sch.; Univ. of Edinburgh (MA); Moray House (PGCE); Heriot-Watt Univ. (PGC Counselling); Aberdeen Coll. (Postgrad. Cert. Pupil Support). Teacher, Viewforth High Sch., Kirkcaldy, 1984–87; Dollar Academy: Housemistress, 1990–93; Hd of Year, 1993–94; Reception Year Hd and Principal Teacher of Guidance, 1994–2001; Loretto School: Housemistress, 2001–06; Sen. Mgt Team, 2006–15; Actg Hd, 2013–14. *Recreations:* singing, music, reading. *Address:* Glenalmond College, Glenalmond, Perth PH1 3RY. *T:* (01738) 880143. *E:* warden@glenalmondcollege.co.uk. *Clubs:* Lansdowne, Caledonian.

LOGAN, Fergus; *see* Logan, J. F. G.

LOGAN, Gabrielle Nicole; broadcaster, presenter and journalist; b Leeds, 24 Jan. 1973; d of Terry and Christine Yorath; m 2001, Kenny Logan; one s one d (twins). *Educ:* Notre Dame Sixth Form Coll., Leeds; Durham Univ. (BA Law 1995). Gymnast; represented Wales in rhythmic gymnastics, Commonwealth Games, Auckland, 1990. Radio broadcaster, Metro FM, 1992–96; football presenter, Sky Sports, 1996–98; with ITV, 1998–2007: presenter, On the Ball, World Cup, Champions League and Premiership football, Boat Race; with BBC, 2007–: Radio 5 Live: Sunday morning show, 2008–09; Gabby Logan Show, 2010–11; BBC One: presenter, Final Score, Inside Sport, Six Nations, Autumn Rugby Internats, Match of the Day, Olympic Games, Beijing, 2008, London, 2012 and Rio de Janeiro, 2016, FIFA World Cup, 2010, 2014, 2018, Eur. Football Championships, 2012; FIFA 2011 Women's World Cup, BBC Three, Commonwealth Games, Glasgow, 2014, Brisbane, 2018; Invictus Games, 2016; Live with Gabby Logan, Channel 5, 2011–12; Sports Personality of the Year, 2014–15; FIFA 2019 Women's World Cup, BBC One; columnist, The Times, 2002–. Chancellor, Leeds Trinity Univ., 2013–18. Patron: Disabilities Trust, 2002–; Prince's Trust, 2002–; Gt Ormond St Hosp., 2002–; Vice Pres., Sparks, 2002–. Hon. DSc Leeds Metropolitan, 2009. *Address:* c/o James Grant Management, 4th Floor, 180 Great Portland Street, W1W 5QZ.

LOGAN, (James) Fergus (Graeme); Chief Executive, PSP Association, 2011–16; b 20 June 1950; s of late James John Forbes Moffat, (Hamish), Logan and Lorna Jane Logan; m 1977, Wendy Elizabeth, d of Maj.-Gen. Frederick Joseph Plaskett, CB, MBE; three s one d. *Educ:* Monmouth Sch. Gen. Sec., Nat. Youth Theatre, 1969–80; Head of Appeals, MENCAP, 1981–86; Head of Ops, UNICEF UK, 1986–88; Develt Dir, Bath Internat. Fest. of the Arts, 1988–90; Dir, Meml Fund for Disaster Relief, 1990; Exec. Dir, Muscular Dystrophy Gp, 1990–97; Chief Exec., Arthritis Res. Campaign, 1998–2009. Founder and Chm., "Batteries not included" (250 charity consortium), 1992–96; Chairman: Exec. Cttee, European Neuromuscular Centre, Baarn, Netherlands, 1992–98; AMRC, 1995–99 (Mem. Exec. Council, 1992–95); Res. for Health Charities Gp, 1996–98. Trustee, Neuromuscular Centre, Winsford, Ches., 1991–97. *Recreations:* family, sport, books, beer, sloth. *Address:* Pug Lodge, 1 Queen's Lane, Eynsham, Oxon OX29 4HL. *T:* (01865) 883732.

LOGAN, Joseph Andrew; Chairman, Hay & Kilner, Solicitors, Newcastle, Wallsend and Gosforth, 1998–2001; b 5 Nov. 1942; s of late Joseph Baird Logan and Hellen Dawson Logan (née Wink); m 1964, Heather Robertson; one s one d. *Educ:* Hilton Acad., Aberdeen. Sales Manager: Aberdeen Journals, 1958–69; Newcastle Evening Chronicle, 1969–77; Newcastle Chronicle and Journal: Exec. Asst, 1976–77; Asst Man. Dir, 1979–82; Dir, 1984–89; Man. Dir, 1985–89; Asst Man. Dir, Evening Post, Luton and Evening Echo, Watford, 1977–79; Man. Dir, Peter Reed and Co., 1982; Dep. Man. Dir, Aberdeen Journals, 1982–83 (Dir, 1984); Man. Dir, Scotsman Publications, 1989–94; Pres. and Chief Exec., Thomson Newspaper Corp., Western USA, 1994–97. Director: Weekly Courier Ltd, 1971–89; Thomson Regional Newspapers, 1984–94; Thomson Scottish Organisation Ltd, 1989–94; Northern Rock Building Soc. Scotland, 1989–94 (Dep. Chm., Northern Rock Foundn, 1989–2000). Pres., Scottish Daily Newspaper Soc., 1990–92 (Vice Pres., 1989–90); Trustee, NE Civic Trust, 1984–89; Member: British Airways Consumer Council, 1986–89; Bd, BITC, 1985–89; ScotBIC, 1989–94; Dir, Prince's Scottish Youth Business Trust, 1989–94. Mem. Council, Univ. of Newcastle upon Tyne, 1985–89. *Address:* 5 Burnside, Ponteland, Newcastle upon Tyne NE20 9AQ. *T:* (01661) 822280. *E:* jalogan@onetel.com.

LOGAN, Prof. Malcolm Ian, AC 1996; PhD; Chairman, Education Gateway Holdings Ltd, 1998–2001; b 3 June 1931; m 1954, Antoinette (d 2013), d of F. Lalich; one d. *Educ:* Univ. of Sydney (BA Hons 1951, DipEd 1952, PhD 1965). Lectr in Geography, Sydney Teachers Coll., 1956–58; Lectr in Geog., 1959–64, Sen. Lectr, 1965–67, Univ. of Sydney; Prof. of Geog. and of Urban and Regional Planning, Univ. of Wisconsin, Madison, USA, 1967–71; Monash University: Prof. of Geog., 1971–81; Pro Vice-Chancellor, 1982–85; Dep. Vice-Chancellor, 1986; Vice-Chancellor, 1987–96. Visiting Professor: Univ. of Ibadan, Nigeria, 1970–71; LSE, 1973; Nanyang Univ., Singapore, 1979. Chm., Open Learning Agency, Australia Pty Ltd, 1993–96. Australian Newspaper Australian of the Year, 1996. *Publications:* (jtly) New Viewpoints in Economic Geography, 1966; Studies in Australian Geography, 1968; New Viewpoints in Urban and Industrial Geography, 1971; Urban and Regional Australia, 1975; Urbanisation, the Australian Experience, 1980; (jtly) The Brittle Rim, 1989; contribs to Aust. Geographical Studies, Regional Studies, Land Econs, and Econ. Geography. *Address:* 25 Tasmania Circle, Forrest, ACT 2603, Australia.

LOGAN, Rt Rev. Vincent; Bishop of Dunkeld, (RC), 1981–2012, now Bishop Emeritus; b 30 June 1941; s of Joseph Logan and Elizabeth Flannigan. *Educ:* Blairs College, Aberdeen; St Andrew's Coll., Drygrange, Melrose. Ordained priest, Edinburgh, 1964; Asst Priest, St Margaret's, Davidson's Mains, Edinburgh, 1964–66; Corpus Christi Coll., London, 1966–67 (DipRE); Chaplain, St Joseph's Hospital, Rosewell, Midlothian, 1967–77; Adviser in Religious Education, Archdiocese of St Andrews and Edinburgh, 1967; Parish Priest, St Mary's, Ratho, 1977–81; Episcopal Vicar for Education, Archdiocese of St Andrews and Edinburgh, 1978. *Address:* Croghmore, 10 Arnhall Drive, Dundee DD2 1LU.

LOGES, Corinna; Director of Development and Strategy, Thames Christian School, since 2018; b Nordhorn, Germany, 17 April 1970; d of Wolfgang Loges and Christel Loges; m 2017, James Rae. *Educ:* Hamburger Akademie für Kommunikationsdesign (Dip. Communication Design 1996); Inst. of Commonwealth Studies, London (MSc Human Develt and Security 2006). UK Dir, Media Consulta UK Ltd, 2003–06; Dir, Communications and Fundraising, Christian Solidarity Worldwide, 2007–12; Founder, helping your charity grow, 2012–15; Sen. Consultant, Action Planning, 2015; CEO, Humanitarian Aid Relief Trust, 2016–17. *E:* corinnaloges1@gmail.com.

LOGIE, John Robert Cunningham, PhD; FRCS, FRCSEd, FRCPSGlas; Consultant General Surgeon, Raigmore Hospital, Inverness, 1981–2011; Hon. Senior Lecturer in Surgery, Aberdeen University, 1981–2011; b 9 Sept. 1946; s of Norman John Logie and Kathleen Margaret Cameron Logie (née Neill); m 1st, 1981, Sheila Catherine Will (d 2001); one s one d; 2nd, 2004, Carol Joan MacDonald. *Educ:* Robert Gordon's Coll., Aberdeen; Trinity Coll., Glenalmond; Aberdeen Univ. (MB ChB 1970; PhD 1978). FRCSEd 1974; FRCS 1975; FRCPSGlas 1993. Various jun. surg. hosp. posts, Aberdeen Royal Infirmary, 1970–75; Lectr in Surgery, Aberdeen Univ., 1975–81. Vice Pres., RCSE, 2006–09 (Mem. Council, 1991–2002; Treas., 2002–06). Med. Mem., First-tier Tribunal (Social Entitlement Chamber), 2013–16. JP Grampian, Highlands and Islands, 2010–19. *Recreations:* railways in Britain, opera (especially Wagner). *Address:* The Darroch, Little Cantray Road, Culloden Moor, Inverness IV2 5EY. *T:* (01463) 792090. *E:* john.r.c.logie@lineone.net.

LOGSDAIL, (Christopher) Nicholas (Roald), OBE 2017; owner, founder and Director, Lisson Gallery, since 1967; b 21 June 1945; s of late John Logsdail and Else Logsdail (née Dahl); m 1st, 1968, Fiona McLean (d 2011); one s; 2nd, 1985, Caroline Mockett; two s one d. *Educ:* Bryanston Sch.; Slade Sch., University College London. Opened Lisson Gallery, 1967, two locations in London and two in New York; celebrated 50th anniv., 2017 with major off-site exhibn, Lisson Presents; represents 58 acclaimed artists, including: British sculptors, Tony Cragg, Richard Deacon and Anish Kapoor; minimal and conceptual artists, Richard Long, Carmen Herrera and Dan Graham; prominent internat. artists, Marina Abramovic and Ai Weiwei; next generation of contemp. artists, Ryan Gander, Haroon Mirza. Mem., Soc. of London Art Dealers. *Publications:* (jtly) Artist|Work|Lisson, 2017; over 100 monographs and artists' books, 1970–. *Recreations:* collecting 20th century art and furniture, paleoanthropology, African studies. *Address:* Lisson Gallery, 67 Lisson Street, NW1 5DA. *T:* (020) 7724 2739. *E:* nicholas@lissongallery.com.

LOHN, Matthew Simon; Senior Partner, Fieldfisher (formerly Field Fisher Waterhouse), since 2013; b Brentwood, 19 Nov. 1965; s of Carl William Lohn and Ann Isobel Lohn; m 1992, Johanna Gabriella Miranda Cornwell; one d. *Educ:* Brentwood Sch.; London Hosp. Med. Coll. (BSc Hons 1st Cl. Physiol.; MB BS); Coll. of Law (DipLaw Distinction); Harvard Business Sch. House Officer, Epsom Hosp., 1991–92; Field Fisher Waterhouse, then Fieldfisher, 1994–: Partner, 1998–; Mem., Main Bd, 2004–11; Managing Partner, 2011–13. Member: Determinations Panel, Pensions Regulator, 2013–17; Complaints Panel, 2014–17, Bd, 2019–, IPSO. Chm., Appeal Panel, RFU, 2006–12; Legal Chairman: Disciplinary Panel, British Horseracing Authy, 2008–16; Nat. Anti Doping Panel, 2009–. Dir, Newmarket Racecourse, 2019–. Mem., Licensing Appeals Bd, Dubai Healthcare City Authy, 2014–. Chair, Regulatory Bd, CIPFA, 2016–. *Recreations:* gardening, racing, shooting. *Address:* Oak Farm, Scaldwell, Northants NN6 9JY. *T:* (01604) 889140. *Club:* Boodle's.

LOISELLE, Hon. Gilles; PC (Can.) 1990; Advisor, Power Corporation of Canada, since 1993; b 20 May 1929; s of Arthur Loiselle and Antoinette Lethiecq; m 1962, Lorraine Benoît; one s one d. *Educ:* Sacred-Heart Coll., Sudbury, Ont; BA Laval. Teacher, Tafari Makonnen Sch., Addis Ababa, 1951–53; Journalist, Le Droit, Ottawa, 1953–56; Haile Selassie First Day Sch., Addis Ababa, 1956–62; Dir, Behrane Zarie Néo Inst., Addis Ababa, 1958–62; Canadian Broadcasting Corporation: Editor, TV French Network, 1962–63; Quebec and Paris correspondent, French Radio and TV Network, 1963–67; Counsellor, Quebec House, Paris, 1967–72; Dir Gen. of Quebec Govt Communications, 1972–76; Pres., Intergovtl Deptl Cttee for Olympic Year, 1976; Dir, Interparly Relations, Quebec Nat. Assembly, 1977; Agent General for Quebec in London, with responsibility for Scandinavian countries, Iceland, and Ireland, 1977–83; Dep. Minister for federal provincial relations, 1983–84, for Cultural Affairs, Quebec, 1984–85; Agent Gen. for Quebec in Rome, 1985–88. MP (PC) Langelier, 1988–93; Minister of State for Finance, 1989–93; Pres., Treasury Bd of Canada, 1990–93; Minister of Finance, 1993. Dir, Mines Richmont Inc. Founder Mem., Assoc. France-Québec, 1969–72. Hon. Col, 55th Bde. *Recreation:* reading. *Address:* Power Corporation of Canada, 751 Victoria Square, Montreal, QC H2Y 2J3, Canada.

**LOLE, Simon Richard Anthony;** freelance musician, composer, arranger and broadcaster; Director of Music and Master of the Choristers, Salisbury Cathedral, 1997–2005; *b* 23 Dec. 1957; *s* of late Margaret and of Dennis Lole; *m* 2010, Gwen Carvill; one *s* two *d. Educ:* St Paul's Cathedral Choir Sch.; King's Coll., London (BMus Hons 1978); Guildhall Sch. of Music. ARCO(CHM). Organist and Choirmaster: Barking Parish Church, 1978–80; Croydon Parish Church, 1980–85; Dir of Music, St Mary's Collegiate Church, Warwick, 1985–94; Master of the Music, Sheffield Cathedral, 1994–97; Actg Dir of Music, Jesus Coll., Cambridge, 2005 and 2009. Mem. Council, Incorp. Guild of Church Musicians, 2008–. Hon. FGCM 2005; Hon. ARSCM 2019. *Publications:* many church compositions. *Recreations:* walking, reading, sport. *Address:* Cockhill Farm, Haddon, Sturminster Newton, Dorset DT10 2LB. *E:* simon@simonlole.com. *W:* www.simonlole.com.

**LOLLAR, Barbara S.;** *see* Sherwood Lollar, B.

**LOMAS, Alfred;** *b* 30 April 1928; *s* of Alfred and Florence Lomas; one *s* one *d. Educ:* St Paul's Elem. Sch., Stockport; various further educnl estabs. Solicitor's clerk, 1942–46; Radio Telephony Operator, RAF, 1946–49; various jobs, 1949–51; railway signalman, 1951–59; Labour Party Sec./Agent, 1959–65; Pol Sec., London Co-op., 1965–79. MEP (Lab) London NE, 1979–99; Leader, British Lab Gp, EP, 1985–87. *Publications:* The Common Market—why we should keep out, 1970. *Recreations:* chess, arts, sport. *Address:* 28 Brookway, SE3 9BJ. *T:* (020) 8852 6689. *Club:* Hackney Labour.

**LOMAS, Anthony Victor,** FCA; Chairman, Business Recovery Services, PricewaterhouseCoopers, 2006–18; *b* London, 26 Nov. 1956; *s* of Victor and Patricia Lomas; *m* 1989, Kerry; two *s. Educ:* University Coll. London (BA Geog.). FCA 1982. Joined Price Waterhouse, later PricewaterhouseCoopers, 1978; Lead Administrator: Enron Europe, 2001–18; MG Rover, 2005–18; Lehman UK, 2008–18. Chm., Insolvency Cttee, ICAEW, 2004–14. *Recreations:* family, travel.

**LOMAS, Prof. David Arthur,** ScD, PhD; FRCP, FMedSci, FHEA; Professor of Medicine, since 2013, Head of Medical School, since 2014, and Vice Provost Health and Head, School of Life and Medical Sciences, since 2015, University College London; Academic Director, UCL Partners Academic Health Science Centre, since 2015; *b* 19 Feb. 1962; *s* of Peter Harry Lomas and Margaret Lomas (*née* Halsall); *m* 1987, Judith Amanda Glasbey; three *s. Educ:* Univ. of Nottingham (BMedSci 1983; BM BS Hons 1985); Trinity Coll., Cambridge (PhD 1993); ScD Cambridge 2004. MRCP 1988, FRCP 1997; ILTM 2000. SHO, Central Birmingham HA, 1986–88; Registrar, Gen. Hosp., Birmingham, 1988–90; MRC Trng Fellow, and Mem., Trinity Coll., Cambridge, 1990–93; MRC Clinician Scientist Fellow, Cambridge, 1993–95; Lectr in Medicine, 1995–98, Prof. of Respiratory Biol., 1998–2012, Univ. of Cambridge; Dep. Dir, Cambridge Inst. for Medical Res., 2002–12; Fellow, St John's Coll., Cambridge, 2008–12; Dean, Faculty of Med. Scis, UCL, 2013–15. Hon. Consultant Physician: Addenbrooke's and Papworth Hosps, 1995–2012; UCLH and Royal Free Hosps, 2013–. Sen. Investigator, NIHR, 2014–. Dep. Chief Exec., MRC, 2017–18. Non-exec. Dir, UCLH, 2015–. Director: GMEC, 2015–; MedCity Ltd, 2016–. Member, Board of Directors: Francis Crick Inst., 2015–; African Health Res. Inst., SA, 2016–. Chairman: Grants Cttee, Asthma UK, 2006–10; Grants Cttee, British Lung Foundn, 2010–13; Respiratory Therapy Area Bd, GlaxoSmithKline, 2012–15; MRC Population and Systems Medicine Bd, 2012–16; Grants Cttee, Alpha-1 Foundn (USA), 2008–13 (Mem., 2000–13 and 2016–); Co-Chm., 2004–08). Pres., Assoc. of Physicians GB and Ireland, 2017–18. Med. Trustee, BHF, 2016–19. Mem. Council, Acad. of Med. Scis, 2018–. Croonian Lectr, RCP, 2005; Gordon Cummings Lect., Med. Res. Soc., 2008. MAE 2017. FMedSci 2001; FHEA 2007. Res. Award, BUPA Foundn, 1996; Oon Internat. Prize in Preventative Medicine, Downing Coll., Cambridge, 1996; Biochem. Soc. GSK Prize, 2004. *Publications:* res. on α:-antitrypsin deficiency, conformational diseases and chronic obstructive pulmonary disease in med. jls. *Recreations:* cricket, hill walking, modern literature, opera. *Address:* Vice Provost Health, University College London, 1st Floor, Maple House, 149 Tottenham Court Road, W1T 7NF. *T:* (020) 3108 7929.

**LOMAS, Prof. David John,** FRCP, FRCR; Professor (formerly Amersham Professor) of Clinical Magnetic Resonance Imaging, University of Cambridge, 2001, now Emeritus; *b* 21 March 1957; *s* of Geoffrey and Sheila Lomas; *m* 1986, Rebecca Steward; two *d. Educ:* Emmanuel Coll., Cambridge (MA Engrg; MB BChir). MRCP 1985, FRCP 1998; FRCR 1989. Medical Registrar, Princess Margaret Hosp., Swindon, 1985–87; Radiology Registrar, 1987–93, Hon. Consultant Radiologist and Univ. Lectr, 1993–2001, Addenbrooke's Hosp., Cambridge. Vis. Scientist, Mayo Clinic, USA, 1993. *Publications:* contrib. papers to Clinical Radiol., Radiol., Science, Jl Magnetic Resonance Imaging, British Jl Radiol. *Recreations:* industrial archaeology, photography, plumbing. *Address:* Department of Radiology, University of Cambridge School of Clinical Medicine, Box 218, Cambridge Biomedical Campus, Cambridge CB2 0QQ. *T:* (01223) 336890, *Fax:* (01223) 330915.

**LOMAS, Eric George;** Managing Director, Gatwick Airport, 1994–97; *b* 26 June 1938; *s* of Arthur Edward Lomas and Florence Lomas; *m* 1959, Carol Letitia Davies; two *d. Educ:* Willesden County Grammar School; Templeton Coll., Oxford (Sen. Exec. Leadership Prog.); Cranfield Inst. (Computer Prog.); London Business Sch. (Aviation Prog.). FCIT. PLA, 1954–69; served with RE, 1957–59; Associated Container Transportation, 1969–70; BAA, 1970–86, BAA plc, 1986–97; Man. Dir, Stansted Airport, 1989–94. Trustee Dir, BAA Pension Fund Co. Ltd, 2003–06. Dir, Sussex TEC, 1995–97. Advr, Jedlo Associates. Mem., SE Reg., CBI, 1995–97. Chm., Lapwing Flying Club Ltd, 1979–82; Vice Cdre, British Motor Yacht Club Ltd, 1994–96. Member: Petersham Book Club; Square Rigger Club. *Recreations:* reading, classic car rallies, boating, travel.

**LOMAS, Joanne;** HM Diplomatic Service; High Commissioner to Rwanda and Ambassador (non-resident) to Burundi, since 2018; *b* High Wycombe, 7 Sept. 1970; *d* of Geoffrey Lomas and Judith Lomas; *m* 2008, Christopher Finucane; one *d. Educ:* Univ. of Bristol (BSc Politics). Joined FCO, 1993; Third Sec., Damascus, 1997–2000; Second Sec., UK Mission to the UN, Geneva, 2001–06; Hd, Global Response Centre, FCO, 2009; Dep. Hd of Mission, Sarajevo, 2011–15; High Comr to Namibia, 2015–17. *Recreations:* tennis, hiking, horse riding, the great outdoors. *Address:* c/o Foreign and Commonwealth Office, King Charles Street, SW1A 2AH.

**LOMAS, Ven. John Derrick Percy;** Archdeacon of Wrexham, since 2018; *b* 19 Aug. 1958. *Educ:* St Michael's Coll., Llandaff. Ordained deacon, 1994, priest, 1995; Curate, Parish of Rhyl, 1994–2000; RN Chaplain, 2000–01; Vicar, St James, Holywell, 2001–11; Area Dean, Holywell, 2001–11; Transition Missioner: St Mael and St Sulien, Corwen, 2011–13; St Dunawd, Bangor Monachorum and Benefice of Wrexham, 2013–14; Archdeacon of St Asaph, 2014–18; Rector, St Michael's, Caerwys and St Stephens, Bodfari, 2015–18. Canon Cursal, St Asaph Cathedral, 2008–14.

**LOMAS, Julia Carole;** Partner, since 2002, and National Head, Court of Protection Department, since 2008, Irwin Mitchell, Solicitors (Consultant, 2000–02); *b* 9 Dec. 1954; *d* of Charles James Lomas and Sadie Lomas; *m* 1st (marr. diss.); one *s*; 2nd, 2014, William Frederick Hill. *Educ:* Lanchester Poly. (BA Business Law). Admitted solicitor, 1980. Articled clerk, London Borough of Islington, 1977–80; Dep. Borough Solicitor, London Borough of Waltham Forest, 1980–89; Borough Solicitor, London Borough of Haringey, 1989–94; Public Trustee, and Chief Exec., Public Trust Office, 1994–99. FCMI (FIMgt 1994). *Recreations:* theatre, crosswords, dining out. *Address:* Irwin Mitchell, 40 Holborn Viaduct, EC1N 2PZ.

**LOMAS, Mark Henry;** QC 2003; *b* 17 Nov. 1948; *s* of Keith and Margaret Lomas; *m* 1st, 1980, Caroline Margaret Mary Agnew (marr. diss. 2005); three *d*; 2nd, 2010, Joanna Jane Allen (*née* Wigglesworth) (*d* 2012). *Educ:* Oundle Sch.; Trinity Hall, Cambridge (BA Hons, MA). Called to the Bar, Middle Temple, 1977; in practice as barrister, specialising in professional negligence, 1977–2009; Accredited Mediator, 2001; Mem., London Court of Internat. Arbitration, 2008–; in practice as Commercial Mediator and sitting as Commercial Arbitrator, 2009–. *Recreations:* hunting, shooting, salmon fishing. *Address:* Littleton Chambers, 3 King's Bench Walk North, Temple, EC4Y 7HR. *Club:* Boodle's.

**LOMAX, (Janis) Rachel;** Deputy Governor, Bank of England, 2003–08; *b* 15 July 1945; *d* of William and Dilys Salmon; *m* 1967, Michael Acworth Lomax (marr. diss. 1990); two *s. Educ:* Cheltenham Ladies' Coll.; Girton Coll., Cambridge (MA); LSE (MSc). HM Treasury: Econ. Assistant, 1968; Econ. Advr, 1972; Sen. Econ. Advr, 1978; Principal Pvte Sec. to Chancellor of the Exchequer, 1985–86; Under-Sec., 1986–90; Dep. Chief Econ. Advr, 1990–92; Dep. Sec. (Financial Instns and Markets), 1992–94; Dep. Sec., Cabinet Office, 1994–95; Vice Pres. and Chief of Staff, World Bank, 1995–96; Permanent Secretary: Welsh Office, 1996–99; DSS, then DWP, 1999–2002; DTLR, then DfT, 2002–03. Non-executive Director: HSBC Hldgs, 2008– (Sen. Ind. Dir, 2015–); Heathrow (SP) Ltd (formerly BAA), 2010–; CityUK, 2013–16; Serco, 2014–; Breugel, 2014–; Ditchley Park, 2014–; SETL, 2017–. Pres., IFS, 2007–15. Mem. Bd, RNT, 2002–11. Dep. Chair, British Council, 2018–. Mem. Council, Imperial Coll. London, 2010–. *Address:* 25 Henning Street, SW11 3DR.

**LOMAX, Kevin John;** Founder, Misys plc, 1979 (Chairman, 1985–2005; Chief Executive Officer, 2005–06); *b* 8 Dec. 1948; *s* of late Brig. Kenneth John Lomax and of Mary Lomax (*née* Foley); *m* 1975, Penelope Frances Flynn; one *s* two *d. Educ:* Ampleforth Coll.; Manchester Univ. (BSc Hons 1970). Advanced Project Manager, J & S Pumps Ltd, 1970–73; Asst to Divl Chm., Allied Polymer Gp, 1973–75; Managing Director: British Furnaces Ltd, 1975–77; Wellman Incandescent Ltd, 1977–80; Dir and Divl Chm., Caparo Industries (CMT) Ltd, 1980–83; Dir and Divl CEO, Electronic Components Div., STC plc, 1983–85. Non-exec. Dir, Marks & Spencer, 2000–06. Trustee/Dir, Royal Opera House, 2000–05. Hon. DSc Birmingham, 2003. *Recreations:* golf, shooting, fishing, horse-racing, military history, music. *Address:* Clarence House, The Vineyard, Richmond, Surrey TW10 6AQ.

**LOMAX, Rachel;** *see* Lomax, J. R.

**LOMBARDELLI, Clare;** Chief Economic Advisor and Director General Economics, HM Treasury, since 2018; Joint Head, Government Economic Service, since 2018; *b* Stockport, 20 Nov. 1978; *d* of Dario Lombardelli and Ann Lombardelli. *Educ:* Hazel Grove High Sch.; Magdalen Coll., Oxford (BA PPE); London Sch. of Econs and Political Sci. (MSc Econs). Economist, Bank of England, 2001–05; HM Treasury: joined, 2005; Tech. Advr, IMF, 2010–11; Econ. Affairs Private Sec. to the Prime Minister, 2011–13; Principal Private Sec. to Chancellor of the Exchequer, 2013–15; Dir, Budget, 2015–18. Vis. Prof., KCL, 2018–. *Address:* HM Treasury, 1 Horse Guards Road, SW1A 2HQ.

**LOMBE, Hon. Sir Edward Christopher E.;** *see* Evans-Lombe.

**LOMER, Geoffrey John,** CBE 1985; MA; FREng; FIET; Chairman, Satellite Information Services Ltd, 1993–96; Director (non-executive), Vodafone Group plc, 1992–97; *b* 5 Jan. 1932; *s* of Frederick John Lomer and Dorothy Lomer; *m* 1st, 1955, Pauline Helena May (*d* 1974); one *s* one *d*; 2nd, 1977, Antoinette Ryall (*d* 2003); one step *s* one step *d. Educ:* St Austell Grammar School; Queens' College, Cambridge (MA). FREng (FEng 1984). Research Engineer, EMI Research Laboratories, 1953–57; Head of Radio Frequency Div., Broadcast Equipment Dept, EMI Electronics, 1957–63; Head of Transmitter Lab., Racal Communications, 1963–68; Technical Dir, Racal Mobilcal, 1968–70; Dir in Charge, Racal Communications Equipment, 1970–76; Dep. Man. Dir, Racal Tacticom, 1976–77; Technical Dir, Racal Electronics plc, 1977–92. Vice Pres., IEE, 1991–94; Hon. FIET (Hon. FIEE 1998). *Recreations:* music, theatre. *Address:* Ventana, The Devil's Highway, Crowthorne, Berks RG45 6BJ.

**LONDESBOROUGH,** 9th Baron *cr* 1850; **Richard John Denison;** *b* 2 July 1959; *s* of John Albert Lister, 8th Baron Londesborough, TD, AMICE, and Elizabeth Ann (*d* 1994), *d* of late Edward Little Sale, ICS; *S* father, 1968; *m* 1987, Rikki Morris, *d* of J. E. Morris, Bayswater; one *s* one *d. Educ:* Wellington College; Exeter Univ. *Heir:* *s* Hon. James Frederick Denison, *b* 4 June 1990. *Address:* Edw Cottage, Aberedw, Builth Wells, Powys LD2 3UR.

**LONDON, Bishop of,** since 2018; **Rt Rev. and Rt Hon. Dame Sarah Elisabeth Mullally,** DBE 2005; PC 2018; Prelate of the Order of the British Empire, since 2018; Dean of the Chapels Royal, since 2019; *b* 26 March 1962; *d* of Michael Frederick Mills Bowser and Ann Dorothy Bowser; *m* 1987, Eamonn James Mullally; one *s* one *d. Educ:* Nightingale Sch. of Nursing; S Bank Poly. (BSc Hons Nursing and RGN 1984); MSc Interprofessional Health and Welfare, S Bank Univ., 1992; DipTh Kent 2001; MA Pastoral Theol., Heythrop Coll., London Univ., 2006. Staff Nurse: St Thomas' Hosp., 1984–86; Royal Marsden Hosp., 1986–88; Ward Sister, Westminster Hosp., 1988–90; Sen. Nurse, Riverside HA, 1990–92; Asst Chief Nurse, Riverside Hosps, 1992–94; Dir of Nursing and Dep. Chief Exec., Chelsea and Westminster Healthcare Trust, 1994–99; Chief Nursing Officer, DoH, 1999–2004. Ordained deacon, 2001; NSM, Battersea Fields, 2001–04; Asst Curate, St George, St Saviour and All Saints, Battersea Fields, 2004–06; Team Rector, Sutton, Surrey, 2006–12; Canon Res. and Treas., Salisbury Cathedral, 2012–15; Bishop Suffragan of Crediton, 2015–18. Non-executive Director: Royal Marsden NHS Foundn Trust, 2005–13; Salisbury NHS Foundn Trust, 2013–16. Independent Governor: S Bank Univ., 2005–15; KCL, 2016–. Bencher, Middle Temple, 2019. Hon. Fellow: S Bank Univ., 2000; Christ Church, Canterbury, 2006. Hon. Dr Health Sci.: Bournemouth, 2001; Wolverhampton, 2004; Hon. DSc Herts, 2005.

**LONDON, Archdeacon of;** *see* Miller, Ven. L. J.

**LONDON, Orville Delarno;** High Commissioner of the Republic of Trinidad and Tobago to the Court of St James's, since 2017; *b* Parlatuvier, Tobago, 6 Nov. 1945; *s* of late John London and Doris London; *m* 1992, Brigid McFarlane; three *s* two *d. Educ:* Univ. of the West Indies, St Augustine (BA Hist. and Sociol.; Dip. Internat. Relns; DipEd). Teacher, 1966–79, Vice Principal, 1979–89, Scarsborough Jun. Secondary Sch.; Principal, Signal Hill Sen. Comp. Sch., Tobago, 1989–95. Senator, Parlt of Trinidad and Tobago, 1995–96. Councillor, 1996–2000, Chief Sec., 2001–17, Tobago House of Assembly. Dep. Political Leader, 1998–2016, Tobago Political Leader, 2012–16, People's Nat. Movement. Sports Editor, Tobago News, 1996–2001. *Recreation:* reading. *Address:* 12A Greenaway Gardens,

Hampstead, NW3 7DH. *E:* orvillelondon@hotmail.com; High Commission of the Republic of Trinidad and Tobago, 42 Belgrave Square, SW1X 8NT. *T:* (020) 7245 9351, ext. 234, *Fax:* (020) 7823 1065. *E:* londono@foreign.gov.tt.

**LONDONDERRY**, 10th Marquess of, *cr* 1816; **Frederick Aubrey Vane-Tempest-Stewart;** Baron Londonderry 1789; Viscount Castlereagh 1795; Earl of Londonderry 1796; Baron Stewart 1814; Earl Vane, Viscount Seaham 1823; *b* 6 Sept. 1972; *s* of 9th Marquess of Londonderry and of Doreen Patricia Wells, *qv; S* father, 2012. *Heir: b* Lord Reginald Alexander Vane-Tempest-Stewart [*b* 30 May 1977; *m* 2004, Chloe Belinda Guinness; one *s* two *d*].

**LONDONDERRY, Doreen, Marchioness of;** *see* Wells, D. P.

**LONG,** family name of **Viscount Long.**

**LONG,** 5th Viscount *cr* 1921, of Wraxall; **James Richard Long;** *b* 31 Dec. 1960; *s* of 4th Viscount Long and Margaret Frances Long; *S* father, 2017.

**LONG, Prof. Adrian Ernest**, OBE 2006; PhD, DSc; FREng, FIAE; Professor of Civil Engineering, Queen's University, Belfast, 1976–2006, now Professor Emeritus; Leverhulme Emeritus Research Fellow, 2009–11; *b* 15 April 1941; *s* of Charles Long and Sylvia Long; *m* 1967, Elaine Thompson; one *s* one *d. Educ:* Royal Sch., Dungannon; QUB (BSc 1st cl. Hons (Civil Engrg) 1963; PhD (Structural Engrg) 1967; DSc (Civil Engrg) 1984). Bridge design engr, Foundn Engrg Co. of Canada, Toronto, 1967–68; Asst Prof., Dept of Civil Engrg, Queen's Univ., Kingston, Ont, 1968–71; Queen's University, Belfast: Lectr, 1971–76, Hd, 1977–89, Dept of Civil Engrg; Dean, Fac. of Engrg, 1988–91, 1998–2002; Dir, Sch. of Built Envmt, 1989–98. Pres., ICE, 2002–03. Hon. UK Rep., Tech. Cttee, EU Co-operation Sci. and Technol. Urban Civil Engrg, 1991–2006; Chm., Civil Engrg Sub-Panel, Res. Assessment Exercise for UK, 2008. Ed., Jl of Engrg Structures, 1986–94. Inventor of FlexiArch system, 2004. FREng 1989; FIAE, 1998. Hon. DSc City, 2007. (Jtly) Esso Energy Gold Medal, Royal Soc., 1994; Ewing Medal, ICE and Royal Soc., 2009; ICE Gold Medal, 2010. *Publications:* four patents, incl. for FlexiArch for construction of short-span bridges, 2004 (system used for over 80 arch bridges in UK and Ireland); over 350 tech. papers in jls and procs of confs. *Recreations:* walking, travel, gardening, occasional golf, Elder in a Presbyterian Church in Belfast. *Address:* School of Civil Engineering, Queen's University, Belfast, Belfast BT7 1NN. *T:* (028) 9097 6950, *Fax:* (028) 9097 4278. *E:* a.long@qub.ac.uk.

**LONG, Amanda;** Chief Executive Officer, Morison KSi, since 2019; *b* Herts, 25 March 1969; *m* 1996, Mark Long; one *s* one *d. Educ:* De Montfort Univ. (BA Jt Hons English Lit. and Hist.). Internat. Projects Manager, Birds Eye Wall's Ltd, Unilever plc, 1996–99; Dir and Nat. Rep., Plant Publicity Holland UK and Ireland Bureau, 2000–10; Hd, Corporate Responsibility, Anglian Water Services, 2010–11; CEO, Corporate Culture, 2011–12; Dir, Membership, Mktg and Media, E of England Co-operative Soc., 2012–14; Dir Gen., Consumers Internat., 2014–18. FCIM 2012; FRSA. Responsible Business Game Changer Award, Business in the Community, 2013. *Publications:* (contrib.) Addressing Tipping Points for a Precarious Future, 2013. *Recreations:* sailing, tennis. *Address:* Morison KSi, 6th Floor, 2 Kingdom Street, Paddington, W2 6BD. *E:* amanda@morisonksi.com.

**LONG, Christopher William,** CMG 1986; HM Diplomatic Service, retired; non-executive Director, Gedeon Richter plc, Budapest, 1998–2017; *b* 9 April 1938; *s* of late Eric and May Long; *m* 1972, Patricia, *d* of late Dennis and May Stanbridge; two *s* one *d. Educ:* King Edward's Sch., Birmingham; Balliol Coll., Oxford (Deakin Scholar); Univ. of Münster, W Germany. Served RN, 1956–58. HM Diplomatic Service, 1963–98: FO, 1963–64; Jedda, 1965–67; Caracas, 1967–69; FCO, 1969–74; Budapest, 1974–77; Belgrade (CSCE), 1977; Counsellor, Damascus, 1978–80; Counsellor and Dep. Perm. Rep., UKMIS, Geneva, 1980–83; Head, Near East and N Africa Dept, FCO, 1983–85; Asst Under-Sec. of State (Dep. Chief Clerk and Chief Inspector), FCO, 1985–88; Ambassador: to Switzerland, 1988–92 and also to Liechtenstein, 1992; to Egypt, 1992–95; to Hungary, 1995–98. Dir, Foreign Service Prog., Oxford Univ., 1999–2003. Non-exec. Dir, KFKI Computer Systems Corp., Budapest, 2001–04. Dir, World Faiths Develt Dialogue, 2004–05. Trustee, Orders of St John Care Trust, 2003–10. Gov., Prior Park Coll., Bath, 2000–09. *Recreations:* family, notably grandchildren, Middle East, Hungary and Switzerland, geriatric tennis, growing vegetables and fruit for home consumption. *Club:* Athenæum.

**LONG, Dr Ian Edward,** FRGS; Headmaster, Albyn School, Aberdeen, since 2008; *b* Sutton, Surrey, 26 Aug. 1959; *s* of late Gerald and Mimi Long; *m* 1998, Gwyneth Rogers. *Educ:* King's Coll., Sch., Wimbledon; King's Coll. London (BA Hons Geog., AKC, PGCE, PhD); Birkbeck Coll., London (MA N American Geog. Studies). Work for Shell and in a home for children in care; teacher: Royal Grammar Sch., High Wycombe, 1993–96 (Hd of Dept); Brentwood Sch., Essex, 1996–99 (Hd of Sixth Form); Dep. Hd, City of London Freemen's Sch., 1999–2008. Freeman: City of London; Co. of Educators. FRSA. *Publications:* contrib. Jl Rural Studies. *Recreations:* former oarsman at Molesey, Kingston, Globe Rowing Club, former researcher at King's College London, reading, theatre, keeping warm in the Granite City. *Address:* Albyn School, 17–23 Queen's Road, Aberdeen AB15 4PB. *T:* (01224) 322408. *E:* i.long@albynschool.co.uk. *Club:* Royal Over-Seas League.

**LONG, John Richard,** CBE 1987; *b* 9 March 1931; *s* of late Thomas Kendall Long and Jane Long; *m* 1952, Margaret (*née* Thistlethwaite) (*d* 2017); one *s* two *d. Educ:* Kirkham Grammar School; Dip. in EU Law, KCL, 1993. Clerical Officer, Customs and Excise, 1947; Exec. Officer, Min. of Pensions, subseq. DHSS, 1949; various posts on health functions; Asst Sec., 1978 (posts on regulation and pricing of medicines, maternity and child health, and communicable diseases); Under Sec., 1987 (NHS Personnel Div.), resigned 1988. *Publications:* co-author, articles on regulation of medicines. *Recreations:* family, gardening, writing stories for great grandchildren, fighting technophobia. *Address:* 77 Prospect Road, Farnborough, Hants GU14 8NT. *T:* (01252) 548525.

**LONG, Kieran William John;** Director, Swedish Centre for Architecture and Design, since 2017; *b* Lyndhurst, 19 Aug. 1977; *s* of Colin Long and Margaret Long; *m* 2012, Sofia Lagerkvist. *Educ:* King Edward VI Sch., Southampton; Cardiff Univ. (BA Eng. Lit. 1998). Deputy Editor: Building Design Mag., 1998–2001; Icon Mag., 2003–07; Editor-in-Chief, Architects' Jl and Architectural Rev., 2007–10; Architecture Critic, Evening Standard, 2010–13; Sen. Curator, Contemp. Architecture, Design and Digital, then Keeper, Design, Architecture and Digital, V&A, 2013–17. Television presenter: Restoration Home, 2010–13; The House that £100K Built, 2013–16. Tutor, RCA, 2011–12; Asst Dir, Venice Architectural Biennale, 2012. *Publications:* (ed jtly) Common Ground: a critical reader, 2012. *Recreations:* playing guitar, folk music, American fiction, tennis, cricket, golf. *Address:* Swedish Centre for Architecture and Design, Box 16410, 103 27 Stockholm, Sweden.

**LONG, Martin Paul;** Chairman: Churchill Properties (Southern) Ltd, since 2003; M4 Underwriting Ltd, 2006; Co-Chairman, Crystal Palace Football Club, since 2010; *b* 27 Aug. 1950; *s* of Robert and Alice Long; five *s* one *d. Educ:* St Joseph's Coll., SE19. FCII 1981. Prudential Assce Co., 1968–69; Guardian Royal Exchange Assce Co., 1970–74; Sphere Drake Insce Co., 1975–78; Northern Star Insce Co., 1979–83; Man. Dir, Halifax Insce Co., 1983–84; Dir and Gen. Manager, Direct Line Insce, 1984–87; setting up Churchill Insce Gp, 1987–89; Founder Chm. and CEO, Churchill Insurance Gp plc, 1989–2003; Dep. Chm., Royal Bank of Scotland Insurance, 2003–04; Chairman, Ashworth Mairs Gp, 2005–08; AMG (Chartered Loss Adjusters), 2005–08. Owner of Sweetwoods Park Golf Course, 2008–. *Recreations:* sports (watching and playing), socialising, spending time with my children. *Address:* Churchill Properties (Southern) Ltd, c/o K. A. Jeffries & Co., 18 Melbourne Grove, SE22 8RA. *T:* 07982 273327. *E:* martin@martinlong.co.uk.

**LONG, Naomi Rachel;** Member (Alliance): Belfast East, Northern Ireland Assembly, 2003–10 and since 2016; Northern Ireland, European Parliament, since 2019; *b* 13 Dec. 1971; *d* of James Dobbin Johnston and Olive Emily Johnston; *m* 1995, Michael Andrew Long. *Educ:* Mersey Street Primary Sch.; Bloomfield Collegiate Grammar Sch.; Queen's Univ., Belfast (MEng Dist. Civil Engrg 1994). Asst Engr, Parkman Consulting Engrs, 1994–96; Res. Asst, QUB, 1996–99; Graduate Civil and Envmtl Engr, Mulholland & Doherty, 1999–2003. Mem. (Alliance), Belfast CC, 2001–10 (Lord Mayor of Belfast, 2009–10). Vice Chm., Cttee for Office of First and Dep. First Minister, NI Assembly, 2007–10. MP (Alliance) Belfast E, 2010–15; contested (Alliance) same seat, 2015, 2017. Leader, Alliance Party of NI, 2016– (Dep. Leader, 2006–16). *Recreations:* Guide leader, reading, travel, choral singing. *Address:* Northern Ireland Assembly, Parliament Buildings, Stormont, Belfast BT4 3XX; European Parliament, Rue Wiertz 60, 1047 Brussels, Belgium.

**LONG, Raymond John,** CB 2018; CEng, FBCS, FIET; Director, since 2017, and independent consultant, since 2018, Ray Long Consulting Ltd; Director, Applications Development, Maintenance and Support Programme (formerly Senior Responsible Owner, Infrastructure Modernisation Programme, then Director, Technology Platforms), Department for Work and Pensions, 2014–17 (Chief Executive, Benefits and Pensions Digital Technology Services Ltd, 2016–17); *b* Hemel Hempstead, 21 Aug. 1957; *s* of Allan John Long and Elsie Patricia Long; *m* 1st, 1978, Kathleen Dean (marr. diss. 2005); two *d*; 2nd, 2010, Yvette Radford-Foley. *Educ:* Longdean Sch. (formerly Apsley GS); Ashington High (formerly Co. Grammar) Sch.; City Univ., London (MSc 1989); Open Univ. (BA 1992). CEng 1992; FBCS 2004; FIET 2008. Postal Worker, Post Office, 1975–77; Programmer/Analyst, 1977–82, Telecommunications Analyst, 1983–86, DHSS; Software Consultant, 1982–83, Mem., Govt Data Network Project Team, 1986–88, CCTA; Hd, Business Analysis and Consultancy, then Hd, IT Strategy Support Office, then Asst Dir, IT Strategies, later Asst Dir, IT Applications, MAFF, 1989–97; Dep. Dir, Inf. Services Div., DoH, 1997–99; Hd, IT Services Div., DETR, then DTLR, later DfT and ODPM, 1999–2004; Chief Exec., NI Business Develt Service, 2004–06; Project Manager, Dept of Educn, NI, 2006–07; Prog. Dir, NHS Connecting for Health, 2007–08; Dir, Major Projects, OGC, HM Treasury, then Cabinet Office, 2008–11; Dir, Business Tax Change, 2011–13, Dir, Corporate Services Change, 2013–14, HMRC. Tutor/Associate Lectr, Open Univ., 1993–. Non-exec. Dir, Frimley Health NHS Foundn Trust, 2017–. Mem. Council, Gresham Coll., 2018–. Pres., BCS, 2016–17. FAPM 2014; CDir 2008; FInstD 2009; CITP 2004; FCMI 2006; FRSA 2006. Freeman: City of London, 2007; Information Technologists' Co., 2007 (Liveryman, 2009–; Master, 2019–20). *Recreations:* piano, running, sailing. *Address:* 35 Linersh Wood Close, Bramley, Guildford, Surrey GU5 0EQ. *T:* (01483) 898016. *E:* ray@raylong.com. *Club:* Athenæum.

**LONG, Sir Richard (Julian),** Kt 2018; CBE 2013; RA 2001; artist; *b* 2 June 1945; *s* of Maurice Long and Frances Carpenter; *m* 1969, Denise Johnston (marr. diss. 1999); two *d. Educ:* West of England Coll. of Art, Bristol; St Martin's Sch. of Art, London. Exhibitions include: Mus. of Modern Art, NYC, 1972; Scottish Nat. Gall. of Modern Art, Edinburgh, 1974; Venice Biennale, 1976; Nat. Gall. of Victoria, Melbourne, 1977; Fogg Art Mus., Harvard Univ., 1980; Nat. Gall. of Canada, Ottawa, 1982; Century Cultural Centre, Tokyo, 1983; Guggenheim, NYC (retrospective), 1986; Tate Gall., 1990; Hayward Gall. (retrospective), 1991; ARC, Paris, 1993; Kunstsammlung Nordrhein-Westfalen, Düsseldorf, 1994; Palazzo Dell Esposizioni, Rome, 1994; Guggenheim, Bilbao, 2000; Royal Acad. (one-man), 2004; Scottish Nat. Gall. of Modern Art, 2007; Tate Britain, 2009; Lisson Gall. (solo), 2014; Faena, Buenos Aires, 2014; Alan Cristea Gall. (solo), Arnolfini, Bristol (solo), 2015; Houghton Hall, Norfolk (solo), 2017. Hon. DLitt: Bristol, 1995; St Andrews, 2011. Kunstpreis, Aachen, 1988; Turner Prize, 1989. Chevalier de l'Ordre des Arts et des Lettres (France), 1990; Praemium Imperiale (Japan), 2010. *Publications include:* South America, 1972; Twelve Works, 1981; Countless Stones, 1983; Stone Water Miles, 1987; (with Anne Seymour) Old World New World, 1988; Nile, 1990; Walking in Circles, 1991; Mountains and Waters, 1992; River to River, 1993; Mirage, 1997; A Walk Across England, 1997; Every Grain of Sand, 1999; Midday, 2001; Walking the Line, 2003; Walking and Sleeping, 2005; Dartmoor, 2006; Heaven and Earth, 2009; Karoo Highveld, 2011; Time and Space, 2015. *Address:* c/o Lisson Gallery, 52–54 Bell Street, NW1 5DA.

**LONG, Prof. Stephen Patrick,** PhD; FRS 2013; Stanley O. Ikenberry Endowed University Chair of Plant Biology and of Crop Sciences, University of Illinois, Urbana-Champaign, since 2018; *b* Camden, London, 13 Aug. 1950; *s* of Frederick George Long and Amy Edith Helen Long; *m* 1972, Ann Denise Baron; two *s. Educ:* Pinner Grammar Sch.; Univ. of Reading (BSc 1st Cl. Hons 1972); Univ. of Leeds (PhD 1976). University of Essex: Lectr, 1975–87; Sen. Lectr, 1987–88; Reader, 1988–90; Prof. of Envmtl Physiol., 1990–98; University of Illinois, Urbana-Champaign: Robert Emerson Prof. of Plant Biol. and Crop Scis, 1999–2008; Edward William and Jane Marr Gutgsell Endowed Univ. Prof. of Plant Biol. and of Crop Scis, 2008–18; Center for Advanced Studies Prof., 2013–. Vis. Prof., Chinese Acad. of Scis, Jt Max-Planck Inst. of Computational Biol., Shanghai, 2013; Newton-Abraham Vis. Prof., Univ. of Oxford, and Fellow Lincoln Coll., Oxford, 2017–18; Distinguished Prof. of Crop Scis, Lancaster Univ., 2016–. Chief and Founding Editor, Global Change Biology, 1994–. Lectures: Riley Meml, World Food Prize/AAAS, Washington, DC, 2013; CeBiTec Annual Dist., Univ. Bielefeld, 2013. MNAS 2019. Hon. DSc Lancaster, 2007. Marsh Award for Climate Change Res., British Ecol Soc., 2012; Innovation Award, Internat. Soc. for Photosynthesis Res., 2013. *Publications:* over 300 articles in jls incl. Sci., Nature, Plant Physiol., Plant Cell and Envmt, Ecol., Jl of Experimental Botany. *Recreations:* distance running, triathlons, classical music. *Address:* University of Illinois, 1206 W Gregory Drive, 1408 IGB, Urbana, IL 61801, USA. *T:* (217) 2440881, *Fax:* (217) 2442496. *E:* slong@illinois.edu. *Club:* Royal Over-Seas League.

**LONG, Dr Tracy Elisabeth,** CBE 2016; Founder Director, Boardroom Review Ltd, since 2004; *b* London, 4 June 1962; two *d. Educ:* Froebel Coll., Roehampton Inst. of Higher Educn (BA London); Henley Management Coll. (MBA, DBA). Founder Director: Avalon Prodns, 1987–90; Classic FM, 1990–94; Director: Baring Brothers, 1994–96; BSkyB Ventures, 1997–2000; Botts & Co., 2000–03. Non-exec. Dir, Lowland Investment Co., 2004–09. Non-exec Dir, DCMS, 2009– (Chair, Audit and Risk Cttee, 2009–). Non-exec. Dir, King's Consort, 2005–08; Member: Adv. Bd, LSO, 1996–2010; Develt Bd, RAM, 2000–08; Adv. Dir, Carnegie Hall, 2013–. Trustee: NESTA, 2003–09; Windsor Leadership Trust, 2016–. Mem. Council, Marlborough Coll., 2013–; Trustee, Marlborough Coll. Foundn, 2013–17. Fellow, Cass Business Sch., 2008–11. Hon. ARAM 2008. Keith McMillan Prize for Research, Henley Business Sch., 2005. *Recreations:* music, literature, art, travel. *Address:* 11 Horbury Mews, W11 3NL. *E:* tlong@boardroomreview.com.

**LONG BAILEY, Rebecca**; MP (Lab) Salford and Eccles, since 2015; *b* 22 Sept. 1979; *m*; one *c*. *Educ:* Catholic High Sch., Chester; Manchester Metropolitan Univ. (BA Politics and Sociol.). Landlord and Tenant Solicitor, Halliwells, 2003–07; Solicitor (Healthcare), Hill Dickinson LLP, 2007–. Shadow Chief Sec. to the Treasury, 2016–17; Shadow Sec. of State for Business, Energy and Industrial Strategy, 2017–. *Address:* House of Commons, SW1A 0AA.

**LONGAIR, Deborah Janet**; *see* Howard, D. J.

**LONGAIR, Prof. Malcolm Sim**, CBE 2000; PhD; FRS 2004; FRSE 1981; Jacksonian Professor of Natural Philosophy, 1991–2008, Head of Department of Physics, 1998–2005, and Director of Research, since 2008, Cavendish Laboratory, University of Cambridge; Professorial Fellow, Clare Hall, Cambridge, 1991–2008, now Emeritus; *b* 18 May 1941; *s* of James Sim Longair and Lily Malcolm; *m* 1975, Prof. Deborah Janet Howard, *qv*; one *s* one *d*. *Educ:* Morgan Acad., Dundee; Queen's Coll., Dundee, Univ. of St Andrews (BSc Electronic Physics, 1963); Cavendish Lab., Univ. of Cambridge (MA, PhD 1967). Res. Fellow, Royal Commn for Exhibn of 1851, 1966–68; Royal Soc. Exchange Fellow to USSR, 1968–69; University of Cambridge: Res. Fellow, 1967–71, and Official Fellow, 1971–80, Clare Hall; Univ. Demonstrator in Phys., 1970–75; Univ. Lectr in Phys., 1975–80; Astronomer Royal for Scotland, Regius Prof. of Astronomy, Univ. of Edinburgh, and Dir, Royal Observatory, Edinburgh, 1980–90. Visiting Professor: of Radio Astronomy, Calif Inst. of Technol., 1972; of Astronomy, Inst. for Advanced Study, Princeton, 1978; Space Telescope Sci. Inst., 1997; Regents' Fellow, Carnegie Inst., Harvard Univ., 1990. Pres., RAS, 1996–98 (Editor, Monthly Notices, 1974–78). Ed.-in-Chief, Biographical Memoirs of Fellows of the Royal Society, 2016–. Foreign Member: Accad. Nazionale dei Lincei, 2000; Istituto Veneto di Scienze, Lettere ed Arte, 2007. Hon. LLD Dundee, 1982; Hon. DSc: Edinburgh, 2013; St Andrews, 2017. Britannica Award, 1986. *Publications:* (ed) Confrontation of Cosmological Theories with Observational Data, 1974; (ed with J. Einasto) The Large-Scale Structure of the Universe, 1978; (with J. E. Gunn and M. J. Rees) Observational Cosmology, 1978; (ed with J. Warner) The Scientific Uses of the Space Telescope, 1980; High Energy Astrophysics: an informal introduction, 1980, 3rd edn 2011; (ed with H. A. Brück and G. Coyne) Astrophysical Cosmology, 1982; Theoretical Concepts in Physics, 1984, 2nd edn 2003; Alice and the Space Telescope, 1989; The Origins of Our Universe, 1991; (with A. R. Sandage and R. G. Kron) The Deep Universe, 1995; Our Evolving Universe, 1996; Galaxy Formation, 1998, 2nd edn 2008; The Cosmic Century: a history of astrophysics and cosmology, 2006; Quantum Concepts in Physics, 2013; Maxwell's Enduring Legacy: a scientific history of the Cavendish Laboratory, 2016; (ed with H. Kragh) The Oxford Handbook of the History of Modern Cosmology, 2019; over 200 papers, mostly in Monthly Notices of RAS. *Recreations:* music, art, architecture, mountain walking. *Address:* c/o Cavendish Laboratory, J. J. Thomson Avenue, Cambridge CB3 0HE. *T:* (01223) 765777.

**LONGBOTHAM, His Honour Tom**; a Circuit Judge, 1999–2010; *b* 9 Aug. 1942; *s* of George Ferrand Longbotham and Elizabeth Ann Longbotham; *m* 1964, Eirlys Thomas; one *s* (and one *s* decd). *Educ:* Rossall Sch.; Bristol Univ. (LLB). Admitted Solicitor, 1966; Sen. Litigation Partner, Bishop Longbotham & Bagnall, Solicitors, until 1999; Asst Recorder, 1990–95; a Recorder, 1995–99. *Recreations:* golf, gardening, hill walking, theatre. *Club:* West Wiltshire Golf.

**LONGBOTTOM, Julia Margaret, (Mrs Julia Sciver)**, CMG 2019; HM Diplomatic Service; Director, Consular Services, Foreign and Commonwealth Office, since 2016; *b* Keighley, 13 July 1963; *d* of Roy Desmond Longbottom and Pauline Mary Longbottom; *m* 1990, Richard Sciver; one *s* two *d*. *Educ:* Jesus Coll., Cambridge (BA Mod. and Medieval Langs 1986; MA 1989). Joined FCO, 1986; Desk Officer, W Africa Dept, FCO, 1986–87; Second Sec., Tokyo, 1990–93; Hd, Nationality and Immigration Section, Hong Kong Dept, FCO, 1994–97; First Sec. (Political/EU), The Hague, 1998–2002; Consul Gen. and Dir, Trade and Investment, Warsaw, 2003–06; Strategy Dir, UKTI, 2006–09; Hd, Far Eastern Dept, later China Dept, FCO, 2009–12; Minister and Dep. Hd of Mission, Tokyo, 2012–16. *Recreations:* tennis (Cambridge blue, 1984), golf, pilates, alpine activities including ski-ing, modern art, travel, England Women's Cricket supporter. *Address:* Foreign and Commonwealth Office, King Charles Street, SW1A 2AH.

**LONGBOTTOM, Simon David**; Chief Executive Officer, Stonegate Pub Co. Ltd, since 2014; *b* Leeds, 4 June 1971; *s* of David and Cynthia Longbottom; *m* 2019, Holly Bland; one *s* one *d*. *Educ:* Berkhamsted Sch.; Nottingham Univ. (BA Hons Hist.). Ops Dir, Mill House Inns, 1995–2000; Dir-Gen. Manager, Mitchells & Butlers, 2000–04; Commercial Dir, Coral Eurobet, 2004–07; Managing Director: Gala Gaming, 2007–10; Greene King, 2010–14. *Recreations:* travel, Rugby, football, cricket, running, music. *Address:* Stonegate Pub Co., Porter Tun House, 500 Capability Green, Luton, Beds LU1 3LS. *E:* simon.longbottom@stonegatepubs.com. *Club:* Lansdowne.

**LONGDEN, Wilson**; industrial relations consultant, 1987–2005; *b* 26 May 1936; *s* of late Harold and Doris Longden; *m* 1st, 1966 (marr. diss. 1982); two *s*; 2nd, 1985 (marr. diss. 1993). *Educ:* Chesterfield Grammar Sch.; Univ. of Hull (BA Hons, Dip Ed); Univ. of Bradford (MSc). National service, RAF, 1955–57; Teacher, Northmount High Sch., Canada, 1961–62; Lecturer: Matthew Boulton Tech. Coll., Birmingham, 1962–66; Bingley Coll. of Educn, 1966–67; Margaret McMillan Coll. of Educn, 1967–68; Hatfield Polytechnic, 1968–69; Coventry (Lanchester) Polytechnic, 1969–73; Vice-Principal, Barnfield College, Luton, 1973–87. Sec., Assoc. of Vice-Principals of Colleges, 1986–87 (Pres., 1982–84). Comr, MSC, 1983–85. JP Luton, 1980; Mem., Beds Magistrates' Courts Cttee, 1998–2000. *Publications:* The School Manager's and the School Governor's Handbook, 1977; Meetings, 1977, 2nd edn 1997; Making Secondments Work, 1990; My Longden Family, 2016; My Longden Lineage, 2017; The Tragic Tricketts, 2018; My Barker Family, 2019. *Recreations:* music, playing the piano, family history, travel. *Address:* 311 Turnpike Drive, Luton LU3 3RE. *T:* (01582) 658695. *E:* wilsonlongden@hotmail.com.

**LONGDON, Patricia Joyce**; Director, Trish Longdon Associates, 2008–15; *b* 19 Jan. 1952; *d* of Fred and Nell Morgan; *m* 1st (marr. diss. 1987); 2nd, 1995, Mick Penny; one step *s* two step *d*. *Educ:* Brighton and Hove High Sch.; UCL (BSc 1st cl. Hons 1973); Sch. of Envmtl Studies, London (MPhil 1977). DoE, 1973–80; London Rape Crisis Centre, 1980–83; Asst Dir, Local Govt Ombudsman, 1983–89; Dir, People Develt, Audit Commn, 1989–2003; Dep. Parly and Health Service Ombudsman, 2003–08. Independent Complaints Monitor: Criminal Records Bureau, 2009–12; Disclosure and Barring Service, 2012–14. Non-exec. Dir, Hammersmith and Fulham NHS, 2009–12; Mem., Appts Cttee, GDC, 2010–12 (Chair, 2012–14); Vice Chair, NW London NHS Cluster Bd, 2012–13; Lay Mem., Hammersmith and Fulham CCG, 2013–; Chair, Strategic Lay Forum, Imperial Coll. Hosp. Trust, 2019–. *Recreations:* family and friends, reading, listening to classical music, climbing mountains, exploring the world.

**LONGFIELD, Anne Elizabeth**, OBE 2000; Children's Commissioner for England, since 2015; *b* 5 July 1960; *d* of James Vincent Longfield and Jean Elizabeth Longfield; *m* 2003, Richard Reeve; one *s*. *Educ:* Prince Henry's Grammar Sch., Otley; Univ. of Newcastle upon Tyne (BA Hons History). Researcher, Save the Children Fund, 1982–83; community develt in London, 1983–87; Develt, Kids' Clubs Network, 1987–93; Dir, then Chief Exec., Kids' Clubs Network, later 4Children, 1994–2015. Policy advr, Performance and Innovation Unit, Cabinet Office, 2001–02. Non-exec. Dir, Social Investment Business, 2009–11. Trustee, Early Intervention Foundn, 2012–15. Hon. DCL Newcastle upon Tyne, 2016. Freeman, City of London, 2014. *Publications:* policy and research reports on children, families and communities. *Recreations:* family, gardening, cycling, heritage. *Address:* Office of the Children's Commissioner, Sanctuary Buildings, Great Smith Street, SW1P 3BT.

**LONGFORD, Earldom of**; *cr* 1785; title not used by 8th Earl (*see* Pakenham, T. F. D.).

**LONGHURST, Andrew Henry**, FCIB; FBCS; Deputy Chairman, Royal London Assurance Society Ltd, 2000–02; *b* 23 Aug. 1939; *s* of Henry and Connie Longhurst; *m* 1962, Margaret; one *s* two *d*. *Educ:* Nottingham University (BSc Hons). FBCS 1968; FCIB (FCBSI 1990). Computer systems consultancy, 1961; Cheltenham & Gloucester Building Society: Data Processing Manager, 1967; Asst Gen. Manager (Admin), 1970; Dep. Gen. Manager, 1977; Chief Exec. and Dir, 1982–95; Cheltenham & Gloucester plc: Chief Exec., 1995–96; Dir, 1995–98; Chm., 1997–98; Gp Dir Customer Finance, and Dir, Lloyds TSB Group plc, 1997–98; Chm., United Assurance Gp plc, 1998–2000. Director: Lloyds Bank plc, 1995–98; TSB Bank plc, 1995–98; Chairman, 1997–98: Lloyds UDT Ltd; Lloyds Bowmaker Ltd; United Dominions Trust Ltd; Dir, Cardnet Merchant Services Ltd, 1997–98. Non-executive Director: Hermes Focus (formerly Hermes Lens) Asset Management, 1998–2009 (Chm., 2008–09); Thames Water Plc, 1998–2000; Abbey National plc, 2005–08. Mem. Council, Univ. of Glos, 2004–12. CCMI (CBIM 1989); FRSA. Chm., Council of Mortgage Lenders, 1994. *Recreation:* golf. *Address:* Riverhaven, Riverside Road East, Newton Ferrers, Plymouth PL8 1AE.

**LONGHURST, Prof. James William Stuart**, PhD; CSci, CEnv, FIEnvSc; Professor of Environmental Science, since 1996, and Assistant Vice Chancellor, Environment and Sustainability, since 2011, University of the West of England; *b* 25 Feb. 1958; *s* of late Leonard Longhurst, DFC and bar, and Isabella (*née* Laing); *m* 1984, Denise Barlow; two *d*. *Educ:* Univ. of Plymouth (BSc Hons Envmtl Sci. 1980); Univ. of Aston (MSc Resource Utilisation and Envmtl Sci. 1981); Univ. of Birmingham (PhD 1983). Envmtl Officer, Gtr Manchester Council, 1984–86; Dir, Atmospheric Res. and Inf. Centre, Dept of Envmtl and Geographical Scis, Manchester Poly., later Manchester Metropolitan Univ., 1986–96; University of the West of England: Associate Dean and Hd, Dept of Envmtl Scis, 1996–2001; Associate Dean: Res. and Ext. Affairs, 2001–03; (Academic), Faculty of Applied Scis, 2003–07; (Envmt and Ext. Affairs), 2007–10, (Learning, Teaching and the Student Experience), 2010–15, Faculty of Envmt and Technol.; Co-Dir, Inst. for Sustainability, Health and Envmt, 2008–14. Visiting posts: Swedish Envmtl Protection Agency, 1988; Academia Istropolitana, Bratislava, 1994; Univ. Poly. Catalonia, Barcelona, 1996. Series Ed., Advances in Air Pollution, 1997–2007; Mem., Scientific Adv. Cttee, Advances in Transport, 2000–03; Mem., Editl Adv. Bd, The Environmentalist, 1995–2015. Mem., 1999–2000, Chm., 2006–08, QAA Benchmarking Rev. Panel for Earth Scis, Envmtl Scis and Envmtl Studies. Higher Education Academy: Co-Chair, Adv. Bd for Geog., Earth and Envmtl Scis Subject Centre, 2008–09; Mem., 2012–, Chair, 2013–14, Educn for Sustainable Develt Adv. Gp. Portuguese Foundation for Science and Technology: Chair: Natural and Envmtl Scis Panel for Nat. Scis. Unit Evaluation Unit, 2015; Envmt and Global Change Panel, 2012–13, 2015. Member: Gp Western Res. Sustainability Panel, 2005–11 (Chm., 2008–11); Low Carbon South West (formerly Bristol Envmtl Technology Partnership Bd), 2007–12; Low Carbon Consensus Panel, Acad. of Sci. of S Africa, 2009–11; NUS Responsible Future Adv. Bd, 2014–15; Ind. Academic Mem., Bristol Green Capital 2015 Strategic Grants Panel, 2014; Interim Chair and UWE Bd Mem., Bristol Green Capital Partnership CIC, 2015–; Mem., Bristol Resilience Sounding Bd, 2016–17. Mem. Bd, Science Council, 2001–03. Mem., 1982–, Fellow, 1994, Chm. Council, 2000–06, Vice Pres., 2006–, Instn of Envmtl Scis; Co. Sec., Instn of Envmtl Scis Ltd, 2009–16; Mem., Environmental Protection, UK (formerly Nat. Soc. for Clean Air and Envmtl Protection), 1986– (Hon. Vice Pres., 2016–); Founder Mem., Inst. Air Quality Mgt, 2002–. Vice Chm., 2002–04, Chm., 2004–06, 2007–09, Cttee of Heads of Envmtl Scis. Mem., Bd of Dirs, Soc. of the Envmt, 2004–06. MIEnvSc 1982, FIEnvSc 1994; FHEA (ILTM 2001); CEnv 2004; CSci 2011; Fellow, Wessex Inst. of GB, 2004; Hon. FSE 2017. *Publications:* editor: Acid Deposition: sources, effects and controls, 1989; Acid Deposition: origins, impacts and abatement strategies, 1991; Air Pollution VIII, 2000; Air Quality Management, 2000; Local and Regional Aspects of Air Quality Management, 2004; (with C. A. Brebbia et al.) Air Pollution VIII, 2000, XIV, 2006, XVI, 2008, XVIII, 2010, XIX, 2011, XX, 2012, XXI, 2013, XXII, 2014, XXIII, 2015, XXIV, 2016, XXV, 2017, XXVI, 2018; Urban Transport and the Environment, 2012; Sustainable Development and Planning, 2017; contrib. numerous refereed scientific papers to learned jls incl. Atmospheric Envmt, Envmtl Pollution, Jl Envmtl Mgt, Urban Studies, Water, Air and Soil Pollution, Local Envmt, Jl of Envmtl Planning and Mgt. *Recreations:* reading, walking in the Alps, football (sadly now only watching West Ham United). *Address:* University of the West of England, Frenchay Campus, Coldharbour Lane, Bristol BS16 1QY; 8 Kent Road, Bishopston, Bristol BS7 9DN.

**LONGHURST, William Jesse**; HM Diplomatic Service; Deputy Head of Mission and Consul-General for Switzerland and Liechtenstein, since 2019; *b* Chelmsford, 7 Feb. 1967; *s* of late William Peter Longhurst and of Gillian Carey Longhurst (*née* Hardwick); *m* 2006, Kathryn Scheding; one *s* three *d*. *Educ:* King Edward VI Grammar Sch., Chelmsford; Univ. of Sheffield (BA Hons Japanese and Business Studies). Joined Diplomatic Service, 1990; Third Sec., 1992–93, Second Sec., 1993–95, Seoul; First Sec., Tokyo, 1995–98; Hd, Exports to Japan Unit, DTI, London (on secondment), 1998–2001; First Sec., UK Mission to the UN, NY, 2001–06; Dep. Hd of Mission and HM Consul-Gen., Belgrade, 2007–11; Dep. Hd, ASEAN Dept, FCO, 2011–13; Ambassador to Cambodia, 2014–18; full-time lang. trng, FCO, 2019. *Recreations:* cello, piano, tennis, squash, badminton, golf (badly). *Address:* c/o Foreign and Commonwealth Office, King Charles Street, SW1A 2AH. *E:* bill.longhurst@fco.gov.uk.

**LONGLEY, Mrs Ann Rosamund**; Head Mistress, Roedean School, 1984–97; *b* 5 March 1942; *d* of late Jack Gilroy Dearlove and of Rhoda E. M. Dearlove (*née* Billing); *m* 1964, Stephen Roger Longley (*d* 1979); one *s* two *d*. *Educ:* Walthamstow Hall School, Sevenoaks; Edinburgh University (MA 1964); PGCE Bristol University, 1984. Wife and mother, 1964–; Teacher, Toorak Coll., Victoria, Australia, 1964–65; Asst Housemistress, Peninsula C of E Sch., Victoria, 1966–67; Residential Teacher, Choate School, Conn, USA, 1968–73; Teacher, Webb School, Calif, 1975–78; Headmistress, Vivian Webb School, Calif, 1981–84. FRSA 1987. DUniv Sussex, 1991. *Recreations:* film, theatre, fishing, walking.

**LONGLEY, Most Rev. Bernard**; *see* Birmingham, Archbishop of, (RC).

**LONGLEY, Clifford Edmund**; journalist, author, novelist, broadcaster, lecturer and consultant; *b* 6 Jan. 1940; *s* of Harold Anson Longley and Gladys Vera (*née* Gibbs); *m* 1, 1962, Anne Patricia Clough; 2nd, 1980, Elizabeth Anne Holzer; one *s* two *d*. *Educ:* Trinity Sch., Croydon; Univ. of Southampton (BSc Eng.). Reporter: Essex and Thurrock Gazette, 1961–64; Portsmouth Evening News, 1964–67; The Times, 1967–92 (Religious Affairs Ed., 1972–92; Asst Ed. (Leaders), 1990–92); leader writer and columnist, Daily Telegraph,

1992–95; editorial consultant and columnist, The Tablet, 1996– (Actg Ed., 1996); columnist, Daily Telegraph, 1995–2000; freelance broadcaster and author; regular contributor, BBC Radio 4: Thought for the Day, 2002–; The Moral Maze, 2005–12. Chm., Portsmouth Br., NUJ, 1966–67; Father of The Times NUJ Chapel, 1972–74 and 1986–89; Chm., Docklands Br., NUJ, 1988–89. Consultant, RC Bishops' Conf. of England and Wales, 1996–. Mem. Adv. Council, Three Faiths Forum, 1995–. Select Preacher, Oxford Univ., 1988. Principal author of reports: The Common Good, for Catholic Bishops' Conf. of England and Wales, 1996; Prosperity with a Purpose, for CTBI, 2005; Choosing the Common Good, for Catholic Bishops' Conf. of England and Wales, 2010. Member, Steering Committee: True Wealth of Nations Project, Inst. for Advanced Catholic Studies, Univ. of S California, 2006–10; Centre for Catholic Social Thought and Teaching, 2013–; Blueprint for Better Business, 2011–14. Pres., Bromley Neighbourhood Watch Assoc., 2010–. Hon. Fellow, St Mary's UC Strawberry Hill, Surrey Univ., 1999. MLitt Lambeth, 2012. Specialist Writer of the Year, British Press Awards, 1986; Gold Medallist, Peace Through Dialogue, Internat. CCJ, 2006. JP Bromley, 1999, transf. Supplementary list, 2010. *Publications:* The Times Book of Clifford Longley, 1991; The Worlock Archive, 1999; Chosen People, 2002; The Babylon Contingency (novel), 2013; Just Money: how Catholic social teaching can redeem capitalism, 2014; numerous articles and book chapters. *Recreations:* classical music (piano), grandchildren, reading, theology, musicology, pilot, Biggin Hill (general aviation). *Address:* 24 Broughton Road, Orpington, Kent BR6 8EQ. *T:* (01689) 853189. *E:* clifford.longley@ntlworld.com.

**LONGLEY, Prof. Edna Mary,** FBA 2006; Professor of English Literature, Queen's University Belfast, until 2002, now Emerita; *b* 24 Dec. 1940; *d* of Timothy Stanislaus Broderick and Agnes Watson McDiarmid; *m* 1964, Michael George Longley, *qv*; one *s* two *d*. *Educ:* Trinity Coll. Dublin (BA). Lectr, Sch. of English, QUB, 1963, then Reader. MRIA 2000. *Publications:* Poetry in the Wars, 1986; Louis MacNeice: a study, 1988; The Living Stream: literature and revisionism in Ireland, 1994; Poetry and Posterity, 2000; (ed) The Bloodaxe Book of 20th Century Verse, 2000; (with Declan Kiberd) Multiculturalism: the view from the two Irelands, 2001; (contrib.) Cambridge Companion to the Literature of the First World War, 2005; Yeats and Modern Poetry, 2013; *edited:* Edward Thomas: first and last poems, 1972; Selected Paul Durcan, 1982; A Language Not to be Betrayed: selected prose of Edward Thomas, 1985; (jtly) Across a Roaring Hill: the Protestant imagination in modern Ireland, 1985; Marin Sorescu: the biggest egg in the world, 1987; Dorothy Hewett: Alice in wormland: selected poems, 1990; Culture in Ireland: division or diversity?, 1991; (jtly) Yeats Annual No 12: that accusing eye - Yeats and his Irish Readers, 1996; (jtly) Ireland (Ulster) Scotland: concepts, contexts, comparisons, 2003; Edward Thomas: the annotated collected poems, 2008; (jtly) Modern Irish and Scottish Poetry, 2011; (jtly) Incorrigibly Plural: Louis MacNeice and his legacy, 2012. *Address:* Seamus Heaney Centre for Poetry, School of English, Queen's University Belfast, Belfast BT7 1NN.

**LONGLEY, Michael George,** CBE 2010; freelance writer, since 1991; *b* 27 July 1939; *s* of Richard Cyril Longley and Constance Evelyn (*née* Longworth); *m* 1964, Edna Mary Broderick (*see* E. M. Longley); one *s* two *d*. *Educ:* Royal Belfast Academical Instn; Trinity Coll., Dublin (BA). Teacher, secondary schs in Dublin, Belfast and London, 1963–69; Combined Arts Dir, Arts Council of NI, 1970–91. Ireland Prof. of Poetry, 2007–10. Freeman, City of Belfast, 2015. Hon. LLD: QUB, 1995; TCD, 1999; Open, 2004. Literary prizes include: Eric Gregory Award, 1966; Cholmondeley Award, 1991; Queen's Gold Medal for Poetry, 2001; PEN Pinter Prize, 2017. *Publications:* Poems 1963–1983, 1985; Gorse Fires (Whitbread Prize), 1991; The Ghost Orchid, 1995; Louis MacNeice: selected poems, 1998; The Weather in Japan (Hawthornden Prize, T. S. Eliot Prize), 2000; Snow Water (Librex Montale Prize), 2004; Collected Poems, 2006; (jtly) John Hewitt: selected poems, 2007; A Hundred Doors, 2011; (ed) Robert Graves: selected poems, 2013; The Stairwell (Griffin Prize), 2014; Angel Hill, 2017; Sidelines: selected prose 1962–2015, 2017. *Recreations:* jazz, classical music, ornithology, botany, cooking. *Address:* c/o Lucas Alexander Whitley, 14 Vernon Street, W14 0RJ. *T:* (020) 7471 7900.

**LONGLEY-COOK, Robert Edward;** Chief Executive, Hft (formerly Home Farm Trust), 2010–19; *b* Midhurst, Sussex, 7 Dec. 1958; *s* of Hilary Longley-Cook and Virginia Longley-Cook (*née* Firth); *m* 1984, Sarah Waters; one *s* two *d*. *Educ:* Wellington Coll.; Bristol Univ. (BSc Hons Chem. 1980). With BP, 1980–2006; Exec. Dir, Fundraising, Mktg and Communication, WRVS, 2007–10. Non-exec. Dir, Waste and Resources Action Prog., 2015–. *Recreations:* running, fishing, theatre, golf.

**LONGMAN, Gary Leslie;** Headteacher, King's (The Cathedral) School (formerly King's Cathedral School), Peterborough, 1994–2014; *b* 14 April 1954; *s* of late Bernard Longman and Betty Longman; *m* 1977, Alison Mary Shepherd; one *s* one *d*. *Educ:* Univ. of Nottingham (BSc Hons Botany; PGCE). FCollP 1994. Assistant science teacher: Dayncourt Sch., Nottingham, 1977–79; Queen Elizabeth's Sch., Mansfield, 1979–82; Hd of Biology, 1982–85, Hd of Sci., 1985–88, Toot Hill Sch., Bingham, Notts; Dep. Head Teacher, Heysham High Sch., Morecambe, Lancs, 1988–94. *Recreations:* my family, travel, walking, gardening, cooking, wine-tasting, DIY. *Address:* The Ridings, Station Road, Barnack, Stamford, Lincs PE9 3DW.

**LONGMAN, Michael James; His Honour Judge Longman;** a Circuit Judge, since 2006; *b* 5 July 1955; *s* of late Geoffrey James Longman and Beatrice Isobel Longman (*née* Dixon); *m* 1989, Gillian Sheila Nicholas; two *s* one *d*. *Educ:* Highgate Sch.; St John's Coll., Cambridge (Open Exhibn; BA 1977; MA). Called to the Bar, Middle Temple, 1978; in practice, S Eastern Circuit, 1978–90, Western Circuit, 1991–2006; Recorder, 2000–06. *Recreations:* family, walking, sailing, diving. *Address:* The Law Courts, Small Street, Bristol BS1 1DA. *T:* (0117) 976 3030. *E:* HHJ.Michael.Longman@ejudiciary.net.

**LONGMAN, Peter Martin;** Consultant, The Theatres Trust, 2006–08 (Trustee, 1991–95; Director, 1995–2006); *b* 2 March 1946; *s* of Denis Martin Longman and Mary Joy Longman; *m* 1976, Sylvia June Prentice; two *d*. *Educ:* Huish's School, Taunton; University College, Cardiff; Univ. of Manchester. Finance Dept and Housing the Arts Officer, Arts Council, 1968–78; Dep. Dir, Crafts Council, 1978–83; Dep. Sec., 1983–84, Dir, 1984–95, Museums and Galleries Commn. Director: Caryl Jenner Productions Ltd, 1983–87; Scottish Museums Council, 1986–95; Walpole Foundn, 1997–2005; Orange Tree Theatre Ltd, 2004–10 (Chm., 2008–10); Scarborough Th. Trust, 2005–11; Charcoalblue LLP (formerly Ltd), 2006–18; Member: Council, Textile Conservation Centre Foundn (formerly Ltd), 1983–2011 (Chm., 1998–2000; Dep. Chm., 2000–11; Mem., Exec. Cttee, 1983–85, 1996–99); BTA Heritage Cttee, 1991–95; Exec., Council for Dance Educn and Trng, 1996–97; Adv. Council, Art in Churches, 1996–98; Chichester Fest. Theatre Trust, 1998–2003; Develt Cttee, ENO, 1999–2004; Covent Garden Area Trust, 2001–03; Theatre Planning and Historical Res. Cttee, Assoc. of British Theatre Technicians, 2006–. Trustee, Ken Stradling Collection, 2017–. FRSA 1989. Hon. FMA 1995. *Publications:* Working Party Reports: Training Arts Administrators, Arts Council, 1971; Area Museum Councils and Services, HMSO, 1984; Museums in Scotland, HMSO, 1986; Act Now!, Theatres Trust, 2003; (contrib.) Theatre Buildings: a design guide, 2010; articles on theatre,

the arts, museums. *Recreations:* discovering Britain, listening to music, studio ceramics, avoiding having to mow the lawn. *Address:* 37 Castle Road, Walton St Mary, Clevedon BS21 7DA. *T:* (01275) 544039.

**LONGMORE, Rt Hon. Sir Andrew (Centlivres),** Kt 1993; PC 2001; a Lord Justice of Appeal, 2001–19; *b* 25 Aug. 1944; *s* of John Bell Longmore and Virginia Longmore (*née* Centlivres); *m* 1979, Margaret Murray McNair; one *s*. *Educ:* Winchester College; Lincoln College, Oxford (MA; Hon. Fellow, 2001). Called to the Bar, Middle Temple, 1966, Bencher, 1990. QC 1983; a Recorder, 1992–93; a Judge of the High Court, QBD, 1993–2001. Chm., Law Reform Cttee, Bar Council, 1987–90. Pat Saxton Meml Lectr, British Insce Law Assoc., 2001. *Publications:* (co-editor) MacGillivray and Parkington, Law of Insurance, 6th edn 1975, 9th edn 1997. *Recreation:* fell-walking.

**LONGRIGG, Anthony James,** CMG 1992; HM Diplomatic Service, retired; Governor, Montserrat, 2001–04; *b* 21 April 1944; *m* 1967, Jane Rosa Cowlin; three *d*. Joined FCO, 1972; Second, later First, Sec., Moscow, 1975; FCO 1978; Brasilia, 1981; First Sec., FCO, 1985; Counsellor, Moscow, 1987; Counsellor, Madrid, 1991; Head, S Atlantic and Antarctic Dept, FCO, 1995–97; Minister, Moscow, 1997–2000.

**LONGSDON, Col (Robert) Shaun,** LVO 2006; Lieutenant, Queen's Body Guard of the Yeomen of the Guard, 2002–06; *b* 5 Dec. 1936; *s* of Wing Comdr Cyril Longsdon, Foxcote, Warwicks, and Evadne (*née* Flower); *m* 1968, Caroline Susan, *d* of late Col Michael Colvin Watson, OBE, MC, TD; three *s* one *d*. *Educ:* Eton. Regular Army Officer, 17th/21st Lancers, 1955–81: Adjt, Sherwood Rangers Yeo., 1959–61; ADC to CIGS, 1961–62; Adjt, 17th/21st Lancers, 1965–67; Sen. Mil. Asst to CGS, 1975–77; CO, 17th/21st Lancers, 1977–79; GSO1 DS, NDC, 1979–81. Dir of Mktg, Knight Frank & Rutley, 1981–95; Man. Dir, Visual Insurance Protection Ltd, 1995–97. Queen's Body Guard of Yeomen of the Guard, 1985–2006: Ensign, 1987; Clerk of the Cheque and Adjutant, 1993. Col of Regt, 17th/21st Lancers, 1988–93. Gov., 1982–99, Mem. Council, 1988–99, RSC; Chm., Leonard Cheshire Home, Glos, 1995–99; Trustee, Leonard Cheshire Foundn, 2000–07. Chm., Glos Br., SSAFA Forces Help, 2004–08. *Recreation:* country sports. *Address:* The Old Bakehouse, Eastleach, Cirencester, Glos GL7 3NQ. *T:* (01367) 850284. *E:* longsdon_shaun@hotmail.com. *Clubs:* White's, Pratt's, Cavalry and Guards.

**LONGSTAFF, Lana Claire;** *see* Wood, L. C.

**LONGSTAFF, Suzanne Kathryn,** MA; Headmistress, Putney High School, GDST, since 2015; *b* Leamington Spa, 14 June 1969; *d* of John and Valerie Ellis; *m* 2010, George Longstaff; two *d* and two step *s* one step *d*. *Educ:* Abbots Bromley Sch. for Girls; Durham Univ. (BA Econs 1990); Homerton Coll., Cambridge (PGCE Maths 1998); Bath Univ. (MA Educn 2015). Advertising Manager, Haymarket Publishing, 1991–94; Mem., British Olympic Rowing Team, 1994–99; Coxswain, British Women's Olympic VIII, Atlanta, 1996; Captain, Thames Rowing Club, 1995; Coxswain, Cambridge Univ. Boat Club Goldie, 1997 and 1998; Shiplake College, Henley on Thames: Teacher of Maths, 1999; Teacher of Maths and ICT, 1999–2000; Hd, Key Skills, 2000; Hd, ICT and Key Skills, 2001–04; Rowing Coach of J16, 1999–2001; Coach of 1st Rowing VIII, 2001–04; Kingston Grammar School: Teacher of ICT and Business Studies, 2004–06; Hd, ICT, and Asst Hd of Sixth Form, 2006–08; Putney High School, GDST: Hd of Sixth Form, 2009–13; Dep. Hd (Acad.), 2013–14; Actg Headmistress, 2014–15. ISI Inspector, 2017–. Governor: Waldegrave Sch., 2015–; Old Vicarage Sch., 2017–. *Recreations:* family, sailing, running, allotment gardening. *Address:* Putney High School, GDST, 35 Putney Hill, SW15 6BH. *T:* (020) 8788 4886. *E:* heads.secretary@put.gdst.net.

**LONGSTONE, Lesley,** CB 2010; Chief Executive and Registrar, General Optical Council, since 2018; *b* 9 Dec. 1964; *d* of John and June Broomhead; *m* 1985, Paul Longstone; two *s* one *d*. *Educ:* Univ. of Sheffield (BSc Hons Probability and Stats 1986). Civil Service: Manpower Services Commn, then Employment Service, later DfEE, 1985–2001; on secondment to Australian Dept of Employment, 2000–01; Department for Education and Skills, later Department for Children, Schools and Families, then Department for Education: Divl Manager, Sch. Diversity, 2001–03; Actg Dir, Secondary Educn, 2003–04; Higher Educn Bill Manager and Dir, Internat. Strategy, 2004–05; Dir, Schs White Paper Implementation, subseq. Sch. Formation, 2006–07; Director General: Young People, 2007–10; Infrastructure and Funding, 2010–11; DfE, 2018; Chief Exec. and Sec. for Educn, Ministry of Educn, NZ, 2011–13; Lead Investigator, MoD, 2013–14; Chief Exec., Ind. Police Complaints Commn, 2014–17; interim CEO, Crown Prosecution Service, 2017–18. Trustee, Ambitious about Autism, 2014– (Vice Chair, 2017–; Chair, Schs Trust, 2017–). *Recreations:* Church, family. *Address:* General Optical Council, 10 Old Bailey, EC4M 7NG.

**LONGWORTH, Ian Heaps,** CBE 1994; PhD; FSA, FSAScot; Keeper of Prehistoric and Romano-British Antiquities, British Museum, 1973–95; *b* 29 Sept. 1935; *yr s* of late Joseph Longworth and Alice (*née* Heaps); *m* 1967, Clare Marian Titford; one *s* one *d*. *Educ:* King Edward VII, Lytham; Peterhouse, Cambridge. Open and Sen. Scholar, Matthew Wren Student, 1957, MA, PhD, Cantab. Temp. Asst Keeper, Nat. Museum of Antiquities of Scotland, 1962–63; Asst Keeper, Dept of British and Medieval Antiquities, Brit. Mus., 1963–69; Asst Keeper, Dept of Prehistoric and Romano-British Antiquities, Brit. Mus., 1969–73. Member: Ancient Monuments Bd for England, 1977–84; Ancient Monuments Adv. Cttee, Historic Buildings and Monuments Commn, 1991–94. Chairman: Area Archaeol. Adv. Cttee for NW England, 1978–79; Standing Conf. of London Archaeol., 2003–05. Hon. Sec., 1966–74, Vice-Pres., 1976–80, Hon. Life Mem., 2002, Prehistoric Soc.; Sec., 1974–79, Vice-Pres., 1985–89, Soc. of Antiquaries of London. Chm. Adv. Bd, Alexander Keiller Mus., Avebury, 1999–2005. *Publications:* Yorkshire (Regional Archaeologies Series), 1965; (with G. J. Wainwright) Durrington Walls—excavations 1966–68, 1971; Collared Urns of the Bronze Age in Great Britain and Ireland, 1984; Prehistoric Britain, 1985; (with I. A. Kinnes) Catalogue of the Excavated Prehistoric and Romano-British Material in the Greenwell Collection, 1985; (ed with J. Cherry) Archaeology in Britain since 1945, 1986; (with A. Ellison and V. Rigby) Excavations at Grimes Graves, Norfolk, 1972–76, Fasc. 2, 1988, (*et al.*) Fasc. 3, 1991, Fasc. 4, 1992, Fasc. 5, 1996, Fasc. 6, 2012; articles in various learned jls on topics of prehistory. *Address:* 2 Hurst View Road, South Croydon, Surrey CR2 7AG. *T:* (020) 8688 4960.

**LONGWORTH, John;** media commentator; Chairman, Leave Means Leave, since 2016; Member (Brexit) Yorkshire and the Humber Region, European Parliament, since 2019; *b* Bolton, 14 May 1958; *s* of Norman and Edith Longworth; *m* 1983, Sheila McGivern; one *s* one *d*. *Educ:* Smithills Moor Grammar Sch.; Univ. of Salford (BSc Hons; MSc; Postgrad. Cert. Microbiol.); Univ. of London (Chartered Co. Sec. 1987). ACIS 1987. Asst Sec. and Dir, Trade Liaison, CWS Ltd, 1983–90; Dir, Tesco Stores Ltd, 1991–2003; Executive Director: Asda Stores, 2003–08; Asda Financial Services Ltd, 2004–08; Barts and the London NHS Hosp. Trust, 2008–10; Dir Gen., British Chambers of Commerce, 2011–16. Chm., SVA Ltd, 2008–15. Non-executive Director: Cooperative Food Ltd, 2009–14; Nichols plc, 2010–17. Chm., Vote Leave Business Council, 2016. Hon. PhD BPP, 2013. *Publications:* Due Diligence in Relation to Consumer Products, 2000. *Recreations:* opera, arts, theatre, cycling, running, travel. *Club:* Reform.

**LONGWORTH, Peter,** CMG 2001; HM Diplomatic Service, retired; independent government affairs consultant, since 2012; *b* 26 May 1942; *y s* of late Frank Longworth and Edith E. (*née* Robinson); *m* 1975, Christina Margareta, *d* of late Folke Wallin and Gun Wallin, Växjö. *Educ:* Chislehurst and Sidcup Grammar Sch.; Univ. of Sheffield (BA). Journalist, 1963–74: Labour and Ind. Corresp., Bristol Evening Post, 1964–66; Lobby Corresp., Western Daily Press., 1966–68; Diplomatic Corresp., Westminster Press., 1968–74; joined FCO, 1974; First Secretary: FCO, 1974–77; (Econ.), Bonn, 1977–81; Head of Chancery and HM Consul, Sofia, 1981–84; FCO, 1984–87; Counsellor (Econ. and Commercial), Copenhagen, 1987–91; Dep. Hd of Mission, Counsellor (Econ. and Commercial) and Consul Gen., Seoul, 1991–94; Consul-Gen., Johannesburg, and Dir of UK Trade Promotion and Investment, S Africa, 1994–98; High Comr, Zimbabwe, 1998–2001. Dir, Corporate and Govt Affairs, 2002–12, Interim Dir-Gen. and CEO, 2012–13, Commonwealth Business Council. Govt and Strategy Advr, Oval Observer Foundn, 2014–. Mem., Adv. Bd, Nollywood Business Frontiers, Lagos, 2008–. Mem., Royal African Soc. *Club:* Reform.

**LÖNNGREN, Thomas;** Strategic Adviser, NDA Advisory Services Ltd, since 2011; *b* Sweden, 16 Dec. 1950; *m* 1988, Ann-Charlotte Fondelius; one *s* one *d*. *Educ:* Univ. of Uppsala (MSc Social Pharmacy 1976); Stockholm Sch. of Econs (Advanced Course in Health Econ. 1999). Pharmacist, 1976; Lectr, Pharmaceutical Faculty, Uppsala Univ., 1976–78; Sen. Pharmaceutical Officer, Dept of Drugs, Nat. Bd of Health and Welfare, Sweden, 1978–90; Sen. Pharmaceutical Consultant for Swedish health co-operation prog. in Vietnam, 1982–94; Dir of Ops, 1990–98, Dep. Dir Gen., 1998–2000, Med. Products Agency, Sweden; Exec. Dir, EMEA, 2001–11.

**LONSDALE, 8th Earl of,** *cr* 1807 (UK); **Hugh Clayton Lowther;** Baron and Viscount Lowther, 1797; Bt 1764; *b* 27 May 1949; *s* of 7th Earl of Lonsdale and Tuppina Cecily, *d* of late Captain G. H. Bennet; *S* father, 2006; *m* 1971, Pamela Middleton; *m* 1986, Angela M., *d* of Captain Peter J. Wyatt, RN and Mrs Christine Wyatt; *m* 1999, Elizabeth Margaret, *d* of Stanley Frazer Arnison. *Heir:* half-*b* Hon. William James Lowther [*b* 9 July 1957; *m* 1999, Angela Ann Tinker].

**LONSDALE, Anne Mary,** CBE 2004; President, New Hall, Cambridge, 1996–2008; Deputy High Steward, Cambridge University, since 2009 (Pro-Vice-Chancellor, 1998–2003; Deputy Vice-Chancellor, 2003–08); Provost, Nazarbayev University, Astana, Kazakhstan, 2010–12 and 2015–16 (Trustee, 2013–15 and since 2016); *b* 16 Feb. 1941; *d* of Dr Alexander Menzies and Mabel Menzies; *m* 1st, 1962, Geoffrey Griffin (*d* 1962); 2nd, 1964, Roger Harrison Lonsdale, *qv* (marr. diss. 1994); one *s* one *d*. *Educ:* St Anne's Coll., Oxford (BA Hons Lit. Hum. 1962; BA Hons Chinese (Oriental Studies) 1965; MA 1965; Hon. Fellow, 1996). Oxford University: Davis Sen. Schol. and Lectr in Chinese, St Anne's Coll., 1965–74; Univ. Adminr, 1974–90; Dir, External Relations, 1990–93; Sen. Associate Mem., St Antony's Coll., 1991–2011; Sec.-Gen., Central European Univ., Budapest, Prague, and Warsaw, 1993–96. Chairman: Conf. of Univ. Admin, UK and Ireland, 1991–93; Interdisciplinary Envmtl Studies Cttee, 1996–2001; Jt Chm., Assoc. of Univ. Admin, 1993–94; Member: Commonwealth Scholarships Commn, 1996–2002; Council of Senate, Cambridge Univ., 1997–2004; Council for At-Risk (formerly Assisting Refugee) Academics, 2006– (Hon. Sec., 2008; Chm., 2009–). Trustee: Open Society (formerly Inter-Univ.) Foundn, 1988–2014; Cambridge Commonwealth Trust, 1995–2005; Cambridge Overseas Trust, 1996–2005; Cambridge European Trust, 1998–2007; Newton Trust, 1999–2008; Moscow Sch. of Social and Econ. Scis, 1999–2008; British Assoc. for Central and Eastern Europe, 2000–08; Camfed Internat., 2006–10 (Chm., 2008–10); European Humanities Univ., Vilnius, 2007–. Chm., Syndics, Fitzwilliam Mus., 2002–08; Syndic, CUP, 2006–08; Chm., Mgt Cttee, Kettle's Yard, 2012–. Hon. Dr Tashkent State Univ. for Oriental Studies, 2001; Liverpool Hope, 2014. Cavaliere, Order of Merit (Italy), 1988; Officier, Ordre des Palmes Académiques (France), 2002; Dostyk (Kazakhstan), 2016. *Recreation:* travelling. *Address:* 74 French's Road, Cambridge CB4 3LA. *T:* (01223) 362131.
*See also* C. J. Lonsdale.

**LONSDALE, Charles John;** Deputy Director, Conflict Prevention Centre, Organisation for Security and Co-operation in Europe, since 2016; *b* Oxford, 5 July 1965; *s* of Prof. Roger Harrison Lonsdale, *qv* and Anne Mary Lonsdale, *qv*; *m* 2011, Maria Sadoyan; one *d*. *Educ:* Merton Coll., Oxford (BA Mod. Hist. 1987). Joined FCO, 1987; Vienna, 1988–89; FCO, 1989; Third, later Second Sec., Budapest, 1990–93; FCO, 1995; First Sec., Moscow, 1998–2003; Dep. Hd, Afghanistan Gp, 2003–05, Dep. Hd, Human Rights, Democracy and Governance Gp, 2005–08, FCO; Ambassador to Armenia, 2008–11; Dep. Hd of Mission, UK Delegn, OSCE, Vienna, 2012–16. *Recreations:* music, travelling. *Address:* c/o Organisation for Security and Co-operation in Europe, Wallnerstrasse 6, Vienna, Austria.

**LONSDALE, Prof. Roger Harrison,** DPhil; FBA 1991; Fellow and Tutor in English, Balliol College, Oxford, 1963–2000, now Fellow Emeritus; Professor of English Literature, University of Oxford, 1992–2000; *b* 6 Aug. 1934; *s* of Arthur John Lonsdale and Phebe (*née* Harrison); *m* 1st, 1964, Anne Mary Menzies (*see* A. M. Lonsdale) (marr. diss. 1994); one *s* one *d*; 2nd, 1999, Nicoletta Momigliano. *Educ:* Hymers Coll., Hull; Lincoln Coll., Oxford (BA 1st class Hons 1957); DPhil (Oxon) 1962. National Service, RAF, commnd as Navigator, 1952–54. English Dept, Yale Univ., 1958–60; Oxford University: Bradley Jun. Res. Fellow, Balliol Coll., 1960–63; Reader in English Literature, 1990–92. *Publications:* Dr Charles Burney: a literary biography, 1965; *edited:* The Poems of Gray, Collins and Goldsmith, 1969; Vathek, by William Beckford, 1970; Dryden to Johnson, 1971; The New Oxford Book of Eighteenth-century Verse, 1984; The Poems of John Bampfylde, 1988; Eighteenth-century Women Poets: an Oxford anthology, 1989; The Lives of the English Poets, by Samuel Johnson, 2006. *Recreations:* music, book-collecting.
*See also* C. J. Lonsdale.

**LONZARICH, Prof. Gilbert George,** PhD; FRS 1989; Professor of Condensed Matter Physics, since 1997, Director of Research, since 2012, and Fellow of Trinity College, since 1977, University of Cambridge. *Educ:* Univ. of California (BA 1967); Univ. of Minnesota (MS 1970); PhD British Columbia 1973; MA Cantab 1977. University of Cambridge: Demonstrator, Physics Dept, 1978–81; Lectr in Physics, 1981–90; Reader in Physics, 1990–97. *Address:* Department of Physics, Cavendish Laboratory, J. J. Thomson Avenue, Cambridge CB3 0HE. *T:* (01223) 764454; Trinity College, Cambridge CB2 1TQ; 6 Hicks Lane, Girton, Cambridge CB3 0JS. *T:* (01223) 742056.

**LOOMBA,** family name of **Baron Loomba.**

**LOOMBA, Baron** *cr* 2011 (Life Peer), of Moor Park in the County of Hertfordshire; **Rajinder Paul Loomba, (Raj),** CBE 2008; Founder and Executive Chairman, Loomba Group of Companies (formerly Rinku Group), since 1981; *b* Dhilwan, Punjab, India, 13 Nov. 1943; *s* of late Shri Jagiri Lal Loomba and Shrimati Pushpa Wati Loomba; *m* 1966, Veena; one *s* two *d*. *Educ:* DAV Coll., Jalandhar, Punjab, India; State Univ. of Iowa, USA. Founder and Chairman of Trustees: Shrimati Pushpa Wati Loomba Meml Foundn, 1997–; British Indian Golden Jubilee Banquet Fund, 1999–2014; India First Ltd (formerly India First plc), 1999–. Mem. Council, RIIA, 2002–09. Member: Bd, 2000–04, Pres.'s Council, 2004–06, London First; Bd of Develt, Oxfam, 2008–11; Vice President: Barnardo's, 2005–; Safer London Foundn, 2006–12; Chm., Friends of Three Faiths Forum, 2007–10. Mem., All Party Parly Gp on India, on UN Women. Founding Patron, World Punjabi Orgn, 2002–; Patron, Patrons Council, Youth Business Internat., 2007–11; Vice Pres. for Europe, Global Orgn for People of Indian Origin, 2008–11. Mem., CPA. Mem., Bd of Govs, UEL, 2008–12. Freeman, City of London, 2000. FRSA 2004; MInstD. Paul Harris Fellow, Rotary Internat., 2001. Hind Rattan Award, India, 1991; Priyadarshni Acad. Global Award, 2006; Philanthropy Award, Forbes India, 2012; Lifetime Achievement Award, UN Assoc. of NY, 2014; Parman Patra Award, Punjab State, 2015. Pravasi Award (India), 2015. *Recreations:* travelling, reading, cooking. *Address:* Loomba House, 622 Western Avenue, W3 0TF. *T:* (020) 8102 0351. *E:* raj@loomba.com, loombar@parliament.uk. *Clubs:* Royal Automobile, Rotary of London.

**LOOMES, Prof. Graham,** FBA 2010; Professor of Economics and Behavioural Science, University of Warwick, since 2009; *b* London, 5 Aug. 1950; *s* of Frederick and Gladys Loomes; one *s* two *d*. *Educ:* Christ's Hosp., Horsham; Westminster City Sch.; Essex Univ. (BA (Econ) 1970); Birkbeck Coll., Univ. of London (MSc (Econ) 1978). School teacher, 1970–77; Res. Officer, Dept of Econs, then Lectr, Health Care Res. Unit, Univ. of Newcastle upon Tyne, 1978–84; University of York: Sen. Lectr and Dir of Graduate Prog. in Health Econs, Dept of Econs and Related Studies, 1984–88; Sen. Lectr, 1988–91; Prof. of Econs, 1991; Co-Dir, Centre for Experimental Econs, 1988–95, (part-time) 1996, 1999–2000; Prof. of Econs and Co-Dir, Centre for the Analysis of Safety Policy and Attitudes to Risk, Univ. of Newcastle upon Tyne, (part-time) 1996, 1999–2000; Prof. of Econ. Behaviour and Decision Theory, UEA, 2001–09. *E:* g.loomes@warwick.ac.uk.

**LOOSEMORE, Thomas;** Partner, Public Digital Ltd, since 2015; *b* Solihull, 22 May 1971; *s* of Geoff and Jean Loosemore; *m* 2003, Jo Angell; one *s* one *d*. *Educ:* Bristol Univ. (MEng Civil Engrg). Internet ed., Wired UK mag., 1995–97; web ed., Capital Radio, 1997–98; Sen. Producer, BBC News Online, 1998–99; Dir of Applications, Chello Broadband, 1999–2001; Hd of Broadband, BBC New Media, 2001–07; Digital Media Strategist, Ofcom, 2007–08; Hd of 4IP, Channel 4, 2008–10; Dep. Dir, Govt Digital Service, Cabinet Office, 2011–15; Gp Dir of Digital Services, Co-operative Gp, 2015–17. *Recreation:* dinghy sailing.

**LOOSLEY, Brian;** a District Judge (Magistrates' Courts) (formerly Metropolitan Stipendiary Magistrate), 1989–2010; *b* 20 Dec. 1948; *s* of late Bernard Allan Loosley and Barbara Clara Randle; *m* 1971, Christine Mary Bat; one *s* one *d*. *Educ:* Sir William Borlase Grammar Sch., Marlow; Leeds Univ. (LLB 1971). Admitted Solicitor 1974; Prosecuting Solicitor, Thames Valley Police, 1975–78; practised privately, 1978–89. *Recreations:* history, foreign travel.

**LOPES,** family name of **Baron Roborough.**

**LOPES CARDOZO KINDERSLEY, Lydia Helena, (Lida),** MBE 2015; owner, Cardozo Kindersley Workshop, since 1981 (co-owner, 1981–95 and since 1998); *b* 22 July 1954; *d* of late Prof. Dr Paul Lopes Cardozo and of Ottoline Baronesse van Hemert tot Dingshof; *m* 1st, 1986, David Kindersley, MBE (*d* 1995); three *s*; 2nd, 1998, Graham F. Beck. *Educ:* Royal Acad. of Fine Arts, Den Haag, Netherlands. David Kindersley's Workshop: Lettercutter, 1976; Partner, 1981; Founder Editor, Cardozo Kindersley Editions, 1989. Associate Mem., 1999–2003, Life Mem., 2003, Clare Hall, Cambridge. Member: Assoc. Typographique Internationale, 1974–; Wynkyn de Worde Soc., 1978– (Chm., 1988); Hon. Fellow, 2001); Double Crown Club, 1996–; Cttee, Hazlitt Soc., 2005–06. Patron, Michaelhouse Project, Cambridge, 1999–2013. Gov., Impington Village Coll., 1997–2000. Brother, Art Workers Guild, 2000–. Fellow, 1994, Honoured Fellow, 2007, Calligraphy and Lettering Arts Soc. Hon. Fellow, Magdalene Coll., Cambridge, 2014. *Publications:* Glass & Engraver, 1983; (with David Kindersley) Letters Slate Cut, 1981, 3rd edn 2004; (with R. McKitterick) Lasting Letters, 1992; Oxford Handwriting Practice, 1993, 2nd edn 2006; The Cardozo Kindersley Workshop: a guide to commissioning work, 1996, 4th edn 2013; (with Emma Lloyd-Jones) Letters for the Millennium, 1999; (with W. Graham Cannon) Kindersley at Addenbrooke's Hospital, 2000; (jtly) Optical Letter Spacing, 2001; (jtly) Apprenticeship, 2003; (with Michael Wheeler) The kindest cut of all, 2005; The Annotated Capital, 2009; (ed) Red Letters All, 2015; with Tom Sherwood: Cutting through the Colleges, 2010; Cutting across Cambridge, 2011; Cutting around Cambridgeshire, 2012; (with Lottie Hoare and Tom Sherwood) Cutting into the Workshop, 2013; (with David Meara) Remembered Lives, Personal Memorials in Churches, 2013; (ed) Mr Eric Gill, 2014; (with Fiona Boyd and Tom Sherwood) David Kindersley, vol. I, The Boy, 2015, vol. 2, The Man, 2016; (jtly) I Ask About the Sky, 2016; (jtly) Cutting It in Oxford, 2017; (with Els Bottema) The Shingle Street Shell Line, 2018; Cutting through Nature, 2018; (with Dr Frank King) Sundials: cutting time, 2019. *Recreations:* letter writing, religion. *Address:* Cardozo Kindersley Workshop, 152 Victoria Road, Cambridge CB4 3DZ. *T:* (01223) 362170. *Club:* Athenæum.

**LOPEZ, Julia Louise;** MP (C) Hornchurch and Upminster, since 2017; *née* Dockerill; *m* 2017. *Educ:* Queens' Coll., Cambridge. Mem. (C), Tower Hamlets LBC, 2014–. Mem., Internat. Trade Select Cttee, 2017–. *Address:* House of Commons, SW1A 0AA.

**LOPEZ, Paul Anthony; His Honour Judge Lopez;** a Circuit Judge, since 2014; a Deputy High Court Judge (Family and Queen's Bench Divisions), since 2014; Nominated Judge, Court of Protection, since 2015; *b* Wolverhampton, 22 Oct. 1959; *s* of Anthony William Lopez and late Lilian Lopez (*née* Rowley); *m* 1984, Diana Douglas Black; two *d*. *Educ:* Pendeford High Sch., Wolverhampton; Univ. of Birmingham (LLB Hons). Called to the Bar, Middle Temple, 1982; in practice as a barrister, St Ives Chambers, Birmingham, 1983–2014; a Recorder, 2001–14; a Dep. High Court Judge (Family), 2013. Member: Nelson Soc.; 1805 Club. *Recreations:* history, working, collecting Nelson memorabilia, my family. *Address:* Wolverhampton Combined Courts Centre, Pipers Row, Wolverhampton WV1 3LQ. *T:* (01902) 481000.

**LOPEZ CABALLERO, Alfonso;** Ambassador of Colombia to Russia, since 2016; *b* 17 Aug. 1944; *s* of Alfonso Lopez Michelsen and Cecilia Caballero de Lopez; *m* 1969, Josefina Andreu de Lopez; one *d*. *Educ:* Sch. of Foreign Service, Georgetown Univ., Washington (BSFS Internat. Affairs); INSEAD, Fontainebleau (MBA); Columbia Univ., NY (MA, MPhil Econs). Asst Manager, First Nat. City Bank of NY; Business Consultant, Arthur Young & Co.; Congressman, Colombia, 1986–90; Senator, 1990–94; Ambassador of Colombia to France, 1990–91; Minister of Agriculture, 1991–92; Ambassador to Canada, 1994–97; Minister: of the Interior, 1997–98; i/c Presidential functions (during several Presidential trips abroad); Govt negotiator with FARC guerrillas during peace process, 2000–01; Ambassador to UK, 2002–06. *Publications:* Un nuevo modelo de desarrollo para el campo, 1988. *Club:* Jockey (Bogota).

**LOPEZ-FABREGAT, Fernando;** Ambassador of Uruguay to the Court of St James's and to Republic of Ireland and Iceland, since 2014; *b* Montevideo, Uruguay; *m* 1987, Maria Carolina Silveira; one *s* one *d*. *Educ:* Catholic Univ. of Uruguay (Master in Human Resources Mgt); Univ. of Republic of Uruguay (law degree). First Secretary: Pretoria, SA, 1991–93; Quito, 1993–97; Counsellor, Ottawa, 1999–2004; Dir, HR, Min. of Foreign

Affairs, Uruguay, 2004–06; Consul Gen., Toronto, 2006–12; Dir Gen. for Internat. Econ. Affairs, Ministry of Foreign Affairs, 2012–14. *Address:* Embassy of Uruguay, 150 Brompton Road, SW3 1HX. *T:* (020) 7584 4200. *E:* urureinounido@mrree.gub.uy.

**LOPPERT, Max Jeremy;** writer on music, musicologist; *b* Johannesburg, 24 Aug. 1946; *m* 1972, Delayne Aarons. *Educ:* Univ. of Witwatersrand, Johannesburg (BA 1966); Univ. of York (BA Music 1971). Chief Music Critic, FT, 1980–96; Associate Editor, Opera, 1986–97. Vis. Music Schol., Univ. of Natal, 1998–99; residency: Rockefeller Foundn Study Center, Bellagio, Italy, 2004; Centro Studi Ligure, Bogliasco, Italy, 2005. Founder, Opera Sch. and Voice Acad., Music Sch., Univ. of Natal, 1999 (opened 2002). Hon. Res. Fellow, Univ. of Kwa Zulu Natal, 2007–15. *Publications:* contrib. to: Opera on Record (ed Alan Blyth), 3 vols, 1979, 1983, 1984; The New Grove Dictionary of Music and Musicians, 1980; The New Grove Dictionary of Opera, 1992; Who's Who in Hollywood, 1993; (ed) Words and Music, 2003. *Recreations:* cinema, cooking, pottery. *Address:* Via Buonabitacolo 15/6, 31053 Pieve di Soligo, Italy.

**LOPRESTI, Jack;** MP (C) Filton and Bradley Stoke, since 2010; *b* Bristol, 23 Aug. 1969; *s* of Domenico and Grace Lopresti; *m* 2017, Andrea Marie Jenkyns, *qv;* one *s*. *Educ:* Brislington Comprehensive Sch. Worked for family catering and ice cream business, 1985–97; consultant and manager, financial services and residential property, 1997–2007. Mem. (C) Bristol CC, 1999–2007. Mem., NI Affairs Cttee, 2010–, Defence Cttee, 2016–17; PPS, MoD. Contested: (C) Bristol E, 2001; SW, Eur. Parlt, 2004. Territorial Army, 2006–12: gunner, 266 Battery, RA (Glos Vol. Artillery); served with 29 Commando RA in Afghanistan. Mem., RUSI, 2013–. Member: Gen. George Patton Histl Soc.; Internat. Churchill Centre. *Recreations:* running, hill-walking, military and political history. *Address:* House of Commons, SW1A 0AA. *T:* (020) 7219 7070. *E:* jack.lopresti.mp@parliament.uk.

**LORAINE-SMITH, Nicholas George Edward; His Honour Judge Loraine-Smith;** a Circuit Judge, since 2002; *b* 24 Jan. 1953; *s* of Maj. Bernard Lawson Loraine-Smith, MC, and Rachel Anne Loraine-Smith; *m* 1980, Annabelle Catherine Schicht; two *d*. *Educ:* Eton Coll.; Oriel Coll., Oxford (BA English). Called to the Bar, Inner Temple, 1977; Jun. Treasury Counsel, 1994–99, Sen. Treasury Counsel, 1999–2002, Central Criminal Court; Asst Recorder, 1997–2000; a Recorder, 2000–02; a Circuit Judge, Court of Appeal Criminal Div., 2005–11; Coroner, inquests into deaths of 30 British nationals who died in terrorist attack, Sousse, Tunisia, 2015.

**LORAM, Mary Caroline;** QC 2018; a Recorder, since 2016; *b* Wirral, 18 Jan. 1970; *d* of Ronald Geoffrey Loram and Caroline Loram; partner, L. C. Cooper; one *s* one *d*. *Educ:* Birkenhead High Sch. for Girls GPDST; Brasenose Coll., Oxford (BA Hons Juris.); Sidney Sussex Coll., Cambridge (MA Criminol.). Called to the Bar, Inner Temple, 1995. *Recreations:* food and wine, friends, walking both children and dog. *Address:* The Thatch, Butts Green, Clavering, Saffron Walden CB11 4RT. *T:* 07767 685984. *E:* mloram@36crime.co.uk.

**LORD,** family name of **Baron Framlingham.**

**LORD, Alan,** CB 1972; Deputy Chairman and Chief Executive, Lloyd's of London, 1986–92; *b* 12 April 1929; *er s* of Frederick Lord and Anne Lord (*née* Whitworth), Rochdale; *m* 1953, Joan Ogden; two *d*. *Educ:* Rochdale; St John's Coll., Cambridge (BA 1950 (1st Cl. Hons); MA 1987). Entered Inland Revenue, 1950; Private Sec. to Dep. Chm. and to Chm. of the Board, 1952–54; HM Treasury, 1959–62; Principal Private Sec. to First Secretary of State (then Rt Hon. R. A Butler), 1962–63; Comr of Inland Revenue, 1969–73, Dep. Chm. Bd, 1971–73; Principal Finance Officer to DTI, subseq. to Depts of Industry, Trade, and Prices and Consumer Protection, 1973–75; Second Permanent Sec. (Domestic Econ.), HM Treasury, 1975–77. Man. Dir, 1980, Chief Exec., 1982–84, Dunlop Hldgs plc; formerly: Exec. Dir, Dunlop Hldgs; Man. Dir, Dunlop Internat. AG, 1978. Director: Allied-Lyons plc, 1979–86; Bank of England, 1983–86; Johnson Matthey Bankers, 1985–86. Chm., CBI Taxation Cttee, 1979–81. Mem. Council of Management, Henley Centre for Forecasting, 1977–82. Gov., NIESR, 1975–2013. Pres., Johnian Soc., 1985–86. *Publications:* A Strategy for Industry (Sir Ellis Hunter Meml Lecture, Univ. of York), 1976; Earning an Industrial Living (1985 Johnian Society Lecture). *Recreations:* reading, music, gardening. *Address:* Mardens, Hildenborough, Tonbridge, Kent TN11 8PA. *Club:* Reform.

**LORD, Hon. Bernard,** ONB 2007; Chairman, Ontario Power Generation, since 2014; Chief Executive Officer, Medavie Inc., since 2016; *b* 27 Sept. 1965; *s* of Ralph and Marie-Émilie Lord; *m* 1990, Diane Haché; one *s* one *d*. *Educ:* Mathieu-Martin High Sch., Dieppe; Univ. of Moncton, Canada (BScSoc Econs 1988; LLB 1992). Called to the Bar, New Brunswick, 1993; in private law practice, Founding Partner, LeBlanc, Desjardins, Lord, Moncton, 1995–99; Counsel, McCarthy Tétrault, 2007. MLA (Progressive C) Moncton E, NB, 1998–2007; Leader of Opposition, 1998–99; Premier of NB, 1999–2006; Pres., Exec. Council and Minister, 1999–2006: Intergovtl Affairs; resp. for NB Adv. Council on Youth; resp. for council on status of disabled persons. Leader, Progressive Cons. Party of NB, 1997–2006. Pres. and Chief Exec., Canadian Wireless Telecommunications Assoc., 2008–16. Hon. LLD New Brunswick, 2001; St Thomas Univ.; Mt Allison Univ.; Hon. Dr Pol Sci. Moncton, 2002. Grand Officier, Ordre de la Pléiade, Internat. Assoc. of Francophone Parliamentarians, 2001. *Recreations:* golf, chess.

**LORD, (Charles) Edward,** OBE 2011; JP; Managing Director, Edward Lord Ltd, since 2015 (Principal, Edward Lord Consultants, 2002–15); *b* Littleborough, Lancs, 13 Jan. 1972; *s* of Charles Andrew Lord and Vivienne Marie Lord (*née* Fairbank, now Brittain); partner 2003–09, Laura Willoughby, MBE; partner 2012–18, Dr Meg-John Barker. *Educ:* Bury Grammar Sch.; Univ. of Essex (BA Public Policy and Public Mgt 1994); BPP Law Sch. Mem., Nat. Exec., NUS, 1994–96. Dir, John Moores Univ. Trust, 1998–2000; Develt Dir, City Univ., 2000–02. Chair: Public Private Partnerships Prog., 2005–09; Local Partnerships LLP, 2009–12 (non-exec. Dir, 2012–17); Dep. Chair, Whittington Hosp. NHS Trust, 2008–10. Chair: Capital Ambition, 2011–18; Megalith Realty Ltd, 2016–18; Social Care Housing Ltd, 2018–; non-executive Director: London Strategic Housing Ltd, 2006–09; Parkwood Hldgs plc, 2011–12; Social Investment Business Ltd, 2013–17. Mem. Bd, and Lead Mem. for Equality, LGA, 2004–13; Mem., Leaders' Cttee, London Councils, 2011–18. Chair, Ap Gp Bd, Amateur Swimming Assoc., 2013–15; Chair, Inclusion Adv. Gp, London FA, 2013–17; Mem., Inclusion Adv. Bd, FA, 2013–14; Ind. Dir, British Basketball League, 2018–; Dir, Middlesex CCC, 2019–. Member: Council, Coll. of Optometrists, 2000–03; Council for Registration of Forensic Practitioners, 2006–09. Mem. Court, Univ. of Essex, 2011– (Mem., Audit and Risk Mgt Cttee, 2017–). Chair, Sir John Cass's Foundn Sch., 2001–03; Governor: GSMD, 2002–09; City of London Sch., 2009–; Univ. of Northampton, 2018–. Estate Gov., Bury Grammar Schs, 2004–08. Trustee: British Youth Council, 1995–97; Trust for London, 2001–05 and 2015–; Anne Frank Trust, 2006–09; Albert Kennedy Trust, 2012–13; Nat. Campaign for the Arts, 2012–16; BiCon Continuity Ltd, 2014–16. JP Central London, 2002. Mem., Court of Common Council, City of London, 2001– (Mem., Policy and Resources Cttee, 2009–; Chair: Licensing Cttee, 2010–13; Standards Cttee, 2013–16; Establishment Cttee, 2018–; Dep. Chair, Capital Bldgs Cttee, 2018–; Mem. Bd, Barbican Centre, 2017–18; Mem., Jt Grand Gresham Cttee,

2017–). Freeman: City of London, 2000; Leathersellers' Co., 2002; Liveryman, Broderers' Co., 2011. *Publications:* (ed) Civic Ceremonial: advice on protocol to the Mayors of the London Boroughs, 2009. *Recreations:* contemporary and classical music, theatre, cinema, watching sport, urban and country walking, swimming, reading, good food, travel. *Address:* 2 Union House, 6 Martin Lane, EC4R 0DP. *E:* contact@edwardlord.org. *Clubs:* Guildhall, MCC, Soho House, Ned's; Middlesex County Cricket, Rochdale Association Football.

**LORD, David William;** QC 2009; *b* Farnborough, Kent, 28 Sept. 1964; *s* of John and Pat Lord; *m* 2004, Julia Fitzpatrick; two *s* one *d* and one step *d*. *Educ:* King's Sch., Rochester; Bristol Univ. (LLB Hons). Called to the Bar: Middle Temple, 1987; BVI, 2000. *Recreations:* ski-ing, golf. *Address:* 3 Stone Buildings, Lincoln's Inn, WC2A 3XL. *T:* (020) 2242 4937, *Fax:* (020) 3405 3896. *E:* dlord@threestone.law.

**LORD, Edward;** *see* Lord, C. E.

**LORD, Geoffrey,** OBE 1989; Founder Trustee, 1989–2008, and Vice President, 2000–08, Adapt Trust (Founder Director, 1989–96); *b* 24 Feb. 1928; *s* of Frank Lord and Edith Lord; *m* 1955, Jean; one *s* one *d*. *Educ:* Rochdale Grammar Sch.; Univ. of Bradford (MA Applied Social Studies). AIB. Midland Bank Ltd, 1946–58; Probation and After-Care Service, 1958–76: Dep. Chief Probation Officer, Greater Manchester, 1974–76; Sec. and Treas., Carnegie UK Trust, 1977–93. Chairman: Unemployed Voluntary Action Fund (Scotland), 1990–95; Pollock Meml Missionary Trust, 1985–2004; Pres., Centre for Envmtl Interpretation, 1984–97. Member, Scottish Arts Lottery Bd, 1994–98; Council, NYO of Scotland, 1998–2013. Trustee: Home-Start (formerly Home-Start Consultancy) UK, 1993–98; Faith in Older People Trust, 2007–13; Murrayfield Dementia Project, 2008–13; BSS Ltd, 2009–15; Sec. and Trustee, Edin. Vol. Orgns' Trusts, 1996–2015. FRSA 1985. Hon. Fellow, Manchester Metropolitan Univ. (formerly, Manchester Poly.), 1987. St Cuthbert Award, Scottish Episcopal Ch, 2017. *Publications:* The Arts and Disabilities, 1981; Access for Disabled People to Arts Premises: the journey sequence, 2003; Cathedrals for the Curious, 2011. *Recreations:* Church of the Good Shepherd Edinburgh, philately, walking, appreciation of the arts. *Address:* 9 Craigleith View, Ravelston, Edinburgh EH4 3JZ. *T:* (0131) 337 7623. *Club:* New (Edinburgh).

**LORD, Prof. Graham Michael,** PhD; FRCP; FRSB; FMedSci; Vice-President, and Dean, Faculty of Biology, Medicine and Health, University of Manchester, since 2019; *b* Manchester; *s* of Brian and Margaret Lord; *m* 1997, Jane Howard; two *s* one *d*. *Educ:* Kingsway Comprehensive Sch., Manchester; Fitzwilliam Coll., Cambridge (BA Med. Scis 1988; MB BChir 1991; MA 1992); Imperial Coll. London (PhD Molecular Immunol. 2000); Cert. of Completion of Specialist Trng and Bd Cert. in Nephrology, Transplantation and Gen. (Internal) Medicine. MRCP 1993, FRCP 2008; FRSB 2011. NHS training to SHO and Registrar at Hammersmith Hosp., John Radcliffe Hosp., Oxford, Royal Brompton Hosp. and Addenbrooke's Hosp., Cambridge, 1991–96; Imperial College London: MRC Trng Fellow, 1996–99; Renal Lectr and MRC Clinician Scientist, 2000–03 (MRC Clinician Scientist Fellow, 2000); Sen. Lectr and Hon. Consultant in Renal Medicine, Imperial Coll. London and Hammersmith Hosps NHS Trust, 2003–05; Prof. of Medicine, KCL, 2005–19; Dir, Translational Res., and Co-Dir, NIHR Comprehensive Biomedical Res. Centre, Guy's and St Thomas' Hosp. and KCL, 2007–11; Dir, NIHR Biomedical Res. Centre, Guy's and St Thomas' NHS Foundn Trust and KCL, 2012–19; NIHR Sen. Investigator, 2013–. Vis. Scientist, Harvard Univ., 2003–08. FMedSci 2016; Fellow King's Coll. Sch., 2017. Sue McCarthy Prize for Young Investigator of Year, Med. Res. Soc., 1999; NHS Nat. Clin. Scientist Award, 2002; Mary Evelyn Lucking Prize in Medicine, Cambridge Univ., 2002; Nat. Clin. Excellence Award (Silver), 2011, 2015. *Publications:* (jtly) Genome Wide Polymorphism Association Analysis in Organ Transplantation, 2010; *contributor:* (jtly) Textbook of Immunology, 1998; Allogeneic Immunotherapy for Malignant Diseases, 1998; Acute Renal Failure in Practice, 2001; Cytokines and Chemokines in Infectious Diseases, 2002; (and ed jtly) Yearbook of Intensive Care and Emergency Medicine, 2004; (jtly) Principles of Mucosal Immunology, 2011; The Oxford Textbook of Clinical Nephrology, 2015; contribs to peer reviewed jls. *Recreations:* cricket, football, tennis, motorcycling, ocean sailing, playing clarinet and guitar. *Address:* Faculty of Biology, Medicine and Health, Room 1.016, Core Technology Facility, 46 Grafton Street, University of Manchester, Manchester M13 9NT. *T:* (0161) 306 0533. *E:* profgraham.lord@gmail.com. *Club:* Medical Research.

**LORD, Jonathan George Caladine;** MP (C) Woking, since 2010; *b* Oldham, 17 Sept. 1962; *s* of His Honour John Herent Lord and of (June) Ann Lord (*née* Caladine); *m* 2000, Caroline Commander; one *s* one *d*. *Educ:* Shrewsbury Sch.; Kent Sch., Connecticut (Schol.); Merton Coll., Oxford (BA Hist. 1985). Dir, Saatchi & Saatchi, 1998–2000; campaign manager, Anne Milton, MP, gen. election, 2005. Member (C): Westminster CC, 1994–2002 (Dep. Leader, 1998–2000); Surrey CC, 2009–11. Contested (C) Oldham W and Royton, 1997. Chm., Guildford Cons. Assoc., 2006–10; Dep. Chm., Surrey Area Conservatives, 2007–09. *Recreations:* cricket, theatre, walking in the Surrey Hills. *Address:* House of Commons, SW1A 0AA. *T:* (020) 7219 6913. *E:* jonathan.lord.mp@parliament.uk.

**LORD, Peter Duncan Fraser,** CBE 2006; Co-founder (with D. Sproxton), owner and Creative Director, Aardman Animations, since 1972; *b* 4 Nov. 1953; *s* of Peter and Margaret Lord; *m* 1976, Karen Jane Bradshaw; two *s* one *d*. *Educ:* Univ. of York (BA 1976). Films directed include: The Amazing Adventures of Morph, 1981–83; Conversation Pieces, 1982–83; Wat's Pig, 1996; Chicken Run, 2000; The Pirates!, 2012. Hon. Fellow, BKSTS, 2000. Hon. Dr Design UWE, 1995; DUniv York, 2003; Hon. LLD Exeter, 2007. Chevalier, Ordre des Arts et des Lettres (France), 2001. *Publications:* Cracking Animation, 1999, 3rd edn 2010; Aardman: an epic journey, 2018. *Recreations:* cricket, comic books, walking. *Address:* Aardman Animations, Gas Ferry Road, Bristol BS1 6UN. *T:* (0117) 9848485. *Club:* MCC.

**LORD, Richard Denyer;** QC 2002; *b* 2 Jan. 1959; *s* of Arthur James Lord and Daphne Anne Lord (now Beaumont); *m* 1992, Alexandra Barnes; one *s* one *d*. *Educ:* Stowe Sch.; Sidney Sussex Coll., Cambridge (MA). Called to the Bar, Inner Temple, 1981. Trustee: Web of Hope, 2003–; Wychwood Project Oxon, 2009–. *Publications:* Controlled Drugs: law and practice, 1984; (with Simon Salzedo) Guide to the Arbitration Act 1996, 1996; (with R. Aikens and M. Bools) Bills of Lading, 2006, 2nd edn 2016; (ed jtly) Climate Change Liability, 2011. *Recreations:* cricket, reggae music, planting trees. *Address:* Brick Court Chambers, 7–8 Essex Street, WC2R 3LD. *T:* (020) 7379 3550, *Fax:* (020) 7379 3558. *E:* richard.lord@brickcourt.co.uk. *Club:* MCC.

**LORD, Stuart;** Lay Member, Fitness to Practise Panel, General Medical Council, 2006–14; *b* 10 Feb. 1951; *yr s* of William Ughtred Lord and Sybil Lord (*née* Greenhalgh); *m* 1970, Dwynwen Williams; one *s* one *d*. *Educ:* Manchester Grammar Sch.; University Coll. of Swansea (BScEcon Hons). DHSS, later DSS, then Department for Work and Pensions, 1972–2002; Principal Private Sec. to Sec. of State, 1988–91; Asst Sec. seconded to DoE, 1991; seconded to Prudential Life and Pensions, 1993; Head of Security, Benefits Agency, 1993–94; Head of Planning and Finance Divisions, and Prin. Finance Officer, 1994–98; Head of Transport and Corporate Directorate, Govt Office for London (on secondment), 1998–2000; Dir, Modernisation Strategy, Service Strategy and Commercial Partnerships,

2000–02. Non-exec. Dir, Richmond and Twickenham PCT, 2003–07. *Publications:* (contrib.) Economics of Unemployment, 1981. *Recreations:* travel, photography, consumer electronics. *Address:* 49 Ditton Reach, Thames Ditton, Surrey KT7 0XB.

**LORD, Hon. Timothy Michael;** QC 2008; *b* Cambridge, 10 Feb. 1966; *s* of Baron Framlingham, *qv*; *m* 2001, Amanda Jane Green; two *s*. *Educ:* Bedford Modern Sch.; Christ's Coll., Cambridge (BA 1st Cl. Hons Law 1987; MA). Admitted solicitor, 1991; Slaughter & May, 1989–92. Called to the Bar, Inner Temple, 1992; in practice at the Bar, 1993–. Sec., London Common Law and Commercial Bar Assoc., 2000–06. *Recreations:* Rugby (Cambridge blue 1986), cricket (playing Mem., MCC), sailing, ski-ing, golf. *Address:* Brick Court Chambers, 7–8 Essex Street, WC2R 3LD. *T:* (020) 7379 3550, *Fax:* (020) 7379 3558. *Club:* MCC.

**LOREN, Sophia;** film actress; *b* 20 Sept. 1934; *d* of Ricardo Scicolone and Romilda Villani; *m* 1957, Carlo Ponti (*d* 2007), film producer (marriage annulled in Juarez, Mexico, Sept. 1962; marriage in Paris, France, April 1966); two *s*. *Educ:* parochial sch. and Teachers' Institute, Naples. First leading role in, Africa sotto i Mari, 1952; acted in many Italian films, 1952–55; subsequent films include: The Pride and the Passion, Boy on a Dolphin, Legend of the Lost, 1957; The Key, Desire under the Elms, Houseboat, 1958; The Black Orchid (Venice Film Festival Award, 1958), That Kind of Woman, 1959; It Started in Naples, Heller in Pink Tights, A Breath of Scandal, 1960; The Millionairess, Two Women (Cannes Film Festival Award, 1961), Madame sans Gêne, El Cid, 1961; Boccaccio 70, 1962; Five Miles to Midnight, 1963; Yesterday, Today and Tomorrow, The Fall of the Roman Empire, Marriage, Italian Style, 1964; Operation Crossbow, Lady L, 1965; Judith, Arabesque, 1996; A Countess from Hong Kong, 1967; Sunflower, 1970; The Priest's Wife, 1971; Man of La Mancha, 1972; The Voyage, 1973; The Verdict, 1974; A Special Day, The Cassandra Crossing, 1977; Firepower, 1979; Blood Feud, 1980; Running Away, 1989; Saturday, Sunday and Monday, 1990; Prêt-à-Porter, 1994; Between Strangers, 2003; Nine, 2009. Chevalier, Legion of Honour (France), 1991. *Publications:* Eat with Me, 1972; Sophia Loren on Woman and Beauty, 1984; Yesterday, Today, Tomorrow: my life, 2014; *relevant publication:* Sophia: living and loving, by A. E. Hotchner, 1979. *Address:* Case Postale 430, 1211 Geneva 12, Switzerland.

**LORENZ, Andrew Peter Morrice;** Chairman, Financial Communications Group, FTI Consulting (formerly Financial Dynamics), since 2006 (Managing Director and Head of Industrials Group, 2001–06); *b* 22 June 1955; *s* of Hans Viktor Lorenz and Catherine Jesse Cairns Lorenz (*née* James); *m* 1988, Helen Marianne Alway; two *s*. *Educ:* Stamford Sch., Lincs; Worcester Coll., Oxford (MA Mod. Hist.). The Journal, Newcastle: News Reporter, 1978–80; Educn Correspondent, 1980–81; Industrial Correspondent, 1981–82; Business Correspondent, The Scotsman, 1982–86; City Correspondent, 1986–88, Dep. City Editor, 1988–89, Sunday Telegraph; Industrial Editor, 1989–95, Business Editor, 1995, Sunday Times; joined FTI Strategic Communications, London, 2000. Business Journalist of the Year, UK Press Awards, 1999; Business Journalist of the Year, Corp. of London, 2000. *Publications:* A Fighting Chance: British manufacturing industry in the 1980s, 1989; BZW: the first ten years, 1997; Lurssen: the story of a shipbuilder, 1997; Rover Reborn: the road to BMW, 1999; (jtly) End of the Road: BMW and Rover – a brand too far, 2000, 2nd edn as End of the Road: the true story of the downfall of Rover, 2005; Kumar Bhattacharyya: the unsung guru, 2002; GKN: the making of a business, 1759–2009, 2009; The View from the Bridge: an industrial journey, by Sir John Parker, 2018; (contrib.) Oxford DNB. *Recreations:* film, music, sport. *Address:* 4 Skindles Reach, Mill Lane, Taplow, Bucks SL6 0AG.

**LORIMER, Prof. (Andrew) Ross,** CBE 2004; MD; FRCP, FRCPE, FRCPGlas, FMedSci; President, Royal College of Physicians and Surgeons of Glasgow, 2000–03; *b* 5 May 1937; *s* of James Lorimer and Katherine Lorimer (*née* Ross); *m* 1963, Fiona Marshall; three *s*. *Educ:* Uddingston Grammar Sch.; High Sch. of Glasgow; Univ. of Glasgow (MD Hons 1976). FRCPGlas 1972; FRCP 1978; FRCPE 1981. Res. Fellow in Medicine, Vanderbilt Univ., Nashville, 1961–63; Registrar in Medicine, Royal Infirmary, Glasgow, 1963–66; Lectr in Cardiol., Glasgow Univ., 1966–71; Consultant Cardiologist, Royal Infirmary, Glasgow, 1971–91; Hon. Prof. of Medicine, Glasgow Univ., 1991–2001. FMedSci 1998; FACP 2001; FFPH (FFPHM 2001); FRCPI 2002; Fellow, Bangladesh Coll. of Physicians and Surgeons, 2002; FRCS, FRCSE, 2003; FRACP 2004; FRCSI 2004; FCP(SoAf) 2004. DUniv Glasgow, 2001. *Publications:* Preventive Cardiology, 1988. *Recreations:* golf, cricket, hill-walking. *Address:* Woodlands Cottage, 12 Uddingston Road, Bothwell, Glasgow G71 8PH.

**LORIMER, Sir Desmond;** *see* Lorimer, Sir T. D.

**LORIMER, Prof. George Huntly,** FRS 1986; Distinguished University Professor, Department of Chemistry and Biochemistry, University of Maryland, since 1998; *b* 14 Oct. 1942; *s* of late Gordon and Ellen Lorimer; *m* 1970, Freia (*née* Schulz-Baldes); one *s* one *d*. *Educ:* George Watson's College, Edinburgh; Univ. of St Andrews (BSc); Univ. of Illinois (MS); Michigan State Univ. (PhD). Scientist, Max-Planck Society, Berlin, 1972–74; Research Fellow, Inst. for Advanced Studies, ANU, Canberra, 1974–77; Scientist, Society for Radiation and Environmental Research, Munich, 1977; Prin. Investigator, then Res. Leader, E. I. Du Pont de Nemours & Co., 1978–91; Dupont Fellow, Central Res. Dept, Dupont Co., Delaware, 1991–97. Mem., NAS, USA, 1997. Res. Award, Alexander von Humboldt Foundn, 1997. *Publications:* contribs to Biochemistry, Jl of Biological Chemistry, Nature, Science. *Recreations:* music, political history. *Address:* 7705 Lake Glen Drive, Glenn Dale, MD 20769–2028, USA. *T:* (home) (301) 3523679, (office) (301) 4051828. *E:* glorimer@umd.edu.

**LORIMER, Ross;** *see* Lorimer, A. R.

**LORIMER, Sir (Thomas) Desmond,** Kt 1976; Chairman, Northern Bank Ltd, 1986–97 (Director, 1983–97; Deputy Chairman, 1985); *b* 20 Oct. 1925; *s* of Thomas Berry Lorimer and Sarah Ann Lorimer; *m* 1957, Patricia Doris Samways; two *d*. *Educ:* Belfast Technical High Sch. Chartered Accountant, 1948; Fellow, Inst. of Chartered Accountants in Ireland, 1957. Practised as chartered accountant, 1952–74; Sen. Partner, Harmood, Banner, Smylie & Co., Belfast, Chartered Accountants, 1960–74; Chairman: Lamont Holdings PLC, 1973–96; Northern Ireland Electricity, 1991–94; Dir, Irish Distillers PLC, 1986–98. Chm., Industrial Develt Bd for NI, 1982–85; Pres., Inst. of Chartered Accountants in Ireland, 1968–69; Chairman: Ulster Soc. of Chartered Accountants, 1960; NI Housing Exec., 1971–75; Mem., Rev. Body on Local Govt in NI, 1970. *Recreations:* gardening, golf. *Address:* Windwhistle Cottage, 6A Circular Road West, Cultra, Holywood, Co. Down BT18 0AT. *T:* (028) 9042 3323. *Clubs:* Royal Belfast Golf, Royal Co. Down Golf (Co. Down).

**LORNE, Marquess of; Archie Frederick Campbell;** *b* 9 March 2004; *s* and *heir* of Duke of Argyll, *qv*. A Page of Honour to the Queen, 2015–18.

**LOSOWSKY, Prof. Monty Seymour,** FRCP; Professor of Medicine and Head of University of Leeds Department of Medicine, St James's University Hospital, Leeds, 1969–96, now Emeritus Professor; *b* 1 Aug. 1931; *s* of Dora and Solomon (Myer) Losowsky; *m* 1971, Barbara Malkin; one *s* one *d*. *Educ:* Coopers' Company's Sch., London; Univ. of Leeds (Hons MB, ChB; MD). House appts, Leeds Gen. Infirmary, 1955–56; Registrar in Medicine, Epping, 1957–59; Asst, Externe Hôpital St Antoine, Paris, 1960; Research Fellow, Harvard Med. Unit, 1961–62; Lectr, Sen. Lectr, Reader in Medicine, 1962–69, Dean, Faculty of Medicine, 1989–94, Univ. of Leeds. Member: Leeds Eastern Health Authy, 1981–89; Specialist Adv. Cttee on General (Internal) Medicine, 1984–88; Systems Bd Grants Cttee B, MRC, 1984–88; Panel of Studies Allied to Medicine, UGC, 1982–89; British Digestive Foundn Sci. and Res. Awards Cttee, 1987–90; Yorks RHA, 1989–90; Working Gp, France Steering Gp on Undergrad. Medical and Dental Educn, DoH, 1990–94; Council, British Nutrition Foundn, 1991–2014 (Mem. Scientific Adv. Cttee, 1987–91; Scientific Governor, 1991–2014); GMC, 1991–96; CVCP Rep., Acad. and Res. Staff Cttee of DoH Jt Planning and Adv. Cttee, 1990–94 (Mem., General Purposes Working Gp, 1989–94); Chm., Other Studies and Professions Allied to Medicine Panel, HEFCE, 1995–97. Lectures: Watson Smith, RCPE, 1995; Simms, RCP, 1996. Pres., British Soc. of Gastroenterol., 1993–94. Chm., Coeliac Trust, 1983–95; Governor: Coeliac Soc., 1975–2005 (Chm., Med. Adv. Council, 1995–2003); British Liver Trust, 1999–2001 (Chm., Med. Adv. Cttee, 1999–2001). Examr for Membership, RCP, 1982–96; Academic Observer and Ext. Examr, Utd Examining Bd, 1994–96. Trustee, 1995–2012, Exec. Chm., 1997–2012, Life Pres., 2012–, Thackray Med. Mus. Gov., Leeds GS, 1988–2005. Leeds Award, Leeds CC, 2014. *Publications:* (jtly) Malabsorption in Clinical Practice, 1974; (ed) The Gut and Systemic Disease, 1983; (ed jtly) Advanced Medicine, 1983; (jtly) The Liver and Biliary System, 1984; (jtly) Clinical Nutrition in Gastroenterology, 1986; (jtly) Gut Defences in Clinical Practice, 1986; (jtly) Gastroenterology, 1988; Consensus in Clinical Nutrition, 1994; Getting Better: stories from the history of medicine, 2007; chapters and papers relating to haematology, hepatology, gastroenterology and history of medicine. *Recreations:* golf, medical history, walking, DIY, medical biography. *Club:* Royal Society of Medicine.

**LOTEN, Graeme Neil;** Executive Director, Imbabazi NGO, Rubavu, Rwanda, 2013–15; *b* 10 March 1959; *s* of Richard Maurice Loten and Brenda Ivy Elizabeth Loten. *Educ:* Portsmouth Grammar Sch.; Liverpool Univ. (BA). Entered Diplomatic Service, 1981; Private Sec. to Ambassador to NATO, 1983–86; Third Sec., Khartoum, 1986–87; Second Sec., The Hague, 1988–92; Dep. Head of Mission, Almaty, 1993–97; Ambassador: to Rwanda and (non-resident) to Burundi, 1998–2001; to Mali, 2001–03; on temp. attachment to Dio. of Cyangugu, Rwanda, 2003–04; Ambassador to Tajikistan, 2004–09; Country Representative: Fondation Hirondelle, Sierra Leone, 2009–11; Fondation Hirondelle, Democratic Republic of Congo, 2011–12. Trustee and volunteer with Rwanda-orientated charities incl. Cricket Builds Hope. *Recreations:* travel, Portsmouth FC. *Address:* c/o 12 Brunswick Gardens, Havant, Hants PO9 3HZ.

**LOTERY, Prof. Andrew John,** MD; FRCOphth; Professor of Ophthalmology, University of Southampton, since 2002; *b* 6 Dec. 1965; *s* of John Samuel Lotery and Caroline Lotery; *m* 1993, Helen Elizabeth Gore; two *s* one *d*. *Educ:* Queen's Univ., Belfast (MD 1997). FRCOphth 1994. Jun. hosp. appts, Belfast, 1989–91; trng in ophthalmology, Belfast, 1991–98; Molecular Ophthalmology Fellowship, 1998–2000, Asst Prof. of Ophthalmology, 2000–02, Univ. of Iowa. Current research developing novel treatments for age related macular degeneration. *Publications:* res. articles in jls incl. New England Jl of Medicine, Nature Genetics. *Recreations:* time with family, reading, running, travel. *Address:* Southampton Eye Unit, Southampton General Hospital, Tremona Road, Southampton SO16 6YD. *T:* (023) 8179 4590, *Fax:* (023) 8179 4120.

**LOTHIAN,** 13th Marquess of, *cr* 1701; **Michael Andrew Foster Jude Kerr, (Rt Hon. Michael Ancram);** PC 1996; DL; QC (Scot.) 1996; Lord Newbottle, 1591; Earl of Lothian, 1606; Lord Jedburgh, 1622; Earl of Ancram, Baron Kerr of Nisbet, Longnewton and Dolphinstoun, 1633; Viscount of Briene, Baron Ker of Newbattle, 1701; Baron Ker (UK), 1821; Baron Kerr of Monteviot (Life Peer), 2010; *b* 7 July 1945; *s* of 12th Marquess of Lothian, KCVO and Antonella (OBE 1997), *d* of Maj.-Gen. Sir Foster Newland, KCMG, CB; *S* father, 2004; *m* 1975, Lady (Theresa) Jane Fitzalan-Howard (*see* Lady Herries of Terregles); two *d* (and one *d* decd). *Educ:* Ampleforth; Christ Church, Oxford (BA); Edinburgh Univ. (LLB). Advocate, Scottish Bar, 1970. Contested (C): W Lothian, 1970; Edinburgh S, 1987. MP (C): Berwickshire and East Lothian, Feb.–Sept. 1974; Edinburgh S, 1979–87; Devizes, 1992–2010. Parly Under-Sec. of State, Scottish Office, 1983–87, NI Office, 1993–94; Minister of State, NI Office, 1994–97; Opposition front bench spokesman on constitutional affairs, 1997–98; Dep. Leader of the Opposition and Shadow Foreign Sec., 2001–05; Shadow Sec. of State for Internat. Affairs, 2003–05, for Defence, 2005. Member: Select Cttee on Energy, 1980–83; Public Accounts Cttee, 1992–93; Intelligence and Security Cttee, 2006–. Chairman: Cons. Party in Scotland, 1980–83 (Vice-Chm., 1975–80); Cons. Party, 1998–2001. Chm., Northern Corporate Communications, 1989–91; Dir, CSM Parly Consultants, 1988–92; Mem. Bd, Scottish Homes, 1988–90. Chairman: Global Strategy Forum, 2006–; Gulf Policy Forum, 2007–. Vice-Pres., Anglo-Jordanian Soc., 2015–. Pres., Royal Highland Show, 2019. Grand Prior (England and Wales), Order of St Lazarus of Jerusalem, 2013–. DL Roxburgh, Ettrick and Lauderdale, 1990. Freeman: Devizes, 2010; City of Gibraltar, 2010. GCLJ 2013. *Publications:* The Magical Gardens of Monteviot, 2018; pamphlets for Global Strategy Forum. *Recreations:* ski-ing, photography, folksinging, gardening. *Heir:* *b* Lord Ralph William Francis Joseph Kerr [*b* 7 Nov. 1957; *m* 1st, 1980, Lady Virginia FitzRoy (marr. diss. 1987); 2nd, 1988, Marie-Claire Black; four *s* two *d*]. *Address:* Monteviot, Jedburgh TD8 6UH. *Clubs:* Beefsteak, Pratt's, White's; New (Edinburgh).

*See also* Rt Hon. N. R. Hurd.

**LOTHIAN, Prof. Niall,** OBE 2012; Professor, Graduate Business School, Heriot-Watt University, 1996–2011; President, Institute of Chartered Accountants of Scotland, 1995–96; *b* 27 Feb. 1948; *s* of Rev. Thomas Lothian and Jean Morgan Lothian (*née* Henderson); *m* 1971, Carol Miller; one *s* one *d*. *Educ:* Daniel Stewart's Coll.; Heriot-Watt Univ. (BA 1971). CA 1972. Lectr, Sen. Lectr, 1973–88, Prof. of Accounting, 1988–96, Director, 1991–93, Business School, Heriot-Watt Univ. Visiting Professor: IMEDE, Lausanne, 1979–80; Univ. of Witwatersrand, 1984; Mem., internat. vis. faculty, INSEAD, Fontainebleau, 1984–2018; Consultant: UNIDO, China, 1980; NZ Soc. of Accountants, 1992. Mem., Internat. Exec. Adv. Bd, Coll. of Finance and Accountancy, Budapest. Chm., Chiene + Tait, CA, 2005–08; non-exec. Dir, Stoddard Internat. plc, 1998–2002. Chm., Adv. Audit Bd, Scottish Parly Corp. Body, 2002–09. Chm., Inspiring Scotland, 2009–17. Mem. Council, Edinburgh Internat. Fest., 2011– (Chm., 2016–). Trustee, Lloyds TSB Charitable Foundn for Scotland, 1997–99. Governor: George Watson's Coll., 1991–2004 (Chm., 1999–2004); RSAMD, later Royal Conservatoire of Scotland, 2007–11. *Publications:* How Companies Manage R&D, 1984; Measuring Corporate Performance, 1987; (jtly) Accounting, 1991; (contrib.) Ernst and Young Manager's Handbook, 2nd edn 1992; articles in professional jls. *Recreations:* graveyards, golf. *Address:* 30 Granby Road, Edinburgh EH16 5NL. *T:* (0131) 667 4429. *Clubs:* New (Edinburgh); Royal & Ancient Golf; Luffness New Golf.

**LOTINGA, Stephen Andrew;** Chief Executive Officer, Publishers Association, since 2016; *b* Scarborough, 29 Dec. 1980; *s* of David Lotinga and Ann Lotinga. *Educ:* Keele Univ. (BA Politics and Econs 2003); Univ. of Manchester (MA Politics 2004). Parly Res. Asst to Tom Brake, MP, 2005; Parly Researcher to Don Foster, MP, 2006–07; Sen. Political Advr to Liberal Democrats, 2007–10; Man. Dir and Partner, Bell Pottinger, 2010–14; Dep. Dir, Govt Communications, 2014–15. *Recreations:* books, travel, politics, Arsenal. *Address:* Publishers Association, First Floor, 50 Southwark Street, SE1 1UN. *T:* (020) 7378 0504. *E:* slotinga@publishers.org.uk.

**LOTON, Brian Thorley,** AC 1989; FTS; Chairman: Broken Hill Proprietary Co. Ltd, 1992–97; Atlas Copco Australia Pty Ltd, 1996–2001; Director, Australian Foundation Investment Co. Ltd, 1993–2001; *b* Perth, WA, 17 May 1929; *s* of Sir (Ernest) Thorley Loton and Grace (*née* Smith); *m* 1956, Joan Kemelfield (*d* 2016); two *s* two *d*. *Educ:* Hale Sch., Perth; Trinity Coll., Melbourne Univ. (BMetEng 1953). Joined BHP as Cadet 1954; Technical Asst, 1959; Asst Chief Engr, 1961; Gen. Manager Planning and Develt, 1969, Gen. Manager Newcastle Steel Works, 1970; Exec. Gen. Manager Steel Div., 1973; Dir, 1976; Chief Gen. Manager, 1977; Man. Dir, 1982; Chief Exec. Officer, 1984, Dep. Chm., 1991. Director: Nat. Australia Bank, 1988–99; Amcor Ltd, 1992–99. President: Aust. Inst. of Mining and Metallurgy, 1982; Australian Mining Industry Council, 1983–84; Business Council of Aust., 1990–92; Vice-Chairman: Internat. Iron and Steel Inst., 1988, 1992–94 (Chm., 1991–92); Defence Industry Cttee, 1976–88; Member: Aust. Sci. and Technol. Council, 1977–80; Aust. Manufg Council, 1977–81; Vict. Govt Long Range Policy Planning Cttee, 1980–82; Aust. Council on Population and Ethnic Affairs, 1980–82. Internat. Counsellor, The Conf. Bd, 1984–97. Pres., Vic. Br., Scout Assoc. of Australia, 1997–2002. Mem. Faculty Engrg, Melbourne Univ., 1980–83. FIE (Aust) 1984 (Hon. Fellow); FAIM 1973; FIDA 1980. *Clubs:* Melbourne, Australian (Melbourne).

**LOTT, Dame Felicity (Ann Emwhyla),** DBE 1996 (CBE 1990); soprano; *b* 8 May 1947; *d* of John Albert Lott and Whyla (*née* Williams); *m* 1st, 1973, Robin Mavesyn Golding (marr. diss. 1982); 2nd, 1984, Gabriel Woolf; one *d*. *Educ:* Pate's Grammar Sch. for Girls, Cheltenham; Royal Holloway Coll., Univ. of London (BA Hons French; Hon. Fellow, 1995); Royal Acad. of Music (LRAM; ARAM 1976; FRAM 1986). Début: ENO, 1975; Covent Garden, 1976; Glyndebourne, 1977. Particularly associated with Mozart and Richard Strauss, whose operas she has sung in Glyndebourne, Covent Garden, Cologne, Hamburg, Brussels, Paris, Vienna, Munich, Dresden, Milan, NY, Chicago and Japan; gives recitals worldwide; many recordings. Pres., British Youth Opera, 2012–. Founder Mem., The Songmakers' Almanac. Hon. FGS 2014; Hon. FRCM 2006. Dr *hc*: Sussex, 1989; Sorbonne, 2010; Hon. DLitt Loughborough, 1996; Hon. DMus: London, 1997; RSAMD 1998; Leicester, 2000; Oxford, 2001. Wigmore Hall Medal, 2010. Bayerische Kammersängerin, 2003; Distinguished Musician Award, ISM, 2014. Officier, Ordre des Arts et des Lettres (France), 2000 (Chevalier, 1993); Chevalier de la Légion d'Honneur (France), 2001. *Recreations:* reading, gentle gardening. *Address:* c/o Askonas Holt Ltd, 15 Fetter Lane, EC4A 1BW. *T:* (020) 7400 1700.

**LOTT, Timothy;** novelist and journalist; teacher of Creative Writing, Guardian Master Classes, since 2011; *b* Southall, Middx, 23 Jan. 1956; *s* of Jack and Jean Lott; *m* 1st, 1991, Sarigna Lavigna (*d* 2000); 2nd, 2007, Rachael Newberry (marr. diss. 2018); four *d*. *Educ:* Greenford Co. Grammar Sch.; London Sch. of Econs and Pol Sci. (BA Govt and Hist. 1986). Reporter, Uxbridge Gazette, 1976–77; feature writer: Sounds, 1977–78; Record Mirror, 1978–79; Founder and publisher, Flexipop, 1980–83; researcher and producer, Mentorn Films, 1988–89; feature writer, Sunday Corresp. mag., 1989–90; teacher of creative writing: Brunel Univ., 2011; Faber Acad., 2012–15; Guardian Masterclasses, 2015–18. *Publications:* The Scent of Dried Roses (memoir), 1996 (PEN/J. R. Ackerley Prize for Autobiog., Penguin Modern Classics); *novels:* White City Blue, 1999 (Whitbread First Novel Award); Rumours of Hurricane, 2002; The Love Secrets of Don Juan, 2003; The Seymour Tapes, 2005; Under the Same Stars, 2012; The Last Summer of the Water Strider, 2015; When We Were Rich, 2019; *for young adults:* Fearless, 2007; How to be Invisible, 2013. *Recreations:* navel gazing, fence sitting, eating, tweeting, shopping, talking, dozing, observing, some racquet sports, occasional cigarette, cheese, theatre, Zen. *Address:* Flat 69, NoKo, 3–6 Banister Road, W10 4AR. *T:* 07812 043453. *E:* timlott@me.com. *Club:* Academy.

**LOUDON, Prof. Andrew Stewart Irvine,** PhD; FMedSci; Beyer Professor of Animal Biology, University of Manchester, since 1995; *b* Oxford, 27 March 1950; *s* of Irvine Loudon and Jean Loudon (*née* Norman); *m* 1972, Bente Schroeder; two *s* one *d*. *Educ:* Abingdon Sch., Abingdon; Pembroke Coll., Oxford (BA Zool. 1972); Univ. of Edinburgh (PhD 1979). University of Edinburgh: Res. Fellow, 1979; demonstrator, 1979–82; Lectr in Animal Biol., 1983; MRC Res. Fellow, 1983–91, Dir, Reproductive Biol. Gp, 1992–95, Inst. of Zool., Univ. of London. Vis. Prof., Dept of Biol., UCL, 1993–95; Vis. Res. Schol., Univ. of Virginia, Charlottesville, 1991. FMedSci 2015. *Publications:* Reproductive Energetics in Mammals, 1987; res. papers, reviews and commentaries. *Recreations:* motorcycling, fly fishing, wood turning. *Address:* A. V. Hill Building, Faculty of Biology, Medicine and Health, University of Manchester, Manchester M13 9PT. *T:* (0161) 275 3888. *E:* andrew.loudon@manchester.ac.uk.

**LOUDON, Deborah Jane, (Mrs H. R. Woudhuysen);** Partner, Saxton Bampfylde (formerly Saxton Bampfylde Hever), 2010–17; Director General, Civilian Personnel, Ministry of Defence, 2005–07; *b* 4 June 1955; *d* of Joseph Buist Loudon and Joan Katherine Loudon (*née* Ede); *m* 1987, Prof. Henry Ruxton Woudhuysen, *qv*; two *s*. *Educ:* Malvern Girls' Coll.; Somerville Coll., Oxford (MA PPE). Home Office, 1977–2003: Private Sec. to Minister of State, 1983–84; Principal, Prison Service, 1984; Grade 5, Police Dept, 1993–99; HR Dir, 2000–03; Dir Gen., Security and Safety, MoD, 2003–05. Member: Adv. Bd, Apeldoorn, 2016–; Bd, Centre for Econs and Business Res., 2016–. Trustee: Crime Reduction Initiatives, then CGL (Change, Grow, Live), 2011–16; Services Sound and Vision Corp., 2016–; Charity for Civil Servants, 2016–. Gov., Combe C of E Primary Sch., 2017–. FCIPD 2002. *E:* deborahloudon55@gmail.com.

**LOUDON, Maj. Gen. Euan;** *see* Loudon, Maj. Gen. W. E. B.

**LOUDON, George Ernest;** Chairman: Altius Holdings Ltd, 1999–2014; Pall Mall Capital Ltd, since 2001; *b* 19 Nov. 1942; *m* 1968, Angela Mary Goldsbrough; one *s* one *d*. *Educ:* Christelijk Lyceum, Zeist; Balliol Coll., Oxford (BA); Johns Hopkins Univ., Washington (MA). Lazard Frères & Cie, Paris, 1967–68; Ford Foundn, New York and Jakarta, 1968–71; McKinsey & Co., Amsterdam, 1971–76; Amro Bank, Amsterdam: Gen. Man., 1976–83; Mem., Bd of Man. Dirs, 1983–88; Dir, Midland Group, 1988–92; Chief Exec., 1988–92, Chm., 1991–92, Midland Montagu; Chairman: Helix Associates Ltd, 1993–2005; GAM Diversity Inc., 2014–18. Non-executive Director: M&G Gp, 1993–94; Arjo-Wiggins Appleton, 1993–2000; Harrison/Parrott Ltd, 1993–; Global Asset Management, 1994–99; Logica CMG (formerly CMG) plc, 1998–2007; Evolution (formerly Beeson Gregory) Gp plc, 2001–04. Member, Board: Multiple Sclerosis Internat. Fedn, 1999–2007; TNC UK Foundn Ltd, 2019–. Trustee and Chm., Finance Cttee, Royal Botanic Gardens, Kew, 2007–15; Mem. Bd, Founds and Friends of Royal Botanic Gdns, Kew, 2009–. *Publications:* Object Lessons, 2015.

**LOUDON, James Rushworth Hope;** DL; Chairman, Caledonia Investments plc, 2008–12 (non-executive Director, 1995–2012); *b* Newbury, Berks, 19 March 1943; *s* of late Francis William Hope Loudon and Lady Prudence Katharine Patton Loudon (*née* Jellicoe); *m* 1975, Jane Gavina Fryett; two *s* one *d*. *Educ:* Eton Coll.; Magdalene Coll., Cambridge (BA Hons 1965); Stanford Business Sch., Calif (MBA 1971). RTZ Corp. Ltd, 1966–69; Samuel Montagu & Co. Ltd, 1971–72; Cons. Central Office, 1972–75; Overseas Containers Ltd, 1975–77; Blue Circle Industries plc, 1977–2001, Gp Finance Dir, 1987–2001. Non-executive Director: Lafarge Malayan Cement, 1989–2004; James Hardie Industries NV, 2002–08. Mem., Kent CC, 1977–81. Ind. Mem., Selection Panel, Kent Police Authy, 1994–98. Mem., Ind. Monitoring Bd, HMP Swaleside, 2013–18. Mem., Fundraising Adv. Council, VSO, 1994–99. Governor: Univ. of Greenwich, 2001–10 (Dep. Chm., 2008–10); Royal Sch. for Deaf Children, 2002–05; Caldecott Foundn, 2002–12. Trustee: Kent, Surrey and Sussex Air Ambulance Trust, 2005–19; Canterbury Cathedral Trust, 2005– (Dep. Chm., 2008–). High Sheriff, 2004–05, DL, 2011, Kent. DUniv Greenwich, 2011. *Recreations:* golf, cricket, ski-ing, opera, cabinet making. *Address:* Little Olantigh, Wye, Kent TN25 5DH. *T:* (01233) 812294. *Clubs:* MCC; Rye Golf, Royal St George's Golf.

**LOUDON, John Duncan Ott,** OBE 1988; FRCSE, FRCOG, FFSRH; retired; Consultant Obstetrician and Gynaecologist, Eastern General Hospital, Edinburgh, 1960–87; Senior Lecturer, University of Edinburgh, 1962–87; *b* 22 Aug. 1924; *s* of late James Alexander Law Loudon and Ursula (*née* Ott); *m* 1953, Nancy Beaton (*née* Mann) (OBE 1992) (*d* 2009); two *s*. *Educ:* John Watson's Sch., Edinburgh; Wyggeston Sch., Leicester; Univ. of Edinburgh (MB, ChB 1947). FRCSE 1954; FRCOG 1973 (MRCOG 1956); FFSRH 1995. National Service, RAF, 1948–50. House appts, Edinburgh and Cambridge, 1948–52; Registrar, Sen. Registrar and Consultant Obstetrician and Gynaecologist, Simpson Maternity Pavilion and Royal Infirm., Edinburgh, 1954–66. Formerly Examiner in Obstetrics and Gynaecology: Univs of Cardiff, Manchester, Leeds, Dundee, Glasgow, Aberdeen, Newcastle upon Tyne, Cape Town, RCSI, RCSE, RCOG and RACOG. Adviser in Family Welfare to Govt of Malta, 1976–81. Vice Pres., RCOG, 1981–84 (Mem. Council, 1966–72 and 1976–81). Member: Interim Licensing Authority for IVF, 1985–91; GMC, 1986–92. *Publications:* papers to obstetric and gynaecol jls. *Recreations:* bridge, reading. *Address:* 13/10 Ravelston Terrace, Edinburgh EH4 3TP. *T:* (0131) 332 4288. *Club:* Bruntsfield Links Golfing Society (Edinburgh).

**LOUDON, Prof. Rodney,** FRS 1987; Professor of Physics, Essex University, 1967–2008, now Emeritus; *b* 25 July 1934; *s* of Albert Loudon and Doris Helen (*née* Blane); *m* 1960, Mary Anne Philips; one *s* one *d*. *Educ:* Bury Grammar Sch.; Brasenose Coll., Oxford (MA, DPhil). Postdoctoral Fellow, Univ. of California, Berkeley, 1959–60; Scientific Civil Servant, RRE Malvern, 1960–65; Member, Technical Staff: Bell Labs, Murray Hill, NJ, 1965–66, 1970; RCA Labs, Zurich, 1975; Essex University: Reader in Physics, 1966–67; Dean of Sch. of Physical Scis, 1972–74; Chm. of Physics Dept, 1976–79 and 1988–89. Visiting Professor: Yale Univ., 1975; Univ. of California, Irvine, 1980; Ecole Polytechnique, Lausanne, 1985; Univ. of Rome, 1988 and 1996; Univ. of Strathclyde, 1998–2012. Chm., Bd of Editors of Optica Acta, 1984–87. Fellow, Optical Soc. of America, 1994. Thomas Young Medal and Prize, Inst. of Physics, 1987; Max Born Award, Optical Soc. of Amer., 1992; Alexander von Humboldt Prize, 1998. *Publications:* The Quantum Theory of Light, 1973, 3rd edn 2000; (with W. Hayes) Scattering of Light by Crystals, 1978; (ed with V. M. Agranovich) Surface Excitations, 1984; (with D. J. Barber) An Introduction to the Properties of Condensed Matter, 1989; papers in Nature, Phys. Rev., Jl Mod. Opt., Jl Phys., etc. *Recreations:* music, gardening. *Address:* 3 Gaston Street, East Bergholt, Colchester, Essex CO7 6SD. *T:* (01206) 298550.

**LOUDON, Maj. Gen. (William) Euan (Buchanan),** CBE 2004 (OBE 1991); Chief Executive, St Andrews Links Trust, since 2011; *b* 12 March 1956; *s* of David Christie Buchanan Loudon and Doreen Mary Loudon; *m* 1981, Penelope Jane Head. *Educ:* Uddingston Grammar Sch.; Royal Military Acad., Sandhurst. Commnd Royal Highland Fusiliers, 1975; Adjt 1st Bn, 1980–83; Exchange Officer, CTC RM, 1983–85; Army Staff Coll., 1988; Bde Maj. 7th Armoured Bde, 1989–91; UN Monitoring Orgn, Zagreb, 1995; CO 1RHF, 1995–97; Mil. Sec. (A), 1997–99; HCSC, 1999; Comdr 39th Inf. Bde, 1999–2001; COS and Comdr Force Troops HQ NI, 2001–03; GOC 2nd Div., and Gov., Edinburgh Castle, 2004–07; Chief Exec., Edinburgh Military Tattoo, later Royal Edinburgh Military Tattoo, 2007–11. Chairman: St Andrews Links Ltd, 2012–; Tom Morris Ltd, 2016–. FCMI 2003. QCVS 2002. *Recreations:* field sports, fishing, golf, music, farming. *Clubs:* Caledonian; New (Edinburgh).

**LOUDOUN, 15th Earl of,** *cr* 1633; **Simon Michael Abney-Hastings;** Lord Campbell of Loudoun, 1601; Lord Tarrinzean and Mauchline, 1633; *b* 29 Oct. 1974; *s* of 14th Earl of Loudoun and Noelene Margaret (*née* McCormick) (*d* 2002); *S* father, 2012; *co-heir* to Baronies of Botreaux 1368, Stanley 1456 and Hastings 1461. Patron: Repton Coll. (Life Hereditary Gov.), 2012–; Friends of Loudoun Kirk, Galston, 2012–; Ashby de la Zouch Mus., 2012–; Ringwood Highland Games Inc., Melbourne, Vic, 2017–; Barnet 1471 Soc., 2017–; Australia Day Council; Australian Monarchist League; Clan Campbell Soc. of Australia. Gov., Bd of St Andrew's First Aid Australia, 2018–. *Heir: b* Hon. Marcus William Abney-Hastings, *b* 1 Sept. 1981. *Address:* Wangaratta, Vic 3677, Australia; Melbourne, Vic 3001, Australia.

**LOUGH, Paula Jane;** *see* Radcliffe, P. J.

**LOUGHBOROUGH, Lord;** Jamie William St Clair-Erskine; *b* 28 May 1986; *s* and *heir* of Earl of Rosslyn, *qv*. *Educ:* Eton Coll.; Bristol Univ.

**LOUGHBOROUGH, Bishop of,** since 2017; **Rt Rev. Dr Gulnar Eleanor, (Guli), Francis-Dehqani;** *b* Isfahan, Iran, 18 June 1966; *d* of Hassan and Margaret Dehqani-Tafti; *m* 1991, Lee Francis; two *s* one *d*. *Educ:* in Iran; Clarendon Sch., Beds; Univ. of Nottingham (BA Music 1989); Univ. of Bristol (MA Religious Studies 1994; PhD 1999). Studio Manager, BBC World Service Radio, 1989–91; Producer, BBC Religious Dept, 1991–92; ordained deacon, 1998, priest, 1999; Curate, Mortlake and East Sheen Team Ministry, 1998–2002; Chaplain (pt-time), Royal Acad. of Music and St Marylebone C of E Secondary Sch., 2002–04; Interfaith Res. Asst (pt-time), Univ. of Northampton, 2009–10; Curate Trng Officer, 2011–17, Advr for Women's Ministry, 2012–17, Dio. of Peterborough. Hon. Canon, Peterborough Cathedral, 2016–17. Mem., Gen. Synod, 2012–17. *Publications:* Religious Feminism in an Age of Empire, 2000; (contrib.) The Church Mission Society and World Christianity 1799–1999, 2000; (contrib.) Voices of This Calling, 2002; (contrib.) Women, Religion and Culture in Iran, 2002; (contrib.) A Faithful Presence: essays for Kenneth Cragg, 2003; (contrib.) Edinburgh 2010: mission then and now, 2009; (contrib.) Putting Names with Faces: women's impact in mission history, 2012; articles in jls incl. Anglican Theol Rev. *Recreations:* Persian culture and cuisine, contemporary fiction, music, family life. *Address:* Bishop's Lodge Annexe, 12 Springfield Road, Leicester LE2 3BD. *T:* (0116) 2708985. *E:* bishop.loughborough@leccofe.org.

**LOUGHBOROUGH, Archdeacon of;** *see* Wood, Ven. C.

**LOUGHHEAD, John Neil,** CB 2018; OBE 2011; FREng, FIMechE, FIET; Chief Scientific Adviser, Department for Business, Energy and Industrial Strategy (formerly Department of Energy and Climate Change), since 2014; *b* Derby, 24 Sept. 1948; *s* of Neil Loughhead and late Mary Charlotte Loughhead; *m* 2007, Ellen Tingle. *Educ:* Bemrose Sch., Derby; Imperial Coll., London (BSc (Eng), MSc; DIC). CEng 1984; FIMechE 1988; FIET

1995; FREng 2008. Res. technologist, GEC Mech. Engrg Lab., 1975–83; Manager, Thermofluids Div., 1983–87, Man. Dir, 1987–92, GEC Engrg Res. Centre; R&D Dir, GEC Alsthom, 1992–98; Vice-Pres., Alstom Gp, 1998–2004; Exec. Dir, UK Energy Res. Centre, 2004–15. Non-executive Director: R&D Bd, MoD, 2008–15; Carbon Mgt Canada Ltd, 2011–; Samad Power Ltd, 2014–17. Focal Point UK-China energy collaboration, BIS, 2013–15. Member: EPSRC, 2003–05 (Chm., User Panel, 2004–05); Eur. Adv. Gp for Energy, 2008–15; Comité Energie, Agence Nat. de Recherche, France, 2011–16. Co-Chair, Internat. Partnership for Hydrogen Econ., 2007–10; Founding Mem., Eur. Energy Res. Alliance, 2008–15; Chair, Steering Cttee, Mission Innovation, 2019–20. Mem., Univ. Industrial Adv. Bds at Cardiff Univ., Loughborough Univ., QMUL, Sheffield Univ., Leeds Univ. and Durham Univ. Hon. Prof., Cardiff Univ., 2009–. Mem. Council, 2012–14, Trustee Bd, 2014–15, RAEng. President: IET, 2007–08; City & Guilds Coll. Assoc., 2009–10. FCGI 2007; FRSA; Foreign FTSE 2011. Freeman, City of London, 2009; Liveryman, Engineers' Co., 2009. Hon. Fellow, QMUL, 2009. Hon. DSc Keele, 2013. *Recreations:* travel, gardening, cooking, cherishing an MGB. *Address:* Department for Business, Energy and Industrial Strategy, 1 Victoria Street, SW1H 0ET. *T:* (0300) 068 6591.

**LOUGHLIN, Prof. John Patrick,** PhD; FRHistS, FAcSS, FLSW; Professor of Politics, Cardiff University, 1995–2010, Emeritus Professor, 2015; Director, Von Hügel Institute 2010–15, now Emeritus Director, and Fellow, St Edmund's College, Cambridge, 2010–15, now Emeritus Fellow; Research Fellow, Blackfriars, Oxford, since 2015; *b* Belfast, 9 Sept. 1948; *s* of John Patrick Loughlin and Margaret Loughlin; one *d*. *Educ:* St Malachy's Coll., Belfast; Our Lady of Bethlehem Abbey, NI; Ulster Poly. (BA Hons 1982); European University Inst., Florence (PhD 1987); MA Cantab 2015. Army, 1964–68; Cistercian monk, 1968–74; religious orgns, 1974–78; Lectr, Univ. of Ulster, 1985–91; Associate Prof., Erasmus Univ., Rotterdam, 1991–95. Tutor, Maryvale Inst., Birmingham, 2017–. Visiting Professor: Eur. Univ. Inst., Florence, 1994; Inst. d'Etudes Politiques, Paris, 1999–2002; Univ. of Umeå, 2003–07; Univ. of Santiago da Compostela, 2005; Inst. d'Etudes Politiques, Aix-en-Provence, 2005–12; Univ. Libre de Bruxelles, 2012–13 (Chaire Ganshof van der Meersch, 2013–14); St Mary's Univ., Twickenham, 2017–; Visiting Fellow: Eur. Univ. Inst., Florence, 2001–02; Eur. Studies, St Antony's Coll., Oxford, 2006–07; St Edmund's Coll., Cambridge, 2009; Dist. Vis. Res. Fellow, QMUL, 2009; Vis. Res. Fellow, Merton Coll., Oxford, 2004; Sen. Vis. Res. Scholar, Centre for Contemp. Hist., Univ. of Oxford, 2005–06; Vis. Scholar, Nuffield Coll., Oxford, 2009–10; Mem., Residential Colloquium, Centre of Theol Inquiry, Princeton, 2010. FRHistS 2007; FAcSS (AcSS 2008); FRSA 2008; Fellow, Eur. Acad. of Scis and Arts, 2013; FLSW 2014. Hon. PhD Umeå, 2009. Officier, Ordre des Palmes Académiques (France), 2010. *Publications:* Public Policy in Northern Ireland, 1995; The Political Economy of Regionalism, 1997; Regional and Local Democracy in the EU, 1999; Subnational Democracy in the EU, 2001; Albania and the EU, 2007; Subnational Government: the French experience, 2007; The Oxford Handbook of Local and Regional Democracy in Europe, 2010; The Routledge Handbook of Regionalism and Federalism, 2013; The UK's 'Big Society' Programme and Catholic Social Teaching, 2013; Human Dignity in the Judaeo-Christian Tradition: Catholic, Orthodox, Anglican and Protestant perspectives, 2019; numerous articles and book chapters. *Recreations:* travel, music, choral singing, reading. *Address:* School of Law and Politics, Cardiff University, Law Building, Museum Avenue, Cardiff CF10 3AX. *T:* 07779 297052. *Clubs:* Oxford and Cambridge, Victory Services.

**LOUGHLIN, Prof. Martin,** FBA 2011; Professor of Public Law, London School of Economics and Political Science, since 2000 (Head, Department of Law, 2009–12); *b* Birtley, Co. Durham, 16 July 1954; *s* of Martin Loughlin and Ann Loughlin (née Casey); *m* 1982, Christine Foley; two *d*. *Educ:* St Bede's Sch., Lanchester; London Sch. of Econs and Pol Sci. (LLB 1975); Univ. of Warwick (LLM 1977); Law Sch., Harvard Univ. (LLM 1977). Lecturer: Osgoode Hall Law Sch., York Univ., Toronto, 1977–78; in Law, Univ. of Warwick, 1978–84; in Law, LSE, 1984–88; John Millar Prof. of Public Law, Univ. of Glasgow, 1988–91; Prof. of Law, Univ. of Manchester, 1991–2000 (Dean of Faculty, 1998–2000). Leverhulme Trust Maj. Res. Fellow, 2000–02; Fellow, Wissenschaftskolleg zu Berlin, 2007–08; Law and Public Affairs Fellow, Princeton Univ., 2012–13; Eur. Inst. for Advanced Study Sen. Fellow, Freiburg Inst. of Advanced Studies, Freiburg Univ., 2016–17; MacCormick Fellow, Edinburgh Univ., 2019. Hon. LLD Edinburgh, 2015. *Publications:* Local Government in the Modern State, 1986; Public Law and Political Theory, 1992; Administrative Accountability in Local Government, 1992; Legality and Locality: the role of law in central-local government relations, 1996; Sword and Scales: an examination of the relationship between law and politics, 2000; The Idea of Public Law, 2003; Foundations of Public Law, 2010; The British Constitution: a very short introduction, 2013; Political Jurisprudence, 2017. *Address:* Law Department, London School of Economics and Political Science, Houghton Street, WC2A 2AE. *T:* (020) 7849 4642. *E:* m.loughlin@lse.ac.uk.

**LOUGHRAN, Sir Gerald (Finbar),** KCB 2002; Head, Northern Ireland Civil Service, 2000–02; *b* 22 Feb. 1942; *m* Gemma, (Her Honour Judge Gemma Loughran); one *s* one *d* (and one *s* decd). *Educ:* St Malachy's Coll., Belfast; QUB (BSc (Econ)). Northern Ireland Civil Service: posts in Dept of Econ. Develt and Dept of Envmt; Perm. Sec., Dept of Econ. Develt, 1991–2000. Director: Baird Gp, 2003–; Irish Inst., Louvain, 2003–. Mem. Bd, Educn Authy for NI, 2015–. Hon. Prof., QUB. Hon. DLitt Ulster, 2004.

**LOUGHRAN, James,** CBE 2010; conductor; *b* 30 June 1931; *s* of James and Agnes Loughran; *m* 1st, 1961, Nancy Coggon (marr. diss. 1983; she *d* 1996); one *s* (and one *s* decd); 2nd, 1985, Ludmila (née Navratil). *Educ:* St Aloysius' Coll., Glasgow; Bonn, Amsterdam and Milan. FRNCM 1976; FRSAMD 1983. 1st Prize, Philharmonia Orchestra's Conducting Competition, 1961. Associate Conductor, Bournemouth SO, 1962–65; Principal Conductor: BBC Scottish SO, 1965–71; Bamberg SO, 1979–83; Prin. Conductor and Musical Advr, 1971–83, Conductor Laureate, 1983–91, Hallé Orchestra; Musical Dir, English Opera Gp, 1966 (Festivals of Drottningholm, Versailles and Aldeburgh); Chief Conductor, 1996–2003, Principal Guest Conductor, 2003–11, Aarhus SO, Denmark. Guest conductor of principal orchestras of Europe, America, Australasia and Japan; conducted opera at Sadler's Wells, Royal Opera House, Scottish Opera, Netherlands Opera and Montpellier Opera; Guest Conductor, Stockholm Philharmonic, 1977–92; Guest Conductor, 1980–, Permanent Guest Conductor, 1993–, Hon. Conductor, 2006, Japan Philharmonic SO; Chief Guest Conductor, BBC Welsh SO, 1987–90. Internat. festivals and tours with Bamberg and Hallé orchestras, as well as Munich Philharmonic, BBC Symphony, Stockholm Philharmonic, London Philharmonic and Scottish Chamber orchestras; conductor, BBC Proms, 1965–89, incl. 5 last nights. Many recordings, including complete Beethoven, Brahms and Elgar symphonies. Gold Disc, EMI, 1983. Freeman, City of London, 1991; Liveryman, Musicians' Co., 1992. Hon. DMus: Sheffield, 1983; RSAMD, 2005. *Address:* 18 Hatfield Drive, Glasgow G12 0YA.

**LOUGHRAN, Rear-Adm. Terence William,** CB 1997; Chief Executive, Sabrage Enterprises, since 1998; conference chairman and after dinner speaker; *b* Newcastle-upon-Tyne, 27 March 1943; parents decd; *m* (marr. diss. 1988); one *s* two *d*; *m* 1995, Philippa Mary Vernon. *Educ:* Devonport High Sch.; Britannia Royal Naval Coll. FRAeS 1997. Qualified as: rotary wing pilot, 1967; flying instructor, 1971; graduated Canadian Forces Comd and Staff Coll., 1976; i/c 706 Naval Air Sqdn, 1976–77; Comdr 1979; i/c HMS Phoebe, 1980–81; Executive Officer: HMS Bristol, 1983–84; HMS Intrepid, 1984–85; Captain 1986; i/c HMS Gloucester and Comdr Armilla Patrol, Arabian Gulf Task Unit, 1986–88; Dep. Dir, Internat. Affairs in Naval Staff Duties, 1988–90; Dir, Naval Manpower Planning, 1990–92; i/c HMS Ark Royal and Comdr, Grapple Adriatic Task Gp, 1993–94; Rear-Adm., 1995; Flag Officer, Naval Aviation, 1995–98. Mem., Rona Trust, 1991– (Skipper Emeritus, 2004); Chairman of Trustees: FAA Mus., 2005–15; Fly Navy Heritage Trust, 2005–15 (Hon. Life Vice Pres., 2015); Founder Mem. and Trustee, Nat. Mus. of the RN, 2008–15. Gov., Countess Gytha Sch., 1996–2005. *Publications:* (contrib.) Royal United Services Inst. Jl, Defence Mgt Jl. *Recreations:* sailing, motor cycling, spinning yarns. *Address:* Court Lodge, St Margarets Road, Tintinhull, Somerset BA22 8PL. *T:* and *Fax:* (01935) 824298. *E:* terry@sabrage.com. *Clubs:* Royal Navy; Travellers (Newcastle); Yeovil Beefsteak and Kidney Pudding.

**LOUGHREY, (Stephen Victor) Patrick;** Warden, Goldsmiths, University of London, 2010–19; *b* 29 Dec. 1955; *s* of Eddie Loughrey and Mary Loughrey (née Griffin); *m* 1978, Patricia Kelly; one *s* two *d*. *Educ:* Loreto Coll., Milford; Univ. of Ulster (BA); Queen's Univ. (MA). Res. student, Trent Univ., Canada, 1977; teacher, St Colm's Draperstown, 1978–84; BBC: Producer, Educn, 1984–88; Hd, Educnl Broadcasting, 1988–91; Hd of Progs, NI, 1991–94; Controller, NI, 1994–2000; Dir, Nations and Regions, 2000–09. Fellow, Radio Acad., 2004–. Trustee, Teaching Awards Trust, 2008–12. Jt Editor, Ulster Local Studies, 1988–91. FRSA. *Publications:* People of Ireland, 1988. *Recreations:* walking, talking. *Clubs:* Athenæum, Century.

**LOUGHTON, David Clifford,** CBE 2010; Chief Executive: The Royal Wolverhampton Hospitals NHS Trust, since 2004; National Institute for Health Research (West Midlands), since 2014; Chair, West Midlands Cancer Alliance, since 2018; *b* 28 Jan. 1954; *s* of late Clifford Loughton and Hazel Loughton; *m* 1986, Deborah Wellington (marr. diss. 2015); one *s* one *d*. *Educ:* Roxet Manor Sch., Harrow; tech. colls in Harrow, Watford and Southall. MIHospE 1974; MIPlantE 1976, TEng (CEI) 1978; MHSM 1993. Asst hosp. engr, Hillingdon AHA, 1974–76; hosp. engr, Herts AHA, 1976–78; Dir and Gen. Manager, Ducost Ltd, 1978–83; Divl Manager, GEC Electrical Projects, 1984–86; Chief Exec., Walsgrave Hosps, subseq. Univ. Hosps Coventry and Warwicks, NHS Trust, 1986–2002; Develt Dir, InHealth Gp, 2002–04. Chm., Coventry and Warwicks Educn and Trng Consortium, 1996–2001; Member: NHS Confedn Nat. Council, 2007–; Adv. Bd, NHS Nat. Inst. for Health Res., 2007–. Hon Dr Wolverhampton, 2019. *Recreations:* home improvements, walking, sport. *Address:* The Royal Wolverhampton Hospitals NHS Trust, Hollybush House, New Cross Hospital, Wolverhampton WV10 0QP. *T:* (01902) 695951.

**LOUGHTON, Timothy Paul,** FSA; MP (C) East Worthing and Shoreham, since 1997; *b* 30 May 1962; *s* of late Rev. Michael Loughton and Pamela Dorothy Loughton (née Brandon); *m* 1992, Elizabeth Juliet MacLauchlan; one *s* two *d*. *Educ:* Priory Sch., Lewes; Univ. of Warwick (BA 1st cl. Hons); Clare Coll., Cambridge. Joined Montagu Loebl Stanley, then Fleming Private Asset Mgt, 1984, Dir 1992–2000. Formerly: Member: Wandsworth CHC; Substance Misuse Cttee, Wandsworth HA; Battersea Sector Policing Gp; Vice-Chm., Wandsworth Alcohol Gp. Joined Conservative Party, 1977; various posts in local assocs in Lewes, Warwick Univ., Cambridge Univ. and Battersea, 1978–91; Dep. Chm., Battersea Cons. Assoc., 1994–96. Contested (C) Sheffield Brightside, 1992. Opposition spokesman: for envmt, transport and the regions, 2000–01; for health, 2001–07; for children, 2003–10; Parly Under-Sec. of State for Children and Families, DFE, 2010–12. Member: Finance Bill Standing Cttee, 1997–98; Envmtl Audit Select Cttee, 1997–2001; Eur. Standing Cttee C, 1999–2001; Jt House Cttee on Financial Services and Markets Bill, 1999; Home Affairs Select Cttee, 2014–; Treasurer: Parly Maritime Gp, 1997–2008; Parly Animal Welfare Gp, 2001–07; Chairman: Cons. Disability Gp, 1998–2006; Parly Archaeology Gp, 2013– (Treas., 2002–10); Jt Chm., Parly Mental Health Gp, 2005–10; All Party Parliamentary Groups: Vice Chairman: Child Protection, 2013–17; Youth; Digital Crime; Missing Persons; Ethiopia; Looked After Children; Parents and Families; Foetal Alcohol; Chairman: Wholesale Financial Mkts, 2005–10; British Mus.; Tibet; 1001 Critical Days; Wine and Spirits; Co-Chairman: Archaeology; Children; Mindfulness; Secretary: Switzerland; Young People and Social Technol. Mem., Exec. Cttee, Inter Parly Union (UK), 2006–10 and 2013–17. Captain, Commons and Lords Hockey Team, 2003–. Member: Sussex Archaeol Soc.; BM Soc. Patron: Positive for Youth Awards; Fatherhood Inst.; Grandparents' Assoc.; St Barnabas Hospice, Worthing; Worthing Hockey Club; campaign for Worthing and Adur to become Fairtrade Town; W Grinstead and Dist. Ploughing and Agricl Soc.; Electric Storm Youth; Canadian Roots UK; Guild Care, Worthing; President: Shoreham and Adur FC; Shoreham Cons. Club; Southwick Camera Club; Lancing Art Club; Vice-Pres., League of Friends, Worthing Hosp.; Ambassador, Ambition. Chm. Trustees, Parent and Infant Partnership. Mem. Ct, Sussex Univ. FSA 2015. *Recreations:* archaeology, classics, wine, ski-ing, tennis, hockey. *Address:* House of Commons, SW1A 0AA.

**LOUIS, Prof. (William) Roger,** Hon. CBE 1999; DLitt; FBA; Kerr Professor of English History and Culture, since 1985, Distinguished Teaching Professor, since 1998, University of Texas at Austin; Supernumerary Fellow, St Antony's College, Oxford, 1986–96 (Hon. Fellow, since 1996); *b* 8 May 1936; *s* of Henry Edward and Bena May Louis; *m* 1st, 1960, Patricia Ann Leonard; one *s* one *d*; 2nd, 1983, Dagmar Cecilia Friedrich. *Educ:* Univ. of Oklahoma (Phi Beta Kappa, BA 1959; Dist. Alumnus, 2013); Harvard (Woodrow Wilson Fellow; MA 1960); St Antony's Coll., Oxford (Marshall Scholar; DPhil 1962); DLitt Oxon 1979; Cert. Arabic, Oman, 2014. FRHistS 1984; Corresp. FBA 1993. Asst and Associate Prof., Yale, 1962–70; Humanities Research Center, University of Texas: Prof. of History and Curator, Historical Collections, 1970–85; Dir, British Studies, 1975–; Teaching Awards, 1984, 1992, 1993, 1998; National Endowment Humanities: Sen. Fellow, 1974–75; Dir, Seminars, 1985–2000. Guggenheim Fellow, 1979–80; Vis. Fellow, 1979–80, 2004, Chichele Lectr, 1990, 2002, 2003, 2006, 2010, All Souls Coll., Oxford; Vis. Fellow, Balliol Coll., Oxford, 2005; Fellow/Lecturer: Churchill Coll., Cambridge, 1985; Brookings Instn, 1989; LSE, 1992; Woodrow Wilson Internat. Center for Scholars, 1994–95, 2000 (Global Fellow, 2012–); lectures: Cust, Univ. of Nottingham, 1995; British Acad. Inaugural Elie Kedourie Meml, 1996; Churchill Meml, Westminster Coll., Fulton, Mo, 1998; Antonius, Oxford Univ., 2002; Leonard Stein, Oxford, 2005; Strelitz, Tel Aviv, 2008; Bancroft Meml, US Naval Acad., 2016; Weizmann Meml, 2016. Dist. Visitor, Dept of Hist., Univ. of Peking, 1998; Dist. Vis. Prof., Amer. Univ. in Cairo, 2001. Founding Dir, Nat. History Center, 2001–13. Chm., US Dept of State Histl Adv. Cttee, 2001–08; Member: Scholars' Council, 2006–16, Kluge Chair, 2010, Liby of Congress; Amer. Acad. of Arts and Scis, 2011. Pres., Amer. Historical Assoc., 2001–02. Trustee, British Empire Mus., Bristol, 2005–13. Editor, British Documents on the End of Empire, 1988–2008; Editor-in-Chief, Oxford History of the British Empire, 1992–. Hon. DPhil Westminster Coll., 1998. Prof. of the Year, 2009, Civitatis Award, 2018, Univ. of Texas at Austin; Benson Medal, Royal Soc. of Literature, 2015. *Publications:* Ruanda-Urundi, 1963; Germany's Lost Colonies, 1967; (ed with P. Gifford) Britain and Germany in Africa, 1967; (with J. Stengers) Congo Reform Movement, 1968; British Strategy in the Far East, 1971; (ed with P. Gifford) France and Britain in Africa, 1971; (ed) National Security and International Trusteeship in the Pacific, 1972; (ed) A. J. P. Taylor and his Critics, 1972; (ed) Imperialism: the Robinson and Gallagher controversy, 1976; Imperialism at Bay, 1977; (ed with W. S. Livingston) Australia, New Zealand and the Pacific Islands, 1979; (ed with P. Gifford) The Transfer of

Power in Africa, 1982; The British Empire in the Middle East 1945–51, 1984 (Amer. Hist. Assoc. Prize); (ed with R. Stookey) The End of the Palestine Mandate, 1986; (ed with H. Bull) The Special Relationship, 1986; (ed with P. Gifford) Decolonization in Africa, 1988; (ed with J. A. Bill) Musaddiq, Nationalism and Oil, 1988; (ed with R. Owen) Suez 1956, 1989; (ed with R. Fernea) The Iraqi Revolution, 1991; In the Name of God Go! Leo Amery and the British Empire, 1992; (ed with R. Blake) Churchill, 1993; (ed) Adventures with Britannia: personalities, politics and culture in Britain, 1995; (ed) More Adventures with Britannia, 1998; (ed with Michael Howard) The Oxford History of the Twentieth Century, 1998; (ed with J. M. Brown) The Oxford History of the British Empire, vol. IV: the twentieth century, 1999; (ed with Roger Owen) A Revolutionary Year: the Middle East in 1958, 2002; (ed) Still More Adventures with Britannia, 2003; (ed) Yet More Adventures with Britannia, 2005; (ed) Burnt Orange Britannia, 2005; Ends of British Imperialism, 2006; (ed) Penultimate Adventures with Britannia, 2007; Ultimate Adventures with Britannia, 2009; Resurgent Adventures with Britannia, 2011; (ed with Avi Shlaim) The 1967 Arab-Israeli War: origins and consequences, 2012; (ed) History of Oxford University Press, 1896–1970, 2013; (ed) Irrepressible Adventures with Britannia, 2013; (ed) Resplendent Adventures with Britannia, 2015; (ed) Effervescent Adventures with Britannia, 2017; Indispensable Reading: 1001 books from Arabian Nights to Zola, 2018; (ed) Serendipitous Adventures with Britannia, 2019; *festschrift*: (ed Robert King and Robin Kilson) The Statecraft of British Imperialism: essays in honor of Wm Roger Louis, 1999. *Recreation*: a German wife. *Address*: Humanities Research Center, University of Texas, Austin, TX 78712, USA. *Clubs*: Reform; Century (NY), Metropolitan (Washington).

**LOUISY, Dame (Calliopa) Pearlette,** Grand Cross, Order of St Lucia, 1997; GCMG 1999; Governor General, St Lucia, 1997–2017; *b* 8 June 1946; *d* of Rita Louisy. *Educ*: St Joseph's Convent; Univ. of West Indies (BA); Université Laval, Quebec (MA); Univ. of Bristol (PhD 1994). Principal, St Lucia A-Level Coll., 1981–86; Sir Arthur Lewis Community College: Dean, 1986–94; Vice Principal, 1994–95; Principal, 1996–97. Paul Harris Fellow, 2001. FRSA 1999. Hon. LLD: Bristol, 1999; Sheffield, 2003; Univ. of W Indies, 2011. DStJ 2001; DSG 2002. Internat. Woman of the Year, 1998, 2001; Woman of Great Esteem, QKingdom Ministries, 2003; Caribbean Luminary Award, 2007; Woman of Distinction Global Leadership Award, 2016. *Recreations*: horticulture, performing arts, reading.

**LOUSTAU-LALANNE, Bernard Michel;** barrister; international copyright consultant; *b* 20 June 1938; *s* of Michel Loustau-Lalanne, OBE, and Madeleine (*née* Boullé); *m* 1974, Debbie Elizabeth Grieve (*née* Temple-Brown) (marr. diss. 1982); one *d*. *Educ*: Seychelles Coll.; St Mary's Coll., Southampton; Imperial Coll., London. Called to the Bar, Middle Temple, London, 1969. Assistant Inspector, Northern Rhodesia Police, 1962–64; Crown Counsel, Seychelles, 1970–72; Sen. State Counsel and Official Notary, 1972–76; Attorney-General, Seychelles, 1976–78; High Comr for Seychelles, in London, 1978–80; concurrently Seychelles Ambassador to USA, and Seychelles Perm. Rep. to UN; Internat. Rep., PRS, 1980–90; Sec.-Gen., Eur. Fedn of Mgt Consulting Assocs, 1991–92. *Recreations*: international affairs, French literature, theatre, tennis. *Address*: 2 Albert Mansions, Luxborough Street, W1U 5BQ.

**LOUTH, 17th Baron** *cr* 1541 (Ire.); **Jonathan Oliver Plunkett;** *b* 4 Nov. 1952; *s* of 16th Baron Louth and Angela Patricia Plunkett (*née* Cullinane); *S* father, 2013; *m* 1981, Jennifer Hodgetts (separated 2000; marr. diss. 2015); one *s* one *d*. *Educ*: De La Salle Coll., Jersey; Hautlieu Sch., Jersey; Univ. of Hull (BSc 1975). MIET. Diamond Jubilee Medal, 2012. *Heir*: *s* Hon. Matthew Oliver Plunkett [*b* 22 Dec. 1982; *m* 2008, Jenna Maree Baker; two *s*]. *Club*: St Helier Yacht (Jersey).

**LOUTH, Very Rev. Prof. Andrew,** DD; FBA 2010; FSA; Professor of Patristic and Byzantine Studies, Durham University, 1998–2010, now Emeritus; *b* Louth, Lincs, 11 Nov. 1944; *s* of Cecil George Louth and Mary Louth; *m* 1st, 1966, Janet Sisson (marr. diss. 1990); one *s* two *d*; 2nd, 1991, Carol Harrison (marr. diss. 2010); one *s*. *Educ*: Queen Elizabeth Grammar Sch., Wakefield; Waterloo Grammar Sch., Liverpool; St Catharine's Coll., Cambridge (BA 1965); Univ. of Edinburgh (MTh 1968); Univ. of Oxford (DD 1991). Fellow and Chaplain, Worcester Coll., Oxford, 1970–85; Goldsmiths College, London: Sen. Lectr, 1985–89, Reader, 1989–91, in Religious Studies; Prof., 1992–96; Reader in Greek Patristics, Durham Univ., 1996–98. Vis. Prof. of Eastern Orthodox Theol., Free Univ., Amsterdam, 2010–14 (Hon. Fellow, Faculty of Theol., 2015–). Ordained priest, Russian Orthodox Ch, Moscow Patriarchate, 2003; archpriest, 2014. Pres., Ecclesiastical Hist. Soc., 2009–10. FSA 2001. *Publications*: The Origins of the Christian Mystical Tradition: from Plato to Denys, 1981, 2nd edn 2007; Discerning the Mystery: an essay on the nature of theology, 1983; Denys the Areopagite, 1989, 2nd edn 2001; The Wilderness of God, 1991, 2nd edn 2003; Maximus the Confessor, 1996; St John Damascene: tradition and originality in Byzantine theology, 2002; Greek East and Latin West: the Church AD 681–1071, 2007; Introducing Eastern Orthodox Theology, 2013; Modern Orthodox Thinkers: from the Philokalia to the present, 2015. *Recreations*: reading, playing and listening to music, walking. *Address*: 13 Uplands Road, Darlington DL3 7SZ. *T*: (01325) 481080. *E*: louth.andrew@gmail.com.

**LOVAT, 18th Lord** (S) *cr* 1458–1464 (*de facto* 16th Lord, 18th but for the attainder); **Simon Fraser;** Baron (UK) 1837; commodities analyst, Carmignac Group, since 2011; *b* 13 Feb. 1977; *er s* of Hon. Simon Augustine Fraser, Master of Lovat (*d* 1994) and of Virginia Fraser (who *m* 1998, Frank Robert Johnson, journalist (*d* 2006)), *d* of David Grose; *S* grandfather, 1995; *m* 2016, Petra, *d* of Baron Palumbo, *qv*. *Educ*: Harrow; Edinburgh Univ. *Heir*: *b* Jack Fraser, Master of Lovat, *b* 22 Aug. 1984.

**LOVE, Andrew;** *b* 21 March 1949; *s* of late James Love and Olive Love (*née* Mills); *m* 1983, Ruth, *d* of late Jack and Esther Rosenthal. *Educ*: Strathclyde Univ. (BSc Hons). FCIS. Parly Officer, Co-operative Party, 1993–97. Mem. (Lab), Haringey LBC, 1980–86 (Chairman: Finance, 1984–85; Housing, 1985–86). Mem., NE Thames RHA, 1988–90. Contested (Lab and Co-op) Edmonton, 1992. MP (Lab and Co-op) Edmonton, 1997–2015. PPS to Minister of State: DoH, 2001–03; for Industry and the Regions, DTI, 2003–05; for Local Govt, 2008–10. Member: Public Accounts Cttee, H of C, 1997–2001; Deregulation Select Cttee, 1999–2001; Regulatory Reform Select Cttee, 2001–05; Treasury Select Cttee, 2005–15. Chairman: All Party Bldg Socs and Financial Mutuals Gp (formerly All Party Building Socs Gp), 1997–2002; All Party Lebanon Gp, 2005–15; PLP Backbench Treasury Cttee, 2010–15; Co-Chairman: All Party Homelessness and Housing Needs Gp, 2000–08; All Party Sri Lanka Gp, 2004–15 (Sec., 1999–2004); Vice Chm., All Party Small Businesses Gp, 2010–15 (Sec., 2000–05; Chm., 2005–10); Sec., All Party Opera Gp, 2010–15 (Vice Chm., 2005–10). Trustee, Industrial Common Ownership Finance, 1991–; Chairman: Citizens Advice Haringey, 2015–; Peter Bedford Housing Assoc., 2015–. FRSA. *Publications*: (contrib.) Parliament in the 21st Century, 2004; (contrib.) More Homes for Rent: stimulating supply to match growing demand, 2006. *Recreations*: golf, opera, reading, history. *Address*: Flat 2, Cumberland House, 16 Highbury Crescent, N5 1RT. *E*: andylove1949@gmail.com.

**LOVE, Graham Carvell,** FCA; Senior Adviser (formerly Principal), Chertoff Group, since 2010; *b* 18 March 1954; *s* of Peter and Nancy Love; *m* (marr. diss.); one *s* one *d*. *Educ*: Fitzwilliam Coll., Cambridge (BA Hons Eng. 1975; MA). FCA 1979; CCIM 2007; FRAeS 2008. Gp Financial Controller, Shandwick plc, 1988–92; Finance Dir, Defence Res. Agency, 1992–96; Chief Exec., Comax Secure Business Services, 1996–99; Chief Financial Officer, 2001–05, Chief Exec., 2005–09, QinetiQ. Chairman: Racing Green Cars, 1999–; LGC Science Gp, 2010–16; Eversholt Rail Gp, 2011–14; 2e2 Gp, 2011–13; SLR Consulting, 2012–18; Xendo BV, 2017–18; TVR Parts Ltd, 2017–; Royal Mint, 2019–. *Recreations*: historic motor racing, shooting, ski-ing, sailing. *Address*: 39 Smith Street, SW3 4EP. *E*: gclove15@yahoo.co.uk.

**LOVE, Prof. Philip Noel,** CBE 1983; Vice Chancellor, University of Liverpool, 1992–2002; *b* 25 Dec. 1939; *o s* of Thomas Isaac and Ethel Violet Love; *m* 1st, 1963, Isabel Leah (*d* 1993), *yr d* of Innes Taylor and Leah Wallace Mearns; three *s*; 2nd, 1995, Isobel, *widow* of David Pardey. *Educ*: Aberdeen Grammar Sch.; Aberdeen Univ. (MA 1961, LLB 1963). Admitted Solicitor in Scotland, 1963; Advocate in Aberdeen, 1963–; Partner, Campbell Connon, Solicitors, Aberdeen, 1963–74, Consultant, 1974–2004. University of Aberdeen: Prof. of Conveyancing and Professional Practice of Law, 1974–92; Dean, Faculty of Law, 1979–82, 1991–92; Vice Principal, 1986–90. Law Society of Scotland: Mem. Council, 1975–86; Examr, 1975–83 (Chm. Examrs, 1977–80); Vice-Pres., 1980–81; Pres., 1981–82. Local Chm., Rent Assessment Panel for Scotland, 1972–92; Chairman: Sec. of State for Scotland's Expert Cttee on house purchase and sale, 1982–84; Scottish Conveyancing and Executry Services Bd, 1991–96; Vice-Pres., Scottish Law Agents Soc., 1970; Member: Jt Standing Cttee on Legal Educn in Scotland, 1976–85 (Chm., 1976–80); Rules Council, Court of Session, 1968–92; Council, Internat. Bar Assoc., 1983–87 (Vice-Chm., Legal Educn Div., 1983–87); Jt Ethical Cttee, Grampian Health Bd, 1984–92 (Vice-Chm., 1985; Chm., 1986–92); Scottish Law Commn, 1986–95; Council, CVCP, then UUK, 1996–2002. Chairman: Univs and Colls Employers Assoc., 1995–2002; NW Univs Assoc., 2001–02. Chm., Aberdeen Home for Widowers' Children, 1971–92. Pres., Aberdeen Grammar Sch. Former Pupils' Club, 1987–88. Hon. Sheriff of Grampian, Highland and Islands, 1978–. Chm., Registers of Scotland Customer Adv. Gp, 1990–92. Trustee: Grampian and Islands Family Trust, 1988–92; St George's Hall Trust, 1996–2013; Merseyside Police and High Sheriff's Charitable Trust, 1998–2009; Liverpool Charity and Voluntary Services (formerly Council of Social Service), 2003–11; Liverpool Philharmonic Foundn, 2005–11. Chairman: Mersey Partnership, 1995–98; NW Regl Assembly, Knowledge Economy Gp, 2000–02; Mem., NW Sci. Council, 2001–02. Gov., Inst. of Occupational Medicine Ltd, 1990–2013; Gov., Liverpool Coll., 2003–10; Mem., Liverpool Coll. Ind. Schs Trust, 2013–17. Dir, Rising Stars Growth Fund Ltd, 2001–05. Mem., Editl Consultative Bd for Scotland, Butterworth & Co. (Publishers) Ltd, 1990–95. DL 1997, High Sheriff, 2007–08, Merseyside. FAcSS (AcSS 2002). Hon. Fellow, Liverpool John Moores Univ., 2002. Hon. LLD: Abertay Dundee, 1996; Aberdeen, 1997; Liverpool, 2002; Hon. DLitt Chester, 2013. *Address*: 111 King's Gate, Aberdeen AB15 4ES. *T*: (01224) 048936. *Clubs*: New (Edinburgh); Aberdeen Grammar School Former Pupils' Club Centre, Royal Northern and University (Aberdeen).
*See also* S. A. Love.

**LOVE, Rear Adm. Robert Thomas,** CB 2011; OBE 2004; FREng; Chief Executive Officer, AE2A Maritime Engineering and Programme Management Consultancy, since 2018; Chief Naval Engineer Officer, 2008–11; *b* 21 July 1955; *s* of late Bill and Ellen Love; *m* 1983, Jean Francis; two *s* one *d*. *Educ*: Ashton-in-Makerfield Grammar Sch.; RNEC (BSc 1978). CEng 1984; FIMarEST 1987; CMarEng 2006; FREng 2011; FAPM 2007; FIET 2011. HM Yacht Britannia, 1982–84; Comdr E HMS Ark Royal, 1992–94; Desk Officer, DN Plans, MoD, 1994–96; SMEO to Flag Officer Sea Trng, 1997–98; Captain 1998; Team Leader Major Warships, 2001; recovered HMS Nottingham from grounding off coast of Australia, 2003; Cdre 2003; Defence Advr to Australia, 2003–06; Team Leader, Carrier Vessel Future and Maritime Airborne Surveillance and Control, later Capital Ships Dir, incl. Future Carriers, 2007–08, Dir Ships, 2008–11, Defence Equipment and Support, MoD. Dep. CEO, Babcock Pty Ltd (Australia), 2011–17; consultant, BMT, 2017–18. Pres., RN Golf Assoc., 2009–11. Mem., MENSA. *Publications*: papers at various confs. *Recreations*: cricket, golf, Rugby, fitness, food, wine, music. *Address*: 22A Edith Street, Leichhardt, Sydney, NSW 2040, Australia. *Club*: MCC.

**LOVE, Prof. Rosalind Claire,** PhD; Elrington and Bosworth Professor of Anglo-Saxon, University of Cambridge, since 2019; Fellow of Robinson College, Cambridge, since 1993; *b* Chipping Sodbury, 29 June 1966; *d* of John Love and Pamela Love; *m* 1998, Nicholas Moir; one *s* one *d*. *Educ*: Haberdashers' Monmouth Sch. for Girls; St John's Coll., Cambridge (BA Hons Classics and Anglo-Saxon, Norse, and Celtic 1984; PhD Anglo-Saxon, Norse, and Celtic 1992). University of Cambridge: Lectr, Dept of Anglo-Saxon, Norse, and Celtic, 2000–07; Sen. Lectr, 2008–12; Reader in Insular Latin, 2012–19. Gen. Editor, Oxford Medieval Texts, 2004–; Mem., Editl Bd, Anglo-Saxon England, 2012–. *Publications*: Three Anglo-Latin Saints' Lives, 1996; Goscelin of Saint-Bertin: the hagiography of the female saints of Ely, 2004; (with S. DeGregorio) trans., Bede, On First Samuel, 2019. *Recreations*: family, choral singing, classical music concert-going, reading, Street Pastor. *Address*: Department of Anglo-Saxon, Norse and Celtic, University of Cambridge, 9 West Road, Cambridge CB3 9DP. *E*: rcl10@cam.ac.uk; Robinson College, Cambridge CB3 9AN.

**LOVE, Prof. Seth,** PhD; FRCP, FRCPath; Professor of Neuropathology, University of Bristol, since 2001; *b* Johannesburg, SA; *s* of Frank and Dora Love; *m* 1978, Lynn Hirschowitz; one *s* one *d*. *Educ*: Univ. of Witwatersrand (MB BCh *cum laude* 1978); Inst. of Neurol., Univ. of London (PhD 1984). MRCP 1980, FRCP 1996; MRCPath 1985, FRCPath 1996. Internships, Johannesburg Gen. Hosp., 1979; Lectr, Inst. of Neurol., 1980–83, Sen. Registrar, 1983–85, Nat. Hosp. for Nervous Diseases, London; Fogarty Fellow, Univ. of Calif, San Diego, 1985–87; Consultant in Neuropathol., 1987–2001, Hon. Consultant in Neuropathol., 2001–, Frenchay Hosp., N Bristol NHS Trust; Hon. Prof. of Neuropathol., Univ. of Bristol, 1995–2001. Dir, MRC Brain Banks UK Network, 2013–. Ed.-in-Chief, Brain Pathol., 2014–. *Publications*: (ed with D. Ellison) Neuropathology, 1998, 3rd edn 2013; (ed) Current Topics in Pathology: neuropathology, 2001; (contrib.) Greenfield's Neuropathology, 7th edn 2002, 9th edn (ed jtly) 2015. *Recreations*: music, walking, cycling, ski-ing. *Address*: Medical School (Translational Health Sciences), University of Bristol, Learning and Research Level 2, Southmead Hospital, Bristol BS10 5NB. *T*: (0117) 414 2402. *E*: seth.love@bris.ac.uk.

**LOVE, Steven Andrew;** QC (Scot.) 2016; *b* Aberdeen, 25 March 1965; *s* of Prof. Philip Noel Love, *qv* and late Isabel Leah Love (*née* Mearns); *m* 1991, Pauline Elizabeth Brooks; two *d*. *Educ*: Robert Gordon's Coll., Aberdeen; Aberdeen Univ. (LLB 1986; DipLP 1987). Trainee Solicitor, Allan McDougall & Co., Solicitors, 1987–89; Asst Solicitor, 1989–94, Partner, 1994–97, Simpson & Marwick, WS; Partner, Ledingham Chalmers, Solicitors, 1997–99; called to the Scottish Bar, 2001. Mem., Scottish Malt Whisky Soc. *Recreations*: hill walking, fishing, golf, wine. *Address*: The Mount, 23 Ferryhills Road, North Queensferry, Fife KY11 1HE. *E*: steve.love@compasschambers.com.

**LOVE, Stuart;** Chief Executive, Westminster City Council, since 2018; b South Africa. Educ: Univ. of Natal (BCom). Director: Economy and Envmt, IoW Council, 2006–14; Place, Southampton CC, 2014–15; Exec. Dir, City Mgt and Communities, Westminster CC, 2015–18. Address: Westminster City Council, Westminster City Hall, 64 Victoria Street, SW1E 6QP.

**LOVEDAY, Mark Antony;** Senior Partner, Cazenove & Co., 1994–2001; b 22 Sept. 1943; s of George Arthur Loveday and Sylvia Mary Loveday; m 1981, Mary Elizabeth Tolmie; one s one d. Educ: Winchester Coll.; Magdalen Coll., Oxford (MA). Cazenove & Co., 1966–2001; Partner, 1974–2001. Chm., Foreign & Colonial Investment Trust PLC, 2002–10 (Dir, 2001–10). Chm., Grosvenor Pension Plan, 2008–15. Trustee: Magdalen Coll. Develt Trust, 1982–2019 (Chm., 2006–17); Grosvenor Estate, 1999–2008; Westminster Foundn, 2008–16. Liveryman, Skinners' Co., 1972 (Mem. Court, 2014–18; Third Warden, 2016, 2018); Dir, Skinners' Almshouse Charity. Fellow, Winchester Coll., 2008–14; Hon. Fellow, Trinity Laban Conservatoire of Music and Dance, 2013. Recreations: golf, trekking. Address: 42 Royal Avenue, SW3 4QF. T: (office) (020) 7730 6335. Clubs: Boodle's, City University, Hurlingham, MCC; Royal St George's Golf.

**LOVEGROVE, Ross Nigel,** RDI 2003; FCSD; Principal, Lovegrove Design Studio, London, since 1990; b 16 Aug. 1958; s of Herbert William John Lovegrove, OBE and Mary Eileen Lovegrove; m 1997, Maria (née Miller); one s. Educ: Manchester Polytech. (BA 1st cl. Industrial Design 1980); Royal Coll. of Art (MDes 1983). FCSD 1990. Designer, Frog Design, W Germany, working on projects, e.g. Walkmans for Sony, computers for Apple Computers, 1980s; Consultant, Knoll Internat., Paris, 1984–87; with Atelier de Nimes, consultants to Cacharel, Louis Vuitton, Hermes and Dupont, etc, 1984–86; London, 1986–: projects for clients including Airbus Industries, Driade, Peugeot, Apple Computers, Issey Miyake, Olympus Cameras, Yamagiwa Corp., Tag Heuer, Hackman, Herman Miller, Japan Airlines, Toyo Ito Architects, Japan, Lasvit, Vondom, and Renault. Has exhibited in MOMA, NY, Guggenheim Mus., NY, Axis Centre, Japan, Pompidou Centre, Paris and Design Mus., London; work in permanent collections including: MOMA, NY; Design Mus., London; Vitra Design Mus., Weil Am Rhein, Basel; solo exhibitions include: Danish Mus. of Decorative Art, Copenhagen; Stockholm; Idee, Tokyo; Yamagiwa Corp., Tokyo; Rheinauen Space, Cologne, 2001; Designosaurs, Segheria, Milan, 2004; Superliquidity, Le Bain Gall., Tokyo, 2005; Endurance, Phillips de Pury New York Chelsea Galls, 2007; Solar Tree, Vienna, 2007; Cellular Automation, Tokyo 2008; Liquid Space, Miami, 2008; Primordial, Istanbul, 2009; Endless, Milan, 2011; UFO, Lille, 2012; Future Primitives, Kortrijk, 2012. Hon. Fellow, UWIC, 2002. Numerous internat. awards, including: D&AD Silver Medal, 1997; Médaille de la Ville de Paris, 1998; George Nelson Award, 1998; iF Industrie Forum Design Award, Hanover, 1999; Good Design Award, ID mag., 2000; G Mark Federal Design Prize, Japan, 2001; Janus, Paris, 2004; World Technol. Prize, San Francisco, World Technol. Network, 2005; Condé Nast Traveller Ecology Prize, 2007; Product Designer of the Year, FX, 2012. Publications: Designing the 21st Century, 1998; (ed) International Design Yearbook, 2002, 2003; Supernatural: the work of Ross Lovegrove, 2004; (contrib.) Designers on Design, 2005. Recreations: evolution, biomimicry, paleontology, materials technology, digital architecture, form related sculpture, travel. Address: Lovegrove Design Studio, 21 Powis Mews, W11 1JN. T: (020) 7229 7104, Fax: (020) 7229 7032. E: general@rosslovegrove.com. Club: Groucho.

**LOVEGROVE, Sir Stephen Augustus,** KCB 2019 (CB 2013); Permanent Secretary, Ministry of Defence, since 2016; b Solihull, 30 Nov. 1966; s of John Lovegrove and Zenia Stewart Lovegrove; m 1997, Kate Constantia Brooke; two d. Educ: Warwick Sch.; Corpus Christi Coll., Oxford (BA 1989). Consultant, Hydra Associates, 1990–94; Man. Dir, Morgan Grenfell, Deutsche Bank, 1995–2004; Dir, Shareholder Exec., DTI, subseq. BERR, 2004–07; Chief Exec., Shareholder Exec., BERR, later BIS, 2007–13; Perm. Sec., DECC, 2013–16. Member, Board: LOCOG, 2007–13; Grosvenor (Britain and Ireland), 2016–. Trustee, CAF, 2010–16. Recreations: bricolage, reading detective stories. Address: Ministry of Defence, Whitehall, SW1A 2HB. Clubs: Brooks's, Tapper's Cricket.

**LOVEJOY, Joseph Reginald;** freelance football writer and author; b 23 June 1951; s of Reginald Henry Lovejoy and Ivy May Lovejoy; m 1st, 1973, Cynthia Turner (marr. diss. 1990); one s one d; 2nd, 1995, Lesley Griffiths. Educ: Bancroft's Sch., Woodford Green; Portsmouth Tech. Coll. (NCTJ Proficiency). Reporter: Kentish Observer, 1969–73; Doncaster Evening Post, 1973; Derby Evening Telegraph, 1973–77; South Wales Echo, 1977–83; Mail on Sunday, 1983–86; Independent, 1986–94; Football Correspondent, Sunday Times, 1994–2009. Publications: Bestie: portrait of a legend, 1998; Sven Goran Eriksson, 2002; (jtly) Giggs: the autobiography, 2005; Glory, Goals, and Greed: 20 years of the Premier League, 2011; The Auschwitz Goalkeeper, 2013. Recreations: reading, watching Rugby. Address: 30 Twmpath Road, Pontypool, Gwent NP4 6AQ. Clubs: Pontypool Rugby Football, Pontypool Working Men's.

**LOVELL, Alan Charles;** DL; FCA; FSA; Chairman, Safestyle, since 2018; Senior Independent Director, SIG plc, since 2018; b Winchester, 19 Nov. 1953; s of William George Lovell and Mary Kerr Lovell (née Briant); m 1982, Hon. Virginia, d of Baron Weatherill, PC; two d. Educ: Winchester Coll.; Jesus Coll., Oxford (MA Lit. Hum. 1976). FCA 1979. Price Waterhouse, 1976–80; Plessey, 1980–89; Finance Dir, 1989–91, Chief Exec., 1991–92, Conder; Finance Dir, 1992–95, Chief Exec., 1995–97, Costain; Finance Dir, 1997–2004, Chief Exec., 2004, Dunlop Slazenger; Chief Executive: Jarvis, 2004–06; Infinis, 2006–09; Chm., 2011–15, Chief Exec., 2011–13, Tamar Energy. Chairman: Sepura plc, 2016–17; Flow Gp, 2017–18. Chair, Consumer Council for Water, 2015–19. Non-executive Member: Council, Lloyd's, 2007–16; Assoc. of Lloyd's Members, 2006– (Chm., 2012–). Gov., Univ. of Winchester, 2009– (Chm., 2016–). Chairman: Blue Lamp Trust, 2010–16; Hants Cultural Trust, 2014–; Trustee: Mary Rose Trust, 2006– (Chm., 2015–); Winchester Cathedral, 2010– (Mem. Council, 2008–17). FSA 2009. High Sheriff, 2010–11, DL 2012, Hants. Recreations: sport, especially Real tennis, opera and theatre, forestry and gardening. Address: The Palace House, Bishop's Lane, Bishop's Waltham, Hants SO32 1DP. T: (01489) 892838, 07767 874052. E: alan.lovell@philtd.com. Clubs: Garrick, All England Lawn Tennis, MCC, Queen's.

**LOVELL, Dr (Julian Patrick) Bryan,** OBE 1989; CGeol; Senior Research Fellow in Earth Sciences, University of Cambridge, since 1996; President, Geological Society of London, 2010–12; b Bath, 10 Feb. 1942; s of Sir (Alfred Charles) Bernard Lovell, OBE, FRS and Mary Joyce Lovell; m 1964, Caroline Stansfield; two s one d. Educ: King's Sch., Macclesfield; New Coll., Oxford (BA Geol. 1963; MSc Geol. 1964); Harvard Univ. (PhD Geol. 1968). CGeol 1991. Teaching Fellow, Harvard Univ., 1965–68; Lectr in Geol., Univ. of Edinburgh, 1969–81; BP Exploration: Chief Sedimentologist, 1981–84; Exploration Manager, Ireland, 1984–87; Gen. Manager, Ireland, 1987–89; Internat. Exploration Manager, with responsibility for ME and N Africa, 1989–92; Manager, Petrotechnical Resource Develt, 1992–94; Hd, Recruitment, BP Gp, 1994–96. Chm., Petrological Services Edinburgh Ltd, 1980–81; Dir, Lovell Consultants Hertford Ltd, 2002–. Mem. Bd, British Geol Survey, 1996–2000. Energy spokesman, Scottish Liberal Party, 1978–79. Contested (L) Edinburgh S, 1979. Publications: The British Isles Through Geological Time: a northward drift, 1977; Challenged by Carbon: the oil industry and climate change, 2009; contrib. articles to learned jls. Recreations: cricket, gardening, racing, beer, poetry, Hertfordshire Puddingstone. Address: 7 The Avenue, Hertford SG14 3DQ. T: and Fax: (01992) 551737. E: lovell@esc.cam.ac.uk.

**LOVELL-BADGE, Dr Robin Howard,** CBE 2018; FRS 2001; Group Leader, Stem Cell Biology and Developmental Genetics, Francis Crick Institute, since 2015; b 14 June 1953; s of Don Lovell-Badge and Eileen Betty Cator (née Daniels). Educ: Norwich Sch. (King Edward VI); University Coll. London (BSc Hons Zool. 1975; PhD Embryol. 1978). Postdoctoral research: Dept of Genetics, Univ. of Cambridge, 1978–81; EMBO Long Term Fellow, Institut Jacques Monod, Univ. Paris VII, 1981–82; Member: Scientific Staff, MRC Mammalian Develt Unit, UCL, 1982–88; MRC Scientific Staff, NIMR, 1988–2015; Hd, Div. of Develt Genetics, then Div. of Stem Cell Biol. and Develtl Genetics, MRC NIMR, 1993–2015. Hon. Sen. Res. Fellow, subseq. Hon. Prof., Dept of Biomedical Scis (formerly Dept of Anatomy and Develtl Biol.), UCL, 1994–; University of Hong Kong: Vis. Prof., Dept of Biochem., 1996–; Dist. Vis. Prof., 2009–15; Special Vis. Prof., 2015–. Pres., Inst. of Animal Tech., 2006–. Mem., EMBO, 1993. FMedSci 1999. Louis Jeantet Prize for Medicine, 1995; Amory Prize, Amer. Acad. Arts and Scis, 1996; Wilhelm Feldberg Prize, Feldberg Foundn, 2008; Waddington Medal, British Soc. for Develtl Biol., 2010. Publications: contribs to learned jls. Recreations: drawing, painting, sculpture, cooking, good food and wine. Address: Francis Crick Institute, 1 Midland Road, NW1 1AT. E: robin.lovell-badge@crick.ac.uk.

**LOVELL-PANK, Dorian Christopher;** QC 1993; a Chairman, Police Appeals Tribunals (formerly Police Discipline Appeal Tribunals), since 1991; b 15 Feb. 1946; s of late Christopher Edwin Lovell-Pank, Madrid and Jean Alston de Oliva-Day (née McPherson), Cape Town and Buenos Aires; m 1983, Diana, d of late Michael Cady Byford and Sonia Byford, Claret Hall, Clare, Suffolk; one s one d. Educ: Downside; Colegio Sarmiento, Buenos Aires; LSE; Inns of Court Sch. of Law. Called to the Bar: Inner Temple, 1971, Bencher, 1998; Cayman Is, 2011; Gibraltar, 2013; in practice SE Circuit; Junior, Middlesex Bar Mess, 1977–80; Asst Recorder, 1985–89; Recorder, 1989–2006. Vis. Prof. of Law and Advocacy, Loyola Univ., Chicago, 2018–. Member: Cttee, Criminal Bar Assoc., 1989–2006 (Chm., Internat. Relations Sub-Cttee, 1993–2006); Gen. Council of Bar, 1989–92, 1998–2005 (Chm., Internat. Relations Cttee, 2001–05); Internat. Bar Assoc., 1993– (Mem. Council, 2001–05); Human Rights Inst., 1996– (Mem. Council, 2000–04); British Spanish Law Assoc., 2001–; FCO Pro Bono Lawyers Panel, 2002–. Associate Mem., ABA, 1997–. Chm., Bar Conf., 1999. Recreations: travel, reading, things latin. Address: 6 KBW, 21 College Hill, EC4R 2RP. T: (020) 3301 0910, Fax: (020) 3301 0911. E: dorian.lovell-pank@6kbw.com. Club: RNVR Yacht.

**LOVELOCK, Derek John;** non-executive Chairman: Jack Wills, 2016–17; Joe Browns Ltd, since 2017; b Sutton, Surrey, 1 Jan. 1950; m 1976, Deborah Susan; one s one d. Educ: King's Coll. Sch., Wimbledon; Enfield Coll. of Technol. (BA Hons). C&A, 1972–84: Mgt Trainee; Mktg Manager; Buyer, Co-ordinates; Buyer, Clockhouse; Buying Team Leader; Storehouse Gp plc, 1985–92: Buying and Merchandise Controller, then Dir, Richards; Chief Exec., Richards; Chief Exec., Mothercare; Chief Exec., Sears Clothing, Sears plc, 1992–99; Chief Exec., Mosaic Fashions Ltd, 1999–2009; CEO, 2009, Exec. Chm., 2009–14, Aurora Fashions; Executive Chairman: Karen Millen, 2011–12; Mamas & Papas, 2015–17. Ind. Dir, Spartoo.com, 2015–.

**LOVELOCK, Prof. James Ephraim,** CH 2003; CBE 1990; FRS 1974; independent scientist, since 1964; Senior Research Fellow, Green Templeton College (formerly Green College), Oxford, since 2012 (Hon. Visiting Fellow, 1994–2012); Fellow, Birkbeck, University of London, since 2007; b 26 July 1919; s of Tom Arthur Lovelock and Nellie Ann Elizabeth (née March); m 1st, 1942, Helen Mary Hyslop (d 1989); two s two d; 2nd, 1991, Sandra Jean Orchard. Educ: Strand Sch., London; Manchester and London Univs. BSc, PhD, DSc, ARIC. Staff Scientist, Nat. Inst. for Med. Research, 1941–61; Rockefeller Fellow, Harvard Univ., 1954–55; Yale Univ., 1958–59; Prof. of Chemistry, Baylor Univ. Coll. of Medicine, Texas, 1961–64. Vis. Prof., Univ. of Reading, 1967–90. Pres., Marine Biol Assoc., 1986–90 (Founding Hon. Fellow, 2014). Mem. Sigma Xi, Yale Chapter, 1959. Hon. ScD East Anglia, 1982; Hon. DSc: Exeter, 1988; Plymouth Poly., 1988; Stockholm, 1991; Edinburgh, 1993; Kent, 1996; E London, 1996; Colorado, 1997; KCL, 2008; Goldsmiths Coll., London, 2011. Amsterdam Prize, Roy. Netherlands Acad. of Arts and Scis, 1990; Prize, Volvo Envmt Prize Foundn, 1996; Nonino Prize, Italy, 1996; Blue Planet Prize, Asahi Glass Foundn, Tokyo, 1997; Wollaston Medal, Geol Soc., 2006; John Collier, IChemE, 2006; Edinburgh Medal, 2006; Basile J. Luyet Medal, Soc. for Cryobiology, 2010; Climate Change Award, Foundn of Prince Albert II of Monaco, 2010; Pioneering Achievement in Exobiology, NASA, 2010; Observer Lifetime Ethical Achievement Award, 2011. Publications: Gaia, 1979; (with Michael Allaby) The Great Extinction, 1983; (with Michael Allaby) The Greening of Mars, 1984; The Ages of Gaia, 1988; Gaia: the practical science of planetary medicine, 1991; Homage to Gaia: the life of an independent scientist (autobiog.), 2000; The Revenge of Gaia, 2006; The Vanishing Face of Gaia, 2009; A Rough Ride to the Future, 2014; Novacene: the coming age of hyperintelligence, 2019; numerous papers and patents. Recreations: walking, digital photography, reading. Address: Matthew Cottage, The Old Coastguards, Abbotsbury, Dorset DT3 4LB.

**LOVELUCK, Paul Edward,** CBE 1993; Parliamentary Boundary Commissioner for Wales, since 2011; b 3 Feb. 1942; s of Edward Henry Loveluck and Elizabeth Loveluck (née Treharne); m 1965, Lynne Gronow; one s one d. Educ: Maesteg Grammar Sch.; UCW, Cardiff (BA). Board of Trade, 1963–69; Welsh Office, 1969–84 (Asst Sec., 1975–84); Chief Executive: Wales Tourist Bd, 1984–95; Countryside Council for Wales, 1996–2002. Chm., Wales New Deal Task Force, 1999–2003; Pres., Nat. Mus and Galls of Wales, later Nat. Mus. Wales, 2002–11. Trustee: Clwyd-Powys Archaeol Trust; Archaeol Orgns Pension Scheme Trust; Nat. Zoological Soc. of Wales. JP Cardiff, 1982–2006, Dyfed-Powys, 2006–12. Recreations: music, grandparenting. Address: Dôl Awel, 8 Corndon Drive, Montgomery, Powys SY15 6RE.

**LOVEMAN, Stephen Charles Gardner;** Under Secretary, Department of Employment, then Department for Education and Employment, 1989–96; b 26 Dec. 1943; s of Charles Edward Loveman and Edith Mary Gardner; m 1972, Judith Pamela Roberts; one s one d. Educ: Arnold Sch., Blackpool; Emmanuel College, Cambridge (BA). Dept of Employment, 1967; Private Sec. to Minister of State for Employment, 1972–74; Health and Safety Exec., 1974–77; Dept of Employment, 1977–80; Manpower Services Commn, 1980–87; Dept of Employment, 1987–88; Cabinet Office, 1988–89. Recreations: TV, cinema, theatre, opera, reading, walking, French, keeping fit, voluntary work (witness support).

**LOVENDUSKI, Prof. Joni,** PhD; FBA 2007; Anniversary Professor of Politics, Birkbeck College, University of London, 2006–, now Professor Emerita; b 19 May 1945; d of Austin Lovenduski and Teresa Lovenduski (née Allan); m 1993, Prof. Alan Ware; one s, and one step s. Educ: Manchester Univ. (BSc Hons Econ. 1970; MA Govt 1976); Loughborough Univ. (PhD Politics 1986). Loughborough University: Lectr, then Sen. Lectr, in Politics, 1972–88; Reader in Politics, 1988–92; Prof. of Comparative Politics, 1992–94; Prof. of Politics, Southampton Univ., 1995–2000. Dir, British Candidate Study, 1992, British Representation Study, 1997, 2001, 2005. European Consortium for Political Research: Publications Dir, Exec. Cttee, 1997–2000; Vice-Chair, 2000–03; Founding

Mem. and Convener, Standing Gp on Women and Politics, 1985. Mem., Res. Council, Eur. Univ. Inst., 2003–08. Founding Mem. and Convener, Women's Gp, Pol Studies Assoc. UK, 1977–. AcSS 2009. Hon. DSSc Edinburgh, 2017. Prize for Best Achievement in Study of Politics, Pol Sci. Assoc., 2008; Gender and Politics Award, 2009, Lifetime Achievement Award for outstanding work in pol sci., 2017, Eur. Consortium for Pol Res.; Sir Isaiah Berlin Award for lifetime contribn to Pol Sci., Pol Studies Assoc., 2013. Chm. Editl Bd, Pol Quarterly, 2009–; Member, Editorial Board: British Jl of Pol Sci., 1995–; French Politics, 2003–; British Politics, 2006–; Eur. Pol Sci. Review, 2010–; Former Member, Editorial Board: Pol Studies, Politics and Gender, Social Movt Studies. *Publications:* (ed jtly) The Politics of the Second Electorate, 1981; (ed jtly) The New Politics of Abortion, 1986; Women and European Politics: contemporary feminism and public policy, 1986; (jtly) Politics and Society in Eastern Europe, 1987; (jtly) Contemporary Feminist Politics, 1993; (ed jtly) Gender and Party Politics, 1993; (ed jtly) Different Voices, Different Lives: gender and politics, a reader, 1994; (jtly) Political Recruitment: gender, race and class in the British Parliament, 1995 (George H. Hallett Award, Amer. Pol Sci. Assoc., 2018); (ed jtly) Women in Politics in Britain, 1996; (ed) Feminism and Politics, 2 vols, 2000; Feminizing Politics, 2005; (ed) State Feminism and Political Representation, 2005; (jtly) Women in Parliament, 2005; Gendering Politics, Feminizing Political Science, 2014; contribs to British Jl Political Sci., Political Studies, Party Politics, Political Qly, Parly Affairs, Govt & Opposition, W Eur. Politics. *Recreations:* Italy, reading, gardening, bridge. *Address:* Department of Politics, Birkbeck, University of London, Malet Street, WC1E 7HX.

**LOVERANCE, Rowena Kathryn;** writer and consultant; Head of Outreach and Learning Resources, then Head of e-learning, British Museum, 2001–07; *b* 4 Sept. 1952; *d* of Maurice and Wilfreda Loverance. *Educ:* Manchester High Sch. for Girls; Somerville Coll., Oxford (BA Hons Modern History; Dip. Archaeol.). Res. Fellow, Univ. of Birmingham, 1979–80; Lectr, Dept of Ancient History and Classical Archaeology, Univ. of Sheffield, 1980–83; Education Officer, 1985–98, Head of Educnl IT, 1998–2001, BM. Trustee, Culture24 (formerly 24 Hour Museum), 2005–13. Chm., Publications Cttee, Soc. for Promotion of Byzantine Studies, 2008–18. Pres., Churches Together in England, 1998–2001 (Chair, Bd of Trustees). *Publications:* Byzantium, 1988, rev. edn 2004; The British Museum Christ, 2004; Christian Art, 2007. *Recreations:* Byzantine studies, archaeology.

**LOVERING, John David,** CBE 2016; farmer; *b* 11 Oct. 1949; *s* of John George and Ruby Beatrice Lovering; *m* 1971, Brenda Joan Wotherspoon; two *s* one *d*. *Educ:* Dulwich Coll.; Exeter Univ. (BA Hons); Manchester Business Sch. (MBA 1975). Planning Manager, Spillers Internat. Div., 1975–78; Corporate Strategy Manager, Lex Service plc, 1978–83; Grand Metropolitan plc, Commercial Dir, Express Dairy Ltd, 1983–85; Head of Gp Finance and Planning, Imperial Gp plc, 1985–86; Finance Dir, Sears plc, 1986–93; Chief Operating Officer, Tarmac plc, 1993–95; Chairman: Birthdays Gp Ltd, 1996–2002; Fired Earth Ltd, 1998–2001; Homebase Ltd, 2001–02; Debenhams plc, 2003–10; Somerfield Ltd, 2005–09; Mitchells & Butlers plc, 2010–11; RetailCURe, 2015–17. Sen. Partner, Echelon Capital LLP, 2005–12; Partner, Montagu Private Equity Advrs, 2011–15. Non-executive Chairman: Peacock Gp Ltd, 1997–2004; Odeon Cinemas Ltd, 2000–03; Laurel Pub Co., 2002–04; Fitness First, 2003–05; GO Outdoors, 2010–11; Retail Trust, 2011–14; Maplin Electronics, 2011–14; Jamella plc, 2011–13; Host Europe Ltd Gp, 2012–13; EmiTel, Poland, 2012–13; itim, 2013–14; Vice-Chm., Barclays Capital, 2007–08; Director: Aga Foodservice, 2003–06; Meyer Department Stores Pty, Australia, 2006–09. Trustee and Dir, SCF, 1990–96; Chm., Hastings Pier Charity, 2012–17; Committee Member: Mending Broken Hearts Appeal, BHF, 2009–12; Retail Leadership Gp, Prince's Trust, 2009–11; Diamond Woods Adv. Gp, Woodland Trust, 2010– (Ambassador for Woodland Trust, 2013–); Trustee: Bexhill Acad., 2015–17; Durrell Wildlife Conservation Trust, 2015–17; Holburne Gall., Bath, 2016–; United World Schs, 2018–. Mem., Tonbridge Sch. Foundn, 2003–06; Dir, Dulwich Coll. Enterprises, 2008–17; Gov., Dulwich Coll., 2010–17. Outstanding Alumnus Award, Manchester Business Sch., 2010; Legend Award, Retail Trust, 2017. *Recreations:* sport, walking, farming. *Club:* Alleyn (Dulwich).

**LOVERING, Prof. John Francis,** AO 1993; FAA; FTSE; Chairman: WaterEd Australia Pty Ltd, 2003–07; WaterSmart, 2004–06; Uniwater, since 2007; Board Member, Southern Rural Water, 2001–07; *b* 27 March 1930; *s* of George Francis Lovering and Dorothy Irene Mildwater; *m* 1954, Jennifer Kerry FitzGerald; two *s* one *d*. *Educ:* Canterbury High Sch., Sydney; Univ. of Sydney (MSc); Univ. of Melbourne (MSc); California Inst. of Technology (PhD). FAA 1982; FTSE (FTS 1993). Asst Curator of Minerals, Australian Museum, 1951–55; Research Fellow, Fellow and Sen. Fellow, Dept of Geophysics and Geochemistry, ANU, 1956–69; Chief Investigator of Lunar Sample Analyses from Apollo 11, 1969 to Apollo 17, 1972, NASA; University of Melbourne: Prof. of Geology, 1969–87; Dean of Science, 1983–85; Dep. Vice-Chancellor (Research), 1985–87; Vice-Chancellor and Prof. of Geology, Flinders Univ. of SA, 1987–95. Professorial Fellow, Sch. of Earth Scis, Univ. of Melbourne, 1999–. Presiding Officer, Natural Resources Council of SA, 1992–94; Chairman: Australian Antarctic Sci. Adv. Cttee, 1985–89; Envmt Conservation Council of Victoria, 1998–2002; Australian Nat. Seismic Imaging Resource, 1998–2001; Gippsland Res. Coordination Gp, 1999–2001; Office for Environmental Programs: Chm., Academic Adv. Bd, 1999–2013; Mem., Community and Industry Adv. Bd, 1999–2013. Chairman of Directors: Comlabs Ltd, 1985–93; Geotrack International Pty Ltd, 1987–93; Open Learning Technology Corp., 1992–96. Pres., Murray-Darling Basin Commn, 1994–99. President: Royal Soc. of Victoria, 1977–79 (Mem. Bd, 1969–2014); and Mem. Bd, Internat. Geol Correlation Prog., 1981–87; Vice Pres., Internat. Union of Geol Scis, 1990–96. Hon. DSc: Flinders Univ., 1995; Melbourne Univ., 1999. Chevalier des Palmes Académiques, 1981. *Publications:* Last of Lands: Antarctica (with J. R. V. Prescott), 1979; contribs to learned jls. *Recreations:* music, wine, food. *Address:* 9 Park Square, Port Melbourne, Vic 3207, Australia. *Clubs:* Melbourne, Wallaby (Melbourne).

**LOVESEY, Peter Harmer;** crime writer, since 1970; *b* 10 Sept. 1936; *s* of Richard Lear Lovesey and Amy Lovesey (née Strank); *m* 1959, Jacqueline Ruth Lewis; one *s* one *d*. *Educ:* Hampton Grammar Sch.; Reading Univ. (BA Hons 1958). Flying Officer, RAF, 1958–61; Lectr, Thurrock Technical Coll., 1961–69; Head of Gen. Educn Dept, Hammersmith & West London Coll., 1969–75. Crime Writers' Association: Chm., 1991–92; Cartier Diamond Dagger, 2000. Grand Prix de Littérature Policière (French Crime Writers' Assoc.), 1985; Vikelas Plaque, Internat. Soc. of Olympic Historians, 2008; Grand Master: Swedish Acad. of Detection, 2010; Mystery Writers of America, 2018. *Publications:* Wobble to Death, 1970 (televised 1980); The Detective Wore Silk Drawers, 1971 (televised 1980); Abracadaver, 1972 (televised 1980); Mad Hatter's Holiday, 1973 (televised 1981); Invitation to a Dynamite Party, 1974 (televised 1981); A Case of Spirits, 1975 (televised 1980); Swing, Swing Together, 1976 (televised 1980); Waxwork (Silver Dagger), 1978 (televised 1979); The False Inspector Dew (Gold Dagger), 1982; Keystone, 1983; Rough Cider, 1986; Bertie and the Tinman, 1987; On the Edge, 1989 (televised as Dead Gorgeous, 2002); Bertie and the Seven Bodies, 1990; The Last Detective, 1991; Diamond Solitaire, 1992; Bertie and the Crime of Passion, 1993; The Summons (Silver Dagger), 1995; Bloodhounds (Silver Dagger), 1996; Upon a Dark Night, 1997; The Vault, 1999; The Reaper, 2000; Diamond Dust, 2002; The House Sitter, 2003; The Circle, 2005; The Secret Hangman, 2007; The Headhunters, 2008; Skeleton Hill, 2009; Stagestruck, 2011; Cop to Corpse, 2012; The Tooth Tattoo, 2013; The Stone Wife, 2014; Down Among the Dead Men, 2015; Another One Goes Tonight, 2016; Beau Death, 2017; Killing with Confetti, 2019; *short stories:* Butchers and Other Stories of Crime, 1985; The Crime of Miss Oyster Brown and Other Stories, 1994; Do Not Exceed the Stated Dose, 1998; The Sedgemoor Strangler and Other Stories of Crime, 2001; Murder on the Short List, 2008; *non-fiction:* The Kings of Distance, 1968; (jtly) The Guide to British Track and Field Literature, 1969; The Official Centenary History of the Amateur Athletic Association, 1979; (jtly) An Athletics Compendium: an annotated guide to the UK literature of track and field, 2001; (jtly) British Athletics 1866–80, 2016; *as Peter Lear:* Goldengirl, 1977 (filmed 1979); Spider Girl, 1980; The Secret of Spandau, 1986. *Recreations:* researching athletics history, visiting teashops. *Address:* c/o Vanessa Holt Ltd, 59 Crescent Road, Leigh-on-Sea, Essex SS9 2PF. *Club:* Detection.

**LOVESTONE, Sir Simon Harold,** Kt 2017; Vice President, Disease Area Stronghold Lead for Neurodegeneration, Janssen; Professor of Translational Neuroscience (part-time), University of Oxford, since 2014; *b* 16 Feb. 1961. *Educ:* Univ. of Sheffield (BSc Microbiol. 1982); Univ. of Southampton (BM 1986); PhD London 1998. MRCPsych. Sen. Lectr, 1995–99, Reader, 1999–2000, in Old Age Psychiatry, Prof. of Old Age Psychiatry, 2000–14, Inst. of Psychiatry, London Univ.; Hon. Consultant, Maudsley Hosp., 1995–2014. Dir, NIHR Biomedical Res. Centre for Mental Health, 2007–14; Dir of Res., King's Health Partners, 2010–14. Chm., Sci. Adv. Bd, Alzheimer's Res. Trust, 2004–09. *Publications:* scientific papers on old age psychiatry and neuroscience. *Address:* Department of Psychiatry, University of Oxford Medical Sciences Division, Warneford Hospital, Oxford OX3 7JX.

**LOVILL, Sir John (Roger),** Kt 1987; CBE 1983; DL; Chairman, Sloane Square Investments, 1980–99 (Director, 1960–99); *b* 26 Sept. 1929; *s* of Walter Thomas Lovill and Elsie Lovill (née Page); *m* 1958, Jacqueline (née Parker); two *s* (one *d* decd). *Educ:* Brighton, Hove and Sussex Grammar School. S. G. Warburg, 1951–55; Dep. Gen. Manager, Securicor Ltd, 1955–60; Dir, Municipal Gen. Insce Co., 1984–95; Managing Trustee, Municipal Mutual Insce, 1988–2013 (Chm., 1993–2013); Chm., Nationwide Small Business Property Trust, 1988–96; Chm., Prime Health Ltd, 1992–94. Contested (C) Ebbw Vale, 1966; Mem., East Sussex CC, 1967–89, Leader, 1973–77; Chairman: Sussex Police Authority, 1976–79; Local Authority Conditions of Service Adv. Bd, 1978–83; ACC, 1983–86; Pres., Sussex Assoc. of Local Councils, 1987–97; Vice Pres., Nat. Assoc. of Local Councils, 1991–93; Leader, Conservative Assoc. of County Councils, 1981–83. DL E Sussex 1983. *Recreations:* opera, politics, marine paintings. *Address:* 34 Sadlers Way, Ringmer, Lewes, Sussex BN8 5HG.

**LOW,** family name of **Barons Aldington** and **Low of Dalston**.

**LOW OF DALSTON,** Baron *cr* 2006 (Life Peer), of Dalston in the London Borough of Hackney; **Colin MacKenzie Low,** CBE 2000; Vice-President, Royal National Institute of Blind People (formerly Royal National Institute for the Blind), since 2009 (Chairman, 2000–09); President, International Council for Education of People with Visual Impairment, 2010–16 (Member, Executive Committee, 1987–2010); *b* 23 Sept. 1942; *s* of Arthur Eric Low and Catherine Cameron (née Anderson); *m* 1969, Jill Irene Coton; one *s* one *d*. *Educ:* Worcester Coll. for the Blind; Queen's Coll., Oxford (BA Juris, MA 1987); Churchill Coll., Cambridge (Dip. Criminol.). Lectr in Law, Univ. of Leeds, 1968–84; Dir, Disability Resource Team, GLC and London Boroughs, 1984–94; Sen. Res. Fellow, 1994–2000, Vis. Prof., 2000–, City Univ. Member: Special Educnl Needs Tribunal, 1994–2007; Nat. Disability Council, 1996–2000; Disability Rights Task Force, 1997–99; Disability Rights Commn, 2000–02. Chm., Low Commn on Future of Advice and Legal Support, 2012–16. President: European Blind Union, 2003–11; Skill, 2008–11 (Mem. Council, 1975–2003; Vice-Pres., 2003–08); Disability Alliance, 2010–11 (Mem. Cttee, 1974–2011; Chm., 1991–97; Vice-Pres., 1997–2010); Visionary (formerly Nat. Assoc. of Local Socs for Visually Impaired People), 2010–; Mem. Council, St Dunstan's, 2000–10. *Publications:* contrib. articles to learned periodicals. *Recreations:* music, wine appreciation. *Address:* Royal National Institute of Blind People, 105 Judd Street, WC1H 9NE. *T:* (020) 7392 2205. *E:* colin.low@rnib.org.uk.

**LOW, Dr (George) Graeme (Erick),** CBE 1989; Member, 1986–91, Managing Director, Site Operations, 1990–91, United Kingdom Atomic Energy Authority; *b* Palmerston North, NZ, 29 Nov. 1928; *s* of George Eric Low and Evelyn Edith Low (née Gillman); *m* 1st, 1952, Marion Townsend (marr. diss. 1977); two *d*; 2nd, 1985, Joan Kathleen Swinburne. *Educ:* New Plymouth Boys' High Sch., NZ; Canterbury Coll., Univ. of NZ (BSc, MSc); Univ. of Reading (PhD, DSc). FInstP. Special Branch, RNZN, 1952–58; Research Scientist, 1958–68, Head of Materials Physics Div., 1968–70, AERE Harwell; Special Asst to Dir, UKAEA Research Gp, 1970–73; Programme Dir (Applied Nuclear), 1973–76, Research Dir (Industry), 1976–81, Dir of Environmental Research, 1981–83, AERE Harwell; Dir, AEE, Winfrith, 1983–86; Dir, AERE Harwell, 1986–87; Mem. for Estabts, UKAEA, 1987–90. Dir, UK Nirex Ltd, 1986–91. *Publications:* papers on semiconductors, neutron beam studies of the solid state, magnetism and management. *Recreations:* reading, walking, family and friends. *Address:* 21 New Road, Reading RG1 5JD.

**LOW, Gillian;** Head Mistress, The Lady Eleanor Holles School, Hampton, 2004–14; *b* 21 Feb. 1955; *d* of William Edward Coysh and Elizabeth Joyce Coysh (née Legge); *m* 1st, 1980 (marr. diss. 2001); one *s* two *d*; 2nd, 2016, Kenneth Drummond Grimshaw. *Educ:* North London Collegiate Sch.; Somerville Coll., Oxford (Emma Clarke Beilby Schol.; BA Hons 1977, MA 1982); Trinity Coll., Cambridge (Tripos Prize; PGCE 1981). Mgt trainee, Courtaulds Ltd, 1977–79; teacher of English as foreign lang., British Coll., Reggio di Calabria, Italy, 1979–80; Asst English Teacher, then Dep. Hd of Dept, Claverham Community Coll., Battle, 1981–88; Hd of English, then Dir of Studies, Bishop Ramsey Sch., Ruislip, 1989–94; Dep. Headmistress, Godolphin and Latymer Sch., Hammersmith, 1994–98; Headmistress, Francis Holland Sch., N London, 1998–2004. Mem., Humanities Ext. Adv. Panel, Univ. of Oxford, 2013–14. Member: ASCL (formerly SHA), 1994–2014; GSA, 1998–2014 (Pres., 2010; Vice-Pres., 2011; Hon. Mem., 2014–16; Fellow, 2016–; representative: Council, Internat. Confedn of Principals, 2008–13; Ind. Schs Travel Assoc., 2008–14 (Trustee, 2010–14); Ind. Schs Inspectorate, 2014–15); GSA/HMC Educn and Acad. Policy Cttee, 2004–08; GSA/HMC Universities Cttee, 2009–12. Governor: Sarum Hall Sch., Hampstead, 2003–05; Moat Sch., Fulham, 2003–06 (Chm., Educn Cttee, 2004–06); Queen's Coll., London, 2006–14; St Paul's Girls' Sch., 2015– (Mem., Educn Cttee, 2015–); Warwick Ind. Schs Foundn, 2015–19 (Mem., Educn Cttee, 2015–19; Chm., King's High Sch. Cttee, 2016–19). *Recreations:* travel, reading, the arts, photography. *Club:* Lansdowne.

**LOW, Sir John (Menzies),** Kt 2017; CBE 2008; PhD; Chief Executive, Charities Aid Foundation, since 2007; *b* 1 July 1953; *s* of late David Low and Helen Low (née Menzies); *m* 1977, Alison Jean Donald; two *d*. *Educ:* Aberdeen Acad.; Robert Gordon's Inst. of Technol. (BSc); Univ. of Aberdeen (MSc, PhD); Templeton Coll., Oxford. CEng, FIET. John Brown Engrg (UDI), 1979–84; Wm McGeogh, Birmingham, 1984–87; Booker plc (Sortex), 1988–93; Bühler AG (Sortex), 1993–99; with RNID, 1999–2007, Chief Exec., 2002–07. Mem., Assoc. of Offshore Diving Contractors Task Force on safe use of electricity underwater, 1983–84. Ind. Mem., H of L Appts Commn, 2008–13. Chm., BBC Appeals Adv. Cttee, 2018–. Chm., Disability Charities Consortium, 2003–07; non-executive Director: Euclid Network of European Third Sector Leaders, 2007–17 (Pres., 2015–17); CAF Bank Ltd, 2007–. Trustee: ACEVO, 2003–09 (Chm., 2005–09); Charity Bank, 2010–. Ind. Mem. Council, City, Univ. of London (formerly City Univ.), 2011–. Deacon: Gilcomston Park Baptist Ch, 1977–84; Hertford Baptist Ch, 1991–2003 (Treas., 1994–2003). CCMI. FRSA. *Publications*: 6 patents in optics and automated sorting; contrib. articles on speech fluency, auditory feedback, image processing, marketing and voluntary sector; commentator on social investment, philanthropy, economy and civil society. *Address*: Charities Aid Foundation, 10 St Bride Street, EC4A 4AD. *T*: 0300 012 3010. *E*: jlow@cafonline.org.

**LOW, Sir Richard Walter Morrison-**, 4th Bt *cr* 1908, of Kilmaron, co. Fife; *b* 4 Aug. 1959; *o s* of Sir James Richard Morrison-Low, 3rd Bt and Ann Rawson Morrison-Low (*née* Gordon); *S* father, 2012; *m* 1994, Sandra Scott Newman; one *s* one *d*. *Heir*: *s* Rory James Morrison-Low, *b* 1997. *Address*: Kilmaron Farm, Cupar, Fife KY15 4NE.

**LOWCOCK, His Honour Andrew Charles;** a Circuit Judge, 2001–16; *b* 22 Nov. 1949; *s* of late Eric and Elizabeth Lowcock; *m* 1st, 1976, Patricia Anne Roberts (marr. diss. 1985); 2nd, 1985, Sarah Elaine Edwards; two *s*. *Educ*: Malvern Coll.; New Coll., Oxford (MA). Called to the Bar, Middle Temple, 1973; barrister, specialising in criminal and family law, Northern Circuit, 1974–2001; Asst Recorder, 1993–97; Recorder, 1997–2001. Governor: The Ryleys School, 1996–2007; Malvern Coll., 2017–. *Recreations*: music, theatre, watching cricket and football. *Clubs*: MCC; Lancashire County Cricket, Nefyn Golf.

**LOWCOCK, Sir Mark (Andrew),** KCB 2017 (CB 2011); Under Secretary General for Humanitarian Affairs, Office for the Coordination of Humanitarian Affairs, and Emergency Relief Co-ordinator, United Nations, since 2017; *b* 25 July 1962; *s* of Brian Lowcock and Stella Connolly; *m* 1991, Dr Julia Watson; two *s* one *d*. *Educ*: Christ Church, Oxford (BA Hons 1985); Birkbeck Coll., Univ. of London (MSc Econs Dist. 1988). Grad. Fellow, Boston Univ., 1989. Mem. CIPFA 2007. Overseas Development Administration, then Department for International Development, 1985: Private Sec. to Minister for Overseas Develt, 1992–94; Dep., then Hd, Central Africa, Harare, 1994–97; Hd, EU Dept, 1997–99; Hd, Eastern Africa, 1999–2001; Dir, Finance and Corporate Performance, 2001–03; Director General: Corporate Performance and Knowledge Sharing, 2003–06; Policy and International, 2006–08; Country Progs, 2008–11; Perm. Sec., DFID, 2011–17. *Recreations*: Manchester United Football Club, Africa, reading. *Address*: Office for the Co-ordination of Humanitarian Affairs, United Nations, New York, NY 10017, USA.

**LOWDEN, Prof. John Hopkins,** PhD; FBA 2013; Professor of the History of Art, Courtauld Institute of Art, London, 2002, now Emeritus; *b* 1 May 1953; *s* of Eric Walter and Muriel Florence Amelia Lowden; *m* 1980, Joanna Louise Cannon; one *s* one *d*. *Educ*: Leys Sch., Cambridge (Schol.); Emmanuel Coll., Cambridge (Exhibnr) MA (English) 1974; Hon. Fellow 2011); Courtauld Inst. of Art, London (MA 1977; PhD (Hist. of Art) 1980). Jun. Fellow, Dumbarton Oaks, 1979–80; Temp. Lectr, Univ. of St Andrews, 1981; Lectr, 1982–94, Reader, 1994–2002, Courtauld Inst. of Art, London. Leverhulme Sen. Res. Fellow, 1992–93; Grinfield Lectr, Univ. of Oxford, 1996–98. MAE 2006. Corresp. Fellow, Medieval Acad. of America, 2010. Otto Gründler Prize, Western Michigan Univ., 2002. *Publications*: Illuminated Prophet Books, 1988; The Octateuchs, 1992; Early Christian and Byzantine Art, 1997, 6th edn 2008 (trans. French, Greek, Japanese, Korean); The Making of the 'Bibles Moralisées', vol. I, The Manuscripts, vol. II, The Book of Ruth, 2000; (with Alixe Bovey) Under the Influence, 2007; (with John Cherry) Medieval Ivories and Works of Art, 2008; The Jaharis Gospel Lectionary, 2009; (with Eberhard König) Biblia Moralizada de los Limbourg, 2010; (with Scot McKendrick and Kathleen Doyle) Royal Manuscripts: the genius of illumination, 2011; Medieval and Later Ivories in the Courtauld Institute, 2013; numerous contribs, primarily on manuscript illumination, to scholarly jls, standard ref. works, conf. procs, exhibn catalogues, etc. *Recreation*: family. *Address*: Courtauld Institute of Art, Somerset House, Strand, WC2R 0RN. *T*: (020) 7848 2668, *Fax*: (020) 7848 2410. *E*: John.Lowden@courtauld.ac.uk.

**LOWE, Prof. (Alan) Vaughan;** QC 2008; barrister; Chichele Professor of Public International Law, University of Oxford, 1999–2012, now Emeritus; Fellow of All Souls College, Oxford, 1999–2012, now Emeritus; *b* 1952; *m* Sally. *Educ*: UWIST (LLB 1973; LLM 1978; PhD 1980); MA Cantab 1991; MA Oxon 1999. Called to the Bar, Gray's Inn, 1993, Bencher, 2008; in practice at the Bar, Essex Court Chambers, 1993–. Lectr, Cardiff Law Sch., 1973–79; Lectr, 1979–86, Sen. Lectr, 1986–88, Manchester Univ.; Cambridge University: Lectr, 1988–94; Reader in Internat. Law, 1994–99; Fellow of Corpus Christi Coll., 1988–99; Warden of Leckhampton, 1998–99. Visiting Professor: Duke Law Sch., USA, 1990; Tulane Law Sch., USA, 2000. Mem., Institut de droit international, 2013 (Associé, 2005); Judge, European Nuclear Energy Tribunal, 2006–; *ad hoc* Judge, ECHR, 2009–10. Pres. or Mem., various arbitral tribunals, 2004–. Order of the Rising Sun, Gold Rays with Neck Ribbon (Japan), 2008; Cavaler, Ordinul Nat. Serviciul Credincios, Romania, 2009; Darjah Paduka Seri Laila Jasa Yang Amat Berjasa (Darjah Ke-Dua), Brunei, 2010; Grand Cross, Order of El Sol Del Perú, 2017. *Publications*: Extraterritorial Jurisdiction, 1983; (jtly) The Law of the Sea, 1983, 3rd edn 1999; (jtly) Fifty Years of the International Court of Justice, 1996; (jtly) The Settlement of International Disputes, 1999; International Law, 2007; A Very Short Introduction to International Law, 2015; papers in jls. *Recreations*: ambling, rambling, music. *Address*: Essex Court Chambers, 24 Lincoln's Inn Fields, WC2A 3EG. *T*: (020) 7813 8000.

**LOWE, Anthony Marshall; His Honour Judge Anthony Lowe;** a Circuit Judge, since 2018; *b* Wolverhampton, 21 Feb. 1953; *s* of Thomas Marshall Lowe and Anstice Beryl Lowe; *m* 1994, Tracy Price; three *s* and one step *s*. *Educ*: Municipal Grammar Sch., Wolverhampton; Christ Church, Oxford (MA Hons). Called to the Bar, Middle Temple, 1976; a Recorder, 2005–18. *Recreations*: music, both rock and classical, most sport (sadly now only spectating), ornithology, spending time with good friends. *Clubs*: Worcestershire Ambassadors; Tettenhall 41.

**LOWE, Charlotte Merilyn;** see Skene Catling, C. M.

**LOWE, Prof. Christopher Robin,** OBE 2011; PhD; FREng; Fellow, Trinity College, Cambridge, since 1984; Director of Biotechnology, 1988–2013, Director, Institute of Biotechnology, 1988–2013, and Professor of Biotechnology, 1999–2013, University of Cambridge; *b* 15 Oct. 1945; *s* of late Thomas Lowe and of Hilda Lowe (*née* Moxham); *m* 1974, Patricia Margaret Reed; one *s* one *d*. *Educ*: Univ. of Birmingham (BSc 1967; PhD Biochem., 1970). FREng 2005. Postdoctoral Research Associate: Dept of Biochem., Univ. of Liverpool, 1970–73; Pure and Applied Biochem., Univ. of Lund, Sweden, 1973–74; Lectr in Biochem., 1975–82, Sen. Lectr, 1982–84, Univ. of Southampton. Visiting Professor: Univ. of Lund, 1995–; Univ. of Bath, 1996–. *Publications*: Affinity Chromatography, 1974; An Introduction to Affinity Chromatography, 1979; numerous contribs to learned jls; 83 patents. *Recreations*: antiques, travel. *Address*: Institute of Biotechnology, University of Cambridge, Tennis Court Road, Cambridge CB2 1QT. *T*: (01223) 334160; The Limes, Hempstead, Saffron Walden, Essex CB10 2PW. *T*: (01799) 599307.

**LOWE, David Alexander;** QC 1984; *b* Kilbirnie, Ayrshire, 1 Nov. 1942; *o s* of late David Alexander Lowe and Rea Sadie Aitchison Lowe (*née* Bridges); *m* 1972, Vivian Anne Langley (*d* 2017); three *s* one *d* (and one *d* decd). *Educ*: Pocklington Sch., York; St John's Coll., Cambridge (schol.; MA; MacMahon Law Student). Called to Bar, Middle Temple, 1965 (Harmsworth Schol.; Bencher, 1992), *ad eundem*; Lincoln's Inn, 1975. In practice at the Chancery Bar, 1966–. *Address*: Three Stone Chambers, Lincoln's Inn, WC2A 3XL.

**LOWE, Hon. Douglas Ackley,** AM 2000; Chairman: Premier's Physical Activity Council, 2004–07; Board of Governance, GP Assist Tasmania, 2004–11; Executive Officer, Tasmanian Branch, Australian Medical Association, 1992–2004; *b* 15 May 1942; *s* of Ackley Reginald Lowe and Dulcie Mary Lowe (*née* Kean); *m* 1963, Pamela June (*née* Grant); two *s* two *d*. *Educ*: St Virgil College, Hobart. Mem. Tasmanian House of Assembly, for Franklin, 1969–86: ALP, 1969–82; Ind., 1982–86. Minister for Housing, 1972; Chief Secretary, 1974; Deputy Premier, 1975–77; Chief Sec. and Minister for Planning and Reorganisation, 1975; Premier, 1977–81; Treasurer, 1980–81; Minister for: Industrial Relations, Planning and the Environment, 1976; Industrial Relations and Health, Aug. 1976; Industrial Relations and Manpower Planning, 1977–79; Economic Planning and Development, 1979–80; Energy, 1979–81; MLC (Ind.) Buckingham, Tas., 1986–92; Dep. Leader for Govt, Legislative Council, 1989–92. Australian Labor Party: State Sec. 1965–69, State Pres. 1974–75, Tasmanian Section. Tasmanian Deleg. to Aust. Constitutional Convention, 1973–85. Senator, Jaycees Internat. State Pres., Tasmanian Swimming Inc., 1990–98; Mem. Panel, Australian Swimming Disciplinary Tribunal, 1996–98. Patron, Australia Fujian Assoc., Tasmania, 2016–. Treas., 2011–12, Sec., 2012–17, Mem. Mgt Cttee, 2017–, Berriedale Bowls Club Inc. Silver Jubilee Medal, 1977; Australian Sports Medal, 2000; Centenary Medal (Tasmania), 2003; President's Award, AMA, 2004. *Publications*: The Price of Power, 1984. *Address*: 1 Michele Court, Berriedale, Tas 7011, Australia.

**LOWE, Sir Frank (Budge),** Kt 2001; Founder, 1981, and Chairman Emeritus, since 2003, Lowe and Partners Worldwide (formerly Lowe Howard Spink); *b* 23 Aug. 1941; *s* of Stephen and Marion Lowe; two *s* one *d*. *Educ*: Westminster School. Vis. Prof., UCL, 1990–. Founder: Queen's Club Pre-Wimbledon Grass Ct Championships, 1974; Octagon Sports Marketing Gp, 1996; Founder and Chm. of Trustees, Capital City Acad., 2003–. FRSA.

**LÖWE, Dr Jan,** FRS 2008; Director, MRC Laboratory of Molecular Biology, University of Cambridge, since 2018; Fellow, Darwin College, Cambridge, since 2012; *b* 14 July 1967. *Educ*: Univ. of Hamburg (BSc Chem. 1992); Max-Planck-Inst. for Biochem. (PhD 1996). MRC Laboratory of Molecular Biology, University of Cambridge: Fellow, 1996–98; tenure-track Gp Leader, Bacterial Cytoskeleton Gp, 1998–2002; tenured Gp Leader, 2002–; Jt Hd, Structural Studies Div., 2010–18. Mem., EMBO, 2004. Mem., German Nat. Acad. Scis, Leopoldina, 2013. Young Investigator Award, 2001, Gold Medal, 2007, EMBO. *Publications*: contribs to jls incl. Nature, Science, Cell, Annual Revs in Biochem. *Address*: MRC Laboratory of Molecular Biology, Francis Crick Avenue, Cambridge CB2 0QH. *E*: jyl@mrc-lmb.cam.ac.uk.

**LOWE, Janet,** CBE 2003; FRSE 2010; Principal, Lauder College, Dunfermline, 1996–2005 (Depute Principal, 1992–95); *b* South Normanton, 27 Sept. 1950; *d* of George Frederick and Sheila Lowe; *m* 1982, Dr Donald Thomas Stewart. *Educ*: Swanwick Hall Grammar Sch.; Univ. of Hull (BA Hons French and Italian 1973); Univ. of Dundee (MBA 1990); Univ. of Stirling (EdD 2005). Immigration Officer, Home Office, 1973–76; Personnel Asst, Univ. of Hull, 1976–80; Adminr, Lothian Regl Council, 1980–82; Personnel Officer, 1982–86, Asst Registrar, 1986–88, Napier Univ.; Sec. and Registrar, Duncan of Jordanstone Coll. of Art, 1988–92. Member: Bd of Mgt, Scottish Further Educn Unit, 1993–2001; Scottish Consultative Council on the Curriculum, 1995–99; Scottish Cttee, Nat. Cttee of Inquiry into Higher Educn, 1996–97; Bd, Scottish Enterprise, 1998–2004; Bd, Assoc. of Scottish Colls, 2002–05; Ind. Rev. of Local Govt Finance, 2004–07; SFC, 2005–13; Bd, Skills Develt Scotland, 2008–13. US/UK Fulbright Comr, 2009–12. Asst Regl Co-ordinator, Rotary Foundn, 2017–19. Hon. Prof. of Applied Social Scis, Univ. of Stirling, 2010–15. Trustee: Carnegie Trust for Univs of Scotland, 2005–15; Dundee Botanic Garden Endowment Trust, 2015–18. Member of Court: Heriot-Watt Univ., 1999–2005; Univ. of Dundee, 2005–13. FRSE 2010. Hon. DEd Queen Margaret Univ., Edinburgh, 2007. *Recreations*: Rotary (Pres., Rotary Club of Dunfermline Carnegie, 2008–09; Foundn Chm., District 1010, 2012–16; Asst Regl Rotary Foundn Co-ordinator, Zone 17, 2017–), gardening, reading novels, photography, travel. *Address*: 42 Gamekeepers Road, Kinnesswood, Kinross KY13 9JR. *T*: (01592) 840277. *E*: janetlowe@aol.com.

**LOWE, Prof. (Joseph) John,** PhD; CGeol, FGS, FRGS; Gordon Manley Professor of Geography (formerly Professor of Geography and Quaternary Science), Royal Holloway, University of London, 1992–2013, now Emeritus; Leverhulme Trust Emeritus Fellow, 2014–16; *b* 12 June 1946; *s* of Joseph Lowe and Margaret (*née* Rooney); *m* 1969, Jeanette P. Bell; two *s*. *Educ*: Univ. of St Andrews (MA 1st Cl. Hons Geog. 1970); Univ. of Edinburgh (PhD 1977). City of London Polytechnic: Lectr, 1973–77; Sen. Lectr, 1977–85; Principal Lectr and Reader, 1985–88; Prof. and Hd, Dept of Geog., 1988–89; Royal Holloway and Bedford New College, University of London: Sen. Lectr, 1989–90; Reader, 1990–92; Dean of Science, 1997–2000; Dir, Centre for Quaternary Res., Univ. of London, 1989–97 and 2006. Pres., UK Quaternary Res. Assoc., 2005–08 (Vice-Pres., 1992–97); Sen. Vice-Pres., Internat. Union of Quaternary Assocs, 2011–15 (Vice-Pres., 2007–11). Chm., Earth Scis Cttee, NERC, 1993–96. Univ. of Helsinki Medal, 1996; Coke Medal, Geol Soc. of London, 2003; Victoria Medal, RGS, 2011; Croll Medal, Quaternary Res. Assoc., 2013. *Publications*: Studies in the Scottish Lateglacial Environment, 1977; Studies in the Lateglacial Environment of North-West Europe, 1980; (with M. J. C. Walker) Reconstructing Quaternary Environments, 1984, 3rd edn 2015; contrib. to Nature, Jl Geol Soc., Jl Ecology, Phil. Trans Royal Soc., Quaternary Sci. Rev. and others. *Recreations*: music, hill-walking, soccer (training). *Address*: Department of Geography, Royal Holloway, University of London, Egham, Surrey TW20 0EX. *T*: (01784) 443565. *E*: j.lowe@rhul.ac.uk.

**LOWE, Matthew Justin; His Honour Judge Matthew Lowe;** a Circuit Judge, since 2018; *b* Birmingham, 7 May 1968; *s* of Richard Lowe and Ann Lowe; *m* 2012, Anita; three *s*. *Educ*: Abbeydale Grange Sch., Sheffield; Univ. of Exeter (LLB). Called to the Bar, Inner Temple, 1991; barrister, 1991–2018; a Recorder, 2009–18. *Recreations*: running, fishing. *Address*: Peterborough Crown Court, Combined Court Centre, Crown Buildings, Rivergate, Peterborough PE1 1EJ.

**LOWE, (Nicholas) Mark;** QC 1996; a Recorder, since 2000; *b* 17 June 1947; *s* of late John Lancelot Lowe, solicitor, and Margaret Janet Lowe (*née* Hucklesby); *m* 1975, Felicity Anne Parry-Williams; two *s* one *d*. *Educ*: Colchester Royal Grammar Sch.; Leicester Univ. (LLB 1969). Called to the Bar, Gray's Inn, 1972, Bencher, 2004; in practice at the Bar, 1973–; Head of Chambers, 2006–11. *Recreations*: fishing (occasional), walking, birdwatching, gardening, allotment bashing, Friary rebuilding. *Address*: Cornerstone Barristers, 2–3 Gray's Inn Square, WC1R 5JH. *T*: (020) 7242 4986.

**LOWE, Paul Edward;** Chief Executive, Keeper, and Registrar General, National Records of Scotland, since 2018; *b* Edinburgh, 15 April 1972; *m* 2018, Lisa Tweedle. Case Manager, Scottish Court Service, 2000–02; Hd, Business Mgt, Crown Office and

Procurator Fiscal Service, 2002–15; Chief Exec., Student Awards Agency, Scotland, 2015–18. *Address:* HM General Register Office, Edinburgh EH1 3YY. *T:* (0131) 5351314. *E:* rg-keeper@scotland.gsi.gov.uk.

**LOWE, Peter Alexander;** Group Applications Director, Department for Work and Pensions, until 2013; *b* 1 March 1955; *s* of James Thomas Lowe and Dorothy Jean Bell Lowe; one *s* one *d*; *m* 2009, Marion Chuter. *Educ:* Wallace Hall Acad.; Heriot-Watt Univ. (BSc Hons Mech. Engrg). ESSO/EXXON, 1977–99: Maintenance Manager, Fawley Refinery, 1996–97; Prog. Manager, EXXON Year 2000, 1998–99; Principal Consultant, Booz Allen Hamilton, 1999–2003; Dir, IT, Home Office, 2003–06; Chief Inf. Officer and Dir, Inf. and Workplace Services, DTI, later BERR, 2006–09; Change and Transformation Dir, Pension, Disability and Carers Service, DWP, 2009. *Recreations:* golf, running. *Club:* Bramley Golf.

**LOWE, Prof. Philip David,** OBE 2003; Duke of Northumberland Professor of Rural Economy, University of Newcastle upon Tyne, 1992–2014, now Professor Emeritus; Director, UK Research Councils' Rural Economy and Land Use Programme, 2003–12; *b* 29 March 1950; *s* of Wilf and Lena Lowe; *m* 1972, Veronica Gibbins; one *s* one *d*. *Educ:* Exeter Coll., Oxford (MA); Manchester Univ. (MSc); Univ. of Sussex (MPhil). Res. Officer, Union of Internat. Assocs, Brussels, 1973; Lectr in Countryside Planning, 1974–89, Reader in Envmtl Planning, 1989–92, UCL; Founder and Dir, Centre for Rural Economy, Univ. of Newcastle upon Tyne, 1992–2004. Vis. Fellow, Science Centre, Berlin, 1983; Res. Fellow, Woodrow Wilson Internat. Center for Scholars, Washington, 1985. Expert Advr, H of C Select Cttee on the Envmt, 1996–99; Member: Minister of Agriculture's Adv. Gp, 1997–98; Science Adv. Council, DEFRA, 2004–09; Chm., Vets' Working Gp, DEFRA, 2007–09. Mem. Bd, Countryside Agency, 1999–2006; Chm., Market Towns Adv. Forum, 2001–06. FAcSS (AcSS 2009). Hon. DSc UEA, 2014. Bertebos Prize, Royal Swedish Acad. of Agriculture and Forestry, 2013. *Publications:* Environmental Groups in Politics, 1983; Locality and Rurality, 1984; Countryside Conflicts, 1986; Deprivation and Welfare in Rural Areas, 1986; Rural Studies in Britain and France, 1990; Rural Restructuring, 1990; The Voluntary Principle in Conservation, 1990; Rural Enterprise, 1991; Labour and Locality, 1992; Constructing the Countryside, 1993; European Integration and Environmental Policy, 1993; Gender and Rurality, 1994; Regulatory Agriculture, 1994; Moralising the Environment, 1997; British Environmental Policy and Europe, 1998; CAP Regimes and the European Countryside, 2000; Technological Change and the Rural Environment, 2000; Professionals and Volunteers in the Environmental Process, 2001; The Differentiated Countryside, 2003; The Ageing Countryside, 2006; Unlocking Potential: veterinary expertise in food animal production, 2009. *Recreations:* cycling, cinema.

**LOWE, Sir Philip (Martin),** KCMG 2014; Director General for Energy, European Commission, 2010–14; *b* 29 April 1947; *s* of late Leonard Ernest Lowe and Marguerite Helen Lowe (*née* Childs); *m* 1st, 1967, Gillian Baynton Forge (marr. diss. 1980); two *s*; 2nd, 1984, Nora Mai O'Connell. *Educ:* Leeds Grammar Sch.; Reading Sch.; St John's Coll., Oxford (MA in PPE); London Business Sch. (MSc Business Studies). Tube Investments, 1968–73; Commission of the European Communities, later European Commission: Directorate-Gen. for Credit and Investments, Luxembourg, 1973–82; Mem., Cabinet of President Gaston Thorn, 1982–85, of Alois Pfeiffer, 1985–86; Directorate-Gen. for Co-ordination of Structural Instruments, 1986–89; Chef de Cabinet to Rt Hon. Bruce Millan, Comr for regl policy, 1989–91; Dir, Rural Develt, 1991–93; Dir, Merger Task Force, 1993–95; Chef de Cabinet to Rt Hon. Neil Kinnock, Comr for transport, 1995–97, Vice-Pres. for admin. reform, 2000–02; Director-General: Develt, 1997–2000; Competition, 2002–10. Non-exec. Dir, UK Competition and Mkts Authy, 2013–16. Chair: Trilemma Initiative, World Energy Council; Competition Law Wkg Gp, Florence European Univ. Inst., 2010–. Sen. Advr, Oxera Consulting. *Recreations:* music, running, hill-walking. *Address:* 5 Columbus House, Trossachs Drive, Bathampton, Bath BA2 6RP. *T:* 07857 221766. *E:* philiplowe7@icloud.com.

*See also* Rt Rev. S. R. Lowe.

**LOWE, Dr Robert David;** Dean, St George's Hospital Medical School, 1971–82; Medical Research Consultant, National Heart Foundation of Australia, 1986–89; *b* 23 Feb. 1930; *s* of John Lowe and Hilda Althea Mead; *m* 1952, Betty Irene Wheeler; one *s* three *d*. *Educ:* Leighton Park Sch.; Emmanuel Coll., Cambridge; UCH Medical School. BCh, MB, MA, MD, PhD Cantab; FRCP, LMSSA. Medical Research Council, RAMC, 1955–59; Research Asst, UCH Med. Sch., 1959–61; St George's Hosp. Med. Sch.: MRC Res. Fellow, 1961–62; Wellcome Sen. Res. Fellow in Clinical Science, 1963–64; Sen. Lectr in Medicine, St Thomas' Hosp. Med. Sch., 1964–70; Hon. Consultant to St Thomas' Hosp., 1966–70. AUCAS: Exec. Mem., 1967; Chm., 1972–78. *Publications:* (with B. F. Robinson) A Physiological Approach to Clinical Methods, 1970; papers on peripheral circulation, hypertension, adrenergic mechanisms, central action of angiotensin, control of cardiovascular system. *Recreations:* bridge, squash, hill-walking, sailing. *Address:* 54 Drovers, Sturminster Newton, Dorset DT10 1QY.

**LOWE, Roger Stephen Richard;** Partner, Capstar Advisers, since 2019; *b* Epsom, Surrey, 12 Sept. 1966; *s* of Stephen and Margaret Lowe; *m* 1998, Sandra Hey; one *s* one *d*. *Educ:* Epsom Coll.; Peterhouse, Cambridge (BA Hons 1987). Asst Dir, Lazard, 1987–98; Gp Dir of Corporate Finance, TI Gp plc, 1998–2001; Dir, Poyry Capital, 2001–10; Exec. Dir, 2010–12, Dir, Royal Mail and Post Office Unit, 2012–14, Shareholder Exec., BIS; Dir, Portfolio Unit, Shareholder Exec., BIS, then Dir, Portfolio, UK Govt Investments, HM Treasury, 2014–19. Non-exec. Dir, Highways England, 2016–. *Recreations:* cycling, tennis, reading, ski-ing. *Address:* 54 Poland Street, W1F 7NU.

**LOWE, Rosalynde Cathryn Anne,** CBE 2011; Chair, Queen's Nursing Institute, 2003–12 (Patron and Member of Council, since 2012); *b* High Wycombe, 1 Dec. 1948; *d* of Thomas Pearce and Florence Evans Pearce; *m* 1st, 1968, James Lowe (marr. diss. 1980); one *s* one *d*; 2nd, 1993, Peter Farmer (*d* 2012). *Educ:* Didcot Girls' Grammar Sch.; Newcastle upon Tyne Poly. (BA Nursing; RGN 1980); New Coll., Durham (RHV 1981). Health Visitor, Gateshead, 1981–87; Dir, Community Nursing Services, Tower Hamlets, 1987–89; Dep. Gen. Sec., Health Visitors' Assoc., 1989–90 (Chm., 1986–88); Regl Nurse, NW Thames, 1990; Dir, Operational Services and Hd, Nursing, Hillingdon Hosp., 1992–97; Chief Exec., Hounslow and Spelthorne NHS Trust, 1997–2002. Member: UKCC, 1988–93; English Nat. Bd for Nurses, Midwives and Health Visitors, 1988–93; Audit Commn, 1995–2001; Associate Fellow, King's Fund, 2001–06; Chm., Govt Review of Health Visiting (Facing the Future), 2007. Consultant to WHO in Serbia and Moscow, 2000–07. Gov., Univ. of Brighton, 2008–17; Mem., Jt Bd, Brighton and Sussex Med. Sch., 2008–14. *Recreations:* grandchild-bothering whenever possible, unofficial theatre critic, travelling, theatre, cinema, art galleries, walking, friends, books, art history. *Address:* Apt 74 New River Head, 173 Rosebery Avenue, EC1R 4UP.

**LOWE, Rupert William Manley; His Honour Judge Lowe;** a Circuit Judge, since 2016; *b* Berden, Essex, 25 June 1963; *s* of Simon and Jenny Lowe; *m* 1995, Caroline Franks; one *s* two *d*. *Educ:* Oakham Sch., Rutland; Trinity Hall, Cambridge (BA 1st Cl. Hons 1985; MA); Univ. of Bristol (PGCE 1993); Univ. of the West of England (DipLaw 1997). Language teacher, Paris, Prato, Perugia, Rome, Milan, Lugano, 1985–92; Head Teacher,

Bath Small Sch., 1993–96; called to the Bar, Inner Temple, 1998; in practice as barrister, Bristol, 1998–2016; a Recorder, 2012–16. *Publications:* (trans.) Abducting Diana, by Dario Fo, 1986. *Address:* Canterbury Crown Court, Chaucer Road, Canterbury, Kent CT1 1ZA. *T:* (01227) 319200. *E:* listing@canterbury.crowncourt.gsi.gov.uk.

**LOWE, Stephen;** playwright; Artistic Director, Meeting Ground Theatre, since 1984; *b* 1 Dec. 1947; *s* of Harry Wright and Minnie Wright; *né* Stephen James Wright; changed name to Stephen Lowe; *m* 1st, 1975, Tina Barclay (marr. diss. 1985); one *s*; 2nd, 1999, Tanya Myers; two *d*. *Educ:* Birmingham Univ. (BA English and Theatre Studies; MA). Actor, Scarborough Theatre in the Round, 1974–78; Sen. Lectr, Writing for Performance, Dartington Coll., 1978–82; Resident Playwright, Riverside Studios, London, 1982–84. Chm., Year of Artist Adv. Gp (E Midlands), 2001–02; actg Chm., E Midlands Arts, 2001–02; Mem., Arts Council of England, then Arts Council England, and Chm., E Midlands Regl Arts Council, 2002–06; Chair, Artists taking the Lead, Culture Olympiad/ Arts Council England, 2009–. Special Lectr, Nottingham Univ., 2011–. Hon. DLitt Nottingham, 2011. *Publications:* Touched, 1981; Ragged Trousered Philanthropists, 1983; Divine Gossip/Tibetan Inroads, 1984; Moving Pictures and Other Plays, 1985; (ed) Peace Plays, vol. 1, 1985, vol. 2, 1990; Revelations, 2004; Old Big 'Ead in the Spirit of the Man, 2007; The Fox & Empty Bed Blues, 2009. *Recreations:* Buddhism, walking, snooker, history. *Address:* c/o Howard Gooding, Judy Daish Associates, 2 St Charles Place, W10 6EG. *T:* (020) 8964 8811, *Fax:* (020) 8964 8966.

**LOWE, Most Rev. Stephen Marmion;** *see* Hamilton, (NZ), Bishop of, (RC).

**LOWE, Rt Rev. Stephen Richard;** Bishop Suffragan of Hulme, 1999–2009; Bishop for Urban Life and Faith, 2006–09; an Honorary Assistant Bishop: Diocese of St Asaph, 2009–17; Diocese of Liverpool, since 2015; *b* 3 March 1944; *s* of Leonard Ernest Lowe and Marguerite Helen Lowe; *m* 1967, Pauline Amy Richards; one *s* one *d*. *Educ:* Leeds Grammar School; Reading School; Birmingham Poly. (BSc London); Ripon Hall, Oxford. Curate, St Michael's Anglican Methodist Church, Gospel Lane, Birmingham, 1968–72; Minister-in-Charge, Woodgate Valley Conventional District, 1972–75; Team Rector of East Ham, 1975–88; Archdeacon of Sheffield, 1988–99; Priest-in-Charge, St Mary Towyn, St Asaph, 2011–12; Mission Area Leader, Aled Mission Area, St Asaph, 2016–17. Hon. Canon, Chelmsford Cathedral, 1985–88; Chelmsford Diocesan Urban Officer, 1986–88. A Church Comr, 1992–99, 2001–08 (Member: Bd of Govs, 1994–99, 2001–08; Bishoprics Cttee, 1995–99, Dep. Chm., 2001–08); General Synod: Mem., 1991–99, 2000–09; Member: Exec., Central Bd of Finance, 1993–96; House of Bishops, 2000–09; Urban Bishops' Panel, 2001–09 (Chm., 2006–09); Bd for Social Responsibility, 2000–02. Member: Churches Council for Britain and Ire., 1991–96; Bishoprics and Cathedrals Cttee, 1991–2009 (Dep. Chm., 2002–09); Archbishop's Commn on Orgn of C of E, 1994–95; Bishops' Adv. Gp on urban priority areas, 1993–97; Archbishops' Commn on Urban Life and Faith, 2004–06; Trustee, Church Urban Fund, 1991–97 (Chm., Grants Cttee, 1993–96). Chairman: Sheffield Somalian Refugees Trust, 1990–94; William Temple Foundn, 2006–09. Mem., Standards Cttee, Salford CC, 2010–. Mem., Duke of Edinburgh Commonwealth Study Conf., 1989. Travelling Fellowship, Winston Churchill Meml Trust, 1980; Paul Cadbury Travelling Fellowship on Urban Empowerment, 1996. Regular contributor, Stephen Nolan Show, BBC Radio 5, 2009–; Panellist, The Big Questions, BBC 1, 2009–; paper reviewer, BBC1 Breakfast, 2012–16. *Publications:* The Churches' Role in the Care of the Elderly, 1974; What Makes a Good City, 2009. *Recreations:* watching football, cinema, theatre, travel, photography, broadcasting. *Address:* 2 Pen-y-Glyn, Bryn-y-maen, Colwyn Bay LL28 5EW. *T:* (01492) 533510. *E:* lowehulme@btinternet.com.

*See also* Sir P. M. Lowe.

**LOWE, Sir Thomas (William Gordon),** 4th Bt *cr* 1918, of Edgbaston, City of Birmingham; QC 2008; *b* 14 Aug. 1963; *s* of Sir Francis Reginald Gordon Lowe, 3rd Bt and of Franziska Cornelia, *d* of Siegfried Steinkopf; *S* father, 1986; *m* 1996, Mozhgan, *d* of Hassan Asilzadeh; one *s*. *Educ:* Stowe School; London School of Economics (LLB 1984); Jesus Coll., Cambridge (LLM 1986). Called to the Bar, Inner Temple, 1985. *Publications:* articles in various legal periodicals. *Heir: s* Theodore Christopher William Lowe, *b* 23 Aug. 2000. *Address:* Wilberforce Chambers, 8 New Square, Lincoln's Inn, WC2A 3QP.

**LOWE, Rear Adm. Timothy Miles,** CBE 2017; National Hydrographer, since 2015, and Chief Executive and Accounting Officer, since 2019, UK Hydrographic Office (Deputy Chief Executive, 2015–19); *b* Folkestone, 31 July 1963; *s* of Colin Lowe and Gillian Lowe; *m* 1985, Lynda Jane Beard; one *s*. *Educ:* Harvey Grammar Sch., Folkestone; BRNC. Joined Royal Navy, 1981; PWO, 1992; specialist navigator, 1994; in command: HMS Sandpiper, 1989–91; jsdc 1997; i/c HMS Sheffield, 1999–2001; Office of Dep. SACEUR, 2004–06; i/c HMS Albion, 2006–08; UK Maritime Component Comdr Bahrain, 2008–10; i/c Maritime Warfare Sch. and HMS Collingwood, 2010–12; Dep. FOST, 2012; Dep. Comdr Striking Force NATO, 2012–15. Pres., Sutton Sea Cadets, TS Puma, 2008–. Trustee, Bastion Baton Charity, 2012–15. QCVS 2010. *Recreations:* family, DIY, classic vehicles, reading history of nautical charting, local history. *Address:* c/o Naval Secretary, Navy Command Headquarters, Mail Point 3.1, Leach Building, Whale Island, Portsmouth PO2 8BY. *T:* (023) 9262 5542. *E:* navsec-navsec@mod.uk.

**LOWE, Vaughan;** *see* Lowe, A. V.

**LOWE, Veronica Ann;** a Judge of the First-tier Tribunal (Immigration and Asylum Chamber) (formerly Immigration Appeals Adjudicator, later Immigration Judge), since 2001, and a Judge of the First-tier Tribunal (Social Entitlement Chamber), since 2011; *b* 29 June 1951; *d* of late Arthur Ernest Bagley and Agatha (*née* Blackham); *m* 1977, Ian Stanley Lowe; one *d*. *Educ:* King Edward VI Grammar Sch. for Girls, Handsworth, Birmingham; St Hugh's Coll., Oxford (MA); Oxford Polytechnic (MIL Exams); City of Birmingham Polytechnic. Articled Clerk, Ryland, Martineau & Co., Birmingham, 1976–78; Lectr in Labour Law, Univ. of Aston in Birmingham, 1978–80; admitted solicitor, 1979; solicitor in private practice, 1979–86; Asst Area Dir, Legal Aid Area No 8, 1986–88; Area Dir (W Midlands), Legal Aid Area No 6, 1988–89; Gp Manager (Midlands), Legal Aid Bd, 1989–90; Dir, Solicitors' Complaints Bureau, 1990–95; Chief Exec., Valuation Office Agency, 1996–97; mgt consultant and author, 1998–; solicitor, Pinsent Curtis, 1999–2000; Hd of Legal Services, Oxford Brookes Univ., 2000; Sen. Legal Counsel, 2000–03, European Legal Affairs Consultant, 2003–07, Mayne Pharma (formerly Faulding Pharmaceuticals) plc. Mem. Bd, Eur. Generic Medicines Assoc., 2002–07 (Mem., Legal Affairs Cttee, 2002–07). *Publications:* contribs to publications on law for accountants and businessmen; articles on intellectual property law, generic medicines, Eur. legislation and CPD in immigration, asylum and human rights law. *Recreations:* cooking, eating and drinking, reading, writing unfinished novels, listening to music, travel, talking, current affairs, being with my daughter, all historical subjects. *Address:* Phoenix Cottage, 6 Rugby Road, Dunchurch, Warwicks CV22 6PE.

**LOWEN, Barry Robert;** HM Diplomatic Service; Ambassador to Algeria, since 2017; *b* 9 Jan. 1964; *s* of Robert Lowen and Pamela Lowen; *m* 1989, Karin (*née* Blizard); three *s*. *Educ:* Jesus Coll., Oxford (MA PPE); Open Univ. (MBA). Joined HM Diplomatic Service, 1986: Arab-Israeli Desk Officer, FCO, 1986; Arabic trng, 1987–89; Second Sec., Kuwait,

1989–93; Head of Section: Non-Proliferation Dept, FCO, 1993–95; ME Dept, FCO, 1995–97; First Sec., UKMIS, NY, 1997–2001; Dep. Hd, ME Dept, FCO, 2001–03; Dir, Trade and Investment, 2003–04, Dep. Hd of Mission, 2004–06, Riyadh; Hd, Engaging with the Islamic World Gp, FCO, 2006–07; Dir Asia, UK Trade and Investment, 2008–10; Dir, Trade and Investment, New Delhi, 2010–14; Hd, Econ. Growth and Business Dept, FCO, 2014–16; Hd, Trade Diplomacy Unit, FCO and DIT, 2016–17. *Recreations:* cycling, ski-ing, hang-gliding, family. *Address:* c/o Foreign and Commonwealth Office, King Charles Street, SW1A 2AH. *E:* bklowen@yahoo.com.

**LOWEN, David Travers;** Director, International TV and Media Consulting, since 1998; *b* London, 20 June 1946; *s* of Norman Frederick Lowen and Beatrice Lowen; *m* 1970, Jennifer Durston; one *s* one *d*. *Educ:* Queen Elizabeth's Sch., Barnet; Emmanuel Coll., Cambridge (BA 1967; Hon. Fellow 2009). Newspaper journalist, Kent Messenger Gp, 1968–71; Southern TV, 1971–74; Hd of News, Westward TV, 1974–77; Yorkshire TV: producer, 1977–92; Dir, Network Prog. Develt, 1992–95; Dir, Corporate Develt, 1995–98; Dir, Millbank TV Studios, 1995–98. Dir Gen., Euronews, 2003. Non-exec. Chm., Sysmedia Gp plc, 2003–; non-executive Director: Palm FM, 2006–13; Radio Plymouth, 2008–13; Green Gaia Films Ltd, 2012–15; Formal Futures Ltd, 2013–; Dir, Media Local Solutions Ltd, 2007–14. Chm., Bd of Govs, Leeds Beckett Univ., 2014–; Chair, Council, UCAS, 2018–; Dep. Chm., Cttee of Univ. Chairs, 2016–. Trustee and Hon. Sec., RTS, 2000– (Fellow, 1995). Chm., Emmanuel Soc. Mem., ESU. FRSA. *Publications:* Stay Alive with Eddie McGee, 1979; Fighting Back: a woman's guide to self-defence, 1982. *Recreations:* cricket, horse-racing. *E:* d_lowen@btinternet.com. *Club:* Lord's Taverners.

**LOWEN, His Honour Jonathan Andrew Michael;** a Circuit Judge, 2000–13; *b* 16 Aug. 1943; *s* of George Lowen, QC and Vera Fanny Lowen; *m* 1974, Eve Susan Karpf; two *s*. *Educ:* Witwatersrand Univ., Johannesburg (BA); Christ Church, Oxford (MA). Called to the Bar, Gray's Inn, 1972; a Recorder, 1995–2000.

**LOWENSTEIN, Paul David;** QC 2009; *b* London, 31 Dec. 1963; *s* of John and Vivien Lowenstein; *m* 1st, 1991, Nadine Shenton (marr. diss. 2010); three *s*; 2nd, 2010, Carolyn Greene; two *s*. *Educ:* Manchester Univ. (LLB Hons 1986); Queens' Coll., Cambridge (LLM 1987). Called to the Bar, Middle Temple, 1988, Bencher, 2017; in practice as barrister, specialising in commercial, financial and business litigation, 1989–; Accredited Mediator, 2000. Chm., Bar Disciplinary Tribunals, 2017–. International Law Book Facility: Chm., Operating Cttee, 2005–; Trustee, 2010–; Chm. Trustees, 2016–. *Recreations:* sailing, Cornwall. *Address:* 20 Essex Street, WC2R 3AL. *T:* (020) 7842 1200, *Fax:* (020) 7842 1270. *E:* pdl@20essexst.com. *Clubs:* United and Cecil; St Mawes Sailing.

**LOWER, Adrian Christopher;** a District Judge (Magistrates' Courts), since 2012; *b* Newton Abbot, 9 May 1970; *s* of Geoffrey McDougall and Georgina Rosemary Lower; two *s*. *Educ:* Colfox Sch., Bridport; Univ. of Southampton (LLB Hons); Coll. of Law, Chester. Higher Rights of Audience (Criminal), 2001. Admitted as solicitor, 1994; Crown Prosecution Service: Crown Prosecutor, 1994–96; Sen. Crown Prosecutor, 1996–2004; District Crown Prosecutor, 2004–10; Hd of Complex Casework Unit, S Yorks and Humberside, 2010–11; Legal Asst to Principal Legal Advr to DPP, CPS HQ, 2011–12; a Dep. Dist Judge (Civil), 2010–12. Mem., Adv. Bd, Sch. of Law, Univ. of Sheffield, 2009–. Mem., Editl Bd, Criminal Law Week, 2019–. *Recreations:* cricket, current affairs, funding sons. *Address:* York Magistrates' Court, Clifford Street, York YO1 9RE. *T:* (01904) 818300.

**LOWMAN, Ven. David Walter;** Archdeacon of Chelmsford, 2013–16, now Archdeacon Emeritus; *b* 27 Nov. 1948; *s* of Cecil Walter Lowman and Queenie Norah Lowman. *Educ:* Crewkerne Sch., Somerset; City of London Coll. (Dip. in English Civil Law 1970); King's Coll. London (BD 1973; AKC 1973). Estate Duty Office, Inland Revenue, 1966–70. Ordained deacon, 1975, priest, 1976; Curate: Notting Hill Team Ministry, 1975–78; St Augustine, Kilburn, 1978–81; Vocations Adviser and Selection Sec., ACCM, and Chaplain, Church House, Westminster, 1981–86; Team Rector, Wickford and Runwell, Dio. Chelmsford, 1986–93; Diocesan Dir of Ordinands, and Non-residentiary Canon of Chelmsford Cathedral, 1993–2001; Archdeacon of Southend, 2001–13. Mem. Wkg Pty, House of Bishops (reported on marriage in church after divorce), 1999. Chair: Vocations Adv. Panel, Ministry Div., Archbishops' Council, 2001–08; N Thames Ministerial Trng Course, 2001–06. Trustee: SE Essex Christian Hospice, 2001–06; Clergy Support Trust (formerly Corp. of Sons of the Clergy and Friends of the Clergy), 2012–; Vice Chair, Trustees, St Mellitus Coll., 2008–16. Gov., Brentwood Sch., 2001–. *Recreations:* cricket, travel (France, Italy, USA, Cyprus), opera, red wine. *Address:* 16 Kelvin Court, Fourth Avenue, Frinton-on-Sea CO13 9DT. *T:* (01255) 676793.

**LOWNIE of Largo, Andrew James Hamilton,** FRHistS; literary agent; Proprietor, Andrew Lownie Literary Agency Ltd, since 1988; writer; *b* 11 Nov. 1961; *s* of His Honour Dr Ralph Hamilton Lownie of Largo; *m* 1998, Angela Doyle; one *s* one *d*. *Educ:* Fettes Coll.; Asheville Sch., NC (ESU Schol.); Westminster Sch.; Magdalene Coll., Cambridge (MA); Edinburgh Univ. (MSc); Coll. of Law, London; Edinburgh Univ. (PhD). Pres., Cambridge Union Soc., 1984. Graduate trainee, Hodder & Stoughton Publishers, 1984–85; John Farquharson Literary Agents, 1985–88 (Dir, 1986–88); Director: Denniston & Lownie Ltd, 1991–93; Thistle Publishing, 1996–. Literary Agent to PEN, 2001–04. Archives Bye-Fellow, Churchill Coll., Cambridge, 2016. Contested (C) Monklands West, 1992. Vice-Chm., Cons. Gp for Europe, 1992–95. Mem., Adv. Bd, Biographers' Internat. Orgn, 2012–. Sec., 1998–2008, Pres., 2008–, Biographers' Club. Trustee: Iain MacLeod Award, 1986–; Campaign for Freedom of Information, 2017–. FRHistS 2017. *Publications:* (ed) North American Spies, 1991; The Edinburgh Literary Guide, 1992; John Buchan: the Presbyterian Cavalier, 1995; (ed) John Buchan's Collected Poems, 1996; (ed) John Buchan: the complete short stories, vols 1–3, 1996–97; (ed) John Buchan: shorter Scottish fiction, 1997; The Literary Companion to Edinburgh, 2000; The Edinburgh Literary Companion, 2005; Stalin's Englishman, 2015 (Intelligence Bk of the Year Award, St Ermin's Hotel, 2017); The Mountbattens, 2019. *Recreations:* history, music, tennis, travel. *Address:* Andrew Lownie Literary Agency Ltd, 36 Great Smith Street, SW1P 3BU. *T:* (020) 7222 7574, *Fax:* (020) 7222 7576. *E:* Lownie@globalnet.co.uk. *Club:* Beefsteak.

**LOWRY-CORRY,** family name of **Earl of Belmore.**

**LOWSON, Rt Rev. Christopher;** see Lincoln, Bishop of.

**LOWSON, Sir Ian (Patrick),** 2nd Bt *cr* 1951; *b* 4 Sept. 1944; *s* of Sir Denys Colquhoun Flowerdew Lowson, 1st Bt and Hon. Patricia, OStJ, *yr d* of 1st Baron Strathcarron, PC, KC; *S* father, 1975; *m* 1979, Mrs Tanya Du Boulay, *d* of R. F. A. Judge; one *s* one *d*. *Educ:* Eton; Duke Univ., USA. OStJ. *Heir: s* Henry William Lowson [*b* 10 Nov. 1980; *m* 2009, Rocio R. Acal Mendez; two *s*]. *Address:* 23 Flood Street, SW3 5ST. *Clubs:* Boodle's, Pilgrims, Brook (NY).

**LOWSON, Robert Campbell;** independent consultant, since 2014; Director, Regulation, Department for Environment, Food and Rural Affairs, 2007, on secondment to European Environment Agency, 2007–11; *b* 7 March 1949; *s* of late George Campbell Lowson and Betty Lowson (*née* Parry); *m* 1973, Hilary Balsdon; one *s* one *d*. *Educ:* Gravesend Grammar Sch.; Brasenose Coll., Oxford (BA History 1970). Joined Ministry of Agriculture, Fisheries and Food, 1970: UK Mission, Geneva, 1977; Principal Private Sec. to Minister of Agric., Fisheries and Food, 1982; successively Head of Cereals, Milk, Animal Health, and Agric. Resource Policy Divs, 1983–94; Under Sec., 1994; Minister, UK Repn Brussels, on loan to FCO, 1995–99; Dir of Communications, MAFF, subseq. DEFRA, 1999–2001; Dir of Envmt Protection Strategy, later Envmt Strategy, DEFRA, 2001–07. Consultant on space and research questions: Technol. Strategy Bd, 2011–14; Evenflow Consultants, 2016–. Mem. Bd, NIAB, 2019–. Jt Chm., Cambridge for Europe campaign, 2016. *Recreations:* all the usual things. *Club:* Athenæum.

**LOWTHER,** family name of **Earl of Lonsdale** and **Viscount Ullswater.**

**LOWTHER, James;** Vice Lord-Lieutenant of Northamptonshire, since 2018; Founding Partner, M&C Saatchi (UK), 1995–2016 (Chairman, 2000–06); *b* 27 Jan. 1947; *s* of George Hugh Lowther and Sheila Rachel Isabelle Lowther; *m* 1987, Karen Healey Wallace; one *s* three *d*. *Educ:* Eton Coll.; Keble Coll., Oxford (MA Hons Hist.). Saatchi & Saatchi, 1977–95, Creative Dir and Dep. Chm., 1991–95. Dir, Lowther Productions, 2003–. Dir, British Television Advertising Awards, 1992–2012; Exec. Producer, Britain's Brilliant Prodigies, 2002, 2003. Mem., Mgt Bd, Northants Surprise. Trustee, Children in Crisis, 2000–10; Develt Cttee, Mayor of London's Fund for Young Musicians, 2012–14. DL Northants, 2016. *Publications:* (contrib.) The Copy Book, 1995; (contrib.) The 22 Irrefutable Laws of Advertising (and When to Violate Them). *Recreations:* listening to, playing and writing music, restoring beautiful but hungry historic house, promoting the wonders of Northamptonshire. *Address:* 4 Fawcett Street, SW10 9HZ. *T:* (020) 7352 2735; Holdenby House, Northampton NN6 8DJ. *T:* (01604) 770241. *Club:* Bluebird.

**LOWTHER, Merlyn Vivienne;** a Director, 2011–14, and Chairman of Risk Committee, 2012–13, Co-operative Banking Group; *b* 3 March 1954; *d* of Norman Edward Douglas Humphrey and Joan Margaret Humphrey (*née* Hewitt); *m* 1975, David John Lowther; one *s* one *d*. *Educ:* Manchester High Sch. for Girls; Univ. of Manchester (BSc Hons Maths 1975); London Business Sch. (MSc Econs 1981); Central Sch. of Speech and Drama (MA Actor Trng and Coaching 2007). FCIB 1999. Bank of England, 1975–2004: Sen. Dealer, Gilt Edged Div., 1985–87; Head, Banking Div. and Dep. Chief Cashier, 1991–96; Personnel Dir, 1996–98; Dep. Dir and Chief Cashier, 1999–2004; Schroders plc: a Dir, 2004–13; Chm., Audit and Risk Cttee (formerly Audit Cttee), 2010–13. Trustee: Henry Smith's Charity, 1999–2017; Winston Churchill Meml Trust, 2003–. Mem. Council, Salford Univ., 2018–. Gov., Manchester High Sch. for Girls, 2015–. FRSA 1996. Hon. LLD Manchester, 1999. *Recreations:* theatre, singing, reading, family.

**LOWTHER, Sir Patrick William,** 7th Bt *cr* 1824; *b* 15 July 1977; *s* of Sir Charles Douglas Lowther, 6th Bt and Florence Rose Lowther (*née* Cramsie); *S* father, 2018, but his name does not appear on the Official Roll of the Baronetage; *m* 2006, Sarah Jane, *o d* of William Davis; two *s*. *Heir: s* Hugo Charles Sandy Lowther, *b* 2 Dec. 2008.

**LOWTHER-PINKERTON, (Anthony) James (Moxon),** LVO 2013 (MVO 1986); MBE 1990; DL; Extra Equerry to the Duke and Duchess of Cambridge and the Duke of Sussex (formerly Prince Henry of Wales), since 2014; *b* 28 Sept. 1960; *s* of Anthony Hull Lowther-Pinkerton and Sue Lowther-Pinkerton (*née* Leslie-Smith); *m* 1995, Susannah Lucy (*née* Richards); one *s* three *d*. *Educ:* Eton Coll.; RMA Sandhurst. Irish Guards, 1979–98: Equerry to HM Queen Elizabeth the Queen Mother, 1984–86; 22 SAS Regt, 1987–94; sc 1995; Balkans desk officer, Directorate of Mil. Ops, MoD, 1996–98. Dir, Objective Team Ltd, 2001–09; Sen. Consultant, Kroll Security Gp, 2004–06. Private Sec. to Prince William of Wales, later as Duke of Cambridge and Prince Henry of Wales, 2005–12, and to Duchess of Cambridge, 2011–12; Principal Private Sec. to Duke and Duchess of Cambridge and Prince Henry of Wales, 2012–14. Consultant: GEMS Educn, 2013–19; Audley, 2019–. Director: Peregrine Partners Fund, 2018–; Time Partners, 2019–. Mem., Adv. Council, Cranemere Gp Ltd, 2013–15; Strategic Partner, C5 Investments, 2015–; Advr, DS-48, 2015– (Chm., 2018–). Member: RIIA, 2014–; Atlantic Partnership, 2016–. Chairman: Adv. Cttee, Invictus Games, 2014–16; Cloud Leadership Centre, 2016–. Trustee: HALO Trust, 2005–15 (Mem., Adv. Council, 2015–); Sentebale - The Princes' Fund for Lesotho, 2006–09, 2010–13; Royal Foundn of Duke and Duchess of Cambridge (formerly Charitable Foundn of Prince William and Prince Harry, then Royal Foundn of Duke and Duchess of Cambridge and Prince Harry, then the Duke and Duchess of Sussex), 2009–; Varkey Foundn, 2014–19; Waterloo Uncovered, 2016–; Endeavour Fund, 2016–; Gerry Holdsworth Special Forces Charitable Trust, 2018–. Pres., RBL, Suffolk Co., 2015–. Mem. Council, Irish Guards, 2015–. Fellow, British American Project. FRGS. Hon. Bencher, Middle Temple, 2012. DL Suffolk, 2013. *Recreations:* Nelson, castles, the Suffolk coast, watercolour painting. *Address:* Methersgate Hall, Sutton, Woodbridge, Suffolk IP12 3JL. *T:* (01394) 385928. *Clubs:* Pratt's, 1805, White's, Pitt.

**LOXDALE, Prof. Hugh David,** MBE 2007; DPhil; CBiol; FLS; FRSB; Editor-in-Chief, Brambleby Books (UK) Ltd, since 2012; Professor of Ecology, Institute of Ecology, Friedrich Schiller University and Max Planck Institute for Chemical Ecology, Jena, Germany, 2009–11 (Senior Research Fellow in Entomology, 2006–09); *b* 9 Sept. 1950; *s* of late John David Loxdale and Phyllis Marjorie Loxdale (*née* Duke); *m* 1993, Nicola von Mende, MSc, PhD. *Educ:* Apsley Grammar Sch., Hemel Hempstead; Univ. of Reading (ARC Bursary; BSc Hons (Zool. with Biochem. and Physiol.) 1974); Linacre Coll., Oxford (DPhil 1980). MIBiol 1974, FRSB (FIBiol 2001); CBiol 1979. Entomologist, Rothamsted Experimental Station, subseq. Rothamsted Research: scientific asst, 1969–71; returned to Rothamsted, 1977; SO, 1977; HSO, 1979; SSO, 1985; Principal Res. Scientist, 1991–2005. Hon. Vis. Prof., Cardiff Sch. of Biosciss, Cardiff Univ., 2015–. Lectr in field; Special Lectr in insect molecular ecol., Sutton Bonington, Univ. of Nottingham, 1993–96. Mem., Co-ordination Cttee, ESF network, PARTNER (Parthenogenesis Network), 2003–05. Royal Entomological Society: Fellow, 1985; Mem. Council and Trustee, 2000–03; Vice Pres., 2003; Pres., 2004–06; Hon. Treas., 2011–16; Hon. Fellow, 2016. Mem. Council, Systematics Assoc., 1986–89. Beds, Essex and Herts Branch, Institute of Biology: Mem. Cttee, 1998–99; Sec., 1999–2003; Chm., 2003–06. Life Gov., ICRF, 1989–2003; Hon. Fellow, CRUK, 2003–. FLS 2002. Hon. FRES. Freeman, Shrewsbury, 1993. Ed.-in-Chief, The Entomologist (Jl of Royal Entomol. Soc.), 1987–89; Member, Editorial Board: Molecular Ecol., 2000–05; Molecular Ecol. Resources, 2000–16; Subject Ed., 2002–05, Associate Ed., 2010–13, Bulletin Entomol Res.; English Lang. Ed. and Mem., Editl Bd, Eur. Jl Entomol., 2012–14; Asst Ed., Royal Entomological Soc. Bulletin, Antenna, 2016–. *Publications:* (ed with J. Den Hollander) Electrophoretic Studies on Agricultural Pests, 1989; (ed with G. Lushai) Intraclonal Genetic Variation: ecological and evolutionary aspects, 2003; *natural history poetry:* The Eternal Quest: a celebration of nature in poetry, 1988, 2nd edn 2003; Blue Skies in Tuscany, 2000, 2nd edn 2003; Fascinating Felines: sixty cat poems, 2002; Bird Words: poetic images of wild birds, 2003; The Jena Poems, 2010; Love and the Sea, 2010; Nevisian Days: poetry from a Caribbean Isle, 2011; Bird of Paradise: selected poems, 1968–2011, 2011; Zoooo… Living Poems for Children, 2012; Red Tulips: selected poems 1999–2016, 2017; numerous contribs to internat. scientific jls, res. and review papers, book chapters and popular articles, esp. about insect migration using molecular markers, clonality and generalism in nature. *Recreations:* natural history, genealogy, history, writing poetry, walking, debating. *Address:* 15 Lyngford Square, Taunton, Somerset TA2 7ES. *T:* (01823) 259615. *E:* Loxdale@web.de.

**LU, Prof. Gaoqing, (Max),** AO 2017; DL; PhD; FAA; FTSE; President and Vice-Chancellor, University of Surrey, since 2016; *b* China, 8 Nov. 1963; *s* of Bensheng Lu and Huailan Change; *m* 1987, Dr Lianxiang Liu; one *s* one *d. Educ:* Northeastern Univ., China (BEng, MEng); Univ. of Queensland (PhD 1991). Lectr, Nanyang Technol Univ., Singapore, 1991–94; Sen. Lectr, 1994–98, Associate Prof., 1998–2000, Prof., 2000–03, Sch. of Chem. Engrg, Univ. of Qld; Dir, ARC Centre of Functional Nanomaterials, Australia, 2003–09; University of Queensland: Pro Vice-Chancellor, Res. Linkages, 2008–09; Dep. Vice-Chancellor (Res.), 2009–13; Provost and Sen. Vice-Pres., 2014–16. Member: Council for Sci. and Technol., 2017–; Bd, UK Res. and Innovation, 2017–. DL Surrey, 2017. FTSE 2002; FAA 2013. *Publications:* over 500 contribs to learned scientific jls. *Recreations:* swimming, tennis, walking. *Address:* Senate House, University of Surrey, Guildford, Surrey GU2 7XH. *T:* (01483) 689249. *E:* vice-chancellor@surrey.ac.uk.

**LUBA, Jan Michael Andrew;** QC 2000; **His Honour Judge Luba;** a Circuit Judge, since 2015; a Senior Circuit Judge and Designated Civil Judge, since 2019; *b* 12 Feb. 1957; *s* of Zenon and Marlene Luba; *m* 1978, Adriana; two *d. Educ:* London Sch. of Economics (LLB); Univ. of Leicester (LLM). Called to the Bar, Middle Temple, 1980, Bencher, 2009; Legal Officer, CPAG, 1987–89; Nat. Housing Law Service, 1990–92; private practice at the Bar, England and Wales, 1992–2015; a Recorder, 2000–15; a Judge of the Employment Appeal Tribunal (pt-time), 2002–15. Patron, Croydon Housing Aid Soc., 2003–10. Chair, Zacchaeus 2000 Trust, 2013–16 (Patron, 2016–). *Publications:* Repairs: Tenant's Rights, 1986, 6th edn (with Catherine O'Donnell and Giles Peaker) 2016; Housing and the Human Rights Act, 2000; (jtly) Defending Possession Proceedings, 1987, 8th edn 2016; The Homelessness Act 2002, 2002, 2nd edn (with Liz Davies) 2003; (jtly) Housing Allocation and Homelessness, 2006, 5th edn (with Liz Davies) 2018. *Recreations:* spending time with my family, walking. *Address:* County Court at Central London, Royal Courts of Justice, Thomas More Building, Strand, WC2A 2LL.

**LUBBOCK,** family name of **Baron Avebury.**

**LUBBOCK, John David Peter,** OBE 2015; FRAM; Founder and Musical Director, Orchestra of St John's, since 1967; Founder and Director, Music for Autism, since 2000; *b* 18 March 1945; *s* of Michael Lubbock and Diana (*née* Crawley); *m* 1st, 1977, Eleanor Sloan (marr. diss.); two *s*; 2nd, 1991, Christine Cairns; two *s. Educ:* St George's Choir Sch., Windsor Castle (Chorister); Radley Coll.; Royal Acad. of Music (FRAM 1999). Mem., Swingle Singers, 1971–74. Guest conductor, USA, Canada, Europe. Trustee: Music of Life Foundn; Clear Sky Foundn; Thornley Hall Activity Centre; My World Autistic Day Centre. *Recreation:* tennis. *Address:* 7 Warborough Road, Shillingford, Oxon OX10 7SA. *T:* (01865) 858210.

**LUCAN, 8th Earl of,** *cr* 1795 (Ire.); **George Charles Bingham;** Bt 1632; Baron Lucan 1776; Baron Bingham (UK) 1934; *b* 21 Sept. 1967; *s* of 7th Earl of Lucan and Veronica Mary Bingham (*née* Duncan); his father's Death Certificate was issued in the High Court on 3 Feb. 2016 under the Presumption of Death Act 2014; *m* 2016, Anne-Sofie Foghsgaard, one *d. Educ:* Eton; Trinity Hall, Cambridge. *Clubs:* Turf, White's, Pratt's.
*See also* Lady C. Bingham.

**LUCAS,** family name of **Baron Lucas of Chilworth.**

**LUCAS OF CHILWORTH, 3rd Baron** *cr* 1946, of Chilworth; **Simon William Lucas;** *b* 6 Feb. 1957; *er s* of 2nd Baron Lucas of Chilworth and Ann-Marie (*née* Buck); *S* father, 2001; *m* 1993, Fiona, *yr d* of Thomas Mackintosh, Vancouver; two *s. Educ:* Leicester Univ. (BSc); RMA Sandhurst. Late RE. *Heir: s* Hon. John Ronald Muir Lucas, *b* 21 May 1995.

**LUCAS OF CRUDWELL, 11th Baron** *cr* 1663, **AND DINGWALL, 14th Lord** *cr* 1609; **Ralph Matthew Palmer;** *b* 7 June 1951; *s* of 10th Baroness Lucas of Crudwell and 13th Lady Dingwall and of Maj. the Hon. Robert Jocelyn Palmer, MC, 3rd *s* of 3rd Earl of Selborne, PC, CH; *S* mother, 1991; *m* 1st, 1978, Clarissa Marie (marr. diss. 1995), *d* of George Vivian Lockett, TD and Alice Jeannine Lockett; one *s* one *d*; 2nd, 1995, Amanda Atha (*d* 2000); 3rd, 2001, Antonia Vera Kennedy, *d* of late Anthony Benno John Stanley Rubinstein and Anne Langford Dent; one *d. Educ:* Eton; Balliol Coll., Oxford (BA (Hons) Physics). BDO Binder Hamlyn, 1972–76; S. G. Warburg & Co. Ltd, 1976–88. A Lord in Waiting (Govt Whip), 1994–97; Govt spokesman on educn, 1994–95, social security and Wales, 1994–97, agric. and envmt, 1995–97; Opposition spokesman on internat. develt, 1997–98; elected Mem., H of L, 1999. Ed., Good Schs Guide, 2000–; Chm., Good Careers Guide, 2014–. *Heir: s* Hon. Lewis Edward Palmer, *b* 7 Dec. 1987. *Address:* House of Lords, SW1A 0PW. *T:* (020) 7219 4177. *E:* lucasr@parliament.uk.

**LUCAS, Adrian Paul,** FRCO(CHM); freelance conductor, organist, animateur, adjudicator and examiner; Head of Choral Studies and Chief Examiner, Royal School of Church Music, since 2015; *b* 14 March 1962; *s* of Kenneth David Lucas and Kathleen Lucas (*née* Mash); *m* 1986, Joanna Louise Harrison; one *s* one *d. Educ:* St John's Coll., Cambridge (Organ Schol.; MA). FRCO(CHM) 1990. Actg Asst Organist, Salisbury Cathedral, 1980; Asst Organist, Norwich Cathedral, 1983–90; Tutor, UEA, 1985–90; Organist, Portsmouth Cathedral, 1990–96; Organist and Master of the Choristers, Worcester Cathedral, 1996–2011. Musical Director: Worcester Fest. Choral Soc., 1997–2011; Worcs SO, 2000–02; City of Birmingham Choir, 2002–; Millennium Youth Choir, 2015–. Pres., Cathedral Organists' Assoc., 2003–05. Guest Conductor: Philharmonia Orch., 2000–; Classic FM Live, 2010. Examr, Associated Bd, RSM, 1989–; former Ext. Examr, RAM; Ext. Examr, Birmingham Conservatoire, 2000–. Freelance recitalist, broadcaster and conductor, incl. Three Choirs Fest. Founder, Acclaim Prodns, 2011–. Recordings incl. 4 solo organ discs and choral works with Portsmouth and Worcester Cathedral Choirs, and Choirs of Three Choirs Fest. Responsible for installation of new organ at Worcester Cathedral, 2008. *Publications:* various musical compositions, incl. Noël for boys' voices, harp and organ, 1998 (also recorded), Creation Canticles, 2004; contrib. to musical training books. *Recreations:* flying (Eur. Aviation Safety Agency Private Pilot Licence for Single-engine Piston aircraft), bread making, wine. *Address:* 2 Field Terrace, Worcester WR5 3BN. *T:* (01905) 352136.

**LUCAS, Prof. Alan,** MD; FRCP, FRCPCH, FMedSci; MRC Clinical Research Professor, MRC Childhood Nutrition Research Centre, 1996, and concurrently Professor of Paediatric Nutrition, 2001, Institute of Child Health, University College London; Fellow, Clare College, Cambridge, since 1982; *b* 30 June 1946; *s* of late Dr Saul H. Lucas, Maj., RAMC, and Dr Sophia Lucas; *m* 1st, 1967, Sally Wedeles (marr. diss.); 2nd, 1978, Penny Hodgson; one *s* two *d. Educ:* Bedales Sch., Hants; Clare Coll., Cambridge (Foundn Schol.; BA Med. & Natural Sci. Tripos 1st Cl. Hons 1968; BChir 1971, MB 1972; MA 1985); MD Cantab 1991; Oxford Univ. Med. Sch. FRCP 1991; FRCPCH 1997. Jun. posts, Radcliffe Infirmary, Oxford and Addenbrooke's Hosp., Cambridge, 1971–77; Lector, Trinity Coll., Cambridge, 1972–76; University of Oxford: Wellcome Res. Fellow, Dept of Paediatrics, 1977–79; Lectr, St Edmund Hall, 1977–80; University of Cambridge: Clinical Lectr, 1980–82, Hon. Consultant, 1982–96, Dept of Paediatrics; Dir, Med. Studies, Peterhouse, 1980–86; Dir, Studies in Medicine and in Anatomy, Clare Coll., 1982–97; Hd, Infant and Child Nutrition, MRC Dunn Nutrition Unit, Cambridge, 1982–96; Dir, MRC Childhood Nutrition Res. Centre, Inst. of Child Health, UCL, 1996–2011; Hon. Consultant, Gt Ormond St Hosp. for Children, 1996–. Lectures include: McCance, 1995, George Alexander Gibson, Widdowson, 2009, Neonatal Soc., London; Edna Park, Toronto; Telford, Manchester, 2011. Member: Panel on Child Nutrition, DHSS, 1988–96; Wkg Gp on Infant Formula, EEC, 1988; Standing Cttee on Nutrition, BPA, subseq. RCPCH, 1988–2000 (Mem., Acad. Bd, 1989–94); Physiol Medicine and Infections Bd, 1992–96, Wkg Gp on Fluoride and Osteoporosis, 1994 (Chm.) and Health Services Res. Bd, 1995–96, MRC. FMedSci 2000. Hon. Citizen, Georgia, USA (for educnl services), 1994. Guthrie Medal, RCPCH, 1982. *Publications:* over 400 scientific papers and articles, and contrib. to books, on child health, nutrition and metabolism, notably long term health effects of early nutrition. *Recreations:* art, art history, music, sports.

**LUCAS, Andrew,** FRCO; Master of the Music, Cathedral and Abbey Church of St Alban, since 1998; *b* 19 Aug. 1958; *s* of Richard John Lucas and Vera Mary Lucas (*née* Lawrence). *Educ:* Wakeman Sch., Shrewsbury; Royal Coll. of Music (GRSM 1979; BMus (London) 1981); Sweelinck Conservatoire, Amsterdam. FRCO 1979. Dir of Music, St James's, Sussex Gardens, London, 1981–85; St Paul's Cathedral: organ student, 1980–84; Asst Sub-Organist, 1985–89; Sub-Organist and Asst Dir of Music, 1990–98; Acting Organist and Master of Choristers, St Andrew's Cathedral, Sydney, Aust., 1997. Conductor, St Albans Bach Choir, 1998–; Artistic Dir, St Albans Internat. Organ Fest., 1999–2007. Pres., Asst Cathedral Organists' Assoc., 2002– (Chm., 1993–98); Mem. Council, RCO, 1997–2006. Liveryman, Co. of Musicians, 1998–. Hon. FGCM 2006. *Recreations:* theatre, travel, architecture, gardens, good food and coffee. *Address:* Cathedral and Abbey Church of St Alban, St Albans, Herts AL1 1BY. *T:* (01727) 568721. *E:* andrewl01@aol.com; 31 Abbey Mill Lane, St Albans, Herts AL3 4HA.

**LUCAS, Anne Katharine;** *see* Stevenson, A. K.

**LUCAS, Prof. Arthur Maurice,** AO 2005; CBE 2002; PhD; Professor of Science Curriculum Studies, 1980–2003, now Emeritus, and Principal, 1993–2003, King's College, London; *b* 26 Oct. 1941; *s* of Joseph Alfred Percival Lucas and May Queen Lucas (*née* Griffin); *m* 1970, Paula Jean Williams; one *s* one *d. Educ:* Univ. of Melbourne (BSc 1963; BEd 1968); Ohio State Univ. (PhD 1972; Fulbright Award). FRSB (FIBiol 1981); FACE 1995. Appts at Yallourn and Newborough High Schs, 1964–66; Flinders Univ. of SA, 1967–70; Ohio State Univ., 1970–72; Warrnambool Inst. of Advanced Educn, 1973; Flinders University: Lectr in Sci. Educn, 1974–80; Sen. Lectr, 1976; Vice-Chm., 1976, Chm., 1977–79, Sch. of Educn; King's College, London: Asst Principal, 1987–89; Vice-Principal, 1991–93; Actg Principal, 1992; London University: Chm., Bd of Educnl Studies, 1986–88; Mem. Council, 1995–2003; Chm., Mgt Bd, Marine Biol. Stn, Millport, 1995–2002; Dep. Vice Chancellor, 1997–2002. Hon. Vis. Prof., Sch. of Educn, UEA, 2005–12. Mem., Lord Chancellor's Adv. Council on Nat. Records and Archives, 2006–15. Member, Council: Commonwealth Assoc. for Sci., Maths and Technol. Educn, 1981–89; Zoological Soc. of London, 1992–93 (Vice Pres., 1993); Royal Instn, 1998–2004; British Soc. for History of Sci., 1999–2002; Member: Exec. Cttee, Field Studies Council, 1986–92, 1994–2000, 2002–07; COPUS, 1993–95; Bd, Univs and Colls Employers Assoc., 1996–2003; Bd, QAA, 2002–08; Parly and Scientific Cttee, 2002–03. Chm., Medicine and Soc. Panel, Wellcome Trust, 1998–2002. Mem., SE Thames RHA, 1993–94. Pres., 2006–09, Hon. Mem., 2010, Soc. for Hist. of Natural Hist. Trustee, Samuel Courtauld Trust, 1997–2002. Mem. Cttee, Wymondham Arts Forum, 2009–15; Chm., Wymondham Arts Centre, 2009–15. *Publications:* Review of British Science Curriculum Projects (with D. G. Chisman), 1973; Environment and Environmental Education, 1979; (ed jtly) New Trends in Biology Education, 1987; (ed with P. J. Black) Children's Informal Ideas in Science, 1993; (ed jtly) Regardfully Yours: selected correspondence of Ferdinand von Mueller, vol. 1 1840–1859, 1998, vol. 2 1860–1875, 2002, vol. 3 1876–1896, 2006; numerous articles in learned jls. *Recreations:* reading, getting to know Devon. *Club:* Athenæum.

**LUCAS, Ven. Canon Brian Humphrey,** CB 1993; author; Chaplain-in-Chief, and Archdeacon of the Royal Air Force, 1991–95, Archdeacon Emeritus, 1996; *b* 20 Jan. 1940; *s* of Frederick George Humphrey Lucas and Edith Mary Lucas; *m* 1966, Joy Penn, BA, MEd, FRGS; two *s* one *d. Educ:* St David's Coll., Lampeter (BA); St Stephen's House, Oxford. Ordained deacon 1964, priest 1965: Curate: Llandaff Cathedral, 1964–67; Parish of Neath, 1967–70; Royal Air Force: Chaplain, 1970–87; Asst Chaplain-in-Chief, 1987–91; Canon and Prebendary of Lincoln Cathedral, 1991–95, now Emeritus; Priest-in-charge, St Clement Danes, 1991–95; Priest-in-charge, 1996–2000, Rector, 2000–03, of Caythorpe, Fulbeck, and Carlton Scroop with Normanton, Diocese of Lincoln. QHC, 1989–95. Mem., Gen. Synod of C of E, 1991–95. Hon. Chaplain: Assoc. of London Clubs, 2004–; Bomber Command Assoc., 2004–; Coastal Command Assoc., 2005–; Horners' Co., 2011–18, now Emeritus; Hon. Pres., No. 3 Welsh Wing, ATC, 2007–; Chaplain to High Sheriff of Lincs, 2005–06. Vice-Pres., Clergy Orphan Corp., 1991–95; Visitor, Soldiers' and Airmen's Scripture Readers Assoc., 1991–95; Mem. Council, Bible Reading Fellowship, 1992–95. Mem. Council, RAF Benevolent Fund, 1991–95. Chm., Governing Body, Sir William Robertson Acad., Welbourn, 2012–18; Chm., Bd of Dirs, Aspire Schs Trust, 2018–. FRSA 1993. *Publications:* Reflections in a Chalice: the memoirs of a practical priest, 2011; A Glimpse of Glory in the Gothic Cathedrals of France, vol. 1, 2014, vol. 2, 2017; Alive in Christ: selected sermons, 2019. *Recreations:* archaeology of the Near East, travel (excluding tourist areas), watching Welsh Rugby football, researching Gothic architecture. *Address:* Pen-y-coed, 6 Arnhem Drive, Caythorpe, Lincs NG32 3DQ. *Clubs:* Savage (Hon. Sec., 1998–2008), Trustee, 2016–18; Hon. Life Mem., 2018), Royal Air Force, Civil Service.

**LUCAS, Bridget Ann;** QC 2018; *b* Albrighton, Sept. 1965; *d* of John Lucas and Ann Lucas (*née* Coles); *m* 1996, Lt Col Simon Hall. *Educ:* Gordonstoun; Worcester Coll., Oxford (BA Hons 1st Cl. Juris. 1987). Called to the Bar, Inner Temple, 1989; in practice as a barrister, Thirteen Old Square Chambers, 1990–98, Fountain Court Chambers, 1998–, specialising in chancery and commercial law. CEDR Mediator, 2004. Mem., Licensing Cttee, British Horseracing Authy, 2012–17. *Address:* Fountain Court Chambers, Temple, EC4Y 9DH. *T:* (020) 7583 3335.

**LUCAS, Dr Caroline;** MP (Green) Brighton Pavilion, since 2010; Co-Leader, Green Party, 2016–18 (Leader, 2008–12); *b* 9 Dec. 1960; *d* of Peter and Valerie Lucas; *m* 1991, Richard Le Quesne Savage; two *s. Educ:* Exeter Univ. (BA English Lit. 1983; PhD 1989). Oxfam: Press Officer, 1989–91; Communications Officer for Asia, 1991–93; Policy Adviser on trade and envmt, 1993–97; on secondment to Trade Team, DFID, 1997–98; Team Leader, Trade and Investment Policy Team, 1998–99. Mem., Oxford CC, 1993–97. European Parliament: Mem. (Green) SE Region, England, 1999–2010; Mem., Cttee on Internat. Trade, 1999–2010, on Transport and Tourism, 1999–2004, on Envmt, Public Health and Food Safety, 2004–10; Mem., Palestine Delegn, 1999–2010. Mem., Envmtl Audit Cttee, H of C, 2010–. Green Party: Mem., 1986–; Nat. Press Officer, 1987–89; Co-Chair, 1989–90. *Publications:* (as Caroline Le Quesne): Writing for Women, 1989; Reforming World Trade: the social and environmental priorities, 1996; (as Caroline Lucas): (with Mike

Woodin) Green Alternatives to Globalisation, 2004; Honourable Friends?: Parliament and the fight for change, 2015. *Recreations:* gardening, walking, piano playing. *Address:* House of Commons, SW1A 0AA.

LUCAS, **Christopher Tullis**, CBE 1994; Chairman, Wonderful Beast, 2012–16; *b* 20 Dec. 1937; *s* of late Philip Gaddesden Lucas, GM and Maise Lucas; *m* 1962, Tina Colville; two *d. Educ:* Winchester Coll. Apprenticeship with Thomson McLintock & Co.; CA 1965; Chief Exec., ICEM Ltd, 1966–72; Sen. Radio Officer, IBA, 1972–74; first Man. Dir, Radio Forth, Edinburgh, 1974–77; Dir and Sec., RSA, and Sec., Faculty of Royal Designers for Industry, 1977–94. Founder and Dir, Animarts, 2000–03; Founder, 2004, Dir, 2005–07, Chm., 2010–13, Eastfeast. Leader, Saxmundham Mkt Hall Develt Plan, 2014–. *Recreation:* Suffolk and Saxmundham. *Address:* The Clock House, Church Street, Saxmundham, Suffolk IP17 1ER.

LUCAS, **Sir Colin (Renshaw)**, Kt 2002; DPhil; FRHistS; Chief Executive, Rhodes Trust and Warden of Rhodes House, 2004–09 (Trustee, Rhodes Trust, 1995–2004); Fellow, All Souls College, Oxford, 2001–09; Vice-Chancellor, University of Oxford, 1997–2004; *b* 25 Aug. 1940; *s* of Frank Renshaw Lucas and Janine (*née* Charpentier); *m* 1st, 1964, Christiane Berchon de Fontaine Goubert (marr. diss. 1975); one *s*; 2nd, 1990, Mary Louise Hume. *Educ:* Sherborne Sch.; Lincoln Coll., Oxford (MA, DPhil; Hon. Fellow 1995). FRHistS 1974. Asst Lectr, then Lectr, Sheffield Univ., 1965–69; Vis. Asst Prof., Indiana Univ., 1969–70; Lectr, Manchester Univ., 1970–73; Fellow, Balliol Coll., Oxford, and Lectr in Modern History, Oxford University, 1973–90; Prof., 1990–94, and Dean, Div. of Social Scis, 1993–94, Chicago Univ.; Master of Balliol Coll., Oxford, 1994–2001 (Hon. Fellow, 2001). Chm. Bd, BL, 2006–10 (Mem., 2004–10). Trustee: Andrew W. Mellon Foundn, 2001–13; Eur. Inst. for Innovation and Technol. Foundn, 2010–15. Member: Hong Kong UGC, 2003–14; Academic Adv. Council, Heidelberg Univ., 2006–; Lay Mem. Council, Univ. of Liverpool, 2008–17. Hon. Dr of University: Lyon, 1989; Princeton, 2002; Peking, 2002; Heidelberg, 2013; Hon. DLitt: Sheffield, 2000; Western Australia, 2000; St Francis Xavier, 2003; Oxford Brookes, 2004; Hon. LLD: Glasgow, 2001; Warwick, 2006; Hon. DCL Oxford, 2003. Officier: Ordre des Arts et des Lettres (France), 1989; Légion d'Honneur (France), 2005 (Chevalier, 1998); Chevalier, Ordre du Mérite (France), 1994; Bronze Bauhinia Star (Hong Kong), 2014. *Publications:* The Structure of the Terror, 1973; (with G. Lewis) Beyond the Terror, 1983; (ed) The Political Culture of the French Revolution, 1988; numerous articles.

LUCAS, **Cristina;** *see* Odone, C.

LUCAS, **Geoffrey Haden;** Secretary, Headmasters' and Headmistresses' Conference, 2000–11; *b* 1 Sept. 1951; *s* of Alfred Philip Lucas and Joyce Lucas; *m* 1974, Elaine Jean Helsby; two *s* one *d. Educ:* Northgate Grammar Sch. for Boys, Ipswich; Univ. of Birmingham (BA Hons); Univ. of Leeds (MEd Dist.); Trinity and All Souls Coll., Leeds (PGCE). Asst teacher, then Hd of Dept, George Dixon Sch., Birmingham, 1974–80; Sen. Lectr, then Principal Lectr and Dir, PGCE Secondary Course, Trinity and All Souls Coll., Leeds, 1980–89; Professional Officer, Modern Langs/Teacher Educn, Nat. Curriculum Council, York, 1989–93; Asst Chief Exec., SCAA, 1993–97; Hd, Corporate Policy and Dir, Special Projects, QCA, 1997–2000. *Recreations:* walking, gardening, cooking, wine tasting, travel, family holidays. *Club:* East India.

LUCAS, **George;** film director, producer and screenwriter; Chairman: Lucasfilm, 1974–2012 (Creative Consultant, since 2012); George Lucas Educational Foundation; *b* 14 May 1944; *s* of George and Dorothy Lucas; *m* 2013, Mellody Hobson. *Educ:* Univ. of Southern California (Bachelor of Fine Arts), 1966). Asst to Francis Ford Coppola on The Rain People, 1967 (winner, Grand Prize, Nat. Student Film Festival for short film, THX-1138, 1967); director, co-author of screenplays: THX-1138, 1970; American Graffiti, 1973; director, author, executive producer: Star Wars, 1977; director, author, executive producer: Star Wars, Episode I: The Phantom Menace, 1999; Star Wars, Episode II: Attack of the Clones, 2002; Star Wars, Episode III: The Revenge of the Sith, 2005; executive producer, author: More American Graffiti, 1979; The Empire Strikes Back, 1980; Return of the Jedi, 1983; Indiana Jones and the Temple of Doom, 1984; Willow, 1988; The Young Indiana Jones Chronicles (TV series), 1992–93; Indiana Jones and the Kingdom of the Crystal Skull, 2008; Star Wars: The Clone Wars, 2008; co-executive producer: Raiders of the Lost Ark (and co-author), 1981; Land Before Time, 1988; Indiana Jones and the Last Crusade, 1989; executive producer: Mishima, 1985; Howard the Duck, 1986; Labyrinth, 1986; Tucker, the Man and his Dream, 1988; Radioland Murders, 1994; Red Tails, 2012. Irving G. Thalberg Meml Award, Acad. of Motion Picture Arts and Scis, 1992; Lifetime Achievement Award, Amer. Film Inst. *Publications:* Star Wars, 1976. *Address:* Lucasfilm Ltd, PO Box 29901, San Francisco, CA 94129–0901, USA.

LUCAS, **Prof. Ian Albert McKenzie**, CBE 1977; Principal, 1977–88, Fellow, since 1992, Wye College, Professor, 1988, University of London, now Professor Emeritus; *b* 10 July 1926; *s* of Percy John Lucas and Janie Inglis (*née* Hamilton); *m* 1950, Helen Louise Langerman; one *s* two *d. Educ:* Clayesmore Sch.; Reading Univ.; McGill Univ. BSc, MSc; CBiol, FRSB; FRAgS. Lectr, Harper Adams Agricl Coll., 1949–50; pig nutrition res., Rowett Res. Inst., Aberdeen, 1950–57 and 1958–61; Res. Fellow, Ruakura Res. Station, New Zealand, 1957–58; Prof. of Agriculture, UCNW, Bangor, 1961–77. Chm., Agricl and Vet. Cttee, British Council, 1978–87. Member: Jt Cttee on use of antibiotics in animal husbandry and vet. medicine, 1967–69; MAFF Adv. Council for Agric. and Hort., 1969–79; Agric. and Vet. Sub-Cttee, UGC, 1972–77; CVCP, 1985–88; Cttee, Internat. Co-operation in Higher Educn, British Council, 1986–90. President: Sect. M, BAAS, 1983; Agricl Educn Assoc., 1987; Rural Educn and Develt Assoc., 1994. Member Governing Body: Grassland Res. Inst., 1970–79; Rydal Sch., 1975–77; RVC, 1978–88; E Malling Res. Station, 1978–87; Hadlow Agric. Coll., 1978–88; Inst. for Grassland and Animal Production Research, 1987–89. Hon. Life Mem., British Council, 1987. Hon. DSc McGill, 1996. *Publications:* scientific papers in Jl Agricl Science, Animal Production, Brit. Jl Nutrition and others. *Recreation:* gardening. *Address:* Valley Downs, Brady Road, Lyminge, Folkestone, Kent CT18 8DU. *T:* (01303) 863053.

LUCAS, **Ian Colin;** MP (Lab) Wrexham, since 2001; *b* 18 Sept. 1960; *s* of Colin and Alice Lucas; *m* 1986, Norah Anne (*née* Sudd); one *s* one *d. Educ:* New Coll., Oxford (BA Jurisprudence). Articled Clerk, then Solicitor, Russell-Cooke, Potter and Chapman Solicitors, Putney and Kingston, 1983–85; Solicitor: Percy, Hughes and Roberts, Chester, 1985–86; Lees, Moore and Price, Birkenhead, 1986–87; Kirwan Nicholas Jones, then Roberts Moore Nicholas Jones, Birkenhead and Wrexham, 1987–92; D. R. Crawford, Oswestry, 1992–97; Sole Principal, Crawford Lucas, Oswestry, 1997–2000; Partner, Stevens Lucas, Oswestry and Chirk, 2001. Contested (Lab) N Shropshire, 1997. An Asst Govt Whip, 2008–09; Parly Under-Sec. of State, BIS, 2009–10; Shadow Minister: BIS, 2010–11; FCO, 2011–14; Defence, 2014–15. Mem., Culture, Media and Sport, subseq. Digital, Culture, Media and Sport, Select Cttee, 2015–. Non-exec. Dir, Robert Jones and Agnes Hunt Hosp., Gobowen, Shropshire, 1997–2001. *Recreations:* history, sport, art. *Address:* (office) Vernon House, 41 Rhosddu Road, Wrexham LL11 2NS. *T:* (01978) 355743.

LUCAS, **Irene, (Mrs John Hays),** CBE 2008; private consultant, since 2011; Chair, Hays Travel Group, since 2011; Senior Adviser, Newton Europe, since 2011; *b* Newcastle upon Tyne, 4 Feb. 1954; *d* of Vincent and Isabelle Lucas; *m* 1997, John Hays; one *s* one *d. Educ:* Univ. of Sunderland (MBA). Sunderland City Council, 1977–2002: various posts incl. Asst Dir, and Dir, Community and Cultural Services; Asst Chief Exec., 1999–2002; Chief Exec., South Tyneside Metropolitan BC, 2002–09; Dir Gen., Local Govt and Regeneration and Actg Perm. Sec., DCLG, 2009–11; Chief Exec., Sunderland CC, 2017–19. Chair, Mgt Bd, Educn and Skills Funding Agency, 2019–; non-exec. Dir, DfE, 2018–. *Recreations:* family, football, travel. *Address:* Whitburn House, 47 Front Street, Whitburn, Sunderland SR6 7JD.

LUCAS, **Iris Grace;** *see* Burton, I. G.

LUCAS, **John Randolph**, FBA 1988; Fellow and Tutor of Merton College, Oxford, 1960–96; *b* 18 June 1929; *s* of late Rev. E. de G. Lucas, sometime Archdeacon of Durham, and Joan Mary Lucas; *m* 1961, Morar Portal, *er d* of Sir Reginald Portal, KCB, DSC; two *s* two *d. Educ:* St Mary's Coll., Winchester; Balliol Coll., Oxford (1st cl. Maths Mods; 1st cl. Lit.Hum. 1951; John Locke Schol., 1952; MA 1954). Jun. Res. Fellow, Merton Coll., Oxford, 1953–56; Fellow and Asst Tutor, Corpus Christi Coll., Cambridge, 1956–59; Reader in Philosophy, Oxford Univ., 1990–96. Jane Eliza Procter Vis. Fellow, Princeton Univ., 1957–58; Leverhulme Res. Fellow, Leeds Univ., 1959–60. Chm., Oxford Consumers' Gp, 1961–63, 1965. Member: Archbishops' Commn on Christian Doctrine, 1967–76; Lichfield Commn on Divorce and Remarriage, 1975–78. Pres., British Soc. for the Philosophy of Sci., 1991–93. Lectures: (jtly) Gifford, Univ. of Edinburgh, 1971–73; Margaret Harris, Univ. of Dundee, 1981; Harry Jelema, Calvin Coll., Grand Rapids, 1987; Darwin, Cambridge Univ., 2000. *Publications:* Principles of Politics, 1966, 2nd edn 1985; The Concept of Probability, 1970; The Freedom of the Will, 1970; (jtly) The Nature of Mind, 1972; (jtly) The Development of Mind, 1973; A Treatise on Time and Space, 1973; Essays on Freedom and Grace, 1976; Democracy and Participation, 1976 (trans. Portuguese 1985); On Justice, 1980; Space, Time and Causality, 1985; The Future, 1989; (jtly) Spacetime and Electromagnetism, 1990; Responsibility, 1993; (with M. Griffiths) Ethical Economics, 1997, 2nd edn 2016; The Conceptual Roots of Mathematics, 1999; (jtly) An Engagement with Plato's Republic, 2003; Reason and Reality, 2006; Economics as a Moral Science, 2012, rev. edn 2014; Heretical Orthodoxy, 2019; various articles in learned jls. *Recreations:* walking and talking. *Address:* Lambrook House, East Lambrook, South Petherton, Somerset TA13 5HW. *T:* (01460) 240413. *E:* john.lucas@merton.ox.ac.uk. *W:* http://users.ox.ac.uk/~jrlucas.
See also C. Odone.

LUCAS, **Matt;** actor and writer; *b* London, 1974; *s* of John and Diana Lucas. *Educ:* Haberdashers' Aske's Sch. for Boys, Elstree; Univ. of Bristol. Started in stand-up comedy, 1992; television includes: as actor and writer: Sir Bernard's Stately Homes, 1999; Rock Profile, 1999–2000; Da Ali G Show, 2000; Little Britain, 2003–06 (Best Comedy Perf., RTS, 2003; Best TV Comedy, British Comedy Awards, 2004; Best Comedy Prog., 2003, 2004, Best Comedy Perf., 2004, BAFTA); Little Britain USA, 2008; Come Fly With Me, 2010; (host) The Matt Lucas Awards, 2012, 2013; as actor: The Smell of Reeves and Mortimer, 1995; Shooting Stars, 1995–2003 and 2009; Catterick, 2004; Casanova, 2005; The Wind in the Willows, 2006; Kröd Mändoon and the Flaming Sword of Fire, 2009; Portlandia (USA), 2012; Super Fun Night (USA), 2013–14; Fresh Off the Boat (USA), 2015; Dr Who, 2015–17; A Midsummer Night's Dream, 2016; as actor, writer and director: Pompidou, 2015; *theatre* includes: Troilus and Cressida, Oxford Stage Co., 2000; Taboo, 2002; Little Britain Live, UK and Australian tour, 2005–07; Prick Up Your Ears, Comedy, 2009; Les Miserables 25th Anniv. Concert, O2, 2010; Les Miserables, Queen's, 2011; Me and My Girl, Chichester, 2018; *films* include: Shaun of the Dead, 2004; Alice in Wonderland, Infidel, 2010; Bridesmaids, 2011; Gnomeo and Juliet, 2011; The Look of Love, 2013; The Harry Hill Movie, 2013; In Secret, 2013; Small Apartments, 2013; Paddington, 2014; Alice Through the Looking Glass, 2016; How to Talk to Girls at Parties, 2017; A Futile and Stupid Gesture, 2018. Hon. DLitt Bristol, 2017. *Publications:* Little Me: my life from A to Z, 2017. *Recreations:* eating crisps, watching football, eating chocolate, watching stage musicals, sleeping, eating crumpets. *Address:* c/o Troika Talent, 180 Great Portland Street, W1W 5QZ. *Club:* Arsenal Football Supporters.

LUCAS, **Neil Raymond;** author; Director, Knoll Gardens Ltd, since 2013 (Owner, 1994–2012); *b* London, 6 June 1957; *s* of Ian Raymond Edwin Lucas and Janet Elizabeth Lucas; *m* 1985, Susan Deidre Smith (marr. diss. 1995). *Educ:* Bassingbourn Village Coll.; Cambridge Coll. of Arts. MCIHort (MIHort 2004). With MoD, 1975–77; Gardens Manager, S Devon Health Trust, 1977–93. Chm., Knoll Gdns Foundn, 2008–13. Mem. Council, RHS, 2012–. *Publications:* Designing with Grasses, 2011; contribs to horticultural jls and periodicals. *Recreations:* gardening, walking, photography. *Address:* Knoll Gardens, Hampreston, Wimborne, Dorset BH21 7ND. *T:* (01202) 873931, *Fax:* (01202) 870842. *E:* neil@knollgardens.co.uk.

LUCAS, **Noel John Mac;** QC 2008; **His Honour Judge Lucas;** a Circuit Judge, since 2014; Resident Judge, Wood Green Crown Court; *b* Asansol, India, 5 Dec. 1952; *s* of Armenian parents, John Joseph Lucas and Aroosiak Lucas (*née* Sarkies); *m* 1994, Sylvia Hagopian; two *s. Educ:* King's Sch., Ely; Queen Mary Coll., Univ. of London (BSc Biol.). Called to the Bar, Middle Temple, 1979; in practice as a barrister, 187 Fleet St, 1981–2005, Red Lion Chambers, 2005–14. *Recreations:* sailing, ski-ing, walking, reading, classic cars, motorcycling. *Address:* Wood Green Crown Court, Woodall House, Lordship Lane, Wood Green, N22 5LF. *T:* (020) 8826 4100.

LUCAS, **Prof. Robert Emerson**, PhD; John Dewey Distinguished Service Professor of Economics, University of Chicago, 1980, now Professor Emeritus; *b* 15 Sept. 1937; *s* of Robert Emerson Lucas and Jane Templeton Lucas; *m* 1959, Rita Cohen (marr. diss.); two *s. Educ:* Roosevelt High Sch., Seattle; Univ. of Chicago (BA 1959; PhD 1964). Lectr, Dept of Econs, Univ. of Chicago, 1962–63; Asst Prof. of Econs, Carnegie Inst. of Technol., 1963–67; Associate Prof., 1967–70; Prof. of Econs, 1970–74, Carnegie-Mellon Univ.; University of Chicago: Ford Foundn Vis. Res. Prof., 1974–75; Prof. of Econs, 1975–80; Vice-Chm., 1975–83, Chm., 1986–88, Dept of Econs. Fellow, Amer. Acad. of Arts and Scis, 1980; Mem., NAS, USA, 1981. Nobel Prize for Economics, 1995. *Publications:* Studies in Business-cycle Theory, 1981; (with T. J. Sargent) Rational Expectations and Econometric Practice, 1981; Models of Business Cycles, 1987; (with N. L. Stokey) Recursive Methods in Economic Dynamics, 1989; Customer Service: skills and concepts for business, 1996; Lectures on Economic Growth, 2002; papers on growth theory, public finance and monetary theory. *Address:* Department of Economics, University of Chicago, 1126 East 59th Street, Chicago, IL 60637, USA.

LUCAS, **Prof. Sebastian Brendan**, FRCP, FRCPath; Professor of Clinical Histopathology, King's College London School of Medicine, 1995–2012, now Emeritus; Consultant Histopathologist, Guy's and St Thomas' NHS Foundation Trust, since 2012; *b* London, 12 Sept. 1947; *s* of Edward and Branwen Lucas; *m* 1970, Susan Jay; one *s* one *d. Educ:* King's Coll. Sch., Wimbledon; Magdalen Coll., Oxford (BA); University Coll. Hosp. Med. Sch. (BM BCh). FRCPath 1990; FRCP 1992. Wellcome Trust Res. Fellow, 1979, 1982; Sen. Lectr, Univ. of Nairobi, 1980–82; Sen. Lectr and Consultant Pathologist, UCH and Hosp. for Tropical Diseases, 1983–. Hon. Prof., LSHTM, 2005–. Adviser: to UK Govt on coronial autopsy practice; on pathology develt in Africa. Expert morbid anatomical witness on maternal death, sickle cell disease, HIV disease, sepsis and perioperative complications. *Publications:* contrib. articles to jls and textbook chapters on infectious diseases, HIV pathology, tuberculosis, leprosy, maternal mortality, sickle cell disease, autopsy practice and governance, sepsis, error in medicine, and the coronial system. *Recreations:* classical music, opera, family, Trollope, western civilisation, church bell ringing, Gothic cathedrals, tree-planting, bee-keeping, challenging political correctness in medicine. *Address:* Department of Cellular Pathology, St Thomas' Hospital, Lambeth Palace Road, SE1 7EH. *E:* sebastian.lucas@kcl.ac.uk.

**LUCAS, Stephen Bryan;** Partner, Kirkland & Ellis International LLP, since 2014; *b* London, 14 Dec. 1968; *s* of John and Pamela Lucas; *m* 2002, Dina, *d* of Michael Charles Flesch, *qv*; three *s*. *Educ:* University Coll. London (LLB 1st Cl. Hons 1990; LLM Dist. 1991; PhD Soviet Corporate Law 2002); Harvard Univ. Law Sch. (Fulbright Schol.; LLM 1992). Mem., NY State Bar, 1993; admitted Solicitor, England and Wales, 1996. Associate, 1992–2002, Partner, 2002–04, Clifford Chance LLP; Partner: Linklaters LLP, 2004–11; Weil, Gotshal & Manges LLP, 2011–14. Pres., UCL Law Soc., 1990. *Recreations:* Shakespeare, Russia, history, football. *Address:* Kirkland & Ellis International LLP, 30 St Mary Axe, EC3A 8AF. *T:* (020) 7469 2233.

**LUCAS, Sir Thomas (Edward),** 5th Bt *cr* 1887; MA; research engineer, scientist, author, lecturer, mind-body consultant and chairman; *b* 16 Sept. 1930; *s* of late Ralph John Scott Lucas (killed in action, Libya, 1941), and Dorothy (*d* 1985), *d* of late H. T. Timson, Tatchbury Mount, Hants; *S* cousin, 1980; *m* 1st, 1958, Charmian (*d* 1970), *d* of late Col J. S. Powell; one *s*; 2nd, 1980, Ann Graham Moore. *Educ:* Wellington College; Trinity Hall, Cambridge; Farnborough Sch. of Gas Turbine Technol. Engr, Bristol Cars Ltd; Develt Engr, Rolls-Royce-Bristol Aero Engines Ltd; Tech. Dir, Vacuum Research (Cambridge) Ltd; Founder, Engineering Capacity Exchange (London); Consultant to European Commn DG XIII, INCRA Inc., The Hale Clinic, RTZ plc, and to other orgns; formerly Director: SGF Industries plc; Columbia Industrial Gp; Vacuum Metallizing Processes Inc.; EMDI Ltd; Digital Health Research Ltd, and other cos. Senior Trustee and Chairman: Inlight Trust, 1995–2019; Truemark Trust, 1995–2019. *Recreations:* motor sport, art, architecture, traditional Eastern medicines. *Heir: s* Stephen Ralph James Lucas [*b* 11 Dec. 1963; *m* 1993, Charlotte Johnson; one *s* one *d*]. *Address:* c/o Drummonds Bank, 49 Charing Cross, SW1A 2DX.

**LUCAS-TOOTH, Sir (Hugh) John,** 2nd Bt *cr* 1920, of Bught; *b* 20 Aug. 1932; *s* of Sir Hugh Vere Huntly Duff Munro-Lucas-Tooth of Teananich, 1st Bt and Laetitia Florence, OBE (*d* 1978), *er d* of Sir John Ritchie Findlay, 1st Bt, KBE; *S* father, 1985; *m* 1955, Hon. Caroline, *e d* of 1st Baron Poole, PC, CBE, TD; three *d*. *Educ:* Eton College; Balliol Coll., Oxford. *Address:* Parsonage Farm, East Hagbourne, Didcot, Oxon OX11 9LN. *Clubs:* Brooks's, Beefsteak.

**LUCE,** family name of **Baron Luce**.

**LUCE, Baron** *cr* 2000 (Life Peer), of Adur in the co. of West Sussex; **Richard Napier Luce,** KG 2008; GCVO 2000; Kt 1991; PC 1986; DL; Lord Chamberlain of HM Household, 2000–06; a Permanent Lord in Waiting to the Queen, since 2007; High Steward of Westminster Abbey, 2011–16; *b* 14 Oct. 1936; *s* of late Sir William Luce, GBE, KCMG, and Margaret, *d* of late Adm. Sir Trevylyan Napier, KCB; *m* 1961, Rose, *d* of Sir Godfrey Nicholson, 1st Bt; two *s*. *Educ:* Wellington Coll.; Christ's Coll., Cambridge (2nd cl. History; Hon. Fellow, 2005); Wadham Coll., Oxford. Nat. Service officer, 1955–57, served in Cyprus. Overseas Civil Service, served as District Officer, Kenya, 1960–62; Brand Manager, Gallaher Ltd, 1963–65; Marketing Manager, Spirella Co. of GB; Dir, National Innovations Centre, 1968–71; Mem. European Adv. Bd, Corning Glass International, 1975–79; Director: Booker Tate, 1991–96; Meridian Broadcasting, 1991–96. Vice-Chancellor, Univ. of Buckingham, 1992–96. Contested (C) Hitchin, 1970. MP (C) Arundel and Shoreham, April 1971–74, Shoreham, 1974–92. PPS to Minister for Trade and Consumer Affairs, 1972–74; an Opposition Whip, 1974–75; an Opposition spokesman on foreign and commonwealth affairs, 1977–79; Parly Under Sec. of State, 1979–81, Minister of State, 1981–82 and 1983–85, FCO; Minister of State, Privy Council Office (Minister for the Arts), 1985–90. Governor and C-in-C, Gibraltar, 1997–2000. Chm., Crown Nominations Commn for See of Canterbury, 2012. Chairman: Commonwealth Foundn, 1992–96; Atlantic Council of the UK, 1993–96. Mem., Royal Motor Ad. Cttee, 2000–06. Chancellor, Univ. of Gibraltar, 2015–. President: Voluntary Arts Network, 1993–2013; King George V Fund for Actors and Actresses, 2007–12; Commonwealth Youth Orch., 2010–12, Emeritus President, 2013. Gov., RSC, 1994–2003. Mem., Bd of Trustees, Royal Collection Trust, 2000–06; Trustee, Geographers' A–Z Map Trust, 1993–2016; Emeritus Trustee, RA, 2001–. Patron, Sir William Luce Meml Trust, 1994–; Founding Patron, Voluntary Arts Network, 2013–. DL W Sussex, 1991. *Publications:* Ringing the Changes: a memoir, 2007. *Recreations:* painting, piano, reading, walking. *Address:* House of Lords, SW1A 0PW. *Club:* Royal Over-Seas League (Pres., 2002–).

**LUCE, Thomas Richard Harman,** CB 1996; Member, Regulatory Decisions Committee, Financial Services Authority, 2001–08 (a Deputy Chairman, 2004–08); *b* 11 July 1939; *er* of late Air Cdre Charles Luce, DSO, and Joyce Marjorie Elizabeth Luce (*née* Johnson); *m* 1991, Virginia Manson Hunt; two step *s*. *Educ:* Clifton Coll.; Christ's Coll., Cambridge (BA Hons); Indiana Univ., USA. HM Inspector of Taxes, 1965–67; Asst Principal, Ministries of Aviation and Technology, 1967–69; Principal, CSD, 1969–72; Department of Health and Social Security: Principal, 1972–75; Asst Sec., 1975–84; Under Sec., 1984; seconded to HM Treasury (Head of Management Policy and Running Costs Gp), 1987–90; Dep. Dir, NHS Finance, 1990; Under Sec., Community Services Div., 1990–94, Hd of Social Care Policy, 1995–99, DoH. Chm., Home Office Review of Coroners, 2001–03. Hon. Mem., Coroners' Soc. of England and Wales, 2018. Trustee and Council Mem., CSV, 1999–2003; Trustee, Internat. Social Services (UK), 2001–04. Trustee, Hampstead and Highgate Fest., 1997–2001 (Chm. Trustees, 1997–2000). A music critic, Crosscut, Seattle, 2007–12. *Publications:* articles on coroner and death certification reform; music criticism. *Recreations:* music, reading, walking, swimming. *Address:* 6 Morpeth Mansions, Morpeth Terrace, SW1P 1ER. *T:* (020) 7834 6835; 1301 Spring Street, Apt 7A, Seattle, WA 98104, USA. *E:* tom.luce@btinternet.com. *Clubs:* Athenæum; Seattle Monday.

**LUCHFORD, Diana Frances,** CB 2017; Senior Director, Windrush, Home Office, since 2018; *b* Amersham, Bucks, 29 May 1964; *d* of Arthur Francis Smith and Barbara Rosemary Smith; *m* 1992, Mike Luchford; two *s*. *Educ:* Dr Challoner's High Sch.; Portsmouth Poly. (BA Hons). Joined Home Office, 1987, Immigration Dept, 1987–89; Duty Clerk, No 10 Downing St, 1989–91; various posts, Home Office and HM Prison Service, 1991–2002; Principal Private Sec. to Perm. Sec., 2002–05, Hd, Juvenile Offenders Unit, 2005–07, Home Office; Hd, Jt Youth Justice Unit, MoJ, 2007–09; Home Office: Hd, Anti-Social Behaviour and Youth Crime, 2009–12; Hd, Border Force Transformation, 2012–13; Dir, Crime, 2013–17; Interim Dir Gen., Policing and Crime, 2017. *Recreations:* reading, writing, cinema. *Address:* Home Office, 2 Marsham Street, SW1Y 4DF. *E:* diana.luchford@homeoffice.gov.uk. *Club:* Balham Football.

**LUCIE, Gary Allan;** a District Judge (Magistrates' Courts), since 2011; *b* 16 Jan. 1966; *s* of late David Lucie and Patricia Lucie (*née* Jones). *Educ:* Broomfield Secondary Sch.; Havant Coll.; Local Govt Training Bd (Dip. Trading Standards 1988); Manchester Univ. (LLB Hons 1993). Trading Standards Officer, various appts, 1984–95; called to the Bar, Middle Temple, 1994; in practice as a barrister, 1995–2011; a Dep. Dist Judge (Magistrates' Courts), 2009–11. *Recreations:* astronomy, hiking, travel, socialising. *Address:* c/o Portsmouth Magistrates' Court, Winston Churchill Avenue, Portsmouth, Hants PO1 2DQ.

**LUCIE-SMITH, (John) Edward (McKenzie);** poet, art critic and photographer; *b* Kingston, Jamaica, 27 Feb. 1933; *s* of John Dudley Lucie-Smith and Mary (*née* Lushington); unmarried. *Educ:* King's Sch., Canterbury; Merton Coll., Oxford (MA). Settled in England, 1946. Education Officer, RAF, 1954–56; subseq. worked in advertising and as free-lance journalist and broadcaster. Curator of a number of exhibns, UK and USA, 1977–. Digital projects include: (with Zavier Ellis), 100 London Artists, 2014. FRSL. *Publications:* A Tropical Childhood and other poems, 1961 (jt winner, John Llewellyn Rhys Mem. Prize); winner, Arts Council Triennial Award); (ed, with Philip Hobsbaum) A Group Anthology, 1963; Confessions and Histories, 1964; (with Jack Clemo, George MacBeth) Penguin Modern Poets 6, 1964; (ed) Penguin Book of Elizabethan Verse, 1965; What is a Painting?, 1966; (ed) The Liverpool Scene, 1967; (ed) A Choice of Browning's Verse, 1967; (ed) Penguin Book of Satirical Verse, 1967; Thinking about Art, 1968; Towards Silence, 1968; Movements in Art since 1945, 1969; (ed) British Poetry Since 1945, 1970; (with Patricia White) Art in Britain 69–70, 1970; (ed) A Primer of Experimental Verse, 1971; (ed with S. W. Taylor) French Poetry: the last fifteen years, 1971; A Concise History of French Painting, 1971; Symbolist Art, 1972; Eroticism in Western Art, 1972; The First London Catalogue, 1974; The Well Wishers, 1974; The Burnt Child (autobiog.), 1975; The Invented Eye (early photography), 1975; World of the Makers, 1975; (with Celestine Dars) How the Rich Lived, 1976; Joan of Arc, 1976; (with Celestine Dars) Work and Struggle, 1977; Fantin-Latour, 1977; The Dark Pageant (novel), 1977; Art Today, 1977, revd edn 1999; A Concise History of Furniture, 1979; Super Realism, 1979; Cultural Calendar of the Twentieth Century, 1979; Art in the Seventies, 1980; The Story of Craft, 1981; The Body, 1981; A History of Industrial Design, 1983; Art Terms: an illustrated dictionary, 1984; Art in the Thirties, 1985; American Art Now, 1985; Lives of the Great Twentieth Century Artists, 1986, rev. edn 2009; Sculpture since 1945, 1987; (ed) The Essential Osbert Lancaster, 1988; (with Carolyn Cohen, Judith Higgins) The New British Painting, 1988; Art in the Eighties, 1990; Art Deco Painting, 1990; Fletcher Benton, 1990; Jean Rustin, 1991; Harry Holland, 1992; Art and Civilisation, 1992; (ed) The Faber Book of Art Anecdotes, 1992; Andres Nagel, 1992; Wendy Taylor, 1992; Alexander, 1992; British Art Now, 1993; Race, Sex and Gender: issues in contemporary art, 1994; (with Elisabeth Frink) Elisabeth Frink: a portrait, 1994; American Realism, 1994; Art Today, 1995; Visual Arts in the Twentieth Century, 1996; Ars Erotica: an arousing history of erotic art, 1997; Adam, 1998; Zoo, 1998; (with Judy Chicago) Women and Art: contested territory, 1999; Judy Chicago: an American vision, 2000; Flesh and Stone (photographs), 2000; Flora, 2001; Art Tomorrow, 2002; Changing Shape (poems), 2002; Roberto Marquez, 2002; Carlo Bertocci, 2002; Stefano di Stasio, 2002; Paola Gandolfi, 2003; Ricardo Cinalli, 2004; Philip Pearlstein, 2004; John Kirby, 2004; Elias Rivera, 2006; Harry Holland, 2006; Censoring the Body, 2007; The Glory of Angels, 2009; (with Dominique Nahas) Margaret Evangeline, 2011; The Face of Jesus, 2011; Milos Sobaïc, 2012; Jamil Naqsh: the painted word, 2013; contribs to Times, Sunday Times, Independent, Mail-on-Sunday, Listener, Spectator, New Statesman, Evening Standard, Encounter, London Magazine, Illustrated London News, etc. *Recreation:* the Internet. *Address:* 104 West Kensington Court, Edith Villas, W14 9AB.

**LUCIER, Pierre;** President, University of Quebec, 1996–2003; Fernand-Dumont Professor, Institut National de la Recherche Scientifique, Centre Urbanisation, Culture et Société, Quebec, 2006–10, now Associate Professor; *b* 15 Oct. 1941. *Educ:* Univ. of Montreal (BA 1963; LRelSc 1970); Jesuit Coll. Maximum (MA Philosophy 1965; MA Theology 1971); Univ. des Sciences Humaines, Strasbourg (Dr d'Etat (Phil.) 1975). Prof., Faculty of Theology, Univ. of Montreal, 1970–75; Sen. Researcher, Center for Res. in Educn, Montreal, 1975–78; Sen. Counselor, Cultural and Scientific Develt Secretariat, Exec. Council, Quebec, 1978–80; Asst Dep. Minister of Educn, Quebec, 1980–84; President: Superior Council for Educn, Quebec, 1984–89; Council of Univs, Quebec, 1989–90; Dep. Minister of Higher Educn and Sci., Quebec, 1990–93; Dep. Minister of Educn, Quebec, 1993–96. Canadian Member: Centre for Educnl Res. and Innovation, OECD, Paris, 1984–86; Cttee of Educn, OECD, Paris, 1996–97; Chm., Council of Canadian Dep. Ministers of Educn, 1993–95; Member: Sci. and Technology Council of Quebec, 1990–96; Standing Adv. Cttee for Univ. Res., Assoc. of Univs and Colls of Canada, 1998–2003; Vice-Pres., Bd of Dirs and Council of Govs, Agence Universitaire de la Francophonie, 1998–2003; Pres., Conf. of Univ. Rectors and Principals of Quebec, 2001–03 (Vice-Pres., 1997–2001). *Publications:* approx. 150 pubns, incl. a treatise on logical empiricism, and papers and articles on culture, epistemology, educn, educnl systems, instnl evaluation and higher learning. *Recreations:* reading, travelling, cinema. *Address:* INRS Urbanisation, Culture et Société, 490 rue de la Couronne, Quebec, QC G1K 9A9, Canada.

**LUCK, Air Vice-Marshal Christopher James,** CB 2019; MBE 1996; Group Chief Executive Officer, Shaw Trust, since 2019; *b* London, 1965; *s* of Leonard and Frances Luck; *m* 1999, Sara Cook (*née* Newhouse); one *s* two *d*. *Educ:* Central Flying Sch. (Helicopter Instructor (A2 grade) 1994); Sch. of Advanced Air and Space Studies, Montgomery, USA (MA 2003; MPhil 2007). Joined RAF, 1984; initial officer trng, RAF Coll., Cranwell, 1984; flying trng, 1985–87; 33 Sqdn, 1987–92; 230 Sqdn, 1992–96; Flight Comdr, 33 Sqdn Puma Operational Conversion Unit, 1996–98; staff appts, HQ Strike Comd and HQ Jt Helicopter Comd, 1998–2001; loan service to Kuwait Air Force, 2001–03; Exchange Instructor, Air Comd and Staff Coll., Air Univ., USAF, 2004–06; Sqdn Comdr, 33 Sqdn, 2007–09; DACOS, J5 Middle East, 2009–11; Stn Comdr, RAF Shawbury, 2011–13; Comdt, RAF Coll., Cranwell, and Dir, Recruiting and Initial Trng, RAF, 2013–16; Comdt Jt Services Comd and Staff Coll., and CEO, Defence Acad., 2017–19. Pres., RAF Equitation, 2014–; Vice Pres., RAF Polo, 2014–; Vice-Chm., UK Armed Forces Polo, 2016–. Hon. Pres., 936 Sqdn ATC, 2017–. Chm. Govs, Welbeck Defence Sixth Form Coll., 2018–. Trustee: Internat. Bomber Comd Meml Trust, 2018–; SkillForce (Prince William Award) Charity, 2018–. FCMI 2007, CCMI 2018; FRSA 2012; FRAeS 2015. *Publications:* (contrib.) Changing War: the British Army, the hundred days campaign and the birth of the Royal Air Force, 1918, 2013; contrib. to RAF Histl Soc. Jl, Air Power Rev. *Recreations:* equitation (show jumping, polo), motorbike racing, ski-ing, trail running, sub-aqua, reading. *Address:* Shaw Trust, Shaw Trust House, 19 Elmfield Road, Bromley, Kent BR1 1LT. *E:* christopher.luck@shaw-trust.org.uk. *Clubs:* Royal Automobile, Royal Air Force.

**LUCK, Keith Frank;** Operations Director (Commercial), MACE Group Ltd, since 2018; *b* 18 July 1960; *s* of Jack Luck and Mauree Luck (*née* Campbell); *m* 1987, Michelle Susan Harris; one *s* one *d*. *Educ:* Sidney Sussex Coll., Cambridge (BA Hons 1981; MA 1985). ACMA 1986, FCMA 1993; Associate Mem., ACT, 1994; CGMA 2011. Internal audit, then financial accounting, BT, 1981–85 (CIMA Inst. Prize and Harold Wilmot Prize, 1985); BT Schol., RAPC, Worthy Down, 1983–85; Head of Financial Training, BT Mgt Coll., 1986–87; Consultant, Deloitte, Haskins & Sells, 1987–89; Business Systems Manager,

1989–90, Project Dir, 1990–91, Financial Controller, 1991–93, Midland Bank; Head of Corporate Finance, 1993–94, Asst Dir (Corporate Finance and Property) and Chief Internal Auditor, 1994–97, Tower Hamlets LBC; Dir of Finance and Support Services, Lewisham LBC, 1997–99; Dir, Support Services, Accord plc, 1999–2000; Dir of Resources, Metropolitan Police Service, 2000–06; Dir Gen., Finance, FCO, 2007–10; Strategic Advr to Govt of Cayman Islands, 2011; Serco plc: Dir, Strategic Progs, 2011–14; Finance and Commercial Dir, Strategic Partnerships Div., 2014–15; Chief Operating Officer, MoD's Defence Business Service (on secondment), 2012; Commercial Dir, Central Govt, Serco plc, 2015–17. Dir, Northern Rail Ltd, 2014–14. Chartered Institute of Management Accountants: Member: Adv. Panel, 2005–09; Internat. Develt/Global Markets Cttee, 2006–11; Exec. Cttee, 2010–16; Members' Services Cttee, 2011–12; Appts Cttee, 2012–16; Vice Pres., 2012–13; Dep. Pres., 2013–14; Pres., 2014–15. Dep. Chm., Jt Venture Bd for Global CGMA Designation with AICPA, 2015–16; Mem., AICPA Internat. Nomination Cttee, 2016–18. Mem., Professional Accountants in Business, 2007–12, Bd Observer, 2014–17, IFAC; Mem., Assoc. of Internat. Professional Certified Accts, 2012–. Pres., Comets (Met. Police Sports and Social Club), 2002–06. Conservator, Wimbledon and Putney Commons, 2015–18 (Chm. Conservators, 2015–16). Trustee: Civil Staff Welfare Fund, 2001–06; London Gdns Scheme, 2005–06. Mem. Court, City Univ., 2009–14; Anthony Howitt Lecture Trust, 2012–16. FCMI (FIMgt 1987); FRSA 2000; FInstD 2010 (MInstD 2006); Fellow, ACT, 2015. Editl Advr, Excellence in Leadership, 2006–11. Business Leader of Year, CIMA, 2004. *Recreations:* family, local history, historical geography, archaeology, distance running, swimming. *Address:* SW20. *E:* keith.luck@yahoo.co.uk. *Club:* Oxford and Cambridge.

**LUCKETT, Dr Richard;** Fellow, 1978–2012, now Emeritus Fellow, and Pepys Librarian, 1982–2012, Magdalene College, Cambridge; *b* 1 July 1945; *s* of late Rev. Canon Gerald Archer Luckett and of Margaret Mary Luckett (*née* Chittenden). *Educ:* St John's Sch., Leatherhead; St Catharine's Coll., Cambridge (MA, PhD). Lectr, RMA, Sandhurst, 1967–69; Cambridge University: Res. Fellow, 1970–72, Fellow, 1972–78, Dean, 1974–78, St Catharine's Coll.; Univ. Asst Lectr in English, 1973–78; Lectr, 1978–2001; Precentor, Magdalene Coll., 1982–94. *Publications:* The White Generals, 1971, 2nd edn 1988; The Fabric of Dryden's Verse (Chatterton Lect.), 1981; (ed with C. Hogwood) Music in Eighteenth Century England, 1983; (contrib.) The Pepys Companion, 1983; Handel's Messiah: a celebration, 1992; (ed) The Cryes of London, 1994. *Address:* 20 Eagle Road, Rye, E Sussex TN31 7NB.

**LUCKHURST, Prof. Timothy Colin Harvey;** Professor of Journalism, and Founder and Head, Centre of Journalism, University of Kent, since 2007; *b* Sheffield, 8 Jan. 1963; *s* of Colin Luckhurst and Barbara Luckhurst (*née* Harvey); *m* 1989, Dorothy Ann Williamson; one *s* three *d. Educ:* Peebles High Sch.; Robinson Coll., Cambridge (BA Hist. 1983). Parly Res. Asst to Rt Hon. Donald Dewar, MP, 1986–89; Broadcast Journalist, Today Prog., BBC Radio 4, 1989–93; Washington Producer, BBC News, 1992; Asst Ed., BBC Radio 5 Live, 1993–95; Ed., News Progs, BBC Scotland, 1995–97; The Scotsman: Asst Ed., News, 1997–98; Dep. Ed., 1998–2000; Ed., 2000; columnist and contrib. to Scottish Daily Mail, Independent, Times, Guardian and New Republic, 2000–07. Dir, KMTV, 2016–. FRSA. *Publications:* This is Today: a biography of the Today Programme, 2001; (contrib.) Afghanistan, War and the Media: frontlines and deadlines, 2010; (contrib.) Face the Future: tools for the modern media age, 2011; (contrib.) The Phone Hacking Scandal: journalism on trial, 2012; Responsibility Without Power: Lord Justice Leveson's constitutional dilemma, 2012; (contrib.) Routledge Companion to British Media History, 2014; contribs to jls incl. Ethical Space, British Journalism Rev., Contemporary British History, THES, Eur. Jl of Communication and Journalism Studies, Jl of George Orwell Studies. *Recreations:* walking, playing guitar, motorcycling. *Address:* Centre for Journalism, University of Kent, Gillingham Building, Chatham Maritime ME4 4AG. *T:* (01634) 202913. *E:* Journalism@kent.ac.uk. *Club:* Frontline.

**LUCKIN, Prof. Rosemary Helen,** PhD; Professor of Learner Centred Design, Institute of Education, University College London (formerly Institute of Education, University of London), since 2006; *b* Leatherhead, 8 June 1958; *d* of Marcel Galster and Gladys Galster; one *s* one *d. Educ:* Rosebery Sch., Epsom; Univ. of Sussex (BA Hons 1st Cl. Computer Sci. and Artificial Intelligence 1993; PhD 1997). ACIB 1982. Midland Bank, 1978–83. University of Sussex: Lectr, 1999–2002, Reader, 2002–04, in Computer Sci. and Artificial Intelligence; Director: Undergraduate Studies, 2002–04; Human Centre Technol. Gp, 2002–04; Pro-Vice-Chancellor, 2004–06. Non-exec. Dir, British Educnl Communications and Technol. Agency, 2006–11. Gov., St Paul's Sch., 2011–. FRSA. *Publications:* Re-Designing Learning Contexts, 2010; Machine Learning and Human Intelligence, 2018; articles in learned jls on technol. and learning design and use; learning contexts. *Recreations:* family, the sea, walking, cinema, politics. *Address:* UCL Knowledge Lab, UCL Institute of Education, 23–29 Emerald Street, WC1N 3QS. *T:* (020) 7763 2176, 2164, *Fax:* (020) 7763 2138. *E:* r.luckin@ucl.ac.uk.

**LUCKING, Adrienne Simone;** QC 2014; **Her Honour Judge Lucking;** a Circuit Judge, since 2015. *Educ:* De Montfort Univ. (LLB Hons). Called to the Bar, Inner Temple, 1989; in practice as barrister, specialising in crime, 1989–2015; a Recorder, 2009–15. *Address:* Northampton Crown Court, 85–87 Lady's Lane, Northampton NN1 3HQ.

**LUCRAFT, Mark;** QC 2006; **His Honour Judge Lucraft;** a Circuit Judge, since 2012; Chief Coroner, since 2016; a Senior Circuit Judge, Central Criminal Court, since 2017; *b* 28 Dec. 1961; *s* of Rev. Cyril William Lucraft and Ann Elizabeth Lucraft; *m* 1985, Fiona Carmel Ovington; three *s. Educ:* Wood Green Sch.; Univ. of Kent at Canterbury (BA Hons Law 1983). Called to the Bar, Inner Temple, 1984, Bencher, 2017; in practice as a barrister, 1985–2012; Recorder, 2003–12. Mem. Standards Cttee, Bar Standards Bd, 2005–11; Chm., Remuneration Cttee, Bar Council, 2012 (Vice Chm., 2010–12); Legal Assessor: Gen. Optical Council, 2008–12; GMC, 2010–12. Mem., Founders' Co., 2018–. *Publications:* (contrib.) Archbold: Criminal Pleading, Evidence and Practice, 1996–2018, Gen. Ed., 2019–; (ed jtly) Encyclopedia of Road Traffic Law and Practice, 2002–; Fraud: criminal law and procedure, 2009; (consultant ed.) Halsbury's Laws of England, Road Traffic, 4th edn 2007, 5th edn 2011; (ed jtly) Crown Court Index, 2015–. *Recreations:* cricket, classical music, gardening, good food and wine. *Address:* Central Criminal Court, Old Bailey, EC4M 7EH. *Club:* MCC.

**LUCY, Sir Edmund John William Hugh Cameron-Ramsay F.;** *see* Fairfax-Lucy.

**LUDEMAN, Keith Lawrence;** Chairman: Bristol Water Company plc, since 2012; Eversholt Rail Group, since 2014; HS1 Ltd, since 2018; Luton Airport, since 2019; *b* 28 Jan. 1950; *s* of Joseph William Lawrence and Joan Violet Ludeman (*née* Dopson); *m* 1974, Diane June Eatock; two *d. Educ:* Newcastle Univ. (BA Hons Geog. 1971); Salford Univ. (MSc Transport Engrg and Planning 1973). Area Traffic Manager, Gtr Manchester Transport, 1974–82; Sen. Transport Officer, Hong Kong Govt, 1982–85; Sen. Consultant, MVA Consultancy, 1985–86; Managing Director: Burnley & Pendle Transport & Viscount Central, 1986–88; London Gen. Transport, 1988–96; London Bus Div., Go-Ahead Gp, 1996–99; Thameslink Rail and Thames Trains, 1999–2000; Chief Exec., Rail, 2000–06, Exec. Dir, 2003–06, Gp Chief Exec., 2006–11, Go-Ahead Gp; Dir, ATOC Ltd, 2003–11; non-executive Director: Interserve plc, 2011–18; Network Rail, 2011–14 (Sen. Ind. Dir, 2012–14). Mem. Council, Confedn of Passenger Transport, 1997–2000; Mem., British Transport Police Authy, 2003–05. Chm., Assoc. Train Operating Cos, 2003–05. Chm. Trustees, London Transport Mus., 2017–. FCILT; Fellow, Inst. of Railway Operators. Hon. DSc Salford, 2010. *Recreations:* sailing, scuba diving, swimming. *E:* ludemankd@aol.com. *Club:* Royal Automobile.

**LUDER, (Harold) Owen,** CBE 1986; architect and construction industry consultant; Founder and Principal, Owen Luder Consultancy (specialising in communication in construction, expert witness, mediation and advice on construction disputes), since 1987; President, Royal Institute of British Architects, 1981–83 and 1995–97; *b* Islington, London, 7 Aug. 1928; *s* of Ellen Clara Mason and adopted *s* of Edward Charles Luder; *m* 1st, 1951, Rose Dorothy (Doris) Broadstock (marr. diss. 1988; she *d* 2010); four *d* (one *s* decd); 2nd, 1989, Jacqueline Ollerton (*d* 2008). *Educ:* Ecclesbourne Rd Sch., Islington; Deptford Park Primary Sch.; Peckham Sch. for Girls; Brixton Sch. of Building; Regent St Evening Sch. of Architecture. ARIBA 1954, FRIBA 1967. Private practice in architecture, 1957–87; Owen Luder Architect, 1957–65; Founder and Sen. Partner, Owen Luder Partnership, 1965–78, when it became one of the first architectural partnerships to convert to an unlimited co., Chm. and Man. Dir, 1978–87; on withdrawal from architectural practice, set up Owen Luder Consultancy (specialising in communication in construction), 1987; Dir, Communication in Construction Ltd, 1990–2004. Non-executive Director: The Investment Company PLC, 1975–80; Jarvis PLC, 1995–2003. Principal architectural works in commercial and industrial architecture and environmental and urban planning in UK and abroad; consultant: to NCB for Vale of Belvoir coal mining project, 1975–87; to BR for re-use of Engrg Works, Shildon and Swindon, 1985–86; Consultant Architect, RCS, 1974–87; Architect/Planning Consultant, Marine Soc., 1990–99; Architect for: Trinity Square Shopping Centre and Car Park, Gateshead, 1960; Tricorn Centre, Portsmouth, 1965; Dunston Rocket, Gateshead, 1974; Tiaf City Hall, Saudi Arabia; Nat. Stadium, Abuja, Nigeria; extension to Craig-y-Don, Laugharne, 2015; unbuilt major schemes: Super Stadium for Sunderland FC, 1970; Hayes Wharf alongside HMS Belfast, 1975; Nat. Olympic Stadium, Docklands, 1973 for submission for Olympics, 1978; Channel Bridge, 1978. Gave evidence to US Congress Cttee on Urban Develt, 1967; Mem., UK Govt Delegation to the Conference on Cities, Indianapolis, 1971. Royal Institute of British Architects: Mem. Council, 1967–97, 2010–16; Hon. Treasurer, 1975–78; Vice-Pres., Membership Communications, 1989–90; Pres., Doric Club, 1994–2016; Hon. Sec./Treasurer, Commonwealth Assoc. of Architects, 1985–87; Chm. Organising Cttee, IUA Congress 1987; Vice-Chm., 1997–2002, Chm., 2003, Architects Registration Bd; Chm., Internat. Bldg Study Gp, 2010–12. Pres., Norwood Soc., 1981–92. Columnist: Building magazine, 1969–78, 1983–90; Building Design magazine, 1978–81, 1994–95; Editor and Presenter, Architectural Practice Video Magazine, 1987–90; Consultant and Presenter: RIBA Technical Seminar Prog., 1985–93; Building Design Update Seminars, 1994–2004. Regular lecturer: UCL Bartlett Sch. of Architecture; Oxford Brookes Univ. Occasional radio and TV broadcaster, UK and USA; featured in documentary film, Get Luder, 2010. British Kart Racer, 1961–63; survivor, Lakonia cruise-liner disaster, 1963. FRSA 1984. Mem., British Acad. of Experts, 1991 (Vice Chm., 1997–99); expert witness; qualified mediator. Trustee, Children Nationwide, 1997–2001. Freeman: City of London, 2010; Architects' Co., 1994 (Liveryman, 2010). RIBA Architecture Bronze Medal (for Eros House, Catford), 1963; various Civic Trust architectural and housing awards and commendations; Silver Jubilee Medal, for Housing Strategy for the 80s, Town Planning Assoc., 1981; Business Columnist of the Year, Publisher magazine, 1985. Arkansas Traveller, USA, 1971; Freedom, State of Arkansas, 1971. Audio biog. in BL Oral Hist. Collection, Architects' Lives. *Publications:* Sports Stadia after Hillsborough, 1990; Keeping out of Trouble, 1999, 4th edn 2012; contribs on architectural, planning and building matters to various jls. *Recreations:* live theatre, collecting art, supporting Arsenal avidly, enjoying my ever-expanding 'United Nations' family, No 34 on the family birthday card list 2019. *Address:* (office) 702 Romney House, 47 Marsham Street, Westminster, SW1P 3DS; Craig-y-Don, Cliff Road, Laugharne, Carmarthen SA33 4SD.

**LUDER, Ian David,** CBE 2010; JP; freelance independent non-executive director and advisor; Chairman, Basildon and Thurrock University Hospitals NHS Foundation Trust, 2012–15; Lord Mayor of London, 2008–09; *b* London, 13 April 1951; *s* of late Mark Luder and of Frances Luder (*née* Stillerman); *m* 1999, Lin Jane Surkitt. *Educ:* Haberdashers' Aske's Sch.; University Coll. London (BSc Econ.; Fellow 2009). FCA 1980; FTII 1983. Tax Partner: Arthur Andersen, 1989–2002; Grant Thornton UK LLP, 2002–09. Mem., Bedford BC, 1976–99. Contested (UK Ind) S Basildon and E Thurrock, 2015. Mem. Council, Chartered Inst. of Taxation, 1983–97 (Pres., 1994–95). City of London: Mem., Court, Common Council, 1998–; Chm., Finance Cttee, 2003–06; Member: Audit and Risk Mgt Cttee, 2011– (Chm., 2017–); Open Spaces Cttee, 2012– (Chm., 2013–16); Alderman, Castle Baynard Ward, 2005–; Sheriff, City of London, 2007–08; Liveryman: Coopers' Co., 1999– (Master, 2016–17); Tax Advisers' Co., 2005–; Art Scholars' Co., 2014– (Master, 2014–15). JP City of London, 2002. Hon. Fellow, GSMD, 2009. Hon. DSc City, 2008. KStJ 2009. *Recreations:* cricket, Rugby, gardening. *Clubs:* City Livery, MCC, East India.

**LUDER, Owen;** *see* Luder, H. O.

**LUDFORD,** Baroness *cr* 1997 (Life Peer), of Clerkenwell in the London Borough of Islington; **Sarah Ann Ludford;** *b* 14 March 1951; *m* 1982, Stephen Hitchins. *Educ:* Portsmouth High Sch.; London Sch. of Economics (BSc Econ; MSc Econ); Inns of Court Sch. of Law. Called to the Bar, Gray's Inn, 1979. With European Commn, 1979–85; European Advr, Lloyd's of London, 1985–87; Vice Pres., Corporate External Affairs, American Express Europe, 1987–90. Mem. (Lib Dem) Islington LBC, 1991–99. Mem., Lib Dem Federal Policy Cttee, 1990– (Vice Chm., 1992–98, 2017–); Vice Chm., London Lib Dems, 1990–94. Contested: (L) Wight and Hampshire E, 1984, (Lib Dem) London Central, 1989 and 1994, EP elections; (Lib Dem) Islington N, 1992, Islington S and Finsbury, 1997. Mem. (Lib Dem) London Reg., EP, 1999–2014; contested same seat, 2014. *Address:* House of Lords, SW1A 0PW.

**LUDLOW, Bishop Suffragan of,** since 2009; **Rt Rev. Alistair James Magowan;** Archdeacon of Ludlow, since 2009; *b* 10 Feb. 1955; *s* of Samuel and Marjorie Magowan; *m* 1979, (Margaret) Louise Magowan (*née* Atkin); one *s* two *d. Educ:* King's Sch., Worcester; Leeds Univ. (BSc Hons Animal Physiol. and Nutrition); Trinity Coll., Bristol (DipHE); MTh Oxon 2002. Ordained deacon, 1981, priest, 1982; Curate: St John the Baptist, Owlerton, Sheffield, 1981–84; St Nicholas, Durham, 1984–89; Chaplain, St Aidan's Coll., Durham Univ., 1984–89; Vicar, St John the Baptist, Egham, 1989–2000; RD, Runnymede, 1993–98; Archdeacon of Dorset, 2000–09. Canon, Salisbury Cathedral, 2000–09; Prebendary, Hereford Cathedral, 2010–. Chairman: Guildford Diocesan Bd of Educn, 1995–2000; Salisbury Diocesan Bd of Educn, 2003–09. *Recreations:* walking, fly fishing, oil painting, stamp collecting. *Address:* The Bishop's House, Corvedale Road, Craven Arms, Shropshire SY7 9BT.

**LUDLOW, Archdeacon of;** *see* Ludlow, Bishop Suffragan of.

**LUDMAN, Harold,** FRCS; Consultant Surgeon in Neuro-otology, National Hospital for Neurology and Neurosurgery, 1967–98; Consultant Surgeon to Ear, Nose and Throat Department, King's College Hospital, 1965–94; *b* 23 Feb. 1933; *s* of Nathan Ludman and

Fanny Dinah Jerome; m 1957, Lorraine Israel; one s one d. Educ: Bradford Grammar Sch.; Sidney Sussex Coll., Cambridge (BA 1954; MB, BChir 1957; MA 1958). FRCS 1961. House Physician, UCH, 1957; House Surgeon: Royal Ear Hosp., UCH, 1957; Edgware Gen. Hosp., 1958; Royal Marsden Hosp., 1958–59; Registrar and Sen. Registrar, Ear, Nose and Throat Dept, KCH, 1960–65. President: British Assoc. Otolaryngology, 1990–93; Section of Otology, RSocMed, 1985; Chm., Soc. Audiology Technicians, 1967–75. Chm., Specialist Adv. Cttee in Otolaryngology, Jt Cttee Higher Surgical Trng, 1988–91; Mem., Intercollegiate Bd in Otolaryngology, RCS (formerly Mem. Court of Examiners); Chm., working party on deafness, MRC, 1973–77; formerly Mem., Hearing Aid Council. W. J. Harrison Prize, RSocMed, 1987; W. Jobson Horne Prize, BMA, 1990. *Publications:* (jtly) Diseases of the Ear, 1963, 6th edn 1997; (contrib.) Scott-Brown's Diseases of the Ear, Nose and Throat, 4th edn 1979 to 6th edn 1996; ABC of Ear, Nose and Throat, 5th edn 2007 to 6th edn 2012; contribs to books on ear diseases; numerous papers to learned jls on diseases of the ear. *Recreations:* photography, computers, reading, theatre, bird watching.

**LUDWIG, Christa;** singer; *b* Berlin, 16 March; *d* of Anton Ludwig, singer, stage director and opera general manager and Eugenie (*née* Besalla), singer; *m* 1st, 1957, Walter Berry (marr. diss. 1970), baritone; one *s*; 2nd, 1972, Paul-Emile Deiber (*d* 2011), actor and stage-director. *Educ:* Matura. Staedtische Buehnen, Frankfurt; Landestheater Darmstadt; Landestheater, Hannover; Vienna State Opera; guest appearances in New York, Chicago, London, Berlin, Munich, Tokyo, Milan, Rome, Lucerne, Salzburg, Epidauros, Zürich, Holland, Los Angeles, Cleveland, Saratoga, Bayreuth, Copenhagen, Gent, Montreal, Prague, Budapest and others. Hon. Prof., Senat Berlin, Germany, 1995. Dr *hc* Warsaw, 2008. Kammersängerin, Austria, 1962; Grand Prix du Disque, 1966; Grammy Award, 1967; Mozart Medal, Mozartgemeinde, Vienna, 1969; First Class Art and Science, Austria, 1969; Deutscher Schallplattenpreis, 1970; Orphée d'Or, 1970; Prix des Affaires Culturelles, 1972; Vienna Philharmonic Silver Rose, 1980; Hugo Wolf Medal, 1980; Gustav Mahler Medal, 1980; Ehrenring, Staatsoper Vienna, 1980, Hon. Mem., 1981, Fidelio Medal, 1991; Golden Medal, City of Salzburg, 1988, and Vienna, 1988; Echo Prize, Germany, 1994; Musician of the Year, Musical America, 1994; Hugo Wolf Medal, 2010. Grosses Bundesverdienstkreuz (Germany), 2004. Commandeur: des Arts et des Lettres (France), 1988; Légion d'Honneur (France), 2011; Grosses Ehrenzeichen (Austria), 1994; Silver Great Honour (Austria), 2007; Grand Officier, Ordre pour le Mérite (France), 2016 (Commandeur, 1997). *Publications:* Und ich wäre so gern Primadonna gewesen (autobiog.), 1994 (French edn 1996, US edn 1999); Leicht Muss Man Sein, 2018. *Recreations:* listening to music, theatre, concerts, reading.

**LUDWIG, Karen Heather;** *see* Vousden, K. H.

**LUESLEY, Prof. David Michael,** MD; FRCOG; Lead Cancer Clinician, Sandwell and West Birmingham NHS Trust, 2016–18 (Group (formerly Divisional) Director of Women's and Children's Health, 2010–14); Director, Pan-Birmingham Gynaecological Cancer Centre, City Hospital, Birmingham, 2005–16; Consultant Gynaecologist and Gynaecological Oncologist, BMI Priory Hospital and BMI Edgbaston Hospital, 2016–18; *b* 14 Feb. 1952; *s* of Michael James Joseph and Elizabeth Margaret Luesley; *m* 1996, Gabrielle Patricia Downey; two *d*. *Educ:* Queen Elizabeth Grammar Sch., Wakefield; Downing Coll., Cambridge (BA 1972; MA); Birmingham Univ. (MB ChB 1975; MD 1985). FRCOG 1993. University of Birmingham: Sen. Lectr, 1986–93, Reader, 1993–96, in Obstetrics and Gynaecol.; Prof. of Gynaecol Oncology, 1996–2003; Lawson-Tait Prof. of Gynaecol Oncology, 2003–12, now Emeritus. Hon. Consultant Gynaecol Oncologist, Birmingham Women's Hosp., 2000–05. *Publications:* Intraepithelial Neoplasia of the Lower Genital Tract, 1995; Handbook of Colposcopy, 1996, 2nd edn 2002; Understanding Gynaecology: a problem solving approach, 1997; Cancer and Pre-Cancer of the Cervix, 1998; Cancer and Pre-Cancer of the Vulva, 1999; Handbook of Gynaecological Oncology, 2000. *Recreations:* food, wine, painting, photography.

**LUETCHFORD, Teresa Jane;** *see* Kingham, T. J.

**LUFF, Rev. Canon Alan Harold Frank;** Canon Residentiary of Birmingham Cathedral, 1992–96, Canon Emeritus, 1996; *b* 6 Nov. 1928; *s* of late Frank Luff and Elsie Lilian Luff (*née* Down), Bristol; *m* 1956, Enid Meirion, *d* of late Robert Meirion Roberts and Daisy Harker Roberts; three *s* one *d*. *Educ:* Bristol Grammar School; University Coll., Oxford (BA 1951, Dip. Theol. 1952, MA 1954); Westcott House, Cambridge. ARCM 1977. Deacon, 1956; priest, 1957; Assistant Curate: St Matthew, Stretford, Manchester, 1956–59; St Peter, Swinton, Manchester (with charge of All Saints, Wardley), 1959–61; Precentor of Manchester Cathedral, 1961–68; Vicar of Dwygyfylchi (otherwise Penmaenmawr), Gwynedd, dio. Bangor, 1968–79; Precentor, 1979–92, also Sacrist, 1979–86, Westminster Abbey; licensed to officiate, dio. Llandaff, 1996–. Chm., Hymn Soc. of Great Britain and Ireland, 1987–93 (Hon. Sec., 1973–86; Hon. Vice Pres., 2014–); Vice Pres., Internat. Arbeitsgemeinschaft für Hymnologie, 1999–2009. Chm., Pratt Green Trust, 1988–2006. Hon. FGCM 1993 (Warden, 1984–97; Vice Pres., 1997–); ARSCM 2000. Editor, Hymn Quest, 2000–. *Publications:* Hymns and Psalms (composer and author), 1981; Welsh Hymns and their tunes, 1990; (ed) Story Song, 1993; (ed) Sing His Glory, 1997; (ed and trans.) Ann Griffiths, Hymns and Letters, 1999; (ed) Strengthen for Service: 100 years of the English Hymnal, 2005; contribs to New Christian, Musical Times, Choir and Organ, etc. *Recreations:* singing, conducting, cooking. *Address:* Lakeside House, 37 Wedal Road, Cardiff CF14 3QX.

**LUFF, Sir Peter (James),** Kt 2014; Chair, National Heritage Memorial Fund and National Lottery Heritage (formerly Heritage Lottery) Fund, since 2015; *b* 18 Feb. 1955; *s* of Thomas Luff and Joyce (*née* Mills); *m* 1982, Julia Jenks; one *s* one *d*. *Educ:* Windsor Grammar Sch.; Corpus Christi Coll., Cambridge (MA Econs). Research Asst to Rt Hon. Peter Walker, 1977–80; Head of Private Office to Rt Hon. Edward Heath, 1980–82; Dir, Good Relations Public Affairs, 1982–87; Special Advr to Rt Hon. Lord Young of Graffham, 1987–89; Sen. Consultant, Lowe Bell Communications, 1989–90; Asst Man. Dir, Good Relations Ltd, 1990–92. MP (C) Worcester, 1992–97, Mid Worcestershire, 1997–2015. PPS to Minister for Industry and Energy, 1993–96, to Lord Chancellor, 1996–97, to Minister of State, Home Office, 1996–97; an Opposition Whip, 2000–05; Opposition Asst Chief Whip, 2002–05; Parly Under-Sec. of State, MoD, 2010–12 (Minister for Defence Equipment, Support and Technol.). Chairman: Agriculture Select Cttee, 1997–2000; Trade and Industry Select Cttee, 2005–07; Business and Enterprise Select Cttee, 2007–09; Business, Innovation and Skills Cttee, 2009–10; Mem., Internat. Develt Cttee, 2014–15; Dep. Chm., All-Party India Gp, 2006–15; Chair, Speakers' Adv. Cttee on 2015 Anniversaries, 2014–15. Chm., Cons. Parly Friends of India, 2001–05. Mem., Exec. Cttee, CPA, 2001–06. Patron, Conservative Students, 1995–98. Vice-Pres., Severn Valley Railway, 1997–. Chm., Worcester Cathedral Council, 2002–08. FCIPR (FIPR 1998; Hon. Fellow, 2008). *Recreations:* performing arts, shooting, photography. *E:* peter@peterluff.com.

**LUFF, Peter John Roussel,** FRGS; *b* Brussels, 14 Sept. 1946; *s* of Edward and Yvonne Luff; *m* 1969, Carolyn Watson; three *s* one *d* (and one *d* decd). *Educ:* Eltham Coll.; Swansea Univ. (BA Hons Politics and Internat. Relns); Sch. of African and Oriental Studies, Univ. of London (MA 2013). FRGS 1971. Asst Dir, Amnesty Internat. UK, 1974–78; originated and co-produced first two shows in The Secret Policeman's Ball comedy series, 1976–77; Dir, All-Party Parly Human Rights Gp, 1976–78; Asst Producer, BBC TV, 1978–81; Funding and Mktg Dir, SDP, 1981–86; Dir, Eur. Movement UK, 1986–92; Vice Pres., Internat. Eur. Movement, 1992–95; Partner, Matrix Communications Ltd, 1995–97; Dir Gen., Royal Commonwealth Soc., 1997–2001; Consultant, Umeed health prog., Punjab, 2001–03; Exec. Dir, Action for a Global Climate Community, 2003–12. Chm., Eur. Movement, 2007–12. Vice Chair: Congress, World Federalist Movement/Inst. of Global Policy, 2004–; Coalition for Creation of Internat. Court for Envmt, 2009–; Member: Bd, One World Trust, 2000–06 (Trustee, 2019–); Bd, China Dialogue, 2016–. Trustee: Responding to Conflict, 2002–10; Mass Extinction Meml Observatory, 2012–19. FRSA. *Publications:* The Simple Guide to Maastricht, 1992; A Brilliant Conspiracy?, 1997. *Recreations:* travel, theatre, cinema, boating, walking, exploring Greece. *Address:* 46 St Marks Road, Henley-on-Thames, Oxon RG9 1LW. *E:* peterluff@hotmail.com. *Clubs:* Athenæum, Chelsea Arts, Two Brydges.

**LUFFINGHAM, Prof. John Kingley,** FDSRCSE; Professor of Orthodontics, University of Glasgow, 1976–93, now Emeritus; *b* 14 Aug. 1928; *s* of Alfred Hulbert Carr Luffingham and Frances Tugby; *m* 1968, Elizabeth Margaret Anderson; two *s* one *d*. *Educ:* Haileybury; London Hosp. Med. Coll. (BDS, PhD London); Dip. Orth RCSE. House Surgeon, London Hosp. Med. Coll., 1957–58; Registrar, KCH, 1959–61; Clinical Research Fellow, MRC, 1961–64; Sen. Registrar, Guy's Hosp., 1965–67; Lectr, Glasgow Univ., 1968–76; Consultant Orthodontist, Greater Glasgow Health Board, 1968–76. *Publications:* articles in dental jls, incl. British Jl of Orthodontics, European Jl of Orthodontics, Archives of Oral Biology. *Recreation:* golf.

**LUGG, Nigel John;** Group Executive Chairman and Chief Executive Officer, Prominent Europe, since 2002; *b* Bristol, 16 June 1956; *s* of late Rev. Stewart John Lugg and of Margaret Naomi Lugg; *m* 1984, Susie Mary Brett; two *d*. *Educ:* Wells Cathedral Sch. Retail Buyer: Liberty, 1974–80; House of Fraser, 1980–90; Managing Director: Warnaco Men's Apparel, 1990–93; Prominent Europe, 1993–2002. Chairman: Chester Barrie Savile Row, 1997–; Quantum Clothing, 2012–16. Chm., UK Fashion and Textiles Assoc., 2015–. Chm., Harringworth Educnl Trust, 2012–. *Recreations:* ski-ing, golf, fashion, the arts. *Address:* Shotley House, Shotley, Harringworth, Corby NN17 3AG. *T:* 07771 667920. *E:* nlugg@paleu.com.

**LUK, Margrit Alexandra, (Sandy);** Chief Executive Officer, Marine Conservation Society, since 2016; *b* Tübingen, Germany, 17 March 1969; *d* of Wilfried Otto Keutsch and Elina Muriel Keutsch; *m* 1997, Sin Min Luk; one *s* one *d*. *Educ:* Manchester Univ. (LLB Hons 1992); Guildford Law Sch. (Law Soc. Finals 1993); Sch. of Oriental and African Studies, Univ. of London (LLM 1994). Intern, Field, 1993–94; trainee solicitor, Cameron Markby Hewitt, 1995–97; admitted as a solicitor, 1997; Solicitor: Garretts, 1997–98; Corporate and Envmtl Law, Rowe & Main, 1998–99; Regulatory and Envmtl Law, Anglian Water, 1999–2000; Policy Officer, RSPB, 2002–07; Dir, EPPAC Ltd, 2007–10; Hd, Biodiversity, then Dir of Progs, ClientEarth, 2010–16. RSPB volunteer, 2001. *Publications:* chapters and appendices: Improving Compliance with International Environmental Law, 1996; The Habitats Directive in its EU Environmental Law Context: European nature's best hope, 2015; contrib. to Internat. Marine Conservation Congress, 2014. *Recreations:* mountain walking, dancing, Duke of Edinburgh expeditions. *Address:* Marine Conservation Society, Overross House, Ross Park, Ross-on-Wye HR9 7US. *T:* (01989) 566017. *E:* sandy.luk@mcsuk.org.

**LUKE, 4th Baron** *cr* 1929, of Pavenham, co. Bedford; **Ian James St John Lawson Johnston;** *b* 3 Oct. 1963; *s* of 3rd Baron Luke and Silvia Maria Lawson Johnston (*née* Roigt); *S* father, 2015; *m* 1998, Rowena Jane, *y d* of John Aldington; two *s* one *d*. *Educ:* Eton. *Heir:* *s* Hon. Samuel Arthur St John Lawson Johnston, *b* 12 Oct. 2000.

**LUKE, Iain Malone;** *b* 8 Oct. 1951; *m* 1987, Marie (*d* 2009). *Educ:* Dundee Coll.; Univ. of Dundee (MA 1980); Univ. of Edinburgh (DipBA 1981); Jordanhill Teacher Trng Coll. (FE Teaching Qualif.). Asst Collector of Taxes, Inland Revenue, 1969–74; Asst Sales Manager, Brown & Tawse Steel Stockholder, 1974–75; Asst Bar Manager, 1981–83; Lectr, then Sen. Lectr, Dundee Coll. of Further Educn, 1983–2001. Member (Lab): Dundee DC, 1984–96; Dundee CC, 1995–2001. MP (Lab) Dundee E, 2001–05; contested (Lab) same seat, 2005. JP Dundee, 1996–2001.

**LUKE, Robert Haydon Vernon,** CVO 2015; Group Director of Operations and External Affairs, Social Communications, since 2018; *b* 9 Sept. 1974; *m* Louise Elwell; two *s* one *d*. *Educ:* St George's Sch., Harpenden; St Catharine's Coll., Cambridge (BA 1995). Grant Scheme Manager, Millennium Commn, 1997–2000; joined FCO, 2000; Desk Officer, Middle East Peace Process Section, Nr East and N Africa Dept, FCO, 2000–01; on secondment to Brazilian Diplomatic Inst., 2002; Second Sec. (Pol/Press and Public Affairs), Brasilia, 2002–05; Hd, War Crimes Section, Internat. Orgns Dept, FCO, 2005–08; on secondment to French Immigration Ministry, 2008; Counsellor, Justice and Home Affairs, Paris, 2009–12; High Comr, Malta, 2012–16; Dep. Comr (Policy), Inf. Comr's Office, 2017.

**LUKES, Prof. Steven Michael,** DPhil; FBA 1987; Professor of Sociology, New York University, since 1998; *b* 8 March 1941; *o s* of S. Lukes; *m* 1977, Nina Vera Mary Stanger (*d* 1999); two *s* one *d*; *m* 2006, Katha Pollitt. *Educ:* Royal Grammar School, Newcastle upon Tyne; Balliol Coll., Oxford (MA 1965; DPhil 1968). Student, 1962–64, Res. Fellow, 1964–66, Nuffield Coll., Oxford; Fellow of Balliol Coll., Oxford, 1966–88; Lectr in Politics, Oxford Univ., 1967–88; Prof. of Political and Social Theory, European Univ. Inst., Florence, 1987–95; Prof. of Moral Philosophy, Univ. of Siena, 1995–2000. Vis. Centennial Prof., LSE, 2001–03. *Publications:* (ed jtly) The Good Society, 1972; Emile Durkheim: his life and work, 1972; Individualism, 1973; Power: a radical view, 1974, 2nd enlarged edn 2005; Essays in Social Theory, 1976; (ed) Durkheim: Rules of Sociological Method, 1982; (ed jtly) Rationality and Relativism, 1982; (ed jtly) Durkheim and the Law, 1984; Marxism and Morality, 1985; (jtly) No Laughing Matter: a collection of political jokes, 1985; (ed) Power, 1986; Moral Conflict and Politics, 1991; The Curious Enlightenment of Professor Caritat: a comedy of ideas, 1995; Liberals and Cannibals: the implications of diversity, 2003; Moral Relativism, 2009. *Recreation:* playing jazz piano. *Address:* Department of Sociology, New York University, 295 Lafayette Street, 4th Floor, New York, NY 10012, USA. *E:* steven.lukes@nyu.edu; 175 Riverside Drive, Apartment 13G, New York, NY 10024, USA.

**LUKIES, Alastair,** CBE 2014; Founding Partner, Origination, Motive Partners, since 2016; Founder and Chief Executive Officer, Pollinate International, since 2017; *b* Harlow, 26 Sept. 1973; *s* of Robert Lukies and Melanie Harris (*née* Carver); *m* 2003, Helen Reeves; one *s*. *Educ:* Bishops Stortford Coll. Rugby player for Saracens and London Irish; Dir, Asia Pacific, Internat. Communications Mgt Commonwealth Games Hospitality Div., 1999–2000; Co-founder, ePolitix, 2000–03; Co-founder and Chief Exec., Monitise, 2003–15. Non-exec. Chm., Innovate Finance, 2014–17. UK Business Ambassador for Financial Services, 2014–19; Mem., Prime Minister's Business Council, 2019–; Chm., Fintech Alliance, 2019–. Member, UK Trade and Investment delegation: to Africa, 2011; to Indonesia, 2012; to China, 2013. Entrepreneur of Year, Growing Business Awards, 2011. *Recreations:* Rugby, swimming, ski-ing, Baptist Church, family roast dinners, long walks with wife Helen and son Jacob.

**LUKŠIĆ, Igor**, PhD; Director for Southeast Europe, PricewaterhouseCoopers, since 2016; *b* Bar, Montenegro, 14 June 1976; *s* of Božidar and Nada Lukšić; *m* 2005, Nataša Bajović; one *s* two *d*. *Educ:* Univ. of Montenegro (BA 1998; MA 2002; PhD 2005). Docent and Lectr, Faculty of Internat. Econs, Finance and Business, Univ. of Montenegro; Sec., Min. of Foreign Affairs, 2001. MP (Democratic Party of Socialists) Montenegro, 2001–16; Finance Minister, 2004–10; Dep. Prime Minister, 2008–10; Prime Minister, 2010–12; Dep. Prime Minister and Minister of Foreign Affairs and Eur. Integration, 2012–16. *Publications:* Book of Laughter (poetry and prose), 2001; (jtly) The Quest for Economic Freedoms, 2010; Fear, 2011; Book of Fear, 2013. *Recreations:* occasional basketball and tennis. *Address:* PricewaterhouseCoopers, The Capital Plaza, 98 Dzordza Vasingtona Boulevard, 20000 Podgorica, Montenegro.

**LUMLEY**, family name of **Earl of Scarbrough**.

**LUMLEY, Joanna Lamond**, OBE 1995; FRGS; actress; *b* Kashmir, India, 1 May 1946; *d* of late Maj. James Rutherford Lumley, 6th Gurkha Rifles and Thyra Beatrice Rose Lumley (*née* Weir); one *s*; *m* 1st, Jeremy Lloyd (marr. diss. 1971; he *d* 2014); 2nd, 1986, Stephen William Barlow, *qv*. Theatre includes: Don't Just Lie There, Say Something, Garrick, 1972; Private Lives, tour, 1983; Hedda Gabler, Dundee, 1985; Blithe Spirit, Vaudeville, 1986; An Ideal Husband, Chichester, 1989; The Cherry Orchard, 1989; Vanilla, Brighton, transf. Lyric, 1990; The Revengers' Comedies, Strand, 1991; Who Shall I Be Tomorrow?, Greenwich, 1992; The Letter, Lyric, Hammersmith, 1995; The Cherry Orchard, Crucible, Sheffield, 2007; La Bête, Comedy, transf. NY, 2010; The Lion in Winter, Th. Royal, Haymarket, 2011; *television* includes: General Hospital, 1973; Coronation Street, 1973; Steptoe and Son; The New Avengers, 1976–78 (BAFTA Special Award, 2000); Sapphire and Steel, 1979; The Weather in the Streets, 1983; Mistral's Daughter; Oxbridge Blues, 1984; The Glory Boys; guest presenter, Wogan; A Perfect Hero, 1989; Lovejoy, 1992; Absolutely Fabulous, 1992–96, 2001–03, 2011 (2 BAFTA Awards; British Comedy Award, 1993); Class Act, 1994; Coming Home, A Rather English Marriage, 1998; Nancherrow, Dr Willoughby, MD, 1999; Mirrorball, 2000; (co-prod) The Cazalets, 2001; Up in Town, 2002; Born to be Wild, 2002; Sensitive Skin, 2005, 2007; Last Chance to Save, 2005; Jam and Jerusalem, 2006; Mistresses, 2010; The Making of a Lady, 2012; documentaries: White Rajahs of Sarawak, 1991; Girl Friday, 1994; Joanna Lumley in the Kingdom of the Thunder Dragon, 1997; Joanna Lumley's Nile, 2010; Joanna Lumley on Broadway, 2011; Joanna Lumley's Greek Odyssey, 2011; Joanna Lumley in search of Noah's Ark, 2013; Joanna Lumley meets Will.i.am, 2014; Joanna Lumley's Trans-Siberian Adventure, 2015; Joanna Lumley: Elvis and me, 2015; Joanna Lumley's Japan, 2016; Joanna Lumley's Postcards, 2017; Joanna Lumley's India, 2017; Joanna Lumley's Silk Road Adventure, 2018; *radio* includes: The Psychedelic Spy, 1990; The Fortunes of War, 2008; *films* include: On Her Majesty's Secret Service; The Satanic Rites of Dracula; Trail of the Pink Panther; Curse of the Pink Panther; Shirley Valentine, 1989; Innocent Lies, 1995; James and the Giant Peach, Cold Comfort Farm, 1996; Prince Valiant, 1997; Sweeney Todd, 1998; Parting Shots, Mad Cows, 1999; Maybe Baby, 2000; Ella Enchanted, The Cat's Meow, 2004; The Magic Roundabout, 2005; Corpse Bride, 2005; Boogie Woogie, 2010; The Wolf of Wall Street, 2014; She's Funny That Way, 2015; Me Before You, 2016; Absolutely Fabulous: the Movie, 2016; Finding Your Feet, 2018. Hon. Patron, Trinity Coll. Dublin Philosophical Soc., 2007. Hon. DLitt: Kent, 1995; St Andrews, 2006; DUniv Oxford Brookes, 2000. BAFTA Fellowship, 2017. *Publications:* (ed) Peacocks and Commas, 1983; Stare Back and Smile (autobiog.), 1989; Forces Sweethearts, 1993; Girl Friday, 1994; In the Kingdom of the Thunder Dragon, 1997; No Room for Secrets (autobiog.), 2004; Absolutely: a memoir, 2011; articles in jls. *Recreations:* reading, music, travelling, granddaughters, daydreaming. *Address:* c/o Conway Van Gelder Grant Ltd, 8–12 Broadwick Street, W1F 8HW.

**LUMLEY, Karen Elizabeth**; *b* 28 March 1964; *d* of Derek and Sylvia Allott; *m* 1984, Richard Gareth Lumley; one *s* one *d*. *Educ:* Rugby High Sch. for Girls; E Warwicks Coll., Rugby. Trainee accountant, Ford Motor Co., 1982–84; Co. Sec., RKL Geological Services Ltd, 1985–. Member (C): Wrexham BC (Gp Leader, 1991–96); Clwyd CC, 1993–96; Redditch BC, 2001–03. Contested (C) Delyn, 1997; Redditch, 2001, 2005. MP (C) Redditch, 2010–17. *Recreations:* knitting, cooking, reading.

**LUMLEY, Nicholas James Henry**; QC 2012; a Recorder, since 2008; *b* Nottingham, 29 March 1969; *s* of Henry Lumley and Christine Lumley (*née* Rodger); *m* 1st, 1997 (marr. diss. 2007); one *d*; 2nd, 2012, Ruth Phillips; one *s* one *d*, and one step *d*. *Educ:* Pocklington Sch.; Newcastle Univ. (LLB Hons); Inns of Court Sch. of Law. Called to the Bar, Lincoln's Inn, 1992; Jun., 1997–98, Sec., 2004–11, N Eastern Circuit. Mem., Merchant Taylors' Co., York, 2013–. Vigneron d'honneur, St Emilion, 2005. *Recreations:* perusing wine lists, pottering, perfecting the art of embarrassing my children. *Address:* New Park Court Chambers, 16 Park Place, Leeds LS1 2SJ. *T:* (0113) 243 3277, *Fax:* (0113) 242 1285. *E:* nicholas.lumleyqc@newparkcourt.co.uk. *Clubs:* Northern Counties; Primary Cricket, Armstrong Rugby Football (Newcastle).

**LUMLEY-SAVILE**, family name of **Baron Savile**.

**LUMSDAINE, Nicola Frances**; *see* LeFanu, N. F.

**LUMSDEN, Prof. Andrew Gino**, PhD; FRS 1994; Professor of Developmental Neurobiology, King's College London School of Biomedical and Health Sciences (formerly United Medical and Dental Schools of Guy's and St Thomas' Hospitals, then Guy's, King's and St Thomas' Hospitals' Medical and Dental School, King's College London), London University, 1989–2016, now Emeritus; Director, MRC Centre for Developmental Neurobiology, 2000–14; *b* 22 Jan. 1947; *s* of Dr Edward Gilbert Sita-Lumsden, MD and Stella Pirie Lumsden; *m* 1st, 1970, Anne Farrington Roberg (marr. diss. 1996); two *d*; 2nd, 2002, Kathleen Marie Wets. *Educ:* Kingswood Sch., Bath; St Catharine's Coll., Cambridge (BA 1968; MA 1972; Frank Smart Scholar); Yale Univ.; PhD London 1978. Fulbright Scholar, 1968–70; Lectr in Anatomy, 1973–87, Reader in Craniofacial Biology, 1987–89, Guy's Hosp. Med. Sch. Miller Foundn Vis. Prof., Univ. of California, Berkeley, 1994; Lectr, Coll. de France, Paris, 1991; Yntema Lectr, SUNY, 1993; Howard Hughes Internat. Res. Scholar, 1993–98; Jenkinson Meml Lectr, Univ. of Oxford, 1994; Seymour Kreshover Lectr, NIH, 1996; Brooks Lectr, Harvard Univ., 1996; Ferrier Lectr, Royal Soc., 2001. Mem., EMBO, 2008–. Founder FMedSci 1998; FKC 1999. Freeman, 2006, Liveryman, 2016, Clockmakers' Co. W. Maxwell Cowan Prize, Soc. for Neurosci., 2007. Médaille de la Ville de Paris, 1986. *Publications:* (jtly) The Developing Brain, 2001; (jtly) Principles of Development, 2015; reports in learned jls. *Recreations:* mechanical engineering, natural history, Lotus Sevens, bridge, horology, ski-ing. *Address:* Department of Developmental Neurobiology, King's College London, SE1 1UL.

**LUMSDEN, Andrew Michael**; Organist and Director of Music, Winchester Cathedral, since 2002; *b* 10 Nov. 1962; *s* of Sir David James Lumsden, *qv*. *Educ:* Winchester Coll.; Royal Scottish Acad. of Music and Drama; St John's Coll., Cambridge (MA Hons). ARCO 1979. Asst Organist, Southwark Cathedral, 1985–88; Sub-organist, Westminster Abbey, 1988–91; Organist and Master of the Choristers, Lichfield Cathedral, 1992–2002. Ext. Examr, Birmingham Conservatoire, RNCM, 1995–2005. Hon. FRCO 2004; Hon. FGCM 2008. *Recreations:* travel, flying, wine. *Address:* Cathedral Office, 9 The Close, Winchester SO23 9LS. *T:* (01962) 857200, *Fax:* (01962) 857201. *E:* andrew.lumsden@winchester-cathedral.org.uk.

**LUMSDEN, Sir David (James)**, Kt 1985; Principal, Royal Academy of Music, 1982–93; *b* Newcastle upon Tyne, 19 March 1928; *m* 1951, Sheila Daniels; two *s* two *d*. *Educ:* Dame Allan's Sch., Newcastle upon Tyne; Selwyn Coll., Cambridge (Hon. Fellow, 1986). Organ scholar, Selwyn Coll., Cambridge, 1948–51; BA Class I, 1950; MusB (Barclay Squire Prize) 1951; MA 1955; DPhil 1957. Asst Organist, St John's Coll., Cambridge, 1951–53; Res. Student, 1951–54; Organist and Choirmaster, St Mary's, Nottingham, 1954–56; Founder and Conductor, Nottingham Bach Soc., 1954–59; Rector Chori, Southwell Minster, 1956–59; Dir of Music, Keele, 1958–59; Prof. of Harmony, Royal Academy of Music, 1959–61; Fellow and Organist, New Coll., Oxford (Hon. Fellow, 1996), and Lectr in the Faculty of Music, Oxford Univ., 1959–76; Principal, RSAMD, Glasgow, 1976–82. Conductor: Oxford Harmonic Soc., 1961–63; Oxford Sinfonia, 1967–70; BBC Scottish Singers, 1977–80; Organist, Sheldonian Theatre, 1964–76; Choragus, Oxford Univ., 1968–72. Harpsichordist to London Virtuosi, 1972–75. Member of Board: Scottish Opera, 1977–83; ENO, 1983–88. President: Inc. Assoc. of Organists, 1966–68; ISM, 1984–85; RCO, 1986–88; Chairman: NYO, 1985–94; Early Music Soc., 1985–89. Hugh Porter Lectr, Union Theological Seminary, NY, 1967; Vis. Prof., Yale Univ., 1974–75. Hon. Editor, Church Music Soc., 1970–73. Mem., Royal Soc. of Musicians, 1984. Hon. FRCO 1976; Hon. RAM 1978; FRCM 1980; FRNCM 1981; FRSAMD 1982; Hon. GSM 1984; FLCM 1985; FRSA 1985; FRSCM 1987; Hon. FTCL 1988; FKC 1991. Hon. DLitt Reading, 1990. *Publications:* An Anthology of English Lute Music, 1954; Thomas Robinson's Schoole of Musicke, 1603, 1971; Articles in: The Listener; The Score; Music and Letters: Galpin Soc. Jl; La Luth et sa Musique; La Musique de la Renaissance, etc. *Recreations:* reading, theatre, photography, travel, hill-walking, etc. *Address:* 26 Wyke Mark, Dean Lane, Winchester SO22 5DJ. *E:* lumsdendj@aol.com.
*See also* A. M. Lumsden.

**LUMSDEN, Iain Cobden**, FFA; Group Chief Executive, Standard Life Assurance Co., 2002–04; *b* 6 June 1946; *s* of John A. Lumsden and Helen H. Lumsden (*née* Foster); *m* 1970, Rosemary Hoey; one *s* one *d*. *Educ:* Exeter Coll., Oxford (BA 1967; MA). FFA 1971. Standard Life Assurance Co., 1967–2004: Gp Finance Dir, 1990–2001.

**LUMSDEN, Prof. Keith Grant**, FRSE; Director, Edinburgh Business School, 1995–2016; *b* 7 Jan. 1935; *s* of Robert Sclater Lumsden and Elizabeth Brow; *m* 1st, 1961, Jean Baillie Macdonald (*d* 2005); one *s*; 2nd, 2009, Ruth Edith Reid. *Educ:* Univ. of Edinburgh (MA Hons Econ 1959); Stanford Univ., California (PhD 1968). FRSE 1992. Stanford University: Instructor, Dept of Econs, 1960–63; Asst Prof., Graduate Sch. of Business, 1964–67; Research Associate, Stanford Res. Inst., 1965–71; Associate Prof., Grad. Sch. of Business, 1968–75; Dir, Esmée Fairbairn Res. Centre, Heriot-Watt Univ., 1975–95. Vis. Prof., Heriot-Watt Univ., 1969–70; Affiliate Prof. of Econs, INSEAD, 1975; Acad. Dir, Sea Transport Exec. Programme, 1979; Prof. of Econs, Advanced Management Coll., Stanford Univ., 1971. Director: Economic Educn Project, 1969–74; Behavioral Res. Labs, 1970–72; Capital Preservation Fund, 1971–75; Nielsen Engineering Research, 1972–75; Hewlett-Packard Ltd, 1981–92. *Publications:* The Free Enterprise System, 1963; The Gross National Product, 1964; International Trade, 1965; (jtly) Macroeconomics, 1966, 4th edn 1981; (ed) New Development in the Teaching of Economics, 1967; Excess Demand and Excess Supply in World Tramp Shipping Markets, 1968; (ed) Recent Research in Economics Education, 1970; (jtly) Basic Economics: theory and cases, 1973, 2nd edn 1977; (ed) Efficiency in Universities: the La Paz papers, 1974; (jtly) Division Management Simulation, 1978; (jtly) Economics Education in the UK, 1980; (jtly) Basic Macroeconomic Models, 1981; (jtly) Running the British Economy, 1981, 6th edn 1990; (jtly) Managing the Australian Economy, 1985; (jtly) Shipping Management Model—Stratship, 1983; (jtly) Macroeconomic Database, 1984; (jtly) Strategies for Life—Stratlife, 1988; Economics, 1991; articles in professional jls. *Recreations:* golf, deep sea game fishing. *Address:* 40 Lauder Road, Edinburgh EH9 1UE. *Clubs:* Waverley Lawn Tennis & Squash (Edinburgh); Archerfield Links Golf.

**LUMSDEN, Prof. Mary Ann**, OBE 2017; MD; Professor of Medical Education and Gynaecology, University of Glasgow, since 2004; *b* Suffolk, 31 May 1952; *d* of John and Mary Welbon; *m* 1978, Ian George Lumsden; one *s* two *d*. *Educ:* Ipswich High Sch.; Queens' Coll., London; St Mary's Hosp. Med. Sch., Imperial Coll., London (BSc Hons Biochem. 1974; MB BS 1977; MD 1984). FRCOG 1998. MRC Fellow, Edinburgh, 1981–84; trainee in obstetrics and gynaecol., 1985–93 (Registrar, then Sen. Registrar (pt-time), Edinburgh Royal Infirmary and Western Gen. Hosp., Edinburgh, 1987–93); Sen. Lectr, 1993–2001, Reader, 2001–04, in Obstetrics and Gynaecol., Univ. of Glasgow; Hon. Consultant in Obstetrics and Gynaecol., N Glasgow Hosps NHS Trust, subseq. NHS Gtr Glasgow and Clyde, 1993–. Sen. Vice Pres. (Strategy), RCOG, 2016–19. Chair, British Menopause Soc., 2009–11; Pres. Internat. Menopause Soc., 2016–18. Member: Gynaecol Visiting Soc.; Friends of Covent Gdn; Friends of Scottish Opera. *Publications:* (jtly) Menstrual Problems for the MRCOG, 1997; (ed jtly) Complete Women's Health, 2000; (jtly) The Menopause in Practice, 2002; (ed) Best Practice and Research - Clinical Obstetrics and Gynaecology, 2009; (jtly) Menstrual Problems for the MRCOG and Beyond, 2014; contrib. papers on menstrual disorders and menopausal medicine to jls incl. BMJ and Lancet. *Recreations:* opera and chamber music, gardens, family, reading, food and wine, tennis, ski-ing. *Address:* Myretoun House, Menstrie, Clackmannanshire FK11 7EB. *T:* (01259) 761453. *E:* maryann.lumsden@glasgow.ac.uk. *Club:* New (Edinburgh).

**LUMSDEN-COOK, Lucy**; Producer, Director and Managing Director, Yellow Door Productions, since 2016; *b* London, 24 Oct. 1968; *d* of Joseph Andrew Christopher Hoare and Lady Christina Alice Hoare; *m* 2002, Mark Lumsden-Cook; one *s* one *d*. *Educ:* King's Sch., Canterbury; Univ. of Edinburgh (MA Hist. of Art). Production roles, Comic Strip Ltd, Red Rooster Films and Big Talk Prodns, 1992–99; Commissioning Exec., 2000–05, Controller of Comedy Commissioning, 2005–09, BBC; Hd of Comedy, Sky plc (formerly BSkyB), 2009–15. *Recreations:* drawing, children's illustration (illustrator for Daunt Books), family history, tennis, writing, theatre, funny people. *E:* lucy.lumsden@sky.com.

**LUMSDON, Katherine Jane**; QC 2018; *b* London, 1969; *d* of John Lumsdon and Gill Lumsdon; *m* 1997, Andrew; two *c*. *Educ:* King's Sch., Worcester; Univ. of Manchester (BA Hons); Univ. of Westminster (CPE). Called to the Bar, Middle Temple, 1993. *Address:* 23 Essex Street, WC2R 3AA. *T:* (020) 7413 0353. *E:* KateLumsdonQC@23es.com.

**LUNA MENDOZA, Ricardo Victor**; Minister of Foreign Affairs, Peru, since 2016; *b* 19 Nov. 1940; *s* of Ricardo Luna and Victoria Mendoza; *m* 1969, Margarita Proaño; one *d*. *Educ:* Princeton Univ. (BA Hons Politics 1962); Columbia Univ., NY (Master Internat. Affairs 1964); Peruvian Diplomatic Acad. Diplomatic Service of Peru: served in London, Tel-Aviv, Geneva, Washington, Paris, Quito and NY, 1966–86; Ambassador, 1986; Under-Sec., Multi-lateral Affairs, Lima, and Co-ordinator, Contadora-Apoyo and Rio Gps, 1987–89; Ambassador: to UN, NY, 1989–92; to USA, 1992–99; Weinberg Vis. Prof. of Foreign Affairs, Princeton Univ., 2000–01; Tinker Vis. Prof. of Foreign Affairs, Columbia Univ., NY, 2002; Prof. of Internat. Affairs, Govt Inst., San Martín de Porres Univ., Lima, 2003; Advr to Peruvian Finance Minister for Internat.

Affairs, 2004; Cogut Vis. Prof. of Internat. Affairs, Brown Univ., 2005; Vis. Prof. of Internat. Affairs and Co-ordinator, Latin-American Area, Fletcher Sch. of Law and Diplomacy, Tufts Univ., 2005–06; Ambassador to UK and concurrently to Ireland, 2006–10. Kluge Distinguished Schol., Liby of Congress, Washington DC, 2011–12. Fellow, Centre for Internat. Affairs, 1980–81, Inst. of Politics, 2006, Harvard Univ. Pan American Order, Panamerican Foundn, 1990. Commander: Order de Mayo (Argentina); Order Rio Branco (Brazil); Orden del Sol (Peru). *Publications:* Política Exterior del Perú, 1981; Carlos García Bedoya, 1993; Revaluación de la Idea del Hemisferio Occidental, 2002; contribs to jls. *Address:* Ministerio de Relaciones Exteriores del Peru, Jirón Lampa 545, Lima 1, Peru. *Clubs:* Athenæum, Travellers; University, Cosmos (Washington); Harvard (New York); Colonial (Princeton Univ.); Phoenix (Lima).

**LUNAN, Very Rev. David Ward;** Moderator of the General Assembly of the Church of Scotland, 2008–09; *b* London, 29 Feb. 1944; *s* of Andrew Lunan and Jean Lunan (*née* Orr); *m* 1974, Margaret Ann Fiddes Young; four *s*. *Educ:* Glasgow High Sch.; Univ. of Glasgow (MA 1965; BD 1968). Ordained C of S, 1970; Asst Minister, Calton New Parish, 1969–75; Minister: St Andrews Lhanbryd, Moray, 1975–87; Renfield St Stephens, Glasgow, 1987–2002; Clerk to Presbytery of Glasgow, 2002–08. Moderator: Presbytery of Moray, 1985–86; Presbytery of Glasgow, 2000–01. Hon. DLitt Strathclyde, 2010; Hon. DD Glasgow, 2011. *Recreations:* hill walking, music, reading, travel, family. *Address:* c/o Church of Scotland, 121 George Street, Edinburgh EH2 4YN. *T:* (0131) 225 5722. *E:* amurray@cofscotland.org.uk.

**LUND, Helge;** Chairman, BP, since 2019 (non-executive Director, since 2018); *m*; two *c*. *Educ:* Norwegian Sch. of Econs and Business Admin (MA); INSEAD (MBA). Dep. CEO and Chief Financial Officer, pharmaceutical div., Hafslund Nycomed; Chief Executive: Aker Kvaerner; Statoil, 2004–14; Chief Exec., BG Gp, 2015–16. Non-exec. Dir, Schlumberger Ltd, 2016–18; Advr, Clayton, Dubilier & Rice, 2016–.

**LUND, Ven. Karen Belinda;** Archdeacon of Manchester, since 2017; *b* West Middx, 1962; *d* of Theodore Best and Monica Agatha Best (*née* Francis); *m* 2014, Richard Einar John Lund; one *s*. *Educ:* Elthorne High Sch., W Ealing; Canterbury Christ Church Coll. (BA Hons Theol.). Ordained deacon, 1994, priest, 1995; Asst Curate, St John, Southall Green, 1994–97; Associate Vicar, St Barnabas, Northolt Park, 1997–2000; Vicar: St Barnabas, Gillingham, 2000–08; St Michael and All Angels, Roxwell, 2008–14; Episcopal Lay Discipleship Advr, Dio. of Chelmsford, 2008–14; Team Vicar, Turton Moorland Ministry, 2014–16. *Recreations:* health and fitness, felting, vintage fashion. *Address:* 14 Moorgate Avenue, Withington, Manchester M20 1HE. *T:* (0161) 445 9458. *E:* archmanchester@manchester.anglican.org.

**LUND, Mark Joseph;** consultant; Chairman, MyCSP Trustee Company Ltd, since 2012; *b* 1 July 1957; *s* of Joseph and Maureen Lund; *m* 1986, Karen Will; two *s* one *d*. *Educ:* Liverpool Polytech. (BA Hons Social Studies); Univ. of Leeds (MA Transport Econs). Transport economist, BR, 1983–84; Management Consultant: Spicer & Oppenheim, 1984–89; Booz Allen Hamilton, 1989–91; Dir, Henderson Investors plc, 1991–2001; Chief Executive: J. P. Morgan Fundshub, 2001–03; St James's Place Capital, later St James's Place plc, 2004–07; Money Portal Ltd, later Honister Capital Ltd, 2008–11. Chm., Equiniti Financial Services Ltd, 2015–; non-executive Director: MyCSP Ltd, 2012–; Skipton Building Soc. (formerly Financial Services) Ltd, 2014– (Sen. Ind. Dir, 2018–); Coutts & Co., 2015–; Sen. Ind. Dir, GB Snowsport (formerly British Ski and Snowboard), 2013–. Chartered FCSI 2011. *Recreations:* family activities, cycling, ski-ing.

**LUND, Prof. Raymond Douglas,** PhD; FRS 1992; Hatch Professor of Ophthalmology and Research Director, Moran Eye Center, University of Utah, 2000–06, now Professor Emeritus; *b* 10 Feb. 1940; *s* of Henry Douglas Lund and Rose Lund; *m* 1963, Jennifer Sylvia Hawes; two *s*. *Educ:* University College London (BSc 1st cl. Hons, PhD). LRAM. Asst Lectr, then Lectr, Anatomy Dept, UCL, 1963–66; Res. Associate, Univ. of Pennsylvania, 1966–67; Asst Prof., Anatomy Dept, Univ. of Stanford, 1967–68; Asst Prof., then Prof., Depts of Biological Structure and Neurological Surgery, Univ. of Washington, 1968–79; Prof. and Chm., Dept of Anatomy, Univ. of S Carolina, 1979–83; Prof. and Chm., Dept of Neurobiology, Anatomy and Cell Sci., Univ. of Pittsburgh, 1983–91 (Dir, Centre for Neuroscience, 1984–87); Prof. and Head of Dept of Anatomy, and Fellow of Clare College, Cambridge, 1992–95; Duke-Elder Prof. of Ophthalmology, Inst. of Ophthalmol., UCL, 1995–2000. Adjunct Prof. of Ophthalmology, Casey Eye Inst., Oregon Health and Sci. Univ., 2006–11. Chm. Scientific Cttee, Internat. Spinal Res. Trust, 1994–97; Trustee, Corporate Action Trust, 1997–2008. Founder FMedSci 1998. NIH Merit Award, 1988. *Publications:* Development and Plasticity of the Brain, 1978; contribs to learned jls. *Recreation:* music. *Address:* 1799 SE Wall Street, Astoria, OR 97103, USA; 541 Willoughby House, EC2Y 8BN.

**LUND, Prof. Valerie Joan,** CBE 2008; FRCS, FRCSEd; Professor of Rhinology, University College London, 1995, now Emeritus; *b* Wallasey, Cheshire, 9 May 1953; *d* of George Andrew Lund and Joan Lund (*née* Henry); *m* 2010, David John Howard. *Educ:* Charing Cross Hosp. Med. Sch., Univ. of London (MB BS 1977; MS 1987). Final FRCS Otolaryngol. 1982; FRCS *ad eundem* 1993; FRCSEd *ad eundem*. Trained RNTNEH, 1980–84, Charing Cross Hosp., 1984–86; Lectr, Inst. of Laryngol. and Otol., 1986–87; Sen. Lectr, 1987–93, Reader, 1993–95, UCL. Hon. Consultant: RNTNEH, 1987–; Moorfields Eye Hosp., 1990–; UCH, 2005–; Imperial Coll. NHS Trust, 2009–. Pres., British Assoc. of Otolaryngology-Head Neck Surgery, 2012–15. Mem., German Nat. Acad. of Scis Leopoldina, 2009–. Hon. Member: Internat. Rhinologic Soc., 2017; Eur. Rhinologic Soc., 2018; ENT-UK, 2019. Hon. Fellow, Amer. Coll. of Surgeons, 2017. Hon. DMed Sussex, 2016. Co-Ed., EPOS, 2005–20. *Publications:* (with A. G. D. Maran) Clinical Rhinology, 1990; (with D. F. N. Harrison) Tumours of the Upper Jaw, 1993; (jtly) Nasal Polyps, 1997; (jtly) Endonasal Sinus Surgery, 1999; (with G. K. Scadding) Investigative Rhinology, 2004; (contrib. and vol. ed.) Rhinology: Scott Brown's Otolaryngology, 2008, 8th edn 2014; (ed) Cumming's Otolaryngology Head and Neck Surgery, 2010, (vol. ed.) 7th edn 2018; Tumors of the Nose, Paranasal Sinuses and Nasopharynx, 2014; contrib. 92 chapters in books and over 325 peer-reviewed papers. *Recreations:* cooking and eating. *Address:* Royal National Throat, Nose and Ear Hospital, 330 Gray's Inn Road, WC1X 8DA. *T:* (020) 3456 5197.

**LUNGHI, Cherie Mary;** actress; *b* 4 April 1952; *d* of late Allessandro Lunghi and Gladys Corbett Lee; one *d* by Roland Joffé. *Educ:* Arts Educnl Trust, London; Central Sch. of Speech and Drama. *Theatre includes:* The Three Sisters, Owners, Newcastle, 1973; She Stoops to Conquer, Nottingham Playhouse, 1974; Teeth 'n' Smiles, Royal Court, 1975; RSC, 1976–80: Much Ado About Nothing; The Winter's Tale; King Lear; Destiny; Bandits; As You Like It; Saratoga; Twelfth Night; Uncle Vanya, RNT, 1982; Holiday, Old Vic, 1987; The Homecoming, Comedy, 1991; Arcadia, RNT, 1993; Passion Play, Donmar, 1999; Afterplay, Pushkin House, 2010; The Syndicate, Chichester, 2011; Steel Magnolias, New Alexandra Th., 2012; The Importance of Being Earnest, Harold Pinter Th., 2014; Off the King's Road, Jermyn Street Th., 2016. *Films include:* Excalibur, 1980; King David, 1984; The Mission, 1986; To Kill a Priest, 1987; Jack and Sarah, 1995; Mary Shelley's Frankenstein, 1995; Patrick, 2018. *Television includes: series and serials:* The Praying Mantis, 1982; Master of the Game, 1984; The Monocled Mutineer, 1986; Ellis Island, 1987; The Manageress, 1988, 1989; The Buccaneers, 1995; Little White Lies, 1998; The Knock, 1999; Hornblower, 1999; David Copperfield, 1999; Cutting It, 2003; Casualty 1906, 2006; Casualty 1907, 2007; Secret Diary of a Call Girl, 2007; A Touch of Frost, 2008; Casualty 1909, 2009; Starlings, 2013; Pat and Cabbage, 2013; Unforgotten, 2015; *plays and films:* The Misanthrope, 1978; Oliver Twist, 1983; Much Ado About Nothing, 1984; Letters to an Unknown Lover, 1986; The Lady's Not for Burning, 1987; The Canterville Ghost, 1995; Le Vipère au Poing, 2004. *Address:* c/o Creative Artists Management, 55–59 Shaftesbury Avenue, W1D 6LD.

**LUNN, Rt Rev. David Ramsay;** an Honorary Assistant Bishop, Diocese of York, 1998–2014; *b* 17 July 1930. *Educ:* King's College, Cambridge (BA 1953; MA 1957); Cuddesdon College, Oxford. Deacon 1955, priest 1956, Newcastle upon Tyne; Curate of Sugley, 1955–59; N Gosforth, 1959–63; Chaplain, Lincoln Theological College, 1963–66; Sub-Warden, 1966–70; Vicar of St George, Cullercoats, 1970–75, Rector, 1975–80; Rural Dean of Tynemouth, 1975–80; Bishop of Sheffield, 1980–97. *Address:* Rivendell, 28 Southfield Road, Wetwang, Driffield, E Yorks YO25 9XX. *T:* (01377) 236657.

**LUNN, Virginia;** Chief Executive Officer, Coram Beanstalk (formerly Beanstalk), children's literacy charity, since 2015; *b* Boston, Lincs, 24 Jan. 1963; *d* of John and Joyce Lunn; civil partnership 2010, Margaret Paterson (*d* 2015). *Educ:* Univ. of Leeds (BA English and Media; PGCE). Primary sch. teacher, 1988–92; Programme Developer, Youthreach, Republic of Ireland, 1992–99; Director: Strategy and Policy, Prince's Trust, 1999–2011; UK Progs, Save the Children, 2012–14. *Recreations:* swimming, walking. *Address:* Coram Beanstalk, Coram Campus, 41 Brunswick Square, WC1N 1AZ. *T:* (020) 7729 4087. *E:* ginny.lunn@beanstalkcharity.org.uk.

**LUNNON, Jane Teresa;** Head, Wimbledon High School, since 2014; *b* 17 Aug. 1969; *d* of Dr Barry Cullen and Margaret Cullen; *m* 1997, Neill Lunnon; one *s* one *d*. *Educ:* North London Collegiate Sch.; Univ. of Bristol (BA English 1990). Hd of English, 1997–2003, Asst Dir of Studies, 2003–05, Wellington Coll.; Hd of Sixth Form, 2005–06, Dep. Hd, 2005–10, Prior's Field Sch.; Dep. Hd, Wellington Coll., 2010–14. Governor: St Andrew's Prep. Sch., Woking, 2007–14; Newland Hse Sch., 2016–; King Edward's Sch., 2018–. *Recreations:* reading, writing, drama of all kinds, running, dancing, walking, swimming (especially in cold, Dorset seas). *Address:* Wimbledon High School, Mansel Road, SW19 4AB. *T:* (020) 8971 0920. *E:* Jane.lunnon@wim.gdst.net.

*See also* J. A. Brown.

**LUNT, Beverly Anne; Her Honour Judge Lunt;** a Circuit Judge, since 2004; *b* 8 March 1954; *d* of late Thomas Gordon Lunt and of Mary Lunt. *Educ:* Oxford Poly. (BA). Called to the Bar, Gray's Inn, 1977, Bencher, 2018; in practice as a barrister, 1977–2004, Hd of Chambers, Kingsgate Chambers, Manchester, 1990–2004. *Recreations:* reading, cinema, walking, theatre, supporting animal charities (Dogs Trust, Battersea Dogs Home, PDSA, Mare and Foal Sanctuary, Guide Dogs). *Address:* Preston Crown Court, Openshaw Place, Preston PR1 2LL.

**LUNTS, David;** Executive Director, Housing and Land, Greater London Authority, since 2012; *b* 31 Oct. 1957; *s* of Lawrence Henry Lunts and Kvetinka Sonja Lunts; *m*; one *s*. *Educ:* Univ. of Manchester (BA Hons Pols and Mod. Hist.). Chm., Hulme Regeneration Ltd, 1992–95; Chief Executive: Urban Villages Forum, 1995–98; Prince's Foundn, 1998–2002; Dir, Urban Policy Unit, ODPM, 2002–05; Exec. Dir, Policy and Partnerships, GLA, 2005–08; Exec. Dir, London, Homes and Communities Agency, 2008–11. Mem., Urban Task Force, 1997–99. *Recreations:* cinema, cycling, food. *Address:* Greater London Authority, City Hall, The Queen's Walk, SE1 2AA. *E:* David.Lunts@london.gov.uk.

**LUPTON,** family name of **Baron Lupton.**

**LUPTON, Baron** *cr* 2015 (Life Peer), of Lovington in the County of Hampshire; **James Roger Crompton Lupton,** CBE 2012; Senior Advisor, Greenhill Europe, since 2017 (Chairman, 2011–17); *b* Whalley, Lancs, 15 June 1955; *s* of Alec William and Margaret Crompton Lupton; *m* 1983, Béatrice Marie-Françoise Delaunay; one *s* three *d*. *Educ:* Sedbergh Sch., Yorks; Lincoln Coll., Oxford (MA Juris.). Admitted as solicitor, 1979; Baring Brothers, 1980–88 (Dep. Chm., 1995–98); Greenhill & Co., 1998–. Mem., Internat. Adv. Bd, Global Leadership Foundn, 2011–; non-exec. Dir, Lloyds Banking Gp, 2017–; Chm., Lloyds Bank Corporate Mkts, 2017–. Co-Treas., Cons. Party, 2013–16. Trustee: Dulwich Picture Gall., 1997–2011 (Chm., 2006–11); BM, 2012–. Mem., Adv. Bd, Grange Park Opera, 1997–2011. Gov., Downe Hse Sch., 1998–2006. *Recreations:* collecting art, opera, shooting, ski-ing. *Address:* Greenhill & Co., Lansdowne House, 57 Berkeley Square, W1J 6ER. *T:* (020) 7198 7401. *E:* jlupton@greenhill.com. *Club:* Brooks's.

**LUPU, Radu,** CBE 2016; pianist; *b* 30 Nov. 1945; *s* of late Meyer Lupu, lawyer, and Ana Gabor, teacher of languages. *Educ:* Moscow Conservatoire. Debut at age of twelve with complete programme of own music; studied with Florica Muzicescu, Cella Delavrancea, Heinrich Neuhaus and Stanislav Neuhaus. 1st prize: Van Cliburn Competition, 1966; Enescu Internat. Competition, 1967; Leeds Internat. Pianoforte Competition, 1969; Abbiati Prize, Italian Critics' Assoc., 1989, 2006; Premio Internazionale Arturo Benedetti Michelangeli, 2006. Débuts: London, 1969; Berlin, 1971; NY and Chicago, 1972. Numerous recordings include complete Mozart violin and piano sonatas, complete Beethoven Piano Concertos, 1979. *Recreations:* history, art, sport. *Address:* c/o Barbara Golan, Stettbachstrasse 131H, 8051 Zurich, Switzerland. *T:* 443220704. *E:* golan@bluewin.ch.

**LURIE, Prof. Alison;** writer; Professor of English, Cornell University, 1976–2006, now Professor Emerita; *b* 3 Sept. 1926; *d* of Harry Lurie and Bernice Stewart; *m* 1st, 1948, Jonathan Bishop (marr. diss. 1985); three *s*; 2nd, 1995, Edward Hower. *Educ:* Radcliffe Coll., Cambridge, Mass (AB). Mem., AAAL 2005. *Publications:* Love and Friendship, 1962; The Nowhere City, 1965; Imaginary Friends, 1967 (televised, 1987); Real People, 1969; The War Between the Tates, 1974; Only Children, 1979; Foreign Affairs, 1984 (Pulitzer Prize, 1985); The Truth About Lorin Jones, 1988; (ed) The Oxford Book of Modern Fairy Tales, 1993; Women and Ghosts (short stories), 1994; The Last Resort, 1998; Truth and Consequences, 2005; *non-fiction:* The Language of Clothes, 1981; Don't Tell the Grown-ups, 1990; Familiar Spirits, 2001; Boys and Girls Forever, 2003; The Language of Houses, 2014; Reading for Fun, 2017; Words and Worlds, 2019; *children's books:* Clever Gretchen, 1980; The Heavenly Zoo, 1980; Fabulous Beasts, 1981. *Address:* c/o English Department, 263 Goldwin Smith Hall, Cornell University, Ithaca, NY 14853–3201, USA.

**LUSBY, John Martin;** Adjudicator (panel member), Tribunals Service, Criminal Injuries Compensation Appeals Panel, 1997–2008; Tribunal Member, First-tier Tribunal (Social Entitlement Chamber), 2008–09; *b* 27 April 1943; *s* of late William Henry Lusby and Florence Mary (*née* Wharam); *m* 1966, (Mary) Clare, *d* of late John Gargan and Ellen (*née* Myers); one *s* one *d*. *Educ:* Marist Coll., Hull; Ushaw Coll., Durham; Maryvale Inst., Birmingham (DipTh (with commendation) 1997); Open Univ. (MA Theol. (with distinction) 1998). DipHSM 1972; MHSM (AHA 1972). Proofreader, Plough Publicity (Hull) Ltd, 1961; entered NHS, 1961; junior appointments: De la Pole Hosp., Hull, Hull 'B' Gp HMC, 1961–66; County Hosp., York, York 'A' Gp HMC, 1966–67; Kettering Gen. Hosp., Kettering and District HMC, 1967–68; Admin. Asst, United Sheffield Hosps,

1968–70; Dep. Hosp. Sec., E Birmingham Hosp., E Birmingham HMC, 1970–72; Hosp. Sec., Pontefract Gen. Infirmary and Headlands Hosp., Pontefract, Pontefract, Castleford and Goole HMC/Wakefield AHA, 1972–74; Area Gen. Administrator, Kirklees AHA, 1974–76; Asst Dist Administrator (Patient Services), 1976–79, Dist Administrator, Wandsworth and E Merton Dist, 1979–81, Merton, Sutton and Wandsworth AHA(T); Area Administrator, Doncaster AHA, 1981; Dist Administrator, 1981–84, Dist Gen. Man., 1984–90, Exec. Dir, 1990, Doncaster HA; Mem., 1990–91, Gen. Manager, 1990–95, and Exec. Dir, 1991–95, Lothian Health Bd; Chm., Ind. Review Panel, NHS Complaints Procedure, Northern and Yorks Reg., NHS Exec., 1996–97. Member: Scottish Council for Postgrad. Med. and Dental Educn, 1992–95; Health Services and Public Health Res. Cttee, Chief Scientist Orgn, SHHD, 1993–95; Scottish Implementation Gp, Jun. Doctors and Dentists Hrs of Work, 1993–95; Jt Wkg Gp on Information Services, NHS in Scotland, 1993–95. Trustee: Dementia Services Develt Centre, Univ. of Stirling, 1991–95; Scottish Dementia Appeal Trust, 1994–95. Member: Catholic Theol Assoc. of GB, 1997–2008; Catholic Biblical Assoc. of GB, 1998–; Catholic Inst. for Internat. Relations, 1999–2004; Soc. for the Study of Theology, 2000–08; European Soc. for Catholic Theology, 2004–08; Catholic Union of GB, 2012–15. *Recreations:* study of theology, music, reading, travel. *Address:* Flat A, Copper Beech, 31 North Grove, N6 4SJ. *T:* (020) 8341 3426. *E:* john.lusby@sky.com. *Club:* Middlesex CC.

**LUSCOMBE, Christopher David;** theatre director; *b* Ashtead, Surrey, 6 Nov. 1963; *s* of late David and of Jill Luscombe. *Educ:* King's Coll. Sch., Wimbledon; Pembroke Coll., Cambridge (BA 1985; MA 1989). Actor: Cambridge Footlights, 1984–85; repertory th., 1985–90; Kean, Old Vic, 1990; RSC, 1991–98; Half Time, Donmar Warehouse, 1994; Peter Pan, NT, 1998; Chichester Fest. Th., 1999–2000; Art, Whitehall, 2002; The Iron Lady (film), 2011; plays directed include: The Shakespeare Revue, RSC, 1994, Vaudeville, 1995; Star Quality, Apollo, 2001; Home and Beauty, Lyric, 2002; Fascinating Aïda: One Last Flutter, Comedy, 2003; The Rocky Horror Show, Playhouse, 2006 and 2015, tour, 2006–18; The Comedy of Errors, Shakespeare's Globe, 2006; A Midsummer Night's Dream, Regent's Park, 2007; The Merry Wives of Windsor, Shakespeare's Globe, 2008, 2010; Enjoy, Gielgud, 2009; Alphabetical Order, Hampstead, 2009; When We Are Married, Garrick, 2010; The Madness of George III, Apollo, 2011; Travels with my Aunt, Menier Chocolate Factory, 2013; Love's Labour's Lost, Love's Labour's Won, RSC, 2014, Th. Royal Haymarket, 2016; Nell Gwynn, Shakespeare's Globe, 2015, Apollo, 2016, tour, 2017; Travels with my Aunt (musical), Chichester Fest. Th., 2016; While the Sun Shines, Th. Royal, Bath, 2016; Love's Labour's Lost/Much Ado About Nothing, Chichester Fest. Th., 2016; Twelfth Night, RSC, 2017; The Argument, Th. Royal, Bath, 2019; others include: Masterpieces, Birmingham Rep., 2002; Little Shop of Horrors, 2003, The History Boys, 2010, W Yorks Playhouse; Things We Do For Love, Harrogate, 2004; Candida, Oxford Stage Co., 2004; The Likes of Us, Sydmonton, 2005; Arms and the Man, Salisbury, 2006; A Small Family Business, Watford, 2007; Hobson's Choice, Sheffield Crucible, 2011; Hay Fever, Minneapolis, 2012; Henry V, 2014, Nell Gwynn, 2018, Chicago; While the Sun Shines, Bath, 2016; Candide, Grange Fest., 2018; The Winter's Tale, Cincinatti, 2019; Falstaff, Grange Fest., 2019; tours of: The Importance of Being Earnest, Tell Me on a Sunday, The Lady in the Van, 2004; Lord Arthur Savile's Crime, 2005, 2010; Single Spies, 2008; Spamalot, 2010–12 (then Harold Pinter Th., 2012, Playhouse, 2012–14, UK tour, 2015); Dandy Dick, Blue/Orange, 2012. Trustee: Actors' Benevolent Fund, 2001–; Noël Coward Foundn, 2002–17; Royal Theatrical Support Trust, 2012–. *Publications:* The Shakespeare Revue (with M. McKee), 1994; Star Quality (adapted from play by Noël Coward), 2001; Dandy Dick (adapted from play by Arthur Wing Pinero), 2012. *Recreations:* reading, music, travel, learning Italian. *Address:* c/o Nicki Stoddart, United Agents Ltd, 12–26 Lexington Street, W1F 0LE. *T:* (020) 3214 0800. *E:* nstoddart@unitedagents.co.uk. *Clubs:* Royal Automobile, Soho House.

**LUSCOMBE, Prof. David Edward,** LittD; FSA; FRHistS; FBA 1986; Professor of Medieval History, 1972–95, Leverhulme Personal Research Professor of Medieval History, 1995–2000, Research Professor of Medieval History, 2000–03, now Emeritus, University of Sheffield; *b* 22 July 1938; *s* of Edward Dominic and Nora Luscombe; *m* 1960, Megan Phillips; three *s* one *d*. *Educ:* St Michael's Sch., North Finchley; Finchley Grammar Sch.; King's Coll., Cambridge (BA, MA, PhD, LittD). Fellow, King's Coll., Cambridge, 1962–64; Fellow and Dir of Studies in History, Churchill Coll., Cambridge, 1964–72; Sheffield University: Head of Dept of History, 1973–76, 1979–84; Dep. Dean, 1983–85, Dean, 1985–87, Faculty of Arts; Pro-Vice-Chancellor, 1990–94; Chm., Humanities Res. Inst., 1992–2003; Res. Dir for Arts and Humanities, 1994–2003. Vis. Prof., Univ. of Connecticut, 1993; Leverhulme European Fellow, 1973; Vis. Fellow, All Souls Coll., Oxford, 1994; British Acad./RSC Exchange Visitor to Canada, 1991; British Acad./Japan Acad. Exchange Visitor to Japan, 1996. Raleigh Lectr, British Acad., 1988. External examiner for higher degrees in Univs of Cambridge, Oxford, London, Liverpool, Bangor, Lancaster, ANU, Toronto, Groningen, for BA degrees at Bangor, Leicester and Leeds. Dir, Historical Assoc. Summer Vacation Sch., 1976 and 1992. Member: Governing Body, later Assoc. St Edmund's House, Cambridge, 1971–84; Cttee, Ecclesiastical History Soc., 1976–79; Council, RHistS, 1981–85; Council, British Acad., 1989–97 (Publications Sec., 1990–97; Member: Medieval Texts Cttee, 1982– (Chm., 1991–2004); Publications Cttee, 1987–97 (Chm., 1990–97); Postgrad. Studies Cttee, 1988–90; Humanities Res. Bd, 1994–96); Cttee on Acad. Res. Projects, 1990–97; Commonwealth Scholarships Commn in UK, 1994–2000; Auditor, HEQC, 1994–97. Mem. Council, Worksop Coll. and Ranby House, 1996–2008. Fellow, later Hon. Fellow, Woodard Corp. Hon. Pres., Soc. internat. pour l'étude de la philosophie médiévale, 2002– (Vice-Pres., 1987–97; Pres., 1997–2002); Mem. Cttee, Soc. for Study of Medieval Langs and Lit., 1991–96. Trustee, Church Burgesses Educnl Foundn, Sheffield, 2012–. Hon. LittD Sheffield, 2013. Gen. Editor, Cambridge Studies in Medieval Life and Thought, 4th series, 1988–2004 (Adv. Editor, 1983–88); Mem., Jt Supervisory Cttee, British Acad./OUP for Oxford DNB, 1992–99 (Associate Editor, 1993–2004). British Acad. Medal for Outstanding Academic Achievement, 2014; Franklin Jameson Award, Amer. Hist Assoc., 2015. *Publications:* The School of Peter Abelard, 1969; Peter Abelard's Ethics, 1971 (trans. Italian 1976); (ed jtly) Church and Government in the Middle Ages, 1976; (ed jtly) Petrus Abaelardus 1079–1142: Person, Werk und Wirkung, 1980; (jtly) David Knowles Remembered, 1991; (ed jtly) Anselm: Aosta, Bec and Canterbury, 1996; Medieval Thought, 1997 (trans. Portuguese 2000, Greek 2007); The Twelfth-Century Renaissance: monks, scholars and the shaping of the European mind, (in Japanese) 2000; (ed jtly) Peter Abelard, Expositio in Hexameron, 2004; (ed jtly) The New Cambridge Medieval History, vol. 4, *c* 1024–*c* 1198, parts 1 and 2, 2004; (ed jtly) Peter Abelard, Sententie, 2006; (ed jtly) A Monastic Community in Local Society: the Beauchief Abbey Cartulary, 2011; (ed and rev. trans.) The Letter Collection of Peter Abelard and Heloise, 2013; Peter Abelard and Heloise: collected studies, 2019; articles in learned jls and contribs to books. *Recreations:* family and grandchildren, lunches with colleagues, working in my study, using libraries, cooking for two (or three max). *Address:* 28 Endcliffe Hall Avenue, Sheffield S10 3EL. *T:* (0114) 222 2555.

**LUSCOMBE, Rt Rev. Lawrence Edward;** Bishop of Brechin, 1975–90; Primus of the Episcopal Church in Scotland, 1985–90; *b* 10 Nov. 1924; *s* of Reginald John and Winifred Luscombe; *m* 1946, Doris Carswell Morgan, BSc, MB, ChB (*d* 1992); one *d*. *Educ:* Torquay Grammar Sch.; Kelham Theological Coll.; King's Coll., London; Univ. of Dundee (MA; MPhil 1991; PhD 1993). CA 1952, ASAA 1957. FSAScot 1980. Served Indian Army, 1942–47, Major. Partner, Galbraith, Dunlop & Co., Chartered Accountants, Glasgow, 1952–63. Ordained deacon, 1963; priest, 1964; Curate, St Margaret's, Glasgow, 1963–66; Rector, St Barnabas', Paisley, 1966–71; Provost of St Paul's Cathedral, Dundee, 1971–75. Hon. Canon, Trinity Cathedral, Davenport, Iowa, 1983. A Trustee, Scottish Episcopal Ch, 1985–. Hon. Res. Fellow, Dundee Univ., 1993–. Chm. of Council, Glenalmond Coll., 1987–94. FRSA 1987. Hon. DLitt Geneva Theological Coll., 1972; Hon. LLD Dundee, 1987. OStJ 1986; ChStJ 1996. *Publications:* Matthew Luscombe, Missionary Bishop, 1992; A Seminary of Learning, 1994; The Scottish Episcopal Church in the 20th Century, 1996; Episcopacy in an Angus Glen, 2003; Steps into Freedom, 2004; Hands Across the Sea, 2006; Episcopacy in the Heart of Dundee, 2009. *Address:* Woodville, Kirkton of Tealing, by Dundee DD4 0RD. *T:* (01382) 380331.

**LUSH, His Honour Denzil Anton;** Senior Judge, Court of Protection, 2007–16 (Master, 1996–2007); *b* 18 July 1951; *s* of Dennis John Lush, MBE and late Hazel June Lush (*née* Fishenden). *Educ:* Devonport High Sch., Plymouth; University Coll. London (BA, MA); Corpus Christi Coll., Cambridge (LLM); Coll. of Law, Guildford. Admitted Solicitor, England and Wales, 1978; in private practice, 1978–96; admitted Solicitor and Notary Public, Scotland, 1993. Chm., Social Security Appeals Tribunals, 1994–96. Member: Law Soc. Mental Health and Disability Sub-Cttee, 1993–96; BMA Steering Gp on advance statements about medical treatment, 1994; Judicial Mem., Soc. of Trust and Estate Practitioners, 1996– (Geoffrey Shindler Award for Outstanding Contrib. to the Profession, 2009; Lifetime Achievement Award, 2016). Hon. Member: Assoc. of Contentious Trust and Probate Specialists, 1998–; Japan Adult Guardianship Assoc., 2013–. Trustee: Pan-European Org. of Personal Injury Lawyers Foundn, 2003–06; Action on Elder Abuse, 2016–; Headway UK, 2017–; Patron, Solicitors for the Elderly, 2003–. Lay Reader, 1982–98. FRSocMed 2001. Mem., Devon and Exeter Instn. *Publications:* Cohabitation and Co-Ownership Precedents, 1993, 5th edn as Cohabitation Law Practice and Precedents, 2012; Elderly Clients: a precedent manual, 1996, 5th edn 2016; (with Stephen Cretney) Enduring Powers of Attorney, 4th edn 1996, 6th edn, as Cretney & Lush on Lasting and Enduring Powers of Attorney, 2009, 8th edn 2017; numerous contribs to legal publications. *Recreations:* supporting Plymouth Argyle FC, collecting commemorative and parliamentary pottery. *Address:* 3 Pennsylvania Park, Exeter, Devon EX4 6HB. *E:* denzillush@gmail.com. *Club:* Athenæum.

**LUSH, Ian Frank;** Chief Executive, Imperial Health Charity (formerly Imperial College Healthcare), since 2014; *b* 13 July 1960; *s* of late Cecil Lush and Dolly Lush; *m* 1st, 1985, Margaret Clare Hindle (marr. diss. 2002); one *d*; 2nd, 2005, Ceri-Louise Hunter; one *s* one *d*. *Educ:* King Alfred Sch., Hampstead; Univ. of York (BA Hons (Music) 1981, MA (Music) 1982); City Univ., London (Dip. Arts Admin 1986). ARCM 1982. Co-Principal Viola, Iceland SO, 1982–83; rank and file Viola, Royal Liverpool Philharmonic Orch., 1983–85; Mktg Manager, Philharmonia Orch., 1986–87; Barbican Centre: Mktg and Promotions Manager, 1987–91; Mktg Dir, 1991–93; Hd of Mktg, LSO, 1993–95; Man. Dir, London Mozart Players, 1995–2003; CEO, Architectural Heritage Fund, 2003–14. Chm., NI Built Heritage Forum, 2006–14; Dep. Chm., Heritage Alliance (formerly Heritage Link), 2006–12; Director: Croydon Marketing and Development Ltd, 1996–2001; Croydon Partnership, 1997–2001; Innovative Enterprise Action, 2006–09. Co-Chair, Maddox Gp, 2015–. Member: Welsh Assembly Govt Historic Envmt Gp, 2005–14; Prince's Regeneration Trust Adv. Gp, 2005–14; Gt Ormond St Hosp. Foundn Trust Members' Council (formerly Forum), 2008–15 (Lead Councillor, 2012–15). FRSA. *Publications:* more than 120 concert progs and CD sleeve notes; articles for English Heritage Conservation Bulletin, SPAB Cornerstone magazine, Local Government Rev. and others. *Recreations:* sport (especially fanatical devotion to Chelsea Football Club), playing tennis (Stormont Lawn Tennis Club), theatre, cinema and concert going, urban and rural walking, cooking. *Address:* Imperial Health Charity, 178–180 Edgware Road, W2 2DS. *T:* 07970 123106. *E:* ian.lush@imperialcharity.org.uk.

**LUSH, Jane Elaine;** Joint Managing Director, Kalooki Pictures, since 2013; *b* 10 Aug. 1952; *d* of Sidney and Rebecca Lush; *m* 1974, Peter Tenenbaum, landscape designer; one *s* one *d*. *Educ:* Camden Sch. for Girls. Joined BBC as trainee, 1970; BBC Television: Exec. Prod., Features Dept, 1989–90; Ed., Holiday, Commissioning Exec., Have I Got News For You, 1990; Dep. Hd, Features, 1995–2000; Controller: Daytime Television, 1998–2001; Entertainment Commissioning, 2002–05; Jt Man. Dir, Splash Media, 2005–13. *Recreations:* my children, family, friends, reading, holidays, Tottenham Hotspur.

**LUSHINGTON, Sir John (Richard Castleman),** 8th Bt *cr* 1791, of South Hill Park, Berkshire; *b* 28 Aug. 1938; *s* of Sir Henry Edmund Castleman Lushington, 7th Bt and Pamela Elizabeth Daphne, *er d* of Major Archer Richard Hunter; *S* father, 1988; *m* 1966, Bridget Gillian Margaret, *d* of late Colonel John Foster Longfield; three *s*. *Educ:* Oundle. *Publications:* From Gavelkinders to Gentlemen: a history of the Lushington family in East Kent from 1200–1700, 2012; From Men of Kent to Men of the World, 2018. *Heir: s* Richard Douglas Longfield Lushington, BA, Wing Comdr RAF, retd [*b* 29 March 1968; *m* 1st, 2001, Christianne Jane Tipping, Flight Lieut RAF (marr. diss. 2004); 2nd, 2006, Sarah Alice Butler; one *s* two *d* (of whom one *s* one *d* are twins)]. *Address:* Kent House, Barrington, Ilminster, Somerset TA19 0JP.

**LUSK, (Ormond) Felicity (Stewart);** Head, Abingdon School, 2010–16; *b* 25 Nov. 1955; *d* of late Harold Stewart Lusk, QC (NZ), and Janet Kiwi Lusk; *m* 1976 (marr. diss. 1996); two *s*. *Educ:* Marsden Coll., Wellington, NZ; Victoria Univ. (BMus); Massey Univ. (DipEd); Christchurch Teachers' Coll. (Dip Teaching); Univ. of York (Cert. Mus. Educn). Head of Music Department: Wellington E Girls' Coll., NZ, 1980–86; Aotea Coll., NZ, 1986–89; Hasmonean High School, London: Sen. Teacher and Head of Music Dept, 1990–93; Dep. Headteacher, 1993–96; Headmistress, Oxford High Sch., 1997–2010. Vice Pres., Educn, GEMS, Dubai, 2016–. Woolf Fisher Fellowship, NZ, 1985. Councillor, London Borough of Enfield, 1990–94. Mem., Standards Cttee, City of London Corporation, 2009–16. Member: SHA, 1993–99; GSA, 1997–2010; Forum UK, 2009–; HMC, 2010–16. Member: Court, Oxford Brookes Univ., 1999–2010; Council, 2013–16, Finance and Gen. Purposes Cttee, 2014–16, Univ. of Buckingham. Gov., GSMD, 1999–2010. Mem., Adv. Council, Oxford Philomusica, 2002–. Trustee, Oxfordshire Youth, 2017–. Freeman, City of London, 2010. *Recreations:* reading, music, trekking, travel, theatre, New Zealand history.

**LÜST, Prof. Reimar;** President, Alexander von Humboldt Foundation, Bonn, 1989–99, now Hon. President; Director General, European Space Agency, 1984–90; *b* 23 March 1923; *s* of Hero Lüst and Grete (*née* Strunck); *m* 1986, Nina Grunenberg; two *s* by a previous marriage. *Educ:* Univ. of Frankfurt; Univ. of Göttingen (Dr rer. nat.). Max-Planck-Institut of Physics: Staff Scientist, 1950–60; Head of Astrophysics Dept, 1960–63; Dir, Max-Planck-Institut of Extraterrestrial Physics, 1963–72; Pres., Max-Planck-Gesellschaft zur Förderung der Wissenschaften, 1972–84. Vis. Prof., Univs of Princeton, Chicago, New York, MIT, CIT, 1955–63; Hon. Prof., Technical Univ. of Munich, 1965; Hon. Prof., Univ. of Hamburg, 1992. Chm., German Science Council, 1969–72. Chm., Bd of Govs, Internat. Univ., Bremen, 1999–2004, Hon. Chm., 2005–. Mem. and Hon. Mem. of eight academies. Dr *hc:* Sofia, 1991; Birmingham 1993. Planet No 4386 named

Lüst, 1991. Adenauer-de Gaulle Prize, 1994. Grand Cross, Order of Merit (FRG), 1984; Officier, Légion d'Honneur (France), 1984; Grand Cross of Merit with Star and Shoulderblade (FRG), 1990. *Publications*: Hydrodynamik, 1955; articles in scientific jls. *Recreations*: tennis, history, ski-ing. *Address*: Max-Planck-Institute of Meteorology, Bundesstrasse 53, 20146 Hamburg, Germany. *T*: (40) 41173300.

LUSTIG, Robin Francis; journalist and broadcaster; *b* 30 Aug. 1948; *s* of late Fritz Lustig and Susan (*née* Cohn); *m* 1980, Ruth Kelsey; one *s* one *d*. *Educ*: Univ. of Sussex (BA Politics). With Reuters, 1970–77: Madrid, 1971–72; Paris, 1972–73; Rome, 1973–77; The Observer, 1977–89: reporter, 1977–81; News Ed., 1981–85; ME Corresp., 1985–87; Home Affairs Ed., 1987–88; Asst Ed., 1988–89; BBC, 1989–2012; progs on Radio 4 and World Service; Presenter, The World Tonight, BBC Radio 4, 1989–2012. Hon. DLitt Sussex, 2015. *Publications*: Is Anything Happening?, 2017.

LUSZTIG, Prof. George, PhD; FRS 1983; Professor of Mathematics, Massachusetts Institute of Technology, Cambridge, USA, since 1978; *b* 20 May 1946; *s* of Akos and Erzsébet Lusztig; *m* (marr. diss.); two *d*; *m* 2003, Gongqin Li. *Educ*: Univ. of Bucharest, Rumania; Princeton Univ. (MA, PhD). Asst, Univ. of Timisoara, Rumania, 1969; Mem., Inst. for Advanced Study Princeton, 1969–71; Univ. of Warwick: Res. Fellow, 1971–72; Lectr in Maths, 1972–74; Prof. of Maths, 1974–78. Mem., US Nat. Acad. of Scis, 1992. *Publications*: The Discrete Series of $GL_n$ over a Finite Field, 1974; and Characters of Reductive Groups over a Finite Field, 1984; Introduction to Quantum Groups, 1993; Hecke Algebras with Unequal Parameters, 2003. *Address*: 106 Grant Avenue, Newton, MA 02459, USA.

LUTHER, Anne Margaret, (Mrs A. N. Brearley-Smith); Director General, Action Research, 1990–2001; *b* 19 Jan. 1946; *d* of Dermot William Richard O'Leary and Eva Margaret (*née* Christie); *m* 1st, 1969, Philip John Luther (marr. diss. 1988); two *d*; 2nd, 1992, Andrew Neville Brearley-Smith. *Educ*: Ursuline Convent, Ilford; Chelsea Coll., London (BSc 1967). King's Fund Trainee, 1967–69; PA to House Governor, Westminster Hosp., 1969–71; Dir of Res., Action Research, 1982–90. Association of Medical Research Charities: Hon. Sec., 1982–87; Mem., Exec. Council, 1991–95. Mem., Prince of Wales Adv. Gp on Disability, 1990–95. Trustee, Common Investment Funds for Charities, 1991–98. Mem., Ashridge Mgt Coll. Assoc., 1984–2001. MInstD 1994–2001. FRSocMed, 1982–2008. *Recreations*: music, watercolours, theatre, cookery.

LUTON, Jean-Marie; Officier de la Légion d'Honneur; Commandeur de l'Ordre National du Mérite; Chairman, Arianespace, 2002–07 (Chief Executive Officer, 1997–2002); Chief Executive Officer, Starsem, 2002–06, now Hon. President; *b* Chamalières, 4 Aug. 1942; *m* 1967, Cécile Robine; three *s*. *Educ*: Ecole Polytechnique. Centre National de la Recherche Scientifique: researcher, 1964–71; Chargé de Recherches, 1971–74; Chargé de Mission, Service des Programmes des Organismes de Recherche, Min. for Industrial and Scientific Develt, 1971–73; Centre National d'Etudes Spatiales: Hd, Res. Progs Div., Progs and Indust. Policy Directorate, 1974–75; Hd, Planning and Projs Div., Progs and Indust. Policy Directorate, 1975–78; Dir, Progs and Planning, 1978–84; Dep. Dir Gen., 1984–87; Dir for Space Progs, Space Systems Div., Aérospatiale, 1987–89; Director General: Centre National d'Etudes Spatiales, 1989–90; ESA, 1990–97. Mem., Internat. Acad. of Astronautics, 1986. Astronautics Prize, French Assoc. for Aeronautics and Astronautics, 1985. *Recreations*: tennis, sailing. *Address*: c/o Arianespace, boulevard de l'Europe, 91006 Evry, France.

LUTZ, Marianne Christine, (Mrs C. A. Whittington-Smith); Headmistress, Sheffield High School for Girls (Girls' Public Day School Trust), 1960–83; *b* 9 Dec. 1922; *d* of Dr H. Lutz; *m* 1981, Charles Alexander Whittington-Smith, LLM, FCA (*d* 1997). *Educ*: Wimbledon High Sch., GPDST; Girton Coll., Cambridge (Schol.; MA Historical Tripos); University of London (DipEd, DipTh). Asst Mistress (History) at: Clergy Daughters' Sch., Bristol, 1946–47; South Hampstead High Sch., GPDST, 1947–59. Former Member: History Textbooks Panel for W Germany (under auspices of FO and Unesco); Professional Cttee, Univ. of Sheffield; Historical Assoc.; Secondary Heads' Assoc. *Publications*: several in connection with Unesco work and Historical Assoc. *Recreations*: crosswords, opera, art, theatre. *Address*: Evona House, Hydro Close, Baslow, Bakewell, Derbyshire DE45 1SH. *T*: (01246) 582152.

LUXMOORE-BALL, Simon Coryndon, FRAeS; independent adviser; Chief Executive, Royal Aeronautical Society, 2009–18; *b* Chew Magna, 9 April 1951; *s* of Cecil Michael and Felicity Luxmoore-Ball; *m* 2011, Pauline Sirrell. *Educ*: Millfield Sch., Som; Univ. of Bath (MBA); Univ. of West of England. Dowty Aerospace: Hd, Design Engrg, 1991–94; Mktg, Sales and Product Support Dir, 1995–97; Mktg Dir, 1998, Vice Pres., Business Develt, 1999–2000, Messier-Dowty Europe; Pres., Messier Dowty Ltd and Gp Vice Pres., Boeing and military business, 2001–04; Sen. Vice Pres. and Dep. Chief Exec., Messier Dowty, 2004–08. Non-executive Director: Aero Vodochody, 2009–13; Beagle Aerospace, 2010–15; non-exec. Chm., Vets 1 Gp. Mem. Council, Air League, 2012–17. Trustee, Kennel Club, 2011–16 (Chm., 2015–18); Pres., Welsh Kennel Club, 2016–. FRAeS 2003. Patron, Canadian Eskimo Dog Club, 2016–. *Publications*: The Complete Siberian Husky, 2002. *Recreations*: sled dogs and gun dogs, general canine interests including judging, sport in general but in particular Rugby and cricket, countryside activities, voluntary work, reading. *Address*: Hushwig Barn, Magdalen High Road, Wiggenhall St Mary Magdalen, King's Lynn, Norfolk PE34 3BG. *T*: (01553) 812277. *E*: simon.luxmoore@btinternet.com. *Clubs*: Royal Air Force; Kennel.

LUXON, Benjamin Matthew, CBE 1986; FGS; narrator and performer; *b* Camborne, Cornwall, 1937; US citizen, 2002; *m* 1969, Sheila Amit; two *s* one *d*; *m* 2002, Susan Crofut. *Educ*: Truro Sch.; Westminster Trng Coll.; Guildhall Sch. of Music. Teacher of Physical Education until becoming professional singer (baritone), 1963; due to severe hearing loss in 1996, eventually finished career as a professional singer. Repertoire included lieder, folk music, Victorian songs and duets, oratorio (Russian, French and English song), and operatic rôles at major opera houses at home and abroad. Major rôles included: Eugene Onegin, Don Giovanni, Wozzeck, Papageno, Julius Caesar, Posa, Gianni Schicchi, Falstaff. Numerous recordings. Appointed Bard of the Cornish Gorsedd, 1974. Third prize, Munich Internat. Festival, 1961; Gold Medal GSM, 1963. FGS (FGSM 1970); Hon. RAM 1980; Hon. DMus: Exeter, 1980; RSAMD, 1996; Canterbury Christ Church Coll., 1997. *Recreations*: collecting English water-colours and drawings, tennis, swimming.

LUZIO, Prof. (John) Paul, PhD; FRCPath; FMedSci; Professor of Molecular Membrane Biology, 2001–14, now Emeritus, and Voluntary Director of Research, since 2014, University of Cambridge; Master, St Edmund's College, Cambridge, 2004–14 (Fellow, 1987–2004; Hon. Fellow 2014); *b* 15 Aug. 1947; *s* of (Fadri Gian) John Luzio and Brenda Luzio (*née* Barnwell); *m* 1st, 1977, Alison Turner (*née* Ford) (marr. diss. 1981); one *s*; 2nd, 1986, Toni Copeland (*née* Stanton) (marr. diss. 1991); 3rd, 1992, Jane Edson (*née* Geering). *Educ*: Shene Grammar Sch., London; Clare Coll., Cambridge (BA 1968; PhD 1974). MRCPath 1991, FRCPath 1998; FRSB (FIBiol 2004). Lectr, Dept of Med. Biochem. (Chem. Pathol.), Welsh Nat. Sch. of Medicine, 1974–77; University of Cambridge: Sen. Res. Associate, Dept of Clin. Biochem., 1977–79; Lectr in Clinical Biochem., 1979–96; Reader in Molecular Membrane Biol., 1996–2001; Dir, Cambridge Inst. for Med. Res., 2002–12; Dep. Head, Sch. of Clinical Medicine, 2012–14; Sen. Tutor, St Edmund's Coll., 1991–96. Chm., MRC Molecular and Cellular Medicine Bd, 2007–12. FMedSci 1999; FHEA (ILTM 2002). Foundn Award, Assoc. of Clinical Biochemists, 2005. *Publications*: contribs to professional jls in biochem. and molecular cell biology. *Recreations*: gardening, fishing. *Address*: Pippin Meadow, 32 Lowfields, Little Eversden, Cambridge CB23 1HJ. *T*: (office) (01223) 336780. *E*: jpl10@cam.ac.uk.

LUZZATTO, Prof. Lucio, MD; FRCP, FRCPath; Hon. Professor of Haematology, University of Firenze, since 2011 (Professor of Haematology, 2006–11); Professor of Haematology, Muhimbili University of Health and Allied Sciences, Dar-es-Salaam, Tanzania, since 2015; *b* 28 Sept. 1936; *s* of Aldo and Anna Luzzatto; *m* 1963, Paola Caboara; one *s* one *d*. *Educ*: Genoa Univ. (MD 1959); Pavia Univ. (Spec. Haematology 1962); Lib. Doc. Italy, 1968. FRCPath 1982; FRCP 1983. Research Fellow in Haematology, Columbia Univ., 1963–64; Lectr, then Prof. of Haematology, Univ. of Ibadan, 1964–74; Dir, Internat. Inst. of Genetics and Biophysics, Naples, 1974–81; Prof. of Haematology, RPMS, 1981–94; Hon. Dir, MRC Leukaemia Res. Fund's Leukaemia Unit, 1987–93; Chm., Dept of Human Genetics, Meml Sloan-Kettering Cancer Center, NY, 1994–2000; Scientific Dir, Nat. Inst. for Cancer Res., Italy, 2000–04; Prof. of Haematology, Univ. of Genoa, 2002–06; Scientific Dir, Istituto Toscano Tumori, Italy, 2005–15. Pres., Italian Fedn of Life Scis, 2008–11. Foreign Mem., Amer. Acad. of Arts and Scis, 2004. Hon. DSc Ibadan, 1998; Hon. MD Patras, 2006. Pius XI Medal, 1976; Laurea ad hon., Univ. of Urbino, 1990; Chiron award, Italian Acad. of Medicine, 1995; Accademia Lincei Prize for Biology, 2016. *Publications*: Understanding Cancer, 2006 (G. M. Pace Prize, 2008); 403 contribs to learned jls and scientific pubns. *Address*: Department of Haematology, Muhimbili University of Health and Allied Sciences, POB 65001, Dar-es-Salaam, Tanzania. *T*: (255) 684751346.

LYALL, Andrew Gardiner, CMG 1976; Under Secretary, Department of Transport, 1981–86, retired; *b* 21 Dec. 1929; *s* of late William and Helen Lyall (*née* Gardiner); *m* 1953, Olive Leslie Gennoe White; one *s* one *d*. *Educ*: Kirkcaldy High Sch. Joined MoT, 1951; Asst Shipping Attaché, British Embassy, Washington, DC, 1961–64; Principal, Nationalised Industry Finance and Urban Transport Planning, 1965–70; Asst Sec., Railways Div., 1970–72; seconded to FCO as Counsellor, UK Representation to European Communities, 1972–75; Assistant Secretary: Land Use Planning, DoE, 1975–76; Central Unit on Environmental Pollution, 1976–77; Under Sec., PSA, 1978–81. *Recreations*: reading, mind games. *Address*: Apartment 20, The Hawthorns, 4 Carew Road, Eastbourne, E Sussex BN21 2BF.

LYALL, John Adrian, FRIBA; Director, Lyall Bills & Young Architects, since 2011 (Managing Director, John Lyall Architects Ltd, 1991–2011); *b* 12 Dec. 1949; *s* of Keith Lyall and Phyllis Lyall; *m* 1991, Sallie Jean Davies; one *s* one *d*. *Educ*: Southend High Sch. for Boys; Architectural Association Sch. of Architecture, London. RIBA 1980; FRIBA 2016. Partner, Alsop & Lyall, 1980–91. Major completed projects include: Leeds Corn Exchange, 1990; Cardiff Bay Visitor Centre, 1992; White Cloth Hall, Leeds, 1992; Tottenham Hale Station, 1992; N Greenwich Jubilee Line Station, 1999; Crystal Palace Park, 2000; Hammersmith Pumping Station, 2007; Cranfields Mill Develt, Ipswich, 2009; Jerwood Dance House, Ipswich, 2009; Pudding Mill Pumping Station, 2009; pumping stations, Olympic site, Stratford, 2011; Goldsmiths Centre, Clerkenwell, 2012; Pop-Up Gall., The Waste Land, Southend-on-Sea and touring, 2015. Member: Design Panel, Cardiff Bay Develt Corp., 1989–95; Nat. Design Adv. Panel, English Partnerships, 1998–2005; Acad. of Urbanism, 2011–; Quality Rev. Panel, London Legacy Develt Corp., 2012–17 (Vice-Chm., 2012–17); Oxford City Design Panel, 2014–; Haringey Design Rev. Panel, 2015–17; Chairman: Thurrock Design Panel, 2016–; Design Rev. Panel, Highways England, 2017– (Mem., Strategic Design Panel, 2018–); Vice Chm., Nat. Design Adv. Panel, CABE, 2007–11; Built Envmt Expert, Design Council, and Vice Chm., Design Rev. Panel, CABE, 2011–. Sir Bannister Fletcher Vis. Prof., UCL, 1998. Vice Pres., RIBA, 1997, 1999; Vice Chm., RIBA Trust, 2004–08; Council Mem., AA, 2005–10. Founder Mem., Architects 4 Education, 2007. Organiser: Polyark 2, 2009–10; Polyark 3, 2013; Polyark 4, 2018. External Examiner: Univ. of Greenwich, 2011–; Univ. of Brighton, 2015–18; London Metropolitan Univ., 2015–; Bartlett Sch. of Architecture, UCL, 2016–; New Course Scrutineer, UCL, 2018. FRSA. *Publications*: (with W. Alsop) Architecture Projects & Drawings, 1984; (jtly) John Lyall: contexts and catalysts, 1999; contrib. Architecture Today, RIBA Jl, Architects Jl and Building Design. *Recreations*: choral singing, cycling, gardening, fruit trees. *Address*: Lyall Bills & Young, Studio D2, 400 Caledonian Road, N1 1DN. *T*: (020) 7253 1630. *E*: john.lyall@lbyarchitects.com. *Club*: Chelsea Arts.

LYALL, Katharine Elizabeth; see Whitehorn, K.

LYALL GRANT, Maj.-Gen. Ian Hallam, MC 1944; Director General, Supply Co-ordination, Ministry of Defence, 1970–75; retired; *b* 4 June 1915; *s* of Col H. F. Lyall Grant, DSO and Lucy Ellinor (*née* Hardy); *m* 1951, Mary Jennifer Moore (*d* 2007); one *s* two *d*. *Educ*: Cheltenham Coll.; RMA, Woolwich; Gonville and Caius Coll., Cambridge (MA). CEng, MICE 1968; FGA 1978. Regular Commission, RE, 1935; service in: India, Burma and Japan, 1938–46 (MC; twice mentioned in despatches); Cyprus and Egypt, 1951–52; CO 131 Para Engr Regt (TA), 1954–56; Instructor, JSSC, 1957–58; Imperial Defence Coll., 1961; Aden, 1962–63; Comdt, Royal School of Mil. Engineering, 1965–67; Maj.-Gen. 1966; Dep. QMG, 1967–70, retired 1970. Col Comdt, RE, 1972–77. President: Bengal Sappers Officers' Assoc., 1987–95; Burma Campaign Fellowship Gp, 1996–2002 (Chm., 1991–96). Proprietor, Zampi Press, 1991–2011. *Publications*: Burma: the turning point, 1993; (with Kazuo Tamayama) Burma 1942: the Japanese Invasion, 1999. *Recreations*: travel, writing. *Club*: Naval and Military.
*See also* Sir M. J. Lyall Grant.

LYALL GRANT, Sir Mark (Justin), GCMG 2018 (KCMG 2006; CMG 2003); HM Diplomatic Service, retired; Visiting Professor, King's College, London, since 2017; consultant in geostrategic and security affairs; *b* 29 May 1956; *s* of Maj.-Gen. I. H. Lyall Grant, *qv*; *m* 1986, Sheila Jean Tresise; one *s* one *d*. *Educ*: Eton; Trinity Coll., Cambridge (MA Law). Called to the Bar, Middle Temple, 1980, Bencher, 2011; joined FCO, 1980; Second Sec., Islamabad, 1982–85; FCO, 1985–87; Private Sec. to Minister of State, FCO, 1987–89; First Sec., Paris, 1990–93; FCO 1993; seconded to European Secretariat, Cabinet Office, 1994–96; Dep. High Comr and Consul Gen., S Africa, 1996–98; Hd, EU Dept (Internal), FCO, 1998–2000; Dir, Africa, FCO, 2000–03; High Comr to Pakistan, 2003–06; Political Dir, FCO, 2007–09; Permanent Representative to the UN, 2009–15; Nat. Security Advr, 2015–17. Fellow, Eton Coll., 2017. *Recreations*: golf, tennis, sailing, bridge. *Clubs*: Royal Automobile; Royal Mid Surrey Golf.

LYDON, Prof. Julie Elspeth, OBE 2014; FLSW; Vice Chancellor and Chief Executive, University of South Wales (formerly University of Glamorgan), since 2010; *b* Builth Wells, Powys, 14 June 1954; *d* of Dennis and Rosalind Hodges; *m* 1985, Stephen Lydon; two *s*. *Educ*: Wolverhampton Poly. (BA Hons Econs 1975); Part 1, ICMA, 1977; Cert. of Proficiency, Chartered Insce Inst., 1987; Univ. of Wolverhampton (MBA 2000). Graduate mgt trainee, then Computer Systems Analyst/Programmer, TI Gp, 1975–79; Mktg and Sales Rep., 1980–82, Sales and Mktg Manager, 1982–85, TI Accles & Pollock; Regl and Project Manager, MAI plc, 1986–89; Wolverhampton Polytechnic, later University of Wolverhampton: Sen. Lectr, Inf. Mgt, 1989–92; Principal Lectr, Inf. Mgt and Strategic

Mgt, and Dep. to Hd of Undergrad. Studies, 1992–97; Associate Dean, Business Sch., 1997–2002; Asst Vice Chancellor, UWE, 2003–06; Dep. Vice Chancellor, Univ. of Glamorgan, 2006–10. Director: RWCMD, 2010–; Merthyr Tydfil Coll., 2010–. FHEA 2007; CCMI 2013; FRSA 2013; FLSW 2016. *Publications:* (contrib.) The Evolving Academic e-Learning Endeavour: the impact of using technology in learning and teaching, 2008; (contrib.) Collaborative Working in Higher Education: the social academy, 2009; contribs to Jl Applied Res. in Higher Educn. *Recreations:* walking, theatre, travel. *Address:* University of South Wales, Pontypridd CF37 1DL. *T:* (01443) 482001. *E:* julie.lydon@southwales.ac.uk.

**LYDON, Dr Nicholas B.;** FRS 2013; Co-Founder, Member, Therapeutic Advisory Board and Director, AnaptysBio Inc., since 2006; Co-Founder and Director, Blueprint Medicines, since 2011; *b* 27 Feb. 1957. *Educ:* Univ. of Leeds (BSc Biochem. 1978); Univ. of Dundee (PhD 1982). Charge de Recherché, Schlering-Plough Corp., Lyon and Paris, 1982–85; Team Leader, Tyrosine Protein Kinase Inhibitors, Ciba-Geigy AG, Basel, 1985–97; Founder and CEO, Kinetix Pharmaceuticals Inc., Boston, 1997–2000; Vice Pres., Drug Discovery and Res. Informatics, Amgen Inc., 2000–02; Founder, Granite Biopharma LLC; Advr and Mem., Bd of Dirs, Ambit BioSci., 2004–09. Hon. LLD Dundee, 2011. (Jtly) Warren Alpert Foundn Prize, 2001; Amer. Assoc. Cancer Res.—Bruce F. Cain Meml Award, 2002; Charles F. Kettering Prize, Gen. Motors Cancer Res. Foundn, 2002; (jtly) Lasker-DeBakey Award for Clin. Med. Res., 2009; (jtly) Japan Medal, Japan Prize Foundn, 2012. *Publications:* contribs to learned jls incl. New England Jl Medicine, Jl Pharmacol., Clin. Cancer Res., Blood, Bioorganic and Medicinal Chem. Letters, Nature Medicine, Biochem. Jl. *Address:* Blueprint Medicines, 45 Sidney Street, Cambridge, MA 02139, USA.

**LYE, David William Frederick;** freelance consultant, since 2011; Fellow, since 2011 and Director, since 2014, SAMI Consulting; *b* 13 Jan. 1958; *s* of Frederick Hayle Lye and Barbara Criddle Lye; *m* 2008, Jacqueline Helen Warwick Karas. *Educ:* Radley Coll.; Lincoln Coll., Oxford (BA Hons Modern Hist. 1979). Joined Civil Service, 1985; Hd, NHS Trusts Unit, DoH, 1991–93; Dir, Performance Mgt, NHS W Midlands, 1993–98; Project Dir, Children and Family Court Adv. and Support Service, 1999–2001; Chief Exec., Public Guardianship Office, 2001–04; Department of Health: Project Manager, Social Care, Local Govt and Care Partnerships Directorate, DoH, 2004–07; Hd of Dental and Eye Care Services, 2007–11. Associate Mem., Primary Care Commng, 2011–. MInstD 2017. *Publications:* contrib. articles to various NHS-related jls. *Recreations:* travel, cookery, armchair sports. *Address:* 6 Clock Tower Mews, N1 7BB. *E:* lye_david@hotmail.com.

**LYGO, Kevin Antony;** Director of Television, ITV, since 2016; *b* 19 Sept. 1957; *s* of Adm. Sir Raymond Derek Lygo, KCB and Pepper Lygo (*née* Van Osten); *m* 1999, Suzy Solomon; one *d*, and one step *s*. *Educ:* Cranbrook Sch.; Durham Univ. (BA Psychol.). BBC TV: comedy scriptwriter, 1981–83; gen. trainee, 1983–85; Producer, Omnibus, Wogan, 1985–96; Head of Ind. Commng Gp, 1996–97; Head of Entertainment, Channel 4, and Controller, E4, 1998–2001; Dir of Progs, Five (formerly Channel Five TV), 2001–03; Dir of TV, 2003–07, Dir of TV and Content, 2007–10, Channel 4; Man. Dir, ITV Studios, 2010–16. *Recreations:* Islamic art, Tibetan culture, tennis. *Address:* ITV plc, 2 Waterhouse Square, 138–142 Holborn, EC1N 2AE.

**LYKIARDOPOULOS, Andrew Nicolas;** QC 2014; *b* Bucks, 27 Jan. 1968; *s* of late Nico and of Margaret Lykiardopoulos; *m* 1993, Amanda Mary Heaslip; three *s*. *Educ:* Beacon Sch., Chesham Bois; Radley Coll.; Bristol Univ. (BA 1st Cl. Hons Hist. 1990); Coll. of Law, Lancaster Gate. Admitted as solicitor, 1994; Partner, Bristows Solicitors, 2000–04; in practice as solicitor advocate, 2000–04; called to the Bar, Middle Temple, 2004; in practice as barrister, specialising in intellectual property, 2004–. *Recreations:* music, history, travel, family. *Address:* 8 New Square, Lincoln's Inn, WC2A 3QP. *T:* (020) 7405 4321. *E:* andrew.lykiardopoulos@8newsquare.co.uk.

**LYLE, Alexander Walter Barr, (Sandy),** MBE 1987; professional golfer, since 1977; *b* 9 Feb. 1958; *s* of late Alex and Agnes Lyle; *m* (marr. diss.); two *s*; *m* 1989, Brigitte Jolande Huurman; one *s* one *d*. *Educ:* Shrewsbury local sch. Rookie of the Year, 1978; 1st in European order of merit, 1979, 1980, 1985; Open Champion, Royal St George's, 1985; won US Masters, 1988. *Publications:* Learning Golf the Lyle Way, 1986; To the Fairway Born, 2006. *Recreation:* cars.

**LYLE, Sir Gavin Archibald,** 3rd Bt *cr* 1929; estate manager, farmer; company director; *b* 14 Oct. 1941; *s* of late Ian Archibald de Hoghton Lyle and Hon. Lydia Yarde-Buller (who *m* 1947, as his 2nd wife, 13th Duke of Bedford; marr. diss. 1960; then Lydia Duchess of Bedford), *d* of 3rd Baron Churston; *S* grandfather, 1946; *m* 1967, Suzy Cooper (marr. diss. 1985; she *d* 2011); five *s* one *d*. Heir: *s* (Ian) Abram Lyle [*b* 25 Sept. 1968; *m* 2016, Lorna Violet, *d* of Hon. George and Sarah Lopes]. *Address:* Wester Gourdie House, Glendelvine Estate, Caputh, Perthshire PH1 4LG.

**LYLE, Jonathan Henry,** CB 2017; RCNC; Chief Executive, Defence Science and Technology Laboratory, 2012–17 (Director, Programme Office, 2010–12); *b* 25 Feb. 1959; *s* of John Henry Turner Lyle and Gillian Lucy Lyle; *m* 1981, Beverley Nichola Uren; one *s* one *d*. *Educ:* Kingswood Sch., Bath; Royal Naval Engrg Coll., Plymouth (BSc Electrical and Electronic Engrg 1979); University Coll. London (MSc Microwaves and Mod. Optics 1980). FIET 2009 (MIEE 1984); CEng 1984. RCNC 1976; Procurement Exec., MoD, 1982–91; Cabinet Office, 1991–95; DTI, 1995–96; Defence Procurement Agency: Directorate of Mil. Aircraft Projects, 1996–2000; Integrated Project Team Leader, 2000–04; Ops Dir, Air and Weapon Systems, 2004–07; Dir Gen., Helicopters, Defence Equipment and Support, MoD, 2007; Dir, Defence Acad.—Coll. of Mgt and Technol. (formerly Comdt, Defence Coll. of Mgt and Technol., Defence Acad.), 2007–10; Hd, RCNC, 2007–12. FREng 2015. *Recreations:* orienteering, watching Bath Rugby, inland waterways. *Club:* Bristol Orienteering.

**LYLE, Richard;** Member (SNP) Uddingston and Bellshill, Scottish Parliament, since 2016 (Scotland Central, 2011–16); *b* Bothwellhaugh, Lanarkshire, 12 June 1950; *s* of Richard and Margaret Lyle; *m* 1973, Marion Smith; one *s* one *d*. *Educ:* Lawmuir Sch.; Bellshill Acad. Grocer, 1965–79; credit advr, 1979–90; Area Manager, Royal Bank of Scotland, 1990–2000; credit advr, 2000–11. Joined SNP, 1966; Member (SNP): Motherwell DC, 1976–96 (Leader, SNP Gp, 1976–96); N Lanarks Council, 1996–2012 (Leader, SNP Gp, 1996–2011). Leader, COSLA SNP Gp, 2007–09. *Recreations:* politics, reading. *Address:* Scottish Parliament, Edinburgh EH99 1SP. *T:* (0131) 348 6394. *E:* richard.lyle.msp@parliament.scot. *Club:* Orbiston Bowling (Hon. Pres.).

**LYLE, Sandy;** see Lyle, A. W. B.

**LYMBERY, Philip John;** Chief Executive, Compassion in World Farming, since 2005; *b* Luton, 23 Sept. 1965; *s* of Rev. Peter Lymbery and Evelyn Lymbery; *m* 2011, Helen Roberts; one step *s*. *Educ:* Vandyke Upper Sch. and Coll., Leighton Buzzard. Packaging Designer, Bowater, 1987–90; Campaigns Dir, Compassion in World Farming, 1990–2000; freelance strategist, 2000–02; Dir, Communications, WSPA, 2003–05. Vis. Prof., Univ. of Winchester, 2015–. Wildlife tour leader, Gullivers Natural History Holidays, 1995–2005. FRSA; MInstD. *Publications:* (with Isabel Oakeshott) Farmageddon: the true cost of cheap meat, 2014; Dead Zone: where the wild things were, 2017; Farmageddon in Pictures, 2017.

*Recreations:* birdwatching, walking, song-writing, landscape and wildlife photography, guitar, my dog, gardening. *Address:* c/o Compassion in World Farming, River Court, Mill Lane, Godalming, Surrey GU7 1EZ. *T:* 07818 071918. *E:* philip.lymbery@ciwf.org.

**LYMINGTON, Viscount; Oliver Henry Rufus Wallop;** *b* 22 Dec. 1981; *s* and *heir* of Earl of Portsmouth, *qv*; *m* 2016, Flora Grace, *d* of George Pownall; one *d*. *Educ:* Eton. *Recreations:* shooting, cars. *Club:* White's.

**LYNAGH, Richard Dudley;** QC 1996; a Recorder, 2000–10; *b* 14 Nov. 1952; *s* of Charles Lynagh and Mary Browne; *m* 1979, Regula Wegmann (*d* 2004); two *s* one *d*. *Educ:* Kettering Grammar Sch.; University Coll. London (LLB Hons). Called to the Bar, Gray's Inn, 1975, Bencher, 2004; an Asst Recorder, 1999–2000. *Address:* 2 Crown Office Row, Temple, EC4Y 7HJ.

**LYNAM, Desmond Michael,** OBE 2008; broadcaster; *b* 17 Sept. 1942; *s* of Edward Lynam and Gertrude Veronica Lynam (*née* Malone); *m* 1st, 1965, Susan Eleanor Skinner (marr. diss. 1974); one *s*; 2nd, 2011, Rosemary Elizabeth Diamond. *Educ:* Varndean Grammar Sch., Brighton; Brighton Business Coll. ACII. Business career in insurance, until 1967; also freelance journalist; reporter for local radio, 1968–69; reporter, presenter and commentator, BBC Radio, 1969–78; presenter and commentator, BBC TV Sport, 1978–99, incl. Grandstand, Sportsnight, Match of the Day, Commonwealth and Olympic Games, and World Cup; presenter: Holiday, BBC TV, 1988–89; How Do They Do That?, BBC TV, 1994–96; The Des Lynam Show, BBC Radio, 1998–99; ITV Sport, 1999–2004; Des Meets…, BBC Radio, 2004–05; We'll Meet Again, BBC TV, 2005; The World's Greatest Sporting Legend, Sky One, 2005; Des At Wimbledon, BBC Radio, 2005; Are You Younger Than You Think?, BBC TV, 2005; Countdown, Channel 4, 2005–06; Touchline Tales, BBC Radio, 2010, 2011. TV Sports Presenter of the Year, TRIC, 1985, 1987, 1988, 1993, 1997; Radio Times Male TV Personality, 1989; RTS Sports Presenter of the Year, 1994, 1998; Richard Dimbleby Award, BAFTA, 1994; Variety Club of GB Media Award, 1997; RTS Lifetime Achievement Award, 2003. *Publications:* Guide to Commonwealth Games, 1986; The 1988 Olympics, 1988; The 1992 Olympics, 1992; I Should Have Been At Work! (autobiog.), 2005. *Recreations:* golf, tennis, Brighton and Hove Albion, reading, theatre. *Address:* c/o Jane Morgan Management Ltd, Argentum, 2 Queen Caroline Street, W6 9DX. *T:* (020) 3178 8071.

**LYNAS, Mark;** climate author and environmentalist; *b* Suva, Fiji, 11 April 1973; *s* of Bryan Donald Theodore Lynas and Valerie Margaret Lynas (*née* Wilson); *m* 2005, Maria Elizabeth Padget; one *s* one *d*. *Educ:* Teesdale Comp. Sch., Barnard Castle; Univ. of Edinburgh (1st Cl. MA Hons Politics and Mod. Hist. 1994). Editor, OneWorld.net, 1994–2000; freelance writer and envmtl campaigner, 2000–. Vis. Fellow, Cornell Alliance for Sci., Cornell Univ., 2013–. *Publications:* High Tide, 2004; Six Degrees, 2007; The God Species, 2011; Nuclear 2.0, 2013; Seeds of Science, 2018. *Recreations:* fell running, mountain climbing, ultimate frisbee. *T:* 07811 456824. *E:* marklynas36@gmail.com.

**LYNCH, Christopher Charles B.;** see Balogun-Lynch.

**LYNCH, His Honour David;** a Circuit Judge, 1990–2005; *b* 23 Aug. 1939; *s* of Henry and Edith Lynch; *m* 1974, Ann Knights; two *s*. *Educ:* Liverpool Collegiate Grammar School. LLB London (ext.); Liverpool John Moores Univ. (MRes; PhD 2015). Served RAF, 1958–61. Sharman & Sons, Solicitors, 1955–57; Bremner Sons & Corlett, Solicitors, 1961–66; Schoolmaster, 1966–68. Called to the Bar, Middle Temple, 1968, Bencher, 2016; Northern Circuit; Asst Recorder, 1983–88; a Recorder, 1988–90; Liaison Judge: St Helens Justices, 1991–2005; Liverpool John Moores Univ., 1994–2005 (Hon. Fellow, 2003). Pres., Mental Health Review Tribunals (restricted patients), 1991–2001. Northern Circuit Remembrancer, 2006–. Vis. Res. Fellow, Liverpool John Moores Univ., 2015–18. Hon. Vice Pres., Merseyside Br., Magistrates' Assoc., 1991–2005. Associate, Designer Bookbinders, 1999–. Member: Soc. of Bookbinders, 1998– (Trustee, 2000–14; Hon. Sec., 2009–14); Selden Soc., 2000–. *Publications:* (contrib.) A Century of Liverpool Lawyers, 2002; Northern Circuit Directory 1876–2004, 2005; Northern Circuit Directory Supplement, 2005–2015, 2016; The Role of the Circuit Courts in the Formation of United States Law: following Supreme Court Justices Washington, Livingston, Story and Thompson, 2018. *Recreations:* classical guitar, golf, bookbinding, photography, history of the Northern Circuit, early United States legal history. *Address:* c/o The Queen Elizabeth II Law Courts, Derby Square, Liverpool L2 1XA. *T:* (0151) 473 7373. *Clubs:* Victory Services, Union Jack; Caldy Golf.

**LYNCH, David Keith;** film director and producer; *b* Missoula, MT, USA, 20 Jan. 1946; *m* 1st, 1967, Peggy Reavey (marr. diss. 1974); one *d*; 2nd, 1977, Mary Fisk (marr. diss. 1987); one *s*; 3rd, 2006, Mary Sweeney (marr. diss.); one *s*; 4th, 2009, Emily Stofle; one *d*. *Educ:* Sch. of Mus. of Fine Arts, Boston; Pennsylvania Acad. of Fine Arts. Fellow, Center for Advanced Film Studies, Amer. Film Inst., 1970. *Films:* writer and director: Eraserhead (also prod.), 1977; The Elephant Man, 1980; Dune, 1984; Blue Velvet, 1986; Wild at Heart, 1990; Twin Peaks: Fire Walk with Me (also prod.), 1992; Lost Highway, 1997; Mulholland Drive, 2002; Inland Empire, 2006 (also prod.); dir, The Straight Story, 1999; prod., Surveillance, 2008; *television series:* writer, director and producer: Twin Peaks, 1990; On the Air, 1992; Twin Peaks: The Return, 2017. Recorded albums: Crazy Clown Time, 2011; The Big Dream, 2013. Exhibn, The Factory Photographs, Photographers' Gall., London, 2014. Founder, 2005, and Chm. Bd of Trustees, David Lynch Foundation for Consciousness-Based Education and World Peace. *Publications:* Catching the Big Fish: meditation, consciousness and creativity, 2006; The Factory Photographs, 2014; (jtly) Room to Dream, 2018.

**LYNCH, Holly Jamie;** MP (Lab) Halifax, since 2015; *b* Northowram, 8 Oct. 1986; *m* 2014, Chris Walker. *Educ:* Brighouse High Sch.; Lancaster Univ. With Matrix Technol. Solutions; Communications Officer for Linda McAvan, MEP. Shadow Minister for Flooding and Coastal Communities, 2017–. Co-Chair, All Party Parly Gp on Population, Develt and Reproductive Health, 2015–; Mem., Envmtl Audit Cttee, 2015. *Address:* House of Commons, SW1A 0AA.

**LYNCH, Prof. James Michael,** OBE 2007; PhD, DSc; CSci, CChem, FRSC, CBiol, FRSB, FIBiotech, CEnv, FRGS; Distinguished Professor of Life Sciences, University of Surrey, 2003–06, now Emeritus; Head of Global Landscapes, Earth-i, since 2017; *b* 24 Nov. 1945; *s* of James Michael Lynch and Constance Violet Lynch; *m* 1971, Mary Elizabeth Gibbons; two *s* two *d*. *Educ:* Wilson's Grammar Sch., London; Loughborough Univ. (BTech Chem. 1968); King's Coll. London (PhD 1971, DSc 1984, Microbiol.). CChem 1975; FRSC 1984; CBiol 1984; FRSB (FIBiol 1984); FIBiotech 1993; CSci 2005; CEnv 2016; FRGS 2016. Microbiologist, Letcombe Lab., 1971–83; Hd, Microbiol. and Crop Protection, Horticultural Res. Internat., 1983–93; Prof. of Biotechnol., and Head, Sch. of Biomed. and Life Scis, Univ. of Surrey, 1993–2003. Vis. Lectr, Univ. of Oxford, 1980–84; Visiting Professor: Washington State Univ., 1981–83; KCL, 1986–93; Oregon State Univ., 1995; Univ. of Reading, 2007–11; Univ. of Helsinki, 2009–12. Mem., editl bds of scientific jls, 1978–. Chm., Internat. Union of Soil Sci., Soil Biol. Commn, 1990–94. Co-ordinator, OECD Prog. on Biol Resource Mgt for Sustainable Agricl Systems, 1989–2006. Dir, Internat. Inst. of Biotechnol., 1998–2008; Bd Mem., Eur. Forestry Inst., 2006–; Chief

Exec., Forest Research, 2007–10; Sen. Advr, Thames Gateway Inst. for Sustainability, 2007–10; Dir of Forestry, DMC Internat. Imaging, 2011–13. Mem. Bd, Council for Frontiers of Knowledge, Africa, 2010–. Vice-Chm., Blasker Award Cttee, USA, 1996–2001. Chair of Govs, Univ. of Chichester, 2014–18. FRSA 1997; MInstD 2004. Freeman, City of London, 2019. Res. Award for Foreign Specialists, Japanese Govt, 1987, 1991; Prize for Microbiol. (Carlos J. Finlay Award), UNESCO, 1993. *Publications:* Soil Biotechnology: microbiological factors in crop productivity, 1983; (ed) The Rhizosphere, 1990; joint editor: Microbial Ecology: a conceptual approach, 1979; Contemporary Microbial Ecology, 1980; Microbial Adhesion to Surfaces, 1980; Microbiological Methods for Environmental Biotechnology, 1984; Micro-organisms in Action: concepts and applications in microbial ecology, 1988; Terrestrial Gene Exchange: mathematical modelling and risk assessment, 1994; Biocontrol Agents: benefits and risks, 1995; Ecotoxicology: responses, biomarkers and risk assessment, 1997; Environmental Biomonitoring: the biotechnology ecotoxicology interface, 1998; Biological Resource Management: connecting science and policy, 2000; Innovative Soil-Plant Systems for Sustainable Agricultural Practices, 2003; Remote Sensing for Agriculture and the Environment, 2004; Forestry and Climate Change, 2007; contrib. numerous review articles and res. papers. *Recreations:* running, cycling, sailing, gardening, walking, music, kayaking, golf. *Address:* Tudor Close, 12 The Drive, Angmering on Sea, W Sussex BN16 1QH. *T:* (01903) 785534. *E:* j.lynch@surrey.ac.uk. *Clubs:* English-Speaking Union, London Athletic.

**LYNCH, Jerome Cecil Alfonso;** QC 2000; *b* 31 July 1955; *s* of late Clifford James Lynch and Loretta Rosa Lynch; *m* 1983, Jacqueline Theresa O'Sullivan (marr. diss. 2011); two *s*. *Educ:* Lancashire Poly. (BA Hons). Called to the Bar, Lincoln's Inn, 1983, Bencher, 2008; in practice at the Bar, 1983–. Co-Presenter, Nothing But the Truth, Channel 4, 1998, 1999; Presenter, Crime Team, Channel 4, 2001, 2002; Co-Presenter, The People's Court, ITV1, 2005. Fellow, Univ. of Central Lancs, 2005. *Recreations:* ski-ing (well), golf (badly), drinking good wine. *Address:* Charter Chambers, 33 John Street, WC1N 2AT. *T:* (020) 7618 4400. *Club:* Royal Automobile.

**LYNCH, Prof. Michael,** PhD; FRSE; Sir William Fraser Professor of Scottish History and Palaeography, University of Edinburgh, 1992–2005, then Research Professor, now Hon. Professorial Fellow; *b* 15 June 1946; *s* of Francis J. and Kathleen Lynch. *Educ:* Aberdeen Grammar Sch.; Univ. of Aberdeen (MA Eng. Lit. and Hist. 1st cl. hons 1969); Inst. of Historical Res., Univ. of London (PhD 1977). Lectr in History, UCNW, Bangor, 1971–79; Lectr, 1979–88; Sen. Lectr, 1988–92, Dept of Scottish History, Univ. of Edinburgh. Chm., Ancient Monuments Bd for Scotland, 1996–2003; Publications Sec., Scottish History Soc., 1990–93; President: Historical Assoc. of Scotland, 1992–2002; Soc. of Antiquaries of Scotland, 1996–99. Trustee, Nat. Mus Scotland (formerly Nat. Mus of Scotland), 2002–10. FRHistS 1982; FRSE 1995. Editor, The Innes Review, 1984–92. *Publications:* Edinburgh and the Reformation, 1981; The Early Modern Town in Scotland, 1986; The Scottish Medieval Town, 1987; Mary Stewart: Queen in three kingdoms, 1988; Scotland: a new history, 1991, 2nd edn 1992; (ed with Julian Goodare) The Reign of James VI, 2000; (ed) The Oxford Companion to Scottish History, 2002; Aberdeen before 1800: a new history, 2002. *Address:* School of History, Classics and Archaeology, University of Edinburgh, William Robertson Wing, Old Medical School, Teviot Place, Edinburgh EH8 9AG.

**LYNCH, Michael Francis,** CBE 2008; AO 2017 (AM 2001); Chief Executive Officer, West Kowloon Cultural District Authority, 2011–15; Interim Director, National Art School, 2016–17; *b* 6 Dec. 1950; *s* of late Wilfred Brian Lynch and Joan Margaret Lynch; *m* 1976, Jane Scott (marr. diss. 1987); one *d*; *m* 1990, Christine Josephine Sharp; two step *s*. *Educ:* Marcellin Coll., Randwick; Univ. of Sydney. Australia Council for the Arts, 1973; Gen. Manager, King O'Malley Theatre Co., Australian Theatre for Young People; Administrator, Aust. Nat. Playwrights Conf.; Gen. Manager, Nimrod Th., 1976–78; Casting Dir and Man. Partner, Forcast Pty Ltd, 1981–89; General Manager: Sydney Th. Co., 1989–94; Australia Council for the Arts, 1994–98; Chief Executive: Sydney Opera House, 1998–2002; South Bank Centre, London, 2002–09; Dir, Australian Broadcasting Corp., 2009–11. Chair, Sydney Community Foundn, 2016–. Mem. Bd, Visit London, 2004–09. Prod., film, Raw Nerve, 1988. Garrett Award, Arts & Business, 2008.

**LYNCH, Michael Richard,** OBE 2006; DL; PhD; FRS 2014; FREng; Founder, Invoke Capital, since 2012; *b* 16 June 1965; *s* of Michael and Dolores Lynch. *Educ:* Christ's Coll., Cambridge (BA; PhD 1991; Hon. Fellow). Founder, Cambridge Neurodynamics, 1991; Founder and Gp CEO, Autonomy Corp. plc, 1996–2012; founding investor, Bridges Venturing. Non-executive Director: BBC, 2007–12; Cambridge Enterprise, 2010–. Member, Board: British Library, 2011–14; Create the Change campaign, Francis Crick Inst., 2012–. Member: Council for Sci. and Technol., 2011–; Investment Cttee Adv. Bd, Tech City; Adv. Bd, Turing Inst.; Advr, Prince's Trust Technol. Gp. Mem. Council, RAEng. Trustee: NESTA, 2009–12; Foundn for Sci. and Technol. FREng 2008. DL Suffolk 2012. *Recreations:* jazz saxophone, preserving rare breeds.

**LYNCH, Niamh;** see Cusack, N.

**LYNCH, Noel;** Member (Green) London Assembly, Greater London Authority, May 2003–04; *b* 20 Jan. 1947; *s* of William and Nancy Lynch; *m* 1976, Angela Enright (marr. diss. 1988); one *d*; *m* 2018, Diane Burstein. *Educ:* Kilmallock Nat. Sch.; Charleville Christian Brothers Sch., Co. Cork; University Coll. Cork (night classes) (Dip. Social Studies). Freelance auctioneer, 1986–2004; shopkeeper, E Finchley, 1992–2003. Member: Metropolitan Police Authy, 2003–04; London Fire and Emergency Planning Authy, 2003–04. Chm., Standards, GLA, 2003–04. Co-ordinator, 2001–03, 2004–15, 2017–18, Membership Officer, 2000–17, London Green Party. Director: Green Room Charity Shop, 1994–; Chaville Press, 2018–. *Publications:* Setting up Green Secondhand Shops, 1989. *Recreation:* conducting charity auctions. *E:* noellynch@tiscali.co.uk.

**LYNCH, Sir Patrick (Joseph),** KNZM 2015; QSO 1991; education consultant; Chief Executive Officer, New Zealand Catholic Education Office and Association of Proprietors' of Integrated Schools, 1994–2016; *b* Otahuhu, Auckland, NZ, 18 March 1942; *s* of James David Lynch and Mavis Amelia Lynch (*née* Wilson). *Educ:* De La Salle Coll., Mangere, Auckland; Auckland Univ. (BA 1972); Massey Univ. (DipEd 1977). Primary Teacher, St Mary's Boys' Sch., 1963–66; De La Salle College, Auckland: Dean of Form 4, 1976–77; Dep. Principal, 1978; Principal, 1979–93. Comr, NZ Nat. Commn for UNESCO, 1996–2008. Pres., Secondary Principals' Assoc. NZ, 1991–93. *Recreations:* walking, music, gardening. *Address:* 81 Gray Avenue, Mangere East, 2158 Auckland, New Zealand. *T:* (9) 0274905396; PO Box 86099, Mangere East, 2158 Auckland, New Zealand.

**LYNCH, Roderick Robertson;** aviation industry consultant; Director and Vice President, GSS Ltd, 2015–16 (Chairman and Chief Executive, 2001–15); *b* 22 May 1949; *s* of Nanson Lynch and Catherine (*née* Robertson); *m* 1972, Christina Williams; two *s*. *Educ:* Perth Acad.; Dundee Univ. (MA 1971). Served RAC, 1966–67. British Airways, 1971–89; Gen. Manager, Southern Europe, 1983–84; Man. Dir, British Airtours, 1984–86; Head, Customer Service, 1986–89; Man. Dir, Air Europe, 1989–91; Dir, Forte Hotels, 1991–93; Man. Dir, then Chief Exec., Resources, BBC, 1993–99; CEO, Olympic Airways, 1999–2000. Bd Mem., CAA, 1993–99; Dir, NATS Ltd, 1996–99. *Recreations:* Rugby football, military history, music, aviation. *Club:* Caledonian.

**LYNCH, Sarah Jane; Her Honour Judge Lynch;** a Circuit Judge, since 2012. Admitted as solicitor, 1989; solicitor: Edward Fail Bradshaw & Waterson, 1989–90; Wake Smith & Tofields, 1990–2008; Howells, 2008–12; a Recorder, 2008–12. *Address:* Leeds Combined Court Centre, The Court House, 1 Oxford Row, Leeds LS1 3BG. *T:* (0113) 306 2800.

**LYNCH-BLOSSE, Sir Richard Hely,** 17th Bt *cr* 1622; general medical practitioner, since 1985 (senior partner, since 2000); *b* 26 Aug. 1953; *s* of Sir David Edward Lynch-Blosse, 16th Bt, and of Elizabeth, *er d* of Thomas Harold Payne, Welwyn Garden City; *S* father, 1971; *m* 1st, 1976, Cara (marr. diss. 1999), *o d* of late George Sutherland, St Ives, Cambs; two *d*; 2nd, 2000, Jacqueline, *o d* of late Gordon Francis, Yardley Gobion, Northants. *Educ:* Royal Free Hosp. Sch. of Medicine (MB BS 1979). LRCP MRCS 1978; DRCOG 1983; MRCGP 1984. Commnd RAMC, 1975, served, 1975–85. Medical Officer: European Sch., Culham, 1987–2012; Oxon ACF, 1993–2018. Med. Referee, S Oxon Crematorium. Mem., Soc. of Ornamental Turners, 1992–. *Publications:* contrib. to Jl of RAMC. *Heir:* cousin David Ian Lynch-Blosse [*b* 14 Jan. 1950; *m* 1st, 1984, Mrs Barbara Susan McLaughlin (*d* 1985); 2nd, 1989, Nadine, *d* of John Baddeley; one *s* one *d*]. *Address:* The Surgery, Watery Lane, Clifton Hampden, Oxon OX14 3EL.

**LYNCH-ROBINSON, Sir Dominick (Christopher),** 4th Bt *cr* 1920, of Foxrock, co. Dublin; novelist and creative consultant; Global Creative Director, J. Walter Thompson, 2004–13; *b* 30 July 1948; *s* of Sir Niall Lynch-Robinson, 3rd Bt, DSC, and Rosemary Seaton; *S* father, 1996; *m* 1973, Victoria, *d* of Kenneth Weir; one *s* one *d*, and one step *d*. Podcasts: Brand Stories from Brand Champions; The Amazing Adventures of Lenny the Lizard. *Publications:* My Name is Charlie and I Don't Think Right (memoir), 2016. *Recreations:* reading, cinema, writing, travel. *Heir:* *s* Christopher Henry Jake Lynch-Robinson, *b* 1 Oct. 1977.

**LYNDEN-BELL, Ruth Marion,** PhD, ScD; FRS 2006; Professor of Condensed Matter Simulation, Queen's University, Belfast, 1995–2003, now Emeritus; *b* 7 Dec. 1937; *d* of David and Priscilla Truscott; *m* 1961, Prof. Donald Lynden-Bell, CBE, FRS (*d* 2018); one *s* one *d*. *Educ:* Newnham Coll., Cambridge (BA 1959, MA 1962; PhD 1962; ScD 1989). FRSC; FInstP. Fellow, New Hall, Cambridge, 1962–65; Lectr, Univ. of Sussex, 1965–72; Fellow, New Hall, Cambridge, 1972–95, now Emerita; Coll. Lectr, St John's Coll., Cambridge, 1975–95. Acting Pres., Murray Edwards Coll., Cambridge, 2012–13. Lennard-Jones Lectr, Thermodynamics and Stats Mechanics Gp, RSC, 2018. Paul Walden Award, German Res. Foundn, 2012. *Publications:* (with R. K. Harris) Nuclear Magnetic Resonance Spectroscopy, 1969; numerous articles in scientific jls. *Recreations:* gardening, walking. *Address:* Department of Chemistry, Lensfield Road, Cambridge CB2 1EW.

**LYNDHURST, Nicholas;** actor, since 1971; *b* 20 April 1961; *m* 1999, Lucy Smith; one *s*. *Theatre includes:* Harding's Luck, Greenwich; Trial Run, Oxford Playhouse, 1980; Black Comedy (tour); The Private Ear (tour); The Foreigner, Albery, 1987; Straight and Narrow, Wyndham's, 1992; The Dresser, Duke of York's, 2005; The Tempest, Haymarket Th. Royal, 2011; Carousel, Coliseum, 2017; Man of La Mancha, Coliseum, 2019. *Television includes:* Going Straight, 1978; Spearhead, 1978; Butterflies, 1978–83; Father's Day, 1979; To Serve Them All My Days, 1980; Fairies; Losing Her; Only Fools and Horses, 1981–91; It'll All Be Over in Half an Hour, 1983; The Two of Us, 1986–90; The Piglet Files, 1990; Goodnight Sweetheart, 1993–99 (one-off revival, 2016); Gulliver's Travels, 1996; David Copperfield, 1999; Thin Ice, 2000; Murder in Mind, 2003; After You've Gone, 2007; Rock and Chips, 2010–11; New Tricks, 2013–15. *Radio includes:* My First Planet, BBC Radio 4, 2012. *Address:* c/o Chatto & Linnit Ltd, 17 Old Park Lane, W1K 1QT.

**LYNE, Prof. Andrew Geoffrey,** PhD; FRS 1996; FRAS; Langworthy Professor of Physics, University of Manchester, 2002–08, now Hon. Professor of Physics; *b* 13 July 1942; *s* of Lionel Geoffrey Lyne and Kathleen Elizabeth Lyne; *m* 1st, Jennifer Anne Duckels; two *d*; 2nd, 1994, Diane Elizabeth Stanway; one step *s* one step *d*. *Educ:* Portsmouth GS; St John's Coll., Cambridge (MA); Manchester Univ. (PhD). Manchester University: Lectr in Radio Astronomy, 1969–79; Sen. Lectr, 1979–90; Prof. of Radio Astronomy, 1990–2002. Dir, Nuffield Radio Astronomy Labs, subseq. Jodrell Bank Observatory, 1998–2006. Vis. Scientist, CSIRO Div. of Radiophysics, Sydney, 1975–76; Leverhulme Fellow, Royal Soc., 1994. Mem., PPARC, 1997–2000. Herschel Medal, RAS, 1992; Sir George Thomson Gold Medal, Inst. of Measurement and Control, 1993; Descartes Prize for Res., EC, 2005. *Publications:* Pulsar Astronomy, 1990, 4th edn 2012; contrib. Nature, Monthly Notes of RAS and other scientific jls. *Recreations:* tennis, golf, walking, sailing. *Address:* Tall Trees, New Road, Moreton, Congleton, Cheshire CW12 4RX.

**LYNE, Colin Gwaynten;** Commercial Director, Department for Constitutional Affairs, 2003–06; *b* 10 Feb. 1945; *s* of William Henry Lyne and Ada Lilian Lyne (*née* Brownsell); *m* 1978, Hilary Janet Luscombe; two *s* one *d*. *Educ:* Humphry Davy Grammar Sch., Penzance; Bristol Univ. (Open Schol.). Various posts in NHS, 1973–85; Co. Supplies Officer, 1985–88, Dir, Commercial Services, 1988–93, Surrey CC; Director: Commercial Services, Essex CC, 1993–99; Purchasing and Contract Mgt, LCD, 1999–2003. Non-exec. Dir, Investment and Implementation Bd, Office of Govt Commerce, HM Treasury, 2005–07. Chm., 1992–93, Pres., 1994–95, Chartered Inst. Purchasing and Supply. Chm., Eur. Council of Purchasing and Supply, 2000–02. Mem., Bd of Advrs, Southampton Univ. Sch. of Mgt, 2005–07. FCIPS 1990. FRSA 1995. *Recreations:* golf, bridge, genealogy.

**LYNE, Kevin Douglas;** HM Diplomatic Service, retired; consultant, since 2014; *b* 6 Nov. 1961; *s* of Douglas Lyne and Anne Lyne; *m* 1988, Anne Dabbadie; two *d*. *Educ:* Richard Hale Sch., Hertford; Portsmouth Poly. (BA Hons Latin Amer. Studies); Univ. of Essex (MA Govt and Politics). Res. Cadre, FCO, 1988–91; Second Sec., Santiago, 1991–94; Principal Res. Officer, FCO, 1994–96; First Secretary: FCO, 1996–98; UK Mission to UN, Geneva, 1998–2003; Dep. Hd of Mission, Rabat, 2003–07; Ambassador to Montenegro, 2007–09; Conflict Team Leader, Res. Analysts, FCO, 2010–11; UK Stabilisation Planner, ISAF, 2011; FCO, 2012; Stabilisation Advr, Stabilisation Unit, 2013–14. *Recreation:* fishing. *Address:* 64130 Idaux-Mendy, France.

**LYNE, Richard John;** HM Diplomatic Service, retired; High Commissioner to Solomon Islands, 2004–08; *b* 20 Nov. 1948; *s* of late John Arthur Lyne and Sylvia Mary Raven Lyne (*née* Knott); *m* 1977, Jennifer Anne Whitworth; one *s* one *d*. *Educ:* Kimbolton Sch. RAPC, 1967–70; joined HM Diplomatic Service, 1970; Archivist and Communications Officer, Belgrade, 1972–74; Accountant and Dep. Mgt Officer, Algiers, 1974–76; Third Sec., Damascus, 1977–80; Second Sec., New Delhi, 1984–87; Second, later First Sec., Stockholm, 1987–91; Dep. High Comr, Port of Spain, Trinidad, 1997–2000; Deputy Head: Conf. and Visits Gp, FCO, 2000–02; Personnel Services Dept, FCO, 2002–04. Church Warden, St Peter and St Sigfried Anglican Ch, Stockholm, 1989–91. Chm., St Albans Dio. Property Cttee, 2010–18. Mem., St Albans Diocesan Synod, 2013–18; Dir, St Albans Dio. Property Co., 2013–18. Mem., St John Boxmoor PCC, Hemel Hempstead, 1994–96, 2000–04 and 2009–16; Mem. Bd and Trustee, Music at St John's, Boxmoor,

Hemel Hempstead, 2009–. *Recreations:* family, reading, genealogy, watching sport. *Address:* 12 Campion Road, Chaulden Vale, Hemel Hempstead HP1 2DN. *Club:* Royal Over-Seas League.

**LYNE, Rt Hon. Sir Roderic (Michael John),** KBE 1999; CMG 1992; PC 2009; HM Diplomatic Service, retired; consultant and lecturer; *b* 31 March 1948; *s* of Air Vice-Marshal Michael Dillon Lyne, CB, AFC and Avril Joy, *d* of Lt-Col Albert Buckley, CBE, DSO; *m* 1969, Amanda Mary, *d* of Sir Howard Frank Trayton Smith, GCMG; two *s* one *d*. *Educ:* Legbourne County Primary Sch., Lincs; Highfield Sch., Hants; Eton Coll.; Leeds Univ. (BA Hist. 1970). FCO 1970; Army Sch. of Langs, 1971; Moscow, 1972–74; Dakar, 1974–76; Eastern European and Soviet Dept, FCO, 1976–79; Rhodesia Dept, FCO, 1979; Asst Pvte Sec. to Sec. of State for Foreign and Commonwealth Affairs, 1979–82; UK Mission to UN, NY, 1982–86; Vis. Res. Fellow, RIIA, 1986–87; Counsellor and Hd of Chancery, Moscow, 1987–90; Hd of Soviet Dept, 1990–92, Hd of Eastern Dept, 1992–93, FCO; Pvte Sec. to Prime Minister, 1993–96 (on secondment); Dir for Policy Develt, CIS ME and Africa, British Gas, 1996 (on secondment); UK Perm. Rep. to Office of UN and other internat. orgns, Geneva, 1997–2000; Ambassador to Russia, 2000–04. Hon. Prof., Moscow Sch. of Social and Economic Studies, 2001; Vis. Prof., Faculty of Business and Law, 2005–11, Mem., 2007–13 and Chm., 2011–13, Bd of Govs, Kingston Univ. Stephen Roskill Meml Lect., Churchill Coll., Cambridge, 2016. Non-executive Director: Accor, 2006–09; Aricom, 2006–09; Petropavlovsk plc (formerly Peter Hambro Mining), 2009–16, 2018– (Chm., 2018–); JPMorgan Bank Internat. LLC, 2013–19; Mem., Strategic Adv. Gp, QucomHaps Hldgs Ltd, 2005–18; Special Adviser: HSBC, 2004–07; BP, 2005–09; Chm., Internat. Adv. Bd, Altimo, 2006–07; Special Rep., ITE Gp plc, 2005–10; Special Advr, JPMorgan Chase Bank, 2007–10. Member: Bd, Russo-British Chamber of Commerce, 2006–09; Exec. Cttee, UK/Russia Round Table, 2005–07; Trilateral Commn's Task Force on Russia, 2005–07; Oxford Univ. Task Force on Energy, the Envmt and Develt, 2006–07; Iraq Inquiry Cttee, 2009–16; Dep. Chm., Council, RIIA, 2009–16; Chm., Adv. Cttee, Centre for E European Language Based Area Studies, 2007–16. Mem. Bd, Internat. Early Music Trust, St Petersburg, 2007–10. Hon. Vice-Pres., GB-Russia Soc., 2005–. Patron, AMUR, 2001–16. Trustee, World Race Trust, 2004–07. Gov., Ditchley Foundn, 2005–11. Hon. Dr Rostov State Construction Univ., 2001; Hon. LLD Leeds, 2002; Hon. DBA Kingston, 2004; Hon. DLit Heriot-Watt, 2004; DUniv Birmingham, 2012. *Publications:* (jtly) Engaging with Russia: the next phase, 2006; (contrib.) Russia: the challenges of transformation, 2011. *Recreations:* sport, grandchildren. *Address:* 39 Richmond Park Road, East Sheen, SW14 8JU. *Club:* Travellers.

**LYNE, William Macquarie,** CBE 2002 (MBE 1986); AM 2002; Director, Wigmore Hall, 1966–2003 (Assistant Manager, 1957–66), Director Emeritus, since 2006; *b* 28 Nov. 1932; *s* of Harold Baden Lyne and Marie Veronica Lyne (*née* Catalano). *Educ:* Canterbury High Sch., Sydney, Australia. Transcription Officer, Australian Broadcasting Commn, 1951–56. Mem. Bd, Henry Wood Hall, 1991–2013; Trustee, Geoffrey Parsons Meml Trust, 1995–2012; Internat. Artistic Advr, Melbourne Internat. Chamber Music Competition, 2007–17; Mem. Cttee, Queen's Medal for Music, 2004–. Hon. FTCL 1997; Hon. GSM 1997; Hon. RAM 1999; Hon. RCM 1999. Evening Standard Award for Outstanding Achievement for Classical Music, 1997; Ambassador for London Award for lifetime achievement, 1997; Cobbett Medal for Services to art of chamber music, Musicians' Co., 2001; Internat. Artists' Mgt Assoc. award, 2003; Queen's Medal for Music, 2016. Chevalier, Ordre des Arts et des Lettres (France), 1996; Grand Cross of Honour (First Class) for Sci. and the Arts (Austria), 2001. *Publications:* (contrib.) Wigmore Hall 1901–2001: a celebration, 2001. *Recreations:* collecting gramophone records, incl. vintage; cinema, esp. films from the thirties; reading, visiting art galleries, fell walking, travel, theatre, concerts, opera. *Address:* c/o Wigmore Hall, 36 Wigmore Street, W1U 2BP. *E:* wmlyne@outlook.com. *Club:* Reform.

**LYNES, Robert Christopher,** CMG 2017; Adviser, Future Hope, since 2018; *b* Huddersfield, 12 Dec. 1961; *s* of Hubert Lynes and Patricia Lynes; *m* 1991, Marta Antál; two *d*. *Educ:* King James's Grammar Sch., Almondbury; Univ. of Lancaster (MA Applied Linguistics 1995); RAF Sch. of Languages (Russian and Polish). Linguist, RAF, 1980–86; Dep. Dir, 1987–91, Exec. Dir, 1991–94, Internat. House, Hungary; British Council: Sen. Trng Consultant, Saudi Arabia, 1995–96; Asst Dir, Eastern Province, Saudi Arabia, 1996–98; Asst Dir, Poland, 1998–2000; Regl Dir, Europe and Americas, Educnl Enterprises, 2000–04; Regl Dir, Middle East, 2004–08; Dep. Dir, Global Ops, 2008–11; Director: India, 2011–16; UK, 2016–18. *Publications:* Teaching English in Eastern and Central Europe, 1996. *Recreations:* painting, golf, reading. *Address:* 4 Doune Terrace, Edinburgh EH3 6DY. *E:* robmartalynes@hotmail.com.

**LYNK, Roy,** OBE 1990; consultant in human resources, since 1996; National President, Union of Democratic Mineworkers, 1987–93; General Secretary, Nottingham Section, 1985–93; *b* 9 Nov. 1932; *s* of John Thomas Lynk and Ivy Lynk; *m* 1978, Sandra Ann; three *s* three *d*. *Educ:* Station Road Higher Sch. and Healdswood Sch., Sutton-in-Ashfield; Nottingham Univ. Cert. in Industrial Relations. Miner at Teversal Colliery, Nottingham, 1947; RN 1948; Miner at various collieries, Nottingham, 1950–79. National Union of Mineworkers: Branch Sec., Sutton Colliery, 1958–79; full time Area Official, Nottingham, 1979–83; Financial Sec., Nottingham Area, 1983–85, Gen. Sec., 1985; Union of Democratic Mineworkers: formed, Dec. 1985; Nat. Gen. Sec., 1985–86. Member: European Coal and Steel Community's Consultative Cttee, 1988–93; Industrial Appeal Tribunal, Nottingham, 1993–; Board, Coal Authy, 1995–98. *Recreation:* watching football. *Address:* Columbia House, 143 Huthwaite Road, Sutton-in-Ashfield, Notts NG17 2HB.

**LYNN, Bishop Suffragan of,** since 2011; **Rt Rev. (Cyril) Jonathan Meyrick**; *b* 23 April 1952; *s* of late Christopher and Isolde Meyrick; *m* 1984, Rebecca Keatley; one *s* two *d*. *Educ:* Lancing Coll.; St John's Coll., Oxford (BA Hons 1973, MA 1977); Salisbury and Wells Theol Coll. Ordained deacon, 1976, priest, 1977; Curate, Bicester, 1976–78; Domestic Chaplain to Bishop of Oxford, 1978–81; Tutor in Old Testament Studies, Codrington Coll., Barbados, 1981–84; Team Vicar, Taplow, Burnham Team Ministry, 1984–90; Team Rector, Tisbury, 1990–98; RD, Chalke Valley, 1997–98; Canon Residentiary, Rochester Cathedral, 1998–2005; Acting Dean, Rochester, 2003–05; Dean of Exeter, 2005–11. Provost, Colleges of Lancing, Hurstpierpoint and Ardingly, and of Lancing Prep. Schs, Hove and Worthing, 2017–; Chaplain to High Sheriff of Herts, 2018–19. Chairman: Cathedrals Plus (formerly Pilgrims Assoc.), 2008–11; Papua New Guinea Church Partnership, 2013–16; Mem., Cathedral Fabric Commn for England, 2016–. Trustee, Emmaus Exeter, 2010–11. Regular columnist, Exeter's Express and Echo, 2008–11. Released charity CD, The Rocking Bishop: everlasting smiles from the 60s, 2013. Hon. DEd Plymouth, 2011. *Publications:* Old Testament Syllabus for Developing Ministries Programme, Diocese of Rochester, 2001; (contrib.) Cultural Diversity Guide, 2001, rev. edn 2003; Rochester Cathedral Official Guidebook, 2004; A Carol of Hope, 2008; (contrib.) The Church in the City, 2008. *Recreations:* acting, singing, punting, croquet, tennis. *Address:* The Old Vicarage, Priory Road, Castle Acre, Kings Lynn, Norfolk PE32 2AA. *T:* (office) (01760) 755553. *E:* bishop.lynn@diocesofnorwich.org. *Clubs:* Garrick; Norfolk (Norwich).

**LYNN, Archdeacon of;** *see* Bentley, Ven. I. R.

**LYNN, Inez Therese Philomena Alice,** MBE 2018; Librarian, The London Library, 2002–17; *b* 15 March 1960; *d* of Jack Basil Lynn and Mari Therese Philomena Josephine Patricia Lynn (*née* Prendergast). *Educ:* La Sagesse Convent High Sch., Newcastle upon Tyne; Univ. of Liverpool (BA); Univ. of Toronto; Pembroke Coll., Oxford (MLitt); University Coll. London (DipLib). MCLIP (ALA 1992). SCONUL trainee, Warburg Inst., 1984–86, Inst. of Advanced Legal Studies, 1986–88, Univ. of London; London Library: Cataloguer, 1988–90; Chief Cataloguer, 1990–93; Prin. Asst Librarian, 1993–94; Dep. Librarian, 1994–2001. Trustee: Maitland Trust, 2002–06; R. M. Chambers Settlement Trust, 2002–10; London Library Trust, 2002–12; London Library Staff Superannuation Fund, 2002–17. Trainee teacher, F. Matthias Alexander Technique, Alexander Technique Studio, London, 2018–. *Publications:* (contrib.) Libraries: case studies in re-planning and refurbishment, 2009. *Recreations:* editing Medieval Latin poetry, dressage.

**LYNN, Jonathan Adam;** director, writer and actor; *b* 3 April 1943; *s* of Robin and Ruth Lynn; *m* 1967, Rita Merkelis; one *s*. *Educ:* Kingswood Sch., Bath; Pembroke Coll., Cambridge (MA). Acted in Cambridge Circus, New York, 1964; TV debut, Ed Sullivan Show, 1964; actor in repertory, Leicester, Edinburgh and Bristol Old Vic, and in London; performances include: Green Julia, 1965; Fiddler on the Roof, 1967–68; Blue Comedy, 1968; The Comedy of the Changing Years, 1969; When We Are Married, 1970; Dreyfus, 1982; actor in TV comedy programmes and plays, including: Barmitzvah Boy, 1975; The Knowledge, 1979; Outside Edge, 1982; Diana, 1984; actor in films including: Prudence and the Pill, 1967; Into the Night, 1984; Three Men and a Little Lady, 1990; Greedy (also dir.), 1994; Artistic Dir, Cambridge Theatre Co., 1977–81 (dir. 19 prodns); *director: London:* The Plotters of Cabbage Patch Corner, 1970; The Glass Menagerie, 1977; The Gingerbread Man, 1977 and 1978; The Unvarnished Truth, 1978; The Matchmaker, 1978; Songbook, 1979 (SWET Award, and Evening Standard Award, for Best Musical, 1979); Tonight at 8.30, 1981; Arms and the Man, 1981; Pass the Butler, 1982; Loot, 1984; The Patriotic Traitor (also wrote), 2016; *National Theatre:* A Little Hotel on the Side, 1984; Jacobowski and the Colonel, 1986; Three Men on a Horse, 1987 (Olivier Award for Best Comedy); *RSC:* Anna Christie, Stratford 1979, London 1980; *Broadway:* The Moony Shapiro Songbook, 1981; Yes, Prime Minister (also co-wrote), Chichester Festival Th., 2010, Gielgud Th., 2010, Apollo Th., 2011, Trafalgar Studios, 2012, LA, 2013 (WhatsOnStage Award for Best Comedy); Cosi fan tutte, Pasadena Opera (also wrote adaption), 2017; *films:* Mick's People (also wrote), 1982; Clue (also wrote), 1984; Nuns on the Run (also wrote), 1990; My Cousin Vinny, 1991; The Distinguished Gentleman, 1992 (Envmtl Media Award, 1993); Greedy (also acted), 1994; Sgt Bilko, 1996; Trial and Error, 1997; The Whole Nine Yards, 2000; The Fighting Temptations, 2003 (NAACP Image Award for Best Dir); Wild Target, 2008; *screenplay:* The Internecine Project, 1974; *TV scriptwriter:* situation comedies, including: My Brother's Keeper, 2 series, 1974 and 1975 (also co-starred); Yes, Minister (also radio scripts), 3 series, 1980, 1981 and 1982; Yes, Prime Minister, 1986, 1987, 2013; Life After Life, 1990. Hon. MA Sheffield, 1987; Hon. PsyD Amer. Behavioral Studies Inst., 2000. Writer's Award, BAFTA, 1987; Pye TV Writers Award (for Yes, Minister and Yes, Prime Minister), 1981, 1986; Broadcasting Press Guild Award, 1980, 1986; ACE Award for Amer. Cable TV Best Comedy Writing (for Yes, Prime Minister), 1988; Diamond Jubilee Award for Best Political Satire, Pol Studies Assoc., 2010; Outstanding Career Achievement Award, Anaheim Internat. Film Fest., 2010; Friends of Film Lifetime Achievement Award, 2011. *Publications:* A Proper Man (novel), 1976; Mayday (novel), 1993, 25th Anniv. edn 2018; Comedy Rules!, 2011; Samaritans (novel), 2017; with Antony Jay: Yes, Minister, The Diaries of a Cabinet Minister: Vol. I, 1981; Vol. II, 1982; Vol. III, 1983; The Complete Yes Minister, 1984; Yes, Prime Minister, the Diaries of the Rt Hon. James Hacker: Vol. I, 1986; Vol. II, 1987; The Complete Yes Prime Minister, 1989; Mayday (novel), 1993; Yes, Prime Minister (play), 2010; The Patriotic Traitor (play), 2016. *Recreation:* changing weight. *Address:* (writing) c/o Alan Brodie Representation, Paddock Suite, The Courtyard, 55 Charterhouse Street, EC1M 6HA; (directing) c/o Simon Beresford, Dalzell and Beresford, Paddock Suite, The Courtyard, 55 Charterhouse Street, EC1M 6HA.

**LYNN, Michael David;** Corporate Development Director, The Stationery Office Ltd, 1996–99; *b* 18 July 1942; *s* of Martin and Dorothy Lynn; *m* 1965, Hilary Smyth; one *s* one *d*. *Educ:* Lincoln Sch. Joined HMSO 1960; Director: Publications Distribution, 1980; Finance, 1983; Print Procurement, 1984; Dir–Gen., Corporate Services, 1987; Dep. Chief Exec., 1989; Controller and Chief Exec., 1995–96. *Recreations:* chess, crosswords.

**LYNN, Prof. Richard,** PhD; FBPsS; Professor of Psychology, University of Ulster, 1972–95; President, Ulster Institute for Social Research, since 1995; *b* 20 Feb. 1930; *s* of Prof. Sydney Cross Harland, FRS and Ann Lynn; *m* 1st, 1956, Susan Maher (marr. diss. 1978); one *s* two *d*; 2nd, 1990, Susan Hampson (*d* 1998); 3rd, 2004, Joyce Dora Walters, *qv*. *Educ:* Bristol Grammar Sch.; King's Coll., Cambridge (BA 1953; PhD 1956; Passingham prizeman). FBPsS 1965. Lectr in Psychology, Univ. of Exeter, 1956–67; Prof. of Psychology, Dublin Economic and Social Res. Inst., 1967–72. US Mensa Award for Excellence, for work on intelligence, 1985, 1988, 1993. *Publications:* Attention, Arousal and the Orientation Reaction, 1966; The Irish Braindrain, 1969; The Universities and the Business Community, 1969; Personality and National Character, 1971; An Introduction to the Study of Personality, 1972; The Entrepreneur, 1974; (ed) Dimensions of Personality, 1981; Educational Achievement in Japan, 1987; The Secret of the Miracle Economy, 1991; Dysgenics: genetic deterioration in modern populations, 1996, 2nd rev. edn 2011; Eugenics: a reassessment, 2001; The Science of Human Diversity, 2001; The Chosen People: Jewish IQ and achievement, 2011; (with E. Dutton) Race and Sport, 2015; Race Differences in Psychopathic Personality, 2018; (with D. Becker) The Intelligence of Nations, 2019; with T. Vanhanen: IQ and the Wealth of Nations, 2002; Race Differences in Intelligence, 2005, 2nd rev. edn 2015; IQ and Global Inequality, 2006; The Global Bell Curve, 2008; Intelligence: a unifying construct for the social sciences, 2012; articles on personality, intelligence and social psychology. *Recreations:* do-it-yourself house renovation, bridge. *Address:* 4 Longwood, Clevedon Road, Bristol BS8 3TL. *E:* Lynnr540@aol.com. *Club:* Oxford and Cambridge.

**LYNN, Dame Vera, (Dame Vera Margaret Lewis),** CH 2016; DBE 1975 (OBE 1969); singer; *b* 20 March 1917; *d* of Bertram Samuel Welch and Annie Welch; *m* 1941, Harry Lewis; one *d*. *Educ:* Brampton Rd Sch., East Ham. First public appearance as singer, 1924; joined juvenile troupe, 1928; ran own dancing school, 1932; broadcast with Joe Loss and joined Charlie Kunz, 1935; singer with Ambrose Orch., 1937–40, then went solo; voted most popular singer, Daily Express comp., 1939, and named Forces Sweetheart; own radio show, Sincerely Yours, 1941–47; starred in Applesauce, London Palladium, 1941; sang to troops in Burma, etc, 1944 (Burma Star, 1985); subseq. Big Show (radio), USA; London Laughs, Adelphi; appeared at Flamingo Hotel, Las Vegas, and many TV shows, USA and Britain, including own TV series on Rediffusion, 1955; BBC TV, 1956; BBC 2, 1970; also appearances in Holland, Denmark, Sweden, Norway, Germany, Canada, NZ and Australia; in seven Command Performances, also films and own shows on radio. 14 Gold Records; records include Auf Wiederseh'n (over 12 million copies sold), became first British artiste to top American Hit Parade. Pres., Printers' Charitable Corp., 1980. Internat. Ambassador, Variety Club Internat., 1985. Founder and Pres., Dame Vera Lynn Trust for Children with Cerebral Palsy, 2001–. Hon. Citizen: Winnipeg, 1974; Nashville, Tennessee, 1977.

Freedom: City of London, 1978; City of Corner Brook, Newfoundland, 1981. FInstD. Fellow, Univ. (formerly Poly.) of E London, 1990. Hon. LLD Memorial Univ. of Newfoundland, 1977 (founded Lynn Music Scholarship, first award, 1982); Hon. MMus London, 1992. Show Business Personality of the Year, Grand Order of Water Rats, 1973; Music Publishers' Award, 1975; Ivor Novello Award, 1975; Humanitarian Award, Variety Club Internat., 1985; BBC TV Woman of the Year, 1994; Lillian K. Keil Award for outstanding service by a woman during World War II, 2005; Women of the Year Lifetime Achievement Award, 2009; Nordoff Robbins Icon of the Century Award, 2010; Classic BRIT Lifetime Achievement Award, 2018. Dutch War Veteran Medal, 2010. Comdr, Order of Orange-Nassau, Holland. *Publications*: Vocal Refrain (autobiog.), 1975; (jtly) We'll Meet Again, 1989; Unsung Heroines, 1990; Some Sunny Day: my autobiography, 2009; (jtly) Keep Smiling Through: my wartime story, 2017. *Recreations*: gardening, painting, sewing, swimming.

**LYNNE, Elizabeth, (Liz)**; Member (Lib Dem) West Midlands Region, European Parliament, 1999–Feb. 2012; *b* 22 Jan. 1948. *Educ*: Dorking Co. Grammar Sch. Actress, 1966–89; numerous theatre appearances in repertory and West End, and television, film and radio roles. Speech consultant, 1989–92 and 1997–99. Contested (L) Harwich, 1987. MP (Lib Dem) Rochdale, 1992–97; contested (Lib Dem) same seat, 1997. Lib Dem spokesperson: on health and community care, 1992–94; on social security and disability, 1994–97. Vice-Pres., Eur. Employment and Social Affairs Cttee, EP, 2004–12. Mem. Bd, EEF, 2012–15. Mem., Lib Dem Federal Conf. Cttee, 2012–; Pres., Mid-Worcs Lib Dems, 2013–; Vice-Pres., Lib Dem Women, 2014–. *Recreation*: tennis.

**LYNTON, Michael Mark;** Chairman, Snap Inc., since 2017; *b* London, 1 Jan. 1960; *s* of Mark O. L. Lynton and Marion Lynton; *m* 1994, Elizabeth Jamie Alter; three *d*. *Educ*: Harvard Coll. (BA 1982); Harvard Business Sch. (MBA 1987). Associate, First Boston Corp., 1982–87; Pres., Disney Publg, 1987–92, Hollywood Pictures, 1992–96, Walt Disney Co.; Chm. and CEO, Penguin Gp, 1996–2000; Pres., America Online Internat., 2000–03; CEO, AOL Europe, 2001–02; Pres., Internat., AOL Time Warner, subseq. Time Warner, 2002–03; Chm. and Chief Exec., Sony Pictures Entertainment, 2004–17; CEO, Sony Entertainment, 2012–17. Ind. Dir, Pearson, 2018–. Trustee, Tate, 2017–. *Recreations*: tennis, ski-ing. *Address*: Snap Inc., 2772 Donald Douglas Loop North, Santa Monica, CA 90405, USA.

**LYON;** *see* Bowes Lyon.

**LYON, Christina Margaret; Her Honour Judge Lyon;** a Circuit Judge, since 2007; *b* 12 Nov. 1952; *d* of Edward Arthur Harrison and Kathleen Joan Harrison; *m* 1976, His Honour Adrian Pirrie Lyon (*d* 2017); one *s* one *d*. *Educ*: Wallasey High Sch. for Girls; University Coll. London. LLB (1st Cl. Hons) 1974; admitted Solicitor, 1977. Tutor and sometime Lectr in Law, University Coll. London, 1974–75; Trainee and Asst Solicitor, Bell & Joynson, 1975–77; Liverpool University: part-time Tutor in Law, 1976–77; Lectr in Law, 1977–80; Manchester University: Lectr in Law and Law and Social Work, 1980–86; Sub-Dean, Law Faculty, 1986; Prof. of Law, Head of Dept and of Sch. of Law, Keele Univ., 1987–93; Liverpool University: Prof. of Common Law, 1993–98; Head, Dept of Law, 1993–97; Dean, Faculty of Law, 1994–97; Dir, Centre for the Study of the Child, the Family and the Law, 1995–2007; Queen Victoria Prof. of Law, 1998–2007, now Emeritus. Asst Recorder, 1998–2000; Recorder, 1999–2007. Member: ESRC Res. Grants Bd, 1988–91; Child Policy Review Gp, Nat. Children's Bureau, 1989–; Chm., Independent Representation for Children in Need, 1991–; Member: Nat. Exec. Cttee and Fundraising Cttee, Relate, 1990–94 (Pres., N Staffs Relate, 1987–93); Merseyside Panels of Guardians *ad Litem*, 1993–2002 (Vice-Chm., 1993–97); Child Protection and Family Justice Cttee, Nuffield Foundn, 1994–. Dr Barnardo's Research Fellow, 1987–92. Advisory Editor, Jl of Social Welfare and Family Law (formerly Jl of Social Welfare Law) (Jt Ed., 1984); Mem. Editl Bd, Representing Children, 1996–. FRSA 1991. *Publications*: Matrimonial Jurisdiction of Magistrates' Courts, 1981; Cohabitation without Marriage, 1983; (ed) Butterworth's Family Law Service Encyclopaedia, 1983, rev. edn 2006; Law of Residential Homes and Day Care Establishments, 1984; (ed) Child Abuse, 1990, 3rd edn 2003; The Law Relating to Children in Principles and Practice of Forensic Psychiatry, 1990; (ed with A. P. Lyon) Butterworth's Family Law Handbook, 1991; Atkins Court Forms on Infants, vols I and II, 1992; The Law Relating to Children, 1993; Legal Issues Arising from the Care and Control of Children with Learning Disabilities who also Present Severely Challenging Behaviour, vol. I, Policy Guidance, vol. II, A Guide for Parents and Carers, 1994; Child Protection and the Civil Legal Framework in The Child Protection Handbook, 1995; Children's Rights and The Children Act 1989 in Children's Rights, 1995; Working Together: an analysis of collaborative inter-agency responses to the problem of domestic violence, 1995; Law and Body Politics, 1995; (jtly) Effective Support Services for Children, 1998; (jtly) A Trajectory of Hope, 2000; Loving Smack, Lawful Assault: a contradiction in human rights and law, 2000. *Recreations*: riding, swimming, foreign travel, reading, theatre, opera.

**LYON, Rt Hon. Clare;** *see* Short, Rt Hon. C.

**LYON, Dr (Colin) Stewart (Sinclair),** FIA; FSA, FRNS; General Manager (Finance), Group Actuary and Director, Legal & General Group Plc, 1980–87; *b* 22 Nov. 1926; *s* of late Col Colin Sinclair Lyon, OBE, TD and Mrs Dorothy Winstanley Lyon (*née* Thomason); *m* 1958, Elizabeth Mary Fargus Richards; four *s* one *d*. *Educ*: Liverpool Coll.; Trinity Coll., Cambridge (MA; PhD 2004). FIA 1954; FSA 1972; FRNS 1955. Chief Exec., Victory Insurance Co. Ltd, 1974–76; Chief Actuary, Legal & General Assurance Soc. Ltd, 1976–85. Director: Lautro Ltd, 1987–92; Cologne Reinsurance Co. Ltd, 1987–97; City of Birmingham Touring Opera Ltd, 1987–90; Ætna Internat. (UK) Ltd, 1988–91; Pearl Gp PLC, 1991–97; UK Bd, AMP and London Life, 1991–97. Member: Occupational Pensions Bd, 1979–82; Inquiry into Provision for Retirement, 1983–85; Treasure Trove Reviewing Cttee, 1986–93. President: Inst. of Actuaries, 1982–84 (Gold Medal, 1991); British Numismatic Soc., 1966–70 (Vice-Pres., 1976–2008 and 2010–; Sanford Saltus Gold Medal, 1974). Trustee, Disablement Income Gp Charitable Trust, 1967–84; Dir, Disablement Income Gp, 1984–94 (Vice-Pres., 1995–2002); Trustee, Independent Living Fund, 1988–93. *Publications*: (with C. E. Blunt and B. H. I. H. Stewart) Coinage in Tenth-Century England, 1989; Sylloge of Coins of the British Isles 68: the Lyon collection of Anglo-Saxon coins, 2016; papers on Anglo-Saxon coinage, particularly in British Numismatic Jl; contrib. Jl of Inst. of Actuaries and Trans Internat. Congress of Actuaries. *Recreations*: numismatics, music, amateur radio (call sign GW3EIZ). *Address*: Ardraeth, Malltraeth, Bodorgan, Anglesey LL62 5AW. *T*: (01407) 840273. *Club*: Actuaries'.

**LYON, David;** *see* Lyon, J. D. R.

**LYON, George;** Senior Consultant, Hume Brophy, since 2015; *b* 16 July 1956; *s* of Alister and Mary Lyon; *m* (marr. diss.); three *d*. *Educ*: Rothesay Acad. Family business, farming, A. H. Lyon, 1972–94, A. K. Farms, 1994–2010, Isle of Bute. Mem., NFU Scotland, 1990– (Pres., 1997–99). Mem. (Lib Dem) Argyll and Bute, Scottish Parlt, 1999–2007. Dep. Minister for Parly Business and for Finance and Public Services Reform, Scottish Exec., 2005–07. MEP (Lib Dem) Scotland, 2009–14; contested (Lib Dem) same seat, 2014. Dir, Agricl and Horticultural Develt Bd, 2015–. FRAgS 2000. *Recreations*: football, reading, cycling. *Club*: Farmers.

**LYON, (John) David (Richard),** MBE 2009; Chief Executive, Rexam plc (formerly Bowater Industries, then Bowater plc), 1987–96; *b* 4 June 1936; *s* of John F. A. Lyon and Elizabeth Lyon (*née* Owen); *m* 1st, 1960, Nicola M. E. Bland (marr. diss. 1986); two *s* (and one *s* decd); 2nd, 1987, Lillis Lanphier. *Educ*: Wellington College; Magdalen College, Oxford (BA Modern History 1959); Harvard Business Sch. (Advanced Management Programme, 1973). 1st Bn The Rifle Brigade, Kenya and Malaya, 1954–56 (despatches). Courtaulds, 1959–70; Rank Organisation, 1970–71; Redland, 1971–87 (Dir, 1976; Man. Dir, 1982); Dir, Smiths Industries, 1991–94. Chm., Stocks Austin Sice, 1997–2002. Mem., Adv. Cttee on Business and the Envmt, 1991–93. Col Comdt, SAS Regt, 1994–2000. Non-executive Member: Field Army Command Gp, 2003–11; Land Forces Command Gp, 2011–12. Trustee, Army Museums Ogilby Trust, 1998–2011. Royal Geographical Society: Hon. Treas., 2002–08; Hon. Fellow, 2012. *Recreations*: blacksmithing, woodworking, gardening. *Address*: Oak Tree House, Church Street, Amberley, W Sussex BN18 9ND.

**LYON, John MacDonald,** CB 2003; Director, Strategy and Implementation, Woolf Institute, Cambridge, 2015–18; Parliamentary Commissioner for Standards, 2008–12; *b* 12 April 1948; *m* Juliet Christine Southall (*see* J. C. Lyon); one *s* one *d*. *Educ*: Selwyn Coll., Cambridge (BA, MA). Home Office, 1969; Principal, 1974; Asst Sec., 1982; Grade 3, 1991; Director General: Police Policy, 1999; Policing and Crime Reduction Gp, 2000–03; Legal and Judicial Services Gp and Sec. of Commns, LCD, later DCA, then MoJ, 2003–07. Lay Mem., Bar Tribunals and Adjudication Service, 2013–. Mem. Council, Nat. Trust, 2013– (Chm. Nominations Cttees for Council Elections, 2014, for Trustee appts, 2015–18). Sen. Mem., St Edmund's Coll., Cambridge, 2016–. Expert advr, parly standards, OSCE, 2013. Trustee, Somerset Community Foundn, 2016–. FRSA 2000.

**LYON, Juliet Christine,** CBE 2009; Director, Prison Reform Trust, 2000–16; Chair, Independent Advisory Panel on Deaths in Custody, since 2016; *b* 8 April 1950; *d* of Christopher Redhead Southall and Jewel Eugenie Carr; *m* 1986, John MacDonald Lyon, *qv*; one *s* one *d*. *Educ*: Univ. of Exeter (BA Comb. Hons 1971); Univ. of London (MA Rights Dist.); Tavistock Inst. of Human Relns. Head: Adolescent Unit Sch., Exevale Hosp., 1973–76; Community Educn, Court Fields Sch., Somerset, 1976–79; Regl Manager, Richmond Fellowship Therapeutic Communities, 1980–90; Associate Dir, Trust for Study of Adolescence, 1990–99. Hon. Res. Fellow, QUB, 1994–99. Justice in Wales Comr, 2017–19. Vis. Prof., Sch. of Law, Birkbeck, Univ. of London, 2016–. Social Exclusion Unit Advr, 2001–02. Professional Advr, Childline, 1993–2003. Trustee: Children's Express, 1997–2000; Hadley Trust, 2019–; AB Charitable Trust, 2019–; Mem. Council, Winston Churchill Meml Trust, 2016–. Sec. Gen., Penal Reform Internat., 2007–16; Women's Nat. Comr, 2008–10. Vice-Pres., British Assoc. of Counselling and Psychotherapy, 2009–. Part-time columnist and broadcaster, 2000–. *Publications*: Tell Them So They Listen: messages from young people in custody, 2000; jl articles and chapters. *Recreations*: gardening, theatre, bee-keeping. *E*: juliet.lyon@bbk.ac.uk.

**LYON, Maj.-Gen. Robert,** CB 1976; OBE 1964 (MBE 1960); Bursar, Loretto School, Musselburgh, 1979–91; *b* Ayr, 24 Oct. 1923; *s* of David Murray Lyon and Bridget Lyon (*née* Smith); *m* 1st, 1951, Constance Margaret Gordon (*d* 1982); one *s* one *d*; 2nd, 1992, Rosemary Jane (*d* 2019), *d* of G. H. Allchin, Torquay. *Educ*: Ayr Academy. Commissioned, Aug. 1943, Argyll and Sutherland Highlanders. Served Italy, Germany, Palestine, Greece; transf. to Regular Commn in RA, 1947; Regtl Service, 3 RHA in Libya and 19 Field in BAOR, 1948–56; Instr, Mons Officer Cadet Sch., 1953–55; Staff Coll., 1957; DAQMG, 3 Div., 1958–60; jssc, 1960; BC F (Sphinx) Batt. 7 PARA, RHA, 1961–62 (Bt Lt-Col); GSO1, ASD2, MoD, 1962–65 (Lt-Col); CO 4 Lt Regt, RA, 1965–67, Borneo (despatches), UK and BAOR (Lt-Col); as Brig.: CRA 1 Div., 1967–69, BAOR; IDC, 1970; Dir Operational Requirements, MoD, 1971–73; DRA (Maj.-Gen.), 1973–75; GOC SW District, 1975–78; retired 1979. Pres., Army Hockey Assoc., 1974–76; Chm., Army Golf Assoc., 1977–78. Chm., RA Council of Scotland, 1984–90. Col Comdt RA. Director: Braemar Civic Amenities Trust, 1986–90; Edinburgh Military Tattoo Ltd, 1988–98; Financial Forum, 1996–2000. Regl Dir Scotland, Manufacturing Forum, 1994–2000. HM Comr, Queen Victoria Sch., Dunblane, 1984–95. Pres., La Punta Urbanisation, Los Cristianos, 1995–98. FCMI 1982 (MBIM 1978). *Publications*: Irish Roulette, 1991. *Recreations*: golf, writing, gardening. *Address*: Woodside, Braemar, Aberdeenshire AB35 5YT. *T*: and *Fax*: (013397) 41667. *E*: RandRLyon@btinternet.com.

**LYON, Stewart;** *see* Lyon, C. S. S.

**LYON-DALBERG-ACTON,** family name of **Baron Acton**.

**LYON-DALBERG-ACTON, Edward David Joseph;** *see* Acton, E. D. J. L.-D.

**LYONS, Maj.-Gen. Adrian William,** CBE 1994; Director General, Railway Forum, 2001–06; *b* 26 Dec. 1946; *s* of late Gp Capt. W. M. Lyons and M. P. Lyons (*née* Willis); *m* 1993, Rosemary Ann Farrer (marr. diss. 2017); one *d*. *Educ*: Merchant Taylors' Sch. Commnd RCT, 1966, transf. RAOC, 1972; various logistic mgt and planning appts, largely MoD based, 1977–94; psc 1980, jsdc 1986, rcds 1995; Dep. UK Mil. Rep., Brussels, 1996–98; Dir Gen. Logistic Support (Army), then Defence Logistic Support, MoD, 1998–2000. Col Comdt RLC, 2000–06; Hon. Col 168 Pioneer Regt RLC(V), 2001–07. Dir, Armed Forces Common Investment Fund, 2015–. Member: Railway Safety Adv. Bd, 2001–06; Strategy and Policy Steering Cttee, BSI, 2005–13; Adv. Bd, Railway Heritage Trust, 2011–. Chairman: Hong Kong Locally Enlisted Personnel Trust, 1998–2001; Lady Grover's Fund, 2007–18; Drapers' Acad., 2009–13. Librettist for opera, Reluctant Highwayman, music by Sir Nicholas Jackson, Bt, first performed Broomhill Fest., 1995. Master, Drapers' Co., 2010–11; Liveryman, Carmen's Co., 1998–. Chm. of Govs, Bancroft's Sch., 2003–08. Pres., Rail Study Assoc., 2004–05. Trustee, RLC Assoc., 2012–. Pres., RAOC Officers' Club, 2012–. Hon. Fellow, QMUL, 2012. *Recreations*: theatre, travel, collecting (almost) anything that makes the past come alive, esp. coins (FRNS; Council Mem., British Numismatic Soc., 2005–08, 2009–12). *Address*: 52 Mandarin Drive, Newbury, Berks RG14 7WE. *T*: (01635) 36072. *Club*: Cavalry and Guards.

**LYONS, Alastair David,** CBE 2001; non-executive Chairman: Dwr Cymru (Welsh Water), since 2016; Harworth Group, since 2018; Vitality Health, since 2018; Admiral Europe, since 2018; *b* 18 Oct. 1953; *o s* of late Alexander Lyons and of Elizabeth (*née* Eynon); *m* 1980, Judith Shauneen Rhodes; one *s* two *d*. *Educ*: Whitgift Sch.; Trinity Coll., Cambridge (Sen. Schol.; MA 2nd Cl. Hons). With Price Waterhouse & Co., 1974–79; N. M. Rothschild & Sons Ltd, 1979; H. P. Bulmer Holdings PLC, 1979–89: Gp Treas. 1979–82; Gp Financial Controller, 1983–88; Actg Gp Finance Dir, and Finance Dir, H. P. Bulmer Drinks Ltd, 1988–89; Divl Dir, Corporate Finance, Asda Gp PLC, 1989–90; Finance Dir, ASDA Stores Ltd, 1990–91; Finance Dir, 1991–94, Chief Exec., 1994–96, Nat. & Provincial Building Soc.; Man. Dir, Insurance, and Exec. Dir, Abbey National plc, 1996–97; Chief Exec., NPI, 1997–99; Dir of Corporate Projs, Nat. Westminster Gp, 1999–2000. Non-executive Chairman: Admiral Gp plc, 2000–17; Legal Mktg Services Ltd, 2002–17; In Retirement Services Ltd, 2003–09; Equity Release Services Ltd, 2003–09; Health & Case Mgt Ltd, 2003–08; Buy-as-you-View Ltd, 2004–07; Higham Gp plc, 2005–07; Cardsave Ltd, 2007–10; Serco Gp plc, 2010–15; Towergate Insce Gp, 2011–15; Dep. Chm., Bovis Homes Gp plc, 2008–18; Sen. Ind. Dir, Phoenix Gp plc, 2010–13; non-executive Director: Wishstream Ltd, 2001–02; Sesame Group Ltd, 2003–04. Non-executive Director: Benefits Agency, 1994–97; DSS, 1997–2001; DWP, 2001–02; DFT, 2002–05. Mem., Yorks Regl Cttee, NT, 1994–96. Gov., Giggleswick Sch., 1994–97. *Recreations:* cycling, hill walking, ski-ing, collecting antiques.

**LYONS, Claire;** *see* Hanna, C.

**LYONS, Dr Gerard Patrick;** independent economist, author and public speaker; *b* London, 31 March 1961; *s* of Francis Joseph Lyons and Anne Lyons (*née* Moran); *m* 1990, Annette Lambert; one *s* two *d*. *Educ:* St Mary's Primary Sch., Kilburn; Cardinal Vaughan Sch., Kensington; Univ. of Liverpool (BA Econs 1982); Univ. of Warwick (MA Econs 1983); Univ. of London (PhD Econs 1985). Registered Rep. of Stock Exchange 1987. Economist, Chase Manhattan Bank, 1985–86; Chief UK Economist: Savory Milln Stockbrokers, 1986–87; Swiss Bank Corp., 1987–89; Chief Economist and Exec. Dir, DKB Internat., 1989–99; Chief Economist, Gp Hd of Global Res. and Econ. Advr, Bd of Standard Chartered Bank, 1999–2012; Chief Econ. Advr to Mayor of London, 2013–16; Econ. Advr, Parker Fitzgerald, 2015–; Chief Econ. Strategist, Netwealth Investments, 2016–. Dir, CityUK, 2015–16 (Chair, Ind. Economists Gp, 2012); Ind. non-exec. Dir, Bank of China (UK), 2016–. Chief Economic Adviser: Policy Exchange, 2016–17; Centre for Social Justice, 2016–18 (Mem., Cttee on UK Productivity, 2016–17; Sen. Econ. Advr, Report on the Future of Work, 2018). Mem., Commn on £ Sterling, 1999 (Co-author of Report, Britain and the Pound). Member: Global Agenda Council on Banking and Capital Mkts, 2009–14, on Global Investment Flows, 2009–10, on Financing and Capital, 2013–14, WEF; Expert Cttee, Annual Financial Develt Report, WEF, 2010–13; Taskforce on Gold and the Internat. Monetary System, Chatham House, 2011–12; Informal Network of China Experts, EC, 2011–13; Adv. Council, Official Monetary and Financial Instns Forum, 2012–; Adv. Bd, Open Europe, 2012–; Internat. Adv. Bd, ANA Airways, 2014–15; Adviser: Business Council for Britain, 2007–08; Vivid Economics, 2016–. Ex-officio Mem., London Finance Commn, 2012–13. Comr, London Stansted Cambridge Growth Commn, 2015–16. Co-founder, Economists for Brexit, 2016. Co-Chair, UK-Hong Kong Business Partnership, 2006; Vice-Chm., 48 Gp Club, 2009–. Chm., Steering Cttee, Asia Study at RIIA, 2002–05; Member: Council, Warwick Univ., 2006–12; Adv. Bd, Grantham Inst., LSE and Imperial Coll. London, 2008–; Adv. Bd, Warwick Univ. Business Sch., 2014–; Exec. Dir, Centre for Econ. Policy Res. Member, Council: REconS, 2010–15; RSAA, 2015–. Mem. Cttee, Hong Kong Assoc., 2007–. Fellow, Soc. of Business Economists, 2010. FRSA. Trustee, Benenden Sch., 2004–15. *Publications:* The Consolations of Economics, 2014; The EU Referendum: how to make a success of leaving the European Union, 2017; (with Liam Halligan) Clean Brexit: how to make a success of leaving the European Union, 2017; academic papers, econ. reports for internat. banks, contribs on econ., monetary and financial issues to books, newspapers, etc. *Recreations:* being with the family, watching Fulham FC, ballet, travel, reading, watching stand-up comedy, public speaking, giving talks about economic affairs to students, walking. *Address:* Netwealth Investments Ltd, 60 Charlotte Street, W1T 2NU. *E:* drgerardlyons@yahoo.com. *W:* www.twitter.com/DrGerardLyons.

**LYONS, Sir John,** Kt 1987; FBA 1973; Master of Trinity Hall, Cambridge, 1984–2000; *b* 23 May 1932; *s* of Michael A. Lyons and Mary B. Lyons (*née* Sullivan); *m* 1959, Danielle J. Simonet; two *d*. *Educ:* St Bede's Coll., Manchester; Christ's Coll., Cambridge. MA; PhD 1961; LittD 1988. Lecturer in Comparative Linguistics, SOAS, 1957–61; in General Linguistics, Univ. of Cambridge, 1961–64; Prof. of General Linguistics, Edinburgh Univ., 1964–76; Prof. of Linguistics, 1976–84, Pro-Vice-Chancellor, 1981–84, Sussex Univ. DèsL (*hc*): Univ. Catholique de Louvain, 1980; Toulouse, 2009; Hon. DLitt: Reading, 1986; Edinburgh, 1988; Sussex, 1990; Antwerp, 1992. *Publications:* Structural Semantics, 1964; Introduction to Theoretical Linguistics, 1968; New Horizons in Linguistics, 1970; Chomsky, 1970, 3rd edn 1991; Semantics, vols 1 and 2, 1977; Language and Linguistics, 1981; Language, Meaning and Context, 1981, 2nd edn 1991; Natural Language and Universal Grammar, 1991; Linguistic Semantics, 1995; articles and reviews in learned journals.

**LYONS, John;** *b* 11 July 1949; one *s* one *d*. *Educ:* Woodside Secondary Sch.; Stirling Univ. (MSc 2000). Mechanical engr, 1971–88; Officer UNISON, 1988–2001. MP (Lab) Strathkelvin and Bearsden, 2001–05. Mem., Forth Valley Health Bd, 1999–2001.

**LYONS, Prof. Malcolm Cameron;** Sir Thomas Adams's Professor of Arabic, University of Cambridge, 1985–96; Fellow, Pembroke College, Cambridge, since 1957 (President, 1989–93); *b* Indiana, 11 Feb. 1929; *s* of Harold William Lyons and Florence Katharine (*née* Cameron); *m* 1961, Ursula Schedler. *Educ:* Fettes Coll.; Pembroke Coll., Cambridge (Major Open Classical Schol., 1946; John Stewart of Rannoch Classical Schol. in Latin and Greek, 1948; Browne Medallist, 1948; 1st cl. hons Pts I and II, Classical Tripos, 1948, 1949; 1st cl. hons Pts I and II, Oriental Studies, Arabic and Persian, 1953; E. G. Browne Prize, 1953; MA 1954; PhD 1957; LittD 1997). RAF, 1949–51, commissioned 1950. University of Cambridge: Asst Lectr in Arabic, 1954–59; Lectr, 1959–84; Reader in Medieval Islamic Studies, 1984–85. Seconded to FO as Principal Instructor, MECAS, Lebanon, 1961–62. Founder Editor: Arabic Technical and Scientific Texts, 1966–78; Jl of Arabic Literature, 1970–. *Publications:* Galen on Anatomical Procedures (with W. Duckworth and B. Towers), 1962; In Hippocratis de Officina Medici, 1963, and De Partibus Artis Medicativae, De Causis Contentivis, De Diaeta in Morbis Acutis (in Corpus Medicorum Graecorum), 1967; An Arabic Translation of Themistius' Commentary on Aristotle's De Anima, 1973; Aristotle's Ars Rhetorica, Arabic version, 1982; (with E. Maalouf) The Poetic Vocabulary of Michel Trad, 1968; (with J. Riley-Smith and U. Lyons) Ayyubids, Mamlukes and Crusaders, 1971; (with D. Jackson) Saladin, The Politics of the Holy War, 1982; (jtly) Meredith Dewey: diaries, letters, writings, 1992; The Arabian Epic, 1995; Identification and Identity in Classical Arabic Poetry, 1999; (with U. Lyons) The Thousand and One Nights: a new translation, 2008; The Man of Wiles in Popular Arabic Literature, 2012; Tales of the Marvellous and News of the Strange: a translation, 2014; articles and reviews in learned jls. *Recreation:* golf. *Address:* Pembroke College, Cambridge CB1 2RF. *Club:* Royal and Ancient Golf (St Andrews).

**LYONS, Sir Michael (Thomas),** Kt 2000; Chairman: English Cities Fund, since 2002; SQW Ltd, since 2013 (Director, since 2007); consultant and adviser; *b* West Ham, 15 Sept. 1949; *s* of Thomas Lyons and Lilly Lyons (*née* Stafford); *m* 1976, Gwendolene Jane Calvert; two *s* one *d*. *Educ:* Stratford Grammar Sch.; Middlesex Polytechnic (BA Soc. Scis Hons); Queen Mary Coll., London (MSc Econ; Hon. Fellow, 2003). Street market trader, 1970–72; Brand Manager, Crookes-Anestan, 1971–72; Lectr in Econs, Walbrook Coll., London, 1972–73; Lectr and Res. Fellow, Dept of Industrial Econs, Univ. of Nottingham, 1973–75; Sen. Res. Officer, DoE, 1975–78; W Midlands County Council: Principal Economist, 1978–82; Dep. Dir and Dir, Economic Develt, 1982–85; Chief Executive: Wolverhampton MBC, 1985–90; Notts CC, 1990–94; Birmingham CC, 1994–2001. Birmingham University: Dir, Inst. of Local Govt Studies, 2001–06; Prof. of Public Policy, 2001–06; Hon. Prof., 1999–. Sec., W Midlands Regl Chamber, 1998–2001. Councillor, Birmingham City Council, 1980–83. Non-executive Director: Mouchel (formerly Parkman) plc, 2001–12; Wragge & Co., 2001–13; ITV (Central Ind. Television), 2002–06; Redrow, 2015–; Sage Housing, 2018–19. Chairman: BBC Trust, 2007–11; Tindal Street Press, 2010–13; Participle Ltd, 2010–13; YourTV Ltd, 2012–14; Sage Partnerships, 2018–.

Mem., Public Services Productivity Panel, HM Treasury, 2000–07; Dep. Chm., 2003–05, Acting Chm., 2005–06, Audit Commn. Strategic Advr, CBRE, 2011–. Mem., Ind. Review of the Fire Service, 2002; conducted: Ind. Review of Public Sector Relocation, 2004 (report, 2004); Ind. Review of Mgt of Public Assets, 2004 (report, 2004); Ind. Review of Council Tax and the Funding of Local Govt, later Lyons Inquiry into Local Govt, 2005–07 (final report, 2007); Lyons Housing Review for Lab. Party, 2013–14 (report, 2014); Chm., Cardiff CC Corporate Governance Commn, 2004. Chm., CBSO, 2001–07; Gov., RSC, 1999–2005, 2006–. Vice Chair, Lunar Soc., 2017–. FRSA. Hon. Dr: Middlesex, 1997; UCE, 2001; Wolverhampton, 2004; Birmingham, 2009. *Publications:* (ed with A. Johnson) The Winning Bid, 1992; (with Sir Ian Byatt) The Role of External Review in Improving Performance, 2001; (ed jtly and contrib.) What More Can be Done to Build the Homes We Need, 2017; contribs to professional jls. *Recreations:* music, theatre, cinema, walking. *Address:* 48 Hartopp Road, Four Oaks, Sutton Coldfield B74 2QR. *E:* m.t.lyons@btconnect.com.

**LYONS, Roger Alan;** Joint General Secretary, Amicus, 2002–04; consultant on business services and public policy, since 2005; *b* 14 Sept. 1942; *s* of late Morris and Phyllis Lyons; *m* 1971, Kitty Horvath; two *s* two *d*. *Educ:* Roe Green Junior Sch., Kingsbury; Christ's Coll., Finchley; University Coll. London (BSc Hons Econ.; Fellow, 1996). Voter Organiser, Mississippi Civil Rights Project, 1965. Regional Officer, ASSET, then ASTMS, 1966–70; Nat. Officer 1970–87, Asst Gen. Sec. 1987–89, ASTMS; Asst Gen. Sec., 1989–92, Gen. Sec., 1992–2002, MSF; MSF merged with AEEU to form Amicus, 2002. Exec., European Metalworker Fedn, 1987–2004; Mem., Gen. Council, 1990–2004, Pres. 2003–04, TUC. Member: Central Arbitration Cttee, 2002–13; Employment Appeal Tribunal, 2003–12. Advr, Anti-Apartheid Movt, 1964–. EU Observer, first free S African elections, 1994. Mem., Design Council, 1998–2004. Mem., Council, UCL, 1997–2005. Patron: Envmtl Industries Commn, 2000–; Burma Campaign, 2003–. Chm., Trade Union Friends of Israel, 2004–14. *Recreations:* family, take-aways, cinema, football (Arsenal in particular). *Address:* 22 Park Crescent, N3 2NJ. *T:* (020) 8346 6843, 07768 737475. *E:* rogerlyons22@hotmail.com.

**LYONS, His Honour Shaun,** CBE 2004; a Circuit Judge, 1992–2015; a Senior Circuit Judge, 2002–15; Resident Judge, Wood Green Crown Court, 1995–2015; *b* 20 Dec. 1942; *s* of late Jeremiah Lyons and of Winifred Ruth Lyons; *m* 1970, Nicola Rosemary, *d* of late Capt. D. F. Chilton, DSO, RN; one *s* one *d*. *Educ:* Portsmouth Grammar Sch.; Inns of Court Sch. of Law. Joined RN, 1961; Lt 1966; Lt Comdr 1974; called to the Bar, Middle Temple, 1975, Bencher, 2008; Comdr 1981; Captain 1988; Chief Naval Judge Advocate, 1989–92; retd RN, 1992. Asst Recorder and Recorder, 1988–92. Mem., Parole Bd, 2010–17. Chm., Middx Adv. Cttee for Magistrates, 2004–07 (Dep. Chm., 1996–2004). *Clubs:* Army and Navy; Royal Yacht Squadron.

**LYONS, Stuart Randolph,** CBE 1993; Chairman: Airsprung Group (formerly Airsprung Furniture Group) plc, 2005–17; J. E. Beale plc, 2015–17 (Director, 2013); *b* 24 Oct. 1943; 3rd *s* of late Bernard Lyons, CBE and Lucy Lyons; *m* 1969, Ellen Harriet Zion; two *s* one *d*. *Educ:* Rugby; King's Coll., Cambridge (Major Scholar, Classics; Fellow Commoner, 2014); Wharton Sch., Univ. of Pennsylvania (AMP 1991); Open Univ. (LLB Hons 2014). Man. Dir, John Collier Tailoring Ltd, 1969–74 (Chm., 1975–83); Dir, UDS Group plc, 1974–83 (Man. Dir, 1979–83); Chm., Colmore Trust Ltd, 1984–; Chief Exec., Royal Doulton plc, 1985–97 (Chm., 1987–93); Director: British Ceramic Res. Ltd, 1987–94; Hogg Robinson plc, 1998–2000; Aurora Computer Services Ltd, 1999–2003; Chairman: Gartmore Absolute Growth & Income Trust plc, 2004–06 (Dir, 2000–06); The Wensum Co. plc, 2003–09 (Dir, 2001–09). Member: Leeds CC, 1970–74; Yorkshire and Humberside Econ. Planning Council, 1971–75; Clothing EDC, 1976–79; Ordnance Survey Review Cttee, 1978–79; Monopolies and Mergers Commn, 1981–85; Council, CBI, 1991–96; Nat. Manufacturing Council, 1992–95; Dir, Staffs TEC, 1990–93. Pres., BCMF, 1989–90; Chairman: British Ceramic Confedn, 1989–95; Staffs Develt Assoc., 1992–95; DTI Tableware Strategy Group, 1994–96; W Midlands Develt Agency, 1995–99; Vice-Chm., Industry 96 (W Midlands Fest. of Industry and Enterprise), 1994–96. Mem. Council, Keele Univ., 1989–97; Gov., Staffs Univ. (formerly Staffs Poly.), 1991–97; Chm., Develt Bd, King's Coll., Cambridge, 2010–13. Mem., Vice-Chancellor's Circle, Univ. of Cambridge, 2014. Contested (C) Halifax, Feb. and Oct. 1974. Chief Policy Advr to Shadow Sec. of State for Trade and Industry, then Health and Educn, subseq. Transport and the Envmt, 2003–05. Hon. DLitt Keele, 1994. *Publications:* The Fleeting Years: Odes of Horace, 1996; Can Consignia Deliver?, 2001; A Department for Business, 2001; Harnessing our Genius, 2003; Horace's Odes and the Mystery of Do-Re-Mi, 2007; Music in the Odes of Horace, 2010; contrib. articles to classical and industrial jls. *Address:* 50 Seymour Walk, SW10 9NF. *T:* (020) 7352 3309. *E:* stuartlyons.cbe@gmail.com. *Club:* Hurlingham.

**LYONS, Prof. Terence John,** DPhil; FRS 2002; FRSE; FLSW; Wallis Professor of Mathematics, University of Oxford, since 2000; Fellow, St Anne's College, Oxford, since 2000; Director, Oxford-Man Institute of Quantitative Finance, 2011–15; *b* 4 May 1953; *s* of late Peter Lyons and Valerie (*née* Hardie); *m* 1975, Barbara, *d* of late Joseph and Barbara Epsom; *m*; one *s* one *d*. *Educ:* St Joseph's Coll., W Norwood; Trinity Coll., Cambridge (BA Maths 1975 and 1976); Christ Church, Oxford (DPhil 1980). FRSE 1988. Jun. Res. Fellow, Jesus Coll., Oxford, 1979–81; Lectr in Maths, Imperial Coll., London, 1981–85; Colin Maclaurin Prof. of Maths, 1985–93, Hd, Dept of Maths and Stats, 1988–91, Univ. of Edinburgh; Prof. of Maths, Imperial Coll., London, 1993–2000; Dir, Wales Inst. of Mathematical and Computational Scis, 2007–10. Hendrick Vis. Asst Prof., UCLA, 1981–82; Visiting Professor: Univ. of BC, 1990; Univs of Paris VI and XI; Univ. of Toulouse; Inst. des Hautes Etudes Scientifiques. Sen. Fellow, EPSRC, 1993–98. Vice Pres., 2000–02, Pres., 2013–15, LMS. FIMS 2005; FLSW 2011. Hon. Fellow: Aberystwyth Univ., 2010; Cardiff Univ., 2012. Dr *hc* Univ. Paul Sabatier, France, 2007. Rollo Davidson Prize, 1985, Jun. Whitehead Prize, 1986, Polya Prize, 2000, LMS; Humboldt Res. Award, Humboldt Foundn, 2015. *Recreations:* reading, cycling, computer programming, family life. *Address:* c/o Petrona Winton, Mathematical Institute, Andrew Wiles Building, Radcliffe Observatory Quarter, Woodstock Road, Oxford OX2 6GG. *T:* (01865) 611500; Oxford-Man Institute of Quantitative Finance, Eagle House, Walton Well Road, Oxford OX2 6ED. *T:* (01865) 616611. *E:* tlyons@maths.ox.ac.uk.

**LYONS, Dr Timothy John;** QC 2003; *b* 27 Dec. 1957; *s* of Kenneth Sidney Lyons and late Margaret Winifred Lyons (*née* Sim); *m* 1993, Patricia Ann Webb. *Educ:* Bristol Univ. (LLB Hons 1979); Queen Mary Coll., Univ. of London (LLM 1981); Queen Mary and Westfield Coll., Univ. of London (PhD 1991). CTA (Fellow) (FTII 1996). Called to the Bar, Inner Temple, 1980; joined Lincoln's Inn, 1994; Mem., Hon. Soc. of King's Inns and called to the Bar, Ireland, 1998; in private practice, specialising in revenue, customs, trade law and EU matters. Mem. and Co-Rapporteur, Expert Gp on Taxation of Individuals, EC, 2014–16. Visiting Professor: Law Dept, LSE, 2008–17; Law Faculty, Univ. of Porto, 2010–. Regular lectr, UK and continental Europe. Gen. Ed., European Cross-Border Estate Planning (formerly Capital Taxes and Estate Planning in Europe), 1991–; Asst Ed. (European Law), British Tax Review, 2004–. *Publications:* (ed) Chapman's Inheritance Tax, 7th edn, 1987, 8th edn 1990; Insolvency: law and taxation, 1989; Inheritance Tax Planning through Insurance, 1990; (jtly) Historic Buildings and Maintenance Funds, 1991; (jtly) Capital Gains Tax Roll Over Relief for Business Assets, 1993; (ed jtly) The International

Guide to the Taxation of Trusts, 1999; EC Customs Law, 2002, 3rd edn 2018; (contrib.) Value Added Tax: commentary and analysis, 2009; (contrib.) De Voil Indirect Tax Service, 2012; contrib. articles to jls incl. British Tax Rev., EC Tax Jl, European Taxation, Global Trade and Customs Jl. *Recreations:* reading, music, collecting antiquarian maps. *Address:* 39 Essex Chambers, 81 Chancery Lane, WC2A 1DD. *T:* (020) 7832 1111.

**LYSAGHT,** family name of **Baron Lisle**.

**LYSCOM, David Edward;** HM Diplomatic Service, retired; Policy Director, Chartered Institute of Internal Auditors, 2012–15; *b* 8 Aug. 1951; *s* of late William Edward Lyscom and Phyllis Edith May Lyscom (*née* Coyle); *m* 1973, Dr Nicole Ward; one *s* two *d*. *Educ:* Latymer Upper Sch.; Pembroke Coll., Cambridge (BA 1972). Joined HM Diplomatic Service, 1972; Vienna, 1973–76; Ottawa, 1977–79; FCO, 1979–83; First Secretary: Bonn, 1984–87; Riyadh, 1988–90; Asst Head, Aid Policy Dept, FCO, 1990–91; Counsellor, Science, Technology and Envmt, Bonn, 1991–95; Head of Envmt, Science and Energy Dept, FCO, 1995–98; Ambassador to Slovak Republic, 1998–2001; FCO, 2002–03; UK Perm. Rep. to OECD, Paris, 2004–08; Chief Exec., ISC, 2008–11. Treas., Sherborne Artslink, 2016–. *Recreations:* music, theatre, squash, tennis, golf.

**LYSTER, Simon,** PhD; DL; conservationist, lawyer; Chief Executive (formerly Executive Director), LEAD International, 2005–11 (Director of Development and Programmes, 2003–05); *b* 29 April 1952; *s* of John Neal Lyster and Marjorie Aird, (Peggy), (*née* Everard); *m* 1990, Sandra Elizabeth (*née* Charity); one *s* one *d*. *Educ:* Radley Coll.; Magdalene Coll., Cambridge (MA Hons; PhD). Admitted solicitor, 1978; Slaughter and May, 1976–78; Envmtl Defense Fund, NY, 1978–79; admitted to NY Bar, 1979; Defenders of Wildlife, Washington, 1979–81; Dir, Falklands Conservation, 1982–86; Hd, Conservation Policy, WWF UK, and Internat. Treaties Officer, WWF Internat., 1986–95; Dir-Gen., The Wildlife Trusts, 1995–2003. Non-exec. Dir, Northumbrian Water Ltd, 2006–. Mem., Darwin Adv. Cttee, 1997–2003; Mem. Bd, Natural England, 2014–; Trustee: Kilverstone Wildlife Charitable Trust, 2002–; World Land Trust, 2004–17 (Chm., 2014–17; Mem. Council, 2017–); Conservation Internat. - UK, 2005– (Chm., 2018–); Rural Community Council of Essex, 2013–. DL Essex, 2013. *Publications:* International Wildlife Law, 1985; numerous articles in mags and newspapers and contribs to books. *Recreations:* natural history, tennis, cricket, walking, golf. *Address:* Great Prestons Farm, Stock, Essex CM4 9RN. *Club:* Queen's.

**LYSTER-BINNS, Benjamin Edward Noël;** HM Diplomatic Service; Head, Somalia Unit, Foreign and Commonwealth Office; *b* 19 Oct. 1965; *m* 1995, Belinda Hunter Blair; one *s* two *d*. Entered FCO, 1989; Desk Officer, Non-Proliferation Dept, FCO, 1989–91; Third Secretary: (Develt) Lilongwe, 1991–94; (Chancery/Inf.), Muscat, 1994–98; Desk Officer, Human Rights Policy Dept, FCO, 1998–2000; Dep. Eur. Corresp. and Hd, EU Gen. Affairs and Ext. Relns Council/G8 Team, Common Foreign and Security Policy Dept, FCO, 2000–03; Dep. Hd of Mission, Lisbon, 2003–07; Policy Advr, Counter Terrorism Dept, FCO, 2007–10; Dep. Hd, Internat. Orgns Dept, FCO, 2010–12; Ambassador to Uruguay, 2012–16. *Address:* c/o Foreign and Commonwealth Office, King Charles Street, SW1A 2AH.

**LYTHELL, Jane;** *see* Clarke, J.

**LYTHGO, Adrian;** Chief Executive, Kirklees Metropolitan Borough Council, 2010–17; *b* Cyprus, 3 Dec. 1962; *s* of Derek and Beryl Lythgo; *m* 1996, Melanie Pilbrough; one *s* one *d*. *Educ:* Edgbarrow Sch., Crowthorne; Univ. of Loughborough (BSc). CPFA 1990. Audit Commn, 1984–88; Royal Bor. of Windsor and Maidenhead, 1989–90; Audit Commn, 1990–92; KPMG, 1993–95; Dist Auditor, Audit Commn, 1995–99; Associate Partner, KPMG, Leeds, 1999–2009; Dir of Finance, Kirklees MBC, 2009–10; Hd, Paid Service, W Yorks Combined Authy, 2014–16. Mem., Audit Cttee, Leeds City Coll., 2010–15. Chair, NW Regl Flood and Coastal Cttee, 2017–. Special Advr, Regl Engagement and Partnerships, Univ. of Huddersfield, 2017–. *Recreations:* Rugby nut, sliding down mountains.

**LYTTELTON,** family name of **Viscounts Chandos** and **Cobham**.

**LYTTELTON, Hon. Richard Cavendish;** Chairman: Help Musicians UK (formerly Musicians Benevolent Fund), 2008–14; Artis, 2010–14; *b* Pershore, Worcs, 24 July 1949; 3rd *s* of 10th Viscount Cobham, KG, GCMG, GCVO, TD, PC and Elizabeth Alison, *d* of J. R. Makeig-Jones, CBE; *m* 1971, Romilly Sybil Barker; one *s* one *d*. *Educ:* Eton Coll.; Birmingham Sch. of Music. Founder, Richard Lyttelton Hldgs, 1969–74; Manager, New Projects, EMI Leisure Enterprises Ltd, 1974–76; Man. Dir, Oy EMI Finland AB, 1977–80; Dir, Internat. Ops, EMI Records (UK) Ltd, 1980–83; Gp Man. Dir, EMI S Africa, 1984–86; President: Capitol Records, EMI Canada, 1986–88; EMI Classics and Jazz, 1988–2006. Chm., English Touring Opera, 2003–09. Pres., Royal Albert Hall, 2010–11. Mem. Council, RCM, 2009–. Trustee: EMI Archive Trust, 2003–; Universal Music UK (formerly EMI Music) Sound Foundn, 2007–. Mem., Ct of Assts, Musicians' Co. *Recreations:* music, shooting, fishing, theatre, opera. *Address:* 5 Queens Gate Place Mews, SW7 5BG. *T:* (020) 7823 8128. *E:* richard.lyttelton@gmail.com.
*See also* Viscount Cobham.

**LYTTLE, Brian;** *see* Lyttle, J. B. C.

**LYTTLE, Christopher;** Member (Alliance) Belfast East, Northern Ireland Assembly, since 2010; *b* Belfast, 19 Jan. 1981; one *c*. *Educ:* Queen's Univ., Belfast (BA Hons 1st Cl. Pols 2003). Frank Knox Fellow in Public Policy, Kennedy Sch. of Govt, Harvard Univ., 2006. Constituency and Res. Asst to Naomi Long, 2007–10. *Recreation:* Association Football. *Address:* Parliament Buildings, Stormont, Belfast BT4 3XX. *T:* (028) 9047 2004. *E:* chris.lyttle@allianceparty.org.

**LYTTLE, (James) Brian (Chambers),** OBE 1996; Secretary, Probation Board for Northern Ireland, 1987–97; *b* 22 Aug. 1932; *s* of late James Chambers Lyttle and Margaret Kirkwood Billingsley; *m* 1957, Mary Alma Davidson; four *d*. *Educ:* Bangor Grammar Sch.; Trinity Coll., Dublin (BA 1st Cl. Hons Classics). Entered NI Civil Service as Asst Principal, 1954; Private Sec. to Minister of Commerce, 1960–62; Chief Exec., Enterprise Ulster, 1972–75; Dir, Employment Service, Dept of Manpower Services, 1975–77; Dir, Industrial Develt Orgn, Dept of Commerce, 1977–81; Under Secretary, Dept of Commerce, later Dept of Economic Develt, 1977–84; Under Sec., Dept of Finance and Personnel, 1984–87. Mem., Prison Arts Foundn, 1996–2010. *Recreations:* reading, walking, music, poetry.

**LYTTLE,** family name of **Earl of Lytton**.

**LYTTON, 5th Earl of,** *cr* 1880; **John Peter Michael Scawen Lytton;** Baron Wentworth, 1529; Bt 1838; Baron Lytton, 1866; Viscount Knebworth, 1880; DL; chartered surveyor, Lawrence Foote & Partners, since 2014; *b* 7 June 1950; *s* of 4th Earl of Lytton, OBE, and Clarissa Mary, *d* of Brig.-Gen. C. E. Palmer, CB, CMG, DSO, RA; *S* father, 1985; *m* 1980, Ursula Alexandra (*née* Komoly); two *s* one *d*. *Educ:* Downside; Reading Univ. (BSc, Estate Management). FRICS 1987 (ARICS 1976); IRRV 1990. Sole practitioner, John Lytton & Co. Ltd, Chartered Surveyors and Valuers, 1988–2015. President: Sussex Assoc. of Local Councils, 1997–2014; Nat. Assoc. of Local Councils, 1999–2014; Chm., Leasehold Adv. Service (formerly Leasehold Enfranchisement Adv. Service), 1994–2000. Member: Council, CLA, 1993–99 (Exec., 1994–99); Bd, Sussex Rural Community Council, 2000–09; Council, S of England Agricl Soc., 2004–; Chm., Rights of Way Rev. Cttee, 2012–. Pres., Newstead Abbey Byron Soc., 1988–. Elected Mem., H of L, 2011. Member: Information Cttee, H of L, 2012–14; Built Envmt ad hoc Cttee, H of L, 2015–16. DL W Sussex, 2011. Hon. FBEng 1997. *Heir:* s Viscount Knebworth, *qv*. *Address:* Newbuildings Place, Shipley, Horsham, West Sussex RH13 8GQ. *T:* (01403) 741650.

**LYTTON COBBOLD,** family name of **Baron Cobbold**.

**LYVEDEN, 8th Baron** *cr* 1859, of Lyveden, co. Northampton; **Colin Ronald Vernon;** freezer hand; *b* Te Aroha, New Zealand, 3 Feb. 1967; *s* of 7th Baron Lyveden and Lynette June Vernon (*née* Lilley); *S* father, 2017; *m* 2009, Rachel Marie Rainey. *Educ:* Te Aroha Coll. K. Manning, 1983–87; Lowe Walker, 1987–95; Richmond Ltd, 1996–2005; PPCS, 2006–08; Silver Fern Farms, 2008–. *Recreations:* hunting, fishing, horse racing, golf. *Address:* 8 Cynthia Crescent, Te Aroha, Matamata-Piako, Waikato 3320, New Zealand. *E:* bigcol@xtra.co.nz.

# M

**MA Tao Li, Hon. Geoffrey,** GBM 2012; Chief Justice, Court of Final Appeal of the Hong Kong Special Administrative Region of the People's Republic of China, since 2010; *b* Hong Kong, 11 Jan. 1956; *s* of late George Ma and Margaret Ma (*née* Wei); *m* 1984, Maria Candace Yuen, (Madam Justice Yuen); one *d*. *Educ*: Altrincham Grammar Sch.; Univ. of Birmingham (LLB 1977). Called to the Bar: Gray's Inn, 1978 (Hon. Bencher 2004); Hong Kong, 1980: State of Vic., Australia, 1983; Singapore, 1990; QC (Hong Kong) 1993. Legal Consultant to Messrs David Chong & Co., Singapore, Advocates and Solicitors, 1995–2001; Hd of Chambers, Temple Chambers, Hong Kong, 1999–2001; High Court of Hong Kong: a Recorder, 2000–01, Judge, 2001–02, Court of First Instance; Justice of Appeal, Court of Appeal, 2002–03; Chief Judge, 2003–10. Adjudicator, Registration of Persons Tribunal, Hong Kong, 1987–96. Hon. Lectr, Dept of Professional Legal Educn, Univ. of Hong Kong, 1987–. Dep. Chm., Bd of Review (Inland Revenue), 1997–2000. Chm., Appeal Tribunal Panel (Bldgs), 1994–2001; Mem., Hong Kong Futures Exchange Disciplinary Appeal Tribunal, 1994–2001. Chm., Judicial Officers Recommendation Commn, 2010–; Member: Criminal and Law Enforcement Injuries Compensation Bd, 1991–2001; Law Reform Commn, 2010–; Dep. Chm., Appeals Panel, 1999–2001, Takeovers Appeals Cttee, 1999–2001, Securities and Futures Commn. Hong Kong International Arbitration Centre: Member: Appt Adv. Bd, 1997–; Arbitration Ordinance Rev. Cttee, 1998–; Internat. Adv. Bd, 2011–. Mem., Wkg Party on Civil Justice Reform, 2000–01; Chairman: Steering Cttee on Civil Justice Reform, 2004–09; Monitoring Cttee on Civil Justice Reform, 2009–10; Rules Cttee, Court of Final Appeal, 2010–; Wkg Gp on Use of Chinese, 2010–; Steering Cttee on Relocation of Court of Final Appeal, 2010–15; Chief Justice's Cttee on Community-Related Projects, 2011–; Hong Kong Judicial Inst., 2013–; Mem., Civil Court Users Cttee of Judiciary, 1993–2001; Mem., 1994–97, Vice Chm., 1997–98, Mgt Cttee, Consumer Legal Action Fund. Mem., Bar Council, Hong Kong Bar Assoc., 1982–84 and 1992–96. Patron: Hong Kong Acad. of Law, Law Soc. of Hong Kong, 2010–; Soc. of Rehabilitation and Crime Prevention, Hong Kong, 2010–; Bingham Centre for Rule of Law, 2010–; Hong Kong Inst. of Arbitrators, 2011–; Internat. Advocacy Trng Council, Hong Kong, 2012–. Pres., Scout Assoc. of Hong Kong, 2008–18. Hon. Fellow, Harris Manchester Coll., Oxford, 2012. Hon. Bencher, Middle Temple, 2016. Hon. LLD: Birmingham, 2011; Chinese Univ., 2016; Hong Kong, 2019. Officier, Légion d'Honneur (France), 2015. *Publications*: (contributing and adv. ed.) Hong Kong Civil Procedure, 2001; (contrib.) Litigation in the Commercial List: 2002 Law Lectures for Practitioners, 2002; (contrib.) The Interpretation of Hong Kong's Constitution: a personal view, 2013; Editor-in-Chief: Arbitration in Hong Kong: a practical guide, 2003, 3rd edn 2014; Professional Conduct and Risk Management in Hong Kong, 2007. *Recreations*: badminton, golf, tennis, films. *Address*: Court of Final Appeal, 8 Jackson Road, Central, Hong Kong. *T*: 21230011. *E*: enquiry@judiciary.gov.hk. *Clubs*: Chinese Recreation, Victoria Recreation, Hong Kong; Hong Kong Golf, Shek O Golf and Country, Hong Kong Jockey, Hong Kong Cricket.

**MA YING-JEOU;** President of Taiwan, 2008–16; *b* Hong Kong, 13 July 1950; *s* of late Ma Ho-ling and of Chin Hou-hsiu; *m* Chow Mei-Ching; two *d*. *Educ*: National Taiwan Univ. (LLB 1972); New York Univ. (LLM 1976); Harvard Law Sch. (SJD 1981). Legal Consultant, First Nat. Bank of Boston, 1980–81; Res. Consultant, Sch. of Law, Univ. of Maryland, 1980–81; Associate Lawyer, Cole & Deits, NY, 1981; Government of Taiwan: Dep. Dir-Gen., First Bureau, Office of the Pres., 1981–88; Sen. Sec., Office of the Pres., 1982; Minister, Res., Develt and Evaluation Commn, 1988–91; Sen. Dep. Minister and spokesperson, Mainland Affairs Council, 1991–93; Minister of Justice, 1993–96; Minister without Portfolio, 1996–97; Associate Prof. of Law, Nat. Chengchi Univ., 1997–98; Mayor, Taipei City, 1998–2006. Mem., National Assembly, 1992–96. Kuomintang: Dep. Sec.-Gen., 1984–88, Mem., 1993–97, Central Club Clique; Mem., Central Standing Cttee, 1999–2001; Vice-Chm., 2004–05; Chm., 2005–07, 2009–14. *Publications*: Legal Problems of Seabed Boundary Delimitation in the East China Sea, 1984; Two Major Legal Issues Relating to the International Status of the Republic of China, 1986; Taipei-Beijing Relations and East Asian Stability: implications for Europe, 1993; The Republic of China (Taiwan)'s Entry into the World Trade Organisation: problems and prospects, 1996.

**MA, Yo-Yo;** 'cellist; *b* Paris, 7 Oct. 1955; of Chinese parentage; *m* 1978, Jill A. Horner; one *s* one *d*. *Educ*: Harvard Univ.; Juilliard Sch. of Music, NY. First public recital at age of 5 years; winner Avery Fisher Prize, 1978; has performed under many distinguished conductors with all major world orchestras including: Berlin Philharmonic; Boston Symphony; Chicago Symphony; Israel Philharmonic; LSO; NY Philharmonic; also appears in chamber music ensembles; regular participant in festivals at Tanglewood, Edinburgh, Salzburg and other major European fests. Founder and Artistic Dir, Silk Road Ensemble (formerly Silk Road Project), 1998–. Has made numerous recordings. Dr *hc*: Northeastern, USA, 1985; Harvard, 1991. Numerous Grammy Awards. Presidential Medal of Freedom, 2010. *Address*: c/o Opus 3 Artists, 470 Park Avenue South, 9th Floor North, New York, NY 10016, USA. *T*: (212) 5847500.

**MA Zhengang;** President, China Arms Control and Disarmament Association; Chairman, Chinese National Committee, Council for Security Cooperation in the Asia Pacific; *b* 9 Nov. 1940; (to a worker's family); *m* 1972, Chen Xiaodong; one *s*. *Educ*: Beijing Foreign Langs Univ.; post-grad. study at Ealing Tech. Coll. and LSE. Staff Mem., N American and Oceanian Affairs Dept (NAOAD), Min. of Foreign Affairs, China, 1967–70; Staff Mem., then Attaché, Yugoslavia, 1970–74; Attaché, NAOAD, 1974–81; Consul, Vancouver, 1981–85; Dep. Dir, then Dir, NAOAD, 1985–90; Counsellor, Washington, 1990–91; Dep. Dir-Gen., then Dir-Gen., NAOAD, 1991–95; Vice-Minister, Foreign Affairs Office of State Council, 1995–97; Ambassador of China to the Court of St James's, 1997–2002; Ambassador, Min. of Foreign Affairs, 2002–04; Pres., China Inst. of Internat. Studies, 2004–10. *Recreations*: table tennis, bridge, literature. *Address*: China Arms Control and Disarmament Association, 3 Toutiao, Taijichang, Beijing 100005, People's Republic of China.

**MAAN, Bashir Ahmed,** CBE 2000; JP; DL; Member, Scottish Constitutional Convention, 1988–98; Judge, City of Glasgow District Courts, 1968–97; *b* Maan, Gujranwala, Pakistan, 22 Oct. 1926; *s* of late Choudhry Sardar Khan Maan and Mrs Hayat Begum Maan; *m*; one *s* three *d*. *Educ*: D. B. High Sch., Qila Didar Singh; Panjab Univ.; Strathclyde Univ. (MSc 1994). Involved in struggle for creation of Pakistan, 1943–47; organised rehabilitation of refugees from India in Maan and surrounding areas, 1947–48; emigrated to UK and settled in Glasgow, 1953; Glasgow Founder Sec., Pakistan Social and Cultural Soc., 1955–65, Pres., 1966–69; Pres., Islamic Centre, Glasgow, 2007–10; Vice-Chm., Glasgow Community Relations Council, 1970–75; Pres., Standing Conf. of Pakistani Orgns in UK, 1974–77; a Dep. Chm., Commn for Racial Equality, 1977–80; Founder Chm., Scottish Pakistani Assoc., 1984–98; Pres., Nat. Assoc. of British Pakistanis, 2000–07; Member: Overseas Pakistanis Adv. Council, Govt of Pakistan, 2001–04; President's Task Force on Human Develt of Pakistan, 2001–04; Scottish rep., Muslim Council of Britain, 1998–2008; Convenor, Muslim Council of Scotland, 2007–10; Chairman: Strathclyde CRC, 1987–93 and 1994–96; Strathclyde Interpreting Services Adv. Cttee, 1988–96; Council of Ethnic Minority Orgns Scotland, 2002–11 (Pres., 2012–). Member: Immigrants Prog. Adv. Cttee, BBC, 1972–80; Gen. Adv. Cttee, BBC, 1991–95; Scottish Selecting Panel, BBC, 1992–96. Hon. Res. Fellow, Univ. of Glasgow, 1988–91. Councillor, Glasgow Corp., 1970–75, City of Glasgow Dist, 1974–84 (Bailie, 1980–84); Mem., Glasgow City Council, 1995–2003 (Bailie, 1996–99); Magistrate, City of Glasgow, 1971–74; Vice-Chm. 1971–74, Chm. 1974–75, Police Cttee, Glasgow Corp.; Police Judge, City of Glasgow, 1974–75; Mem., 1995–2003, Convenor, 1999–2003, Strathclyde Jt Police Bd. Mem. Exec. Cttee, Glasgow City Labour Party, 1969–70. Contested (Lab) East Fife, Feb. 1974. Convener, Pakistan Bill Action Cttee, 1973; Member: Nat. Road Safety Cttee, 1971–75; Scottish Accident Prevention Cttee, 1971–75; Scottish Gas Consumers' Council, 1978–81; Greater Glasgow Health Bd, 1981–91; Hon. Pres., SCVO, 2001–06 (Mem., Mgt Bd, 1988–95). Chm., Organising Cttee, Glasgow Internat. Sports Festival Co. Ltd, 1987–89. Mem. Bd of Governors, Jordanhill Coll. of Educn, Glasgow, 1987–91. JP 1968, DL 1982, Glasgow. Hon. Fellow, Glasgow Caledonian Univ., 2003–07. Hon. LLD Strathclyde, 1999; DUniv Glasgow, 2001; Hon. DLitt Glasgow Caledonian, 2002. *Publications*: The New Scots, 1992; The Thistle and the Crescent, 2008; Muslims in Scotland, 2014; articles, contrib. to press. *Recreations*: golf, reading. *Address*: 8 Riverview Gardens, Flat 6, Glasgow G5 8EL. *T*: (0141) 429 7689.

**MAAS, Rupert Nicholas;** Managing Director, Maas Gallery, since 1993; *b* Chelsea, 23 July 1960; *s* of late Jeremy Maas and of Antonia Maas; *m* 1991, Tamar Seaborn; three *d*. *Educ*: Sherborne Sch.; Essex Univ. (BA Art Hist.). Joined Maas Gall., 1983. Expert in English painting, Antiques Roadshow, BBC, 1996–. Brand Ambassador, Ballantine's Whisky, China, 2009–12. *Recreations*: mending things, sailing, playing the piano in secret, harassing the Council. *Address*: Maas Gallery, 15a Clifford Street, W1S 4JZ. *T*: (020) 7734 2302. *E*: mail@maasgallery.com.

**MABB, David Michael;** QC 2001; *b* 12 June 1956; *s* of Kenneth George Mabb and Joyce Madeline Mabb. *Educ*: King James' Grammar Sch., Almondbury; St Nicholas Grammar Sch., Northwood; Gonville and Caius Coll., Cambridge (BA 1978; MA 1982). Called to the Bar, Lincoln's Inn, 1979. Mem., Financial Reporting Rev. Panel, 2009–. *Address*: Erskine Chambers, 33 Chancery Lane, WC2A 1EN. *T*: (020) 7242 5532.

**MABB, Katherine Anne;** *see* Green, K. A.

**MABEY, Richard Thomas,** FRSL; writer and broadcaster; *b* 20 Feb. 1941; *s* of late Thomas Gustavus Mabey and Edna Nellie (*née* Moore). *Educ*: Berkhamsted Sch.; St Catherine's Coll., Oxford (BA Hons 1964, MA 1971). Lectr in Social Studies, Dacorum Coll. of Further Educn, 1963–65; Sen. Editor, Penguin Books, 1966–73; freelance writer, 1973–; columnist: BBC Wildlife, 1984–2015; The Times, 2004–06. Mem. Mgt Cttee, Soc. of Authors, 1998–2000. Presenter: Tomorrow's World, BBC TV, 1995; Mabey in the Wild, BBC Radio 4, 2013. Member: Nature Conservancy Council, 1982–86; Council, Botanical Soc. of the British Isles, 1981–83; President: London Wildlife Trust, 1982–92; Richard Jefferies Soc., 1995–98; Norfolk and Norwich Naturalists' Soc., 2005–06; Waveney and Blyth Arts, 2010–; Vice-Pres., Open Spaces Soc., 2003–. Dir, Common Ground, 1988–2016. Patron: Thomas Bewick Trust, 1986–; John Clare Soc., 2006–; Mem. Adv. Council, Plantlife, 1992–96. Leverhulme Trust Res. Award, 1983–84; Leverhulme Res. Fellowship, 1993–94; Writer-in-Residence, New Writing Partnership, UEA, 2008; Burrows Lectr, Univ. of Essex, 2013; Derek Brewer Vis. Fellow, Emmanuel Coll., Cambridge, 2014. FRSL 2012. Hon. DSc St Andrews, 1997; DUniv Essex, 2007; Hon. DLitt UEA, 2011. Granted a civil list pension, 2008. Peter Scott Meml Award and Hon. Fellow, British Naturalists' Assoc., 2012. *Publications*: (ed) Class, 1967; The Pop Process, 1969; Food for Free, 1972, 2nd edn 1989; Children in Primary School, 1972; The Unofficial Countryside, 1973; The Pollution Handbook, 1973; The Roadside Wildlife Book, 1974; Street Flowers, 1976 (TES Inf. Book Award); Plants with a Purpose, 1977; The Common Ground, 1980; The Flowering of Britain, 1980; (ed) Landscape with Figures, 1983; Oak and Company, 1983 (NY Acad. of Sci. Children's Book Award, 1984); In a Green Shade, 1983; Back to the Roots, 1983; (ed) Second Nature, 1984; The Frampton Flora, 1985; Gilbert White: a biography, 1986 (Whitbread Biography Award); Gen. Ed., The Journals of Gilbert White, 1986–89; (ed) The Gardener's Labyrinth, 1987; The Flowering of Kew, 1988; Home Country, 1990; (ed) The Flowers of May, 1990; A Nature Journal, 1991; Whistling in the Dark, 1993; Landlocked, 1994; (ed) The Oxford Book of Nature Writing, 1995; Flora Britannica (British Bk Awards Illustrated Book of the Year), 1996; Selected Writings 1974–1999, 1999; Nature Cure, 2005; (with Mark Cocker) Birds Britannica, 2005; Fencing Paradise, 2005; Beechcombings: the narratives of trees, 2007; The Full English Cassoulet, 2008; (with Peter Marren) Bugs Britannica, 2010; A Brush with Nature, 2010; Weeds, 2010; The Barley Bird, 2010 (E Anglian Book Award, 2010); The Perfumier and the Stinkhorn, 2011; A Good Parcel of English Soil, 2013; Turned Out Nice Again: on living with the weather, 2013; The Ash and the Beech: the drama of woodland change, 2013; Dreams of the Good Life: the life of Flora Thompson and the creation of Lark Rise to Candleford, 2014; The Cabaret of Plants: botany and imagination, 2015; Turning the Boat for Home: a life writing about nature, 2019. *Recreations*: food, meandering, early music. *Address*: c/o Sheil Land Associates, 52 Doughty Street, WC1N 2LS. *W*: www.richardmabey.co.uk.

**MABEY, Roger Stanley,** CMG 1997; non-executive Director, Sweett Group (formerly Cyril Sweett Group) Ltd, 2003–16; *b* 11 Aug. 1944; *s* of Stanley Mabey and Edith Mabey (*née* Stride); *m* 1968, Margaret Marian Watkins; one *s* one *d. Educ:* Cleeve Sch., Cheltenham; Gloucestershire Coll. of Technology (HND 1964); Lancaster Coll. of Technology, Coventry; Eur. Centre of Continuing Educn, INSEAD. Joined Bovis, 1967; Project Manager, Bristol, 1967–73; Regl Dir, Harrow office, 1973–79; a Divl Dir, 1979–86; Dir, Bovis Construction Ltd, 1986–93; Asst Man. Dir, 1993–94, Man. Dir, 1994–97, Bovis Internat. Ltd; Executive Director: Bovis Construction Gp, 1998–2000; Bovis Lend Lease Ltd, 2000–03. Chm., Housing Solutions Gp, 2011–14 (Vice Chm., 2005–11). Member: DTI Adv. Gps on India, 1994, and S Africa; Market Gp, Cttee for S African Trade, 1996; BOTB, 1998. Vice Chm., Cookham Soc., 1998–2000. FCIOB 1980; FRSA 1998. *Recreations:* travel, gardening, painting, food, music, athletics, family, ski-ing.

**MABLY, Louis Asa Luke Alexis Dylan;** QC 2017; Senior Treasury Counsel, Central Criminal Court, since 2015; *b* Welwyn Garden City, 21 June 1974; *s* of late Michael Mably and of Sheila Mably (*née* Eaves); *m* 2003, Nina Wilson; two *s. Educ:* Monk's Walk Sch.; Univ. of Leeds (BA 1st Cl. Hons Hist. 1995); City Univ. (DipLaw 1996); Inns of Court Sch. of Law. Called to the Bar, Lincoln's Inn, 1997; Jun. Treasury Counsel, Central Criminal Court, 2009–15. *Recreations:* history, books, cycling, cricket, Liverpool FC, Sadler's Wells Dining Club. *Address:* 6KBW College Hill, 21 College Hill, EC4R 2RP. *T:* (020) 3301 0910. *E:* clerks@6kbw.com. *Club:* MCC.

**MABUZA, Lindiwe;** High Commissioner for the Republic of South Africa to the United Kingdom, 2001–09; *b* Natal, 13 Aug. 1938. *Educ:* Grailville Community Coll., Ohio (Dip. Home Econs 1959); Roma, Lesotho, Univ. of S Africa (BA 1961); Stanford Univ., Calif (MA English 1966); Univ. of Minnesota (MA American Studies 1968); Diplomatic Trng, Kuala Lumpur (Dip. 1993). Teacher, English and Zulu Lit., Manzini Central Sch., Swaziland, 1962–64; Lectr, Dept of Sociol., Univ. of Minnesota, 1968–69; Asst Prof. of Lit. and Hist., Ohio Univ., 1969–77; radio journalist with ANC's Radio Freedom (broadcasting into SA from Zambia), 1977–79; Chief Representative of ANC: to Scandinavia, based in Sweden, 1979–87 (opened ANC offices in Denmark, Norway and Finland); to US, 1989–94; Mem., first democratic Parliament, SA, 1994–95; first Ambassador for S Africa to Germany, 1995–99; High Commissioner: to Malaysia, 1999–2001 (also to Brunei and the Philippines (non-resident)). Ed., Voice of Women, Jl by ANC women, 1977–79. Chm., ANC Cultural Cttee, Lusaka, 1977–79. Hon. PhD Durban-Westville, 1997. Yari Yari Award, New York Univ., 1997; Lifetime Achievement Award for Arts Advocacy, Arts and Culture Trust, 2017. *Publications:* (ed) Malibongwe: poetry by ANC women, 1980 (trans. German and Russian); (ed) One Never Knows: short stories by ANC women in exile, 1989; From ANC to Sweden: Olof Palme poem in English and Swedish 1986 (trans. Norwegian and Finnish); Letter to Letta: selected poetry from 1970–1987, 1993; Africa to Me: poetry from 1976–1996 in English and German, 1998; Voices that Lead: poetry selection from 1976–1996, 1998; Footprints and Fingerprints, 2008; Tambo Lenyoka, 2018; contrib. to various poetry and short story anthologies. *Address:* c/o South African High Commission, Trafalgar Square, WC2N 5DP.

**MAC;** *see* McMurtry, S.

**McADAM, Douglas Baxter;** HM Diplomatic Service, retired; Consul General, Hamburg, 1999–2004; *b* 25 June 1944; *s* of late John Watson McAdam and Jean Cook McAdam; *m* 1965, Susan Clare Jarvis; one *s* one *d. Educ:* Musselburgh Burgh Sch.; Musselburgh Grammar Sch. Entered Foreign Office, 1961; served Ulan Bator, Luanda, New Delhi and FCO, 1966–78; Dep. Hd of Mission, Ulan Bator, 1978; Vice-Consul, Rio de Janeiro, 1979–82; 2nd, later 1st Sec., UK Delegn MBFR, Vienna, 1983–87; FCO, 1987–90; 1st Sec., Lagos, 1990–94; FCO, 1994–95; Ambassador to Kazakhstan and Kyrgyzstan (resident in Almaty), 1996–99. Mem., RSAA, 1997. Pres., Fiscal Council, Assoc. of Foreign Property Owners in Portugal, 2010–. Mem. Bd. Madrugada Assoc., 2015–. Chieftain, St Andrew's Soc. of the Algarve, 2010–. *Recreations:* fly fishing, swimming, eating well. *Address:* Colinas Verdes Lote 105, 8600–074 Bensafrim, Lagos, Portugal.

**McADAM, Dr Ellen;** Director, Birmingham Museums Trust, since 2013; *b* Dumfries, 23 May 1952; *d* of William McAdam and Helen Robertson McAdam; partner, Mark Richard Roberts; one *s. Educ:* Dumfries Acad.; Univ. of Edinburgh (MA); Somerville Coll., Oxford (DPhil 1982); HNC Computer Studies 1987. Katherine and Leonard Woolley Jun. Res. Fellow, Somerville Coll., Oxford, 1977–79; excavations and post-doctoral res., 1982–84; Res. Fellow, British Sch. of Archaeology in Iraq, 1984–86; Gp Manager, Gtr Manchester Archaeol Unit, 1988–89; Post-excavation Manager, Oxford Archaeol Unit, 1990–95; Academic Ed., English Heritage, 1995–98; Hd, Specialist Services, Mus. of London, 1998–2001; Collections Services Manager, 2001–09; Hd of Museums and Collections, 2009–13, Glasgow Museums. Member: Council, British Inst. for Study of Iraq, 2014–; Exec. Cttee, Nat. Mus. Dirs Council, 2014–; Humanities Ext. Adv. Bd, Univ. of Oxford, 2015–16; Adv. Panel, Nat. Railway Mus., 2015–; Designation Panel, Arts Council England, 2015–; Cttee, Archaeol Archives Gp, Chartered Inst. for Archaeologists, 2015–17; Bd, Culture Central, 2015–; Cttee, Birmingham and Warwicks Archaeol Soc., 2017– (Pres., 2018–). Member: Women Leaders in Museums Network, 2008–15; Transitions and Develt Gp, 2015–. Hon. Research Fellow: Univ. of Birmingham, 2014–; UCL, 2016–. MCIfA (MIFA 1994). FSAScot 1972. *Publications:* contribs to jls on British and Near East archaeol. *Recreations:* opera, theatre, gardening, cooking, small fat terriers. *Address:* Birmingham Museums, Chamberlain Square, Birmingham B3 3DH. *T:* (0121) 348 8008. *E:* ellen.mcadam@birminghammuseums.org.uk.

**McADAM, John David Gibson;** Chairman, ConvaTec Group, since 2019; *b* 30 April 1948; *s* of John McAdam and Sarah McAdam (*née* Gibson); *m* 1979, Louise Mary Mann; one *s* one *d. Educ:* Kelsick Grammar Sch., Ambleside; Lakes Secondary Sch., Windermere; Manchester Univ. (BSc 1st Cl. Hons Chem. Physics; Dip. Adv. Studies in Science (Physics) 1971; PhD 1973). MRC Fellowship, Manchester and Cambridge Univs; Sen. Vice Pres., Quest Internat., 1987–90; Tech. Dir, Birds Eye Walls Ltd, 1990–93; Chairman and Chief Executive Officer: Unichema Internat., 1993–97; Quest Internat., 1997; Exec. Vice-Pres., ICI plc, 1997–98; Chm. and CEO, ICI Paints, 1998–2003; Dir, 1999–2008, Chief Exec., 2003–08, ICI plc. Chairman: United Utilities, 2008–19; Rentokil Initial, 2008–19; non-executive Director: Severn Trent plc, 2000–05; Sara Lee Corp., 2008–12; Rolls Royce, 2008–17; Senior non-executive Director: J. Sainsbury plc, 2005–16; Electra plc, 2017–18; Cobham plc, 2017–; Senior Adviser: TPG Capital, 2008–16; Royal Bank of Canada, 2015–17. *Publications:* scientific papers in scientific jls on macromolecular motion in solutions. *Recreations:* Rugby, cricket, soccer (now as a spectator), walking, listening to music.

**McADAM, Prof. Keith Paul William James;** DL; FRCP, FWACP; Special Advisor for East, Central and Southern Africa, Royal College of Physicians, since 2013 (Associate International Director, 2010–13); Wellcome Professor of Tropical Medicine, London School of Hygiene and Tropical Medicine, London University, 1984–2004, now Emeritus (Head of Department of Clinical Sciences, 1988–94); *b* 13 Aug. 1945; *s* of Sir Ian William James McAdam, OBE, FRCS, of Mrs L. M. Hrothgaarde Bennett (*née* Gibson); *m* 1968, Penelope Ann (*née* Spencer); three *d. Educ:* Prince of Wales School, Nairobi; Millfield School, Som.; Clare Coll., Cambridge (MA, MB BChir); Middlesex Hosp. Med. Sch.; FRSTM&H; Dip. Amer. Bd of Internal Medicine, Dip. Amer. Bd of Allergy and Clinical Immunology. Medical posts at Middlesex Hosp., Royal Northern Hosp., Brompton Hosp., Nat. Hosp. for Nervous Diseases, 1969–73; Lectr in Medicine, Inst. of Med. Research, Goroka, Papua New Guinea, 1973–75; MRC Travelling Fellow, 1975–76; Vis. Scientist, Immunology Branch, Nat. Cancer Inst., NIH, Bethesda, 1976–77; Asst Prof., Tufts Univ. Sch. of Medicine, 1977–82; Associate Prof., Divs of Allergy, Exptl Medicine and Geographic Medicine, Tufts Univ., 1982–84; Consultant Physician, Hosp. for Tropical Diseases, NW1, 1984–95; Dir, MRC Labs, The Gambia, 1995–2003 (on secondment); Dir, Infectious Diseases Inst., Mulago Hosp., Makerere Univ. Med. Sch., Kampala, Uganda, 2004–07; Member: Academic Alliance for AIDS Care and Prevention in Africa, 2007–; Internat. Bd of Dirs, African Medical and Res. Foundn, 2011–15. Adjunct Professor: Tufts New England Med. Center, Boston, 2004–07; Univ. of Minnesota Med. Sch., 2006–14. Fellow, Coll. of Physicians (E, Central and Southern Africa). Trustee, BBC Media Action, 2013–19. Founder: NAMWEZA (life skills trng prog. for people living with HIV), 2008; Music for My Mind, 2016 (Chm., Trustee Bd, 2016–). DL Herts, 2013. *Publications:* scientific articles on immunology and tropical medicine, esp. on amyloidosis, acute phase proteins, leprosy, tuberculosis, AIDS, malaria, inflammation. *Recreations:* cricket, tennis, golf, gardening. *Address:* Oakmead, 70 Luton Lane, Redbourn, Herts AL3 7PY. *T:* (01582) 792833. *Clubs:* MCC, Jesters.

**MACADIE, Jeremy James;** HM Diplomatic Service, retired; Chief Executive Officer, Ainsley International (Norway) Ltd, since 2014; *b* 10 July 1952; *s* of Donald Jaimeson Macadie and Olga May Sheck; *m* 1975, Chantal Andrea Jacqueline Copiatti; one *d. Educ:* Yeovil Grammar Sch. Joined FCO, by open competition, 1972; Dakar, 1975; Addis Ababa, 1980; Sana'a, 1984; Dep. Hd of Mission, Antananarivo, 1987; Foreign Office Spokesman, 1990; Asst Private Sec. to Minister for Europe, 1995; Dep. Hd of Mission, Algiers, 1997; on secondment to African Directorate, French Ministry of Foreign Affairs, 2003; Ambassador to Republics of Rwanda and Burundi, 2004–07; Consul General, Erbil, Iraq, 2009–11; FCO, 2011–12. Dir, RTEC Security Ltd, 2013–. Commnd TAVR (Intelligence and Security Gp), 1983. *Recreations:* country pursuits, turning wine into water.

**McAFEE, Raymond Noel,** CB 2002; consultant in international trade; Managing Director, UK Division, GlobalLink Trade Consulting, Washington, 2004–07; Associate Director, GlobalLink Border Solutions, 2007–08; *b* 15 Dec. 1943; *s* of late James Hill and Sarah McAfee (*née* O'Kane); *m* 1966, Margot McGowan; one *s* one *d. Educ:* Strabane Coll.; Portadown Coll. Joined HM Customs and Excise, 1963: Officer, 1963–74; Surveyor, 1974–79; Asst Collector, 1979–85; Sen. Principal, HQ London, 1985–89; Collector, NI, 1989–93; Asst Sec., HQ London, 1993–96; Dir, Central Ops, 1996–99; Comr, 1996–2003; Dir, Outfield, 1999–2001; Dir, Regl Business Services, 2001–03; Acting Dir Gen., 2003. Mem., Standards Cttee, Tunbridge Wells BC, 2004–. Reviewer of mgt articles for Chartered Mgt Inst., 2012–. FIMMM (FIM 1991). *Recreations:* golf, theatre, music. *E:* ray.mcafee@btinternet.com.

**McAFEE, Maj.-Gen. Robert William Montgomery,** CB 1999; *b* 8 Nov. 1944; *s* of Andrew Montgomery McAfee and Jane Beryl McAfee; *m* 1967, Erica-May MacLennan; one *s* one *d. Educ:* Inverness Royal Academy; Mons Officer Cadet Sch. Commnd, RTR, 1965; served Aden, BAOR, NI (despatches), Cyprus, Gulf, Bosnia; CO 2nd RTR, 1982–84; Instructor, Staff Coll., 1985–86; Col, Higher Command and Staff Course, 1987; Comdr 6 Armd Bde, 1988–89; ACOS (Land), HQ British Forces, ME, 1990; COS HQ 1 (BR) Corps, 1991–92; RCDS 1993; DG, Army Training, 1993–95; Comdr, Multi Nat. Div. (Central), 1996–99, retired. Dir of Admin, Norton Rose, 1999–2004. Rep. Col Comdt, RTR, 1995–99; Hon. Col Westminster Dragoons, 2003–09. Chm., RAC War Meml Benevolent Fund, 2004–11. Comr, Duke of York's Royal Mil. Sch., 2004–10. Chm., British Bobsleigh Assoc., 1998–2000; Dep. Pres., Army Rugby Union, 1994–99. *Recreations:* golf, ski-ing, watching Rugby and motor racing. *Address:* c/o Clydesdale Bank, 15 Academy Street, Inverness IV1 7JN. *Club:* Army and Navy (Chm., 2009–12).

**MACAIRE, Robert Nigel Paul,** CMG 2009; HM Diplomatic Service; Ambassador to Iran, since 2018; *b* 19 Feb. 1966; *s* of late James Macaire and of Tatiana Macaire; *m* 1996, Alice Mackenzie; two *d. Educ:* Cranleigh Sch.; St Edmund Hall, Oxford (BA Modern Hist.). Gen. Staff Secretariat and Policy Studies Secretariat, MoD, 1987–90; entered FCO, 1990; Falkland Is Dept, FCO, 1990–91; Bucharest, 1992–95; Near East and N Africa Dept, then Africa Dept Southern, FCO, 1995–98; First Sec., Washington, 1998–2002; Hd, Counter Terrorism Policy Dept, FCO, 2002–04; Counsellor (Political), New Delhi, 2004–06; Dir, Consular Services, FCO, 2006–08; High Comr, Kenya, 2008–11; on leave of absence as Dir, Political Risk, BG Gp, 2011–16. *Recreations:* sailing, riding, polo. *Address:* c/o Foreign and Commonwealth Office, King Charles Street, SW1A 2AH. *Club:* Royal Ocean Racing.

**McALEENAN, Rt Rev. Paul;** an Auxiliary Bishop of Westminster, (RC), since 2016; Titular Bishop of Mercia, since 2016; *b* Belfast, 15 July 1951. *Educ:* St Gabriel's Secondary Sch., Belfast; St Patrick's Coll., Thurles. Worked in engineering until 1979; ordained priest, 1985; Asst Priest, Our Lady of Grace and St Edward, Chiswick, 1985–87; Asst Priest, St Aidan's, E Acton and Hospital Chaplain, Hammersmith Hosp., 1987–90; Asst, Stevenage Team Ministry, 1990–94; Parish Priest: St Scholastica's, Clapton, 1994–2001; Holy Rood, Watford, 2001–16. Mem., Cathedral Chapter, 2010–. *Address:* Archbishop's House, Ambrosden Avenue, SW1P 1QJ. *T:* (020) 7798 9381.

**McALEER, Declan Martin;** Member (SF) West Tyrone, Northern Ireland Assembly, since July 2012; *b* Omagh, 10 July 1973; *s* of Barney and Kathleen McAleer; *m* 2001, Geraldine Rafferty; two *s* one *d. Educ:* Univ. of Ulster (BSc Hons Social Psychol. and Sociol.; PGCFHE; MSc Applied Psychol.). Lectr in Psychol., Omagh Coll., 1999–2012; teacher in Psychol. and Health and Social Care, Dean Maguire Coll., 2003–07. Mem., Western Educn Liby Bd, 2006–12. Chair and Dir, Loughmacrory Community Develt Assoc., 2011–. *Recreations:* community development, Gaelic football. *Address:* 4 James Street, Omagh, Co. Tyrone BT78 1DH. *T:* (028) 8225 3040. *E:* declanmcaleer@ymail.com.

**McALEESE, Mary Patricia, (Mrs Martin McAleese);** President of Ireland, 1997–2011; Professor of Children, Religion and Law, University of Glasgow, since 2018; *b* 27 June 1951; *d* of Patrick Leneghan and Claire (*née* McManus); *m* 1976, Martin McAleese; one *s* two *d. Educ:* QUB (LLB 1973); TCD (MA 1986); Dip. in Spanish, Inst. of Linguists, 1994; Nat. Univ. of Ireland (MA Theol. 2010); Pontifical Gregorian Univ., Rome (Lic. Canon Law 2012; DCL 2018). AIL. Called to the Bar: N Ireland, 1974; King's Inns, Dublin, 1978. Barrister, NI, 1974–75; Reid Prof. of Criminal Law, Criminology and Penology, TCD, 1975–79 and 1981–87; journalist and TV presenter, Radio Telefís Eireann, 1979–81 (part-time presenter, 1981–85); Queen's University, Belfast: Dir, Inst. of Professional Legal Studies, 1987–97; Pro Vice-Chancellor, 1994–97. Chair, Von Hugel Inst., Univ. of Cambridge, 2012–. Burns Schol., Boston Coll., 2013; Vis. Fellow, 2014–15, Exec. Fellow, 2015–, Keough Sch. of Global Affairs, Univ. of Notre Dame, Indiana; Dist. Vis. Prof., St Mary's Univ., London, 2016. Chair, EC High Level Gp on Modernisation of Third Level Educn, 2012–15. Director: Northern Ireland Electricity, 1991–97; Channel 4 Television, 1992–97; Royal Gp of Hospitals HSS Trust, Belfast, 1996–97. Patron: Bob Hawke Res. Inst., Univ. of S Australia, 2014–; Mayo-Roscommon Hospice, 2017–. *Publications:* (jtly) Reports on Irish Penal System, 1981; Children in Custody (ed Stewart and Tutt), 1987;

(jtly) Sectarianism: a discussion document, 1993; Reconciled Being, 1997; Building Bridges, 2011; Quo Vadis? Collegiality in the Code of Canon Law, 2012; The Moral Heart of Public Service, 2017; contrib. legal and religious jls. *Recreations:* hill-walking, set dancing, reading, theology.

**McALINDEN, Hon. Sir Gerald (Joseph),** Kt 2018; **Hon. Mr Justice McAlinden;** a Judge of the High Court, Northern Ireland, since 2018; *b* Larne, Co. Antrim, 4 Dec. 1962; *s* of James and Marjorie McAlinden; *m* 1987, Eileen Finnegan; two *s* one *d. Educ:* MacNissi's Coll.; Queen's Univ. Belfast (LLB). Called to the Bar, NI, 1986, Bencher, 2016; QC (NI) 2011. Pres., Mental Health Rev. Tribunal, 2015–18. Chm., Bar Council of NI, 2014–16. *Recreations:* astronomy, flying, jogging. *Address:* Royal Courts of Justice, Chichester Street, Belfast BT1 3JF. *Club:* Ulster Flying (Newtownards).

**McALISKEY, (Josephine) Bernadette, (Mrs Micheal McAliskey);** Co-ordinator, South Tyrone Empowerment Programme; *b* 23 April 1947; *d* of late John James Devlin and Elizabeth Devlin; *m* 1973, Micheal McAliskey; three *c. Educ:* St Patrick's Girls' Acad., Dungannon; psychology student at Queen's Univ., Belfast, 1966–69. Youngest MP in House of Commons when elected at age of 21; MP (Ind. Unity) Mid Ulster, April 1969–Feb. 1974. Founder Member and Mem. Exec., Irish Republican Socialist Party, 1975–76. Former Chm., Ind. Socialist Party, Ireland. Contested: (Ind) N Ireland, European Parlt, 1979; (People's Democracy), Dublin N Central, Dáil Eireann, Feb. and Nov. 1982. *Publications:* The Price of my Soul (autobiog.), 1969. *Recreations:* walking, folk music, doing nothing, swimming.

**McALISTER, William Harle Nelson;** Associate Director, Media Trust, since 2013; independent arts producer; *b* 30 Aug. 1940; *s* of Flying Officer William Nelson, DFC (*d* 1940) and late Marjorie Isobel (*née* McIntyre); adopted by late William Edwyn McAlister (whom she *m* 2nd); *m* 1968 (marr. diss. 1985); two *s* two *d;* one *s. Educ:* Sorbonne, Paris; Univ. of Copenhagen; University Coll. London (BA Hons Psychology, 1967). Dir, Almost Free Theatre, 1968–72; Dep. Dir, Inter-Action Trust, 1968–72; Founder Dir, Islington Bus Co., 1972–77; Director: Battersea Arts Centre, 1976–77; ICA, 1977–90; Creative Research Ltd, 1989–91; Beaconsfield Gall., 1999–; Ambient TV Ltd, 2000–; hiddenart.com, 2002–. Dir, Sense of Ireland Fest., 1980; Bd Dir, London International Theatre Fest., 1983; Chm. for the Arts, IT 82 Cttee, 1982. Chm., Recreational Trust, 1972–88; Co-Founder, Fair Play for Children, 1974–75; Advr, Task Force Trust, 1972–74; Cultural Policy Advr, Soros Foundns, 1992–97; Sen. Advr, Tonguesten, 2013–. Trustee: Circle 33 Housing Trust, 1972–75; Moving Picture Mime Trust, 1978–80; Shape (Arts for the Disadvantaged), 1979–81. Trustee: International House, 1989–; Africa Centre, 1990–2000; World Circuit Arts, 1996–2000. Governor: Holloway Adult Educn Inst., 1974–76; Byam Shaw Sch. of Art, 2000–. Patient Gov., UCL Hosp. Foundn Trust, 2011–15. Mem. Court, RCA, 1980–90. CSCE British Deleg., Krakow, Poland, 1991. *Publications:* Community Psychology, 1975; EEC and the Arts, 1978; (contrib.) Art and Society, 1999; articles on arts policy. *Recreations:* mycology, angling, tennis, travel. *Address:* 151c Grosvenor Avenue, N5 2NH. *T:* 07956 229796. *E:* bill.mcalister@gmail.com.

**McALLION, John;** Member (Lab) Dundee East, Scottish Parliament, 1999–2003; *b* 13 Feb. 1948; *s* of Joseph and Norah McAllion; *m* 1971, Susan Jean Godlonton; two *s. Educ:* St Augustine's Comprehensive School, Glasgow; St Andrews Univ. (MA Hons 2nd cl. Modern and Medieval Hist. 1972); Dundee Coll. of Education. Civil Servant, Post Office, 1967–68; History Teacher, St Saviour's High Sch., Dundee, 1973–78; Social Studies Teacher, Balgowan Sch., Dundee, 1978–82; Research Asst to Bob McTaggart, 1982–86. Regional Councillor, 1984–87, Convener, 1986–87, Tayside Regional Council. MP (Lab) Dundee East, 1987–2001. Contested (Lab) Dundee E, Scottish Parlt, 2003. *Recreations:* sport, reading, music. *Address:* 3 Haldane Street, Dundee DD3 0HP. *T:* (01382) 826678.

**McALLISTER, Adrian,** OBE 2019; Chief Executive, Office of Police Ombudsman for Northern Ireland, 2013–18; *b* Walsall, W Midlands, 20 Sept. 1962; *s* of Peter Ernest McAllister and Patricia Hilda McAllister; *m* 2007, Julie Winfield; one *d. Educ:* Streetly Comprehensive Sch.; Univ. of Loughborough (BA Hons Politics with Econs); Univ. of Manchester (MA Police and Public Sector Mgt); Univ. of Cambridge (Dip. Applied Criminol.). With W Midlands Police, 1985–97; Detective Superintendent, Merseyside Police, 1997–2000; Lancashire Police: Detective Chief Superintendent, 2000–02; Asst Chief Constable, 2002–05; Actg Dep. Chief Constable, 2005–07; Chief Exec., Ind. Safeguarding Authy, 2007–12. *Recreations:* sport, football, squash, golf, cycling, contemporary music, cooking, current affairs.

**McALLISTER, Dominic James;** HM Diplomatic Service; Deputy High Commissioner, Bangalore, since 2015; *b* Mtarfa, Malta, 12 Feb. 1964; *s* of late John Michael Kevin Patrick McAllister and of Eileen McAllister (*née* Reid); *m* 1993, Hei Yee Chan; two *s* two *d. Educ:* King's Coll. London (BSc Chem. 1985; AKC); Sch. of Oriental and African Studies, Univ. of London (MA Chinese Area Studies 1990). Joined FCO, 1990; Third Secretary: (Consular) Gulf Emergency Unit, 1991; Asst Japan Desk Officer, 1991–92; EU Liaison Officer, Belgrade, 1992; Press and Public Affairs Officer, Riyadh, 1995–97; Second Sec., Desk Officer, Nigeria, 1997; Dir of Admin, British Trade and Commerce Office, Taipei, 1998–2001; Desk Officer, Thailand, Cambodia and Laos, 2001–04; First Sec. and Hd, UKTI, Caracas, 2004–08; Sen. Policy Advr, Internat. Sci. and Innovation Unit, DIUS (on secondment), 2008; First Sec. and Hd, Sci. and Innovation, 2008–11, Counsellor, Econ., Climate, Sci., 2011–12, Seoul; Counsellor, Sci. and Innovation (Gulf), 2012–15. *Recreations:* second hand bookshops, National Trust properties, botanical gardens, family holidays, family history, growing vegetables, reading, theatre. *Address:* British Deputy High Commission, Prestige Takt, 23 Kasturba Road Cross, Bangalore 560001, Karnataka, India. *Club:* Bangalore.

**McALLISTER, Sir Ian (Gerald),** Kt 2008; CBE 1996; Chairman, Carbon Trust, 2001–11; *b* 17 Aug. 1943; *s* of Ian Thomas McAllister and Margaret Mary McAllister (*née* McNally); *m* 1968, Susan Margaret Frances Mitchell; three *s* one *d. Educ:* Thornleigh College, Bolton; University College London (BScEcon; Fellow, 2009). Ford Motor Co.: operations and marketing appts, 1964–79; Director: Parts Sales, 1980; Product and Marketing Parts Ops, 1981; Car Sales Ops, 1983; Marketing Plans and Programmes, 1984; Sales, Ford Germany, 1987; Gen. Marketing Manager, Lincoln Mercury Div., USA, 1989; Man. Dir, 1991–2002, and Chm. and Chief Exec., 1992–2002, Ford. Vice-President: Inst. of the Motor Industry, 1992–2002; SMMT (Pres., 1996–98). Mem. Bd and Council, BITC, 1974–2002. Non-executive Director: Scottish & Newcastle plc, 1996–2008; UCL Business Bd, 2007–16. Mem. Adv. Bd, Victim Support, 1994. Member: Adv. Cttee on Business and the Envmt, 1996–2004; Welfare to Work Task Force, 1997–2001; Bd, QCA, 1997–2003 (Dep. Chm., 2000–03); Co-Chm., Cleaner Vehicles Task Force, 1997–2000; Chairman: Greater Essex Prosperity Forum, 2007–09; Essex Economic Bd, 2009–10. Hon. PhD: E London, 1993; Loughborough, 1999; Hon. LLD Nottingham, 1995. *Recreation:* reading.

**McALLISTER, John Brian;** Chairman, Selbourne Care Ltd, 2004–17; *b* 11 June 1941; *s* of late Thomas McAllister and of Jane (*née* McCloughan); *m* 1st, 1966, Margaret Lindsay Walker (*d* 2002); two *d;* 2nd, 2004, Lynne Patricia Oldham. *Educ:* Royal Belfast Academical Instn; Queen's Univ., Belfast (BA Hons). Joined NI Civil Service as Asst Principal, Dept of Educn, 1964; Dep. Principal, Higher Educn Div., 1968; Principal: Secondary Schs Br., 1969; Re-Organisation of Local Govt Br., 1970; Principal, Dept of Finance, 1971, Dept's Central Secretariat, 1972; Asst Sec. 1973, Sen. Asst Sec. 1976, Dep. Sec., 1978–80, Dept of Educn; Dep. Sec., later Under Sec., Dept of Finance, 1980–83; Under Sec., DoE, NI, 1983–84; Dep. Chief Exec., 1984–85, Chief Exec., 1985–88, Industrial Develt Bd for NI; Chief Exec., Crestacare (formerly Cresta Hldgs Ltd), 1990–93 (Gp Man. Dir, 1988–90); consultant, 1993–94; Chief Exec., 1994–96, Chm. 1996–99, Craegmoor Healthcare; Chief Exec., Sapphire House Ltd, 1999–2006. *Recreations:* watching sport of all kinds, reading, travel.
See also Dame J. I. Harbison.

**McALLISTER, Prof. Laura Jean,** CBE 2016; PhD; FLSW; Professor of Public Policy and the Governance of Wales, Cardiff University, since 2016; *b* Bridgend, Wales, 10 Dec. 1964; *d* of William Keith McAllister and Ann Eiluned McAllister; partner, 2002, Llinos Jones. *Educ:* Bryntirion Comprehensive Sch., Bridgend; London Sch. of Econs and Pol Sci. (BSc (Econ) Hons 1988); Cardiff Univ. (PhD 1996; Hon. Fellow, 2013). Prof. of Governance, Univ. of Liverpool, 2004–16. Chair, Sport Wales, 2010–16; Board Member: FAW Trust (Welsh Football Trust), 2004–; UK Sport, 2010–16; Dep. Chair, UEFA Women's Football Cttee, 2017–. Mem., Welsh Assembly Remuneration Bd, 2014–15; Chair, Expert Panel on Electoral Reform, Nat. Assembly for Wales, 2016–17. Chair, Inst. of Welsh Affairs Women, 2009–13; Board Member: Inst. of Welsh Affairs, 2009–; Wales Adv. Cttee, British Council, 2011–; Stonewall, 2012–15. Chm., Welsh Sports Hall of Fame, 2018–. FLSW 2015; FRSA 2017. Hon. Fellow: Bangor Univ., 2011; Cardiff Metropolitan Univ., 2014; Trinity St David's Univ., 2017. Hon. Dr Glamorgan, 2011; Hon. DSc Swansea, 2016. *Publications:* Plaid Cymru: the emergence of a political party, 2001; Women, Politics and Constitutional Change, 2006; contribs to internat. jls. *Recreations:* sport, football, Wales. *T:* (029) 2087 5426. *E:* McAllisterL3@cardiff.ac.uk. *Clubs:* Cardiff City Amateur Football, Cardiff City Ladies Football.

**McALLISTER, Sophie Jane;** *see* Lamb, S. J.

**McALLISTER, Susan,** CB 2017; Prisons and Probation Ombudsman, since 2018; *b* Grimethorpe, S Yorks, 23 April 1961; *d* of Kenneth Wilks and Patricia Wilks; *m* 1990, Daniel Francis McAllister (CBE 2009); one *s* one *d. Educ:* Willowgarth High Sch., Grimethorpe; Univ. of St Andrews (MA Arabic 1983); Open Univ. (BSc 2000). GCHQ, 1983–86; National Offender Management Service, 1986–2011: Gov., HMP Gartree, 2000–02; Gov., HM Young Offender Instn Onley, 2002–04; Hd, Security Gp, 2004–05; Area Manager, W Midlands, 2005–09; Hd, Public Sector Bids Unit, 2009–11; Dir Gen., NI Prison Service, 2012–16. Hon. Vis. Fellow, Univ. of Leicester, 2014–. *Recreations:* walking, running, travel, reading, family. *Address:* Thorpe Langton, Leics. *E:* sue1mcallister@btinternet.com.

**McALPINE, Sir Andrew (William),** 7th Bt *cr* 1918, of Knott Park; *b* London, 22 Nov. 1960; *s* of Sir William Hepburn McAlpine, 6th Bt and Jill Benton McAlpine; *S* father, 2018; *m* 1991, Caroline Claire Hodgson; four *s* (incl. twins). *Educ:* Stowe Sch. Dir, Sir Robert McAlpine Enterprises Ltd, 1990–. *Recreations:* country sports, motor racing. *Heir: s* Frederick William Edwin McAlpine, *b* 25 Aug. 1993. *Address:* 33 Great Portland Street, W1W 8QF. *T:* 0333 566 3301. *E:* sirandrew@SRM.com. *Clubs:* British Racing Drivers; Northern Counties (Newcastle upon Tyne).

**McALPINE, Joan;** Member (SNP) Scotland South, Scottish Parliament, since 2011; *b* Gourock, Renfrewshire, 28 Jan.; *d* of James Campbell McAlpine and Mary Esther McAlpine (*née* McCourt); *m* 1987, Patrick Kane (marr. diss. 2016); two *d. Educ:* St Columba's Comprehensive Sch., Greenock; Univ. of Glasgow (MA Hons Econ. Hist. and Scottish Hist. 1985); City Univ., London (Postgrad. Dip. Newspaper Journalism). Writer: Greenock Telegraph, 1987–89; Scotsman, 1989–95; Daily Record, 1995–96; writer, columnist, then Ed., Sunday Times Scotland, 1996–2001; Dep. Ed., The Herald, 2001–07; columnist and Ed. of Features, Sunday Times Scotland, 2007–10. *Recreations:* family, reading, the arts. *Address:* Scottish Parliament, Edinburgh EH99 1SP. *T:* (0131) 348 6885. *E:* joan.mcalpine.msp@parliament.scot.

**McALPINE, Rear Adm. Paul Anthony, (Paddy),** CBE 2014 (OBE 2006); Principal Consultant, Castleforth Ltd, since 2018; Director, PADMC Consulting Ltd, since 2018; *b* Enniskillen, NI, 20 Nov. 1962; *s* of Niall McAlpin and Sonia McAlpin; *m* 1989, Janette Elstob; one *s* one *d. Educ:* Portora Royal Sch., Enniskillen; BRNC, Dartmouth; King's Coll. London (MA Defence Studies 1999). Joined RN, 1982; served Gulf War, 1991 (Despatches); CO HMS Somerset, 2000–01; Commander: Sea Trng, 2003–05; Task Gp 58.1, 2005–06; Dir Jt Tactical Exercise Planning Staff, 2006–08; CO HMS Daring, 2008–10; Dep. Flag Officer Sea Trng, 2011–12; Commander: UK Task Gp, UK/ Netherlands Amphibious Task Gp, 2012–14; Portsmouth Flotilla, 2014–15; Dep. Comdr, Naval Striking and Support Forces, NATO, 2015–17. ADC to the Queen, 2012–15. Younger Brother, Trinity House, 2012–. Vice Pres., RN Rugby Union, 2011–18; Chm., UK Armed Forces Rugby (formerly Combined Services Rugby), 2012–18; Mem., Portsmouth Services Fly Fishing Assoc. *Recreations:* Rugby, golf, fly fishing. *Address:* Chichester, West Sussex. *Club:* Chichester Rugby Football (Vice Pres., 2011–; Chm., 2018–).

**McALPINE, Robert James,** FCIOB; Director, Alfred McAlpine plc, 1957–94 (Chairman, 1983–92); *b* 6 May 1932; *s* of late Alfred James McAlpine and of Peggy (*née* Saunders); *m* 1st, Mary Jane Anton; two *s* one *d;* 2nd, Angela Bell (*née* Langford Brooke) (*d* 2016); one *d. Educ:* Harrow Sch. FCIOB. Director: Chester Racecourse Co., 1976–2008 (Chm., 1994–2008; Pres., 2008–); Haynes Hanson & Clark, 1978–2018 (Chm., 1993–2018); Hall Engrg plc, 1985–99; Aintree Racecourse Co., 1988–2007. Chm., Export Gp for Constructional Industries, 1975–77. Mem., Jockey Club. High Sheriff, Cheshire, 1994–95. *Recreations:* racing, shooting, golf, bridge. *Address:* Rose Hall, Dairy Lane, Aston Juxta Mondrum, Nantwich, Cheshire CW5 6DS. *Clubs:* White's, Turf, Portland, MCC.

**MACAN, Thomas Townley;** HM Diplomatic Service, retired; Governor, British Virgin Islands, 2002–06; *b* 14 Nov. 1946; *o s* of late Dr Thomas Townley Macan and Zaida Bindloss (*née* Boddington); *m* 1976, Janet Ellen Martin, Hollidaysburg, Penn; one *s* one *d. Educ:* Shrewsbury Sch.; Univ. of Sussex (BA Hons Econs; Pres., Students' Union, 1967–68). MCIL (MIL 1982). Joined HM Diplomatic Service, 1969; UN Dept, FCO, 1969–71; Bonn, 1971–74; Brasilia, 1974–78; Maritime, Aviation and Envmt Dept, FCO, 1978–81; Press Sec., Bonn, 1981–86; Hd, Commonwealth Co-ordination Dept, FCO, 1986–88; Hd, Trng Dept, FCO, 1988–90; Counsellor, Lisbon, 1990–94; Ambassador to Lithuania, 1995–98; on secondment to BOC Group, 1998–99; Minister and Dep. High Comr, New Delhi, 1999–2002. Mem., Inst. of Tourist Guiding, 2011–; Blue Badge Guide for Cumbria, 2011–. *Recreations:* steam boats, sailing, church architecture, walking. *Address:* Stevney, Outgate, Ambleside, Cumbria LA22 0NH. *Clubs:* Naval; Royal British Virgin Islands Yacht.

**McANALLY, Vice Adm. John Henry Stuart,** CB 2000; LVO 1983; Naval Adviser, 2001–05; Senior Military Advisor, 2006–10, to VT Flagship (formerly Flagship Training Ltd); National President, Royal Naval Association, since 2001; *b* 9 April 1945; *s* of late Arthur Patrick McAnally and Mrs Basil Hamilton Stuart McAnally. *Educ:* Willington Prep. Sch., Putney; Westminster Sch. FNI 1999; FRIN 1999. BRNC (RN Scholarship); HM Ships Wizard, Ashanti, Walkerton, Leverton, 1963–67; USS Moale (Exchange), 1967–68; HMS Eskimo, 1968–69; HMA Ships Melbourne and Torrens, 1971–73; CO HMS Iveston, 1973–75; Adv. Navign Course, 1975; HMS Fife, 1976–77; Staff Course, 1978; HMS Birmingham and HMY Britannia, 1979–81; MoD, 1982–83; Comd HM Ships Torquay and Alacrity, 1984–86; Staff of C-in-C Fleet, 1986–87; Captain Sixth Frigate Sqdn and CO HM Ships Ariadne and Hermione, 1987–89; Asst Dir (Warfare), Dir Naval Plans, 1989–91; RCDS 1992; HCSC 1993; Dir, Naval Logistics Staff Duties and Naval Staff Duties, MoD, 1993–95; Flag Officer Trng and Recruiting, and Chief Exec., Naval Recruiting and Trng Agency, 1996–98; Comdt, RCDS, 1998–2001. Ind. Chm., Retired Officer Selection Bds, 2001–03. Pres., Internat. Maritime Confedn, 2009–11. Gov., Corps Security, 2010–; Gov. and Trustee, Corps of Commissionaires Mgt Ltd and Trustees Ltd, 2010–. President: TS Barrosa, 2001–; RN Golf Soc., 2009–14. Mem., Hon. Co. of Master Mariners, 2002. Younger Brother, Trinity House. *Recreation:* golf. *Clubs:* Naval and Military (Vice Chm., 2010–12; Chm., 2012–19), National Liberal; Royal Naval and Royal Albert Yacht, Portsmouth Sailing (Portsmouth); Hayling Golf; Rye Golf; Liphook Golf; Leckford Golf.

**MacANDREW,** family name of **Baron MacAndrew.**

**MacANDREW,** 3rd Baron *cr* 1959, of the Firth of Clyde; **Christopher Anthony Colin MacAndrew;** farmer, 1968–2015; *b* 16 Feb. 1945; *s* of 2nd Baron MacAndrew and Ursula Beatrice (*née* Steel) (*d* 1986); *S* father, 1989; *m* 1975, Sarah (marr. diss. 2005), *o* d of Lt-Col P. H. and Mrs Brazier; one *s* two d. *Educ:* Malvern. Tax Comr, 1996–2009. *Recreations:* follower of cricket, football, Rugby, golf, tennis and motor racing. *Heir: s* Hon. Oliver Charles Julian MacAndrew, *b* 3 Sept. 1983. *Address:* 54B Sutherland Avenue, W9 2QU.

**McANDREW, Daisy Candida Leslie;** freelance reporter, presenter and journalist, since 2013; Special Correspondent, ITV News, 2011–13; *b* London, 20 May 1972; *d* of Alistair and Camilla Sampson; *m* 2005, John McAndrew; one *s* one d. *Educ:* Wycombe Abbey Sch.; Cambridge Coll. of Sixth Form Studies. Researcher for Sir Patrick Cormack, MP, 1991; political journalist, Press Gall., H of C, 1992–99; Man. Ed., House Mag., 1995–97; Press. Sec. to Charles Kennedy, MP, 1999–2001; Co-presenter, Daily Politics prog. and political corresp., Breakfast News, BBC TV, 2001–05; presenter, Drivetime, LBC Radio, 2005; Chief Political Corresp., 2005–08, Econs Ed., 2008–11, ITV News. *Publications:* (consultant) BBC's A–Z of Politics, 2000; (ed) The Politics Companion, 2004. *Recreations:* entertaining friends and family, playing with my children.

**McANDREW, Deborah Louise;** playwright and actor; Creative Director, Claybody Theatre, since 2013; *b* Huddersfield, 11 Oct. 1967; *d* of John and Rita McAndrew; *m* 1999, Conrad Nelson; one d. *Educ:* Cardinal Heenan High Sch., Leeds; Manchester Univ. (BA Hons Drama 1989); Bretton Hall Coll. (PGCE 1990). Actor: Coronation St, ITV, 1990–93 and 1997; dramas for BBC Radio; theatre incl. classical touring co., Northern Broadsides, 1995–2000; *plays:* Vacuum, 2006; Flamingoland, 2008; King Macbeth, 2010; Losing the Plot, 2012; Beyond the Veil, Ugly Duck, 2013; Till the Cows Come Home, An August Bank Holiday Lark, 2014 (UK Th. Award for Best New Play, Manchester Th. Award for Best New Play, 2014); Digging In, One of Each, 2015; Dirty Laundry, 2017; Hot Lane, 2018; The D-Road, 2019; *adaptations:* The Bells, 2004; Accidental Death of an Anarchist, 2008; Oliver Twist, 2009; David Copperfield, 2010; A Government Inspector, 2012; The Grand Gesture, 2013; Cyrano, The Tenant of Wildfell Hall, Anna of the Five Towns, A Christmas Carol, 2017; Hard Times, The Chester Mystery Plays, They Don't Pay? We Won't Pay!, 2018; Peter Pan, 2019. Chancellor, Leeds Trinity Univ., 2018–. Hon. DArts Staffs, 2018. *Publications:* Flamingoland, 2002; A Government Inspector, 2012; The Grand Gesture, 2013; An August Bank Holiday Lark, 2014; Cyrano, 2017; Hard Times, 2018. *Recreations:* choral singing, tenor horn, beekeeping. *Address:* c/o Giles Smart, United Agents, 12–26 Lexington Street, W1F 0LE. *T:* (020) 3214 0800. *E:* GSmart@unitedagents.co.uk.

**McANDREW, Nicolas;** Chairman, Murray Johnstone Ltd, 1992–99; *b* 9 Dec. 1934; *s* of late Robert Louis McAndrew and Anita Marian McAndrew (*née* Huband); *m* 1960, Diana Leonie Wood (*d* 2015); two *s* one d. *Educ:* Winchester Coll. CA 1961. Commnd Black Watch, 1953–55. With Peat, Marwick, Mitchell & Co., 1955–61; S. G. Warburg & Co. Ltd, 1962–78: Dir, 1969–78; Chm., Warburg Investment Mgt, 1975–78; Dir, Mercury Securities Ltd, 1975–78; N. M. Rothschild & Sons Ltd, 1979–88 (Man. Dir, 1980–88); Murray Johnstone Ltd, 1988–99 (Man. Dir, 1988–92). Board Member: Highlands & Islands Enterprise, 1993–97; N of Scotland Water Authy, 1995–2002. Deputy Chairman: Burn Stewart Distillers PLC, 1991–99; Liverpool Victoria Friendly Soc., 1995–2005; Chairman: Martin Currie Enhanced Income Trust (formerly Moorgate Investment Trust) PLC, 1996–2005; Guinness Flight Extra Income Trust, 1995–2002; Derby Trust PLC, 1999–2003. Chairman: Highlands and Is Rivers Assoc., 2001–05; Beauly Dist Fishery Bd, 2003–12. Master, Grocers' Co., 1978–79. *Recreations:* shooting, fishing, golf, bridge. *Address:* Ard-na-Coille, Ruisaurie, by Beauly, Inverness-shire IV4 7AJ. *T:* (01463) 782524. *Club:* White's.

**MACAPAGAL-ARROYO, Dr Gloria;** Member for 2nd District of Pampanga, since 2010, and a Deputy Speaker, House of Representatives, Republic of the Philippines; *b* 5 April 1947; *d* of Diosdado Macapagal (former Pres. of the Philippines), and Dr Evangelina Macaraeg-Macapagal; *m* Jose Miguel Arroyo; two *s* one d. *Educ:* Georgetown Univ. (BA Econs); Assumption Coll. (BSc Commerce *magna cum laude*); Ateneo de Manila Univ. (MA Econs); Univ. of the Philippines (PhD Econs). Chair, Econs Dept, Assumption Coll.; Asst Prof., Ateneo de Manila Univ.; Sen. Lectr, Sch. of Econs, Univ. of the Philippines; Asst Sec., 1986–89, Under-Sec., 1989, DTI, Philippines; Sec., Dept of Social Welfare and Develt, 1998; Vice-Pres., 1998–2001, Pres., 2001–10, Republic of the Philippines. Exec. Dir, Garments and Textiles Bd, 1987. Mem., Senate of the Philippines, 1992–98. Hon. Mem., Philippine Mil. Acad. Cl. of 1978. Hon. Dr: Tsinghua, China, 2001; Chulalongkorn, Thailand, 2002; Hon. LLD Waseda, Japan, 2002. *Publications:* (with V. M. Cunanan) Socio-Economic Impact of Tourism: a measurement and analysis system, 1979; (with M. San Buenaventura) The Economic and Social Impact of Tourism, 1983; The Services Sector in the Philippines, 1984; Getting Our Act Together: a President's campaign against the sexual exploitation of children, 2001; contrib. papers on tourism. *Recreations:* playing golf with my husband, watching movies, reading good books. *Address:* House of Representatives, Constitution Hills, Quezon City 1126, Philippines.

**MACARA, (John David) Murray;** QC (Scot.) 2008; Partner, Beltrami & Co., since 1975; *b* Glasgow, 22 July 1949; *s* of Alexander Macara and Mary Hamilton Macara (*née* Smillie); *m* 1981, Elaine Graham; one d. *Educ:* Loretto Sch., Musselburgh; Univ. of Glasgow (LLB 1970). Admitted solicitor, 1973; Solicitor Advocate, 1993. *Recreations:* golf, travel, the company of friends. *Address:* 10 Rowan Road, Glasgow G41 5BS. *T:* (0141) 427 4060. *E:* macara@btinternet.com. *Club:* Pollok Golf.

**McARDLE, Tony,** TD 1990; Lead Commissioner, Northamptonshire County Council, since 2018; *b* 31 Jan. 1958; *s* of William and Olive McArdle; one *s* two d. *Educ:* Knockbreda Primary Sch., Belfast; Methodist Coll., Belfast; Univ. of Essex (BA Hons Govt). Free Trade Dept, Adnams plc, 1980–85; East Cambridgeshire District Council: Emergency Planning Officer, 1985–87; Asst to Chief Exec., 1987–89; Corp. Support Manager, 1989–92; Hd, Community Services, 1992–95; Asst Chief Exec., 1995–98; Chief Exec., Wellingborough BC, 1998–2005; Chief Exec., Lincs CC, 2005–18. Territorial Army, 1977–99: commnd; Royal Anglian Regt, 1979; regtl appts, 1979–95; Second i/c, Cambridge Univ. OTC, 1995–98; CO 49 Bde BSTT, 1998–99.

**McAREAVEY, Most Rev. John;** *see* Dromore, Bishop of, (RC).

**McARTHUR, Surgeon Rear Adm. Calum James Gibb,** FRCGP; Commander Joint Medical Command, and Medical Director General (Naval) and Chief Naval Medical Officer, 2012–14; *b* Glasgow, 10 Nov. 1956; *s* of James McArthur and Joan McArthur; *m* 1989, Barbara Halliday. *Educ:* Glasgow Acad.; Royal Coll. of Surgeons in Ireland (MB BCh 1980; BAO 1980; LRCPI 1980). MRCGP 1986, FRCGP 2005; DRCOG 1990; Dip. Occupational Medicine 1995. PMO HM Naval Base Portsmouth and Advr in Gen. Practice, RN, 2001–04; rcds 2005; Dep. ACOS Med. PJHQ, 2005–07; Standing Jt Comdr Med., 2007–09; Comdr Defence Med. Gp, 2009–11; Hd Med. Operational Capability, 2011–12; QHP 2011–15. Non-exec. Dir, Poole Hosp. NHS Foundn Trust, 2014–. *Recreations:* antiques, paintings, gardening, keeping fit. *Address:* c/o Naval Secretary, Fleet Headquarters, Whale Island, Portsmouth PO2 8BY. *T:* (020) 7807 0471. *E:* cjgmcarthur@gmail.com. *Club:* Army and Navy.

**McARTHUR, Douglas Brown,** OBE 2001; Chairman, UK Online Measurement Ltd, since 2010; Managing Consultant, Planning for Results, since 2006; *b* Dundee, March 1951; *s* of Ronald McArthur and Edith McArthur; *m* 2006, Miranda Kennett; three d. *Educ:* Univ. of Glasgow (BSc Hons 1st Cl.). Marketing Manager: Procter & Gamble, 1973–75; Scottish and Newcastle, 1976–79; Founder, Town Art and Design, 1979–79; Sales and Mktg Dir, Radio Clyde, 1983–85; Dir, Baillie Marshall Advertising, 1986–90; Dir, Mktg, Campbell's Soups, 1990–92; Founder and CEO, Radio Advertising Bureau, 1992–2006. Mem., Marketing Soc. *Recreations:* trekking, theatre, arts. *Clubs:* 30; Marketing Gp of GB; Solus.

**MACARTHUR, Dame Ellen (Patricia),** DBE 2005 (MBE 2001); former professional offshore sailor; *b* 8 July 1976; *d* of Kenneth John Macarthur and Avril Patricia Macarthur. *Educ:* Anthony Gell Sch., Wirksworth. RYA Yachtmaster Commercial; RYA Yachtmaster Instructor. Winner: Class II (Open 50) Route du Rhum solo trans-Atlantic race, 1998, Class I (Open 60), 2002; (Open 60) Europe 1 New Man STAR solo trans-Atlantic race, 2000; EDS Atlantic Challenge, 2001; 2nd overall, Vendée Globe non-stop solo round-the-world race, 2001; fastest solo circumnavigation of the globe (World Record, 71 days, 14 hours, 18 mins and 33 secs), 2005. Founder: Ellen MacArthur Cancer Trust, 2002–; Founder and Chair of Trustees, Ellen Macarthur Foundn, 2009–. Young Sailor of the Year, 1995, Yachtsman of the Year, 1999, Yachting Journalists' Assoc.; FICO World Champion, 2001; ISAF World Champion Woman Sailor, 2001. Freeman, Skye and Lochalsh, 2006. Chevalier, Légion d'Honneur (France), 2008. *Publications:* Taking on the World (autobiog.), 2002; Race Against Time, 2005; Full Circle, 2010.

**McARTHUR, Dr John Duncan,** FRCPGlas; Consultant Cardiologist, Western Infirmary, Glasgow, 1978–2003; *b* 7 Jan. 1938; *s* of Neil McPhail McArthur and Elizabeth Duncan; *m* 1st, 1963, Elizabeth Agnew Bowie (*d* 2004); two *s* one d; 2nd, 2014, Elizabeth, (Betty) Gray King. *Educ:* Univ. of Glasgow (BSc Hons 1960; MB ChB Hons 1963); DM Madras 1970. DObstRCOG 1965; MRCP 1966; MRCPGlas 1966, FRCPGlas 1980; MRCPE 1967, FRCPE 1994. Junior House Officer, Glasgow Royal Infirmary and Ayrshire Hosps, 1963–65; Senior House Officer and Registrar, Glasgow Royal Inf., 1965–67; Lectr, Sen. Lectr, Reader, Christian Med. Coll. Hosp., Vellore, India, as Missionary, Church of Scotland, 1968–73; Sen. Registrar, Medicine/Cardiology, Glasgow Teaching Hosps, 1973–78; Consultant Cardiologist, Nuffield Hosp., Glasgow, 1985–2007. Retired Elder, Ch of Scotland. *Publications:* articles on valvular heart disease and pacemakers. *Recreations:* DIY, gardening. *E:* jd.mcarthur@gmail.com.

**MacARTHUR, Judy Anne;** *see* MacArthur Clark, J. A.

**McARTHUR, Liam Scott;** Member (Lib Dem) Orkney, Scottish Parliament, since 2007; *b* 8 Aug. 1967; *s* of William Archibald McArthur and Susan Margaret McArthur; *m* 1998, Tamsin Bailey; two s. *Educ:* Sanday Jun. High Sch.; Kirkwall Grammar Sch.; Univ. of Edinburgh (MA Pols 1990). Res. Asst to Jim Wallace, MP, 1990–92; Stagiaire, External Affairs, EC, 1992–93; Account Dir, APCO Worldwide, London and Brussels, 1995–2002; Special Advr to Dep. First Minister, Scottish Exec., 2002–05. Scottish Parliament: Lib Dem spokesman on enterprise, energy and tourism, 2007–08, on envmt, rural develt and energy, 2008–11, on educn, skills and energy, later energy, educn and young people, 2011, on justice, energy and envmt; Member: Finance Cttee, 2007–08; Rural Affairs and Envmt Cttee, 2008–11; Educn and Culture Cttee, 2011–16; Justice Cttee, 2016–. Mem., Scottish Lib Dem Policy Cttee, 2007–. *Recreations:* football, music. *Address:* Scottish Parliament, Edinburgh EH99 1SP. *T:* (0131) 348 5815. *E:* liam.mcarthur.msp@parliament.scot.

**McARTHUR, Dr Thomas Burns, (Tom);** English teacher, since 1959; feature writer, since 1962; lecturer and writer on yoga and Indian philosophy, since 1962; author and language consultant, since 1970; Editor, English Today, 1984–2007; *b* 23 Aug. 1938; *s* of Archibald McArthur and Margaret Burns; *m* 1st, 1964, Fereshteh Mottahedin (*d* 1993); one *s* two d; 2nd, 2001, Jacqueline Lam Kam-mei. *Educ:* Glasgow Univ. (MA 1958); Edinburgh Univ. (MLitt 1970; PhD 1978). Officer-Instr, RAEC, 1959–61; Asst Master, Riland Bedford Sch., Warwicks, 1961–63; Head of English, Cathedral and John Connon Sch., Bombay, India, 1965–67; Vis. Prof. in the English of the Media, Rajendra Prasad College of Mass Communication (Bharatiya Vidya Bhavan), Univ. of Bombay, 1965–67; Dir of Extra-Mural English Language Courses, Univ. of Edinburgh, 1972–79; Associate Prof. of English, Université du Québec à Trois-Rivières, Canada, 1979–83; Recognised Teacher (pt-time), 1986–2001, Res. Fellow, 1992–2001, Exeter Univ. Co-founder (with Reinhard Hartmann), Internat. Lexicography Course, Univ. of Exeter, 1987–2001. Consultant: Min. of Educn, Quebec, 1980–81; Société pour la promotion de l'enseignement de l'anglais (langue seconde) au Québec, 1980–83; Henson International Television (the Muppets), 1985–86; Dictionary Res. Centre, Exeter Univ., 1987–90; BBC Policy Planning Unit, 1992; also on dictionaries, encyclopedias and ELT books published by Century Hutchinson, Chambers, Collins, CUP, Longman, Macmillan, OUP and Time-Life. The Story of English (BBC radio series with D. Crystal), 1987. Member, Editorial Board: Internat. Jl of Lexicography, 1988–98; World Englishes, 1993–; Editl Advr, The Good Book Guide, 1992–; Mem., Internat. Adv. Bd, Logos, 1994–96. Hon. PhD Uppsala, 1999. *Publications:* Patterns of English series, 1972–74; English for Students of Economics, 1973; (with Beryl Atkins) Collins Dictionary of English Phrasal Verbs, 1974; (ed with A. J. Aitken) Languages of Scotland, 1979; Longman Lexicon of Contemporary English, 1981; A Foundation Course for Language Teachers, 1983; The Written Word, Books 1 and 2, 1984; Worlds of Reference, 1986; Yoga and the Bhagavad-Gita, 1986; Understanding Yoga, 1986; Unitive Thinking, 1988 (Beyond Logic and Mysticism, USA, 1990); The English Language as Used in Quebec: a survey, 1989; (ed) The Oxford Companion to the English Language, 1992, concise edn 1998; (ed with Ilan Kernerman) Lexicography in Asia, 1998; Living Words: language, lexicography and the knowledge revolution, 1998; The English Languages, 1998; The Oxford Guide to World English, 2002. *Recreations:* reading, television, walking, cycling, travel. *Address:* 22–23 Ventress Farm Court, Cherry Hinton Road, Cambridge CB1 8HD. *T:* (01223) 245934.

**MacARTHUR CLARK, Dr Judy Anne**, CBE 2004; FRSB; FRCVS; Executive Director: JMC Consultancy, since 1991; Solomon Foundation, since 2007; UK Government International 3Rs Programme Leader, since 2014; JMC Welfare International, since 2018; *b* 18 Nov. 1950; *d* of Archibald Alastair Cameron MacArthur and Elinore Muriel MacArthur (*née* Warde); *m* 1991, David Wayne Clark; two *s* two *d*. *Educ:* Orton Longueville Grammar Sch.; Glasgow Univ. (BVMS 1973); MRCVS 1973; DLAS 1985; DipECLAM 2001; DACLAM 2007. Vet. Officer, UFAW, 1974–76; SSO, MoD, 1976–82; Director: G. D. Searle, 1982–86; Pfizer, UK, 1986–91; Vet. Dir, BioZone Ltd, 1992–2005; Vice-Pres., Worldwide Comparative Medicine, Pfizer, USA, 2005–07; Chief Inspector, Animals Scientific Procedures Inspectorate, 2007–11; Hd, Animals in Sci. Regulation Unit, Home Office, 2011–16. Mem., BBSRC, 1996–99; Chair: Farm Animal Welfare Council, 1999–2004; Bd of Trustees, Soulsby Foundn, 2017–. Pres., RCVS, 1992–93. Mem., Trustee Bd, RSTM&H, 2015–20. FRSB (FIBiol 1997); FRAgS 2007 (ARAgS 2002); FRSTM&H 2015; FRCVS 2016. Hon. FBPhS 2016. Hon. DVMS Glasgow, 2001. *Publications:* contribs to scientific and policy pubns. *Recreations:* gardening, exploring remote places, especially with my family. *Address:* Aynsley Court, Strand Street, Sandwich, Kent CT13 9DU. *T:* (01304) 619665. *E:* judymacarthurclark@gmail.com. *Clubs:* Farmers, Royal Society of Medicine.

**MACARTNEY, Sir John Ralph**, 7th Bt *cr* 1799, of Lish, Co. Armagh; *b* 24 July 1945; *o s* of Sir John Barrington Macartney, 6th Bt and Amy Isobel Reinke; *S* father, 1999, but his name does not appear on the Official Roll of the Baronetage; *m* 1966, Suzanne Marie Fowler; four *d*. *Heir: cousin* John Alexander Macartney [*b* 1961; *m* 1986, Robyn Mary Norling (marr. diss. 2003)].

**MacASKILL, Ewen**; Defence and Security Correspondent, The Guardian, 2013–18 (US Bureau Chief, 2007–13); *b* 29 Oct. 1951; *s* of John Angus MacAskill and Catherine Euphemia MacAskill (*née* MacDonald); *m* 1976, Sarah Anne Hutchison; three *s*. *Educ:* Woodside Secondary Sch., Glasgow; Glasgow Univ. (MA Hons Modern History and Politics). Reporter, Glasgow Herald, 1973–77; VSO, working as journalist, Nat. Broadcasting Commn, Papua New Guinea, 1978–79; journalist: Reuters, 1980; Scotsman, 1981–83; China Daily, Beijing, 1984–85; Political Correspondent, 1986–90, Political Editor, 1990–96, Scotsman; Chief Pol Correspondent, 1996–99, Diplomatic Ed., 2000–07, The Guardian. Lawrence Sterne Fellow, Washington Post, 1986. Mem., St Margarets Film Club. Member: Scoop of the Year team, What the Papers Say awards, 1999; Pulitzer Prize team for public service, 2014; Emmy Award team, 2014. Scotland's Young Journalist of Year, 1974; (jtly) George Polk Award for nat. security reporting, Long Island Univ., NY, 2013; (jtly) Investigative Reporters and Editors Award, 2013; (jtly) Walkley Award, Walkley Foundn, 2014. *Recreations:* mountaineering, film, books. *Club:* Junior Mountaineering of Scotland.

**MacASKILL, Kenneth Wright**; solicitor; Member (SNP) Edinburgh Eastern, Scottish Parliament, 2011–16 (Lothians, 1999–2007, Edinburgh East and Musselburgh, 2007–11); *b* 28 April 1958; two *s*. *Educ:* Linlithgow Acad.; Edinburgh Univ. (LLB Hons). Cabinet Secretary for Justice, Scottish Parlt, 2007–14. Mem., SNP, 1981– (Mem., Nat. Exec., 1984–2003; Treas., until 1999). Contested (SNP): Livingston, 1983, 1987; Linlithgow, 1992, 1997; Scotland Mid and Fife, EP elecns, 1989. *Publications:* Building a Nation: post devolution nationalism in Scotland, 2004; (with H. McLeish) Global Scots: making it in a modern world, 2005; (with H. McLeish) Wherever the Saltire Flies, 2006; The Lockerbie Bombing: the search for justice, 2016; Glasgow 1919: the rise of red Clydeside, 2019.

**McASLAN, John Renwick**, CBE 2012; RSA 2014; RIBA; FRIAS; FRICS; FICE; Executive Chairman, John McAslan + Partners, since 1996; *b* Glasgow, 16 Feb. 1954; *s* of Prof. T. Crawford McAslan and Jean McAslan; *m* 1981, Dava Sagenkahn; one *s* two *d*. *Educ:* Dunoon Grammar Sch.; Dollar Acad.; Edinburgh Univ. (MA; DipArch). RIBA 1982; FRIAS 2014; FRICS 2013; FICE 2013. With Cambridge Seven Associates, Boston, 1978–79; Richard Rogers and Partners, 1980–83; Troughton McAslan, 1984–95. Teaching, throughout UK and worldwide, 1990–; Prof., Welsh Sch. of Architecture, Univ. of Wales, 1998–2001; Architectural Advr to Govs, Dollar Acad., 2006–12; Prof., Sch. of Architecture and Design, Univ. of Ulster, 2009–11. Chm., Architect Adv. Panel, RBK&C, 2008–; Mem. Council, Tate Britain, 2008–14. Hon. Consul for Haiti in London, 2012–13; Goodwill Ambassador, Port-au-Prince, Haiti, 2016–. Numerous exhibns, 1984–. Chm., many cttees and awards gps. Internat. Associate, AIA, 2000; Mem., Japan Inst. of Architects, 1993. Founding Mem., Volubilis Foundn, Morocco, 2001. Foundation Trustee: Whitechapel Art Gall., 1989–96; John McAslan Family Charitable Trust, 1997–; RIBA/ICE McAslan Bursary, 2004–; Trustee, Photographer's Gall., 2005–09; Chm., Dunoon Burgh Hall Trust, 2009–. Mem., Clinton Global Initiative, 2007–11. Regent, Univ. of Edinburgh, 2013–. FRSA 1989. Hon. FAIA 2016. Dr *hc* Edinburgh, 2016. *Completed* works include: *London:* RSA; Friends House; Heals; John Roan Sch.; Christopher Place Sch.; Fenchurch St; 28 Dorset Square; Goldsmiths Coll. Masterplan; Mus. of Methodism; Al Jazeera Media Network; Trinity Coll. of Music; Swiss Cottage Liby; Peter Jones; Roundhouse; Royal Acad. of Music; Harris Acad.; King's Cross Station; Thomas Tallis Sch., Greenwich; London Olympics Energy Centres; Wellington House; Dulwich Coll. Masterplan; RMA Woolwich; SOAS; Art Fund HQ; *other:* Engrg Bldg, Charles Carter Bldg, Postgrad. Centre, Masterplan, Lancs Univ.; De La Warr Pavilion, Bexhill-on-Sea; 78–82 Derngate, Northampton; Kingston Univ.; Student Centre and Sch. of Nursing, Masterplan, Manchester Univ.; Oasis Acad., Enfield; RSA Acad., Tipton; Surgeon's Hall Museums, Edinburgh; *international:* St Catherine's Coll., Kobe; Yapi Kredi HQ, Istanbul; Florida Southern Coll.; Max Mara HQ, Reggio Emilia; British Embassy, Algiers; Delhi Metro; Iron Market, Port-au-Prince, Haiti; Cultural Forum, Doha; Jumaa Mosque, Doha; Msheireb Museums, Doha; Kericho Cath., Kenya; British Sch., Rio de Janeiro; *ongoing* works include: *London:* Cross Rail Bond Street Station; St Paul's Girls Sch.; Nat. Hist. Mus.; Millbank Tower; Sloane St Masterplan; *other:* Saïd Business Sch., Oxford; Clore Music Studios, Oxford; Nat. Collections Facility, Nat. Galls of Scotland; St Albans Mus. and Art Gall.; Belfast Transport Hub; Health and Innovation Campus, Lancs Univ.; Burrell Collection, Glasgow; BM Arc, Berks; *international:* Memorial Centre, Rwanda; Malawi Schs; Mandarin Oriental Hotel, Doha; Msheireb Acad., Doha; Park Hyatt Hotel, Doha; Doha Metro; Varanasi Station, India; Taj Palace, Mumbai; Ciftciler Towers, Istanbul; Royal BC Mus., Vic, Canada; Sydney Central Station, Australia; British Sch., Rio de Janeiro. Numerous internat. architectural awards incl. Architectural Practice of the Year, Builder Gp, 1998, 1999, 2002; Civic Trust Award, 1999, 2000, 2008 (4 awards), 2009, 2012 (2 awards), 2015, 2017 (2 awards), 2018 (2 awards); Millennium Award, Design Council, 2000; British Construction Industry Award, 2000, 2007, 2010, 2012; 2015, 2016; Concrete Soc. Award, 2001, 2002; AIA Merit Award, 2001, 2003, Commendation 2016; RIBA Award for Architecture, 1996, 2002, 2005 (3 awards), 2007 (3 awards), 2008 (3 awards), 2009, 2011 (3 awards), 2013 (3 awards), 2014 (2 awards), 2015 (3 awards); Royal Fine Art Commn Trust Award, 2004; Roses Award, 2004, Roses Gold Award, 2009; EU Cultural Heritage Prize (Europa Nostra), diploma 2006, medal 2007, award 2013; English Heritage Award, 2006; Camden Design Award, 2006, 2015; Architect of the Year, 2006, Masterplanning Architect of the Year, 2006, Retail Architect of the Year, 2007, World Architect of the Year, 2009, Transport Architect of the Year, 2009, Building Design; Internat. Property Award, 2011, 2012, 2016; Chicago Athenæum Award, 2011, 2017; ICE Award, 2012; Elle Decoration Awards, 2012; Nat. Rail Award, 2012; Nat. Transport Award, 2012; IStructE Award (2 awards), 2012; Internat. Architecture Award, 2012, 2015; British Design Award, 2012; AJ Retrofit Award, 2012; AJ Value Excellence Award, 2012; Network Rail Partnership Award, 2012; Outstanding Achievement in Station Design and Construction, 2012; RICS Award, 2012; Brick Award, 2012; Combined Heat and Power Assoc., 2012; Commercial Real Estate Award, 2012 (2 awards); BCIA Award, 2012, 2015, 2016; New London Awards, 2012 (2 awards), 2013; London Transport Award, 2013; London Planning Awards, 2013 (2 awards), 2016 (2 awards); German Design Council Awards, 2013; AJ 100 Building of the Year, 2013; Building Awards, 2013; AIA UK Design Awards, 2013; MIPIM Awards (2 awards), 2013; European Property Awards, 2013; Nat. Railway Heritage Award, 2013; UK Property Award, 2013; Iconic Award, 2013; Internat. Design Award, 2014; Queen's Award for Enterprise, 2014; Placemaking Award, 2014; Sir Henry Royce Meml Foundn Award, 2014; ULI Global Award, 2015; Faith and Form Award, 2016 (2 awards); AIA Internat. Design Award, 2017; Religious Art and Architecture Award, 2017. *Publications:* numerous articles and monographs. *Recreation:* spending time with family. *Address:* John McAslan + Partners, 7–9 William Road, NW1 3ER. *T:* (020) 7313 6000. *E:* j.mcaslan@mcaslan.co.uk. *Clubs:* Athenæum; Caledonian; Stoke Park (Stoke Poges); Royal Bombay Yacht.

**McATASNEY, Philippa Mary**; QC 2006; *b* 29 Sept. 1962; *d* of Patrick Anthony McAtasney and Mary Dianne McAtasney (*née* Swateridge); *m* 2003, Richard George Leach; two *d*. *Educ:* Brookfield Comp. Sch.; Itchen Sixth Form Coll.; London Sch. of Econs and Pol Sci. (LLB Hons 1984). Called to the Bar, Lincoln's Inn, 1985, Bencher, 2012; in practice specialising in law of sexual offences, violent crime, fraud, judicial review and police discipline work; Mem., SE and W Circuits. *Recreations:* theatre, cinema, reading, swimming, socialising with family and friends. *Address:* Furnival Chambers, 30–32 Furnival Street, EC4A 1JQ. *T:* (020) 7405 3232.

**McATEER, Rev. Bruce James**; General Secretary of the General Synod, Anglican Church of Australia, 2004–08; Rector, St Luke's Anglican Church, Mosman, 2008–14; *b* 21 Dec. 1946; *s* of Alwyn James McAteer and Olive Ellen McAteer (*née* Child); *m* 1970, Margaret Lorraine Pocock; one *s* one *d*. *Educ:* Australian Coll. of Theol. (DipTh); Charles Sturt Univ. (Grad. Dip. Ch Leadership and Mgt). Accountant, 1962–71; CA 1973. Ordained deacon, 1973, priest, 1975; parochial appts, dios Newcastle and Grafton, NSW, 1972–89; Gen. Manager and Bishop's Registrar, Anglican Dio. Grafton, 1989–2004; Canon in Residence, and Hon. Associate Priest, 1991–2004, Hon. Canon, 2004–08, Christ Church Cathedral, Grafton. Hon. Chaplain, TS Shropshire, Grafton, 1991–2004. *Recreations:* reading, listening to music, walking. *Address:* 571/8 Carrak Road, Kincumber, NSW 2251, Australia. *E:* bmcateer@tpg.com.au. *Clubs:* NSW Masonic (Sydney); Davistown RSL.

**McATEER, Michael**; Founder Director, Financial Inclusion Centre, since 2007; Deputy Chair, General Consumer Council of Northern Ireland, since 2016; *b* Derry, NI, 19 Nov. 1962; *s* of Patrick McAteer and Margaret McAteer (*née* McLaughlin); *m* 2002, Margaret Donnelly; one *s*. *Educ:* St Columb's Coll., Derry, NI. Henderson Investors, 1986–89; Framlington Investment Mgt, 1989–91; business advr, 1991–93; Principal Policy Advr, Consumers' Assoc., 1994–2006. Founder Dir, Hackney Credit Union, 2005–07. Non-executive Director: Pensions Adv. Service, 2007–10; FSA, 2009–13; Financial Conduct Authy, 2013–16. Member: Professional Oversight Bd, Financial Reporting Council, 2009–12; Registry Trust Consumer Panel, 2012–16 (non-exec. Dir, 2016–; Dep. Chm., 2018–). Mem., Financial Users Expert Panel, EC, 2007–10 (Chair, 2010); Chm., EC Financial Services Users Gp, 2011–17 (Mem., 2018–). Member, Consultative Panel: Cttee of Eur. Insce and Occupational Pension Supervisors, 2006–10; Cttee of Eur. Banking Supervisors, 2009–10; Cttee of Eur. Securities Regulators, 2010–11; Adv. Bd, CARITAS Westminster, 2012–; European Securities and Markets Authy Financial Innovation Consultative Wkg Gp, 2017–19. Chm., Z2K, 2016–. Trustee, Share Action, until 2019. *Recreations:* reading (European history), running, experimental cinema, following Manchester United, Member of Mildmay Club and Institute Union. *Address:* Financial Inclusion Centre, 19 Albion Road, N16 9PG.

**McAULAY, Ian James**; Chief Executive, Southern Water, since 2017; *b* Glasgow, 25 April 1965; *s* of John McAulay and Suzanne McAulay; two *d*. *Educ:* Univ. of Strathclyde (BEng Civil Engrg 1988); Harvard Business Sch. (AMP 2001). Sen. Engr, Crouch, Hogg, Waterman, 1988–94; Business Dir, 1994–2005, Man. Dir, 2005–07, MWH UK Ltd; Exec. Dir, United Utilities plc, 2007–10; Chief Strategy Officer, MWH Global Inc., 2010–13; Chief Exec., Viridor Ltd, 2013–16; Exec. Dir, Pennon Gp plc, 2013–16. *Recreations:* football, golf, Rugby, reading. *Address:* Southern Water, Southern House, Yeoman Road, Worthing, W Sussex BN13 3NX.

**MacAUSLAN, Harry Hume**; Vice Chairman, Europe, Middle East and Africa, Leo Burnett, 2004; *b* London, 2 Oct. 1956; *s* of John and Constance MacAuslan; *m* 1981, Fiona Caroline (*née* Boag); two *s* one *d*. *Educ:* Charterhouse; Manchester Univ. (BA Hons Hist.). Mktg Exec., De La Rue, 1979–80; JWT: Advertising Exec., 1980–89; Bd Dir, 1989–96; Dep. Chm., 1996–2004. Non-executive Director: Octopus Investments, 2007–; Perfect Pizza, 2009–. Trustee, Mental Health Foundn, 2009–. Trustee and Gov., Sadler's Wells, 1996– (Vice Chm., 2009–). Chm., Russell Maliphant Dance Co., 2010–12. *Recreation:* portrait painting. *E:* harry@macauslan.co.uk. *T:* 07770 735907.

**McAVAN, Linda**; Member (Lab) Yorkshire and the Humber Region, European Parliament, 1999–2019 (Yorkshire South, May 1998–99). *Educ:* St Joseph's RC Coll., Bradford; Heriot-Watt Univ. (BA Hons Interpreting and Translation 1984); Univ. Libre de Bruxelles (MA Internat. Relns 1991). Work in Brussels for various European agencies, 1984–91; European Officer, Coalfield Communities Campaign, Barnsley, 1991–95; Sen. Strategy Officer on European Affairs, Barnsley BC, 1995–98. European Parliament: Lab spokesman on Envmt, Food Safety and Public Health, 2004–14; Socialist and Democrat Gp Spokesperson/Coordinator on Envmt, Food Safety and Public Health, 2009; Mem., Temp. Cttee on Climate Change, 2007–09; Chairman: Fair Trade Wkg Gp, 2004–19; Cttee for Internat. Develt, 2014–19; Vice Chair, Afro-Caribbean and Pacific Cttee, 2009–12; Dep. Leader, European Parly Lab. Party, 1999–2004; Mem., PES, 2004–19 (Treas., 2004–06; Vice Pres. (climate change portfolio), 2006–09). Mem., Convention on the Future of Europe, 2002–03. British European Woman of the Year, 2002.

**McAVEETY, Francis**; Member (Lab) Glasgow City Council, since 2012; *b* 27 July 1962; *s* of Philip and Anne Marie McAveety; *m* 1985, Anita Mitchell; one *s* one *d*. *Educ:* Strathclyde Univ. (BA Jt Hons English and History 1983); St Andrew's Coll. of Educn, Glasgow (post grad. teaching qualification, 1984). Teacher: Glasgow, 1984–94; Renfrewshire, 1994–99. Member (Lab): Glasgow DC, 1988–95; Glasgow City Council, 1995–99 (Convener, Arts and Culture, 1995–97; Leader, 1997–99). Mem. (Lab) Glasgow Shettleston, Scottish Parlt, 1999–2011. Scottish Executive: Dep. Minister for Local Govt, 1999–2000, for Health,

2002–03; Minister for Tourism, Culture and Sport, 2003–04; Shadow Minister for Sport, 2007–10; Convenor, Public Petitions Cttee, Scottish Parlt, 2007–10. Contested (Lab) Glasgow Shettleston, Scottish Parlt, 2011. DL Glasgow 1998. *Recreations:* sport, reading, record collecting. *Address:* 156 Glenbuck Avenue, Glasgow G33 1LW.

**McAVOY,** family name of **Baron McAvoy**.

**McAVOY,** Baron *cr* 2010 (Life Peer), of Rutherglen in Lanarkshire; **Thomas McLaughlin McAvoy,** PC 2003; *b* 14 Dec. 1943; *m* 1968, Eleanor Kerr; four *s*. Employee, Hoover, Cambuslang; shop steward, AEU. Mem., Strathclyde Regl Council, 1982–87; former Chm., Rutherglen Community Council. MP (Lab and Co-op) Glasgow, Rutherglen, 1987–2005, Rutherglen and Hamilton W, 2005–10. An Opposition Whip, 1990–93; Comptroller of HM Household, 1997–2008; Treasurer of HM Household (Dep. Chief Whip), 2008–10. House of Lords: an Opposition Whip, 2011–15; Opposition spokesman on Scotland, 2012–18, on NI, 2012–18; Opposition Dep. Chief Whip, 2015–18; Opposition Chief Whip, 2018–. *Address:* House of Lords, SW1A 0PW; 30 Southhill Avenue, Rutherglen, Lanarkshire G73 3TB.

**McAVOY, Prof. Brian Ramsay,** MD; FRCP, FRCGP, FRACGP, FRNZCGP, FAChAM; Addiction Medicine Specialist, Alcohol and Drug Service, Department of Health and Human Services, Tasmania, since 2010; *b* 2 Jan. 1949; *s* of Thomas Ramsay McAvoy and Christine McMillan McAvoy. *Educ:* Eastwood Sen. Secondary Sch., Glasgow; Univ. of Glasgow (BSc; MB ChB); Leicester Univ. (MD). FRCGP 1988; FRCP 1992; FRNZCGP 1999; FRACGP 2000; FAChAM 2005. Vocational Trainee in Gen. Practice, Southern Gen. Hosp. Scheme, Glasgow, 1973–76; Teaching Fellow, Dept of Family Medicine, McMaster Med. Sch., Hamilton, Ont, 1976–77; Principal in General Practice: Byfield, Northants, 1977–84; Leicester, 1984–89; Guidepost, Northumberland, 1994–2000; Lectr, 1977–84, Sen. Lectr, 1984–89, in General Practice, Univ. of Leicester; Elaine Gurr Foundation Prof. of General Practice, Univ. of Auckland, NZ, 1989–94; William Leech Prof. of Primary Health Care, Univ. of Newcastle upon Tyne, 1994–2000; GP, Melbourne, 2000–06; Dir, Res. and Practice Support, RACGP, 2000–01; Dep. Dir, Nat. Cancer Control Initiative, Melbourne, 2002–06; Specialist Med. Officer, Auckland Community Alcohol and Drug Service, 2006–10; Addiction Medicine Specialist, Capri Hosp. Trust, Auckland, 2012–14. Adjunct Prof. of Gen. Practice, Univs of Melbourne and Queensland, 2000–; Hon. Professor of General Practice: Monash Univ., 2000; Auckland Univ., 2006–. *Publications:* (ed jtly) Asian Health Care, 1990; (contrib.) Clinical Method: a general practice approach, 1988, 2nd edn 1992; (jtly) General Practice Medicine: an illustrated colour text, 2003; articles on addiction, workplace bullying, med. educn, health care delivery, cancer, ethnic minority health, alcohol and health promotion to jls incl. British Jl Gen. Practice. *Recreations:* cycling, walking, music, reading. *Address:* Department of General Practice and Primary Health Care, University of Auckland, Auckland, New Zealand.

**McBAIN, (David) Malcolm,** LVO 1972; HM Diplomatic Service, retired; Founder, British Diplomatic Oral History Programme, at Leicester University, 1995–97, Churchill Archives Centre, Churchill College, Cambridge, since 1997; *b* 19 Jan. 1928; *s* of David Walker McBain and Lilian J. McBain; *m* 1951, Audrey Yvonne Evison; one *s* three *d*. *Educ:* Sutton County School; London School of Economics (evening student). Min. of Civil Aviation appts in Tripoli, Libya, 1949–51, New Delhi, 1953–54; Diplomatic Service: New Delhi, 1958–61; Kenya, 1963–67; Thailand, 1968–75; Brunei, 1978–81; Texas, 1981–84; Ambassador to Madagascar, 1984–87. Order of Crown of Thailand, 1972. *Address:* 7 Charter Court, Gigant Street, Salisbury, Wilts SP1 2LH.

**McBARNET, Prof. Doreen Jean,** CBE 2006; PhD; Professor of Socio-Legal Studies, University of Oxford, 2004–14, now Emeritus; Fellow, Wolfson College, Oxford, since 1977. *Educ:* Dunoon Grammar Sch., Argyll; Univ. of Glasgow (MA 1st Cl. Hons Hist. and Sociol.; PhD 1980). Lectr in Sociol., Univ. of Glasgow, 1969–77; University of Oxford: Res. Fellow in Socio-Legal Studies, 1977–85; Sen. Res. Fellow, 1985–2000; Reader, 2000–04. Adjunct Prof., Res. Sch. of Social Scis, ANU, 2002–05; Vis. Prof., Sch. of Law, Edinburgh Univ., 2008–14. *Publications:* Conviction: law, the state and the construction of justice, 1981; (ed jtly) Law, State and Society, 1981; (with C. Whelan) Creative Accounting and the cross-eyed javelin thrower, 1999; Crime, Compliance and Control (collected essays), 2004; (ed jtly) The New Corporate Accountability: corporate social responsibility and the law, 2007; contrib. articles to learned jls incl. Internat. Jl Sociol. of Law, British Jl Criminol., British Jl Sociol., Modern Law Rev., Jl Law and Society, Criminal Law Rev., Accounting Orgns and Society. *Address:* Centre for Socio-Legal Studies, University of Oxford, Manor Road, Oxford OX1 3UQ.

**MacBEATH, Prof. John Ernest Carmichael,** OBE 1997; Professor of Educational Leadership, 2000, now Emeritus, and Director of Leadership for Learning: the Cambridge Network, and Wallenberg Research Centre, University of Cambridge; Fellow of Hughes Hall, Cambridge, 2000; *b* Bolobo, Congo, 23 May 1940; *m* Sandra; two *d*. *Educ:* Univ. of Glasgow (MA, MEd); Jordanhill Coll. (PGCE). Prof., Dept of Educnl Studies, and Dir, Quality in Educn Centre, Univ. of Strathclyde, until 2000. Mem., Govt Task Force on Standards, 1997–2001. Consultant: OECD; UNESCO; ILO; EC; Scottish Exec.; Educn Dept, HK; Govt of Switzerland; Bertelsmann Foundn; Prince's Trust; Varkey Gp, Dubai. Hon. Dr Edinburgh. *Publications:* (ed) Effective School Leadership: responding to change, 1998; (with K. Myers) Effective School Leaders, 1999; Schools Must Speak for Themselves: arguments for school self-evaluation, 1999; (jtly) Self-evaluation in European Schools: a story of change, 2000; (with P. Mortimore) Improving School Effectiveness, 2001; (with A. McGlynn) Self-evaluation: what's in it for schools?, 2002; (jtly) Self-evaluation in the Global Classroom, 2002; (ed with L. Moos) Democratic Learning, 2003; (jtly) School Inspection and Self-evaluation, 2006; (ed with Neil Dempster) Connecting Leadership and Learning, 2008; Learning In and Out of School: the selected works of John MacBeath, 2012; (ed with Mike Younger) A Common Wealth of Learning, 2013; Education and Schooling: myth, heresy and misconception, 2014; Strengthening the Connections Between Leadership and Learning, 2017. *Address:* Faculty of Education, 184 Hills Road, Cambridge CB2 8PQ.

**McBRATNEY, Samuel;** writer, since 1976; *b* Belfast, NI, 1 March 1943; *s* of Samuel and Verina McBratney; *m* 1964, Maralyn Green; two *s* one *d*. *Educ:* Friends' Sch., Lisburn; Trinity Coll., Dublin (BA Modern Hist. and Pol Sci. 1965). Teaching appts at primary, secondary and further educn levels, 1965–93. *Publications:* over 100 books and scripts, mainly children's fiction, including: Mark Time, 1976; The Chieftain's Daughter, 1993; Guess How Much I Love You, 1994; You're All My Favourites, 2004; There, There, 2013 for adults: Lagan Valley Details, 1976; One Grand Sweet Song, 1999. *Recreations:* watching sport, playing chess badly, viniculture (7 vines). *Address:* Shirping World Resources Ltd, 101 Antrim Road, Lisburn, Northern Ireland BT28 8EA. *E:* sam@mcbratney.org.uk.

**McBREARTY, Anthony;** regeneration consultant, since 2008; Senior Research Fellow, University of East London, since 1997; *b* 26 April 1946; *s* of Patrick and Mary McBrearty; *m* 1969, Heather McGowan (marr. diss. 1994; she *d* 2003), solicitor; one *s*; two *d* by former partner Lesley Seary. Councillor (Lab) London Borough of Haringey, 1975–86 (Chm. of Personnel Cttee, 1976–79; Chm. of Housing Cttee, 1979–82); Mem. (Lab) Enfield N, 1981–86, Chm., Housing Cttee, 1982–86, GLC. Contested (Lab) W Herts, 1987. Mem., Central Technical Unit, 1986–88; Hd of Policy, London Bor. of Newham, 1988–96; Dep. Chief Exec., Thames Gateway London Partnership, 2002–08. Mem., Mgt Cttee, Thames Reach (formerly Thames Reach Bondway) Housing Assoc., 1987–. Special Advr for the Public Sector, London Metropolitan Univ., 2008–. *Recreations:* politics, history. *Address:* 56 First Avenue, Manor Park, E12 6AN. *T:* 07503 246751. *E:* tony.mcbrearty@tiscali.co.uk.

**McBRIDE, Brian James;** Chairman: Wiggle, since 2015; Trainline, since 2019; *b* Glasgow, 15 Oct. 1955; *s* of Alexander and Maire McBride; *m* 1980, Linda Wilson; two *d*. *Educ:* Lourdes Secondary Sch., Glasgow; Univ. of Glasgow (MA Hons). Salesman, Xerox, 1977–81; IBM, 1981–93; Man. Dir, Crosfield Electronics, 1993–95; Pres., Europe, Madge Networks, 1996–98; Vice Pres., Dell Computers, 1998–2002; Man. Dir, T-Mobile UK, 2003–05; Vice-Pres. and Man. Dir, Amazon.co.uk, 2006–11. Sen. Venture Partner, then Sen. Advr, Scottish Equity Partners, 2011–; Sen. Advr, Lazard. Non-executive Director: SThree plc, 2001–08; Celtic plc, 2005–09; BBC, 2012–14; Kinnevik AB, 2019–; Senior Independent non-executive Director: Computacenter plc, 2011–15; AO.com, 2014–19; Chm., Asos plc, 2012–18. Member, Advisory Board: Huawei UK, 2011–14; Numis plc, 2011–14. Trustee, In Kind Direct, 2009–12. *Recreations:* golf, tennis, watching football, music. *Clubs:* Camberley and District; Camberley Heath Golf.

**McBRIDE, Dianne Gwenllian;** *see* Nelmes, D. G.

**McBRIDE, Prof. Ian Richard,** PhD; Foster Professor of Irish History, University of Oxford, since 2016; Fellow, Hertford College, Oxford, since 2016; *b* Armagh, NI, 13 May 1967; *s* of George and Gloria McBride; *m* 2006, Emily Wolfe; one *d*. *Educ:* Royal Sch., Armagh; Jesus Coll., Oxford (BA Hons Hist.); University Coll. London (PhD). Res. Fellow, Corpus Christi Coll., Cambridge, 1993–96; Lectr, Dept of Hist., Univ. of Durham, 1996–2000; King's College London: Lectr, 2000–05; Sen. Lectr, 2005–12; Prof., 2012–16. *Publications:* The Siege of Derry in Ulster Protestant Mythology, 1997; Scripture Politics: Ulster Presbyterians and Irish radicalism in the late eighteenth century, 1998; (ed with T. Claydon) Protestantism and National Identity: Britain and Ireland, *c.* 1650–*c.* 1850, 1998; History and Memory in Modern Ireland, 2001; Eighteenth Century Ireland: the isle of slaves, 2009; (ed with R. Bourke) The Princeton History of Modern Ireland, 2016. *Recreation:* London life. *Address:* Hertford College, Oxford OX1 3BW. *T:* (01865) 279400. *E:* Ian.McBride@hertford.ox.ac.uk.

**McBRIEN, Philippa Jill Olivier;** *see* Harris, Dame P. J. O.

**McBURNEY, Simon Montagu,** OBE 2005; actor, director and writer, since 1980; *s* of late Prof. Charles B. M. McBurney and Anne F. E. McBurney (*née* Charles). *Educ:* Peterhouse, Cambridge (BA 1980); École Lecoq, Paris. Founder and Artistic Director, Theatre de Complicite, 1983–: *performer*: Put it on Your Head; A Minute Too Late, 1987, Dir, revival, NT, 2005; More Bigger Snacks Now; Please, Please, Please; Burning Ambition; The Winter's Tale; *director/adaptation*: The Street of Crocodiles, 1992; Out of a house walked a man…; Shun-kin, 2008, 2010; A Dog's Heart (opera), 2010; The Master and Margarita, 2011–13; The Magic Flute (opera), 2012–13; Beware of Pity, Schaubühne, Berlin, 2015, Barbican, 2017; The Kid Stays in the Picture, Royal Court, 2017; *director/ adaptation/performer*: The Three Lives of Lucie Cabrol, 1994; To the Wedding; *director/ performer*: The Visit (co-dir); The Caucasian Chalk Circle; Mnemonic, 1999; Endgame, 2009; The Encounter, 2015–17; *director*: The Chairs, NY, 1998; Light, 2000; The Noise of Time, 2001; Genoa 01, 2002; The Elephant Vanishes, 2003; Measure for Measure, 2004; Strange Poetry (for LA Philharmonic Orch.); A Disappearing Number, 2007, 2008, 2010; A Dog's Heart, 2010, The Magic Flute, 2018 (for ENO); *freelance director*: French and Saunders Live, Apollo, Hammersmith, 2000; The Resistible Rise of Arturo Ui, NY, 2002; So Much Things to Say, Wyndham's, 2003; All My Sons, NY; *actor*: *films* include: Kafka, 1991; Tom and Viv, 1994; Cousin Bette, 1998; Skaggerak, 2003; Bright Young Things, 2003; The Manchurian Candidate, 2004; The Last King of Scotland, 2006; The Golden Compass, 2007; Body of Lies, 2008; The Duchess, 2008; Tinker, Tailor, Soldier, Spy, 2011; Jane Eyre, 2011; Magic in the Moonlight, 2014; Mission Impossible: Rogue Nation, 2015; Allied, 2016; The Mercy, 2018; *television* includes: The Comic Strip Presents, 1992–93; The Vicar of Dibley, 1994–2004; Rev, 2010–12; The Loudest Voice, 2019; *writer and producer*: Mr Bean's Holiday (film), 2007. *Publications:* Who You Hear It From, 2012; contrib. Guardian, Independent, The Times and Telegraph. *Address:* c/o Complicite, 14 Anglers Lane, NW5 3DG.

**MACCABE, Christopher George,** CB 2004; consultant and lecturer on peace processes and political development; British Joint Secretary, British-Irish Intergovernmental Conference, and Political Director (formerly Associate Political Director), Northern Ireland Office, 2000–08; *b* 17 Dec. 1946; *s* of late Max Maccabe, FRSA and Gladys Maccabe (*née* Chalmers), MBE; *m* 1974, Jenny Livingston; one *s* two *d*. *Educ:* Royal Belfast Academical Instn; Univ. of London (LLB); Queen's Univ., Belfast (LLM). Civil Servant, 1968–2008: Researcher: NI Cabinet Office, 1971–72; NI Office, 1972–73; Asst Private Sec. to Chief Minister, NI Power Sharing Exec., 1973–74; Private Sec. to Minister of State, NI Office, 1974–77; NI Office, 1977–80; seconded as Special Asst to Chief Constable, RUC, 1980–84; NI Office, 1984–88; Dir of Regimes, NI Prison Service, 1988–92; Hd, Political Affairs Div., NI Office, 1992–2000. Mem., Assessment Team assessing Minister of Justice's agreement with dissident republican prisoners in Maghaberry Prison, 2010–. Chm., Belfast Conflict Resolution Consortium, 2015–. Director: Forum for Cities in Transition (Belfast) Ltd, 2014–; Centre for Democracy and Peace Building, 2016–. UK Special Envoy to Sri Lanka peace process, 2006–09; Mem., Internat. Verification Commn to monitor ETA ceasefire, 2011–17. Mem. Adv. Bd, Centre for Advancement of Women in Politics, QUB, 2001–06. Gov., Victoria Coll., Belfast, 1989–2017 (Chm., 2002–09). FRSA 2001. Hon. Fellow, Inst. of Irish Studies, Univ. of Liverpool, 2009. *Publications:* (contrib.) The British and Peace in Northern Ireland, ed G. Spencer, 2015. *Recreations:* golf, Rugby Union, reading, Anglo-Zulu War of 1879. *Clubs:* Instonians Rugby, Dunmurry Golf (Belfast).

**MacCABE, Prof. Colin Myles Joseph;** Distinguished Professor of English and Film, University of Pittsburgh, since 2002 (Professor of English, 1985–2002); Chairman (formerly Executive Producer), Derek Jarman Lab, Birkbeck, Univ. of London, since 2012; *b* 9 Feb. 1949; *s* of Myles Joseph MacCabe and Ruth Ward MacCabe; *m* 2009, Flavia Mary Lambert; two *s* one *d*. *Educ:* Trinity College, Cambridge (BA English and Moral Scis 1971, MA 1974, PhD 1976); Ecole Normale Supérieure, 1972–73 (pensionnaire anglais). University of Cambridge: Research Fellow, Emmanuel College, 1974–76; Fellow, King's College, 1976–81; Asst Lectr, Faculty of English, 1976–81; Prof. of English Studies, 1981–85, Vis. Prof., 1985–91, Strathclyde Univ.; Head of Production, 1985–89, Head of Res., 1989–98, BFI; Prof. of English, Univ. of Exeter, 1998–2006 (Vis. Prof., 2006–16; Hon. Prof., 2016–); Prof. of English and Humanities, Birkbeck, Univ. of London, 2006–10. Chm., 1995–2005, Associate Dir, 2006–12, London Consortium. Chm., John Logie Baird Centre for Research in Television and Film, 1985–91 (Dir, 1983–85). Vis. Fellow, Sch. of Humanities, Griffith Univ., 1981, 1984; Mellon Vis. Prof., Univ. of Pittsburgh, 1985; Vis. Prof., Birkbeck Coll., Univ. of London, 1992–2006; Vis. Fellow, All Souls Coll., Oxford, 2014; Vis. Schol., English and Foreign Langs, Univ. of Hyderabad, 2011; Vis. Prof., UCL, 2014–. Mem., Editl Bd, Screen, 1973–81; Editor, Critical Qly, 1990– (Critical Editor, 1987–90). *Publications:* James Joyce and the Revolution of the Word, 1979, 2nd edn 2002; Godard: Images,

Sounds, Politics, 1980; (ed) The Talking Cure: essays in psychoanalysis and language, 1981; (ed) James Joyce: new perspectives, 1982; Theoretical Essays: film, linguistics, literature, 1985; (ed jtly) The BBC and Public Sector Broadcasting, 1986; (ed) High Theory/Low Culture: analysing popular television and film, 1986; (ed) Futures for English, 1987; (ed jtly) The Linguistics of Writing, 1987; (with Isaac Julien) Diary of a Young Soul Rebel, 1991; (ed jtly) Who is Andy Warhol?, 1996; Performance, 1998; The Eloquence of the Vulgar, 1999; Godard: a portrait of the artist at 70, 2003; T. S. Eliot, 2006; The Butcher Boy, 2007; (ed jtly) True to the Spirit: adaptation and the question of fidelity, 2011; (ed jtly) Cinema and Empire: film and the end of the empire, 2012; (ed jtly) Godard's Contempt: essays from the London Consortium, 2013; Perpetual Carnival: essays on film and literature, 2017; (with A. Bartos) Studio: a remembrance of Chris Marker, 2017. *Recreations:* eating, drinking, talking.

**McCABE, Eamonn Patrick;** portrait photographer and television presenter; Picture Editor, The Guardian, 1988–2001; *b* 28 July 1948; *s* of James and Celia McCabe; *m* 1st, 1972, Ruth Calvert (marr. diss. 1993); one *s*; 2nd, 1997, Rebecca Smithers; one *d*. *Educ:* Challoner School, Finchley; San Francisco State Coll. FRPS 1990. Freelance photographer on local papers and with The Guardian for one year; staff photographer, The Observer, 1977–86 and 1987–88; official photographer for the Pope's visit to England, 1982; Picture Editor, Sportsweek, 1986–87. Dir, Newscast, 2001–06. Presenter, BBC TV series, Britain in Focus: a history of photography, 2017. Works held in Nat. Portrait Gall. Hon. Prof., Thames Valley Univ., 1994; Sen. Vis. Lectr in Photography, Univ. Campus Suffolk, then Univ. of Suffolk, 2011–. Fellow in Photography, Nat. Mus. of Photography and TV, Bradford, 1988. Hon. DLit UEA, 2007; DUniv Staffordshire, 2010. Sports photographer of the year, RPS and Sports Council, 1978, 1979, 1981, 1984; News photographer of the year, British Press Awards, 1985; Picture Editor of the Year, Nikon Press Awards, 1992, 1993, 1995, 1997, 1998. *Publications:* Sports Photographer, 1981; Eamonn McCabe, Photographer, 1987; The Making of Great Photographs, 2006; Artists and Their Studios, 2008; Decade, 2010. *Recreations:* running, cinema, taking photographs, golf. *Address:* c/o The Guardian, Kings Place, 90 York Way, N1 9AG. *Club:* Chelsea Arts.

**McCABE, Ven. (John) Trevor,** RD 1976; Archdeacon of Cornwall, 1996–99, now Emeritus; *b* 26 Jan. 1933; *s* of John Leslie McCabe and Mary Ena McCabe; *m* 1959, Mary Thomas; three *s* one *d*. *Educ:* Falmouth Grammar Sch.; Nottingham Univ. (BA Hons); St Catherine's Coll., Oxford; Wycliffe Hall, Oxford (DipTh). Ordained, 1959; served Plymouth and Exeter; Vicar of Capel, Surrey, 1966–71; Chaplain, Isles of Scilly, 1971–81; Residentiary Canon, Bristol Cathedral, 1981–83; Vicar, Manaccan St Anthony and St Martin in Meneage, Helston, 1983–96; RD of Kerrier, 1987–90 and 1993–96; Hon. Canon of Truro, 1993–99. Non-exec. Dir, Cornwall Partnership Trust, 1999–2005. Chm., NHS Trust for Learning Disability, 1990–99. Served RNVR/RNR, 1955–57, 1963–83. *Recreations:* shrub gardening, local Cornish history. *Address:* Sunhill, School Lane, Budock, Falmouth TR11 5DG. *T:* (01326) 378095.

**McCABE, Prof. Mary Margaret Anne,** PhD; FBA 2017; Professor of Ancient Philosophy, King's College, London, 1998–2014, now Emerita; Keeling Scholar in Residence and Hon. Professor, University College London, 2014–17; Bye Fellow, Newnham College, Cambridge, 2014–17; *b* 18 Dec. 1948; *d* of late Edward McCabe and Sarah Frances McCabe; *m* 1993, Martin William Denton Beddoe, *qv*; two *d*. *Educ:* Oxford High Sch. for Girls; Newnham Coll., Cambridge (BA 1970; MA 1973; PhD 1977). Fellow in Classics, New Hall, Univ. of Cambridge, 1981–90; King's College, London: Lectr in Philosophy, 1990–92; Reader in Philosophy, 1992–98; Leverhulme Trust Major Res. Fellow, 2005–08. Vis. Res. Fellow, Dept of Philosophy, Princeton Univ., 2015; Vis. Prof., Dept of Philosophy, Yale Univ., 2015; Sather Prof., Dept of Classics, Univ. of Calif, Berkeley, 2016–17; Leventis Vis. Prof. in Classics, Univ. of Edinburgh, 2019. President: British Philosophical Assoc., 2009–12; Mind Assoc., 2016–17 (Vice-Pres., 2015–16). Trustee and Chair, Philosophy in Prison, 2018–. *Publications:* (as M. M. Mackenzie) Plato on Punishment, 1981; (ed jtly, as M. M. Mackenzie) Images of Authority, 1989; Plato's Individuals, 1994; (ed jtly) Form and Argument in Late Plato, 1996; Plato and his Predecessors: the dramatisation of reason, 2000; (ed jtly) Perspectives on Perception, 2007; (ed jtly) Aristotle and the Stoics reading Plato, 2010; Platonic Conversations, 2015. *Recreation:* brass band and orchestral percussion. *Address:* Department of Philosophy, King's College London, Strand, WC2R 2LS. *T:* (020) 7848 2309. *E:* mm.mccabe@kcl.ac.uk.

**McCABE, Michael Benedict;** Owner, Michael McCabe Productions Ltd, since 2009; Co-owner, The Marketing Department London Ltd, since 2019; *b* Brighton, 1 June 1965; *s* of Timothy and Jill McCabe; civil partnership 2011, *m* 2015, Anthony J. McNeill. *Educ:* Shoreham Coll. Man. Dir, Michael McCabe Associates, 1998–2003; Internat. Mktg Dir, 1998–2004, Associate Producer, 2003–04, Mamma Mia!; Producer, Spring Awakening, London, 2009; Associate Producer, Promises, Promises, NY, 2010; Producer: Million Dollar Quartet, London, 2011; How to Succeed in Business Without Really Trying, NY, 2011–12; Sweeney Todd, London, 2012; Wicked The Musical, London, 2006–, UK and internat. tours, 2013–19; An American In Paris, London, 2017–18. Trustee, English Touring Th., 2015–. *Recreations:* theatre, cinema, opera, literature, travel. *Address:* Michael McCabe Productions Ltd, c/o The Marketing Department, 60 St Martin's Lane, WC2N 4JS. *T:* (020) 7183 5019. *E:* mailbox@michaelmccabe.net. *W:* www.michaelmccabe.net. *Club:* Ivy.

**McCABE, Primrose Smith;** *see* Scott, P. S.

**McCABE, Prof. Richard Anthony,** PhD; FBA 2007; Professor of English Language and Literature, University of Oxford, since 2002; Fellow, Merton College, Oxford, since 1993 (Sub-Warden, 2008–10); *b* 2 Sept. 1954; *s* of Edward McCabe and Jenny (*née* Synnott). *Educ:* Trinity Coll., Dublin (Foundn Schol.; BA 1976 (Gold Medallist)); Pembroke Coll., Cambridge (PhD 1980). Robert Gardiner Meml Schol., Univ. of Cambridge, 1976–78. Drapers' Res. Fellow, Pembroke Coll., Cambridge, 1978–82; Lecturer: UCD, 1982–86; TCD, 1986–93; Reader in English Lang. and Lit., Univ. of Oxford, 1996–2002. Chatterton Lectr in Poetry, 1991, Res. Reader, 1999, British Acad. Major Leverhulme Fellow, 2011–14. Mem. Council, British Acad., 2014–17. Chm. Council, Friends of Bodleian Library, 2009–19. *Publications:* monographs: Joseph Hall: a study in satire and meditation, 1982; The Pillars of Eternity: time and providence in The Faerie Queene, 1989; Incest, Drama and Nature's Law 1550–1700, 1993; Spenser's Monstrous Regiment: Elizabethan Ireland and the poetics of difference, 2002; Ungainfully Arte: poetry, patronage and print in the early modern era, 2016; editor: (with H. Erskine-Hill) Presenting Poetry: Composition, Publication, Reception: essays in honour of Ian Jack, 1995; Edmund Spenser, The Shorter Poems, 1999; (with D. Womersley) Literary Milieux: essays in text and context presented to Howard Erskine-Hill, 2007; The Oxford Handbook of Edmund Spenser, 2010. *Recreations:* book collecting, theatre going, writing, walking. *Address:* Merton College, Oxford OX1 4JD. *T:* (01865) 276289. *E:* Richard.mccabe@ell.ox.ac.uk.

**McCABE, Stephen James;** MP (Lab) Birmingham Selly Oak, since 2010 (Birmingham, Hall Green, 1997–2010); *b* 4 Aug. 1955; *s* of late James and Margaret McCabe; *m* 1991; one *s* one *d*. *Educ:* Univ. of Bradford (MA); Moray House Coll., Edinburgh (Dip. and CQSW). Social worker, Generic Team, 1977–79, Intermediate Treatment Worker, 1979–83, Wolverhampton; Manager, The Priory, Newbury, 1983–85; Lectr in Social Services, NE Worcs Coll., 1986–89; social policy researcher, BASW, and part-time child care worker, Solihull, 1989–91; Educn Advr, CCETSW, 1991–97. An Asst Govt Whip, 2006–07; a Lord Comr, HM Treasury (Govt Whip), 2007–10; Shadow Minister for Educn, 2013–15. Member: Panel of Chairs, 2015–; Work and Pensions Cttee, 2015–. *Recreations:* cooking, hill-walking, reading, football. *Address:* House of Commons, SW1A 0AA. *T:* (020) 7219 3509.

**McCABE, Ven. Trevor;** *see* McCabe, Ven. J. T.

**McCAFFER, Prof. Ronald,** FREng; FRSE; Professor of Construction Management, Loughborough University (formerly Loughborough University of Technology), 1986–2009, now Emeritus; Chairman, European Construction Institute, 2007–10 (Finance Director, 1990–2007); *b* 8 Dec. 1943; *s* of late John Gegg McCaffer and Catherine Turner (*née* Gourlay); *m* 1966, Margaret Elizabeth, *d* of late Cyril Warner and Mary Huntley (*née* Mason); one *s*. *Educ:* Albert Sch., Glasgow; Univ. of Strathclyde (BSc 1965; DSc 1998); PhD Loughborough 1977. FICE 1988; FCIOB 1988; FREng (FEng 1991); Eur Ing 1990; FRSE 2009. Design Engr, Babtie, Shaw & Morton, 1965–67; Site Engineer: Nuclear Power Gp, 1967–69; Taylor Woodrow Construction Ltd, 1969–70; Loughborough University of Technology: Lectr, 1970–78; Sen. Lectr, 1978–83; Reader, 1983–86; Head of Civil Engrg, 1987–93; Dean of Engineering, 1992–97; Loughborough University: Sen. Pro-Vice-Chancellor, then Dep. Vice-Chancellor, 1997–2002; Dir, Strategic Business Partnership Innovation and Knowledge Transfer, 2002–06. Chairman: Loughborough University Utilities Ltd, 1997–2002; Loughborough Univ. Enterprises Ltd, 2002–06; Loughborough Univs Innovation Center Ltd, 2002–06; Construction Industry Simulations Ltd, 2006–; Director: Loughborough Consultants Ltd, 1997–2003; Peterborough HE Co. Ltd, 1997–2002; Innovative Projects Worldwide Ltd, 1998–2004; Emman Ltd, 2002–06; Imago Ltd, 2003–06. Mem., Programme Cttee, 1992–95, Educn, Trng and Competence to Practise Cttee, 1995–98, Strategy Rev. Gp, 1996, Royal Acad. of Engrg. Member: Engrg Construction Industry Trng Bd, 1994–2003; Technical Opportunities Panel, EPSRC, 2000–04; Civil Engrg Panel, 2001 RAE; Civil Engrg Sub-Panel, 2008 RAE; Associate Parly Gp for Engrg Develt, 1995–2009; Council Mem., E Midlands Innovation, 2005–09; Engrg Sectional Cttee, RSE, 2011–14. Member: BIM, later Chartered Mgt Inst., 1989–2010; ASCE, 1999–2010; Smeatonian Soc. Civil Engrs, 2011–. Visiting Professor: Univ. of Moratuwa, Sri Lanka, 1986–92; Technol Univ. of Malaysia, 1996, 2000, 2007, 2008, 2010; Sch. of Built and Natural Envmt, Glasgow Caledonian Univ., 2007–10. Mem., Bd of Trustees and Advr, British Univ. in Egypt, 2005–10. Moderating Examr, Engrg Council, 1988–92; past and present examr, univs in UK and overseas. Fellow, Instn of Shipbuilders and Engrs in Scotland, 2012–. Mem., Incorporation of Hammermen of Glasgow, 2015–; a Burgess and Guild Brother and Freeman Citizen of Glasgow, 2015–. Editor, Engineering, Construction and Architectural Management, 1994–2014. *Publications:* Modern Construction Management, 1977, 7th edn 2013; Worked Examples in Construction Management, 1978, 2nd edn 1986; Estimating and Tendering for Civil Engineering Works, 1984, 2nd edn 1991; Management of Construction Equipment, 1982, 2nd edn 1991; International Bid Preparation, 1995; International Bidding Case Study, 1995; Management of Off-highway Plant and Equipment, 2002; jl articles and conf. papers. *Recreations:* being patient with administrators, cooking. *Address:* Department of Civil Engineering, Loughborough University, Loughborough, Leics LE11 3TU. *T:* (01509) 222600, 07710 975495, *Fax:* (01509) 223980. *E:* ronald@mccaffer.com. *W:* www.mccaffer.com.

**McCAFFERTY, Christine;** *b* 14 Oct. 1945; *d* of late John and Dorothy Livesley; *m* 1st, Michael McCafferty; one *s*; 2nd, David Tarlo. *Educ:* Whalley Range Grammar Sch. for Girls, Manchester; Footscray High Sch., Melbourne. Welfare Worker (Disabled), CHS Manchester, 1963–70; Educn Welfare Officer, Manchester Educn Cttee, 1970–72; Registrar of Marriages, Bury Registration Dist, 1978–80; Project worker, Calderdale Well Women Centre, 1989–96. Member: Calderdale MBC, 1991–97; W Yorks Police Authy, 1994–97. MP (Lab) Calder Valley, 1997–2010. Mem., Select Cttee on Internat. Develt, 2001–05; Chair, All-Pty Parly Gp on Population, Develt and Reproductive Health, 1999–2010, on Guides, 2000–10, on Compassion in Dying, 2007–10. Mem., Council of Europe/WEU, 1999–2010; Chm., Social Health and Family Affairs Cttee, Council of Europe, 2008–10. Dir, Royd Regeneration Ltd, 1996–2012. Mem. Exec., N Reg. Assoc. for the Blind, 1993–96. Gov., Luddenden Dene Sch.

**McCAFFERTY, Ian Alexander,** CBE 2019; Member, Monetary Policy Committee, Bank of England, 2012–18; Senior Adviser, Oxford Economics; *b* London, 1 July 1956; *s* of William John Edward McCafferty and Mary McCafferty (*née* Cutts); *m* 1982, Susan Jean Craig (*d* 2016); two *s*. *Educ:* Dulwich Coll.; Univ. of Durham (BA Hons Econ 1978); Univ. of Amsterdam (Dip. European Integration 1979). Economist, ICC, 1980–83; Head: Statistics, The Economist, 1983–85; Economic Trends, CBI, 1985–88; Chief Internat. Economist, Baring Securities, 1987–92; Dir, Internat. Econs, NatWest Markets, 1993–97; Hd, Macroeconomics, BP, 1998–2001; Chief Econ. Advr, CBI, 2001–12. Vis. Prof., KCL. FRSA. Hon. DEcon Nottingham Trent, 2012. *Recreations:* golf, Rugby, cooking, music, France. *Address:* 6 Selwyn House, Manor Fields, Putney, SW15 3LR. *T:* 07764 974552. *E:* mccafferty@talk21.com. *Club:* Sundridge Park Golf.

**McCAFFERTY, Lynne;** QC 2018; *b* Motherwell, 12 April 1974; *d* of Brian McCafferty and Linda McCafferty. *Educ:* Richmond Sch., N Yorks; Lincoln Coll., Oxford (BA Eng. Lit. and Lang. 1995); City Univ. (Grad. Dip. Law 1996). Called to the Bar, Middle Temple, 1997; pupil barrister, 4–5 Gray's Inn Sq., 1997–98, in practice as a barrister, 5 Paper Bldgs, 1998–2000, 4 Pump Court, 2000–, specialising in construction, energy, professional negligence, and technol. and telecoms law. *Publications:* Civil Appeals: principle and procedure, 2010, 2nd edn 2014. *Recreations:* family, friends, literature, theatre, football. *Address:* 4 Pump Court, Temple, EC4Y 7AN. *T:* (020) 7842 5555.

**McCAFFERY, Prof. Peter,** PhD; Director, PMHE Consulting Ltd, since 2017; *b* Durham, 2 Nov. 1952; *s* of Lawrence McCaffery and Margaret McCaffery (*née* Byrne); *m* 1977, Carol Stapleton; two *s*. *Educ:* St Bede's Grammar Sch., Lanchester; Univ. of Ulster (BA Hons Hist.); Swansea Univ. (MSc (Econ) Modern Social Hist.); Keele Univ. (PGCE); Univ. of Pennsylvania, Philadelphia; London Sch. of Econs and Political Sci. (PhD). QTS 1977. Hist. and politics teacher, Worthing Sixth Form Coll., 1978–84; Lectr, then Sen. Lectr, later Principal Lectr, Hist. and Amer. Studies, Ealing Coll. of HE, 1984–92; Associate Dean, Faculty of Creative, Cultural and Social Studies, 1992–96, Dean, Faculty of Educ., Internat. and Social Studies, 1996–99, Thames Valley Univ.; Vice Principal, Bolton Inst. of HE, 1999–2003; Pro-Vice Chancellor, London South Bank Univ., 2004–09; Vice Chancellor and Chief Exec., Univ. of Cumbria, 2009–10; Dep. Vice Chancellor, London Metropolitan Univ., 2011–17, now Emeritus Prof. Assessor, QAA, 1996–98. Mem. Bd, UCAS, 2010–. Idlewild Internat. Teaching Fellow, Univ. of Pennsylvania, Philadelphia, 1981–82; Churchill Fellow, 1997; Nat. Fellow, Leadership Foundn for HE, 2005. USA Politics Analyst, Sky News, 2015–. Gov., Holland Park Acad. Sch., 2013–. FCMI 2000; FRSA 2002; FCIPD 2003. *Publications:* When Bosses Ruled Philadelphia: the emergence of the Republican machine, 1867–1933, 1993; The HE Manager's Handbook: effective leadership and management in universities and colleges, 2004, 3rd edn 2018; 38 articles and reviews in Jl of Interdisciplinary Hist., Urban Hist., etc. *Recreations:* swimming (internat. masters swimmer), literature, music, theatre, Newcastle United Football Club. *T:* (01784) 886034. *E:* peter.mccaffery@londonmet.ac.uk.

**McCAHILL, Patrick Gerard;** QC 1996; **His Honour Judge McCahill;** a Circuit Judge, since 2001; a Specialist Chancery Circuit Judge, since 2007; a Judge, Business and Property Courts, since 2017; a Senior Judge, Sovereign Base Areas of Akrotiri and Dhekelia, Cyprus, since 2019; *b* 6 May 1952; *s* of John McCahill and Josephine McCahill (*née* Conaghan); *m* 1979, Liselotte Gabrielle Steiner; two *d. Educ:* Corby GS; St Catharine's Coll., Cambridge (1st cl. Hons; MA); LLM London ext. 2003; BSc (1st cl. Hons) Open Univ. 2004. FCIArb 1992. Called to the Bar: Gray's Inn, 1975 (Bacon Schol., 1973; Atkin Schol., 1975), Bencher, 2014; King's Inns, Dublin, 1990; Asst Dep. Coroner for Birmingham and Solihull, 1984–99; Asst Recorder, 1993–97; a Recorder, 1997–2001. Member: Mental Health Review Tribunal, 2000–07; Parole Bd, 2004–07. *Recreations:* humour, family history, sport. *Address:* Birmingham Civil and Family Justice Centre, Priory Courts, 33 Bull Street, Birmingham B4 6DS.

**McCAIG, Callum;** Special Adviser to the First Minister of Scotland, since 2017; *b* 6 Jan. 1985. *Educ:* Cults Acad.; Edinburgh Univ. (MA Politics). Parly Asst to Maureen Watt, MSP, 2006. Mem. (SNP) Aberdeen CC, 2007–15 (Leader of Council, 2011–12; Leader, SNP Gp, 2011–15). MP (SNP) Aberdeen S, 2015–17; contested (SNP) same seat, 2017.

**McCAIG, Prof. Colin Darnley,** PhD; FRSE; Regius Professor of Physiology, University of Aberdeen, since 2002 (Head, School of Medical Sciences, 2003–15); *b* 26 June 1953. *Educ:* Univ. of Edinburgh (BSc); Univ. of Glasgow (PhD). Beit Meml Res. Fellow, Univ. of Edinburgh, 1983–86; University of Aberdeen: MRC Sen. Fellow, 1986–88; Wellcome Trust Univ. Award Lectr, 1988–93; Lectr, 1993–95; Sen. Lectr, 1995–99; Prof., 1999–2002; Hd, Dept of Biomed. Scis, 1998–2003. FRSE 2007. *Address:* School of Medicine, Medical Sciences and Nutrition, Institute of Medical Sciences, University of Aberdeen, Foresterhill, Aberdeen AB25 2ZD.

**McCALL, Dame Carolyn, (Dame Carolyn Frawley),** DBE 2016 (OBE 2008); Chief Executive, ITV plc, since 2018; *b* 13 Sept. 1961; *d* of late Colleen and of Arthur McCall; *m* 1986, Peter Frawley; two *s* one *d. Educ:* Univ. of Kent (BA Hons Hist. and Politics); Inst. of Educn, Univ. of London (PGCE); Univ. of London (MA Politics). Risk Analyst, Costain Gp plc, 1984–86; The Guardian: planner, 1986–88; advertising exec., 1988–89; advertising manager, 1989–91; Product Develt Manager, 1991–92; Display Advertising Manager, 1992; Advertising Dir, Wire UK, 1992–94; Dep. Advertising Dir, 1994–95; Advertising Dir, 1995–97; Commercial Dir, 1997–98; Guardian Newspapers Ltd: Dep. Man. Dir, 1998–2000; Dir/Chief Exec., 2000–06; Chief Exec., Guardian Media Gp plc, 2006–10; Chief Exec., easyJet plc, 2010–17. Non-executive Director: New Look plc, 1999–2005 and 2010; Tesco plc, 2005–08; Lloyds TSB Gp, then Lloyds Banking Gp plc, 2008–09. Non-exec. Dir, BEIS, 2017–. Chair, Opportunity Now, 2005–09. Member: WACL, 1995–; Mktg Gp of GB. *Address:* ITV plc, 2 Waterhouse Square, 138–142 Holborn, EC1N 2AE.

**McCALL, Christopher Hugh;** QC 1987; *b* 3 March 1944; *yr s* of late Robin Home McCall, CBE and Joan Elizabeth McCall; *m* 1981, Henrietta Francesca Sharpe. *Educ:* Winchester (Scholar); Magdalen Coll., Oxford (Demy; BA Maths, 1964; Eldon Law Scholar, 1966). Called to the Bar, Lincoln's Inn, 1966, Bencher, 1993. Second Jun. Counsel to the Inland Revenue in chancery matters, 1977–87; Jun. Counsel to Attorney Gen. in charity matters, 1981–87. Mem., Bar Council, 1973–76. Trustee, British Mus., 1999–2004. Lifetime Achievement Award, Soc. of Trust and Estate Practitioners, 2015. *Recreations:* music, travel, Egyptomania. *Address:* Maitland Chambers, 7 Stone Buildings, Lincoln's Inn, WC2A 3SZ. *T:* (020) 7406 1200; Sphinx Hill, Ferry Lane, Moulsford on Thames OX10 9JF. *T:* (01491) 652162. *Clubs:* Alpine; Leander (Henley-on-Thames).

**McCALL, Rt Rev. David;** *see* McCall, Rt Rev. W. D. H.

**McCALL, David Slesser,** CBE 1988; Chairman, Anglia Television Ltd, 1994–2001 (Director, 1970–2001; Chief Executive, 1976–94); *b* 3 Dec. 1934; *s* of Patrick McCall and Florence Kate Mary Walker; *m* 1968, Lois Patricia Elder. *Educ:* Robert Gordon's Coll., Aberdeen. Mem., Inst. of Chartered Accountants of Scotland, 1958. National Service, 1959–61. Accountant, Grampian Television Ltd, 1961–68; Company Sec., Anglia Television Ltd, 1968–76; Dir, 1970–98, Chief Exec., 1986–94, Chm., 1994–98, Anglia Television Gp. Chairman: Oxford Scientific Films Ltd, 1982–89; Greene King plc, 1995–2005; United Trustees Ltd, 1997–; United Exec. Trustee Ltd, 1998–; 99.9 Radio Norwich Ltd, 2006–; Director: ITN, 1978–86, 1991–96; Ind. Television Publications Ltd, 1971–89; Ind. Television Assoc. Ltd, 1976–96; Sodastream Holdings Ltd, 1978–85; Norwich City Football Club, 1979–85; Channel Four Television Co., 1981–85; Radio Broadland, 1984–91; Super Channel Ltd, 1986–88; British Satellite Broadcasting, 1987–90; Regl Adv. Bd, National Westminster Bank, 1988–92; TSMS Group Ltd, 1989–96; Hodder & Stoughton Holdings Ltd, 1992–93; Cosgrove Hall Films, 1993–96; MAI plc, 1994–96; MAI Media UK Ltd, 1995–96; Meridian Broadcasting Ltd, 1994–96; Satellite Inf. Services, 1994–96; Village Roadshow Ltd, Australia, 1994–96; Bakers Dozen Inns Ltd, 1996–2006; Anglia FM Ltd, 1996–99; Anglo Welsh Group PLC, 1996–2000; Bernard Matthews Gp PLC, 1996–2000; Granada Pension Trust Co. Ltd, 2000–03; Bernard Matthews Hldgs Ltd, 2002–13; Bernard Matthews Ltd, 2009–13. Chm., Forum Trust Ltd (formerly Norfolk and Norwich Millennium Bid), 1996–2005; Dep. Chm., United Broadcasting and Entertainment, 1996. Mem., ITCA, subseq. Ind. Television Assoc., 1976–95 (Chm., 1986–88); Pres., Cinema and Television Benevolent Fund, 1998–2001 (Trustee, 1995–2016). Pres., Norfolk and Norwich Chamber of Commerce, 1988–90 (Dep. Pres., 1986–88); Chm., Norwich Playhouse Theatre, 1992–98. Treas., 1995–97, Chm. Council, 1997–2006, UEA. FRTS 1988; FRSA 1993. CCMI (CBIM 1988). DL Norfolk, 1992. Hon. DCL UEA, 2006. *Recreations:* sport, travel. *Address:* Woodland Hall, Redenhall, Harleston, Norfolk IP20 9QW. *T:* (01379) 854442.

**McCALL, Duncan James;** QC 2008; *b* 8 May 1965; *s* of John Berry McCall and Stella McCall. *Educ:* Magdalen Coll., Oxford (BA). Called to the Bar, Gray's Inn, 1988; in practice as barrister, 1989–. *Address:* 4 Pump Court, Temple, EC4Y 7AN. *T:* (020) 7842 5555, *Fax:* (020) 7583 2036. *E:* dmccall@4pumpcourt.com.

**McCALL, William;** General Secretary, Institution of Professional Civil Servants, 1963–89; *b* 6 July 1929; *s* of Alexander McCall and Jean Corbet Cunningham; *m* 1955, Olga Helen Brunton; one *s* one *d. Educ:* Dumfries Academy; Ruskin College, Oxford. Civil Service, 1946–52; Social Insurance Dept, TUC, 1954–58; Asst Sec., Instn of Professional Civil Servants, 1958–63; Mem., Civil Service Nat. Whitley Council (Staff Side), 1963–89, Chm. 1969–71, Vice-Chm. 1983. Hon. Treasurer, Parly and Scientific Cttee, 1976–80; Part-time Mem., Eastern Electricity Board, 1977–86; Member: Cttee of Inquiry into Engrg Profession, 1977–79; PO Arbitration Tribunal, 1980–90; TUC Gen. Council, 1984–89; Pay and Employment Policy Cttee, CVCP, 1990–94; Police Complaints Authority, 1991–94. Member Council: Univ. of London, 1994–97 (Mem. Ct, 1984–94); Goldsmiths' Coll., 1989–95 (Hon. Fellow, 1996). *Address:* Foothills, Gravel Path, Berkhamsted, Herts HP4 2PF. *T:* (01442) 864974.

**McCALL, Rt Rev. (William) David (Hair);** Bishop of Bunbury, 2000–10; *b* 29 Feb. 1940; *s* of late Rt Rev. Theodore Bruce McCall, ThD, Bishop of Wangaratta, and Helen Christie McCall; *m* 1969, Marion Carmel le Breton; two *s* three *d. Educ:* Launceston and Sydney Grammar Schools; Saint Michael's House, Crafers. Deacon 1963, priest 1964, dio. Riverina; Assistant Curate: St Alban's, Griffith, 1963–64; St Peter's, Broken Hill, 1965–67; Priest-in-charge, Barellan-Weethalle, 1967–73; Rector: St John's, Corowa, 1973–78; St George's, Goodwood, 1978–87; Pastoral Chaplain, St Barnabas' Theol Coll., 1980–87; Bishop of Willochra, 1987–2000. Bishop assisting Archbishop of Adelaide, 2010–15; Priest-in-Charge, St Cyprian's, N Adelaide, 2010–15; Locum Tenens Priest: Mount Gambier, Dio. of Murray, 2016–17; Sempahore, Dio. of Adelaide, 2017–18. *Recreations:* reading, walking, gardening.

**McCALL SMITH, Prof. Alexander,** CBE 2007; PhD; FRSE, FMedSci; writer; Professor of Medical Law, University of Edinburgh, 1995–2005, now Emeritus; *b* 24 Aug. 1948; *s* of Sandy McCall Smith and Daphne McCall Smith (*née* Woodall); *m* 1982, Dr Elizabeth Parry; two *d. Educ:* Christian Brothers Coll., Bulawayo; Univ. of Edinburgh (LLB; PhD). Admitted to Faculty of Advocates, 2010. Lectr in Law, Queen's Univ., Belfast, 1973–74; Lectr in Law, subseq. Reader in Law, Univ. of Edinburgh, 1974–95; Hd, Dept of Law, Univ. of Botswana, 1981 (on secondment). Vis. Prof. of Law, Law Sch., Southern Methodist Univ., Dallas, 1988. Vice-Chm., Human Genetics Commn, 2000–04; Mem., Internat. Bioethics Cttee, UNESCO, 1997–2004. FRSE 2001; FMedSci 2005. Hon. FRCPE 2004. Hon. DIur Parma, 2005; Hon. DLitt: Napier, 2005; Aberdeen, 2006, BC, 2006; Southern Methodist Univ., Dallas, 2009; Leicester, 2008; QUB, 2009; Buckingham, 2010; St Andrews, 2015; Hon. LLD Edinburgh, 2007; Queen's Univ., Ont, 2015; Hon. DSc UEA, 2007; DUniv Stirling, 2015. Saga Award, 2004; Author of the Year, British Book Awards, 2004; Gold Medal, American Acad. of Achievement, 2009; Burke Medal, Trinity Coll. Dublin Histl Soc., 2012; Duke LEAF Award, Nicholas Sch. of Envmt, Duke Univ., 2013; Bollinger Everyman Wodehouse Prize for Comic Fiction, 2015; 49th Annual Medal of Honor for Achievement in Lit., Nat. Arts Club, NYC, 2017. Presidential Order of Meritorious Service (Botswana), 2010. *Publications:* over 80 books including: (with J. K. Mason) Law and Medical Ethics, 1983, 6th edn 2002; (with K. Frimpong) The Criminal Law of Botswana, 1991; (with C. Shapiro) Forensic Aspects of Sleep, 1997; (with A. Merry) Errors, Medicine and the Law, 2001; What W. H. Auden Can Do For You, 2013; A Work of Beauty: Alexander McCall Smith's Edinburgh, 2014; *fiction:* Portuguese Irregular Verbs, 1997; The Finer Points of Sausage Dogs, 1998; 2½ Pillars of Wisdom, 2002; At the Villa of Reduced Circumstances, 2003; The Girl Who Married a Lion (short stories), 2004; Dream Angus, 2006; La's Orchestra Saves the World, 2008; Unusual Uses for Olive Oil, 2011; Trains & Lovers, 2012; The Forever Girl, 2014; Emma: a modern retelling, 2014; The Good Pilot Peter Woodhouse, 2017; My Italian Bulldozer, 2017; The Second Worst Restaurant in France, 2019; The Department of Sensitive Crimes, 2019; *The No 1 Ladies' Detective Agency series:* The No 1 Ladies' Detective Agency, 1998; Tears of the Giraffe, 2000; Morality for Beautiful Girls, 2001; The Kalahari Typing School for Men, 2002; The Full Cupboard of Life, 2003; In the Company of Cheerful Ladies, 2004; Blue Shoes and Happiness, 2006; The Good Husband of Zebra Drive, 2007; The Miracle at Speedy Motors, 2008; Tea Time for the Traditionally Built, 2009; The Double Comfort Safari Club, 2010; The Saturday Big Tent Wedding Party, 2011; The Limpopo Academy of Private Detection, 2012; The Minor Adjustment Beauty Salon, 2013; The Handsome Man's De Luxe Cafe, 2014; The Woman Who Walked in Sunshine, 2015; Precious and Grace, 2016; The House of Unexpected Sisters, 2017; The Colours of All the Cattle, 2018; To the Land of Long Lost Friends, 2019; *The Sunday Philosophy Club series:* The Sunday Philosophy Club, 2004; Friends, Lovers, Chocolate, 2005; The Right Attitude to Rain, 2006; The Careful Use of Compliments, 2007; The Comfort of Saturdays, 2008; The Lost Art of Gratitude, 2009; The Charming Quirks of Others, 2010; The Forgotten Affairs of Youth, 2011; The Uncommon Appeal of Clouds, 2012; The Novel Habits of Happiness, 2015; A Distant View of Everything, 2017; The Quiet Side of Passion, 2018; *The 44 Scotland Street series:* 44 Scotland Street, 2005; Espresso Tales, 2005; Love Over Scotland, 2006; The World According to Bertie, 2007; The Unbearable Lightness of Scones, 2008; The Importance of Being Seven, 2010; Bertie Plays the Blues, 2011; Sunshine on Scotland Street, 2012; Bertie's Guide to Life and Mothers, 2013; The Revolving Door of Life, 2015; The Bertie Project, 2016; A Time of Love and Tartan, 2017; The Peppermint Tea Chronicles, 2019; *Corduroy Mansions series:* Corduroy Mansions, 2009; The Dog Who Came in from the Cold, 2010; A Conspiracy of Friends, 2011; books for children include: Precious and the Puggies, 2011; Precious and the Monkeys, 2012; Precious and the Mystery of Meerkat Hill, 2012; The Great Cake Mystery, 2012; Precious and the Zebra Necklace, 2015; *School Ship Tobermory series:* School Ship Tobermory, 2015; The Sands of Shark Island, 2016; The Race to Kangaroo Cliff, 2018; *librettos:* The Okavango Macbeth, 2011; A Tapestry of Many Threads, 2012; The Tumbling Lassie, 2018. *Recreations:* wind instruments, sailing. *Clubs:* New, Scottish Arts (Edinburgh).

**McCALLA, Hon. Zaila Rowena,** OJ 2007; Chief Justice of Jamaica, 2007–18; *b* Westmoreland, Jamaica, 31 Jan. 1948; *d* of Herbert and Beryl Morris; *m* Adolph Holness (marr. diss.); *m* 1981, William McCalla; two *s* one *d. Educ:* Univ. of West Indies (LLB Hons); Norman Manley Law Sch. (Cert. Legal Educn). Manager, Montego Bay Co-op. Credit Union, 1971–72; Dep. Clerk of Courts, 1976–77; Clerk of Courts, 1977–80; Crown Counsel, Office of the DPP, 1980–85; Actg Asst DPP, 1985; Resident Magistrate, 1985–96; Sen. Resident Magistrate, 1996; Actg Master in Chambers, 1993–96, Master in Chambers, 1996–97; Judge, Supreme Court of Jamaica, 1997; Actg Judge, Grand Court of Cayman Is, 2006; Actg Judge of Appeal, 2004–06, Judge of Appeal, 2006–07. Chm., Judicial Service Commn. Chairman: Supreme Court Rules Cttee; Queen's Counsel Cttee; Resident Magistrates' Rules Cttee; Archives Adv. Cttee; Co-Chm., Consultative Cttee, Jamaican Bar Assoc. and Bench; Member: Cttee reviewing Legal Aid system; Cttee formulating Code of Conduct for Justice of the Peace, 2006. Bencher, Middle Temple, 2016. Chancellor, Anglican Dio. Jamaica and Cayman Is, 2014–. Former Pres., Resident Magistrates' Assoc. Chm., Justice Trng Inst. Adv. Bd. Mem., Council of Legal Educn. Keeper of Records, Island Record Office. Mem., Editl Bd, Caribbean Civil Court Practice. Mem., St Margaret Anglican Ch. *Recreations:* gardening, cooking, reading.

**McCALLION, Elisha;** MP (SF) Foyle, since 2017; *b* Galliagh, Co. Derry, 1 Jan. 1982; *m* Declan Aaron McCallion; three *s.* Welfare rights advr, Galliagh Integrated Advice Service, then Galliagh Develt Trust. Member, (SF) Foyle, NI Assembly, 2017. Member (SF): Derry CC, 2005–15; Derry and Strabane DC, 2015 (Mayor, 2015). *Address:* c/o Sinn Féin, 55 Falls Road, Belfast BT12 4PD.

**McCALLUM, His Honour Alastair Grindlay;** a Circuit Judge, 1992–2012; *b* 28 Feb. 1947; *s* of William and Catherine McCallum; *m* 1969, Lindsay Sheila Watkins; two *d. Educ:* Gilbert Rennie, Northern Rhodesia; Leeds Univ. (LLB, LLM (Com.)). Called to the Bar, Inner Temple, 1970; Asst Recorder, 1984; Recorder, 1989; Head of Chambers, 1990. *Recreations:* golf, travel, reading. *Club:* Bradford.

**McCALLUM, Helen Mary;** Director General, Consumers International, 2011–13; *b* 23 Dec. 1952; *d* of late Edward James Ward and of Pauline Ward; *m* 1980, Duncan Peter Finlay McCallum; two *d. Educ:* Queen Elizabeth's Girls' Grammar Sch., Barnet; Nottingham Univ. (BA Hons English Lit.). Sabbatical Sec., Students' Union, Univ. of Nottingham,

1973–74; Admin. Asst (PR), Univ. of Sheffield, 1974–78; PRO, Univ. of Salford, 1978–81; freelance publications work, 1981–85; Alumni Officer, Univ. of Sheffield, 1985–88; Sen. PR Manager, 1989–92, Hd of Communications, 1992–94, E Anglian RHA; Hd of Communications, NHS Exec., 1994–98; Dir of Communications, DoH, 1999–2001; Dir of Corporate Affairs, Envmt Agency, 2001–07; Dir, Policy, 2007–08, Dir, Policy, Campaigns and Communications, 2008–11, Which? (Consumers' Assoc.). Mem., Assoc. of Health Care Communicators, 1989. Chm., Cambs and Peterborough Arts and Minds, 2015–. Trustee: Keep Britain Tidy, 2007–12; Diabetes UK, 2014–. *Recreations:* amateur dramatics, keeping moderately fit. *Address:* 79 Gilbert Road, Cambridge CB4 3NZ.

McCALLUM, Martin; producer; theatre designer and consultant; *b* 6 April 1950; *s* of Raymond and Jessie; *m* 1st, 1971, Lesley Nunnerley (marr. diss.); one *s* one *d*; 2nd, 1986, Julie Edmett (marr. diss.); one *d*; 3rd, 1989, Mary Ann Rolfe (marr. diss.); two *s*. *Educ:* Barfield Sch., Surrey; Frensham Heights Sch., Surrey. Entered theatre as student asst stage manager, Castle Th., Farnham, 1967; worked throughout rep. system; Prodn Manager, NT at Old Vic, 1971–75; prodns incl. Merchant of Venice, Long Day's Journey into Night, Saturday Sunday Monday; moved to S Bank, 1975; founder and Prodn Manager, The Production Office, West End, 1978–84; prodns incl. Filumena, Evita, Sweeney Todd, Cats; Man. Dir, 1981–2000, Vice-Chm., 2000–03, Cameron Mackintosh Ltd; prodns incl. Les Miserables, Phantom of the Opera, Miss Saigon, Oliver!; Director: Donmar Warehouse Th., 1992–2008 (Chm., 1996–2004); Philip Quast: live`at the Donmar, 2002; Sydney Theatre Co., 2005–14; prod., Edward Scissorhands, London and world tour, 2005, UK tour, 2014–15 (New York Drama Desk Award, 2007); exec. prod., Spider-Man Turn Off the Dark, NY, 2011, The Cripple of Inishmaan, NY, 2014; prod., Dirty Dancing, Australian tour, 2014–15, Hughie, NY, 2016. Consultant: to Glyndebourne Fest. Opera, 1980–81; to Regl Th. Scheme, Arts Council, 1980. Theatre designer and consultant: Old Fire Station Th., Oxford, 1991; Musical Hall, Stuttgart, 1994; Musical Th., Duisburg, 1996; Schaumburg Village Th., Ill, 2002; restorations: Prince Edward Th., London, 1993; Capital Th., Sydney, 1995; Th. Royal, Sydney, 1998; Auditorium Th., Chicago, 2001; Fine Arts Bldg Theatres, Chicago, 2003; Prince of Wales' Th., London, 2004; Montecasino Th., Johannesburg, 2007. Initiated Wyndham Report (on economic importance of West End theatre), 1998; initiated Theatre 2001 - Future Directions, inaugural jt theatre conference of SOLT/TMA/ITC, 2001. Hon. Lifetime Mem., SOLT, 1999– (Pres. 1999–2002). Member: Drama Panel, 1999–2004, Adv. Task Gp, 2003–05, Arts Council England (formerly Arts Council of England); London's Cultural Strategy Gp, 2000–04; Th. Mus. Cttee, V&A, 2002–06. FRSA 1995. Mem., Broadway League (formerly League of Amer. Theatres and Producers), 1988–2011. *Recreations:* the performing arts, music, art, gardens.

McCAMLEY, Sir Graham (Edward), KBE 1986 (MBE 1981); owner, cattle properties, since 1954; *b* 24 Aug. 1932; *s* of Edward William George and Ivy McCamley; *m* 1956, Shirley Clarice Tindale (*d* 2010); one *s* two *d*. *Educ:* Rockhampton Grammar Sch. President: Aust. Brahman Breeders, 1971–74; Central Coastal Graziers, 1974–75; Cattlemen's Union of Australia, 1976–78. Mem. Producer of Australian Meat and Livestock Co., 1982–84; Chm., Beeflands Australia Pty Ltd, 1994–97. *Recreations:* tennis, flying helicopter and fixed wing aircraft. *Clubs:* Queensland (Brisbane); Rockhampton and District Masonic.

McCANDLESS, Air Vice-Marshal Brian Campbell, CB 1999; CBE 1990; Chief Executive, Murchison Villas Ltd, since 2017; Air Officer Communications and Information Systems and Air Officer Commanding Signals Units, Royal Air Force, 1996–99; *b* 14 May 1944; *s* of Norman Samuel McCandless and Rebecca Campbell; *m* 1969, Yvonne Haywood; one *s*. *Educ:* Methodist Coll., Belfast; RAF Tech. Coll., Henlow (BSc 1967); Birmingham Univ. (MSc 1972); RAF Staff Coll. RAF, 1962–99: posts included: OC 26 Signals Unit, 1985–87; OC RAF Henlow, 1987–89; Dep. Chief, Architecture and Plans Div., NATO CIS Agency, Brussels, 1989–92; Dir, Comd Control and Management Inf. Systems, RAF, 1992–93; Dir, Communications and Inf. Systems, RAF, 1993–95. Dir, Business Develt, EMEA, Oracle Corp., 1999–2002. Chm., Fiordland Retirement Housing Trust, 2016–. *Recreations:* bridge, music, sailing, hill walking. *Club:* Royal Air Force.

McCANN, Michael; *b* Glasgow, 2 Jan. 1964; *s* of Charles and Bridget McCann; *m* 1989, Tracy Anne Thomson; one *s* one *d*. *Educ:* St Bride's High Sch.; St Andrew's High Sch. Admin. Officer, ODA, 1982–92; Scottish Officer, CPSA, 1992–98; Dep. Scottish Officer, PCS, 1998–2008. Mem. (Lab) S Lanarks Council, 1999 (Vice-Chair: E Kilbride Area Cttee, 1999–2003; Social Work Resources, 2003–07; Depute Leader, 2007–10). MP (Lab) E Kilbride, Strathaven and Lesmahagow, 2010–15; contested (Lab) same seat, 2015. *Recreations:* golf, football (watching it!).

McCANNY, Prof. Sir John (Vincent), Kt 2017; CBE 2002; FRS 2002; FREng; Regius Professor of Electronics and Computer Engineering, 2016–17, now Emeritus (Professor of Microelectronics Engineering, 1988–2016), Director, Institute of Electronics, Communications and Information Technology, 2001–17, and Principal Investigator, Centre for Secure Information Technology, 2009–17, Queen's University of Belfast; *b* 25 June 1952; *s* of Patrick Joseph McCanny and Kathleen Brigid McCanny (*née* Kerr); *m* 1979, Maureen Bernadette Mellon; one *s* one *d*. *Educ:* Univ. of Manchester (BSc Physics Hons 1973); Univ. of Ulster, Coleraine (PhD Solid State Physics 1978); Queen's Univ., Belfast (DSc Electronics Eng 1998). CPhys, MInstP 1982, FInstP 1992; CEng, MIEE 1985, FIET (FIEE 1992); IEEE Fellow 1999; FREng 1995; MRIA 2000; FIAE 2006; FIEI 2006. Lectr in Physics, Univ. of Ulster, Coleraine, 1977–79; Higher SO, 1979–82, SSO, 1982–84, PSO, 1984, RSRE, Malvern; Queen's University of Belfast: EPSRC IT Res. Lectr, Sch. of Electrical and Electronic Engrg, 1984–87; Reader in VLSI Signal Processing, 1987–88; Hd, Digital Signal Processing and Telecommunications Res. Div., 1988–2004; Hd, Sch. of Electronics, Electrical Engrg and Computer Sci., 2005–10. Guest Prof., Shanghai Univ., 2010–. Founder, 1988, Dir, 1988–96, Audio Processing Technology Ltd; Founder, 1994, pt-time Chief Technology Officer, 1994–2004, Amphion Semiconductor Ltd (formerly Integrated Silicon Systems Ltd). Dir, Inst. of Advanced Microelectronics in Ireland, 1989–91. Royal Society: Mem., Sectl Cttee 4, 2004–06 and 2011–14 (Chm., 2005, 2006); Mem., Hook Cttee, 2010–13; Co-Chair, Cyber Security Res. Policy Cttee, 2013–16 (report, 2016); Mem., Sci., Industry and Translation Cttee, 2018–Dec. 2020; Mem., Community of Interest Cttee, 2018–; Royal Academy of Engineering: Member: Council, 2008–11; Internat. Cttee, 2009–13; Dowling Rev. on more effective collaborations between businesses and univ. researchers in UK, 2015 (report, 2015); Cttee, Investing in Innovation Report, 2015; Judging Panel, MacRobert Award, 2018–Oct. 2020; Mem. Bd, Nat. Tyndall ICT Inst., Ireland, 2004–11; Member: Sub-Panel 24, Electrical and Electronics Engrg, 2008 RAE, HEFCE, 2005–08; IT Strategic Adv. Team, EPSRC, 2006–11; Emerging Technols and Industries Strategy Gp, UK Technol. Strategy Bd, 2010–; Sub-Panel 13, Electrical and Electronic Engrg, Metallurgy and Materials, HEFCE REF, 2011–14. Mem. Council, Royal Irish Acad., 2012–13 (Mem., Assessment Panel, US/ Ireland Res. Innovation Awards, 2015). Mem., Internat. Adv. Bd, German Excellence Initiative Centre for Ultra High Speed Mobile Information and Communication, RWTH Aachen Univ., 2007–13; Mem., Judging Panel, Blavatnik Award for Young Scientists in UK, NY Acad. of Scis, 2018, 2019. Silver Medal, Royal Acad. of Engrg, 1996; Millennium Medal, IEEE, 2000; Boyle Medal, Royal Dublin Soc./Irish Times, 2003; IT Professional of the Year, BCS (Belfast Br.), 2004; Faraday Medal, IET, 2006; Cunningham Medal, RIA, 2011; Lifetime Achievement Award, QUB, 2017; Parson's Medal, Irish Acad. of Engrg, 2018. *Publications:* (ed jtly) VLSI Technology and Design, 1987; (ed jtly) Systolic Array Processors, 1989; (ed jtly) VLSI Systems for DSP and Control, 1991; (ed jtly) Signal Processing Systems: design and implementation, 1997; (with Maire McLoone) System-on-Chip Architectures and Implementation for Private-Key Data Encryption, 2003; 360 scientific papers in major internat. jls and confs; 25 patents. *Recreations:* golf, soccer, Rugby, cricket, guitar, photography, films. *Address:* Institute of Electronics, Communications and Information Technology, Queen's University of Belfast, Northern Ireland Science Park, Queen's Road, Queen's Island, Belfast BT3 9DT. *Club:* Clandeboye Golf.

McCARRY, Frances Jane; *see* McMenamin, F. J.

McCARTAN, Patrick Anthony, CBE 2008; Chair, Police Pensions Board for Northern Ireland, since 2015; *b* Belfast, 28 Dec. 1945; *s* of Henry McCartan and Margaret McCartan (*née* Gillespie); *m* 1972, Margaret Petrea Owens; one *s* one *d*. *Educ:* Queen's Univ. Belfast (Trade Union studies); Henley Mgt Coll.; Univ. of Ulster (MSc Dist. 1988). FCIPD 1991. NI Civil Service, 1962–72; NI Area Sec., APEX, 1972–90; Sen. Lectr and Hd of Dept, Centre for Mgt Educn, Univ. of Ulster, 1990–2002; Chairman: NW Belfast HSS Trust, 2001–06; Labour Relns Agency, 2002–08. Chairman: Belfast Health and Social Care Trust, 2006–12; Ind. Financial Rev. Panel, NI Assembly, 2011–16; Mem., Police Remuneration Rev. Bd, 2018–. Trustee, NHS Confedn, 2005–11. Consultant, employment relns and mgt develt, 1990–. Chm. and Mem. Bd, Co-operation Ireland, 1991–2004; Member Board: SE Educn and Liby Bd, 1976–83; NI Econ. Council, 1978–82; IDB, 1982–89; Council for Catholic Maintained Schs, 1996–2004, 2014–. Mem. Bd, St Columbanus Coll., Bangor, 1976– (Chm., 2000–08, 2013–). *Recreations:* motorcycling (former road racer), golf, playing guitar badly, lutherie (making instruments). *E:* mccartan@btinternet.com. *T:* (028) 9146 7691.

McCARTHY, Anthony David; consultant on leadership, change, productivity and performance; *b* 14 April 1956; *s* of Robert Alan and Ena Mary McCarthy; *m* 1983, Patricia Barbara Blakey; one *s* one *d* (and one *d* decd). *Educ:* Sheffield Poly. (BA Hons (Business Studies) 1978); Salford Univ. (Postgrad. Dip. 1982). MCIPD 1980. British Aerospace, subseq. BAESYSTEMS, 1978–2003: various human resource appts; HR Dir, Royal Ordnance, 1995–97; Chm., Royal Ordnance Pensions Trustees, 1997–98; Gp HR Dir, 2001–03; Gp Dir People, Royal Mail Gp, 2003–07; Dir, People and Orgnl Effectiveness, British Airways, 2007–11. *Recreations:* golf (not very well!), most sports as spectator, keen supporter of Burnley FC. *Club:* Preston Golf.

McCARTHY, Arlene, OBE 2015; Executive Director, AMC Strategy, since 2014; *b* 10 Oct. 1960; *d* of J. J. McCarthy and F. L. McCarthy. *Educ:* Dunmurry Primary; Friends' Sch., Lisburn; Univ. of Manchester; Freie Universität Berlin; South Bank Poly. (BA Hons); Stuttgart Univ.; Univ. Clermont-Ferrand. Researcher and Press Officer to Leader of European PLP, 1990–91; Lectr in Politics, Freie Univ., Berlin, 1991–93; Head of European Affairs, Kirklees MBC, W Yorks, 1992–94. MEP (Lab) Peak Dist, 1994–99, NW Reg., 1999–2014. European PLP (formerly Socialist Gp and European PLP) spokesperson on regl affairs, 1994–99; on internat. mkt and legal affairs, 1999–2004; on internal mkt and consumer protection, 2004–14; on legal affairs, 2004–14. Mem., Internal Mkt and Consumer Protection Cttee, EP, 2004–09 (Chm., 2006–09); Vice Chm., EP Cttee on Econ. and Monetary Affairs, 2009–14; Mem., EP Delegn for US Relns, 1999–2009, EP Delegn for Relns with Switzerland, Iceland and Norway and to Eur. Econ. Area Jt Parly Cttee, 2009–14; Substitute Mem., EP Delegn to EU-Turkey Jt Parly Cttee, 2009–14. Non-executive Director: Bloomberg Trade Repository Ltd, 2014–19; Bloomberg Trading Facility Ltd, 2014–. Non-exec. Dir, Regulatory Bd, ICAEW, 2016–17. Member: Adv. Bd, Global Witness, 2014–; EC High-Level Expert Gp on Sustainable Finance, 2017–18; European Corporate Reporting Lab Steering Gp, 2018–. *Publications:* (ed jtly) Changing States: a Labour agenda for Europe, 1996; EP reports on post 2008 financial crisis reform, reform of structural funds, gen. provisions of structural funds and on intellectual property. *E:* amcstrategy@icloud.com.

McCARTHY, Sir Callum, Kt 2005; PhD; Chairman, Financial Services Authority, 2003–08; Member of Court, Bank of England, 2003–08; *b* 29 Feb. 1944; *s* of Ralph and Nan McCarthy; *m* 1966, Penelope Ann Gee; two *s* one *d*. *Educ:* Manchester Grammar Sch.; City of London Sch.; Merton Coll., Oxford (BA 1965); Stirling Univ. (PhD 1971); Grad. Sch. of Business, Stanford Univ. (Sloan Fellow; MS 1982). Operations Res., ICI, 1965–72; various posts from Economic Adv. to Under Sec., DTI, 1972–85; Dir, Kleinwort Benson, 1985–89; Man. Dir, BZW, 1989–93; CEO, Barclays Bank, Japan, 1993–96, Barclays Bank, N America, 1996–98; Dir Gen. subseq. Chief Exec., Ofgem, 1999–2003 (Gas Supply, 1998–2003, Electricity Supply, 1999–2003); Chm., Gas and Electricity Mkts Authy, 2000–03; European Chm., JC Flowers, 2009–12. Freeman, City of London, 2008. *Publications:* (with D. S. Davies) Introduction to Technological Economics, 1967. *Recreations:* walking, cooking, reading, beekeeping.

*See also* T. P. McCarthy.

MacCARTHY, Fiona, OBE 2009; biographer and cultural historian; *b* 23 Jan. 1940; *m* 1966, David Mellor (*d* 2009), CBE, RDI; one *s* one *d*. *Educ:* Wycombe Abbey Sch.; Lady Margaret Hall, Oxford (MA Hons Eng. Lang. and Lit.); Hon. Fellow, 2007). FRSL 1997. Design Correspondent, Guardian, 1963–69; Women's Editor, Evening Standard, 1969–70; Literary Critic: The Times, 1980–90; Observer, 1990–98; an Associate Editor, Oxford DNB, 1998–2005. Curator, exhibitions: Homespun to Highspeed: British Design, 1860–1960, Sheffield Mus and Art Galls, 1979; The Omega Workshops: Decorative Arts of Bloomsbury, Crafts Council, 1984; Eye for Industry, V&A Mus., 1986; Byron, NPG, 2002; Anarchy and Beauty: William Morris and his Legacy, NPG, 2014. Sen. Fellow, RCA, 1997 (Hon. Fellow, 1990). Hon. FRIBA 2012. Hon. DLitt Sheffield, 1996; DUniv Sheffield Hallam, 2001. Bicentenary Medal, RSA, 1986. *Publications:* All Things Bright and Beautiful: British design 1830 to today, 1972; The Simple Life: C. R. Ashbee in the Cotswolds, 1981; The Omega Workshops: decorative arts of Bloomsbury, 1984; Eric Gill, 1989; William Morris: a life for our time, 1994 (Wolfson History Prize; Yorkshire Post Art Book Award; Writer's Guild Non-Fiction Award); Stanley Spencer: an English vision, 1997; Byron: life and legend, 2002; Last Curtsey: the end of the debutantes, 2006; The Last Pre-Raphaelite: Edward Burne-Jones and the Victorian Imagination, 2011 (James Tait Black Prize, 2012); Anarchy and Beauty: William Morris and his legacy, 2014; Walter Gropius: Visionary Founder of the Bauhaus, 2019; articles in The Guardian, TLS, New York Review of Books. *Recreations:* museums, theatre, looking at buildings. *Address:* The Round Building, Hathersage, Sheffield S32 1BA. *T:* (01433) 650220. *E:* fionamccarthy@davidmellordesign.co.uk.

McCARTHY, Frances Ellen; Senior Partner, Pattinson & Brewer Solicitors; *b* London, 30 Sept. 1956; *d* of Dr John Walter McCarthy and Doreen McCarthy; *m* 1992, Charles Peter Fenton; three *s*. *Educ:* Poles Convent, Ware; Univ. of Hull (LLB). Admitted solicitor, 1981; solicitor, Pattinson & Brewer Solicitors. Dir, Trust Mediation. Former mem., Civil Justice Council. Pres., Assoc. of Personal Injury Lawyers, 2000–02; former Chair, Internat. Section, Assoc. of Trial Lawyers of America. Mem., Lord Woolf's Wkg Party. Member, Board: Catholic Children's Soc.; Internat. Performers Aid Trust. Former Mem., Editl Bd,

Jl of Personal Injury Law. *Publications:* (ed jtly) APIL Personal Injury: law, practice and precedents. *Recreations:* supporting Irish Rugby (Munster in particular), family. *Address:* Pattinson & Brewer Solicitors, Mermaid House, 2 Puddle Dock, EC4V 3DB. *T:* (020) 7653 3203, *Fax:* (020) 7653 3201. *E:* fmccarthy@pattinsonbrewer.co.uk.

**McCARTHY, Hui Ling Sarita;** QC 2018; *b* London, 2 Feb. 1981; *d* of Peter Daniel McCarthy and Janet Khoo Phaik Choo McCarthy; partner, 2009, Jonathan Sinclair Grant Bremner, *qv. Educ:* Godolphin and Latymer Sch.; Durham Univ. (BSc Maths 2001). Northumberland Univs OTC, 1998–2001. Corporate Finance, Bear Stearns Internat. Inc., 2001; called to the Bar, Inner Temple, 2005, Bencher, 2018; in practice as barrister, 2007–. Mem., Assoc. of Tax Technicians, 2005. *Recreations:* former ultra-marathoner, former Channel swimmer, current mountaineer (3/7 Seven Summits), cinema goer and popcorn eater, Facebooker (but not Tweeter). *Address:* 11 New Square, Lincoln's Inn, WC2A 3QB. *T:* (020) 7242 4017. *E:* hlm@11newsquare.com. *Clubs:* Royal Automobile; Ski of GB.

**McCARTHY, John Patrick,** CBE 1992; journalist; *b* 27 Nov. 1956; *yr s* of late Pat and Sheila McCarthy; *m* 1999, Anna Ottewill; one *d. Educ:* Haileybury; Hull Univ. (BA 1979). Joined UPITN (later WTN) as journalist, 1982. Kidnapped and held hostage in Beirut, 17 April 1986–8 Aug. 1991. BBC TV series (with Sandi Toksvig), Island Race, 1995; ITV series: It Ain't Necessarily So, 2001; John Meets Paul, 2003; Faultlines, 2003; ITV documentary, Out of the Shadows, 2004; BBC Radio 4 series: John McCarthy's Bible Journey, 1999; A Place Called Home, 2000. Patron, Medical Foundn for the Care of Victims of Torture. Hon. DLitt Hull, 1991. *Publications:* (with Jill Morrell) Some Other Rainbow, 1993; (with Sandi Toksvig) Island Race: improbable voyage around the coast of Britain, 1995; (with Brian Keenan) Between Extremes, 1999; A Ghost Upon your Path, 2002; You Can't Hide the Sun: a journey through Israel and Palestine, 2012. *Address:* c/o LAW, 14 Vernon Street, W14 0RJ.

**McCARTHY, John Sidney,** MBE 1984; FCIOB; Executive Chairman, 1990–2000, non-executive Chairman, 2001–03, McCarthy & Stone; *b* 31 Dec. 1939; *s* of John James McCarthy and Helen Caroline McCarthy; *m* 1982, Gwendoline Joan Holmes; three *s* one *d.* McCarthy & Stone: Joint Founder, 1963; Chief Exec./Chm., 1963–90. Founder, 1987, and Trustee, 1996–98, McCarthy Foundn. Non-exec. Dir, Churchill Retirement Living plc, 2004–. *Publications:* Building a Billion, 2011. *Recreations:* ski-ing, golf, shooting, polo, sailing, subaqua diving, furniture making, big game hunting. *Clubs:* Royal Ocean Racing; Royal Guernsey Golf; Salisbury and S Wilts Golf; Remedy Oak Golf.

**McCARTHY, Kerry;** MP (Lab) Bristol East, since 2005; *b* 26 March 1965; *d* of late Oliver Thomas Haughney and of Sheila Ann Rix (*née* Smith); name changed to McCarthy, 1992. *Educ:* Univ. of Liverpool (BA Hons Russian, Politics and Linguistics); City of London Poly. Legal Asst, S Beds Magistrates' Court, 1986–87; Litigation Asst, Neves (Solicitors), 1988–89; trainee, Wilde Sapte, 1992–94; admitted solicitor, 1994; Lawyer, Abbey National Treasury Services plc, 1994–96; Sen. Counsel, Merrill Lynch Europe plc, 1996–99; Lawyer, Labour Party, 2001; Regl Dir, Britain in Europe, 2002–04; Hd, Public Policy, Waterfront Partnership, 2004–05. Dir, London Luton Airport Ltd, 1999–2003. PPS to Minister of State, Dept of Health, 2007, to Sec. of State for Internat. Develt, 2007–09; an Asst Govt Whip, 2009–10; Shadow Minister for Work and Pensions, 2010; Shadow Econ. Sec. to HM Treasury, 2010–11; Shadow Foreign Office Minister, 2011–15; Shadow Sec. of State for Envmt, Food and Rural Affairs, 2015–16. Member: Treasury Select Cttee, 2005–07; Envmtl Audit Cttee, 2016–; Envmt, Food and Rural Affairs Cttee, 2016–. Mem. (Lab) Luton BC, 1995–96 and 1999–2003. *Recreations:* travel, scuba-diving, music. *Address:* House of Commons, SW1A 0AA. *T:* (020) 7219 4510. *E:* kerry.mccarthy.mp@parliament.uk; (constituency) The King Centre, 16–18 Kings Square, Bristol BS2 8AZ. *T:* (0117) 939 9901. *Club:* St George Labour (Bristol).

**McCARTHY, Kieran;** JP; Member (Alliance) Strangford, Northern Ireland Assembly, 1998–2016; *b* 9 Sept. 1942; *s* of James and Elizabeth McCarthy; *m* 1967, Kathleen Doherty; two *s* two *d. Educ:* Newtownards Coll. of Technol. Formerly textile worker and sales clerk; joint partner, discount drapery, 1965–87; retailer, 1987. Councillor, 1985–2013, Alderman, 1997–2013, Ards BC. Contested (Alliance) Strangford, 2005. JP Ards, 1990. *Recreations:* gardening, reading, cycling. *Address:* Loughedge, 3 Main Street, Kircubbin, Newtownards, Co. Down BT22 2SS. *T:* (028) 4273 8221.

**McCARTHY, Prof. Mark Ian,** MD; FRCP, FMedSci; Robert Turner Professor of Diabetic Medicine, University of Oxford, since 2002; Fellow of Green Templeton College (formerly Green College), Oxford, since 2002; *b* 18 July 1960; *s* of Roy Allen McCarthy and Marion Eluned McCarthy. *Educ:* Pembroke Coll., Cambridge (BA 1981; MB BChir 1985; MD 1995); St Thomas's Hosp. Med. Sch. FRCP 1999. MRC Clin. Trng Fellow, London Hosp. Med. Coll., 1991–94; MRC Travelling Fellow, Whitehead Inst., Cambridge, Mass, 1994–95; Sen. Lectr in Molecular Genetics, 1995–98, Reader, 1998–2000, Prof. of Genomic Medicine, 2000–02, Imperial Coll., Univ. of London. Hon. Consultant, Oxford Radcliffe Hosps NHS Trust, 2002–. Mem. Council, Human Genome Orgn, 2008. FMedSci 2006. *Address:* Diabetes Research Laboratories, Oxford Centre for Diabetes, Endocrinology & Metabolism, Churchill Hospital, Headington, Oxford OX3 7LJ.

**McCARTHY, Nicholas Melvyn,** OBE 1983; HM Diplomatic Service, retired; High Commissioner to Cameroon, and also Ambassador (non-resident) to Gabon, Chad, Equatorial Guinea and the Central African Republic, 1995–98; *b* 4 April 1938; *s* of Daniel Alfred McCarthy and Florence Alice McCarthy; *m* 1961, Gillian Eileen Hill; three *s* one *d. Educ:* Queen Elizabeth's Sch., Faversham; London Univ. (BA Hons). Attaché, Saigon, 1961–64; Language Student, then Second Sec., Tokyo, 1964–69; FCO, 1969–73; First Sec., Brussels, 1973–78; FCO, 1978–80; Head of Chancery, Dakar, 1980–84; FCO, 1984–85; Consul-Gen., Osaka, 1985–90; Dep. Hd of Mission, Consul-Gen. and Counsellor, Brussels, 1990–94. *Recreations:* golf, bridge, opera, tennis, Japanese pottery, writing, cooking. *Address:* The Old Rectory, 34 Cross Street, Moretonhampstead, Devon TQ13 8NL.

**McCARTHY, Richard John,** CBE 2009; FCIH; FRICS; Senior Director, Government Affairs (formerly Strategic Services), Capita plc, since 2016; Chairman: Smart Meters DCC, since 2013; Fera Science, since 2017; Axelos, since 2018; *b* 28 April 1958; *s* of John Anthony McCarthy and Anna Patricia (*née* Sheehan); *m* 1983, Judith Karen McCann; two *s* one *d. Educ:* Richard Challoner Sch., New Malden; Univ. of Southampton (BA Hons Geog.); Hackney Coll. FCIH 1987; FRICS 2013. Housing Officer etc, 1979–87, Ops Dir, 1987–94, Hyde Housing Assoc.; Chief Executive: S London Family Housing Assoc., 1994–99; Peabody Trust, 1999–2003; Director General: Sustainable Communities, ODPM, subseq. Places, Planning and Communities, DCLG, 2003–06; Progs, Policy and Innovation, later Housing and Planning, then Neighbourhoods, DCLG, 2006–11; Exec. Dir, Capita Symonds, later Capita Property and Infrastructure, then Capita Local Govt, Health and Property Services, 2012–16. Chm., Care and Repair, 1986–93. Non-exec. Dir, Funding Affordable Homes, 2017– (Chm., 2015–17). Member: Council, Nat. Housing Fedn, 1998–2003 (Chm., 2000–03); Bd, 1066 Housing Assoc., 2000–03; Housing Panel, Audit Commn, 2003. Chm., Company of Dreams, 2016–. Columnist, Building mag., 2012–. *Publications:* articles in various housing jls. *Recreations:* theatre, music, opera, tennis, football, watching Rugby. *Address:* Capita plc, 71 Victoria Street, Westminster, SW1H 0XA. *T:* (020) 7654 2183. *E:* richard.mccarthy@capita.co.uk.

**MacCARTHY, Very Rev. Robert Brian,** PhD; Dean of St Patrick's Cathedral, Dublin, 1999–2012 (Prebendary, 1994–99); *b* 28 March 1940; *o c* of Richard Edward MacCarthy and Dorothy MacCarthy (*née* Furney), Clonmel. *Educ:* St Columba's Coll., Rathfarnham; Trinity Coll., Dublin (BA, MA, PhD 1983); St John's Coll., Cambridge; Trinity Coll., Oxford (MA); Cuddesdon Theol Coll.; MA NUI 1965. Ordained deacon, 1979, priest, 1980; Curate, Carlow, 1979–81; Librarian, Pusey House, and Fellow, St Cross Coll., Oxford, 1981–82; Curate, 1982–83, Team Vicar, 1983–86, Bracknell; Curate, Kilkenny, 1986–88; Bp's Vicar in Kilkenny Cath., 1986–88; Domestic Chaplain to Bp of Ossory, 1986–89; Rector, Castlecomer, and RD of Carlow, 1988–95; Rector, St Nicholas' Collegiate Church, Galway and Provost of Tuam, 1995–99. *Publications:* The Estates of Trinity College, Dublin, 1992; Ancient and Modern, 1995; How Shall They Hear, 2002; John Henry Bernard 1860–1927, 2008. *Recreation:* architectural history. *Address:* Suirmount, Clonmel, Co. Tipperary, Ireland. *T:* (52) 6136395. *Clubs:* Kildare Street and University (Dublin); Royal Irish Yacht (Dun Laoghaire).

**McCARTHY, Shaun Patrick,** OBE 2013; Owner and Director, Action Sustainability, since 2006; *b* London, 2 Aug. 1957; *s* of Terence McCarthy and Ethel McCarthy; *m* 1983, Kay (*d* 2018); one *d* (one *s* decd). *Educ:* Lanchester Poly. (HND Mech. Engrg 1981). MCIPS 1992; MIEMA 2005, FIEMA 2017. Apprentice Mechanical Fitter, Esso Petroleum Co., 1973–77; Applications Engr, Worthington Pumps, 1981–83; Sales Engr, Sulzer UK, 1983–85; Procurement Manager, Shell UK Ltd, 1986–95; BAA plc: Hd, Procurement Develt, 1995–2000; Hd, Utilities, 2000–03; Hd, Utilities and Sustainability, 2003–06. Chm., Commn for a Sustainable London 2012, 2006–13; Mem., London Sustainable Develt Commn, 2004–15. Trustee, Greenshoots Fund, 2011–. MInstD. FRSA. *Publications:* Principles and Practice of Sustainable Procurement, 2011; (with C. Berry) Guide to Sustainable Procurement in Construction, 2011; contribs to reports for Commn for a Sustainable London 2012. *Recreations:* family, music, boating. *E:* shaun.mccarthy@actionsustainability.com.

**McCARTHY, Shona Mary;** Chief Executive, Edinburgh Festival Fringe Society, since 2016; *b* Co. Down, 17 Jan. 1968; *d* of Don and Elizabeth McCarthy; partner, Bobby Gordon; two *d. Educ:* Univ. of Ulster (BA Hons Film, Media and English 1989; Postgrad. Dip. Cultural Mgt 1997). Chief Executive: Cinemagic, 1991–2001; Imagine Belfast 2008, 2001–02; Exec. Dir, Rubyblue, 2002–09; Dir, British Council NI, 2009–11; Chief Exec., Culture Co. 2013, 2011–14. Dir, Foyle Film Fest., 1995–98. Chair: Oh Yeah Music Centre, 2015–; Walk the Plank, 2015–. *Recreations:* walking, cinema, music, food, theatre, reading. *Address:* Edinburgh Fringe Festival, 180 High Street, Edinburgh EH1 1QS. *T:* (0131) 226 0021. *E:* admin@edfringe.com.

**McCARTHY, Steven Scott,** CBE 2019; Minister (Defence and Materiel), British Defence Staff, British Embassy, Washington, DC, 2014–18; *b* Caterham, Surrey, 29 June 1958; *s* of Leslie McCarthy and Cynthia McCarthy; *m* 1988, Dawn Oliver; two *d. Educ:* de Stafford Sch., Caterham. Joined MoD, 1977; Asst Private Sec. to Sec. of State for Defence, 1988–89; Hd, Net Assessment Unit, MoD, 1989–92; Sec., Equipment Approvals Cttee, 1992–96; Private Sec. to Chief of Defence Procurement, 1996–98; Counsellor (Defence Equipment), Washington, DC, 1998–2002; Sec., Defence Procurement Agency, 2002–08; Dir, Change, 2008–10, COS, 2010–11, Defence Equipment and Support; Dir, Internat. Security Policy, MoD, 2011–14. *Publications:* (with M. Gilbert) The Crystal Palace Dinosaurs, 1994. *Recreations:* military history (especially tramping battlefields), gardening, (watching) sport, supporting Liverpool FC, just being with my wife. *Address:* Gloucestershire.

**McCARTHY, Suzanne Joyce;** Deputy Chairman, Valuation Tribunal Service, since 2018; Chairman, Fire Standards Board, since 2019; *b* 21 Nov. 1948; *d* of Leo and Lillian Rudnick; *m* 1990, Brendan McCarthy. *Educ:* New York Univ. (BA 1970; Phi Beta Kappa); Wolfson Coll., Cambridge (Dip Social Anthropol. 1971); Lucy Cavendish Coll., Cambridge (LLM 1986); Univ. of E London (MSc 2010). Admitted Solicitor, 1976; Solicitor in private practice, 1977–86; Lectr in Law, Univ. of Manchester, 1986–89; joined Civil Service, 1989; posts with Home Office (incl. Private Sec. to Home Sec.), Treasury, Civil Service Coll. (Dir, Policy, Govt and Europe), 1989–96; Chief Executive: HFEA, 1996–2000; Financial Services Compensation Scheme, 2000–04. Immigration Services Comr, 2005–15. Chm., Depaul UK, 2015–; Trustee, Depaul Internat., 2015–17. Dir, Senet Gp, 2015–16. Chm., Jt Audit Panel, Mayor's Office of Policing and Crime and Metropolitan Police Service, 2016–19; Member: Determinations Panel Pensions Regulator, 2005–13; Conduct Disciplinary Cttee, CIMA, 2006–08; Council, GMC, 2009–12; Disciplinary and Regulatory Cttees, Assoc. of Chartered Certified Accountants, 2011–; UK and Ireland Regulatory Bd, RICS, 2012–16; Adv. Bd, LSE Centre for Analysis of Risk and Regulation, 2014–; Advertising Standards Authy, 2015–March 2020; Gender Equality Adv. Gp, City Univ., 2015–18; Marshall Aid Commemoration Commn, 2016–19; Architects Registration Bd, 2016–March 2020; Ind. Adv. Panel, Coll. of Policing, 2016–18; Bd, Acad. of Medical Royal Colls, 2017–; Faculty, Healthcare Leadership Acad., 2016–; IPSO, 2017–; Dir, Fundraising Regulator, 2016–20; Gangmasters and Labour Abuse Authy, 2019–; Independent Appointed Person: GLA, 2012–20; London Emergency and Fire Planning Authy, 2012–17. Chairman: Gen. Chiropractic Council, 2013–16; Southwark and Lambeth Integrated Partnership, 2017–19. Non-executive Director: Royal Brompton and Harefield NHS Trust, 1998–2006; Candoco Dance Co., 2000–04; RIBA, 2004–14; Public Guardian Bd, 2007–12; Human Tissue Authy, 2010–16. Chm. Adv. Cttee, Vopulus, 2017–. Chm., European Forum of Deposit Insurers, 2002–04 (Hon. Chm. 2008); Mem. Exec. Council, British and Irish Ombudsman Assoc., 2008–12. Mem. Panel (Dance), SOLT (Laurence Olivier) Awards, 2002. Trustee, RNIB, 2002–04. University of London: Mem. Council, 2003–08 (Dep. Chm., 2006–08); Mem., Bd of Trustees, 2008–16; Mem., Res. Ethics Panel, Sch. of Advanced Studies, 2016–; Hon. Fellow, 2018. Freeman, City of London, 2006; Yeoman, 2006–08, Liveryman, 2008–, Co. of Ironmongers. *Recreations:* learning French, dance, Italian and French cookery. *Club:* Athenæum.

**McCARTHY, Thomas Patrick;** novelist; *b* Stirling, 22 May 1969; *s* of Sir Callum McCarthy, *qv*; *m* 2009, Eva Stenram; two *d. Educ:* Dulwich Coll.; New Coll., Oxford (BA Hons 1990). Writer and conceptual artist. *Publications: novels:* Remainder, 2005; Men in Space, 2007; C, 2010, Satin Island, 2015; *non-fiction:* Tintin and the Secret of Literature, 2006; Typewriters, Bombs, Jellyfish: essays, 2017. *Recreation:* listening to Test Cricket. *Address:* c/o Jonathan Pegg Literary Agency, 67 Wingate Street, SW4 0AF.

**McCARTHY, William Joseph Anthony;** Deputy Vice-Chancellor, Operations, and Honorary Professor of Health Policy, University of Bradford, since 2014; North West Regional Director, NHS Executive Group, since 2019; *b* Leeds, 14 June 1963; *s* of Shaun and Patricia McCarthy; *m* 1986, Rose Coady; four *s* one *d. Educ:* Prior Park, Bath; Queen Mary Coll., Univ. of London (BSc Econ.); London Sch. of Econs (MSc). Asst Economist, DoH, 1986–88; Analyst, Herts CC and ACC, 1988–91; rejoined Department of Health, 1991: Principal, 1991–94; Asst Sec., Primary Care, 1994–97; Head: of Public Expenditure Survey Br., 1997–99; of Finance and Performance Div. A, NHS Exec., 1999–2000; Dir of

Planning and Performance, Leeds Teaching Hosps NHS Trust, 2000–02; Dir, Strategic Develt, W Yorks Strategic HA, 2002–06; Dir, Policy and Strategy, DoH, 2006–07; Chief Executive: York CC, 2007–09; Yorks and the Humber Strategic HA, 2009–11; Man. Dir, NHS Commissioning Bd, 2011–13; Nat. Dir, Policy, NHS England, 2013–14. Chair, Bradford Teaching Hosps NHS Foundn Trust, 2016–19. *Recreations:* playing with the children, eating out, weekends away, watching sport.

**McCARTHY-FRY, Sarah;** Finance Director, Cowes, Isle of Wight and Western Approach, Bristol, GKN Aerospace Services, since 2012 (Financial Controller, Cowes, Isle of Wight, 2010–12); *b* 4 Feb. 1955; *d* of Sidney and Constance Macaree; *m* 1st, 1973, Roger Fry (marr. diss. 1997); one *s* one *d*; 2nd, 1997, Anthony McCarthy. *Educ:* Portsmouth High Sch.; BPP Coll., Southampton. ACMA 2004. Financial Accountant, FPT Industries, Portsmouth, 1988–2000; GKN Aerospace Services: Financial Analyst, Farnham, 2000–03; Financial Controller, Cowes, IoW, 2003–05. Dep. Leader, Portsmouth CC, 1995–2000. MP (Lab and Co-op) Portsmouth N, 2005–10; contested (Lab and Co-op) same seat, 2010. Parly Under-Sec. of State, DCSF, 2008–09, DCLG, 2009; Exchequer Sec. to HM Treasury, 2009–10. *Recreations:* tap dancing, dog walking.

**McCARTIE, Rt Rev. (Patrick) Leo;** Bishop of Northampton, (RC), 1990–2001, now Emeritus; *b* 5 Sept. 1925; *s* of Patrick Leo and Hannah McCartie. *Educ:* Cotton College; Oscott College. Priest, 1949; on staff of Cotton College, 1950–55; parish work, 1955–63; Director of Religious Education, 1963–68; Administrator of St Chad's Cathedral, Birmingham, 1968–77; Aux. Bp of Birmingham, and Titular Bp of Elmham, 1977–90. Pres., Catholic Commn for Racial Justice, 1978–83; Chm., Cttee for Community Relations, Dept for Christian Responsibility and Citizenship, Bishops' Conf. on Eng. and Wales, 1983–90; Mem., Churches Main Cttee, 1996–2002. Church Representative: Churches Together in England, 1990; Council of Churches for Britain and Ireland, 1990. *Recreations:* music, walking.

**McCARTNEY, Gordon Arthur;** consultant; Managing Director, Gordon McCartney Associates, since 1991; *b* 29 April 1937; *s* of Arthur and Hannah McCartney; *m* 1st, 1960, Ceris Ysobel Davies (marr. diss. 1987); two *d*; 2nd, 1988, Wendy Ann Vyvyan Titman. *Educ:* Grove Park Grammar Sch., Wrexham. Articled to Philip J. Walters, MBE (Town Clerk, Wrexham), 1954–59; admitted solicitor, 1959. Asst Solicitor, Birkenhead County Bor. Council, 1959–61; Asst Solicitor, 1961–63, Sen. Asst Solicitor, 1963–65, Bootle County Bor. Council; Dep. Clerk, Wrexham RDC, 1965–73; Clerk, Holywell RDC, 1973–74; Chief Exec., Delyn Bor. Council, 1974–81; Sec., Assoc. of Dist Councils, 1981–91; Associate, Succession Planning Associates, 1991–94. Dir, Nat. Transport Tokens Ltd, 1984–92. Secretary-General, British Section, IULA/CEMR, 1984–88; Chairman: CEMR Individual Members Gp, 1992–97; Local Govt Gp for Europe, 1997–2005 (Hon. Sec., Local Govt Gp for Europe, later Local Govt Section, Eur. Movt, 2006–17); Co. Sec., Local Govt Internat. Bureau, 1988–91. Mem., Hansard Soc. Commn on Legislative Process, 1991–93. Director: Leisure England Ltd, 1993–; White Rock Developments Ltd, 1996–97. Organist, Elton Methodist Ch, 1991–2015; Dep. Organist, Falmouth Methodist Church, 2018–. *Recreations:* cricket, music. *Address:* 21 Challenger Quay, Falmouth TR11 3YL. *T:* 07951 703992. *Club:* MCC.

**McCARTNEY, Rt Hon. Sir Ian;** Kt 2010; PC 1999; *b* 25 April 1951; *s* of late Hugh McCartney and Margaret McCartney (née McDonald); *m* (marr. diss.); two *d* (one *s* decd); *m* 1988, Ann Parkes (née Kevan). *Educ:* State primary, secondary schools; Tech. Colls. Led paper boy strike, 1965; joined Labour Party, 1966; joined trade union, 1966; seaman, local govt manual worker, chef, 1966–71; unemployed, 1971–73; Labour Party Organiser, 1973–87. Councillor, Wigan Borough, 1982–87. MP (Lab) Makerfield, 1987–2010. Hon. Parly Adviser: to Greater Manchester Fire and Civil Defence Authy, 1987–92 (Mem., 1986); to Nat. Assoc. for Safety in the Home, 1989–92. Opposition spokesperson on NHS, 1992–94, on employment, 1994–96, chief spokesperson on employment, 1996–97; Minister of State: DTI, 1997–99; Cabinet Office, 1999–2001; Minister for Pensions, DWP, 2001–03; Minister without Portfolio and Chair, Labour Party, 2003–06; Minister of State, FCO and DTI, 2006–07. Mem., Parly Select Cttee on Health and Social Security, 1991–92; Sec., All Party Parly Gp on Credit Unions, 2007–10. Chm., T&GWU Parly Gp, 1989–91. Sponsored by TGWU. Prime Minister's Rep., Socialist Internat., 2008–10. Mem., Nat. Constitutional Cttee, Lab. Party, 2012–. Hon. Pol Sec. Nat. Union of Labour and Socialist Clubs, 2013–. Pres., 2007–10, Ambassador, 2012–, Money Advice Trust. UK Comr-Gen., Shanghai Expo 2010, 2007–10. Advr, Drop in and Share, 2012–; Chair, Healthwatch Wigan, 2013–16. Hon. President: Wigan Wheelchair Fund 1987–; Mencap, Ashton, Lowton and Golborne, 2012–16. *Recreations:* Wigan Rugby League fanatic (supports Wigan Warriors); head of McCartney family, a family of proud working class stock.

**McCARTNEY, Sir (James) Paul,** CH 2017; Kt 1997; MBE 1965; musician, composer; *b* Allerton, Liverpool, 18 June 1942; *s* of James McCartney and Mary McCartney; *m* 1st, 1969, Linda Eastman (*d* 1998); one *s* two *d*, and one step *d*; 2nd, 2002, Heather Mills (marr. diss. 2008); one *d*; 3rd, 2011, Nancy Shevell. *Educ:* Liverpool Inst. Mem., skiffle group, The Quarry Men, 1957–59; toured Scotland with them and Stuart Sutcliffe as the Silver Beetles, 1960; first of five extended seasons in Hamburg, Aug. 1960; made 1st important appearance as the Beatles at Litherland Town Hall, nr Liverpool, Dec. 1960; appeared as mem. of Beatles: UK, Sweden, and Royal Variety perf., London, 1963; UK, Netherlands, Sweden, France, Denmark, Hong Kong, Australia, NZ, Canada, 1964; TV appearances, USA, and later, coast-to-coast tour, 1964; UK, France, Italy, Spain, USA, Canada, 1965; West Germany, Japan, Philippines, USA, Canada, 1966; Beatles disbanded 1970; formed MPL group of cos, 1970, and own group, Wings, 1971; toured: UK, Europe, 1972–73; UK, Australia, 1975; Europe, USA, Canada, 1976; UK, 1979; Wings disbanded 1981; Europe, UK, Canada, Japan, USA, Brazil, 1989/90; USA, 2002; UK, Europe, 2003; USA, 2005; USA, Europe, UK, 2009; USA, UK, 2010; USA, Europe, UK, 2011; Europe, S America, 2012; Europe, 2015. Wrote (with Carl Davis) Liverpool Oratorio, 1991; *symphony:* Standing Stone, 1997; Ecce Cor Meum (oratorio), 2006; Ocean's Kingdom (ballet), 2011. *Songs* with John Lennon include: Love Me Do; Please Please Me; From Me To You; She Loves You; Can't Buy Me Love; I Want to Hold Your Hand; I Saw Her Standing There; Eight Days a Week; All My Loving; Help!; Ticket to Ride; I Feel Fine; I'm A Loser; A Hard Day's Night; No Reply; I'll Follow The Sun; Yesterday; For No One; Here, There and Everywhere; Eleanor Rigby; Yellow Submarine; Penny Lane; All You Need Is Love; Lady Madonna; Hey Jude; We Can Work It Out; Day Tripper; Paperback Writer; When I'm Sixty-Four; A Day in the Life; Back in the USSR; Hello, Goodbye; Get Back; Let It Be; The Long and Winding Road; subseq. *songs* include: Maybe I'm Amazed; My Love; Band on the Run; Jet; Let 'Em In; Silly Love Songs; Mull of Kintyre; Coming Up; Ebony and Ivory; Tug of War; Pipes of Peace; No More Lonely Nights; My Brave Face. *Albums* with the Beatles: Please Please Me, 1963; With The Beatles, 1963; A Hard Day's Night, 1964; Beatles for Sale, 1964; Help!, 1965; Rubber Soul, 1965; Revolver, 1966; Sgt Pepper's Lonely Hearts Club Band, 1967; Magical Mystery Tour, 1967; The Beatles (White Album), 1968; Yellow Submarine, 1969; Abbey Road, 1969; Let it Be, 1970; Anthology I, II and III, 1995–96; other albums: McCartney, 1970; Ram, 1971; Wild Life, 1971; Red Rose Speedway, 1973; Band on the Run, 1973; Venus and Mars, 1975; Wings at the Speed of Sound, 1976; Wings over America, 1976; London Town, 1978; Wings Greatest, 1978; Back to the Egg, 1979; McCartney II, 1980; Tug of War, 1982; Pipes of Peace, 1983; Give My Regards to Broad Street, 1984; Press to Play, 1986; All the Best!, 1987; CHOBA B CCCP, 1988; Flowers in the Dirt, 1989; Tripping the Live Fantastic, 1990; Unplugged: The Official Bootleg, 1991; Paul McCartney's Liverpool Oratorio, 1991; Off The Ground, 1993; Paul Is Live, 1993; Flaming Pie, 1997; Standing Stone, 1999; Run Devil Run, 1999; Wingspan, 2001; Driving Rain, 2001; Chaos and Creation in the Back Yard, 2005; Memory Almost Full, 2007; Electric Arguments, 2008; Kisses on the Bottom, 2012; New, 2013; Egypt Station, 2018. *Films* (with the Beatles): A Hard Day's Night, 1964; Help!, 1965; Magical Mystery Tour (TV), 1967; Yellow Submarine, 1968; Let It Be, 1970; (with Wings) Rockshow, 1981; (wrote, composed score, and acted in) Give My Regards To Broad Street, 1984; (wrote, composed score and produced) Rupert and the Frog Song, 1984 (BAFTA award, Best Animated Film); Get Back, 1991. *Film scores:* The Family Way, 1966; Live and Let Die, 1973 (title song only); Twice In A Lifetime, 1984 (title song only); Spies Like Us, 1985 (title song only); *TV scores:* Thingumybob (series), 1968; The Zoo Gang (series), 1974. One-man art exhibn, Walker Gall., Liverpool, 2002. Live Russian 'phone link-up, BBC Russian Service, 1989. FRCM 1995. Numerous Grammy Awards, Nat. Acad. of Recording Arts and Scis, USA, incl. Lifetime Achievement Awards, 1990 and (for The Beatles), 2014; Ivor Novello Awards include: for Internat. Achievement, 1980; for Internat. Hit of the Year (Ebony and Ivory), 1982; for Outstanding Contrib. to Music, 1989; PRS special award for unique achievement in popular music, 1990; Kennedy Center Honor, 2010. Officier de la Légion d'honneur (France), 2012. Freeman, City of Liverpool, 1984. Fellow, British Acad. of Composers and Songwriters, 2000. DUniv Sussex, 1988. *Publications:* The Beatles Anthology (with George Harrison and Ringo Starr), 2000; Paintings, 2000; Blackbird Singing: poems and lyrics 1965–1999, 2001; Wingspan: Paul McCartney's band on the run, 2002; (jtly) The Meat-Free Monday Cookbook, 2016; *for children:* (jtly) High in the Clouds, 2005; Hey Grandude!, 2019.
See also M. A. *McCartney,* S. *McCartney.*

**McCARTNEY, Jason Alexander;** Head of Public Affairs, Huddersfield University, since 2017; *b* Harrogate, 29 Jan. 1968; *s* of Wing Comdr Robert McCartney and Jean McCartney; two *d*. *Educ:* Lancaster Royal Grammar Sch.; RAF Coll., Cranwell; Leeds Trinity University Coll. (Postgrad. Dip. Broadcast Journalism). Officer, RAF, 1988–97; journalist, Radio Cleveland and Leeds, BBC, 1997–98; journalist and presenter, ITV Yorkshire, 1998–2007; Sen. Lectr, Leeds Metropolitan Univ., 2008–10. MP (C) Colne Valley, 2010–17; contested (C) same seat, 2017. Member: Transport Select Cttee, 2013–15; Culture, Media and Sport Cttee, 2015–17; 1922 Exec. Cttee, 2013–17. NATO Parly Assembly, 2010–17. Dir, fairandfunky CIC, 2018–. Member: One Community Foundn Trust, 2017–; Bd, Mid Yorks Chamber of Commerce, 2018–. Hon. Pres., Huddersfield Br., RAF Assoc., 2011–. *Recreations:* Huddersfield Town AFC, Huddersfield Giants RLFC, Yorkshire CCC, tennis. *W:* jasonmccartney.com. *Club:* Royal Air Force.

**McCARTNEY, Joanne;** Member (Lab) Enfield and Haringey, since 2004, and Deputy Mayor, since 2016, London Assembly, Greater London Authority. *Educ:* Univ. of Warwick (LLB); Univ. of Leicester (LLM). Barrister, specialising in employment law; adjudicator, Housing Ombudsman. Mem. (Lab) Enfield BC, 1998–2006. Mem., Metropolitan Police Authy, 2004–12; Chair, Police and Crime Cttee, GLA, 2012–16. *Address:* Greater London Authority, City Hall, Queen's Walk, SE1 2AA.

**McCARTNEY, Karl Ian;** JP; *b* St Catherine's, Birkenhead, 25 Oct. 1968; *s* of John McCartney and Brenda McCartney (née Weir); *m* 1999, Cordelia Pyne; two *s*. *Educ:* Woodfall Lane Prim. and Jun. Schs; Birkenhead Sch. for Boys; Neston High Sch.; Willink Sch.; St David's University Coll., Wales (BA Hons Geog. 1991; Pres., Student Union, 1991–92); Kingston Business Sch., Kingston Univ. (MBA 1998). Logistics Analyst, Hasbro, 1992–93; Agent and Researcher, Conservative Central Office, 1993–96; Corporate Affairs, Corp. of London, 1996–2001. Dir, MLSystems, mgt consultancy, 1999–. Campaign Dir, 2007–10, Dep. Chm., 2010–12, Sir Keith Park Meml Campaign. Contested (C) Lincoln, 2005. MP (C) Lincoln, 2010–17; contested (C) same seat, 2017. Member: Transport Select Cttee, 2012–17; Exiting EU Select Cttee, 2016–17; 1922 Exec. Cttee, 2012–17. JP Dartford, later Maidstone, then Lincoln, 1999–. *Recreations:* myriad of sports—football, Rugby, cricket, croquet, snowboarding, shooting; classic cars, green laning, trains, gardens, architecture, history, dance music, relaxing with family and friends, cooking.

**McCARTNEY, Mary Anna;** freelance photographer; author; *b* London, 1969; *d* of Sir (James) Paul McCartney, *qv; m* 2010, Simon Aboud; two *s*, and two *s* by a previous marriage. Solo exhibitions: Off Pointe, Royal Opera House, 2004, Dimbola Lodge, I of W, 2005, Crane Kalman Gall., Brighton, 2007; Playing Dress Up, Goss Michael Foundn, Dallas, 2007; Backup, OXO Tower Wharf, London, 2007; British Style Observed, Natural Hist. Mus., 2008; Collective Works, Nunnington Hall, Yorks, 2009; From Where I Stand, NPG and Michael Hoppen Gall., 2010, Staley Wise Gall., NY, 2010, Contributed, Berlin, 2011, Tres Hombres, Sweden, 2012; Developing, Lowry Galls, Manchester, Izzy Gall., Toronto, 2013; Monochrome & Colour, de Pury de Pury, 2014; Mother Daughter, Gagosian, NY, 2015; group exhibitions: NPG, 1995, 2009; Plymouth Arts Centre, 2004; RCA and Waterfront, NY, 2007. Trustee, NPG, 2011–15. *Publications:* From Where I Stand, 2010; Food, 2012; Monochrome & Colour, 2014; At My Table, 2015; (jtly) The Meat-Free Monday Cookbook, 2016; Twelfth Night, 2018; The White Horse, 2018; Paris Nude, 2019.
See also S. *McCartney.*

**McCARTNEY, Sir Paul;** see McCartney, Sir J. P.

**McCARTNEY, Robert Law;** QC (NI) 1975; Member (UKU) North Down, Northern Ireland Assembly, 1998–2007; *b* 24 April 1936; *s* of William Martin McCartney and Elizabeth Jane (née McCartney); *m* 1960, Maureen Ann Bingham; one *s* three *d*. *Educ:* Grosvenor Grammar Sch., Belfast; Queen's Univ., Belfast (LLB Hons 1958). Admitted solicitor of Supreme Court of Judicature, NI, 1962; called to NI Bar, 1968. MP (UKU) N Down, June 1995–2001; contested (UKU) same seat, 2001; contested (UKU) N Down, NI Assembly, 2007. Chm., Nat. Grammar Schs Assoc., 2008–. *Publications:* Liberty and Authority in Ireland, 1985; Liberty, Democracy and the Union, 2001; political reports and pamphlets. *Recreations:* reading (biography and military history), walking. *Address:* St Catherines, 2 Circular Road East, Cultra, Holywood, Co. Down, Northern Ireland BT18 0HA.

**McCARTNEY, Stella,** OBE 2013; fashion designer; *b* 13 Sept. 1971; *d* of Sir (James) Paul McCartney, *qv; m* 2003, Alasdhair Willis; two *s* two *d*. *Educ:* Central St Martin's Coll. of Art and Design. Set up own clothing line, London, 1995; Creative Dir, Chloe, Paris, 1997–2001; estabd own fashion house, in partnership with Gucci Gp, 2001–; opened stores in NY, 2002, London, and Los Angeles, 2003. Creative Dir, Team GB, London Olympics, 2012, Rio de Janeiro Olympics, 2016. British Designer of the Year, 2007, 2012; Red Carpet Award, 2011, Designer Brand of the Year, 2012, British Fashion Awards. *Publications:* (jtly) The Meat-Free Monday Cookbook, 2016.
See also M. A. *McCartney.*

**McCARTNEY, Thomas;** Sheriff of North Strathclyde at Paisley, since 2012; *b* Glasgow, 9 Aug. 1958; *s* of Thomas McCartney and Theresa McCartney (*née* Logan); *m* 1982, Patricia Frances Potts. *Educ:* St Aloysius Coll., Glasgow; Univ. of Glasgow (LLB 1979). Admitted Solicitor, 1981; Partner, Fitzpatrick & Co., solicitors, Glasgow, 1983–99; sole practitioner, 1999–2009; Sheriff of Tayside Central and Fife at Falkirk, 2009–12. A pt-time Chm., Appeals Service, 2001–09; Mem., Scottish Solicitors' Discipline Tribunal, 2005–09. *Recreations:* golf, running, ski-ing, Scottish art. *Address:* c/o Paisley Sheriff Court, St James Street, Paisley PA3 2AW.

**McCARTY, Marie Elizabeth;** *see* Mallon, M. E.

**McCASKILL, Prof. Margaret,** PhD; Pro Vice-Chancellor, De Montfort University, 2000–02; *b* 29 April 1946; *d* of late Roderick McKay Campbell McCaskill and Gladys May McCaskill (*née* Ireland); *m* 1st, 1967, Anthony Howell (marr. diss.); two *d*; 2nd, 1978, Alan Fearn (marr. diss.); 3rd, 1985, Herbert Kinnell (marr. diss.); 4th, 1989, Gwynne Evans (marr. diss.). *Educ:* Nottingham Poly. (BA CNAA); Leicester Poly. (MBA CNAA); Loughborough Univ. (PhD); Nottingham Univ. (PGCE). FCLIP (FLA 1994; FIInfSc 1995). Librarian: Nottingham City Libraries, 1964–65; Notts Co. Libraries, 1967–69; Sutton in Ashfield Libraries, 1971–73; antiquarian bookseller, 1973–75; Loughborough University: Lectr, 1979–88; Sen. Lectr, 1988–94; Prof. of Information Studies, 1994–2000; Hd of Dept of Information and Liby Studies, 1994–98; Dean, Sci. Faculty, 1998–2000. *Publications:* (jtly) Book acquisition and use by young people: a review of recent research initiatives, 1988; (ed) Planned Public Relations for Libraries, 1989; (ed) The Learning Experiences of Overseas Students, 1990; (ed) Managing Fiction in Libraries, 1991; All Change?: public library management strategies for the 1990s, 1991; (jtly) Managing Library Resources in Schools, 1994; (jtly) Meeting the marketing challenge: strategies for public libraries and leisure services, 1994; (jtly) Continuity and Innovation in the Public Library, 1996; (jtly) Marketing in the Not-for-profit Sector, 1997; (jtly) Learning support for special educational needs: potential for progress, 1997; (jtly) Adult reading promotion in UK public libraries, 1998; Northern Working Lives from the 18th to 20th centuries, 2013; numerous other books, reports and articles. *Recreations:* Jamie, Lizzie, Flossie, Tom, animals, HWL for Southwell Choral Society.

**McCAUGHRAN, John;** QC 2003; *b* 24 April 1958; *s* of Desmond McCaughran and Elizabeth McCaughran (*née* Miller); *m* 1985, Catherine Françoise Marie Mondange; one *s*. *Educ:* Methodist Coll., Belfast; Trinity Hall, Cambridge (MA 1980). Called to the Bar, Gray's Inn, 1982, Bencher, 2009. *Recreations:* reading, weeding, la vie française. *Address:* One Essex Court, Temple, EC4Y 9AR. *T:* (020) 7583 2000, *Fax:* (020) 7583 0118. *E:* jmccaughran@oeclaw.co.uk.

**McCAUGHREAN, Geraldine Margaret,** FRSL, FEA; author; *b* 6 June 1951; *d* of Lesley Arthur Jones and Ethel Jones (*née* Thomas); *m* 1988, John McCaughrean; one *d*. *Educ:* Enfield County Grammar Sch. for Girls; Southgate Technical Coll.; Christ Church Coll. of Educn, Canterbury (BEd Hons 1977; Hon. Fellow, Canterbury Christ Church Univ., 2006). Sec., Thames TV, 1970–73; Sec. 1977–79, and Sub-Editor, 1983–88, Marshall Cavendish; Editorial Asst, Rothmans Internat., 1980–82; Editor, Banbury Focus, 1982. Radio play, Last Call, 1991; stage play, Dazzling Medusa, Polka Children's Theatre, 2005. FRSL 2010; FEA 2010. *Publications:* over 190 titles, various trans. into 49 languages in 62 countries, including: *for children:* A Little Lower than the Angels (Whitbread Children's Book Award), 1987; A Pack of Lies (Guardian Children's Award, Carnegie Medal), 1988; Gold Dust (Whitbread Children's Book Award), 1994; Plundering Paradise (Smarties Bronze Award), 1996; Forever X (UK Reading Assoc. Award), 1997; The Stones are Hatching, 1999; Britannia, 1999; (new version) A Pilgrim's Progress, 1999 (Blue Peter Book of the Year, 2000); The Kite Rider (Smarties Bronze Award), 2001; Stop the Train (Smarties Bronze Award), 2001; Gilgamesh the Hero, 2002 (staged Bristol Old Vic, 2006); Bright Penny, 2003; The Jesse Tree, 2003; Smile! (Smarties Bronze Award), 2004; Questing Knights of the Faerie Queen, 2004; Cyrano, 2005; Peter Pan In Scarlet, 2006 (trans. 42 langs); Tamburlaine's Elephants, 2007; The Death Defying Pepper Roux, 2009; Pull Out All the Stops, 2010; Monacello, 2011; Pittipat's Saucer of Moon, 2012; Monocello - The Wish Bringer, 2012; The Nutcracker Moving Picture Book, 2012; The Positively Last Performance, 2013; Go! Go! Chichico!, 2013; The Middle of Nowhere, 2013; *for teenagers:* Not the End of the World (Whitbread Children's Book Award), 2004 (staged Bristol Old Vic, 2007); The White Darkness, 2005 (Michael L. Printz Award, 2008); Where the World Ends, 2017 (CILIP Carnegie Medal, Ind. Bookshop Week Book Award, 2018); *for adults:* The Maypole, 1989; Fire's Astonishment, 1990; Vainglory, 1991; Lovesong, 1996; The Ideal Wife, 1997; contribs to anthologies for children and young people. *Recreation:* theatre. *Address:* c/o David Higham Associates, 6th Floor, Waverley House, 7–12 Noel Street, W1F 8GQ. *W:* www.geraldinemccaughrean.co.uk.

**McCAUL, Colin Brownlie;** QC 2003; *b* 21 Oct. 1954; *s* of Ian and Elizabeth McCaul; *m* 1988, Claire Louise Carden; two *s* three *d*. *Educ:* Dulwich Coll.; University Coll. London (LLB Hons). Called to the Bar, Gray's Inn, 1978, Bencher, 2006. *Recreations:* horses, West Ham United, English history. *Address:* 39 Essex Chambers, 81 Chancery Lane, WC2A 1DD. *T:* (020) 7832 1111, *Fax:* (020) 7353 3978. *E:* colin.mccaul@39essex.com.

**McCAUSLAND, Benedict Maurice Perronet T.;** *see* Thompson-McCausland.

**McCAUSLAND, Nelson;** Member (DemU) Belfast North, Northern Ireland Assembly, 2003–17; *b* N Belfast, 1951; *m* Mary. *Educ:* Belfast Royal Acad.; Worcester Coll., Oxford; Queen's Univ., Belfast (DipEd). Teacher of Science, Belfast; NI Sec., Lord's Day Observance Soc., 1983–93; Chm., 1995–97, Dir, 1997–2003, Ulster-Scots Heritage Council. Minister for Culture, Arts and Leisure, 2009–11, for Social Develt, 2011–14, NI. Contested (DemU) Belfast N, 2017. Mem., Belfast CC, 1989–2010 (Ind U, 1989–93; UU, 1993–2001; DemU, 2001–10); High Sheriff of Belfast, 1997–98.

**McCAVE, Prof. (Ian) Nicholas,** FGS; Woodwardian Professor of Geology, University of Cambridge, 1985–2008, now Emeritus; Fellow, St John's College, Cambridge, since 1986; *b* 3 Feb. 1941; *s* of Thomas Theasby McCave and Gwendoline Marguerite McCave (*née* Langlois); *m* 1972, Susan Caroline Adams (*née* Bambridge); three *s* one *d*. *Educ:* Elizabeth Coll., Guernsey; Hertford Coll., Oxford (MA, DSc); Brown Univ., USA (PhD). FGS 1963. Fulbright Scholar, 1963–67; Instructor in Geology, Brown Univ., 1967; NATO Research Fellow, Netherlands Inst. for Sea Research, 1967–69; Lectr 1969–76, Reader 1976–84, UEA, Norwich; Hd, Dept of Earth Scis, Univ. of Cambridge, 1988–98. Visiting Professor: Oregon State Univ., 1974; MIT, 1999; Columbia Univ., NY, 2007; Adjunct Scientist, Woods Hole Oceanographic Instn, 1978–87. Chm., Atmospheric and Aquatic Physics Sci. Cttee, NERC, 1982–85; Mem., Scientific Cttee on Oceanic Res., ICSU, 1989–2001 (Pres., 1992–96). Leverhulme Emeritus Res. Fellow, 2008–10. Shepard Medal for Marine Geol., US Soc. for Sedimentary Geol., 1995; Huntsman Medal for Marine Scis, Canada, 1999; Lyell Medal, Geol Soc. of London, 2009. *Publications:* (ed) The Benthic Boundary Layer, 1976; (ed) The Deep Sea Bed, 1990; over 180 papers in jls. *Recreations:* pottering about in the garden, rough carpentry, travel. *Address:* Marlborough House, 23 Victoria Street, Cambridge CB1 1JP.

**McCAWLEY, Leon Francis;** concert pianist, since 1989; Professor of Piano, Royal College of Music, since 2008; *b* Culcheth, 12 July 1973; *s* of Bernard McCawley and Marian McCawley; *m* 1996, Anna Hyunsook Paik. *Educ:* Chetham's Sch. of Music, Manchester; Curtis Inst. of Music, Philadelphia (BMus 1995). ARCM (Hons) 1991. Royal Festival Hall début with LPO, 1991; performances with leading orchestras worldwide incl. Philadelphia, Vienna Symphony, RPO, LPO, Philharmonia, BBC Philharmonic, Netherlands Philharmonic; notable recitals incl. Wigmore Hall, QEH, Lincoln Center, NY, Rudolfinum, Prague and Philharmonie, Berlin. Numerous recordings. Winner, Piano Section, BBC Young Musician of the Year, 1990; First Prize, Internat. Beethoven Piano Competition, Vienna, 1993. *W:* www.leonmccawley.com. *Club:* Garrick.

**McCLARAN, Anthony Paul;** Chief Executive Officer, Tertiary Education Quality and Standards Agency, since 2015; *b* 5 Nov. 1957; *s* of John Edwin McClaran and Sheila Margaret McClaran (*née* Rayner); *m* 1986, Mary-Ann Helen Smith; two *s* two *d*. *Educ:* The John Lyon Sch., Harrow-on-the-Hill; Univ. of Indiana (scholarship, 1979–80); Univ. of Kent (BA 1st cl. Hons (English and American Lit.) 1981). University of Warwick: Admin. Asst, 1985–89; Asst Registrar, 1989–92; Sen. Asst Registrar, 1992; University of Hull: Acad. Registrar, 1992–95; Actg Registrar and Sec., 1995; Universities and Colleges Admissions Service: Hd, Acad. Services and Develt, 1995–96; Dep. Chief Exec., 1996–2003; Actg Chief Exec., Jan.–Dec. 2003; Chief Exec., 2003–09. Man. Dir, UCAS Media Ltd (formerly UCAS Enterprises), 1996–2009; Chm., SDS Ltd, 2003–09; Chief Exec., QAA, 2009–15; Man. Dir, QAA Enterprises Ltd (formerly Partners in Quality Ltd), 2011–15. Member: Bd of Dirs, Hero UK, 2001–06; Exec. Cttee, AUA, 2003–06; Leadership Council, Nat. Centre for Univs and Business (formerly Council for Industry and Higher Educn), 2009–15; UK HE Internat. Unit Strategic Adv. Bd, 2010–15; Bd, Eur. Assoc. for Quality Assurance in Higher Educn, 2013–15; Internat. Educn Council, 2013–15; Internat. Network for Quality Assurance Agencies in Higher Educn, 2015–18; Adv. Council, Internat. Quality Gp, Council for Higher Educn Accreditation, 2015–; Audit Cttee, Aust. Accounting Standards Bd, 2017–; Nat. Review of Teacher Registration, 2018. University of Gloucestershire: Mem. Council, 1997–2005; Chair of Council, 2007–09; Pro-Chancellor, 2007–09. Chm., Employment and Skills Adv. Panel, Gloucestershire First, 2009–11; Mem. Bd, Glos Develt Agency, 2010–11. Trustee: Inspiring Futures Foundn, 2007–13; Summerfield Trust, 2010–15. Governor: St Edward's Sch., Cheltenham, 2003–09; Nat. Star Coll., 2006–09; Cheltenham Kingsmead Sch., 2007–09; John Lyon Sch., 2008–15 (Dep. Chm., 2013–15); John Lyon's Foundn (formerly Harrow Sch. Foundn), 2011–15; All Saints' Acad., Cheltenham, 2011–15 (Chm., 2011–15). FCMI 2007. Mem., 2007–, Trustee, 2012–15, Hon. Co. of Gls. Freeman: Co. (formerly Guild) of Educators, 2007; City of London, 2012. *Publications:* reviews, chapters and articles on higher educn policy and practice. *Recreations:* polyphony, tennis, parkrun. *Address:* Tertiary Education Quality and Standards Agency, GPO Box 1672, Melbourne, Vic 3001, Australia. *T:* (3) 83062411. *E:* anthony.mcclaran@teqsa.gov.au. *Clubs:* Athenæum; Royal Automobile of Victoria (Melbourne); Melbourne Football.

**McCLARKIN, Emma;** Member (C) East Midlands, European Parliament, 2009–19; *b* Stroud, 9 Oct. 1978; *d* of George McClarkin and Maria McClarkin. *Educ:* Stroud Girls High Sch.; Bournemouth Univ. (LLB (Hons) Business Law 2001). Legal clerk, Goldinghams solicitors, Stroud, 2001–02; Press Officer, East Midlands MEPs, 2002–04; Pol Advr to MEP (C) for E Midlands, 2004–08; Govt Relns Exec., Rugby Football Union, 2008–09. Contested (C) E Midlands, EP, 2019. *Recreations:* countryside walking, photography, Rugby, kayaking, ski-ing.

**McCLEAN, Maj. Gen. Colin Thomas,** CBE 2017 (MBE 2003); FIMechE; Director, Land Equipment, Defence Equipment and Support, since 2017; *b* Tywyn, 30 Aug. 1968; *s* of James Lough McClean and late Elizabeth Ann McClean (*née* collins); *m* 1997, Joanne Kimber; one *s* one *d*. *Educ:* Campbell Coll., Belfast; Sidney Sussex Coll., Cambridge (BA 1991); RMA, Sandhurst; Cranfield Univ. (MSc). FIMechE 2008. Commissioned into Army, 1987; CO, 3 Bn, REME, Operation Herrick, 2008–09; Hd, Equipment, Army HQ, 2015–16. Chm., Bd of Trustees, Team Army Sports Foundn Charitable Fund, 2017–. Chm., Army Water Sports, 2017–. *Recreations:* mountaineering, ski-ing, travel, gardening. *Address:* Director Land Equipment, MoD Abbey Wood, Bristol BS34 8JH. *E:* mcclean.colin@sky.com.

**McCLEAN, Prof. (John) David,** CBE 1994; FBA 2003; Professor of Law, 1973–2004, now Emeritus, Public Orator, 1988–91 and 1994–2007, University of Sheffield; *b* 4 July 1939; *s* of Major Harold McClean and Mrs Mabel McClean; *m* 1966, Pamela Ann Loader; one *s* one *d*. *Educ:* Queen Elizabeth's Grammar Sch., Blackburn; Magdalen Coll., Oxford (DCL, 1984). Called to the Bar, Gray's Inn, 1963, Bencher, 2001. University of Sheffield: Asst Lectr, 1961; Lectr, 1963; Sen. Lectr, 1968; Dean, Faculty of Law, 1978–81, 1998–2002; Pro-Vice-Chancellor, 1991–96. Vis. Lectr in Law, Monash Univ., Melbourne, 1968, Vis. Prof., 1978. Chancellor: Dio. of Sheffield, 1992–2014; Dio. of Newcastle, 1998–2009. Vice-Chm., C of E Bd for Social Responsibility, 1978–80. Member: Gen. Synod of C of E, 1970–2005 (Vice-Chm., House of Laity, 1979–85, Chm. 1985–95); Crown Appts Commn, 1977–87. Pres., Eur. Consortium for Church and State Res., 1995. Hon. QC 1995. Hon. LittD Sheffield, 2012. *Publications:* Criminal Justice and the Treatment of Offenders (jtly), 1969; (contrib.) Halsbury's Laws of England, Vol. 8, 4th edn 1974, re-issue 1996, Vol. 2 (re-issue), 4th edn 1991; The Legal Context of Social Work, 1975, 2nd edn 1980; (jtly) Defendants in the Criminal Process, 1976; (ed jtly) Shawcross and Beaumont, Air Law, 4th edn 1977, and loose-leaf issues, 1977– (Gen. Ed., 2000–); (jtly) Recognition and Enforcement of Judgments, etc, within the Commonwealth, 1977; (ed jtly) Dicey and Morris, Conflict of Laws, 10th edn 1980 to 15th edn (as Dicey Morris and Collins, Conflict of Laws) 2012; Recognition of Family Judgments in the Commonwealth, 1983; International Judicial Assistance, 1992, 2nd edn 2002 as International Co-operation in Civil and Criminal Matters, 3rd edn 2012; (ed) Morris, The Conflict of Laws, 4th edn 1993 to 9th edn 2016; (contrib.) Chitty, Contracts, 27th edn 1994 to 33rd edn 2019; Transnational Organized Crime, 2007; (contrib.) Mithani, Directors' Disqualification; (contrib.) Tolley's Insolvency Law; (contrib.) State and Church in the European Union, 1995, 3rd edn 2019. *Recreation:* detective fiction. *Address:* Hall House, Ingrams, Sturminster Newton, Dorset DT10 1FR.

**McCLEARY, Dame Ann Heron;** *see* Gloag, Dame A. H.

**McCLEARY, (William) Boyd,** CMG 2010; CVO 2004; HM Diplomatic Service, retired; Partner, The Ambassador Partnership, since 2014; Mediator, 39 Essex Chambers, since 2015; *b* 30 March 1949; *s* of Robert McCleary and Eleanor Thomasina McCleary (*née* Weir); *m* 2000, Jeannette Ann Collier; three *d*. *Educ:* Queen's Univ., Belfast (BA 1st Cl. Hons German Lang. and Lit. 1972). Asst, then Dep. Principal, Dept of Agric. for NI, 1972–75; First Sec. (Agric., then Chancery), Bonn, 1975–80; Western European Dept, then EC Dept (Ext.), FCO, 1981–85; First Sec., Hd of Chancery and Consul, Seoul, 1985–88; Asst Hd, Far Eastern Dept, FCO, 1988–89; Dep. Hd of Mission and Dir of Trade Promotion, Ankara, 1990–93; Counsellor (Econ. and Trade Policy), Ottawa, 1993–97; Hd, Estate Dept, FCO, 1997–2000; Consul-Gen., Düsseldorf, and Dir-Gen., Trade and Investment in Germany, 2000–05; Dir for Global Rollout of Oracle System, FCO, 2005–06; High Comr to Malaysia, 2006–10; Gov., British Virgin Islands, 2010–14. Lay

Mem., Special Immigration Appeals Commn, 2015–. Member: Council, UK Overseas Territories Forum, 2014–; Adv. Bd, Official Monetary and Financial Institutions Forum, 2014–; Bd of Trustees, SE Asian Rainforest Res. Prog., 2015–. Hon. Prof. of Diplomacy and Internat. Relns, Univ. of Nottingham, 2015–18. Hon. LLD Nottingham, 2010. *Recreations:* spending time with my family, tennis, walking, reading. *Address:* Sycamore House, Bentworth, Alton, Hants GU34 5RB. *Club:* Royal Over-Seas League.

**McCLELLAND, Hon. Douglas**, AC 1987; Chairman, Australian Political Exchange Council, 1993–95; *s* of Alfred McClelland and Gertrude Amy Cooksley; *m* Lorna Belva McNeill (*d* 2016); one *s* two *d*. Mem. NSW ALP Executive, 1956–62; Hon. Dir, St George Hosp., Sydney, 1957–68. Member, Australian Senate for NSW, 1962–87; Senate appointments: Minister for the Media, 1972–75; Manager, Govt Business, 1974–75; Special Minister of State, June–Nov. 1975; Opposition spokesman on Admin. Services, 1976–77; Manager, Opposition Business, 1976–77; Dep. Leader of Opposition, May–Dec. 1977; Dep. Pres. and Chm. of Cttees, 1981–82; Pres. of the Australian Senate, 1983–87; High Commissioner in UK, 1987–91; Comr-Gen., Australian Pavilion, Expo '92, Seville, Spain, 1992. Chm., Old Parliament House Redevelt Cttee, 1993–95. Australian rep., Commonwealth War Graves Commn, 1987–91. Chm., Bobby Limb Foundn, 1999–2002; Member: Bd of Govs, St George Foundn, 1993–2002; Bd of Govs, Mick Young Trust, 1998–2002. Patron: Intellectual Disability Foundn of St George, 1995– ; St George Illawarra Rugby League FC, 2002– (Chm., 1998–2000). Queen's Jubilee Medal, 1977; Centenary Medal (Australia), 2001; Citizen of the Year, Kogarah, NSW, 2010. *Recreations:* reading, films, Rugby league, making friends. *Address:* 103/172 Russell Avenue, Dolls Point, NSW 2219, Australia. *Clubs:* City Tattersalls (Life Mem.), St George Leagues (Life Mem.), St George Rugby League Football (Life Mem.), St George Motor Boat (Veteran Mem.), Georges River Sailing (Botany Bay) (Veteran Mem. and Patron); Cronulla RSL.

**McCLEMENT, Vice Adm. Sir Tim(othy Pentreath)**, KCB 2006; OBE 1990; non-executive Chairman: Marine Rescue Technologies, since 2013 (non-executive Director, since 2012); Mobilarm, 2013–19; Protection Group International, 2013–18; CTruk Group, 2016–17; *b* 16 May 1951; *s* of late Capt. Reginald McClement, RN retd, and of Winnifred McClement (née Pentreath); *m* 1980, Lynne Laura Gowans; two *s*. *Educ:* Douai Sch., Berks. Joined Royal Navy, 1971: appts in various submarines, 1975–81; passed SMCC 1981; 2nd i/c HMS Conqueror during Falklands Conflict, 1982; in command: HMS Opportune, 1983–84; Staff of Captain Submarine Sea Training as a Command Sea Rider, 1984–87; CO, SMCC, 1987–89 (Comdr); HMS Tireless, 1989–92 (surfaced at North Pole, 8 May 1990, and played cricket); HMS London, 1992–94 (Capt., Wilkinson Sword of Peace, 1993); HMS Cornwall, 1999–2001 (led Task Gp around world, May–Nov. 2000); Rear-Adm. 2001; ACNS, 2001–03; COS (Warfare) and Rear-Adm. Surface Ships, 2003–04; Vice Adm. 2004; Dep. C-in-C Fleet, 2004–06. Man. Dir, Flagship Superyacht Acad., 2007–09. Dir, World Defence Forum, 2010–11. Dir, Pentreath Enterprises Ltd, 2007–. Non-exec. Chm., Protection Vessels Internat., 2011–13. Non-exec. Dir, CWind, 2012–16. Mem. Defence Adv. Bd, Babcock Internat., 2010–12. Chm. Trustees, RN Submarine Mus., 2011–14. Younger Brother, Trinity House, 2006. Freeman, City of London, 1993. *Recreations:* keeping fit, improving my golf, gig rowing. *Clubs:* Royal Navy of 1765 and 1785, Special Forces.

**MACCLESFIELD, 9th Earl of**, *cr* 1721; **Richard Timothy George Mansfield Parker**; Baron Parker, 1716; Viscount Parker, 1721; *b* 31 May 1943; *s* of 8th Earl of Macclesfield and Hon. Valerie Mansfield (*d* 1994), *o d* of 4th Baron Sandhurst, OBE; *S* father, 1992; *m* 1967, Tatiana Cleone, *d* of Major Craig Wheaton-Smith; three *d* (including twins); *m* 1986, Mrs Sandra Hope Mead. *Educ:* Stowe; Worcester Coll., Oxford. *Heir: b* Hon. (Jonathan) David (Geoffrey) Parker [*b* 2 Jan. 1945; *m* 1968, Lynne Valerie Butler; one *s* two *d*]. *Address:* Rectory Farmhouse, Church Lane, North Stoke, Wallingford, Oxon OX10 6BQ.

**MACCLESFIELD, Archdeacon of;** *see* Bishop, Ven. I. G.

**McCLEVERTY, Prof. Jon Armistice**; Professor of Inorganic Chemistry, 1990–2003, now Emeritus, and Senior University Research Fellow, 2003–07, University of Bristol; *b* 11 Nov. 1937; *s* of John and Nessie McCleverty; *m* 1963, Dianne Barrack; two *d*. *Educ:* Univ. of Aberdeen (BSc 1960); Imperial College, London (DIC, PhD 1963); Massachusetts Inst. of Technology. Asst Lectr, part-time, Acton Coll. of Technology, 1962–63; Asst Lectr, then Lectr, Sen. Lectr, and Reader, Univ. of Sheffield, 1964–80; Prof. of Inorganic Chem., 1980–90, and Head of Dept of Chem., 1984–90, Univ. of Birmingham. Chairman: Cttee of Heads of Univ. Chem. Depts, 1989–91; Internat. Cttee, RSC, 1994–97; Chemistry Cttee, SERC, 1990–93; Vice-Chm., Chairman of Eur. Res. Council Chemistry Cttees, 1992–93, 1995, 1997–99 (Chm., 1996–97); Member: Science Bd, SERC, 1990–93; Technical Cttee for Chemistry, Co-operation in Sci. and Technol. in Europe, EU, 1990–96; Physical Scis and Technol. Panel, NATO Sci. Affairs Div., 1999–2002 (Chm., 2001). Royal Society of Chemistry: Pres., Dalton Div., 1999–2001; Chm., Sci. and Technol. Bd, 2001–05; Chm., Awards Cttee, 2006–. Tilden Lectr, 1981, Sir Ronald Nyholm Lectr, 2001–02, RSC. RSC Medal, for work on chem. and electrochem. of transition metals, 1985. Golden Order of Merit (Poland), 1990. *Publications:* numerous articles, principally in Jl of Chem. Soc. *Recreations:* gardening, travel, music of the 20s, 30s and 40s. *Address:* School of Chemistry, University of Bristol, Cantock's Close, Bristol BS8 1TS.

**McCLINTOCK-BUNBURY,** family name of **Baron Rathdonnell**.

**McCLOSKEY, Dr Brian Gerald**, CBE 2013; FFPH; Consultant in Global Health Security, Public Health England, since 2016 (Director, Global Health, 2013–16); *b* Derry, NI, 20 Oct. 1952; *né* Bernard Gerald McCloskey, changed name to Brian, 2013; *m* 1976, Oonagh McConaghy. *Educ:* St Columb's Coll., Derry; Trinity Coll., Dublin (MB BCh BAO 1976; MA; MD 1988). FFPH 1995. Dir, Public Health, Worcestershire, 1988–2002; Dep. Regl Dir, Public Health, West Midlands, 2002–04; Health Protection Agency: Dep. Dir, Local and Regl Services, 2004–06; Advr to Chief Exec., 2006–08; Regl Dir, London, 2008–13. Advr to UN Special Envoy on Ebola, 2014. Sen. Consulting Fellow, Centre on Global Health Security, RIIA (Chatham House), 2016–. Hon. Prof., Faculty of Epidemiol. and Population Health, LSHTM, 2017–. *Recreations:* rowing, eating, theatre. *Address:* Centre for Global Health Security, Royal Institute of International Affairs, Chatham House, 10 St James's Square, SW1Y 4LE.

**McCLOUD, Victoria Helen**, DPhil; a Master of the Senior Court, Queen's Bench Division, since 2010; *b* 13 Oct. 1969; *d* of Ronald Henry Williams and Valerie Margaret Josephine Williams; civil partnership 2006, Dr Annie Siobhan McCloud. *Educ:* Christ Church, Oxford (BA Hons Experimental Psychol. 1990; DPhil Experimental Psychol. 1993); City Univ. (DipLaw 1994); Central Lancs Univ. (Cert. Astrobiol. 2013). Called to the Bar, Lincoln's Inn, 1995; in practice as a barrister, 1995–2010; a Dep. Costs Judge, 2006–10, 2017–; Dep. Adjudicator to HM Land Registry, 2007–10. Mem., Bar Equality and Diversity Cttee, 2004–10. FZS 2012. *Publications:* (as Williams until 2009, then McCloud): (ed) The White Book, 2000–; Civil Procedure Handbook (annually), 2004–12; The Surveillance and Intelligence Law Handbook, 2006; Personal Injury Pleadings, 2008.

*Recreations:* American constitutional history and Revolutionary War history, history of transatlantic cable telecommunications, nature conservation, biotechnology, computing, flying, jazz, hiking. *Address:* Royal Courts of Justice, Strand, WC2A 2LL. *T:* (020) 7947 6000. *Club:* Reform.

**McCLOY, Dr Elizabeth Carol**, FRCP, FFOM; Chief Medical Officer and Medical Services Director, UNUM Ltd, 1997–98; *b* 25 April 1945; *d* of Edward Bradley and Ada Entwisle; *m* 1969, Rory McCloy (marr. diss. 1989); two *s*. *Educ:* Guildford Grammar Sch.; University Coll. and UCH, London (BSc Hons 1966; MB BS Hons 1969). MFOM 1988, FFOM 1993; FRCP 1995. Clinical Asst, Medicine, W Middlesex Univ. Hosp., 1972–83; Manchester Royal Infirmary: Sen. Clinical MO, Occupational Health, 1984–88; Consultant in Occupational Medicine, 1988–93; Dir of Occupational Health and Safety, Central Manchester Healthcare Trust, 1988–93; Chief Exec. and Dir, CS Occupational Health Service, later CS Occupational Health and Safety Agency, and Med. Advr to CS, 1993–96. Pres., Soc. of Occupational Medicine, 1993–94. *Publications:* (ed jtly) Practical Occupational Medicine, 1994; (contrib.) Hunters Diseases of Occupations, 7th edn 1987, 8th edn 1994; (contrib.) Oxford Textbook of Medicine, 1994; articles on hepatitis. *Recreations:* theatre, gardening, antiques.

**McCLURE, Prof. John**, OBE 2007; MD; FRCPath, FFPath, RCPI; Procter Professor of Pathology, University of Manchester, 1987–2003, now Emeritus; *b* 2 May 1947; *s* of Richard Burns McClure and Isabella McClure (née Nelson); *m* 1970, Sheena Frances Tucker; three *d*. *Educ:* Queen's Univ. Belfast (BSc Hons, MB, BCh, BAO, MD, DMJPath). FRCPath 1990; FFPath, RCPI 2017. Training posts in Pathology, QUB, 1972–78; Clinical Sen. Lectr and Specialist/Sen. Specialist in Pathology, Univ. of Adelaide and Inst. of Med. and Vet. Sci., Adelaide, 1978–83; University of Manchester: Sen. Lectr and Hon. Consultant in Histopathology, 1983–87; Head of Pathological Scis, 1987–95; Associate Dean, Faculty of Medicine, 1995–98. Dir, Laboratory Medicine, Central Manchester Healthcare Trust, 1996–2001. British Red Cross: Chm., Northern Regl Council, 1998–99; Mem., Nat. Bd of Trustees, 1998–2006 (Chm., 2001–07); Pres. and Trustee, Gtr Manchester Br., 1994–99. Hon. Prof., Univ. of Ulster, 2003–07. *Publications:* papers in med. and path. jls. *Recreations:* DIY, microscopy, beekeeping. *Address:* Rushfield, 8 Drumquin Road, Castlederg, Co. Tyrone BT81 7PX. *T:* (028) 8167 1999.

**McCLURE, Dr Judith**, CBE 2003; FSAScot; Head of St George's School, Edinburgh, 1994–2009; Convener, Scotland-China Educational Network, 2006–18; *b* 22 Dec. 1945; *d* of James McClure and Vera (née Knight); *m* 1977, Roger John Howard Collins, DLitt, FRHistS, FSAScot. *Educ:* Newlands GS, Middlesbrough; Coll. of Law, London; Somerville Coll., Oxford (Shaw Lefevre Scholar; BA 1st Cl. Hons 1973; MA 1977; DPhil 1979). Canoness of St Augustine, Les Oiseaux, Westgate, Kent, 1964–70; Sir Maurice Powicke Meml Res. Fellow, LMH, Oxford, 1976–77; Lecturer: in Medieval Latin and Medieval History, Univ. of Liverpool, 1977–79; in History, Jesus, Somerville and Worcester Colls, Univ. of Oxford, 1979–81; School of St Helen and St Katharine, Abingdon: teacher of History and Politics, 1981–83; Head, History and Politics Dept, 1983–84; Asst Head, Kingswood Sch., Bath, 1984–87, Dir of Studies, 1986–87; Head, Royal Sch., Bath, 1987–93. Dir, 48 Gp Club, 2015–17 (Mem. Cttee, 2014–17; Acting Chm., 2016–17). Mem., Sch. Reform Commn, Scotland, 2011–13. Member: Governing Body, 1995–2007, Mgt Cttee, 1998–2007 (Chm., 2001–07), Scottish Council of Ind. Schs; Regl Standing Cttee for Scotland, UCAS, 1997–99; Bd of Mgt, Scottish Qualifications Authy, 1999–2000; Scottish Ministerial Strategy Cttee on Continuing Professional Develt of Teachers, 2000–03 (Chm., Leadership and Mgt Pathways Subgroup, 2001–03); Scottish Adv. Cttee on Continuing Professional Develt of Teachers, 2004–07; Commn for Sch. Reform, 2012–18; Chair, Adv. Bd, Scottish Centre for Studies in Sch. Admin, 2012–16; Chm., Scottish Region, and Mem. Council, GSA, 1996–99. Member: Judicial Studies Cttee, 2006–13; China Forward Planning Gp, Scottish Exec., 2006–08; Cross-Pty Working Gp on China, Scottish Parlt, 2009– (Sec., 2013–16); Scottish Schs Adv. Gp on China, 2010–12; Lay Mem., Judicial Inst. for Scotland Adv. Council, 2013–16; Mgt Cttee, Scottish Chs China Gp, 2014–15; Adv. Gp, China-Scotland Business Forum, 2014–. Convener: Scottish Leadership, Mgt and Admin Soc., 2004–10; Asia Connections Network Scotland, 2015–18; Japanese Lang. Gp Scotland, 2015–17. Mem. Adv. Cttee, Edinburgh Youth Transition and Crime Survey, 2002–08. Mem., Court, Bath Univ., 1989–92; Heriot-Watt University: Mem., Gen. Convocation, 1994–2012; Mem., Court, 2003–13 (Convener, Staffing Strategy Cttee, 2009–13); Member: Adv. Bd, Open Univ. in Scotland, 2000–08; Bd, Inst. of Sci. Educn in Scotland, 2003–08; Bd, Confucius Inst., Univ. of Edinburgh, 2006–; Educn Cttee, RSE, 2010–13; Adv. Bd, Swire Chinese Lang. Centre for Excellence, George Watson's Coll., Edinburgh, 2016–18; Member, Board of Governors: Selwyn Schs, Gloucester, 1988–90; Clifton Hall Sch., Lothian, 1995–99; Merchiston Castle Sch., 1999–2006; The New Sch., Butterstone, 2004–05. Trustee: Hopetoun House Preservation Trust, 1997–2003; Soc. of Antiquaries Scotland, 2010–12; Scottish Internat. Educn Trust, 2013–. Jt Pres., Royal Sch. Association, 1994–. Chm., Women of Lothian Lunch, 1998–2001. FRSA 1997; FSQA 2009. DUniv Heriot-Watt, 2014. Scotland Icebreaker Award and Fellow, 48 Group Club, 2009. *Publications:* Gregory the Great: exegesis and audience, 1979; Thinking About Snow (memoir), 2018; Introduction and notes to Bede's Ecclesiastical History, 1994; articles in Jl Theol Studies, Peritia, Papers of Liverpool Latin Seminar, Prep. School and in Festschriften. *Recreations:* reading, travel, e-mails. *Address:* 12A Ravelston Park, Edinburgh EH4 3DX. *Club:* New (Edinburgh) (Mem., Cttee of Managers, 2018–).

**McCLURE, Roger Niall**; Chief Executive, Scottish Funding Councils for Further and Higher Education, later Scottish Further and Higher Education Funding Council, 2002–08; Honorary Research Associate, University of Cambridge, since 2010; *b* 28 Dec. 1950; *s* of late Rev. Canon Hugh Norman McClure and Jane Paterson Brown; *m* 1974, Catherine Lynne Thomas; four *d*. *Educ:* King Edward VI Sch., Norwich; Corpus Christi Coll., Cambridge (MA); Corpus Christi Coll., Oxford (Postgrad. Dip); City of London Polytechnic (Dip Public Finance & Accountancy). CPFA 1982. Auditor, Nat. Audit Office, 1978–84; Sen. Consultant, then Manager, Deloitte Haskins & Sells Mgt Consultancy, 1984–88; seconded as Financial Advr to UGC, 1985–87; Dir of Finance, PCFC, 1988–92; Dir of Finance, FEFC, 1992–96; Pro-Rector, London Inst., 1996–2002; Chief Exec., Learning and Skills Improvement Service, 2008–09; Chm., JANET (UK), 2008–12. Harkness Fellow, Center for Higher Educn Studies, Univ. of California, Berkeley, 1990–91; Special Advr, H of C Educn Sub-Cttee, 1997–98; Member, Council: KCL, 1988–97; Business and Technol. Educn Council, 1995–98; City Literary Inst., 1998–2002; Inst. for Employment Studies, 2004–13 (Mem. Bd, 2008–13); Mem. Bd, JISC, 2008–12. Chm., Capel Manor Coll., 2017–. CCMI 2003. *Publications:* (contrib.) Further Education Reformed, 2000. *Recreations:* music, sport, current affairs, reading, cinema. *E:* mcclure.roger@gmail.com.

**McCLURE, Ven. Timothy Elston**; Archdeacon of Bristol, 1999–2012; *b* 20 Oct. 1946; *s* of late Kenneth Elston McClure and Grace Helen McClure (née Hoar); *m* 1969, Barbara Mary Marchant; one *s* one *d*. *Educ:* Kingston Grammar Sch.; St John's Coll., Durham (BA); Ridley Hall, Cambridge. Deacon 1970, priest 1971; Curate, Kirkheaton Parish Church, Huddersfield, 1970–73; Marketing Mgr, Agrofax Labour Intensive Products Ltd, Harrow, Middx, 1973–74; Chaplain, Manchester Poly., 1974–82; Curate, St Ambrose, Chorltonon-Medlock, 1974–79; Team Rector, Parish of Whitworth, Manchester and Presiding Chaplain, Chaplaincies to Higher Educn in Manchester, 1979–82; Gen. Sec., SCM, 1982–92; Dir, Churches' Council for Industry and Social Responsibility, Bristol, 1992–99; Hon. Canon, Bristol Cathedral, 1992–2012; Lord Mayor's Chaplain, Bristol, 1996–99. Chairman: Traidcraft plc, 1990–97; Christian Conference Trust, 1998–2003. *Recreations:* cooking, gardening, living sustainably, cider making, walking, beekeeping. *Address:* Park House, Denton, Gilsland, Brampton, Cumbria CA8 7AG. *T:* (01697) 747415.

**McCLUSKEY, Len;** General Secretary, Unite, since 2011 (Assistant General Secretary, 2007–10; General Secretary designate, 2010–11); *b* 23 July 1950; *s of* Leonard and Margaret McCluskey. *Educ:* Cardinal Godfrey High Sch., Merseyside. Dockworker, 1968–79; Transport and General Workers' Union: District Official, Merseyside, 1979–89; Political Officer, NW Region, 1985–89; Nat. Sec., 1990–2004; Nat. Organiser, 2004–05; Asst Gen. Sec., 2005–07, when T&GWU merged with Amicus to form Unite. Mem., TUC Gen. Council and Exec., 2007–. Alumnus, Duke of Edinburgh's 8th Commonwealth Study Conf., 1998. FRSA 2013. *Recreations:* football, sport, reading, politics, chess, poetry. *Address:* Unite, 128 Theobalds Road, Holborn, WC1X 8TN.

**McCLUSKIE, John Cameron,** CB 1999; QC (Scot.) 1989; Consultant Parliamentary Counsel to Irish Government, 2006–08; *b* 1 Feb. 1946; *m* 1970, Janis Mary Helen McArthur; one *s* one *d*. *Educ:* Hyndland Sch., Glasgow; Glasgow Univ. (LLB Hons 1967). Admitted Solicitor, Scotland, 1970; admitted Faculty of Advocates, 1974. Apprentice Solicitor, Boyds, Glasgow, 1967–69; Asst Town Clerk, Burgh of Cumbernauld, 1969–70; Legal Assistant: Macdonald, Jameson and Morris, Glasgow, 1970; SSEB, 1970–72; Asst, then Sen. Asst, Legal Sec. and Parly Draftsman, Lord Advocate's Dept, 1972–89; Legal Sec. to Lord Advocate, 1989–99; First Scottish Parly Counsel, later First Parly Counsel, Scottish Exec., 1989–2006. Trustee and Co. Sec., Leuchie, 2011–18. *Recreations:* watching mogs, walking dogs, cutting logs. *Address:* Law View, Redside Farm Steading, North Berwick, East Lothian EH39 5PE.

**McCLYMONT, Dr Gregg;** Head of Retirement Savings, Aberdeen Asset Management, since 2015; *b* Glasgow, 3 June 1976; *s of* Hugh Forbes McClymont and Sheila McClymont (*née* McGalliard). *Educ:* Cumbernauld High Sch.; Glasgow Univ. (MA Hons); Univ. of Pennsylvania (AM); St John's Coll., Oxford (DPhil 2006; MA 2007). Fellow in History, St Hugh's Coll., Oxford, 2007–10; Vis. Fellow, Nuffield Coll., Oxford, 2014–. MP (Lab) Cumbernauld, Kilsyth and Kirkintilloch E, 2010–15; contested (Lab) same seat, 2015.

**McCOLGAN-NUTTALL, Elizabeth,** MBE 1992; athletic coach; Director: Athletic Zones, since 2014; Doha Athletic Club, since 2014; RunDohaRun, since 2014; *b* 24 May 1964; *d of* Martin and Elizabeth Lynch; *m* 1987 (marr. diss. 2013); three *s* two *d*; *m* 2014, John Nuttall. *Educ:* St Saviour's High Sch., Dundee; Univ. of Alabama. Athletic achievements include: Commonwealth Games: Gold Medal, 10,000m, Edinburgh, 1986, Auckland, 1991; Bronze Medal, 3,000m, Auckland, 1991; World Cross Country Championships: Silver Medal, Warsaw, 1987; Bronze Medal, Antwerp, 1991; Silver Medal, 10,000m, Olympic Games, Seoul, 1988; Silver Medal, 3,000m, World Indoor Championships, Budapest, 1989; Gold Medal, 10,000m, World Championships, Tokyo, 1991; Gold Medal, World Half-Marathon Championships, 1992; Marathons: winner, NYC, 1991; winner, 1992, 3rd, 1996, Tokyo; 3rd, 1993, 5th, 1995, winner, 1996, 2nd, 1997 and 1998, London; retd 2001. Chair, Scottish Athletics, 2003–05. Patron, Leukaemia and Lymphoma Res. (formerly Leukaemia Res. Fund). Hon. DLaws Dundee, 2007; Hon. Dr Abertay. BBC Sports Personality of the Year Award, 1991. *Recreations:* cinema, reading, writing, keeping fit. *Address:* c/o Silver Fox Media, 3 Sauncey Wood, Harpenden, Herts AL5 5DP.

**McCOLL,** family name of **Baron McColl of Dulwich**.

**McCOLL OF DULWICH,** Baron *cr* 1989 (Life Peer), of Bermondsey in the London Borough of Southwark; **Ian McColl,** CBE 1997; MS, FRCS, FACS, FRCSE; Professor of Surgery, University of London at Guy's, King's and St Thomas' School of Medicine of King's College London (formerly United Medical Schools of Guy's and St Thomas' Hospitals), 1971–98, now Emeritus; Director of Surgery, 1985–98, and Consultant Surgeon, 1971–98, Guy's Hospital; Consultant Surgeon to Mercy Ships, since 2000; *b* 6 Jan. 1933; *s of* late Frederick George McColl and Winifred E. McColl, Dulwich; *m* 1st, 1960, Dr Jean Lennox (*d* 2012), 2nd *d of* Arthur James McNair, FRCS, FRCOG; one *s* two *d*; 2nd, 2015, Dr Evy Lise Kaarvang, *d of* Dr Kristian Kaarvang and Evy Ugland Kaarvang, Oslo. *Educ:* Hutchesons' Grammar Sch., Glasgow; St Paul's Sch., London; Guy's Hosp., London. MB, BS 1957; FRCS 1962; FRCSE 1962; MS 1966; FACS 1975. Junior staff appts at St Bartholomew's, Putney, St Mark's, St Peter's, Great Ormond Street, Barnet, St Olave's and Guy's Hosps, 1957–67; Research Fellow, Harvard Med. Sch., and Moynihan Fellowship, Assoc. of Surgeons, 1967; Reader in Surgery, St Bartholomew's Hosp. Med. Coll., 1967 (Sub Dean, 1969–71). Visiting Professor: Univ. of South Carolina, 1974; Johns Hopkins Hosp., 1976. Consultant Surgeon: KCH, 1971–98 (FKC 2001); Edenbridge Dist Meml Hosp., 1978–91; Lewisham Hosp., 1983–90; Hon. Consultant in Surgery to the Army, 1982–98. External examiner in Surgery to Univs of Newcastle upon Tyne and Cardiff, QUB, TCD and NUI. Royal College of Surgeons: Examr in Pathology, 1970–76; Regl Advr, SE Reg., 1975–80; Mem. Council, 1986–94; Arris and Gale Lectr, 1964, 1965; Erasmus Wilson Lectr, 1972; Haig Gudenian Meml Lectr, 1988; Henry Cohen Meml Lectr, 1994; Lettsomian Lectr, Med. Soc. of London, 1993; Cotter Cruikshank Meml Lect., 2019. Medical Advisor, BBC Television, 1976–92. PPS (Lord's) to the Prime Minister, 1994–97; a Dep. Speaker, H of L, 1994–2004; opposition spokesman on health, 1997–2010. Member: Central Health Services Council, 1972–74; Standing Medical Adv. Cttee, 1972–82; Management Cttee, King Edward VII Hospital Fund (Chm., R&D Cttee), 1975–80; Council, Metrop. Hosp. Sunday Fund, 1986–91; Council, Imperial Cancer Res. Fund, 1986–94; Exec. Council, British Limbless Ex-Service Men's Assoc., 1991–; Chairman: King's Fund Centre Cttee, 1976–86; Govt Wkg Pty on Artificial Limb and Appliance Centres in England, 1984–86; Vice Chm., SHA for Disablement Services, 1987–91. Hon. Sec., British Soc. of Gastroenterology, 1970–74. President: Soc. of Minimally Invasive Gen. Surgery, 1991–94; Limbless Assoc. (formerly Nat. Assoc. for Limbless Disabled), 1992– (Patron and Hon. Consultant, 1989–); Internat. Wheelchair Fedn, 1991–; Assoc. of Endoscopic Surgeons of GB and Ireland, 1994–98; The Hospital Saving Assoc., 1994–2001; Leprosy Mission, 1996–; REMEDI, 1996–99; Royal Med. Foundn of Epsom Coll., 2001–; Vice-Pres., Livability (formerly John Grooms Assoc. for Disabled People), 1990–. Governor-at-Large for England, Bd of Governors, Amer. Coll. of Surgeons, 1982–88. Pres., 1985–94, Chm. Bd of Govs, 1994–2002, Mildmay Mission Hosp.; Chm., Mercy Ships UK, 2005–; Vice Chm., Mercy Ships Internat. and Surgeon to Mercy Ships, 2005–. Governor: Dulwich Coll. Prep. Sch., 1978–2002; James Allen's Girls' Sch., 1994–2004 (Chm., 1998–2004); St Paul's Sch., 2001–11 (Pres., Old Pauline Club, 2005–07); Pres., King's Coll. Alumni, 2010–12. Trustee, Wolfson Foundn, Dulwich Estate, 1994–; Chm., Dulwich Estate Trustees, 2007–08 (Chm., Mgt Cttee, 2003–07). Master, Barbers' Co., 1999–2000. FKC 2002. Hon. FDSRCS 2007. Edenbridge Medal for Services to the Community, 1992; George and Thomas Hutcheson's Award, 2000; Great Scot Award, 2002; Dist. Award, Nat. Maritime Assoc., NY, 2003. *Publications:* (ed jtly) Intestinal Absorption in Man, 1975; Talking to Patients, 1982; NHS Data Book, 1984; (contrib.) 60 Years of the NHS, 2008; med. articles, mainly on gastroenterology, rehabilitation and NHS management. *Recreations:* forestry, ornithology, uxoriousness. *Address:* House of Lords, SW1A 0PW. *Clubs:* Royal College of Surgeons Council, Royal Society of Medicine.

**McCOLL, (Christopher) Miles;** a District Judge (Magistrates' Courts) (formerly Provincial Stipendiary Magistrate), Birmingham, 1993–2009; *b* 18 April 1946; *s of* John Parr McColl and Lilian McColl (*née* Oddy); *m* 1971, Susan Margaret Rathbone; three *d*. *Educ:* Liverpool Coll. Admitted solicitor, 1971. Articled clerk in private practice, St Helens, 1965–69; trainee, Court Clerk, then Principal Court Clerk, Manchester City Magistrates' Court, 1969–74; Dep. Clerk to Stockport Justices, 1974–78; Clerk to Leigh Justices, 1978–93. Sec., Gtr Manchester Justices' Clerks and Courts Liaison Cttee, 1984–90; Member: Magistrates' Courts Rev. of Procedure Cttee, 1989–91; Magistrates' Courts Consultative Council, 1992–93; Children Act Procedure Adv. Gp, 1989–90; Pres. of Family Division's Cttee, 1990–92; Legal Aid Steering Cttee, 1992; Pre-trial Issues Steering Gp, 1992–93; Legal Cttee, Dist Judges (Magistrates' Cts) (formerly Jt Council of HM Stipendiary Magistrates), 1997–2009 (Chm., 2000–09); Magistrates' Cts Rule Cttee, 2001–09; Consultee, Sentencing Adv. Panel, 1998–2009. Secretary: S Lancs Br., Magistrates' Assoc., 1979–85; British Juvenile and Family Courts' Soc., 1980–81; Justices' Clerks' Society: Mem. Council, 1988–93; Chm., Parly Cttee, 1989; Chm., Professional Purposes Cttee, 1989–93; Pre-trial Issues Nat. Action Manager, 1991–93; Vice-Pres., Duchy of Lancaster Br., 1993. Ed., 1979–87, Jt Ed., 1987–2004, Family Law. *Publications:* Court Teasers: practical situations arising in magistrates' courts, 1978; contrib. to legal jls. *Recreations:* sport, reading, music, British countryside.

**McCOLL, Sir Colin (Hugh Verel),** KCMG 1990 (CMG 1983); HM Diplomatic Service, retired; Head of MI6, 1988–94; *b* 6 Sept. 1932; *s of* Dr Robert McColl and Julie McColl; *m* 1st, 1959, Shirley Curtis (*d* 1983); two *s* two *d*; 2nd, 1985, Sally Morgan; one *s*. *Educ:* Shrewsbury School; The Queen's College, Oxford (BA; Hon. Fellow 1996). Foreign Office, 1956; Third Secretary, Bangkok, 1958, Vientiane, 1960; Second Secretary, FO, 1962; First Secretary, Warsaw, 1966; Consul and First Secretary (Disarmament), Geneva, 1973; Counsellor, FCO, 1977. Chm., Pimpernel Trust, 1997–2014. *Recreations:* music, walks, classics.

**MacCOLL, Gavin Lachlan;** QC (Scot.) 2017; *b* Edinburgh, Feb. 1973; *s of* John and Helen MacColl; *m* 2000, Catherine; one *d*. *Educ:* Daniel Stewart's and Melville Coll., Edinburgh; Pembroke Coll., Cambridge (BA 1994; MA 1998); Edinburgh Univ. (LLB). Admitted as advocate, 2000. Chm., Governance Standing Cttee, Scottish Rugby Union, 2018–. *Recreations:* Rugby, reading. *Address:* Advocates Library, Parliament House, Edinburgh EH1 1RF. *Club:* Carlton.

**McCOLL, Isabella Garden;** Sheriff of Lothian and Borders at Edinburgh, 2005; *b* 7 Nov. 1952; *m* Alexander James; one *s* two *d*. *Educ:* James Gillespie's High Sch.; Edinburgh Univ. Admitted: Solicitor, 1975; Advocate, 1993; Sheriff of Tayside, Central and Fife at Dunfermline, 2000–05.

**McCOLL, Gen. Sir John Chalmers,** KCB 2008; CBE 1997 (OBE 1994); DSO 2002; Executive Chairman, Confederation of Service Charities, since 2017; *b* 17 April 1952. Commnd Royal Anglian Regt, 1973; sc, 1984; Staff Officer, Germany; Rifle Co. Comdr, 2nd Bn, 1987; 3rd Royal Tank Regt, 1989; Mem., Directing Staff, Staff Coll., Camberley, 1990; Comdr, 2nd Bn, 1992; COS 1st (UK) Armoured Div., 1995; mentioned in dispatches, 1995; Comdr, 1st Mechanized Bde, 3rd (UK) Div., 1997–99; ACOS Commitments, HQ Land Comd, 1999–2000; GOC 3rd (UK) Div., 2000–03; Comdr Internat. Security Assistance Force, Afghanistan, 2002; Comdt, JSCSC, 2003–04; Sen. British Mil. Rep., Iraq, subseq. Dep. Comdg Gen. Multinational Corps, Iraq, 2004; Comdr, Regl Forces Land Comd, 2004–07; Prime Minister's Special Envoy to Afghanistan, 2004–05; Dep. Supreme Allied Comdr Europe, 2007–11. Lt-Gov. and C-in-C, Jersey, 2011–16, Col Comdt, Queen's Div., 2002–10. KStJ 2016. Officer, Legion of Merit (USA), 2006.

**McCOLL, Miles;** see McColl, C. M.

**McCOLLUM, Prof. Charles Nevin,** MD; FRCS, FRCSE; Professor of Surgery, University of Manchester, and Hon. Consultant Surgeon, Manchester University NHS Foundation Trust (formerly South Manchester University Hospitals NHS Trust, later University Hospital of South Manchester NHS Foundation Trust), since 1989; *b* 17 April 1950; *m*; two *d*. *Educ:* Tettenhall Coll.; Millfield Sch.; Medical Sch., Univ. of Birmingham (MB ChB 1972; MD 1981). Cert. Higher Surgical Trng 1981. FRCS 1976; FRCSE 1976. Registrar in Surgery, St James's Univ. Hosp., Leeds, 1976–78; Lectr in Surgery, Univ. of Birmingham, 1978–83; Sen. Lectr, 1983–88, Reader in Surgery, 1988–89, Charing Cross and Westminster Hosp. Med. Sch., London; Hon. Consultant Surgeon, Charing Cross Hosp., 1983–89. Chairman: IVS Ltd; VTE Ltd; McCollum Consultants Ltd; Director: Manchester Surgical Res. Trust; Rinicare Ltd; Puir Imaging AG; Tomorrow Cardiovascular Screening Ltd. Dir, Gtr Manchester AAA Screening Prog., 2008–. Examiner in Surgery: Univ. of London; Univ. of Manchester; Univ. of Glasgow. NIHR Sen. Investigator, 2012–17. Treas. and Cttee Mem., Surg. Res. Soc. of GB and Ire; Scientific Cttee, Internat. Soc. on Thrombosis and Haemostasis. Editd Bd, British Jl of Surgery. Hunterian Prof., RCS, 1985. Moynihan Prize, Assoc. of Surgeons of GB and Ire., 1979; Patey Prize, Surg. Res. Soc. of GB and Ire., 1983, 1995. *Publications:* 44 chapters; over 420 papers on original res. *Recreations:* tennis, country sports, riding, ski-ing, sailing. *Address:* Academic Surgery Unit, Education and Research Centre, Wythenshawe Hospital, Southmoor Road, Manchester M23 9LT. *T:* (0161) 291 5853, *Fax:* (0161) 291 5854. *E:* charles.mccollum@manchester.ac.uk. *Clubs:* Manchester Tennis and Racquet, Alderley Edge Tennis, Wilmslow Golf.

**McCOLLUM, Rt Hon. Sir William Paschal, (Rt Hon. Sir Liam McCollum),** Kt 1988; PC 1997; a Surveillance Commissioner, 2004–10; *b* 13 Jan. 1933; *s of* Patrick McCollum and Mary Ellen McCollum (*née* Strain); *m* 1958, Anne Bernadette Fitzpatrick (CBE 1995); six *s* two *d*. *Educ:* Waterside School; St Columb's Coll., Derry; University College Dublin (BA 1953; LLB 1954). Called to the Bar of N Ireland, 1955; called to Irish Bar, 1963; QC 1971; High Court Judge, NI, 1987–97; a Lord Justice of Appeal, Supreme Court of Judicature, NI, 1997–2004.

**McCOMB, Christina Margaret,** OBE 2018; Chairman, One Family Assurance, since 2014; *b* 6 May 1956; *d of* Patrick William John McComb and Margaret McComb; *m* 1980, Peter John Linacre; two *s* one *d*. *Educ:* London Sch. of Econs (BA French and Russian 1978); London Business Sch. (MBA 1989). FCO, 1978–88; Director: 3i plc, 1989–2003; Shareholder Exec., DTI, 2003–06; Partnerships UK plc, 2004–06; CEO, C5 Capital Ltd, 2011–13. Non-executive Director: Engage Mutual Assce, 2005–15 (Chm., 2014–15); Nexeon Ltd, 2007–; Baronsmead VCT2, 2011–17; Big Society Capital, 2017–; Senior Independent Director: Standard Life European Private Equity Trust plc, 2013–; British Business Bank, 2013–. Trustee, Land Restoration Trust, 2010–14. *Recreations:* running, travel.

**McCOMB, Paul John;** Director-General, Department for International Trade, Hong Kong and Macau, since 2017; *b* Downpatrick, 15 Nov. 1967; *s* of Robert and Evelyn McComb; *m* 1991, Chris Pascoe; two *s*. *Educ:* Univ. of York (MA Social Policy); Univ. of Leicester (MSc Crime and Security); Open Univ. (BSc Computer Sci.). Adminr, DHSS, 1985–88; Sec., Cttee on Rev. of Medicines, 1989–90; Exec., DSS, 1991–97; Inspector, Benefit Fraud Inspectorate, 1997–2000; HM Inspector, Magistrates' Courts Inspectorate, 2001–03; Jobcentre Plus: Regl Fraud Manager, 2004–05; Dep. Dir, 2006–09; Dir, Working Age Benefits, 2009–11; Dep. Dir, Welfare Policy, DWP, 2011; Principal Private Sec. to Sec. of State, DWP, 2011–16; Dir, UKTI, subseq. DIT, 2016–17. *Recreations:* travel, ski-ing, watersports, cycling, running. *Address:* British Consulate General, 1 Supreme Court Road, Admiralty, Hong Kong.

**McCOMBE, Rt Hon. Sir Richard (George Bramwell),** Kt 2001; PC 2012; **Rt Hon. Lord Justice McCombe;** a Lord Justice of Appeal, since 2012; *b* 23 Sept. 1952; *s* of Barbara Bramwell McCombe, MA, FCA; *m* 1st (marr. diss.); 2nd, 1986, Carolyn Sara Birrell (marr. diss. 2009); one *s* one *d*; 3rd, 2013, Jill Margaret Black (*see* Rt Hon. Lady Black of Derwent). *Educ:* Sedbergh Sch.; Downing Coll., Cambridge (MA; Hon. Fellow 2013). Called to the Bar, Lincoln's Inn, 1975, Bencher, 1996 (Treas., 2019); admitted (*ad hoc*) to Bars of Singapore, 1992, Cayman Is, 1993. Second Jun. Counsel to Dir-Gen. of Fair Trading, 1982–87, First Jun. Counsel, 1987–89; QC 1989; an Asst Recorder, 1993–96, Recorder, 1996–2001; Attorney Gen., Duchy of Lancaster, 1996–2001; a Dep. High Ct Judge, 1998–2001; a Judge of the High Court of Justice, QBD, 2001–12; Presiding Judge, Northern Circuit, 2004–07. Mem., Senate of Inns of Court and of Bar Council, 1981–86; Chm., Young Barristers' Cttee, Bar Council, 1983–84; Co-opted Mem., Bar Council Cttees, 1986–89; Mem., Gen. Council of the Bar, 1995–97 (Chm., Internat. Relns Cttee, 1997); Chm., Assoc. of High Court Judges, 2008–09. Head of UK Delegn to Council, Bars and Law Socs of EC, 1996–98. Inspector into affairs of Norton Group PLC, 1991–92 (report, with J. K. Heywood, 1993). Mem., Singapore Acad. of Law, 1992. Pres., Assoc. of Lancastrians in London, 2008. Gov., Sedbergh Sch., 2002–13. Chm., Oversight Cttee, RCSE, 2012–16. Trustee, Duke of Lancaster Housing Trust, 2008–14. Hon. FRCS 2015. *Publications:* (ed jtly) Performance Appraisal of the Judiciary and Judicial Independence, 2014. *Recreations:* cricket, Rugby, flying light aircraft. *Address:* Royal Courts of Justice, Strand, WC2A 2LL. *Clubs:* Garrick, Royal Automobile, MCC; London Scottish Football, Lancs CC.

**McCOMBIE, John Alexander Fergusson,** FRICS; General Manager, Glenrothes Development Corporation, 1993–96; *b* 13 Sept. 1932; *s* of Alexander William McCombie and Charlotte Mary McCombie (*née* Fergusson); *m* 1959, Seana Joy Cameron Scott; two *s* one *d*. *Educ:* Perth Acad.; Coll. of Estate Management. ARICS 1968, FRICS 1982; IRRV 1969. Nat. service, RAF, 1955–57 (MEAF). E Kilbride Develt Corp., 1959–67; Irvine Develt Corp., 1968–70; Glenrothes Develt Corp., 1970–96: Chief Estates Officer, 1970–74; Commercial Dir, 1975–93. Director: Glenrothes Enterprise Trust, 1983–94; Mid-Fife Business Trust, 1994–2003 (Chm., 1997–2003); Chairman and Director: Age Concern Glenrothes Ltd, 1996–2010; Leven Valley Develt Trust, 1997–2018; Ecowise Fife Ltd, 1999–2002; GIA Properties Ltd, 1999–2018; Chm., Scottish Gp, 1999–, Vice Pres., 2017–, Wolseley Register; Dir and Sec., 1996–2015, Chm., 1997–2011, Fife Historic Bldgs Trust. Mem. Bd of Mgt, Glenrothes Coll., 1999–2003. *Recreations:* gardening, golf, philately, reading, classic cars. *Address:* 13 Carnoustie Gardens, Glenrothes, Fife KY6 2QB. *T:* (01592) 345470. *Club:* Balbirnie Park Golf.

**McCONNELL,** family name of **Baron McConnell of Glenscorrodale.**

**McCONNELL OF GLENSCORRODALE,** Baron *cr* 2010 (Life Peer), of the Isle of Arran in Ayrshire and Arran; **Jack Wilson McConnell;** PC 2001; Member (Lab) Motherwell and Wishaw, Scottish Parliament, 1999–2011; Founder and Chairman, McConnell International Foundation, since 2012; *b* 30 June 1960; *s* of William Wilson McConnell and Elizabeth McEwan McConnell; *m* 1990, Bridget Mary McLuckie (*see* B. M. McConnell); one *s* one *d*. *Educ:* Arran High Sch., Isle of Arran; Stirling Univ. (BSc 1983; DipEd 1983). Mathematics Teacher, Alloa, 1983–92; Gen. Sec., SLP, 1992–98. Mem. (Lab) Stirling DC, 1984–93 (Treas., 1988–92; Leader, 1990–92). Contested (Lab) Perth and Kinross, 1987. Scottish Executive: Minister for Finance, 1999–2000; Minister for Educn, Europe and External Affairs, 2000–01; First Minister, 2001–07. Special Rep. of the Prime Minister on Peacebuilding, 2008–10. Member: COSLA, 1988–92; Scottish Constitutional Convention, 1990–98; Bd, Inst. for Cultural Diplomacy; Adv. Bd, UK-Japan 21st Century Gp, PwC, 2010–. Pres., Gp of EU Regions with Legislative Powers, 2003–04. Chm., SSE Sustainable Develt Fund. Professorial Fellow, 2014–, Chancellor, 2019–, Univ. of Stirling. Fellow, UK-China 48 Gp Club. Ambassador, Action for Children UK; Chm., Radio Clyde Cash for Kids; Vice Pres., Unicef UK, 2014–. Patron: Positive Women; Diana Awards. Chair, Great Scot Awards; Judge, Internat. Peacebuilding Awards. DUniv Stirling, 2008; Hon. DSocSc Edinburgh, 2015. *Publications:* political articles in newspapers, jls and booklets. *Recreations:* music, gardening, golf, other sports. *Address:* House of Lords, SW1A 0PW.

**McCONNELL, Prof. Alison Kay,** PhD; CSci; Professor of Exercise Science, Bournemouth University, since 2015; *b* Singapore, 17 Oct. 1961; *d* of late Ian Harrison McConnell and of Audrey McConnell; civil partnership 2008, Melanie Varvel. *Educ:* Chase High Sch., Malvern; Univ. of Birmingham (BSc Biol Scis 1983); King's Coll., London (MSc Human and Applied Physiol. 1984; PhD Respiratory Physiol. 1989). CSci 2014. Res. Fellow, Univ. of Birmingham, 1986–89; Lectr, Loughborough Univ., 1989–94; Dir, Centre for Sports Medicine, Univ. of Birmingham, 1994–98; Res. Dir, IMT Technologies Ltd, 1996–2000; Reader, 2000–05, Prof., 2005–15, Brunel Univ. Fellow: Amer. Coll. Sports Medicine, 2006; British Assoc. of Sport and Exercise Scis, 2010. *Publications:* Breathe Strong, Perform Better, 2011; Respiratory Muscle Training: theory and practice, 2013; contrib. articles to learned jls; five patents. *Recreations:* cycling, running, free diving, dog walking, fast cars, inventing useful stuff that improves people's lives (e.g. POWERbreathe® and Brythm). *E:* hello@breathestrong.com.

**McCONNELL, Bridget Mary, (Lady McConnell of Glenscorrodale),** CBE 2015; EdD; Chief Executive, Glasgow Life (formerly Culture & Sport Glasgow), since 2007; *b* 28 May 1958; *d* of Robert Rankin McLuckie and Patricia McLuckie (*née* Airlie); *m* 1990, Jack Wilson McConnell (*see* Baron McConnell of Glenscorrodale); one *s* one *d*. *Educ:* St Patrick's Jun. Secondary Sch., Kilsyth; Our Lady's High Sch., Cumbernauld; St Andrews Univ. (MA Hons 1982); Dundee Coll. of Commerce (DIA 1983); Stirling Univ. (MEd 1992; EdD 2009). Curator, Doorstep Gall., Fife Regl Council, 1983–84; Arts Officer, Stirling DC, 1984–88; Principal Arts Officer, and Arts in Fife, Fife Regl Council, 1988–96; Service Manager, Community Services/Arts, Libraries, Museums, Fife Council, 1996–98; Dir, Cultural and Leisure Services, 1998–2005, Exec. Dir (Culture and Sport), 2005–07, Glasgow CC. Chair, Scottish Assoc. of Dirs of Leisure Services, 2001–02. Member: Bd, Workshop and Artists Studio Provision Scotland Ltd, 1985–90; Combined Arts Cttee, Scottish Arts Council, 1988–94; Heritage Lottery Fund Cttee for Scotland, 2004–10; Bd, 2014 Commonwealth Games Organising Cttee, 2008–; Bd, UNESCO City of Music, 2009–. Chair, Scottish Youth Dance Fest., 1993–96 (Founder Mem., 1988); Co-ordinator, Fourth Internat. Conf. in Adult Educn and the Arts, 1995. Chm., Vocal - Voice of Chief Officers of Cultural, Community and Leisure Services in Scotland, 2002–04. Mem. Bd of Govs, 2001–, Vice Chm., 2007–13, RSAMD, later Royal Conservatoire of Scotland. FRSE 2017. DHC Aberdeen, 2008; Hon. DLitt St Andrews, 2008; Hon. Dr Royal Conservatoire of Scotland, 2013; DUniv Glasgow, 2014. *Publications:* (contrib.) Modernising Britain: creative futures, 1997; internat. conf. papers, ed conf. proceedings. *Recreations:* walking, playing the piano, swimming, reading. *Address:* (office) 220 High Street, Glasgow G4 0QW. *T:* (0141) 287 5058.

**McCONNELL, Carmel Bridget,** MBE 2016; Founder, Magic Breakfast, 2001 (Chief Executive Officer, 2001–17); *b* Romford, Essex, 17 Aug. 1961; *d* of Gerald McConnell and Patricia Donaghey; civil partnership, Catherine Purkiss. *Educ:* Sacred Heart Convent, Dagenham; Cass Business Sch. (MBA). Technologist, BT plc, 1989–94; mgt consultant, Holistic Mgt, 1995–2001. Hon. Dr Open, 2018. *Publications:* Change Activist, 2001, 2002; Soul Trader, 2002; (jtly) Float You, 2003; Make Money Be Happy, 2004; The Happiness Plan, 2007. *Recreations:* open water swimming, guitar, creating the national will to end child hunger. *Address:* Magic Breakfast, 190 High Holborn, WC1V 7BH. *E:* carmel@magicbreakfast.com.

**McCONNELL, Prof. (Francis) Ian,** PhD; FRSE; Professor of Veterinary Science and Director of Research, Centre for Veterinary Science, Department of Veterinary Medicine (formerly of Clinical Veterinary Medicine), University of Cambridge, 1994, now Professor Emeritus; Professorial Fellow of Darwin College, Cambridge, 2003, now Emeritus; *b* 6 Nov. 1940; *s* of Edward McConnell and Pearl McConnell (*née* Quigley); *m* 1967, Anna Farren; three *s* two *d*. *Educ:* St Aloysius' Coll., Glasgow; Univ. of Glasgow (BVMS 1965); St Catharine's Coll., Cambridge (Scholar; BA 1st Cl. Hons 1967; MA 1970; PhD 1970). MRCVS 1965; MRCPath 1981, FRCPath 1992. Fellow, Clare Hall, Cambridge, 1967–72; Wellcome Trust Res. Fellow, Inst. of Animal Physiology, Cambridge, 1970–72; Sen. Lectr in Immunology, RPMS, Hammersmith Hosp., 1972–76; MRC Sen. Scientist, MRC Lab. of Molecular Biology, Cambridge, 1976–83; Hon. Associate Lectr in Pathology, Dept of Pathology, Univ. of Cambridge, 1976–83; Prof. and Hd of Dept of Vet. Pathology, Univ. of Edinburgh, 1983–94. Member: Selbourne Cttee of Enquiry into Vet. Res., 1996–98; Wellcome Trust Vet. Medicine Interest Panel, 1998–; Govt's Spongiform Encephalopathy Adv. Cttee (SEAC), 2000–; HEFCE Panel of Experts for 2001 RAE; Working Gp on TSE, Royal Soc. and Acad. of Med. Scis, 2001–02; Adv. Gp on use of Genetically Modified Animals, Royal Soc., 2001–02; Inquiry into Infectious Diseases in Livestock, Royal Soc., 2001–02; Nuffield Council for Bioethics Wkg Party on the Ethics of Res. Involving Animals, 2004–. Mem., Governing Body, Inst. for Animal Health, 1988–94. FRSE 1987; FMedSci 1998; FRSocMed 2000. Wellcome Trust Medal for Vet. Res., 1997. *Publications:* (with M. J. Hobart) The Immune System: a course on the molecular and cellular basis of immunity, 1976, 2nd edn (with A. J. Munro and H. Waldmann) 1981; res. papers in immunology, pathology and veterinary sci. *Recreations:* ski-ing, mountain walking, family. *Address:* Department of Veterinary Medicine, University of Cambridge, Madingley Road, Cambridge CB3 0ES. *T:* (01223) 337654, *Fax:* (01223) 337671. *E:* im200@cam.ac.uk.

**McCONNELL, Prof. James Desmond Caldwell,** FRS 1987; Professor of the Physics and Chemistry of Minerals, Department of Earth Sciences, University of Oxford, 1986–95, now Emeritus (Head of Department, 1991–95); Fellow of St Hugh's College, Oxford, 1986–95 (Hon. Fellow, 1995); *b* 3 July 1930; *s* of Samuel D. and Cathleen McConnell; *m* 1956, Jean Elspeth Ironside; one *s* two *d*. *Educ:* Queen's Univ. of Belfast (BSc, MSc 1952); Univ. of Cambridge (MA 1955; PhD 1956); MA Oxon 1986. Univ. of Cambridge: Demonstrator, 1955; Lectr, 1960; Reader, 1972–82; Churchill College: Fellow, 1962–82; Extraordinary Fellow, 1983–88; Head of Dept of Rock Physics, Schlumberger Cambridge Research, 1983–86. Alex von Humboldt Prize, Alexander von Humboldt Stiftung, Germany, 1996. *Publications:* Principles of Mineral Behaviour (with A. Putnis), 1980, Russian edn, 1983; papers in physics jls and mineralogical jls. *Recreations:* local history, singing. *Address:* 19 Gilmerton Court, Cambridge CB2 9HQ. *T:* (01223) 843711.

**McCONNELL, John,** RDI 1987; FCSD; graphic designer; freelance design practice, McConnell Design, 1963–74 and since 2005; Director, Pentagram Design, 1974–2005; *b* 14 May 1939; *s* of Donald McConnell and Enid McConnell (*née* Dimberline); *m* 1963, Moira Rose Macgregor; one *s* one *d*. *Educ:* Borough Green Secondary Modern School; Maidstone College of Art (NDD). FCSD (FSIAD 1980). Employed in advertising and design, 1959–62; Lectr, Colchester College of Art, 1962–63; co-founder, Face Photosetting, 1968. Design consultant, Boots, 1984–2002; design adviser to John Lewis Partnership, 2001–10, to British Museum, 2010–. Mem., Post Office Stamp Adv. Cttee, 1984–2012; Pres., D&AD, 1985 (President's Award, 1985); served on design competition juries, D&AD. FRSA. Gold medallist at Biennale, Warsaw; Special Commendation, Prince Phillip Designer's Prize, 2002. *Publications:* (jtly) Living by Design, 1978; (jtly) Ideas on Design, 1986; (jtly) The Compendium, 1993; (ed jtly) Pentagram Book 5, 1999; Editor, Pentagram Papers. *Recreations:* house restoration, cooking. *Address:* 12 Orme Court, W2 4RL.

**McCONNELL, Philippa Mary;** *see* Harrison, P. M.

**McCONNELL, (Sir) Robert Shean,** (4th Bt *cr* 1900); *S* father, 1987, but does not use the title; *b* Belfast, 23 Nov. 1930. *Educ:* Stowe; Queens' Coll., Cambridge (MA Urban Estate Management); Regent St Polytech. (DipTP); Univ. of BC (MSc Community and Regl Planning). FRTPI; MRICS; MCMI. Worked as a trainee surveyor in Belfast and as a town planner in UK, Canada and USA. Lectured in town planning and principles of management at univs in UK and Australia. Chm., Lambeth Race Scrutiny Commn, 2002–03. Member: London SE Valuation Tribunal, 1995–2002; Community Police Consultative Gp for Lambeth, 1995–2005; S Metropolitan (W Norwood) Cemetery Adv. Gp, 1998–2006; Health Scrutiny Cttee for Lambeth and Southwark, 2002–06; Health Watch, Lambeth and Southwark, 2012–15; Trustee, Lambeth Patient Participation Gp Network, 2015–18 (Mem., Lambeth Link Patient Participation Gp, 2012–15); Chm., Patient Participation Gp, Stockwell Practice, 2013–. Mem., Bruce House Appeal Cttee, 1984–86. Governor: South Bank Poly., 1973–75; Tulse Hill Sch., 1976–90; Stockwell Infant Jun. Sch., 1983–88; Norwood Park Primary Sch., 1996–2002; Crown Lane Primary Sch., 2003–12. Councillor (Lib Dem) Lambeth BC, 1996–2006. Voluntary Manager, St Michael's Church Hall, Stockwell, 2012–17; Mem., Parochial Ch Council, Stockwell Parish, 2015–18. Zeta Psi Fraternity (Canada), 1957. *Publications:* Theories for Planning, 1981; (contrib.) Planning Ethics, ed Hendler, 1995; (contrib.) Housing: the essential foundations, ed Balchin and Rhoden, 1998; The Peace Bug, 2010; articles in professional jls on planning matters; unsuccessful playwright and novelist. *Recreations:* gardening. *Heir: nephew* Terence Reade McConnell [*b* 16 Nov. 1959; *m* 1987, Lorel Natalie Willetts (marr. diss. 2004); one *s* one *d*].

**McCONNELL, Wendy Jane;** *see* Miles, W. J.

**McCORKELL, George Alexander,** CB 2002; management consultant, G. A. McCorkell Ltd, 2004–08; Director, Pensions Change Programme, Department for Work and Pensions, 2001–04; *b* 6 Jan. 1944; *s* of Samuel Robert McCorkell and Sarah McCorkell; *m* 1967, Nuala McCarthy; two *s*. *Educ:* Foyle Coll., Londonderry, NI; BA Math. Open, 1978; MSc Information Systems, LSE, 1982. Computer Programmer, MoD, 1967–69; Systems Analyst: Min. of Finance, 1970–74; DHSS, 1974–76; Liaison Officer, CCTA, 1976–79; Department of Health and Social Security, later Department of Social Security: Operational

Systems Team Leader, 1979–83; Principal, 1983–86; Sen. Principal, 1987–88; Director: ITSA, 1988–95; Benefits Agency, 1995–99; Chief Exec., ITSA, 1999–2000; Chief Inf. Officer, 2000–01; Hd of Inf. Systems and Commercial Mgt Div., 2001, DSS. *Recreation:* golf. *Address:* 46 West Drive, Thornton-Cleveleys, Lancs FY5 2BH.

**McCORMAC, Prof. Francis Gerard, (Gerry),** PhD; FSA; Principal and Vice Chancellor, University of Stirling, since 2010; *b* Belfast, 1 Aug. 1958; *s* of Francis Gerald McCormac and Jane Philomena McCormac; *m* 1982, Catherine Marie Louise Gormley; three *s*. *Educ:* Ulster Poly. (BSc Hons 1980); Univ. of Southampton (PhD Physics 1984); London Business Sch. (Sen. Exec. Prog. 2005). Lectr in Physics, Ulster Poly., 1985–86; Post-doctoral Res. Fellow, Space Physics, 1986–87, Asst Res. Scientist, Space Physics, 1987–90, Univ. of Michigan; Queen's University of Belfast: Lectr in Carbon Dating/Envmtl Monitoring, 1990–94, Sen. Lectr, 1994–99; Dir, Radiocarbon Res. Facility/CHRONO Centre, 1990–2010; Hd, Sch. of Archaeol. and Palaeoecol., 1998–2001; Prof., Science Based Archaeol., 1999–2010; Pro Vice-Chancellor, 2001–10. Dir, NI Sci. Park, 2007–10. Dir and Chm. Mgt Bd, QUBIS Ltd, 2006–10. Member: Inter-agency Strategy Gp, Belfast CC, 2004–10; HE/FE Business Alliance, 2004–10; Bd, Business in the Community, 2005–10; Econ. Develt Forum, 2006–10; MATRIX, NI Sci. and Ind. Panel, 2007–10; Bd, Invest NI, 2008–14. Member: Bd, Universities UK, 2010–; Universities Scotland, 2010–; Scottish Cttee, Univs and Colls Employers' Assoc., 2010–; UCEA, 2015–. Mem., Carnegie Trust for Univs of Scotland, 2010–. FHEA 1998; FRSA 1999; FSA 2001; FRSE 2017. *Publications:* (contrib.) Advances in the Astronautical Sciences, 1992; (contrib.) Energy and the Environment: geochemistry of fossil, nuclear and renewable resources, 1998; (with B. Maloney) A 30,000-year pollen, radiocarbon and $d^{13}C$ record from Highland North Sumatra and South China Deep Sea Core: 17940 results compared, 2000; (contrib.) Hambledon Hill, Dorset, England: excavation and survey of a Neolithic monument complex and its surrounding landscape, 2008; (contrib.) Radiocarbon Dates, 2008; contribs to learned jls incl. Radiocarbon, Geophysics Res. Letters, Space Sci., Jl Geophysics Res., The Holocene. *Address:* Principal's Office, University of Stirling, Stirling FK9 4LA. *T:* (01786) 467012. *E:* principal@stir.ac.uk. *Club:* Caledonian.

**McCORMACK, Rev. Canon Kevan Sean;** Rector, St Mary the Virgin, Woodbridge, since 2000; a Chaplain to the Queen, 2014–Feb. 2020; *b* Whitby, 13 Feb. 1950; *s* of Kenneth Basil McCormack and Marion McCormack. *Educ:* Univ. of Southampton (CTh 1983). Ordained deacon, 1980, priest, 1981; Assistant Curate: Ross-on-Wye, 1980–83; Leominster, 1983–84; Team Vicar, Leominster Team Ministry, 1984–87; Chaplain, 1987–2000, 6th Form Housemaster, 1991–96, Royal Hospital Sch., Holbrook. Officiating Chaplain to the Military, 2010–. Honorary Chaplain: Ipswich Town FC, 2000–; Suffolk Coastal District Council, 2002–19; Woodbridge RBL, 2002–; Seckford Foundn (The Seckford Chapel), 2003–; Hon. Canon, Cathedral Church of St James and St Edmund, 2009–. Masonic Provincial Grand Chaplain for Suffolk, 2011–; Asst Grand Chaplain, United Grand Lodge of England, 2018–19. Hon. Freeman, Woodbridge, 2014–. *Recreations:* cooking, eating out, reading, music, animals, travel, cinema, gardening, Masonic life and activities. *Address:* St Mary's Rectory, 11 Church Street, Woodbridge IP12 1DS. *T:* (01394) 610424. *E:* rector@stmaryswoodbridge.org.

**McCORMACK, Margaret;** a District Judge (Magistrates' Courts), since 2018; *b* Manchester, 10 Jan. 1963. *Educ:* Manchester Metropolitan Univ. (LLB Hons). Admitted solicitor, 1995; Berry & Berry Law, subseq. HCB Berry & Berry Ltd: joined as trainee solicitor, 1993; a Dir, until 2018; a Dep. District Judge (Magistrates' Courts), 2012–18. *Recreations:* running, tag Rugby. *Address:* Doncaster Magistrates' Court, College Road, Doncaster DN1 3HT.

**McCORMACK, Rev. Dr Philip John,** MBE 2011; Principal, Spurgeon's College, London, since 2017; *b* Bangor, NI, 1963; *s* of John and Alice McCormack; *m* 1987, Karen McCartney; one *s*. *Educ:* Irish Baptist Coll. (DipTh 1992); Queen's Univ., Belfast (BD 1993; PhD 2001); Cardiff Univ. (MTh (Dist.) 2006); Cranfield Univ. (PhD 2015). Mech. engr, Harland and Wolff, 1979–89; Pastor, Carryduff Baptist Ch, 1993–97; Chaplain, HM Land Forces, 1997–2017: SO1 Ethics, 2013–17; Asst Chaplain Gen., Army Recruiting and Trng Div., 2016–17. Vis. Prof. of Practical Ethics, Univ. of Worcester, 2015–. Principal Fellow, Higher Educn Acad., 2017–. Pres., Naval and Military Bible Soc., 2018–. Served (pt-time) UDR, 1982–86. *Publications:* contrib. Army Doctrine Publication Operations. *Recreations:* cinema, art, golf, family. *Address:* Spurgeon's College, South Norwood Hill, SE25 6DJ. *T:* (020) 8653 0850. *E:* p.mccormack@spurgeons.ac.uk.

**McCORMICK, Dr Andrew Graham,** FGS; Director General, International Relations, Executive Office, Northern Ireland, since 2018; *b* 26 Aug. 1957; *s* of Jackson and Helen McCormick; *m* 1981, Alison Griffiths; one *s*. *Educ:* University Coll., Oxford (BA 1st Cl. Geol. 1978; MA 1989); Queen's Univ., Belfast (PhD Geochem. 1989). Joined NI Civil Service, 1980; Dept of Finance and Personnel, 1980–93; Sen. Civil Service, Dept of Educn, 1993–98; Dep. Sec., 1998–2002; Second Perm. Sec., Dept of Finance and Personnel, 2002–05; Perm. Sec., Dept of Health, Social Services and Public Safety, 2005–14; Perm. Sec., Dept of Enterprise, Trade and Investment, then Dept of the Economy, 2014–18. FGS 2005. *Publications:* co-author several res. papers in geochemistry. *Recreations:* hill-walking, photography, classical music. *Address:* Executive Office, Northern Ireland Executive, Stormont Castle, Belfast BT4 3TT.

**McCORMICK, Prof. Barry,** CBE 2010; PhD; Fellow, Centre for Health Service Economics and Organisation, Department of Economics, University of Oxford (Director, 2010); *b* 3 Aug. 1949; *s* of Leonard McCormick and Lucy Adelaide McCormick; *m* 1975, Doreen Foti; two *s*. *Educ:* Co. High Sch., Arnold, Nottingham; Manchester Univ. (BA, MA); MIT (PhD 1976). Harkness Fellow, 1972–74, Instructor, 1974–75, MIT; Asst Lectr, Univ. of Cambridge, and Fellow, Robinson Coll., Cambridge, 1976–80; Southampton University: Lectr, 1981–87; Sen. Lectr, 1987–89; Reader, 1989–90; Prof. of Econs, 1991–2002; Prof. Emeritus, 2009; Chief Economist and Dir, Econs and Ops Res., DoH, 2002–04; Chief Analyst, DoH, 2004–10. Sir Norman Chester Vis. Fellow, Nuffield Coll., Oxford, 1989. Academic Consultant to HM Treasury, 2001–02. Mem. Council, REconS, 2003–08. *Publications:* (with G. Hughes) Housing Policy and Labour Market Performance, 2000; (jtly) Immigration Policy and the Welfare State, 2002; scientific papers and govt reports on policy in labour markets, develt and health. *Recreations:* music, theatre, art, walking, watching cricket. *Address:* Flat 9A, Vincent House, Vincent Square, SW1P 2NB. *T:* (020) 7821 6433. *E:* barry.mccormick@phc.ox.ac.uk.

**McCORMICK, Caroline;** Founder and Director, Achates Philanthropy, since 2014; *b* 14 Oct. 1971; *d* of Anthony and Marie McCormick; *m* 1st, 2001, Ian Whitaker (marr. diss. 2008); 2nd, 2015, Bill Swainson. *Educ:* Astbury Primary Sch.; Heathfield High Sch.; Univ. of Sheffield (BA Hons Eng. Lit. 1993; MA Contemp. Writing 1995). Res. Officer, Rotherham TEC, 1995–96; Trust Fundraising Manager, RNID, 1996–97; Hd, Trust Fundraising, Nat. Th., 1997–99; Dir, Develt, Coin Street Community Builders, 1999–2001; Hd, Develt, Natural Hist. Mus., 2001–05; Dir, Internat. PEN, 2005–10. Established strategy and fundraising consultancy in 2005. Board Member: DanceEast, 2010–12; The Green Belt Movement, 2010–13; Old Vic Th. Develt Council, 2013–16. Founder, Achates Philanthropy Prize, 2016; Founder and Chair, Achates Philanthropy Foundn, 2016–. *Recreations:* reading, writing, thinking, talking, swimming, theatre, film. *E:* caroline@achatesphilanthropy.com.

**McCORMICK, Prof. Francis Patrick,** PhD; FRS 1996; Director, Helen Diller Family Comprehensive Cancer Center, 1997–2014, David A. Wood Distinguished Professor of Tumor Biology and Cancer Research, since 1997, and E. Dixon Heise Distinguished Professor in Oncology, University of California, San Francisco (Director, Cancer Research Institute, 1997–2009); *b* 31 July 1950; *s* of late David and of Jane McCormick; *m* 1979, Judith Anne Demske (marr. diss. 1995). *Educ:* Univ. of Birmingham (BSc 1972); St John's Coll., Cambridge (PhD 1975). Post-doctoral Fellow: SUNY, 1975–78; ICRF, London, 1978–81; Scientist, 1981–89, Vice-Pres., Res., 1989–90, Cetus Corp.; Vice-Pres., Res., Chiron Corp., 1991–92; Founder and Vice-Pres., Res., Onyx Pharmaceuticals, 1992–96. Associate Dean, Sch. of Medicine, UCSF, 1997–. Mem., Inst. of Medicine, 2005. *Publications:* (jointly): Origins of Human Cancer, 1991; The GTPase Superfamily, 1993; The ras Superfamily of GTPases, 1993. *Recreations:* motor racing, African history. *Address:* Helen Diller Family Comprehensive Cancer Center, UCSF School of Medicine, 1450 3rd Street, Room 371, San Francisco, CA 94158, USA.

**McCORMICK, John,** FRSE; Member for Scotland, UK Electoral Commission, 2008–16; Chairman, Commission on Parliamentary Reform (Scotland), 2016–17; *b* 24 June 1944; *s* of Joseph and Roseann McCormick; *m* 1973, Jean Frances Gibbons; one *s* one *d*. *Educ:* St Michael's Acad., Irvine; Univ. of Glasgow (MA Modern History with Econ. History 1967; MEd 1970). Teacher, St Gregory's Secondary Sch., Glasgow, 1968–70; Education Officer, BBC School Broadcasting Council, 1970–75; Senior Education Officer, Scotland, 1975–82; Sec., and Head of Information, BBC Scotland, 1982–87; The Sec. of the BBC, 1987–92; Controller of BBC Scotland, 1992–2004; Chm., Scottish Qualifs Authy, 2004–09. Chm., Edinburgh Internat. Film Fest., 1996–2008; Mem., Edinburgh Fests Forum, 2009–16; Mem. Bd, 1997–2003, Vice-Chm., 2003–05, Scottish Screen; Chm., Screen Sector Leadership Gp, Creative Scotland, 2015–18. Non-exec. Dir, Lloyds TSB Scotland, 2005–09. Mem. Bd, Skillset, 2002–04. Mem., Lay Adv. Cttee, RCPE, 2010–15. Member: Glasgow Sci. Centre Charitable Trust, 1999–2005; Bd, Glasgow Sch. of Art, 2004–07; Bd, Scottish Opera, 2005– (Vice-Chm., 2008–). Director: Irvine Bay Urban Regeneration Co., 2006–13; Glasgow Life, 2013–. Mem. Court, Univ. of Strathclyde, 1996–2002; Gov., RSAMD, 2003–08. FRTS 1998; FRSE 2003. Hon. DLitt Robert Gordon Univ., Aberdeen, 1997; Hon. LLD Strathclyde, 1999; DUniv: Glasgow, 1999; Paisley, 2003. *Recreation:* newspapers.

**McCORMICK, John St Clair,** OBE 2002; FRCSE; Medical Director, Dumfries and Galloway Royal Infirmary, 1994–2001; *b* 20 Sept. 1939; *s* of James McCormick and Dianne Anne McCormick (*née* Diskett-Heath); *m* 1964, Fiona Helen McLean; two *s*. *Educ:* St Paul's Cathedral Choir Sch.; Sedbergh Sch.; Univ. of Edinburgh (MB ChB 1964). FRCSE 1967. Consultant Surgeon: Dunfermline, 1974–79; Dumfries and Galloway Royal Infirmary, 1979–99. Royal College of Surgeons of Edinburgh: Mem. Council, 1994–2003; Dir of Standards, 1997–2002; Vice Pres., 2000–03. Mem., Clinical Standards Bd, Scotland, 1999–2002. Liveryman, Co. of Wax Chandlers, 1962. *Address:* Ivy Cottage, Kirkpatrickdurham, Castle Douglas DG7 3HG.

**McCORMICK, Peter David Godfrey,** OBE 2000; Founding and Senior Partner, McCormicks Solicitors, since 1983; Chairman, Football Board and Chairman, Legal Advisory Group, Premier League, since 1996; Member Board, since 2015 and Vice Chairman, since 2017, Football Association; *b* Leeds, 27 June 1952; *s* of Ronald McCormick and Paulina McCormick; *m* 1981, Kathryn Gill; one *s* one *d*. *Educ:* Ashville Coll., Harrogate; King's Coll. London (LLB Law 1973). Admitted solicitor, 1976; articled clerk, 1974–76, solicitor, 1976–78, Partner, 1978–83, J. Levi & Co. Solicitors, Leeds. Chm., Premier League, 2014–15. Chairman: Football Stadia Improvement Fund Ltd, 2008–; Sport Resolutions (UK), 2008–; Yorkshire Young Achievers Foundn, 2010–; War Memorials Trust, 2012–; Trustee, Football Foundn, 2008–. *Publications:* Sport, Business and the Law, 1999. *Recreations:* football, food, wine, opera, theatre, film. *Address:* McCormicks Solicitors, 35–37 East Parade, Harrogate HG1 5LQ. *T:* (01423) 530630. *E:* p.mccormick@mccormicks-solicitors.com.

**McCORQUODALE, David Alexander;** Partner, 1993–2017, and UK Head of Retail, 2012–17, KPMG; *b* Aberdeen, 19 April 1962; *s* of Duncan McCorquodale and Helen Margaret McCorquodale (*née* Macdonald); *m* 1987, Kay Roslyn Mackintosh; three *d*. *Educ:* West End Primary Sch., Elgin; Blairmore Prep. Sch., Huntly; Merchiston Castle Sch., Edinburgh; Univ. of Edinburgh (LLB; DipLP). CA 1987. With Thomson McLintock, subseq. KPMG, 1984–2017: on secondment to Takeover Panel, 1990–92; UK Hd, Consumer Mkts for Corporate Finance, 2002–12; Mem. Bd, KPMG Corporate Finance in US, 2008–10. University of Edinburgh: Mem., Campaign Bd, 2007–12; Regent, 2012–. Trustee, Retail Trust, 2018– (Ambassador, 2014–18); Ambassador, Pennies Charity, 2014–17. *Recreations:* golf, sport in general, family, travel.

**McCOSKER, Penelope Anne;** *see* Wensley, P. A.

**McCOURT, Arthur David,** CBE 2004; Chief Executive, The Highland Council, 1995–2007; *b* 11 July 1947; *s* of Thomas McCourt and Thomasina (*née* Taylor); *m* 1994, Jan McNaughton Smith; two *d*. *Educ:* Bell Baxter High Sch.; Edinburgh Coll. of Art; Heriot-Watt Univ. (BSc Hons Town and Country Planning, 1971). Planner, Northumberland CC, 1974–76; Team Leader, Central Regl Council, 1976–87; Sen. Policy Advr, Stirling DC, 1987–90; Asst Chief Exec., Tayside Regl Council, 1990–95. *Recreation:* keen mountaineer and walker. *Address:* Westcroft, Newtonhill, Lentran, Inverness IV3 8RN.

**McCOURT, Martin;** Chairman: Venture Founders, since 2015 (non-executive Director, since 2015); The Learning Curve Group, since 2016; Glen Dimplex Group, since 2016; Lightfoot Ltd, since 2018; *b* Glasgow, 29 Dec. 1956; *s* of Donald and Roseanne McCourt; *m* 2009, Liane; two *d* and one step *s* one step *d*. Cartographic draughtsman, MoD Mapping and Charting Estabt, 1974–77; Develt Exec., Mars Confectionery, 1977–80; Nat. Sales Manager, Personnel Manager, Sales Ops Manager, Sales Trng Manager, Nat. Accounts Manager, Duracell, 1980–87; Gen. Manager, Audiovisual, Toshiba, 1987–88; Sales and Mktg Dir, Office Internat., 1988–91; Man. Dir, Marcus Bohn Associates, 1991–95; Gen. Manager and Internat. Account Dir, Pelikan, 1995–97; Dyson Ltd, 1997–2012: Gp Commercial Dir; Man. Dir, Floorcare; Internat. Man. Dir; Chief Exec., 2001–12; Dir, Montagu Private Equity Associates, 2012–15. Non-executive Director: Your Life, 2014–; Headbox, 2015–; Weber Stephen, 2019–. Mem., Charting and Cartographic Inst. 1975. Orange Business Leader of Year, 2010. *Recreation:* tennis.

**McCOWAN, Sir David William Cargill,** 4th Bt cr 1934, of Dalwhat, Dumfries; b 28 Feb. 1934; s of Sir David James Cargill McCowan, 2nd Bt and Muriel Emma Annie, d of W. C. Willmott; S brother, 1998, but his name does not appear on the Official Roll of the Baronetage; m 1995, Jean, d of A. R. McGhee; one s one d. Heir: s David James Cargill McCowan, b 2 June 1975. Address: Auchendennan Farm, Alexandria, Dunbartonshire G83 8RB.

**McCOY, Sir Anthony Peter,** Kt 2016; OBE 2010 (MBE 2003); National Hunt jockey, retired 2015; Presenter, ITV Racing, since 2017; b 4 May 1974; m 2006, Chanelle Burke; one s one d. Apprentice, Jim Bolgers Stables. Champion Nat. Hunt Jockey, 1995–96, 1996–97, 1997–98, 1998–99, 1999–2000, 2000–01, 2001–02, 2002–03, 2003–04, 2004–05, 2005–06, 2006–07, 2007–08, 2008–09, 2009–10, 2010–11, 2011–12, 2012–13, 2013–14, 2014–15. Winner: Cheltenham Gold Cup on Mr Mulligan, 1997, on Synchronised, 2012; Hennessy Gold Cup on Carlingford Lough, 2015; Champion Hurdle on Make A Stand, 1997, on Brave Inca, 2006, on Binocular, 2010; Scottish Grand National on Belmont King, 1997; Grand Annual Chase on Edredon Bleu, 1998; Champion Chase on Edredon Bleu, 2000; King George VI Chase on Best Mate, 2002; Irish Grand National on Butler's Cabin, 2007; Grand National on Don't Push It, 2010. Record 1700 Nat. Hunt wins, 2002; record 18 championships, 2013; first jockey to ride 2,000 Nat. Hunt winners in UK, 2004 and first to ride 3,000 winners, 2009 and 4,000 winners, 2013. Pres., Injured Jockeys Fund, 2016–. Hon. Dr QUB, 2002; Hon. DSc Ulster, 2014. BBC Sports Personality of the Year, 2010. Publications: (with Claude Duval) The Real McCoy: my life so far, 1998; McCoy: the autobiography, 2002; (with Donn McClean) My Autobiography, 2011; Taking the Fall (novel), 2013; Winner: my racing life (autobiog.), 2015. Recreations: golf, football. Address: Lodge Down Stables, Lambourn Woodlands, Hungerford, Berks RG17 7BJ.

**McCRACKEN, Guy;** see McCracken, P. G.

**McCRACKEN, (James) Justin;** Chief Executive, Health Protection Agency, 2008–13; b 28 April 1955; s of late Dermot and Margaret McCracken; m 1st (marr. diss.); two s one d, 2nd, 2010, Lynn Frances Colleran. Educ: Rugby Sch.; Jesus Coll., Oxford (MA Physics). Res. scientist, ICI, 1976–91; Business Manager, ICI Acrylics, 1991–97; Man. Dir, ICI Katalco, 1997–98; Regl Dir, Envmt Agency, 1998–2002; Dep. Dir Gen. (Ops), then Dep. Chief Exec. (Ops), Health and Safety Executive, 2002–08. Non-exec. Ind. Dir, Ombudsman Services, 2013–; non-exec. Dir, Office of Rail and Road (formerly Rail Regulation), 2014–. Non-exec. Dir, Entrust, 2014–. Recreation: sailing. Club: Coniston Sailing.

See also R. H. J. McCracken.

**McCRACKEN, (Philip) Guy,** LVO 2004; Chairman, Branston Ltd, since 2010; b 25 Nov. 1948; m 1972, Frances Elizabeth Addison; one s two d. Educ: Clee Humberston Foundn Sch., Cleethorpes; Nat. Coll. of Food Technology, Reading Univ. (BSc 1st Class Hons Food Technology). Production Manager, Mars, 1972–73; Product Development Manager, Imperial Foods, 1973–75; Marks & Spencer, 1975–2000: Man. Dir, Food Div., 1993–98; Exec. Dir, Internat. Retail and IT, 1999–2000; Chief Exec., Food Retail, Co-operative Gp, 2005–08. Chm., Duchy Originals, 1997–2004. Mem., Council of Food Policy Advrs, 2008–10. Gov., Nuffield Health, 2010–. Recreations: golf, ski-ing, food, travel.

**McCRACKEN, Robert Henry Joy;** QC 2003; b 15 March 1950; s of late Dermot McCracken, FRCP and Margaret McCracken, MB BCh. Educ: Rugby Sch.; Worcester Coll., Oxford (MA). Called to the Bar: Inner Temple, 1973; Lincoln's Inn (ad eundem), 1978, Bencher, 2014; barrister practising in public, envmtl and planning law. Mem., Animal Procedures Cttee advising Home Sec., 1999–2003. Chm., UK Envmtl Law Assoc., 1995–97; Sec., Planning and Envmtl Bar Assoc., 1992–94. Vis. Prof., KCL, 2018. Publications: (jtly) Statutory Nuisance, 2000, 3rd edn 2012; contribs to Judicial Rev., Jl Planning and Envmtl Law. Recreations: painting, natural science, fell-walking. Address: Francis Taylor Building, Inner Temple, EC4Y 7BY. Clubs: Reform; Cyclists' Touring, Coniston Sailing.

See also J. J. McCracken.

**McCREA,** family name of **Baron McCrea of Magherafelt and Cookstown.**

**McCREA OF MAGHERAFELT AND COOKSTOWN, Baron** cr 2018 (Life Peer), of Magherafelt in the County of Londonderry and Cookstown in the County of Tyrone; **Robert Thomas William McCrea;** Minister, Magherafelt Free Presbyterian Church of Ulster, since 1969; b 6 Aug. 1948; s of Robert T. and Sarah J. McCrea; m 1971, Anne Shirley McKnight; two s three d. Educ: Cookstown Grammar Sch.; Theol Coll., Free Presbyterian Church of Ulster. Civil servant, 1966; Free Presbyterian Minister of the Gospel, 1967–. Dist Councillor, Magherafelt, 1973–2011; Mem. (DemU) Mid Ulster, NI Assembly, 1982–86 and 1998–2007, Antrim S, 2007–10. MP (DemU) Mid Ulster, 1983–97 (resigned seat Dec. 1985 in protest against Anglo-Irish Agreement; re-elected Jan. 1986); contested (DemU): Mid Ulster, 1997; Antrim S, 2001; MP (DemU) S Antrim, Sept. 2000–2001 and 2005–15; contested (DemU) same seat, 2015. Dir, Daybreak Recording Co., 1981–. Gospel singer and recording artist; Silver, Gold and Platinum Discs for record sales. Hon. DD Marietta Bible Coll., Ohio, 1989. Publications: In His Pathway—the story of the Reverend William McCrea, 1980. Recreations: music, horse riding.

See also I. McCrea.

**McCREA, Diane,** MBE 2016; Chair, Natural Resources Wales, 2015–18; b Usk, 27 Aug. 1954; d of late Colin Davies McCrea and Eileen McCrea. Educ: Pontypool Girls' Grammar Sch.; University Coll., Cardiff (BEd Hons 1976); Queen Elizabeth Coll., Univ. of London (MSc 1977). Lectr, Coll. of All Saints, Tottenham, 1978–82; Sen. Lectr, Middx Poly., 1982–89; London Food Commn Seconded Researcher, 1986–87; Course Hd, Middx Univ., 1989–92; Hd, Food and Health Res., Which? Mag., 1992–97; consultant, food and consumer affairs, 1997–2005. Winston Churchill Travelling Fellow, USA, 1990; Chair, Welsh Assoc. of Churchill Fellows, 2019–. Consumer Council for Water: Chair, Wales Cttee, 2005–15; Vice Chair, 2011–15. Chair, Scrutiny Cttee, Soil Assoc. Certification Ltd, 2010–16. Member: UK food adv. cttees (incl. Spongiform Encephalopathy Adv. Cttee), 1997–2015; Bd, Assured Food Standards UK, 2004–08; Bd, Transport Focus, 2013–17; Consumer Expert Panel, Office of Rail and Road, 2017–. Chair, Shelter Cymru, 2011–17; Trustee, Cynnal Cymru, 2019–. Dir, All Saints Educnl Trust, 1997–. Hon. Fellow, Univ. of Wales, Trinity St David, 2017. Publications: (ed with S. Wright) The Handbook of Organic Food Processing and Production, 1994, 2nd edn 2000; (ed with S. Wright) The Handbook of Organic and Fair Trade Food Marketing, 2007; contrib. articles on food safety, BSE, internat. food trade and consumer issues. Recreations: walking the Wales Coast Path with my dog, opera, jazz, fine food, wine and friends, my VW Camper van.

**McCREA, Ian;** Member (DemU) Mid-Ulster, Northern Ireland Assembly, 2007–16; b 12 June 1976; s of Rev. Dr (Robert Thomas) William McCrea (see Baron McCrea of Magherafelt and Cookstown); m 1998, Wanita Cardwell; two s one d. Educ: Magherafelt Controlled Primary Sch.; Rainey Endowed Grammar Sch.; NE Inst. for Further and Higher Educn, Magherafelt. Unipork, Cookstown, 1996–97; alarm and security installation engr, 1997–99; PA to Dr William McCrea, MP, 1997–2007. Mem. (DemU) Cookstown DC, 2001–15 (Vice Chm., 2005–06; Chm., 2007–08). Contested (DemU): Mid-Ulster, 2010, 2015; Mid-Ulster, NI Assembly, 2016. Dir, Cookstown Local Strategy Partnership, 2001–; Chm., Cookstown Dist Policing Partnership, 2006–07; Mem., Northern Ireland Policing Bd, 2011–13; Mem. Bd, Loughs Agency, 2015–; Mem., Flags, Identity, Culture and Tradition Commn, 2016–.

**McCREADIE, Robert Anderson;** QC (Scot.) 2003; PhD; Sheriff of Tayside Central and Fife at Perth, 2004–13; b 17 Aug. 1948; s of John Walker McCreadie and Jean J. M. McCreadie (née Ramsay). Educ: Univ. of Edinburgh (LLB Hons); Christ's Coll., Cambridge (PhD 1981). Lecturer in Law: Univ. of Dundee, 1974–78; Univ. of Edinburgh, 1978–92; called to Scottish Bar, 1992; Standing Junior Counsel: Dept of Transport, 1994–95; SHHD/Justice Dept, 1995–2000; Advocate Depute, 2000–02; Standing Jun. Counsel, Advocate Gen. for Scotland, 2002–03; pt-time Sheriff, 2003–04. Recreations: Scottish history, music, walking. Address: 18 Merchiston Park, Edinburgh EH10 4PN. T: (0131) 667 1383.

**McCREADY, John Francis;** Managing Director, Government Property Unit, Cabinet Office, 2010–12; b Southborough, Kent, 21 March 1956; s of John Robert McCready and Ann McCready (née Baxendale); m 1986, Alison Julie Perreau; two d (and one d decd). Educ: Eton Coll.; City of London Poly. (Dip. Accounting); INSEAD (MBA 1986). ACA 1983. Arthur Young McLelland Moores, 1978–83; Securicor plc, 1983–85; Goldman Sachs Internat., 1987–89; Arab Banking Corp. Internat., 1989–91; Man. Dir, Bluewater Park plc, 1994–96; Chief Exec., Whitecliff Properties, 1996–2000; Hd, Mergers and Acquisitions, Blue Circle Industries plc, 2000–01; Partner, Ernst & Young LLP, 2001–09. Chairman: Architecture Centre, 2001–09; London and SE Industrial Develt Bd, 2002–09. Recreations: tennis, reading, history, flying, countryside, conservation, Swahili. Address: Eastbury House, Eastbury, Hungerford, Berks RG17 7JJ. Clubs: Turf; Old Etonian Rifle.

**McCREADY, Prof. (Victor) Ralph,** DSc; FRCR, FRCP; Hon. Consultant, Royal Sussex County Hospital, since 2007; Emeritus Professor, Institute of Cancer Research, since 2002; b 17 Oct. 1935; s of Ernest and Mabel McCready; m 1964, Susan Margaret Mellor; two d. Educ: Ballyclare High Sch., NI; Queen's Univ., Belfast (MB BCh; BAO 1960; BSc 1957; DSc 1987); Guy's Hosp., London Univ. (MSc 1964); Dip. Med. Radiodiagnosis 1963. MRCP 1974, FRCP 1994; FRCR 1975. Mem., Scientific Staff, Inst. of Cancer Res., London, 1964–74, 1998–2002; Consultant, Royal Marsden Hosp., 1974–98; Hon. Consultant, Royal Marsden NHS Trust, 1998–2002; Emeritus Hon. Consultant, Hammersmith Hosp., 2004–11. Civilian Consultant, RN, 1993–2010. Hon. Mem., Japanese Radiological Soc., 2002. Hon. FFR, RCSI, 1992. Barclay Prize, British Inst. of Radiology, 1973. Publications: (ed jtly) A History of Radionuclide Studies in the UK, 2016; med. articles, books and contribs to books on nuclear medicine, ultrasound and magnetic resonance. Recreations: aviation, music. Address: Nuclear Medicine Department, Royal Sussex County Hospital, Eastern Road, Brighton BN2 5BE. Club: Royal Automobile.

**McCREATH, His Honour Alistair William;** a Circuit Judge, 1996–2017; a Senior Circuit Judge and Resident Judge, Southwark Crown Court, 2011–17; b 6 June 1948; s of late James McCreath and Ruth Mary McCreath (née Kellar); m 1976, Julia Faith Clark; one s one d. Educ: St Bees Sch.; Univ. of Keele (BA Hons). Called to the Bar, Inner Temple, 1972, Bencher, 2008; in practice at the Bar, 1973–96; Asst Recorder, 1986–90; Recorder, 1990–96; Resident Judge, Worcester Crown Court, 2006–11. Hon. Recorder: of Worcester, 2007–11; of Westminster, 2012–17. Course Dir, Criminal Continuation (Judicial Studies Bd), 2007–10. Judicial Member: Sentencing Council, 2010–13; Parole Bd, 2018–. Recreations: golf, theatre, playing on computers. Clubs: Athenæum; Royal Troon Golf.

**McCREDIE, Fionnuala Mary Constance;** QC 2013; b London, 15 Jan. 1965; d of Peter McCredie and Rosemary McCredie; partner, Michael John Mylonas, qv; two d. Educ: North London Collegiate Sch.; Univ. of Manchester (BSc (Hons) Geog. 1986); Brunel Univ. (MA Public and Social Admin 1990); Middlesex Poly. (CPE 1991). Called to the Bar, Middle Temple, 1992, Bencher, 2016; in practice as barrister, specialising in construction and procurement. Mem. Bd, 2012–16, Mem., Develt Cttee, 2016–, Coin Street Community Builders. Publications: (contrib. researcher) Keating on Construction Contracts, 9th edn 2012. Recreations: family, ski-ing, horses. Address: Keating Chambers, 15 Essex Street, WC2R 3AA. T: (020) 7544 2600. E: fmccredie@keatingchambers.com.

**McCREDIE, Ian Forbes,** CMG 2004; OBE 1984; Chief Executive, Forbes Research Group, since 2010; b 28 Dec. 1950; s of John and Diana McCredie; m 1998, Katherine Heiny; two s, and one s one d from previous marriage. Educ: Churchill Coll., Cambridge (BA 1972; MA 1975); Sch. of Oriental and African Studies, Univ. of London. Entered FCO, 1975; Third Sec., 1975; Third, later Second Sec. (Econ.), Lusaka, 1976–79; FCO, 1979–81; First Secretary: (Econ./Commercial), Tehran, 1981–83; FCO, 1983–85; Copenhagen, 1985–89; FCO, 1989–92; Counsellor: UKMIS, NY, 1992–97; FCO, 1997–99; Washington, 1999–2004; Vice Pres., Corporate Security, Royal Dutch Shell, 2004–10. Dir, GMTL LLP. Mem., Internat. Adv. Bd, Constellis Gp. Recreations: squash, military history.

**McCREESH, Paul;** Founder, Director and Conductor, Gabrieli Consort & Players; Principal Conductor and Artistic Adviser, Gulbenkian Orchestra, Lisbon, since 2013; b 24 May 1960; s of Patrick Michael McCreesh and Valerie McCreesh (née Connors); m 1983, Susan Hemington Jones; one s one d. Educ: Manchester Univ. (MusB 1981; Alumnus of Yr, 2012). Freelance conductor; founded Gabrieli Consort & Players, internat. ensemble specialising in choral and orchestral music, 1982; Artistic Dir, Wratislava Cantans Fest., Poland, 2006–12. Dir, Brinkburn Music, 1994–2013; Founder, Winged Lion, record label, 2010. Guest conductor of modern orchs incl. Budapest Fest., Gothenburg Symphony, Orch. Philharmonique de Radio France, Orch. di Santa Cecilia di Roma, Basel Chamber Orch., Zurich Tonhalle, Nederlands Philharmonic Orch., Bergen Philharmonic, Spanish Nat. Orch., Sydney SO, Leipzig Gewandhaus, St Paul Chamber, Hong Kong Philharmonic, Teatro Real Madrid, Royal Danish, Komische Oper Berlin, Vlaams Opera, Verbier Fest., Berlin Konzerthaus. Numerous recordings and internat. recording awards. Hon. LLD Loughborough, 2005. Recreations: countryside, walking, family. Address: c/o Rayfield Allied, Studio 26 China Works, 100 Black Prince Road, SE1 7SJ. T: (020) 3176 5500.

**McCREEVY, Charlie;** Member, European Commission, 2004–10; b 30 Sept. 1949; s of Charles McCreevy and Eileen Mills; m Noeleen Halligan; three s, and one s three d by a previous marriage. Educ: University Coll., Dublin (BComm). FCA 1973. Partner, Tynan, Dillon and Co., Chartered Accountants, 1974–92. Mem., Kildare CC, 1979–85. TD (FF) Kildare, 1977–2004; Minister for: Social Welfare, 1992–93; Tourism and Trade, 1993–94; frontbench spokesperson on Finance, 1995–97; Minister for Finance, Republic of Ireland, 1997–2004. Non-executive Director: Ryanair, 2010–18; Sports Direct, 2011–14. Recreations: golf, horse-racing, Gaelic Athletic Association. Address: Blundell House, Millicent, Sallins, Co. Kildare, Ireland.

**McCRICKARD, Donald Cecil**, FCIB; Director, American Express International Inc., 1978–83; Chairman, Hill Samuel Bank, 1990–92; *b* 25 Dec. 1936; *s* of late Peter McCrickard and Gladys Mary McCrickard; *m* 1st, 1960, Stella May, JP (marr. diss.), *d* of Walter Edward Buttle, RN retd; two *d*; 2nd, 1991, Angela Victoria Biddulph, JP, *d* of late Robert Biddulph Mitchell and of Mary Buckley Mitchell. *Educ:* Hove Grammar Sch.; LSE; Univ. of Malaya. FCIB 1988. Financial, marketing and gen. management appts to 1975; Chief Exec., American Express Co. UK, 1975, American Express Co. Asia, Pacific, Australia, 1980; Man. Dir, UDT Holdings, later TSB Commercial Holdings, 1983; Chairman: Swan National, 1983; UDT Bank, 1983; Dir, and Dep. Group Man. Dir, 1987, Chief Exec., Banking, 1988, Gp Chief Exec., 1990–92, TSB Group plc; Chief Exec., TSB Bank plc, 1989–92. Non-executive Chairman: London Town plc, 1995–2003; TM Group Holdings Ltd, 1996–98; Verdandi Ltd (formerly SGi Gp), 1998–2006; Digitalbrain plc, 1999–2004; non-executive Director: Carlisle Gp, 1993–96; Nat. Counties Building Soc., 1995–2007 (Vice Chm., 2001–07); Allied London Properties, 1997–2000; Sen. non-exec. Dir, Brit Insurance Hldgs PLC (formerly Benfield & Rea Investment Trust), 1995–2006. Mem., Deposit Protection Bd, Bank of England, 1990–92. Chm., Barnet Enterprise Trust, 1985–88. Mem., Exec. Cttee, British Bankers Assoc., 1989–92. Trustee: Crimestoppers (formerly Community Action) Trust, 1991–2004; Industry in Educn, 1993–2005. *Recreations:* cricket (Vice Pres., Sussex Cricket Foundn, Sussex CCC), photography, theatre, writing, restaurants, the countryside. *Club:* Royal Automobile.

**McCRIRRICK, (Thomas) Bryce**, CBE 1987; FREng; FIET; Director of Engineering, BBC, 1978–87; *b* 19 July 1927; *s* of late Alexander McCrirrick and Janet McCrirrick (*née* Tweedie); *m* 1953, Margaret Phyllis Yates; two *s* (and one *s* decd). *Educ:* Galashiels Academy; Heriot-Watt Coll., Edinburgh; Regent Street Polytechnic, London. BBC Radio, Studio Centres in Edinburgh, Glasgow and London, 1943–46; served RAF, 1946–49; BBC Television, 1949; Engineer-in-Charge Television Studios, 1963; Head of Engineering Television Recording, and of Studio Planning and Installation Dept, 1969; Chief Engineer, Radio Broadcasting, 1970; Asst Dir of Engrg, 1971; Dep. Dir of Engrg, 1976. Technical Assessor, Investigation into Clapham Junction Rly Accident, 1989. Pres., Soc. of Electronic and Radio Technicians, 1981–85 (Vice-Pres., 1979–80); Vice-Pres., IERE, 1985–88; Pres., IEE, 1988–89 (Dep. Pres., 1986–88, Vice-Pres., 1982–86); Hon. FIEE 1995); Mem. Council, Fellowship of Engrg, 1989–92. Gov., Imperial Coll., 1985–99; Mem. Court, Heriot-Watt Univ., 1991–94; Mem. Senate, London Univ., 1992–94. FRTS 1980; FREng (FEng 1981); FBKSTS 1982; FSMPTE 1989; Hon. FIET (Hon. FIEE 1995). Hon. DSc Heriot-Watt, 1987. *Recreation:* theatre. *Address:* 5 Coach House Gardens, Fleet, Hants GU51 4QX. *T:* (01252) 623422.

**McCRONE, Prof. David**, FBA 2005; FRSE; Professor of Sociology, 1996–2011, now Emeritus, and Co-Director, Institute of Governance, 1997–2011, University of Edinburgh; *b* 8 Oct. 1945; *s* of Alexander McCrone and Mary McCrone; partner, Prof. Janette Webb. *Educ:* Univ. of Edinburgh (MA Hons 1969, MSc 1971). Lectr, 1975–85, Sen. Lectr, 1985–92, Reader, 1992–96, in Sociology, Univ. of Edinburgh. FRSE 2002. *Publications:* (jtly) Property and Power in a City, 1989; Understanding Scotland, 1992, 2nd edn 2001; (jtly) Scotland: the brand, 1995; The Sociology of Nationalism, 1998; (jtly) Living in Scotland: social and economic change since 1980, 2004; (jtly) National Identity, Nationalism and Constitutional Change, 2009; (jtly) National Days: constructing and mobilising national identity, 2009; (jtly) Revolution or Evolution?: the 2007 Scottish elections, 2009; (jtly) The Crisis of Social Democracy, 2013; (jtly) Understanding National Identity, 2015; The New Sociology of Scotland, 2017. *Recreations:* walking, reading, gardening. *Address:* Institute of Governance, University of Edinburgh, Chisholm House, High School Yards, Edinburgh EH1 1LZ. *T:* (0131) 650 2459. *E:* d.mccrone@ed.ac.uk.

**McCRONE, Robert Gavin Loudon**, CB 1983; FRSE 1983; General Secretary, Royal Society of Edinburgh, 2005–07 (Vice-President, 2002–05); Hon. Fellow, Europa Institute, University of Edinburgh, since 1992; *b* 2 Feb. 1933; *s* of Robert Osborne Orr McCrone and Laura Margaret McCrone; *m* 1st, 1959, Alexandra Bruce Waddell (*d* 1998); two *s* one *d*; 2nd, 2000, Olive Pettigrew Moon (*née* McNaught); two step *d*. *Educ:* St Catharine's Coll., Cambridge (Economics Tripos; MA); University Coll. of Wales, Aberystwyth (Milk Marketing Bd Research Schol. in agricl economics; MSc 1959); Univ. of Glasgow (PhD 1964). Fisons Ltd, 1959–60; Lectr in Applied Economics, Glasgow Univ., 1960–65; Economic Consultant to UNESCO, 1964; Fellow of Brasenose Coll., Oxford, 1965–72; Mem. NEDC Working Party on Agricl Policy, 1967–68; Economic Adviser to House of Commons Select Cttee on Scottish Affairs, 1969–70; Special Economic Adviser to Sec. of State for Local Govt and Regional Planning, 1970; Head of Econs and Statistics Unit, 1970–72, Under-Sec. for Regional Develt, 1972–80, Chief Econ. Advr, 1972–92, Scottish Office; Secretary: Industry Dept for Scotland, 1980–87; Scottish Office Envmt Dept (formerly Scottish Develt Dept), 1987–92. Prof. of Economics, Centre for Housing Res., Glasgow Univ., 1992–94; Vis. Prof., Dept of Business Studies, later Mgt Sch., Edinburgh Univ., 1994–2005. Member: Adv. Cttee, Constitution Unit (formerly Inquiry into Implementation of Constitutional Reform), 1995–97; Steering Gp for Review of Resource Allocation for NHS in Scotland (Arbuthnott Cttee), 1997–2000. Chm., Cttee of Inquiry into Professional Conditions of Service for Teachers' in Scotland, 1999–2000; Vice Chairman: RSE Inquiry into Foot and Mouth Disease, 2001–02; RSE Inquiry into Future of Scottish Fishing Industry, 2003–04; Chm., RSE Inquiry into the Future of Hills and Island Areas in Scotland, 2007–08. Comr, Parly Boundary Commn for Scotland, 1999–2006. Deputy Chairman: Royal Infirmary of Edinburgh NHS Trust, 1994–99; Lothian Univs Hosps NHS Trust, 1999–2001. Member, Council: Royal Economic Soc., 1977–82; Scottish Economic Soc., 1982–91; ESRC, 1986–89. Member, Board: Scottish Opera, 1992–98; Queen's Hall, Edinburgh, 1999–2002; Trustee: Scottish Opera Endowment Trust, 1999–2011; Scottish Housing Assocs Charitable Trust, 1992–93. Hon. FRSGS 1993. Hon. LLD Glasgow 1986. Bicentenary Medal, RSE, 2008. *Publications:* The Economics of Subsidising Agriculture, 1962; Scotland's Economic Progress 1951–60, 1963; Regional Policy in Britain, 1969; Scotland's Future, 1969; (with Mark Stephens) Housing Policy in Britain and Europe, 1995; European Monetary Union and Regional Development, 1997; Scottish Independence: weighing up the economics, 2013, 2nd enlarged edn 2014; contribs to various economic jls. *Recreations:* music, walking. *Address:* 11A Lauder Road, Edinburgh EH9 2EN. *T:* (0131) 667 4766. *Club:* New (Edinburgh).

**McCRORIE, Linda Esther, (Mrs Peter McCrorie);** *see* Gray, L. E.

**McCRUDDEN, Prof. (John) Christopher**, CBE 2019; DPhil, DCL; FBA 2008; Professor of Human Rights and Equality Law, Queen's University Belfast, since 2011; *b* 29 Jan. 1952; *s* of Gerard and Theodora McCrudden; *m* 1990, Caroline Mary Pannell; one *s* one *d*. *Educ:* Queen's Univ., Belfast (LLB 1974); Yale Univ. (Harkness Fellow, 1974–76; LLM 1975); MA 1980, DPhil 1981, DCL 2017, Oxon. MRIA 2018. Called to the Bar: Gray's Inn, 1996; NI, 2006; Ireland, 2019; non-resident Tenant, Blackstone Chambers, 2009–. University of Oxford: Lectr in Law, 1976–77, Jun. Res. Fellow, 1976–80, Balliol Coll.; CUF Lectr, 1980–96; Fellow, Lincoln Coll., 1980–2011; Reader in Law, 1996–99; Prof. of Human Rights Law, 1999–2011. Visiting Professor: QUB, 1994–98; Univ. of Texas Sch. of Law, 1996; Univ. of Haifa, 1996; Univ. of Michigan Law Sch., 1998–2009; Univ. of Oxford, 2011–14; Vis. Sen. Fellow, PSI, 1987–89; Vis. Fellow and Lectr, Yale Law Sch., 1986; William W. Cook Global Law Prof., Univ. of Michigan Law Sch., 2009–; Leverhulme Maj. Res. Fellow, 2011–14; Jt Straus/Sen. Emile Noël Fellow, Straus Inst. for Advanced Study of Law and Justice, 2013–14, Vis. Fellow, Center for Constitutional Transitions, 2013–14, NYU; Fellow, 2014–15, Chm., Adv. Cttee, 2017–, Wissenschaftskolleg zu Berlin. Mem., NI Judicial Studies Bd, 2019–. Member: Sec. of State for NI's Standing Adv. Commn on Human Rights, 1984–88; Expert Network on Application of Equality Directives, EC, 1986–; NI Procurement Bd, 2003–08; Brexit Stakeholders Gp, 2017–, Cttee on Human Rights, 2019–, Dept of Foreign Affairs, Ireland; Specialist Advr, NI Affairs Select Cttee, H of C, 1999; Mem., Public Procurement Implementation Gp, NI Exec., 2001. Mem., Adv. Cttee, ESRC Res. Unit on Ethnic Relns, 1982–85. Jt Ed., Law in Context series, 1978–2018; Member, Editorial Board: Oxford Jl Legal Studies, 1983–; Internat. Jl Discrimination and the Law, 1996–; Jl Internat. Econ. Law, 1998–2015; European Public Law, 2003–. Hon. LLD QUB, 2006. *Publications:* (with R. Baldwin) Regulation and Public Law, 1987; (ed) Women, Employment and European Community Law, 1988; (ed) Fair Employment Handbook, 1990, 3rd edn 1995; (jtly) Racial Justice at Work: the enforcement of the Race Relations Act 1976 in employment, 1991; Equality in Law between Men and Women in the European Community: United Kingdom, 1994; (ed with G. Chambers) Individual Rights and the Law in Britain, 1994; (ed) Equality between Women and Men in Social Security, 1994; (ed) Regulation and Deregulation, 1998; Buying Social Justice, 2007 (Cert. of Merit, Amer. Soc. of Internat. Law, 2008); (with B. O'Leary) Courts and Consociations, 2013; (ed) Understanding Human Dignity, 2013; (ed jtly) Reasoning Rights, 2014; (ed jtly) Law's Ethical, Global and Theoretical Contexts, 2015; Litigating Religions, 2018. *Recreation:* my family. *Address:* School of Law, Queen's University Belfast, 27–30 University Square, Belfast BT7 1NN. *T:* (028) 9097 3339.

**McCRUM, (John) Robert;** writer; Associate Editor, The Observer, 2008–18; *b* 7 July 1953; *s* of late Michael William McCrum, CBE, and of Christine Mary Kathleen (*née* fforde); *m* 1st, 1979, Olivia Timbs (marr. diss. 1984); 2nd, 1995, Sarah Lyall; two *d*. *Educ:* Sherborne Sch.; Corpus Christi Coll., Cambridge (Schol.; BA 1st Cl. Hons Hist.; MA); Univ. of Pennsylvania (Thouron Fellow; MA); PhD Cantab 2012. House Reader, Chatto & Windus, 1977–79; Faber and Faber Ltd: Editl Dir, 1979–89; Editor-in-Chief, 1990–96; Literary Ed., The Observer, 1996–2008. Scriptwriter and co-producer, The Story of English, BBC TV, 1980–86. Patron, Different Strokes, 2000–. Chair, Norwich Writer's Centre, 2009–12. By-Fellow, Churchill Coll., Cambridge, 2001–03; Beckett Fellow, Reading Univ., 2018–19. Hon. DLitt: Heriot-Watt, 2011; Exeter, 2018. Tony Godwin Prize, 1979; Peabody Award, 1986; Emmy Award, 1987. *Publications:* In the Secret State, 1980; A Loss of Heart, 1982; The Fabulous Englishman, 1984; The Story of English, 1986; The World is a Banana, 1988; Mainland, 1991; The Psychological Moment, 1993; Suspicion, 1996; My Year Off, 1998; Wodehouse: a life, 2004; Globish: how the English language became the world's language, 2010; The 100 Best Novels, 2015; Every Third Thought, 2017. *Recreations:* music and dance. *Address:* 15 Bracknell Gardens, NW3 7EE. *Club:* Groucho.

**McCUBBIN, Henry Bell;** Joint Editor, Scottish Left Review, 2000–15; *b* 15 July 1942; *s* of Henry McCubbin and Agnes (*née* Rankine); *m* 1967, Katie M. Campbell; three *d*. *Educ:* Allan Glen's Sch., Glasgow; BA Hons Open Univ. Film Cameraman: BBC TV, 1960–77; Grampian TV, 1977–89. MEP (Lab) Scotland NE, 1989–94; contested (Lab) Scotland NE, Eur. Parly elecns, 1994. Head, European Office, Assoc. of Gtr Manchester Authorities, 1996–99. *Recreations:* theatre, hill walking, politics.

**McCUE, Jason Daniel;** Senior Partner, McCue and Partners LLP, since 2011; *b* Warrington, 4 June 1969; *s* of Terrence McCue and Janet McCue; *m* 2003, Mariella Frostrup, *qv*; one *s* one *d*. *Educ:* Stockton Heath Secondary Sch.; Queen Mary Coll., Univ. of London (LLB 1990); Coll. of Law. Admitted solicitor, 1992; Mishcon de Reya, 1991–96; Co-founder and Sen. Partner, H2O Law LLP, 1997–2011. Dir, Rigel Ltd, 2016–. Advr on law, human rights, peace process, transitional justice, conflict resolution, counter terrorism, state building, asset recovery, crisis mgt and private/public/foreign affairs to internat. leaders, govts, political parties, business orgns and NGOs, 1993–; business, develt, security and investment interests and experience in Africa and Middle E. Humanitarian campaigner: Chm., Adv. Council, Crisis Action, 2007–; Ambassador for Femmes Africa Solidarité, 2007–; Mandate Darfur, 2008–09; Communications Bd, Oxfam, 2009–10; Dir, The GREAT Initiative (formerly FAST Foundn), 2010–; Hd (non govt) liaison with FCO Libyan Reconciliation and Co-ordination Team, 2009–; UN facilitator to Sudan Peace Process, 2011–12; Special Envoy to Govt of Somaliland, 2013. Hon. LLD Chester, 2011. UK Solicitor of the Year Private Practice, Law Soc., 2009. *Recreations:* family, travelling, gardening, fishing, shooting, fires. *Address:* c/o McCue and Partners LLP, 4th Floor, 158 Buckingham Palace Road, SW1W 9TR. *E:* jason.mccue@mccue-law.com.

**McCUE, Mariella;** *see* Frostrup, M.

**McCULLAGH, Keith Graham**, PhD; non-executive Chairman: Xention Pharma (formerly Xention) Ltd, 2008–10 and since 2016 (Executive Chairman, 2010–16); Torpedo Factory (formerly Phenomenon) Group Ltd, since 1999; Ario Pharma (formerly Provesica) Ltd, since 2010; Metrion Biosciences Ltd, since 2015; *b* 30 Nov. 1943; *s* of John Charles McCullagh and Kathleen Doreen McCullagh (*née* Milne); *m* 1967, Jean Elizabeth Milne; one *s* two *d*. *Educ:* Latymer Upper Sch.; Univ. of Bristol (BVSc 1965); St John's Coll., Cambridge (PhD 1970). MRCVS 1965. Royal Soc. Leverhulme Schol., 1966; Medical Research Council: Mem., External Staff, Uganda, 1967; Mem., Scientific Staff, Dunn Nutrition Lab., Cambridge, 1967–69; Cleveland Clinic Foundation, USA: Res. Fellow, 1970; Mem., Res. Staff, 1971–73; Lectr in Veterinary Pathol., Univ. of Bristol, 1974–80; G. D. Searle & Co. Ltd: Dir of Biol., 1980–84; Dir of Res., 1984–86; Founder and Chief Exec., British Biotech plc, 1986–98; Pres. and Chief Exec., Santaris Pharma A/S, 2004–08. Chm., Action Medical Research, 2007–09; Director: MVM Ltd (formerly Medical Ventures Management Ltd), 1998–2005 (Mem., Investment Cttee, MVM LLC, 2006–10); Isis Innovation Ltd, 1998–99; Pharmacy2U Ltd, 2012– (non-exec. Chm., 2000–12); Taconic Biosciences Inc. (formerly Taconic Farms Inc.), 2013–15. Non-executive Chairman: Affitech A/S, 2008–10 (Vice Chm., 2010–); Clavis Pharma ASA, 2009–10. Chm., HM Treasury Wkg Gp on Financing of High Technol. Businesses, 1998; Mem., DTI Adv. Gp on Competitiveness and the Single Mkt, 1997–98. Chm., BioIndustry Assoc., 1993–96. Vice Chm., European Assoc. of BioIndustries, 1996–98. Chm., British Admiral's Cup Sailing Team, 1999. *Publications:* numerous scientific articles and reviews in learned jls. *Recreations:* visiting grandchildren in California, New Zealand and the UK, playing many sports poorly, forestry, building companies. *Address:* Cuddington Mill, Cuddington, Bucks HP18 0BP. *E:* keith.mccullagh@btinternet.com. *Clubs:* Royal Automobile; Ellesborough Golf (Aylesbury); Royal Ocean Racing (Cowes and London); Cowes Corinthian Yacht.

**McCULLAGH, Prof. Peter**, PhD; FRS 1994; John D. MacArthur Distinguished Service Professor, Department of Statistics, University of Chicago, since 2003; *b* N Ireland, 8 Jan. 1952; *s* of John A. McCullagh and Rita McCullagh (*née* Devlin); *m* 1977, Rosa Bogues; one *s* three *d*. *Educ:* Univ. of Birmingham (BSc 1974); Imperial Coll., London (PhD 1977). Vis. Asst Prof., Univ. of Chicago, 1977–79; Lectr, Imperial Coll., London Univ., 1979–85; Prof., 1985–, Chm., 1992–98, Dept of Stats, Univ. of Chicago. FIMS, FAAAS. President's

Award, Cttee of Presidents of Statistical Socs of N Amer., 1990. *Publications:* Generalized Linear Models (with J. A. Nelder), 1983, 2nd edn 1989; Tensor Methods in Statistics, 1987. *Recreation:* swimming. *Address:* Department of Statistics, University of Chicago, 5734 South University Avenue, Chicago, IL 60637, USA. *T:* (312) 7028340.

**McCULLIN, Sir Donald,** Kt 2017; CBE 1993; freelance photojournalist; *b* 9 Oct. 1935; *m* 1959 (marr. diss. 1987); two *s* one *d*; one *s* by Laraine Ashton; *m* 1995, Marilyn Bridges; *m* 2002, Catherine, *er d* of Sir Patrick Fairweather, *qv*; one *s*. *Educ:* Tollington Park Secondary Sch., Morden; Hammersmith Jun. Art Sch. Started work at 15 yrs of age after death of father; National Service (RAF), 1954–56; first pictures published by The Observer, 1958; thereafter began photographic career; worked for The Sunday Times for 18 yrs, covering wars, revolutions and travel stories. *Exhibitions* include: V&A, 1982; Maison de la Photographie, Paris, 2004; Shaped by War, Imperial War Mus. North, 2010; Tate Britain, 2011, (retrospective) 2019; Conflict-People-Landscape, Hauser & Wirth, Somerset, 2015; Rencontres D'Arles, 2016. Master of Photography, Photo London 2016. Hon. Fellow, Hereford Coll. of Arts, 2009. Hon. FRPS 1977. DUniv: Bradford, 1993; Open, 1994; Hon. DA: Lincoln, 2005; Bath, 2011; Hon. LittD Glos, 2008. *Publications:* Destruction Business, 1971; Is Anyone Taking Any Notice, 1971; The Palestinians, 1979; Homecoming, 1979; Hearts of Darkness, 1980; Battle Beirut, a City in Crisis, 1983; Perspectives, 1987; Skulduggery, 1987; Open Skies, 1989; (with Lewis Chester) Unreasonable Behaviour (autobiog.), 1990; Sleeping with Ghosts, 1995; India, 1999; Don McCullin, 2001; Cold Heaven; Don McCullin on AIDS in Africa, 2001; In England, 2007; Shaped by War, 2010; Southern Frontiers, 2010; Irreconcilable Truths, 3 vols, 2016. *Recreations:* protecting the English countryside, travelling the world, blackberry picking, antiques.

**McCULLOCH, Alexander Patton;** Director, Ardwall Farms Ltd, since 1988; Vice Lord-Lieutenant, Stewartry of Kirkcudbright (Dumfries and Galloway), since 2015; *b* Edinburgh, 10 May 1946; *s* of Walter Jameson McCulloch and Katharine Harriet McCulloch (née Inglis); *m* 1980, Fiona Margaret Gillespie; two *s* two *d*. *Educ:* Loretto Sch., Musselburgh; West of Scotland Agricl Coll. (Scottish DipAgr). Agriculture, 1968–. Pres., Assoc. of Scottish Philatelic Socs, 2011–12; Mem., Royal Philatelic Soc. of London. DL Stewartry of Kirkcudbright (Dumfries and Galloway), 2012. *Recreations:* philately, hiking, cycling, golf. *Address:* Ardwall, Gatehouse of Fleet, Castle Douglas DG7 2EN. *T:* (01557) 814553.

**McCULLOCH, Andrew Grant;** Sheriff of Tayside, Central and Fife at Kirkcaldy, since 2008; Appeal Sheriff, Sheriff Appeal Court, since 2017; President, Law Society of Scotland, 1996–97; *b* 10 Feb. 1952; *s* of late Frederick McCulloch and of Jean McCulloch (later McGregor); *m* 1988, Mave Curran; one *s* one *d*. *Educ:* Glasgow Acad.; Edinburgh Univ. (LLB, BSc SocSci). Joined Drummond & Co., Edinburgh, 1974; Partner, Drummond Miller, WS, 1979–2004; Solicitor-Advocate, 1994. Part-time Sheriff, 2003–04; Sheriff of Tayside, Central and Fife at Dundee, 2004–08. *Recreations:* golf, opera, wine. *Address:* Bracarmi, Cammo Parkway, Edinburgh EH4 8EP.

**McCULLOCH, Dr Andrew William;** Director, McCulloch and Muijen Associates, since 2017; *b* 21 April 1956; *s* of Ian Robert McCulloch and Marguerite Elizabeth McCulloch; partner, Louise Villeneau; one *s* one *d*. *Educ:* Eltham Coll.; Peterhouse, Cambridge (BA Natural Scis 1978); Univ. of Southampton (PhD Psychol. 1986). Principal, 1987–92, Asst Sec., 1992–96, DoH; Dir of Policy, Sainsbury Centre for Mental Health, 1996–2001; Chief Executive: Mental Health Foundn, 2002–13; Picker Inst. Europe, 2013–17. Non-exec. Dir, Haringey Healthcare NHS Trust, 1998–2001. Chair: Mental Health Media, 1999–2002; Children and Young People's Mental Health Coalition, 2009–10; Future Visions Alliance, 2009–13; Mem., Public Health Bd, NIHR, 2011–12; non-exec. Dir, Social Work England, 2018–. Chair, GMC Services Internat., 2017–. Member: Workforce Numbers Adv. Bd, DoH, 2002–04; Ministerial Adv. Gp on Vulnerable Children, 2004–05; Ministerial Adv. Gp on Mental Health, 2007–09 and 2011–13; Expert Advr to Council of Europe, 2007–08. Dir, HM Govt, 2018. Mem. Bd, Healthwatch England, 2018–; Trustee: UK Council for Psychotherapy, 2009–12; Future Care Capital, 2016–18. Patron, Healthy Minds: Calderdale Wellbeing, 2013–; Vice Patron, Family Action, 2015–. President's Medal, RCPsych, 2011. *Publications:* (contrib.) Developing a National Mental Health Policy (Maudsley monograph), 2002; numerous articles on gerontology and on mental health. *Recreations:* birdwatching, reading, wine, cinema, Italy, dining, art.

**MacCULLOCH, Prof. Diarmaid Ninian John,** Kt 2012; DD; FBA 2001; FSA, FRHistS; Professor of the History of the Church, University of Oxford, 1997–2019, now Emeritus; Fellow, St Cross College, Oxford, 1995–2019, now Emeritus; *b* 31 Oct. 1951; *s* of Rev. Nigel MacCulloch and Jennie (née Chappell). *Educ:* Stowmarket Grammar Sch.; Churchill Coll., Cambridge (MA, PhD 1977); Univ. of Liverpool (Dip. Archive Admin 1973); DipTh Oxon 1987; DD Oxon 2001. FSA 1978; FRHistS 1981. Jun. Res. Fellow, Churchill Coll., Cambridge, 1976–78; Tutor in Hist., Librarian and Archivist, Wesley Coll., Bristol, 1978–90; Lectr, Faculty of Theol., Oxford Univ., 1995–; Sen. Tutor, St Cross Coll., Oxford, 1996–2000. Ordained deacon, 1987. Presenter: TV series: A History of Christianity, 2009; How God Made The English, 2012; Sex and the Church, 2015; TV documentary, Thomas Cromwell, 2013. Pres., C of E Record Soc., 2001–; Vice-Pres., British Acad., 2016–. Co-patron, No Anglican Covenant Coalition, 2012–. Co-Ed., Jl Ecclesiastical Hist., 1995–2014. Histl Project Dir, Bishop Auckland Castle Faith Heritage Exhibn, 2011–. Member: Jury, Specialist Factual, BAFTA, 2016; Judges' Panel, Wolfson History Prize, 2016–. Freeman, Barbers' Co., 2009 (Liveryman, 2012). Hon. LittD UEA, 2003; Hon. DD: Virginia Theol Seminary, 2011; Univ. of South at Sewanee, 2012; St Andrews, 2013. *Publications:* Suffolk and the Tudors: politics and religion in an English county (Whitfield Prize, RHistS), 1986; Groundwork of Christian History, 1987, rev. edn 1994; The Later Reformation in England 1547–1603, 1990, rev. edn 2000; (ed) The Reign of Henry VIII: politics, policy and piety, 1995; Thomas Cranmer: a life (Whitbread Biography Prize, Duff Cooper Prize, James Tait Black Prize), 1996; Tudor Church Militant: Edward VI and the Protestant Reformation, 1999; Reformation: Europe's house divided 1490–1700 (Wolfson History Prize, British Academy Prize, Nat. Book Critics' Circle of US Award for non-fiction), 2003; A History of Christianity: the first three thousand years, 2009 (Hessell-Tiltman Prize, Cundill Prize, 2011); Silence: a Christian history, 2013; All Things Made New: writings on the Reformation, 2016; Thomas Cromwell: a life, 2018. *Recreations:* church architecture, music. *Address:* St Cross College, Oxford OX1 3LZ. *T:* (01865) 278458. *Club:* Athenæum.

**McCULLOCH, Prof. Gary James,** PhD; Brian Simon Professor of the History of Education, Institute of Education, University College London (formerly Institute of Education, University of London), since 2003; *b* 13 March 1956; *s* of late Edward Joseph McCulloch and Vera Evelyn McCulloch (née Saunders); *m* 1984, Sarah Margaret Buyekha; one *s*. *Educ:* Caldecot Primary Sch., London; Wilson's Grammar Sch., London; Christ's Coll., Cambridge (MA, PhD History 1981). Res. Fellow, Sch. of Educn, Univ. of Leeds, 1981–83; Lectr, 1983–88, Sen. Lectr, 1988–91, in Educn, Univ. of Auckland, NZ; Prof. of Educnl Res., Lancaster Univ., 1991–94; Prof. of Educn, Univ. of Sheffield, 1994–2003; Institute of Education, University of London: Dean of Res. and Consultancy, 2004–07, Asst Dir (Res., Consultancy and Knowledge Transfer), 2007–08; Head, Dept of Humanities and Social Scis, 2012–15. Vis. Prof., Univ. of Worcester, 2019–. Member: Council, British Educnl Res. Assoc., 2012–20 (Vice-Pres., 2016–17, 2019–20; Pres., 2017–19); Exec. Cttee, Internat. Standing Conf. for History of Educn, 2012–15; Exec. Cttee, Soc. for Educnl Studies, 2014–. Pres., Hist. of Educn Soc. of GB, 2005–07 (Vice-Pres., 2002–04). Editor: History of Education, 1996–2003; British Jl of Educnl Studies, 2014–; Jt Editor, Secondary Education in a Changing World, 2003–15. FRHistS 1995; FRSA 2006; FAcSS (AcSS 2010). *Publications:* (jtly) Technological Revolution?, 1985; The Secondary Technical School, 1989; (jtly) Schooling in New Zealand, 1990; Philosophers and Kings, 1991; (ed) The School Curriculum in New Zealand, 1992; Educational Reconstruction, 1994; (ed jtly) Teachers and the National Curriculum, 1997; Failing the Ordinary Child?, 1998; (jtly) The Politics of Professionalism, 2000; (jtly) Historical Research in Educational Settings, 2000; Documentary Research in Education, History and the Social Sciences, 2004; (ed) The Routledge Falmer Reader in the History of Education, 2005; (jtly) Succeeding with your Doctorate, 2005; Cyril Norwood and the Ideal of Secondary Education, 2007; (ed jtly) Politics and Policy-Making in Education, 2007; (ed jtly) The Death of the Comprehensive High School?, 2007; (ed jtly) Routledge International Encyclopedia of Education, 2008; (ed jtly) Social Change in the History of British Education, 2008; (ed jtly) International Perspectives on Veteran Teachers, 2010; The Struggle for the History of Education, 2011; (jtly) Coming of Age?: secondary education and the school leaving age, 2013; (ed jtly) Education: war and peace, 2016; (jtly) A Social History of Educational Studies and Research, 2018; (ed) Educational Reform Legislation in the 20th Century, 2018. *Recreations:* cinema, reading, travel, walking. *Address:* UCL Institute of Education, University College London, 20 Bedford Way, WC1H 0AL.

**McCULLOCH, James Macdonald;** Chief Inquiry Reporter, 2002–09, and Director for Planning and Environmental Appeals, 2007–09, Scottish Government (formerly Scottish Executive); Principal, James McCulloch Consulting, 2009–14; *b* Dec. 1948; *s* of Thomas and Jane McCulloch; *m* 1992, Jennifer Hay; three *s*. *Educ:* Hardye's Sch., Dorchester; Lanchester Polytechnic, Coventry (BA Hons Urban & Regl Planning). MRTPI 1973–2016. Planning Asst, Coventry Corp., 1971–73; Sen. Planner, then Prin. Planner, Scottish Develt Dept, 1973–84; Inquiry Reporter, then Prin. Reporter, subseq. Dep. Chief Reporter, Scottish Executive (formerly Scottish Office) Inquiry Reporters' Unit, 1984–2002. Mem., Specialist Accreditation Panel for Planning Practitioners, Law Soc. of Scotland, 2009–14. *Recreations:* walking, travel, eating, the people and landscapes of Spain, motorcycling, dry-stone walling, contemplation, mostly futile. *E:* james.mcculloch100@gmail.com.

**McCULLOCH, James Rae,** OBE 2001; HM Diplomatic Service, retired; Ambassador to Iceland, 1996–2000; *b* 29 Nov. 1940; *s* of William McCulloch and Catherine (née Rae); *m* 1965, Margaret Anderson; two *s*. *Educ:* Ardrossan Acad. Joined FO, 1958; Bamako, Mali, 1962; NY, 1964; Lusaka, 1967; FCO 1969; Algiers, 1972; Kabul, 1973; Second Sec., FCO, 1977; Luanda, 1980; Second, subseq. First Sec. (Commercial), Bangkok, 1982; First Sec., UKMIS to UN, Geneva, 1986; FCO, 1990; Dep. Hd of Mission, Hanoi, 1992–96.

**MacCULLOCH, Prof. Malcolm John,** MD; FRCPsych; Emeritus Professor, Wales College of Medicine, Biology, Health and Life Sciences, Cardiff University (Professor of Forensic Psychiatry, University of Wales College of Medicine, and Hon. Consultant Forensic Psychiatrist, Caswell Clinic, Bridgend & District NHS Trust, 1997–2001); *b* 10 July 1936; *s* of William MacCulloch and Constance Martha MacCulloch; *m* 1962, Mary Louise Beton (marr. diss. 1975); one *s* one *d*; *m* 1975, Carolyn Mary Reid; two *d*. *Educ:* King Edward VI Sch., Macclesfield, Cheshire; Manchester Univ. (MB, ChB, DPM, MD). Consultant Child Psychiatrist, Cheshire Child Guidance Service, 1966–67; Director Univ. Dept, Child Psychiatry and Subnormality, Birmingham Univ., 1967–70; Sen. Lectr, Adult Psychiatry, Univ. of Liverpool, 1970–75; PMO, DHSS, 1975–78; SPMO, Mental Health Div., DHSS, 1979–80; Dir, Special Hosps Res. Unit, London, 1979–86; Med. Dir, Park Lane Hosp., Liverpool, 1979–89; Res. Psychiatrist, Ashworth Hosp., Merseyside, 1990–93. Advr to Ontario Govt on Forensic Psychiatric Services, 1988–92. Vis. Prof., Clarke Inst. of Psychiatry, Toronto, 1987–88. Ed.-in-Chief, Jl of Forensic Psychiatry and Psychology, 2002–07. *Publications:* Homosexual Behaviour: therapy and assessment, 1971; Human Sexual Behaviour, 1980; numerous med. papers on aspects of psychiatry and forensic psychiatry. *Recreations:* cars, inventing, playing music. *Address:* 31 Polo Drive, Lime Tree Village, Dunchurch, Rugby CV22 7YW.

**McCULLOCH, Prof. Malcolm Thomas,** PhD; FRS 2010; FAA; Professor, School of Earth and Environment, Premier's Research Fellow and Deputy Director, ARC Centre of Excellence for Coral Reef Studies, since 2009, University of Western Australia; *b* Collie, WA, 9 Sept. 1950. *Educ:* Western Australia Inst. of Technol. (BAppSc; MAppSc); Calif Inst. of Technol. (PhD). Trainee teacher, WA, 1968–72; Teacher of Sci., Governor Stirling Sen. High Sch., WA, 1972; Sen. Tutor, Physics Dept, WA Inst. of Technol., 1972–74; Grad. Res. Asst, Div. of Geol. and Planetary Scis, CIT, 1974–80; Research School of Earth Sciences, Australian National University: Res. Fellow, 1980–83; Fellow, 1983–90; Sen. Fellow, 1990–96; Prof. and Hd, Envmt Geochem. and Geochronol. Res., 1996–2009. FAA 2004; Fellow: Amer. Geophysical Union, 2002; Geol Soc. of Australia, 2007; Geochem. Soc., 2008. Jaeger Medal, Australian Acad. Scis, 2009. *Publications:* contribs to scientific jls incl. Science, Nature. *Address:* School of Earth and Environment, University of Western Australia, 35 Stirling Highway, Crawley, WA 6009, Australia.

**McCULLOCH, Margaret;** Member (Lab) Scotland Central, Scottish Parliament, 2011–16; *b* Glasgow, 9 May 1952; *d* of Joseph Gorman and Margaret Gorman; *m* 1994, Ian McCulloch; two *s*. *Educ:* Holyrood Sen. Secondary Sch.; South Lanarkshire Coll. (HNC IT); Glasgow Caledonian Univ. (Post Grad. Cert. Electronic Business). Trng Exec., Univ. of Strathclyde, 1992–2009; owner, ITC, 2009–10; Dir, Independent Training Consultants Ltd, 2010–11. Contested (Lab) Hamilton, Larkhall and Stonehouse, Scottish Parlt, 2016. *Recreations:* family, socialising with family and friends, reading, gardening.

**McCULLOCH, Michael Cutler;** Member, Investment Committee, Europolis AG (formerly Europolis Invest), 2002–11; *b* 24 April 1943; *s* of late Ian James McCulloch and Elsie Margaret Chadwick; *m* 1st, 1968, Melody Lawrence (marr. diss. 1975); 2nd, 1975, Robin Lee Sussman; two *d*. *Educ:* Prince of Wales Sch., Nairobi; Clare Coll., Cambridge (BA History 1964; MA 2004); Yale Univ. (Mellon Fellow, 1964–66; MA Internat. Relations 1967). ODM, Asst Principal, 1969; Asst Private Sec. to Minister for Overseas Develt, 1972–73, Principal, 1973, ODA; First Sec. (Aid), Dhaka, FCO, 1976–78; Resident Observer, CSSB, 1978–79; Overseas Development Administration: Rayner Scrutiny and Mgt Review Team, 1979–80; E Africa Dept, 1980–83; EC Dept, 1983–84; Principal Private Sec. to Minister for Overseas Develt, 1984–85; Asst Sec., 1985; Head: Evaluation Dept, 1985–86; British Develt Div. in E Africa, 1986–89; Finance Dept, 1990–92; Know How Fund for former Soviet Union, FCO, 1992–97; UK Exec. Dir, 1997–2001, Advr to the Pres., 2003–04, EBRD. Trustee: BBC World Service Trust, 2001–11; British Consultancy Charitable Trust, 2006–11; BBC Media Action, 2011–13; Internat. Union for Conservation of Nature UK, 2015–; Chairman of Trustees: BEARR Trust, 2003–08 (Trustee, 2001–08); Riders for Health, 2003–10 (Trustee, 2001–13). Pres., Bishopsgate Ward Club, 2012–13. Co-Chair, Bledington Community Shop Ltd, 2015–. Gov.,

Bledington Primary Sch., 2008–13. FRSA 1995. *Recreations:* Baroque to Romantic classical music, African wildlife and photography, walking, garden design. *Address:* New Oak Barn, The Green, Bledington, Chipping Norton OX7 6XQ. *T:* (01608) 658941. *E:* mcmcculloch@btinternet.com. *Club:* Lansdowne.

**McCULLOCH, Rt Rev. Nigel Simeon,** KCVO 2013; Lord High Almoner to the Queen, 1997–2013; Bishop of Manchester, 2002–13; an Honorary Assistant Bishop, Diocese of Carlisle, since 2013; *b* 17 Jan. 1942; *s* of late Pilot Officer Kenneth McCulloch, RAFVR, and of Audrey Muriel McCulloch; *m* 1974, Celia Hume Townshend, *d* of Canon H. L. H. Townshend; two *d. Educ:* Liverpool College; Selwyn Coll., Cambridge (Kitchener Schol., BA 1964, MA 1969); Cuddesdon Coll., Oxford. Ordained, 1966; Curate of Ellesmere Port, 1966–70; Chaplain of Christ's Coll., Cambridge, 1970–73; Director of Theological Studies, Christ's Coll., Cambridge, 1970–75; permission to officiate, Dio. of Liverpool, 1970–73; Diocesan Missioner for Norwich Diocese, 1973–78; Rector of St Thomas' and St Edmund's, Salisbury, 1978–86; Archdeacon of Sarum, 1979–86; Bishop Suffragan of Taunton, 1986–92; Bishop of Wakefield, 1992–2002. Prebendary of Ogbourne, Salisbury Cathedral, 1979–86, of Wanstrow, Wells Cathedral, 1986–92; Canon Emeritus of Salisbury Cathedral, 1989. Took his seat in H of L, 1997; Mem., H of L Select Cttee, on BBC Charter Review, 2005–06, on Communications, 2007–10. Mem., House of Bishops, Gen. Synod of C of E, 1990–2013. Chairman: Finance Cttee, ACCM, 1988–92; Decade of Evangelism Steering Gp, 1989–96; C of E Communications Unit, 1993–2011; C of E Mission, Evangelism and Renewal Cttee, 1996–99; Gen. Synod Legislation Gp on Women Bishops, 2006–12; CCJ, 2006–15. Chaplain to Council of St John: Somerset, 1987–92; SW Yorks, 1992–2002; Greater Manchester, 2009–13; Hon. Nat. Chaplain, 2001–15, Hd of Remembrance, 2015–17, RBL. Chairman: Sandford St Martin Trust, 1999–2008; Greater Manchester Poverty Commn, 2011–13. Member, Council: Marlborough Coll., 1984–91; RSCM, 1984–2007. Chm., Somerset County Scout Assoc., 1988–92; Pres., Central Yorks Scouts, 1992–2002. President: Somerset Rural Music Sch., 1986–92; St Anne's Hospice, Gtr Manchester, 2003–13; Selwyn Coll. Cambridge Alumni Assoc., 2015–16. Governor: King's Bruton, 1988–91; Bolton Univ., 2008– (Chm., Bd of Govs, 2013–). Hon. Vice-Pres., Brighouse and Rastrick Band, 1993–. Hon. Canon, Mara Cathedral, Tanzania, 1996–. Hon. DCL Huddersfield, 2003; Hon. DLitt Salford, 2013; Hon. DEd Manchester Metropolitan, 2013. OStJ 2012; Knight of St Hadrian 2013. Alan Turing Meml Award, Lesbian and Gay Foundn, 2013. *Publications:* A Gospel to Proclaim, 1992; Barriers to Belief, 1994; Broadcasting - a service?, 2007. *Recreations:* music, brass bands, walking in the Lake District. *Address:* Stonelea, 1 Heads Drive, Grange-Over-Sands LA11 7DY.

**McCULLOUGH, Angus Maxwell Thomas;** QC 2010; *b* 14 July 1966; *s* of Sir (Iain) Charles (Robert) McCullough and of Margaret Joyce McCullough; *m* 2002, Sarah Barclay; one *s* one *d. Educ:* Pembroke Coll., Oxford (BA Zool. 1987; MA). Pres., Oxford Union, Michaelmas, 1986. Safari guide, Zambia, 1987–88, 1990; called to the Bar: Middle Temple, 1990 (Harmsworth Entrance Exhibnr, 1989; Inns of Ct Studentship, 1989), Bencher, 2016; NI, 2016; Treasury Counsel (Civil), 1997–2010; Special Advocate in nat. security cases, 2003–; Arbitrator, Personal Injury and Clinical Negligence Arbitration Service, 2016–. Trustee: Kasanka Trust, 1999–; Barristers' Benevolent Assoc., 2009–; Internat. Trust for Zool Nomenclature, 2003–14; Buglife, 2010–. FLS 2011. *Publications:* (contrib.) Burnett-Hall on Environmental Law, 2nd edn 2009, 3rd edn 2012; contrib. papers on entomology (hoverflies and butterflies). *Address:* 1 Crown Office Row, Temple, EC4Y 7HH.

**McCULLOUGH, (David) Mark;** Principal, Rainey Endowed School, since 2012; *b* Ballymena, Co. Antrim, 2 March 1975; *s* of Stewart and Mary McCullough; *m* 2000, Cara; five *s* one *d. Educ:* Cambridge House Boys' Grammar Sch.; Queen's Univ., Belfast (BA 1st Cl. Hons French/Hist.; PGCE Modern Langs); Homerton Coll., Cambridge (Cert. Professional Studies 2005). Teacher of Modern Foreign Langs and Hist., St Michael's Sch., Watford, 1998–2001; Hd of Year, Asst Principal, Actg Principal and Hd of Sch., Samuel Ward Acad., 2001–12. *Recreations:* cinema, walking, family time, travel, school governor (primary). *Address:* Rainey Endowed School, 79 Rainey Street, Magherafelt, Co. Derry BT45 5DB. *E:* mmccullough028@c2kschools.net.

**McCULLY, Andrew John,** CB 2019; OBE 2001; Director General, Early Years and Schools, Department for Education, since 2018; *b* 14 Nov. 1963; *s* of John McCully and Lilian McCully; partner, Nicholas Howard. *Educ:* Birkenhead Sch.; Worcester Coll., Oxford (BA Hons 1986). Joined Dept of Employment as Admin. Trainee, 1986; Department for Education and Employment: Sec. to New Deal Task Force, 1997–99; Manager, Learning and Skills Bill, 1999–2000; Dep. Dir, Children and Young People's Unit, 2000–02; Divl Manager, Pupil Standards Div., DFES, 2002–04; Dir, Sch. Standards Gp, DFES, subseq. DCSF, 2004–08; Dir, Supporting Children and Young People Gp, DCSF, subseq. DFE, 2008–10; Department for Education: Dir, Academies Delivery Gp, 2010–11; Acting Dir Gen., Sch. Infrastructure and Funding Directorate, 2011–13; Dir Gen., Infrastructure and Funding Directorate, 2013–18. *Recreations:* listening to music, shopping for, cooking and eating food. *Address:* 26 Carysfort Road, N16 9AL. *T:* (020) 7254 0639. *E:* andrew.mccully@education.gov.uk.

**McCURDY, Ven. Hugh Kyle;** Archdeacon of Huntingdon and Wisbech, since 2005; *b* 9 March 1958; *s* of William Eric McCurdy and Elenor Anne McCurdy; *m* 1984, Ruth Searle; one *s* two *d. Educ:* Portsmouth Poly. (BA Econs 1980); Trinity Coll., Bristol (DipHE 1983); Univ. of Wales (PGCE 1984). Ordained deacon, 1985, priest, 1986; Curate: St John's, Egham, 1985–88; St John's, Woking, 1988–91; Vicar, St Andrew's, Histon, 1991–2005; Priest-in-charge, St Andrew's, Impington, 1998–2005; RD N Stowe, 1994–2005. Hon. Canon, Ely Cathedral, 2004–. Mem., Gen. Synod of C of E, 2010–. Mem. Council, Ridley Hall Cambridge, 2003–; Gov., Wisbech Grammar Sch. 2006–. Trustee: Cambridgeshire ACRE, 2007–; Beds and Cambs Rural Support Gp, 2012–. Pres., Huntingdon Soc. for the Blind, 2013–. *Recreations:* eating, laughing, Dr Who, cycling, travel, family. *Address:* Whitgift House, The College, Ely, Cambs CB7 4DL. *E:* archdeacon.handw@elydiocese.org.

**McCURLEY, Anna Anderson;** freelance communications consultant; Partner, Hamilton Anderson Solutions; *b* 18 Jan. 1943; *d* of George Gemmell and Mary (*née* Anderson); *m* (marr. diss.), one *d. Educ:* Glasgow High Sch. for Girls; Glasgow Univ. (MA); Jordanhill Coll. of Educn (Dip. in Secondary Educn); Strathclyde Univ. Secondary history teacher, 1966–72; College Methods Tutor, Jordanhill Coll. of Educn, 1972–74. Strathclyde Regional Councillor, Camphill/Pollokshaws Div., 1978–82. Sen. Exec., Dewe Rogerson, 1987–89; Head of Govt Affairs, Corporate Communications Strategy, 1990–92. Contested: (C) Renfrew W and Inverclyde, 1987; (Scottish Lib Dem) Eastwood, Scottish Parlt, 1999. MP (C) Renfrew W and Inverclyde, 1983–87. Mem., Scottish Select Cttee, 1984–87. Mem., Horserace Betting Levy Bd, 1988–97. Trustee, Nat. Galleries of Scotland, 1996–99. *Recreations:* music, cookery, cats.

**McCUSKER, Malcolm James,** AC 2012 (AO 2005); CVO 2011; QC 1982; Governor of Western Australia, 2011–14; *b* Perth, WA, 6 Aug. 1938; *s* of Sir James Alexander McCusker and Mary Martindale McCusker; *m* 2006, Tonya Batalin; one *d* and two step *s*; one *s* and two *d* from previous marriage. *Educ:* Perth Modern Sch.; Hobart High Sch.; Univ. of Western Australia (LLB). Admitted to practice, 1961; in practice as barrister, 1961–2019. Chairman: Legal Aid Commn of WA, 1984–2011; Adv. Bd, WA Constitutional Centre, 1997–2011; Parly Inspector, Corruption and Crime Commn of WA, 2004–08; Ministerial Expert Panel on Voluntary Assisted Dying, 2018–19; Law Access, 2018–19; WA Health Translation Network, 2016–19. Hon. LLD WA, 2008; DUniv: Edith Cowan, 2009; Curtin, 2015; Hon. LLD Murdoch, 2011. Civil Justice Award, Australian Lawyers' Alliance, 2007; Australian of Year, WA, 2010. *Recreations:* surf ski, farming, reading, family. *Address:* Level 3, 45 St George's Terrace, Perth, WA 6000, Australia. *T:* (8) 93232222. *E:* mccuskerqc@iinet.net.au. *Club:* North Cottesloe Surf Lifesaving.

**McCUTCHEON, Alison;** see Allden, A.

**McCUTCHEON, Prof. John Joseph,** CBE 1994; PhD, DSc; FFA; FRSE; Professor of Actuarial Studies, Heriot-Watt University, 1975–2001; *b* 10 Sept. 1940; *s* of James Thomson McCutcheon and Margaret (*née* Hutchison); *m* 1978, Jean Sylvia Constable. *Educ:* Glasgow Acad.; St John's Coll., Cambridge (schol.; Wright's Prize, 1960, 1962; MA 1966); Univ. of Liverpool (PhD 1969, DSc 1990). FFA 1965. Scottish Amicable Life Assce Soc., 1962–65; Consulting Actuary, Duncan C. Fraser and Co., 1965–66; Demonstrator, then Sen. Demonstrator in Pure Maths, Univ. of Liverpool, 1966–70; Associate Prof., Univ. of Manitoba, 1970–72; Heriot-Watt University: Sen. Lectr, 1972–75; Dean, Faculty of Science, 1995–98. Pres., Faculty of Actuaries in Scotland, 1992–94. FRSE 1993. *Publications:* (with W. F. Scott) An Introduction to the Mathematics of Finance, 1986; various papers on mathematics, actuarial science, mortality studies. *Recreations:* tennis, cycling, opera, reading, travel. *Address:* 14 Oswald Court, Edinburgh EH9 2HY. *T:* (0131) 667 7645. *Club:* Colinton Lawn Tennis.

**McCUTCHEON, Dr William Alan,** FSA, MRIA; archaeologist (industrial), historian (industry, technology, engineering, transport), archivist, author; Hon. Senior Research Fellow, School of Geography (formerly of Geosciences), Queen's University, Belfast, 1999–2004; *b* 2 March 1934; *s* of late William John and Margaret Elizabeth McCutcheon; *m* 1956, Margaret Craig; three *s. Educ:* Royal Belfast Academical Instn; The Queen's University of Belfast (Hugh Wisnom Scholar, 1960; BA (Hons Geog.) 1955, MA 1958, PhD 1962). FRGS (1958–94); FSA 1970; MRIA 1983. School Teacher (Geography Specialist), Royal Belfast Academical Instn, 1956–62; Director, N Ireland Survey of Industrial Archaeology, 1962–68; Keeper of Technology and Local History, Ulster Museum, Belfast, 1968–77; Dir, Ulster Museum, 1977–82; sch. teacher (geography specialist), Ditcham Park Sch., Petersfield, 1986–93. Vis. Master, Glenalmond Coll., 1984, 1986. Chairman: Historic Monuments Council (NI), 1980–85; Jt Cttee on Industrial Archaeology (NI), 1981–85; Member: Malcolm Cttee on Regional Museums in Northern Ireland, 1977–78; Industrial Archaeol. Cttee, Council for British Archaeol., 1981–85. Created major Industrial Heritage Archive, 1982 and 2010, now with NI Envmt Agency, Belfast. Lifetime Achievement Award (Silver Medal), Industrial Heritage Assoc. of Ireland, 2015. *Publications:* The Canals of the North of Ireland, 1965; Railway History in Pictures, Ireland: vol. 1 1969, vol. 2 1970; (contrib.) Travel and Transport in Ireland, 1973; (contrib.) Folk & Farm, 1976; Wheel and Spindle—Aspects of Irish Industrial History, 1977; The Industrial Archaeology of Northern Ireland, 1980 (Library Assoc. high commendation as an outstanding reference book); (contrib.) Some People and Places in Irish Science and Technology, 1985; (contrib.) An Economic and Social History of Ulster 1820–1939, 1985; numerous papers and articles. *Recreations:* reading, Schubert lieder, landscape photography, gardening. *Address:* Ardmilne, 25 Moira Drive, Bangor, Co. Down BT20 4RW. *T:* (028) 9146 5519.

**MacDAID, Most Rev. Liam Sean;** Bishop of Clogher, (RC), 2010–16, now Bishop Emeritus; *b* Dublin, 19 July 1945; *s* of William MacDaid and Mary Ellen MacDaid (*née* Kerrigan). *Educ:* St Patrick's Coll., Maynooth (BA 1965; BD 1968; HDipEd 1970; DD 2010); University Coll. Dublin (Dip. Career Guidance and Counselling 1978). Ordained priest, 1969; Tutor, Accord, Omagh, 1979–85 (Vice Pres., 2011); Pres., St Macartan's Coll., Monaghan, 1981–89; Diocese of Clogher: Diocesan Sec., 1993–2010; Chancellor, 1993–2010. Chair, Council for Marriage and the Family, 2013–16; Mem. Bd, Towards Healing, 2012–16. Chm., Council of Priests, Clogher, 1979–89; Regl Chair, Assoc. of Mgt of Catholic Secondary Schs, 1984–89. *Recreations:* swimming, cycling, walking, theatre, music. *Address:* Drumhirk, Castleblayney Road, Monaghan, H18 YE30, Ireland. *T:* (47) 82208. *E:* LSMacDaid@gmail.com.

**McDERMID, Prof. John Alexander,** OBE 2010; PhD; FREng; FIET; Professor of Software Engineering, since 1987, and Director, Lloyd's Register Foundation, Assuring Autonomy International Programme, since 2018, University of York (Head of Department of Computer Science, 2006–12 and 2016–17); *b* 5 Oct. 1952; *s* of John Alexander McDermid and Joyce Winifred McDermid (*née* Whiteley); *m* 1980, Heather Mair Denly (marr. diss. 2015); two *d. Educ:* Trinity Coll., Cambridge (BA 1975); Univ. of Birmingham (PhD 1981). CEng 1980, FIET (FIEE 1986). MoD student engr, then res. scientist, RSRE, Malvern, 1971–82; Computing Consultant, then Divl Manager, Systems Designers, 1982–87. Non-exec. Dir, High Integrity Solutions, 2002–08; Dir, Origin Consulting (York), 2003–. Mem., DSAC, 2004–10, 2011–14. FBCS 1988; FRAeS 1998; FREng 2002; FSaRS 2009. *Publications:* (with K. Ripken) Life Cycle Supporting in the Ada Environment, 1984; (ed) Integrated Project Support Environments, 1985; (ed) The Theory and Practice of Refinement, 1989; (ed and contrib.) Software Engineers Reference Book, 1991; (jtly) Software Engineering Environments, 1992; numerous articles in jls. *Recreations:* reading, music, walking, badminton. *Address:* Department of Computer Science, University of York, Deramore Lane, York YO10 5GH. *T:* (01904) 325400, *Fax:* (01904) 325699. *E:* john.mcdermid@york.ac.uk; 3 Heworth Parade, Mill Lane, York YO31 7AA. *Club:* Athenæum.

**MacDERMOT, Prof. John,** MD, PhD; FRCP, FWACP, FMedSci; Head of Undergraduate Medicine, Imperial College, London, 2002–06, now Professor Emeritus of Clinical Pharmacology; Hon. Medical Advisor (formerly Undergraduate Medical Academic Links Co-ordinator), Tropical Health and Education Trust, since 2006; International Director, Royal College of Physicians, 2008–12; Hon. Secretary, Palestine Exploration Fund, since 2016; *b* 24 March 1947; *s* of Niall and Violet MacDermot; *m* 1976, Kay Krnakova; one *d. Educ:* Imperial Coll. of Sci. and Technol.; Charing Cross Med. Sch.; Univ. of London (MD 1979); PhD Inst. of Neurology, London, 1977. FRCP 1989; FWACP 2011. Fogarty Internat. Fellow, Lab. of Biochemical Genetics, NIH, 1977–78; Wellcome Sen. Clinical Res. Fellow, RPMS, 1981–87; Professor: of Pharmacology, Univ. of Birmingham, 1987–88; of Clinical Pharmacology, RPMS, later Imperial Coll., Univ. of London, 1989–99; of Medicine and Therapeutics, ICSM, 2000–02. FMedSci 1999. *Publications:* papers on processes involved in signalling from one cell to another. *Recreation:* tour guide at British Museum (Mesopotamia). *Address:* Palestine Exploration Fund, 5–6 Dreadnought Walk, Greenwich, SE10 9FP. *E:* john@thet.org.

**MacDERMOTT, Alasdair Tormod;** HM Diplomatic Service, retired; *b* 17 Sept. 1945; *s* of late Norman MacDermott and Mary MacDermott; *m* 1st, 1966 (marr. diss. 1992); two *d*; 2nd, 1994, Gudrun Geiling. *Educ:* University Coll. Sch., Hampstead; lang. trng, SOAS, Univ. of London; Open Univ. (DipCS 2009). Entered FO, later FCO, 1966; Kabul, 1971–72; FCO, 1973; Accra, 1973–77; FCO, 1977; lang. trng, Tokyo, 1978; Second Secretary: Tokyo, 1979–82; Accra, 1982–83; Political Sec., Colombo, 1983–86; First Secretary: Press Officer, Tokyo, 1986–91; FCO, 1991–95; Turkish lang. trng, 1995;

(Commercial), Ankara, 1995–98; Southern African Dept, FCO, 1998–2002; High Comr, Namibia, 2002–07. Internat. Policy Advr, Europe, Leonard Cheshire Internat., 2008–09; Brussels Rep., Electoral Reform Services Internat., Brussels, 2010–11. Mem., Royal Union of Action and Intelligence Services, Belgium, 2018–. Recorder, British Diplomatic Oral History Prog., 2015–. Pres., SOAS Alumni Assoc., Belgium, 2010–12. *Recreations:* carving wooden sculptures, Maigret, researching WWII evasion lines from Belgium to Spain, the history of Spain. *Address:* Midgard, North Shian, Appin, Argyll PA38 4BA. *Clubs:* Royal Over-Seas League; Hill (Nuwara Eliya, Sri Lanka); Ceylon Sea Anglers (Sri Lanka).

**McDERMOTT, Gerard Francis;** QC 1999; a Deputy High Court Judge, since 2008; *b* 21 April 1956; *s* of late Joseph Herbert McDermott, BSc, and Winifred Mary McDermott (*née* Limon); *m* 1992, Fiona Johnson. *Educ:* De La Salle Coll., Salford; Manchester Univ. (LLB Hons 1977). Called to the Bar, Middle Temple, 1978, Bencher, 2005; Barrister, Manchester, 1979–; Attorney-at-Law, NY, 1990; a Recorder, 1999–2014. General Council of the Bar: Mem., 1983–88, 1990–96, 1998–99, 2003–08 and 2015–17; Chm., Internat. Relns Cttee, 1999–2000. Pres., Amer. Counsel Assoc., 2003–04; Leader, European Circuit of the Bar, 2006–08. Fellow, Amer. Bar Foundn, 2010. Presidential Citation, ABA, 2015. *Recreations:* travel, music, classic cars. *Address:* Outer Temple Chambers, 222 Strand, WC2R 1BA. *T:* (020) 7353 6381; Kings Chambers, 36 Young Street, Manchester M3 3FT. *T:* 0345 034 3444. *Club:* Athenæum.

**McDERMOTT, Jennifer;** Partner and Head of Media and Public Law, Withers LLP, 2007–13; *b* Sunderland, 1957; *d* of Stanley Keith Harding and Elizabeth Harding; *m* 1983, Thomas Francis McDermott (marr. diss. 2003; he *d* 2015); one *s* one *d. Educ:* University Coll. London (LLB Hons 1979). With Lovell, White & King, 1979–2004, Partner, 1989–2004, Hd, Media and Public Law, 1995–2004; Hd, Media and Public Law, Addleshaw Goddard, 2004–07. Exec. Bd, Justice, 2004–15, now Friend. Patron, Tim Bull and Jonathan Parry Peace Foundn, 2009–15. *Recreations:* swimming, walking two Cavalier King Charles spaniels. *T:* 07715 820398.

**MacDERMOTT, Rt Hon. Sir John Clarke,** Kt 1987; PC 1987; a Lord Justice of Appeal, Supreme Court of Judicature, Northern Ireland, 1987–98; *b* 1927; *s* of Baron MacDermott, PC, PC (NI), MC, and of Louise Palmer, *o d* of Rev. J. C. Johnston, DD; *m* 1953, Margaret Helen, *d* of late Hugh Dales, Belfast; four *d. Educ:* Campbell Coll., Belfast; Trinity Hall, Cambridge (BA); QUB. Called to Bar, Inner Temple and Northern Ireland, 1949; QC (NI) 1964. Judge, High Court of NI, 1973–87. *Address:* 6 Tarawood, Holywood, Co. Down BT18 0HS.

**McDERMOTT, Julie;** *see* Clemitson, J.

**McDEVITT, Conall;** Chief Executive, Hume Brophy Dublin, since 2013; *b* Dublin; *s* of late Rory McDevitt and Cathy McDevitt; *m* 1997, Dr Joanne Murphy; two *s* one *d. Educ:* Instituto de Bachillerato Mixto, Fuengirola, Malaga. Political Asst to Joan Burton, TD; Dir, Communications, SDLP, 1996–99; Hd, Communications, Viridian Gp, 1999–2000; Special Advr to Minister for Agric. and Rural Develt, NI, 2000–02; Public Relns Consultant, 2002–06, Man. Dir, 2006–09, Weber Shandwick, NI. Mem. (SDLP) S Belfast, NI Assembly, Jan. 2010–Sept. 2013. Chm., CIPR NI, 2007. Nat. Sec., Labour Youth, 1993; Vice Pres., Eur. Young Socialists, 1994. *Recreations:* running, cycling, Gaelic football, soccer. *Address:* Hume Brophy, 14 Herbert Street, Dublin 2, Ireland.

**McDEVITT, Prof. Denis Gordon,** MD, DSc; Professor of Clinical Pharmacology, University of Dundee, 1984–2002, now Emeritus; Hon. Consultant Physician, Dundee teaching hospitals, 1984–2002; *b* 17 Nov. 1937; *s* of Harry and Vera McDevitt; *m* 1967, Anne McKee; two *s* one *d. Educ:* Queen's Univ., Belfast (MB ChB, BAO Hons 1962; MD 1968; DSc 1978). FRCPI 1977; FRCP 1978; FRCPE 1984. House Physician and Surg., 1962–63, SHO, 1963–64, Royal Victoria Hosp., Belfast; SHO, Registrar, Sen. Registrar, Dept of Therapeutics and Pharmacology, QUB and Belfast teaching hosps, 1964–68; Asst Prof. of Medicine and Cons. Physician, Christian Med. Coll., Ludhiana, India, 1968–71; Cons. Physician, Belfast teaching hosps, 1971–83; Queen's University, Belfast: Sen. Lectr, 1971–76, Reader, 1976–78, in Clin. Pharmacology and Therapeutics; Prof. of Clin. Pharmacology, 1978–83; Dean, Faculty of Medicine, Dentistry and Nursing, Univ. of Dundee, 1994–97. Merck Internat. Fellow in Clin. Pharmacology, Vanderbilt Univ., 1974–75. Civil Cons. in Exptl Medicine, RAF, 1987–2002. Member: British Pharmacol Soc., 1972– (SKF Medal and Lecture, 1975; Hon. FBPhS 2007); Assoc. of Physicians, 1978– (Pres., 1987–88; Hon. Mem., 1988–); Medicines Commn, 1986–95 (Vice-Chm., 1992–95); GMC, 1997–2003 (Treas., 2001–03; Associate, 2003–07 and 2009–16); Council, RCPE, 2003–08; Faculty Bd, FPM, 2003–08; Chm., Specialist Adv. Cttee on Clin. Pharmacol. and Therapeutics, 1980–83; Vice-Chm., Ethics Cttee, Centre for Human Scis, DERA, 1994–2003. FFPM 1990; FRSE 1996; FRSocMed 1996; Founder FMedSci 1998. Man. Editor, European Jl of Clin. Pharmacology, 1998–2002. *Publications:* papers on clin. pharmacology in learned jls. *Recreations:* golf, music, opera. *Address:* Mariners View, 10 Ogilvie Road, Broughty Ferry, Dundee DD5 1LU. *T:* (01382) 739483. *Club:* Royal and Ancient Golf.

**MACDIARMID, Hugh Finlay,** CB 2003; Solicitor to Advocate General for Scotland, 1999–2005; *b* 1 Aug. 1944; *s* of Finlay Macdiarmid and Winifred Stalker Macdiarmid; *m* 1976, Catherine Rose Smith; two *s. Educ:* Morrison's Acad., Crieff; St Andrews Univ. (MA); Edinburgh Univ. (LLB). Admitted as solicitor, 1974; Office of Solicitor to Sec. of State for Scotland, 1974–99, Divl Solicitor, 1986–99. Legal Mem., Mental Health Tribunal for Scotland, 2005–14. *Recreations:* reading, contemplating. *Address:* 27/22 Maxwell Street, Edinburgh EH10 5FT.

**McDIARMID, Ian;** actor, director; Joint Artistic Director, Almeida Theatre, 1989–2002; *b* 11 Aug. 1944; *s* of Frederick McDiarmid and Hilda (*née* Emslie). *Educ:* Morgan Acad.; St Andrews Univ.; Royal Scottish Acad. of Music and Dramatic Art (Gold Medal, 1968). *Theatre* includes: Mephisto, Round House, 1981; Insignificance, Royal Court, 1982; Tales from Hollywood, NT, 1983; The Black Prince, Aldwych, 1989; Royal Shakespeare Company: joined, 1978; Shylock in Merchant of Venice, Henry V, The Party, 1984; Red, Black and Ignorant, War Plays, The Castle, 1985; The Danton Affair, 1986; A Life of Galileo, 2013, tour, 2014; Royal Exchange, Manchester: The Wild Duck, 1983; Edward II, 1986; Don Carlos, 1987; Associate Dir, 1986–88; Jonah and Otto, 2008; Almeida: Volpone, The Rehearsal (dir), Scenes from an Execution (dir), 1990; Hippolytos, Lulu (dir), 1991; Terrible Mouth (opera), A Hard Heart (dir), 1992; School for Wives, 1993; Siren Song (opera) (dir), 1994; Tartuffe, 1996; The Cenci (opera), The Government Inspector, 1997; The Doctor's Dilemma, 1998; The Jew of Malta, 1999; The Tempest, 2000; Faith Healer, 2001, Dublin and NY, 2006 (Tony Award for best featured actor); The Embalmer, 2002; The Merchant of Venice, 2014; The Soldier's Tale, LSO, 1987; The King Goes Forth to France, Royal Opera House, 1987; Henry IV, Donmar, 2004; Lear, Crucible, Sheffield, 2005; John Gabriel Borkman, Donmar, 2007; Six Characters in Search of an Author, Minerva, Chichester, transf. Gielgud, 2008; Be Near Me, Donmar, transf. Nat. Theatre of Scotland (and adapted), 2009; The Prince of Homburg, Donmar, 2010; Emperor and Galilean, NT, 2011; The Faith Machine, Royal Court, 2011; Timon of Athens, Chicago Shakespeare, 2012; Bakersfield Mist, Duchess Th., 2014; What Shadows, Birmingham Repertory Th., 2016, transf. London, 2017; Faust x2 (and adapted), Watermill Th., 2017;

*films* include: The Return of the Jedi, 1983; Restoration, 1996; Star Wars, Episode I: The Phantom Menace, 1999; Sleepy Hollow, 2000; Star Wars, Episode II: Attack of the Clones, 2002, Episode III: Revenge of the Sith, 2005; The Lost City of Z, 2017; *television:* Karaoke, 1996; Hillsborough, 1996; Great Expectations, 1999; All the King's Men, 1999; Crime and Punishment, 2002; Charles II: The Power and the Passion, 2003; Elizabeth I, 2005; Our Hidden Lives, 2005; City of Vice, 2008; Margaret, 2009; 37 Days, 2014; Utopia 2, 2014; Britannia, 2017; *radio* includes: King Lear, 2016. *Address:* c/o Troika Talent, 180 Great Portland Street, W1W 5QZ.

**McDONAGH,** Baroness *cr* 2004 (Life Peer), of Mitcham and of Morden in the London Borough of Merton; **Margaret Josephine McDonagh;** management consultant; Founder and Chair, The Pipeline, since 2013; *b* 26 June 1961; *d* of Cumin McDonagh and Breda McDonagh (*née* Doogue). *Educ:* Brunel Univ. (BSc); Kingston Business Sch. (MA); Harvard Business Sch. (AMP). Labour Party: Gen. Election Co-ordinator, 1997; Gen. Sec., 1998–2001; Gen. Manager, Express Newspapers, 2001–02. Chm., iPublic, 2004; Director: TBI plc, 2004–14; Standard Life plc, 2007–12; CareCapital plc, 2008–10; Chair, Smart Energy, 2013–15. Chair, Standard Life Charitable Trust, 2009–12; Dir, AFC Wimbledon Foundn; SW London Elective Orthopaedic Centre. *Address:* House of Lords, SW1A 0PW. *See also* S. A. McDonagh.

**MacDONAGH, Lesley Anne;** Managing Partner, Lovells (formerly Lovell White Durrant), Solicitors, 1995–2005; *b* 19 April 1952; *d* of Arthur George Payne and Agnes Dowie Scott; *m* 1st, 1975, John Belton (marr. diss. 1985); one *d*; 2nd, 1987, Simon Michael Peter MacDonagh; three *s. Educ:* Queen Elizabeth I Sch., Wimborne; College of Law, Guildford and London. Admitted Solicitor, 1976; Partner, Lovell White Durrant, subseq. Lovells, 1981–2006, Support Dir and Solicitor, 2005–07. Member: Council, Law Society, 1992–2001 (Mem., Planning and Envmtl Cttee, 1988–95); Lands Tribunal Consultative Cttee, 1991–95; Property Adv. Gp, 1993–98. Non-executive Director: Bovis Homes plc, 2003–13; SEGRO (formerly Slough Estates plc), 2007–09; Ogier, 2009–11; BDO (formerly BDO Stoy Hayward), 2009–17; Charles Russell Speechly (formerly Speechly Bircham), 2010–17; Univ. of Law, 2013–16; non-exec. Chm., T. P. Bennett Architects, 2015–. Trustee, Citizenship Foundn, 1991. Vice-Chm., Envmt Cttee, Knightsbridge Assoc., 1991–2010. Former Gov., LSE. Liveryman, Solicitors' Co., 1982– (Mem. Court, 1997–2006). Hon. Fellow, Soc. for Advanced Legal Studies, 1998. *Recreations:* family life, painting, theatre, dining.

**McDONAGH, Robert, (Bobby);** commentator and columnist; Deputy Secretary General, Department of Foreign Affairs, Ireland, 2017–18; *b* Washington, DC, 29 June 1954; *s* of Robert and Roisín McDonagh; *m* 1979, Mary Garvey; four *d. Educ:* Gonzaga Coll., Dublin; Balliol Coll., Oxford (MA Classics). Pres., Oxford Union. Entered Dept of Foreign Affairs, Ireland, 1977; Third Secretary: Political Div., 1977–80; Luxembourg, 1980–83; Gen. Secretariat of EP, 1983–85 (on special leave); First Secretary: Econ. Div., 1985–87; Perm. Representation of Ireland to EU, Brussels, 1987–90; Mem. Cabinet of Raymond McSharry, 1990–92, Dep. Chef de Cabinet of Padraig Flynn, EC, 1993–94 (on special leave); Counsellor, Econ. Div., 1995–2000; Ambassador to Malaysia, also accredited to Laos, Thailand and Vietnam, 2000–01; Asst Sec., EU Div., 2001–05; Perm. Rep. to EU, Brussels, 2005–09; Ambassador: to the Court of St James's, 2009–13; to Italy, 2013–17. *Publications:* Original Sin in a Brave New World: the paradox of Europe, 1998; (contrib.) Genesis and Destiny of the European Constitution, 2007.

**McDONAGH, Siobhain Ann;** MP (Lab) Mitcham and Morden, since 1997; *b* 20 Feb. 1960; *d* of Cumin McDonagh and Breda McDonagh (*née* Doogue). *Educ:* Holy Cross Convent; Essex Univ. (BA Hons 1981). Clerical Officer, DHSS, 1981–82; Wandsworth Council: Admin. Asst, 1982–83; Receptionist, Homeless Persons Unit, 1983–86; Housing Advr, Housing Aid Centre, 1986–88; Develt Co-ordinator, Battersea Churches Housing Trust, 1988–97. An Asst Govt Whip, 2007–08. Mem., South Mitcham Community Centre, 1988. *Recreations:* shopping, music, women's magazines. *Address:* 1 Crown Road, Morden SM4 5DD. *T:* (020) 8542 4835.
*See also* Baroness McDonagh.

**MACDONALD,** family name of **Barons Macdonald, Macdonald of River Glaven** and **Macdonald of Tradeston**.

**MACDONALD,** 8th Baron *cr* 1776; **Godfrey James Macdonald of Macdonald;** JP; DL; Chief of the Name and Arms of Macdonald; *b* 28 Nov. 1947; *s* of 7th Baron Macdonald, MBE, TD, and Anne (*d* 1988), *o d* of late Alfred Whitaker; *S* father, 1970; *m* 1969, Claire, *e d* of Captain T. N. Catlow, CBE, RN, Gabriel Cottage, Tunstall, Lancs; one *s* three *d.* JP Skye and Lochalsh, 1979; DL Ross and Cromarty, Skye and Lochalsh, 1986. *Heir: s* Hon. Godfrey Evan Hugo Thomas Macdonald of Macdonald, yr, *b* 24 Feb. 1982. *Address:* Kinloch Lodge, Isle of Skye. *Club:* New (Edinburgh).

**MACDONALD OF RIVER GLAVEN,** Baron *cr* 2010 (Life Peer), of Cley-next-the-Sea in the County of Norfolk; **Kenneth Donald John Macdonald,** Kt 2007; QC 1997; Warden, Wadham College, Oxford, since 2012; *b* 4 Jan. 1953; *s* of late Dr Kenneth Macdonald, scientist, and Maureen Macdonald (*née* Sheridan); *m* 1980, Linda Zuck, television producer; two *s* one *d. Educ:* St Edmund Hall, Oxford (BA Hons PPE 1974; Hon. Fellow, 2012). Called to the Bar, Inner Temple, 1978, Bencher, 2004. A Recorder, 2001–03 and 2010–17; Dir of Public Prosecutions, 2003–08; Mem., Matrix Chambers, 2000–03, 2008–; a Dep. High Court Judge, 2010–. Mem., Treasury Counsel Selection Cttee, Central Criminal Court, 2001–03. Criminal Bar Association: Mem. Cttee, 1997–2003; Chm., Educn Sub-Cttee, 1999–2001; Vice Chm., 2002–03; Chm., 2003; Member: Bar Council, 2000; Bar Public Affairs Gp, 2001–03 (Vice-Chm., 2001–02); Sentencing Guidelines Council, 2003–08; Criminal Procedure Rules Cttee, 2003–08; Nat. Criminal Justice Bd, 2003–08; Ind. Commn on Youth Crime, 2008–11; H of L Constitution Cttee, 2012–13. Vis. Prof. of Law, LSE, 2009–12; Mem., Adv. Bd, Centre for Criminol., Univ. of Oxford, 2010–19. Chair, Reprieve, 2011–17. Mem. Council, ICA, 2012–13. Trustee, Index on Censorship, 2009–12. Chair: Orwell Prize, 2015–17; Orwell Foundn, 2017–. *Recreations:* 20th century history, crime fiction, film noir. *Address:* Wadham College, Oxford OX1 3PN.

**MACDONALD OF TRADESTON,** Baron *cr* 1998 (Life Peer), of Tradeston in the City of Glasgow; **Angus John Macdonald,** CBE 1997; PC 1999; *b* 1940; *s* of Colin and Jean Macdonald; *m* 1963; two *d. Educ:* Allan Glen's Sch., Glasgow. Marine fitter, 1956–63; Circulation Manager, Tribune, 1964–65; journalist, The Scotsman, 1965–67; producer, presenter and Executive, Granada Television, 1967–85; Presenter, Right to Reply, Channel 4, 1982–88; Dir of Progs, 1985–90, Man. Dir, 1990–96, Chm., 1996–98, Scottish Television, subseq. Scottish Media Gp. Chm., Taylor & Francis Group, 1997–98; Director: GMTV, 1991–97; Bank of Scotland, 1998; Scottish Enterprise, 1998. Mem., H of L, 1998–2017. Parly Under-Sec. of State (Minister for Business and Industry), Scottish Office, 1998–99; Minister of State (Minister for Transport), DETR, 1999–2001; Minister for the Cabinet Office and Chancellor of the Duchy of Lancaster, 2001–03; Mem., Select Cttee on Econ. Affairs, 2004–08, on Communications, 2008–12, on Digital Skills, 2014–15, H of L; Mem., Cabinet Office Adv. Cttee on Business Appts, 2009–13. Chm., All Party Parly Humanist Gp, 2005–10. Mem., OECD Futures Project on Global Infrastructure, 2004–07 and 2009–11. Sen. Advr, Macquarie Gp, 2004–16. Non-exec. Dir, Scottish Power, 2009–15. Chm., Cairngorms Partnership Bd, 1997–98. Founder Chm., Edinburgh Television Festival, 1976; Chairman: Edinburgh Film Fest., 1994–96; ITV Broadcasting Bd, 1992–94. Governor: Nat. Film and Television Sch., 1986–97; BFI, 1997–98. Chancellor, Glasgow Caledonian Univ., 2007–12; Mem. Council, Univ. of Sussex, 2006–08. Patron, Dystonia Soc., 2006–16. DUniv: Stirling, 1992; Glasgow, 2001; Hon. DLitt: Napier, 1997; Robert Gordon, 1998; Hon. DBA Lincoln, 2007. BAFTA Award, Best Factual Series (World In Action), 1973; Chairman of the Year, and Business Leader of the Year, Scottish Business Elite Awards, 1997; BAFTA Scotland Lifetime Achievement Award, 1997. *Publications:* Camera: Victorian eyewitness, 1979. *Recreations:* music, pictures, sports.

**McDONALD, Very Rev. Alan Douglas;** Moderator of the General Assembly of the Church of Scotland, 2006–07; Minister, St Leonard's and Cameron, St Andrews, 1998–2016; *b* 6 March 1951; *s* of Douglas Gordon McDonald and Ray Lindsay Bishop McDonald (*née* Craig); *m* 1975, Dr Judith Margaret McDonald (*née* Allen); one *s* one *d*. *Educ:* Glasgow Acad.; Strathclyde Univ. (LLB 1972); Edinburgh Univ. (BD 1978; MTh 1996). Legal apprentice, Biggart Baillie & Gifford, 1972–74; Solicitor, Farquharson Craig, 1974–75. Community Minister, Pilton, Edinburgh, 1979–83; Minister, Holburn Central, Aberdeen, 1983–98. Convener, Church and Nation Cttee, Gen. Assembly of C of S, 2000–04. Mem. Bd, Christian Aid, 2012–. Hon. DLitt Strathclyde, 2007; Hon. DD St Andrews, 2007. *Recreations:* music, poetry, hillwalking, golf. *Address:* 7 Duke Street, Cromarty, Ross-shire IV11 8YH. *T:* (01381) 600954. *E:* alan.d.mcdonald@talk21.com.

**MACDONALD, Sir Alasdair (Uist),** Kt 2008; CBE 2001; Advocate for the Pupil Deprivation Grant (Welsh Government), since 2014, and Advisor on Leadership to Welsh Government, since 2016; Headteacher, Morpeth School, Tower Hamlets, 1992–2013; *b* Glasgow, 15 July 1949; *s* of William Uist and Patricia Joan Macdonald; *m* 1981, Susan Catherine Roberts; two *s*. *Educ:* Morgan Primary Sch.; Morgan Acad., Dundee; Aberdeen Univ. (MA Hons Geog.); Leeds Univ. (PGCE). Teacher of English, Nkhota Kota Secondary Sch., Malawi, 1971–73; Project Manager, Christian Service Cttee, Blantyre, Malawi, 1973–74; Teacher of Geog., 1975–77, Hd of Geog., 1977–80, Dep. Hd, 1980–82, George Green's Sch., Tower Hamlets; Dep. Principal, 1983–85, Principal, 1986, Passam Nat. High Sch., Wewak, PNG; Dep. Headteacher, Quintin Kynaston Sch., Westminster, 1987–92. Consultant, Nat. Coll. of Sch. Leadership, 2006–12; educational consultant for London Bor. of Tower Hamlets, 2013–; Member, Board: Tower Hamlets Educn Partnership, 2016–; Ind. Review of Welsh Sch. Teachers' Pay and Conditions, 2018. Chair, New Visions Educn Gp, 2015–; Trustee, Into Film, 2013–; Mem. Bd, Drum Works, 2016–. Unilever Fellow, London Leadership Centre, 2000. Hon. DEd E London 2008. *Recreations:* travelling with family, hiking, theatre, education, Dundee United FC, East and Central Africa. *Address:* 55 Hervey Road, SE3 8BS. *T:* (020) 8856 5684. *E:* uistmac@aol.com.

**MACDONALD, Alastair John Peter,** CB 1989; a Civil Service Commissioner, 2001–07; Director General, Industry (formerly Deputy Secretary), Department of Trade and Industry, 1992–2000; *b* 11 Aug. 1940; *s* of late Ewen Macdonald and Hettie Macdonald; *m* 1969, Jane, *d* of late T. R. Morris; one *s* two *d*. *Educ:* Wimbledon Coll.; Trinity Coll., Oxford. Editorial staff of Spectator, 1962; Financial Times, 1963–68: Washington DC, 1965–66; Features Editor, 1966–68; joined Home Civil Service as Asst Principal, DEA, 1968; Principal, DTI, 1971; Sec., Lord Devlin's Commn into Industrial and Commercial Representation, 1971–72; Asst Sec., DoI, 1975; RCDS, 1980; Under Sec., DTI, 1981. Dep. Sec., DTI, 1985–90; Dep. Under Sec. of State, MoD (PE), 1990–92. Non-exec. Dir, Parity Gp plc, 2002–08. Mem., Design Council, 2001–04. Pres., BCS, 2000–01. FBCS 1999. Trustee, Chatham Historic Dockyard Trust, 2001–09. *Address:* 13 Burbage Road, SE24 9HJ.

**MACDONALD, Alison Catherine;** QC 2017; *b* Nottingham, 28 May 1977; *d* of Dr John Macdonald and Dr Elspeth Macdonald; *m* 2012, Adam Thirlwell; one *d*. *Educ:* Wellington Sch., Ayr; Queens' Coll., Cambridge (BA Juris. 1998); Wadham Coll., Oxford (BCL 1999). Fellow, All Souls Coll., Oxford, 1999–2006. Called to the Bar, Gray's Inn, 2000; in practice as barrister, 2000–. *Recreations:* photography, ballet, yoga. *Address:* Matrix Chambers, Griffin Building, Gray's Inn, WC1R 5LN. *T:* (020) 7404 3447, *Fax:* (020) 7404 3448. *E:* alisonmacdonald@matrixlaw.co.uk.

**MacDONALD, Hon. Sir Alistair William Orchard,** Kt 2015; **Hon. Mr Justice MacDonald;** a Judge of the High Court of Justice, Family Division, since 2015; Family Division Liaison Judge, Northern Circuit, since 2019; *b* Sudbury, Suffolk, 22 Feb. 1970; *s* of Murray and Mary MacDonald; *m* 2000, Penelope Melville. *Educ:* Nottingham Univ. (BA Hons Archaeol. 1991); City Univ. (DipLaw 1994). Field Archaeologist, Trent and Peak Archaeol Trust, 1992–93. Called to the Bar, Inner Temple, 1995; barrister, specialising in family law, 1995–2015; a Recorder, 2009–15; QC 2011. Dep. Hd, Internat. Family Justice, 2017–. *Publications:* The Rights of the Child: law and practice, 2011, annotated materials, 2014; (contrib.) Family Court Practice (annually), 2012–. *Recreations:* amateur astronomy, ski-ing, biography. *Address:* Royal Courts of Justice, Strand, WC2A 2LL.

**MACDONALD, Andrew;** producer; Head: DNA Films, since 1997; DNA TV, since 2013; *b* Glasgow, 1 Jan. 1966; *s* of William Macdonald and Angela Pressburger; *m* 1997, Rachael Fleming; four *s* one *d*. Producer: Shallow Grave, 1994; Trainspotting, 1996; A Life Less Ordinary, 1997; The Beach, 2000; The Parole Officer, 2001; Alien Love Triangle, 2002; 28 Days Later, 2002; Sunshine, 2007; 28 Weeks Later, 2007; Never Let Me Go, 2010; Dredd, 2012; Sunshine on Leith, 2013; Ex Machina, 2015; Far From The Madding Crowd, 2015; T2 Trainspotting, 2017; Annihilation, 2018; Executive Producer: Twin Town, 1997; Beautiful Creatures, 2000; Strictly Sinatra, 2001; Heartlands, 2002; The Final Curtain, 2002; The Last King of Scotland, 2006; Notes on a Scandal, 2006; The History Boys, 2006; The Sweeney, 2012. *Recreations:* food, football, film. *Address:* DNA Films, 10 Amwell Street, EC1R 1UQ. *T:* (020) 7843 4410, *Fax:* (020) 7843 4411. *E:* info@dnafilms.com.

**McDONALD, Dr Andrew John,** CB 2015; Chair, Scope, since 2014; *b* 27 June 1962; *s* of A. J. W. McDonald and Eileen McDonald (*née* Sharkey); *m* 1992, Louise London (marr. diss. 2017); one *d*. *Educ:* St John's Coll., Oxford (BA Hons (Modern Hist.) 1983; MA 1989); Bristol Univ. (PhD 1988). PRO, 1986–2000 (Mem., Management Bd, 1997–2000); Client Services Dir/Actg Chief Exec., Public Guardianship Office, 2000–01; Tribunals Prog. Dir, LCD, 2001–02; Constitution Dir, DCA, 2003–05; Chief Exec., Govt Skills, Cabinet Office, then at DIUS, later at BIS, 2006–09; Chief Exec., Ind. Parly Standards Authy, 2009–14. Chm., Chapter Two Gp, 2017–. Gwilym Gibbon Fellow, Nuffield Coll., Oxford, 1996–97; Fulbright Fellow, Inst. of Govtl Studies, Univ. of Calif, Berkeley, 2005–06; Vis. Fellow, 2006, Academic Visitor, 2017, ANU; Associate, Inst. for Govt, 2015–; Associate Mem., History Faculty, Univ. of Oxford, 2017–; Mem., Sen. Common Room, St John's Coll., Oxford, 2018–. FRHistS 2000. FRSA 1999–2010. Hon. Fellow, Sch. of Public Policy, UCL, 1998–. Trustee: Action for Children, 2007–14; Cure Parkinson's Trust, 2012–15. *Publications:* (ed with G. Terrill) Open Government, 1998; (ed) Reinventing Britain, 2007; A Long and Winding Road: improving communication with patients in the NHS, 2016; Alderney's Choices, 2016; (jtly) The Human Right, 2018; articles on modern hist. and public policy. *Recreations:* history, sport, walking, travel, writing, swimming. *Club:* MCC.

**McDONALD, Andrew Joseph;** MP (Lab) Middlesbrough, since Nov. 2012; *b* Middlesbrough, 8 March 1958; *m* 1987, Sally. *Educ:* Leeds Poly. (BA Hons). Admitted Solicitor, 1990. Wilson-McDonald Solicitors, 1990–94; McDonald Solicitors, 1994–99; Thompson's Solicitors, 1999–2012. PPS to Shadow Attorney Gen., 2013, to Shadow Minister for Business, Innovation and Skills, 2013–15; Shadow Minister for Transport, 2016; Shadow Sec. of State for Transport, 2016–. Mem. (Lab) Middlesbrough Council, 1995–99. Governor: Abingdon Primary Sch., Middlesbrough, 1995–2010; Middlesbrough Coll., 2012–. *Address:* House of Commons, SW1A 0AA; (office) Unit 4 Broadcasting House, Newport Road, Middlesbrough TS1 5JA.

**MacDONALD, Angus;** Member (SNP) Falkirk East, Scottish Parliament, since 2011; *b* Stornoway, 11 Oct. 1963; *s* of William James MacDonald and Enid MacDonald; *m* 2014, Linda Sim; one *s*. *Educ:* Keil Sch.; Grangemouth High Sch.; Coll. of Estate Mgt. Agriculture, until 1992. Member (SNP): Falkirk DC, 1992–96; Falkirk Council, 2004–12. Parliamentary Liaison Officer: to Cabinet Sec. for Rural Affairs, Climate Change and Envmt, 2012–16; to Minister for Envmt and Climate Change, 2012–16. Gov., Stirlingshire Educn Trust, 2007–12. JP, 1992–96. *Address:* Scottish Parliament, Edinburgh EH99 1SP. *T:* (0131) 348 5489.

**MACDONALD, His Honour Angus Cameron;** a Circuit Judge, 1979–98; *b* 26 Aug. 1931; *o s* of late Hugh Macdonald, OBE, and Margaret Cameron Macdonald (*née* Westley); *m* 1956, Deborah Anne, *d* of late John Denny Inglis, DSO, MC, JP, and Deborah Margary Meiklem Inglis (*née* Thomson); two *d* (and one *d* decd). *Educ:* Bedford Sch.; Trinity Hall, Cambridge (BA 1954; MA 1960). Nat. service, 1950–51, commissioned, TA, 1951–57. Called to Bar, Gray's Inn, 1955; Resident Magistrate, then Crown Counsel, Nyasaland Govt, 1957–65; Sen. State Counsel, Malawi Govt, 1965–67; practised, NE Circuit, 1967–79; a Recorder of the Crown Court, 1974–79. *Recreations:* singing, fishing, shooting. *Clubs:* Northern Counties (Newcastle upon Tyne); New (Edinburgh).

**MACDONALD, Angus David;** Headmaster, Lomond School, 1986–2009; *b* Edinburgh, 9 Oct. 1950; *s* of Iain and Molly Macdonald; *m* 1976, Isabelle Marjory; two *d*. *Educ:* Jesus Coll., Cambridge (BA 1972); Edinburgh Univ. (DipEd). Teacher: Alloa Acad., 1972; Edinburgh Acad., 1973–82; Kings Sch., Paramatta, NSW, 1978; Dep. Hd, George Watson's Coll., 1982–86. *Recreations:* outdoor ed., gardening, piping. *Address:* Shenavail, Camserney, Aberfeldy, Perth and Kinross PH15 2JF. *T:* (01887) 820728. *E:* angusmacdonald910@btinternet.com.

**McDONALD, Prof. Arthur Bruce,** CC 2015 (OC 2006); OOnt 2012; ONS 2016; PhD; FRSC; FRS 2009; PEng (Ont); Director, Sudbury Neutrino Observatory Collaboration, since 1989, and Gordon and Patricia Gray Professor of Particle Astrophysics, 2006–13, now Emeritus; Queen's University, Ontario; *b* 29 Aug. 1943; *m* Janet; four *c*. *Educ:* Dalhousie Univ., Halifax (BSc 1964; MSc 1965; Hon. LLD 1997); Calif Inst. of Technol. (PhD 1969; Distinguished Alumnus, 2018). Chalk River Nuclear Laboratories, Atomic Energy of Canada Ltd: Postdoctoral Fellow, 1969–70; Asst Res. Officer, 1970–75; Associate Res. Officer, 1975–80; Sen. Res. Officer, 1980–82; Prof. of Physics, Princeton Univ. and Co-Principal Investigator, Princeton Cyclotron, 1982–89; Queen's University, Ontario: Prof. of Physics, 1989–2013; Univ. Res. Chair in Physics, 2002–06; Dir, 1991–2003, 2006–09, Associate Dir, 2009–13, Sudbury Neutrino Observatory Inst. Rutherford Meml Fellow, 1969–70; Killam Res. Fellow, 1998–2000. Associate, Cosmology and Gravity Prog., Canadian Inst. for Advanced Res., 2000– (Chair, Adv. Bd, 2000–05). Member: Canadian Assoc. of Physicists, 1964; Professional Engrs of Ontario, 2004; Foreign Associate, NAS, 2017. Fellow, APS, 1983; FRSC 1998. Hon. LLD: Cape Breton, 1999; St Francis Xavier, 2009; Hon. DSc: Royal Military Coll., 2001; Chicago, 2006; Alberta, 2011; Waterloo, 2012; Mount Allison, 2016; British Columbia, 2016; McGill, 2017; Queen's, 2017; Toronto, 2017; Hon. DSc Laurentian, 2018. Tom W. Bonner Prize in Nuclear Physics, APS, 2003; Medal for Lifetime Achievement in Physics, Canadian Assoc. of Physicists, 2003; Herzberg Medal, NSERC, 2003; Bruno Pontecorvo Prize, Jt Inst. for Nuclear Res. Dubna, 2005; (jtly) J. C. Polanyi Award, NSERC, 2006; (jtly) Benjamin Franklin Medal in Physics, 2007; Killam Prize in Nat. Scis, 2010; Tory Medal, RSC, 2011; Cocconi Prize, Eur. Physical Soc., 2013; (jtly) Nobel Prize in Physics, 2015; (jtly) Breakthrough Prize in Fundamental Physics, 2016; W. B. Lewis Medal, Canadian Nuclear Soc., 2017. *Publications:* more than 150 pubns on nuclear and particle physics in scientific jls. *Address:* Department of Physics, Engineering Physics and Astronomy, Queen's University, Kingston, ON K7L 3N6, Canada.

**MACDONALD, Prof. Averil Mary,** OBE 2015; PhD; CPhys, FInstP; Professor of Science Communication, University of Reading, 2007–14, now Emeritus; Chair, UK Onshore Oil and Gas, since 2015; *b* Walsall, 15 Oct. 1957; *d* of late Joseph Henry and Clara Eleanor Frost; *m* 1986, George Macdonald (marr. diss. 1998); two *d*, *m* 2001, Prof. Alun Vaughan. *Educ:* Univ. of York (BSc Physics 1980); Open Univ. (MA Educn Mgt 1996); Southampton Univ. (PhD Chem. 2004). CPhys 1987; FInstP 1999. Teacher of physics, Ingatestone, Essex, 1981–86; Hd of Physics, Kenilworth Sch., 1986–93; Lectr (pt-time), Univ. of Reading, 1996–2007. Educnl Consultancy business, 1996–. Trustee, Science Mus. Gp (formerly NMSI), 2008–16. Freeman, Horners' Co. Bragg Medal, Inst. Physics, 1999; Woman of Outstanding Achievement in Sci., UK Res. Council for Women in Sci., 2007; Plastics Industry Award for Personal Contribn to the Plastics Industry 2007. *Publications:* jointly: Reading into Science: physics, 2003; Fantastic Plastic; co-author of school textbooks in series incl. Science Web Readers, GCSE Modular Science, GCSE Gateway Science, Salters A-level Physics, Science Through Hydrogen, Essential Physics Revision. *Recreations:* talking to husband in pubs (when time permits), keeping tropical fish, 2 cats, 2 daughters and 1 husband.

**MACDONALD, Dr Calum Alasdair;** Executive Director, Point and Sandwick Power, since 2006; Development Director, An Teallach Energy, since 2010; *b* 7 May 1956; *s* of Malcolm and Donella Macdonald. *Educ:* Bayble Sch.; The Nicolson Inst.; Edinburgh Univ.; Univ. of California at Los Angeles (PhD). MP (Lab) Western Isles, 1987–2005; contested (Lab) Na h-Eileanan An Iar, 2005. Parly Under-Sec. of State, Scottish Office, 1997–99. Chm., Forestry Commn Scotland, 2006–09. Vice-Chm., Point Power & Energy Co. Ltd, 2006. Member: TGWU; Scottish Crofting Foundn (formerly Crofters Union). *Address:* 21 New Garrabost, Isle of Lewis HS2 0PH.

**MACDONALD, Charles Adam;** QC 1992; **His Honour Judge Macdonald;** a Circuit Judge, since 2005; *b* 31 Aug. 1949; *s* of late Alasdair Cameron Macdonald, VRD, MB ChB, FRCP, FRCPGlas and of Jessie Catherine Macdonald, BA; *m* 1978, Dinah Jane Manns; three *d*. *Educ:* Glasgow Academy; New Coll., Oxford (MA Hons Jurisp.). Called to the Bar, Lincoln's Inn, 1972. An Asst Recorder, 1996–99; a Recorder, 1999–2005. Mem. Panel, Lloyd's Salvage Arbitrators, 2000–05. Tribunal Mem., Mental Health Review Tribunal Restricted Patients Panel, 2009–13; Mem., Parole Bd for England and Wales, 2010–13. *Publications:* Butterworths Commercial Court and Arbitration Pleadings, 2005. *Recreation:* owns sport horses. *Address:* Maidstone Combined Court, Barker Road, Maidstone, Kent ME16 8EQ.

**MACDONALD, Clare Mary;** *see* Moriarty, C. M.

**MacDONALD, Colin Cameron**, CB 1999; Secretary, Sound of Iona Harbours Committee, 2004–14; Chairman, South West Mull and Iona Development Company Ltd, since 2014; *b* 13 July 1943; *s* of Captain Colin D. C. MacDonald and Ann MacDonald (*née* Hough); *m* 1969, Kathryn Mary Campbell. *Educ*: Allan Glen's Sch., Glasgow; Univ. of Strathclyde (BA Hons Econ. 1967). Scottish Development Department, 1967–92: Asst Sec., Housing Div., 1988–91, Management Orgn, 1991–92; Under Sec. and Principal Estab. Officer, Scottish Office, then Scottish Exec., 1992–2000; Man. Dir, Colmcille Fisheries (Iona), 2000–03. Non-exec. Dir, TSB Bank Scotland, 1994–98. *Recreations*: tennis, fishing, music. *Address*: Caol Ithe, Iona, Argyll PA76 6SP. *T*: (01681) 700344.

**McDONALD, David Arthur**; Chairman, Willow Housing and Care Ltd, 2004–05 and 2006–11; *b* 16 Jan. 1940; *s* of late Campbell and Ethel McDonald; *m* 1st, 1963, Barbara MacCallum (marr. diss.); one *d*; 2nd, 1971, Mavis Lowe (*see* Dame Mavis McDonald); one *s*. *Educ*: Campbell College, Belfast; Trinity College, Dublin. BA (Moderatorship) Classics. Asst Master, Classics, Methodist College, Belfast, 1963–66; Press Sec. to Minister of Education, N Ireland, 1967–68; joined Min. of Housing and Local Govt, later DoE, 1970; Asst Private Sec. to Sec. of State for the Envmt, 1974–76; Asst Sec., Local Govt Finance Divs, 1977–82; Dir of Information, 1982–87; Under Sec., Construction Industry, and Sport and Recreation, Directorates, 1987–90; Dir of Information, 1990–92; Under Sec., Urban Develt and Relocation Directorate, 1992–94; Under-Sec., Cities, Countryside and Private Finance Directorate, 1994. Mem., Local Govt Area Cost Adjustment Rev. Panel, 1995–96. Chm., Network Housing Assoc., later Stadium Housing Assoc., 1996–2006; Vice-Chm., London Strategic Housing Ltd, 1999–2002; Mem. Bd, Network Housing Gp, 2003–11 (Chm. Council, 2003–08; Ind. Mem., Investment Cttee, 2011–15). *Recreations*: golf, watching sport. *Clubs*: Middlesex CC; London Scottish Rugby.

**MACDONALD, David Cameron**; Chairman, National Kidney Foundation of New Zealand, 1998–2003; *b* 5 July 1936; *s* of James Fraser Macdonald, OBE, FRCS and Anne Sylvia Macdonald (*née* Hutcheson); *m* 1st, 1968, Melody Jane Coles (marr. diss. 1980); two *d*; 2nd, 1983, Mrs Sally Robertson; one *s* one *d*. *Educ*: St George's Sch., Harpenden; Newport Grammar Sch. Admitted a solicitor with Slaughter and May, 1962; joined Philip Hill Higginson Erlangers, later Hill Samuel & Co. Ltd, 1964: Dir, 1968; Dep. Chm., 1979–80; Dir, Hill Samuel Gp Ltd, 1979–80; Chief Exec., Antony Gibbs Holdings Ltd and Chm., Antony Gibbs & Sons, 1980–83; Chairman: Bath and Portland Gp, 1982–85; Pittards, 1985–97 (Dir, 1984); Sound Diffusion, 1987–89; Director: Coutts and Co., 1980–95; Sears, 1981–97; Merivale Moore, 1985–98; Cogent Elliott, 1986–97; Foster Yeoman Ltd, 1993–95. Sen. UK Advr, Credit Suisse First Boston, 1983–91. Dir Gen., Panel on Takeovers and Mergers, 1977–79. Adviser to Govt on Upper Clyde Shipbuilders crisis, 1971. Chm., Issuing Houses Assoc., 1975–77. Mem., BTA, 1971–82. Trustee, London City Ballet, 1983–87. *Recreations*: music, fishing. *Address*: Laburnum Cottage, Westcombe, Shepton Mallet, Som BA4 6ER. *T*: (01749) 838724.

**McDONALD, David John, (David Tennant)**; actor; *b* 18 April 1971; *s* of late Very Rev. Alexander McDonald and Essdale Helen McDonald (*née* McLeod); *m* 2011, Georgia Moffett; one *s* two *d*, and one step *s*. *Educ*: Royal Scottish Acad. of Music and Drama (BA). *Theatre* includes: appearances with 7:84 Theatre Co.; Royal Shakespeare Co.: As You Like It, 1996; Romeo and Juliet, 2000; Comedy of Errors, 2000; Hamlet, 2008; Love's Labour's Lost, 2008; Lobby Hero, Donmar and New Ambassadors, 2002; Much Ado About Nothing, Wyndham's, 2011; Richard II, Stratford, 2013, Barbican, 2016; Don Juan in Soho, Wyndham's, 2017; *films* include: Bright Young Things, 2003; Harry Potter and the Goblet of Fire, 2005; Glorious 39, St Trinian's 2: the Legend of Fritton's Gold, 2009; Fright Night, 2011; What We Did On Our Holiday, 2014; Mad to be Normal, 2017; Bad Samaritan, 2018; How to Train your Dragon: the hidden world, 2019; Mary Queen of Scots, 2019; *television* includes: He Knew He Was Right, 2004; Blackpool, 2004; Casanova, 2005; The Doctor in Doctor Who, 2006–10; Recovery, 2007; Hamlet, 2009; Single Father, 2010; United, 2011; This Is Jinsy, 2011; Spies of Warsaw, 2013; Broadchurch, 2013, 2015, 2017; The Politician's Husband, 2013; The Escape Artist, 2013; There She Goes, 2018; Camping, 2019; Good Omens, 2019; Criminal, 2019; *radio*: The Purple Land, Kafka: The Musical, 2011; Love, Virtually, 2012. *Address*: c/o Independent Talent Group Ltd, 40 Whitfield Street, W1T 2RH.

**MACDONALD, Prof. David Whyte**, CBE 2010; DPhil, DSc; FRSE; FRGS, FRSB; Founding Director, Wildlife Conservation Research Unit, since 2004, and Professor of Wildlife Conservation, since 2004, University of Oxford; Senior Research Fellow in Wildlife Conservation, Lady Margaret Hall, Oxford, since 1986; *b* Oxford, 30 Sept. 1951; *s* of Dr William Alexander Fraser Macdonald and Williamina Stirrat (*née* Whyte), Glasgow; *m* 1975, Jennifer Mary Wells (marr. diss. 2015); one *s* two *d*; partner, Dr Dawn Burnham. *Educ*: St Lawrence Coll., Ramsgate; Wadham Coll., Oxford (Wells Schol.; BA 1972); Balliol Coll., Oxford (DPhil 1977; DSc Oxon 2004. FRGS 1978; FRSB (FIBiol 1990). University of Oxford: Jun. Res. Fellow, Balliol Coll., 1976–79; Ernest Cook Res. Fellow, 1979–84, Nuffield Res. Fellow, 1984–87, Dept of Zool. A. D. White Prof.-at-Large, Cornell Univ., 1997–2003; Vis. Prof., Imperial Coll., London, 2004–. Department for Environment, Food and Rural Affairs: Mem., Adv. Cttee on Pesticides, 2002–05 (Mem., Envmtl Panel, 2003–05); Advr to UK Biodiversity Res. Adv. Gp, 2002–; Mem., 2003–04, Chm., 2004–, Darwin Adv. Cttee. Advr to Burns Inquiry into hunting with hounds, 2000; Comr, Ind. Supervisory Authy for Hunting, 2000–05. Biodiversity Advr to Esmée Fairbairn Foundn, 2002–11. Founding Chm., IUCN/Species Survival Commn Canid Specialist Gp, 1985–2005. Member: Council, English Nature, 2003–05; Bd, Natural England, 2005–14 (Chm., Sci. Adv. Cttee, 2006–14); Council, Wildfowl and Wetlands Trust, 2005–10; Inter Agency Climate Change Forum, JNCC, 2007–10. Trustee, Macaulay Land Use Res. Inst., 1999–2003; Mem., NERC Peer Rev. Coll., 2006–08. Vice-President: Royal Soc. of Wildlife Trusts, 1999–; RSPCA, 2001–05. Zoological Society of London: Scientific Fellow, 1993; Mem. Council, 2001–06; Vice-Pres., 2003–06. FRSE 2008; Emer. Fellow, IUCN Survival Commn, 2005. Vice Pres., Eur. Soc. of Mammalogists, 1993–2004; Mem. Council, Fauna and Flora Internat., 1995–2002. Trustee: Earthwatch Europe, 2007– (Chm., 2009–); WWF UK, 2008–. Natural history films: The Night of the Fox, BBC TV, 1976; Meerkats United, BBC TV, 1987 (Wildscreen Award, 1988); One for All, All for One, 1988; The Velvet Claw (series), BBC TV, 1992. T. H. Huxley Prize, Zool Soc., 1978; Dawkins Prize for Animal Conservation and Welfare, Balliol Coll., Oxford, 2004; Merriam Prize for res. in mammalogy, Amer. Soc. of Mammalogists, 2006; Medal for outstanding services to mammalogy, Mammal Soc. of GB, 2007; Silver Medal for contribs to understanding and appreciation of zoology, Zool Soc. London, 2010. *Publications*: Rabies and Wildlife: a biologist's perspective, 1980; *joint editor*: A Handbook on Biotelemetry and Radio Tracking, 1979; Social Odours in Mammals, vols 1 and 2, 1985; Carnivore Conservation, 2001; The Biology and Conservation of Wild Canids, 2004; Key Topics in Conservation Biology, 2007; Wildlife Conservation on Farmland (2 vols), 2015; *popular science*: Vulpina: story of a fox, 1977; Expedition to Borneo, 1980; Running with the Fox, 1987 (Natural Hist. Author of Year Award); The Velvet Claw: a natural history of the carnivores, 1992; Field Guide to Mammals of Britain and Europe, 1993; European Mammals: evolution and behaviour, 1995 (Natural Hist. Author of Year Award); Meerkats, 1999; Foxes, 2000; (ed) Encyclopedia of Mammals, 3rd edn 2006; contrib. learned jls incl. Nature and Science.
*Recreations*: farming (sheep and sheep dogs), Burns' poetry, photography, rowing, golf, surviving. *Address*: Wildlife Conservation Research Unit, Department of Zoology, University of Oxford, Recanati-Kaplan Centre, Tubney House, Tubney, Oxon OX13 5QL. *T*: (01865) 611100, *Fax*: (01865) 393101. *E*: david.macdonald@zoo.ox.ac.uk, wcru@zoo.ox.ac.uk. *Club*: Athenæum.

**MACDONALD, Dame Denise (Assunta)**; *see* Coia, Dame D. A.

**MACDONALD, Prof. Ewan Beaton**, OBE 2002; FRCP, FRCPE, FRCPGlas, FFOM, FFOMI; Professor and Head, Healthy Working Lives Group, Public Health and Health Policy Section, University of Glasgow, since 2004 (Senior Lecturer, 1990–2004); *b* 11 Jan. 1947; *s* of Dr Duncan Macdonald, MBE and Isabel Dow Macdonald; *m* 1971, Patricia Malloy; three *s* one *d*. *Educ*: Keil Sch.; Univ. of Glasgow (MB ChB). FFOM 1988; FRCPGlas 1992; FRCP 1994; FRCPE 1996; FFOMI 1997. General medicine, Western Infirmary, Glasgow, 1971–75; National Coal Board: MO, 1975–80; PMO, Yorks, 1980–85; Hon. Consultant in Rehabilitation, Firbeck Hosp., 1980–85; IBM UK: SMO, 1986; CMO, 1987–90; Chm., IBM European Occupational Health Bd, 1988–90; Dir, SALUS (Lanarks Occupnl Health and Safety Service), 1990–2011. Dean, Faculty of Occupational Medicine, RCP, 1994–96; Pres., Sect. of Occupnl Medicine, Union of Eur. Med. Specialists, 2001–05 (Sec., 1997–2001). Mem., Bevan Commn, 2012–. Founder and Chm., Kinloch Castle Friends Assoc., 1996–. Deacon, Incorporation of Cordiners of Glasgow, 2018–19. Hon. Col, 225 Med. Regt (V), 2007–13. *Publications*: numerous articles and chapters on occupational health. *Recreations*: mountaineering, sailing, fishing. *Address*: Public Health and Health Policy Section, 1 Lilybank Gardens, University of Glasgow, Glasgow G12 8RZ. *T*: (0141) 330 3719. *E*: ewan.macdonald@glasgow.ac.uk. *Club*: Loch Lomond Sailing.

**MACDONALD, Very Rev. Dr Finlay Angus John**; Principal Clerk, 1996–2010, Moderator, 2002–03, General Assembly of the Church of Scotland; an Extra Chaplain to the Queen in Scotland, since 2015 (a Chaplain to the Queen, 2001–15); *b* 1 July 1945; *s* of late Rev. John Macdonald, AEA, MA and Eileen Ivy Sheila (*née* O'Flynn); *m* 1968, Elizabeth Mary Stuart; two *s*. *Educ*: Dundee High Sch.; Univ. of St Andrews (MA 1967; BD 1970; PhD 1983). Pres. Students' Representative Council, St Andrews Univ., 1968–69. Licensed by Presbytery of Dundee, 1970; ordained by Presbytery of Stirling and Dunblane, 1971; Minister: Menstrie Parish Ch, 1971–77; Jordanhill Parish Ch, Glasgow, 1977–96. Convener, Business Cttee, Gen. Assembly, 1988–92. Mem., Scottish Inter-Faith Council, 2005–08. Co-leader, Scottish Inter-Faith Pilgrimage, 2008. Chm., Iona Cathedral Trust, 2005–. Gov., Jordanhill Coll., 1988–93; Lay Mem. Court, Strathclyde Univ., 1993–96 (Fellow, 2002). Hon. DD St Andrews, 2002. *Publications*: Confidence in a Changing Church, 2004; Luke Paul, 2012; Luke Paul and the Mosque, 2013; From Reform to Renewal: Scotland's Kirk century by century, 2017. *Recreations*: music, gardening, hill-walking. *Address*: 8 St Ronan's Way, Innerleithen, Peeblesshire EH44 6RG. *T*: (01896) 831631.

**MacDONALD, Gavin**; *see* MacDonald, S. G. G.

**McDONALD, Gillian Clare, (Jill)**; Managing Director, Clothing, Home and Beauty, Marks and Spencer Group plc, 2017–19; *b* Birmingham, 15 May 1964; *d* of John and Mavis Manaton; *m* 2001, David McDonald; two *s*. *Educ*: Sevenoaks Sch.; Brighton Univ. (BA 1st Cl. Hons Business Studies). Mktg posts with Colgate Palmolive, 1987–90; mktg and gen. mgt rôles with British Airways, 1990–2006; McDonald's Restaurants: Chief Mktg Officer, UK and Northern Europe, 2006–10; UK CEO and Pres., Northern Europe, 2010–13; Pres., NW Div., Europe, 2014–15; Chief Exec., Halfords Gp plc, 2015–17.

**MACDONALD, Howard**; *see* Macdonald, J. H.

**MACDONALD, Prof. (Hugh) Ian**, OC 1977; Professor of Economics and Public Policy, Schulich School of Business (formerly Faculty of Administrative Studies), since 1974, Director, Programme in Public Administration, since 1992, York University, Toronto; President Emeritus, York University, since 1984; *b* Toronto, 27 June 1929; *s* of Hugh and Winnifred Macdonald; *m* 1960, Dorothy Marion Vernon; two *s* three *d*. *Educ*: public schs, Toronto; Univ. of Toronto; Oxford Univ. BCom (Toronto), MA (Oxon), BPhil (Oxon). Univ. of Toronto: Lectr in Economics, 1955; Dean of Men, 1956; Asst Prof., Economics, 1962. Govt of Ontario: Chief Economist, 1965; Dep. Provincial Treas., 1967; Dep. Treas. and Dep. Minister of Economics, 1968; Dep. Treas. and Dep. Minister of Economics and Intergovernmental Affairs, 1972. Pres., York Univ., 1974–84; Dir, York Internat., 1984–94. Director: the AGF Cos, 1982–2014; McGraw-Hill Ryerson Ltd, 1984–2014 (Chm., 1996–2014). Hon. Prof., Hunan Univ., 2009–. Member: Canadian Economics Assoc.; Amer. Economics Assoc.; Canadian Assoc. for Club of Rome; Inst. of Public Admin of Canada; Lambda Alpha Fraternity (Land Economics); Amer. Soc. for Public Admin. President: Empire Club of Canada, 1969–70; Ticker Club, 1971–72; Couchiching Inst. of Public Affairs, 1975–77; Canadian Rhodes Scholars Foundn, 1986–92; World Univ. Service of Canada, 1992–93; Chairman: Toronto Men's Br. of CIIA, 1959–61; Inst. for Political Involvement, 1974–76; Bd, Corp. to Promote Innovation Develt for Employment Advancement (Govt of Ontario), 1984–86; Commn on Financing of Elementary and Secondary Educn in Ontario, 1984–87; Ont. Municipal Trng and Educn Adv. Council, 1984–86; Hockey Canada, 1987–94; Annual Fund Appeal in Canada of Balliol Coll., Oxford Univ., 1992–98; The Commonwealth of Learning, 1994–2003 (Fellow, 2004). Member: Attorney General's Cttee on Securities Legislation, 1963–65; Economic Council of Canada, 1976–79; Bd, Council for Canadian Unity, 1978–99; Admin. Bd, Internat. Assoc. of Univs, 1980–90; Council and Exec. Cttee, Interamerican Orgn for Higher Educn, 1980–88 (Vice-Pres., Canada); Canadian Exec. Service Orgn, 1998–2001. Advr, Commonwealth Assoc. for Public Admin and Mgt, 2004–. Hon. Councillor, Internat. Orgn for Higher Educn, 1992. Hon. Life Mem., Canadian Olympic Assoc., 1997. KLJ 1978; Citation of Merit, Court of Canadian Citizenship, 1980. Hon. LLD Toronto, 1974; DUniv Open, 1998; Hon. DLitt: Sri Lanka Open, 1999; Dr B. R. Ambedkar Open, Hyderabad, 2001; York, 2008. Canada Centennial Medal, 1967; Silver Jubilee Medal, 1977; Commemorative Medal, 125th Anniversary of Confedn of Canada, 1992; Award of Merit, Canadian Bureau for Internat. Educn, 1994; Vanier Medal, for distinction in public service and excellence in public admin, Inst. of Public Admin of Canada, 2000; Senator Peter Boorsma Award, S Eastern Conf. for Public Admin, 2006; President's Award, Lambda Alpha Internat. Land Use Soc., 2010; Special Award, Commonwealth Assoc. for Public Admin and Mgt, 2014. Golden Jubilee Medal, 2002; Diamond Jubilee Medal, 2012. *Recreations*: hockey, tennis; public service in various organizations. *Address*: 7 Whitney Avenue, Toronto, ON M4W 2A7, Canada. *T*: (416) 9212908; York University, 4700 Keele Street, Toronto, ON M3J 1P3, Canada. *T*: (416) 7365632.

**MACDONALD, Prof. Hugh John**; Avis Blewett Professor of Music, Washington University, St Louis, 1987–2011, now Emeritus (Chair, Music Department, 1997–99); *b* 31 Jan. 1940; *s* of Stuart and Margaret Macdonald; *m* 1st, 1963, Naomi Butterworth; one *s* three *d*; 2nd, 1979, Elizabeth Babb; one *s*. *Educ*: Winchester College; Pembroke College, Cambridge (MA; PhD). FRCM 1987. Cambridge University: Asst Lectr, 1966–69; Lectr, 1969–71; Fellow, Pembroke Coll., 1963–71; Lectr, Oxford Univ., 1971–80, and Fellow, St John's Coll.; Gardiner Prof. of Music, Glasgow Univ., 1980–87. Vis. Prof., Indiana

Univ., 1979. Gen. Editor, New Berlioz Edition, 1966–2006. Szymanowski Medal, Poland, 1983. Ordre National du Mérite (France), 2013. *Publications*: Berlioz Orchestral Music, 1969; Skryabin, 1978; Berlioz, 1981; (ed) Berlioz Selected Letters, 1995; Berlioz's Orchestration Treatise, 2002; Beethoven's Century, 2008; Music in 1853, 2012; Bizet, 2014; Shakespeare in Modern English: three plays, 2016; Saint-Saëns and the Stage, 2019; articles in New Grove Dict. of Music and Musicians, Musical Times, Music and Letters, Revue de Musicologie. *Recreation*: bridges. *Address*: 18 Fishergate, Norwich NR3 1SE.

**MACDONALD, Iain Smith**, CB 1988; MD; FRCPE, FFPH; Chief Medical Officer, Scottish Home and Health Department, 1985–88, retired; *b* 14 July 1927; *s* of Angus Macdonald, MA and Jabina Urie Smith; *m* 1958, Sheila Foster; one *s* one *d*. *Educ*: Univ. of Glasgow (MD, DPH). Lectr, Univ. of Glasgow, 1955; Deputy Medical Officer of Health: Bury, 1957; Bolton, 1959; joined Scottish Home and Health Dept, 1964, Dep. Chief Med. Officer, 1974–85. Mem., MRC, 1985–88. QHP 1984–87. *Publications*: Glencoe and Beyond: the sheep-farming years 1780–1830, 2005. *Address*: 4 Skythorn Way, Falkirk FK1 5NR. *T*: (01324) 625100.

**MACDONALD, Ian;** *see* Macdonald, H. I.

**MACDONALD, Ian Alexander;** QC 1988; *b* 12 Jan. 1939; *s* of late Ian Wilson Macdonald and Helen Nicolson, MA; *m* 1st, 1968, Judith Roberts (marr. diss.; *d* 2018); two *s*; 2nd, 1978, Jennifer Hall (marr. diss.); one *s*; 3rd, 1991, Yasmin Sharif (marr. diss.); 4th, 2008, Brigid Baillie; one step *s*. *Educ*: Glasgow Acad.; Cargilfield Sch., Edinburgh; Rugby Sch.; Clare Coll., Cambridge (MA, LLB). Called to the Bar, Middle Temple, 1963 (Astbury Scholar, 1962–65; Bencher, 2002); SE Circuit. Lectr in Law, Kingston Polytechnic, 1968–72; Senior Legal Writer and Research Consultant, Incomes Data Services Ltd, 1974–80 (monitoring develts in employment law). Mem., Cttee of Inquiry into disappearance of Gen. Humberto Delgado, 1965; Chm., Ind. Inquiry into Racial Violence in Manchester Schs, 1987–88. Special Advocate, Special Immigration Appeals Commn, 1999–2004. Pres., Immigration Law Practitioners' Assoc., 1984–2014. Mem. Editl Adv. Bd, Immigration and Nationality Law and Practice. Grand Cross, Order of Liberty (Portugal), 1995. *Publications*: Resale Price Maintenance, 1964; (with D. P. Kerrigan) The Land Commission Act 1967, 1967; Race Relations and Immigration Law, 1969; Immigration Appeals Act 1969, 1969; Race Relations: the new law, 1977; (with N. Blake) The New Nationality Law, 1982; Immigration Law and Practice, 1983, 9th edn 2015, Supplements, 2017, 2018; Murder in the Playground: report of Macdonald Inquiry into Racial Violence in Manchester Schools, 1990; (contrib.) Family Guide to the Law, 1971, 1972; articles in professional jls. *Recreations*: swimming, watching football, reading, visiting 5 grandchildren. *Address*: Garden Court Chambers, 57–60 Lincoln's Inn Fields, WC2A 3LS. *T*: (020) 7993 7600. *Club*: Cumberland Lawn Tennis.

**MACDONALD OF SLEAT, Sir Ian Godfrey B.;** *see* Bosville Macdonald of Sleat.

**MACDONALD, Prof. Ian Grant,** FRS 1979; Professor of Pure Mathematics, Queen Mary College, subsequently Queen Mary and Westfield College, University of London, 1976–87, now Professor Emeritus, Queen Mary, University of London; *b* 11 Oct. 1928; *s* of Douglas Grant Macdonald and Irene Alice Macdonald; *m* 1954, Margaretha Maria Lodewijk Van Goethem; two *s* three *d*. *Educ*: Winchester Coll.; Trinity Coll., Cambridge (MA). Asst Principal and Principal, Min. of Supply, 1952–57; Asst Lectr, Univ. of Manchester, 1957–60; Lectr, Univ. of Exeter, 1960–63; Fellow, Magdalen Coll., Oxford, 1963–72; Fielden Prof. of Pure Maths, Univ. of Manchester, 1972–76. *Publications*: Introduction to Commutative Algebra (with M. F. Atiyah), 1969; Algebraic Geometry, 1969; Symmetric Functions and Hall Polynomials, 1978, 2nd edn 1995; Symmetric Functions and Orthogonal Polynomials, 1998; Affine Hecke Algebras and Orthogonal Polynomials, 2003; articles in math. jls. *Address*: 56 High Street, Steventon, Abingdon, Oxon OX13 6RS.

**McDONALD, Iona Sara MacIntyre,** OBE 2019; Lord Lieutenant for Ayrshire and Arran, since 2017; Sheriff of North Strathclyde at Kilmarnock, since 2002; *b* 18 Nov. 1954; *d* of Thomas and Isabella MacIntyre; *m* 1978, Colin Neale McDonald (*d* 2001); one *s* one *d*. *Educ*: Glasgow Univ. (MA 1976; LLB 1978). NP 1980. Admitted solicitor, 1980; Partner, Messrs Mathie-Morton Black & Buchanan, Solicitors, Ayr, 1982–2000; Reporter to the Court, Safeguarder and Curator ad Litem, 1985–2000; Temp. Sheriff, 1995, Hon. Sheriff at Ayr, 1995–2000; All Scotland Floating Sheriff, 2000–02. Mem., Scottish Court Service Bd, 2010–. DL Ayrshire and Arran, 2013. *Recreations*: gardening, ski-ing, walking, travel. *Address*: Kilmarnock Sheriff Court, St Marnock Street, Kilmarnock KA1 1ED. *T*: (01563) 520211.

**MACDONALD, Most Rev. James Hector,** DD; CSC; Archbishop of St John's (Newfoundland), (RC), 1991–2000, now Emeritus; *b* 28 April 1925; *s* of Alexander and Mary Macdonald. *Educ*: St Joseph's Univ., 1944–45. Ordained priest, 1953. Congregation of the Holy Cross: Mission Bank, 1954–56; Dir, Holy Cross Minor Seminary, St Joseph's, NB, 1956–62; Sec., Provincial Council, 1956–63; Dir of Vocations, 1962–63; Superior, Holy Cross House of Studies, 1964–69; Asst Provincial, 1966–72; Pastor, St Michael's, Waterloo, Ont., 1969–77; Dean, Waterloo County Priests, dio. of Hamilton, 1974–77; Aux. Bishop of Hamilton, 1978–82; Bishop of Charlottetown, 1982–91.

**MacDONALD, James Iain,** FRICS; Chief Executive, Architecture and Design Scotland, since 2010; *b* Portree, Isle of Skye, 9 Feb. 1966; *s* of John and Sylvia Macdonald; *m* 1996, Anne-Marie O'Hara; two *d*. *Educ*: Portree High Sch.; Edinburgh Univ. (BSc Hons); University Coll. London (MPhil). MRTPI; FRICS 2012. Casework Manager, English Heritage, 1990–94; Conservation Officer, City of Westminster, 1994–99; Sen. Officer, N Lanarks Council, 1999–2001; Principal Officer, Glasgow CC, 2001–07; Dep. Chief Inspector, Historic Scotland, 2007–10. Trustee, Edinburgh World Heritage, 2012–. Dir, Skye Connect, 2018–; Chair, Old Town Projects Ltd, 2018–. FRSA 2014. Hon. FRIAS. *Recreations*: cricket, hill walking, yoga, opera, cooking, bonfires. *Address*: Architecture and Design Scotland, 9 Bakehouse Close, 146 Canongate, Edinburgh EH8 8DD. *T*: (0131) 556 6699. *E*: jim.macdonald@ads.org.uk.

**McDONALD, Sir James (Rufus),** Kt 2012; PhD; FREng, FIET, FInstP; FRSE; Principal and Vice-Chancellor, University of Strathclyde, since 2009; President, Royal Academy of Engineering, since 2019; *b* 1957. *Educ*: Univ. of Strathclyde (BSc, MSc, PhD). Electricity supply industry; University of Strathclyde, 1984–: Sen. Lectr, Dept of Electronic and Electrical Engrg; Rolls Royce Prof. of Electrical Power Systems, 1994–; Chm., Rolls Royce Univ. Technol. Centre, 1997–; Dir, Inst. for Energy and Envmt, 2001–; Dep. Principal, 2006–09. Chm., Scottish Energy Technol. Partnership, 2007–; Co-Chair, Energy Adv. Bd in Scotland; Co-Director: Centre for Sustainable Electricity and Distributed Generation, DTI, later BERR, 2004; Scottish Res. Partnership in Energy Exec., 2006–. Non-exec. Dir, Weir Gp plc, 2014–. Member: Scottish Enterprise Bd; Scottish Sci. Adv. Cttee, 2008; Energy Excellence Bd, UK Trade and Investment. Trustee and Vice Pres., IET, 2012–15. FREng 2003; FRSE 2003. *Publications*: three books; contrib. jl and conf. papers. *Address*: University of Strathclyde, 16 Richmond Street, Glasgow G1 1XQ.

**McDONALD, Jane Elizabeth;** *see* Cross, J. E.

**McDONALD, Jill;** *see* McDonald, G. C.

**MacDONALD, Maj.-Gen. John Donald,** CB 1993; CBE 1986 (OBE 1981); DL; Chief Executive (formerly General Secretary): The Earl Haig Fund, 1994–2003; Officers Association Scotland, 1994–2003; *b* 5 April 1938; *s* of Lt-Col John MacDonald, OBE; *m* 1964, Mary (*d* 2016), *d* of Dr Graeme M. Warrack, CBE, DSO, TD; one *s* two *d*. *Educ*: George Watson's Coll., Edinburgh; RMA Sandhurst. Commnd, 1958; saw service with KOSB, RASC, RCT and Airborne Forces Berlin, UK, BAOR, N Africa, India (Defence Services Staff Coll.), 1958–71; ndc, 1976; Turkey NATO HQ Izmir, CO 4 Armoured Div., Transport Regt RCT, 1978–80; Instr Australian Comd and Staff Coll., 1980–82; Chief Instr and Comdt, RCT Officers' Sch., 1983; DCS 3 Armoured Div., 1983–86; Col Personnel Br. Sec., MoD, 1987–88; Comdr Transport, 1st BR Corps and Garrison Comdr Bielefeld, 1988–91; DG Transport and Movements, MoD, 1991–93. Col Comdt RLC, 1993–2003. Hon. Col, Scottish Transport Regt plc, 1997–2004. Gen. Sec., RBL, Scotland, 1994–2000. Chm., Sportsmatch, Scotland, 1993–98; Mem., Sports Council, Scotland, 1994–99. Queen's Councillor, Queen Victoria Sch., Dunblane, 1994–2004. Chm., Combined Services Rugby, 1991–93. Freeman, City of London, 1991; Hon. Mem. Ct of Assts, Carmen's Co., 1991. DL City of Edinburgh, 1996. *Recreations*: Rugby (played for Scotland, Barbarians, Combined Services and Army), ski-ing, golf, travel, music, collecting. *Clubs*: Army and Navy; London Scottish, Royal & Ancient (St Andrews), Honourable Co. of Edinburgh Golfers (Muirfield), Rugby Internationalists Golfing Society.

**MACDONALD, (John) Howard,** CA; FCT; Director: BOC Group plc, 1991–2002; Weir Group plc, 1991–2001; *b* 5 June 1928; *s* of John and Helen Macdonald; *m* 1961, Anne Hunter; three *d*. *Educ*: Hermitage, Helensburgh. CA 1954. Thomson McLintock & Co. (served articles), 1949–55; Walter Mitchell & Sons, 1955–58; Aircraft Marine Products, 1958; Finance Manager, Keir & Cawdor Arrow Drilling, 1958–60; Royal Dutch Shell Group, 1960–83, Group Treasurer, 1978–83; Chairman and Chief Executive: Dome Petroleum, 1983–88; NatWest Investment Bank, 1989–91; Director: National Westminster Bank, 1989–91; McDermott Internat. Inc., 1985–97; J. Ray McDermott Inc., 1985–97; Reed Internat., until 1983. Financial Advr to new Hong Kong Airport, 1991–93. Mem., Assoc. of Corporate Treasurers, 1979. *Recreations*: golf, theatre. *Address*: Blackdown Border, Tennysons Lane, Haslemere, Surrey GU27 3AF. *T*: (01428) 654953. *Club*: Caledonian.

**MACDONALD, John Reginald;** QC 1976; barrister-at-law; Commercial, Chancery and Administrative Lawyer; *b* 26 Sept. 1931; *s* of Ranald Macdonald and Marion Olive (*née* Kirkby); *m* 1958, Erica Stanton; one *s* one *d*. *Educ*: St Edward's Sch., Oxford; Queens' Coll., Cambridge. Called to Bar, Lincoln's Inn, 1955, Bencher, 1985; called to Bar of Eastern Caribbean, 1988. Represented: the people of Ocean Island, 1975; Yuri Orlov, the Soviet dissident, 1977–86; Canadian Indians, 1982; the Ilios, who were removed from Diego Garcia to make way for a US base, 1983; appeared for the people of Barbuda at the Antigua Ind. Conf. at Lancaster House in 1980; represented majority shareholders in battle fought in Nevis and BVI for control of only co. producing oil in Belize, and advised Seigneur of Sark and acted for major shareholder in closing stages of contest for control of three of London's leading hotels, 2010–13; represented Barbuda MP and Council in battle with Antigua Govt over peoples' land rights in Barbuda, 2018–19; Mem., Internat. Commn of Jurists missions to investigate violence in S Africa, 1990, 1992, 1993. Drafted written constitution for the UK (We the People), proposed by Liberal Democrats, 1990, revised 1993; Mem., Jt Lib Dem Labour Cttee on Constitutional Reform, 1996–97. Contested: Wimbledon (L) 1966 and 1970; Folkestone and Hythe (L) 1983, (L/Alliance) 1987; E Kent (Lib Dem), Eur. election 1994. Chm. Council, New Kent Opera, 1996–2008. *Publications*: (ed with Clive H. Jones) The Law of Freedom of Information, 2003, 3rd edn with Ross Grail) as Macdonald on the Law of Freedom of Information, 2016. *Recreation*: the theatre. *Address*: 12 New Square, Lincoln's Inn, WC2A 3SW. *T*: (020) 7419 8000. *Club*: MCC.

**MACDONALD, Sir John Ronald M.;** *see* Maxwell Macdonald, Sir J. R.

**MacDONALD, John William;** HM Diplomatic Service, retired; *b* 13 June 1938; *s* of John MacDonald and Anne MacDonald (*née* Richards); *m* 1960, Margaret Millam Burns. *Educ*: Boteler Grammar Sch.; NDC; Manchester Business Sch. Foreign Office, 1955, and 1959–94; Royal Navy, 1957–59; Diplomatic Service appts include Cairo, Tokyo, Dhaka, Dar es Salaam; Consul-Gen., Shanghai, 1991–94. *Recreations*: walking, cooking, listening to music. *Address*: 12 Snells Wood Court, Little Chalfont, Bucks HP7 9QT.

**MACDONALD, Sir Kenneth (Carmichael),** KCB 1990 (CB 1983); Chairman, Raytheon Systems Ltd (formerly Cossor Electronics, later Raytheon Cossor Ltd), 1991–2000; *b* 25 July 1930; *s* of William Thomas and Janet Millar Macdonald; *m* 1960, Ann Elisabeth (*née* Pauer); one *s* two *d*. *Educ*: Hutchesons' Grammar Sch.; Glasgow Univ. MA (Hons Classics). RAF, 1952–54. Asst Principal, Air Ministry, 1954; Asst Private Sec. to Sec. of State, 1956–57; Private Sec. to Permanent Sec., 1958–61; HM Treasury, 1962–65; MoD, 1965; Asst Sec., 1968; Counsellor (Defence), UK Delegn to NATO, 1973–75; Asst Under-Sec. of State, 1975, Dep. Under-Sec. of State, 1980, Second Perm. Under-Sec. of State, 1988–90, MoD. Chairman: Raytheon (Europe) Ltd, 1991–94, 1995–2000; Internat. Military Services Ltd, 1993–2005. Chm., Council of Voluntary Welfare Work, 1993–2005. Trustee, Chatham Historic Dockyard Trust, 1992–2000. *Recreation*: golf. *Address*: c/o Barclays Bank, 27 Regent Street, SW1Y 4UB. *Club*: Royal Air Force.

**McDONALD, Most Rev. Kevin John Patrick;** Archbishop of Southwark, (RC), 2003–10, now Archbishop Emeritus; *b* 18 Aug. 1947. *Educ*: St Joseph's Coll., Stoke; Birmingham Univ. (BA Latin); Ven. English Coll., Rome; Gregorian Univ. (STL); Angelicum Univ. (STD). Ordained priest, 1974; Asst Priest, All Saints, Stourbridge, 1975–76; Lectr in Moral Theol., St Mary's Coll., Oscott, 1976–85; official with resp. for Anglican and Methodist relns, Pontifical Council for Promoting Christian Unity, Rome, 1985–93; Parish Priest, English Martyrs, Sparkhill, Birmingham, 1993–98; Rector, Oscott Coll., 1998–2001; Bishop of Northampton, 2001–03. Chairman: Ecumenical Commn, Archdio. Birmingham, 1980–85; Archdiocesan Commn for Inter-Religious Dialogue, 1998–2001; Bishops' Conf. Cttee for Catholic-Jewish Relns, 2001–; Bishops' Conf. Cttee for Other Faiths, 2001–; Bishops' Conf. Dept of Dialogue and Unity, 2004–; Consultor to Holy See Commn for Religious Relns with the Jews, 2008–. Canon, St Chad's Cathedral, Birmingham, 1998–2001. Hon. DD Birmingham, 2005. *Recreations*: music, reading, walking.

**MACDONALD, Lewis;** Member (Lab) Scotland North East, Scottish Parliament, since 2011 (Aberdeen Central, 1999–2011); *b* 1 Jan. 1957; *s* of late Rev. Roderick Macdonald and Margaret Macdonald (*née* Currie); *m* 1997, Sandra Inkster; two *d*. *Educ*: Inverurie Acad.; Univ. of Aberdeen (MA, PhD). Parly Researcher, office of Frank Doran, MP, 1987–92 and 1997–99; Adviser to Tom Clarke, MP, 1993–97. Mem., Exec. Cttee, SLP, 1997–99. Dep. Minister for Transport and Planning, 2001, for Enterprise, Transport and Lifelong Learning, 2001–03, for Enterprise and Lifelong Learning, 2003–04, for Envmt and Rural Develt, 2004–05, for Health and Community Care, 2005–07, Scottish Exec. Convenor, Health and Sport Cttee, Scottish Parlt, 2018–. Convenor, Holyrood Progress Gp, 2000–01. Contested (Lab) Moray, 1997. *Recreations*: walking, football, history. *Address*: (office) 70 Rosemount Place, Aberdeen AB25 2XJ. *T*: (01224) 646333. *E*: Lewis.Macdonald.msp@parliament.scot.

**MacDONALD, Madeleine Mary**; see Arnot, M. M.

**MACDONALD, Dame Mary (Beaton)**, DBE 2005; Headteacher, Riverside Primary School, North Shields, 1994–2010; *b* 29 July 1950; *d* of Robert Beaton Skinner and Mary Ann Skinner (*née* Gregory); *m* (marr. diss.); two *s* one *d*. *Educ*: Jordanhill Coll., Glasgow (DipEd (Scotland)). Primary teacher, Isle of Bute, 1970–75; career break (short-term supply work), 1975–87; Sen. Teacher, Hawthorn Primary Sch., Newcastle upon Tyne, 1987–90; Dep. Hd, Montagu Primary Sch., Newcastle upon Tyne, 1990–94. Nat. Leader of Educn, Nat. Coll. for Sch. Leadership, 2008. DUniv Strathclyde, 2006. *Recreations*: reading, gardening.

**McDONALD, Dame Mavis**, DCB 2004 (CB 1998); Permanent Secretary, Office of the Deputy Prime Minister, 2002–05; Chairman, Catalyst Housing Group Ltd, 2005–11; *b* 23 Oct. 1944; *d* of late Richard Henry and of Elizabeth Lowe; *m* 1971, David Arthur McDonald, *qv*; one *s*. *Educ*: Chadderton Grammar Sch. for Girls; London Sch. of Econs and Pol Science (BSc Econ). Min. of Housing and Local Govt, later DoE, then DETR, 1966–2000: Asst Private Sec. to Minister for Housing and Local Govt, 1969–70, to Sec. of State for the Environment, 1970–71; Private Sec. to Perm. Sec., 1973–75; Asst Sec., Central Policy Planning Unit, 1981–83; Head of Personnel Management (Envmt) Div., 1983–86; Finance, Local Authority Grants, 1986; Dep. Dir, Local Govt Finance, 1987; Under Secretary: Directorate of Admin. Resources, 1988–90; Directorate of Personnel Management, 1990–91; Directorate of Housing Resources and Management, 1990–93; Directorate of Local Govt, 1994–95; Prin. Estab. Officer, 1995; Sen. Dir, Housing, Construction, Planning and Countryside, then Dir Gen., Housing, Construction, Regeneration and Countryside Gp, 1995–2000; Perm. Sec., Cabinet Office, 2000–02. Non-exec. Dir, Tarmac Housing Div., 1988–91. Member: Cttee of Mgt, Broomleigh Housing Assoc., 1995–96; Bd, Ealing Family Housing Assoc., 2001–02. Hon. MCIH 2001. Trustee, Joseph Rowntree Foundn, 2006–16. Ext. Mem. Council, Univ. of Cambridge, 2009–14 (Dep. Chm., 2011–14); Mem., Finance and Infrastructure Cttee, New Model in Technol. and Engrg, 2018–. Lay Gov., Birkbeck Coll., London, 1999–2008 (Fellow, Birkbeck, Univ. of London, 2009).

**McDONALD, Prof. Michael**, PhD; CEng, FICE; Professor of Transportation, 1992–2008, now Emeritus, and Director, Transportation Research Group, 1986–2008, University of Southampton; *b* 10 Dec. 1944; *s* of late Douglas Frederick McDonald and Joyce Mary Kathleen McDonald (*née* Burke); *m* 1970, Millicent Elizabeth Agnew; three *s*. *Educ*: Univ. of Newcastle upon Tyne (BSc); Univ. of Southampton (PhD 1981). MCIHT (MIHT 1973); MICE 1975; CEng 1975; FCILT (FCIT 1998); FICE 2004. University of Southampton: Rees Jeffreys Lectr in Highway and Traffic Engrg, 1971–86; Sen. Lectr, 1986–88; Reader in Transportation, 1988–92; Hd, Dept of Civil and Envmtl Engrg, 1996–99. Consultant, Roughton & Partners, 1985–2005 (Exec. Dir, 1990–95); Chm., ITSUK, 2004–07. Member: European Road Transport Res. Adv. Council (Vice Chm., 2004–09); Strategic Bd, Local Authy and Res. Councils' Initiative, 2009–10. Hills Rees Award, ITS UK, 2009; CIHT Award, 2010. *Address*: School of Civil Engineering and the Environment, University of Southampton, Highfield, Southampton SO17 1BJ.

**MACDONALD, Michael Christopher Archibald**, FBA 2016; Research Associate, Khalili Research Centre, University of Oxford, since 2013; Academic Director, Online Corpus of Inscriptions of Ancient North Arabia, since 2013; *b* London, 25 May 1947; *s* of Archibald James Florence Macdonald and Hon. Elspeth Ruth Macdonald, *d* of 2nd Baron Craigmyle; *m* 1977, Ann Searight (marr. diss. 1989). *Educ*: University Coll. Sch., Hampstead; Merton Coll., Oxford (BA 1970; MA 1975). Asst to Gerald Lankester Harding, Lebanon and Jordan, 1975–79; Res. Fellow, Centre for Jordanian Studies, Yarmouk Univ., Jordan, 1979–84; Founder and First Dir, Corpus of Inscriptions of Jordan Project, 1979–84; ind. res. on Ancient N Arabian langs, scripts and hist. of nomads of ancient Syria and Arabia, 1985–94; Leverhulme Res. Fellow, Faculty of Oriental Studies, Univ. of Oxford, 1995–97; full-time ind. res., 1997–; Supernumerary Fellow, Wolfson Coll., Oxford, 1997–2014, Hon. Fellow, 2014. Mem., Steering Cttee Seminar for Arabian Studies, 1984–89, 2009–. Creator, Safaitic Database Project, 1994–97; Co-director: Safaitic Epigraphic Survey prog., Syria, 1995–2003; Namara Rescue Survey, Syria, 1996; Acad. Dir, Ancient Arabia: Langs and Cultures project, Khalili Res. Centre, Univ. of Oxford, 2011–; Dir, Badia Epigraphic Survey Project (formerly N Badia Survey Project), North-Eastern Jordan, 2015–; Leader, British team, Epigraphy and Landscape in the Hinterland of Tayma Project, Saudi Arabia, 2015–. Associate Foreign Mem., UMR 8167 Orient et Méditerranée, Centre Nat. de la Recherche Scientifique, Paris, 1993–. Mem., Internat. Adv. Cttee on Archaeol Res., Oman, 1999–2004. Founder Trustee, and Hon. Sec., British Foundn for Study of Arabia, 2011–19; Trustee, Internat. Assoc. for Study of Arabia, 2019–; Ed., *Proc. Seminar for Arabian Studies*, 2004; ISA 1988–2019. Hon. DLitt Chicago, 2018. *Publications*: (ed with C. S. Phillips) *A. F. L. Beeston at the Arabian Seminar, and other papers*, 2005; *Literacy and Identity in Pre-Islamic Arabia*, 2009; (ed) *The Development of Arabic as a Written Language*, 2010; (ed) *Languages, Scripts and their Uses in Ancient North Arabia*, 2018; contrib. articles to learned jls. *Recreations*: medieval history, theatre, opera. *Address*: Wolfson College, Linton Road, Oxford OX2 6UD.

**MACDONALD, Morag, (Mrs Walter Simpson)**, CBE 1993; PhD; Secretary of the Post Office, 1985–94; *b* 8 Feb. 1947; *d* of Murdoch Macdonald Macdonald and Isobel Macdonald (*née* Black); *m* 1st, 1970, Adam Somerville; 2nd, 1983, Walter Simpson; one *d*. *Educ*: Bellahouston Academy, Glasgow; Univ. of Glasgow (LLB Hons 1968; PhD 2002); College of Law, London; King's Coll., London (BA 1997). Called to the Bar, Inner Temple, 1974. Joined Post Office as graduate trainee, 1968; posts in Telecommunications and Corporate HQ, 1969–79; PA to Managing Dir, Girobank, 1980; Dep. Sec., Post Office, 1983–85. Mem. Management Cttee, Industry and Parlt Trust, 1986–94. Council Mem., St George's Hosp. Med. Sch., 1994–97. Chairman: Adamson Trust, 2007–11; Glasgow City Heritage Trust, 2011–14 (Trustee, 2006–14; Vice-Chm., 2009–11); Scottish Commn for Learning Disability (formerly Scottish Consortium for Learning Disability), 2013–17. Gen. Council Assessor, 2014–; Mem. Bd, Chancellor's Fund Adv. Bd, 2015–, Univ. of Glasgow. FRSA 1990. *Recreations*: walking, embroidery, very indifferent piano playing. *Address*: 7 Lancaster Crescent, Glasgow G12 0RR. *Club*: Western (Glasgow).

**MACDONALD, Muir**, FREng; owner, muirmacdonald.com Ltd, since 2018; *b* Leamington Spa, 6 Jan. 1958; *s* of Keith Macdonald and Cynthia Macdonald; *m* 1988, Siân Davies; two *s*. *Educ*: University Coll. London (MSc Naval Arch. 1980). RCNC 1980; Ministry of Defence: Asst Constructor, 1981–86; Constructor, 1987–94; Asst Dir Warship Integration, 1994–97; rcds 1998; Dir Procurement Policy, 1999–2002; Dir Attack Submarines Proj., 2002–06; BMT Defence Services Ltd (on secondment), 2006–07; Dir Gen. Air Support, 2007–08; Man. Dir, BMT Defence Services Ltd, 2008–17; Strategic Pursuit Dir, Defence and Security, BMT Gp Ltd, 2017–18. FREng 2014; CDir 2015. *Recreation*: the outdoors. *Address*: muirmacdonald.com Ltd, 141 Englishcombe Lane, Bath BA2 2EL. *T*: (01225) 445507. *E*: muir.macdonald@gmail.com.

**McDONALD, Neil Kevin**; independent adviser and commentator on housing and planning issues, since 2011; *b* 1 April 1957; *s* of Eric and Margaret McDonald; *m* 1982, Barbara Moyser; two *s* one *d*. *Educ*: Kingsbury High Sch.; Newcastle-under-Lyme High Sch.; St John's Coll., Cambridge (BA 1979). Entered Civil Service, 1979; Admin. Trainee, Depts of Trade and Industry, 1979–82; Department of Transport, 1982–97: Principal: civil aviation, 1984–87; Driver Testing Review, 1987; LT, 1987–91; Asst Sec., Railways, 1991–93; on secondment to Office of Passenger Rail Franchising, 1994–97; Department of the Environment, Transport and the Regions: Divl Manager, Roads Policy, 1997–2000; Ed., Urban White Paper, 2000; Divl Manager, Local Authy Housing, 2000–02; Prog. Dir, Communities Plan, ODPM, 2002–03; Dir, Housing, ODPM, later DCLG, 2003–06; Department for Communities and Local Government: Dir, Home Inf. Pack Implementation, 2006–07; Dir, Planning Policy, 2007–08; Dir, Planning for Major Infrastructure, 2008–09; Chief Exec., Nat. Housing and Planning Advice Unit, 2009–10; Dir, Housing Mgt, Homelessness and Support, DCLG, 2010–11. Vis. Fellow, Cambridge Centre for Housing and Planning Res., 2012–15. *Recreations*: classic car restoration, walking, cycling. *E*: neilkmcdonald@gmail.com.

**MACDONALD, Nigel Colin Lock**; Partner, Ernst & Young, 1976–2003; *b* 15 June 1945; *s* of late Trevor William and Barbara Evelyn Macdonald; *m* 1st, 1972, Elizabeth Ruth Leaney (*d* 1981); 2nd, 1983, Jennifer Margaret Webster; one *d*. *Educ*: Cranleigh Sch.; Inst. of Chartered Accountants of Scotland. Thomson McLintock & Co., 1962–68; Whinney Murray & Co., 1968–70; Whinney Murray Ernst & Ernst, Netherlands, 1970–72; Whinney Murray, later Ernst & Whinney, then Ernst & Young, 1972–2003. Dir, James Lock & Co., 1976– (Chm., 1986–). Bd Mem., Coca-Cola Hellenic (formerly Coca-Cola HBC), 2005–16. Accounting Advr, Internat. Oil Pollution Compensation Fund, 2002–11. Mem. Council, 1989–93, Pres., 1993–94, Inst. of Chartered Accountants of Scotland. Member: Cadbury Cttee on corporate governance, 1991; Review Panel, Financial Reporting Council, 1991–2006; Bd, BSI, 1992–2004; Industrial Develt Adv. Bd, 1995–2001; Competition (formerly Monopolies and Mergers) Commn, 1998–2005. Chairman: Royal Museums Greenwich Foundn, 2013–; Awareness Foundn, 2014–. Trustee: Nat. Maritime Mus., 2003–13; Scottish Chartered Accountants' Trust for Educn, 2006–11; Scottish Accountancy Trust for Educn and Res., 2006–11 (Chm., 2006–11). FRSA 1993. Mem., Mission Council, URC, 2005–08; Elder, St Andrew's URC, Cheam, 1978– (Sec., 2013–). *Recreations*: old cars, swimming, topography. *Address*: 10 Lynwood Road, Epsom, Surrey KT17 4LD. *T*: (01372) 720853. *Clubs*: Royal Automobile, City of London.

**McDONALD, Dr Oonagh**, CBE 1998; international regulatory and public policy consultant, since 1989; Director, Oonagh McDonald Ltd, since 2008; *b* Stockton-on-Tees, Co. Durham; *d* of Dr H. D. McDonald, theologian. *Educ*: Roan Sch. for Girls, Greenwich; East Barnet Grammar Sch.; Univ. of London (BD Hons 1959; MTh 1962, PhD 1974, King's Coll.). Teacher, 1959–64; Lectr in Philosophy, Bristol Univ., 1965–76. Gwilym Gibbon Res. Fellow, Nuffield Coll., Oxford, 1988–89; Sen. Res. Fellow, Univ. of Warwick, 1990. Contested (Lab): S Glos, Feb. and Oct. 1974; Thurrock, 1987. MP (Lab) Thurrock, July 1976–87. PPS to Chief Sec. to Treasury, 1977–79; Opposition front bench spokesman on defence, 1981–83, on Treasury and economic affairs, 1983–87, on Civil Service, 1983–87. Consultant, Unity Trust Bank plc, 1987–88. Non-executive Director: Investors' Compensation Scheme, 1992–2001; SAGA Gp, 1995–98; Gen. Insce Standards Council, 1999–2005; British Portfolio Trust plc, 1999–2008; Gibraltar Financial Services Commn, 1999–; Scottish Provident, 1999–2001; Skandia, 2001–04; Dresdner RCM Global Investors, 2001–09. Director: FSA (formerly SIB), 1993–98 (Chm., Consumer Panel, 1994–95); FSA Ombudsman Scheme, 1998–2001; Bd for Actuarial Standards, 2010–13. Complaints Commissioner: London Metal Exchange, 2001–10; Virt-x, 2001–09; ICE Futures (formerly IPE), 2001–; ICE Clear Europe Ltd, 2008–. Chair: Public Inquiry into Property Valuation, 2013–14 (report, 2014); Fair Banking Panel, 2014–. Editor, Jl of Financial Regulation and Compliance, 1998–2008. *Publications*: (jtly) *The Economics of Prosperity*, 1980; *Own Your Own: social ownership examined*, 1989; *Parliament at Work*, 1989; *The Future of Whitehall*, 1992; *The Future of European Retail Banking: the view from the top*, 2002; *Fannie Mae and Freddie Mac: turning the American dream into a nightmare*, 2012; *Lehman Brothers: a crisis of value*, 2015; *Holding Bankers to Account*, 2019. *Address*: Washington, DC, USA. *E*: oonagh@oonaghmcdonald.com. *W*: www.oonaghmcdonald.com.

**McDONALD, Patrick Anthony**, CChem, CEng, FRSC, FIChemE; Director, Department for Business, Innovation and Skills, 2011; *b* 22 June 1958; *s* of late Patrick Bernard and Mary Ellen McDonald; *m* 1980, Anne Holtham. *Educ*: Rutherford Comp. Sch.; Kingston Poly. (BSc Hons Applied Chem.). CChem 1983; CEng; FRSC 2005; FIChemE. Forensic Scientist, Lab. of Govt Chemist, 1980–87; Department of Trade and Industry: Administrator, 1987–93; Dep. Dir, 1993–2002; Dir, Key Business Technols, 2002–04; Technology Dir, 2004–06; Chief Scientific Advr, HSE, 2006–11. Dir, Britech Foundn, 2004–06. Lay Mem., Res. Awards Cttee, Stroke Assoc., 2012–. *Publications*: papers in Jl of Forensic Sci. *Recreations*: travel, early music, good food, playing cricket, drinking beer. *T*: 07599 505966. *E*: pmac.holmdene@googlemail.com. *Clubs*: Erith Cricket, Statics Cricket.

**MACDONALD, Patrick James**; Managing Partner, Calton Hill Partners, since 2007; Chairman (formerly Partner), School for CEOs, since 2011; Chairman, Corona Corporate Solutions, since 2018; *b* 14 May 1962; *s* of Charles Patrick Macdonald and Frances Gillian Macdonald; *m* 1987, Jacqueline Ann Willis; one *s* two *d*. *Educ*: Stowe Sch.; Oriel Coll., Oxford (BA Hons Engrg Sci.); INSEAD, Fontainebleau (MBA with dist.). CEng 1990; MIMechE 1990; MIET (MIEE 1990). RCNC, 1984–85; Project Manager, Unilever, 1985–91; Manager, Boston Consulting Gp, 1993–97; Vice-Pres., Sourcing, GE Capital, Gen. Electric, 1997–2002; Chief Exec., John Menzies plc, 2003–07; Chief. Exec., Reconomy, 2009–11 (Chm., 2011–18); CEO, Dalestone Energy, 2012–14. Chm., Inenco, 2016–17; non-exec. Dir, NatureSpace Partnership, 2017–. Vice Chm., Scottish Adv. Cttee, Duke of Edinburgh's Award, 2005–. Trustee, Woodland Trust, 2012–. FRSA; CCMI 2004. *Recreations*: ski-ing, hill-walking, canoeing, sailing, rowing, extreme gardening. *Address*: School for CEOs, 6 Castle Street, Edinburgh EH2 3AT.

**MacDONALD, Philip Geoffrey**; Headmaster, City of London Freemen's School, 2007–15; *b* Bath, 30 Jan. 1956; *s* of Philip MacDonald and Margaret MacDonald; *m* 1990, Michelle Spencer; two *s* two *d*. *Educ*: St Brendan's Coll., Bristol; Hertford Coll., Oxford (BA Classics); Bristol Univ. (PGCE). Teacher of English, Venice, 1978–80; Classics Teacher, Rougemont Sch., 1982–85; Hd of Classics/Dir of Studies, Douai Sch., 1985–92; Dep. Hd, Marist Sch., 1993–98; Headmaster, Mount St Mary's Coll., 1998–2007. Mem., HMC, 1998–2015. *Publications: translations*: Don Luigi Orione, *The Restless Apostle*, 1981; Cecilia Vianelli, *The Way of the Carts*, 1982. *Recreations*: music (listening), family, church, woodwork, Italian opera. *Address*: Ferndale House, Church Road, Chavey Down, Ascot, Berks SL5 8RR. *E*: philip.macdonald@tiscali.co.uk.

**MACDONALD OF CLANRANALD, Ranald Alexander**; 24th Chief and Captain of Clanranald; formerly Chairman and Managing Director, Tektura Ltd; *b* 27 March 1934; *s* of late Captain Kenneth Macdonald of Inchkenneth, DSO, and late Marjory Broad Smith, Basingstoke; *S* kinsman as Chief of Clanranald, 1944; *m* 1961, Jane Campbell-Davys, *d* of late I. E. Campbell-Davys, Llandovey, Carms; two *s* one *d*. *Educ*: Christ's Hospital. Founded: Fairfix Contracts Ltd, 1963; Tektura Wallcoverings, 1970. Chm., British Contract Furnishing Assoc., 1975–76. Lieut (TA) Cameron Highlanders, 1958–68. Mem., Standing Council of Scottish Chiefs, 1957–; Pres., Highland Soc. of London, 1988–91 (Dir,

1959–80); Chief Exec., Clan Donald Lands Trust, 1978–80; Chm., Museum of the Isles, 1981–90; Founding Trustee, Lord of the Isles Galley Proj., 1989–. Vice Pres., Les Avants Bobsleigh and Toboggan Club, 1987–. *Recreation:* avoidance of boredom. *Heir: s* Ranald Og Angus Macdonald, younger of Clanranald, *b* 14 Sept. 1963. *Address:* 13 Eccleston Street, Belgravia, SW1W 9LX. *Clubs:* Beefsteak, Pratt's; New, Puffin's (Edinburgh); British (Bangkok).

**MACDONALD, Richard Auld,** CBE 2002; Director General, National Farmers' Union, 1996–2009; *b* 31 Oct. 1954; *s* of Anthony Macdonald and Gillian Macdonald (*née* Matthews); *m* 1980, Susan Jane Reynolds; two *d. Educ:* Bishop's Stortford Coll.; Queen Mary Coll., London Univ. (BSc Hons Biology). National Farmers' Union: Parly Sec., 1978–85; County Sec., Devon, 1985–89; Regl Dir, SW, 1989–92; Dir, 1992–96. Chm., Better Regulation Task Force on food and farming, DEFRA, 2010–13. Chairman: Associa Ltd, 2001–09; SALSA, 2010–15; Sidai Internat., 2015–; Bd, Acting on Campylobacter Together, 2015–; Strategic Advr, Moy Park Ltd, 2010–18; non-executive Director: Dairy Crest plc, 2010–; NIAB Ltd, 2011– (Vice Chm., 2014–). Mem. Bd, Envmt Agency, 2013–May 2020 (Dep. Chm., 2016–May 2020). Trustee: Farm Africa, 2009– (Chm., 2010–); Earth (formerly Northmoor) Trust, 2011–18. Gov., Royal Agricl Univ. (formerly Coll.), Cirencester, 2010–16. FRASE 2005. *Recreations:* golf, cricket, Rugby, travel. *Address:* Woodpeckers, Hithercroft, South Moreton, Oxon OX11 9AL. *E:* richard.macdonald@woodpeckers.biz. *Clubs:* Farmers; Moreton Cricket; Springs Golf; South Moreton Boxing.

**MACDONALD, Roderick Francis;** *see* Uist, Hon. Lord.

**MACDONALD, Dr Rosemary Gillespie,** FRCP, FRCA; Dean, Post-graduate Medical Education (Yorkshire), University of Leeds and Northern and Yorkshire NHS Executive, 1992–2001, now Emeritus; *b* 25 March 1944; *d* of John Mackenzie Paterson and Mary McCauley Paterson; *m* 1968, Hamish Neil Macdonald; one *s* one *d* (twins). *Educ:* Univ. of Glasgow (MB ChB); Univ. of Bradford (PhD 1976). FRCA 1971; FRCP *ad eund.* 1998. Lectr in Anaesthesia, Univ. of Leeds, 1973–76; Consultant Obstetric Anaesthetist, St James's Univ. Hosp., Leeds, 1976–92. Chair, St Gemma's Hospice, 2010– (Trustee, 2003–). Hon. FRCPsych 2002. Life Fellow, Univ. of Leeds, 1992. *Publications:* contribs to British Jl Anaesthesia, Anaesthesia, BMJ, etc. *Recreations:* cooking, walking, opera, ballet, art, human beings. *Address:* The Hawthorns, Moreton OX9 2HX. *T:* (01844) 761067.

**MacDONALD, Sally;** Director, Museum of Science and Industry, since 2014; *b* Carlisle, 18 June 1959; *d* of Neil MacDonald and Helen MacDonald; *m* 1987, Hilary James Young; two *s. Educ:* Cheadle Hulme Sch.; Univ. of Bristol (BA Jt Hons 1st Cl. Latin, Archaeol. and Ancient Hist. 1980); Study Centre, London (Dip. Hist. of Architecture, Fine and Decorative Arts (Dist.) 1983); Museums Assoc. (Dip. 1987). FMA 1998. Asst Keeper, Decorative Arts, Manchester City Art Galls, 1984–87; Asst Curator, and Actg Dep. Dir, Geffrye Mus., 1987–89; Principal Mus Officer, London Bor. of Croydon, 1989–98; University College London: Manager, Petrie Mus. of Egyptian Archaeol., 1998–2005; Project Manager, Inst. for Cultural Heritage, 2005–06; Dir, Public and Cultural Engagement, 2006–14; Member: Bd, UCL-Qatar, 2011–14; UK-Qatar Year of Culture 2013 Steering Gp, 2013–14. Co-Founder and Co-Dir, Heritage Without Borders, 2011–14; Co-Chm., Women Leaders in Mus Network, 2012–15. Member, Board: Culture Unlimited, 2003–11; Jewish Mus., 2011–13; Mus Assoc., 2011–13; Bloomsbury Fest., 2012–14; North Council, Arts Council England, 2017–; Mem., Our Mus Steering Gp, Paul Hamlyn Foundn, 2011–. FRSA 2008. *Publications:* articles in jls and book chapters on public engagement with univ. and public museums, touch and object handling in museums, and 3D scanning applications in museums; mus. catalogues on design hist. and decorative arts. *Recreations:* visiting places I think I won't like in order to confound my expectations, outdoor swimming. *Address:* Museum of Science and Industry, Liverpool Road, Manchester M3 4FP.

**MACDONALD, Sharman;** playwright, screenwriter and novelist; *b* 8 Feb. 1951; *d* of Joseph Henry Hosgood Macdonald and Janet Rowatt Williams; *m* 1976, Kevin William Knightley; one *s* one *d. Educ:* Hutchesons' Girls' GS, Glasgow; George Watson's Ladies' Coll., Edinburgh; Univ. of Edinburgh (MA 1972). *Theatre:* When I Was a Girl I Used to Scream and Shout, 1984; The Brave, 1988; When We Were Women, 1988; All Things Nice, 1990; Shades, 1992; The Winter Guest, 1995; Borders of Paradise, 1995; After Juliet, 1999; The Girl With Red Hair, 2005; Broken Hallelujah, 2005; *radio:* Sea Urchins, 1997 (Bronze Sony Drama Award; adapted for stage, 1998); Gladly My Cross-eyed Bear, 2000; Soft Fall the Sounds of Eden, 2004; *opera libretto:* Hey Persephone!, 1998; *films:* Wild Flowers, 1989; The Winter Guest, 1998; The Edge of Love, 2008. Most Promising Playwright Award, Evening Standard Awards, 1984. *Publications:* plays: When I Was a Girl I Used to Scream and Shout, 1984; When We Were Women, 1988; The Brave, 1988; All Things Nice, 1990; Shades, 1992; Sharman Macdonald Plays I, 1995; Sea Urchins, 1998; After Juliet, 1999; The Girl with Red Hair, 2005; *novels:* The Beast, 1986; Night Night, 1988. *Recreation:* body boarding. *Address:* c/o United Agents, 12–26 Lexington Street, W1F 0LE.

**MacDONALD, Prof. (Simon) Gavin (George),** FRSE; Professor of Physics, University of Dundee, 1973–88, now Emeritus; *b* 5 Sept. 1923; *s* of Simon MacDonald and Jean H. Thomson; *m* 1948, Eva Leonie Austerlitz; one *s* one *d. Educ:* George Heriot's Sch., Edinburgh; Edinburgh Univ. (MA (1st Cl. Hons) Maths and Nat. Phil); PhD (St Andrews). FIP 1958, FRSE 1972. Jun. Scientific Officer, RAE, Farnborough, 1943–46; Lectr, Univ. of St Andrews, 1948–57; Senior Lecturer: University Coll. of the West Indies, 1957–62; Univ. of St Andrews, 1962–67; Visiting Prof., Ohio Univ., 1963; University of Dundee: Sen. Lectr, then Prof., 1967–88; Dean of Science, 1970–73; Vice-Principal, 1974–79. Convener, Scottish Univs Council on Entrance, 1977–83 (Dep. Convener, 1973–77); Chm., Stats Cttee, UCCA, 1989–93 (Mem. Exec. Cttee, 1977–93; Chm., Technical Cttee, 1979–83; Dep. Chm., 1983–89). Chm., Bd of Dirs, Dundee Rep. Th., 1975–89; Chm., Fedn of Scottish Theatres, 1978–80. *Publications:* Problems and Solutions in General Physics, 1967; Physics for Biology and Premedical Students, 1970, 2nd edn 1975; Physics for the Life and Health Sciences, 1975; *novels:* Death is My Mistress, 2007; The Crime Committee, 2007; Publish and Be Dead, 2007; My Frail Blood, 2007; Swallow Them Up, 2008; Dishing the Dirt, 2008; A Family Affair, 2009; Playing Away, 2009; Bloody and Invisible Hand, 2009; The Truth in Masquerade, 2009; I Spy, I Die, 2010; Bow at a Venture, 2010; Passport to perdition, 2010; The Plaintive Numbers, 2010; The Root of All Evil, 2011; Pay the Price, 2011; The Forsyth Saga, 2011; Murder at the Museum, 2012; The Second Forsyth Saga, 2012; Mysteries of Space and Time, 2013; Murder of an Unknown, 2013; The Long Arm, 2014; A Further Forsyth Saga, 2014; Amorphous, 2014; Double Jeopardy, 2014; Rendezvous with Death, 2015; A Forsyth Duo, 2015; The Man Who Died Twice, 2015; Forsyth Triumphant, 2015; Encore Forsyth, 2016; Green Pastures, 2017; A Winter's Tale, 2017; Pools, Poison and Pressure, 2018; Bridge: could you have played or defended better?, 2018; articles in physics jls. *Recreations:* bridge, golf, fiction writing. *Address:* 7A Windmill Road, St Andrews KY16 9JJ. *T:* (01334) 478014.

**McDONALD, Sir Simon (Gerard),** KCMG 2014 (CMG 2004); KCVO 2015; Permanent Under-Secretary of State, Foreign and Commonwealth Office and Head of the Diplomatic Service, since 2015; *b* 9 March 1961; *s* of James B. McDonald and Angela (*née* McDonald); *m* 1989, Hon. Olivia Mary, *o d* of Baron Wright of Richmond, *qv;* two *s* two *d. Educ:* De La Salle Coll. Grammar Sch., Salford; Pembroke Coll., Cambridge (MA; Hon. Fellow, 2016). Joined FCO, 1982; Jedda, 1985; Riyadh, 1985–88; Bonn, 1988–90; FCO, 1990; Private Sec. to Perm. Under-Sec. of State, FCO, 1993–95; First Sec., Washington, 1995–98; Counsellor, Dep. Hd of Mission and Consul-Gen., Riyadh, 1998–2001; Principal Private Sec. to Sec. of State for Foreign and Commonwealth Affairs, 2001–03; Ambassador to Israel, 2003–06; Dir, Iraq, FCO, 2006–07; Foreign Policy Advr to Prime Minister and Hd, Overseas and Defence Secretariat, later Foreign and Defence Policy Secretariat, Cabinet Office, 2007–10; Ambassador to Germany, 2010–15. *Address:* c/o Foreign and Commonwealth Office, King Charles Street, SW1A 2AH. *E:* the6mcdonalds@yahoo.co.uk.

**McDONALD, Stewart Malcolm;** MP (SNP) Glasgow South, since 2015; *b* Glasgow, 24 Aug. 1986. *Educ:* Govan High Sch. Tour guide, Canary Is; work on campaigns and res. for MSPs. SNP spokesperson for Defence, 2017–. Member: Transport Select Cttee, 2015–17; Cttee on Standards, 2019–; Cttee on Privileges, 2019–. *Address:* House of Commons, SW1A 0AA.

**McDONALD, Stuart Campbell;** MP (SNP) Cumbernauld, Kilsyth and Kirkintilloch East, since 2015; *b* Glasgow, 2 May 1978. *Educ:* Kilsyth Acad.; Univ. of Edinburgh (LLB Hons; DipLP 2001). Legal trainee, Simpson and Marwick, Solicitors, 2001–03; Solicitor, NHS Central Legal Office, 2003–05; Human Rights Solicitor, Immigration Adv. Service, 2005–09; Researcher, then Sen. Researcher, Scottish Parlt, 2009–13; Sen. Researcher and Hd of Information, Yes Scotland HQ, 2013–14; work for anti-racism charity, 2014–15. SNP spokesperson on immigration, asylum and border control, 2015–. Mem., Home Affairs Select Cttee, 2015–. *Address:* House of Commons, SW1A 0AA.

**MACDONALD, Very Rev. Susan Elizabeth;** Rector, Christ Church, Morningside, since 2007; *b* 11 July 1951. *Educ:* Edinburgh Theol Coll. Ordained deacon, 1996, priest, 1997; Asst Curate, St John's, Jedburgh, 1996–98; Priest, St Peter, Galashiels, 1998–2001; Priest-in-charge, Gordon Chapel, Fochabers, 2001–04; Mission 21 Co-ordinator, Dio. of Moray, Ross and Caithness, 2001–04; Mission and Ministry Officer, Dio. of Aberdeen and Orkney, 2005–07; Dean of Edinburgh, 2012–16. Canon, St Andrew's Cath., Inverness, 2003–04; Hon. Canon, St Mary's Cath., Edinburgh, 2017–. *Address:* 4 Morningside Road, Edinburgh EH10 4DD. *T:* (0131) 229 0090.

**McDONALD, Sir Trevor,** Kt 1999; OBE 1992; DL; newscaster, 1990–2005, presenter, News at Ten, ITN, 1992–99, and ITV News at Ten, 2001–05 and 2008; *b* Trinidad, 16 Aug. 1939; *m;* two *s* one *d.* Work on newspapers, radio and television, Trinidad, 1962–69; producer for Caribbean Service and World Service, BBC Radio, London, 1969–73; Independent Television News: reporter, 1973–78; sports corresp., 1978–80; diplomatic corresp., 1980–82; diplomatic corresp. and newscaster, 1982–87, Diplomatic Ed., 1987–89, Channel Four News; newscaster, News at 5.40, 1989–90; presenter: The ITV Evening News, 1999–2001; Tonight with Trevor McDonald, 1999–2007; presenter, TV series: The Secret Caribbean with Trevor McDonald, 2009; The Secret Mediterranean with Trevor McDonald, 2011; The Mighty Mississippi, 2012; The Mafia with Trevor McDonald, 2015; Las Vegas with Trevor McDonald, 2015; Mafia Women with Trevor McDonald, 2017; Death Row 2018 with Trevor McDonald, 2018; Martin Luther King by Trevor McDonald, 2018; Trevor McDonald and the Killer Nurse, 2018; Babes in the Wood, 2019. Trustee, Historic Royal Palaces, 2007–. Gov. ESU, 2000–06. DL Greater London, 2006. Chancellor, London South Bank (formerly S Bank) Univ., 1999–2012. Fellow, BAFTA, 2011. Newscaster of the Year, TRIC, 1993, 1997, 1999; Gold Medal, RTS (for outstanding contrib. to television news), 1998. *Publications:* Clive Lloyd: a biography, 1985; Vivian Richards: a biography, 1987; Queen and Commonwealth, 1989; Fortunate Circumstances (autobiog.), 1993; (ed) Trevor McDonald's Favourite Poems, 1997; Trevor McDonald's World of Poetry (anthology), 1999. *Address:* c/o ITN, 200 Gray's Inn Road, WC1X 8XZ.

**MACDONALD, Valerie Frances;** *see* Gooding, V. F.

**MACDONALD-DAVIES, Isobel Mary;** Deputy Registrar General for England and Wales, 1994–2005 (Registrar General, April–June 2000); *b* 7 Feb. 1955; *d* of Henry Alexander Macdonald and Freda Matilda Macdonald; *m* 1977, Peter Davies; one *s* two *d. Educ:* Bar Convent Grammar Sch., York; St Andrews Univ. (BSc 1977). CStat 1993. Asst Statistician, OPCS, 1977–84; Statistician, Dept of Educn and OPCS, 1984–94. Mem. Mgt Exec. Bd, ONS, 2001–04. *Recreations:* family, music, reading.

**McDONNELL,** family name of **Earl of Antrim.**

**McDONNELL, Dr Alasdair;** general medical practitioner, since 1979; *b* Cushendall, Co. Antrim, 1 Sept. 1949; *s* of Charles McDonnell and Margaret (*née* McIlhatton); *m* 1998, Olivia Nugent; two *s* two *d. Educ:* St MacNissi's Coll., Garron Tower; University Coll. Dublin Med. Sch. (MB, BCh, BAO 1974). Jun. hosp. med. posts, 1975–79. Mem. (SDLP) Belfast CC, 1977–2001; Dep. Mayor, Belfast, 1995–96. Mem. (SDLP) Belfast S, Northern Ireland Assembly, 1998–June 2015. MP (SDLP) Belfast S, 2005–17; contested (SDLP) same seat, 2017. Contested (SDLP) Belfast S, 1979, 1982, 1983, 1987, 1992, 1997, 2001. Dep. Leader, 2004–10, Leader, 2011–15, SDLP. *Address:* 22 Derryvolgie Avenue, Belfast BT9 6FN.

**McDONNELL, David Croft,** CBE 2005; DL; Vice Lord-Lieutenant of Merseyside, 2010–18; *b* 9 July 1943; *s* of late Leslie and Catherine McDonnell; *m* 1967, Marieke (*née* Bos); three *d. Educ:* Quarry Bank High School, Liverpool. FCA. Qualified Chartered Accountant, 1965; Partner, Thornton Baker, later Grant Thornton, 1972; Nat. Managing Partner, Grant Thornton, 1989–2001; Chief Exec. Worldwide, Grant Thornton, 2001–09. Chm. Bd of Trustees, Nat. Museums Liverpool (formerly Nat. Museums and Galls on Merseyside), 1995–2005; Chm., Arena and Convention Centre, Liverpool, 2010–16; Trustee, Aintree Racecourse, 2011–. Pres., 2007–14, Pro Chancellor, 2015–17, Univ. of Liverpool. DL 2003, High Sheriff, 2009–10, Merseyside. *Recreations:* sailing, motor racing (spectating), mountain walking. *Address:* Burn Lea, 18 The Serpentine, Grassendale, Liverpool L19 9DT. *Clubs:* Athenæum; Artists' (Liverpool).

**McDONNELL, John Beresford William;** QC 1984; DL; *b* 26 Dec. 1940; *s* of Beresford Conrad McDonnell and Charlotte Mary McDonnell (*née* Caldwell); *m* 1968, Susan Virginia, *d* of late Wing Comdr H. M. Styles, DSO and of Audrey (*née* Jorgensen, who *m* 2nd, 1947, Gen. Sir Charles Richardson, GCB, CBE, DSO); two *s* one *d. Educ:* City of London School (Carpenter Scholar); Balliol College, Oxford (Domus Scholar; Hon. Mention, Craven Scholarship, 1958; 1st Cl. Hon. Mods 1960; 2nd LitHum 1962, 2nd Jurisp 1964: MA); Harvard Law Sch. (LLM 1965). Called to the Bar, Inner Temple, 1968; Bencher, Lincoln's Inn, 1993; a Dep. High Ct Judge, 1993–. Pres., Oxford Union Soc. and Amer. Debating Tour, 1962; Harkness Fellowship, 1964–66; Amer. Political Science Assoc. Congressional Fellowship, 1965–66 (attached Rep. Frank Thompson Jr, NJ and Senator George McGovern, SDak); Cons. Research Dept, 1966–69; HM Diplomatic Service, 1969–71, First Sec., Asst Private Sec. to Sec. of State for Foreign and Commonwealth

Affairs, 1970–71; practising at Chancery Bar, 1972–. Cllr, Lambeth Borough Council, 1968–69. Cons. Candidate for Grimsby, 1974–75. Trustee: Trireme Trust, 1980; Bowes Mus., 2000–08; Auckland Castle Trust, 2011–16. Gov., Inns of Ct Sch. of Law, 1995–2000. London Rowing Club Grand VIII, Henley, 1958. FRSA 1994. DL Durham, 2012. *Recreation:* sculling. *Address:* The Lodge, Rushall SN9 6EN. *T:* (01980) 630300; 17 Rutland Street, SW7 1EJ. *T:* (020) 7584 1498; 3 Stone Buildings, Lincoln's Inn, WC2A 3XL. *T:* (020) 7242 4937. *Club:* Athenæum.

**McDONNELL, John Martin;** MP (Lab) Hayes and Harlington, since 1997; *b* 8 Sept. 1951; *s* of Robert and Elsie McDonnell; *m* 1st, 1971, Marilyn Jean Cooper (marr. diss. 1987); two *d*; 2nd, 1995, Cynthia Marie Pinto; one *s. Educ:* Great Yarmouth Grammar Sch.; Burnley Technical Coll.; Brunel Univ. (BSc); Birkbeck Coll., Univ. of London (MSc Politics and Sociology). Prodn worker, 1968–72; Research Assistant: NUM, 1976–78; TUC, 1978–82; full-time GLC Councillor, Hillingdon, Hayes and Harlington, 1982–86; Dep. Leader, GLC, 1984–85; Chm., GLC F and GP Cttee, 1982–85; Prin. Policy Advr, Camden Bor. Council, 1985–87; Secretary: Assoc. of London Authorities, 1987–95; Assoc. of London Govt, 1995–97. Editor, Labour Herald, 1985–88. Member: Gtr London Lab. Party Regl Exec. Cttee, 1982–87; for Gtr London, Lab. Party Nat. Policy Forum, 1993–; Chairman: Lab. Party Irish Soc.; Labour Repn Cttee. Advr, Guildford Four Relatives Campaign, 1984–; Chair, Britain and Ireland Human Rights Centre, 1992–; Founding Mem., Friends of Ireland, 1998–. Contested (Lab): Hampstead and Highgate, 1983; Hayes and Harlington, 1992. Shadow Chancellor of Exchequer, 2015–. Secretary: All Pty Britain-Kenya Gp of MPs, 1997–; All Pty Kurdish Gp, 1997–; All Pty Irish in Britain Parly Gp, 1999–; All Pty Gp on Endometriosis; Chair, All Party Punjabi Community in Britain Gp of MPs, 1999–; Secretary: Fire Brigades Union Parly Gp; Justice Unions Parly Gp; NUJ Parly Gp; PCS Trade Union Gp; Chair: Socialist Campaign Gp of MPs, 1998–; PCS Parly Gp; Labour Repn Cttee; Left Economists Adv. Panel; Co-ordinator, RMT Parly Gp. Housefather (pt-time) of family unit, children's home, 1972–87. Chairman: Hayes and Harlington Community Develt Foundn, 1997–; Barra Hall Regeneration Cttee; Friends of Lake Farm; Friends of Minet Country Park; Mem., Hayes Horticultural Show Assoc.; Hon. Vice Pres., Hayes FC; Patron, Hayes CC. *Publications:* (ed) Economics for the Many, 2018; articles and pamphlets incl. contribs to Labour Herald, Briefing, Tribune, Campaign News. *Recreations:* gardening, reading, cycling, music, theatre, cinema, Wayfarer dinghy sailing, supporting Liverpool, Hayes and Yeading Football Clubs, football refereeing; generally fermenting the overthrow of capitalism. *Address:* House of Commons, SW1A 0AA; Beverley, Cedar Avenue, Hayes, Middx UB3 2NE. *Clubs:* London Irish, Blues West 14; Hillingdon Irish Society; St Claret's, Working Men's (Hayes); Hayes and Harlington Community Centre.

**McDONOUGH, David Fergus,** OBE 1998; Founder and Chairman, Sanctuary Counsel Ltd, since 2019; *b* Eastbourne, Sussex, 7 June 1953; *s* of Alan James and Shirley McDonough. *Educ:* Stowe Sch.; Merton Coll., Oxford (MA Hons). Special Advr to Basil Feldman, 1975–79; Man. Dir, McDonough Associates Ltd, 1979–90; Sen. Consultant, 1990–2001, Dep. Chm., 2001–03, Bell Pottinger Consultants; Chm., McDonough Associates Ltd, 2003–18. Mem., First World War Centenary Adv. Gp, 2013–18; Ambassador, Winston Churchill Meml Trust, 2017–; Trustee, Normandy Meml Trust, 2017–. Patron, The Cares Family, 2017–. Life Pres., October Club, 2005. Hon. Fellow, Harris Manchester Coll., Oxford, 2010. OStJ 2002. *Recreations:* reading, theatre, painting, poetry. *Address:* Flat 10, 17–20 Embankment Gardens, SW3 4LW. *T:* (020) 7349 7533. *E:* david.mcdonough@sanctuarycounsel.com. *Clubs:* White's, Pratt's, Boodle's, Garrick.

**McDOUGALL, Hon. Barbara Jean;** PC (Can.) 1984; OC 2001; Advisor, Aird & Berlis LLP, 2004; *b* Toronto, 12 Nov. 1937; *m* 2005, Adam Hartley Zimmerman, OC, FCA. *Educ:* Univ. of Toronto (BA Hons Econ. and Pol Sci. 1960). Chartered Financial Analyst, 1973. Worked in financial sector in Vancouver, Edmonton and Toronto; Exec. Dir, Canadian Council Financial Analysts, 1982–84; financial columnist, national magazines and on TV. MP (PC) St Paul's, Toronto, 1984–93; Minister of State: Finance, 1984–86; Privatisation, 1986–88; Minister Responsible for Status of Women, 1986–90 and for Regulatory Affairs, 1986–88; Minister, Employment and Immigration, 1988–91; Sec. of State for External Affairs, 1991–93; Chairperson, Cabinet Cttee on Foreign Affairs and Defence Policy, 1991–93; Member Cabinet Cttees: Planning and Priorities, 1991–93; Canadian Unity and Constitutional Negotiations, 1991–93. Chairperson: Morguard Real Estate Investment Trust, 1997–99; AT&T Canada Corp., 1996–99; Pres. and CEO, Canadian Inst. of Internat. Affairs, 1999–2004. Director: Corel Corp., 1998–2003; Bank of Nova Scotia, 1999–2008; Stelco, Inc., 1999–2006; Sun Media Corp., 1999–2001; Unique Design Solutions, Halifax, 2001–11; Imperial Tobacco Ltd, 2004–10. Dir, 2004–13, Emeritus Dir, 2014, Inst. for Res. on Public Policy; Chm., Internat. Develt Res. Centre, 2008–12; Director: Canadian Opera Co., 1993–2007; Inter-Amer. Dialogue, 1994–2008; Internat. Crisis Gp, 1995–2006; Ind. Order of Foresters, 1998–2009. Mem., Internat. Adv. Bd, Council on Foreign Relns, NY, 1995–2002. Governor, York Univ., 1995–2006. Hon. LLD St Lawrence, 1992.

**McDOUGALL, Douglas Christopher Patrick,** OBE 2001; Chairman: Law Debenture Corporation plc, 2000–13 (Director, 1998–2000); Independent Investment Trust plc, since 2000; *b* 18 March 1944; *s* of late Patrick McDougall and Helen (*née* Anderson); *m* 1986, Hon. Carolyn Jane Griffiths, *d* of Baron Griffiths, MC, PC; two *d. Educ:* Edinburgh Acad.; Christ Church, Oxford (MA; Hon. Student 2008). Partner, 1969–89, Sen. Partner, 1989–99, Baillie Gifford & Co., Investment Managers, Edinburgh. Chairman: Eur. Investment Trust plc (formerly Foreign and Colonial Eurotrust plc), 1999–2017; 3i Bioscience Investment Trust plc, 2001–06 (Dep. Chm., 2000–01); Scottish Investment Trust plc, 2003–16 (Dir, 1998–2016); Dep. Chm., Sand Aire Investments plc, 1999–2003; Director: Provincial Insce plc, 1989–94; Baillie Gifford Japan Trust plc, 1989–99; Pacific Horizon Trust plc, 1993–2017; Stramongate Assets plc, 2003–11; Monks Investment Trust plc, 1999–; Herald Investment Trust plc, 2002–16. Chairman: Institutional Fund Managers Assoc., 1994–96; Assoc. Investment Trust Cos, 1995–97; IMRO, 1997–2000 (Dir, 1988–2000). Mem., Investment Bd, Cambridge Univ., 2005–11. *Address:* Linplum House, Haddington, East Lothian EH41 4PE. *T:* (01620) 810242. *Clubs:* Brooks's; New (Edinburgh); Honourable Company of Edinburgh Golfers.

**McDOUGALL, Ellen Rose Eva;** Artistic Director, Gate Theatre, London, since 2017; *b* Enfield, 17 July 1983; *d* of Robert and Sheila McDougall; *m* 2011, Jonah Russell. *Educ:* N London Collegiate Sch.; Edinburgh Univ. and Univ. of Calif, San Diego (1st Cl. Hons English Lit.). Staff Dir, NT, 2009–10; Associate Dir, Gate Th., 2012; Dir, Secret Th., Lyric Hammersmith, 2013–14; plays directed include: Ivan and the Dogs, Soho Th., 2010; Henry the Fifth, Unicorn, 2013; Idomeneus, Gate, 2014; Nutcracker, Unicorn, 2014; Anna Karenina, Manchester Royal Exchange, 2015; The Glass Menagerie, Headlong, 2015; Cinderella, Lyric Hammersmith, 2015; The Rolling Stone, Manchester Royal Exchange and Orange Tree, Richmond, 2015; The Remains of Maisie Duggan, Abbey Th. Dublin, 2016; Aladdin, Lyric Hammersmith, 2016; Othello, Shakespeare's Globe, 2017; The Unknown Island, Gate, 2017; Effigies of Wickedness, Gate, 2018; The Wolves, Th. Royal, Stratford East, 2018; Dear Elizabeth, Gate, 2019; Our Town, Regent's Park Open Air Th., 2019. *Address:* Gate Theatre, 12 Pembridge Road, W11 3HQ. *T:* (020) 7229 5387.

**MacDOUGALL, Hugh;** see MacDougall, R. H.

**MACDOUGALL, Neil;** Justice of Appeal, 1989–95, and Vice-President of the Court of Appeal, 1993–95, Supreme Court of Hong Kong; *b* 13 March 1932; *s* of Norman Macdougall and Gladys Clare Kennerly; *m* 1987, Helen Lui. *Educ:* Aquinas Coll., Perth, WA; Univ. of Western Australia (LLB 1954). Admitted Barrister and Solicitor of Supreme Court, WA, 1957, and of High Court of Australia, 1958; Solicitor of Supreme Court of England, 1976, and of Supreme Court of Hong Kong, 1977. Crown Counsel, Hong Kong, 1965; Director of Public Prosecutions, Hong Kong, 1978; a Judge of the High Court, Hong Kong, 1980; Comr, Supreme Court of Brunei, 1987; a Non-Permanent Judge, Court of Final Appeal, Hong Kong, 1997–2003. Chairman: Insider Dealing Tribunal, Hong Kong, 1987–88; Air Transport Licensing Authy, Hong Kong, 1992–95. *Recreations:* classical music, study of natural history, physical training. *Club:* Hong Kong (Hong Kong).

**MACDOUGALL, Patrick Lorn,** FCA; Chairman: Arlington Securities plc, 1999–2005; West Merchant Bank Ltd (formerly Standard Chartered Merchant Bank, then Chartered WestLB), 1989–98 (Chief Executive, 1985–97); *b* 21 June 1939; *s* of late James Archibald Macdougall, WS, and Valerie Jean Macdougall; *m* 1st, 1967, Alison Noel Offer (marr. diss. 1982); two *s*; 2nd, 1983, Bridget Margaret Young; three *d. Educ:* schools in Kenya; Millfield; University Coll., Oxford (MA Jurisprudence). FCA 1976. Called to the Bar, Inner Temple, 1962. Manager, N. M. Rothschild & Sons Ltd, 1967–70; Exec. Dir, Amex Bank (formerly Rothschild Intercontinental Bank Ltd), 1970–77, Chief Exec., 1977–78; Exec. Dir, Jardine Matheson Holdings Ltd, 1978–85; Gp Exec. Dir, Standard Chartered PLC, 1988–89. Member: Internat. Adv. Bd, Creditanstalt-Bankverein, Vienna, 1982–85; Mem., Sen. Adv. Council, Seagull Energy Inc., Houston, 1996–99; Director: Global Natural Resources Inc., USA, 1994–96; Nuclear Electric plc, 1994–96; Panmure Gordon & Co. Ltd, 1996–98 (Dep. Chm., 1997–98); National Provident Instn, 1997–99; Chm., China Private Equity Investment Hldgs Ltd, 2009–13. Dir and Trustee, SANE, 2001–17 (Chm., 2002–06). FRSA 1988. *Recreations:* opera, bridge, tough crosswords. *Address:* 110 Rivermead Court, SW6 3SB. *T:* (020) 7736 3506. *Clubs:* Athenæum, Hurlingham; Hong Kong, Shek O (Hong Kong).

**MacDOUGALL, Prof. (Robert) Hugh,** FRCSE, FRCR, FRCPE; Bute Professor of Medicine, Head, School of Medicine (formerly Bute Medical School), and Dean, Faculty of Medicine, University of St Andrews, 2002–14; Hon. Consultant Clinical Oncologist, Edinburgh Cancer Centre, Lothian University Hospitals, 1986–2014; *b* 9 Aug. 1949; *s* of Dr John David Bathgate MacDougall and Isabella Williamson MacDougall (*née* Craig); *m* 1977, Moira Jean Gray; one *s* two *d. Educ:* High Sch. of Dundee; Univ. of St Andrews (MB ChB 1972); Univ. of Edinburgh (DMRT 1979). FRCSE 1977; FRCR 1981; FRCPE 1996. House physician and house surgeon, Dundee Royal Infirmary, 1972–73; Registrar in Surgery, Aberdeen Royal Infirmary, and Hon. Clin. Tutor in Surgery, Univ. of Aberdeen, 1976–77; Lectr in Clin. Oncol., Univ. of Edinburgh, 1979–82; Consultant Radiotherapist and Oncologist, Tayside Health Bd, and Sen. Lectr, Univ. of Dundee, 1982–86; Sen. Lectr in Oncol., Univ. of Edinburgh, 1986–2002. Vis. Prof., Coll. of Medicine, Univ. of Edinburgh, 2014–18. HM Inspector of Anatomy for Scotland 2014–18. Lay Mem. Bd, Scottish Courts and Tribunals Service, 2014–. Gov., St Columba's Hospice, Edinburgh, 2012–. *Publications:* (jtly) Helpful Essential Links to Palliative Care, 1992, 5th edn 1999; contribs to internat. jls on neutron therapy. *Recreations:* reading, music, project management. *Address:* 21 GF Belgrave Crescent, Edinburgh EH4 3AJ. *Club:* New (Edinburgh).

**McDOUGALL, Prof. Trevor John,** AC 2018; FRS 2012; FAA; FInstP; FRSN; Professor of Ocean Physics, School of Mathematics and Statistics, UNSW Sydney (formerly University of New South Wales, then UNSW Australia), since 2012; *b* Adelaide, 1 July 1952; *s* of Jack Ronald McDougall and Violet Holly McDougall; *m* 1978, Brita Kathryn Hack; one *s* two *d. Educ:* Unley High Sch., Adelaide; Univ. of Adelaide (BE 1st cl. Hons Mech. Engrg 1973); St John's Coll., Cambridge (PhD 1978). Queen's Fellow in Marine Sci., 1978–80, Res. Fellow, 1980–83, Res. Sch. of Earth Scis, ANU; CSIRO: Sen. Res. Scientist, subseq. Sen. Principal Res. Scientist, Div. of Oceanography, Hobart, 1983–96; Chief Res. Scientist, 1996–2006, CSIRO Fellow, 2007–11, Div. of Marine and Atmospheric Res. Chm., Scientific Cttee on Oceanic Res. and Internat. Assoc. of Phys. Scis of Ocean Wkg Gp 127 on Thermodynamics and Equation of State of Seawater, 2005–11. FAA 1997; Fellow, Aust. Meteorol and Oceanographic Soc., 2004; FInstP 2012; FRSN 2015; Fellow, American Geophysical Union, 2018. Frederick White Prize, 1988, Jaeger Medal, 2015, Aust. Acad. of Scis; Centenary Medal (Australia), 2003; A. G. Huntsman Award, Bedford Instn of Oceanography, 2005; Anton Bruun Medal and Meml Lect., IOC, Paris, 2009; Prince Albert I Medal and Meml Lect., Internat. Assoc. for Phys. Scis of Oceans, 2011; Royal Soc. of Tasmania Medal, 2013; NSW Premier's Prize for Excellence in Maths, Earth Scis, Chemistry and Physics, 2017. *Recreations:* bush walking, cycling, boot camp. *Address:* School of Mathematics and Statistics, UNSW Sydney, Sydney, NSW 2052, Australia. *T:* (2) 93853498, *Fax:* (2) 93857123. *E:* Trevor.McDougall@unsw.edu.au.

**McDOWALL, His Honour Andrew Gordon;** a Circuit Judge, 1998–2018; *b* 2 Sept. 1948; *s* of William Crocket McDowall and Margery Haswell McDowall (*née* Wilson); *m* 1976, Cecilia Clarke; one *s* one *d. Educ:* Glasgow Acad.; Queen's Coll., Oxford (Open Hastings Schol.; BCL, MA). Called to the Bar, Gray's Inn, 1972; in practice at the Bar, 1972–98; a Recorder, 1993–98; South Eastern Circuit. *Recreations:* reading, music (London Orpheus Choir), squash, paronomasia. *Address:* c/o 1 King's Bench Walk, Temple, EC4Y 7DB.

**McDOWALL, Maj. Gen. David,** CBE 2009 (MBE 1993); Chief Executive and Lieutenant Governor, Royal Hospital Chelsea, 2014–15; Senior Defence Advisor, Leonardo (MW) Ltd; *b* 16 Aug. 1954; *s* of David and Mary McDowell; *m* 1977, Valerie King; two *s* one *d. Educ:* Rephad Primary Sch.; Stranraer Acad.; RMA Sandhurst; RMCS. CO 7th Signal Regt, 1993–96; Comdr 1st Signal Bde, 2000–02; Signal Officer in Chief, 2002–04; Dir Comd and Battlespace Mgt (Army), 2004–07; GOC Second Div., 2007–09. FIET 2004; FBCS 2005. Chm., Army Football Assoc. *Recreations:* golf, bagpipes. *Club:* Army and Navy.

**MacDOWALL, Dr David William,** MA, DPhil; FSA, FRAS; Chairman, Society for South Asian Studies (formerly Society for Afghan Studies), 1982–98 (Hon. Secretary, 1972–82; Hon. Fellow, 1999); Hon. Research Fellow, Centre for Research in East Roman Studies, University of Warwick, since 1993; *b* 2 April 1930; *o s* of late William MacDowall and Lilian May MacDowall (*née* Clarkson); *m* 1962, Mione Beryl, *yr d* of late Ernest Harold Lashmar and Dora Lashmar; two *d. Educ:* Liverpool Inst.; Corpus Christi Coll., Oxford; British Sch. at Rome. Hugh Oldham Scholar 1947, Pelham Student in Roman History 1951; Barclay Head Prize for Ancient Numismatics, 1953 and 1956. 2nd Lieut Royal Signals, 1952. Asst Principal, Min. of Works, 1955; Asst Keeper, Dept of Coins and Medals, British Museum, 1956; Principal, Min. of Educn, 1960; Principal, Univ. Grants Cttee, 1965; Asst Sec. 1970; Master of Univ. Coll., Durham, 1973–78; Hon. Lectr in Classics and in Oriental Studies, Univ. of Durham, 1975; Asst Dir, 1978–80, Dir, 1980–85, Polytechnic of N London. Hon. Treasurer, Royal Numismatic Soc., 1966–73; Vice-Pres., British Archaeol Assoc., 1993–95 (Hon. Treas., 1989–93); Pres., Royal Asiatic Soc., 1994–97 (Vice-Pres., 1993–94, 1997–2000). Mem. Governing Body, SOAS, 1990–97. Trustee, UK Trust, Indian Nat. Trust for Architectl and Cultural Heritage, 1994–2009. Corresponding Member: Istituto Italiano per il Medio ed Estremo Oriente, 1987; Amer. Numismatic Soc.,

1991. Hon. Fellow, Asiatic Soc. of Mumbai, 2004. *Publications:* Coin Collections, their preservation, classification and presentation, 1978; The Western Coinages of Nero, 1979; (contrib.) Mithraic Studies, 1975; (contrib.) The Archaeology of Afghanistan, 1978, rev. edn 2019; (ed jtly) Indian Numismatics: history, art and culture, 1992; (jtly) The Roman Coins, Republic and Empire up to Nerva, in the Provinciaal Museum G. M. Kam at Nijmegen, 1992; (ed jtly) Foreign Coins Found in the Indian Sub-Continent, 2003; (jtly) A Catalogue of Coins from the Excavations at Bir-kot-Ghwandai 1984–1992, 2004; articles in Numismatic Chron., Jl Numismatic Soc. India, Schweizer Münzblätter, Acta Numismatica, S Asian Archaeology, Afghan Studies, S Asian Studies, Numismatic Digest, Res Orientales, etc. *Recreations:* travel, antiquities, photography, natural history, gardening, genealogy. *Address:* High Trees, 106 Whitedown Lane, Alton, Hants GU34 1QR. *Club:* Athenæum.

**McDOWALL, Keith Desmond,** CBE 1988; Chairman, Keith McDowall Associates, 1988–2001; *b* 3 Oct. 1929; *s* of William Charteris McDowall and Edna Florence McDowall; *m* 1st, 1957, Shirley Margaret Russell Astbury (marr. diss. 1985); two *d*; 2nd, 1988, Brenda Dean (Baroness Dean of Thornton-le-Fylde, PC) (*d* 2018). *Educ:* Heath Clark Sch. Croydon, Surrey. Served RAF, National Service, 1947–49. South London Press, 1947–55; Daily Mail, 1955–67: Indust. Corresp., 1958; Indust. Editor, 1961–67; Man. Dir, Inca Construction (UK) Co. Ltd, 1967–69; Govt Information Service: successively Chief Inf. Officer, DEA, BoT, Min. of Housing and Local Govt, DoE, and Home Office, 1969–72; Dir of Inf., NI Office, 1972–74; Dir of Inf., Dept of Employment, 1974–78; Man. Dir Public Affairs, British Shipbuilders, 1978–80. Dir, Govan Shipbuilders Ltd, 1978–80. Dir of Information, 1981–86, Dep. Dir Gen., 1986–88, CBI. Chm., Kiss FM Radio, 1990–92 (Chm., steering cttee, 1989–90). Freeman, City of London, 1997; Liveryman: Shipwrights' Co., 1998–; Stationers' Co., 2018–. *Publications:* Before Spin (memoirs), 2016; articles in newspapers and various pubns. *Recreations:* classic cars, cricket, jazz, mingling. *Address:* 2 Malvern Terrace, N1 1HR. *Clubs:* Reform (Mem., Gen. Council, 2013–), MCC; Royal Cornwall Yacht (Falmouth).

**MacDOWALL, Simon Charles,** CD 1985; self-employed communications consultant and author, since 2013; *b* 18 July 1956; *s* of Joseph and Oonagh MacDowall; *m* 1981, Gabriele Kuzaj (marr. diss. 2010); one *s* one *d*; partner, Caroline Gay Way. *Educ:* Collège Militaire Royal, St Jean, Quebec (BA 1978). Royal Canadian Dragoons, 1978–87; Canadian Army: Public Affairs Officer, 1987–91; Regl Communications, NW Canada, 1991–93; NATO: Press Officer, SHAPE, Belgium and Bosnia, 1993–94; UN Spokesman, Sarajevo, 1994; Chief of Press and Inf., Allied Forces NW Europe, 1995–99; Communications Director: DSS, 1999–2001; DWP, 2001–06; Dir Gen., Media and Commns, MoD, 2006–07; Director: Communications and Mktg, HMRC, 2007–11; Emic Communications, 2011–13. *Publications:* Late Roman Infantryman, 1994; Late Roman Cavalryman, 1995; Germanic Warrior, 1996; Battle of Adrianople, 2001; Battle of the Catalaunian Fields, 2015; The Vandals, 2016; The Goths, 2017; The Franks, 2018. *Recreations:* travel, walking, good food and wine, painting historical figurines, study of military history. *Clubs:* Reform, Frontline, Blacks.

**McDOWALL, Stuart,** CBE 1984; Chairman, Fife Healthcare NHS Trust, 1994–96; economic consultant; Senior Lecturer in Economics, University of St Andrews, 1967–91; *b* 19 April 1926; *s* of Robert McDowall and Gertrude Mary Collister; *m* 1951, Margaret Burnside Woods Gyle; three *s*. *Educ:* Liverpool Institute; St Andrews University (MA Hons 1950). Personnel Manager, Michael Nairn & Co., 1955–61; Lectr in Econs, St Andrews Univ., 1961–67; Master, United Coll. of St Salvator and St Leonard, 1976–80. Dep. Chm., Central Arbitration Cttee, 1976–96; Local Govt Boundary Comr for Scotland, 1983–99; Member: Monopolies and Mergers Commn, 1985–89; Restrictive Practices Court, 1993–96. Econ. Consultant to UN in Saudi Arabia, 1985–89. Sec., Scottish Economic Soc., 1970–76. *Publications:* (with P. R. Draper) Trade Adjustment and the British Jute Industry, 1978; (with H. M. Begg) Industrial Performance and Prospects in Areas Affected by Oil Developments, 1981; articles on industrial economics and regional economics. *Recreations:* golf, hill walking. *Club:* Royal and Ancient Golf (St Andrews).

**McDOWELL, Alexander Blair,** RDI 2006; production designer, since 1980; *b* 11 April 1955; *s* of late (Hamilton) Blair McDowell and Pamela McDowell (*née* Howe); *m* 1995, Kirsten Everberg; one *s* one *d*. *Educ:* Downs Sch., Colwall; Bootham Sch., York; Central Sch. of Art, London. Graphic Designer and owner, Rocking Russian Design, 1977–86; production designer: *films* designed include: The Crow, 1994; Fear and Loathing in Las Vegas, 1998; Fight Club, 1999; Minority Report, 2002; The Terminal, 2004; Charlie and the Chocolate Factory, 2005; Corpse Bride, 2005; Breaking and Entering, 2006; Watchmen, 2009; Man of Steel, 2013. Adv. Bd, University Art Mus., Long Beach, CA, 2005–. Vis. Artist, MIT Media Lab, 2006–11. Founder, Matter Art and Science, 2002–. Founder and Co-Dir, 5D Immersive Design Conference, 2008–. *Recreations:* art, reading, food, walking. *E:* alexmcdowell1@mac.com.
  *See also* J. B. McDowell.

**McDOWELL, Rt Rev. (Francis) John;** *see* Clogher, Bishop of.

**McDOWELL, Prof. Gary Linn,** PhD; FRHistS; Tyler Haynes Professor of Leadership Studies, Political Science and Law, University of Richmond, USA, 2005–18, now Emeritus (Tyler Haynes Professor of Leadership Studies and Political Science, 2003–05); *b* 4 June 1949; *s* of Samuel Earl McDowell and Violet Marie McDowell (*née* Harris); *m* 1990, Brenda Jo Evans. *Educ:* Univ. of S Florida (BA 1972); Memphis State Univ. (MA 1974); Univ. of Chicago (AM 1978); Univ. of Virginia (PhD 1979). Social Studies Teacher, Dunedin Jun. High Sch., 1972–73; Asst Prof. of Political Sci., Dickinson Coll., 1979–83; Liberal Arts Fellow, Harvard Law Sch., 1981–82; Asst Prof., 1983–85, Associate Prof., 1985–86, of Political Sci., Tulane Univ.; Dir, Office of the Bicentennial of the Constitution, Nat. Endowment for the Humanities, 1984–85; Associate Dir of Public Affairs, US Dept of Justice, 1985–87; Resident Schol., Center for Judicial Studies, 1987–88; Fellow, Woodrow Wilson Internat. Center for Scholars, 1987–88; Vice Pres., Nat. Legal Center for Public Interest, 1988–89; Bradley Vis. Schol., Harvard Law Sch., 1990–92; Lectr, Harvard Univ., 1992; Dir, Inst. of US Studies, 1992–2003, and Prof. of American Studies, 1993–2003, Univ. of London. Fellow, Nat. Endowment for the Humanities, 2007–08. Mem., Fulbright Commn, 1997–2003. Member: Bd, Landmark Legal Foundn, 1992–; Bd of Visitors, Pepperdine Univ. Sch. of Public Policy, 2000–04; Soc. of Scholars, James Madison Prog. in American Ideals and Instns, Princeton Univ., 2002–. FRHistS 1996. FRSA. Dist. Educator Award, 2005, Jepson Sch. of Leadership Studies Award for Leadership and Service, 2018, Univ. of Richmond. *Publications:* (ed jtly and contrib.) The American Founding, 1981; (ed jtly and contrib.) Taking the Constitution Seriously, 1981; Equity and the Constitution, 1982; Curbing the Courts, 1988; (jtly) Justice vs Law, 1993; (ed jtly and contrib.) Our Peculiar Security, 1993; (ed jtly and contrib.) Reason and Republicanism, 1997; (ed jtly) Juvenile Delinquency in the United States and the United Kingdom, 1999; (ed jtly and contrib.) America and Enlightenment Constitutionalism, 2006; (ed jtly and contrib.) Lincoln's Legacy of Leadership, 2010; The Language of Law and the Foundations of American Constitutionalism, 2010; (ed jtly) Executive Power in Theory and Practice, 2012; numerous contribs to learned jls and other publications. *Recreations:* walking, reading, bluegrass music, martinis, mint juleps and Cuban cigars. *Address:* 10230 Sioux Road, Richmond, VA 23235, USA. *T:* (804) 5140557. *Club:* Reform.

**McDOWELL, Rt Rev. John;** *see* McDowell, Rt Rev. F. J.

**McDOWELL, Prof. John Henry,** FBA 1983; FAAAS; Distinguished University Professor of Philosophy, University of Pittsburgh, since 2009 (Professor of Philosophy, 1986–88; University Professor of Philosophy, 1988–2009); *b* 7 March 1942; *s* of Sir Henry McDowell, KBE and Norah, *d* of Walter Slade Douthwaite; *m* 1977, Andrea Lee Lehrke. *Educ:* St John's College, Johannesburg; University College of Rhodesia and Nyasaland; New College, Oxford (MA); BA London. FAAAS 1993. Fellow and Praelector in Philosophy, UC, Oxford, 1966–86, Emeritus Fellow, 1988, Hon. Fellow, 2007; Univ. Lectr (CUF), Oxford Univ., 1967–86. James C. Loeb Fellow in Classical Philosophy, Harvard Univ., 1969; Visiting Professor: Univ. of Michigan, 1975; Univ. of California, Los Angeles, 1977; Univ. of Minnesota, 1982; Jadavpur Univ., Calcutta, 1983; John Locke Lectr, Oxford Univ., 1991. Sen. Fellow, Council of Humanities, Princeton Univ., 1984. Hon. DHumLit Chicago, 2008; Hon. DLit UCD, 2013; Hon. Dr Human Scis Patras, 2015. Dist. Achievement Award, Andrew W. Mellon Foundn, 2011. *Publications:* Plato, Theaetetus (trans. with notes), 1973; (ed with Gareth Evans) Truth and Meaning, 1976; (ed) Gareth Evans, The Varieties of Reference, 1982; (ed with Philip Pettit) Subject, Thought, and Context, 1986; Mind and World, 1994; Mind, Value, and Reality (collected articles), 1998; Meaning, Knowledge, and Reality (collected articles), 1998; Having the World in View (collected articles), 2009; The Engaged Intellect (collected articles), 2009; articles in jls and anthologies. *Recreations:* reading, music, gardening. *Address:* c/o Department of Philosophy, University of Pittsburgh, Pittsburgh, PA 15260, USA. *T:* (412) 6245792.

**McDOWELL, Jonathan Bruce,** RIBA; architect; Director, Matter Architecture Ltd, since 2016; *b* 18 March 1957; *s* of late Hamilton Blair McDowell and Pamela (*née* Howe); *m* 2001, Rebecca Wells; two *d*. *Educ:* The Downs Sch.; Bootham Sch.; Downing Coll., Cambridge (MA, DipArch); Graduate Sch. of Design, Harvard Univ. RIBA 1985. Julyan Wickham Architects; Sansom Cross Architects; Terry Farrell Partnership, 1983–86; Associate, Munkenbeck & Marshall, 1986–90; Principal, Jonathan McDowell Architects, 1991–96; Partner, McDowell+Benedetti, 1996–2016; Dir, McDowell+Benedetti Ltd, 1998–2016: main projects include: Oliver's Wharf Penthouse, Wapping, 1996; Assoc. of Photographers, New Gall., London, 1998; Nursing Home for Merchant Taylors' Co., Lewisham, 2002; Suncourt Hse, 2002; Springboard Centre, Stokesley, 2005; Castleford Bridge, 2008; JCB Uttoxeter Masterplan, 2008–; Claremont Fan Court Sch. Masterplan, Esher, 2013; Scale Lane Bridge, Hull, 2013; Brunner showroom, 2013; Eleventh Church of Christ Scientist, London, 2016. Member: CABE Enabling Panel, 2001–11; Hackney Design Review Panel, 2007–; Yorks and Humber Reg. Design Review Panel, 2009–13; Islington Design Rev. Panel, 2015–; Design SE Rev. Panel, 2015–; HS2 Ind. Design Panel, 2018–. Professional Studies Advr, Cambridge Univ., 2002–; Ext. Examiner, Univ. of E London, 2014–17. RIBA Competitions Architect Advr, 2015–. FRSA 1999. *Recreation:* Balinese, Javanese and contemporary gamelan. *Address:* (office) Studio G03, Pillbox, 115 Coventry Road, E2 6GG.
  *See also* A. B. McDowell.

**McDOWELL, Kathryn Alexandra,** CBE 2011; DL; Managing Director, London Symphony Orchestra, since 2005; *b* 19 Dec. 1959; *d* of late John McDowell and (Kathleen) Avril McDowell; *m* 1997, Ian Charles Stewart Ritchie, qv. *Educ:* Belfast High Sch.; Univ. of Edinburgh (BMus 1982); Stranmillis Coll. of Education (PGCE 1983). LTCL 1980, Hon. FTCL 1996; ARCM 1981; Hon. RCM 1999. Marketing and Educn Assistant, WNO, 1984–85; Develt Manager, Scottish Chamber Orch., 1985–89; Dep. Gen. Manager, Ulster Orch., 1989–92; Music Officer, Arts Council, 1992–94; Music Dir, Arts Council of England, 1994–99; Chief Exec., Wales Millennium Centre, 1999–2001; Dir, City of London Festival, 2001–05. Chair: Family Arts Campaign, 2012–15; Assoc. of British Orchestras, 2014–17. Member, Council: Royal Philharmonic Soc., 1999–2008; St Paul's Cathedral, 2008–. Trustee, Leeds Internat. Piano Competition, 2017–. Governor, GSMD, 2008–16. Hon. FGS 2013. DL Greater London, 2009. *Recreations:* tennis, walking, travel. *Address:* London Symphony Orchestra, Barbican Centre, Silk Street, EC2Y 8DS.

**McDOWELL, Prof. Linda Margaret,** CBE 2016; PhD, DLitt; FBA 2008; Professor of Human Geography, University of Oxford, 2004–16, now Emerita; Professorial Fellow, St John's College, Oxford, 2004–16, now Emerita Research Fellow; *b* 1 Jan. 1949; *d* of Frederick Herbert Leigh and Olive Morgan Leigh (*née* Nicholson); *m* 1972, Christopher James McDowell; one *s* one *d*. *Educ:* Newnham Coll., Cambridge (BA Hons 1971); Bartlett Sch., University Coll. London (MPhil 1973; PhD 1986); Univ. of Oxford (DLitt 2011). Res. Fellow, Centre for Res. in Soc. Scis, Univ. of Kent, Canterbury, 1973–76; Res. Officer, Inst. of Community Studies, London, 1976–78; Open University: Lectr, then Sen. Lectr in Geog., 1978–92; Dep. Dean, Soc. Scis Faculty, 1989–92; University of Cambridge: Univ. Lectr in Geog., 1992–99; Fellow and Coll. Lectr, 1992–99, Vice Principal, 1997–99, Newnham Coll.; Prof. of Human Geog., LSE, 1999–2000; Prof. of Econ. Geog., UCL, 2000–04. Visiting Lecturer: Univ. of Southampton, 1976; Univ. of Kent, 1978; UCLA, 1990; UCL, 1991. Hon. Prof. of Geog., Univ. of Exeter, 2017–. FAcSS (AcSS 2001). Hon. Fellow, Gender Inst., LSE, 2000–. Back Award, 2001, Victoria Medal, 2008, RGS. *Publications:* (with D. Morgan) Patterns of Residence, 1979; (ed jtly) Urban Change and Conflict, 1981; (ed jtly) City, Economy and Society, 1981; (ed jtly) Geography and Gender, 1984; (ed jtly) Divided Nation: social and cultural change in Britain, 1989; (ed jtly) The Changing Social Structure, 1989; (with J. Allen) Landlords and Property, 1989; (jtly) The Transformation of Britain, 1989; (ed jtly) Defining Women: social institutions and gender divisions, 1992; Capital Culture: gender at work in the City, 1997; Undoing Place?, 1997; (ed jtly) Space, Gender, Knowledge, 1997; (ed jtly) A Feminist Glossary of Human Geography, 1999; Gender, Identity and Place, 1999; Redundant Masculinities?: employment change and white working class youth, 2003; Hard Labour: the forgotten voices of Latvian 'volunteer' workers, 2005; (ed jtly) Gender Divisions and Working Time in the New Economy, 2005; Working Bodies, 2009; (ed jtly) Sage Handbook of Qualitative Research in Human Geography, 2010; (ed jtly) A Companion to Economic Geography, 2011; Working Lives, 2013; Migrant Women's Voices, 2016; contrib. numerous book chapters and to learned jls. *Recreations:* cities, cycling, contemporary fiction, gardening. *Address:* School of Geography and the Environment, University of Oxford, South Parks Road, Oxford OX1 3QY. *T:* (01865) 275843. *E:* linda.mcdowell@geog.ox.ac.uk; St John's College, Oxford OX1 3JP. *T:* (01865) 277300.

**McDOWELL, Malcolm, (Malcolm Taylor);** actor; *b* 13 June 1943; *m* 1992, Kelley Kuhr; two *s*; one *s* one *d* from former marriage. *Educ:* Leeds. *Stage:* RSC Stratford, 1965–66; Entertaining Mr Sloane, Royal Court, 1975; Look Back in Anger, NY, 1980; In Celebration, NY, 1984; Holiday, Old Vic, 1987; Another Time, NY, 1993; *films:* If, 1969; Figures in a Landscape, 1970; The Raging Moon, 1971; A Clockwork Orange, 1971; O Lucky Man, 1973; Royal Flash, 1975; Aces High, 1976; Voyage of the Damned, 1977; Caligula, 1977; The Passage, 1978; Time After Time, 1979; Cat People, 1981; Blue Thunder, 1983; Get Crazy, 1983; Britannia Hospital, 1984; Gulag, 1985; Cross Creek,

1985; Sunset, 1988; Assassin of the Tsar, 1991; Milk Money, 1993; Star Trek Generations, 1994; Tank Girl, 1995; Exquisite Tenderness, 1995; Mr Magoo, 1998; Gangster No 1, 2000; Just Visiting, 2002; I Spy, 2003; The Company, 2004; Rag Tale, 2005; Never Apologise, 2008; Bolt, 2008; Easy A, 2010; The Artist, 2011; Sanitarium, 2013; Some Kind of Beautiful, 2015; 31, 2016; Yamasong: March of the Hollows, 2018; *television:* Our Friends in the North, 1996; Entourage (series), 2005–11; Heroes (series), 2007–08; Franklin & Bash (series), 2011–14. *Address:* c/o Markham, Froggatt and Irwin, 4 Windmill Street, W1T 2HZ.

**McDOWELL, Michelle Janet,** MBE 2010; FREng, FICE; Chair, Civil and Structural Engineering, BDP, since 2004; *b* Coleraine, NI, 6 April 1963; *d* of Ronald McDowell and Doris McDowell; partner, Jason Mark Fox; two *s. Educ:* Coleraine High Sch.; Bristol Univ. (BSc Hons Civil Engrg 1984). MICE 1990, FICE 1999. Engineer: W. S. Atkins & Partners, 1984–87; John Laing Construction, 1988; Associate, Whitby, Bird & Partners, 1989–97; Associate Dir, 1997–2003, Company Dir, 2003–, BDP. Vice Pres., ICE, 2000. FREng 2011. Hon. DEng Bristol, 2012. *Recreations:* travel, cooking, piano playing. *Address:* BDP, 16 Brewhouse Yard, EC1V 4LJ. *T:* (020) 7812 8000. *E:* michellejmcdowell@gmail.com.

**McDOWELL, Paul Duncan;** Partner, Lower Elmsford Farm, since 2015; *b* Luton, 15 Aug. 1962; *s* of Thomas Morris McDowell and Christine Anne McDowell (*née* Moore, now Burgess); *m* 2001, Janine Marcelle Morris; two *s* one *d. Educ:* Queensbury Sch., Dunstable; Univ. of Central England (Dip. Criminal Justice, Policy and Practice 1998); Fitzwilliam Coll., Cambridge (MSt Applied Criminology and Mgt 2003). Served HMP Gartree, Prison Service Coll., HMP Wellingborough, HMP Woodhill, HM YOI Stoke Heath, 1990–2000; Prison Minister's Private Office, Home Office, 2000–01; Dep. Gov., HM YOI Feltham, 2001–03; Governor: HMP Coldingley, 2003–06; HMP Brixton, 2006–09; CEO, Nacro, 2009–14; HM Chief Inspector of Probation, 2014–15. Member: Enquiry Panel, Community or Custody, Make Justice Work Nat. Enquiry, 2009–12; Adv. Gp, Young Offender Acad., 2009–13; Adv. Gp, Impetus Trust, 2010–11. Trustee, Prison Radio Assoc., 2010–; Mem., Bd of Trustees, Eisenhower Foundn, Washington, DC, 2010–18. FRSA. DUniv Birmingham City, 2015. *Recreations:* supporting Luton Town Football Club, attending Glastonbury Festival, collecting music, sport, travel, family.

**McDOWELL, Stanley;** Town Clerk and Chief Executive, Belfast City Council, 1989–92; *b* 14 June 1941; *s* of William McDowell and Annie Storey; *m* 1966, Charlotte Elizabeth Stockdale; three *d. Educ:* Royal Belfast Academical Instn; Queen's Univ. of Belfast (BSc Econ). FCIS. Belfast City and Dist Water Comrs, 1959–70; Asst Sec. (Actg), Antrim County Council, 1971–73; Roads Service Divl Finance Officer, DoE (NI), 1973–79; Belfast City Council, 1979–92; Asst Town Clerk (Admin), 1979–89. Non-exec. Dir, Ulster Community and Hosps Trust, 1998–2002 (Chm., Audit Cttee, 1998–2002); Chm., Belfast Abbeyfield Soc. Ltd, 2011–18 (Dep. Chm., 2002–11). *Address:* 7 Rannoch Road, Holywood, N Ireland BT18 0NA. *T:* (028) 9042 5132.

**MACDUFF, Earl of;** *see* Duke of Fife.

**MacDUFF, Hon. Sir Alistair (Geoffrey),** Kt 2008; a Judge of the High Court of Justice, Queen's Bench Division, 2008–15; *b* 26 May 1945; *s* of late Alexander MacDonald MacDuff and Iris Emma Jarvis (*née* Gardner); *m* 1st, 1969, Susan Christine Kitchener (*d* 1991); two *d*; 2nd, 1993, Katherine Anne Buckley; one *s* one *d. Educ:* Ecclesfield Grammar Sch., Sheffield; LSE (LLB 1965); Sheffield Univ. (LLM 1967). Called to the Bar, Lincoln's Inn, 1969, Bencher, 2003. QC 1993; Asst Recorder, 1983–87; Recorder, 1987–97; Circuit Judge, 1997–2008; Sen. Circuit Judge, 2002–08; Designated Civil Judge, Birmingham Gp, 2000–08. *Recreations:* theatre, opera, wine, Rugby football. *Clubs:* East India; Painswick Rugby Football.

**McDUFF, Prof. (Margaret) Dusa,** PhD; FRS 1994; Helen Lyttle Kimmel '42 Chair of Mathematics, Barnard College, Columbia University, since 2008; *b* 18 Oct. 1945; *d* of Conrad Hal Waddington and Margaret Justin (*née* Blanco White); *m* 1st, 1968, David William McDuff (marr. diss. 1978); one *d*; 2nd, 1984, John Willard Milnor; one *s. Educ:* Univ. of Edinburgh (BSc Hons); Girton Coll., Cambridge (PhD 1971). Lecturer: Univ. of York, 1972–76; Univ. of Warwick, 1976–78; Asst Prof., 1978–80, Associate Prof., 1980–84, Prof. of Maths, 1984–98, Dist. Prof. of Maths, 1998–2008, SUNY at Stony Brook. Asst Prof., MIT, 1974–75; Mem., Inst. for Advanced Study, Princeton, 1976 and 1977; Vis. Prof., Univ. of Calif, Berkeley, 1993. Fellow, Amer. Acad. of Arts and Scis, 1995; Member: NAS, USA, 1999; Amer. Philosophical Soc., 2013. Hon. FKC, 2015; Hon. Mem., LMS, 2007. Corresp. Mem., RSE, 2008. Hon. DSc: Edinburgh, 1997; York, 2000; Louis Pasteur, Strasbourg, 2008; St Andrews, 2014; Warwick, 2017; Hon. Dr Pierre et Marie Cure, Paris, 2016. Sen. Berwick Prize, LMS, 2010: (jtly) Steele Prize for Mathematical Exposition, Amer. Mathematical Soc., 2017. *Publications:* (with D. Salamon): J-Holomorphic Curves and Quantum Cohomology, 1994; Introduction to Symplectic Topology, 1995; J-Holomorphic Curves and Symplectic Topology, 2004. *Recreations:* chamber music, reading, walking. *Address:* Mathematics Department, Columbia University, 2990 Broadway, New York, NY 10027, USA.

**MACE, Andrew Stephen;** Senior UK Government Relations Officer, Bill & Melinda Gates Foundation, since 2014; *b* Woolwich, 31 Dec. 1973; *s* of Raymond and Pauline Mace. *Educ:* Chislehurst and Sidcup Grammar Sch.; Emmanuel Coll., Cambridge (BA 1995). Entered FCO, 1995; Asst Desk Officer, EU Dept (Internal), FCO, 1995–97; Mem., UK Representation to EU, 1997–99; Pol Sec., Copenhagen, 1999–2003; Hd of Pol Team, UN Dept, 2003–05, Dep. Hd, Conflict Issues Gp, 2005–07, FCO; Pol Counsellor, Monrovia, 2007–08; Ambassador to Cambodia, 2008–11; Hd of Sudan Unit, FCO, 2011–14. *Address:* Bill & Melinda Gates Foundation, 62 Buckingham Gate, SW1E 6AJ.

**MACE, Brian Anthony;** Director, Revenue Policy: Employment Initiatives, Board of Inland Revenue, 2002–04; *b* 9 Sept. 1948; *s* of late Edward Laurence Mace and Olive (*née* Bennett); *m* 1973, Anne Margaret Cornford. *Educ:* Maidstone Grammar Sch.; Gonville and Caius Coll., Cambridge (MA Mathematics). Admin. trainee, Bd of Inland Revenue, 1971–73; seconded to Secretariat, Inflation Accounting Cttee, 1974–75; Inland Revenue: Principal, 1975–82; Asst Sec., 1982–90; Under Sec., 1990–2004; Dir, Savings and Investment Div., 1990–98, and Capital and Valuation Div., 1995–98; Dir, Personal Tax, 1998–2000; Dir, Study of Personal Tax, 2000–02. Mem., Tax Law Rev. Cttee, 2007–. *Recreations:* opera, chamber music and song, theatre, cricket, historic buildings. *Address:* 406 Faraday Lodge, Renaissance Walk, SE10 0QL. *T:* (020) 8305 0420.

**MACE, Dame Georgina (Mary),** DBE 2016 (CBE 2007; OBE 1998); DPhil; FRS 2002; Professor of Biodiversity and Ecosystems, and Director, Centre for Biodiversity and Environment Research, University College London, since 2012; *m* 1985, Roderick O. Evans; one *s* two *d. Educ:* Univ. of Liverpool (BSc Hons 1976); Univ. of Sussex (DPhil 1979). Postdoctoral Fellow, Smithsonian Instn, Washington, DC, 1980–81; Sir James Knott Res. Fellow, Dept of Zoology, Univ. of Newcastle upon Tyne, 1981–83; Res. Fellow, Inst. of Zoology, and Hon. Fellow, Dept of Biology, UCL, 1983–89; Institute of Zoology, Zoological Society of London: Pew Scholar in Conservation and the Envmt, 1991–94; NERC Advanced Fellow, 1994–99; Dir of Sci., 2000–06; Prof. of Conservation Sci., 2006–12, Dir, NERC Centre for Population Biology, 2006–10, Imperial Coll. London. Mem., NERC, 2011–18. Member: Natural Capital Cttee, DEFRA, 2012–18; Cttee on Climate Change, 2018–. Member Council: Durrell Wildlife Conservation Trust, 1998–2004; RSPB, 2000–04; Royal Soc., 2005–06, 2013–16; WWF-UK, 2015–. Trustee: Nat. Hist. Mus., 2004–12; Eden Project, 2018–; Linnean Soc. of London, 2018–. *Publications:* (jtly) Creative Conservation: interactive management of wild and captive animals, 1993; (ed jtly) Conservation in a Changing World, 1999; (ed jtly) Conservation of Exploited Species, 2001; articles in learned jls. *Address:* Division of Biosciences, Darwin Building, University College London, Gower Street, WC1E 6BT.

**MACE, Lt-Gen. Sir John (Airth),** KBE 1990 (OBE 1974; MBE 1967); CB 1986; New Zealand Chief of Defence Force, 1987–91; *b* 29 June 1932; *m* 1962, Margaret Theodocia (*née* McCallum); one *s* one *d. Educ:* Ashburton High Sch., NZ; Nelson Coll., NZ; RMC Duntroon, Australia. Commissioned NZ Army, 1953; NZ SAS, 1955–57; active service in Malayan Emergency (despatches, 1958); Comd SAS Sqdn, 1960–62 and 1965; Comd Co. of 1 RNZIR 1st Bn, Borneo, 1966; Vietnam, 1967; appts include: Dir of Infantry and NZ SAS; CO, 1st Bn RNZIR, Singapore; Dir, Officer Postings; Comdr, Army Logistics Support Gp; Comdr, 1st Inf. Bde Gp; Army Staff Coll., Camberley; JSSC, Canberra; Comdr, NZ Force SE Asia, 1979–80; RCDS 1981; Dep. Chief of Defence Staff, 1982–84; Chief of General Staff, 1984–87. Hon. Col, First Bn, Royal NZ Inf. Regt, 2005–08. *Recreations:* golf, walking, reading.

**MACE, Prof. Ruth,** DPhil; FBA 2008; Professor of Evolutionary Anthropology, University College London, since 2004; *b* London, 9 Oct. 1961; *d* of David Mace and Angela Mace; partner, Prof. Mark Pagel, *qv*; two *s. Educ:* South Hampstead High Sch. for Girls; Westminster Sch.; Wadham Coll., Oxford (BA Zool. 1983; DPhil Zool. 1987). Res. Fellow, Imperial Coll. London, 1987–89; Lectr, Univ. of East Anglia, 1989–91; Lectr, then Reader in Evolutionary Anthropol., UCL, 1991–2004. Ed.-in-Chief, Evolution and Human Behavior, 2005–10; Founding Ed.-in-Chief, Evolutionary Human Scis, 2019–. Visiting Professor: Chinese Acad. of Scis, Beijing, 2014–15; Lanzhou Univ., 2016–. *Publications:* The Conservation of Biological Resources, 1998; The Evolution of Cultural Diversity: a phylogenetic approach, 2005; Substitute Parents, 2008; over 100 jl articles and book chapters. *Recreation:* failing to learn Mandarin. *Address:* Department of Anthropology, University College London, 14 Taviton Street, WC1H 0BW. *T:* (020) 7679 8845. *E:* r.mace@ucl.ac.uk.

**McEACHRAN, Colin Neil,** MBE 2018; QC (Scot.) 1982; *b* 14 Jan. 1940; *s* of Eric Robins McEachran and Nora Helen Bushe; *m* 1967, Katherine Charlotte Henderson; two *d. Educ:* Trinity Coll., Glenalmond; Merton Coll., Oxford (BA 1961); Univ. of Glasgow (LLB 1963); Univ. of Chicago (Commonwealth Fellow; JD 1965). Admitted Solicitor, 1966; admitted to Faculty of Advocates, 1968. Advocate Depute, 1975–78. Mem., Scottish Legal Aid Bd, 1990–98; Pres., Pension Appeal Tribunals for Scotland, 1995–2013. Chm., Commonwealth Games Council for Scotland, 1995–99. *Recreations:* target rifle shooting (Silver Medal, Commonwealth Games, NZ, 1974), golf. *Address:* 13 Saxe-Coburg Place, Edinburgh EH3 5BR. *T:* (0131) 332 6820.

**MACEDO, Prof. Helder Malta,** Comendador, Ordem de Santiago da Espada (Portugal), 1993; PhD; Camoens Professor of Portuguese, University of London at King's College, 1982–2004, now Professor Emeritus; *b* 30 Nov. 1935; *s* of Adelino José de Macedo and Aida Malta de Macedo; *m* 1960, Suzette Armanda (*née* de Aguiar). *Educ:* Faculty of Law, Univ. of Lisbon; King's Coll., Univ. of London (BA, PhD); FKC 1991. Lectr in Portuguese and Brazilian Studies, KCL, 1971–82; Sec. of State for Culture, Portuguese Govt, 1979. Visiting Professor: Harvard Univ., 1981; Ecole des Hautes Etudes et Sciences Sociales, Paris, 1992, 1995; Res. Fellow, Univ. of Oxford, 2016–. President: Internat. Assoc. of Lusitanists, 1994–99 (Hon. Pres., 2002); Modern Humanities Res. Assoc., 2009–10. Fellow, Academia das Ciências de Lisboa, 1987. Grã-Cruz, Ordem do Infante D. Henrique (Portugal), 2018. Editor, Portuguese Studies Jl, 1985–2002. *Publications:* Nós, Uma Leitura de Cesário Verde, 1975, 4th edn 1999; Do Significado Oculto da 'Menina a Moça', 1977, 2nd edn 1999; Poesia 1957–77, 1978; Camões e a Viagem Iniciática, 1980; The Purpose of Praise: Past and Future in The Lusiads of Luís de Camões, 1983; Cesário Verde: O Romântico e o Feroz, 1988; Partes de Africa, 1991; Viagem de Inverno, 1994; Pedro e Paula, 1998, 2nd edn 1998 (Brazilian edn, 1999); Viagens do Olhar, 1998; Vícios e Virtudes, 2000, 2nd edn 2001 (Brazilian edn, 2002); Sem Nome, 2004 (Brazilian edn, 2006); Trinta Leituras, 2007; Natália, 2009 (Brazilian edn, 2010); Poemas Novos e Velhos, 2011; Tão Longo Amor Tão Curta A Vida, 2013 (Brazilian edn, 2013); Romance, 2015 (Brazilian edn, 2016); Resta Ainda A Face, 2015; Camões e Outros Contemporâneos, 2017; Cada Um Com O Seu Contrário Num Sujeito, 2019. *Address:* Department of Spanish, Portuguese and Brazilian Studies, King's College London, Strand, WC2R 2LS. *T:* (020) 7873 2507.

**McELDUFF, Barry;** *b* Carrickmore, 16 Aug. 1966; *m* Paula Kelly; one *s* two *d. Educ:* Christian Brothers Grammar Sch., Omagh; Queen's Univ., Belfast (BA Hons Political Sci. and Celtic Studies). Mem. (SF) W Tyrone, NI Assembly, 1998–2017. Mem. (SF), Omagh DC, 2000–10. MP (SF) W Tyrone, 2017–Jan. 2018. Mem. (SF), Fermanagh and Omagh DC, 2019–. *Publications:* Keep 'Er Lit, 2012; Sustain the Flame, 2015.

**McELVOY, Anne;** Senior Editor and Director, Economist Audio, The Economist, since 2015; columnist, Evening Standard, since 2002; broadcaster; *b* 25 June 1965; *d* of Alexander and Mary McElvoy; *m* 1994, Martin Paul Ivens, *qv*; two *s* one *d. Educ:* St Bede's RC Comprehensive Sch., Lanchester; Wadham Coll., Oxford (MA German and Philosophy); Humboldt Univ., Berlin. Foreign corresp., The Times, 1989–94; Dep. Ed., Spectator, 1995–97; Executive Editor: Independent, 1997–2002; Evening Standard, 2002–09; Public Policy Ed., The Economist, 2011–15. Presenter: Free Thinking (formerly Night Waves), BBC Radio 3, 2009–; Start the Week, BBC Radio 4, 2013–. Mem., Global Adv. Council, WEF, 2014–. Mem., Educn Bd, Royal Opera Hse, 2012–. *Publications:* The Saddled Cow: East Germany's life and legacy, 1991; Man Without a Face: the memoirs of Markus Wolf, 1995. *Recreations:* herding teenagers, theatre. *Address:* The Economist, 10 John Adam Street, WC2N 6HG. *W:* www.twitter.com/annemcelvoy.

**McENERY, Judith Mary;** *see* Chessells, J. M.

**McENERY, Peter;** actor; Associate Artist, Royal Shakespeare Co.; *b* 21 Feb. 1940; *s* of Charles and Mary McEnery; *m* 1978; one *d. Educ:* various state and private schs. First stage appearance, Brighton, 1956; first London appearance in Flowering Cherry, Haymarket, 1957; *stage:* rôles with RSC include, 1961–: Laertes, Tybalt, Johnny Hobnails in Afore Night Come, Bassanio, Lorenzaccio, Orlando, Sachs in The Jail Diary of Albie Sachs, Pericles, Brutus, Antipholus of Ephesus, Godber in A Dream of People; other rôles include: Rudge in Next Time I'll Sing to You, Criterion, 1963; Konstantin in The Seagull, Queen's, 1964; Harry Winter in The Collaborators, Duchess, 1973; Trigorin in The Seagull, Lyric, 1975; Edward Gover in Made in Bangkok, Aldwych, 1986; Fredrik in A Little Night Music, Chichester, transf. Piccadilly, 1989; Torvald in The Doll's House, Robert in Dangerous Corner, Chichester, 1994; Menelaus in Women of Troy, NT, 1995; Hector Hushabye in Heartbreak House, Almeida, 1997; Claudius in Hamlet, RNT, 2000; directed: Richard III, Nottingham, 1971; The Wound, Young Vic, 1972; devised and performed Walter & Lenny, Chichester Fest. Th., 2015. *Films* include: Tunes of Glory, 1961; Victim,

1961; The Moonspinners, 1963; Entertaining Mr Sloane, 1970; *television:* Clayhanger, 1976; The Jail Diary of Albie Sachs, 1980; Pictures, 1983; The Collectors, 1986; The Mistress, 1986; Witchcraft, 1992. *Recreations:* steam railway preservation, ski-ing, American football. *Address:* c/o United Agents Ltd, 12-26 Lexington Street, W1F 0LE.

**McENROE, John Patrick**; tennis player and commentator; *b* Wiesbaden, 16 Feb. 1959; *s* of John Patrick McEnroe and Katherine, (Kay), McEnroe (*née* Tresham); *m* 1st, 1986, Tatum O'Neal (marr. diss. 1994); two *s* one *d*; 2nd, 1997, Patty Smyth; two *d*, and one step *d*. *Educ:* Trinity High Sch., NYC; Stanford Univ., Calif. Amateur tennis player, 1976–78, turned professional, 1978; winner of 77 singles titles and 77 doubles titles, including: US Open (singles) 1979, 1980, 1981, 1984, (doubles) 1979, 1981, 1983, 1989; Wimbledon (singles) 1981, 1983, 1984, (doubles) 1979, 1981, 1983, 1984, 1992; Grand Prix Masters 1979, 1983, 1984. Mem., US Davis Cup team, 1978–84, 1987–89, 1991, 1992, Captain, 1999–2000. Tennis commentator, USA TV, 1992–, BBC TV, 2000–; host, TV quiz show, The Chair, 2002. Owner, John McEnroe Gall., NY. *Publications:* (with James Kaplan) Serious (autobiog.), 2002; But Seriously (autobiog.), 2017. *Address:* The John McEnroe Gallery, 41 Greene Street, New York, NY 10013, USA.

**McEVOY, His Honour David Dand**; QC 1983; a Circuit Judge, 1996–2008; *b* 25 June 1938; *s* of David Dand McEvoy and Ann Elizabeth McEvoy (*née* Breslin); *m* 1974, Belinda Anne Robertson; three *d*. *Educ:* Mount St Mary's Coll.; Lincoln Coll., Oxford. BA (PPE). 2nd Lieut The Black Watch, RHR, 1958–59. Called to the Bar, Inner Temple, 1964; a Recorder, 1979–96. *Recreations:* golf, fishing. *Clubs:* Garrick; Blackwell Golf; Seniors Golfing Society; Highland Brigade.

**McEWAN, Hon. Lord; Robin Gilmour McEwan**; a Senator of the College of Justice in Scotland, 2000–08; *b* 12 Dec. 1943; *s* of late Ian G. McEwan and Mary McEwan, Paisley, Renfrewshire; *m* 1973, Sheena, *d* of late Stewart F. McIntyre and Lilian McIntyre, Aberdour; two *d*. *Educ:* Paisley Grammar Sch.; Glasgow Univ. (1st Cl. Hons LLB; PhD). Faulds Fellow in Law, Glasgow Univ., 1965–68; admitted to Faculty of Advocates, 1967; QC (Scot.) 1981. Standing Jun. Counsel to Dept of Energy, 1974–76; Advocate Depute, 1976–79; Sheriff of S Strathclyde, Dumfries and Galloway, at Lanark, 1982–88, at Ayr, 1988–2000; Temp. Judge, Court of Session and High Court of Justiciary, 1991–99. Chm., Industrial Tribunals, 1981–82; Mem., Scottish Legal Aid Bd, 1989–96. Dep. Chm., Boundary Commn for Scotland, 2007–08. Mem., Scottish Civil Courts Review, 2007–09. Chancellor, dio. of Glasgow and Galloway, 2005–18. *Publications:* Pleading in Court, 1980, 2nd edn 1995; (with Ann Paton) A Casebook on Damages in Scotland, 1983; contrib. Stair Memorial Encyclopaedia of the Laws of Scotland, 1987. *Recreation:* golf. *Clubs:* New (Edinburgh); Prestwick Golf.

**McEWAN, Ian Russell**, CBE 2000; FRSL; author; *b* 21 June 1948; *s* of late Major (retd) David McEwan and Rose Lilian Violet Moore; *m* 1982, Penny Allen (marr. diss. 1995); two *s* two *d*; *m* 1997, Annalena McAfee. *Educ:* Woolverstone Hall Sch.; Univ. of Sussex (BA Hons Eng. Lit.); Univ. of East Anglia (MA Eng. Lit.). Began writing, 1970. Hon. Member: Amer. Acad. of Arts and Scis, 1996; Amer. Acad. of Arts and Letters, 2006. FRSL 1982; FRSA. Hon. DLitt Sussex, 1989; Hon. DLit London, 1998; Hon. LittD: E Anglia, 1993; UCL, 2008; Hull, 2009. Shakespeare Prize, FVS Foundn, Hamburg, 1999. *Films:* The Ploughman's Lunch, 1983; Last Day of Summer, 1984; Soursweet, 1988; The Innocent, 1993; The Good Son, 1994. *Publications:* First Love, Last Rites, 1975 (filmed, 1997); In Between the Sheets, 1978; The Cement Garden, 1978 (filmed, 1993); The Imitation Game, 1981; The Comfort of Strangers, 1981 (filmed, 1991); Or Shall we Die? (oratorio; score by Michael Berkeley), 1982; The Ploughman's Lunch (film script), 1985; The Child in Time, 1987 (Whitbread Award; Prix Fémina, 1993; filmed, 2017); Soursweet (film script), 1989; The Innocent, 1990; Black Dogs, 1992; The Daydreamer, 1994; The Short Stories, 1995; Enduring Love, 1997 (filmed, 2004); Amsterdam, 1998 (Booker Prize, 1998); Atonement, 2001 (filmed, 2006); Rose Blanche, 2004; Saturday, 2005 (James Tait Black Meml Prize, 2006); On Chesil Beach, 2007 (film script, 2018); For You (opera libretto; score by Michael Berkeley), 2008; Solar, 2010; Sweet Tooth, 2012; The Children Act, 2014 (filmed, 2018); Nutshell, 2016; Machines Like Me, 2019; The Cockroach (novella), 2019. *Recreations:* hiking, tennis, cooking. *Address:* c/o Jonathan Cape, Random Century House, 20 Vauxhall Bridge Road, SW1V 2SA.

**McEWAN, Leslie James**; JP; independent consultant, 2004–15; Associate Consultant, Care and Health Ltd, 2004–09; *b* 26 Feb. 1946; *s* of Charles and Ann McEwan; *m* 1966, Catherine Anne Currie; two *s*. *Educ:* Lasswade High Sch.; St Andrews Univ. (MA); Dundee Univ. (Dip Social Admin); Univ. of Edinburgh (Dip Social Work). Midlothian, East Lothian and Peebles: Child Care Officer, Children's Dept, 1967–69; Social Worker, 1969–71; Sen. Social Worker, 1971–74; Social Work Advr, 1974–75; Divisional Director of Social Work: Midlothian-Lothian Reg., 1975–80; West Lothian, 1980–85; Lothian Region: Depute Dir of Social Work, 1985–90; Sen. Depute Dir, 1990–95; Dir, 1995–96; Dir of Social Work, City of Edinburgh Council, 1996–2003. Chm., FAIR charity, Edinburgh, 2007–17; Mem. Bd, MYPAS charity, Midlothian, 2007–16. Volunteer woodturning instructor, Grassmarket Community Project, Edinburgh, 2011–. Mem., Bonnyrigg and Lasswade Burgh Council, 1969–75 (Baillie, 1972–75). JP Midlothian, 1975–2007, Edinburgh, Lothian and Borders, 2007–. *Recreations:* fly-fishing, golf, woodturning, choral music. *Address:* 1 Eskglades, Dalkeith, Midlothian EH22 1UZ.

**McEWAN, Morag Barbara**; *see* Wise, M. B.

**McEWAN, Robin Gilmour**; *see* McEwan, Hon. Lord.

**MacEWEN, Dr Caroline Jan**, MD; FRCSE, FRCPE, FRCOphth, SFFMLM; Consultant Ophthalmologist, Ninewells Hospital, Dundee, since 1992; President, Royal College of Ophthalmologists, 2014–17; Chair, Academy of Medical Royal Colleges, 2017–July 2020; *b* Glasgow, 23 Feb. 1958; *d* of Charles and Jan MacEwen; *m* 1990, Stuart Pringle; one *s* two *d*. *Educ:* Laurel Bank Sch., Glasgow; Univ. of Dundee (MB ChB 1981; MD 1994). FRCSE 1986; FRCOphth 1988; FRCPE 2015; SFFMLM 2018. Ophthalmology Registrar, Glasgow, Dundee and London, 1983–91; Associate Post-grad. Dean, NHS Educn for Scotland, 2001–; University of Dundee: Hon. Prof., 2011–; Hd, Dept of Ophthalmol., Sch. of Medicine, 2003–. Ophthalmol. Speciality Advr to Scottish CMO, 2009–. Hon. FFSEM 2012; Hon. FCOptom 2017; Hon. FRCGP 2018. *Publications:* A Textbook of Sports Vision, 1995; (with R. Gregson) A Manual of Strabismus Surgery, 2003. *Recreations:* ski-ing, cycling, gardening, walking, theatre.

**McEWEN, Dame Hilary Mary**; *see* Mantel, Dame H. M.

**McEWEN, Prof. James**, FRCP, FFPH, FFOM, FDSRCS, FMedSci; Professor of Public Health, University of Glasgow, 1989–2002, now Emeritus (Henry Mechan Professor of Public Health, 1989–2000); President, Faculty of Public Health Medicine, Royal Colleges of Physicians of the United Kingdom, 1998–2001; *b* 6 Feb. 1940; *s* of Daniel McEwen and Elizabeth Wells (*née* Dishington); *m* 1964, Elizabeth May Archibald; one *s* one *d*. *Educ:* Dollar Acad.; Univ. of St Andrews (MB ChB 1963). FFPH (FFPHM 1981); FFOM 1990; FRCPGlas 1991; FRCP 1999; FRCPE 1999; FDSRCS 2003. Asst MO of Health, City of Dundee, 1965–66; Lectr, Univ. of Dundee, 1966–74; Sen. Lectr, Univ. of Nottingham, 1975–81; CMO, Health Educn Council, 1981–82; Prof. of Community Medicine, King's Coll. Sch. of Medicine and Dentistry, Univ. of London, 1983–89. Hon. Consultant in Public Health Medicine, Gtr Glasgow Health Bd, 1989–2002; Hon. Civilian Advr in Public Health to the Army, 2001–06; non-exec. Dir, Glasgow Royal Infirmary and Univ. NHS Trust, 1994–99. Chm., Health Protection Adv. Gp, Scotland, 2005–13. Mem., NRPB, 1996–2003. Distinguished Visitor, Univ. of Tucuman, Argentina, 1993. Hon. Chairman: UK Register for Public Health (formerly UK Voluntary Register for Public Health Specialists), 2003–09; Pharmacy Health Link, 2004–07. Chm., Dunhill Medical Trust, 2016–. Chair, Bd of Govs, Dollar Acad., 2014– (Hon. Vice-Chm., 2003–14). FCPS (Pak), 1996; Founder FMedSci 1998. Hon. FFPHMI 1997. Hon. DSc Glasgow Caledonian, 2008. *Publications:* (with A. Finlayson) Coronary Heart Disease and Patterns of Living, 1977; (jtly) Measuring Health Status, 1986; (ed jtly) Oxford Textbook of Public Health, 3rd edn 1997, 4th edn 2002; contrib. articles on public health, health services and quality of life. *Recreations:* Church, gardening, architectural heritage. *Address:* Auchanachie, Ruthven, Huntly AB54 4SS. *T:* (01466) 760742. *Club:* Royal Society of Medicine.

**McEWEN, Sir John (Roderick Hugh)**, 5th Bt *cr* 1953; actor and writer; *b* 4 Nov. 1965; *s* of Sir Robert Lindley McEwen, 3rd Bt, of Marchmont and Bardrochat, and of Brigid Cecilia, *d* of late James Laver, CBE, and Veronica Turleigh; *S* brother, 1983; *m* 2000, Rachel, *er d* of Gerald Soane, Wallington, Surrey; two *s* two *d*. *Educ:* Ampleforth; University Coll. London; Glasgow Univ. (MPhil 1999). Comdr of Clan MacEwen. *Heir:* s Joseph Mungo James McEwen, *b* 18 Oct. 2008. *Address:* The Steadings, Polwarth, Berwickshire TD10 6YR.

**MACEY, Air Vice-Marshal Eric Harold**, OBE 1975; Director General of Training (Royal Air Force), 1989–91, retired; *b* 9 April 1936; *s* of Harold Fred and Katrina Emma Mary Macey; *m* 1957, Brenda Ann Bracher; one *s* one *d*. *Educ:* Shaftesbury Grammar School; Southampton Tech. Coll. Asst Sci. Officer, Min. of Supply, 1953–54; RAF, 1954; commissioned, 1955; Pilot's Wings, 1956; RAF Staff Coll., 1966; RCDS 1983; AOC and Comdt, RAF Coll., Cranwell, 1985–87; ACDS (Policy and Nuclear), 1987–89. Vice-President: 214 Sqdn Assoc., 1990–; 101 Sqdn Assoc., 1999–; Bomber Comd Assoc., 1998–2016. *Recreation:* music. *Address:* Ebblemead, Homington, Salisbury, Wilts SP5 4NL.

**MACEY-DARE, Thomas Charles**; QC 2018; *b* London, 11 Sept. 1969; *s* of Dr Barry L. Macey-Dare and Dr Mitzi Macey-Dare (*née* Coyle); *m* 1996, Karon Cook; two *s* two *d*. *Educ:* Stonyhurst Coll.; Trinity Coll., Cambridge (BA 1990; LLM 1991; MA 1994); Cornell Law Sch. (LLM 1992). Called to the Bar, Middle Temple, 1994; in practice as a barrister, 2 Essex Court, later Quadrant Chambers, 1994–; Attorney and Counselor at Law, New York, 1995. Middle Temple Advocacy Faculty, 2013–. *Publications:* (ed) Atkin's Court Forms: Arbitration, 1998–2016; (contrib. ed) Marsden and Gault on Collisions at Sea, 14th edn 2016. *Recreations:* music, sport, spending time with my family. *Address:* Quadrant Chambers, 10 Fleet Street, EC4Y 1AU. *T:* (020) 7583 4444. *E:* thomas.macey-dare@quadrantchambers.com. *Club:* Travellers.

**McFADDEN, Rev. Mgr Andrew**, QHC 2011; Vicar-General (Bishopric of the Forces) and Principal Roman Catholic Chaplain (Naval), since 2011; Principal Chaplain, HM Naval Base Portsmouth, since 2016 (Chaplaincy Team Leader, 2011–14); *b* Glasgow, 26 March 1964; *s* of Samuel Gerard McFadden and Frances Mary McFadden (*née* McAnulty). *Educ:* St Vincent's Coll., Langbank; Blairs Coll., Aberdeen; Pontifical Scots Coll., Rome; Gregorian Univ., Rome (PhB 1984; STL 1989). Ordained priest, Dio. Paisley, 1989; Assistant Priest: St Mary's, Paisley, 1990; St Andrew's, Larkfield, 1990–93; St Mirin's Cathedral, Paisley, 1993–96; St Margaret's, Johnstone, 1996–98. Dio. Scout Chaplain, 1990–93; Hosp. Chaplain and Chaplain, Reid Kerr Coll., 1993–96. Royal Naval Chaplain: Royal Naval Hosp., Haslar, 1998; Fourth Frigate Sqdn, 1999–2000; HMS Sultan, and Parish Priest, St Benedict's Catholic Naval Community, 2000–03; HMS Nelson, 2003–05; HMS Ocean, 2005–07; HMS Raleigh, 2007–09; Cdre Faslane Flotilla, 2009–11; Principal, Armed Forces Chaplaincy Centre, 2014–16. Prelate of Honour to HH Pope Benedict XVI, 2012. *Recreations:* music, art, hill-walking, all things Italian, steamers of the Clyde and the Western Isles. *Address:* RN Catholic Chaplaincy, Bldg 1/020, NW Admiralty House, PP13 HM Naval Base, Portsmouth PO1 3LR. *E:* andrew.mcfadden375@mod.gov.uk.

**McFADDEN, Prof. Daniel L.**, PhD; E. Morris Cox Professor of Economics, 1991, now Emeritus, and Director, Econometrics Laboratory, 1991–95 and 1996, University of California, Berkeley (Head, Department of Economics, 1995–96); Presidential Professor of Health Economics, University of Southern California, since 2011; *b* Raleigh, NC, 29 July 1937; *s* of Robert Sain McFadden and Alice Little McFadden; *m* 1962, Beverlee Tito Simboli; two *s* one *d*. *Educ:* Univ. of Minnesota (BS 1957; PhD 1962). Asst Prof. of Econs, Univ. of Pittsburgh, 1962–63; Asst Prof., 1963–66, Associate Prof., 1966–68, Prof. 1968–77, of Econs, Univ. of Calif, Berkeley; Prof. of Econs, 1977–84, James R. Killian Prof. of Econs, 1984–91, Dir, Statistics Center, 1986–88, MIT. (Jtly) Nobel Prize for Economics, 2000. *Publications:* (ed jtly) Essays on Economic Behavior Under Uncertainty, 1974; (jtly) Urban Travel Demand: a behavioural analysis, 1975; (ed jtly) Production Economics: a dual approach to theory and applications (2 vols), 1978; (ed jtly) Structural Analysis of Discrete Data with Econometric Applications, 1981; (jtly) Microeconomic Modeling and Policy Analysis: studies in residential energy demand, 1984; (ed jtly) Preferences, Uncertainty and Optimality: essays in honor of Leonid Hurwicz, 1990; (ed jtly) Handbook of Econometrics, vol. IV, 1994; contrib. learned jls. *Address:* Department of Economics, University of California, Berkeley, CA 94720–3880, USA.

**McFADDEN, Jean Alexandra**, CBE 1992; JP; DL; MA, LLB; Senior Lecturer in Law, 1992–2006, Visiting Lecturer, 2006–15, University of Strathclyde; Vice Lord Lieutenant of City of Glasgow, 1980–92; *b* 26 Nov. 1941; *d* of John and Elma Hogg; *m* 1966, John McFadden (*d* 1991). *Educ:* Univ. of Glasgow (MA 1st Cl. Hons Classics); Univ. of Strathclyde (LLB 1st Cl. Hons). Principal Teacher of Classics, Strathclyde Schools, 1967–86; part-time Lectr in Law, Univ. of Glasgow, 1991–92. Entered Local Govt as Mem. of Glasgow Corp. for Cowcaddens Ward, 1971 then (following boundary changes) Mem., Glasgow DC for Scotstoun Ward, 1984–96; Mem., City of Glasgow Council, 1995–2012 (Convener, 1995–96; Chair: Labour Gp, 1995–2012; Social Strategy Cttee, 1996–99; Exec. Mem. for Corporate Governance, 2007–10, for Educn, 2010–12); Chm., Manpower Cttee, 1974–77; Leader, Labour Gp, 1977–86, 1992–94; Leader, 1980–86, 1992–94, Treas., 1986–92, Glasgow DC. Convener, Scottish Local Govt Information Unit, 1984–2003; Pres., Convention of Scottish Local Auths, 1990–92; Member Board: SDA, 1989–91; Legal Services Agency, 1992– (Convener, 2015–); Glasgow Develt Agency, 1992–2000. Convener, Strathclyde Police Jt Bd, 2003–07. Chm., Scottish Charity Law Commn, 2000–01; Member: Health Appts Adv. Cttee, Scottish Exec. (formerly Scottish Office), 1995–2000; Ancient Monuments Bd for Scotland, 2000–03. Member, Council: Royal Glasgow Inst. Fine Arts, 2007–15 (Pres., 2014–15); Royal Philosophical Soc. of Glasgow, 2016–. Chm., W of Scotland Jt Archaeol Cttee, 1997–2012. Chm., Mayfest (Glasgow Internat. Arts Fest.), 1983–97. JP 1972, DL 1980, Glasgow. *Recreations:* theatre, walking, golf, West Highland terriers, Italian language and literature, Modern Greek. *Address:* 16 Lansdowne Crescent, Glasgow G20 6NQ. *T:* (0141) 334 3522.

**McFADDEN, Rt Hon. Patrick**; PC 2008; MP (Lab) Wolverhampton South East, since 2005; *b* 26 March 1965; *s* of James and Annie McFadden; *m* Marianna; one *s* one *d*. *Educ*: Holyrood Sec. Sch., Glasgow; Univ. of Edinburgh (MA Hons Pols 1988). Res. Asst to Rt Hon. Donald Dewar, MP, 1988–93; Advr to Rt Hon. John Smith, MP, 1993–94; Policy Advr to Rt Hon. Tony Blair, MP, 1994–2001; Political Sec. to the Prime Minister, 2002–05. Parly Sec. (Minister for Social Exclusion), Cabinet Office, 2006–07; Minister of State, BERR, later BIS, 2007–10; Shadow Sec. of State for Business, 2010; Shadow Minister of State for Europe, 2014–16. Member: Treasury Select Cttee, 2011–14; Cttee on Exiting the EU, 2016–. *Recreations*: sport, reading. *Address*: House of Commons, SW1A 0AA. *T*: (020) 7219 4036, *Fax*: (020) 7219 5665.

**McFADYEAN, Colin William**; teacher, Gloucestershire, 2003–15; Deputy Headteacher, Ilminster Avenue Primary School, Knowle West Bristol, 1999–2003; *b* 11 March 1943; *s* of Captain Angus John McFadyean, MC, 1st Bn London Scottish Regt (killed in action, 1944) and late Joan Mary McFadyean (*née* Irish); *m* 1970, Jeanette Carol Payne; one *s*. *Educ*: Plymouth Coll.; Bristol Grammar Sch.; Loughborough Coll. of Education; Keele Univ. (DLC Hons, Adv. DipEd). Phys. Educn teacher, Birmingham, 1965–67; Phys. Educn Lectr, 1967–72, Sen. Lectr, 1972–74, Cheshire; Dep. Dir, Nat. Sports Centre, Lilleshall, 1974–78; Chief Coach, Jubilee Sports Centre, Hong Kong, 1979–82; Sports Master and House Master, Dulwich Coll., 1983–85; Dir Gen., NPFA, 1985–87; with Croydon Educn Authy, 1988–90; teacher, Avon, then Bristol Educn Authy, 1991–98; Dep. Headteacher, Oldbury Court Primary Sch., 1998–99. Dir Coaching, Bristol FC (Rugby Union), 1990–91; Coach: Moseley FC, 1991–93; Cleve RFC, 1992–99. Internat. Rugby career includes: 11 England caps, 1966–68; 4 Tests British Lions *v* NZ, 1966; (captain) *v* Ireland, 1968; (captain) *v* Wales, 1968; scored 5 tries, 1 dropped goal (in 15 Tests); other sport: coach to Hong Kong disabled team to Olympics, Arnhem, 1980; Adviser, Hong Kong table tennis team to World Championships, Yugoslavia, 1981. Mem., Adv. Gp, RCM, 2004–07. Broadcaster with Hong Kong TV and commercial radio. Hon. BA Loughborough, 2009. *Recreations*: golf, music, theatre, gardening; supporter of Plymouth Argyle FC, 1952–. *Clubs*: British Sportsman's; England Rugby Internationals; Rugby Internationals Golf; Moseley Football (Vice-Pres.); Cleve Rugby Football (Vice-Pres.).

**MacFADYEN, Alasdair Lorne**; Sheriff of South Strathclyde, Dumfries and Galloway at Hamilton, since 2012; Appeal Sheriff, Sheriff Appeal Court, since 2015; *b* 18 Sept. 1955; *s* of Iain Archibald MacFadyen and Anna MacFadyen; *m* 1978, Lynne Ballantyne; two *d*. *Educ*: High Sch., Glasgow; Glasgow Univ. (LLB). Solicitor in private practice, 1978–2001. Temp. Sheriff, 1995–2000; pt-time Sheriff, 2000–01; all Scotland Floating Sheriff, 2001–02; Sheriff of Grampian, Highland and Islands at Dingwall and Inverness, 2002–12. Pt-time Chm., Employment Tribunals, 2000–01. *Recreations*: sailing in tall ships, music. *Address*: Sheriff Court, 4 Beckford Street, Hamilton ML3 0BT.

**MACFADYEN, (David) Matthew**; actor, since 1995; *b* Great Yarmouth, 17 Oct. 1974; *s* of Martin Macfadyen and Meinir Macfadyen (*née* Owen); *m* 2004, Keeley Hawes; one *s* one *d*, and one step *s*. *Educ*: Oakham Sch.; Royal Acad. of Dramatic Art. *Theatre* includes: The Duchess of Malfi, Cheek by Jowl, 1995; A Midsummer Night's Dream, RSC, 1996; Much Ado About Nothing, Cheek by Jowl, 1998; The School for Scandal, RSC, 1998; Battle Royal, NT, 1999; Henry IV, Parts 1 and 2, NT, 2004; The Pain and the Itch, Royal Court, 2007; Private Lives, Vaudeville, 2009; Perfect Nonsense, Duke of York's, 2013. *Television* includes: Wuthering Heights, 1998; Warriors, 1999; Perfect Strangers, 2001; The Way We Live Now, 2001; Spooks, 2002–04; The Project, 2002; Secret Life (Best Actor, RTS Award, 2008); Little Dorrit, 2008; Enid, 2009; Criminal Justice, 2009 (Best Supporting Actor, BAFTA Award, 2010); The Pillars of the Earth, 2010; Any Human Heart, 2010; Ripper Street (5 series), 2012–17; Ambassadors, 2013; The Enfield Haunting, 2015; The Last Kingdom, 2015; Churchill's Secret, 2016; Howards End, 2017; Succession, 2018, 2019. *Films* include: Maybe Baby, 2000; Enigma, 2001; The Reckoning, 2003; In My Father's Den, 2004; Pride and Prejudice, 2005; Middletown, 2006; Death at a Funeral, 2007; Incendiary, 2008; Frost/Nixon, 2008; Robin Hood, 2010; The Three Musketeers, 2011; Anna Karenina, 2012; Lost in Karastan, 2016; The Nutcracker and the Four Realms, 2018; The Current War, 2019. *Address*: c/o Christian Hodell, Hamilton Hodell, 20 Golden Square, W1F 9JL. *T*: (020) 7636 1221. *E*: info@hamiltonhodell.co.uk. *Club*: Garrick.

**MACFADYEN, Air Marshal Sir Ian (David)**, KCVO 2014; CB 1991; OBE 1984; Constable and Governor of Windsor Castle, 2000–14; *b* 19 Feb. 1942; *s* of Air Marshal Sir Douglas Macfadyen, KCB, CBE and Lady Macfadyen (*née* Dafforn, later Mrs P. A. Rowan); *m* 1967, Sally Harvey; one *s* one *d*. *Educ*: Marlborough; RAF Coll., Cranwell. Joined RAF, 1960; Cranwell cadet, 1960–63 (Sword of Honour); 19 Sqdn, 1965–68; HQ RAF Strike Command, 1969; Flying Instructor, RAF Coll., Cranwell, 1970–73; RAF Staff Coll., 1973; 111 Sqdn, 1974–75; Flt Comdr, 43 Sqdn, 1975–76; HQ TWOATAF, RAF Germany, 1976–79; comd 29 Sqdn, 1980–84; comd 23 Sqdn, 1984; MoD, 1984–85; comd RAF Leuchars, Fife, 1985–87; RCDS, 1988; MoD, 1989–90; COS, then Comdr, HQ British Forces ME, Riyadh, 1990–91; ACDS, Op. Requirements (Air Systems), 1991–94; Dir Gen., Saudi Arabia Armed Forces Project, 1994–98; retd, 1999. Lt Gov., IOM, 2000–05; Nat. Pres., RBL, 2006–09. Mem., Royal Air Sqdn, 1984–; Chm., Geoffrey de Havilland Flying Foundn, 2002–; Trustee: RAF Mus., 1998–2003 (Chm. Trustees, 1999–2001); Bentley Priory Battle of Britain Trust, 2006–; Chairman: IOM Bd, Prince's Trust, 2001–05; IOM Golden Jubilee Trust, 2002–05; Pres., Popular Flying Assoc., 2004–06. Mem. Council, St George's House, 2009–15. Patron: GAIN (formerly Guillain-Barré Syndrome Support Gp), 2010–; Alexander Devine Children's Cancer Trust, 2010–; Vice Patron, Gallantry Medallists League, 2010–18. Hon. Air Cdre, 606 (Chiltern) Sqdn, RAuxAF, 2007–19. Hon. Inspector Gen., RAuxAF, 2009. Liveryman, Hon. Co. of Air Pilots (formerly GAPAN), 1999–; Hon. Liveryman Lightmongers' Co., 2011–. President: Windsor Fest., 2009–14; Lucifer Golfing Soc., 2012–. QCVSA 1974. OStJ 2001. *Recreations*: aviation history, flying, golf, photography, shooting, watercolour painting. *Address*: Collyns Mead, Hawkesbury Upton, S Glos GL9 1BB. *Clubs*: Royal Air Force; Royal & Ancient (St Andrews).

**McFADYEN, Jock**; RA 2012; painter; *b* Paisley, 18 Sept. 1950; *s* of James Lachlan McFadyen and Margaret McFadyen (*née* Owen); *m* 1st, 1972, Carol Hambleton (marr. diss. 1987); one *s*; 2nd, 1991, Susie Honeyman; one *s* one *d*. *Educ*: Chelsea Sch. of Art (BA 1976; MA 1977). Artist-in-Residence, Nat. Gall., 1981; Lectr (pt-time), Slade Sch. of Fine Art, 1985–2004; designed sets and costumes for The Judas Tree, Royal Opera Hse, 1992; est. Grey Gall., 2007; Co-ordinator, RA Summer Exhibn, 2019. *Solo exhibitions* include: Nat. Gall., 1982; Camden Arts Centre, 1988; Imperial War Mus., 1991; Talbot Rice Gall., Univ. of Edinburgh, 1998; Pier Arts Centre, Orkney, 1999; Agnew's Gall., London, 2001; Rude Wercs, London, 2005; Grey Gall., Edinburgh Fest., 2007; Clifford Chance, London, 2010; Bourne Fine Art, Edinburgh, 2011, 2012; Fine Art Soc., 2012; Fleming Collection, London, 2012; Eleven Spitalfields, 2012; Marsden Woo Gall., London, 2014; *group exhibitions* incl. John Moores Univ., Hayward annual, British Art Show, Five Centuries of Scottish Portraits at Fine Art Soc. and Bourne Fine Art, 2011, Cohen Collection at Chatsworth Hse, 2012; Estuary, Mus. of London, Docklands, 2013; Holbourne Mus., Bath, 2013; Sainsbury Centre for Visual Art, 2014; Walker Art Gall., 2015; Endarkenment, Dovecot Studios, Edinburgh, 2016; Now, Scottish Nat. Gall. of Modern Art, 2017; *work in public collections* incl. Tate Gall., Nat. Gall., V&A, BM, Scottish Nat. Gall. of Modern Art and private and corporate collections in Britain, Europe and America. *Recreations*: cycling, motorcycling, exploring Scotland, music. *E*: info@jockmcfadyen.com. *Club*: Vintage Motorcycle.

**MACFADYEN, Matthew**; see Macfadyen, D. M.

**McFALL OF ALCLUITH**, Baron *cr* 2010 (Life Peer), of Dumbarton in Dunbartonshire; **John Francis McFall**; PC 2004. MP (Lab and Co-op) Dumbarton, 1987–2005, W Dunbartonshire, 2005–10. An Opposition Whip, 1989–91; Opposition front bench spokesman: for education and home affairs, 1992; on Scottish Affairs, 1992–97; a Lord Comr of HM Treasury (Govt Whip), 1997–98; Parly Under-Sec. of State, NI Office, 1998–99. Member, Select Committee: on Defence, 1988; on Sittings of the House, 1991; on Information, 1990–97; Chm., HM Treasury Select Cttee, 2001–10; Mem. Exec. Cttee, Parly Gp for Energy Studies, 1988–97; Secretary: Retail Industry Gp, 1992–97; Hon. Sec., Parly and Scientific Cttee, 1989–92. Sen. Dep. Speaker, H of L, 2016–; Mem., Parly Commn on Banking Standards, 2012–13. Founder and non-exec. Chm., New City Agenda, 2013–. Dep. Chm., Banking Standards Bd, 2014–16. Visiting Professor: Strathclyde Business Sch., Univ. of Strathclyde, 1991–; Glasgow Univ. Business Sch., 2004–. Hon Dr: Strathclyde, 2010; Stirling, 2011; Glasgow, 2011; W of Scotland, 2012; Hon. DBA BPP Business Sch., 2011. *Recreations*: running, golf, reading. *Address*: House of Lords, SW1A 0PW.

**McFARLAND, Alan**; see McFarland, R. A.

**McFARLAND, Prof. David John**, DPhil; Professor of Biological Robotics, University of the West of England, 2000–02; Fellow, Balliol College, Oxford, 1966–2000, now Emeritus; *b* 31 Dec. 1938; *s* of John Cyril and Joan Elizabeth McFarland; *m* 1st, 1962, Frances Jill Tomlin; one *s* one *d*; 2nd, 2013, Penelope Jane Farmer. *Educ*: Leighton Park Sch., Reading; Liverpool Univ. (BSc 1st Cl. Hons Zoology, 1961); Oxford Univ. (DPhil Psychology, 1965). Lectr in Psychology, Durham Univ., 1964; Oxford University: Lectr in Psychology, 1966–74; Reader in Animal Behaviour, 1974–2000; Tutor in Psychology, Balliol Coll., 1966–2000. Hofmeyer Fellow, Univ. of the Witwatersrand, 1974; Visiting Professor: Dalhousie Univ., 1968; Rutgers Univ., 1971; Univ. of Penn, 1977; SUNY, Stonybrook, 1978; Univ. of Oregon, 1978; Univ. of Münster, Germany, 1989. Pres., Internat. Ethological Conf., 1981. Pres., Assoc. of Teachers in the Arts and Scis, Lanzarote, 2004–. Editor, Animal Behaviour, 1969–74. *Publications*: (with J. McFarland) An Introduction to the Study of Behaviour, 1969; Feedback Mechanisms in Animal Behaviour, 1971; (ed) Motivational Control Systems Analysis, 1974; (ed) The Oxford Companion to Animal Behaviour, 1981; (with A. Houston) Quantitative Ethology: the state space approach, 1981; (ed) Functional Ontogeny, 1982; Animal Behaviour, 1985, 3rd edn 1999; Problems of Animal Behaviour, 1989; Biologie des Verhaltens, (Germany) 1989, 2nd edn 1999; (with T. Bosser) Intelligent Behavior in Animals and Robots, (USA) 1993; Le Comportement Animal, (France) 2001; (with O. Holland) Artificial Ethology, 2001; The Oxford Dictionary of Animal Behaviour, 2006, 2nd edn 2014; Guilty Robots, Happy Dogs: the question of alien minds, 2008; Death by Eating: the evolution of human food, 2010; God's Own Geneticist: a fable of our times, 2011; The Biology of Time, 2012; The Biological Bases of Economic Behaviour, 2016; articles in scientific learned jls. *Recreations*: writing, potter. *Address*: 7 Drake Court, Scotts Road, W12 8HG; Calle La Escorta, El Golfo, Yaiza 35570, Lanzarote, Spain.

**McFARLAND, Prof. Ian Alexander**, PhD; Regius Professor of Divinity, University of Cambridge, since 2015; Fellow, Selwyn College, Cambridge, since 2015; *b* Hartford, Conn, 26 July 1963; *s* of Rodney C. and Sandra K. McFarland; *m* 1994, Ann Elizabeth Lillya; two *d*. *Educ*: Trinity Coll., Hartford, Conn (BA Classics 1984); Union Theol Seminary, NY (MDiv 1989); Lutheran Sch. of Theol., Chicago (ThM 1991); Yale Univ. (MPhil 1994; PhD 1995); Cambridge Univ. (MA 2015). Clerk, Music Center, Hawaii, 1995–97; Chaplaincy Staff, Queen's Med. Center, Honolulu, 1997–98; Lectr, 1998–2003, Sen. Lectr, 2003–05, in Systematic Theol., Univ. of Aberdeen; Candler School of Theology, Emory University: Associate Prof., 2005–11, Prof., 2011–13, of Systematic Theol.; Bp Mack B. and Rose Stokes Prof. of Theol., 2013–15; Associate Dean, Faculty and Acad. Affairs, 2012–15. Gillespie Vis. Associate Prof. of Religion, Coll. of Wooster, Ohio, 2003–04. *Publications*: Listening to the Least: doing theology from the outside, 1998; Difference and Identity: a theological anthropology, 2001; The Divine Image: envisioning the invisible God, 2005; In Adam's Fall: a meditation on the Christian doctrine of original sin, 2010; From Nothing: a theology of creation, 2014. *Recreations*: hill walking, classical music, opera. *Address*: Faculty of Divinity, University of Cambridge, West Road, Cambridge CB3 9BS. *T*: (01223) 763036. *E*: iam33@cam.ac.uk.

**McFARLAND, Sir John (Talbot)**, 3rd Bt *cr* 1914, of Aberfoyle, Londonderry; TD 1967; Chairman: Malvay Ltd (formerly Lanes (Business Equipment)), 1977–2001; J. T. McFarland Holdings, 1984–2001; Information and Imaging Systems Ltd, 1994–2001; *b* 3 Oct. 1927; *s* of Sir Basil Alexander Talbot McFarland, 2nd Bt, CBE, ERD, and Anne Kathleen (*d* 1952), *d* of late Andrew Henderson; *S* father, 1986; *m* 1957, Mary Scott, *d* of late Dr W. Scott Watson, Londonderry; two *s* two *d*. *Educ*: Marlborough College; Trinity Coll., Oxford. Captain RA (TA), retired 1967. Chm., R. C. Malseed & Co. Ltd, 1957–90; Chairman, 1977–84: Lanes (Derry) Ltd; Lanes (Fuel) Oils Ltd; Lanes Patent Fuels Ltd; Holmes Coal Ltd; Alexander Thompson & Co. Ltd; Nicholl Ballintyne Ltd; J. W. Corbett Ltd; Wattersons Ltd. Chm., Londonderry Lough Swilly Railway Co., 1978–81; Director: Londonderry Gaslight Co., 1958–89; Donegal Holdings Ltd, 1963–85; G. Kinnaird & Son Ltd, 1981–95; Windy Hills Ltd, 1994–95; Wallcoatings Dublin Ltd, 1995–98; Taughboyne Develt Assoc., 1998–2007. Member: Londonderry County Borough Council, 1955–69; NW HMC, 1960–73; Londonderry Port and Harbour Comrs, 1965–73. Jt Chm., Londonderry and Foyle Coll., 1971–76. High Sheriff, Co. Londonderry 1958, City of County of Londonderry 1965–67; DL Londonderry 1962, resigned 1982. *Recreations*: golf, shooting. *Heir*: *er s* Anthony Basil Scott McFarland [*b* 29 Nov. 1959; *m* 1988, Anne Margaret, BA, ACA, *d* of T. K. Laidlaw, Gernonstown, Slane, Co. Meath. *Educ*: Marlborough Coll.; Trinity College, Dublin (BA). ACA]. *Address*: Dunmore House, Carrigans, Lifford, Co. Donegal, Ireland. *T*: (91) 40120, *Fax*: (91) 40336.

**McFARLAND, (Robert) Alan**; Chairman, Somme Association, since 2015; *b* 9 Aug. 1949; *s* of Dr Albert John Black McFarland and Mary Elizabeth Florence McFarland (*née* Campbell); *m* 1979, Celia Mary Sharp; one *s* two *d*. *Educ*: Rockport Sch., Craigavad, Co. Down; Campbell Coll., Belfast; RMA, Sandhurst. Commnd RTR, 1975; various regtl appts, 1975–81 (despatches, 1981); SO, Orgn and Deployment, HQ 4th Armd Div., 1981–83; Sqn Ldr, Challenger Tank Sqn and HQ Sqn 2nd RTR, 1983–86; SO, Public Relns, HQ SW Dist and UK Mobile Force, 1987–89; Mgt Consultant, MoD, 1989–92; retd in rank of Major, 1992. Parly Asst to Rev. Martin Smyth, MP and Rt Hon. James Molyneaux, MP, H of C, 1992–95; Dir, Somme Heritage Centre, Newtownards, 1996–98. Mem., NI Policing Bd, 2002–06. Mem., N Down, NI Assembly (UU, 1998–2010, Ind, 2010–11); contested (Ind) same seat, 2011. European Co-ordinator, Three Worlds Meet, 2013–. Trustee: Nat. Mus NI, 2013–; Scotch Irish Trust of Ulster, 2016–. Presenter, Robert Campbell: Mountain Man, BBC, 2018. *Recreations*: American fur trade history, military history, genealogy, folk and country music.

**MACFARLANE,** family name of **Baron Macfarlane of Bearsden.**

**MACFARLANE OF BEARSDEN,** Baron *cr* 1991 (Life Peer), of Bearsden in the district of Bearsden and Milngavie; **Norman Somerville Macfarlane,** KT 1996; Kt 1983; DL; FRSE; Hon. Life President: Macfarlane Group PLC, 1999 (Chairman, 1973–98, Managing Director, 1973–90); United Distillers PLC (Chairman, 1987–96); Lord High Commissioner, General Assembly, Church of Scotland, 1992, 1993 and 1997; *b* 5 March 1926; *s* of Daniel Robertson Macfarlane and Jessie Lindsay Somerville; *m* 1953, Marguerite Mary Campbell; one *s* four *d*. *Educ*: High Sch. of Glasgow. Commnd RA, 1945; served Palestine, 1945–47. Founded N. S. Macfarlane & Co. Ltd, 1949; became Macfarlane Group (Clansman) PLC, 1973. Underwriting Mem. of Lloyd's, 1978–97; Chairman: The Fine Art Society PLC, 1976–98 (Hon. Life Pres., 1998); American Trust PLC, 1984–97; Guinness PLC, 1987–89 (Jt Dep. Chm., 1989–92); Director: Clydesdale Bank PLC, 1980–96 (Dep. Chm., 1993–96); General Accident Fire & Life Assce Corp. plc, 1984–96; Edinburgh Fund Managers plc, 1980–98. Dir, Glasgow Chamber of Commerce, 1976–79; Member: Council, CBI Scotland, 1975–81; Bd, Scottish Develt Agency, 1979–87. Chm., Glasgow Develt Agency (formerly Glasgow Action), 1985–92. Mem., H of L, 1991–2016. Scottish Ballet: Dir, 1975–87; Vice Chm., 1983–87; Hon. Pres., 2001–12; Dir, Scottish National Orch., 1977–82; Pres., Royal Glasgow Inst. of the Fine Arts, 1976–87; Mem., Royal Fine Art Commn for Scotland, 1980–82; Scottish Patron, National Art Collection Fund, 1978–; Governor, Glasgow Sch. of Art, 1976–87 (Hon. Fellow, 1993; Hon. Pres., 2001–12); Trustee: Nat. Heritage Meml Fund, 1984–97; Nat. Galls of Scotland, 1986–97; Dir, Culture & Sport Glasgow, 2007–12. Dir, Third Eye Centre, 1978–81. Hon. Pres., Tenovus Scotland, 2006–. Hon. Pres., Charles Rennie Mackintosh Soc., 1988–. Hon. Pres., High Sch. of Glasgow, 1992– (Chm. Govs, 1979–92); Mem. Court, Univ. of Glasgow, 1979–87; Regent, RCSE, 1997–. President: Stationers' Assoc. of GB and Ireland, 1965; Co. of Stationers of Glasgow, 1968–70; Glasgow High Sch. Club, 1970–72. Patron, Scottish Licensed Trade Assoc., 1992–; Hon. Patron, Queen's Park FC. Vice Pres., PGA. Hon. Life Mem., Scottish Football League, 2006. DL Dunbartonshire, 1993. Freeman: Dumfries and Galloway, 2006; City of Glasgow, 2007. FRSE 1991; CCMI (CIMgt 1996). HRSA 1987; HRGI 1987; Hon. FRIAS 1984; Hon. FScotvec 1991; Hon. FR.CPSGlas 1992. Hon. LLD: Strathclyde, 1986; Glasgow, 1988; Glasgow Caledonian, 1993; Aberdeen, 1995; DUniv Stirling, 1992; Dr (*hc*) Edinburgh, 1992. St Mungo Prize, City of Glasgow, 2005; Goodman Award, Art & Business, 2007. *Recreations*: golf, cricket, theatre, art. *Address*: Macfarlane Group PLC, Clansman House, 21 Newton Place, Glasgow G3 7PY; 50 Manse Road, Bearsden, Glasgow G61 3PN. *Clubs*: Glasgow Art (Glasgow); Hon. Co. of Edinburgh Golfers, Glasgow Golf.

**MACFARLANE, Prof. Alan Donald James,** FRAI; FRHistS; FBA 1986; Professor of Anthropological Science, University of Cambridge, 1991–2009, now Emeritus; Fellow, King's College Cambridge, 1981–2008, now Life Fellow; *b* 20 Dec. 1941; *s* of Donald Kennedy Macfarlane and Iris Stirling Macfarlane; *m* 1st, 1966, Gillian Ions; one *d*; 2nd, 1981, Sarah Harrison. *Educ*: Dragon Sch., Oxford; Sedbergh School; Worcester College, Oxford (MA, DPhil); LSE (MPhil); SOAS (PhD). University of Cambridge: Senior Research Fellow in History, King's College, 1971–74; Univ. Lectr in Social Anthropology, 1975–81; Reader in Historical Anthropology, 1981–91. Lectures: Frazer Meml, Liverpool Univ., 1974; Malinowski Meml, LSE, 1978; Radcliffe-Brown Meml, Univ. of Lancaster, 1992; Marett Meml, Univ. of Oxford, 1995; F. W. Maitland Meml, Univ. of Cambridge, 2000; Maruyama, Univ. of Calif. Berkeley, 2006; Sir Li Ka Sheng Dist., China, 2006; Wang Gouwei Meml, Tsinghua Univ., Beijing, 2011. Rivers Meml Medal, 1984; Huxley Meml Medal, 2012, RAI; William J. Goode Award, Amer. Sociol Assoc., 1987. Principal consultant and presenter, The Day the World Took Off (millennium series), C4, 2000. *Publications*: Witchcraft in Tudor and Stuart England, 1970; The Family Life of Ralph Josselin, 1970; Resources and Population, 1976; (ed) The Diary of Ralph Josselin, 1976; Reconstructing Historical Communities, 1977; Origins of English Individualism, 1978; The Justice and the Mare's Ale, 1981; A Guide to English Historical Records, 1983; Marriage and Love in England, 1986; The Culture of Capitalism, 1987; The Cambridge Database System User Manual, 1990; (jtly) The Nagas: hill peoples of North-east India, 1990; (ed and trans. with S. Harrison) Bernard Pignède, The Gurungs of Nepal, 1993; The Savage Wars of Peace, 1997; The Riddle of the Modern World, 2000; The Making of the Modern World, 2001; (with Gerry Martin) The Glass Bathyscaphe, 2002; (with Iris Macfarlane) Green Gold: the empire of tea, 2003; Letters to Lily: on how our world works, 2005; Japan Through the Looking Glass, 2007; Reflections on Cambridge, 2009; The Invention of the Modern World (in Chinese), 2012; (with J. Bruce Lockhart) Dorset Days, 2012; (with J. Bruce Lockhart) Dragon Days, 2012; Individualism, Capitalism and the Modern World (essays), 2013; Thomas Malthus and the Making of the Modern World, 2013; The Invention of the Modern World, 2014; China, Japan, Europe and the Anglosphere, 2018; How do we know?, 2018; How to Understand Each Other, 2018; Intelligent Machines, 2018; How to Discover the World, 2018; A Modern Education, 2018; The Survival Manual, 2018; Learning to be Modern, 2018; How to Study the World, 2018; On How to Investigate Mysteries, 2018; King's College, Cambridge: a personal view, 2018; Oxford Undergraduate, 2019; Oxford Postgraduate, 2019; Sedbergh Schooldays, 2019; Lakeland Life, 2019. *Recreations*: walking, gardening, second-hand book hunting. *Address*: 25 Lode Road, Lode, near Cambridge CB25 9ER. *T*: (01223) 811976. *W*: www.alanmacfarlane.com.

**MacFARLANE, Sir Alistair (George James),** Kt 2002; CBE 1987; FRS 1984; FREng; FRSE; Principal and Vice-Chancellor of Heriot-Watt University, 1989–96; *b* 9 May 1931; *s* of George R. MacFarlane; *m* 1st, 1954, Nora Williams (*d* 2005); one *s*; 2nd, 2008, Anwen Tudor Davies. *Educ*: Hamilton Academy; Univ. of Glasgow. BSc 1953, DSc 1969, Glasgow; PhD London 1964; MSc Manchester 1973; MA 1974, ScD 1979, Cantab. FIET; FREng (FEng 1981); FRSE 1990. Metropolitan-Vickers, Manchester, 1953–58; Lectr, Queen Mary Coll., Univ. of London, 1959–65, Reader 1965–66; Reader in Control Engrg, Univ. of Manchester Inst. of Sci. and Technology, 1966–69, Prof. 1969–74; Prof. of Engrg and Hd of Information Engrg Div., Univ. of Cambridge, 1974–88; Fellow, 1974–88, Vice-Master, 1980–88, Hon. Fellow, 1989–, Selwyn Coll., Cambridge. Chm., Cambridge Control Ltd, 1985–90; Non-executive Director: Lothian and Edinburgh Enterprise Ltd, 1990–96; British Nuclear Fuels plc, 1995–2000. Member: Council, SERC, 1981–85; Computer Board, 1983–88; Adv. Cttee for Safety of Nuclear Installations, 1987–90; Engrg Tech. Adv. Cttee, DTI, 1991–93; BT Adv. Forum, 1997–98. Chm., Res. Councils' High Performance Computing Strategy Gp, 1995–98. Comr, Nat. Commn on Educn, 1991–93; Academic Advr, 1997–2000, CEO and Dir, 2000–01, Univ. of Highlands and Islands project; Rector, UHI Millennium Inst., 2002–04. Chairman: Scottish Univs Wkg Party on Teaching and Learning in an Expanding Higher Educn System, 1991–92 (MacFarlane Report, 1992); Scottish Council for Res. in Educn, 1992–98; Scottish Library and Information Council, 1994–98. Royal Society: Vice-Pres., 1997–99; Mem. Council, 1997–99; Chm., Educn Cttee, 2000–04. Trustee, Scottish Internat. Educn Trust, 1994–2010. Hon. DEng: UMIST, 1995; Glasgow, 1995; Heriot-Watt, 1997; Paisley, 1997; Hon. DSc Abertay Dundee, 1998; Hon. DLitt Lincolnshire and Humberside, 1999. Medals: Centennial, ASME, 1980; Sir Harold Hartley, Inst. of Measurement and Control, 1982; Achievement, IEE, 1992; Faraday, IEE, 1993; Oldenburger, ASME, 2004. *Publications*: Engineering Systems Analysis, 1964; Dynamical System Models, 1970; (with I. Postlethwaite) A Complex Variable Approach to the Analysis of Linear Multivariable Feedback Systems, 1979; (ed) Frequency-Response Methods in Control Systems, 1979; (ed) Complex Variable Methods for Linear Multivariable Feedback Systems, 1980; (with S. Hung) Multivariable Feedback: a quasi-classical approach, 1982; (with G. K. H. Pang) An Expert Systems Approach to Computer-Aided Design of Multivariable Systems, 1987. *Address*: Apartment 4, Horfield Lodge, Kellaway Avenue, Bristol BS7 8SU. *E*: alistairmacfarlane33@gmail.com.

**McFARLANE, Rt Hon. Sir Andrew (Ewart),** Kt 2005; PC 2011; President of the Family Division, since 2018; *b* 20 June 1954; *s* of Gordon McFarlane and Olive McFarlane (*née* Davies); *m* 1981, Susanna Jane Randolph (DL Herefords); four *d*. *Educ*: Shrewsbury Sch.; Durham Univ. (BA Hons Law 1975); Univ. of Wales (LLM Canon Law 1998). Called to the Bar, Gray's Inn, 1977, Bencher, 2003 (Chm., Mgt Cttee, 2014); QC 1998; an Asst Recorder, 1995–99; a Recorder, 1999–2005; a Dep. High Court Judge, 2000–05; a Judge of the High Court of Justice, Family Div., 2005–11; Family Div. Liaison Judge, Midland Circuit, 2006–11; a Lord Justice of the Appeal, 2011–18. Member: Family Justice Review Panel, 2010–11; Family Procedure Rules Cttee, 2016–. Chm., Tribunal Appts Bd, Council of Inns of Court, 2012–17. Chm., Family Law Bar Assoc., 2001–03. Pres., Clergy Discipline Tribunals, 2014–18; Chairman: Clergy Discipline Commn, 2014–18; Council, Hereford Cathedral, 2016–. Chm., Adv. Bd, Durham Univ. Law Sch., 2017–; Mem., Adv. Bd, UCL Judicial Inst., 2011–. Trustee, Young Minds, 2001–08. Patron, HOPE Family Centre, Bromyard, 2010–. Dep. Chancellor, Dio. of Wakefield, 2004–06; Chancellor, Dio. of Exeter, 2006–. Hon. DCL Durham, 2018. Canterbury Cross for Services to C of E, 2019. *Publications*: (with David Hershman) Children: law and practice, 1991; (contrib.) Family Court Practice, 1993–; (with Madeleine Reardon) Child Care and Adoption Law, 2006, 2nd edn 2010, 3rd edn as Child Protection and the Family Court, 2019. *Recreations*: family life, theatre, vegetable gardening, beekeeping. *Address*: c/o Royal Courts of Justice, Strand, WC2A 2LL.

**MACFARLANE, Anne Bridget;** Master of the Court of Protection, 1982–95; *b* 26 Jan. 1930; *d* of late Dr David Griffith and Dr Grace Griffith; *m* 1957, James Douglas Macfarlane (*d* 1999); two *d*. *Educ*: nine schools; Bristol Univ. (LLB). Admitted Solicitor, 1954. HM Land Registry, 1966–75; Registrar, Bromley County Court, 1975–82. *Publications*: (contrib.) Atkin's Court Forms, 2nd edn 1983; Older Adults' Decision-Making and the Law, 1996. *Recreation*: collecting Victorian tiles. *Club*: Law Society (Hon. Life Mem., 1996).

**MACFARLANE, Major Charles Keble;** Harbinger, Her Majesty's Body Guard of the Honourable Corps of Gentlemen at Arms, since 2018; *b* Ardingly, Sussex; *s* of Peter Macfarlane and Richenda Macfarlane (*née* Guy); *m* 1980, Diana Wake-Walker; one *s* one *d*. *Educ*: Marlborough Coll. Served Army, Coldstream Guards, 1971–85; Temp. Equerry to the Queen, 1979–82; Co. Comdr, Falkland Islands, 1983; Hd of Business Develt, Robert Fleming & Co., 1985–99; Private Sec. to Lord Mayor of Westminster, 2013–14; Trustee: St Bart's Hosp. Med. Coll. Trust; Cynthia Dickinson Trust; Bullough Tompson Trust. *Recreations*: golf, family, gardening, current affairs. *Clubs*: Pratt's; City of London; Royal St George's Golf; Berkshire Golf; MCC; I Zingari.

**MACFARLANE, Christine Anne;** *see* Salt, C. A.

**MACFARLANE, Sir (David) Neil,** Kt 1988; Chairman, Associated Nursing Services, 1994–2004; *b* 7 May 1936; *yr s* of late Robert and of Dulcie Macfarlane; *m* 1961, June Osmond King, Somerset; two *s* one *d*. *Educ*: St Aubyn's Prep. Sch.; Bancroft's Sch., Woodford Green. Short Service Commission, Essex Regt, 1955–58; served TA, 265 LAA, RA, 1961–66. Joined Shell Mex and BP, 1959; contested (C): East Ham (North), 1970; Sutton and Cheam, by-election, 1972. Parly Under-Sec. of State (Dep. Minister for the Arts), DES, 1979–81; Parly Under-Sec. of State, DoE, 1981–85 (with spec. responsibility for Sport, 1981–85, for Children's Play, 1983–85). Mem., All Party Select Cttee on Science and Technology, 1974–79; MP (C) Sutton and Cheam, Feb. 1974–1992. Chairman: Rushman Lloyd PLC, 1994–97; Securicor plc, 1995–2003 (Dir, 1992–2003); Director: RMC, 1987–2001; Bradford and Bingley Bldg Soc., 1987–2000. Chairman: Sports Aid Foundn, 1986–87; Golf Fund PLC; Vice-Pres. PGA, 1985–. Trustee, England and Wales Cricket Foundn, 1997–. Mem., National Trust, 1976–. Pres., Reading Cons. Assoc. Freeman, City of London, 2000; Founder Master, 1999–2002, Guild of Security Professionals (now Security Professionals' Co.). *Publications*: Sport and Politics: a world divided, 1986. *Recreations*: golf, cricket-watching. *Address*: Beechwood House, Pangbourne, West Berks RG8 7AT. *Clubs*: MCC; Lord's Taverners; Essex County Cricket; Royal & Ancient Golf, Huntercombe Golf.

**McFARLANE, Prof. Duncan Campbell,** PhD; Professor of Industrial Informational Engineering, University of Cambridge, since 2010; Fellow, St John's College, Cambridge, since 1996; *b* 3 May 1963; *m* 1993, Meredith Lillian Bhathal (*d* 2008); one *s* one *d*. *Educ*: Trinity Coll., Univ. of Melbourne (BEng Hons 1984); Queens' Coll., Cambridge (PhD 1988). BHP Co. Ltd: Cadet, 1980; Res. Officer, 1985–92; Co-ordinator, 1992–94; University of Cambridge: Lectr, 1995–2000, Sen. Lectr, 2000–03, Reader, 2003–06, in Automation Systems; Prof. of Service and Support Engrg, 2006–11; Mem., Steering Bd, Cambridge Centre for Smart Infrastructure and Construction, 2011–; Dep. Hd, Res., Cambridge Inst. for Manufg, 2017–. Vis. Prof., 2008, 2010, Vis. Professorial Fellow, 2017–, Univ. of Melbourne. Dir, Distributed Automation and Inf. Lab., 2000–; Res. Dir, Auto ID Centre, 2000–03; Dir, Cambridge Auto ID Lab., 2003–07. Chm., RedBite Solutions Ltd, 2007–. Mem. Mgt Bd, Centre for Digital Build Britain, 2018–. *Publications*: (with K. Glover) Robust Controller Design Using Normalised Coprime Factor Plant Descriptions, 1990; (ed jtly) Holonic and Multi-Agent Systems for Manufacturing, 2003; (with N. Chokshi) A Distributed Coordination Approach to Reconfigurable Process Control, 2008; over 100 jl and conf. papers. *Recreations*: walking, swimming, cricket, green Penguins (collecting), bottle-top collecting, poetry, cartoons. *Address*: St John's College, Cambridge CB2 1TP. *Club*: Melbourne Cricket.

**MACFARLANE, Ian John,** AC 2004; Governor, Reserve Bank of Australia, 1996–2006; *b* 22 June 1946; *s* of Gordon H. and Lilias E. M. Macfarlane; *m* 1970, Heather (*née* Payne); one *s* one *d*. *Educ*: Monash Univ. (BEc Hons; MEc). Inst. of Econs and Stats, Oxford Univ., 1971–72; OECD, Paris, 1973–78; Reserve Bank of Australia, 1979–2006: various posts, 1979–88; Head, Res. Dept, 1988–90; Asst Gov. (Economic), 1990–92; Dep. Gov., 1992–96. Non-executive Director: Australia and NZ Banking Group Ltd, 2007–16; Leighton Hldgs, 2007–13. Dir, Woolworths Ltd, 2007–15. International Adviser: Goldman Sachs, 2007–16; China Banking Regulatory Commn, 2010–14. FASSA. Hon. DSc: Sydney; UNSW Sydney; Hon. DLitt Macquarie; Hon. DCom Melbourne; Hon. LLD Monash. Centenary Medal, 2003.

**McFARLANE, Rt Rev. Janet Elizabeth;** *see* Repton, Bishop Suffragan of.

**McFARLANE, John,** OBE 1995; Chairman, Barclays plc, 2015–19; *b* Dumfries, 14 June 1947; *s* of John McFarlane and Margaret Campbell; *m* Anne; three *d*. *Educ*: Dumfries Acad.; Univ. of Edinburgh (MA); Cranfield Univ. (MBA). Man. Dir, Citicorp, UK Reg., 1975–93; Exec. Dir, Standard Chartered plc, 1993–97; CEO, ANZ Banking Gp Ltd,

1997–2007. Chairman: Aviva plc, 2012–15; FirstGroup plc, 2014–15; non-executive Director: Capital Radio plc, 1995–98; Royal Bank of Scotland plc, 2008–12; Westfield Corp., 2008–; Old Oak Hldgs Ltd, 2008–. Chm., TheCityUK, 2015–. Ext. Mem., Financial Services Trade and Investment Bd, 2015–. Centenary Medal (Australia), 2003.

**MACFARLANE, Prof. John Thomson**, DM; FRCP, FRCPGlas, FRCGP; Professor of Respiratory Medicine, University of Nottingham, 2004–08, Emeritus Professor, 2013; Consultant General and Respiratory Physician, Nottingham University Hospitals, 1982–2008; *b* 21 Nov. 1948; *s* of Sir George Gray Macfarlane, CB and of Barbara Grant Macfarlane; *m* 1971, Rosamund MacInnes, medical researcher and photographer; two *s*. *Educ*: Merton Coll., Oxford (BA Hons 1970); Oxford University Med. Sch. (BM BCh 1973; MA 1983; DM 1983). MRCP 1976, FRCP 1989; MRCGP 1999, FRCGP 2008; FRCPGlas 2009. LRPS 2009; DPAGB 2012; AFIAP 2013; PPSA 2013, EPSA 2015; ARPS 2019. Med. trng posts in Oxford, Brompton Hosp., London, and Ahmadu Bello Univ. Hosp., Zaria, Nigeria, 1974–82. Vis. Prof., Faculty of Life Scis, Univ. of Manchester, 2010–. Chm., British Thoracic Soc., 2006–08; Trustee and Mem. Council, RCP, 2006–08. UK Representative: on Council, Eur. Respiratory Soc., 2003–06; to Fedn of Eur. Respiratory Socs, 2006–08. *Publications*: (jtly) Legionella Infections, 1986; (jtly) Colour Atlas of Respiratory Infections, 1993; many articles, revs, guidelines and chapters in major jls and internat. textbooks, incl. Oxford Textbook of Medicine, mainly on pneumonia, legionnaires' disease and lung infections. *Recreations*: photography, travel, wildlife, mountain walking, cooking, story telling, history. *Address*: Watergate Barn, Loweswater, Cumbria CA13 0RU. *T*: (01900) 85289. *E*: jtmacfarlane@gmail.com.
See also R. G. *Macfarlane*.

**MACFARLANE, Sir Neil;** *see* Macfarlane, Sir D. N.

**MacFARLANE, Neil;** *see* MacFarlane, S. N.

**MACFARLANE, Patricia Mary, (Trisha);** *see* Greenhalgh, P. M.

**MACFARLANE, Dr Robert Grant;** writer; Reader in English, University of Cambridge, since 2016; Fellow, Emmanuel College, Cambridge, since 2003; *b* Oxford, 15 Aug. 1976; *s* of Prof. John Thomson Macfarlane, *qv*; *m* 2000, Julia Lovell; two *s* one *d*. *Educ*: Nottingham High Sch.; Pembroke Coll., Cambridge (BA 1997; PhD); Magdalen Coll., Oxford (MPhil). Lectr, 2006–11, Sen. Lectr, 2011–16, in English, Univ. of Cambridge. Hon. DLitt: Gloucestershire, 2013; Aberdeen, 2014. *Publications*: Mountains of the Mind, 2003; Original Copy, 2007; The Wild Places, 2007; The Old Ways, 2012; (jtly) Holloway, 2013; Landmarks, 2015; The Lost Words, 2017; Underland: a deep time journey, 2019. *Recreations*: mountaineering and hill walking, conservation. *Address*: Emmanuel College, St Andrew's Street, Cambridge CB2 3AP. *T*: (01223) 334200.

**MACFARLANE, Ross Paul;** QC (Scot.) 2016; Summary Sheriff, South Strathclyde, Dumfries and Galloway at Hamilton, since 2017; *b* Glasgow, 13 April 1958; *s* of Colin and Elizabeth Macfarlane; *m* 2011, Dr Lesley-Anne Barnes; three *s* two *d*. *Educ*: Holyrood Sen. Secondary Sch., Glasgow; Edinburgh Univ. (LLB); Strathclyde Univ. (DipLP); Nat. Inst. of Trial Advocacy, USA (Dip. Trial Advocacy; Dip. Teaching Advocacy Skills). Advocate, 1994; Accredited Mediator, 2006; Advocate Depute, 2014–16. Mem. Council, Faculty of Advocates, 1999–2002. Chair: Scottish Child Law Centre, 1998–2001; Stepfamily Scotland, 2004–08. Founding Ed., Green's Family Law Reports, 1996–. *Recreations*: writing, family, charity fundraising. *Address*: Advocates Library, Parliament House, Edinburgh EH1 1EW. *E*: inqdesk@advocates.org.uk.

**MacFARLANE, Prof. (Stephen) Neil**, DPhil; Lester B. Pearson Professor of International Relations, since 1996, and Head, Department of Politics and International Relations, 2005–10, University of Oxford; Fellow, St Anne's College, Oxford, since 1996; *b* 7 March 1954; *s* of David Livingstone MacFarlane and Gertrude Cecile (*née* Straight); *m* 1981, Anne Church Bigelow; three *s* one *d*. *Educ*: Dartmouth Coll., NH (AB); Balliol Coll., Oxford (MA, MPhil, DPhil 1982). University of Virginia, USA: Asst Prof., 1984–87; Associate Prof., 1987–91; Dir, Center for Russian and E European Studies, 1990–91; Queen's University, Kingston, Ontario: Prof. of Political Studies, 1991–96; Dir, Centre for Internat. Relns, 1995–96; Dir, Centre for Internat. Studies, Oxford, 1997–2002. *Publications*: Intervention and Regional Security, 1985; The Idea of National Liberation, 1985; Western Engagement in the Caucasus and Central Asia, 1999; Politics and Humanitarian Action, 2000; Intervention in Contemporary World Politics, 2002; The United Nations and Human Security: a critical history, 2006; articles in Internat. Affairs, Internat. Jl, Survival, Post-Soviet Affairs, World Politics, Security Studies, Third World Qly. *Address*: St Anne's College, Oxford OX2 6HS. *T*: (01865) 274800.

**McFEE, Bruce James;** Director, Environmental Services Pest Control Ltd, Paisley, since 2005; *b* 18 May 1961; *s* of James and Ellen Margaret McFee; *m* 1997, Iris Lille; one *s* (and one twin *s* decd). *Educ*: Johnstone High Sch. Formerly Customer Service Manager, Scotland's largest ind. pest control co. Member (SNP): Renfrew DC, 1988–96 (Sec., 1988–92, Leader, 1992–96, SNP Gp); Renfrewshire Council, 1995–2003 and 2007–12 (Leader, SNP Gp, 1995–2003). MSP (SNP) Scotland West, 2003–07. Est. ABR Scotland, 2012; Ed., www.abrscotland.com. *Recreations*: travel, DIY. *Address*: 36 Troubridge Avenue, Kilbarchan, Johnstone PA10 2AU.

**McFEELY, Elizabeth Sarah Ann C.;** *see* Craig-McFeely.

**McFERRAN, Arthur Joseph,** CBE 2005; Managing Director, 1999–2015, and Vice President, 2013–15, Allstate Northern Ireland Ltd (formerly Northbrook Technology of NI Ltd); *b* 30 May 1951; *s* of Dr Francis Michael Joseph McFerran and Margaret Mary Ethna McFerran; *m* 1974, Patricia McNally; two *s* one *d*. *Educ*: St Malachy's Coll., Belfast; Queen's Univ., Belfast. Salesperson, Rank Xerox, 1972–79; Man. Dir, Logicom Ltd, 1979–97; Vice-Pres., Sales and Mktg, IMR global inc., 1997–99; Vice Pres., Allstate Corp., 2013–15. Non-executive Director: Northern Bank Ltd, 2005–14; Strategic Investment Bd, NI, 2009–15. Board Member: Springvale Trng Ltd, 1999–2016; BITC NI, 2005–16; NI Sci. Park Foundn, 2010–. Pres., NI Chamber of Commerce and Industry, 2008–10 (Vice-Pres., 2006–08). Hon. DSc Ulster, 2010. *Recreations*: golf, ski-ing, walking. *E*: bromcferranis@gmail.com. *Clubs*: Fortwilliam Golf (Belfast), Golfe do Levante, Quinta da Ria (Portugal).

**McGAGH, John Michael,** CEng, EurEng; FIChemE; President, Institution of Chemical Engineers, 2017–18; *b* Rotherham, 18 Nov. 1956; *s* of John McGagh and Elizabeth McGagh (*née* Hale); *m* 1987, Sharon Ward; one *s* two *d*. *Educ*: Univ. of Bradford (BEng Chem. Engrg and Mgt Econs). CEng 1984; EurEng 1984; FIChemE 2003. Grad. Mgt Trainee, RTZ Chemicals, 1980–84; Marketing Officer, Hamersley Iron, London, 1984–87; Perth, Australia, 1987–89; Manager, Polished Sales Services, 1989–94, Business Analysis Ops, 1994–97, Argyle Diamond Mines; Managing Director: Rio Tinto Procurement/Supply Chain, 1997–2007; Rio Tinto Innovation, 2007–16; on secondment as Chief Operating Officer, Quadrem, 1999; Chief Digital Officer, Snowy Hydro Pty Ltd, 2016–18. Dir, Interlate Pty Ltd, 2016–. Member, Advisory Board: Micromone Pty Ltd, 2015–; Equinor (Digital), 2017–. Adjunct Prof., 2011–, Chair, Inst. of Social Sci. Res., 2017–, Univ. of Qld. Chair, Minerals and Mining Cttee, Australian Acad. Technol. and Engrg, 2019–. Chair, Australian Acads rev. of Res. Educn Sector, 2015. FTSE 2013. *Publications*: (contrib.) Extracting Innovations: mining, energy and technological change in the digital age, 2018. *Recreations*: extensive reading, regular travel to off-beat places to experience new cultures, family life, boating, business interactions in start ups, restoring vintage motor vehicles and motor enthusiast interactions. *Address*: 58 Enderley Road, Clayfield, Qld 4011, Australia. *T*: 408983761. *E*: john@mcgagh.com. *Clubs*: Royal Queensland Yacht Squadron; Queensland Jaguar Owners.

**McGAHAN, Bernard Joseph, (Barney),** CBE 2014; Permanent Secretary, Department for Regional Development, Northern Ireland, 2014; Interim Chief Executive, Northern Ireland Policing Board, 2015; *b* 19 March 1954; *s* of Patrick and Rita McGahan; *m* 1976, Teresa Corrigan (marr. diss. 2012); three *d*. *Educ*: Queen's Univ., Belfast (BSc Maths and Computer Sci. 1976). FCCA 1986. Dir, Financial Mgt, Dept of Health and Social Services, NI, 1991–98; Dir, Ops, NI Social Security Agency, 1999–2003; Chief Exec., NI Child Support Agency, 2004–06; Dep. Sec., Dept for Social Develt, 2006–11, Dept for Regl Develt, 2011–14, NI. Chm., Armagh Coll. of Further and Higher Educn, 2002–06. Gov., St Mary's UC, Belfast, 2010–15. *Recreations*: chess, gardening, walking.

**McGAHEY, Cathryn Margaret;** QC 2016; *b* Liverpool, 2 Jan. 1967; *d* of Peter Richard McGahey and Constance Margaret McGahey; *m* 2017, Michael Andrew Nadin Clarke. *Educ*: Howell's Sch., Llandaff; Queens' Coll., Cambridge (BA 1988). Called to the Bar, Inner Temple, 1990; in practice as a barrister, specialising in public law, 1990–. Trustee, Ashbourne and Dist Animal Welfare Soc., 2016–. Gov., Howell's Sch., Llandaff, 2019–. *Recreation*: animal rescue and welfare. *Address*: Temple Garden Chambers, 1 Harcourt Buildings, EC4Y 9DA. *T*: (020) 7583 1315. *E*: cmcgahey@tgchambers.com.

**McGANN, Gary,** FCCA; Chairman: Flutter Entertainment (formerly Paddy Power Betfair) plc, since 2015 (non-executive Director, since 2014); Aryzta AG, since 2016; *b* Dublin, 25 Aug. 1950; *s* of Liam and Rita McGann; *m* 1972, Moira; three *d*. *Educ*: University Coll., Dublin (BA); Trinity Coll., Dublin (MA Mgt Sci.). Gp Financial Controller, Irish cos of L. M. Ericsson Ltd; Gilbeys of Ireland Gp, 1988–94 (CEO, 1991–94); Gp CEO, Aer Lingus, 1994–98; Smurfit Kappa Group plc: Chief Financial Officer, 1998–2000; Chief Operations Officer, 2000–02; CEO, 2002–15. Chairman: AON Ireland; Sicon Ltd. Hon. Fellow, Nat. Coll. of Ireland, 2008. Order of Merit (Colombia), 2016. *Recreations*: golf, music, theatre, grandchildren. *Address*: Flutter Entertainment, Belfield Office Park, Beech Hill Road, Clonskeagh, Dublin 4, Ireland. *E*: gmcgoffice@gmail.com. *Clubs*: K (Co. Kildare); Royal Irish Automobile; Fitzwilliam Lawn Tennis (Dublin); Las Brisas Golf (Marbella).

**McGANN, Heidi-Louise;** *see* Thomas, H.-L.

**McGANN, Prof. Jerome John,** PhD; John Stewart Bryan University Professor, University of Virginia, since 1997 (John Stewart Bryan Professor of English, 1987–97); *b* 22 July 1937; *s* of John J. McGann and Marie V. McGann (*née* Lecouffe); *m* 1960, Anne Lanni; two *s* one *d*. *Educ*: Le Moyne Coll. (BS); Syracuse Univ. (MA); Yale Univ. (PhD 1966). Asst Prof., then Prof., Univ. of Chicago, 1966–75; Professor: Johns Hopkins Univ., 1975–81; CIT, 1981–87. Fulbright Fellow, 1965–66; Guggenheim Fellow, 1970–71 and 1976–81; NEH Fellow, 1975–76 and 1987–89. Co-founder: Inst. for Advanced Technol. in the Humanities, 1992; Speculative Computing Lab., 2001; Founding Dir, Networked Infrastructure for Nineteenth-century Electronic Scholarship, 2003–08. Lectures: Clark, Trinity Coll., Cambridge, 1988; Carpenter, Univ. of Chicago, 1988; Alexander, Univ. of Toronto, 1986; Beckman, Univ. of Calif (Berkeley), 1992; Lansdowne, Univ. of Victoria, 1994; Patten, Indiana Univ., 1995; Byron, Univ. of Nottingham, 1998; Hulme, Univ. of London, 1998; James Murray Brown, Univ. of Aberdeen, 2007. Fellow: Amer. Acad. of Arts and Scis, 1994; Amer. Philosophical Soc., 2014. Hon. DHL Chicago, 1997; Hon. DPhil Athens, 2009. Melville Kane Award, Amer. Poetry Soc., 1973; Distinguished Schol. Award, Byron Soc., 1989; Wilbur Cross Medal, Yale Univ., 1994; Richard Lyman Award, Nat. Humanities Center, 2002; James Russell Lowell Award, MLA, 2002; Lifetime Achievement Award, Mellon Foundn, 2003; Thomas Jefferson Award, Univ. of Virginia, 2016. *Publications*: Fiery Dust: Byron's poetic development, 1969; (ed) Pelham, or The Adventures of a Gentleman, by Edward Bulwer-Lytton, 1972; Swinburne: an experiment in criticism, 1972; Don Juan in Context, 1976; Air Heart Sermons (poems), 1976; (with J. Kauffman) Writing Home (poems), 1978; (with J. Kahn) Nerves in Patterns (poems), 1979; (ed) Byron: the complete poetical works, Vol. I 1980, Vols II and III 1981, Vols IV and V 1986, Vol. VI 1991, Vol. VII 1993; The Romantic Ideology: a critical investigation, 1983; A Critique of Modern Textual Criticism, 1983, 2nd edn 1992; The Beauty of Inflections: literary investigations in historical method and theory, 1985; (ed) Textual Studies and Literary Interpretation, 1985; (ed jtly) The Manuscripts of the Younger Romantics: Byron, Vol. I 1985, Vol. II 1986, Vols III and IV 1988; (ed) Historical Studies and Literary Criticism, 1985; (ed) The Oxford Authors Byron, 1986; Social Values and Poetic Acts, 1987; Towards a Literature of Knowledge, 1989; (ed) Victorian Connections, 1989; (ed) Postmodern Poetries, 1990; The Textual Condition, 1991; (ed) The New Oxford Book of Romantic Period Verse, 1993; Black Riders: the visible language of modernism, 1993; (ed) A Symposium on Russian Postmodernism, 1993; (ed) Byron: the Oxford poetry library, 1994; Four Last Poems (poems), 1996; Poetics of Sensibility: a revolution in literary style, 1997; (ed jtly) Letitia Elizabeth Landon: selected writings, 1997; Complete Writings and Pictures of Dante Gabriel Rossetti: a hypermedia research archive, 1999; D. G. Rossetti and The Game that Must be Lost, 2000; Radiant Textuality: literature since the World Wide Web, 2001; Byron and Romanticism, 2002; The Collected Writings of Dante Gabriel Rossetti, 2003; Algernon Charles Swinburne: major poems and selected prose, 2004; The Scholar's Art: literature and criticism in a managed world, 2006; The Point is to Change It: poetry and criticism in the continuing present, 2007; Are the Humanities Inconsequent?: an interpretation of Marx's Riddle of the Dog, 2009; Byron's Manfred, 2009; (ed) The Black Riders and Other Lines, by Stephen Crane, 2009; (ed) Online Humanities Scholarship: The Shape of Things to Come, 2010; The Invention Tree, 2012; (ed) Poe and the Remapping of Antebellum Print Culture: a new republic of letters, memory and scholarship in the age of digital republication, 2013; The Poet Edgar Allan Poe: alien angel, 2014; (ed) Martin Delaney's Blake; or The Huts of America, 2016. *Recreations*: squash, yoga. *Address*: 303 Poplar Glen Court, Charlottesville, VA 22903, USA.

**McGARRY, Ian;** General Secretary, British Actors' Equity Association, 1991–2005; *b* 27 Feb. 1941; *s* of John and Jean McGarry; *m* 1964, Christine Smith (marr. diss. 1989); one *s*. *Educ*: Chichester High Sch.; Lewes County Grammar Sch. Labour Party Constituency Agent, Putney, 1964–76; Asst General Sec., Equity, 1976–91. *Recreations*: golf, football (spectator), horse racing. *Address*: The White Cottage, Barrington, Ilminster, Som TA19 0JB. *T*: (01460) 55243.

**McGARRY, Natalie;** *b* Fife, 7 Sept. 1981; *m* David Meikle; one *c*. *Educ*: Univ. of Aberdeen (law degree). Policy advr in voluntary sector. Columnist: Scotsman, Herald. MP (SNP) Glasgow E, 2015–17. SNP spokesperson on disabilities, 2015.

**McGARVA, John, (Jack);** a District Judge (Magistrates' Courts), since 2010; *b* Lancaster, 23 Nov. 1961; *s* of John and Dorothy McGarva; *m* 1991, Tracey Worrall; two *s* two *d*. *Educ*: Queen's Park High Sch., Chester; Sheffield Univ. (LLB Hons 1983). Admitted as solicitor, 1987; Asst Solicitor, 1987–91, Partner, 1991–97, Wayman-Hales, Solicitors; Partner, Hill

Dickinson, Solicitors, 1997–2009. Independent Chair: Standards Cttee, Chester CC, 2008–09; Standards Cttee, Cheshire West and Chester, 2009–10. *Recreation:* rowing. *Address:* Liverpool Magistrates' Court, Queen Elizabeth II Law Courts, Derby Square, Liverpool L2 1XA. *Club:* Royal Chester Rowing.

**McGARVEY, Alan;** independent specialist in local community economic and industrial development, 1996–2012; *b* 22 June 1942; *s* of William and Rosina McGarvey; *m* 1st, 1967, Eileen Cook (*d* 1992); 2nd, 1997, Shirlee Gleeson. *Educ:* Wallsend Grammar Sch.; Rutherford Coll. of Further Educn; Univ. of Newcastle (BSc); Cranfield Sch. of Management (MBA). C. A. Parsons, 1958–64 (apprentice); junior management positions: RTZ, 1968–71; Decca Gp, 1972–76; MK Electric, 1976–78; Director, Small Company Div., NEB, 1978–82; Chief Exec., Greater London Enterprise Bd, 1982–86; management consultant, 1986–88; Chief Exec., Greater Manchester Econ. Develt Ltd, 1987–90; ind. regl/local develt specialist, 1990–93; specialist, Regl and Small and Medium Enterprises Develt, EC, 1993–96. Labour Party, 1974–2013; Mem., Wandsworth Borough Council, 1981–86 (Dep. Opposition Leader, 1982–83); Chm., Battersea Constituency Labour Parties, 1978–82. Exec. Mem., Wandsworth CRC, 1973–82; Board Member: Battersea Arts Centre Trust, 1982–88; Northern Chamber Orch., 1988–93; Member: Jt Governing Board, Centre for Development of Industry (EEC-ACP Lomé), 1981–90; Adv. Council, Cttee for Industrial Co-operation (EEC-ACP), 1990–96. Sch. Gov., 1973–91; Gov., Poynton High Sch., 2013–17. *Recreations:* painting (pictures not walls!), Tai Chi, reading (lots and lots and varied), Multi-Academy Trustee, going to a gym twice a week (ah well, somebody has to do it!). *Address:* Cheadle Hulme, Cheadle, Stockport SK8 7AQ. *T:* 07544 409725. *E:* alanmcgarvey4@gmail.com.

**McGAUGHRIN, Anne,** CBE 2018; Legal Director, Government Legal Department. *Educ:* York Univ. (BA Jt Hons English and Hist.). Admitted solicitor, 1986; Adviser: Plumstead Law Centre, 1979–84; Cullen & Co., 1984–88; PR, Canon Inc., Tokyo, 1988–91; Legal Advr, Govt Legal Service, 1992–. *Publications:* (ed and contrib.) Exploring Japan, 1991. *Recreations:* enjoying family, friends, the arts and the great outdoors.

**McGEACHY, Alistair Laird,** WS; a Judge of the Upper Tribunal (Immigration and Asylum Chamber) (formerly a Vice President, Immigration Appeal Tribunal, later a Senior Immigration Judge, Asylum and Immigration Tribunal), 2004–17; *b* 2 April 1949; *s* of William Laird McGeachy and Alice McGeachy (*née* Hill); *m* 1978, Jennifer Heather Macleod; two *s* one *d*. *Educ:* Strathallan Sch.; Univ. of Edinburgh (LLB Jt Hons Law and Hist.). Admitted solicitor: Scotland, 1974; England, 1982; WS 1975; with Fyfe Ireland, 1974–76; Refugee, then Tribunal, Counsellor, UKIAS, 1976–82; with Manches and Co., 1982–84; Partner, Macdonald Stacey, subseq. incorporated in Kidd Rapinet, 1984–97; Adjudicator of Immigration Appeals, 1997–2004; Judge, Special Immigration Appeals Commn, 2013–17. Liveryman, Gardeners' Co., 1990 (Clerk, 1985–90). *Recreations:* reading, visiting art galleries, travel.

**McGee, Rt Rev. Brian Thomas;** *see* Argyll and the Isles, Bishop of, (RC).

**McGEE, Prof. James O'Donnell,** FMedSci; Professor of Morbid Anatomy, University of Oxford, 1975–99, now Emeritus; Fellow of Linacre College, Oxford, 1975, now Emeritus; *b* 27 July 1939; *s* of Michael and Bridget McGee; *m* 1961, Anne Lee (*d* 2012); one *s* two *d*. *Educ:* Univ. of Glasgow. MB, ChB, PhD, MD; MA (Oxon). FRCPath 1986; FRCPGlas 1989. Various appts in Univ. Dept of Pathology, Royal Infirmary, Glasgow, 1962–69; Roche Inst. of Molecular Biology, Nutley, NJ: MRC Fellow 1969–70; Vis. Scientist 1970–71; Distinguished Vis. Scientist, 1981 and 1989; Dept of Pathology, Royal Infirmary, Glasgow: Lectr, 1971–74; Sen. Lectr, 1974–75. Member: Scientific Cttee, 1978–88, Grants Cttee, 1988–92, Cancer Res. Campaign; Cttee on Safety of Medicines, 1987–89 (Safety and Efficacy Sub Cttee, 1984–87). Mem., Bd of Dirs, 2003–10, Sen. Special Advr, 2011–14, Internat. Soc. for Telemedicine and eHealth. Kettle Meml Lectr, RCPath, 1980; Annual Guest Lecturer: Royal Coll. of Physicians, Ireland, 1986; Royal Acad. of Medicine (Ireland), 1985. Founder FMedSci 1998. Bellahouston Gold Medal, Glasgow Univ., 1973. *Publications:* Biopsy Pathology of Liver, 1980, 2nd edn 1988; In Situ Hybridisation: principles and practice, 1990; Oxford Textbook of Pathology, 1992: vol. 1, Principles of Pathology, vols 2a, 2b, Pathology of Systems; The Natural Immune System: The Macrophage, 1992; The Natural Killer Cell, 1992; Diagnostic Molecular Pathology, vols 1 and 2, 1992; papers in scientific jls on liver disease, breast and cervical cancers, telematics/telepathology in health care. *Recreations:* talking with my family, swimming. *Address:* Linacre College, Oxford OX1 3JA.

**McGEECHAN, Sir Ian (Robert),** Kt 2010; OBE 1990; coaching consultant; Chairman, Rugby Coaches Association, since 2012; *b* 30 Oct. 1946; *s* of Bob McGeechan and Hilda (*née* Shearer); *m* 1969, Judy Fish; one *s* one *d*. *Educ:* Carnegie Coll. of Physical Educn (DipPE). Teacher: Moor Grange High Sch., 1968–72; and Hd of Humanities, Fir Tree High Sch., 1972–90; Rugby player: Scottish Internat., 1972–79; Barbarians, 1973–78; British Lions, SA, 1974, NZ, 1977; coach: Headingley, 1980–83; Scotland under 21s, 1981–83; Scotland B, 1983 and 1985–88; Northampton, 1994–99; Asst Coach, Scotland, 1985–88; Nat. Coach, Scotland, 1988–93 and 1999–2003 (incl. Scotland Grand Slam, 1990, 4th place, World Cup, 1991); British Lions Coach: Australia, 1989 (won 2–1); NZ, 1993 (lost 2–1); SA, 1997 (won 2–1); SA, 2009 (lost 2–1); Asst Coach (midweek), NZ, 2005; Director of Rugby: London Wasps, 2005–09; Bath Rugby, 2010–12. Mem. Bd, Sports Coach UK, 1996– (Chm., 2005–08). Chm., 2012–14, Pres., 2014–19, Yorkshire Carnegie (formerly Leeds Carnegie) Rugby. Sports journalist, The Telegraph, 2012–. Hon. MA Nottingham, 1998; Hon. DArts Leeds Metropolitan, 2004. Parly Rugby Medal, 2004. *Publications:* Scotland's Grand Slam, 1990; So Close to Glory: Lions New Zealand, 1993; Winning Lions, South Africa, 1997; Lion Man (autobiog.), 2009; The Lions: when the going gets tough, 2017. *Recreations:* photography, hill-walking with wife and two dogs. *E:* ianmcgeechan@hotmail.com.

**McGEEHAN, Prof. Joseph Peter,** CBE 2004; PhD; FREng; Professor of Communications Engineering, Department of Electrical and Electronic Engineering, 1985, now Emeritus, and Director, Centre for Communications Research, since 1987, University of Bristol; Managing Director, Telecommunications Research Laboratory, Bristol, 1998–2011, Senior General Adviser, since 2011, Toshiba Research Europe Ltd; *b* 15 Feb. 1946; *s* of Joseph McGeehan and Rhoda Catherine McGeehan; *m* 1970, Jean Lightfoot; two *d*. *Educ:* Univ. of Liverpool (BEng Hons Electrical Engrg and Electronics 1967; PhD 1971; DEng 2003). FREng 1994. Sen. Scientist, Allan Clark Res. Centre, Plessey Co. Ltd, Caswell, 1970–72; Lectr, then Sen. Lectr, in Electrical Engrg, Sch. of Electrical Engrg, Univ. of Bath, 1972–85; University of Bristol: Hd, Dept of Electrical and Electronic Engrg, 1991–98; Dean of Engrg, 1998–2003. Founding Chm. and non-exec. Dir, Wireless Systems International Ltd, 1995–98; non-executive Director: Renishaw plc, 2001–10; 3CR, 2003. Non-exec. Dir, Technology Foresight Mobile Virtual Centre of Excellence, 1996–98, 2001–07, 2011–12. Chair, W of England Inward Investment Bd, 2012–. Mem., SW Sci. and Industry Council, 2009–11; Industry Mem., LEP, 2010–. Ambassador, SW England RDA, 2003–12. Governor: Bristol Grammar Sch., 2003–04; Colston Sch., Bristol, 2007–. *Publications:* more than 350 articles in internat. acad. jls and confs. *Recreations:* keeping fit, cycling, watching sport (particularly cricket, Rugby Union and F1), amateur photography, theatre, concerts.

**McGEGAN, (James) Nicholas,** OBE 2010; Music Director, Philharmonia Baroque Orchestra, San Francisco, since 1985; Principal Guest Conductor, Pasadena Symphony Orchestra, since 2013; *b* 14 Jan. 1950; *s* of late (James Edward) Peter McGegan and Christine Mary McGegan (*née* Collier); civil partnership 2006, *m* 2013 (Calif), 2015 (UK), David von Recklinghausen Bowles. *Educ:* Corpus Christi, Cambridge (BA, MA); Magdalen Coll., Oxford. LTCL 1969. Royal College of Music: Prof., 1973–79; Dir, Early Music, 1976–80; Artist-in-Residence, Washington Univ., St Louis, Mo, 1979–85; Principal Conductor, Drottningholm Court Th., Sweden, 1993–96 (Vänners Hederstecken, 1996); Principal Guest Conductor, Scottish Opera, 1993–98. Artistic Dir, Göttingen Handel Fest., Germany, 1991–2011; Baroque series Dir, St Paul Chamber Orch., 1999–2004. Hon. Prof., Georg-August Univ., Göttingen, 2006. Hon. DMus San Francisco Conservatory of Music, 2013. Hon. RCM 1978. Has made numerous recordings, incl. opera and oratorios. Handel Prize, Halle, Germany, 1993. Cross of Order of Merit of Lower Saxony (Germany), 2011. *Publications:* (ed) Philidor, Tom Jones, 1978. *Recreations:* history, cooking, good wine. *Address:* 722 Wildcat Canyon Road, Berkeley, CA 94708, USA. *T:* (510) 5280862; 1 Kew Terrace, Glasgow G12 0TD. *T:* (0141) 339 0786. *Clubs:* East India, Savile.

**McGEOCH, Dr Duncan James,** FRSE; Director, Medical Research Council Virology Unit, Glasgow, 1995–2009; *b* 13 Sept. 1944; *s* of Peter and Christina McGeoch; *m* 1971, Jennifer A. Wylie; two *s*. *Educ:* Hutchesons' Grammar Sch., Glasgow; Univ. of Glasgow (BSc 1967; PhD 1971). FRSE 1987. Jane Coffin Childs Postdoctoral Fellow, Dept of Microbiology and Molecular Genetics, Harvard Med. Sch., 1971–73; Researcher, Virology Div., Dept of Pathology, Univ. of Cambridge, 1973–76; Mem. of Scientific Staff, MRC Virology Unit, Glasgow, 1976–95. Hon. Prof., Univ. of Glasgow, 1996–2009. Editor-in-Chief, Jl of General Virology, 1988–92. Fleming Award, Soc. for Gen. Microbiology, 1980. *Publications:* scientific papers. *Recreations:* reading, mountains and sea, ski-ing, walking, sailing.

**McGEORGE, Alistair Kenneth;** Chairman, The Original Factory Shop, since 2016; *b* Glasgow, 6 May 1959; *s* of late Sam McGeorge and Wendy McGeorge; *m* 1984, Caroline Herbert; one *s* one *d*. *Educ:* Bramhall Grammar Sch.; Manchester Poly. (BA Hons 1980). FCA 1984. Chartered Accountant, Deloitte, Haskins & Sells, 1980–94; Littlewoods Group: various financial roles incl. Home Shopping Finance Dir, 1994–98; Gp Financial Services Dir, 1998–2000; Gp Supply Chain Dir, 2000–01; CEO, 2001–05; CEO, Matalan, 2006–10; Exec. Chm., New Look Retailers Ltd, 2011–14, 2017–19; Man. Dir, BIG W, 2014–15. Chm., Bd of Trustees, Retail Trust, 2018–. *Recreations:* golf, keeping fit, family.

**McGEOUGH, Prof. Joseph Anthony,** CEng, FREng, FIMechE; Regius Professor of Engineering, University of Edinburgh, 1983–2005, now Professor Emeritus (Head, Department of Mechanical Engineering, 1983–91; Honorary Professorial Fellow, 2007–April 2020); *b* 29 May 1940; *s* of late Patrick Joseph McGeough and Gertrude (*née* Darroch); *m* 1972, Brenda Nicholson; two *s* one *d*. *Educ:* St Michael's Coll., Irvine; Glasgow Univ. (BSc, PhD); Aberdeen Univ. (DSc). Research Demonstrator, Leicester Univ., 1966; Sen. Res. Fellow, Queensland Univ., 1967; Res. Metallurgist, International Research & Development Co. Ltd, Newcastle upon Tyne, 1968–69; Sen. Res. Fellow, Strathclyde Univ., 1969–72; Lectr 1972–77, Sen. Lectr 1977–80, Reader 1980–83, Dept of Engineering, Aberdeen Univ. Royal Society/SERC Industrial Fellow, 1987–89; Hon. Prof., Nanjing Univ. of Aeronautics and Astronautics, 1992–; Visiting Professor: Univ. degli Studi di Napoli Federico II, 1994; Glasgow Caledonian Univ., 1997–2003; Tokyo Univ. of Agric. and Technol., 2004; Monash Univ., 2005; Manchester Univ., 2018–19. Institution of Mechanical Engineers: Chm., Scottish Br., 1993–95; Mem. Council, 2000–03; Mem., Trustee Bd, 2004–10; Vice-Pres., 2006–10; Pres., 2019–20. Chm., CIRP UK Bd, 2000–03 (Mem. Council, 2006–08). Editor: Procs of Internat. Confs on Computer-aided Prodn Engrg, 1986–; Processing of Advanced Materials, 1991–94; CIRP Ed., Jl of Materials Processing Technol., 1995–2005; Ed.-in-Chief, Procs IMechE, 2014–17; Ed.-in-Chief, Jl Nanomaterials, Nanoengrg and Nanosystems, 2014–17. Fellow, Internat. Acad. Prodn Engrg, 1987 (Emeritus Fellow, 2019); FRSE 1990. FREng 2009; Fellow, Internat. Soc. for Nanomanufacturing, 2018. *Publications:* Principles of Electrochemical Machining, 1974; Advanced Methods of Machining, 1988; (ed) Micromachining of Engineering Materials, 2001; The Engineering of Human Joint Replacements, 2013; papers mainly in Journal of Mech. Engrg Science, Proc. IMechE; contrib. Encyclopaedia Britannica, Encyclopaedia of Electrochemistry, Encyclopaedia of Production Engineering. *Recreations:* golf, hill-walking. *Address:* 39 Dreghorn Loan, Colinton, Edinburgh EH13 0DF. *T:* (0131) 441 1302.

**McGHEE, George Arnott;** Programming Director, Snap-B TV, 2013–14; *b* 8 March 1956; *s* of Douglas and Myra McGhee. *Educ:* Ravensbourne Coll. of Art and Design (Dip. Media and Gen. Art Studies). Asst Film Ed., later Broadcast Exec., Scottish TV, 1979–93; Hd of Acquisitions, Channels TV Max and Max 1, Czech Republic, 1993–94; Carlton Cinema: Hd of Acquisitions, 1994–98; Dir, 1998–2003; Controller, BBC Programme Acquisition, 2003–09. *Recreations:* cinema, theatre, music, ski-ing, entertaining, collecting.

**McGHEE, John Alexander;** QC 2003; barrister; *b* 11 Feb. 1962; *s* of Alastair Orr McGhee and Joyce Alison McEwen McGhee (*née* Gall); *m* Marianne Richards; one *s* one *d* from a previous marriage. *Educ:* University Coll., Oxford (MA). Called to the Bar, Lincoln's Inn, 1984. *Publications:* Snell's Equity, 30th edn (ed.) 1999 to 33rd edn (gen. ed.) 2015. *Recreation:* flute playing. *Address:* Maitland Chambers, 7 Stone Buildings, Lincoln's Inn, WC2A 3SZ.

**McGHEE, Prof. Patrick,** CPsychol; Assistant Vice-Chancellor, University of Bolton, since 2014; *b* Glasgow, 3 Feb. 1962; *s* of Patrick and Bridgid McGhee; *m* 1992, Marianne Keirle; two *s*. *Educ:* All Saints' Secondary Sch., Glasgow; Univ. of Glasgow (MA 1st Cl. Hons Psychol. 1983); Wolfson Coll., Oxford (DPhil Psychol. 1987); Harvard Business Sch. (Global Leadership Prog. (CPD) 2009); ACCA Cert. in Internat. Accounting 2013; Univ. of Bolton (Postgrad. Dip. Cognitive Behavioural Therapies 2016). CPsychol 1989. Res. Fellow in Psychol., St George's Hosp. Med. Sch., Univ. of London, 1986–87; Lectr, Edge Hill, 1987–91; Sen. Tutor and Consultant, Open Univ., 1987–2000; Sen. Lectr, Sheffield City Poly., 1991–92; Hd of Psychol., Univ. of Derby, 1992–97; Associate Dean, 1997–2000, Dean of Learning Support and Develt, 2000, Bolton Inst.; Dean, 2000–02, Pro-Vice-Chancellor, 2003–04, Dep. Vice-Chancellor, 2005–10, Univ. of Central Lancs; Vice-Chancellor, Univ. of E London, 2010–13. Man. Dir, Hampshire Global Ltd, 2013–. Vis. Prof., Univ. of Wolverhampton, 2013–; Vis. Scholar, MIT, Cornell Univ. and Yale Univ., 2017–18. Non-executive Director: Transformation Bd, Northants Police and Crime Comr, 2013–15; Knowledge Centre for Materials Chemistry, 2015–. Trustee, Creative Support, 2016– (Chair, Finance and Audit Cttee, 2016–). TEF Assessor, HEFCE, 2016–18. Nat. Teaching Fellow. FRSA 1996; FHEA 2002. Columnist: Guardian, 2010–; BBC News, 2015. *Publications:* (jtly) Accounting for Relationships, 1987; Thinking Psychologically, 2001; The Academic Quality Handbook, 2007. *Recreation:* chess.

**McGHIE, Hon. Lord;** James Marshall McGhie; Chairman, Scottish Land Court, 1996–2014; President, Lands Tribunal for Scotland, 1996–2014; Judge, Abu Dhabi General Market Court, since 2016; *b* 15 Oct. 1944; *s* of James Drummond McGhie and Jessie Eadie Bennie; *m* 1968, Ann Manuel Cockburn; one *s* one *d*. *Educ:* Perth Acad.; Edinburgh Univ.

(LLB Hons). Called to the Scottish Bar, 1969; QC (Scot.) 1983; Advocate-Depute, 1983–86; pt-time Judge, Inner Hse, Ct of Session, 2012–17. Pt-time Chm., Medical Appeal Tribunal, 1987–92; pt-time Mem., Criminal Injuries Compensation Bd, 1992–96. *Recreations:* various.

**McGHIE, Duncan Clark,** CA; Chairman: Scottish Ballet, 1999–2004; Scottish Opera, 1999–2004; *b* 6 Dec. 1944; *s* of William and Helen McGhie; *m* 1969, Una Gray Carmichael; one *s* one *d*. *Educ:* George Watson's Coll., Edinburgh. BSC, 1967–78 (Financial Controller, Scottish Div., 1975–78); Gp Finance Dir, Wm Collins Plc, 1978–84; Partner, Mgt Consultancy, Coopers & Lybrand, subseq. PricewaterhouseCoopers, 1984–2000. Mem., Inland Waterways Adv. Council, 2006–11 (Vice Chm., 2009–11). Mem., ICAS, 1967–. Elder, Ch of Scotland. *Recreations:* golf, music. *Address:* 65 Corrour Road, Newlands, Glasgow G43 2ED. *T:* (0141) 632 4502, *Fax:* (0141) 649 9030. *E:* duncan.mcghie@ntlworld.com. *Clubs:* Pollok Golf, Western Gailes Golf.

**McGHIE, James Marshall;** *see* McGhie, Hon. Lord.

**MacGIBBON, Dr Barbara Haig, (Mrs John Roberts),** CB 1988; FRCPath; Chairman, Commission on Environmental Health, 1996–97; Assistant Director (Medical), National Radiological Protection Board, 1988–93; *b* 7 Feb. 1928; *d* of Ronald Ross MacGibbon and Margaret Fraser; *m* 1954, John Roberts; one *s* one *d*. *Educ:* Lady Margaret Hall, Oxford; University College Hosp. Registrar, then Res. Assistant, Dept of Haematology, Royal Postgraduate Med. Sch., 1957–64; Sen. Registrar, Sen. Lectr/Hon. Consultant, then Sen. Res. Fellow, Dept of Haematology, St Thomas' Hosp. Med. Sch., 1969–79; SMO, then PMO, Toxicology and Environmental Health, DHSS, 1979; SPMO, DHSS, 1983–88. Chm., Panel on Energy, WHO Commn on Health and Envmt, 1990–92; Consultant, MRC Inst. for Envmt and Health, 1994–97. *Publications:* (ed) Concern for Europe's Tomorrow: health and environment in the WHO European region, 1995; articles in various med. jls.

**MacGIBBON, Ross Arthur;** freelance television director and producer, since 2009; *b* Bromley, Kent, 29 Jan. 1955; *s* of Prof. Iain Campbell MacGibbon and Dawn Eleanor MacGibbon; *m* 1984, Julie Cooper Kavanagh; two *s*. *Educ:* Daniel Stewart's Coll., Edinburgh; Royal Ballet Sch. Dancer with Royal Ballet, 1973–86; Ed. and Dir, Dancelines Prodns, 1986–91; Dir, Landseer Films, 1991–2002; Exec. Producer, Dance, BBC TV, 2002–07; Exec. Dir, ScreenStage Prodns, 2007–09. Mem., Dance Panel, Arts Council England, 1993–98. Board Member: Royal Opera House, 1999–2002; Rambert Dance Co., 2001–; Birmingham Royal Ballet, 2013–19. Gov., Royal Ballet Cos, 2002–08. Trustee, Council for Dance Educn and Trng, 2008–13. *Recreations:* golf, Clarice Cliff, photography. *Address:* Flat 6, 41 St George's Square, SW1V 3QN. *T:* (020) 7821 1117. *E:* rossmacgibbon@btinternet.com.

**McGIBBON, Susanna Justine;** Director General, Government Legal Department, since 2018; *b* 11 Nov. 1967; *d* of Ian and Gwen McGibbon; *m* 2004, Patrick Spencer. *Educ:* Bolton Co. Grammar Sch.; Canon Slade Sch., Bolton; Univ. of Sheffield (LLB Hons 1989); Inns of Court Sch. of Law. Called to the Bar, Lincoln's Inn, 1990; in private practice at the Bar, 1990–93; FCO, 1993–98; Treasury Solicitor's Dept, 1998–2006: MoD, 1998–2000; DfES, 2000–02; Cabinet Office, 2002–06; Dir, Legal Services B, DTI, later BERR, 2006–08; Dir, Legal Services A, BERR, later BIS, 2008–09; Legal Dir, DCLG, 2009–12; Dir, Litigation Gp, Treasury Solicitor's Dept, then Govt Legal Dept, 2012–18. *Recreations:* travel, particularly Europe and Asia; music, including returning to the piano; generally enjoying London life. *Address:* c/o Government Legal Department, 102 Petty France, SW1H 9AJ.

**MACGILL, His Honour Kerry Michael Peter;** a Circuit Judge, 2000–12; *b* 30 April 1950; *s* of Alan and Betty Macgill; *m* 1973, Janet Hazeldine; one *s* one *d*. *Educ:* Holborn Coll. of Law (LLB Hons London, 1971). Asst Solicitor, T. I. Clough & Co., 1975–77; Partner, Lumb & Kenningham, which later became Lumb & Macgill, criminal law practice, 1977–2000. *Recreations:* walking, golf, sailing.

**McGILL, Robin William,** CEng; Director, McGill Advisory Services, 2015–18; Vice President, HSE, Quality, Engineering and Business Excellence, Fosroc Inc., 2016–19; *b* 19 Aug. 1955; *s* of William Robertson McGill and Catherine Meikle Leitch; *m* 1977, Susan (*née* McMorran); one *s* one *d*. *Educ:* Univ. of Edinburgh (BSc 1st cl. Hons Engrg Sci. 1977). CEng, MIMechE, 1981, FIMechE; FIET. BP Chemicals, Scotland, 1977–88, Engr, then operational roles, subseq. Polythene Ops Manager; Business Manager, Boron Nitride, Carborundum Inc., Buffalo, NY, 1988–92; BP plc, 1992–2006: Strat. and Projs Manager, BP Chemicals; Distribution Sen. Bus. Advr, BP Oil Internat.; Mktg Div. Manager, Pittsburgh Pa, BP America Inc.; Mergers & Acquisitions Proj. Manager, BP Chemicals Ltd; Business Unit Leader: Plastic Fabrications Gp, BP Amoco Ltd; European Polymers, BP Chemicals Ltd; CEO, BP Solvay HDPE, 2001–04; Man. Dir, BP Grangemouth, 2004–06; Chief Exec. and Sec., IET, 2007–09; Man. Dir, Atomic Weapons Establishment, Aldermaston, 2009–10; Dir, Energy Oil and Gas Europe, Exova Gp Ltd, 2012–14. Mem. Council, CBI Scotland, 1981–.

**McGILL, Stephen Phillip,** CBE 2014; Director, Hartford Financial Services, since 2017; *b* 18 Feb. 1958; *s* of late Maj. James Osmond McGill and Joyce Courteney McGill; *m* Elizabeth Mawbey; one *s* two *d*. *Educ:* Gordon's Boys' Sch., West End, Woking. ACII 1980. Sedgwick, 1977–81; Director: Fenchurch Gp Brokers Internat., 1981–86; Willis Internat., 1986–89; Lloyd Thompson Ltd, 1989–97; Dir, 1997–2002, Gp Chief Exec., 2002–04, Jardine Lloyd Thompson Gp plc; CEO, Aon Global, 2005–06, CEO, Aon Risk Services Americas, 2006–08, Aon Corporation. Dir, Internat. Insce Soc. Inc., 2002–05; Pres., Insce Inst. of London, 2005–06; Chm. and CEO, Aon Risk Solutions, 2008–17; Gp Pres., Aon plc, 2012–17. Mem., Internat. Adv. Bd, British American Business, 2010–. Trustee, Find a Better Way, 2011–16. *Recreations:* ski-ing, swimming, tennis.

**MacGILLIVRAY, Prof. Ian,** MD, FRCP, FRCOG; Regius Professor of Obstetrics and Gynæcology, University of Aberdeen, 1965–84 (Dean of Medical Faculty, 1976–79), now Emeritus Professor; *b* 25 Oct. 1920; *yr s* of W. and A. MacGillivray; *m* 1950, Edith Mary Margaret Cook; one *s* twin *d*. *Educ:* Vale of Leven Academy, Alexandria; University of Glasgow (MB, ChB 1944; MD 1953); MRCOG 1949, FRCOG 1959; FRCPGlas 1973. Gardiner Research Schol., 1949–51, Lectr in Midwifery, 1951–53, Univ. of Glasgow; Senior Lecturer: in Obstetrics and Gynæcology, Univ. of Bristol, 1953–55; in Midwifery and Gynæcology, Univ. of Aberdeen, 1955–61; Prof. of Obstetrics and Gynæcology, University of London, at St Mary's Hospital Medical Sch., 1961–65. Mem., GMC, 1979–84. Founder Pres., Internat. Soc. for Study of Hypertension in Pregnancy, 1976–80; Pres., Internat. Soc. for Twin Studies, 1980–83; Mem. Council, RCOG, 1974–80. *Publications:* Outline of Human Reproduction, 1963; Combined Textbook of Obstetrics and Gynæcology, 1976; Human Multiple Reproduction, 1976; Pre-eclampsia: the hypertensive disease of pregnancy, 1983; contrib. to: British Medical Journal, Lancet, Journal of Obstetrics and Gynæcology of the British Empire; Clinical Science. *Address:* Devonshire Nursing Home, 95 Carlisle Road, Eastbourne BN20 7TB.

**McGILLIVRAY, Laura Susan;** Chief Executive, Norwich City Council, since 2006; *b* 29 Dec. 1953; *d* of late William Watson McGillivray and Marjory Joan McGillivray (*née* Cameron); *m* 1999, Paul Robert Golding Chaplin (marr. diss. 2014); two *d*. *Educ:* Liverpool Univ. (BA Sociol. 1975); Birmingham Univ. (MBA Public Service Mgt 1994). Dir and Sen. Consultant, CAG Consultants, 1985–88; Dir, Manor Gdns Health and Community Centre, Islington, 1988–91; Milton Keynes Council: Community Devmt Mgr, 1991–94; Asst Dir, Local Govt Reorganisation, 1994–96; Hd of Policy and Communications, 1996–2000; Strategic Dir, Community Services, Dacorum BC, 2000–03; Dep. Chief Exec., City of York Council, 2003–05; Chief Exec., Gt Yarmouth BC, 2014. Chm., Bd of Trustees, Pregnancy Adv. Service, Greater London, 1985–91. Member: Council, UEA, 2006–; Bd, Sainsbury Centre for the Visual Arts, 2006–; Adv. Bd, Inst. of Local Govt, Univ. of Birmingham, 2010–12; Stakeholder Bd, Norwich Res. Park, 2011–; Bd, Norwich Univ. of Arts, 2013–18; Chm., Norfolk Community Safety Partnership, 2012–; Trustee, SOLACE Foundn, 2012–15. Mem. RSA. *Recreations:* networking, spending time with family and friends, supporting Norwich as UNESCO City of Literature, sea kayaking and other adventures. *Address:* Norwich City Council, City Hall, Norwich NR2 1NH. *T:* (01603) 212001, *Fax:* (01603) 213001. *E:* lauramcgillivray@norwich.gov.uk. *Club:* Druidstone (Pembrokeshire).

**McGIMPSEY, Michael;** Member (UU) Belfast South, Northern Ireland Assembly, 1998–2016; *b* 1 July 1948; *s* of Henry and Isabel McGimpsey; *m* 1970, Maureen Elisabeth Speers; one *s* one *d*. *Educ:* Regent House Grammar Sch.; Trinity Coll., Dublin (BA 1970). Mem. (UU), Belfast CC, 1993–2011. Minister of Culture, Arts and Leisure, 1999–2002, of Health, Social Services and Public Safety, 2007–11, NI. Contested (UU) Belfast S, 2005. *Recreations:* reading, gardening, walking.

**McGINLEY, Aideen,** OBE 2000; Trustee for Northern Ireland, BBC Trust, 2012–17; *b* 31 May 1954; *d* of Joseph Slevin and Terry Slevin (*née* O'Brien); *m* 1975, James McGinley; two *s* one *d*. *Educ:* Salford Univ. (BSc Hons Envmtl Sci. 1975); Univ. of Ulster (MSc Social Policy, Admin and Planning 1983). Community Services Officer: Fermanagh DC, 1976; Strabane DC, 1976–89; Fermanagh District Council: Principal Officer, Policy and Planning, 1989–92; Dir of Devmt, 1992–95; Chief Exec., 1995–2000; Permanent Secretary: Dept of Culture, Arts and Leisure, NI, 1999–2006; Dept for Employment and Learning, NI, 2006–09; Chief Exec., Ilex, 2009–12. Chair, Galway 2020, 2017–19; Trustee: Carnegie UK Trust, 2015–; Nat. Trust, 2019–. Hon. Mem. RSUA, 2004. DUniv Ulster, 1998. *Recreation:* family.

**McGINN, Conor Patrick;** MP (Lab) St Helens North, since 2015; *b* Co. Armagh, 31 July 1984; *m*; one *s* one *d*. Worked in charity sector and managed health projects; Pol Advr to Labour defence team. An Opposition Whip, 2015–16. Member: Defence Select Cttee, 2015; NI Affairs Cttee, 2017–; Foreign Affairs Cttee, 2019–. *Address:* House of Commons, SW1A 0AA. *Clubs:* Ulster Reform; Windle Labour.

**McGINN, Gerry,** CBE 2017; Chairman: Strategic Investment Board Ltd, since 2013; HNH Group, since 2014; *b* 4 May 1957. *Educ:* QUB; Columbia Graduate Business Sch., NY. Joined Nat. Westminster Bank, London; Bank of Ireland: Chief Exec., Corporate and Internat. Banking, 1990–94; Chief Exec., NI, 1994–99; Chief Exec., UK, 1999–2001; Permanent Secretary: Dept of Educn, NI, 2001–05; Dept for Regl Devlpt, NI, 2006–07; Hd, Goodbody Stockbrokers, NI, 2007–09; Chief Exec., Irish Nationwide Building Soc., 2009–11; Man. Dir, 2011–14, Regl Exec. Dir, 2014, First Trust Bank. Non-executive Director: Progressive Building Soc., 2015–; Link (formerly Capita) Asset Services (Ireland), 2014–19 (Chm.).

**McGINTY, Kevin Charles Patrick,** CBE 2012; HM Chief Inspector, Crown Prosecution Service, since 2015; *b* Swansea, 16 June 1957; *s* of Laurence Patrick McGinty and Joan McGinty (*née* Thomas). *Educ:* St Joseph's Comprehensive Sch., Port Talbot; Poly. of N London (BA). Called to the Bar: Gray's Inn, 1982, Bencher, 2013; NI, 1998; in practice, CPS, 1988–92; Attorney Gen.'s Office, 1992–96; Bank of England, 1996–97; Attorney Gen.'s Office, 1997–2015, Dep. Legal Sec., 2011–15. *Address:* HM Crown Prosecution Service Inspectorate, 102 Petty France, SW1H 9EA. *T:* (020) 7210 1185. *E:* kevin.mcginty@hmcpsi.gov.uk.

**McGINTY, Lawrence Stanley;** Health and Science Editor, ITN, 1989–2014 (Science Editor, 1987–89); *b* 2 July 1948; *s* of Lawrence McGinty and Hilda (*née* Hardman); *m* 1st, 1969, Joan Allen (*d* 2008); 2nd, 2011, Kate Evans. *Educ:* Stand Grammar Sch., Whitefield, Bury; Liverpool Univ. (BSc Zoology). Asst Editor, Chemistry in Britain, 1971–72; Technology Editor, then Health and Safety Editor, later News Editor, New Scientist, 1972–82; Science Correspondent, Channel 4 News, 1982–87. Guest Lectr, Ecole Polytechnique, Paris, 1984. Special Advisor: WHO, 2000; IAEA, 2001–03. Chm., Medical Journalists' Assoc., 2014–. Hon. DLitt Liverpool, 2012. Silver Jubilee Medal, 1977; Lifetime Achievement Award, RTS, 2015. *Recreations:* fine wine, books, walking.

**McGIVAN, Alec John;** Head, BBC Outreach, 2007–13; *b* 8 Sept. 1953; *s* of Ronald McGivan and Nancy McGivan (*née* Richards); *m* 1992, Elizabeth Ann Astill; one *s* one *d*. *Educ:* Bristol Cathedral Sch.; Wadham Coll., Oxford (MA Modern Hist.). Nat. Organiser, SDP, 1981–88; Events Dir, Corp. of London, 1988–90; Chief Exec., Shakespeare Globe Trust, 1990–91; Hd of Communications, Chapter One, 1991–94; Football Association: Media/Events Manager, Euro 96, 1994–96; Campaign Dir, World Cup Bid 2006, 1996–2000; Dir, Internat. Mktg, Interclubnet, 2000–02; Dir of Sport, DCMS, 2002–04; Hd, Charter Review Campaign, BBC, 2004–07. Trustee: Comic Relief, 2007–11; BBC Performing Arts Fund, 2007–13; Elizabeth R Broadcasting Fund, 2007–15; Children's Univ., 2012– (Chm., 2016–). *Recreations:* gardening, music, all sport, Bristol City FC, family and friends. *E:* alec.mcgivan@gmail.com.

**McGIVERN, Eugene,** CB 1997; Under Secretary, Board of Inland Revenue, 1986–98; *b* 15 Sept. 1938; *s* of late James and Eileen McGivern; *m* 1960, Teresa Doran; two *s* one *d*. *Educ:* St Mary's Grammar School, Belfast. Joined Inland Revenue, 1955; seconded to Welsh Office as Private Sec. to Minister of State, 1967–69; Inland Revenue, 1969–98. Mem., CSAB, 1998–2004; Tribunal Mem., AIDB, subseq. AADB, 2005–14. Papal Medal Benemerenti, 2016.

**McGLADE, Prof. Jacqueline Myriam,** PhD; Professor: Institute for Global Prosperity and Faculty of Engineering, University College London, since 2000; Maasai Mara University, Kenya, since 2017; Chief Scientist, and Director, Division of Early Warning and Assessment, United Nations Environment Programme, 2014–17 (Special Adviser to Executive Director, 2013–14); *b* 30 May 1955; *d* of Bryan Maurice Cox and Maria Alphonsonia (*née* LeClair); *m* 1977, James McGlade (marr. diss. 1994); two *d*. *Educ:* UCNW (BSc; Hon. Fellow, Univ. of Wales, 1999); Univ. of Guelph, Canada (PhD 1981). FRICS 1989. Sen. Res. Scientist, Federal Govt of Canada, 1981–87; Adrian Fellow, 1987–90, Fellow, 1990–, Darwin Coll., Cambridge; Associate Prof., Cranfield Inst. of Technology, 1987–88; Schol., Internat. Fedn of Insts of Advanced Studies, Maastricht, 1988–93; Dir, and Prof. of Theoretical Ecology, Forschungszentrum Jülich, 1988–92; Prof. of Biol Scis, Univ. of Warwick, 1992–98 (Hon. Prof., 1998–2003); Dir, Centre for Coastal and Marine Scis, NERC, 1998–2000; Prof., Dept of Maths, 2000–10, Dept of Earth Scis, 2010–17. Exec.

Dir, EEA, 2003–13. Member: Bd, Envmt Agency, 1998–2003; Marine Foresight Panel, 1999–2002; UK–China Forum, 1999–; UK-Japan 21st Century Gp, 2002–; Adv. Cttee on Earth Observation, ESA, 2016–. Trustee: Earth Centre, 1990–2003; Natural Hist. Mus., 2002–11. Hon. Mem., Internat. Inst. for Dynamical Systems, 1991. FRSA 1997; FLS 1998. Hon. DSc Kent, 2004. Jubileum Award, Chalmers Univ., Sweden, 1991; Minerva Prize, FZ Jülich, Germany, 1992; Masaryk Gold Medal, Univ. of Brno, 2005; Global Citizen Award, Global Spatial Data Infrastructure Assoc., 2013; Il Monitor del Giardino Award, Italy, 2013. Knight, Order of St James (Monaco), 2010. *Publications:* Advanced Ecological Theory, 1999; Gulf of Guinea Large Marine Ecosystem, 2002; papers on math. biology, marine sci. informatics and governance. *Recreations:* sailing, diving, ski-ing, climbing, flying. *Address:* 10 The Coach House, Compton Verney, Warwick CV35 9HJ.

**MacGLASHAN, Maureen Elizabeth,** CMG 1997; HM Diplomatic Service, retired; indexer, since 1987; Ambassador to the Holy See, 1995–98; *b* 7 Jan. 1938; *d* of Kenneth and Elizabeth MacGlashan. *Educ:* Luton High Sch.; Girton Coll., Cambridge (MA, LLM). Joined FO, 1961; 2nd Sec., Tel Aviv, 1964–67; FCO, 1967–72; Head of Chancery, East Berlin, 1973–75; UK Representation to EEC, 1975–77; seconded to Home Civil Service, 1977–82; Counsellor, Bucharest, 1982–86; Asst Dir, Res. Centre for Internat. Law, and bye-Fellow, Girton Coll., Cambridge Univ., 1986–90; Counsellor, Consul-Gen. and Dep. Head of Mission, Belgrade, 1990; Head, Western European Dept, FCO, 1991–92; on secondment to CSSB, 1992–95. Pres., Soc. of Indexers, 2002–05. Ed., The Indexer, 2005–18. *Publications:* (trans.) Weil, Maritime Delimitation, 1989; Consolidated Index and Tables to the International Law Reports, vols 1–125, 2004, vols 1–160, 2017. *Club:* Royal Over-Seas League.

**McGLONE, (John) Alistair (Philip),** CBE 2007; international law consultant, since 2013; *b* 21 Feb. 1956; *s* of Walter and Anne McGlone; *m* 1993, Rosanna Heralall; two *s*. *Educ:* Queen's Coll., Oxford (MA). Admitted solicitor, 1981; Department for Environment, Food and Rural Affairs: Legal Advr, 2001–02; Head: Internat. and Biotechnol. Legal team, 2002–06; Water, Soil and Ecology Legal team, 2006–09; Legal Dir, 2009–10; Hd, Internat. Law, 2010–13. *Recreations:* cookery, cycling, walking, supporting Arsenal FC. *Address:* 55 Aberdeen Park, N5 2AZ. *T:* (020) 7359 8616, 07545 306789. *E:* alistairmcglone@virginmedia.com.

**McGONIGAL, His Honour Christopher Ian;** North Eastern Circuit Mercantile Judge, 1997–2003; a Deputy High Court Judge, 2003–05; *b* 10 Nov. 1937; *s* of Harold Alfred Kelly McGonigal and Cora McGonigal (*née* Bentley); *m* 1961, Sara Ann Sander; three *s* one *d*. *Educ:* Ampleforth Coll., York; Corpus Christi Coll., Oxford (MA). Coward Chance: articled clerk, 1963–65; Asst Solicitor, 1965–68; Sen. Litigation Partner, 1969–79, 1983–87; Sen. Resident Partner, Dubai, Sharjah, Bahrain and Jeddah offices, 1979–83; Clifford Chance: Jt Sen. Litigation Partner, 1987–95; Sen. Partner, Contentious Business Area, 1995–97. Asst Recorder, 1990–95; Recorder, 1995–97. *Recreations:* gardening, opera, local history. *Address:* 90 Seabrook Road, Hythe, Kent CT21 5QA.

**McGOUGAN, Donald,** OBE 2012; Director of Finance, City of Edinburgh Council, 1995–2011; *b* 26 Dec. 1950; *s* of Louis and Sidney McGougan; *m* 1991, Mandy Dodgson; one *s* one *d*. *Educ:* Hermitage Acad., Helensburgh. CPFA 1976. Trainee Accountant, Midlothian CC, 1971–75; Professional Asst, City of Edinburgh DC, 1975–77; Falkirk District Council: Sen. Accountant, 1977–79; Principal Asst, 1979–81; Depute Dir of Finance, 1981–87; City of Edinburgh District Council: Depute Dir of Finance, 1987–95; acting Dir of Finance, 1995–96. *Recreations:* family, golf, Rugby.

**McGOUGH, Rt Rev. David;** Auxiliary Bishop of Birmingham, (RC), and Titular Bishop of Cunavia, since 2006; *b* 20 Nov. 1944; *s* of Clement and Ethel McGough. *Educ:* Cotton Coll., N Staffs; Oscott Coll., Birmingham; Ven. English Coll., Rome; Gregorian Univ., Rome (STL 1969); Pontifical Biblical Inst., Rome (LSS 1977). Ordained priest, 1970; Lectr in Biblical Studies, Oscott Coll., Birmingham, 1975–90; Parish Priest: Christ the King, Birmingham, 1986–90; Our Lady & All Saints, Stourbridge, 1990–2006; Canon of Chapter, St Chad's Cathedral, Birmingham, 2002–. Vis. Lectr, Maryvale Inst., Birmingham, 1990–2007. *Recreations:* walking, cricket. *Address:* The Rocks, 106 Draycott Road, Tean, Stoke-on-Trent ST10 4JF. *T:* (01538) 722433.

**McGOUGH, Roger,** CBE 2004 (OBE 1997); FRSL; poet; *b* 9 Nov. 1937; *s* of Roger Francis and Mary Agnes McGough; *m* 1st, 1970 (marr. diss. 1980); two *s*; 2nd, 1986, Hilary Clough; one *s* one *d*. *Educ:* St Mary's Coll., Crosby, Liverpool; Hull Univ. (BA, Grad. Cert. Ed.). Fellow of Poetry, Univ. of Loughborough, 1973–75. Mem. Exec. Council, 1989–; Pres., 2011–, Poetry Soc. Hon. Prof., Thames Valley Univ., 1993; Hon. Fellow, John Moores Univ., 1999. FRSL 2005. Hon. MA Nene Coll., 1998; Hon. DLitt: Hull, 2004; Roehampton, 2006; Liverpool, 2006; Nottingham, 2015; DUniv Open, 2009. *Television:* Kurt, Mungo, BP and Me (BAFTA Award), 1984. Presenter, Poetry Please, BBC Radio 4, 2007–. Lyrics for Wind in the Willows, Broadway, 1985–86; The Elements (RTS Award), 1993. *Publications:* Watchwords, 1969; After The Merrymaking, 1971; Out of Sequence, 1972; Gig, 1972; Sporting Relations, 1974; In The Glassroom, 1976; Summer with Monika, 1978; Holiday on Death Row, 1979; Unlucky For Some, 1981; Waving at Trains, 1982; Melting into the Foreground, 1986; Selected Poems 1967–1987, 1989; You at the Back, 1991; Defying Gravity, 1992; The Spotted Unicorn, 1998; The Way Things Are, 1999; Everyday Eclipses, 2002; Collected Poems, 2003; Said and Done (autobiog.), 2005; Selected Poems, 2006; That Awkward Age, 2009; As Far As I Know, 2012; It Never Rains, 2014; joinedupwriting, 2019; *play adaptations:* Molière: Tartuffe, 2008; The Hypochondriac, 2009; The Misanthrope, 2013; *children's books:* Mr Noselighter, 1977; The Great Smile Robbery, 1982; Sky in the Pie, 1983; The Stowaways, 1986; Noah's Ark, 1986; Nailing the Shadow, 1987; An Imaginary Menagerie, 1988; Helen Highwater, 1989; Counting by Numbers, 1989; Pillow Talk, 1990; The Lighthouse That Ran Away, 1991; My Dad's a Fire-eater, 1992; Another Custard Pie, 1993; Lucky, 1993; Stinkers Ahoy!, 1995; The Magic Fountain, 1995; The Kite and Caitlin, 1996; Bad, Bad Cats, 1997; Until I Met Dudley, 1997; Good Enough to Eat, 2002; Moonthief, 2002; What on Earth?; Dotty Inventions, 2002; The Bee's Knees, 2003; All the Best, 2003; (with Brian Patten) The Monsters' Guide to Choosing a Pet, 2004; Slapstick, 2008; Mind the Gap, 2010; Poetry Pie, 2015; If Only We had a Helicopter, 2015; I Never Liked Wednesdays, 2015; '80' Poems, 2017; Merry-go-Round, 2020; Crocodile Tears, 2020; contributed to: Penguin Modern Poets, No 10, Mersey Sound, 1967, rev. edn 1983; Oxford Book of 20th Century Verse, 1973; The Norton Anthology of Modern Poetry, 1973; Penguin Modern Poets, No 4 (new series), 1995; edited: Strictly Private, 1981; Kingfisher Book of Comic Verse, 1986; The Kingfisher Book of Poems about Love, 1997; The Ring of Words (anthology), 1998; Wicked Poems, 2002; Sensational, 2004; You Have Been Warned, 2008; Happy Poems, 2018. *Address:* c/o United Agents, 12–26 Lexington Street, W1F 0LE. *T:* (020) 3214 0800. *Club:* Chelsea Arts (Chm., 1984–86; Trustee, 1992–).

**McGOVERN, Alison;** MP (Lab) Wirral South, since 2010; *b* 30 Dec. 1980; *d* of Mike and Ann McGovern; *m* 2008, Ashwin Kumar; one *d*. *Educ:* Wirral Grammar Sch. for Girls; University Coll. London (BA Philosophy). Researcher, H of C, 2002–06; Public Affairs Manager: Network Rail, 2006–08; Art Fund, 2008–09; Creativity, Culture and Educn, 2009. Mem. (Lab) Southwark LBC, 2006–10. PPS to Rt Hon. Gordon Brown, MP, 2010–13. *Address:* House of Commons, SW1A 0AA.

**McGOVERN, James Christopher;** *b* 17 Nov. 1956; *s* of Thomas McGovern and Alice McGovern; *m* 1991, Norma Ward. *Educ:* Lawside RC Acad., Dundee. Apprentice glazier, 1973–77, glazier, 1977–87, Solaglas; glazier, Dundee DC, 1987–97; trade union organiser, GMB, 1997–2005. Mem., Tayside Regl Council, 1994–96. Chm., Dundee E Labour Party, 1999–2001. MP (Lab) Dundee W, 2005–15. *Recreations:* fitness club, watching football (Celtic FC).

**McGOVERN, Jimmy;** screenwriter; *b* Liverpool, 1949. Writer for television dramas and series: Brookside, 1983–89; Cracker, 1993, 1994, 1995, 2006; Heart and Minds, 1995; Hillsborough, 1996; The Lakes, 1997, 1999; Dockers, 1999; Sunday, 2002; Gunpowder, Treason and Plot, 2004; (also prod.) The Street, 2006, 2007, 2009; Moving On, 2009, 2010, 2011, 2013, 2014, 2016; 2018; Accused, 2010, 2012; Common, 2014; Banished, 2015; Reg, 2016; Broken, 2017; Care, 2018; films: Priest, 1994; Go Now, 1995; Heart, 1999; Liam, 2001; musical stage show, King Cotton, Lowry, 2007. *Address:* c/o The Agency, 24 Pottery Lane, Holland Park, W11 4LZ.

**McGOWAN,** family name of **Baron McGowan**.

**McGOWAN,** 4th Baron *cr* 1937; **Harry John Charles McGowan;** *b* 23 June 1971; *o s* of 3rd Baron McGowan and Lady Gillian Angela Pepys, *d* of 7th Earl of Cottenham; *S* father, 2003; *m* 2001, Emma, *d* of Duncan Hattersley Smith; four *d* (incl. twin *d*). *Educ:* Harrow. *Heir:* *uncle* Hon. Dominic James Wilson McGowan [*b* 26 Nov. 1951; *m* 1982, Brigitta Papadimitriou (marr. diss.)].

**MACGOWAN, Christopher John,** OBE 2008; Chief Executive, Society of Motor Manufacturers and Traders, 1999–2007; *b* 26 April 1947; *s* of Rev. John Macgowan and Dorothy Macgowan; *m* 1st, 1968, Victoria Lindey (*d* 1989); two *d*; 2nd, 1995, Amanda Fuller (*d* 2003). *Educ:* Orwell Park; Marlborough Coll. Export Rep. (Canada), British Leyland, 1965–73; PR Manager, Massey-Ferguson, 1973–90; Sales Dir, Ransomes, 1990–94; Chief Exec., Retail Motor Ind. Fedn, 1994–99. Chm., inpixnow, 2013–16; Dir, Alcraft Motor Co. Ltd, 2015–16 (Advr, 2013–15). Vis. Prof., Univ. of Buckingham, 2008–14; External Assessor, Loughborough Univ., 2009–12. Member: DfT Motorists' Forum, 2003–; Public Policy Cttee, RAC Foundn, 2008–16. Trustee: Nat. Motor Museum, 1999–; BEN Automotive Benevolent Fund, 2000–14; Farleigh Hospice, 2007–09. Hon. Treas., Caravan Club, 2011–. Freeman, City of London, 1997. *Recreations:* social media, information technology, National Hunt racing, travel. *Club:* Royal Automobile.

**McGOWAN, Prof. David Alexander,** PhD; Professor of Oral Surgery, University of Glasgow, 1977–99, now Emeritus; Hon. Consultant in Oral Surgery, Greater Glasgow Health Board, 1977–99; *b* 18 June 1939; *s* of George McGowan, MBE, and Annie, (Nan), Hall McGowan (*née* Macormac); *m* 1968, Margaret Vera Macauley; one *s* two *d*. *Educ:* Portadown Coll.; QUB (BDS 1961; MDS 1970); London Hosp. Med. Coll., London Univ. (PhD). FDSRCS 1964; FFDRCSI 1966; FDSRCPSGlas 1978; FDSRCSE 1999. Oral Surgery trng, Royal Victoria Hosp., Belfast and Aberdeen Royal Infirmary, 1961–67; Lectr in Dental Surgery, QUB, 1968; Department of Oral and Maxillo-Facial Surgery, London Hospital Medical College: Lectr, 1968–70; Sen. Lectr, 1970–77; Sen. Tutor, 1970–73; Consultant, 1971–77; Dep. Head, 1973–77. Chm., Nat. Dental Adv. Cttee, Scotland, 1995–99. Post-grad. Advr in Dentistry for W Scotland, 1977–90; Dean: Dental Faculty, RCPSG, 1989–92; Glasgow Univ. Dental Sch., 1990–95; Senate Assessor, Court, Univ. of Glasgow, 1995–99; Mem., GDC, 1989–99 (Dep. Chm., Educ., 1995–99). Founder Ed., Dental History Mag., 2007–12. Univ. Fellow, Univ. of Western Australia, 1986; Caldwell Lectr, Univ. of Glasgow, 1993. Pres., Lindsay Soc. for History of Dentistry, 2016–18. Gold Medal, Bulgarian Acad. of Medicine, 1992; University Medal: Malta, 1999; Helsinki, 2000. *Publications:* (jtly) Outline of Oral Surgery, part 1, 1985; An Atlas of Minor Oral Surgery, 1989 (trans. Italian 1991, trans. French 1993), 2nd edn 1999; (jtly) The Maxillary Sinus and its Dental Implications, 1993; (jtly) Outline of Oral Surgery, parts 1 and 2, 1998; (jtly) Apprenticeship to Life-Long Learning: dental education through the centuries, 2015; numerous articles in jls. *Recreations:* painting, photography, dog-walking, reading novels, listening to music. *Address:* Glenderry, 114 West King Street, Helensburgh, Argyll G84 8DQ. *T:* (01436) 676688.

**McGOWAN, Ian Duncan;** Librarian, National Library of Scotland, 1990–2002; *b* 19 Sept. 1945; *s* of Alexander McGowan and Dora (*née* Sharp); *m* 1971, Elizabeth Ann Weir; two *d*. *Educ:* Liverpool Inst.; Exeter Coll., Oxford (BA 1st Cl. Hons Russian Lang. and Lit., 1967); Sch. of Slavonic and E European Studies, Univ. of London. National Library of Scotland: Asst Keeper, 1971–78; Keeper (Catalogues and Automation), 1978–88; Sec. of the Library, 1988–90. Chm., Nat. Preservation Adv. Cttee, 1994–96; President: Scottish Library Assoc., 1998 (Vice-Pres., 1996–97); Edinburgh Bibliographical Soc., 2010–13 (Vice-Pres., 2004–10). Editor, Alexandria: jl of nat. and internat. liby and inf. issues, 2003–11. Chm., Britain-Russia Centre, Scotland, 1999–2002; Hon. Treas., Scotland-Russia Forum, 2003–13. Chm., 2006–08, Treas., 2008–18, Scottish Working People's History Trust. Founding Fellow, Inst. of Contemporary Scotland, 2000. FRSA 1999. IFLA Medal, 2002. *Recreations:* books, gardens. *Address:* 23 Blackford Road, Edinburgh EH9 2DT. *T:* (0131) 667 2432. *Club:* New (Edinburgh).

**McGOWAN, John;** Sheriff in Ayr, 2000–12; *b* 15 Jan. 1944; *s* of Arthur McGowan and Bridget McCluskey; *m* 1966, Elise Smith; two *s*. *Educ:* St Joseph's Acad., Kilmarnock; Glasgow Univ. (LLB). Admitted Solicitor, 1967; Partner, Black Hay & Co., 1970–93. Temp. Sheriff, 1986–93; Sheriff in Glasgow, 1993–2000. Chm., DHSS Appeal Tribunal, 1980–86. Mem. Council, Law Soc. of Scotland, 1982–85. *Recreations:* golf, reading, choral singing, theatre. *Address:* 20 Auchendoon Crescent, Ayr KA7 4AS. *T:* (01292) 260139.

**McGOWAN, Prof. Margaret Mary, (Mrs Sydney Anglo),** CBE 1998; PhD; FBA 1993; Professor of French, 1974–99, Senior Pro-Vice-Chancellor, 1992–97, Research Professor, since 1997, and 50th Anniversary Fellow, since 2012, University of Sussex; *b* 21 Dec. 1931; *d* of George McGowan and Elizabeth (*née* McGrail); *m* 1964, Prof. Sydney Anglo, *qv*. *Educ:* Stamford High Sch.; Univ. of Reading (BA, PhD). Lecturer: Univ. of Strasbourg, 1955–57; Univ. of Glasgow, 1957–64; University of Sussex: Lectr, 1964–68; Reader, 1968–74; Dean, Sch. of European Studies, 1977–80; Pro-Vice-Chancellor (Arts and Social Studies), 1981–86. Leopold Delisle Lectr, Bibliothèque nationale de France, 2012. Mem. Bd, European Strategic Mgt Unit, 1995–2003. Vice-President: British Acad., 1996–98; Early Dance Circle, 2012–. Chm., Adv. Council, Warburg Inst., Univ. of London, 2013–17 (Chm. of Review of Warburg Inst., 2006–07). Vice-Chm. Bd, British Inst. in Paris, 1978–99; Gov., Ardingly Coll., 1994–2004. FRSA 1997. Freeman, City of Tours, 1986. Hon. DLitt Sussex, 1999. *Publications:* L'Art du Ballet de Cour, 1963; Montaigne's Deceits, 1974; Ideal Forms in the Age of Ronsard, 1985; Louis XIII's Court Ballets, 1989; Moy qui me voy: studies of the self, 1990; The Vision of Rome in Late Renaissance France, 2000; Dance in the Renaissance: European fashion, French obsession, 2008 (Wolfson History Prize, 2008); Sources livresques et albums d'images: la danse à la Renaissance, 2012; Dynastic Marriages 1612/1615: a celebration of the Hapsburg and Bourbon unions, 2013; Festival and Violence: princely entries in the context of war, 1480–1635, 2019. *Recreations:* music, cooking, tennis. *Address:* 59 Green Ridge, Withdean, Brighton BN1 5LU.

**McGOWAN, Hon. Mark;** MLA (ALP) Rockingham, Western Australia, since 1996; Premier of Western Australia, since 2017; *b* Newcastle, NSW, 13 July 1967; *s* of Dennis McGowan and Mary McGowan; *m* 1996, Sarah; two *s* one *d*. *Educ*: Univ. of Queensland (BA, LLB). Legal Officer, Aust. Royal Navy, 1989–96. Western Australia: Parly Sec. to the Premier, 2001–05; Minister: for Tourism, Racing and Gaming, Youth, Peel, and SW, 2005–06; for Envmt, and Racing and Gaming, 2006; for Educn and Trng, and SW, 2007–08; Leader of the Opposition, 2012–17; Minister for Public Sector Mgt, State Develt, Jobs and Trade, and State and Federal Relns, 2017–. Gov.-Gen.'s Commendation for Brave Conduct, 1997. *Recreations*: camping, spending time with family at the beach. *E*: wa-government@dpc.wa.gov.au.

**McGOWAN, Hon. Dame Maura Patricia,** DBE 2014; **Hon. Mrs Justice McGowan;** a Judge of the High Court, Queen's Bench Division, since 2014; *b* 27 Jan. 1957; *d* of Matthew Vincent McGowan and Bridget McGowan (née Helebert). *Educ*: Virgo Fidelis Convent, London; St Mary's Coll., Leeds; Manchester Univ. (LLB Hons). Called to the Bar, Middle Temple, 1980, Bencher, 2005; called to the Irish Bar, 1990, to the Bar of NI, 2013; in practice, specialising in criminal law; a Recorder, 1996–2014; QC 2001; a Dep. High Court Judge, 2010–14; Presiding Judge, SE Circuit, 2016–19. Member: Sentencing Council of England and Wales, 2017–; Sentencing Adv. Cttee, Supreme Ct of Eastern Caribbean, 2017–. Chm., Bar Council, 2013. *Recreations*: cricket, fishing, opera, theatre, reading. *Address*: Royal Courts of Justice, Strand, WC2A 2LL.

**McGOWAN, Michael;** *b* 19 May 1940; *m*; two *s* one *d*. *Educ*: Leicester University. Formerly: lecturer; BBC journalist; co-operative employment development officer, Kirklees Council, to 1984. MEP (Lab) Leeds, 1984–99.

**McGOWAN, Dr Neal Lowson;** educational consultant, speaker and presenter on school leadership and education; Headteacher, William de Ferrers School, Chelmsford, 2013–16; *b* 12 May 1963; *s* of late John McGowan and Elizabeth (née Taylor). *Educ*: Moray House Coll. of Educn, Edinburgh (Dip Tech. Ed); Univ. of Edinburgh (MEd); Univ. of Stirling (EdD 2016). Teacher, Wester Hailes Educn Centre, 1985–88; Asst Principal Teacher, Lasswade High Sch., 1988–90; Principal Teacher, 1990–93, Asst Head Teacher, 1993–96, Musselburgh Grammar Sch.; Depute Rector, Selkirk High Sch., 1996–97; Head Teacher, Gracemount High Sch., Edinburgh, 1997–2002; Rector, Banchory Acad., Aberdeenshire, 2002–04; Rector, Larbert High Sch., Falkirk, 2004–09; Headteacher, Cherwell Sch., Oxford, 2009–10; Headmaster, Dulwich Coll. Beijing, 2011–12. Sec. to Ministerial Discipline Task Gp, 2001. *Publications*: Standard Grade Technological Studies Revision Notes, 1990; Higher Grade Technological Studies Revision Notes, 1991; Practice Questions for Higher Grade Technological Studies, 1993. *Recreations*: golf, travel, eating out, keep fit, everything 'Apple', West End Theatre.

**McGRAIL, Prof. Seán Francis,** FSA; Professor of Maritime Archæology, University of Oxford, 1989–93, now Emeritus; Visiting Professor of Maritime Archaeology, University of Southampton, since 1991; Chief Archaeologist, National Maritime Museum, 1976–86; *b* 5 May 1928; *m* 1955, Ursula Anne Yates, BA; one *s* three *d*. *Educ*: Royal Navy (Master Mariner); Univ. of Bristol (BA); Univ. of London (PhD); Campion Hall, Oxford (MA 1987); DSc Oxon 1989. FSA 1981; MCIfA (MIFA 1983). Served RN, 1946–68: Seaman Officer; awarded Wings (pilot), 1952; qualified as Air Warfare Instr, 1954, as Instrument Rating Examr, 1958; comd 849 Sqdn, FAA, 1962–63. Undergrad., Univ. of Bristol, 1968–71 (Harry Crook Scholar, 1969–71); Postgrad. Student, Inst. of Archaeology, London, 1972–73; Postgrad. Student (pt-time), UCL, 1973–78; National Maritime Museum, 1972–86, Hd of Archaeol Res. Centre, 1976–86. Leverhulme Res. Fellow, 1991–94; Visiting Professor: of Maritime Archæology, Oxford Univ., 1986–89; Danish Nat. Museum's Centre for Maritime Archaeology, Roskilde, 1994; Univ. of Haifa, 1995. Mem., Adv. Cttee on Historic Wrecks, Dept of Nat. Heritage (formerly DoE), 1974–98. Mem., Wardour Catholic Cemetery Trust, 1976–2014 (Treas., 1999–2014); Vice-Chm., Trust for Preservation of Oxford Coll. Barges, 1987–95. Prehistoric and medieval excavations, Norway, Denmark, Orkney, Ireland and Britain, 1974–93; maritime ethnographic fieldwork, Bangladesh and east coast of India, 1994–2001. Mem. Editl Bd, Mary Rose Trust, 1998–2002, 2004–12. *Publications*: Building and Trials of a Replica of an Ancient Boat, 1974; Logboats of England and Wales, 1978; Rafts, Boats and Ships, 1981; Ancient Boats, 1983; Ancient Boats of North West Europe, 1987, 2nd edn 1998; Medieval Boat and Ship Timbers from Dublin, 1993; Studies in Maritime Archaeology, 1997; Boats of the World, 2001, 2nd edn 2004; Boats of South Asia, 2003; (with N. Nayling) Barland's Farm Romano-Celtic Boat, 2004; Ancient Boats and Ships, 2006; Early Ships and Seafaring: water transport in European waters, 2014; Water Transport beyond Europe, 2015; *edited*: Sources and Techniques in Boat Archaeology, 1977; Medieval Ships and Harbours, 1979; Paul Johnstone, Seacraft of Prehistory, 1980, 2nd edn 1988; Brigg 'raft' and her Prehistoric Environment, 1981; Woodworking Techniques before 1500, 1982; Aspects of Maritime Archaeology and Ethnography, 1984; (with J. Coates) Greek Trireme of 5th Century BC, 1984; (with E. Kentley) Sewn Plank Boats, 1985; Maritime Celts, Saxons and Frisians, 1990; articles in archaeological and maritime jls. *Recreations*: strategic gardening, real ale specialist. *Address*: Institute of Archaeology, 36 Beaumont Street, Oxford OX1 2PG. *T*: (01865) 278240.

**McGRATH, Prof. Alister Edgar,** DD, DLitt; Andreas Idreos Professor of Science and Religion and Director, Ian Ramsey Centre for Science and Religion, University of Oxford, since 2014; Fellow, Harris Manchester College, Oxford, since 2014; *b* 23 Jan. 1953; *s* of Edgar P. McGrath and Annie J. M. McGrath (née McBride); *m* 1980, Joanna Ruth Collicutt; one *s* one *d*. *Educ*: Wadham Coll., Oxford (BA 1975); Linacre Coll., Oxford; Merton Coll., Oxford (MA, DPhil 1978; BD 1983; DD 2001; DLitt 2013); St John's Coll., Cambridge. Ordained deacon, 1980, priest, 1981; Curate, St Leonard's Ch, Wollaton, Nottingham, 1980–83; Lectr, 1983–95, Principal, 1995–2004, Wycliffe Hall, Oxford; Titular Prof. of Historical Theology, 1999–2008, Dir, Centre for Evangelism and Apologetics, subseq. Oxford Centre for Christian Apologetics, 2004–06, Univ. of Oxford; Sen. Res. Fellow, Harris Manchester Coll., Oxford, 2006–14; Prof. of Theol., Ministry and Educn, KCL, 2008–14. Gresham Prof. of Divinity, 2015–18. FRSA 2005. Hon. DD: Virginia Theol Seminary, 1996; Union Theol Seminary, Belfast, 2005; Wycliffe Coll., Univ. of Toronto, 2007. *Publications*: Explaining Your Faith… Without Losing Your Friends, 1988; Justification by Faith, 1988; Justitia Dei: history of the Christian doctrine of justification, Vol. I 1989, Vol. II 1993; Doubt: handling it honestly, 1990; Luther's Theology of the Cross: Martin Luther's theological breakthrough, 1990; Cloud of Witnesses: ten great Christian thinkers, 1990; Genesis of Doctrine, 1990; Life of John Calvin: a study in the shaping of Western culture, 1990; Affirming Your Faith: exploring the Apostles' Creed, 1991; Bridge Building: creative Christian apologetics, 1992; Intellectual Origins of the European Reformation, 1992; Making Sense of the Cross, 1992; Reformation Thought: an introduction, 1992; Roots that Refresh, 1992; Suffering, 1992; (with J. McGrath) Dilemma of Self Esteem: the Cross and Christian confidence, 1992; (ed) Blackwell Encyclopedia of Modern Christian Thought, 1993; Christian Theology: an introduction, 1993; Making of Modern German Christology: from the Enlightenment to Pannenberg, 1993; Renewal of Anglicanism, 1993; Jesus: who He is and why He matters, 1994; Evangelicalism and the Future of Christianity, 1994; A Passion for Truth, 1996; (ed jtly) Doing Theology for the People of God, 1996; J. I. Packer: a biography, 1997; The Foundations of Dialogue in Science and Religion, 1998; Historical Theology: an introduction to the history of Christian thought, 1998; T. F. Torrance: an intellectual biography, 1999; Theology for Amateurs, 2000; The Unknown God: searching for spiritual fulfilment, 2000; The Journey: a pilgrim in the lands of the spirit, 2000; (ed) Christian Literature: an anthology, 2000; In the Beginning: the story of the King James Bible, 2001; Knowing Christ, 2001; The Future of Christianity, 2001; A Scientific Theology: vol. 1, Nature, 2001, vol. 2, Reality, 2002, vol. 3, Theory, 2003; Glimpsing the Face of God, 2002; A Brief History of Heaven, 2002; The Re-enchantment of Nature, 2002; The Twilight of Atheism, 2004; Dawkins' God, 2004; Theology—The Basics, 2004; Creation, 2005; Incarnation, 2005; The Science of God: an introduction to scientific theology, 2005; The Order of Things: explorations in scientific theology, 2006; (with J. McGrath) The Dawkins' Delusion, 2007; Christianity's Dangerous Idea: the Protestant revolution, a history from the sixteenth century to the twenty-first, 2007; Resurrection, 2008; The Open Secret: a new vision for natural theology, 2008; The Christian Vision of God, 2008; Heresy: a history of defending the truth, 2009; A Fine Tuned Universe: the quest for God in science and theology, 2009; Mere Theology: Christian faith and the discipleship of the mind, 2010; Darwinism and the Divine: evolutionary thought and natural theology, 2011; Why God Won't Go Away: engaging with the new atheism, 2011; Surprised by Meaning: science, faith and and the search for meaning, 2012; C. S. Lewis: a life, 2013; The Intellectual World of C. S. Lewis, 2013; Christian Belief for Everyone: faith and creeds, vol. 1, 2013; The Living God, vol. 2, 2014; Lord and Saviour: Jesus of Nazareth, vol. 3, 2014; Deep Magic, Dragons and Talking Mice: how C. S. Lewis can change your life, 2014; Inventing the Universe: why we can't stop talking about science, 2015; Mere Apologetics: how to help seekers and sceptics find faith, 2016; Re-Imagining Nature: the promise of a Christian natural theology, 2016; Enriching our Vision of Reality: theology and the natural sciences in dialogue, 2016; The Great Mystery: God and the human quest for meaning, 2017; The Landscape of Faith: an explorer's guide to Christian faith, 2018; Mere Discipleship: on growing in wisdom and hope, 2018; Richard Dawkins, C. S. Lewis and the Meaning of Life, 2019; The Territories of Human Reason: science and theology in an age of multiple rationalities, 2019; contrib. articles to learned jls. *Recreations*: walking, French. *Address*: Harris Manchester College, Mansfield Road, Oxford OX1 3TD.

**McGRATH, Colin Paul;** Member (SDLP) South Down, Northern Ireland Assembly, since 2016; *b* Downpatrick, Co. Down, 21 Oct. 1975; *s* of Brian and Rosemary McGrath. *Educ*: St Patrick's Grammar Sch., Downpatrick; Univ. of Ulster (BSc Hons Community Youth Work 1998). Youth worker, Patrician Youth Centre, Downpatrick, 1999–2016. Member (SDLP): Down DC, 2005–14 (Chm. Council, 2008–09); Newry, Mourne and Down Council, 2014–16. Gov., St Mary's High Sch., Downpatrick. *Recreations*: community development, health campaigning, reading, walking. *Address*: 23 Ardmeen Green, Downpatrick, Co. Down BT30 6JJ. *T*: 07720 429805. *E*: colin.mcgrath@mla.niassembly.gov.uk.

**McGRATH, Prof. Elizabeth,** FBA 1998; Curator, Photographic Collection, 1991–2010, and Professor of the History of Art, 2000–10, Warburg Institute, University of London, now Professor Emeritus and Hon. Fellow; *b* 20 March 1945; *d* of Thomas McGrath and Emilie McGrath (née Melvin). *Educ*: St Joseph's High Sch., Kilmarnock; Glasgow Univ. (MA 1967); PhD London 1971. Photographic Collection, Warburg Inst., London Univ., 1970–2010; Joint Editor: Jl of Warburg and Courtauld Insts, 1977–2010; Corpus Rubenianum (Antwerp), 2010–. Durning Lawrence Lectr, UCL, 1989; Slade Prof. of Fine Art, Oxford Univ., 1990. Mem., Flemish Acad. for Arts and Scis, 2003. Hans Reimer Prize, Hamburg Univ., 1996; Mitchell Prize for the History of Art, 1998; Eugène Baie Prize for Flemish Cultural History, Province of Antwerp. *Publications*: Rubens: Subjects from History, vol. XIII in *Corpus Rubenianum*, 1997; (ed and contrib.) The Slave in European Art: from Renaissance trophy to Abolitionist emblem, 2012; (ed and contrib.) Rubens: Mythological Subjects, vol. XI 1 in *Corpus Rubenianum*, 2016; contrib. to Jl of Warburg and Courtauld Insts, Burlington Mag., etc. *Address*: Warburg Institute, University of London, Woburn Square, WC1H 0AB. *T*: (020) 7862 8949.

**McGRATH, Sir Harvey (Andrew),** Kt 2016; Chairman, Big Society Capital Ltd, since 2014; *b* Belfast, 23 Feb. 1952; *m* 1978, Allison Baird; one *s* one *d*. *Educ*: Methodist Coll., Belfast; St Catharine's Coll., Cambridge (BA Geog. 1974). Asst Treas. and Second Vice Pres., Chase Manhattan Bank, 1974–80; Finance Dir, 1980–86, Pres., 1986–90, Farr Man & Co. Inc.; Gp CEO, 1990–2000, Chm., 2000–07, Man Gp plc. Chairman: E London Business Alliance, 2003–08; London First, 2004–08; London Develt Agency, 2008–12; Prudential plc, 2009–12; Prince's Teaching Inst., 2009–17; Funding London, 2014–; Nat. Adv. Bd on Impact Investing, 2018–; West London Zone, 2018–; Vice Chm., London Skills & Employment Bd, 2005–12; Dep. Chair, London Enterprise Panel, 2012–16. Trustee: New Philanthropy Capital, 2002–; Royal Anniversary Trust, 2003–13; Mayor's Fund for London, 2010–19; Pres. and Trustee, Children and Families Across Borders (formerly Internat. Social Service UK), 2008–17; Chm., icould, 2008–19. Chm., Bd of Govs, Birkbeck, Univ. of London, 2010–. *Recreations*: music, theatre, reading, ski-ing.

**McGRATH, Ian;** *see* McGrath, J. C.

**McGRATH, James Aloysius;** reporter and presenter, At The Races, since 2006; Hotspur, Racing Correspondent of the Daily Telegraph, 1991–2014; *b* 13 June 1952; *s* of Brian James McGrath and Kathleen May McGrath; *m* 1977, Anita Lee; two *s* two *d*. *Educ*: Xavier Coll., Melbourne. Cadet racing writer, The Australian, 1972–73; Racing Corresp., China Mail (Hong Kong), 1973–74; Chief Racing Writer, South China Morning Post (Hong Kong), 1975–86; writer, Racing Post, 1986–90; Racing Corresp., Sunday Telegraph, 1988–95. Racing Commentator: BBC, 1992–2012 (Sen. Racing Commentator, 1997–2012); Satellite Information Services, 1993–97. Clive Graham Award for Racing Journalist of the Year, Horserace Writers' Assoc., 1992; Sports Commentator of the Year, RTS, 2001. *Publications*: (with Trevor Marmalade) Great Racetracks of the World, 2014. *Recreations*: golf, ski-ing, watching cricket. *Address*: The Travers, Chobham, Woking, Surrey GU24 8SZ. *T*: (01276) 857155. *Clubs*: Carbine (founding Pres., 1997–2000); Hong Kong Jockey, Hong Kong Golf, Hong Kong Football (Hong Kong).

**McGRATH, John Brian;** Chairman, The Boots Co. plc, 2000–03 (non-executive Director, 1998–2003); Chief Executive Officer, Diageo, 1997–2000; *b* 20 June 1938; *m* 1964, Sandy Watson; one *s* one *d*. *Educ*: Brunel Univ. (BSc 1st Cl. Hons Applied Physics). UKAEA, 1962–65; NCB, 1965–67; Ford Motor Co., 1967–71; Jaguar Cars, 1971–75; Stone-Platt, 1976–82; Man. Dir, Construction and Mining Div. and Chief Exec., Compair, 1982–85; joined Grand Metropolitan PLC, 1985: Gp Dir, Watney Mann & Truman Brewers Ltd, 1985; Chm. and Man. Dir, Grand Metropolitan Brewing, 1986–88; Jt Man. Dir, Internat. Distillers & Vintners, 1988–91; IDV Ltd: Man. Dir and Chief Operating Officer, 1991–92; Chief Exec., 1992–93; Chm. and Chief Exec., 1993–96; Gp Chief Exec., Grand Metropolitan PLC, 1996–97. Non-executive Director: Carlton Communications plc, 2003–04; ITV plc, 2004–07. Chm., Scotch Whisky Assoc., 1995–2000. Chm., Cicely Saunders International (formerly Foundn), 2001–. Mem. Council, Brunel Univ., 2004–12. Trustee, Tetbury Hosp. Trust, 2013–17. *Address*: c/o Cicely Saunders Institute, Bessemer Road, SE5 9PJ.

**McGRATH, Prof. John Christie, (Ian);** pharmacologist and physiologist; Editor-in-Chief, British Journal of Pharmacology, 2009–15 (Senior Editor, 2001–07); *b* 8 March 1949; *s* of John Christie McGrath and Margaret Gilmour Cochrane McGrath (*née* Murray); *m* 1970, Wilma Nicol (*d* 2007); one *s* one *d*; partner, 2008, Elspeth Mary McLachlan. *Educ:* Cross Arthurlie Primary Sch.; John Neilson Instn; Univ. of Glasgow (BSc 1st class Hons 1970; PhD 1974). FRSB (FSB 2013). Wellcome Interdisciplinary Research Fellowship, Dept of Pharmacology and Univ. Dept of Anaesthesia, Glasgow Royal Infirmary, Univ. of Glasgow, 1973–75; Institute of Biomedical and Life Sciences (formerly Institute of Physiology), University of Glasgow: Lectr, 1975; Wellcome Trust Research Leave Fellowship, 1982; Sen. Lectr, Reader, Titular Prof., 1983–91; Regius Prof. of Physiology, 1991–2012; Hd, Dept of Physiol., 1991–94; Co-Dir, Clinical Res. Initiative, 1994–99; Hd, Div. of Neurosci. and Biomed. Systems, 1997–2004; Hd, Div. of Integrated Biol., 2008–10. Chm. Standing Cttee, Heads of UK Physiology Depts, 2000–04. Chm., Physiolog. Soc., 2006–08 (Mem., 1978; Mem. Cttee, 1988–94; Mem. Council, 2004–10; Vice-Chm., 2004–06; Chm., Publications Cttee, 2007–10; Hon. Mem., 2017); Mem. Council, Bioscis Fedn, 2007–10. Member: British Pharmacol Soc. 1975 (Sandoz Prize, 1980; FBPhS (FBPharmacolS 2007); JR Vane Medal, 2011; Hon. FBPhS 2017); Internat. Soc. for Heart Research, 1989; Amer. Soc. for Pharmacology and Experimental Therapeutics, 1991; Amer. Physiol Soc., 1994; British Neurosci. Assoc., 1994. Hon. Sen. Res. Fellow, Neuroscience Australia, Sydney, 2009; Hon. Prof. of Pharmacology, Univ. of Sydney, 2013. Hon. Mem., Australian Soc. for Clinical and Experimental Pharmacology and Toxicology, 2012. Mem., Labour Party, 1983–. Member Editorial Board: British Jl of Pharmacology, 1985–91, 2018–; Jl of Cardiovascular Pharmacology, 1988–2010; Pharmacological Reviews, 1990–98; Jl of Vascular Res., 1991–; Jl of Hypertension, 2006–10. 1st Pfizer Award for Biology, 1983. *Publications:* contribs to learned jls in fields of pharmacology and physiology. *Recreations:* running, cycling, politics, travel, grandsons Dylan and Rory, swimming. *Address:* 7 Horselethill Road, Glasgow G12 9LX.

**McGRATH, Kevin David,** OBE 2016; DL; Chairman: M&M Property Asset Management LLP, since 2012; Regional REIT, since 2016; *b* London, 1963; *s* of Sean and Caroline McGrath; *m* 2000, Kate Wormald; one *s* one *d*. *Educ:* Christopher Wren Secondary Sch.; South Bank Poly. (BSc Estate Mgt 1989). MRICS 1991. Sen. Surveyor, Hermes Investment, 1989–96; Founding Equity Partner, Reit Asset Mgt, 1996–2007; Man. Dir, F&C Reit Asset Mgt, 2007–12. Chm., McGrath Charitable Trust, 2000–; Founder and Vice Chm., Clink Prison Restaurant charity, 2009–. Chm., Lyric Th., 2011–15; Trustee: Old Vic, 2012–; Arts Ed Sch., 2019–. Dir, 2002–05, Chm., 2003, QPR FC; Chm., QPR Ladies FC, 2012–; Vice Chm., QPR Community Trust, 2015–. DUniv Surrey, 2017. High Sheriff, Gtr London, 2014–15; DL Hammersmith and Fulham, 2015. *Recreations:* QPR FC, tennis, swimming, piano, theatre, family, public service. *Address:* 19 Elm Avenue, Ealing Common, W5 3XA. *T:* 07768 145757. *E:* kevinmcgrath@themct.co.uk. *Club:* Hurlingham.

**McGRATH, Patrick;** novelist, since 1979; lecturer, since 2007; *b* 7 Feb. 1950; *s* of Patrick G. McGrath and Helen McGrath (*née* O'Brien); *m* 1991, Maria Penelope Katharine Aitken, qv; one step *s*. *Educ:* City of Birmingham Coll. of Commerce; Univ. of London (external BA Hons 1971). Visiting Professor: Univ. of Texas, 2006; New Sch. of Social Research, NY, 2007–18; Hunter Coll., NY, 2010–12; Lectr, Princeton Univ., 2013–16. FRSL 2002. Hon. Fellow, Manchester Metropolitan Univ., 2009. Hon. DLitt Stirling, 2018. *Publications:* Blood and Water and Other Tales, 1987; The Grotesque, 1988; Spider, 1990; Dr Haggard's Disease, 1993; Asylum, 1996; Martha Peake, 2000; Port Mungo, 2004; Ghost Town: tales of Manhattan then and now, 2005; Trauma, 2008; Constance, 2013; The Wardrobe Mistress, 2017; Writing Madness, 2017. *Address:* 25 Broad Street, 19–i, New York, NY 10004, USA. *T:* (212) 7661690. *E:* pmcg277@gmail.com. *Club:* Groucho.

**McGRATH, Stephen John,** CPhys; Chief Executive, Soil Association Certification Ltd, 2010–11; *b* 24 Jan. 1954; *s* of late John Patrick McGrath and of Helena Mary McGrath; *m* 1977, Stephanie Doreen (*née* Powell); three *s*. *Educ:* Southampton Univ. (BSc Hons 1976, MSc 1977). CPhys, MInstP 1978. British Gas, 1978–96: Director: Business Gas, 1993–95; Gas Supplies and Transportation, 1995–96; Ops, 1996; Operations Director: AccuRead, 1996–2001; Serviceteam, 2001–02; Chief Operating Officer, Spark Response, 2002–03; Dir, Nat. Insurance Contribns Office, Bd of Inland Revenue, subseq. HMRC, 2003–06; Chief Exec., Meat Hygiene Service, 2007–10; Interim Dir of Ops, Food Standards Agency, 2010. MInstD 1997. *Recreations:* coastal sailing, campanology, motor bike.

**MacGREGOR,** family name of **Baron MacGregor of Pulham Market**.

**MacGREGOR OF PULHAM MARKET,** Baron *cr* 2001 (Life Peer), of Pulham Market in the County of Norfolk; **John Roddick Russell MacGregor,** OBE 1971; PC 1985; *b* 14 Feb. 1937; *s* of late Dr. N. S. R. MacGregor; *m* 1962, Jean Mary Elizabeth Dungey; one *s* two *d*. *Educ:* Merchiston Castle Sch., Edinburgh; St Andrews Univ. (MA, 1st cl. Hons); King's Coll., London (LLB; FKC 1988). Univ. Administrator, 1961–62; Editorial Staff, New Society, 1962–63; Special Asst to Prime Minister, Sir Alec Douglas-Home, 1963–64; Conservative Research Dept, 1964–65; Head of Private Office of Rt Hon. Edward Heath, Leader of Opposition, 1965–68. MP (C) S Norfolk, Feb. 1974–2001. An Opposition Whip, 1977–79; a Lord Comr of HM Treasury, 1979–81; Parly Under-Sec. of State, DoI, 1981–83; Minister of State, MAFF, 1983–85; Chief Sec. to HM Treasury, 1985–87; Minister of Agriculture, Fisheries and Food, 1987–89; Sec. of State for Educn and Sci., 1989–90; Lord Pres. of the Council and Leader of H of C, 1990–92; Sec. of State for Transport, 1992–94. Mem., H of L, 2001–19. Hill Samuel & Co. Ltd, 1968–79 (Dir, 1973–79), Dep. Chm., 1994–96; Director: Associated British Foods, 1994–2007; Slough Estates, 1995–2006; UK Food and Agric. Adv. Bd, Rabobank Gp, 1995–2011 (Jt Chm., 2006–11); Uniq (formerly Unigate), 1996–2005; London & Manchester Gp, 1997–98; Friends Provident, 1998–2007; European Supervisory Bd, DAF Trucks NV, 2000–09. Chm., Pension Fund Trustees of EDF (formerly British Energy), 2007–14, of SEGRO, 2006–10, of Anglian Water Gp, 2009–12, and of Eggborough Power Ltd, 2010–16. Chairman: Fedn of University Cons. and Unionist Assocs, 1959; Bow Group, 1963–64; 1st Pres., Conservative and Christian Democratic Youth Community, 1963–65; Vice-President: ACC, 1995–97; LGA, 1997–99. Mem., Cttee on Standards in Public Life, 1997–2003. Chm., Assoc. of Cons. Peers, 2012–16. Member, Council: KCL, 1996–2002; IOD, 1996–2006; Mem., 2002–, Chm., 2007–, Cathedral Council, Norwich Cathedral (High Steward, 2007–); Chm., Friends of Norwich Cathedral, 2007–. Dep. Chm., GBA, then Assoc. of Governing Bodies of Independent Schs, 1998–2006. Trustee, Royal Norfolk Agricl Assoc., 2007–10. Chm., St Andrew's (Ecumenical) Trust, 2005–12. Hon. LLD Westminster, 1995. *Publications:* contrib. The Conservative Opportunity; also pamphlets. *Recreations:* music, reading, travelling, gardening, conjuring (Member: Magic Circle, 1989; Inner Magic Circle, 2000).

**McGREGOR, Prof. Alan Michael,** MD; FRCP, FMedSci; Professor of Medicine, 1986–2013, now Emeritus, and Dean of Research, 1996–2000, King's College London School of Medicine (formerly King's College School of Medicine and Dentistry, subseq. Guy's, King's and St Thomas' School of Medicine, King's College London) (Head of Department of Diabetes, Endocrinology and Internal Medicine, 1996); Dean, Denmark Campus, King's College London, 2005–13; *b* 3 Aug. 1948. *Educ:* Selwyn Coll., Cambridge (BA 1971; MB, BChir 1974; MA 1982; MD 1982). DTM&H 2014; MSc Tropical Medicine 2014. MRCP 1977, FRCP 1985. MRC Trng Fellow, Royal Victoria Infirmary, Newcastle upon Tyne, 1977–80; Lectr, 1980, Wellcome Sen. Res. Fellow, 1981–86, Dept of Medicine, Univ. of Wales Coll. of Medicine. Hon. Consultant Physician, KCH NHS Trust, later KCH NHS Foundn Trust (non-exec. Dir, 2005–12). Vis. Prof. of Medicine, Univ. of Zimbabwe, Harare, 2015–18. Mem., MRC, 1995–2000 (Chm., Physiological Medicine and Infections Bd). FKC 1997; Founder FMedSci, 1998. *Publications:* (ed) Immunology of Endocrine Diseases, 1986; contrib. learned jls. *Address:* 5 Colebrooke Row, N1 8DB.

**McGREGOR, Rev. Alexander Scott;** Chief Legal Adviser to the Archbishops' Council and the General Synod, since 2019 (Deputy Legal Adviser, 2009–19); Official Solicitor to the Church Commissioners, since 2019 (Deputy Official Solicitor, 2017–19); *b* London, 23 Oct. 1972; *s* of Donald and Irene McGregor. *Educ:* John Lyon Sch., Harrow; Christ Church, Oxford (MA Ancient and Modern History 2000); Coll. of Law, London; Inns of Court Sch. of Law; St Albans and Oxford Ministry Course. Called to the Bar, Lincoln's Inn, 1996; 3 Temple Gardens, 1996–98; Clarendon Chambers, 1998–2005; Legal Advr, Legal Office of Nat. Instns of C of E, 2006–09; Dep. Chancellor, 2007–13, Chancellor, 2013–19, Dio. of Oxford. Ordained deacon, 2006, priest, 2007; Assistant Curate (non-stipendiary): St Mary, Harrow on the Hill, 2006–09; St Barnabas, Pimlico, 2009–15; Our Most Holy Redeemer, Clerkenwell, 2015–. Mem., Dacorum BC, 1999–2007; Chm. of Dirs, Dacorum Sports Trust, 2003–07. *Recreations:* history, music, conversation. *Address:* Legal Office, Church House, Great Smith Street, SW1P 3AZ. *T:* (020) 7898 1748. *E:* alexander.mcgregor@churchofengland.org.

**McGREGOR, Rev. Alistair Gerald Crichton;** QC (Scot.) 1982; WS; Minister, North Leith Parish Church, Edinburgh, 1987–2002; *b* 15 Oct. 1937; *s* of late James Reid McGregor, CB, CBE, MC, and Dorothy McGregor; *m* 1965, Margaret Lees or McGregor; two *s* one *d*. *Educ:* Charterhouse; Pembroke Coll., Oxford (BA (Hons) Jurisprudence); Edinburgh Univ. (LLB; BD). Intelligence Corps, 1956–58. Solicitor and WS, 1965–66; Advocate, 1967–82. Clerk to Court of Session Rules Council, 1972–75; Standing Junior Counsel to: SHHD, 1977–79; Scottish Develt Dept, 1979–82. Chm., Family Care (Scotland), 1983–88; Director: Apex (Scotland), 1988–98; Kirk Care Housing Assoc., 1994–97; Palcrafts (UK) Ltd, 2003– (Chm., 2011–). Governor: Dean Orphanage Trust, 1998–; Loretto Sch., 2000–06. Gen. Trustee, Ch of Scotland, 2004–14; Chm., Friends of St Andrew's Ch, Jerusalem, 2014–. Licensed, Church of Scotland, 1986. Pastoral Minister, St Andrew's and St George's West Ch, Edinburgh, 2004–18. *Recreations:* squash, tennis. *Address:* 22 Primrose Bank Road, Edinburgh EH5 3JG. *T:* (0131) 551 2802.

**McGREGOR, Hon. Alistair John;** QC 1997; *b* 11 March 1950; *s* of Baron McGregor of Durris; *m* 1985, Charlotte Ann East; one *s* one *d*. *Educ:* Haberdashers' Aske's Sch., Elstree; Queen Mary Coll., London Univ. (LLB Hons). Called to the Bar, Middle Temple, 1974, Bencher, 2011. *Recreations:* music, sport. *Club:* Garrick.

**McGREGOR, Ewan Gordon,** OBE 2013; actor; *b* 31 March 1971; *s* of James and Carol McGregor; *m* 1995, Eve Mavrakis; four *d*. *Theatre:* What the Butler Saw, Salisbury Playhouse, 1992; Little Malcolm, Comedy, 1998–99; Guys and Dolls, Piccadilly, 2005; Othello, Donmar Warehouse, 2007; The Real Thing, NY, 2014; *films:* Family Style, Being Human, 1993; Shallow Grave, 1994; Trainspotting, Swimming with the Fishes, Emma, The Pillow Book, Brassed Off, 1996; The Serpent's Kiss, Blue Juice, A Life Less Ordinary, 1997; Nightwatch, Velvet Goldmine, Little Voice, Desserts, Anno Domini, 1998; Star Wars, Episode I: The Phantom Menace, Rogue Trader, Eye of the Beholder, Tube Tales (also dir.), 1999; Nora (co-producer, 2000); Moulin Rouge, 2001; Black Hawk Down, Star Wars, Episode II: Attack of the Clones, 2002; Young Adam, Down with Love, 2003; Big Fish, 2004; Star Wars, Episode III: Revenge of the Sith, The Island, 2005; Stay, Stormbreaker, Scenes of a Sexual Nature, 2006; Miss Potter, 2007; Deception, Cassandra's Dream, Incendiary, 2008; The Men Who Stare At Goats, 2009; I Love You Phillip Morris, The Ghost, 2010; Beginners, Perfect Sense, 2011; Haywire, Salmon Fishing in the Yemen, 2012; The Impossible, Jack the Giant Slayer, 2013; August: Osage County, 2014; Mortdecai, Son of a Gun, 2015; Miles Ahead, Jane Got a Gun, Our Kind of Traitor, American Pastoral (also dir), 2016; T2: Trainspotting, Beauty and the Beast, 2017; Christopher Robin, 2018; Doctor Sleep, 2019; *television* includes: Lipstick on Your Collar, Scarlet and Black, 1993; Doggin' Around, 1994; Karaoke, 1996; Solid Geometry, 2002; Long Way Round (series), 2004; Long Way Down (series), 2007; The Battle of Britain, 2010; Fargo (series), 2017 (Best Actor, Golden Globe Awards 2018). Hon. DLitt Ulster, 2001. *Publications:* (with Charley Boorman) Long Way Round, 2004. *Recreation:* motor bikes. *Address:* c/o Lindy King, United Agents, 12–26 Lexington Street, W1F 0LE.

**MacGREGOR OF MacGREGOR, Fiona;** *see* Armstrong, F.

**McGREGOR, Gillian Elizabeth,** CBE 2016; Director, Office of the Secretary of State for Scotland, since 2017; *b* Montrose, 10 May 1963; *d* of Charles Sharpe and Elizabeth Sharpe; *m* 1991, Roderick McGregor. *Educ:* Montrose Acad.; Univ. of Aberdeen (MA 1st Cl. Hons Psychol. 1985). Home Office: Immigration Caseworker, 1985–92; Asst Private Sec. to Lord Privy Seal (on secondment), 1992–95; Policy Advr, Royalty and VIP Protection, 1995–97; Asst Dir, Immigration Service, 1997–2001; Policy and Ops Officer, Office for Security and Counter-Terrorism, 2001–09; Principal Private Sec. to Home Sec., 2009–11; Dir, Immigration Enforcement, 2011–17. *Recreations:* reading, sewing, walking. *Address:* Scotland Office, 1 Melville Crescent, Edinburgh EH3 7HW. *T:* (0131) 244 9022. *E:* gillian.mcgregor@scotlandoffice.gsi.gov.uk.

**McGREGOR, Prof. Graham Alexander,** CBE 2019; FRCP; FMedSci; Professor of Cardiovascular Medicine, Wolfson Institute of Preventive Medicine, Queen Mary University of London, since 2009; *b* St Albans, 1 April 1941; *s* of Alexander MacGregor and Sybil MacGregor (*née* Hawkey). *Educ:* Trinity Hall, Cambridge (BA 1964); Middlesex Hosp. Med. Sch. (MB BChir 1968). MRCP 1969, FRCP 1982. HP, Middlesex Hosp., SHO, Hammersmith Hosp., then Registrar, St Thomas' Hosp., 1967–71; Sen. Registrar, 1973–76, MRC Fellow, 1976–79, Charing Cross Hosp.; Sen. Lectr and Hon. Consultant Physician, Blood Pressure and Metabolic Unit, Charing Cross and Westminster Med. Sch., London, 1979–89; Prof. of Cardiovascular Medicine, and Dir, Blood Pressure Unit, St George's Hosp. Med. Sch., Univ. of London, 1989–2009. Hon. Consultant, Barts Health NHS Trust, 2009–. Chairman: Consensus Action on Salt and Health, 1996–; World Action on Salt and Health, 2005–; Action on Sugar, 2014–. FAHA 1999; FMedSci 2003. *Publications:* contrib. papers to scientific jls on blood pressure, salt and obesity. *Address:* Wolfson Institute of Preventive Medicine, Charterhouse Square, EC1M 6BQ. *T:* (020) 7882 6217. *E:* g.macgregor@qmul.ac.uk. *Club:* Hurlingham.

**McGREGOR, Prof. Heather Jane,** CBE 2015; PhD; Executive Dean, Edinburgh Business School, Heriot Watt University, since 2016; *b* London, 27 March 1962; *d* of Peter and Barbara Gosden; *m* 1988, Rowan Alexander McGregor; three *s*. *Educ:* Newcastle Univ. (BSc Hons Agricl Mktg); London Business Sch. (MBA); Univ. of Hong Kong (PhD 2002). Acct Planner, Boase Massimi Pollitt, 1984–85, Charles Barker City Ltd, 1985–87; Hd, Investor Relns, Cortecs plc, 1987–92; Investment Analyst, ABN Amro Hoare Govett, 1992–2000; CEO and Majority Shareholder, Taylor Bennett, 2000–16. Non-executive

Director: NSF plc, 2015–; IGT plc, 2017–. Mrs Moneypenny columnist, FT, 1999–2016. Mem., Honours Cttee for the Economy, 2017–. Jt Mem., Steering Cttee, 30% Club, 2010–17. Trustee, Career Ready, 2007–15 (Chair, 2011–15). Hon. Dr E London, 2008. *Publications:* Survival in the City, 2003; Careers Advice for Ambitious Women, 2012; Financial Advice for Independent Women, 2014. *Recreations:* reading The Economist, the study of the life and times of Lachlan Macquarie (1762–1824), general aviation (holder of a PPL). *Address:* Edinburgh Business School, Heriot Watt University, Riccarton, Edinburgh EH14 4AS. *Club:* University Women's.

**MacGREGOR, Heather Margaret;** District Judge, Central Family Court (formerly Principal Registry, Family Division), 2004–17; *b* 14 June 1952; *d* of James Gibson and Annie Gibson (*née* Ferry); *m* 1977, Dr Arthur MacGregor; one step *s. Educ:* Birmingham Univ. (BA); City Univ. (Dip. Law). Archaeologist, York Archaeol Trust, 1975–79; called to the Bar, Gray's Inn, 1982; in practice as barrister, London, 1982–2004; Dep. Dist Judge, Principal Registry, Family Div., 1999–2004.

**MACGREGOR, Sir Ian Grant,** 8th Bt *cr* 1828, of Savile Row, Middlesex; *b* 22 Feb. 1959; *s* of Sir Edwin Robert Macgregor, 7th Bt and (Margaret Alice) Jean Macgregor (*née* Peake); *S* father, 2003, but his name does not appear on the Official Roll of the Baronetage; *m* Cheryl, *d* of Stephen Macdonald. *Heir: uncle* Arthur Joseph Macgregor [*b* 7 Sept. 1933; *m* 1st, 1957, Carole Isabel Valens (*d* 1984); two *d*; 2nd, 1985, Brenda Margaret Hanson].

**McGREGOR, James Stalker;** Chairman, Honeywell Ltd, 1981–89; *b* 30 Oct. 1927; *s* of John McGregor and Jean McCabe; *m* 1953, Iris Millar Clark; one *s. Educ:* Dumfries Acad.; Royal Tech. Coll., Glasgow (ARTC); Glasgow Univ. BSc (Hons), CEng, MIMechE. Production Engr, Rolls Royce Ltd, 1952–56; Sales Engr, Sandvik Swedish Steels, 1956–57; Honeywell Control Systems: Assembly Manager, later Production Control Manager and Admin Manager, 1957–65; Divl Dir, Temperature Controls Gp, 1965–71; Man. Dir, 1971–86. CCMI. Hon. LLD Strathclyde, 1984. *Recreation:* golf.

**MacGREGOR, Joanna Clare,** CBE 2019 (OBE 2012); FTCL, FRAM; concert pianist, conductor and curator; Head of Piano, Royal Academy of Music, since 2011; Artistic Director, Dartington International Summer School, 2015–19; *b* 16 July 1959; *d* of Alfred MacGregor and Angela (*née* Hughes); *m* 1986, Richard Williams; (one *d* decd). *Educ:* S Hampstead Sch. for Girls; New Hall, Cambridge (BA Hons; Hon. Fellow); Royal Acad. of Music; Birkbeck, Univ. of London (MA Medieval Lit. and Medieval Studies, 2016). Gresham Prof. of Music (jtly), 1997–2000. Has appeared as a soloist with leading orchestras, including: LSO, Philharmonia, BBC SO, NYO, Sydney SO, NY Philharmonic, Chicago Philharmonic; has toured worldwide, incl. Europe, Africa, Australia, NZ, S America, USA and Far East. Classical repertoire, also jazz, electronica and new music (has commissioned and premiered over 100 new works); jtly organised Platform Fest. of New Music, ICA, 1991–93; Artistic Dir, SoundCircus, Bridgewater Hall, Manchester, 1996 and creator, SoundCircus recording label, 1998; Guest Artistic Dir, Britten Sinfonia, 2002–04; Artistic Director: Bath Internat. Fest., 2006–12; Deloitte Ignite Fest., 2013; ROH, 2010; Dir, Aventures+, Luxembourg Philharmonie, 2012–13; has made numerous recordings. Vis. Fellow, Oriel Coll., Oxford, 2015–16. Member: Arts Council of England, 1998–2003; Adv. Bd, British Council, 2002–04. Chair, Paul Hamlyn Composers Awards, 2015–20; Booker Prize Judge, 2019. Presenter, Strings, Bow and Bellows (series), BBC TV, 1995. Hon. FTCL (FTCL 1995); Hon. FRAM (FRAM 1991). FRSA 2002. Hon. DMus: Open, 2004; Bath, 2008; Cambridge, 2016; Hon. DLitt Bath Spa, 2011. European Encouragement Prize for Music, 1995; South Bank Show Award for Classical Music, 2000; Royal Philharmonic Soc. Prize, 2003. *Publications:* Joanna MacGregor's Piano World (5 vols), 1999. *Address:* c/o Annette Förger, Music Inter Alia, Augustinian Centre, 55 Fulham Palace Road, W6 8AU. *E:* annette@musicinteralia.com. *W:* www.soundcircus.com.

**MACGREGOR, John Malcolm,** CVO 1992; HM Diplomatic Service, retired; Visiting Professor, since 2011 and Senior Fellow, Centre for European Studies, since 2016, Canterbury Christchurch University; Board Chair, ORBIS Africa, since 2017; *b* 3 Oct. 1946; *s* of late Dr D. F. Macgregor and K. A. Macgregor (*née* Adams); *m* 1982, Judith Anne Brown (*see* Dame J. A. Macgregor); three *s* one *d. Educ:* Kibworth Beauchamp Grammar Sch., Leics; Balliol Coll., Oxford (BA 1967; MA 2010); Birmingham Univ. (Cert. Ed. 1969). ARCO 1965. Taught at Cranleigh Sch., Surrey, 1969–73; joined HM Diplomatic Service, 1973; 2nd Sec., UN Affairs, 1973–74; 1st Sec. (political), New Delhi, 1975; FCO, 1979; Pvte Sec. to Minister of State, FCO, 1981; speechwriter to Sec. of State, FCO, 1982; Assistant, Soviet Dept, FCO, 1983; Dep. Head of Mission, Prague, 1986; Head of Chancery, Paris, 1990–93; Head of EU Dept (Ext.), 1993–95; Dir Gen. for Trade Promotion in Germany and Consul-Gen., Düsseldorf, 1995–98; Ambassador to Poland, 1998–2000; Dir, Wider Europe, FCO, 2000–02; Ambassador to Austria, 2003–07; UK Perm. Rep. to UN in Vienna and UK Gov. to IAEA, 2006–07. Dean, Univ. of Kent at Brussels, 2007–09. Partner, Ambassador Partnership LLP, 2010–16. Occasional Lectr, Diplomatic Acad., Vienna, 2009–. Trustee: Shannon Trust, 2007–12; I Fagiolini Trust, 2007–. Gov., Chichester Univ., 2008–13. *Recreations:* music, languages, bricolage, travel. *E:* jmalcolmgarg@gmail.com.

**MACGREGOR, Dame Judith (Anne),** DCMG 2016 (CMG 2012); LVO 1992; DL; HM Diplomatic Service, retired; High Commissioner to South Africa, 2013–17, and (non-resident) to Lesotho and Swaziland, 2014–17; *b* 17 June 1952; *d* of John Richard Brown and Beatrice Brown; *m* 1982, John Malcolm Macgregor, *qv*; three *s* one *d. Educ:* St Saviour's and St Olave's Grammar Sch.; Lady Margaret Hall, Oxford (BA 1st cl. Hons (Modern Hist.) 1974; Hon. Fellow). Entered FCO, 1976; First Secretary: Belgrade, 1978–81; FCO, 1981–86; Prague, 1989; Paris, 1992–93; Dep. Hd, Western European Dept, FCO, 1993–95; Counsellor and Hd, Security Strategy, FCO, 2001–03; FCO Chair, CSSB, 2003–04; Ambassador to Slovakia, 2004–07; Dir for Migration, FCO, 2007–09; Ambassador to Mexico, 2009–13. Non-exec. Dir, Fresnillo, 2017–. Mem. Bd, VisitBritain, 2017–; Mem., AHRC, 2018–. Mem., Adv. Council, Lady Margaret Hall, Oxford, 2018–; Vice-Chair, Governing Council, Univ. of Southampton, 2018–. Hon. Bencher, Middle Temple, 2017. DL Hants, 2018. *Recreations:* walking, reading, gardening.

**MacGREGOR OF MacGREGOR, Sir Malcolm (Gregor Charles),** 7th Bt *cr* 1795, of Lanrick, co. Perth; 24th Chief of Clan Gregor; writer, photographer; *b* 23 March 1959; *er s* of Brig. Sir Gregor MacGregor of MacGregor, 6th Bt, ADC and of Fanny (*née* Butler); *S* father, 2003; *m* 1st, 1988, Cecilia Campbell (marr. diss. 2004); 2nd, 2005, Fiona Armstrong, *qv. Educ:* Eton; Cranfield Univ. (MBA). Major, Scots Guards, retd. Mem., Queen's Body Guard for Scotland (Royal Co. of Archers). FRGS; FRPS; ABIPP. *Publications:* Wilderness Oman, 2002; Rob Roy's Country, 2003; Light over Oman, 2004; The Outer Hebrides, 2007; Oman: eloquence and eternity, 2009; Mull, Iona and Staffa, 2010. *Heir: b* Ninian Hubert Alexander MacGregor [*b* 30 June 1961; *m* 1999, Fiona Graham; one *s* one *d*].

**McGREGOR, Menna Lyn;** charity adviser, since 2015; Clerk to Governors, Alleyn's School, since 2018; *d* of late William Beasley, MD, FRCPath and Elizabeth Beasley; *m* 1976, Bruce McGregor; two *d. Educ:* Ardwyn Grammar Sch., Aberystwyth; University Coll. of Wales, Aberystwyth (LLB). Called to the Bar, Lincoln's Inn, 1973; Co. Sec. and Dir, private property develt and investment cos, 1986–91; Bd and Co. Sec., RNT, 1993–2007; Sec., Trustees of RNT Foundn, 1994–2007; Co. Sec., Mercers' Co., 2007–08.

Mem., Bd Develt team, Clore Leadership Prog., 2007–11. Mem. Council, Gresham Coll., 2009–13. Trustee: Nat. Foundn for Youth Music, 1999–2012; Wales Millennium Centre, 2006–09; Public Catalogue Foundn, 2009–12; Royal Ballet Sch. Endowment Fund, 2014–; Nat. Centre for Early Music, 2014–; Wilton's Music Hall, 2017–18; Shakespeare Schs Foundn, 2017–. Clerk to: Govs and Co. Sec., St Paul's Girls' Sch., 2007–12; Mercers' Co., 2008–15. Governor: Royal Central Sch. of Speech and Drama, 2012–; Royal Ballet Sch., 2013–. *Recreations:* music, theatre, opera, walking.

**MacGREGOR, Neil;** *see* MacGregor, R. N.

**MacGREGOR, Robert Murray Robertson;** Senior Partner (Europe, Middle East and Africa), Bryan Cave Leighton Paisner (formerly Berwin Leighton Paisner) LLP, since 2018 (Partner and Head of Real Estate, 2004–18, and Chairman, 2012–18); *b* London, 14 Jan. 1960; *s* of Ian and Pamela MacGregor; *m* 2000, Sally Gladwell; one *s* one *d. Educ:* Berkhamsted Sch.; Nottingham Univ. (LLB Hons). With Titmus, Sainer & Webb, 1983–90 (Partner, 1989–90); Clifford Chance, 1990–2004 (Partner, 1992–2004). *Recreations:* sailing, classic cars. *Address:* Bryan Cave Leighton Paisner LLP, Adelaide House, London Bridge, EC4R 9HA. *E:* robert.macgregor@bclplaw.com. *Clubs:* Goodwood Road Racing; Itchenor Sailing (W Sussex).

**MacGREGOR, (Robert) Neil,** OM 2010; a Founding Director, Humboldt Forum, 2016–18; Director, British Museum, 2002–15; *b* 16 June 1946; *s* of Alexander MacGregor and Anna (*née* Neil). *Educ:* Glasgow Acad.; New Coll., Oxford (Hon. Fellow); Ecole Normale Supérieure, Paris; Univ. of Edinburgh; Courtauld Inst. of Art. Mem., Faculty of Advocates, Edinburgh, 1972. Lectr in History of Art and Architecture, Univ. of Reading, 1976; Editor, The Burlington Magazine, 1981–86; Dir, Nat. Gallery, 1987–2002. Trustee: Pilgrim Trust, 1990–2006; Courtauld Inst. of Art, 2002–08. Member: Supervisory Bd, Rijksmuseum, Amsterdam, 1995–2004; Internat. Adv. Bd, Hermitage, St Petersburg, 1997–; Museums, Libraries and Archives Council, 2003–05; Arts and Humanities Res. Council (formerly Bd), 2003–09; Bd, NT. Presenter: TV series: Seeing Salvation, 2000; Making Masterpieces; Painting the World; radio series: A History of the World in 100 Objects, 2010; Living With The Gods, 2017; As Others See Us, 2019. Hon. Mem., Royal Scottish Acad., 1995; Hon. FBA 2000. DUniv York, 1992; Dr *hc:* Edinburgh, 1994; Reading, Leicester, 1997; Exeter, Strathclyde, Glasgow, 1998; Hon. DLitt: Oxford, 1998; London, 1999. *Publications:* (jtly) Seeing Salvation: images of Christian art, 2000; (jtly) Britain's Paintings: the story of art through masterpieces in British collections, 2003; A History of the World in 100 Objects, 2010; Shakespeare's Restless World, 2012; Germany: memories of a nation, 2014; Living with the Gods, 2018.

**MacGREGOR, Susan Katriona, (Sue),** CBE 2002 (OBE 1992); Presenter for BBC Radio Four: Woman's Hour, 1972–87; Today, 1984–2002; A Good Read, 2003–10; The Reunion, since 2003; *b* 30 Aug. 1941; *d* of late Dr James MacGregor and Margaret MacGregor. *Educ:* Herschel School, Cape Province, South Africa. Announcer/producer, South African Broadcasting Corp., 1962–67; BBC Radio reporter, World at One, World This Weekend, PM, 1967–72; Presenter: Tuesday Call, 1973–86; Conversation Piece, 1978–94; Around Westminster, BBC TV, 1990–92. Vis. Prof. of Journalism, Nottingham Trent Univ., 1995–2003. Mem. Bd, RNT, 1998–2003. Member: RCP Cttee on Ethical Issues in Medicine, 1985–2000; Marshall Aid Commemoration Commn, 1989–98. Chair: Jury, Orange Prize for Fiction, 2002; Jury, BBC4 Samuel Johnson Prize for Non-Fiction, 2005; Jury, Art Fund Museum Prize, 2008; BBC Nat. Short Story Award, 2011; Mem., Jury, Orwell Literary Prize, 2014. Trustee: John Ellerman Foundn, 2002–12; Young Classical Artists Trust (formerly Young Concert Artists' Trust), 2013–; UNICEF UK, 2004–13 (Vice-Chm., 2011–13). FRSA 1983; Hon. MRCP 1995. Hon. Fellow, Harris Manchester Coll., Oxford, 2002. Hon. DLitt: Nottingham, 1996; Nottingham Trent, 2000; Staffordshire, 2001; London Metropolitan, 2002; Hon. LLD Dundee, 1997. *Publications:* Woman of Today (autobiog.), 2002. *Recreations:* theatre, cinema, ski-ing. *Address:* c/o Knight Ayton Management, 29 Gloucester Place, W1U 8HX. *T:* (020) 3795 1806.

**McGREGOR, Wayne,** CBE 2011; choreographer and director; Founder and Artistic Director, Studio Wayne McGregor (formerly Wayne McGregor | Random Dance), since 1992 (resident company of Sadler's Wells, since 2001); Resident Choreographer, Royal Ballet, since 2006; *b* 12 March 1970; *s* of Lawrence and Ella McGregor. *Educ:* Bretton Hall Coll., Univ. of Leeds (BA 1st Cl. Hons Dance); José Limon Sch., NY. AHRB/Arts Council England Res. Fellow in Cognition and Choreography, Sch. of Exptl Psychol., Univ. of Cambridge, 2003; Innovator in Residence, UCSD, 2009; Prof. of Choreography, Trinity Laban Conservatoire of Music and Dance, 2014–. Choreographer in Residence, The Place Th., London, 1992–99; productions for Company Wayne McGregor (formerly Wayne McGregor | Random Dance Co.) include: The Millennarium, 1997, Sulphur 16, 1998, and Aeon, 2000, commnd RFH; digit01 (commnd The Place), 2001; Nemesis (co-commnd S Hill Park, Swindon Dance, Sadler's Wells, DanceEast), 2002; Alpha, Polar Sequences (co-commnd The Place, PACT Zollverein), 2003; Ataxia (co-commnd Sadler's Wells, PACT Zollverein), 2004; AMU (co-commnd Sadler's Wells, Wellcome Trust), 2005; Entity (co-commnd Sadler's Wells, Het Muziektheater, Biennale de la Danse, Dance East, Swindon Dance) 2008; Dyad 1909 (In the Spirit of Diaghilev) (commnd Sadler's Wells), 2009; FAR (co-produced by Sadler's Wells and Peak Performances), 2010; Undance (commnd Sadler's Wells), 2011; Big Dance Trafalgar Square (commnd Big Dance), 2012; Rain Room, Barbican, 2012; Atomos, 2013; Tree of Codes (co-commnd Park Ave Armory, Manchester Internat. Fest., Paris Opera Ballet, Sadler's Wells and FAENA ART Milan), 2015; +/- Human, Roundhouse, 2017; Autobiography, 2017; independent commissions include: Telenoia (Canary Wharf), 2000; (with V. Durante) Fleur de Peux, Symbiont(s) (Royal Ballet, Covent Gdn), 2001; Detritus (Rambert Dance Co.), 2001; Brainstate (Royal Ballet/Random Dance), 2001; PreSentient (Rambert Dance Co.), 2002; 2 Human (English Nat. Ballet), Nautilus (Stuttgart Ballet), 2003; Qualia (Royal Ballet), 2004; Eden/Eden (Stuttgart Ballet), Engram (Royal Ballet), 2005; Skindex (NDT1), 2006; Chroma (Royal Ballet), 2006; Genus (Paris Opera Ballet), 2007; Nimbus (Royal Ballet), 2007; Infra (Royal Ballet), 2008; Re:Nature (NDT1), 2008; Limen (Royal Ballet), 2009; Dyad 1929 (Australian Ballet), 2009; Yantra (Stuttgart Ballet), 2010; Outlier (NY City Ballet), 2010; L'Anatomie De La Sensation (Paris Opera Ballet), 2011; Live Fire Exercise (Royal Ballet), 2011; Carbon Life (Royal Ballet), 2012; Machina (co-commnd Royal Ballet and Nat. Gallery), 2012; Raven Girl (Royal Ballet), 2013; Borderlands (San Francisco Ballet), 2013; Tetractys - The Art of Fugue (Royal Ballet), 2014; Woolf Works (Royal Ballet), 2015 (Olivier Award for Best New Dance Prodn, 2016); Kairos (Ballett Zürich), 2015; Alea Sands (Paris Opera Ballet), 2015; Obsidian Tear (Royal Ballet, Covent Gdn), 2016; Multiverse (Royal Ballet), 2016; Witness (NY City Center), 2016; Yugen (Royal Ballet), 2018; Sunyata (Bayerisches Staatsballett), 2018; AFTERITE (Amer. Ballet Th.), 2018; *theatre* includes: A Little Night Music, RNT, 1995; Cleansed, Royal Court, 1998; Antony and Cleopatra, RNT, 1998; Genus (Paris Opera Ballet), 2007; Cloaca, 2004, Aladdin, 2005, Old Vic; You Never Can Tell, Much Ado About Nothing, Peter Hall Co., 2005; Kirikov et Karaba, 2007; Ring Round the Moon, West End, 2008; Breakfast at Tiffany's, West End, 2009; Closer, Donmar Warehouse, 2015; Sweet Charity, Donmar Warehouse, 2019; *opera* includes: Orpheus and Eurydice, 1993, Marriage of Figaro, 1995, Scottish Nat. Op.; Rinaldo, The Mikado, Grange Pk Op., 2000; Hansel and Gretel, Scottish Nat. Op., 2000; Manon, English Touring Op., 2001; La Bohème, Scottish Nat. Op., 2004; The Midsummer

Marriage, Chicago Lyric Op., 2005; Salome, ENO, 2005; (dir.) Dido and Aeneas, La Scala, 2006; Dido and Aeneas/Acis and Galatea (Royal Opera/Royal Ballet), 2009; (dir) Twice Through the Heart, Sadler's Wells, 2011; SUM (commnd ROH2), 2012; Noye's Fludde (ENO), Th. Royal Stratford East, 2019; Orpheus and Eurydice, ENO, 2019; contribs to TV progs and films include: Bent (C4), 1996; Chrysalis, 2002; Dice Life (C4), 2004; Tremor (C4), 2005; Harry Potter and the Goblet of Fire, 2005; La Danse - The Paris Opera Ballet, 2009; Wayne McGregor - A Moment In Time, 2010; Wayne McGregor - Going Somewhere, 2011; The Legend of Tarzan, Fantastic Beasts and Where to Find Them, 2016; Fantastic Beasts: The Crimes of Grindelwald, 2018; Mary Queen of Scots, 2019; Lotus Flower music video (Radiohead), 2011; (dir) Ingenue music video (Atoms for Peace), 2013; exhibns incl. Thinking with the Body, Wellcome Collection, 2013. Mem., Grand Jury, RIBA Internat. Prize, 2018. Hon. Fellow: British Acad. Assoc., 2017; Northern Sch. of Contemp. Dance, 2017; Cultural Fellow, KCL, 2016. Hon. DSc Plymouth, 2012; Hon. LittD Leeds, 2016. Outstanding Achievement in Dance Award, 2001, 2003, Outstanding Choreography Award, 2002, Time Out Live Awards; IMZ Dance Screen Award, 2002; Excellence in Internat. Dance, Internat. Theatre Inst., 2009; Choreographer of the Year, Ballet Tanz, 2009; Movimentos Award, 2009; Dance Magazine Award, 2014. *Address:* Studio Wayne McGregor, Broadcast Centre, Here East, 10 East Bay Lane, Queen Elizabeth Olympic Park, E15 2GW. *T:* (020) 7278 6015.

**McGREGOR-JOHNSON, His Honour Richard John;** a Circuit Judge, 1998–2017; Resident Judge, Isleworth Crown Court, 2004–17; a Senior Circuit Judge, 2010–17; *b* 11 July 1950; *s* of Maxwell and Pamela McGregor-Johnson; *m* 1974, Elizabeth Weston; one *s* one *d. Educ:* Dean Close Sch., Cheltenham; Bristol Univ. (LLB 1972). Called to the Bar, Inner Temple, 1973, Bencher, 2001; an Asst Recorder, 1990–94; a Recorder, 1994–98. Hon. Recorder, RBK&C, 2012–17. *Recreations:* choral singing, sailing.

**McGREGOR-SMITH,** Baroness *cr* 2015 (Life Peer), of Sunninghill in the Royal County of Berkshire; **Ruby McGregor-Smith,** CBE 2012; Chair, Office for Tackling Injustices, since 2019; *b* Lucknow, India. *Educ:* Kingston Univ. (BA 1985). ACA 1991. Operational and financial roles with Serco, 1991–2002; Financial Dir, 2002–05, Chief Operating Officer, 2005–07, Chief Exec., 2007–16, MITIE Gp PLC. Non-exec. Dir, Michael Page plc, 2007–17; Chm., Q3 Services Gp, 2017–. Sen. Advr, Mace Gp, 2016–. Non-exec. Dir, DFE, 2015–. Mem., Women's Business Council, 2012– (Chm., 2012–16). Mem. Council, Univ. of Bath, 2017–. Hon. Dr: UWE; Kingston; Cranfield.

**McGRIGOR, Sir James (Angus Rhoderick Neil),** 6th Bt *cr* 1831, of Campden Hill, Middlesex; Member (C) Highlands and Islands, Scottish Parliament, 1999–2016; *b* 19 Oct. 1949; *er s* of Sir Charles Edward McGrigor, 5th Bt, and of Mary Bettine, *e d* of Sir Archibald Edmonstone, 6th Bt; *S* father, 2007; *m* 1st, 1987, Caroline Roboh (marr. diss. 1993); two *d*; 2nd, 1997, Emma Mary Louise Fellowes; one *s* three *d. Educ:* Cladich Sch., Argyll; Sunningdale Sch., Berks; Eton College. Shipping, 1969–71; stockbroking, 1971–74; farmer, 1975–. Mem., Queen's Body Guard for Scotland, Royal Co. of Archers, 1990. Kentucky Col, 2010. Contested (C) Argyll and Bute, 2005. Mem. (C), Argyll and Bute Council, 2017–. Vice Pres., ESU, 2008. Chair, Loch Awe Improvement Assoc., 1992–. Hon. President: Highland Disabled Ramblers' Assoc., 2004–; Clyde Fishermen's Assoc., 2011–. *Recreations:* fishing, music, literature. *Heir:* is Alexander James Edward Lyon McGrigor, *b* 5 Aug. 1998. *Address:* Ardchonnel, by Dalmally, Argyll PA33 1BW. *Clubs:* Chelsea Arts, Pratt's; New (Edinburgh); Edinburgh Trout Anglers.

**McGROUTHER, Prof. (Duncan) Angus,** MD; FRCS, FRCSGlas, FRCSE; FMedSci; Professor of Plastic and Reconstructive Surgery, University of Manchester, 2001, now Emeritus; Hon. Consultant Surgeon, South Manchester University Hospitals, since 2001; Clinical Director, Manchester Integrating Medicine and Innovative Technology, 2010, now Ambassador; Senior Consultant, Singapore General Hospital; *b* 3 March 1946; *s* of Dr John Ingram McGrouther and Margot Christina Cooke Gray; *m*; one *s* one *d*; *m* 2005, Gillian Fletcher-Williams. *Educ:* Glasgow High Sch.; Univ. of Glasgow (MB ChB 1969; MD Hons 1988); Univ. of Strathclyde (MSc Bioengineering 1975). Glasgow Royal Infirmary, 1969–74; Cruden Med. Res. Fellow, Bioengrg Unit, Univ. of Strathclyde, 1972–73; Registrar and Sen. Registrar in Plastic Surgery, Canniesburn Hosp., Glasgow, 1975–78; Assistenzart, Klinikum Rechts der Isar, Munich, 1978; Consultant Plastic Surgeon: Shotley Bridge Gen. Hosp. and Sunderland Dist Gen. Hosp., 1979–80; Canniesburn Hosp., 1981–89; Prof. of Plastic and Reconstructive Surgery (first estabd British chair), UCL, 1989–2001. Christine Kleinert Vis. Prof., Univ. of Louisville, 1988. Mem. Council, RCS, 2010–. Pres., British Soc. for Surgery of the Hand, 2010–11. FMedSci 2005. Kay-Kilner Prize, British Assoc. of Plastic Surgeons, 1979; Pulvertaft Prize, British Soc. for Surgery of the Hand, 1981. *Publications:* (jtly) Principles of Hand Surgery, 1990; (ed jtly) Dupuytren's Disease, 1990; contributor to: Current Surgical Practice, vol. 6, 1992; Microvascular Surgery and Free Tissue Transfer, 1993; Gray's Anatomy, 38th edn, 1995; Bailey and Love's Short Practice of Surgery, 22nd edn, 1995; Green's Operative Surgery, 4th edn 1998, 5th edn 2004; papers on anatomy, biomechanics, plastic surgery, hand surgery, microsurgery, and wound healing. *Recreations:* mountains, sea, books. *Address:* University of Manchester, Stopford Building, Oxford Road, Manchester M13 9PT.

**McGUCKIAN, John Brendan;** Chairman, UTV Media plc (formerly Ulster Television), 1990–2012; *b* 13 Nov. 1939; *s* of late Brian McGuckian and of Pauline (*née* McKenna); *m* 1970, Carmel, *d* of Daniel McGowan; two *s* two *d. Educ:* St MacNissi's Coll., Garrontower; Queen's Univ. of Belfast (BSc). Chairman: Cloughmills Mfg Co., 1967–; Tedcastle Hldgs, 1999–2001; Irish Continental Gp (formerly Irish Ferries) plc, 2004– (Dir, 1988–); Cooneen By Design Ltd (formerly Cooneen Textiles); Director: Munster & Leinster Bank, 1972–2007; Allied Irish Bank plc, 1976–2007; Harbour Group Ltd, 1978–; Aer Lingus plc, 1979–84; Unidare plc, 1987–2006; United Dairy Farmers, 2001–08; TVC Hldgs; Derry Development Commn, 1968–71; Dep. Chm., Laganside Corp., 1988–92; and other directorships. Chairman: Internat. Fund for Ireland, 1990–93; IDB for NI, 1991–98. Former Sen. Pro-Chancellor and Chm. of Senate, QUB. Hon. DLaws QUB, 2000. *Address:* Ardverna, Cloughmills, Ballymena, Co. Antrim, Northern Ireland BT44 9NL. *T:* (028) 2763 8121; Lisgoole Abbey, Culkey, Enniskillen BT92 2FP.

**McGUCKIN, Stephen Augustine;** Global Managing Director (formerly Managing Director), Turner & Townsend LLP, since 2009; *b* Eton, 1961; *s* of Augustus McGuckin and Sarah McGuckin; partner, Linda Cartwright; one *s* one *d. Educ:* Univ. of Brighton (BA Hons 1982); Univ. of Bradford (MBA 1986); Univ. of Reading (MSc Proj. Mgt 1991); Univ. of Sheffield (MA Arch. 2001). George Wimpey plc, 1979–85; Associate Dir, Fitch & Co. plc, 1986–89; Proj. Dir, Nicholas Grimshaw & Partners, 1989–92; Dir, Mace Ltd, 1992–2001; Develt Dir, Land Securities plc, 2001–09. Mem., London 2012 Panel, CABE, 2007–11; Trustee: V&A Mus., 2008–17; Architectural Assoc. Foundn, 2019–. RIBA 1990; RICS 2004. *Recreations:* ski-ing, scuba diving, motorcycles, history of art, architecture. *Address:* Turner & Townsend LLP, One New Change, EC4M 9AF. *T:* (020) 7544 4554. *E:* steve.mcguckin@turntown.com.

**McGUFFIN, Prof. Peter,** CBE 2016; PhD; FRCP, FRCPsych, FMedSci; Professor of Psychiatric Genetics, Institute of Psychiatry, King's College London, 1998–2013, now Emeritus (Director, MRC Social, Genetic and Developmental Psychiatry Research Centre, 1998–2006 and 2010–12; Dean, Institute of Psychiatry, 2007–10); *b* 4 Feb. 1949; *s* of Captain W. B. McGuffin, RD, RNR and M. M. McGuffin; *m* 1972, Prof. Anne E. Farmer; one *s* two *d. Educ:* Univ. of Leeds (MB ChB); Univ. of London (PhD). MRCP 1976, FRCP 1988; MRCPsych 1978, FRCPsych 1990. St James Univ. Hosp., Leeds, 1972–77; Registrar, Sen. Registrar, Maudsley Hosp., 1977–79; MRC Fellow, MRC Sen. Clinical Fellow, Inst. of Psychiatry, 1979–86; Hon. Consultant, Maudsley and King's Coll. Hosps, 1983–86; Prof. of Psychological Medicine, Univ. of Wales Coll. of Medicine, 1987–98. Vis. Fellow, Washington Univ., St Louis, 1981–82. Founder FMedSci 1998. Pres., Internat. Soc. of Psychiatric Genetics, 1996–2000. Member: S Wales Guitar Soc.; Cyfeillion Amgueddfa Cymru. *Publications:* Scientific Principles of Psychopathology, 1984; A Psychiatric Catechism, 1987; Schizophrenia, the Major Issues, 1988; The New Genetics of Mental Illness, 1991; Seminars in Psychiatric Genetics, 1994; (ed jtly) Essentials of Postgraduate Psychiatry, 1997, 4th edn as Essentials of Psychiatry, 2008; (jtly) Behavioral Genetics, 4th edn 2001, 5th edn 2008; Measuring Psychopathology, 2002; Psychiatric Genetics and Genomics, 2002; Behavioural Genetics in the Postgenomic Era, 2002; (ed jtly) Beyond Nature and Nurture in Psychiatry, 2006; (ed jtly) Schizophrenia: the final frontier, 2011; articles, research papers on psychiatry and genetics. *Recreations:* classical guitar, music, running, horse riding, dysgu Cymraeg, sailing. *Clubs:* Brading Haven Yacht; Rhyddid Riding.

**McGUGAN, Irene Margaret;** Assistant Director, Barnardo's Scotland, 2007–12; *b* 29 Aug. 1952; *d* of late James Millar Duncan and Phyllis Margaret Duncan (*née* Smith, later Mrs John Nicoll); *m* 1971, James McGugan; one *s* one *d. Educ:* Robert Gordon's Inst. of Technol. (CQSW 1982; Dip. Social Work 1982); Dundee Univ. (Advanced Cert. in Child Protection Studies 1991). VSO, India, 1970–71; full-time mother and voluntary worker, 1971–80; Social Work Dept, Tayside Regl Council, 1985–96, Angus Council, 1996–99 (Manager, Community Support, 1998–99); Project Dir, Children's Services, Aberdeen CC, 2003–07. Mem. (SNP) NE Scotland, Scottish Parlt, 1999–2003. Contested (SNP) Dundee W, Scottish Parlt, 2003. Elder, Church of Scotland, 1985; Mem., Church of Scotland Social Care Council, 2012–. *Recreations:* hill walking and keeping fit, visiting Scottish islands, books, music, theatre, cycling, grandchildren. *E:* irene.mcgugan@btinternet.com.

**McGUIGAN, Finbar Patrick, (Barry),** MBE 1994; journalist and commentator on boxing; *b* 28 Feb. 1961; *s* of late Patrick McGuigan and of Catherine, (Kate), McGuigan; *m* 1981, Sandra Mealiff; three *s* one *d. Educ:* St Louis Convent, Clones, Co. Monaghan; Largy Sch., Clones; St Patrick's High Sch., Clones. Started boxing, 1973, Wattle Bridge ABC, then Smithborough ABC; winner: Ulster and Irish title (Juvenile), 1977; Irish Sen. title, 1978; Commonwealth Gold Medal, 1978; represented Ireland at Olympic Games, Moscow, 1980; turned professional, 1981; winner: British and European Featherweight titles, 1983; World WBA Featherweight title, 1985; made two successful defences, then lost title on third defence, 1986; retd 1989. Pres. and Founder, Professional Boxing Assoc. (formerly Professional Boxers' Assoc., subseq. British Boxers' Assoc.), 1993–. *Publications:* (jtly) Leave the Fighting to McGuigan, 1985; (jtly) McGuigan—The Untold Story, 1991. *Recreations:* fitness, reading, etymology, relaxing with my family. *Address:* PO Box 233, Faversham, Kent ME13 9WP.

**McGUIGAN, Rupert Iain Sutherland;** HM Diplomatic Service, retired; *b* 25 June 1941; *s* of Hugh and Sue McGuigan; *m* 1968, Rosemary Rashleigh Chaytor; two *d. Educ:* Marlborough Coll.; Magdalene Coll., Cambridge (MA Law). With BP Ltd, 1964–72; HM Diplomatic Service, 1972–97: First Secretary: New Delhi, 1974–77; Kingston, Jamaica, 1978–81; Permanent Under-Secretaries Dept, FCO, 1981–85; Bridgetown, 1985–88; Counsellor: Lagos, 1989–93; Kingston, Jamaica, 1994–96. Private Sec. to the Princess Royal, 1997–99. Man. Dir, Private Trust Corporation (East Africa) Ltd, 1999–2007. *Recreations:* most ball games, amateur dramatics, philately, travel to unusual places. *Address:* Goodhope, Halls Lane, Waltham St Lawrence, Berks RG10 0JB. *T:* (0118) 934 0989. *Clubs:* Hawks (Cambridge); Castle Royle Golf; Muthaiga Country (Nairobi).

**McGUIGAN BURNS, Rt Hon. Sir Simon (Hugh);** see Burns, Rt Hon. Sir Simon H. McG.

**McGUINESS, Robert Clayton,** PhD; Chief Executive, UK Central Government, Serco Group plc, 2013–14; *b* 31 Dec. 1951; *s* of Robert McGuiness and Agnes McGuiness; *m* 1982, Beate Winkelmann; two *d. Educ:* Univ. of Glasgow (BSc (Hons) 1973; PhD 1976). ICI plc, 1976–2000: ICI Paints, 1976–93; Gen. Manager Marketing and Planning, ICI Autocolor, 1993–96; Vice Pres., Refinish, Glidden Co., N America, 1996–98; Chief Exec., ICI Autocolor, 1999–2000; Man. Dir, NPL Mgt Ltd, 2000–05; Chief Exec., Serco Science, 2005–06; CEO, Serco Defence, Sci. and Technol., 2006–10; Director: Serco Ltd, 2002–09; AWEML, 2003–09; Serco Global Services (India), 2010–13; SRL Ltd, 2011–12; CEO, Serco Africa, Middle E, Asia and Australasia, 2010–13; Hd, Corporate Renewal, Serco, 2013. *Recreations:* golf, ski-ing. *Address:* Oak Lodge, Bray Road, Maidenhead, Berks SL6 1UF. *T:* (01628) 621699. *Clubs:* Maidenhead Golf; DLF Golf and Country (Haryana, India).

**McGUINNESS, Andrew Peter;** Chief Executive Officer, Ellipsis, since 2017; Chairman, Seven Dials PR, since 2013; *b* Southport, 22 April 1970; *s* of Gerald and Zita McGuinness; *m* 2000, Isabella Wesolowska; one *s* two *d. Educ:* St Dominic, Harpenden; Nicholas Breakspear RC Comprehensive Sch., St Albans; Univ. of Salford (BA Hons). Graduate Account Dir, J. Walter Thompson, 1993–97; Gp Account Dir, M&C Saatchi, Sydney, 1997–2000; Gp Account Dir, 2000–01, Man. Dir, 2001–02, CEO, 2002–05, TBWA, Omnicom; Founding Partner, Beattie McGuinness Bungay, 2005–14; CEO, freuds, 2014–16. Non-exec. Dir, Chorion plc, 2005–06. Chairman, Advertising Assoc., 2009–12. Mem., Mktg Gp of GB, 2007. FIPA 2009; Fellow, Mktg Soc., 2008. *Recreations:* photography, politics, football. *Address:* Ellipsis, 5 Elstree Gate, Elstree Way, Borehamwood, Herts WD6 1JD. *Clubs:* Ivy, Thirty.

**McGUINNESS, Maj.-Gen. Brendan Peter,** CB 1986; consultant in education and training, now retired; Adviser on Engineering to Schools and Colleges, University of Birmingham, 1994–96; Director of Education and Training Liaison, Engineering Employers' Federation, West Midlands, 1988–94 (Head of Educational Liaison, 1987–88); *b* 26 June 1931; *s* of Bernard and May McGuinness; *m* 1968, Ethne Patricia (*née* Kelly) (*d* 2013); one *s* one *d. Educ:* Mount St Mary's College. psc, rcds. Commissioned Royal Artillery, 1950; regimental duty, 1950–60; Staff, 1960–62; *sc* 1963; Adjutant, 1964–65; Staff, 1965–68 (despatches, Borneo, 1966); Battery Comdr, 1968–70; Staff Coll. Directing Staff, 1970–72; CO 45 Medium Regt, 1972–75; CRA 1st Armd Div., 1975–77; RCDS 1978; MoD Staff, 1979–81; Dep. Comdr, NE District, 1981–83; GOC W Dist, 1983–86. Hon. Col, Birmingham Univ. OTC, 1987–97; Hon. Regtl Col, 45 Field Regt, 1985–91. Mem. Cttee, Hereford and Worcester Br., STA, 1991–96. Project Dir, 1987–88, Gov., 1988–2015, CTC Kingshurst Acad. (formerly The City Technol. Coll., Kingshurst); Mem. Court, Birmingham Univ., 1992–94; Governor: King's Coll. for the Arts and Technol., Guildford, 1999–2013; King's Internat. Coll. for Business and the Arts, Camberley, 2000–10; Guest Gov., Cirencester Coll., 1998–2006. Dir, Acafess Community Trust, Birmingham, 1992–94 (Chm., 1992). *Recreations:* Scottish country dancing (reeling), hill walking, beagling. *Address:* 4 St Monica Court, Cote Lane, Westbury-on-Trym, Bristol BS9 3TL. *T:* (0117) 949 4704. *Club:* Army and Navy.

**McGUINNESS, Frank**; playwright; Professor of Creative Writing, School of English, University College, Dublin, since 2007 (Writer in Residence, 1997–2007); *b* 29 July 1953; *s* of Patrick McGuinness and Celine O'Donnell-McGuinness. *Educ*: University College, Dublin (BA 1974; MPhil 1976). *Plays*: The Factory Girls, 1982; Observe the Sons of Ulster Marching Towards the Somme, Baglady, 1985, Abbey Th.; Innocence, Gate Th., 1986; Carthaginians, Abbey, 1988; Peer Gynt (version), Gate, 1988; Mary and Lizzie, RSC, 1989; Three Sisters (version), Gate, 1990; Someone Who'll Watch Over Me, Vaudeville, transf. NY, 1992, Chichester, 2015; The Bird Sanctuary, Abbey, 1994; A Doll's House (version), Playhouse, transf. NY, 1996; Mutabilitie, Caucasian Chalk Circle (version), 1997, RNT; Electra (version), Donmar, transf. NY, 1997; The Storm (version), Almeida, 1998; Dolly West's Kitchen, Abbey, transf. Old Vic, 1999; Miss Julie (version), Haymarket, 2000; Gates of Gold, Gate Th., Dublin, 2002; The Wild Duck, Abbey Th., 2003; Hecuba (version), Donmar, 2004; Rebecca (version), Th. Royal, Newcastle upon Tyne, 2005; Speaking Like Magpies, RSC, 2005; Phaedra, Donmar, 2006; Yerma (trans.), Arcola Th., 2006; There Came a Gypsy Riding, Almeida, 2007; The Lady from the Sea (version), Almeida, 2008; Oedipus, RNT, 2008; The Master Builder, New York, 2008; Helen, Globe, 2009; Greta Garbo Came to Donegal, Tricycle Th., 2010; Ghosts, Duchess, 2010; John Gabriel Borkman (version), Abbey Th., Dublin, 2010; The Match Box, Liverpool Playhouse, 2012, transf. Tricycle Th., 2013; Damned By Despair, RNT, 2012; The Dead, 2012, The Hanging Gardens, 2013, Abbey Th., Dublin; libretto for Thebans, London Coliseum, 2014; Donegal, Abbey Th., Dublin, 2016; De Profundis (adaptation), Vaudeville, 2018; *television*: Scout, 1987; The Hen House, 1989; A Short Stay in Switzerland, 2009 (Broadcast Award, Best Single Drama, 2010); A Song for Jenny, 2015; *films*: Talk of Angels, 1998; Dancing at Lughnasa, 1998; The Stronger, 2008. HRHA, 2009. Freeman of Buncrana, 2011. Hon. DLitt Ulster, 2000. Evening Standard Award, 1986; Ewart-Biggs Prize, 1987; NY Critics Circle Award, 1992; Writers' Guild Award, 1992; Ireland Fund Literary Award, 1992; Tony Award, 1997; Lifetime Achievement Award for Irish Writing, Sunday Tribune, 2007; British Classical Assoc. Prize, 2011; Irish PEN Award, 2014; Ulysses Medal, UCD, 2019. Officier de la République française, 1996. *Publications*: The Factory Girls, 1982; Observe the Sons of Ulster Marching Towards the Somme, 1986; Innocence, 1987; Carthaginians, and Baglady, 1988; Mary and Lizzie, 1989; Someone Who'll Watch Over Me, 1992; Booterstown (poems), 1994; Plays, vol. 1, 1996; Mutabilitie, 1997; Dolly West's Kitchen, 1999; The Sea With No Ships (poems), 1999; Plays, vol. 2, 2002; Gates of Gold, 2002; The Stone Jug: poems, 2003; Dulse (poems), 2008; Greta Garbo Came to Donegal, 2010; The Match Box, 2012; The Hanging Gardens, 2013; Arimathea (novel), 2013; Thebans (libretto), 2014; Donegal, 2016; The Woodcutter and his Family (novel), 2017; The Wedding Breakfast (poems), 2019; *versions*: Peer Gynt, 1990; Three Sisters, 1990; A Doll's House, 1996; Electra, 1997; The Storm, 1998; Miss Julie, 2000; Speaking Like Magpies, 2005; There Came a Gypsy Riding, 2007; Oedipus, 2008; The Lady from the Sea, 2008; Helen, 2009; Ghosts, 2010; John Gabriel Borkman, 2010; Damned By Despair, 2012; In A Town of Five Thousand People, 2012; The Dead: a version, 2012. *Recreations*: walking, horse-racing, Irish art. *Address*: Department of Anglo-Irish Literature, University College, Dublin, Belfield, Dublin 4, Ireland.

**McGUINNESS, Patrick Joseph**, CMG 2014; OBE 1997; Founder and Director, Hudhud Associates Ltd, since 2018; *b* Oxford, 27 April 1963; *s* of Prof. Bernard Francis McGuinness and Prof. Rosamond Ziegler, (Corky), McGuinness; *m* 1994, Susannah Mills; one *s* two *d*. *Educ*: Ampleforth Coll., York; Balliol Coll., Oxford (BA Mod. Hist.). Foreign and Commonwealth Office, 1985–2013: Second Sec., Sana'a, 1988–91; First Sec., Abu Dhabi, 1994–96; Counsellor: Cairo, 1996–99; Rome, 2003–06. Dep. Nat. Security Advr (Intelligence, Security, Resilience), Cabinet Office, 2014–18. Sen. Advr, Brunswick Gp; Mem., Adv. Bd, Glasswall Solutions. Comr, Oxford Commn on Elections and Technol. Chair of Trustees, St Joseph's Hospice, Hackney. *Recreations*: dogs, Rugby Union, classical music, sybaritism. *Clubs*: Athenæum, Special Forces.

**McGUINNESS, Prof. Patrick Robert Anthony**, DPhil; FLSW; Professor of French and Comparative Literature, University of Oxford, since 2010; Fellow and Tutor in French, St Anne's College, Oxford, since 1998; *b* Tunis, 2 June 1968; *s* of Kevin McGuinness and Monique McGuinness (*née* Lejeune); partner, Angharad Price; one *s* one *d*. *Educ*: Clifton Coll., Bristol; Downing Coll., Cambridge (BA 1990); Univ. of York (MA 1991); Magdalen Coll., Oxford (DPhil 1994). Fellow and Tutor in French, Jesus Coll., Oxford, 1995–98. FLSW 2010. Chevalier: Ordre des Palmes Académiques (France), 2009; Ordre des Arts et des Lettres (France), 2011. *Publications*: (ed) T. E. Hulme: selected writings, 1998; Maurice Maeterlinck and the Making of Modern Theatre, 2000; Symbolism, Decadence and the fin de siècle, 2000; (ed) Lynette Roberts: collected poems, 2006; Other People's Countries: a journey into memory (memoir), 2014 (Duff Cooper Prize, 2014); Poetry and Radical Politics in fin de siècle France, 2015; *poetry*: The Canals of Mars, 2004; 19th Century Blues, 2006; Jilted City, 2010; *fiction*: The Last Hundred Days, 2011 (Wales Book of the Year, Writers' Guild Fiction Prize, 2012); Throw Me to the Wolves, 2019. *Address*: St Anne's College, Oxford OX2 6HS. *T*: (01865) 274836. *E*: patrick.mcguinness@st-annes.ox.ac.uk.

**McGUIRE, Prof. Alistair James**, PhD; Professor of Health Economics, London School of Economics, since 2002; *b* Coventry, 6 Nov. 1956; *s* of Terence McGuire and Charlotte McGuire (*née* Dolan); one *s* one *d*, and two step *d*. *Educ*: Royal High Sch., Edinburgh; Heriot-Watt Univ. (BA Hons Econs); Univ. of Aberdeen (MLitt Econs; PhD Econs 1987). Res. Fellow, Univ. of Aberdeen, 1980–87; Oxford University: Sen. Res. Fellow, Centre for Socio-Legal Studies, Wolfson Coll., 1987–92; Res. Fellow and Teaching Tutor, Pembroke Coll., 1987–92; Reader, 1992–97, Prof. of Econs, 1997–2002, City Univ. *Publications*: (jtly) Economics of Health Care, 1988; (with G. Mooney) Medical Ethics and Economics in Health Care, 1988; (jtly) Providing Health Care, 1991; (with P. Annand) Issues in the Reformed NHS, 1997; (with M. Drummond) Economic Evaluation in Health Care, 2001; (jtly) The Economics of New Health Care Technologies, 2009. *Recreations*: music, sleeping, walking. *Address*: London School of Economics, Houghton Street, WC2A 2AE. *T*: (020) 7955 6375, *Fax*: (020) 7955 6308. *E*: a.j.mcguire@lse.ac.uk.

**McGUIRE, Rt Hon. Dame Anne (Catherine)**, DBE 2015; PC 2008; *b* 26 May 1949; *d* of Albert Long, CBE and Agnes Long (*née* Coney); *m* 1972, Leonard F. McGuire; one *s* one *d*. *Educ*: Our Lady and St Francis Sch., Glasgow; Univ. of Glasgow (MA Hons 1971); Notre Dame Coll. of Educn. Registrar and Sec., Court's Dept, Univ. of Glasgow, 1971–74; teacher, 1983–85; fieldworker, 1985–89, Nat. Council, Scotland, 1989–93, CSV; Dep. Dir, Scottish Council for Voluntary Orgns, 1993–97. MP (Lab) Stirling, 1997–2015. PPS to Sec. of State for Scotland, 1997–98; an Asst Govt Whip, 1998–2001; a Lord Comr of HM Treasury (Govt Whip), 2001–02; Parly Under-Sec. of State, Scotland Office, 2002–05; Minister for Disabled People, DWP, 2005–08; PPS to Leader of the Opposition, 2010–11; Shadow Minister for Disabled People, 2011–13. Hon. Dr Stirling, 2018. *Recreations*: walking, Scottish traditional music, reading.

**McGUIRE, Prof. William Joseph**, PhD; FGS; academic, writer, broadcaster, blogger and activist; Professor of Geophysical and Climate Hazards, University College London, 1997–2012, now Emeritus (Co-Director, UCL Environment Institute, 2010–12); Co-Director, New Weather Institute, since 2018; *b* 1 Dec. 1954; *s* of late John McMillan McGuire and of Audrey McGuire (*née* Wade Owens); *m* 2000, Anna Taylor; one *s* and one adopted *s*. *Educ*: St Michael's Coll., Hitchin; University Coll. London (BSc Geol 1976); CNAA (PhD 1980). FGS 1977. Lectr in Igneous Petrology and Geochem., W London Inst. of Higher Educn, 1981–90; Lectr, 1990–93, Sen. Lectr, 1993–95, Reader, 1995–97, in Volcanology and Igneous Petrology, Cheltenham and Gloucester Coll. of Higher Educn; Dir, Aon Benfield (formerly Benfield) UCL Hazard Res. Centre, 1997–2010. Dir, DisasterMan Ltd, 2000–; consultant on natural hazards and climate change, HSBC Gp, 2006–; Mem., Adv. Bd, Contraction and Convergence Foundn, 2011–. Member: UK Govt Natural Hazard Working Gp, 2005; UK Govt Scientific Adv. Gp in Emergencies for Icelandic ash crisis, 2010. Chm. Volcanic Studies Gp, 1993–96, Council Mem., 1997–99, Geol. Soc. of London; Mem., Sci. Media Panel, Royal Instn, 2002–. UK Nat. Corresp., Internat. Assoc. of Volcanology and Chemistry of the Earth's Interior, 1993–96; UK Rep., Eur. Volcanology Proj. Cttee, ESF, 1994; Mem., 1993–95, Sec., 1996–2000, UK Panel, IUGG. Presenter: radio: Disasters in Waiting (series), 2000, Scientists Under Pressure (series), 2001; television: The End of the World (series), 2006. Sci. Advr, Footprint Friends, 2009–; blogs: Bill McGuire's Climate Bombshells (Extinction Rebellion); Weather Bombs (New Weather Inst.). FRI 2003. Member, Editorial Board: Volcanology and Seismology, 1994–98; Acta Vulcanologica, 1995–2000; Disasters, 2002–15; BBC Focus Magazine, 2005–11. *Publications*: (ed jtly) Monitoring Active Volcanoes: strategies, procedures and techniques, 1995; Volcanoes of the World, 1997; Apocalypse: a natural history of global disasters, 1999; Italian Volcanoes, 2001; (jtly) Natural Hazards and Environmental Change, 2002; Raging Planet, 2002; A Guide to the End of the World: everything you never wanted to know, 2002; (with Robert Kovach) Guide to Global Hazards, 2003; (jtly) World Atlas of Natural Hazards, 2004; Surviving Armageddon: solutions for a threatened planet, 2005; Global Catastrophes: a very short introduction, 2005, rev. edn 2014; Seven Years to Save the Planet, 2008; Waking the Giant: how a changing climate triggers earthquakes, tsunamis and volcanoes, 2012; Climate Forcing of Geological Hazards, 2013; (contrib. short story) Knock Twice: 25 modern folk tales for troubling times, 2017; (ed jtly) Observing the Volcano World, 2018; learned papers in Nature, Phil Trans of Royal Soc., etc. *Recreations*: playing with sons Fraser and Jake, and cats Dave, Toby and Cashew, growing vegetables, walking and mountain biking in the Peaks, worrying about the future of our planet, our race and my sons, organising 'Warm Wet & Windy'—the Peak District Climate Change and Eco Festival. *Address*: UCL Hazard Centre, Department of Earth Sciences, University College London, Gower Street, WC1E 6BT. *T*: (020) 7679 3449, *Fax*: (020) 7679 2390. *E*: w.mcguire@ucl.ac.uk.

**McGUIRK, Stephen John Paul**, CBE 2005; QFSM 2002; DL; Chairman, Warrington and Halton Hospitals NHS Foundation Trust, since 2015; *b* 16 July 1960; *m* 1983, Julie Bennion; two *d*. *Educ*: Southbank Univ. (BSc, MA); Open Univ. (BA Hons). Served: Gtr Manchester Co. Fire Service, 1976–86; Royal Berks Fire Service, 1986–89; W Midlands Fire Service, 1989–98; Chief Fire Officer, Cheshire Fire Service, 1999–2009; County Fire Officer and Chief Exec., Gtr Manchester Fire and Rescue Service, 2009–15. FIFireE. DL Gtr Manchester, 2011. Long Service Medal, 1996. *Recreations*: running, fitness generally, reading. *Address*: Warrington and Halton Hospitals NHS Foundation Trust, Warrington Hospital, Lovely Lane, Warrington WA5 1QG.

**McGURK, John Callender**; writer, media consultant, broadcaster; *b* 12 Dec. 1952; *s* of John B. McGurk and Janet McGurk; *m* 1984, Karen Patricia Anne Ramsay (marr. diss. 2005); one *s* one *d*. *Educ*: Tynecastle Sen. Secondary Sch., Edinburgh. Trainee Journalist, Scottish County Press, 1970–74; Reporter: Evening Post, Nottingham, 1974–75; Scottish Daily News, 1975; Reporter and Broadcaster, Radio Clyde, 1975–78; Sunday Mail: Reporter, 1978–84; News Editor, 1984–88; Dep. Editor, 1988–89; Editor, Sunday Sun, Newcastle, 1989–91; Dep. Editor, Daily Record, 1991–94; broadcaster, BBC Radio Scotland, and media consultant, 1994–95; Editor: Evening News, Edinburgh, 1995–97; Scotland on Sunday, 1997–2001; Editl Dir, The Scotsman Pubns Ltd, 2001–04; Ed., The Scotsman, 2004–06; Gp Man. Ed., Daily Telegraph and Sunday Telegraph, 2006. Chm., Editors' Cttee, Scottish Daily Newspaper Soc., 2001. Mem., Press Complaints Commn, 1999–2001. *Recreations*: newspapers, dining out, travel. *E*: jcmcgurk@blueyonder.co.uk.

**McGURK, Ven. Michael Joseph Patrick**; Archdeacon of Liverpool, since 2017; *b* 1968. *Educ*: St John's Coll., Nottingham. Ordained deacon, 2007, priest, 2008; Curate, St Mary the Virgin, Haughton, 2007–09; Curate, 2009–10, Rector, 2010–17, Christ Church, Harpurhey; Area Dean, Manchester North, 2012–17. *Address*: c/o Diocese of Liverpool, St James' House, 20 St James Road, Liverpool L1 7BY. *T*: (0151) 709 9722.

**MACH, David Stefan**, RA 1998; sculptor; *b* 18 March 1956; *s* of Joseph Mach and Martha (*née* Cassidy); *m* 1979, Lesley June White (*d* 2014). *Educ*: Buckhaven High Sch.; Duncan of Jordanstone Coll. of Art (Dip. and Post Dip. in Art); Royal Coll. of Art (MA). Full-time sculptor and occasional vis. lectr, 1982–; Associate Prof., Sculpture Dept, Edinburgh Coll. of Art, 1999; Prof. of Sculpture, Royal Acad., 2000–08; Prof. of Inspiration and Discovery, Univ. of Dundee, 2004–. Work includes Train, Darlington, largest contemp. sculpture in the UK, 1998; sculptures exhibited at galleries in England, Scotland, NY, São Paulo Biennale, Venice Biennale, Paris, Hong Kong, Seoul, Dubai. Trustee, NPG, 2006–10. City of Glasgow Lord Provost Prize, 1992. *Recreations*: music, film, ski-ing, tennis. *Address*: 8 Havelock Walk, Forest Hill, SE23 3HG. *T*: (020) 8699 5659. *E*: davidmach@davidmach.com. *Club*: Chelsea Arts.

**McHALE, His Honour Keith Michael**; a Circuit Judge, 1980–2000; *b* 26 March 1928; *s* of late Cyril Michael McHale, MC and Gladys McHale; *m* 1966, Rosemary Margaret Arthur; one *s* one *d*. Called to the Bar, Gray's Inn, 1951. *Address*: 1 D'Arcy Place, Bromley, Kent BR2 0RY.

**McHARG, Anne Carla**; see Ferguson-Smith, A. C.

**MACHELL, John William**; QC 2012; *b* Maidstone, 9 Feb. 1970; *s* of Paul and Jill Machell; *m* 1994, Helen Cheetham; one *s* one *d*. *Educ*: St Albans Sch.; Univ. of Southampton (LLB). Called to the Bar, Inner Temple, 1993; in practice as a barrister, specialising in chancery and commercial law, 1993–. *Publications*: The Law of Limited Liability Partnership, 2001, 4th edn 2016. *Recreations*: basketball, golf, tennis. *Address*: Serle Court, 6 New Square, Lincoln's Inn, WC2A 3QS. *T*: (020) 7242 6105. *E*: jmachell@serlecourt.co.uk.

**McHENRY, Rev. Brian Edward**, CBE 2008; Vicar, All Saints', Orpington, 2011–17; permission to officiate, Diocese of Canterbury, since 2018; Day Chaplain, Canterbury Cathedral, since 2018; *b* 12 Dec. 1950; *s* of late Alexander Edward McHenry and of Winifred Alice McHenry (*née* Wainford); *m* 1979, Elizabeth Anne Lipsey; two *s*. *Educ*: Dulwich Coll.; New Coll., Oxford (MA); SE Inst. for Theol Educn (Dip. in Applied Christian Theol.); Canterbury Christ Church (BA Ministerial Theol.). Called to the Bar, Middle Temple, 1976. Treasury Solicitor's Dept, 1978–92, 2000; legal advr, Monopolies and Mergers Commn, 1992–96; Solicitor: N Wales Tribunal of Inquiry into Child Abuse, 1996–97; BSE Inquiry, 1998–2000; Chief Legal Advr, Competition Commn, 2000–04; Office of Fair Trading: Solicitor, 2004–06; Gen. Counsel, 2006–08. Mem., Crown Appts Commn, 1997–2002. General Synod of Church of England: Mem., 1980–85 and 1987–2005; Vice-Chm., House of Laity, 2000–05; Chm., Standing Orders Cttee, 1991–99; Member: Standing Cttee, 1990–95; Legislative Cttee, 1981–85, 1991–95 and 2001–05 (Dep. Chm., 2001–05); Business Cttee, 1999–2005; Archbishops' Council, 1999–2005; Lay Vice-Pres., Southwark Diocesan Synod, 1988–96 and 1997–99; Hon. Lay Canon,

2004–08, Mem., Chapter, 2010–12, Southwark Cathedral; Rector of Rochester Chapter, 2012–15, Sec. of Canterbury Chapter, 2018–, Soc. of Catholic Priests. Trustee: Churches Conservation Trust, 2008–13; Orpington Christian Counselling Service, 2012–16; Vice Pres., Churches Together in Orpington, 2013–16; Chm., Canterbury Christian Aid Gp, 2018–; Dep. Chm., Thomas More Fellowship (St Dunstan's Canterbury), 2019–; Mem. Cttee, E Kent Justice for Palestinians, 2019–. A Reader, C of E, 1976–2008; ordained deacon, 2008, priest, 2009; Curate, St Paul's, Deptford, 2008–11. Chaplain: Orpington Br., RBL, 2011–17; to Mayor, London Bor. of Bromley, 2015–16. Governor: Burwood Sch., Orpington, 2012–14; St Olave's and St Saviour's Grammar Sch., Orpington, 2013–17. Volunteer guide, Walmer Castle, 2017–. *Recreations:* swimming, walking, travel, Arsenal FC, reading widely especially classic fiction and history, art gallery and museum exhibitions, family and friends. *Address:* 14 Richmond Gardens, Canterbury CT2 8ES. *T:* (01227) 781899, 07780 308220.

**McHENRY, Donald F.;** Distinguished Professor in the Practice of Diplomacy, School of Foreign Service, Georgetown University, 1998–2014 (University Research Professor of Diplomacy and International Affairs, 1981–98); *b* 13 Oct. 1936; *s* of Limas McHenry and Dora Lee Brooks; *m* Mary Williamson (marr. diss.); one *s* two *d*. *Educ:* Lincoln Senior High Sch., East St Louis, Ill; Illinois State Univ. (BS); Southern Illinois Univ. (MSc); Georgetown Univ. Taught at Howard Univ., Washington, 1959–62; joined Dept of State, 1963; Head of Dependent Areas Section, Office of UN Pol Affairs, 1965–68; Asst to Sec. of State, US, 1969; Special Asst to Counsellor, Dept of State, 1969–71; Lectr, Sch. of Foreign Service, Georgetown Univ.; Guest Scholar, Brookings Inst., and Internat. Affairs Fellow, Council on Foreign Relations (on leave from State Dept), 1971–73; resigned from State Dept, 1973; Project Dir, Humanitarian Policy Studies, Carnegie Endowment for Internat. Peace, Washington, 1973–76; served in transition team of President Carter, 1976–77; Ambassador and Deputy Rep. of US to UN Security Council, 1977–79, Permanent Rep., 1979; US Ambassador to UN, 1979–81. Founder and Co-Pres., IRC Gp, LLC, 1981–; Director: Internat. Paper Co., 1981; Fleet Boston Financial Co.; Bank of Boston Corp., 1981–2004; GlaxoSmithKline (formerly SmithKline Beecham) plc, 1982–2004; Coca-Cola, 1982–2014; American Telephone and Telegraph, 1987–2005; Inst. for Internat. Economics, 1999. Dir, American Ditchley Foundn; Chm., Bd of Dirs, Africare, 1989–2004; Mem. Bd of Govs, UNA of USA. Mem., American Acad. of Arts and Scis, 1992. Hon. degrees: Dennison, Duke, Eastern Illinois, Georgetown, Harvard, Illinois State, Michigan, Princeton, Southern Illinois, Tufts, and Washington Univs; Amherst, Bates, Boston and Williams Colleges. Superior Honor Award, Dept of State, 1966. Mem. Council on Foreign Relations and Editorial Bd, Foreign Policy Magazine. *Publications:* Micronesia: Trust Betrayed, 1975. *Address:* c/o Georgetown University, 37th and O Streets, NW, Washington, DC 20057, USA.

**MACHIN, David;** Under Treasurer, Gray's Inn, 1989–2000; *b* 25 April 1934; *s* of late Noel and Joan Machin; *m* 1963, Sarah Mary, *yr d* of late Col W. A. Chester-Master, DL; two *d*. *Educ:* Eton (Oppidan Scholar); Trinity Coll., Cambridge. National Service, 1952–54 (2nd Lieut Welsh Guards). Editor, William Heinemann Ltd, 1957–66; Literary Agent, Gregson & Wigan Ltd and London International, 1966–68; Partner, A. P. Watt & Son, 1968–70; Director: Jonathan Cape Ltd, 1970–78; Chatto, Bodley Head and Jonathan Cape Ltd, 1977–78, 1981–87; Jt Man. Dir, 1981, Man. Dir, 1982–87, The Bodley Head Ltd; Dir, Triad Paperbacks Ltd, 1983–86; Gen. Sec., The Society of Authors, 1978–81. Chm. of Trustees, Inns of Court Gainsford Trust, 1992–2000. Vice-Chm., Hammersmith Democrats, 1988–89. Chm., Lansdown Crescent Assoc., 2003–06 (Trustee, 2010–13). Hon. Bencher, Gray's Inn, 2000. *Publications:* (contrib.) Outlook, 1963; (ed) Gray's Inn 2000: a millennium record, 2002; (ed) Simon Phipps: a portrait, 2003; contrib. The Oldie. *Address:* 11 Deanery Walk, Avonpark, Limpley Stoke, nr Bath, Wilts BA2 7JQ. *Club:* Garrick.

**MACHIN, His Honour John Vessey;** DL; a Circuit Judge, 1997–2009; *b* 4 May 1941; *s* of late William Vessey Machin and Dona Machin (*née* Pryce), Worksop; *m* 1967, Susan Helen, *d* of Edgar Frank Emery; one *s* one *d*. *Educ:* Dragon Sch., Oxford; Westminster Sch. Called to the Bar, Middle Temple, 1965; Midland and Oxford Circuit; Asst Recorder, 1990–94; Recorder, 1994–97. Chm., Agricl Land Tribunal (Eastern Area), 1999–2013 (Dep. Chm., 1986–99); Regl Judge (part-time), First-tier Tribunal (Property Chamber), 2013–14. Judicial Mem., Lincs Probation Bd, 2006–08. Governor: Worksop Coll., Notts, 1986–2012; Ranby House Sch., 1986–2012; Fellow and Midland Dir, Woodard Schs, 1988–2012 (Hon. Fellow, 2012); Foundn Gov., St Matthew's C of E Primary Sch., Normanton-on-Trent, 2005–15. DL Notts, 2011. *Recreations:* rural pursuits especially canambulation and trees. *Address:* Normanton Hall, Normanton-on-Trent, Newark, Notts NG23 6RP. *Clubs:* Garrick, Farmers; Newark Rowing.

**MACHIN, His Honour Kenneth Arthur;** QC 1977; a Judge, International Criminal Tribunal for Rwanda, United Nations, 2003–09; *b* 13 July 1936; *o s* of Thomas Arthur Machin and Edith May Machin; *m* 1983, Amaryllis Francesca (former ballet dancer and Member of Court of Common Council, Cripplegate Ward, City of London), *o d* of Dr Donald and Lucille Bigley. *Educ:* St Albans School. Called to the Bar, 1960; South Eastern Circuit; Central Criminal Court, 1985–90 and 2001; a Recorder of the Crown Court, 1979–83; a Circuit Judge, 1983–90; a Sen. Circuit Judge, 1990–2001; a Dep. Circuit Judge, 2001. Chief Social Security and Child Support Comr, 1990–2000. Mem., Judicial Studies Bd and Chm., Tribunals Cttee, 1992–99. Freeman, City of London. *Recreations:* painting, Martello Towers.

**MACHIN, Prof. Stephen Jonathan,** PhD; FBA 2006; Professor of Economics and Director, Centre for Economic Performance, London School of Economics and Political Science, since 2016 (Research Director, Centre for Economic Performance, 2004–16); *b* 23 Dec. 1962; *s* of Raymond Edward Machin and Betty Patricia Machin; *m* 2001, Kirstine Hansen; one *s*. *Educ:* Wolverhampton Grammar Sch.; Wolverhampton Poly. (BSc 1st cl. Econs) 1985); Univ. of Warwick (PhD 1988). Lectr, 1988–93, Reader, 1993–96, Prof. of Econs, 1996–2016, UCL. Dir, Centre for Econs of Educn, 2000–09. Visiting Professor: Harvard Univ., 1993–94; MIT, 2001–02. Hon. PhD Wolverhampton, 2010. Editor: Economic Jl, 1998–2013; Economica, 2016–. *Publications:* papers in leading academic jls, inc. Qly Jl of Econs, Rev. of Econ. Studies, Econ. Jl, Industrial and Labor Relns Rev. and Jl of European Econ. Assoc. *Address:* Department of Economics, London School of Economics and Political Science, Houghton Street, WC2A 2AE.

**MACHIN, Thomas Paul Edwin;** Director: MacGregor Associates, since 2000; Fraser Otis Ltd, since 2000; *b* 14 Sept. 1944; *s* of late Thomas Edwin Machin and Elizabeth Pamela Machin (*née* Collett); *m* 1970, Elizabeth-Ann Suttle. *Educ:* St Joseph's Coll., Stoke-on-Trent; London Sch. of Economics (BSc Econ). Plessey Co., 1966–69; Massey Ferguson, 1969–74; joined British Leyland, 1974; Dir, Engrg Services, 1980–82; Personnel Dir, Cowley, 1983–87; Eur. Employee Relns and Mgt Develt Dir, Lawson Mardon Gp (Europe), 1987–91; Human Resources Dir, James Neill Hldgs Ltd, 1991–92; CEO, States of Jersey Estabt Cttee, 1992–95; Chief Executive, BPIF, 1995–2000. Consultant: Negotiating Solutions, 2002–05; First Class Partnerships, 2002–12. Chairman: Indust. Relns Cttee, BPIF, 1989–91; Trade Assoc. Council, CBI, 2000; Pres., Yorks Publicity Assoc., 1998. Chartered FCIPD (FIPD 1986); FRSA 1996. Freeman, City of London,

1998; Liveryman, Co. of Stationers and Newspaper Makers, 1998–2002. *Recreations:* retired Association Football referee, weight training, spectator sports (especially horse racing and Association Football), investment - business and sports, sports politics, skidelling, current affairs, travelling. *Address:* 24 Rowallan Castle, Kilmarus, East Ayrshire KA3 2DP.

**MACHO, Louise June;** *see* Sweet, L. J.

**MACHRAY, Alastair Hulbert;** Editor, Liverpool Echo, since 2005; Editor-in-chief, Reach plc (formerly Trinity Mirror), Merseyside, since 2009, and North Wales and Cheshire, since 2012; *b* 19 June 1961; *s* of Douglas Basil Machray and June Hulbert; *m* 1987, Lynne Elizabeth Ward; one *s* one *d*. *Educ:* Glasgow Acad.; Greencroft Comprehensive. Reporter, Sunderland Echo, 1979–82; sports journalist, Journal, Newcastle, 1982–85; editor, Football Pink, Newcastle, 1985–86; sports journalist, Today, 1986–88; Evening Chronicle, Newcastle: Sub Editor, 1988; Asst Chief Sub Editor, 1988–89; Dep. Chief Sub Editor, 1989–90; Design Editor, 1990–93; Asst Editor, Liverpool Echo, 1994–95; Editor: Liverpool Daily Post, 1995–2002; Daily Post in Wales, 2002–05; Ed.-in-Chief, Trinity Mirror North Wales, 2002–05. *Recreations:* golf, cricket, family, wine, cookery. *Address:* PO Box 48, Old Hall Street, Liverpool L69 3EB.

**MACIEJEWSKI, Brig. Justin Charles Władysław,** DSO 2008; MBE 2004; Director, National Army Museum, since 2018; *b* Croydon, 7 July 1966; *s* of Bogusław Maciejewski and Liesel Maciejewska; *m* 1993, Rebecca Charlotte Pilcher; three *s*. *Educ:* St Edward's Sch., Oxford; Selwyn Coll., Cambridge (BA Hist. 1988); RMA, Sandhurst; King's Coll., London (MA 1999). Served Royal Green Jackets: Regtl Duty, Germany, NI and NATO HQ, 1990–98 (ADC to UKMILREP, 1993–95); SO, 1st (UK) Armd Div., Herford, Germany, Bulford, Oman and Iraq, 2001–04; SO2 G3 (Ops, Orgn and Deployment); MA to Surgeon Gen., MoD, 2004; CO, 1st Bn Royal Green Jackets/2nd Bn The Rifles, UK, Kosovo, Iraq, 2004–07; COS, 3rd (UK) Div., 2007–09; HCSC 2008; Comdr, 12th Mechanized Bde, 2009–11; Dir Combat, Army HQ, Andover, 2011–12; Mgt Consultant, McKinsey and Co., 2013–18. Vis. Fellow in Hist., Univ. of Oxford, 2012. *Publications:* (contrib.) British Generals in Blair's Wars, 2013. *Recreations:* Italian history, culture and language. *Address:* National Army Museum, Royal Hospital Road, Chelsea, SW3 4HT. *Clubs:* Cavalry and Guards; Rifles Officers'.

**McILROY, David Thomas;** HM Diplomatic Service; Ambassador to the Republic of Guinea, since 2019; *b* Ballymena, 3 March 1968; *s* of George and Beth McIlroy; *m* 2000, Victoria Stone; one *s* one *d*. *Educ:* Coleraine Academical Instn; Selwyn Coll., Cambridge (BA Hons Law 1990; MA 1994). Served NI Civil Service, Belfast and London, 1990–2000; entered FCO, 2000; Hd, Gibraltar and Justice and Home Affairs Sections, EU (Internal) Dept, 2000–02; Serbian lang. trng, 2002–04; Dep. Hd of Mission and Consul Gen., Belgrade, 2004–07; Hd, Borders, Managed Migration, Multilateral and Develt, Migration Directorate, 2007–09; on secondment to Secretariat, Iraq Inquiry, Cabinet Office, 2009–11; Dep. Perm. Rep., UKMIS to UN and Other Internat. Orgns, Vienna, 2011–15; Deputy Head: Counter Proliferation Dept, and Hd, State Progs Team, 2015–16; Stabilisation Unit, 2016–18. *Recreations:* Christian ministry, family adventures, walking, landscape photography. *Address:* British Embassy, Lansébounjdi, Corniche Sud, PO 6729, Conakry, Republic of Guinea. *T:* 626264040. *E:* david.mcilroy@fco.gov.uk.

**McILVEEN, David;** Member (DemU) North Antrim, Northern Ireland Assembly, 2011–16; *b* Belfast, 11 Feb. 1981; *s* of David McIlveen and Mary McIlveen. Mem., NI Policing Bd, 2015–16. Contested (DemU) N Antrim, NI Assembly, 2016. *Recreations:* golf, music, travelling, motorcycling.

**McILVEEN, Michelle Elizabeth;** Member (DemU) Strangford, Northern Ireland Assembly, since 2007; *b* 21 Jan. 1971; *d* of Henry and Elizabeth McIlveen. *Educ:* Queen's Univ., Belfast (BSSc, MSSc; PGCE). Teacher of hist. and politics, 1994–97; business manager, 1997–2007. Mem. (DemU) Ards BC, 2005. Jun. Minister, Office of First Minister and Dep. First Minister, 2015, Minister for Regl Develt, 2015–16, Minister for Agriculture, Envmt and Rural Affairs, 2016–17, NI. *Address:* Constituency Office, 7 The Square, Town Parks, Comber, Co. Down, Northern Ireland BT23 5DX. *T:* (028) 9187 1441, *Fax:* (028) 9187 1494. *E:* michelle.mcilveen@niassembly.gov.uk.

**McILVRIDE, Rhoderick Robert;** QC (Scot.) 2014; *b* Campbeltown, Argyll, 19 Jan. 1957; *s* of Daniel McIlvride and Catherine McIlvride (*née* Brownie); *m* 1978, Miriam Frances Haig; one *s* three *d*. *Educ:* Kelvinside Acad., Glasgow; Univ. of Glasgow (LLB Hons). Admitted Solicitor, 1981; in practice as solicitor, 1981–2004; Licensed Insolvency Practitioner, 1988–2004; Solicitor Advocate, 1997–2004; Advocate, 2005–; standing jun. to Advocate Gen. for Scotland (Home Office), 2009–15. Mem., Arbitrators Panel, Sport Resolutions, 2017–. *Recreations:* reading, opera, football, dining out. *Address:* Advocates Library, Parliament House, Edinburgh EH1 1RF. *E:* clerks@terrafirmachambers.com.

**McILWHAM, Fiona May Joan;** HM Diplomatic Service; Private Secretary to the Duke and Duchess of Sussex, since 2019; *b* Guildford, 31 Dec. 1973; *d* of John McIlwham and Ann McIlwham; partner, Daniel Korski. *Educ:* St John's Coll., Cambridge (BA Pt 1 Philos. Pt 2 Social and Pol Scis 1995); Sch. of Oriental and African Studies, Univ. of London (MSc Develt Econs 1998). NGO field work, Bangladesh, 1995, Sudan, 1997; EC, 1996; joined FCO, 1998; Second Sec. (Pol and Press), Sarajevo, 2000–02; Hd, British Embassy Office, Banja Luka, 2002–03; EU Presidency team, London, 2004–06; First Sec., Baghdad and Basra, 2006; seconded to US Dept of State, Washington, 2006–07; First Sec. (Pol), Washington, 2007; Ambassador to Republic of Albania, 2009–12; Sen. Advr to Dir Gen. of Enlargement, EC (on secondment), 2012–14; Dir, Western Balkans, FCO, 2015–18; RCDS, 2019. *Recreations:* reading, film, theatre, ski-ing, hiking.

**McINDOE, Very Rev. John Hedley;** Minister of St Columba's Church, Pont Street, London, 1988–2000; Moderator of the General Assembly of The Church of Scotland, 1996–97; *b* 31 Aug. 1934; *s* of William McIndoe and May (*née* Hedley); *m* 1960, Evelyn Kennedy Johnstone (*d* 2006); three *d*. *Educ:* Greenock Acad.; Glasgow Univ. (MA Hons (Classics), 1956; BD (with distinction), 1959); Hartford Seminary, Conn, USA (STM, 1960). Ordained, 1960; Asst Minister, Paisley Abbey, 1960–63; Minister: Park Church, Dundee, 1963–72; St Nicholas Parish Church, Lanark, 1972–88. Hon. DD Glasgow, 2000. *Recreations:* theatre, films. *Address:* 5 Dunlin, Westerlands Park, Glasgow G12 0FE. *T:* (0141) 579 1366.

**McINERNEY, Prof. John Peter,** OBE 1995; Glanely Professor of Agricultural Policy and Director of Agricultural Economics Unit, University of Exeter, 1984–2002, now Emeritus; *b* 10 Jan. 1939; *s* of Peter McInerney and Eva McInerney; *m* 1961, Audrey M. Perry; one *s* one *d*. *Educ:* Colyton Grammar Sch., Colyford, Devon; Univ. of London (BScAgric Hons); Univ. of Oxford (DipAgricEcons); Iowa State Univ. (PhD). Lectr in Agricl Econs, Wye Coll., Univ. of London, 1964–66; Lectr and Sen. Lectr in Agricl Econs, Univ. of Manchester, 1967–78; Prof. of Agricl Econs and Management, Univ. of Reading, 1978–84. Research Economist and Cons., World Bank, Washington, 1972–97. Visiting Professor: Res. Sch. of Animal Prodn and Health, Royal Vet. and Agricl Univ., Copenhagen, 1999–2005; RAC, 2001–09. President: Agricl Econs Soc., 1996–97; Rural Educn and Develt Assoc., 1996–97; Member: Dunnet Cttee on TB, Cattle and Badgers, MAFF, 1984–86; Mgt Cttee, MAFF/DTI LINK Sustainable Livestock Prog., 1996–2002; Farm

Animal Welfare Council, MAFF, 1996–2004; Bd, UK Register of Organic Food Standards, 1996–2003; Independent Scientific Gp on Cattle TB, MAFF, subseq. DEFRA, 1998–2007; Econs Panel, SW RDA, 2001–06; Econs and Social Studies Prog. Adv. Gp, TB res., DEFRA, 2008–10. Trustee, Farm Animal Welfare Trust, 2008–. Governor, Silsoe Res. Inst., 1996–2003. Phi Kappa Phi 1964, Gamma Sigma Delta 1964. FRSA 1995. Hon. FRASE 1999. Massey Ferguson Nat. Agricl Award, 1998; Agricl Econs Soc. Award, 2011. *Publications:* The Food Industry: economics and policy (jtly), 1983; Badgers and Bovine Tuberculosis (jtly), 1986; Disease in Farm Livestock: economics and policy (jtly), 1987; Diversification in the Use of Farm Resources, 1989; Economic Analysis of Milk Quotas, 1992; Agriculture at the Crossroads, 1998; Who Cares?: a study of farmers' involvement in countryside management, 2000; What's the Damage?: costs of countryside management on farms, 2001; Animal Welfare: economics and policy, 2004; chapters in: Current Issues in Economic Policy, 1975, 2nd edn 1980; Resources Policy, 1982; Grassland Production, 1999, etc; articles in Jl of Agricl Econs, Amer. Jl of Agricl Econs, Canadian Jl of Agricl Econs, Outlook on Agric., Jl of RASE, Farm Mgt, Preventive Vet. Medicine, Agricl Progress, Nature, Jl Applied Ecol. *Recreations:* doing it myself, tentative farming, introspection. *Address:* Mundens Field, Horsley Road, Nailsworth, Stroud, Glos GL6 0JR. *T:* 07764 516964. *E:* J.P.McInerney@exeter.ac.uk. *Club:* Templeton Social.

**McINNES OF KILWINNING,** Baron *cr* 2016 (Life Peer), of Kilwinning in the County of Ayrshire; **Mark McInnes,** CBE 2016; Director, Scottish Conservative Party, since 2003; *b* Paisley, 4 Nov. 1976; *s* of Eric McInnes and Irene McInnes (*née* Wardrop). *Educ:* Kilwinning Acad.; Univ. of Edinburgh (MA Hons 1998). Cons. Party Agent, NE Fife and Edinburgh Pentlands, 1999–2003. Mem. (C), Edinburgh CC, 2003–17. Constitutional Advr to Sec. of State for Scotland, 2018–; Co-Chair, All Party Parly Gp on Turkey, 2019–. Mem. Bd, Better Together, 2013–15. Gov., George Watson's Coll., 2007–16. Curator of Patronage, Edinburgh Univ., 2007–17; Regl Champion, British Mus., 2019–. Elder, Morningside Parish Ch, 2004–. *Recreations:* Ottoman and Byzantine history, Middle Eastern and US politics, hill walking. *Address:* 9/2 Steel's Place, Edinburgh EH10 4QR. *T:* (0131) 524 0030. *E:* mark.mcinnes@scottishconservatives.com.

**MacINNES, Dame Barbara Mary;** *see* Stocking, Dame B. M.

**McINNES, Elizabeth Anne;** MP (Lab) Heywood and Middleton, since Oct. 2014; *b* Oldham, Lancs, 30 March 1959; *d* of George McInnes and Margaret Elizabeth McInnes; partner, Stephen John Duxbury; one *s. Educ:* Hathershaw Comp. Sch., Oldham; St Anne's Coll., Oxford (BA Hons Biochem. 1981); Surrey Univ. (MSc Clin. Biochem. 1983). Trainee Clin. Scientist, Greenwich District Hosp., 1981–83; Basic Grade Biochemist, Royal Hallamshire Hosp., Sheffield, 1983–87; Sen. Clin. Scientist, Pennine Acute Hosps NHS Trust, 1987–2014. Chair, Nat. Health Sector Cttee, Unite, 2013–14. Mem., Rossendale BC, 2010–14. Shadow Minister for Communities and Local Govt, 2015–16, for Foreign and Commonwealth Affairs, 2016–. *Recreations:* hill-walking, camping, art, music. *Address:* House of Commons, SW1A 0AA. *T:* (020) 7219 0684. *E:* mcinnesl@parliament.uk.

**MacINNES, Hamish,** OBE 1979; BEM; Founder and Leader, Glencoe Mountain Rescue Team, 1960–94; author and film consultant, major movies; Director, Glencoe Productions Ltd, since 1989; *b* 7 July 1930. Dep. Leader, British Everest Expedition, 1975. Hon. Dir, Leishman Meml Res. Centre, Glencoe, 1975–92; Mountain Rescue Cttee for Scotland (Past Sec.). Founder and Hon. Pres., Search and Rescue Dog Assoc.; Co-founder, Snow and Avalanche Foundn of Scotland, 1988; Past Pres., Alpine Climbing Group; Pres., Guide Dogs for the Blind Adventure Gp, 1986–. Patron, Equal Adventure, 2005–. Designer of climbing equipment, incl. the first all metal ice axe, terrodactyl ice tools, the MacInnes stretchers, etc. Hon. Member: Scottish Mountaineering Club; Alpine Club. Hon. LLD: Glasgow, 1983; Dundee, 2004; Hon. DSc: Aberdeen, 1988; Heriot-Watt, 1992; DU Stirling, 1997. Mem., Scottish Sports Hall of Fame, 2003. *Publications:* Climbing, 1964; Scottish Climbs, 2 vols, 1971, 2nd edn (1 vol.) 1981; International Mountain Rescue Handbook, 1972, 5th edn 2005; Call-Out: mountain rescue, 1973, 4th edn 1986; Climb to the Lost World, 1974; Death Reel (novel), 1976; West Highland Walks, vols 1 and 2, 1979, Vol. 3, 1983, Vol. 4, 1988; Look Behind the Ranges, 1979; Scottish Winter Climbs, 1980; High Drama (stories), 1980; Beyond the Ranges, 1984; Sweep Search, 1985; The Price of Adventure, 1987; My Scotland, 1988; The Way Through the Glens, 1989; Land of Mountain and Mist, 1989; Mammoth Book of Mountain Disaster, 2003; Murder in the Glen (novel), 2008; Errant Nights (novel), 2011; Cabin by the Sea, 2018; books have been translated into Russian, Japanese, Italian and German. *Address:* Tigh A'Voulin, Glencoe, Argyll PH49 4HX.

**McINNES, Prof. Iain Blair,** CBE 2019; PhD; FRCPE, FRCPGlas, FMedSci; FRSE; Muirhead Professor of Medicine, since 2012, Arthritis Research UK Professor of Rheumatology, since 2014, Director, Institute of Infection, Immunity and Inflammation, since 2010, and Honorary Consultant Rheumatologist, since 2002, University of Glasgow; *b* Glasgow, 19 Oct. 1964; *s* of John McInnes and Janice McInnes; *m* Karin; two *d. Educ:* Hutchesons' Grammar Sch.; Univ. of Glasgow (BSc Immunol. 1st Cl. Hons 1986; MB ChB Hons 1989; PhD 1996). MRCP 1992; Accredited Clin. Rheumatol., 1999; FRCPGlas 2003; FRCPE 2010. Residencies in Medicine/Surgery, Glasgow Royal Inf. and Western Inf., Glasgow, 1989–90; SHO Med. Rotation, Western Inf., Glasgow, 1990–92; SHO III Rheumatol. and Gen. Medicine, Centre for Rheumatic Diseases, Univ. Dept of Medicine, Glasgow, 1992–93; Wellcome Clin. Fellow, Univ. of Glasgow, 1993–96; Arthritis Res. Campaign Travelling Fellow to Arthritis and Rheumatism Br., NIH, Bethesda, Md, 1996–98; University of Glasgow: Lectr in Rheumatol., 1998–99; Sen. Lectr in Rheumatol. and Hon. Consultant Rheumatologist, Centre for Rheumatic Diseases, 1999–2002; Hd, Div. of Immunol., Infection and Inflammation, 2008–10. FRSE 2008; FMedSci 2012. *Publications:* (ed) Kelley's Textbook of Rheumatology, 8th edn 2007 to 9th edn 2012; over 200 scientific articles in learned jls. *Recreations:* golf, music. *Address:* Institute of Infection, Immunity and Inflammation, College of Medical, Veterinary and Life Sciences, University of Glasgow, 120 University Place, Glasgow G12 8TA. *T:* (0141) 330 8412, *Fax:* (0141) 330 4297. *E:* iain.mcinnes@glasgow.ac.uk.

**MacINNES, Keith Gordon,** CMG 1984; HM Diplomatic Service, retired; Ambassador and UK Permanent Representative to OECD, Paris, 1992–95; *b* 17 July 1935; *s* of late Kenneth MacInnes and Helen MacInnes (*née* Gordon); *m* 1st, 1966, Jennifer Anne Fennell (marr. diss. 1984); one *s* one *d;* 2nd, 1985, Hermione Pattinson. *Educ:* Rugby; Trinity Coll., Cambridge (MA); Pres., Cambridge Union Soc., 1957. HM Forces, 1953–55. FO, 1960; Third, later Second Secretary, Buenos Aires, 1961–64; FO, 1964 (First Sec., 1965); Private Sec. to Permanent Under-Sec., Commonwealth Office, 1965–68; First Sec. (Information), Madrid, 1968–70; FCO, 1970–74; Counsellor and Head of Chancery: Prague, 1974–77; Dep. Perm. Rep., UK Mission, Geneva, 1977–80; Head of Information Dept, FCO, 1980–83; Asst Under-Sec. of State and Principal Finance Officer, FCO, 1983–87; Ambassador to the Philippines, 1987–92. *Recreations:* golf, bridge.

**McINTOSH,** family name of **Baroness McIntosh of Hudnall.**

**McINTOSH OF HUDNALL,** Baroness *cr* 1999 (Life Peer), of Hampstead in the London Borough of Camden; **Genista Mary McIntosh;** arts consultant; *b* 23 Sept. 1946; *d* of late Geoffrey Tandy and Maire Tandy; *m* 1971, Neil Scott Wishart McIntosh, *qv* (marr. diss.); one *s* one *d. Educ:* Univ. of York (BA Philosophy and Sociology). Press Sec., York Festival of Arts, 1968–69; Royal Shakespeare Co.: Casting Dir, 1972–77; Planning Controller, 1977–84; Sen. Administrator, 1986–90; Associate Producer, 1990; Exec. Dir, RNT, 1990–96 and 1997–2002; Chief Exec., Royal Opera House, Covent Gdn, 1997; Principal, Guildhall Sch. of Music and Drama, 2002–03. Hon. Paramount Management Ltd, 1984–86. Bd Mem., RSC, 2010–. Trustee: Southbank Sinfonia, 2003–; Artis Foundn, 2017–. Hon. Fellow, Goldsmiths Coll., Univ. of London, 2003. DUniv: York, 1998; Middlesex, 2002; City, 2002. *Address:* House of Lords, SW1A 0PW.

**McINTOSH OF PICKERING,** Baroness *cr* 2015 (Life Peer), of the Vale of Pickering in the County of North Yorkshire; **Anne Caroline Ballingall McIntosh;** *b* 20 Sept. 1954; *d* of late Dr Alastair Ballingall McIntosh and Grete-Lise McIntosh; *m* 1992, John Harvey. *Educ:* Harrogate Coll., Harrogate, Yorks; Univ. of Edinburgh (LLB Hons); Univ. of Aarhus, Denmark. Admitted to Faculty of Advocates, 1982. Stagiaire, EEC, Brussels, 1978; legal advr in private EEC practice, Brussels, 1979–80; Bar apprentice with Simpson and Marwick, WS, and devilling at Scottish Bar, 1980–82; private legal practice, Brussels, specialising in EEC law, 1982–83; Secretariat Mem., responsible for transport, youth, culture, educn and tourism, and relations with Scandinavia, Austria, Switzerland and Yugoslavia, EDG, Eur. Parlt, 1983–89. European Parliament: Mem. (C), NE Essex, 1989–94; Essex N and Suffolk S, 1994–99; a Jun. Whip, EDG, 1989–92; Mem., Transport and Legal Affairs Cttees; EDG Spokesman on Rules Cttee, 1989–95, Transport and Tourism Cttee, 1992–99; Mem., Norway Parly Delegn, 1989–95, Polish Parly Delegn, 1995–97, Czech Parly Delegn, 1997–99. MP (C) Vale of York, 1997–2010, Thirsk and Malton, 2010–15. Shadow Minister: for Culture, Media and Sport, 2001–02; for Transport, 2002–03; for Envmt and Transport, 2003–05; for Foreign Affairs, 2005; for Work and Pensions, 2005–06; for Educn, 2006–07; for Envmt, 2007–10; Opposition frontbench spokesman on envmt, food and rural affairs, 2007–10. Chairman: Select Cttee on Envmt, Food and Rural Affairs, 2010–15 (Mem., 2007–10); Post Legislative Scrutiny Cttee on Licensing Act 2003, H of L, 2016–17; Member: Select Cttee on Envmt, Transport and the Regions, 1999–2001, on Transport, Local Govt and the Regions, 2001–02, on Transport, 2003–05; Exec., 1922 Cttee, 2000–01; European Scrutiny Cttee, 1999–2003; European Standing Cttee; Co Chm., All-Party Parly Gp on Water, 2015–. President: Anglia Enterprise in Europe, 1989–99; Yorkshire First, Enterprise in Yorks, 1995–99. Former Member: Governing Council, Anglia Poly. Univ.; Senate, Univ. of Essex; Gov., Writtle Coll. Hon. LLD Anglia Poly. Univ., 1997. *Recreations:* swimming, cinema, walking. *Address:* House of Lords, SW1A 0PW.

**McINTOSH, Alisdair Douglas;** Policy and External Relations Director, Chartered Institute of Internal Auditors, since 2015; *b* Addlestone, 19 July 1963; *s* of Alexander and Doreen McIntosh; *m* 1998, Sarah Mary Burnett; one *s* one *d. Educ:* Strode's Sch., Egham; Durham and Paris Univs (BA Hons French 1986); Birkbeck Coll., Univ. of London (MA Romance Langs and Lits 1991); INSEAD, Fontainebleau (AMP 2007). Policy official, HM Treasury, 1987–91; Econ. and Financial Attaché, UK Perm. Repn to EU, Brussels, 1991–96; Sen. Policy Advr, Cabinet of Vice-Pres., Eur. Commn, 1997–99; Hd of Secretariat, Cttee of Enquiry into Teachers' Pay and Conditions, Edinburgh, 1999–2000; Scottish Government: Hd of Access to Justice, 2000–03; Hd of Antisocial Behaviour Unit, 2003–05; Hd of Regeneration, 2005–09; Director: Scotland Office, 2009–12; Public Bodies and Public Service Reform, 2012–13; Housing, Regeneration and Welfare, 2013; Dir, Business for New Europe, 2014–15. Non-executive Director: Scottish Urban Regeneration Forum, 2005–09; Real Life Options, 2008–13; Advr, TheCityUK, 2015. *Recreations:* hills, books, visual arts. *Address:* 81 St John's Road, Edinburgh EH12 6NN.

**McINTOSH, David Angus;** Senior Partner, Davies Arnold Cooper, Solicitors, 1978–2007; Consultant, Warren's Law and Advocacy (formerly Rodney Warren & Co.), since 2009; President, Law Society, 2001–02; *b* 10 March 1944; *s* of late Robert Angus McIntosh and of Monica Joan (*née* Hillier, now Sherring); *m* 1968, Jennifer Mary Dixon; two *d. Educ:* Selwood Co. Sch., Frome; Coll. of Law, London. Admitted solicitor, 1969. Joined Davies Arnold Cooper, 1963. Consultant, Fox Solicitors, 2007–09. Mem., Legal Consultative Panel, Dept of Constitutional Affairs, 2003–04. Law Society of England and Wales: Mem. Council, 1996–; Chm., Exec. Cttee, 2000–; Member: Court of Appeal Users' Cttee, 1998–2000; Interim Exec. Cttee, 1999; Vice-Chm., 1997–98, Chm., 1999–2000, Civil Litigation Cttee. Chm., Cttee on Consumer Affairs, Advertising, Unfair Competition and Product Liability, Internat. Bar Assoc., 1995–99; Mem., Exec. Cttee (US), Internat. Assoc. Defense Counsel, 1995–98. Chair, City of London Law Society, 2004–10. Chm., Solicitors Indemnity Fund Ltd, 2006–; Chair, Legal and Professional Claims Ltd, 2008–. Chm., Professional Standards Bd, Chartered Insurance Inst., 2006–. Mem. Council, Sch. of Pharmacy, Univ. of London, 2003–04. Master, City of London Solicitors' Co., 2013–14. Hon. QC 2009; Hon. FCII 2014. *Publications:* Personal Injury Awards in EC Countries, 1990; Civil Procedures in EC Countries, 1993; Personal Injury Awards in EU and EFTA Countries, 1994, 2003; numerous contribs on compensation, insurance and products liability to learned jls. *Recreations:* golf, trying to keep fit, choosing ties! *Address:* c/o Warren's Law and Advocacy, Map House, 34–36 St Leonard's Road, Eastbourne, E Sussex BN21 3UT. *T:* (01323) 430430. *Clubs:* Chigwell Golf; Real Sotogrande Golf (Spain).

**McINTOSH, John Charles,** CBE 2013 (OBE 1996); Headmaster, The London Oratory School, 1977–2007; *b* 6 Feb. 1946; *s* of Arthur and Betty McIntosh. *Educ:* Ebury Sch.; Shoreditch Coll.; Sussex Univ. (MA). The London Oratory School: Asst Master, 1967–71; Dep. Headmaster, 1971–77. Additional Mem., HMC, 1986–2007; Member: Centre for Policy Studies Educn Gp, 1982–99; Inst. of Econ. Affairs Educn Adv. Council, 1988–91; Health Educn Council, 1985–88; Nat. Curriculum Council, 1990–93; Adv. Cttee, Nat. Curriculum Rev., 2010–13; Teachers' Standards Rev. Cttee, 2010–11; Skills Tests Rev. Panel, 2012–13; Bd, Nat. Coll. for Sch. Leadership, 2012–13; Adv. Cttee, Nat. Coll. for Teaching and Leadership (formerly Teaching Agency), 2012–14; Chm., Commn on Assessment Without Levels, 2015–. Associate Mem. (formerly Consultant Dir), Reform, 2007–. Advr to Leader, Hammersmith and Fulham LBC, 2007–12 (Chm., Bilingual Mgt Cttee, 2009–12); Advr on Free Sch. Applications, 2011–, Mem., Panel of Experts on Assessment, 2015, DfE. University of Buckingham: Vis. Tutor, 2004–10; Mem., Council, 2014– (Vice Chm., 2014–); Prof. of Professional Practice in Educn, 2018–. Member: Abbot's Adv. Council, Ampleforth Coll., 1997–2010 (Chm., Educn Cttee, 2007–10); Educn Cttee, David Ross Educn Trust, 2013–15; Interim Exec. Bd, Hurlingham and Chelsea Sch., 2014–15; Interim Exec. Bd, Langford Sch., 2014–; Chm., Mgt Intervention Bd, St Francis of Assisi Sch., Kensington, 2013–15. Dean, Acad. of St Cecilia, 2005– (Hon. Fellow, 2000); Trustee: The Oratory, Oxford, 2003–; English Schs Orch. and Choir, 2007–; London Oratory Schola Foundn, 2007–13; Trustee/Director: WLFS Multi Academy Trust, 2013–15; Hackney New Schs Trust, 2016–. Governor and Trustee: St Philip's Prep. Sch., 1985– (Chm., 2007–); More House Sch., 2008–; Governor: W London Free Sch., 2011–13 (Advr, Steering Cttee, 2010–11); Holy Cross Primary Sch., 2011–13. Hon. Pres., Knowledge Schs Trust (formerly W London Free Sch. Trust), 2014–. Mem., Catholic Union of GB, 1978–. FRSA 1981. Hon. FCP 1998; FCollT 2017. Hon.

DLitt Westminster, 2016. Knight of Merit with Star, Sacred Military Constantinian Order of St George, 2011 (Mem., Council of Delegn of GB and Ireland, 2015). *Recreations:* music, opera, ballet, theatre, playing the organ, architecture and design, photography. *Address:* Apartment 1602, 251 Southwark Bridge Road, SE1 6FL. *E:* cantemus@mac.com. *Club:* Athenæum.

**MACINTOSH, Rt Hon. Kenneth;** PC 2016; Member for Scotland West, Scottish Parliament; Presiding Officer, Scottish Parliament, since 2016; *b* 15 Jan. 1962; *s* of Dr Farquhar Macintosh, CBE; *m* 1998, Claire, *d* of Douglas and Deirdre Kinloch Anderson; two *s* four *d*. *Educ:* Royal High Sch., Edinburgh; Edinburgh Univ. (MA Hons History). Sen. Broadcast Journalist in News and Current Affairs, BBC, 1987–99. MSP (Lab) Eastwood, 1999–2016, Scotland W, 2016, when elected Presiding Officer. *Recreations:* sport (including football, tennis and golf), music, reading. *Address:* Suite 10, 1 Spiersbridge Way, Thornliebank, Glasgow G46 8NG. *T:* (0141) 620 6310.

**McINTOSH, Lyndsay June;** JP; Chairman, Central Scotland Rape Crisis and Sexual Abuse Centre, 2003–08; *b* 12 June 1955; *d* of Lawrence S. and Mary Clark (*née* Calderwood); *m* 1981, Gordon McIntosh; one *s* one *d*. *Educ:* Duncanrig Sen. Secondary Sch.; Dundee Coll. of Technology (Dip. Mgt Studies). Legal Secretary, 1973–75; Civil Servant, Inland Revenue, 1975–84; business consultant, 1996–99. Lay Inspector of Schools, 1994–99. Mem. (C) Central Scotland, Scottish Parlt, 1999–2003; Cons. spokesman on justice, 1999–2001, on social justice, equal opportunities and women's issues, 2001–03; Dep. Convenor, Justice 2 Cttee, 2001. Sec., Assoc. of former Mems of Scottish Parlt, 2003–18. Mem., N Lanarks Justices Cttee, 2004–08. JP: N Lanarks, 1993–2008; S Strathclyde, Dumfries and Galloway, 2008. Sec., Tannochside Action Gp. *Publications:* articles on social affairs in newspapers and magazines. *Recreations:* reading, weeding, feeding, travel, stadium concerts, karaoke, Rock Choir, Scottish Police Community Choir, supporting Sir Andy Murray. *Address:* 35 Lynnhurst, Uddingston, Glasgow G71 6SA.

**McINTOSH, Melinda Jane Frances;** *see* Letts, M. J. F.

**McINTOSH, Dr Neil;** Edward Clarke Professor of Child Life and Health, University of Edinburgh, 1987–2007, now Emeritus; *b* 21 May 1942; *s* of William and Dorothy McIntosh; *m* 1967, Sheila Ann Clarke; two *s* one *d*. *Educ:* University College Hosp., London (MB BS; DSc Med 1995); Univ. of Southampton (BSc). Sen. Registrar in Paediatrics, UCH, 1973–78; Res. Fellow in Paediatric Endocrinology, Univ. of Calif, San Francisco, 1975–76; Sen. Lectr and Consultant Paediatrician, St George's Hosp. and Med. Sch., 1978–87; Hon. Consultant Paediatrician, Royal Hosp. for Sick Children, Edinburgh, 1987–2007; Hon. Neonatologist, Royal Infirmary, Edinburgh, 1987–2007. Consultant Advr in Neonatology to British Army, 1984–2007. Pres., European Soc. for Pediatric Res., 1993–94; Trustee, Internat. Pediatric Res. Foundn, 1993–97 (Chm., 1995–96); Scientific Vice-Pres., RCPCH, 2002–07. Editor, Current Topics in Neonatology, 1996–2000. *Publications:* (ed with A. G. M. Campbell) Forfar and Arneil's Textbook of Paediatrics, 4th edn 1993, 7th edn (ed with P. Helms and R. Smyth) 2008. *Recreations:* music, family. *Address:* 33 Thomas More House, Barbican, EC2Y 8BT. *T:* (020) 7374 2771.

**McINTOSH, Neil Scott Wishart,** CBE 2013; Chief Executive, CfBT Education Trust (formerly Centre for British Teachers), 1990–2012; *b* 24 July 1947; *s* of William Henderson McIntosh and Mary Catherine McIntosh; *m* 1st, 1971, Genista Mary Tandy (*see* Baroness McIntosh of Hudnall) (marr. diss. 1990); one *s* one *d*; 2nd, 1991, Melinda Jane Frances Letts, *qv*; one *s* one *d*. *Educ:* Merchiston Castle Sch., Edinburgh; Univ. of York (BA Politics); London Sch. of Econs (MSc Industrial Relations). Res. Associate, PEP, 1969–73; Res. Dir, Southwark Community Develt Proj., 1973–76; Dir, Shelter, 1976–84; Dir, VSO, 1985–90. Councillor, London Bor. of Camden, 1971–77; Chm., Housing Cttee, 1974–76. Dir, Stonham Housing Assoc., 1982–98. Vice Pres., BSA, 1985–91. Founder and Chm., Homeless Internat., 1988–91; Chm., Campaign for Freedom of Information, 2008– (Treas., 1984–2008; Co-Chm., 1997–2008); Mem., Independent Broadcasting Telethon Trust, 1987–94. Trustee: HOST, 2004–10; CfBT Advice and Guidance, 2012–18; Chair, Trustees, Access Project, 2013–18; President: CfBT Schs Trust, 2013–; Centre for Educn Econs (formerly Centre for the Study of Market Reform of Educn), 2015–. Governor: Langtree Sch., Oxon, 2006–; St Andrews Sch., Pangbourne, 2010–; All Saints Free Sch., Reading, 2013–15; Chair of Govs, Oakfield Sch., Dulwich, 2012. Hon. Fellow, Dept of Educn, Univ. of Oxford, 2010–19. *Publications:* The Right to Manage?, 1971, 2nd edn 1976. *Recreations:* golf, sailing, theatre. *E:* nswmcintosh@gmail.com. *Clubs:* Goring and Streatley Golf; Plockton Sailing.

**McINTOSH, Sir Neil (William David),** Kt 2000; CBE 1990; New Zealand Honorary Consul for Scotland, since 2014; *b* 30 Jan. 1940; *s* of Neil and Beatrice McIntosh; *m* 1965, Marie Elizabeth Lindsay; one *s* two *d*. *Educ:* King's Park Sen. Secondary Sch., Glasgow. ACIS 1967; FCIPD (FIPM 1987). J. & P. Coats, 1957–59; Outward Bound, Moray Sea Sch., 1958 (Gold Award); Honeywell Controls, 1959–62; Berks, Oxford and Reading Jt O&M Unit, 1962–64; Stewarts & Lloyds, 1964–66; Sen. O&M Officer, Lanark CC, 1966–69; Estabt/O&M Officer, Inverness CC, 1969–75; Personnel Officer, 1975–81, Dir of Manpower Services, 1981–85, Highland Regl Council; Chief Executive: Dumfries and Galloway Regl Council, 1985–92; Strathclyde Regl Council, 1992–96; Convener, Scottish Council for Voluntary Orgns, 1996–2001. Chairman: Commn on Local Govt and Scottish Parlt, 1998–99; Judicial Appts Bd for Scotland, 2002–08. Mem. Bd, British Telecom, Scotland, 1998–2003. Chm., Nat. Cos Contact Gp, 1996–98; Hd, COSLA Consultancy, 1996–99. Scottish Advr, Joseph Rowntree Foundn, 2000–05; Expert Advr, NI Review of Public Admin, 2002–05; Ind. Reviewer, Scottish Parlt MSP Expenses Scheme, 2009; Mem., Scottish Parlt Ind. Budget Review Panel, 2010. Chief Counting Officer, Scottish Parlt Referendum, 1997; Mem., UK Electoral Commn, 2001–08; Civil Service Comr, 2008–13. Trustee: Nat. Museums Scotland (formerly Nat. Museums of Scotland), 1999–2008; Dumfries Theatre Royal Trust, 2003–06. Member: Comunn na Gàidhlig Wkg Gp on Status of Gaelic Lang., 2000–03; BBC Audience Council for Scotland, 2008–11; Bd, Nat. Library of Scotland, 2014– (Vice-Chm., 2016–18); Ind. Mem., Crichton Campus Liaison Gp, 2011–17. DL Dumfries, 1998. FRSA 1989. Hon. DHL Syracuse Univ., USA, 1993; Hon. LLD Glasgow Caledonian, 1999. *Recreations:* antique bottle collecting, bowling, local history, hill walking, dry stane dyking, curling.

**McINTOSH, Dr Robert,** CBE 2013; Director, Forestry Commission Scotland (formerly Director, Scottish Forestry Commission), 2003–15, and Director, Environment and Forestry, Scottish Government, 2012–15; *b* 6 Oct. 1951; *s* of Robert Hamilton McIntosh and Kathleen McIntosh. *Educ:* Linlithgow Acad.; Edinburgh Univ. (BSc Hons 1973; PhD 1985); MICFor 1974. Dist Officer, 1973–78, Res. Project Leader, 1979–84, Forestry Commn; Forest Dist Manager, Kielder Forest, 1984–94; Forest Enterprise: Dir, Ops, 1994–97; Chief Exec., 1997–2003. Mem. Bd, Highlands and Is Enterprise, 2016–. Tenant Farming Comr, Scottish Land Commn, 2017–. *Publications:* papers and articles in forestry jls. *Recreations:* shooting, stalking, farming. *Club:* Farmers.

**MacINTOSH, Sarah,** CMG 2009; HM Diplomatic Service; UK Permanent Representative, UK Delegation to NATO, since 2017; *b* 7 Aug. 1969. Entered FCO, 1991; Third Sec., UK Mission to UN, Vienna, 1994–95; Second Sec. (Econ./EU), Madrid, 1996–97; First Sec., FCO, 1997–2000, UK Mission to UN, NY, 2000–02; FCO, 2002–04; UN Interim Admin Mission, Kosovo, 2004–05; High Comr to Sierra Leone, and Ambassador (non resident) to Liberia, 2006–08; Fellow, Weatherhead Center for Internat. Affairs, Harvard Univ., 2008–09; Dir, Defence and Internat. Security, FCO, 2011–14; Dir Gen., Defence and Intelligence, FCO, 2014–17. *Address:* c/o Foreign and Commonwealth Office, King Charles Street, SW1A 2AH.

**McINTOSH, Stuart;** Senior Telecoms Advisor, KPMG, since 2015; *b* Bellshill, Scotland, 28 Oct. 1951; *s* of Peter and Mary McIntosh; *m* 1996, Helen Jean Brass; one *d*. *Educ:* London Sch. of Econs (BSc Econs, MSc Econs). Partner, Coopers & Lybrand, then PricewaterhouseCoopers, 1990–2000; Sen. Vice Pres., Adventis, 2000–04; Partner, IBM Global Consulting Services, 2004–08; Partner, Competition, and Bd Mem., Ofcom, 2008–14. *Recreations:* guitar, theatre, reading, running. *T:* 07834 432065.

**MacINTYRE, Prof. Alasdair Chalmers;** Research Professor of Philosophy, 2000–10, now Emeritus and Senior Fellow, Center for Ethics and Culture, since 2010, University of Notre Dame; Senior Fellow, Centre for Contemporary Aristotelian Studies in Ethics and Politics, London Metropolitan University, since 2010; *b* 12 Jan. 1929; *o s* of Eneas John MacIntyre, MD (Glasgow), and Margaret Emily Chalmers, MB, ChB (Glasgow); *m* 1977, Lynn Sumida Joy; one *s* three *d* by previous marriages. *Educ:* Epsom Coll. and privately; Queen Mary Coll., Univ. of London (Fellow, 1984); Manchester Univ. BA (London); MA (Manchester); MA (Oxon). Lectr in Philosophy of Religion, Manchester Univ., 1951–57; Lectr in Philosophy, Leeds Univ., 1957–61; Research Fellow, Nuffield Coll., Oxford, 1961–62; Sen. Fellow, Council of Humanities, Princeton Univ., 1962–63; Fellow and Preceptor in Philosophy, University Coll., Oxford, 1963–66; Prof. of Sociology, Univ. of Essex, 1966–70; Prof. of History of Ideas, Brandeis Univ., 1970–72; Univ. Prof. in Philos. and Political Sci., Boston Univ., 1972–80; Luce Prof., Wellesley Coll., 1980–82; W. Alton Jones Prof. of Philosophy, Vanderbilt Univ., 1982–88; McMahon/Hank Prof. of Philosophy, Univ. of Notre Dame, Indiana, 1988–94; Arts and Scis Prof. of Phil., Duke Univ., 1995–2000. Mem., Amer. Philosophical Soc., 2006; Pres., Eastern Div., Amer. Phil Assoc., 1984. Fellow, Amer. Acad. of Arts and Scis, 1985; Corresp. FBA, 1994. Hon. Mem., Phi Beta Kappa, 1973. Hon. MRIA 2000. Hon. DHL: Swarthmore, 1983; New School, 1996; Duke, 2010; Hon. DLit: QUB, 1988; Williams Coll., Mass, 1993; Marquette, 2000; Aberdeen, 2001; UCD, 2009; DU Essex, 1990; Hon. DPhil Maynooth, 2002. *Publications:* Marxism and Christianity, 1954 (revised, 1968); New Essays in Philosophical Theology (ed, with A. G. N. Flew), 1955; Metaphysical Beliefs (ed), 1956; The Unconscious: a conceptual analysis, 1958; A Short History of Ethics, 1965; Secularisation and Moral Change, 1967; Marcuse: an exposition and a polemic, 1970; Sociological Theory and Philosophical Analysis (ed with D. M. Emmet), 1971; Against the Self-Images of the Age, 1971; After Virtue, 1981; Whose Justice? Which Rationality?, 1988; Three Rival Versions of Moral Enquiry, 1990; Dependent Rational Animals, 1999; Edith Stein: a philosophical prologue, 2005; The Tasks of Philosophy: selected essays vol. 1, 2006; Ethics and Politics: selected essays vol. 2, 2006; God, Philosophy, Universities, 2009; Ethics in the the Conflicts of Modernity, 2016. *Address:* Philosophy Department, University of Notre Dame, 100 Malloy Hall, Notre Dame, IN 46556, USA.

**McINTYRE, Sir Alister;** *see* McIntyre, Sir M. A.

**McINTYRE, Anthea Elizabeth Joy, (Mrs Frank Myers);** Member (C) West Midlands, European Parliament, since Dec. 2011; *b* London, 29 June 1954; *d* of David Scott McIntyre and Joy Irma Stratford McIntyre; *m* 1999, Frank Myers, MBE. *Educ:* Claremont Sch., Esher; Queens Coll., Harley St, London. Partner, Wythall Estate, 1976–; MCP Systems Consultants (formerly MCP Management Consultants): consultant, 1985–91; Partner, 1991–2011; Dir, 2011–; Dir, Myers Rd Safety Ltd, 2018–. Vice Pres. and Mem. Bd, Cons. Party, 2016–18. *Recreations:* gardening, wildlife photography, family, Scottish country dancing, cooking. *Address:* Wythall, Walford, Ross-on-Wye HR9 5SD. *T:* (01989) 769544. *E:* anthea@antheamcintyre.com.

**MACINTYRE, Benedict Richard Pierce;** writer; Associate Editor, since 1995, and Writer at Large, since 2001, The Times; *b* Oxford, 25 Dec. 1963; *s* of Angus Macintyre and Joanna Macintyre; *m* 1993, Kate Muir (marr. diss. 2017); two *s* one *d*. *Educ:* Abingdon Sch.; St John's Coll., Cambridge (BA Hist. 1985); Columbia Univ., NY (MA Internat. Affairs 1990). The Times: New York Corresp., 1991–95; Paris Corresp., 1995–98; Chief, Washington Bureau, 1998–2001. Pres., Johnian Soc., 2011–13. *Publications:* Forgotten Fatherland, 1992; Napoleon of Crime, 1997; A Foreign Field, 2001; Josiah the Great, 2004; Agent Zigzag, 2007; For Your Eyes Only, 2008; The Last Word, 2009; Operation Mincemeat, 2010; Double Cross, 2012; A Spy Among Friends: Kim Philby and the great betrayal, 2014; SAS Rogue Heroes, 2016; The Spy and the Traitor: the greatest espionage story of the Cold War, 2018. *Recreations:* cricket, sheep farming. *Address:* The Times, 1 London Bridge Street, SE1 9GF. *T:* (020) 7782 5000. *Club:* MCC.

**McINTYRE, Blanche Phoebe Katharine;** theatre director; *b* London, 5 Sept. 1980; *d* of Grant James McIntyre and Dame Helen (Jean Sutherland) Fraser, *qv*. *Educ:* St Paul's Girls' Sch., London; Corpus Christi Coll., Oxford (BA Hons 1st cl. Lit.Hum. 2003). Productions include: Accolade, Foxfinder, Finborough, 2011 (Most Promising Newcomer, Critics' Circle Awards, 2011); The Birthday Party, Royal Exchange, Manchester, 2013; Ciphers, Out of Joint, 2013; The Seagull, Headlong, Nuffield, 2013 (Best Dir, UK Theatre Awards, 2013); The Comedy of Errors, Shakespeare's Globe, 2014; Tonight at 8:30, Nuffield, 2014; Accolade, St James, 2014; Arcadia, Theatre Royal, Brighton, 2015; As You Like It, Shakespeare's Globe, 2015; The Oresteia, Home, Manchester, 2015; Welcome Home, Captain Fox!, Donmar Warehouse, 2016; Noises Off, Nottingham Playhouse, 2016; The Two Noble Kinsmen, RSC, 2016; Tosca, English Touring Opera, 2017; Titus Andronicus, RSC, 2017; The Norman Conquests, Chichester Fest. Th., 2017; The Marriage of Figaro, English Touring Opera, 2018; The Writer, Almeida, 2018; The Winter's Tale, Shakespeare's Globe, 2018; Women in Power, Nuffield, 2018; Tartuffe, Lyttelton Th., 2019; Bartholomew Fair, Sam Wanamaker Th., 2019. Winner, Leverhulme Bursary for Emerging Th. Dirs (inaugural), 2009. *Address:* c/o United Agents, 12–26 Lexington Street, W1F 0LE.

**McINTYRE, Derrick William McEwen,** TD 1980; Sheriff of Lothian and Borders at Jedburgh and Duns, 2013–14 (at Edinburgh, 2000–13); *b* 16 June 1944; *s* of Lt Col Donald and Rosemary McIntyre; *m* 1973, Janet Anna Fraser; one *d* (and one *s* one *d* decd). *Educ:* Wellington Coll.; St Andrews Univ. (LLB). Lieut, 6th Gurkha Rifles, 1966–68; Major, Black Watch (RHR), 1969–85. Solicitor in private practice, 1973–2000; Temp. Sheriff, 1982–2000. Mem., Queen's Body Guard for Scotland (Royal Co. of Archers), 1994–. *Recreations:* riding, shooting, fishing, golf. *Address:* Mainsfield, Mainsfield Avenue, Morebattle, Kelso, Roxburghshire TD5 8QW. *T:* (01573) 440254.

**McINTYRE, Sir Donald (Conroy),** Kt 1992; CBE 1985 (OBE 1977); opera singer, free-lance; *b* 22 Oct. 1934; *s* of George Douglas McIntyre and Mrs Hermyn McIntyre; *m*; three *d*; *m* 2014, Bettina Jablonski. *Educ:* Mount Albert Grammar Sch.; Auckland Teachers' Trng Coll.; Guildhall Sch. of Music. Debut in Britain, Welsh National Opera, 1959; Sadler's Wells Opera, many roles, 1960–67; Royal Opera, Covent Garden, from 1967; also Vienna, Bayreuth, La Scala, Milan and Metropolitan, NY. Principal roles: Barak, in Die Frau Ohne Schatten, Strauss; Wotan and Wanderer, in The Ring, Wagner; Hollander, Wagner; Hans

Sachs, in Die Meistersinger von Nürnberg, Wagner; Heyst, in Victory, Richard Rodney Bennett; Macbeth, Verdi; Scarpia, in Tosca, Puccini; Count, in Figaro, Mozart; Doctor, in Wozzeck, Berg; title role in Cardillac, Hindemith; Rocco, in Fidelio; Prospero, in Un Re in Ascolto, Berio; Balstrode, in Peter Grimes, Britten; Bayreuth: Wotan, Wanderer, Hollander; Telramund, in Lohengrin; Klingsor, Amfortas and Gurnemanz in Parsifal; Bayreuth Centenary Ring, 1976–81. *Video and films include:* Der Fliegende Holländer, 1975; Electra, 1976; Die Meistersinger, 1984; Bayreuth Centenary Ring, 1976–81; recordings include Pelléas et Mélisande, Il Trovatore, The Messiah, Oedipus Rex, The Ring, Beethoven's 9th Symphony, Damnation of Faust, Bayreuth Centenary Ring. Fidelio Award, 1989. *Publications:* The Only Way is Up, 2019. *Recreations:* gardening, swimming, tennis, farming.

**MACINTYRE, Donald John;** journalist and author; *b* 27 Jan. 1947; *s* of Kenneth Mackenzie Campbell Macintyre and Margaret Macintyre (*née* Freeman); one *s*. *Educ:* Bradfield Coll.; Christ Church, Oxford (BA Lit.Hum.); UC, Cardiff (Dip. Journalism Studies). Reporter, Sunday Mercury, 1971–75; Industrial Reporter, Daily Express, 1975–77; Labour Corresp., The Times, 1977–83; Labour Editor: Sunday Times, 1983–85; The Times, 1985–86; Independent, 1986–87; Political Editor: Sunday Telegraph, 1987–89; Sunday Correspondent, 1989–90; Independent on Sunday, 1990–93; Independent: Pol Ed., 1993–96; Chief Pol Commentator, 1996–2004; Asst Ed., 2003–04; Jerusalem Correspondent, 2004–12; Parly Sketchwriter, 2012–15. Academic Visitor, St Antony's Coll., Oxford, 2016–17. New Century Foundn Peace Through Media Award, 2011. *Publications:* Talking about Trade Unions, 1979; (jtly) Strike!, 1985; Mandelson and the Making of New Labour, 1999; Gaza: preparing for dawn, 2017. *Recreations:* cinema, swimming, bad chess. *Address:* 29 Crescent Grove, SW4 7AF. *Clubs:* Garrick, Soho House.

**McINTYRE, Dame Helen Jean Sutherland;** *see* Fraser, Dame H. J. S.

**MACINTYRE, Iain Melfort Campbell,** MD; FRCSE, FRCPE; FSAScot; Consultant Surgeon, Edinburgh, 1979–2004; Surgeon to the Queen in Scotland, 1997–2004; *b* 23 June 1944; *s* of John Macintyre, MA, BD, FSAScot and Mary (née Campbell); *m* 1969, Tessa Lorna Mary Millar; three *d*. *Educ:* Daniel Stewart's Coll., Edinburgh; Edinburgh Univ. (MB ChB 1968; MD 1992). FRCSE 1974; FRCPE 1997. FSAScot 1997. Lectr in Surgery, Edinburgh Univ., 1974–78; Vis. Prof., Univ. of Natal, 1978–79; Consultant Surgeon: Leith Hosp., 1979–85; Western Gen. Hosp., 1985–2002; Royal Infirmary, Edinburgh, 2002–04. Royal College of Surgeons of Edinburgh: Mem. Council, 1991–2000; Dir of Educn and Wade Prof., 1997–2000; Hon. Sec., 2000–04; Vice Pres., 2003–06. Mem., Nat. Med. Adv. Cttee, 1992–95. Treas., Scottish Soc. of the Hist. of Medicine, 2010–15; Pres., British Soc. for the Hist. of Medicine, 2015–17.

**McINTYRE, Jennifer Louise;** *see* Armstrong, J. L.

**McINTYRE, (John) Paul;** Managing Director, E-Serve, Office of Gas and Electricity Markets, 2010–11; *b* 4 Dec. 1951; *s* of John McIntyre and Julia McIntyre; *m* 1984, Jennifer Eastabrook; two *d*. *Educ:* Austin Friars, Carlisle; Churchill Coll., Cambridge (BA Econs); King's Coll. London (MA Mod. Hist. 2013). Joined HM Treasury, 1974: on secondment to: UK Delegn to IMF/IBRD, Washington, 1977–78; Hambros Bank, City of London, 1983–85; Assistant Secretary: Social Security Policy, 1987–90; Monetary and Debt Mgt Policy, 1990–94; Dir, European Policy, 1995–99; Department of Trade and Industry: Dep. Dir Gen., Enterprise and Innovation, Regions (Business Gp), 2000–03; Hd, British Energy Team, 2003–04; Dir, Energy Strategy Unit (Energy Gp), 2004–05; Hd, Energy Policy Rev. Team, 2005–07; Hd, Energy Strategy and Internat. Unit, then Dir, Energy Security and Mkts, DTI, later BERR, then DECC, 2007–09; Dir, Resilience and Risk, DECC, 2009–10. *Recreations:* family, cricket, reading, history, music. *Clubs:* MCC; Mandarins Cricket.

**McINTYRE, Sir (Meredith) Alister,** Kt 1992; Chairman, Agency for Reconstruction and Development, Grenada, 2004–05; Chief Technical Advisor, Caribbean Regional Negotiating Machinery, Kingston, Jamaica, 1998–2001; *b* Grenada, 29 March 1932; *s* of Meredith McIntyre and Cynthia Eileen McIntyre; *m* Marjorie Hope; three *s* one *d*. *Educ:* LSE (BSc (Econ) 1st Cl. Hons 1957); Nuffield Coll., Oxford (BLitt 1963). Fulbright-Hays Fellow, Columbia Univ., 1963–64; Asst Prof., Woodrow Wilson Sch. of Public Affairs, Princeton Univ., 1962; University of the West Indies: Lectr in Economics, 1960–64; Sen. Lectr and Chm. of Social Scis, 1964–67; Dir, Inst. of Social and Econ. Res., 1964–74; Sec.-Gen., Caribbean Community Secretariat, 1974–77; Dir, Commodities Div., UNCTAD, 1977–82; Dep. Sec.-Gen., UNCTAD, 1982–87; Asst Sec.-Gen., UN, 1987–88. Vice-Chancellor, Univ. of West Indies, 1988–98. Hon. LLD: West Indies, 1980; Sheffield, 1995; Toronto, 1996. Comdr, Order of Distinction (Jamaica), 1975; Cacique's Crown of Honour (Guyana), 1978; Order of Merit (Jamaica), 1992; Order of the Caribbean Community, 1994. *Publications:* The Caribbean and the Wider World: commentaries on my life and career, 2016. *Recreations:* swimming, sailing, reading.

**McINTYRE, Michael;** *see* McIntyre, T. M.

**McINTYRE, Prof. Michael Edgeworth,** PhD; FRS 1990; Professor of Atmospheric Dynamics, Cambridge University, 1993–2008, now Emeritus; Co-director, Cambridge Centre for Atmospheric Science, 1992–2003; *b* 28 July 1941; *s* of Archibald Keverall McIntyre and Anne Hartwell McIntyre; *m* 1968, Ruth Hecht; one step *d* two step *s*. *Educ:* King's High School, Dunedin, NZ; Univ. of Otago, NZ; Trinity Coll., Cambridge. PhD Cantab 1967 (geophysical fluid dynamics); postdoctoral Fellow, Woods Hole Oceanographic Inst., 1967. Research Associate, Dept of Meteorology, MIT, 1967; Cambridge University: Asst Dir of Research, 1969; Res. Fellow, St John's Coll., 1968–71; Univ. Lectr, 1972; Reader in Atmospheric Dynamics, 1987; SERC, then EPSRC, Sen. Res. Fellow, 1992–97. Member: Atmospheric Sci. Cttee, NERC, 1989–94; Sci. Steering Gp, UK Univs Global Atmos. Modelling Prog., NERC, 1990–2002; Workshop on Tropical Cyclone Disasters, IUTAM/IUGG/ICSU, 1990–91; Scientific Steering Cttee, STRATEOLE experiment, 1992–2002; Scientific Adv. Cttee and Organizing Cttee, Prog. on Maths of Atmosphere and Ocean Dynamics, Isaac Newton Inst., 1995–96. Member: Academia Europaea, 1989; Eur. Geophys. Soc., later Eur. Geoscis Union (Julius Bartels Medal, 1999); Amer. Geophys. Union (Fellow, 2011); FRMetS; Fellow, Amer. Met. Soc., 1991 (Carl-Gustaf Rossby Res. Medal, 1987; Haurwitz Meml Lect., 2013); FAAAS 1999. *Publications:* numerous papers in professional jls, incl. papers on lucidity principles. *Recreation:* music. *Address:* Centre for Mathematical Sciences, Wilberforce Road, Cambridge CB3 0WA. *W:* www.atm.damtp.cam.ac.uk/people/mem.

**McINTYRE, Prof. Neil,** FRCP; Professor of Medicine, Royal Free Hospital School of Medicine, 1978–99; Hon. Consultant Physician, Royal Free Hospital, 1968–99; *b* 1 May 1934; *s* of John William McIntyre and Catherine (née Watkins); *m* 1966, Wendy Ann Kelsey; one *s* one *d*. *Educ:* Porth County School for Boys; King's Coll. London (BSc 1st Cl. Hons Physiol); King's Coll. Hosp. (MB BS (Hons), MD). House Officer: KCH, 1959; Hammersmith Hosp., 1960; RAF Med. Br. (Flt Lieut), 1960–63; MRC Res. Fellow, Registrar, Lectr in Medicine, Royal Free Hosp., 1963–66; MRC Travelling Fellowship, Harvard Med. Sch., 1966–68; Royal Free Hospital School of Medicine: Sen. Lectr 1968–73, Reader in Medicine 1973–78; Chm., Dept of Medicine, 1983–94; Vice Dean, 1993–96; Dir of Med. Educn, UCL Med. Sch. and Royal Free Hosp. Sch. of Med., 1993–95. Non-exec. Dir, N Middlesex Hosp. NHS Trust, 1991–96. Pres., Hist. of Medicine Soc. of Wales, 2007. FRSocMed 1968. Liveryman, Soc. of Apothecaries, 1971–. Mem., Bd of Govs, Amer. Osler Soc., 2003–06. Sam E. Roberts Medal, Univ. of Kansas Med. Sch., 1980. *Publications:* Therapeutic Agents and the Liver, 1965; The Problem Orientated Medical Record, 1979; Lipids and Lipoproteins, 1990; Clinical Hepatology, 1991; How British Women became Doctors: the story of the Royal Free Hospital and its medical school, 2014; papers on liver disease, lipoprotein metabolism, med. educn, med. history. *Recreations:* reading, medical history, photographing medical statues, golf. *Address:* 7 Butterworth Gardens, Woodford Green, Essex IG8 0BJ. *Club:* Athenæum.

**McINTYRE, Paul;** *see* McIntyre, J. P.

**MACINTYRE, Dame Sarah Jane, (Dame Sally),** DBE 2011 (CBE 2006; OBE 1998); PhD; FRSE; Professor of Social and Public Health Sciences, 2008–14, now Emeritus, and Director, Institute of Health and Wellbeing, 2011–14, University of Glasgow; *b* 27 Feb. 1949; *d* of late Rev. Angus Macintyre and Evelyn Macintyre; *m* 1980, Dr Guy Paul Muhlemann. *Educ:* Univ. of Durham (BA 1970); Bedford Coll., London (MSc 1971); Univ. of Aberdeen (PhD 1976). FRSE 1998. Res. Fellow, Aberdeen Univ., 1971–75; non-clinical scientist, 1975–84, Dir, 1984–2014, MRC Social and Public Health Sciences (formerly Med. Sociology) Unit, Glasgow. Honorary Professor: Univ. of Glasgow, 1991–2008; Univ. of Strathclyde, 2007–10. Member: MRC, 2008–16; Human Tissue Authy, 2016–19. Founder FMedSci 1998. Hon. Fellow, LSHTM, 2003. Hon. MFPHM 1993. Hon. DSc: Aberdeen, 2005; UCL, 2013; Lancaster, 2013. *Publications:* Single and Pregnant, 1977; (jtly) Antenatal Care Assessed, 1985; contrib. jl articles on sociological and public health topics. *Recreations:* mountaineering, rock-climbing, ski-ing, yoga, running. *Address:* c/o Institute of Health and Wellbeing, University of Glasgow, 1 Lilybank Gardens, Glasgow G12 8RZ. *Club:* Pinnacle.

**McINTYRE, (Theodore) Michael;** Senior Executive, HSBC Private Banking, 1996–2001; *b* 9 Dec. 1941; *s* of James Penton McIntyre and Susan E. M. McIntyre; *m* 1969, Jill Yvonne Mander; one *s* one *d*. *Educ:* Marlborough Coll. Hongkong and Shanghai Banking Corporation Ltd: E Malaysia, Kowloon, Japan, Hong Kong and Brazil, 1959–91; Dep. CEO, 1991–92; CEO, 1992–96, UK. SBStJ 1989. *Recreations:* reading, fishing, gardening. *Address:* The Old School House, Everleigh, Marlborough, Wilts SN8 3EY. *T:* (01264) 850512.

**MACINTYRE, William Ian,** CB 1992; Chairman, Council: Incorporated Froebel Educational Institute, 2003–12 (Council Member, 1999–2012); Froebel Trust, 2012–15; *b* 20 July 1943; *s* of late Robert Miller Macintyre, CBE and Florence Mary Macintyre; *m* 1967, Jennifer Mary Pitblado; one *s* two *d*. *Educ:* Merchiston Castle School, Edinburgh; St Andrews University. MA. British Petroleum Co. Ltd, 1965–72; ECGD, 1972–73; DTI, later Dept of Energy, 1973–77; seconded to ICFC, 1977–79; Asst Sec., Dept of Energy, Gas Div., 1979–83; Under-Sec. 1983, Dir-Gen., Energy Efficiency Office, 1983–87; Under Sec., Electricity Div., 1987–88, Electricity Div. B, 1988–91, Dept of Energy; Under Sec., Coal Div., Dept of Energy, then DTI, 1991–94; Head, Telecoms Div., 1994–95, Communications and Inf. Industries Directorate, 1996–2002, DTI. Dir, Templeton Estates, 2002–12. Dep. Chm., Froebel Inst., 2001–03 (Mem. Council, 1999–2012). Pro-Chancellor, Univ. of Roehampton (formerly Univ. of Surrey Roehampton), 2006–11 (Mem. Council, 2000–06; Hon. Fellow, 2012); Governor: Froebel Coll., 2001–07; Ibstock Sch., 2001–12 (Chm. of Govs, 2002–03).

**McISAAC, Ian,** FCA; Finance Director and Registered Treasurer, Conservative Party, 2006–10; *b* Surbiton, 13 July 1945; *s* of Archibald McIsaac and Elsie McIsaac (née Sampson); *m* 1983, Debrah Ball; one *s* one *d*, and one *s* one *d* from previous marriage. *Educ:* Charterhouse (Scholar). FCA 1969. Touche Ross & Co., later Deloitte: Partner, 1979–2005; UK Chm., DTT Emerging Markets, 2000–04; Man. Partner, Global Risk Mgt, Deloitte Touche Tohmatsu, 2003–05. Director: C&UCO Properties Ltd, 2006–11; Jubilee Managing Agency Ltd, 2008–10 (Chm., 2010). Dir, City Disputes Panel, 2004–07. Member: Policy Adv. Gp, DFID, 2004–05; Investment Cttee, NESTA, 2007–09. Founder Chm., Inst. for Turnaround, 2001–04 (Fellow, 2004). UK Chm., Care Internat., 1997–2004. Gov., Sutton's Hosp. in Charterhouse, 2006–13. Trustee, Legacy List, 2012–13. Freeman, City of London, 1993; Liveryman, Chartered Accountants' Co., 1993. *Recreations:* golf, photography, travel, cookery. *Address:* 3 Lennox House, Twickenham, Middx TW1 2TA. *T:* 07770 312518; Parsonage Farm, Pitton, Wilts SP5 1DT. *E:* imcisaac47@gmail.com. *Clubs:* Carlton, Hurlingham; Royal Mid-Surrey Golf.

**McISAAC, Shona;** *b* 3 April 1960; *d* of late Angus McIsaac and of Isa McIsaac; *m* 1994, Peter Keith. *Educ:* St Aidan's Coll., Durham (BSc Geography). Formerly: Lifeguard, Tooting Pool; Sub-Editor: Chat; Bella; Woman; food writer, Slimmer. Mem. (Lab) Wandsworth BC, 1990–98. MP (Lab) Cleethorpes, 1997–2010; contested (Lab) same seat, 2010. Parliamentary Private Secretary: NI Office, 2001–05; to Minister of State, Home Office, 2004–05; to Minister of State, DTI, 2005–06; to Minister of State, DoH, 2006–07. Mem., Select Cttee on Standards and Privileges, 1997–2001. *Recreations:* family and local history, food, football, cycling, archaeology.

**MacIVER, Matthew Macleod,** CBE 2008; UK Independent Member, Committee of Experts, European Charter for Regional or Minority Languages, Council of Europe, since 2013; *b* Portnaguran, Isle of Lewis, 5 July 1944; *s* of Donald and Henrietta MacIver; *m* 1972, Katrina Robertson; one *s* one *d*. *Educ:* Aird Primary Sch.; Nicolson Inst., Stornoway; Edinburgh Univ. (MA 1968; DipEd 1969; MEd 1979). Teacher, Kilmarnock Acad., 1969–71; teacher, 1971–72, Principal Teacher, 1972–80, Craigmount High Sch., Edinburgh; Asst Rector, Royal High Sch., Edinburgh, 1980–83; Depute Head Teacher, Balerno High Sch., Edinburgh, 1983–86; Rector: Fortrose Acad., Ross-shire, 1986–89; Royal High Sch., Edinburgh, 1989–98; Depute Registrar (Educn), 1998–2001, Chief Exec. and Registrar, 2001–08, Gen. Teaching Council for Scotland. Winston Churchill Travelling Fellow, 1998. Chairman: Teachers' Action Gp on Gaelic Medium Educn, 2005; Bòrd na Gàidhlig (Gaelic Lang. Bd), 2006–08. Chm., Gaelic Broadcasting Cttee, 1996–2001; Member: Gaelic Television Cttee, 1991–95; for Scotland, Ofcom Content Bd, 2003–06; BBC Audience Council for Scotland, 2011–17. Mem., Cross Party Gp on Higher and Further Educn, 2009–, on Gaelic, 2009–; Scottish Parlt. Chm., Highlands and Is Educnl Trust, 1994–. Gov., George Watson's College, 2009–17; Chm., Bd of Govs, UHI Millennium Inst., subseq. Univ. Court, UHI, 2009–14. Mem. Cttee, Scottish Assoc. of Churchill Fellows, 2009–13. Mem., Urras Brosnachaidh na Gaidhlig (Gaelic Lang. Promotion Trust), 2017–. Hon. Prof., UHI, 2008 (Hon. Fellow, 2013). Hon. Life Mem., Scottish Secondary Teachers' Assoc., 2008. FEIS 2004. Hon. Dhc Aberdeen, 2008; Hon. DEd Edinburgh, 2008. *Publications:* (with A. Hogg) Industry-Coal and Iron 1700–1900, 1977; (contrib.) Scottish Education, 2nd edn 2003, 3rd edn 2008; (contrib.) Report of the Gaelic Medium Teachers' Action Group, 2005; (ed with M. Nicolson) Policy and Practice in Education: Gaelic Medium Education, Series 10, 2006, trans. as Foghlam tro Mheadhan na Gàidhlig, 2007; Playing for the Red Jersey: a history of Point Football Club, 1934–2014,

2014; The Influence of the Church on Gaelic Education in Lewis, 2017. *Recreations:* reading, Gaelic culture, writing a monthly article for The Rudhach (community newspaper in Lewis), watching Hibernian FC. *Address:* 21 Durham Road, Edinburgh EH15 1NY. *T:* (0131) 669 5029. *Club:* New (Edinburgh).

McIVOR, (Frances) Jane; District Judge (Magistrates' Courts), London, since 2001; *b* NI, 22 Oct. 1959; *d* of Rt Hon. (William) Basil McIvor, OBE, PC (NI) and (Frances) Jill McIvor, CBE; *m* 1988, Girish Thanki; one *s* one *d*. *Educ*: sch. in Belfast; Univ. of E Anglia (LLB 1982). Called to the Bar, Inner Temple, 1983; in practice on S Eastern Circuit; Actg Metropolitan Stipendiary Magistrate, 1998–2001. Chm., Connexional Discipline Cttee, Methodist Church, 2005–. *Recreations:* golf, cooking. *Address:* Thames Magistrates' Court, 58 Bow Road, E3 4DJ.

McIVOR, Sarah Oonagh; see Rapson, S. O.

MACK, Prof. (Brian) John, DPhil; FBA 2009; FSA; Professor of World Art Studies, University of East Anglia, since 2004 (Head, School of World Art and Museology, 2009–12; Chairman, Sainsbury Institute for Art, 2011–15); *b* 10 July 1949; *s* of late Brian Mack and Joan Alexandra Mack (*née* Kelly); *m* 1975, Caroline Jenkins, *d* of late Rev. Dr D. T. Jenkins; one *s* one *d*. *Educ*: Campbell Coll., Belfast; Univ. of Sussex (MA); Merton Coll., Oxford (DPhil 1975). FSA 1994. Res. Asst, 1976, Asst Keeper, 1977, Keeper, 1991–99 and 2002–04, Sen. Keeper, 1998–2002, Dept of Ethnography, BM. Vis. Prof., UCL, 1996–. Member: Council, British Inst. in Eastern Africa, 1981–2017 (Pres., 2005–11; Hon. Life Vice-Pres., 2017); Council, RAI, 1983–86; Council, African Studies Assoc., 1986–88; British Acad. Bd for Academy-sponsored Insts and Schs, 1996–2003; Conseil d'orientation de l'établissement publique de Musée du Quai Branly, Paris, 1999–2000; Pitt-Rivers Cttee, Univ. of Oxford, 2000–12. Trustee: Horniman Mus. and Public Park, 1998–2010; S Asian Decorative Arts and Crafts Collection, Norwich, 2014–; Mem. Bd, Sainsbury Centre for the Visual Arts, 2009–. Chm., Editl Bd, World Art, 2011–; Member, Editorial Board: Art History, 1982–91; Jl of Art Historiography, 2009–. FRSA 2005. Nat. Art Collections Fund Award for Images of Africa, BM, 1991. *Publications:* (with J. Picton) African Textiles (Craft Adv. Council Book of the Year), 1979, 2nd edn 1989; Zulus, 1980; (with P. T. Robertshaw) Culture History in the Southern Sudan, 1982; (with M. D. McLeod) Ethnic Sculpture, 1984; Madagascar, Island of the Ancestors, 1986; Ethnic Jewellery, 1988; Malagasy Textiles, 1989; Emil Torday and the Art of the Congo 1900–1909, 1990; (with C. Spring) African Textile Design, 1991; Masks, the Art of Expression, 1994; (with K. Yoshida) Images of Other Cultures, 1997; Africa, Arts and Cultures, 2000; Museum of the Mind: art and memory in world cultures, 2003; The Art of Small Things, 2007; (with K. Yoshida) Preserving the Cultural Heritage of Africa: crisis or renaissance, 2008; The Sea: a cultural history, 2011; (jtly) From Here to There: the art of Michael Buhler, 2013; The Artfulness of Death in Africa, 2019; articles and revs in learned jls. *Address:* Sainsbury Research Unit, Sainsbury Institute for the Visual Arts, University of East Anglia, Norwich NR4 7TJ. *T:* (01603) 592463.
See also K. M. Jenkins, Sir S. D. Jenkins.

MACK, Prof. Peter, PhD; FBA 2012; Professor of English, University of Warwick, 2001–18. *Educ*: St Peter's Coll., Oxford (BA English Lang. and Lit. 1976); Warburg Inst. (MPhil Combined Histl Studies 1978; PhD 1983); Warwick Univ. (DLitt). Leverhulme Eur. Student, Inst. of Philosophy, Univ. of Rome and Vatican Liby, 1978–79; University of Warwick: Lectr in English and Comparative Lit., Sen. Lectr, then Reader, 1979–2001; Chair: Arts Faculty, 1995–98; English Dept, 2001–04; Prof. of History of Classical Tradition, Univ. of London and Dir, Warburg Inst., 2010–14 (on secondment). Ed., Rhetorica, 1998–2002. *Publications:* (ed with E. Chaney) England and the Continental Renaissance, 1990; Renaissance Argument: Valla and Agricola in the traditions of rhetoric and dialectic, 1993; (ed with C. Walton) The General Prologue to the Canterbury Tales, 1994, 2nd edn 2008; (ed) Renaissance Rhetoric, 1994; (ed with C. Walton) The Miller's Tale, 1995, 2nd edn 2007; (ed with A. Hawkins) The Nun's Priest's Tale, 1996, 2nd edn 2006; Elizabethan Rhetoric: theory and practice, 2002; (contrib.) Medieval Rhetoric, 2004; (contrib.) A Concise Companion to English Renaissance Literature, 2006; (contrib.) The Cambridge Companion to Ancient Rhetoric, 2009; Reading and Rhetoric in Montaigne and Shakespeare, 2010; (contrib.) The Classical Tradition, 2010; A History of Renaissance Rhetoric 1380–1620, 2011; Rhetoric's Questions, Reading and Interpretation, 2017; Reading Old Books: writing with traditions, 2019; articles in jls. *Address:* Humanities Building, University of Warwick, Coventry CV4 7AL.

MACKAY, family name of **Earl of Inchcape, Lord Reay** and **Barons Mackay of Clashfern** and **Tanlaw**.

MACKAY OF CLASHFERN, Baron *cr* 1979 (Life Peer), of Eddrachillis in the District of Sutherland; **James Peter Hymers Mackay**, KT 1997; PC 1979; FRSE 1984; Editor-in-Chief, Halsbury's Laws of England, 1998–2015; Lord High Commissioner, General Assembly, Church of Scotland, 2005–06 and 2006–07; Lord Clerk Register of Scotland and Keeper of the Signet, since 2007; *b* 2 July 1927; *s* of James Mackay and Janet Hymers; *m* 1958, Elizabeth Gunn Hymers; one *s* two *d*. *Educ*: George Heriot's Sch., Edinburgh; Edinburgh Univ. (MA Hons Maths and Nat. Philosophy 1948). Lectr in Mathematics, Univ. of St Andrews, 1948–50; Major Schol., Trinity Coll., Cambridge, in Mathematics, 1947, taken up 1950; Senior Schol. 1951; BA (Cantab) 1952; MA 2016; LLB Edinburgh (with Distinction) 1955. Admitted to Faculty of Advocates, 1955; QC (Scot.) 1965; Standing Junior Counsel to: Queen's and Lord Treasurer's Remembrancer; Scottish Home and Health Dept; Commissioners of Inland Revenue in Scotland; Sheriff Principal, Renfrew and Argyll, 1972–74; Vice-Dean, Faculty of Advocates, 1973–76; Dean, 1976–79; Lord Advocate of Scotland, 1979–84; a Senator of Coll. of Justice in Scotland, 1984–85; a Lord of Appeal in Ordinary, 1985–87; Lord High Chancellor of GB, 1987–97. Chancellor, Heriot-Watt Univ., 1991–2005. Commissary, Univ. of Cambridge, 2003–16. Part-time Mem., Scottish Law Commn, 1976–79. Chairman: Commn for rev. of Law of Mauritius, 1997–98; Commn on Admin of Justice, Trinidad and Tobago, 2000. Mem., Ethics Rev. Cttee, 2006–09, Chm., Wkg Party preparing Guide to Sponsored Res., Internat. Agency for Res. on Cancer, 2006. Hon. Master of the Bench, Inner Temple, 1979. Dir, Stenhouse Holdings Ltd, 1976–77. Mem., Insurance Brokers' Registration Council, 1977–79. A Comr of Northern Lighthouses, 1975–84; Elder Brother of Trinity House, 1990. Fellow: Internat. Acad. of Trial Lawyers, 1979; Amer. Coll. of Trial Lawyers, 1990; Hon. Fellow, Chartered Inst. of Taxation (Fellow, Inst. of Taxation, 1981). Hon. Mem., SPTL, 1986; Hon. Pres., Assoc. of Cons. Peers. Hon. Fellow: Trinity Coll., Cambridge, 1989; Girton Coll., Cambridge, 1990; Hon. FRCSE 1989; Hon. FRCPE 1990; Hon. FRCOG 1996; Hon. FICE 1988. Hon. LLD: Edinburgh, 1983; Dundee, 1983; Strathclyde, 1985; Aberdeen, 1987; St Andrews, 1989; Cambridge, 1989; Coll. of William and Mary, Va, 1989; Birmingham, 1990; Nat. Law Sch. of India, 1994; Bath, 1994; Glasgow, 1994; Leicester, 1996; De Montfort, 1999; Hon. DCL: Newcastle, 1990; Oxford, 1998; Northumbria, 2017; Hon. Dr jur Robert Gordon, 2000. Royal Medal, RSE, 2003. *Publications:* Armour on Valuation for Rating, 5th edn (Consultant Editor), 1985. *Recreations:* walking, travel. *Address:* House of Lords, SW1A 0PW. *Clubs:* Athenæum; Caledonian; New (Edinburgh).

MACKAY, Prof. Alan Lindsay, FRS 1988; Professor of Crystallography, Birkbeck College, University of London, 1986–91, now Emeritus; *b* 6 Sept. 1926; *s* of Robert Lindsay Mackay, OBE, MC, BSc, MD and Margaret Brown Mackay, OBE, MB ChB, JP; *m* 1951, Sheila Thorne Hague, MA; two *s* one *d*. *Educ*: Wolverhampton Grammar Sch.; Oundle Sch.; Trinity Coll., Cambridge (BA, MA); Univ. of London (BSc, PhD, DSc). Lectr, Reader, Prof., Dept of Crystallography, Birkbeck Coll., 1951–91. Visiting Professor: Univ. of Tokyo, 1969; Univ. of Tsukuba, 1980; Korean Advanced Inst. of Sci. and Tech., 1987; Hon. Professor: Central China Univ.; Sichuan Inst. of Sci. Studies; China Inst. for Sci. Studies. Foreign Member: Academia Mexicana de Ciencias, 1998; Korean Acad. of Sci. and Technol., 1999. Oliver E. Buckley Prize for Condensed Matter Physics, APS, 2010. *Publications:* The Harvest of a Quiet Eye, 1977; (with A. N. Barrett) Spatial Structure and the Microcomputer, 1987; (ed) A Dictionary of Scientific Quotations, 1991; (with E. A. Lord and S. Ranganathan) New Geometries for New Materials, 2006; papers in learned jls. *Recreation:* Asian studies. *Address:* 22 Lanchester Road, N6 4TA. *T:* (020) 8883 4810.

MacKAY, Rt Hon. Andrew (James); PC 1998; *b* 27 Aug. 1949; *s* of Robert James MacKay and Olive Margaret MacKay; *m* 1st 1975, Diana Joy (*née* Kinchin) (marr. diss. 1996); one *s* one *d*; 2nd, 1997, Julie Kirkbride, *qv*; one *s*. *Educ*: Solihull. MP (C) Birmingham, Stechford, March 1977–1979; contested (C) same seat, 1979; MP (C) Berkshire E, 1983–97, Bracknell, 1997–2010. PPS to Sec. of State for NI, 1986–89, to Sec. of State for Defence, 1989–92; an Asst Govt Whip, 1992–93; a Lord Comr of HM Treasury (Govt Whip), 1993–95; Vice Chamberlain of HM Household, 1995–96; Treasurer of HM Household (Dep. Govt Chief Whip), 1996–97; Opposition front bench spokesman on NI, 1997–2001; Sen. Political and Parly Advr to Leader of Opposition, 2005–09. Member: Environment Select Cttee, 1985–86; Standards and Privileges Cttee, 2002–05; Foreign Affairs Select Cttee, 2004–05; Sec., Cons. Parly For. Affairs Cttee, 1985–86. Dep. Chm., Cons. Party, 2004–05; Mem., Cons. Party Nat. Exec., 1979–82. *Recreations:* golf, tennis, good food. *Clubs:* Berkshire Golf; Aberdovey Golf; Royal & Ancient Golf (St Andrews).

MACKAY, Andrew John, OBE 2006; Regional Director, British Council, European Union, since 2019; *b* 28 July 1960; *s* of John and Margaret Mackay; *m* 1990, Margaret Allport; one *d*. *Educ*: Exeter Univ. (BA Combined Hons 1982); Reading Univ. (MA Dist. 1989); Durham Univ. (MBA 1996). British Council: Asst Dir, Teaching Centre, Cairo, 1983–87; Lang. Advr, London, 1988–89; English Lang. Officer, Peru, 1989–92; Director: Dubai, 1992–96; Barcelona, 1996–2001; USA, 2001–06; Spain, 2015–19; Hd of Strategy and Evaluation, Public Diplomacy Gp, FCO, 2006–08 (on secondment); Hd, Corporate Affairs, and Sec. to British Council, 2008–12; Dir Operations, 2013–15. FRSA 2002. *Recreations:* cinema, literature, Hispanic cultures, walking. *Address:* British Council, Paseo General Martinez Campos 31, 28010 Madrid, Spain. *E:* andrewjmackay@hotmail.com.

MacKAY, Angus; Director, Policy, Partnership and Strategic Direction, MacKay Hannah Ltd, since 2003; *b* 10 Sept. 1964. *Educ*: St Augustine's High Sch., Edinburgh; Edinburgh Univ. (MA Hons Politics and History, 1986). Formerly Campaign Officer, Shelter (Scotland); Parly Asst to Dr Mo Mowlam, 1990–92. Mem. (Lab) City of Edinburgh Council, 1995–99 (Convener, Finance Cttee, 1997–99). Member (Lab) Edinburgh S, Scottish Parlt, 1999–2003; Dep. Minister for Justice, 1999–2000; Minister for Finance and Local Govt, 2000–01. Contested (Lab) Edinburgh S, Scottish Parlt, 2003. *Address:* MacKay Hannah Ltd, Suite 54, Bonnington Bond, 2 Anderson Place, Edinburgh EH6 5NP.

MACKAY, Dr Angus Victor Peck, OBE 1997; PhD; FRCPE, FRCPsych; Chair, Advisory Board on Homeopathic Products, since 2014 and Member, Expert Advisory Group on Patient and Public Engagement, since 2012, Medicines and Healthcare Products Regulatory Agency (Board Member, 2003); Member, Mental Health Tribunal for Scotland, 2005–17; Director, Mental Health Services, Lomond and Argyll Primary Care NHS Trust, 1999–2005; *b* 4 March 1943; *s* of Victor P. Mackay and Christine Mackay (*née* Peck); *m* 1969, Elspeth Margaret Whitton Norris; two *s* two *d*. *Educ*: George Heriot's Sch., Edinburgh; Univ. of Edinburgh (BSc 1st Cl. Hons Pharmacol.; MB ChB 1969); Churchill Coll., Cambridge (PhD 1973). FRCPsych 1983; FRCPE 1989; TPsych 1994. Jun. Res. Fellow, 1970–73, Clin. Res. Fellow, 1973–76, Sen. Clin. Scientist, then Dep. Dir, 1976–80, MRC Neurochem. Pharmacol. Unit, Cambridge; Lector in Pharmacol., Trinity Coll., Cambridge, 1976–80; Physician Superintendent, Argyll and Bute Hosp., 1980–2005. Hon. Fellow in Neurosci., Univ. of Edinburgh, 1999–; Hon. Prof. (formerly MacIntosh Lectr in Psychol Medicine), Glasgow Univ., 1982–. Member: Res. Cttee, Mental Health Foundn UK, 1981–88; Health Services Res. Cttee, 1981–90 (Vice-Chair); Cttee on Safety of Medicines and associated cttees, 1984–2002; Sec. of State's NHS Policy Bd, 1987; UK Panel of Experts to Eur. Cttee on Proprietary and Medicinal Products, 1990–; Scottish Medicines Consortium, 2001–04 (Chm., Appeals Panels, 2012–17); UK Monitoring Gp on Creutzfeldt-Jacob Disease, DHSC (formerly DoH)/MRC, 2002–; Scottish Adv. Cttee on Distinction Awards, 1998–2007; Commn on Human Medicines, 2010–12; Chairman: Wkg Gp on Res. into Care of Dementing Elderly, 1986–87; Scottish Wkg Gp on Mental Illness Services, 1992–96; Wkg Gp on Health Technol. Assessment for Scotland, 1999; Health Technol. Bd for Scotland, 2000–03; Sec. of State for Health's Ind. Scrutiny Panel on Health Services along the Clyde, 2007–09. Mem., Nat. Prion Cohort Steering Cttee, 2009–. Chm., Scientific Adv. Cttee, Sackler Inst. of Psychobiology, 2005–. Member: George Heriot's First Four (stroke) (Scottish Schs Rowing Champions), 1959–62 (Capt. of Boats, George Heriot's Sch.); Edinburgh Univ. First Eight, 1963–66; First Eight, 1970–73, Coxless Pair, 1976–80, Churchill Coll., Cambridge. Jun. Cdre, Fisherrow Yacht Club, 1960–61. Mem., British Dragon Assoc. *Publications:* over 90 contribs to text books and articles in learned jls, on various aspects of neurochem. and neuropharmacol. (particularly schizophrenic illness and drug-associated movement disorder), mental health service organisation, health technology assessment, and medicines regulation. *Recreations:* rowing, sailing (International Dragon), rhododendrons (Mem., American Rhododendron Soc.). *Address:* Tigh-an-Rudha, Ardrishaig, Argyll PA30 8ER. *T:* (01546) 603272, *Fax:* (01546) 602332. *E:* angus.mackay@nhs.net. *Club:* Ardrishaig Boat.

MACKAY, Charles Dorsey, CBE 2013; Chairman, Opera Holland Park, since 2015; *b* 14 April 1940; *s* of late Brig. Kenneth Mackay, CBE, DSO and Evelyn Maud (*née* Ingram); *m* 1964, Annmarie Joder-Pfeiffer; one *s* one *d* (and one *s* decd). *Educ*: Cheltenham Coll.; Queens' Coll., Cambridge (MA); INSEAD (MBA). British Petroleum Co., 1957–69; commercial apprentice, 1957–59; univ. apprentice, Cambridge, 1959–62; marketing assistant, London, 1962–63; Regl Sales Manager, Algeria, 1963–65; Commercial Dir, Burundi/Rwanda/Congo, 1965–68; sponsored at INSEAD, France, 1968–69; McKinsey & Co. Inc., 1969–76: Consultant; Sen. Engagement Manager, 1972–76; worked in London, Paris, Amsterdam, Dar es Salaam; Pakhoed Holding NV, Rotterdam, 1976–81: Dir, 1976–77, Chm., 1977–81, Paktrans Div.; Chloride Group plc, 1981–86: Dir, 1981–86; Chm., Overseas Div., 1981–85; Chm., Power Electronics Div., 1985–86; Inchcape plc, 1986–96: Dir, 1986–96; Chief Exec., 1991–96; Dep. Chm., 1992–96; Chm., Inchcape (Hong Kong) Ltd and Dodwell and Co. Ltd, 1986–87; Chm. and Chief Exec., Inchcape Pacific Ltd, 1987–91. Chairman: DSL Gp Ltd, 1996–97; TDG plc, 2000–08; Eurotunnel Gp, 2001–04 (non-exec. Dir, 1997–2004; Dep. Chm., 1999–2001); Production Services Network Ltd, 2009–11; Dep. Chm., Thistle Hotels plc, 1996–2003; non-executive Director: Union Insurance Soc. of Canton Ltd, 1986–91; Hongkong and Shanghai Banking Corp. Ltd, 1986–92; Midland Bank plc, 1992–93; HSBC Holdings plc, 1992–98; British

Airways plc, 1993–96; Johnson Matthey plc, 1999–2008 (Sen. Ind. Dir); Member: Supervisory Bd, Gucci Gp NV, 1997–2001; Business Bd, House of Habib, 2007–17; Bd, 2000–11, Adv. Council, 2011–, INSEAD. Chm., 2006–15, Hon. Pres., Campaign Bd, 2015–, Historic Royal Palaces. Trustee, Develt Trust (for the mentally handicapped), 1993–2017. *Recreations:* restoring old buildings, travel, fly-fishing, tennis, ski-ing, opera, classical music. *Address:* 4 Ormonde Gate, SW3 4EU. *T:* 07803 796295. *E:* charlesmackay8@gmail.com. *Clubs:* Brooks's, Piscatorial Society; Hong Kong (Hong Kong).

**MacKAY, Colin,** CBE 2001; FRCS, FRCSE, FRCSGlas, FRCP, FRCPI, FFPH, FRCPE; Consultant Surgeon, Western Infirmary/Gartnavel General Hospital, Glasgow, 1982–96; *b* 8 Nov. 1936; *s* of Kenneth MacKay and Margaret Blair Dawson MacKay; *m* 1966, Dr Helen Paul Miskimmin; one *s* two *d*. *Educ:* Univ. of Glasgow (BSc Hons; MB ChB (Commendation)). FRCS 1966; FRCSE 1966; FRCSGlas 1966; FRCP 1999; FRCPI 1999; FFPH (FFPHM 1999); FRCPE 2000. Surgical trng, Western Infirmary, Glasgow, 1961–69; MRC Travelling Fellow, Boston Univ., 1969–70; Sen. Lectr in Surgery, Univ. of Glasgow, 1970–82. Royal College of Physicians and Surgeons of Glasgow: Mem. Council, 1972–; Hon. Treas., 1976–86; Vice Pres., Surgical, 1992–94; Visitor, 1996–97; Pres., 1997–2000. Chm., Bd of Govs, UHI Millennium Inst., 2001–09. FACP 1998; FCMSA 1998; Fellow, Acad. of Medicine, Singapore 1998. *Publications:* (with I. McA. Ledingham) Textbook of Surgical Physiology, 1978, 2nd edn 1988; contribs to med. jls in field of surgical gastroenterology, in general, and peptic ulcer and gallstone disease, in particular. *Recreations:* travel, walking. *Address:* 73 Buchanan Drive, Bearsden, Glasgow G61 2EP. *T:* (0141) 942 8759, 07712 667834.

**MACKAY, Hon. Sir Colin (Crichton),** Kt 2001; a Judge of the High Court, Queen's Bench Division, 2001–13; *b* 26 Sept. 1943; *s* of Sir James Mackerron Mackay, KBE, CB, and Katherine Millar Crichton Mackay (*née* Hamilton); *m* 1969, Rosamond Diana Elizabeth Collins; one *d* two *s*. *Educ:* Radley Coll.; Corpus Christi Coll., Oxford (Open Classical Schol.; MA). Harmsworth Entrance Exhibnr, 1965, and Astbury Schol., 1967; called to the Bar, Middle Temple, 1967, Bencher, 1995; QC 1989, a Recorder, 1992–2001. Member: Special Immigration Appeals Commn, 2003–13; Parole Bd for England and Wales, 2005–11. Mem., Lambeth Horticultural Soc., 2002–. *Recreations:* opera, growing vegetables, Scotland. *Club:* Vincent's (Oxford).

**McKAY, Colin Graham;** Sheriff of North Strathclyde at Kilmarnock, 2001–07; part-time Sheriff, 2007–16; *b* 20 Jan. 1942; *s* of Patrick Joseph McKay and Mary Kieran; *m* 1966, Sandra Anne Coli; one *d* one *s*. *Educ:* St Aloysius' Coll., Glasgow; Clongowes Wood Coll., by Dublin; Univ. of Glasgow (MA, LLB). Admitted Solicitor, 1966; in private practice, 1966–90; Temporary Sheriff, 1985–90; Sheriff of N Strathclyde: (floater), 1990–95; at Oban and Fort William, 1995–2001.

**McKAY, Daithí Gerard;** Head of Advocacy and Campaigns, Royal Society for the Protection of Birds, Northern Ireland, since 2018; *b* 2 March 1982; *s* of Gerard and Anne McKay. *Educ:* St Patrick's Primary Sch., Rasharkin; St Louis Grammar Sch., Ballymena; N Eastern Inst. of Further and Higher Educn, Ballymena; Open Univ. (Dip Soc Scis). Customer Advr, Ulster Bank, 2001–03; Political Advr to Philip McGuigan, MLA, 2003–05. Mem. (SF) Ballymoney BC, 2005. Contested (SF) N Antrim, 2010, 2015. Mem. (SF) N Antrim, NI Assembly, 2007–16. Chm., Finance and Personnel Cttee, NI Assembly, 2012–16. Sen. Engrg Recruitment Consultant, CpI Solutions Internat., 2017–18. Mem., Gaelic Athletic Assoc. *Recreations:* Gaelic games, reading, keeping fit, travelling. *E:* daithimckay@btinternet.com.

**MACKAY, David James,** FCILT; Chief Executive, John Menzies plc, 1997–2003; *b* 20 May 1943; *s* of David Mackay and Lena Mackay (*née* Westwater); *m* 1966, Jane Brown Hunter; one *s* one *d*. *Educ:* Kirkcaldy High Sch.; post experience programmes at Edinburgh and Bradford Univs. FCILT (FCIT 1993). Various exec. posts in John Menzies plc, 1964–2003, including: Transport Manager, NI, 1965; Asst Regl Dir, Southern & London, 1973; Ops Dir, Edinburgh, 1978; Man. Dir, Wholesale, 1984. Chairman: Malcolm Gp, 2003–06; Transport Edinburgh Ltd, 2006–09; Lothian Buses plc, 2010. Mem., Nat. Employer Adv. Bd, 2007–14. Chm., Adv. Gp, Glasgow's Commonwealth Games Bid, 2004–05. CCMI (CIMgt 1998). Hon. Col, Scottish Transport Regt, 2004–11. Pres., Friends of Scottish Rugby, 2014– (Vice Pres., 2004). Chieftain, Inverkeithing Highland Games, 2003–06. *Recreations:* golf, walking. *Address:* 4 East Harbour Road, Charlestown, Fife KY11 3EA. *Clubs:* Caledonian; Bruntsfield Golf (Edinburgh); Aberdour Golf (Fife).

**MACKAY, Derek;** Member (SNP) Renfrewshire North and West, Scottish Parliament, since 2011; Cabinet Secretary for Finance, Economy and Fair Work (formerly Cabinet Secretary for Finance and the Constitution), since 2016; *m*; two *c*. *Educ:* Renfrew High Sch.; Glasgow Univ. Mem. (SNP), Renfrewshire Council, 1999–2011 (Leader, 2007). Researcher for Bruce McFee, MSP, 2003–05. Minister for Local Govt and Planning, 2011–14, for Transport, 2014–16, Scottish Parlt. Non-exec. Dir, Gtr Glasgow and Clyde Health Bd, 2003–11; Chm., Renfrewshire Community Health Partnership, 2007–11. *Address:* Scottish Parliament, Edinburgh EH99 1SP.

**MACKAY, Donald George;** Hon. Research Fellow, Aberdeen University, since 1990; *b* 25 Nov. 1929; *s* of William Morton Mackay and Annie Tainsh Higgs; *m* 1st, 1965, Elizabeth Ailsa Barr (*d* 1999); two *s* one *d*; 2nd, 2005, Catherine Anne McDonald (*d* 2011). *Educ:* Morgan Academy, Dundee; St Andrews Univ. (MA); Aberdeen Univ. (PhD). Assistant Principal, Scottish Home Dept, 1953; Principal, SHHD, 1962–66; Sec., Royal Commission on Local Govt in Scotland, 1966–69; Asst Sec., Scottish Develt Dept, 1969–79; Asst Sec., 1980–83, Under Sec., 1983–85, Dept of Agric. and Fisheries for Scotland; Under Sec., Scottish Develt Dept, 1985–88. Mem., Scottish Agricl Wages Bd, 1991–97. *Publications:* (contrib.) Rural Land Use: Scotland and Ireland, 1994; Scotland's Rural Land Use Agencies, 1995. *Recreations:* hill walking, photography, music. *Address:* 25 Melville Street, Perth PH1 5PY. *T:* (01738) 621274. *E:* dgmac29@gmail.com.

**MACKAY, Douglas Ian;** QC (Scot.) 1993; *b* 10 Aug. 1948; *s* of Walter Douglas Mackay and Karla Marie Anna Fröhlich; *m* 1970, Susan Anne Nicholson; two *s* one *d*. *Educ:* Inverness High Sch.; Aberdeen Univ. (LLB). Admitted advocate, 1980. *Recreations:* Scottish art, travel, mountaineering, game fishing. *Address:* St Ann's House, Lasswade, Midlothian EH18 1ND. *T:* (0131) 660 2634; Mount Pleasant Farm, Fortrose, Ross-shire IV10 8SH; Plantation Village, St Ann's Bay, St Ann, Jamaica, WI.

**MACKAY, Eileen Alison, (Lady Russell),** CB 1996; FRSE; Principal Finance Director, Scottish Office, 1992–96; *b* 7 July 1943; *d* of Alexander William Mackay and Alison Jack Ross; *m* 1983, (Alastair) Muir Russell (*see* Sir A. M. Russell). *Educ:* Dingwall Acad.; Edinburgh Univ. (MA Hons Geography). FRSE 2002. Dept of Employment, Scottish HQ, 1965–72; Scottish Office, 1972–78; HM Treasury, 1978–80; CPRS, Cabinet Office, 1980–83; Scottish Office, 1983–96: Under Sec., Housing, Envmt Dept, 1988–92. Chm., Castlemilk Partnership, 1988–92; Director: Moray Firth Maltings, 1988–99; Royal Bank of Scotland Gp plc, 1996–2005; Edinburgh Investment Trust plc, 1996–2005; Scottish TV (Regional) Ltd, 1998–99; Lothian and Edinburgh Enterprise Ltd, subseq. Scottish Enterprise Edinburgh and Lothian, 1998–2002; Scottish Financial Enterprise Ltd, 2000–06. Chm., Standing Adv. Cttee on Trunk Road Assessment, 1996–99. Mem., Commn on Local Govt and the Scottish Parlt, 1998–99. Member: Bd, Scottish Screen, 1997–99; ESRC, 1999–2003; Scottish Business and Biodiversity Gp, 1999–2002; Accountancy Review Bd, 2000–03; Bd, British Library, 2003–11; Bd of Govs, Royal Conservatoire of Scotland (formerly RSAMD), 2007–16 (Vice-Chair, 2013–16); Court, UHI (formerly Bd, UHI Millennium Inst.), 2009–17. Mem. Bd, Margaret Blackwood Housing Assoc., 1996–2001; Trustee: David Hume Inst., 1996–2008 (Chm. Trustees, 2002–08); Carnegie Trust for Univs of Scotland, 2000–16. Mem. Court, Univ. of Edinburgh, 1997–2003. *Club:* New (Edinburgh).

**MACKAY, Sir Francis Henry,** Kt 2003; FCCA; Founding Member, Graysons Ltd, since 2007; *b* 24 Oct. 1944; *m* 1963, Christine Leach; one *s* two *d*. FCCA 1967. Compass Group: Finance Dir, 1986–91, Chief Exec. and Dep. Chm., 1991–99; Chm., 1999–2006; Jt Dep. Chm., Granada Compass, 2000–01; Chm., Kingfisher, 2001–06. Chairman: ISS, 2006–08; Carlton Partners, 2006–12; non-exec. Dir, Centrica, 1997–2001.

**MACKAY, Air Vice-Marshal (Hector) Gavin,** CB 2002; OBE 1987; AFC 1982; FRAeS; defence and training consultant, since 2012; Senior Military Adviser (formerly Military Deputy) to Head of Defence Export Services, 2002–09; *b* 3 Oct. 1947; *s* of John MacLean Mackay and Isobel Margaret Mackay (*née* Mackay); *m* 1971, Elizabeth Stark Bolton; one *s* one *d*. *Educ:* Dingwall Acad.; Glasgow Univ. (BSc Civil Engrg 1970); RAF Coll., Cranwell. FRAeS 1997. Qualified Flying Instructor, RAF Linton-on-Ouse, 1973–75; Harrier Pilot: No 20 Sqdn, RAF Wildenrath, 1976–77; No 3 (F) Sqdn, RAF Gutersloh, 1977–79; Flight Comdr, No 1 (F) Sqdn, RAF Wittering, 1979–82; RNSC, 1982; Central Tactics and Trials Orgn, 1983–84; OC Examng Wing, CFS, 1984–87; Concept Studies and Operational Requirements, MoD, 1987–90; Station Comdr, RAF Gutersloh, 1991–93; Dep. Dir Air Offensive, MoD, 1993; rcds 1994; ACOS Ops, HQ AIRCENT, 1995–96; Comdt, CFS, 1996–99; Hd, Jt Force Harrier 2000 Implementation Team, 1999–2000; AOC, and Comdt, RAF Coll., Cranwell, 2000–02. Qualified Flying Instructor, No 16(R) Sqdn, RAF Cranwell, 2009–12. Pres., CFS Assoc., 2012–. Hon. Air Cdre 2503 (Co. of Lincoln) Sqdn, RAuxAF Regt, 2005–16. Mem. Council, Bishop Grosseteste Univ., Lincoln, 2014–. Liveryman, Hon. Co. of Air Pilots (formerly GAPAN), 2002–. High Sheriff, Lincs, 2015–16. *Recreations:* flying, golf, walking, fishing, guide at Lincoln Cathedral, delighting in his grandchildren (Monty, Martha, Freddie and Joe). *Club:* Royal Air Force.

**MACKAY, Ian Stuart,** FRCS; Consultant Otorhinolaryngologist, Royal Brompton Hospital and Charing Cross Hospital, London, 1977–2003; Hon. Consultant, King Edward VII Hospital for Officers, 1995–2014; Responsible Officer, Independent Doctors Federation, since 2014 (Chairman, 2012–14); *b* 16 June 1943; *s* of Rev. Gordon Mackay and Sylvia Mackay (*née* Spencer); *m* 1981, Madeleine Hargreaves (*née* Tull); one step *d*, and one *s* one *d* from former marriage. *Educ:* Kearsney Coll., Natal, South Africa; Royal Free Hosp. Sch. of Medicine, London (MB BS 1968). FRCS 1974. Cons. Otorhinolaryngologist, Metropolitan ENT Hosp., 1977–86. Hon. Senior Lecturer: Nat. Heart and Lung Inst., 1985–; Inst. of Laryngology and Otology, Univ. of London, 1985–. Vis. Prof., Mayo Clinic, 1996. Hon. Treas., European Acad. of Facial Surgery, 1978–93; Master, British Academic Conf. in Otolaryngology, 2012–15 (Hon. Treas., 1992–99); Mem. Council, Laryngology and Rhinology Section, RSocMed, 1996– (Pres., 2002–03); Founder Mem., British Allergy Foundn, 1995; Pres., British Assoc. of Otolaryngologists, 1999–2002 (Pres.-elect, 1996–99); Chm., Fedn of Surgical Specialty Assocs, 2001–03. Mem. Editl Bd, Amer. Jl of Rhinology, 1995–2014. *Publications:* (ed) Scott-Brown's Otolaryngology, Rhinology Vols, 5th edn 1987, 6th edn 1997; (contrib.) Facial Plastic Surgery, 1986; Otolaryngology, 1987, 2nd edn 1997; (ed) Rhinitis: mechanisms and management, 1989; chapters in books and papers, mainly on rhinoplasty and endoscopic sinus surgery. *Recreations:* fell walking, carpentry, house restoration. *Address:* Foxhills Farmhouse, Swerford OX7 4BQ. *T:* 07836 555424. *Clubs:* Sloane, Royal Society of Medicine.

**MacKAY, Julie;** *see* Kirkbride, J.

**McKAY, Sir Neil (Stuart),** Kt 2009; CB 2001; independent health care management consultant, since 2013; Associate Partner, GE Healthcare Finnamore, since 2013; Chief Executive, NHS Midlands and East (formerly East of England Strategic Health Authority), 2006–13; *b* 19 Feb. 1952; *s* of late Roy McKay and of Alison Maude McKay (*née* Dent); *m* 1978, Deirdre Mary McGinn; two *s*; *m* 2018, Wendy Elizabeth Hewitt. *Educ:* Dame Allan's Boys' Sch., Newcastle upon Tyne. Trainee Adminr, Newcastle upon Tyne Univ. HMC, 1970–72; Asst Hosp. Sec., Dunston Hill Hosp., Gateshead HMC, 1972–74; Admin. Asst, Gateshead AHA, 1974–75; Unit Adminr, Dryburn Hosp., Durham AHA, 1975–76; Commng Officer, St George's Hosp., Merton, Sutton and Wandsworth AHA, 1976–80; Dist Planning Adminr, 1980–82, Hosp. Adminr, Springfield Hosp., 1982–85, Wandsworth HA; Gen. Manager, Doncaster Royal Infirmary, 1985–88; Gen. Manager, 1988–91, Chief Exec., 1991–96, Northern Gen. Hosp. NHS Trust, Sheffield; Regl Dir, Trent Regl Office, 1996–2000, Dep. Chief Exec., 2000, NHS Exec., DoH; Chief Operating Officer, DoH, 2000–02; Chief Exec., Leeds Teaching Hosps NHS Trust, 2002–06. Hon. LLD Sheffield, 2000. *Recreations:* sport of all kinds (especially following Sunderland AFC), reading, gardening.

**MACKAY, Neville Patrick,** Vice Convener, Scottish Council for Voluntary Organisations, 2015; *b* 22 June 1958; *s* of Edward William Charles Mackay and Constance Evelyn Mackay; *m* 1996, Gillian Anne Prole; two *d*. *Educ:* Brentwood Sch.; Lancaster Univ. (BA Hons Geog. 1979); University Coll. London. Researcher, DoE, 1983–90; DFE, 1990–92; Department for National Heritage, later Department for Culture, Media and Sport: 1992–99; Dep. Hd, Heritage Div., 1995–97; Hd, Libraries and Inf. Div., 1997–99; Chief Exec., Resource: Council for Museums, Archives and Libraries, 2000–02; Hd, Voluntary Issues Unit, Scottish Exec., 2002–04; Chief Exec., Scottish Public Pensions Agency, 2004. *Recreations:* motor sports, walking, camping, being with my family.

**MacKAY, Prof. Norman,** CBE 1997; MD; FRCPGlas, FRCPE, FRCSE, FRCGP, FRCP; Dean of Postgraduate Medicine and Professor of Postgraduate Medical Education, University of Glasgow, 1989–2001; *b* 15 Sept. 1936; *s* of Donald MacKay and Catherine MacLeod; *m* 1961, Grace Violet McCaffer; two *s* two *d*. *Educ:* Glasgow Univ. (MB ChB, MD). FRCPGlas 1973; FRCPE 1975; FRCSE 1993; FRCGP 1993. Junior posts, Glasgow hosps, 1959–66; Lectr in Medicine, Nairobi, 1966–67; Sen. Registrar, Victoria Infirmary, Glasgow, 1967–68; Acting Sen. Lectr, Materia Medica, Univ. of Glasgow, 1968–72; Acting Consultant Physician, Falkirk, 1972–73; Consultant Physician, Victoria Infirmary, 1973–89, Hon. Consultant, 1989–94. Mem., GMC, 1999–2003. Pres., RCPSG, 1994–97 (Hon. Sec., 1973–83; Visitor, 1992–94). Vice-Chm., Copmed, 1999–2001. FCPS (Pak) 1993; FRACP; FAMS; FRCPI; FAMM; Hon. FACP 1995; Hon. FCPS Bangladesh; Hon. FRCS. *Publications:* articles in med. jls. *Recreations:* gardening, golf, soccer. *Address:* 5 Edenhall Grove, Newton Mearns, Glasgow G77 5TS. *T:* (0141) 616 2831.

**MACKAY, Peter,** CB 1993; Chairman, Local Government Boundary Commission for Scotland, 2007–13; b Arbroath, 6 July 1940; s of John S. Mackay, FRCS, and Patricia M. Atkinson; m 1964, Sarah Holdich; one s two d. Educ: Glasgow High Sch.; St Andrews Univ. (MA 1st Cl. Hons Political Economy). Teacher, Kyogle High Sch., NSW, 1962–63; joined Scottish Office as Asst Principal, 1963; various posts, incl. Private Sec. to successive Ministers of State, 1966–68 and Secs of State, 1973–75; Nuffield Travelling Fellow, Canada, Australia and NZ, 1978–79; seconded: as Dir for Scotland, MSC, 1983–85; as Under Sec., Manpower Policy, Dept of Employment, London, 1985–86; Under Sec., Further and Higher Educn, Scottish Educn Dept, 1987–89; Principal Establishment Officer, Scottish Office, 1989–90; Sec. and Chief Exec., Scottish Office Industry Dept, 1990–95. Director: British Linen Bank, 1996–2000; Business Banking Div., Bank of Scotland, 1999–2001; Pacific Horizon Investment Trust plc, 2001–10 (Chm., 2004–10). Member: Competition (formerly Monopolies and Mergers) Commn, 1996–2002; Bd, Scottish Natural Heritage, 1996–2003; Cairngorms Outdoor Access Forum, 2014–; Comr, Northern Lighthouse Bd, 1999–2008 (Chm., 2005–07); Director: Scottish Forest Alliance, 2000–10; Cairngorm Outdoor Access Trust, 2009–13; Chm., Northern Lighthouse Heritage Trust, 2014–17. Mem. Court, Napier Univ., 1996–2004. Hon. LLD Robert Gordon's, 1996. Recreations: sea canoeing, sculling, Scottish hills in all seasons. Address: Silverwood, Kincraig, by Kingussie, Inverness-shire PH21 1QE. Club: Loch Lomond Sailing.

**MacKAY, Hon. Peter Gordon;** PC (Can.) 2006; QC (Can.) 2006; Partner, Baker & McKenzie, since 2016; b New Glasgow, NS, 27 Sept. 1965; s of Hon. Elmer M. MacKay, PC (Can.), QC (Can.) and Macha MacKay; m 2012, Nazanin Afshin-Jam; two s one d. Educ: Carleton Univ.; Acadia Univ., NS (BA 1987); Dalhousie Univ., NS (LLB 1990). Called to the Nova Scotia Bar, 1991; in private practice specialising in criminal and family law, New Glasgow, NS, 1991–93; Crown Attorney for Central Reg., NS, 1993–97. MP (PC) Pictou-Antigonish-Guysborough, 1997–2004, (C) Central Nova, 2004–15. House Leader, 1997–2003, Leader, 2003–04, PC Party of Canada; Dep. Leader, Cons. Party of Canada, 2004–15; Minister: of Foreign Affairs, 2006–07; Atlantic Canada Opportunities Agency, 2006–10; for the Atlantic Gateway, 2008–10; of Nat. Defence, 2007–13; of Justice, 2013–15. Nat. Ambassador for Adopt-a-Liby Literacy Prog., Pictou Co., NS, 2000–. Member, Board: Special Olympics Canada, 2015; Boost Child; Youth Advocacy Center; Wounded Warrior Canada. Golden Jubilee Medal, 2002; Diamond Jubilee Medal, 2012; Afghanistan Civilian Service Medal, 2012; Belgium Civilian Service Medal, 2012. Recreations: silviculture, painting, Rugby, baseball, football, ice hockey. Address: Baker & McKenzie LLP, Brookfield Place, Bay/Wellington Tower, 181 Bay Street, Suite 2100, Toronto, ON M5J 2T3, Canada. T: (416) 8656889, Fax: (416) 8636275. E: peter.mackay@bakermckenzie.com.

**McKAY, His Honour Randal Joseph;** QC (NI) 1989; a County Court Judge, Armagh and South Down Division, Northern Ireland, 1994–2009; b Larne, 16 April 1943; s of Hugh and Josephine McKay; m 1974, Brenda O'Neill; three s. Educ: Queen's Univ., Belfast (LLB 1969; BL 1970). In practice as barrister, 1970–94. Recreations: boxing, pistol shooting, crosswords, motor racing, deflating egos.

**MacKAY, Prof. Robert Sinclair,** PhD; FRS 2000; FInstP, FIMA; Professor of Mathematics, University of Warwick, since 2000; President, Institute of Mathematics and its Applications, 2012–13; b 4 July 1956; s of Donald MacCrimmon MacKay and Valerie MacKay (née Wood); m 1992, Claude Noëlle Baesens; one s. Educ: Trinity Coll., Cambridge (BA Math.; MA; MMath); Princeton (PhD Astrophys. Sci 1982). Res. Asst, QMC, 1982–83; Vis. Researcher, Institut des Hautes Etudes Scientifiques, Bures-sur-Yvette, France, 1983–84; Lectr, 1984–90, Reader, 1990–93, Prof., 1993–95, Mathematics, Univ. of Warwick; Prof. of Nonlinear Dynamics, and Fellow of Trinity Coll., Univ. of Cambridge, 1995–2000. Nuffield Foundn Sci. Res. Fellow, 1992–93; Res. Associate 1994–95, Vis. Prof., 1995, CNRS, Université de Bourgogne, France; Prof. invité, Institut des Hautes Etudes Scientifiques, Bures-sur-Yvette, 2006; Vis. Prof., Physics, Université Libre de Bruxelles, 2010–11; Turing Fellow, Alan Turing Inst., 2017–19. FInstP 2000; FIMA 2003. (First) Stephanos Pnevmatikos Internat. Award for Res. in Nonlinear Phenomena, 1993; Jun. Whitehead Prize, 1994, Sen. Whitehead Prize, 2015, London Math. Soc. Publications: Hamiltonian Dynamical Systems, 1987; Renormalisation in area-preserving maps, 1993; over 140 papers in learned jls. Address: Mathematics Institute, University of Warwick, Coventry CV4 7AL.

**MACKAY, Ronald David;** see Eassie, Rt Hon. Lord.

**MACKAY, Prof. Trudy Frances Charlene, (Mrs R. R. H. Anholt),** PhD; FRS 2006; Self Family Endowed Chair of Human Genetics, Department of Genetics and Biochemistry, and Director, Clemson Center for Human Genetics, Clemson University, since 2018; b 10 Sept. 1952; d of Charles Edward Mackay and Jean Somerville Mackay; m 1990, Robert R. H. Anholt. Educ: Dalhousie Univ. (BSc Hons 1974, MSc 1976); Univ. of Edinburgh (PhD 1979). Lectr, Dept of Genetics, Univ. of Edinburgh, 1980–87; North Carolina State University: Associate Prof., 1987–93, Prof., 1993–96, Dept of Genetics; William Neal Reynolds and Dist. Univ. Prof., Dept of Genetics, subseq. Dept of Biol Scis, 1996–2018. FAAAS 2003; Fellow: Amer. Acad. of Arts and Scis, 2005; NAS, USA, 2010. N Carolina Award for Sci., 2011. Wolf Prize in Agriculture, Wolf Foundn, 2016. Publications: over 200 peer-reviewed articles in scientific jls. Recreations: dressage and carriage driving, listening to opera, reading mystery novels. Address: Clemson Center for Human Genetics, Self Regional Hall, 114 Gregor Mendel Circle, Greenwood, SC 29646, USA. E: tmackay@clemson.edu.

**McKAY, Sir William (Robert),** KCB 2001 (CB 1996); Clerk of the House of Commons, 1998–2002; b 18 April 1939; s of late William Wallace McKay and Margaret H. A. Foster; m 1962, Rev. Margaret M., d of late E. M. Fillmore, OBE; twin d. Educ: Trinity Academy, Leith; Edinburgh Univ. (MA Hons). Clerk in the House of Commons, 1961; Clerk of Financial Cttees, H of C, 1985–87; Clerk of the Journals, H of C, 1987–91; Clerk of Public Bills, H of C, 1991–94; Clerk Asst, H of C, 1994–97. Secretary: to the House of Commons Commn, 1981–84; to the Public Accounts Commn, 1985–87. Chm., Commn on the Consequences of Devolution for H of C, 2012–13. Lay Observer, Law Soc. of Scotland, 2006–11. Mem., Legal Questions Cttee, Church of Scotland, 2006–11. Hon. Prof., Univ. of Aberdeen, 2003–07. Mem. Council, Scottish History Soc., 2012–16. Publications: (ed) Erskine May's Private Journal 1883–86, 1984; Secretaries to Mr Speaker, 1986; Clerks in the House of Commons 1363–1989: a biographical list, 1989; (ed) Observations, Rules and Orders of the House of Commons: an early procedural collection, 1989; (ed jtly) Erskine May's Parliamentary Practice, 22nd edn 1997, (sole editor) 23rd edn 2004; (contrib.) Stair Memorial Encyclopaedia of the Laws of Scotland, rev. edn 2002; (with M. M. McKay) A United Parish, 2002; (contrib.) Halsbury's Laws of England, 4th edn; (with C. W. Johnson) Parliament and Congress: representation and scrutiny in the twenty-first century, 2010; contrib. historical jls. Recreation: reading Scottish history. Address: 2 Mackenzie Gardens, Dornoch, Sutherland IV25 3RU. Club: New (Edinburgh).

**MACKAY-DICK, Maj.-Gen. Sir Iain (Charles),** KCVO 1997; MBE 1981; Clerk to the Trustees and Chief Executive, Morden College, 1997–2011; b 24 Aug. 1945; s of late John and Margaret Mackay-Dick; m 1971, Carolynn Hilary Holmes; three d. Educ: St Edmund's Sch., Hindhead; Sherborne Sch.; RMAS; Staff Coll., Camberley (psc, hcsc). Commnd, Scots Guards, 1965; served Malaysia, Borneo, Germany, Cyprus and UK to 1986, and Falkland Is, 1982; Comdr, Jun. Div. Staff Coll., Warminster, 1986–88; Comdr, 11 Armoured Bde, 1989–91; Dep. Mil. Sec. (A), 1991–92; GOC 1st Armoured Div., Verden, 1992–93; GOC Lower Saxony Dist, Verden, 1993; Comdr British Forces Falkland Is, 1993–94; GOC London Dist and Maj. Gen. commanding Household Div., 1994–97. Mem., RUSI, 1979–2006. Hon. Col, 256 (City of London) Field Hosp., RAMC(V), 2000–07. Member: Public Schools Old Boys LTA; South Atlantic Medal Assoc. Mem., Gov. Council, Union Jack Club, 2011–17. Freeman, City of London, 2000. DL Greater London, 2011–14. FCMI 1996–2011 (FIMgt 1996). Trustee, Falkland Is Meml Chapel, Pangbourne, 2005–18; Chm., Guards Chapel Cttee, 2011–17. Publications: (contrib.) Central Region versus Out of Area (essays), 1990. Recreations: most sports (represented Army in lawn tennis and squash (Army Squash Champion, 1971)), walking, gardening, military history. Address: c/o Lloyds Bank, Cox's and Kings, 39 Piccadilly, W1V 0AA. Clubs: Edinburgh Angus (Edinburgh); Jesters; Third Guards; Guards' Golfing Society, Army Golfing Society.

**MacKEAN, His Honour Thomas Neill;** a Circuit Judge, 1993–2004; b 4 March 1934; s of late Andrew Neill MacKean and Mary Dale MacKean (née Nichol); m 1962, Muriel Hodder; three d (and one d decd). Educ: Sherborne; Trinity Hall, Cambridge (BA). 2nd Lt, Royal Hampshire Regt, 1952–54. Partner, Hepherd Winstanley & Pugh, solicitors, Southampton, 1960–93; HM Coroner, Southampton and New Forest, 1990–93; a Recorder, 1991–93. Recreations: sailing, walking. Club: Royal Cruising.

**McKEARNEY, Philip,** CMG 1983; HM Diplomatic Service, retired; b 15 Nov. 1926; s of Philip McKearney, OBE; m 1950, Jean Pamela Walker; two s. Educ: City of London Sch.; Hertford Coll., Oxford. 4/7th Dragoon Guards, 1946–53; joined HM Diplomatic Service, 1953; 3rd Sec., British Embassy, Damascus, 1955–56; 1st Sec., British Legation, Bucharest, 1959–62; British Political Agent, Qatar, 1962–65; Counsellor and Consul-Gen., Baghdad, 1968–70; Counsellor, Belgrade, 1970–74; Inspector, FCO, 1975–77; Consul-General: Zagreb, 1977–80; Boston, Mass, 1980–83; Amb. to Romania, 1983–86; Dir, Foreign Service Prog., Oxford Univ., 1987–88.

**McKECHIN, Ann;** Head, Corporate Social Responsibility, Scottish Power, since 2017; b 22 April 1961; d of late William Joseph McKechin and Anne McKechin (née Coyle). Educ: Strathclyde Univ. (LLB, DLP). Solicitor, 1983–; Partner, Pacitti Jones, Glasgow, 1990–2000. MP (Lab) Glasgow, Maryhill, 2001–05, Glasgow N, 2005–15; contested (Lab) same seat, 2015. Parly Under Sec. of State, Scotland Office, 2008–10; Shadow Sec. of State for Scotland, 2010–11. Mem., Business, Innovation and Skills Select Cttee, 2011–15. Vice Chair, Westminster Foundn for Democracy, 2013–15. Trustee, UN Women Nat. Cttee UK, 2016–. Mem. Court, Univ. of West of Scotland, 2016–. Convenor, Scottish Grantmakers Assoc., 2018–. Recreations: films, dancing, art history. E: mckechina@gmail.com. W: www.twitter.com/AnnMcKechin2.

**McKECHNIE, Aileen Mary;** Director, Advanced Learning and Science, Scottish Government, since 2015; b Paisley, 22 Nov. 1966; d of Hugh McHale and Celine McHale; m 2002, William McKechnie; two s. Educ: Holyrood Secondary Sch.; Univ. of Glasgow (MA Hons French and German; MBA). Senior Development Manager: Glasgow CC, 1990–94; Scottish Homes, 1994–96; Thistle Housing Assoc., 1996–98; Scottish Executive, subseq. Scottish Government: Head: Local Econ. Develt, 1998–2002; Higher Educn Strategy and Funding, 2002–04; Further and Adult Educn Div., 2004–09; Innovation, Investment and Industries Div., 2009–12; Director: Culture and External Affairs, 2012–13; Culture and Heritage, 2013–14. Dir (pt-time), Scottish Arbitration Centre, 2011–13. Recreations: reading, walking, ballet, art, cinema, theatre, spending quality time with family. Address: Scottish Government, 5 Atlantic Quay, Glasgow G2 8LU. T: 0300 244 1264. E: aileen.mckechnie@gov.scot.

**MACKECHNIE, Sir Alistair (John),** Kt 1993; financial consultant, since 1992; b 15 Nov. 1934; s of Frank Harper McIvor Mackechnie and Ellen Annie (née Brophy); m 1961, Countess Alexandra Kinsky, er d of Count Frederick-Carl Kinsky; three d. Educ: St Patrick's Coll., Wellington, NZ; Victoria Univ. of Wellington, NZ. ACA 1957. Nat. Service: commnd NZ Scottish Regt, 1955. Director: Henderson Admin, 1976–88; BSI-Thornhill Investment Mgt, 1989–2000; Hori Construction Ltd, 2000–; Carlton Club (London) Ltd, 2008–; Carlton Trustees (London) Ltd, 2008–. Twickenham Conservative Association: Chm., 1985–88; Pres., 1989–2017; Greater London Area Conservatives: Dep. Chm., 1988–90; Chm., 1990–93; Mem., Exec. Cttee, Nat. Union of Cons. and Unionist Assocs, 1988–96. Mem. Council, Back Care (formerly Nat. Back Pain Assoc.), 1994–2009. Governor: St Mary's UC, 1997–2006; St Catherine's Sch., Twickenham, 1997–2006. Recreations: theatre, travel, bird-watching, hill-walking. Club: Carlton.

**McKECHNIE, George;** Director of Participation and Communications, Education and Learning Wales, 2001–04 (Consultant, 2004–06); b 28 July 1946; m 1971, Janequin (née Morris); two s. Educ: Portobello Sen. Secondary Sch., Edinburgh; Swansea Univ. (MA 2008; PhD 2012). Reporter: Paisley and Renfrewshire Gazette, 1964–66; Edinburgh Evening News, 1966; Scottish Daily Mail, 1966–68; Daily Record, 1968–73; Dep. News Editor and News Editor, Sunday Mail, 1974–76; Asst Editor, 1976–81, Editor, 1981–94, Evening Times, Glasgow; Editor, The Herald, Glasgow, 1994–97; Dir of Public Affairs, Beattie Media, 1998–99; Dir of Communications, Council of Welsh TECs, 1999–2001. Director: George Outram & Co., 1986–92; Caledonian Newspaper Publishing, 1992–97. Mem., Press Complaints Commn, 1992–94. Recreations: reading, walking, cinema, Hearts FC.

**McKECHNIE, Stuart Iain William;** QC 2018; b Toowoomba, Australia, 2 Sept. 1974; s of Michael and Rosemary McKechnie; m 2006, Louise Bass; two s. Educ: Hewett Comprehensive Sch., Norwich; Nottingham Univ. (LLB 1996); Inns of Court Sch. of Law (Inner Temple Scholar). Called to the Bar, Inner Temple, 1997; in practice as barrister, specialising in personal injury and clinical negligence, 1997–. Contributor and Mem., Editl Bd, Judicial Coll. Guidelines for Assessment of Gen. Damages in Personal Injury Cases, 2012–. Publications: (contrib. and Gen. Ed.) Jordan's APIL Guide to Catastrophic Injury Cases, 2010, 3rd edn 2019; (contrib.) Kemp: Practice and Procedure. Recreations: time with family, restaurants, following Norwich City Football Club, cricket, Rugby, golf. Address: 9 Gough Square, EC4A 3DG. T: (020) 7832 0500. E: smckechnie@9goughsquare.co.uk.

**McKEE, Prof. (Clifford) Martin,** CBE 2005; MD, DSc; FRCP, FRCPE, FRCPI, FFPH, FMedSci; Professor of European Public Health, since 1997, and Medical Director, since 2014, London School of Hygiene and Tropical Medicine, University of London; b Belfast, 12 July 1956; s of Dr Clifford McKee and Dr Anna McKee (née Martin); m 1987, Dorothy McCrory; two d. Educ: Royal Belfast Academical Instn; Queen's Univ., Belfast (MB BCh BAO 1979; MD 1990; DSc 2006); Univ. of London (MSc 1986). MRCP 1982, FRCP 1995; MFCM 1988, FFPH (FFCM 1994); FRCPI 1997; FRCPE 2010. Jun. med. posts, Belfast City Hosp., Royal Victoria Hosp., Islington HA, 1979–89; Lectr, Sen. Lectr, then Reader, LSHTM, Univ. of London, 1987–97. Ed., Eur. Jl of Public Health, 1993–2009. Founding Director: WHO Collaborating Centre on Health of Socs in Transition, 1997–2014; Res. Policy, Eur. Observatory on Health Systems and Policies, 1998–; Chm., WHO Eur. Adv. Cttee on Health Res., 2008–13. Member: Public Health sub-bd, 1998–2004; Global Health Adv. Cttee, 2004–15 (Chm., 2010–15), Open Society Inst.; BUPA Med. Adv. Panel, 1999–2012; Expert Panel on Effective Ways of Investing in Health, EC, 2013–; Bd of Sci., BMA, 2014–17. Mem. Council, UK Public Health Assoc., 2009–10; Chm., Soc. for Social Medicine, 2010; Pres., European Public Health Assoc., 2014–16. Visiting Professor: Univs of Belgrade and Zagreb, 2005; LSE, 2009–; Taipei Med. Univ., 2010. Lectures: Ferenc Bojan, EUPHA, 1997; Sir Stanley Davidson, RCPE, 2003; Salvatore Lucia, UCSF, 2004; Milroy, RCP, 2005; DARE, FPH, 2006; Cochrane, Soc. for Social Medicine, 2006; Victor Horsley, BMA, 2010; Thackrah, Leeds Univ., 2011; Hjelt, Helsinki Univ., 2011; Duncan, Liverpool Univ., 2012; Sir Thomas and Lady Edith Dixon, Ulster Med. Soc., 2015; Albert Neuberger, Hebrew Univ., 2015; Sandy Macara, BMA, 2016; Netherlands Scientific Council, 2016; Litchfield, Univ. of Oxford, 2017; Dr Andrew Duncan, RCPE, 2017; Schorstein, QMUL, 2018; Teddy Chester, Manchester Univ.. FMedSci 2000; FRSocMed 1985. Hon. Member: Romanian Acad. of Med. Scis, 1999; Italian Soc. of Hygiene, Preventive Medicine and Public Health, 2015; For. Associate Mem., US Nat. Acad. (formerly Inst.) of Medicine, 2006. MAE 2018. Hon. Dr: Debrecen, 1998; Maastricht, 2006; Karlstad, 2010; Nordic Sch. of Public Health, 2013; Athens Sch. of Public Health, 2016; QUB, 2019. Andrija Stampar Medal, Assoc. of Schs of Public Health in the Eur. Region, 2003; Alwyn Smith Prize, FPH, 2014; Donabedian Internat. Award, 2015. *Publications:* (ed jtly) International Co-operation and Health, 2001; (ed with Judith Healy) Hospitals in a Changing Europe, 2002; (with Elias Mossialos) EU Law and the Social Character of Health Care, 2002; (jtly) The Impact of EU Law on Health Care Systems, 2002; (ed with Judith Healy) Accessing Health Care: responding to diversity, 2004; (jtly) Health Policy and European Union Enlargement, 2004; (ed with Joceline Pomerleau) Issues in Public Health, 2005; (jtly) Human Resources for Health in Europe, 2005; (jtly) Health: a vital investment for economic development in eastern Europe and central Asia, 2007; (jtly) Responding to the Challenge of Cancer in Europe, 2008; (jtly) Health Systems and the Challenge of Communicable Disease: experiences from Europe and Latin America, 2008; (with Ellen Nolte) Caring for People with Chronic Conditions: a health system perspective, 2008; (jtly) Investing in Hospitals of the Future, 2009; (with Johan Mackenbach) Successes and Failures of Health Policy in Europe, 2013; (with Ingrid Wolfe) European Child Health: services and systems, 2013; over 1100 papers in learned jls, esp. on health and health policy in Europe. *Recreations:* reading, ski-ing, complaining about politicians, running through airports, damage control on daughters' credit cards. *Address:* London School of Hygiene and Tropical Medicine, 15–17 Tavistock Place, WC1H 9SH. *T:* (020) 7927 2229. *E:* martin.mckee@lshtm.ac.uk. *Club:* Athenæum.

**McKEE, David John;** writer, illustrator, painter and film maker; *b* 2 Jan. 1935; *m* Barbara Ennuss (decd); two *s* one *d. Educ:* Tavistock Grammar Sch.; Plympton Grammar Sch.; Plymouth Coll. of Art; Hornsey Coll. of Art. Freelance cartoonist, 1955–; films incl. Mr Benn (14 films), 1970; Founder and Dir, King Rollo Films Ltd, 1979–2004; Dir, Rollo Rights Ltd, 2004–. Hon. Dr Open, 2012; Hon. DArts Plymouth, 2012. *Publications:* include: Bronto's Wings, 1964; Two Can Toucan, 1964; Mr Benn series, 1967–; Elmer series, 1968–; Melric the Magician, 1970; Two Admirals, 1977; Tusk Tusk, 1978; King Rollo, 1979; Adventures of King Rollo, 1982; Not Now Bernard, 1980; I Hate My Teddy Bear, 1982; Further Adventures of King Rollo, 1983; Two Monsters, 1985; King Rollo's Letter and Other Stories, 1986; Sad Story of Veronica Who Played the Violin, 1988; Snow Woman, 1989; Zebra's Hiccups, 1991; Isabel's Noisy Tummy, 1994; Charlotte's Piggy Bank, 1996; Monster and the Teddy Bear, 1997; Prince Peter and the Teddy Bear, 1999; Mary's Secret, 1999; King Rollo's New Stockings, 2001; The Conquerors, 2004; Three Monsters, 2006; Four Red Apples, 2006; Denver, 2010; (with Brett McKee) Sir Ned and the Nasties, 2017; Belinda Brown, 2018. *Address:* c/o Andersen Press, 20 Vauxhall Bridge Road, SW1V 2SA.

**McKEE, Dr Ian Hume,** MBE 2006; Member (SNP) Lothians, Scottish Parliament, 2007–11; *b* 2 April 1940; *s* of late John and Marjory McKee; *m* 1992, Penelope Ann Watson (née Bartlett); one *s* two *d*, and one step *s* one step *d. Educ:* Fettes Coll., Edinburgh; Univ. of Edinburgh (MB ChB 1965); DRCOG 1970. House Officer: Ingham Infirmary, South Shields, 1965–66; Royal Infirmary, Edinburgh, 1966; MO, RAF, 1966–71; Gen. Med. Practitioner, Sighthill and Wester Hailes Health Centres, 1971–2006. Man. Dir, Hermiston Publications Ltd, 1979–95; Dir, One City Trust Ltd, 2007–08. Scottish Advr, ABPI, 1985–2002. Medical Columnist: Daily Record, 1990–97; Scotsman, 2003–06. Columnist, Scotsman, 2008–09. Mem., Lord Provost of Edinburgh's Commn on Social Exclusion, 1999–2002. Scottish Parliament: Dep. Convener, Subordinate Legislation Cttee, 2008–11, End of Life Assistance Bill Cttee, 2010–11; Mem., Health-Sport Cttee, 2007–11. Fellow, Soc. of Medical Writers, 2007–. Mem., Medical Journalists' Assoc., 1982–. Dir, St Mary's Music Sch., Edinburgh, 2011–15. Mem., Merchants' Co., City of Edinburgh, 1982–; Burgess and Freeman, City of Edinburgh, 2007. Friend of Foreign Service Medal (Taiwan), 2011. *Recreations:* hill walking, boating, supporting unsuccessful football clubs, admiring finer things in life, making marmalade. *Address:* Flat 1, 4 The Cedars, Edinburgh EH13 0PL. *Clubs:* Royal Air Force; Scottish National Party (Edinburgh).

**McKEE, Ivan;** Member (SNP) Glasgow Provan, Scottish Parliament, since 2016; Minister for Trade, Investment and Innovation, since 2018; *b* Helensburgh, 1963. *Educ:* Univ. of Strathclyde (BSc BEng Manufg Scis and Engrg 1986); Newcastle Univ. (MBA). VSO, Bangladesh, 1986–89; work in manufg cos; estabd internat. manufg consultancy, 2005–09; investment in and turning around failing manufg businesses, 2009–15. *Address:* Scottish Parliament, Edinburgh EH99 1SP.

**McKEE, Martin;** see McKee, C. M.

**McKEE, Richard Anthony;** a Judge of the Upper Tribunal (Immigration and Asylum Chamber) (formerly a Senior Immigration Judge, Asylum and Immigration Tribunal), 2006–14; *b* 28 Sept. 1948; *s* of Ian and Ilse McKee. *Educ:* Campbell Coll., Belfast; Jesus Coll., Cambridge (BA Classics 1971); Sch. of Oriental and African Studies, London (MA Linguistics 1983). Lectr in Linguistics, PCL, Central Sch. of Speech and Drama, and Goldsmiths' Coll., London Univ., 1984–90. Called to the Bar, Inner Temple, 1991; in practice as barrister, 1993–2000, 2015–; Immigration Adjudicator, 2000–06. Mem., Editl Adv. Bd, Jl of Immigration, Asylum and Nationality Law, 1997–2014; Gen. Ed., 2010–14, Contributing Ed., 2015–, Butterworth's Immigration Law Service; Dep. Ed., Immigration Case Rev., 2011–13. *Publications:* (jtly) United Kingdom Asylum Law in its European Context, 1999; (contrib.) Butterworths Immigration Law Service, 1999–; (contrib.) Jackson & Warr's Immigration Law and Practice, 2001– (Co-Ed., 2013–); compiler, Immigration Law Update, 2002–10; numerous articles on immigration and asylum law in various jls. *Recreations:* assiduous gym membership - in vain attempt to combat the effects of wining, dining and general conviviality, theatre critic for PlaysToSee. *Address:* 71A Victoria Road, NW6 6TB. *Club:* Savage.

**McKEEVER, Prof. Ian,** RA 2003; artist; Professor in Painting, University of Brighton, since 2001; Professor of Drawing, Royal Academy School of Arts, London, 2006–11; Chairman, Collections and Library Committee, 2009–15 and Member of Council, 2013–15, Royal Academy of Arts; *b* 30 Nov. 1946; *m* 1991, Gerlinde Gabriel; one *s* one *d. Educ:* Withernsea High Sch.; Avery Hill Coll. of Educn, London (DipEd). DAAD Scholar, Berlin, 1989–90. Exhibitions include: (first solo exhibn) ICA, 1973; Kunsthalle, Nuremberg, 1982; Moderna Museet, Stockholm, 1985; Kunstverein, Braunschweig, 1987; Kunst Forum, Städtische Galerie im Lenbachhaus, Munich, 1989; Whitechapel Art Gall., 1990; Haggerty Mus. of Art, Milwaukee, 1994; Museo Nacional Centro de Arte, Reina Sofia, Madrid, 1996; Museo d'Art Contemporani, Barcelona, 1996; Kunsthallen Brandts Klaedefabrik, Odense, 2001, 2007; Horsen Kunstmus., Horsens, 2002, 2014; Kettle's Yard, Cambridge, 2004; China Art Gall., Beijing and Nat. Gall., Shanghai, 2005; Morat Inst. für Kunst und Kunstwissenschaft, Freiburg, 2005, 2007; Ny Carlsberg Glyptotek, Copenhagen, 2006; Kings Place Gallery, London, 2009; Galerie Forsblom, Helsinki, 2009; Galleri Andersson Sandström, Stockholm, 2009, 2013; Galleri Susanne Ottesen, Copenhagen, 2010, 2014; RA, 2010, Mus. Sønderjylland, Tønder, 2011, 2015; Tate Britain, 2011; Seongnam Arts Center, S Korea, 2011; Nat. Mus. of Art, Oslo, 2012; Josef Albers Mus., Quadrat Bottrop, Germany, 2012; Queen's Gall., Buckingham Palace, 2013; HackelBury Fine Art, London, 2014; Kunst-Station Sankt Peter, Cologne, 2014; work in collections, including: Tate Gall., London; BM; Govt Art Collection; British Council; Arts Council of GB; Scottish Nat. Gall. of Modern Art; Metropolitan Mus. of Modern Art, NY; Brooklyn Mus.; Boston Mus. of Fine Arts; Cincinnati Mus. of Modern Art; Louisiana Mus., Denmark; Mus. des 20 Jahrhunderts, Vienna; Ny Carlsberg Glyptotek, Copenhagen; Mus. of Contemp. Art, Helsinki; Yale Center for British Art, Connecticut; Royal Acad. of Arts; Royal Collection Trust, London. Hon. Fellow, Arts Inst., Bournemouth, 2002. *Publications:* In Praise of Painting: three essays, 2005; *relevant publications:* Ian McKeever - Paintings, by M. Allthorpe-Guyton, M. Tucker and C. Lampert, 2009; Artists' Laboratory - Ian McKeever: Hartgrove paintings and photographs, 2010; Black and Black Again… Paintings 1987–2010, 2011; Ian McKeever: Hartgrove, 2012. *Address:* c/o Royal Academy of Arts, Burlington House, Piccadilly, W1J 0BD.

**MacKEITH, Prof. Margaret Anne,** CBE 1997; PhD; FRTPI; FRGS; town planning consultant; Consultant, MacKeith Dickinson & Partners Ltd, 2000–11; Pro Vice-Chancellor, University of Central Lancashire (formerly Lancashire Polytechnic), 1995–99; *b* 26 June 1939; *d* of James and Gertrude Crane; *m* 1962, Charles Gordon MacKeith (*d* 2018); two *s. Educ:* Shirebrook Grammar Sch., Derbyshire; Univ. of Manchester (DipTP, MA); Heriot-Watt Univ. (PhD). FRTPI 1980; FRGS 1976; MIEnvSc 1977. Planning Officer, Lancs CC, 1961–63; Consultant to MacKeith Dickinson and Partners, 1963–74; Lancashire Polytechnic: Sen., then Principal, Lectr, 1975–87; Hd, Sch. of Construction and Surveying, 1987–90; Dean, Faculty of Technol., 1987–90, Faculty of Design and Technol., 1990–95. Mem., Royal Fine Art Commn, 1993–99. Member: BTEC Cttees, 1988–93; NW Cttee, OFFER, 1990–93; Landscape Adv. Cttee, Dept of Transport, 1991–93; NRA NW Cttee, 1994–97. Trustee, Nat. Museums Liverpool (formerly Nat. Museums and Galls on Merseyside), 2000–09. Hon. Prof., Transylvania Univ., Romania, 1998. FRSA 1990. Dr hc Cluj, Romania, 1994. *Publications:* Shopping Arcades 1817–1939, 1985; History and Conservation of Shopping Arcades, 1986; articles and conf. papers on conservation, engrg educn and women in engrg and technol. *Recreations:* travel, architectural history, music, opera. *Address:* 104 Breck Road, Poulton-le-Fylde, Lancs FY6 7HT. *T:* (01253) 884774; 4 Breton House, Barbican, EC2Y 8DQ.

**McKELLAR, Prof. Quintin Archibald,** CBE 2011; PhD, DVM; FRSB, FRAgS, FRCVS; FRSE; Vice Chancellor, University of Hertfordshire, since 2011; *b* 24 Dec. 1958; *s* of Quintin and Elizabeth McKellar; *m* 1984, Patricia Law; one *s* three *d. Educ:* Glasgow Univ. (BVMS 1981; PhD 1984; DVM 2002); Eur. Coll. Vet. Pharmacol. and Toxicol. (DipECVPT). MRCVS 1981, FRCVS 2017; FRSB (FIBiol 2001); FRAgS 2003. University of Glasgow: Lectr, 1984–96; Prof. of Veterinary Pharmacol., 1996–97; Chief Exec. and Scientific Dir, Moredun Res. Inst., 1997–2004; Prof. of Veterinary Pharmacol. and Principal, RVC, Univ. of London, 2004–10. Chm., Regulatory Agencies Strategy Bd, 2005–08; Member: Veterinary Products Cttee, 1993–2001; Council, BBSRC, 2005–11; Science Adv. Council, DEFRA, 2011–14; non-exec. Dir, Animal and Plant Health Agency, 2013–17. Gov., Inst. Animal Health, 2003–09 and 2011–13; Chm. of Trustees, Pirbright Inst., 2014–. Gov., Queenswood Sch., 2011–16. FRSE 2003. *Publications:* numerous contribs to scientific literature. *Recreation:* rowing. *Address:* University of Hertfordshire, College Lane, Hatfield, Herts AL10 9AB. *Clubs:* Athenæum; Leander (Henley-on-Thames).

**McKELLEN, Sir Ian (Murray),** CH 2008; Kt 1991; CBE 1979; actor and director, since 1961; *b* 25 May 1939; *s* of late Denis Murray McKellen and Margery (née Sutcliffe). *Educ:* Wigan Grammar Sch.; Bolton Sch.; St Catharine's Coll., Cambridge (BA; Hon. Fellow, 1982). Cameron Mackintosh Prof. of Contemporary Theatre, Univ. of Oxford, 1991–92. Pres., Marlowe Soc., 1960–61. Elected to Council of Equity, 1971–72. Hon. DLitt Nottingham, 1989. 1st appearance (stage): Belgrade Theatre, Coventry, in a Man for all Seasons, Sept. 1961; Arts Theatre, Ipswich, 1962–63; Nottingham Playhouse, 1963–64; 1st London stage appearance, Duke of York's in A Scent of Flowers, 1964 (Clarence Derwent Award); Recruiting Officer, Chips with Everything, Cambridge Theatre Co., 1971; Founder Mem., Actors Company: Ruling the Roost, 'Tis Pity She's a Whore, Edin. Fest., 1972; Knots, Wood-Demon, Edin. Fest., 1973, and with King Lear, Brooklyn Acad. of Music, Wimbledon Theatre season, 1974; *London stage appearances:* A Lily in Little India, St Martin's; Man of Destiny/O'Flaherty VC, Mermaid Theatre; Their Very Own and Golden City, Royal Court, 1966; The Promise, Fortune, 1967 (also Broadway); White Lies/Black Comedy, Lyric; Richard II, Prospect Theatre Co., 1968 (revived with Edward II, Edin. Fest., British and European tours); Hamlet, Cambridge, 1971 (British and European tours); Ashes, Young Vic, 1975; Bent, Royal Court, Criterion, 1979 (SWET Award, 1979); Short List, Hampstead, 1983; Cowardice, Ambassadors, 1983; Henceforward, Vaudeville, 1988; Dance of Death, Lyric, 2003; Aladdin, Old Vic, 2004, 2005; The Cut, Donmar Warehouse, 2006; Waiting for Godot, UK tour then Theatre Royal Haymarket, 2009, internat. tour, 2010, NY 2013; No Man's Land, NY, 2013, UK tour then Wyndham's, 2016; Shakespeare, Tolkien, Others and You (one man show), Park Th., 2017; Ian McKellen on Stage, UK tour, 2019; *with Royal National Theatre:* Much Ado About Nothing, Old Vic, 1965; Armstrong's Last Goodnight, Trelawney of the Wells, Chichester Fest., 1965; Venice Preserv'd, Wild Honey (Laurence Olivier Award, Plays and Players Award; Los Angeles and NY, 1986–87), Coriolanus (London Standard Award), South Bank, 1984–85; as Assoc. Dir, produced and acted in The Duchess of Malfi, The Real Inspector Hound with The Critic, The Cherry Orchard (Paris and Chicago), 1984–85; Bent, 1990 (also Garrick); Kent in King Lear, and title role, Richard III, 1990 (Laurence Olivier Award; Assoc. Prod. for world tour, 1990–91); Napoli Milionaria, 1991; Uncle Vanya, 1992; Richard III, US tour, 1992; An Enemy of the People, Peter Pan, 1997–98; *with Royal Shakespeare Co.:* Dr Faustus, Edin. Fest. and Aldwych, 1974; Marquis of Keith, Aldwych, 1974–75; King John, Aldwych, 1975; Too Good to be True, Aldwych and Globe, 1975; Romeo and Juliet, The Winter's Tale, Macbeth (Plays and Players Award, 1976), Stratford, 1976–77; Every Good Boy Deserves Favour, RFH, 1977, Barbican, 1982; Romeo and Juliet, Macbeth, Pillars of the Community (SWET Award, 1977), Days of the Commune, The Alchemist (SWET Award, 1978), Aldwych and RSC Warehouse, 1977–78; King Lear, The Seagull, Stratford and world tour, 2007; Prod. RSC Tour, 1978: Three Sisters, Twelfth Night, Is There Honey Still for Tea; Iago in Othello, The Other Place, Stratford and Young Vic, 1989, BBC TV (Evening Standard and London Critics' Award); *with W Yorks Playhouse, Leeds:* The Seagull, Present Laughter, 1998; The Tempest, 1999; *Directed:* Liverpool Playhouse, 1969; Watford and Leicester, 1972; A Private Matter, Vaudeville, 1973; The Clandestine Marriage, Savoy, 1975; *other performances include:* Words, Words, Words (solo recital), Edin. Fest. and Belfast Fest., 1976 (with Acting Shakespeare, Edin. and Belfast, 1977); Amadeus, Broadhurst, NY, 1980–81 (Drama Desk, NY Drama League, Outer Critics' Circle and Tony Awards); A Knight Out, NY, S Africa, UK, 1994–95; Dance of Death, NY, 2001; The Syndicate, Chichester Festival Th., 2011; King Lear, Chichester, 2017, transf. Duke of York's, 2018; *Acting Shakespeare tours:* Israel, Norway, Denmark, Sweden, 1980; Spain, France, Cyprus, Israel, Poland, Romania, 1982; Los Angeles and Ritz, NYC (Drama Desk Award), 1983; San Francisco, Washington DC, Los Angeles, Olney, Cleveland, San Diego, Boston (Elliot Norton Award), 1987 Playhouse, London, 1987–88. *Films:* A Touch of Love, Alfred the Great, 1968; The Promise, 1969; Priest of Love, 1979; Scarlet Pimpernel, 1982; Plenty, Zina, 1985; Scandal, 1988; The Ballad of Little Jo, 1992; Six Degrees of Separation, Last Action Hero, 1993; The Shadow, Jack and Sarah, 1994; Restoration, 1995; Richard III (European Actor of the Year, Berlin Film Fest.), Swept from the Sea, 1996; Apt Pupil, Bent, 1997; Gods and Monsters, 1998; X-Men, 2000; The Fellowship of the Ring, 2001; The Two Towers, 2002; X-Men 2, Return of the King, 2003; Emile, 2004; Asylum, Sprung!, 2005; The Da Vinci Code, X-Men: The Last Stand, Neverwas, Flushed Away, 2006; Stardust, The Golden Compass, 2007; The Hobbit: An Unexpected Journey, 2012; The Hobbit: The Desolation of Smaug, 2013; X-Men: Days of Future Past, The Hobbit: The Battle of the Five Armies, 2014; Mr Holmes, 2015; Beauty and the Beast, 2017; All is True, The Good Liar, Cats, 2019. Has appeared on television, 1966–, incl. Walter, 1982 (RTS Performance Award for 1982); Walter and June, 1983; Mister Shaw's Missing Millions, 1993; Tales of the City, 1993; Cold Comfort Farm, 1995; Rasputin, 1996 (Golden Globe Award); The Prisoner, 2010; Vicious, 2013, 2015, 2016; The Dresser, 2015; radio performances include Walter Now, 2009. Hon. DLitt Cambridge, 2014. *Address:* c/o Independent Talent Group Ltd, 40 Whitfield Street, W1T 2RH. *T:* (020) 7636 6565, *Fax:* (020) 7323 0101. *W:* www.mckellen.com.

**McKELVEY, Very Rev. Houston;** *see* McKelvey, Very Rev. R. S. J. H.

**McKELVEY, Rev. Dr Robert John;** Principal, Northern College, Manchester, 1979–93; Moderator, General Assembly of the United Reformed Church, 1994–95; *b* 12 Oct. 1929; *s* of Robert John McKelvey and Eleanor McMaster McKelvey (*née* Earls); *m* 1957, Martha Esther Skelly; two *s* one *d*. *Educ:* Paton Congregational Coll.; Nottingham Univ. (BA 1955); Pittsburgh Theol Seminary (MTh 1956); Mansfield Coll., Oxford (DPhil 1959). Tutor, 1959–67, Principal, 1968–74, Adams United Coll., S Africa; Pres., Federal Theol Seminary of S Africa, 1970–71; Dir, Internship Trng, United Congregational Church of S Africa, 1975–78; Pres., Northern Fedn for Trng in Ministry, 1984–86. *Publications:* The New Temple: the Church in the New Testament, 1969; The Millennium and the Book of Revelation, 1999; contributor to: New Bible Dictionary, 1962; The Illustrated Bible Dictionary, 1980; New 20th Century Encyclopedia of Religious Knowledge, 2nd edn 1991; New Dictionary of Biblical Theology, 2000; Studies in the Book of Revelation, 2001; Pioneer and Priest: Jesus Christ in the Epistle to the Hebrews, 2013; learned jls incl. NT Studies, Jl of Theol Studies. *Recreations:* gardening, walking, travel, oddjobbery. *Address:* 64 Brooklawn Drive, Withington, Manchester M20 3GZ. *T:* (0161) 434 4936.

**McKELVEY, Very Rev. Dr (Robert Samuel James) Houston,** OBE 2010; TD 1983; QVRM 2000; Dean of Belfast, 2001–11; *b* 3 Sept. 1942; *s* of Robert and Annie McKelvey; *m* 1969, Eileen Roberta; one *s*. *Educ:* Queen's Univ., Belfast (BA 1965; MA (Ed) 1988); TCD; Garrett-Evangl Theol Seminary, Evanston, Ill. (DMin 1993; Hon. DHL 2003). Ordained deacon, 1967, priest, 1968; Curate, Dunmurry, 1967–70; Rector, Kilmakee, 1970–82; Sec., Gen. Synod Bd of Educn (NI), 1982–2001. Hon. Chaplain, RN Reserve, 2010–15. Ed., Ch of Ire. Gazette, 1975–82. CF (TAVR), 1970–99. *Publications:* Forty Days with Jesus, 1991; The Apostles' Creed, 1992; Children at the Table, 1993; In Touch with God, 1997; God, our Children, and Us, 1999. *Recreations:* sailing, photography, travel. *Address:* 9 College Park, Coleraine BT51 3HE. *T:* (028) 7035 3621. *Club:* Ulster (Belfast).

**McKELVIE, Anne;** *see* Neville, A.

**McKELVIE, Christina;** Member (SNP) Hamilton, Larkhall and Stonehouse, Scottish Parliament, since 2011 (Scotland Central, 2007–11); Minister for Older People and Equalities, since 2018; *b* Glasgow, 4 March 1968; *d* of David and Roseann Curran; two *s*. *Educ:* HNC Social Care. Learning Disability Services, then Learning and Develt Officer, Social Work Services, Glasgow City Council. Convenor, Eur. and External Relations Cttee, Scottish Parlt, 2011–16. *Recreations:* painting, hill walking, reading. *Address:* Scottish Parliament, Edinburgh EH99 1SP. *T:* (0131) 348 6680. *E:* Christina.McKelvie.msp@parliament.scot.

**McKELVIE, Peter,** FRCS, FRCSE; Consultant Ear, Nose and Throat Surgeon: London Hospital, 1971–98 (Hon. Consulting Surgeon, Bart's and the London (formerly Royal Hospitals) NHS Trust, since 1998); Royal National Throat, Nose and Ear Hospital, London, 1972–95 (Hon. Consulting Surgeon, since 1995); *b* 21 Dec. 1932; *s* of William Bryce McKelvie, MD, ChM, FRCSE, DLO, and Agnes E. McKelvie (*née* Winstanley), Headmistress; *m* Myra Chadwick, FRCP, Cons. Dermatologist; one *d*. *Educ:* Manchester Grammar Sch.; Rugby Sch.; Univ. of Manchester (MB ChB, MD, ChM). FRCS 1962, FRCSE 1989. House Surgeon: Manchester Royal Inf., 1957; Royal Nat. Throat, Nose and Ear Hosp., London, 1958; Lectr in Anatomy, KCL, 1959; Casualty Surg., St Mary's Hosp., London, 1960; Reader in Laryngology, UCL, 1968–70; Dean, Inst. of Laryngology and Otology, London, 1984–89. Examiner: London Univ.; Royal Colls of Surgeons of England, Edinburgh and Glasgow. MRSM 1966 (Pres., Laryngology Sect., 1992–93). *Publications:* numerous, on head and neck cancer. *Recreations:* mirth, watching young surgeons develop, Mediterranean Basin. *Address:* 9 Drakes Drive, Northwood, Middx HA6 2SL. *T:* (01923) 823544.

**McKENDRICK, Emma Elizabeth Ann;** Headmistress, Downe House, since 1997; *b* 24 June 1963; *d* of Ian and Ann Black; *m* 1987, Iain Alastair McKendrick; two *s*. *Educ:* Bedford High Sch.; Univ. of Liverpool (BA Hons German with Dutch); Univ. of Birmingham (PGCE). Royal School, Bath: Teacher of German, 1986–88; Head of Sixth Form and Careers, 1988–90; Housemistress for Sixth Form, 1989–90; Dep. Head, 1990–93; Headmistress, 1994–97. Member: Exec., Ind. Schs Exam. Bd, 2008–11; Educn Cttee, GSA, 2011–; HMC, 2015–. Governor: Hatherop Castle Prep. Sch., 1997–2002; Study Sch., Wimbledon, 1998–2006; Manor Prep. Sch., Oxford, 1998–2006; Godstowe Prep. Sch., 2000–11; Cheam Prep. Sch., 2002–13; King's Sch., Canterbury, 2003–; Sandroyd Prep. Sch., 2006–; Radley Coll., 2008–; Lambrook Sch., 2011–18; Elstree Sch., 2018–. FRSA 2008. *Recreations:* travel, theatre. *Address:* St Peter's House, Downe House, Cold Ash, Thatcham, Berks RG18 9JJ. *T:* (01635) 200286. *Club:* Lansdowne.

**McKENDRICK, Prof. Ewan Gordon;** Professor of English Private Law, University of Oxford, since 2000 (Chair of Board, Faculty of Law, 2004–06; Pro-Vice-Chancellor, 2006–10; Registrar, 2011–18); Fellow, Lady Margaret Hall, Oxford, since 2000; Professor of Anglo-American Private Law, University of Leiden, since 2018; *b* 23 Sept. 1960; *s* of Norman and Muriel McKendrick; *m* 1983, Rosemary Grace Burton-Smith; four *d*. *Educ:* Univ. of Edinburgh (LLB Hons); Pembroke Coll., Oxford (BCL). Lecturer in Law: Central Lancashire Poly., 1984–85; Univ. of Essex, 1985–88; LSE, 1988–91; Fellow, St Anne's Coll., Oxford and Linnells Lectr in Law, Univ. of Oxford, 1991–95; Prof. of English Law, UCL, 1995–2000; called to the Bar, Gray's Inn, 1998, Bencher, 2009; in practice as barrister, 1998–. Mem., AHRC, 2010–14. Mem. Bd, Rosalind Franklin Inst. Hon. QC 2015. Deleg., 2005–15, Chair, Finance Cttee, 2018–, OUP; Chair, Oxford Pastorate. Gov., Emmanuel Christian Sch., Oxford. Gen. Editor, Oxford Jl of Legal Studies, 2006–09. *Publications:* Contract Law, 1990, 13th edn 2019; (with A. Burrows and J. Edelman) Cases and Materials on the Law of Restitution, 1997, 2nd edn 2005; (with N. E. Palmer) Interests in Goods, 1993, 2nd edn 1997; (ed) Chitty on Contracts, 27th edn 1995 to 32nd edn 2015; Sale of Goods, 2000; Contract Law: text, cases and materials, 2003, 8th edn 2018. *Recreations:* reading, travel. *Address:* Lady Margaret Hall, Oxford OX2 6QA. *T:* (01865) 274380; 3 Verulam Buildings, Gray's Inn, WC1R 5NT. *T:* (020) 7831 8441.

**McKENDRICK, John Dempster;** QC 2016; *b* Alexandria, W Dunbartonshire, 31 Aug. 1976; *s* of Ian and Dorothy McKendrick; partner, 2004, Vladimir Antonio Bernal Cedeno. *Educ:* Strathblane Primary Sch.; Kelvinside Acad.; London Sch. of Econs and Pol Sci. (LLB); St Antony's Coll., Oxford (MSc); Catholic Univ. of Leuven (LLM). Called to the Bar: Inner Temple, 1999; Eastern Caribbean Supreme Court, 2013; admitted Faculty of Advocates, Edinburgh, 2008; Tribunal Judge (Convener) (pt-time), Addnl Support Needs Tribunal for Scotland, 2011–15; Mem., Attorney Gen.'s Panel of Counsel, 2012–16; Standing Jun. to Advocate Gen. of Scotland, 2012–15; Attorney Gen., Anguilla, 2016–18. Associate Prof., Catholic Univ. of Santa Maria La Antigua, Panama City, 2005–06; Vis. Scholar, City Univ., Hong Kong, 2019. FRGS 2002. *Publications:* (contrib.) Lissack and Horlick on Bribery, 2nd edn 2014; Darien: a journey in search of empire, 2016; contrib. Eur. Rev. of Private Law. *Recreations:* eating and drinking, all things Latin American, travel in the tropics. *Address:* Outer Temple Chambers, 222 The Strand, WC2R 1BA. *T:* (020) 7353 6381. *E:* jmqc@outertemple.com.

**McKENDRICK, Prof. Melveena Christine,** PhD, LittD; FBA 1999; Professor of Spanish Golden Age Literature, Culture and Society, 1999–2008, and Pro-Vice-Chancellor for Education, 2004–08, University of Cambridge; Fellow of Girton College, Cambridge, since 1967; *b* 23 March 1941; *d* of James Powell Jones and Catherine Letitia Jones (*née* Richards); *m* 1967, Neil McKendrick, *qv*; two *d*. *Educ:* Neath Girls' Grammar Sch.; Dyffryn Grammar Sch., Port Talbot; King's Coll., London (BA 1st cl. Hons Spanish); Girton Coll., Cambridge (PhD 1967); LittD Cantab, 2002. Girton College, Cambridge: Jex-Blake Res. Fellow, 1967–70; Tutor, 1970–83; Sen. Tutor, 1974–81; Dir of Studies in Modern Langs, 1984–95; Lectr in Spanish, 1980–92, Reader in Spanish Lit. and Soc., 1992–99, Univ. of Cambridge; British Acad. Reader, 1992–94. Vis. Prof., Univ. of Victoria, 1997. Member: Gen. Bd, Cambridge Univ., 1993–97 (Chair, Educn Cttee, 1995–97); Humanities Res. Bd, British Acad., 1996–98; Arts and Humanities Res. Bd, 1998–99. Consultant Hispanic Ed., Everyman, 1999–99; Member, Editorial Board: Donaire, 1994–; Revista Canadiense de Estudios Hispánicos, 1995–; Bulletin of Spanish Studies (formerly Hispanic Studies (Glasgow)), 1998–. Hon. DLitt South Wales, 2013. *Publications:* Ferdinand and Isabella, 1968; A Concise History of Spain, 1972; Woman and Society in the Spanish Drama of the Golden Age, 1974; Cervantes, 1980 (trans. Spanish 1986); (ed) Golden-Age Studies in Honour of A. A. Parker, 1984; Theatre in Spain 1490–1700, 1989 (trans. Spanish 1994); (jtly) El Mágico Prodigioso, 1992; The Revealing Image: stage portraits in the theatre of the Golden Age, 1996; Playing the King: Lope de Vega and the limits of conformity, 2000; Identities in Crisis: essays on honour, gender and women in the Comedia, 2002; contributed to: Critical Studies of Calderón's Comedias, 1973; Women in Hispanic Literature, 1983; El mundo del teatro en el siglo de oro, 1989; Teatro y prácticas escénicas en los siglos XVI y XVII, 1991; Feminist Readings on Spanish and Spanish-American Literature, 1991; Hacia Calderón, 1991; The Comedia in the Age of Calderón, 1993; Teatro y Poder, 1994; Heavenly Bodies, 1996; Texto e Imagen en Calderón, 1996; Calderón 1600–1681, 2000; Calderón: protagonista eminente del barroco europeo, 2000; Spanish Theatre: studies in honour of Victor F. Dixon, 2001; Never-Ending Adventure: studies in medieval and early modern Spanish literature in honour of Peter N. Dunn, 2002; Approaches to Teaching Early Modern Spanish Drama, 2006; Rhetoric and Reality in Early Modern Spain, 2006; articles on Early Modern Spanish theatre in many jls. *Address:* The Manor House, 3 High Street, Burwell, Cambridge CB25 0HB.

**McKENDRICK, Neil,** FRHistS; historian; Master, 1996–2005, Fellow, 1958–96 and since 2005, Gonville and Caius College, Cambridge; Reader in Social and Economic History, University of Cambridge, 1995–2002; *b* 28 July 1935; *s* of late Robert Alexander McKendrick and Sarah Elizabeth Irvine; *m* 1967, Melveena Jones (*see* M. McKendrick); two *d*. *Educ:* Alderman Newton's Sch., Leicester; Christ's Coll., Cambridge (Entrance Schol.; BA 1st cl. Hons (with distinction) History, 1956; MA 1960; Hon. Fellow, 1996). FRHistS 1971. Cambridge University: Res. Fellow, Christ's Coll., 1958; Asst Lectr in History, 1961–64; Lectr, 1964–95; Sec. to Faculty Bd of History, 1975–77; Chm., History Faculty, 1985–87; Gonville and Caius College: Lectr in History, 1958–96; Dir of Studies in History, 1959–96; Tutor, 1961–69. Lectures: Earl, Univ. of Keele, 1963; Inaugural, Wallace Gall., Colonial Williamsburg, 1985; Chettyar Meml, Univ. of Madras, 1990. Member: Tancred's Charities, 1996–; Sir John Plumb Charitable Trust, 1999–; Properties Cttee, Nat. Trust, 1999–2005; Dr E. N. Williams' Meml Fund, Dulwich Coll., 2003–; Vice-Pres., Caius Foundn in America, 1998–; Chm., Glenfield Trust, 2002–. *Publications:* (ed) Historical Perspectives: studies in English thought and society, 1974; (jtly) The Birth of a Consumer Society: the commercialization of eighteenth century England, 1982, 3rd edn 2018; (ed jtly) Business Life and Public Policy, 1986; L'Impressa Industria Commercio Banca XIII–XVIII, 1991; The Birth of Foreign & Colonial: the world's first investment trust, 1993; Il Tempo Libero Economia e Societa Secc XIII–XVIII, 1995; (jtly) 'F & C': a history of Foreign & Colonial Investment Trust, 1999; contributed to: Essays in Economic History, ed E. M. Carus Wilson, 1962; Rise of Capitalism, ed D. S. Landes, 1966; Changing Perspectives in the History of Science, ed M. Teich and R. M. Young, 1971; The Historical Development of Accounting, ed B. S. Yamey, 1978; Science and Culture in the Western Tradition, ed J. Burke, 1987; Industry and Modernization, ed Wang Jue-fei, 1989; The Social History of Western Civilization, ed R. Golden, 1992; The Other Side of Western Civilization, ed P. Stearns, 1992; The History of Enterprise, ed S. Jones and J. Inggs, 1993; The Industrial Revolution in Britain, ed J. Hoppit and E. A. Wrigley, 1994; Europäische Konsumgeschichte, ed H. Siegrist, H. Kaelble and J. Kocka, 1997; The Modern Historiography Reader: western sources, ed A. Budd, 2008; Hunting Scraps: the hunting diary of Charles James Cropper, 2013; Sir John Plumb: the hidden life of a great historian—a personal memoir, 2019; articles in learned jls, mainly on Josiah Wedgwood and the Industrial Revolution. *Recreations:* gardening, antiques, claret, photography, my wife and daughters. *Address:* Gonville and Caius College, Cambridge CB2 1TA. *T:* (01223) 332404; The Manor House, 3 High Street, Burwell, Cambridge CB25 0HB. *T:* (01638) 742312. *E:* nm10000@cam.ac.uk. *Club:* Athenæum.

**McKENNA, Alison Jayne;** Judge, Upper Tribunal (Tax and Chancery Chamber), since 2009, and Upper Tribunal (Administrative Appeals Chamber), since 2009; President, First-tier Tribunal (General Regulatory Chamber), since 2018; *b* Redhill, Surrey, 12 Nov. 1963; *d* of Peter and Evelyn Lee; *m* 1st, 1998, Jack McKenna (marr. diss. 2011); one *d*; 2nd, 2015, Richard Corden. *Educ:* Our Lady's Abingdon; Poly. of the South Bank (LLB 1987); Inns of Court Sch. of Law (Bar Finals). Called to the Bar, Middle Temple, 1988; in practice as a barrister, 1988–93; Investigator, Commn for Local Admin in England, 1993–96; Legal Adviser: Criminal Appeals Office, 1996–97; Charity Commn, 1997–2002; Hd, Charities Dept, Wilsons LLP, 2002–08; admitted Solicitor-Advocate, 2003. Principal Judge, First-tier Tribunal (Charity) (formerly Pres., Charity Tribunal), 2008–18; Pres., First-tier Tribunal (War Pensions and Armed Forces Compensation Chamber), 2014–16; Principal Judge (Gen. Regulatory Chamber), 2016–18. Member: Mental Health Act Commn, 1996–2002; Judicial Appts Commn, 2012–14. *Recreations:* anything involving horses. *Address:* General Regulatory Chamber, PO Box 9300, Leicester LE1 8DJ. *E:* presidentsoffice.grc@justice.gov.uk.

**McKENNA, Anna Louise;** QC 2017; *b* Lytham St Annes, 12 Dec. 1968; *d* of Joseph and Marie McKenna; *m* 1999, Ian Upton; two *d. Educ:* Leeds Univ. (BA Hons Econ. and Social Hist.). Called to the Bar, Middle Temple, 1994; in practice as barrister, specialising in family law, 1994–. *Recreations:* mountain walking, running, theatre. *Address:* 1 King's Bench Walk, Temple, EC4Y 7DB.

**McKENNA, Hon. Francis Joseph, (Frank);** PC (Can.) 1987; OC 2008; Deputy Chairman, TD Bank Financial Group, since 2006; *b* 19 Jan. 1948; *s* of Durward and Olive McKenna; *m* Julie Friel; two *s* one *d. Educ:* Sussex High Sch.; St Francis Xavier Univ. (BA); Queen's; Univ. of New Brunswick (LLB). Lawyer; Mem., NB and Canadian Bar Assocs. MLA (L) Chatham, NB, 1982–97; Leader, NB Liberal Party, 1985–97; Premier of NB, 1987–97. Counsel, McInnes Cooper, 1998; Ambassador of Canada to the USA, 2005–06. Hon. DSP Moncton, 1988; Hon. LLD New Brunswick, 1988. Vanier Award, 1988. *Address:* TD Bank Financial Group, TD Tower, 66 Wellington Street West, Toronto, ON M5K 1A2, Canada.

**McKENNA, Geraldine Martina Maria;** Advisor, Cedar Capital Partners, since 2014 (Partner, 2009–14); *b* 9 Aug. 1955; *d* of late John and Mary McKenna. *Educ:* Loreto Convent, Omagh, NI. British Airways, NI, 1976–81; Enterprise Travel (Aer Lingus), Florida, 1981–84; Belfast City Airport, 1984–87; Inter-Continental Hotel Corp., 1987–96; Gp Dir, Mktg and Sales, Savoy Gp, 1996–2002; Chief Exec., Maybourne Hotel Gp (formerly Savoy Gp), 2002–06. Non-exec. Dir, GuestInvest, 2006–; Advr, Fraser Giles Partnership, 2008–. Mem., British Airways Internat. Business Adv. Bd, 2013–. FRSA 2002. Hon. DHL Schiller Internat., 2004. *Recreations:* sailing, horse-riding, travel. *E:* Gmmmckenna@gmail.com.

**McKENNA, Rev. Lindsay Taylor Francis;** Vicar, St Andrew the Apostle, Catford, since 2011 (Priest-in-charge, 2010–11); *b* Glasgow, 7 July 1962; *s* of Francis Christopher McKenna and Elizabeth Colquhoun McKenna (née Taylor). *Educ:* Univ. of Glasgow (MA Hons 1983); Univ. of Aberdeen (BD 1986); Edinburgh Theol Coll. Ordained deacon, 1987, priest, 1988; Curate, St Mary's, Broughty Ferry, 1987–90; Senior Curate, Wantage, 1990–93; Vicar, St Mary the Virgin, Illingworth, 1993–99; Pastor-Dir, CARA Trust, 1999–2002; Vicar, All Saints, Hanworth, 2002–08; Rector and Provost, St Paul's Cathedral, Dundee, 2008–09. *Recreations:* gardening, keeping fit, cooking, the company of friends, Modern Spanish history, lunch.

**McKENNA, His Honour Martin Nicholas;** a Circuit Judge, 2000–19; a Senior Circuit Judge, 2008–19; *b* 19 Nov. 1955; *s* of Bernard Malcolm McKenna and Anne Rose McKenna; *m* 1st, 1979, Deborah Jane Scott (marr. diss. 1995); two *d*; 2nd, 1996, Sarah Louise Malden; two step *d. Educ:* Birmingham Univ. (LLB 1st Cl. Hons); Lincoln Coll., Oxford. Admitted Solicitor, 1980. Joined Evershed & Tomkinson, Solicitors, 1978: Associate, 1984–87; Partner, 1987–2000; Head of Litigation Dept, 1994–99. Midland Circuit. *Recreations:* Rugby, cricket, sailing, ski-ing, cycling. *Club:* East India.

**McKENNA, Maureen,** OBE 2015; Executive Director of Education (formerly Service Director Education), Glasgow City Council, since 2007; *b* Edinburgh, 2 July 1960; *d* of Adrian and Sheila Hynes; *m* Jack McKenna; two *s* one *d. Educ:* Bearsden Acad.; Univ. of Glasgow (BSc Hons Maths); Jordanhill Coll. (PGCE). Maths teacher, Dyce Acad., 1982–85; Asst Principal Teacher, Ellon Acad., 1985–89; Principal Teacher, Northfield Acad., 1989–91; Principal Teacher, 1991–97, Asst Head Teacher, 1997–2000, Kilsyth Acad.; HM Inspector of Educn, 2000–07. Pres., Assoc. of Dirs of Educn, 2015–19. Hon. Vice Pres., Basketball Scotland, 2009. *Recreation:* basketball referee (qualified 1980; international referee, 1990; retired 2009). *E:* maureen.mckenna@education.glasgow.gov.uk.

**McKENNA, Prof. Patrick Gerald, (Gerry)** DL; PhD; geneticist; Vice-Chancellor and President, University of Ulster, 1999–2006; *b* 10 Dec. 1953; *s* of late Gerald Joseph McKenna and Mary Teresa (née Smyth); *m* 1976, Philomena Winifred McArdle; two *s. Educ:* Univ. of Ulster (BSc 1st Cl. Hons 1976); PhD Genetics, QUB, 1979. FIBMS 1982; FRSB (FIBiol 1988); MRIA 2001; CSci 2006. Lectr, Human Biology, NUU, 1979–84; University of Ulster: Sen. Lectr, Biology, 1984–88; Dir, Biomedical Scis Res. Centre, 1985–88; Prof. and Head of Dept of Biol and Biomed. Scis, 1988–94; Dean, Faculty of Science, 1994–97; Pro-Vice-Chancellor (Res.), 1997–99. Visiting Professor: Univ. Kebangsaan, Malaysia, 1992; Univ. of Malaya, 1993; Univ. of Calif, Berkeley, 2005. Chairman: NI Foresight, Life and Health Technologies Panel, 1995–99; Heads of Univ. Centres Biomed. Sci., 1995–97 (Pres., Emeritus, 2000–; Hon. Exec. Sec., 2011–); UU-Online.com, 2000–05; Univ. of Ulster Sci. Res. Parks Ltd, 2002–04; Univs Ireland, 2003–05; Founder: UU Step Up Programme, 1999; UU e-learning (Campus One), 2001; Harry Ferguson Engineering Village, Jordanstown, 2004; Co-Founder: Universities Ireland, 1993; NI Centre for Diet and Health, 1995; non-executive Director: NI Med. Physics Agency, 1995–2001; (Co-Founder) NI Sci. Park Foundn, 1999–2005; UK eUnivs Worldwide, 2000–06; eUniv. Hldg Co., 2001–06; UUTECH Ltd, 1997–2005 (Chair, 2002–05); Bd Mem., ILEX, 2003–05. Advr, Biomedical Scis Dept, 2011–17, Chair, Health Technol. and Informatics Adv. Cttee, 2017–, Hong Kong Polytechnic Univ.; REF 2014 advr to UK univs, 2012–. Member: Council, Inst. of Biomed. Sci., 1996–2002; Jt Med. Adv. Cttee, 2003–04; Founding Bd Mem., UK Health Educn Partnership, 2003–05. Mem., Shadow Bd for E-nursing educn, 2001–02. Member: US-Ireland R&D Taskforce, 2002–04; Bd, BITC NI, 2002–03; Sci., Engrg and Envmt Adv. Cttee, British Council, 2003–05; Science All-Party Gp, Stormont, 2012–; Exec. Cttee, Heads of Univ. Biosciences, 2013–; Educn Policy Adv. Cttee, Soc. of Biol., 2014–; QAA Benchmarking Wkg Gp, Biocsis, 2014–16, Biomed. Scis, 2014–16; Internat. Adv. Bd, JMD MARBLE; Chm., Ind. Adv. Gp, Doctoral Trng Alliance, University Alliance, 2015–. Royal Irish Academy: Member: North-South Standing Cttee, 2012– (Chair, 2018–); All-island and Internat. Working Gp, 2013–; Standing Cttee for Council-nominated Members, 2014–; Steering Cttee on Govtl Structure for HE and Res., 2015; Coordinator, Rev. of HE Funding in NI, 2016; Vice Pres. and Mem. Council, 2017–; Chair, NI Brexit Wkg Gp, 2017. Vice-Chm., Ulster Cancer Foundn, 1999–2005; Chairman: Servite Priory Liby Project Bd, 2011–; Mgt Bd, Benburb Priory Liby and Mus., 2016–. Mem., Internat. Adv. Bd, Univ. of Kufa, 2013–. Chm., Review Gp, British Jl of Biomed. Sci., 2013. Mem., Armagh Rotary Club, 2015–19. Freedom, Borough of Coleraine, 2001; Keys to City of Portland, Maine, 2003. DL Co. Londonderry, 2002. FRSA 1999. Hon. DSc NUI, 2001; Hon. LLD QUB, 2002. Honoree: Friends of Harvard Celtic Studies, 2002; Flax Trust, New York, 2003. *Publications:* Diet, Lifestyle and Health in Northern Ireland, 1989; Biotechnology and Industry—Present and Future, 1994; Celebrating Age, 1996; Research Training in Healthcare Professions, 2003; Management Challenges for a 21st Century University, 2004; (contrib.) Dictionary of Irish Biography, 2015, 2016; over 200 articles, books and chapters on genetics, DNA repair, diet and health, and higher educn and research policy. *Recreations:* reading, the turf. *Address:* Lemneigh, 20 Tobermesson Road, Dungannon, Northern Ireland BT71 7QE. *T:* 07766 745511. *E:* mckenna.gerry@rocketmail.com. *Club:* Reform.

**McKENNA, Rosemary,** CBE 1995; *b* 8 May 1941; *d* of Cornelius Harvey and Mary (née Crossan); *m* 1963, James S. McKenna; three *s* one *d. Educ:* St Augustine's, Glasgow; Notre Dame Coll. (Dip. Primary Educn). Private sec., 1958–64; teacher, various primary schs, 1974–94. Member (Lab): Cumbernauld and Kilsyth DC, 1984–96 (Leader, 1984–88 and 1992–94; Provost, 1988–92); N Lanarks Council, 1995–97. Pres., COSLA, 1994–96. MP (Lab) Cumbernauld and Kilsyth, 1997–2005, Cumbernauld, Kilsyth and Kirkintilloch E, 2005–10. PPS to Minister of State for Foreign and Commonwealth Affairs, 1998–2001. Member, Select Committee: on culture, media and sport, 2001–10; on procedure, 2001–10; Chm., Cttee of Selection, 2005–10. Mem., Cttee of Regions of EU, 1994–98; Chm., UK and European Standing Cttees, CEMR, 1996–98. Chm., Scottish Libraries and Inf. Council, 1998–2002. Member, Management Board: Cumbernauld Coll., 2011–; New College, Lanarkshire, 2014–. *Recreations:* reading, travelling, family gatherings. *Address:* 7 Scott Drive, Cumbernauld G67 4LB.

**MACKENZIE,** family name of **Earl of Cromartie** and **Barons MacKenzie of Culkein** and **Mackenzie of Framwellgate**.

**MACKENZIE of Gairloch;** see Inglis of Glencorse.

**MacKENZIE OF CULKEIN,** Baron *cr* 1999 (Life Peer), of Assynt in Highland; **Hector Uisdean MacKenzie;** Associate General Secretary, UNISON, 1993–2000; *b* 25 Feb. 1940; *s* of George MacKenzie and Williamina Budge Sutherland; *m* 1961, Anna Morrison (marr. diss.); one *s* three *d. Educ:* Nicolson Inst., Stornoway, Isle of Lewis; Portree High Sch., Skye; Leverndale School of Nursing, Glasgow; West Cumberland School of Nursing, Whitehaven. RGN, RMN. Student Nurse, Leverndale Hosp., 1958–61; Asst Lighthouse Keeper, Clyde Lighthouses Trust, 1961–64; Student Nurse, 1964–66, Staff Nurse, 1966–69, West Cumberland Hosp.; Confederation of Health Service Employees: Asst Regl Sec., 1969; Regl Sec., Yorks and E Midlands, 1970–74; Nat. Officer, 1974–83; Asst Gen. Sec., 1983–87; Gen. Sec., 1987–93. Co. Sec., UIA Insurance Ltd, 1996–2000. Pres., TUC, 1998–99. *Recreations:* reading, aviation, maritime issues, travel. *Address:* House of Lords, SW1A 0PW. *T:* (020) 7219 8515, *Fax:* (020) 7219 8712.

**MACKENZIE OF FRAMWELLGATE,** Baron *cr* 1998 (Life Peer), of Durham in the co. of Durham; **Brian Mackenzie,** OBE 1998; *b* 21 March 1943; *s* of Frederick George Mackenzie and Lucy Mackenzie (née Ward); *m* 1965, Jean Seed (marr. diss.); two *s. Educ:* Eastbourne Sch., Darlington; London Univ. (LLB Hons 1974); FBI Nat. Acad. (graduate 1985). Durham Constabulary, 1963–98: Constable, 1963; Sgt (Trng), 1970; Det. Insp., Hd of Drug Squad, 1976; Chief Insp., Hd of Crime Computer Unit, 1979; Supt (Det.), attached to Home Office, 1980; Territorial Comdr Supt, 1983; Divl Comdr, Chief Supt, 1989–98. Nat. Pres., Police Superintendents' Assoc. of England and Wales, 1995–98 (Vice Pres., 1993–95). Vice Pres., BALPA, 2004–08. Studied and lectured extensively on police methods, visiting Europe, USA and Canada. Regular broadcasts on TV and radio on law and policing issues. *Publications:* Two Lives of Brian (memoir), 2004; articles in legal and policing jls. *Recreations:* after-dinner speaking, swimming, music, travel. *Address:* House of Lords, SW1A 0PW. *W:* www.lordmackenzie.com.

**McKENZIE OF LUTON,** Baron *cr* 2004 (Life Peer), of Luton in the County of Bedfordshire; **William David McKenzie;** *b* 24 July 1946; *s* of Donald McKenzie and Elsie May McKenzie (née Doust); *m* 1972, Diane Joyce (née Angliss). *Educ:* Bristol Univ. (BA Hons Econs and Accounting). ACA 1971, FCA 1979. Partner, Price Waterhouse UK, 1980–86, Price Waterhouse, Hong Kong, 1993–98 (Partner-in-charge, Vietnam, 1996–98). Mem. (Lab) Luton BC, 1976–92, 1999–2005 (Leader, 1999–2003). Contested (Lab) Luton S, 1987, 1992. A Lord in Waiting (Govt Whip), 2005–07; Parly Under-Sec. of State, DWP, 2007–10, DCLG, 2009–10. Pres., RoSPA, 2015–. *Recreations:* swimming, reading, music. *Address:* 6 Sunset Drive, Luton, Beds LU2 7TN. *T:* and *Fax:* (01582) 455384. *E:* mckenziew@parliament.uk.

**MACKENZIE, Sir Alexander Alwyne Henry Charles Brinton M.;** see Muir Mackenzie.

**McKENZIE, Alistair William,** MBE 1980; HM Diplomatic Service, retired; *b* 19 Feb. 1945; *s* of late James McKenzie and Barbara McKenzie (née Anderson); *m* 1968, Margaret Emily Young; two *s. Educ:* Leith Acad., Edinburgh. Entered FCO, 1965; Budapest, 1967–69; Singapore, 1969–72; Brasilia, 1972–75; FCO, 1975–78; Vice Consul: San Salvador, 1978–80; San Jose, 1980–82; Commercial Attaché, Madrid, 1982–84; W Africa Dept, 1984–86; Dep. High Comr and Hd of Chancery, Banjul, 1986–89; Consul-Gen., Bilbao, 1990–94; First Sec., Lagos, 1994–98; Dir, British Trade Internat., 1998–2001; Counsellor and Dep. Head of Mission, Abu Dhabi, 2001–05. Chief of Protocol, Shaheen Business and Investment Gp, Amman, 2006–07; CEO, Pearl Capital LLC, Abu Dhabi, 2007–09. *Recreations:* golf, photography. *Club:* Royal Over-Seas League.

**MACKENZIE, Amanda Felicity,** OBE 2014; Chief Executive, Business in the Community, since 2016; *b* Yorks, 6 Dec. 1963; *d* of Frazer Mackenzie and Rachel Mackenzie. *Educ:* Wakefield Girls' High Sch.; Bedford Coll., Univ. of London (BSc Psychol.); INSEAD (AMP). Graduate trainee, WCRS, 1986–88; Bd Dir, DMBB, 1988–98; Mktg Dir, British Airways Air Miles, 1998–2001; Brand and Mktg Dir, BT, 2001–04; Commercial Dir, British Gas, 2005–08; Chief Marketing Officer, Aviva plc, 2008–16. Non-executive Director: Mothercare plc, 2011–17; Lloyds Banking Gp, 2018–. Member: Govt Strategic Mktg Adv. Bd, 2009–11; Steering Gp, Lord Davies of Abersoch's ind. rev. into Women on Bds, 2010–16; Adv. Bd, Royal Mail, 2014–. Pres., Marketing Soc., 2011–13. Mem. Bd, NYO, 2007–16; In Kind Direct, 2017–18. Hon. DLit Winchester, 2018. *Address:* Business in the Community, 137 Shepherdess Walk, N1 7RQ.

**MACKENZIE, Prof. Andrew Peter,** PhD; FRS 2015; Director, Max Planck Institute for Chemical Physics of Solids, Dresden, since 2012; Professor of Condensed Matter Physics, University of St Andrews, since 2001; *b* Elderslie, 7 March 1964; *s* of Alexander Colin Mackenzie and Bridget Mary Mackenzie (née Gordon); *m* 1991, Olga Maria Dunin-Borkowski; one *s* two *d. Educ:* Hutchesons' Grammar Sch., Glasgow; Univ. of Edinburgh (BSc Hons Phys 1986); Trinity Coll., Cambridge (PhD Phys 1991). Researcher, CERN, Geneva, 1986–87; Res. Associate, 1991–93, Royal Soc. Univ. Res. Fellow, 1993–97, Univ. of Cambridge; Royal Soc. Univ. Res. Fellow and Univ. Reader, Univ. of Birmingham, 1997–2001. *Publications:* 132 res. and review papers in learned jls. *Recreations:* golf, hiking, ski-ing, travel. *Address:* Max Planck Institute for Chemical Physics of Solids, Nöthnitzer Strasse 40, 01187 Dresden, Germany. *T:* (351) 46465900, *Fax:* (351) 46465902. *E:* mackenzie@cpfs.mpg.de.

**MACKENZIE, Andrew Stewart,** PhD; FRS 2014; Chief Executive Officer, BHP Group Ltd (formerly BHP Billiton Ltd), since 2013; *b* UK, 20 Dec. 1956; *s* of Hugh Mackenzie and Mary Mackenzie; *m* 1977, Liz Allan; two *d. Educ:* St Andrews Univ. (BSc Geol. 1st Cl. 1977); Univ. of Bristol (PhD Organic Chem. 1981). Postdoctoral Fellow, Univ. of Bristol,

1981; Humboldt Fellow, Nuclear Res. Centre, Jülich, 1981–82; British Petroleum, 1983–2004: Chief Reservoir Engr, 1993–95; Hd of Corporate Affairs, 1995–96; Chief Technol. Officer, 1997–2001; Gp Vice Pres., Petrochemicals, 2001–04; Product Gp Hd, Diamonds and Minerals, Rio Tinto, 2004–07; Gp Exec., CEO Non Ferrous, and Hd of London Office, BHP Billiton Ltd, 2008–13. Non-exec. Dir, Centrica, 2005–13. Mem., RAE Panel 2008. Treas., 1994–2004, Chm., Bd of Trustees, 2005–07, Demos. Trustee, Mus. of Sci. and Industry, Chicago, 2002–04. Member: Geol Soc., 1982; Soc. of Petroleum Engrs, 1987. Hon. DSc Bristol, 2011. *Address*: BHP Group Ltd, 171 Collins Street, Melbourne, Vic 3000, Australia. *T*: 3 9609 3464; BHP Group Ltd, Nova South, 160 Victoria Street, SW1E 5LB. *T*: (020) 7802 4000. *E*: andrew.mackenzie@bhpbilliton.com. *Clubs*: Reform; British Sub-Aqua.

MacKENZIE, Prof. Angus Buchanan, PhD; Professor, 2005, and Director, 2007–12, Scottish Universities Environmental Research Centre; *b* Glasgow, 23 Jan. 1950; *s* of Hugh C. MacKenzie and Christina MacKenzie; *m* 1983, Shelagh Stenhouse MacKay; one *s* one *d*. *Educ*: Shawlands Acad., Glasgow; Univ. of Glasgow (BSc 1st Cl. Hons Chem.; PhD Chem. 1977). CChem 1979; MRSC 1979, FRSC 1989. Res. Officer, CEGB, 1976–77; Scottish Universities Research and Reactor Centre, later Scottish Universities Environmental Research Centre: Lectr, 1977–91; Sen. Lectr, 1991–99; Reader, 1999–2005. *Publications*: contribs to jls and conf. procs. *Recreations*: walking, fitness, gardening, reading, travel, DIY. *Address*: 11 Claremount Avenue, Giffnoch, Glasgow G46 6UT. *T*: (0141) 569 9566.

MACKENZIE, Colin Douglas; Chief Executive, Aberdeenshire Council, 2008–15; *b* Tripoli, N Africa, 10 March 1950; *s* of late Major John Mackenzie, MC, RA and of Elsie Mackenzie (*née* Stewart); *m* 1976, Lesley Adam, MA, CQSW; five *s*. *Educ*: Forfar Acad.; Strathclyde Univ. (BA 1973); Glasgow Univ. (DipSW, CQSW 1975). Trainee social worker, Dundee City Corp., 1973–75; Child Care Specialist, 1975–77, Area Team Leader, 1977–82, Tayside Regl Council; Social Work Manager, 1982–85, Divl Officer, 1985–96 (Lead Officer, Piper Alpha Disaster response, 1988–90), Grampian Regl Council; Hd of Service, 1996–2000, Dir of Housing and Social Work, 2000–08, Aberdeenshire Council. Mem., 21st Century Rev. of Social Work, 2004–05. Non-exec. Dir, Scottish Prison Service, 2007–08; Jt Chair, Scottish Govt Delivery Gp, Health and Social Care, 2012–15. Pres., ADSW, 2005–06. Dir, NE Scotland Preservation Trust, 2015–. *Recreations*: Rugby, swimming, gardening, good company, family.

MACKENZIE, Colin Scott, OBE 2019; DL; Sheriff of Grampian, Highland and Islands at Lerwick and Kirkwall, 1992–2003; part-time Sheriff, 2004–09; Retired Sheriff, Grampian Highlands and Islands, 2009–13, now Honorary Sheriff; Vice Lord-Lieutenant, Western Isles, 1984–92; *b* 7 July 1938; *s* of late Major Colin Scott Mackenzie, BL and Mrs Margaret S. Mackenzie, MA; *m* 1966, Christeen Elizabeth Drysdale McLauchlan. *Educ*: Nicolson Inst., Stornoway; Fettes Coll., Edinburgh; Edinburgh Univ. (BL 1959). Admitted Solicitor and Notary Public, 1960; Procurator Fiscal, Stornoway, 1969–92; Temporary Sheriff, 1992. Clerk to the Lieutenancy, Stornoway, 1975–92. Dir, Harris Tweed Assoc. Ltd, 1979–95; Trustee, Western Isles Kidney Machine Trust, 1977–. Council Mem. for Western Isles, Orkney, Shetland etc, Law Soc. of Scotland, 1985–92. General Assembly, Church of Scotland: Comr, Presbytery of Lewis, 1991–92; Mem., Bd of Social Responsibility, 1991–95; Convenor, Study Gp into Young People and the Media, 1991–93; Mem., Judicial Commn, 2011–. Council Mem., Sheriffs' Assoc., 2002–03. DL Islands Area of Western Isles, 1975. Pres., Probus Club, Isle of Lewis, 2010–11; Hon. Mem., Rotary Club, Stornoway, 1992– (Pres., 1976–77). *Publications*: The Last Warrior Band, 2002; Personal Reflections on Shetland, Orkney and Western Isles, 2010; Eaglais na h-Aoidhe, the Overlooked Jewel in our Crown, 2012; Gael Force over Gallipoli, 2016; contrib. Stair Memorial Encyclopaedia of Laws of Scotland, 1987. *Recreations*: amateur radio, reading, local history, travel and other more sedentary pursuits. *Address*: Park House, 8 Matheson Road, Stornoway, Western Isles HS1 2NQ. *T*: (01851) 702008. *Club*: New (Edinburgh).

McKENZIE, Dan Peter, CH 2003; PhD; FRS 1976; BP Professor of Earth Sciences, Cambridge University, 2006–12, now Emeritus (Royal Society Professor of Earth Sciences, 1996–2006); Fellow of King's College, Cambridge, 1965–73 and since 1977; *b* 21 Feb. 1942; *s* of William Stewart McKenzie and Nancy Mary McKenzie; *m* 1971, Indira Margaret Misra; one *s*. *Educ*: Westminster Sch.; King's Coll., Cambridge (BA 1963, PhD 1966). Cambridge University: Sen. Asst in Res., 1969–75; Asst Dir of Res., 1975–79; Reader in Tectonics, 1979–84; Prof. of Earth Scis, 1984–96. Hon. Mem., Japan Acad., 2015 Hon. MA 1966, Hon. DSc 2014, Cambridge. (Jtly) Geology and Geophysics Prize, Internat. Balzan Foundn of Italy and Switzerland, 1981; (jtly) Japan Prize, Science and Technology Foundn of Japan, 1990; Royal Medal, 1991, Copley Medal, 2011, Royal Soc.; Gold Medal, RAS, 1992; Crafoord Medal, Royal Swedish Acad. of Scis, 2002. *Publications*: papers in learned jls. *Recreation*: gardening. *Address*: Bullard Laboratories, Madingley Road, Cambridge CB3 0EZ. *T*: (01223) 337177.

MacKENZIE, Prof. Donald Angus, PhD; FBA 2004; FRSE; Professor of Sociology, University of Edinburgh, since 1992; *b* 3 May 1950; *s* of Angus MacKenzie and Anne MacKenzie; *m* 1998, Caroline Bamford; one *s* one *d*. *Educ*: Univ. of Edinburgh (BSc 1972; PhD 1978). Lectr, 1975–88, Reader, 1988–92, in Sociology, Univ. of Edinburgh. Vis. Prof. of Hist. of Sci., Harvard Univ., 1997. FRSE 2002. *Publications*: Statistics in Britain 1865–1930, 1981; Inventing Accuracy, 1990; Knowing Machines, 1995; Mechanizing Proof, 2001; An Engine, not a Camera, 2006; Material Markets, 2009. *Recreations*: cycling, walking, chess. *Address*: School of Social and Political Science, University of Edinburgh, Chrystal Macmillan Building, George Square, Edinburgh EH8 9LD.

MacKENZIE, George Paterson; Keeper of the Records of Scotland, 2001–12; Registrar General for Scotland, 2011–12; Chairman, Scottish Ancestral Tourism Group, since 2013; *b* 22 Sept. 1950; *s* of James Sargent Porteous MacKenzie and Flora Black MacKenzie; *m* 1st, 1972, Elizabeth Hamilton (marr. diss. 1988); 2nd, 1995, Katherine Barratt (marr. diss. 2003); 3rd, 2005, Caroline Morgan. *Educ*: Univ. of Stirling (BA 1972; MLitt 1978). Asst history teacher, Larbert High Sch., 1974–75; Res. Asst, Scottish Record Office, 1975–83; Departmental Records Officer, General Register Office for Scotland, 1984–85; Hd of Records Liaison, then Preservation Services, Scottish Record Office, 1986–94; Dep. Sec. Gen., Internat. Council on Archives, Paris, 1995–96; Dir of External Relns, Nat. Archives of Scotland, 1997–2000. Adviser: on protection of archives in former Yugoslavia for UNESCO, 1995–97; on archives for World Bank, 1998–99; External Examiner in archives and records mgt, Univ. of Liverpool, 1998–2002, Univ. of Dundee, 2014–. Pres., Scottish Record Soc., 2014–. *Publications*: articles and conf. papers on protection of archives in armed conflict, electronic records and archives mgt. *Recreations*: reading, travel, cooking. *Address*: Clachan Seil, Oban.

MacKENZIE, Gillian Rachel, (Mrs N. I. MacKenzie); *see* Ford, G. R.

MACKENZIE, Sir Guy; *see* Mackenzie, Sir J. W. G.

McKENZIE, Iain; *b* Greenock, 4 April 1959; *s* of Adam McKenzie and Isobel McKenzie; *m* 1982, Alison Stewart; two *s*. *Educ*: Greenock High Sch.; James Watt Coll. Apprentice mechanic; manufacturing line technician, debug technician, quality assurance officer and large enterprise procurement officer, IBM; Wise Gp. Mem. (Lab), Inverclyde Council, 2003–11 (Leader, 2011). MP (Lab) Inverclyde, July 2011–2015; contested (Lab) same seat, 2015. Mem., River Clyde Homes, 2008–10.

MacKENZIE, James Alexander Mackintosh, CB 1988; FREng; Chief Road Engineer, Scottish Development Department, 1976–88, retired; *b* Inverness, 6 May 1928; *m* 1970, Pamela Dorothy Nixon; one *s* one *d*. *Educ*: Inverness Royal Acad. FICE, FCIHT; FREng (FEng 1982). Miscellaneous local govt appts, 1950–63; Chief Resident Engr, Durham County Council, 1963–67; Dep. Dir, 1967–71, Dir, 1971–76, North Eastern Road Construction Unit, MoT, later DoE. *Recreations*: golf, fishing. *Address*: Pendor, 2 Dean Park, Longniddry, East Lothian EH32 0QR. *T*: (01875) 852643.

MACKENZIE, Sir James William Guy, 5th Bt *cr* 1890, of Glen Muick, Aberdeenshire; Chairman, Kerrier Direct Services, 1995–98 (Vice-Chairman, 1994–95); *b* 6 Oct. 1946; *s* of Lt-Col Eric Dighton Mackenzie, CMG, CVO, DSO (*d* 1972), 4th *s* of Sir Allan Russell Mackenzie, 2nd Bt, and Elizabeth Kathrine Mary, *d* of Captain James William Guy Innes, CBE; *S* cousin, 1993; *m* 1st, 1972, Paulene Patricia Simpson (marr. diss. 1980); two *d*; 2nd, 1996, Sally Ann (*née* Howard). *Educ*: Stowe. Mem. (Ind) Kerrier DC, 1993–2003. *Recreations*: watching cricket and football, walking, music, collecting popular music memorabilia; historic buildings. *Heir*: *b* Allan Walter Mackenzie, *b* 6 Nov. 1952.

MACKENZIE, Ven. Janet; Archdeacon of Hertford, since 2016; *b* 1962. *Educ*: Westminster Coll., Oxford (BEd 1986); Westcott House, Cambridge; Anglia Ruskin Univ. (BA 2008). Ordained deacon, 2006, priest, 2007; Curate, St Swithun, Sandy, 2006–10; Priest-in-charge, 2010–14, Vicar, 2014–16, St Augustine of Canterbury, Luton; Area Dean, Luton, 2012–16. *Address*: Glebe House, St Mary's Lane, Hertingfordbury SG14 2LE.

McKENZIE, Ven. Jennifer Gaines; Archdeacon of Wigan and West Lancashire, since 2015; *b* 1963. *Educ*: Auburn Univ., Alabama (BA 1988); Virginia Theol Seminary (MDiv 2004). Ordained deacon, 2004, priest, 2005; Curate: St David's, Washington, DC, 2004–07; Christ Church, Alexandria, Va, 2007–09; Church of the Good Shepherd, Burke, Va, 2011–12; Priest-in-charge, Oak Hill, Epiphany, Va, 2012–15. *Address*: 33 Elmers Green, Skelmersdale, Lancs WN8 6RZ.

MACKENZIE, Gen. Sir Jeremy (John George), GCB 1998 (KCB 1992); OBE 1982; Chairman and owner, Tan Trax International Ltd, since 2015; *b* 11 Feb. 1941; *s* of late Lt-Col John William Elliot Mackenzie, DSO, QPM and of Valerie (*née* Dawes); *m* 1969, Elizabeth Lyon (*née* Wertenbaker); one *d* (one *s* decd). *Educ*: Duke of York Sch., Nairobi, Kenya. psc, HCSC. Commnd Queen's Own Highlanders, 1961; Canadian Forces Staff Coll., 1974; Bde Major, 24 Airportable Bde, 1975–76; CO 1 Queen's Own Highlanders, NI and Hong Kong, 1979–82; Instructor, Staff Coll., 1982–83; Col Army Staff Duties 2, 1983–84; Comdr 12th Armoured Bde, 1984–86; Service Fellowship, King's Coll., Univ. of London, 1987; Dep. Comdt, 1987–89, Comdt, 1989, Staff Coll.; GOC 4th Armoured Div., BAOR, 1989–91; Comdr 1st (British) Corps, 1991–92; Comdr, Ace Rapid Reaction Corps, 1992–94; Dep. SACEUR, 1994–98; ADC Gen. to the Queen, 1997–98. Gov., Royal Hospital, Chelsea, 1999–2006. Director: SIRVA plc, 2003–07; SELEX Communications Ltd, 2004–13; Main Bd, Blue Hackle Security, 2012– (Mem., 2006–, Chm., 2011–14, Adv. Bd); Secure Accommodation, 2013–18; Dir and shareholder, AC Cars (England) Ltd, 2016–19; Main Bd, Allies Corp., 2016–18 (Sen. Mil. Advr, 2016–18); Fort Monroe Reimagined LLC, 2018–. Senior Military Adviser: Beretta, 2007–14; Benteler Automotive, 2011–13. Colonel Commandant: WRAC, 1990–92; AGC, 1992–98; Colonel: Highlanders Regt, 1994–2001; APTC, 1997–2012. Lieut, Queen's Bodyguard for Scotland, Royal Company of Archers, 2013 (Mem., 1986–; Brig., 2001–08; Ensign, 2008–13). Pres., Services Br., British Deer Soc., 1993–2015; Life Vice-Pres., Combined Services Winter Sports Assoc., 2001. DL Greater London, 2006; Citizen and Gunmaker, City of London, 2009–. OStJ 2003. Comdr, US Legion of Merit, 1997, 1st Oak Leaf Cluster, 1998; Cross of Merit 1st Class (Czech Republic), 1998; Officers' Cross, Order of Merit (Hungary), 1998; Order of Madara Horseman, 1st Cl. (Bulgaria), 1999; Officers' Gold Medal of Merit (Slovenia), 2002. *Publications*: The British Army and the Operational Level of War, 1989. *Recreations*: shooting, fishing, classic cars. *Address*: The Old Bell, 20 Long Street, Cerne Abbas, Dorset DT2 7JF. *Club*: Sloane.

MACKENZIE of Gairloch, John Alexander; landowner, Gairloch and Conon estates, since 1980; Vice Lord-Lieutenant of Ross and Cromarty, 2013–19; *b* Muir of Ord, Ross-shire, 27 May 1944; *s* of late Brig. William Alexander Mackenzie of Gairloch, DSO, OBE and Marjory Kythé Mackenzie (*née* Stirling); *m* 1969, Frances Marian Williams; one *s* one *d*. *Educ*: Gordonstoun. 2nd Lt, Queen's Own Highlanders, 1962–65. Export Dir, James Buchanan & Co. Ltd, 1966–80. Chm., Black Isle Grain Ltd, 1987–90. Mem., Red Deer Commn, 1987–98. Chm., Highland Reg., Scottish Landowners Fedn, 1990–95. DL Ross, Cromarty, Skye and Lochalsh, 1984. *Address*: Conan House, Conon Bridge, Ross-shire IV7 8AL. *T*: (01349) 861101.

McKENZIE, Prof. John Crawford; Founding Governor, University of the Arts London (formerly The London Institute), since 1996 (Rector, 1986–96, now Emeritus Professor); *b* 12 Nov. 1937; *s* of late Donald Walter McKenzie and Emily Beatrice McKenzie; *m* 1960, Ann McKenzie (*née* Roberts); two *s*. *Educ*: London School of Economics and Political Science (BScEcon); Bedford Coll., London (MPhil). Lecturer, Queen Elizabeth Coll., Univ. of London, 1961; Dep. Director, Office of Health Econs, 1966; Market Inf. Manager, Allied Breweries Ltd, 1968; various posts, Kimpher Ltd, 1969, finally Chief Exec., Kimpher Marketing Services, 1973; Head of Dept, London Coll. of Printing, 1975; Principal: Ilkley Coll., 1978; Bolton Inst. of Higher Educn, 1982; Rector, Liverpool Poly., 1984. Visiting Professor: Queen Elizabeth Coll., 1976–80; Univ. of Newcastle, 1981–87. Director: Antiquarian Pastimes Ltd, 1984–; New Frontiers in Educn Ltd, 1993–; Ringmaster Holdings plc, 2001–. Chm., Leeds Utd plc, 2003. Mem., Adv. Council, Univ. of Sarawak, Malaysia, 1994–; Advr, Japan Coll. of Foreign Langs, Tokyo, 1997–; Mem. Consultative Cttee, Eastern Visual Arts and Design Univ. of China, Shanghai, 2002; Sen. Vice-Pres., Shanghai Univ. of Visual Arts, 2003–. Special Advr, Shanghai Metropolitan Govt, 2002–. Chevalier de l'Ordre des Arts et des Lettres (France), 1992. *Publications*: (ed jtly) Changing Food Habits, 1964; (ed jtly) Our Changing Fare, 1966; (ed jtly) The Food Consumer, 1987; many articles in Proc. Nutrition Soc., British Jl Nutrition, Nutrition Bull., etc. *Recreations*: collecting antiquarian books and works of art, contract bridge. *Address*: c/o TSB Bank plc, PO Box 99 BX4 7SB. *Clubs*: Athenæum, Chelsea Arts.

McKENZIE, Julia Kathleen, (Mrs Jerry Harte), CBE 2018; actress, singer and director; *b* 17 Feb. 1941; *d* of Albion McKenzie and Kathleen Rowe; *m* 1972, Jerry Harte. *Educ*: Guildhall School of Music and Drama. Hon. FGSM, 1988. *Stage*: Maggie May, Adelphi, 1966; Mame, Drury Lane, 1969; Promises, Promises, Prince of Wales, 1970; Company, Her Majesty's, 1972; Cowardy Custard, Mermaid, 1972; Cole, Mermaid, 1974; Norman Conquests, Globe, 1975; Side by Side by Sondheim, Wyndhams, 1976, NY 1977; Ten Times Table, Globe, 1978; Outside Edge, Queens, 1979; On the 20th Century, Her Majesty's, 1980; Guys and Dolls, NT, 1982; Schweyk in 2nd World War, NT, 1982;

Woman in Mind, Vaudeville, 1986; Follies, Shaftesbury, 1987; Into the Woods, Phoenix, 1990; Sweeney Todd, NT, 1993; Communicating Doors, Gielgud, 1995; Kafka's Dick, Piccadilly, 1998; The Royal Family, Th. Royal, Haymarket, 2001; The Philadelphia Story, Old Vic, 2005; directed: Stepping Out, Duke of York's, 1984; Steel Magnolias, Lyric, 1989; Just So, Watermill, Bagnor, Berks, 1989; Putting it Together, Old Fire Station, Oxford, 1992, NY, 1993; A Little Night Music, Tokyo, 1999; Honk! The Ugly Duckling, NT, 1999; Peter Pan, the Musical, RFH, 2001; Fuddy Meers, Arts Th., 2004; *films*: Ike: the War Years, 1978; Shirley Valentine, 1989; The Old Curiosity Shop, 1994; Bright Young Things, 2003; Notes on a Scandal, 2006; *television films*: Those Glory Glory Days, 1980; Hotel Du Lac, 1986; Adam Bede, 1992; Jack and the Beanstalk—the Real Story, 2001; Celebration, 2006; You Can Choose Your Friends, 2007; The Mystery of Edwin Drood, 2012; Gangsta Granny, 2013; *television series*: Maggie and Her, 1977–79; Fame is the Spur, 1982; Blott on the Landscape, 1985; Fresh Fields, 1984–86; French Fields, 1989–91; Death In Holy Orders, 2003; Cranford, 2007; Marple, 2008–13; Cranford II, 2009; The Town, 2012; The Casual Vacancy, 2015; Gold Digger, 2019; *television plays*: Dear Box No, 1983; Sharing Time, 1984; Absent Friends, 1985; Julia and Company (TV special), 1986; The Shadowy Third, 1995; The Last Detective, 2002; numerous TV musicals; *radio*: Sweeney Todd, 1994, The Country Wife, A Room With a View, 1995; Mame, 1996; Follies, Gigi, 1997; Water Babies, 1998; Two Planks and a Passion, 1999; Woman in Mind, She Stoops to Conquer, 2000; On the Town, Past Forgetting, 2001; Pal Joey, On Your Toes, 2002; The Old Curiosity Shop, 2003; *directed for radio*: Rosalind, 2002; A Well Remembered Voice, Barbara's Wedding, Call Me Madam, 2003. *Recreations:* cooking, gardening. *Address:* c/o The Artists Partnership, 21–22 Warwick Street, W1B 5NE. *T:* (020) 7439 1456, *Fax:* (020) 734 6530.

**MacKENZIE, Kelvin Calder;** *b* 22 Oct. 1946; *m* 1st, 1969, Jacqueline (marr. diss. 2006); two *s* one *d*; 2nd, 2008, Sarah McLean (marr. diss. 2017). Editor, The Sun, 1981–94; Man. Dir, British Sky Broadcasting, 1994; Dir, 1994–98, Gp Man. Dir, 1998, Mirror Group plc; Chm. and Chief Exec., Wireless Gp plc, 1998–2005; Chm., Base79.com (formerly MyVideoRights.com), 2008–12. Founder: A Spokesman Said, 2014–; Love Sport Radio, 2018–.

**MacKENZIE, Rev. Kenneth Ian;** DL; Minister, Parish of Braemar and Crathie, since 2005; Domestic Chaplain to the Queen in Scotland, since 2007; *b* 7 April 1959; *s* of Ian Kenneth MacKenzie and Margaret Vera Matheson; *m* 1987, Jayne Louise Lovett; one *s* three *d*. *Educ*: RAC, Cirencester; Christ's Coll., Univ. of Aberdeen (BD Hons). Managing Partner, Moy Estate, Inverness, 1981–83; ordained, 1990; Asst Minister, Dyce Parish Church, Aberdeenshire, 1988–91; Associate Pastor, First Presbyterian Church, Burlingame, Calif, USA, 1991–94; Associate Minister, North Church, Perth, 1994–99; Minister, St Columba's, Budapest, 1999–2005. DL Aberdeenshire, 2013. Knight's Cross, Order of Merit (Hungary), 2013. *Recreations:* community building projects, fostering through Barnardo's, charitable work in Romania, field sports, hill walking, cycling. *Address:* The Manse, Crathie, Ballater, Aberdeenshire AB35 5UL.

**MacKENZIE, Kenneth John,** CB 1996; Chairman: Historic Scotland Foundation, 2001–12; Edinburgh City Centre Churches, 2010–12; Secretary, Scottish Executive (formerly Scottish Office) Development Department, 1998–2001; *b* 1 May 1943; *s* of John Donald MacKenzie and Elizabeth Pennant Johnston Sutherland; *m* 1975, Irene Mary Hogarth; one *s* one *d*. *Educ:* Woodchurch Road Primary School, Birkenhead; Birkenhead School; Pembroke College, Oxford (Exhibnr; MA Mod. Hist.); Stanford Univ., Calif (AM Hist.). Scottish Home and Health Dept, 1965; Private Sec. to Jt Parly Under Sec. of State, Scottish Office, 1969–70; Scottish Office Regional Develt Div., 1970–73; Scottish Educn Dept, 1973–76; Civil Service Fellow, Glasgow Univ., 1974–75; Principal Private Sec. to Sec. of State for Scotland, 1977–79; Asst Sec., Scottish Economic Planning Dept, 1979–83; Scottish Office: Finance Div., 1983–85; Principal Finance Officer, 1985–88; Under Sec., Home and Health Dept, 1988–91; Under Sec., 1991–92, Sec., 1992–95, Agric. and Fisheries Dept; Cabinet Office (on secondment): Dep. Sec. (Hd of Economic and Domestic Affairs Secretariat), 1995–97; Hd, Constitution Secretariat, 1997–98. Mem., BBSRC (formerly AFRC), 1992–95. Quinquennial Reviewer for the Court Service, LCD, 2001–02. Mem., British Waterways Scotland Gp, 2002–07; Mem., Christian Aid Bd, 2005–08. Hon. Prof., Dept of Politics and Internat. Relations, Univ. of Aberdeen, 2001–04. Associate Consultant, Public Admin Internat., 2002–08. Elder, St Cuthbert's Parish Church, 1971–. *Address:* 23C/1 Ravelston Park, Edinburgh EH4 3DX.

**MACKENZIE, Lorimer David Maurice;** Director, Development Strategy for Enterprises, European Commission, 1996–2002; *b* 4 Aug. 1940; *s* of William David Beveridge Mackenzie and Elizabeth Reid (née Peters); *m* 1959, Penelope Marsh Happer; two *s* two *d*. *Educ:* Hermitage Park Sch., Leith; Royal High Sch., Edinburgh; Edinburgh Univ. (MA Hons Mental Philosophy). Department of Agriculture and Fisheries, Scottish Office: Asst Principal, 1964–68; Principal, 1968–73; Commission of the European Communities: Head of Division: Agricl Res., 1973–77; Food Aid, 1978–82; Develt of Trade, 1982–92; Dir, Budget and Gen. Affairs, Directorate Gen. of Fisheries, 1992–96. Member: Scottish Council, Eur. Movt, 2003–09; Council, Saltire Soc., 2004–12 (Chm., 2010–12). Mem., Editl Bd, Internat. Jl of Entrepreneurship and Innovation, 2001–. Chevalier de l'Ordre National du Mérite (France), 2002. *Recreation:* Scottish history and literature. *Address:* Achadh Na Sgiath, Duror, Argyll PA38 4DA. *Clubs:* New, Scottish Arts (Edinburgh).

**MacKENZIE, Madeleine;** Parliamentary Counsel (formerly Scottish Parliamentary Counsel), since 2002; *b* 27 Aug. 1963; *er d* of William Gordon MacKenzie and late Veronica Dorothy Rachel MacKenzie. *Educ:* Inverness High Sch.; Univ. of Aberdeen (LLB Hons; DipLP). Solicitor in private practice, 1986–90; Asst Scottish Parly Counsel, then Depute Scottish Parly Counsel, 1990–2002. *Publications:* (contrib.) Craies on Legislation, 10th edn 2012; (ed jtly) Thring's Practical Legislation, 3rd edn 2015. *Recreations:* bridge, reading, music. *Address:* (office) Victoria Quay, Edinburgh EH6 6QQ. *T:* (0131) 244 1667. *E:* madeleine.mackenzie@gov.scot. *Clubs:* Athenæum; New, Scottish Arts (Edinburgh).

**MACKENZIE, Mary Margaret;** see McCabe, M. M. A.

**McKENZIE, Michael,** CB 1999; QC 1991; Master of the Crown Office and Queen's Coroner and Attorney, Registrar of Criminal Appeals and of the Courts Martial Appeal Court, and Master of the Queen's Bench Division, High Court of Justice, 1988–2003; *b* Hove, Sussex, 25 May 1943; *s* of Robert John McKenzie and Kitty Elizabeth McKenzie; *m* 1964, Peggy Dorothy, *d* of Thomas Edward William Russell and Dorothy Mabel Russell; three *s*. *Educ:* Varndean Grammar Sch., Brighton. Town Clerk's Dept, Brighton, 1961–63; Asst to Clerk of the Peace, Brighton Quarter Sessions, 1963–67; Sen. Clerk of the Court, 1967–70, Dep. Clerk of the Peace, 1970–71, Middlesex Quarter Sessions; called to the Bar, Middle Temple, 1970, Bencher, 1993; Deputy to Courts Administrator, Middlesex Crown Court, 1972–73; Courts Administrator (Newcastle), NE Circuit, 1974–79; Courts Administrator, Central Criminal Court, and Coordinator for Taxation of Crown Court Costs, S Eastern Circuit, 1979–84; Dep. Circuit Administrator, SE Circuit, 1984–86; Asst Registrar, Ct of Appeal Criminal Div., 1986–88. Registrar, Internat. Civil and Commercial Court and Regulatory Tribunal, Qatar Financial Centre, 2006–11. Adjunct Lectr, SOAS, 2000–03; Adjunct Prof. of Law, Wake Forest Univ., NC, 2002–05. British representative: Internat. Great Debates on Criminal Law, 1987–2003; at internat. judicial conferences in USA, Canada, Aust. and Tasmania, 1990–2003. Mem., Criminal Cttee, Judicial Studies Bd, 1988–2003. Mem., Ind. Monitoring Bd, Lewes Prison, 2004–06. Life Mem., Litigation Section, State Bar, California, 2002. Freeman, City of London, 1979. FRSA 1990. Mem., NY Acad. of Scis, 1992. Hon. Fellow, Kent Sch. of Law, Canterbury Univ., 1991. *Publications:* (ed) Rules of Court: criminal procedure, annually 1994–97; (with Lord Woolf) A Review of the Working Methods of the European Court of Human Rights, 2005. *Recreations:* Northumbrian stick dressing, fell walking. *Address:* Selwyns Wood House, Cross in Hand, East Sussex TN21 0QN.

**MACKENZIE, Michael Philip;** Director-General, Food and Drink Federation, 1986–2001; *b* 26 June 1937; *s* of Brig. Maurice Mackenzie, DSO, and Mrs Vivienne Mackenzie; *m* 1966, Jill (née Beckley); one *s* one *d*. *Educ:* Downside Sch.; Lincoln Coll., Oxford (BA); Harvard Business Sch., USA. United Biscuits plc, 1966–86: Prodn Dir, various businesses within United Biscuits, 1974–83; Man. Dir, D. S. Crawford Bakeries, 1983–86. *Recreations:* walking, gardening, opera, theatre. *Address:* Ebony Cottage, Reading Street, near Tenterden, Kent TN30 7HT. *Club:* Travellers.

**MACKENZIE, Sir Peter Douglas,** 13th Bt *cr* 1673 (NS), of Coul, Ross-shire; *b* 23 April 1949; *s* of Henry Douglas Mackenzie (*d* 1965) and Irene Carter Freeman; *S* kinsman, 1990, but his name does not appear on the Official Roll of the Baronetage; *m* 1st, 1982, Jennifer, *d* of Ridley Boyce (marr. diss.); two *d*; 2nd, 2000, Margo Lamond, *d* of Albert Gordon. *Heir: kinsman* Miles Roderick Turing Mackenzie [*b* 18 April 1952; *m* 1983, Hiroko Sato].

**MACKENZIE, Polly Janet;** Chief Executive, Demos, since 2018; *b* Gloucester, 8 Dec. 1980; *d* of Ian David Mackenzie and Nicolette Hibbin (née Mills); *m* 2010, Nicholas Tyrone; two *s* one *d*. *Educ:* Builth Wells High Sch.; New Hall, Cambridge (BA Hons). Journalist, United Business Media, 2002–04; Policy Advr, Liberal Democrats, 2004–10; Dir of Policy to Dep. Prime Minister, 2010–15; Founding Dir, Women's Equality Party, 2015–16; Dir, Money and Mental Health Policy Inst., 2016–18. *Recreations:* running, reading, family. *Address:* Demos, 76 Vincent Square, SW1P 2PD. *E:* polly.mackenzie@ demos.co.uk.

**MACKENZIE, Richard Hill,** CB 2002; Member, Boundary Commission for Northern Ireland, 2002–13; *b* 21 Feb. 1942; *s* of late Richard H. Mackenzie and Mary Mackenzie; *m* 1966, Jane Valerie Holmes; two *s* one *d*. *Educ:* Grosvenor High Sch., Belfast; Queen's Univ., Belfast (BSc Econs). Dep. Sec., DoE (NI), 1987–2000. Jt Sec., North/South Ministerial Council, NI, 2002–02. Local Govt Boundaries Comr, 2006–09. Vis. Prof. in Planning, Univ. of Ulster, 2002–. Hon. MRTPI 2000. *Recreation:* choral singing. *Clubs:* Ulster Reform (Belfast); Grosvenor Rugby.

**MACKENZIE, Sir Roderick McQuhae,** 12th Bt *cr* 1703, of Scatwell; FRCP(C); medical practitioner, pediatrician; *b* 17 April 1942; *s* of Captain Sir Roderick Edward François McQuhae Mackenzie, 11th Bt, CBE, DSC, RN and Marie Evelyn Campbell (*d* 1993), *oc* of late William Ernest Parkinson; *S* father, 1986, but his name does not appear on the Official Roll of the Baronetage; *m* 1970, Nadezhda, (Nadine), Baroness von Rorbas, *d* of Georges Frederic Schlatter, Baron von Rorbas; one *s* one *d*. *Educ:* Sedbergh; King's College London. MB, BS; MRCP; DCH. *Recreations:* classical music (violin, viola), horseback riding (3-Day eventing), windsurfing. *Heir: s* Gregory Roderick McQuhae Mackenzie, *b* 8 May 1971. *Address:* 2431 Udell Road NW, Calgary, AB T2N 4H4, Canada.

**MACKENZIE, Ruth,** CBE 2013 (OBE 1995); Artistic Director and Joint Chief Executive Officer, Théâtre du Châtelet, since 2017; Chair, London Area Council, Arts Council England, since 2018; *b* 24 July 1957; *d* of Kenneth Mackenzie and Myrna Blumberg. *Educ:* South Hampstead High Sch.; Sorbonne, Paris; Newnham Coll., Cambridge (MA English 1982). Editor's Asst, Time Out magazine, 1980–81; Co-founder, Dir and writer, Moving Parts Theatre Co., 1980–82; Fellow in Theatre, and Dir, Theatre in the Mill, Bradford Univ., 1982–84; Drama Officer, Arts Council of GB, 1984–86; Head of Strategic Planning, South Bank Centre, 1986–90; Exec. Dir, Nottingham Playhouse, 1990–97; Gen. Dir, Scottish Opera, 1997–99; Special Advr to Sec. of State for Culture, Media and Sport, 1999–2002; Dir, Time/Room Prodns, 2002–17. Artistic Dir, Bradford Multicultural Fest., 1983–84; Artistic Programmer, Theatr Clwyd, 1995–96; Theatre Programmer, Barbican Centre, 1995–97; Artistic Dir, Chichester Fest. Theatre, 2002–06; Gen. Dir, Manchester Internat. Fest., 2006–07; Consultant Dramaturg, Vienna Fest., 2007–10; Dir, Cultural Olympiad, 2010–12; Interim CEO and Creative Dir, The Space, 2013–15; Artistic Dir, Holland Fest., 2014–18. Expert Advr, DCMS, 2007–10; Advisor: 14-18 Now, 2013–19; Abu Dhabi Louvre, 2019–. Member: Bd, Women in Entertainment, 1987–89; Bd, Paines Plough Theatre Co., 1990–96; Touring Panel, 1992–95, Lottery Panel, 1994–97, Arts Council of GB, later Arts Council of England, subseq. Arts Council England; Dance and Drama Panel, British Council, 1992–97; Bd, London Internat. Fest. of Theatre, 1993–97; Nat. Develt Forum, ABSA, 1994–96; Bd, New Millennium Experience Co., 1997–99; Panel 2000, 1998–99; QCDA (formerly QCA) Cttee on Creativity, 2001–12; Chancellor's Forum, London Inst., 2001–; Adv. Council, Tate Modern, 2014–; Warwick Commn, 2014–15; Nat. Campaign for the Arts, 2014–; Bd, Serpentine Gall., 2017–; Chm., Improbable, 2013–18. Vis. Prof., City Univ., 2007–. Trustee, Cass Sculpture Foundn (formerly Sculpture at Goodwood), 2005–07, 2013–17. Governor: Trinity Coll. of Music, 2002–05; Royal Northern Coll. of Music, 2007. FRSA. Hon. Fellow: Univ. of Nottingham, 1994; QMUL, 2013. Hon. DLitt: Nottingham Trent, 1994; Nottingham, 1997.

**MACKENZIE, Dr Ursula Ann;** Chairman, Little, Brown Book Group, 2015–16 (Chief Executive Officer, 2006–15); *b* Burton-on-Trent, 11 Dec. 1951; *d* of late Ian Alexander Ross Mackenzie and Phyllis Mackenzie (née Naismith); one *s* by Michael Johnson. *Educ:* Malvern Girls Coll.; Nottingham Univ. (BA Jt Hons English and American Studies; PhD American Lit. 1976). Lectr in English and American Lit., Univ. of Hong Kong, 1976–79; Internat. Scripts (literary agency), 1979–80; Rights Manager, Granada Publishing, 1980–84; Transworld Publishers: Editl and Rights Manager, 1985–86, Editl and Rights Dir, 1986–87, Publishing Dir, 1987–95, Hardcover Publisher, Bantam Press and Doubleday, 1995–2000; Publisher, Little, Brown Book Gp, 2000–05. Chair, Trade Publishers' Council, 2006–11. Publishers' Association: Officer, 2011–14; Pres., 2012–13; Mem. Council, 2014–16. *Recreations:* theatre, travel, swimming, cooking. *E:* ursula.mackenzie@outlook.com.

**MACKENZIE, Wallace John,** OBE 1974; Director, Slough Estates plc, 1972–91 (Group Managing Director, 1975–86); *b* 2 July 1921; *s* of Wallace D. Mackenzie and Ethel F. Williamson; *m* 1951, Barbara D. Hopson; two *s* one *d*. *Educ:* Harrow Weald County Grammar Sch. Gen. Manager, Slough Estates Canada Ltd, 1952–72; Dep. Man. Dir, Slough Estates Ltd, 1972–75. Dir, Investors in Industry plc, 1982–86; Chm., Trust Parts Ltd, 1986–94 (Dir, 1985). Member: Commn for New Towns, 1978–94; London Residuary Body, 1985–95. Trustee, Lankelly Foundn, 1985–2005. *Recreations:* golf, bridge.

**MacKENZIE-BEEVOR, Col Christopher David,** CBE 1996 (OBE 1989); Vice President, Mahfouz Foundation, since 2017; Lieutenant, Her Majesty's Body Guard of the Honourable Corps of Gentlemen at Arms, since 2018 (Member, since 2002); Clerk of the Cheque and Adjutant, 2016–17; *b* London, 10 April 1949; *s* of Mary Beevor and step *s* of Rt Rev. Humphry Beevor; *m* 1st, 1974, Gail Susan Paterson (*d* 2016); one *s* two *d*; 2nd, 2017, Lynn Bultitude. *Educ:* King's Coll., Taunton; RMA, Sandhurst. Commnd 1st Queen's Dragoon Guards, 1971; COS, 1st Inf. Bde, 1982–83; MA to C-in-C, UKLF, 1985–88; CO, Queen's Dragoon Guards, 1990–92; MA to Chm., NATO Mil. Cttee, 1993–96. Director: Westminster Sound Systems, then SONUS Ltd, 1996–2006; English Courtyard Assoc., then Cognatum Ltd, 2007–12; Macbee Consultancy, 2012–18; Chief Exec., William and Elizabeth Morris Foundn, 2013–15. Col, 1st Queen's Dragoon Guards, 2002–07. Chm., Queen's Dragoon Guards Regtl Trust, 2009–15; Trustee, Veterans Aid, 2018–. *Recreations:* sailing, ski-ing, fishing, shooting, music, vinology. *E:* cmb49@me.com. *Club:* Cavalry and Guards (Chm., 2011–15; Trustee, 2015–).

**McKENZIE JOHNSTON, Henry Butler,** CB 1981; Vice-Chairman, Commission for Local Administration in England, 1982–84 (Commissioner, 1981–84); *b* 10 July 1921; *er s* of late Colin McKenzie Johnston and late Bernardine (*née* Fawcett Butler); *m* 1949, Marian Allardyce Middleton (*d* 2009), *e d* of late Brig. A. A. Middleton and late Winifred (*née* Salvesen); one *s* two *d*. *Educ:* Rugby. Served with Black Watch (RHR), 1940–46; Adjt 6th Bn, 1944–45; Temp. Major 1945. Staff of HM Embassy, Athens, 1946–47; entered Foreign (subseq. Diplomatic) Service, 1947; Paris, 1948–51; British High Commn, Germany, 1951–54; FO, 1954–56; 1st Sec. (Commercial), Montevideo, 1956–60; FO, 1960–63; Counsellor (Information), Mexico City, 1963–66; Dep. High Comr, Port of Spain, 1966–67; seconded to Min. of Overseas Develt, 1968–70; Consul-Gen., Munich, 1971–73; seconded to Office of Parly Comr for Admin, 1973–79, transferred permanently, 1979–81; Dep. Parly Comr for Admin, 1974–81. Mem., Broadcasting Complaints Commn, 1986–90. Mem., Social Security Appeal Tribunal, Kensington, subseq. Central London, 1985–88. Chm., British-Mexican Soc., 1977–80. *Publications:* Missions to Mexico: a tale of British diplomacy in the 1820s, 1992; Ottoman and Persian Odysseys: James Morier, creator of Hajji Baba of Ispahan, and his brothers, 1998. *Address:* 6 Pembroke Gardens, W8 6HS. *Clubs:* Athenæum, Hurlingham.

**McKENZIE-PRICE, Isobel Clare;** content strategy consultant, since 2017; *b* 11 Jan. 1956; *d* of Edward Charles Price and Patricia Price (*née* Edgeley); *m* 1st, 1977, Andrew James Alistair McKenzie (marr. diss. 1981); 2nd, 1983, William Woods; one *s* three *d*. *Educ:* Horsham Girls High Sch.; Univ. of Leeds (BA Hons). Homes Editor, Over 21, 1979–80; Dep. Editor, Wedding and Home, 1983–85; Mem., Launch Team, Country Living, 1985–86; Dep. Editor, Essentials, 1986–90; Editor: Mother and Baby, 1990–91; Parents, 1991–92; Period Living, 1993–94; Editor in Chief, Elle Decoration, and Period Living, 1994–96; Publishing Consultant, Inspirations, 1997; Exec. Editor, Prima, and Launch Editor, Your Home, 1997–98; Ed.-in-Chief, then Editl Dir, IPC Home Interest Magazines (Ideal Home, Living etc, 25 Beautiful Homes, Homes & Gardens, Country Homes & Interiors), 1998–2004; Ed.-in-Chief, All You mag., Time Inc., NY, 2004–07; Editl Dir, housetohome.co.uk and Ideal Home mag., 2007–15; Content Strategy Dir, Homes Network, TimeInc. UK, 2015–16. *Recreations:* family, new media, country walking. *E:* isobel.mckenzie.price@gmail.com.

**McKENZIE SMITH, Ian,** CBE 2009 (OBE 1992); PPRSA (RSA 1987; ARSA 1973); PPRSW (RSW 1981); artist (painter); *b* 3 Aug. 1935; *y s* of James McKenzie Smith and Mary Benzie; *m* 1963, Mary Rodger Fotheringham; two *s* one *d*. *Educ:* Robert Gordon's Coll., Aberdeen; Gray's Sch. of Art, Aberdeen; Hospitalfield Coll. of Art, Arbroath; Aberdeen Coll. of Educn. SSA 1960; AAS 1963; FSAScot 1970; ASIAD 1975; FMA 1987. SED Travelling Scholarship to France, Italy, Belgium and Netherlands, Gray's Sch. of Art, 1958–59. Teacher of art, 1960–63; Educn Officer, Council of Industrial Design, Scottish Cttee, 1963–68; Dir, Aberdeen Art Gall. and Museums, 1968–89 (Hon. Mem., Friends of Aberdeen Art Gall., 2000); City Arts and Recreation Officer, City of Aberdeen, 1989–96. Work in permanent collections: Scottish Nat. Gall. of Modern Art; Scottish Arts Council; Arts Council of NI; Contemp. Art Soc.; Aberdeen Art Gall. and Museums; Glasgow Art Gall. and Museums; City Art Centre, Edinburgh; Perth Art Gall.; McManus Gall., Dundee; Abbot Hall Art Gall., Kendal; Hunterian Mus., Glasgow; Nuffield Foundn; Carnegie Trust; Strathclyde Educn Authority; Lothian Educn Authority; RSA; DoE; Robert Fleming Holdings; IBM; Deutsche Morgan Grenfell; Grampian Hosps Art Trust; Lord Chancellor; British Library. Mem., Cttee of Enquiry into Econ. Situation of Visual Artists, Gulbenkian Foundn, 1978. Trustee, Nat. Galls of Scotland, 1999–2007. Member: Scottish Arts Council, 1970–77 (Chm., Art Cttee, 1975–77); Scottish Museums Fedn, 1970–86; Scottish Museums Council, 1980–87 (Chm., Industrial Cttee, 1985–87); Aberdeen Univ. Museums Cttee and Music Cttee, 1970–96; ICOM Internat. Exhibns Cttee, 1986–96; Museums and Galls Commn, 1997–2000; Nat. Heritage, Scottish Gp, 1977–99; Bd of Mgt, Grampian Hosps Art Project, 1987–2000; Adv. Council on Export of Works of Art, 1991–2007; Curatorial Cttee, 1991–2001, Council, 1996–99, Bldgs Cttee, 1998–2001, NT for Scotland; RGI, 1998–. Arts Advr, COSLA, 1976–85. Pres., RSW, 1988–98. Royal Scottish Academy: Dep. Pres. and Treas., 1990–91; Sec., 1991–98; Pres., 1998–2007. Governor: Edinburgh Coll. of Art, 1976–88; The Robert Gordon Univ. (formerly Robert Gordon Inst. of Technology), 1989–93. External Assessor: Glasgow Sch. of Art, 1982–86; Duncan of Jordanstone Coll. of Art, 1982–86; Scottish Arts Council Gifting Scheme, 1997. Board Member: RSA Enterprises, and Friends of RSA, 1972–2007; Scottish Sculpture Workshop, 1979–2000; Aberdeen Maritime Mus. Appeal, 1981–98; Aberdeen Art Gall. Redevelt Project, 2009–. Vice Pres., NADFAS, 2000–04. Trustee: Painters Workshop (Scotland), 1975–89; John Kinross Fund, 1990–2007; Alexander Naysmith Fund, 1990–2007; Spalding Fund, 1990–2007; Sir William Gillies Fund, 1990–2007; Hospitalfield Trust, 1991–2007; Royal Scottish Acad. Foundn, 2015–. Chm., Marguerite McBey Trust, 2000–. FSS 1981; FRSA 1973; FRSE 2003. Hon. RA 1999; Hon. RHA 1999; Hon. RUA 1999; Hon. RWA 2000. Hon. Mem., Peacock Printmakers, 1993. Hon. LLD Aberdeen, 1991; Hon. DArt Robert Gordon, 2000. Inst. of Contemp. Prints Award, 1969; Guthrie Award, 1971, Gillies Award, 1980, RSA; ESU Thyne Scholarship, 1980; Eduardo Paolozzi Medal, Nat. Galls of Scotland, 2007; Sir William Gillies Award, RSW, 2008; Arts and Business Scotland Award, Arts and Business Scotland, 2011. *E:* i.mckenziesmith@btinternet.com. *Clubs:* Royal Over-Seas League, Scottish Arts (Edinburgh); Royal Northern (Aberdeen).

**MACKENZIE SMITH, Peter;** Chairman, Getenergy Ltd, since 2014; *b* 12 Jan. 1946; *s* of late Antony and of Isobel Mackenzie Smith; *m* 1973, Sandra Gay-French; three *d*. *Educ:* Downside; Jesus Coll., Cambridge (BA Classical Tripos). Teacher: British Inst., Oporto, 1967–68; Internat. House, London, 1969; British Council, 1969–97: Asst Rep., Lagos, 1969–72; Asst Cultural Attaché, Cairo, 1972–77; Regl Dir, Southampton, 1977–80; Educnl Contracts Dept, 1980–83; Dep. Rep., Cairo, 1983–87; Director: Educnl Contracts, 1987–89; Projects Div., 1989–92; Nigeria and W Africa, 1992–94; Export Promotion, 1994–96; Africa and S Asia, 1996–97; Dir of Educn, General Electric Co., subseq. Marconi plc, 1997–2003; Export Promoter for Educn and Training, Trade Partners UK, 2001–03; Man. Dir, Prothero Ltd, 2003–12. Mem., Methodology Soc., 2000–. *Address:* Backfields End, Winchelsea, E Sussex TN36 4AB. *Club:* Athenæum.

**McKEON, Andrew John;** Chair, Nuffield Trust, since 2016 (Acting Chief Executive, 2013–14; Senior Policy Fellow, 2014–16); *b* 22 Sept. 1955; *s* of Kenneth and Maurine McKeon; *m* 1989, Hilary Neville; one *s* one *d*. *Educ:* William Hulme's Grammar Sch., Manchester; St Catharine's Coll., Cambridge. Joined DHSS, 1976; Hd of Medicines, Pharmacy and Industry Div., 2000–02, Dir of Policy and Planning, 2002–03, DoH; Man. Dir (Health), Audit Commn, 2003–12. Non-executive Director, NICE, 2009–17; EMIS, 2013–. Trustee, Nuffield Trust, 2008–13. Adjunct Prof., Inst. of Global Health Innovation, Imperial Coll. London, 2011–15.

**McKEON, Simon Vincent,** AO 2012; Chairman, Commonwealth Scientific and Industrial Research Organisation, 2010–15; Chairman, AMP Ltd, 2014–16 (Director, since 2013); Consultant, Macquarie Group Ltd, since 2014; *b* Dandenong, Vic. *Educ:* Univ. of Melbourne (BCom 1976; LLB 1978). Solicitor, Blake Dawson Waldron, Sydney, 1980–83; with Macquarie Group Ltd, 1983–2014: Exec., 1984; Manager, 1985; Associate Dir, 1987; Divl Dir, Macquarie Corp. Finance Ltd, 1988; Exec. Chm., Melbourne Office, 2004–14. Chairman: MYOB, 2006–09; In2Science, 2013–16; Arthurs Seat Eagle Pty Ltd, 2015–; Summer Housing Ltd, 2016–; South East Melbourne, 2017–. Mem., Editl Bd, Companies and Securities Law Jl, 1988–2011. Founding Pres., Australian Takeovers Panel, 1999–2010; Pres., Rev. Panel for Australian banking industry's Banking and Finance Oath, 2013–. Chair, Strategic Rev. of Health and Med. Res., 2011–13. Chairman: Business for Millennium Develt, 2007–15; Global Poverty Project Australia, 2012–15; Dir, Global Poverty Project Inc., 2009–14. Mem., Adv. Panel on Human Rights Grants Scheme, Australian Govt, 2009–13. Founding Chair, MS Res. Australia, 2004–10; Director: World Vision Australia, 1994–2005; Vision Fund, World Vision Internat., 2003–13; MS Soc. Australia, 2001–05; Red Dust Role Models, 2008–16; Spotless Gp Ltd, 2016–; Rio Tinto plc, 2019–; Rio Tinto Ltd, 2019–; Member, Advisory Board: PGA Mgt Pty Ltd, 2005–; Big Issue, 2008–; BlackMagic Design Pty Ltd, 2016–; Mem., Business Engagement Steering Cttee, AusAid, 2011–13. Mem., Strategic Adv. Bd, Univ. of Melbourne Law Grad. Prog., 2001–09; Chancellor, Monash Univ., 2016–; Chm., Industry and Innovation Bd, Gp of Eight Australia, 2016–. Australia Day Ambassador, Govt of Vic, 2007–. Chm., Point Nepean Community Trust, 2004–09. Patron: Australian Cttee, UN Year of Microcredit, 2005; Australian Olympic Sailing Team, 2006–. FAICD 2005. Hon. DPH La Trobe, 2015. Australian of Year, 2011. Acad. Medal, Australian Acad. Sci., 2014. *Recreations:* yachting, bushwalking. *Clubs:* MCC; McCrae Yacht.

**McKEOWEN, David;** *see* Wills, Baron.

**McKEOWN, Most Rev. Donal;** *see* Derry, Bishop of, (RC).

**McKEOWN, Prof. Patrick Arthur,** OBE 1991; MSc; FREng, FIMechE; Professor of Precision Engineering, 1974–91, now Emeritus, Director of Cranfield Unit for Precision Engineering, 1969–96, Cranfield University (formerly Institute of Technology); *b* 16 Aug. 1930; *s* of Robert Matthew McKeown and Augusta (*née* White); *m* 1954, Mary Patricia Heath; three *s*. *Educ:* Cambridge County High Sch. for Boys; Bristol Grammar Sch.; Cranfield Inst. of Technol. (MSc). CEng, MIMechE 1969; FIET (FIProdE 1971); FREng (FEng 1986). National Service, RE, 1949–51; Suez Campaign, 1956: Captain RE; port maintenance. Student apprentice, Bristol Aircraft Co. Ltd, Bristol, 1951–54 (HNC National State Scholarship); Cranfield Inst. of Technol., 1954–56; Société Genevoise, Newport Pagnell and Geneva, 1956–68 (Technical and Works Dir, 1965); Hd of Dept for Design of Machine Systems, Cranfield Inst. of Technol., 1975–85. Chairman: Cranfield Precision Systems Ltd, 1984–87; Cranfield Moulded Structures Ltd, 1984–91; Cranfield Precision Engrg Ltd, 1987–95 (Chief Exec., 1987–92); non-executive Director: Control Techniques plc, 1990–95; AMTRI, 1990–92; Cranfield Aerospace Ltd, 2001–03. Vice-Pres., Inst. of Quality Assurance, 1976; Pres., CIRP (Internat. Instn for Prodn Engrg Res.), 1988–89 (Fellow, 1975). Member: Evaluation Panel, National Bureau of Standards, Washington, USA; Metrology and Standards Requirements Bd, DTI, 1983–86; Advanced Manufg Technol. Cttee, DTI, 1983–87; Vis. Cttee, RCA, 1984–87; ACARD working gp, 1987–88. Internat. Advr, Gintic Inst. of Manufg Technology, Singapore, 1991–97. Vis. Prof., Univ. of Calif, Berkeley, 1994. Mem., Adv. Bd, Kimberley STEM Coll., 2013–16. Clayton Meml Lectr, IMechE, 1986. Pres., Eur. Soc. for Precision Engrg and Nanotechnol., 1998–2000. Charter Fellow, Soc. of Manufacturing Engineers, 1985. FSME, USA; Hon. FIED 1990. Hon. DSc: Connecticut, 1996; Cranfield, 1996. Fulbright Award (Vis. Prof. of Mechanical Engrg, Univ. of Wisconsin-Madison), 1982; F. W. Taylor Award, Soc. of Manufacturing Engrs, 1983; Thomas Hawksley Gold Medal, IMechE, 1987; Mensforth Gold Medal, IProdE, 1988; Life Achievement Award, Amer. Soc. for Precision Engrg, 1998; Faraday Medal, IEE, 1999; Life Achievement Award, European Soc. for Precision Engrg and Nanotechnol., 2002; Internat. Prize, Japan Soc. for Precision Engrg, 2003; Georg Schlesinger Preis, Senate, State of Berlin, 2006; James Clayton Prize, IMechE, 2007; M. Eugene Merchant Manufg Medal, ASME/SME USA, 2009. Freedom, City of London, 2007; Liveryman, Co. of Engrs, 2008–. *Publications:* papers in CIRP Annals; project reports and lectures for Royal Acad. of Engrg. *Recreations:* walking, travel, enjoyment of wine, good food, classical music, theatre. *T:* (01234) 267678. *E:* patmckeown37@gmail.com.

**McKERNAN, Prof. James,** PhD; FRS 2011; Charles Lee Powell Professor of Mathematics, University of California at San Diego, since 2012; *b* 1964. *Educ:* Trinity Coll., Cambridge (BA 1985); Harvard Univ. (PhD 1991). Instructor: Univ. of Utah; Univ. of Texas; Vis. Asst Prof., Oklahoma State Univ., 1994–95; Prof. of Maths, UCSB, 1995–2007; Prof. of Maths, 2007–09, Norbert Wiener Prof. of Maths, 2009–12, MIT. Clay Res. Award, Clay Maths Inst., 2007; (with C. Hacon) Frank Nelson Cole Prize in Algebra, Amer. Maths Soc., 2009. *Address:* Department of Mathematics, University of California at San Diego, 9500 Gilman Drive, La Jolla, CA 92093–0112, USA.

**McKERNAN, Ruth Mitchell,** CBE 2013; PhD; Chief Executive, Innovate UK, 2015–18; *b* Alyth, Scotland, 19 March 1958; *d* of Dr William Mitchell McKernan and Catherine McKernan; *m* 1996, Dr Gerard Dawson; one *s* one *d*. *Educ:* Prendergast Grammar Sch., London; King's Coll. London (BSc (Hons I) Pharmacol. and Biochem.); Inst. of Psychiatry, Univ. of London (PhD Neurosci. 1984). Post-doctoral Fellow, UCSD, 1985–87; Scientist, Biochemistry Dept, Merck Res. Labs, 1987–2005 (Dept Hd, 1997–2002); Site Hd, 2002–05); Vice Pres., Pfizer, 2005–11; Chief Scientific Officer, Neusentis and Sen. Vice Pres., Pfizer, 2011–15. Member: MRC, 2012–17; Bd, Cancer Res. Technol., 2013–15. Vis. Prof., KCL, 2003–15. Patron, Internat. Spinal Res. Trust, 2013– (Trustee, 2003–13); Trustee, Alzheimer's Res. UK. FMedSci 2015. Hon. FBPhS 2017. *Publications:* Billy's Halo, 2006; 120 articles in scientific jls. *Recreation:* walking round the garden with a glass of wine.

**MacKERRON, Prof. Gordon Stewart;** Professor of Science and Technology Policy, SPRU - Science and Technology Policy Research, University of Sussex, since 2014; *b* 15 Jan. 1947; *s* of James and Jessie MacKerron; *m* 1997, Kara Smith; one *s* one *d*. *Educ:* St John's Coll., Cambridge (BA Econs 1968); Univ. of Sussex (MA Develt Econs). Econ. planner, ODI-Nuffield Fellow, Malawi, 1969–71; Fellow, SPRU, Univ. of Sussex, 1974–76; Lectr, Griffith Univ., Brisbane, 1976–78; Sen. Fellow, SPRU, Univ. of Sussex, 1978–2000; Dep. Dir, Energy Rev. Team, Perf. and Innovation Unit, Cabinet Office, 2001; Associate Dir, NERA Econ. Consulting, 2001–05; Dir, Sussex Energy Gp, 2005–08, Dir, 2008–13, SPRU, Univ. of Sussex. Chm., Cttee on Radioactive Waste Mgt, 2003–07; Mem., Royal

Commn on Envmtl Pollution, 2010–11. *Publications:* (ed) The UK Energy Experience: a model or warning, 1996; (ed) The International Experience, 2000; contrib. jls incl. Energy Policy, Energy Jl, Revue de l'Energie. *Recreations:* singing, salsa (dance), history. *Address:* Science and Technology Policy Research Unit, Jubilee Building, University of Sussex, Falmer, Brighton BN1 9SL. *T:* (01273) 876584, *Fax:* (01273) 685865. *E:* g.s.mackerron@sussex.ac.uk.

**McKERROW, June;** charity advisor; Director, Mental Health Foundation, 1992–2000; *b* 17 June 1950; *d* of late Alexander Donald and Lorna McKerrow; one adopted *d. Educ:* Brunel Univ. (MPhil 1977). Housing management in local govt and housing assocs, 1967–80; Dir, Stonham Housing Assoc., 1980–92. Mem. Cttee, English Rural Housing Assoc., 1997–99. Trustee and Vice-Chm., Shelter, 1985–93; Trustee: Homeless Internat., 1988–93; Cherwell Housing Trust, 1992–97; Charity Projects, 1993–97; Comic Relief, 1995–97; Donnington Doorstep, 2002–09; Winston's Wish, 2002–04; Change of Scene, 2008–11; Dir, Soundabout, 2003–13; Mentor, Prince's Trust, 2011–. Patron, Revolving Doors Agency, 1993–99; Chm., Housing Assocs Charitable Trust, 1998–2002; Mem. Bd, Advance Housing and Support, 2001–03. Mem., British Council, UN Internat. Year of Shelter for the Homeless, 1987. Non-exec. Dir, Oxfordshire and Buckinghamshire Mental Health Trust (formerly Oxfordshire Mental Healthcare NHS Trust), 2000–07. Mem. Court, Oxford Brookes Univ., 1999–2007. *E:* junemckerrow@me.com.

**McKERROW, Neil Alexander Herdman;** *b* 17 May 1945; *s* of late Anderson Herdman McKerrow, TD, MB ChB and of Joan Ysobel Cuthbertson (*née* Clark); *m* 1st, 1971, Penelope Mackinlay (*née* Chiene) (marr. diss. 2018); one *s* two *d*; 2nd, 2018, Vivien Henderson (*née* Langford). *Educ:* Sedbergh Sch.; Emmanuel Coll., Cambridge (MA). Reckitt & Colman (Overseas) Ltd, 1968–69; commnd 1st Bn Queen's Own Highlanders (Seaforth and Camerons), service in Trucial-Oman States, BAOR, 1969–73 (Capt.); Marketing Manager, Distillers Co., 1973–75; Macdonald Martin Distilleries, later Glenmorangie plc: Export Dir, 1975–81; Sales Marketing Dir, 1981–87; Man. Dir, 1987–94; Chief Exec., Forest Enterprise, Forestry Commn, 1995–96. Bursar and Clerk to the Govs, Sedbergh Sch., 1997–2006. Director: Welsh Whisky Co., 2006–15; Royal Lyceum Theatre Co., 2007–10. Dep. Dir, Atlantic Salmon Trust, 2006–10. Member: Royal Scottish Pipers Soc., 1971–2015; High Constabulary, Port of Leith, 1976– (Moderator, 2007–08); Incorp. of Malt Men, 1990–. Liveryman, Co. of Distillers, 2006–. Gov., Belhaven Hill Sch., Dunbar, 1997–2004. Pres., Old Sedberghian Club, 2013–15. *Recreations:* fishing, outdoor pursuits, most sports, malt whisky, local history, traditional jazz. *Clubs:* London Scottish; New (Edinburgh); Hawks (Cambridge); Royal & Ancient Golf (St Andrews).

**MACKESON, Sir Rupert (Henry),** 2nd Bt *cr* 1954; *b* 16 Nov. 1941; *s* of Brig. Sir Harry Ripley Mackeson, 1st Bt, and Alethea, Lady Mackeson (*d* 1979), *d* of late Comdr R. Talbot, RN; *S* father, 1964; *m* 1968, Hon. Camilla Keith (marr. diss. 1973), *d* of Baron Keith of Castleacre. *Educ:* Harrow; Trinity Coll., Dublin (MA). Captain, Royal Horse Guards, 1967, retd 1968. *Publications:* (as Rupert Collens): (jtly) 'Snaffles' on Racing and Point-to-Pointing, 1988; (jtly) 'Snaffles' on Hunting, 1989; Look at Cecil Aldin's Dogs and Hounds, 1990; 25 Legal Luminaries from Vanity Fair, 1990; Cecil Aldin's Dog Models, 1994; (as Rupert Mackeson): Bet Like a Man (novel), 2001; Flat Racing Scams and Scandals, 2004. *Recreations:* art, racing. *Heir:* none. *Address:* 25 Thirlmere Road, Weston-super-Mare, Somerset BS23 3UY.

**MACKESON-SANDBACH, Antoinette, (Mrs M. R. Sherratt);** MP for Eddisbury, since 2015 (C, 2015–19; Ind, since 2019); *b* London, 15 Feb. 1969; *d* of Ian and Annie Mackeson-Sandbach; one *d* (one *s* decd); *m* 2012, Matthew Robin Sherratt. *Educ:* West Heath; Haileybury Coll.; Nottingham Univ. (BA Hons Law; LLM Internat. Law). Called to the Bar, Lincoln's Inn, 1993; in practice as barrister, 9 Bedford Row, 1995–2006; farmer, 2006–11. Mem. (C) Wales N, Nat. Assembly for Wales, 2011–15; Shadow Minister for Rural Affairs, 2011–14; for Envmt and Energy, 2014–15. Mem., BEIS Select Cttee, 2017–; Mem., 1922 Cttee, 2015. *Address:* House of Commons, SW1A 0AA. *T:* (020) 7219 3000. *E:* antoinette.sandbach.mp@parliament.uk.

**MACKEY, Allan Robert;** Project Director, International Association of Refugee Law Judges, since 2011; *b* 24 April 1942; *s* of Albert George Mackey and Eileen Annie Mackey; *m* 1966, Mary Anne Kirkness; two *s* one *d. Educ:* Otahuhu Coll., Auckland; Auckland Univ. (LLB 1966); Cranfield Univ. (MBA 1976). Barrister and Solicitor, NZ, 1966; Solicitor, NSW, 1968; Barrister and solicitor, Auckland, 1966–68 and 1970–74; Solicitor, Sydney, Australia, 1968–70; Mktg Manager, Todd Motors Ltd, NZ, 1975–79; Gen. Manager, Mazda Motors, NZ, 1980–86; Solicitor/Consultant, Auckland, Hong Kong, Dubai, 1987–91; Mem., Residence, Removal and Refugee Appeal Authy of NZ, 1991–94; Chm., Refugee and Residence Appeal Authorities of NZ, 1994–2001; Legal Chair, Immigration Appeal Tribunal, UK, 1999–2001; Sen. Immigration Judge (formerly a Vice-Pres., Immigration Appeal Tribunal), UK, 2001–07; Chair, Refugee Status Appeals Authy, NZ, 2007–10; Dep. Chair, Immigration and Protection Tribunal, NZ, 2010–12. Vis. Prof., Univ. of Tokyo, 2006. Pres., Internat. Assoc. of Refugee Law Judges, 2002–05 (Vice Pres., 2000–02). *Recreations:* yachting, walking. *Address:* c/o International Association of Refugee Law Judges, PO Box 1621, 2003 BR Haarlem, Netherlands. *T:* (9) 5287660. *E:* arm.mam@gmail.com. *Club:* Wellington (Wellington, NZ).

**MACKEY, Sir Craig (Thomas),** Kt 2018; QPM 2009; Deputy Commissioner, Metropolitan Police Service, 2012–18; *b* Ibadan Town, Nigeria, 26 Aug. 1962; *m* Debbie; one *d. Educ:* Open Univ. (BSc Hons); Postgrad. Dip. Econs; Postgrad. Dip. Criminal Justice. Served Merchant Navy, with BP, 1980–84; joined Police Service, 1984; with Wilts Police, 1984–99; specialist staff inspector, HM Inspector of Constabulary, Home Office, 1999–2001; Asst Chief Constable, 2001–05, Dep. Chief Constable, 2005–07, Glos Constabulary; Chief Constable, Cumbria Constabulary, 2007–12. Member: British Transport Police Authy, 2019–; Civil Nuclear Police Authy, 2019–. FCMI. *Recreations:* walking, reading, Rugby, mountain biking.

**MACKEY, Sir James,** Kt 2019; Chief Executive Officer, Northumbria Healthcare NHS Foundation Trust, since 2003 (on secondment as Chief Executive Officer, NHS Improvement (formerly Monitor and NHS Trust Development Authority), 2015–17); *b* Hebburn, Tyne and Wear, 11 Oct. 1966; *s* of James and Hazel Mackey; *m* 1991, Victoria Merina Trotter. *Educ:* Hebburn Comprehensive Sch.; New Coll., Durham. CIPFA 1990. Finance trainee in local govt, 1985–90; finance roles, latterly as Dep. Finance Dir, 1990–96; Finance Dir, Northumbria Healthcare, 1996–2000; Regl Finance Dir, Northern and Yorkshire Reg., DoH, 2000–01; Chief Operating Officer, Northumbria Healthcare NHS Trust, 2001–03. *Recreations:* swimming, running, walking, cycling. *Address:* 7 Edgewood, Darras Hall, Ponteland, Newcastle upon Tyne NE20 9RY. *T:* 07768 485106. *E:* jimmackey@live.co.uk. *Club:* Lansdowne.

**MACKEY, Prof. James Patrick;** Thomas Chalmers Professor of Theology, 1979–99, now Emeritus, and Director of Graduate School and Associate Dean, 1995–99, University of Edinburgh (Hon. Fellow, Faculty of Divinity, 1999–2002); *b* 9 Feb. 1934; *e s* of Peter Mackey and Esther Mackey (*née* Morrissey); *m* 1973, Hanorah Noelle Quinlan; one *s* one *d. Educ:* Mount St Joseph Coll., Roscrea; Nat. Univ. of Ireland (BA); Pontifical Univ., Maynooth (LPh, BD, STL, DD); Queen's Univ. Belfast (PhD); postgraduate study at Univs of Oxford, London, Strasbourg. Lectr in Philosophy, QUB, 1960–66; Lectr in Theology, St John's Coll., Waterford, 1966–69; Associate Prof. and Prof. of Systematic and Philosophical Theol., Univ. of San Francisco, 1969–79; Dean, Faculty of Divinity, Edinburgh Univ., 1984–88. Visiting Professor: Univ. of California, Berkeley, 1974; Dartmouth Coll., NH, 1989; TCD, 1999–2010; Curricular Consultant, UC Cork, 1999–2003. Member: Ind. Assessment Panel for NI Policing Bd, 2005; Consultative Gp on the Past (NI), 2007–09. Mem., Centre for Hermeneutical Studies, Univ. of California, Berkeley, 1974–79. Organiser, Internat. Conf. on the Cultures of Europe, Derry, 1992. *Television series:* The Hall of Mirrors, 1984; The Gods of War, 1986; Perspectives, 1986–87; radio programmes. Associate Editor: Herder Correspondence, 1966–69; Concilium (church history section), 1965–70; Horizons, 1973–79; Founding Editor, Studies in World Christianity, 1995–2002. *Publications:* The Modern Theology of Tradition, 1962; Life and Grace, 1966 (trans. Spanish 1969); Tradition and Change in the Church, 1968 (trans. French 1969, Polish 1974); Contemporary Philosophy of Religion, 1968; (ed) Morals, Law and Authority, 1969 (trans. Italian 1973); The Church: its credibility today, 1970; The Problems of Religious Faith, 1972; Jesus: the man and the myth, 1979 (trans. German 1981); The Christian Experience of God as Trinity, 1983; (ed) Religious Imagination, 1986; Modern Theology: a sense of direction, 1987; (with Prof. J. D. G. Dunn) New Testament Theology in Dialogue, 1987; (ed) Introduction to Celtic Christianity, 1989; Power and Christian Ethics, 1993; (ed) The Cultures of Europe, 1994; The Critique of Theological Reason, 2000; (ed) Religion and Politics in Ireland, 2003; Christianity and Creation, 2006; The Scientist and the Theologian, 2007; Jesus of Nazareth, 2008; contribs to theol. and philosoph. jls. *Recreations:* yachting; rediscovery of original Celtic culture of these islands. *Address:* 15 Glenville Park, Dunmore Road, Waterford, Eire.

**MACKEY, Air Vice-Marshal Jefferson;** Chief Executive, Defence Dental Agency, 1996–97; *b* 24 Oct. 1936; *s* of late James Mackey and of Cicely (*née* Hitchman); *m* 1959, Sheila Mary Taylor; one *s* two *d. Educ:* Latymer Upper Sch.; Guy's Hosp. (BDS, LDS RCS). Asst Dir, Defence Dental Services, 1982–86; Officer Comdg RAF Inst. of Dental Health and Trng, 1986–87; Principal Dental Officer, RAF Support Command, 1987–90; Dir, RAF Dental Services, 1990–94; Dir, Defence Dental Services, 1992–96. QHDS 1987–97. FInstLM; FCMI; FRGS. *Address:* Takali, Oxford Road, Stone, Bucks HP17 8PB. *T:* (01296) 748823. *Clubs:* Royal Air Force; Mentmore Golf and Country.

**McKIBBIN, Sir (David) Malcolm,** KCB 2016; DPhil; Head of the Northern Ireland Civil Service, 2011–17; *b* Belfast, 20 Nov. 1956; *s* of Desmond and Iris McKibbin; *m* 1981, Susan Crook; two *d. Educ:* Univ. of Southampton (BSc Hons Civil Engrg 1978); Univ. of Ulster (DPhil 1987; MBA 1991). CCE 1982. Various posts, NI Roads Service, 1978–98; Dir, Transport Policy Div., 1998–99, Regl Transport Strategy Div., 1992–2002, Dept for Regl Develt; Chief Exec., NI Roads Service, 2002–07; Perm. Sec., Dept of Agriculture and Rural Develt, 2007–10, Dept for Regl Develt, 2010–11, NI. Mem., Bd of Govs, Royal Belfast Academical Instn, 2004–11. *Recreations:* Rugby (played for many years for Instonians Rugby Club and coached Under 21 and First team squads, former Mem. Ulster Rugby Squad), playing tennis (at Belfast Boat Club and for Ulster Veterans). *Clubs:* Instonians Rugby; Belfast Boat.

**McKIBBIN, Dr Ross Ian,** FBA 1999; Fellow, St John's College, Oxford, 1972–2005, now Emeritus; *b* 25 Jan. 1942; *s* of Arnold Walter McKibbin and Nance Lilian (*née* Spence). *Educ:* Univ. of Sydney (BA, MA); St Antony's Coll., Oxford (DPhil 1970). Lectr in Hist., Univ. of Sydney, 1968–70; Jun. Res. Fellow, Christ Church, Oxford, 1970–72; CUF Lectr, Univ. of Oxford, 1972–2005; Tutor in Modern Hist., St John's Coll., Oxford, 1972–2005. *Publications:* The Evolution of the Labour Party 1910–1924, 1974, 2nd edn 1991; The Ideologies of Class, 1990; Classes and Cultures: England 1918–1951, 1998; (ed) M. Stopes, Married Love, 2004; Parties and People: England 1914–1951, 2010; Democracy and Political Culture: studies in modern British history, 2019. *Recreation:* gardening. *Address:* St John's College, Oxford OX1 3JP. *T:* (01865) 277300.

**MACKIE, (Ann) Louise;** *see* Heathwaite, A. L.

**MACKIE, Anne;** Director of Programmes, UK National Screening Committee, since 2007; *b* Yorkshire, 8 Aug. 1962; *d* of William Mackie and Jean Mackie; *m* 2006, Jo Mackie; one *d. Educ:* Moor End Comprehensive Sch., Huddersfield; King's Coll., London (MB BS 1985). MFPHM 1995, FFPHM 2001. Registrar, SE London HA, 1986–89; Dep. Dir, E London and the City HA, 1987–93; Director of Public Health: Kent and Medway SHA, 1995–2004; SW London SHA, 2004–07; London SHA, 2007–. *Publications:* contribs to BMJ, Heart, Jl of Public Health and annual reports. *Recreations:* family, cycling, literature, modern art, gastronomy. *Address:* UK National Screening Committee, Public Health England, Skipton House, SE1 6LH. *T:* (020) 3312 6927.

**MACKIE, His Honour David Lindsay,** CBE 2004; QC 1998; a Deputy High Court Judge, 1998–2016; Senior Circuit Judge, 2004–15, Judge in charge, London Mercantile Court, 2006–15; *b* 15 Feb. 1946; *s* of Air Cdre Alastair Cavendish Lindsay Mackie, CBE, DFC; *m* 1971 (marr. diss.); two *s* one *d; m* 2015, Katherine Reece. *Educ:* St Edmund Hall, Oxford. FCIArb 1990. Admitted Solicitor, 1971. Joined Allen & Overy, 1968, Partner, 1975–2004, Hd of Litigation, 1988–2004. A Recorder, 1992–2004. Trustee, Royal Courts of Justice Advice Bureau, 1998–. Pres., Financial Markets Tribunal, Dubai Internat. Financial Services Authy, 2014–. *Recreation:* climbing.

**MACKIE, Eileen Philomena Carroll;** *see* Carroll, E. P.

**MACKIE, George,** DFC 1944; RSW 1968; RDI 1973; freelance graphic artist and painter; Head of Design, Gray's School of Art, Aberdeen, 1958–80 (retd); *b* 17 July 1920; *s* of late David Mackie and late Kathleen Grantham; *m* 1952, Barbara Balmer, RSA, RSW, RGI (*d* 2017); two *d.* Served Royal Air Force, 1940–46. Consultant in book design to Edinburgh University Press, 1960–87. Paintings in various private and public collections incl. HRH the Duke of Edinburgh's and Scottish Nat. Gall. of Modern Art. Major retrospective exhibitions: Books, mostly scholarly, and some Ephemera, Nat. Library of Scotland, 1991; Dartmouth Coll., NH, USA, 1991. *Publications:* (ed) Lynton Lamb: Illustrator, 1979. *Address:* 32 Broad Street, Stamford, Lincs PE9 1PJ. *T:* (01780) 753296.

**MACKIE, Prof. George Owen,** FRS 1991; FRSC; DPhil; Professor of Biology, University of Victoria, 1968–94, Professor Emeritus since 1995; *b* 20 Oct. 1929; *s* of late Col (Frederick) Percival Mackie, CSI, OBE, IMS and Mary E. H. Mackie (*née* Owen); *m* 1956, Gillian V. Faulkner; three *s* two *d. Educ:* Oxford (BA 1954; MA 1956; DPhil 1956). FRSC 1982. Univ. of Alberta, 1957–68; Univ. of Victoria, 1968–; Chm., Biol. Dept, 1970–73. Killam Res. Fellow, 1986–88. Editor, Canadian Jl of Zoology, 1980–89. Fry Medal, Canadian Soc. of Zoologists, 1989. *Publications:* (ed) Coelenterate Ecology and Behavior, 1976; numerous research articles in books and jls. *Recreations:* chamber music ('cello), earthenware pottery. *Address:* 2173 Tryon Road, North Saanich, BC V8L 5H6, Canada. *T:* (250) 6564291.

**MACKIE, Joyce Grant,** MBE 2014; Vice Lord-Lieutenant of Aberdeenshire, 2009–15; partner, farming business, since 1963; *b* Forfar, Angus, 7 May 1940; *d* of Jay Grant Clark and Winifred Bertram Clark (*née* Wood); *m* 1963, (Bruce) Stephen Mackie (*d* 2011); two *s* two *d*. *Educ*: Montrose Primary Sch.; St Margaret's Sch. for Girls, Aberdeen; Moray House Coll. of Educn, Edinburgh (Cert Ed 1961); Open Univ. (BA Hons 1992). National Trust for Scotland: Member: Council, 1974–79, 1985–90; Exec. Cttee, 1976–86, 1986–2003; Regl Cttee, 1976– (Chm. 1976–2000); Vice-Pres., 1988–2003; Hon. Founder Pres., Chm. and Mem. Cttee, NE Aberdeenshire Members' Centre, 1976–. Member: Aberdeen Cttee, RSSPCC, 1966–96; Agricl Adv. Cttee, BBC, 1976–84; Trustee, David Gordon Meml Trust, 1977–; Pres., 2005–13, Patron, 2013–, NE Scotland and Northern Isles Br., British Red Cross. Dir, Lathallan Prep. Sch., Montrose, 1979–2001 (Chm., 1990–98); Mem. Council, Glenalmond Coll., 1991–2004 (Mem. Cttee, 2001–04), Fellow, 2006 (Pres., Glenalmond Fellows, 2017–); Mem. Exec. Cttee, Aberdeen Univ. Quincentenary Campaign, 1993–96. Mem., Nomination Cttee, Church of Scotland, 1985–88. DL Aberdeenshire, 1992. *Recreations*: art, art history, gardens, National Trust for Scotland. *Address*: Balquhindachy, Methlick, Ellon, Aberdeenshire AB41 7BY. *T*: (01651) 806373, *Fax*: (01651) 806875. *Clubs*: Farmers; New (Edinburgh).

**MACKIE, Karl Joseph,** CBE 2010; PhD; Founder President, Centre for Effective Dispute Resolution, since 2017 (Chief Executive, 1990–2017); *s* of John Mackie and Ethel Mackie (*née* Freedman); *m* 1st, 1968, Ann Douglas (marr. diss.); one *s* one *d*; 2nd, 2001, Eileen Philomena Carroll, *qv*; one step *d*. *Educ*: Buckhaven High Sch.; Univ. of Edinburgh (MA Hons), DipEd; Univ. of London (LLB ext.); Univ. of Nottingham (PhD 1987); Open Univ. (MBA 1990). CPsychol 1989; FCIArb 1992. Accredited Mediator, CEDR. Called to the Bar, Gray's Inn, 1982; Res. Associate, Univ. of Edinburgh, 1971–72; various posts, 1972–73; Lectr, then Sen. Lectr, Law and Social Psychology, Univ. of Nottingham, 1973–90; Partner, Network Associates Strategy Consultants, 1985–90. Hon. Prof. in Alternative Dispute Resolution, Univ. of Birmingham, 1994–2001; Special Prof. in Law, Univ. of Westminster, 2003–09. Vice-Chm., Civil Mediation Council, 2003–10. Chief Adjudicator, OFSTED Ind. Complaints Service, 2009–17; Standing Arbitrator, govt dept, 2015–. Ombudsman, LIFFE NYSE Euronext, 2011–14. Member: Panel of Independent Mediators and Arbitrators, ACAS, 1980–; Singapore Internat. Commercial Mediators Panel, 2001–; Panel of Dist. Neutrals, Internat. Inst. for Conflict Prevention and Resolution, 2007–; Panel of Internat. Mediators, China Internat. Economic and Trade Arbitration Commn, 2012–; Panel of Mediators, UN Staff Mgt Commn, 2017–; Adv. Council, All Pty Parly Gp on Conflict, 2007–. Member: Educn Cttee, Bar Assoc. for Commerce, Finance and Industry, 1987–90; Law Soc. Specialisation Cttee, 1989–92. Chm., Write Away, 2003–06. FRSA 1993. Mem. editl cttee, various jls. *Publications*: (ed jtly) Learning Lawyers' Skills, 1989; Lawyers in Business and the Law Business, 1989; (ed) A Handbook of Dispute Resolution, 1991; (jtly) Commercial Dispute Resolution, 1995, 3rd edn as The ADR Practice Guide, 2007; (with E. Carroll) International Mediation: the art of business diplomacy, 2000, 3rd edn as International Mediation: breaking business deadlock, 2016; (ed jtly) The EU Mediation Atlas, 2004. *Recreations*: film, photography, swimming, ski-ing, writing. *Address*: Centre for Effective Dispute Resolution, 70 Fleet Street, EC4Y 1EU. *T*: (020) 7536 6000.

**MACKIE, Lily Edna Minerva, (Mrs John Betts),** OBE 1986; Head Mistress, City of London School for Girls, 1972–86; *b* 14 April 1926; *d* of Robert Wood Mackie and Lilian Amelia Mackie (*née* Dennis); *m* 1985, John Betts (*d* 1992). *Educ*: Plaistow Grammar Sch.; University Coll., London (BA); Lycée de Jeunes Filles, Limoges; Université de Poitiers. Asst Mistress; Ilford County High Sch. for Girls, 1950–59; City of London Sch. for Girls, 1960–64; Head Mistress: Wimbledon County Sch., 1964–69; Ricards Lodge High Sch., Wimbledon, 1969–72. *Recreations*: reading, film, music, bridge. *Address*: Flat 49, 246 Kingston Road, SW20 8DA.

**MACKIE, Prof. Neil,** CBE 1996; FRSE; international concert tenor; Professor, Fine Arts Faculty, University of Agder, Kristiansand, Norway, 2004–14; Professor of Singing, Royal Academy of Music, 2009–19; *b* 11 Dec. 1946; *yr s* of late William Fraser Mackie and Sheila Roberta (*née* Taylor); *m* 1973, Kathleen Mary Livingstone, soprano; two *d*. *Educ*: Aberdeen Grammar Sch.; Royal Scottish Acad. of Music and Drama (DipMusEd, DipRSAMD; FRSAMD 1992); Royal Coll. of Music (Foundn Scholar 1970; ARCM Hons; FRCM 1996). London recital début, Wigmore Hall, 1972; London concert début with English Chamber Orch., 1973; world premières include works by Peter Maxwell Davies, Britten, Henze, Judith Weir and Kenneth Leighton; numerous recordings. Prof. of Singing, 1985–2008, Head of Vocal Studies, 1994–2006, Royal Coll. of Music. Artistic Dir, Mayfield Internat. Fest., E Sussex, 2004–12. Hon. RAM 2011. Hon. Mem., Agder Acad. of Scis and Letters, 2012. Hon. DMus Univ. of Aberdeen, 1993. CStJ 1996. *Recreations*: reading, charity work, gardening. *Address*: 70 Broadwood Avenue, Ruislip, Middx HA4 7XR. *T*: (01895) 632115. *E*: neilmackie@talktalk.net. *Club*: Athenæum.

**McKIE, Peter Halliday,** CBE 1995; CChem, FRSC, CEng; Chairman, PHM Associates (NI) Ltd, 1996–2017; *b* 20 March 1935; *s* of Harold and Winifred McKie; *m* 1959, Jennifer Anne Parkes; three *s* one *d*. *Educ*: Bangor Grammar Sch.; Queen's Univ., Belfast (BSc Chem., Hon. DSc 1993). CChem, FRSC 1988; FCQI (FIQA 1987); CEng 1993. Shift Supervisor, Courtaulds Ltd, 1956–59; Supervisor, Du Pont Mfg, Londonderry, 1959–77; Manager, Du Pont Waynesbro Orlon Plant, USA, 1977–79; Asst Works Dir, Du Pont, Londonderry, 1979–81; Man. Dir, Du Pont Scandinavia and Du Pont Finland, 1981–84; Prodn Manager, Du Pont Europe, 1984–87; Chm., Du Pont (UK) Ltd, 1987–96; Manager, Du Pont Belle Plant, W Virginia, USA, 1995–96; Chm., QUBIS Ltd, 1998–2005. Chm., Industrial Res. & Technol. Unit, Dept of Econ. Develt, NI, 1994–2001. Chm., HSE, NI, 2005–11. Vis. Prof., Dept of Engrg, QUB, 1991–2005. FInstD 1987. *Recreations*: photography, sport, classic cars and motor cycles. *Address*: 3 The Rookery, Killinchy, Co. Down BT23 6SY.

**McKIE, Robin Lewis;** Science Editor, The Observer, since 1982; *b* Glasgow, 25 June 1950; *s* of Thomas McKie and Doreen McKie (*née* Pearson); *m* 1993, Sarah Ann Mitchell; one *s* one *d* (and one *d* decd). *Educ*: High Sch. of Glasgow; Univ. of Glasgow (BSc Hons). Trainee, Scotsman Pubns, 1974–78; Science corresp., THES, 1978–82. *Publications*: Genetic Jigsaw, 1988; (with W. Bodmer) The Book of Man, 1994; (with C. Stringer) African Exodus, 1996; Apeman, 2000; Face of Britain, 2006. *Recreations*: photography, walking, travelling on trains. *Address*: 36 Trinity Gardens, SW9 8DP. *T*: (020) 7733 7386. *E*: robin.mckie@observer.co.uk. *Club*: Grafton Tennis.

**MacKIE, Prof. Rona McLeod, (Lady Black),** CBE 1999; MD, DSc; FRCP, FRCPath, FMedSci; FRSE; Professor of Dermatology, 1978–2001, Professorial Research Fellow, since 2001, Department of Public Health and Health Policy, University of Glasgow; *b* Dundee, 22 May 1940; *d* of late Prof. (James) Norman Davidson, CBE, FRS and Morag McLeod, PhD; *m* 1st, 1962, Euan Wallace MacKie (marr. diss. 1992); one *s* one *d*; 2nd, 1994, Sir James Whyte Black, OM, FRS (*d* 2010). *Educ*: Channing Sch., London; Laurel Bank Sch., Glasgow; Univ. of Glasgow (MB ChB 1963; MD with commendation 1970; DSc 1994). FRCPath 1984; FRCP 1985. Junior hosp. posts, Glasgow, 1964–70; Lectr in Dermatology, Glasgow. Univ., 1971–72; Consultant Dermatologist, Greater Glasgow Health Bd, 1972–78. Pres., British Assoc. of Dermatologists, 1994–95 (Sir Archibald Gray Medal, 1999); FRSE 1983 (Meeting Sec., 1994–97; Internat. Convener, 2002–07); FMedSci 1998. Bicentenary Medal, RSE, 2007; Medal for Dermatological Res., British Soc. for Investigative Dermatology, 2011. *Publications*: textbooks and contribs to learned jls in field of skin cancer, particularly malignant melanoma. *Recreations*: family, opera, golf, gardening. *Address*: c/o University of Glasgow, Glasgow G12 8RZ. *E*: ronamblack@hotmail.com. *Club*: Glasgow Art.

**MACKILLIGIN, David Patrick Robert,** CMG 1994; HM Diplomatic Service, retired; Governor, British Virgin Islands, 1995–98; *b* 29 June 1939; *s* of R. S. Mackilligin, CMG, OBE, MC and Patricia (*née* Waldegrave); *m* 1976, Gillian Margaret Zuill Walker; two *d*. *Educ*: St Mary's Coll., Winchester; Pembroke Coll., Oxford (2nd Cl. Hons PPE). Asst Principal, CRO, 1961–62; Third, later Second Sec., Pakistan, 1962–66; Asst Private Sec. to Sec. of State for Commonwealth Relations, 1966–68; Private Sec. to Minister Without Portfolio, 1968–69; Dep. Comr, Anguilla, 1969–71 (Actg Comr, July–Aug. 1970); First Sec., Ghana, 1971–73; First Sec., Head of Chancery and Consul, Cambodia, 1973–75 (Chargé d'Affaires at various times); FCO, 1975–80 (Asst Head of W African Dept, 1978–80); Counsellor (Commercial and Aid), Indonesia, 1980–85; NATO Defence Coll., Rome, 1985–86; Counsellor (Economic and Commercial), and Dir of Trade Promotion, Canberra, 1986–90; High Comr, Belize, 1991–95. *Recreations*: walking and swimming in remote places, ruins, second-hand bookshops, theatre, literature. *Address*: c/o Foreign and Commonwealth Office, King Charles Street, SW1A 2AH. *Clubs*: Oxford and Cambridge, Reform.

**McKILLOP, Elizabeth Dorothy;** Director of Collections, 2007–16, and Deputy Director, 2010–16, Victoria and Albert Museum, now Honorary Senior Research Fellow; *b* 28 May 1953; *d* of Norman R. and Mary M. McConochie; *m* 1973, Andrew C. McKillop; one *s* one *d*. *Educ*: Univ. of Glasgow (MA 1972); Churchill Coll., Cambridge (MA 1975); University Coll. London (MSc 2004). Ed., BBC Monitoring Service, 1979–81; Curator: Chinese Collection, BL, 1981–90; Samsung Gall. of Korean Art, V&A, 1990–93; Korean Collection, BL, 1993–2004; Keeper, Dept of Asia, V&A, 2004–10; Tutor, Rare Book Sch., Univ. of Virginia, 2019–. Pres., Oriental Ceramic Soc., 2018–. *Publications*: Korean Art and Design, 1992; North Korean Culture and Society, 2004. *Recreations*: food, travel. *Address*: 179 Engadine Street, SW18 5DU. *T*: (020) 3509 9370. *E*: bethmckillop@hotmail.com.

**McKILLOP, Prof. James Hugh,** FRCP, FRCR, FMedSci; Muirhead Professor of Medicine, University of Glasgow, 1989–2011; *b* 20 June 1948; *s* of Patrick McKillop and Helen Theresa McKillop (*née* Kilpatrick); *m* 1972, Caroline Annis Oakley; two *d*. *Educ*: St Aloysius' Coll.; Univ. of Glasgow (BSc, MB ChB; PhD 1979). FRCPGlas 1986; FRCPE 1990; FRCP 1992; FRCR 1994. University of Glasgow: Lectr in Medicine, 1975–82; Sen. Lectr in Medicine, 1982–89; Associate Dean for Med. Educn, 2000–03; Hd, Undergraduate Med. Sch., 2003–06; Dep. Exec. Dean of Medicine, 2007–10; Dep. Hd, Sch. of Medicine, 2010–11. Harkness Fellow, Stanford Univ., California, 1979–80. Chairman: Intercollegiate Standing Cttee on Nuclear Medicine, 1995–99; Admin of Radioactive Substances Adv. Cttee, DoH, 1996–2004; Scottish Med. and Scientific Adv. Cttee, 2001–07; NHS Educn Scotland Med. Adv. Gp, 2004–11; Scottish Deans Med. Curriculum Gp, 2005–09; Expert Adv. Panel, British Polio Fellowship, 2008–12. General Medical Council: Team Leader, GMC Quality Assurance of Basic Med. Educn, 2003–08; Mem., 2009–16; Chair: Undergrad. Educn Bd, 2009–12; Audit and Risk Cttee, 2014–16; Pensions Trustee Bd, 2017–. Pres., British Nuclear Medicine Soc., 1990–92; Congress Pres., Eur. Assoc. of Nuclear Medicine, 1997; Mem., Exec. Cttee, Assoc. of Physicians of UK and Ire., 2000–03. Vestry Sec., 2011–, Provost's Warden 2017–, St Mary's Episcopal Cathedral, Glasgow (People's Warden, 2016–17). FMedSci 1998. Hon. FAcadMed 2011. Hon. Dr Örebro 2011; Hon. MD Internat. Med. Univ. (KL) 2017. *Publications*: (with D. L. Citrin) Atlas of Technetium Bone Scans, 1978; (with A. G. Chalmers and P. J. Robinson) Imaging in Clinical Practice, 1988; (with I. Fogelman) Clinicians' Guide to Nuclear Medicine: benign and malignant bone disease, 1991; 250 papers mainly on nuclear medicine and cardiology. *Recreations*: opera (esp. Verdi), reading fiction, soccer, digital photography, looking at art. *Address*: Flat 1, 6 Kirklee Gate, Glasgow G12 0SZ.

**McKILLOP, Murdoch Lang,** CA; Partner, Talbot Hughes McKillop (formerly Talbot Hughes McKillop, then Kroll Talbot Hughes) LLP, 2002–13; *b* 30 Oct. 1947; *s* of Graham Lang McKillop and Margaret Morris (*née* Stark); *m* 1972, Elizabeth Leith; two *d*. *Educ*: Kelvinside Acad., Glasgow; Univ. of Strathclyde (BA Hons 1971). CA 1975; FSPI 1996. Joined Arthur Andersen, subseq. Andersen, Glasgow, as grad. trainee, 1971; Partner, 1984; Jt Administrator, Maxwell Private Gp, 1991; Joint Administrative Receiver: Leyland Daf Ltd, 1993; Ferranti Internat. plc, 1994, and others; Worldwide Head, Corporate Recovery and Turnaround, Arthur Andersen, 1996–98. Pres., Soc. of Practitioners of Insolvency, 1998–99; Institute of Chartered Accountants of Scotland: Jun. Vice-Pres., 2001–02; Sen. Vice-Pres., 2002–03; Pres., 2003–04; Convenor, Investigation and Professional Conduct Enforcement Cttee, 2004–10. Dir, Celsa UK Holdings, 2013–. *Recreation*: sailing. *Address*: Flat 501 Fennel Apartments, 3 Cayenne Court, SE1 2PJ. *Club*: Royal Yacht Squadron.

**McKILLOP, Sir Thomas Fulton Wilson, (Sir Tom),** Kt 2002; PhD; FRS 2005; FRSE; FMedSci; Chief Executive, AstraZeneca plc, 1999–2006; President, Science Council, 2007–11; *b* 19 March 1943; *s* of Hugh McKillop and Annie (*née* Wilson); *m* 1966, Elizabeth Kettle; one *s* two *d*. *Educ*: Irvine Royal Acad.; Univ. of Glasgow (BSc 1st Cl. Hons; PhD Chem. 1968). Centre de Mécanique Ondulatoire Appliquée, Paris. Res. scientist, ICI Corporate Lab., 1969–75; ICI Pharmaceuticals: Hd, Natural Products Res., 1975–78; Res. Dir, France, 1978–80; Chemistry Manager, 1980–84; Gen. Manager, Res., 1984–85; Develt, 1985–89; Technical Dir, 1989–94; Zeneca Gp, then AstraZeneca: CEO, Zeneca Pharmaceuticals, 1994–99; Dir, 1996–2006. Dep. Chm., 2005–06, Chm., 2006–09, Royal Bank of Scotland Gp. Non-executive Director: Amersham Internat. PLC, 1992–97; Nycomed Amersham PLC, 1997–2000; Lloyds TSB Gp PLC, 1999–2004; BP PLC, 2004–09; Almirall SA, 2007–; UCB, 2009–16; Evolva SA, 2010–17 (Chm., 2012–17); Theravectys SAS, 2011–15; Alere Inc., 2013–17. Adv. Bd, Alsbridge PLC, 2010–12. Pres., European Fedn of Pharmaceutical Industries and Assocs, 2002–04. Trustee, Council for Industry and Higher Educn, 2002–09. Pro-Chancellor and Mem. Gen. Council, Univ. of Leicester, 1998–2007. MRI; MACS; Mem., Soc. for Drug Res. Trustee, Darwin Trust of Edinburgh, 1995–. FMedSci 2002; FRSE 2003. Hon. Fellow, Univ. of Lancs, 2004; Hon. FIChemE 2006; Hon. FRSC 2002. Hon. LLD: Manchester, 1999; Dundee, 2003; Hon. DSc: Glasgow, Leicester, Huddersfield, 2000; Nottingham, 2001; St Andrews, Salford, 2004; Manchester, 2005; Lancaster, 2007; Hon. Dr: Middx, 2000; Paisley, 2006; Hon. DLitt Heriot-Watt, 2006. Royal Medal, RSE, 2007. *Recreations*: music, sport, reading, walking, carpentry. *Address*: Moss Cottage, Lowes Lane, Gawsworth, Cheshire SK11 9QR. *Club*: Wilmslow Golf.

**MACKINLAY, Andrew Stuart;** *b* 24 April 1949; *s* of Danny Mackinlay and late Monica (*née* Beanes); *m* 1972, Ruth Segar; two *s* one *d*. *Educ*: Salesian Coll., Chertsey. ACIS; DMA. A clerk, Surrey CC, 1965–75; Nalgo official, 1975–92. MP (Lab) Thurrock, 1992–2010. An Opposition Whip, 1992–93; Member: Transport Select Cttee, 1992–97; Foreign Affairs Select Cttee, 1997; Chm., All-Party Poland Gp, 1997. *Recreations*: studying battlefields of World War I in France and Belgium, non-league football, Ireland and Poland. *Club*: Chadwell Working Men's.

**MACKINLAY, Craig;** JP; MP (C) South Thanet, since 2015; *b* Chatham, 7 Oct. 1966; *s* of Colin Francis Mackinlay and Margaret Elizabeth Mackinlay; *m* 2011, Katalin Madi. *Educ:* Rainham Mark Grammar Sch., Rainham; Univ. of Birmingham (BSc Hons Zool. and Comparative Physiol.). FCA 1992; CTA 1993. Mackinlay Chartered Accountants, 1995–2011; self-employed Partner, Beak Kemmenoe, Chatham, 2011–. Mem. (C), Medway Council, 2007–15. JP N Kent, 2006. *Recreations:* sailing, shooting, travel. *Address:* House of Commons, SW1A 0AA. *T:* (020) 7219 4442. *E:* craig@craigmackinlay.com. *Clubs:* Carlton; Castle (Rochester).

**MACKINLAY, (Jack) Lindsay;** DL; Canon Treasurer, York Minster, 2000–07, now Canon Emeritus; *b* 24 Jan. 1936; *m* 1961, Catherine Elizabeth Houston; one *s* one *d.* FCA, FCMA. Rowntree plc, 1964–89 (Dir, 1973–89); Dir, 1990–2002, Chm., 1995–2002, Bradford & Bingley Bldg Soc., subseq. Bradford & Bingley plc. Dir, Argos, 1990–97; Chm., RPC Gp, 1992–2000. DL N Yorks, 2005. *Recreations:* golf, music. *Address:* The Cottage, Main Street, Stillington, York YO61 1JU.

**McKINLAY, Peter,** CBE 1998; Chairman, Wise Group, 1998–2001; *b* 29 Dec. 1939; *s* of late Peter McKinlay and of Mary Clegg (*née* Hamill); *m* 1963, Anne Rogerson Aitken Thomson; two *s* one *d. Educ:* Univ. of Glasgow (MA Hons). GPO HQ, Edinburgh, 1963–67; Scottish Office, 1967–91: Private Sec. to Minister of State, 1974–75; Director, Scottish Prison Service, 1988–91; Chief Executive, Scottish Homes, 1991–99. Nat. Exec., First Div. Assoc., 1977–80. Non-exec. Dir, D. S. Crawford Ltd, 1984–86; Chm., Bute Beyond 2000 (formerly Bute Partnership), 1993–98; Member: Bd, Cairngorms Partnership, 1998–99; Accounts Commn for Scotland, 2003–06. Dir, Common Purpose, 1993–97. FRSA 1998. Hon. DBA Napier, 1999. *Recreations:* family, friends, garden, TV, reading, food, drink. *Club:* Machrihanish Golf.

**McKINLAY, Robert Murray,** CBE 1993; FREng, FRAeS; President, Bristol Chamber of Commerce and Industry, 1994–97; *b* 12 Jan. 1934; *s* of Robert Graham McKinlay and Mary Murray; *m* 1957, Ellen Aikman Stewart; two *s. Educ:* Vale of Leven Acad.; Royal Tech. Coll., Glasgow (BSc Hons, ARTC). Flight testing and project engineering, Bristol Helicopters and Westlands, 1956–66; British Aircraft Corporation, 1966–79: Systems Develt Manager; Designer in charge; Asst Chief Engr; Asst Dir, Flight Test; Concorde Design Dir; British Aerospace, 1979–94: Dir, Airbus; Gp Dir, Man. Dir, Airbus Div.; Man. Dir, Commercial Aircraft; Chm., Airbus, 1991–94. Non-exec. Dir, B. F. Goodrich, Aerospace, Europe, 1998–2003 (Consultant, 2003–06). FREng (FEng 1992). Hon. DTech Bristol, 1991; Hon. DEng Glasgow, 2001. British Gold Medal, RAeS, 1995. *Recreations:* travelling, golf, piano, woodworking. *Address:* 43 Glenavon Park, Bristol BS9 1RW. *T:* (0117) 968 6253. *Club:* Society of Merchant Venturers (Bristol).

**McKINNEL, Rt Rev. Nicholas Howard Paul;** *see* Plymouth, Bishop Suffragan of.

**McKINNELL, Catherine;** MP (Lab) Newcastle upon Tyne North, since 2010; *b* Newcastle upon Tyne, 8 June 1976; *d* of John Grady and Agnes Grady (*née* Miller); *m* 2006, James Rhys McKinnell; one *s* one *d. Educ:* Sacred Heart Comprehensive Sch., Fenham, Newcastle upon Tyne; Univ. of Edinburgh (MA Hons Politics and Hist.); Univ. of Northumbria (Postgrad. DipLaw, CPE and Legal Practice Course). Admitted Solicitor 2004; Dickinson Dees LLP, 2002–09. Shadow Solicitor Gen., 2010–11; Shadow Minister for Children, 2011–13; Shadow Treasury Minister, 2013–15; Shadow Attorney Gen., 2015–16. Member: Northumbria Assoc.; Unite the Union. Mem., Tyneside Cinema. *Recreations:* swimming, gardening, travel. *Address:* House of Commons, SW1A 0AA. *T:* (020) 7219 7115. *Club:* Tyneside Irish Centre.

**McKINNELL, Soraya Jane; Her Honour Judge McKinnell;** a Circuit Judge, since 2018; *b* 1969. *Educ:* Univ. of Exeter (LLB Hons). Called to the Bar, Middle Temple, 1991; Dep. District Judge, 2010–14; District Judge, 2014–18.

**McKINNEY, Rt Rev. Patrick Joseph;** *see* Nottingham, Bishop of, (RC).

**MacKINNON, Charles Archibald,** CB 2005; freelance change management consultant, since 2008; *b* 1 July 1950; *s* of Ian MacDougall MacKinnon and Colina (*née* Beaton); *m* 1972, Jane Halpin; one *s* two *d. Educ:* Woodside Sen. Secondary Sch.; Sheffield Hallam Univ. (MBA). Various field operational mgt roles, 1968–84; Hd of Section, Policy and Planning, MSC, 1984–86; Project Manager, then Sen. Manager, various large projects in Employment Service, 1986–98; Benefits Agency: Dir, Field Ops (Scotland and N England), 1998–2000; Dep. Chief Exec., 2000–02; Chief Operating Officer, Pension Service, 2002–04; Transformation Dir, Pension Service, DWP, 2004–08. *Recreations:* theatre, gardening, reading, chess, current affairs, sport spectating.

**McKINNON, Rt Hon. Sir Donald (Charles),** GCVO 2009; ONZ 2008; PC 1992; Commonwealth Secretary-General, 2000–08; *b* 27 Feb. 1939; *s* of Maj.-Gen. Walter Sneddon McKinnon, CB, CBE and Anna Bloomfield McKinnon (*née* Plimmer); *m* 1st, 1964, Patricia Maude Moore (marr. diss. 1995); three *s* one *d*; 2nd, 1995, Clare de Lore; one *s. Educ:* Lincoln Univ., New Zealand. AREINZ. Farm Manager, 1964–72; Farm Management Consultant, 1973–78; Real Estate Agent, 1974–78. MP (Nat. Party) NZ, 1978–99, for Albany, 1978–96; Dep. Leader of the Opposition, 1987–90; Dep. Prime Minister, 1990–96; Leader of the House, 1990–96; Minister: of External Relations, then Foreign Affairs, and Trade, 1990–99; of Pacific Island Affairs, 1991–98; for Disarmament and Arms Control, 1996–99; i/c War Pensions, 1998–99. Chairman: Regl Facilities, Auckland, 2011–; NZ-China Council, 2012–. Member: Asia Foundn; Waitangi Nat. Trust. Interim Dir, Auckland War Meml Mus., 2010–11. *Publications:* Six Months in Wyoming, 2006; In The Ring: a Commonwealth memoir, 2013. *Recreations:* enthusiastic jogger and tennis player, horse riding. *Address:* 49 Dell Road, Waiau Pa RD 4, Pukekohe 2679, New Zealand.

**MacKINNON, Kenneth Alasdair,** CVO 2011; RD 1971; WS; NP; JP; Lord-Lieutenant of Argyll and Bute, 2002–11 (Clerk of Lieutenancy, 1974–95; Vice Lord-Lieutenant, 2001–02); *b* 8 March 1936; *s* of Neil MacKinnon, WS and Janet Alison Mackenzie; *m* 1963, Anne Clare Valentine; one *s* two *d. Educ:* Edinburgh Acad.; Fettes Coll. (Pres., Old Fettesian Assoc., 1989–91); Pembroke Coll., Cambridge (BA 1959); Edinburgh Univ. (LLB 1961). Nat. Service, RN, 1954–56; Midshipman, RNVR, 1955; Lt Comdr, RNR, 1956–86. Apprentice Solicitor, Messrs Dundas & Wilson, CS, 1959–62; WS, 1962; D. M. MacKinnon, Oban: Asst Solicitor, 1962–63; Partner, 1963–96; Sen. Partner, 1989–96. Dean, Oban Faculty of Solicitors, 1995–97. Dir, Glasgow Local Bd, Commercial Union Assce, 1981–83. Hon. Sheriff, N Strathclyde at Oban, 1997. Council Member: WS Soc., 1993–96; Macmillan Cancer Relief, subseq. Macmillan Cancer Support, 2002–05 (Chm., Oban and Dist Br., 1993–2007). Pres., Oban Sea Cadet Unit, 2007–. Elder, C of S, 1975–2007. DL 1996, JP 2002, Argyll and Bute. Sec., 1963–76, Trustee, 2002–12, Argyllshire Gathering; Patron, Oban War and Peace Mus., 2009–. *Recreations:* motoring, watching Rugby. *Address:* Ardcuan, Gallanach Road, Oban, Argyll PA34 4PE. *T:* (01631) 562325. *Club:* Royal Highland Yacht (Cdre, 1988–89, Trustee, 2003–11).

**McKINNON, Prof. Kenneth Richard,** AO 1995; FACE; Chairman: McKinnon Walker Pty Ltd, since 1995; IMB Pty Ltd, 2000–04; Chairman, Australian Press Council, 2000–09; *b* 23 Feb. 1931; *s* of Charles and Grace McKinnon; *m* 1st, 1956 (marr. diss.); one *s*; 2nd, 1981, Suzanne H., *d* of W. Milligan. *Educ:* Univ. of Adelaide; Univ. of Queensland (BA; BEd); Harvard Univ. (EdD). FACE 1972. Teacher, headmaster and administrator, 1957–65; Dir of Educn, Papua New Guinea, 1966–73; Chm., Australian Schs Commn, 1973–81; Vice-Chancellor, 1981–95, and Prof. Emeritus, Univ. of Wollongong; Vice-Chancellor: James Cook Univ. of N Qld, 1997; Northern Territory Univ., 2002–03. Chairman: Bd of Educn, Vic, 1982–85; Australian Nat. Commn for UNESCO, 1984–88; Illawara Technology Corp., 1983–; Marine Sci. and Technol. Review, 1988; Nuclear Res. Reactor Review, 1993; Reviewer, Marine Scis Orgns, 1993. Pres., AVCC, 1991–92. Member: Australia Council, 1974–77 (Dep. Chm., 1976–77); Primary Industries and Energy Res. Council, 1991–92; Prime Minister's Science Council, 1991–92. Consultant in the Arts, Aust. Govt, 1981. Dir, Coll. of Law, NSW, 1993–. Hon. DLitt: Wollongong, 1994; Deakin, 1994; NSW, 1995; DUniv James Cook, 1998. *Publications:* Realistic Educational Planning, 1973; Oceans of Wealth, 1988; Benchmarking in Universities, 2000; articles in jls and papers. *Recreations:* swimming, theatre, music, reading. *Address:* Unit 703, Links Seaside, 1 Ross Street, Wollongong, NSW 2500, Australia. *T:* (2) 42250506.

**McKINNON, Malcolm;** *see* McKinnon, W. M.

**MACKINNON, Neil Joseph;** Sheriff of Glasgow and Strathkelvin at Glasgow, 2014–20; *b* 24 Jan. 1956; *s* of late Donald Patrick Mackinnon and Catriona Traese Mackinnon (*née* Sinclair); *m* 1990, Anne Helen Gavagan; one *d. Educ:* St Aloysius' Coll., Glasgow; Univ. of Glasgow (LLB Hons 1978). Admitted solicitor, Scotland, 1980; Advocate, Scots Bar, 1984. Floating Sheriff, Edinburgh, 2000–05; Sheriff of Tayside Central and Fife at Falkirk, 2005–09; Sheriff of Lothian and Borders at Edinburgh, 2009–14. Mem., Rules Council, Court of Session, 1997–99. *Recreations:* travel, hill-walking. *Address:* 10 Merrylee Road, Glasgow G43 2SH. *T:* (0141) 6331716.

**MacKINNON, Prof. Roderick,** MD; John D. Rockefeller Jr Professor and Head of Laboratory of Molecular Neurobiology and Biophysics, Rockefeller University, since 1996; *b* 19 Feb. 1956; *m* Alice Lee. *Educ:* Brandeis Univ. (BA 1978); Tufts Univ. (MD 1982). Harvard Univ., 1985–86; Brandeis Univ., 1986–89; Asst, later Prof., Dept of Neurobiol., Harvard Med. Sch., 1989–96; Investigator, Howard Hughes Med. Inst., 1997–. (Jtly) Nobel Prize for Chemistry, 2003. *Address:* Laboratory of Molecular Neurobiology and Biophysics, Rockefeller University, 1230 York Avenue, New York, NY 10065, USA.

**MacKINNON, Rowan Dorothy;** *see* Pelling, R. D.

**McKINNON, Sir Stuart (Neil),** Kt 1988; a Judge of the High Court of Justice, Queen's Bench Division, 1988–2009; *b* 14 Aug. 1938; *s* of His Honour Neil Nairn McKinnon, QC; *m* 1st, 1966, Rev. Helena Jacoba Sara (*née* van Hoorn) (marr. diss. 1999); two *d*; 2nd, 2001, Michelle Jean Mary Withers. *Educ:* King's Coll. Sch., Wimbledon; Council of Legal Educn; Trinity Hall, Cambridge (BA, LLB 1963; MA 1967). Called to the Bar, Lincoln's Inn, 1960, Bencher, 1987; Junior at the Common Law Bar, 1964–80; QC 1980; a Recorder, 1985–88. Chm., Lord Chancellor's Middx Adv. Cttee on JPs, 1990–97. Pres., Cambridge Univ. Law Soc., 1962–63. *Recreation:* watching cricket and golf.

*See also* His Honour W. N. McKinnon.

**McKINNON, His Honour Warwick Nairn;** a Circuit Judge, 1998–2017; a Senior Circuit Judge, 2010–17; Resident Judge, Croydon Crown Court, 2006–17; *b* 11 Nov. 1947; *s* of His Honour Neil McKinnon, QC; *m* 1978, Nichola Juliet Lloyd; one *s* one *d. Educ:* King's Coll. Sch., Wimbledon; Christ's Coll., Cambridge (MA). Called to the Bar, Lincoln's Inn, 1970, Bencher, 2010; in practice on SE Circuit; Asst Recorder, 1991–95; Recorder, 1995–98. Chm., Essex Criminal Justice Strategy Cttee, 1999–2001; IT Liaison Judge for Kent, 2001–06; Magistrates Liaison Judge and Chm., Area Judicial Forum for SE London, 2006–13. Hon. Recorder, Croydon, 2008–17. *Recreations:* music, painting, travel, gardening, golf.

*See also* Sir S. N. McKinnon.

**McKINNON, (William) Malcolm;** Chief Executive, SITPRO Ltd, 2005–10; *b* Ilford, Essex, 14 Dec. 1953; *s* of William Malcolm McKinnon and Maureen Helena Margaret McKinnon; *m* 1978, Christine Elizabeth Platt; two *d. Educ:* Southend High Sch. for Boys; Inst. of Export (MIEx (Grad.) 1982). DTI, then Dept of Trade, subseq. DTI, 1973–2005; EO, Gen. Export Services, 1973–80; Third Sec., Consulate-Gen., Vancouver, 1977–78; EO, Commercial Relns with Republic of Korea, 1980–82; HEO, Internat. Trade Policy, 1983–86; Private Sec., 1987–88; Head: Trade with Soviet Union, 1988–90; EU Insce Policy, 1990–94; WTO Trade in Services, 1994–2005. Mem., Borough of Southend Swimming and Trng Club (Chm., 1992–2000 and 2003–08). Freeman, City of London, 2007. *Recreations:* travel, photography, hill and coastal walking, music, learning to ski and play golf, swimming.

**MACKINTOSH,** family name of **Viscount Mackintosh of Halifax**.

**MACKINTOSH OF HALIFAX,** 3rd Viscount *cr* 1957; **John Clive Mackintosh,** FCA, Bt 1935; Baron 1948; *b* 9 Sept. 1958; *s* of 2nd Viscount Mackintosh of Halifax, OBE, BEM; *S* father, 1980; *m* 1st, 1982, Elizabeth Lakin (marr. diss. 1993); two *s*; 2nd, 1995, Claire Jane, *y d* of Stanislaw Nowak; one *d. Educ:* The Leys School, Cambridge; Oriel College, Oxford (MA in PPE). FCA 1995. Pres., Oxford Univ. Conservative Assoc., 1979. Chartered accountant. Partner, Price Waterhouse, then PricewaterhouseCoopers, 1992–2017. *Recreations:* cricket, bridge, golf. *Heir: s* Hon. Thomas Harold George Mackintosh, *b* 8 Feb. 1985. *Clubs:* MCC, Royal Automobile, Beefsteak; Ocean Reef (Key Largo).

**MACKINTOSH, Dr Andrew John,** FInstP; Chairman, Sphere Fluidics Ltd, since 2010; *m*; two *d. Educ:* King's Sch., Canterbury (Schol.); Univ. of Bristol (BSc 1st Cl. Hons Chem. Physics 1976); Darwin Coll., Cambridge (PhD Condensed Matter Physics 1983). FInstP 2000. Royal Soc. Res. Fellow, Kyoto Univ., Japan, 1983–84; Res. Fellow, Univ. of Cambridge, 1984–85; Oxford Instruments plc, 1985–2005, Chief Operating Officer, 1996–98, Chief Exec., 1998–2005; Chief Exec., Royal Soc. Enterprise Fund, 2008–14. Member, Board: CoSector Ltd, 2014–16; Ploughshare Innovations, 2016–; Oxford Quantum Circuits, 2018–. Member: Diplomatic Excellence Panel, FCO, 2013–18; Steering Bd, Intellectual Property Office, 2015–18; Expert Lead, HM Treasury initiative on knowledge asset exploitation, 2019–. Trustee, Design Council, 2016–. Fellow, Hughes Hall, Cambridge, 2018–. *Recreations:* playing the bassoon, Real tennis. *E:* andrew.mackintosh@wolfson.ox.ac.uk. *Club:* Athenæum.

**MACKINTOSH, Sir Cameron (Anthony),** Kt 1996; producer of musicals; Chairman, Cameron Mackintosh Ltd, since 1981; Director, Delfont/Mackintosh, since 1991; *b* 17 Oct. 1946; *s* of late Ian Mackintosh and of Diana Mackintosh. *Educ:* Prior Park Coll., Bath. Hon. Fellow, St Catherine's Coll., Oxford, 1990; Hon. DDra Royal Conservatoire of Scotland, 1998. Decided to be producer of musical stage shows at age 8, after seeing Slade's Salad Days; spent brief period at Central Sch. of Speech and Drama; stage hand at Theatre Royal, Drury Lane; later Asst Stage Manager; worked with Emile Littler, 1966, with Robin Alexander, 1967; produced first musical, 1969. Owner of Prince Edward, Prince of Wales,

Novello (formerly Strand), Gielgud, Sondheim (formerly Queen's), Wyndhams, Noël Coward (formerly Albery), Victoria Palace and Ambassadors Theatres. *London productions:* Little Women, 1967; Anything Goes, 1969; Trelawny, 1972; The Card, 1973, 1994; Winnie the Pooh, 1974; Owl and Pussycat Went to See, 1975; Godspell, 1975; Diary of a Madam, 1975; Out on a Limb, 1976; Side by Side by Sondheim, 1976; Oliver!, 1977, 1994, 2008; Gingerbread Man, 1978; My Fair Lady, 1979, 2001; Oklahoma!, 1980, 1999; Tomfoolery, 1980; Jeeves Takes Charge, 1980; Cats, 1981; Song and Dance, 1982; Blondel, 1983; Little Shop of Horrors, 1983; Abbacadabra, 1983; The Boyfriend, 1984; Les Misérables, 1985, 2019; Café Puccini, 1985; Phantom of the Opera, 1986; Follies, 1987; Miss Saigon, 1989, 2015; Just So, 1990; Five Guys Named Moe, 1991; Moby Dick, 1992; Putting It Together, 1992; Carousel, 1993; Martin Guerre, 1996; The Fix, 1997; The Witches of Eastwick, 2000; Mary Poppins, 2004; Avenue Q, 2006; Hair, 2010; Betty Blue Eyes, 2011; Half a Sixpence, 2016; Hamilton, 2017. Nat. Enjoy England Award for Excellence for Outstanding Contribution to Tourism, 2006. *Recreations:* taking holidays, cooking. *Address:* Cameron Mackintosh Ltd, 1 Bedford Square, WC1B 3RB. *T:* (020) 7637 8866. *Club:* Groucho.

**MACKINTOSH, Catherine Anne, (Mrs C. D. Peel)**, FRCM, FRSAMD; violinist; teacher; *b* 6 May 1947; *d* of late Duncan Robert Mackintosh and Mary Isa Mackintosh; *m* 1973, Charles David Peel; one *s* one *d*. *Educ:* Cranborne Chase Sch.; Dartington Coll. of Arts; Royal Coll. of Music (ARCM; FRCM 1994). FRSAMD 1998. Prof. of Baroque and Classical Violin and Viola, Royal Coll. of Music, 1977–99. Visiting Professor of Early Music: RSAMD, later Royal Conservatoire of Scotland, 1989–; RCM, 2000–; RAM, 2003–; Zagreb Acad., 2007–; Prof. of Baroque Violin, Koninklijk Conservatorium, 2008–11; Vis. Prof., Sydney Conservatorium of Music, 2013–; chamber music coach, Wellington, NZ, 2011–. Leader, Acad. of Ancient Music, 1973–87; Mem., Julian Bream Consort, 1978–88; Founding Mem., Purcell Quartet, 1984–; Founding Mem., 1986–2013, and Co-Leader, 1987–2007, Orch. of Age of Enlightenment; Artistic Dir, Aestas Musica Internat. Summer Sch. of Music and Dance, Croatia, 1996–2007; violinist of Duo Amadè with Geoffrey Govier, 2003–. *Recreations:* trombone playing, crosswords, theatre, knitting, friendly string quartet playing. *Address:* 15 Ranelagh Road, W5 5RJ. *W:* www.catherinemackintosh.com.

**MACKINTOSH, David James**; *b* Northampton, 2 April 1979; *s* of James Mackintosh and Dolores Mackintosh. *Educ:* Roade Sch., Northants; Univ. of Durham. Member (C): Northamptonshire CC, 2009–17; Northampton BC, 2011–15 (Leader, 2011–15). MP (C) Northampton S, 2015–17. Chair, All Party Parly Gp for Ending Homelessness, 2016–17, for Sweden, 2016–17. Vice-Pres., Cons. Friends of Bangladesh, 2015–. Mem., Franco-British Council Young Leader's Prog., 2017–18. Patron: Hope Centre, Northampton, 2014–; Caring and Sharing Trust, Northants, 2015–. Kt, Order of St George, House of Habsburg, 2017. *E:* info@davidmackintosh.org.uk.

**MACKINTOSH, Ian**, FCA, FCPA; Chair: Financial Reporting Advisory Board, HM Treasury, since 2016; Corporate Reporting Dialogue, since 2017; *b* 18 Feb. 1946; *s* of Angus John Mackintosh and Jean Elizabeth Mackintosh (*née* Sanders); *m* 1970, Patricia Caroline (*née* McMahon) (*d* 2006); two *s*. *Educ:* Auckland Grammar Sch.; Auckland Univ. (BComm). Partner, Coopers & Lybrand, Australia, 1976–96, Consultant, 1996–2000; Chief Accountant, Australian Securities & Investment Commn, 2000–02; Manager, Financial Mgt, World Bank, 2002–04; Chm., Accounting Standards Bd (UK), 2004–11; Vice Chair, Internat. Accounting Standards Bd, 2011–16. Advr, Huawei Technology Ltd, 2016–. Adjunct Prof., Univ. of Canberra, 2000–06. Chm., Public Sector Cttee, Internat. Fedn of Accountants, 2000–03. *Recreations:* golf, swimming, music, reading.

**MACKINTOSH, Nicola Ann**; Founder, 2011, and Sole Director, since 2019, Mackintosh Law (Sole Principal, 2011–19); *b* Norwich, 30 July 1966; *d* of Athole Spalding Mackintosh and Ellen Mackintosh; *m* 2016, Gordon Gapper; three step *d*. *Educ:* Oxford Poly. (BA Law and Psychol. 1988). Admitted solicitor, 1992; asst solicitor, two London legal aid firms, 1992–99; Co-Founder and Partner, Mackintosh Duncan, 1999–2011. Accredited Legal Rep. (Mental Capacity Welfare), 2017–. Mem., Civil Justice Council, 2003–11. Co-Chm., Legal Aid Practitioners Gp, 2012–. Mem., Bach Commn, 2016–17. Mem., Mental Health and Disability Cttee, 2000–, Mem. Council, 2013–17, 2018–, Law Soc. Hon. QC 2014. Hon. Bencher, Middle Temple, 2018. *Recreation:* driving around the Apennines listening to The Bonzo Dog Doo Dah Band, plotting next stage of fight against injustice. *Address:* Mackintosh Law, 103 Borough High Street, SE1 1NL. *T:* (020) 7357 6464. *E:* info@ macklaw.co.uk.

**McKINTOSH, Peter Finlay**; theatre set and costume designer, since 1993; *b* Liverpool, 22 Jan. 1967; *s* of Peter Ewan McKintosh and Beryl Elizabeth McKintosh; *m* 2016, Oliver John Bartholomew Rowe. *Educ:* Plymouth Coll.; Univ. of Warwick (BA Hons Theatre Studies 1990); Bristol Old Vic Theatre Sch. *Theatre* includes: National Theatre: Honk!, Widowers' Houses, 2000; The Doctor's Dilemma, 2012; Our Country's Good, 2015; Royal Shakespeare Company: Alice in Wonderland, 2001, Pericles, Brand, The Merry Wives of Windsor, 2002; King John, 2006; Donmar Warehouse: Boston Marriage, 2001; The Cryptogram, 2005; John Gabriel Borkman, 2007, The Chalk Garden, 2008; Be Near Me, 2009; Serenading Louie, 2010; Luise Miller, 2011; My Night With Reg, 2014; Splendour, 2015; The Resistible Rise of Arturo Ui, 2017; The York Realist, 2018; Measure for Measure, 2018; St Nicholas, 2018; Almeida Theatre: Romance, 2005; Cloud Nine, 2007; Waste, 2008; House of Games, 2010; The Knot of the Heart, 2011; The Turn of the Screw, 2013; West End: A Woman of No Importance, 2003; The Birthday Party, The Home Place, 2005; The 39 Steps, 2005, UK tours, NY and worldwide, 2005–; Donkeys' Years, 2006; Fiddler on the Roof, The Dumb Waiter, 2007; Entertaining Mr Sloane, Prick Up Your Ears, 2009; Educating Rita, Shirley Valentine, Love Story, 2010; Butley, Noises Off, 2011; Viva Forever!, 2012; The Winslow Boy (also Broadway), Relatively Speaking, 2012; Dirty Rotten Scoundrels, Another Country, 2014; Hay Fever, Harvey, The Importance of Being Earnest, 2015; Guys and Dolls, 2016; The Wind in the Willows, 2017; Open Air Theatre, Regent's Park: Hello Dolly!, 2009; Crazy for You, 2011, transf. West End (Olivier Best Costume Design Award, 2012); The Sound of Music, 2013; Seven Brides for Seven Brothers, 2015; On the Town, 2017; The Heretic, Royal Court, 2011; Guys and Dolls, Chichester, 2014, Théâtre Marigny, Paris, 2019; 42nd Street, Châtelet, Paris, 2016; The Jungle Book, UK tour, 2018; Chess, Copenhagen and tour, 2018; God of Carnage, Th. Royal Bath, 2018; Shadowlands, Chichester, 2019; King Hedley II, Th. Royal Stratford E, 2019; The Deep Blue Sea, Chichester, 2019; Funny Girl, Théâtre Marigny, Paris, 2019; *Opera* includes: The Handmaid's Tale (world premiere), Royal Danish Opera, 2000, ENO, 2003, Canadian Opera, 2004; Love Counts, 2006, The Silent Twins, 2007, Almeida; The Marriage of Figaro, ENO, 2011; Hansel and Gretel, ENO, 2019. *E:* petermckintosh@ mac.com. *W:* www.petermckintosh.com.

**McKITTERICK, Dr David John**, FSA, FRHistS; FBA 1995; Fellow, Trinity College, Cambridge, since 1986 (Librarian, 1986–2015; Vice-Master, 2012–16); *b* 9 Jan. 1948; *s* of Rev. Canon J. H. B. McKitterick and Marjory McKitterick (*née* Quarterman); *m* 1976, Rosamond Deborah Pierce (*see* R. D. McKitterick); one *d*. *Educ:* King's Coll. Sch., Wimbledon; St John's Coll., Cambridge (Scholar; BA 1969; MA 1973; LittD 1994); University College London (DipLib 1971). Staff, Cambridge Univ. Library, 1969–70, 1971–86; Fellow, Darwin Coll., Cambridge, 1978–86; Hon. Prof. of Historical Bibliography, Cambridge Univ., 2006–15. Lyell Reader in Bibliography, Univ. of Oxford, 2000; Sandars Reader in Bibliography, Univ. of Cambridge, 2001–02. Panizzi Lectr, BL, 2015. Syndic, CUP, 2000– (Chm. Pubns Cttee, 2011–). Hon. Curator, Early Printed Books, Fitzwilliam Mus. Vice-Pres., 1990–98, Pres., 1998–2000, Bibliog. Soc.; Pres., Cambridge Bibliog. Soc., 1991–; Pubns Sec., British Acad., 2002–09. Chm., Nat. Manuscripts Conservation Trust, 2018–; Trustee, Dove Cottage, 2019–. MAE 2011. Gold Medal, Bibliographical Soc., 2005. *Publications:* The Library of Sir Thomas Kynvett of Ashwellthorpe 1539–1618, 1978; (ed) Stanley Morison and D. B. Updike: Selected Correspondence, 1979; (ed) Stanley Morison: selected essays on the history of letter forms in manuscript and print, 1981; (with John Dreyfus) A History of the Nonesuch Press, 1981; Four Hundred Years of University Printing and Publishing at Cambridge 1584–1984, 1984; Cambridge University Library: a history: the eighteenth and nineteenth centuries, 1986; A New Specimen Book of Curwen Pattern Papers, 1987; (ed jtly) T. F. Dibdin: *Horae Bibliographicae Cantabrigiensis*, 1988; Wallpapers by Edward Bawden, 1989; (ed) Andrew Perne: quatercentenary studies, 1991; Catalogue of the Pepys Library at Magdalene College, Cambridge, VII: facsimile of Pepys's catalogue, 1991; A History of Cambridge University Press, vol. 1: printing and the book trade in Cambridge 1534–1698, 1992, vol 2: scholarship and commerce 1698–1872, 1998, vol. 3: new worlds for learning 1873–1972, 2004; (ed) The Making of the Wren Library, 1995; Print, Manuscript and the Search for Order 1450–1830, 2003; (ed) The Trinity Apocalypse, 2005; (ed) The Cambridge History of the Book in Britain, 1830–1914, 2009; Old Books, New Technologies: the representation, conservation and transformation of books since 1700, 2013; The Invention of Rare Books, 2018; contribs to learned jls. *Address:* Trinity College, Cambridge CB2 1TQ. *T:* (01223) 338463. *Clubs:* Roxburghe, Double Crown (President, 1994–95).

**McKITTERICK, Prof. Rosamond Deborah**, FRHistS, FSA; Professor of Mediaeval History, University of Cambridge, 1999–2016, now Emerita; Fellow, Sidney Sussex College, Cambridge, since 2007 (Vice-Master, 2013–16); *b* Chesterfield, Derbys, 31 May 1949; *d* of Rev. Canon C. A. Pierce, OBE, MA, BD and Melissa (*née* Heaney); *m* 1976, David John McKitterick, *qv*; one *d*. *Educ:* Univ. of WA (BA 1st cl. Hons 1970); Univ. of Cambridge (MA 1977; PhD 1976; LittD 1991); Univ. of Munich (Graduate Student). FRHistS 1980; Fellow, European Medieval Acad., 1993; FSA 2017. University of Cambridge: Asst Lectr, 1979–85; Lectr, 1985–91; Reader, 1991–97; Prof. of Early Mediaeval European Hist., 1997–99; Newnham College: Fellow, 1974–2006; Dir of Studies in Anglo-Saxon, Norse and Celtic, 1979–93; Vice-Principal, 1996–98. British School at Rome: Hugh Balsdon Fellow, 2001–02; Chair, Faculty of Archaeol., History and Letters, 2011–. Fellow in Residence, Netherlands Inst. of Advanced Study, 2005–06; Fellow, Scaliger Inst., 2005–06, Scaliger Fellow, 2010, Univ. of Leiden; Scholar in Residence, American Acad. in Rome, 2011; LECTIO Chair, KU Leuven, 2015; Leverhulme Emeritus Fellow, 2018–19. Guest Lectr in univs in Germany, Austria, USA, Australia, Denmark, Eire, France, Netherlands, Norway, Belgium, Estonia, Italy, Russia and New Zealand, 1978–; lecture tours: USA, 1982, 1990, 1994; Germany, 1987; UK; speaker, internat. confs on early medieval studies, Belgium, France, Netherlands, Germany, Switzerland, Turkey, Italy, USA, UK, Eire, Austria, Luxembourg, Czech Republic and Finland; Guest Prof., Dept of Culture and Civilisation, Univ. of Verona, 2019. Corresponding Fellow: Monumenta Germaniae Historica, Germany, 1999; Medieval Acad. of America, 2006; philosophisch-historische Klasse, Austrian Acad. Scis, 2006; Associé correspondant étranger, Société nationale des Antiquaires de France, 2016–. MAE 2011. FRSA 2001. Vice-Pres., RHistS, 1994–98, 2000–03; Pres., Ecclesiastical History Soc., 2018–19. Editor: Cambridge Studies in Medieval Life and Thought; Cambridge Studies in Palaeography and Codicology, 1989–2003; Corresp. Ed., Early Medieval Europe, 1999– (Editor, 1992–99). Dr A. H. Heineken Prize in History, Heineken Foundn and Royal Dutch Acad., 2010. *Publications:* The Frankish Church and the Carolingian Reforms 789–895, 1977; The Frankish Kingdoms under the Carolingians 751–987, 1983; The Carolingians and the Written Word, 1989; The Uses of Literacy in early medieval Europe, 1990; (with Lida Lopes Cardozo) Lasting Letters, 1992; Carolingian Culture: emulation and innovation, 1993; Books, Scribes and Learning in the Frankish Kingdoms, Sixth to Ninth Centuries, 1994 (trans. Polish 2011); (ed and contrib.) The New Cambridge Medieval History II, 700–900, 1995; Frankish Kings and Culture in the Early Middle Ages, 1995; (ed jtly and contrib.) Edward Gibbon and Empire, 1996; (ed and contrib.) The Short Oxford History of Europe: the early middle ages 400–1000, 2001 (trans. Spanish 2001, Polish 2010); (ed and contrib.) The Times Atlas of the Medieval World, 2003; History and Memory in the Carolingian World, 2004 (trans. French 2009); Perceptions of the Past in the Early Middle Ages, 2006; Charlemagne: the formation of a European identity, 2008 (trans. German 2008); (ed jtly and contrib.) La culture des élites au haut moyen âge, 2009; (ed jtly and contrib.) Ego Trouble: authors and their identities in the early middle ages, 2010; (ed with C. Bolgia and J. Osborne) Rome across Time and Space c.500–1400: cultural transmission and exchange of ideas, 2011; (jtly) Turning Over a New Leaf: change and development in the medieval book, 2012; (ed jtly) Old St Peter's, Rome, 2013; (ed jtly and contrib.) The Resources of the Past in Early Medieval Europe, 2015; articles in many collections of essays and conf. proc. and jls, incl. English Hist. Rev., Library, Studies in Church History, Trans of RHistS, Early Medieval Europe, Francia, Scriptorium, Papers of British Sch. at Rome; reviews for TLS and English and continental learned jls. *Recreations:* music, fresh air. *Address:* Sidney Sussex College, Cambridge CB2 3HU. *T:* (01223) 338800.

**McKITTRICK, Ven. Douglas Henry**; Archdeacon of Chichester, 2002–18; *b* 18 Feb. 1953; *s* of Joseph Henry McKittrick and Doreen Mary (*née* Davidson). *Educ:* John Marley Sch., Newcastle upon Tyne; St Stephen's House, Oxford (BTh). Ordained deacon, 1977, priest, 1978; Curate: St Paul's, Deptford, 1977–80; St John's, Tuebrook, Liverpool, 1980–81; Team Vicar, St Stephen's, Grove Street, Liverpool, 1981–89; Vicar: St Agnes, Toxteth Park, 1989–97; St Peter's, Brighton with Chapel Royal, Chichester, 1997–2002. RD, Brighton, 1998–2002; Preb., 1998–2002, and Canon, 1998–, Chichester Cathedral. Member: Gen. Synod, 2005–; Council, Additional Curates Soc., 2005–; Nat. Healthcare Chaplaincies Council, 2006–; Ecclesiastical Law Soc., 2003–. *Recreations:* long country/coastal walks, cooking, theatre, wine, Brighton and Hove Albion FC.

**McKITTRICK, His Honour Neil Alastair**; DL; a Circuit Judge, 2001–11; Resident Judge, Peterborough and Huntingdon Crown Court, 2009–11; *b* 1 Jan. 1948; *s* of late James Arthur McKittrick and of Mary Patricia McKittrick (*née* Hobbs); *m* 1975, Jean Armstrong; one *s* one *d*. *Educ:* King's Sch., Ely; College of Law, Guildford. LLB London. Solicitor, 1972. Articled Clerk and Asst Solicitor, Cecil Godfrey & Son, Nottingham, 1967–73; Prosecuting Solicitor, Notts, 1973–77; Clerk to the Justices, 1977–89 (Darlington 1977, E Herts 1981, N Cambs 1986–89); Stipendiary Magistrate, subseq. Dist Judge (Magistrates' Courts), Middx, 1989–2001; a Recorder, 1996–2001; Resident Judge, Ipswich Crown Court, 2006–09; Magistrates' Liaison Judge, Suffolk, 2007–09. Member: Council, Justices' Clerks' Soc., 1985–89 (Chm., Professional Purposes Cttee, 1987–89); Middlesex Probation Cttee, 1990–2001. Mem., Chapter, Peterborough Cathedral, 2015–17. DL, 2011, High Sheriff, 2019–March 2020, Cambs. Editor, Justice of the Peace, 1985–89; Licensing Editor, Justice of the Peace Reports, 1983–2003; Editor, Jl of Criminal Law, 1990–2000 (Mem., Editl Bd, 1985–2000). *Publications:* (ed jtly) Wilkinson's Road

Traffic Offences, 14th edn to 18th edn, 1997; (with Pauline Callow) Blackstone's Handbook for Magistrates, 1997, 2nd edn 2000; (contrib.) Confronting Crime, 2003; papers and articles in learned jls. *Recreation:* visiting churches. *Address:* c/o Peterborough Combined Courts Centre, Rivergate, Peterborough PE1 1EJ.

**MACKLE, Joanna, (Mrs David Utterson);** a Deputy Director, British Museum, since 2013; *b* Belfast, 7 April 1958; *d* of Henry Mackle and Rosemary Campbell; *m* 1991, David Utterson; one *s* one *d*. *Educ:* Ursuline Convent Sch., Wimbledon; Univ. of Manchester (BA Hons French 1981). Faber and Faber: publicity asst, 1982–85; Publicity Manager, 1985–87; Publicity Dir, 1987–93; Publishing Dir, 1993–2002; British Museum: Hd of Communications, 2003–07; Dir of Public Engagement, 2007–13. Member: Speaker's Adv. Council on Public Engagement, 2012–15; Bd of Dirs, Knowledge Quarter, 2017–. Gov., Latymer Upper Sch., 2013–. Trustee, Forward Arts Foundn, 1994–; Mem. Bd, Shakespeare's Globe, 2015–. *Recreations:* walking, reading, travelling. *Address:* British Museum, Great Russell Street, WC1B 3DG. *T:* (020) 7323 8345. *E:* jmackle@britishmuseum.org.

**MACKLOW-SMITH, Roxanna;** see Panufnik, R.

**MACKNEY, Paul Leon John;** General Secretary, National Association of Teachers in Further and Higher Education, 1997–2006; Founder and Joint General Secretary, University and College Union, 2006–07; Member, Trades Union Congress General Council, 2002–07; *b* 25 March 1950; *s* of Rev. L. E. Mackney and Margaret Mackney; *m* 1st, 1969, Rosemary A. Draper (marr. diss. 1974); one *s*; 2nd, 1982, Cherry M. Sewell; one *d*. *Educ:* Exeter Univ. (BA Hons); Birmingham Poly. (RSA DipTEFL); Wolverhampton Poly. (FE CertEd); Warwick Univ. (MA Industrial Relns 1986). Trainee probation officer, 1971–73; General Studies Lectr, Poole Tech. Coll., 1974–75; Hall Green Technical College: ESOL Organiser, 1975–79; Trade Union Studies Tutor, 1980–85; Head, Birmingham Trade Union Studies Centre, S Birmingham Coll., 1986–92; W Midlands Regl Official, NATFHE, 1992–97; Associate Gen. Sec., Univ. and Coll. Union, 2007; Associate Dir for Further Educn, NIACE, 2008–09. Pres., Birmingham TUC, 1980–84 (Life Mem.). Vice-Chair: Unite Against Fascism, 2004–11; Coalition of Resistance, 2010–15; Founding Mem., People's Assembly, 2015–; Co-Chair, Greece Solidarity Campaign, 2012–; Co-ordinator, Campaigning Alliance for Lifelong Learning, 2008–11. TUC Gold Badge, 1977. *Publications:* Birmingham and the Miners' Strike, 1986; numerous articles. *Recreations:* music, singing, spending time with my children, Sean and Ruby, and my granddaughter, Thea, researching family history, learning Modern Greek. *T:* 07974 353709. *E:* paulmackney@btinternet.com.

**McKNIGHT, Samuel;** hair stylist, since 1980; *b* Irvine, Scot. *Educ:* Cumnock Acad. Miss Selfridge Salon, 1975–76; Elizabeth Arden Salon, 1976–77; Molton Brown Salon, 1977–80. Personal hairdresser to Diana, Princess of Wales, 1990–97; Ambassador for Pantene, 2002–13; Creative Dir for GHD, 2013–15. Collaborations: with photographers incl. Nick McKnight, Tim Walker, Patrick Demarchelier, Craig McDean, Mario Testino; with designers incl. Karl Lagerfeld, Chanel, Vivienne Westwood, Fendi, Balmain, Burberry, Dolce & Gabbana, DSquared2. Clients incl. Cate Blanchett, Tilda Swinton, Kate Moss, Cara Delevingne. Magazines: over 200 Global Vogue covers, Harpers Bazaar, Vanity Fair, I-D, LOVE, SHOWstudio, V Mag., W Mag., Garage. Exhibn, Hair by Sam McKnight, Somerset House, 2016–17. Product launch, Hair by Sam McKnight, 2017. *Publications:* Hair by Sam McKnight, 2016. *Recreations:* gardening, yoga. *Address:* c/o Premier Hair and Makeup, 8 Royalty Studios, 105–109 Lancaster Road, W11 1QF. *T:* (020) 7221 2333. *E:* lindsay@premierhairandmakeup.com.

**McKONE, Sophie Helena; Her Honour Judge McKone;** a Circuit Judge, since 2019; *b* Morley, 9 June 1967; *d* of Eric Drake and Deanna Drake; *m* 1994, Mark McKone; two *s* one *d*. *Educ:* Morley High Sch.; Univ. of Leicester (LLB). Called to the Bar, Gray's Inn, 1990; barrister, 1990–2019; a Recorder, 2009–19. *Recreations:* family, dog walking, wine tasting. *Address:* Liverpool Crown Court, Queen Elizabeth II Building, Derby Square, Liverpool L2 1XA. *E:* HHJ.Sophie.McKone@ejudiciary.net.

**MACKRELL, Judith Rosalind;** dance writer and author; Chief Dance Critic, The Guardian, 1995–2018; *b* 26 Oct. 1954; *d* of Alec Mackrell and Margaret (*née* Atkinson, later Halsey); *m* 1977, Simon Henson; two *s*. *Educ:* York Univ. (BA 1st Cl. Hons Eng. and Philosophy); Oxford Univ. Part-time Lectr in English and Dance at various estabts incl. Oxford Univ., Oxford Poly. and Roehampton Inst., 1981–86; Dance Critic, Independent, 1986–94. Freelance dance writer and arts broadcaster, 1986–. Hon. Fellow, Laban Centre for Dance, 1996. *Publications:* Out of Line, 1994; Reading Dance, 1997; (with Darcey Bussell) Life in Dance, 1998; (ed with Debra Craine) The Oxford Dictionary of Dance, 2000; Bloomsbury Ballerina: Lydia Lopokova, imperial dancer and Mrs John Maynard Keynes, 2008; Flappers: six women of a dangerous generation, 2013; The Unfinished Palazzo: life, love and art in Venice, 2017. *Recreations:* travel, food, music, reading, my family. *Address:* 79 Greenwood Road, E8 1NT. *T:* (020) 7249 5553. *W:* www.twitter.com/judithmackrell.

**MACKRELL, Keith Ashley Victor;** Chairman, LSE Enterprise, 1992–2004; Vice Chairman, Duke Corporate Education Ltd, 2004–14; *b* 20 Oct. 1932; *s* of late Henry George Mackrell and Emily Winifred Mackrell (*née* Elcock); *m* 1960, June Yvonne Mendoza, *qv*; one *s* three *d*. *Educ:* Peter Symonds Sch.; London School of Economics (Harold Laski Schol.; BSc Econs 1953; Hon. Fellow, 1999). Director: Shell International, 1976–91 (Regl Co-ordinator, East and Australasia, 1979–91); BG plc, 1994–2005 (Dep. Chm., 2000–05). Non-executive Director: Standard Chartered Bank, 1991–2002; Regalian Properties, 1991–2002; Rexam (formerly Bowater) plc, 1991–98; Fairey Gp plc, 1993–99; Dresdner Emerging Markets Investment Trust, 1998–2002; Gartmore Asia Pacific (formerly Govett Asian Recovery Trust), 1998–2006; Aberdeen All Asia Trust, 2006–07. Gov., LSE, 1991–2009, now Emeritus Gov. Gov. and Trustee, NIESR, 2015–. FInstD 1976; CCMI (CBIM 1978). Hon. LLD Nat. Univ. of Singapore, 1991. *Recreations:* tennis, theatre, reading. *Clubs:* Hurlingham, Wimbledon.

**MACKWORTH, Sir Alan (Keith),** 11th Bt *cr* 1776, of The Gnoll, Glamorganshire; FRSC; Professor of Computer Science, University of British Columbia, since 1984 (Canada Research Chair in Artificial Intelligence, 2001–14); *b* 18 Oct. 1945; *s* of Norman Humphrey Mackworth and Jane Felicity Mackworth (*née* Thring), *S* kinsman, 2018; *m* 1969, Marian Elizabeth; *d* of J. V. Fry; one *d*. *Educ:* Toronto Univ. (BSc 1966); Harvard Univ. (AM 1967); Sussex Univ. (DPhil 1974). Lectr, Univ. of Toronto, 1976–70; Asst Prof., 1974, Associate Prof., 1979, UBC. Chm., Canadian Soc. for Computational Studies of Intelligence, 1980–82; Pres., American Assoc. for Artificial Intelligence, 2005–07. FRSC 2009; FAAAI; Fellow, Canadian Inst. for Advanced Res. *Publications:* (jtly) Computational Intelligence: a logical approach, 1998; (jtly) Artificial Intelligence: foundations of computational agents, 2010, 2nd edn 2017; articles in jls. *Heir: b* Hugh Francis Mackworth [*b* 1958; *m* 1988, Josefina del Carmen, *d* of Mario Gonzalez de Mendoza y Vinent; one *s*].

**MACKWORTH, Rosalind Jean,** CBE 1994; Social Fund Commissioner for Great Britain, 1987–96, and for Northern Ireland, 1987–96; Consultant, Ashley Wilson LLP (formerly Mackworth Rowland), Solicitors; *b* 10 Aug. 1928; *d* of Rev. Albert Walters, FRMetS and Alma Walters, sometime Comptroller to Archbishop of Canterbury; *m* 1960, Richard Charles Audley Mackworth, MA, MSc, DIC, CEng (*d* 2014); two *d*. *Educ:* twelve small schools, following father's postings; Queen's Univ. Belfast (BA); Girton Coll., Cambridge (MA); Law Soc. professional exams. Joined Gregory Rowcliffe, Solicitors, 1956; set up own practice, 1967; amalgamated practice, Mackworth Rowland, 1982, Ashley Wilson, 2005. Mem., VAT Tribunals, 1976. Chm., Judicial Commn, Eur. Union of Women, 1984–87 (Vice-Chm., British Section, 1986–87). *Recreation:* everything except golf. *Address:* Ashley Wilson Solicitors LLP, 26 St Ives Street, Knightsbridge, SW3 2ND. *T:* (020) 7802 4802.

**MACKWORTH-YOUNG, Prof. Charles Gerard,** MD; FRCP; Consultant Physician, Rheumatology and General Medicine, Charing Cross Hospital, since 1990; Professor of Practice (Rheumatology), Imperial College London, since 2017; *b* Menton, France, 6 July 1954; *s* of Sir Robert Christopher, (Sir Robin), Mackworth-Young, GCVO and Rosemarie Mackworth-Young (*née* Aue); *m* 1981, Lady Iona Lindsay, *d* of Earl of Crawford and Balcarres, *qv*; one *s* two *d*. *Educ:* Magdalene Coll., Cambridge (BA 1975; MB BChir 1979; MD 1987); St Bartholomew's Hosp. Med. Coll., London; Medizinische Hochschule, Hanover. MRCP 1980, FRCP 1995. Jun. appts, St George's, Brompton and Hammersmith Hosps, 1981–90; Res Fellow, Tufts Univ., Boston, 1984–86; Consultant Physician, 1992–2016, Hd of Rheumatol., 1993–97, Westminster Hosp., subseq. Chelsea and Westminster Hosp.; Chief of Service for Specialist and Gen. Medicine, Hammersmith Hosps, 1998–2008; King Edward VII's Hospital Sister Agnes: Physician, 1992–; Chairman: Med. Audit Cttee, 2001–06; Med. Cttee, 2006–18; Trustee and Gov., 2001–18; Dep. Med. Dir, 2001–05; Med. Dir, 2006–18. Chairman: Riverside Res. Ethics Cttee, 1998–2004; Fulham (formerly Charing Cross) Res. Ethics Cttee, 2004–15; Dir, Peer Rev. Cttee, Imperial Coll. London, 2009–; Comr, Royal Hosp. Chelsea, 2018–. British Society for Rheumatology: Mem. Council, 2001–04; Chm., Educn and Trng Cttee, 2007–10; Trustee and Exec. Mem., 2007–10. Rheumatol. Continuing Med. Educn Rep., RCP, 2003–. Liveryman: Apothecaries' Society, 1991 (Master, 2017–18; Vice-Chm., 2006–09, Chm., 2009–12, Exams Bd); Goldsmiths' Co., 2003 (Mem. Court, 2011–). Michael Mason Prize for Res., British Soc. for Rheumatol., 1994. *Publications:* original articles, reviews and chapters, mainly on autoimmunity and rheumatology. *Recreations:* music, ski-ing. *Address:* Charing Cross Hospital, Fulham Palace Road, W6 8RF; King Edward VII's Hospital Sister Agnes, Beaumont Street, W1G 6AA. *Clubs:* Travellers, Pratt's, Hurlingham.

**McLACHLAN, Dr Andrew David,** FRS 1989; Scientific Staff, Medical Research Council Laboratory of Molecular Biology, Cambridge, 1967–2000; Fellow of Trinity College, Cambridge, since 1959; *b* 25 Jan. 1935; *s* of late Donald Harvey McLachlan and Katherine (*née* Harman); *m* 1959, Jennifer Margaret Lief Kerr; three *s*. *Educ:* Winchester Coll. (Schol.); Trinity Coll., Cambridge (BA, MA, PhD, ScD). Res. Fellow, Trinity Coll., 1958; Harkness Fellow, USA, 1959–61; Lectr in Physics, Trinity Coll., 1961–87; Lectr in Chemistry, Cambridge Univ., 1965–67. Visiting Professor: CIT, 1964; Brandeis Univ., 1975; UCLA, 1989. *Publications:* (with A. Carrington) Introduction to Magnetic Resonance, 1967; papers in various jls, including Jl of Molecular Biology, Nature, and Acta Crystallographica. *Recreations:* walking, music, camping. *Address:* Trinity College, Cambridge CB2 1TQ; 12 Dane Drive, Cambridge CB3 9LP. *T:* (01223) 361318. *E:* andrew_mclachlan@fastmail.fm.

**McLACHLAN, Edward Rolland;** freelance cartoonist, illustrator and designer, since 1966; *b* 22 April 1940; *m* 1964, Shirley Ann Gerrard; one *s* three *d*. *Educ:* Humberstone Village Jun. Sch.; Wyggeston Boys' Grammar Sch.; Leicester CAT. Cartoonist for Punch, Private Eye, Spectator, Saga mag., The Oldie, The Cartoonist, Regenerate (formerly Building), Roof, Property Week, IFG; cartoonist and illustrator for The Salisbury Review; illustrator for Document mag.; cartoonist of numerous books for publishers, incl. Methuen, Macmillan Heinemann, Profile, John Wiley & Sons, Pearson, Penguin, OUP, Longmans, Cornelsen, and Sound Foundations educnl books for children; television cartoon series, ITV: Simon and the Land of Chalk Drawings, 1977, and Canada, 2001; Bangers and Mash, 1989; titling design for BBC TV series, Just William, 2010; greetings cards for Cardmix Ltd; work for many advertising agencies. Heneage Cup, Cartoon Art Trust, 2011. Exhibn, On the Edge, Chris Beetles Gall., London, 2018. DLitt Leicester, 2017. *Publications:* writer and illustrator: (series for children) Simon in the Land of Chalk Drawings, 1969, Simon and the Chalk Drawing Army, 1971, Simon and the Moon Rocket, 1972, Simon and the Dinosaur, 1973, reissued as Simon in the Land of Chalk Drawings: four stories that inspired the TV series!, 2016; McLachlan Book of Cartoons, 2000; illustrator: Sorry I'm British, by B. Crystal and A. Russ, 2010; 117 'For Dummies' books. *Recreations:* cycling, weight-training, gardening, pubs, Everyone Active gym Oadby. *Address:* 3 Spinney View, Coverside Road, Great Glen, Leics LE8 9EP. *T:* (0116) 259 2632; c/o Chris Beetles Gallery, 8–10 Ryder Street, St James's, SW1Y 6QB. *T:* (020) 7839 7551. *E:* gallery@chrisbeetles.com; Folio, 10 Gate Street, Lincoln's Inn Fields, WC2A 3HP. *E:* mail@edmclachlan.co.uk. *W:* www.edmclachlan.co.uk.

**McLACHLAN, Hon. Ian (Murray),** AO 1989; Managing Director, Tupra Pastoral Co., since 1990; Minister for Defence, Australia, 1996–98; Chairman, Australian Wool Innovation Ltd, 2002–08; *b* 2 Oct. 1936; *s* of I. McLachlan; *m* 1964, Janet Lee; two *s* one *d*. *Educ:* Collegiate Sch. of St Peter, SA; Jesus Coll., Cambridge (cricket blue, 1957–58). Played cricket for SA, 1961–64. Director: SA Brewing, 1978–90 (Dep. Chm., 1983–90); Elders IXL, 1980–90. MP (L) Barker, SA, 1990–98. Pres., Nat. Farmers' Fedn, 1984–88. Pres., SA Cricket Assoc., 1999–2013; Dir, Cricket Australia, 2004–12; Dir, Adelaide Oval Stadium Mgt Authy, 2014–. (Chm., 2009–14). *Address:* 5 Fuller Court, Walkerville, Adelaide, SA 5081, Australia.

**McLACHLAN, Malcolm Orde,** MBE 2007; HM Diplomatic Service; Vice President, International Relations, ASR Group, since 2012; *b* 10 Sept. 1963; *m* 2005, Dr Mary Oswana; one *s* two *d*. Entered FCO, 1981; Archivist and Entry Clearance Officer, Karachi, 1984–87; Third Sec., Guatemala City, 1988–93; Second Sec., EU Directorate, FCO, 1993–96; First Sec. and Hd, Political Sect., Nairobi, 1996–2001; Press Officer, Harare, 2000; Dep. Hd of Mission, Hanoi, 2001–05; Migration Envoy, Horn of Africa, FCO, 2005–06; Dep. Hd, SE Asia and Pacific Gp, FCO, 2006–08; High Comr to Fiji, and concurrently to Tonga, Vanuatu, Tuvalu, Kiribati and Nauru, 2009–11.

**McLACHLAN, Marjory Jane,** CVO 2017; Lord-Lieutenant of Stirling and Falkirk, 2005–17; *b* 15 Feb. 1942; *d* of Walter and Kate Alexander; *m* 1962, Colin McLachlan; two *d*. *Educ:* St Leonard's Sch., St Andrews. Pres., Ladies' Br., Royal Caledonian Curling Club, 1989–90; Scottish Rep., World Curling Fedn, 1991–99. JP Falkirk, 2006. CStJ 2008. *Recreations:* family, bridge, curling, golf, travel. *Address:* Dromore, 23 Majors Loan, Falkirk FK1 5QG. *T:* (01324) 622633. *E:* marjmcl@sky.com.

**McLACHLIN, Rt Hon. Beverley,** CC 2018; PC 2000; Chief Justice of Canada, 2000–17; *b* Pincher Creek, Alberta, 7 Sept. 1943; *m* 1st, 1967, Roderick McLachlin (*d* 1988); one *s*; 2nd, 1992, Frank E. McArdle. *Educ:* Univ. of Alberta (MA 1968, LLB 1968). Called to the Bar: Alberta, 1969; BC, 1971; practised law: with Wood, Moir, Hyde and Ross, Edmonton, 1969–71; with Thomas, Herdy, Mitchell & Co., Fort St John, BC, 1971–72; with Bull, Housser and Tupper, Vancouver, 1972–75; Lectr, 1974–75, Associate Prof.,

1975–78, Prof., 1981, Univ. of BC, 1974–81; Judge: County Court of Vancouver, 1981; Supreme Court of BC, 1981–85; Court of Appeal, BC, 1985–88; Chief Justice, Supreme Court of BC, 1988–89; Judge, Supreme Court of Canada, 1989–2000. Hon. LLD: BC, 1990; Alberta, 1991; Toronto, 1995; York, 1999; Law Soc. of Upper Canada, Ottawa, Calgary, Brock, Simon Fraser, Victoria, Alberta, 2000; Lethbridge, Bridgewater State Coll., 2001; Mt St Vincent, Prince Edward Island, 2002; Montreal, 2003; Manitoba, QUB, Dalhousie, Carleton, 2004; Maine at Fort Kent, 2005; Ateneo de Manila Univ., 2006. *Publications*: Full Disclosure (novel), 2018; contrib. to learned jls.

**McLAREN,** family name of **Baron Aberconway**.

**McLAREN, David John;** Chief Executive, London Oncology Clinic, 2006–11; Chairman, McLaren and Partners Ltd, since 2008; *b* 14 April 1944; *s* of late Charles Claude McLaren and Eileen Patricia (*née* Shanley); *m* 2002, Anna Maria Jacobson; one *s* three *d*. *Educ*: Merchant Taylors' Sch., Crosby; QMC, KCL, and Courtauld Inst., Univ. of London (BA 1965; Dip. Hist. of Art and Architecture, 1967). Mather & Crowther, 1965–67; Radio Newsroom, BBC, 1967–68; Ogilvy & Mather, 1968–70; KMP Partnership, 1970–82 (Man. Dir, 1974–82); Man. Dir, Collett Dickenson Pearce, 1982–91; Hill & Knowlton: CEO, 1994–2000; Chm., 2000–04. Global Co-ordinator, WPP, 2000–04. Chairman: Gainmedium Ltd, 1992–2008; Cohn & Wolfe, 2005–07. Non-executive Director: Corney and Barrow Ltd, 1991–2017; London Metabolic Services, 2015–; Private Cellar Ltd, 2017–. Council Member: IPA, 1984–89; Advertising Assoc., 1984–89; Dir, PRCA, 2003–06. Trustee, 2006–11, Strategic Advr, 2011–, Oxford Literary Festival. Member: Thames & Solent Cttee, NT, 1999–2008; Nat. Campaign Bd, Maggie's Centres, 2004–11; Business Adv. Bd, Ashmolean Mus., 2005. Trustee: Photographers' Gall., 1986–90; River & Rowing Mus., 2000–09 (Chm., Develt Bd, 1999–2003); Chair, Global Foundn to Eliminate Domestic Violence, 2015–16. Dir, Orch. of St John's, 2012–. FIPA 1987. FRSA 1997. *Recreations*: motoring, opera, wine, shooting, fishing, photography, books, architecture. *Clubs*: Cavalry and Guards, Groucho.

**MacLAREN of MacLaren, Donald;** Chief of the Clan MacLaren; HM Diplomatic Service; Ambassador to Georgia, 2004–07; *b* 22 Aug. 1954; *s* of late Donald MacLaren of MacLaren, (The MacLaren of MacLaren) and Margaret Sinclair (*née* Miller); *m* 1978, Maida-Jane Aitchison; three *s* two *d*. Joined FCO, 1978; BMG, Berlin, 1980–83; First Secretary: Moscow, 1984–87; FCO, 1987–91; Dep. Hd of Mission, Cuba, 1991–94; FCO, 1994–97; Dep. Hd of Mission, Venezuela, 1997–2000; Consul-Gen. and Dep. Hd of Mission, Ukraine, 2000–04. Contested (Ind) Kirkcaldy and Cowdenbeath, 2010. *Address*: c/o Foreign and Commonwealth Office, King Charles Street, SW1A 2AH.

**McLAREN, Iain Archibald;** President, Institute of Chartered Accountants of Scotland, 2011–12; *b* Edinburgh, 21 Feb. 1951; *s* of Hugh McLaren and Margaret McLaren; *m* Fiona Gillian Coulter (*née* Maclachlan); two *s* two *d*. *Educ*: Daniel Stewart's Coll., Edinburgh; Heriot-Watt Univ. (BA). Mem. ICAS 1974. CA, Peat Marwick Mitchell, 1971–78; Hd, Internal Audit, Miller Gp, 1978–80; Peat Marwick Mitchell, then Peat Marwick McLintock, subseq. KPMG: Audit Partner, 1981–97; Sen. Partner, Scotland, 1998–2004; Chm., Infrastructure and Govt, 2005–08. Dir, Cairn Energy plc, 2008– (Chm., Audit Cttee, 2008–); Chm., Investors Capital Trust plc, 2010–. Dir, Scottish Enterprise, 2010–15. *Recreations*: golf, hill walking, arts. *Address*: 9 Ravelston Dykes, Edinburgh EH4 3EA. *T*: (0131) 332 3000. *E*: mclaren.ia@gmail.com.

**McLAREN, Ian Alban Bryant;** QC 1993; a Recorder, 1996–2010 (an Assistant Recorder, 1992–96); *b* 3 July 1940; *yr s* of Alban McLaren and Doris (*née* Hurst); *m* 1964, Margaret Middleton, BA; two *s* one *d*. *Educ*: Sandbach Sch., Blackpool Grammar Sch.; Univ. of Nottingham (LLB 1961). Called to the Bar, Gray's Inn, 1962 (Macaskie Schol.; Bencher, 2004); in practice at the Bar, 1962–2009; Law Tutor, Univ. of Nottingham, 1962–64; Hd of Ropewalk Chambers, 2000–06. Mem., Standards Cttee, Notts CC, 2009–12. Pres., Notts Medico-Legal Soc., 1997–98. Fellow, Soc. for Advanced Legal Studies, 2000–. Hon. LLD Nottingham Trent, 2005. *Recreations*: gardening, photography. *Address*: c/o Ropewalk Chambers, 24 The Ropewalk, Nottingham NG1 5EF. *T*: (0115) 947 2581.

**McLAREN, Melanie Elizabeth;** Executive Director, Audit and Actuarial Regulation, Financial Reporting Council, 2016–18 (Executive Director, Codes and Standards, 2012–16); *b* 1 April 1963; partner, James Hind; two *s* one *d*. *Educ*: Univ. of St Andrews (MA Arabic Studies and German). ACA 1990. Coopers & Lybrand, later PricewaterhouseCoopers, 1985–2008, Partner, Financial Services Practice, 1999–2008; Friends Provident, then Friends Life Group: interim Chief Risk Officer, 2010; Business Risk Dir, 2010–11; interim Chief Risk Officer, 2011–12.

**McLAREN, Hon. Michael Duncan;** QC 2002; *b* 29 Nov. 1958; *s* of 3rd Baron Aberconway and Ann Lindsay (*née* Aymer); *m* 1985, Caroline Jane, *d* of Air Chief Marshal Sir (William) John Stacey, KCB, CBE, FRAeS; two *s* one *d*. *Educ*: Eton Coll.; Christ's Coll., Cambridge (MA 1st Cl. Law 1980). Called to the Bar, Middle Temple, 1981, Bencher, 2012; in practice at the Bar, 1981–, specialising in regulatory and commercial law (aviation, insurance, etc). Dir, Bodnant Garden, 2003–. Prime Warden, Fishmongers' Co., 2015–16. *Recreations*: horticulture, music, travel, architecture. *Address*: Fountain Court Chambers, Temple, EC4Y 9DH. *T*: (020) 7583 3335, *Fax*: (020) 7353 0329. *E*: mmclaren@fountaincourt.co.uk.

**MacLAREN, Prof. Robert Edward,** DPhil; FRCSE, FRCOphth, FMedSci, FACS; Professor of Ophthalmology, University of Oxford, since 2009; Consultant Ophthalmologist, Oxford Eye Hospital, since 2009; Bodley Fellow and Lecturer in Human Anatomy, Merton College, Oxford, since 1992; Civilian Consultant Advisor to the Royal Navy, since 2011; *b* Epsom, Surrey, 14 Nov. 1966; *s* of late Michael Gordon MacLaren and Penelope Gael MacLaren (*née* Newbery); *m* 2002, Lucy Amelia Pester; two *s* one *d*. *Educ*: Angmering Sch.; Chichester Coll.; Univ. of Edinburgh (MB ChB 1990); Merton Coll., Oxford (DPhil 1996). FRCSE 1998; FRCOphth 2005. SHO, Guy's Hosp., London, 1991–92; Demonstrator, Univ. of Oxford, 1992–93; MRC Clin. Trng Fellow, 1993–95; Captain, 16 Armoured Field Ambulance, RAMC, 1995–96, temp. Regtl MO, 1 Worcs and Sherwood Foresters Regt, 26 Regt RA, Queen's Royal Hussars, Bosnia Herzegovina, 1996; SHO in Ophthalmol., Reading and Oxford, 1996–99; Moorfields Eye Hospital: Registrar and Fellow in Vitreoretinal Surgery, 1999–2004; Res. Fellow in Med. Retina, 2004–06; Hon. Consultant Vitreoretinal Surgeon, 2006–. Hon. Prof. of Ophthalmol., Inst. of Ophthalmol., UCL, 2009–. Commnd RAMC (Vol.), 1992; Regtl MO, 5th (Vol.) Royal Green Jackets, 1994–95 and 1996–98; MO, 306 Field Hosp. RAMC (Vol.), 1998–2000; Surgeon Maj., HAC, London, 2000–04; Locum Surgeon Maj., Household Cavalry Mounted Regt, London, 2002–03. Lectures: King James IV Professorship of Surgery and Medal, RCSE, 2007; Percival Hay Medal, Northern England Ophthalmol Soc., 2011; Euretina, 2014. FACS 2017; FMedSci 2018. Research Gold Medal, Moorfields Eye Hosp., 2005; ARVO Camras Award, 2013; Richardson-Gross Medal, South Western Ophthalmol Soc., 2017; Sir Adrian Cadbury Medal, Midland Ophthalmol Soc., 2018; Keeler Medal, Royal Coll. of Ophthalmologists, 2019. *Publications*: articles on ophthalmology, gene therapy, stem cell research, electronic retinal implants and cataract surgery. *Recreations*: tennis, military history. *Address*: Merton College, Oxford OX1 4JD. *T*: (01865) 276310, *Fax*: (01865) 276361. *Club*: Honourable Artillery.

**MacLAREN, Hon. Roy;** PC (Can.) 1983; High Commissioner for Canada in the United Kingdom, 1996–2000; *b* 26 Oct. 1934; *s* of Wilbur MacLaren and Anne (*née* Graham); *m* 1959, Alethea (*née* Mitchell) (*d* 2015); one *s* (and one *s* one *d* decd); *m* 2018, Rev. Dr Susan Montgomery. *Educ*: schs in Vancouver, Canada; Univ. of BC (BA); Univ. of Cambridge (MA); Univ. of Harvard; Univ. of Toronto (MDiv). With Canadian Diplomatic Service, in Saigon, Hanoi, Prague, Geneva, NY (UN) and Ottawa, 1957–69; Dir, Public Affairs, Massey Ferguson Ltd, 1969–73; President: Ogilvy & Mather (Canada) Ltd, 1974–76; Canadian Business Media Ltd, 1977–93; Director: Deutsche Bank (Canada), 1984–93; London Life Assurance, 1984–93; Royal LePage Ltd, 1985–93. MP (L) Etobicoke N, 1979–96; Parly Sec., Energy, 1980–82; Minister of: State Finance, 1983; Nat. Revue, 1984; Internat. Trade, 1993–96. Non-executive Director: Standard Life, 2001–04; Brookfield (formerly Brascan), 2001–09; Canadian Tire, 2001–03; Patheon, 2001–06; Algoma Central, 2001–10; Wilton Petroleums, 2008–. Commissioner: Commonwealth War Graves Commn, 1996–2000; Trilateral Commn, 2001–17; Trustee, Imperial War Mus., 1996–2000; Dir, Bletchley Park Trust, 2001–08; Mem. Adv. Cttee, Scott Polar Res. Inst., 1998–2000; Gov., Ditchley Foundn, 2004–. Mem. Council, IISS, 2001–08; Chairman: Canadian Inst. of Internat. Affairs, 2001–05; Canada-Europe Round Table, 2001–; Canada-India Business Council, 2001–14; Atlantic Council of Canada, 2003–06. Sen. Fellow, Massey Coll., Univ. of Toronto, 2013–. Hon. Col, 7th Toronto Regt, Royal Canadian Artillery, 1995–2005. Hon. DSL Toronto, 1996; Hon. DCL N Alabama, 2000; Hon. DLitt New Brunswick, 2001; Hon. LLD Prince Edward Island, 2003. *Publications*: Canadians in Russia 1918–1919, 1976; Canadians on the Nile 1882–1898, 1978; Canadians Behind Enemy Lines 1939–1945, 1981; Honourable Mentions, 1986; African Exploits: the diaries of William Stairs 1887–1892, 1997; Commissions High, 2006; The Fundamental Things Apply, 2011; Empire and Ireland, 2015; Mackenzie King in the Age of the Dictators: Canada's imperial and foreign policies, 2019. *Address*: 425 Russell Hill Road, Toronto, ON M5P 2S4, Canada. *Clubs*: White's, Pratt's; Rideau (Ottawa); Toronto; Royal Canadian Yacht.

**McLATCHIE, Cameron,** CBE 1996 (OBE 1988); Chairman, 1988–2016, Chief Executive, 1988–2003, Consultant, 2016–17, British Polythene Industries plc (formerly Scott & Robertson); *b* 18 Feb. 1947; *s* of Cameron McLatchie and Maggie McLatchie (*née* Maxwell Taylor); *m* 1973, Leslie Mackie; two *s* one *d*. *Educ*: Univ. of Glasgow (LLB). Apprentice CA, Whinney, Murray & Co., 1968–70; Admin. Asst, subseq. Prodn Manager, then Prodn Dir, Thos Boag & Co. Ltd, 1971–74; Managing Director: Anaplast Ltd, 1975–83; Scott & Robertson plc, 1983–88. Non-executive Director: Motherwell Bridge Hldgs Ltd, 1993–97; Hiscox Select plc, 1993–98 (Chm.); Royal Bank of Scotland Gp, 1998–2002. Dep. Chm., Scottish Enterprise, 1997–2000 (Mem. Bd, 1990–95). Member: Adv. Cttee on Business and the Envmt, 1991–93; Sec. of State for Scotland's Adv. Gp on Sustainable Develt, 1994–95; Bd, Scottish Envmtl Protection Agency, 1995–97. DUniv Paisley 2000. *Recreations*: golf, bridge, gardening.

**McLAUCHLAN, Prof. Keith Alan,** PhD; FRS 1992; Professor of Chemistry, Oxford University, 1996–2002, now Emeritus; Fellow of Hertford College, Oxford, 1965–2002, now Emeritus; *b* 8 Jan. 1936; *s* of Frederick William McLauchlan and Nellie (*née* Summers); *m* 1958, Joan Sheila Dickenson; one *s* one *d*. *Educ*: Queen Elizabeth's Hosp., Bristol; Univ. of Bristol (BSc, PhD); Univ. of Oxford (MA). Post-doctoral Fellow, NRCC, Ottawa, 1959–60; Post-doctoral Fellow, then Sen. Scientific Officer, NPL, Teddington, 1960–65. Oxford University: Lectr, 1965–94; Reader in Physical Chemistry, 1994–96; Chairman: Inter-deptl Cttee for Chemistry, 1990–93; Cttee of Heads of Sci. Depts, 1991–93; Member: Gen. Bd, 1993–97; Hebdomadal Council, 1998–2000. Erskine Fellow, Univ. of Christchurch, NZ, 1991; Eminent Scientist, RIKEN, Tokyo, 2000–01. Visiting Professor: Tata Inst., Bombay, 1986; Univ. of Konstanz, Germany, 1990; Univ. of Padua, 1998; Ecole Normale Supérieure, Paris, 1998; George Willard Wheland Vis. Prof., Univ. of Chicago, 1998. Chm., Electron Spin Resonance Discussion Gp, RSC, 1989–92. Pres., Internat. Soc. for Electron Paramagnetic Resonance, 1993–96. Mem., Scientific Adv. Bd, Electro Magnetic Field Biol Res. Trust, 1995–2001. Fellow, IES, 2005. Silver Award for Chemistry, 1993, Gold Award, 2002, IES; Bruker Prize, RSC, 1997; Zavoisky Prize for Electron Spin Resonance, Tatarstan, 2001. Radio and television appearances. *Publications*: Magnetic Resonance, 1972; Molecular Physical Chemistry: a concise introduction, 2004; contrib. chaps in books; papers and review articles in Molecular Physics, Chemical Physics Letters, etc. *Recreations*: gardening, walking, reading.

**McLAUCHLAN, Dr Sylvia June,** FFPH; Director General, The Stroke Association, 1993–97; *b* 8 June 1935; *d* of Sydney George Smith and Muriel May (*née* Treweek); *m* 1960, Derek John Alexander McLauchlan, CBE (*d* 2009); two *d*. *Educ*: High Sch. for Girls, Chichester; Univ. of Bristol (MB ChB 1959); Univ. of Manchester (MSc 1981). FFPH (FFPHM 1989). GP, Bristol, 1960–66; MO, Dept of Public Health, Portsmouth, 1970–76; Clinical MO, Macclesfield, 1976–77; Community Medicine Dept, NW RHA, 1977–86; Public Health Dept, SW Thames RHA, 1986–91; Dir of Public Health, Ealing HA, 1991–93. Chm., Primary Care Facilitation Trust, 2000–03; Trustee, East Thames Care, 2000–04. Gov., Treloar Sch., 2001–03. *Recreations*: theatre, gardening, cooking. *Address*: 7 Holmwood Close, East Horsley, Surrey KT24 6SS.

**McLAUGHLIN, Anne,** *see* McLaughlin, E. A.

**McLAUGHLIN, Christopher John;** Editor at Large, Tribune, since 2018 (Editor, 2004–18); *b* 11 Oct. 1955; *s* of Patrick Thomas McLaughlin and Norah Mary McLaughlin (*née* Walsh). *Educ*: St Helen's, Plaistow; St Bonaventure's, Forest Gate. Gen. reporter, Barking and Dagenham Advertiser, then Newham Recorder, 1974–78; Foreign Ed., 1978–81, Lobby Corresp., 1981–87, Labour Weekly; Parly Corresp. and Dep. Political Ed., 1987–93, European Ed., 1993–96, Scotsman; Political Corresp., Mail on Sunday, 1996–2000; Parly Columnist, Big Issue, 1999–2005; Political Ed., Sunday Mirror, 2000–04. Mem. (Lab) Newham LBC, 1978–82. *Address*: c/o Tribune, Press Gallery, House of Commons, SW1A 0AA. *T*: 07775 337001. *Club*: Soho House.

**McLAUGHLIN, Eleanor Thomson;** JP; DL; Lord Provost and Lord Lieutenant of Edinburgh, 1988–92; *b* 3 March 1938; *d* of Alexander Craig and Helen Thomson; *m* 1959, Hugh McLaughlin; one *s* two *d*. *Educ*: Broughton School. Mem. (Lab), Edinburgh District Council, 1974–96. Chairman: Edinburgh Festival Soc., 1988–92; Edinburgh Military Tattoo Ltd, 1988–92. JP Edinburgh, 1975; DL Edinburgh, 1993. *Recreations*: Shetland lace knitting, gardening (Alpine plants). *Address*: 28 Oxgangs Green, Edinburgh EH13 9JS. *T*: (0131) 445 4052.

**McLAUGHLIN, (Elizabeth) Anne;** *b* Greenock, 8 March 1966; *d* of John Robert McLaughlin and Elizabeth Fulton McLaughlin (*née* Purdie). *Educ*: Port Glasgow High Sch.; Royal Scottish Acad. of Music and Drama and Univ. of Glasgow (BA Dramatic Studies 1987). Anniversary Co-ordinator, Sense Scotland, 1994–96; Scottish Fundraising Manager, ICRF, 1996–2000; Staff Fundraiser, ScottishPower, 2000–01; Man. Dir, Business for Scotland, 2001–06; Internal Communications Exec., SNP HQ, 2002–06; Political Advr to Aileen Campbell, MSP, 2007–08; Communications Manager, Community Business Technol. Developers, Galle, Sri Lanka, 2008; Campaign Co-ordinator, SNP, Glasgow E by-election, 2008; Political Advr to Robert Doris, MSP, 2008–09. MSP (SNP) Glasgow,

Feb. 2009–2011; contested (SNP): Glasgow Provan, Scottish Parlt, 2011; Inverclyde, June 2011. MP (SNP) Glasgow NE, 2015–17; contested (SNP) same seat, 2017. *Publications:* (ed) Tall Tales, Short Stories, 1995. *Recreations:* blogging, travel, languages, creative writing, photography.

**McLAUGHLIN, Léonie Anne;** Parliamentary Counsel, since 2003; *b* 15 Nov. 1963; *d* of Timothy Edward Nodder, *qv*; *m* 1996, Wing Comdr Andrew McLaughlin. *Educ:* Christ's Coll., Cambridge (BA English Lit. and Law 1984). Admitted solicitor, 1988; solicitor's articles with May, May & Merrimans, Gray's Inn, 1986–88; Asst, then Sen. Asst, then Dep., Parly Counsel, Parly Counsel Office, 1988–96, 2000–03; self-employed Parly draftsman, 1996–2000. *Recreations:* books, fine art, gardening. *Address:* Parliamentary Counsel Office, 1 Horse Guards Road, SW1A 2HQ. *Club:* Royal Air Force.

**McLAUGHLIN, Dr Mark Hugh;** Executive Director of Finance, Northamptonshire County Council, 2017–18; *b* 20 March 1962; *s* of Raymond and Helen McLaughlin; *m* 1988, Clare Louise Hennessy; three *s*. *Educ:* Univ. of St Andrews (BSc Hons (Zool.) 1983); Univ. of Nottingham (PhD (Zool.) 1988). Res. Fellow, Inst. of Neurol., 1987; Auditor, Audit Commn, 1987–91; Principal Auditor, City of Westminster, 1991–93; Borough of Broxbourne: Asst Dir of Finance, 1993–95; Dir of Resources, 1995–98; Dir of Finance, London Borough of Hammersmith and Fulham, 1998–2001; Dir of Finance and Corporate Resources, London Borough of Enfield, 2001–07; Exec. Dir, Finance and Performance, Identity and Passport Service, 2007–09; Exec. Dir of Finance, Envmt Agency, 2009–15; Chief Finance Officer, DEFRA, 2015–17. Non-exec. Dir, Camden and Islington NHS Trust, 2018–. *Address:* Department for Environment, Food and Rural Affairs, 2 Marsham Street, SW1P 4DF.

**McLAUGHLIN, Prof. Martin Leonard,** DPhil; Agnelli Serena (formerly Fiat Serena) Professor of Italian Studies, University of Oxford, 2001–17; Fellow, Magdalen College, Oxford, 2001–17, now Emeritus; *b* 4 Dec. 1950; *s* of George Vincent McLaughlin and Ann Josephine McLaughlin; *m* 1974, Catherine Ann Gallagher; one *d*. *Educ:* St Aloysius' Coll., Glasgow; Glasgow Univ. (MA); Balliol Coll., Oxford (MA; DPhil 1984). Lectr, Italian Dept, Edinburgh Univ., 1977–90; Lectr in Italian, and Student, Christ Church, Oxford, 1990–2001; Dir, Eur. Humanities Res. Centre, 2002–04, 2011–14, Res. Dir, Faculty of Medieval and Mod. Langs, 2014–17, Univ. of Oxford. Reviews Ed., Italian Studies, 1989–94; Italian Ed., 1994–2001, Gen. Ed., 2001–03, Modern Lang. Rev.; Chm., Editl Bd, Legenda, 2002–09. Member, Executive Committee: Soc. for Italian Studies, 1987–94 (Chm., 2004–10); MHRA, 1994–2004 (Hon. Life Mem., 2004). John Florio Prize for Translation, 2000; Serena Medal, British Acad., 2017. Commendatore dell' Ordine della Stella della Solidarietà Italiana, 2008. *Publications:* (ed jtly) Leopardi: a Scottis Quair, 1987; Literary Imitation in the Italian Renaissance, 1995; Italo Calvino, 1998; (trans.) Italo Calvino, Why Read the Classics?, 1999; (ed) Britain and Italy from Romanticism to Modernism, 2000; (trans.) Italo Calvino, Hermit in Paris, 2003; (trans.) Umberto Eco, On Literature, 2005; (ed jtly) Biographies and Autobiographies in Modern Italy, 2007; (ed jtly) Image, Eye and Art in Calvino: writing visibility, 2007; (ed jtly) Petrarch in Britain: interpreters, imitators and translators over 700 years, 2007; (ed jtly) Sinergie Narrative: cinema e letteratura nell'Italia contemporanea, 2008; (trans.) Italo Calvino, The Complete Cosmicomics, 2009; (ed jtly) Dante the Lyric and Ethical Poet: Dante lirico e etico, 2010; (ed jtly) Dante in Oxford: the Paget Toynbee Lectures, 2011; (trans.) Italo Calvino: Into the War, 2011; Letters 1941–1985, 2013; Collection of Sand, 2013; (ed jtly) Authority, Innovation and Early Modern Epistemology: essays in honour of Hilary Gatti, 2015; Leon Battista Alberti: la vita, l'umanesimo, le opere letterarie, 2016; (ed jtly) Machiavelli's 'Prince': traditions, text and translations, 2017. *Recreations:* football, travel, cinema, walking. *Address:* Magdalen College, Oxford OX1 4AU.

**McLAUGHLIN, Mary,** CBE 2007; Head Teacher, Notre Dame High School, Glasgow, 1990–2007; Principal, Notre Dame New Learning Community, 2003–07; *b* 18 Aug. 1948; *d* of Philip McGachey and Mary McGachey (*née* Ashe); *m* 1972, William McLaughlin; one *d*. *Educ:* Our Lady and St Joseph's Primary Sch., Glenboig; St Patrick's High Sch., Coatbridge; Univ. of Glasgow (MA); Notre Dame Coll. (DipEd). Principal Teacher, Modern Langs, St Margaret's High Sch., Airdrie, 1975–84; Asst Head, Taylor High Sch., New Stevenson, 1984–90. Member: Bd, Anniesland Coll., 1993–97; Bd, Curriculum for Excellence Prog., 2005–. Leadership in Learning Award, Becta, 2005; Glasgow Archdio. Medal for Services to Educn, 2007. *Recreations:* reading, walking, travel, theatre. *Address:* Notre Dame High School, 160 Observatory Road, Glasgow G12 9LN. *T:* (0141) 582 0190, *Fax:* (0141) 582 0191.

**McLAUGHLIN, Mitchel;** Member for South Antrim, 2007–16 (Foyle, 1998–2007) (SF, 1998–2015, when elected Speaker), and Speaker, 2015–16, Northern Ireland Assembly (Deputy Speaker, 2013–15); *b* 29 Oct. 1945; *m* 1975, Mary-Lou Fleming; three *s*. Mem. (SF) Derry CC, 1985–99. Sinn Féin: Mem., Nat. Exec., 1981–; Nat. Chairperson, 1994–2015; peace negotiator, 1997–. Member: Civil Rights Assoc., 1968–; Nat. H-Blocks/ Armagh Cttee, 1980–81. Contested (SF): Foyle, 2005; S Antrim, 2010. Hon. Prof. in Peace Studies, QUB, 2018–.

**McLAUGHLIN, Niall,** RA 2019; Principal, Niall McLaughlin Architects, since 1990; *b* Geneva, 17 Feb. 1962; *s* of John McLaughlin and Mairin McLaughlin (*née* Cryan); *m* 2006, Mary Miller; one *s* one *d*. *Educ:* St Michael's Coll., Dublin; University Coll. Dublin (BArch 1984). Architect, Scott Tallon Walker, 1984–89. Projects include: student residence, Somerville Coll., Oxford, 2011; chapel, Ripon Coll., Cuddesdon, 2013; accommodation, res. facilities and auditorium, Jesus Coll., Cambridge, 2017; Sultan Nazrin Shah Centre, Oxford, 2017. Visiting Professor: Bartlett Sch. of Architecture, UCL, 2007–; UCLA, 2012–13; Lord Norman Foster Vis. Prof. of Architecture, Yale Univ., 2014–15. Hon. RDI 2015. *Address:* Niall McLaughlin Architects, 3rd Floor, Bedford House, 125–133 Camden High Street, NW1 7JR.

**MacLAURIN,** family name of **Baron MacLaurin of Knebworth**.

**MacLAURIN OF KNEBWORTH,** Baron *cr* 1996 (Life Peer), of Knebworth in the county of Hertfordshire; **Ian Charter MacLaurin,** Kt 1989; DL; Chairman, Chartwell Group, 2004–10; *b* Blackheath, 30 March 1937; *s* of Arthur George and Evelina Florence MacLaurin; *m* 1st, 1961, Ann Margaret (*née* Collar) (*d* 1999); one *s* two *d*; 2nd, 2002, Paula Elizabeth Brooke (*née* Morris). *Educ:* Malvern Coll., Worcs. Served in RAF, 1956–58. Joined Tesco, 1959; Dir, 1970; Man Dir, 1973–85; Dep. Chm., 1983–85; Chm., 1985–97. Vodafone (then Vodafone AirTouch, subseq. reverted to Vodafone): non-exec. Dir, 1997–2006; Chm., 1998–99, 2000–06; Dep. Chm., 1999–2000; Chm., Vodafone Gp Foundn, 2006–09; non-executive Director: Enterprise Oil, 1984–90; Guinness PLC, 1986–95; National Westminster Bank plc, 1990–97; Gleneagles Hotels plc, 1992–97; Whitbread plc, 1997–2001 (Dep. Chm., 1999–2001); Evolution Gp plc, 2004–11; Heineken NV, 2006–11. Chm., TCCB, then ECB, 1996–2002. Chm., Food Policy Gp, Retail Consortium, 1980–84; Pres., Inst. of Grocery Distribution, 1989–92. Mem., H of L, 1996–2017. Trustee, Royal Opera House Trust, 1992. Governor and Mem. Council, Malvern Coll. (Chm. Council, 2003–15); Chancellor, Univ. of Hertfordshire, 1996–2005. FRSA 1986; FIMMM (FIM 1987); Hon. FCGI 1992. Liveryman, Carmen's Co., 1982–.

DL Herts, 1992, Wilts, 2007. Hon. Fellow, Univ. of Wales, Cardiff, 1996. DUniv: Stirling, 1987; Bradford, 2001; Hon. LLD Hertfordshire, 1995. *Publications:* Tiger by the Tail (memoirs), 1999. *Recreations:* golf, cricket. *Clubs:* MCC (Mem. Cttee, 1986–96; Pres., 2017–18), Lord's Taverners, XL, Band of Brothers; Royal & Ancient Golf (St Andrews).

**MACLAY,** family name of **Baron Maclay**.

**MACLAY,** 3rd Baron *cr* 1922, of Glasgow; **Joseph Paton Maclay;** Bt 1914; Group Marketing Executive, Acomarit Group, 1993–99; *b* 11 April 1942; *s* of 2nd Baron Maclay, KBE, and Nancy Margaret, *d* of R. C. Greig, Hall of Caldwell, Uplawmoor, Renfrewshire; *S* father, 1969; *m* 1976, Elizabeth Anne, *o d* of G. M. Buchanan, Delamere, Pokataroo, NSW; two *s* one *d*. *Educ:* Winchester; Sorbonne Univ. Managing Director: Denholm Maclay Co. Ltd, 1970–83; Denholm Maclay (Offshore) Ltd, 1975–83; Triport Ferries (Management) Ltd, 1975–83; Dep. Man. Dir, Denholm Ship Management Ltd, 1982–83; Man. Dir, Milton Timber Services Ltd, 1984–90; Dir, Denholm Ship Management (Holdings) Ltd, 1991–93. Director: Milton Shipping Co. Ltd, 1970–83; Marine Shipping Mutual Insce Co., 1982–83; Altnamara Shipping PLC, 1994–2002; Pres., Hanover Shipping Inc., 1982–83. Director: British Steamship Short Trades Assoc., 1978–83; N of England Protection and Indemnity Assoc., 1976–83. A Comr of Northern Lighthouses, 1996–2003 (Vice Chm., 2001–01, Chm., 2001–03, Bd). Chm., Scottish Br., British Sailors Soc., 1979–81; Vice-Chm., Glasgow Shipowners & Shipbrokers Benevolent Assoc., 1982–83 and 1996–97 (Pres., 1998–99); Chm., Scottish Nautical Welfare Soc., 2002–04. Chm., Scottish Maritime Mus., 1998–2005. Trustee: Cattanach Charitable Trust, 1991– (Chm., 2009–11); Western Isles Fisheries Trust, 2004–06; Western Isles Salmon Fishing Bd, 2004–06; Younger Benmore Trust, 2018–. DL Renfrewshire, 1986–2008. *Heir: s* Hon. Joseph Paton Maclay [*b* 6 March 1977; *m* 2008, Kathryn Meyricka Bruton Good]. *Address:* Milton House, Kilmacolm, Renfrewshire PA13 4RP.

**McLAY, Hon. Sir James Kenneth, (Sir Jim),** KNZM 2015 (CNZM 2003); QSO 1987; Consul General of New Zealand in Honolulu, 2016–17; Managing Director and Principal, J. K. McLay Ltd (international business consultants), since 1987; Executive Chair, Macquarie New Zealand, 1982–2009; New Zealand Ambassador and Permanent Representative to United Nations, New York, 2009–15; *s* of late Robert McLay and Joyce McLay; *m* 1983, Marcy Farden. *Educ:* St Helier's Sch.; King's Sch.; King's Coll.; Auckland Univ. (LLB 1967); Pennsylvania State Univ. (EMP 1987). Solicitor in practice on own account, 1971; barrister 1974. MP (National Party) for Birkenhead, NZ, 1975–87; Attorney-Gen. and Minister of Justice, 1978–84; Government Spokesperson for Women, 1979–84; Dep. Prime Minister, 1984; Leader, National Party and Leader of the Opposition, 1984–86. Mem., Ministerial Wkg Party on Accident Compensation and Incapacity, 1990–91; NZ Comr, Internat. Whaling Commn, 1993–2002. Chairman: Wholesale Electricity Market Study, 1991–92; Wholesale Electricity Market Develt Gp, 1993–94. Chairman: OMNIPORT Napier Ltd, 1988–2001; Roading Adv. Gp, 1997; Project Manukau Audit Gp, 1998–2009; Pharmacybrands Ltd, 1999–2007; Just Water International Ltd, 2004–; Goodman (NZ) Ltd, 2005–; Metlifecare Ltd, 2006–; Director: Evergreen Forests Ltd, 1995–2002; Motor Sport New Zealand Ltd, 1996–99; Mem. Adv. Bd, Westfield NZ Ltd, 1998–2002. Founder Chm., 2004, and Patron, 2005–09, NZ Council for Infrastructure Develt. Hon. NZ Chm., Trans-Tasman Business Circle, 2004–08, 2015–. NZ deleg., Australia/NZ Leadership Forum, 2004–08, 2018–; NZ Rep. to Palestinian Authy, 2015–17; Special Advr to Min. of Foreign Affairs, and Special Envoy for Prime Minister, 2015–17. Advr, UK Cons. Party Commn on Bank of England, 1999–2000. *Recreation:* trout fishing. *Address:* PO Box 94, Matakana, Warkworth 0948, New Zealand.

**MacLEAN, Rt Hon. Lord; Ranald Norman Munro MacLean;** PC 2001; a Surveillance Commissioner, 2010–16; a Senator of the College of Justice in Scotland, 1990–2005; *b* 18 Dec. 1938; *s* of late John Alexander MacLean, CBE; *m* 1963, Pamela Ross (marr. diss. 1993); two *s* one *d* (and one *s* decd). *Educ:* Inverness Royal Acad.; Fettes Coll.; Clare Coll., Cambridge Univ. (BA); Edinburgh Univ. (LLB); Yale Univ., USA (LLM). Called to the Scottish Bar, 1964; QC (Scot.) 1977; Advocate Depute, 1972–75, Home Advocate Depute, 1979–82; Standing Jun. Counsel, Health and Safety Exec. (Scotland), 1975–77; Member: Council on Tribunals, 1985–90 (Chm., Scottish Cttee, 1985–90); Scottish Legal Aid Bd, 1986–90; Scottish Judicial Appts Bd, 2002–05. Member: Stewart Cttee on Alternatives to Prosecution, 1977–82; Parole Bd for Scotland, 1998–2000, 2003; Chairman: Cttee on Serious Violent and Sexual Offenders, 1999–2000; Sentencing Commn for Scotland, 2003–05; Billy Wright Inquiry, Banbridge, NI, 2005–10; Vale of Leven Hosp. Inquiry, Glasgow, 2009–14. Mem., Ind. Rev. Commn on Scottish Football, Scottish Football Assoc., 1995–97. Trustee, Nat. Liby of Scotland, 1967–90. Chm. of Council, Cockburn Assoc., 1988–96. Chm. Govs, Fettes Coll., 1996–2006. FSAScot 1994; FRSE 2000. Hon. LLD Aberdeen, 2003. *Publications:* (ed jtly) Gloag and Henderson, Introduction to the Law of Scotland, 7th edn 1968, 8th edn 1980. *Recreation:* trying to enjoy life for as long as I can. *Address:* 67/3 Grange Loan, Edinburgh EH9 2EG. *Club:* New (Edinburgh).

**MACLEAN, Alan John;** QC 2009; *b* Glasgow, 6 Aug. 1969; *s* of Dr John and Jean Maclean; *m* 2001, Sarah Joanne Corkish; two *s*. *Educ:* Lenzie Acad., Glasgow; University Coll., Oxford (BA 1st Cl. PPE); Harvard Univ. (Kennedy Meml Schol.); City Univ. London (CPE with Dist.); Inns of Court Sch. of Law. Called to the Bar, Gray's Inn, 1993; in practice as barrister, 1993–. Mem., Attorney Gen.'s Panel of Counsel, 1999–2009. *Recreations:* theatre, tennis, enjoying the frustrations of devotion to Arsenal FC and Glasgow Tigers. *Address:* Blackstone Chambers, Blackstone House, Temple, EC4Y 9BW. *T:* (020) 7822 7351. *E:* alanmaclean@blackstonechambers.com.

**McLEAN, Alan William David;** QC (Scot.) 2008; *b* London, 27 Dec. 1963; *s* of David Colin Hugh McLean and Deborah McLean (*née* Packe); *m* 1993, Katharine Jane Colwell; one *s* one *d*. *Educ:* Harrow Sch., Middx; Gonville and Caius Coll., Cambridge (BA 1985; MA 1989); Edinburgh Univ. (LLB 1987; DipLP 1988). Solicitor, 1990–92; Advocate, 1993; Stable Dir, Hastie Stable, Faculty of Advocates, 2010–13. Gov., Fettes Coll., 2015–. *Publications:* (contrib.) Court of Session Practice, 2005. *Address:* Advocates' Library, Parliament House, Edinburgh EH1 1RF. *T:* (0131) 226 5071.

**MACLEAN of Dochgarroch, Very Rev. Canon Allan Murray;** historian; Provost of St John's Cathedral, Oban, 1986–99; *b* 22 Oct. 1950; *o s* of late Rev. Donald Maclean of Dochgarroch and Loraine Maclean of Dochgarroch (*née* Calvert); *m* 1990, Anne (*née* Cavin), *widow* of David Lindsay; two *s* one *d*. *Educ:* Dragon School, Oxford; Trinity College, Glenalmond; Univ. of Edinburgh (MA 1st cl. Hons Scottish History); Cuddesdon Coll. and Pusey House, Oxford. Ordained deacon 1976, priest 1977; Chaplain of St Mary's Cathedral, Edinburgh, 1976–81; Rector of Holy Trinity, Dunoon, 1981–86; Exam. Chaplain to Bishop of Argyll and the Isles, 1983–93. Hon. Canon, St John's Cathedral, Oban, 1999–. Pres., Clan Maclean Assoc., 1994–98, 2009–14 (Vice-Pres., 1982–94); Chm., Clan Maclean Heritage Trust, 2001–07; Chm., Clan Chattan Assoc., 2007–10. Editor: Clan Maclean, 1975–85, 2001–04, 2010–; Argyll and the Isles, 1984–93; Edge, 2006–13. *Publications:* Telford's Highland Churches, 1989. *Recreations:* topography, history, genealogy, architecture. *Address:* 5 North Charlotte Street, Edinburgh EH2 4HR. *T:* (0131) 225 8609; Hazelbrae House, Glen Urquhart, Inverness IV63 6TJ. *T:* (01456) 476267. *Clubs:* New, Puffin's (Edinburgh).

**McLEAN, Dame Angela Ruth, (Dame Angela van Oss),** DBE 2018; PhD; FRS 2009; Professor of Mathematical Biology, University of Oxford, since 2004; Senior Research Fellow in Theoretical Life Sciences, All Souls College, Oxford, since 2008; Chief Scientific Advisor, Ministry of Defence, since 2019; *b* Kingston, Jamaica, 31 May 1961; *d* of Andre and Elizabeth McLean; *m* 1986, David van Oss; two *d*. *Educ:* Mary Datchelor Girls' Sch.; Somerville Coll., Oxford (BA Maths 1982); Imperial Coll., London (PhD Biomaths 1986). Royal Soc. Res. Fellow, Zool. Dept, Univ. of Oxford, 1990–98; Hd, Mathematical Biol., Inst. for Animal Health, Compton, 1998–2000; Lectr in Biodiversity, Zool. Dept, Univ. of Oxford and Tutorial Fellow, St Catherine's Coll., Oxford, 2000–08. *Publications:* (jtly) SARS: a case study in emerging infections, 2005; (jtly) Theoretical Ecology, Principals and Applications, 2007; contrib. articles to biol jls on infectious disease dynamics, evolution and immune responses. *Address:* All Souls College, Oxford OX1 4AL. *T:* (01865) 271210, *Fax:* (01865) 310447. *E:* angela.mclean@zoo.ox.ac.uk.

**MACLEAN of Dunconnel, Sir Charles (Edward),** 2nd Bt *cr* 1957, of Dunconnel, co. Argyll; *b* 31 Oct. 1946; *s* of Sir Fitzroy Hew Maclean of Dunconnel, 1st Bt, KT, CBE and Hon. Veronica Fraser, *d* of 16th Lord Lovat, KT, GCVO, KCMG, CB, DSO and *widow* of Lt Alan Phipps, RN; *S* father, 1996; *m* 1986, Deborah, *d* of Lawrence Young; four *d*. *Educ:* Eton; New Coll., Oxford. *Publications:* Island on the Edge of the World: story of St Kilda, 1972; The Wolf Children, 1977; The Watcher, 1983; (with C. S. Sykes) Scottish Country, 1993; Romantic Scotland, 1995; The Silence, 1996; Home Before Dark, 2008. *Heir: b* Alexander James Simon Aeneas Maclean [*b* 9 June 1949; *m* 1st, 1983, Sarah (marr. diss. 1989), *d* of Hugh Janson; 2nd, 1993, Sarah, *d* of Nicolas Thompson; two *s*]. *Address:* Strachur House, Strachur, Cairndow, Argyll PA27 8BX.
See also Maj.-Gen. J. J. J. Phipps.

**MacLEAN, Colin Ross;** Chairman, Partnership Commission on Childcare Reform (Scotland), 2014–15; *b* 22 May 1951; *s* of Maurice MacLean and Freda MacLean; *m* 1974, Ilse Youngman; two *s* one *d*. *Educ:* Univ. of Edinburgh (BSc Pure Maths 1972; DipEd (Sec. Educn) 1973; MSc Microelectronics 1980). Teacher of Maths, Edinburgh, 1973–79; Lothian Region: Asst Advr in Microelectronic Technology, 1980–82; Advr in Educnl Computing, 1982–85; Scottish Office: HM Inspector of Schs, 1985–96; Chief Statistician, 1996–99; Scottish Executive Education Department: HM Depute Sen. Chief Inspector of Schs, 1999–2000; Depute Hd, Schs Gp, 2000–02; Acting Hd of Dept, 2007; Hd, then Dir, Children, Young People and Social Care, Scottish Exec. Educn Dept, later Scottish Govt, 2002–08; Dir, Schs, then Learning, 2008–11, Dir, Financial Strategy, 2011–13, Scottish Govt. Trustee: Barnardo's, 2014–15 (Chair, Scotland Cttee, 2014–15); Barnardo's Staff Pension Scheme, 2018–; Mem. Bd and Trustee, Streetwork UK, 2014–15. Mem. Court, Heriot-Watt Univ., 2014–15 (Mem., Audit and Risk Cttee, 2014–15). Volunteer: Edinburgh Cyrenians, 2013–15; Phone Credit for Refugees, 2018–. *Publications:* Computing in Schools, 1985. *Recreations:* golf, chess, badminton. *E:* crmacl@btinternet.com.

**MACLEAN, Colin William,** OBE 2000; FRCVS; Director General, Meat and Livestock Commission, 1992–99 (Technical Director, 1988–92); Chairman, Royal Berkshire NHS Foundation Trust (formerly Royal Berkshire and Battle Hospitals NHS Trust), 2000–12; *b* 19 June 1938; *s* of late Kenneth Percy Maclean and Elsie Violet (*née* Middleton); *m* 1959, Jacqueline Diana Brindley; two *d*. *Educ:* William Hulme's Grammar Sch., Manchester; Liverpool Univ. Sch. of Vet. Sci. (BVSc; MVSc 1971). MRCVS 1961, FRCVS 1969. Veterinary Surgeon and Partner, veterinary practice, Thornbury, Glos, and Wickham, Hants, 1961–66; Unilever Ltd: Chief Vet. Advr, 1966–72; Manager, Pig Breeding, 1972–74; Man. Dir, Farm Mark Ltd and Masterbreeders Ltd, 1974–76; Area Gen. Manager (S), BOCM Silcock Ltd, 1980–83; Glaxo Group: Dep. Man. Dir, 1983–88; Product Devolt Dir, Glaxo Animal Health Ltd, 1983–88. Non-exec. Dir, Solutions for Public Health, 2009–. Special Trustee, Moorfields Eye Hosp., 2012–15; Trustee, Moorfields Eye Charity, 2016–; Chm., My Cancer My Choices, 2014–; Mem. Council, Assoc. of NHS Charities, 2013– (Chm., 2017–). *Publications:* contrib. to Veterinary Record (William Hunting Silver Medal, BVA, 1965, 1967), Res. Vet. Sci., Jl Comparative Pathology. *Recreations:* squash, Rugby, theatre, travel, private pilot's licence. *Address:* Crackwillow, Cock Lane, Bradfield, Reading RG7 6HW. *Club:* Farmers.

**McLEAN, Hector John Finlayson,** CBE 1995; Secretary, Crown Appointments Commission, and Archbishops' Appointments Secretary, 1987–95; a Civil Service Commissioner, 1996–2001; *b* 10 Feb. 1934; *s* of late Dr Murdoch McLean, MB ChB and Dr Edith Muriel Finlayson McLean (*née* McGill), MB ChB, DPH, DOMS; *m* 1959, Caroline Elizabeth Lithgow; one *s* two *d*. *Educ:* Dulwich Coll.; Pembroke Coll., Cambridge (BA Hons 1958; MA 1997); Harvard Business Sch., Switzerland (SMP6 1976). Chartered FCIPD (FIPM 1965). 2nd Lieut, KOSB, 1954–55. Imperial Chemical Industries, 1958–87: Central Staff Dept, 1958; various personnel and admin. posts in Dyestuffs and Organics Divs, 1959–72; Personnel Manager, Organics Div., 1972–74; Polyurethanes Business Area Manager, 1974–75; Dir, Agricl Div., 1975–86. Non-exec. Chairman: People & Potential Ltd, 1987–97; Positive People Develt (formerly Teesside Positive People), 1987–94. Mem. Exec. Cttee, N of England Develt Council, 1978–83; Teesside Industrial Mission: Mem., Management Cttee, 1978–85; Chm., 1982–85; Dir, Cleveland Enterprise Agency, 1982–87. Mem., Northern Regl Council, CBI, 1981–85; Trustee: NE Civic Trust, 1976–88; Northern Heritage Trust, 1984–87; mediationplus (formerly Family Mediation Service (N Wilts)), 2000–10 (Chm., 2004–09; Pres., 2010–16). Mem., Chemical and Allied Products ITB, 1979–82. Chm., Selection Panel, Wilts Police Authy, 1997–2003. Gov. Teesside Polytechnic, 1978–84; Mem. Council, Newcastle Univ., 1985–87. FRSA 1991–2010. Pres., Alleyn Club, 1997–98 (Vice Pres., 1996–97). Hon. DSc Aston, 2004. *Recreations:* family, music (especially choral music), travel, gardening, walking more gently. *Address:* College Farm House, Purton, near Swindon, Wilts SN5 4AE. *T:* (01793) 770525.

**McLEAN, Prof. Iain Sinclair,** DPhil; FBA 2008; FRSE; Professor of Politics, University of Oxford, and Fellow, Nuffield College, Oxford, since 1993; *b* 13 Sept. 1946; *s* of John and Louisa McLean; *m* 1984, Dr Jo Poulton; one *s* one *d*. *Educ:* Royal High Sch., Edinburgh; Christ Church, Oxford (MA, MPhil; DPhil 1972). Res. Fellow in Politics, Nuffield Coll., Oxford, 1969–71; Lectr in Politics, Univ. of Newcastle upon Tyne, 1971–78; Fellow and Praelector in Politics, University Coll., Oxford, 1978–91; Prof. of Politics, Univ. of Warwick, 1991–93. Visiting Professor: Stanford Univ., 1990; ANU, 1996, 2002; Yale Univ., 2001; Internat. Center for Jefferson Studies, Monticello, Va, 2010. Vice-Pres. for Public Policy, British Acad., 2012–16. Member: (Lab) Tyne and Wear MCC, 1973–79; (SDP) Oxford CC, 1982–86. Chm., 2013–14, Vice-Chm., 2014–, Welshpool and Llanfair Light Railway. FRSE 2012. *Publications:* Keir Hardie, 1975; Elections, 1976, 3rd edn 1983; Dealing in Votes, 1982; The Legend of Red Clydeside, 1983, 2nd edn 2000; Public Choice: an introduction, 1987; Democracy and New Technology, 1989; (ed, trans. and introd with F. Hewitt) Condorcet: foundations of social choice and political theory, 1994; (ed, trans. and introd with A. B. Urken) Classics of Social Choice, 1995; (gen. ed and contrib.) Concise Oxford Dictionary of Politics, 1996, 2nd edn 2003; (jtly) A Mathematical Approach to Proportional Representation: Duncan Black on Lewis Carroll, 1996; (ed with D. Butler) Fixing the Boundary: defining and redefining single-member electoral districts, 1996; (ed jtly) The Theory of Committees and Elections by Duncan Black and Committee Decisions with Complementary Valuation by Duncan Black and R. A. Newing, 1998; (with M. Johnes) Aberfan: government and disasters, 2000, rev. edn 2019; Rational Choice and British Politics: an analysis of rhetoric and manipulation from Peel to Blair, 2001; (jtly) International Trade and Political Institutions: instituting trade in the long nineteenth century, 2001; The Fiscal Crisis of the United Kingdom, 2005; Adam Smith, 2006; What's Wrong with the British Constitution?, 2009; (ed jtly) Governing England, 2018; numerous articles in learned jls. *Recreations:* steam railway preservation, walking, choral music. *Address:* Nuffield College, Oxford OX1 1NF.

**MACLEAN, Prof. Ian Walter Fitzroy,** DPhil; FRHistS; FBA 1994; Titular Professor of Renaissance Studies, Oxford University, 1996–2014, now Emeritus; Fellow, All Souls College, Oxford, 2012–15, now Emeritus (Senior Research Fellow, 1996–2012); Hon. Professor, School of History, University of St Andrews, since 2018; *b* 9 Feb. 1945; *s* of James Walter Maclean and Elsie May Maclean (*née* Davis); *m* 1971, Pauline Jennifer Henderson; one *s* two *d*. *Educ:* Christ's Hosp.; Wadham Coll., Oxford (BA 1st Cl. Hons Mod. Lang. 1966; MA, DPhil 1971). FRHistS 1989. Sen. Scholar, Wadham Coll., Oxford, 1967–69; Lectr in French, Univ. of Leeds, 1969–72; Oxford University: CUF Lectr in French, 1972–93; Reader in French, 1994–96; Fellow, 1972–96, Supernumerary Fellow, 1996–, Queen's Coll.; Dir, European Humanities Res. Centre, 1994–99; Lyell Reader in Bibliography, 2009–10. Vis. Fellow, Humanities Res. Centre, Canberra, 1983; Vis. Scholar, Herzog August Bibliothek, Wolfenbüttel, 1986, 1995, 2008; Visiting Professor: Catholic Univ. of Nijmegen, 1993; Collège de France, 2005; Ecole Pratique des Hautes Etudes, Paris, 2007; Dist. Vis. Schol., Centre for Renaissance and Reformation Studies, Victoria Univ., Univ. of Toronto, 1994. MAE 1998. Officier, Ordre des Arts et des Lettres (France), 2005. *Publications:* Woman Triumphant: feminism in French literature, 1977; The Renaissance Notion of Woman, 1980; (ed and contrib.) Montaigne, 1982; (ed and contrib.) The Political Responsibility of Intellectuals, 1990; Meaning and Interpretation in the Renaissance: the case of law, 1992; (trans.) Potocki, The Manuscript Found in Saragossa, 1995; Montaigne philosophe, 1996; Logic, Signs and Nature in the Renaissance: the case of learned medicine, 2001; (ed and contrib.) Res et verba in the Renaissance, 2002; (ed) Cardano, De Libris Propriis, 2005; (ed and contrib.) Heterodoxy in Early Modern Science and Religion, 2006; (ed and contrib.) Transmitting Knowledge: words, images and instruments in Early Modern Europe, 2006; Le monde et les hommes selon les médecins de la Renaissance, 2006; (trans.) Descartes, A Discourse on the Method, 2006; Learning and the Market Place: essays in the history of the early modern book, 2009; Scholarship, Commerce, Religion: the learned book in the age of confessions, 1560–1630, 2012; articles and essays in learned jls, collective vols, etc. *Recreations:* music, fishing, wine. *Address:* All Souls College, Oxford OX1 4AL. *T:* (01865) 279379.

**McLEAN, Irwin;** see McLean, W. H. I.

**MACLEAN, Kate;** Member (Lab) Dundee West, Scottish Parliament, 1999–2007; *b* 16 Feb. 1958; *d* of late Alexander Robertson and Sarah Robertson; *m* 1978 (marr. diss.); one *s* one *d*. *Educ:* Craigie High Sch., Dundee. Mem. (Lab) Dundee City Council, 1988–99 (Leader, 1992–99). Convener, Equal Opportunities Cttee, Scottish Parliament, 1999–2007. Vice-Pres., COSLA, 1996–99. *Address:* c/o Scottish Parliament, Edinburgh EH99 1SP.

**McLEAN, Keith Richard,** FCCA; Chairman: Harrogate Training and Development, 2004–07; Centre for Performance Measurement and Innovation Ltd, 2007–14; *b* 27 Oct. 1947; *s* of Bertie and Elsie McLean; *m* 1973, Patricia Ann Morrell; one *d*. *Educ:* J. Rowntree Sch., York. FCCA 1975; CPFA (IPFA 1989); MHSM 1992. Hospital Management Committees: Clerical Officer, York B, 1964–67; Higher Clerical Officer, Leicester No 4, 1967–68; Internal Auditor, Nottingham No 4, 1968–70; Sen. Accountant, Huddersfield, 1970–74; Dep. Area Treas., Calderdale HA, 1974–79; Dist Finance Officer, Derbys AHA, 1979–82; North Derbyshire Health Authority: Dist Treas., 1982–85; Dist Treas. and Dep. Dist Gen. Manager, 1985–87; Dir of Finance and Corporate Strategist, Leics HA, 1987–89; Yorkshire Regional Health Authority: Regl Dir of Finance, 1990–91; Regl Gen. Manager, 1991–94; Regl Gen. Manager, Trent RHA and Regl Dir, NHS Exec., Trent, 1994–96. Director: Harrogate Mgt Centre Ltd, 1996–2004; Key Health Marketing Ltd, 1998–2004; 22/44 The Shambles Ltd, 2008–12; Vintage York Ltd, 2010–12; Partner: Key Health Consulting, 1998–2005; Birchfield Associates, 2004–08; owner, The Shambles Tavern, York, 2014–. Principal Res. Fellow, Sheffield Univ., 1996–2000; Fellow, Nottingham Univ., 1995. Nat. Chm., Healthcare Financial Mgt Assoc., 1992–93; Mem., Inst. of Healthcare Mgt, 1995. FRSA 1994. *Recreation:* golf.

**MacLEAN, Kenneth Walter;** QC 2002; *b* 9 Feb. 1959; *s* of Walter and Mary MacLean; *m* 1994, Jane Elizabeth; three *c*. *Educ:* Rugby Sch.; Trinity Hall, Cambridge (MA); Harvard Law Sch. (LLM). Called to the Bar, Gray's Inn, 1985. *Recreations:* ski-ing, Rugby, piping. *Address:* One Essex Court, Temple, EC4Y 9AR. *T:* (020) 7583 2000, *Fax:* (020) 7583 0118. *E:* kmaclean@oeclaw.co.uk. *Club:* Harvard (New York).

**MACLEAN, Hon. Sir Lachlan Hector Charles,** 12th Bt *cr* 1631 (NS), of Duart and Morvern; CVO 2000; Major, Scots Guards, retired; 28th Chief of Clan Maclean; *b* 25 Aug. 1942; *s* of Baron Maclean, KT, GCVO, KBE, PC and of Elizabeth, *er d* of late Frank Mann; *S* to baronetcy of father, 1990; *m* 1st, 1966, Mary Helen (*d* 2007), *e d* of late W. G. Gordon; two *s* two *d* (and one *d* decd); 2nd, 2010, Rosemary, *widow* of Lt-Col Richard Mayfield, DSO, LVO. *Educ:* Eton. *Heir: s* Malcolm Lachlan Charles Maclean [*b* 20 Oct. 1972; *m* 1998, Anna, *e d* of Giles Sturdy; three *s*]. *Address:* Duart Castle, Isle of Mull, Argyll PA64 6AP.

**MACLEAN, Mavis,** CBE 2002; Founding Director, Oxford Centre for Family Law and Policy, Department of Social Policy and Intervention (formerly Social Policy and Social Work), University of Oxford, since 2001; Senior Research Fellow of St Hilda's College, Oxford, since 2005; *b* 31 Dec. 1943; *m* 1967, Robert Maclean; two *d*. *Educ:* St Hilda's Coll., Oxford (BA (Hist.) 1965); LSE (MSc (Econs) 1967); Univ. of N London (LLB 1990). Res. Fellow, Centre for Socio-Legal Studies, Univ. of Oxford, 1974–2001. Academic Advr to LCD, later DCA, then MoJ, 1997–; Panel Mem., Bristol Royal Infirmary Inquiry, 1998–2001. Hon. Bencher, Middle Temple, 2014. FAcSS (AcSS 2012). *Publications:* (with J. Eekelaar) The Parental Obligation, 1997; (ed jtly) Cross Currents, 2000; (jtly) Family Lawyers, 2000; Family Law and Family Values, 2005; Parenting after Partnering, 2008; (with J. Eekelaar) Family Law Advocacy, 2009; (with Jacek Kurczewski Hart) Making Family Law, 2011; (with J. Eekelaar) Family Justice, 2013; (ed with J. Eekelaar) Managing Family Law in Diverse Societies, 2013; (with J. Eekelaar and B. Bastard) Delivering Family Justice in the 21st Century, 2015; (with J. Eekelaar) Lawyers and Mediators: the brave new world of services for separating families, 2016; (with J. Eekelaar) After the Act: access to family justice after LASPO, 2019; contribs to Family Law, Internat. Jl Law, Policy and the Family, Law and Soc., Jl of Social Welfare and Family Law. *Recreation:* music. *Address:* Department of Social Policy and Intervention, Oxford Centre for Family Law and Policy, 32 Wellington Square, Oxford OX1 2ER. *E:* mavis.maclean@spi.ox.ac.uk. *Club:* Athenæum.

**McLEAN, Miller Roy;** Group Secretary, 1994–2010, and Group General Counsel, 2003–10, Royal Bank of Scotland Group; *b* Dumbarton, 4 Dec. 1949; *s* of David Peter Miller McLean and Jane Roy McLean (*née* Stenhouse); *m* 1973, Anne Gourlay; one *s* one *d*. *Educ:* Vale of Leven Acad.; Glasgow Univ. (MA); Edinburgh Univ. (LLB with Dist.). MCIBS 1972, FCIBS 1992; NP 1980; FIBI 2007; WS 2009. Royal Bank of Scotland: grad.

trainee, 1970; Sec., 1983–88; Gp Sec., 1988–91; Dir, Legal and Regulatory Affairs, 1991–2000; Gp Dir, Legal and Regulatory Affairs, 2000–03. Trustee, 2000–16, Chm., 2003–16, Royal Bank of Scotland Gp Pension Fund; Trustee, 2006–, Chm., 2007–, Direct Line Gp (formerly Royal Bank of Scotland Insurance) Pension Fund. Director: Banco Santander Portugal SA, 1991–2003 (Vice Chm., 1993–2003); Adam & Co. Gp plc, 1998–2017 (Chm., 2010–17); Newton Mgt Ltd, 1998; Ulster Bank Gp, 2001–10. Member, Supervisory Board: ABN AMRO Holdings NV, 2009–11; ABN AMRO Bank NV, 2009–11. Mem., Financial Issues Adv. Gp, Scottish Parlt, 1998–2000; Dir, 1999–2012, Chm., 2001–12, Whitehall and Industry Gp; Dir, Scottish Parlt and Business Exchange, 2001–08. Industry and Parliament Trust: Corporate Fellow, 1989–; Mem. Council, 1990–99 (Chm. Council, 1996–99); Trustee, 2000–10. Chartered Institute of Bankers in Scotland: Mem. Council, 1997–2013; Vice-Pres., 2002–07; Pres., 2007–09. Mem. Council, Soc. of Writers to Signet, Edinburgh, 2009–12. Trustee: National Museums Scotland, 2010–18; Acad. of Med. Royal Colls, 2016–; David Livingstone Trust, 2018– (Mem. Exec. Cttee, 2016–). Gov., Queen Margaret Univ. Coll., 2000–03; Mem. Court, Queen Margaret Univ., 2011–17; Member, Audit and Risk Committee: Abertay Univ., 2018–; Scottish Rural Coll., 2018–. *Recreations:* golf, reading, music, gardening. *Club:* New (Edinburgh).

**MACLEAN, Sir Murdo,** Kt 2000; Director, Anuua Ltd, 2014–16; *b* 21 Oct. 1943; *s* of late Murdo Maclean and of Johanna (*née* Martin). *Educ:* Glasgow. Min. of Labour Employment Exchange, Govan, Glasgow, 1963–64; BoT, 1964–67; Prime Minister's Office, 1967–72; Dept of Industry, 1972–78; Private Sec. to Govt Chief Whip, 12 Downing St, 1978–2000; Chief Exec., Tridos Solutions Ltd, 2000–02; Chm., SiScape Technology Ltd, 2001–02. Advr, CH2M HILL, 2007–12. Dir, Landau Forte Charitable Trust, 2010–16; Vice Patron, Ricci Foundn, 2009–; Trustee, Columba 1400 Foundation, 2003–05. Freeman, City of London, 1994. FRSA 1990. *Clubs:* Garrick; Western (Glasgow).

**MACLEAN of Pennycross, Nicolas Wolfers Lorne,** CMG 2002; 8th Chieftain of Maclean of Pennycross; Chief Executive, MWM (Asia) and MWM (Strategy), since 1999; *b* 3 Jan. 1946; *s* of late Marcel Wolfers and Audrey Wolfers (*née* Maclean of Pennycross); named Nicolas Lorne Maclean Wolfers; *S* kinsman as Maclean of Pennycross, 1993; *m* 1978, Qamar Aziz; two *s. Educ:* Eton; Oriel Coll., Oxford (MA PPE 1967); Univ. of Santander (Cert. Spanish). Grad. Trainee, later Manager, Eur. and Japanese Investment Section, J. Henry Schroder Wagg & Co. Ltd, 1967–71; Manager, P. N. Kemp Gee & Co., 1971–72; Samuel Montagu & Co. Ltd: Manager, London Continental Pension Unit Trust, 1972–74; Asst Dir, Project and Export Finance, 1974–82; Asst Dir, Public Finance Dept, 1982–85; Gp Advr, Midland Bank Gp, 1985–93; Sen. Advr, China, Robert Fleming PLC, 1994–97; Gp Advr, Prudential Corp. PLC and Exec. Dir, Prudential Corp. Asia Ltd, 1997–99. Initiated Wolfers Prog. with Japan (subseq. Japan Exchange and Teaching Prog.), 1976. Chairman: Japan Festival Educn Trust, 2002–03 (Dep. Chm., 1992–2002); Council, Project Trust, 2012–; Co-Chm., Japan400, 2012–. Member: RIIA, 1967–; IISS, 2002– (Sen. Fellow, 2000–07); Bd, Canada-UK Council (formerly Canada-UK Colloquia), 2007–. Fellow Emeritus, British Assoc. of Japanese Studies, 2003. *Publications:* (all jointly): Trading with China: a practical guide, 1979; Journey into Japan 1600–1868, 1981; The Eurobond and Eurocurrency Markets, 1984; Mongolia Today, 1988. *Recreations:* history, etymology, performing and visual arts, rowing, broadcasting, international affairs, Scotland, grandparenthood. *Heir:* s Mark Maclean, yr of Pennycross, *b* 19 July 1982. *Address:* 30 Malwood Road, SW12 8EN. *T:* (020) 8675 6725, *Fax:* (020) 8675 6886. *E:* nmatmwm@hotmail.com. *Club:* Beefsteak.

**MACLEAN, Prof. Norman;** JP; PhD; FRSB, FLS; Professor of Genetics, University of Southampton, 1992–2004, now Emeritus (Head of Department of Biology, 1993–97); *b* 23 Sept. 1932; *s* of late Alexander Maclean and Christine Walker; *m* 1962, Dr Jane Kay Smith; one *s* one *d. Educ:* George Heriot's Sch., Edinburgh; Edinburgh Sch. of Agriculture; Edinburgh Univ. (SDA, BSc 1st cl. Hons, PhD 1962). FRSB (FIBiol 1990); FLS 1992. Asst Lectr in Zoology, Edinburgh Univ., 1961–64; Sir Henry Wellcome Travelling Fellow, 1964–65; Res. Associate, Rockefeller Inst., NY, 1964; Lectr in Biology, Sen. Lectr and Reader, Southampton Univ., 1965–92. Molecular Scis Ed., Jl Fish Biol., 2006–. Mem., Scientific Adv. Cttee, Aquagene Inc., Fla, 1999–. Advr, Eur. Food Safety Authy, 2008–. Hon. Scientific Advr, Marwell Preservation Trust (Trustee, 1995–2004). Dir, Test and Itchen Assoc. Ltd, 2006–. Edinburgh University: MacGillivray Prize in Zoology, 1956; Moira Lindsay Stuart Prize in Zoology, 1957; Gunning Victoria Jubilee Prize, 1960. JP Southampton, 1976. *Publications:* Control of Gene Expression, 1976; The Differentiation of Cells, 1977; Haemoglobin, 1978; Trout and Grayling: an angler's natural history, 1980; (jtly) DNA, Chromatin and Chromosomes, 1981; (ed jtly) Eukaryotic Genes: structure, activity and regulation, 1983; (ed) Oxford Surveys on Eukaryotic Genes, vols 1–7, 1984–90; (jtly) Cell Commitment and Differentiation, 1987; Macmillan Dictionary of Genetic and Cell Biology, 1987; Genes and Gene Regulation, 1989, 3rd edn 1992; Animals with Novel Genes, 1994; Silent Summer: the state of wildlife in Britain and Ireland, 2010; A Less Green and Pleasant Land: our threatened wildlife, 2015; (ed jtly) Austral Ark: the state of wildlife in Australia and New Zealand, 2015; articles in learned jls. *Recreations:* gardening, fly fishing, tennis, reading. *Address:* 10 Russell Place, Southampton SO17 1NU. *T:* (023) 8055 7649. *E:* nm4@soton.ac.uk.

**McLEAN, Peter Standley,** CMG 1985; OBE 1965; Head of East Asia Department, Overseas Development Administration, 1985–87; *b* 18 Jan. 1927; *s* of late William and Alice McLean; *m* 1954, Margaret Ann Minns (*d* 2002); two *s* two *d. Educ:* King Edward's Sch., Birmingham; Wadham Coll., Oxford (MA). Served Army, 1944–48; Lieut, 15/19th King's Royal Hussars. Colonial Service, Uganda, 1951–65, retired from HMOCS as Permanent Sec., Min. of Planning and Economic Develt; Ministry of Overseas Development: Principal, 1965; Private Sec. to Minister for Overseas Develt, 1973; Head of Eastern and Southern Africa Dept, 1975; Head of Bilateral Aid and Rural Develt Dept, 1979; Minister and UK Perm. Rep. to FAO, Rome, 1980. Chm., Africa Grants Cttee, Comic Relief, 1989–92. Chm., Internat. Health Solutions Trust, 1997–2019. Vice-Chm., Overseas Service Pensioners Benevolent Soc., 2001–14. *Recreations:* watching sport, DIY, painting. *Address:* 1 Claverton, Woodfield Lane, Ashtead, Surrey KT21 2BJ. *T:* (01372) 278146.

**McLEAN, Rachel;** Director General and Chief Financial Officer, Ministry of Housing, Communities and Local Government, since 2018; *b* Coventry, 2 June 1967; *m* 2015, Brian McLean; one *d. Educ:* Durham Univ. (BA Hons); Sheffield Hallam Univ. (MSc). FCMA; CPFA. Ford Motor Co., 1987–91; British Rail, 1992–97; AEA Technology plc, 1997–2007; Hd of Finance, then Dir of Finance, Rail and Underground, Transport for London, 2007–15; Finance Dir, HMRC Customer Services, 2015–18. *Recreations:* walking Scamp the dog, travel, reading. *E:* rachel.mclean@communities.gov.uk.

**MACLEAN, Rachel Helen;** MP (C) Redditch, since 2017; *b* Madras, 3 Oct. 1965; *d* of David Cooke and Anthea Cooke (now Kaan); *m* 1992, David Maclean; three *s* one *d. Educ:* St Hugh's Coll., Oxford (BA Experimental Psychol.); Aston Univ. (MSc Work and Organisational Psychol. 2002). Internat. Officer, HSBC, 1988–91; Sales Manager, Computer Manuals Ltd, 1991–92; Sales Manager, Wrox Press Ltd, 1994–99; Hd, Sales, 2005–07, Hd, People and Culture, 2005–13, Packt Publishing; Hd, Orgnl Develt, Hollywood Monster Ltd, 2015–16; Co-Founder and Chief Operating Officer, Air, 2016–17. Founder, Skilled and Ready, 2012–17. Mem., Business, Energy and Industrial Strategy Cttee, H of C, 2017–. Contested (C) Birmingham Northfield, 2015. *Recreations:* long dog walks in mountainous, rainy terrain throughout British Isles, Scouting, grassroots political campaigning. *Address:* House of Commons, SW1A 0AA. *T:* (020) 7219 1848. *E:* rachel.maclean.mp@parliament.uk. *Clubs:* Carlton, Oxford and Cambridge.

**MacLEAN, Ranald Norman Munro;** *see* MacLean, Rt Hon. Lord.

**McLEAN, Prof. Sheila Ann Manson,** PhD; FRSE; FRCPE; International Bar Association Professor of Law and Ethics in Medicine, 1990–2013, now Emerita, and Director, Institute of Law and Ethics in Medicine, 1985–2005, Glasgow University; *b* 20 June 1951; *d* of late William Black and of Bethia Black (*née* Manson); *m* 1976, Alan McLean (marr. diss. 1987). *Educ:* Glasgow High Sch. for Girls; Glasgow Univ. (LLB 1972; MLitt 1978; PhD 1987). FRSE 1996; FRCPE 1997. Area Reporter, Children's Panel, 1972–75; Lectr, 1975–85, Sen. Lectr, 1985–90, Sch. of Law, Glasgow Univ. Chm., Scottish Criminal Cases Review Commn, 1999–2002. Chairman: Review of consent provisions of Human Fertilisation and Embryology Act, DoH, 1997–98; Ind. Review Gp on Organ Retention at Post Mortem, 2000–03; Member: UK Xenotransplantation Interim Regulatory Authy, 1997–2002; Wellcome Trust Biomedical Ethics Panel, 2002–06; Internat. Fedn of Obstetrics and Gynaecol. Ethics Cttee, 2003–06; UNESCO Biomed. Ethics Cttee, 2006–09; Crown Office Inspectorate Review of Organ Retention Practices, 2005–06; Vice Chair, Multi-Centre Res. Ethics Cttee for Scotland, 1997–98. Member: Ethics Cttee, BMA, 2000–10; Ethics and Governance Council, UK Biobank, 2004–06; Adv. Cttee, ESRC Genomics Policy and Res. Forum, 2004–06; Expert Panel, Parly Inquiry into End of Life Choices, 2009–11, Expert Panel on Assisted Dying, 2013–15, Royal Soc. of Canada; Expert Gp on Med. Assistance in Dying, Council of Canadian Acads, 2017–18. UK Rep., Intergovtl Bioethics Cttee, UNESCO. Member: UKCC, 1993–98; SHEFC, 1996–98; AHRC Peer Review Coll., 2005. Mem., Broadcasting Council for Scotland, 1991–96. FMedSci 2006. FRSA 1996. Hon. FRCGP 2003. Hon. LLD: Abertay Dundee, 2002; Edinburgh, 2002. *Publications:* (jtly) Medicine, Morals and the Law, 1983; A Patient's Right to Know: information disclosure, the doctor and the law, 1989; (jtly) The Case for Physician Assisted Suicide, 1997; Old Law, New Medicine, 1999; (jtly) Legal and Ethical Aspects of Healthcare, 2003; (jtly) Xenotransplantation: law and ethics, 2005; Modern Dilemmas: choosing children, 2006; (jtly) Disability and Impairment: law and ethics at the beginning and end of life, 2006; Assisted Dying: reflections on the need for law reform, 2007 (Minty Prize, Soc. of Authors, 2008; RSocMed Book Award, 2008); Autonomy, Consent and the Law, 2009; *edited:* Legal Issues in Medicine, 1981; (jtly) Human Rights: from rhetoric to reality, 1986; (jtly) The Legal Relevance of Gender, 1988; Legal Issues in Human Reproduction, 1989; Law Reform and Human Reproduction, 1992; Compensation for Personal Injury: an international perspective, 1993; Law Reform and Medical Injury Litigation, 1995; Law and Ethics in Intensive Care, 1996; Death, Dying and the Law, 1996; Contemporary Issues in Law, Medicine and Ethics, 1996; Medical Law and Ethics, 2002; Genetics and Gene Therapy, 2005; First Do No Harm, 2006; Regulating Pre-Implantation Genetic Diagnosis: a comparative and theoretical analysis, 2013. *Recreations:* playing guitar, singing, reading.

**McLEAN, Dr Thomas Pearson,** CB 1990; FRSE; CPhys, FInstP; Professor of Electrical Engineering and Science, Royal Military College of Science, Shrivenham, 1992–95; *b* Paisley, 21 Aug. 1930; *s* of Norman Stewart McLean and Margaret Pearson McLean (*née* Ferguson); *m* 1957, Grace Campbell Nokes; two *d. Educ:* John Neilson Instn, Paisley; Glasgow Univ. (BSc, PhD); Birmingham Univ. Royal Radar Estabt (becoming Royal Signals and Radar Estabt, 1976), 1955–80: Head of Physics Gp, 1973–77; Dep. Dir, 1977–80; Ministry of Defence: Under Sec., Dir Gen. Air Weapons and Electronic Systems, 1980–83; Dir, RARDE, 1984–86; Dep. Controller, Aircraft, 1987; Dir, Atomic Weapons Estabt, 1987–90. Member: Physics Cttee, SRC, 1968–73; Optoelectronics Cttee, Rank Prize Funds, 1972–81; Council, Inst. of Physics, 1980–84. Hon. Prof. of Physics, Birmingham Univ., 1977–80. Dep. Editor, Jl of Physics C, 1976–77. *Publications:* papers in Physical Rev., Jl of Physics, etc. *Recreations:* music, mathematics, computing.

**McLEAN, Prof. (William Henry) Irwin,** PhD, DSc; FRS 2014; FRSE, FMedSci; Professor of Human Genetics, 2002–19, now Emeritus, Principal Investigator, Division of Biological Chemistry and Drug Discovery, 2015–19, and Scientific Director, Centre for Dermatology and Genetic Medicine, 2012–19, University of Dundee; *b* Ballymoney, Co. Antrim, 9 Jan. 1963; *s* of Henry McLean and Rosetta McLean (*née* McAleese). *Educ:* Queen's University Belfast (BSc Hons Microbiol. 1985; PhD Human Genetics 1988; DSc Human Genetics 1999). Res. Asst, 1985–88, Postdoctoral Res. Asst, 1988–91, Dept of Med. Genetics, QUB; Res. Dir, Ångström Labs, Larne, 1991–92; Postdoctoral Res. Fellow, CRC Cell Structure Res. Gp, Univ. of Dundee, 1992–96; Associate Prof., Dept of Dermatol. and Cutaneous Biol., Jefferson Med. Coll., Philadelphia, 1996–98; University of Dundee: Wellcome Trust Sen. Res. Fellow and Sen. Lectr, 1998–2002; Hd, Human Genetics Res., Human Genetics Unit, Div. of Pathol. and Neurosci., Ninewells Med. Sch., 1998–2008; Hd, Div. of Molecular Medicine, 2008–15. Hon. NHS Clin. Scientist, 2000–06; Hon. Consultant Clinical Scientist in Dermatol., 2006–, in Human Genetics, 2010–, NHS Tayside. FRSE 2005; FMedSci 2009. Chanel-CERIES Dermatol. Award, 2006; Gerson-Unna Dermatol. Award, 2007; Wolfson Merit Award, Royal Soc., 2007; Achievement Award, Amer. Skin Assoc., 2009; Buchanan Medal, Royal Soc., 2015. *Publications:* book chapters; contrib. res. articles to learned jls, incl. Nature Genetics; eight patents. *Recreations:* electronic music, photography, hill-walking, fishing, astronomy, geology, cinema, science fiction.

**MACLEAN, Prof. William James,** MBE 2006; RSA 1991; RSW 1997; Professor of Fine Art, 1995–2001, now Emeritus Professor of Visual Art, and Research Professor, Visual Research Centre, since 2001, University of Dundee; *b* 12 Oct. 1941; *s* of Capt. John Maclean and Mary Isabella (*née* Reid); *m* 1968, Marian Leven, RSA; two *s* one *d. Educ:* Inverness Royal Acad.; HMS Conway MN Cadet Trng Sch., N Wales; Gray's Sch. of Art, Aberdeen (DA 1966; Post-Grad. Dip. 1967). Midshipman, Blue Funnel Line, 1957–59; school teacher, 1971–81; Lectr in Drawing and Painting, Dundee Coll. of Art, 1981–94. Solo exhibns in GB and abroad; *work in Collections of:* Arts Council of GB; British Mus.; Nat. Art Collection; Fitzwilliam Mus. and Art Gall., Cambridge; Yale Centre for British Art; Scottish Nat. Gall. of Modern Art, etc. FRSE, 2010. Hon. Fellow, UHI, 2008. Hon. DLitt: St Andrews, 2000; Aberdeen, 2009. *Publications:* Will Maclean: sculptures and box constructions, 1987; Will Maclean: different meridians, 2009; (jtly) Catechism of the Laws of Storms, 2015; *relevant publications:* Symbols of Survival: the art of Will Maclean, by Prof. Duncan Macmillan, 1992; Will Maclean Collected Works 1970–2010, 2011. *Recreations:* reading, walking.

**MacLEARY, Alistair Ronald;** surveyor, retired; Hon. Professor, Heriot-Watt University, 2004–10; *b* 12 Jan. 1940; *s* of Donald Herbert MacLeary and Jean Spiers (*née* Leslie); *m* 1967, Mary-Claire Cecilia (*née* Leonard); one *s* one *d. Educ:* Inverness Royal Acad.; Coll. of Estate Management, London; Edinburgh Coll. of Art, Heriot-Watt Univ.; Strathclyde Univ. MSc, DipTP; FRICS, FRTPI. Gerald Eve & Co., 1963–65; Murrayfield Real Estate Co., 1965–67; Dept of Environment (on secondment), 1971–73; Wright, Partners, 1967–76; MacRobert Prof. of Land Economy, 1976–89, Dean, Faculty of Law, 1982–85, Aberdeen

Univ. Univ. of Auckland Foundn Visitor and Fletcher Challenge Vis. Fellow, 1985; Memorialist, Macaulay Inst. for Soil Science, 1986–87. Mem., Cttee of Inquiry into Acquisition and Occupancy of Agricl Land, 1977–79; Chm., Watt Cttee, Energy Working Gp on Land Resources, 1977–79; Mem., Exec. Cttee, Commonwealth Assoc. of Surveying and Land Economy, 1980–85 (Chm., Bd of Surveying Educn, 1981–90); Member: Home Grown Timber Adv. Cttee, Forestry Commn, 1981–87; NERC, 1988–91 (Chm., Terrestrial and Freshwater Sci. Cttee, 1990–91); Lands Tribunal for Scotland, 1989–2005; Administrative Justice & Tribunals Council (formerly Council on Tribunals), 2005–09 (Chm., Scottish Cttee, 2005–09). Mem., Gen. Council, RICS, 1983–87 (Pres., Planning and Develt Divl Council, 1984–85). Mem., MacTaggart Chair Adv. Bd, Glasgow Univ., 1992–2000. FRSA. Hon. Fellow, Commonwealth Assoc. of Surveying and Land Economy, 1992. Founder and Editor, Land Development Studies, subseq. Jl of Property Research, 1983–90. *Publications:* (ed with N. Nanthakumeran) Property Investment Theory, 1988; National Taxation for Property Management and Valuation, 1990. *Recreations:* hill walking, field sports, golf. *Address:* 20 Victoria Crescent Road, Glasgow G12 9DD. *T:* (0141) 339 2738. *Club:* Western Baths (Glasgow).

*See also* D. W. Bentham-MacLeary.

**MacLEARY, Donald Whyte;** *see* Bentham-MacLeary, D. W.

**McLEAY, Hon. Leo Boyce;** *b* 4 Oct. 1945; *s* of Ron and Joan McLeay; *m* 1969, Janice Delaney; three *s*. *Educ:* De La Salle Sch., Marrickville; North Sydney Technical Coll. Telephone technician, 1962–76; Asst Gen. Sec., ALP (NSW), 1976–79. MP (Lab) Grayndler, 1979–93, Watson, 1993–2004, NSW; Dep. Speaker, 1986–89, Speaker, 1989–93, House of Representatives; Chief Govt Whip, 1993–96; Chief Opposition Whip and Dep. Manager, Opposition business, 1996–2001. Dir, Enhance Gp, 2005–09. Dir, Mary MacKillop Foundn, 2006–11; Chm., Catholic Cemeteries Bd, 2011–17; Trustee, Sydney Harbour Fedn Trust, 2011–16. *Recreations:* fishing, reading, boating. *Address:* 702/185 Macquarie Street, Sydney, NSW 2000, Australia. *Club:* Canterbury Rugby League (NSW).

**MacLEHOSE, Christopher Colin,** CBE 2011; Publisher, MacLehose Press, since 2006; *b* Edinburgh, 12 July 1940; *s* of Alexander MacLehose and Elizabeth Hope MacLehose (*née* Bushell); *m* 1985, Koukla Dorange; two *s*. *Educ:* Shrewsbury Sch.; Worcester Coll., Oxford (MA). Literary Ed., The Scotsman, 1964–67; Editor, Cresset Press, Barrie & Rockliff, Cresset Press, then Barrie & Jenkins, 1967–72; Editl Dir, Chatto & Windus, 1973–79; Ed. and Ed.-in-Chief, William Collins, 1979–83; Publisher, Harvill Press, 1983–2004. *Recreations:* dogs, roses. *Address:* 3 Westbourne Road, N7 8AR; Santa Elena, 3 chemin de la Tour des Sarrazins, 83820 Le Rayol-Canadel, France.

**McLEISH, Rt Hon. Henry (Baird);** PC 2000; Member (Lab) Fife Central, Scottish Parliament, 1999–2003; *b* 15 June 1948; *s* of Harry McLeish and late Mary McLeish; *m* 1968, Margaret Thomson Drysdale (*d* 1995); one *s* one *d*; *m* 1998, Julie Fulton (marr. diss. 2011); *m* 2012, Caryn Nicolson. *Educ:* Heriot-Watt Univ. (BA Hons planning). Research Officer, Social Work Dept, Edinburgh, 1973–74; Planning Officer, Fife County Council, 1974–75; Planning Officer, Dunfermline DC, 1975–87; part time Lectr/Tutor, Heriot-Watt Univ., 1973–87; part-time employment consultant, 1984–87. Member: Kirkcaldy DC (Chm., Planning Cttee, 1974–77); Fife Regl Council (Chm., Further Educn Cttee, 1978–82; Leader, Council, 1982–87). MP (Lab) Central Fife, 1987–2001. Minister of State, Scottish Office, 1997–99; Scottish Executive: Minister for Enterprise and Lifelong Learning, 1999–2000; First Minister, 2000–01. Commnd by SFA to produce Review of Scottish Football, 2009 (report publd 2010). *Publications:* Scotland First: truth and consequences, 2004; Global Scots: voices from afar, 2005. *Recreations:* reading, malt whisky (history and development of), history, life and works of Robert Burns, Highlands and Islands of Scotland, astronomy, history of great speeches.

**McLEISH, Prof. Thomas Charles Buckland,** PhD; FRS 2011; CPhys, FInstP; FRSC; Professor of Natural Philosophy, University of York, since 2018; *b* Farnborough, Kent, 1 May 1962; *s* of late Ian Buckland McLeish and of Susan Jane McLeish; *m* 1984, Dr Julie Elizabeth King; two *s* two *d*. *Educ:* Sevenoaks Sch., Kent; Emmanuel Coll., Cambridge (BA 1984; MA 1987; PhD 1987). CPhys 2003; FInstP 2003; FRSC 2008. Lectr in Physics, Univ. of Sheffield, 1989–93; Prof. of Polymer Physics, Univ. of Leeds, 1993–2008; Prof. of Physics, 2008–18, Pro-Vice-Chancellor for Res., 2008–14, Durham Univ. Vis. Prof., Univ. of Calif, Santa Barbara, 2002. Chair, Educn Cttee, Royal Soc., 2015–. *Publications:* (ed) Theoretical Challenges in the Dynamics of Complex Fluids, 1997; (jtly) The Dimensions of Colour: Robert Grosseteste's De Colore, 2013; Faith and Wisdom in Science, 2014; Let There Be Science, 2017; The Poetry and Music of Science, 2019; contrib. articles to jls incl. Physics, Nature, Science, Physical Rev. Letters. *Recreations:* music (French horn, singing), walking, sailing, scuba-diving. *Address:* Department of Physics, University of York, Heslington, York YO10 5DD. *E:* tom.mcleish@york.ac.uk.

**McLELLAN, Alasdair Ewan;** photographer; *b* Doncaster, 6 March 1974; *s* of Terence McLellan and Christina McLellan. *Educ:* Edlington Comp. Sch.; Nottingham Trent Univ. (BA Hons Photography). Exhibitions include: The Palace, ICA, 2016; Here We Are, 2017. *Publications:* Ultimate Clothing Company, 2013; Ceremony, 2016; The Palace, 2016.

**MacLELLAN, Maj.-Gen. (Andrew) Patrick (Withy),** CB 1981; CVO 1989; MBE 1964; Resident Governor and Keeper of the Jewel House, HM Tower of London, 1984–89; *b* 29 Nov. 1925; *y s* of late Kenneth MacLellan and Rachel Madeline MacLellan (*née* Withy); *m* 1954, Kathleen Mary Bagnell; one *s* twin *d*. *Educ:* Uppingham. Commnd Coldstream Guards, 1944; served Palestine 1945–48, N Africa 1950–51, Egypt 1952–53, Germany 1955–56; psc 1957; DAA&QMG 4th Guards Brigade Group, 1958–59; Mil. Asst to Chief of Defence Staff, 1961–64; Instructor, Staff Coll., Camberley, 1964–66; GSO1 (Plans) Far East Comd, 1966–67; CO 1st Bn Coldstream Guards, 1968–70; Col GS Near East Land Forces, 1970–71; Comdr 8th Inf. Brigade, 1971–72; RCDS 1973; Dep. Comdr and COS, London District, 1974–77; Pres., Regular Commns Bd, 1978–80. Vice-Patron (formerly Vice-Pres.), Officers' Assoc., 1993–. Mem. Cttee, Royal Humane Soc., 1980–2010; Vice-Pres., First Aid Nursing Yeomanry (The Princess Royal's Volunteer Corps), 2004– (Mem., 1979–2003, Chm., 1997–2003, Adv. Council). FCMI (FBIM 1970). Mem. (Walbrook Ward), Court of Common Council, City of London, 1989–2000 (Chm., Police Cttee, 1995–97). Freeman: City of London, 1984; Co. of Watermen and Lightermen; Liveryman, Fletchers' Co., 1986– (Master, 1997–98). Chevalier de la Légion d'Honneur, 1960; Order of the Sacred Treasure (Japan), 1998. *Address:* c/o Bank of Scotland, 33 Old Broad Street, EC2N 1NZ. *Clubs:* White's, Pratt's.

**McLELLAN, Very Rev. Andrew Rankin Cowie,** CBE 2009; HM Chief Inspector of Prisons for Scotland, 2002–09; Moderator of the General Assembly of the Church of Scotland, 2000; *b* 16 June 1944; *s* of Andrew Barclay McLellan and Catherine Hilda McLellan (*née* Cowie); *m* 1975, Irene Lamont Meek; twin *s*. *Educ:* Kilmarnock Acad.; Madras Coll., St Andrews; St Andrews Univ. (MA 1965); Glasgow Univ. (BD 1968); Union Theol Seminary, NY (STM 1969; Unitas Award, 2008). Asst Minister, St George's West, Edinburgh, 1969–71; Minister: Cartsburn Augustine, Greenock, 1971–80; Viewfield, Stirling, 1980–86; Parish Church of St Andrew and St George, Edinburgh, 1986–2002; Locum Minister, Edinburgh Morningside, 2017–18. Tutor, Glasgow Univ., 1978–82; Chaplain, HM Prison, Stirling, 1982–85. Dir, Scottish Television, 2004–07. Chairman: George St Assoc. of Edinburgh, 1990–93; Scottish Religious Adv. Cttee, BBC, 1996–2001; Commn to Investigate Safeguarding in the Catholic Church in Scotland, 2013–15; Steering Gp, Scottish Nat. Prison Visitors' Centre, 2017–. Convener, Church and Nation Cttee, 1992–96, Parish Develt Fund, 2002–06, World Mission Council, 2010–14, Gen. Assembly of the Church of Scotland. Nat. Chaplain, Boys' Bde, 2013–16 (Hon. Vice-Pres.). Warrack Lectr on Preaching, Divinity Faculties of Scotland, 2000. Mem., Inverclyde DC, 1977–80. Hon. DD St Andrews, 2000. *Publications:* Preaching for these People, 1997; Gentle and Passionate, 2001. *Recreations:* sport, travel, books, gardening. *Address:* 4 Liggars Place, Dunfermline, Fife KY12 7XZ. *T:* (01383) 725959. *E:* iamclellan4@gmail.com.

**McLELLAN, Prof. David,** DPhil; Visiting Professor of Political Theory, Goldsmiths (formerly Goldsmiths College), University of London, since 1999; Professor of Political Theory, University of Kent, 1975–99; *b* 10 Feb. 1940; *s* of Robert Douglas McLellan and Olive May Bush; *m* 1967, Annie Brassart; two *d*. *Educ:* Merchant Taylors' Sch.; St John's Coll., Oxford (MA, DPhil). University of Kent: Lectr in Politics, 1966–71; Sen. Lectr in Politics, 1972–73; Reader in Political Theory, 1973–75. Vis. Prof., State Univ. of New York, 1969; Guest Fellow in Politics, Indian Inst. of Advanced Studies, Simla, 1970. Hon. Fellow, Goldsmiths Coll., Univ. of London, 2004. *Publications:* The Young Hegelians and Karl Marx, 1969 (French, German, Italian, Spanish and Japanese edns); Marx before Marxism, 1970, 2nd edn 1972; Karl Marx: The Early Texts, 1971; Marx's Grundrisse, 1971, 2nd edn 1973; The Thought of Karl Marx, 1971 (Portuguese and Italian edns); Karl Marx: His Life and Thought, 1973, 2nd edn 1976 (German, Italian, Japanese, Swedish and Dutch edns); Marx (Fontana Modern Masters), 1975; Engels, 1977; Marxism after Marx, 1979, 4th edn 2007 (rev. Chinese edn 2013); (ed) Marx: the first hundred years, 1983; Karl Marx: the legacy, 1983; Ideology, 1986; Marxism and Religion, 1987; Simone Weil: Utopian pessimist, 1989; Christianity and Politics, 1990; Religion and Public Life, 1992; Unto Caesar: the political relevance of Christianity, 1993; Case Law and Political Theory, 1996; (ed) Political Christianity, 1997; Karl Marx: a biography, 2006; Marxism, Religion and Ideology: themes from David McLellan, 2016. *Recreations:* chess, Raymond Chandler, hill walking. *Address:* c/o Goldsmiths, University of London, Lewisham Way, New Cross, SE14 6NW.

**McLELLAN, John Crawford;** Director, Scottish Newspaper Society, since 2013; *b* Glasgow, 8 Feb. 1962; *s* of John and Margaret McLellan; *m* 1993, Patricia Vasey; two *s* one *d*. *Educ:* High Sch. of Glasgow; Hutchesons' Grammar Sch., Glasgow; Univ. of Stirling (BA 1983); Preston Poly. Sports Ed., NW Evening Mail, 1988–90; Asst Ed., The Journal, 1991–93; Edinburgh Evening News: Dep. Ed., 1993–97; Ed., 1997–2001 and 2004–09; Ed., Scotland on Sunday, 2002–04; Ed.-in-Chief, Scotsman Pubns, and Ed., The Scotsman, 2009–12; Dir, Communications, Scottish Conservatives, 2012–13. Member: Defence, Press and Broadcasting Cttee, 2000–04, 2006–12; Press Complaints Commn, 2009–12; Chm., Editors' Cttee, Scottish Newspaper Soc. Hon. Prof., Univ. of Stirling, 2010–. Mem. (C). Edinburgh CC, 2017–. Trustee, Radio Forth Cash for Kids appeal, 2005–10. *Recreation:* watching Watsonian Rugby and hockey.

**MacLELLAN, Maj.-Gen. Patrick;** *see* MacLellan, A. P. W.

**MACLEMAN, Hugh;** a Judge of the Upper Tribunal, Immigration and Asylum Chamber (formerly a Senior Immigration Judge, Asylum and Immigration Tribunal), since 2009; *b* Elgin, 24 Dec. 1953; *s* of William Patience Macleman and Isabella Margaret Macleman (*née* Macmillan); *m* 1980, Dianne Isobel Duncan; two *d*. *Educ:* Lossiemouth High Sch.; Elgin Acad.; Aberdeen Univ. (MA Hons Hist.); Glasgow Univ. (LLB). Admitted solicitor, 1979; solicitor, Elgin, 1979–82; Procurator Fiscal Depute, Elgin, 1982–86; advocate, 1986; Principal Magistrate and Chm. of Trade Disputes Panel, Solomon Is, 1988–91; Sen. Crown Counsel, Turks and Caicos Is, 1991–92; solicitor, Grantown on Spey, 1992–2002; Immigration Adjudicator, part-time 1999–2002, full-time, 2002–05; Immigration Judge, Asylum and Immigration Tribunal, 2005–09. *Recreations:* golf, scuba diving. *Address:* Upper Tribunal (Immigration and Asylum Chamber), Eagle Building, 215 Bothwell Street, Glasgow G2 7EZ. *Clubs:* Royal Over-Seas League; Grantown-on-Spey Golf.

**MACLENNAN,** family name of **Baron Maclennan of Rogart.**

**MACLENNAN OF ROGART,** Baron *cr* 2001 (Life Peer), of Rogart in Sutherland; **Robert Adam Ross Maclennan;** PC 1997; Barrister-at-Law; *b* 26 June 1936; *e s* of late Sir Hector Maclennan and Isabel Margaret Adam; *m* 1968, Mrs Helen Noyes, *d* of late Judge Ammi Cutter, Cambridge, Mass, and *widow* of Paul H. Noyes; one *s* one *d*, and one step *s*. *Educ:* Glasgow Academy; Balliol Coll., Oxford; Trinity Coll., Cambridge; Columbia Univ., New York City. Called to the Bar, Gray's Inn, 1962. MP Caithness and Sutherland, 1966–97 (Lab, 1966–81, SDP, 1981–88, Lib Dem, 1988–97), (Lib Dem) Caithness, Sutherland and Easter Ross, 1997–2001. Parliamentary Private Secretary: to Secretary of State for Commonwealth Affairs, 1967–69; to Minister without Portfolio, 1969–70; an Opposition Spokesman: on Scottish Affairs, 1970–71; on Defence, 1971–72; Parly Under-Sec. of State, Dept of Prices and Consumer Protection, 1974–79; opposition spokesman on foreign affairs, 1980–81; SDP spokesman on agriculture, fisheries and food, 1981–87; Leader, SDP, 1987–88; Jt Leader, SLD, 1988; Lib Dem spokesman on home affairs and the arts, 1988–94, on constitutional affairs and culture, 1994–2001; on Cabinet Office, Civil Service and Scotland (formerly Scotland and the Civil Service), H of L, 2005–. Member: H of C Estimates Cttee, 1967–69; Select Cttee on Scottish Affairs, 1969–70; Public Accounts Cttee, 1979–99; EU Select Cttee, H of L, 2005–. Pres., Lib Dems, 1994–98. Alternate Mem., Convention on Future of Europe, 2002–03; UK Chm., European Cultural Foundn, 2001–07. Mem., Latey Cttee on Age of Majority, 1968. *Publications:* libretti: The Lie, 1992; Friend of the People, 1999. *Recreations:* theatre, music, visual arts. *Address:* House of Lords, SW1A 0PW.

**MacLENNAN, Dr David Herman,** OC 2001; OOnt 2008; PhD; FRS 1994; FRSC 1985; University Professor, University of Toronto, 1993–2015; *b* 3 July 1937; *s* of Douglas Henry MacLennan and Sigridur MacLennan (*née* Sigurdson); *m* 1965, Linda Carol Vass (*d* 2013); two *s* (one *d* decd). *Educ:* Swan River Collegiate Inst., Canada; Univ. of Manitoba (BSA 1959); Purdue Univ. (MS 1961; PhD 1963). Postdoctoral Fellow, 1963–64, Asst Prof., 1964–68, Inst. for Enzyme Res., Univ. of Wisconsin; Banting and Best Department of Medical Research, University of Toronto: Associate Prof., 1969–74; Prof., 1974–93; Acting Chm., 1978–80; Chm., 1980–90; J. W. Billes Prof. of Med. Res., 1987–2007. Principal Investigator, Canadian Genetic Diseases Network, 1991–2005; Consultant, Merck, Sharp & Dohme, PA, 1992–98. Member: Med. Adv. Bd, Muscular Dystrophy Assoc., Canada, 1976–87; Scientists' Review Panel, MRC Canada, 1988–90; Univ. of Ottawa Heart Inst. Res. Review Panel, 1991–94; Chm., Molecular Biol. and Pathol. Cttee, Heart and Stroke Foundn of Canada, 1995–99; Member: Gairdner Foundn Review Panel, 1999–2001; Gairdner Foundn Med. Adv. Bd, 2001–05. Founding Fellow, Internat. Soc. Heart Res., 2001; For. Associate, NAS, USA, 2001; Hon. Mem., Japanese Biochemical Soc., 2004; For. Hon. Mem., Amer. Acad. Arts and Scis, 2015. Hon. DSc Manitoba, 2001. Awards include: Ayerst Award, Canadian Biochem. Soc., 1974; Nat. Lectr Award, Biophys. Soc., 1990; Gairdner Foundn Internat. Award, 1991; Izaak Walton Killam Meml Prize for Health Scis, Canada Council, 1997; Jonas Salk Award, Ontario March of Dimes, 1998; Royal Soc. Glaxo Wellcome Prize, Medal and Lecture, 2000; Salute to the City Award, Toronto, 2002;

Rick Gallop Award, Heart and Stroke Foundn of Ontario, 2002. Canadian Medical Hall of Fame, 2013. Golden Jubilee Medal, 2002; Diamond Jubilee Medal, 2012. *Publications:* ed and contrib. to numerous learned jls, esp. on study of calcium regulation by muscle membranes. *Recreations:* collecting and restoring Canadian antique furniture, reading fiction and non-fiction, listening to classical music, gardening, ski-ing.

**MacLENNAN, David Ross;** HM Diplomatic Service, retired; Ambassador and Consul General, Qatar, 2002–05; *b* 12 Feb. 1945; *s* of David Ross MacLennan and Agnes McConnell; *m* 1964, Margaret Lytollis; two *d*. *Educ:* West Calder High Sch. FO, 1963; ME Centre for Arab Studies, 1966–69; Third, later Second Sec., Aden, 1969–71; Second, later First Sec., FCO, 1972–75; First Sec., UK Delegn to OECD, Paris, 1975–79; First Sec., Hd of Chancery, Abu Dhabi, 1979–82; Asst Hd, N America Dept, FCO, 1982–84; EEC, Brussels, 1984–85; Counsellor, Kuwait, 1985–88; Dep. High Comr, Nicosia, 1989–90; Consul Gen., Jerusalem, 1990–93; Counsellor, Head of Africa Dept (Equatorial), FCO, and Comr, British Indian Ocean Territory, 1994–96; Ambassador to Lebanese Republic, 1996–2000. *Recreations:* conservation, gardening. *Address:* c/o Foreign and Commonwealth Office, SW1A 2AH.

**MACLENNAN, Prof. Duncan,** CBE 1997; FRSE; FAcSS; Professor of Strategic Urban Finance and Management (part-time), University of St Andrews, since 2014 (Professor of Economic Geography and Director, Centre for Housing Research, 2009–14); *b* 12 March 1949; *s* of James Dempster Maclennan and Mary Mackechnie (*née* Campbell); *m* 2005, Sharon Chisholm; one *s* one *d* by a previous marriage. *Educ:* Allan Glen's Sch., Glasgow; Univ. of Glasgow (MA, MPhil). FRSE 1999. Lectr in Pol Econ., Aberdeen Univ., 1976–79; Glasgow University: Lectr in Applied Econs, 1979–81; Sen. Lectr, 1981–84; Titular Prof., 1984–88; Prof. of Urban Studies, 1988–90; Mactaggart Prof. of Land Economics and Finance, 1990–2004; Chief Economist: Dept of Sustainability and Envmt, Govt of Vic, Australia, 2004–05; Dept for Infrastructure and Communities, Canada, 2005–09. Special Advr to First Minister of Scotland, 1999–2003. Director: Centre for Housing Res. and Urban Studies, 1983–96; Cities Programme, ESRC, 1996–99. Susman Prof. of Real Estate Finance, Wharton Bus. Sch., 1988; Regent's Prof., Univ. of Calif at Berkeley, 1996; Prof. of Housing and Urban Econs, RMIT, 2004; Prof. of Public Policy, Univ. of Glasgow, 2014–. Chm., Care and Repair (Scotland), 1987–94; Dir, Joseph Rowntree Res. Programme, 1988–94; Chairman: Joseph Rowntree Area Regeneration Steering Gp, 1996–2000; Cttee on Easing Shortages of Housing, Joseph Rowntree Foundn, 2007. Trustee, David Hume Inst., 1998–2005. FRSA 1993; FAcSS (AcSS 2010). Hon. MRTPI 2001; Hon. MCIH 2001. *Publications:* Regional Policy in Britain, 1979; Housing Economics, 1982; Paying for Britain's Housing, 1990; The Housing Authority of the Future, 1991; Fairer Subsidies, Faster Growth, 1992; Fixed Commitments, Uncertain Incomes, 1997; Changing Places, Engaging People, 2000; Cities, Competition and Economic Success, 2006; contribs to Urban Studies, Housing Studies, Economic Jl, Applied Econs. *Recreations:* walking, cooking, cycling. *Address:* School of Management, University of St Andrews, The Gateway, North Haugh, St Andrews, Fife KY16 9RJ. *E:* dm103@st-andrews.ac.uk.

**MacLENNAN, Graeme Andrew Yule,** CA; Director, Phillips & Drew Fund Management, 1990–93; *b* 24 Aug. 1942; *s* of Finlay and Helen MacLennan; *m* 1st, 1973, Diane Marion Gibbon (*née* Fyfe) (marr. diss. 1989); two *s* two *d*; 2nd, 1989, Diana Rosemary Steven (*née* Urie). *Educ:* Kelvinside Academy, Glasgow. Asst Investment Manager, Leopold Joseph & Sons Ltd, London, 1964–68; Investment Man., Murray Johnstone & Co., Glasgow, 1969–70; Edinburgh Fund Managers: Investment Man., 1970; Dir, 1980, Jt Man. Dir, 1983–88; Investment Dir, Ivory & Sime plc, 1988–90; Hd, Investment Trust Business, LGT Asset Management, 1995–98; non-executive Director: HTR Japanese Smaller Cos Trust, 1993–96; Premium Trust, 1993–2006 (Chm., 2001–06); Noble, then Cornelian, Asset Managers, 1998–2005 (Chm. 2000–05); TriVen VCT, 1999–2003; Financial Services Compensation Scheme, 2000–06; TriVest VCT, 2000–03. *Recreations:* golf, travel.

**MacLENNAN, Prof. Ian Calman Muir,** CBE 2005; PhD; FRCP, FRCPath, FMedSci; FRS 2012; Professor of Immunology, 1979–2004, Professor Emeritus, 2005, and Director, MRC Centre for Immune Regulation, 1999–2004 (Deputy Director, 2005–09), University of Birmingham; *b* Inverness, 30 Dec. 1939; *s* of late Calman MacLennan and Mary Helen MacLennan (*née* Muir, subseq. Roxburgh) and step *s* of William Alexander Roxburgh; *m* 1965, Pamela Bennett; two *s*. *Educ:* Guy's Hosp. Med. Sch., Univ. of London (BSc Anatomy 1962; MB BS 1965; PhD 1970). FRCPath 1985; FRCP 1995. SHO, MRC Rheumatism Res. Unit, Taplow, 1966–69 (ARC Res. Fellow); Lectr, Nuffield Dept of Clin. Medicine, Oxford Univ., 1969–79; Hd, Dept of Immunology, 1979–98, Hd, Div. of Immunity and Infection, 1998–2000, Univ. of Birmingham. Medical Research Council: Co-ordinator, trials in Multiple Myeloma, 1980–98; Chm., Wkg Party on Leukaemia in Adults, 1982–92; Dep. Chm., Cell Biol. and Disorders Bd, 1983–87 (Chm., Grants Cttee A, 1982–84); Mem. Council, and Chm., Molecular and Cellular Medicine Bd, 2000–04. Sec., British Soc. for Immunol., 1973–79. Founder FMedSci, 1998. Mem., Birmingham Med. Res. Expeditionary Soc., 1986–. Hon. Life Mem., Scandinavian Soc. Immunol., 1995. *Publications:* Walking the Alps from Mediterranean to Adriatic, 2014; Mountains of the Provençal Rim 2017; numerous contribs to learned jls, incl. Immunological Reviews, Nature, Annual Rev. of Immunol., Jl Exptl Medicine. *Recreations:* hill walking, observing the natural world, listening to and supporting the City of Birmingham SO. *Address:* College of Medical and Dental Sciences, University of Birmingham, Birmingham B15 2TT.

**McLENNAN, William Patrick,** CBE 1997; AM 1992; Australian Statistician, Australian Bureau of Statistics, 1995–2000; *b* 26 Jan. 1942; *s* of William Freeman McLennan and Linda Maude Shannon; *m* 1st, 1968, Christine Elizabeth Alexander (marr. diss. 2006); one *s* one *d*; 2nd, 2008, Bronwyn Jayne Driscoll. *Educ:* Australian National University (BEcon Hons). Statistician, Aust. Bureau of Statistics, 1960–92; Dep. Aust. Statistician, 1986–92; Dir, CSO, and Head of Govt Statistical Service, UK, 1992–95. Vis. Fellow, Nuffield Coll., Oxford, 1992–95. Centenary Medal, Aust., 2003. *Recreation:* golf. *Address:* 325 Hindmarsh Drive, Rivett, ACT 2611, Australia. *E:* bill.mclennan@mac.com.

**MACLEOD, Alison Margaret;** *see* Cornwell, A. M.

**McLEOD, Prof. David,** FRCS, FRCOphth; Professor of Ophthalmology, 1988–2006, now Emeritus, and Head of Department of Ophthalmology, 1988–98, University of Manchester; Hon. Consultant Ophthalmologist, Manchester Royal Eye Hospital, since 1988; Hon. Civilian Consultant Ophthalmologist, Royal Air Force, since 2003; *b* 16 Jan. 1946; *s* of Norman McLeod and Anne McLeod (*née* Heyworth); *m* 1967, Jeanette Allison Cross; one *s* one *d*. *Educ:* Univ. of Edinburgh (BSc 1st cl. Hons Physiology 1966; MB ChB Hons 1969). FRCS 1974; FRCOphth 1989. House Physician and Surg., Edinburgh Royal Infirmary, 1969–70; Sen. House Officer and Res. Fellow, Princess Alexandra Eye Pavilion, Edinburgh, 1970–72; Moorfields Eye Hospital: RSO, 1972–75; Fellow in Vitreoretinal Surgery and Ultrasound, 1975–78; Consultant Ophthalmic Surg., 1978–88. Civilian Consultant Ophthalmologist, RAF, 1984–2003. Vis. Prof., UMIST, 1996–2006. Vice-Pres., Royal Coll. of Ophthalmologists, 1997–2001. Mem., Club Jules Gonin, Lausanne.

*Publications:* over 180 publications on retinal vascular disease, diabetic retinopathy, vitreoretinal surgery, vitreous pathology. *Recreations:* golf, ballroom dancing. *Address:* Langdale, 370 Chester Road, Woodford, Stockport, Cheshire SK7 1QG. *Clubs:* Brookdale, Probus (Bramhall); Bramall Park Golf.

**McLEOD, Prof. (David) Hugh,** PhD; FBA 2008; Professor of Church History, University of Birmingham, 1994–2010, now Emeritus. *Educ:* Trinity Hall, Cambridge (BA Hist. 1966; PhD 1971). Res. Fellow in Modern Hist., Birmingham Univ., 1970; Lectr in History, Univ. of Warwick, 1972–73; University of Birmingham: Lectr in Church History, 1973–86; Sen. Lectr, 1986–94; Hd, Dept of Theol., 1995–97. Vis. posts at Univs of Amsterdam and Uppsala; Fellow, Swedish Collegium for Advanced Studies, Uppsala, 2010. Vonhoff Lectr, Univ. of Groningen, 2004; Hulsean Lectr, Univ. of Cambridge, 2008. Ed., Christianity and Society in the Modern World series, 1983–. President: Ecclesiastical Hist. Soc., 2002–03; Commn Internat. d'Histoire et d'Etudes du Christianisme, 2005–10. *Publications:* Class and Religion in the late Victorian City, 1974; Religion and the People of Western Europe 1789–1970, 1981, rev. edn as Religion and the People of Western Europe 1789–1989, 1997; Religion and Society in England 1850–1914, 1996; Piety and Poverty: working class religion in Berlin, London and New York 1870–1914, 1996; Secularisation in Western Europe 1848–1914, 2000; (ed with W. Ustorf) The Decline of Christendom, 2003; (ed and contrib.) The Cambridge History of Christianity, vol. 9, 2006; The Religious Crisis of the 1960s, 2007; (ed with D. Hempton) Secularization and Religious Innovation in the North Atlantic World, 2017. *Address:* Department of History, Arts Building, University of Birmingham, Edgbaston, Birmingham B15 2TT. *E:* d.h.mcleod@bham.ac.uk.

**MacLEOD, David Scott G.;** *see* Gordon-MacLeod.

**MacLEOD, Donald Alexander;** HM Diplomatic Service, retired; *b* 23 Jan. 1938; *er s* of late Col Colin S. MacLeod of Glendale, OBE, TD, and of Margaret Drysdale Robertson MacLeod; *m* 1963, Rosemary Lilian Abel (*née* Randle); two *s* two *d*. *Educ:* Edinburgh Academy; Pembroke Coll., Cambridge, 1958–61 (BA). National Service, Queen's Own Cameron Highlanders, 1956–58. HM Foreign Service, 1961; School of Oriental and African Studies, London, 1961–62; British Embassy, Rangoon, 1962–66; Private Sec. to Minister of State, Commonwealth Office, 1966–69; First Secretary, Ottawa, 1969–73; FCO, 1973–78; First Sec./Head of Chancery, Bucharest, 1978–80; Counsellor (Econ. and Commercial), Singapore, 1981–84. Dep. High Comr, Bridgetown, 1984–87; Hd of Protocol Dept, FCO, 1987–89. *Address:* 10a Drummond Place, Edinburgh EH3 6PH.

**MacLEOD, Donald Roderick;** QC (Scot.) 2005; *b* 24 Sept. 1948; *s* of Ian MacCrimmon MacLeod, MB, ChB and Mairi M. E. MacLeod, MA Hons; *m* 1978, Susan Mary Fulton, LLB, solicitor; two *d*. *Educ:* High Sch. of Stirling; Univ. of Glasgow (LLB). Dip. FMS. Solicitor, 1973–77; called to Scottish Bar, 1978; in practice as counsel, 1978–. Temp. Sheriff, 1998–2000. Mem. Bd, Scottish Medico-Legal Soc.; Sec., Faculty of Advocates Criminal Bar Assoc. Contested (Lab) Kinross and W Perthshire, 1979. Founder Mem., Circle of Willis. *Publications:* The Law of Firearms and Related Legislation, 2007; contrib. occasional articles to professional jls. *Recreations:* opera, music, angling (Mem., Cobbinshaw Angling Assoc.), tying classic salmon flies, book-collecting, especially first editions of Neil M. Gunn, studying the natural history of the Highlands and Islands of Scotland and their Gaelic culture, place-names and language, hill-walking, golf, wildfowling, supporting Labour's serious and purposeful politicians, visiting historic buildings and enjoying the landscape of Scotland, savouring malt whisky. *T:* (0131) 260 5607. *E:* donald.macleod@advocates.org.uk.

**McLEOD, Fiona Grace;** Member (SNP) Strathkelvin and Bearsden, Scottish Parliament, 2011–16; *b* 3 Dec. 1957; *d* of John McLeod and Irene McLeod (*née* Robertson); *m* 1979, Dr Andrew David Rankine; one *s*. *Educ:* Glasgow Univ. (MA Hons Medieval and Modern Hist.); Strathclyde Univ. (Postgrad. DipLib). MCLIP. Librarian: Balfron High Sch., 1983–87; Glasgow North Coll. of Nursing, 1987–90; Marie Curie Centre Huntershill Liby, 1995–98; British Homeopathic Library, 2004–08. Partnership Officer, E Dunbartonshire CVS, 2004. MSP (SNP), West of Scotland, 1999–2003. Contested (SNP) Strathkelvin and Bearsden, 2003, Paisley S, 2007, Scottish Parlt. Acting Minister for Children and Young People, Scottish Govt, 2014–15. Mem., Commn for Parly Reform, Scotland, 2016–17. Orgn Convener, 2015–18, Convenor, Candidate Assessment Panel, 2016–17, SNP. Chm., E Dunbartonshire Children's Panel Adv. Cttee, 2004–08; Mem., Adv. Cttee for Scotland, Ofcom, 2004–06. Peer Support Worker, Carers Link E Dunbartonshire, 2009–10. Chair, Scottish Liby and Information Council, 2011–14. Trustee, Scottish Book Trust, 2017–19. *Recreations:* Scottish castles, walking.

**MACLEOD, Sir Hamish;** *see* Macleod, Sir N. W. H.

**McLEOD, Hugh;** *see* McLeod, D. H.

**MACLEOD, Sir Iain,** KCMG 2017; HM Diplomatic Service; Legal Adviser, Foreign and Commonwealth Office, since 2011; *b* 15 March 1962; *s* of Rev. Allan Macleod and Peggy Macleod (*née* Mackay); *m* 1988, Dr Alison M. Murchison; two *s* two *d*. *Educ:* Portree High Sch., Isle of Skye; Glasgow Univ. (LLB Hons 1983; Dip. Prof. Legal Practice 1985); University Coll. London (LLM 1984). Trainee solicitor, Dundas & Wilson CS, Edinburgh, 1985–87; admitted solicitor, Scotland, 1987, England & Wales, 2007; joined HM Diplomatic Service, 1987; Asst Legal Advr, FCO, 1987–91; First Sec. (Legal), UK Repn to EC, Brussels, 1991–95; Asst Legal Advr, FCO, 1995–96; Legal Counsellor: FCO, 1996–97; on loan to Law Officers' Dept, 1997–2000; FCO, 2000–01; UK Mission to UN, NY, 2001–04; FCO, 2004–05; on loan as Dep. Legal Advr, Home Office and NI Office, 2005–09; on loan as Dir, Central Adv. Div., Treasury Solicitors, 2009–11. *Publications:* (jtly) The External Relation of the European Communities, 1995. *Address:* Foreign and Commonwealth Office, King Charles Street, SW1A 2AH.

**MacLEOD, Prof. Iain Alasdair,** PhD; CEng, FICE, FIStructE, FIES; Professor of Structural Engineering, University of Strathclyde, 1981–2004, now Emeritus Professor; *b* 4 May 1939; *s* of Donald and Barbara MacLeod; *m* 1967, Barbara Jean Booth; one *s* one *d*. *Educ:* Lenzie Acad.; Univ. of Glasgow (BSc 1960, PhD 1966). CEng 1968; FIStructE 1982; FICE 1984. Asst Engr, Crouch & Hogg, Glasgow, 1960–62; Asst Lectr in Civil Engrg, Univ. of Glasgow, 1962–66; Structural Engineer: H. A. Simons Internat., Vancouver, Canada, 1966–67; Portland Cement Assoc., Skokie, USA, 1968–69; Lectr in Civil Engrg, Univ. of Glasgow, 1969–73; Prof. and Head of Dept of Civil Engrg, Paisley Coll. of Technol., 1973–81. Vice-Pres., IStructE, 1989–90; Mem., Standing Cttee on Structural Safety, IStructE and ICE, 1990–97; Pres., IES, 2012–14 (Vice Pres. and Sec., 2010–12). FIES 2006. Lewis Kent Award, IStructE, 1998. *Publications:* Analytical Modelling of Structural Systems, 1990; Modern Structural Analysis, 2005; over 100 published papers. *Recreations:* sailing, hill walking. *Address:* c/o Department of Civil Engineering, University of Strathclyde, Glasgow G1 1XJ.

**McLEOD, Brig. Ian,** CMG 1999; OBE 1983; MC 1965; Division for Relations with Armed and Security Forces, International Committee of the Red Cross, since 1999; *b* 19 June 1941; *s* of David Drummond McLeod and Eleanor McLeod (*née* Williams); *m* 1966, Janet Edith Prosser Angus (*d* 2004); one *s* two *d*. *Educ:* Rhondda Co. Grammar Sch.; RMA

Sandhurst; sc 1973; ndc 1991; Open Univ. (BA 1990); Univ. of Buckingham (MA 2012). Commnd Parachute Regt, 1961; service in 3 Para, UK, Gulf and Aden, 1961–67; Jungle Warfare Sch., Malaya, 1967–69; 2 Para, 1969–71; SC, 1971–73; HQ 44 Para Bde (V), 1974–75; 82 AB Div., US Army, 1976–77; Co. Comd, 3 Para, BAOR, 1977–79; GSO2, Defence Ops Analysis Estabt, 1979–81; CO 1 Para, 1981–84; SO1, SC, 1984–86; Col Operational Requirements, MoD, 1986–87; UK Liaison Officer, US Army, 1987–89; Comd, 42 Inf. Bde, 1989–91; Defence Advr, British High Commn, Islamabad, 1992–94; retd 1995; Mem., EC Monitor Mission to former Yugoslavia, 1995–97; Dep. Hd, Regl Office in Brcko of High Rep. for Bosnia, 1997–98; Mem., Kosovo Verification Mission, OSCE, 1998–99. Mem., Pakistan Soc., 2003–. Freeman, City of London, 1992. *Recreations:* travel, military history. *Address:* c/o HSBC, 33 The Borough, Farnham, Surrey GU9 7NJ.

**MACLEOD, Rear Adm. James Norman,** CEng; Defence Services Secretary, and Assistant Chief of Defence Staff (Personnel Capability), since 2019; *b* Mirfield, 17 March 1970; *s* of Norman and Elaine Macleod; *m* 2009, Charlotte Amy Lewis; one *s* one *d. Educ:* RNEC Manadon (BEng Hons); Cranfield Univ. (MSc Systems Engrg); King's Coll. London (MA Defence Studies). CEng, MIET 1998. Joined RN, 1989; Comdr, Weapon Engrg, HMS Illustrious, 2008–09; DACOS, Integrated Change Prog., 2014–15; Hd, Armed Forces Remuneration, 2016–19. FCIPD 2019. *Recreations:* gardening, family, woodwork. *Address:* Ministry of Defence, Main Building, Whitehall, SW1A 2HB. *T:* (020) 7218 6340.

**McLEOD, Sir James (Roderick Charles),** 4th Bt *cr* 1925, of The Fairfields, Cobham, Surrey; Trainer, Blacklion Training and Coaching Consultancy Ltd, since 2016; *b* Haslemere, 26 Sept. 1960; *o s* of Sir Charles Henry McLeod, 3rd Bt and Ann Gillian McLeod (*née* Bowlby); *S* father, 2012, but his name does not appear on the Official Roll of the Baronetage; *m* 1990, Helen M. Cooper; one *s* one *d. Educ:* Eton Coll. Certified Master Coach, Internat. Coaching Council; Certified Exec. Coach, Internat. Coaching Fedn. Man. Dir, Internat. Herald Tribune, 1989–98; Pres., Redwood Publishing International, 1998–2005; Assoc. Publisher, World's Best Hotels, 2005–09; Certified Master Coach, CONCHIUS, Shanghai, 2009–14. *Recreations:* marathon running (64 completed), cricket. *Heir: s* Rory Andrew McLeod, *b* 7 July 1994. *Club:* MCC.

**MACLEOD, Jane Margaret;** Vice Lord-Lieutenant for Argyll and Bute, since 2017; *b* Glasgow, 27 Feb. 1953; *d* of Duncan Macneill and Margaret May Macneill (*née* Mathieson); *m* 1976, Murdoch Macleod (*d* 2017); four *d. Educ:* Jordanhill Coll. Sch.; Strathclyde Univ. (LLB 1973). Admitted solicitor, 1975; Partner, Macarthur Stewart-Orr, 1976–98; sole practitioner, Jane Macleod Solicitors, 1998–. Dir, M & K Macleod Ltd, 2017–. Sec., Mid-Argyll Chamber of Commerce, 1986–. Chair, Developing Young Workforce Argyll, 2017–. Director: Argyll-Bute Family Mediation, 2002–; Argyll-Bute CAB, 2006–. Hon. Sheriff, N Strathclyde, 2009–; DL Argyll and Bute, 2016. *Recreations:* swimming, cycling, hill walking, boats, reading. *Address:* Achnaba House, Lochgilphead PA31 8RY. *T:* (01546) 606666, 07919 214997. *E:* jane@janemacleod.co.uk.

**MACLEOD, Jean Grant;** *see* Scott, Jean G.

**McLEOD, Rev. John;** Minister of Resolis and Urquhart, 1986–93; Chaplain to the Queen in Scotland, 1978–96, an Extra Chaplain, since 1996; *b* 8 April 1926; *s* of Angus McLeod and Catherine McDougall; *m* 1958, Sheila McLeod; three *s* two *d. Educ:* Inverness Royal Academy; Edinburgh Univ. (MA); New Coll., Edinburgh. Farming until 1952; at university, 1952–58; ordained, Inverness, 1958. Missionary in India: Jalna, 1959–68; Poona, 1969–74; involved in rural development with special emphasis on development and conservation of water resource; also responsible for pastoral work in Church of N India, St Mary's, Poona, 1970–74; Church of Scotland Minister, Livingston Ecumenical Team Ministry, 1974–86. *Recreation:* gardening. *Address:* Benview, 19 Balvaird, Muir of Ord, Ross-shire IV6 7RQ. *T:* (01463) 871286.

**MacLEOD, Hon. Sir (John) Maxwell (Norman),** 5th Bt *cr* 1924, of Fuinary, Morven, Co. Argyll; Chief Executive Officer: Edinburgh Energy Consultants, since 2014; Fair Winds for Scotland, 2014–15; *b* 23 Feb. 1952; *s* of Baron MacLeod of Fuinary (Life Peer), MC and Lorna Helen Janet (*d* 1984), *er d* of late Rev. Donald Macleod; *S* to baronetcy of father, 1991. *Educ:* Gordonstoun; Bede Coll., Durham; Lady Spencer Churchill Coll., Oxford. Teacher of the deaf, journalist, cartoonist for The Herald, and property developer. A Founder and Chm., Hebridean Whale and Dolphin Trust, 2010. Mem., Speculative Soc. *Heir: b* Hon. Neil David MacLeod, *b* 25 Dec. 1959. *Address:* Dowies Mill House, Dowies Mill Lane, Cramond, Edinburgh EH4 6DW; Fuinary, Morven, Argyll. *Club:* New (Edinburgh).

**McLEOD, Kirsty, (Mrs Christopher Hudson);** author and journalist; *b* 23 Dec. 1947; *d* of late Alexander McLeod and Elizabeth Davidson McLeod; *m* 1978, Christopher Hudson; one *s. Educ:* St Leonard's Sch., St Andrews; St Anne's Coll., Oxford (MA). Editorial staff, IPC Magazines, 1970–73; Editor, Fontana Books, 1974–76; Columnist, Daily Telegraph, 1991–93. English Heritage: Comr, 1995–2001; Chm., Historic Parks and Gardens Adv. Cttee, 1998–2001 (Mem., 1995–2001). Trustee, Kent Gardens Trust, 2002–03. *Publications:* The Wives of Downing Street, 1976; Drums and Trumpets: the House of Stuart, 1977; The Last Summer: May to September 1914, 1983; A Passion for Friendship: Sibyl Colefax and her circle, 1991; Battle Royal: Edward VIII and George VI, 1999; The Best Gardens in Italy: a traveller's guide, 2011; numerous newspaper articles. *Recreations:* architecture, visiting Italian gardens, armchair mountaineering. *Address:* Domons, Higham Lane, Northiam, E Sussex TN31 6JT. *T:* (01797) 252007.

**MACLEOD, Dr Malcolm David,** FIET, FREng; Chief Scientist, CIT Division, and Dean of Fellows, QinetiQ Ltd, since 2013; *b* Cathcart, 26 Sept. 1953; *s* of Angus and Mary Macleod; two *d. Educ:* Hampton Grammar Sch.; Peterhouse, Cambridge (BA 1974; MA 1978; PhD 1979). FIET 2002; CEng 2004; FREng 2014. Cambridge Consultants: Engr, 1978–82; Gp Leader, 1982–85; Consultant, 1985–88; Fellow, Queens' Coll., Cambridge, 1984–2002; Lectr, 1988–95, Dir of Res., 1995–2002, Engrg Dept, Univ. of Cambridge; Principal Scientist, QinetiQ, 2002–13. Vis. Prof., Univ. of Strathclyde, 2007–. Sen. Mem., IEEE, 2013. FIMA 2014. *Publications:* contrib. jl papers, book chapters and conf. papers. *Recreations:* choral director, singer, organist, accompanist. *Address:* QinetiQ Ltd, St Andrews Road, Malvern, Worcs WR14 3PS. *T:* (01684) 543796. *E:* mmacleod@qinetiq.com.

**McLEOD, Prof. Malcolm Donald,** CBE 2006; FRSE; FSAScot; Professor of African Studies, 1994–2006, Vice-Principal, 1999–2005 and Pro Vice-Principal, 2005–06, Glasgow University; Director, Hunterian Museum and Art Gallery, Glasgow, 1990–99; *b* 19 May 1941; *s* of Donald McLeod and Ellen (*née* Fairclough); *m;* two *s* one *d. Educ:* Birkenhead Sch.; Hertford and Exeter Colls, Oxford (MA, BLitt). FRSE 1995; FSAScot 2012. Lectr, Dept of Sociology, Univ. of Ghana, 1967–69; Asst Curator, Museum of Archaeology and Ethnology, Cambridge, 1969–74; Lectr, Girton Coll., Cambridge, 1969–74; Fellow, Magdalene Coll., Cambridge, 1972–74; Keeper of Ethnography, British Museum, 1974–90. Member: Hist. and Current Affairs Selection Cttee, Nat. Film Archive, 1978–84; Council, Museums Assoc., 1983–86; UK Unesco Cultural Adv. Cttee, 1980–85; Unesco Scotland Cttee, 2008–; Chairman: Scottish Mus Council, 1996–2001; Caledonian Foundn, USA, 2003–08; Trustee: Nat. Mus Scotland (formerly Nat. Mus of Scotland), 2005–13; Borders Sculpture Park, 2013–. Consultant, Manhyia Palace Mus., Kumasi, Ghana, 1994–99; Curator, RSE, 1999–2002; Museum Consultant to Opuku Ware II, King of Asante. Hon. Lecturer: Anthropology Dept, UCL, 1976–81; Archæology Dept, Glasgow Univ., 1991–2006. Lectures: Marett, Exeter Coll., Oxford, 1982; Sydney Jones, Liverpool Univ., 1984; Arthur Batchelor, UEA, 1987; Rivers, Cambridge, 1993. Trustee: Sainsbury Unit, UEA, 1991–2000; Oriental Mus., Univ. of Durham, 1994–2000; Hunterian Collection, London, 1998–; Scottish Mus. of the Year Awards, 1999–2002; Opuku Ware Foundn Award, Ghana, 2005. *Publications:* The Asante, 1980; Treasures of African Art, 1980; (with J. Mack) Ethnic Art, 1984; (with E. Bassani) Jacob Epstein: collector, 1987; An English-Kriolu, Kriolu-English Dictionary, 1990; Collecting for the British Museum, 1994; (with Hector MacLeod) Peter Manuel, Serial Killer, 2009; articles and reviews in learned jls. *Address:* The Schoolhouse, Oxnam, Jedburgh TD8 6NB. *Club:* Athenæum.

**McLEOD, (Margaret) Kirsty;** *see* McLeod, K.

**MacLEOD, Mary;** Senior Client Partner, Board and CEO Services, Korn Ferry, since 2016; *b* London. *Educ:* Glasgow Univ. (MA Hons). Mgt Consultant, Andersen Consulting, later Accenture, 1990–2002; Man. Dir, MCG, 2002–10, appts incl. Chief Operating Officer for Gp Ops, ABN AMRO, 2003–07, Gp Communications Hd of Transition, RBS, 2007–10. Policy Advr to the Queen's Private Office, Buckingham Palace, 1998–99. Contested (C) Ross, Skye and Inverness W, 1997. MP (C) Brentford and Isleworth, 2010–15; contested (C) same seat, 2015, 2017. Parliamentary Private Secretary: to Minister for Policing and Justice, 2010–12; to Sec. of State for Culture, Media and Sport, 2012–14; to Minister for Women and Equalities, 2012–14; to Sec. of State for Northern Ireland, 2014–15. Mem., Home Affairs Select Cttee, 2010; Chm., All-Party Parly Gp for Women in Parlt, 2010–15 (Chair, Inq. for Improving Parlt, 2014–15); Vice Chm., All Party Parly Gp for Microfinance, 2012–15. Prime Minister's Small Business Ambassador for London, 2012–15; Mem., No 10 Policy Bd with resp. for Home and Constitutional Affairs, Justice, Culture, Media and Sport, 2014–15; Grad. Mem., Armed Forces Parly Scheme (RAF), 2010–15. Special Advr to Sec. of State for Scotland, 2015–16. Non-exec. Dir, Lewis PR, 2014–. Member, Advisory Board: Learning for Life, 2010–15; Kupambana Foundn, 2014–16; Mem., Social Integration Commn, 2014–15; Trustee, Career Ready (formerly Career Acads UK) (Mem., Adv. Bd, 2012–19). Pres., Chiswick, RBL, 2010–18. Fellow, Sporting Equals, 2011–14; Community Champion for Brentford FC Community Sports Trust, 2011–15. Trustee: Holland Park Sch. Trust, 2009–16; Industry Parlt Trust, 2012–15; Hounslow Shelter Project, 2014–; UK Parlt Choir, 2018–. Ambassador, London's Women Forum, 2017– (Patron, 2014–16); Ambassador, Villa di Geggiano, Chiswick, 2015–. FRSA 2007. *Address:* Korn Ferry, Ryder Court, 14 Ryder Street, SW1Y 6QB. *T:* (020) 3819 1920. *E:* mary.macleod@kornferry.com.

**MacLEOD, Hon. Sir Maxwell;** *see* MacLeod, Hon. Sir J. M. N.

**MacLEOD, Murdo Angus;** QC (Scot.) 2008; *b* 21 Oct. 1967; *s* of Murdo Alexander MacLeod, DA and Dolina MacLeod (*née* Macdonald); *m* 2010, Laura-Anne van der Westhuizen. *Educ:* Nicolson Inst., Stornoway; Univ. of Aberdeen (LLB Hons 1989; DipLP 1990). Admitted to Faculty of Advocates, 1994; Crown Counsel, 2001–03; Sen. Crown Counsel, 2004–05; Counsel to Billy Wright Inquiry, 2005–10; called to the Bar, Middle Temple, 2011; Sheriff (part-time), 2011–. UK delegate to Criminal Law Cttee, Council of Bars and Law Socs of Europe, 2012–. Mem. Bd, Glasgow Print Studio, 2007–13. *Recreations:* art, golf, music. *Address:* Compass Chambers, Parliament House, Edinburgh EH1 1RF. *T:* (0131) 260 5648. *E:* murdo.macleod@advocates.org.uk; Temple Garden Chambers, 1 Harcourt Buildings, Temple, EC4Y 9DA. *T:* (020) 7583 1315. *Clubs:* Scottish Arts (Edinburgh); Bruntsfield Links Golfing Soc.

**MACLEOD, Sir (Nathaniel William) Hamish,** KBE 1994 (CBE 1992); Financial Secretary, Hong Kong, 1991–95; *b* 6 Jan. 1940; *s* of George Henry Torquil Macleod and Ruth Natalie Wade; *m* 1970, Fionna Mary Campbell; one *s* one *d. Educ:* Univ. of St Andrews (MA Soc. Sci. Hons); Univ. of Bristol (Dip. Soc. Sci. Sociology); Birmingham Coll. of Commerce. FCIS 1995. Commercial trainee, Stewarts & Lloyds, Birmingham, 1958–62; Hong Kong Government: Admin. Officer, 1966; Dir of Trade and Chief Trade Negotiator, 1983–87; Secretary for Trade and Industry, 1987–89; Sec. for the Treasury, 1989–91. Director: Scottish Community (formerly Caledonian) Foundation, 1995–2002; Highland Distilleries, 1995–99; Scottish Oriental Smaller Cos Trust, 1995–2011; Chm., JP Morgan Fleming Asian Investment Trust (formerly Fleming Asian Investment Trust), 1997–2003. *Recreations:* golf, walking. *Address:* 20 York Road, Trinity, Edinburgh EH5 3EH. *T:* (0131) 552 5058. *Clubs:* Bruntsfield Links Golf; Hong Kong, Royal Hong Kong Yacht.

**MacLEOD, Prof. Norman,** PhD; FGS, FLS; Dean, Post-graduate Education and Training, Department of Earth Sciences, 2012–16, Researcher, 2016–19, Natural History Museum, London; Professor, School of Earth Sciences and Engineering, Nanjing University, since 2019; *b* 23 Feb. 1953; *s* of Archibald Alexander MacLeod and Helen Chester MacLeod; *m* 1988, Dr Cecilia McDonald (marr. diss. 2019); one *d. Educ:* Univ. of Missouri, Columbia (BSc Geol. 1976); Southern Methodist Univ., Dallas (MSc Palaeontol. 1980); Univ. of Texas at Dallas (PhD Palaeontol. 1986). FGS 2002; FLS 2003. Sci. teacher (physics, geol., astronomy, ecol.), H. Grady Spruce High Sch., Segoville, Texas, 1976–78; owner, Boreas Technical Photographers, Dallas, 1982–86; Consultant, Atlantic Richfield (ARCO) Oil and Gas, Richardson, Texas, 1984–86; Michigan Soc. Fellow and Vis. Asst Prof., Dept of Geol Scis, Univ. of Michigan, Ann Arbor, 1986–89; Researcher, Dept of Geol and Geophysical Scis, Princeton Univ., 1989–93; Natural History Museum, London, 1993–2019: Scientific Officer, 1993–94; SSO, 1994–96; Stratigraphy and Correlation Prog. Leader, 1995–2001; Researcher, 1996–99; Petroleum Sector Leader, 1997–2001; Associate Keeper of Palaeontol., 2000–01; Actg Keeper of Palaeontol., 2001; Keeper of Palaeontol., 2001–12. Hon. Professor: UCL, 2004–19; Nanjing Inst. of Geol. and Palaeontol., Chinese Acad. of Sci., 2011–; Univ. of Manchester, 2016; Vis. Prof., Univ. of Chicago, 2011. Member: Soc. Systematic Biol., 1981; Centre for Evolution and Ecol., 1998; Systematics Assoc., 2001; Palaeontol Assoc., 2003–09 (Trustee, 2005–09; Vice Pres., 2007–09); Geol Soc. London, 2002. Trustee, Scarborough Mus Trust, 2004–13. *Publications:* The Cretaceous-Tertiary Mass Extinction: biotic and environmental changes, 1996; Morphometrics, Shape and Phylogenetics, 2002; Automated Taxon Identification in Systematics: theory, approaches and applications, 2007; The Great Extinctions: what causes them and how they shape life, 2013; (Ed.-in-Chief) Grzimek's Animal Life Encyclopedia: extinctions (2 vols), 2013; (ed) Issues in Paleobiology, 2014; contrib. numerous peer reviewed technical articles, technical reports and reviews. *Recreations:* music, writing, cooking, gardening, theatre, wine, dining. *Address:* School of Earth Sciences and Engineering, Nanjing University, 163 Xianlin Avenue, Nanjing, Jiangsu 210023, China. *T:* (258) 9680700, *Fax:* (258) 3686016.

**MACLEOD, (Roderick) James (Andrew) R.;** *see* Robertson-Macleod.

**MacLEOD, Roderick John;** *see* Minginish, Hon. Lord.

**MacLEOD, Sian Christina,** OBE 2002; HM Diplomatic Service; Ambassador to Serbia, since 2019; *b* 31 May 1962; *m* Richard Robinson. *Educ:* Royal Acad. of Music (BMus 1983). Joined FCO, 1986; Desk Officer, S African Dept, 1986–87; Third, then Second Sec., Moscow, 1988–92; Dep. Hd of Mission, Vilnius, 1992; Foreign and Commonwealth Office: Hd, Russia Section, Jt Assistance Unit, 1992; Hd of Section, Arms Control and Disarmament Dept, 1993–94; Personnel Mgt Dept, 1995–96; First Sec., The Hague, 1996–2000; Dep. Hd, Counter Terrorism Policy Dept, FCO, 2000–01; on loan to Cabinet Office, 2002–04; Political Counsellor, 2004–05, Minister and Dep. Hd of Mission, 2005–07, Moscow; Hd, Whitehall Liaison Dept, FCO, 2007–08; Ambassador to the Czech Republic, 2009–13; Dir, British Council Triennial Rev., 2013–14; Additional Dir, Eastern Europe and Central Asia, FCO, 2014–15; Ambassador and Hd of UK Delegn to OSCE, Vienna, 2015–19. *Recreations:* music, gardening, cross-country ski-ing. *Address:* c/o Foreign and Commonwealth Office, King Charles Street, SW1A 2AH.

**MacLEOD, Tracey Ann;** Restaurant Critic, The Independent, 1997–2016; Guest Critic, MasterChef, BBC, since 2010; Director, KBJ Management, since 2007; *b* Ipswich, 30 Oct. 1960; *d* of Donald MacLeod and Colleen MacLeod; partner, Harry Ritchie; two *s*. *Educ:* Ipswich High Sch.; Durham Univ. (BA Eng. Lang. and Lit.). Writer, The Stage, 1984–85; researcher, BBC TV, 1985–87; reporter and producer, Network 7, Channel 4, 1987–88; producer and presenter, The Late Show, BBC, 1989–95; Dir, Planet 24 Prodns, 1997–99. *Recreations:* walking in Suffolk, eating in London. *Address:* c/o KBJ Management, 22 Rathbone Street, W1T 1LA. *E:* tracey@kbjmanagement.co.uk.

**MACLEOD CLARK, Prof. Dame Jill,** DBE 2000; PhD; Professor of Nursing, University of Southampton, 1999–2009, now Emeritus Professor in Health Sciences (Dean of Nursing and Health Sciences, 2000–12); *b* 11 June 1944; *d* of late George William Charles Tearle Gibbs and Edith Vera Macleod Gibbs; *m* 1st, 1967, Andrew William Clark (marr. diss. 1983); two *s*; 2nd, 1989, William Arthur Bridge. *Educ:* UCH (RGN 1965); LSE (BSc Hons 1972); KCL (PhD 1982). FRCN 1997. Various clin. posts, London, Birmingham and Bedford, 1965–76; Nursing Officer, DoH, 1976–78; Res. Fellow, 1978–81, Lectr in Nursing, 1981–86, Chelsea Coll., London Univ.; King's College London: Sen. Lectr in Nursing, 1986–90; Prof. of Nursing, 1990–93; Dir, Nightingale Inst., 1993–99; University of Southampton: Hd, Sch. of Nursing and Midwifery, 1999–2009; Dep. Dean, Faculty of Medicine, Health and Life Scis (formerly Faculty of Medicine and Health), 1999–2011. Adjunct Prof., Univ. of Toronto, 2015–; Hon. Prof., Univ. of Western Australia, 2018–. Trustee and Professional Advr, Florence Nightingale Foundn, 2018–. FQNI 2004. Hon. DSc: Brighton, 2004; UEA, 2005; QUB, 2010; Robert Gordon, 2013; City, 2014. *Publications:* Research for Nursing, 1979; Communication in Nursing Care, 1981; Further Research for Nursing, 1989; Adult Nursing Care: putting evidence into practice, 2012; numerous res. based papers in learned jls on health promotion, smoking cessation, health prof. educn and communication in health care. *Recreations:* sailing, singing. *Address:* 31 Pacific Close, Ocean Village, Southampton SO14 3TX. *Club:* Royal Southampton Yacht.

**McLERNAN, Kieran Anthony;** Sheriff of Grampian, Highland and Islands at Aberdeen, 2000–11; *b* 29 April 1941; *s* of James John McLernan and Delia (*née* McEvaddy); *m* 1979, Joan Doherty Larkins; one *s* three *d*. *Educ:* St Aloysius' Coll., Glasgow; Glasgow Univ. (MA 1961; LLB 1965). Admitted solicitor, 1965; Tutor, Glasgow Univ., 1985–91. Temp. Sheriff, 1986–91; Sheriff of Grampian, Highland and Islands at Banff and Peterhead, 1991–2000. KCHS 1998 (KHS 1990). *Recreations:* golf, hockey, ski-ing, etc.

**McLINTOCK, Michael George Alexander;** Chairman: Associated British Foods, since 2018 (non-executive Director, since 2017); Grosvenor Group Ltd, since 2018 (Director, since 2012); *b* 24 March 1961; *s* of Sir (Charles) Alan McLintock and of Sylvia Mary McLintock; *m* 1996, Nicola Fairles Ogilvy Watson; one *s* two *d*. *Educ:* Malvern Coll.; St John's Coll., Oxford (scholar; BA 1st cl. hons Mod. History and Econs). Morgan Grenfell & Co. Ltd, 1983; Baring Brothers & Co. Ltd, 1987; M&G Group plc, 1992, Chief Exec., 1997–99; Chief Exec., Prudential M&G Asset Mgt, then M&G Group Ltd, 1999–2016. Director: Prudential plc, 2000–16; Close Brothers Gp plc, 2001–08. Trustee, Grosvenor Estate, 2008–. Mem., Takeover Appeal Bd, 2016–. *Recreations:* family, friends, good wine. *Address:* Associated British Foods, Weston Centre, 10 Grosvenor Street, W1K 4QY. *Clubs:* Army and Navy, Boodle's, MCC (Member: Finance Cttee, 2005–18; Develt Cttee, 2009–11).

**McLINTOCK, Sir Michael (William),** 4th Bt *cr* 1934, of Sanquhar, Co. Dumfries; *b* 13 Aug. 1958; *s* of Sir William Traven McLintock, 3rd Bt and Andrée, *d* of Richard Lonsdale-Hands; *S* father, 1987; *m* 1991, Jill Andrews; one *s* one *d*. *Heir: s* James Kieron McLintock, *b* 14 Feb. 1995.

**McLOUGHLIN, Catherine Mary Anne,** CBE 1998; independent management consultant; Vice-President, Age UK, since 2009 (Chair, Age Concern England, 2005–09); *b* 26 July 1943; *d* of Peter Patrick McLoughlin and Catherine (*née* McHugh). *Educ:* Ravenswell Convent, Bray, Co. Wicklow. Gen. nurse trng, N Middx Hosp., 1961–64; post-registration psychiatric trng, 1965–66, then specialist posts, 1966–73, Bethlem Royal and Maudsley Hosp.; Principal Nursing Officer, Bexley Hosp., 1973–77; Dep. Area Nursing Officer, Oxon, 1977–79; Chief Nursing Officer, Paddington and N Kensington HA, 1979–85; Dist Gen. Manager, Haringey HA, 1985–89; Dir of Nursing and Dep. Chief Nursing Officer, DoH, 1989–90, retd. Chair: Bromley FHSA, 1992–94; Bromley HA, 1994–99; NHS Confedn, 1997–2000; St George's Healthcare NHS Trust, 1999–2003. Chair: Nat. Network Art in Health, 2000–06; Age Concern Bromley, 2002–05. Dr *hc* Middx 1995. *Recreations:* reading, art, walking, swimming. *Address:* 53 South Croxted Road, West Dulwich, SE21 8BA. *T:* 07768 252300.

**McLOUGHLIN, Elizabeth Mary,** CBE 1997; Command Secretary, HQ Land Command, Ministry of Defence, 2003–06; *b* 10 April 1947; *d* of late Donald Norwood Menzies and Doreen Mary Menzies (*née* Collinson); *m* 1976, John McLoughlin; three *s*. *Educ:* South Hampstead High Sch.; University College London (BA Hons History). Res., 1969–72; joined MoD, 1972; various posts, 1972–88; Sen. Civil Service, 1988; Comd Sec., Adjutant Gen., 1997–2002; Dir Gen., Service Personnel Policy, 2002–03. Non-executive Director: Great Western Ambulance NHS Trust, 2006–13 (Dep. Chm., 2006–13); Bd, Nat. Offender Mgt Service, MoJ, 2010–16; Bd, Valuation Office Agency, HMRC, 2011–14; Cabinet Office proj. and prog. assurance reviewer, 2009–. Gov., King's Sch., Bruton, and Hazlegrove Prep. Sch., 2004–18 (Sen. Warden, 2012–14). *Recreations:* gardening, reading, walking the dog, music. *E:* emmcloughlin@btinternet.com.

**McLOUGHLIN, Sir Frank,** Kt 2015; CBE 2009; Associate Director for Leadership, Education and Training Foundation, since 2016; Associate Fellow, Saïd Business School, University of Oxford, since 2017; *b* London, 30 May 1956; *s* of Patrick McLoughlin and Mary McLoughlin; *m* 1997, Fiona Wallace; one *s* one *d*. *Educ:* Leeds Univ. (BA Hons Pol Studies); London Univ. (PGCE). Range of unskilled jobs before univ.; part-time lectr, Hammersmith and West London Coll., 1979–81; Lectr, then Sen. Lectr, North London Coll., 1981–93; Curriculum Manager, then Dep. Principal, City and Islington Coll., 1993–2002; Principal, City and Islington Coll., 2002–16. Chm., Commn on Adult Vocational Learning, 2012–13. Fellow: City Univ., 2013; UCL, 2016. Trustee, Royal Anniv. Trust, 2017–. *Recreations:* Irish music and culture, reading, travel, London. *Address:* Education and Training Foundation, 157–197 Buckingham Palace Road, SW1W 9SP.

**McLOUGHLIN, Rt Hon. Sir Patrick (Allen),** CH 2019; Kt 2016; PC 2005; MP (C) Derbyshire Dales, since 2010 (West Derbyshire, May 1986–2010); *b* 30 Nov. 1957; *s* of Patrick and Gladys Victoria McLoughlin; *m* 1984, Lynne Newman; one *s* one *d*. *Educ:* Cardinal Griffin Roman Catholic Sch., Cannock. Mineworker, Littleton Colliery, 1979–85; Marketing Official, NCB, 1985–86. PPS to Sec. of State for Trade and Industry, 1988–89; Parly Under-Sec. of State, Dept of Transport, 1989–92, Dept of Employment, 1992–93, DTI, 1993–94; an Asst Govt Whip, 1995–96; a Lord Comr of HM Treasury (Govt Whip), 1996–97; Opposition Pairing Whip, 1997–98; Dep. Opposition Chief Whip, 1998–2005; Opposition Chief Whip, 2005–10; Parly Sec. to HM Treasury (Govt Chief Whip), 2010–12; Sec. of State for Transport, 2012–16; Chancellor of the Duchy of Lancaster, 2016–18. Chm., Cons. Party, 2016–18. *Address:* House of Commons, SW1A 0AA.

**McLURE, Donald Keith;** Strategic Director for Corporate Resources, Derby City Council, since 2018; *b* Gateshead, 23 Dec. 1955; *s* of Donald Hall McLure and Florence McLure; *m* 1977, Jacqueline; two *d*. *Educ:* Blaydon Comp. Sch. IRRV; CIPFA. Asst Dir of Finance, Gateshead Council, 1991–2002; Asst Dir of Resources, 2002–07, Strategic Dir of Resources, 2007–10, Derby CC; Corporate Dir of Resources, Durham CC, 2010–16. *Recreations:* keen golfer for nearly 50 years, football fan of Newcastle United and Derby, walking, family including two young grandsons. *Clubs:* Brancepeth Castle Golf, Kedleston Park Golf.

**MACLURE, Sir John (Robert Spencer),** 4th Bt *cr* 1898; Headmaster, Croftinloan School, Pitlochry, Perthshire, 1978–92 and 1997–98; *b* 25 March 1934; *s* of Sir John William Spencer Maclure, 3rd Bt, OBE, and Elspeth (*d* 1991), *er d* of late Alexander King Clark; *S* father, 1980; *m* 1964, Jane Monica, *d* of late Rt Rev. T. J. Savage, Bishop of Zululand and Swaziland; four *s*. *Educ:* Winchester College. DipEd. 2nd Lt, 2nd Bn KRRC, 1953–55, BAOR; Lt, Royal Hampshire Airborne Regt, TA. Assistant Master: Horris Hill, 1955–66 and 1974–78; St George's, Wanganui, NZ, 1967–68; Sacred Heart Coll., Auckland, NZ, 1969–70; St Edmund's, Hindhead, Surrey, 1971–74. *Heir: s* John Mark Maclure [*b* 27 Aug. 1965; *m* 1996, Emily, *d* of Peter Frean; two *s* one *d*]. *Address:* Seaward, Crescent Close, Widemouth Bay, Bude, Cornwall EX23 0AE. *Clubs:* Royal Green Jackets; Royal N Devon Golf.

**McMAHON, Prof. Andrew Paul,** PhD; FRS 2007; W. M. Keck Professor and Chair, Department of Stem Cell Biology and Regenerative Medicine, and Director, Edythe and Eli Broad Center for Regenerative Medicine and Stem Cell Research, University of Southern California, since 2012. *Educ:* St Peter's Coll., Oxford (BA Zool. 1978); University Coll. London (PhD 1981). Postdoctoral Fellow, Div. of Biol., CIT; Staff Scientist, NIMR, London; Adjunct Prof., Dept of Genetics and Biol Scis, Columbia Univ.; Mem., Dept of Cell and Develtl Biol., Roche Inst. of Molecular Biol.; Prof. of Molecular and Cellular Biol., 1993, Frank B. Baird, Jr Prof. of Sci., 2001–12, Chm., Dept of Molecular and Cellular Biol., 2001–04, Harvard Univ. Associate Mem., EMBO. Fellow, Amer. Acad. Arts and Scis, 2003. *Publications:* contribs to jls incl. Science, Develt, Develtl Cell, Cell, Genes & Develt. *Address:* Edythe and Eli Broad Center for Regenerative Medicine and Stem Cell Research, Keck School of Medicine, University of Southern California, 1425 San Pablo Street, Los Angeles, CA 90033–9080, USA.

**McMAHON, Prof. April Mary Scott,** PhD; FBA 2005; FRSE, FLSW; Deputy Vice-Chancellor Education, and Professor of English Language and Linguistics, University of Kent, since 2016; *b* 30 April 1964; *d* of Irene Dugan (*née* Grant); *m* 1984, Robert McMahon; two *s* one *d*. *Educ:* Univ. of Edinburgh (MA 1986; PhD 1990). Lectr in Linguistics, and Fellow, Selwyn Coll., Cambridge, 1988–2000; Prof. of English Lang. and Linguistics, Univ. of Sheffield, 2000–04; Forbes Prof. of English Lang., 2005–11, Vice-Principal, Planning and Res. Planning, 2009–11, Univ. of Edinburgh; Vice-Chancellor, Aberystwyth Univ., 2011–16. Member, Council: AHRC, 2005–10; British Acad., 2008–11. Pres., Linguistics Assoc. of GB, 2000–05. FRSE 2003; FLSW 2012. *Publications:* Understanding Language Change, 1994; Lexical Phonology and the History of English, 2000; Change, Chance and Optimality, 2000; (ed jtly) Time-depth in Historical Linguistics, 2 vols, 2000; An Introduction to English Phonology, 2001; (with R. McMahon) Language Classification by Numbers, 2005; (ed jtly) The Handbook of English Linguistics, 2006; (with R. McMahon) Evolutionary Linguistics, 2012. *Recreations:* walking, cooking, Scottish country dancing. *Address:* University of Kent, Canterbury, Kent CT2 7NZ.

**McMAHON, Sir Christopher William, (Sir Kit),** Kt 1986; Director, Angela Flowers, 1992–2006; *b* Melbourne, 10 July 1927; *s* of late Dr John Joseph McMahon and late Margaret Kate (*née* Brown); *m* 1st, 1956, Marion Kelso; two *s*; 2nd, 1982, Alison Barbara Braimbridge, *d* of late Dr J. G. Cormie and late Mrs B. E. Cormie. *Educ:* Melbourne Grammar Sch.; Univ. of Melbourne (BA Hons Hist. and English, 1949); Magdalen Coll., Oxford. 1st cl. hons PPE, 1953. Tutor in English Lit., Univ. of Melbourne, 1950; Econ. Asst, HM Treasury, 1953–57; Econ. Adviser, British Embassy, Washington, 1957–60; Fellow and Tutor in Econs, Magdalen Coll., Oxford, 1960–64 (Hon. Fellow, 1986); Tutor in Econs, Treasury Centre for Admin. Studies, 1963–64; Mem., Plowden Cttee on Aircraft Industry, 1964–65; entered Bank of England as Adviser, 1964; Adviser to the Governors, 1966–70; Exec. Dir, 1970–80; Dep. Governor, 1980–85; Chief Exec. and Dep. Chm., 1986–87, Chm. and Chief Exec., 1987–91, Midland Bank. Director: Eurotunnel, 1987–91; Hongkong and Shanghai Banking Corp., 1987–91; Royal Opera House, 1989–97; Taylor Woodrow, 1991–2000 (Dep. Chm., 1997–2000); Newspaper Publishing, 1993–94; Aegis, 1993–99; FI Gp, 1994–2001; HistoryWorld, 2001–; Chairman: Coutts Consulting Gp, 1992–96; Pentos, 1993–95; Arc Dance Co., 2000–03. Mem., Gp of Thirty, 1978–84; Chairman: Working Party 3, OECD, 1980–85; Young Enterprise, 1989–92; Centre for Study of Financial Innovation, 1993–95. Mem. Court, Univ. of London, 1984–86; Gov., Birkbeck Coll., 1991–2003. Trustee: Whitechapel Art Gall., 1984–92; Royal Opera House Trust, 1984–86. Hon. Fellow, UCNW, 1988. Hon. Mem., Antiquarian Booksellers' Assoc., 2000. Chevalier, Légion d'Honneur (France), 1990. *Publications:* Sterling in the Sixties, 1964; (ed) Techniques of Economic Forecasting, 1965. *Recreations:* looking at pictures, buying books, going to the movies. *Address:* 134 Cranmer Court, Whiteheads Grove, SW3 3HE. *Club:* Garrick.

**McMAHON, Harvey Thomas,** PhD; FRS 2008; Programme Leader, MRC Laboratory of Molecular Biology, Cambridge, since 1995; *b* Belfast, 31 Aug. 1965; *s* of William McMahon and Sarah Jean McMahon (*née* McCrea); *m* 1995, Kelly Lynn Hammonds; two *s*. *Educ:* Trinity College, Dublin (BA Mod. Biochem. 1987); Dundee Univ. (PhD 1990). Res. Asst, Dundee Univ., 1990–91; Postdoctoral Fellow, Howard Hughes Med. Inst., Dallas, 1991–95. *Publications:* regular contribs of papers, reviews and book chapters in scientific literature. *Recreations:* hill walking, travelling, ornithology, gardening (mostly growing weeds), community work. *Address:* MRC Laboratory of Molecular Biology, Neurobiology Division, Francis Crick Avenue, Cambridge CB2 0QH. *T:* (01223) 402311, *Fax:* (01223) 402310. *E:* hmm@mrc-lmb.cam.ac.uk.

**McMAHON, Hugh Robertson;** UK Political Editor, World Parliamentarian magazine, since 1999; Lecturer in Social Sciences, James Watt College, 1999–2011; Lecturer in Politics, University of Edinburgh, 2002–10; *b* 17 June 1938; *s* of Hugh McMahon and Margaret Fulton Robertson; *m* 1986, Helen Grant; one *s* one *d*. *Educ:* Glasgow University (MA Hons); Jordanhill College. Assistant Teacher: Largs High School, 1962–63; Stevenston High School, 1963–64; Irvine Royal Academy, 1964–68; Principal Teacher of History, Mainholm Academy, Ayr, 1968–71; Principal Teacher of History and Modern Studies, 1971–72, Asst Head Teacher, 1972–84, Ravenspark Academy, Irvine. MEP (Lab) Strathclyde W, 1984–99; contested (Lab) Scotland, 1999. European Parliament: Mem., Budgetary Control Cttee, 1987–92; Social Affairs, Employment and Working Envmt Cttee, 1984–99 (Vice Chm., 1992–94); Fisheries Cttee, 1994–99; Mem., Interparly Delegn with Czech Republic, 1997–99. Formerly Rep. of Scottish MEPs, Scottish Exec. Cttee, Labour Party. Chm., Paisley Bids Gp, 2011–. Mem. Bd, Centre for Russian, Central and Eastern European Studies, 2007–; Member: European Movement, 1999–; Scotland Russia Forum, 2009–; Labour Movement in Europe, 2015–. *Recreations:* golf, reading, walking, languages, foreign travel. *Address:* 47 Roffey Park Road, Paisley PA1 3JL. *T:* (0141) 889 0885, *Fax:* (0141) 889 4790. *E:* breakplough@btinternet.com. *Clubs:* Saltcoats & Kilbirnie Labour; Irvine Bogside Golf.

**McMAHON, James,** OBE 2015; MP (Lab Co-op) Oldham and Royton, since Dec. 2015; *b* Manchester, 7 July 1980; *s* of William McMahon and Alicia McMahon (*née* O'Rourke); partner, Charlene Duerden; two *s*. Univ. of Manchester, 1997–2004; Bolton at Home, 2004–05; Groundwork Trust, 2005–08; Town Centre Manager, 2008–12; Gtr Manchester Combined Authy, 2011–16. Mem. (Lab) Oldham MBC, 2003–16. Shadow Minister for Devolution, 2016–. FRSA 2015. *Recreations:* family, food, reading. *Address:* House of Commons, SW1A 0AA. *T:* (020) 7219 6039. *E:* jim.mcmahon.mp@parliament.uk.

**McMAHON, Kate;** private prosecution fraud specialist; Founding Partner, Edmonds Marshall McMahon, since 2012; *b* Denowa, Australia; *d* of Patrick and Carmel McMahon. *Educ:* Queensland Univ. of Technol. (BA/LLB 2006). Sen. Caseworker, Law Soc. of England and Wales, 2005–06; Public Prosecutor, Dept of Public Prosecutions, 2007–08; Sen. Prosecution Lawyer, 2008–12. UK Mem., Fraudnet (ICC Fraud and Asset Trng), 2017–; Dep. Hd, Asset Recovery Sub-cttee, IBA, 2018–. *Publications:* contrib. articles to jls. *Recreations:* swimming, running, reading. *Address:* Edmonds Marshall McMahon, 35 Cock Lane, EC1A 9BW. *T:* (020) 3780 2266, *Fax:* (020) 7681 2248. *E:* katemcmahon@emmlegal.com.

**McMAHON, Sir Kit;** *see* McMahon, Sir C. W.

**McMAHON, Most Rev. Malcolm Patrick;** *see* Liverpool, Archbishop of, (RC).

**McMAHON, Michael Joseph;** Member (Lab) Uddingston and Bellshill, Scottish Parliament, 2011–16 (Hamilton North and Bellshill, 1999–2011); *b* 18 Sept. 1961; *s* of Patrick McMahon and Bridget Clarke; *m* 1983, Margaret Mary McKeown; one *s* two *d*. *Educ:* Glasgow Caledonian Univ. (BA Hons Social Scis (Politics and Sociology) 1996). Welder, Terex Equipment Ltd, 1977–92; freelance socio-political researcher, 1996–99. Contested (Lab) Uddingston and Bellshill, Scottish Parlt, 2016. *Recreations:* swimming, hill walking, supporting Celtic FC. *Address:* 7 Forres Crescent, Bellshill, Lanarkshire ML4 1HL. *T:* (01698) 306112.
*See also* S. M. McMahon.

**McMAHON, Sir Patrick John Westropp,** 9th Bt *cr* 1817; *b* 7 Feb. 1988; *s* of late Shaun Desmond McMahon and of Jill Rosamund McMahon; *S* uncle, 2018. *Heir:* *b* Charles Beresford McMahon, *b* 1989.

**McMAHON, Richard James;** QC (Guernsey) 2009; Deputy Bailiff of Guernsey, since 2012; *b* Farnborough, Kent, 1 May 1962; *s* of James Ronald McMahon and Alice Rose McMahon (*née* Skipp); *m* 1998, Sue-Yin Elizabeth Chan; one *s* one *d*. *Educ:* Abingdon Sch.; Univ. of Liverpool (LLB 1984); Emmanuel Coll., Cambridge (LLM 1985); Univ. of Caen (Certificat d'Etudes Juridiques Françaises et Normandes). Called to the Bar: Middle Temple, 1986; Guernsey, 1998; Lectr, Univ. of Reading, 1987–95; Legislative Draftsman, Guernsey, 1995–99; Crown Advocate, Guernsey, 2000–09; HM Comptroller, Guernsey, 2009–12. *Publications:* (contrib.) Blackstone's Criminal Practice, 1995–. *Recreations:* music, reading, Ireland. *Address:* Bailiff's Chambers, Royal Court House, St Peter Port, Guernsey GY1 2PB. *T:* (01481) 726161, *Fax:* (01481) 713861. *E:* Deputy.Bailiff@gov.gg.

**McMAHON, Siobhan Marie;** Member (Lab) Scotland Central, Scottish Parliament, 2011–16; *b* Bellshill, North Lanarks; *d* of Michael Joseph McMahon, *qv*. *Educ:* Glasgow Caledonian Univ. (BA Social Scis Pols with Hist. 2006). Researcher to Rt Hon. James Murphy, MP and Kenneth Macintosh, MSP, 2007–11; Office Manager, Labour Support Unit, Scottish Parlt, 2010–11. *Recreation:* Celtic supporter and season ticket holder.

**McMAHON, Rt Rev. Thomas;** Parish Priest, Stock, since 1969; Bishop of Brentwood, (RC), 1980–2014, now Emeritus; *b* 17 June 1936. *Educ:* St Bede's GS, Manchester; St Sulpice, Paris. Ordained priest, 1959; Asst Priest, Colchester, 1959–64; Priest, Westcliff-on-Sea, 1964–69; Chaplain, Univ. of Essex, 1972–80. Hon. Ecumenical Canon, Chelmsford Cathedral, 2005–. Former Member: Nat. Ecumenical Commn; Internat. Commn on English in the Liturgy, 1983–2001; Mem., Churches Together in Essex & E London, 1991– (Chm., 1984–93); Chairman: Brentwood Ecumenical Commn, 1979; Cttee for Pastoral Liturgy, 1983–97; Essex Churches Consultative Council, 1984–; Cttee for Church Music, 1985–2001; Bishop's Patrimony Cttee, 2001–12; Mem., London Church Leaders Gp, 1980–; Rep. of Bps' Conf. on Council of St George's House, Windsor, 2005–. Founder Mem., Movt for Christian Democracy, 1999–. President: Essex Show, 1992; Essex Club, 2009; Friends of Essex Churches, 2017. Vice-President: Pax Christi, 1987–; Friends of Cathedral Music, 2005–; Historic Churches Preservation Trust, 2007–. Hon. Fellow, Hertford Coll., Oxford, 2004. DU: Essex, 1991; Anglia, 2001. Freeman, City of London, 2013. *Address:* Bishop's House, Stock, Ingatestone, Essex CM4 9BU. *T:* (01277) 840268.

**McMANNERS, (Joseph) Hugh;** author, since 1984; singer-songwriter guitarist, since 2018; Director, Scars of War Foundation, Queen's College, Oxford, since 2011; *b* Oxford, 9 Dec. 1952; *s* of Rev. Prof. John McManners, CBE, FBA and of Sarah McManners; *m* 1989; two *s*. *m* 2018, Megan. *Educ:* Oadby Beauchamp Upper Sch.; RMA Sandhurst; St Edmund Hall, Oxford (BA Geog. 1978; MA 1980). Commnd RA 1972; served 148 Cdo Forward Observation Battery with Special Boat Sqdn, Falklands War, 1982 (mentioned in despatches); sc Camberley 1984; Battery Comdr, 17 (Corunna) Field Battery, 1986–89; resigned Commn, 1989. Independent television producer, 1991–96; Defence Corresp., Sunday Times, 1995–2000. Vis. Res. Fellow, Changing Character of War Prog., Univ of Oxford, 2013. *Television:* co-productions include: Thinking of the Soldier, 1991, P Company, 1992, Inside the Glasshouse, 1994, Cutting Edge Films; series: Battle Cries, 1992; Commando; Top Guns; The Cinderellas; co-presenter, Bare Necessities, 1999–2001. Writer and presenter, BBC Radio 4 series: Taking the Crown, 1990; The Psychology of War, 1994. Band leader and guitarist, 1992–; songwriter, 2010–; solo singer-songwriter, 2014–; guitarist and singer, Linden Tree Band, 2018–. *Publications:* Falklands Commando, 1984; Crowning the Dragon, 1986; The Scars of War, 1993, 2nd 2014; Commando Survival Manual, 1994; Commando, 1995; The Backpacker's Handbook, 1995; The Children's Outdoor Training Book, 1996; Top Guns, 1996; Outdoor Survival Guide, 1999; Forgotten Voices of the Falklands War, 2002; Gulf War One, 2011. *Recreations:* trips off-grid, dreaming of vintage Harley Davidsons, red wine. *E:* hugh@hughmcmanners.com. *W:* www.hughmcmanners.com, music.hughmcmanners.com.

**McMANUS, Christopher;** *see* McManus, I. C.

**McMANUS, Declan Patrick Aloysius, (Elvis Costello),** OBE 2019; musician and composer; *b* 25 Aug. 1954; *s* of late Ross McManus and of Lillian McManus (*née* Costello); *m* 1974, Mary; one *s*; *m* 1986, Cait O'Riordan; *m* 2003, Diana Krall; two *s* (twins). Formed Elvis Costello and the Attractions, 1977; has collaborated with, amongst others, Brodsky Quartet, Swedish Radio Symphony Orchestra and Burt Bacharach. Dir, S Bank Centre Meltdown, 1995. Presenter, TV series, Spectacle, 2008–. Recordings include: *albums:* My Aim is True, 1977; This Year's Model, 1978; Armed Forces, 1979; Trust, 1981; Almost Blue, 1981; Imperial Bedroom, 1982; Punch the Clock, 1983; Blood and Chocolate, 1986; Spike, 1989; Mighty Like the Rose, 1991; (with Brodsky Quartet) The Juliet Letters, 1993; Brutal Youth, 1994; Extreme Honey, 1997; Painted from Memory, 1998; (with Anne Sofie von Otter) For the Stars, 2001; When I Was Cruel, 2002; North, 2003; The Delivery Man, 2004; Il Sogno, 2004; Momofuku, 2008; Secret, Profane and Sugarcane, 2009; National Ransom, 2010; The Return of the Spectacular Spinning Songbook, 2011; (with The Roots) Wise Up Ghost, 2013; Look Now, 2018; *singles:* Alison, 1977; Watching the Detectives, 1977; (I Don't Want to Go to) Chelsea, 1978; Oliver's Army, 1979; Accidents Will Happen, 1979; Good Year for the Roses, 1981; Everyday I Write the Book, 1983; Pills and Soap, 1983; The People's Limousine, 1985; Little Atoms, 1996; She, 1999. *Publications:* Unfaithful Music and Disappearing Ink (autobiog.), 2015.

**McMANUS, Francis Joseph;** solicitor; *b* 16 Aug. 1942; *s* of Patrick and Celia McManus; *m* 1971, Carmel V. Doherty, Lisnaskea, Co. Fermanagh; two *s* one *d*. *Educ:* St Michael's, Enniskillen; Queen's University, Belfast. BA 1965; Diploma in Education, 1966. Subsequently a Teacher. MP (Unity) Fermanagh and S Tyrone, 1970–Feb. 1974. Founder Mem. and Co-Chm., Irish Independence Party, 1977. *Address:* Lissadell, 40 Drumlin Heights, Enniskillen, Co. Fermanagh, N Ireland BT74 7NR. *T:* (028) 6632 3401.

**McMANUS, Prof. (Ian) Christopher,** PhD, MD; FRCP, FRCPEd, FMedSci; Professor of Psychology and Medical Education, University College London, since 1997; *b* 1 March 1951; *s* of Robert Victor McManus and June McManus; *m* 2007, Christine Pleines; one *s* two *d*. *Educ:* Harrow Co. Grammar Sch.; Christ's Coll., Cambridge (BA 1972, MA 1977; PhD 1979); Univ. of Birmingham (MB ChB 1975); Univ. of London (MD 1985). FRCP 1998; FRCPEd 2007. University of London: Lectr in Psychol. as Applied to Medicine, Dept of Psychol., Bedford Coll., then UCL, and Dept of Psychiatry, St Mary's Hosp. Med. Sch., 1979–88; Sen. Lectr in Psychol. as Applied to Medicine, Dept of Psychol., UCL, and Dept of Psychiatry, St Mary's Hosp. Med. Sch., ICSTM, 1988–93; Prof. of Psychol., Dept of Psychol., UCL, and Dept of Psychiatry, ICSM at St Mary's, 1993–97. Examr and Educnl Advr, MRCP(UK), 1999–. Vis. Prof., Univ. of Vienna, 2012. Lectures: C. S. Myers, BPsS, 2005; G. J. Burton, Applied Vision Assoc., 2009; Lord Cohen, ASME, 2011. Pres., Psychol. Section, British Assoc., 2002. Fellow, Internat. Assoc. Empirical Aesthetics, 2000. Ed., Laterality, 1996–2016. FMedSci 2007. Hon. Fellow, Acad. of Medical Educators, 2014. Ig Nobel Prize, 2002. *Publications:* Psychology in Medicine, 1992; (ed jtly) Cambridge Handbook of Psychology, Health and Medicine, 1997, 3rd edn 2019; Right Hand, Left Hand, 2002 (Wellcome Trust Prize, 1999; Aventis Prize, 2003); The Right Hand and the Left Hand of History, 2010. *Recreations:* all things aesthetic, all things Italian. *Address:* Department of Psychology, University College London, Gower Street, WC1E 6BT. *T:* (020) 7679 5390, *Fax:* (020) 7436 4276. *E:* i.mcmanus@ucl.ac.uk.

**McMANUS, Dr James John;** human rights consultant specialising in prisons and detention conditions, since 1988; Professor of Criminal Justice, Glasgow Caledonian University, 2004–09; *b* 23 June 1950; *s* of David McManus and Alice McManus (*née* Vallely); *m* 1974, Catherine MacKellaig; one *s* four *d*. *Educ:* Our Lady's High Sch., Motherwell; Univ. of Edinburgh (LLB); Univ. of Dundee (PhD 1985). Lectr, UC, Cardiff, 1972–74; Lectr, 1974–76, Sen. Lectr, 1976–2004, Univ. of Dundee. Comr, Scottish Prisons Complaints Commn, 1994–99; Chm., Parole Bd for Scotland, 2000–06; Vice Convenor, Risk Mgt Authy, 2005–13. Expert Advr, 1992–2009 and 2019–, Mem., 2009–17, European Cttee for Prevention of Torture. *Publications:* Lay Justice, 1992; Prisons, Prisoners and the Law, 1994; (with Dr Lindsay Thomson) Mental Health and Scots Law in Practice, 2005. *Recreation:* walking. *Address:* Heathbank, Coupar Angus Road, Blairgowrie PH10 6JY.

**McMANUS, John Andrew;** HM Diplomatic Service, retired; UK Representative, Mauritania, 2013–15; *b* 20 May 1955; *s* of Andrew McManus and Winifred (*née* Hazzard). *Educ:* Univ. of Sussex (BA Econs and Europ. Studies 1977). Joined FCO, 1977; Vice-Consul, Algiers, 1984–85; Commercial Attaché, Moscow, 1988–91; Presidency Co-ordinator, UK Perm. Repn to EU, Brussels, 1992; First Sec., Press and Public Affairs, Berne, 1993–97; Hd of Political Section, Brussels, 2000–04; Ambassador to Guinea, 2004–08; Dep. Dir, 2009–10, Acting Dir, 2010–11, Shanghai Expo 2010; Administrator, British Indian Ocean Territory, 2011–13. *Recreations:* athletics, food, languages. *E:* john_mcmanus1066@hotmail.com.

**McMANUS, Jonathan Richard;** QC 1999; *b* 15 Sept. 1958; *s* of Frank Rostron McManus and Benita Ann McManus. *Educ:* Neale Wade Comprehensive, March; Downing Coll., Cambridge (MA). Called to the Bar, Middle Temple, 1982; in practice as barrister, 4–5 Gray's Inn, 1983–2013. *Publications:* Education and the Courts, 1998, 3rd edn 2012; contrib. Economic, Social and Cultural Rights: their implementation, in United Kingdom Law, ed Burchill, Harris and Owers, 1999; (consultant ed) Judicial Review: principles and procedures, 2013. *Recreations:* music, travel, photography. *Address:* 262 Liverpool Road, Islington, N1 1LG.

**McMANUS, Prof. Richard James,** PhD; FRCGP, FRCP; Professor of Primary Care Research, University of Oxford, since 2012; Fellow, Green Templeton College, Oxford, since 2012; *b* London, 17 April 1967; *s* of Peter McManus and late Margaret S. S. McManus; two *d*. *Educ:* St Mary's Coll., Southampton; Peter Symonds Coll., Winchester; St Mary's Hosp. Med. Sch., Univ. of London (BSc Hons Biol and Clin. Scis 1990; MB BS 1991); Univ. of Birmingham (MSc 2000; PhD 2004). MRCGP 1997, FRCGP 2006; FRCP 2016. Jun. med. posts, St Mary's Hosp., London, 1991–94, Glos, 1994–97; jun. res. posts, 1997–2009, Prof. of Primary Care, 2009–11, Univ. of Birmingham; General Practitioner (part-time): Greenridge Surgery, Birmingham, 1999–2012; The Surgery, Beaumont St, Oxford, 2013–. *Publications:* contribs to jls incl. Lancet, Jl Amer. Med. Assoc., BMJ, British Jl Gen. Practice. *Recreations:* music, both playing (trombone and guitar) and listening, cycling. *Address:* Nuffield Department of Primary Care Health Sciences, University of Oxford, Radcliffe Observatory Quarter, Woodstock Road, Oxford OX2 6GG.

**McMASTER, Sir Brian (John),** Kt 2003; CBE 1987; Director, Edinburgh International Festival, 1991–2006. International Artists' Dept, EMI Ltd, 1968–73; Controller of Opera Planning, ENO, 1973–76; Gen. Administrator, subseq. Man. Dir, WNO, 1976–91; Artistic Dir, Vancouver Opera, 1984–89. *Address:* Apartment 40, 1 Lambs Passage, EC1Y 8AB.

**McMASTER, Hughan James Michael;** Chief Architect and Director of Works, Home Office, 1980–87, retired; *b* 27 July 1927; *s* of William James Michael and Emly McMaster; *m* 1950; one *s* two *d*. *Educ:* Christ's Coll., Finchley; Regent Street Polytechnic (DipArch). ARIBA 1951. Served RAF, India and Far East, 1946–48. Joined Civil Service, 1961; Navy Works, 1961–69; Whitehall Development Gp, Directorate of Home Estate Management and Directorate of Civil Accommodation, 1969–76; Defence Works (PE and Overseas), 1976–80. *Recreations:* gardening, reading, theatre, music.

**McMASTER, Prof. Paul;** Professor of Hepatobiliary Surgery and Transplantation, and Consultant Surgeon, Queen Elizabeth Hospital, University of Birmingham, 1980–2005; *b* 4 Jan. 1943; *s* of Dr James McMaster and Sarah Jane McMaster (*née* Lynn); *m* 1969, Helen Ruth Bryce; two *s* one *d*. *Educ:* Liverpool Coll.; Univ. of Liverpool (MB ChB 1966); ChM 1979); MA Cantab 1978. FRCS 1971. House Surgeon, subseq. House Physician, Liverpool Royal Infirmary, Univ. of Liverpool, 1966–67; SHO in Urology and Transplantation, RPMS, Hammersmith Hosp., 1967–68; Registrar in Surgery, Addenbrooke's Hosp., 1969–72; Sen. Registrar and Res. Fellow, 1972–76, Sen. Lectr in Surgery, 1976–80, Univ. Dept of Surgery, Addenbrooke's Hosp., Cambridge Univ. Visiting Professor: Univs of Rome, Genoa, Cairo, Concepción; RACS Foundn, 1998. FICS. *Publications:* numerous articles on immuno suppression, liver transplantation, develt of laparoscopic and hepatobiliary surgery, advances in major hepatic and biliary surgery. *Recreations:* gardening, sailing, reading. *Address:* c/o Liver Unit, Queen Elizabeth Hospital, Edgbaston, Birmingham B15 2TH.

**McMASTER, Peter,** CB 1991; Member, Lord Chancellor's Panel of Independent Inspectors, 1991–2001; *b* 22 Nov. 1931; *s* of Peter McMaster and Ada Nellie (*née* Williams); *m* 1955, Catherine Ann Rosborough; one *s* one *d*. *Educ:* Kelvinside Academy, Glasgow; RMA Sandhurst; RMCS Shrivenham. BScEng London. Called to the Bar, Middle Temple, 1969. Commissioned into Royal Engineers, 1952; served Middle and Far East; retired (major), 1970; joined Civil Service, 1970; W Midland Region, Ordnance Survey, 1970–72; Caribbean Region, Directorate of Overseas Survey, 1972–74; Headquarters, 1974–91, Dir Gen., 1985–91, Ordnance Survey. Vis. Prof., Kingston Polytechnic, subseq. Kingston Univ., 1991–93. Member Council: BCS, 1983–92; RGS, 1990–93. FIIM 1990. *Recreations:* travel, walking, chess. *Address:* Hillhead, Stratton Road, Winchester, Hampshire SO23 0JQ. *T:* (01962) 862684.
*See also Peter McMaster.*

**McMASTER, Peter;** QC 2008; *b* Dhekelia, Cyprus, 10 Jan. 1959; *s* of Peter McMaster, *qv*; *m* 1992, Natalie Ann Adams; three *s*. *Educ:* North Bromsgrove High Sch.; Winchester Coll.; King's Coll. London (LLB 1980). Called to the Bar, Middle Temple, 1981. *Recreations:* reading, walking, shooting, cooking, paddleboarding.

**McMEIKAN, Kennedy;** businessman and investor; Chief Executive, Brakes Group, 2013–17; *b* Dumfries, 13 May 1965; *s* of Robert Allan Henry McMeikan and Jessie Anne McMeikan; three *s* two *d*; *m* 2012, Melanie Burton. *Educ:* Stranraer Acad. Joined RN, 1981, Electronic Warfare Operator, 1981–86; Retail Manager, Sears plc, 1986–90; Tesco plc, 1990–2004: Store Manager, then Stores Dir, later CEO, Europa Foods; CEO, Tesco Japan; Retail Dir, J Sainsbury plc, 2004–08; Chief Exec., Greggs plc, 2008–13. Prince of Wales' Ambassador for the NE, 2010–12; Chm., NE, CBI, 2010–12. Mem., Policy Cttee, Inst. of Grocery Distribution, 2013–17. Trustee: Meals and More; Alnwick Garden. *Recreations:* family life, ski-ing, golf, music, EGLST open water swimming.

**McMENAMIN, Frances Jane, (Mrs Ian McCarry);** QC (Scot.) 1998; *b* 21 May 1951; *d* of Francis and Agnes McMenamin; *m* 1991, Ian McCarry. *Educ:* Our Lady of Lourdes Primary Sch., Glasgow; Notre Dame High Sch., Glasgow; Strathclyde Univ. (BA 1971; LLB 1974). Mgt trainee, GKN Ltd, 1971–72. Admitted Solicitor, 1976; admitted to Faculty of Advocates, 1985. Legal Apprentice, Hughes, Dowdall & Co., Solicitors, 1974–76; Procurator Fiscal Depute, 1976–84; advocate specialising in criminal law, 1985–; Temp. Sheriff, 1991–97; Advocate Depute, 1997–2000. Member: Adv. Gp on rape and other sexual offences, Scottish Law Commn, 2005–06; Scottish Criminal Cases Review Commn, 2010–19; Lord Justice Gen.'s Criminal Courts Rules Council, 2011–14, 2015–17; Rt Hon. Lord Bonomy's Post-Corroboration Rev. Gp, 2014–15; Direct Access Gp, 2015–17, Professional Standards Cttee, 2015–17, Faculty of Advocates; Audit Cttee, Police Investigations and Rev. Commn, 2018–; Scottish Govt's Governance Gp on Jt Investigative Interviews, 2018–; Lord Justice Clerk's Rev. Gp on Mgt of Sexual Offences Cases, 2019–. Vis. Lectr, Scottish Police Coll., Tulliallan Castle, 1991–2015. Mem., Law Sch. Adv. Panel, 2002–, Mem. of Ct, 2005–09, Univ. of Strathclyde. Dir, Faculty Services Ltd, 2003–07. Mem., Merchants' House of Glasgow, 2015– (Dir, 2016–). DUniv Strathclyde, 2009. *Recreations:* spending time with husband, family and friends, reading, travelling. *Address:* (home) 59 Hamilton Drive, Glasgow G12 8DP. *T:* (0141) 339 0519; Advocates' Library, Parliament House, Parliament Square, Edinburgh EH1 1RF. *T:* (0131) 226 5071. *Club:* Hole in the Head (Edinburgh).

**McMICHAEL, Sir Andrew (James),** Kt 2008; FRS 1992; Director, 1998–2000, Hon. Director, 2000–10, Medical Research Council Human Immunology Unit, John Radcliffe Hospital, Oxford; Professor of Molecular Medicine and Director, Weatherall Institute of Molecular Medicine, Oxford University, 2000–12, now Emeritus; Fellow of Corpus Christi College, Oxford, 2000–12; *b* 8 Nov. 1943; *s* of Sir John McMichael, FRS and Sybil McMichael; *m* 1968, Kathryn Elizabeth Cross; two *s* one *d*. *Educ:* St Paul's Sch., London; Gonville and Caius Coll., Cambridge (MA; BChir 1968; MB 1969); St Mary's Hosp. Med. Sch., London. PhD 1974; MRCP 1971; FRCP 1985. House Physician, St Mary's Hosp., Royal Northern Hosp., Hammersmith Hosp. and Brompton Hosp., 1968–71; MRC Jun. Res. Fellow, National Inst. for Med. Res., 1971–74; MRC Travelling Fellow, Stanford Univ. Med. Sch., 1974–76; Oxford University: Wellcome Sen. Clin. Fellow, Nuffield Depts of Medicine and Surgery, 1977–79; University Lectr in Medicine and Hon. Consultant Physician, 1979–82; MRC Clinical Res. Prof. of Immunology, 1982–98; Prof. of Immunology, 1999–2000; Fellow, Trinity Coll., 1983–2000 (Hon. Fellow). Member: Adv. Bd, Beit Meml Trust, 1984–; MRC AIDS Steering Cttee, 1988–94; Res. Grants Council, Hong Kong, 1999–; Council, Royal Soc., 1998–99. Founder FMedSci 1998. Hon. Fellow, Harris Manchester Coll., Oxford. *Publications:* (ed with J. W. Fabre) Monoclonal Antibodies in Clinical Medicine, 1982; articles on genetic control of human immune response, antiviral immunity and AIDS. *Recreation:* walking and ski-ing in France.

**MACMILLAN,** family name of **Earl of Stockton.**

**MACMILLAN OF OVENDEN, Viscount; Daniel Maurice Alan Macmillan;** *b* 9 Oct. 1974; *s* and *heir* of Earl of Stockton, *qv*. Dir, Project Zoltar Ltd, 2002–. *Publications:* (with Kieron Livingstone) Zoltar the Magnificent: 33, 2013.

**McMILLAN, Alan Austen,** CB 1986; Solicitor to the Secretary of State for Scotland, 1984–87; *b* 19 Jan. 1926; *s* of Allan McMillan and Mabel (*née* Austin); *m* 1949, Margaret Moncur; two *s* two *d*. *Educ:* Ayr Acad.; Glasgow Univ. Served in Army, 1944–47. Qualified Solicitor in Scotland, 1949; Legal Assistant, Ayr Town Council, 1949–55; Scottish Office: Legal Assistant, 1955–62; Sen. Legal Assistant, 1962–68; Asst Solicitor, 1968–82, seconded to Cabinet Office Constitution Unit, 1977–78; Dep. Solicitor, 1982–84. *Recreations:* reading, music, theatre.

**McMILLAN, David Loch,** FRAeS, FCILT; Director General, European Organisation for the Safety of Air Navigation (EUROCONTROL), 2008–12; *b* 16 Sept. 1954; *s* of David and May McMillan; *m* 1977, Frances Beedham; one *s* two *d*. *Educ:* Royal High Sch., Edinburgh; Univ. of Edinburgh (MA French and Spanish). FCO, 1976; Rabat, 1978; Harare, 1980; Principal, Dept of Transport, 1984–87; First Sec. (Transport), Washington, 1987–92; Hd, Information, Dept of Transport, 1993–97; Hd, Air Traffic Div., DETR, 1997–2001; Dir, Rail Restructuring, DETR, 2001–02; Dir, Strategy and Delivery, 2002–04, Dir Gen., Civil Aviation, 2004–07, DfT. Non-exec. Dir, Gatwick Airport Ltd, 2013–. Mem., Bd of Govs, Flight Safety Foundn, 2008–15 (Chm., 2012–15); Chair: Air Traffic Mgt Cttee, RaeS, 2016–; Air Traffic Mgt Policy Inst., 2016–. Trustee: Bd of Govs, British Sch. of Brussels, 2009–12; BAA Communities Trust, 2008–13 (Chm., 2012–13). FRAeS 2008; FCILT 2010. Médaille de l'Aéronautique (France), 2010. *Recreations:* travel, reading, cricket.

**MacMILLAN, Prof. David W. C.,** PhD; FRS 2012; James S. McDonnell Distinguished University Professor of Chemistry, since 2011, Director, Merck Center for Catalysis, since 2006, and Chair, Department of Chemistry, since 2010, Princeton University; *b* Bellshill, Scotland, 1968. *Educ:* Univ. of Glasgow (BSc Chem. 1991); Univ. of Calif, Irvine (PhD 1996). Postdoctoral Res. Fellow, Harvard Univ., 1996–98; res. at Univ. of Calif, Berkeley, 1998–2000; Dept of Chem., CIT, 2000–06, Earle C. Anthony Prof. of Chem., 2004–06; A. Barton Hepburn Prof. of Chem., Princeton Univ., 2006. Sloan Fellow, 2002. Scientific Consultant: Abbott Res. Labs, 2000–; Johnson & Johnson, 2000–; Bayer Pharmaceuticals, 2001–; Merck Res. Labs. 2001–; Amgen Pharmaceuticals, 2002–; Gilead Pharmaceuticals, 2003–; Constellation Pharmaceuticals, 2009–. Ed.-in-Chief and Mem., Editl Adv. Bd, Chem. Sci. jl, 2010–; Member, Editorial Advisory Board: Tetrahedron & Tetrahedron Letters, 2001–; Chem. Communications, 2004–; Chem., an Asian jl, 2005–; Advanced Synthesis & Catalysis, 2009–. Mem., Amer. Acad. Arts and Scis, 2012. Corday-Morgan Medal, RSC, 2005; Thieme-IUPAC Prize in Organic Synthesis, 2006; Mukaiyama Award, Soc. of Synthetic Organic Chem., Japan, 2007; Harrison Howe Award, Amer. Chem. Soc., 2014. *Publications:* contribs to Jl Amer. Chem. Soc. *Address:* Princeton University, Frick Laboratory, Washington Road, Princeton, NJ 08544, USA.

**MACMILLAN, Deborah Millicent, (Lady Macmillan);** artist; *b* Boonah, Qld, 1 July 1944; *d* of Dr Dudley Williams and Nina Deborah (*née* Darvall); *m* 1st, 1966, Denis Allard (marr. diss. 1973); 2nd, 1974, Sir Kenneth Macmillan (*d* 1992); one *d*. *Educ:* Wenona, N Sydney; Nat. Art Sch., E Sydney (Painting and Sculpture). Member: Bd, Royal Opera House, 1993–96; Exec. Cttee, Royal Acad. Dancing, 1994–97; Council, Arts Council of England, 1996–98 (Chm., Dance Panel, 1996–98); Chm., Friends of Covent Gdn, 1995–96. Mem., Nat. Cttee, Houston Ballet, 1993–96; Hon. Mem. Bd, American Ballet Theatre, 1993–. Gov., Nat. Youth Dance Trust, 1999–2004; Trustee, Wimbledon Coll. (formerly Sch.) of Art, 2000–08. Custodian, Sir Kenneth Macmillan's choreography, 1992–. Man. Dir, KM Ballet Prodns, 2014–17; Sen. Partner, Kenneth MacMillan and Partner, 1993–; Dir, Avlaki Ltd Superb Organic Olive Oils, 2014–. *Exhibitions:* solo shows: Charlotte Lampard Gall., 1984; Turtle Key Arts Centre, 1992, 1995; Chelsea Arts Club, 1999; Gall. 27 Cork St, 2005; Water and Light Gall., 2005; oils and watercolours, Gall. 27 Cork St, 2011; *group shows:* Camden Arts Centre, 1990; Royal Acad. Summer Exhibn, 1990; Accrochage, Fischer Fine Art, 1990; Contemporary Art Soc. Mkt, 1990; Drawing Show, Thumb Gall., 1990; Art for Equality, ICA, 1991; Leicestershire Collection, 1992; Gillian Jason Contemporary Portraits Real and Imagined, 1993; Jason Rhodes Gp Show, 1995; Glyndebourne Fest. Opera, 1997–2003; Glyndebourne Ten for Ten Anniv. exhibn, 2004; Astana Opera and Ballet (Expo), 2017. Represented by BinghamFrench Ltd. *Recreations:* gardening, any displacement activity.

**MACMILLAN, Duncan;** *see* Macmillan, J. D.

**MACMILLAN, Very Rev. Gilleasbuig Iain,** KCVO 2014 (CVO 1999); FRSE; Minister of St Giles', The High Kirk of Edinburgh, 1973–2013; Chaplain to the Queen in Scotland, 1979–2014; Dean of the Order of the Thistle, 1989–2014; an Extra Chaplain to the Queen in Scotland, since 2014; *b* 21 Dec. 1942; *s* of Rev. Kenneth M. Macmillan and Mrs Mary Macmillan; *m* 1965, Maureen Stewart Thomson; one *d*. *Educ:* Oban High School; Univ. of Edinburgh. MA, BD. Asst Minister, St Michael's Parish, Linlithgow, 1967–69; Minister of Portree Parish, Isle of Skye, 1969–73. Extra Chaplain to the Queen in Scotland, 1978–79. Hon. Chaplain: Royal Scottish Academy, 1973–; Royal Coll. of Surgeons of Edinburgh, 1973–2014; Soc. of High Constables of City of Edinburgh, 1973–2014. FRSE 2005. Hon. FRCSE 1998. Hon. DD: Alma Coll., 1997; St Andrews, 2003; Dr *hc* Edinburgh, 1998. *Publications:* A Workable Belief, 1993; Understanding Christianity, 2004. *Address:* 207 Dalkeith Road, Edinburgh EH16 5DS. *T:* (0131) 667 5732. *Club:* New (Edinburgh).

**McMILLAN, Hamilton;** *see* McMillan, N. H.

**McMILLAN, Sir Iain (Macleod),** Kt 2015; CBE 2003; DL; Chairman, Skill Force Development Ltd, since 2016; Director, CBI Scotland, 1995–2014 (Assistant Director, 1993–95); *b* 25 April 1951; *s* of late William Catterall McMillan and Helen Macleod McMillan (*née* Paterson); *m* 1975, Giuseppina Silvana Pellegrini; three *s*. *Educ:* Bearsden Acad., Glasgow. AIB 1976, FCIB 1991; AIB (Scot) 1981, FCIBS 1997; FAIA 2004. Bank officer and various mgt and sen. mgt posts, TSB Gp plc, 1970–93; Liaison Officer for Scotland and Northern England, Royal Jubilee and Prince's Trusts, 1984–85 (on secondment). Board Member: Scottish Qualifications Authy, 1997–2006 (Vice Chm., 2004–06); Young Enterprise Scotland, 1999–2003; Scottish N Amer. Business Council, 1999–2015 (Chm., 2009–15); British Amer. Business Council, 2010–16 (Mem., Exec. Cttee, 2010–17); Chm., Scottish Business Educn Coalition, 2001–07; Member: Scottish Adv. Bd, Equal Opportunities Commn, 1995–2001; Cttee of Review into Careers Service, Scottish Exec., 1999–2000; Adv. Bd, Scottish Co-investment Fund, 2003–08; Adv. Bd, Scottish Enterprise Investments, 2008–10; Commn on Scottish Devolution, 2008–09; Literacy Commn, 2008–10; Standing Literacy Commn, 2011–15; Competition Appeal Tribunal, 2017–; Chm., Ind. Commn for Competitive and Fair Taxation in Scotland, 2015–16. Non-exec. Dir, Special Health Bd, Scottish Ambulance Service, 2000–08. Chm., Adv. Bd, Business Sch. (formerly Grad. Sch. of Business), Univ. of Strathclyde, 2005–. Trustee: Industrial Mission Trust, 2000–13 (Chm., 2008–13); Teaching Awards Trust, 2007–13; Carnegie Trust for Univs of Scotland, 2010–19; Grangemouth Spitfire Meml Trust, 2012–16; Chm., Work Place Chaplaincy Scotland, 2014–16. Mem., Skillforce Scottish Adv. Cttee, 2015–; mem. or former mem., various adv. bodies and public policy cttees and working gps in Scotland. FRSA 1994; CCMI 2002; FSQA 2007. Hon. Air Cdre, 602 (City of Glasgow) Sqdn, RAuxAF, 2009–; Selected Air Mem., Lowland Reserve Forces' and Cadets' Assoc., 2010–. Freeman, City of Glasgow, 2011. DL Stirling and Falkirk, 2019. *Recreations:* walking, reading. *Club:* Royal Air Force.

**MacMILLAN, Sir James (Loy),** Kt 2015: CBE 2004; PhD; composer and conductor; Professor of Theology, Imagination and the Arts, University of St Andrews, since 2015; Professor, Royal Conservatoire of Scotland, since 2014; b 16 July 1959; s of James MacMillan and Ellen MacMillan (née Loy); m 1983, Lynne Frew; one s two d. Educ: Edinburgh Univ. (BMus); Durham Univ. (PhD 1987). Lectr, Univ. of Manchester, 1986–88; Featured Composer: Musica Nova, Glasgow, 1990; Huddersfield Contemp. Music Fest., 1991; Edinburgh Fest., 1993; Raising Sparks Fest., S Bank and Barbican, 1997; Artistic Dir, Philharmonia, Music of Today, 1992–2002; composer/conductor, BBC Philharmonic, 2000–09; Principal Guest Conductor, Netherlands Radio Kamer Filharmonie, 2010–13. Founder and Artistic Dir, Cumnock Tryst, music festival, 2014–. FRSAMD 1996; FRNCM 2001; FRSCM 2001; FRSE 2007. Hon. FRIAS 1997. DUniv: Paisley, 1995; Open, 2001; Hon. DLitt: Strathclyde, 1996; UMIST, 2001; Hon. DMus: St Andrews, 2001; Glasgow, 2001; Abertay Dundee, 2004; Edinburgh, 2005; RSAMD, 2005; Newman Coll., Leicester, 2006; Durham, 2007; RCM, 2011. Gramophone Award, 1993; Classic CD Award, 1994; British Classical Music Award, 2006; British Composer Award, 2008; Ivor Novello Classical Music Award, 2009; Royal Medal, RSE, 2010; Assoc. of British Orchestras' Award, 2011. *Compositions* include: Busquéda (music theatre), 1988; Tryst (for orch.), 1989; The Berserking (piano concerto no 1), 1990; Confession of Isobel Gowdie (for orch.), 1990; Veni, Veni Emmanuel (percussion concerto), 1992; Visitatio Sepulchri (one-act opera), 1993; Seven Last Words (chorus and strings), 1994; Ines de Castro (opera), 1996; The World's Ransoming (concerto for cor anglais), 1996; 'Cello Concerto, 1996; Ninian (clarinet concerto), 1997; 14 Little Pictures (for piano trio), 1997; Vigil (symphony), 1997; Raising Sparks (for mezzo-sop. and ensemble), 1997; Quickening (for chorus, orch., boys' choir and four soloists), 1999; Symphony no 2, 1999; Mass (chorus and organ), 2000; Parthenogenesis (for soprano, baritone, actress and small ensemble), 2000; A Deep but Dazzling Darkness (for solo violin, ensemble and tape), 2002; O Bone Jesu (a cappella chorus), 2002; Symphony no 3, 2003; Piano Concerto No. 2, 2004; A Scotch Bestiary (for organ and orch.), 2004; Tenebrae Responsaries (a cappella chorus), 2006; Stomp (with Fate and Elvira) (concert overture for orch.), 2006; From Ayrshire (for violin and orch.), 2006; The Sacrifice (opera), 2007 (Royal Philharmonic Soc. Award, 2008); St John Passion (for baritone, chorus and orch.), 2008; Violin Concerto, 2009; Oboe Concerto, 2010; Clemency (chamber opera), 2011; Woman of the Apocalypse (full orch.), 2011–12; Gloria, 2012; Canite Tuba (brass band), 2012; Since it was the day of preparation… (bass solo, choir and 5 piece ensemble), 2012; Cecilia Virgo (a cappella chorus), 2012; He Rose (solo cello), 2012; St Luke Passion (two choirs, orch. and organ), 2013; Death of Oscar (orch.), 2013; Viola Concerto, 2014; Percussion Concerto No 2, 2014; A Rumoured Seed (a cappella chorus); Seven Angels (chorus and ensemble), 2014; Symphony No 4 (for orch.), 2014–15; Little Mass (children's chorus and orch.), 2015; Stabat Mater (a cappella chorus), 2016; European Requiem, 2016; Trombone Concerto, 2017; Saxophone Concerto, 2018; All the Hills and Vales Along (for solo tenor, chorus, brass band and strings), 2018; O Virgo Prudentissima, 2018; Symphony No 5 - Le grand inconnu, 2019. *Address*: c/o Boosey & Hawkes Music Publishers Ltd, Aldwych House, 71–91 Aldwych, WC2B 4HN. *T*: (020) 7054 7200.

**MACMILLAN, Prof. (John) Duncan,** PhD; FRSE; Curator, Talbot Rice Gallery, 1979–2004, and Professor of History of Scottish Art, 1994–2001, now Emeritus, University of Edinburgh; b 7 March 1939; s of late William Miller Macmillan and Mona Constance Mary Tweedie; m 1971, Vivien Rosemary Hinkley; two d. Educ: Gordonstoun Sch.; St Andrews Univ. (MA Hons 1961); Courtauld Inst., London (Dip. Hist. of Art 1964); Edinburgh Univ. (PhD 1974). Lectr, 1964–81, Curator of Univ. Collections, 1987–2002, Edinburgh Univ. Curator, RSE, 2008–12. Art critic: The Scotsman, 1994–2000, 2002–; Business am, 2000–02. Visiting Fellow: Yale Centre for British Art, 1991; Japan Soc. for Promotion of Science, 1995. Convener, Scottish Univ. Museums Gp, 1992–99; Chm., Edinburgh Galls Assoc., 1995–98; Vice-Chm., European Union Cultural Forum; Chm., Torvean Project Steering Gp, 1997–2000; Member: Council, Edinburgh Fest. Soc., 1991–97; Cttee, Univ. Museums Gp, 1992–99; Heritage Unit Adv. Bd, Robert Gordon Univ.; comité consultatif, French Inst., Edinburgh, 1997–. Member Editorial Board: Scotlands, 1994–98; British Art Jl, 1999–; Dundee Univ. Press, 2005–08. Hon. Keeper of Portraits, RCSE. Hon. RSA; FRSA; FRSE 2005 (Henry Duncan Prize, 2004). Hon. LLD Dundee, 2004. Andrew Fletcher of Saltoun Prize, Saltire Soc., 2005; Sir Walter Scott Medal, RSE, 2019. *Publications*: (jtly) Miró in America, 1983; Painting in Scotland: the Golden Age 1707–1843, 1986; Scottish Art 1460–1990, 1990 (Scottish Book of the Year, Saltire Soc., 1992), 2nd edn 2002; The Paintings of Steven Campbell: the story so far, 1993; Scottish Art in the Twentieth Century, 1994 (Scottish Arts Council Book Award, 1995), 2nd edn as Scottish Art in the Twentieth Century: 1890–2001, 2001; (jtly) Peter Brandes: stained glass, 1994; (jtly) Eugenio Carmi, 1996; Elizabeth Blackadder, 1999; (with Tom Hewlett) F. C. B. Cadell, 2011; Victoria Crowe, 2012; Scotland's Shrine: the Scottish National War Memorial, 2014; numerous exhibn catalogues, articles, etc. *Recreations*: walking, landscape photography. *Address*: 20 Nelson Street, Edinburgh EH3 6LJ. *T*: (0131) 556 7100; Wester Balnagrantach, Glen Urquhart, Inverness-shire. *T*: (01456) 450727.

**MACMILLAN, John Kenneth;** Regional Employment Judge (formerly Regional Chairman, Industrial, later Employment Tribunals), Nottingham, 1999–2012; fee-paid Employment Judge, East Midlands Region, 2012–18; b 8 July 1946; s of late Kenneth Lionel Macmillan, OBE and Marjorie Ethel Macmillan; m 1st, 1972, Mary Lister (marr. diss.); 2nd, 1977, Dawn Nelson (marr. diss.); one d; 3rd, 1995, Pauline Anne Swain; two step d. Educ: Carlton le Willows Grammar Sch., Nottingham. Admitted Solicitor, 1970; Asst Solicitor, 1970, Litigation Partner, 1971–84, Haden and Stretton, Solicitors. Pt-time Chm., 1981–87, full-time Chm., 1987–97, Industrial Tribunals, Birmingham; Mem., President's Trng Panel, 1992–2000. Ed., Employment Tribunals Members Handbook, 1999–2006; Principal Consulting Ed., Blackstone's Employment Law Practice, 2007–14 (a Consulting Ed., 2006–07). Co. Sec., Stafford Rangers FC Ltd, 2014–17. Hon. Sec., RSNC, 1992–2003. Trustee, Staffs Wildlife Trust, 1982–99, 2005–09; Chm., Colton Local Nature Reserve, 2014–. *Publications*: (contrib.) Sweet & Maxwell's Employment Court Practice, 2007; Blackstone's Guide to the Employment Tribunals Rules 2013 and the Fees Order, 2013. *Recreations*: bird watching, theatre, gardening, fly fishing, philosophy, non-league football. *Address*: c/o Employment Tribunals, Nottingham Justice Centre, Carrington Street, Nottingham NG2 1EE.

**MacMILLAN, Lt-Gen. Sir John Richard Alexander,** KCB 1988; CBE 1978 (OBE 1973); former fruit farmer; General Officer Commanding Scotland and Governor of Edinburgh Castle, 1988–91; b 8 Feb. 1932; m 1964, Belinda Lumley Webb; one s two d. Educ: Trinity Coll., Cambridge (BA 1953; MA 1958); rcds, psc. Commnd Argyll and Sutherland Highlanders, 2nd Lieut, 1953; GSO2 (Ops Int. Trng), Trucial Oman Scouts, 1963–64; BM, HQ 24 Inf. Bde, 1967–69; Chief Recruiting and Liaison Staff, Scotland, 1970; CO, 1st Bn The Gordon Highlanders, 1971–73; GSO1 (DS), Staff Coll., 1973–75; Col GS, Mil. Ops 4, 1975–76; Brig., 1976; Bde Comd, 39 Inf. Bde, 1977–78; RCDS 1979; COS, 1 (Br.) Corps, 1980–82; Maj.-Gen., 1982; GOC Eastern Dist, 1982–84; ACGS, MoD, 1984–87; Lt-Gen., 1988. Col, The Gordon Highlanders, 1978–86; Col Comdt, Scottish Div., 1986–91; Hon. Col, Aberdeen Univ. OTC, 1987–97. Chm. Exec. Cttee, Scottish Conservation Projects Trust, 1992–98; Chairman: Erskine Hosp. (formerly Princess Louise Scottish Hosp.), 1995–2000; HM Comrs for Queen Victoria Sch., Dunblane, 2000–03. DL Stirling and Falkirk, 1998–2007. *Address*: 14 Main Street, Thornhill, Stirling FK8 3PN.

**MacMILLAN, Prof. Margaret Olwen,** CH 2018; CC 2015 (OC 2005); DPhil; Warden, St Antony's College, Oxford, 2007–17; Professor of International History, University of Oxford, 2007–18, now Emeritus; Professor of History, University of Toronto, since 2003; b 23 Dec. 1943; d of Robert and Eluned MacMillan. Educ: Univ. of Toronto (BA Hons Mod. Hist. 1966); St Hilda's Coll., Oxford (BPhil Pols 1968; Hon. Fellow, 2007); St Antony's Coll., Oxford (DPhil 1974; Hon. Fellow, 2003). Prof. of Hist., 1975–2002, Chair, Hist. Dept, 1987–92, Ryerson Univ.; University of Toronto: Fellow, 1999, Provost, 2002–07, Hon. Fellow, 2009, Trinity Coll.; Sen. Fellow, Massey Coll., 2003. Trustee: Central European Univ., 2018–; Imperial War Mus., 2019–. Co-Editor (pt-time), Internat. Jl, 1995–2003. FRSL 2003. Hon. Fellow, Lady Margaret Hall, Oxford, 2017. Hon. FBA 2019. Hon. DCL: King's Coll., Halifax, 2004; Royal Mil. Coll., Kingston, 2004; Western Ontario, 2012; Bishop's, 2018; Hon. LLD Ryerson, 2005; Hon. DL: Calgary, 2015; Toronto, 2017; Memorial Univ., Newfoundland, 2018. *Publications*: Women of the Raj, 1988; (ed jtly) Canada and NATO: uneasy past, uncertain future, 1990; (ed jtly) The Uneasy Century: international relations 1900–1990, 1996; Peacemakers: the Paris Conference of 1919 and its attempt to end war, 2001, revised as Paris, 1919: six months that changed the world (Samuel Johnson Prize), 2002; (ed jtly and contrib.) Parties Long Estranged: Canadian-Australian relations, 2003; (jtly) Canada's House: Rideau Hall and the invention of a Canadian home, 2004; Seize the Hour: when Nixon met Mao, 2006; The Uses and Abuses of History, 2008; Stephen Leacock, 2009; The War that Ended Peace, 2013; History's People: personalities and the past, 2016. *Recreations*: opera, films, tennis, ski-ing, hiking. *Address*: St Antony's College, Oxford OX2 6JF. *Clubs*: Athenæum; Toronto Lawn Tennis.
*See also P. J. Snow.*

**MACMILLAN, Maureen;** Member (Lab) Highlands and Islands, Scottish Parliament, 1999–2007; b 9 Feb. 1943; m 1965, Michael Muirdon Macmillan, LLB; two s two d. Educ: Oban High Sch.; Edinburgh Univ. (MA Hons); Moray House. English Teacher, 1983–99. Co-founder, Ross-shire Women's Aid, 1980. Mem., EIS, 1980–.

**McMILLAN, Neil Macleod,** CMG 1997; Director of Political Affairs and Trade, EuroCommerce, since 2015; b 21 Oct. 1953; s of John Howard McMillan, CBE and Ruby Hassell McMillan (née Meggs); m 1st, 1978, Karin Lauritzen (marr. diss. 1985); 2nd, 1994, Lena Madvig Madsen; one s. Educ: Westminster City Sch.; Univ. of Regensburg; Univ. of Kiel, Germany; Exeter Univ. (BA Hons Mod. Langs 1977). Admin. Trainee, Dept of Prices and Consumer Protection, 1978–79; Dept of Industry, 1980–81; HEO (Develt), Dept of Trade, 1981–82; Private Sec. to Minister for Industry and IT, 1982–84; seconded to Govt Commn on Telecommunications Reform, Federal Min. of Research, Bonn, 1985; Principal, DTI, 1986–87; First Sec., UK Representation to EU, Brussels, 1987–91; Department of Trade and Industry: Dir, Internat. Communications Policy, 1991–98; Dir, EU Internal Trade Policy, 1998–2000; Dep. Perm. Rep., UK Mission to UN, Geneva, 2001–05; Dir, Europe, DTI, 2005–06; Dir and Dep. Hd, European Secretariat, Cabinet Office, 2006–08; Head, Nabucco Political Strategy, RWE Supply and Trading GmbH, 2008–11; Partner, Brunswick Gp LLP, 2011–14. Mem. Bd, Amer. Chamber of Commerce to EU, Brussels, 2013–15. Chairman: European Telecommunications Regulatory Cttee, 1992–96; WTO Negotiating Gp on Basic Telecommunications Services, 1994–97; World Telecommunications Policy Forum, 1998; WTO Budget Cttee, 2002–03. *Recreations*: reading, church architecture. *Club*: Athenæum.

**McMILLAN, (Norman) Hamilton,** CMG 1997; OBE 1984; Managing Director, Zwischenzug Ltd, 2006–16; b 28 Oct. 1946; s of Neil McMillan and Alma McMillan (née Hall); m 1969, Dr Carolyn Vivienne Barltrop; one s one d. Educ: Brentwood Sch.; Balliol Coll., Oxford. Joined HM Diplomatic Service, 1968; Third Sec., FCO, 1968–70; Third, later Second Sec., Vienna, 1970–72; Second, later First Sec., FCO, 1972–77; First Secretary: Rome, 1977–81; Dhaka, 1981–84; Cairo, 1984–86; Counsellor: (Chancery), Vienna, 1989–93; FCO, 1993–97. Dir of Ops, CIEX Ltd, subseq. Penumbra, 1997–2003; Gp Security Advr, ABN-AMRO Bank, Amsterdam, 2003–06. *Recreations*: board games, music with bite, cosmology, ceramics. *Club*: Oriental.

**McMILLAN, Stuart;** Member (SNP) Greenock and Inverclyde, Scottish Parliament, since 2016 (Scotland West, 2007–16); b 6 May 1972; s of Henry McMillan and Janet McMillan; m 2003, Alexandra; two d. Educ: Univ. of Abertay Dundee (BA Hons Europ. Business Mgt and Langs; MBA Europ. 1997). Supply Analyst, IBM UK Ltd, 1998–2000; Parly Researcher, SNP Westminster Gp, 2000–03; Office Manager to Bruce McFee, MSP, 2003–07. *Recreations*: play bagpipes, football, music, travel, reading. *Address*: (office) 26 Grey Place, Greenock PA15 1YF. *T*: (01475) 720930. *E*: stuart.mcmillan.msp@parliament.scot.

**McMILLAN, Prof. Trevor John,** PhD; Vice-Chancellor, Keele University, since 2015; b Gateshead, 2 Oct. 1959; s of Emmerson McMillan and Margaret McMillan; m 1982, Christine Hanglow; one d. Educ: Lord Lawson Comp. Sch., Birtley; Lancaster Univ. (BSc Biol Scis 1981); Inst. of Cancer Res., Univ. of London (PhD Biophys 1984). Res. Fellow, ICRF, London, 1984–87; Hd, DNA Damage and Repair Lab., Inst. of Cancer Res., Surrey, 1987–95; Lancaster University: Reader, 1995–97, Peel Prof. of Cancer Biol., 1997–2013; Dean, Inst. of Envmtl and Nat. Scis, 2001–05; Pro Vice-Chancellor (Res.), 2005–13; Dep. Vice-Chancellor and Provost, Keele Univ., 2014–15. Member: Cttee on Med. Aspects of Radiation in Envmt, DoH, 1998–2006; Adv. Gp on Ionising Radiation, HPA, 2006–14; Nat. Adv. Gp on Concordat for Early Careers Researchers, 2010–; Adv. Gp on Genomics in Medicine, Health Educn England, 2014–; Res. and Knowledge Exchange Strategic Adv. Bd, HEFCE, 2014–18; non-executive Director: Parly Counsel Office, Cabinet Office, 2008–11; N Lancs Teaching PCT, 2008–12; Lancs Teaching Hosps Foundn Trust, 2011–13. Chairman: Res. Adv. Cttee, NW Univs Assoc., 2008–12; Exec. Mgt Cttee, N8 Gp of N Res. Intensive Univs, 2008–13; Res. and Enterprise Gp, 1994 Gp of Univs, 2009–13. Member: Bd, British Oncol Assoc., 1995–2000 (Treas., 1995–2000); Council, BIR, 1996–99 (Chm., Biol. Cttee, 1996–99); Educn and Res. Cttees, RCR, 1997–2009; Council, Internat. Assoc. of Radiation Res., 2002–08; Chm., Assoc. of Radiation Res., 1998–2000. FRSB (FSB 2011). Hon. MRCP 2002; Hon. FRCR 2007. *Publications*: (jtly) Molecular Biology for Clinical Oncologists, 1993, 2nd edn 1996; articles on DNA damage and repair in relation to use of ionizing radiation in cancer treatment and harmful effects of long wavelength UV light. *Recreations*: family, theatre, golf. *Address*: Vice-Chancellor's Office, Claus Moser Building, Keele University, Newcastle Under Lyme, Staffs ST5 5BG. *T*: (01782) 733333, *Fax*: (01782) 734181. *E*: t.j.mcmillan@keele.ac.uk.

**McMILLAN-SCOTT, Edward;** Member, Yorkshire and the Humber Region, 1999–2014 (C, 1999–2009, Ind C, 2009–10, Lib Dem, 2010–14), and Vice-President, 2004–14, European Parliament (York, 1984–94; North Yorkshire, 1994–99); b 15 Aug. 1949; s of late Walter Theodore Robin McMillan-Scott, ARIBA and Elizabeth Maud Derrington Hudson; m 1972, Henrietta Elizabeth Rumney Hudson, solicitor; two d. Educ: Blackfriars School, Llanarth; Blackfriars School, Laxton; Exeter Technical College. Tour director in

Europe, Scandinavia, Africa and USSR, 1968–75; PR exec., then parly consultant, 1976–84; political adviser to Falkland Islands Govt, London office 1983–84. European Parliament: Member: For. Affairs and Security Cttee, 1989–2004; Transport Cttee, 1989–92; Chm., 1979 Cttee (Cons. back-bench cttee), 1994–95; Leader, Conservatives in EP, 1997–2001 (Treas., 1995); Founder, 1990, and Rapporteur, EU Initiative for Democracy and Human Rights; Chm., Audit Panel, 2004–12; Vice-Pres. (Human Rights and Democracy portfolio), 2004–14; Chm., Election Observer Missions, Palestine 2005 and 2006, Egypt 2005. Founder, 2011, Patron, 2014–, campaign for Single Seat in Brussels; Coordinator, Where Next for Brexit? forum, 2017–. Contested (Lib Dem): Yorks and the Humber Reg., EP, 2014; Normanton, Pontefract and Castleford, 2015; W Worcs, 2017. Mem. Bd, Cons. Party, 1998–2001. Trustee, BBC World Service Trust, 1999–2009. Patron, European Movt UK, 2014–. *Recreations:* music, reading. *Address:* Wick House Farm, Wick, Pershore, Worcestershire WR10 3NU.

**McMORRIN, Anna Rhiannon;** MP (Lab) Cardiff North, since 2017; two *d*; partner, Alun Davies, *qv. Educ:* Univ. of Southampton (BA French); Cardiff Univ. (Postgrad. Dip. Journalism). Advr to Welsh Govt, 2008–14. Mem., Envmtl Audit Cttee, 2017–, Welsh Affairs Cttee, 2017–, H of C. *Address:* House of Commons, SW1A 0AA.

**McMULLAN, Rt Rev. Gordon;** Bishop of Down and Dromore, 1986–97; *b* 1934; *m* 1957, Kathleen Davidson; two *s. Educ:* Queen's Univ., Belfast (BSc Econ 1961, PhD 1971); Ridley Hall, Cambridge; Dipl. in Religious Studies (Cantab) 1978; ThD Geneva Theol Coll., 1988; MPhil TCD, 1990; DMin Univ. of the South, USA, 1995; DPhil Ulster, 2004. Deacon 1962, priest 1963, dio. Down; Curate of Ballymacarrett, 1962–67; Central Adviser on Christian Stewardship to Church of Ireland, 1967–70; Curate of St Columba, Knock, Belfast, 1970–71; Bishop's Curate, St Brendan's, East Belfast, 1971–76; Rector of St Columba, Knock, Belfast, 1976–80; Archdeacon of Down, 1979–80; Bishop of Clogher, 1980–86. Merrill Fellow/Resident Fellow, Harvard Divinity Sch., 1997–98. Hon. DCL Univ. of the South, USA, 2001. *Publications:* A Cross and Beyond, 1976; We are called …, 1977; Everyday Discipleship, 1979; Reflections on St Mark's Gospel, 1984; Growing Together in Prayer, 1990; Reflections on St Luke's Gospel, 1994; Opposing Violence/Building Bridges, 1996; The Story of Saint Martin's Church and the Southern Church Mission to Ballymacarrett, 2008. *Address:* Abbeyfield House, 2A Ward Avenue, Bangor, Co. Down, N Ireland BT20 5JW.

**McMULLAN, Lynda;** Director of Commercial and Finance, Metropolitan Police, since 2014; *b* Belfast, 1966; *d* of Noel McMullan and Pamela McMullan; *m* 1998, Phillip Drysdale; one *d. Educ:* Simon Langton Girls' Grammar Sch.; Newcastle Univ. (BA Hons Finance and Accounting). Mem. CIPFA 1992. Gp Accountant, Nottingham CC, 1989–96; Hd, Corporate Finance, Southwark LBC, 1996–2000; Actg Dir of Finance, Hammersmith and Fulham LBC, 2000–02; Co. Finance Manager, 2002–06, Dir of Finance and Procurement, 2006–11, Kent CC; Asst Auditor Gen., Nat. Audit Office, 2011–13; Dir of Public Resources and Perf., Mayor of London's Office for Policing and Crime, 2013–14. *Recreations:* running, reading, enjoying friends and family. *Address:* Metropolitan Police, New Scotland Yard, Victoria Embankment, SW1A 2JL. *T:* (020) 7230 4321. *E:* Lynda.McMullan@met.police.uk.

**McMULLEN, Prof. David Lawrence,** FBA 1994; Professor of Chinese, University of Cambridge, 1989–2006, now Professor Emeritus; Fellow of St John's College, Cambridge, since 1967; *b* 10 Aug. 1939; twin *s* of late Alexander Lawrence McMullen and Muriel Felicité McMullen (*née* Sikes); *m* 1983, Sarah Jane Clarice Croft; two *d. Educ:* Monkton Combe Sch., Bath; St John's Coll., Cambridge (BA, MA, PhD). National Service, RAF, 1957–59. Taiwan Min. of Educn Schol., 1963–64; Harkness Commonwealth Fellowship, 1965–67; Asst Lectr 1967, Lectr 1972, in Chinese Studies, Cambridge Univ. Pres., British Assoc. for Chinese Studies, 1985–87. *Publications:* Concordances and Indexes to Chinese Texts, 1975; State and Scholars in T'ang China, 1988; contribs to jls of E Asian studies. *Recreation:* gardening. *Address:* Grove Cottage, 35 High Street, Grantchester, Cambridge CB3 9NF. *T:* (01223) 840206.

*See also* I. J. McMullen.

**McMULLEN, Dr Ian James,** FBA 2001; Lecturer in Japanese, University of Oxford, 1972–2006 (Pro-Proctor, 1986–87); Fellow, Pembroke College, Oxford, 1989–2006 (Vicegerent, 2003–04), Fellow Emeritus, since 2006; Fellow Emeritus, St Antony's College, Oxford, since 2009; *b* 10 Aug. 1939; twin *s* of late Alexander Lawrence McMullen and Muriel Felicité McMullen (*née* Sikes); *m* 1970, Bonnie Shannon; one *s. Educ:* Monkton Combe Sch., Bath; St John's Coll., Cambridge (BA, MA; PhD 1969). Nat. Service, RAF, 1957–59. Schol., Min. of Educn, Japan, 1963–64; Lectr, 1965, Asst Prof., 1966–70, Associate Prof., 1970–72, Univ. of Toronto; Fellow, St Antony's Coll., Oxford, 1972–89. Pres., British Assoc. Japanese Studies, 1997–98. *Publications:* Genji Gaiden: the origins of Kumazawa Banzan's commentary on the Tale of Genji, 1991; Idealism, Protest and the Tale of Genji, 1999; (ed) Murasaki Shikibu's, The Tale of Genji, 2019; The Worship of Confucius in Japan, 2019; contribs to jls of E Asian studies. *Recreation:* gardening. *Address:* Wilton Lodge, 44 Osberton Road, Oxford OX2 7NU. *T:* (01865) 559859.

*See also* D. L. McMullen.

**McMURRAY, Dr Cecil Hugh,** CBE 2002; FRSC, FIFST; Managing Director, Sci-Tec Consultancy, 2003–18; *b* 19 Feb. 1942; *s* of late Edwin McMurray and Margaret McMurray (*née* Smyth); *m* 1967, Ann Stuart; two *s* one *d. Educ:* Royal Belfast Academical Instn; Greenmount Agricl Coll.; Queen's University, Belfast (BSc 1965; BAgr 1966); PhD Bristol, 1970. FRSC 1981; FIFST 1987. Res. Fellow, Dept of Chem., Harvard Univ., 1970–72; Head of Biochem. Dept, Vet. Res. Lab., Dept of Agric. for NI, 1972–84; Prof. of Food and Agricl Chem., QUB, and concurrently DCSO, Dept of Agric. for NI, 1984–88; CSO, Dept of Agric. and Rural Develt for NI, 1988–2002. Hon. Prof., QUB, 1998–. Expert Advr, WHO, 1983, 1986; Assessor to: AFRC, 1988–94; Priorities Bd for R&D in Agric. and Food, 1988–93; Technology Bd for NI, 1988–92; NERC, 1992–93; Adv. Cttee on microbiol safety of food, 1992–2002; Dir, NI Public Sector Overseas, 1994–2002. Delivered overseas projects on behalf of World Bank and EU in Azerbaijan, Uzbekistan, Tajikistan, Kazakhstan (also for Min. of Agriculture in Kazakhstan), Serbia, Montenegro, Kyrgyz Republic, Philippines, Jamaica and Cambodia. Mem., Steering Gp on chem. aspects of food surveillance, 1992–95. Pres., Agricl Gp, BAAS, 1986–87. Non-exec. Dir, Agri-Food and Biosciences Institute, 2012–17; Ind. Mem. (Sci.), TB Strategic Partnership Gp, 2014–17. Mem. Cttee, Coronary Prevention Gp, 1985–89. Trustee, Agricl Inst. for NI, 1985–2002; Mem. Governing Body, Rowett Res. Inst., Aberdeen, 1986–89, 1993–2003. Mem. Editl Bd, Fertiliser Res., 1985–92. *Publications:* (ed jtly) Detection Methods for Irradiated Foods: current status, 1996; over 100 scientific publications incl. articles in Biochemical Jl, Jl of Amer. Chemical Soc., Clin. Chem., CIBA Foundn Symposia, Jl of Chromatography, British Vet. Jl, Vet. Record, Jl Assoc. of Analytical Chem., Trace Metals in Man and Domestic Animals, Biology of Total Envmt. *Recreations:* reading, photography, walking. *Address:* 6 Pinehill Road, Bangor, Co. Down BT19 6SA.

**McMURTRY, Sir David (Roberts),** Kt 2001; CBE 1994; RDI 1989; FRS 2011; CEng, FREng, FIMechE; Co-founder and Executive Chairman, Renishaw plc (formerly Renishaw Electrical Ltd), since 1973 (Chief Executive, 1973–2018); *b* Dublin, 5 March 1940. FREng 2001. Formerly with Rolls Royce plc. *Address:* Renishaw plc, New Mills, Wotton-under-Edge, Glos GL12 8JR.

**McMURTRY, Hon. (Roland) Roy,** OC 2009; OOnt 2007; Senior Counsel, Hull & Hull LLP, since 2014; Chief Justice of Ontario, 1996–2007 (Associate Chief Justice, 1991–94, Chief Justice, 1994–96, Ontario Court of Justice (General Division)); *b* 31 May 1932; *s* of Roland Roy McMurtry and Doris Elizabeth Belcher; *m* 1957, Ria Jean Macrae; three *s* three *d. Educ:* St Andrew's Coll., Aurora, Ont; Trinity Coll., Univ. of Toronto (BA Hons); Osgoode Hall Law Sch., Toronto (LLB). Called to the Bar of Ontario, 1958; QC 1970. Partner: Benson, McMurtry, Percival & Brown, Toronto, 1958–75; Blaney, McMurtry, Stapells, 1988–91; Counsel, Gowling Lafleur Henderson LLP, until 2014. Elected to Ontario Legislature, 1975; re-elected, 1977 and 1981; Attorney General for Ontario, 1975–85; Solicitor General for Ontario, 1978–82. High Comr in UK, 1985–88. Chancellor, York Univ., Canada, 2008–14. Freeman, City of London, 1986. Hon. LLD: Ottawa, 1983; Law Soc. of Upper Canada, 1984; Leeds, 1988; York, 1991; Toronto, 1998. *Recreations:* painting, ski-ing, tennis. *Address:* Hull & Hull LLP, 141 Adelaide Street West, Suite 1700, Toronto, ON M5H 3L5, Canada. *Clubs:* Albany, York (Toronto).

**McMURTRY, Stanley, (Mac),** MBE 2004; social and political cartoonist, Daily Mail, 1970–2018; *b* 4 May 1936; *s* of Stanley Harrison McMurtry and Janet Lind McMurtry; *m* 1st, 1958, Maureen Flaye (marr. diss. 1980); one *s* one *d;* 2nd, 1981, Janet Elizabeth Rattle (marr. diss. 2002); 3rd, 2003, Elizabeth Mary Vaughan (*d* 2017). *Educ:* Sharmans Cross Secondary Sch., Birmingham; Birmingham Coll. of Art. Cartoon film animator, 1956–65; social and political cartoonist, Daily Sketch, 1968–70; freelance cartoonist, for Punch and other magazines, 1966–; TV scriptwriter with Bernard Cookson, for Tommy Cooper and Dave Allen, 1973–76. Social and Political Cartoonist of the Year, 1983, Master Cartoonist, 2000, Cartoonists Club of GB; Cartoonist of Year Award, 1982, 1984 and 1999, UK Press Gazette; Cartoonist of the Year, What the Papers Say Awards, 2003, 2007; Political Cartoonist of the Year, 2007, Lifetime Achievement Award, 2010, Cartoon Art Trust; Cartoonist of Year, Soc. of Editors, 2016, 2018. *Publications:* The Bunjee Venture (for children), 1977 (cartoon film, 1979); Mac's Year Books, annually, 1980–; contrib. short story to Knights of Madness, ed Peter Haining, 1998. *Recreations:* golf, writing. *Clubs:* Chelsea Arts, Saints and Sinners (Chm., 2015–16).

**McNAB, Angela;** Chief Executive, Camden and Islington Foundation Trust, since 2016; *b* London, 1 April 1957; *d* of Bernard and Doris Hammond; *m* 1st; two *s* one *d;* 2nd, 2005, Carl Powell. *Educ:* Open Univ. (BA Hons); South Bank Univ. (MSc). Nat. Hosps Coll. of Speech Scis (LCST). Speech and language therapist, 1978–92; gen. manager posts, Mid Essex Community and Mental Health Trust, 1992–99; Sen. Policy Manager, Nat. Sexual Health and HIV Strategy, DoH, 1999–2001; Chief Executive: Chingford, Wanstead and Woodford PCT, 2001–02; HFEA, 2002–08; on secondment as Dir of Public Health Delivery, DoH, 2007–08; Chief Executive: NHS Luton, and NHS Bedfordshire, 2008–12; Kent and Medway NHS and Social Care Partnership Trust, 2012–16. Mem. Bd, Council for Registration of Forensic Practitioners, 2006–10. Mem. Council, Univ. of Kent, 2014–. *Publications:* contrib. health and scientific jls, incl. Cell Stem Cell. *Recreations:* running, theatre, family. *T:* 07860 114553. *E:* angela.mcnab@me.com.

**MACNAB of Macnab, James William Archibald;** The Macnab; 24th Chief of Clan Macnab; Director, Country House Sales, Savills, since 1999; *b* Edinburgh, 22 March 1963; *er s* of James Charles Macnab of Macnab and Hon. Diana Mary Macnab of Macnab, *er d* of Baron Kilmany (Life Peer), 1st Bt, MC, PC; *S* father, 2013; *m* 1994, Dr Jane Louise Mackintosh; one *s* one *d. Educ:* Glenalmond Coll.; RAC Cirencester. MRICS. With Savills, 1987–. Mem., Royal Co. of Archers, Queen's Bodyguard in Scotland. Mem. Exec., Standing Council of Scottish Clan Chiefs. *Recreations:* golf, walking, Rugby, travel. *Heir: s* James David Macnab, younger of Macnab, *b* 27 Dec. 2000. *Address:* 22 Royal Crescent, Edinburgh EH3 6QA. *T:* (0131) 247 3711. *E:* jmacnab@savills.com. *Clubs:* Royal & Ancient Golf (St Andrews); Craigielaw Golf (East Lothian).

**McNAB, John Stanley;** Chief Executive, Port of Tilbury London Ltd (formerly Port of Tilbury (Port of London Authority)), 1987–96; *b* 23 Sept. 1937; *s* of Robert Stanley McNab and Alice Mary McNab; *m* 1st, 1961, Carol Ford (marr. diss. 1978); two *d;* 2nd, 1980, Jacqueline Scammell (marr. diss. 1997); 3rd, 2001, Susan Cole. *Educ:* Gravesend Grammar Sch. FCCA 1976; FCIT 1992. Nat. Service, Royal Engineers, Libya, 1956–58. Port of London Authority: joined 1954; Accountant, India and Millwall Docks, 1965, Upper Docks, 1970; Man. Dir, PLA (Thames) Stevedoring, 1973; Dir, Upper Docks, 1974; Exec. Dir (Manpower) and Group Board Mem., 1978; Dir, Tilbury, 1983. Director: Internat. Transport Ltd, 1992–96; Airflights Direct Ltd, 2000–08. FRSA 1991; MCMI (MBIM 1970). Freeman: City of London, 1988; Co. of Watermen and Lightermen of River Thames, 1988. *Recreations:* golf, swimming, DIY, learning Spanish and Portuguese. *Address:* 48 Daines Way, Thorpe Bay, Essex SS1 3PQ. *T:* (01702) 587060.

**MACNAGHTEN, Sir Malcolm Francis,** 12th Bt *cr* 1836, of Bushmills House, co. Antrim; *b* 21 Sept. 1956; *s* of Sir Patrick Alexander Macnaghten, 11th Bt and of Marianne (*née* Schaefer); *S* father, 2007; *m* 1991, Yvonne Sonia-Louise Greenfield; three *d. Heir: b* Edward Alexander Macnaghten [*b* 24 July 1958; *m* 1992, Kon Foong, *d* of Fook Pang; one *s* one *d*].

**MACNAGHTEN, Prof. Philip Martin,** PhD; Professor of Technology and International Development, Knowledge, Technology and Innovation Group, Wageningen University, Netherlands, since 2015; *b* 6 Aug. 1965; *s* of Antony Martin Macnaghten and Catherine Frances Macnaghten (*née* Young); *m* 2005, Simone Clementino Soares; two *d*, and one step *s. Educ:* Univ. of Southampton (BA Psychol. 1987); Univ. of Exeter (PhD Psychol. 1991). University of Lancaster: Res. Associate, Centre for Study of Envmtl Change, 1992–94; British Acad. Postdoctoral Fellow, 1995–97; Lectr, 1998–2002; Sen. Lectr, 2003–06; University of Durham: Dir, Inst. of Hazard and Risk Res., 2006–08; Prof. of Geography, 2006–15. Vis. Prof., Dept of Sci. and Technol. Policy, Univ. of Campinas, 2012–15. Coordinator, Deepening Ethical Engagement and Participation in Emerging Nanotechnologies proj., 2006–09; GM Futuros proj., 2012–14. Mem., Strategic Adv. Panel, EPSRC, 2011–14. FRSA. *Publications:* (jtly) Uncertain World: GMOs, food and public attitudes in Britain, 1997; (with J. Urry) Contested Natures, 1998; (jtly) Wising Up: the public and new technologies, 2000; (ed with J. Urry) Bodies of Nature, 2001; Embodying the Environment in Everyday Life Practices, 2003; Nanotechnology, Governance and Public Deliberation: what role for the social sciences; (jtly) Reconfiguring Responsibility: deepening debate on nanotechnology, 2009; (jtly) Developing a framework for responsible innovation, 2013; (ed with S. Carro-Ripalda) Governing Agricultural Sustainability: global lessons from GM crops, 2015. *Recreations:* reading, travel, film, cooking, hiking, dog walking. *Address:* Knowledge, Technology and Innovation Group, Leeuwenborch, Hollandseweg 1, 6706 KN Wageningen, Netherlands. *E:* philip.macnaghten@wur.nl.

**McNAIR,** family name of **Baron McNair**.

**McNAIR**, 3rd Baron *cr* 1955, of Gleniffer; **Duncan James McNair**; Chairman and Managing Director, Applied Learning Techniques International Ltd, 2004; *b* 26 June 1947; *s* of 2nd Baron McNair and Vera, *d* of Theodore James Faithfull; *S* father, 1989. *Educ*: Bryanston. Former Mem., Parly Gps on Drug Misuse, Alcohol Misuse, Population Develt and Reproductive Health; Vice Chm., Parly Waterways Gp, 1995–99. Mem., Sub-Cttee E (Envmt), EC Select Cttee, H of L, 1990–92. Dir, British Anti-Trafficking Orgn Ltd, 2000–. Member: Resource Use Institute Ltd, 1994–; Adv. Bd, Effective Educn Assoc., 1996–; Council for Human Rights and Religious Freedom, 1996–; Exec. Cttee, Health Freedom Movt UK, 2002–; Exec. Cttee, Commonwealth Forum for Project Mgt, 2002–. Dir, Chelkin Ltd, 2001. Chm., Unitax Assoc., 1994–. Co-Vice-Patron, Nat. Police Community Trust, 2001–. *Heir: b* Hon. William Samuel Angus McNair [*b* 19 May 1958; *m* 1981, Emma Procter (marr. diss. 1990); one *s* one *d*].

**MACNAIR, Charles Neville**; QC (Scot.) 2002; Sheriff of Tayside, Central and Fife at Dunfermline, since 2014 (at Cupar, 2009–14, at Dundee, 2014); *b* 18 March 1955; *s* of late James T. H. Macnair, MC, and of Dr Margaret E. Macnair (*née* Cameron); *m* 1987, Patricia Anne Dinning; two *d*. *Educ*: Bryanston Sch.; Aberdeen Univ. (LLB). Commnd Queen's Own Highlanders, 1977–80. Apprentice solicitor, Simpson & Marwick WS, Edinburgh, 1980–82; Solicitor: Brodies WS, Edinburgh, 1982–85; Peterkins, Aberdeen, 1985–87; Advocate, 1988–; Sheriff (pt-time), 2005–06; Floating Sheriff of Tayside, Central and Fife, 2006–09. Mem., Youth Court Feasibility Project Gp, Scottish Exec., 2002. Chm., Child and Family Law Gp, Faculty of Advocates, 2002–06. Served TA, 1980–87 and 1990–92. *Recreations*: reading, walking, sailing. *Address*: Sheriff Court House, 1/6 Carnegie Drive, Dunfermline, Fife KY12 7HJ.

**McNAIR-WILSON, Sir Patrick (Michael Ernest David)**, Kt 1989; consultant; *b* 28 May 1929; *s* of Dr Robert McNair-Wilson; *m* 1953, Diana Evelyn Kitty Campbell Methuen-Campbell (*d* 2015), *d* of Hon. Laurence Methuen-Campbell; one *s* four *d*. *Educ*: Eton. Exec. in French Shipping Co., 1951–53; various appointments at Conservative Central Office, 1954–58; Staff of Conservative Political Centre, 1958–61; Director, London Municipal Society, 1961–63; Executive with The British Iron and Steel Federation, 1963–64. Partner, Ferret PR and Public Affairs, 1995–2000. Dir, Photo-Me International Plc, 1996–2005. MP (C): Lewisham W, 1964–66; New Forest, Nov. 1968–1997. Opposition Front Bench Spokesman on fuel and power, 1965–66; Vice-Chm., Conservative Parly Power Cttee, 1969–70; PPS to Minister for Transport Industries, DoE, 1970–74; Opposition Front Bench Spokesman on Energy, 1974–76; Chm., Jt Lords and Commons Select Cttee on Private Bill Procedure, 1987–88; Mem., Select Cttee on Members' Interests, 1985–86. Editor of The Londoner, 1961–63. *Recreations*: sailing, pottery, flying. *Address*: Godfrey's Farm, Beaulieu, Hants SO42 7YP.

**McNAIRNEY, John Walter**; Chief Planner, Scottish Government, since 2012; *b* East Calder, West Lothian, 12 Sept. 1957; *s* of John McNairney and Grace McNairney; *m* 1989, Ellen Parr; one *s* one *d*. *Educ*: St Mary's Acad., Bathgate; Dundee Univ. (BSc Town and Regl Planning); Edinburgh Napier Univ. (MBA). Consultant, Montgomery Forgan Associates, 1984–87; Town Planner, Fife Council, 1987–99; Policy Manager, Transport Gp, Scottish Office, 1999–2002; Hd, Freedom of Information Br., 2002–05, Asst Chief Planner, 2005–12, Scottish Exec., subseq. Scottish Govt. *Recreations*: walking, reading, football. *Address*: 2–H–73, Scottish Government, Victoria Quay, Edinburgh EH6 6QQ. *T*: (0131) 244 7528, 07795 618393. *E*: john.mcnairney@gov.scot.

**McNALLY**, family name of **Baron McNally**.

**McNALLY, Baron** *cr* 1995 (Life Peer), of Blackpool in the county of Lancashire; **Tom McNally**; PC 2005; *b* 20 Feb. 1943; *s* of John P. McNally and Elizabeth May (*née* McCarthy); *m* 1st, 1970, Eileen Powell (marr. diss. 1990); 2nd, 1990, Juliet Lamy Hutchinson; two *s* one *d*. *Educ*: College of St Joseph, Blackpool; University Coll., London (BScEcon; Fellow 1995). President of Students' Union, UCL, 1965–66; Vice-Pres., Nat. Union of Students, 1966–67; Asst Gen. Sec. of Fabian Society, 1966–67; Labour Party researcher, 1967–68; Internat. Sec. of Labour Party, 1969–74; Political Adviser to: Foreign and Commonwealth Sec., 1974–76; Prime Minister, 1976–79. Public Affairs Adviser, GEC, 1983–84; Dir-Gen., Retail Consortium, and Dir, British Retailers Association, 1985–87; Head of Public Affairs, Hill & Knowlton, 1987–93; Head of Public Affairs, 1993–96, Vice-Chm., 1996–2004, Shandwick Consultants, then Weber Shandwick Worldwide, subseq. Weber Shandwick. MP (Lab 1979–81, SDP 1981–83) Stockport S; contested (SDP) Stockport, 1983. SDP Parly spokesman on educn and sport, 1981–83. Mem., Select Cttee on Industry and Trade, 1979–83. House of Lords: Dep. Leader, 2001–04, Leader, 2004–13, Lib Dems; Dep. Leader, 2010–13; Minister of State, MoJ, 2010–13. Chm., Youth Justice Bd, 2014–17. Trustee, Nat. Liberal Club. Mem. of Court, Univ. of Hertfordshire, 2006–. FRSA; FCIPR. Hon. LLD Hertfordshire, 2010. *Recreations*: watching sport, reading political biographies. *Address*: House of Lords, SW1A 0PW. *E*: mcnallyt@parliament.uk.

**McNALLY, Eryl Margaret**; Chairman, National Energy Foundation, 2004–07; *b* 11 April 1942; *d* of late Llywelyn Williams, MP and Elsie Williams; *m* 1964, James Frederick McNally; one *s* one *d*. *Educ*: Newbridge Grammar Sch.; Bristol Univ. (BA Langs); University Coll., Swansea (PGCE); Open Univ. (BSc 2006; BSc Hons Psychol. 2013; MSc 2016). Modern langs teacher, 1964–84; advisory work, Bucks CC, 1985–93; freelance schools inspector, OFSTED, 1993–94; MEP (Lab) Beds and Milton Keynes, 1994–99, Eastern Region, England, 1999–2004. Councillor: Abbots Langley Parish Council, 1970–73; Watford RDC, 1972–74; Three Rivers DC, 1973–77; Herts CC, 1986–95. Hon. LLD Herts, 2000; Hon. DSc Cranfield, 2003. Chevalier, Légion d'Honneur (France), 2002. *Publications*: articles on language teaching and teacher training in professional jls. *Recreations*: learning languages, reading, world music, films. *Address*: 30 Follet Drive, Abbots Langley, Herts WD5 0LP. *T*: (01923) 662711.

**McNALLY, John**; MP (SNP) Falkirk, since 2015; *b* Denny, 1 Feb. 1951; *s* of John and Rose McNally; *m* 1980, Sandra Chalmers; one *s* one *d*. *Educ*: St Patrick's Primary Sch., Denny; St Modan's High Sch., Stirling. Hairdresser, 1965–; salon owner, 1970–. Mem. (SNP), Falkirk Council, 2005–15. *Recreations*: cycling, golf. *Address*: House of Commons, SW1A 0AA. *T*: (020) 7219 6525.

**McNALLY, Shaun George**, CBE 2008; Chief Executive Officer, and Director, Legal Aid Casework, Legal Aid Agency, since 2016; *b* Newcastle-upon-Tyne, 8 June 1967; *s* of William and Jane Bruce McNally; *m* 1993, Karen Leah Ruddy; one *s* one *d*. *Educ*: St Edmund Campion RC Comprehensive Sch.; Univ. of Westminster (Postgrad. Dip. Business Admin and Mgt (Dist.) 1996); Major Projects Leadership Acad., Univ. of Oxford. Admin Officer, Newcastle County Court, 1985–90; Asst to HEO Personnel and Finance Officer, 1990–92; Finance and Perf. Manager (HEO), 1992–97; Temp. Gp Manager, Court Service, 1997–98; Finance and Perf. Manager, Wales and Chester Circuit, 1998–2001; Court Service, then HM Courts Service, later HM Courts and Tribunal Service: Gp Manager, Lancs and Cumbria, 2001–04; Area Dir, Merseyside, 2004–06; Area Dir, Cheshire and Merseyside, 2006–08; Regl Dir, NW, 2008; Dir, Ops and Performance, 2008–11; Dir, Crime, 2011–12; Dir, Case Mgt, Legal Aid Agency, 2012–16. *Recreations*: walking the dog, keeping fit, squash, football, horse riding, reading, cooking. *Address*: Legal Aid Agency, 102 Petty France, SW1H 9AJ. *T*: 07870 856079. *E*: shaun.mcnally@justice.gov.uk.

**McNAMARA, Prof. John Michael**, DPhil; FRS 2012; Professor of Mathematics and Biology, University of Bristol, 1995–2015, now Emeritus. *Educ*: Univ. of Oxford (BA Maths 1971; DPhil 1977); Sussex Univ. (MSc Astronomy 1972). Postdoctoral Fellow, Univ. of Sussex, 1976–79; Lectr in Stats, 1979–90, Reader in Stats, 1990–95, Univ. of Bristol. Tage Erlander Vis. Prof., Univ. of Gothenburg, 2007–08; Vis. Prof., Royal Netherlands Acad. of Arts and Scis, 2009–10; Hon. Vis. Prof., Univ. of Exeter. Hon. DSc Sussex, 2012. (Jtly) Hamilton Award, Internat. Soc. Behavioural Ecol., 2008; (jtly) Assoc. for Study of Animal Behaviour Medal, 2013; Weldon Meml Prize, Univ. of Oxford, 2014; Sewall Wright Award, Amer. Soc. of Naturalists, 2018; Frink Medal, Zool Soc. of London, 2019. *Publications*: articles in jls. *Address*: School of Mathematics, University of Bristol, University Walk, Clifton, Bristol BS8 1TW.

**McNANEY, Peter Francis**, CBE 2013; Chairman, Belfast Health and Social Care Trust, since 2014; *b* 8 Feb. 1959; *m* 1987, Karen McMillen; two *s* two *d*. *Educ*: Manchester Univ. (LLB Hons); Univ. of Ulster (DMS); Queen's Univ., Belfast (Cert Prof. Legal Studies; Cert Adv. Advocacy for Solicitors). Belfast City Council: Asst Solicitor, 1983–85; Sen. Solicitor, 1985–91; Asst Town Solicitor, 1991–94; Dir, Legal Services, 1994–2002; Chief Executive, Belfast City Council, 2002–14. Member: Bd, Chief Execs' Forum, 2003–; NI Econ. Develt Forum, 2005–; NI Local Govt Taskforce, 2006–; Bd, Invest NI. Mem. Editl Bd, Local Authorities Chief Execs Imprint Foundn, 2004–. *Address*: Belfast Health and Social Care Trust, Trust Headquarters, A Floor, Belfast City Hospital, Lisburn Road, Belfast BT9 7AB. *T*: (028) 9504 0101. *E*: peter.mcnaney@belfasttrust.hscni.net.

**McNAUGHT, Captain Ian**, CVO 2019; Deputy Master, Corporation of Trinity House, since 2011; *b* Sunderland, 27 Aug. 1954; *s* of Andrew McNaught and Kathleen Olive McNaught; *m* 1980, Susan Sproxton; one *s*. *Educ*: Monkwearmouth Grammar Sch.; Fleetwood Nautical Coll. Pre-Sea Boys; South Tyneside Nautical Coll. (professional certs of competency leading to Master Mariner). Cadet, BP Tanker Co., 1972–76; Third Officer, Bibby Line, 1976–79; Second Officer, then Chief Officer, Hullgates Shipping, 1979–87; Cunard Line: joined as Second Officer, 1987; Master: Sea Goddess I, 2001; QE2, 2003–08; Queen Victoria, 2009; Seabourn Spirit, 2010; Seabourn Odyssey, 2010; Seabourn Cruises, 2010, 2011; Seabourn Pride, 2011. Younger Brother, Trinity House, Newcastle upon Tyne, 2003–. FNI 2017. Merchant Navy Medal, 2013. *Recreations*: maritime history, fell walking in the Lake District. *Address*: Corporation of Trinity House, Trinity House, Tower Hill, EC3N 4DH.

**McNAUGHT, His Honour John Graeme**; a Circuit Judge, 1987–2006; *b* 21 Feb. 1941; *s* of Charles William McNaught and Isabella Mary McNaught; *m* 1966, Barbara Mary Smith; two *s* one *d*. *Educ*: King Edward VII Sch., Sheffield; The Queen's Coll., Oxford (BA Jurisprudence, 1962). Bacon Scholar, Gray's Inn, 1962; called to the Bar, Gray's Inn, 1963; a Recorder, 1981–87; Hon. Recorder, Devizes, 1996–. Judge, High Court of St Helena, 1998–2006. Mem., Parole Bd for England and Wales, 1998–2004; Pres., Mental Health Review Tribunal, 2001–05. Chm., Wilts Criminal Justice Strategy Cttee, 2000–02. UK Council Mem., Commonwealth Magistrates' and Judges' Assoc., 1997–2000. DL Wilts, 2006. *Address*: c/o Swindon Combined Court, Islington Street, Swindon SN1 2HG.

**McNAUGHTON, Andrew George**, FREng; Director, Clarke McNaughton Associates Ltd, since 2018; Technical Director (formerly Chief Engineer), High Speed Two Ltd, 2009–17 (Member of Board, 2013–14; Strategic Technical Adviser (part-time), since 2018); *b* 26 July 1956; *s* of late Arthur Alfred George, (Ian), McNaughton and Betty McNaughton; *m* 1984, Jane Evelyn Merriott; two *s*. *Educ*: Univ. of Leeds (BSc Civil Engrg 1978). CEng 1981; FICE 2001; FREng 2007; FCILT 2010; FRGS 2012; FIET 2017. Civil Engr, SE British Rail, 1991–94; Railtrack plc: Manager, E Anglia, 1994–96; Hd, Prodn, 1997–99; Dir, Great Western, 1999–2001; Chief Engr, Network Rail, 2001–09. Chm. Adv. Bd, Rail Research UK, 2004–09; non-exec. Dir, Great Central Railway Develt Ltd, 2011–13; Dir, Rail2050 Ltd, 2011–13. Mem., Eur. Rail Res. Council, 2004–12 (Chm., 2008–12); Mem., Railway Heritage Cttee, 2006–12; Chairman: Infrastructure Commn, 2006–10, InterCity and High Speed Forum, 2016–, Internat. Railway Union; World High Speed Rail Cttee, 2016–; FastRail Panel, Govt of NSW, 2018–; Vice Chm., EU Transport Adv. Gp, 2006–12. Advr on High Speed Rail to Govt of Czech Rep., 2017–. Pres., Railway Study Assoc., 2010–11. Hon. Prof. (formerly Special Prof.), Rail Engrg, Univ. of Nottingham, 2006–; Vis. Prof., Imperial Coll. London, 2010–; Vis. Prof., 2011–18, Professorial Fellow, 2018–, Southampton Univ. Trustee, ICE, 2018–. Asst, Engineers' Co., 2009–. FPWI 1975. Mem., Smeatonian Soc., 2013. *Recreations*: mountain walking, road cycling, growing vegetables. *Address*: 25 Kenwood Drive, Beckenham, Kent BR3 6QX. *T*: (020) 7944 0773. *E*: andrew.mcnaughton@clarkemcnaughton.com.

**MacNAUGHTON, Joan**, CB 2005; adviser globally on energy and environmental policies; Chair, The Climate Group, since 2016; *b* 12 Sept. 1950; *d* of Duncan McNaughton and Marion McNaughton (*née* Caldwell); *m* 1979, William Alexander Jeffrey (*see* Sir W. A. Jeffrey). *Educ*: Notre Dame Coll. Sch., Liverpool; Warwick Univ. (BSc Hons Physics). Home Office: Admin. Trainee, 1972–74; HEO (Develt), 1974–76; Asst Sec. to Royal Commn on Criminal Procedure, 1976–80; Criminal Policy Dept, 1981–85; Prin. Private Sec. to Dep. Prime Minister and Lord Pres. of the Council, 1985–87; Head, Women and Young Offenders Div., Prison Service, 1987–89; Dir, Prison Service Industries and Farms, 1989–91; Head, Criminal Policy Div., 1991–92; Prin. Private Sec. to Home Secretary, 1992–95; Chief Exec., Police IT Orgn, 1996–99; Director General: Policy, LCD, 1999–2002; Energy, DTI, 2002–06; Internat. Energy Security, DTI, 2006–07; Sen. Vice Pres., Power and Envmtl Policies, Alstom Power (formerly Alstom Power Systems), 2007–11; Exec. Chair, Energy and Policy Assessment (Trilemma), World Energy Council, 2011–16, now Hon. Chair. Chm., Governing Bd, Internat. Energy Agency, 2004–05. Mem., Strategic Adv. Bd, Engie UK, 2016–. Non-exec. Dir, Quintain Estates and Development plc, 2004–10; Mem. Bd, En+ Gp plc, 2019–. Sen. Vis. Res. Fellow, Oxford Inst. for Energy Studies, Oxford Univ., 2006–13; Distinguished Fellow: Inst. of Energy Economics, Japan, 2016; Global Fedn of Competitiveness Councils, 2016. Member, Council: Energy Inst., 2008–14 (Vice Pres., 2009–10; Pres. elect, 2010–11; Pres., 2011–13); Warwick Univ., 2014–; Member, Board: Internat. Emissions Trading Assoc., 2010–12; Carbon Capture and Storage Assoc., 2010–13; James Hutton Inst., 2015– (Chair, Nominations and Remuneration Cttee, 2016–). Chm., Internat. Adv. Bd, New Energy Coalition of Europe (formerly Energy Acad. of Europe), 2013–; Vice Chm., UN High Level Panel on Policy Dialogue on the Clean Develt Mechanism, 2012; Member: Adv. Council, Jt Inst. for Strategic Energy Analysis, Colo, 2014–; UK Energy Res. Centre, 2015–; Bd, Energy Savings Trust, 2018–. Mem., Bd of Govs, Argonne Nat. Lab., Univ. of Chicago, 2007–13 (Chm., Admin and Budget Cttee, 2010–13; Co-Chm., Strategic Rev. of Lab. Operations, 2010–13). Trustee, Climate Gp, 2014–. Hon. FEI 2006; Hon. Fellow,

Nat. Emissions Trading Assoc., 2014. *Publications:* (contrib.) The New Economic Diplomacy, 2nd edn 2007, 3rd edn 2011; articles on energy and climate change. *Recreations:* reading, hill walking, watching football, crosswords, bridge. *Address:* c/o The Climate Group, County Hall, Belvedere Road, SE1 7PB. *Club:* Reform.

**McNAUGHTON, Prof. Peter Anthony,** DPhil; FMedSci; Professor of Pharmacology, King's College London, since 2013; *b* 17 Aug. 1949; *s* of Anthony Henry McNaughton and Dulcie Helen McNaughton; *m* 1985, Linda Ariza; two *s* two *d. Educ:* Univ. of Auckland, NZ (BSc 1970); Balliol Coll., Oxford (DPhil 1974); MA Cantab 1976. University of Cambridge: Res. Fellow, Clare Coll., 1974–78; Physiological Laboratory: Elmore Med. Res. Student, 1977–78; Univ. Demonstrator, 1978–83; Univ. Lectr, 1983–91; Fellow, Christ's Coll., 1983–91; Nuffield Sci. Res. Fellow, 1988–89; King's College London: Halliburton Prof. of Physiology, and Head of Physiology, 1991–99; Dean of Basic Med. Scis, 1993–96. Hon. Prof., Dept of Optometry and Vision Scis, Univ. of Wales, Cardiff, 1998–2002; Sheild Prof. and Hd, Dept of Pharmacol., Univ. of Cambridge, 1999–2013; Fellow, Christ's Coll., Cambridge, 1999–2013. Biotechnology and Biological Sciences Research Council: Member: Biochem. and Cell Biology Panel, 1996–2000; Neurone Initiative Panel, 2001–04; Inst. Assessment Panel, 2001; Chm., Bio-imaging Initiative Panel, 1998–2002; Member: Neurosci. Panel, Wellcome Trust, 1998–2001; Adv. Bd, MRC, 2001–06; Performance Based Res. Fund Panel, NZ, 2003. Member: Physiological Soc., 1979– (Mem. Cttee, 1988–92); British Pharmacological Soc., 1999– (FBPhS 2017). FMedSci 2013. *Publications:* articles in fields of physiology, pharmacology and neuroscience in learned jls. *Address:* Wolfson Centre for Age-related Diseases, King's College London, Guy's Campus, SE1 1UL.

**MacNEE, Prof. William,** MD; FRCPE; Professor of Respiratory and Environmental Medicine, University of Edinburgh, 1997–2018, now Emeritus; Hon. Consultant Physician, NHS Lothian, 1987; *b* Glasgow, 18 Dec. 1950; *s* of James and Elsie MacNee; *m* 1976, Edna Marina Kingsley; one *s* one *d. Educ:* Coatbridge High Sch.; Univ. of Glasgow (MB ChB 1975; MD Hons 1985). MRCPGlas 1978; FRCPE 1990. Hse Physician and Hse Surgeon, Glasgow and Paisley, 1975–76; SHO/Registrar in Medicine, Western Infirmary and Gartnavel Hosps, Glasgow, 1976–79; Registrar in Respiratory Medicine, City Hosp., Edinburgh, 1979–80; MRC Res. Fellow and Hon. Registrar, Dept of Respiratory Medicine, Royal Infirmary, Edinburgh, 1980–82; Lectr, Dept of Respiratory Medicine, City Hosp., Edinburgh, 1982–83; Sen. Registrar, Respiratory Medicine and Medicine, Lothian Health Bd, 1983–87; Sen. Lectr in Respiratory Medicine, 1987–93, Reader in Medicine, 1993–97, Univ. of Edinburgh; Hd, Cardiovascular/Thoracic Service, Royal Infirmary of Edinburgh, 1998–99. Clinical Director, Respiratory Medicine: Lothian Univ. Hosps NHS Trust, 1992–97; Lothian Hosps NHS Trust, 1992–2002. MRC Res. Fellow, Univ. of BC, Vancouver, 1985–86; Vis. Prof., Sch. of Life Scis, Napier Univ., Edinburgh. Mem. Council, Scottish Thoracic Soc., 1990–93; Vice Pres., British Lung Foundn, 2007– (Hon. Sec., Scotland, 1993–2004; Chm., Scientific Cttee, 1997–2000). European Respiratory Society: Chm., Scientific Prog. Cttee, 1990–2003; Congress Chair, 2003–04; Pres., 2006–07. *Publications:* Chronic Obstructive Lung Disease, 2002, 2nd edn 2008; The Year in Respiratory Medicine, 2003; Chronic Obstructive Pulmonary Disease, 2nd edn 2003; Fast Facts Chronic Obstructive Pulmonary Disease, 2004; Clinical Management of Chronic Obstructive Pulmonary Disease, 2004; contrib. scientific papers and rev. articles on respiratory medicine topics. *Recreations:* music, walking, reading. *Address:* c/o Centre for Inflammation Research, Queen's Medical Research Institute, Edinburgh BioQuarter, 47 Little France Crescent, Edinburgh EH16 4TJ.

**MacNEIL, Angus Brendan;** MP (SNP) Na h-Eileanan An Iar, since 2005; *b* 21 July 1970; *m* 1998, Jane Douglas (marr. diss.). *Educ:* Castlebay Secondary Sch., Isle of Barra; Nicolson Inst., Stornoway; Strathclyde Univ. (BEng 1992); Jordanhill Coll. (PGCE 1996). Civil Engr, Lilley Construction Ltd, 1992–93; reporter, BBC Radio, Inverness, 1993–95; teacher, Salen Primary Sch., Mull, 1996–98; Gaelic Develt Officer, Lochaber, 1998–99; Lectr in Educn (part-time), Inverness Coll., 1999–2000; teacher, various schs incl. Lochaber and Fort William, 2000–03; teacher and crofter, Isle of Barra, 2009–. Contested (SNP) Inverness E, Nairn and Lochaber, 2001. Chm., Internat. Trade Select Cttee, 2016–. *Recreation:* keeping flock of sheep on croft in Hebrides. *Address:* (office) 31 Bayhead Street, Stornoway, Isle of Lewis, Outer Hebrides HS1 2DU; House of Commons, SW1A 0AA.

**McNEIL, Duncan;** Member (Lab) Greenock and Inverclyde, Scottish Parliament, 1999–2016; *b* 7 Sept. 1950; *m* Margaret; one *s* one *d.* Apprentice, Cartsdyke Shipyard; shipbuilder; Officer, GMB. Mem., Labour Party Scottish Exec.; Chm., Local Govt Cttee. Mem., Health Cttee, 2003–07, Scottish Parly Corporate Body, 2003–07, Scottish Parlt.

**McNEIL, Keith,** FRACP; Assistant Deputy Director General, and Chief Medical Information Officer, Queensland Health, since 2017; *b* London, 28 July 1957; *s* of David Loudon and Pauline Ann McNeil; *m* 1984, Sharyn Lee; one *s* two *d. Educ:* Caringbah High Sch.; Cairns State High Sch.; Univ. of Queensland (MB, BS 1981). FRACP 1991. Intern/ Jun. Hse Officer, Mater Misericordiae Hosp., Brisbane, 1982–83; Bn MO, 2/4 RAR Australian Infantry, 1984–85, MO, Special Warfare, 1985, Field Ambulance, 1986. Specialist Trng Registrar, 1987–93; Sen. Transplant Fellow, Papworth Hosp., 1993–95; Consultant Transplant Physician: Prince Charles Hosp., Brisbane, 1995–96; Papworth Hosp., 1996–2002; Hd, Heart and Lung Transplantation, Prince Charles Hosp., Brisbane, 2002–07; Chief Executive Officer: Royal Brisbane & Women's Hosp., Brisbane, 2007–08; Metro Health Service, Brisbane, 2008–13; Chief Exec., Cambridge Univ. Hosps NHS Foundn Trust, 2013–15; Chief Clinical Inf. Officer, Health and Social Care, and Hd of IT, NHS England, 2016–17. *Publications:* contribs to text books; scientific articles. *Recreations:* running, classical guitar. *E:* profkeithmcneil@gmail.com. *Clubs:* Royal Society of Medicine; University of Queensland Cricket.

**McNEIL, Paul;** Partner, Fieldfisher (formerly Field Fisher Waterhouse), since 1995; *b* Irvine, Scotland, 26 July 1958; *s* of Hugh and Margaret McNeil; *m* 1990, Elizabeth; one *s* two *d. Educ:* All Saints' Comprehensive Sch., Huddersfield; Sheffield Univ. (LLB). Admitted Solicitor; personal injury and clin. negligence solicitor, Taylor Joynson Garrett, 1987–92; Field Fisher Waterhouse, subseq. Fieldfisher: Mem., Mgt Bd, 2005–; Hd, Personal Injury and Med. Negligence, 2008–. *Publications:* (contrib.) International Product Liability; (ed) Handbook on Medical Negligence; (contrib.) Expert Witness. *Recreations:* cycling, ski-ing, cooking. *Address:* 103 Deodar Road, SW15 2NU. *T:* (020) 7861 4019, *Fax:* (020) 7488 0084. *E:* paul.mcneil@fieldfisher.com.

**McNEIL, Rupert Kenneth;** Government Chief People Officer, since 2016; *b* Marylebone, London, 24 April 1967; *s* of Andrew Ross McNeil and Barbara Cordelia McNeil (*née* Collins); *m* 1994, Nicole Sochor; one *s* one *d. Educ:* Robert Gordon's Coll., Aberdeen; St Catherine's Coll., Oxford (Victor Blank Schol. in Law, 1985; Hons Mods in Jurisprudence 1986; MA Politics and Philosophy); Harvard Business Sch. (AMP 2010). Internship, Office of Senator Paul Simon, USA, 1988; Confederation of British Industry: Asst Trng Policy Advr, 1989–90; Trng Policy Advr, 1990–92; Hd of Remuneration Policy, 1992–94; Hd of Pay and Employment Markets, 1994–95; Arthur Andersen: Semi-Senior, then Senior, 1995; Experienced Senior, 1996–97; Manager, 1997–99; Sen. Manager, 1999–2001; Partner, 2001–02; Partner, Deloitte, 2002–05; Exec. Mgt Dir, HR, 2005–07, HR Dir, Global Retail and Commercial Banking, 2007–09, Barclays Bank plc; UK HR Dir, Aviva, 2010–12; Gp HR Dir, Lloyd's Banking Gp, 2012–15. Mem., Assoc. of Tax Technicians, 1998. FCIPD 2014 (Licenciate 2007). *Publications:* Reward Governance for Senior Executives, 2007. *Recreations:* reading, cycling, family. *Address:* 33 Briardale Gardens, NW3 7PN. *T:* 07767 834755. *E:* rupertmcneil@gmail.com. *Club:* Civil Service.

**MacNEILL, Calum Hector Sinclair;** QC (Scot.) 2007; *b* Elgin, 19 May 1964; *s* of late Malcolm Torquil MacNeill and of Morag MacNeill (*née* McKinnon). *Educ:* Robert Gordon's Coll., Aberdeen; Univ. of Aberdeen (LLB Hons 1985; DipLP 1986). Called to the Scottish Bar, 1992; Advocate Depute, 1998–2001; Standing Jun. Counsel to Scottish Exec., 2003–06. Accredited Mediator, CEDR, 2005. Mem. Panel, Police Appeals Tribunal, 2013–. MCIArb 2014, FCIArb 2017. *Address:* Advocates Library, Parliament House, Parliament Square, Edinburgh EH1 1RF. *T:* (0131) 226 5071. *E:* calum.macneill@ westwateradvocates.com. *Club:* New (Edinburgh).

**McNEILL, (Elizabeth) Jane;** QC 2002; a Recorder, since 2005; *b* 18 March 1957; *d* of David McNeill and Margaret McNeill (*née* Lewis); *m* 1990, David Adams; two *s. Educ:* St Hilda's Coll., Oxford (BA Hons Mod. Langs); City Univ., London (Dip Law). Called to the Bar, Lincoln's Inn, 1982, Bencher, 2007. Fee-paid Employment Judge, 2000–. Mem. Council, ACAS, 2014–. Hon. Fellow, Lucy Cavendish Coll., Cambridge, 2015. *Recreations:* reading, cooking, bridge, walking, singing. *Address:* Old Square Chambers, 10–11 Bedford Row, WC1R 4BU. *T:* (020) 7269 0300.

**McNEILL, James Walker;** QC (Scot.) 1991; Judge of the Courts of Appeal of Jersey and Guernsey, since 2006; *b* 16 Feb. 1952; *s* of late James McNeill and Edith Anna Howie Wardlaw; *m* 1986, Katherine Lawrence McDowall; two *s* one *d. Educ:* Dunoon Grammar Sch.; Cambridge Univ. (MA); Edinburgh Univ. (LLB); Open Univ. (BMus, MMus). Advocate 1978; Standing Junior Counsel: to Dept of Transport in Scotland, 1984–88; to Inland Revenue in Scotland, 1988–91. Chm., Disciplinary Appts Cttee, Inst. and Faculty of Actuaries, 2013–19. Mem., Judicial Appts Bd for Scotland, 2012–19. Mem. Council, Commonwealth Lawyers' Assoc., 2005–11. Church of Scotland: Procurator to Gen. Assembly, 2000 and 2005; Mem., Fergusson Commn on Structural Reform, 2018–19; Admin. Trustee, Assembly Trustees, 2019–. Session Clerk, St Andrew's and St George's Parish Ch, Edinburgh, 1999–2003; Sec., Edinburgh City Centre Churches Together, 2012–18. Mem. Bd and Chm., Music Cttee, Scottish Internat. Piano Competition, 2004–10; Dir, New Town Concerts Soc. Ltd, 2018–. *Publications:* (ed) A Practical Guide to Charity Law in Scotland, 2016. *Recreations:* music, ski-ing, cycle touring, travel. *Address:* 28 Kingsburgh Road, Edinburgh EH12 6DZ. *Clubs:* New (Edinburgh); Hon. Company of Edinburgh Golfers.

**McNEILL, Jane;** *see* McNeill, E. J.

**McNEILL, Prof. John,** PhD; Director Emeritus, Royal Ontario Museum, Toronto, since 1997 (Director, 1991–97); Hon. Associate, Royal Botanic Garden, Edinburgh, since 1998 (Regius Keeper, 1987–89); *b* 15 Sept. 1933; *s* of Thomas McNeill and Helen Lawrie Eagle; *m* 1st, 1961, Bridget Mariel Winterton (marr. diss. 1990); two *s*; 2nd, 1990, Marilyn Lois James. *Educ:* George Heriot's, Edinburgh; Univ. of Edinburgh (BSc Hons, PhD 1960). Asst Lectr and Lectr, Dept of Agricl Botany, Univ. of Reading, 1957–61; Lectr, Dept of Botany, Univ. of Liverpool, 1961–69; Plant (later Biosystematics) Research Institute, Agriculture Canada, Ottawa: Res. Scientist, 1969–77, Chief, Vascular Plant Taxonomy Sect., 1969–72; Sen. Res. Scientist, 1977–81; Prof. and Chm., Dept of Biology, Univ. of Ottawa, 1981–87; Associate Dir Curatorial, Royal Ontario Mus., Toronto, 1989–90, Acting Dir, 1990–91; Dir, George R. Gardiner Mus. of Ceramic Art, Toronto, 1991–96. Hon. Prof., Univ. of Edinburgh, 1989; Prof., Dept of Botany, Univ. of Toronto, 1990–2006; Adjunct Prof., Univ. of Ottawa, 1987–91. Mem. Editl Cttee, 1985–2003, Chm. Mgt Cttee, 1998–2001, Mem. Bd of Dirs, 2003–06, Emeritus Mem., 2006–, Flora North America Association; Rapporteur-général, Nomenclature section, Internat. Botanical Congresses, 1997–2012 (Vice-rapporteur, 1982–94); Ed., Nomenclature section, 2000–11, Technical Nomenclature sections, 2011–, Taxon (jl of Internat. Assoc. for Plant Taxonomy). *Publications* include: Phenetic and phylogenetic classification (jt ed), 1964; (jtly) Grasses of Ontario, 1977; (jt ed) International Code of Botanical Nomenclature, 1983, 1988, 1994, 2000, 2006; (jtly) Preliminary Inventory of Canadian Weeds, 1988; (jt ed) Flora of North America north of Mexico, vols 1 and 2, 1993, vol. 3, 1997, vol. 22, 2000, vol. 26, 2002, vol. 23, 2003; (jt ed) International Code of Nomenclature for Cultivated Plants, 1995, 7th edn 2004; (jt ed) International Code of Nomenclature for algae, fungi, and plants, 2012, 2018, Appendices, II–VIII, 2015; over 20 chapters or sections of sci. books and over 90 contribs to sci. res. jls. *Recreation:* botanical nomenclature. *Address:* Royal Botanic Garden, 20A Inverleith Row, Edinburgh EH3 5LR.

**McNEILL, Johnston David John;** Chief Executive, Rural Payments Agency, 2001–06; *b* 15 Aug. 1956; *s* of David McNeill and Mary McNeill (*née* Kane); *m* 1983, Jennifer Fowler (marr. diss. 1997); one *s* one *d. Educ:* Lurgan Coll.; Southampton Coll. of Technology (HND Mech. Engrg); Univ. of Ulster (BA); Univ. of Central Lancashire (MBA); Portsmouth Univ. (PGDipPM, MA); PGDipM. Marine engr, 1974–79; mgt posts, private sector cos, 1979–88; Dep. Gen. Manager, Lancs CC, 1988–90; Asst Dir, Southampton CC, 1990–92; Dir of Contract Services, Belfast CC, 1992–94; Chief Executive: Meat Hygiene Service, MAFF, 1994–2000; Food Standards Agency, 2000–01. FIPD. Freeman, City of London; Liveryman, Butchers' Co. *Recreations:* ski-ing, rowing, yacht sailing, guitar, socialising with friends and family. *Club:* Farmers.

**McNEILL, Pauline Mary;** Member (Lab) Glasgow, Scottish Parliament, since 2016; *b* 12 Sept. 1962; *d* of John Patrick McNeill and Teresa Ward or McNeill; *m* 1999, William Joseph Cahill; two step *s. Educ:* Glasgow Coll. of Building and Printing (Dip. 1986); Strathclyde Univ. (LLB 1999). NUS, 1986–88; Regl Orgnr, GMB Scotland, 1988–99. MSP (Lab) Glasgow Kelvin, 1999–2011; contested same seat (Lab), 2011. Dir of Legal and Public Affairs, Nationwide Milk Services Ltd, 2014; Co-founder and Partner, McNeill & Stone, 2015. *Recreations:* guitar, singing, rock music, keep fit. *Address:* Scottish Parliament, Edinburgh EH99 1SP.

**McNEISH, Prof. Alexander Stewart,** PhD; FRCP, FMedSci; Emeritus Professor of Clinical Science, London University, since 2001; Hon. Professor, School of Medicine, Birmingham University, since 2003; *b* 13 April 1938; *s* of Angus Stewart McNeish and Minnie Howieson (*née* Dickson); *m* 1963, Joan Ralston (*née* Hamilton); two *s* (one *d* decd). *Educ:* Glasgow Acad.; Univ. of Glasgow (MB, MPhil 2005); Univ. of Birmingham (MSc); Queen Mary, Univ. of London (PhD 2011). FRCP 1977; FRCPGlas 1985; FRCPCH 1996. Sen. Lectr in Paediatrics and Child Health, Univ. of Birmingham, 1970–76; Foundn Prof. of Child Health, Univ. of Leicester, 1976–80; University of Birmingham: Leonard Parsons Prof. of Paediatrics and Child Health, 1980–95; Dir, Inst. of Child Health, 1980–93; Dean, Faculty of Medicine and Dentistry, 1987–92; Dir of R&D, W Midlands RHA, 1992–95; Dir, MRC Clinical Scis Centre, Hammersmith Hosp., 1995–97; London University: Warden, St Bart's and Royal London Sch. of Medicine and Dentistry, 1997–2001; Vice Principal, 1997–99, Dep. Principal, 1999–2001, QMW. Mem., GMC,

1984–95. Founder FMedSci 1998. Hon. Fellow, QMUL, 2007. *Publications:* papers on paediatric gastroenterology in Lancet, BMJ and in Archives of Disease in Childhood. *Recreations:* golf, music. *Address:* 128 Westfield Road, Edgbaston, Birmingham B15 3JQ. *T:* (0121) 454 6081. *Clubs:* Athenæum; Blackwell Golf, Rye Golf.

**McNELLY, Rev. Nicola;** Rector, St Cuthbert's Church, Colinton, since 2017; *b* Tredegar, 1 May 1962; *d* of Eric Calder and Beryl Calder (*née* Stock); *m* 1984, Iain McNelly; two *d*. *Educ:* Ebbw Vale Grammar Sch.; Cranmer Hall, St John's Coll., Durham (DipTh and Ministry 2009). Intelligence Corps, WRAC, 1980–84; Sch. Sec., Mountbatten Sch., Celle, W Germany, 1986–89; PA to Customer Services Dir, Magnet Kitchens, 1990–93; SSAFA Forces Help: Admin. positions in Cyprus and NI, 2001–04; Volunteer Develt Manager, NI, 2004–07; Chair, In-Service Cttee, Edinburgh, 2009–11; ordained deacon, 2009, priest, 2010; Chaplain, St Mary's Cath., Edinburgh, 2009–12; Provost, St John the Divine Cathedral, Oban, 2012–17; Rector, St James', Arkbrecknish, 2012–17; Canon, Cathedral of the Isles and Collegiate Ch of the Holy Spirit, Isle of Cumbrae, 2013–17. *Recreations:* trekking in Nepal, raising money for AGE/Nepal (A Genuine Effort Nepal, sch. for children with neurological disorders). *Address:* The Rectory, 6 Westgarth Avenue, Colinton, Edinburgh EH13 0BD. *T:* 07825 440580. *E:* nicki.mcnelly@gmail.com.

**McNICOL,** family name of **Baron McNicol of West Kilbride**.

**McNICOL OF WEST KILBRIDE,** Baron *cr* 2018 (Life Peer), of West Kilbride in the County of Ayrshire; **Iain MacKenzie McNicol;** General Secretary, Labour Party, 2011–18; *b* Kilwinning, 17 Aug. 1969; *s* of Iain and Zoe McNicol; *m* 1995, Shelley; one *s* one *d*. *Educ:* Dundee Inst. of Technol. (HND Bldg Mgt 1991). Pres., Dundee Inst. of Technol. Students' Union (on sabbatical), 1991–93; Campaigns and Membership Officer, Labour Students (on sabbatical), 1993–94; Organiser and Agent, Labour Party, 1994–97; Organiser, 1997–2004, Nat. Political Officer, 2004–11, GMB Union. Mem. Bd, Nat. Citizen Service Trust, 2018–. *Recreations:* karate, playing the bagpipes, golf, cooking. *Address:* House of Lords, SW1A 0PW. *E:* mcnicoli@parliament.uk.

**McNICOL, Prof. Donald;** Vice-Chancellor and Principal, University of Tasmania, 1996–2002; *b* 18 April 1939; *s* of Ian Robertson McNicol and Sadie Isabelle Williams; *m* 1963, Kathleen Margaret Wells; one *s* two *d*. *Educ:* Unley High Sch.; Univ. of Adelaide (BA 1964); St John's Coll., Cambridge (PhD 1967). Fellow, Aust. Psych. Soc. Lectr in Psychology, Univ. of Adelaide, 1967–71; Research Fellow, St John's Coll., Cambridge, 1968–69; Sen. Lectr in Psych., Univ. of NSW, 1971–74; Associate Prof. in Psych., Univ. of NSW, 1975–81; Prof. of Psych., Univ. of Tasmania, 1981–86, now Emeritus Prof.; Comr for Univs and Chm., Univs Adv. Council, Commonwealth Tertiary Educn, 1986–88; Vice-Chancellor, Univ. of New England, NSW, 1988–90; Vice-Chancellor and Principal, Univ. of Sydney, 1990–96. President: AVCC, 1994–95; Assoc. of Univs of Asia Pacific, 1998–99; AHEIA, 2000–01. *Publications:* A Primer of Signal Detection Theory, 1972, repr. 2005. *Recreations:* walking, jazz, reading. *Address:* PO Box 1155, Sandy Bay, Tas 7006, Australia.

**McNICOL, Judith Kenzie;** Director, National Railway Museum, since 2017; *b* Inverness, 22 Aug. 1970; *d* of Michael and Margaret Whitaker; *m* 2011, Colin McNicol. *Educ:* Thorpe Hse Sch. for Girls, Norwich; Norwich City Coll. (HND Business Studies 1992). Ops Dir, Chiron Werke UK Ltd, 1996–99; Dir, Results Internat. plc, 1999–2002; Ops Dir, Coach Europ, 2002–03; Dir, 2003–10, Change Dir, 2010–15, Dir, People and Culture, 2015–18, Science Mus. Gp. *Recreations:* gardening, land management. *Address:* National Railway Museum, Leeman Road, York YO26 4XJ. *E:* judith.mcnicol@railwaymuseum.org.uk.

**MACNICOL, Malcolm Fraser,** FRCSE, FRCPE, FRCSE(Orth); Consultant Orthopaedic Surgeon: Royal Hospital for Sick Children and Royal Infirmary, Edinburgh, 1979–2007; Spire Murrayfield Hospital, Edinburgh, 1984–2010; *b* 18 March 1943; *s* of Roy Simson Macnicol and Eona Kathleen Macnicol (*née* Fraser); *m* 1972, Anne Morag Docherty; two *s* one *d*. *Educ:* Royal High Sch., Edinburgh (Capt. of Sch., Dux in English and Biol.); Edinburgh Univ. (BSc Hons 1966, MB ChB 1969); MChOrth Liverpool 1979. FRCSE 1973; FRCSE(Orth) 1979; Dip. Sports Med., RCSE, 1998; FRCPE 2002. Research Fellow: Stanford Univ., 1966; Harvard Univ., 1970–71; Lectr in Orthopaedics, Edinburgh Univ., 1976–78; Sen. Orthopaedic Lectr, Univ. of W Australia, 1978–79; Sen. Orthopaedic Lectr (pt-time), Univ. of Edinburgh, 1982–. Treas., RCSE, 1987–90. Pres., British Orthopaedic Assoc., 2001–02 (Chm., Medico-legal Sub Cttee, 1998–2003; Mem., Robert Jones Orthopaedic Club); Member: Medico-Chirurgical Soc., 1984–; British Soc. for Children's Orthopaedic Surgery, 1985–; British Assoc. for Surgery of the Knee, 1985–; British Orthopaedic Res. Soc., 1985–; Scottish Soc. of Hist. of Medicine, 2010–. Patron, Scottish Post-Polio Network, 2006–. Hon. Med. Advr, Scottish RU, 2004–08. Mem., Malt Whisky Tasting Soc., 2000–. Hon. Fellow, British Orthopaedic Assoc., 2016. *Publications:* Princess Margaret Rose Orthopaedic Hospital 1932–1982, 1982, 2nd edn 2002; Aids to Orthopaedics, 1984; Basic Care of the Injured Hand, 1984 (Italian edn 1986); Problem Knee, 1986, 3rd edn 2011; Color Atlas and Text of Osteomy of the Hip, 1995 (Portuguese edn 1997); Children's Orthopaedics and Fractures, 1994, 3rd edn 2010; The Red Sandstone Buildings of Edinburgh, 2009; contrib. numerous peer-reviewed papers and book chapters. *Recreations:* tennis, walking, water-colour painting, theatre, architecture. *Address:* Red House, 1 South Gillsland Road, Edinburgh EH10 5DE. *Clubs:* Robert Jones; Harveian Soc. (Edinburgh); Harvard Research.

**McNICOLL, Iain Walter,** CB 2006; CBE 2000; business director, since 2011; *b* 3 May 1953; *s* of Walter McNicoll and Maida Cameron McNicoll (*née* Readdie); *m* 1980, Wendelien Henriëtte Maria van den Biggelaar; one *s* two *d*. *Educ:* Dundee High Sch.; Univ. of Edinburgh (BSc 1975). Commnd RAFVR, 1973, RAF, 1975; XV Sqn, 1978–81; qwi 1979; Tornado Weapons Conversion Unit 45 (Reserve) Sqn, 1982–85; 17 (Fighter) Sqn, 1985–86; 16 Sqn, 1986–89; RAF Staff Coll., 1990; PSO to Dep. C-in-C, Strike Command, 1991–92; OC 17 (Fighter) Sqn, 1992–95; MoD, 1995–98; Station Comdr, Brüggen, 1998–2000; Dir, Force Development, MoD, 2000–02; DG, Jt Doctrine and Concepts, MoD, 2002–05; AOC No 2 Gp, 2005–07; Dep. C-in-C Ops Air Comd, 2007–10; retd as Air Marshal, 2010. Associate Partner, Defence Strategy & Solutions LLP, 2010–11. Non-executive Director: Jee Ltd, 2009–16; NATS, 2013–. FRAeS 2001. QCVSA 1989. *E:* iain_mcnicoll@hotmail.com. *Club:* Royal Air Force.

**MacNISH, Alastair Jesse Head,** OBE 2008; Chairman, Accounts Commission for Scotland, 2001–07; Chairman of Board, Audit Scotland, 2001–07; *b* 4 Feb. 1947; *m* 1970, Jean Ferguson Bell; one *s* two *d*. *Educ:* Gourock High Sch. FCCA 1972. Chief Auditor, Renfrew CC, 1973–75; Strathclyde Regional Council: Principal Accountant, 1975–77; Asst Dir of Educn, 1977–87; Depute Dir of Social Work, 1987–95; Chief Exec., S Lanarks Council, 1995–99; Chm., Leadership Adv. Panel, Scottish Exec., 1999–2000. Clerk: Strathclyde Jt Fire Bd, 1995–99; Lanarkshire Jt Valuation Bd, 1995–99. Member: Scotland Adv. Cttee, EOC, 1996–2000; Scottish Govt's Ministerial Panel on Fire & Rescue Services, 2007–. Member, Board: Glasgow Housing Assoc., 2009–11; Wheatley Housing Gp, 2012– (Chm., 2015–); Chm., Greenock Med. Aid Soc., 2013–17. Chm., Bd of Dirs, Royal Caledonian Curling Club, 1999–2002, 2013–. MCIPD (MIPD 1994). *Recreations:* golf, curling, bridge. *Club:* Gourock Golf (Capt. 1998–99).

**McNISH, Althea Marjorie, (Althea McNish Weiss),** CMT 1976; freelance textile designer, since 1957; *b* Trinidad; *d* of late J. Claude McNish, educnl reformer, and late Margaret (*née* Bourne); *m* 1969, John Weiss. *Educ:* Port-of-Spain, by her father and others; London Coll. of Printing; Central School of Arts and Crafts; Royal Coll. of Art. NDD, DesRCA; FCSD (FSIA 1968, MSIA 1960). Painted throughout childhood; after design educn in London, freelance practice in textile and other design; commns from Ascher and Liberty's, 1957; new techniques for laminate murals, for SS Oriana and hosp. and coll. in Trinidad; Govt of Trinidad and Tobago travelling schol., 1962; interior design (for Govt of Trinidad and Tobago) in NY, Washington and London, 1962; Cotton Bd trav. schol. to report on export potential for British printed cotton goods in Europe, 1963; collection of dress fabric designs for ICI and Tootal Thomson for promotion of Terylene Toile, 1966; special features for Daily Mail Ideal Home Exhibn, 1966–78; (with John Weiss) etched silver dishes, 1973–; interior design for Sec.-Gen. of Commonwealth, 1975; bedlinen collection for Courtaulds, 1978; (with John Weiss) textile design develt for BRB, 1978–81; textile hangings for BRB Euston offices, 1979; banners for Design Centre, 1981; (with John Weiss) improvements to London office of High Comr for Trinidad and Tobago, 1981; advr on exhibn design for Govt of Trinidad and Tobago, Commonwealth Inst., 1982–84; fashion textile designs for Slovene textile printers, 1985–91; furnishing textile designs for Fede Cheti, Milan, 1986–91; murals and hangings for Royal Caribbean Cruise Line: MS Nordic Empress, 1990; MS Monarch of the Seas, 1991. Paintings and various work in exhibitions include: individual and gp exhibns, London, 1954–; with Caribbean Artists Movt, Th. Royal, Stratford, 1967, Digby Stuart Coll., LSE and H of C, 1968; Caribbean Artists in England, Commonwealth Inst., 1971; Island Pulse: five Caribbean-born artists, Islington Arts Factory, 1996; solo exhibn, RCA Hockney Gall., 1997; Trinidad & Tobago Through the Eye of the Artist, Commonwealth Inst., 1997; Fine Arts Soc., 198 Gall. and Six into One: Artists from the Caribbean, Morley Gall., 1998; Glebe Place, 2000; paintings, Jamaica, 1975; hangings, Kilkenny, 1981; hangings, individual exhibn, Peoples Gall., 1982; hangings, Magazine Workspace, Leicester, 1983; textile designs in exhibitions: Inprint, Manchester and London, 1964–71; Design Council/BoT, USA and Sweden, 1969, London, 1970, London and USA, 1972; Design-In, Amsterdam, 1972–74; Design Council, 1975–80; The Way We Live Now, V&A Mus., 1978; Afro-Caribbean Art, Drum Arts Centre, London, 1978; Indigo, Lille, 1981–82; Commonwealth Fest. Art Exhibn, Brisbane, 1982; Designs for British Dress and Furnishing Fabrics, V&A Mus., 1986; Make or Break, Henry Moore Gall., 1986; Surtex, New York, 1987; Ascher, V&A Mus., 1987; Transforming the Crown: African, Asian and Caribbean Artists in Britain 1966–96, NY, 1996; Trade and Empire: Remembering Slavery, Whitworth Art Gall., Manchester, 2008; Shirley Craven and Hull Traders: Revolutionary Post-War Fabrics and Furniture, Ferens Art Gall., Hull, 2009, Bankfield Mus., Halifax, Arts Centre, King's Lynn, 2010, Harris Mus. and Art Gall., Preston, 2011; RCA Black: Past, Present and Future, RCA, 2011; work represented in permanent collections of V&A Mus. and Whitworth Art Gall., Univ. of Manchester. Vis. Lecturer: Central Sch. of Art and Crafts and other colls and polytechnics, 1960–; USA, 1972; Italy, W Germany and Slovenia, 1985–; Advisory Tutor in Furnishing and Surface Design, London Coll. of Furniture, 1972–90. External assessor for educnl and professional bodies, incl. CSD and NCDAD/CNAA, 1966–; Mem. jury for Leverhulme schols, 1968; Judge: Portuguese textile design comp., Lisbon, 1973; 'Living' Design Awards, 1974; Carnival selection panels, Arts Council, 1982 and 1983. Vice-Pres., SIAD, 1977–78; Design Council: Mem., selection panels for Design Awards and Design Index, 1968–80; Mem. Bd, 1974–81; Mem., Jubilee Souvenir Selection Panel, 1976; Mem., Royal Wedding Souvenir Selection Panel, 1981. Member: Fashion and Textiles Design Bd, CNAA, 1975–78; London Local Adv. Cttee, IBA, 1981–; Formation Cttee, London Inst., ILEA, 1985. Mem. Governing Body, Portsmouth Coll. of Art, 1972–81. *BBC-TV:* studio setting for Caribbean edn of Full House, 1973. Has appeared, with work, in films for COI and Gas Council. Hon. Dr Fine Arts, Trinidad and Tobago, 2006. Chaconia Medal (Gold) (Trinidad and Tobago), 1976, for service to art and design; Scarlet Ibis Award (Trinidad and Tobago), 1993; Award for Achievement in the Arts (Trinidad and Tobago), 2012. *Publications:* textile designs produced in many countries, 1957–; designs and paintings illustrated in: J. Laver, The Liberty Story, 1959; L. Carson, The Stage Year Book, 1964; Top Symbols and Trademarks of the World: Great Britain, Ireland, Benelux, 1973; W. Mahabir, In and Out of Politics, 1978; A. Ali, Westindians in Britain, 1979; Costumes, Masks and Jewellery of the Commonwealth, ed J. Debayo, 1982; Young Blood, Britain's Design Schools Today and Tomorrow, ed K. Baynes, 1983; V. D. Mendes and F. M. Hinchcliffe, Ascher, 1987; Did Britain Make It?, ed P. Sparke, 1986; M. Schoeser, Fabrics and Wallpapers, 1986; M. Schoeser and C. Rufey, English and American Textiles from 1790 to the Present, 1989; B. Philips, Fabrics and Wallpapers, 1991; S. Calloway, The House of Liberty, 1992; A. Walmsley, The Caribbean Artists Movement 1966–1972, 1992; A Select Bibliography of Contemporary Afro-Caribbean and Asian British Art, 1996; A Life in Exile, 1999; N. Ikoku, The Victoria and Albert Museum's Textile Collection, 1999; N. Ikoku, British Textile Design from 1940 to the Present, 1999; L. Jackson, The Sixties: decade of design revolution, 2000; M. Paton, The Best of Women: the history of Women of the Year, 2000; A. Donnell, Companion to Contemporary Black British Culture, 2002; B. Alleyne, Radicals Against Race, 2002; L. Jackson, 20th Century Pattern Design: textile and wallpaper pioneers, 2002; S. Courtman, Beyond the Blood, the Beach and the Banana, 2004; L. Morrison, A Century of Black Journalism in Britain, 2007; M. Schoeser, Silk, 2007; E Baxter Wright and Z. Rhodes, Vintage Fashion, 1900–1990, 2007; The Oxford Companion to Black History, 2007; Neo-classicism to Pop, vol. 2, 2008; Africa and the Americas: culture, politics and history: a multi-disciplinary encyclopedia, 2008; L. Jackson, Shirley Craven and Hull Traders: Revolutionary Fabrics and Furniture 1957–1980, 2009; Building Britannia: life experience with Britain, 2009; A. Buruma, Liberty and Co. in the Fifties and Sixties: a taste for design, 2009; A. Rice, Creating Memorials, Building Identities: the politics of memory in the black Atlantic, 2010; Denis Williams: a life in works: new and collected essays, 2010; A. Rice et al., Trade and Empire: remembering slavery, 2011; N. Albrechtsen and F. Solanke, Scarves, 2011; V&A Pattern: Modern British Designers, ed S Safer, 2012; V&A Pattern: Sanderson 1954–74, ed M. Schoeser, 2012; Artists' Textiles, 1940–1976, 2012; J. Kelman, And the Judge Said…, 2012; L. Jackson, Alastair Morton and Edinburgh Weavers: Visionary Textiles in Modern Art, 2012; W. Schwarz, West Indian Intellectuals in Britain, 2013; G. Collier, D. Walcott, The Journeyman Years, vol. 1, 2013; E. Chambers, Black Artists in British Art, 2014; The Handbook of Textile Culture, 2015; River of Freedom, 2016; R. Rowe, Imagining Caribbean Womanhood, 2016; published in Race Today, Decorative Art, Designers in Britain, Penrose Annual and art and design jls. *Recreations:* ski-ing, travelling, music, gardening. *E:* althea.mcnish@virgin.net. *Club:* Soroptimist.

**MACNIVEN, Duncan,** CBE 2012; TD 1985; Registrar General for Scotland, 2003–11; *b* 1 Dec. 1950; *s* of late John and Jenny Macniven; *m* 1976, Valerie Margaret Clark; two *d*. *Educ:* Melville Coll., Edinburgh; Aberdeen Univ. (MA 1973; MLitt 1978). Joined Scottish Office, 1973; Principal, 1978–85; Asst Sec., 1986–90; Dep. Dir, Historic Scotland, 1990–95; Head of Police Div., 1995–97; Head of Police, Fire and Emergencies Gp, 1997–99; Comr and Hd of Corporate Services, Forestry Commn, 1999–2003. RE, TA, 1969–85 (Major, 1983–85). Trustee, John Muir Trust, 2015–. Asst Scout Leader, 2014–.

Hon. LLD: Robert Gordon, 2008; Aberdeen, 2012. *Recreations:* active church membership, being outdoors, walking, ski-ing, Scottish history, family history. *Address:* Ashestiel, Kenmore Street, Aberfeldy, Perthshire PH15 2BL.

**McNULTY, Rt Hon. Anthony James;** PC 2007; *b* 3 Nov. 1958; *s* of James Anthony McNulty and Eileen Anne McNulty; *m* 2002, Christine Gilbert. *Educ:* Univ. of Liverpool (BA Hons); Virginia Poly. Inst. and State Univ. (MA); City Univ. London (MA Dist.). Business School, Polytechnic of North London: Research Asst, 1983–85; Res. Fellow and part-time Lectr, 1985–86; part-time Lectr, PCL and Kingston Poly., 1984–86; Sen. Lectr, then Principal Lectr, Business Sch., Poly. of N London, later Univ. of N London, 1986–97. MP (Lab) Harrow E, 1997–2010; contested (Lab) same seat, 2010. Mem. (Lab), Harrow LBC, 1986–97 (Dep. Leader, 1990–96, Leader, 1996–97, Labour Gp). Mem., Regl Exec., Gtr London Labour Party, 1985–87. Mem., NI Grand Cttee. PPS to Min. of State, DfEE, 1997–99; an Asst Govt Whip, 1999–2001; a Lord Comr of HM Treasury (Govt Whip), 2001–02; Parliamentary Under-Secretary of State: ODPM, 2002–03; DfT, 2003–04; Minister of State: DfT, 2004–05; Home Office, 2005–08; DWP, 2008–09; Minister for London, 2008–09. *Publications:* various academic works on local govt, public sector mgt, trng and small firms. *Recreations:* eating out, theatre, films, Rugby, current affairs.

**McNULTY, Des(mond);** Deputy Director, Policy Scotland, since 2014, and Assistant Vice-Principal (Economic Development and Civic Engagement), since 2017, University of Glasgow; *b* Stockport, 28 July 1952; *m*; two *s*. *Educ:* St Bede's Coll., Manchester; York Univ.; Glasgow Univ. Subject Leader in Sociology, 1990–97, Head of Strategic Planning, 1997–99, Glasgow Caledonian Univ. Non-exec. Dir, Gtr Glasgow Health Bd, 1998–99. Member (Lab): Strathclyde Regl Council, 1990–96; Glasgow City Council, 1995–99. Mem. (Lab) Clydebank and Milngavie, Scottish Parlt, 1999–2011; contested (Lab) same seat, 2011. Dep. Minister for Communities, Scottish Exec., 2002–03, 2006–07. Scottish Parliament: shadow spokesman on transport, 2007–09; Shadow Cabinet Sec. for Educn and Lifelong Learning, 2009–11; Member: Transport and Envmt Cttee, 1999–2003; Corporate Body, 1999–2001; Enterprise and Lifelong Learning Cttee, 2000–01; Rural and Environment Cttee, 2007–08; Transport Infrastructure and Climate Change Cttee, 2008–11; Convenor, Finance Cttee, 2001–02, 2003–06. Chairman: Glasgow Healthy City Partnership, 1999–; Glasgow 1999 Fest. of Architecture and Design. Board Member: Wise Gp, 1995–; Tron Theatre Ltd, 2005–12. Mem. Ct, Glasgow Univ., 1994–99. *Address:* 12A The Square, University of Glasgow G12 8QQ.

**McNULTY, Sir (Robert William) Roy,** Kt 1998; CBE 1992; Deputy Chairman, Gatwick Airport Ltd, 2017–18 (non-executive Director, 2011–18; Chairman, 2013–16); *b* 7 Nov. 1937; *s* of Jack and Nancy McNulty; *m* 1963, Ismay Ratcliffe Rome; one *s* two *d*. *Educ:* Portora Royal School, Enniskillen; Trinity College, Dublin (BA, BComm). Audit Manager, Peat Marwick Mitchell & Co., Glasgow, 1963–66; Accounting Methods Manager, Chrysler UK, Linwood, 1966–68; Harland & Wolff, Belfast: Management Accountant, 1968–72; Computer Services Manager, 1972–74; Management Services Manager, 1975–76; Sen. Management Consultant, Peat Marwick Mitchell & Co., Belfast, 1977–78; Short Brothers plc: Exec. Dir, Finance and Admin, 1978–85; Dep. Managing Dir, 1986–88; Man. Dir and Chief Exec., 1988–92; Pres., Shorts Gp, Bombardier Aerospace, 1992–96; Chm., 1996–99. Chairman: The Odyssey Trust Co. Ltd, 1997–99; NATS Ltd, 1999–2001; CAA, 2001–09 (Mem. Bd, 1999–2000); Ilex URC, 2007–12; Advantage West Midlands, 2009–12; Dep. Chm., Olympic Delivery Authy, 2007–14 (Acting Chm., 2006–07); non-executive Director: Norbrook Laboratories Ltd, 1990–2016 (Chm., 2014–16); Ulster Bank Ltd, 1996–2000; Monarch Hldgs Ltd, 2012–16 (Chm., 2014). Mem., Council, SBAC, 1988–99 (Pres., 1993–94; Treas., 1995–99). Member: IDB for NI, 1992–98; Steering Gp for UK Foresight Programme, 1997–2000; Chairman: NI Growth Challenge, 1993–98; Technology Foresight Defence and Aerospace Panel, 1994–95; DTI Aviation Cttee, 1995–98; Rail Value for Money Study, 2010–11. Industrial Prof., Dept of Engineering, Univ. of Warwick. Vice Pres., EEF, 1997–2001. CCMI; FIMI. Hon. FRAeS 1995; Hon. DSc QUB, 1999; Hon. DTech Glamorgan, 2011. *Recreations:* walking, golf, reading.

**McPARTLAND, Stephen;** MP (C) Stevenage, since 2010; *b* 9 Aug. 1976; *m* Emma. *Educ:* Liverpool Coll.; Liverpool Univ. (BA Hist. 1997); Liverpool John Moores Univ. (MSc Technol. Mgt 1998). Agent, NE Herts Cons. Assoc., 2001–08; Membership Dir, British Amer. Business, 2008–10. *Address:* House of Commons, SW1A 0AA.

**McPARTLIN, Anthony David,** OBE 2016; actor and presenter; *b* Newcastle upon Tyne, 18 Nov. 1975. Music career, 1993–97 (14 Top 20 hits; UK, European and world tours); *television:* actor: Byker Grove, 1989–93; A Tribute to the Likely Lads, 2002; presenter of series with Declan Donnelly, *qv* as Ant and Dec: The Ant and Dec Show, 1995; Ant and Dec Unzipped, 1997; SM:TV Live, 1998–2001 (British Comedy Award, 2000; RTS Award, 2001); CD:UK, 1998–2001; Ant and Dec's Secret Camera Show, 2000; Friends Like These, 2000; Slap Bang with Ant and Dec, 2001; Pop Idol, 2001–03; Ant and Dec's Saturday Night Takeaway, 2002– (British Comedy Awards, 2003, 2004, 2005; Nat. TV Awards, 2007, 2010; British Acad. TV Award, 2014; Best Entertainment Perf., BAFTA, 2014, 2015); I'm a Celebrity… Get Me Out of Here!, 2002– (British Comedy Award, 2004; Best Entertainment Perf., BAFTA, 2010; Nat. TV Awards, 2011–18; TRIC Special Award, 2013; RTS Award, 2013); Gameshow Marathon, 2005; Pokerface, 2006–07; Britain's Got Talent, 2007–; Wanna Bet? (USA), 2008; Push the Button, 2010–11; Red or Black?, 2011–12; When Ant and Dec Met the Prince, 2016; host (with Declan Donnelly) Brit Awards, 2001, 2015, 2016; *film:* Alien Autopsy, 2006. Awards with Declan Donnelly include: Most Popular Entertainment Presenter of Year, annually, 2001–08 and 2010–15, Best TV Presenter, 2016–19, Landmark Award, 2014, Nat. TV Awards; Best Entertainment Personality, British Comedy Awards, 2003, 2004; Best Entertainment Performers, RTS Awards, 2011; Personality of the Year, Freesat Free TV Awards, 2014; TV Personality of the Year, TRIC Awards, 2013, 2014; UK TV Legends, Nickelodeon Kids' Choice Awards, 2015; TV Personality of the Year, TV and Radio Industry Club Awards, 2016, 2018; TV Times Favourite Presenter, 2017; Guinness World Record for Most Nat. TV Awards Won Consecutively, 2019. *Publications:* (with D. Donnelly) Ooh! What a Lovely Pair: our story, 2009. *Address:* c/o YMU Group, 4th Floor, 180 Great Portland Street, W1W 5QZ. *T:* (020) 8742 4950.

**McPHAIL, Dr Alastair David,** CMG 2014; OBE 2005; HM Diplomatic Service; Ambassador to Ethiopia and to Djibouti (non-resident), and Permanent Representative of the United Kingdom to the African Union, since 2019; *b* 2 March 1961; *m* 1989, (Pamela) Joanne Davies; two *s*. *Educ:* Univ. of Otago (Modern Langs); Univ. of Edinburgh (PhD Russian). Lectr in Russian, Nottingham Univ.; work in publishing; entered FCO, 1994; Nuclear Weapons Desk Officer, Security Policy Dept, FCO, 1994–95; Arabic lang. trng, 1995–96; First Sec. (Pol/Mil), Ankara, 1996–2000; Hd, Egypt, Libya and Sudan Section, Near East and N Africa Dept, 2000–02, Hd, Sudan Unit, 2002–04, FCO; UK Special Rep. for Sudan, 2004–05; Italian lang. trng, 2005; Minister and Dep. Hd of Mission, Rome, 2006–09; UK Special Envoy to Mali and Hd, Crisis Mgt Team, Bamako, 2009; Consul Gen., S Sudan, 2011; Ambassador to S Sudan, 2011–13; Consul Gen., Jerusalem, 2014–17.

**McPHAIL, Angus William,** MA, MLitt; Warden, Radley College, 2000–14; *b* 25 May 1956; *s* of Peter Bigham McPhail and Sylvia Bridget McPhail (née Campbell); *m* 1980, Elizabeth Hirsch; two *s* one *d*. *Educ:* Abingdon Sch.; University Coll., Oxford (BA Hons 1978; MA 1982); Univ. of St Andrews (MLitt 2015). Overseas Dept, Bank of England, 1978–82; Asst Master, Glenalmond Coll., 1982–85; Head of Econs and Housemaster, Sedbergh Sch., 1985–93; Headmaster, Strathallan Sch., 1993–2000. *Recreations:* cricket, golf, music, walking. *Clubs:* Vincent's (Oxford); Cryptics Cricket.

**MacPHAIL, Sir Bruce (Dugald),** Kt 1992; FCA; Managing Director, Peninsular and Oriental Steam Navigation Co., 1985–2003; *b* 1 May 1939; *s* of late Dugald Ronald MacPhail and Winifred Marjorie MacPhail; *m* 1st, 1963, Susan Mary Gregory (*d* 1975); three *s*; 2nd, 1983, Caroline Ruth Grimston Curtis-Bennett (née Hubbard). *Educ:* Haileybury Coll.; Balliol Coll., Oxford (MA); Harvard Business Sch., Mass, USA (MBA 1967). FCA 1976. Articled, Price Waterhouse, 1961–65; Hill Samuel & Co. Ltd, 1967–69; Finance Director: Sterling Guarantee Trust Ltd, 1969–74; Town & City Properties Ltd, 1974–76; Man. Dir, Sterling Guarantee Trust, 1976–85. Non-executive Director: Chelsfield Plc, 1999–2004; Chelsfield Partners, 2006–18; Intelligent Engrg Ltd, 2005–16; Scarborough Minerals, 2006–08. Gov., Royal Ballet Sch., 1982–99; Life Gov., 1992, and Mem. Council, 1992–2004, Haileybury Coll.; Chairman: Council, Templeton Coll., Oxford, 1993–95; Council for Sch. of Management Studies, Univ. of Oxford, 1995–2001; Business Adv. Forum, Saïd Business Sch., Univ. of Oxford, 2001–08. Barclay Fellow, Green Templeton Coll. (formerly Templeton Coll.), Oxford, 1995–2012 (Hon. Fellow, 2012). Trustee, Sir Jules Thorn Charitable Trust, 1994–. *Recreations:* reading, wine, scuba diving. *Address:* Thorpe Lubenham Hall, Lubenham, Market Harborough, Leics LE16 9TR.

**McPHATE, Very Rev. Gordon Ferguson,** MD, FRCPE; Dean of Chester, 2002–17; *b* 1 June 1950; *s* of David and Grace McPhate; one adopted *s*. *Educ:* Aberdeen Univ. (MB, ChB 1974); Fitzwilliam Coll., Cambridge (BA 1977, MA 1981, MD 1988); Surrey Univ. (MSc 1986); Edinburgh Univ. (MTh 1994); Westcott House Theol Coll., Cambridge. Dip. RCPath 2019. FRCPE 1998. Ordained deacon, 1978, priest, 1979. Tutor in Physiol., Clare Coll., Cambridge, 1975–77; Lectr in Physiol., Guy's Hosp. Med. Sch., London Univ., 1978–84; Registrar in Pathol., Guildford Hosps, 1984–86; Lectr in Pathol., 1986–93, Sen. Lectr, 1993–2002, St Andrews Univ.; Fife Hospitals: Hon. Sen. Registrar in Pathol., 1988–96; Hon. Consultant Chem. Pathologist, 1996–2002; Consultant Chem. Pathologist, 2001–02. External Mem., GMC, 2000–15. Hon. Curate, Sanderstead, 1978–80; Hon. Minor Canon, Southwark Cathedral, 1980–86; Hon. Chaplain, St Andrews Univ., 1986–2002. Vis. Prof. of Theol. and Medicine, Univ. of Chester (formerly UC Chester), 2003–; Hon. Reader in Medicine, Univ. of Liverpool, 2005–08. FHEA 2007. Hon. DD Chester, 2017. *Publications:* articles in learned jls. *Recreations:* classical and choral music, 18th and 19th century Western art, cinema, reading history and biography. *Address:* 50 Llys Onnen, Llandudno, Conwy, N Wales LL31 9EZ.

**McPHEE, Robin Alasdair; His Honour Judge McPhee;** a Circuit Judge, since 2019; *b* 3 Sept. 1958; *s* of Kenneth Alfred McPhee and Margaret Thorpe McPhee; *m* 1982, Beverley Jayne Leggatt; one *s* one *d*. *Educ:* Goffs Sch., Cheshunt. Admitted as solicitor, 1983; Clerk: Tottenham Magistrates' Court, 1977–83; Harlow, Epping and Ongar Magistrates' Court, 1983–88; Partner, Attwater & Liell, Solicitors, Harlow, Essex, 1988–2002; a District Judge (Magistrates' Cts), 2002–19. *Recreations:* reading, ski-ing, hill walking. *Address:* Watford County Court and Family Court, 3rd Floor, Cassiobury House, 11–19 Station Road, Watford WD17 1EZ.

**MACPHERSON,** family name of **Barons Macpherson of Drumochter, Macpherson of Earl's Court** and **Strathcarron**.

**MACPHERSON OF DRUMOCHTER,** 3rd Baron *cr* 1951; **James Anthony Macpherson;** *b* London, 27 Feb. 1979; *o s* of 2nd Baron Macpherson of Drumochter and of Catherine Bridget Macpherson (née MacCarthy); *S* father, 2008; *m* 2009, Kirsty, *y d* of Mrs Katalin Zetenyi Budai, Budapest; two *s* one *d*. *Educ:* Napier Univ., Edinburgh (BA Hons Business Studies 2002); Aberdeen Univ. (Master of Land Econ. 2010). Dir, Games and Movies, 2003–07; Property Co-ordinator, Alba Residential, 2007–08; Dir, Tomatin Firewood, 2011–. Trustee, Lord Macpherson Trust, 2015–. *Recreations:* tennis, field sports, travel, restaurants, films, photography. *Heir: s* Hon. Daniel Thomas Macpherson, *b* 23 Jan. 2013. *Address:* Ardachy House, Tomatin, Inverness-shire IV13 7YA. *T:* 07527 883606. *E:* Thelordmacpherson@googlemail.com.

**MACPHERSON OF EARL'S COURT,** Baron *cr* 2016 (Life Peer), of Earl's Court in the Royal Borough of Kensington and Chelsea; **Nicholas Ian Macpherson,** GCB 2015 (KCB 2009); Chairman, C. Hoare & Co., since 2016; *b* 14 July 1959; *s* of Ewen Macpherson and Nicolette Macpherson (née Van der Bijl); *m* 1983, Suky Jane Appleby; two *s*. *Educ:* Eton Coll.; Balliol Coll., Oxford; University Coll. London. Economist; CBI, 1982–83; Peat Marwick and Mitchell, 1983–85; joined HM Treasury, 1985; Principal Private Sec. to Chancellor of the Exchequer, 1993–97; Head of Work Incentives Policy, 1997–98; Dep. Dir, then Dir, (Welfare Reform), Budget and Public Finances, 1998–2001; Man. Dir, Public Services, 2001–04, Budget and Public Finances, 2004–05; Perm. Sec., 2005–16. Non-executive Director: HM Revenue and Customs, 2005–07; Scottish American Investment Co., 2016–; British Land, 2016–. Vis. Fellow, Nuffield Coll., Oxford, 2007–15; Visiting Professor: QMUL, 2012–16; KCL, 2014–. Trustee, Royal Mint Mus., 2015–. *Address:* House of Lords, SW1A 0PW. *Clubs:* Athenæum, MCC.

**MACPHERSON, (Agnes Lawrie Addie) Shonaig, (Mrs S. Cairns),** CBE 2006; FRSE; Chairman, Royal Lyceum Theatre Company, since 2012; *b* 29 Sept. 1958; *d* of Harry Dempster Baird Macpherson and Margaret Douglas McClure; *m* 2002, Scott Cairns; two *s* by Roger Brown. *Educ:* Univ. of Sheffield (LLB Hons); Coll. of Law, Chester; Open Univ. (BA Hons). Admitted solicitor: England and Wales (Dist.), 1984; Scotland, 1992; Solicitor: Norton Rose, 1982–85; Corporate Dept, Knapp Fisher, 1985–87; Asst Co. Sec., Storehouse plc, 1987; Hd, Legal Dept, Harrods Ltd, 1987–89; Partner, Calow Easton, 1989–91; McGrigor Donald, later McGrigors, Solicitors: Hd, IP/Technol. Team, 1991–2004; Man. Partner, Edinburgh, 1996–2001; Sen. Partner, 2001–04. Co. Sec., 2012–16, Chm., 2015, Macpherson Coaches Ltd. Chairman: SCDI, 2004–09 (Mem. Bd, 2000–09); Nat. Trust for Scotland, 2005–10. Director: ITI Scotland Ltd, 2003–09 (Chm., 2005–09); Edinburgh Internat. Conf. Centre Ltd, 2005–14; Braveheart Ventures, 2005–08; Braveheart Investment Gp, 2005–08; Edinburgh Military Tattoo Ltd, later Royal Edinburgh Military Tattoo, 2008–15 (Dep. Chm., 2010–15); Euan's Guide Ltd, 2015–18; non-exec. Dir, Futurelearn Ltd, 2016–19. Mem., Scottish Adv. Bd, BT plc, 2002–19 (Chm., 2008–19). Mem., Calman Commn on Scottish Devolution, 2009–10. Scottish Executive: non-exec. Mem., Mgt Gp, 2001–07; Culture Comr, 2004–05; Mem., Jt Mgt Bd, Scotland Office and Office of Advocate Gen., 2015– (Lead non-exec. Dir, 2019–). Chm., Scottish Council Foundn, 2000–09. Pres., Edinburgh Chamber of Commerce, 2002–04; Dep. Pres., British Chambers of Commerce, 2004–06. Mem. Bd, Edinburgh Internat. Film Fest., 2000–09. Mem. Ct, Univ. of Edinburgh, 2001–07; Governor: Edinburgh Coll. of Art, 2000–11; Heriot-Watt Univ., 2009–15; Royal Conservatoire of Scotland, 2015–18; Mem. Council, Open Univ., 2009–17; Chm., Edinburgh Business Sch., 2015–17. Chm., Prince's Scottish YBT, 2007–12; Trustee: Robertson Trust, 2005–

(Dep. Chm., 2014–17; Chm., 2017–); Prince's Trust Scotland, 2005–10 (Chm., 2007–10); Prince's Trust, 2007–10; Dunedin Consort, 2012–18; Scottish Chamber Orch. Trust, 2010–. CCMI 2009. FRSE 2004; FRSA 2000. DUniv: Glasgow, 2007; Heriot Watt, 2018. *Recreations:* theatre, golf, film, walking, 20th century literature. *Address:* Lochcote, Linlithgow, W Lothian EH49 6QE. *Fax:* (01506) 655231. *E:* shonaigm@btconnect.com.

**McPHERSON, Prof. Andrew Francis;** Professor of Sociology, 1989–96, now Emeritus, and Director, Centre for Educational Sociology, 1972–96, University of Edinburgh; *b* 6 July 1942; *m* 1st, 1965, Eldwyth Mary Boyle (*d* 2000); one *s* one *d*; 2nd, 1989, Alison Jean Elphinstone Edward or Arnott (*d* 2002). *Educ:* Ripon Grammar Sch.; The Queen's Coll., Oxford (BA Hist.). DPSA; FEIS; FSCRE. Lectr in Sociology, Univ. of Glasgow, 1965; University of Edinburgh: Res. Fellow in Education, 1968; Lectr in Sociology, 1973; Sen. Lectr, 1978; Reader, 1983. FRSE 1994; FBA 1993–2003. *Publications:* (with G. Neave) The Scottish Sixth, 1976; (with L. Gow) Tell Them from Me, 1980; (jtly) Reconstructions of Secondary Education, 1983; (with C. Raab) Governing Education, 1988; academic articles on history and sociology of education. *Recreations:* music, sport, art history.

**MACPHERSON, Prof. Fiona Elizabeth,** PhD; FRSE; Director, Centre for Study of Perceptual Experience, since 2004, and Professor of Philosophy, since 2011, University of Glasgow (Head of Philosophy, 2014–17); *b* Irvine, Scotland, 19 Oct. 1971; *d* of Matthew Macpherson and Margaret Hyndman Macpherson (*née* Taylor, now Arthur). *Educ:* Ardrossan Acad.; Univ. of Glasgow (MA 1st Cl. Hons 1993); Univ. of St Andrews (MLitt 1995); Univ. of Stirling (PhD 2000). ALCM 1988. Vis. Fellow, Harvard Univ., 1998–99; Teaching Fellow, Univ. of St Andrews, 2000–02; Rosamund Chambers Res. Fellow in Philosophy, Girton Coll., Cambridge, 2002–04; Lectr, 2004–08, Sen. Lectr, 2008–11, Univ. of Glasgow; Res. Fellow, ANU, 2005–06, 2008, 2009; Co-Dir, CenSes: Centre for Study of the Senses, Inst. of Philosophy, Sch. of Advanced Study, Univ. of London, 2009–. Visiting Professor: Umeå Univ., 2011; Univ. of London, 2013; Trnava Univ., 2015; Dept of Philosophy, Univ. of Kentucky, 2017; Vis. Faculty, Nat. Endowment for Humanities Summer Inst. on Presuppostion and Perception, Cornell Univ., 2016. Mem., AHRC, 2014–. Trustee, Kennedy Meml Trust, 2014–. Pres., British Philosophical Assoc., 2019–. MAE 2018. FRSE 2017. *Publications:* (ed with A. Haddock) Disjunctivism: perception, action, knowledge, 2008; (ed with K. Hawley) The Admissible Contents of Experience, 2011; (ed) The Senses: classical and contemporary philosophical perspectives, 2011; (ed with D. Platchias) Hallucination: philosophy and psychology, 2013; (ed with F. Dorsch) Perceptual Imagination and Perceptual Memory, 2018; (ed with F. Dorsch) Phenomenal Presence, 2018; (ed with D. Brown) The Routledge Handbook of the Philosophy of Colour, 2019; (ed) Sensory Substitution and Augmentation, 2018; contrib. papers to philosophy and psychol. jls. *Recreations:* blethering and getting stocious with friends, vegan gastronomy, science, walking, travel, music, art, film, Partick Thistle Football Club. *Address:* Department of Philosophy, 67–69 Oakfield Avenue, University of Glasgow, Glasgow G12 8QQ. *E:* fiona.macpherson@glasgow.ac.uk.

**McPHERSON, Graeme Paul;** QC 2008; barrister; licensed racehorse trainer; *b* Dartford, Kent, 23 Sept. 1970; *s* of Ian Bernard McPherson and Maureen Ethel McPherson (*née* Larkins); *m* 2002, Mary Seanin Gilmore; one *s* two *d*. *Educ:* Canford Sch.; Emmanuel Coll., Cambridge (BA Hons 1992; MA 1995). Called to the Bar, Gray's Inn, 1993; in practice as barrister specialising in professional indemnity and sports law. Judicial Officer, FA, 2018–; Mem., Panel of Arbitrators, Sports Resolutions, 2017–. Holder of public licence to train racehorses, 2006. *Publications:* (ed) Jackson and Powell on Professional Indemnity, 5th edn 2002, 6th edn 2007. *Recreations:* training racehorses, dreaming of winners. *Address:* 4 New Square, Lincoln's Inn, WC2A 3RJ. *T:* (020) 7822 2000, *Fax:* (020) 7822 2001. *E:* g.mcpherson@4newsquare.com.

**McPHERSON, Ian Andrew,** QPM 2009; Partner, Advisory, KPMG LLP, Denver, since 2015; *b* Lancs, 25 March 1961; *s* of Ian Douglas McPherson and Mary Elizabeth McPherson (*née* Simpson); *m* 1984, Wendy Spence; one *s* one *d*. *Educ:* Univ. of Central Lancashire (MBA 1999); Cambridge Univ. (Dip. Applied Criminol. 2000). Various ranks, Lancs Constabulary, 1979–2001 (Divl Comdr, Burnley, Pendle and Rossendale, 1999–2001); Asst Chief Constable, Merseyside Police, 2001–05; Dep. Chief Constable, N Yorks Police, 2005–06; Chief Constable, Norfolk Constabulary, 2006–10; Asst Comr of Territorial Policing, Metropolitan Police Service, 2010–11; Partner, Justice and Security, KPMG Canada, 2012–15. National Lead: Business Area for Children and Young People, ACPO, 2008–; Police Support Help for Heroes, 2011–. Hon. Fellow, Univ. of Central Lancs, 2008. *Recreations:* running, walking, ski-ing, keen follower of Rugby and supporter of Preston North End FC. *Address:* KPMG LLP, Suite 800, 1225 17th Street, Denver, CO 80202–5598, USA.

**McPHERSON, Katherine;** Strategy and Marketing Director, Fieldfisher LLP (formerly Field Fisher Waterhouse), since 2016 (Marketing Director, 2013–16); *b* 23 May 1964; *d* of Ezra Balaraj and Rebecca Balaraj (*née* Jacobs); *m* 1997, Alasdair McPherson; twin *d*. *Educ:* Nat. Univ. of Singapore (BA); Univ. of Kent, Canterbury (MBA). Ernst & Young: Project Manager, 1987–88, Mktg Manager, 1988–90, Exec. Consultant, 1990–92, Mgt Consultants, Singapore; Sen. Manager, Nat. Sales and Mktg, UK, 1992–95; Hd of Sales and Mktg, Media and Resources Office, 1996–98; Nat. Hd of Sales and Mktg, Technol., Communications and Entertainment, 1998–99; Project Dir, BBC, 1999 (on secondment); Mgt Consultant, Cap Gemini Ernst & Young, 1999–2001; Business Develt Manager, 2001–02, Ops Dir, 2002, Lambeth, Lewisham and Southwark YMCA; Dir of Business Develt and Marketing, Europe, Middle East and Africa, White & Case, 2002–04; Head of Business Develt, Corporate, 2004–05, Europe, 2005–07, Herbert Smith; Head of Winning Business, 2007–10, Dir, Global Mkts, 2010–13, KPMG. Mediator, 2013. Mem., S London Bd, Prince's Youth Business Trust, 2000–02. Vis. Prof., Univ. of Law, 2018–. Church of England: Member: Archbishops' Council, 2003–09 (Mem., HR Panel, 2003–09); Dir, Central Bd of Finance, 2003–09; Mem., Gen. Synod, 2003–09; Mem., Strategic Investment Bd, 2017–. Mem., PCC, St John's Ch, Blackheath, 2006–09, 2017–. *Recreations:* reading, cooking, walking, music. *E:* mcpherson.katherine@gmail.com.

**MACPHERSON, (Philip) Strone (Stewart);** Chairman, Close Brothers Group plc, 2008–17 (non-executive Director, 2003–08); *b* Edinburgh, 21 July 1948; *s* of Brig. George Philip Stewart Macpherson and Elizabeth Margaret Cameron Smail; *m* 1981, Hon. Alexandra Grace Baring; one *s* two *d*. *Educ:* Summer Fields, Oxford; Fettes Coll., Edinburgh; Oriel Coll., Oxford (MA Juris. 1970); INSEAD (MBA 1975). Chairman: JP Morgan Smaller Companies Investment Trust plc, 1990–2013; Tribal Gp, 2004–10; British Empire Securities and General Trust, 2007–17; Estover Energy Ltd, 2010–; Exec. Dep. Chm., Misys, 1991–2002; former Dir, Flemings; non-executive Director: Axa plc; Kleinwort Benson Private Bank, 2003–10. Trustee Mem., Audit Cttee and Chm., Investment Cttee, 2009–18, King's Fund. Chm., Audit Cttee and Mem., Develt Trust, Oriel Coll., Oxford; Mem. Ct, Heriot Watt Univ., 2012–17. Mem., Highland Soc. *Recreations:* restoring listed buildings, early motor cars, Scottish pictures, travel, active country pursuits. *Clubs:* Caledonian; 20 Ghost.

**MACPHERSON, Shonaig;** *see* Macpherson, A. L. A. S.

**MACPHERSON, Strone;** *see* Macpherson, P. S. S.

**MACPHERSON, Prof. Stuart Gowans,** OBE 2007; FRCSGlas, FRCSE, FRCS, FRCP, FRCGP; Professor of Postgraduate Medical Education, University of Edinburgh, 1999–2010, now Emeritus; *b* 11 July 1945; *s* of John Buchanan Macpherson and Elizabeth Doris Macpherson (*née* Gowans); *m* 1970, Norma Elizabeth Carslaw; two *s* one *d*. *Educ:* Allan Glen's Sch., Glasgow; Univ. of Glasgow (MB ChB with Commendation 1968). FRCSGlas 1972; FRCPE 2000; FRCSE 2001; FRCS 2002; FRCGP 2005. Res. Fellow, Harvard Med. Sch., 1973–74; University of Glasgow: Sen. Lectr in Surgery, 1977–99; Associate Undergrad. Dean (Admissions), 1991–99; Associate Postgrad. Dean, 1994–99; Postgrad. Dean, SE Scotland, 1999–2009; Hon. Consultant Surgeon, Western Infirmary, Glasgow, 1977–99. Mem. Bd, 2003–08, Chm., 2008–10, Postgraduate Med. Educn and Trng Bd; Mem., Postgraduate Bd, GMC, 2010–11. Convener, Business Cttee, Gen. Council, Univ. of Edinburgh, 2016–. Hon. FAcadMed 2009. *Publications:* articles on surgery, transplantation and med. educn in med. jls. *Recreations:* family, golf, travel, Isle of Arran. *Address:* 33/4 Blackford Road, Edinburgh EH9 2DT. *T:* (0131) 668 4574. *Clubs:* New (Edinburgh); Shiskine Golf and Tennis, Bruntsfield Links Golfing Society.

**MACPHERSON OF CLUNY (and Blairgowrie), Sir William (Alan),** Kt 1983; TD 1966; Cluny Macpherson; 27th Chief of Clan Macpherson; Judge of the High Court of Justice, Queen's Bench Division, 1983–96; *b* 1 April 1926; *s* of Brig. Alan David Macpherson, DSO, MC, RA (*d* 1969) and late Catharine Richardson Macpherson; *m* 1962, Sheila McDonald Brodie (*d* 2003); one *s* one *d* (and one *s* decd). *Educ:* Wellington Coll., Berkshire; Trinity Coll., Oxford (MA; Hon. Fellow, 1991). Called to Bar, Inner Temple, 1952; Bencher, 1978; QC 1971; a Recorder of the Crown Court, 1972–83; Presiding Judge, Northern Circuit, 1985–88; Pres., Interception of Communications Tribunal, 1990–2000; Chm., Stephen Lawrence Inquiry, 1997–99. Mem., Bar Council and Senate, 1981–83; Hon. Mem., Northern Circuit, 1987. Served, 1944–47, in Scots Guards (Capt.). Commanded (Lt-Col) 21st Special Air Service Regt (TA), 1962–65, Hon. Col, 1983–91; Mem., Queen's Body Guard for Scotland, Royal Co. of Archers, 1977–2006, Lieut 2004. Gov., Royal Scottish Corporation, 1972–96 (Vice-Pres., 1989–2005). Mem., Tay Dist Salmon Fisheries Bd, 1996–99. *Recreations:* golf, fishing, archery; Past Pres., London Scottish FC. *Heir:* *s* James Brodie Macpherson yr of Cluny and Blairgowrie. *Address:* Newton Castle, Blairgowrie, Perthshire PH10 6SU. *Clubs:* Caledonian, Highland Society of London (Pres., 1991–94); New (Edinburgh); Blairgowrie Golf.

**McQUAID, James,** CB 1997; PhD; FREng, FIMMM; Director, Science and Technology, and Chief Scientist, Health and Safety Executive, 1996–99; *b* 5 Nov. 1939; *s* of late James and Brigid McQuaid; *m* 1968, Catherine Anne, *d* of late Dr James John Hargan and Dr Mary Helen Hargan; two *s* one *d*. *Educ:* Christian Brothers' Sch., Dundalk; University Coll., Dublin (BEng); Jesus Coll., Cambridge (PhD); DSc NUI 1978. MIMechE 1972; FIMMM (FIMinE 1986); FREng (FEng 1991). Graduate engrg apprentice, British Nylon Spinners, 1961–63; Sen. Res. Fellow 1966–68, Sen. Scientific Officer 1968–72, PSO 1972–78, Safety in Mines Res. Estabt; seconded as Safety Advr, Petrochemicals Div., ICI, 1976–77; Health and Safety Executive: Dep. Dir, Safety Engrg Lab., 1978–80, Dir, 1980–85; Res. Dir, 1985–92; Dir, Strategy and Gen. Div. and Chief Scientist, 1992–96. Mem., Envmtl Security Panel, NATO Sci. Cttee, 2005–08 (Chm., 2007–08). Chm., Electrical Equipment Certification Management Bd, 1985–92; Member: Safety in Mines Res. Adv. Bd, 1985–92; Council, Midland Inst. of Mining Engrs, 1987–98 (Vice-Pres., 1991–93, Pres., 1993–94); Council, IMinE, 1991–95; Council, Royal Acad. Engrg, 1995–98; Adv. Bd for Mech. Engrg, Univ. of Liverpool, 1987–92; Exec. Cttee, RoSPA, 1992–94; Standing Cttee on Scientific Aspects of Internat. Security, Royal Soc., 2006–08; Health Protection Adv. Gp, HPA, 2006–09. Mem. Court, 1985–2003, Mem. Council, 1993–2003, Vis. Prof. of Mechanical Engrg, 1996–2017, Univ. of Sheffield; Visiting Professor: of Sustainable Develt, Ulster Univ., 1999–2002; of Civil Engrg, QUB, 2002–05. Pres., Sheffield Trades Hist. Soc., 1989–91. Mem., Council, S Yorks Trades Hist. Trust, 1989– (Chm., 1999–2016). Mem., Bd of Govs, EC Jt Res. Centre, 2001–07. FRSA 2000; FIAE 2001. Hon. DEng Sheffield, 2000. *Publications:* numerous papers in technical jls. *Recreations:* ornamental turning, model engineering, industrial archaeology, theatre. *Address:* 61 Pingle Road, Sheffield S7 2LL. *T:* (0114) 236 5349.

**MacQUARRIE, (John) Kenneth;** Director, Nations and Regions, BBC, since 2016; *b* 5 June 1952; *s* of Duncan and Peggy MacQuarrie; *m* 1977, Angela Sparks; one *s* two *d*. *Educ:* Oban High Sch.; Univ. of Edinburgh (MA Eng. and Hist. 1973); Moray House Coll. of Educn, Edinburgh (DipEd 1974). BBC Scotland: joined as researcher, 1975; radio producer, BBC Highland, 1976–79; producer, TV, 1979–88; Head: of Gaelic, 1988–92; of Gaelic and Features, 1992–97; of Broadcast, 1997–2000; of Progs, 2000–04; Controller, later Dir, 2004–16. Board Member: Scottish Film Council, 1990–97; Gaelic Media Service, 2004–08; Vice Chm., Celtic Film and TV Assoc., 1986–93; Founder Mem., Scottish Screen Forum, 1986. Chm., Nat. Bd, Skillset Scotland, 2009–13. *Recreations:* sailing, reading, walking. *E:* ken.macquarrie@bbc.co.uk.

**McQUATER, Ewan Alan;** QC 2003; *b* 30 Oct. 1962; *s* of Angus and Doreen McQuater; *m* 1999, Caroline Hudson; two *s*. *Educ:* Robinson Coll., Cambridge (MA 1st cl. Hons Law 1984). Called to the Bar, Middle Temple, 1985; barrister practising in commercial law, 1986–. Asst Ed., Encyclopaedia of Banking Law, 1985–2005. *Recreations:* Rugby, blues piano. *Address:* 3 Verulam Buildings, Gray's Inn, WC1R 5NT. *T:* (020) 7831 8441, *Fax:* (020) 7831 8479. *E:* emcquater@3vb.com. *Club:* Belsize Park Rugby Football.

**McQUAY, Prof. Henry John,** DM; FRCA, FRCPE; Nuffield Professor of Clinical Anaesthetics, University of Oxford, 2007–10, now Emeritus; Fellow, Balliol College, Oxford, 1987–2010, now Emeritus; *b* 16 Sept. 1948; *s* of T. A. I. and M. D. McQuay; *m* 1st, 1971, Meryl Rhys Jones (marr. diss. 2001); two *d*; 2nd, 2002, Maureen Richfield. *Educ:* Sedbergh Sch.; Balliol Coll., Oxford (MA, BM BCL 1974; DM 1985). FRCA 1979; FRCPE 2002. Clin. Reader in Pain Relief, 1985–98, Prof. of Pain Relief, 1998–2007, Oxford Pain Relief Unit, Nuffield Dept of Anaesthetics, Univ. of Oxford. Consultant, Churchill Hosp., Oxford. Dir, R&D, Oxford Regl HA, 1992–94. Praefectus, Holywell Manor, 1997–2000. *Publications:* An Evidence-based Resource for Pain Relief, 1998; Bandolier's Little Book of Pain, 2003; Bandolier's Little Book of Making Sense of The Medical Evidence, 2006; scientific papers. *Address:* Nuffield Department of Anaesthetics, John Radcliffe Hospital, Headley Way, Oxford OX3 9DU.

**MACQUEEN, Angus Donald;** Director, Ronachan Films, 2005–06 and since 2008; *b* 20 Oct. 1958; *s* of Angus and Elizabeth Macqueen; *m* 2004, Fiona Marie Currie; one *s*. *Educ:* Lincoln Coll., Oxford (BA English 1980). Lectr, Univ. of Wrocław, Poland, 1981–84; British Council Lectr, Univ. of Novosibirsk, USSR, 1984–85; Dir, October Films, 2000–05; Hd of Documentaries, Channel 4 TV, 2006–08. Documentary Director: The Hand of Stalin, 1990; The Second Russian Revolution, 1991; The Death of Yugoslavia, 1995; The People's Century, 1997; Dancing for Dollars, 1998; Gulag, 1999; Vodka, 2000; The Last Peasants, 2003; Cocaine, 2005; (also presenter) Our Drugs War (series), 2010; 2320 Days in the Jungle, 2010; 17 Days Buried Alive, 2011; Aung San Suu Kyi: the choice, 2012; The Legend of Shorty, 2014; First Contact: the lost tribe of the Amazon, 2016; The End of Eden, 2016; Oink: man loves pig, 2017; Executive Producer: Leonora Carrington, the Lost Surrealist, 2018; Working with Weinstein, 2018; Il Testigo: Cain i Abel, 2018. *Recreations:* being in Kintyre, Scotland.

**MacQUEEN, Prof. Hector Lewis,** CBE 2019; PhD; FBA 2006; FRSE; Professor of Private Law, University of Edinburgh, since 1994; Commissioner, Scottish Law Commission, 2009–18; *b* 13 June 1956; *s* of late Prof. John MacQueen and Winifred W. MacQueen (*née* McWalter); *m* 1979, Frances Mary Young; two *s* one *d. Educ:* George Heriot's Sch., Edinburgh; Univ. of Edinburgh (LLB Hons; PhD). Lectr, 1979–91, Sen. Lectr, 1991–94, Reader, 1994, Univ. of Edinburgh. Visiting Professor: Cornell Univ., 1991; Utrecht Univ., 1997; Stetson UC of Law, Florida, 2007–09. Mem., Adv. Panel on Public Sector Information, Cabinet Office, later MoJ, 2004–11. Mem., Co-ordinating Cttee, Eur. Civil Code Study Gp, 1999–2008. Chairman: Scottish Records Adv. Council, 2001–08; Scottish Medievalists, 2007–11; David Hume Inst., 2012–15. Literary Dir, Stair Soc., 1999–2016. Law Section Convener, British Acad., 2016–. Pres., Soc. of Legal Scholars, 2012–13; Vice-Pres. (Humanities), RSE, 2018–21; Vice-Pres., Scottish Text Soc., 2008–. FRSE 1995. *Publications:* Common Law and Feudal Society in Medieval Scotland, 1993, repr. 2016; Atlas of Scottish History to 1707, 1996; Copyright, Competition and Industrial Design, 1989, 2nd edn 1995; Studying Scots Law, 1993, 4th edn 2012; (with J. Thomson) Contract Law in Scotland, 2000, 4th edn 2016; Unjustified Enrichment, 2004, 3rd edn 2013; (jtly) Contemporary Intellectual Property: law and policy, 2007, 2nd edn 2010; (ed with J. N. Adams) Atiyah's Sale of Goods, 12th edn 2010, 13th edn (ed with C. Twigg-Flessner and R. Canavan) 2016; (ed with Rt Hon. Lord Eassie) Gloag & Henderson, The Law of Scotland, 13th edn 2012, 14th edn 2017; (ed) White & Willock, The Scottish Legal System, 5th edn 2013. *Recreations:* walking, sometimes with golf clubs, more often with the wife and a camera, cricket, Scotland, conviviality. *Address:* School of Law, University of Edinburgh, Old College, South Bridge, Edinburgh EH8 9YL. *T:* (0131) 650 4596. *E:* hector.macqueen@ed.ac.uk. *Club:* Heriot's Former Pupils Cricket.

**McQUEEN, Steve Rodney,** CBE 2011 (OBE 2002); artist; *b* 1969. *Educ:* Chelsea Sch. of Art; Goldsmiths' Coll.; Tish Sch. of Arts, NY Univ. Works incorporate film, photography and sculpture. Exhibitions in Europe and USA; solo exhibitions include: ICA, 1999; Thomas Dane Gall., 2004, 2007, 2014; Espace Louis Vuitton, Tokyo, 2014; Whitney Mus. of Contemp. Art, NY, Galerie Marian Goodman, Paris, 2016; ICA, Boston, 2017; represented GB, Venice Biennale, 2009. Works include: Bear, 1993; Five Easy Pieces, 1995; Stage, 1996; Just Above My Head, 1996; Deadpan, 1997; Drumroll, 1998; Cold Breath, 2000; Queen and Country, 2007; Ashes, 2014. Films: Hunger, 2008 (Carl Foreman Award, BAFTA, 2009); Shame, 2012; 12 Years a Slave, 2013 (Best Film, BAFTA, 2014); Widows, 2018. Turner Prize, 1999. *Address:* c/o Tate Gallery, Millbank, SW1P 4RG.

**McQUEEN, William Robert James,** CBE 2008; Deputy Chief Executive, Crown Office and Procurator Fiscal Service, Scottish Government (formerly Executive) Justice Department, 2005–08; *b* 19 April 1951; *s* of William Robert McQueen and Mary Jane McQueen (*née* Gregson); *m* 1989, Maureen Frances Hall; two *d. Educ:* Queen Mary Coll., London Univ. (BSc Hons Geog.); Univ. of Calif, Los Angeles (MA); Univ. of Strathclyde (MBA). Res. Officer, Local Govt Boundary Commn for Scotland, 1974–78; Scottish Office: Sen. Res. Officer, Central Res. Unit, 1979–85; Principal: Develt Dept, 1985–88; Agric. and Fisheries Dept, 1988–91; Industry Dept, 1991; Central Services, 1991–92; Hd of Mgt and Orgn Div., 1992–95; Head, Transport Div., Scottish Exec. Develt Dept, 1995–2001; Dir, Corporate Services, Crown Office and Procurator Fiscal Service, 2001–05. Member: Accounts Commn for Scotland, 2008–14; Scottish Legal Aid Bd, 2010–18; Lay Mem., Employment Tribunal Service, 2009–18; non-executive Director: Disclosure Scotland Agency, 2010–13; Scottish Fire and Rescue Service, 2012–; NHS Lothian, 2018–. *Recreations:* tennis, ski-ing, cooking. *Address:* 91 Trinity Road, Edinburgh EH5 3JX. *T:* (0131) 552 0876.

**MACQUIBAN, Rev. Timothy Stuart Alexander,** PhD; Director, Methodist Ecumenical Office Rome, and Minister, Pont Sant'Angelo Methodist Church, 2014–19; Research Director, Englesea Brook Museum of Methodism, Crewe, since 2019; *b* 11 Jan. 1952; *s* of late Gordon and Beryl Macquiban; *m* 1975, Angela (*née* Spencer). *Educ:* King's Sch., Chester; Jesus Coll., Cambridge (MA); Univ. of Liverpool (DipSRAA 1974); Univ. of Bristol (MA 1986); Univ. of Birmingham (PhD 2000). Asst Archivist, Wigan MBC, 1974–77; Borough Archivist, Doncaster MBC, 1977–84; Minister, Halifax Methodist Circuit, 1987–90; Tutor in Hist., Wesley Coll., Bristol, 1990–93; Dir, Wesley and Methodist Studies Centre, Westminster Coll., Oxford, 1993–2002; Principal, Sarum Coll., Salisbury, 2002–08; Sarum Canon, 2004–08; Minister, Wesley Methodist Church, Cambridge, 2008–14; Chaplain, Wesley House, Cambridge, 2008–11; Hon. Chaplain and Sen. Mem., Wolfson Coll., Cambridge, 2009–14; Mem., Select Preacher's Syndicate, Univ. of Cambridge, 2011–14; Superintendent, Cambridge Methodist Circuit, 2012–14. Dep. Chm., E Anglia Dist, Methodist Ch, 2013–14. Chm., English Cttee, Waldensian Church Missions, 2011 (Dep. Chm. 1999–2006). British Sec., subseq. Co-Chm., Oxford Inst. for Methodist Theol Studies, 1993–2013; Co-Chm., Internat. Dialogue of Baptists and Methodists, 2014–; Vice President: World Methodist Historical Soc., 1996–2006; Charles Wesley Soc., 2004–11; Member: Methodist Church Heritage Cttee, 2009–12; Eur. Methodist Council, 2014–; World Methodist Council, 2016– (Chm., Ecumenical Relationships Cttee, 2016–). Gov., Ley's Foundn, Cambridge, 2009–14. Mem. Council, Univ. of Roehampton, 2019–. Vis. Prof., Pontifical Univ. of St Thomas Aquinas, Rome. Hon. Fellow, Westminster Inst. of Educn, Oxford Brookes Univ., 2008–14. *Publications:* Methodist Prison Chaplains, 1994; Pure Universal Love, 1995; Methodism and Education, 2000; contributions to: Historical Dictionary of Methodism, 1996; A Dictionary of British and Irish Methodism, 2000; Studies in Church History, 2002, 2004; An Encyclopedia of Protestantism, 2004; Oxford DNB, 2004; Our Calling to Fulfill, 2009. *Recreations:* choral singing, collecting Wesleyana and Methodist ephemera. *Address:* 7 Willow Hey, Saughall, Chester CH1 6BW. *E:* tmacquiban@gmail.com, tmacquiban@live.co.uk.

**McQUIGGAN, John,** MBE 1955; Executive Director, United Kingdom-South Africa Trade Association Ltd, 1978–86; retired at own request from HM Diplomatic Service, 1977; *b* 24 Nov. 1922; *s* of John and Sarah Elizabeth McQuiggan; *m* 1950, Doris Elsie Hadler; three *s* one *d. Educ:* St Edward's Coll., Liverpool. Served War, in RAF, 1942–47 (W Africa, Europe and Malta). Joined Dominions Office, 1940; Administration Officer, British High Commission, Canberra, Australia, 1950–54; Second Sec., Pakistan, Lahore and Dacca, 1954–57; First Sec. (Inf.), Lahore, 1957–58; Dep. Dir, UK Inf. Services, Australia (Canberra and Sydney), 1958–61; Dir, Brit. Inf. Services, Eastern Nigeria (Enugu), 1961–64; Dir, Brit. Inf. Services in Uganda, and concurrently First Sec., HM Embassy, Kigali, Rwanda, 1964–69; W African Dept, FCO, 1969–73; HM Consul, Chad, 1970–73 (first London based Consul); Dep. High Comr and Counsellor (Econ. and Commercial), Lusaka, Zambia, and sometime Actg High Comr, 1973–76. Dir-Gen., Brit. Industry Cttee on South Africa, 1986. Mem., Royal African Soc. FInstD. Benemerenti Medal awarded by Pope Benedict XVI, 2012. *Publications:* A Time to Heal (for use at Eucharist services), 2001; Prayers for the Sick (USA), 2003; booklets and contribs to trade and economic, technical woodworking, and religious jls. *Recreations:* tennis, carpentry, craftwork, research (current affairs). *Address:* 7 Meadowcroft, Bickley, Kent BR1 2JD. *T:* (020) 8467 0075. *Club:* Royal Over-Seas League.

**McQUILLAN, Stephen;** Chief Executive, Avingtrans plc, since 2008; *b* Glasgow, 6 Aug. 1961; *s* of Joseph McQuillan and Helen McQuillan (*née* Curran); *m* 1988, Sheena Lang; one *s. Educ:* Univ. of Glasgow (BSc Hons Electronics and Electrical Engrg). MIET 1998; FInstP 2006. Engr, Conoco Inc., 1982–85; Mars, Inc.: Proj. Engr, 1985–88; Sen. Mgt Scientist, 1988–90; Internat. Distributor Manager, 1990–91; European Sales Develt Manager, 1992–94; Sales Dir, W Eur., 1994–97; Business Unit Dir, Sodeco Cash Mgt Systems, 1995–97; Global Sales Dir, Marconi Instruments, 1997–98; Man. Dir, Oxford Instruments Superconductivity Ltd, 1998–2004; Chief Exec., NPL, 2005–08. Member Board: Serco Science, 2005–06; Serco Defence Ops, 2007–08; (non-exec.) UKAEA, 2010–15; (non-exec.) EEF Ltd, 2016–18. Mem. Bd, Assoc. of Ind. Res. and Technol. Orgns, 2007–08. FCMI 2008; FInstD 2009. *Recreations:* running, cycling, ski-ing, cinema, theatre, biographies, travel, learning, Celtic FC, Robert Burns poetry. *Address:* Avingtrans plc, Chatteris Business Park, Chatteris, Cambs PE16 6SA. *T:* (01354) 692391. *E:* smcquillan@avingtrans.plc.uk.

**MacQUITTY, (Joanna) Jane;** freelance wine writer and broadcaster, since 1982; Wine and Drink Correspondent, The Times, since 1982; *b* 14 Oct. 1953; *d* of late William Baird MacQuitty and Betty (*née* Bastin); *m* 1988, Philip Killingworth Hedges; one *s* two *d. Educ:* Benenden Sch. Wine and food writer, House & Garden, 1975–82; Editor, Which Wine Guide, and Which Wine Monthly, 1982–84; Wine Editor, Good Housekeeping, 1984–2000. Wine Lectr and Judge, 1982–. Member: Circle of Wine Writers, 1977–; Soc. of Authors, 1982–. Patron, Urology Foundn, 2014–. Glenfiddich Awards: Wine Writer of the Year, 1981; Whisky Writer of the Year, 1981; Special Award (for Which Wine Guide), 1983; Portuguese Wine Journalist of the Year, 2014. *Publications:* Which Wine Guide, 1983, rev. edn 1984; Jane MacQuitty's Guide to Champagne and Sparkling Wines, 1986, 3rd edn 1993; Jane MacQuitty's Guide to Australian and New Zealand Wines, 1988. *Recreations:* my family, eating, drinking, talking, sleep. *Address:* c/o The Times Weekend, The Times, 1 London Bridge Street, SE1 9GF.

**McQUOID, Judith Mary;** *see* Eve, J. M.

**MacRAE, Sir (Alastair) Christopher (Donald Summerhayes),** KCMG 1993 (CMG 1987); HM Diplomatic Service, retired; *b* 3 May 1937; *s* of Dr Alexander Murray MacRae and Dr Grace Maria Lynton Summerhayes MacRae; *m* 1963, Mette Willert; two *d. Educ:* Rugby; Lincoln Coll., Oxford (BA Hons English); Harvard (Henry Fellow in Internat. Relations). RN, 1956–58. CRO, 1962; 3rd, later 2nd Sec., Dar es Salaam, 1963–65; ME Centre for Arab Studies, Lebanon, 1965–67; 2nd Sec., Beirut, 1967–68; FCO, 1968–70; 1st Sec. and Head of Chancery: Baghdad, 1970–71; Brussels, 1972–76; attached Directorate-Gen. VIII, European Commn, Brussels, on secondment from FCO, 1976–78; Ambassador to Gabon, 1978–80, and to São Tomé and Príncipe (non-resident), 1979–80; Head of W Africa Dept, FCO, 1980–83, and Ambassador (non-resident) to Chad, 1982–83; Political Counsellor and Head of Chancery, Paris, 1983–87; Minister and Head of British Interests Section, Tehran, 1987; Vis. Fellow, IISS, 1987–88; Support Services Scrutiny, FCO, 1988; Under Sec. (on secondment), Cabinet Office, 1988–91; High Comr to Nigeria, and concurrently Ambassador (non-resident) to Benin, 1991–94; High Comr to Pakistan, 1994–97; Sec. Gen., Order of St John, 1997–2000. Asst Prof., Amer. Grad. Sch. of Internat. Relns and Diplomacy, Paris, 2005–08. KStJ 1997. *Address:* 23 Chemin Carboussan, Mormoiron 84570, France.

**MACRAE, Prof. (Colin) Neil,** PhD, DSc; FBA 2011; FRSE; Professor of Social Cognition, University of Aberdeen. *Educ:* Univ. of Aberdeen (BSc 1987; PhD 1990; DSc 2006). Prof. of Psychol. and Brain Scis, Dartmouth Coll., NH, USA; Reader in Psychol., Univ. of St Andrews, 2005. Wolfson Fellow, Royal Soc. FRSE 2008; FAcSS. Spearman Medal, BPsS, 1997. *Publications:* (jtly) Stereotypes and Stereotyping, 1996; (ed with S. T. Fiske) The SAGE Handbook of Social Cognition, 2012; contribs to scientific jls. *Address:* School of Psychology, University of Aberdeen, William Guild Building, Room F6, King's College, Old Aberdeen AB24 3FX.

**McRAE, Dame Frances Anne;** *see* Cairncross, Dame F. A.

**McRAE, Hamish Malcolm Donald;** Associate Editor, The Independent, since 1991; *b* 20 Oct. 1943; *s* of Donald and Barbara McRae (*née* Budd); *m* 1971, Frances Anne Cairncross (*see* Dame F. A. Cairncross); two *d. Educ:* Fettes College; Trinity College, Dublin (BA Hons Economics and Political Science, MA). Liverpool Post, 1966–67; The Banker, 1967–72 (Asst Editor, 1969, Dep. Editor, 1971); Editor, Euromoney, 1972–74; Financial Editor, The Guardian, 1975–89; Business and City Editor, The Independent, 1989–91. Visiting Professor: UMIST, 1999–2004; Univ. of Lancaster, 2005–10; Adjunct Prof., TCD, 2012–15. Mem. Council, REconS, 2005–10. Wincott Foundn financial journalist of the year, 1979; David Watt Prize, RTZ awards, 2005; Business and Finance Journalist of the Year, British Press Awards, 2006. *Publications:* (with Frances Cairncross) Capital City: London as a financial centre, 1973, 5th edn 1991; (with Frances Cairncross) The Second Great Crash, 1975; Japan's role in the emerging global securities market, 1985; The World in 2020, 1994; (with Tadashi Nakamae) Wake-up, Japan, 1999; What Works: the secrets of the world's best organisations and communities, 2010. *Recreations:* walking, ski-ing, cooking. *Address:* The Independent, Northcliffe House, 2 Derry Street, W8 5HF.

**MACRAE, John Esmond Campbell,** CMG 1986; DPhil; HM Diplomatic Service, retired; *b* 8 Dec. 1932; *s* of Col Archibald Campbell Macrae, IMS, and Euretta Margaret Skelton; *m* 1962, Anne Catherine Sarah Strain (marr. diss. 2018); four *s. Educ:* Sheikh Bagh Sch., Kashmir; Fettes Coll., Edinburgh; Christ Church Oxford (Open Scholar; MA; DPhil Radiation Chem. 1960); Princeton, USA. Atomic Energy and Disarmament Dept, Foreign Office, 1959–60; 2nd Sec., British Embassy, Tel Aviv, 1961–64; 1st Secretary: Djakarta, 1964; Vientiane, 1964–66; FO, NE African Dept, 1966; Central Dept, 1967–69; Southern African Dept, 1970–72; UK Mission to the UN, New York (dealing with social affairs, population and outer space), 1972–75; Counsellor, Science and Technology, Paris, 1975–80; Head of Cultural Relns Dept, FCO, 1980–85; RCDS, 1985; Ambassador: to Senegal, and (non-resident) to Mali, Cape Verde, Guinea, Guinea-Bissau and Mauritania, 1985–90; to Morocco and to Mauritania, 1990–92. *Recreations:* music, hill walking, picnics in unusual places.

**MacRAE, His Honour Kenneth Charles;** a Circuit Judge, 1990–2009; *b* 14 March 1944; *s* of William and Ann MacRae; *m* 1981, Hilary Vivien Williams; one *d. Educ:* Redruth County Grammar School; Cornwall Tech. Coll.; Fitzwilliam Coll., Cambridge (BA Hons). Called to the Bar, Lincoln's Inn, 1969; a Recorder of the Crown Court, 1985. *Recreations:* gardening, walking, music.

**McRAE, Lindsay Vere;** *see* Duncan, L. V.

**MACRAE, Neil;** *see* Macrae, C. N.

**McRAE, Steven;** Principal Dancer, Royal Ballet, since 2009; *b* Sydney; *s* of Phillip McRae and Dianne McRae; *m* 2011, Elizabeth Harrod; one *s* one *d. Educ:* Royal Ballet Sch.; Royal Acad. of Dance (Solo Seal); Open Univ. (BA Hons Business Mgt and Leadership). Dip. in Dance. Joined Royal Ballet Co., 2004. Prix de Lausanne, 2003; Best Male Dancer, Critics'

**MACREADY, Sir Charles Nevil**, 4th Bt *cr* 1923, of Cheltenham, co. Gloucester; vineyard consultant and contract manager, since 2012; *b* Ripley, Surrey, 19 May 1955; *s* of Sir Nevil John Wilfrid Macready, 3rd Bt, CBE and Emma Macready, *d* of Sir (John) Donald (Balfour) Fergusson, GCB; *S* father, 2014; *m* 2001, Jillian Simms; one *s* one *d* from previous marriage. *Educ*: Downside Sch., Somerset. Area supervisor, Augustus Barnett, wine merchants, 1985–87; owner/manager, The Brasserie Restaurant and Wine Cellars, Bury St Edmunds, 1987–92; Wyken Vineyard, 1992– (manager, 1995–); manager, Wyken's Leaping Hare Restaurant, 1992–2001; owner/manager, Ickworth Vineyard, 1995–2012. *Recreations*: classical piano music, motorcycling. *Heir*: *s* James Nevil Macready, *b* 26 Nov. 1982. *Address*: Fortlands, Sicklesmere Road, Bury St Edmunds, Suffolk IP33 2BN. *E*: charles@treesforgardens.co.uk.

**MacROBBIE, Prof. Enid Anne Campbell**, FRS 1991; FRSE; Professor of Plant Biophysics, University of Cambridge, 1987–99, now Emeritus Professor; Fellow of Girton College, since 1958; *b* 5 Dec. 1931; *d* of late George MacRobbie and Agnes Kerr MacRobbie (*née* Campbell). *Educ*: Mary Erskine Sch., Edinburgh; Univ. of Edinburgh (BSc, PhD); MA, ScD Cantab. FRSE 1998. Res. Fellow, Univ. of Copenhagen, 1957–58; Cambridge University: Res. Fellow, Botany Sch., 1958–62; Demonstrator in Botany, 1962–66; Lectr in Botany, 1966–73; Reader in Plant Biophysics, 1973–87. Mem., BBSRC, 1996–99. Foreign Associate, Nat. Acad. of Scis, USA, 1999. *Publications*: papers in sci jls. *Address*: Girton College, Cambridge CB3 0JG. *T*: (01223) 338999.

**MACRON, Emmanuel Jean-Michel Frédéric**; President of France, since 2017; *b* Amiens, 21 Dec. 1977; *s* of Jean-Michel Macron and Françoise Macron (*née* Noguès); *m* 2007, Brigitte Trogneux. *Educ*: La Providence Jesuit Sch.; Lycée Henri-VI, Paris; Nanterre Univ. (DEA Philos); Sciences Po Univ. (Dip. Political Studies); École Nat. d'Admin (Dip. 2004). Inspector of Finances, 2004–07, Hd of Service, 2007–08, Inspectorate Gen. of Finances; Dep. Rapporteur, Commn to improve French econ. growth, 2007–08; Associate, Rothschild & Cie Banque, 2008–11; Dep. Sec. Gen., Office of the Pres. of France, 2012–14; Minister of the Economy, Industry and Digital Affairs, 2014–16. Founder, En Marche!, later La République En Marche!, 2016. *Address*: Palais d'Elysée, 55 rue du Faubourg Ste-Honoré, 75008 Paris, France.

**MacRORY, Avril**; Chief Executive Officer, Silverapples Media, since 2001; *b* 5 April 1956; *d* of Patrick Simon MacRory and Elizabeth (*née* Flynn); *m* 1983, Val Griffin; one *s*. *Educ*: University College, Dublin (BA Hons 1978). Producer and Director, RTE, 1979; Head of Variety, RTE, 1986; Commissioning Editor, Music, Channel 4, 1988; Head of Music Progs, 1993–98, of Millennium Event Progs, 1998–2000, BBC TV. Advr, Programming, Hello! TV. Mem., Exec. Cttee, Women's Irish Network. Pres., Internat. Music Zentrum, Vienna, 1992–. *Recreations*: sailing, music, reading.

**MACRORY, Prof. Richard Brabazon**, CBE 2000; Professor of Environmental Law, University College, London, 1999–2017, now Emeritus; Barrister-at-law; *b* 30 March 1950; *s* of Sir Patrick Macrory and Lady Marjorie Elizabeth Macrory; *m* 1979, Sarah Margaret Briant; two *s*. *Educ*: Westminster Sch.; Christ Church, Oxford (BA 1972; MA 1976). Called to the Bar, Gray's Inn, 1974, Bencher, 2010; Legal Advr, Friends of the Earth Ltd, 1975–78; Imperial College, London: Lectr, 1980–89; Reader in Envmtl Law, 1989–91; Denton Hall Prof. of Envmtl Law, 1991–94; Dir, Envmtl Change Unit, Univ. of Oxford, 1994–95; Prof. of Envmtl Law, Imperial Coll., London, 1995–99. Leader, Review of Regulatory Sanctions, Cabinet Office, 2005–06. Chairman: UK Envmtl Law Assoc., 1986–88 (Patron, 2007–; Co-Chair, Brexit Task Force, 2017–18); Steering Cttee, European Envmtl Adv. Councils, 2001–02; Hon. Standing Counsel, CPRE, 1981–92; Member: Envmtl Adv. Bd, Shanks and McKewan plc, 1989–91; UK Nat. Adv. Cttee on Eco-labelling, 1990–91; Royal Commn on Envmtl Pollution, 1991–2003; Expert Strategy Panel, Inter-Agency Cttee for Global Envmtl Change, 1995–96; Bd, Envmt Agency, 1999–2004; Gen. Electric Ecomagination Bd, 2006–10; Sullivan Working Gp on Access to Envmtl Justice, 2007–08. Specialist Adviser: H of L Select Cttee on EC, 1991–92, and 1996–97; H of C Select Cttee on Envmt, 1989–92, 1993–99. Hon. Chm., Merchant Ivory Prodns Ltd, 1992–2005; Chm., Lady Sale Prodns LLP, 2009–. Hon. Pres., Nat. Soc. for Clean Air, 2004–05. Rapporteur, UK Nat. Biotechnology Conf., 1996; UK nominated expert arbitrator, Law of the Sea Convention, 1998–2003. Fernand Braudel Sen. Fellow, Eur. Univ. Inst., Florence, 2009; Sen. Global Res. Fellow, NYU Sch. of Law, 2010. Hon. QC 2008. Editor, Jl of Envmtl Law, 1988–2006; Legal Corresp., Ends Report, 1982–2019. Elizabeth Haub Prize for Envmtl Law, Internat. Council for Envmtl Law, 2014. *Publications*: Nuisance, 1982; Water Law: principles and practice, 1985; Water Act 1989, 1989; (with D. Gilbert) Pesticide Related Law, 1989; (with S. Hollins) Bibliography of Community Environmental Law, 1995; (ed) Principles of European Environmental Law, 2004; (ed) Reflections on 30 years of EU Environmental Law, 2005; Regulation, Enforcement, and Governance of Environmental Law, 2008, 2nd edn 2014; (ed with R. Stewart and I. Havercroft) Legal Aspects of Carbon Capture and Storage, 2011, 2nd edn 2018; (ed jtly) National Courts and EU Environmental Law, 2013; First Afghan War, 2016; (Consultant Ed.) Halsbury's Laws Environmental Law, 2019; articles and reviews in legal and tech. jls. *Recreations*: cinema, conjuring, cycling. *Address*: Crossing Farmhouse, Tackley, Oxford OX5 3AT. *T*: (01869) 331151; Brick Court Chambers, 7–8 Essex Street, WC2R 3LD. *T*: (020) 7379 3550, *Fax*: (020) 7379 3558; Faculty of Laws, University College, Bentham House, Endsleigh Gardens, WC1H 0EG. *T*: (020) 7679 1543. *E*: r.macrory@ucl.ac.uk. *Clubs*: 2 Brydges, Polish Hearth.

**MacROW-WOOD, Ven. Antony Charles**; Archdeacon of Dorset, since 2015; *s* of David and Mary Wood; *m* 1987, Dawn MacRow-Hill; one *s* two *d*. *Educ*: Bishop Wordsworth's Grammar Sch., Salisbury; Univ. of York (BA Hons 1982); Jesus Coll., Cambridge (BA 1991); Univ. of Winchester (MA 2017). ACA 1985. Articled Clerk, Deloitte Haskins and Sells, 1982–87; Finance Manager, Rolls Royce plc, 1987–89; ordained deacon, 1992, priest, 1993; Curate, Parks and Walcot, Swindon, 1992–96; Team Vicar, Weymouth, 1996–2004; Team Rector, North Poole Ecumenical Team, 2004–15. President: Assoc. of British Credit Unions Ltd, 2009–12; Churches' Mutual Credit Union, 2015–. *Recreations*: golf, gardening, walking the dog. *T*: 07775 574971. *E*: amacrowwood@mac.com.

**MacSHANE, Denis**, PhD; Senior Advisor, Avisa Partners, Brussels, since 2014; *b* 21 May 1948; *e s* of late Jan Matyjaszek and of Isobel McShane; *m* 1987, Nathalie Pham Minh Duong (marr. diss. 2003); one *s* three *d* (and one *d* decd). *Educ*: Merton Coll., Oxford (MA); Birkbeck Coll., London. (PhD; Hon. Fellow, 2005). BBC reporter, 1969–77; Pres., NUJ, 1978–79; Policy Dir, Internat. Metalworkers Fedn, 1980–92; Dir, European Policy Inst., 1992–. MP (Lab) Rotherham, May 1994–Nov. 2012. PPS, 1997–2001, Parly Under-Sec. of State, 2001–02, Minister of State, 2002–05, FCO. UK Delegate: Council of Europe, 2005–10; NATO Parly Assembly, 2005–10. Vis. Parly Fellow, St Antony's Coll., Oxford, 1998–99. Mem. Council, RIIA, 1998, 2001, 2005–11; Chm., Fabian Soc., 2001–02. Vice Pres., German-British Forum, 2018–. Contributing Ed., Globalist, 2014–. *Publications*: Solidarity: Poland's Independent Trade Union, 1981; François Mitterrand: a political Odyssey, 1982; Black Workers, Unions and the Struggle for Democracy in South Africa, 1984; International Labour and the Origins of the Cold War, 1992; Britain's Steel Industry in the 21st Century, 1996; Edward Heath, 2006; Globalising Hatred: the new antisemitism, 2008; Why Kosovo Still Matters, 2011; Prison Diaries, 2014; Brexit: how Britain will leave Europe, 2015; Brexit, No Exit: why (in the end) Britain won't leave Europe, 2017. *Recreations*: family, the Alps, poetry, friends.

**McSHANE, Mark**; Headteacher, Stroud High School, since 2014; *b* Cuckfield, E Sussex, 23 Feb. 1974; *s* of John McShane and Pauline McShane; *m* 2001, Alison Healey; one *s* two *d*. *Educ*: Uckfield Community Coll.; Univ. of Essex (BA Hons Govt and Politics); Univ. of Wales Inst., Cardiff (PGCE). Teacher of Hist. and Politics, Ribston Hall High Sch., 1997–2000; Teacher of Hist. and Politics, 2000–07, Asst Headteacher, 2008–10, Pate's Grammar Sch.; Dep. Headteacher, Denmark Road Sch., 2010–13. *Recreations*: following all sports, keen cyclist, love of reading, enjoy spending time with family. *Address*: Stroud High School, Beards Lane, Stroud, Glos GL5 4HF. *T*: (01453) 764441. *E*: head@stroudhigh.gloucs.sch.uk.

**McSHANE, Martin David**, FRCS; Chief Medical Officer (UK), Optum International, since 2016; *b* 27 Jan. 1957; *s* of late Jan Matyjaszek and of Isobel Matyjaszek (*née* McShane); *m* 1989, Dr Linda Jewes; one *s* one *d*. *Educ*: St Benedict's Sch., Ealing; University Coll. London and University Coll. Hosp. Med. Sch. (BSc Anatomy 1978; MB BS 1981); Univ. of London (MS 1989); Sheffield Hallam Univ. (MA Writing 1998); Teesside Univ. (Postgrad. Performance Develt Coaching 2013). Gen. and vascular surgical trng and res., 1981–89 (Musgrove Park Hosp., Taunton, Edgware Gen. Hosp., London, Leicester Royal Infirmary, Southampton Gen. Hosp., Sheffield Gen. Hosp., Rotherham Dist Gen. Hosp.); trainee, 1990–92, Partner, 1992–2014, Moss Valley Med. Practice, Eckington; Chair, NE Derbys PCG, 1999–2001; Professional Exec. Chair, 2001–04, Chief Exec., 2004–06, N Eastern Derbys PCT; Dir of Strategy and Health Outcomes, and Dep. Chief Exec., Lincs Teaching PCT, 2006–12; Dir, Domain 2 (Enhancing quality of life for people with long term conditions), NHS England, 2012–15. Vice Chair, E Midlands Specialised Commng Gp, 2006–12. Mem., Nat. Patient Safety Forum, 2007–10. *Publications*: papers on Duplex Ultrasound of femorodistal bypass grafts. *Recreations*: cycling, dog walking. *Address*: c/o Optum, 10th Floor, 5 Merchant Square, Paddington, W2 1AS. *E*: martin.mcshane@optum.com.

**McSHARRY, Deirdre**; Editor-in-Chief and Launch Editor, Country Living, 1986–89; *b* 4 April 1932; *d* of late Dr John McSharry and Mrs Mary McSharry. *Educ*: Dominican Convent, Wicklow; Trinity Coll., Dublin. Woman's Editor, Daily Express, 1962–66; Fashion Editor, The Sun, 1966–72; Editor, Cosmopolitan, 1973–86; Consultant, Nat. Magazine Co., and Magazine Div., The Hearst Corp., 1990–95; Ed., Countryside mag., NY, 1991–92. Curated exhibitions: American Museum in Britain, Bath: Inspirations: the textile tradition, 2001; Quilt Bonanza, 2003; Victoria Art Gallery, Bath: Blue and White Show, 2008; Newark Park, Ozleworth: Bringing Home the East, 2010. Mem. Council and Chm., Bath Friends of American Museum in Britain, 1995–2004; Trustee, 2003–05. Patron, Holburne Mus., Bath, 2007–08. Contrib., Edwardian Revival, BBC2, 2007. Magazine Editor of the Year, PPA, 1981, 1987; Mark Boxer Lifetime Achievement Award, British Soc. of Magazine Editors, 1992. *Publications*: contrib. Selvedge, You mag., Bath Life mag., Bath Mag., America in Britain. *Recreations*: the arts, textiles, costume and fashion. *Address*: 5 Sion Hill Place, Sion Hill, Bath BA1 5SJ.

**MacSHARRY, Raymond**; Chairman, London City Airport, 1996–2006; Director, Ryanair, 1993–2006 (Chairman, 1993–96); *b* Sligo, April 1938; *m* Elaine Neilan (*d* 2008); three *s* three *d*. *Educ*: St Vincent's Nat. Sch., Sligo; Ballincutranta Nat. Sch., Beltra, Co. Sligo; Marist Brothers Nat. Sch., Sligo; Summerhill Coll., Sligo. TD (FF) for Sligo Leitrim, 1969–89; opposition front bench spokesman on Office of Public Works, 1973–75; Mem., Cttee of Public Accts, 1969–77; Minister of State, Dept of Finance and the Public Service, 1977–79; Minister of Agriculture, 1979–81; opposition spokesman on Agric., 1981–82; Tánaiste and Minister for Finance, 1982; Minister for Finance and the Public Service, 1987–88. Mem., Commn of EC, 1989–92. Formerly Member: New Ireland Forum; Nat. Exec., Fianna Fáil Party (later, also an Hon. Treas.). Mem. for Connaught/Ulster, Eur. Parlt, 1984–87; Mem., Council of Ministers, 1984–87. Governor, Eur. Investment Bank, 1982. Director: Jefferson Smurfit Gp, 1993–2002; Bank of Ireland, 1993–2005; Chairman: Telecom Éireann, 1999–2001; Irish Forestry Board, 1999–2002. Councillor, Sligo CC, 1967–78; Chairman: Bd of Management, Sligo Reg. Tech. Coll., 1970–78; Sligo Hosp. Exec. Cttee, 1972–78; NW Health Bd, 1974–75 (Mem., 1971–78); Member: Sligo Corp., 1967–78 (Alderman, 1974–78); Town of Sligo Vocational Educn Cttee, 1967–78; Bd of Management, Sligo-Leitrim Reg. Develt Org., 1973–78; Sligo Jun. Chamber, 1965–2005 (PP). Freeman, Borough of Sligo, 1993. Hon. Dr NUI, 1994; Hon. DEconSc Limerick, 1994. Grand Cross, Order of Leopold II (Belgium), 1993. *Address*: Alcantara, Pearse Road, Sligo, Eire.

**McSHERRY, (John) Craig (Cunningham)**; Sheriff at Dunfermline, since 2006; *b* 21 Oct. 1949; *s* of John and Janet McSherry; *m* 1972, Elaine Beattie; two *s*. *Educ*: Ardrossan Acad.; Univ. of Glasgow (LLB Hons 1972). Lead singer, The Wilderness, 1967–68. Solicitor, 1972–92; Sen. Partner, McSherry Halliday, Solicitors, 1983–92; Advocate, 1993; Temp. Sheriff, 1997–99; Pt-time Sheriff, 2000–03; Immigration Appeals Adjudicator (pt-time), 2001–03; All Scotland Floating Sheriff, Edinburgh, 2003–05. Mem. Council, Law Soc. of Scotland, 1982–85. *Recreations*: country pursuits, ski-ing, music (classical, rock, folk), bridge, golf. *Address*: 2 Heriot Row, Edinburgh EH3 6HU. *T*: (0131) 556 8289. *E*: jccmcs@hotmail.com. *Club*: New (Edinburgh).

**MACTAGGART, Rt Hon. Fiona**; PC 2015; Chair, Fawcett Society, since 2018; *b* 12 Sept. 1953; *d* of Sir Ian Auld Mactaggart, 3rd Bt of Rosemary, *d* of Sir Herbert Williams, 1st Bt, MP. *Educ*: Cheltenham Ladies' Coll.; King's Coll., London (BA Hons); Inst. of Educn, London (MA). Gen. Sec., London Students' Organisation, 1977–78; Vice-Pres., 1978–80, Nat. Sec., 1980–81, NUS; Gen. Sec., Jt Council for Welfare of Immigrants, 1982–86. Mem. (Lab) Wandsworth BC, 1986–90 (Leader of the Opposition, 1988–90). Teacher, Lyndhurst Sch., Camberwell, 1988–92; Lectr, Inst. of Educn, 1992–97. MP (Lab) Slough, 1997–2017. PPS to Sec. of State for Culture, Media and Sport, 1997–2001; Parly Under-Sec. of State, Home Office, 2003–06. Member: Public Admin Cttee, 1997–98; Educn and Skills, then Children, Schs and Families Cttee, 2006–10; Jt Cttee on Human Rights, 2009–10; Health Cttee, 2010; Public Accounts Cttee, 2011–14; Intelligence and Security Cttee, 2014–17. Chm., PLP Women's Cttee, 2001–03, 2008–10, 2011–17. Chm., Liberty (NCCL), 1994–96.

**MACTAGGART, Sir John (Auld)**, 4th Bt *cr* 1938, of King's Park, City of Glasgow; *b* 21 Jan. 1951; *s* of Sir Ian Auld Mactaggart, 3rd Bt and of Rosemary, *d* of Sir Herbert Williams, 1st Bt, MP; *S* father, 1987; *m* 1st, 1977, Patricia (marr. diss. 1990), *y d* of late Major Harry Alastair Gordon, MC; 2nd, 1991, Caroline (marr. diss. 2014), *y d* of Eric Williams; two *s* two *d*. *Educ*: Shrewsbury; Trinity Coll., Cambridge (MA). Chm., Western Heritable Investment Company, 1987–. *Heir*: *s* Jack Auld Mactaggart, *b* 11 Sept. 1993. *Address*: 2 Babmaes Street, SW1Y 6HD.
*See also Rt Hon. F. Mactaggart.*

**MacTHOMAS OF FINEGAND, Andrew Patrick Clayhills;** 19th Chief of Clan MacThomas (MacThomaidh Mhor); *b* 28 Aug. 1942; *o s* of late Captain Patrick Watt MacThomas of Finegand and Elizabeth Cadogan Fenwick MacThomas (*née* Clayhills-Henderson); *S* father, 1970; *m* 1985, Anneke Cornelia Susanna, *o d* of late Albert and Susanna Kruyning-Van Hout; one *s* one *d*. *Educ:* St Edward's, Oxford. FSA (Scot.) 1973. Hd, Barclaycard/Visa (Scotland), 1975–82; Dir, Scotworld, 1982–85; Public Relations, S Africa, 1985–90; Hd of Govt Relns, Barclays Bank, 1990–97; Public Affairs Dir, Barclays PLC, 1997–2005; Develt Dir, Industry and Parliament Trust, 2005–07. Mem., Exec. Cttee, Standing Council of Scottish Chiefs, 2010–; Pres., Clan MacThomas Soc., 1970–; Hon. Vice-Pres., Clan Chattan Assoc., 1970–. *Publications:* History of the Clan MacThomas, 2009. *Recreations:* Clan, politics, wine and wit. *Heir: s* Thomas David Alexander MacThomas, Yr of Finegand, *b* 1 Jan. 1987. *Address:* c/o Barclays Bank, 22 Hide Hill, Berwick-upon-Tweed, Northumberland TD15 1AF. *Club:* Hurlingham.

**McTIER, Duncan Paul;** international double bass soloist, chamber musician and teacher; Member: Nash Ensemble, 1994–2014; Fibonacci Sequence, since 1995; *b* Stourbridge, 21 Nov. 1954; *s* of John and May McTier; *m* 1984, Yuko Inoue (marr. diss. 2010); one *s* one *d*. *Educ:* King Edward VI Grammar Sch., Stourbridge; Bristol Univ. (BSc Math. Scis 1975). ARCM Hons 1974. With BBC SO, 1975–77; Principal Double Bass, Netherlands Chamber Orch., 1977–84; Sen. Tutor of Double Bass, RNCM, 1984–96; Lectr in Double Bass, RAM, 1996–2014; Professor of Double Bass: Univ. of Limerick, 2000–02; Zürcher Hochschule der Künste, Winterthur, 2002–; Escuela Superior de Música Reina Sofia, Madrid, 2007–. Guest Prof., Utrecht Conservatorium, 1994–96. Double Bass Tutor, NYO of GB, 1983–2002 and 2007–09; Double Bass Consultant, RSAMD, 1991–2000. Vis. Master, Double Bass, Codarts, Hogeschool voor de Kunsten, Rotterdam, 2007–10. FRNCM 1994. Hon. RAM 1998. First Prize, IOM Internat. Double Bass Competition, 1982. Recognition Award for Solo Perf., Internat. Soc. of Bassists, 2005. *Publications:* Daily Exercises for Double Bass, 1994; Tips & Tricks, Vol. 1, Preparation and Practice, Vol. 2, The Koussevitsky Concerto, 1999. *Recreations:* golf, cycling, other sports, walking, theatre, good food and wine.

**McTIGHE, (Robert) Michael;** Member, Office of Communications, 2007–15; *b* Stourbridge, 17 Oct. 1953; *s* of Glenville McTighe and Mary McTighe; partner Terry Vega; two *s* one *d* from previous marriages. *Educ:* University Coll. London (BSc Hons Electrical Engrg 1975). GEC Machines Ltd, 1975–76; Thorn EMI plc, 1976–80; GE Medical Systems, 1980–90; Motorola Inc.: Gen. Manager, UK Manuf. Ops, 1990–91, Dir, Eur. Manuf. Ops, 1991–92, Gen. Manager, Original Equipment Manufacturer Mkts, 1992–93, Gen. Manager, Area III, 1993–94, Eur. Cellular Subscriber Div.: Dir, Ops, Asia/Pacific Cellular Subscriber Div., 1994–95; Philips Electronics NV: Man. Dir, Philips Consumer Communications, Le Mans, 1995–97; Pres. and CEO, Philips Consumer Communications LP, NJ, 1997–98; consultant, 1998–99; Cable & Wireless plc: Exec. Dir and CEO, Global Ops, 1999–2001; Exec. Dir, Strategy and Business Develt, 2001; Chm. and CEO, Carrier1 International SA, 2001–02. Chairman: Pace plc, 2001–11; Red M Gp Ltd, 2001–05; Enition SA, 2002–03; Via Networks, Inc., 2002–05; Radiant Networks plc, 2003–04; Alphamosaic Ltd, 2003–04; Corvil Ltd, 2003–08; Am Beo Ltd, 2004–05; Phyworks Ltd, 2004–10; Frontier Silicon Hldgs Ltd, 2004–11; Nujira Ltd, 2005–15; Cambridge Semiconductors Ltd, 2006–10; Perpetuum Ltd, 2006–09; Volex Gp plc, 2008–13; WYG plc, 2009–17; Together Financial Services (formerly Jerrold Hldgs) Ltd, 2010–; JJB Sports plc, 2010–12; Quinn Gp Holdco Ltd, 2012–; Openreach Ltd, 2017–; Igas Energy plc, 2017– (Dep. Chm., 2016–17); non-executive Director: European Telecom plc, 1998–2002; Alliance & Leicester plc, 2000–08; Arran Isle Ltd, 2009– (Chm., 2013–); Dir, London Metal Exchange Hldgs Ltd, 2002–08; Sen. Ind. Dir, Betfair Ltd, 2008–14. *Recreations:* gardening, ski-ing, scuba diving. *Address:* Flat 1, 3 Eaton Place, SW1X 8BN. *T:* (020) 7823 1124, 07957 806158. *E:* mike@mctighe.net.

**MACUR, Rt Hon. Dame Julia,** DBE 2005; PC 2013; **Rt Hon. Lady Justice Macur;** a Lady Justice of Appeal, since 2013; Senior Presiding Judge of England and Wales, 2018–19 (Deputy Senior Presiding Judge, 2016–17); *b* 17 April 1957; *d* of Boleslaw Macur and Betsy Macur; *m* 1981; two *s*. *Educ:* Sheffield Univ. (LLB 1978). Called to the Bar, Lincoln's Inn, 1979 (Bencher, 2005); Midland and Oxford Circuit; QC 1998; a Recorder, 1999–2005; a Judge of the High Ct of Justice, Family Div., 2005–13; Presiding Judge, Midland Circuit, 2008–11. Sen. Judicial Comr, Judicial Appts Commn, 2013–. *Address:* Royal Courts of Justice, Strand, WC2A 2LL.

**McVAY, Leslie Elizabeth;** *see* Evans, L. E.

**McVEIGH, Charles Senff,** III; Chairman, Corporate and Investment Banking-Global Wealth Management Partnership, Citigroup (formerly Chairman, Salomon Brothers International Ltd, subseq. Salomon Smith Barney, and then Co-Chairman Schroder Salomon Smith Barney, subseq. European Investment Bank, Citigroup), 1987–2013; Senior Advisor, since 2013 and Deputy Chairman, European Advisory Board, Citigroup Private Bank; *b* New York, 4 July 1942; *s* of Charles S. McVeigh, Jr and Evelyn B. McVeigh; *m* 1st, 1964, Pamela Osborn (marr. diss. 1991); one *s* three *d*; 2nd, 1993, Jennifer Champneys; two *s* one *d*. *Educ:* Univ. of Virginia (BA); Long Island Univ. (MBA). Officer, Morgan Guaranty Trust Co., 1965–71; joined Salomon Brothers, 1971: Vice-Pres. and Manager, NY Internat. Dept, 1974–75; Hd, Salomon Bros Internat., London, 1975–87; General Partner, 1977–81; Mem., European Mgt Cttee, 1981. Chm., Rubicon Fund Mgt LLP, 2015–18; non-executive Director: Witan Investment Trust, 1998–2006; Savills plc, 2000–; Petropavlovsk (formerly Peter Hambro Mining) PLC, 2009–17. Mem., Fulbright Commn, 1993–2005. Member Board: LIFFE, 1983–89; London Stock Exchange, 1986–92; Clearstream (formerly CEDEL), 1994–2005; Member: City Capital Mkts Cttee, 1989–94; Legal Risk Rev. Cttee, 1990–92. Trustee, Landmark Trust, 2010–. *Recreations:* field sports, gardening. *Address:* Samways Farm, Alvediston, Salisbury, Wilts SP5 5LQ. *Clubs:* White's, Beefsteak, Pratt's; The Brook, Anglers' (NYC).

**McVEIGH, (Robert) Desmond;** Chairman: Westwind Partners, 2004–08; N. T. Energy Inc., 2005–07; Advisory Board, Oriental Minerals Inc., 2007–10; *b* 10 Jan. 1939; *s* of late Rev. Robert Walker McVeigh and Evelyn Mary (*née* McCoubrey); *m* 1966, Gillian Ann Nash; two *s* one *d*. *Educ:* Methodist Coll., Belfast; QUB (LLB Hons); Univ. of Michigan (LLM). Citibank, London, 1967–71; GATX, London, 1971–72; Citibank, 1972–74; First Nat. Bank, Dallas, 1974–77; Saudi Internat. Bank, London, 1977–85; Lloyds Merchant Bank, 1985–87; independent consultant, 1987–92; Chief Exec., IDB for NI, 1993–95; Man. Dir, Longdown Financial Services Ltd, 1995–2002; Official Econ. Advr, Jilin Province, N China, 1996–2008; Chm. and CEO, SE Asian Business Adv. Services, 1997–2015; Exec. Chm., Asia Broadbent Inc., 2001–03; Dep. Chm., Richard Kleinwort Consultancy Group, 2002–; non-executive Director: Viking Internat. Petroleum plc, 2003–05; Kate Energy, 2018–. Vis. Prof. of Finance and Industrial Relations, Warsaw Univ., 1994–97. CCMI (CIMgt 1994). *Recreations:* golf, tennis, music. *T:* 07710 305380. *E:* dmlfcl@gmail.com. *Clubs:* Royal Over-Seas League; Automobile de Monaco.

**McVEY, Rt Hon. Esther (Louise);** PC 2014; MP (C) Tatton, since 2017; Minister of State, Ministry of Housing, Communities and Local Government, since 2019; *b* Liverpool, 24 Oct. 1967; *d* of James and Barbara McVey. *Educ:* Belvedere Acad., Liverpool; Queen Mary and Westfield Coll., Univ. of London (LLB Hons 1990); City Univ., London (postgrad. course in radio journalism 1991); John Moores Univ. (MSc Corporate Governance (Dist.; N of England Excellence Award 2009)). CBBC, BBC 1, 1991; BBC Radio 5, 1992; Reportage, BBC2, 1993; Live TV and Meridian TV, 1994; Living TV, 1995; How Do They Do That?, BBC1, 1996; Nothing but the Truth, Channel 4, 1997; 5's Company, Channel 5, 1998; GMTV, 1999; BBC 1, 2000; Man. Dir, Making It (UK) Ltd, 2002–10. Founder, Winning Women (women's business network), 2003–10. Chair, British Transport Police Authy, 2015–17. Contested (C) Wirral W, 2005. MP (C) Wirral W, 2010–15; contested (C) same seat, 2015. Parly Under-Sec. of State, 2012–13, Minister of State, 2013–15, DWP; Treasurer of HM Household (Dep. Chief Whip), 2017–18; Sec. of State for Work and Pensions, 2018. Mem., Home Affairs Select Cttee, 2017–. Hon. Fellow, Univ. of Liverpool. *Publications:* If Chloe Can series, 2010. *Recreations:* charity work, gardening, theatre, walking, cinema. *Address:* House of Commons, SW1A 0AA.

**McVICAR, Sir David,** Kt 2012; freelance opera director; *b* Glasgow, 1 June 1966; *s* of John and Morag McVicar; partner, Andrew George. *Educ:* Royal Scottish Acad. of Music and Drama (Acting Dip. 1998; Fellow 2003). Full-time specialist in opera direction, 1993–; prodns at houses incl. Royal Opera Hse, Metropolitan Opera, NY and Glyndebourne. *Recreations:* cookery, reading, music. *Address:* c/o Judy Daish Associates, 2 St Charles Place, W10 6EG. *T:* (020) 8964 8811. *E:* tracey@judydaish.com.

**McVICAR, Jessica Francis, (Jekka);** organic herb farmer, since 1985; author, since 1993; *b* Bristol, 21 Feb. 1951; *d* of John Oliver Stanley-Clarke and Clare Stanley-Clarke (*née* Lowinsky); *m* 1976, Ian McVicar; one *s* one *d*. *Educ:* Cranborne Chase; Somerset Coll. of Art. Flautist and clarinettist with Marsupilami, heavy progressive pop gp, 1969–71; Prodn Office, Drama Serials, BBC TV, 1971–74; Dir and Prod., Community TV, 1974–79; Dir, Prod. and Unit Manager, Avon and Somerset Constabulary Video Unit, 1979–81. Presenter: Herbs Pure and Simple (2 series), BBC Radio 4, 1999, 2000; Sunday Gardening, BBC Radio Bristol, 2005–. Lecture and book tours: South Africa, 2007; Australia, 2008. Royal Horticultural Society: Mem. Council, 2005–15; Member: Fruit, Veg. and Herb Cttee, 1998–2014 (Hon. Mem., 2016); Conservation and Envmt Adv. Cttee, 2003–11; RHS Three Counties Agricl Soc. Jt Cttee, 2007–18 (Jt Chm., 2011–14); Nominations and Appts Cttee, 2009–14; Judge, Floral Exhibits, 1998; Chm., Judging, 2011–15, 2018, Chelsea Flower Show; RHS Ambassador, 2016–; Vice Pres., 2016–. Mem., Horticulture Standards Cttee, Soil Assoc., 2011–17. President: W of England Herb Gp, 2006–; Herb Soc., 2013–14 (Vice Pres., 2015–); Friends of Univ. of Bristol Botanic Garden, 2014–. Contrib., BBC Gardeners' World Mag., 2002–. 62 Gold Medals, RHS, 1993–2019, incl. 14 Gold Medals, Chelsea Flower Show, 1995–2009; Tudor Rose Award, Hampton Court Palace Flower Show, 2007, 2008; Colin Spires Herb Trophy, RHS, 2004–09; Lawrence Medal, RHS, 2009; Lifetime Achievement Award, Garden Media Guild, 2012; VMH 2017. *Publications:* Jekka's Complete Herb Book, 1994, 9th edn 2009; Good Enough to Eat, 1997, 2nd edn as Cooking with Flowers, 2003; Seeds: the ultimate guide to growing successfully from seed, 2001, 3rd edn 2008; The New Book of Herbs, 2002, 2nd edn as Grow Herbs, 2010; The Complete Book of Vegetables, Herbs and Fruit, 2002, 5th edn 2009; Jekka's Herb Cookbook, 2010; A Pocketful of Herbs, 2019. *Recreations:* music (classical and modern), cooking, gardening, plant photography. *Address:* Rose Cottage, Shellards Lane, Alveston, Bristol BS35 3SY. *T:* (01454) 418878. *E:* Sales@jekkas.com.

**McVICAR, Dr Malcolm Thomas;** DL; Group Chief Executive, University of Central Lancashire, 2013–14 (Vice-Chancellor, 1998–2013); *b* 16 June 1946; *s* of Thomas Frederick McVicar and Rose Edith McVicar; two *s*; *m* 2002, Alison Smith; two step *s*. *Educ:* Univ. of Exeter (BA, MA); Univ. of London (PGCE 1975; DPA 1978; PhD 1989). Portsmouth Polytechnic: Prin. Lectr, then Hd of Dept; Dean, 1989–92; Pro-Vice-Chancellor, Univ. of Portsmouth, 1993–98. DL Lancs, 2011. *Recreations:* ski-ing, sailing.

**McVIE, Prof. (John) Gordon,** MD; Chairman, Cancer Intelligence Ltd, since 2011 (Director, 2003–11); Clinical Advisor, Institute of Molecular Oncology, Milan, since 2016; *b* 13 Jan. 1945; *s* of John McVie and Lindsaye Woodburn McVie (*née* Mair); *m* 1998, Claudia Joan Burke; three *s* by previous marriage. *Educ:* Royal High Sch., Edinburgh; Univ. of Edinburgh (BSc Hons; MB, ChB; MD 1978) MRCP 1971. Edinburgh University: MRC Fellow, 1970–71; Lectr in Therapeutics, 1971–76; CRC Sen. Lectr in Oncology, Glasgow Univ., 1976–80; Netherlands Cancer Institute, Amsterdam: Hd, Clinical Res. Unit, 1980–84; Clinical Res. Dir, 1984–89; Scientific Dir, CRC, 1989–96; Dir Gen., CRC, 1996–2002, Jt Dir Gen., Cancer Res. UK, 2002. Sen. Consultant, Eur. Inst. of Oncol., Milan, 2003–15; Consultant to Dir, Internat. Agency for Res. on Cancer, WHO, Lyon, 2006–08. Chairman: Oncology Research Internat. Ltd, Aust., 2009–; Proton Partners Internat. Ltd, 2015–17. Visiting Professor: BPMF, London Univ., 1990–96; Univ. of Glasgow, 1996–2001; Univ. of Wales, Cardiff, 2003–10; Univ. of Milan, 2011–17; Sch. of Medicine, KCL, 2014–. Non-exec. Dir, Nanovi, Denmark, 2015–; Dir, Ellipses Pharma Ltd, 2017–. Member: Council, Scottish Action for Smoking and Health, 1975–80; Royal College of Physicians: Collegiate Mems Cttee, 1975–80; Standing Cttee on Smoking, 1976–80; MRC Cancer Therapy Cttee UK, 1984–92; Bd of Dirs, Netherlands Cancer Inst., 1984–89; Permanent Cttee on Oncology, Min. of Health, Netherlands, 1986–89; European Organisation for Research and Treatment of Cancer: Chairman: Lung Cancer Co-operation Gp, 1981–88; Pharmacokinetics and Metabolism Gp, 1984–87 (Mem., 1981–87); Protocol Rev. Cttee, 1984–91 (Pres., 1994). Examiner: RCPE, 1976–94; RCPSG, 1978–84. Chm., UICC Fellowships Prog., 1990–98. Member: Nat. Review of Resource Allocation, Scottish Office, 1998–99; Internat. Scientific Cttee, Italian Govt, 1998; Steering Cttee, Alliance of World Cancer Res. Orgns; Co-Chair, Eur. Alliance on Personalised Medicine, 2015– (Sec., 2012). Mem., editl bds of numerous jls related to cancer; Editor-in-Chief, European Cancer News, 1987–97; European Ed., Jl Nat. Cancer Inst., 1994–2003; Founder, ecancer.org, 2007; Founding Editor, ecancermedicalscience, 2007–18; Editor, ecancerpatient, 2015–18. FRCPE 1981; FRCPSGlas 1987; FRCP 1997; FMedSci 1999: Fellow: Eur. Acad. of Cancer Scis, 2014; Assoc. of Cancer Physicians (UK), 2017. Hon. FRCSE 2001. Hon. DSc: Abertay Dundee, 1996; Nottingham, 1997; Portsmouth, 1999; Napier Edinburgh, 2002; Ghent, 2005; Bath, 2014. *Publications:* Cancer Assessment and Monitoring, 1979; Autologous Bone Marrow Transplantation and Solid Tumours, 1984; Microspheres and Drug Therapy, 1984; Clinical and Experimental Pathology and Biology of Lung Cancer, 1985; 360 chapters and peer reviewed articles. *Recreations:* opera, theatre, wine, grandchildren.

**McVITTIE, Dame Joan (Christine),** DBE 2013; Head Teacher, Woodside High School, Haringey, 2005–15; *b* Lanark, Scotland, 15 Sept. 1952; *d* of James Smith Docherty and Anne Frances Docherty; *m* 1977, David McVittie (marr. diss. 2000); two *d*. *Educ:* Hollies Convent Grammar Sch.; Birmingham Univ. (BSc Hons); Open Univ. (MA). Teacher of Biology: Burnage High Sch., Manchester, 1974–77; Loreto Sixth Form Coll., Manchester, 1977–82; Newham FE Coll. and Waltham Forest Coll., 1988–90; Hd of Biology, Ilford Ursuline Sch., 1990–94; Sen. Teacher, St Bonaventure's Sch., 1994–96; Deputy Head Teacher: Langdon Sch., 1996–98; Eastlea Sch., 1998–99; Head Teacher, Leytonstone Sch., 2000–06. Pres., ASCL, 2011–12. Trustee, Youth Sports Trust, 2012–. Gov., Nat. Coll. of Sch. Leadership, 2006–12. *Publications:* contrib. Jl Anatomy. *Recreations:* family, reading, cinema, theatre, gym. *E:* damejoanmcvittie@gmail.com.

**McWALTER, Tony**; philosopher; Teacher of Key Stage 5 Mathematics, Thomas Alleyne Academy, Stevenage, since 2016; *b* 20 March 1945; *s* of late Joe McWalter and Anne Murray; *m* 1991, Karry Omer; one *s* two *d*. *Educ*: UC Wales, Aberystwyth (BSc 1968); McMaster Univ., Canada (MA 1969); University Coll., Oxford (BPhil 1971; MLitt 1983); Inst. of Educn, London Univ. (QTS 2010). School teacher, Cardinal Wiseman Sch., Greenford, 1963–64; lorry driver, E. H. Patterson Transport, 1964; Lecturer in Philosophy: Thames Poly., 1972–74; Hatfield Poly., then Univ. of Hertfordshire, 1974–97 (Dir of Computing, 1989–92); Associate Lectr in Maths, Open Univ., 2007–10; Teacher: of Maths and Physics, Thomas Alleyne Sch., Stevenage, 2008–14; of Economics and Maths, Barclay Sch., Stevenage, 2014–16. MP (Lab and Co-op) Hemel Hempstead, 1997–2005; contested same seat, 2005. Member, Select Committee: NI, 1997–2000; Sci. & Technol., 2001–05; Procedure, 2003–05. Treas., Nat. Cttee for Philosophy, 1984–97. Mem., External Adv. Bd, Faculty of Lit. Hum., Oxford Univ., 2000–; Board Member: Council for Economic and Social Aspects of Genomics, 2003–05; British Philosophical Assoc., 2004–05 (Exec. Mem., 2003–06). Hon. Vice-Pres., Herts Conservation Soc., 1997–2006. Educn consultant, 2005–. *Publications*: (ed jtly) Kant and His Influence, 1990. *Recreations*: tennis, bridge, croquet, theatre. *Address*: 56 St Giles Road, Codicote, Hitchin, Herts SG4 8XW. *Club*: Reform.

**McWEENY, Prof. Roy**; Professor of Theoretical Chemistry, University of Pisa, 1982–97, Professor Emeritus, since 1998; *b* 19 May 1924; *o s* of late Maurice and Vera McWeeny; *m* 1947, Patricia M. Healey (marr. diss. 1979); one *s* one *d*; *m* 1982, Virginia Del Re. *Educ*: Univ. of Leeds; University Coll., Oxford. BSc (Physics) Leeds 1945; DPhil Oxon 1949. Lectr in Physical Chemistry, King's Coll., Univ. of Durham, 1948–57; Vis. Scientist, Physics Dept, MIT, USA, 1953–54; Lectr in Theoretical Chemistry, Univ. Coll. of N Staffs, 1957–62; Associate Dir, Quantum Chemistry Gp, Uppsala Univ., Sweden, 1960–61; Reader in Quantum Theory, 1962–64; Prof. of Theoretical Chemistry, 1964–66, Univ. of Keele; Prof. of Theoretical Chem., 1966–82, and Hd of Chemistry Dept, 1976–79, Sheffield Univ. Vis. Prof., America, Japan, Europe. Mem., Acad. Européenne des Scis, des Arts et des Lettres, 1988. Spiers Meml Medal, RSC, 2006. *Publications*: Symmetry, an Introduction to Group Theory and its Applications, 1963, repr. 2002; (with B. T. Sutcliffe) Methods of Molecular Quantum Mechanics, 1969, 2nd edn as sole author, 1989; Spins in Chemistry, 1970, repr. 2004; Quantum Mechanics: principles and formalism, 1972, repr. 2003; Quantum Mechanics: methods and basic applications, 1973; Coulson's Valence, 3rd rev. edn 1979; (contrib. and Associate Ed.) Handbook of Molecular Physics and Quantum Chemistry, 3 vols, 2002; (Series Ed. and author) Basic Books in Science, 2005–13; contrib. sections in other books and encyclopædias; many research papers on quantum theory of atomic and molecular structure in Proc. Royal Soc., Proc. Phys. Soc., Phys. Rev., Revs. Mod. Phys., Jl Chem. Phys., etc. *Recreations*: drawing, sculpture, travel. *Address*: Via Venanzo Nisi 2, 56125 Pisa, Italy.

**McWHA, Prof. James Alexander**, AO 2011; Pro-Chancellor and Provost, Lincoln University, New Zealand, since 2019 (Vice-Chancellor, 2018); Founding Vice-Chancellor and President, University of Rwanda, 2013–15; *b* 28 May 1947; *s* of David McWha and Sarah Isabel McWha (*née* Caughey); *m* 1970, Jean Lindsay Farries; one *s* two *d*. *Educ*: Queen's Univ., Belfast (BSc, BAgr Hons); Glasgow Univ. (PhD Plant Physiol. 1973); PhD *aeg* Adelaide, 2002. Lectr in Plant Physiol., 1973–79, Hd, Dept of Plant and Microbial Scis, 1980–85, Univ. of Canterbury; Prof. of Agricl Botany, QUB and Dep. CSO, Dept of Agriculture for NI, 1985–89; Dir, DSIR Fruit and Trees (NZ), 1989–92; CEO, Horticulture and Food Res. Inst., NZ, 1992–95; Vice-Chancellor and President: Massey Univ., NZ, 1996–2002; Univ. of Adelaide, 2002–12. Member: Council, NIAB, Cambridge, 1986–89; Bd, NZ Foundn for Res. Sci. and Technol., 1992–95; Bd, NZ Dairy Res. Inst., 1995–98; Gen. Bd, Amer. Chamber of Commerce in NZ, 2000–02. Association of Commonwealth Universities: Mem. Council, 2000–02 (NZ Rep.), 2006–07, 2011–12 (Aust. Rep.); Hon. Treas., 2007–; Exec. Cttee, 2007–17; Convenor, SA Vice-Chancellors' Cttee, 2002, 2007–08; Sec. Gen., Internat. Assoc. of Univ. Presidents, 2002–05, Sec. Gen. Emeritus, 2005; Mem., Universities Australia (formerly Australian Vice-Chancellors' Cttee), 2002–12; Dir, Aust. Univs Quality Agency, 2003–09; Mem., Exec. Cttee, Inter-Univ. Council for East Africa, 2014–16. Director: Industrial Res. Ltd, 1996–2001; Gp of Eight Ltd (Aust.), 2002–12; Martindale Hldgs Pty Ltd, 2008–12. Patron, Children's Univ. of Australasia, 2013–; Chancellor, Children's Univ. of NZ, 2018–. Hon. DSc Massey, 2004; DUniv Adelaide, 2012. Centenary Medal (Aust.), 2003. *Publications*: numerous scientific and educnl articles. *Recreations*: classic cars, rallying, motor sport, Rugby Union. *Address*: Wellington, New Zealand. *Clubs*: Wellington (Wellington); Adelaide.

**McWHINNEY, Jeffrey Harold**; Chairman: Significan't (UK) Ltd, since 2013; Vortex Consulting Ltd, since 2014; *b* 9 May 1960; *s* of late Harold George McWhinney and Mabel Joan McWhinney (*née* Carlisle); *m* 1989, Brigitte François; three *s* one *d*. *Educ*: Jordanstown Schs, Belfast; Mary Hare Grammar Sch., Newbury; Kingston Univ. (Cert. Mgt 1992; Dip. Mgt 1993). Develt Officer, Breakthrough Trust, 1984–87; Head of Community Services, Disability Resources Team, 1987–91; Sen. Economic Develt Officer, Economic Develt Office, Wandsworth BC, 1991–94; Dir, Greenwich Assoc. of Disabled People, 1994–95; Chief Exec., British Deaf Assoc., 1995–2004; Man. Dir, Significan't (UK) Ltd, 2004–13. Dir, Sign Campaign, 1993–2003; Chief Exec., Big D Trading Co., 1996–2002; Chm., Greater London Initiatives for Disabled Entrepreneurs, 2003–05. Specialist Mem., Special Educnl Needs and Disability Tribunal, 2002–05; Mem., Adv. Cttee, Deafness Cognition and Language Res. Centre, UCL, 2011–; UK Council on Deafness (formerly Telecom Action Group): Trustee, 2001–03; Mem., Deaf Access to Communication, 2007–; Dir, 2015–; Trustee, RNID, 2006–09. Chm., Technol. Expert Cttee, 2006–10, Mem., ICT Experts Wkg Gp, 2011–, Eur. Union of the Deaf; Mem., Experts in Design for All, World Fedn of the Deaf, 2008–12. Mem., ACEVO (formerly ACENVO), 1995–2005. Dir, British Sign Lang. Broadcasting Trust, 2012–15. Winston Churchill Travel Fellow, 2007. MInstD 1996. Deaf Acad. Award, 1996. *Publications*: Deaf Consciousness, 1992; numerous articles in various professional and specialist jls. *Recreations*: golf, reading, family activities, travel, sailing, Charlton Athletic FC. *Address*: Significan't (UK) Ltd, St Agnes House, 6 Cresswell Park, SE3 9RD. *Club*: Greenwich Yacht.

**MACWHIRTER, Iain**; political commentator and broadcaster; *b* 24 Sept. 1952; *s* of Robert Archibald Macwhirter and Christina Ann Macwhirter (*née* McKean); *m* 1991, Christina Harley (marr. diss. 2006); one *s* two *d*. *Educ*: George Heriot's Sch., Edinburgh; Univ. of Edinburgh (MA Hons Pols). Postgrad. Res. in politics, Univ. of Edinburgh, 1976–78; BBC Researcher, 1979; TV current affairs reporter, 1980–87; Scottish Political Corresp., 1987–89; Westminster Corresp., 1989–90; presenter, political television: Westminster, 1990–99; Holyrood, 1999–2006; presenter, The Road to Referendum (series), 2013. Columnist: Scotland on Sunday, 1990–94; Observer, 1995–96; Scotsman, 1995–99; political commentator, Sunday Herald, 1999–. Rector, Univ. of Edinburgh, 2009–12. Blog, iainmacwhirter.wordpress.com, 2006–. *Publications*: Road to Referendum, 2013; Disunited Kingdom: how Westminster won a referendum but lost Scotland, 2014; Tsunami: Scotland's democratic revolution, 2015; contribs to numerous books and other publications incl. Guardian, New Statesman and Public Finance. *Recreations*: hill walking, yoga, children, travel. *Address*: 19 Lilyhill Terrace, Edinburgh EH8 7DR. *T*: (0131) 667 0845, 07714 667871. *E*: iainmacwhirter@mac.com.

**McWHIRTER, Prof. John Graham**, PhD; FRS 1999; FREng; Distinguished Research Professor in Engineering, Cardiff University, 2007–19; *b* 28 March 1949; *s* of late Francis David McWhirter and Elizabeth McWhirter (*née* Martin); *m* 1973, Avesia Vivianne Wolfe; one *s* one *d*. *Educ*: Newry High Sch.; Queen's Univ., Belfast (BSc 1st Cl. Hons Maths 1970; PhD 1973). CMath, FIMA 1988; FIET (FIEE 1994); FREng (FEng 1996); FInstP 1999. Royal Signals and Radar Establishment: Higher Scientific Officer, 1973–77; SSO, 1977–80; PSO, 1980–86; SPSO, 1986–96. Sen. Fellow, Signal Processing Gp, DERA, later QinetiQ Ltd, 1996–2007. Visiting Professor: Electrical Engrg Dept, Queen's Univ., Belfast, 1986–; Sch. of Engrg, UC, Cardiff, 1997–2019. Pres., IMA, 2002–03 (Vice Pres., 1998–99; Chm. and Proceedings Ed., IMA Internat. Conf. on Maths in Signal Processing, 1988, 1992, 1996, 2000 and 2004); Mem. Council, Royal Soc., 2011–12. Hon. DSc: QUB, 2000; Edinburgh, 2002. J. J. Thomson Medal, IEE, 1994. *Publications*: over 200 res. papers; inventor or jt inventor of 30 UK, European, US and Canadian patents. *Recreations*: swimming for exercise, building and flying radio-controlled model gliders. *Club*: Malvern Soaring Association.

**McWILLIAM, Sir Michael (Douglas)**, KCMG 1996; Director, School of Oriental and African Studies, University of London, 1989–96 (Hon. Fellow, 1997); *b* 21 June 1933; *s* of Douglas and Margaret McWilliam; *m* 1st, 1960, Ruth Arnstein (*d* 2009); two *s*; 2nd, 2010, Thalia Sybil Stone. *Educ*: Cheltenham Coll.; Oriel Coll., Oxford (MA; Hon. Fellow 2012); Nuffield Coll., Oxford (BLitt). Kenya Treasury, 1958; Samuel Montagu & Co., 1962; joined Standard Bank, subseq. Standard Chartered Bank, 1966; Gen. Manager, 1973; Gp Man. Dir, 1983–88. Member: Bd, Commonwealth Development Corp., 1990–96; Council, ODI, 1991–94. Chm., Superannuation Fund, London Univ., 1990–97. Hon. Vice Pres., Royal African Soc., 2004–18 (Mem. Council, 1979–91; Chm., 1996–2004); Vice-Pres., Royal Commonwealth Soc., 2002 (Dep. Chm., 1982–91; Chm., 1996–2002, 2009); Chm., Centre for the Study of African Economies, Oxford, 1998–2012. Trustee: British Empire and Commonwealth Mus., Bristol, 2003–12 (Dep. Chm., 2003–06; Chm., 2006–08); David Vaisey Trust, 2016–; Chm., Bryanston Sq. Trust, 2012–17. Chm., Cheltenham Festivals, 2007–11 (Dep. Chm., 2006). Pres. Council, Cheltenham Coll., 1988–92 (Mem., 1977–92). Mem., Hon. Co. of Gloucestershire, 2010– (Mem. Court, 2013–17). Mem., Brimpsfield Parish Council, 2019–. *Publications*: The Development Business: a history of the Commonwealth Development Corporation, 2001. *Address*: Yew Tree Farm, Brimpsfield, Glos GL4 8LD. *Club*: New (Cheltenham).

**McWILLIAMS, Douglas Francis**; Deputy Chairman, Centre for Economics and Business Research, since 2017 (Chief Executive, 1993–2013; Chairman, 2013–15; President, 2015–17); *b* Leigh, Lancs, 24 Nov. 1951; *s* of Sir Francis McWilliams, *qv*; *m* 1979, Ianthe Wright. *Educ*: Stonyhurst Coll.; Lincoln Coll., Oxford (MA; MPhil Econs). Economist, CBI, 1974–85; Chief Economist, IBM UK, 1985–88; Chief Econ. Advr, CBI, 1988–92. Gresham Prof. of Commerce, Gresham Coll., 2012–14. *Publications*: Basic Economics (with T. Congdon), 1975; The Flat White Economy, 2015; The Inequality Paradox—How to Make Capitalism Work for Everyone, 2018. *Recreations*: classic cars, historic car rallying, cricket. *Address*: 18 Kent Terrace, NW1 4RP. *T*: (020) 7724 7951. *Club*: MCC.

**McWILLIAMS, Sir Francis**, GBE 1992; FREng; conciliator and arbitrator, since 1978; Chairman, Centre for Economics and Business Research, 1992–2002; Lord Mayor of London, 1992–93; *b* 8 Feb. 1926; *s* of John J. and Mary Anne McWilliams; *m* 1950, Winifred (*née* Segger); two *s*. *Educ*: Holy Cross Acad., Edinburgh; Edinburgh Univ. (BSc Eng 1945); Inns of Court Sch. of Law. Engineer in local govt, 1945–54; Town Engineer, Petaling Jaya New Town, Malaysia, 1954–64; Consulting Civil and Struct. Engineer, Kuala Lumpur, 1964–76. Bar student, 1976–78; called to the Bar, Lincoln's Inn, 1978, Bencher, 1993. Dir, Hong Kong & Shanghai Bank (Malaysia), 1993–99. Chm., British/Malaysian Soc., 1994–2001. Mem., Common Council, City of London, 1978–80; Alderman, Ward of Aldersgate, 1980–96; Sheriff, City of London, 1988–89. Master: Arbitrators' Co., 1985–86; Engineers' Co., 1990–91; Loriners' Co., 1995–96; Pres., Aldersgate Ward Club, 1980–96. Chm., St John's Ambulance City Br., 1992–96. Pres., Instn of Incorp. Exec. Engrs, 1994–97. Vice Chm. Trustees, Foundn for Manufg and Industry, 1994–2000. FCGI; FREng (FEng 1991). Hon. FICE. Hon. DCL City; Hon. DEng Kingston, 1994; Dr *hc* Edinburgh, 1994. KStJ 1992; KSG 1993. PJK, Selangor, Malaysia, 1963; Dato Seri Selera, Selangor, 1973. Order of Merit (Senegal), 1989; Order of Independence (CI. III) (UAE), 1989; Grande Official da Ordem do Infante Dom Henrique (Portugal), 1993. *Publications*: Pray Silence for "Jock" Whittington (autobiog.), 2002. *Recreations*: golf, ski-ing. *Address*: Flat 7, Whittingehame House, Whittingehame, E Lothian EH41 4QA. *T*: and *Fax*: (01368) 850619. *Clubs*: Hon. Company of Edinburgh Golfers, Muirfield; Royal Selangor Golf (Kuala Lumpur).

*See also* D. F. McWilliams.

**MADAN, Arvind Kumar**; Director of Primary Care and Deputy Medical Director, NHS England, 2015–18; *b* London, 11 Jan. 1968; *s* of Surinder and Santosh Madan; *m* 1993, Ashu; two *s*. *Educ*: Dulwich Coll.; Leicester Univ. (MB ChB 1991). DRCOG 1994; MRCGP 1996. St Thomas' Hosp., London; GP Partner, Hurley Gp, 1996–. *Recreations*: club cricket, club tennis, travel, reading, family.

**MADDEN, Sir Charles (Jonathan)**, 4th Bt *cr* 1919, of Kells, co. Kilkenny; Technical Director, Wind-Ways Pty Ltd, since 2007; *b* 11 Aug. 1949; *yr s* of Lt-Col John Wilmot Madden, MC, RA, *yr s* of 1st Bt, and Beatrice Catherine (*née* Sievwright); *S* brother, 2006; *m* 1st, 1980, Kirsteen Victoria Ronald Noble (marr. diss. 2003); one *s* one *d*; 2nd, 2006, Dr Margaret Elaine Taylor. *Educ*: Blundell's; Portsmouth Poly. (BSc Engrg 1974); Loughborough Univ. (MTech Design 1975); San Diego Univ. (MBA Marketing 1984). *Recreations*: playing the 'cello (Unley SO, Adelaide), sailing. *Heir*: *s* Samuel Charles John Madden, *b* 22 Sept. 1984. *Address*: 3 Sea View, Lynton, SA 5062, Australia. *E*: charlie.madden@internode.au.net.

**MADDEN, Rt Rev. Cuthbert**, OSB; Abbot of Ampleforth, since 2005; *b* 12 Feb. 1955; *s* of late James and Joan Madden. *Educ*: Middlesex Hosp. Med. Sch. (MB BS). MRCP 1982. House Surgeon, W Norwich Hosp., 1978–79; House Physician, 1979, SHO, 1979–80, Middlesex Hosp.; Rotating SHO in Medicine, Bath Utd Hosps, 1980–82; Rotating Registrar in Medicine, Royal Hallamshire Hosp., Sheffield, 1982–84; Ampleforth: entered monastic community, 1984; solemn profession, 1988; ordained priest, 1990; Housemaster, St John's, 1997–2005. Hon. FRCP 2006. *Address*: Ampleforth Abbey, York YO62 4EN. *T*: (01439) 766700/710.

**MADDEN, Sir David (Christopher Andrew)**, KCMG 2003 (CMG 1996); HM Diplomatic Service, retired; Senior Member, St Antony's College, Oxford, since 2012 (Distinguished Friend, 2016); *b* 25 July 1946; *s* of late Dr (Albert) Frederick (McCulloch) Madden and (Alice) Margaret Madden; *m* 1970, Penelope Anthea Johnston; one *s* two *d*. *Educ*: Magdalen Coll. Sch., Oxford; Merton Coll., Oxford (Postmaster; MA); Courtauld Inst. of Art, London Univ. (MA). FCO, 1970–72; British Mil. Govt, Berlin, 1972–75; Cabinet Office, 1975–77; Moscow, 1978–81; Athens, 1981–84; FCO, 1984–87; Counsellor, 1987; Dep. Hd of Mission, Belgrade, 1987–90; Head, Southern European Dept, FCO, 1990–94; High Comr, Republic of Cyprus, 1994–99; Ambassador to Greece, 1999–2004; Pol Advr to OC EU Force, Bosnia and Hercegovina, 2004–05. Accredited Mediator, ADR Gp, 2009–13. Chair, SEESOX Steering Cttee, 2018– (Chm., Develt Cttee, SE Eur. Studies at Oxford, 2012–17). Trustee: Brooke Hosp. for Animals, 2008–16;

Compassion in World Farming, 2010–; Patron, Voice for Ethical Research at Oxford, 2008–. Hon. Dr London Metropolitan, 1999. *Publications:* The Mystery of Edwin Drood, by Charles Dickens (completion of an unfinished book), 2011; (ed jtly) Balkan Legacies of the Great War: the past is never dead, 2016. *Recreations:* animal welfare, cricket, tennis, reading, writing. *Address:* 5 Rawlinson Road, Oxford OX2 6UE.

**MADDEN, Dr (John) Lionel,** CBE 1999; Librarian, National Library of Wales, 1994–98; *b* 8 Aug. 1938; *s* of late Cyril Madden and Edith (*née* Mottram); *m* 1965, Georgina Mary Hardwick; one *s* one *d*. *Educ:* King Edward VII Grammar Sch., Sheffield; Lincoln Coll., Oxford (MA 1964); University Coll. London (DipLib 1963); Univ. of Leicester (PhD 1970). ALA 1964. Asst Librarian, Univ. of Hull, 1963–67; Bibliographer, Univ. of Leicester Victorian Studies Centre, 1967–72; Sen. Lectr, Coll. of Librarianship, Wales, 1973–87; Keeper of Printed Books, Nat. Liby of Wales, 1987–94. Mem., Pubns Bd, Leicester Univ. Press, 1968–72; Chm., Pubns Bd, Tennyson Soc., 1973–77. Pres., Welsh Liby Assoc., 1994–98; Chairman: Welsh Books Council, 1996–2005 (Vice-Chm., 1994–96); Liby and Inf. Services Council, Wales, 1998–2001; Capel (Welsh Chapels Heritage Soc.), 1999–2009 (Hon. Pres., 2010–). Trustee, St Deiniol's Liby, Hawarden, 1994–2009. Hon. Fellow, Dept of Inf. and Liby Studies, Univ. of Wales, Aberystwyth, 1989–93, Hon. Prof., 1993–; Hon. Fellow, Univ. of Wales, Lampeter, 1998. Hon. FCLIP (Hon. FLA 1998). Hon. Mem., Gorsedd Beirdd Ynys Prydain, 1995–. *Publications:* Thomas Love Peacock, 1967; How to Find Out about the Victorian Period, 1970; Robert Southey: the critical heritage, 1972; Sir Charles Tennyson: an annotated bibliography, 1973; The Nineteenth Century Periodical Press in Britain, 1976; Primary Sources for Victorian Studies, 1977; (ed jtly) Investigating Victorian Journalism, 1990; Methodism in Wales, 2003; articles in learned jls. *Recreation:* walking. *Address:* Hafren, Cae'r Gog, Aberystwyth SY23 1ET. *T:* (01970) 617771.

**MADDEN, John Philip;** film director; *b* 8 April 1949; *s* of William John Raleigh Madden and Jean Elizabeth Hunt Mills; *m* 1975, Penelope Jane Abrahams; one *s* one *d*. *Educ:* Clifton Coll., Bristol; Sidney Sussex Coll., Cambridge (MA; Hon. Fellow 2000). Artistic Dir, Oxford and Cambridge Shakespeare Co., 1970–73; Associate Prof., Yale Sch. of Drama, 1977–80. *Stage:* Wings, The Bundle, Measure for Measure, The Suicide, Terry by Terry, Grownups, Beyond Therapy, Salonika, Cinders, Between East and West, An American Comedy, Ivanov, Mrs Warren's Profession, Caritas, Proof; *films:* Ethan Frome, 1992; Golden Gate, 1994; Mrs Brown, 1997; Shakespeare in Love, 1998 (seven Academy Awards, four BAFTA Awards, 1999); Captain Corelli's Mandolin, 2001; Proof, 2005; Killshot, 2008; The Debt, 2011; The Best Exotic Marigold Hotel, 2012; The Second Best Exotic Marigold Hotel, 2015; Miss Sloane, 2017; *television:* Poppyland, A Wreath of Roses, Sherlock Holmes, After the War, Widowmaker, Inspector Morse (four films), Prime Suspect: The Lost Child, Meat, Truth or Dare (BAFTA Scotland Award, Best Single Drama, 1997); Masters of Sex, 2013; *radio:* US National Public Radio: Wings (Prix Italia, 1978), Star Wars, The Empire Strikes Back, Return of the Jedi. Hon. DLitt Portsmouth, 2006. *Recreations:* cooking, walking, sailing. *Address:* c/o Jenne Casarotto, Casarotto Ramsay Ltd, Waverley House, 7–12 Noel Street, W1F 8GQ.

**MADDEN, Lionel;** *see* Madden, J. L.

**MADDEN, Max;** *b* 29 Oct. 1941; *s* of late George Francis Leonard Madden and Rene Frances Madden; *m* 1972, Sheelagh Teresa Catherine Howard (*d* 2007). *Educ:* Lascelles Secondary Modern Sch.; Pinner Grammar Sch. Journalist: East Essex Gazette; Tribune (political weekly); Sun, London; Scotsman, London; subseq. Press and Information Officer, British Gas Corp., London; Dir of Publicity, Labour Party, 1979–82. MP (Lab): Sowerby, Feb. 1974–1979; Bradford West, 1983–97.

**MADDEN, Michael;** Under Secretary, Ministry of Agriculture, Fisheries and Food, 1985–96, retired; *b* 12 Feb. 1936; *s* of late Harold Madden and Alice Elizabeth (*née* Grenville); *m* 1st, 1960, Marion Will (marr. diss. 1977); two *s* one *d*; 2nd, 1994, Angela Grace Abell (*d* 2012). *Educ:* King Edward VII Sch., Sheffield. Exec. Officer, Min. of Transport and Civil Aviation, 1955; Ministry of Agriculture, Fisheries and Food: Asst Principal, 1963–67; Asst Private Sec. to Minister, 1966–67; Principal, 1967; Asst Sec. (as Head, Tropical Foods Div.), 1973; Under Sec., 1985; Head, Management Services Gp, 1985; Flood Defence, Plant Protection and Agricl Resources, 1990; Envmt Policy Gp, 1991–96. *Recreations:* walking, music, theatre going. *Address:* 89 Corinium Gate, Cirencester GL7 2PX. *T:* (01242) 641423. *Club:* Farmers.

**MADDEN, Prof. Paul Anthony,** DPhil; FRS 2001; FRSE; Provost, Queen's College, Oxford, 2008–19; Pro-Vice-Chancellor, University of Oxford, 2011–19; *m*; five *c*. *Educ:* St Bede's Catholic Grammar Sch., Bradford; Univ. of Sussex (BSc, DPhil). Fellow, Magdalene Coll., Cambridge, 1974–82; Lectr in Chemistry, then Prof. of Chemistry, 1984–2004, Univ. of Oxford; Fellow, Queen's Coll., 1984–2004; Prof. of Chemistry, 2005–06, Joseph Black Prof. of Chemistry, 2006–08, and Dir, Centre for Sci. at Extreme Conditions, 2005–08, Univ. of Edinburgh. Chair, Conf. of Oxford Colleges, 2015–17. FRSE 2006. Eli Burstein Lect., Univ. of Philadelphia, 2004. Tilden Medal, 1993/94, Medal for Statistical Mechanics and Simulation, 2002, RSC; Robert S. Mulliken Award, Univ. of Chicago, 2002. *Address:* Queen's College, Oxford OX1 4AW.

**MADDEN, Paul Damian,** CMG 2013; FRGS; HM Diplomatic Service; Ambassador to Japan, since 2017; *b* 25 April 1959; *s* of Antony Angus Thomas Madden and Doris May Madden (*née* Brewer); *m* 1989, Sarah Pauline Thomas; two *s* one *d*. *Educ:* King's School, Ottery St Mary; Gonville and Caius Coll., Cambridge (BA Geog. 1980, MA 1983); Sch. of Oriental and African Studies, Univ. of London; Durham Univ. Business Sch. (MBA 2002). DTI, 1980–87, Private Sec. to Minister, 1984–86; Japanese Lang. Studies, SOAS and Kamakura, 1987–89; entered Diplomatic Service, 1989; First Secretary: Tokyo, 1989–92; FCO, 1992–96; Washington, 1996–2000; Dep. High Comr, Singapore, 2000–03; Hd, Public Diplomacy Dept, FCO, 2003–04; Gp Dir, UK Trade and Investment, 2004–07; High Comr, Singapore, 2007–11; High Comr, Australia, 2011–15; Additional Dir, Asia Pacific, FCO, 2015. Member, Court: Imperial Coll. London, 2004–07; Cranfield Univ., 2004–07. *Publications:* Raffles: lessons in business leadership, 2003. *Recreations:* travel, family. *Address:* c/o Foreign and Commonwealth Office, King Charles Street, SW1A 2AH.

**MADDEN, Penelope Jane;** QC 2016; Co-Chair, International Arbitration, and Partner, Gibson Dunn, since 2013; *b* Canterbury, Kent, 19 Jan. 1969; *d* of Sidney John Rogers and Christine Hildegard Irene Elizabeth Rogers; *m* Col David Alexander Grevile Madden, MBE; one *s* one *d*. *Educ:* Simon Langton Sch. for Girls; St Hugh's Coll., Oxford (BA Hist.); Guildford Coll. of Law (CPE). Trainee, then Associate, Clifford Chance, 1992–2000; Associate, then Counsel, Shearman & Sterling, 2000–07; Counsel, then Partner, Skadden Arps, 2007–13. *Publications:* (jtly) Covered Investment, Investment Treaty Arbitration Review, 2016; contrib. articles to Commercial Dispute Resolution, Financier Worldwide. *Recreations:* equestrian, ski-ing, tennis, opera. *Address:* The Manor House, Chilthorne Domer, Som BA22 8RD. *T:* (01935) 840255. *E:* penny_madden@icloud.com. *Club:* Cavalry and Guards.

**MADDERS, Rev. Mgr (Brian) Richard,** MBE 1996; Parish Priest (RC), St John the Evangelist, Tadworth, since 2016; *b* 12 Aug. 1949; *s* of Mervyn and Eleanor Madders. *Educ:* Mayfield Coll.; St John's Seminary, Wonersh; Heythrop Coll., London. Employee, National Bank, 1969–71; ordained priest, 1978; Assistant Priest: Banstead, 1978–81; Brighton, 1981–84; Worthing, 1984–85; Chaplain, RN, 1985–2007: First Flotilla (Seagoing), 1986–87; HMS Sultan, 1987–90; Third Flotilla (Seagoing), 1990–93; Staff Chaplain, FO Surface Flotilla, 1993–95; HMS Raleigh, 1995–99; Australian Defence Force Acad., 1999; HMS Nelson, 2000–01; HMS Drake, 2001–02; Principal RC Chaplain (Naval), VG for Bishopric of the Forces (RC), and Dir, Naval Chaplaincy Service (Training and Progs), 2002–07; Parish Priest (RC), Camberley and Bagshot, 2007–16. QHC, 2002–07. Pres., RN Motorcycle Club, 1989–2000. Trustee, Apostleship of the Sea, 2014–. Travelled to 103 countries and territories. Gulf War Medal, 1992; Golden Jubilee Medal, 2002; NATO Former Yugoslavia Medal, 2003. *E:* pp@stjohnstadworth.org.uk.

**MADDERS, Justin;** MP (Lab) Ellesmere Port and Neston, since 2015; *b* Manchester, 22 Nov. 1972; *m* Nicole Meardon; three *s*. *Educ:* Univ. of Sheffield. Solicitor, 1998–2015. Member (Lab): Ellesmere Port and Neston BC, 1998–2009 (Leader, 2007–09); Cheshire W and Chester Council, 2009–15 (Leader of Opposition, 2011–14). Shadow Minister for Health, 2015–19. *Address:* House of Commons, SW1A 0AA. *T:* (020) 7219 6584. *E:* justin.madders.mp@parliament.uk.

**MADDICOTT, David Sydney, (Syd);** HM Diplomatic Service, retired; Partner and Director, DORIS Resources LLP, since 2013; Chairman, Co-ordinating Committee on Remuneration, since 2015; *b* 27 March 1953; *s* of Patrick McCagh and Eileen Hannigan, and adopted *s* of Sydney Walter Maddicott and Catherine O'Brien; *m* 1980, Elizabeth Wynne; four *s* one *d*. *Educ:* University Coll. London (BA Hons English 1976); Univ. of Exeter (MA Classics and Ancient History 2010). Various sales and mktg appts, Rank Xerox (UK) Ltd, 1976–89; Gen. Sales and Mktg Manager, Pitney Bowes (Ireland) Ltd, 1989–90; postgrad. studies, UC, Dublin, 1990–92; self-employed consultant, 1992–94; joined FCO, 1994; Hd of Section, Econ. Relns Dept/UN Dept, 1994–96; on attachment to Canadian Dept of For. Affairs and Internat. Trade, Ottawa, 1996–97; Hd, Pol, Media and Public Affairs Section, High Commn, Ottawa, 1997–2000; Dep. Hd, Latin America and Caribbean Dept, 2000–03, and Hd, Caribbean Unit, 2001–03, FCO; Sen. Duty Manager, FCO Response Centre, 2003–06; High Comr to Cameroon and Ambassador (non-resident) to Central African Republic, Chad and Gabon, 2006–09. *Recreations:* singing, reading, speedway, cricket. *Clubs:* Deddington Cricket, New Edinburgh Cricket (Ottawa).

**MADDICOTT, Dr John Robert Lewendon,** FBA 1996; FSA; Fellow and Lecturer in Modern History, Exeter College, Oxford, 1969–2006, now Emeritus; *b* Exeter, 22 July 1943; *e s* of late Robert Maddicott, Ipplepen, Devon, and Barbara (*née* Lewendon); *m* 1965, Hilary, *d* of late Thomas and Violet Owen; two *d*. *Educ:* Cheltenham Grammar Sch.; King Edward's Sch., Bath; Worcester Coll., Oxford (BA 1st cl. 1964; DPhil 1968). FSA 1980. Jun. Lectr, Magdalen Coll., Oxford, 1966–67; Asst Lectr, Univ. of Manchester, 1967–69; Sub-Rector, Exeter Coll., Oxford, 1988–90. Vis. Prof., Univ. of S Carolina, 1983. Raleigh Lectr, British Acad., 2001; Ford's Lectr in British Hist., Oxford, 2004; Selden Soc. Lectr, 2011. Jt Editor, English Hist. Review, 1990–2000. *Publications:* Thomas of Lancaster 1307–22, 1970; The English Peasantry and the Demands of the Crown, 1294–1341, 1975; Law and Lordship: Royal Justices as Retainers in Thirteenth- and Fourteenth-Century England, 1978; Simon de Montfort, 1994; The Origins of the English Parliament, 924–1327, 2010; Founders and Fellowship: the early history of Exeter College, Oxford, 1314–1592, 2014; contribs to learned jls. *Recreations:* hill walking, poetry, book collecting. *Address:* Exeter College, Oxford OX1 3DP.

**MADDICOTT, Syd;** *see* Maddicott, D. S.

**MADDISON, Jane Hope;** *see* Kennedy, J. H.

**MADDOCK,** family name of **Baroness Maddock**.

**MADDOCK,** Baroness *cr* 1997 (Life Peer), of Christchurch in the co. of Dorset; **Diana Margaret Maddock;** President, Liberal Democrats, 1998–99; *b* 19 May 1945; *d* of Reginald Derbyshire and Margaret Evans; *m* 1st, 1966, Robert Frank Maddock (marr. diss. 2001); two *d*; 2nd, 2001, Rt Hon. Sir Alan Beith (*see* Baron Beith). *Educ:* Brockenhurst GS; Shenstone Training Coll.; Portsmouth Polytechnic. Teacher: Weston Park Girls' Sch., Southampton, 1966–69; Extra-Mural Dept, Stockholm Univ., 1969–72; Sholling Girls' Sch., Southampton, 1972–73; Anglo-Continental Sch. of English, Bournemouth, 1973–76; Greylands Sch. of English, Southampton, 1990–91. Member: (L, subseq. Lib Dem), Southampton CC, 1984–93; (Lib Dem), Northumberland CC, 2005–08; (Lib Dem) Berwick-upon-Tweed BC, 2007–09. Contested (Lib Dem) Southampton Test, 1992. MP (Lib Dem) Christchurch, July 1993–1997; contested (Lib Dem) same seat, 1997. Lib Dem spokesman on housing, H of L, 1997–2004. Chm., Lord Speaker's Adv. Panel on Works of Art (formerly Works of Art Cttee), H of L, 2014–; Member: Cttee on Standards in Public Life, 2003–09; H of L Merits of Statutory Instruments Cttee, 2005–09; Finance Sub-Cttee, H of L Europe Select Cttee, 2010–14; Co-Chm., All-Party Anglo-Swedish Gp, 2010–; Vice Chm., All-Party Univ. Gp, 2010–. A Vice-Pres., Nat. Housing Fedn, 1997–2010; President: Anglo-Swedish Soc., 2000–; Sustainable Energy Assoc. (formerly Micropower Council), 2005–17; Vice President: Nat. Energy Action, 2000–; Local Government Association, 2010–; Pres., Nat. Home Improvement Council, 2016– (Vice Pres., 2004–16). *Recreations:* theatre, music, reading, travel. *Address:* House of Lords, SW1A 0PW.

**MADDOCK, Stephen David,** OBE 2017; Chief Executive, City of Birmingham Symphony Orchestra, since 1999; *b* Lichfield, Staffs, 18 Sept. 1968; *s* of David Maddock and Betty Maddock; *m* 1994, Kathryn Heeley; one *s* one *d*. *Educ:* Durrington High Sch., Worthing; Worthing Sixth Form Coll.; New Coll., Oxford (BA PPE 1990). Prodn Asst, BBC Radio 3, 1990–93; Planning Asst, 1993–95, Administrator, 1995–99, BBC Proms. Member, Board: Henry Barber Trust, 2002–; Assoc. of British Orchs, 2003–09; Marketing Birmingham, 2005–17; Culture Central, 2016–. Gov., Hodge Hill Sch., 2002–06. Patron, Schola Cantorum of Oxford, 2017–. Mem., Midlands team, Round Britain Quiz, BBC Radio 4, 2003–. *Recreations:* cinema, theatre, reading, football, family, TV, cycling, politics. *Address:* City of Birmingham Symphony Orchestra, CBSO Centre, Berkley Street, Birmingham B1 2LF. *T:* (0121) 616 6500. *E:* smaddock@cbso.co.uk.

**MADDOCKS, Anne Mary Catherine;** *see* Ashworth, A. M. C.

**MADDOCKS, Arthur Frederick,** CMG 1974; HM Diplomatic Service, retired; Ambassador and UK Permanent Representative to OECD, Paris, 1977–82; *b* 20 May 1922; *s* of late Frederick William Maddocks and Celia Elizabeth Maddocks (*née* Beardwell); *m* 1945, Margaret Jean Crawford Holt; two *s* one *d*. *Educ:* Manchester Grammar Sch.; Corpus Christi Coll., Oxford. Army, 1942–46; Foreign (later Diplomatic) Service, 1946–82: Washington, 1946–48; FO, 1949–51; Bonn, 1951–55; Bangkok, 1955–58; UK Delegn to OEEC, 1958–60; FO, 1960–64; UK Delegn to European Communities, Brussels, 1964–68; Political Adviser, Hong Kong, 1968–72; Dep. High Comr and Minister (Commercial), Ottawa, 1972–76. Mem., OECD Appeals Tribunal, 1984–89. *Address:* Lynton House, 83 High Street, Wheatley, Oxford OX33 1XP. *Club:* Hong Kong (Hong Kong).

**MADDOCKS, His Honour Bertram Catterall;** a Circuit Judge, 1990–2005; *b* 7 July 1932; *s* of His Honour George Maddocks and of Mary Maddocks (*née* Day); *m* 1964, Angela Vergette Forster; two *s* one *d*. *Educ*: Malsis Hall, near Keighley; Rugby; Trinity Hall, Cambridge (schol.; MA; Law Tripos Part 2 1st Cl. 1955). Nat. Service, 2nd Lieut, RA, 1951; Duke of Lancaster's Own Yeomanry (TA), 1958–67. Called to the Bar, Middle Temple, 1956; Harmsworth Schol.; Mem., Lincoln's Inn; a Recorder, 1983–90. Pt-time Chm., VAT Tribunals, 1977–92. *Recreations*: real tennis, bridge, croquet. *Address*: Moor Hall Barn, Prescot Road, Aughton, Lancashire L39 6RT. *T*: (01695) 228612. *Clubs*: Cavalry and Guards; Manchester Tennis and Racquet, Southport and Birkdale Croquet.

**MADDOCKS, Fiona Hamilton;** Classical Music Critic, The Observer, 1997–2002, and since 2008. News trainee, Producer and Sen. Producer, LBC, 1979–82; Founder Editor, Comment, 1982–85, Asst Commng Editor, Music, 1985–86, Channel 4; The Independent: Dep. Arts Editor, 1986–88, and writer; Music Editor and Associate Arts Editor, 1988–91; Founding Editor, BBC Music Magazine, 1992–97; Editor, BBC Proms Guide, 1998–99; Exec. Editor, LSO Living Music Magazine, 1998–2003; Chief Opera Critic, Music Critic and Arts Feature Writer, Evening Standard, 2002–08. Writer in Residence and Fellow, Salzburg Global Seminar, 2011. Board Member: Opera magazine, 1998–; Unknown Public, 2006–10; Adviser: Editl Bd, RA mag., 2008–; Wild Plum Arts, 2018–. Member: Exec. Cttee, SPNM, 1990–91; Critics' Circle, 1995 (Mem. Council, 1997–99); Cttee, Kim Scott Walwyn Prize, 2003–13; Pimlico Opera, 2012–. Gov., Sherborne Sch., 2001–11. Dir's Visitor, Inst. for Advanced Study, Princeton, 2008–11. Patron, SWAP'ra, 2019–. *Publications*: Hildegard of Bingen, 2001; Harrison Birtwistle: wild tracks, 2014; Music for Life: 100 works to carry you through, 2016; Twentieth Century Music, 2018. *Address*: c/o The Observer, Kings Place, 90 York Way, N1 9GU.

**MADDOX, Bronwen Maria;** Director, Institute for Government, since 2016; *b* 7 May 1963; *d* of Sir John Royden Maddox and Brenda Power Maddox; writer; one *d*. *Educ*: Westminster Sch.; St Paul's Girls' Sch.; St John's Coll., Oxford (BA PPE 1985). Analyst, Charterhouse Venture Capital, 1985–86; Dir and Hd, Media Investment Team, Kleinwort Benson Securities, 1986–91; investigative reporter, then leader writer, FT, 1991–96; The Times: US Editor and Washington Bureau Chief, 1996–99; Foreign Editor, 1999–2006; Chief Foreign Commentator, 2006–10; Editor and Chief Exec., Prospect, 2010–16. Non-exec. Mem. Bd, Law Commn, 2016–. Mem. Council, Chatham House, 2010–16; Trustee, Imperial War Mus., 2010–14; Trustee, 2013–19, Gov., 2019–, Ditchley Foundn. Bencher, Middle Temple, 2019. *Publications*: In Defence of America, 2008. *Recreations*: cooking, hiking. *Address*: Institute for Government, 2 Carlton Gardens, SW1Y 5AA.

**MADDOX, Air Vice Marshal Nigel David Alan,** CBE 1999; Chief of Staff (Operations), Headquarters Air Command, 2007–09; *b* 1 April 1954; *s* of Albert and Beverly Maddox; *m* 1979, Sue Elizabeth Armitage; one *d*. *Educ*: Clark's Grammar Sch.; Westcliff High Sch. for Boys; MBA Open Univ. Flight Comdr, No 12 Sqdn, 1987; RNSC, Greenwich, 1988; PSO, AOC No 18 Gp, 1989; OC Ops Wing, RAF Mount Pleasant, Falkland Is, 1990; OC No 12 Sqdn, RAF Lossiemouth, 1991; Asst Dir W, ACDS(Ops), MoD, 1993–96; Sen. RAF Officer, Germany, and Stn Comdr, RAF Brüggen, 1996–99; Air Cdre Maritime, 1999–2002; AOC No 2 Gp, 2002–05; Comdt, Jt Services Comd and Staff Coll., 2005–07. *Recreations*: squash, golf. *Club*: Royal Air Force.

**MADDOX, Stephen,** OBE 2008; DL; Chief Executive, Metropolitan Borough of Wirral, 1997–2010; *b* Merseyside. *Educ*: Univ. of Kent (BA 1974). Joined Wirral MBC as articled clerk, 1974; admitted as solicitor, 1977; Dep. Borough Solicitor and Sec., Wirral MBC, 1991–98. Chm., Wirral Mind, 2015–. Freedom, Bor. of Wirral, 2010. DL Merseyside, 2011. *Address*: 8 Fairfield Road, Hoole, Chester CH2 3RN.

**MADDRELL, (Catherine) Siân;** Head Teacher, The Grey Coat Hospital, since 2011; *b* St Asaph, 19 Nov. 1966; *d* of late Geoffrey Keggen Maddrell, OBE; *m* 2003, Richard Paul Germond; two *s*. *Educ*: Surbiton High Sch.; Durham Univ. (BA Hons French); Exeter Coll., Oxford (PGCE Modern Langs); Inst. of Educn, Univ. of London (NPQH Nat. Coll. for Teaching and Leadership). Buyer, Fenwick Ltd, 1990–91; The Grey Coat Hospital: Teacher of Modern Foreign Langs, 1992–2000; Hd of Year, 1993–95; Hd of Modern Langs, 1995–2000; Hd of Langs and Lang. Coll. Manager, Elliott Sch., 2000–01; Asst Head Teacher, Acland Burghley Sch., 2001–08; First Vice Principal, Pimlico Acad., 2008–11. *Recreations*: family, travel, languages, reading, theatre, art, ski-ing, snowboarding, swimming, tennis. *Address*: The Grey Coat Hospital, Greycoat Place, SW1P 2DY.

**MADDRELL, Simon Hugh Piper,** PhD, ScD; FRS 1981; Fellow of Gonville and Caius College, Cambridge, 1964–2007, now Life Fellow; Hon. Professor of Integrative Physiology, Cambridge University, 2003–08, now Emeritus Hon. Professor; *b* 11 Dec. 1937; *s* of late Hugh Edmund Fisher Maddrell and Barbara Agnes Mary Maddrell; *m* 1st, 1961, Anna Myers (marr. diss. 1985, she *d* 1997); three *s* one *d*; 2nd, 1990, Katherine Mona Mapes. *Educ*: Peter Symonds' Sch., Winchester; St Catharine's Coll., Cambridge. BA, MA, PhD 1964, ScD 1978. Res. Fellow, Dalhousie Univ., Canada, 1962–64; SPSO, AFRC Unit of Invertebrate Chem. and Physiology, subseq. Unit of Insect Neurophysiology and Pharmacology, Cambridge Univ., 1968–90; College Fellow and Lectr, Gonville and Caius Coll., Cambridge, 1968–2007; Hon. Reader, Univ. of Cambridge, 1991–2003. Manager of Finances and Investments (formerly Financial Sec. and Investments Manager), 1965–2010, Dir, 2010–, Co. of Biologists Ltd. Scientific Medal, Zool Soc. of London, 1975. *Publications*: Neurosecretion, 1979; contrib. 120 res. papers. *Recreations*: gardening, planting trees (Dir, I of M Woodland Trust (Chm., 2004–19)), play-reading, cinema, wine-tasting. *Address*: Gonville and Caius College, Cambridge CB2 1TA; Ballamaddrell, Ballabeg, Arbory, Isle of Man IM9 4HD. *T*: (01624) 822787.

**MADEJSKI, Sir (Robert) John,** Kt 2009; OBE 2000; DL; Co-Chairman, Reading Football Club, since 2014 (Chairman, 1990–2014); *b* 28 April 1941; *s* of Zygmunt Madejski and Joan Edith Madejski; two *d*. *Educ*: Reading Collegiate Sch. Encyclopedia salesman, Caxton Press, 1959; biscuit salesman, Huntley & Palmer, 1959–64; various jobs incl. selling Rolls Royce, Jaguar and Aston Martin cars, Calif, 1964–66; sales exec., British Motor Corp., 1966–67; Sales Dir, Stan Hope Mills, 1967–69; Classified Advertising Sales Exec., Reading Evening Post, 1969–76; founder: Auto Trader, 1976; Jt Founder, Hurst Publishing Ltd, 1977–98 (allied with Guardian/Manchester Evening News, 1982). Chairman of companies, including: Goodhead Group plc, 1991–2012; Rentwise Sdn Bhd, 1994–; Malaysian Motor Trader, 1998–2011; Sackville Properties plc, 2001–13; Royal Palm Hotel, Galapagos Is, 2002–; Reading Broadcasting (107 Jack FM Berkshire) (formerly Reading 107 (local radio)), 2002–; Clearview Traffic Gp, 2003–. Chancellor, Univ. of Reading, 2007–16. DL Berks 2000. Charitable funding of art galls, theatres, lecture theatres, including: Falklands Meml Chapel, Pangbourne Coll., 2000; John Madejski Fine Rooms, Royal Acad. of Arts, 2004. Hon. Fellow, Henley Mgt Coll., 2007. *Recreations*: fine dining (owner of Rossini at the Leatherne Bottel Restaurant, Goring-on-Thames), art, swimming. *Address*: Reading Football Club, Madejski Stadium, Junction 11, M4, Reading, Berks RG2 0FL. *Club*: Annabel's.

**MADEL, Sir (William) David,** Kt 1994; *b* 6 Aug. 1938; *s* of late William R. Madel and Eileen Madel (*née* Nicholls); *m* 1st, 1971, Susan Catherine (*d* 2009), *d* late Lt-Comdr Hon. Peter Carew; one *s* one *d*; 2nd, 2014, Susan Margaret Dykes. *Educ*: Uppingham Sch.; Keble Coll., Oxford. MA Oxon 1965. Graduate Management Trainee, 1963–64; Advertising Exec., Thomson Organisation, 1964–70. Contested (C) Erith and Crayford Nov. 1965, 1966. MP (C): S Bedfordshire, 1970–83; Bedfordshire SW, 1983–2001. PPS to Parly Under-Sec. of State for Defence, 1973–74, to Minister of State for Defence, 1974, to Rt Hon. Sir Edward Heath, KG, MBE, MP, 1991–97; an Opposition Whip, 1997–99. Chm., Cons. Backbench Educn Cttee, 1983–85; Vice-Chm., Cons. Backbench Employment Cttee, 1974–81; Member: Select Cttee on Educn, Sci. and Arts, 1979–83, on Transport, 1995–97, on Foreign Affairs, 1999–2001; H of C European Legislation Cttee, 1983–97. Mem. Ind. Monitoring Bd, HM Prison Hollesley Bay, Suffolk, 2004–14. Lay Rep. for Disciplinary Hearings, Council of the Inns of Court, 2005–14; Mem., Arbitration Panel, ACAS, 2009–. Mem. Exec., CCJ, 2002–06. Mem. Court, Univ. of Bedfordshire (formerly Univ. of Luton), 1993–. *Recreations*: cricket, tennis, reading, walking, campanology. *Address*: 40 Westbourne Terrace, W2 3UH. *Club*: Carlton.

**MADELEY, Richard Holt;** television presenter; *b* 13 May 1956; *s* of Christopher Holt Madeley and Mary Claire McEwan; *m* 1st, 1977, Lynda Hooley; 2nd, 1986, Judith Finnigan, *qv*; one *s* one *d*, and two step *s*. *Educ*: Coopers' Co. Grammar Sch., Bow; Shenfield Sch., Essex. Indentured jun. reporter, Brentwood Argus, 1972–74; Asst, then Dep. Ed., E London Advertiser, 1975–76; reporter, 1976–77, producer, 1977–78, BBC Radio Carlisle; reporter: Border TV, 1978–80; and presenter, Yorkshire TV, 1980–82; presenter: Granada Television, 1982–2001; programmes include: Runway, 1987–89; This Morning, 1988–2001; Eye of the Storm, 1997–2000; British Soap Awards, 1999, 2000 and 2001; Channel 4: Richard and Judy, 2001–08; British Book Awards, 2004–; ITV1: Fortune, 2007; Watch: Richard and Judy's New Position, 2008–09; Madeley Meets the Squatters, 2011; Good Morning Britain, 2017–; radio: Sunday Brunch, Radio 2, 2012–; Breakfast, Drivetime, Talk Radio, 2018–. *Publications*: Richard & Judy: the autobiography (with Judith Finnigan), 2001; Fathers and Sons, 2008; Some Day I'll Find You (novel), 2013; The Way You Look Tonight, 2014; The Night Book, 2016; Follow Me, 2019. *Recreations*: cliff-walking in Cornwall, cycling, acoustic guitar, reading. *Address*: c/o James Grant Management, 4th Floor, 180 Great Portland Street, W1W 5QZ. *T*: (020) 8742 4950. *Clubs*: Home House, Ivy.

**MADELIN, Robert;** Chief Strategist, since 2016, and Chairman, since 2017, FIPRA International Ltd; *b* 8 May 1957; *s* of John Madelin and Kathleen Madelin (*née* Webb); *m* 1990, Marie-Christine Jalabert. *Educ*: Royal Grammar Sch., High Wycombe; Magdalen Coll., Oxford (BA (Mod. Hist. and Mod. Langs), MA); Ecole Nationale d'Admin, Paris. Principal, Multilateral Trade Policy, DTI, 1979–88; 1st Sec., UK Perm. Repn, Brussels, 1988–93; Mem., then Dep. Hd, Cabinet of Vice-Pres. of Commn, Sir Leon, later Lord, Brittan, 1993–97; European Commission: Dir, Directorate Gen. of Trade, 1997–2003; Dir Gen. for Health and Consumer Protection, later Health and Consumers, 2004–10, for Inf. Society and Media, later Communication Networks, Content and Technol., 2010–15; Sen. Innovation Advr, Eur. Political Strategy Centre, 2015–16. Hon. FRCP 2007. Dr *hc* Edinburgh, 2016. *Recreations*: walking, running, music. *T*: (Belgium) (4) 98963338. *E*: robert@madelin.one.

**MADELUNG, Prof. Wilferd Willy Ferdinand,** FBA 1999; Laudian Professor of Arabic, University of Oxford, 1978–98; Senior Research Fellow, Institute of Ismaili Studies, London, since 1998; *b* 26 Dec. 1930; *s* of Georg Madelung and Elisabeth (*née* Messerschmitt); *m* 1963, A. Margaret (*née* Arent) (*d* 2018); one *s*. *Educ*: Eberhard Ludwig Gymnasium, Stuttgart; Univs of Georgetown, Cairo, Hamburg. PhD (Hamburg). Cultural Attaché, W German Embassy, Baghdad, 1958–60. Vis. Professor, Univ. of Texas, Austin, 1963; Privatdozent, Univ. of Hamburg, 1963–64; University of Chicago: Asst Prof., 1964; Associate Prof., 1966; Prof. of Islamic History, 1969. Guggenheim Fellowship, 1972–73; Fellow: Inst. of Advanced Studies, Hebrew Univ. of Jerusalem, 2002–; Inst. of Advanced Studies, Princeton Univ., 2011; Academia Ambrosiana, Milan, 2013. Decoration of Republic of Sudan (4th cl.), 1962. *Publications*: Der Imam al-Qāsim ibn Ibrāhīm und die Glaubenslehre der Zaidīten, 1965; Religious Schools and Sects in Medieval Islam, 1985; Religious Trends in Early Islamic Iran, 1988; Religious and Ethnic Movements in Medieval Islam, 1992; The Succession to Muhammad, 1996; Studies in Medieval Shi'ism, 2012; Studies in Medieval Muslim Thought and History, 2013. *Address*: 21 Belsyre Court, Oxford OX2 6HU.

**MADEN, Prof. Margaret;** Professor of Education, Keele University, 1995–2001; *b* 16 April 1940; *d* of Clifford and Frances Maden. *Educ*: Arnold High Sch. for Girls, Blackpool; Leeds Univ. (BA Hons); Univ. of London Inst. of Educn (PGCE). Asst Teacher of Geography, Stockwell Manor Comprehensive Sch., SW9, 1962–66; Lectr, Sidney Webb Coll. of Educn, 1966–71; Dep. Head, Bicester Comprehensive Sch., Oxon, 1971–75; Headmistress, Islington Green Comprehensive Sch., 1975–82; Dir, Islington Sixth Form Centre, 1983–86; Principal Advr, Tertiary Develt, ILEA, 1986–87; Dep. County Educn Officer, 1987–88, County Educn Officer, 1989–95, Warwickshire CC. Mem., Nat. Commn on Educn, 1991–93. Member: Basic Skills Agency, 1998–2007; Prince's Trust Adv. Gp, 2001–02; Bd, Royal Opera House, 2002–11; Chm., BBC Regl Adv. Council (South), 2002–05. Vice-Pres., Oxford Civic Soc., 2017–. Governor: Peers Sch., Oxford, 2006–08; Royal Ballet Sch., 2007–16; St Christopher's C of E Sch., Oxford, 2012–15. Norham Fellow, Dept of Educn, Univ. of Oxford, 2011–15. Hon. Pres., BEMAS, 1995–99. Hon. FCP 1994. *Publications*: (ed jtly) Success Against the Odds, 1995; Shifting Gear: changing patterns of educational governance in Europe, 2000; (ed) Success Against the Odds—5 Years On, 2001; contributions to: Dear Lord James, 1971; Teachers for Tomorrow (ed Calthrop and Owens), 1971; Education 2000 (ed Wilby and Pluckrose), 1979; The School and the University, an International Perspective (ed Burton R. Clark), 1984; Education Answers Back (ed Brian Simon and Clyde Chitty), 1993; School Co-operation: new forms of Governance (ed Ransom and Tomlinson), 1994; Living Education (ed John Tomlinson), 1997; Developing Education: fifteen years on (ed Philip Hunter), 1998; Children and the State: whose problem? (ed Jane Tunstill), 1999; Letters to the Prime Minister (ed Ted Wragg), 2005; A Generation of Radical Educational Change (ed Richard Pring and Martin Roberts), 2016. *Recreations*: European painting, writing and films; politics, opera. *Address*: 12 Dale Close, Oxford OX1 1TU. *T*: (01865) 721372.

**MADGE, His Honour Nicolas John;** writer; photographer; judicial trainer; Circuit Judge, 2004–18; *b* 1953; *s* of John Kenneth Lewis Madge and Lucy Mildred Madge; *m* 2014, Amanda Jane Sigrist West; two *s* by a previous marriage. *Educ*: Cannock Grammar Sch.; St Catharine's Coll., Cambridge (BA 1974). Admitted solicitor, 1978. Solicitor: Camden Community Law Centre, 1978–83; Nash and Dowell, 1984–85; Partner, Bindman and Partners, 1985–95; Dep. Dist Judge (pt-time), 1989–95; Dist Judge, W London Co. Court, 1995–2004; Resident Judge, Peterborough and Huntingdon Crown Courts, 2011–14. Photographic exhibitions: One World, One View, Harrow Crown Court, 2005, Friends Meeting House, London, 2008–09, Jam Factory, Oxford, 2009; Faces of Bangladesh, BM, 2011, Swiss Cottage Gall., 2012. *Publications*: Troubled by the Law?, 1978; Out of School: legal responsibility for children, 1981; (contrib.) Tribunals Practice and Procedure, 1985; (jtly) Defending Possession Proceedings, 1987, 8th edn

2017; (with D. Forbes) Debt and Housing: emergency procedures, 1993; English Roots: a family history, 1995; Housing Law Casebook, 1996, 7th edn 2017; (contrib.) Supreme Court Practice, 1999; (contrib.) Civil Procedure (The White Book), 1999– (Mem., Sen. Edtl Bd, 2004–); Annotated Housing Statutes, 2003, 2nd edn 2005; one world one view (photographs), 2007; contribs to Law Soc. Gazette, New Law Jl, Solicitors' Jl, Legal Action, Justice of the Peace, Jl Housing Law, Civil Justice Qly, Criminal Law Rev., Landlord and Tenant Rev., Jl Commonwealth Magistrates and Judges Assoc. *Recreations:* travel, walking, bridge, family history. *W:* www.nicmadge.co.uk.

**MADONNA;** see Ciccone, M. L. V.

**MADRIGAL FERNÁNDEZ, Prof. (José) Alejandro,** MD, PhD, DSc; FRCP, FRCPath, FMedSci; Scientific Director, Anthony Nolan Research Institute, since 1995; Professor of Haematology, Royal Free Hospital and University College London, since 1997; Hon. Consultant Haematologist, Royal Free Hospital, since 2001; *b* Mexico City, 4 Nov. 1953; *s* of Luis Madrigal and Aurora Fernandez; *m* 1977, Maria Elena Macarty. *Educ:* Univ. del Valle de México (BS 1973); Univ. Nacional Autónoma de México (MD 1978); Imperial Cancer Res. Fund, London (PhD 1989); Univ. of London (DSc 2001). FRCP 1998; FRCPath 2002. WHO Fellow, Dana Farber Cancer Inst., Harvard Univ., 1983–85; Postdoctoral Res. Fellow, Stanford Univ., 1989–93; Hd of Res., Anthony Nolan Res. Inst., 1993–95; Hon. Lectr in Haematol., Royal Free Hosp., 1993–95; Hon. Lectr, RPMS, 1993–95; Hon. Sen. Lectr in Haematol., Imperial Coll. London, 1995–97; Pro-Provost for the Americas, 2011–14, Pro-Vice Provost for the Americas, 2014–15, for Latin America, 2015–, UCL. Pres., Eur. Gp for Blood and Marrow Transplantation, 2010–14. FMedSci 2013. Hon. DSc Nottingham Trent, 2008; Dr *hc* Guadalajara, Mexico, 2017. *Publications:* (ed jtly) Cord Blood Characteristics: rôle in stem cell transplantation, 2000; contribs to scientific peer-reviewed jls. *Recreations:* fiction writing, painting, tennis, violin, music, reading. *Address:* Anthony Nolan Research Institute, Royal Free Hospital, Pond Street, NW3 2QG. *T:* (020) 7284 8315, *Fax:* (020) 7284 8331. *E:* a.madrigal@ucl.ac.uk.

**MAEHLER, Prof. Herwig Gustav Theodor,** FBA 1986; Professor of Papyrology, University College London, 1981–2000, now Emeritus; *b* 29 April 1935; *s* of Ludwig and Lisa Maehler; *m* 1963, Margaret Anderson; two *d*. *Educ:* Katharineum Lübeck (Grammar Sch.); Univs of Hamburg (PhD Classics and Classical Archaeol.), Tübingen and Basel. British Council Schol., Oxford, 1961–62; Res. Assistant, Hamburg Univ., 1962–63, Hamburg Univ. Liby, 1963–64; Keeper of Greek Papyri, Egyptian Mus., W Berlin, 1964–79; Habilitation for Classics, 1975, Lectr in Classics, 1975–79, Free Univ. of W Berlin; Reader in Papyrology, UCL, 1979–81. Corresp. Mem., German Archaeol Inst., 1979; Mem., Accad. Nazionale dei Lincei, Rome, 2000. Hon. Mem., Hungarian Acad. of Scis, Budapest, 2007. Hon. Fellow UCL, 2000. Hon. PhD: Helsinki, 2001; Budapest, 2001; Rome II (Tor Vergata), 2003. *Publications:* Die Auffassung des Dichterberufs im frühen Griechentum bis zur Zeit Pindars, 1963; Die Handschriften des S Jacobi-Kirche Hamburg, 1967; Urkunden römischer Zeit (BGU XI), 1968; Papyri aus Hermupolis (BGU XII), 1974; Die Lieder des Bakchylides, Part 1, 2 vols, 1982, Part 2, 1997; (with G. Cavallo) Greek Bookhands of the Early Byzantine Period, 1987; Bacchylides: a selection, 2004; editions of Bacchylides and Pindar, 1970, 1987, 1989, 1992, 2003; Urkunden aus Hermupolis (BGU XIX), 2005; Schrift, Text und Bild (selected essays), 2006; (with G. Cavallo) Hellenistic Bookhands, 2008; (with P. J. Parsons and F. Maltomini) The Vienna Epigrams Papyrus, 2015; articles in learned jls. *Address:* Zeltgasse 6/12, 1080 Wien, Austria.

**MAFFEY,** family name of **Baron Rugby**.

**MAGAN,** family name of **Baron Magan of Castletown**.

**MAGAN OF CASTLETOWN,** Baron *cr* 2011 (Life Peer), of Kensington in the Royal Borough of Kensington and Chelsea; **George Morgan Magan;** Director, Conservative Party Foundation, 2003–13 (Deputy Chairman, 2009–13); *b* 14 Nov. 1945; *s* of late Brig. William Morgan Tilson Magan, CBE and Maxine, *d* of Sir Kenneth Mitchell, KCIE; *m* 1972, Wendy Anne, *d* of Maj. Patrick Chilton, MC; two *s* one *d*. *Educ:* Winchester Coll. FCA. Peat Marwick Mitchell, 1964–70; Kleinwort Benson Ltd, 1971–74; Dir, Morgan Grenfell & Co. Ltd, 1974–88; Co-Founder and Chm., J. O. Hambro Magan, 1988–96; Chairman: Hawkpoint Partners, 1997–2001; emuse (Dublin), 2001–17; Lion Capital Partners, 2001–08; Mallett plc, 2001–08; Morgan Shipley Ltd (Dubai), 2001–; Director: Asprey plc, 1998–99; Edmiston & Co., 2001–13; Allied Investment Partners (Abu Dhabi), 2007–12. Dir, Bank of Ireland, 2003–09 (Dep. Gov., 2006–09). Dep. Treas., 2002–03, Treas. and Mem. Bd, 2003, Conservative Pty. Mem., Works of Art Cttee, H of L, 2015–17. Trustee: LPO, 1992–2016 (Chm., 1997–2006); Royal Opera House, Covent Garden, 1995–2001; BM Develt Trust, 1999–2003; Foundn of Coll. of St George, Windsor Castle, 2008–15. Chairman: St George's Chapel, Windsor Castle, Develt Appeal, 2007–13; Develt Bd, Royal Albert Hall, 2014–17. Gov., Stowe Sch., 2001–16. *Address:* House of Lords, SW1A 0PW. *Club:* Royal Yacht Squadron.

**MAGARIAN, Michael;** QC 2011; *b* London, 17 June 1964; *s* of Boghos and Ayko Magarian; *m* (marr. diss. 1989); one *d*. *Educ:* City of London Sch.; Trinity Coll., Cambridge (Schol.; BA 1987). Called to the Bar, Gray's Inn, 1988. *Recreation:* épater le bourgeois. *Address:* Drystone Chambers, 35 Bedford Row, WC1R 4JH. *Club:* Blacks.

**MAGDALENA RODRIGUEZ, (Jose) Carlos;** Senior Tropical Botanical Horticulturalist, Royal Botanic Gardens, Kew, since 2006; *b* Gijon, Asturias, Spain, 18 Sept. 1972; *s* of Rafael Magdalena and Edilia Rodriguez; partner, Genieve Gravel; one *s*. *Educ:* Royal Botanic Gardens, Kew (Kew Dip. Botanical Horticulture 2006). Self-employed in design, construction and maintenance of aquariums, ponds and gardens, Asturias, Spain, 1991–95; Envmtl Technician, Ayuntamiento de Gijon, 1999; Hd Sommelier, Le Meridien Hotels, 1999–2003; propagator, Tropical, Temperate and Arboretum Nurseries, Royal Botanic Gardens, Kew, 2003. Hortcil writer for Water Gardeners Internat., Horticultural Week, Garden. *Publications:* The Plant Messiah, 2017; contrib. to acad. papers in Annals of Botany, Conservation Biol., Curtis's Botanical Mag., etc. *Recreations:* nature, wildlife, travelling, swimming, music. *Address:* Flat 2, 64 Boileau Road, Barnes, Richmond, Surrey, SW13 9BL. *T:* 07818 496471. *E:* c.magdalena@kew.org, licantropop@hotmail.com. *W:* www.twitter.com/plantmessiah, www.facebook.com/carlosmagdalena.

**MAGDALINO, Prof. Paul,** DPhil; FBA 2002; Professor of Byzantine History, Koç University, Istanbul, since 2010 (Professor of History, 2006–08); *b* 10 May 1948; *s* of Andrea and Audrey Magdalino; *m* 1973, Ruth Macrides; one *d*; *m* 2011, Krassimira Tzankova. *Educ:* Oriel Coll., Oxford (BA; DPhil Modern Hist. 1976). Jun. Fellow, Dumbarton Oaks Center for Byzantine Studies, Washington, 1974–75; Andrew J. Mellon Fellow in Early Christian Humanism, Catholic Univ. of America, 1976–77; University of St Andrews: Lectr, 1977–94; Reader, 1994–99; Prof. of Byzantine Hist., 1999–2002; Bishop Wardlaw Prof. of Byzantine Hist., 2002–09. Res. Fellow, Alexander von Humboldt Stiftung, at Inst. für Rechtsgeschichte, Frankfurt, 1980–81, and Inst. für Byzantinistik, Munich, 1983; Vis. Fellow, Humanities Res. Centre, Canberra, 1985; Vis. Prof. of Hist., Harvard Univ., 1995–96; Sen. Fellow, Dumbarton Oaks Center for Byzantine Studies, 2001–07. *Publications:* (jtly) Rome and Byzantium, 1977; (ed) The Perception of the Past in Twelfth Century Europe, 1992; The Empire of Manuel I Komnenos, 1143–1180, 1993; (ed) New Constantines, 1994; Constantinople médiévale, 1996; L'Orthodoxie des Astrologues, 2006; Studies in the History and Topography of Medieval Constantinople, 2007; numerous contribs to ed vols and articles to learned jls. *Recreations:* walking, swimming. *Address:* Department of Archaeology and Art History, Koç University, 34450 Sarıyer, Istanbul, Turkey. *T:* (212) 3381755.

**MAGEE, Anna;** see Gregor, A.

**MAGEE, Sir Ian (Bernard Vaughan),** Kt 2006; CB 2002; Senior Fellow, Institute for Government, 2009; *b* 9 July 1946. *Educ:* Leeds Univ. (BA Hist.). Joined DHSS, 1969; Private Sec. to Minister for Social Security, 1976–78; seconded to Cabinet Office Enterprise Unit, 1984–86; Department of Social Security, 1986–98: Dep. to Dir of Personnel, 1986–89; Territorial Dir, Benefits Agency, 1990–93; Chief Exec., IT Services Agency, 1993–98; Chief Exec., Ct Service, LCD, 1998–2003; Second Permanent Sec. and Chief Exec., Ops, LCD, then DCA, 2003–05; Hd, Profession for Operational Delivery across Civil Service, 2004–05. Mem., Adv. Bd, Liaison FS, 2008–. *Recreations:* sport, reading. *Clubs:* MCC (Chm., Membership and Gen. Purposes Cttee, MCC, 2016–), Royal Automobile; Verulam Golf (Chm., 2017–); Yorkshire CC.

**MAGEE, Prof. Jeffrey Norman,** PhD; FREng; FBCS; FCGI; Professor of Computing, since 1999, and President's Envoy, since 2017, Imperial College London (Head, Department of Computing, 2004–11; Dean, Faculty of Engineering, 2011–17); *b* Londonderry, 12 Feb. 1952; *s* of Norman and Athalie Magee; *m* 1991, Judith O'Brien; two *s* one *d*. *Educ:* Foyle Coll., Londonderry; Queen's Univ., Belfast (BSc Hons 1973); Imperial Coll. London (MSc 1978; PhD 1984). FREng 2013. Exec. Engr, Post Office (Telecomms), 1973–79; Lectr, Imperial Coll. London, 1984–99. Vice Pres. and Trustee, BCS, 2014–16. FBCS 2005; FCGI 2010. *Publications:* Concurrency: state models and Java program, 1999, 2nd edn 2006. *Recreations:* sailing, fishing, dog walking, photography. *Address:* Department of Computing, Huxley Building, South Kensington Campus, Imperial College London, SW7 2AZ. *E:* j.magee@imperial.ac.uk.

**MAGERS, Philomene Korinna Kornelia;** Co-owner, Sprüth Magers, contemporary art gallery, since 1998; *b* Bonn, Germany, 18 March 1965; *d* of Wolfgang and Philomene Magers; *m* 1996, Jan Wendish-Garré; two *s*. *Educ:* studies of art hist., philosophy, Christian archaeol. and German philology, Rheinische Friedrich-Wilhelms Univ. Bonn and Ludwig-Maximilians Univ. Munich, 1984–90. Direction and dramaturgy trainee and asst in opera and theatre, Städtische Bühnen, Bonn, 1984–86; curatorial assistant: German Pavilion, 43rd Venice Biennale, 1988; Städtische Galerie, Lehnbachhaus, Munich, 1988; Siemens Arts Program, Munich, 1988–90; Gall. Founder, Philomene Magers, Bonn, 1990, relocated Cologne, 1992; merged with Galerie Monika Sprüth, as Sprüth Magers, Cologne, 1998; Sprüth Magers, Munich, opened 2000, addnl project space for young and emerging art, opened 2002; Sprüth Magers, London, opened 2003, Berlin, 2008, LA, 2016, Hong Kong, 2016. *Address:* Sprüth Magers, Oranienburger Strasse 18, 10178 Berlin, Germany. *E:* info@spruethmagers.com.

**MAGINNESS, Alban Alphonsus;** barrister; Member (SDLP) Belfast North, Northern Ireland Assembly, 1998–2016; *b* 9 July 1950; *s* of Alphonsus and Patricia Maginness; *m* 1978, Carmel McWilliams; three *s* five *d*. *Educ:* St Malachy's Coll., Belfast; Univ. of Ulster (BA Hons Mod. Hist. 1973); Queen's Univ., Belfast (LLM Human Rights 2007). Called to the Bar: NI, 1976; Ireland, 1984; in practice at NI Bar, specialising in civil litigation. Chm., SDLP, 1985–91. Mem. (SDLP) Belfast CC, 1985–2010; Lord Mayor of Belfast, 1997–98 (first SDLP Lord Mayor). Contested (SDLP) Belfast North, 1997, 2001, 2005, 2010. Northern Ireland Assembly: Chairman: Enterprise, Trade and Investment Cttee, 2009–12; Cross-Party Human Trafficking Gp, 2014–16; Member: Cross-Party Pro-Life Gp, 2007–16; Justice Cttee, 2010–16; Envmt Cttee, 2012–16; Procedures Cttee, 2013–16. Member: NI Forum, 1996–98; Forum for Peace and Reconciliation, Dublin, 1994–96; Cttee of the Regions of the EU, 2002–06; NI Assembly Commn, 2007–09; Mem. and Dir, NI Assembly Business Trust, 2012–16. Mem. Bd, Belfast Harbour Comrs, 2006–08. *Recreations:* theatre, history, reading, walking, music. *Address:* 96 Somerton Road, Belfast BT15 4DE. *T:* (028) 9077 0558.

**MAGINNIS,** family name of **Baron Maginnis of Drumglass**.

**MAGINNIS OF DRUMGLASS,** Baron *cr* 2001 (Life Peer), of Carnteel in the County of Tyrone; **Kenneth Wiggins Maginnis;** *b* 21 Jan. 1938; *m* 1961, Joy Stewart; two *s* two *d*. *Educ:* Royal Sch., Dungannon; Stranmillis Coll., Belfast. Served UDR, 1970–81, commissioned 1972, Major. Party spokesman on internal security and defence. Mem., Dungannon District Council, 1981–93 and 2001–05; Mem. (UU) Fermanagh and S Tyrone, NI Assembly, 1982–86 and 1994–98. Contested (UU) Fermanagh and S Tyrone, Aug. 1981. MP (UU) Fermanagh and S Tyrone, 1983–2001 (resigned seat Dec. 1985 in protest against Anglo-Irish Agreement; re-elected Jan. 1986). Mem., H of C Select Cttee on Defence, 1984–86, on NI, 1994–97. Vice Pres., UU Council, 1990–2005; Hon. Treas., UU Party, 2005–08. Chm., Moygashel Community Develt Assoc., 1992–. Chairman: Ind. Review Autism Services (NI), 2007–08; NI Regl Reference Gp on Autism, 2008–11. *Address:* House of Lords, SW1A 0PW; 1 Park Lane, Dungannon BT71 6JL.

**MAGNUS, Sir Laurence (Henry Philip),** 3rd Bt *cr* 1917, of Tangley Hill, Wonersh; Deputy Chairman, Evercore Partners (Europe), since 2011; Chairman, Historic Buildings and Monuments Commission for England (Historic England, formerly English Heritage), since 2013; *b* 24 Sept. 1955; *s* of Hilary Barrow Magnus, QC (*d* 1987), and late Rosemary Vera Anne Magnus (*née* Masefield); *S* uncle, Sir Philip Magnus-Allcroft, 2nd Bt, CBE, 1988; *m* 1983, Jocelyn Mary, *d* of late R. H. F. Stanton; two *s* one *d*. *Educ:* Eton College; Christ Church, Oxford (MA). Corporate Finance Executive, 1977–84, Head of Corporate Finance, Singapore Branch, 1984–87, Samuel Montagu & Co. Ltd; Group Country Manager, Singapore Region, Midland Bank plc (Singapore), 1987–88; Exec. Dir, 1988–95 and Dep. Head, UK Corporate Finance Div., 1994–95, Samuel Montagu & Co. Ltd; Dir, Phoenix Securities Ltd, 1995–97 (acquired by Donaldson, Lufkin & Jenrette, 1997); Managing Director: Donaldson, Lufkin & Jenrette Internat., 1997–2000 (acquired by Credit Suisse First Boston, 2000); Credit Suisse First Boston, 2000–01; Vice Chm., 2001–10, Chm., 2010–11, Lexicon Partners Ltd (acquired by Evercore Partners, 2011). Non-exec. Chm., Xchanging ins-sure Services Ltd (formerly Ins-Sure Services Ltd), 2001–09; Chairman: JP Morgan Income & Capital Trust plc, 2008–18; JP Morgan Multi-Asset Trust plc, 2018–; non-executive Director: Forestry Investment Mgt Ltd, 1997–; TT Electronics plc, 2001–07; J. P. Morgan (formerly J. P. Morgan Fleming) Income & Capital Investment Trust plc, 2001–08; Climate Exchange plc, 2006–10; Cayenne Trust plc, 2006–15; Fidelity Japan Trust (formerly Japanese Values) plc, 2010–; Pantheon International (formerly Pantheon International Participations) plc, 2011– (Chm., 2016–); Aggregated Micro Power plc, 2011–. National Trust: Dep. Chm., 2005–13; Mem., Finance Cttee, 1997–2005 (Chm., 2002–05); Mem., Bd of Trustees, 2005–13. Trustee: Eating Disorders Assoc. ('B-eat'), 2005–13 (Chm., 2005–11); Windsor Leadership Trust, 2006– (Chm., 2015–); Landmark Trust, 2011–16; All Churches Trust, 2013–; English Heritage Trust, 2014–. *Recreations:* reading, fishing, walking. *Heir: s* Thomas Henry Philip Magnus [*b*

30 Sept. 1985; *m* 2018, Clementine Anne, *d* of Michael and Annabel Hendry]. *Address:* c/o Evercore Partners Ltd, 15 Stanhope Gate, W1K 1LN. *T:* (020) 7653 6030, *Fax:* (020) 7653 6001. *E:* laurie.magnus@evercore.com. *Clubs:* Brooks's, Beefsteak, City of London; Millennium.

**MAGNUS, Prof. Philip Douglas,** FRS 1985; R. P. Doherty, Jr-Welch Regents Professor of Chemistry, University of Texas at Austin, 1989–2014, now Emeritus; *b* 15 April 1943; *s* of Arthur Edwin and Lillian Edith Magnus; *m* 1963, Andrea Claire (*née* Parkinson); two *s*. *Educ:* Imperial College, Univ. of London (BSc, ARCS, PhD, DSc). Asst Lectr, 1967–70, Lectr, 1970–75, Imperial College; Associate Prof., Ohio State Univ., 1975–81; Prof. of Chemistry, 1981–87, Distinguished Prof., 1987–88, Indiana Univ. Corday Morgan Medal, RSC, 1978; Janssen Prize, Belgian Chemical Soc. and Janssen Foundn, 1992; Robert Robinson Medal, RSC, 1996. *Publications:* papers in leading chemistry jls. *Recreations:* golf, chess. *Address:* 3111D Windsor Road, Austin, TX 78703, USA. *T:* (512) 4713966.

**MAGONET, Rabbi Prof. Jonathan David;** Editor, European Judaism, since 2005 (Member, Editorial Board, since 1978; Co-Editor, 1992–2005); *b* 2 Aug. 1942; *s* of Alexander Philip and Esther Magonet; *m* 1974, Dorothea (*née* Foth); one *s* one *d*. *Educ:* Westminster Sch.; Middlesex Hosp. Med. Sch. (MB BS). Leo Baeck Coll.; Univ. of Heidelberg (PhD). Junior hosp. doctor, 1966–67; Leo Baeck College, subseq. Leo Baeck College—Centre for Jewish Education: Rabbinic studies, 1967–71; Head of Dept of Bible Studies, 1974–85; Principal, 1985–2005; Prof., 1996–2005, now Emeritus. Vis. Fellow, Tel Aviv Univ., 1990–91; Guest Professor: Kirchliche Hochschule, Wuppertal, Germany, 1992–93, 1995, 2004, 2010; Carl von Ossietzky Univ., Oldenburg, 1999, 2004; Univ. of Luzern, 2004; Seinan Gakuin Univ., Fukuoka, 2010–; Doshisha Univ., Kyoto, 2012; Vis. Prof., Univs of Würzburg and Augsburg, 2008. Co-organiser: Annual Internat. Jewish-Christian Bible Week, Bendorf/Osnabrueck, 1968–; Annual Jewish-Christian-Muslim Student Conf., Bendorf/Wuppertal, 1972–2014. Vice-President: World Union for Progressive Judaism, 1988–2005; Movt for Reform Judaism, 2007–. Member, Editorial Board: Christian-Jewish Relations, 1987–91; Jl of Progressive Judaism, 1993–99. FRSA. Hon. DTheol: Kirchliche Hochschule Wuppertal, 2005; Seinan Gakuin, Fukuoka, 2014; DUniv Open, 2006; Hon. DHL Hebrew Union Coll., 2007. Verdienstkreuz (Germany), 1999. *Publications:* Form and Meaning: studies in literary techniques in the Book of Jonah, 1976; Forms of Prayer, (ed jtly) vol. I, Daily and Sabbath Prayerbook, 1977, (ed) 8th edn 2008, (ed jtly) vol. III, Days of Awe Prayerbook, 1985, (ed jtly) vol. II, Pilgrim Festival Prayerbook, 1995, (ed) vol. IV, Evening Prayers, 2009, (ed) vol. V, Funeral Service, 2009; (ed jtly) The Guide to the Here and Hereafter, 1988; A Rabbi's Bible, 1991, 2nd edn as A Rabbi Reads the Bible, 2004; Bible Lives, 1992; (jtly) How to Get Up When Life Gets You Down, 1992; (ed jtly) The Little Blue Book of Prayer, 1993; A Rabbi Reads the Psalms, 1994, 2nd edn, 2004; (jtly) Kindred Spirits, 1995; (ed) Jewish Explorations of Sexuality, 1995; The Subversive Bible, 1997; (ed) Das Jüdische Gebetbuch, 2 vols, 1997; Mit der Bibel durch das Jüdische Jahr, 1998; The Explorer's Guide to Judaism, 1998; (jtly) Sun, Sand and Soul, 1999; Abraham-Jesus-Mohammed: interreligiöser Dialog aus jüdischer Perspektive, 2000; From Autumn to Summer: a Biblical journey through the Jewish year, 2000; Talking to the Other: Jewish interfaith dialogue with Christians and Muslims, 2003; Einführung ins Judentum, 2004; Schabbat Schalom: Juedische Theologie - in Predigten entfaltet, 2011; Rabbino Seishokaishak: Yudaiyakuo to Kiristokuo no Taiwa (Japanese), 2012; Netsuke Nation: tales from another Japan, 2013; A Rabbi Reads the Torah, 2013; Ghostwalk and Other Poems, 2018; *festschrift:* Welcome to the Cavalcade, ed by E. Cooper and S. Tikvah, 2013. *W:* www.jonathanmagonet.co.uk.

**MAGOS, Adam László,** MD; Consultant Obstetrician and Gynaecologist, and Hon. Senior Lecturer, Royal Free Hospital, London, since 1991; *b* 26 Sept. 1953; *s* of László Pál Aurel Magos and Eva Mária Magos (*née* Benjamin); *m* 1991, Anne Cyprienne Coburn; three *s*. *Educ:* Whitgift Sch., Croydon; KCL (BSc 1975); King's Coll. Hosp. Sch. of Medicine (MB BS 1978; MD 1986). MRCOG 1986, FRCOG 1998. House Officer, KCH, 1980–82; Res. Fellow in Obstetrics and Gynaecol., Dulwich Hosp., 1982–84; Registrar, KCH and Dulwich Hosp., 1984–86; Lectr, Nuffield Dept of Obstetrics and Gynaecology, John Radcliffe Hosp., Univ. of Oxford, 1986–90; Sen. Lectr and Hon. Consultant, Academic Dept of Obstetrics and Gynaecology, Royal Free Hosp., Univ. of London, 1990–91; Consultant Gynaecologist, King Edward VII Hosp. for Officers, later King Edward VII Hosp. Sister Agnes, 1992–2013. Treas., British Soc. for Gynaecol Endoscopy, 1989–92; Member: Wkg Gp on New Technol. in Endoscopic Gynaecol Surgery, RCOG, 1993–94; MAS Trng Sub-Cttee, RCOG, 1998–2001. Hon. Member: Aust. Gynaecol Endoscopy Soc., 1994; Egyptian Soc. for Gynaecol Endoscopy, 1996. Ed., Gynaecological Endoscopy, 1990–93. Syntex Award, Internat. Soc. of Reproductive Medicine, 1988; Veress Meml Medal, Hungarian Soc. for Gynaecol Endoscopy, 1997. *Publications:* (ed jtly) Endometrial Ablation, 1993; contribs to books on premenstrual syndrome, hysteroscopic, laparoscopic and vaginal surgery, and to professional jls. *Recreations:* music, IT. *Address:* Royal Free Hospital, Pond Street, NW3 2QG. *T:* (020) 7794 0500.

**MAGOWAN, Rt Rev. Alistair James;** *see* Ludlow, Bishop Suffragan of.

**MAGOWAN, Maj. Gen. Robert Andrew,** CB 2018; CBE 2013 (MBE 2004); Assistant Chief of Defence Staff (Capability and Force Design), since 2018; *b* Tenterden, Kent, 12 Sept. 1967; *s* of Ronald and Colette Magowan; *m* 1999, Charlotte Bendy; two *d*. *Educ:* Queen Elizabeth's Sch., Faversham; Univ. of Southampton (BSc Chem. 1989); US Marine Corps Base Quantico (Master of Mil. Studies 2000). Joined RM, 1989; CO, 30 (IX) Commando, RM, 2006–08; COS, UK Nat. Contingent Comdr, Kabul, 2012–13; Dir, Naval Personnel Strategy, 2013–15; Comdr, Jt Forces Intelligence Gp, 2015–16; Comdt Gen. RM, Comdr UK Amphibious Forces and Operational Comdr, EU Naval Force Operation Atalanta, 2016–17; ACNS (Capability) and COS Navy Comd HQ, 2017–18. *Recreations:* climbing and mountaineering, running, cooking, reading European history. *Club:* Naval and Military.

**MAGUIRE, Adrian Edward;** National Hunt jockey, retired 2002; trainer, 2005–18; *b* 29 April 1971; *s* of Joseph Maguire and of late Phyllis Maguire; *m* 1995, Sabrina; one *s* one *d*. *Educ:* Kilmessan Nat. Sch.; Trim Vocational Sch. Winner: Irish Grand National, on Omerta, 1991; Hennessy Gold Cup, on Sibton Abbey, 1992; Cheltenham Gold Cup, on Cool Ground, 1992; King George VI Chase, on Barton Bank, 1993, on Florida Pearl, 2001; Queen Mother Champion Chase, on Viking Flagship, 1994; Scottish National, on Baronet, 1998, on Paris Pike, 2000; Whitbread Gold Cup, on Call It A Day, 1998; rode 1,000th winner in British racing, 2001. *Address:* Laharn Cross, Lombardstown, Mallow, Co. Cork, Ireland.

**MAGUIRE, Prof. David John,** PhD; PFHEA, FRGS; Vice-Chancellor, University of Greenwich, since 2011; *b* Lancaster, 22 Aug. 1958; *s* of Alfred Maguire and Anne Maguire; *m* 1983, Heather Knubley; one *d*. *Educ:* Lancaster Royal Grammar Sch.; Univ. of Exeter (BSc 1979); Univ. of Bristol (PhD 1983). Lecturer: Univ. of Plymouth, 1984–86; Univ. of Leicester, 1987–91; Chief Scientist and Dir of Products, ESRI, 1990–2008; Pro-Vice-Chancellor, Birmingham City Univ., 2008–11. FRGS 1998; PFHEA 2016. Hon. Dr Univ. of Agricl Scis and Vet. Med., Bucharest, 2009. *Publications:* Computers in Geography, 1989; (jtly) Geographical Information Systems: principles, techniques, management and applications, 1991, 2nd edn 2005; (jtly) Geographic Information Systems and Science, 2001, 4th edn 2016; (jtly) Proving the Business Benefits of GIS: an ROI approach, 2008. *Recreations:* guitar music, wine, walking, squash. *Address:* University of Greenwich, Old Royal Naval College, Park Row, Greenwich, SE10 9LS. *E:* d.maguire@gre.ac.uk.

**MAGUIRE, Prof. Eleanor Anne,** PhD; CPsychol; FRS 2016; FBA 2018; FMedSci; Professor of Cognitive Neuroscience, since 2007, and Deputy Director, Wellcome Centre for Human Neuroimaging (formerly Wellcome Trust Centre for Neuroimaging), since 2010, University College London; Hon. Neuropsychologist, Department of Neuropsychology, National Hospital for Neurology and Neurosurgery, since 1999; *b* Dublin, 27 March 1970; *d* of Patrick Maguire and Anne Maguire. *Educ:* University College Dublin (BA Hons Psychol. 1990; PhD 1995); Univ. of Wales, Swansea (MSc Clinical and Experimental Neuropsychol. 1991). CPsychol 2002. Richmond Institute for Neurology and Neurosurgery, Beaumont Hospital, Dublin: Clin. Neuropsychologist, 1991–93; Clin. Neuropsychologist, Epilepsy Surgery Prog., 1993–94; Institute of Neurology, University College London: Postdoctoral Res. Fellow and Neuropsychologist, 1995–97, Sen. Res. Fellow and Neuropsychologist, 1997–99, Wellcome Dept of Cognitive Neurol.: Lectr, 1999–2003, Sen. Lectr, 2003–07, Wellcome Dept of Imaging Neurosci.; Wellcome Trust Centre for Neuroimaging: Wellcome Trust Sen. Res. Fellow in Basic Biomed. Sci., 2003–13; Wellcome Trust Principal Res. Fellow, 2013–. Hon. MRIA 2018. FMedSci 2011. Ig Nobel Prize for Medicine, 2003; Young Investigator Award, Cognitive Neurosci. Soc., 2004; Rosalind Franklin Award, Royal Soc., 2008; Feldberg Foundn Prize, 2011; Kemali Prize, 2012; Joan Mott Prize in Physiol., Physiol Soc., 2013; Foundn Day Alumni Award for Res., Innovation and Impact, UCD, 2016. *Publications:* over 150 articles in jls and book chapters on the cognitive neuroscience of memory and navigation. *Recreations:* comedy lover, long-suffering supporter of Crystal Palace Football Club, getting lost. *Address:* Wellcome Centre for Human Neuroimaging, UCL Queen Square Institute of Neurology, University College London, 12 Queen Square, WC1N 3AR. *E:* e.maguire@ucl.ac.uk.

**MAGUIRE, Kevin John;** Associate Editor, Daily Mirror, since 2005; *b* South Shields, 20 Sept. 1960; *s* of John Maguire and Jennie Maguire; *m* 1986, Emma Burstall; two *s* one *d*. *Educ:* Harton, South Shields; Univ. of York (BA Politics 1982); Cardiff Univ. (Dip. Journalism 1984). Western Morning News, 1984–87; New Civil Engineer, 1987; Press Assoc., 1988–89; Daily Telegraph, 1990–94; Daily Mirror, 1994–99; The Guardian, 1999–2005. Hon. DArts Sunderland, 2018. *Publications:* (with Matthew Parris) Great Parliamentary Scandals, 2004. *Recreations:* beer, history, sport, the outdoors. *Address:* Daily Mirror, Press Gallery, House of Commons, SW1A 0AA. *T:* (020) 7293 3000. *E:* kevin.maguire@mirror.co.uk. *Club:* Sunderland Association Football.

**MAGUIRE, Mairead C.;** *see* Corrigan-Maguire.

**MAGUIRE, Maria Bernadette, (Mrs G. R. Nicholson);** QC (Scot.) 2002; *b* 19 Sept. 1961; *d* of late Robert Miller Maguire, Police Inspector, and of Mary Maguire (*née* Tanham); *m* 1991, Gavin Robert Nicholson; one *s* one *d*. *Educ:* Aberdeen Univ. (LLB; DLP). Admitted to Faculty of Advocates, 1987. Standing JC to Home Office, 1999–2002. *Address:* Advocates' Library, Parliament House, Parliament Square, Edinburgh EH1 1RF. *T:* (0131) 226 5071. *E:* maria.maguire@advocates.org.uk.

**MAGUIRE, Hon. Sir Paul (Richard),** Kt 2012; **Hon. Mr Justice Maguire;** a Judge of the High Court, Northern Ireland, since 2012; *b* Belfast, 10 Nov. 1952; *s* of Patrick and Lucy Maguire; *m* 1994, Patricia Mary Coburn; one *s* one *d*. *Educ:* London Sch. of Econs and Pol Sci. (LLB). Called to the Bar, NI, 1978; Lectr in Public Law, QUB, 1976–82; Jun. Crown Counsel for NI, 2000–04; QC (NI) 2006; Sen. Crown Counsel for NI, 2009–12. Mem. (APNI) N Belfast, NI Assembly, 1982–86. *Publications:* contribs to books and jls in the field of public law. *Recreations:* golf, reading. *Address:* Royal Courts of Justice, Chichester Street, Belfast BT1 3JF.

**MAHARAJH, Julia L.;** *see* Lalla-Maharajh, J.

**MAHAREY, Hon. Steven,** CNZM 2009; independent director, commentator and consultant, since 2016; Vice-Chancellor, Massey University, 2008–16; *b* Palmerston North, NZ, 3 Feb. 1953; *s* of William Wood Maharey and Irene Maharey; partner, Bette Flagler. *Educ:* Massey Univ. (BA Sociol. 1974; MA Hons Sociol. 1976). Jun. Lectr in Business Admin, 1976–78, Lectr, then Sen. Lectr in Sociol., 1979–90, Massey Univ. Mem. (Ind) Palmerston N CC, 1986–90. MP (Lab) Palmerston N, 1990–2008; Minister: of Social Services and Employment, 1999–2002; for Community and Voluntary Sector, 1999–2002; for Social Develt and Employment, and Associate Minister of Educn, 2002–04; of Broadcasting, 2002–07; of Housing, 2003–05; for Res., Sci. and Technol., 2004–07; for Educn, 2005–07. *Publications:* contrib. articles and chapters on media studies, cultural studies and politics. *Recreations:* mountain and road biking, walking, dog (Hazel), reading, film, cooking, music, travel.

**MAHATHIR bin MOHAMAD, Tun Dr;** MHR for Langkawi, since 2018 (for Kubang Pasu, 1974–2003); Prime Minister of Malaysia, 1981–2003 and since 2018; *b* 20 Dec. 1925; *m* Tun Dr Siti Hasmah bt Mohamad Ali; seven *c*. *Educ:* Sultan Abdul Hamid Coll.; College of Medicine, Singapore (MB BS). Medical Officer, Kedah and Perlis, 1953–57; in private practice, 1957–64. MHR for Kota Star Selatan, 1964–69; Mem., Senate, 1972–74; Minister of: Education, 1974–77; Trade and Industry, 1977–81; Home Affairs, 1986–99; Dep. Prime Minister, 1976–81. President, United Malays Nat. Orgn, 1981–2003 (Mem., Supreme Council, 1972–2003). Chairman: Parti Pribumi Bersatu Malaysia, 2016–; Pakatan Harapan Coalition, 2017–. Chancellor, Universiti Teknologi Petronas, 2004–16. *Publications:* The Malay Dilemma, 1969; The Way Forward (essays), 1998; A Doctor in the House: the memoirs of Tun Dr Mahathir Mohamad, 2011.

**MAHER, Christina Rose,** OBE 1994; Co-founder and Director, Plain English Campaign, since 1979; *d* of late Fred Lewington and Maureen Lewington; *m* 1959, George Bernard Maher; three *s* one *d*. *Educ:* St Cecilia's Sch., Liverpool. Community worker, 1969–98. Founder: Tuebrook Bugle (first community newspaper), 1971; Liverpool News (first newspaper for people with learning difficulties), 1974. Chm., Impact Printers Foundn, 1974–98; Founder, Salford Form Market (for NCC), 1975. Hon. Fellow, Liverpool John Moores Univ., 2010. Hon. MA Manchester, 1995; DUniv Open, 1997. Public Affairs Achiever of the Year, and Outstanding Achiever, Women in Public Life Awards, 2010. *Publications:* (jtly) Plain English Story, 1980; How to Write Letters/Reports in Plain English, 1995; Decade of Drivel, 1996; Language on Trial, 1996; A to Z for Lawyers, 1996. *Recreations:* swimming, dance, theatre, keep fit.

**MAHER, Prof. Eamonn Richard,** MD; FRCP, FRSB, FMedSci; Professor of Medical Genetics and Genomic Medicine, and Head, Department of Medical Genetics, University of Cambridge, since 2013; Consultant in Clinical Genetics, Addenbrooke's Hospital, Cambridge, since 2013; *b* 20 July 1956; *s* of Richard and Edna Maher; *m* 1980, Helen Marie (*née* Jackson); two *s* three *d*. *Educ:* Salesian High Sch., Bootle; Univ. of Manchester (BSc 1st Cl. Hons Physiol. 1977; MB ChB Hons 1980; MD 1988); Univ. of Cambridge (MA 1996). MRCP 1983, FRCP 1996. Clinical Lectr, 1988–91, Univ. Lectr, 1991–96, in Med. Genetics, Univ. of Cambridge; Consultant in Med. Genetics, Addenbrooke's Hosp.,

Cambridge, 1991–96; Prof. of Med. Genetics, and Hd, Dept of Med. and Molecular Genetics, 1996–2013, Dir, Centre for Rare Diseases and Personalised Medicine, 2010–13, Univ. of Birmingham; Consultant in Clin. Genetics, W Midlands Regl Genetics Service, Birmingham Women's Health Care NHS Trust, 1996–2013. Ed., Jl of Med. Genetics, 1998–2009. FMedSci 2006; FRSB (FSB 2012). *Publications:* A Practical Guide to Human Cancer Genetics (with S. V. Hodgson), 1994, 4th edn (with S. V. Hodgson, W. D. Foulkes and C. Eng) 2013; over 400 scientific articles and book chapters on clinical and molecular aspects of cancer and med. genetics. *Recreations:* Everton Football Club, taxi driver for children. *Address:* Department of Medical Genetics, University of Cambridge, Addenbrooke's Treatment Centre, Addenbrooke's Hospital, Cambridge CB2 0QQ. *T:* (01223) 746714, *Fax:* (01223) 746777. *E:* erm1000@medschl.cam.ac.uk, E.R.Maher@bham.ac.uk.

**MAHER, (Elizabeth) Jane, (Mrs Peter Krook),** FRCP, FRCPE, FRCR; Consultant Clinical Oncologist, Mount Vernon Cancer Centre and Hillingdon Hospital, since 1986; Joint Chief Medical Officer, Macmillan Cancer Support (formerly Macmillan Cancer Relief), since 2014 (Chief Medical Officer, 1999–2014); *b* 31 March 1953; *d* of Matthew Gerard Maher and Stella Marie Maher (*née* Griffiths); *m* 1987, Peter Arthur Larson Krook (*d* 2011); one *d. Educ:* Edgbaston C of E Coll. for Girls; King's Coll., London; Westminster Med. Sch. (MB BS 1976); Westminster Hosp.; Middlesex Hosp.; Harvard Univ.; Massachusetts Gen. Hosp. MRCP 1979, FRCP 1997; FRCR 1982; FRCPE 1998. Sen. Clinical Lectr, UCL, 1990–; Med. Dir, Lynda Jackson Macmillan Centre, and Dir, Psychosocial Res., 1998–. Chairman: Nat. Cancer Inst. Consensus Meeting, palliative radiotherapy, 1992; Maher Cttee, mgt of adverse effects of radiotherapy, 1995; London Cancer Task Force, 2000–04; Lead Clinician, Cancer Services Improvement, 2000–12. Vis. Prof. of Cancer and Supportive Care, Complexity Management Centre, Hertfordshire Univ., 2005–. *Publications:* articles on breast cancer and psychosocial oncology. *Recreations:* detective fiction, medieval churches. *Address:* Lynda Jackson Macmillan Centre, Mount Vernon Hospital, Rickmansworth Road, Northwood, Middx HA6 2RN. *T:* (01923) 844681, *Fax:* (01923) 844172. *Club:* Blacks.

**MAHER, His Honour Terence;** a Circuit Judge, 1995–2006; *b* 20 Dec. 1941; *s* of late John Maher and of Bessie Maher; *m* 1965 (marr. diss. 1983); two *d. Educ:* Burnley Grammar Sch.; Univ. of Manchester (LLB Hons). Admitted Solicitor, 1966; articled to Town Clerk, Burnley; Asst Solicitor, City of Bradford, 1966–68; Prosecuting Solicitor, Birmingham Corp., 1968–70; Dep. Pros. Solicitor, Thames Valley Police, 1970–73; Asst Solicitor and partner, Cole & Cole, Oxford, 1973–83; Metropolitan Stipendiary Magistrate, 1983–95; a Chm., Inner London Juvenile, subseq. Youth, Courts and Family Proceedings Court, 1985–95; a Recorder, 1989–95. Gen. Sec., Univ. of Manchester Students' Union, 1962–63; Chm., Chipping Norton Round Table, 1975–76; Treas./Vice-Chm. and Chm., Oxford and District Solicitors' Assoc., 1980–83; Mem., Law Society Standing Cttee on Criminal Law, 1980–85. Mem. Editl Bd, Jl of Criminal Law, 1982–95. *Recreations:* walking, reading, anything to do with France and the French. *Address:* c/o Luton Crown Court, 7 George Street, Luton LU1 2AA. *Club:* Frewen (Oxford).

**MAHER, Terence Anthony,** FCCA; Founder, Chairman and Chief Executive, Pentos plc, 1972–93; *b* 5 Dec. 1935; *s* of late Herbert and Lillian Maher; *m* 1960, Barbara (*née* Grunbaum); three *s. Educ:* Xaverian Coll., Manchester. ACCA 1960, FCCA 1970. Carborundum Co. Ltd, 1961–69; First National Finance Corp., 1969–72; Chairman: Dillons Bookstores, 1977–93; Athena Internat., 1980–93; Ryman, 1987–93; Tempus Publishing (formerly Chalford Publishing) Co. Ltd, 1994–98; Maher Booksellers Ltd, 1995–2008; Race Dynamics Ltd, 1998–2008. Mem., Adv. Council on Libraries, 1997–98. Contested (L): Accrington, 1964; Runcorn, 1966. Founder Trustee, Lib Dem, 1988–2001. Trustee, Photographers' Gall., 1994–97. FRSA 1988. Led successful campaign to abolish price control on books. *Publications:* (jtly) Counterblast, 1965; (jtly) Effective Politics, 1966; Against My Better Judgement (business memoir), 1994; Unfinished Business (novel), 2003; Grumpy Old Liberal: a political rant, 2005; What Would a Liberal Do?: a polemic, 2010; One of Lowry's Children (personal memoir), 2015. *Recreations:* reading, ski-ing, tennis, walking, music, bridge. *Address:* 27 Bryanston Square, W1H 2DT. *T:* (020) 7723 4254. *Clubs:* Savile, Portland.

**MAHMOOD, Khalid;** MP (Lab) Birmingham Perry Barr, since 2001; *b* 13 July 1961. Formerly: engr, advr, Danish Internat. Trade Union. Mem., Birmingham CC, 1990–93. Shadow Minister for Europe, 2016–. *Address:* c/o House of Commons, SW1A 0AA.

**MAHMOOD, Shabana;** MP (Lab) Birmingham Ladywood, since 2010; *b* Small Heath, Birmingham, 17 Sept. 1980; *d* of Mahmood Ahmed. *Educ:* Lincoln Coll., Oxford (LLB). Called to the Bar, Gray's Inn, 2004; employed as barrister, Berrymans Lace Mawer, 2004–07. Shadow Home Office Minister, 2010–11; Shadow Minister: for Higher Educn, BIS, 2011–13; for Univs and Sci., BIS, 2013; for the Treasury, 2013–15; Shadow Chief Sec. to the Treasury, 2015. Member: Work and Pensions Select Cttee, 2010; Public Accounts Cttee, 2017–. *Address:* House of Commons, SW1A 0AA.

**MAHON, Alexandra Rose;** Chief Executive Officer, Channel 4, since 2017; *b* England, 29 Oct. 1973; *d* of Thomas A. Mahon and Isobel S. Edwards (*née* Harris); *m* 2003, Richard C. Barker; three *s* one *d. Educ:* St Margaret's Sch., Edinburgh; Gillespie's Sch., Edinburgh; Imperial Coll. London (BSc 1st Cl. Physics; ARCS); Imperial Coll. and Inst. of Cancer Res. (PhD Physics 1998). Mitchell Madison Gp, 1998–2000; Sen. Strategy Exec., RTL Gp, 2000–02; Dir, Commercial Develt and Strategy, FremantleMedia Gp Ltd, 2002–04; Chief Operating Officer, talkbackTHAMES, 2004–06; Chief Executive Officer: Shine Gp, 2006–15; Foundry, 2015–17; Sen. Ind. Dir, Ocado plc, 2012–17. Mem. Bd, Pact, 2010–12. Appeal Chair, Scarfree Foundn, 2014–17. Non-exec. Dir, Edinburgh Fest., 2007–17. Chm., RTS Awards, 2015–17. Fellow, Royal Commn for Exhibn of 1951, 1994; RTS Fellow, 2013. *Recreations:* reading, learning, listening, watching, arts/technology/visual media. *Address:* Channel 4, 124 Horseferry Road, SW1P 2TX. *E:* amahon@channel4.co.uk.

**MAHON, Alice;** *b* 28 Sept. 1937; *m*; two *s. Educ:* Bradford Univ. (BA Hons). Lectr, Bradford and Ilkley Community Coll. Member: Calderdale Bor. Council, 1982–87; Calderdale DHA. MP (Lab) Halifax, 1987–2005. PPS to Sec. of State for Culture, Media and Sport, 1997. Mem., Select Cttee on Health, 1991–97. Mem., Nato Parly (formerly N Atlantic) Assembly, 1992–2005. *Address:* 125 The Hough, Northowram, Halifax, W Yorks HX3 7DE.

**MAHON, Seán Patrick Lauritson;** Independent Director, International Board and Global Board, DLA Piper, 2007–17; Chairman, Scottish Coal Group, 2009–12; *b* 16 April 1946; *s* of John Patrick Mahon and Peggy Lauritson Mahon; *m* 1968, Pauline Kathleen Starling; one *s* two *d* (and one *d* decd). *Educ:* Ratcliffe Coll. FCA 1969. Partner, Coopers & Lybrand, subseq. PricewaterhouseCoopers, 1969–2000; Member: UK Bd, Coopers & Lybrand, 1992–98; UK Supervisory Bd, PricewaterhouseCoopers, 1998–2000; Chief Exec., Cattles plc, 2001–07. Chairman: Jerrold Hldgs, 2007–09; Scottish Resources Gp, 2008–10. Accreditation Bd, ICAEW, 1982–88; Pres., Sheffield Soc. of Chartered Accountants, 1990–91. Careers Adv. Bd, Univ. of Sheffield, 1982–88. Dir, S Yorks Ambulance Trust, 1991–97; Chairman: Leeds Cares, 1998–2004; National Cares, 2004–07; HRH Prince of Wales's Ambassador for Yorks Businesses, 2004–07; Vice-Chm., St Luke's Hospice Capital Appeal, 2012–15. Vice Pres., Boys & Girls Clubs of S Yorks (formerly Clubs for Young People), 1984–. Pres., Sheffield Irish Soc., 1990–91. DUniv Sheffield Hallam, 2005. *Recreations:* golf, fishing, shooting. *Address:* Wyngrove, 41 Stumperlowe Crescent Road, Sheffield S10 3PR. *T:* 07802 470100. *Clubs:* Royal Automobile; Woolley Park Golf; Wykeham Shoot Syndicate.

**MAHON, Colonel Sir William (Walter),** 7th Bt *cr* 1819 (UK), of Castlegar, Co. Galway; LVO 2011; *b* 4 Dec. 1940; *s* of Sir George Edward John Mahon, 6th Bt and Audrey Evelyn (*née* Jagger) (*d* 1957); *S* father, 1987; *m* 1968, Rosemary Jane, *yr d* of late Lt-Col M. E. Melvill, OBE, Symington, Lanarks; one *s* two *d. Educ:* Eton. Commnd Irish Guards, 1960; served UK, Germany, Malaysia, Aden, Hong Kong, Pakistan, Spain. HM Body Guard, Hon. Corps of Gentlemen at Arms: Mem., 1993; Clerk of the Cheque and Adjutant, 2006–08; Standard Bearer, 2008–10. Fundraising, Macmillan Cancer Relief, 1993–2002. Chm., Nat. Army Museum Develt Trust, 2003–18. *Publications:* Waterloo Messenger: the life of Henry Percy, 2017. *Recreations:* shooting, collecting, military history. *Heir: s* James William Mahon [*b* 29 Oct. 1976; *m* 2004, Antonia Williams; one *s* one *d*].

**MAHONEY, Prof. Craig,** PhD; CPsychol; Principal and Vice-Chancellor, University of the West of Scotland, since 2013; *b* Tasmania, 13 April 1957; *s* of Bruce Gordon Mahoney and Vida Doreen Mahoney. *Educ:* Tasmanian Coll. of Advanced Educn (BEd Chem., Maths, Biol.; Tasmanian Teaching Cert.); Univ. of Birmingham (MA Sport and Exercise Scis); Queen's Univ., Belfast (PhD Psychol. 1995). Teacher of Maths, Sci. and Computing, Tasmania, 1980–86; Queen's University, Belfast: Res. Associate, 1988–92; Lectr, 1992–95; Sen. Lectr, Leeds Metropolitan Univ., 1995–96; Hd, Sport Studies, Roehampton Inst., 1997–99; Prof. of Applied Sport Psychol. and Dean of Sch., Univ. of Wolverhampton, 1999–2007; Dep. Vice-Chancellor, Northumbria Univ., 2007–10; Chief Exec., Higher Education Acad., 2010–13. Dist. Scholar, Olabisi Onabanjo Univ., 2010; Vis. Prof. of Higher Educn Strategy, Univ. of Huddersfield, 2012–. AFBPsS 2007; Fellow, British Assoc. of Sport and Exercise Scis, 2010. FRSA; FInstD 2005. Hon. DArts Abertay Dundee. Outstanding Service to Higher Educn Award, Internat. Higher Educn Teaching and Learning Assoc., 2013. *Publications:* articles in jls on children's fitness, health, sport, exercise, performance and educn. *Recreations:* former semi-professional squash player, coached and managed squash teams in Australia, Sweden and Ireland, qualified squash referee. *Address:* University of the West of Scotland, High Street, Paisley PA1 2BE. *T:* (0141) 848 3000.

**MAHONEY, Dennis Leonard;** Executive Chairman, RFIB Holdings Ltd, since 2015; *b* 20 Sept. 1950; *s* of late Frederick Mahoney; *m* 1st, Julia McLaughlin (marr. diss.); one *s* one *d*; 2nd, 1988, Jacqueline Fox; one *s* two *d. Educ:* West Hatch Technical High School; Harvard Business Sch. (PMD 1983). Chm. and CEO, Aon Group Ltd, subseq. Aon Ltd, 1997–2007; Chm., Aon Global, 2007–09. Dir, Ironshore Inc., 2012–.

**MAHONEY, Rev. Prof. John Aloysius, (Jack),** SJ; Emeritus Professor of Moral and Social Theology, University of London, since 1999; Emeritus Professor, Gresham College, London, since 2007; *b* Coatbridge, 14 Jan. 1931; *s* of Patrick Mahoney and Margaret Cecilia Mahoney (*née* Doris). *Educ:* Our Lady's High Sch., Motherwell; St Aloysius' Coll., Glasgow; Univ. of Glasgow (MA 1951). LicPhil 1956; LicTheol 1963; DTheol *summa cum laude*, Pontifical Gregorian Univ., Rome, 1967. Entered Society of Jesus, 1951; ordained priest, 1962; Jesuit Tertianship, NY, 1963–64. Lectr in Moral and Pastoral Theology, Heythrop Coll., Oxon, 1967–70, and Heythrop Coll., London, 1970–86; Principal, Heythrop Coll., London, 1976–81 (Fellow, 2000); F. D. Maurice Prof. of Moral and Social Theology, KCL, 1986–93; Founding Dir, KCL Business Ethics Res. Centre, 1987–93; Dean, Faculty of Theol., London Univ., and Faculty of Theol. and Religious Studies, KCL, 1990–92; Dixons Prof. of Business Ethics and Social Responsibility, London Business Sch., 1993–98; Founding Dir, Lauriston Centre for Contemporary Belief and Action, Edinburgh, and Hon. Fellow, Faculty of Divinity, Edinburgh Univ., 1998–2005; Sen. Res. Associate Dir, Heythrop Inst. for Religion, Ethics and Public Life, Heythrop Coll., Univ. of London, 2005–06; Mount Street Jesuit Centre, London, 2006–08. Mercers' Sch. Meml Prof. of Commerce, Gresham Coll., London, 1987–93; Dist. Prof. of Theol., Georgetown Univ., Washington, DC, 2008; Martin D'Arcy Meml Lectr, Campion Hall, Oxford, 1981–82. Vis. Scholar, Boston Coll., Mass, 2005. Mem., Internat. Theol. Commn, Rome, 1974–80; Sector Pres., Nat. Pastoral Congress, 1980; Mem., Internat. Study Gp on Bioethics, Internat. Fedn of Catholic Univs, 1984–93. Pres., Catholic Theolog. Assoc., 1984–86. Chaplain to Tablet Table, 1983–98; Domestic Chaplain to Lord Mayor of London, 1989–90. CCMI (CMgt 1993). Hon. Fellow: Gresham Coll., City of London, 1999–2000; St Mary's UC, Strawberry Hill, 1999; Hon. Fellow and Guestmaster, Campion Hall, Oxford, 2014–18. Governor, St Aloysius' Coll., Glasgow, 1999–2005 (Chm., 2000–05). Founding Editor, Business Ethics, A European Review, 1992–98. Hon. DD London, 2004. President's Medal, Georgetown Univ., Washington, DC, 2003. *Publications:* Seeking the Spirit, 1981; Bioethics and Belief, 1984; The Making of Moral Theology, 1987; The Ways of Wisdom, 1987; Teaching Business Ethics in the UK, Europe and USA, 1990, 2nd edn 2013; (ed) Business Ethics in a New Europe, 1992; The Challenge of Human Rights: origin, development and significance, 2006; Christianity in Evolution: an exploration, 2011; Glimpses of the Gospels, 2019. *Address:* Jesuit Residence, 114 Mount Street, W1K 3AH. *T:* (020) 7529 4814. *E:* jmahoney663@gmail.com.

**MAHY, Brian Wilfred John,** PhD, ScD; Senior Scientific Adviser, Coordinating (formerly National) Center for Infectious Diseases, Centers for Disease Control and Prevention, Atlanta, Georgia, 2000–10; Adjunct Professor, Emory University, 1993–2010; *b* 7 May 1937; *s* of Wilfred Mahy and Norah Dillingham; *m* 1st, 1959, Valerie Pouteaux (marr. diss. 1986); two *s* one *d*; 2nd, 1988, Penny Scott (*née* Cunningham). *Educ:* Elizabeth Coll., Guernsey; Univ. of Southampton (BSc, PhD); Univ. of Cambridge (MA, ScD 1982). Res. Biologist, Dept of Cancer Res., London Hosp. Med. Coll., Univ. of London, 1962–65; Asst Dir, Res. Virology, Dept of Pathology, Cambridge Univ., 1965–79; Fellow and Tutor, University (Wolfson) Coll., 1967–84; Librarian, Wolfson Coll., 1975–80; Huddersfield Lectr in Special Path. (Virology), 1979–84; Head, Div. of Virology, Cambridge, 1979–84; Head, Pirbright Lab., AFRC Inst. for Animal Health (formerly Animal Virus Res. Inst. and AFRC Inst. for Animal Disease Res.), 1984–89; Dir, Div. of Viral and Rickettsial Diseases, Centers for Disease Control and Prevention, Atlanta, GA, 1989–2000. Vis. Prof., Univ. of Minnesota, 1968; Eleanor Roosevelt Internat. Cancer Fellow, Dept of Microbiol., Univ. of California, San Francisco, 1973–74; Vis. Prof., Inst. für Virologie, Univ. of Würzburg, 1980–81. Convener, Virus Group, 1980–84, Mem. Council, 1983–87, Soc. for General Microbiology; Vice-Chm., 1987–90, Chm., 1990–93, Past Chm., 1994–96, Virology Div. Vice Pres., 1995–99, Pres., 1999–2002, Past Pres., 2002–05, Internat. Union of Microbiol Socs. FRSocMed 1985; Fellow: Infectious Diseases Soc. of America, 1992; Amer. Acad. of Microbiol., 1998–2010. Hon. DSc Southampton, 2001. Editor-in-Chief, Virus Research, 1983–2011; US Editor: Jl of Med. Virology, 1994–2010; Reviews in Med. Virology, 2000–10; Sen. Associate Ed., Emerging Infectious Diseases, 2008–16; Virology Ed. Reference Module in Biomed. Scis, 2013–16. *Publications:* (jtly) The Biology of Large RNA Viruses, 1970; Negative Strand Viruses, 1975; Negative Strand Virus and the Host Cell, 1978; Lactic Dehydrogenase Virus, 1975; A Dictionary of Virology, 1981, 4th edn 2009; Virus Persistence, 1982; The Microbe 1984: pt 1, Viruses, 1984; Virology: a practical approach, 1985; The Biology of Negative Strand Viruses, 1987; Genetics and Pathogenicity of Negative Strand Viruses, 1989; Concepts in Virology: from Ivanovsky to the present, 1993; Virology Methods Manual, 1996; Immunobiology and Pathogenesis of Persistent Virus Infections, 1996; (ed jtly) Topley & Wilson's Microbiology and Microbial Infections, 9th edn, Vol. 1, 1998, 10th edn, Vol. 1 and Vol. 2, 2005; Encyclopedia of Virology, 3rd edn 2008; (ed jtly) Desk Encyclopedias of General Virology, Plant and Fungal Virology, Human and Medical Virology, and Animal and Bacterial Virology, 2010; over 200 articles on virology in learned jls. *Recreations:* music, reading. *Address:* Herringbone Cottage, Rede Road, Whepstead, Bury St Edmunds IP29 4ST. *E:* bwjmahy@gmail.com.

**MAHY, Helen Margaret**, CBE 2015; Chairman, The Renewables Infrastructure Group Ltd, since 2013; *b* Guernsey, 4 March 1961; *d* of Donald Gregory Mahy and Mary Margaret Mahy; *m* 1993, Mark Roy Hughes; two step *s*. *Educ:* Guernsey Ladies Coll.; Univ. of Manchester (LLB Hons). Called to the Bar, Middle Temple, 1982; insurance broker, Hogg Robinson plc, 1982–86; Commercial Manager, Crown Agents, 1986–93; Babcock International Group plc: legal and commercial roles, 1993–99; Gp Gen. Counsel and Co. Sec., 1999–2002; Co. Sec., 2002–03, Gen. Counsel, 2003–13, Lattice, subseq. Nat. Grid plc. Mem., Equality and Human Rights Commn, 2018–. Non-executive Director: Aga Rangemaster, 2003–09; Stagecoach Gp plc, 2010–16; Bonheur ASA, 2013–; SVG Capital plc, 2014–17; SSE plc, 2016–; Medicx Fund Ltd, 2017–19; Primary Health Properties plc, 2019– (Dep. Chm., 2019–). Patron, Social Mobility Business Partnership, 2019–. FRSA. Freeman, Tallow Chandlers' Co., 2011–. *Publications:* The Adventures of Basil the Spaniel, 3 vols, 2010–11. *Recreations:* husband, spaniels, sleeping, family, travelling, collecting dolls, opera, musical theatre, speaking Norwegian. *Address:* The Renewables Infrastructure Group Ltd, East Wing, Trafalgar Court, Les Banques, St Peter Port, Guernsey GY1 3PP. *T:* 07500 706540. *E:* helen.mahy@equalityhumanrights.com.

**MAI, Prof. Yiu-Wing**, AM 2010; PhD, DSc, DEng; FRS 2008; FREng, FAA, FTSE; University Chair, since 2004, Professor of Mechanical Engineering, since 2007, and Director, Centre for Advanced Materials Technology, 1988–2011, University of Sydney; *b* Hong Kong, 5 Jan. 1946; *s* of Lam Mai and Yuet-Yau Tsui; *m* 1980, Louisa Kit-Ling. *Educ:* Univ. of Hong Kong (BSc Engrg 1969; PhD 1972; DSc 1999); Univ. of Sydney (DEng 1999). Mgt and Technol. Trainer, Hong Kong Productivity Council, 1973; Postdoctoral Research Assistant: Univ. of Michigan, 1974–75; Imperial Coll., London, 1975–76; University of Sydney: Lectr, 1976–78; Sen. Lectr, 1978–82; Associate Prof., 1983–87; Prof. of Mechanical Engrg, 1987–2002; Associate Dean, R&D, 1990–93; Dir, Graduate Sch. of Engrg, 1995–98; Dir, Defence Sci. and Technol. Orgn—Airframes and Engines Div. Centre for Expertise in Damage Mechanics, 1997–2003; Pro-Dean, 1998–2004; ARC Federation Fellow, 2002–07. Prof., HKUST, 1993–95; Chair, City Univ. of Hong Kong, 2000–02; Dist. Vis. Prof., Univ. of Hong Kong, 2003–04, 2014–18; IAS Vis. Prof., Hong Kong Univ. of Sci. and Technol., 2013–18. Pres., Australian Fracture Gp Inc., 1997. Mem. Council, Asian-Australian Assoc. for Composite Materials, 1999– (Founder Pres., 1997–98); Pres., Internat. Congress on Fracture, 2002–05 (Vice-Pres., 1997–2001). FTSE 1992; FAA 2001; FHKAES 2003. Mem., Eur. Acad. of Scis, 2008; Foreign Mem., Chinese Acad. of Engrg, 2017. FASME 1999 (Life Fellow 2013); Internat. FREng 2011. Hon. DSc Hong Kong, 2013. *Publications:* (with A. G. Atkins) Elastic and Plastic Fracture, 1985; (with B. Cotterell) Fracture Mechanics of Cementitious Materials, 1996; (with J. K. Kim) Engineered Interfaces in Fibre-Reinforced Composites, 1998; (with S.-Y. Fu and B. Lauke) Science and Engineering of Short Fibre Reinforced Polymers, 2009; (with X.-H. Chen) Fracture Mechanics of Electromagnetic Materials, 2013; (with E. H. Wong) Robust Design of Microelectronics Assemblies against Mechanical Shock, Temperature and Moisture, 2015; (jtly) Polymer Nanocomposites: towards multi-functionality, 2016; over 800 articles in scientific jls. *Recreations:* reading mainly Chinese literature, practising Chinese calligraphy, walking. *Address:* School of Aerospace, Mechanical and Mechatronic Engineering, Mechanical Engineering Building J07, University of Sydney, Sydney, NSW 2006, Australia. *T:* (2) 93512290, *Fax:* (2) 93513760. *E:* yiu-wing.mai@sydney.edu.au.

**MAIANI, Prof. Luciano**; President, Consiglio Nazionale delle Ricerche, Rome, 2008–11; Professor of Theoretical Physics, University of Rome, 1984, now Emeritus; Director General, Organisation Européenne pour la Recherche Nucléaire (CERN), 1999–2003 (President of Council, 1997); *b* 16 July 1941. *Educ:* Univ. of Rome (degree in Physics 1964). Research Associate: Istituto Superiore di Sanità, 1964; Univ. of Florence, 1964; Fellow, Lyman Lab. of Physics, Univ. of Harvard, 1969; Prof., Inst. of Theoretical Physics, Univ. of Rome, 1976; Vis. Prof., Ecole Normale Supérieure, Paris, 1977; Vis. Prof., 1979–80, 1985–86, Mem. Council, 1993–97, CERN. Pres., Istituto Naz. di Fisica Nucleare, Italy, 1993–98. Fellow, APS, 1991 (J. Sakurai Prize, 1987; E. Fermi Prize, 2003).

**MAIBAUM, Prof. Thomas Stephen Edward**, PhD; CEng, FIET; Professor, Foundations of Software Engineering, and Canada Research Chair, Department of Computing and Software, McMaster University, Canada, 2004–17, now Emeritus; *b* 18 Aug. 1947; *s* of Leslie Maibaum and Olga Maibaum (*née* Klein); *m* 1971, Janet Hilless; one *s* one *d*. *Educ:* Toronto Univ. (BSc); PhD London Univ. Postdoctoral Fellow, 1973, Asst Prof., 1974–81, Univ. of Waterloo; Imperial College, University of London: Lectr, Dept of Computing, 1981–86; Reader in Computing Science, 1986–90; Hd, Dept of Computing, 1989–97; Prof., Foundns of Software Engrg, 1990–99; King's College London: Prof., Foundns of Software Engrg, 1999–2004; Hd, Dept of Computer Sci., 2001–03. Vis. Prof., Pontifícia Universidade Católica de Rio do Janeiro, 1977, 1981 (Hon. Prof., 1992); Royal Soc./ SERC Industrial Fellow, 1984; Marie Curie Fellowship (EU), Univ. of Lisbon, 1997–98. MIEEE; MCIPS; FRSA. Engrg Foresight Award, Royal Acad. Engrg, 1998; Dr Luis Federico Leloir Prize for Internat. Cooperation in Sci., Technology and Innovation, Govt of Argentina. *Publications:* (jtly) The Specification of Computer Programs, 1987; (ed jtly) Handbook of Logic in Computer Science, vol. I, 1992, vol. II, 1992, vol. III, 1995, vol. IV, 1995, vol. V, 2000. *Recreations:* memorising the films of Mel Brooks, music, opera, travel, literature. *Address:* Department of Computing and Software, McMaster University, 1280 Main Street West, Hamilton, ON L8S 4K1, Canada; 4 Green Square, Wadhurst, East Sussex TN5 6BU.

**MAIDEN, Sir Colin (James)**, Kt 1992; ME, DPhil; Chairman, Tower Insurance Ltd (formerly National Insurance Company of New Zealand Ltd), 1988–2002; Vice-Chancellor, University of Auckland, New Zealand, 1971–94; *b* 5 May 1933; *s* of Henry A. Maiden; *m* 1957, Jenefor Mary Rowe; one *s* three *d*. *Educ:* Auckland Grammar Sch.; Univ. of New Zealand (ME); Rhodes Scholar (NZ) 1955; Exeter Coll., Oxford (DPhil; Hon. Fellow, 1994). Post-doctorate research, Oxford Univ. (supported by AERE, Harwell), 1957–58; Head of Hypersonic Physics Section, Canadian Armament Research and Develt Estabt, Quebec City, Canada, 1958–60; Sen. Lectr in Mechanical Engrg, Univ. of Auckland, 1960–61; Head of Material Sciences Laboratory, Gen. Motors Corp., Defense Research Laboratories, Santa Barbara, Calif, USA, 1961–66; Manager of Process Engineering, Gen. Motors Corp., Tech. Centre, Warren, Michigan, USA, 1966–70. Chairman: NZ Synthetic Fuels Corp. Ltd, 1980–90; Fisher & Paykel Industries Ltd, 1989–2001 (Dir, 1978); Sedgwick Gp (NZ) Ltd, 1996–98 (Dir, 1994–98); Transpower NZ Ltd, 1997–2004 (Dir, 1994–2004); DB Gp Ltd, 2003–08 (Dir, 1994–2008); Director: Mason Industries Ltd, 1971–78; Farmers Trading Co. Ltd, 1973–86; Winstone Ltd, 1978–88; Wilkins & Davies Co. Ltd, 1986–89; NZ Steel Ltd, 1988–92; Independent Newspapers Ltd, 1989–2004 (Chm., 1994–2001); ANZ Banking Gp (NZ) Ltd, 1990–93; NZ Refining Co. Ltd, 1991–2007; Progressive Enterprises Ltd, 1992–2000; Tower Ltd, 1995–2003; Foodland Associated Ltd (WA), 2000–05; Fisher & Paykel Healthcare Corp. Ltd, 2001–11. Chairman: NZ Energy R&D Cttee, 1974–81; Liquid Fuels Trust Bd, 1978–86. Chm., NZ Vice-Chancellors' Cttee, 1977–78, and 1991; Hon. Treasurer, ACU, 1988–98. Member: Spirit of Adventure Trust Bd, 1972–80; NZ Metric Adv. Bd, 1973–77. NZ Agent for Joint NZ/US Sci. and Technol Agreement, 1974–81. Hon. FIPENZ 1999. Hon. LLD Auckland, 1994. Thomson Medal, Royal Soc. NZ, 1986; Medal, Univ. of Bonn, 1983; Symons Award, ACU, 1999. Silver Jubilee Medal, 1977. *Publications:* An Energetic Life (autobiog.), 2008; (with Des Mataga) Two Inspiring Deans: TDJ Leech and CJG Dalton, 2019; numerous scientific and technical papers. *Recreation:* tennis. *Address:* Apt 503, 10 Middleton Road, Remuera, Auckland, New Zealand. *T:* (9) 5247412. *Clubs:* Vincent's (Oxford); Northern (Auckland); Remuera Racquets, International Lawn Tennis of NZ, Auckland Golf.

**MAIDEN, Prof. Martin David**, PhD; FBA 2003; Professor of the Romance Languages, since 1996, and Director, Oxford Research Centre for Romance Linguistics, since 2007, University of Oxford; Fellow of Trinity College, Oxford, since 1996; *b* 20 May 1957; *s* of Kenneth Henry Maiden and Betty Maiden (*née* Liddiard); *m* 2005, Liliana Buruiana; one step *d*. *Educ:* King Edward VI Sch., Southampton; Trinity Hall, Cambridge (MA, MPhil, PhD). Lectr in Italian, Univ. of Bath, 1982–89; Univ. Lectr in Romance Philology, and Fellow of Downing Coll., Cambridge, 1989–96. Delegate, OUP, 2004–14. Pres., Società Internazionale di Linguistica e Filologia Italiana, 1989–91; Mem. Council, Philological Soc., 1996–2000, 2003–10; Vice-Pres., Società di Linguistica Italiana, 2004–06. Associate Member: Centre for Res. on Lang. Contact, York Univ., Toronto, 2005; Associazione Italiana di Romenistica, 2006; Hon. Member: Asociația culturală Alexandru Philippide (Iași, Romania), 2005–; Dacoromania, 2006–. Hon. Dip., Linguistics Inst., 2009, Dip. for Academic Merit, 2012, Romanian Acad.; Dr *hc* Bucharest, 2013. Consultant Editor: Revue romanes, 2001–; Diachronica, 2002–; Bollettino linguistico campano, 2002–; Legenda Publications, 2002–; Troubadour Publications, 2002–; L'Italia dialettale, 2006–; Rivista italiana di linguistica, 2006–; Current Issues in Linguistic Theory (Benjamins), 2006; Italian Jl of Linguistics, 2007–13; Linguistica (Zagreb), 2008–; Revue roumaine de linguistique, 2015–; Series Ed., Oxford Guides to the World's Languages, 2013–. Comdr, Nat. Order for Faithful Service (Romania). *Publications:* Interactive Morphonology: metaphony in Italy, 1991; (ed with J. C. Smith) Linguistic Theory and the Romance Languages, 1995; A Linguistic History of Italian, 1995; (ed with M. Parry) The Dialects of Italy, 1997; Storia linguistica dell' italiano, 1998; (with C. Robustelli) A Reference Grammar of Modern Italian, 2000, 2nd edn 2007; (ed with J. C. Smith and A. Ledgeway) Cambridge History of the Romance Languages, Vol. 1, 2011, Vol. 2, 2013; (ed jtly) Morphological Autonomy: perspectives from Romance inflectional morphology, 2011; (consultant ed.) The Grammar of Romanian, 2013; (consultant ed.) The Syntax of Old Romanian, 2016; (ed with S. Cruschina and J. C. Smith) The Boundaries of Pure Morphology, 2013; (ed with A. Ledgeway) The Oxford Guide to the Romance Languages 2016; articles in various jls, incl. Romance Philology, Zeitschrift für romanische Philologie, Jl of Linguistics. *Recreation:* travel. *Address:* 62 Cunliffe Close, Oxford OX2 7BL. *T:* (01865) 511753.

**MAIDEN, Robert Mitchell**, FCIBS; Managing Director, Royal Bank of Scotland plc, and Executive Director, Royal Bank of Scotland Group plc, 1986–91; *b* 15 Sept. 1933; *s* of Harry and Georgina Maiden; *m* 1st, 1958, Margaret Mercer (*née* Nicolson) (*d* 2012); 2nd, 2018, Dr Pamela Molyneaux (*née* Whitby). *Educ:* Montrose Acad., Tayside, Scotland. Royal Bank of Scotland: various appts, 1950–74; Supt of branches, 1974–76; Treasurer, 1976–77; Chief Accountant, 1977–81; Gen. Man. (Finance), 1981–82; Exec. Dir, 1982–86. Vice-Chm., CC-Bank AG, Germany, 1991–93; Chm., Lothian and Edinburgh Enterprise, 1994–96. Member: Accounts Commn for Scotland, 1992–99; Scottish Panel of Adjudicators, Investors in People, Scotland, 1996–2001. Gov., Napier Univ. (formerly Napier Poly.), 1988–98. Trustee, C of S Pension Scheme, 1991–96. FCMI; FRSA. *Recreations:* music, golf, reading. *Address:* 51 Dick Place, Edinburgh EH9 2JA.

**MAIDLOW DAVIS, Richard Cuthbert Tolley, (Dom Leo)**, OSB; monk, since 1975, and Monastery Guest Master, Downside Abbey (Prior Administrator, 2014–18); Assistant Parish Priest, St Benedict's, Stratton-on-the-Fosse; *b* 22 April 1954; *s* of Michael Maidlow Davis and Yvette Maidlow Davis (*née* Tolley). *Educ:* Downside Sch.; Magdalene Coll., Cambridge (BA 1975); Univ. of London (BD 1982); Gregorianum, Rome (STL 1986). Professed, 1979; ordained priest, 1981; Downside School: Teacher of Classics and Religious Studies, 1982–2014; Novice Master, 1986–91; House Master, Smythe House, 1991–2000; Editor, Raven (Downside Sch. Mag.), 1992–2000; Novice Master, 2000–02; Headmaster, 2003–14. Curate, Midsomer Norton, 1982–84. *Recreations:* calligraphy, botany, sundials, riding his racing bike around the local countryside, gardening. *Address:* Downside Abbey, Stratton-on-the-Fosse, Radstock, Bath, Som BA3 4RJ. *T:* (01761) 235107.

**MAIDMENT, Francis Edward, (Ted)**; Headmaster, Shrewsbury School, 1988–2001; *b* 23 Aug. 1942; *s* of late Charles Edward and Olive Mary Maidment. *Educ:* Pocklington Sch., York; Jesus Coll., Cambridge (Scholar; MA). Asst Master, Lancing Coll., 1965–81 (Housemaster, 1975–81); Headmaster, Ellesmere Coll., Shropshire, 1982–88. Trustee, Rekindle Charitable Trust, 2001–09; Chm., Sanata Charitable Trust (UK), 2009–15. *Recreations:* lecturing and speaking, singing, medieval history, modest tennis. *Address:* Linden Cottage, Astley, Shrewsbury SY4 4BP. *Club:* East India, Devonshire, Sports and Public Schools.

**MAIDMENT, Neil**, CMG 1996; Executive Director, Glaxo Wellcome plc (formerly Glaxo Holdings plc), 1993–95 (responsible for Asia Pacific, 1993–95, and for Africa, Middle East and Turkey, 1994–95); *b* Oxford, 18 Aug. 1938; *s* of late Kenneth John Maidment, Founding Vice-Chancellor, Univ. of Auckland and Isobel Felicity Maidment (*née* Leitch); *m* 1983, Sandie Shuk-Ling Yuen. *Educ:* Christ Church Cathedral Sch., Oxford; Magdalen Coll. Sch., Oxford; King's Sch., Auckland; King's Coll., Auckland; Univ. of Auckland (Life Mem., Students' Assoc.) (Joynt Scroll Debating Shield, NZ Univs, 1956; Controller, NZ Univs Tournament, 1959). Evacuated to USA with Oxford Univ. children's gp, 1940–45. Compulsory Mil. Trng, 1st Field Regt, RNZA Signals, 1958. South British Insurance Co. Ltd, Auckland, Singapore, Calcutta, Bombay, 1958–65; Glaxo Group: Far Eastern Surgical Rep., Singapore, Kuala Lumpur, 1965–68; Manager: Hong Kong, 1968–70; Manila, 1971; Director and General Manager: Glaxo Hong Kong Ltd, 1971–93; Glaxo China Ltd, 1988–93; Area Dir, North Asia, 1990–93; Dir, Glaxo India, 1990–93. Member: Pharmacy and Poisons Appeal Tribunal, Hong Kong, 1979–88; Sub-Cttee on Biotechnology, Hong Kong, 1988–89; UK/Hong Kong Scholarships Cttee, 1988–94. Pres., Hong Kong Assoc. of Pharmaceutical Industry, 1977–78; Chm., British Chamber of Commerce, Hong Kong, 1989–90. Non-exec. Dir, Hong Kong Inst. of Biotechnol. Ltd, Hong Kong, 1996–2002. *Publications:* (with H. Scrimgeour and H. Williams) Arthur Scrimgeour—a life, 1990. *Address:* PO Box 23022, Wanchai, Hong Kong. *Clubs:* Hong Kong, Hong Kong Jockey (Hong Kong); Saturday (Calcutta).

**MAIDMENT, Ted;** *see* Maidment, F. E.

**MAIDSTONE, Viscount; Tobias Joshua Stormont Finch Hatton;** *b* 21 June 1998; *s* and *heir* of Earl of Winchilsea and Nottingham, *qv*.

**MAIDSTONE, Bishop Suffragan of,** since 2015; **Rt Rev. Roderick Charles Howell Thomas;** an Honorary Assistant Bishop: Dioceses of Exeter, London and Southwark, since 2015; Dioceses of Chelmsford, Chester, Ely, Manchester, Norwich, Rochester and Sheffield, since 2016; Dioceses of Birmingham, Bristol and Lichfield, since 2017; Diocese of Oxford, since 2018; *b* 7 Aug. 1954; *s* of Alan and Edna Thomas; *m* 1981, Lesley Easton; two *s* one *d*. *Educ:* London Sch. of Econs and Pol Sci. (BSc 1975); Wycliffe Hall, Oxford. Dir of Employment and Envmtl Affairs, CBI, 1986–91; ordained deacon, 1993, priest, 1994; Curate, St Andrew, Plymouth with St Paul, Stonehouse, 1993–99; Priest-in-charge, 1999–2005, Vicar, 2005–15, St Matthew, Elburton; Preb., Exeter Cathedral, 2012–15. Mem., Gen. Synod, 2000–15. Chm., Reform, 2007–15. *Address:* The Old Vicarage, 29 St John's Meadow, Blindley Heath, Lingfield, Surrey RH7 6JU. *T:* 07906 331110. *E:* rod.thomas@bishopofmaidstone.org.

**MAIDSTONE, Archdeacon of;** *see* Taylor, Ven. S. R.

**MAIER, Prof. John Paul,** DPhil; FRS 1999; Professor of Physical Chemistry, University of Basel, since 1991; *b* 15 Nov. 1947; *s* of Dr H. E. Maier and S. Maier; three *d* (one *s* decd). *Educ:* Univ. of Nottingham (BSc Hons Chemistry 1966); Balliol Coll., Oxford (DPhil Physical Chemistry 1972). University of Basel: Royal Soc. Fellow, 1973–74; Res. Associate 1975–78; Lectr in Chemistry, 1978–81; Associate Prof. in Physical Chemistry, 1982–90. Werner Prize, Swiss Chem. Soc., 1979; Marlow Medal, RSC, 1980; Chemistry Prize, Göttingen Sci. Acad., 1986; Nat. Latsis Prize, Swiss Nat. Sci Foundn, 1987; ERC Advanced Investigator Grant, 2010; Humboldt Res. Award, 2011; SASP Erwin Schrödinger Medal, 2012; Wheland Award, Univ. of Chicago, 2017. *Recreations:* bridge, golf. *Address:* Department of Chemistry, University of Basel, Klingelbergstrasse 80, 4056 Basel, Switzerland. *T:* (61) 2673826, *Fax:* (61) 2673855. *E:* j.p.maier@unibas.ch.

**MAIER, Juergen,** CBE 2019; Chief Executive, Siemens plc, since 2014; *b* Karlsruhe, Germany, 12 Jan. 1964; *s* of Horst Maier and Sigrun Trotter; civil partnership 2007, Richard Madgin. *Educ:* Allerton Grange High Sch.; Trent Poly. (BSc Hons Prodn Engrg 1986). Siemens: Prodn Engr, 1986–87, Prodn Manager, 1987–94, Prodn Control Manager, 1994–95, Manufg Manager, 1995–96, Automation and Drives Div.; Ops Dir, Birmingham, 1996–97; Gen. Manager, Manchester, 1997–2000; eBusiness Dir, Corporate UK, 2000–01; Man. Dir, Siemens Shared Services, 2001–04; Dir, Sales Europe, 2004–06; Man. Dir, Automation and Drives Div., 2006–08; Man. Dir, Industry Sector, UK, Ire. and Nigeria, 2008–14. Non-exec. Dir, BIS, 2014–16. Chm., Industrial Digitalisation Rev., 2017–. Chm., NW Business Leadership Team, 2009–; non-executive Director: Sci., Engrg, Manufg and Technols Alliance, 2009–15; EEF, 2010–15; High Value Manufg Catapult, 2011–14; Internat. Innovative Technologies, 2011–; Mem., Gtr Manchester LEP, 2013–. Hon. Prof., Univ. of Manchester, 2014. FIET 2014; FREng 2017. *Recreations:* ski-ing, walking, mountains. *Address:* Siemens plc, Faraday House, Sir William Siemens Square, Frimley, Camberley, Surrey GU16 8QD.

**MAILER, Joanna Mary;** *see* Shapland, J. M.

**MAIN, Very Rev. Prof. Alan,** TD 1982; PhD; Professor of Practical Theology, Aberdeen University, 1980–2001; Master, Christ's College, Aberdeen, 1992–2001; Moderator of the General Assembly of the Church of Scotland, 1998–99; *b* 31 March 1936; *s* of James E. W. Main and Mary A. R. Black; *m* 1960, Anne Louise Swanson; two *d*. *Educ:* Robert Gordon's Coll., Aberdeen; Aberdeen Univ. (MA 1957; BD 1960; PhD 1963); Union Theol Seminary, NY (STM 1961). Minister, Chapel of Garioch Parish, Aberdeenshire, 1963–70; Chaplain to Univ. of Aberdeen, 1970–80. Pres., Boys' Bde, 2005–07. Patron, Seven Incorp. Trades of Aberdeen, 2000–. Hon. DD Aberdeen, 2006. *Publications:* Worship Now, 1989; (ed) But Where Shall Wisdom Be Found?, 1995; (ed) Northern Accents, 2001; articles in jls on pastoral care and counselling, military ethics, medical ethics. *Recreations:* music (piano and organ), golf, bee-keeping. *Address:* Kirkfield, Barthol Chapel, Inverurie AB51 8TD. *Club:* Royal Northern and University (Aberdeen).

**MAIN, Anne;** MP (C) St Albans, since 2005; *b* 17 May 1957; *d* of late George and of Rita Wiseman; *m* 1st, 1978, Stephen Tonks (*d* 1991); one *s* two *d*; 2nd, 1995, Andrew Jonathan Main; one *s*. *Educ:* Bishop of Llandaff Secondary Sch., Cardiff; Univ. Coll. of Wales, Swansea (BA 1978); Univ. of Sheffield (PGCE 1978). Teacher of English and Drama, Feltham Comp. Sch., 1979–80; supply posts, Bristol, 1991–94. Member (C): Beaconsfield Parish Council, 1999–2002; S Bucks DC, 2001–05. *Address:* (office) 104 High Street, London Colney, St Albans, Herts AL2 1QL; House of Commons, SW1A 0AA.

**MAIN, Air Vice-Marshal John Bartram,** CB 1996; OBE 1979 (MBE 1977); FREng; Military Adviser, Matra Marconi Space/Astrium, 1996–2001; *b* 28 Jan. 1941; *s* of late Wing Comdr James Taylor Main, OBE and Nellie Ethel Toleman; *m* 1965, Helen Joyce Lambert; two *d*. *Educ:* Portsmouth Grammar Sch.; Birmingham Univ. (BSc Elect. Eng.); RAF Tech. Coll., Henlow. CEng 1968; MIEE 1968, FIET (FIEE 1983), Hon. FIET 2015; FRAeS 1984; FREng 2001. Commissioned Engr Branch, RAF, 1960; served Benson, Hiswa (Aden), Thorney Island; mentioned despatches, 1968; Dir of Sci. and Tech. Intell., MoD, 1970–73; OC No 33 Signals Unit, Cyprus, 1974–76; 72 Advanced Staff Course, RAF Staff Coll., 1977; CO RAF Digby, 1977–79; Directing Staff, RAF Staff Coll., 1979–80; RAF Signals Engrg Estabt, 1980–83; Head, Tech. Intell. (Air), 1983–87; RCDS 1986; Dep. Comd Aerosystems Engr, HQ Strike Comd, 1987–88; Comdt, RAF Sigs Engrg Estabt and Air Cdre Sigs, HQ RAF Support Comd, 1988–89; Dir, Command, Control, Communication and Inf. Systems (Policy and Op. Requirements), 1989–93; DG Support Services (RAF), 1993–94; AO Communications and Inf. Systems, and AOC Signals Units, HQ Logistics Comd, 1994–96. *Recreations:* gardening, cycling, sailing, reading. *Address:* Robin's Mead, 120 Manor Way, Aldwick Bay, West Sussex PO21 4HN. *Club:* Royal Air Force.

**MAIN, Monica Maitland,** FRCGP; Lord-Lieutenant of Sutherland, since 2005; *b* 9 Aug. 1952; *d* of Kenneth Morrison and Gwenneth Morrison (*née* Austin); *m* 1975, William George Main; one *s* one *d*. *Educ:* Dingwall Acad.; Univ. of Aberdeen (MB ChB 1975). DRCOG 1978; MRCGP 1979, FRCGP 2011. General Practitioner: Kingsmills Practice, Inverness, 1982–86; Brora Med. Practice, 1992–2011. *Recreations:* gardening, walking. *Address:* Ballamhor, 35 Golf Road, Brora, Sutherland KW9 6QS. *T:* (01408) 621234.

**MAIN, His Honour Peter Ramsay;** QC 2003; a Circuit Judge, 2008–17; a Deputy High Court Judge, 2008–17; *b* 17 May 1958; *s* of late Henry James Main and of Rosemary Ina Main (*née* Anderson); *m* 1988, Valerie Marie Ramsden; one *s* one *d*. *Educ:* Repton Sch.; LSE (LLB 1980); Centre for Petroleum and Mineral Law Studies, Univ. of Dundee (Dip Pet. Law 1982). Called to the Bar, Inner Temple, 1981; in practice as a barrister, Manchester, 1983–2008; Junior, Northern Circuit, 1986; Asst Recorder, 1999–2001; Recorder, 2001–08; Designated Civil Judge, Staffs and W Mercia, 2010–15; Civil Judge, Manchester Civil Justice Centre, 2015–17. *Recreations:* avid sports watcher, golf, Rhodesian ridgebacks, winter sports.

**MAIN, Dr Sarah,** FRSB; Executive Director, Campaign for Science and Engineering, since 2013; *b* Chelmsford, 20 Nov. 1975; *d* of Robert Sutherland Drayton and Sheila Margaret Drayton; *m* 2006, Peter William George Main; one *s* one *d*. *Educ:* King's Coll., Cambridge (BA 1997); University Coll. London (PhD 2003). FRSB 2018. Investigator Scientist and Career Devel. Fellow, MRC Cancer Cell Unit, 2003–08; Charles and Katherine Darwin Res. Fellow, Darwin Coll., Cambridge, 2004–07; Sen. Post-doctoral Scientist, MRC Lab. for Molecular Cell Biol., 2008–09; Res. Coordination Manager (Policy and Strategy), 2009–12, Prog. Manager, 2012–13, MRC Head Office; Sen. Policy Advr, BIS, 2012–13. Hon. Prof., UCL, 2018. Trustee, British Sci. Assoc., 2017–. *Recreation:* singing. *Address:* Campaign for Science and Engineering, Gordon House, 29 Gordon Square, WC1H 0PP. *T:* (020) 7679 4994. *E:* sarah@sciencecampaign.org.uk.

**MAINE, Steven;** Chief Executive, WiSpire, 2015–16; *b* 7 Dec. 1951; *s* of Gerald Ivor Gordon Maine and Jean Maine; *m* 1990, Sarah Anne Kennard. *Educ:* Oriel Coll., Oxford (MA). BT, 1974–95 (Dir, Visual and Broadcast, 1988–94, India, 1994–95); Chief Executive: Kingston Communications (Hull) plc, 1997–2003; Solaris Mobile, 2008–11; Deputy Chairman: Spiritel plc, 2006–10; Six Degrees Gp, 2011–15; non-executive Director: SMG plc, 2000–07; Orion Farming Gp, 2013–. Chm., Regl CBI Yorks and Humber, 2000–03. Dir, Urban Regeneration Co., Hull, 2002–03. *Recreations:* golf, cycling, photography.

**MAINES, James Dennis,** CB 1998; CEng, FIET; Director General, Command Information Systems, Ministry of Defence, 1995–97; *b* 26 July 1937; *s* of Arthur Burtonwood Maines and Lilian Maines (*née* Carter); *m* 1st, 1960, Janet Enid Kemp (marr. diss. 1997); three *s*; 2nd, 1997, Janet Elizabeth Bussey (*née* Franks); two step *d*. *Educ:* Leigh Grammar School; City University (BSc). Joined RSRE (then RRE), Malvern, 1956 (Sandwich course in applied physics, 1956–60); Head of Guided Weapons Optics and Electronics Group, 1981; Head, Microwave and Electro-optics Group, 1983; Head, Sensors, Electronic Warfare and Guided Weapons, ARE, Portsdown, 1984–86; Dep. Dir (Mission Systems), RAE, 1986–88; Dir Gen., Guided Weapons and Electronics Systems, MoD, 1988–95. Wolfe Award for outstanding MoD research (jtly), 1973. *Publications:* (jtly) Surface Wave Filters (ed Matthews), 1977; papers in learned jls. *Recreations:* sailing, cricket, golf, music, painting, non-labour intensive gardening. *Address:* Hollybush Cottage, Folly Hill, Farnham, Surrey GU9 0DR.

**MAINI, Prof. Philip Kumar,** DPhil; FRS 2015; FRSB; FIMA; FMedSci; Director, Wolfson Centre for Mathematical Biology (formerly Centre for Mathematical Biology), since 1998, and Professor of Mathematical Biology, since 2005, Mathematical Institute, University of Oxford; Fellow, St John's College, Oxford, since 2005; *b* Magherafelt, Co. Londonderry, 16 Oct. 1959; *s* of late Panna Lal Maini and of Satya Wati Maini (*née* Bhandari). *Educ:* Rainey Endowed Sch., Magherafelt; Balliol Coll., Oxford (BA Hons, MA, DPhil 1985). FRSB (FSB 2013). Asst Master, Eton Coll., 1986; Jun. Res. Fellow, Wolfson Coll., Oxford, 1987–88; Asst Prof., Dept of Maths, Univ. of Utah, Salt Lake City, 1988–90; Lectr in Math. Biol., 1990–2005, Titular Prof. of Math. Biol., 1998–2005, Math. Inst., Univ. of Oxford; Tutorial Fellow, Brasenose Coll., Oxford, 1990–2005. Adjunct Professor: Sch. of Math. Scis, Qld Univ. of Technol., 2006–09; Lincoln Univ., Christchurch, NZ, 2010–12. Visiting Professor: Williams Coll., Mass, 1995; Inst. for Maths and its Applications, Univ. of Minn, 1998; Hon. Guest Prof., Univ. of Electronic Sci. and Technol. of China, 2005–; Vis. Fellow, 2001, Vis. Prof., 2004, Qld Univ. of Technol.; Vis. Fellow, Clare Hall, Cambridge, 2001; Tewkesbury Bequest Internat. Visitor, Univ. of Melbourne, 2008; Walker Ames Guest Schol., Univ. of Washington, Seattle, 2011. Royal Soc. Leverhulme Trust Sen. Res. Fellow, 2001–02; Dist. For. Vis. Fellow, Res. Inst. for Electronic Sci., Hokkaido Univ., 2002; Wolfson Res. Merit Award, Royal Soc., 2006–11; Dist. Res. Fellow, African Inst. of Math. Scis, 2010–13; Fellow, SIAM, 2012. Corresp. Mem., Academia Mexicana de Ciencias, 2011; For. Mem., Indian Nat. Sci. Acad., 2017. FIMA 2003; FMedSci 2017. (Jtly) Bellman Prize, Math. Bioscis jl, 1997; Naylor Prize and Lectureship, LMS, 2009; Arthur T. Winfree Prize, Soc. for Math. Biol., 2017. *Publications:* (ed jtly and contrib.) Experimental and Theoretical Advances in Biological Pattern Formation, 1993; (ed jtly and contrib.) Mathematical Models for Biological Pattern Formation, 2000; (ed jtly and contrib.) Morphogenesis and Pattern Formation in Biological Systems: experiments and models, 2003; (ed jtly) Multiscale Modeling of Developmental Systems, 2008; (ed jtly) Mathematical Biology, 2009. *Recreations:* football, travel, volunteer dog-walking. *Address:* Wolfson Centre for Mathematical Biology, Mathematical Institute, Andrew Wiles Building, Radcliffe Observatory Quarter, Woodstock Road, Oxford OX2 6GG. *T:* (01865) 280497. *E:* maini@maths.ox.ac.uk.

**MAINI, Sir Ravinder (Nath),** Kt 2003; FRCP, FMedSci; FRS 2007; Professor of Rheumatology, Imperial College School of Medicine at Charing Cross Hospital Campus (formerly Charing Cross and Westminster Medical School), University of London, 1989–2002, now Emeritus Professor; Visiting Professor, University of Oxford, since 2011; *b* 17 Nov. 1937; *s* of Sir Amar (Nath) Maini, CBE and Saheli (*née* Mehra); *m* 1st, 1963, Marianne Gorm (marr. diss. 1986); one *s* one *d* (and one *s* decd); 2nd, 1987, Geraldine Room; two *s*. *Educ:* Sidney Sussex Coll., Cambridge (BA; MB, BChir 1962; Hon. Fellow, 2004). MRCP 1966, FRCP 1977; FRCPE 1994. Jun. med. appts, Guy's, Brompton and Charing Cross Hosps, 1962–70; Consultant Physician: St Stephen's Hosp., London, 1970–79; Rheumatology Dept, Charing Cross Hosp., 1970–81; Hon. Consultant Physician, Charing Cross Hosp., Hammersmith Hosps NHS Trust, 1981–2007; Prof. of Immunology of Rheumatic Diseases, and Hd, Dept of Immunology of Rheumatic Diseases, Charing Cross and Westminster Med. Sch., 1981–89; Dir, Kennedy Inst. of Rheumatology, 1990–2000 then Head, Kennedy Inst. of Rheumatology Div., Imperial Coll. Sch. of Medicine at Charing Cross Hosp. Campus, 2000–02 (Head, Clinical Immunology Div., 1979–2002). President: Brit. League Against Rheumatism, 1985–89; Brit. Soc. Rheumatology, 1989–90 (Heberden Orator, 1988); Med. Protection Soc., 2015–17; Kennedy Trust for Rheumatology Res. (formerly Kennedy Inst. of Rheumatology Trust), 2013– (Trustee, 2002–17); Chm., Res. Subcttee, 1980–85, and Mem., Scientific Co-ordinating Cttee, 1985–95, Arthritis and Rheumatism Council; Chm., Standing Cttee for Investigative Rheumatology, European League Against Rheumatism, 1992–98; Mem., Exec. Cttee, Assoc. Physicians of GB and Ire., 1988–91; Chm., Rheumatology Cttee, RCP, 1992–96 (Croonian Lectr, 1995; Lumleian Lectr, 1998); Mem., European Union of Medical Specialists, 1991– (Pres., Sect. of Rheumatology, 1994–98; Chm., Eur. Bd of Rheumatology, 1996–99). Samuel Hyde Lectr, 1998, Hon. Fellow, 2004, RSocMed. FMedSci 1999; Fellow, British Soc. for Rheumatol., 2003. Member: Slovakian Rheumatol. Soc., 2003–; (Life) Indian Rheumatol. Assoc., 2003; For. Associate, NAS, USA, 2010. Hon. Member: Australian Rheumatism Assoc., 1987; Norwegian Soc. for Rheumatology, 1987; Amer. Coll. of Rheumatology, 1988 (Master, 2004; Klemperer Lect., 2017); Hellenic Rheumatology Soc., 1989; Hungarian Rheumatology Soc., 1990; Scandinavian Soc. for Immunology, 1996; Mexican Soc. for Rheumatology, 1996; Eur. League Against Rheumatism, 1997 (jtly, Meritorious Service Award in Rheumatology, 2005); British Soc. for Immunology, 2010; Czech Soc. of Rheumatology, 2012. Trustee, Sir Jules Thorn Trust, 2004–; Guardian, Wellcome-Beit Fellowship, 2009–16. Dr *hc* Univ. René Descartes, Paris, 1994; Hon. DSc Glasgow, 2004. Dist. Investigator Award, Amer. Coll. of Rheumatology, 1999; EULAR Courtin-Clarins Prize (with Prof. M. Feldmann and Prof. J.-M. Dayer), Assoc. de Recherche sur la Polyarthrite, 2000; Outstanding Achievement in Clin. Res. Award, Inst. Clin. Res., 2004; Fothergillian Medal, Med. Soc. of London, 2004; Ambuj Nath Bose Prize, RCP, 2005; Galen Medal, Soc. of Apothecaries, 2006; Semmelweis Budapest Award, Univ. of Semmelweis, 2017; with Sir Marc Feldmann: Carol

Nachman Prize for rheumatology, city of Wiesbaden, 1999; Craford Prize, Royal Swedish Acad. of Scis, 2000; Albert Lasker Clin. Med. Res. Award, 2003; Cameron Prize, Edinburgh Univ., 2004; Japan Rheumatism Foundn Internat. Rheumatoid Arthritis Award, 2007; Dr Paul Janssen Award for Biomed. Res., Johnson & Johnson, 2008; Ernst Schering Prize, Ernst Schering Foundn, 2010; Canada Gairdner Internat. Award, 2014. *Publications:* Immunology of Rheumatic Diseases, 1977; (ed) Modulation of Autoimmune Disease, 1981; (contrib.) Textbook of the Rheumatic Diseases, 6th edn 1986; (ed) T cell activation in health and disease, 1989; (ed) Rheumatoid Arthritis, 1992; (contrib.) Oxford Textbook of Rheumatology, 1993; (section ed.) Rheumatology, 1993; (ed jtly) Manual of Biological Markers of Disease, Sect. A, Methods of Autoantibody Detection, 1993, Sect. B, Autoantigens, 1994, Sect. C, Clinical Significance of Autoantibodies, 1996; (contrib.) Oxford Textbook of Medicine, 2001, 4th edn 2003; articles in learned jls. *Recreations:* music appreciation, walking. *Address:* 103 Faulkner House, Tierney Lane, W6 9AT. *Club:* Reform.

**MAINLAND, Kathleen Mary,** CBE 2014; Executive Director, Melbourne Festival, since 2016; *b* Aberdeen, 30 May 1969; *d* of Tommy and Bertha Mainland. *Educ:* Stromness Acad., Orkney; Glasgow Univ. (MA 1990); Strathclyde Univ. (Dip. Accounting 1991). Edinburgh Festival Fringe Soc., 1991–96; Gen. Manager, Assembly Th. Ltd, 1997–2004; Gen. Manager, 2005, Admin. Dir, 2006–09, Edinburgh Internat. Book Fest.; Chief Exec., Edinburgh Festival Fringe Soc., 2009–15. Freelance prodn co-ordinator and project manager working on events incl. Edinburgh's Hogmanay, MTV Eur. Music Awards, UEFA Champions League, NVA Virtual World Orch., 1996–2005. *Address:* Melbourne Festival, PO Box 10 Flinders Lane, Melbourne, Vic 8009, Australia. *T:* (3) 96624242. *E:* k.mainland@festival.melbourne.

**MAIR,** family name of **Baron Mair**.

**MAIR, Baron** *cr* 2015 (Life Peer), of Cambridge in the County of Cambridgeshire; **Robert James Mair,** CBE 2010; PhD; FRS 2007; FREng, FICE; Sir Kirby Laing Professor of Civil Engineering (formerly Professor of Geotechnical Engineering), 1998–2017, and Head of Civil and Environmental Engineering, 1998–2016, University of Cambridge; Master of Jesus College, Cambridge, 2001–11; Founding Director, Geotechnical Consulting Group, London, since 1983; *b* 20 April 1950; *s* of late Prof. William Austyn Mair, CBE; *m* 1981, Margaret Mary Plowden O'Connor; one *s* one *d. Educ:* Leys Sch.; Clare Coll., Cambridge (MA 1975; PhD 1979). FICE 1990; FREng (FEng 1992). Scott Wilson Kirkpatrick and Partners, Consulting Engineers: Engr, London and Hong Kong, 1971–76; Sen. Engr, London, 1980–83; Res. Asst, Dept of Engrg, Univ. of Cambridge, 1976–79; Fellow, St John's Coll., Cambridge, 1998–2001. Special Prof., Dept of Civil Engrg, Univ. of Nottingham, 1994–97; Royal Acad. of Engrg Vis. Prof., Univ. of Cambridge, 1997–98. Principal Investigator, Cambridge Centre for Smart Infrastructure and Construction, 2011–; Chief Engrg Advr, Laing O'Rourke Gp, 2012–. Member: Commn of Enquiry into Collapse of Toulon Tunnel, French Govt, 1997; Adv. Bd, Rome Metro, 2008–; Adv. Bd, Barcelona Metro, 2009–; Construction Industrial Strategy Adv. Council, 2013–; Chm., Adv. Bd of Govt of Singapore on Underground Construction Projects, 2004–15. Mem., Select Cttee on Sci. and Technol., H of L, 2016–. Mem., Royal Commn for Exhibn of 1851. Sen. Vice-Pres., RAEng, 2008–11; Chm., Royal Soc./RAEng Report to UK Govt on Shale Gas, 2012; Pres., ICE, 2017–18 (Mem. Council, and various cttees, 1993–95; Gold Medal, 2004). Lectures: Rankine, British Geotech. Soc., 2007; Muir Wood, Internat. Tunnelling Assoc., Helsinki, 2011. Hon. Prof., Tongji Univ., Shanghai, 2008–. Hon. DSc Nottingham, 2011. Singapore Public Service Medal, 2011. *Publications:* (with D. M. Wood) Pressuremeter Testing: methods and interpretation, 1987; technical papers, mainly in jls of soil mechanics and geotechnical engrg; conf. proceedings, principally on underground construction and tunnelling. *Recreations:* supporting QPR, sailing, golf, long walks, Asian cities, theatre. *Address:* Department of Engineering, Trumpington Street, Cambridge CB2 1PZ. *T:* (01223) 332631, *Fax:* (01223) 339713. *E:* rjm50@cam.ac.uk.

**MAIR, Alexander,** MBE 1967; Chief Executive and Director, Grampian Television Ltd, 1970–87, retired; *b* 5 Nov. 1922; *s* of Charles Mair and Helen Dickie; *m* 1953, Margaret Isobel Gowans Rennie. *Educ:* Skene, Aberdeenshire; Webster's Business Coll., Aberdeen; Sch. of Accountancy, Glasgow. Fellow, CIMA, 1992 (Associate, 1953). Chief Accountant, Bydand Holdings Ltd, 1957–60; Company Sec., Grampian Television, 1961–70; apptd Dir, 1967; Director: ITN, 1980–87; Cablevision (Scotland) Ltd, 1983–88; TV Publication Ltd, 1970–87. Chairman: British Regional Television Assoc., 1973–75; ITCA Management Cttee, 1980–87; RGIT Ltd, 1989–98. Pres., Aberdeen Junior Chamber of Commerce, 1960–61; Mem. Council, Aberdeen Chamber of Commerce, 1973–96 (Vice-Pres., 1987–89; Pres., 1989–91). Gov., Robert Gordon's Coll., Aberdeen, 1987–2002. FRSA 1973. FRTS 1987. *Recreations:* golf, ski-ing, gardening. *Address:* Ravenswood, 66 Rubislaw Den South, Aberdeen AB15 4AY. *T:* (01224) 317619. *Club:* Royal Northern (Aberdeen).

**MAIR, Alexander Stirling Fraser, (Alistair),** MBE 1987; Chairman, 1991–98, and Managing Director, 1977–98, Caithness Glass Ltd; *b* 20 July 1935; *s* of Alexander W. R. Mair and Agnes W. (*née* Stirling); *m* 1st, 1961, Alice Anne Garrow (*d* 1975); four s; 2nd, 1977, Mary Crawford Bolton; one *d. Educ:* Robert Gordon's Coll., Aberdeen; Aberdeen Univ. (BSc (Eng)); BA Hist. Open Univ. 2001. SSC, RAF, 1960–62. Rolls-Royce, Glasgow: grad. apprentice, 1957–59; various appts, until Product Centre Manager, 1963–71; Man. Dir, Caithness Glass, Wick, 1971–75; Marketing Dir, Worcester Royal Porcelain Co., 1975–77. Director: Grampian Television, 1986–2001; Crieff Hydro Ltd, 1994–2003 (Chm., 1996–2003); Murray VCT 3 PLC, 1998–2006. Vice Chm., Scottish Cons. and Unionist Party, 1992–93; Chairman: Perth Cons. and Unionist Assoc., 1999–2004; Ochil and S Perthshire Cons. and Unionist Assoc., 2005–09. Mem. Council, CBI, 1985–92 (Chm., Scotland, 1989–91). Pres., British Glass Manufacturers' Confedn, 1997 and 1998; Chm., Crieff and Dist Aux. Assoc. (Richmond House), 1993–99. Hon. Pres., Perth and Kinross Assoc., Duke of Edinburgh's Award Scheme, 1993–. Mem. Court, Aberdeen Univ., 1993–2010 (Convener, Jt Planning, Finance and Estates Cttee, 1998–2004; Chancellor's Assessor and Vice Chm., 2000–10); Chm., Cttee of Chairmen of Scottish Higher Educn Instns, 2001–07. Chm. Trustees, Superannuation and Life Assce Scheme, Univ. of Aberdeen, 2000–15; Trustee, Univ. of Aberdeen Develt Trust, 2011–18. Gov., Morrison's Acad., Crieff, 1985–2006 (Chm., 1996–2006); Comr, Queen Victoria Sch., Dunblane, 1992–97. FRSA 1986. DL Perth and Kinross, 1993–2010. Hon. LLD Aberdeen, 2004. *Recreations:* walking, gardening, current affairs, history. *Address:* Woodend, Madderty, by Crieff, Perthshire PH7 3PA. *T:* and *Fax:* (01764) 683210. *Club:* Royal Northern and University (Aberdeen).

**MAIR, Colin David Robertson,** MA; Rector, High School of Glasgow, 2004–15; *b* 4 Aug. 1953; *s* of late Colin James Robertson Mair and Catherine Barbara Mair (later Welsh). *Educ:* Kelvinside Acad.; St Andrews Univ.; Glasgow Univ. (MA); Jordanhill Coll. (Cert Ed). High School of Glasgow: teacher of Latin, 1976–79; Head of Rugby, 1977–88; of Latin, 1979–85; Bannerman Housemaster, 1982–85; Asst Rector, 1985–96; Dep. Rector, 1996–2004. Member: Council, Sch. Leaders Scotland (formerly Headmasters' Assoc. of Scotland), 1997–2014; UCAS Standing Gp, Scotland, 2013–15; Bd, SCIS, 2013–15. Member: Commonweal Cttee, Trades House of Glasgow, 2005–06; Merchants House of Glasgow, 2014–. Mem., Gen. Convocation, Univ. of Strathclyde, 2009–10. Trustee,

Cricket Develt Trust Scotland, 2017–. Fellowship Award, Scottish Qualifications Authy, 2014. *Recreations:* cricket, golf, Rugby, walking, watching Partick Thistle. *Address:* 17 Ladywood, Milngavie, Glasgow G62 8BE. *T:* (0141) 956 5792. *Clubs:* Ross Priory; W of Scotland Cricket (Chm., Bd of Dirs, 2016–), W of Scotland Football (Glasgow); XL.

**MAIR, Eddie;** journalist and broadcaster; Presenter, Eddie Mair Show, LBC, since 2018; *b* 12 Nov. 1965; *s* of Hubert Nicolson Mair and Mary Balneaves Mair. *Educ:* Whitfield Primary Sch., Dundee; Whitfield High Sch., Dundee. Broadcast Asst, Radio Tay, Dundee, 1983–87 (Host, Tay-Talk-In and Breakfast Show, 1985–87); joined BBC, 1987: sub-ed., News, Glasgow, 1987–89, Presenter, Good Morning Scotland, 1989–93, BBC Radio Scotland; Presenter: Reporting Scotland, BBC TV Scotland, 1989–93; Eddie Mair Live, BBC Radio Scotland, 1993–94; Breakaway, Radio Four, 1993–94; Midday with Mair, Radio Five Live, 1994–98; (jtly) The World, World Service/WGBH Boston, 1996–98; PM, 1998–2018, Broadcasting House, 1998–2003, iPM, 2007–18, Radio Four; Newsnight, BBC2, 2004, 2012, 2013; (jtly) The Robert Peston Interview Show (with Eddie Mair), Radio 4, 2015; host, Seven O'Clock News, BBC3, 2004–05. Diarist, The Guardian, 2001–04; columnist, Radio Times, 2010–19. Award for Best Breakfast Show, Eddie Mair Live, 1994, Gold Award, News Journalist of Year, 1994, 2005, Gold Award for Speech Broadcaster of the Year, 2006, Interview of the Year, 2012, Gold Award for Speech Radio Broadcaster of the Year, 2013, Sony Radio Awards; Winner, Radio Prog. of Year for Broadcasting House, 2002, Radio Broadcaster of Year, 2009, BPG. *Publications:* A Good Face for Radio: confessions of a radio head (memoir), 2017. *Address:* c/o Anita Land Ltd, 10 Wyndham Place, W1H 2PU. *E:* anita@anitaland.com. *Club:* Soho House.

**MAIRS, Christopher John,** CBE 2014; FREng; Venture Partner, Entrepreneur First, since 2014; *b* 14 Feb. 1957; *s* of late Gordon Mairs and Dinah Mairs (*née* Hipkin); *m* 2012, Shirley Donald. *Educ:* Nottingham High Sch.; Churchill Coll., Cambridge (BA 1st Cl. Hons Computer Sci. 1979). FREng 2006; FBCS 2006. Dir, Data Connection Ltd, 1984–2007, Sen. Vice-Pres., Product Mgt, 2004–05, Chief Technical Officer, 2005–11; Chief Scientist, 2011–16, Mem. Bd, 2016–18, Metaswitch Networks Ltd. Chairman: a-technic, 2001–18; Code Club World Ltd, 2014–15 (Bd Mem., 2013–14); Spontly Ltd, 2014–; Magic Pony Technol. Ltd, 2015–16; Kheiron Med. Technologies, 2016–; GTN Ltd, 2017–; Phoelex Ltd, 2017–; Indigo Ltd, 2017–; Nodes & Links, 2018–; Board Member: Elastera Ltd, 2014–18; Procedural Ltd, 2015–; Cloud NC, 2018–; Proportunity, 2018–; Metomic, 2018–; Raspberry Pi Trading, 2019–. Chm., UK Forum for Computer Educn, 2013–15. Patron, Fight for Sight, 2012–; Trustee: Thomas Pocklington Trust, 2013–17; Raspberry Pi Foundn, 2015–. *Publications:* various papers and lectures on telecommunications, digital technology and inclusive design. *Recreations:* water ski-ing (including captaining British Disabled Waterski Team to victory in 3 world championships, 1989, 1997, 2001), tandem cycling (including Land's End to John O'Groats, Transamerica, 2017). *Address:* Horton's House, 15 Church Street, Bradford on Avon, Wilts BA15 1LN. *T:* (01225) 866037.

**MAIRS, Robin Gordon James; His Honour Judge Mairs;** a Circuit Judge, since 2015; *b* Northern Ireland, 10 April 1969; *s* of Gordon Mairs and Elizabeth Mairs (*née* Waugh); *m* 1998, Gaynor Barbara, *d* of late James Crawford and Barbara Crawford; one *s* one *d. Educ:* Wallace High Sch., Lisburn; Manchester Univ. (LLB 1991); Hughes Hall, Cambridge (LLM 1993). Called to the Bar, Gray's Inn, 1992 (Sir Raymond Phillips Award); in practice, SE and NE Circuit, 1994–2015; a Recorder, 2009–15; a Judge, First-tier Tribunal, Health, Educn and Social Health Chamber (Mental Health - Restricted Patients' Panel), 2011–. *Recreations:* Rugby, history, food. *Address:* Leeds Combined Court Centre, The Courthouse, 1 Oxford Row, Leeds LS1 3BG. *E:* customerenquiries@leeds.crowncourt.gsi.gov.uk. *Club:* West Park Leeds Rugby Union Football.

**MAISEY, Prof. Michael Norman,** BSc, MD; FRCP; FRCR; FBIR; Professor of Radiological Sciences, Guy's, King's and St Thomas' Hospitals' School of Medicine, King's College London (formerly United Medical and Dental Schools of Guy's and St Thomas's Hospitals), 1984–2002, now Emeritus; *b* 10 June 1939; *s* of Harold Lionel Maisey and Kathleen Christine Maisey; *m* 1965, Irene Charlotte (*née* Askay); two *s. Educ:* Caterham Sch.; Guy's Hosp. Med. Sch. (BSc, MD). ABNM 1972; FRCP 1980; FRCR 1989. House appts, 1964–66; Registrar, Guy's Hosp., 1966–69; Fellow, Johns Hopkins Med. Instns, 1970–72; Guy's Hospital: Sen. Registrar, 1972–73; Consultant Physician, Endocrinology and Nuclear Medicine, 1973–; Med. Dir and Chm. of Mgt Bd, 1991–93; Med. Dir, Guy's and St Thomas's Hosp. NHS Trust, 1993–96. Hon. Consultant to the Army in Nuclear Medicine, 1978–. Chairman: ROC and ROCME Ltd, 2004–08; Medical Imaging Gp Ltd, 2006–11; Dir, e-locum Services Ltd, 2003–07. Pres., BIR, 2000–01. Chm., SE London Support Gp, Freedom from Torture charity, 2011–. FBIR 2008. Freeman, City of London, 2018; Liveryman, Turners' Co., 2019. *Publications:* Nuclear Medicine, 1980; (ed jtly) Clinical Nuclear Medicine, 1983, 3rd edn 1998; (jtly) An Atlas of Normal Skeletal Scintigraphy, 1985; (jtly) An Atlas of Clinical Nuclear Medicine, 1988, 2nd edn 1994; (jtly) New Developments in Myocardial Imaging, 1993; Clinical Positron Emission Tomography, 1999; (jtly) Atlas of Clinical Positron Emission Tomography, 2006; books and papers on thyroid diseases, nuclear medicine and medical imaging. *E:* michael@maisey.org.uk.

**MAITLAND,** family name of **Earl of Lauderdale**.

**MAITLAND, Viscount,** Master of Lauderdale; **John Douglas Maitland;** *b* 29 May 1965; *s* and *heir* of Earl of Lauderdale, *qv*; *m* 2001, Rosamund (marr. diss. 2006), *yr d* of Nigel Bennett. *Educ:* Emanuel School; Radley College; Van Mildert College, Durham (BSc). *Recreations:* cycling, camping, sailing. *Address:* 150 Tachbrook Street, SW1V 2NE.

**MAITLAND, Charles Alexander,** (10th Bt *cr* 1918, of Clifton, Midlothian); *b* 3 June 1986; *s* of Sir Richard John Maitland, 9th Bt (*d* 1994). Has not yet established his claim to the title and his name does not appear on the Official Roll of the Baronetage.

**MAITLAND, Prof. Geoffrey Colin,** CBE 2019; DPhil; CEng, FREng; FIChemE; CChem, FRSC, FEI; Professor of Energy Engineering, Imperial College London, since 2005; President, Institution of Chemical Engineers, 2014–15 (Deputy President, 2013–14); *b* Stoke-on-Trent, Staffs, 25 Feb. 1947; *s* of Colin and Betty Maud Maitland; *m* 1969, Margot Yvonne Marks; one *s* two *d. Educ:* Hanley High Sch., Stoke-on-Trent; St Catherine's Coll., Oxford (MA; DPhil Chem. 1972). CChem 1987, FRSC 1987; CEng 2004, FREng 2006; FIChemE 2004; CSci 2005; FEI 2006. ICI Res. Fellow, Dept of Physical Chem., Univ. of Bristol, 1972–74; Lectr, 1974–83, Sen. Lectr in Chem. Engrg, 1983–86, Imperial Coll. London; Schlumberger Cambridge Research: Sen. Res. Scientist, 1986–87; Dept Hd, 1987–96; Res. Dir, 1999–2005; Chef de Métier, Schlumberger Paris, 1996–98; Sen. Mem., Hughes Hall, Cambridge, 2000–07. Founding Dir, Qatar Carbonates and Carbon Storage Res. Centre, Imperial Coll. London, 2008–14; Dir, Shell-Imperial Digital Rocks Lab., 2016–. Chm., UK Offshore Oil and Gas Regulatory Regime Ind. Rev., 2011. Pres., British Soc. Rheology, 2002–05. Trustee: RSC, 2016–; RAEng, 2017–. Gov., St Paul's Sch., Cambridge, 2001–05. Churchwarden, St Benet's Church, Cambridge, 2017–. Hutchison Medal, IChemE, 1998; Chem. Engrg Envoy Award, IChemE, 2010; Rideal Lecture Award, RSC/Soc. of Chem. Industry, 2012; Imperial Coll. Medal, 2017; Leverhulme Medal, Soc. of Chem. Industry, 2017. *Publications:* (with G. G. Slinn) Ceramicists' Handbook, 1973; (jtly) Intermolecular Forces: their origin and determination,

1981; (jtly) The Forces Between Molecules, 1986; (ed with L. J. Struble) Flow and Microstructure of Dense Suspensions, 1993; contrib. res. papers to scientific jls. *Recreations:* amateur drama, opera and choral singing, football (Stoke City), cricket (England, Middlesex, Somerset); theatre, British coins, grandchildren. *Address:* Department of Chemical Engineering, Imperial College London, SW7 2AZ. *T:* (020) 7594 1830, *Fax:* (020) 7594 5629. *E:* g.maitland@imperial.ac.uk.

**MAITLAND, Lady (Helen) Olga, (Lady Olga Hay);** journalist, public affairs consultant; Chief Executive Officer, Money Transfer International, 2008–14; *b* 23 May 1944; *er d* of 17th Earl of Lauderdale and Stanka (*née* Lozanitch); *m* 1969, Robin Hay, *qv*; two *s* one *d*. *Educ:* Sch. of St Mary and St Anne, Abbots Bromley; Lycée Français de Londres. Reporter, Fleet St News Agency, Blackheath and Dist Reporter, 1965–67; columnist, Sunday Express, 1967–91, Daily Mail, 1998–2001. CEO, Internat. Assoc. of Money Transfer Networks, 2006–08. Consultant: Kroll Security Internat., 2004–; Sovereign Strategy, 2004–07; Dir, Earthport plc, 2008–12. ILEA Candidate, Holborn and St Pancras, 1986; contested (C) Bethnal Green and Stepney, 1987. MP (C) Sutton and Cheam, 1992–97; contested (C) same seat, 1997, 2001. PPS to Minister of State, NI Office, 1996. Member, Select Committee: on Procedure, 1992–95; on Educn, 1992–96; on Social Security, 1995–96; on Health, 1996–97. Formerly Sec., Cons. back bench Defence Cttee; Sec., Cons. back bench NI Cttee, 1992–97. Chm., Copenhagen Compliance UK, 2015–. Founder and Chm., Families for Defence, 1983–; Pres., Defence and Security Forum, 1992–. Chm., Algeria British Business Council, 2005–. *Publications:* Margaret Thatcher: the first ten years, 1989; Faith in the Family, 1997; (contrib.) Peace Studies in our Schools, 1984; (contrib.) Political Indoctrination in Schools, 1985. *Recreations:* family, the arts, travel. *Address:* 21 Cloudesley Street, N1 0HX. *T:* (020) 7837 9212.

**MAITLAND, Prof. Kathryn,** PhD; FMedSci; Professor of Paediatric Tropical Infectious Diseases, Imperial College London, since 2009; *b* Liverpool, 8 Nov. 1962; *d* of Raymond Maitland and Yvonne Ann Maitland (*née* Christie); *m* 1993, Prof. Thomas Neil Williams; two *s* (and one *s* decd). *Educ:* St Bartholomew's Med. Sch., London (MB BS 1986); Univ. of London (PhD 2000). MRCPCH 1991, FRCPCH 2015. House surgeon, Hackney-Homerton Hosp., London, 1986–87; House Physician, 1986–87, SHO, 1987–88, Whipps Cross Hosp., London; SHO/CMO in Paediatrics, Queen Elizabeth Children's Hosp., London, 1988–89; SHO in Neonatal Care, UCH, 1988; Paediatric Registrar, Alder-Hey Regl rotation, Liverpool, 1989–90; Sen. Registrar, Paediatrics, Edgware Gen. Hosp., London, 1990–91; Clin. Scientist, Epidemiol studies, Vanuatu, 1991–94; Wellcome Trust Res. Fellow, Centre for Infectious Diseases, Dept of Zool., Univ. of Oxford, 1995–96; Wellcome Trust Res. Fellow, 1998–99, Specialist Registrar in Paediatrics, 1998, in Microbiol., 1998–99, John Radcliffe Hosp., Oxford; Clin. Lectr in Tropical Paediatric Infectious Diseases, St Mary Hosp., London, 1999–2000; Imperial College London: Clin. Lectr, 2000–04; COSMIC Clin. Lectr, 2004–06; Sen. Lectr in Tropical Paediatric Infectious Diseases, 2006–09. FMedSci 2016. *Publications:* book chapters and articles in jls incl. Nature, New England Jl of Medicine, Jl of the Amer. Medical Assoc., BMJ, Lancet. *Address:* KEMRI-Wellcome Trust Programme, PO Box 230, Kilifi, Kenya. *E:* k.maitland@imperial.ac.uk.

**MAITLAND-CAREW, Captain Hon. Gerald (Edward Ian),** CVO 2016; Lord-Lieutenant of Roxburgh, Ettrick and Lauderdale, 2007–16; *b* 28 Dec. 1941; *s* of 6th Baron Carew, CBE and Lady Sylvia Maitland (*d* 1991), *o d* of 15th Earl of Lauderdale; assumed by Deed Poll, 1971, the surname Maitland-Carew; *m* 1972, Rosalind Averil Speke; two *s* one *d*. *Educ:* Heatherdown Prep. Sch.; Harrow Sch. Served 15th/19th King's Royal Hussars, 1960–72, Captain 1963; ADC to GOC Home Counties, 1964–67. Ran family estate and Thirlestane Castle, 1970–2014. Chairman: Lauderdale and Galawater Br., RBL, Scotland, 1974–2004; Gurkha Welfare Trust Scotland, 1996–2004 (Pres., 2004–). Racecourse Steward: Cheltenham, Newmarket, Newcastle, Ayr, Musselburgh, Kelso, 1976–2016. Chm. and host, Scottish Horse Trials Championships, Thirlestane Castle, 1982–2009; Chairman: Lauderdale Hunt, 1980–2000; Musselburgh Racecourse, 1988–98; Mem., Jockey Club, 1987–; Vice President: Internat. League for the Protection of Horses, 2006– (Chm., 1999–2006); World Horse Welfare, 2008–; Border Union Agricl Soc., 2016–. Church of Scotland: an Elder, 1977–; Mem. Architectl and Artistic Cttee, 1986–96. Trustee: Thirlestane Castle Trust, 1982–; Mellerstain House Charitable Trust, 1983–. Brig., Royal Co. of Archers, Queen's Bodyguard for Scotland, 2003–16 (Mem., 1979–2003). DL Roxburgh, Ettrick and Lauderdale, 1989. Pres., Royal Burgh of Lauder Golf Club, 2009–. Pres., Small Bore Rifle Championships of Scotland, 1985–. *Recreations:* horses, shooting, racing. *Address:* The Garden House, Thirlestane Castle, Lauder, Berwickshire TD2 6PD. *T:* (01578) 722254. *Clubs:* Cavalry and Guards, Pratt's; Royal Caledonian Hunt, Jed Forest Hunt.

**MAITLAND DAVIES, Keith Laurence;** a District Judge (Magistrates' Courts) (formerly Metropolitan Stipendiary Magistrate), 1984–2003; *b* 3 Feb. 1938; *s* of Wyndham Matabele Davies, QC and Enid Maud Davies; *m* 1964, Angela Mary (*née* Jenkins); two *d* one *s*. *Educ:* Winchester; Christ Church, Oxford (MA). Called to the Bar, Inner Temple, 1962; private practice, 1962–84. *Address:* c/o Hammersmith Magistrates' Court, 181 Talgarth Road, W6 8DN.

**MAITLIS, Emily, (Mrs M. Gwynne);** Presenter: Newsnight and News 24, BBC, since 2006; This Week's World, since 2016; *b* 6 Sept. 1970; *d* of Prof. Peter Michael Maitlis, *qv*, *m* 2000, Mark Gwynne; two *s*. *Educ:* Queens' Coll., Cambridge (BA Hons English Lit. and Medieval Italian 1992). Documentary programme-maker, Radio 1, TVB, 1995–97; Channel 4 producer, Hong Kong handover, 1997; Business corresp., NBC, Hong Kong, 1997–98; presenter and business corresp., Sky News, 1998–2001; presenter, BBC, 2001–. *Publications:* Airhead: the imperfect art of making news, 2019. *Address:* c/o Noel Gay, 19 Denmark Street, WC2H 8NA. *E:* emily.maitlis@bbc.co.uk. *Clubs:* Soho House (Mem. Cttee); Foreign Correspondents' (Hong Kong).

**MAITLIS, Prof. Peter Michael,** FRS 1984; Professor of Inorganic Chemistry, 1972–97, Research Professor, 1997–2002, now Emeritus, Sheffield University; *b* 15 Jan. 1933; *s* of Jacob Maitlis and Judith Maitlis; *m* 1959, Marion (*née* Basco); three *d*. *Educ:* Univ. of Birmingham (BSc 1953); Univ. of London (PhD 1956, DSc 1971). Asst Lectr, London Univ., 1956–60; Fulbright Fellow and Res. Associate, Cornell Univ., 1960–61, Harvard Univ., 1961–62; Asst Prof., 1962–64, Associate Prof., 1964–67, Prof., 1967–72, McMaster Univ., Hamilton, Ont, Canada. Chm., Chemistry Cttee, SERC, 1985–88. Fellow, Alfred P. Sloan Foundn, USA, 1968–70; Tilden Lectr, RSC, 1979–80; Sir Edward Frankland Prize Lectr, RSC, 1985; Ludwig Mond Lectr, RSC, 1996–97; Van der Kerk Lectr, Netherlands, 1999; Paolo Chini Lectr, Italy, 2001; Glenn T. Seaborg Meml Lectr, Univ. of Calif, Berkeley, 2004–05. Vis. Prof., Australia, Belgium, Brazil, Canada, France, Israel and Japan; Assessor for nat. res. assessments, UK, Holland, Italy, Israel and Portugal. Member: Royal Soc. of Chemistry (formerly Chem. Soc.), 1952 (Pres., Dalton Div., 1985–87; Fellow); Amer. Chemical Soc., 1963; Council, Royal Soc., 1991–93; BBC Sci. Consultative Gp, 1989–93. Foreign Mem., Accademia Nazionale dei Lincei, Italy, 1999. E. W. R. Steacie Prize (Canada), 1971; Medallist, RSC (Noble Metals and their Compounds), 1981; Kurnakov Medal, Russian Acad. of Scis, 1998. *Publications:* The Organic Chemistry of Palladium, vols 1 and 2, 1971; (jtly) Metal-catalysis in Industrial Organic Processes, 2006;

Greener Fischer-Tropsch Processes, 2013; many research papers in learned jls. *Recreations:* travel, music, writing, conversation. *Address:* 18 Tor Court, Kensington, W8 4HX. *E:* p.maitlis@sheffield.ac.uk.
See also E. Maitlis.

**MAJOR;** *see* Henniker-Major, family name of Baron Henniker.

**MAJOR, Rt Hon. Sir John,** KG 2005; CH 1999; PC 1987; Prime Minister and First Lord of the Treasury, and Leader of the Conservative Party, 1990–97; *b* 29 March 1943; *s* of late Thomas Major and Gwendolyn Minnie Coates; *m* 1970, Norma Christina Elizabeth Johnson (*see* Dame N. C. E. Major); one *s* one *d*. *Educ:* Rutlish. AIB. Banker, Standard Chartered Bank: various executive posts in UK and overseas, 1965–79. Member, Lambeth Borough Council, 1968–71 (Chm. Housing Cttee, 1970–71). Contested (C) St Pancras North (Camden), Feb. 1974 and Oct. 1974. MP (C) Huntingdonshire, 1979–83, Huntingdon, 1983–2001. PPS to Ministers of State at the Home Office, 1981–83; an Asst Govt Whip, 1983–84; a Lord Comr of HM Treasury (a Govt Whip), 1984–85; Parly Under-Sec. of State for Social Security, DHSS, 1985–86; Minister of State for Social Security, DHSS, 1986–87; Chief Sec. to HM Treasury, 1987–89; Sec. of State for Foreign and Commonwealth Affairs, 1989; Chancellor of the Exchequer, 1989–90. Jt Sec., Cons. Parly Party Environment Cttee, 1979–81. Pres., Eastern Area Young Conservatives, 1983–85. Mem., Cons. Party Adv. Council, 2003–05. Mem., European Adv. Bd, 1998–2005, Chm., European Bd, 2001–05, Carlyle Gp; Chairman: European Adv. Council, Emerson Electric Co., 1999–2015; Internat. Adv. Bd, Nat. Bank of Kuwait, 2007–14; Adv. Bd, Global Infrastructure Partners, 2007–; Global Adv. Bd, AECOM, 2011–16; Sen. Adv., Credit Suisse (formerly Credit Suisse First Boston), 2001–; non-exec. Dir, Mayflower Corporation, 2000–03; Mem. European Bd, Siebel Systems, Inc., 2001–03. Chm., Ditchley Council, 2000–09; Jt Pres., Chatham House, 2009– (Chm., Panel of Sen. Advrs, 2011–); Pres., Bow Gp, 2012–14. Chm., Campaign Bd, KCL, 2010–. Mem., InterAction Council, Tokyo, 1998–2008. President: Asthma UK (formerly Nat. Asthma Campaign), 1998–; British and Commonwealth Cricket Charitable Trust, 2002–; Res. Action Fund, Prostate Cancer UK, 2009–; Sir Edward Heath Charitable Foundn Centenary Campaign for Arundells, Educn and the Arts, 2014–; Vice-President: Macmillan Cancer Relief, 2001–; Inst. of Sports Sponsorship, 2001–; Gtr London Fund for the Blind, 2005–; Hon. Pres., Sight Savers Appeal, 2001–; Chairman: World Questions King's Answers Campaign, KCL, 2010–; Queen Elizabeth Diamond Jubilee Trust, 2011–. Patron: Mercy Ships; Support for Africa 2000; Atlantic Partnership, 2001–; FCO Assoc., 2001–; Professional Cricketers' Assoc., 2001–; Deafblind UK, 2002–; Consortium for Street Children, 2002–; 21st Century Trust, 2002–; Goodman Fund, Chicago, 2002–; Norfolk Cricket Umpires and Scorers Assoc., 2002–; Foundation for Peace (formerly Tim Parry Johnathan Ball Trust, then Tim Parry Johnathan Ball Foundn for Peace), 2004–; Dickie Bird Foundn, 2004–; SeeAbility Sight Pioneers, 2006–13 (Vice President, 2013–); Tory Reform Gp, 2009–; Margaret Thatcher Scholarship Trust, 2012–; British Music Hall Soc., 2012–; Hoxton Hall, 2012–; British Gymnastics, 2013–; Ladybird Boat Trust, 2014–; Conservative Alumni, 2014–; Churchill Alliance, 2015–; Oxford Univ. Cons. Assoc., 2015–; Cromwell Mus. Trust, 2015–; Street Child Cricket World Cup, 2017–; Vice-Patron, Atlantic Council of UK; Ambassador: Chance to Shine, 2005–; Right to Sight Prog., Vision 2020, 2005–. Mem. Bd, Warden Housing Assoc., 1975–83. Member: Bd of Advrs, Baker Inst., Houston, 1998–2005; Internat. Bd of Govs, Peres Center for Peace, Israel, 1997–. Pres., Surrey CCC, 2000–02, now Hon. Life Vice-Pres. Hon. Bencher, Middle Temple, 1993. Hon. Freeman, Merchant Taylor's Co., 2002. Hon. Comr, Sir John A Macdonald Bicentennial Commn, 2012–. Hon. FCIB; Hon. FCGI. Freedom, City of Cork, 2008. Elder Brother, Corp. of Trinity House, 2013. Outstanding Contribn to Ireland Award, Business and Finance Irish Business Awards, 2014; Sir Winston Churchill Award, Internat. Churchill Soc., 2017. Grand Cordon, Order of the Rising Sun (Japan), 2012. *Publications:* The Autobiography, 1999; More Than a Game: the story of cricket's early years, 2007; My Old Man: a personal history of music hall, 2012. *Recreations:* music, theatre, opera, reading, travel, cricket and other sports. *Address:* PO Box 38506, SW1P 1ZW. *Clubs:* Buck's, Carlton, Farmers, Pratt's, MCC (Mem. Cttee, 2001–04, 2005–08, 2009–11), Surrey CC.

**MAJOR, John,** LVO 1998; General Manager, Borde Hill Estate, 2001–06; Regional Surveyor, Country Land and Business Association, 2007–09; *b* 16 June 1945; *s* of John Robert Major and Vera Major; *m* 1967, (Mary) Ruth Oddy; one *s* one *d*. *Educ:* Wellingborough Sch.; RAC, Cirencester. FRICS 1980. Partner, Osmond Tricks, Bristol, 1980–85; Land Agent, Castle Howard, N Yorks, 1986–91; Land Agent to HM the Queen, Sandringham Estate, 1991–98; Partner, Chm., Clegg Kennedy Drew, Land Agents and Chartered Surveyors, 1998–99; Dir, F. P. D. Savills, 2000–01; consultant surveyor, 2002–07. *Recreations:* travelling, gardening, reading, plant collecting. *Address:* Rabbit Wood, Hadnock Road, Monmouth NP25 3NJ.

**MAJOR, Kathryn Elizabeth; Her Honour Judge Major;** a Circuit Judge, since 2018; *b* Penzance, Cornwall, 29 Sept. 1969; *d* of John Major and Susan Major; *m* 2015, Lt Col Leigh Christopher Jackson; one *d*. *Educ:* Cape Cornwall Comp. Sch.; Penwith Sixth Form Coll.; Univ. of Kent (BA Hons Law). Admitted solicitor, 1994; a District Judge, 2011–18.

**MAJOR, Lee E.;** *see* Elliot Major.

**MAJOR, Dame Malvina (Lorraine),** ONZ 2012; GNZM 2009 (PCNZM 2008); DBE 1991 (OBE 1985); opera singer; Senior Fellow, University of Waikato, New Zealand, since 2012; *b* 28 Jan. 1943; *d* of Vincent William Major and Eva Gwendolen (*née* McCaw); *m* 1965, Winston William Richard Fleming (*d* 1990); one *s* two *d*. *Educ:* Hamilton Technical Coll.; London Opera Centre. ATCL, LTCL; LRSM. Studied with Dame Sister Mary Leo, Auckland; winner: NZ Mobil Song Quest, 1963; Melbourne Sun Aria Contest, Australia, 1964; Kathleen Ferrier Award, London, 1966. Camden Fest., London; Salzburg Fest., 1968 (internat. début as Rosina in Barber of Seville), 1969, 1991; returned to NZ, 1970; La Finta Giardiniera, Th. de la Monnaie, Brussels, 1985; Vienna, Amsterdam, New York, Antwerp, Salt Lake City, 1986; Don Giovanni, Drottningholm, Brighton Fest., 1987; Covent Garden début as Rosalinde in Die Fledermaus, 1990; with Australian Opera, and in E Berlin, 30 rôles, including: La Bohème; Madame Butterfly; Faust; Il Seraglio; Rigoletto; Don Pasquale; Lucia di Lammermoor; Magic Flute; Tosca; Merry Widow; La Traviata; Eugene Onegin; Elisabetta Regina d'Inghilterra; Marriage of Figaro; also extensive concert repertoire, TV and recordings. Established Dame Malvina Major Foundn for educn in performing arts, 1992. Prof. of Voice, Univ. of Canterbury, Christchurch, 2003–11. Hon. DLitt Massey, 1993; Hon. Dr Waikato, 1994. Entertainer and Internat. Performer of the Year, NZ, 1992; NZ Classical Disc Award, 1993 and 1994. *Relevant publication:* Viva Malvina, by Joy Tonks, 2003. *Recreations:* golf, sewing, family. *Address:* c/o Dame Malvina Major Foundation, PO Box 9976, Wellington 6141, New Zealand.

**MAJOR, Mark,** RIBA; RDI 2012; FRIAS; FIALD; Founding Partner and Director, Speirs + Major, Designers, since 1996; *b* Worthing, Sussex, 13 Nov. 1961; *s* of Colin and Nina Major; *m* 1990, Riel Meredith Karmy-Jones, *qv*; one *s* one *d*. *Educ:* Hurstpierpoint Coll.; Brighton Poly.; Edinburgh Univ. (BA Hons); DipArch. RIBA 1988; IALD 1999, FIALD. Lighting Design Partnership, 1986–88; HKPA Architects, 1988–90; Principal, Major-Rossen Architects, 1990–95; Tutor (pt-time), Univ. of Brighton, 1989–95. Projects include lighting of: Millennium Dome, London, 2000; 30 St Mary Axe, London, 2004; interior, St Paul's Cathedral, 2007; current projects: King's Cross redevelt, 2006–; Battersea Power Station, 2014–; interior, Norwich Cathedral, 2015–18; interior, Westminster Abbey, 2016–. Lighting Design Advr, London Olympics, 2009–12; Lighting Vision, City of London, 2016–18. FRIAS 2012. *Publications*: Made of Light: the art of light and architecture, 2005. *Recreations*: art, music, reading. *Address*: Speirs + Major, 8 Shepherdess Walk, N1 7LB. *T*: (020) 7067 4700, *Fax*: (020) 7067 4701. *E*: info@speirsandmajor.com.

**MAJOR, Dame Norma (Christina Elizabeth),** DBE 1999; *b* 12 Feb. 1942; *d* of late Norman Wagstaff and Edith Johnson; *m* 1970, Rt Hon. Sir John Major, *qv*; one *s* one *d*. *Educ*: Peckham Sch. for Girls; Battersea Coll. of Domestic Science (Teachers' Cert.). Teacher, Sydenham Sch. and St Michael and All Angels Sch., Camberwell, 1963–70. Campaigned with husband, 7 Gen. Elecns, 1974–97. A Nat. Vice Pres., Mencap, 1995– (Pres., Mencap Challenge Fund, 1992–2002. Mem., Archives Cttee, Churchill Archives Centre, Churchill Coll., Cambridge, 2011–. Pres., Huntingdon, Mencap, 1987–2009 (Hon. Pres., 2013); Patron, Cambs Mencap, 2009–13); Patron, Bd, WNO, 1999–2003; Mem., League of Mercy, 2004–; Patron: Crossroads Care, 1991–2013; Renton Foundn, 1992–2015; English Schs Orch., 2005–; Spinal Res. Trust, 1996–2011; Rowan Foundn, 1998–; Mercy Ships; Penfold Trust, 2000–; Shakespeare at The George, Huntingdon, 2006–; Pepys Hse Appeal, 2015–; Hon. Patron, Joan Sutherland and Richard Bonynge Opera Foundn, 2011–. Hon. Fellow, Harris Manchester Coll., Oxford, 2012. FRSA 2004. Paul Harris Fellow, Rotary Club, 2007. *Publications*: Joan Sutherland, 1987; Chequers: the Prime Minister's country house and its history, 1996. *Recreations*: opera, theatre, reading. *Address*: PO Box 38506, SW1P 1ZW.

**MAJOR, Pamela Ann;** HM Diplomatic Service, retired; self-employed coach, since 2010; *b* 4 March 1959; *d* of Arthur and Mary Major; *m* 1992, (Robert) Leigh Turner, *qv*; one *s* one *d*. *Educ*: Hertford Coll., Oxford (BA Russian and French 1981); Bradford Univ. (Postgrad. Dip. Interpreting and Translating 1982); Leicester Univ. (MA Employment Relns and Labour Law 2000). Entered FCO, 1982; Second Sec., Beijing, 1986–88; FCO, 1988–92; First Sec., Moscow, 1992–95; FCO, 1995–2002 (special unpaid leave, 1998–2002); Counsellor (EU and Econ.), Berlin, 2002–06; Equality and Human Rights Commn (on secondment), 2007; Hd of Coaching and Asst Dir, Recruitment and Develt, FCO, 2008–10. Accredited coach, Internat. Coach Fedn, 2009. *Recreations*: theatre and amateur dramatics, rowing, walking, bird-watching, reading.

**MAJOR, Riel Meredith;** *see* Karmy-Jones, R. M.

**MAK, Alan;** MP (C) Havant, since 2015; *b* York, 19 Nov. 1983. *Educ*: St Peter's Sch., York; Peterhouse, Cambridge (BA Hons Law 2005); Oxford Inst. of Legal Practice (DipLP 2006). Admitted as solicitor, 2009. Parly researcher, Hon. Ed Vaizey, MP, 2006–07; Trainee Solicitor, Solicitor, 2009–14, Clifford Chance LLP; Founder, two small businesses, 2014. PPS MoJ, 2017–18; BEIS, 2018–. Chairman: All Party Parly Gp for Entrepreneurship, 2015–18; All Party Parly Gp on Fourth Industrial Revolution, 2016–; Co-Chm., All Party Parly Gp for Apprenticeships, 2016–18. Trustee, Magic Breakfast, 2009–15 (Pres., 2011–15); Founder and Chm., Young Professionals' Br., RBL, 2011–15. FRSA 2008. *Recreations*: spending time with family and friends, watching sport, films, travel. *Address*: House of Commons, SW1A 0AA. *T*: (020) 7219 3000. *E*: alan.mak.mp@parliament.uk.

**MAK, Prof. Tak Wah,** OC 2000; OOnt 2007; FRS 1994; FRSC 1986; University Professor, University of Toronto, since 1997, Senior Scientist and Director, Advanced Medical Discovery Institute, since 2002, and Director, Campbell Family Institute for Breast Cancer Research, Ontario Cancer Institute, since 2004, University Health Network, Toronto; *b* Canton, China, 4 Oct. 1946; *s* of Kent and Linda Mak; *m* 1969, Shirley Lau; two *d*. *Educ*: Univ. of Wisconsin (BSc 1967; MSc 1969); Univ. of Alberta (PhD 1972). Research Assistant: Univ. of Wisconsin, Madison, 1967–69; Univ. of Alberta, 1969–72; University of Toronto: Postdoctoral Fellow, 1972–74; Asst Prof., 1974–78; Associate Prof., 1978–84; Prof., 1984–. Founding Dir, Amgen Inst., 1993–2002. Chm., Croucher Foundn, 2011–. Gairdner Internat. Award, Gairdner Foundn, 1989; Novartis Immunol. Prize, Novartis Inc., 1998; Killam Prize, Canada Council, 2003. *Publications*: (ed) Molecular and Cellular Biology of Hemopolitic Stem Cell Differentiation, 1981; (ed) Molecular and Cellular Biology of Neiplasia, 1983; (ed) Cancer: perspective for control, 1986; (ed) The T Receptor, 1987; (ed) AIDS: ten years later, 1991; (with J. L. Simard) Handbook of Immune Response Genes, 1998; (jtly) The Gene Knockout Facts Book, 1998; contrib. Cell, Science, Nature and other learned jls. *Address*: (office) Princess Margaret Hospital, 620 University Avenue, Room 7–706, Toronto, ON M5G 2C1, Canada.

**MAKAREM, Dr Rima, (Mrs Jonathan Cumming);** Managing Director, Healthpeak Ltd, 2011; Chairman, National Travel Health Network and Centre, 2015–19; *b* London, 5 Aug. 1969; *d* of Riad Makarem and Dolly Makarem; *m* 2000, Jonathan Cumming; one *s* one *d*. *Educ*: Lycée Français Charles de Gaulle; Girton Coll., Cambridge (BA Hons Nat. Scis 1990); Univ. of Manchester (PhD Biochem. 1994); INSEAD (MBA 1999). Sen. Res. Associate, RPMS, 1994–95; Consultant, Arthur Andersen, 1995–98; Sen. Consultant, Gemini Consulting, 1999–2001; GlaxoSmithKline: Dir, Global Commercial Strategy, 2001–03; Dir, Competitive Excellence, 2003–07. Non-executive Director and Audit Chair: NHS Haringey, 2007–10; NHS London, 2010–13; University Coll. London Hosps NHS Foundn Trust, 2013–19; NICE, 2016– (Sen. Ind. Dir, 2019–); H of C Commn, 2018–; non-exec. Dir, Hillingdon Hosps NHS Foundn Trust, 2019–; Mem., Audit and Risk Cttee, MRC, 2011–14; Chm., Risk Assurance Cttee, Health Educn S London, 2013–16. Lay Mem., Gen. Pharmaceutical Council, 2019–. Mem. Council, St George's, Univ. of London, 2016–19. Dir, Anchor Trust, 2012–17; Trustee, UCLH Charities, 2013–19. *Recreations*: running around after two 'tweenies', chasing the family up hills and into kayaks, relaxing at the cinema and theatre. *E*: rima_makarem@hotmail.com.

**MAKAROVA, Natalia;** dancer and choreographer; *b* Leningrad, 21 Nov. 1940; *m* 1976, Edward Karkar (*d* 2013); one *s*. *Educ*: Vaganova Ballet Sch.; Leningrad Choreographic Sch. Mem., Kirov Ballet, 1959–70; London début, as Giselle, Covent Garden, 1961; joined American Ballet Theatre, 1970; formed dance co., Makarova & Co., 1980; Guest Artist: Royal Ballet, Covent Garden, 1972; London Festival Ballet, 1984. Has danced many classical and contemporary rôles in UK, Europe and USA, 1970–92; appearances include: La Bayadère (which she also staged, and choreographed in part), NY Met, 1980, Manchester, 1985, Royal Opera House, Covent Gdn, 1989; On Your Toes, London and NY, 1984–86; choreographed new productions: Swan Lake, for London Fest. Ballet, London and tour, 1988; Sleeping Beauty, La Bayadère, for Royal Ballet, 2003. Honoured Artist of RSFSR, 1970; Kennedy Center Honors, 2012. *Publications*: A Dance Autobiography, 1979; On Your Toes, 1984. *Address*: 323 Marina Boulevard, San Francisco, CA 94123–1213, USA.

**MAKEHAM, Peter Derek James,** CB 2003; independent consultant, since 2011; Director General, Strategy (formerly Performance) and International, Home Office, 2006–11; *b* 15 March 1948; *s* of Derrick James Stark Makeham and Margaret Helene Makeham; *m* 1972, Carolyne Rosemary Dawe (marr. diss. 2002); one *s* three *d*. *Educ*: Chichester High Sch. for Boys; Nottingham Univ. (BA); Leeds Univ. (MA Lab Econs). Economist, Dept of Employment, 1971–82; on secondment to Unilever, 1982–83; HM Treasury, 1983–84; Enterprise Unit, Cabinet Office, 1984–85; Dept of Employment, 1985–87; DTI, 1987–90; Department of Employment, then Department for Education and Employment, subseq. Department for Education and Skills, 1990–2006: Head of Strategy and Employment Policy Div., 1992–95; Director: Employment and Adult Trng, 1995–97; School Orgn and Funding, 1997–99; Teachers Gp, 1999–2000; Dir Gen., Finance and Analytical Services, 2000–06; Dir Gen., Strategy and Reform, 2006–11.

**MAKEKA, Felleng Mamakeka;** High Commissioner of Lesotho in the United Kingdom, also accredited to Spain, Portugal, Malta and Cyprus, 2013–15; *b* Thaba Phatsoa, Lesotho, 11 Feb. 1953; *d* of Nchocho Ntšekhe; *m* 1975, Sen. Advocate Thabo Romeo Makeka (*d* 2012); three *s* one *d*. *Educ*: Univ. of Botswana, Lesotho and Swaziland (Dip. Develt Studies); Univ. of Dist of Columbia (BA Econs); City Univ. of New York (MA Econs). Sen. Economist, Lesotho Nat. Develt Corp., 1988–2003; Economist, Lesotho Investment Promotion Centre, 1996; Dir, Investment Promotion, 2003–05, Actg Chief Exec., 2005–06, Lesotho Tourism Develt Corp.; Vice-Chm., Queen's Nat. Trust Fund, Lesotho, 2006–07; Founder, Owner, Business and Investment Facilitation Services, 2007–08; Owner, Manager, Felleng's Blooming Place (garden centre and events venue), 2006–. Internat. PR Officer, Fedn of Lesotho Women Entrepreneurs, 2011–. *Recreations*: debating international political economy issues, listening to political and parliamentary debates, gardening, entertaining family and friends, reading.

**MAKEPEACE, John,** OBE 1988; FCSD; FRSA; designer and furniture maker, since 1961; Founder and Director, The Parnham Trust and Parnham College (formerly School for Craftsmen in Wood), 1977–2000; *b* 6 July 1939; *m* 1st, 1964, Ann Sutton (marr. diss. 1979); 2nd, 1983, Jennie Moores (*née* Brinsden). *Educ*: Denstone Coll., Staffs. Study tours: Scandinavia 1957; N America, 1961; Italy, 1968; W Africa, 1972; USA, 1974; Japan, 1994; Yunnan, China, 2005. Fellow: Arts Univ., Bournemouth, 2007; Hereford Coll. of Arts, 2013. Goodison Lect., Fitzwilliam Mus., 2017. Furniture in private and corporate collections in Europe, USA, Asia and S Africa. *Public collections*: Cardiff Museum; Fitzwilliam Museum, Cambridge; Leeds Museum; Court Room, Worshipful Co. of Innholders; Board Room, Grosvenor Estate Holdings; Art Inst., Chicago; Museum für Kunsthandwerk, Frankfurt; Royal Museum of Scotland; V & A Museum; Lewis Collection, Richmond, USA; Banque Générale du Luxembourg; Crab Tree Farm, Chicago; Chatsworth, 2017. *Exhibitions*: Herbert Art Gall., Coventry, 1963; New Art Centre, London, 1971; Fine Art Soc., London, 1977; Interior, Kortrijk, Belgium, 1978, 1992, 1994; Royal Show, Stoneleigh, 1981–87; Crafts Council Open, 1984; National Theatre, 1980, 1986; Parnham at Smiths Gall., 1988–91; Sotheby's, 1988, 1992, 1993, 1997; New Art Forms, Chicago, 1989–92; Tokyo, 1990; ARCO, Madrid, 1993; Chicago Contemporary Art Fair, 1993–96; Art '93, London; Conservation by Design, Providence, USA, 1993; Creation, Claridge's, 1994; Banque de Luxembourg, 1995; British Embassy, Brussels, 1995; Smithsonian Instn, 1996; Rotunda, Hong Kong, 1996; Chicago Design Show, 1997; Mayor Gall., 1997; Great British Design, Cologne, 1997; Crafts Council, 1999, 2002; Maastricht Fair, 1999–2001; Sotheby's Contemporary Decorative Arts, 2000; Modern Collectibles, London, 2003; Collect, London at Saatchi Gall., 2004, 2007, 2008, 2014, 2015, 2017, 2018; Grosvenor House Art and Antiques Fair, 2005; Internat. Expo. of Sculpture, Objects and Functional Art, Chicago, 2007; Arts Council Retrospective, John Makepeace: Enriching the Language of Furniture (tour), 2010–11; Somerset House, 2011; The Power of Making, V&A Mus., 2012; British Design 1948–2012, V&A Mus., 2012; Gall. NAGA, Boston, 2012; Pritam and Eames Gall., E Hampton, NY, 2012; Design, Shanghai, 2014; Masterpiece, Royal Hosp. Chelsea, 2019. *Consultancies/Lectures*: Crafts Council (and Mem.), 1972–77; India Handicrafts Bd, 1975; Jammu and Kashmir Govt, 1977; Belgrade Univ., 1978; Artist in Context, V&A Mus., 1979; Chm., Wood Programme, World Crafts Conf., Kyoto, Japan, 1979; Australian Crafts Council, 1980; Oxford Farming Conf., 1990; Cheongju Internat. Craft Biennale 2001, Korea. Trustee, V & A Mus., 1987–91. *Films*: Made by Makepeace (filmed by John Read), 1975; History of English Furniture, 1978; Heritage in Danger, 1979; First Edition, 1980; Touch Wood, 1982; Tomorrow's World, 1986; Essays in Wood, 2010; Objects of Desire, 2012; Crafting a Legacy, Plymouth Univ., 2016. Winner, Observer Kitchen Design, 1971; Hooke Park Winner, UK Conservation Award, 1987; British Construction Industry Award, 1990; Amer. Inst. of Archts Award, 1993; Award of Distinction, 2002, Lifetime Achievement Award, 2004, Furniture Soc. of USA; Claxton Stevens Award, 2009, Lifetime Achievement Award, 2010, Furniture Makers' Co.; Prince Philip Designer Prize, 2016. *Publications*: Beyond Parnham, 2017; *relevant publications*: John Makepeace: a spirit of adventure in craft and design, by Prof. Jeremy Myerson, 1995; Furniture with Soul, by David Savage, 2011; Handmade in Britain, by Joanna Norman, 2012. *Recreations*: friends, travel, garden design, sylviculture, contemporary art. *Address*: Farrs, Beaminster, Dorset DT8 3NB. *T*: (01308) 862204. *W*: www.johnmakepeacefurniture.com. *Club*: Athenæum.

**MAKEPEACE, Peter Anthony;** QC 2016; a Recorder, since 2008; *b* Lancs, 9 Nov. 1965; *s* of Peter and Margaret Makepeace; partner, Patricia Andrews. *Educ*: Northallerton Grammar Sch., N Yorks; Univ. Coll. of Wales, Aberystwyth (LLB Hons). Called to the Bar, Lincoln's Inn, 1988. *Address*: Dere Street Barristers Chambers, 14 Toft Green, York YO1 6JT. *T*: (01904) 620048. *E*: p.makepeaceqc@derestreet.co.uk.

**MAKEPEACE, Richard Edward,** CMG 2011; HM Diplomatic Service, retired; Registrar, Oxford Centre for Islamic Studies, since 2011; Fellow, St Cross College, Oxford, since 2011; *b* 24 June 1953; *s* of late Edward Dugard Makepeace and of Patricia Muriel Makepeace; *m* 1980, Rupmani Catherine Pradhan; two *s*. *Educ*: St Paul's Sch.; Keble Coll., Oxford. Joined FCO, 1976; MECAS, 1977–78; Muscat, 1979–81; Prague, 1981–85; FCO, 1985–86; Private Sec. to Parly Under-Sec. of State, FCO, 1987–88; UK Perm. Repn to EC, 1989–93; Dep. Head, Personnel Mgt Dept, FCO, 1993–95; Counsellor and Dep. Hd of Mission, Cairo, 1995–98; Ambassador to Sudan, 1999–2002; Ambassador to UAE, 2003–06; Consul-Gen., Jerusalem, 2006–10. *Recreations*: travel, reading, scuba diving. *Address*: Oxford Centre for Islamic Studies, Marston Road, Oxford OX3 0EE.

**MAKGILL,** family name of **Viscount of Oxfuird**.

**MAKGOBA, Most Rev. Thabo Cecil;** *see* Cape Town, Archbishop of.

**MAKHLOUF, Gabriel;** Governor, Central Bank of Ireland, since 2019; *b* 3 Feb. 1960; *s* of Antoine Makhlouf and Aïda Makhlouf (*née* Lazian); *m* 1984, Sandy Cope; one *s*. *Educ*: Prior Park Coll., Bath; Univ. of Exeter (BA Hons Econs); Univ. of Bath (MSc Industrial Relns). Board of Inland Revenue: HM Inspector of Taxes, 1984–89; Policy Advr, 1989–92; Head of Secretariat, Change Mgt Gp, 1992–93; Head of Direct Tax Br., Fiscal Policy, HM Treasury, 1993–95; Asst Dir, Personal Tax Div., Bd of Inland Revenue, 1995–97; Principal Private Sec. to Chancellor of Exchequer, 1997–98, Head, Work Incentives and Poverty Analysis, 1998, HM Treasury; Dir, Internat., 1998–2003, Capital and Savings, 2003–05, Bd of Inland Revenue; Dir, Debt Mgt and Banking, 2005–08, Dir, Banking Services, 2008–10, HMRC; Dep. Chief Exec., 2010–11, Chief Exec. and Sec., 2011–19, NZ Treasury. Chm., Cttee on Fiscal Affairs, OECD, 2000–04. Hon. FICM. *Address*: Central Bank of Ireland, New Wapping Street, North Wall Quay, Dublin 1, Ireland.

**MAKHOUL, Prof. Bashir,** PhD; Vice-Chancellor, University for the Creative Arts, since 2017; *b* Akko, Israel, 13 Aug. 1963; *s* of late Wadia Makhoul and of Salwa Makhoul; *m* 2006, Prof. Annie Lu; three *s*. *Educ:* Liverpool Poly. (BA Hons Fine Art 1990); Manchester Metropolitan Univ. (MA Fine Art 1992; PhD Contemp. Palestinian Art 1995). Lectr, Liverpool Sch. of Art, 1994–95, Post-doctoral Res. Fellow and Dir, Centre for Internat. Art Res., 1996–97, Liverpool John Moores Univ.; Sen. Lectr, Sch. of Cultural Studies and Dir, res. degrees in Fine Art, 1997, Subject Leader for Painting and Printmaking, 1999, Sheffield Hallam Univ.; Hd, Dept of Art and Design, 2002–04, Hd, Sch. of Media, Art and Design and Dir, Res. Inst. of Media, Art and Design, 2004–05, Univ. of Luton; Prof. of Art and Design and Hd of Sch., Winchester Sch. of Art, 2005–13, Rector, Winchester Campus, 2009–13, Univ. of Southampton; Pro Vice-Chancellor, 2013–15, Dep. Vice-Chancellor, 2015–17, Birmingham City Univ. Visiting Professor: Dalian Poly. Univ., China, 2005–; Tsinghua Univ., Beijing, 2009–; Xiamen Univ., China, 2012–. FRSA 2019. Hon. DArt Manchester Metropolitan, 2019. *Solo exhibitions:* Alhijara, UK touring, 1993–94; New Paintings, Studio iM Gall., Berlin, 1995; Signs and Significance, UEL Gall./Hayward Gall., 1997; Hold I and Hold II, internat. touring, 1999–2001; Return in Conflict, internat. touring, 2007–09; New Work, Mus. of St Petersburg, 2009; Enter Ghost Exit Ghost, internat. touring, 2011–13; Palestinian Pavilion, 55th Venice Biennale, 2013; House of Cards, Granada Studios, Manchester, 2014; House of Cards II, Xiamen Cultural Center, China, 2015; Floating Free, Birzeit Univ. Mus., Ramallah Al-Hoash Mus. and Art Gall., Jerusalem and installations in Jerusalem Old City, 2015; The Punishment of Luxury, Umm el-Fahem Art Gall., Israel, 2018–19. *Publications:* (with G. Hon) Found in Conflict, 2012; (ed) Palestinian Video Art: constellation of the moving image, 2013; (with G. Hon) The Origins of Palestinian Art, 2013; (ed with A. Mitha) Conflict and Compassion: a paradox of difference in contemporary Asian art, 2016; (ed with J. Harris) Contemporary Art and Visual Culture in Global Asia, vol. 1, 2017; contrib. chapters in books and articles in jls. *Recreation:* violin playing. *Address:* University for the Creative Arts, Falkner Road, Farnham, Surrey GU9 7DS. *T:* (01252) 892600. *E:* bmakhoul@uca.ac.uk.

**MAKHULU, Most Rev. Walter Paul Khotso,** CMG 2000; Archbishop of Central Africa, 1980–2000, now Emeritus; Bishop of Botswana, 1979–2000; an Honorary Assistant Bishop, Diocese of London, since 2003; *b* Johannesburg, 1935; *m* 1966, Rosemary Sansom; one *s* one *d*. *Educ:* St Peter's Theological Coll., Rosettenville; Selly Oak Colls, Birmingham. Deacon 1957, priest 1958, Johannesburg; Curate: Johannesburg, 1957–60; Botswana, 1961–63; St Carantoc's Mission, Francistown, Botswana, 1961–63; St Andrew's Coll., Selly Oak, Birmingham, 1963–64; Curate: All Saints, Poplar, 1964–66; St Silas, Pentonville, with St Clement's, Barnsbury, 1966–68; Vicar of St Philip's, Battersea, 1968–75; Secretary for E Africa, WCC, 1975–79. A President: WCC, 1983–91; All Africa Conf. of Churches, 1981–86. Hon. DD: Kent, 1988; Gen. Theol Seminary, NY, 1990. Officier, Ordre des Palmes Académiques (France), 1981; PH 2000; Order of St Mellitus, 2008; Order of the Companions of O. R. Tambo (South Africa), 2019.

**MAKIN, Claire Margaret,** FRICS; business consultant; *b* 21 March 1951; *d* of late James Ernest Makin, CBE and Mary Makin (*née* Morris); *m* 1978, David Anthony Bowman. *Educ:* City Univ. (MBA). FRICS 1988; ACIArb 1985. Partner, Richard Ellis, 1978–90; Consultant, Price Waterhouse, 1990–91; Partner, Bernard Thorpe, 1991–93; Dir, DTZ Debenham Thorpe, 1993–95; Chief Exec., RICS, 1995–97; Chambers Dir, 13 King's Bench Walk, 1998–2001. FRSA 1991. *Recreations:* travelling, food and wine, restoring old houses.

**MAKINS,** family name of **Baron Sherfield**.

**MAKINSON, John Crowther,** CBE 2001; Chairman, Penguin Random House, 2013–16 (Chairman and Chief Executive, Penguin Group, 2002–13); *b* 10 Oct. 1954; *s* of Kenneth Crowther Makinson and Phyllis Georgina Makinson (*née* Miller); *m* 1st, 1985, Virginia Clare Macbeth (marr. diss. 2012); two *d*; 2nd, 2012, Nandana Dev Sen. *Educ:* Repton Sch.; Christ's Coll., Cambridge (BA Hons). Journalist: Reuters, 1976–79; Financial Times, 1979–86; Vice Chm., Saatchi & Saatchi (US), 1986–89; Partner, Makinson Cowell, 1989–94; Man. Dir, Financial Times, 1994–96; Finance Dir, Pearson plc, 1996–2002. Chm. Trustees, IPPR, 2008–10. Chm., Nat. Th., 2010–15. *Recreations:* music, cooking. *Address:* 1965 Broadway, Apt 12B, New York City, NY 10023, USA.

**MAKKAWI, Dr Khalil;** Chevalier, Order of Cedar, Lebanon; Chairman, Lebanese Palestinian Dialogue Committee, 2005–10; Ambassador and Permanent Representative of Lebanon to the United Nations, New York, 1990–94; *b* 15 Jan. 1930; *s* of Abdel Basset Makkawi and Rosa Makkawi; *m* 1958, Zahira Sibaei; one *s* one *d*. *Educ:* Amer. Univ. of Beirut (BA Polit. Science); Cairo Univ. (MA Polit. Science); Columbia Univ., NY, USA (PhD Internat. Relations). Joined Lebanese Min. of Foreign Affairs, 1957; UN Section at Min., 1957–59; Attaché to Perm. Mission of Lebanon to UN, New York, 1959, Dep. Perm. Rep., 1961–64; First Sec., Washington, 1964–66; Chief of Internat. Relations Dept, Min. of For. Affairs, Beirut, 1967–70; Counsellor, London, 1970–71; Minister Plenipotentiary, London, 1971–73; Ambassador to: German Democratic Republic, 1973–78; Court of St James's, and Republic of Ireland, 1979–83; Dir of Political Dept, Min. of Foreign Affairs, Beirut, 1983–85; Amb. to Italy, and Permanent Rep. to UNFAO, 1985–90. Mem., Lebanese Delegn to UN Gen. Assembly Meetings, 14th–39th Session; Chairman of Lebanese Delegations to: Confs and Councils, FAO, 1985–89; Governing Councils, IFAD, 1985–89; 16th Ministerial Meeting, Islamic conf. in Fès, 1986; 8th Summit Conf. of Non-Aligned Countries, Harare, 1986; Ministerial Meeting, Mediterranean Mems, Non-Aligned Countries, Brioni, Yugoslavia, 1987; IMO Conf., Rome, 1988; Vice-Pres., Lebanese delegn to ME peace negotiations, Washington, 1993–94. A Vice-Chm., Exec. Bd, UNICEF, 1993–95, Pres., 1995–96. Pres., Worldwide Alumni assoc., Amer. Univ. of Beirut, 2007–11. Pres., Lebanese Circle of Ambassadors, 2013–. Grand Cross of Merit (Italian Republic). *Recreations:* sports, music. *Address:* c/o Ministry of Foreign Affairs, Beirut, Lebanon.

**MAKLOUF, Raphael David;** sculptor; painter; Chairman, Tower Mint, since 1975; *b* Jerusalem, 10 Dec. 1937; *m* 1968, Marillyn Christian Lewis, *d* of Gwilym Hugh Lewis, DFC; two *s* one *d*. *Educ:* studied art at Camberwell School of Art, under Karel Vogel, 1953–58. Official commissions: Tower of London, Carnegie Hall, NY, etc. Portrait effigy of the Queen on all UK and Commonwealth coinage minted 1985–97, on Britannia gold coins minted 1989–97. Bronze portraits of the Queen, 1988, at Royal Nat. Theatre, Richmond Riverside Develt and Westminster Sch. Science Building, unveiled by the Queen. 15 Stations of Cross for new Brentwood Cathedral, 1992. Sitters have included: HM Queen; HRH Prince Philip; Rt Hon. Margaret Thatcher. Designs for National Trust and English Heritage. FRSA 1985. Fellow, Univ. of the Arts London, 2003. *Address:* 3 St Helena Terrace, Richmond, Surrey TW9 1NR. *Clubs:* City Livery, Garrick, Chelsea Arts; Riverside Racquets Centre.

**MAKSYMIUK, Jerzy;** conductor; Chief Conductor, 1983–93, Conductor Laureate, 1993, BBC Scottish Symphony Orchestra; *b* Grodno, Poland, 9 April 1936. *Educ:* Warsaw Conservatory. First Prize, Paderewski Piano Comp., 1964; worked at Warsaw Grand Theatre, 1970–72; founded Polish Chamber Orchestra, 1972; UK début, 1977; toured all over world incl. European festivals of Aix-en-Provence and Vienna and BBC Promenade concerts; Principal Conductor, Polish Nat. Radio Orch., 1975–77; toured extensively in E Europe and USA; has conducted orchestras in Europe, USA and Japan including: Orch. Nat. de France, Tokyo Metropolitan Symphony, Ensemble Orchestral de Paris, Israel Chamber Orch., Rotterdam Philharmonic and Hong Kong Philharmonic; in UK has conducted BBC Welsh and BBC Philharmonic Orchs, CBSO, LSO, London Philharmonic, ENO, Bournemouth Sinfonietta and Royal Liverpool Phil. Orch.; début for ENO with Don Giovanni, London Coliseum, 1990. Has made numerous recordings. Hon. DLitt Strathclyde, 1990. Commander's Cross, Order of Merit (Poland).

**MALAHIDE, Patrick;** *see* Duggan, P. G.

**MALAM, Colin Albert;** freelance football writer, Sunday Mirror, 2009–14; *b* 16 Oct. 1938; *s* of Albert and Irene Malam; *m* 1971, Jacqueline Cope; four *s*. *Educ:* Liverpool Inst. High Sch. for Boys; Sidney Sussex Coll., Cambridge (BA Hons History). Trainee, Liverpool Daily Post and Echo, 1961–64; News Reporter, Birmingham Post, 1964–65; Press Officer: Westward TV, 1965–66; GEC (Telecommunications) Ltd, Coventry, 1966; Football Writer, later Football Correspondent, Birmingham Post, 1966–70; Football and Athletics Writer, The Sun, 1970–73; Football and Boxing Correspondent, 1973–2003, freelance football writer, 2003–09, Sunday Telegraph. *Publications:* World Cup Argentina, 1978; Gary Lineker: strikingly different, 1993; (with Terry Venables) The Best Game in the World, 1996; The Magnificent Obsession: Keegan, Sir John Hall, Newcastle and sixty million pounds, 1997; (with Malcolm Macdonald) Supermac: my autobiography, 2003; Clown Prince of Soccer?: the Len Shackleton story, 2004; The Boy Wonders: Wayne Rooney, Duncan Edwards and the changing face of football, 2006. *Recreations:* DIY, listening to music, especially jazz, reading anything, watching cricket. *E:* c.malam@btinternet.com.

**MALAND, David;** barrister; *b* 6 Oct. 1929; *s* of Rev. Gordon Albert Maland and Florence Maud Maland (*née* Bosence); *m* 1953, Edna Foulsham (*d* 2016); two *s*. *Educ:* Kingswood Sch.; Wadham Coll., Oxford (BA Hons Mod. Hist., 1951; MA 1957; Robert Herbert Meml Prize Essay, 1959); City Univ. (Dip. Law (ext.) 1985). Nat. service commn RAF, 1951–53. Asst Master, Brighton Grammar Sch., 1953–56; Senior History Master, Stamford Sch., 1957–66; Headmaster: Cardiff High Sch., 1966–68; Denstone Coll., 1969–78; High Master, Manchester Grammar Sch., 1978–85. Schoolmaster Commoner, Merton Coll., Oxford, 1975. Chm., Assisted Places Sub-Cttee of Headmasters' Conf., 1982–83. Called to the Bar, Gray's Inn, 1986; in practice, 1987–95. Gen. Gov., British Nutrition Foundn, 1987–95. Governor: Stonyhurst Coll., 1973–80; Abingdon Sch., 1979–91; GPDST, 1984–88. *Publications:* Europe in the Seventeenth Century, 1966; Culture and Society in Seventeenth Century France, 1970; Europe in the Sixteenth Century, 1973; Europe at War, 1600–1650, 1980; (trans.) La Guerre de Trente Ans, by Pagès, 1971; articles and reviews in History. *Address:* Flat 9, Meadsway, Staveley Road, Eastbourne BN20 7LH. *Club:* Athenæum.

**MALBON, Vice-Adm. Sir Fabian (Michael),** KBE 2001; Lieutenant Governor and Commander-in-Chief of Guernsey, 2005–11; *b* 1 Oct. 1946; *s* of Rupert Charles Malbon and June Marion Downie; *m* 1969, Susan Thomas; three *s*. *Educ:* Brighton, Hove and Sussex Grammar Sch. Joined RN, Dartmouth, 1965; jun. postings, 1969–82; CO, HMS Torquay, 1982–84; MoD, 1984; Comdr Sea Training, 1985–87; CO, HMS Brave, 1987–88; Dir, Naval Service Conditions, MoD, 1988–90; RCDS 1991; CO, HMS Invincible, 1992–93; Naval Sec. and CE Naval Manning Agency, MoD, 1996–98; Dep. C-in-C, Fleet, 1999–2001; Dir, TOPMAST, 2001–02. President: CCF Assoc., 2003–08; Royal Naval Benevolent Trust, 2007–13; Union Jack Club, 2011–19. Trustee, Chesil Sailing Trust, 2014–19. Mem., RNSA. *Recreations:* sailing, walking.

**MALCOLM, Rt Hon. Lord; Colin Malcolm Campbell;** PC 2015; a Senator of the College of Justice in Scotland, since 2007; *b* 1 Oct. 1953; *s* of Malcolm Donald Campbell and Annabella Ferguson or Campbell; *m* 1977, Fiona Anderson; one *s* one *d* (and one *d* decd). *Educ:* Grove Acad., Broughty Ferry; Univ. of Dundee (LLB). Passed Advocate, 1977; QC (Scot.) 1990. Lectr, Dept of Scots Law, Univ. of Edinburgh, 1977–79; Standing Junior Counsel: to Scottish Develt Dept (all matters other than Planning), 1984–86; to Scottish Develt Dept (Planning), 1986–90. Vice-Dean, Faculty of Advocates, 1997–2001 (Dean of Faculty, 2001–04). Part-time Mem., Mental Welfare Commn for Scotland, 1997–2001; Mem., Judicial Appts Bd for Scotland, 2002–05. *Address:* Supreme Courts, Parliament House, 11 Parliament Square, Edinburgh EH1 1RQ. *T:* (0131) 225 2595.

**MALCOLM, Prof. Alan David Blair,** DPhil, CBiol, FRSB, FRSC, FIFST; Chief Executive, Institute of Biology, 1998–2009; *b* 5 Nov. 1944; *s* of late David Malcolm and Helena Malcolm (*née* Blair); *m* 1972, Susan Waller (*d* 2015); two *d*. *Educ:* King's Coll. Sch., Wimbledon; Merton Coll., Oxford (MA, DPhil 1970). FIFST 1994; FRSB (FIBiol 1997); FRSC 2004. Demonstrator, Oxford Univ., 1969–72; EMBO Fellow, Max-Planck-Institute, 1971; Lectr, Univ. of Glasgow, 1972–76; St Mary's Hospital Medical School: Lectr, 1976–79; Sen. Lectr, 1979–81; Reader, 1981–84; Prof. of Biochem., Charing Cross and Westminster Med. Sch., 1984–92; Dir Gen., Flour Milling and Baking Res. Assoc., 1992–94; Dir, BBSRC Inst. of Food Res., 1994–98. Vis. Fellow, Yale Univ., 1982; Hon. Res. Fellow, UCL, 1984–89. Vice-Chm., Technol. Foresight Food and Drink Panel, 1995–99; Member: MAFF Food Adv. Cttee, 1995–2001; EU Standing Cttee on Fruit and Vegetables, 1998–; Adv. Cttee on Novel Foods and Processes, 2002–07; UK Deleg. to Eur. Cttee of Biol Assocs, 1998–; Council, Parly and Scientific Cttee, 2000–17, now Life Mem. (Vice-Pres., 2003–12; Exec. Sec., 2012–17); Expert Advisor: H of C Select Cttee on Genetically Modified Organisms, 1999; H of L Eur. Affairs Cttee on GM Labelling, 2002. Chm., Res. and Scientific Cttee, Arthritis and Rheumatism Council, 1990–92; Mem., Royal Soc. Cttee on Genetically Modified Organisms, 1998; Scientific Gov., 1995–, Vice-Chm. Council, 1996–98, Chm. 1998–2000 and 2010–12, British Nutrition Foundn; Director: Assured Food Standards, 2002–; Sci. Council, 2003–; Chairman: Adv. Bd, ESRC Centre for Econ. and Social Aspects of Genomics, 2008–; Trustees, British Nut Foundn, 2010–12. Dir, Oxford Internat. Biomed. Centre, 2008–12. Chm., Biochemical Soc., 1992–95. Mem. Court, ICSTM, Univ. of London, 1998–2007. Member Editorial Board: Internat. Jl Food Science Nutrition, 1997–; Pesticide Outlook, 1998– (Chm., 2002–03); Outlook on Agriculture, 1999–; Science in Parliament, 2003– (Ed., 2012–). *Publications:* Enzymes, 1971; Molecular Medicine, vol. 1, 1984, vol. 2, 1987; numerous articles, symposia, etc. *Address:* 12 Earl's Court Square, SW5 9DP. *T:* (020) 7373 9505.

**MALCOLM, Col Sir Alexander James Elton,** 13th Bt *cr* 1665 (NS), of Balbedie and Innertiel, co. Fife; OBE 2000; Secretary: Turf Club, since 2012; Pratt's, since 2018; *b* 30 Aug. 1956; *er s* of Sir James William Thomas Alexander, 12th Bt and Gillian Heather (*née* Humpherus); *S* father, 2012; *m* 1982, Virginia Elizabeth Coxon; two *s* one *d*. *Educ:* Eton; RMA Sandhurst. Col Welsh Guards. *Heir: s* Edward Alexander Humpherus Malcolm [*b* 28 Sept. 1984; *m* 2015, Fiona Louise, *d* of Iain Heggie; one *s*].

**MALCOLM, Derek Elliston Michael;** Film Critic: The Guardian, 1971–97; London Evening Standard, 2003–15; Huffington Post UK, since 2016; President: International Film Critics, 1990–2001 (Chairman, UK Section, since 1982); British Federation of Film Societies, since 1993; *b* 12 May 1932; *s* of J. Douglas Malcolm and Dorothy Taylor; *m* 1st, 1962, Barbara Ibbott (marr. diss. 1966); one *d*; 2nd, 1994, Sarah Gristwood. *Educ:* Eton; Merton College, Oxford (BA Hons Hist.). Actor, amateur rider (National Hunt), 1953–56; Drama Critic, Gloucestershire Echo, 1956–62; Sub-Editor, The Guardian, 1962–69;

Racing correspondent, The Guardian, 1969–71. Dir, London Internat. Film Fest., 1982–84. Gov., BFI, 1989–92. Pres., Critics' Circle of UK, 1980 (Chm., Film Section, 1978–81). Internat. Publishing Cos Critic of the Year, 1972. *Publications:* Robert Mitchum, 1984; A Century of Films, 2001; Family Secrets, 2003. *Recreations:* cricket, tennis, squash, music. *Address:* 28 Avenue Road, Highgate, N6 5DW. *T:* (020) 8348 2013; The Dower House, Hull Place, Sholden, Kent CT14 0AQ. *T:* (01304) 364614. *E:* derekmalcolm32@gmail.com.

**MALCOLM, Dr Graeme Peter Alexander,** OBE 2015; FREng; FRSE; FInstP; Founder and Chief Executive Officer, M-Squared Lasers Ltd, since 2006; *b* Edinburgh, 17 Sept. 1968; *s* of Alexander and Patricia Malcolm; *m* 2002, Kellie Yarranton; three *s* ond. *Educ:* Eastwood High Sch., Glasgow; Univ. of Strathclyde (BSc 1st Cl. Hons Laser Physics and Optoelectronics 1989; PhD Diode-Pumped Solid-State Lasers 1992). FInstP 2016. Man. Dir and Founder, Microlase Optical Systems, 1992–99; Dir, Product Business Mgt, Coherent Inc., 2000–05; Man. Dir, Coherent Scotland, 2000–05. Vis. Prof. and Entrepreneur in Residence, Inst. of Photonics, Univ. of Strathclyde, 2010–. Industrial Mem., Quantum Technol. Flagship Expert Gp, EC; Member: Adv. Bd, Quantum Technologies Special Interest Gp UK; Mkt Opportunities Panel, Quantum Enhanced Imaging Hub, Glasgow Univ.; Translation of DFB Lasers Panel, Quantum Technol. Hub for Sensors and Metrol., Birmingham Univ.; Quantum Engrg Skills Hub, Imperial Coll. London. FRSE 2016; FREng 2017. *Publications:* contrib. jl papers and conf. proc. on subjects relating to photonics. *Recreations:* hill walking, swimming, golf. *Address:* M-Squared, 1 Kelvin Campus, West of Scotland Science Park, Glasgow G20 0SP. *T:* (0141) 945 0500. *E:* graeme.malcolm@m2lasers.com.

**MALCOLM, Helen Katharine Lucy;** QC 2006; a Recorder, since 2005; a Deputy High Court Judge, since 2013; *b* 2 Jan. 1962; *d* of Dugald Malcolm and Patricia Malcolm; *m* 1987; one *s* two *d*. *Educ:* New Coll., Oxford (BA 1983). Called to the Bar, Gray's Inn, 1983, Bencher, 2011. *Recreations:* food, horses, ski-ing. *Address:* 3 Raymond Buildings, Gray's Inn, WC1R 5BH. *T:* (020) 7400 6400. *E:* helen.malcolm@3rblaw.com.

**MALCOLM, James Ian,** OBE 1995; HM Diplomatic Service, retired; travel photographer, including of the Panama Canal; *b* 29 March 1946; *e s* of late William Kenneth Malcolm and Jennie Malcolm (*née* Cooper); *m* 1967, Sheila Nicholson Moore; one *s* one *d*. *Educ:* Royal High Sch., Edinburgh. Joined Foreign Office, 1966; UKDEL NATO, Brussels, 1969–72; Burma, 1972–74; FCO, 1974–77; Commercial Attaché, Kenya, 1977–80; Consul, Syria, 1980–83; Second Sec. (Commercial), Angola, 1983–85; Second, later First, Sec., FCO, 1985–87; First Secretary: (Political/Econ.), Indonesia, 1987–94; FCO, 1994–97; Dep. High Comr, Jamaica, 1997–2001; Ambassador, Panama, 2002–06. Has exhibited as photographer, incl. Edinburgh Fringe Fest. 2010 and contrib. Panama Passages exhibn, Smithsonian Mus., Washington DC, 2009–10; photographer, Panama Maritime Rev., 2007–. Orden de Vasco Nunez de Balboa (Panama), 2007. *Recreations:* riding motorcycles, photography. *Address:* Apartment 6, West Hill House, Frome, Som BA11 3AD. *Club:* Royal Over-Seas League.

**MALCOLM, Sir Noel Robert,** Kt 2014; PhD; FBA 2001; historian; Fellow of All Souls College, Oxford, since 2002; *b* 26 Dec. 1956. *Educ:* Eton; Peterhouse, Cambridge (BA 1978; Hon. Fellow, 2010); Trinity Coll., Cambridge; Gonville and Caius Coll., Cambridge (MA 1981; PhD 1983). Fellow, Gonville and Caius Coll., Cambridge, 1981–83; political columnist, 1987–91, Foreign Editor, 1991–92, The Spectator; political columnist, Daily Telegraph, 1992–95. Vis. Fellow, St Antony's Coll., Oxford, 1995–96; Vis. Lectr, Harvard, 1999; Carlyle Lectr, Oxford, 2001. Chm., Bosnian Inst., 1997–. FRSL 1997. *Publications:* De Dominis 1560–1624, 1984; George Enescu: his life and music, 1990; Sense on Sovereignty, 1991; Bosnia: a short history, 1994; (ed) The Correspondence of Thomas Hobbes, 2 vols, 1994; The Origins of English Nonsense, 1997; Kosovo: a short history, 1998; (jtly) Books on Bosnia: a critical bibliography, 1999; Aspects of Hobbes, 2002; Agents of Empire: knights, corsairs, jesuits and spies in the sixteenth-century Mediterranean world, 2015; Useful Enemies, 2019. *Address:* All Souls College, Oxford OX1 4AL.

**MALCOLM of Poltalloch, Robin Neill Lochnell;** Chief of Clan Malcolm; Vice Lord-Lieutenant of Argyll and Bute, 1996–2001; *b* 11 Feb. 1934; *s* of Lt-Col George Ian Malcolm of Poltalloch, A&SH and Enid Gaskell; *m* 1962, Susan Freeman (*d* 2004); two *s* two *d*; *m* 2010, Patricia Currie (*née* Burness). *Educ:* Eton; North of Scotland Coll. of Agriculture. National Service, 1 Argyll and Sutherland Highlanders, 1952–54; TA service, 8 A&SH, 1954–64. Shipping, and British Iron & Steel Co., 1955–62; farming at Poltalloch, 1963–. Convenor, Highlands and Islands Cttee, NFU, 1972–74; Member: HIDB Consultative Council, 1973–77, 1988–91; Bd, Argyll and Isles Enterprise, 1991–98; Bd, SW Region, Scottish Natural Heritage, 1993–99. Pres., Scottish Agricl Orgn Soc. Ltd, 1983–86. Mem., Argyll and Bute DC, 1976–92. Argyll and Bute: DL, 1974–2004; JP 1976–2004. *Recreations:* shooting, swimming. *Address:* Duntrune Castle, Kilmartin, Argyll PA31 8QQ. *T:* (01546) 510283.

**MALCOMSON, Prof. James Martin,** PhD; FBA 2000; Professor of Economics, University of Oxford, 1999–2013, now Emeritus; Fellow, All Souls College, Oxford, 1999–2013, now Emeritus; *b* 23 June 1946; *s* of E. Watlock Malcomson and Madeline Malcomson (*née* Stuart); *m* 1979, Sally Claire Richards; (one *d* decd). *Educ:* Gonville and Caius Coll., Cambridge (BA, MA); Harvard Univ. (MA, PhD 1973). Res. Fellow in Econs, 1971–72, Lectr 1972–83, Sen. Lectr, 1983–85, Univ. of York; Prof. of Econs, Univ. of Southampton, 1985–98. Vis. Fellow, Université Catholique de Louvain, Belgium, 1983–84. Fellow, Econometric Soc., 2005. *Publications:* (contrib.) Efficiency Wage Models of the Labor Market, 1986; (contrib.) Handbook of Labor Economics, 1999; (contrib.) Handbook of Health Economics, 2000; (contrib.) Handbook of Organizational Economics, 2013; numerous articles in learned jls. *Recreations:* walking, music, film, theatre. *Address:* All Souls College, Oxford OX1 4AL. *T:* (01865) 279379.

**MALCOMSON, Mark,** CBE 2017; Principal, City Literary Institute (City Lit), since 2011; *b* Lagos, Nigeria, 29 Nov. 1963; *s* of John and Sandra Malcomson; one *d* with Tony Traxler. *Educ:* Birkenhead Sch.; Univ. of Edinburgh (LLB); Univ. of Strathclyde (DipLP); Univ. of Kent (MA Internat. Relns). Man. Dir, DC Gardner Trng, 1997–2000; Pres., NY Inst. of Finance, 2000–06; Dir, Exec. Educn, London Business Sch., 2007–11. *Recreations:* American political history, cooking, travel. *Address:* City Lit, 1–10 Keeley Street, Covent Garden, WC2B 4BA. *T:* (020) 7492 2593. *E:* mark.malcomson@citylit.ac.uk.

**MALCOMSON, Thomas Herbert;** HM Diplomatic Service, retired; Vice-President, Board of Directors, British-Peruvian Cultural Association, since 2014 (Executive Director, 2005–14); *b* 9 Oct. 1937; *m* 1st, 1960, Barbara Hetherington (marr. diss. 1985); one *s* two *d*; 2nd, 1986, Blanca Ruiz de Castilla; twin *d*. *Educ:* Univ. of Glasgow. Joined FO, subseq. FCO, 1961; Bangkok, 1963; São Paulo, 1967; FCO, 1971; Colombo, 1972; Consul, Chiang Mai, 1975; FCO, 1978; Dep. High Comr, Brunei, 1981; Acting High Comr, Solomon Is, 1984; Lima, 1985; FCO, 1989; Ambassador to Panama, 1992–96. *Address:* Av. La Floresta 331 apto. 101, Chacarilla, San Borja, Lima 41, Peru.

**MALE, Anthony Hubert, (Tony),** CMG 1997; National Executive Adviser for Languages, Department for Education and Skills (formerly Department for Education and Employment), 2001–02; Director, Central Bureau for Educational Visits and Exchanges, 1986–99, and Secretary, UK Centre for European Education, 1989–99, British Council; *b* 16 March 1939; *s* of Hubert Edward Male and Louise Irene Lavinia (*née* Thomas); *m* 1960, Françoise Andrée Germaine Pinot, LèsL, PGCE; one *s* one *d*. *Educ:* Yeovil Sch.; Exeter Univ. (BA, PGCE); Sorbonne. FCIL (FIL 1990). Housemaster, 1962–74; Head, Comparative Internat. Studies, 1970–74, Tiverton GS; Central Bureau for Educational Visits and Exchanges: Head, Teacher and Sch. Exchange, Europe, 1974–76; Asst Dir, 1976–78; Dep. Dir, 1978–84; Sec., 1984–86. Expert, Eur. Commn, 1977–99; Consultant, Council of Europe, 1982–99. Chm., Langs Nat. Working Gp, 2001. Pres., Fédn Internat. des Organisations de Correspondances et d'Echanges Scolaires (FIOCES), 1986–94. Member: Adv. Panel, Langs Lead Body, 1991–98; Council, Inst. Linguists, 1997–99. Member: Bd of Dirs, Nat. Youth Jazz Orch., 1975–2004 (Hon. Vice-Pres., 2004–18); Jury, Concours Internat. de Guitare, Radio France, 1993–2000; Concours Internat. de Guitare Classique, Barbezieux, France, 2007–09. Trustee, Amer. Field Service, 1981–86; Internat. House, 1989–98; Lefèvre Trust, 1991–93; Technol. Colls Trust, 1996–99. Academic Gov., Richmond Coll., 1990–99. Life FRSA (FRSA 1985). Hon. FCP 1993; Hon. Fellow, Westminster Coll., Oxford, 1999. Hon. Mem., British Council, 1999. Chevalier, 1977, Comdr, 1992, Ordre des Palmes Académiques (France); Chevalier, Ordre National du Mérite (France), 1984; Chevalier, Ordre de Léopold II (Belgium), 1981; Comdr, Orden del Mérito Civil (Spain), 1999. *Publications:* contrib. articles on inter-cultural exchange, modern langs and internat. dimension in education. *Recreations:* music, flamenco and jazz guitar, travel, photography (www.thenomadcamera.com, www.ralphfry.com). *E:* tony.male@orange.fr. *Club:* Travellers.

**MALE, Peter Royston, (Roy),** CBE 2003; Chief Executive, Blackpool, Fylde & Wyre Hospitals NHS Trust, 2002–05; *b* 16 March 1948; *s* of Royston Stanley Male and Patricia Male (*née* Kennedy); *m* 1975, Susan Bootle; one *s*. *Educ:* Nottingham High Sch.; King's Coll. Sch., Wimbledon; St John's Coll., Cambridge (BA 2nd Cl. Hons 1970; MA 1974). MHSM 1974; DipHSM 1974; MIPD 1987. Grad. trainee, NHS, Sheffield Reg., 1970–72; Doncaster Royal Infirmary, 1972–73; Fazakerley Hosp., 1973–75; Dist Personnel Officer, S Sefton, 1975–77; Area Personnel Officer, Norfolk HA, 1977–87; Director: of Personnel and Admin, Liverpool HA, 1987–90; of Personnel, Cambridge HA, 1990–92; Dep. Chief Exec., 1992–98, Chief Exec., 1998–2002, Addenbrooke's NHS Trust. Independent Member: Standards Cttee, Lancs Combined Fire and Rescue Authy, 2005–12; Disciplinary Tribunals, Inst. of Legal Execs, 2005–14; Chm., Probation Bd, Lancs Probation Trust (formerly Nat. Probation Service, Lancs), 2007–14; Dir, Cumbria and Lancs Community Rehabilitation Co., 2014–15. Dir, Probation Assoc. Ltd, 2008–11. *Publications:* papers and contribs to jls. *Recreations:* Rotary, keyboard, gardening.

**MALEK, Ali;** QC 1996; a Deputy High Court Judge, 2008; *b* 19 Jan. 1956; *s* of late Ali Akbar Malek and Irene Elizabeth (*née* Johnson); *m* 1989, Francesca Shoucair; two *d*. *Educ:* Bedford Sch.; Keble Coll., Oxford (MA, BCL). Called to the Bar, Gray's Inn, 1980, Bencher, 2003 (Vice-Treas., 2020); in practice at the Bar, 1980–; Asst Recorder, 1998–2000; Recorder, 2000; Hd of Chambers, 2009–16. Chm., Commercial Bar Assoc., 2007–09. *Publications:* (jtly) Jack: documentary credits, 4th edn, 2009; various articles on banking law. *Recreations:* running, ski-ing, golf, music. *Address:* 3 Verulam Buildings, Gray's Inn, WC1R 5NT. *T:* (020) 7831 8441. *Club:* Vincent's (Oxford).
See also H. M. Malek.

**MALEK, Hodge Mehdi;** QC 1999; a Recorder, since 2005; *b* 11 July 1959; *s* of late Ali Akbar Malek and Irene Elizabeth Malek (*née* Johnson); *m* 1st, 1986, Inez Dies Louise Vegelin van Claerbergen (marr. diss. 2010); two *s* one *d*; 2nd, 2010, Azadeh Malek; one *s* one *d*. *Educ:* Bedford Sch.; Sorbonne, Univ. of Paris; Keble Coll., Oxford (MA 1981; BCL 1982). Called to the Bar, Gray's Inn, 1983 (Birkenhead Schol.; Atkin Schol.; Band Schol.), Bencher, 2004; in practice at the Bar, 1983–. Chm., Competition Appeal Tribunal, 2013–; acting Deemster, IOM, 2017. Member: Supplementary Treasury Panel (Common Law), 1995–99; Bar Disciplinary Tribunal, 2001–11; Inns of Ct Conduct Cttee, 2010–15. *Publications:* Gen. Ed.; Phipson on Evidence, 15th edn, 2nd supp., 2002 to 19th edn, 2018; (contrib.) Atkins Court Forms, 2003, vol. 1, Administrative Court, 2012, 2016, vol. 15, Disclosure and Information Requests, 2014, vol. 19(5), Financial Services, 2014, vol. 21(3), Human Rights, 2014; (with P. B. Matthews): Discovery, 1992; Disclosure, 2001, 5th edn 2017; (contrib.) Information Rights, 2004; The Dābūyid Ispahbads and Early 'Abbāsid Governors of Tabaristān, 2004; Arab-Sanian Numismatics and History during the Early Islamic Period in Iran and Iraq, 2019; articles on law and history. *Recreations:* swimming, ski-ing, history. *Address:* 3 Verulam Buildings, Gray's Inn, WC1R 5NT. *T:* (020) 7831 8441.
See also A. Malek.

**MALES, Rt Hon. Sir Stephen Martin,** Kt 2012; PC 2019; **Rt Hon. Lord Justice Males;** a Lord Justice of Appeal, since 2019; *b* 24 Nov. 1955; *s* of Dennis Albert Males and Mary Winifred Males (*née* Bates); *m* 1982, Daphne Clytie Baker; three *s*. *Educ:* Skinners' Sch.; St John's Coll., Cambridge (MA). Called to the Bar, Middle Temple, 1978, Bencher, 2007; QC 1998; Asst Recorder, 1999–2000; Recorder, 2000–12; Deputy High Court Judge, 2008–12; a Judge of the High Ct of Justice, QBD, 2012–18; a Presiding Judge, NE Circuit, 2015–18. Lay Canon, Rochester Cathedral, 2008–. *Address:* Royal Courts of Justice, Strand, WC2A 2LL.

**MALET, Sir Harry (Douglas St Lo),** 9th Bt *cr* 1791, of Wilbury, Wiltshire; JP; farmer, Australia and England; *b* 26 Oct. 1936; *o s* of Col Sir Edward William St Lo Malet, 8th Bt, OBE and Baroness Benedicta von Maasburg (*d* 1979); S father, 1990; *m* 1967, Julia Gresley, *d* of Charles Harper, Perth, WA; one *s*. *Educ:* Downside; Trinity Coll., Oxford (BA Eng. Lit.). Lt QRIH, 1958–61. JP W Somerset, 1982. *Recreation:* equestrian sports. *Heir: s* Charles Edward St Lo Malet [*b* 30 Aug. 1970; *m* 1997, Rachel, *d* of T. P. S. Cane; four *d*]. *Address:* Wrestwood, RMB 184, Boyup Brook, WA 6244, Australia. *Club:* Weld (Perth).

**MALHADO, Noël;** *see* Harwerth, N.

**MALHI, Prof. Yadvinder Singh,** PhD; FRS 2017; Professor of Ecosystem Science, University of Oxford, since 2008; Jackson Senior Research Fellow, Oriel College, Oxford, since 2005; *b* 1968; *s* of Jagat Singh Malhi and Gurdeep Kaur Malhi; *m* 2002, Dr Rachel Barbara Hinton; one *s* one *d*. *Educ:* Southend High Sch. for Boys; Queens' Coll., Cambridge (BA Natural Scis 1990); Univ. of Reading (PhD Meteorol. 1993). Envmtl Scis Ed., Nature, 1994; University of Edinburgh: Postdoctoral Res. Associate, 1995–98; Royal Soc. Univ. Res. Fellow, 1998–2005; University of Oxford: Univ. Lectr, 2005–07; Reader in Terrestrial Ecol., 2007–08. Dir, Oxford Centre for Tropical Forests, 2008–. Patrons' Medal, RGS, 2018. *Publications:* Tropical Forests and Global Atmospheric Change, 2004; numerous articles in jls such as Science, Nature, Philosophical Trans. of Royal Soc. *Recreations:* exploring extraordinary places, finding the extraordinary in the everyday. *Address:* Environmental Change Institute, School of Geography and Environment, University of Oxford, South Parks Road, Oxford OX1 3QY. *T:* (01865) 285188. *E:* yadvinder.malhi@ouce.ox.ac.uk.

**MALHOTRA, Seema**; MP (Lab and Co-op) Feltham and Heston, since Dec. 2011; *b* Hammersmith, London, 7 Aug. 1972; *d* of late Sushil Kumar Malhotra and of Usha Malhotra; *m* 2005, Sushil Saluja. *Educ*: Green Sch., Isleworth; Univ. of Warwick (BA Hons Politics and Philosophy 1994; MBA with Dist. 2016); Univ. of Massachusetts (Schol.); Aston Univ. (MSc Business IT 1995). Mgt Consultant, Accenture, 1995–2003; Sen. Manager, PricewaterhouseCoopers, 2003–07; Advisor: to Minister for W Midlands, 2007–09; to Chair, Council of Regl Ministers, 2008–09; to video games industry on child safety agenda, 2008; Prog. Leader, cross-govt prog. to increase diversity in public appts, 2009–10; Pol Advr to Actg Leader of Opposition, 2010; Strategic Prog. Advr, UK Interactive Entertainment Assoc., 2011. Shadow Minister for Home Office, 2015; Shadow Chief Sec. to Treasury, 2015–16. Member: Justice Select Cttee, 2012–13; Commons Reference Gp on Representation and Inclusion, 2016–; Cttee on Exiting the EU, 2016–; Constitutional Reform Steering Gp, 2018–; Chair: All Pty Parly Gp on Assistive Technol., 2017–; All Pty Parly Gp on Entrepreneurship, 2018–. Comr, Financial Inclusion Commn, 2018–. Chair, Young Fabians, 1999–2000; Fabian Society: Exec. Mem., 2000–; Chair, 2005–06; Founder and Dir, 2005–12, Pres., 2012–, Fabian Women's Network. Fellow, British American Project, 2007. FRSA. *Publications*: (contrib.) Dictionary of Labour Biography, 2001; (contrib.) From the Workhouse to Welfare, 2009. *Recreations*: running, cinema, music, gardening, playing the guitar. *Address*: House of Commons, SW1A 0AA. *T*: (020) 7219 8957. *E*: seema.malhotra.mp@parliament.uk.

**MALIK, Adeeba**, CBE 2015 (MBE 2004); Deputy Chief Executive, QED-UK, since 2002; *b* Bradford, 30 Sept. 1966; *d* of Mohammed Sadiq Malik and Fahmeeda Begum Malik. *Educ*: Grange Sch., Bradford; Humberside Poly. (BEd Hons 1990); Open Univ. Joined QED-UK, 1992. Non-executive Director: Yorkshire Forward, 1998–2004; British Waterways, 2001–04; Nat. Clin. Assessment Authy, 2001–05; Mem., 2000–04, Chair, 2005–07, Ethnic Minority Business Forum; Co Chair, Ethnic Minority Business Task Force, 2007–08; Member: Women and Work Commn, 2004–06; Adv. Bd on Naturalisation and Immigration, Home Office, 2004–08; Nat. Women Muslim Adv. Gp, 2007–10. Gov., Sheffield Hallam Univ., 2011–13. *Recreations*: cinema, music, theatre, family and friends. *T*: 07976 658268. *E*: a.malik@qed-uk.org.

**MALIK, Khalid Taj**; a District Judge, North Eastern Circuit, since 2013; *b* 29 Dec. 1958; *s* of Taj Ahmed Malik and Anwari Begum Malik; *m* 1986, Ruby Shabnam Khalid Malik; three *s* one *d*. *Educ*: Wyndham Primary Sch.; Kenton Comp. Sch., Newcastle upon Tyne; Univ. of Hull (BSc Hons Econs and Accountancy 1980); Newcastle upon Tyne Poly. (Law Soc. finals 1991). Family clothing business, 1980–91; admitted solicitor, 1993; Goldwaters Solicitors, Newcastle upon Tyne, 1991–2006; Dep. Dist Judge, Northern Circuit, 2003–06; District Judge, Principal Registry, Family Div., 2006–13. *Address*: Newcastle upon Tyne Combined Court Centre, The Law Courts, The Quayside, Newcastle upon Tyne NE1 3LA.

**MALIK, Moazzam**, CMG 2019; HM Diplomatic Service; Ambassador to Indonesia (and concurrently to Association of South East Nations and to East Timor), 2014–19; *b* London, 29 May 1967; *s* of Mohammed Amin Malik and Shamim Malik; *m* 1993, Rachel Richardson; one *s* two *d*. *Educ*: London Sch. of Econs (BSc (Econ) Internat. Trade and Develt); Hertford Coll., Oxford (MSc Develt Econs). Chartered Dip., Accounting and Finance, 1996. Advr, Central Bank of Uganda, 1991–94; Consultant, African Develt Bank and EC, 1994; Consultant Economist, London Economics Ltd, 1994–96; Dir, Global Trade Centre, 1996–97; Team Leader, Internat. Econ. Policy Dept, DFID, 1997–99; Man. Dir, Autumn Engrg Ltd, 1999–2001; Department for International Development: Pakistan Prog. Manager, Western Asia Dept, 2001–03; Hd of Dept, Iraq Humanitarian Response, 2003; Principal Private Sec. to Sec. of State, 2003–05; Hd, White Paper Team on Internat. Develt (Eliminating World Poverty), 2005–06; Hd, Dept of Conflict, Humanitarian and Security Affairs, 2006–07; Dir, UN, Conflict and Humanitarian Div., 2007–10; Western Asia and Stabilisation, 2010–13; Acting Dir, Gen. Western Asia, Middle East, Conflict and Humanitarian, 2013–14. *Recreations*: Liverpool FC, cricket (follows Pakistan highs and (many) lows), cooking and eating Asian foods, music, cinema, reading novels and theatre, hacking around municipal golf course, walking around London, holidaying in Scotland. *Address*: c/o Foreign and Commonwealth Office, King Charles Street, SW1A 2AH.

**MALIK, Shahid**; *b* 24 Nov. 1967; *s* of Rafique Malik. *Educ*: London Poly.; Univ. of Durham (BA 1991). E Lancs TEC; Hd of Policy and Develt, Gtr Nottingham TEC; Chief Exec., PMC Gp; Gen. Manager, KYP Ltd; Chief Executive: Haringey Regeneration Agency, 1997–2001; Inclusive Futures. Vice-Chm., UNESCO UK, 1999–2003. Mem., CRE, 1998–2002; Equality Comr for NI, 1999–2002. MP (Lab) Dewsbury, 2005–10; contested (Lab) same seat, 2010. Parliamentary Under-Secretary of State: DFID, 2007–08; MoJ and Home Office, 2008–09; DCLG, 2009–10. Mem., Lab Party NEC, 2004–05. Chm., World Congress of Muslim Philanthropists, 2011–. Chm. of Govs, Caribbean Develt Bank, 2007–08; Governor: Asian Develt Bank, 2007–08; Inter-American Develt Bank, 2007–08.

**MALIM, Prof. Michael Henry**, DPhil; FRS 2007; Professor of Infectious Diseases, since 2001, and Head, School of Immunology and Microbial Sciences, since 2017, King's College London; *b* 4 July 1963; *s* of Anthony and Joan Malim; *m* 1990, Prof. Rebecca J. Oakey; one *s* one *d*. *Educ*: Bristol Univ. (BSc Biochem.); Oxford Univ. (DPhil Biochem. 1987). University of Pennsylvania School of Medicine: Asst Prof., Depts of Microbiol. and Medicine, 1992–98, Associate Prof. (with tenure), 1998–2001; Hd, Dept of Infectious Diseases, 2001–17, Hd, Div. of Immunol., Infection and Inflammatory Disease, 2013–17, KCL. Reported discovery of human anti-HIV gene, APOBEC3G, 2002. Mem., EMBO, 2005. FMedSci 2003; Fellow, Amer. Acad. Microbiol., 2005; FKC 2013. Elizabeth Glaser Scientist, Elizabeth Glaser Pediatric AIDS Foundn, 2001; M. Jeang Retrovirology Prize, 2010. *Publications*: articles and reviews on molecular pathogenesis of HIV/AIDS. *Recreations*: parenting, cuisine, achievable DIY, post-varsity golf, cycling, hiking, bridge. *Address*: c/o Department of Infectious Diseases, King's College London, 2nd Floor, Borough Wing, Guy's Hospital, London Bridge, SE1 9RT. *T*: (020) 7848 9606, 07593 047008. *E*: michael.malim@kcl.ac.uk. *Club*: Oxford and Cambridge Golf Society.

**MALIN, Dr Stuart Robert Charles**; Professor of Geophysics, Bosphorus University, Istanbul, 1994–2001; *b* 28 Sept. 1936; *s* of late Cecil Henry Malin and Eleanor Mary Malin (*née* Howe); *m* 1st, 1963, Irene Saunders (*d* 1997); two *d*; 2nd, 2001, Lindsey Jean Macfarlane. *Educ*: Royal Grammar Sch., High Wycombe; King's College, London (BSc 1958); PhD 1972, DSc 1981, London. FInstP 1971; CPhys 1985; FRAS 1961 (Mem. Council, 1975–78). Royal Greenwich Observatory, Herstmonceux: Asst Exptl Officer, 1958; Scientific Officer, 1961; Sen. Scientific Officer, 1965; Institute of Geological Sciences, Herstmonceux and Edinburgh: PSO, 1970; SPSO (individual merit), 1976, Hd of Geomagnetism Unit, 1981; Hd of Astronomy and Navigation, Nat. Maritime Museum, 1982; Maths teacher: Dulwich Coll., 1988–91, 1992–94; Haberdashers' Aske's Hatcham Coll., 1991–92. Cape Observer, Radcliffe Observatory, Pretoria, 1963–65; Vis. Scientist, Nat. Center for Atmospheric Res., Boulder, Colorado, 1969; Green Schol., Scripps Instn of Oceanography, La Jolla, 1981. Visiting Professor: Dept of Physics and Astronomy, UCL, 1983–2001; Univ. of Cairo, 1996–2002. Consultant, Rahmi M. Koç Müzesi, Istanbul, 1995–2001. Pres., Jun. Astronomical Soc., 1989–91. Associate Editor, Qly Jl, RAS, 1987–92; Editor, Geophysical Jl Internat., 1996–2004. Freeman, City of London, 2003; Liveryman, Clockmakers' Co., 2006– (Freeman, 2003). *Artefacts constructed*: Solar-sidereal mantle clock, 2009; Combined Edo-time and Western-time clock, 2015; Ptolemaic orrery, 2016; Copernican orrery - The Solar System in a Salad Bowl, 2019. *Publications*: (with Carole Stott) The Greenwich Meridian, 1984; Spaceworks, 1985; The Greenwich Guide to the Planets, 1987; The Greenwich Guide to Stars, Galaxies and Nebulae, 1989; The Story of the Earth, 1991; (with Rahmi M. Koç) Rahmi M. Koç Müzesi Tanıtımı, 1997; The Farnol Companion, 2006; In Remembrance of Me, 2013; over 150 contribs to scientific and horological jls. *Recreations*: Jeffery Farnol novels, clocks. *Address*: 30 Wemyss Road, Blackheath, SE3 0TG. *T*: (020) 8318 3712.

**MALINS, Humfrey Jonathan**, CBE 1997; lawyer and consultant; a Recorder, since 1996; *b* 31 July 1945; *s* of late Rev. Peter Malins and Lilian Joan Malins; *m* 1979, Lynda Ann; one *s* one *d*. *Educ*: St John's Sch., Leatherhead; Brasenose Coll., Oxford (MA Hons Law). College of Law, Guildford, 1967; joined Tuck and Mann, Solicitors, Dorking, 1967, qual. as solicitor, 1971; Partner, Tuck and Mann, 1973; an Asst Recorder, 1991–96; Actg Dist Judge (formerly Actg Met. Stipendiary Magistrate), 1992–2015. Councillor, Mole Valley DC, Surrey, 1973–83 (Chm., Housing Cttee, 1980–81). Contested (C): Toxteth Division of Liverpool, Feb. and Oct. 1974; E Lewisham, 1979. MP (C) Croydon NW, 1983–92; contested (C) same seat, 1992; MP (C) Woking, 1997–2010. PPS to Minister of State, Home Office, 1987–89, to Minister of State, DoH, 1989–92; Opposition front bench spokesman on home affairs, 2001–05. Chm. of Trustees, Immigration Adv. Service, 1993–96. *Recreations*: Rugby football, golf, gardening, soup making. *Clubs*: Vincent's (Oxford); Richmond Rugby Football; Walton Heath Golf.
*See also* J. H. Malins.

**MALINS, Julian Henry**; QC 1991; a Recorder, since 2000; *b* 1 May 1950; *s* of late Rev. Peter Malins and (Lilian) Joan Malins; *m* 1972, Joanna Pearce (marr. diss. 2010); three *d*. *Educ*: St John's School, Leatherhead; Brasenose College, Oxford (Boxing Blue; MA). Called to the Bar, Middle Temple, 1972, Bencher, 1996; Member of the Bar: BVI; Cayman Islands; Hd, Malins Chambers. Mem., Court of Common Council, City of London, 1981–2013 (Alderman, 2013–17). Gov., Mus. of London, 1998–2017. *Publications*: The Serpent's Head, 2012. *Recreations*: fishing, walking, conversation. *Address*: 115 Temple Chambers, Temple Avenue, EC4Y 0DA. *T*: 07917 863271. *Club*: Vincent's (Oxford).
*See also* H. J. Malins.

**MALINS, Penelope, (Mrs John Malins)**; *see* Hobhouse, P.

**MALIPHANT, Russell Scott**; Artistic Director and Choreographer, Russell Maliphant Company, since 1996; Associate Artist, Sadler's Wells Theatre, since 2005; *b* Ottawa, 18 Nov. 1961; *m* 2001, Diana Fouras; one *s* two *d*. *Educ*: Royal Ballet Sch. (Upper); Rolfing Structural Integration (Bodywork Practice) (Practitioner Cert. 1994). ARAD 1980. Dancer with Sadler's Wells, Royal Ballet and ind. ballet cos. *Works created* include: Torsion, 2003; (jtly) Critics' Choice, 2003; Critical Mass, 2003; Broken Fall, 2003; Push, 2005; Solo, 2005; Two, 2005; Rise and Fall, 2006; Eonnagata, 2009; Afterlight, 2009; The Rodin Project, 2012; Fallen, 2013; Still/Current, 2013; (jtly) Second Breath, 2014; Here and After, 2015; (jtly) Conceal I Reveal, 2015; Silent Echo, 2016; maliphantworks2, 2018; (jtly) The Thread, 2019; Silent Lines, 2019. Arts Council Fellowship, 2000. Hon. DA Plymouth, 2011. Time Out Live Award for Outstanding Collaboration, 2003; South Bank Show Award for Dance, 2003; Nat. Dance Award for Best Choreography (Modern), Critics' Circle, 2006.

**MALJERS, Floris Anton**, Hon. KBE 1992; Chairman, Unilever NV, and Vice Chairman, Unilever PLC, 1984–94; *b* 12 Aug. 1933; *s* of A. C. J. Maljers and L. M. Maljers-Kole; *m* 1958, J. H. Maljers-de Jongh; two *s* (one *d* decd). *Educ*: Univ. of Amsterdam. Joined Unilever, 1959; various jobs in the Netherlands until 1965; Man. Dir, Unilever-Colombia, 1965–67; Man. Dir, Unilever-Turkey, 1967–70; Chairman, Van den Bergh & Jurgens, Netherlands, 1970–74; Co-ordinator of Man. Group, edible fats and dairy, and Dir of Unilever NV and Unilever PLC, 1974–94. Member: Unilever's Special Committee, 1982–94; Supervisory Bd, KLM Royal Dutch Airlines, 1991–2004 (Vice Chm., 1994; Chm., 2000); Supervisory Bd, Philips Electronics NV, 1993–99 (Chm., 1994); Supervisory Bd, Vendex NV, subseq. Vendex-KBB NV, 1996 (Vice Chm., 1998; Chm., 2000–02); Bd, Rand Europe, 1999–2003; Director: Guinness plc, 1994–98; Amoco Petroleum, Chicago, 1994–98; BP (formerly BP Amoco), 1998–2004; Diageo plc, 1998; Air France-KLM, 2004–10. Gov., Eur. Policy Forum, 1993–. Prof. of Mgt, 1994–2004, Chm., Supervisory Bd, Sch. of Mgt, 1999–2010, Erasmus Univ., Rotterdam. Chm., Concertgebouw, 1987–2003; Mem. Bd, Nat. Mus. of Archaeology, 1993–2004. Chairman: Bd of Trustees, Utrecht Univ. Hosp., 1994–2003; Turkije Inst. of the Netherlands, 2008–13.

**MÄLK, Raul**; Special Diplomatic Representative (formerly Envoy) for the Baltic Sea Region, since 2011; *b* 14 May 1952; *s* of Linda and August Mälk. *Educ*: Tartu State Univ. Res. Fellow, Inst. of Economy, Acad. of Scis, 1975–77; freelance editor, subseq. Editor in Chief, Estonian Radio, 1977–90; Dep. Head and Counsellor, Office of President of Supreme Council, 1990–92; Ministry of Foreign Affairs, Tallinn: Counsellor, 1992–93; Chief of Minister's Office, 1993–94; Dep. Permanent Under Sec. (political affairs, press and inf.), 1994–96; Ambassador to UK, 1996–2001, also (non-resident) to Republic of Ireland, 1996–2003; Minister of Foreign Affairs, Estonia, 1998–99; Ambassador to Portugal (non-resident), 2000–03; Ministry of Foreign Affairs: Dir Gen., Policy Planning Dept, 2001–07; Actg Dep. Perm. Under-Sec. (EU Affairs), 2003–04, 2005–06; Perm. Rep. of Estonia to EU, 2007–11. *Publications*: numerous articles in Estonian newspapers; material for Estonian radio and television broadcasts, incl. comment on internat. and home news, and parly reports. *Recreations*: theatre, music, attending sports events (football, basketball, track and field). *Address*: Ministry of Foreign Affairs, Islandi Väljak 1, 15049 Tallinn, Estonia.

**MÄLKKI, Susanna Ulla Marjukka**; Chief Conductor, Helsinki Philharmonic Orchestra, since 2016; *b* Helsinki, 13 March 1969; *d* of Pentti Mälkki and Liisa Mälkki. *Educ*: Edsberg Inst. of Music (Soloist Dip. 1993); Royal Acad. of Music (Dip. RAM 1994); Sibelius Acad., Helsinki (MA Music (Cello and Conducting) 2000). Principal Cellist, Gothenburg Symphony Orch., 1995–98; Artistic Dir, Stavanger Symphony Orch., 2002–05; Music Dir, Ensemble Intercontemporain, 2006–13; Principal Guest Conductor: Gulbenkian Orch., 2013–17; LA Philharmonic Orch., 2017–. Mem., Royal Swedish Acad. of Music, 2008; FRAM 2010. Pro Finlandia Medal, Order of the Lion of Finland, 2011. Chevalier, Légion d'Honneur (France), 2016. Conductor of Year, Musical America, 2017; Music Prize, Nordic Council, 2017. *Address*: c/o HarrisonParrott Ltd, The Ark, 201 Talgarth Road, W6 8BJ. *T*: (020) 7229 9166. *E*: info@harrisonparrott.co.uk.

**MALKOVICH, John Gavin**; actor and director; *b* Christopher, Ill, 9 Dec. 1953; *s* of late Dan Malkovich and of Joe Anne Malkovich; *m* 1982, Glenne Headley (marr. diss.); partner, Nicoletta Peyran; one *s* one *d*. *Educ*: Eastern Illinois Univ.; Illinois State Univ. Founding Mem., Steppenwolf Theatre Ensemble, Chicago 1976. Theatre includes: True West, 1982; Death of a Salesman, 1984; Burn This, 1987 (transf. London, 1990); Slip of the Tongue, 1992 (transf. London, 1992); Libra, 1994; The Libertine, 1996; The Infernal Comedy, Barbican, 2011; Bitter Wheat, 2019; *director*: Balm in Gilead, 1980, 1984; Coyote Ugly, 1985; Arms and the Man, 1985; The Caretaker, 1986; A Celebration of Harold

Pinter, 2011; Good Canary, 2016. *Films include:* The Killing Fields, Places in the Heart, 1984; Eleni, 1985; Making Mr Right, The Glass Menagerie, 1987; Empire of the Sun, Miles from Home, 1988; Dangerous Liaisons, Jane, La Putaine du Roi, 1989; The Sheltering Sky, 1990; Queen's Logic, The Object of Beauty, 1991; Of Mice and Men, 1992; Shadows and Fog, In the Line of Fire, 1993; Jennifer Eight, Alive, 1994; Beyond the Clouds, The Ogre, 1995; Mary Reilly, Mulholland Falls, 1996; Portrait of a Lady, Con Air, 1997; The Man in the Iron Mask, Rounders, 1998; Time Regained, Ladies Room, Joan of Arc, 1999; Being John Malkovich, 2000; Shadow of the Vampire, Je Rentre à la Maison, 2001; Ripley's Game, 2003; The Hitchhiker's Guide to the Galaxy, The Libertine, 2005; Eragon, 2006; Beowulf, 2007; L'Echange, Burn After Reading, Mutant Chronicles, 2008; Red, Secretariat, 2010; Transformers: Dark of the Moon, 2011; Warm Bodies, Red 2, 2013; Deepwater Horizon, 2016; Extremely Wicked, Shockingly Evil and Vile, 2019; *producer:* The Accidental Tourist, 1988; Somewhere Else, Ghost World, 2000; The Gun Seller, Found in the Street, 2001; *director:* The Dancer Upstairs, 2002. *Television:* actor, The ABC Murders, 2018. *Address:* c/o Finch & Partners, 47–48 Piccadilly, W1J 0DT.

**MALLABER, (Clare) Judith;** *b* 10 July 1951; *d* of late Kenneth Mallaber and Margaret Joyce Mallaber. *Educ:* N London Collegiate Sch.; St Anne's Coll., Oxford (BA Hons). Res. Officer, NUPE, 1975–85; Local Govt Information Unit, 1985–96 (Dir, 1987–95). MP (Lab) Amber Valley, 1997–2010; contested (Lab) same seat, 2010. Mem., Select Cttee on Educn and Employment, 1997–2001. Mem. Adv. Council, Northern Coll., Barnsley, 1995–.

**MALLABY, Sir Christopher (Leslie George),** GCMG 1996 (KCMG 1988; CMG 1982); GCVO 1992; HM Diplomatic Service, retired; *b* 7 July 1936; *s* of late Maj. Gen. Aubertin Walter Sothern Mallaby, CIE, OBE, and Margaret Catherine Mallaby (*née* Jones); *m* 1961, Pascale Françoise Thierry-Mieg; one *s* three *d*. *Educ:* Eton; King's Coll., Cambridge. British Delegn to UN Gen. Assembly, 1960; 3rd Sec., British Embassy, Moscow, 1961–63; 2nd Sec., FO, 1963–66; 1st Sec., Berlin, 1966–69; 1st Sec., FCO, 1969–71; Harvard Business Sch., 1971; Dep. Dir, British Trade Develt Office, NY, 1971–74; Counsellor and Head of Chancery, Moscow, 1975–77; Head of Arms Control and Disarmament Dept, FCO, 1977–79, Head of East European and Soviet Dept, 1979–80, Head of Planning Staff, 1980–82, FCO; Minister, Bonn, 1982–85; Dep. Sec., Cabinet Office, 1985–88; Ambassador to Germany, 1988–92; Ambassador to France, 1993–96. Man. Dir, Warburg Dillon Read, subseq. UBS Warburg, then UBS Investment Bank, 2000–06 (Adviser, 1996–2000 and 2006–10); Adviser to: RMC, 1996–2000; Herbert Smith, 1997–2001; Louis Dreyfus Group, 1998–2003; Mem. Supervisory Bd, Vodafone (formerly Mannesmann) AG, 2000–10; non-executive Director: Sun Life and Provincial Hldgs plc, 1996–2000; Charter Pan-European (formerly European) Investment Trust, 1996–2007. Founder, 1995 and Chm., 2001–08, Entente Cordiale Scholarships (Trustee, 1996–2001). Trustee: Tate Gall., 1996–2002; Thomson-Reuters (formerly Reuters), 1998–2013. Chairman: Primary Immunodeficiency Assoc., 1996–2002, and 2005–06; Adv. Bd, GB Centre, Humboldt Univ., Berlin, 1997–2005 (Hon. Fellow, 2005); Adv. Bd, German Studies Inst., Birmingham Univ., 1998–2005; Somerset House Trust, 2002–06; Adv. Bd, 20/21 British Art Fair, 2011–; Charitable Trust (formerly Foundn) of EORTC, 2001–13 (Hon. Vice Pres., 2013–). Chancellor, Order of St Michael and St George, 2004–11. Hon. LLD Birmingham, 2004. Grand Cross, Order of Merit (Germany), 1992; Grand Officier, Légion d'Honneur (France), 1996; Comdr, Ordre des Palmes Académiques (France), 2004. *Publications:* Living the Cold War: memoirs of a British diplomat, 2017. *Recreation:* grandchildren. *Address:* 112 Ashley Gardens, Thirleby Road, SW1P 1HJ. E: mallabychristopher@gmail.com. *Clubs:* Brooks's, Beefsteak, Grillions.

**MALLALIEU,** Baroness *cr* 1991 (Life Peer), of Studdridge in the County of Buckinghamshire; **Ann Mallalieu;** QC 1988; *b* 27 Nov. 1945; *d* of Sir (Joseph Percival) William Mallalieu and Lady Mallalieu; *m* 1979, Timothy Felix Harold Cassel (marr. diss. 2007) (*see* Sir T. F. H. Cassel, Bt); two *d*. *Educ:* Holton Park Girls' Grammar Sch., Wheatley, Oxon; Newnham Coll., Cambridge (MA, LLM; Hon. Fellow, 1992). (First woman) Pres., Cambridge Union Soc., 1967. Called to the Bar, Inner Temple, 1970, Bencher, 1992; a Recorder, 1985–93. Mem., Gen. Council of the Bar, 1973–75. Opposition spokesman on home affairs and on legal affairs, H of L, 1992–97. Chm., Ind. Council of the Ombudsman for Corporate Estate Agents, 1993–2000; Ind. Mem., British Horseracing Bd, 2004–07. Pres., Countryside Alliance, 1998–. Chm., Suzy Lamplugh Trust, 1997–2000. Pres., Horse Trust, 2010–; Trustee: Racing Welfare, 2010–18; Nat. Assoc. of Stable Staff, 2010–18. *Recreations:* sheep, fishing, hunting, poetry, horseracing. *Address:* House of Lords, SW1A 0PW. *T:* (020) 7219 3000.

**MALLALIEU, Angela Maria;** *see* Brady, A. M.

**MALLET, John Valentine Granville,** FSA; FRSA; Keeper, Department of Ceramics, Victoria and Albert Museum, 1976–89; *b* 15 Sept. 1930; *s* of late Sir Victor Mallet, GCMG, CVO, and Lady Mallet (*née* Andreae); *m* 1st, 1958, Felicity Ann Basset (*d* 2013); one *s*; 2nd, 2016, Diana Lee, *d* of late Robert Emery Edwards and *widow* of Judge Francis D. Murnaghan, Jr. *Educ:* Winchester Coll.; Balliol Coll., Oxford (BA Modern History; Hon. Fellow, 1992). Mil. service in Army: commnd; held temp. rank of full Lieut in Intell. Corps, 1949–50. Messrs Sotheby & Co., London, 1955–62; Victoria and Albert Museum: Asst Keeper, Dept of Ceramics, 1962; Sec. to Adv. Council, 1967–73. Ind. Mem., Design Selection Cttee, Design Council, 1981–89; Member: Exec. Cttee, Nat. Art Collections Fund, 1989–2005; Art Adv. Cttee, Nat. Mus. of Wales, Cardiff, 1991–94; Wissenschaftlicher Beirat, Ceramica-Stiftung, Basel, 1990–; Arts Adv. Panel, Nat. Trust, 1996–2005; Pres., English Ceramic Circle, 1999–2009. Mem., Court of Assistants, Fishmongers' Co., 1970– (Prime Warden, 1983–84). *Publications:* (with F. Dreier) The Hockemeyer Collection: maiolica and glass, 1998; Xanto: pottery-painter, poet, man of the Italian Renaissance (catalogue), 2007 (Art Newspaper/AXA Prize, UK and Eire); (contrib.) Going for a Song, ed Bevis Hillier, 2014; articles on ceramics in Burlington Magazine, Apollo, Trans English Ceramic Circle, and Faenza; poems in Magma, P. N. Rev. and other literary magazines. *Address:* 48 Fitzjames Avenue, W14 0RR.

**MALLETT, Dr Anna Celia;** Chief Executive Officer, ITN, since 2019; *b* Farnborough, Kent, 22 June 1974; *d* of David Mallett and late Margaret Mallett; *m* 2005, Owen Wilson; three *s*. *Educ:* Holy Trinity Convent, Bromley; Eltham Coll.; Durham Univ. (BA 1st Cl. Hons Geog. 1995); Hertford Coll., Oxford (PhD 1998); Harvard Business Sch. (MBA 2003). Project Leader, Boston Consulting Gp, 1998–2006; BBC: Controller, Business Strategy, 2006–12; CEO, Studios and Post Prodn, 2012–14; Chief Operating Officer, Studios Prodn, 2014–18; Chief Operating Officer and Man. Dir, Prodn, BBC Studios, 2018–19. *Recreations:* theatre, television, tennis. *Address:* ITN, 200 Gray's Inn Road, WC1X 8XZ. *Clubs:* Soho House; Sheen Tennis.

**MALLETT, Sarah Jane Victoria;** Her Honour Judge Mallett; a Circuit Judge, since 2016; *b* Sheffield, 27 April 1965; *d* of Michael and Barbara Mallett. *Educ:* Durham Univ. (BA Hons Law). Called to the Bar, Inner Temple, 1988; a Recorder, 2012–16. *Address:* Newcastle Combined Court Centre, Quayside, Newcastle upon Tyne NE1 3LA. *T:* (0191) 201 2000.

**MALLICK, Kamran;** Chief Executive Officer, Disability Rights UK, since 2017; *b* Lahore, Pakistan, 17 Nov. 1972; *s* of Muhammed Saleem Mallick and Rehana Mallick; *m* 2014, Sarah Robinson. *Educ:* Univ. of Hertfordshire (BA Hons Business Studies 2003); Univ. of Westminster (Cisco Certified Network Associate, 2007); Emerging Strategic Leaders Prog., Windsor Leadership. Proj. Develt Officer, Hounslow Social Services, 1994–99; Consultant Dir, Hounslow Bor. Assoc. of Disabled People, 1999–2000; Hd, Trng and IT, Aspire, 2000–04; CEO, Action on Disability, 2004–17. Ind. IT trainer, 1995–2002. Mem., Ind. Disability Adv. Gp, TfL, 2015–18. Trustee, Lyric Hammersmith, 2017–. *Recreations:* all things retro: analogue over digital sound, classic cars over modern and retro games over modern generation, mentoring young disabled leaders. *Address:* Disability Rights UK, Here East, Queen Elizabeth Olympic Park, Stratford, E20 3BS. *T:* 0330 995 0400. *E:* kamran.mallick@disabilityrightsuk.org.

**MALLICK, Sir Netar (Prakash),** Kt 1998; DL; FRCP, FRCPE; Professor of Renal Medicine, University of Manchester, 1994–2000, now Emeritus; Hon. Consultant in Renal Medicine, Manchester Royal Infirmary, 1970–2000; *b* 3 Aug. 1935; *s* of Bhawani Das Mallick and Shanti Devi Mallick; *m* 1960, Mary Wilcockson; three *d*. *Educ:* Queen Elizabeth's Grammar Sch., Blackburn; Manchester Univ. (BSc Hons 1956; MB ChB 1959; Pres., Students' Union, 1958–59). FRCP 1976; FRCPE 1992. Surgical Res. Fellow, Harvard Univ., 1960; Dept of Medicine, Welsh Nat. Sch. of Medicine, 1963–67; Manchester University: Lectr, 1967–72; Sen. Lectr, 1972–92; Hon. Prof. in Renal Medicine, 1992–94; Physician in Charge, Dept of Renal Medicine, Manchester Royal Infirmary, 1973–94. Medical Director: Central Manchester Healthcare NHS Trust, 1997–2000; Adv. Cttee on Distinction Awards, 1999–2003; Adv. Cttee on Clinical Excellence Awards, 2003–07; Mem., Honours Adv. Cttee on Health, Cabinet Office, 2005–11. Vice Chm., Blackburn, Hyndburn and Ribble Valley HA, 1985–90. Advr on Renal Disease to CMO, 1991–97. President: Renal Assoc., 1988–91; Manchester Med. Soc., 2005–06; Chairman: Renal Provision in London, London Implementation Gp, 1991; European Dialysis and Transplantation Assoc. Registry, 1991–94; Rev. of Provision for Renal Disease in Eng. and Wales, DoH, 1992; Union Européenne des Médecins Spécialistes, 1993–98 (Pres., Bd of Nephrology, 1993–97). Member: Wkg Pty on Haemodialysis Provision in the UK, 1966; Ethics Cttee, European Renal Assoc., 2016–. Pres., Manchester Lit. and Phil. Soc., 1986–88, 2014–16. Patron: Nat. Kidney Fedn, 2000–; Indian Assoc., Manchester, 2003–. Chm. of Trustees, Broughton House Home for Veterans, 2013–. Hon. FRCPI 1999; Hon. FRCSE 2005. DL, 1999, High Sheriff, 2002, Greater Manchester. Medal of Honour, Univ. of Manchester, 2014. *Publications:* (ed) Glucose Polymers in Health and Disease, 1977; Renal Disease in General Practice, 1979; (ed) Williams, Colour Atlas of Renal Diseases, 2nd edn 1993; Advances in Nephrology, 1994; Atlas of Nephrology, 1994; papers on renal disease and health provision in learned jls. *Recreations:* theatre, literature, wine and food, cricket. *Address:* 812, W3 51 Whitworth Street West, Manchester M1 5ED. *T:* (0161) 237 5323. *Clubs:* Athenæum; St James's (Manchester).

**MALLIN, Maxwell James;** QC 2017; *b* Wolverhampton, 29 Nov. 1955; *s* of Matthew Mallin and Norma Mallin; *m* 2001, Fiona; one *s* two *d*. *Educ:* Wolverhampton Grammar Sch.; Sidney Sussex Coll., Cambridge (BA Hons 1978). Bankers Trust Internat., 1980–87; Salomon Bros, 1987–89; called to the Bar, Inner Temple, 1993; in practice as a barrister, 11 Stone Bldgs, 1994–2015, Wilberforce Chambers, 2015–. *Recreations:* family, ski-ing, walking, chess. *Address:* 150 Hemingford Road, Islington, N1 1DE. *T:* (020) 7607 1100. *E:* mmallin@wilberforce.co.uk.

**MALLINCKRODT, Georg Wilhelm von;** *see* von Mallinckrodt.

**MALLINSON, Allan Lawrence;** military historian, novelist and defence commentator; *b* Yorks, 6 Feb. 1949; *s* of Alfred Mallinson and Edith Mallinson; *m* 1976, Susan Anne, *yr d* of Major Ronald Routledge; two *d*. *Educ:* various church and state schs; St Chad's Hostel, Hooton Pagnell; St Chad's Coll., Durham; Mons Officer Cadet Sch.; Royal Military Coll. of Sci., Shrivenham; Italian Higher Defence Inst., Rome. Ordinand, 1966. Commnd King's Own Royal Border Regt, 1969, transf. to 13th/18th Royal Hussars (QMO), 1980; Staff Coll., Camberley, 1981; served NI, Far and Near East, Germany, Italy and MoD; Commanded 13th/18th Royal Hussars, 1988–91; retd as Brigadier, 2004. Trustee: Mus. of 13th/18th Royal Hussars, Cannon Hall, Yorks, 2004–15; Light Dragoons' Charitable Trust, 2005–16; Army Mus Ogilby Trust, 2009– (Chm., Grants Cttee, 2014–). Mem., Res. and Collections Panel, Nat. Army Mus., 2018–. Vice Pres., Victorian Military Soc., 2014–. Kt Comdr, Order of Merit (Italy), 2000. *Publications:* non-*fiction:* Light Dragoons, 1992, 2nd edn 2006; The Making of the British Army, 2009, 2nd edn 2010; 1914 Fight the Good Fight, 2013; Too Important for the Generals, 2016; Fight to the Finish, 2018; *fiction:* Matthew Hervey series: A Close Run Thing, 1999; The Nizam's Daughters, 2000; A Regimental Affair, 2001; A Call to Arms, 2002; The Sabre's Edge, 2003; Rumours of War, 2004; An Act of Courage, 2005; Company of Spears, 2006; Man of War, 2007; Warrior, 2008; On His Majesty's Service, 2011; Words of Command, 2015; The Passage to India, 2018. *Recreations:* music, horses, churches. *Address:* c/o Rogers, Coleridge and White, 20 Powis Mews, W11 1JN. *Clubs:* Cavalry and Guards, Beefsteak.

**MALLINSON, Sir James;** *see* Mallinson, Sir W. J.

**MALLINSON, John Russell;** Speaker's Counsel, House of Commons, 1996–2000; *b* 29 June 1943; *s* of Wilfred and Joyce Helen Mallinson; *m* 1968, Susan Rebecca Jane Godfree; one *s* one *d*. *Educ:* Giggleswick Sch.; Balliol Coll., Oxford (Keasbey Schol. 1963; BA). Solicitor (Hons), 1972. Asst Solicitor, Coward Chance, 1972–74; Sen. Legal Assistant, DTI, 1974–79; Assistant Solicitor: Law Officers' Dept, 1979–81; DTI, 1982–84; Under Sec. (Legal), DTI, 1985–89; Corporation of Lloyd's: Gen. Manager, 1989–92; Solicitor, 1992–95; Mem., Lloyd's Regulatory Bd, 1993–95. *Recreations:* reading, conversation, music, film, looking at paintings. *Address:* 4 Nunappleton Way, Hurst Green, Oxted, Surrey RH8 9AW. *T:* (01883) 714775.

**MALLINSON, Sir (William) James,** 5th Bt *cr* 1935, of Walthamstow; DPhil; Senior Lecturer in Sanskrit and Classical Indian Studies, School of Oriental and Asian Studies, University of London, since 2016 (Lecturer, 2013–16); *b* 22 April 1970; *s* of Sir William John Mallinson, 4th Bt and of Rosalind Angela Mallinson (*née* Hoare, now Fishburn); *S* father, 1995; *m* 2002, Claudia Anstice Wright; two *d*. *Educ:* Eton Coll.; St Peter's Coll., Oxford (BA Sanskrit); SOAS, London Univ. (MA); Balliol Coll., Oxford (DPhil). Translator, Clay Sanskrit Liby, 2002–08; teaching Sanskrit, SOAS, 2009–10; Res. Associate, Oriental Inst., Univ. of Oxford, 2012–14. Chair, Centre of Yoga Studies, SOAS. Principal Investigator, Eur. Res. Council Hatha Yoga Project, 2015–. Films: associate prod., Beginners Guide to Yoga, 2007; prod., dir and presenter, Temples in the Clouds, 2009; presenter, West Meets East, 2013. *Publications:* (trans.) Gheranda Samhita, 2004; (trans.) Emperor of the Sorcerers, vols I and II, 2005; (trans.) Shiva Samhita, 2006; Khecarividya, 2007, vol. II 2009; Roots of Yoga, 2017. *Recreations:* juggling, yoga, paragliding. *Heir:* cousin Jonathan Justin Stuart Mallinson [*b* 5 Feb. 1971; *m* 1st, 1998, Leann Alyson Llewellyn (marr. diss. 2001); 2nd, 2005, Caroline Hazel Whelham; one *s* one *d*].

**MALLOCH BROWN,** family name of **Baron Malloch-Brown.**

**MALLOCH-BROWN**, Baron *cr* 2007 (Life Peer), of St Leonard's Forest in the county of West Sussex; **(George) Mark Malloch Brown**, KCMG 2007; PC 2007; Chairman: Smartmatic, since 2014; SGO Corporation Ltd, since 2014; *b* 16 Sept. 1953; s of George Malloch Brown and Ursula (*née* Pelly); *m* 1989, Patricia Cronan; one *s* three *d*. *Educ*: Magdalene Coll., Cambridge (BA 1st Cl. Hons Hist.; Hon. Fellow, 2005); Univ. of Michigan (MA Political Sci.). Political corresp., Economist, 1977–79; i/c field ops for Cambodian refugees, Thailand, 1979–81, Dep. Chief, Emergency Unit, Geneva, 1981–83, Office of UNHCR; Founder and Ed., Economist Develt Report, 1983–86; Lead Internat. Partner, Sawyer-Miller Gp, 1986–94; World Bank: Dir, Ext. Affairs, 1994–96; Vice-Pres., Ext. Affairs and for UN Affairs, 1996–99; Administrator, UNDP, 1999–2005; Chef de Cabinet to Sec.-Gen., UN, 2005–06; Dep. Sec.-Gen., UN, 2006; Vice-Chm., Soros Fund Mgt, 2007; Minister of State (Minister for Africa, Asia and UN), FCO, 2007–09. Dep. Chm., World Economic Forum, 2009–10; Chm., EMEA, FTI Consulting, 2010–14; Chm., Internat. Crisis Gp, 2012–; Sen. Advr, Eurasia Gp, 2016–. Vis. Fellow, Yale Center for the Study of Globalization, 2007. Chm. Council, Marlborough Coll., 2011–. Hon. DLitt: Michigan State, 2002; Catholic Univ. of Peru, 2003; Pace, NY, 2005; Walden Univ., 2008. *Publications*: The Unfinished Global Revolution: the limits of nations and the pursuit of a new politics, 2011. *Address*: House of Lords, SW1A 0AA.

**MALLON, Marie Elizabeth**; a District Judge (Magistrates' Courts), since 2009; *b* Nuneaton, Warwicks, 13 Nov. 1961; *d* of Matthew Christopher and Mary Geraldine Mallon; *m* 1987, John McCarty; one *d*. *Educ*: University Coll., Cardiff (BSc Econ. Hons); Newcastle Poly. (CPE, Law Soc. Finals). Admitted solicitor, 1992; Partner: Askews, 1992–97; Askews Nixon Mallon, 1997–2004; Brown Beer Nixon Mallon, 2004–09; Dep. Dist Judge (Magistrates' Courts), 2006–09. *Recreations*: family, friends, good food and wine, following Middlesbrough FC, jogging. *Address*: Leeds Magistrates' Court, Westgate, Leeds LS1 3JP. *T*: (0113) 245 9653, *Fax*: (01924) 231146.

**MALLON, Seamus**; Member (SDLP) Newry and Armagh, Northern Ireland Assembly, 1998–2003; *b* 17 Aug. 1936; *s* of Francis P. Mallon and Jane O'Flaherty; *m* 1966, Gertrude Cush; one *d*. *Educ*: St Joseph's Coll. of Educn. Member: NI Assembly, 1973–74 and 1982; NI Convention, 1975–76; Irish Senate, 1981–82; New Ireland Forum, 1983–84; Armagh Dist Council, 1973–86. Dep. First Minister (designate), 1998–99, Dep. First Minister, 1999–2001, NI Assembly. Dep. Leader, SDLP, 1978–2001. MP (SDLP) Newry and Armagh, Jan. 1986–2005. Member: Select Cttee on Agric., 1987–97; Anglo-Irish Inter-Parly Body, 1990–2015. Author of play, Adam's Children, prod. radio, 1968, and stage, 1969. *Recreations*: angling, gardening. *Address*: 5 Castleview Road, Markethill, Armagh BT60 1QP. *T*: (028) 3755 1411.

**MALLUCCI, Prof. Giovanna Rachele**, PhD; FRCP; FMedSci; Van Geest Professor of Clinical Neurosciences, University of Cambridge, since 2014; Associate Director, UK Dementia Research Institute at University of Cambridge, since 2017; Fellow, Churchill College, Cambridge, since 2018; Hon. Consultant Neurologist, Addenbrooke's Hospital, Cambridge, since 2012; *b* London, 29 June 1963; *d* of Livio Mallucci and Una Mallucci (*née* Skelly); *m* 2018, Prof. Robin James Milroy Franklin, *qv*; two *s*. *Educ*: Haberdashers' Aske's Sch. for Girls, Elstree; St Hilda's Coll., Oxford (BA Hons Physiol Scis 1985); University Coll. Hosp. and Middlesex Hosp. Med. Sch., London (MB BS 1988); PhD London 2001. MRCP 1991, FRCP 2012. Clin. trng in gen. medicine and neurol. at London hosps, then Nat. Hosp. for Neurol. and Neurosurgery, Queen Sq., 1989–94; Wellcome Trng Fellow in Neurogenetics, Prion Disease Gp, St Mary's Hosp. Med. Sch., Imperial Coll. London, 1995–2000; Gp Leader and Clinician Scientist, 2000–03, MRC Prog. Leader Track, 2003–08, MRC Prion Unit, Inst. of Neurol., Queen Sq.; Hon. Consultant Neurologist, Nat. Hosp. for Neurol. and Neurosurgery, 2005–12; MRC Prog. leader and Hd, Neurobiol., MRC Toxicology Unit, Leicester, 2008–; Prof. of Neurosci., Univ. of Leicester, 2008–14. FMedSci 2017. *Publications*: (contrib.) Cognitive Neurology and Dementia, 2009; contrib. original res. to scientific jls, incl. Nature, Science, Science Translational Medicine, Neuron, EMBO Jl, Proc. NAS, Brain, Acta Neuropathologica, Nature Reviews Neurosci. *Recreations*: hiking, ski-ing, travel, cooking, music, art. *Address*: UK Dementia Research Institute at University of Cambridge, Island Research Building, Cambridge Biomedical Campus, University of Cambridge, Cambridge CB2 0AH. *T*: (01223) 762043. *E*: gm522@cam.ac.uk.

**MALLYON, Catherine Rowena**; Executive Director, Royal Shakespeare Company, since 2012; *b* Cambridge, 28 Jan. 1962; civil partnership, Susan Foster. *Educ*: Impington Village Coll., Cambs; St John's Coll., Oxford (BA). Administrator and Musician, Big Wheel Th. Co., 1984–85; Arbitrage Trader and Credit Analyst, Charterhouse Bank, 1985–90; trng bursary in arts admin, Arts Council, 1990–91; Gen. Manager, Towngate Th., Basildon, 1991–92; Manager, The Screen at Walton on Thames, 1992–93; General Manager: Oxford Playhouse, 1993–99; Arts and Theatres, Reading BC, 1999–2005; Dep. Chief Exec., Southbank Centre, 2005–12. Member: Bd, Coventry and Warwickshire LEP, 2014–18; Nat. Council, Arts Council England, 2018–; Bd, AHRC, 2018–. *Recreations*: violin playing, walking, running, body-boarding, ski-ing. *Address*: c/o Royal Shakespeare Theatre, Stratford-upon-Avon CV37 6BB.

**MALMESBURY, 7th Earl of**, *cr* 1800; **James Carleton Harris**; DL; Baron 1788; Viscount FitzHarris 1800; *b* 19 June 1946; *o s* of 6th Earl of Malmesbury, TD; *S* father, 2000; *m* 1st, 1969, Sally Ann (marr. diss. 2008), *yr d* of Sir Richard Newton Rycroft, 7th Bt; three *s* two *d*; 2nd, 2013, Sally Ann Clare, *d* of William Bruford. *Educ*: Eton; Queen's Coll., St Andrews (MA). DL Hampshire, 1997. *Heir*: *s* Viscount FitzHarris, *qv*. *Address*: Greywell Hill, Greywell, Hook, Hants RG29 1DG. *T*: (01256) 703565.

**MALMESBURY, Archdeacon of**; see Bryan, Ven. C. P.

**MALMSTRÖM, Cecilia**; Member, European Commission, 2010–19; *b* Sweden; *m*; two *c* (twins). *Educ*: Göteborg Univ. (BA; PhD Pol Sci. 1998). Psychiatric nurse, Lillhagen Hosp., Göteborg; social studies teacher, Lindholmen adult secondary educn service, 1991–92; Res. Asst, 1994–98, Sen. Lectr, 1998–99, Dept of Political Sci., Göteborg Univ.; MEP, 1999–2006; Minister for EU Affairs, Sweden, 2006–10. Mem., Västra Götaland Regl Assembly, 1998–2001.

**MALONE, Beverly**; Chief Executive Officer, National League for Nursing, USA, since 2007; *b* Elizabethtown, Ky, 25 Aug. 1948; *d* of Frank Malone and Dorothy Black. *Educ*: Univ. of Cincinnati (BSN 1970; Dr in clinical psychol., 1981); Rutgers State Univ., NJ (MSN, 1972). Surgical staff nurse; own private practice, Detroit, Mich, 1973–96; clinical nurse specialist, Univ. of Cincinnati, 1973–75; Asst Administrator for nursing, Univ. of Cincinnati Hosp., 1981–86; Prof. and Dean, Sch. of Nursing, N Carolina State Univ., 1986–2000; Dep. Asst Sec. for Health, USA, 2000–01; Gen. Sec., Royal Coll. of Nursing, 2001–06. Mem., NHS Modernisation Bd, 2001–06. Pres., American Nurses Assoc., 1996–2000. *Address*: National League for Nursing, The Watergate, 2600 Virginia Avenue NW, Eighth Floor, Washington, DC 20037, USA.

**MALONE, Prof. Caroline Ann Tuke, (Mrs S. K. F. Stoddart)**, FSA; archaeologist; Professor of Prehistory, Queen's University Belfast, since 2013; *b* 10 Oct. 1957; *d* of Lt Col Henry Charles Malone and Margaret Hope (*née* Kayll); *m* 1983, Dr Simon Kenneth Fladgate Stoddart, *qv*; two *d*. *Educ*: St Mary's Sch., St Leonards on Sea; New Hall, Cambridge (MA Hons Archaeol. and Anthropol. 1984); Trinity Hall, Cambridge (PhD Archaeol. 1986). FSA 1993. Italian Govt Scholarship, Rome Univ., 1980–81; Rome Scholarship in Archaeol., Brit. Sch. in Rome, 1981–82; Curator, Alexander Keiller Mus., Avebury, 1985–87; Inspector of Ancient Monuments, English Heritage, 1987–90; Lectr, then Sen. Lectr, Univ. of Bristol, 1990–97; Cambridge University: Tutor in Archaeol., Continuing Educn, 1997–2000; Affiliated Lectr, Dept of Archaeology, 1998–2000, 2005–; Sen. Proctor, 1998–2001; Fellow, New Hall, 1997–2000; Keeper, Dept of Prehistory and Early Europe, British Mus., 2000–03; Sen. Tutor, Hughes Hall, Cambridge, 2003–07; Queen's University Belfast: Sen. Lectr in Prehistorical Archaeol., 2007–10; Reader, 2010–13; Dir of Educn, Archaeology and Paleoecology, 2009–12. Co-Director: Gubbio Archaeol. Project, 1983–88; Gozo Project, Malta, 1987–98; Troina Project, Sicily, 1997–2001; Lismore, Scotland, 2002–08. Res. Associate Prof. of Archaeol., SUNY, Buffalo, 2004–. Principal investigator, Fragility and Sustainability in Restricted Island Contexts project, 2013–18. Mem., BASIS Cttee, British Acad., 2001–09. Ed., 1998–2000, Co-Ed., 2000–02, Antiquity. MCIfA (MIFA 1986). Fellow, McDonald Inst. for Archaeol Res., 1996–2007. *Publications*: (ed with S. Stoddart) Papers in Italian Archaeology, Vols 1–4, 1985; Avebury, 1989; (ed with S. Stoddart) Territory, Time and State, 1994; Neolithic Britain and Ireland, 2001; (with S. Stoddart) Mortuary Customs in Prehistoric Malta: excavations at the Brochtorff Circle at Xaghra 1987–94, 2009; contrib. numerous academic papers, articles and reviews. *Recreations*: gardening, pottery, good books, ancient monuments, antiques, Irish Water Spaniels, art. *Address*: 8 Lansdowne Road, Cambridge CB3 0EU; School of Natural and Built Environment, Queen's University Belfast BT7 1NN.

**MALONE, (Peter) Gerald**; Editor, The Sunday Times Scotland, 1989–90, Editorial Consultant, since 1990; Principal, www.brexRisk.com; *b* 21 July 1950; *s* of P. A. and J. Malone; *m* 1981, Dr Anne S. Blyth; two *s* one *d*. *Educ*: St Aloysius Coll., Glasgow; Glasgow Univ. (MA, LLB). Admitted solicitor, 1972. MP (C): Aberdeen S, 1983–87; Winchester, 1992–97; contested (C) Winchester, 1997. PPS to Parly Under Secs of State, Dept of Energy, 1985, and to Sec. of State, DTI, 1985–86; an Asst Government Whip, 1986–87; Dep. Chm., Cons. Party, 1992–94; Minister of State, DoH, 1994–97. Ind. dir of mutual funds and health care cos, 1997–. Dir of European Affairs, Energy and Envmtl Policy Center, Harvard Univ., 1987–90; Presenter, Talk In Sunday, Radio Clyde, 1988–90. Chm., CGA, 1991. *Recreations*: opera, English church music, history, motoring. *Clubs*: Pratt's; Glasgow Arts; University (New York).

**MALONE, Philip**, LVO 2006 (MVO 1998); HM Diplomatic Service; Ambassador to Mongolia, since 2018; *b* Leeds, 3 Dec. 1961; *s* of James Malone and Sheila Malone; *m* 1999, Yee Whey Sarah Tan; one *s* one *d*. *Educ*: King Edward VII Grammar Sch., King's Lynn; Open Univ. (Professional Cert. Mgt). Joined FCO, 1981; Attaché, Buenos Aires, 1983–86; Third Sec. and Vice Consul, Guatemala City 1986–89; Asst Parly Clerk, FCO, 1989–92; Third Sec., Luxembourg, 1992–95; Second Sec., Bandar Seri Begawan, 1995–99; First Sec., FCO, 1999–2003; Hd, Chancery, Singapore, 2003–08; Dep. Hd of Mission, Helsinki, 2008–12; Ambassador to Laos, 2012–15; Dep. Hd, SE Asia Dept, FCO, 2015–18. Vice-Chm., Bd of Govs, Internat. Sch. of Helsinki, 2009–11. *Recreations*: sports, family, travel, reading. *Address*: c/o Foreign and Commonwealth Office, King Charles Street, SW1A 2AH. *E*: Philip.Malone@fco.gov.uk.

**MALONE, Rt Rev. Vincent**; Auxiliary Bishop of Liverpool, (RC), 1989–2006, now Emeritus; a Vicar General of Archdiocese of Liverpool, since 1989; Titular Bishop of Abora, since 1989; *b* 11 Sept. 1931; *s* of Louis Malone and Elizabeth Malone (*née* McGrath). *Educ*: St Francis Xavier's Coll., Liverpool; St Joseph's Coll., Upholland; Liverpool Univ. (BSc 1959); Cambridge Univ. (CertEd 1960; DipEd 1964). FCP 1967. Chaplain to Notre Dame Training Coll., Liverpool, 1955–59; Curate, St Anne's, Liverpool, 1960–61; Asst Master, Cardinal Allen Grammar School, Liverpool, 1961–71; RC Chaplain to Liverpool Univ., 1971–79; Administrator, Liverpool Metropolitan Cathedral, 1979–89. Hon. DD Liverpool Hope, 2012. *Address*: 17 West Oakhill Park, Liverpool L13 4BN. *T*: (0151) 228 7637, *Fax*: (0151) 228 7637. *E*: vmalone@rcaolp.co.uk.

**MALONE-LEE, Michael Charles**, CB 1995; DPhil; Vice-Chancellor, Anglia Polytechnic University, 1995–2004; *b* 4 March 1941; *s* of late Dr Gerard Brendan and Teresa Malone-Lee; *m* 1971, Claire Frances Cockin; two *s*. *Educ*: Stonyhurst College; Campion Hall, Oxford (MA); University Coll., Oxford (MSt; DPhil 2016). Ministry of Health, 1968; Principal Private Sec. to Sec. of State for Social Services, 1976–79; Asst Sec., 1977; Area Administrator, City and East London AHA, 1979–81; District Administrator, Bloomsbury Health Authy, 1982–84; Under Secretary, 1984, Dir, Personnel Management, 1984–87, DHSS; Prin. Fin. Officer, Home Office, 1987–90; Dep. Sec. (Dir of Corporate Affairs, NHS Management Exec.), DoH, 1990–93; Dep. Sec. (Head of Policy Gp), Lord Chancellor's Dept, 1993–95. Non-exec. Dir, ICI (Agrochemicals), 1986–89. Dir, Essex TEC, 1996–2001; Chairman: BBC E Regl Adv. Council, 1997–99; Essex Learning and Skills Council, 2000–03. Mem., Review Body for Nursing Staff, Midwives, Health Visitors and Professions allied to Medicine, 1998–2001; non-exec. Dir, Mid-Essex PCT, 2006–08; Chm., Mid Essex NHS Hosps Trust, 2009–. Ecumenical Officer, Dio. Brentwood, 2005–09. Chairman Governors: New Hall Sch., 1999–2002; Heythrop Coll., London Univ., 2006–12. DL Essex, 2002. Hon. Fellow, Fachhochschule Für Wirtschaft, Berlin, 2004. Hon. PhD Anglia Poly. Univ., 2005. *Recreations*: natural history, walking.

**MALOUF, David George Joseph**, AO 1987; writer; *b* 1934. *Educ*: Brisbane Grammar Sch.; Univ. of Queensland (BA Hons Eng Lang. and Lit.). Teacher, St Anselm's Coll., Birkenhead, 1962–68; Lectr, Dept of English, Univ. of Sydney, 1968–78. Boyer Lectr, ABC, 1998. Hon. DLitt: Macquarie, 1990; Queensland, 1991; Sydney, 1998. *Publications*: Johnno: a novel, 1975; An Imaginary Life, 1978; Child's Play, 1981; Fly Away Peter, 1981; Harland's Half Acre, 1984; Antipodes (stories), 1985; 12 Edmondstone Street, 1986; The Great World, 1990; Remembering Babylon, 1993; The Conversations at Curlow Creek, 1996; A Spirit of Play (Boyer Lectures), 1998; Untold Tales, 1999; Dream Stuff (stories), 2000; Every Move You Make (stories), 2007; The Complete Stories, 2007; Ransom, 2009; The Happy Life: the search for contentment in the modern world, 2011; A First Place (essays), 2014; The Writing Life (essays), 2015; Being There (essays), 2015; *poetry*: Bicycle and Other Poems, 1970; Neighbours in a Thicket, 1974; First Things Last, 1981; Selected Poems, 1993; Revolving Days: selected poems, 2008; Typewrite Music, 2008; Earth Hour, 2014; *libretti*: Baa Baa Black Sheep, 1993; Jane Eyre, 2000. *Address*: c/o Rogers, Coleridge & White, 20 Powis Mews, W11 1JN.

**MALPAS, Sir Robert**, Kt 1998; CBE 1975; FREng, FIMechE; Chairman, Cookson Group, 1991–98; Co-Chairman, Eurotunnel, 1996–98; *b* 9 Aug. 1927; *s* of late Cheshire Malpas and Louise Marie Marcelle Malpas; *m* 1st, 1956, Josephine Dickenson (*d* 2004); 2nd, 2005, Joan Holloway. *Educ*: Taunton Sch.; St George's Coll., Buenos Aires; Durham Univ. (BScMechEng (1st Cl. Hons)). Joined ICI Ltd, 1948; moved to Alcudia SA (48.5 per cent ICI), Spain, 1963; ICI Europa Ltd, Brussels, 1965; Chm., ICI Europa Ltd, 1973; ICI Main Board Dir, 1975–78; Pres., Halcon International Inc., 1978–82; a Man. Dir, BP, 1983–89;

Chm., PowerGen, 1990. Chm., Ferghana Partners Ltd, 1998–2002; non-executive Director: BOC Group, 1981–96; Eurotunnel, 1987–99; Repsol SA, 1989–2002; Enagas, Spain, 2002–06; Agcert plc, 2005–08. Member: Engineering Council, 1983–88 (Vice-Chm., 1984–88); ACARD, 1983–86; Chairman: LINK Steering Gp, 1987–93; NERC, 1993–96. FREng (FEng 1978; Sen. Vice Pres., 1988–92). Hon. FRSC 1988; Hon. FIMechE 1999. FRSA. Hon. Fellow, Univ. of Westminster, 1992. Hon. DTech Loughborough, 1983; DUniv: Surrey, 1984; Sheffield Hallam, 2001; Hon. DEng Newcastle, 1991; Hon. DSc: Bath, 1991; Durham, 1997. Order of Civil Merit, Spain, 1967. *Recreations:* sport, music, theatre, golf, swimming, walking. *Address:* 2 Spencer Park, SW18 2SX. *Club:* Mill Reef (Antigua).

**MALPASS, Brian William,** PhD; CChem; investor and writer; Chief Executive, De La Rue Co. plc, 1987–89; *b* 12 Sept. 1937; *s* of William and Florence Malpass; *m* 1960, Hazel Anne; two *d. Educ:* Univ. of Birmingham (Open Schol.; Frankland Prize 1960; BScChem 1st Cl. Hons, PhD). MRSC. Passfield Res. Laboratories, 1963–68; De La Rue Co., 1968–89; Finance Dir, 1980–84; Man. Dir, Thomas De La Rue Currency Div., 1984–87. *Publications:* Bluff Your Way in Science, 1993; Bluff Your Way in Chess, 1993; numerous papers in scientific jls, magazine articles and book reviews. *Recreation:* grandchildren. *Address:* 1 Lime Tree Close, Tonbridge, Kent TN9 1LR.

**MALTBY, Colin Charles;** Chairman, Supervisory Board, BBGI SICAV SA (formerly Bilfinger Berger Global Infrastructure SICAV), since 2018 (Director, since 2011); *b* 8 Feb. 1951; *s* of late George Frederick Maltby, MC and Dorothy Maltby; *m* 1983, Victoria Angela Valerie Elton; one *s* two *d. Educ:* George Heriot's Sch., Edinburgh; King Edward's Sch., Birmingham; Christ Church, Oxford (MA, MSc); Stanford Business Sch. Pres., Oxford Union, 1973; Chm., Fedn of Cons. Students, 1974–75. With N. M. Rothschild & Sons, 1975–80; Director: Kleinwort Benson Investment Mgt Ltd, 1984–95 (Chief Exec., 1988–95); Banque Kleinwort Benson SA, Geneva, 1985–88; Kleinwort Benson Gp plc, 1989–95; CCLA Investment Mgt Ltd, 1997–2003 (Chm., 1999–2003); Chm., Kleinwort Overseas Investment Trust plc, 1992–96; Chief Investment Officer, Equitas, 1996–2000; Chief Exec., BP Investment Mgt Ltd, 2000–07; Chairman: Princess Pte Equity Hldg Ltd, 2007–09; Blackrock Absolute Return Strategies Ltd, 2008–14; HarbourVest Sen. Loans Europe Ltd, 2010–14. Director: RM plc, 1997–99; H. Young Hldgs plc, 1997–2001; BACIT Ltd, 2012–14; Ocean Wilsons Hldgs Ltd, 2013–; BH Macro Ltd, 2015–. Investment Adviser: British Coal Staff Superannuation Scheme, 2001–12; British Airways Pension Schemes, 2003–07. Mem., Finance Cttee, Funding Agency for Schs, 1996–99. Fellow, Wolfson Coll., Oxford, 2002–. FRSA 1993. *Recreations:* music, ski-ing. *Address:* 1224 Chêne-Bougeries, Switzerland.

**MALTHOUSE, Christopher Laurie, (Kit);** MP (C) Hampshire North West, since 2015; Minister of State, Home Office, since 2019; *b* Liverpool, 27 Oct. 1966; *s* of John Christopher Malthouse and Susan Malthouse; *m* 2007, Juliana Farha; one *s* one *d*; one *s* by a previous marriage. *Educ:* Liverpool Coll.; Newcastle Univ. (BA Jt Hons Pols and Econs). Mem., ICAEW, 1997. Touche Ross & Co., 1992–97; Finance Officer, Cannock Gp, 1997–2001; Chm., County Hldgs, 2001–; Chief Exec., 2005–08, Finance Dir, 2008–14, Alpha Strategic plc. Contested (C) Liverpool Wavertree, 1997. Mem., Westminster CC, 1998–2006 (Dep. Leader, 2001–05). Mem. (C) W Central, London Assembly, GLA, 2008–16. Dep. Mayor of London, Policing, 2008–12, Business and Enterprise, 2012–15. Parly Under-Sec. of State, DWP, 2018; Minister of State (Minister for Housing), MHCLG, 2018–19. Mem., Treasury Cttee, H of C, 2016–. Chairman: Hydrogen London, 2008–15; London & Partners, 2014–15; Vice Chair, London Enterprise Panel, 2012–15. *Publications:* (contrib.) A Blue Tomorrow, 2001. *Recreations:* baking bread and policies, writing poetry and prose, watching others dance and play, childcare. *Address:* House of Commons, SW1A 0AA.

**MALTMAN, Christopher John;** freelance opera singer (baritone); *b* 7 Feb. 1970; *s* of Robert John Maltman and Christine Maltman; *m* 2000, Leigh Woolf. *Educ:* Warwick Univ. (BSc Hons Biochem.); Royal Acad. of Music (LRAM, Dip. RAM, ARAM; Queen's Commendation for Excellence, 1991). Operatic roles at: Royal Opera House, Covent Gdn; ENO; WNO; Bayerische Staatsoper, Munich; Deutsche Staatsoper, Berlin; La Monnaie, Brussels; Seattle Opera; San Diego Opera; Metropolitan Opera, NY; Salzburg Fest.; Glyndebourne; recitals at: Wigmore Hall; Carnegie Hall, Lincoln Centre, NY; Konzerthaus, Vienna; Concertgebouw, Amsterdam; Schwarzenberg Schubertiade; Edinburgh Fest.; Salzburg Fest.; has made numerous recordings. Lieder Prize, Cardiff Singer of the World, 1997; Young Artist of Year, Royal Philharmonic Soc., 1999; Artist of Year, Seattle Opera, 2000–01. *Recreations:* food, wine, physical fitness. *Address:* c/o Askonas Holt Ltd, 15 Fetter Lane, EC4A 1BW. *T:* (020) 7400 1700, *Fax:* (020) 7400 1799.

**MALTUS, Jonathan Charles Perry,** OBE 2016; winemaker and vigneron; Gérant, Château Teyssier, since 1994; *b* Lagos, Nigeria, 11 June 1955; *s* of John Maltus and Betty Maltus; two *s*; partner, Dr Catherine Clancy. *Educ:* King's Sch., Canterbury. Managing Director: Mecs (Hldgs) Ltd, 1976–81; Unimecs Integrated Ltd, 1981–92. *Recreations:* family, music, history, design, sailing. *Address:* Château Teyssier, Vignonet, 33330 Saint Emilion, France. *Clubs:* 67 Pall Mall, MCC.

**MALVERN,** 3rd Viscount *cr* 1955, of Rhodesia and of Bexley, Kent; **Ashley Kevin Godfrey Huggins;** *b* 26 Oct. 1949; *s* of 2nd Viscount Malvern, and of Patricia Marjorie, *d* of Frank Renwick-Bower, Durban, S Africa; *S* father, 1978. *Heir: uncle* Hon. (Martin) James Huggins, *b* 13 Jan. 1928.

**MALYAN, Hugh David;** Member (Lab), Croydon Borough Council, 1994–2006 (Leader, 2000–05; Hon. Alderman, 2006); *b* 7 June 1959; *s* of late Cyril and Brenda Malyan; *m* 1983, Ruth Margaret; one *s* one *d. Educ:* Strand Grammar Sch., Brixton. Trustee Savings Bank, 1975–78; fireman, London Fire Bde, 1978–92. Chm., Educn Cttee, Croydon BC, 1997–2000. Vice Chm., Assoc. of London Govt, 2002–05; Chm., Commn for London Governance, 2005–06. *Recreations:* amateur dramatics (former Mem., Downsview Players), singing, football (Crystal Palace supporter!).

**MALYNICZ, Simon Spiro;** QC 2016; *b* Barnet, Herts, 15 Dec. 1965; *s* of George Malynicz and Anna Malynicz; *m* 2004, Irina Feskova; two *s* one *d. Educ:* Univ. of Sydney (BA); New School, New York (MA); Birkbeck Coll., Univ. of London (LLB). Called to the Bar, Inner Temple, 1997; in practice as a barrister specialising in intellectual property, 1997–; Attorney-Gen.'s B Panel of Counsel, 2008–13; Attorney Gen.'s A Panel of Counsel, 2014. *Publications:* (jtly) The Modern Law of Trade Marks, 2nd edn 2005 to 3rd edn 2008; (jtly) Gurry on Breach of Confidence, 2nd edn 2012. *Recreations:* travel, tennis, Arsenal FC. *Address:* 3 New Square, Lincoln's Inn, WC2A 3RS. *T:* (020) 7405 1111, *Fax:* (020) 7405 7800. *Club:* Home House.

**MAMET, David Alan;** writer; stage and film director; *b* 30 Nov. 1947; *s* of Bernard Morris Mamet and Lenore June Mamet (*née* Silver); *m* 1st, 1977, Lindsay Crouse (marr. diss.); 2nd, 1991, Rebecca Pidgeon. *Educ:* Goddard College, Plainfield, Vt (BA Eng. Lit. 1969); Neighbourhood Playhouse Sch., NY. Founding Mem. and first Artistic Dir, St Nicholas Theater Co., Chicago, 1974. *Plays: written and produced include:* Sexual Perversity in Chicago, 1975; American Buffalo, 1976; A Life in the Theatre, 1976; The Water Engine, 1976; The Woods, 1977; Lakeboat, 1980; Edmond, 1982; Glen Garry Glen Ross, 1984 (Pulitzer Prize for Drama, 1984; filmed, 1992); Speed the Plow, 1987; Bobby Gould in Hell, 1989; The Old Neighborhood (trilogy), 1990, UK 1998; Oleanna, 1992; The Cryptogram, 1994; *written and directed:* Boston Marriage, 1999, UK, 2001; Dr Faustus, 2004; Bitter Wheat, 2019; *written:* November, 2008; Speed-the-Plow, 2008; Race, 2009; China Doll, 2015; The Penitent, 2017. *Films: written:* The Verdict, 1980; The Untouchables, 1986; Hoffa, 1990; Uncle Vanya on 42nd Street, 1994; The Edge, 1998; Wag the Dog, 1998; (jtly) Hannibal, 2001; *written and directed:* House of Games, 1986; (with Shel Silverstein) Things Change, 1987; Homicide, 1991; State and Main, 2001; Heist, 2001; Spartan, 2004; *directed:* The Winslow Boy, 1999. *Television: written and directed:* The Unit (series), 2006; Phil Spector, 2013. *Publications:* Writing in Restaurants, 1986; Some Freaks, 1989; The Hero Pony, 1990; On Directing Film, 1991; The Cabin, 1992; The Village, 1994; Passover, 1996; True or False—Heresy and Common Sense for the Actor, 1998; The Old Religion, 1998; Wilson: a consideration of the sources, 2000; Three Uses of the Knife, 2002; Bambi vs Godzilla: on the nature, purpose and practice of the movie business, 2007; Theatre, 2010; The Secret Knowledge: on the dismantling of American culture, 2011; Chicago, 2018. *Address:* c/o The Agency (London) Ltd, 24 Pottery Lane, Holland Park, W11 4LZ.

**MAN, Archdeacon of;** *see* Brown, Ven. A.

**MANALO, Enrique Austria;** Undersecretary for Policy, Department of Foreign Affairs, Republic of the Philippines, 2007–10 and since 2016; *b* Manila, 21 July 1952; *s* of Armando Manalo and Jimena Austria; *m* 1986, Pamela Louise Hunt; two *s. Educ:* Univ. of the Philippines, Manila (BA Econs, MA Econs). Department of Foreign Affairs, Manila: Special Asst, Office of the Dep. Minister, 1979–81; Third Sec. and Vice Consul, 1981–84, Second Sec. and Consul, 1984–86, Philippine Mission to UN, Geneva; First Sec. and Consul, Washington, DC, 1986–89; Special Asst to First Undersec., 1989–92; Minister Counsellor, Philippine Mission to UN, NY, 1992–98; Asst Sec. for Eur. Affairs, 1998–2000; Chargé d'Affaires, Philippine Mission to UN, NY, 2003–07; Ambassador and Perm. Rep., Philippine Mission to UN, Geneva, 2003–07; Ambassador to Belgium and Luxembourg, and Head, Philippine Mission to EU, 2010–11; Ambassador to UK and to Ireland (non-resident), 2011–16; Actg Sec. of Foreign Affairs, 2017. Presidential Award, Order of Sikatuna (Philippines), 2010; Gawad Mabini Award (Philippines), 2017; Order of Lakandula (Philippines), 2018. *Recreations:* reading, walking, listening to classical music.

**MANCE,** Baron *cr* 2005 (Life Peer), of Frognal, in the London Borough of Camden; **Jonathan Hugh Mance,** Kt 1993; PC 1999; a Justice, 2009–18, and Deputy President, 2017–18, of the Supreme Court of the United Kingdom (a Lord of Appeal in Ordinary, 2005–09); *b* 6 June 1943; *e s* of late Sir Henry Stenhouse Mance and Lady (Joan Erica Robertson) Mance; *m* 1973, Mary Howarth Arden (*see* Rt Hon. Lady Arden of Heswall); one *s* two *d. Educ:* Charterhouse; University Coll., Oxford (MA; Hon. Fellow 2006). Called to the Bar, Middle Temple, 1965, Bencher, 1989. QC 1982; a Recorder, 1990–93; a Judge of the High Court, QBD, Commercial List, 1993–99; a Lord Justice of Appeal, 1999–2005; Ind. Arbitrator, 2018–. Worked in Germany, 1965. Chm., Banking Appeal tribunals, 1992–93. Dir, Bar Mutual Indemnity Fund Ltd, 1987–94. Member: Consultative Council of European Judges, 2003–11 (Chm., 2000–03); Judicial Integrity Gp, 2008–; Report for Swedish Foundn for Human Rights and All-Party Parly Gp on Gt Lakes Region on impunity in reln to violence against women in Congo, 2008; Ext. Adv. Cttee, Max-Planck Inst. for Comparative and Private Internat. Law, Hamburg, 2012–. Member: H of L Select Cttee on EU, 2007–09 (Chm., Sub-cttee E, Law and Instns, 2007–09); Panel under Article 255 of Treaty on Functioning of EU, 2010–18; Interim Nominating Cttee, Internat. Auditing and Accounting Standards Bd, 2018–19; Chairman: Lord Chancellor's Adv. Cttee on Private Internat. Law, 2009–; H of L Contact Cttee, 2019–. Chm., Hampstead Counselling Service, 2000–. Pres., British Insurance Law Assoc., 2000–02 (Dep. Pres., 1998–2000); Chm., Internat. Law Assoc., 2009–; Pres., British-German Jurists' Assoc., 2009–. Pres., Bar Lawn Tennis Soc., 2014– (Chm., 2000–14). Trustee, European Law Acad., Trier, 2003–11. Vis. Prof., KCL, 2018–. University of Oxford: Mem., Ext. Adv. Cttee, History Faculty, 2018–; High Steward, 2012–18. Hon. Fellow: Liverpool Moores Univ., 2010; John F. Kennedy Univ., Buenos Aires, 2011; Wolfson Coll., Oxford, 2013; Amer. Coll. of Trial Lawyers, 2016–. Hon. Dr Canterbury Christ Church, 2013; Hon. DCL Oxford, 2016. *Publications:* (asst editor) Chalmer's Sale of Goods, 1981; (ed jtly) Sale of Goods, Halsbury's Laws of England, 4th edn 1983; (jtly) Privy Council Practice, 2017; lectures and articles on various legal subjects. *Recreations:* tennis, languages, music, walking. *Address:* House of Lords, SW1A 0PW; 7 King's Bench Walk, Temple, EC4Y 7DS. *Clubs:* Nobody's; Cumberland Lawn Tennis.

**MANCHESTER,** 13th Duke of, *cr* 1719; **Alexander Charles David Drogo Montagu;** Baron Montagu, Viscount Mandeville, 1620; Earl of Manchester, 1626; President, Global Atlantic, since 1983; *b* 11 Dec. 1962; *s* of 12th Duke of Manchester and Mary Eveleen (*née* McClure); *S* father, 2002; *m* 2007, Laura Ann, *d* of Francis Smith, Laguna Beach. *Educ:* Geelong Grammar Sch., Vic; Bancroft Jun. High Sch., Calif.; Kimbolton Grammar Sch., Cambridgeshire. Director: Internal Security, 1991–; Summit Investments, 1994–; Royal Fidelity Trust, 1996–. *Address:* c/o British Consulate-General, 11766 Wilshire Boulevard, Los Angeles, CA 90025–6538, USA; 220 Newport Center Drive, Newport Beach, CA 92660, USA. *E:* globalatlantic@aol.com.

**MANCHESTER, Bishop of,** since 2013; **Rt Rev. Dr David Stuart Walker;** *b* 30 May 1957; *s* of late Fred Walker and Joyce Walker; *m* 1980, Susan Ann (*née* Pearce); one *s* one *d. Educ:* King's Coll., Cambridge (MA 1981); Queen's Coll., Birmingham (DipTh 1982); Warwick Univ. (PhD 2014). Ordained deacon, 1983, priest, 1984; Curate, Handsworth, Sheffield, 1983–86; Team Vicar, Maltby, 1986–91; Industrial Chaplain, 1986–91; Vicar, Bramley and Ravenfield, 1991–95; Team Rector, Bramley and Ravenfield with Hooton Roberts and Braithwell, 1995–2000; Area Bishop of Dudley, 2000–02; Bishop Suffragan of Dudley, 2002–13. A Church Comr, 2014– (Mem., Pastoral Cttee, 2014–15; Dep. Chm., 2017–). Member: Gen. Synod, 2005–; C of E Pensions Bd, 2006–13 (Dep. Vice-Chm., 2010–11; Vice-Chm., 2011–13); C of E Adv. Council on Relns of Bishops and Religious Communities, 2008– (Chm., 2013–); C of E Ethical Investments Adv. Gp, 2014–; Chairman: C of E Remunerations and Conditions of Service Cttee, 2013–16; C of E Ministry Council, 2013–16; Gtr Manchester Police Ethics Cttee, 2014–. Chairman: Housing Justice, 2003–07; Housing Assocs Charitable Trust, 2004–10; Sandwell Homes Ltd, 2011–12. Member: Council, Nat. Housing Fedn, 1996–2002; Govt Policy Action Team on Housing Mgt, 1998–2001; Bd, Wythenshawe Community Housing Gp, 2014– (Chm., 2016–); Member, Lay Advisory Panel: Nat. Police Improvement Agency (formerly Central Police Trng Agency), 2005–13; Homes and Communities Agency, 2009–12. Trustee, Church Urban Fund, 2008–15. FRSA 2008–16. *Publications:* (contrib.) Changing Rural Life, 2005; Communion by Extension, 2006; Belonging to Rural Community and Church, 2006; Marks of Mission and Ways of Belonging, 2010; Prayer and Social Capital, 2011; (contrib.) Rural Life and Rural Church: theological and empirical perspectives, 2012; (contrib.) Exploring Ordinary Theology: everyday Christian believing and the Church, 2013; God's Belongers, 2017; various articles in housing jls. *Recreations:* cricket, hill walking, reading, sudoku puzzles. *Address:* Bishopscourt, Bury New Road, Salford M7 4LE. *E:* bishop.david@manchester.anglican.org.

**MANCHESTER, Dean of;** see Govender, Very Rev. R. M.

**MANCHESTER, Archdeacon of;** see Lund, Ven. K. B.

**MANCHIPP, Amelia Anne Doris;** see Noble, A. A. D.

**MANCROFT,** family name of **Baron Mancroft**.

**MANCROFT,** 3rd Baron *cr* 1937, of Mancroft in the City of Norwich; **Benjamin Lloyd Stormont Mancroft;** Bt 1932; *b* 16 May 1957; *s* of 2nd Baron Mancroft, KBE, TD and Diana Elizabeth (*d* 1999), *d* of late Lt-Col Horace Lloyd, DSO; *S* father, 1987; *m* 1990, Emma Louisa, *e d* of Thomas Peart; two *s* one *d*. *Educ*: Eton. MFH, Vale of White Horse Hunt, 1987–89. Chm., Inter Lotto (UK) Ltd, 1995–2007; Dir and Sen. Vice Pres., ROK Entertainment Gp Inc., USA, 2007– (Dep. Chm., ROK Corp. Ltd, 2003–07); Chairman: New Media Lottery Services plc, Ireland, 2006–09; Phoenix Gaming Ltd, 2007–. Dir, St Martin's Magazines plc, 1991–2008. Chairman: Addiction Recovery Foundn, 1989–2007 (Patron, 2008–); Drug and Alcohol Foundn, 1993–2007; Mentor Foundn UK, 2000–07 (Trustee, Mentor Foundn Internat., 1996–2000); Trustee, Hepatitis C Trust, 2000–06 (Patron, 2006–). Deputy Chairman: British Field Sports Soc., 1993–98; Phoenix House Housing Assoc., 1993–96. Dir, Countryside Alliance, 1998– (Dep. Chm., 2005–). Member Executive: Nat. Union of Cons. and Unionist Assocs, 1989–95; Assoc. of Cons. Peers, 1989–95. Elected Mem., H of L, 1999. Pres., Alliance of Ind. Retailers, 1996–2000. Patron: Sick Dentists' Trust, 1991–; Patsy Hardy Trust, 1991–; Osteopathic Centre for Children, 1996–. *Recreations*: field sports, gardening, reading, travelling. *Heir*: *s* Hon. Arthur Louis Stormont Mancroft, *b* 3 May 1995. *Address*: House of Lords, SW1A 0PW. *Club*: Pratt's.
*See also* S. C. Dickinson.

**MANDELSON,** Baron *cr* 2008 (Life Peer), of Foy in the County of Herefordshire and Hartlepool in the County of Durham; **Peter Benjamin Mandelson;** PC 1998; Chairman: Global Counsel LLP, since 2010; Lazard International, 2012–16 (Senior Adviser, Lazard, since 2016); *b* 21 Oct. 1953; *s* of late George Mandelson and Hon. Mary, *o c* of Baron Morrison of Lambeth, CH, PC. *Educ*: Hendon County Grammar Sch.; St Catherine's Coll., Oxford (Hons degree, PPE). Econ. Dept, TUC, 1977–78; Chm., British Youth Council, 1978–80; producer, LWT, 1982–85; Dir of Campaigns and Communications, Labour Party, 1985–90. MP (Lab) Hartlepool, 1992–Sept. 2004. An Opposition Whip, 1994–95; Opposition spokesman on Civil Service, 1995–97; Minister without Portfolio, Cabinet Office, 1997–98; Sec. of State for Trade and Industry, 1998, for N Ireland, 1999–2001, for Business, Enterprise and Regulatory Reform, later Business, Innovation and Skills, 2008–10; First Sec. of State and Lord Pres. of the Council, 2009–10. Mem., European Commn, 2004–08. Mem. Council, London Bor. of Lambeth, 1979–82. President: Policy Network, 2001–; Great Britain China Centre, 2015–. Chancellor, Manchester Metropolitan Univ., 2016–. Chm. Trustees, Design Mus., 2017–. *Publications*: Youth Unemployment: causes and cures, 1977; Broadcasting and Youth, 1980; (jtly) The Blair Revolution, 1996, 2nd edn 2002; The Third Man: life at the heart of New Labour (autobiog.), 2010. *Recreations*: swimming, country walking. *Address*: House of Lords, SW1A 0PW.

**MANDER, Sir (Charles) Nicholas,** 4th Bt *cr* 1911, of The Mount, Tettenhall, co. Stafford; *b* 23 March 1950; *er s* of Sir Charles Marcus Mander, 3rd Bt and Maria Dolores Beatrice Mander (*née* Brödermann) (*d* 2007); *S* father, 2006; *m* 1972, Karin Margareta, *yr d* of Gustaf Arne Norin; four *s* one *d*. *Educ*: Downside; Trinity Coll., Cambridge (top Scholar; MA); Grenoble Univ. Underwriting Mem. Lloyd's, 1972. Co-founder: Mander Portman Woodward, tutorial coll., London, 1974; Sutton Publishing, Gloucester, 1976; Dir, London & Cambridge Investments, 1985–91; CEO, Flamenco Estates, 1992–2003. Chm., Glos Care Partnership, 2006–14. Founder Chm., Glos County History Trust, 2010–13; Trustee: Woodchester Mansion Trust, 1998–2019; Orders of St John Care Trust, 2006–15; Cllr, St John Ambulance for Glos, 2008–12. Mem., Diocesan Adv. Cttee, 1975–92. FSA 2006. Liveryman, Fishmongers' Co. Kt of Grace and Devotion, SMO Malta, 2002; Kt Jure Sanguinis, Sacred Military Constantinian Order of St George, 2008. Appeared in film, Phantom Thread, 2017. *Publications*: Varnished Leaves: a biography of the Mander family of Wolverhampton 1750–1950, 2004; Country Houses of the Cotswolds, 2008; Borromean Rings, 2011; The Queen of Seven Swords, 2013. *Recreations*: conversation, conservation, dreaming, arts, travelling, forestry. *Heir*: *e s* Charles Marcus Septimus Gustav Mander, *b* 26 July 1975. *Address*: Owlpen Manor, Uley, Glos GL11 5BZ. *T*: (01453) 860261. *E*: nicky@owlpen.com. *Club*: Boodle's.

**MANDER, Prof. Lewis Norman,** AC 2018; FRS 1990; Professor of Chemistry, 1980–2002, Adjunct Professor, 2002–08, now Emeritus Professor, Australian National University; *b* 8 Sept. 1939; *s* of John Eric and Anne Frances Mander; *m* 1965, Stephanie Vautin; one *s* two *d*. *Educ*: Mount Albert Grammar Sch.; Univ. of Sydney (PhD 1965). FRACI 1980; FAA 1983. Postdoctoral Fellow, Univ. of Michigan, 1964–65; Postdoctoral Associate, Caltech, 1965–66; Lectr and Sen. Lectr in Organic Chem., Univ. of Adelaide, 1966–75; Sen. Fellow, 1975–80, Dean, 1981–86 and 1992–95, Res. Sch. of Chem., ANU. Nuffield Commonwealth Fellow, Cambridge, 1972; Fulbright Sen. Schol., Caltech, 1977, Harvard, 1986. H. G. Smith Medal, RACI, 1981; Flintoff Medal and Prize, RSocChem, 1990. *Publications*: numerous articles in learned jls, mainly on synthesis of organic molecules. *Recreations*: bushwalking, speleology. *Address*: Research School of Chemistry, Australian National University, Canberra, ACT 2601, Australia. *T*: (2) 61253761.

**MANDER, Sir Nicholas;** see Mander, Sir C. N.

**MANDERS, Ann Beasley;** see Beasley, A.

**MANDERSON, Marcus Charles William S.;** see Scott-Manderson.

**MANDLER, Prof. Peter,** PhD; FBA 2015; Professor of Modern Cultural History, University of Cambridge, since 2009; Fellow, since 2001 and Bailey Lecturer in History, since 2009, Gonville and Caius College, Cambridge; *b* Boston, USA, 29 Jan. 1958; *s* of George Mandler and Jean Matter Mandler; *m* 1987, Ruth Ehrlich; one *s* one *d*. *Educ*: Point Loma High Sch.; Magdalen Coll., Oxford (BA 1st Cl. Hons Mod. Hist. 1975); Harvard Univ. (AM Hist. 1980; PhD Hist. 1984). Teaching Fellow in Hist., and in Hist. and Lit., Harvard Univ., 1980–82; Asst Prof. of Hist., Princeton Univ., 1984–91; London Guildhall University: Sen. Lectr, 1991–95, Reader, 1995–97, in Mod. Hist.; Prof. of Mod. Hist., 1997–2001; University of Cambridge: Lectr in Hist., 2001–03; Reader in Mod. Brit. Hist., 2003–09; Lectr, Gonville and Caius Coll., 2001–. Hon. Sec., 1998–2002, Vice Pres., 2009–12, Pres., 2012–16, RHistS. Chair, Modern History Section, British Acad., 2018–. Fellow, Amer. Acad. of Arts and Scis, 2015. Editor, Historical Jl, 2002–06 (Chair, Editl Bd, 2016–); mem. of various editl bds and adv. bds. *Publications*: (ed) The Uses of Charity: the poor on relief in the nineteenth-century metropolis, 1990; Aristocratic Government in the Age of Reform: Whigs and Liberals, 1830–52, 1990; (ed with Susan Pedersen) After the Victorians: private conscience and public duty in modern Britain, 1994; The Fall and Rise of the Stately Home, 1997; History and National Life, 2002; (ed) Liberty and Authority in Victorian Britain, 2006; The English National Character: the history of an idea from Edmund Burke to Tony Blair, 2006; (ed with Astrid Swenson) From Plunder to Preservation: Britain and the heritage of Empire, *c* 1800–1940, 2013; Return from the Natives: how Margaret Mead won the Second World War and lost the Cold War, 2013; (ed with David Cesarani) Great Philanthropists: wealth and charity in the modern world, 2017. *Recreations*: reading, theatre, politics, argument. *Address*: Gonville and Caius College, Cambridge CB2 1TA. *T*: (01223) 768779, *Fax*: (01223) 332456. *E*: pm297@cam.ac.uk.

**MANDUCA, Paul Victor Falzon Sant;** Chairman, Prudential plc, since 2012 (Director, 2010; Senior Independent Director, 2011–12); *b* 15 Nov. 1951; *s* of Victor Manduca and Elizabeth Manduca (*née* Johnson); *m* 1982, Ursula Voysey; two *s*. *Educ*: Harrow Sch.; Hertford Coll., Oxford (Hons Mod. Langs). Colegrave & Co., 1973–75; Rowe & Pitman, 1976–79; Hill Samuel Inv. Management, 1979–83; Touche Remnant, 1983–92: Dir 1986; Vice-Chm. 1987; Chm., 1989–92; Dir, Henderson (formerly TR) Smaller Cos Investment Trust (formerly Trustees Corp.), 1986–2006; Man. Dir, TR Industrial & General, 1986–88; Chm., TR High Income, 1989–94; Gp Dep. Man. Dir, Henderson Administration PLC, 1992–94; Chief Executive: Threadneedle Asset Mgt, 1994–99; Rothschild Asset Mgt, 1999–2002; CEO, Deutsche Asset Mgt (Europe), 2002–05. Exec. Chm., Gresham Trust, 1996–99 (Dir, 1994–99); non-executive Chairman: FTSE Trains, 1997–2002; Majid al Futtaim Trust Co., 2007–; Bridgewell Gp, 2006–07; AON UK Ltd, 2008–12 (non-exec. Dir, 2006–08); Microlease plc, 2009–14; RateSetter, 2017–; Director: Eagle Star Hldgs, 1994–99; Allied Dunbar Assce, 1994–99; non-executive Director: Clydesdale Investment Trust, 1987–88; MEPC plc, 1999–2000; Wolverhampton Wanderers FC, 1999–2006; Development Securities plc, 2001–10 (Sen. Ind. Dir, 2006–10); William Morrison Supermarkets plc, 2005–11 (Sen. Ind. Dir, 2006–); Intrinsic Ltd, 2006–12; KazMunaiGaz Exploration & Production plc, 2006–12; JPM Euro Smaller Companies (formerly JPM Euro Fledgeling) Investment Trust plc, 2006–11 (Chm., 2011–12); Henderson Diversified Income plc, 2007–17 (Chm., 2007–17); Chm., UNIQ Pension Fund Trustees Ltd, 2006–09. Mem., Adv. Bd, Alexandra Proudfoot, 2010–12; Chm., Adv. Council, TheCityUK, 2015–. Chm., Assoc. of Investment Trust Cos, 1991–93 (Dep. Chm., 1989–91); Mem., Takeover Panel, 1991–93. Liveryman, Bakers' Co., 1988–. *Recreations*: golf, squash, shooting. *Address*: 22 Rutland Gate, SW7 1BB. *Clubs*: White's, Lansdowne; St George's Hill Golf; Westhill Golf; Royal St George's Golf; Royal Mid-Surrey Golf.

**MANGO, Prof. Cyril Alexander,** FBA 1976; Bywater and Sotheby Professor of Byzantine and Modern Greek, 1973–95, and Emeritus Fellow of Exeter College, Oxford University; *b* 14 April 1928; *s* of Alexander A. Mango and Adelaide Damonov; *m* 1st, 1953, Mabel Grover; one *d*; 2nd, 1964, Susan A. Gerstel; one *d*; 3rd, 1976, Maria C. Mundell. *Educ*: Univ. of St Andrews (MA); Univ. of Paris (Dr Univ. Paris). From Jun. Fellow to Lectr in Byzantine Archaeology, Dumbarton Oaks Byzantine Center, Harvard Univ., 1951–63; Lectr in Fine Arts, Harvard Univ., 1957–58; Visiting Associate Prof. of Byzantine History, Univ. of California, Berkeley, 1960–61; Koraës Prof. of Modern Greek and of Byzantine History, Language and Literature, King's Coll., Univ. of London, 1963–68; Prof. of Byzantine Archaeology, Dumbarton Oaks Byzantine Center, 1968–73. FSA. *Publications*: The Homilies of Photius, 1958; The Brazen House, 1959; The Mosaics of St Sophia at Istanbul, 1962; The Art of the Byzantine Empire, Sources and Documents, 1972; Architettura bizantina, 1974; Byzantium, 1980; Byzantium and its Image, 1984; Le Développement Urbain de Constantinople, 1985; (ed) The Oxford History of Byzantium, 2002. *Address*: 12 High Street, Brill, Aylesbury, Bucks HP18 9ST.

**MANGOLD, Thomas Cornelius;** freelance television and radio correspondent and travel writer, since 2003; author; Senior Correspondent, BBC TV Panorama, 1976–2003; *b* 20 Aug. 1934; *s* of Fritz Mangold and Dorothea Mangold; *m* 1st, 1958, Anne (*née* Butler) (marr. diss. 1970); one *d*; 2nd, 1972, Valerie Ann Hare (*née* Dean) (marr. diss. 1991); two *d*; 3rd, 2000, Kathryn Mary Colleton Parkinson-Smith. *Educ*: Dorking Grammar Sch. Reporter, Croydon Advertiser, 1952. Served RA, 1952–54. Reporter: Croydon Advertiser, 1955–59; Sunday Pictorial, 1959–62; Daily Express, 1962–64; BBC TV News, 1964–70; BBC TV Current Affairs (24 Hours, later Midweek), 1970–76. *Publications*: (jtly) The File on the Tsar, 1976; (jtly) The Tunnels of Cu Chi, 1985; Cold Warrior, 1991; Plague Wars, 1999; Splashed!: a life from print to Panorama, 2016. *Recreations*: writing, playing Blues harp. *Address*: c/o WGM Literary Agency, 12th Floor, Blue Tower, Media City, Manchester M50 2ST. *T*: 07802 880088. *E*: beebtom@aol.com. *W*: www.tommangold.com.

**MANLEY, Andrew Robert,** PhD; Chief Executive, Prolifient Partners Ltd, since 2018; *b* Wallingford, 17 June 1956; *s* of Anthony John Manley and Gillian Kathleen Manley (*née* West); *m* 1980, Pauline Catterall; one *s* one *d*. *Educ*: Bradfield Coll.; Univ. of Wales (BSc 1977; PhD 1980); London Business Sch. (MBA 1991). Cert. Co. Directorship 2006; Dip. Coaching, Birkbeck, Univ. of London, 2015. MCIPS 2010; FRICS 2012. Royal Dutch Shell: Mktg Exec., 1980–92; Chief Exec., Shell Cos, Paraguay, 1993–98; Chm., Forestal Yguazu SRL, 1996–98; Commercial Dir, Shell UK Ltd, 1999–2002; Dir, Shell Gas UK Ltd, 1999–2010; Vice Pres., Latin America, 2003–08; Prog. Dir, Shell Canada Ltd, 2008–09; Dir, Downstream Projects, Shell Internat. Ltd, 2009–10; Commercial Dir, MoD, 2010–11; non-executive Director: Defence Equipment and Support, 2010–11; Defence Estates, 2010–11; Chm. and Chief Exec., Defence Infrastructure Orgn, 2011–14; Exec. Dir, Tidal Lagoon Power plc, 2015–17; Chief Exec., Transcordiant Ltd, 2017–18 (non-exec. Dir, 2014–18). Non-exec. Dir, Symatrix UK Ltd, 2009–. Regl Dir, London, Business Doctors, 2019–. MInstD 2000. FRSA 2018. *Recreations*: hiking, sailing, theatre.

**MANLEY, David Eric;** QC 2003; *b* 30 April 1956; *s* of Eric and May Manley; *m* 1983, Caroline Morgan; one *s* one *d*. *Educ*: Leeds Univ. (BA Hons). Called to the Bar, Inner Temple, 1981; in practice, specialising in planning and environmental law. *Recreations*: gardening, reading, shooting, fishing. *Address*: Kings Chambers, 36 Young Street, Manchester M3 3FT. *T*: (0161) 832 9082, *Fax*: (0161) 835 2139. *E*: clerks@kingschambers.com.

**MANLEY, Hilary; Her Honour Judge Manley;** a Circuit Judge, since 2014; *b* Sheffield, 17 July 1966; *d* of Peter Scott Manley and Alison Manley (*née* Needham); *m* 1998, Jonathan Gregg; one *d*. *Educ*: University Coll. London (LLB (Hons)). Called to the Bar, Gray's Inn, 1996; a Recorder, NE Circuit, 2012–14. *Recreations*: music, photography, history, travel. *Address*: Courts of Justice, Crown Square, Manchester M3 3FL.

**MANLEY, Hon. John (Paul);** PC (Can.) 1993; OC 2009; President and Chief Executive Officer, Business Council of Canada (formerly Canadian Council of Chief Executives), 2010–18; *b* 15 Jan. 1950; *s* of John Joseph and Mildred Charlotte (Scharf) Manley; *m* 1973, Judith Mary Rae; one *s* two *d*. *Educ*: Carleton Univ. (BA 1971); Univ. of Ottawa (Law 1976). Law clerk for Chief Justice of Canada, 1976–77; Partner, Perley-Robertson, Panet, Hill & McDougall, lawyers, 1977–88; Chm., Ottawa-Carleton BoT, 1985–86. MP (L) Ottawa S, 1988–2004; Minister: of Industry, 1993–2000; of Western Econ. Diversification, Atlantic Canadian Opportunities Agency, 1996; of Econ. Develt for Quebec Regs, 1996–2000; of Foreign Affairs, 2000–02; of Infrastructure and Crown Corporations, and of Finance, 2002–03; Dep. Prime Minister of Canada, 2002–03; Political Minister for Ontario, 2002–03; Sen. Counsel, McCarthy Tétrault LLP, 2004–09. Chairman, Cabinet Committees: on Public Security and Anti-Terrorism, 2001–03; on Econ. Union and Social Union, 2002–03. Chm., Ontario Power Gen. Review Cttee, 2004. Dir, Nortel Networks, 2004–09. Newsmaker of Year, Time Mag. of Canada, 2001. *Recreation*: marathon runner.

**MANLEY, Simon John,** CMG 2009; HM Diplomatic Service; Ambassador to Spain and concurrently (non-resident) to Andorra, 2013–19; *b* 18 Sept. 1967; *s of* James and Beryl Manley; *m* 1996, Maria Isabel Fernandez Utgès; three *d. Educ:* Montpelier Primary Sch., Ealing; Latymer Upper Sch., Hammersmith; Magdalen Coll., Oxford (BA Hons Modern Hist.); Yale Univ. Grad. Sch. (MA Internat. Relns). Entered HM Diplomatic Service, 1990; UN Dept, FCO, 1990–93; on secondment to DGIV (Competition), EC, 1993; UKMIS to UN, NY, 1993–98; on secondment to EU Council of Ministers, 1998–2002; Dep. Hd, EU (Internal), FCO, 2002–03; Head: Econ. and Central Europe Team, FCO, 2003–06; Counter-Terrorism Policy Dept, FCO, 2006–07; Dir, Defence and Strategic Threats, FCO, 2007–11; Dir, Europe, FCO, 2011–13. Comdr, Order of Merit (Poland), 2004; Encomienda de Número, Orden de Isabel la Católica (Spain), 2017. *Recreations:* theatre, gardens, history. *Address:* c/o Foreign and Commonwealth Office, King Charles Street, SW1A 2AH.

**MANLY, Timothy John;** Headmaster, Hurstpierpoint College, since 2005; *b* 12 Feb. 1964; *m* 1990, Henrietta Whetstone; two *s* two *d. Educ:* Oriel Coll., Oxford (BA Hons Lit. Hum.); London Sch. of Econs (MSc); Hughes Hall, Cambridge (PGCE). Various appts in commerce, 1987–93; Sevenoaks School: Teacher, 1994–2000; Housemaster, 1996–2000; Hd of Classics Dept, 1996–99; Dep. Headmaster, Oakham Sch., 2000–04. Non-exec. Dir, Harris Fedn of S London Schs, 2007–11; Dir, Dio. of Chichester Academies Trust, 2018–. Governor: Hazelwood Prep. Sch., 2009–18; Dorset House Prep. Sch., 2010–18; Pennthorpe Prep. Sch., 2018–. Chm., Woodard Heads' Assoc., 2011–13. *Recreations:* family, cross-country and distance running, most racquet sports, bridge, books. *Address:* Hurstpierpoint College, Malthouse Lane, Hurstpierpoint, Hassocks, W Sussex BN6 9JS. *T:* (01273) 833636. *E:* headmaster@hppc.co.uk.

**MANN, Hon. Sir Anthony;** see Mann, Hon. Sir G. A.

**MANN, Prof. Anthony Howard,** MD; FRCP, FRCPsych; Professor of Epidemiological Psychiatry, Institute of Psychiatry, King's College London, 1989–2013, now Emeritus; *b* 11 Dec. 1940; *s of* Alfred Haward Mann and Marjory Ethel (*née* Weatherly); civil partnership 2006, Pekka Antero Vaalle. *Educ:* Rugby Sch.; Jesus Coll., Cambridge (MD 1982); St Bartholomew's Hosp. FRCPsych 1984; FRCP 1986. Res. worker, and Sen. Lectr, Inst. of Psychiatry, 1972–80; Sen. Lectr, then Prof. of Psychiatry, Royal Free Hosp., 1980–89. Associate Prof., Montpellier Univ., 2002–03. Hon. FRCGP 2001. *Publications:* In Sunshine and Shadow: the family story of Danny Boy, 2013; numerous contribs to scientific jls on psychiatry of old age, general practice and epidemiology. *Recreations:* friends, France, historical research. *Address:* c/o Hoare and Co., 32 Lowndes Street, SW1X 9HZ.

**MANN, Prof. (Colin) Nicholas (Jocelyn),** CBE 1999; PhD; FBA 1992; Emeritus Professor of Renaissance Studies, since 2007, and Distinguished Senior Fellow, since 2009, School of Advanced Study, University of London; *b* 24 Oct. 1942; *s of* Colin Henry Mann and Marie Elise Mann (*née* Gosling); *m* 1st, 1964, Joëlle Bourcart (marr. diss. 2003); one *s* one *d*; 2nd, 2003, Helen Margaret Stevenson; two *d. Educ:* Eton; King's Coll., Cambridge (MA, PhD). Res. Fellow, Clare Coll., Cambridge, 1965–67; Lectr, Univ. of Warwick, 1967–72; Vis. Fellow, All Souls Coll., Oxford, 1972; Fellow and Tutor, Pembroke Coll., Oxford, 1973–90, Emeritus Fellow, 1991–2006, Hon. Fellow, 2006; University of London: Dir, Warburg Inst., and Prof. of Hist. of Classical Tradition, 1990–2001; Sen. Res. Fellow, Warburg Inst., 2001–07; Dean, Sch. of Advanced Study, 2002–07; Pro-Vice-Chancellor, 2003–07. Visiting Professor: Univ. of Toronto, 1996; Coll. de France, 1998; Univ. of Calabria, 1999–2000. Member Council: Mus. of Modern Art, Oxford, 1984–92 (Chm., 1988–90); Contemporary Applied Arts, 1994–2005 (Chm., 1996–99); British Acad., 1995–98, 1999–2006 (For. Sec., 1999–2006); RHBNC, 1996–98; RCA, 2001–07; Mem., British Library Adv. Council, 1997–2002. Vice-Pres., ALLEA, 2006–11. Trustee: Cubitt Artists, 1996–99; Learning Skills Res., 2010–; Padworth Coll., 2014–19. Fellow: European Medieval Acad., 1993; Fondazione Lorenzo Valla, 2007. Romance Editor, Medium Ævum, 1982–90. Hon. DLitt Warwick, 2006. *Publications:* Petrarch Manuscripts in the British Isles, 1975; Petrarch, 1984; A Concordance to Petrarch's Bucolicum Carmen, 1984; (ed jtly) Lorenzo the Magnificent: culture and politics, 1996; (ed jtly) Medieval and Renaissance Scholarship, 1996; (ed jtly) Giordano Bruno 1583–1585: the English experience, 1997; (ed jtly) The Image of the Individual: portraits in the Renaissance, 1998; (ed jtly) Photographs at the Frontier: Aby Warburg in America 1895–1896, 1998; Carnets de voyage, 2003; Pétrarque: les voyages de l'esprit, 2004; (ed jtly) Britannia Latina: Latin in the culture of Great Britain from the Middle Ages to the twentieth century, 2005; (ed and trans.) Francesco Petrarca, My Secret Book, 2016; articles in learned jls, 1969–2012, 2019. *Recreations:* yoga, poetry, sculpture. *Address:* 34 High Street, Axbridge, Som BS26 2AF. *T:* (01934) 732151.

**MANN, David William,** FBCS; management consultant, 2014–16; Deputy Chairman, Logica plc, 1993–94; *b* 14 June 1944; *s of* William and Mary Mann; *m* 1968, Gillian Mary Edwards; two *s. Educ:* Felixstowe Grammar Sch.; Jesus Coll., Cambridge (MA). CEng; CITP; FBCS. CEIR, 1966–69; Logica: joined 1969; Dir, 1976; Man. Dir, UK Ops, 1979; Dep. Gp Man. Dir, 1982; Gp Man. Dir and Chief Exec., 1987. Chairman: Cambridge Display Technol., 1995–97; Flomerics Gp, 1995–2008; Velti plc, 2006–14; Chm., 1996–2007, Dep. Chm., 2007–14, Charteris plc. Director: Industrial Control Services Gp, 1994–2000; Druid Gp, 1996–2000; Room Solutions (formerly Room Underwriting Systems), 1996–2006; Aveva (formerly Cadcentre) Group, 1999–2010; Eurolink Managed Services, 1999–2000; Ansbacher Hldgs, 2000–04. Special Advr, Technical Rev. Cttee of Bd, NATS, 2010–15. Mem., Engineering Council, 1993–95. Pres., British Computer Soc., 1994–95. Master, Information Technologists' Co., 1997–98 (Chm., 2002–07, Dir, 2007–11, Charitable Trust). Chm., Livery Past Masters' Assoc. 1997/98, 2006–09. CCMI (CIMgt 1994–2008); FInstD 1994–2006. Chm., Epping Forest Wine Soc., 2005–12. *Recreations:* gardening, walking, ski-ing. *Address:* Theydon Copt, Forest Side, Epping, Essex CM16 4ED. *T:* (01992) 575842, 07956 341105. *Club:* Athenæum (Member: Wine Cttee, 2010–16; Gen. Cttee, 2016–; Exec. Cttee, 2017–).

**MANN, Hon. Sir (George) Anthony,** Kt 2004; **Hon. Mr Justice Mann;** a Judge of the High Court of Justice, Chancery Division, since 2004; *s of* George Edgar and Ilse Beate Mann; *m* 1979, Margaret Ann Sherret; two *d. Educ:* Chesterfield Grammar Sch.; Perse Sch., Cambridge; St Peter's Coll., Oxford (BA 1973; MA 1977; Hon. Fellow 2010). Called to the Bar, Lincoln's Inn, 1974, Bencher, 2002; QC 1992; a Recorder, 2002–04. *Recreations:* French horn playing, music, computers. *Address:* Royal Courts of Justice, 7 Rolls Building, Fetter Lane, EC4A 1NL.

**MANN, Prof. Gillian Lesley, (Jill),** FBA 1990; Notre Dame Professor of English, University of Notre Dame, Indiana, 1999–2004, now Emeritus Professor; *b* 7 April 1943; *d* of late Edward William Ditchburn and Kathleen Ditchburn (*née* Bellamy); *m* 1st, 1964, Michael Mann (marr. diss. 1976); 2nd, 2003, Michael Lapidge. *Educ:* Bede Grammar Sch., Sunderland; St Anne's Coll., Oxford (BA 1964; Hon. Fellow, 1990); Clare Hall, Cambridge (MA; PhD 1971). Research Fellow, Clare Hall, Cambridge, 1968–71; Lectr, Univ. of Kent at Canterbury, 1971–72; University of Cambridge: Official Fellow, 1972–88, Professorial Fellow, 1988–98, Life Fellow, 1999, Girton Coll.; Asst Lectr, 1974–78; Lectr, 1978–88; Prof. of Medieval and Renaissance English, 1988–98. British Academy Research Reader, 1985–87. *Publications:* Chaucer and Medieval Estates Satire, 1973; Ysengrimus, 1987; (ed with Piero Boitani) The Cambridge Chaucer Companion, 1986, rev. edn 2003; Geoffrey Chaucer, 1991; Feminizing Chaucer, 2002; (ed) Canterbury Tales, 2005; (ed with Maura Nolan) The Text in the Community, 2006; From Aesop to Reynard, 2009; Life in Words: essays on Chaucer, the Gawain-Poet, and Malory, 2014; articles on Middle English, medieval French and medieval Latin. *Recreation:* travel. *Address:* Girton College, Cambridge CB3 0JG.

**MANN, Jillian Rose,** MBE 2013; FRCP, FRCPCH; Consultant Paediatric Oncologist, Birmingham Children's Hospital, 1979–2002, now Emeritus; *b* 29 April 1939; *d* of William Farmcote Mann and Vera Maud Mann. *Educ:* Pate's Grammar Sch. for Girls, Cheltenham; St Thomas' Hosp. Med. Sch., London (MB BS 1962). LRCP 1962, MRCP 1966, FRCP 1980; MRCS 1962; DCH 1964; FRCPCH 1997, Hon. FRCPCH 2004. Postgrad. trng, St Thomas' and Great Ormond St Children's Hosps, 1963–67, and Birmingham Children's Hosp., 1967–71; Consultant Paediatrician, S Birmingham, and Consultant Associate in Haematological Diseases, Birmingham Children's Hosp., 1972–79. Hon. Prof., Sch. of Medicine, Univ. of Birmingham, 1997–2006. Member: Cttee on Med. Aspects of Radiation in the Envmt, DoH, 1985–89; Standing Med. Adv. Cttee, DoH, 1986–90. Member: Leukaemia in Childhood Wkg party, MRC, 1975–2000; Med. and Scientific Adv. Panel, Leukaemia Res. Fund, 1985–88. Mem. Council, RCP, 1988–91; RCP and RCPCH: Regl Advr, 1994–99; Examr for MRCP/MRCPCH, 1994–2002. Founder Mem., 1977, Sec., 1977–81, Chm., 1983–86, UK Children's Cancer Study Gp; Chm., Educn and Trng Cttee, Soc. Internat. d'Oncologie Pédiatrique Europe and Eur. Soc. of Paediatric Haematol. and Immunol., 2000–03. Trustee, Birmingham Children's Hosp. Charities, 2003–11 (Chm., 2004–09). Mem., Lunar Soc., Birmingham, 1994–2012. Eur. Women of Achievement Award, Humanitarian Section, EUW, 1996; Nye Bevan Lifetime Achievement Award, 2000. *Publications:* numerous book chapters and contribs to learned jls mostly on childhood leukaemia, cancer and blood diseases; numerous abstracts of contribs to nat. and internat. scientific meetings. *Recreations:* music, country pursuits, local history.

**MANN, John;** *b* 10 Jan. 1960; *s of* James Mann and Brenda (*née* Cleavin); *m* 1986, Joanna White; one *s* two *d. Educ:* Manchester Univ. (BA Econ). MIPD. Hd of Res. and Educn, AEU, 1988–90; Nat. Trng Officer, TUC, 1990–95; Liaison Officer, Nat. Trade Union and Lab Party, 1995–2000. Dir, Abraxas Communications Ltd, 1998–2001. Mem. (Lab), Lambeth BC, 1986–90. MP (Lab) Bassetlaw, 2001–Sept. 2019. Mem., Treasury Select Cttee, 2003–05, 2009–19. Ind. govt advr on antisemitism, 2019–. Mem., Editl Adv. Panel, People Management, 2005–. *Publications:* (with Phil Woolas) Labour and Youth: the missing generation, 1985; The Real Deal: drug policy that works, 2006. *Recreations:* football, cricket, hill walking. *Clubs:* Manton Miners'; Worksop Town.
*[Created a Baron (Life Peer), 2019 but title not gazetted at time of going to press.]*

**MANN, John Frederick;** educational consultant; *b* 4 June 1930; *e s of* Frederick Mann and Hilda G. (*née* Johnson); *m* 1966, Margaret (*née* Moore); one *s* one *d. Educ:* Poole and Tavistock Grammar Schs; Trinity Coll., Oxford (MA); Birmingham Univ. Asst Master, Colchester Royal Grammar Sch., 1954–61; Admin. Asst, Leeds County Bor., 1962–65; Asst Educn Officer, Essex CC, 1965–67; Dep. Educn Officer, Sheffield County Bor., 1967–78; Sec., Schools Council for the Curriculum and Exams, 1978–83; Dir of Educn, London Bor. of Harrow, 1983–88. Member: Iron and Steel Industry Trng Bd, 1975–78; Exec., Soc. of Educn Officers, 1976–78; Sch. Broadcasting Council, 1979–83; Council, British Educn Management and Admin Soc., 1979–84; Cttee, Soc. of Educn Consultants, 1990–95 (Sec., 1990–94; Vice Chm., 1994–95). Chm., Standards Cttee, 2002–11, Ind. Person, 2012–13, Brent BC. Governor: Welbeck Coll., 1975–84; Hall Sch., 1985–88. Chm., Brent Samaritans, 1995–99. Sec., London Appreciation Soc., 2016–. Hon. Fellow, Sheffield Polytechnic, 1980; Hon. FCT (Hon. FCP 1986). FRSA. JP Sheffield, 1976–79. *Publications:* Education, 1979; Highbury Fields School, 1994; To Gladly Learn and Gladly Teach, 2004; contrib. to Victoria County History of Essex, Local Govt Studies, and Educn. *Recreations:* travel, books, theatre, gardening. *Address:* 109 Chatsworth Road, NW2 4BH. *T:* (020) 8459 5419.

**MANN, Very Rev. John Owen;** Dean of Belfast, 2011–17; Team Rector, Swanage and Studland Team Ministry, since 2017; *b* Blackheath, 20 March 1955; *s of* Dr Edgar Mann and Joan Mann; *m* 1976, Helen Kneale; one *s* one *d. Educ:* Queen's Univ. Belfast (BD 1977; MTh 1986; MPhil 1998); C of I Theol Coll. Ordained deacon, 1979, priest, 1981; Assistant Curate: Cloughfern, 1979–82; St Columba, Knock, 1982–85; Rector: St John the Baptist, Ballyrashane, 1985–89; Parishes of Bentworth, Shalden and Lasham, Dio. of Winchester, 1989–93; Rural Dean, Alton, 1992–93; Rector: Ascension, Cloughfern, 1993–2002; St John, Malone, 2002–11. Preb. of Clonmethan, Nat. Cathedral of St Patrick's, Dublin, 1999–2011. Hon. DLitt Ulster, 2018. Lambeth Cross for Ecumenism, 2018. *Address:* The Rectory, 12 Church Hill, Swanage, Dorset BH19 1HU.

**MANN, Jonathan Simon;** QC 2015; **His Honour Judge Mann;** a Circuit Judge, since 2018; *b* London, 19 June 1966; *s of* Brian Mann and Ruth Mann; *m* 2001, Pamela Reddy; one *s* one *d. Educ:* Atholl Grammar Sch.; Univ. of Essex (LLB Hons 1987). Called to the Bar, Inner Temple, 1989; in practice as barrister, specialising in criminal defence, fraud and regulatory compliance; a Recorder, 2012–18. Mem., Sentencing Adv. Panel, 2010. Mem., Gen. Cttee, 2006–08, Treas., 2008–10, Criminal Bar Assoc. *Recreations:* study of medieval and Tudor history, study and collection of medieval coinage. *Address:* Woolwich Crown Court, 2 Belmarsh Road, SE28 0EY.

**MANN, Martin Edward;** QC 1983; a Deputy High Court Judge, Chancery Division, 1992–2016; *b* 12 Sept. 1943; *s of* E. S. Mann and M. L. F. Mann; *m* 1966, Jacqueline Harriette (*née* Le Maître); two *d. Educ:* Cranleigh Sch. Called to the Bar, Gray's Inn, 1968 (Lord Justice Holker Sen. Exhibn), Lincoln's Inn, 1973 (*ad eund*); Bencher, Lincoln's Inn, 1991. Mem., Senate of the Inns of Court and the Bar, 1979–82; Chm., Bar Council Fees Collection Cttee, 1993–95; Mem., QC Selection Panel, 2013–17. Member of numerous professional assocs including: Chancery Bar Assoc.; Commercial Bar Assoc.; Bar of Eastern Caribbean Supreme Ct. Consultant Ed., Palmer's Company Law Manual. *Publications:* (jtly) What Kind of Common Agricultural Policy for Europe, 1975; (contrib.) Tolley's Insolvency Law; (contrib.) Blackstone's Guide to the Companies Act, 2006. *Recreations:* farming, the arts. *Address:* XXIV Old Buildings, Lincoln's Inn, WC2A 3UP. *T:* (020) 7691 2424; Kingston St Mary, Somerset. *Club:* Garrick.

**MANN, Nicholas;** see Mann, C. N. J.

**MANN, Paul;** QC 2002; a Recorder, since 1999; *b* 4 Feb. 1958; *s of* George Arthur and Elsie May Mann; *m* 1988, Carol Joy Beddows. *Educ:* Trent Coll., Long Eaton, Derbyshire; Manchester Poly. (BA Hons Law). Called to the Bar, Gray's Inn, 1980, Bencher, 2008; in practice as barrister, specialising in crime, 1981–2016. Treas., 2002–08, Dep. Leader, Nottingham, 2008–11, Midland Circuit. *Recreations:* travel, cycling, open water swimming, gardening, script-writing, local legal history speaker. *Address:* 1 High Pavement, Nottingham NG1 1HF. *T:* (0115) 941 8218.

**MANN, Perminder;** Chief Executive Officer, Bonnier Books UK, since 2017; *b* Hillingdon, Middx, 23 Dec. 1971; *d* of Kanwaljit Singh Gill and Rupjit Kaur Gill; *m* 1999, Permpinder Singh Mann; one *s* one *d*. *Educ:* De Montfort Univ. (BA Arts and Humanities 1993); Kingston Univ. (MBA). Special Sales Mgr, Macmillan Publishers, 1996–98; Gp Sales Develt Mgr, Transworld Publishers, 1998–2002; UK Sales Manager: Hinkler Books, 2002–04; Phidal Publishing, 2004–06; Internat. Sales and Licensing Mgr, Flair Leisure Products, 2006–09; Business Develt Dir, Bonnier Publishing, 2009–12; Managing Director: Autumn Publishing, 2012–14; Blink Publishing, 2014–15; CEO, Kings Rd Publishing, 2015–17. Mem. Cttee, Book Soc., 2017–. *Recreations:* reading, music, Netflix. *Address:* Bonnier Books UK, 4.01 The Plaza, 535 Kings Road, SW10 0SZ. *E:* perminder.mann@bonnierbooks.co.uk.

**MANN, Sir Rupert (Edward),** 3rd Bt *cr* 1905; *b* 11 Nov. 1946; *s* of Major Edward Charles Mann, DSO, MC (*g s* of 1st Bt) (*d* 1959), and Pamela Margaret, *o d* of late Major Frank Haultain Hornsby; *S* great uncle, 1971; *m* 1974, Mary Rose, *d* of Geoffrey Butler, Stetchworth, Newmarket; two *s*. *Educ:* Malvern. *Heir: s* Alexander Rupert Mann, *b* 6 April 1978. *Address:* Billingford Hall, Diss, Norfolk IP21 4HN. *Clubs:* Boodle's, MCC; Norfolk.

**MANN, Scott Leslie;** MP (C) North Cornwall, since 2015; *b* 24 June 1977; *s* of Eugene Mann and Peggy Mann; one *d*. *Educ:* Wadebridge Boys' Sch.; Wadebridge Comp. Sch.; St Austell Coll. (BTEC Business Diploma). Gardener, 1994–97; butcher, 1995–98; postman, 1995–2015; retail worker, 1997–2000. Mem., Cornwall Council, 2009–16. *Recreations:* fishing, road cycling, running (ran London Marathon 2017). *Address:* (office) 10 Market House Arcade, Fore Street, Bodmin, Cornwall PL31 2JA. *T:* (01208) 74337. *E:* scott@scottmann.org.uk. *Club:* Wadebridge Cricket (Hon. Vice Pres., 2013–).

**MANN, Prof. Stephen,** DPhil; FRS 2003; Professor of Chemistry, University of Bristol, since 1998; *b* 1 April 1955; *s* of Harold and Olive Mann; *m* 1977, Jane Lucinda Musgrave; one *s* one *d*. *Educ:* Univ. of Manchester Inst. of Sci. and Technol. (BSc Hons Chem. 1976); Univ. of Manchester (MSc 1978); DPhil Oxford 1981. University of Bath: Lectr in Chem., 1984–88; Reader, 1988–90; Prof. of Chem., 1990–98. Davy Medal, Royal Soc., 2016. *Publications:* Biomineralization: principles and concepts in bioinorganic materials chemistry, 2001; numerous contribs to learned scientific jls. *Recreations:* running, electric guitar, family life. *Address:* School of Chemistry, University of Bristol, Bristol BS8 1TS. *T:* (0117) 928 9935. *E:* s.mann@bristol.ac.uk.

**MANNERS,** family name of **Duke of Rutland** and **Baron Manners**.

**MANNERS,** 6th Baron *cr* 1807, of Foston, co. Lincoln; **John Hugh Robert Manners;** Partner, Macfarlanes, 1987–2014 (Head of Litigation, 2000–08); *b* 5 May 1956; *s* of 5th Baron Manners and Jennifer Selena, *d* of Ian Fairbairn; *S* father, 2008; *m* 2007, Juliet Elizabeth Anthea McMyn; one *s* one *d*, and two *d* by former marriage. *Educ:* Eton. Admitted Solicitor, 1980. Official Verderer, New Forest, 2017–. Chm. Trustees, Fortune Centre of Riding Therapy, 2014–. *Recreations:* shooting, walking, Irish Terriers. *Heir: s* Hon. John Alexander David Manners, *b* 22 Feb. 2011. *Address:* North Ripley House, Avon, Christchurch, Dorset BH23 8EP. *Club:* Pratt's.

**MANNERS, Prof. Ian,** PhD; FRS 2011; FRS(Can); Professor of Inorganic, Macromolecular and Materials Chemistry, since 2006 and European Union Marie Curie Chair, since 2005, University of Bristol; *b* 1961; *m* 1980, Deborah O'Hanlon; one *s* one *d*. *Educ:* Univ. of Bristol (BSc 1st Cl. Hons 1982; PhD Chem. 1985). Postdoctoral res., Dept of Inorganic Chem., Univ. of Aachen, 1986–87; Res. Associate, Dept of Chem., Pennsylvania State Univ., 1988–90; Department of Chemistry, University of Toronto: Asst Prof., 1990–94; Associate Prof., 1994–95; Prof., 1995–; Canada Res. Chair, 2001. Tilden Lectr, RSC, 2007. Alfred P. Sloan Fellow, 1994–98. FRS(Can) 2001. Rutherford Meml Medal in Chem., 1996, Peter Days Award, 2012, RSC; Corday-Morgan Medal, 1997, Wolfson Merit Award, 2005, Royal Soc.; Steacie Prize, E. W. R. Steacie Meml Trust, 2000. *Publications:* Synthetic Metal-Containing Polymers; Metal-Containing and Metallosupramolecular Polymers and Materials; Frontiers in Transition Metal-Containing Polymers; Inorganic Rings and Polymers of the P-Block Elements; contrib. papers to scientific jls, incl. Science, Inorganic Chem., Jl Amer. Chem. Soc.; 11 patents. *Address:* School of Chemistry, University of Bristol, Bristol BS8 1TS.

**MANNERS, Hon. Thomas (Jasper);** Director, Lazard Brothers, 1965–89 (Deputy Chairman, 1986–89); *b* 12 Dec. 1929; *y s* of 4th Baron Manners, MC, and of Mary Edith, *d* of late Rt Rev. Lord William Cecil; *m* 1955, Sarah, *d* of Brig. Roger Peake, DSO; three *s*. *Educ:* Eton. Lazard Brothers & Co. Ltd, 1955–89; Director: Legal & General Gp, 1972–93; Scapa Gp, 1970–96; Davy Corp., 1985–91. *Recreations:* shooting, fishing. *Address:* Holly House, The Paddock, Newbury Road, Kingsclere, Newbury, Berks RG20 5SP. *Club:* White's.

**MANNING, Prof. David Andrew Charles,** PhD; Professor of Soil Science, Newcastle University, since 2000; President, Geological Society of London, 2014–16; *b* Kilwinning, 27 Aug. 1955; *s* of late Leslie Charles Manning and Dorothy Mary Manning; *m* 1978, Lucy Jane Stein; two *s* one *d*. *Educ:* Nottingham High Sch.; Durham Univ. (BSc Geol. 1976); Univ. of Manchester (PhD 1979). CGeol 1993; CSci 2005; EurGeol 2005. Research Fellow: Univ. of Manchester, 1979–81; Centre de Recherches Pétrographiques et Géochimiques, Nancy, 1981–82; Lectr, Newcastle Univ., 1983–88; University of Manchester: Lectr, 1988–92, Sen. Lectr, 1992–96, Reader, 1996–2000, in Geol.; Prof. of Envmtl Geochem., 2000; Acting Hd, Sch. of Civil Engrg and Geoscis, Newcastle Univ., 2016–17. Nuffield Fellow, 1988–89; Leverhulme Res. Fellow, 2001–02. Dir, Mineral Solutions Ltd, 1996–2006. Hon. Prof. of Soil Mineral Processes, Univ. of Edinburgh, 2015–. *Publications:* Introduction to Industrial Minerals, 1995; over 200 articles in jls, book chapters and conf. papers. *Recreations:* being outdoors, rowing, walking, gardening (especially exotic fruit and vegetables), reading Zola in French, fiddle and cello music (Scottish repertoire). *Address:* School of Natural and Environmental Sciences, Drummond Building, Newcastle University, Newcastle upon Tyne NE1 7RU. *T:* (0191) 208 6610, *Fax:* (0191) 208 5322. *E:* david.manning@ncl.ac.uk.

**MANNING, Sir David (Geoffrey),** GCMG 2008 (KCMG 2001; CMG 1992); KCVO 2015 (CVO 2007); HM Diplomatic Service, retired; Ambassador to the United States of America, 2003–07; Registrar, Order of Saint Michael and Saint George, since 2010; *b* 5 Dec. 1949; *s* of John Robert Manning and Joan Barbara Manning; *m* 1973, Catherine Marjory Parkinson. *Educ:* Ardingly Coll.; Oriel Coll., Oxford (Hon. Fellow, 2003); Johns Hopkins Sch. of Advanced Internat. Studies, Bologna (Postgrad. Diploma in Internat. Relations, 1972). FCO, 1972; Warsaw, 1974–76; New Delhi, 1977–80; FCO, 1980–84; First Sec., Paris, 1984–88; Counsellor, seconded to Cabinet Office, 1988–90; Political Counsellor and Head of Political Sect., Moscow, 1990–93; Hd of Eastern Dept, FCO, 1993–94; British Mem., Contact Gp on Bosnia, Internat. Conf. on Former Yugoslavia, April–Nov. 1994; Hd of Policy Planning Staff, FCO, 1994–95; Ambassador to Israel, 1995–98; Dep. Under-Sec. of State, FCO, 1998–2000; Perm. Rep., UK Delegn to NATO, 2000–01; Foreign Policy Advr to Prime Minister, and Hd of Defence and Overseas Secretariat, Cabinet Office, 2001–03. Sen. Advr to Prince William, then to Duke and Duchess of Cambridge, and Prince Harry of Wales, later to Duke and Duchess of Sussex, 2009–19. Non-executive Director: Lloyds Banking Gp, 2008–09; BG Gp, 2008–16; Lockheed Martin UK, 2008–16; Dir, Gatehouse Advisory Partners, 2010–. Member: Panel of Sen. Advrs, Chatham House, 2008–; Internat. Adv. Bd, Hakluyt, 2008–11; Council, IISS, 2009–11; Council, Lloyd's of London, 2010–19; Adv. Bd, Global Strategy Forum, 2014–; Chm., Adv. Bd, IDEAS, LSE, 2010–18. Trustee: Turner Contemporary, 2008–13; Royal Foundn, 2009–17; Fulbright Commn, 2009–15. Patron: Afghan Connection, 2008–; Step Forward (formerly World Wide Volunteering), 2009– (Pres., 2015–). Fisher Family Fellow, Harvard Univ., 2012.

**MANNING, Dr Geoffrey Lewis,** FRCSE; FDSRCS; Chairman, North Staffordshire Hospital NHS Trust, 1993–2002; *b* 21 Sept. 1931; *s* of late Isaac Harold Manning and Florence Hilda Manning; *m* 1978, Patricia Margaret Wilson; one *d*. *Educ:* Rossall Sch., Fleetwood, Lancs; Univ. of Birmingham (LDS, BDS 1953; MB, ChB 1961). FDSRCS 1964; FRCSE 1986. Nat. service, Capt., RADC, 1954–56. Senior Registrar: Central Middx Hosp., 1964–66; Mt Vernon Hosp., 1966–68; Parkland Meml Hosp., Dallas, 1967; Consultant Oral Surgeon, N Staffs Hosp., 1968–93. Mem., N Staffs DHA, 1986–92. Leader, Health Task Force, Prince of Wales Business Leaders Forum, 1993–2000. Hon. DSc Keele, 2000. *Recreations:* gardening, brick-laying, classic cars. *Address:* The Old Hall, Haughton, Stafford ST18 9HB. *T:* (01785) 780273.

**MANNING, Jane Marian,** OBE 1990; freelance concert and opera singer (soprano), since 1965; vocal teacher, coach, writer and lecturer; *b* 20 Sept. 1938; *d* of Gerald Manville Manning and Lily Manning (*née* Thompson); *m* 1966, Anthony Edward Payne, *qv*. *Educ:* Norwich High Sch.; Royal Academy of Music (LRAM 1958); Scuola di Canto, Cureglia, Switzerland. GRSM 1960, ARCM 1962. London début (Park Lane Group), 1964; first BBC broadcast, 1965; début Henry Wood Promenade Concerts, 1972; founded own ensemble, Jane's Minstrels, 1988; regular appearances in leading concert halls and festivals in UK and Europe, with leading orchestras and conductors; many broadcasts and gramophone recordings, lectures and master classes. Specialist in contemporary music (over 300 world premières given); Warsaw Autumn Fest., 1975–78, 1987, 1992; Wexford Opera Fest., 1976; Scottish Opera, 1978; Brussels Opera, 1980. Canadian début, 1977; tours: of Australia and New Zealand, 1978, 1980, 1982, 1984, 1986, 1990, 1996, 2000, 2002; of USA, 1981, 1983, 1985, 1986, 1987, 1988, 1989, 1991, 1993, 1996, 1997. Milhaud Vis. Prof., Mills Coll. Oakland, 1983; Lucie Stern Vis. Prof., Mills Coll., Oakland, 1981 and 1986; Vis. Artist, Univ. of Manitoba, Canada, 1992; Vis. Prof., RCM, 1995–; Hon. Prof., Keele Univ., 1996–2002; AHRC (formerly AHRB) Creative Arts Res. Fellow, 2004–07, Vis. Prof., 2007–11, Kingston Univ. Vice Pres., SPNM, 1984–2009; Res. Fellow, GSM, 2013–. Chm., Eye Music (formerly Nettlefold Fest.) Trust, 1990–; Trustee (formerly Mem., Exec. Cttee), Help Musicians UK (formerly Musicians Benevolent Fund), 1989–2015; Mem., Arts Council Music Panel, 1990–95; Internat. Jury, Gaudeamus Young Interpreters Competition, Holland, 1976, 1979, 1987; Jury, Eur. Youth Competition for Composers, Eur. Cultural Foundn, 1985. Hon. ARAM 1972, FRAM 1984; FRCM 1998. DUniv York, 1988; Hon. DMus: Keele, 2004; Durham, 2007; Hon. DArts Kingston, 2012. Special award, Composers Guild of Gt Britain, 1973; Gold Badge, BASCA, 2013. *Publications:* (chapter in) How Music Works, 1981; New Vocal Repertory, vol. I, 1986, vol. II, 1998; (chapter in) A Messiaen Companion, 1996; Voicing Pierrot, 2012; (contrib.) Cambridge History of Musical Performance, 2012; (chapter in) Creativity in Later Life, 2018; (chapter in) Musicians in the Making, 2018; Vocal Repertoire for the 21st Century (2 vols), 2019; articles in Composer, Music and Musicians, and Tempo. *Recreations:* reading, cinema, ornithology, theatre. *Address:* 2 Wilton Square, N1 3DL. *T:* (020) 7359 1593.

**MANNING, Jeremy James C.;** see Carter-Manning.

**MANNING, Kingsley;** Chair, North West London Pathology, since 2017; *b* Coventry, Feb. 1952; *s* of Alfred Manning and Muriel Manning; *m* 1975, Judy Davies; one *s* one *d*. *Educ:* King Henry VIII Sch., Coventry; Univ. of Birmingham (BSc Biochem.); London Business Sch. (MBA). Founder and Chief Exec., Newchurch Ltd, 1983–2009; Exec. Chm., Tribal Health Services, 2009–11; Sen. Advr, McKinsey & Co., 2011–13. Chm., Health and Social Care Inf. Centre, 2013–16. Director: UK Innovation and Science Seed Fund, 2015–; Silver Link Software Ltd, 2017–. Trustee, Royal Philharmonic Soc., 2015–. *Recreations:* opera, chamber music, vegetable growing, learning French. *Club:* Athenæum.

**MANNING, Lee Antony,** FCA; Partner, ReSolve Advisory Group, since 2019; *b* London, 9 Nov. 1957; *s* of Alan Manning and Judith Manning; *m* 1989, Anne; two *s*. *Educ:* Mill Hill Sch.; Kingston Poly. (BA Hons Accountancy and Finance). FCA 1983; Chartered Accountant; Licensed Insolvency Practitioner. Audit and Insolvency, Touche Ross & Co., 1980–84; Insolvency Gp, Arthur Andersen, 1984–89; Insolvency Partner, Buchler Phillips & Co., 1989–99; Restructuring Partner, Kroll Ltd, 1999–2004; Partner in Restructuring Services, Deloitte LLP, 2004–19. Pres., R3, 2012–13. Mem., Disciplinary Appeals Cttee, ICAEW. Treas., Fulham FC Charitable Foundn. *Recreations:* cycling, swimming, ski-ing, golf, watching football, live music, travel, photography, world cinema. *Address:* ReSolve Advisory Group, 22 York Buildings, corner John Adam Street, WC2N 6JU. *E:* l_manning@sky.com.

**MANNING, Mary Elizabeth;** Executive Director, Academy of Medical Sciences, 2000–09; *b* 1 Nov. 1947; *d* of late Charles Frederick Kent and Marie Lucia Kent (*née* Hall); *m* 1972, Keith Quentin Frederick Manning (*d* 2015); two *d*. *Educ:* Stoodley Knowle Sch. for Girls, Torquay; Bedford Coll., Univ. of London (BA Hons Hist. 1968). Royal Insce Co., 1968–69; Desk Officer, 1969–72, Attaché, British High Commn, Singapore, 1972–73, MoD; English lang. teacher, La Petite Ecole Française, Sofia, 1975–78; Royal Society: Meetings Officer, 1987–95; Manager, Scientific Prog., 1995–97; Hd, Sci. Promotion, 1997–2000. Member: Steering Gp for Public Understanding of Sci., Engrg and Technol. EPSRC, 1999–2001; Council for Assisting Refugee Academics, 2009–15; Steering Gp, Changing Age, Univ. of Newcastle upon Tyne, 2009–11. Mem., British Sci. Assoc. (formerly BAAS), 1995–2010. Mem., Bd for Social Responsibility, C of E, 2001–03. Chm., Royal Soc. Former Staff (formerly Pensioners') Assoc., 2013–18. Trustee and Vice-Chm., Epilepsy Res. UK, 2011–16; Trustee, Holy Rood House Centre for Health and Pastoral Care, 2013–15. *Recreations:* music, walking, family and friends. *Address:* c/o Academy of Medical Sciences, 41 Portland Place, W1B 1QH.

**MANNING, Maurice,** DLitt; Chancellor, National University of Ireland, since 2009; Adjunct Professor of Politics, School of Politics and International Relations, University College, Dublin, since 2007; *b* 14 June 1943; *s* of Thomas and Alicia Manning; *m* 1987, Mary Hayes; one *s*. *Educ:* University Coll., Dublin (BA 1964; MA 1966; DLitt 1998). Lectr in Politics, University Coll., Dublin, 1966–2002. TD (FG), 1981–87; Senator, 1987–2002 (Leader of the Opposition, 1987–94, 1997–2002; Leader of Senate, 1994–97). President: Irish Human Rights Commn, 2002–12; European Group of National Human Rights instns, 2006–11. Chair: Irish Govt Adv. Gp on Centenary of Commemorations, 2012–; Irish Govt Wkg Party on Senate Reform, 2014–. MRIA 2009. Hon. FRCSI 2016. Hon. DHL Toledo, 2012. *Publications:* The Blueshirts, 1970, 3rd edn 2006; Irish Political Parties, 1972; The Irish Electricity Industry, 1987; Betrayal (novel), 1998; James Dillon: a biography,

1999; (ed jtly) The House of the Oireachtas: Parliament in Ireland, 2010; The Kilderry Files (novel), 2017. *Recreations:* tennis, swimming, Gregorian chant, reading. *Address:* 13 Haddington Place, Dublin 4, Ireland. *E:* maurice.a.manning@gmail.com. *Clubs:* Stephen's Green Hibernian, Hypothermia (Dublin).

**MANNING, Paul Andrew,** QPM 1996; Assistant Commissioner, Metropolitan Police, 1994–2000; *b* 29 May 1947; *s* of Owen Manning and Joyce Cynthia Manning (*née* Murgatroyd); *m* 1967, Margaret Anne Bucknall; two *s. Educ:* Forest of Needwood High Sch., Rolleston-on-Dove; Cranfield Inst. of Technology (MSc). Metropolitan Police Cadet, 1964; Constable, 1966, Chief Supt, 1985, Staffordshire Police; Asst Chief Constable, Avon and Somerset Constabulary, 1988; Dep. Chief Constable, Herts Constabulary, 1992. Chm., ACPO Traffic Cttee, 1997–2000 (Sec., 1996–97); ind. advr, Immigration and Nationality Directorate, Home Office, 2001–06. Director: Educnl Broadcasting Services Trust, 1997–2008; Perseus-Global Security Technols, 2006–. Mem., Amwell Rotary Club. Mem., Guild of Freemen, City of London, 1999–. FCILT (FCIT, FILT 2000). *Recreations:* hill walking, Rotary. *Address:* 6 The Chestnuts, Hertford SG13 8AQ. *T:* (01992) 422106. *E:* paul.manning3@ntlworld.com.

**MANNING, Peter;** Artistic Director and Conductor, Manning Camerata, since 2005; Music Director, Mozart Kinderorchester, Salzburg, since 2016; *b* Manchester, 17 July 1956; *s* of Harry and Breda Manning; *m* 1st, 1980, Elizabeth (marr. diss. 1986); one *s* one *d*; 2nd, 1992, Marion; two *s. Educ:* Chetham's Sch., Manchester; Royal Northern Coll. of Music (GRNCM 1978; PPRNCM 1978); Indiana Univ. Prof. of Violin, RNCM, 1981–83; Leader, LPO, 1983–86; Founder and Leader, Britten String Quartet, 1986–96; Leader, RPO, 1997–99; Concertmaster, ROH, Covent Garden, 2000–18; Artistic Dir, Musica Vitae Sweden, 2008–11; Artistic Dir, Three Palaces Fest., Malta, 2016–19. Guest Conductor: Dallas Opera, Texas, 2014–19; Malta Philharmonic, 2019–. Prof. of New Work, Royal Conservatoire of Scotland, 2013–15. Hon. RCM 1989. FRNCM 1992; Internat. Fellow, Royal Conservatoire of Scotland, 2011–16. FRSA. *Recreations:* sailing, fly fishing. *Address:* 52 Stockwell Park Road, SW9 0DA. *E:* peter@manningcamerata.com. *Club:* Garrick.

**MANNINGHAM-BULLER,** family name of **Viscount Dilhorne**.

**MANNINGHAM-BULLER,** Baroness *cr* 2008 (Life Peer), of Northampton in the County of Northamptonshire; **Hon. Elizabeth Lydia Manningham-Buller,** LG 2014; DCB 2005; Director General, Security Service, 2002–07; Chair, Wellcome (formerly Wellcome Trust), since 2015 (Governor, since 2008); *b* 14 July 1948; *d* of 1st Viscount Dilhorne, PC, and Lady Mary Lilian Lindsay, 4th *d* of 27th Earl of Crawford, KT, PC. *Educ:* Benenden Sch.; Lady Margaret Hall, Oxford (MA; Hon. Fellow 2004). Entered Security Service, 1974; Dep. Dir Gen., 1997–2002. Mem. Council, Imperial Coll. London, 2008–15 (Chair, 2011–15). BBC Reith Lectr, 2011. Jt Pres., Chatham Hse (RIIA), 2015–. Hon. Fellow: Univ. of Northampton, 2007; Cardiff Univ., 2010; Hon. FCGI 2012; Hon. FMedSci 2018. DUniv Open, 2005; Hon. DSc Cranfield, 2005; Hon. LLD: St Andrews, 2010; Leeds, 2012; Durham, 2017; Hon. DCL Oxford, 2016; Hon. DLitt Buckingham, 2016. *Address:* House of Lords, SW1A 0PW.

*See also* Viscount Dilhorne.

**MANNION, Rosa;** soprano; Professor of Vocal Studies, Royal College of Music, since 2009; *b* 29 Jan. 1962; *d* of Patrick Anthony Mannion and Maria (*née* MacGregor); *m* 1985, Gerard McQuade; two *s. Educ:* Seafield Grammar Sch., Crosby; Royal Scottish Acad. of Music and Drama (BA). Débuts: Scottish Opera, 1984; Edinburgh Fest., 1985; ENO, 1987; Glyndebourne Fest. Opera, 1988; principal soprano: Scottish Opera, 1984–86; ENO, 1989–92; major rôles include: Gilda in Rigoletto; Violetta in La Traviata; Manon (title rôle); Magnolia in Show Boat; Pamina in Die Zauberflöte; Minka in Le Roi malgré lui; Sophie in Werther; Oscar in A Masked Ball; Atalanta in Xerxes; Constanze in Die Entführung aus dem Serail; Countess in Figaro's Wedding; Sophie in Der Rosenkavalier. Has given many concerts and recitals; has a comprehensive discography. Winner, Internat. Singing Competition, Scottish Opera, 1988. Trustee, Jackdaws Music Educn Trust, 2011–.

**MANOLOPOULOS, Prof. David Eusthatios,** PhD; FRS 2011; Professor of Theoretical Chemistry, University of Oxford, since 2005; Fellow, St Edmund Hall, Oxford, since 1995; *b* Gillingham, Kent, 14 Dec. 1961; *s* of Dimitrios Manolopoulos and Anne Margaret Manolopoulos (*née* Langley); *m* 1988, Clare Elizabeth Collinson; one *d. Educ:* Howard Sch., Gillingham; Girton Coll., Cambridge (BA 1984); Darwin Coll., Cambridge (PhD 1988). Postdoctoral Res. Fellow, Univ. of Texas at Austin, 1988–90; Lecturer: in Physical Chem., Univ. of Nottingham, 1990–95; in Physical and Theoretical Chem., Univ. of Oxford, 1995–2005. Miller Vis. Prof., Univ. of Calif, Berkeley, 2012. Associate Ed., 2008–, Dep. Ed., 2015–, Jl Chemical Physics. *Publications:* (with P. W. Fowler) An Atlas of Fullerenes, 1995; contrib. papers on theoretical chem. to learned jls. *Recreation:* foreign travel. *Address:* Physical and Theoretical Chemistry Laboratory, South Parks Road, Oxford OX1 3QZ.

**MANOR, Prof. James Gilmore,** DPhil; Emeka Anyaoku Professor, Institute of Commonwealth Studies, University of London, 2007–12, now Emeritus; *b* 21 April 1945; *s* of James Manor and Ann (*née* Jones); *m* 1974, Brenda Cohen; one *s. Educ:* Yale Univ. (BA 1967); Univ. of Sussex (DPhil 1975). Asst Lectr in History, Chinese Univ. of Hong Kong, 1967–69; Tutor, SOAS, 1973–75; Lectr in History, Yale, 1975–76; Lectr in Politics, Univ. of Leicester, 1976–85; Prof. of Govt, Harvard, 1985–87; Professorial Fellow, Inst. of Develt Studies, Univ. of Sussex, 1987–2007; Dir, and Prof. of Commonwealth Politics, Inst. of Commonwealth Studies, Univ. of London, 1994–97. V. K. R. V. Rao Prof., Inst. for Social and Economic Change, Bangalore, India, 2006–08. Sen. Res. Fellow, US Nat. Endowment for the Humanities, 1980–81; Vis. Fellow, MIT, 1982. Consultant to: Dutch Govt, 1989–90; World Bank, 1994–97; Swedish Govt, 1995, 2013. Editor, Jl of Commonwealth and Comparative Politics, 1980–88. *Publications:* Political Change in an Indian State, 1977; (ed with P. Lyon) Transfer and Transformation, 1983; (ed) Sri Lanka in Change and Crisis, 1984; The Expedient Utopian, 1989; (ed) Rethinking Third World Politics, 1991; (ed with C. Colclough) States or Markets?, 1991; Power, Poverty and Poison, 1993; Nehru to the Nineties, 1994; Aid that Works, 2006; (with E. Raghavan) Broadening and Deepening Democracy, 2009; (with M. Melo and N. Ng'ethe) Against the Odds, 2012; (with R. Jenkins) Politics and the Right to Work, 2017; Politics and State-Society Relations in India: collected writings, 2017; (with S. Jodhka) Contested Hierarchies, Persisting Influence: caste and power, 2018; (jtly) The Politics of Poverty Reduction in India, 2019. *Recreations:* reading, theatre. *Address:* Institute of Commonwealth Studies, University of London, Senate House, Malet Street, WC1E 7HU. *T:* (020) 7862 8844.

**MANS, Keith Douglas Rowland;** Member (C), since 2009, and Deputy Leader, since 2013, Hampshire County Council; Chief Executive (formerly Director), Royal Aeronautical Society, 1998–2009 (Member, Council, since 2010); *b* 10 Feb. 1946; *s* of Maj.-Gen. Rowland Spencer Noel Mans, CBE and Veeo Mans; *m* 1972, Rosalie Mary McCann; one *s* two *d. Educ:* Berkhamsted School; RAF College Cranwell; Open Univ. (BA). FRAeS. Pilot, RAF, 1964–77 (Flight Lieut); Pilot, RAF Reserve, 1977–2005. Retail Manager, John Lewis Partnership, 1978–87. MP (C) Wyre, 1987–97; contested (C) Lancaster and Wyre, 1997. PPS to Minister of State, Dept of Health, 1990–92, to Sec. of State for Health, 1992–95. Member: H of C Environment Select Cttee, 1987–91; Select Cttee on Defence, 1995–97; Chairman: Parly Envmt Gp, 1993–97; Parly Aerospace Gp, 1994–97; Vice-Chm., Back bench Fisheries Cttee, 1987–96; Secretary: Back bench Aviation Cttee, 1987–90; Back bench Envmt Cttee, 1990–91; All Party Aviation Gp, 1991–94. Public Affairs Advr, Soc. of British Aerospace Cos, 1997–2002. Chm., Air Travel Greener By Design Cttee, 2002–09. Chm., 2009–14, Vice Pres., 2014–, Air League. Mem. Ct, Southampton Univ., 2005–15. Liveryman, Guild of Air Pilots and Navigators, 2005–. FRSA 2005. *Recreation:* flying. *Address:* Rowhurst Cottage, De La Warr Road, Milford on Sea, Lymington, Hants SO41 0PS. *Club:* Royal Air Force.

*See also* Lt Gen. Sir M. F. N. Mans.

**MANS, Lt Gen. Sir Mark (Francis Noel),** KCB 2012; CBE 2005; DL; Chief Royal Engineer, 2013–18; *b* 7 March 1955; *s* of Maj.-Gen. Rowland Spencer Noel Mans, CBE and Veeo Ellen Mans; *m* 1982, Jane Goode; one *s* one *d. Educ:* Berkhamsted Sch. Commnd RE, 1974; CO, 21 Engr Regt, 1993–95; Comdr Engrs, 1999–2001, Asst COS Plans, 2002–04, Land Comd; Dep. Comdg Gen., Multinat. Corps, Iraq, 2005; Dep. Adjt Gen., 2005–08; Military Sec., 2008–09; Comdr Regl Forces, 2009; Adjt Gen., 2009–12. Mem., Scientific Exploration Soc., 1980–. Champion, Defence Med. Welfare Service, 2012–; Patron: Veterans in Action, 2014–; RBL Hants, 2016–; Vice Patron, Ulysses Trust, 2012–. Col Comdt RE, 2005–18. Hon. Vice Pres., Army RU, 2012–. FCMI 1997; FCIPD 2000; FInstRE 2012. DL Hants, 2012. Officer, Legion of Merit (USA), 2006. *Recreation:* sport - sadly increasingly as a spectator.

*See also* K. D. R. Mans.

**MANSEL, Sir Philip,** 15th Bt *cr* 1621; Chairman and Managing Director of Eden-Vale Engineering Co. Ltd, 1962–98, retired; *b* 3 March 1943; *s* of Sir John Mansel, 14th Bt and Hannah, *d* of Ben Rees; *S* father, 1947; *m* 1968, Margaret, *o d* of Arthur Docker; two *s* one *d. Heir: s* John Philip Mansel, *b* 19 April 1982. *Address:* 2 Deyncourt Close, Darras Hall, Ponteland, Northumberland NE20 9JY.

**MANSEL, Dr Philip Robert Rhys;** historian and author; Editor, The Court Historian, 1996–2016; *b* London, 19 Oct. 1951; *s* of Major J. C. Mansel and D. J. Mansel (*née* Hyde-Thomson). *Educ:* Eton Coll. (King's Schol.); Balliol Coll., Oxford (MA); University Coll. London (PhD 1978). Mem., Conseil scientifique, Centre de Recherche, Château de Versailles, 2006– (Pres., 2018–). Fellow, Inst. of Histl Res., 2005. Founding Trustee, Levantine Heritage Foundn, 2011–. Co-founder, Soc. for Court Studies, 1995. Chevalier des Arts et Lettres (France), 2010; Mem., Order of the Crown (Belgium), 2016. *Publications:* Louis XVIII, 1981; Pillars of Monarchy, 1984; The Eagle in Splendour, 1987; Sultans in Splendour, 1988; The Court of France, 1989; Constantinople, 1995; Paris between Empires, 2001; Prince of Europe, 2003; Dressed to Rule, 2005; Levant, 2010; (with T. Riotte) Monarchy and Exile, 2011; Aleppo: the rise and fall of Syria's great merchant city, 2016; King of the World: the life of Louis XIV, 2019. *Recreation:* visiting cities, palaces and museums. *Address:* 13 Prince of Wales Terrace, W8 5PG. *T:* (020) 7937 4734. *E:* philipmansel@compuserve.com. *Club:* Travellers.

**MANSEL, Prof. Robert Edward,** CBE 2006; FRCS; Professor of Surgery, 1992–2015, now Emeritus, and Chairman, Department of Surgery (formerly Department of Surgery, Anaesthetics, Obstetrics and Gynaecology), 2001–16, Cardiff University (formerly University of Wales College of Medicine); *b* 1 Feb. 1948; *s* of Regnier Ranulf Dabridgecourt Mansel and Mary Germaine Mansel (*née* Littlewood); *m* 1987, Elizabeth Clare, *d* of John Francis Skone and Daphne Viola (*née* Rees); two *s* four *d. Educ:* Llandovery Coll.; Charing Cross Hosp. Med. Sch., Univ. of London (MB BS, MS). LRCP 1971; FRCS 1975. Res. Fellow, 1976–78, Lectr and Sen. Lectr, 1979–89, Univ. of Wales Coll. of Medicine; Prof. of Surgery, Univ. of Manchester, 1989–92. Chm., British Breast Gp, 2010–11. Chm., Cttee for Quality Assce and Develt in Breast Cancer, EC, 2014–. Chm., Breast Speciality Gp, 1997–2002, Pres., 2004–06, British Assoc. of Surgical Oncology; Pres., Eur. Soc. of Mastology, 2014–16. Mem., Fitness to Practise Panel, GMC, then MPTS, 2012–. UICC Fellow, Univ. of Texas at San Antonio, 1982–83; Churchill Meml Fellowship, 1982; James IV Fellowship, James IV Assoc., 1989. Hunterian Prof., RCS, 1989. Hon. FRCSE 2003. *Publications:* Fibrocystic Breast Disease, 1986; (with L. E. Hughes and D. J. T. Webster) Benign Breast Disease, 1989, 3rd edn 2009; Atlas of Breast Disease, 1994; contribs to surgical jls. *Recreations:* fishing, Rugby, travel, chess. *Address:* Breast Centre, University Hospital Llandough, Penlan Road, Cardiff CF64 2XX. *E:* manselre@cf.ac.uk.

**MANSEL-JONES, David;** Chairman, Huntingdon Research Centre plc, 1978–86 (Vice-Chairman, 1974–78); *b* 8 Sept. 1926; *o s* of Rees Thomas Jones and Ceinwen Jones; *m* 1952, Mair Aeronwen Davies; one *s. Educ:* St Michael's Sch., Bryn; London Hospital. MB, BS 1950; MRCP 1973; FFPM 1992. Jun. Surgical Specialist, RAMC; Dep. Med. Dir, Wm R. Warner & Co. Ltd, 1957–59; Med. Dir, Richardson-Merrell Ltd, 1959–65; formerly PMO, SMO and MO, Cttee on Safety of Drugs; formerly Med. Assessor, Cttee on Safety of Medicines; Consultant to WHO, 1970–86; Senior PMO, Medicines Div., DHSS, 1971–74. Vis. Prof., Gulbenkian Science Inst., Portugal, 1981; Examiner, Dip. Pharm. Med., Royal Colls of Physicians, UK, 1980–87. *Publications:* papers related to safety of medicines. *Recreations:* music, painting. *Address:* 39 St John's Court, Princes Road, Felixstowe, Suffolk IP11 7SG. *T:* (01394) 275984.

**MANSELL, Ven. Clive Neville Ross;** Archdeacon of Tonbridge, 2002–17, now Archdeacon Emeritus; *b* 20 April 1953; *s* of late (Arthur James) Mervyn Mansell and June Irene Mansell (*née* Duncan); *m* 1980, Jane Margaret (*née* Sellers); one *s* two *d. Educ:* City of London Sch.; Leicester Univ. (LLB Hons 1974); Coll. of Law; Trinity Coll., Bristol (DipHE Theol Studies 1981). Solicitor of the Supreme Court, 1977–81. Ordained deacon, 1982, priest, 1983; Curate, Gt Malvern Priory, 1982–85; Minor Canon, Ripon Cathedral, with pastoral care of parishes of Sharow with Copt Hewick and of Marton-le-Moor, 1985–89; Rector, Kirklington with Burneston, Wath and Pickhill, 1989–2002; Area Dean, Wensley, 1998–2002. Capitular Canon, Ripon Cathedral, 2018–. Mem., Gen. Synod of C of E, 1995–2015; Dep. Prolocutor, House of Clergy, Northern Convocation, 2001–02. Church Comr, 1997–2008. *Recreations:* cricket, music, reading, history, current affairs, photography, enjoying good meals. *Address:* 10 Watermill Lane, North Stainley, Ripon, N Yorks HG4 3LA.

**MANSELL, Nigel Ernest James,** CBE 2012 (OBE 1991); racing driver; *b* 8 Aug. 1953; *s* of Eric and Joyce Mansell; *m* Rosanne Elizabeth Perry; two *s* one *d. Educ:* Wellsbourne and Hall Green Bilateral Schools; Matthew Bolton Polytechnic; Solihull Tech. Coll.; N Birmingham Polytechnic (HND). Engineering apprenticeship with Lucas; lab. technician, Lucas Aerospace, later product manager; senior sales engineer, tractor div., Girling. Began racing in karts; won 11 regional championships, 1969–76; Formula Ford and Formula Three, 1976–79; Formula Two, later Formula One, 1980; Lotus team, 1981–84; Williams-Honda team, 1985–87; Williams-Judd team, 1988; Ferrari team, 1989–90; Williams-Renault team, 1991–92 and 1994 (part time); McLaren team, 1995; first competed in a Grand Prix, Austria, 1980; won 31 Grands Prix, 1980–94 (record); Formula One World Drivers Champion, 1992; American Newman-Haas IndyCar Team, 1993; IndyCar Champion, 1993; won Grand Prix Masters, (inaugural race) Kyalomi, 2005, Qatar, 2006. Mem., Commn for Global Road Safety, 2012–. President: Dream-A-Way Charity, 1995–; UK Youth, 2002–; Inst. of Advanced Motorists, 2005–; Vice Pres., British Racing Drivers

Club, 2009–. Patron: Driving for Disabled, Jersey, 2007–; St Brelade's Youth Project, 2011–. Grand Fellow, MIRCE Akad. for System Operational Sci., 2000. Freedom, City of London, 2015. Hon. DEng Birmingham, 1993; Hon. DSc Worcester, 2015. *Publications:* (with Derick Allsop) Driven to Win, 1988; (with Derick Allsop) Mansell and Williams, The Challenge for the Championship 1992; (with Jeremy Shaw) Nigel Mansell's IndyCar Racing, 1993; (with James Allen) Nigel Mansell, My Autobiography, 1995; Staying on Track: the autobiography, 2015. *Recreations:* golf, flying, cycling.

**MANSELL, Richard Austin;** QC 2009; **His Honour Judge Mansell;** a Circuit Judge, since 2013; *b* Sutton Coldfield, 12 Feb. 1968; *s* of Robert and Lynn Mansell; *m* 2001, Michelle Colborne; one *s* two *d*. *Educ:* Univ. of Leeds (LLB 1st Cl. Hons Law). Called to the Bar, Gray's Inn, 1991; a Recorder, 2005–12. *Recreations:* ski-ing, golf, yoga, cooking, gardening, singing. *Address:* Manchester Crown Court, Crown Square, Manchester M3 3FL.

**MANSELL, Prof. Robin Elizabeth,** PhD; Professor (formerly Dixons Professor) of New Media and the Internet, London School of Economics and Political Science, since 2001 (Interim Deputy Director, 2015–16); *b* Vancouver, 3 Jan. 1952; *d* of Glen Mansell and Esmee Mansell; partner, W. Edward Steinmueller. *Educ:* York House Sch., Vancouver; Univ. of Manitoba (BA Hons Psychol. 1974); London Sch. of Econs and Pol Sci. (MSc Social Psychol. 1976); Simon Fraser Univ. (MA Communication 1980; PhD Communication 1984). Res. Associate, Prog. on Inf. and Communication Technols, ESRC, London, 1985–86; Administrator, Inf., Computers and Communication Policy Div., OECD, Paris, 1986–87; Reader, 1988–94, Prof. in Inf. and Communication Technol. Policy, 1994–2000, Sci. and Technol. Policy Res. Unit, Univ. of Sussex, Hon. Prof., 2001–. Mem., Bd of Dirs, TPRC, 2016–. Trustee: Inst. of Develt Studies, Sussex, 1999–2009; Canadian Centennial Scholarship Fund, 2018–. Hon. Prof., Learning, Inf., Networking Knowledge Centre, Grad. Sch. of Public and Develt Mgt, Univ. of Witwatersrand, 2005–10. *Publications:* The New Telecommunications, 1993; (ed) Communication by Design, 1996; (ed) Knowledge Societies, 1998; Mobilizing the Information Society, 2000; (ed) Trust and Crime in Information Societies, 2005; (ed) The Oxford Handbook of Information and Communication Technologies, 2007; (ed) The Information Society: critical concepts in sociology, 2009; Imagining the Internet: communication, innovation and governance, 2012; (ed jtly) The International Encyclopedia of Digital Communication and Society, 2015. *Recreations:* walking, classical music. *Address:* London School of Economics and Political Science, Houghton Street, WC2A 2AE. *T:* (020) 7955 6380. *E:* r.e.mansell@lse.ac.uk. *Club:* Athenæum.

**MANSELL-JONES, Richard Mansell;** Chairman, Brown, Shipley & Co., 1992–2003; *b* 4 April 1940; *s* of late Arnaud Milward Jones and Winifred Mabel (née Foot); *m* 1st, 1971, Penelope Marion (*d* 2009), *y d* of Major Sir David Henry Hawley, 7th Bt; 2nd, 2018, Hon. Charlotte Mary Ropner (formerly Taddei) (*d* 2018), *d* of 2nd Baron Piercy. *Educ:* Queen Elizabeth's, Carmarthen; Worcester College, Oxford (MA). FCA. Articled to Price, Waterhouse & Co., 1963–68; with N. M. Rothschild & Sons, 1968–72; with Brown, Shipley & Co., 1972–88 (Dir, 1974–84; Dep. Chm., 1984–88); non-exec. Dir, 1982–88, Chm., 1988–2000, Barlow International PLC (formerly J. Bibby & Sons). Director: Brown, Shipley Holdings, 1985–92; Barlow Ltd (formerly Barlow Rand Ltd), 1988–2001; non-executive Director: Barr & Wallace Arnold Trust, 1984–93; Rand Mines Ltd, 1988–93; Barloworld Hldgs, 1990–2003; Standard Bank London, 1992–2005; Standard Internat. Holdings, 2000–05; non-exec. Chm., Amphion Innovations plc, 2005–10, 2016–18. Trustee and Dir, Burlington Magazine Foundn and Burlington Magazine Pubns Ltd, 2009–; Trustee: World Monuments Fund Britain, 2013–17; British Sporting Art Trust, 2013–. Mem. Council, CBI, 1999–2000. Mem. Bd, 2003–08, Treas., 2005–08, Royal Hosp. for Neuro-disability. Patron, Shaw Trust, 1996– (Trustee, 1990–96). MCSI (MSI 1992). *Address:* c/o Private Banking, Brown, Shipley & Co. Ltd, Founders Court, Lothbury, EC2R 7HE. *T:* (020) 7606 9833. *Clubs:* Beefsteak, Boodle's, City of London, Chelsea Arts, Daniel's.

**MANSER, (Peter) John,** CBE 1992; DL; FCA; Chairman, SAB Miller PLC (formerly South African Breweries), 2013–15 (Director, 2001–15; Deputy Chairman, 2012–13); *b* 7 Dec. 1939; *s* of late Peter Robert Courtney Manser and Florence Delaplaine Manser; *m* 1969, Sarah Theresa Stuart (née Todd); two *d*. *Educ:* Marlborough Coll. Man. Dir, Jardine Fleming & Co. Ltd, 1975–79; Chief Exec., Save & Prosper Gp Ltd, 1983–88; Chm., Robert Fleming & Co. Ltd, 1990–97. Chairman: Robert Fleming Hldgs, 1997–2000 (Dir, 1972–; Chief Exec., 1990–97); Delancey Estates, 1998–2001; Intermediate Capital Gp, 2001–10; Shaftesbury, 2004–13 (Dir, 1997–2013); London Asia Chinese Private Equity Fund, 2006–07; Dep. Chm., Colliers CRE (formerly Fitzhardinge), 2002–10; Director: Capital Shopping Centres, 1994–2000; Keppel Tatlee Bank, 2000–01. Dep. Chm., FIMBRA, 1984–85; Dir, SIB, 1986–93; Chm., London Investment Banking Assoc., 1994–98; Vice-Pres., BBA, 1994–98. Mem., Finance Cttee, Royal Commn for Exhibn of 1851, 2008–18. Dir, Cancer Research Campaign, 1985–2000. Chm., Wilts Community Foundn, 1997–2002. Gov., Marlborough Coll., 2008–17; Chm. of Council, Marlborough Coll. Malaysia, 2012–15. Pres., Marlburian Club, 1999–2000. Pres., Devizes Constituency Cons. Assoc., 2018–. DL Wilts, 1999. *Recreations:* gardening, walking, shooting. *Address:* Chisenbury Priory, East Chisenbury, Pewsey, Wilts SN9 6AQ. *Clubs:* Boodle's, MCC.

**MANSFIELD,** family name of **Baron Sandhurst**.

**MANSFIELD AND MANSFIELD,** 9th Earl of, *cr* 1776 (and 10th Earl of, *cr* 1792) (GB); **Alexander David Mungo Murray;** Baron Scone, 1605; Viscount Stormont, 1621; Baron Balvaird, 1641; (Earl of Dunbar, Viscount Drumcairn, and Baron Halldykes in the Jacobite Peerage); Hereditary Keeper of Bruce's Castle of Lochmaben; *b* 17 Oct. 1956; *er s* of 8th and 9th Earl of Mansfield and Mansfield, and of Pamela Joan, *o d* of W. N. Foster, CBE and Millicent Agnes Mary Foster, later Lady Cochrane of Cults; *S* father, 2015; *m* 1985, Sophia Mary Veronica, *o d* of Biden Ashbrooke and Veronica Ashbrooke (née Stourton), St John, Jersey; one *s* three *d*. *Educ:* Eton; Magdalene Coll., Cambridge. Member: Scottish Council, HHA, 1993–2007; Tay and District Salmon Fisheries Bd, 2000–11, 2016–. *Heir: s* Viscount Stormont, *qv*. *Address:* Scone Palace, Perthshire PH2 6BD.

**MANSFIELD, Prof. Averil (Olive), (Mrs J. W. P. Bradley),** CBE 1999; FRCS; FRCP; Professor of Vascular Surgery, Academic Surgical Unit, St Mary's Hospital and Imperial College School of Medicine (formerly St Mary's Hospital Medical School), 1993–2004, now Emeritus (Director, Academic Surgical Unit, 1993–99); Associate Medical Director, St Mary's Hospital, 2002–04 (Consultant Surgeon, 1982–2002); *b* 21 June 1937; *m* 1987, John William Paulton Bradley (*d* 2013). *Educ:* Liverpool Univ. (MB 1960; ChM 1972). FRCS 1966; FRCP 2005. Consultant Surgeon: Royal Liverpool Hosp., 1972–80; Hillingdon Hosp., 1980–82; RPMS, subseq. ICSM, 1980–2002. Royal College of Surgeons: Chm., Court of Examrs, 1990–92; Mem. Council, 1990–2002; Vice-Pres., 1998–2000; President: Assoc. of Surgeons of GB and Ireland, 1992–93; Vascular Surgical Soc. of GB and Ireland, 1996–97; Sect. of Surgery, RSocMed, 1997–98; BMA, 2009–10 (Chm., Bd of Sci., 2010–13). Vice-Chm., 2001–03, Chm., 2004–08, Vice Pres., 2009–, Stroke Assoc. Fellow, Faculty of Medicine, Imperial Coll. London, 2012. Hon. Mem., Liverpool Med. Instn, 2018. Hon. FRACS 1996; Hon. FACS 1998; Hon. FRSocMed 2011; Hon. Fellow, Amer. Surgical Assoc. Hon. MD Liverpool, 1994; Hon. DSc Lancaster, 2010. Aneuryn Bevan Lifetime Achievement Award, NHS Heroes Awards, 2018. *Publications:* Clinical Surgery in General, 1993; articles on vascular surgery. *Recreations:* playing the piano and learning to play the cello, walking in the Lake District, restoring old wrecks. *Address:* 31/32 Radnor Mews, W2 2SA.

**MANSFIELD, David James;** Chairman, Drive Partnership Ltd, since 2011; RAJAR Ltd, since 2008; Visiting Fellow, Oxford University, 2008–15; *b* 12 Jan. 1954; *m* 1979, Alison Patricia Pullin; two *s* one *d*. Gen. Sales Manager, Scottish TV, 1977–85; Sales and Marketing Dir, Thames TV, 1985–93; Capital Radio: Gp Commercial Dir, 1993–97; Gp Man. Dir, May–July 1997; Gp Chief Exec., Capital Radio, then Chief Exec., GCap Media plc, 1997–2006. Non-executive Chairman: 1700 Gp plc, 2008–10; 1801 Gp Ltd, 2010–13; LoveLive TV Ltd, 2010–; HelloU Ltd, 2010–; Music Festivals plc, 2011–12; Discover Digital Ltd, 2012–; Field & Flower Ltd, 2013–; Circus Street Ltd, 2014–; non-executive Director: Carphone Warehouse plc, 2005–10; Game Gp plc, 2010–11; Ingenious Media plc, 2006–13; Results Internat. LLP, 2015–. Hon. Vis. Prof., Cass Business Sch., 2015–.

**MANSFIELD, Guy Rhys John;** QC 1994; a Recorder, 1993–2012; a Deputy High Court Judge, 2008–12; *b* 3 March 1949; *o s* of 5th Baron Sandhurst, DFC and Janet Mary (née Lloyd); *S* father, 2002 as 6th Baron Sandhurst, but does not use the title for public life; *m* 1976, Philippa St Clair Verdon-Roe; one *s* one *d*. *Educ:* Harrow Sch.; Oriel Coll., Oxford (MA). Called to the Bar, Middle Temple, 1972 (Harmsworth Exhibnr, Winston Churchill Pupillage award); Bencher, 2000. Chm., Bar Council, 2005 (Member: Gen. Council of the Bar, 1998–2005; Gen. Mgt Cttee, 1998–2005; Chairman: Remuneration and Terms of Work (formerly Legal Aid and Fees) Cttee, 1998–99; Legal Services Cttee, 2000–03; wkg gp on possible Contingent Legal Aid Fund, 2009–11); Mem., Queen's Counsel Complaints Cttee, 2006–19. Legal Assessor, GMC, 2000–06. Mem. Council, Justice, 2006–18. Lead Counsel for FCO in successful defence of the Kenyan Emergency Gp Litigation, 2013–18. *Publications:* (contrib.) Personal Injury Handbook, 1998, rev. edn 2001; (contrib.) Financial Provision in Family Matters, 1999–2004; (contrib.) An Introduction to Human Rights and the Common Law, 2000. *Recreations:* cricket, opera. *Heir: s* Hon. Edward James Mansfield, *b* 12 April 1982. *Address:* 1 Crown Office Row, Temple, EC4Y 7HH. *T:* (020) 7797 7500. *Clubs:* Reform, MCC, Leander (Henley-on-Thames).

**MANSFIELD, Prof. Michael;** QC 1989; Professor of Law, City, University of London (formerly City University), since 2007; *b* 12 Oct. 1941; *s* of Frank Le Voir Mansfield and Marjorie Mansfield; *m* 1965, Melian Mansfield (née Bordes) (marr. diss. 1992); three *s* one *d* (and one *d* decd); 2nd, 1992, Yvette Vanson; one *s*. *Educ:* Highgate Sch.; Keele Univ. (BA Hons). Called to the Bar, Gray's Inn, 1967, Bencher, 2008. Estabd set of chambers of which head, 1984. Visiting Professor of Law: Westminster Univ., 1997–; Birkbeck, Univ. of London, 2014–. President: Nat. Civil Rights Movt; Haldane Soc.; Amicus. Chair, Bd, Liverpool and Merseyside Theatres Trust, 2016–18. Hon. Fellow, Kent Univ., 1994. Hon. LLD: South Bank, 1992; Keele, 1995; Hertfordshire, 1995; Middx, 1999; Westminster, 2005; Ulster, 2006; Kent, 2007; Wolverhampton, 2010; Huddersfield, 2016. Legal Aid Lawyer of the Yr Award for Outstanding Achievement, 2010, 2016. *Publications:* Presumed Guilty, 1994; The Home Lawyer, 2003; Memoirs of a Radical Lawyer, 2009; The Inquest, 2015. *Recreation:* my children's interests. *Address:* Nexus Chambers, 7 New Square, Lincoln's Inn, WC2A 3QS. *T:* (020) 7404 1147.

**MANSFIELD, Penny,** CBE 2013; Director, OnePlusOne, since 1997; *b* Surrey, 1951; *d* of Stanley Mansfield and Catherine Corry; *m* 1976, Richard George Dowden, *qv*; two *d*. *Educ:* Ursuline Convent, London; Univ. of Surrey (BSc Hons Human Scis). Res. Officer, Univ. of Surrey; Sen. Res. Officer, Marriage Res. Centre, Central Middx Hosp., London; Hd of Res. and Information, then Dep. Dir, OnePlusOne. *Publications:* (with J. Collard) The Beginning of the Rest of Your Life, 1988; contributor: Couple Therapy: a handbook, 1991; Life Stories, 1994; Partners Become Parents, 1996; No Fault No Flaw, 2000; How Helping Works, 2006. *Recreations:* reading, cinema and theatre, art galleries, spending time with friends and family, gardening and general pottering. *Address:* OnePlusOne, Central Working Shoreditch, 6–8 Bonhill Street, EC2A 4BX. *E:* penny.mansfield@oneplusone.org.uk.

**MANSFIELD, Prof. Terence Arthur,** FRS 1987; FRSB; Professor of Plant Physiology, University of Lancaster, 1977–2001, now Emeritus; *b* 18 Jan. 1937; *s* of Sydney Walter Mansfield and Rose (née Sinfield); *m* 1963, Margaret Mary James; two *s*. *Educ:* Univ. of Nottingham (BSc); Univ. of Reading (PhD). FRSB (FIBiol 1984). University of Lancaster: Lectr, then Reader, 1965–77; Dir, Inst. of Envmtl and Biol Scis, 1988–94; Provost of Sci. and Engrg, 1993–96. Member: AFRC, 1989–93; Eur. Envmtl Res. Orgn, 1994–. Hon. Fellow, Univ. of Lancaster, 2007. *Publications:* Physiology of Stomata, 1968; Effects of Air Pollutants on Plants, 1976; Stomatal Physiology, 1981; Plant Adaption to Environmental Stress, 1993; many contribs to books and jls in plant physiology. *Recreations:* cricket, classical music. *Address:* 25 Wallace Lane, Forton, Preston, Lancs PR3 0BA. *T:* (01524) 791338. *Club:* Shireshead and Forton Cricket (Pres., 1993–2002).

**MANSFIELD, Terence Gordon,** CBE 2002; Director, 1993–2004, and a Vice President, 2000–04, Hearst Corporation USA; Consultant, Hearst Corporation UK, since 2003; *b* 3 Nov. 1938; *s* of Archer James Mansfield and Elizabeth Mansfield; *m* 1965, Helen Leonora Russell; two *d*. *Educ:* Maynard Road Jun. Sch., Essex; SW Essex Technical Sch. D. H. Brocklesby, Advertising Agents, 1954; S. H. Benson, Advertising Agents, 1956; served RAF, Christmas Island, 1957–59; Condé Nast Publications, 1960–66; Queen Magazine, 1966; National Magazine Co.: Advertisement Man., Harpers and Queen, 1969; Publisher, Harpers and Queen, 1975; Dep. Man. Dir, 1980, Pres. and CEO, 1982–2003, National Magazine Co.; Chm., COMAG, 1984–2003; Dir, PPA, 1982–. Chm., MOBO Orgn Ltd, 2006–. Chm., Trng Bd, Periodicals Trng Council, 2000–. Member: Marketing Soc., 1975–; British Fashion Council, 1988–; Action Medical Research (formerly Action Res. for the Crippled Child, then Action Res.), 1989–; Campaign Bd, Historic Royal Palaces, 2009–. Chm., Bd of Trustees, Victim Support, 2002–05 (Mem., Adv. Bd, 1996–). Trustee: NewstrAid, 1966–; United World Coll., 1977–; St Bride's Church, 2001–. Chairman: Graduate Fashion, 2006– (Vice Chm., 2005–06); Arts Thread, 2009–. Judge, Shine Sch. Media Awards, 2011–. Freeman, City of London, 1989; Liveryman, Stationers' & Newspaper Makers' Co., 1997–. MInstM 1969; MInstD 1976. FRSA. *Recreations:* family, running, walking dogs. *Address:* The Town House, 5 Grosvenor Gardens Mews North, SW1W 0JP; Hearst, 30 Panton Street, SW1Y 4AJ. *T:* (020) 7565 6666. *W:* www.terrymansfield.co.uk. *Clubs:* Royal Air Force, Solus.

**MANSON, (Christopher John) Justin;** Deputy Chief Executive, UK Government Investments, HM Treasury, since 2016; *b* Woolwich, London, 9 Jan. 1960; *s* of Comdr John Manson and Eve Manson; *m* 1993, Jill Roberts; one *s* two *d*. *Educ:* Trinity Coll., Oxford (BA Hons PPE); Graduate Sch. of Business, Stanford Univ. (MBA); Birkbeck, Univ. of London (MA Philos.). Credit Suisse First Boston, 1982–86; Vice Pres., First Boston Corp., 1989–93; Man. Dir, 1993–2012, Sen. Advr, 2012–13, Morgan Stanley. Dir, Shareholder Exec., 2015–16. Non-executive Director: UK Export Finance, 2015–19; Urenco Gp, 2016–. Dir, National Th. Enterprises, 2003–11; Trustee: National Th. Foundn, 2003–11; Chelsea Academy Foundn, 2014–17. Gov., Chelsea Acad., 2017. *Recreations:* ski-ing, sailing, theatre. *Address:* 18 Lawrence Street, SW3 5NF.

**MANSON, Suzanne Maree**; see Cotter, S. M.

**MANSS, Thomas**, FCSD; designer; Founder and Art Director, Thomas Manss & Company, since 1993; *b* Gütersloh, 11 July 1960; *s* of Karlheinz Manss and Ingrid Manss; two *s*. *Educ*: Luise Hensel Schule (primary); Evangelisch Stiftisches Gymnasium, Gütersloh; Fachhochschule Würzburg (Dipl Des). Metadesign, 1984–85; Sedley Place Design, 1985–89; Pentagram, 1989–93, Associate, 1992–93. Vis. Prof., Corporate Identity, Fachhochschule Potsdam, 1994–97. MSTD; FRSA. *Publications*: Ordnung & Eccentricity, 2002; contributed to: Design: wege zum erfolg, 1994; 26 Letters: illuminating the alphabet, 2004; Corporate Identity and Corporate Design, Neues Kompendium, 2007; Thomas Manss & Company: designers, narrators, myth-makers, fabulators and tellers of tales, 2008. *Address*: Thomas Manss & Company, 3 Nile Street, N1 7LX. *W*: www.manss.com.

**MANSTEAD, Prof. Antony Stephen Reid**, DPhil; FBA 2011; FBPsS; FAcSS; FLSW; Professor of Psychology, Cardiff University, 2004–18, now Emeritus; *b* 16 May 1950; *s* of Dr Stephen K. Manstead and Katharine E. Manstead; *m* 1997, Prof. Stephanie van Goozen; one *s* one *d*. *Educ*: Univ. of Bristol (BSc Hons); Univ. of Sussex (DPhil). FBPsS 1989. Lectr in Social Psychol., Univ. of Sussex, 1974–76; Lectr, 1976–88, Sen. Lectr, 1988–90, Prof. of Psychol., 1990–92, Univ. of Manchester; Prof. of Social Psychol., Univ. of Amsterdam, 1992–2001; Prof. of Psychol. in the Social Scis, and Fellow of Wolfson Coll., Cambridge Univ., 2002–03. FAcSS (AcSS 2004). Fellow: Soc. for Personality and Social Psychol., 2006; Soc. of Experimental Social Psychol., 2009; Assoc. for Psychological Sci., 2010; FLSW 2012. *Publications*: (jtly) The Accountability of Conduct: a social psychological analysis, 1983; (jtly) Introduction to Psychology: an integrated approach, 1984; (ed jtly) Handbook of Social Psychophysiology, 1989; (ed jtly) Blackwell Encyclopedia of Social Psychology, 1995; (ed jtly) Everyday Conceptions of Emotion, 1995; (ed jtly) Blackwell Reader in Social Psychology, 1997; (ed jtly) Emotions and Beliefs: how feelings influence thoughts, 2000; (ed jtly) Feelings and Emotions: the Amsterdam Symposium, 2004; (jtly) Emotion in Social Relations: cultural, group and interpersonal processes, 2005; (ed) Psychology of Emotions, 5 vols, 2008. *Recreation*: photography. *Address*: School of Psychology, Cardiff University, Tower Building, Park Place, Cardiff CF10 3AT.

**MANT, Prof. David Clive Anthony**, OBE 2011; FRCP, FRCGP; Professor of General Practice, University of Oxford, 1998–2010, now Emeritus; Fellow, Kellogg College, Oxford, 1998, now Emeritus. *Educ*: Churchill Coll., Cambridge (BA 1972; MA 1976); Birmingham Univ. (MB ChB 1977); London Sch. of Hygiene and Tropical Medicine (MSc (Community Medicine) 1983). MRCGP 1982, FRCGP 1999; MFPHM 1984; FRCP 1999. Trainee in gen. practice, E Oxford Health Centre, 1981–82; Registrar in Community Medicine, Oxford RHA, 1982–84; Clin. Lectr, 1984–93, and Sen. Scientist, Gen. Practice Res. Gp, 1987–93, Oxford Univ.; Prof. of Primary Care Epidemiology, Southampton University, 1993–98; Dir of R&D, S and W Reg., NHS Exec., DoH, 1996–98 (on secondment). Non-exec. Dir, Oxford Univ. Hospitals NHS Trust, 2010–. Hon. Prof., Bristol Univ., 1996–98. FMedSci 1998.

**MANT, Prof. Jonathan William French**, MD; FFPH, FRCPE, FMedSci; Professor of Primary Care Research, since 2008, and Head, Primary Care Unit, since 2013, University of Cambridge; Honorary Consultant, Addenbrooke's Hospital, since 2008; *b* London, 16 Nov. 1960; *s* of Prof. Arthur Keith Mant and Heather Mant (*née* Smith); *m* 1983, Frances Joy Randall (*d* 2011); one *s* one *d*. *Educ*: Cranleigh Sch.; Millbrook Sch., NY; Corpus Christi Coll., Cambridge (BA 1982; MD 2004); Guy's Hosp., London (MB BS 1985); London Sch. of Hygiene and Tropical Medicine (MSc 1990). MFPHM 1994, FFPH (FFPHM 2003); FRCPE 2012. House Officer, Buckland Hosp., Dover, 1985–86; SHO, Torbay, and Royal Devon and Exeter Hosps, 1986–89; Registrar, then Sen. Registrar, Public Health Medicine, Oxford, 1989–92; Clin. Lectr in Public Health Medicine, Univ. of Oxford, 1992–97; University of Birmingham: Sen. Lectr, 1997–2006; Reader, 2006–07; Prof., 2007–08. NIHR Sen. Investigator, 2015–. Associate Director (Primary Care), Stroke Res. Network, 2005–15. FESC 2010; Fellow: British Hypertension Soc., 2014; Eur. Stroke Orgn, 2015; FMedSci 2018. Académico de Honor, Royal Acad. of Medicine, E Andalucia, 2018. *Publications*: (ed jtly) Evidence Based Practice: a primer for health care professionals, 1999, 2nd edn 2005; (ed jtly) Health Care Needs Assessment: the epidemiologically based needs assessment reviews, 1st series, 2004, 3rd series, 2007; (ed jtly) ABC of Stroke, 2011; contrib. papers on stroke and cardiovascular disease in jls. *Recreations*: amassing unread novels, untidy desks, Tintin memorabilia. *Address*: Primary Care Unit, University of Cambridge, Strangeway's Research Laboratory, Wort's Causeway, Cambridge CB1 8RN. *T*: (01223) 763830. *E*: jm677@medschl.cam.ac.uk.

**MANTEL, Dame Hilary (Mary), (Dame Hilary McEwen)**, DBE 2014 (CBE 2006); author; *b* 6 July 1952; *d* of Henry Thompson and Margaret Mary Thompson (*née* Foster, later Mrs Jack Mantel); *m* 1973, Gerald McEwen. *Educ*: London Sch. of Econs; Sheffield Univ. (BJur). PLR Adv. Cttee, 1997–2003. Vis. Prof., Sheffield Hallam Univ., 2006–09; Hon. Prof., Exeter Univ., 2013. BBC Reith Lectr, 2017 (Best Radio Prog. Award, BPG, 2018). Vice-Pres., RSL, 2015–; Mem. Council, Soc. of Authors, 2015–. Patron: Endometriosis SHE Trust, 2006–09; Scene and Heard, 2016–. FRSL 1990; FEA 2007. Hon. Fellow, RHUL, 2008; Hon. FKC 2011. Hon. LittD Sheffield, 2005; DUniv: Sheffield Hallam, 2009; London, 2013; Hon. DLitt: Exeter, 2011; Kingston, 2011; Cambridge, 2013; QUB, 2013; Bath Spa, 2013; Derby 2014; Open, 2014; Oxford Brookes, 2015; Chester, 2015; Oxford, 2015; Hon. DEcon LSE, 2014. Hon. Bencher, Gray's Inn, 2017. Shiva Naipaul Meml Prize, 1987; Author of the Year, Galaxy Nat. Book Awards, 2010, 2012; David Cohen Award for Lifetime Achievement, 2013; Burke Medal, TCD Historical Soc., 2013; Bodley Medal, 2013; President's Medal, British Acad., 2016; Kenyon Rev. Award for Literary Achievement, 2016; Lions Award, NY Public Library, 2016; Peggy V. Helmerich Dist. Author Award, Tulsa Liby Trust, 2018. *Publications*: Every Day is Mother's Day, 1985; Vacant Possession, 1986; Eight Months on Ghazzah Street, 1988; Fludd (Winifred Holtby Award, RSL; Southern Arts Lit. Prize; Cheltenham Fest. Prize), 1990; A Place of Greater Safety (Book of Year Award, Sunday Express), 1992; A Change of Climate, 1994; An Experiment in Love, 1995 (Hawthornden Prize for Literature, 1996); The Giant, O'Brien, 1998; Giving Up the Ghost: a memoir, 2003 (Book of the Year Award, MIND, 2005); Learning to Talk (short stories), 2003; Beyond Black, 2005 (Yorkshire Post Fiction Prize, 2006); Wolf Hall, 2009 (Man Booker Prize, US Nat. Book Critics Circle Award for Fiction, 2009; Walter Scott Prize for histl fiction, 2010; Ind. Booksellers' Book of the Yr, 2010); Bring Up the Bodies, 2012 (Man Booker Prize, 2012; Costa Book of the Year, 2013; South Bank Sky Arts Award, 2013); The Assassination of Margaret Thatcher and Other Stories, 2014; (with X. Salomon) Holbein's Sir Thomas More, 2018. *Recreation*: sleeping. *Address*: A. M. Heath & Co., 6 Warwick Court, Holborn, WC1R 5DJ.

**MANTELL, Carl Nicholas**; counsellor, since 2015; voluntary work, 2013–18; Director, College of Management and Technology, Defence Academy of the United Kingdom, 2010–12; *b* 2 Feb. 1954; *s* of Charles Henry Purchase Mantell and Edna Joyce Mantell (*née* Bracey); *m* 1st, 1978, Janet Swinford Martin (marr. diss. 2008); two *s* one *d*; 2nd, 2011, Sarah Elizabeth Mitchell (*née* Sansom). *Educ*: Berkhamsted Sch.; Pembroke Coll., Cambridge (MA); Kendal Coll. (Counselling Skills course); Univ. of Cumbria (Postgrad. Dip. Counselling and Psychotherapy 2015). Joined MoD, 1977; Asst Private Sec. to Minister of State for Armed Forces, 1982–83; Principal (procurement finance, procurement policy, Army equipment planning), 1983–92; Hd of Resources and Progs (Mgt Planning), 1992–94; Sec. to Support Mgt Gp, RAF Logistics Comd, 1994–97; Hd of Resources and Progs (Air), 1997–99; Dir, Capability Resources and Scrutiny, 1999–2002; Dir Gen., Central Budget, 2002–05; Command Secretary: RAF PTC, 2005–06; RAF Strike Comd/PTC, 2006–07; Air Command, MoD, 2007–10. Mem., Audit and Risk Cttee, Kendal Coll., 2014–18. *Recreations*: photography, reading, walking, listening to music, military modelling. *E*: carlnicholas@hotmail.co.uk.

**MANTHORPE, John Jeremy**, CB 1994; Chief Executive, 1985–96, and Chief Land Registrar, 1990–96, HM Land Registry; *b* 16 June 1936; *s* of William Broderick and Margaret Dora Manthorpe; *m* 1967, Kathleen Mary Ryan; three *s* one *d*. *Educ*: Beckenham and Penge Grammar School. HM Land Registry: Plans Branch, 1952; Principal Survey and Plans Officer, 1974; Controller (Registration), 1981–85. Consultant and Advr on Land Registration to HM Land Registry, UNECE, World Bank, and govts in Albania, Bahrain, Bermuda, Macedonia and Romania, 1996–2010. Hon. RICS (Hon. ARICS 1992). *Recreation*: walking and watching the Ashdown Forest. *Address*: Beurles, Fairwarp, Uckfield, East Sussex TN22 3BG. *T*: (01825) 712795.

**MANTLE, Anthony Dod**; director of photography; *b* Witney, 14 April 1955; *s* of Charles Ian Mantle and Dorothy Ruth Mantle; *m* 2000, Susanne; one *s*. *Educ*: London Coll. of Printing (BA Hons); National Film Sch. of Denmark (graduated 1989). Freelance work, 1989–; cinematographer: *films* include: Festen/Celebration, 1999; Julien Donkey Boy, 1999; 28 Days Later, 2002; Dogville, 2004; Millions, 2004; Manderlay, 2006; Brothers of the Head, 2006; The Last King of Scotland, 2007; Slumdog Millionaire, 2008 (Academy Award for Best Achievement in Cinematography, BAFTA Award for Best Cinematography, 2009); Antichrist, 2009; 127 Hours, 2010; The Eagle, 2011; Rush, 2013; In the Heart of the Sea, 2015; Our Kind of Traitor, 2016; Snowden, 2016; First They Killed My Father, 2017; T2 Trainspotting, 2017; *television* includes: Wallander (2 episodes), 2008 (BAFTA Award for Best Photography and Lighting, 2009). Member: British Soc. of Cinematographers; Eur. Film Acad. Hon. Mem., Australian Cinematography Soc., 2009. Eur. Cinematographer of the Year, Eur. Film Acad., 2003, 2009. *Recreations*: tennis, golf, family. *Address*: c/o ICM, 10250 Constellation Boulevard, Los Angeles, CA 90067, USA; c/o Independent Talent Group, 40 Whitfield Street, W1T 2RH.

**MANTLE, Richard John**, OBE 2013; DL; General Director, Opera North, since 1994; *b* 21 Jan. 1947; *s* of late George William Mantle, OBE and Doris Griffiths; *m* 1970, Carol June Mountain. *Educ*: Tiffin Sch.; Ealing Coll. of Advanced Technology. Personnel Officer, Beecham Group, 1969–72; Associate Dir, J. Walter Thompson Co., 1973–79; Personnel Dir, then Dep. Man. Dir, ENO, 1980–85; Man. Dir, Scottish Opera, 1985–91; Gen. Dir, Edmonton Opera, Canada, 1991–94. Chm., Walsingham Coll. Trust Assoc. (Yorks Properties), Parcevall Hall (Vice-Chm., 2003). Member: Council, Coll. of the Resurrection, Mirfield, 2009–; Gen. Synod of C of E, 2010–; Archbishops' Council (C of E) Finance Cttee, 2010–; Music Adv. Council, Univ. of York, 2012–. Dir, National Opera Studio, 1995–; Trustee, Opera North Ltd, 2012–. A Guardian, Shrine of Our Lady of Walsingham, 1998–. DL W Yorks, 2012. Hon. DMus Leeds, 2009. *Recreations*: music, reading, the country, English churches. *Address*: 21 Treesdale Road, Harrogate, N Yorks HG2 0LX. *E*: richardmantle@gmail.com. *Club*: Savile.

**MANTON**, 4th Baron *cr* 1922, of Compton Verney; **Miles Ronald Marcus Watson**; *b* 7 May 1958; *s* of 3rd Baron Manton and of Mary Elizabeth, twin *d* of Major T. D. Hallinan; *S* father, 2003; *m* 1984, Elizabeth, *e d* of J. R. Story; two *s* one *d*. *Educ*: Eton. Major, Life Guards. *Heir*: *s* Hon. Thomas Nigel Charles David Watson, *b* 19 April 1985.

**MANTON, Prof. Nicholas Stephen**, PhD; FRS 1996; FInstP; Professor of Mathematical Physics, University of Cambridge, since 1998 (Head, High Energy Physics Group, Department of Applied Mathematics and Theoretical Physics, 2002–17); Fellow, St John's College, Cambridge, since 1997; *b* 2 Oct. 1952; *s* of Franz Eduard Sigmund Manton and Lily Manton (*née* Goldsmith); *m* 1989, Terttu Anneli Aitta; one *s*. *Educ*: Dulwich Coll.; St John's Coll., Cambridge (BA, MA, PhD 1978). FInstP 1996. Joliot-Curie Fellow, Ecole Normale Supérieure, Paris, 1978–79; Res. Fellow, MIT, 1979–81; Asst Res. Physicist, Inst. for Theoretical Physics, Univ. of Calif, Santa Barbara, 1981–84; Cambridge University: Lectr, 1987–94; Reader in Mathematical Physics, 1994–98; St John's College: Sen. Res. Student, 1985–87; Dir of Studies in Applied Maths, 1997–98; Mem., Coll. Council, 2006–09. Vis. Prof., Inst. for Theoretical Physics, SUNY, Stony Brook, 1988; Scientific Associate, CERN, Geneva, 2001. Emilio Segre Dist. Lectr in Physics, Tel Aviv Univ., 2014. Mem. Prog. Cttee, Internat. Centre for Mathematical Scis, Edinburgh, 2005–08. Chm., Res. Meetings Cttee, London Mathematical Soc., 2008–11; Mem., Mgt Cttee, Isaac Newton Inst. for Mathematical Scis, Cambridge, 2011–19. Mem., British Team, Internat. Mathematical Olympiad, 1971. Jun. Whitehead Prize, London Mathematical Soc., 1991; Blaise Pascal Award, Durham Univ., 2010. *Publications*: (with P. M. Sutcliffe) Topological Solitons, 2004; (with N. Mee) The Physical World, 2017; papers in mathematical and theoretical physics in various jls incl. Nuclear Physics, Physics Letters, Physical Rev., Communications in Mathematical Physics, Jl of Mathematical Physics, Jl of Geometry and Physics, arXiv and conf. proceedings. *Recreations*: music, Finland and its culture, binocular astronomy. *Address*: Department of Applied Mathematics and Theoretical Physics, Centre for Mathematical Sciences, University of Cambridge, Wilberforce Road, Cambridge CB3 0WA. *T*: (01223) 765000; St John's College, Cambridge CB2 1TP.

**MANUELLA, Sir Tulaga**, GCMG 1996; MBE 1981; Governor General, Tuvalu, 1994–98; Chancellor, University of the South Pacific, 1997–2000; *b* 26 Aug. 1936; *s* of Teuhu Manuella and Malesa Moevasa; *m* 1957, Milikini Uinifaleti; two *s* three *d*. *Educ*: primary sch., Ocean Is. Gilbert and Ellice Islands Colony: sub-accountant and ledger keeper, 1953–55; clerical officer, 1955–57; Sen. Asst, then Asst Accountant, Treasury, 1957–75; Tuvalu Government: Asst Accountant, Accountant, then Actg Financial Sec., Min. of Finance, 1976–84; Financial Secretary, Financial Division: Church of Tuvalu, 1984–86; Pacific Conf. of Churches, Suva, Fiji, 1987–91; Co-ordinator of Finance and Admin, Ekalesia Kelisiano, Tuvalu, 1992–94. Patron, Pacific Islands Soc. in Britain and Ireland, 1995. *Address*: PO Box 50, Vaiaku, Funafuti, Tuvalu.

**MANVILLE, Lesley Ann**, OBE 2015; actress, since 1972; *b* Brighton, 12 March 1956; *d* of Ronald Leslie Manville and Nora Elizabeth Manville (*née* Edwards); *m* 1988, Gary Oldman, *qv* (marr. diss. 1990); one *s*. *Educ*: St Andrews C of E Primary Sch., Hove; Nevill Secondary Modern Sch., Hove. *Theatre*: RSC Warehouse: Savage Amusement, 1978; The Sons of Light, 1978; Chorus Girls, Th. Royal, Stratford E, 1981; Royal Court: Borderline, 1981; Rita, Sue and Bob Too, 1981; Top Girls, 1982; Falkland Sound, 1983; The Pope's Wedding, 1984; Saved, 1984; Serious Money, 1989; American Bagpipes, 1989; Three Sisters, 1990; RSC: As You Like It, The Philistines, Les Liaisons Dangereuses, 1985; The Wives' Excuse, 1995; The Cherry Orchard, Aldwych, 1989; Miss Julie, Greenwich, 1990; National Theatre: His Dark Materials, 2005; Pillars of the Community, The Alchemist, 2006; Her Naked Skin, 2008; Grief, 2011; All About My Mother, 2007, Six Degrees of Separation, 2010, Old Vic; Ghosts, Almeida, 2013, transf. Trafalgar Studios, 2014 (Best Actress, Critics' Circle Th. Awards; Olivier Award for Best Actress, 2014); Long Day's Journey into Night, Bristol Old Vic, 2016, transf. Wyndham's Th., 2018; *films* include:

Dance with a Stranger, 1985; High Season, 1987; High Hopes, 1988; Secrets and Lies, 1996; Topsy-Turvy, 1999; All or Nothing, 2002 (Critics' Circle Best Actress Award); Vera Drake, 2004; Sparkle, 2007; A Christmas Carol, 2009; Womb, 2010; Another Year, 2010 (Critics' Circle Best Actress Award); Ashes, 2013; Romeo and Juliet, 2013; Spike Island, 2013; Viaggio Sola, 2013; The Christmas Candle, 2013; Maleficent, 2014; Mr Turner, 2014; Rupture, Molly Moon: the incredible hypnotist, 2016; Hampstead, 2017; Phantom Thread, 2018; *television* includes: Emmerdale Farm, 1974–76; The Emigrants, 1976; Grown-Ups, 1980; The Firm, 1988; Soldier Soldier, 1992; Goggle Eyes, 1993; The Mushroom Picker, 1993; Little Napoleons, 1994; Tears Before Bedtime, 1995; The Bite, 1996; Holding On, 1997; Real Women, 1998, Real Women II, 1999; Other Peoples' Children, 2000; The Cazalets, 2001; Bodily Harm, 2002; North & South, 2004; Cranford, 2007; Mayday, 2013; Fleming: The Man Who Would Be Bond, 2014; The Go-Between, 2015; River, 2015; Mum, 2016, 2018, 2019; Harlots, 2017; World on Fire, 2019. *Address:* c/o ARG, 4A Exmoor Street, W10 6BD.

**MANZE, Andrew;** conductor; Principal Conductor, NDR Radio Philharmonic Orchestra, Hannover, since 2014; *b* 14 Jan. 1965; *s of* Vincent and Ann Manze. *Educ:* Bedford Sch.; Clare Coll., Cambridge (MA Classics). Violinist specialising in repertoire 1610–1830; broadcaster, BBC Radio 3, 1994–; Associate Dir, Acad. of Ancient Music, 1996–2003; Artist in Residence, Swedish Chamber Orch., 2001–; Artistic Dir, The English Concert, 2003–07; Principal Conductor, Helsingborg Symphony Orch., 2006–14, now Hon. Conductor. Many recordings incl. Biber Sonatas (Gramophone Award, 1996), Pandolfi Sonatas (Gramophone Award 2000) and music by Bach, Handel, Vivaldi, etc. Rolf Schock Prize, Royal Swedish Acad. of Music, 2004. *Recreations:* music, classics. *Address:* c/o Intermusica Artists' Management, 9 Kingsway, WC2B 6XF. *E:* bemmerson@intermusica.co.uk.

**MANZIE, Dame Stella (Gordon),** DBE 2018 (CBE 2007; OBE 2001); Managing Director Commissioner, Rotherham Metropolitan Borough Council, 2015–16; consultant and researcher, since 2018; *b* 13 June 1960; *d of* Sir (Andrew) Gordon Manzie, KCB and Rosalind Manzie (*née* Clay); partner, Trevor McCarthy. *Educ:* Herts and Essex High Sch. for Girls, Bishop's Stortford; Fettes Coll., Edinburgh; Newnham Coll., Cambridge (MA English 1982); Poly. of Central London (Postgrad. DPA); Univ. of Birmingham (MSocSci 1992). Admin. Asst, ACC, 1982–84; Admin. Officer, SOLACE, 1984–86; Team Leader, Mgt Effectiveness Unit, Birmingham CC, 1987–88; Mgt Consultant, Price Waterhouse Mgt Consultants, 1988–92; Borough Dir, Redditch BC, 1992–97; Chief Executive: W Berks Council, 1997–2001; Coventry CC, 2001–08; Scottish Government: Dir Gen., Finance and Corporate Services, 2008–10; Dir Gen., Justice and Communities, 2010–11; Chief Exec., Barking and Dagenham LBC, 2011–12; Interim Chief Exec., Birmingham CC, 2017–18. Associate, Global Partners Governance, 2013–. Vis. Fellow, Open Univ., 2013–. Mem. Bd, Office of Legal Complaints, 2014–15. Chm., Cambridge Literary Fest., 2013–15. Trustee, Esmée Fairbairn Foundn, 2017–. Kieron Walsh Meml Prize, Birmingham Univ., 1997. *Recreations:* eating, drinking, socialising, travel, watching sport (incl. supporting Heart of Midlothian, Stoke City, Coventry City and Dagenham and Redbridge), reading.

**MANZONI, Charles Peter;** QC 2009; barrister; *b* Birmingham, 17 May 1963; *s of* Michael Manzoni and Julie Manzoni; *m* 1992, Clare Pickering; one *s* three *d*. *Educ:* Uppingham Sch.; Bristol Univ. (BSc Mechanical Engrg); City Univ. (DipLaw). Called to the Bar, Middle Temple, 1988, Hong Kong, 2000; barrister in private practice, 1989–. *Recreations:* sailing, family, ski-ing, music. *Address:* 39 Essex Chambers, 81 Chancery Lane, WC2A 1DD. *Clubs:* Royal Ocean Racing; Royal Hong Kong Yacht.

**MANZOOR,** family name of **Baroness Manzoor**.

**MANZOOR,** Baroness *cr* 2013 (Life Peer), of Knightsbridge in the Royal Borough of Kensington and Chelsea; **Zahida Parveen Manzoor,** CBE 1998; Managing Director, Property Development and Director, Intellisys Ltd, since 2011; *b* 25 May 1958; *d of* Nazir Ahmed and Mahroof Ahmed; *m* 1984, Dr Madassar Manzoor; two *d*. *Educ:* Leeds Univ. (HVCert 1983); Bradford Univ. (MA Applied Social Studies 1989). Student nurse to Staff Nurse, W Suffolk AHA, 1977–80 (SRN 1980); Staff Nurse, then Staff Midwife, Birmingham AHA, 1980–82 (SCM 1981); Health Visitor, Durham AHA, 1983–84; Lectr, Thomas Danby Coll., 1984–86 and 1987–88; NE Regl Prog. Dir, Common Purpose Charitable Trust, 1990–92; Chm., Bradford HA, 1992–97; Regl Chm., Northern and Yorks Regl Office, NHS, DoH, 1997–2001. Co-founder and Dir, Intellisys Ltd, 1996–2003. Legal Services Ombudsman, 2003–11, and Legal Services Complaints Comr, 2004–10, for England and Wales. Comr and Dep. Chm., CRE, 1993–98. Ind. Assessor, FCO, 1998–. Dir, Liberal Democrats Ltd, 2014–16. Lib Dem Spokesperson on Internat. Affairs, 2015–16, for Work and Pensions, 2015–16, H of L; a Baroness in Waiting (Govt Whip), 2018–19. Mem., Race Equality Adv. Panel, Home Office, 2003–. Mem. Bd, Middle East Assoc., 2015–17. Mem., Bradford Congress, 1992–96; Dir, Bradford City Challenge, 1993–96. Trustee: W Yorks Police Community Trust, 1996–98; Uniting Britain Trust, 1996–2000; NSPCC, 1997; Nat. Media Mus., 2008–15. Mem. Ct, Univ. of Bradford, 1992–98; Governor: Sheffield Hallam Univ., 1991–93; Bradford and Airedale Coll. of Health, 1992–93; Keighley Coll., 1994–95. Vice-Patron, Regl Crime Stoppers, 1998. Hon. Fellow, Bolton Inst., 1999. Hon. DSc: Bradford, 1999; Leeds Metropolitan, 2003; Bolton, 2010. *Recreations:* antiques, gardening, painting, historic buildings, photography, travelling, walking. *Address:* House of Lords, SW1A 0PW.

**MAPLE, Graham John;** District Judge, Principal Registry of Family Division, High Court of Justice, 1991–2005; *b* 18 Dec. 1947; *s of* Sydney George and Thelma Olive Maple; *m* 1974, Heather Anderson; two *s*. *Educ:* Shirley Secondary Modern Sch.; John Ruskin Grammar Sch., Croydon; Bedford Coll., London (LLB 1973). Lord Chancellor's Dept, 1968; Sec., Principal Registry of Family Div., 1989. Member: Outer London, Court Service Cttee, 1991–96; Family Courts Forum, 1996–2005. Chm., Tenterden Counselling Service, 2007–14; Mem., Ind. Monitoring Bd, HM Prison/YOI East Sutton Park, 2006– (Chm., 2010–13, 2016–18). Mem. Council, Romney Marsh Historic Churches Trust, 2016–. Church Warden, St Mildred Parish Church, Tenterden, 1992–98. Consulting Editor, Rayden and Jackson on Divorce and Family Matters, 2003–12. *Publications:* (Co-Editor) Rayden and Jackson on Divorce, 12th edn 1974, to 17th edn 2003; (Co-Editor) The Practitioner's Probate Manual, 21st edn 1979; (ed) Holloway's Probate Handbook, 8th edn 1987. *Recreations:* archaeology, Roman Britain, steam and model railways. *Address:* Westbrook, Elmfield, Tenterden, Kent TN30 6RE.

**MAPP, Derek;** DL; Chairman: Sport England, 2006–07; British Amateur Boxing Association, 2008–13; *b* 17 May 1950; *s of* Thomas Mapp and Edna Mapp; *m* 1971, Karen Edmands; two *s* one *d*. *Educ:* Oakwood Primary Sch.; Boteler Grammar Sch. Dir, Mansfield Brewery, 1981–91; Founder and CEO, Tom Cobleigh plc, 1992–97; Chairman: Leapfrog Day Nurseries, 1998–2004; Imagesound plc, 2005–; Dir, Mapp Develts Ltd, 1996–. Non-executive Chairman: Staffline Recruitment plc, 2005–09; Priority Sites Ltd, 2006–07; Concentia Capital Ltd, 2011–; Huntsworth plc, 2014–19; 3aaa Aspire Achieve Advance Ltd, 2014–18; Mitie Gp plc, 2017–; Informa (formerly Taylor and Francis) plc: non-exec. Dir, 1998–2009; Sen. Ind. Dir, 2005–08; Chm., 2008–. Chairman: E Midlands Develt Agency, 1998–2004; Mem. Bd, English Partnerships, 1998–2004. DL 2006, High Sheriff, 2013–14, Derbys. Hon. DTech Loughborough, 2004; Hon. Dr Lincoln, 2004. *Recreations:* sport, reading.

**MAPP, Hon. Dr Wayne Daniel;** Member, Law Commission, New Zealand, 2012–17; *b* Te Kopuru, Northland, NZ, 12 March 1952; *s of* Gordon and Heather Mapp; *m* 1981, Denese Letitia Henare. *Educ:* Univ. of Auckland (LLB Hons); Univ. of Toronto (LLM); Christ's Coll., Cambridge (PhD 1988). Legal practitioner, John Collinge, Solicitor, 1979–82; Associate Prof. and Lectr in Commercial Law, Univ. of Auckland, 1984–96. MP (Nat.) N Shore, NZ, 1996–2011; Minister of Defence, Minister of Res., Sci. and Technol., Associate Minister for Econ. Develt and Associate Minister for Tertiary Educn., 2008–11. *Publications:* (with G. H. Harris) Goods and Services Tax: the application of the Act, 1986; The Iran-United States Claims Tribunal: the first ten years, 1993; contribs to internat. law jls. *Recreations:* flying, sailing, diving, tramping, study of history and politics, astronomy.

**MAPSTONE, Prof. Sally Louise,** DPhil; FRSE; Principal and Vice-Chancellor, University of St Andrews, since 2016; *b* Hillingdon, Middx, 1957; *d of* Thomas John Mapstone and Marjorie Sheila Mapstone (*née* Jones); *m* 2003, Martin Christopher Griffiths-Brayne. *Educ:* Vyners Grammar Sch., Ickenham, Middx; Wadham Coll., Oxford (BA 1st Cl.; Hon. Fellow, 2017); St Cross Coll., Oxford (DPhil 1986; Hon. Fellow, 2017). Ed., Weidenfeld & Nicolson Publishers, London, 1978–81; St Hilda's College, Oxford: Jun. Res. Fellow, 1984–86; Lectr and Supernumerary Fellow, 1986–89; Fellow and Tutor in English, 1989–2016, now Fellow Emeritus; University of Oxford: Jun. Proctor, 2006–07; Reader in Older Scots Lit., 2007–13; Pro Vice-Chancellor (Personnel and Equality), 2009–11, (Educn), 2011–16; Prof. of Older Scots Lit., 2013–16. Pres., Saltire Soc., 2018–. Hon. Pres., Scottish Text Soc., 2012–. FRSE 2019. *Publications:* (with H. Cooper) The Long Fifteenth Century: essays for Douglas Gray, 1997; (ed jtly) A Palace in the Wild: essays on vernacular culture and humanism in late-Medieval and Renaissance Scotland, 2000; (ed) William Dunbar, 'the nobill poyet': essays in honour of Priscilla Bawcutt, 2001; (ed jtly) The European Sun: proceedings of the Seventh International Conference on Medieval and Renaissance Scottish Language and Literature, 2001; (ed) Older Scots Literature, 2005; The Chepman and Myllar Prints: Scotland's first printed texts, 2008; contrib. articles on Older Scots lit. *Recreations:* reading, running. *Address:* Office of the Principal, University of St Andrews, College Gate, North Street, St Andrews, Fife KY16 9AJ. *T:* (01334) 462545. *E:* principal@st-andrews.ac.uk.

**MAR,** Countess of (*suo jure*, 31st in line from Ruadri, 1st Earl of Mar, 1115); Premier Earldom of Scotland by descent; Lady Garioch, *c* 1320; **Margaret of Mar;** *b* 19 Sept. 1940; *er d of* 30th Earl of Mar, and Millicent Mary Salton; *S* father, 1975; recognised in surname "of Mar" by warrant of Court of Lord Lyon, 1967, when she abandoned her second forename; *m* 1st, 1959, Edwin Noel Artiss (marr. diss. 1976); one *d*; 2nd, 1976, (cousin) John Salton (marr. diss. 1981); 3rd, 1982, J. H. Jenkin, MA (Cantab), FRCO, LRAM, ARCM. Lay Mem., Immigration Appeal Tribunal, 1985–2006. Mem., EU Sub-Cttee on environment, health and consumer affairs, H of L, 1995–99, 2001–05; Dep. Speaker, H of L, 1997–2007, 2009–12 and 2014–; elected Mem., H of L, 1999. Mem., Delegated Powers and Regulatory Reform Cttee, H of L, 2013–; Mem., Select Cttee to rev. 2006 NERC Act, 2017–18. Chm., Honest Food, 2000–05. Chm., Environmental Medicine Foundn, 1997–2003. Pres., Guild of Agricl Journalists, 2007–11. Patron: Dispensing Doctors' Assoc., 1985–96; Worcs Mobile Disabled Gp, 1991–2003; Gulf Veterans Assoc., 1995–; Pres., Elderly Accommodation Counsel, 1994–; Chm., Forward-ME, 2008–; patron of several ME/CFS charities; Patron: Global Cabin Air Quality Exec., 2006–; Edith Ellen Foundn, 2016–. Governor, King's Sch., Gloucester, 1984–87. Hon. ARCVS 2006; Hon. Associate, BVA, 2007. *Heir:* *d* Mistress of Mar, *qv*. *Address:* St Michael's Farm, Great Witley, Worcester WR6 6JB. *T:* (01299) 896608.

**MAR, Mistress of; Lady Susan Helen of Mar;** interior designer; *b* 31 May 1963; *d* and *heiress of* Countess of Mar, *qv*; *m* 1989, Bruce Alexander Wyllie; two *d*. *Educ:* King Charles I School, Kidderminster; Christie College, Cheltenham. *Address:* Firethorn Farm Cottage, Plough Lane, Ewhurst Green, Cranleigh, Surrey GU6 7SG.

**MAR,** 14th Earl of, *cr* 1565, **and KELLIE,** 16th Earl of, *cr* 1619; **James Thorne Erskine;** Baron Erskine, 1429; Viscount Fentoun, 1606; Baron Dirleton, 1603; Baron Erskine of Alloa Tower (Life Peer), 2000; Premier Viscount of Scotland; Hereditary Keeper of Stirling Castle; *b* 10 March 1949; *s of* 13th Earl of Mar and 15th Earl of Kellie, and Pansy Constance Erskine, OBE (*d* 1996); *S* father, 1993; *m* 1974, Mrs Mary Mooney, *yr d of* Dougal McD. Kirk. *Educ:* Eton; Moray Coll. of Education, 1968–71; Inverness Coll. (building course, 1987–88). Thistle Page to the Queen, 1962, 1963. Community Service Volunteer, York, 1967–68; Community Worker, Richmond-Craigmillar Parish Church, Edinburgh, 1971–73; Sen. Social Worker, Family and Community Services, Sheffield District Council, 1973–76; Social Worker: Grampian Regional Council, Elgin, 1976–77, Forres, 1977–78; Highland Regional Council, Aviemore, 1979; HM Prison, Inverness, 1979–81; Inverness W, Aug.–Dec. 1981; Community Worker, Merkinch Centre, Inverness, Jan.–July 1982; Community Service Supervisor, Inverness, 1983–87; building technician, 1989–91; project worker, SACRO Intensive Probation Project, Falkirk, 1991–93; boatbuilder, 1993. Mem., sitting as Lib Dem, H of L, 2000–17. Member: H of L Select Cttee on Constitution, 2001–04, on Religious Offences, 2002–03; Ad Hoc Cttee on Barnett Formula, 2008–09; Jt Cttee on Statutory Instruments, 2008–13. Contested (Lib Dem) Ochil, Scottish Parly elecn, 1999. Chm., Strathclyde Tram Inquiry, 1996; Parly Comr, Burrell Collection (lending) Inquiry, 1997. Pilot Officer, RAuxAF, 1979, attached to 2622 Highland Sqdn, RAuxAF Regt; Flying Officer, RAuxAF, 1982–86; RNXS, 1985–89. DL Clackmannan, 1991–2014. *Recreations:* canoeing, hill walking, railways, gardening, restoration of Alloa Tower. *Heir:* *b* Hon. Alexander David Erskine [*b* 26 Oct. 1952; *m* 1977, Katherine Shawford, *e d of* Thomas Clark Capel; one *s* one *d*]. *Address:* Hilton Farm, Alloa, Scotland FK10 3PS. *Club:* Farmers.

**MARA, Solo Naivakarurubalavu;** Ambassador of Fiji to the United States of America, since 2016; *b* Suva, Fiji, 14 Sept. 1967; *s of* Kolinio and Litiana Mara; *m* 2001, Kerry; two *s* two *d*. *Educ:* Univ. of S Pacific, Fiji (BA Pol Scis); Internat. Univ. of Japan (MA Internat. Relns). Counsellor, Brussels, until 2008; Perm. Sec., Min. of Foreign Affairs, Fiji, 2008–11; High Comr of Fiji in UK, also accredited to Republic of Ireland, Germany, Denmark, Egypt, Israel and Holy See, 2012–15. *Address:* Fiji Embassy, 1707 L Street, Suite 200, NW, Washington, DC 20036, USA.

**MARAIS, Prof. Richard,** PhD; FMedSci; FRS 2018; Director, Cancer Research UK Manchester Institute (formerly Paterson Institute for Cancer Research) and Professor of Molecular Oncology, University of Manchester, since 2012; Co-Lead, CRUK Lung Cancer Centre of Excellence, Manchester, since 2014; Scientific Co-Director, Belfast-Manchester Movember Centre of Excellence, since 2014; *b* Witbank, SA, 16 March 1964; *s of* Frans Johannes Marais and Margaret Rose Marais (*née* James); *m* 2000, Katharine Jane Woodward-Nutt. *Educ:* University Coll. London (BSc Genetics and Microbiol. 1985); Ludwig Inst. for Cancer Res. (PhD 1989). Postdoctoral Res. Fellow, ICRF, 1989–92; Institute of Cancer Research: Ind. Postdoctoral Res. Fellow, 1993–98; Team Leader, Signal Transduction Team, 1998–2012; Prof. of Molecular Oncol., 2007–12; Dep. Chair, Section of Cell and Molecular Biol., 2008–11; Hd, Div. of Cancer Biol., 2011–12. Trustee, Melanoma Focus, 2012–. Pres., Eur. Assoc. of Cancer Res., 2014–16; Mem., Bd of Dirs, Amer. Assoc. for Cancer Res., 2015–. *Publications:* contribs to peer-reviewed jls. *Address:* Cancer Research UK Manchester Institute, University of Manchester, Alderley Park, Alderley Edge, Macclesfield SK10 4TG. *T:* (0161) 306 6017. *E:* richard.marais@cruk.manchester.ac.uk. *Club:* Manchester Triathlon.

**MARBER, Patrick;** writer and director; *b* 19 Sept. 1964; *s* of late Brian Marber and of Angela (*née* Benjamin). *Educ:* Wadham Coll., Oxford. *Plays:* Dealer's Choice, RNT and Vaudeville, 1995 (Writers' Guild and Evening Standard Awards, 1995); After Miss Julie, BBC, 1995; Closer, RNT, 1997, transf. Lyric, 1998, NY, 1999 (Evening Standard, Time Out, Critic's Circle and Olivier Best Play Awards, 1998), filmed 2005; Howard Katz, 2001, The Musicians, 2004, RNT; (adapted) Trelawny of the Wells, Donmar, 2013; (adapted) The Beaux' Stratagem, The Red Lion, Three Days in the Country, RNT, 2015; Travesties, Menier Chocolate Factory, 2016; (adapted) Hedda Gabler, NT, 2016; Don Juan in Soho, Wyndham's, 2017; (adapted) Exit the King, NT, 2018. *Publications:* Dealer's Choice, 1995; After Miss Julie, 1995; Closer, 1997; Howard Katz, 2001.

**MARCH AND KINRARA, Earl of; Charles Henry Gordon Lennox;** *b* 20 Dec. 1994; *s* and *heir* of Duke of Richmond, Lennox and Gordon, *qv*.

**MARCH, Prof. Norman Henry;** Coulson Professor of Theoretical Chemistry, University of Oxford, 1977–94; Fellow of University College, Oxford, 1977–94, Emeritus since 1994; *b* 9 July 1927; *s* of William and Elsie March; *m* 1949, Margaret Joan Hoyle (*d* 1994); two *s*. *Educ:* King's Coll., London Univ. University of Sheffield: Lecturer in Physics, 1953–57; Reader in Theoretical Physics, 1957–61; Prof. of Physics, 1961–72; Prof. of Theoretical Solid State Physics, Imperial Coll., Univ. of London, 1973–77. Hon. DTech Chalmers, Gothenburg, 1980; Hon. DPhys Catania, Italy, 2003. *Publications:* The Many-Body Problem in Quantum Mechanics (with W. H. Young and S. Sampanthar), 1967; Liquid Metals, 1968; (with W. Jones) Theoretical Solid State Physics, 1973; Self-Consistent Fields in Atoms, 1974; Orbital Theories of Molecules and Solids, 1974; (with M. P. Tosi) Atomic Dynamics in Liquids, 1976; (with M. Parrinello) Collective Effects in Solids and Liquids, 1983; (with S. Lundqvist) The Theory of the Inhomogeneous Electron Gas, 1983; (with M. P. Tosi) Coulomb Liquids, 1984; (with M. P. Tosi) Polymers, Liquid Crystals and Low-Dimensional Solids, 1984; (with R. A. Street and M. P. Tosi) Amorphous Solids and the Liquid State, 1985; Chemical Bonds outside Metal Surfaces, 1986; (with P. N. Butcher and M. P. Tosi) Crystalline Semiconducting Materials and Devices, 1986; (with B. M. Deb) The Single Particle Density in Physics and Chemistry, 1987; (with S. Lundqvist and M. P. Tosi) Order and Chaos in Nonlinear Physical Systems, 1988; (with J. A. Alonso) Electrons in Metals and Alloys, 1989; Liquid Metals, 1990; Chemical Physics of Liquids, 1990; Electron Density Theory of Atoms and Molecules, 1992; (with J. F. Mucci) Chemical Physics of Free Molecules, 1993; Electron Correlation in Molecules and Condensed Phases, 1996; (with L. S. Cederbaum and K. C. Kulander) Atoms and Molecules in Intense External Fields, 1997; Electron Correlation in the Solid State, 1999; (with C. W. Lung) Mechanical Properties of Metals, 1999; (with M. P. Tosi) Introduction to Liquid State Physics, 2002; (with G. G. N. Angilella) Many-Body Theory of Molecules, Clusters and Condensed Phases, 2010; many scientific papers on quantum mechanics and statistical mechanics in Proceedings Royal Society, Phil. Magazine, Phys. Rev., Jl of Chem. Phys, etc. *Recreations:* music, chess, cricket. *Address:* 11 Oxford Court, Lancaster Road, Carnforth, Lancs LA5 9LE.

**MARCH, Valerie, (Mrs Andrew March);** *see* Masterson, V.

**MARCHAMLEY, 4th Baron** *cr* 1908; **William Francis Whiteley;** *b* 27 July 1968; *o s* of 3rd Baron Marchamley and of Sonia Kathleen Pedrick; *S* father, 1994; *m* 2000, Amy, *yr d* of Douglas Kyle; one *s* one *d*. *Heir: s* Hon. Leon Whiteley, *b* 2004.

**MARCHANT, Clare;** Chief Executive, Universities and Colleges Admissions Service, since 2017; *b* Bournemouth, 16 Aug. 1972; *d* of Philip Mitchell and Elizabeth Mitchell (*née* Kelly, later Styan); *m* 2013, Stephen Marchant; one *s*, and two step *s*. *Educ:* Univ. of Hull (BA Hons Hist. and Politics 1993); Open Univ. (MSc Manufg Mgt and Technol. 1998). Prodn Manager, Rank Hovis McDougall, 1993–97; Manager, Deloitte Consulting, 1997–2003; Chief Deployment Officer, NHS Nat. Prog. for IT, 2003–10; Asst Chief Exec., 2010–14, Chief Exec., 2014–17, Worcs CC. *Recreations:* running marathons (eight), baking, volunteering. *Address:* Universities and Colleges Admissions Service, Rosehill, New Barn Lane, Cheltenham, Glos GL52 3LZ.

**MARCHANT, Clare Wynne;** Director of Social Services and Housing, London Borough of Bromley, 1993–2000; *b* 13 June 1941; *d* of Rev. Glyn Morgan and Elma Morgan; *m* 1980, Harold Marchant. *Educ:* Horley Endowed Sch.; Banbury Grammar Sch.; UC Wales, Aberystwyth (BA Hons Philosophy 1963); UC Wales, Cardiff (DipSocSc 1964); Birmingham Univ. (Dip. Applied Social Sci. 1965). London Borough of Lewisham: Child Care Officer, 1965–67; Team Leader, 1967–71; Social Services Dist Officer, 1971–74; Principal Social Worker, 1974–87; Asst Dir (Social Services), RBK&C, 1987–93. *Publications:* A Vanished Past: Horley, Oxfordshire, vol. 1, 2015, vol. 2, 2015, vol. 3, 2016, vol. 4, 2016. *Recreations:* writing, photography, publishing. *Address:* Shaftesbury House, 15 Royal Circus Street, Greenwich, SE10 8SN.

**MARCHANT, Graham Leslie,** OBE 2011; arts management consultant, since 1989; General Manager, Contemporary Dance Trust, 1994–98; *b* 2 Feb. 1945; *s* of late Leslie and Dorothy Marchant. *Educ:* King's School, Worcester; Selwyn College, Cambridge (MA). Administrator, Actors' Company, 1973–75; General Manager, English Music Theatre, 1975–78; Gen. Administrator, Opera North, 1978–82; Administrator, Tricycle Theatre, 1983–84; Chief Exec., Riverside Studios, 1984; Managing Dir, Playhouse Theatre Co., 1985–86; Dir, Arts Co-ordination, Arts Council, 1986–89; Head of Site Improvement, South Bank Centre, 1989–92. Director: Ballet Rambert Ltd, 1991–93; Lyric Theatre (Hammersmith) Trust, 1993–97; Chairman: London Dance Network, 1998–99; Nat. Dance Co-ordinating Cttee, 2000–03; Director: Shobana Jeyasingh Dance Co., 1999–2001 (Chm., 2011–12). Trustee, Chichester Fest. Th., 2005–06. JP Thames 2003–14. *Recreations:* reading, gardening. *Address:* 43 Canonbury Square, N1 2AW.

**MARCHANT, Ian Derek;** Independent Chairman: Infinis Energy plc, 2013–15; Thames Water, since 2018; *b* 9 Feb. 1961; *s* of Derek William and Rosemary Marchant; *m* 1986, Elizabeth Helen; one *s* one *d*. *Educ:* Trinity Sch., Croydon; Durham Univ. (BA Econs). ACA. Accountant: PricewaterhouseCoopers, 1983–92 (on secondment to Dept of Energy, 1989–90); Southern Electric: Corporate Finance Manager, 1992–96; Finance Dir, 1996–98; Finance Dir, Scottish and Southern Energy plc, 1998–2002; Chief Exec., Scottish and Southern Energy, subseq. SSE plc, 2002–13. Chm., John Wood Gp PLC, 2014–19. Chm., Scotland's 2020 Climate Gp, 2009–15. Pres., Energy Inst., 2013–15. Chm., Maggie's Cancer Caring Centres, 2014–18. *Recreations:* Rugby, reading. *Address:* Dunelm Energy, London House, 20–22 East London Street, Edinburgh EH7 4BQ.

**MARCHANT, Ronald John,** CB 2007; Chief Executive and Comptroller General, Patent Office, 2004–07; *b* 6 Nov. 1945; *s* of Arthur and Bridget Marchant; *m* 1969, Helen Ruth Walker (*d* 2010); one *s* three *d*. *Educ:* West Ham Coll. of Technol. (BSc Hons (Chem.)). Patent Office: Examr, 1969–90; Principal Examr, 1990–92; Dir, Patents, 1992–2004. Non-exec. Dir, Scottish Intellectual Assets Mgt Ltd, 2007–09. Occasional advr for World Intellectual Property Orgn, 2007–, E Europe, Middle East, the Balkans and Central Asia. Mem. (Lab), Colchester BC, 1980–86. Chairman of Governors: Abersychan Sch., 2011–17; Torfaen Assoc., 2012–15. FRSA. *Publications:* contrib. Jl of World Intellectual Property, World Patent Information, Internat. Centre for Trade and Sustainable Develt pubns. *Recreations:* hill walking, reading, conservation, engaging with 9 grandchildren, sailing.

**MARCHBANK, Pearce,** RDI 2004; graphic designer, since 1969; Principal Partner, design consultancy, Pearce Marchbank Studio, since 1980; *b* 14 June 1948; *s* of late Harold George Marchbank and Rachel Pearce Marchbank; *m* 1st, 1975, Sue Miles (marr. diss. 1981); one *s* one *d*; 2nd, 1985, Heather Page (marr. diss. 1996); two *s*; partner, Katie Cornford. *Educ:* Bedford Sch.; Luton Coll. of Art; Central Sch. of Art and Design (BA 1st Cl. Hons). Art Director: Architectural Design mag., 1969–70; Rolling Stone mag., London, 1970; Friends mag., 1970–71; Co-ed. and designer, OZ mag., 1971 and 1974; design of complete editl set-up, style and logo, 1971–74, cover designer, 1971–80 and 1982–84, Time Out mag. (Publishers Assoc. Cover of the Year Award, 1974); Design Dir, Music Sales music publishers, 1974–93 (incl. design of all music books for The Beatles); Dir, Omnibus Press, 1976–79; Design Consultant, Virgin Records, 1978–80; Dir and Designer, Virgin Books, 1979–81; Co-ed. and Design Dir, Event mag., 1980–81; cover designs for Marxism Today mag. up to final issue, 1990–92; Co-ed. and Designer, Les Routiers (UK), 2000–03; Designer, John Lewis Partnership own-brand packaging designs, 2003–08; Design Dir, Booklaunch mag. Clients include: nat. newspapers (designs for mag. sections of Independent, The Times, Guardian, 1988–89); art galls (Berkeley Sq. Gall., Christie's Fine Art, Yale Center for British Art, GroundWork Gall., King's Lynn); music publishers, Chester Music and Novello & Co. (incl. CDs and books for Phillip Glass, Sir John Tavener, Michael Nyman); restaurant designs (Zanzibar, Bank, Corney & Barrow, Opus Birmingham); wine (John Armit, Christian Moueix, Tate Modern, Le Nez Rouge); book design (Yale Centre for British Art, Yale Univ. Press); corporate identities (Eau de Vie Ltd, The Great Tombola nat. lottery); Royal Mail (stamps for Paralympic Games, London, 2012); Compass Pubns (incl. Handbooks for Port of London Authy, for Port of Gibraltar, for Abu Dhabi Port and for Ras Al Khaimah Ports); Norfolk SO; Inskip Gee Architects, London; Storyville Records, Copenhagen; Music Sales Creative, London; Bob Dylan: the complete album collection; V&A Mus. mag.; Yale Centre for British Art; Salk Inst., San Diego. *Publications:* The Wall Sheet Journal, 1969; The Illustrated Rock Almanac, 1977; (ed) With The Beatles, 1982; (concept and design) Objectivity, 2010; Very Flat (monograph), 2014; (ed and designer) The Writing on the Wall, 2015. *Recreations:* landscape photography, Gothic and Modern Movement architecture, driving in continental Europe, slow food, eclectic music, Greece. *Address:* Pearce Marchbank Studio, East End, Newton Road, Castle Acre, Norfolk PE32 2AZ. *T:* (01760) 755886. *E:* mail@pearcemarchbank.com. *W:* www.pearcemarchbank.com.

**MARCHETTI, Federico;** Founder, Yoox, 2000; Chief Executive Officer, Yoox Net-a-Porter Group, since 2015; *b* Ravenna, 21 Feb. 1969. *Educ:* Bocconi Univ. (BA Business Admin); Columbia Univ. (MBA). Advr to chief execs and designers in internat. fashion industry. Leonardo Award for Innovation, Italy, 2012. *Recreations:* art, cinema, travel, sailing. *Address:* Yoox Net-a-Porter Group, Via Morimondo 17, 20143 Milan, Italy.

**MARCHWOOD, 3rd Viscount** *cr* 1945, of Penang and of Marchwood, Southampton; **David George Staveley Penny;** Bt 1933; Baron 1937; Managing Director, 1987–2004, Chairman, 1997–2004, Moët Hennessy UK Ltd (formerly Moët & Chandon (London) Ltd); *b* 22 May 1936; *s* of 2nd Viscount Marchwood, MBE and Pamela (*d* 1979), *o d* of John Staveley Colton-Fox; *S* father, 1979; *m* 1st, 1964, Tessa Jane (*d* 1997), *d* of W. F. Norris; three *s*; 2nd, 2001, Sylva, *widow* of Peter Willis Fleming. *Educ:* Winchester College. 2nd Lt, Royal Horse Guards (The Blues), 1955–57. Joined Schweppes Ltd, 1958, and held various positions in the Cadbury Schweppes group before joining Moët & Chandon. *Recreations:* Real tennis, golf, shooting, racing. *Heir: s* Hon. Peter George Worsley Penny [*b* 8 Oct. 1965; *m* 1995, Annabel, *d* of Rex Cooper; one *s* one *d*]. *Address:* Woodcock Farm, Chedington, Dorset DT8 3JA. *Club:* MCC.

**MARCINIAK, Prof. Stefan John,** PhD; FRCP; Professor of Respiratory Science, University of Cambridge, since 2016; Fellow, St Catharine's College, Cambridge, since 2011; *b* Nottingham, 16 Nov. 1969; *s* of Ignacy Marciniak and Lily Marciniak (*née* Newcombe); *m* 1997, Dominique Manuela Lezmi; one *s* one *d*. *Educ:* Elliott Durham Sch.; Fitzwilliam Coll., Cambridge (BA Hons Med. Sci. 1991; MA 1996; PhD 1996; MB BChir 1997). FRCP 2011. Jun. med. posts, Papworth Hosp. and Royal Brompton Hosp., 1996–99; Registrar: Edinburgh Royal Infirmary, 1999; Eastern Deanery, 2000–06; Res. Fellow, New York Univ., 2002–05; University of Cambridge: Clin. Lectr, 2007–08; MRC Clinician Scientist Fellow, 2008–12, MRC Sen. Clin. Res. Fellow, 2012–17. *Publications:* contribs to scientific and med. jls, incl. eLife, Genes and Develt, Jl Cell Biol., PLoS Pathogens. *Recreations:* dog walking, wine, teaching. *Address:* Cambridge Institute for Medical Research, Cambridge Biomedical Campus, Wellcome-MRC Building, Hills Road, Cambridge CB2 0XY. *T:* (01223) 762660. *E:* sjm20@cam.ac.uk; St Catharine's College, Cambridge CB2 1RL.

**MARCKUS, Melvyn;** communications consultant, since 2018; *b* 1 Jan. 1944; *s* of late Norman Myer Marckus and Violet Frances Mary Marckus (*née* Hughes); *m* 1st, 1970, Rosemary Virden (marr. diss. 1985); one *s* one *d*; 2nd, 1987, Rachel Mary Frances, *d* of Lord King of Wartnaby. *Educ:* Worthing Grammar Sch. Journalist: Scotsman, 1962–66; Daily Mail, 1966–67; Guardian, 1967; Daily Mail, 1967–70; Daily Express, 1970–72; Sunday Telegraph, 1972–82 (Jt Dep. City Editor, 1979–82); Observer, 1982–93: City Editor, 1982–93; Editor, Observer Business, 1984–93; an Asst Editor, 1987–93; Exec. Dir, 1987–93; City Editor, The Times, 1993–96; Columnist, The Express, 1996–99. Consultant, Luther Pendragon, 1996–98; communications consultant associated with Cardew Gp (formerly Cardew & Co.), 1998–2018. Dir, Cavendish Bldgs Ltd, 2016–. Dir, Lorana Sullivan UK Foundn Ltd, 2014–. *Recreations:* fishing, films, literature. *Address:* 18 Musgrave Crescent, SW6 4QD. *Club:* Flyfishers'.

**MARCUS, Ian;** Director, Ian Marcus Consultants Ltd, since 2012; *b* Bournemouth, 16 Jan. 1959; *s* of Monty Marcus and Ruth Marcus; *m* 1984, Beverley Silverman; one *s* one *d*. *Educ:* Westcliff High Sch. for Boys; Fitzwilliam Coll., Cambridge (BA Land Economy 1981). Bank of America, 1981–86; UBS Phillips and Drew, 1986–90; Natwest Markets, 1990–97; Bankers Trust, subseq. Deutsche Bank, 1997–99; Chm., European Real Estate, Credit Suisse, 1999–2012; Chm., Evans Property Gp, 2012; Sen. Ind. non-exec. Dir, Secure Income REIT Plc, 2014–; non-exec. Dir, Town Centre Securities plc, 2015–. Mem., Adv. Bd, Redevco NV, 2013–; Senior Adviser: Eastdil Secured, 2013–; Well Fargo Securities, 2013–. Chm., Commercial Property Forum, Bank of England; a Crown Estate Comr, 2012–. Former Pres., British Property Fedn; Former Chm., Investment Property Forum. Chm., Prince's Regeneration Trust, 2008–. Eminent Fellow, RICS, 2010. Mem., Chartered Surveyors' Co., 2011–. *Recreations:* Rugby (playing and watching), golf, backgammon, Morris Minor driving. *T:* 07747 774290. *Clubs:* Royal Automobile; Old Merchant Taylors' Rugby, Saracens Rugby.

**MARCUS, Prof. Laura**, PhD; FBA 2011; Goldsmiths' Professor of English Literature, University of Oxford, since 2010; Fellow, New College, Oxford, since 2010. *Educ:* Univ. of Warwick (BA); Univ. of Kent (MA, PhD). Prof. of English, Univ. of Sussex; Regius Prof. of Rhetoric and English Lit., Univ. of Edinburgh, 2007–09. Hon. DLitt Kent 2016. Jt Editor, Women: a Cultural Review. *Publications:* Auto/biographical Discourses: theory, criticism, practice, 1994; Virginia Woolf: writers and their work, 1997, 2004; (ed jtly) The Cambridge History of Twentieth-Century English Literature, 2004; The Tenth Muse: writing about cinema in the Modernist Period, 2007 (James Russell Lowell Prize, MLA, 2008); Dreams of Modernity: psychoanalysis, literature and cinema, 2014. *Address:* Faculty of English Language and Literature, University of Oxford, St Cross Building, Manor Road, Oxford OX1 3UL.

**MARCUS, Marshall**; Secretary General (formerly Chief Executive Officer), European Union Youth Orchestra, since 2013; Chief Executive, International Youth Foundation of Great Britain, since 2013; Founder and President, Sistema Europe, since 2012; *b* Leeds, 29 Jan. 1955; *s* of Hyman Marcus and Betty Marcus; *m* 1984, Annia Casagrande; two *d*. *Educ:* Leeds Grammar Sch.; Royal Coll. of Music; Queen's Coll., Oxford (BA Hons Philos. and Experimental Psychol. 1976; Hastings Scholar and Music Exhibnr); Trinity Coll., Cambridge (Cert Ed 1977). ARCM (Hons) 1973. Member: NYO, 1966–72; Leader, Leeds Youth Orch., 1968–72. Mem., BBC SO, 1977–79; Concertmaster, Philharmonica de Caracas, 1979–80; Prof., Venezuelan Youth Orch., 1979–81; Co-Principal viola, Venezuelan SO, 1980–81; freelance violinist, leader and music educationalist with UK orchs and ensembles, 1982–2002; Mem., 1982–2002, Exec. Dir, 1997–2002, Endymion Ensemble; Leader, Orch. of St John's, 1988–94; Principal Mem., Amsterdam Baroque, 1994–97; Orchestra of the Age of Enlightenment: Co-Founder, 1985; Chair, 1994–2002; CEO, 2002–06; Hd, Music, Southbank Centre, 2006–11; Founder and Dir, Orquesta Barroca Juvenil Simón Bolívar, 2011–12. Mem. Council, Assoc. of British Orchs, 2004–06; Mem. Bd, British Assoc. of Concert Halls, 2007–12. Trustee, Sistema England, 2010–; Founder and Adminr, Sistema Evaluation and Res. Archive, 2012–; Advr, Sistema Global, 2012–18. Advr and violin tutor, I, Culture Orch., 2011–12; Advr, Orchs for All, 2013–; Mem., Arts and Creative Economy Adv. Gp, British Council, 2013–18; Mem., Hon. Council, Orch. of the Age of Enlightenment, 2019–. Vice Patron, Kampala Music Sch. Fund, 2012–13. Hon. Fellow, Musicians' Co., 2012–13. *Recreations:* mountain walking, hiking, ski-ing, reading, writing, art, culture, travel. *T:* (office) (020) 7235 7671. *W:* www.twitter.com/marshallmarcus.

**MARCUS, Prof. Rudolph Arthur**; John G. Kirkwood and Arthur A. Noyes Professor of Chemistry, California Institute of Technology, since 2013 (Arthur Amos Noyes Professor of Chemistry, 1978–2013); *b* Montreal, 21 July 1923; *s* of Meyer Marcus and Esther Marcus (*née* Cohen); *m* 1949, Laura Hearne (*d* 2003); three *s*. *Educ:* McGill Univ. (BSc Chemistry 1943; PhD 1946). Postdoctoral research: NRCC, Ottawa, 1946–49; Univ. of N Carolina, 1949–51; Polytechnic Institute, Brooklyn: Asst Prof., 1951–54; Associate Prof., 1954–58; Prof., 1958–64; Acting Head, Div. of Phys. Chem., 1961–62; Prof., 1964–78, Head, Div. of Phys. Chem., 1967–68, Univ. of Illinois. Vis. Prof. of Theoretical Chem., Univ. of Oxford, 1975–76; Linnett Vis. Prof. of Chem., Univ. of Cambridge, 1996; Hon. Professor: Fudan Univ., Shanghai, 1994–; Inst. of Chem., Chinese Acad. of Scis, Beijing, 1995–; Ocean Univ. of China, 2002–; Tianjin Univ., 2002–; Dalian Inst. Chem. Phys., 2005–; Wenzhou Med. Coll., 2005–; Dist. Affiliated Prof., Tech. Univ. of Munich, 2008–; Nanyang Vis. Prof., Nanyang Tech. Univ., Singapore, 2009–14 (Mem., Internat. Panel of Advrs, Inst. of Advanced Studies, 2008–); Hon. Academician, Academia Sinica, Taiwan, 2010–. Mem., Sci. Cttees and Nat. Adv. Cttees, incl. External Adv. Bd, Nat. Sci. Foundn Center for Photoinduced Charge Transfer, 1990–; Internat. Advr in Chem., World Scientific Publishing, 1987; mem., numerous editl bds; Lectr, USA, Asia, Australia, Canada, Europe, Israel, USSR. Mem., Nat. Acad. of Sciences and other learned bodies; Foreign Member: Royal Soc., 1987; RSCan, 1993; Chinese Acad. of Scis, 1998. Hon. MRSC; Hon. Member: Internat. Soc. of Electrochemistry; Korean Chemical Soc., 1996. Hon. Fellow, UC, Oxford, 1995. Hon. DSc: McGill, 1988; Oxford, 1995. Prizes incl. Wolf Prize in Chem., 1985; Nat. Medal of Science, 1989; Nobel Prize in Chem., 1992. *Publications:* contribs to sci jls, incl. articles on electrochemistry, electron transfer, unimolecular reactions, enzymes, quantum dots, mass-independent isotope fractionation and on-water catalysis. *Recreations:* tennis, ski-ing, music. *Address:* Noyes Laboratory of Chemical Physics, Caltech 127–72, Pasadena, CA 91125, USA. *T:* (626) 3956566; 331 S Hill Avenue, Pasadena, CA 91106–3405, USA. *W:* www.cce.caltech.edu/content/rudolph-rudy-marcus.

**MARDELL, Air Vice-Marshal Alison**; Director of Legal Services, Royal Air Force, 2017–18; *b* Bewdley, 23 Sept. 1968; *d* of David Reeve and Gwendoline Reeve. *Educ:* Bristol Poly. (LLB); Birmingham Poly. (Law Soc. Finals); Univ. of Bristol (LLM); King's Coll. London (MA Defence Studies). Legal Officer, Legal Br., RAF, 1997–2018. Trustee, RAF Central Fund, 2016–19. Queen's Golden Jubilee Medal, 2002; Iraq Medal, 2003; Long Service and Good Conduct Medal, 2012; Queen's Diamond Jubilee Medal, 2012. *Club:* Royal Air Force.

**MARDELL, Mark Ian**; Presenter, The World This Weekend and The World at One, BBC Radio 4, since 2014; *b* 10 Sept. 1957; *s* of Donald and Maureen Mardell; *m* 1990, Joanne Veale; two *s* one *d*. *Educ:* Priory Sch., Banstead; Epsom Coll.; Univ. of Kent at Canterbury (BA Hons Politics 1979). Journalist: Radio Tees, 1980–82; Radio Aire, 1982; Ind. Radio News, 1983–87; Industrial Ed. and Reporter, Sharp End (C4), 1987–89; Political Corresp., BBC, 1989–93; Political Ed., Newsnight, 1993–2000; Political Corresp., BBC News at Six, 2000–03; Chief Political Corresp., BBC News, 2003–05; European Political Ed., 2005–09, N America Ed., 2009–14, BBC. Writer, Radio 4 short story, Judgement Day, 2004. *Publications:* How to Get On in TV (for children), 2001. *Recreations:* reading, music, swimming, cooking.

**MARDEN, Nicholas**, LVO 2019; DL; Private Secretary to HRH The Duke of Kent, 2011–18; *b* Colombo, Ceylon, 2 May 1950; *s* of Thomas, (Bob), Marden and Enid Marden; *m* 1977, Melanie Glover; two *d*. *Educ:* Uppingham Sch.; Southampton Univ. (BSc Politics and Law 1971). 2nd Lieut, Devonshire and Dorset Regt, 1971–74. Entered FCO, 1974; Third Sec., FCO, 1974–77; Second Secretary: Nicosia, 1977–80; FCO, 1980–82; First Secretary: Warsaw, 1982–85; FCO, 1985–88; Paris, 1988–93; Counsellor: FCO, 1993–98; Tel Aviv, 1998–2002; FCO, 2002–11. DL Kent, 2019. *Recreations:* sailing, cinema, walking, (watching) Rugby, folk and jazz music.

**MARDER, His Honour Bernard Arthur**; QC 1977; a Circuit Judge, 1983–98; President of the Lands Tribunal, 1993–98 (Member, 1989–98); *b* 25 Sept. 1928; *er s* of late Samuel and Marie Marder; *m* 1953, Sylvia Levy (MBE 1988); one *s* one *d*. *Educ:* Bury Grammar Sch.; Manchester Univ. (LLB 1951). Called to the Bar, Gray's Inn, 1952. A Recorder of the Crown Court, 1979–83. Formerly Asst Comr, Local Govt and Parly Boundary Commns; Chairman: Panel of Inquiry into W Yorks Structure Plan, 1979; Mental Health Review Tribunals, 1987–89. Pres., Land Inst., 1997–99. Mem. Bd, Orange Tree Theatre, 1986–2011; Trustee: Richmond Parish Lands Charity, 1987–96 (Chm., 1993–96); Richmond Museum, 1996–2003; Petersham Meadows Trust, 1999–2010. Hon. FSVA 1994; Hon. RICS 1999. *Recreations:* music, theatre, wine.

**MAREK, John**, PhD; Member for Wrexham, National Assembly for Wales, 1999–2007 (Lab 1999–2003, Ind 2003–07); *b* 24 Dec. 1940; *m* 1964, Anne Pritchard (*d* 2006). *Educ:* King's Coll. London (BSc (Hons), PhD). Lecturer in Applied Mathematics, University College of Wales, Aberystwyth, 1966–83. Mem., Ceredigion DC, 1979–83 (Chair, Finance sub-cttee, 1982–83). MP (Lab) Wrexham, 1983–2001. Opposition frontbench spokesman: on health, 1985–87; on treasury and economic affairs, and on the Civil Service, 1987–92. Dep. Presiding Officer, Nat. Assembly for Wales, 2000–07. Treas., CPA, 2000–03. Mem., IAU. Mem., Audit Cttee, Klimkovice Town Council, Czech Republic, 2018–. *Publications:* various research papers. *E:* johnmarek11@gmail.com.

**MARENBON, John Alexander**, PhD, LittD; FBA 2009; Senior Research Fellow, Trinity College, Cambridge, since 2005; Honorary Professor of Medieval Philosophy, University of Cambridge, since 2010; *b* London, 26 Aug. 1955; *s* of Arthur Marenbon and Zena Marenbon (*née* Jacobs); *m* 1981, Sheila Lawlor; one *s*. *Educ:* Westminster Sch.; Trinity Coll., Cambridge (BA 1976; PhD 1980; LittD 2001). Trinity College, Cambridge: Res. Fellow, 1978; Fellow and Dir of Studies, 1979–2005. Guest Prof., Peking Univ., 2015–16; Vis. Prof., Univ. of Vienna, 2017–18. Hon. ThD Helsinki, 2011. *Publications:* From the Circle of Alcuin to the School of Auxerre, 1981; Early Medieval Philosophy, 1983, 2nd edn 1988; Later Medieval Philosophy, 1987; Aristotle in Britain during the Middle Ages, 1996; The Philosophy of Peter Abelard, 1997; (ed) Routledge History of Philosophy III: medieval philosophy, 1998; Aristotelian Logic, Platonism and the Context of Early Medieval Philosophy in the West, 2000; (ed) Poetry and Philosophy in the Middle Ages, 2001; (ed with Giovanni Orlandi) Peter Abelard: Collationes, 2001; Boethius, 2003; Le Temps, la prescience et les futurs contingents, de Boèce à Thomas d'Aquin, 2005; Medieval Philosophy: an historical and philosophical introduction, 2007; (ed) The Many Roots of Medieval Logic: the Aristotelian and non-Aristotelian Traditions, 2008; (ed) The Cambridge Companion to Boethius, 2009; (ed jtly) Aristotelian Logic East and West, 500–1500: on interpretation and prior analytics in two traditions, 2010; (ed jtly) Methods and Methodologies: Aristotelian Logic East and West, 500–1500, 2011; (ed) Oxford Handbook of Medieval Philosophy, 2012; (ed jtly) Paganism in the Middle Ages: threat and fascination, 2012; Abelard in Four Dimension: a twelfth-century philosopher in his context and ours, 2013; (ed jtly) Aristotle's 'Categories' in the Byzantine, Arabic and Latin Traditions, 2013; Pagans and Philosophers: the problem of paganism from Augustine to Leibniz, 2015; Medieval Philosophy: a very short introduction, 2016; (ed) Relations in the Medieval Traditions of Logic and Metaphysics, 2016. *Recreations:* cooking, listening to music. *Address:* Trinity College, Cambridge CB2 1TQ. *T:* (01223) 338524. *E:* jm258@cam.ac.uk.

**MARFLEET, Jacqueline Elizabeth**; Senate House Librarian, University of London, 2014–17; *b* Lincs, 15 Dec. 1962; *d* of Brian Marfleet and Pauline Marfleet. *Educ:* Univ. of Leeds (BA Jt Hons French and German 1985); Loughborough Univ. (MA Liby and Information Studies 1987). Liby Asst, Simmons & Simmons, 1987–89; Information Manager: Braxton Associates, 1989–91; KPMG Peat Marwick, subseq. KPMG, 1992–96; Vice Pres., J. P. Morgan, 1996–2004; Hd, Reference and Res., BL, 2005–07; Knowledge Manager, Ernst & Young, 2007–08; Hd, Advice and Records Knowledge, Nat. Archives, 2009–14. *Publications:* articles for Business Information Rev. and Electronic Liby. *Recreations:* running, cycling, hill walking, travelling.

**MARGADALE**, 3rd Baron *cr* 1964, of Islay, co. Argyll; **Alastair John Morrison**; DL; *b* 4 April 1958; *er s* of 2nd Baron Margadale, TD and of Clare (*née* Barclay); *S* father, 2003; *m* 1st, 1988, Lady Sophia Louise Sydney Murphy (marr. diss. 1999), *yr d* of 11th Duke of Devonshire, KG, PC, MC and Dowager Duchess of Devonshire, DCVO; one *s* one *d*; 2nd, 1999, Mrs Amanda Wace, *d* of Michael Fuller. *Educ:* Harrow; RAC Cirencester. DL Wilts 2003. *Heir:* *s* Hon. Declan James Morrison, *b* 11 July 1993. *Address:* Estate Office, Fonthill Bishop, Salisbury, Wilts SP3 5SH.

*See also* Viscount Trenchard.

**MARGESSON**, family name of **Viscount Margesson**.

**MARGESSON**, 3rd Viscount *cr* 1942, of Rugby; **Richard Francis David Margesson**; conservationist; *b* 25 Dec. 1960; *o s* of 2nd Viscount Margesson and of Helena Margesson (*née* Backstrom); *S* father, 2014; *m* 1st, 1990, Wendy Maree Hazelton (marr. diss. 2003); one *d*; 2nd, 2003, Roselle Ita Escalona (*née* Rowlands). *Educ:* St Paul's Sch.; Eton; Exeter Univ. (BA Hons Eng. Lit.). Major, Coldstream Guards, retd 2001. *Heir:* none.

**MARGETSON, Sir John (William Denys)**, KCMG 1986 (CMG 1979); HM Diplomatic Service, retired; *b* 9 Oct. 1927; *yr s* of Very Rev. W. J. Margetson and Marion Jenoure; *m* 1963, Miranda, *d* of Sir William Menzies Coldstream, CBE and Mrs Nancy Spender; one *s* one *d*. *Educ:* Blundell's; St John's Coll., Cambridge (choral scholar; MA). Lieut, Life Guards, 1947–49. Colonial Service, District Officer, Tanganyika, 1951–60 (Private Sec. to Governor, Sir Edward Twining, subseq. Lord Twining, 1956–57); entered Foreign (subseq. Diplomatic) Service, 1960; The Hague, 1962–64; speech writer to Foreign Sec., Rt Hon. George Brown, MP, 1966–68; Head of Chancery, Saigon, 1968–70; Counsellor 1971, seconded to Cabinet Secretariat, 1971–74; Head of Chancery, UK Delegn to NATO, 1974–78; Ambassador to Vietnam, 1978–80; seconded to MoD as Senior Civilian Instructor, RCDS, 1981–82; Ambassador and Dep. Perm. Rep. to UN, NY, and Pres., UN Trusteeship Council, 1983–84; Ambassador to the Netherlands, 1984–87; Special Rep. of the Sec. of State for For. and Commonwealth Affairs, 1994–98. Gentleman Usher of the Blue Rod, 1992–2002. Dir, John S. Cohen Foundn, 1988–93. Chm., Foster Parents Plan (UK), 1988–90. Patron, Suffolk Internat. Trade Gp, 1988–90; Jt Pres., Suffolk and SE Cambridgeshire 1992 Club, 1988–90. Chairman: RSCM, 1988–94; Jt Cttee, London Royal Schs of Music, 1991–94; Yehudi Menuhin Sch., 1990–94; Trustee: Fitzwilliam Museum Trust, 1990–98; Ouseley Trust, 1991–97; Music in Country Churches, 1993–2000. Hon. RCM 1992; FRSCM 1994. *Recreation:* music. *Address:* 71b Cumberland Street, Woodbridge, Suffolk IP12 4AG.

**MARGETTS, Prof. Helen Zerlina**, OBE 2019; PhD; FBA 2019; Professor of Society and the Internet, University of Oxford, since 2004 (Director, Oxford Internet Institute, 2011–18); Fellow, Mansfield College, Oxford, since 2004; Turing Fellow and Programme Director for Public Policy, Alan Turing Institute for Data Science and Artificial Intelligence, since 2018; *b* 15 Sept. 1961; *d* of James David Margetts and Helen Jill Scott Margetts (*née* Taylor); partner, Dr Pedro Mascuñán Pérez; one *s*. *Educ:* Univ. of Bristol (BSc Maths 1983); London Sch. of Econs and Pol Sci. (MSc Politics and Public Policy 1990; PhD Govt 1996). Computer programmer/systems analyst, Rank Xerox, 1984–87; Systems Analyst, Amoco Oil Co., 1987–90; Res. Officer, Dept of Govt, LSE, 1991–94; Lectr, then Sen. Lectr in Politics, Dept of Politics and Sociol., Birkbeck Coll., Univ. of London, 1994–99; University College London: Reader, 1999–2001; Prof. of Pol Sci., 2001–04; Dir, Sch. of Public Policy, 2001–04. ESRC Professorial Fellow, 2011–14. Member: Digital Economy Council; Scientific Adv. Council, Home Office; Ada Lovelace Inst., Nuffield Foundn. Friedrich Schiedel Prize for Res. and Res. Leadership in Technol. and Politics, Technical Univ. of Munich, 2018. *Publications:* (ed jtly) Turning Japanese: Britain with a permanent party of government, 1994; (jtly) Making Votes Count: replaying the 1990s General Elections under alternative electoral systems, 1997; Information Technology in Government: Britain and America, 1998; (with P. Dunleavy) Government on the Web,

1999; (with P. Dunleavy) Proportional Representation for Local Government: an analysis, 1999; (jtly) Voices of the People, 2001, 2nd edn 2005; (ed jtly) Challenges to Democracy: ideas, involvement and institutions, 2001; (with P. Dunleavy) Government on the Web II, 2002; (with P. Dunleavy) Digital Era Governance: IT corporations, the State, and e-government, 2006; (with C. Hood) The Tools of Government in the Digital Age, 2007; (with P. Dunleavy) Government on the Internet, 2007; (ed jtly) Paradoxes of Modernization: unintended consequences of public policy reform, 2010; (jtly) Political Turbulence: how social media shape collective action, 2015 (Best Politics Bk Award, Pol Studies Assoc., 2017); contrib. articles to learned jls, incl. Public Admin, Public Policy and Admin, British Jl Politics and Internat. Relns, Internat. Review of Pol Sci., Political Studies, Governance, Jl Public Admin Res. and Theory, Parly Affairs, Jl Theoretical Politics, Internat. Review of Admin. Scis, Eur. Pol Sci. Rev., West Eur. Pols, Royal Soc. Philosophical Trans. *Recreations:* art, painting, reading, writing, talking to my son, sailing. *Address:* Oxford Internet Institute, University of Oxford, One St Giles, Oxford OX1 3JS. *T:* (01865) 287210, *Fax:* (01865) 287211. *E:* Helen.Margetts@oii.ox.ac.uk.

**MARGETTS, Sir Rob(ert John)**, Kt 2006; CBE 1996; FREng; FIChemE; Chairman: Ensus Ltd, since 2006; Energy Technologies Institute, since 2007; Vice Chairman, Venator Materials PLC, since 2017; *b* 10 Nov. 1946; *s* of John William and Ellen Mary Margetts; *m* 1969, Joan Sandra Laws; three *s* one *d. Educ:* Highgate Sch.; Trinity Hall, Cambridge (BA Natural Scis and Chem. Engrg). FIChemE 1985; FREng (FEng 1988). Joined ICI, 1969: Process Design Engr, Agricl Div., Billingham, 1969; subseq. various managerial posts, including: Director: Agricl Div., 1982–85; Petrochemicals and Plastics Div., 1985; Res. and Ops, ICI Chemicals and Polymers Gp, 1987; ICI PLC: Dir, ICI Engrg, 1987–89; Gen. Manager, Personnel, 1989–90; Chm. and Chief Exec., Tioxide Gp PLC, 1991–92; Exec. Dir, 1992–97; Vice Chm., 1998–2000; Chm., ICI Pension Fund Trustee Ltd, 1994–2000. Vice Chm., 1998–2000, Chm., 2000–10, Legal & Gen. Gp PLC (non-exec. Dir, 1996–2010); Chm., Audit Cttee, 1998–2000); Vice Chm., 2001–02, Chm., 2002–06, BOC Gp PLC; Chairman: Ordnance Survey Ltd, 2008–16; Lythe Hill Park Ltd, 2015–; Lythe Hill Park Properties Ltd, 2015–; Dep. Chm., OJSC Uralkali, 2011–18; non-executive Director: English China Clays PLC, 1992–99; Anglo American PLC, 1999–2010 (Chm., Remuneration Cttee, 2001–10; Sen. Ind. Dir, 2003–08); Falck Renewables plc, 2007–10; Huntsman Corp. (USA), 2010– (Chm. Europe, 2000–10); Wellstream, 2010–11; Mem., Internat. Adv. Bd, Teijin, Japan, 2004–06; Neochimiki SA, 2008–09. Chm., NERC, 2001–06. Chm., Govt Industry Forum on Non-Food Crops, 2001–04. Dir, Foundn for Sci. and Technol., 2001–. Gov., and Mem. Finance Cttee, ICSTM, 1991–2004; Member: Bd, CEFIC, 1993–95 and 1998–2000; Council, CIA, 1993–96 and 2001–; Council for Sci. and Technol., 1998–2007; Adv. Cttee on Business and the Envmt, 1999–2001; Chm., Action for Engrg, 1995–97; Trustee, Council for Ind. and Higher Educn, 1992–2010. Vice-Pres., Royal Acad. of Engrg, 1994–97. Mem. Ct, Univ. of Surrey, 2002–. Trustee, Brain Res. Trust, 2002–13. Freeman, City of London, 2004; Hon. Freeman, Salters' Co., 2004. FCGI 2001. Hon. FIC 1999; Hon. Fellow: Univ. of Cardiff, 2007; Energy Inst., 2008; Council for Industry and Higher Educn, 2011. Hon. DEng Sheffield, 1997; Hon. DSc Cranfield, 2003. *Recreations:* sailing, ski-ing, tennis, watersports.

**MARGOLIN, Daniel George**; QC 2015; Partner, Joseph Hage Aaronson LLP, since 2015; *b* 1972; *m* 2001, Sarah Louise Farmer; one *s* one *d. Educ:* Balliol Coll., Oxford (Schol.; Coolidge Pathfinder; BA 1st Cl. Ancient and Modern Hist.); City Univ., London (DipLaw); Inns of Court Sch. of Law (BVC). Called to the Bar, Gray's Inn, 1995; in practice at Chancery Bar, 1996–2015; Jun. Counsel to Crown, 1999–2015. Trustee, RNT Foundn, 2017–. Freeman, City of London, 2012. *Publications:* (Contributing Ed.) Mithani, Directors' Disqualification, 1998–. *Club:* Buck's.

**MARGOLYES, Miriam**, OBE 2002; actress; *b* 18 May 1941; *d* of late Dr Joseph Margolyes and Ruth (*née* Walters). *Educ:* Oxford High Sch.; Newnham Coll., Cambridge; Guildhall Sch. of Music and Drama (LGSM 1959). *Films include:* A Nice Girl Like Me, 1969; Rime of the Ancient Mariner, 1976; Stand Up, Virgin Soldiers, 1977; Little Shop of Horrors, 1986; The Good Father, 1987; Body Contact, 1987; Little Dorrit, 1988; Pacific Heights, 1990; I Love You to Death, 1990; The Butcher's Wife, 1991; As You Like It, 1992; Ed and His Dead Mother, 1993; The Age of Innocence, 1993; Immortal Beloved, 1994; Babe, 1995; Balto, 1995; James and the Giant Peach, 1996; Romeo and Juliet, 1996; Different for Girls, 1996; The IMAX Nutcracker, 1997; The First Snow of Winter, 1998; Left Luggage, 1998; Sunshine, 1999; Dreaming of Joseph Lees, 1999; End of Days, 1999; House!, 2000; Cats and Dogs, 2001; Harry Potter and the Chamber of Secrets, 2002; Being Julia, 2003; Ladies in Lavender, 2004; Life and Death of Peter Sellers, 2004; Harry Potter and the Deathly Hallows, Pt 2, 2011; The Guilt Trip, 2012; The Wedding Video, 2012; (voice) Maya the Bee, 2015; The Man Who Invented Christmas, 2017; *theatre* includes: Dickens' Women (one-woman show), Duke of York's, 1991, world tour, 2012; She Stoops to Conquer, Queen's, 1993; The Killing of Sister George, Ambassador's, 1995; Wicked, Apollo, 2007, NY, 2008; Endgame, Duchess, 2009; Me and My Girl, Sheffield Crucible, 2010; A Day in the Death of Joe Egg, Glasgow Citizens Th., 2011; Dickens' Women, Artsdepot and UK and US tour, 2012; Neighbourhood Watch, Adelaide, 2014; I'll Eat You Last (one-woman show), Melbourne, 2014; The Importance of Being Miriam, Melbourne and tour, 2015; Madame Rubinstein, Park Theatre, 2017; *television* includes: Take a Letter Mr Jones, A Kick Up the Eighties, The History Man, 1981; Blackadder, 1983, 1986, 1988; Oliver Twist, 1985; Poor Little Rich Girl, 1987; The Life and Loves of a She Devil, 1990; Frannie's Turn, 1992; Cold Comfort Farm, 1995; The Phoenix and the Carpet, 1997; Supply & Demand, 1998; Vanity Fair, 1998; Dickens in America, Wallis and Edward, 2005; Miss Fisher's Murder Mysteries, 2012–15; Hebburn, 2013; Nina Needs to Go, 2014; Trollied, 2014; Rake, 2016–18; The Real Marigold Hotel, 2016; Bucket, 2017; Bottersnikes & Gumbles, 2016–17; The Real Marigold Hotel on Tour, 2017, 2019; Miriam's Big American Adventure, 2018; Miriam's Dead Good Adventure, 2019; Call the Midwife, 2019; narrator, Flipping Profit, 2018; *radio performances* include The Queen and I, 1993; Gloomsbury, 2012, 2015, 2018. Best Supporting Actress, LA Critics Circle, 1989; Best Supporting Actress, BAFTA, 1993. *Publications:* (with Sonia Fraser) Dickens' Women, 2011. *Recreations:* reading, talking, eating, Italy. *Address:* c/o United Agents, 12–26 Lexington Street, W1F 0LE.

**MARGRIE, Victor Robert**, CBE 1984; FCSD; studio potter, academic, critic; *b* 29 Dec. 1929; *s* of Robert and Emily Miriam Margrie; *m* 1st, 1955, Janet Smithers (marr. diss. 2005); three *d*; 2nd, 2005, Rosemary Ash. *Educ:* Southgate County Grammar Sch.; Hornsey Sch. of Art (NDD, ATD 1952). FCSD (FSIA 1974). Part-time teaching at various London art colls, 1952–56; own workshop, making stoneware and latterly porcelain, 1954–71; Head of Ceramics Dept, Harrow Sch. of Art, 1956–71 (founded Studio Pottery Course, 1963); Sec., Crafts Adv. Cttee, 1971–77; Founder Dir, Crafts Council, 1977–84; Professorial appt, RCA, 1984–85; own studio, Bristol, 1985. One-man exhibns, British Craft Centre (formerly Crafts Centre of GB), 1964, 1966 and 1969; represented in V&A Mus., Ashmolean Mus. and other collections. Vice-Chm., Crafts Centre of GB, 1965; Member: Cttee for Art and Design, DATEC, 1979–84; Cttee for Art and Design, CNAA, 1981–84; Design Bursaries Bd, RSA, 1980–84; Working Party, Gulbenkian Craft Initiative, 1985–88; Fine Art Adv. Cttee, British Council, 1983–86; UK National Commn for UNESCO, 1984–85 (also Mem., Culture Adv. Cttee); Adv. Council, V&A Mus., 1979–84; Craftsmen Potters Assoc., 1960–89; Internat. Acad. of Ceramics, 1972–; Recording the Crafts (formerly Cttee, Nat. Video and Electronic Archive of the Crafts), 1993–. Ext. Examiner, Royal Coll. of Art: Dept of Ceramics and Glass, 1977; Dept of Silversmithing and Jewellery, 1978–80; Ext. Advisor, Dept of Ceramics, UWE (formerly Bristol Polytechnic), 1987–; Mem., Bd of Studies in Fine Art, Univ. of London, 1989–94; Advr, Faculty of Fine Art, Cardiff Inst. of Higher Educn, 1992–94; Vis. Prof., Univ. of Westminster (formerly Poly. of Central London), 1992–96. Governor: Herts Coll. of Art and Design, 1977–79; Camberwell Sch. of Art and Crafts, 1975–84; W Surrey Coll. of Art and Design, 1978–87; Loughborough Coll. of Art and Design, 1984–89, 1990–93. Associate Editor: Studio Pottery, 1993–2000; Ceramics in Society, 2000–05. *Publications:* contributed to: Oxford Dictionary of Decorative Arts, 1975; Europaische Keramik Seit 1950, 1979; Lucie Rie, 1981; Tradition and Innovation: five decades of Harrow ceramics, 2012; contrib. specialist pubns and museum catalogues. *Address:* 15 Telegraph Street, Shroton (Iwerne Courtney), Blandford Forum, Dorset DT11 8QQ. *T:* (01258) 860944. *E:* margrie@me.com.

**MARINCOWITZ, Dr John**; Headmaster, Queen Elizabeth's School, Barnet, 1998–2011; *b* 19 Dec. 1950; *s* of Nicholas and Diana Marincowitz; *m* 1979, Miriam Salie; one *s* one *d. Educ:* St John's Coll., Johannesburg; Witwatersrand Univ. (BA); UCW, Aberystwyth (BA Hons); SOAS, London Univ. (PhD 1985); Inst. of Educn, London Univ. (NPQH). History teacher, Trafalgar High Sch., Cape Town, 1979–82; Queen Elizabeth's School, Barnet: history teacher, 1985–86; Hd of Year, 1986–88; Hd of Sixth Form, Senior Master, 1988–98. Chm. Govs, Little Heath Sch., Herts, 1994–98. Chairman: Mgt Cttee, Northgate Special Sch., Edgware Hosp., 2007–11; Schools' Finance Forum, London Borough of Barnet, 2007–11; Mem., Boys' Academic State Schs, 2005–11. FRSA 1998. Mem., Cruising Assoc., 1999–. Mem., RYA, 1999. *Recreations:* non-fiction, history of education, creative writing, travel, sailing, historical and abstract art, eclectic music, Rugby Union internationals. *E:* jmarincowitz@gmail.com.

**MARINKER, Prof. Marshall**, OBE 1991; FRCGP; Visiting Professor in General Practice, Guy's, King's and St Thomas' School of Medicine of King's College London (formerly United Medical and Dental Schools of Guy's and St Thomas' Hospitals), 1991–2006; *b* 2 March 1930; *s* of Isidor and Sarah Marinker; *m* 1st, 1955; two *s* one *d*; 2nd, 1978, Jeanette Miller. *Educ:* Haberdashers' Aske's Sch., Hampstead; Middlesex Hosp. Med. Sch., Univ. of London (MB, BS 1956); City Univ. (MA Creative Writing, 2010). FRCGP 1972. Principal in Gen. Practice, Grays, 1959–73; Sen. Lectr, St Mary's Hosp. Med. Sch., 1971–73; Foundation Prof. of Gen. Practice and Head, Dept of Community Health, Univ. of Leicester, 1974–82; Dir, MSD Foundn, 1982–92; Dir of Medical Educn, MSD Ltd, 1992–95. Visiting Professor: Univ. of Iowa, 1973; Univ. of Tampere, 1976; Roche Vis. Prof., NZ Coll. of GPs, 1977; Dozar Prof., Ben Gurion Univ., 1981; Sir James Wattie Meml Vis. Prof., NZ, 1982. Chm., R&D Cttee, High Security Psychiatric Services Bd, NHS, 1996–2000. Royal College of General Practitioners: Res. Registrar, 1967–70; William Pickles Lectr, 1974; Mem. Council, 1974–89; Chm., Educn Div., 1981–84; Chair, Cttee on Med. Ethics, 1987–89; George Abercrombie Prize, 1991. Chm., Council of Europe Wkg Party on the Future of Gen. Practice, 1975–77. Freeman, City of London, 1995. Hon. DM Tampere, 1982. *Publications:* (jtly) Treatment or Diagnosis?, 1970, 2nd edn 1984; (jtly) The Future General Practitioner, 1972; (ed jtly) Practice: a handbook of primary medical care, annually 1978–; (ed jtly) Teaching General Practice, 1981; (ed jtly) Towards Quality in General Practice, 1986; (ed) Medical Audit and General Practice, 1990, 2nd edn 1995; (ed) Controversies in Health Care Policy, 1995; (ed) Sense and Sensibility in Health Care, 1996; (jtly) Clinical Futures, 1998; (ed) Medicine and Humanity, 2001; (ed) Health Targets in Europe, 2002; (ed) Constructive Conversations about Health, 2006; pamphlets, lectures and papers on theory of gen. practice, med. educn, health service policy and med. ethics. *Recreations:* reading, writing, theatre, cinema, music, conversation, walks and conversations with Jeanette over Hampstead Heath and along the towpath of the Regent's Canal. *Address:* 8 St Peter's Church, 124 Dartmouth Park Hill, N19 5HL. *T:* (020) 7263 1586, *Fax:* (020) 7263 6759.

**MARIO, Dr Ernest**; Chairman: Soleno Therapeutics (formerly Capnia), Inc., since 2007 (Chief Executive Officer, 2007–14); Chimerix Inc., since 2013; *b* 12 June 1938; *s* of Jerry and Edith Mario; *m* 1961, Mildred Martha Daume; three *s. Educ:* Rutgers College of Pharmacy, New Brunswick, NJ (BSc Pharmacy); Univ. of Rhode Island (MS; PhD). Vice Pres., Manufacturing Operation, Smith Kline, 1974; E. R. Squibb & Sons: Vice Pres., Manufacturing for US Pharmaceutical Div., 1977; Vice Pres. and Gen. Man., Chemical Div., 1979; Pres., Chemical Engrg Div. and Sen. Vice Pres. of company, 1981; Pres. and Chief Exec. Officer, Squibb Medical Product, 1983; elected to Bd, 1984; joined Glaxo Inc. as Pres. and Chief Exec. Officer, 1986; apptd to Bd of Glaxo Holdings, 1988; Chief Exec., 1989–93; Dep. Chm., 1991–93; Chief Exec., 1993–2001, Co-Chm., 1993–97, Chm., 1997–2001, Alza Corp.; Chm. and CEO, Apothogen Inc., 2002; Chm., IntraBiotics Pharmaceuticals Inc., 2002–03; Chm., 2003–07 and CEO, 2003–06, Reliant Pharmaceuticals Inc. Chairman: Nat. Foundn for Infectious Diseases, Washington, 1989; American Foundn for Pharmaceutical Educn, NY, 1991. *Recreations:* golf, swimming. *Address:* Soleno Therapeutics, Inc., 1235 Radio Road, Suite 110, Redwood City, CA 94065, USA.

**MARJORIBANKS, John Logan**; Chairman, Local Government Boundary Commission for Scotland, 2000–07; *b* 21 Aug. 1944; *s* of William Logan Marjoribanks of that Ilk and Thelma (*née* Williamson); *m* 1976, Andrea Ruth Cox; one *s* two *d. Educ:* Merchiston Castle Sch.; St John's Coll., Cambridge (BA 1965, MA 1982). ACCA 1988, FCCA 1993–2010. Scottish Agricl Industries, 1965–73; Dept of Agric., Zambia, 1973–78; Commonwealth Development Corporation: Lectr, then Sen. Lectr, Mananga Agricl Mgt Centre, Swaziland, 1979–85; Ops Exec., London, 1985–87; Country Mgr, Mozambique and Zimbabwe, 1988–93; Dir, Mananga Mgt Centre, Swaziland, 1993–95; Country Mgr, India, 1995–98; Dir, Public Affairs, 1999–2000. On-line Tutor, Imperial Coll. at Wye, 2001–04. Local Govt Political Restrictions Exemptions Adjudicator for Scotland, 2007–15. Member: Cttee of Mgt, Berwickshire Housing Assoc., 2001–07; E Regl Bd, Scottish Envmtl Protection Agency, 2002–05. Chm., Gavinton, Fogo and Polwarth Community Council, 2012–14. Vice-Chm., Berwickshire Civic Soc., 2002–11. Gov., Macaulay Land Use Res. Inst., 2004–07. *Recreations:* Scots heraldry, bridge. *Address:* 20 Latches Walk, Axminster, Devon EX13 5DQ. *Club:* Axminster Rotary.

**MARK, Sir Alan (Francis)**, KNZM 2009 (DCNZM 2001); CBE 1989; FRSNZ 1978; Professor of Botany, University of Otago, 1975–98, now Emeritus Professor; *b* 19 June 1932; *s* of Cyril Lionel Mark and Frances Evelyn Mark (*née* Marshall); *m* 1958, Patricia Kaye Davie; two *s* two *d. Educ:* Univ. of New Zealand (BSc 1953; MSc 1955); Duke Univ., N Carolina (James B. Duke Fellow, 1957; Phi Beta Kappa, 1958; PhD 1958). Sen. Res. Fellow, 1960–64, Res. Advr, 1965–2000, Chm. Bd of Govs, Hellaby Indigenous Grasslands Res. Trust, 2000–10; University of Otago: Lectr in Botany, 1960–65; Sen. Lectr, 1966–69; Associate Prof., 1969–75. Chm., Guardians of Lakes Manapouri, Monowai and Te Anau, 1973–99; Mem., Fiordland Marine Guardians, 2005–13. Distinguished Life Mem., Royal NZ Forest and Bird Protection Soc., 1998–; Member: NZ Ecol Soc., 1953–2004, now Life Mem.; Ecol Soc. of Amer., 1958–2001, now Emeritus. Hon. DSc Otago, 2014. *Publications:* (with Nancy M. Adams) New Zealand Alpine Plants, 1973, 3rd edn 1995; Above the

Treeline: a nature guide to alpine New Zealand, 2013; over 200 scientific papers. *Recreations:* enjoying the outdoors, nature conservation. *Address:* 205 Wakari Road, Helensburgh, Dunedin, New Zealand. *T:* (3) 4763229, (office) (3) 4797573. *E:* alan.mark@otago.ac.nz. *Club:* New Zealand Alpine (Hon. Mem.).

**MARK, Rear Adm. Robert Alan,** FRIN; Senior Executive Advisor, Strategy& (formerly Booz & Co.), since 2015 (Vice President and Partner, 2011–15); *b* 28 April 1955; *s* of Alexander Mark and Ruby (*née* Oliver); *m* 1978, Wendy Anne Peters; one *s* one *d*. *Educ:* Univ. of Hull (BSc Jt Hons Geol. and Phys. Geog. 1977); London Business Sch., Sloan Prog. (MSc Mgt 2001). Joined RN, 1974; HMS Wolverton, 1976; BRNC 1977; HMS Torquay, 1977–78; HMS Ajax, 1979–80; HMS Fawn (NO), 1980–82; BRNC staff, 1982–84; HMS Hecla (NO), 1984–85; RN Hydrographic Long Course, 1985 (Internat. Hydrographic Bureau Category A Surveyor, 1985); MV Bon Esprit, UK Civil Hydrographic Prog., 1985; CO, HM Survey Motor Launch Gleaner, 1986–87; Exec. Officer, HMS Fox, 1987–89; MA to Dir, US Hydrographic Dept, US Naval Oceanographic Office, 1989–91; CO, HMS Herald, 1991–93; Comdr (H), FO Surface Flotilla, 1993; SO1 (Policy), Directorate, Naval Surveying, Oceanography and Meteorol., UK, MoD, 1994–96; CO, HMS Scott, 1996–98; Asst Dir (Policy), Directorate, Naval Surveying, Oceanography and Meteorol., UK, MoD, 1998–2000; Dir of Strategy, Defence Logistics, MoD, 2001–04; BAE Systems, 2004; Sen. Directing Staff (Navy), RCDS, 2005–07. Booz Allen Hamilton, later Booz & Co., (UK): Principal, 2007–11; Dir, 2011–14. Mem., Council, Nat. Trust, 2016– (Mem., SW Regl Adv. Bd (formerly Wessex Regl Cttee), 2007–17); Trustee, SW Coastal Footpath Assoc., 2017–. MInstD 2004, FInstD 2015; CDir 2006. Freeman, City of London, 2004; Liveryman, Co. of Water Conservators, 2004– (Master, 2009–10). *Recreations:* art, architecture, hill-walking. *E:* bobmark1428@icloud.com. *Club:* Royal Dart Yacht.

**MARKESINIS, Sir Basil (Spyridonos),** Kt 2005; PhD, LLD, DCL; FBA 1997; Conseiller Scientifique du Premier Président de la Cour de Cassation, France, 2002–07; non-executive Director: Alexander S. Onassis Foundation, 2007–10; Alexander S. Onassis Public Benefit Foundation, 2007–10; *b* 10 July 1944; *s* of Spyros B. Markesinis (former Prime Minister of Greece) and Ieta Markesinis; *m* 1970, Eugenie (*née* Trypanis); one *s* one *d*. *Educ:* Univ. of Athens (LLB, DIur); MA, PhD, LLD Cambridge; DCL Oxford. Asst Prof., Law Faculty, Univ. of Athens, 1965–68; Gulbenkian Res. Fellow, Churchill Coll., Cambridge, 1970–74; called to the Bar, Gray's Inn, 1973, Bencher, 1991; Fellow of Trinity Coll., Cambridge, and Univ. Lectr in Law, 1975–86; Denning Prof. of Comparative Law, Univ. of London, at QMC, subseq. QMW, 1986–93; Dep. Dir, Centre for Commercial Law Studies, Univ. of London, 1986–93; Prof. of Eur. Private Law, UCL, 1993–95; University of Oxford: Fellow: LMH, 1995–99; Brasenose Coll., 1999–2000; Clifford Chance Prof. of European Law, 1995–99, of Comparative Law, 1999–2000; Founder Dir, Centre, then Inst., of Eur. and Comparative Law, 1995–2000; Prof. of Common Law and Civil Law, and Chm., Inst. of Global Law, UCL, 2001–07. Prof. of Anglo-Amer. Private Law, Leiden Univ., 1986–2000, and Founder and Dir, Leiden Inst. of Anglo-American Law, 1987–2000. Advocate to Greek Supreme Court, 1976–86. Sen. Advr on European Affairs, Clifford Chance, 1999–2002. Visiting Professor: Univs of Paris I and II; Siena; Rome; Cornell; Michigan (Ann Arbor); Texas (Austin); Francqui Vis. Prof., Univ. of Gent, 1989–90, 2005–06; Jamail Regents' Prof. of Law, Univ. of Texas, Austin, 1998–2014, now Emer. Prof. of Comparative Law. Lectures: Atkin, Reform Club, 1989; Shimizu, LSE, 1989; Lionel Cohen Meml, Hebrew Univ. of Jerusalem, 1993; Wilberforce, 1998; John Maurice Kelly Meml, 2003; Eason-Weinemann, Tulane, 2005; Peter Taylor Meml, Inner Temple, 2006; Denning, Lincoln's Inn, 2007; Andrew David, Hellenic Soc. Trust, 2010; Key note speaker, Suleimania Forum, Amer. Univ. of Kurdistan, 2013. Mem., Council of Management, British Inst. of Internat. and Comparative Law, 1993–2000. Associate Fellow, Internat. Acad. of Comp. Law, 1987–98; Member: Amer. Law Inst., 1989; Acad. Internat. de Droit Comparé, 2004; Foreign Fellow: Royal Belgian Acad., 1990; Royal Netherlands Acad. of Arts and Scis, 1995; Accademia dei Lincei, Rome, 2005; Corresp. Mem., Acad. of Athens, 1994; Corresp. Fellow, Inst. de France, 2004; Hon. Fellow, Greek Archaeol. Soc., 2004; Corresp. Collaborator, UNIDROIT, 1992. Hon. QC 1998. DIur (*hc*): Ghent, 1992; Paris I (Panthéon-Sorbonne), 1998; Munich, 1999; Athens, 2007. Humboldt Forschungspreise, 1996; Univ. Prize, Leiden, 1996; John Fleming Prize, 2008. Officier, Ordre des Palmes Académiques (France), 1992; Comdr, Légion d'Honneur (France), 2004 (Chevalier, 1995; Officier, 2000); Kt Comdr, Order of Merit (Germany), 2003 (Comdr, 1998; Officer's Cross, 1992); Kt Grand Cross, Order of Merit (Italy), 2002 (Kt Comdr, 1999; Officer, 1995); Comdr, Order of Honour (Greece), 2000; Kt, Grand Cross, Order of Merit (France), 2006. *Publications:* The Mother's right to Guardianship according to the Greek Civil Code, 1968; The Theory and Practice of Dissolution of Parliament, 1972 (Yorke Prize); The English Law of Torts, 1976; (jtly) An Outline of the Law of Agency, 1979, 4th edn 1998; (jtly) Richterliche Rechtspolitik im Haftungsrecht, 1981; (jtly) Tortious Liability for un-intentional harm in the Common Law and the Civil Law, 2 vols, 1982; (jtly) Tort Law, 1984, 7th edn 2013; The German Law of Torts: a comparative introduction, 1986, 5th edn (jtly) as The German Law of Torts: a comparative treatise, 2017; (gen. ed. and contrib.) The Gradual Convergence: foreign ideas, foreign influences and English law on the eve of the 21st century, 1994; (ed and contrib.) Bridging the Channel, 1996; Foreign Law and Comparative Methodology: a subject and a thesis, 1997; (jtly) The German Law of Contract and Restitution, 1998; (gen. ed. and contrib.) Protecting Privacy, 1998; The Impact of the Human Rights Bill on English Law, 1998; (jtly) Tortious Liability of Statutory Bodies, 1999; Always on the Same Path: essays on foreign law and comparative methodology, 2001; (gen. ed. and contrib.) The British Contribution to the Europe of the Twenty-First Century, 2002; Comparative Law in the Courtroom and the Classroom: the story of the last thirty-five years, 2003 (trans. French, German, Italian and Chinese); (jtly) Compensation for Personal Injury in English, German and Italian Law: a comparative overview, 2005; The German Law of Contract: a comparative treatise, 2006; (jtly) Foreign Law in National Courts: a new source of inspiration?, 2006 (trans. Italian); Good and Evil in Art and Law, 2007 (trans. Greek 2009, Chinese 2013); Flawed Grandeur: the secret lives of great adventurers (in Greek), 2008; The Duality of Genius: shades, blemishes and vices of great achievers, 2009; (jtly) Engaging with Foreign Law, 2009; Shadows from America: essays in contemporary geopolitics (in Greek), 2009; A New Foreign Policy for Greece (in Greek), 2010; Writing for Myself: stops in a peripatetic life, 2011; Windows to an Author's Soul: nations, peoples, customs and habits through each other's eyes, 2012; The Legacy of Ancient Greek Drama to European Culture (in Greek), 2014, Chinese edn 2016; On the Endurance of Ancient Greek Thought Through the Ages, 2015; The Market Economy and the Rule of Law: how to learn from others, 2015; Massive Immigration: challenges and opportunities, 2016; Ancient Greek Poetry from Homer to Early Roman Times, 3 vols, 2017; Euripides in Macedonia, 2017; Myths, History and Art, 2018; ed. and contrib. many articles in learned jls in Belgium, Canada, England, France, Germany, Greece, Israel, Italy and USA. *Recreations:* painting, music, fund-raising, archaeological digging, chess. *Address:* Michaelsas Cottage, Islip Road, Bletchingdon, Oxon OX5 3DP. *T:* (01869) 343560.

**MARKEY, Air Vice-Marshal Peter Desmond,** OBE 1986; General Manager, NATO Maintenance and Supply Agency, Luxembourg, 1999–2004; *b* 28 March 1943; *s* of Althorpe Hazel Christopher Markey and Marjorie Joyce Markey (*née* Thomas); *m* 1966, Judith Mary Widdowson; one *s* one *d*. *Educ:* RAF Coll. Cranwell; Open Univ. (BA 1980); Cranfield Univ. (MSc 1994). RAF Supply Officer: commissioned 1964; served Singapore, France and UK to 1981; NDC, 1981–82; HQ Strike Comd, 1982–83; HQ AFCENT, Netherlands, 1983–85; MoD Carlisle, 1986–88; Station Comdr, Carlisle, 1988–89; RCDS 1990; MoD Central Staff, 1991; Dept of AMSO, 1991; HQ Logistics Comd, 1994; Dir Gen., Support Mgt, RAF, 1995–97; Dir of Resources, NATO, Luxembourg, 1997–98. Grand Cross, Order of Merit (Luxembourg), 2004. *Publications:* papers and contribs to learned jls. *Recreations:* cycling, mountain walking, travelling. *E:* markeypd@gmail.com.

**MARKHAM, Sir Alexander (Fred),** Kt 2008; PhD, DSc; FRCP, FRCPath; West Riding Medical Research Trust Professor of Medicine, University of Leeds, since 1992; Chairman, Lister Institute of Preventive Medicine, since 2011; *b* 30 Nov. 1950; one *s* one *d*. *Educ:* Univ. of Birmingham (BSc 1971; PhD 1974; DSc 1992); Univ. of London (MB BS 1985). FRCPath 1996; FRCP 1998. ICI Pharmaceuticals, 1979–90; Nuffield Dept of Medicine, Univ. of Oxford, 1990–92; Dir, Molecular Medicine Unit, Univ. of Leeds, 1992; Hon. Consultant Physician, Leeds Teaching Hosps NHS Trust; Chief Executive, Cancer Research UK, 2003–07 (on secondment). Chm., NCRI, 2003–06. FMedSci 2004. *Address:* c/o School of Medicine, University of Leeds, Leeds LS2 9JT.

**MARKHAM, Sir (Arthur) David,** 4th Bt *cr* 1911, of Beachborough Park; Chief Executive Officer, Robin Hurt Ltd, 1993; *b* 6 Dec. 1950; *er s* of Sir Charles Markham, 3rd Bt and Valerie Markham (*née* Barry-Johnston); *S* father, 2006; *m* 1st, 1977, Carolyn Lorna (*née* Park) (marr. diss. 2007); two *d*; 2nd, 2010, Mrs Sarah Leggett. *Educ:* Milton Abbey Sch. Manager, Abercrombie & Kent, 1978–93. *Recreations:* racing, travel. *Heir: b* Richard Barry Markham [*b* 18 April 1954; *m* 1985, Ann Malcolm-Smith; one *s* (and one *s* decd)]. *Clubs:* Muthaiga Country, Jockey (Kenya).

**MARKHAM, Richard Trevelyan;** Principal, Hockerill Anglo-European College, since 2013; *b* Dibden Purlieu, Southampton, 14 Sept. 1971; *s* of David William Markham and Jennifer Ellen Markham (*née* Rees); *m* 1998, Kate Farquhar; one *s* one *d*. *Educ:* King Edward VI Sch., Southampton; Mansfield Coll., Oxford (BA Mod. Hist. 1993; PGCE 1994). Marlborough College: Teacher of History, 1994–2013; Hd, Hist. of Art, 2002–09; IB Coordinator, 2005–09; Dir of Studies, 2009–13. *Recreations:* all sports (particularly hockey, golf and cycling), Welsh hockey international. *Address:* Hockerill Anglo-European College, Dunmow Road, Bishop's Stortford CM23 5HX. *Club:* Vincent's (Oxford).

**MARKHAM, Rudolph Harold Peter, (Rudy),** CMG 2015; Financial Director, Unilever plc, 2000–07; Chief Financial Officer, Unilever NV, 2005–07; Vice Chairman and Senior non-executive Director, Legal & General Group plc, until 2016 (non-executive Director, 2006–17). *Educ:* Christ's Coll., Cambridge (BA Natural Scis 1968). Joined Unilever 1968 as commercial mgt trainee; Financial Dir, Unilever, Zurich; Hd, Finance Dept and Gp Treas., 1986–89; Hd of Ops, E Asia Pacific Reg., 1989–98; Chm., Nippon Lever, Japan, 1992–96; Strategy and Technol. Dir, and Mem., Exec. Cttee, 1998–2007. Non-executive Director: Standard Chartered plc, 2001–14; United Parcel Service Inc., 2007–; AstraZeneca plc, 2008–; FCO, 2010–15. Former Mem. Bd, Financial Reporting Council. Chm., Moorfields Eye Hosp. NHS Foundn Trust, 2008–16. FCMA; Fellow, Assoc. of Corporate Treasurers.

**MARKLAND, John Anthony,** CBE 1999; PhD; Chairman, Scottish Natural Heritage, 1999–2006; *b* 17 May 1948; *s* of late Thomas Henry Markland and Rita Markland (*née* Shippen); *m* 1970, Muriel Harris; four *d*. *Educ:* Bolton Sch., Lancs; Dundee Univ. (MA Geog. 1970; PhD 1975). CDipAF 1979; ACIS 1982. Demographer, Somerset CC, 1974–76; Sen. Professional Asst (Planning Res.), Tayside Regl Council, 1976–79; Fife Regional Council: PA to Chief Exec., 1979–83; Asst Chief Exec., 1983–86; Chief Exec., 1986–95; Chief Exec., Fife Council, 1995–99. Chm., Scottish Br., SOLACE, 1993–95. Chairman: Forward Scotland Ltd, 1996–2000; Scottish Leadership Foundn, 2001–08; Environmental Campaigns, 2003–06. Member: Jt Nature Conservation Cttee, 1999–2006; Scotland Adv. Gp, Woodland Trust, 2011–. Vice Convener, Ct, Edinburgh Univ., 2006–11 (Mem., 2001–11; Convener, Audit Cttee, 2004–06). Dir, Horsecross Arts Ltd, 2007–13. Pres., Old Boltonians' Assoc., 2007. Trustee: Gannochy Trust, 2009–17; Kincarrathie Trust, 2012–; Quilters' Guild of British Isles, 2012–19. Dr *hc* Edinburgh, 2012. *Recreations:* finding the easiest way up Scotland's Munros, attempting to keep fit. *Address:* 3 St Leonard's Bank, Perth PH2 8EB. *T:* (01738) 441798.

**MARKOVA, Prof. Ivana,** PhD; FBA 1999; FRSE; Professor of Psychology, University of Stirling, 1984–2003, now Emeritus. *Educ:* Charles Univ., Prague. Lectr, Sen. Lectr, then Reader, in Psychology, 1970–84, Head of Dept of Psychology, Univ. of Stirling. Vis. Prof., LSE, 2007–. FRSE 1997. *Publications:* (ed) Social Context of Language, 1978; Paradigms, Thought and Language, 1982; Human Awareness: its social development, 1987; (with Klaus Foppa) Dynamics of Dialogue, 1990; (ed with Klaus Foppa) Asymmetries and Dialogue, 1991; (with R. M. Farr) Representations of Health, Illness and Handicap, 1994; (ed jtly) Mutualities in Dialogue, 1995; Dialogicality and Social Representations, 2003; (with Serge Moscovici) The Making of Modern Social Psychology, 2006; The Dialogical Mind: common sense and ethics, 2016. *Address:* Department of Psychology, University of Stirling, Stirling FK9 4LA.

**MARKOWICH, Prof. Peter Alexander;** Distinguished Professor of Applied Mathematics and Computational Science, King Abdullah University of Science and Technology; *b* 16 Dec. 1956; *s* of Otto Markowich and Elfriede Markowich; *m*; one *d*. *Educ:* Technical Univ., Vienna (Diploma 1979; Dr Tech. 1980). Res. Asst, Internat. Inst. for Applied Systems Analysis, Austria, 1979–80; Res. Associate, Math. Res. Center, Univ. of Wisconsin-Madison, 1980–81; Asst Prof., Math. and Computer Sci. Depts, Univ. of Texas at Austin, 1981–82; Asst Prof., 1982–84, Associate Prof., 1984–89, Inst. for Applied and Numerical Math., Technical Univ., Vienna; Professor, Department of Mathematics: Technical Univ. of Berlin, 1989–90, 1991–98; Purdue Univ., 1990–91; Prof. of Math. Analysis, Johannes Kepler Univ. Linz, 1998–99; Prof. of Applied Analysis, Faculty of Math., Univ. of Vienna, 1999–; Prof. of Applied Math., Univ. of Cambridge, 2007; Fellow, Clare Hall, Cambridge, 2009. JSPS Fellow, Kyoto Univ., 2005. Corresp. Mem., Austrian Acad. of Scis, 2005. Wittgenstein Award, Austrian Sci. Fund, 2000; Humboldt Res. Award, Alexander von Humboldt Foundn, 2010. *Publications:* The Stationary Semiconductor Device Equations, 1986; (jtly) Semiconductor Equations, 1990; Applied Partial Differential Equations: a visual approach, 2006; articles in learned jls.

**MARKOWITZ, Prof. Harry M.,** PhD; President, Harry Markowitz Company, since 1984; Adjunct Professor of Finance, Rady School, University of California at San Diego, since 2006; Professor of Finance and Economics, Baruch College, City University of New York, 1982–93; *b* 24 Aug. 1927; *s* of Morris Markowitz and Mildred (*née* Gruber); *m* Barbara Gay. *Educ:* Univ. of Chicago (PhB Liberal Arts 1947; MA 1950, PhD 1954 Econs). Res. Associate, Rand Corp., 1952–60 and 1961–63; Consultant, Gen. Electric Corp., 1960–61; Chm., Bd and Technical Dir, Consolidated Analysis Centres Inc., 1963–68; Prof. of Finance, UCLA, 1968–69; Pres., Arbitrage Management Co., 1969–72; Consultant,

1972–74; Vis. Prof. of Finance, Wharton Bus. Sch., 1972–74; Res. Staff Mem., T. J. Watson Res. Center, IBM, 1974–83; Adj. Prof. of Finance, Rutgers Univ., 1980–82; Consultant, Daiwa Securities, 1990–2000. Director: Amer. Finance Assoc.; TIMS. Fellow: Econometric Soc.; Amer. Acad. Arts and Sciences, 1987. Von Neumann Theory Prize, ORSA/TIMS, 1989; Nobel Prize for Economics, 1990. *Publications:* Portfolio Selection: efficient diversification of investments, 1959, 2nd edn 1991; Simscript: a simulation programming language, 1963; (jtly) Studies in Process Analysis: economy-wide production capabilities, 1963 (trans. Russian 1967); (jtly) The Simscript II Programming Language, 1969; (jtly) The EAS-E Programming Language, 1981; (jtly) Adverse Deviation, 1981; Mean-Variance Analysis in Portfolio Choice and Capital Markets, 1987; Harry Markowitz: selected works (World Scientific-Nobel Laureate Series, Vol. 1), 2008; contrib. chapters to numerous books and papers in professional jls, incl. Jl of Finance, Management Science, Jl of Portfolio Management. *Recreation:* music.

**MARKS**, family name of **Barons Marks of Broughton** and **Marks of Henley-on-Thames**.

**MARKS OF BROUGHTON**, 3rd Baron *cr* 1961, of Sunningdale in the Royal Co. of Berks; **Simon Richard Marks**; *b* 3 May 1950; *s* of 2nd Baron Marks of Broughton and his 1st wife, Ann Catherine (*née* Pinto); *S* father, 1998; *m* 1982, Marion, *o d* of Peter F. Norton; one *s* three *d. Educ:* Eton; Balliol Coll., Oxford (BA 1971). *Heir: s* Hon. Michael Marks, *b* 13 May 1989.

**MARKS OF HENLEY-ON-THAMES**, Baron *cr* 2011 (Life Peer), of Henley-on-Thames in the County of Oxfordshire; **Jonathan Clive Marks**; QC 1995; FCIArb; *b* 19 Oct. 1952; *s* of late Geoffrey Jack Marks, LDS RCS and Patricia Pauline Marks, LLB; *m* 1st, 1982, Sarah Ann Russell (marr. diss. 1991); one *s* one *d*; 2nd, 1993, (Clementine) Medina Cafopoulos; three *s* two *d. Educ:* Harrow; University Coll., Oxford (BA Hons Jurisp.); Inns of Court Sch. of Law. Called to the Bar, Inner Temple, 1975; in practice, Common Law and Commercial Law, Western Circuit. Vis. Lecturer in Advocacy: Univs of Malaya and Mauritius; Sri Lanka Law Coll. Contested (SDP): Weston-Super-Mare, 1983; Falmouth and Camborne, 1987; EP elecn, Cornwall and Plymouth, 1984. Member: Lib Dem Cttee for England, 1988–89; Lib Dem Federal Policy Cttee, 2004–10, 2011–16; H of L Delegated Powers and Regulatory Reform Cttee, 2012–15; Co-Chair, Lib Dem Parly Cttee on Home Affairs, Justice and Equalities, 2012–; Lib Dem spokesman on justice, H of L, 2012–15; Lib Dem spokesman on justice, 2015–. Chm., Lib Dem Lawyers Assoc., 2001–07. Freeman, City of London, 1975; Liveryman, Pattenmakers' Co., 1975– (Mem. Ct Assts, 1998–2004). *Recreations:* tennis, ski-ing, theatre, opera, food, wine, travel. *Address:* 4 Pump Court, Temple, EC4Y 7AN. *T:* (020) 7842 5555; House of Lords, SW1A 0PW. *Clubs:* Royal Automobile, Boodle's.

**MARKS, Alexandra Louise**, CBE 2017; a Recorder, since 2002; a Deputy High Court Judge, since 2010; a First-tier Tribunal Judge (General Regulatory Chamber), since 2017; *b* London, 9 Sept. 1959; *d of* Prof. Vincent Marks and Averil Marks; *m* 1991, Prof. Steven Julius Barnett; two *d. Educ:* Guildford Co. Sch. for Girls; Brasenose Coll., Oxford (BA Hons; Hon. Fellow, 2018); Coll. of Law, London. Articled clerk, 1981–83; admitted as solicitor, 1983; Assistant Solicitor: Rowe & Maw, 1983–84; Linklaters & Paines, 1984–90; Partner: (equity - full-time), Linklaters, 1990–2003; (salaried - pt-time), Linklaters LLP, 2003–11, now Consultant. Solicitors Regulation Authy Adjudicator, 2008–13. Chm., Professional Conduct Cttee, Architects Registration Bd, 2010–16; Legal Assessor, Conduct and Appeals Cttee, RICS, 2011–13; Member: Judicial Appts Commn, 2012–18; Criminal Cases Review Commn, 2013–18. Mem., Adv. Bd, UCL Judicial Inst., 2010–; Statutory Reviewer of Access and Participation Plans, DFE, 2018–. Law Society: Chair: Internat. Human Rights Wkg Gp, 1986–94; Law Reform Bd, 2004–07; Mem. Council, 2003–07; *ex officio* Mem., Corporate Governance Bd, 2004–07; Pres., City of London Law Soc., 2008–09. Chair: Bd of Dirs, Amnesty Internat. Charity Ltd, 2000–10; Centre for Effective Dispute Resolution, 2018–; Mem. Council, Justice, 1986– (Mem. Exec. Bd and Trustee, 1996–2014; Chm., Exec. Bd, 1999–2004; Chm., working party, What is a Court?, 2016); Member, Board and Trustee: Interights, 2006–13; Working Families, 2008–14; Prisoners' Educn Trust, 2010–18 (Chm., 2012–18); Trustee, LawCare, 2018–; Chm., Prisoner Learning Alliance, 2012–18. Dir and Trustee, Hampstead Th. Foundn, 2019–. Mem. Court, Solicitors' Co., 2005– (Master, 2008–09). Sec., Brasenose Soc., 1995– (Pres., 2007–08). Lifetime Achievement Award, Law Soc., 2016. *Recreations:* theatre (as audience), walking, weight-training, tidying up (unsuccessfully). *Address:* c/o Linklaters LLP, One Silk Street, EC2Y 8HQ. *T:* (020) 7456 2000, *Fax:* (020) 7456 2222. *E:* alexandra.marks@linklaters.com

See also L. A. Marks.

**MARKS, Christine**; see Murray, C.

**MARKS, David Francis**, PhD; CPsychol, FBPsS; researcher, editor and author; *b* 12 Feb. 1945; *s* of Victor William Francis Marks and Mary Dorothy Marks; one *d* by Margaret McGoldrick; one *s* by Elsy Cecilia Clavijo. *Educ:* Southern Grammar Sch. for Boys, Portsmouth; Reading Univ. (BSc); Sheffield Univ. (PhD 1970). FBPsS 1984; CPsychol 1988; Chartered Health Psychologist, 1998. Sen. Demonstrator, Sheffield Univ., 1966–69; Lectr, 1970–74, Sen. Lectr, 1978–86, Univ. of Otago, NZ; Middlesex Polytechnic, subseq. University: Prof. of Psychology, 1986–2000; Head, Sch. of Psychology, 1986–91; Head, Health Research Centre, 1989–2000; Prof. of Psychology, 2000–10, Hd, Dept of Psychol., 2002–05, City Univ., London. Visiting Professor: Oregon, 1976; Washington, 1977; Hamamatsu Univ. Sch. of Medicine, Fukuoka Univ., Japan, 1984; Rome, 1997; Hon. Res. Fellow, UCL, 1977. Mem., DoH Scientific Cttee on Tobacco and Health, 1994–98; Convenor, Task Force on Health Psychol., Eur. Fedn of Professional Psychologists' Assocs, 1993–97. Organised internat. confs on mental imagery, 1983, 1985. Consultant to NHS, local govt and EC depts and corps. Sen. Asst Ed., Jl of Mental Imagery, 1987–96; Asst Ed., British Jl of Psychology, 1990–95; Editor: Jl Health Psychol., 1996–; Health Psychol. Open, 2014–. Developer of first smoking cessation prog. on the internet. Gold Disk for Music Therapy, NZ Min. of Health, 1979. *Publications:* The Psychology of the Psychic, 1980, 2nd edn 2000; Theories of Image Formation, 1986; Imagery: current developments, 1990; The Quit for Life Programme, 1993; Improving the Health of the Nation, 1996; Health Psychology: theory, research and practice, 2000, 5th edn 2018 (trans. Chinese 2004, Spanish 2008); Dealing with Dementia, 2000; The Health Psychology Reader, 2002; Research Methods for Clinical and Health Psychology, 2004; Overcoming Your Smoking Habit, 2005 (trans. French 2009); Bryan Poole: contemporary botanical aquatint etchings, 2011; (ed) Mark Baker Portraits, 2011; (ed) Ewan McDougall Paintings, 2011; Obesity: comfort vs discontent, 2016; Stop Smoking Now, 2017; A General Theory of Behaviour, 2018; Psychology and the Paranormal: exploring anomalistic psychology, 2020; numerous book chapters and contribs to Nature, Science, Brit. Jl of Psych., Jl of Mental Imagery, and many other jls. *Recreations:* photography, painting. *Address:* 2 impasse Enclos Reboul, Arles 13200, France. *E:* editorjhp@gmail.com

**MARKS, David Georges Mainfroy**; QC 2009; *b* Manchester, 14 Oct. 1946; *s* of Joseph Marks and Georgette Marks. *Educ:* Manchester Grammar Sch.; Magdalen Coll., Oxford (BA 1968; MA 1972; BCL 1970). Called to the Bar, Gray's Inn, 1974; admitted Illinois State Bar, 1973, US Federal Bar, 1973, Irish Bar, 1998. Dep. Registrar in Bankruptcy,

1985–2013; part-time Tribunal Judge, Administrative Appeals Chamber and Nat. Security Appeals Panel (formerly Dep. Chm., Data Protection and Information Tribunal), 1990–2013. *Publications:* (Gen. Ed) Tolley's Insolvency Law and Practice, 2001–13; (ed jtly) Rowlatt on Principal and Surety, 4th edn 1982 to 6th edn 2011; (contrib. ed.) Lightman and Moss, Law of Administrators and Receivers of Companies, 1986, 5th edn 2011; (contrib. ed.) Moss and Fletcher, The EC Regulation on Insolvency Proceedings, 2002, 2nd edn 2009; (contrib. ed.) Expedited Debt Restructuring, 2007. *Recreations:* theatre, jazz, tennis, wine, music, photography, travel.

**MARKS, Prof. David Ian**, PhD; FRACP, FRCPath; Professor of Haematology and Stem Cell Transplantation, University of Bristol, since 2007; Consultant in Haematology and Bone Marrow Transplantation, University Hospitals Bristol NHS Foundation Trust, since 1996 (Director, Adult Bone Marrow Transplantation Unit, 1998–2017); *b* Melbourne, 6 April 1958; *s of* Dr Brian Marks and Dr Angela Spiers; *m* 1994, Dr Jennifer Bird; one *s* one *d. Educ:* Melbourne Grammar Sch.; Univ. of Melbourne (MB BS 1981; PhD 1990). FRACP 1988; FRCPath 2006. MRC/LRF Fellow to Prof. John Goldman, Hammersmith Hosp., 1990–93; Asst Prof., Haemato-oncol., Hahnemann Univ., Philadelphia, 1993–96. Transplant Coordinator and Dep. Hd, NCRI Acute Lymphoblastic Leukaemia Gp, 2005–; Chair, Tandem BMT meetings, 2016; Med. Dir, Impact, 2017. Pres., British Soc. of Blood and Marrow Transplantation, 2009. *Publications:* chapters in internat. textbooks concerning bone marrow transplantation and leukaemia; over 250 articles in jls incl. New England Jl, Annals of Internal Medicine, Jl of Clinical Investigation, Blood, Jl of Clinical Oncol. *Recreations:* cycling, surfing, football, reading, writing, food, travel. *Address:* 8 Richmond Park Road, Bristol BS8 3AP. *T:* (0117) 946 6396. *E:* David.Marks@uhbristol.nhs.uk. *Club:* Hawthorn Football.

**MARKS, Prof. Isaac Meyer**, MD; FRCPsych; Professor of Experimental Psychopathology, Institute of Psychiatry, University of London, 1978–2000; Professor Emeritus, King's College London, 2000; Clinical Director, CCBT Ltd, since 2005; *b* 16 Feb. 1935; *s* of Morris Norman and Anna Marks; *m* 1957, Shula Eta Winokur (*see* S. E. Marks); one *s* one *d. Educ:* Univ. of Cape Town (MB ChB 1956; MD 1963); Univ. of London (DPM 1963). FRCPsych 1970. Postgrad. teacher and examr in psychiatry, 1964; Lectr, RCN and Home Office Probationer Service, 1966–70; Vis. Consultant and postgrad. teacher, Univ. of Cape Town, 1969; Consultant Psychiatrist and research worker, Bethlem-Maudsley Hosp. and Inst. of Psychiatry, 1978–2000; Director: MRC Prog. Grants, Inst. Psychiatry, 1975–85; Nurse-Therapy Trng Prog., Maudsley Hosp., 1972–2000; Sen. Res. Fellow, Charing Cross Campus and Hon. Consultant Psychiatrist, Charing Cross Hosp., Ealing, Hammersmith and Fulham NHS Trust, 2000–04 (Dir, Stress Self-Help Clinic, 2000–02); Sen. Res. Investigator, 2000–03, Prof. Emeritus, 2001–03, Vis. Prof., 2004–, Imperial Coll. Sch. of Medicine, Univ. of London. Fellow, Center for Advanced Study in Behavioral Scis, Stanford Univ., 1981–82; Sackler Schol., Advanced Studies Inst., Univ. of Tel-Aviv, 1998; Visiting Professor: Univ. of N Carolina, 1967; Univs of Jerusalem and Tel Aviv, 1974; Coll. of Psychiatrists, Australia and NZ, 1978; Univ. of Michigan, Ann Arbor, 1988; Univ. of Wisconsin, 1990; Univ. of Calgary, 1995; Sterne Dist. Prof., Univ. of Indiana, 1981; Roerig Vis. Prof., Mercer Univ., Georgia, USA, 1989; Hon. Prof., Vrije Univ., 2005–08, Vis. Prof., 2008–, Amsterdam. McKerracher Lectr, Univ. of Saskatoon, 1986; Upjohn Lectr, RCPsych, 1991. Ed., annual series, Psychotherapy and Behavior Change, 1971–74; Member Editorial Boards, including: Integrative Psychiatry, 1980–; Jl Anxiety Disorders, 1986–; Community Psychiatric Practice, 1990–; Psychotherapy and Psychosomatics, 1991–; Anxiety, 1993–2004; Jl Technol. in Human Services, 2004–; Current Psychiatry Reviews, 2004–; Annals Depression and Anxiety, 2014–. Coordinator: Taskforce for Common Lang. for Psychotherapy Procedures project, 2002–; www.commonlanguagepsychotherapy.org, 2009–. Psychiatric Panel Advr, BUPA, 1992–94. Chm., British Assoc. for Behavioural Psychotherapy, 1978 (Hon. Fellow, 1993); President: Eur. Assoc. Behavior Therapy, 1979–80; Assoc. Behavioural Clinicians, 1988–94; Member Council: Human and Behavior and Evolution Soc., 1988–90; Inst. for Clin. Psychiatric Res., Netherlands, 1990–95. Starkey Medal and Prize, RSPH, 1969; Salmon Medallist, NY Acad. of Medicine, 1978; Premi Pavlov, Soc. Catalana de Recerca i Therapia del Comportament, Barcelona, 2007; (jtly) E-ward, Trimbos Inst., 2007; E-ward, Internat. Soc. for Res. into Internet Inventions, 2009. Grandes Maestros Psichiatria, Golden Cross Award (Chile), 2007. *Publications:* Patterns of Meaning in Psychiatric Patients, 1965; Fears & Phobias, 1969; (jtly) Clinical Anxiety, 1971; (jtly) Psychotherapy, 1971; (jtly) Nursing in Behavioural Psychotherapy, 1977; Living with Fear, 1978, 2nd edn 2001; Cure and Care of Neuroses, 1981; Psychiatric Nurse Therapists in Primary Care, 1985; Behavioural Psychotherapy, 1986; (jtly) Anxiety and its Treatment, 1986; Fears, Phobias and Rituals, 1987; (ed jtly) Mental Health Care Delivery, 1990; (jtly) Problem-centred care planning, 1995; (jtly) BT Steps—Behavioural self-assessment and self care for OCD, 1996; (jtly) COPE—online self-help for depression, 1998; FearFighter self-help for panic/phobia, 1999; (jtly) Hands-on-Help, 2007; (jtly) Classification of Psychotherapy Procedures, 2013; 460 scientific papers. *Recreations:* hiking, gardening, theatre, cinema, socialising. *Address:* 43 Dulwich Common, SE21 7EU. *T:* (020) 8299 4130.

**MARKS, John Henry**, MD; FRCGP; General Practitioner, Boreham Wood, 1954–90; Medical Director, National Medical Examinations Network Ltd, 1992–2003, later Adviser on Medical Standards; *b* 30 May 1925; *s* of Lewis and Rose Marks; *m* 1954, Shirley Evelyn, *d* of Alic Nathan, OBE; one *s* two *d. Educ:* Tottenham County Sch.; Edinburgh Univ. MD; FRCGP; D(Obst)RCOG. Served RAMC, 1949–51. Chairman: Herts LMC, 1966–71; Herts Exec. Council, 1971–74; Member: NHS Management Study Steering Cttee, 1971–72; Standing Med. Adv. Cttee, 1984–90; Council for Postgrad. Med. Educn, 1984–90. British Medical Association: Fellow, 1976; Member: Gen. Med. Services Cttee, 1968–90 (Dep. Chm., 1974–79); Council, 1973–98 (Chm., 1984–90); GMC, 1979–84, 1990–94; Chairman: Representative Body, 1981–84; Foundn for AIDS, 1987–99. Member, Council: ASH, 1991–99; Assurance Medical Soc., 1999–2004. *Publications:* The Conference of Local Medical Committees and its Executive: an historical view, 1979; The NHS, Beginning, Middle and End? (autobiog.), 2008; The NHS: beginning, middle, and end?, 2008; papers on the NHS and general medical practice. *Recreations:* philately, bridge. *Address:* 62 Eyre Court, 3–21 Finchley Road, NW8 9TU. *T:* (020) 7722 5955.

**MARKS, Julia Barbara**; *see* Barfield, J. B.

**MARKS, Laurence**; writer and producer; *b* 8 Dec. 1948; *s* of late Bernard and of Lily Marks; *m* 1988, Brigitte Luise Kirchheim; one step *s. Educ:* Holloway County Sch., London; Guildhall Sch. of Music, London. Trainee journalist, Thomson Regl Newspapers, 1974; Reporter: N London Weekly Herald, 1975–77; Sunday Times, 1975–76 (freelance) and 1978–79; This Week (TV current affairs prog.), 1977–78; television scriptwriter, 1980–; (with Maurice Gran) creator and writer: Holding the Fort, 1980–82; Roots, 1981; Shine on Harvey Moon, 1982–85, 1995; Roll Over Beethoven, 1985; Relative Strangers, 1985–87; The New Statesman, 1987–91; Birds of a Feather, 1989–98 and 2014–15, Christmas Special, 2017; Snakes and Ladders, 1989; So You Think You've Got Troubles, 1991; Love Hurts, 1991–93; Get Back, 1992–93; Wall of Silence (film), 1993; Goodnight Sweetheart, 1993–99; Unfinished Business, 1997–98; Mosley (film), 1997; Starting Out, 2000; Dirty Work, 2000; Believe Nothing, 2002; Me, My Dad and Moorgate, 2006; Mumbai Calling, 2007; Goodnight Sweetheart Revisited, 2016. Stage plays (with Maurice

Gran): Playing God, 2005; The New Statesman, 2006; Dreamboats and Petticoats (libretto for musical), 2009, 2017; Von Ribbentrop's Watch, 2010; Save the Last Dance for Me (libretto for musical); Birds of a Feather, 2012; Dreamboats and Miniskirts (musical), nat. tour, 2014–15; Love Me Do, Watford Palace, 2014; The Moon's A Balloon, 2017; Early Birds, Edinburgh Fest., 2018; radio plays (with Maurice Gran): My Blue Heaven, 2006; Dr Freud Will See You Now, Mr Hitler, 2007; My Blue Wedding, 2007; Von Ribbentrop's Watch, 2008; Love Me Do, 2014. Founder (with Maurice Gran and Allan McKeown), Alomo Productions, 1988, subseq. pt of Thames TV. Mem., Television Cttee, BAFTA, 2008–. Vis. Lectr, Univ. of York, 2006–. Ambassador, UCARE charity, 2015–. Pres., Pipesmokers' Council of GB, 2000. Freeman, City of London, 1994; Liveryman, Co. of Tobacco Blenders and Briar Pipe Makers, 1994. Pipesmoker of the Year, 1990; Living Legend, British Comedy Assoc., 2015. *Publications*: Moorgate: the anatomy of a disaster, 1976; Ruth Ellis: a case of diminished responsibility, 1977; A Fan for All Seasons, 1999; *with Maurice Gran*: Holding the Fort, 1981; The New Statesman Scripts, 1992; Dorien's Diary, 1993; Shine on Harvey Moon, 1995. *Recreations*: music (saxophone player), reading, English churches, tennis, medieval German, the study of Freud, Jung and Breuer, British politics, oriental philology, artificial intelligence, Russian poetry, the work of Leonhard Euler (mathematician), the life and works of Johann Sebastian Bach, North Korean architecture, a forensic study of the letters of Pyotr Chaadayev. *Address*: c/o Laurie Mansfield International Artistes, Suite 17, Adam House, 7–10 John Adam Street, WC2N 6AA. *T*: (020) 7520 9411. *E*: peter@lmassocltd.com. *W*: www.marksandgran.com. *Clubs*: Reform, Savile, Cryptos, Intelligence Squared, PEN.

**MARKS, Lewis Adam**; QC 2002; *b* 1961; *s* of Prof. Vincent Marks and Averil Marks; *m* 1986, Philippa Johnson; four *s*. *Educ*: City of London Freemen's Sch., Ashtead; Brasenose Coll., Oxford. Called to the Bar, Middle Temple, 1984; in practice, specialising in international divorce and big money financial relief claims. Head of Chambers, 2010–17. *Recreations*: walking, ski-ing (badly), cycling (slowly), music (listening), cricket (watching). *Address*: Imperial Hall, City Road, EC1V 2NR; Queen Elizabeth Building, Temple, EC4Y 9BS. *E*: l.marks@qeb.co.uk.
See also A. L. Marks.

**MARKS, Michael John Paul**, CVO 2014; CBE 1999; Founding Partner, NewSmith Capital Partners LLP, 2003–14; *b* 28 Dec. 1941; *m* 1967, Rosemary Ann Brody; one *s* two *d*. *Educ*: St Paul's Sch. Joined Smith Brothers, subseq. Smith New Court, 1960; Partner, 1969–84; Dir, 1975; Man. Dir, Smith New Court International, 1984–87; Chief Exec., 1987–94, Chm., 1995, Smith New Court PLC; Dep. Chm., Jt Hd of Global Equities, and Mem. Exec. Mgt Cttee, Merrill Lynch Internat., 1995–97; Chief Operating Officer, 1997–98, Exec. Chm., 1998–2003, Merrill Lynch Europe, Middle East and Africa; Exec. Chm., Merrill Lynch Investment Mgrs and Internat. Private Client Gp, 2001–03; Exec. Vice Pres., Merrill Lynch & Co. Inc., 2001–03. Chm., MR Capital Partners; non-executive Director: Rothschilds Continuation, 1990–95; RIT Capital Partners, 2004–. Director: Securities Inst., 1992–93; London Stock Exchange, 1994–2004; Trustee, Stock Exchange Benevolent Fund, 1994–97. Trustee: Prince's Trust, 2003–; Queen's Trust, 2009–.

**MARKS, Peter Vincent**, CBE 2013; Group Chief Executive, Co-operative Group, 2007–13 (Director, 2000–07); *b* Bradford, 27 Oct. 1949; *s* of Vincent Marks and Margaret Marks; *m* 1971, Julia Merry; two *d*. *Educ*: St Bede's Grammar Sch., Bradford; Bradford Coll. (HNC Business Studies). Yorkshire Co-operative Society: mgt trainee, 1967; sen. mgt roles in food and non-food retailing, travel and funeral businesses; Chief Gen. Manager, Retailing, 1996–2000; Chief Exec., 2000–02; Chief Exec., United Co-operatives, 2002–07. Non-exec. Dir, Co-operative Financial Services Ltd, 2009–13. Dir, Greater Manchester LEP, 2011. Member: Policy Issues Council, Inst. of Grocery Distribution, 2008–13; Commn on Ownership, 2009–12. Vice Pres., Action on Hearing Loss (formerly RNID), 2010–17. *Recreations*: family, golf, football, playing drums in a blues band. *Club*: Lansdowne.

**MARKS, Prof. Richard Charles**, PhD; FSA; Professor in Medieval Stained Glass, University of York, 1992–2008, now Emeritus Professor of History of Art (Head, Department of History of Art, 2002–04); Honorary Professor of History of Art, University of Cambridge, 2008–12; Bye-Fellow, since 2008, and Keeper of Works of Art, since 2010, Fitzwilliam College, Cambridge; *b* 2 July 1945; *s* of Major William Henry Marks and Jeannie Eileen Marks (*née* Pigott); *m* 1970, Rita Spratley. *Educ*: Berkhamsted Sch.; Queen Mary Coll., Univ. of London (BA (Hons) History); Courtauld Inst. of Art, Univ. of London (MA, PhD, History of European Art). Research Asst for British Acad. *Corpus Vitrearum Medii Aevi* Cttee, 1970–73; Asst Keeper, Dept of Medieval and Later Antiquities, British Mus., 1973–79; Keeper of Burrell Collection and Asst Dir, Glasgow Museums and Art Galls, 1979–85; Dir, Royal Pavilion, Art Gall. and Museums in Brighton, 1985–92. Pres. Internat. Bd, *Corpus Vitrearum Medii Aevi*, British Academy, 1995–2004. Chm., York Minster East Window Adv. Gp, 2008–. Mem., Adv. Council, Paul Mellon Centre for Studies in British Art, 2012–18. FSA 1977 (Vice-Pres., 1991–94). Trustee, Stained Glass Mus., Ely, 2010–; Vice-Pres., Beds Historical Record Soc., 2010–18. *Publications*: (jtly) British Heraldry from its origins to *c* 1800, 1978; (jtly) The Golden Age of English Manuscript Painting, 1980; Burrell Portrait of a Collector, 1983, 2nd edn 1988; The Glazing of the Collegiate Church of the Holy Trinity, Tattershall, Lincs, 1984; (jtly) Sussex Churches and Chapels, 1989; Stained Glass in England during the Middle Ages, 1993; The Medieval Stained Glass of Northamptonshire, 1998; (jtly) Gothic: art for England 1400–1547, 2003; Image and Devotion in Late Medieval England, 2004; Studies in the Art and Imagery of the Middle Ages, 2012; Windows and Wills, 2019; articles and reviews in learned jls. *Recreations*: opera, cricket, equestrianism, parish churches, travelling in the Levant. *Address*: Hillcroft, 11 Stewkley Road, Soulbury, Bucks LU7 0DH. *Clubs*: Athenæum, MCC.

**MARKS, Richard Leon**; QC 1999; **His Honour Judge Marks**; a Senior Circuit Judge, Central Criminal Court, since 2012; Common Serjeant, City of London, since 2015; *b* 20 Nov. 1953; *s* of Harry and Denise Marks; *m* 1987, Jane Elizabeth Tordoff; one *s* one *d*. *Educ*: Clifton Coll.; Univ. of Manchester (LLB Hons). Called to the Bar, Gray's Inn, 1975, Bencher 2008; Leader, Northern Circuit, 2008–10; an Asst Recorder, 1991–94; a Recorder, 1994–2012. Pres., Restricted Patients Panel, Mental Health Review Tribunal, 2000–15. Deemster, Isle of Man, 2010–12. Mem., Commn of Lieutenancy, City of London, 2015. Liveryman, Cooks' Co., 2017; Hon. Liveryman, Cutlers' Co., 2015. *Recreations*: travel, cinema, Clarice Cliff, MUFC, cookery, collecting modern art. *Address*: Central Criminal Court, Old Bailey, EC4M 7EH. *E*: r.l.marks7@gmail.com.

**MARKS, Sally Hilary**; see Groves, S. H.

**MARKS, Prof. Shula Eta**, OBE 1996; PhD; FBA 1995; Professor of Southern African History, School of Oriental and African Studies, University of London, 1993–2001, now Emeritus; *b* Cape Town, S Africa, 14 Oct. 1936; *d* of Chaim and Frieda Winokur; *m* 1957, Isaac Meyer Marks, *qv*; one *s* one *d*. *Educ*: Univ. of Cape Town (Argus Scholar, 1958–59; BA 1959); PhD London, 1967. Came to London, 1960; Lectr in the History of Southern Africa, SOAS and Inst. of Commonwealth Studies, 1963–76, Reader, 1976–83; Dir, 1983–93, Prof. of Commonwealth Hist., 1984–93, Inst. of Commonwealth Studies, London Univ.; Vice-Chancellor's Visitor to NZ, 1978. Dir, Ford Foundn Grant to Univ. of London on S African History, 1975–78; Mem., Commonwealth Scholarships Commn, 1993–. Member: Adv. Council on Public Records, 1989–94; Humanities Res. Bd, British Acad., 1997–98; AHRB, 1998–2000. Pres., African Studies Assoc. of UK, 1978; Chairman: Internat. Records Mgt Trust, 1989–2004; Council for Assisting Refugee Academics (formerly Soc. for Protection of Sci. and Learning), 1993–2004 (Mem., 1983–2013); Trustee, Canon Collins Educnl Trust for Southern Africa, 2004–14. Editor, Jl of African History, 1971–77; Mem. Council, Jl of Southern African Studies, 1974–2013 (Founding Mem., 1974; Chm. Bd, 1998–2002). Hon. Prof., Univ. of Cape Town, 2006. Dist. Sen. Fellow, Sch. of Advanced Study, 2002, Hon. Fellow, SOAS, 2005, Univ. of London. Hon. DLitt, Cape Town, 1994; Hon. DSocSc Natal, 1996; Hon. DLit Johannesburg, 2012; Witwatersrand, 2017. Dist. Africanist Award, African Studies Assoc. of UK, 2002. *Publications*: Reluctant Rebellion: an assessment of the 1906–8 disturbances in Natal, 1970; (ed with A. Atmore) Economy and Society in Pre-industrial South Africa, 1980; (ed with R. Rathbone) Industrialization and Social Change in South Africa, 1870–1930, 1982; (ed with P. Richardson) International Labour Migration: historical perspectives, 1983; The Ambiguities of Dependence in Southern Africa: class, nationalism and the state in twentieth-century Natal, 1986; (ed) Not either an experimental doll: the separate worlds of three South African women, 1987; (ed with Stanley Trapido) The Politics of Race, Class & Nationalism in Twentieth Century South Africa, 1987; Divided Sisterhood: race, class and gender in the South African nursing profession, 1994; (ed jtly) In Defence of Learning: academic refugees—their plight, persecution and placement, 1933–1980s, 2011; chapters in Cambridge Hist. of Africa, vols 3, 4 and 6, and in Cambridge Hist. of South Africa, vol 2, 2011; contrib. Jl of African Hist. and Jl of Southern African Studies. *Address*: Cypress Tree House, Dulwich Common, SE21 7EU.

**MARKS, Susan Elizabeth, (Ms Susan Jones)**; Headmistress, Withington Girls' School, 2010–16; *b* St Asaph, Flintshire, 14 Oct. 1956; *d* of Edward George Howel Jones and late Anne Jones; *m* 1980 (marr. diss. 2005); one *s* two *d* (and one *d* decd); civil partnership 2016, Susan Rachel Collingridge. *Educ*: Wilmslow Co. Grammar Sch. for Girls; Jesus Coll., Oxford (BA PPE 1978); Univ. of Leicester (Advanced Cert. Educnl Mgt 2000); Univ. of Exeter (Cert. Theol. 2010); Univ. of Nottingham (MA 2018). Corporate Lending Officer, Chemical Bank, 1978–81; Real Estate Lending Officer, Bank of America, 1981–88; Property Team Manager, Kleinwort Benson, 1988–89; a Vice Pres. and Hd, EMEA Airline Div., Bank of America, 1989–91; career break, 1991–95; Hd, Econs and Politics, St George's Coll., Weybridge, 1995–2000; Hd, Sixth Form, 2000–01, Headmistress, 2001–10, Tormead Sch. Reporting Inspector, ISI, 2013–17. Sen. Advr, Governance, RSAcademics, 2017–. Member: GSA, 2001–16 (Hon. Treas., 2007–12; Fellow, 2017); HMC, 2014–16. Trustee, Withington Girls' Sch. Trust; Feoffee, Chetham's Sch. of Music. *Recreations*: reading, postgraduate study. *Club*: Lansdowne.

**MARKS, Victor James**; Cricket Correspondent, The Observer, since 1990; Cricket Writer, since 2006, and Cricket Correspondent, since 2016, The Guardian; *b* 25 June 1955; *s* of late Harold George Marks and Phyllis Joan Marks; *m* 1978, Anna Stewart; two *d*. *Educ*: Blundell's Sch.; St John's Coll., Oxford (BA). Professional cricketer, 1975–89; played for: Oxford Univ., 1975–78 (Capt., 1976 and 1977); Somerset, 1975–89; WA, 1986–87; played in 6 Test Matches and 34 One-Day Internationals for England. Summariser, Test Match Special, BBC, 1989–. Cricket Chm., Somerset CCC, 1999–2016. Mem., Editl Bd, The Cricketer, 1990–2003; Associate Ed., The Wisden Cricketer, 2003–12. *Publications*: Somerset Cricket Scrapbook, 1984; Marks out of XI, 1985; TCCB Guide to Better Cricket, 1987; (with R. Drake) Ultimate One-Day Cricket Match, 1988; Wisden Illustrated History of Cricket, 1989; (with R. Holmes) My Greatest Game, 1994; Original Spin, 2019. *Recreation*: golf. *Address*: c/o The Observer, Kings Place, 90 York Way, N1 9GU.

**MARKUS, Catherine Mary, (Kate)**; QC 2014; a Judge of the Upper Tribunal (Administrative Appeals Chamber), since 2014; a Deputy High Court Judge, since 2016; *b* Billinge, 2 Dec. 1958; *d* of Thomas Markus and Beryl Markus; *m* 1997, Richard Bielby; three *d*. *Educ*: Notre Dame High Sch., Glasgow; Univ. of Manchester (LLB Hons). Called to the Bar, Gray's Inn, 1981; Sen. Legal Advr, Brent Community Law Centre, 1984–94; barrister, Doughty Street Chambers, 1994–2014; a Chm., Employment Tribunals, subseq. an Employment Judge (fee paid), Employment Tribunal, 1998–2014. Member: Exec. Cttee, Law Centres Fedn, 1985–93 (Sec., 1985–88; Chair and Vice-Chair, 1988–93); Legal Aid Bd for England and Wales, 1993–98; Bd, ICSTIS, 1994–2003. Chair, Legal Services Wkg Party, Bar Council, 1998–99. Chair: Public Law Project, 1990–2006; Haldane Soc., 1993–96. Hon. Fellow, Community Law Practice, Univ. of Kent, 1994–98. Case Law Ed., 2006–14, Mem., Editl Bd, 2014–19, Community Care Law Reports. *Publications*: (jtly) Recent Developments in Public Law, Legal Action, 1996–2014; contribs to legal jls and books. *Recreations*: gardening, painting, drawing, walking, reading. *Address*: Upper Tribunal (Administrative Appeals Chamber), 5th Floor, Rolls Building, 7 Rolls Buildings, Fetter Lane, EC4A 1NL.

**MARKWELL, Lisa**; Editor, Code Hospitality, since 2017; Food Editor, Sunday Times, since 2018; *b* Beaconsfield, Bucks, 23 April 1965; *d* of John and Diane Markwell; *m* 1998, John Dempsey; one *s* one *d*. *Educ*: Dr Challoner's High Sch. for Girls; Buckinghamshire Coll. of Higher Educn; Leith's Sch. of Food and Wine (Chef's Dip. (Dist.) 2017). Sunday Correspondent, 1989–90; Commissioning Editor: Sunday Times, 1990–92; Mail on Sunday, 1992–95; Ed., Harvey Nichols Mag., 1996–97; Dep. Ed., Frank, 1997–98; Features Ed., Independent, 1998–2004; Features Dir, Condé Nast, 2004–08; Exec. Ed., i newspaper, Independent, 2008–13; Ed., Independent on Sunday, 2013–16. *Recreations*: high heels and long journeys, good food and sharp knives, rescuing baby robins, championing my children. *Club*: Groucho.

**MARKWELL, Stephen**; Group Chief Executive Officer, National Computing Centre, 2008–17; *b* Northwood, Middx, 25 Nov. 1953; *s* of Edwin and Audrey Markwell; *m* 1st, 1984, Linda Smith (marr. diss. 1996); two *s*; 2nd, 1999, Meera Butterworth (separated 2015); one step *s* one step *d*. *Educ*: Brighton Poly. (BA Business Studies); Kingston Poly. (Postgrad. CNAA DipM). Regl Manager, British Olivetti Ltd, 1977–83; Product Manager, Mcdonnel Inf. Systems, 1983–86; Mktg Manager, Prime Computer, 1986–89; Man. Dir and Founder, Prime Mktg Pubns, 1989–2008. Advr, Coopers & Lybrand, 1989–90. Chm., Inst. of IT Trng, 2008–10. Mem., Adv. Cttee, AQA, 2009–. Chair of Judges, BCS Industry Awards, 2008–. *Publications*: (contrib.) Business: the ultimate resource, 2002. *Recreations*: tennis, table tennis, badminton, golf, classical music, opera. *T*: 07880 788530. *Club*: Lansdowne.

**MARLAND**, family name of **Baron Marland**.

**MARLAND, Baron** *cr* 2006 (Life Peer), of Odstock, in the County of Wiltshire; **Jonathan Peter Marland**; *b* 14 Aug. 1956; *s* of late Peter Greaves Marland and of Audrey Joan Marland (*née* Brierley); *m* 1983, Penelope Mary, *d* of late Richard Anthony Lamb; two *s* two *d*. *Educ*: Shrewsbury Sch. Dir, Lloyd Thompson, then Jardine Lloyd Thompson Ltd, 1982–99; Chairman: Herriot Ltd, 1989–; Commonwealth Enterprise and Investment Council Ltd, 2014–; Eco World Mgt and Adv. Services (UK) Ltd, 2015–; Quale Finance Ltd, 2017–19; Director: Jubilee Hldgs Ltd, 2002–10; C&UCO Properties, 2005–10; Hunter Boot Ltd, 2006–10; Insce Capital Partners LLP, 2006–; W. H. Ireland Ltd, 2008–10; Tamara Mellon Inc., 2013–15; Test Match Extra.com, 2014–. Chm., Kuwait

British Business Council, 2013–15; Member: Adv. Bd, Kuwait Small and Medium Enterprise Fund, 2013–; Adv. Bd, Kuwait Investment Office, 2016–. Treasurer: Cons. Party, 2005–07; Boris Johnson's London Mayoral Campaign, 2007–08. Dir, CChange, 2001–06; Chairman: Harnham Water Meadows Trust, 1990–2010; Tickets for Troops, 2009; Trustee: J. P. Marland Charitable Trust, 1995– (Chm., 1995–); Atlantic Partnership, 2001–; Guggenheim UK Charitable Trust (UK), 2002– (Chm., 2017–); Churchill Centre UK (formerly Internat. Churchill Soc.), 2008– (Chm., 2012–17); Commonwealth Walkway Trust (formerly Outdoor Walkways Trust), 2017–; Member: Adv. Cttee, Airey Neave Refugee Trust, 1992–2007; Exec. Adv. Bd, Peggy Guggenheim Mus., Venice, 2002–; Develt Cttee, RA, 2008–10. Pres., Salisbury Cons. Assoc., 2009–; Patron: Wilts Churches, 2009–; Salisbury and S Wilts Sports Club, 2010–. Contested (C) Somerton and Frome, 1997. Opposition spokesman in H of L on Energy and Climate Change, 2009–10; Parly Under-Sec. of State, DECC, 2010–12, BIS, 2012; Prime Minister's Trade Envoy, 2012–14; Chm., Prime Minister's Business Ambassadors, 2012–14. FRSA. OM (Malta), 2015. *Address:* 78 Belgrave Road, SW1V 2BJ. *T:* (020) 7752 0177. *Clubs:* Brooks's, MCC, Garrick, Pitt.

**MARLAND, Paul;** farmer, since 1967; *b* 19 March 1940; *s* of Alexander G. Marland and Elsa May Lindsey Marland; *m* 1st, 1965, Penelope Anne Barlow (marr. diss. 1982); one *s* two *d*; 2nd, 1984, Caroline Ann Rushton. *Educ:* Gordonstoun Sch., Elgin; Trinity Coll., Dublin (BA, BComm). Hopes Metal Windows, 1964; London Press Exchange, 1965–66. MP (C) Gloucester West, 1979–97; contested (C) Forest of Dean, 1997; contested (C) South West Region, EP elecns, 1999. It PPS to Financial Sec. to the Treasury and Economic Sec., 1981–83, to Minister of Agriculture, Fisheries and Food, 1983–86. Chm., back bench Agric. Cttee, 1989–97. Vice-Pres., 2002–05, Pres., 2005, Nat. Cons. Convention; Mem. Bd, Cons. Party, 2002–05. *Recreations:* ski-ing, shooting, riding, fishing. *Address:* Ford Hill Farm, Temple Guiting, Cheltenham, Glos GL54 5XU.

**MARLAR, Robin Geoffrey;** former cricket journalist and company director; *b* 2 Jan. 1931; *o s* of late E. A. G. Marlar and Winifred Marlar (*née* Stevens); *m* 1st, 1955, Wendy Ann Dumeresque (*d* 2000); two *s* four *d*; 2nd, 1980, Hon. Gill Taylor (*d* 2019), 2nd *d* of Baron Taylor of Hadfield. *Educ:* King Edward Sch., Lichfield; Harrow; Magdalene Coll., Cambridge (BA). Asst Master, Eton Coll., 1953–54; Librarian, Arundel Castle, 1954–59; Captain, Sussex CCC, 1955–59; sportswriter, Daily Telegraph, 1954–60; De La Rue Co., 1960–68; Consultant and Partner, Spencer Stuart and Associates, 1968–71; Cricket Corresp., Sunday Times, 1970–96; Founder, Marlar Group of Consultancies, 1971. Contested (C): Bolsover, 1959; Leicester NE, July 1962; contested (Referendum) Newbury, May 1993. *Publications:* The Story of Cricket, 1978; (ed) The English Cricketers Trip to USA and Canada 1859, 1979; Decision Against England, 1983; Golden Minnows in the World Cup, 2019. *Recreations:* gardening, sport. *Clubs:* Garrick, MCC (Mem. Cttee, 1999–2002; Pres., 2005–06); Sussex CCC (Chm., 1997–98; Pres., 2005–07).

**MARLBOROUGH, 12th Duke of,** *cr* 1702; **Charles James Spencer-Churchill;** Baron Spencer, 1603; Earl of Sunderland, 1643; Baron Churchill, 1685; Earl of Marlborough, 1689; Marquis of Blandford, 1702; Prince of the Holy Roman Empire; Prince of Mindelheim in Suabia; *b* 24 Nov. 1955; *e s* of 11th Duke of Marlborough and Susan Mary Spencer-Churchill (*née* Hornby, later Heber-Percy); *S* father, 2014; *m* 1st, 1990, Rebecca Mary (marr. diss. 2001), *d* of Peter Few Brown; one *s*; 2nd, 2002, Edla, *o d* of Alun Griffiths, OBE; one *s* one *d*. *Educ:* Pinewood; Harrow; RAC, Cirencester; Royal Berks Coll. of Agric. *Heir:* s Marquess of Blandford, *qv. Address:* Blenheim Palace, Woodstock, Oxon OX20 1PP. *E:* marlborough@blenheimpalace.com, duke@blenheimpalace.com. *Clubs:* White's, 5 Hertford Street, Turf, Tramp's, Annabel's; Racquet and Tennis (New York).

**MARLER, David Steele,** OBE 1984; Director, Egypt, British Council, 1997–2001; *b* 19 March 1941; *s* of Steele Edward and Dorothy Marler; *m* 1963, Belinda Mary Handisyde; two *s*. *Educ:* Brighton, Hove and Sussex Grammar Sch.; Merton Coll., Oxford (Postmaster, BA, MA). British Council, 1962–2001: seconded SOAS, 1962–63; Asst Rep., Bombay, 1963; Regional Officer, India, 1967; Dep. Rep., Ethiopia, 1970; Rep., Ibadan, Nigeria, 1974; Dir, Policy Res., 1977; Rep., Cyprus, 1980; seconded SOAS, 1984; National Univ., Singapore, 1985; Rep., China, 1987–90; Director: Asia, Pacific and Americas Div., 1990–92; Turkey, Azerbaijan and Uzbekistan, 1993–97. Chm., British Council Assoc., 2005–12. Mem., Cruising Assoc., 2010–. *Recreations:* sailing, travel, reading, walking, running with the Hash House Harriers. *Address:* 53 The Hall, Foxes Dale, Blackheath, SE3 9BG. *T:* (020) 8318 5874. *Clubs:* Benfleet Yacht; Changi Sailing (Singapore).

**MARLESFORD,** Baron *cr* 1991 (Life Peer), of Marlesford in the County of Suffolk; **Mark Shuldham Schreiber;** DL; political consultant, farmer and journalist; *b* 11 Sept. 1931; *s* of late John Shuldham Schreiber, AE, DL, Marlesford Hall, Suffolk and Maureen Schreiber (*née* Dent); *m* 1969, Gabriella Federica, *d* of Conte Teodoro Veglio di Castelletto d'Uzzone; two *d*. *Educ:* Eton; Trinity Coll., Cambridge. Nat. Service in Coldstream Guards (2nd Lt), 1950–51. Fisons Ltd, 1957–63; Conservative Research Dept, 1963–67; Dir, Conservative Party Public Sector Research Unit, 1967–70; Special Advr to the Govt, 1970–74; Special Adviser to Leader of the Opposition, 1974–75; Editorial Consultant, 1974–91, lobby correspondent, 1976–91, The Economist. Ind. Nat. Dir, Times Newspaper Holdings, 1991–2014; Director: Royal Ordnance Factories, 1972–74; British Railways (Anglia), 1988–92; Eastern Electricity plc, 1990–95. Adviser: Mitsubishi Corp. Internat. NV, 1990–2003; John Swire & Sons Ltd, 1992–2009. Mem., H of L Select Cttee on EU, 2003–07, 2012–14 (Mem., Econ. and Financial sub-cttee, 2001–05, 2010–14; Mem., Home Affairs sub-cttee, 2005–09). Member: Govt Computer Agency Council, 1973–74; Countryside Commn, 1980–92; Rural Development Commn, 1985–93; Chm., CPRE, 1993–98. Pres., Suffolk Preservation Soc., 1997–2018. Mem., East Suffolk CC, 1968–70. DL Suffolk, 1991. *Recreation:* gadfly on bureaucracy. *Address:* Marlesford Hall, Woodbridge, Suffolk IP13 0AU; 5 Kersley Street, SW11 4PR. *Club:* Pratt's.

**MARLING, Sir Charles (William Somerset),** 5th Bt *cr* 1882; *b* 2 June 1951; *s* of Sir John Stanley Vincent Marling, 4th Bt, OBE, and Georgina Brenda (Betty) (*d* 1961), *o d* of late Henry Edward FitzRoy Somerset; *S* father, 1977; *m* 1979, Judi; three *d*.

**MARLOW, Antony Rivers;** *b* 17 June 1940; *s* of late Major Thomas Keith Rivers Marlow, MBE, RE retd, and Beatrice Nora (*née* Hall); *m* 1962, Catherine Louise Howel (*née* Jones) (*d* 1994); three *s* two *d*. *Educ:* Wellington Coll.; RMA Sandhurst; St Catharine's Coll., Cambridge (2nd Cl. Hons (1) Mech Sciences, MA). Served Army, 1958–69; retd, Captain RE; management consultant and industrial/commercial manager, 1969–79. MP (C) Northampton North, 1979–97; contested (C) same seat, 1997. Farming and property design and develt, 1997–. *Recreations:* Rugby spectator, opera, ballet.

**MARLOW, David Ellis;** Chief Executive, 3i Group, 1988–92; *b* 29 March 1935; *m* 1959, Margaret Anne Smith (*d* 2019); one *d* (one *s* decd). Chartered Accountant. Investors in Industry, subseq. 3i, 1960–92. Director: Brixton (formerly Brixton Estate) plc, 1992–2003; Trinity Mirror plc, 1992–2005. *Recreations:* playing tennis, the piano, the organ and the 'cello; ski-ing and scrambling in the Alps. *Address:* The Platt, Elsted, Midhurst, Sussex GU29 0LA. *T:* (01730) 825261. *Club:* Athenæum.

**MARLOW, Prof. Neil,** DM; FRCP, FRCPCH; FMedSci; Professor of Neonatal Medicine, University College London, since 2008 (Director, Institute of Women's Health, 2009–11); *b* Market Harborough, Leics, 10 Nov. 1951; *s* of Wilfred and Daisy Marlow; *m* 1973, Elaine Susan Floyd; three *s* one *d*. *Educ:* Royal Masonic Sch., Bushey; St John's Coll., Oxford (BA Hons 1973; MB BS 1976; DM 1985). FRCP 1994; FRCPCH 1997. Med. trng, Oxford, Sheffield, Manchester, Liverpool, 1977–89; Sen. Lectr in Child Health, Univ. of Bristol, 1989–96; Prof. of Neonatal Medicine, Univ. of Nottingham, 1997–2008; Hon. Consultant Neonatologist, UCLH, 2008–. President: British Assoc. for Perinatal Medicine, 2004–08; Eur. Soc. for Paediatric Res., 2008–12; Internat. Paediatric Res. Foundn, 2008–10. FMedSci 2007. *Publications:* A Neonatal Vade Mecum, 1992, 3rd edn 1998; A Handbook of Neonatalogy, 2001; contribs to academic med. and scientific jls, mainly around the sequelae of preterm birth, randomised trials in perinatal medicine and neonatal care. *Recreations:* British music, opera, hill walking, fine dining. *Address:* Institute for Women's Health, 74 Huntley Street, WC1E 6AU. *T:* (020) 7679 0834. *E:* n.marlow@ucl.ac.uk.

**MARLOW, Timothy John;** art historian, broadcaster and gallery director; Artistic Director (formerly Director of Artistic Programmes), Royal Academy of Arts, since 2014; *b* Long Eaton, Derbys, 18 May 1962; *s* of Preb. W. Geoffrey Marlow and Barbara Anne Marlow (*née* Skinner); *m* 2006, Tanya Hudson; one *s*. *Educ:* King's Coll. London (BA Hons 1984); Pembroke Coll., Cambridge (PGCE 1985); Courtauld Inst. of Art (MA 1988). Vis. Lectr, Winchester Sch. of Art, 1990–2003; Hd, Adult Educn, Tate Gall., 1991–92; Ed., Tate mag., 1993–2002; Creative Dir, Sculpture at Goodwood, 2002–03; Dir of Exhibns, White Cube, 2003–14. Dir, Cultureshock Media Ltd, 2002–. Member: Council, ICA London, 2005–14; Faculty of Fine Arts, British Sch. at Rome, 2015–; Art on the Underground Adv. Panel, TFL, 2015–. Presenter of radio programmes, including: Kaleidoscope, Radio 4, 1991–98; The Ticket, 2006–08, Culture Shock, 2007–09, BBC World Service; presenter of TV arts documentaries, including: The Impressionists, 1998; The Nude, 2000; Great Artists I and II, 2001–03; Easter in Art, 2003; Tim Marlow on…, 2002–; Judgement Day, 2004; Manlow Meets…, 2009–; Tim Marlow: Art's Greatest Failures, 2016; guest presenter: Newsnight Rev., 2006–09; The Review Show, 2010–. Bd Mem./Dir, Sadler's Wells Trust, 2014–; Bd Mem./Trustee, Artichoke Trust, 2015–; Trustee, Imperial War Mus., 2016– (Chm., Art Commn's Cttee, 2016–). Patron, Create, 2017–. FRSA. Special Excellence in Broadcasting Award, Voice of Viewer and Listener, 2005. *Publications:* Egon Schiele, 1991; Auguste Rodin, 1994; Anthony Caro, 1997; Great Artists, 2001; David Bailey's Stardust, 2014; catalogue essays. *Recreations:* cycling, surfing badly, Chelsea FC, modern first editions. *Address:* Royal Academy of Arts, Burlington House, Piccadilly, W1J 0BD. *E:* lisa.jones@royalacademy.org.uk. *Clubs:* Groucho, Shoreditch House.

**MARLOWE, Hugh;** *see* Patterson, Harry.

**MARMION, (John) Piers (Tregarthen);** Chairman: BPA Group (India), since 2010; Wilton & Bain, since 2011; *b* 7 Feb. 1959; *m* 1986, Roxane; two *s* one *d*. *Educ:* Jesus Coll., Cambridge (BA 1981). Founding Dir, NB Selection, and Selector Europe, 1987–90; Chief Operating Officer and Man. Partner, Europe and Asia, Spencer Stuart, 1990–2000; Heidrick & Struggles Inc.: Pres., Internat., Europe and Asia, and Chief Operating Officer, 2000–01; Chm. and CEO, 2001–03; Man. Partner, Whitehead Mann Partnership, later Chm., EMEA, Korn/Ferry Whitehead Mann, 2006–09. Non-executive Director: Blackwell Ltd, 2003–08; Talent Q, 2005–14; Candex Solutions, 2010–16; Chairman: Route2Work Gp, 2017–; Solventis Gp, 2018–. *Recreations:* country pursuits, painting, history, boating in the Mediterranean, classic cars.

**MARMOT, Prof. Sir Michael (Gideon),** Kt 2000; PhD; FRCP, FFPH, FMedSci; Professor of Epidemiology and Public Health, University College London, since 1985 (MRC Professor, 1995–2013); Director, International Institute for Society and Health (formerly International Centre for Health and Society), since 1994, and Director, Institute of Health Equity, since 2011, University College London; *b* 26 Jan. 1945; *s* of Nathan Marmot and Alice Marmot (*née* Weiner); *m* 1971, Alexandra Naomi Ferster; two *s* one *d*. *Educ:* Univ. of Sydney (BSc Hons, MB BS Hons); Univ. of California, Berkeley (PhD Epidemiology). FFPH (FFCM 1989); FRCP 1996. RMO, Royal Prince Alfred Hosp., 1969–70, Fellowship in Thoracic Medicine, 1970–71, Univ. of Sydney; Res. Fellow and Lectr, Dept of Biomedical and Envmtl Health Scis, Univ. of California, Berkeley, 1971–76 (Fellowships from Berkeley and Amer. Heart Assoc., 1972–76); Lectr and Sen. Lectr in Epidemiology, LSHTM, 1976–85. Adjunct Prof., Dept of Soc., Human Develt and Health, Harvard Univ., 2014–2015; Associate, Health Policy and Mgt, Johns Hopkins Univ., 2007–08; Vis. Harvard and Lown Prof., Harvard Univ., 2015–16; Adjunct Prof., Dept of Social and Behavioural Scis, Harvard Univ., 2017–. Hon. Consultant, Public Health Medicine: Camden and Islington (formerly Bloomsbury) HA, 1980–2004; N Central London SHA, 2004–06; SHA for London, 2006–. Vis. Prof., RSocMed, 1987. Chm., DoH Scientific Ref. Gp on tackling inequalities, 2003–; Member: Royal Commn on Envmtl Pollution, 1995–2002; Ind. Inquiry into Inequalities in Health, 1997–98. Chairman: Commn on Social Determinants of Health, WHO, 2005–08; Internat. Adv. Bd, Cancer Res. UK/Bupa Foundn Cancer Prevention Initiative, 2014–. President: BMA, 2010–11; British Lung Foundn, 2013–; WMA, 2015–16. Vice-Pres., Academia Europaea, 2003–. Trustee, Early Intervention Foundn, 2012–. MNAM 2015. Foreign Associate Mem., Inst. of Medicine, NAS, USA, 2002. Founder FMedSci 1998. Hon. FBA 2008; Hon. FRSPH 2008; Hon. FRCPsych 2013; Hon. FRCOG 2015; Hon. Fellow, Amer. Coll. of Epidemiol., 2015; Hon. FRCPCH 2016; Hon. FSS 2016. Jenner Medal, 2010, Gold Medal, 2017, RSocMed; Manchester Doubleday Award, Manchester Sch. of Medicine, 2010; Ambuj Nath Bose Prize, RCP, 2011; Centennial Winslow Medal, Yale Sch. of Public Health, 2015; Prince Mahidol Award for Public Health, 2015; Ihsan Dogramaci Family Health Prize, WHO, 2016; Distinguished Merit Gold Medal, BMA, 2017. *Publications:* (ed jtly and contrib.) Coronary Heart Disease Epidemiology, 1992, 2nd edn 2005; (ed jtly) Social Determinants of Health, 1999, 2nd edn 2006; Status Syndrome, 2004; (contrib.) Food, Nutrition, Physical Activity, and the Prevention of Cancer: a global perspective, 2007; The Health Gap, 2015; contribs to OPCS Medical and Population Studies; numerous papers in learned jls. *Recreations:* tennis, viola. *Address:* Department of Epidemiology and Public Health, University College London, 1–19 Torrington Place, WC1E 6BT.

**MARNEY, Samantha Ruth;** *see* Barrell, S. R.

**MARNOCH, Rt Hon. Lord;** Michael Stewart Rae Bruce; PC 2001; Senator of the College of Justice in Scotland, 1990–2005; *b* 26 July 1938; *s* of late Alexander Eric Bruce, Advocate in Aberdeen, and late Mary Gordon Bruce (*née* Walker); *m* 1963, Alison Mary Monfries Stewart; two *d*. *Educ:* Loretto Sch.; Aberdeen Univ. (MA, LLB). Admitted Faculty of Advocates, 1963; QC Scot. 1975; Standing Counsel: to Dept of Agriculture and Fisheries for Scotland, 1973; to Highlands and Islands Develt Bd, 1973; Advocate Depute, 1983–86. Mem., Criminal Injuries Compensation Bd, 1986–90. Hon. Vice Pres., Salmon and Trout Assoc., 1994–2008 (Chm., Scotland, 1989–94). Hon. LLD Aberdeen, 1999. *Recreations:* fishing, golf. *Clubs:* New (Edinburgh); Honourable Company of Edinburgh Golfers; Rosehall Golf (Turriff), Duff House Royal Golf (Banff).

**MAROIS, Pauline;** Member (Parti Québécois) Charlevoix-Côte-de-Beaupré, National Assembly of Québec, 2007–14; Premier of Québec, 2012–14; *b* Québec City, 29 March 1949; *d* of Grégoire Marois and Marie-Paule Marois; *m* 1969, Claude Blanchet; three *s* one *d*. *Educ:* Univ. Laval (BA Social Work 1971); HEC Montréal (MBA 1976). Budget consultant and training officer, Co-operative Family Economics Assoc., Outaouais, 1971; resp. for Animation-Participation Service, Conseil régional de développement, Outaouais, 1971–73; Co-ordinator and lectr, social work tech. courses, Cégep de Hull, 1973; CEO, Centre local des services communautaires, l'Île-de-Hull, 1973–74; Hd, Childhood Services Div., Centre des services sociaux, Montréal, 1976–78; Press attaché to Minister of Finance, Québec, 1978–79; COS to Minister of State for Status of Women, 1979. Prof., Univ. of Québec, Hull, 1988. Mem. (Parti Québécois) La Peltrie, 1981–85, Taillon, 1989–2006, Nat. Assembly of Québec. Minister: for Status of Women, 1981–83; of Labor and Income Security, 1983–85; Official Opposition critic: for industry and trade, 1989–91; for public admin and Treasury Bd, 1991–93; Chair, Treasury Bd, 1994–95; Minister: for Admin and Public Service, 1994–95; responsible for Family, 1994–97; of Revenue, and of Finance, 1995–96; of Educn, 1996–98; of Child and Family Welfare, 1997–2001; Minister of State: for Health and Social Services, 1998–2001; for the Economy and Finance, 2001–02; Dep. Premier, 2001–08; Minister: of Res., Sci. and Technol., 2001–02; of Industry and Trade, 2002; of Finance, the Economy and Res., 2002–03; Official opposition critic: for educn, 2003–06; for internat. relns, 2006; Leader: Second Opposition Gp, 2007–08; Official Opposition, 2008–12. *Address:* c/o Conseil exécutif, Édifice Honoré-Mercier, 835 boulevard René-Lévesque Est, 3e étage, Québec, QC G1A 1B4, Canada.

**MAROO, Sushil Kumar;** Executive Vice Chairman - Strategic Business, Essar Group, since 2016 (Chief Executive Officer and Director, Essar Energy plc, 2013–14; Managing Director and Chief Executive Officer, Essar Power Ltd, 2014–16); *b* Bhilwara, Rajasthan, India, 5 July 1961; *s* of Nand Singh Maroo and Lalita Maroo; *m* 1990, Dr Preeti; one *s* one *d*. *Educ:* Univ. of Rajasthan (BCom). CA Inst. Chartered Accountants of India. Hindustan Lever, 1983–84; Voltas Ltd (Tata Gp), 1984–87; Nippon Dendrolspat Ltd (Mittal Gp), 1987–90; Chambal Fertilizers & Chemicals Ltd (Birla Gp), 1990–97; RPG Dholpur Power Co. Ltd (RP Goenka Gp), 1997–2008; Deputy Managing Director: Jindal Power Ltd, 2008–12; Jindal Steel & Power Ltd, 2012–13. *Recreations:* lawn tennis, chess, badminton. *Address:* Essar House, 11 K. K. Marg, Mahalaxmi, Mumbai 400 034, India. *T:* 2266601100, *Fax:* 2266102868. *E:* sushil.maroo@essar.com. *Clubs:* Vasant Vihar, Delhi Flying (New Delhi); Noida Golf.

**MARQUAND, Prof. David (Ian),** FBA 1998; FRHistS; FLSW; Principal, Mansfield College, Oxford, 1996–2002, Hon. Fellow, 2002; *b* 20 Sept. 1934; *s* of Rt Hon. Hilary Marquand, PC; *m* 1959, Judith Mary (*née* Reed); one *s* one *d*. *Educ:* Emanuel Sch.; Magdalen Coll., Oxford (BA 1st cl. hons Mod. Hist. 1957); St Antony's Coll., Oxford (Sen. Schol.; Hon. Fellow 2003). FRHistS 1986. Teaching Asst, Univ. of Calif., 1958–59; Leader Writer, The Guardian, 1959–62; Research Fellow, St Antony's Coll., Oxford, 1962–64; Lectr in Politics, Univ. of Sussex, 1964–66. Contested: (Lab) Barry, 1964; (SDP) High Peak, 1983; MP (Lab) Ashfield, 1966–77; PPS to Minister of Overseas Develt, 1967–69; Jun. Opposition Front-Bench Spokesman on econ. affairs, 1971–72; Member: Select Cttee on Estimates, 1966–68; Select Cttee on Procedure, 1968–73; Select Cttee on Corp. Tax, 1971; British Deleg. to Council of Europe, 1970–73. Chief Advr, Secretariat-Gen., European Commission, 1977–78; Prof. of Contemporary History and Politics, Salford Univ., 1978–91; Prof. of Politics, 1991–96 (Hon. Prof., 1997–), and Dir, Political Economy Research Centre, 1993–96, Sheffield Univ. Vis. Scholar, Hoover Instn, Stanford, USA, 1985–86; Vis. Fellow, Dept of Politics and Internat. Relns, Oxford Univ., 2002–: Hon. Dist. Prof., Sch. of Law and Politics, Cardiff Univ., 2015–. Jt Ed., Political Qly, 1987–97. Member: Nat. Steering Cttee, SDP, 1981–88; Policy Cttee, Soc & Lib Dem, 1988–90. Trustee, Aspen Inst., Berlin, 1982–; Member: Adv. Council, Inst. of Contemporary British History, 1987–; Bd of Trustees, IPPR, 1992–2005; Adv. Council, Demos, 1993–; Social Justice Commn, 1993–94; Commn on Wealth Creation and Social Cohesion, 1994–95. Thomas Jefferson Meml Lectr, Univ. of Calif at Berkeley, 1981. FRSA; FLSW 2013. Hon. DLitt: Salford, 1996; Sheffield, 2002; Hon. Dr rer. pol. Bologna, 2002. George Orwell Meml Prize (jtly), 1980; Sir Isaiah Berlin Prize, Pol Studies Assoc., 2001. *Publications:* Ramsay MacDonald, 1977; Parliament for Europe, 1979; (with David Butler) European Elections and British Politics, 1981; (ed) John Mackintosh on Politics, 1982; The Unprincipled Society, 1988; The Progressive Dilemma, 1991, 2nd edn 1999; (ed with Anthony Seldon) The Ideas That Shaped Post-War Britain, 1996; The New Reckoning, 1997; (ed with R. Nettler) Religion and Democracy, 2000; Decline of the Public, 2004; Britain Since 1918, 2008; The End of the West, 2011; Mammon's Kingdom: an essay on Britain, now, 2014; *contributor:* The Age of Austerity, 1964; A Radical Future, 1967; Coalitions in British Politics, 1978; Britain in Europe, 1980; The Political Economy of Tolerable Survival, 1980; The Rebirth of Britain, 1982; European Monetary Union Progress and Prospects, 1982; Social Theory and Political Practice, 1982; The Changing Constitution, 1985; Thatcherism, 1987; The Radical Challenge, 1987; The Ruling Performance, 1987; The Alternative, 1990; Debating the Constitution, 1993; Re-inventing the Left, 1994; The New Social Democracy, 1999; The Market or the Public Domain, 2001; Restating the State, 2004; Building a Citizen Society, 2008; articles and reviews in The Guardian, The Times, The Sunday Times, New Statesman, Encounter, Commentary, Prospect, and in academic jls. *Recreation:* reading thrillers. *Address:* 42 Westbourne Road, Penarth, Vale of Glamorgan CF64 3HF.

**MARQUIS,** family name of **Earl of Woolton**.

**MARR, Andrew William Stevenson;** Presenter: Start The Week, Radio 4, since 2002; The Andrew Marr Show (formerly Sunday AM), BBC TV, since 2005; *b* 31 July 1959; *s* of Donald and Valerie Marr; *m* 1987, Jacqueline Ashley, *qv*; one *s* two *d*. *Educ:* Dundee High Sch.; Craigflower, Fife; Loretto School, Musselburgh; Trinity Hall, Cambridge (BA). Trainee and gen. reporter, 1982–85, Parly Corresp., 1985–86, The Scotsman; Political Corresp., The Independent, 1986–88; Political Editor: The Scotsman, 1988; The Economist, 1989–92; political columnist and Associate Editor, 1992–96, Editor, 1996–98, Editor-in-Chief, 1998, The Independent; columnist, The Observer, and The Express, 1998–2000; Political Editor, BBC, 2000–05; columnist, Daily Telegraph, 2000. Presenter: Andrew Marr's History of Modern Britain (series), BBC2, 2007; The Making of Modern Britain (series), BBC2, 2009; Andrew Marr's Megacities (series), BBC1, 2011; The Diamond Queen, BBC1, 2012; Andrew Marr's History of the World (series), BBC1, 2012; The Making of Merkel with Andrew Marr, BBC2, 2013; Andrew Marr's Great Scots, BBC2, 2014; Andrew Marr on Churchill: blood, sweat and oil paint, BBC4, 2015; Andrew Marr's Paperback Heroes (series), BBC4, 2016; Andrew Marr: my brain and me, BBC2, 2017. Columnist of the Year, What the Papers Say, 1994; Creative Media Journalist of Year, British Press Awards, 2000; Pol Journalist of Year, C4/House Mag., 2001, 2002; Specialist of the Year, RTS Awards, 2001–02; Best Individual TV Performer, Voice of the Listener and Viewer Awards, 2002; Best TV Performer, BPG, 2002; Parly Commentator of the Year, Richard Dimbleby Award, BAFTA, 2004. *Publications:* The Battle for Scotland, 1992; Ruling Britannia, 1995; The Day Britain Died, 2000; My Trade: a short history of British journalism, 2004; A History of Modern Britain, 2007; The Making of Modern Britain, 2009; The Diamond Queen: Elizabeth II and her people, 2011; A History of the World, 2012; A Short Book about Drawing, 2013; Head of State (novel), 2014; Children of the Master (novel), 2015; We British, 2015. *Recreations:* reading, painting, talking. *Address:* c/o BBC, Broadcasting House, Portland Place, W1A 1AA.

**MARR, Douglas,** CBE 2001; HM Inspector of Education, 2004–12; freelance journalist, The Herald and Scottish Review, since 2004; education consultant, since 2004; *b* 7 Feb. 1947; *s* of Douglas N. Marr and Evelyn Marr; *m* 1990, Alison M. Gordon; one *d*. *Educ:* Aberdeen Grammar Sch.; Univ. of Aberdeen (MA Hons 1969, MEd Hons 1982). Teacher of History, Hilton Acad., Aberdeen, 1970–71; Asst Principal Teacher of Hist., Aberdeen GS, 1971–76; Principal Teacher of Hist., Hilton Acad., 1976–81; Asst Rector, Kemnay Acad., 1981–84; Depute Rector, The Gordon Schs, Huntly, 1984–87; Headteacher, Hilton Acad., 1987–88; Rector: St Machar Acad., 1988–95; Banchory Acad., 1995–2002; Schs Mgt and Curriculum Structures Co-ordinator, Aberdeenshire Council, 2002–04; Sen. Teaching Fellow, Sch. of Educn, Univ. of Aberdeen, 2004–06. Sen. Consultant, Acorn Consulting (Scotland), 2004–. Mem., Business Cttee, 2001–06, Ct, 2002–06, Univ. of Aberdeen. Vice Chm., Aberdeen Grammar Sch. Former Pupils' Club, 2014–. *Recreations:* squash, gardening, walking. *Address:* 121 Derbeth Grange, Kingswells, Aberdeen AB15 8UD. *T:* (01224) 744824. *E:* douglas.marr@alford.co.uk. *Club:* Leicestershire CC.

**MARR, (Sir) Leslie Lynn,** (2nd Bt *cr* 1919, but does not use the title); MA Cambridge; painter and draughtsman; late Flight Lieutenant RAF; *b* 14 Aug. 1922; *o s* of late Col John Lynn Marr, OBE, TD, (and *g s* of 1st Bt), and Amelia Rachel, *d* of late Robert Thompson, Overdinsdale Hall, Darlington; *S* grandfather, 1932; *m* 1st, 1948, Dinora Delores Mendelson (marr. diss. 1956); one *d*; 2nd, 1962, Lynn Heneage (marr. diss. 2000); two *d*; 3rd, 2002, Maureen Thelma Monk (*née* Dormer). *Educ:* Shrewsbury; Pembroke Coll., Cambridge. Has exhibited at Ben Uri, Drian, Woodstock, Wildenstein, Whitechapel, Campbell and Franks Galls and Piano Nobile Fine Paintings, London; Art Sch. Gall., Shrewsbury Sch.; Mercer Art Gall., Harrogate; University Gall., Northumbria Univ.; also in Norwich, Belfast, Birmingham, Newcastle upon Tyne, Durham City Art Gall., Bristol and Paris. *Publications:* From My Point of View: personal record of some Norfolk churches, 1979; A Piano Album, 1998; A Second Album for Piano, 1998. *Heir:* cousin Allan James William Marr [*b* 10 Oct. 1965; *m* Dawn, *yr d* of late G. Ridly; two *s*]. *Address:* c/o Piano Nobile Fine Paintings, 129 Portland Road, W11 4LW.

**MARR-JOHNSON, His Honour Frederick James Maugham;** a Circuit Judge, 1991–2006; *b* 17 Sept. 1936; *s* of late Kenneth Marr-Johnson and Hon. Diana Marr-Johnson; *m* 1966, Susan Eyre; one *s* one *d*. *Educ:* Winchester Coll.; Trinity Hall, Cambridge (MA). Called to the Bar, Lincoln's Inn, 1962, Bencher, 1999; practised on SE Circuit, 1963–91. Judge of Mayor's and City of London Court, 1999–2006. *Recreation:* sailing. *Address:* The South Wing, St Paul's Walden Bury, Hitchin SG4 8BP. *T:* (01438) 871617. *Clubs:* Royal Yacht Squadron (Cowes); Bar Yacht (Rear Cdre, 1999–2000).

**MARRA, Jennifer Margaret;** Member (Lab) Scotland North East, Scottish Parliament, since 2011; *b* Dundee, 6 Nov. 1977; *d* of Nicholas James Marra and Eileen Margaret Marra. *Educ:* St John's High Sch., Dundee; Univ. of St Andrews (MA Mod. Hist. 1999); Emory Univ., Atlanta (Bobby Jones Schol.); Univ. of Glasgow (LLB 2008); BPP London (Grad. Dip. Law 2009); Univ. of Dundee (DipLP 2010). Hd of Press, Univ. of Dundee, 2000–05; Spokesperson for Labour MEPs, Brussels and Strasbourg, 2005–06; PR consultant, Glasgow, 2006–08. Scottish Parliament: Shadow Minister for Community Safety and Legal Affairs, 2011–13, for Youth Employment, 2013–; Dep. Shadow Finance Minister, 2013–. *Address:* (office) Office 5/2, Whitehall House, 33 Yeaman Shore, Dundee DD1 4BJ. *T:* (01382) 202584. *E:* jenny.marra.msp@parliament.scot.

**MARRIN, John Wheeler;** QC 1990; a Recorder, 1997–2014; a Deputy High Court Judge, 2008–14; *b* 24 Aug. 1951; *s* of late Dr Charles Ainsworth Marrin and of Cecilia Margaret Marrin (*née* Staveley); *m* 1984, Paquita Carmen Bulan de Zulueta; one *s* three *d*. *Educ:* Sherborne Sch.; Magdalene Coll., Cambridge (MA). CIArb 1998. Called to the Bar, Inner Temple, 1974, Bencher, 2002; Head of Chambers, 2005–10. *Recreations:* music, ski-ing, horse-riding, travel. *Address:* Keating Chambers, 15 Essex Street, WC2R 3AA. *T:* (020) 7544 2600.

**MARRINER, Andrew Stephen;** solo, chamber and orchestral clarinettist; Principal Clarinet, London Symphony Orchestra, 1985–2019; *b* 25 Feb. 1954; *s* of Sir Neville Marriner, CH, CBE; *m* 1988, Elisabeth Anne Sparke; one *s*. *Educ:* King's College Sch., Cambridge (chorister); King's Sch., Canterbury; New Coll., Oxford; Hochschule für Musik, Hannover. Freelance solo, chamber and orchestral clarinettist, 1977–84; Principal Clarinet, Acad. of St Martin-in-the-Fields, 1986–2008; solo and concert appearances at venues incl. RFH and Barbican Hall, and in Paris, Berlin, Vienna, USA, Far East and Australia; concerto work with conductors incl. Sir Neville Marriner, Valery Gergiev, Sir Colin Davis, Leonard Bernstein, Mstislav Rostropovich, Michael Tilson Thomas and Richard Hickox. Numerous recordings. Hon. RAM 1994. *Recreations:* family, cricket. *Address:* 67 Cornwall Gardens, SW7 4BA. *Club:* Lord's Taverners.

**MARRIOTT, Bryant Hayes;** Director of Broadcasting, Seychelles Broadcasting Corporation (formerly Radio Television Seychelles), 1991–93; *b* 9 Sept. 1936; *s* of Rev. Horace Marriott and Barbara Marriott; *m* 1963, Alison Mary Eyles; one *s* two *d*. *Educ:* Tormore Sch., Upper Deal, Kent; Marlborough Coll., Wilts; New Coll., Oxford (MA). Joined BBC, 1961; Studio Manager, 1961; Producer, 1963; Staff Training Attachments Officer, 1973; Chief Asst to Controller Radio 1 and 2, 1976; Head of Recording Services, 1979; Controller, Radio Two, 1983; Controller, Special Duties, Radio BBC, 1990–91. *Recreations:* gardening, sailing, drumming. *Address:* 4 School Pasture, Burnham Deepdale, King's Lynn, Norfolk PE31 8DF. *Club:* Brancaster Staithe Sailing.

**MARRIOTT, Jane,** OBE 2004; HM Diplomatic Service; High Commissioner to Kenya, since 2019; *b* Doncaster, 1976; *d* of Derek Marriott and Patricia Marriott. *Educ:* Danum Comp. Sch.; Durham Univ. (BA Hons 1st Hist. 1997); Darwin Coll., Cambridge (MPhil Internat. Relns 1998). Diversity Policy, Cabinet Office, 1998; Criminal Justice Bill Team, Home Office, 1999; Foreign Policy Secretariat, Cabinet Office, 2000; Hd, Nuclear Non-Proliferation, FCO, 2001–03; Political Advisor: to Coalition Forces, S Iraq, 2003–04; to US-led Combined Coalition Forces, Afghanistan, 2004; Pol-Mil. Team Leader, Iraq Policy Unit, FCO, 2005; Pol-Mil. Counsellor, Baghdad, 2005–06; Dep. Hd, Afghanistan Gp, FCO and Mem., US CENTCOM Assessment Team, 2007–09; Chief Speechwriter, Sec. of State for Defence, 2009; Sen. Political Advr to US Special Rep. for Afghanistan and Pakistan, 2009; Chargé d'Affaires and Dep. Ambassador, Iran, 2010–11; Dep. Dir, Americas, Middle East and Africa, Nat. Security Council, 2012; Ambassador to Yemen, 2013–15; Dir, Gulf, Arabian Peninsula and N Africa, FCO, 2015–16; Dir, Internat. Counter-Terrorism, FCO and Home Office, 2016–19. Chm., British Sch., Tehran, 2010–12. Trustee, Mines Adv. Gp, 2017–. Mil. Campaign Medal, Iraq, 2004, Afghanistan, 2005; Superior Civilian Service Medal (USA), 2005; FCO Civilian Medal, Iraq, 2007. *Publications:* (contrib.) Gender and Diplomacy, ed J. A. Cassidy, 2017. *Recreations:* singing, theatre, travelling/exploring, hiking, writing. *Address:* Foreign and Commonwealth Office, King Charles Street, SW1A 2AH. *T:* 07932 685433. *E:* janemarriott@hotmail.com.

**MARRIOTT, Martin Marriott;** Headmaster, Canford School, 1976–92; *b* 28 Feb. 1932; *s* of late Rt Rev. Philip Selwyn Abraham, Bishop of Newfoundland, and Elizabeth Dorothy Cicely, *d* of late Sir John Marriott; *m* 1956, Judith Caroline Guerney Lubbock; one *s* two *d*. *Educ*: Lancing College; New College, Oxford. MA, DipEd. RAF Educn Branch, 1956–59. Asst Master, Heversham Grammar Sch., 1959–66; Asst Master, Housemaster, Second Master, Acting Master, Haileybury College, 1966–76. Chm., HMC, 1989. *Recreations:* grandchildren, golf, gardening. *Address:* Hillcroft, Meyrick Avenue, Salisbury, Wilts SP2 8ED. *T:* (01722) 330271. *E:* mmarriott32@gmail.com. *Club:* East India.

**MARRIOTT, Michael;** furniture and product designer; Director, Michael Marriott, since 1994; *b* 7 Jan. 1963; *s* of Michael and Jean Marriott. *Educ:* London Coll. of Furniture (HND); Royal Coll. of Art (MA 1993). Work in exhibitions, including: RFH; Crafts Council; ICA, and countries worldwide, including Italy, Germany, Sweden, Japan and USA; work in public collections: Crafts Council; British Council; Design Mus. Jerwood Prize for Furniture, Jerwood Foundn, 1999. *Recreations:* art, architecture, cycling, cities. *Address:* 11 Ramsgate Street, E8 2FD. *E:* mm@ michaelmarriott.com. *W:* www.michaelmarriott.com. *Club:* Hat on Wall.

**MARRIOTT, Maj. Gen. Patrick Claude,** CB 2012; CBE 2003 (OBE 1999); DL; Commandant, Royal Military Academy, Sandhurst, 2009–12; *b* Oxted, Surrey, 23 Feb. 1958; *s* of Captain P. B. Marriott, DSO, DSC, RN and F. J. Marriott; *m* 1989, Karin Henrietta Warde Ingram; two *s* one *d*. *Educ:* Gresham's Sch., Holt. Commnd 17th/21st Lancers, 1977–82; Co. Comdr, Multinat. Force and Observers, Sinai, 1982; Adjt, 17th/21st Lancers, 1982–85; Asst Mil. Asst to VCDS (Personnel & Logistics), 1985–87; Sqdn Ldr, 17th/21st Lancers, 1987–90; psc (Can), 1990; SO2 Instructor, Jun. Div., Staff Coll., 1991–93; Sqdn Ldr, Queen's Royal Lancers, 1993–95; SO2 Tactics/Ops, British Army Trng Unit, Suffield, 1995–97; SO1 Jt Ops Centre (Plans), SHAPE, 1998; CO, Queen's Royal Lancers, 1998–2000; COS, HQ 1 (UK) Armd Div., 2000–04; HCSC (J) 2004; Comdr, 7th Armd Bde, 2005–07; ACOS Ops, PJHQ, 2007–09. Army Rep. to House of Laity in Gen. Synod, 2005–12; Perm. Mem., Service Complaints' Panels, 2015–. Dir, British Forces Foundn, 2009–12. Col, Queen's Royal Lancers, 2011–15. Chairman: Scottish Cttee, Combat Stress, 2013–; Young Karers of E Sutherland (Tykes), 2017–. Gov., Loretto Sch., Musselburgh, 2010–16. DL Sutherland, 2013. QCVS 2006. *Recreations:* field sports, watercolour painting, natural history, rhetoric, keeping pigs and chickens, writing, deer-stalking. *Address:* Fleet Ford, Littleferry, Golspie, Sutherland KW10 6TD. *E:* marriottpckh@hotmail.com.

**MARRIOTT, Sir Peter Francis S.;** *see* Smith-Marriott.

**MARRIOTT, Richard,** CVO 2006; TD 1965; Lord-Lieutenant of East Riding of Yorkshire, 1996–2005; *b* 17 Dec. 1930; *s* of late Rowland Arthur Marriott and Evelyn (*née* Caillard), Cotesbach Hall, Leics; *m* 1959, Janet (Sally) Coles; two *s*. *Educ:* Eton Coll.; Brasenose Coll., Oxford (Schol.). 2nd Lieut, Rifle Bde, 1950–51; Lt-Col comdg 21st SAS Regt (Artists) TA, 1966–69. With Brown Shipley & Co. Ltd, 1954–63; Partner, Mullens & Co. (Govt Brokers), 1964–86; Dir, Mercury Asset Mgt, 1986–96. Mem., Rural Develt Commn, Humberside, 1986–95. Vice-President: Officers' Assoc. (Chm., 1977–86); RUSI, 1993–98; Financial Adviser: Army Benevolent Fund, 1969–97 (Treas., 1997–2000); Airborne Forces Security Fund, 1972–2006; Trustee, Special Air Service Assoc., 1994–2003. Pres., Yorks Agricl Soc., 1995–96. Member Council: Nat. Army Mus., 1991–2005; Hull Univ., 1994–2000. Trustee: Buttle Trust, 1985–98 (Dep. Chm., 1990–96); York Minster Fund, 1987–2000; Nat. Army Mus. Develt Trust, 2006–13; Chm., Burton Constable Foundn, 1992–2008. Mem., Adv. Panel, Greenwich Hosp., 1981–2002. FSA 2013. High Sheriff, Humberside, 1991–92. Hon. Fellow, Sion Coll., 2005–. DUniv Hull, 2003. *Recreations:* books, the arts, travel, field sports. *Address:* Boynton Hall, Bridlington, E Yorks YO16 4XJ. *Clubs:* Beefsteak, Special Forces, White's.

**MARRIS, James Hugh Spencer;** Director: Newcastle Race Course, 1994–2007; Sedgefield Racecourse, 2002–07; *b* 30 July 1937; *s* of Harry V. Marris and Agnes E. Hutchinson; *m* 1963, Susan Mary Husband; one *s* one *d*. *Educ:* King William's College, Isle of Man; Royal Technical College, Salford. ARTCS, CEng, FIGEM. Dir of Engineering, E Midlands Gas, 1978–82; Regional Dep. Chm., Eastern Gas, 1982–83; HQ Dir (Ops), British Gas, 1983–87; Regl Chm., British Gas, Northern, 1988–93. *Publications:* contribs to IGasE Jl. *Recreations:* golf, gardening. *Address:* 3 Apple Tree Rise, Corbridge, Northumberland NE45 5HD. *T:* (01434) 633509.

**MARRIS, Robert;** *b* 8 April 1955; *s* of late Dr Charles Marris and Margaret Chetwode Marris, JP; partner, Julia Pursehouse. *Educ:* St Edward's Sch., Oxford; Univ. of British Columbia (BA Sociology and Hist. (double 1st) 1976; MA Hist. 1979). Trucker, 1977–79; trolley bus driver, 1979–82; law student, Birmingham Poly., 1982–84; articled clerk, 1985–87; solicitor, Manby & Steward, 1987–88; Solicitor and Partner, Thompsons, 1988–2001. Regl Officer, Stafford, NUT, 2011–13. MP (Lab) Wolverhampton SW, 2001–10 and 2015–17; contested (Lab) same seat, 2010. Non-exec. Dir, B. E. Wedge Hldgs Ltd, 2017–. *Recreations:* Wolves, Canadiana, bicycling.

**MARROW, Prof. (Thomas) James,** PhD; James Martin Professor of Energy Materials, University of Oxford, since 2010; Fellow, Mansfield College, Oxford, since 2010; *b* Bromborough, Wirral, 23 Nov. 1966; *s* of John Williams Marrow and Mary Elizabeth Marrow; *m* 1998, Daiva Kojelyte; one *s* one *d*. *Educ:* Wirral Grammar Sch. for Boys; Clare Coll., Cambridge (BA Natural Scis 1988; PhD 1991). Jun. Res. Fellow, Linacre Coll., Oxford, 1992–93; EPSRC Res. Fellow, Birmingham Univ., 1994; Lectr, UMIST, then Univ. of Manchester, 1995–2010. *Publications:* contribs to scientific jls. *Recreations:* ceramics, family. *Address:* Mansfield College, Oxford OX1 3TF. *T:* (01865) 273938. *E:* james.marrow@materials.ox.ac.uk.

**MARS-JONES, Adam;** writer; *b* 26 Oct. 1954; *s* of Hon. Sir William Mars-Jones, MBE. *Educ:* Westminster School; Trinity Hall, Cambridge (BA 1976). Film Critic: The Independent, 1986–99; The Times, 1999–2001; book reviewer: The Observer, 2002–13; London Rev. of Bks, 2013–. Res. Prof. in Creative Writing, Goldsmiths, Univ. of London, 2016–. *Publications:* Lantern Lecture (stories), 1981 (Somerset Maugham Award 1982); (with Edmund White) The Darker Proof (stories), 1987, 2nd edn 1988; Venus Envy (essay), 1990; Monopolies of Loss (stories), 1992; The Waters of Thirst (novel), 1993; Blind Bitter Happiness (essays), 1997; Pilcrow (novel), 2008; Cedilla (novel), 2011; Noriko Smiling (film study), 2011; Kid Gloves (memoir), 2015; Second Sight (selected writing on film), 2019. *Recreations:* cooking, sight-reading piano music I will never be able to play properly. *Address:* 38 Oakbank Grove, Herne Hill, SE24 0AJ. *T:* (020) 7733 9757.

**MARSALIS, Wynton;** trumpeter; Artistic Director, Jazz at Lincoln Center, New York, since 1987; *b* New Orleans, 18 Oct. 1961; *s* of Ellis and Dolores Marsalis. *Educ:* New Orleans Center for the Creative Arts; Berkshire Music Center (Harvey Shapiro Award); Juilliard Sch., NY (Schol.). Mem., Art Blakey's Jazz Messengers, 1980–81; formed own jazz quintet, 1981; has played with major orchestras worldwide, incl. New Orleans Philharmonic, LSO, English Chamber Orch. Music Dir, Lincoln Center Jazz Orch., 1987–. *Compositions* include: In This House, On This Morning; Blood on the Fields, 1997 (Pulitzer Prize for Music, 1997); Knozz-Moe-King; Jazz (ballet score); Concerto in D, 2015. Numerous recordings (Grammy Awards for jazz and classical performances). *Publications:* Sweet Swing Blues on the Road, 1994; Marsalis on Music, 1995; (with C. Vigeland) Jazz in the Bittersweet Blues of Life; (with S. Seyfu Hinds) To a Young Musician: letters from the road, 2004; Jazz ABZ, 2005; (with Geoffrey Ward) Moving to Higher Ground: how jazz can change your life, 2009. *Address:* Wynton Marsalis Enterprises, c/o Jazz at Lincoln Center, 3 Columbus Circle, New York, NY 10023, USA.

**MARSCHALL JONES, Timothy Aidan;** HM Diplomatic Service; Team Leader, Economics Trade and Development, Berlin, since 2013; *b* 5 Sept. 1962; *s* of Dr Derek Hugh Powell Jones and Thelma Anne (*née* Gray); *m* 2001, Dr Christin Marschall; one *s* one *d*. *Educ:* Bexhill Co. Grammar Sch.; Christ's Coll., Cambridge (BA Hons 1984). Joined HM Diplomatic Service, 1984: Vienna (CSCE), 1987–88; The Hague, 1988–92; FCO, 1992–94; EU Admin, Mostar, 1994–95; Dep. Head of Mission, Tehran, 1996–99; Ambassador to Armenia, 1999–2002; Hd of Ops, IT Strategy Unit, FCO, 2003–06; HM Consul Gen., Lille, 2006–08; Principal Advr to EU Counter Terrorism Co-ordinator, 2008–12. *Recreations:* swimming, cycling, idle curiosity. *Address:* c/o Foreign and Commonwealth Office, King Charles Street, SW1A 2AH.

**MARSDEN, Edmund Murray;** Minister (Cultural Affairs), British High Commission, New Delhi, India, and Regional Director, South Asia, British Council, 2000–05; *b* 22 Sept. 1946; *s* of Christopher Marsden and Ruth Marsden (*née* Kershaw); *m* 1975, Christine Vanner (*d* 1980); *m* 1981, Megan McIntyre; one *s*. *Educ:* Winchester College; Trinity College, Cambridge. Partner, Compton Press, Salisbury, 1968–70; Nuffield Foundn Publications Unit, 1970–71; British Council: Ghana, 1971; Belgium, 1973; Algeria, 1975; Management Accountant, 1977; Syria, 1980; Dir, Educn Contracts, 1982; Turkey, 1987; Dir, Corporate Affairs, 1990–93; Asst Dir-Gen., 1993–99; Chm., Intermediate Technol. Develt Gp, 1995–97 and 1998–2000. *Address:* 21755 Ocean Vista Drive, Laguna Beach, CA 92651, USA. *E:* emarsden01@aol.com.

**MARSDEN, Gordon;** MP (Lab) Blackpool South, since 1997; *b* 28 Nov. 1953; *s* of late George Henry Marsden and Joyce Marsden. *Educ:* Stockport Grammar Sch.; New Coll., Oxford (BA 1st cl. Hons History; MA); Warburg Inst., London Univ. (postgrad. res.); Harvard Univ. (Kennedy Schol. in Internat. Relations). Tutor and Associate Lectr, Arts Faculty, Open Univ., 1977–97; PR Consultant, 1980–85; Chief Public Affairs Advr, English Heritage, 1984–85; Editor, History Today, 1985–97; Consultant Ed., New Socialist, 1989–90. Chm., Fabian Soc., 2000–01. Contested (Lab) Blackpool S, 1992. PPS, Lord Chancellor's Dept, 2001–03, to Sec. of State for Culture, Media and Sport, 2003–05, to Sec. of State for Communities and Local Govt, 2009–10; Shadow Minister for Skills and FE, 2010–13, for Transport, 2013–15, for Univs, Skills and FE, 2015–. Mem., Select Cttee on Educn and Employment, 1998–2001, 2005–07, on Innovation, Univs and Skills, 2007–10. Vice-Pres., All Party Arts and Heritage Gp, 2000–15; Chair: All Party Skills Gp, 2006–10; All Party Estonia Gp, 2008–; All Party Veterans Gp, 2010–; Co-Chair: All Party Osteoporosis Gp, 2011–; All Party Arts and Heritage Gp, 2015–; Co-Chm., PLP Educn and Employment Cttee, 1998–2001; Mem., Ecclesiastical Cttee, 1998–2015. Chair, History of Parlt Trust, 2016–. Pres., British Destinations (formerly British Resorts, later British Resorts and Destinations) Assoc., 1998–. Mem. Bd, Inst. of Historical Res., 1995–2001. Trustee, History Today, 2005–14. Vis. Parly Fellow, St Antony's Coll., Oxford, 2003; Centenary Fellow, Historical Assoc., 2006–07. *Publications:* (ed) Victorian Values: personalities and perspectives in Nineteenth Century society, 1990, 2nd edn 1998; (contrib.) The English Question, 2000; (contrib.) The History of Censorship, 2002; (contrib.) Eminent Parliamentarians, 2012; contrib. History Today, Independent, Times, Tribune, TES, FE Week, THES. *Recreations:* world music, travel, medieval culture. *Address:* House of Commons, SW1A 0AA. *T:* (020) 7219 1262.

**MARSDEN, Sir Jonathan (Mark),** KCVO 2017 (CVO 2013; LVO 2003); FSA; Director, Royal Collection Trust and Surveyor of the Queen's Works of Art, 2010–17; *b* 15 Feb. 1960; *s* of Rear-Adm. Peter Nicholas Marsden, *qv*; *m* 2002, Sarah Bernard; two *s*. *Educ:* Sherborne Sch.; Univ. of York (BA Hons Hist.). Asst Curator, The Treasure Houses of Britain exhibn, Nat. Gall. of Art, Washington, 1983–85; Historic Buildings Rep., Nat. Trust N Wales Reg., 1986–92, Thames and Chilterns Reg., 1992–96; Dep. Surveyor of the Queen's Works of Art, 1996–2010. Member: Exec. Cttee, Georgian Gp, 1995–2005; Council, Furniture Hist. Soc., 2002–04 (Hon. Editl Sec., 2005–11); Collections Cttee, RCM, 2003–09; Council, Attingham Trust, 2010–. Trustee: Household Cavalry Mus., 2003–11; Art Fund (formerly NACF), 2005–15; Royal Yacht Britannia Trust, 2007–; City & Guilds of London Art Sch., 2008–; Historic Royal Palaces, 2010–17. FSA 2006. *Publications:* guidebooks to Penrhyn Castle, Stowe Landscape Garden, Cliveden, Chastleton, Clarence House, Buckingham Palace, Windsor Castle; contribs to exhibn catalogues and learned jls. *Recreations:* gardening, music, cricket, family.

**MARSDEN, Paul William Barry;** Business Systems Manager, BAM Nuttall, since 2019; *b* 18 March 1968; *s* of Thomas Darlington Marsden and Audrey Marsden; *m* 1994, Michelle Sarah Bayley (*née* Somerville). (marr. diss. 2005); two *s*; *m* 2009, Elena Sirkina; one step *d*. *Educ:* Open Univ. (Dip. Mgt 1995); Newcastle Coll. (Dip. Business Excellence 2000). Quality Manager: Taylor Woodrow, 1990–94; NatWest Bank, 1994–96; Mitel Telecom, 1996–97. MP (Lab, 1997–2001, Lib Dem 2001–05, Lab, 2005) Shrewsbury and Atcham. Lib Dem spokesman on health, 2002–03, on transport, 2003–05. Mem., Select Cttee on Agric., 1997–2001, on Transport, 2003–05; Chairman: All Party Gp on Mgt, 1998; Equal Access to Cancer Care Parly Cttee, 2000–01; Jt Chair, All Party Parly Road Safety Gp, 2003–04; Associate Life Mem., Inter-Parly Union All Party Gp, 1997. Business consultant and writer, 2005–07; Dir of Policy, British Union for the Abolition of Vivisection, 2007–08; Chief Exec., Painting and Decorating Assoc., 2008–10; Dir, British Security Ind. Assoc., 2010–12; business consultant, 2012–14; Gp SHEQ Systems Manager, Keepmoat Ltd, 2014–15; Hd, Health and Safety, Envmt and Quality, MWH Global, 2015–16; Quality Develt Manager, MBDA, 2016; Hd, Quality, Horizon Nuclear Power, 2017–18. Mem., Continuity and Resilience Cttee, BSI, 2016–. Vice President: Offa's Dyke Assoc., 1997–2005; Heart of Wales Travellers' Assoc., 1997–2005. Member: Shropshire Chamber of Commerce, Trng & Enterprise, 1997–2005; Agric. & Rural Economy Cttee, CLA, 1997–2001; Assoc. of Former MPs, 2010–. Member: DIAL Shropshire, Telford and Wrekin, 2003–05; Shrewsbury and Newport Canals Trust, 2003–05. Dir, Friends of Harmers Wood Trust Ltd, 2015–. Hon. Pres., W Midlands Lib Dem Youth and Students, 2003–05. FCMI (MIMgt 1996); MInstD 2002; Member: Chartered Quality Inst. (CQP), 2014; Eur. Orgn for Quality, 2014; British Standards Soc., 2015. Big Issue Hero of the Year Award, 2001. *Publications:* (contrib.) Voices for Peace, 2001; The Black Friars of Shrewsbury, 2006; Digital Quality Management in Construction, 2019. *Recreations:* history, gardening, politics, family, reading, hill-walking. *E:* paul.marsden1968@gmail.com. *W:* www.twitter.com/paulwbmarsden.

**MARSDEN, Rear-Adm. Peter Nicholas**; *b* 29 June 1932; *s* of Dr James Pickford Marsden and Evelyn (*née* Holman); *m* 1956, Jean Elizabeth Mather; two *s* one *d*. *Educ*: Felsted Sch., Essex. Joined RN, 1950; Commander, 1968; Captain, 1976; Commodore, Admiralty Interview Bd, 1983–84; Sen. Naval Mem., DS, RCDS, 1985–88. Exec. Dir, 21st Century Trust, 1989–92. *Recreations*: golf, gardening. *Address*: c/o National Westminster Bank, Standishgate, Wigan, Lancs WN1 1UE.
See also Sir J. M. Marsden.

**MARSDEN, Dr Philip Bernard**; Deputy Chair, Enforcement Decision Making Committee, Bank of England, since 2018; *b* Rinteln, Germany, 20 Nov. 1965; *s* of Bernard and Patricia Marsden; *m* 1990, Rona; one *s* one *d*. *Educ*: Univ. of Toronto (BA; LLB); Univ. of Leicester (LLM); Univ. of Oxford (DPhil 1999). Official, Competition Bureau, Canada, 1994–96; Competition Lawyer, Linklaters, 1999–2003; Founding Partner and Dir, WTI Advrs Ltd, 2003–10; Dir and Sen. Res. Fellow, British Inst. of Internat. and Comparative Law, 2003–14. Member: Bd, OFT, 2006–14; Financial Conduct Authy, 2016–; Dep. Panel Chair, CMA, 2014–18. Prof. of Law and Econs, Coll. of Europe, 2008–. Ed., Eur. Competition Jl, 2003–. *Publications*: A Competition Policy for the WTO, 2003; (ed) Handbook of Research in Trans-Atlantic Antitrust, 2005. *Recreation*: ultra running. *E*: philip.marsden@bankofengland.gsi.gov.uk. *Club*: Athenæum.

**MARSDEN, Dame Rosalind (Mary)**, DCMG 2010 (CMG 2003); DPhil; HM Diplomatic Service, retired; Ambassador to Sudan, 2007–10; European Union Special Representative for Sudan and South Sudan, 2010–13; *b* 1950; *d* of late Major Walter Stancliffe Marsden and Winifred Howells. *Educ*: Woking County Grammar Sch. for Girls; Somerville Coll., Oxford (BA 1st Cl. Hons Mod. Hist.; Hon. Fellow); St Antony's Coll., Oxford (DPhil). Joined FCO, 1974; Tokyo, 1976–80; Policy Planning Staff, 1980–82; EC Dept (Internal), 1983–84; Bonn, 1985–88; Hong Kong Dept, 1989–91; on secondment to National Westminster Bank Gp, 1991–93; Political Counsellor, Tokyo, 1993–96; Hd, UN Dept, 1996–99, Dir, Asia-Pacific, 1999–2003, FCO; Ambassador to Afghanistan, 2003–06; Consul-Gen., Basra, 2006–07. Associate Fellow, RIIA; Sen. Advr, Centre for Humanity Dialogue. Mem., Adv. Bd, Concordis Internat. Fellow, Rift Valley Inst. Trustee: Conciliation Resources; Waging Peace; Friends of Ibba Girls' Sch. *Recreations*: mountain walking, reading, travel. *E*: rosalindmarsden1@gmail.com.

**MARSDEN, Susan**; campaigner for legal and consumer rights and for the environment; *b* 6 Dec. 1931; *d* of late John Marsden-Smedley and Agatha (*née* Bethell). *Educ*: Downe House Sch.; Girton Coll., Cambridge (BA). Called to the Bar, Middle Temple, 1957. Worked in consumer organisations in Britain and US, 1957–70; Co-founder, 1972, Exec. Dir, 1972–78, and Course Dir, 1978–81, Legal Action Gp (Editor, LAG Bulletin, 1972–78); Sec., Public Sector Liaison, RIBA, 1981–84; Asst Dir, Nat. Assoc. of CAB, 1985–86; part-time Chairman: Social Security Appeal Tribunals (Leeds), 1987–97; Disability Appeal Tribunals, 1992–97. Chair, Greater London CAB Service, 1979–85; Member: Council, National Assoc. of CAB, 1980–84; Royal Commn on Legal Services, 1976–79; Yorks Regional Rivers Adv. Cttee, Nat. Rivers Authority, 1989–96; Council, Leeds Civic Trust, 1989–92. Chair, 1988–93, Trustee, 1998–2004, EYE on the Aire. Sec., Access Cttee, West Riding Ramblers' Assoc., 2001–11. *Publications*: Justice Out of Reach, a case for Small Claims Courts, 1969. *Recreations*: conservation along the River Aire, tree planting and preservation, gardening, walking, looking at modern buildings. *Address*: 28 Newlay Lane, Horsforth, Leeds LS18 4LE. *T*: (0113) 258 0936.

**MARSDEN, Sir Tadgh Orlando Denton**, 5th Bt *cr* 1924, of Grimsby, co. Lincoln; *b* 25 Dec. 1990; *s* of Sir Simon Neville Llewelyn Marsden, 4th Bt and of Caroline Marsden (*née* Stanton); *S* father, 2012, but his name does not appear on the Official Roll of the Baronetage.

**MARSDEN, Prof. Terry Keith**, PhD; Professor of Environmental Policy and Planning, since 1995, Dean of Graduate Studies, since 2008, and Director, Sustainable Places Research Institute, since 2010, Cardiff University; *b* 19 Oct. 1954; *s* of Terence Frederick and Kathleen Marsden; *m* 1982, Mary Anne Speakman; one *s* one *d*. *Educ*: Eccleshall Sec. Mod. Sch., Staffs; Univ. of Hull (BA Hons 1st Cl. Geog. and Sociol. 1976; PhD 1980). MRTPI 1998. Sen. and Principal Lectr in Planning, S Bank Poly., London, 1983–90; Co-Dir, Rural Studies Res. Centre and ESRC Countryside Change Centre, UCL, 1988–93; Reader in Human Geog., Univ. of Hull, 1993–94; Cardiff University: Hd, Sch. of City and Regl Planning, 1999–2009; Dir, Res. and Graduate Sch. in the Social Scis, 2001–02; Mem. Bd, Regeneration Inst., 2000–; Dep. Pro-Vice Chancellor (Res.), 2005–10; Co-Dir, Centre for Business Relationships, Accountability, Sustainability and Society (ESRC Res. Centre), 2002–13. Visiting Professor: Dept of Rural Sociol., Univ. of Wisconsin-Madison, 1990; Econs and Sociol., Univ. of Pernambuco, Brazil, 1993, 1995, 2003; Vis. Internat. Reader in European rural develt, Swedish Sch. of Soc. Scis, Univ. of Helsinki, 2001–03. Special Advisor: Welsh Affairs Select Cttee, 1997–98, 2001; on rural affairs for Nat. Assembly of Wales, 2000–01. Co-Editor, Jl of Environmental Policy and Planning, 1999–. *Publications*: (ed jtly) Critical Perspectives on Rural Change, 6 vols, 1990–94; Constructing the Countryside, 1993; Reconstituting Rurality, 1995; The Condition of Sustainability, 1999; Consuming Interests: the social provision of foods, 2000; (jtly) Worlds of Food, 2006; (ed jtly) The Handbook of Rural Studies, 2006; over 100 refereed jl articles. *Recreations*: running, cycling, squash, gardening, topographical antiquarian books. *Address*: Cardiff School of Planning and Geography, Glamorgan Building, King Edward VII Avenue, Cardiff CF10 3WA. *T*: (029) 2087 5736, *Fax*: (029) 2087 4845. *E*: MarsdenTK@cardiff.ac.uk.

**MARSDEN, William**, CMG 1991; HM Diplomatic Service, retired; conservationist; *b* 15 Sept. 1940; *s* of Christopher Marsden and Ruth (*née* Kershaw); *m* 1964, Kaia Collingham; one *s* one *d*. *Educ*: Winchester Coll.; Lawrenceville Sch., USA; Trinity Coll., Cambridge (MA); London Univ. (BSc Econs). FO, 1962–64; UK Delegn to NATO, 1964–66; Rome, 1966–69; seconded as Asst to Gen. Manager, Joseph Lucas Ltd, 1970; First Sec., FCO, 1971–76; First Sec. and Cultural Attaché, Moscow, 1976–79; Asst Head, European Community Dept, FCO, 1979–81; Counsellor, UK Representation to EEC, 1981–85; Head, E Africa Dept, FCO, and Comr, British Indian Ocean Territory, 1985–88; Ambassador to Costa Rica, and concurrently Ambassador to Nicaragua, 1989–92; Minister (Trade), Washington, 1992–94; Asst Under-Sec. of State, later Dir, (Americas), FCO, 1994–97; Ambassador to Argentina, 1997–2000. Chairman: Diplomatic Service Assoc., 1987–88; Anglo-Central American Soc., 2003–05. Chm., Chagos Conservation Trust, 2002–11. Internat. Advr, Coiba World Heritage Project, 2003–08. Counsellor, ESU, 2012–. Trustee, World Cancer Res. Fund, 2002–08. *Address*: Highwood, Castlegate, Pulborough, W Sussex RH20 2NJ. *T*: (020) 7233 9538.

**MARSDEN THOMAS, Anne**, MBE 2015; organist, organ teacher, author; Director of Music, St Giles Cripplegate Church, Barbican, since 1982; *b* Stanmore, 23 Sept. 1948; *d* of William Marsden Thomas and Margaret Helen Forbes Thomas; *m* 1992, Dr Brian Solomons. *Educ*: Mount Sch., Mill Hill; Copthall Co. Grammar Sch.; Royal Acad. Music (BMus). LRAM, ARAM; Dip. RAM; ARCM. FRCO 1971; FRSCM 1991. Teacher of Music (part-time): Orange Hill Comprehensive Sch., 1974–75; Arts Educnl Sch., 1975–90; Founder/Dir, St Giles Internat. Organ Sch., 1992–2012; Hd, Organ Sch., RCO Acad., 2012–16; teacher, Royal Acad. of Music, 2014–. Liveryman, Musicians' Co., 2015. *Publications*: Organ Practice, 1993; (with A. E. Smoot) The Church Year, 1996; A Graded Anthology for Organ, Book 1: a practical guide to playing the organ, 1997, Books 2–5, 1997; The Organist's Hymnbook, 2000; Oxford Service Music for Organ, Books 1–6, 2010–11; Pedalling for Organists, 2014; Oxford Bach Books for Organ, Books 1–5, 2014; (with Dr Frederick Stocken) Graded Keyboard Musicianship, 2017. *Recreations*: listening to music, sewing. *Address*: 305 Gilbert House, Barbican, EC2Y 8BD. *T*: 07785 533799. *E*: AMT@organschool.com.

**MARSH, Andrew David**, QPM 2018; Chief Constable, Avon and Somerset Constabulary, since 2016; *b* Liverpool, 20 March 1966; *s* of John David Marsh and Carol Marsh (*née* Whipple, now O'Brien); *m* 1990, Nikki Watson; two *d*. *Educ*: Newquay Tretherras Sch., Cornwall; Univ. of Liverpool (BSc Hons Geog. 1987). Joined Avon and Som Constabulary, 1987; Comdr, S Bristol/E Som, 2002–06; Assistant Chief Constable: Wilts Police, 2007–09; Avon and Som Constabulary, 2009–10; Dep. Chief Constable, 2010–13, Chief Constable, 2013–16, Hants Constabulary. *Recreations*: rowing, fly fishing. *Address*: Avon and Somerset Constabulary, PO Box 37, Valley Road, Portishead, Bristol BS20 8QJ.

**MARSH, Barrie**; *see* Marsh, G. B.

**MARSH, David Wayne**, CBE 2000; Co-Founder, 2010, and Chairman, since 2018, Official Monetary and Financial Institutions Forum (Managing Director, 2014–18); *b* Shoreham, Sussex, 30 July 1952; *s* of Dennis and Marguerite Marsh; *m* 1974, Veronika Dangelmayer; two *d*. *Educ*: Hove Grammar Sch.; Queen's Coll., Oxford (BA). With Reuters, 1973–78; FT, 1978–95 (latterly Eur. Ed.); Dir, Eur. Strategy, Robert Fleming, 1995–99; Vice Chm., Hawkpoint Partners, 1999–2001; Man. Dir, London, Droege Mgt Consultants, 2002–05; Dir, then Chm., London and Oxford Capital Mkts, 2005–09. Member: Bd, German British Forum, 1995–2016; Adv. Bd, Centre for Eur. Reform, 1998–2016; Bd, British Chamber of Commerce in Germany, 2010–; Bd, Henderson Eurotrust, 2011–. Honorary Professor: Univ. of Birmingham, 1998; Univ. of Sheffield, 2013; KCL, 2014; Hon. Fellow, S Bank Univ., 1997. Order of Merit (Germany), 2003. *Publications*: The Germans: rich, bothered and divided, 1989, 2nd edn 1990; Germany and Europe: the crisis of unity, 1995; The Bundesbank: the Bank that rules Europe, 1992, 2nd edn 1993; The Euro: the politics of the new global currency, 2009, 2nd edn 2011; Europe's Deadlock: how to solve the Euro crisis and why it won't happen, 2013; (with W. Keegan and R. Roberts) Six Days in September - Black Wednesday, Brexit and the Making of Europe, 2017. *Recreations*: tennis, talking and listening, travel. *Address*: Official Monetary and Financial Institutions Forum, 30 Crown Place, EC2A 4EB. *E*: david.marsh@omfif.org. *Club*: Reform.

**MARSH, Derek Richard**, CVO 1999; Senior Consultant, IRC Ltd, Seoul, since 2009; Director, Marsh Advisers (Asia) Ltd, since 2010; *b* 17 Sept. 1946; *s* of Reginald and Minnie Marsh; *m* 1969, Frances Anne Roberts; one *s* one *d*. *Educ*: Queen's Coll., Oxford (Schol.; MA 1973). Ministry of Defence: Asst Principal, 1968–72; Asst Private Sec. to Minister of State for Defence, 1973–74; Principal, 1974–78; ndc, 1975; Admin. Sec., Sovereign Base Areas, Cyprus, 1978–81; Asst Sec., 1982–86; rcds 1987; Department of Trade and Industry: Head of Air 1 and 2, 1988–91; Director: Companies House, 1991–93; Projects Export Promotion, 1994–97; Dep. Hd of Mission and Consul-Gen., Republic of Korea, 1997–2001; Dir Gen., British Trade and Cultural Office, Taipei, 2002–05. Adviser: UK Trade and Investment, 2006; iFafa Tech (Manila), 2006–08. Non-executive Director: Felixstowe Dock and Railway Co., 1990–91; Bovis Homes Ltd, 1992–93; Haike Chemical Gp Ltd, 2007–13; China Food Co. plc, 2007–11; Auhua Clean Energy plc, 2012–14; Marchwood Mgt (Chichester) Ltd, 2013–16; Pressfit Internat. Enterprise Ltd (Hong Kong), 2014–15; DagangHalal plc, 2017–18; non-exec. Chm., Pressfit Hldgs plc, 2014–15. Vice Chm., British Korean Soc., 2015–17. *Recreations*: travel, reading, walking.

**MARSH, Rt Rev. Edward Frank**; Bishop of Central Newfoundland, 1990–2000; Diocesan Administrator, Diocese of Central Newfoundland, 2005; *b* 25 Oct. 1935; *m* 1962, Emma Marsh; one *s* two *d*. *Educ*: Dalhousie Univ., NS (BCom 1956); Univ. of Newfoundland (BA 1960); Queen's Coll., Newfoundland (LTh 1961; BD 1969). Deacon 1959, priest 1960; Curate, Corner Brook, 1959–63; Incumbent, Harbour Breton, 1963–69; Curate, Wickford, 1969–71; Incumbent, Indian Bay, 1971–73; Curate, St John the Baptist Cathedral, St John's, 1973–77; Rector of Cartwright, Dio. of East Newfoundland, 1977–81; Rector, Holy Trinity, Grand Falls, 1981–90.

**MARSH, Felicity Margaret Sue**; *see* Goodey, F. M. S.

**MARSH, Rev. (Francis) John**, DPhil; Archdeacon of Blackburn, 1996–2001; Priest in Charge, St Michael the Archangel, Emley and St James the Great, Flockton, and Hon. Diocesan Training Officer, 2011–17; *b* 3 July 1947; *s* of William Frederick and Helena Mary Marsh; *m* 1974, Gillian Popely; two *d*. *Educ*: York Univ. (BA 1969; DPhil 1976); Univ. of Cambridge (CTh 1975). ATCL 1965; ARCM 1966; ARCO 1971. Ordained deacon, 1975, priest, 1976; Assistant Curate: St Matthew's, Cambridge, 1975–78; Christ Church, Pitsmoor, Sheffield, 1979–81; Dir of Pastoral Trng, St Thomas', Crookes, Sheffield, 1981–85; Vicar, Christ Church, South Ossett, Wakefield, 1985–96. Rural Dean of Dewsbury, 1993–96. Mem., Gen. Synod of C of E, 1990–96, 1997–2001. Chm. Trustees, Anglican Renewal Ministries, 1989–2001. Mem., Adv. Bd, RSCM, 2000–01. *Address*: Bark House Mews, Bark Close, Shelley, Huddersfield HD8 8JR. *T*: (01484) 981530.

**MARSH, (Graham) Barrie**, FCIArb; solicitor; Partner, Mace & Jones, Solicitors, Liverpool and Manchester, 1959–99 (Senior Partner, 1980–97); *b* 18 July 1935; *s* of Ernest Heaps Marsh and Laura Greenhalgh Marsh; *m* 1961, Nancy Smith; one *s* two *d*. *Educ*: Bury Grammar Sch.; Loughborough Grammar Sch.; Liverpool Univ. (LLB Hons). FCIArb 1982. Admitted as solicitor, 1957. Nat. Chm., Young Solicitors Gp, Law Soc., 1975; President: Liverpool Law Soc., 1978–79; Solicitors' Disciplinary Tribunal, 1988–2001; Liverpool Publicity Assoc., 1980; part-time Chm., Appeals Service, 1989–2008. Chairman: Merseyside Chamber of Commerce and Industry, 1984–86; Radio City PLC, 1988–91. Non-exec. Dir, Liverpool HA, 1996–2000. Trustee, Nat. Museums and Galls on Merseyside, 1998–2006. Hon. Belgian Consul, Liverpool, and for NW, 1987–96. *Publications*: Employer and Employee: a complete and practical guide to the modern law of employment, 1977, 3rd edn 1990; contribs to legal and personnel jls on all aspects of employment law and industrial relations. *Recreations*: Liverpool Football Club, bird-watching, hill-walking. *Address*: Calmer Hey, Benty Heath Lane, Willaston, South Wirral CH64 1SA. *T*: (0151) 327 4863. *E*: g.barrie.marsh@btinternet.com.

**MARSH, Henry Thomas**, CBE 2010; FRCS; Consultant Neurosurgeon, St George's Hospital (formerly Atkinson Morley Hospital), 1987–2015; *b* Oxford, 5 March 1950; *s* of Norman Stayner Marsh and Christiane Christinnecke; *m* 2004, Kate Fox; one *s* two *d* by a previous marriage. *Educ*: Westminster Sch.; University Coll., Oxford (BA PPE 1973); Royal Free Hosp. Sch. of Medicine, Univ. of London (MB BS Hons 1979). FRCS 1984. Neurosurgical Registrar, Royal Free Hosp., 1982–84; Sen. Registrar, Nat. Hosp. for Nervous Diseases and Gt Ormond St Hosp., 1984–87. Clin. Prof. of Neurosurgery, Univ. of Washington, Seattle, 1990–; Hon. Consultant Neurosurgeon: Royal Marsden Hosp., 1995–; University Hosp. of Wales, Cardiff, 1996–. Consultant, Internat. Neurosurgical Centre, Kiev, Ukraine, 1992– (featured in documentary The English Surgeon, 2008). Vis.

Fellow, LMH, Oxford, 2016–19. *Publications:* Do No Harm: stories of life, death and brain surgery, 2014; Admissions: a life in brain surgery, 2017; contrib. articles on neurosurgical topics to jls incl. British Jl Neurosurgery, Jl Neurol. and Neurosurgery. *Recreations:* furniture making, bee keeping.

**MARSH, Jean Lyndsey Torren,** OBE 2012; actress, writer; Artistic Director, Adelphi University Theatre, Long Island, New York, 1981–83; *b* 1 July 1934; *d* of late Henry Charles and of Emmeline Susannah Marsh; *m* 1955, Jon Devon Roland Pertwee (marr. diss. 1960; he *d* 1996). Began as child actress and dancer; *films:* Return to Oz; Willow; danced in Tales of Hoffmann, Where's Charley?, etc; Fatherland, 1995 (Cable Ace Award for Best Supporting Actress, 1996); acted in repertory companies: Huddersfield, Nottingham, etc; Broadway debut in Much Ado About Nothing, 1959; West End debut, Bird of Time, 1961; *stage:* Habeas Corpus, NY, 1975; The Importance of Being Earnest, 1977; Too True to be Good, 1977; Twelfth Night; Blithe Spirit; Whose Life is it Anyway?, NY, 1979; Uncle Vanya; On the Rocks; Pygmalion; Hamlet; The Chalk Garden; Blow Up does Dallas; The Old Country; Boeing, Boeing, Comedy, 2007; Portrait of a Lady, Th. Royal, Bath, 2008; *television:* series, Nine to Five; co-created and co-starred (Rose) in series Upstairs Downstairs, 1971–75 (Emmy, Best Actress, 1975); co-created series, The House of Eliott; Alexei Sayle Show; The Ghost Hunter (3 series); Bremner, Bird and Fortune; Most Mysterious Murder; Sense and Sensibility; Sensitive Skin; The Crooked House; actress: Upstairs Downstairs, 2010, 2012; *radio* incl. Bleak House, The Pier. Hon. DH Maryland Coll., NY, 1980. *Publications:* The Illuminated Language of Flowers, 1978; The House of Eliott, 1993, repr. 2011; Fiennders Keepers, 1996, repr. as Fiennders Abbey, 2011; Iris, 1999, repr. 2012; articles for Sunday Times, Washington Post, New York Times, Los Angeles Times, Daily Telegraph, Times. *Recreations:* walking, reading, cooking, eating, wine, music. *Address:* c/o Lesley Duff, Diamond Management, 31 Percy Street, W1T 2DD.

**MARSH, Dame Jilian Norma;** *see* Matheson, Dame J. N.

**MARSH, Rev. John;** *see* Marsh, Rev. F. J.

**MARSH, John Edward;** Associate Partner, Ernst & Young, since 2008; *b* 18 Dec. 1963; *s* of Keith and Margaret Marsh; *m* 1990, Karen Moors; three *d. Educ:* Ham Dingle Primary Sch., Stourbridge; King Edward VI Coll., Stourbridge; Univ. of Bristol (BA Hons Hist. 1985); Univ. of Warwick (MA Industrial Relns 1986). FCIPD 2006. Home Office, 1986–96, Pvte Sec. to Minister of State, 1994–96; Hd of Voluntary Sector Govt Spending, Dept of Nat. Heritage, 1996–97; Sect. Leader, Public Spending Directorate, HM Treasury, 1997–99; Home Office: Hd of Personnel Mgt, HM Prison Service, 1999–2003; Gp Dir of Human Resources, 2003–07; Dir, Civil Service Capability Gp, Cabinet Office, 2007–08. *Recreations:* football coaching, running, sports, eating out. *Address:* Ernst & Young, 1 More London Place, SE1 2AF.

**MARSH, Kevin John;** Director, OffspinMedia, since 2011; Executive Producer, 7 Digital, since 2017; *b* 14 Nov. 1954; *s* of John Marsh and Elizabeth Jill Marsh; *m* 1979, Melissa Sue Fletcher; one *s* one *d. Educ:* Doncaster Grammar Sch.; Christ Church, Oxford (MA). Joined BBC, 1978; Radio 4: Editor: PM, 1989–92; World at One, 1992–96; World at One and PM, 1996–98; launched Broadcasting House, 1998; Editor, Today, 2002–06; Exec. Editor, BBC Coll. of Journalism, 2006–11. Attended Salzburg Seminar, 1984; panelist and moderator, World Econ. Forum, Davos, 2004, 2005, 2006, Warsaw, 2005. Vis. Fellow, 2005–, Practitioner in Residence, 2013–, Bournemouth Univ. Alumnus, Prince of Wales Business and the Envmt Prog., 2005–. Columnist, Press Gazette, 2009–12. Consultant: Birzeit Univ., Palestine, 2013–16; Geneva Centre for Security Policy, 2012–16; Strategic Asset Recovery Initiative, Washington, 2013; Member, Editorial Board: British Journalism Rev., 2006–15; Jl Applied Journalism and Media Studies, 2012–. Mem., RIIA, 2005–. FRSA. Sony Radio Awards, 1991, 1992, 2003, 2004, 2005; Amnesty Internat. Media Award, 2001. *Publications:* (contrib.) Beyond Trust, 2008; Web Journalism: a new form of citizenship?, 2009; (contrib.) Afghanistan, War and the Media, 2010; (contrib.) Future Tools for Journalism, 2011; (contrib.) Investigative Journalism: dead or alive?, 2011; Stumbling Over Truth, 2012; (contrib.) Journalism: new challenges, 2013; Dust, 2015; (with John Williams) Strategic Communication, 2017; contrib. various articles to jls incl. Political Qly, British Journalism Rev., Jl Applied Journalism and Media Studies, NATO Defence Strategic Communications. *Recreations:* Rugby, opera, playing the lute. *E:* kevinjohnmarsh@gmail.com. *Clubs:* Royal Yachting Association, Wasps Rugby.

**MARSH, Prof. Mark Christopher Pakes,** PhD; Professor of Molecular Cell Biology, since 2000 and Director, Medical Research Council Laboratory for Molecular Cell Biology, since 2006, University College London; *b* Wokingham, Berks, 4 Aug. 1953; *s* of Justyn Marsh and Patricia Marsh; *m* 2000, Victoria Lewis (marr. diss. 2015); three *d. Educ:* Sir Joseph Williamson's Mathematical Sch., Rochester; University Coll. London (BSc Hons 1975; PhD 1979). Royal Soc. Postdoctoral Fellow, EMBL, Heidelberg, 1979–81; EMBO Postdoctoral Fellow, Yale Univ. Med. Sch., New Haven, 1981–85; Group Leader: Inst. of Cancer Res., London, 1985–91; MRC Lab. for Molecular Cell Biol., UCL, 1992–. Mem., EMBO, 2011–. *Publications:* (ed) Frontiers in Molecular Biology, 2001; (ed) Membrane Trafficking in Viral Replication: Current Topics in Microbiology and Immunology, Book 285, 2005; research papers in cell biological and virological jls. *Recreations:* cycling, walking, theatre, opera, cinema, music, reading, daughters and Suryadaya. *Address:* MRC Laboratory for Molecular Cell Biology, University College London, Gower Street, WC1E 6BT. *T:* (020) 7679 7802. *E:* m.marsh@ucl.ac.uk. *Club:* Medical Research (Mem., Exec. Cttee, 2016–).

**MARSH, Dame Mary (Elizabeth),** DBE 2007; Founding Director, Clore Social Leadership Programme, 2008–15; *b* 17 Aug. 1946; *d* of George Donald Falconer and Lesley Mary (*née* Wilson); *m* 1968, Juan Enrique Marsh (*d* 1999); four *s. Educ:* Birkenhead High Sch., GPDST; Univ. of Nottingham (BSc; Hon. Pres., Students Union, 2005–08); London Business Sch. (MBA). Teacher, Icknield High Sch., 1968; St Christopher School, Letchworth: teacher, 1969–72; Dep. Hd, 1980–90; Head: Queens' Sch., Watford, 1990–95; Holland Park Sch., 1995–2000; Dir and Chief Exec., NSPCC, 2000–08. Non-exec. Dir, HSBC Bank plc, 2009– (Mem., Optec Cttee, 2015–18); Mem., Corporate Sustainability Cttee, HSBC Hldgs Bd, 2009–13. Gov., London Business Sch., 2010– (Chair, Internat. Alumni Council, 2010–13); Mem., Asia Adv. Bd, Univ. of Nottingham, 2017–. Chair, Trustees, RCPCH, 2016–; Trustee, Teach First, 2017–. Dir, LSO Bd, 2016–. *Recreations:* music, reading, good company, swimming, walking in mountains and by the sea. *Address:* c/o London Business School, Sussex Place, Regent's Park, NW1 4SA. *Club:* Reform.

**MARSH, Matthew William Brooker;** Master of the High Court, Chancery Division, since 2012; Chief Chancery Master, since 2014; *b* London, 6 June 1953; *s* of Frederick and Elizabeth Marsh; *m* 1981, Andrea Stratford Collins; two *d. Educ:* Sevenoaks Sch.; Kingston Univ. (BA Hons Law). FCIArb 1990. With Sharpe Pritchard, 1975–77; admitted as solicitor, 1977; Stoneham Langton & Passmore, 1977–85; Collyer Bristow, 1985–2012. A Recorder, 2002–12. Hon. Bencher, Gray's Inn, 2016. *Publications:* (ed) Landlord and Tenant Factbook, 2005–11. *Recreations:* tennis, opera, cycling, theatre. *Address:* Royal Courts of Justice, 7 Rolls Building, Fetter Lane, EC4A 1NL. *Club:* Clapham Common All Weather Tennis.

**MARSH, Prof. Paul Rodney;** Professor of Finance, London Business School, 1985–2006, now Emeritus (Professor of Management and Finance, 1985–98, Esmée Fairbairn Professor of Finance, 1998–2002); *b* 19 Aug. 1947; *s* of Harold Marsh and Constance (*née* Miller); *m* 1971, Stephanie (*née* Simonow). *Educ:* Poole Grammar Sch.; London School of Economics (BScEcon, 1st Cl. Hons); London Business Sch. (PhD). Systems Analyst, Esso Petroleum, 1968–69; Scicon, 1970–71; London Business School, 1974–: Bank of England Res. Fellow, 1974–85; Dir, Sloan Fellowship Prog., 1980–83; non-exec. Dir, Centre for Management Develt, 1984–90; Mem. Gov. Body, 1986–90; Faculty Dean, 1987–90; Dep. Principal, 1989–90; Associate Dean, Finance Progs, 1993–2006. Member: CBI Task Force on City-Industry Relationships, 1986–88; Exec. Cttee, British Acad. of Management, 1986–88; FTSE Russell Jury of Appeal, 2012–17. Non-executive Director: M&G Investment Management Ltd, 1989–97; M&G Gp, 1998–99; Majedie Investments, 1999–2006; Aberforth Smaller Cos Trust, 2004–14 (Chm., 2010–14); Dir, Hoare Govett Indices Ltd, 1991–2011. Fellow, CFA Soc. (UK), 2015–. Gov. Examng Bd, Securities Inst., 1994–2002. *Publications:* Cases in Corporate Finance, 1988; Managing Strategic Investment Decisions, 1988; Accounting for Brands, 1989; Short-termism on Trial, 1990; The Millennium Book: a century of investment returns, 2000; Triumph of the Optimists, 2002; Numis (formerly HGSC) Smaller Companies Index, annually 1987–; (with E. Dimson) Global Investment Returns Yearbook, annually 2000–; numerous articles in Jl of Financial Econs, Jl of Finance, Jl of Business, Harvard Business Review, Jl of Inst. of Actuaries, Res. in Marketing, Mergers and Acquisitions, Financial Analysts Jl, Jl of Apples Corporate Finance, Long Range Planning, etc. *Recreations:* gardening, investment. *Address:* London Business School, Regent's Park, NW1 4SA. *T:* (020) 7000 7000. *E:* pmarsh@london.edu.

**MARSH, Peter Ronald;** Managing Director, Peter Marsh Consulting Ltd, since 2011; *b* Basingstoke, 27 Nov. 1969; *s* of Derek and Christine Marsh; civil partnership 2008, Robert Rees. *Educ:* Univ. of Newcastle upon Tyne (BA Hons Econ. and Geog. 1992); New Coll., Durham (CPFA 1996); Univ. of Bedford (PGCE 2012). Auditor, Dist Audit Durham and NE, 1992–96; Audit Manager, KPMG, 1996–97; Deputy Principal: Gateshead Coll., 1997–99; City & Islington Coll., 2000–05; Dir of Resources, 2005–07, Dep. Chief Exec., 2007–08, Housing Corp.; Chief Exec., Tenant Services Authy, 2008–10; Dep. Principal, Fareham Coll., 2012–15. Non-exec. Dir, RHP, 2011–. Trustee, Open Coll. Network London, 2001–11 (Chm., 2005–11). FRSA 2008. *Recreations:* family, sailing, garden. *Address:* Peter Marsh Consulting Ltd, 12 Southgate Street, Winchester SO23 9EF. *T:* (01962) 657157. *E:* peter@petermarshconsulting.com.

**MARSH, Richard St John Jeremy,** PhD; independent charity and travel consultant, since 2017; Director, Global Culture Tours Consultancy Ltd, since 2018; *b* 23 April 1960; *s* of late Gordon Victor Marsh; *m* 1984, Elizabeth Mary Mullins (marr. diss. 2006); one *s* one *d. Educ:* Trinity Sch. of John Whitgift; Keble Coll., Oxford (BA 1982; MA 1986); Coll. of the Resurrection, Mirfield; Durham Univ. (PhD 1991). Ordained deacon 1985, priest 1986; Curate, Grange St Andrew, Runcorn, 1985–87; Chaplain and Solway Fellow, UC, Durham, 1987–92; Asst Sec. for Ecum. Affairs to Abp of Canterbury, 1992–95, Sec., 1995–2001; Canon Residentiary and Dir, Internat. Study Centre, subseq. Canon Librarian and Dir of Educn, Canterbury Cathedral, 2001–05; Dir, Improving Accountability, Clarity and Transparency (ImpACT) Coalition, 2007–09; Chief Exec., Inst. for Food, Brain and Behaviour, 2010–17. Licensed to officiate, Dio. London, 1993–2001; Canon, Dio. Gibraltar in Europe, 1995–2001; Non-Res. Canon, Canterbury Cathedral, 1998–2001. Interim Dir, Intelligent Giving, 2009. Vis. Sen. Lectr, Canterbury Christchurch UC, 2003–05. Chm., St Augustine's Foundn, 2003. Trustee, Rye Arts Fest., 2015–17. Chm., Westport Family and Community Resource Centre, 2018–. FRSA. Licensed to Officiate, Dio. Tuam, Killala and Achonry, 2018–. *Publications:* Black Angels, 1998; (contrib.) Ink and Spirit, 2000; (with Katherine Marshall) Millennium Challenges for Development and Faith Institutions, 2003; (ed) Prayers from the East, 2004. *Recreations:* music, cooking. *Address:* The Yellow House, Kilsallagh Upper, Westport, Co. Mayo, Ireland. *T:* (353) 32451601, 07903 358918. *E:* richard@richardmarsh.org.

**MARSH, Roger,** OBE 2015; Senior Partner, Leeds Office, and Northern Leader, Government and Public Sector, PricewaterhouseCoopers, 2011–13; *b* 19 Sept. 1953; *s* of late Peter Marsh and of Connie Marsh; *m* 1st, 1981, Susan Smith (marr. diss. 2002); three *d*; 2nd, 2010, Sally Thomson; two *d. Educ:* Stockton C of E Grammar Sch.; Univ. of Leeds (BSc Hons Metallurgy 1976). FCA 1990. Price Waterhouse, subseq. PricewaterhouseCoopers: joined, 1976; Partner, 1988; latterly Sen. Business Recovery Partner, Leeds; on secondment as Dir-Gen., Strategic Finance and Ops, Cabinet Office, 2007–09 (Mem. Bd; Chm., Finance Cttee, 2008–09); Sen. Adv. Partner, Govt and Public Sector, 2009–11. Member: Insolvency Licensing Cttee, 1997–2004, Public Sector Adv. Bd, 2009–13, ICAEW; UK Firms Supervisory Bd, 2010–12; HS2 Growth Task Force, 2013–15; W Yorks Combined Authy, 2014–; Transport for the North Partnership Bd, 2015–. Non-exec. Chm., Leeds City Region Enterprise Partnership, 2013–; Chair: Northern Powerhouse Investment Fund Strategic Oversight Bd, 2016–; NP11, 2018–; Expert Challenge Panel, Williams Rev., 2018–. Mem. Council, Leeds Univ., 2013–. Chair, Piece Hall Trust, 2017–; Trustee, Iraq/Afghanistan Meml Project, 2015–17. Mem. Council, IoD, 2016–. DUniv Huddersfield, 2017. *Recreations:* family, fine wines. *Address:* 5 Wedgewood Grove, Roundhay, Leeds LS8 1EG. *E:* r.marsh1953@btinternet.com.

**MARSH, Sarah-Jane;** Chief Executive, Birmingham Women's and Children's NHS Foundation Trust, since 2017 (Chief Executive: Birmingham Children's Hospital NHS Trust, 2009–17; Birmingham Women's NHS Foundation Trust, 2015–17); *b* Dudley, 1 Sept. 1976; *d* of Geoffrey Marsh and Mary Marsh; *m* 2010, Sir David Nicholson, KCB, CBE; one *s* one *d. Educ:* Lancaster Univ. (BA Hons Hist. 1998); Univ. of Birmingham (MA Russian and Eastern Eur. Studies 1999; MSc (distinction) Health Mgt 2004). NHS Graduate Mgt Trng Scheme, 2000–02; Dir's Asst, DoH, 2002–03; Walsall Hospital NHS Trust: Hd, Planning and Develt, 2003–05; Dir, Planning and Productivity, 2003–07; Chief Operating Officer, Birmingham Children's Hosp., 2007–09. *Recreations:* history and politics, reading, swimming, running around after two children. *Address:* Birmingham Women's and Children's NHS Foundation Trust, Steelhouse Lane, Birmingham B4 6NH. *T:* (0121) 333 8406. *E:* sarahjane.marsh@nhs.net.

**MARSH, Susanna;** *see* Nicklin, S.

**MARSHALL, Dr Adam;** Director General, British Chambers of Commerce, since 2016; *b* Washington, DC, 30 July 1978; *s* of Bennett and Dobra Marshall; *m* 2008, Hector Boix-Perales; one *d. Educ:* Yale Univ. (BA 2000); Clare Coll., Cambridge (MPhil 2001; PhD 2004). Industry Prog. Officer, Cambridge-MIT Inst., 2003–04; Res. Fellow, IPPR, 2004–05; Sen. Researcher, 2005–07, Hd, Policy and Develt, 2007–09, Centre for Cities; Exec. Dir, Policy and Ext. Affairs, British Chambers of Commerce, 2009–16. Mem., Gen. Council, World Chambers Fedn, 2017–. Trustee, Industry and Parlt Trust, 2018–. *Address:* British Chambers of Commerce, 65 Petty France, SW1H 9EU. *T:* (020) 7654 5800. *E:* a.marshall@britishchambers.org.uk.

**MARSHALL, Alan Ralph;** Managing Director, ARM Educational Consultants Ltd, 1991–94; *b* 27 July 1931; *s* of Ralph Marshall and Mabel Mills; *m* 1958, Caterina Gattico; one *s* one *d. Educ:* Shoreditch College (Teacher's Cert. 1953); London Univ. (Dip Ed 1959; MPhil 1965); Eastern Washington State Univ. (MEd 1964); Stanford Univ. (MA 1969).

Teacher, schools in UK and USA, 1954–62; Lectr, Shoreditch Coll., 1962–68; Vis. Prof., Eastern Washington State Univ., 1964–65; Field Dir, Project Technology, Schools Council, 1970–72; Editor, Nat. Centre for School Technology, 1972–73; Course Team Chm., Open Univ., 1973–76; HM Inspector, DES, 1976–91, HM Chief Inspector of Schools, 1985–91. Hon. DEd CNAA, 1990. *Publications*: (ed) School Technology in Action, 1974; (with G. T. Page and J. B. Thomas) International Dictionary of Education, 1977; Giving Substance to a Vision, 1990; articles in jls. *Recreations*: painting, reading.

**MARSHALL, Alexander John,** CBE 2018; QPM 2009; General Manager, Anti-Corruption Unit, International Cricket Council, since 2017; *b* Barnet, 7 Dec. 1961; *s* of Clifford and Patricia Marshall; partner, Katherine Pears; two *s* one *d*. *Educ*: Wolfson Coll. and Inst. of Criminol., Univ. of Cambridge (MA Criminol. 2006). Constable to Chief Inspector, Metropolitan Police, 1980–2000; Superintendent to Chief Superintendent, Cambridge Constabulary, 2000–04; Asst Chief Constable, 2004–07, Dep. Chief Constable, 2007–08, Thames Valley Police; Chief Constable, Hants Constabulary, 2008–13; Chief Exec., Coll. of Policing, 2013–17. Cropwood Fellow, Univ. of Cambridge, 1999. *Recreations*: old cars, cricket, exercise. *Address*: International Cricket Council, Street 69, Dubai Sports City, Sheikh Mohammed Bin Zayed Road, PO Box 500 070, Dubai, UAE.

**MARSHALL, Prof. Sir (Arthur) Harold,** KNZM 2009 (DCNZM 2008); PhD; FRSNZ 1995; Group Consultant, Marshall Day Acoustics Ltd, since 1991; principal acoustical designer for concert halls; *b* Auckland, NZ, 15 Sept. 1931; *s* of Arthur Cecil Marshall and Flossie May Marshall; *m* 1956, Shirley Anne Lindsey (*d* 2016); four *s*. *Educ*: King's Coll., Auckland; Auckland Univ. (BArch Hons; BSc Physics and Maths 1956); Inst. of Sound and Vibration Res., Southampton Univ. (PhD 1967). FNZIA 1973; FRAIA 1973. DAAD Fellow, Akademie der Bildenden Künste, Munich, 1958; Sen. Lectr in Architecture, Univ. of Auckland, 1961–67; Sen. Lectr in Building Sci., 1967–70, Associate Prof. in Architecture, 1970–72, Univ. of WA; University of Auckland: Prof. of Architecture, 1973–86; Head, Acoustics Res. Centre, 1983–97; Prof. (Personal Chair), 1986–97. Research Fellow: III Physikalisches Inst., Goettingen, 1977–78; PTB Braunschweig; NRCC. Co-Founder, Marshall Day Associates (Acoustics), 1980; professional work includes: Christchurch Town Hall, NZ, 1972; Michael Fowler Centre, NZ, 1983; Segerstrom Hall, Calif, 1986; Hong Kong Cultural Centre, 1989; Guangzhou Opera House, 2011; La Philharmonie de Paris, 2015. Fellow: Acoustical Soc. of America, 1978; NZ Acoustical Soc., 2013. Sabine Medal, Acoustical Soc. of America, 1994; Pickering Medal, RSNZ, 2013; Rayleigh Medal, Inst. of Acoustics (UK), 2015. *Publications*: (contrib.) Encyclopedia of Acoustics, 1997; (contrib.) Encyclopedia of Building Technology, 1988; contribs to Jl Sound and Vibration, Applied Acoustics, Jl Acoustical Soc. America, AA Jl, Acustica, Jl Audio Engrg Soc., Architecture NZ, Arch. Sci. Rev.; contribs to Landfall, Sport (poetry jls). *Recreations*: fly fishing, poetry, 16 grandchildren and five great-granddaughters. *E*: hmarshall1855@gmail.com.

**MARSHALL, Arthur Stirling-Maxwell,** CBE 1986 (OBE 1979); HM Diplomatic Service, retired; *b* 29 Jan. 1929; *s* of Victor Stirling-Maxwell Marshall and Jeannie Theodora Hunter; *m* 1st, 1955, Eleni Kapralou, Athens (*d* 1969); one *s* two *d*; 2nd, 1985, Cheryl Mary Hookens, Madras; one *d*. *Educ*: Daniel Stewart's Coll., Edinburgh. Served Royal Navy, 1947–59. Foreign Office, 1959; Middle East Centre for Arab Studies, Lebanon, 1959–61; Political Officer, British Political Agency, Bahrain and Registrar of HBM Court for Bahrain, 1961–64; Attaché, Athens, 1964–67; Information Officer, Rabat, Morocco, 1967–69; Commercial Secretary: Nicosia, Cyprus, 1970–75; Kuwait, 1975–79; Deputy High Commissioner, Madras, 1980–83; Counsellor, Kuwait, 1983–85; Ambassador to People's Democratic Republic of Yemen, 1986–89. *Recreations*: music, nature. *Address*: 2 The Larches, Rickmansworth Road, Northwood, Middx HA6 2QY.

**MARSHALL, Prof. Barry James,** AC 2007; FRS 1999; FRACP; Hon. Clinical Professor of Microbiology, University of Western Australia, since 2000; Director, since 2005, and Scientific Officer, since 2013, Ondek Pty Ltd (Chief Executive Officer, 2005–13); *b* 30 Sept. 1951; *s* of Robert and Marjorie Marshall; *m* 1972, Adrienne Joyce Feldman; one *s* three *d*. *Educ*: Univ. of Western Australia (MB BS). FRACP 1983. Clinical asst (res.), Gastroenterology Dept, Royal Perth Hosp., 1985–86; University of Virginia: Res. Fellow in Medicine, Div. of Gastroenterology, 1986–87; Asst Prof. of Medicine, 1988–92, Associate Prof., 1992, Prof., 1993; Clinical Prof., 1993–96; Prof. of Res. in Internal Medicine, 1996–2000; Clinical Prof. of Medicine, 1997–2000, NH&MRC Burnet Fellow and Clinical Prof. of Medicine, 1998–2000, Univ. of WA. Hon. Res. Fellow in Gastroenterology, Sir Charles Gairdner Hosp., 1997. (Jtly) Warren Alpert Prize, Harvard Med. Sch., 1995; Albert Lasker Award, NYC, 1995; (jtly) Paul Ehrlich Prize, Frankfurt, 1997; Kilby Prize, Dallas, 1997; Dr A. H. Heineken Prize for Medicine, Amsterdam, 1998; Florey Medal, Aust. Inst. for Pol Sci., Canberra, 1998; Buchanan Medal, Royal Soc., 1998; Benjamin Franklin Medal for Life Sci., Philadelphia, 1999; Prince Mahidol Award, 2001; (jtly) Nobel Prize in Physiology or Medicine, 2005. *Publications*: Campylobacter pylori, 1988; Helicobacter pylori in peptic ulceration and gastritis, 1991; Helicobacter Pylori, 1990 (Proc. 2nd Internat. Symposium), 1991; Gastroenterology Clinics of North America, 2000; contribs to jls incl. The Lancet, Amer. Jl Gastroenterol., Jl Infectious Diseases, Jl Nuclear Medicine, Jl Clinical Pathol., Digestive Diseases and Scis, Gastroenterol., Scandinavian Jl Gastroenterol., Jl Clinical Microbiol., Alimentary Pharmacol. and Therapeutics. *Recreations*: computers, photography, electronics. *Address*: Helicobacter Pylori Research Laboratory, Department of Microbiology, University of Western Australia, QE2 Medical Centre, Nedlands, WA 6009, Australia. *T*: (8) 93464815.

**MARSHALL, Catriona Frances;** Founder, Transforming Lives, since 2017; *b* Glasgow, 1 March 1967; *d* of Dr David Land and Moira McLean (*née* O'Neill); *m* 2003, Michael Edwin Marshall. *Educ*: Shawlands Acad., Glasgow; Univ. of Dundee (LLB Law). Mktg Manager, Mars Confectionery, 1993–95; Own Brand Dir for UK and Germany, Asda Stores, 1995–2003; Trading and Mktg Dir, Pets at Home, 2003–11; CEO, Hobbycraft, 2011–17; owner, Running Bear Sports Ltd. Chm., Wilmslow Running Fest. *Recreations*: club runner (Wilmslow Running Club), cycling, support for disadvantaged. *Address*: Transforming Lives, Brick Bank, Brick Bank Lane, Knutsford, Cheshire WA16 9LY.

**MARSHALL, Hon. (Cedric) Russell,** CNZM 2001; President, New Zealand Institute of International Affairs, 2007–11; High Commissioner for New Zealand in the United Kingdom, also accredited to Nigeria, and as Ambassador of New Zealand to Ireland, 2002–05; *b* 15 Feb. 1936; *s* of Cedric Thomas Marshall and Gladys Margaret Marshall (*née* Hopley); *m* 1961, Barbara May Watson; two *s* one *d* (and one *s* one *d* decd). *Educ*: Nelson Coll.; Christchurch Teachers' Coll.; Auckland Univ. (DipTeaching, 1966); BA Victoria Univ., 1992. Primary teacher, Nelson, 1955–56; Trinity Methodist Theol Coll., 1958–60; Methodist Minister: Christchurch, Spreydon, 1960–66; Masterton, 1967–71; teacher, Wanganui High Sch., 1972. MP (Lab) Wanganui, 1972–90; Opposition education spokesman, 1976–84; Sen. Opposition Whip, 1978–79; Minister of Education, 1984–87, for the Environment, 1984–86, of Conservation, 1986–87, of Disarmament and Arms Control, 1987–89, of Foreign Affairs, 1987–90, for Pacific Island Affairs, 1988–90. Chairman: Commonwealth Observer Mission to Seychelles election, 1993; Commonwealth Observer Mission to South Africa, 1994; Mem., Commonwealth Observer Mission to Lesotho elections, 1993. Chairman: NZ Commn for UNESCO, 1990–99; Polytechnics Internat. New Zealand, 1994–2001; Education New Zealand, 1998–2002; Tertiary Educn Adv. Commn, 2000–02; Tertiary Educn Commn, NZ, 2005–07; Gbool Ltd, 2011–15; Member: UNESCO Exec. Bd, 1995–99 (Chm., Finance and Admin Commn, 1997–99); Public Adv. Cttee for Disarmament and Arms Control, 1997–2000; Growth and Innovation Adv. Bd, 2005–07; Mem. Council, 1994–2001, Pro-Chancellor, 1999, Chancellor, 2000–01, Hunter Fellow, 2009, Victoria Univ. of Wellington. Mem., 1979–81, Chm., 1981–83, Internat. Affairs Cttee, Christian Conf. of Asia. Chairman: Cambodia Trust (Aotearoa-NZ), 1994–2001; Cambodia Trust (UK), 2002–05 (Trustee, 2000–05); Robson Hanan Trust (Rethinking Crime and Punishment), 2010–11; Gbool Ltd, 2011–; Trustee: Africa Information Centre, 1978–95 (Chm., 1991–95); Mana Educn Centre, 2012–14. Hon. PhD Khon Kaen Univ., 1989. *Recreations*: reading, listening to music, genealogy. *Address*: 36a Upland Road, Kelburn, Wellington 6012, New Zealand. *T*: (4) 2336608, 02115 43753.

**MARSHALL, David;** former transport worker; *b* 7 May 1941; *m*; two *s* one *d*. *Educ*: Larbert, Denny and Falkirk High Schs; Woodside Sen. Secondary Sch., Glasgow. Joined Labour Party, 1962; former Lab. Party Organiser for Glasgow; Mem., TGWU, 1960–. MP (Lab): Glasgow, Shettleston, 1979–2005; Glasgow East, 2005–June 2008. Chairman, Select Committee: Transport, 1987–92 (Mem., 1985–92); Scottish Affairs, 1997–2001 (Mem., 1981–83, 1994–97); Mem., Chairmen's Panel, 2005–08. Former Chairman: All Party ANZAC Gp; British Canadian Gp; S Pacific Gp; Aviation Gp; Gardening and Horticulture Gp. Hon. Sec. and Hon. Treas., Scottish Gp of Labour MPs, 1981–2001. Private Member's Bill, The Solvent Abuse (Scotland) Act, May 1983. Chairman: British Gp, IPU, 1997–2000; Exec. Cttee, UK Br., CPA, 2003–08. Mem., UK Delegn to Council of Europe and WEU, 2001–08. Member: Glasgow Corp., 1972–75; Strathclyde Reg. Council, 1974–79 (Chm., Manpower Cttee); formerly: Chm., Manpower Cttee, Convention of Scottish Local Authorities; Mem., Local Authorities Conditions of Service Adv. Bd. *Recreations*: gardening, music.

**MARSHALL, David Arthur Ambler,** CBE 2003; CEng; FRAeS; Director General, Society of British Aerospace Companies, 1997–2003; *b* 4 April 1943; *s* of Henry R. Marshall and Joan E. Marshall; *m* 1968, Karen Elizabeth Marker; two *d*. *Educ*: Brighton Coll.; Churchill Coll., Cambridge (MA). FRAeS 1994; CEng 2005. Joined Rolls Royce Ltd as Apprentice, 1961; Develt Engr, 1970–73; Co. Rep., Airbus, 1973–75; Manager, Eur. Sales, 1975–78; Commercial Manager, 1978–83; Head of Business Planning, 1983–87; Gen. Manager, Mktg, 1987–89; Dir, Business Planning, 1989–90; Commercial Dir, 1990–93; Dir, Business Develt, 1993–96. President: RAeS, 2007–08; Council of Eur. Aerospace Socs, 2013. Mem., L'Academie de l'air et l'espace, 2011. FRSA 1998. Freeman, City of London, 1999. *Recreations*: garden railways, music. *Address*: 4 Rue Roland Garros, Pechabou 31320, France. *T*: (5) 62161420.

**MARSHALL, Hon. Denis William Anson,** QSO 2000; established Hawkshead Vineyard Partnership, Central Otago, 2005; Secretary-General, Commonwealth Parliamentary Association, 2002–06; *b* 23 Sept. 1943; *s* of Lionel Henry Swainson Marshall and Mabel Alice Okeover Marshall; *m* 1965, Annette Kilmister (separated); one *s* two *d*; partner, Ulrike Kurenbach. *Educ*: Christ's Coll., Christchurch, NZ. Nuffield Farming Schol., 1983. MP (Nat. Party) Rangitikei, NZ, 1984–99; Minister: of Conservation, 1990–96; of Sci., 1990–93; of Lands, 1993–96; of Survey and Land Inf., 1993–96; Associate Minister: of Agric., 1990–96; of Employment, 1990–96. Chairman: NZ Rural Communities Trust, 2000–01; NZ Nat. Parks and Conservation Foundn, 2000–02. *Recreations*: hiking, boating, gardening, reading.

**MARSHALL, Dr Edmund Ian;** Lecturer in Management Science, University of Bradford, 1984–2000; *b* 31 May 1940; *s* of Harry and Koorali Marshall; *m* 1969, Margaret Antill (*d* 2017); one *d*; *m* 2019, Margaret Masding. *Educ*: Magdalen Coll., Oxford (Mackinnon Schol.; Double 1st cl. hons Maths, and Junior Mathematical Prize, 1961); PhD Liverpool, 1965. Various univ. appts in Pure Maths, 1962–66; mathematician in industry, 1967–71. Mem., Wallasey County Borough Council, 1963–65. Contested (L) Louth Div. of Lincs, 1964 and 1966; joined Labour Party, 1967. MP (Lab) Goole, May 1971–1983; PPS to Sec. of State for NI, 1974–76, to Home Sec., 1976–79; Chm., Trade and Industry sub-cttee of House of Commons Expenditure Cttee, 1976–79; Mem., Chairmen's Panel in House of Commons, 1981–82; Opposition Whip, 1982–83; joined SDP, 1985. Contested (SDP/Alliance) Bridlington, 1987. Chair: Wakefield and Dist Lib Dems, 2005; Herts Co-ordinating Cttee, Lib Dems, 2009–10; Sec., Harpenden Lib Dems, 2008–11; rejoined Labour Party, 2015. Non-exec. Dir, Wakefield FHSA, 1990–96; Dir, Wakefield Healthcare Commn, 1994–96. Member: British Methodist Conf., 1969–72, 1980, 1985–97 and 2011–12 (Vice-Pres., 1992); World Methodist Council, 1971; British Council of Churches, 1972–78; Sec., Associate (formerly All-Party) Parly Gp related to Council of Church Colls, 1994–2001; Bishop of Wakefield's Advr for Ecumenical Affairs, 1998–2007. Methodist Local Preacher, 1959–; Reader in C of E, 1994–. Mem., Gen. Synod of C of E, 2000–15. Trustee, Parly Outreach Trust, 2016–. Governor: Woodhouse Grove Sch., Bradford, 1986–94; Wakefield Grammar School Foundn, 1989–97. *Publications*: (jtly) Europe: What Next? (Fabian pamphlet), 1969; Parliament and the Public, 1982; Business and Society, 1993; (jtly) The Times Book of Best Sermons, 1995; various papers in mathematical and other jls. *Recreations*: word games, music, theatre. *Address*: 37 Roundwood Lane, Harpenden, Herts AL5 3BP. *Clubs*: Royal Over-Seas League (Vice-Chm., 2010–12, Chm., 2012–, London Gp); Middlesex CC.

**MARSHALL, Eloïse Mary Katherine Selina;** QC 2018; *b* London, 27 March 1969; *d* of His Honour Laurence Arthur Marshall and of Marion Marshall (later Reynolds); *m* 2003, Alexander Thompson; three *s*. *Educ*: Lycée Français, Kensington; Tudor Hall Sch., Banbury; Durham Univ. (BA Jt Hons Politics and Sociol.); Inns of Court Sch. of Law (BVC). Called to the Bar, Gray's Inn, 1994; in practice as criminal barrister, 1994–. *Recreations*: ceramic restoration, family, theatre. *Address*: 23 Essex Street, WC2R 3AA. *T*: (020) 7413 0353. *E*: Eloisemarshallqc@23es.com.

**MARSHALL, Dr Frank Graham,** FIET; Group Research and Development Director, Colt Group Ltd, 1990–98; technology consultant, 1998–2004; *b* 28 March 1942; *s* of Frank and Vera Marshall; *m* 1965, Patricia Anne (*née* Bestwick); two *s* one *d*. *Educ*: Birmingham Univ. (BSc Physics); Nottingham Univ. (PhD Physics). FIET (FIEE 1984). Joined Royal Signals and Radar Estabt (MoD) (Physics and Electronic Device Res.), 1966; Sen. Principal Scientific Officer, 1975–80; seconded to HM Diplomatic Service as Science and Technology Consultant, Tokyo, 1980–82. Man. Dir, Plessey Electronic Systems Res., later Plessey Res. Roke Manor, 1983–87; Technical Dir, Plessey Naval Systems, 1987–90. (Jtly) IEEE Best Paper award, 1973; (jtly) Wolfe Award, 1973. *Publications*: numerous papers on electronic signal processing devices in various jls. *Recreations*: country life, electronics.

**MARSHALL, Gavin Badenoch;** Director, Treeline Woodlands Ltd, since 1991; Vice Lord-Lieutenant of Tweeddale, since 2017; *b* Edinburgh, 30 May 1955; *s* of Henry Bruce Marshall and Catriona Mary Mackenzie Marshall (*née* Badenoch); *m* 1978, Elaine Patricia Smyth; three *s* one *d*. *Educ*: Trinity Coll., Glenalmond; Royal Agricl Coll., Cirencester. Land Agent, Davidson & Robertson, 1978–84; Acquisitions Officer, Econ. Forestry Gp,

1984–91. Mem., Royal Co. of Archers, Queen's Bodyguard for Scotland, 1996–. DL Tweeddale, 1999. Elder, Church of Scotland, 1994. *Recreations:* sailing, ski-ing, walking, travel, motor sport, reading, music. *Address:* Baddinsgill, West Linton, Peeblesshire EH46 7HL. *T:* (01968) 660698. *E:* gavin@baddinsgill.com. *Club:* Tweeddale Shooting (Chm.).

MARSHALL, Very Rev. Geoffrey Osborne; Dean of Brecon and Warden of Readers, 2008–14; Associate Priest, Morley and Smalley, 2016–18; *b* Rossett, Denbighshire, 5 Jan. 1948; *s* of Dr Harry Marshall and Joan Marshall (*née* Harris); *m* 1972, Hazel Caunce; one *s* two *d*. *Educ:* Repton Sch.; St John's Coll., Univ. of Durham (BA); Coll. of the Resurrection, Mirfield. Ordained deacon, 1973, priest, 1974; Vicar: Christ Church, Belper, 1978–86; Spondon, Derby, 1986–93; Rural Dean, Derby N, 1990–95; Sub-Dean, Derby Cathedral, 1993–2002; Rector, Wrexham, 2002–08; Area Dean, Wrexham, 2002–08; Canon, St Asaph, 2004–08. Trustee, Shelter Cymru, 2002–11. Chaplain, Derby High Sch., 1987–2001. *Recreations:* leading pilgrimages to the Middle East, archaeology, walking, cycling, birdwatching. *Address:* 36 Saundersfoot Way, Oakwood, Derby DE21 2RH. *T:* (01332) 280452. *E:* brecondeanery@btinternet.com.

MARSHALL, Prof. Gordon, CBE 2003; DPhil; FBA 2000; FAcSS; Director, Leverhulme Trust, since 2011; *b* 20 June 1952; *s* of Robert Marshall and Ina Marshall; one *s*; partner, Marion Headicar. *Educ:* Falkirk High Sch.; Univ. of Stirling (BA 1st Cl. Hons Sociol. 1974); Nuffield Coll., Oxford (DPhil 1978). Postdoctoral Res. Fellow, Nuffield Coll., Oxford, 1977–78; Lectr and Sen. Lectr, Dept of Sociol., Univ. of Essex, 1978–90; Prof. of Sociol., Univ. of Bath, 1990–93; Official Fellow in Sociol., Nuffield Coll., Oxford, 1993–99; Chief Exec. and Dep. Chm., ESRC, 2000–02; Vice-Chancellor, Univ. of Reading, 2003–11. Chm., Higher Educn Statistics Agency, 2007–11. British Acad./Leverhulme Trust Sen. Res. Fellow, 1992–93. FAcSS (AcSS 2000); Fellow, Royal Norwegian Soc. of Scis and Letters, 2001. DUniv Stirling, 2001; Hon. DLaws Reading, 2012; Hon. DSc Aberdeen, 2018. *Publications:* Presbyteries and Profits, 1980; In Search of the Spirit of Capitalism, 1982; (jtly) Social Class in Modern Britain, 1987; In Praise of Sociology, 1990; (jtly) Oxford Dictionary of Sociology, 1994, 3rd edn 2005; (jtly) Against the Odds?, 1997; (jtly) Repositioning Class, 1997; contrib. numerous articles to jls and symposia. *Recreation:* in my dreams. *Address:* Leverhulme Trust, 1 Pemberton Row, EC4A 3BG. *T:* (020) 7042 9877. *E:* gmarshall@leverhulme.ac.uk.

MARSHALL, Sir Harold; *see* Marshall, Sir Arthur H.

MARSHALL, Her Honour Hazel Eleanor; QC 1988; a Senior Circuit Judge, 2006–13; a Deputy High Court Judge, 1994–2013; *b* 14 Jan. 1947; *d* of late Geoffrey Briddon and Nancy Briddon; *m* 1st, 1969, Robert Hector Williamson (marr. diss. 1980); 2nd, 1983, Harvey Christopher John Marshall; one step *s*. *Educ:* Wimbledon High Sch.; St Hilda's Coll., Oxford (MA Jurisprudence). FCIArb 1992. Atkin Scholar, Gray's Inn. Called to the Bar, Gray's Inn, 1972, Bencher, 1996; Asst Recorder, 1993–96; a Recorder, 1996–2006. Acting Deemster, IOM, 1999–2006. Judicial Mem., Public Guardian Bd, 2007. Chm., Chancery Bar Assoc., 1994–97. Mem., DfT (formerly DoE, subseq. DETR, then DTLR) Property Adv. Gp, 1994–2003. Hon. Mem., ESU. *Publications:* (with Harvey Marshall) Law and Valuation of Leisure Property, 1994. *Recreations:* gardening, opera, occasional off-shore sailing. *Club:* Royal Over-Seas League (Hon. Mem.).

MARSHALL, Prof. Helen Jane; Vice-Chancellor, University of Salford, since 2015; *b* Cardiff, 31 Oct. 1958; *d* of John Anthony Bond and Marilyn Bond; *m* 1986, Alexander Marshall; two *d*. *Educ:* St Teilo's Ch in Wales High Sch., Cardiff; Univ. of Birmingham (BA Hons, LLM). Lectr in Law, Preston Poly., subseq. Lancashire Poly., then Univ. of Central Lancashire, 1982–2002; Dep. Principal, St Martin's Coll., Lancaster, 2002–07; Pro Vice Chancellor, Univ. of Cumbria, 2007–10; Dep. Vice-Chancellor, Univ. of Glamorgan, subseq. Univ. of South Wales, 2010–13; Dep. Vice-Chancellor, Univ. of Salford, 2013–15. *Publications:* (with Allan Blake) Company Law, 1985, 5th edn 1996; (with Peter Kay) Business Law, 1990, 2nd edn 1992; articles in Jl of Quality in Higher Educn, Jl of Adult and Continuing Educn, Independent Jl of Teaching and Learning, South Africa, Solicitors Jl. *Recreations:* running, horse riding, ski-ing, watching Rugby Union. *Address:* 45 The Crescent, The Old Fire Station, University of Salford, Manchester M5 4WT. *T:* (0161) 295 5050. *E:* vice-chancellor@salford.ac.uk.

MARSHALL, Jeremy Samuel John; Chief Executive, C. Hoare & Co., 2009–16; *b* Hemel Hempstead, Herts, 8 May 1963; *s* of John E. Marshall and Susan E. Marshall (*née* Westcott); *m* 1987, Jeanette Bonsels; two *s* one *d*. *Educ:* Hemel Hempstead Sch.; St John's Coll., Cambridge (BA 1984; MA 1987), INSEAD (MBA 1992). Barclays Bank, 1984–86; Bank of Montreal, 1986–88; Crédit Suisse, 1988–2009: Strategic Planning Internat. Zurich, 1993–95; Hd, Planning and Support, Zurich, 1996–97; Hd, New Business Mgt Support, USA, 1997–2002; CEO, UK Private Banking, 2002–08. Non-exec. Dir, Waterlogic plc, 2011–15. Mem. Bd, BBA, 2014. Chairman: Pastor Training Internat., 2011–; Christian Books Worldwide, 2011–; Christianity Explored, 2013– (Trustee, 2009–13); Trustee: London Theol Seminary, 2003–; Woodland Trust, 2008–17; Allied Schs Trust, 2011–. *Recreations:* cricket, reading, golf.

MARSHALL, Prof. John, MBE 2013; PhD; FRCPath, FMedSci, FRSB; CSci; Frost Professor of Ophthalmology, Institute of Ophthalmology, University College London, since 2011; *b* 21 Dec. 1943; *s* of Henry Thomas George Marshall and Ellen Emily Martha Marshall; *m* 1972, Judith Anne Meadows. *Educ:* Inst. of Ophthalmology, Univ. of London (BSc; PhD 1968). FRCPath 2007; FRSB (FIBiol 2009); CSci 2017. Institute of Ophthalmology: Lectr in Anatomy, 1968–73; Sen. Lectr in Visual Sci., 1973–80; Reader in Exptl Pathology, 1981–83; Sembal Prof. of Exptl Ophthalmology, 1983–91; Frost Prof. of Ophthalmology and Chm., Dept of Ophthalmology, United Med. and Dental Schs of Guy's and St Thomas' Hosps, then Guy's, King's and St Thomas' Sch. of Medicine, KCL, later KCL Sch. of Medicine, 1991–2009; Hon. Consultant in Ophthalmology: St Thomas' Hosp., 1992–2009; Moorfields Eye Hosp., 2012–. Hon. Dist. Prof., Sch. of Optometry and Visual Sci., Univ. of Cardiff, 2008–; Hon. Professor: UCL, 2009–11; Caledonian Univ., 2011–; Hon. Vis. Prof., City Univ., 2011–; Sir Adrian Cadbury Lect., Manchester Eye Hosp., 2016; Dame Ida Mann Lect., Royal Australian and NZ Coll. of Ophthalmologists, 2019. Vice Pres., Nat. Eye Res. Centre, Bristol, 2015–; Dep. Dir, Enterprise Inst. of Ophthalmology, UCL, 2016–. Ed., numerous scientific jls, 1985–. Advr on lasers to WHO, 1974–80, to Internat. Red Cross, 1989–95. Director: DIOMED, 1991–97; Ellex R&D, 2007–11; Ellex Medical Ltd, 2007–11; Laser Inst. of America, 2004–08; Avellino, 2016–; Ellex, 2017. Hon. Pres., Internat. Soc. High Technol. in Ophthalmol., 2018. Trustee: Brit. Retinitis Pigmentosa Soc., 1978–; Devereux House, 1999–; Co. of Spectacle Makers' Charity, 2004–09; Frost Charitable Trust, 2007–; Ambassador, Fight for Sight, 2008–. Gov., Moorfields Eye Hosp., 1988–90. Mem., Ct of Assts, Spectacle Makers' Co., 2001– (Master, 2011–12). Numerous patents on applications of lasers to eye surgery, 1968–. Fellow: Academia Ophthalmologica Europaea, 2004; Assoc. for Res. in Vision and Ophthalmology, 2009; Acad. Translational Medicine Professionals, 2019; FMedSci 2009. FRSA 1989. Hon. Fellow: Coll. of Optometrists, 1997; Univ. of Cardiff, 2005; Hon. FRCOphth, 2005. Hon. DSc: Glasgow Caledonian, 2013; London Metropolitan, 2015. Nettleship Medal, 1980, Ashton Medal, 1993, RCOphth; Mackenzie Medal, Tennant Inst. of Ophthalmol., Glasgow, 1985; Raynor Medal, Intraocular Implant Soc., UK, 1988; Ridley Medal, Internat. Soc. for Cataract and Refractive Surg., 1990; Wilkening Award, Laser Inst. of Amer., 1999 (Fellow, 2003); Ida Mann Medal, Oxford, 2000; Lord Crook Gold Medal, Spectacle Makers' Co., 2001; Doyne Medal, Oxford Congress of Ophthalmol., 2001; Barraquer Medal, 2001, Lifetime Achievement Award, 2009, Internat. Soc. of Refractive Surg.; Euretina Award, European Soc. of Retinal Specialists, 2003; Innovator Award, Amer. Soc. Cataract & Refractive Surgeons, 2004; Lim Medal, Singapore Nat. Eye Centre, 2004; Sen. Achievement Award, Amer. Acad. of Ophthalmol., 2005; Junius-Kuhnt Award and Medal for work on age-related macular degeneration, 2012; Moorfields' Stars Award for Nat. and Internat. Services to Ophthalmol., Moorfields Eye Hosp., 2012; Bowman Medal and Lect., Royal Coll. of Ophthalmologists, 2014; Zivojnovic Award, European Vitreoretinal Soc., 2014; Lifetime Achievement Award, UK Ireland Cataract and Refractive Surgery Soc., 2014; Peter Watson Medal, Cambridge Symposium, 2015; Laser Ambassador Award, Assoc. Industrial Laser Users, 2019. *Publications:* Hazards of Light, 1986; Laser Technology in Ophthalmology, 1988; Vision and Visual Systems, 1991; Annual of Ophthalmic Laser Surgery, 1992; numerous papers in scientific jls, concerning effect of lasers, light and aging on ocular tissues. *Recreations:* work!, reading, cars. *Address:* Wildacre, 27 Cedar Road, Farnborough, Hants GU14 7AU. *T:* (01252) 543473. *Clubs:* Athenæum, Royal Automobile.

MARSHALL, John; *see* Marshall, R. J.

MARSHALL, Prof. John Charles, PhD; FRS 2008; Professor, since 1993, and Cecil and Ida Green Professor of Oceanography, since 2010, Department of Earth, Atmospheric and Planetary Sciences, Massachusetts Institute of Technology; *b* Nottingham, 12 Oct. 1954. *Educ:* Imperial Coll. London (BSc 1st Cl. Hons Physics 1976; PhD 1980). Postdoctoral Researcher: Imperial Coll. London, 1981; Oxford Univ., 1982–83; Lectr in Physics, 1984–89, Reader, 1989–91, Imperial College London; Associate Prof., Dept of Earth, Atmospheric and Planetary Scis, MIT, 1991–92. Fellow, Amer. Meteorol Soc., 2014. L. F. Richardson Prize, 1986, Adrian Gill Prize, 2005, RMetS; Audrey Buyrn and Alan Phillips Ally of Nature Award, 2010; Sverdrup Gold Medal, 2014, Bernhard Haurwitz Prize, 2016, Amer. Meteorol Soc. *Publications:* (with A. Plumb) Atmosphere, Ocean and Climate Dynamics, 2007; contribs to jls incl. Ocean Modelling, Jl Physical Oceanography, Qly Jl RMetS, Nature, Jl Atmospheric Scis, Jl Marine Res., Jl Climate. *Address:* Department of Earth, Atmospheric and Planetary Sciences, Massachusetts Institute of Technology, 77 Massachusetts Avenue, Cambridge, MA 02139–4307, USA.

MARSHALL, John Gibb, (John Sessions); actor, writer; *b* 11 Jan. 1953; *s* of John Marshall and Esmé Richardson. *Educ:* Univ. of Wales (MA). Plays and one-man shows, 1982–85; *television:* Spitting Image, 1986; Porterhouse Blue, 1987; A Day in Summer, 1988; Whose Line is it Anyway?, 1988; Single Voices, 1990; Ackroyd's Dickens, 1990; Jute City, 1991; Life with Eliza, 1992; A Tour of the Western Isles, 1993; Citizen Locke, 1994; The Treasure Seekers, 1996; Tom Jones, 1997; My Night with Reg, 1997; Stella Street (4 series), 1997, 1998, 2000, 2001; In the Red, 1998; The Man, 1999; Gormenghast, 2000; Randall & Hopkirk Deceased, 2000; Murder Rooms, 2001; Well-Schooled in Murder, 2002; Judge John Deed, 2002 and 2005; Midsomer Murders, 2002; The Lost Prince, 2002; Dalziel and Pascoe, 2002; The Key, 2003; George Eliot: a life, 2003; QI, 2003, 2004, 2005; Hawking, 2004; The Legend of the Tamworth Two, 2004; Absolute Power, 2005; The English Harem, 2005; The Moving Finger, 2006; Low Winter Sun, 2006; Jackanory, 2006; The Ronni Ancona Show, 2006; Oliver Twist, 2007; Margaret, 2009; Spies and Lies (NZ), 2009; Mr Selfridge, 2013; Outlander, 2014; Jonathan Strange, 2014; We're Doomed! The Dad's Army Story, 2015; The Rack Pack, 2016; Red Top, 2016; Upstart Crow, 2016; Friday Night Dinner, 2016; Father Brown, 2017; The Loch, 2017; Death in Paradise, 2018; Victoria, 2019; one-man shows: New Year Show, 1988; On the Spot, 1989; Tall Tales, 1991; Likely Stories, 1994; *theatre:* The Life of Napoleon, Albery, 1987; The Common Pursuit, Phoenix, 1988; The American Napoleon, Phoenix, 1989; Die Fledermaus, Royal Opera House, 1990; Travelling Tales, Haymarket, 1991; Tartuffe, Playhouse, 1991; The Soldier's Tale, Barbican, 1993, 2003; My Night with Reg, Royal Court, 1994; Paint, said Fred!, Royal Acad., 1996; Mahler and Me, 2010, Gilbert, 2011, Richmond; Longing, Hampstead Th., 2013; *films:* The Bounty, 1984; Whoops Apocalypse, 1986; Castaway, 1987; Henry V, 1989; Sweet Revenge, 1990; The Pope Must Die, 1991; Princess Caraboo, 1994; In the Bleak Midwinter, 1995; The Scarlet Tunic, 1998; Cousin Bette, 1998; A Midsummer Night's Dream, 1999; One of the Hollywood Ten, 2000; High Heels and Low Life, 2001; Gangs of New York, 2002; A Flight of Fancy, 2002; Stella Street: the movie, 2003; Five Children and It, 2003; The Merchant of Venice, 2004; Rag Tale, 2005; The Good Shepherd, 2006; Intervention, 2007; Inconceivable, 2008; Nativity, 2009; The Last Station, 2010; Made in Dagenham, 2010; The Iron Lady, 2011; The Real American - Joe McCarthy, 2011; Filth, 2013; Pudsey The Movie, 2014; Mr Holmes, 2015; Legend, 2015; Florence Foster Jenkins, 2016; Through the Looking Glass, 2016; Whisky Galore, 2016; Denial, 2017; Finding Your Feet, 2018; *radio:* Whose Line is it Anyway?, 1988; Beachcomber, 1989; Mightier than the Sword, 1992; Figaro gets Divorced, 1993; Poonsh, 1993; The Good Doctor, 1994; Private Passions, 1997–2002; The Reith Affair, 1998; Saturday Night Fry, 1998; The Destiny of Nathalie X, 1998; Season's Greetings, 1999; The Man who came to Dinner, 2000; Reconstructing Louis, 2000; Dante's Inferno, 2001; The Haunting, 2002; The Titanic Enquiry, 2002; In the Company of Men, 2003; St Graham and St Evelyn—Pray for Us, 2003; The Possessed, 2006; Eternal Sunshine, 2008; Let Me Entertain You (presenter), 2008; A Dangerous Thing, 2009; The Babylon Hotel, 2009; Myths and Mystery Cycles, 2010; Electric Ink, 2011; Burns and the Bankers, 2012; A Pact of Silence, 2015; Six Degrees of John Sessions, 2018; The Quanderhorn Xperimentations, 2018; Gloomsbury, 2018; Mrs Sidhu's Deadly Highland Game, 2019. *Recreation:* dinner parties. *Address:* c/o Markham, Froggatt & Irwin, 4 Windmill Street, W1T 2HZ. *T:* (020) 7636 4412. *Club:* Groucho.

MARSHALL, John Leslie; Chairman, Beta Global Emerging Markets Investment Trust plc, 2000–01 (Director, 1990–2001); *b* 19 Aug. 1940; *s* of late Prof. William Marshall and Margaret Marshall; *m* 1978, Susan Elizabeth (marr. diss. 2000), *d* of David Mount, Petham, Kent; two *s*. *Educ:* Glasgow Academy; St Andrews Univ. (MA). ACIS. Asst Lecturer in Economics, Glasgow Univ., 1962–66; Lectr in Economics, Aberdeen Univ., 1966–70; Mem., Internat. Stock Exchange; Carr Sebag & Co., 1979–82; Partner, 1983–86, Dir, 1986–90, Analyst, 1990–93, Carr Kitcat & Aitken; Analyst: London Wall Equities, subseq. Mees Pierson Securities (UK) Ltd, 1993–97; New Japan Securities, 1998–99. Sen. Financial Journalist, Shares mag., 1999–2011. Member (C): Aberdeen Town Council, 1968–70; Ealing Borough Council, 1971–86 (Chm., Finance Bd, 1978–82; Chm., Local Services Cttee, 1982–84); Barnet LBC, 1998– (Chm., Cons. Gp, 1998–2000, 2004–05, 2012–16; Chm., Council Policy Conference, 2002–03; Dep. Mayor, 2004; Cabinet Mem. for Investment in Educn (formerly Educn and Lifelong Learning), 2004–08; Mayor, 2008–09; Chm., Pension Fund Cttee, 2010–11; Chm., Constitution, Ethics and Probity Cttee, 2014–). Contested (C): Dundee East, 1964 and 1966; Lewisham East, Feb. 1974. MEP (C) London N, 1979–89; Asst Whip, EDG, Eur. Parlt, 1986–89. MP (C) Hendon South, 1987–97; contested (C) Finchley and Golders Green, 1997, 2001. PPS to Minister for the Disabled, Dept of Social Security, 1989–90, to Sec. of State for Social Security, 1990–92, to Leader of H of C, 1992–95. Mem., Select Cttee on health, 1995–97; Vice Chm., All Pty Mental Health Gp, 1996–97. Chm., British Israel Parly Gp, 1991–97; Vice Pres., Anglo-

Israel Assoc., 2001– (Chm., 1994–2000). Consultant, Bus and Coach Council, 1991–97. Chairman: Friends of the Northern Line, 1994–97; Dermatrust Appeal, 1998–2005; Barnet Carers Centre, 2011–15; Barnet Blind and Partially Sighted Bowlers, 2011–; Trustee, Mitchell Educnl Charity, 2008–. *Publications*: articles on economics in several professional jls; pamphlets on economic questions for Aims. *Recreations*: watching cricket, football and Rugby; bridge, theatre. *Address*: 3 Westchester Drive, NW4 1RD. *Clubs*: Royal Over-Seas League, MCC; Middlesex County Cricket.

**MARSHALL, John Roger**; Chairman: Building Software Ltd, since 1997; Supply Chain Partnering, since 1996; *b* 20 April 1944; *s* of late John Henry Marshall and of Betty Alaine Rosetta Marshall; *m* (marr. diss.); one *s* two *d*. *Educ*: Rendcomb College; Bristol Univ. (BSc Hons Civil Eng.). MICE, CEng, FCIHT. Balfour Beatty Consultants, W. C. French and R. McGregor & Sons, 1966–70; Mears Construction, 1970–78; Henry Boot, 1978–83; Man. Dir, Mowlem Management, 1983–87; Dir, 1987–95, Man. Dir, 1989–94, Chief Exec., 1994–95, John Mowlem and Co. PLC. Non-executive Director: St Aldwyns Enterprises (subseq. Resources) Ltd, 1996–2002; BRE Ltd, 1998–2001. *Recreations*: painting and giving unwanted advice. *Address*: 118 Bath Road, Cheltenham, Glos GL53 7JX.

**MARSHALL, Katharine Jane, (Mrs H. J. Stevenson); Her Honour Judge Katharine Marshall**; a Circuit Judge, since 2008; *b* 11 Aug. 1958; *d* of Ian David Gordon Lee and Ivy Margaret Lee (*née* Cox); *m* 1st, 1981, David Forrest Marshall (marr. diss. 1985); one *s*; 2nd, 1996, Huw John Stevenson; one *s* one *d*. *Educ*: Sidney Sussex Coll., Cambridge (Taylor Schol.; MA Natural Scis/Law 1980); Council of Legal Educn; Greenwich Univ. (DMS Dist. 1998). Called to the Bar, Inner Temple, 1983; Dep. Justices Clerk, E Berks, 1997–2001; Actg Stipendiary Magistrate, then Dep. Dist Judge, 1999–2002; District Judge (Magistrates' Courts), 2002–06; Recorder, 2007–08; Designated Family Judge, 2012–18. Member: Family Procedure Rule Cttee, 2004–08; Family Justice Council, 2011–16. Mem., Adv. Bd, Cambridge Univ. Alumni, 2010–12. *Publications*: Wilkinson's Road Traffic Referencer, 2007, rev. edn 2008. *Recreations*: living a life I love with those I love, 70's rock music, walking in faraway isolated locations; fascinated by life of Napoleon (particularly exile on St Helena). *Address*: Reading County Court Centre, 160–163 Friar Street, Reading RG1 1HE. *Club*: Oxford and Cambridge.

**MARSHALL, Kathleen Anne**; child law consultant, since 2009; *b* 4 June 1953; *d* of Matthew Gallagher and Christina McEvoy; *m* 1974, Robert Hunter Marshall; two *s* one *d*. *Educ*: Univ. of Glasgow (LLB 1973); Open Univ. (BA Hons 1979); Maryvale Inst., Birmingham (BA Hons (Divinity) 2003). Legal Apprentice, then Solicitor, Glasgow Corp., subseq. Glasgow DC, 1973–77; full-time mother, 1977–89; Co-Dir, then Dir, Scottish Child Law Centre, 1989–94; child law consultant, 1994–2004; Comr for Children and Young People in Scotland, 2004–09. Visiting Professor: Queen's Coll., Glasgow, subseq. Glasgow Caledonian Univ., 1992–95; Glasgow Centre for the Child and Society, Univ. of Glasgow, 1997–2009. Mem., Law Soc. of Scotland, 1975–. *Publications*: Children's Rights in the Balance: the participation-protection debate, 1997; (with Paul Parvis) Honouring Children: the human rights of the child in Christian perspective, 2004; numerous articles in jls. *Recreation*: being a grandmother. *E*: childlaw@btinternet.com.

**MARSHALL, Liza**; Director, Hera Pictures Ltd, since 2017; *b* London, 4 March 1972; *d* of Scott and Denise Marshall; *m* Mark Strong; two *s*. *Educ*: St Paul's Girls' Sch.; Wadham Coll., Oxford (BA Modern Hist.). Script ed. for Lynda La Plante, 1995; storyliner and script ed., London Bridge TV prog., 1995–96; Develt Exec., Carlton TV, 1996; BBC: script ed., serials, 1996–98; Producer, progs incl. The Long Firm, The Sins, Fields of Gold, Eroica, Derailed, 1998–2005; Commng Ed., 2005–07, Hd of Drama, 2007–09, Channel 4; Hd of Film and TV, Scott Free, 2010–14; Jt Man. Dir, Archery Pictures, 2014–16.

**MARSHALL, Margaret Anne**, OBE 1999; concert and opera singer; soprano; *b* 4 Jan. 1949; *d* of Robert and Margaret Marshall; *m* 1970, Dr Graeme Griffiths King Davidson; two *d*. *Educ*: High School, Stirling; Royal Scottish Academy of Music and Drama (DRSAMD). Recital début, Wigmore Hall, 1975; performed regularly with all major British orchs, also with ENO and Scottish Opera; opera début as Euridice, in Orfeo, Florence; major rôles include: Countess Almaviva in The Marriage of Figaro; Fiordiligi in Così fan Tutte; Elvira and Donna Anna in Don Giovanni; Violetta in La Traviata; Marschallin in Der Rosenkavalier; Constanze in Die Seraglio; many concert and opera performances in Europe and N America; numerous recordings. Hon. MusD St Andrews, 2009. First Prize, Munich International Competition, 1974. Gulliver Award, 1992. *Recreations*: squash, golf. *Address*: Armand, Gensac 82120, Tarn et Garonne, France.

**MARSHALL, Mark Anthony**, CMG 1991; HM Diplomatic Service, retired; Ambassador to the Republic of Yemen (formerly Yemen Arab Republic) and the Republic of Djibouti, 1987–93; *b* 8 Oct. 1937; *s* of late Thomas Humphrey Marshall, CMG and of Nadine, *d* of late Mark Hambourg; *m* 1970, Penelope Lesley Seymour; two *d*. *Educ*: Westminster Sch.; Trinity Coll., Cambridge (BA). MECAS, 1958; Third Sec., Amman, 1960; FO, 1962; Commercial Officer, Dubai, 1964; FO, 1965; Aden, 1967; First Sec., 1968; Asst Dir of Treasury Centre for Admin. Studies, 1968; UK Delegn to Brussels Conf., 1970; First Sec./Head of Chancery, Rabat, 1972; First Sec., FCO, 1976; Counsellor: Tripoli, 1979–80; Damascus, 1980–83; Head of Finance Dept, FCO, 1984–87. *Recreations*: swimming, fell walking, bridge.

**MARSHALL, Prof. Martin Neil**, CBE 2005; MD; FRCGP; Professor of Healthcare Improvement, University College London, since 2012; Lead, Improvement Science London, since 2012; Chair, Royal College of General Practitioners, since 2019; *b* 2 Sept. 1961; *s* of Dr Geoffrey Marshall and Mary Marshall; *m* 1988, Susan Miles. *Educ*: University Coll. London (BSc Immunol. 1984); Charing Cross and Westminster Hosp. Med. Sch., Univ. of London (MB BS 1987; MD 1997); Univ. of Exeter (MSc Health Care 1994). DRCOG 1990; DCH 1991; MRCGP 1991, FRCGP 1998. Exeter Vocational Trng Scheme for Gen. Practice, 1988–91; Partner in Gen. Practice, Mt Pleasant Health Centre, Exeter, 1991–99; Lectr in Gen. Practice, Univ. of Exeter, 1994–97; Harkness Fellow in Health Care Policy, Rand Corp., Calif, 1998–99; Hd, Community Health Scis Div., Univ. of Exeter, 1999; University of Manchester: Hon. Res. Fellow, 1998–99, Sen. Clin. Res. Fellow, 2000–01, Nat. Primary Care R&D Centre; Prof. of Gen. Practice, 2001–06; Hd, Div. of Primary Care, 2005–06; Principal in Gen. Practice (pt-time), Robert Darbishire Practice, Manchester, 2000–06; Dep. Chief Med. Officer for England, DoH, 2006–07; Medical Dir, The Health Foundn, 2007–12. Mem., Care Quality Commn, 2009–12. Mem. Council, RCGP, 2005–06, 2007–13. Pres., Eur. Soc. for Quality Improvement in Family Practice, 2005–06. Hon. FRCP 2005; Hon. FFPHM 2005. *Publications*: numerous contribs relating to quality and safety in health care. *Recreation*: being outside.

**MARSHALL, Prof. Mary Tara**, OBE 1997; Director, 1989–2005, Design Associate, 2006–15, Dementia Services Development Centre, University of Stirling, now Professor Emeritus; Senior Consultant, Dementia Centre, HammondCare, since 2015; writer and lecturer in dementia care; *b* 13 June 1945; *d* of Percy Edwin Alan and Phyllis April Trix Johnson-Marshall. *Educ*: Edinburgh Univ. (MA); London School of Economics (DSA); Liverpool Univ. (Dip. in Applied Social Studies). Child Care Officer, Lambeth, 1967–69; Social Worker, Liverpool Personal Service Soc. Project, 1970–74; Organiser, res. project, Age Concern, Liverpool, 1974–75; Lectr in Applied Social Studies, Liverpool Univ.

1975–83; Dir, Age Concern, Scotland, 1983–89. Sessional Inspector, Care Inspectorate (formerly Social Work Inspection Agency), 2007–16. Mem., Royal Commn on Long Term Care for the Elderly, 1998–99. Hon. Prof., Edinburgh Centre for Res. on the Experience of Dementia, Univ. of Edinburgh, 2018–. Member: Liverpool Housing Trust, 1976–; Edinvar Housing Assoc., 1988–; Gov., PPP Foundation (formerly Healthcare Med. Trust Ltd), 1998–2003. Member: Centre for Policy on Ageing, 1986– (Gov., 1994–2000); BASW, 1970–; British Soc. of Gerontology, 1977–; 21st Century Social Work Rev. Gp, 2004–05; Ind. Funding Review of Free Personal and Nursing Care. FRSE 2003. FAcSS (AcSS 1999). FRSA 2003. Hon. DEd Queen Margaret Coll., 1998; Hon. DSocSc Edinburgh, 2004; DUniv Stirling, 2006. Medal for Relief of Suffering, British Geriatric Soc., 2008; Lifetime Achievement Award, Faculty of Old Age Psychiatry, RCPsych, 2010. *Publications*: Social Work with Old People, 1983, 4th edn (with J. Phillips and M. Ray), 2006; "I Can't Place This Place At All": working with people with dementia and their carers, 1996, 2nd edn (with M.-A. Tibbs) as Social Work and People with Dementia, 2006; (ed) Food, Glorious Food: perspectives on food and dementia, 2003; (ed) Perspectives on Rehabilitation and Dementia, 2005; (ed with K. Allan) Dementia: walking not wandering, 2006; (ed with J. Gilliard) Time for Dementia, 2010; Designing balconies, roof terraces and roof gardens for people with dementia, 2010; (with J. Gilliard) Transforming the Quality of Life for People with Dementia through Contact with the Natural World, 2011; (with A. Pollock) Designing Outdoor Spaces for People with Dementia, 2012; Designing Mental Health Units for Older People, 2014; (with J. Gilliard) Creating Culturally Appropriate Outside Spaces and Experiences for People with Dementia, 2014; Toilet Talk: accessible design for people with dementia, 2018; (contrib.) Textbook of Dementia Care: an integrated approach, 2019; book reviews, papers, reports and articles. *Recreations*: birdwatching, photography. *Address*: 24 Buckingham Terrace, Edinburgh EH4 3AE. *T*: (0131) 343 1732.

**MARSHALL, Rt Rev. Michael Eric**, MA; an Hon. Assistant Bishop, Diocese of London, since 1984; *b* Lincoln, 14 April 1936. *Educ*: Lincoln Sch.; Christ's Coll., Cambridge (Tancred Scholar, Upper II: Hist. Pt 1 and Theol Pt 1a, MA); Cuddesdon Theological Coll. Deacon, 1960; Curate, St Peter's, Spring Hill, Birmingham, 1960–62; Tutor, Ely Theological Coll. and Minor Canon of Ely Cath., 1962–64; Chaplain in London Univ., 1964–69; Vicar of All Saints', Margaret Street, W1, 1969–75; Bishop Suffragan of Woolwich, 1975–84; Founding Episcopal Dir, Anglican Inst., St Louis, Missouri, 1984–92; Dir of Evangelism, Chichester Theol Coll., 1991–97; Bishop in Residence, 1997–2012, Rector, 2002–12, Holy Trinity, Sloane Street; Interim Rector, Episcopal Ch of the Heavenly Rest, NY, 2012–13; Preb. of Wightring in Chichester Cathedral and Wightring Theol Lectr, 1990–99; an Asst Bp, Dio. Chichester, 1992–2011. Archbishops' Advr on Evangelism, 1992–97; Leader, Springboard, 1992–97. Founder and Director: Inst. of Christian Studies, 1970; Internat. Inst. for Anglican Studies, 1982; Pres., Awareness Foundn, 2009–14 (Dir, Trinity Inst. for Christianity and Culture, 2003–09; Trustee, Trinity Foundn, 2003–09). Exam. Chap. to Bp of London, 1974. Member: Gen. Synod, 1970, also Diocesan and Deanery Synods; Liturgical Commn; Anglican/Methodist Liaison Commn until 1974; SPCK Governing Body; USPG Governing Body. Hon. Chaplain, 2002, Liveryman, 2008, Wheelwrights' Co. Has frequently broadcast on BBC and commercial radio; also lectured, preached and broadcast in Canada and USA. Hon. DD Nashotah House Seminary, Wisconsin, 2015. *Publications*: A Pattern of Faith, 1966 (co-author); Glory under Your Feet, 1978; Pilgrimage and Promise, 1981; Renewal in Worship, 1982; The Anglican Church, Today and Tomorrow, 1984; Christian Orthodoxy Revisited, 1985; The Gospel Conspiracy in the Episcopal Church, 1986; The Restless Heart, 1987; The Gospel Connection, 1991; The Freedom of Holiness, 1992; Free to Worship, 1996; Flame in the Mind: a journey of spiritual passion, 2002; The Transforming Power of Prayer: from illusion to reality, 2010; Founder and co-editor, Christian Quarterly. *Recreation*: music. *Address*: 18 Grosvenor Court, Sloane Street, SW1X 9PF. *Club*: Athenæum.

**MARSHALL, Maj. Gen. Neil**, OBE 2005; Director, NorScot Consulting Ltd, since 2017; Chief Executive, Forces Pension Society Ltd, since 2019; *b* Aberdeen, 24 May 1965; *s* of William and Dora Marshall; *m* 1989, Trudi Shapland; two *s*. *Educ*: Aboyne Acad.; Merchiston Castle Sch.; RMA, Sandhurst; Cranfield Univ. (MA Defence Studies); Manchester Business Sch., Univ. of Manchester (Advanced Mgt Achievement); Bournemouth Univ. (Internat. Disaster Mgt, 2017). MCMI. Commnd Army, 1985; Regimental Officer: 39 Regt RA, 1986–88; 19 Regt RA, 1988–91; Instructor, RMA, Sandhurst, 1992–94; Battery Comdr, 7 Parachute Regt RHA, 1995–97; JSCSC 1997–98; SO, Dir of Manning (Army), 1998–2000; Battery Comdr, 1st Regt RHA, 2000–02; Staff Officer: HQ Land Forces, 2002–04; Multinat. Forces Iraq/Baghdad, 2004; CO, 1st Regt RHA, 2005–07; Col, MoD, 2007–09; Comdr, RA 3rd (UK) Div., 2009–10; Chief Operating Officer, Army HQ, 2010–12; rcds 2013; Dir, ISAF Jt Comd, Kabul, 2013–14; Dir, HCSC, 2014–15; Sen. British Mil. Advr to US Central Command, 2016–17. Hon. Regimental Colonel: 14 Regt RA, 2012–17; 1st Regt RHA, 2017–. Col Comdt, RA, 2017–. Dir, British Biathlon Union, 2011–15. Trustee, SkillForce, 2018–. *Recreations*: Nordic ski-ing (biathlon and cross country), alpine ski-ing, walking, cycling, family, industrial level gardening in Wiltshire. *E*: neilmarshall24@hotmail.com. *Clubs*: Naval and Military; British Biathlon Supporters.

**MARSHALL, Penelope Jane Clucas**; Social Affairs Editor, ITV News, 2012–14 and since 2015; *b* Addlestone, 7 Nov. 1962; *d* of Alan Marshall and Mary Marshall; *m* 1992, Timothy Ewart; three *d*. *Educ*: St Helen's, Northwood; London Sch. of Econs and Pol Sci. (BA Hist. 1984). Trainee, Surrey and South London Newspaper Gp, 1984–85; ITN: graduate trainee, 1985; Foreign Corresp., ITV News, 1987–2004; freelance journalist and consultant, 2004–07; Special Corresp., ITV News at Ten, 2007–11. Freelance writer and contrib. to BBC Radio 4, The Times, Guardian, Daily Mail, 2006–. Vis. Prof., City Univ., 2006–. *Recreations*: singing, reading, gardening, bird watching, dog walking, opera. *Address*: ITV News, 200 Gray's Inn Road, WC1X 8XZ.

**MARSHALL, Prof. Peter**, DPhil; FBA 2018; Professor of History, University of Warwick, since 2006; *b* Kirkwall, Orkney, 26 Oct. 1964; *s* of George Marshall and Elma Marshall (*née* Fotheringhame); *m* 1986, Alison Cowie; three *d*. *Educ*: Kirkwall Grammar Sch.; University Coll., Oxford (MA Modern Hist. 1986; DPhil Modern Hist. 1990). History Master, Ampleforth Coll., York, 1990–94; University of Warwick: Lectr in Hist., 1994–2001; Sen. Lectr in Hist., 2001–04; Reader in Hist., 2004–06. Ed., English Histl Rev., 2013–. *Publications*: The Catholic Priesthood and the English Reformation, 1994; (ed) The Impact of the English Reformation 1500–1640, 1997; (ed jtly) The Place of the Dead: death and remembrance in late medieval and early modern Europe, 2000; Beliefs and the Dead in Reformation England, 2002; (ed jtly) The Beginnings of English Protestantism, 2002; Reformation England 1480–1642, 2003, 2nd edn 2012; Religious Identities in Henry VIII's England, 2006; (ed jtly) Angels in the Early Modern World, 2006; Mother Leakey and the Bishop: a ghost story, 2007; (ed jtly) Catholic Gentry in English Society: the Throckmortons of Coughton from Reformation to emancipation, 2009; The Reformation: a very short introduction, 2009 (trans. German, 2014, Korean, 2017, Portuguese, 2018); (ed) The Oxford Illustrated History of the Reformation, 2015; Heretics and Believers: a history of the English Reformation, 2017 (Wolfson Hist. Prize, Wolfson Foundn, 2018); 1517: Martin Luther and the invention of the Reformation, 2017; Invisible Worlds: death, religion and the supernatural in England, 1500–1700, 2017; edited books; contrib. articles to learned jls and scholarly collections. *Recreations:* walking, travel, folk music. *Address:* Department of History, University of Warwick, Coventry CV4 7AL. *T:* (024) 7652 3452. *E:* p.marshall@warwick.ac.uk.

**MARSHALL, Sir Peter (Harold Reginald)**, KCMG 1983 (CMG 1974); CVO 2003; Chairman, Joint Commonwealth Societies Council, 1993–2003; *b* 30 July 1924; 3rd *s* of late R. H. Marshall; *m* 1st, 1957, Patricia Rendell Stoddart (*d* 1981); one *s* one *d*; 2nd, 1989, Judith (*d* 2013), widow of E. W. F. Tomlin. *Educ:* Tonbridge; Corpus Christi Coll., Cambridge (Hon. Fellow 1989). RAFVR, 1943–46. HM Foreign (later Diplomatic) Service, 1949–83: FO, 1949–52; 2nd Sec. and Private Sec. to Ambassador, Washington, 1952–56; FO, 1956–60; on staff of Civil Service Selection Board, 1960; 1st Sec. and Head of Chancery, Baghdad, 1961, and Bangkok, 1962–64; Asst Dir of Treasury Centre for Administrative Studies, 1965–66; Counsellor, UK Mission, Geneva, 1966–69, Counsellor and Head of Chancery, Paris, 1969–71; Head of Financial Policy and Aid Dept, FCO, 1971–73; Asst Under-Sec. of State, FCO, 1973–75; UK Rep. on Econ. and Social Council of UN, 1975–79; Ambassador and UK Perm. Rep. to Office of UN and Other Internat. Organisations at Geneva, 1979–83; Commonwealth Dep. Sec. Gen. (Econ.), 1983–88. Chm., Commonwealth Trust and Royal Commonwealth Soc., 1988–92; Pres., Queen Elizabeth House, Oxford, 1990–94; Vice Pres., Council for Educn in World Citizenship, 1985–98; Member: ICRC Consultative Gp of Internat. Experts, 1984–86; Exec. Cttee, Pilgrims, 1986–2001 and 2004–10; Council, VSO, 1989–95; ODI, 1989–99; Governor, E-SU of the Commonwealth, 1984–90; Trustee: King George VI and Queen Elizabeth Foundn of St Catharine's, 1987–2001; Magna Carta Trust, 1993–2004. Patron, Commonwealth Assoc., 2010. Mem., Panel of Judges, WorldAware Business Awards, 1988–2002. Chm., Nikaean Club, 1992–2002. Vis. Lectr, Diplomatic Acad. of London, 1989–2001. Hon. Fellow, Univ. of Westminster, 1992. Hon. Vice-Pres., Aircrew Assoc., 2005. *Publications:* The Dynamics of Diplomacy, 1990; (contrib.) The United Kingdom—The United Nations (ed Jensen and Fisher), 1990; (ed) Diplomacy Beyond 2000, 1996; Positive Diplomacy, 1997; (ed) Are Diplomats Really Necessary?, 1998; (ed) The Information Explosion: a challenge for diplomacy, 1998; (ed) Diplomacy and Divinity, 2006; (contrib.) Strategic Public Diplomacy, 2009; Judith: a memoir, 2013; numerous articles on Commonwealth and EU questions. *Recreations:* television, Euro-gazing. *Address:* 34 Stafford Court, 178–188 Kensington High Street, W8 7DL. *Club:* Travellers.

**MARSHALL, Prof. Peter James**, CBE 2002; DPhil; FBA 1992; Rhodes Professor of Imperial History, King's College, London, 1980–93; now Emeritus; *b* 28 Oct. 1933; *s* of Edward Hannaford Marshall and Madeleine (*née* Shuttleworth). *Educ:* Wellington College; Wadham Coll., Oxford (BA 1957; MA, DPhil 1962; Hon. Fellow, 1997). Military service, King's African Rifles, Kenya, 1953–54. Assistant Lecturer, Lecturer, Reader, Professor, History Dept, King's Coll., London, 1959–80 (FKC 1991). Mem., History Wkg Gp, National Curriculum, 1989–90. Pres., RHistS, 1996–2000 (Vice-Pres., 1987–91; Hon. Vice-Pres., 2000–). Hon. For. Mem., Amer. Historical Assoc., 2003–. Editor, Journal of Imperial and Commonwealth History, 1975–81; Associate Editor, Writings and Speeches of Edmund Burke, 1976–. Hon. DLitt: Bristol, 2008; London, 2008. *Publications:* Impeachment of Warren Hastings, 1965; Problems of Empire: Britain and India 1757–1813, 1968; (ed, with J. A. Woods) Correspondence of Edmund Burke, vol. VII, 1968; The British Discovery of Hinduism, 1972; East India Fortunes, 1976; (ed) Writings and Speeches of Edmund Burke, vol. V, 1981, vol. VI, 1991, vol. VII, 2000, vol. IV (with D. C. Bryant), 2015; (with Glyndwr Williams) The Great Map of Mankind, 1982; Bengal: the British bridgehead (New Cambridge History of India, Vol. II, 2), 1988; Trade and Conquest: studies on the rise of British dominance in India, 1993; (ed) Cambridge Illustrated History of the British Empire, 1996; (ed) Oxford History of the British Empire, Vol. II, The Eighteenth Century, 1998; A Free Though Conquering People: eighteenth-century Britain and its empire, 2003; (ed) The Eighteenth Century in Indian History: evolution or revolution?, 2003; The Making and Unmaking of Empires: Britain, India and America, *c* 1750–1783, 2005; Remaking the British Atlantic: the United States and the British Empire after American independence, 2012; Edmund Burke and the British Empire in the West Indies: wealth, power and slavery, 2019; articles in Economic History Rev., History, Modern Asian Studies, etc. *Address:* 7 Malting Lane, Braughing, Ware, Herts SG11 2QZ. *T:* (01920) 822232.

**MARSHALL, Peter James**, CMG 1996; HM Diplomatic Service, retired; Consul General, Atlanta, USA, 1997–2001; *b* 25 June 1944; *s* of George Aubrey Marshall and Joan Marshall; *m* 1966, Roberta Barlow; one *s* three *d*. *Educ:* Ripon Grammar Sch. Min. of Aviation, 1963–64; CRO, 1964–65; seconded to Commonwealth Secretariat, 1965–67; served Malta, 1967–70; Vice Consul (Commercial), Johannesburg, March–Dec. 1970; 2nd Sec. (Commercial/Information), Kaduna, 1970–74; Vice Consul (Commercial), San Francisco, 1974–79; First Sec., FCO, 1979–83; Dep. High Comr, Malta, 1983–88; First Sec., FCO, 1988–90; Dep. Head, News Dept, FCO, 1990–94; Counsellor, Consul Gen. and Dep. Head of Mission, later Chargé d'Affaires, Algiers, 1994–95; Ambassador to Algeria, 1995–96. *Recreations:* grandchildren, gardening, travel. *Address:* 2 Hemlock Close, Kingswood, Surrey KT20 6QW.

**MARSHALL, Very Rev. Peter Jerome**; Dean of Worcester, 1997–2006, now Emeritus; *b* 10 May 1940; *s* of Guy and Dorothy Marshall; *m* 1965, Nancy Jane Elliott; one *s* two *d*. *Educ:* St John's, Leatherhead; Upper Canada Coll., Toronto; McGill Univ.; Westcott House, Cambridge. Ordained deacon, 1963, priest, 1964; Curate, St Mary, E Ham, 1963–66; Curate, St Mary, Woodford, and Curate i/c, St Philip and St James, S Woodford, 1966–71; Vicar, St Peter, Walthamstow, 1971–81; Dep. Dir of Training, Dio. of Chelmsford, 1981–84; Canon Residentiary, Chelmsford Cathedral, 1981–85; Dio. Dir of Training, Ripon, and Canon Residentiary, Ripon Cathedral, 1985–97. Chm. Pastoral Cttee, Dio. of Worcester, 1997–2006. Chm., Barking and Havering AHA, 1976–82. *Recreations:* swimming, walking, sailing, films, ice-skating, curling. *Address:* 433 Gordon Avenue, Peterborough, ON K9J 6G6, Canada. *T:* (705) 8763381.

**MARSHALL, Philip**; Director, The London Library, since 2017; *b* Taplow, 8 Aug. 1972; *s* of Colin Marshall and Vivien Marshall; *m* 2001, Tamsin Saxton; one *s* two *d*. *Educ:* Desborough Sch.; Univ. of Southampton (LLB Hons); Coll. of Law Guildford (LPC); London Business Sch. (MBA). Admitted solicitor, 1996; Trainee solicitor, then Solicitor, Racal Electronics plc, 1994–97; Commercial Lawyer, Scoot.com plc, 1997–99; Solicitor: EMEA, Galileo Internat. LLC, 1999–2001; Manches, 2001–03; British Museum: Commercial Manager, 2003–05; Hd, Commercial, 2005–13; Dir, Internat. Engagement, 2013–15; Dir, Business Develt, Royal Albert Hall, 2015–16; Dir, Develt, Sadler's Wells, 2017. *Address:* The London Library, 14 St James's Square, SW1Y 4LG. *T:* (020) 7766 4700. *E:* philip.marshall@londonlibrary.co.uk.

**MARSHALL, Philip John**; QC 2012; *b* Crosby, Liverpool, 12 Oct. 1966; *s* of Robert Marshall and Norma Marshall (*née* Middleton). *Educ:* Merchant Taylors' Sch. for Boys; Liverpool Univ. (LLB). Called to the Bar, Gray's Inn, 1989; in practice as barrister, specialising in matrimonial finance, 1989–. Chm., Family Law Bar Assoc., 2016–18 (Vice Chm., 2014–16). Pres., Merchant Taylors' Old Boys' Assoc., 2016–17 (Vice Pres., 2015–16); Trustee, Merchant Taylors' Old Boys' Assoc. Charitable Trust, 2019–. Gov. (Gray's Inn), Inns of Court Coll. of Advocacy, 2018–. *Recreation:* not working. *Address:* 1 King's Bench Walk, Temple, EC4Y 7DB. *T:* (020) 7936 1500. *E:* pmarshall@1kbw.co.uk.

**MARSHALL, Philip Scott**; QC 2003; a Recorder, since 2008; a Deputy High Court Judge, since 2009; *b* 6 June 1965; *s* of Arthur and Elizabeth Marshall; *m* 1993, Barbara James; two *s* one *d*. *Educ:* Merchiston Castle Sch., Edinburgh; Queens' Coll., Cambridge (MA Hons); Harvard Law Sch. (LLM). Called to the Bar, Lincoln's Inn, 1987, Bencher, 2011; Fellow, Queens' Coll., Cambridge, 1991–94; in practice as barrister, specialising in commercial, company and insolvency law, 1991–. *Publications:* Practice and Procedure of the Companies Court, 1997; (contrib.) Civil Appeals, 2002; contribs to various legal jls. *Recreations:* horse racing, golf. *Address:* (chambers) Serle Court, 6 New Square, Lincoln's Inn, WC2A 3QS. *T:* (020) 7242 6105, *Fax:* (020) 7405 4004.

**MARSHALL, Robert David**, FRAeS; Vice Chairman, Marshall of Cambridge (Holdings) Ltd, since 2019 (Chief Executive, 2011–19); *b* Cambridge, 21 July 1962; *s* of Sir Michael John Marshall, CBE; *m* 1st, 1992, Julia Kathleen Hamilton Russell (marr. diss. 2011); one *d*; 2nd, 2013, Sheila Anne Kissane; one *s* one *d*. *Educ:* Eton Coll.; Pembroke Coll., Cambridge (BA English 1984; MA 1988); Harvard Business Sch. (AMP). FRAeS 2005. Res. Associate, Lockheed Martin, 1984–87; Founder, MBL, 1989–94; joined Marshall of Cambridge Aerospace Ltd as Hd of Projects, 1994; Dir, 1998–; Chief Exec., Marshall SV Ltd, 1999–2006; Develt Dir, Marshall Gp, 2000–07; Exec. Chm., Marshall Motor Gp, 2007–08; Chief Operating Officer, Marshall Gp, 2010–11. Mem. Bd, Cambridge Ahead, 2012–; Chm., Cambridge Launchpad, 2013–18. Chairman: Martlet/MarQuity, 2011–; Vantage Power Ltd, 2015–19; Director: e-Go Ltd, 2011–16; Make UK (formerly EEF), 2011–. Mem., Adv. Bd, Founders4Schools, 2015–. Mem., Air League, 1999–. Angel Investor, Cambridge Angels, 2010–. Gov., Hills Road Sixth Form Coll., 2007–11. MInstD. *Recreation:* flying (Private Pilot Licence). *Address:* Marshall of Cambridge (Holdings) Ltd, The Airport, Newmarket Road, Cambridge CB5 8RX. *T:* (01223) 373194. *E:* rdm@marcamb.co.uk. *Club:* Royal Automobile.

**MARSHALL, (Robert) John**; HM Diplomatic Service; Ambassador to Luxembourg, since 2016; *b* Oxford, 19 June 1965; *s* of Robert Marshall and Rosemary Marshall (*née* Simpkins); *m* 2001, (Helen) Marie Glanfield; one *s* two *d*. *Educ:* St Edward's, Oxford; Bristol Univ. (BA Mod. Langs). Joined FCO, 1988; Japanese lang. trng, 1990–92; Second Sec. (Econ.), Tokyo, 1992–95; Hd, India Sect., S Asian Dept, 1995–97; Hd, Pol Sect., UN Dept, 1997–99; First Sec. (Pol, Econ. and Public Diplomacy), Kuala Lumpur, 2000–03; Hd, Caribbean Team, 2003–04; Dep. Hd, Sustainable Develt and Commonwealth Gp, 2004–06; Dep. Hd of Mission, Addis Ababa, 2007–11; Ambassador to Senegal, and concurrently to Guinea-Bissau and Cape Verde, 2011–15. *Recreations:* running, bird watching, travel, diving. *Address:* c/o Foreign and Commonwealth Office, King Charles Street, SW1A 2AH. *E:* john.marshall@fco.gov.uk.

**MARSHALL, Prof. Robin**, PhD; FRS 1995; Professor of Experimental Physics, 1992–2005, Research Professor of Physics and Life Sciences, 2005–08, University of Manchester, now Emeritus Professor of Physics; *b* 5 Jan. 1940; *s* of Robert Marshall and Grace Eileen Marshall (*née* Ryder); *m* 1963 (marr. diss. 2003); two *s* one *d*; *m* 2005, Jennifer (*née* Dodd). *Educ:* Ermysted's Grammar Sch., Skipton; Univ. of Manchester (BSc 1962; PhD 1965). DSIR Research Fellow, 1965–67; Vis. Scientist, Deutsches Elektronen Synchrotron, Hamburg, 1967–68; Res. Scientist, MIT, 1968–70; Scientist, Daresbury Lab., 1970–78; PSO, 1978–86, Sen. Principal (IM), 1986–92, Rutherford Appleton Lab. Dir and Co. Sec., Frontiers Science and Television Ltd, 1999–2005. Mem., Bd of Govs, Museum of Sci. and Industry, Manchester, 2003–08. Proprietor, Champagne Cat publishers. Mem., Find a Better Way charity, 2011–. Max Born Medal and Prize, German Physical Soc., 1997. *Publications:* High Energy Electron-Positron Physics, 1988; Electron-Positron Annihilation Physics, 1990; Three Centuries of Manchester Physics, 4 vols; numerous scientific papers. *Recreations:* writing and painting in the South of France, running the publishing house Champagne Cat. *Address:* 7 impasse des Perrières, 30210 Castillon du Gard, France. *T:* (4) 66209857.

**MARSHALL, Rosamund Margaret**; Chief Executive Officer, Taaleem, Dubai, since 2013; *b* Cheam, Surrey, 5 July 1959; *d* of Kenneth Wilfrid and Christine Mary Samuda; *m* 1989, Geoffrey James Marshall; three *d*. *Educ:* Wallington High Sch. for Girls; Guildford Coll. (OND Instnl Housekeeping and Catering 1977). Gardner Merchant Ltd: Manager, 1977–86; Area Manager, 1986–88; Business Develt Manager, 1988–94; Dep. Divl Dir, 1994–98; Divl Dir, Sodexo, 1998–2002; Man. Dir, Learning Services, 2002–06, Chief Operating Officer, 2006–08, Nord Anglia Educn plc; CEO, Kidsunlimited, 2010–13. Non-exec. Dir, Knightsbridge Schs Internat., 2009–14. Trustee: Nat. Children's Orchestras of GB, 2009–13; British Council, 2012–18. *Recreations:* family, classical music, theatre, opera, ski-ing, walking. *Address:* Springfield House, Chalford, Glos GL6 8NW. *T:* (01453) 887330. *E:* ros.marshall@hotmail.co.uk.

**MARSHALL, Roy Thomas**, PhD; Director of ICT, Hull University, 2011–14; *b* Wolverhampton, 6 Oct. 1955; *s* of Thomas and Brenda Marshall; *m* 1979, Alison Mary Marian Shirley; two *s* one *d*. *Educ:* Univ. of Exeter (BSc 1st cl. Hons Maths and Theoretical Phys 1977; PhD Maths 1980). Geophysicist, BP Exploration, 1980–84; Head, Mapping and Modelling: BP Alaska, 1984–87; BPX London, 1987–92; Head, Systems Integration, Data Services, BPX London, 1992–94; Business Inf. Manager, BP Abu Dhabi, 1994–99; Head, Inf. Systems Gp, National Grid, 1999–2001; Dir, Deanfield Consultancy Ltd, 2003–04; Chief Inf. Officer and Head, ICT, ODPM, subseq. DCLG, 2004–06; Chief Inf. Officer and Dir, Knowledge, Inf. Technol. and Working Envmt, DCLG, 2006–10. Sen. Responsible Officer, Govt Connect, 2006–08. Founder Mem., Govt CIO Council, 2004–. *Recreations:* gardening, DIY.

**MARSHALL, Hon. Russell**; *see* Marshall, Hon. C. R.

**MARSHALL, Valerie Margaret**; Managing Director, Stratagem CFS Ltd, since 2003; *b* 30 March 1945; *d* of Ernest Knagg and Marion Knagg; *m* 1972, Alan Roger Marshall (marr. diss. 1996); two *s* one *d*. *Educ:* Brighton and Hove High Sch.; Girton Coll., Cambridge (MA); London Graduate Sch. of Business Studies (MSc). LRAM. FCSI. Financial Controller, ICFC, 1969–80; Scottish Development Agency: Investment Exec., 1980–84; Investment Man., 1984–88; Head of Business Enterprise, 1988–90; Director: Renfrew Development Co. Ltd, 1988–90; Scottish Food Fund, 1988–90; Grieg, Middleton & Co., 1990–2001; Sitka Capital Partners, 2001–02; Photopharmica Ltd, 2002–03; Fusion Lifestyle (formerly Southwark Community Leisure) Ltd, 2003–. Non-executive Director: Veryan Medical Ltd, 2004–07; Nano Biodesign Ltd, 2006–11. Member: Scottish Cttee, Design Council, 1975–77; Monopolies and Mergers Commn, 1976–81. Chm., Scottish Music Inf. Centre, 1986–90. University of Kent: Mem. Council, 2003–11 (Treas., 2004–05; Chm. 2005–11); Pro-Vice-Chancellor, 2005–11. Governor: Glasgow Sch. of Art, 1989–90; Tonbridge GS for Girls, 1993–97. DCL Kent 2012. *Recreations:* music, ballet, walking, entertaining. *Address:* 6 Egdean Walk, Sevenoaks, Kent TN13 3UQ.

**MARSHALL, Vanessa Juliette**; QC 2018; *b* Walton on Thames, Surrey, 11 April 1967; *d* of Michael and Carol Marshall; *m* 2013, Rupert Charles Mayo, *qv*; one *s* and one step *s* two step *d*. *Educ*: St Thomas' Hosp. (RGN 1989); University Coll. London (LLB Hons 1993). Nurse, St Thomas' Hosp., 1989–94; called to the Bar, Gray's Inn, 1994; in practice as barrister, specialising in criminal, medical and disciplinary law, 1995–. *Recreations*: pig keeping, Burmese cats, walking, appreciating craft gin and shoes. *Address*: 7 Bedford Row, WC1R 4BS. *T*: (020) 7242 3555. *E*: vmarshall@7br.co.uk.

**MARSHALL, Wayne**; organ recitalist and solo pianist, conductor and composer; Principal Conductor, WDR Funkhausorchester, Cologne, since 2014; *b* 13 Jan. 1961; *s* of Wigley Marshall and Costella (née Daniel). *Educ*: Chetham's Sch., Manchester; Royal Coll. of Music; Vienna Hochschule. FRCM 2010. Organ Schol., Manchester Cathedral and St George's Chapel, Windsor. Dir, W11 Opera Gp, 1991; Associate Music Dir and Conductor, Carmen Jones, Old Vic, 1991; Guest Chorus Dir, Royal Opera Hse, 1992; Organist-in-Residence, Bridgewater Hall, Manchester, 1996–; Principal Guest Conductor, Orch. Sinfonica di Milano Giuseppe, 2007–. Organ, solo piano, and duo recitals throughout UK, and overseas incl. US, European and Far East concert series; conductor and soloist with leading orchestras in UK and overseas, incl. CBSO, RPO, Philharmonia, London SO, London Philharmonic, BBCSO, Berlin Philharmonic, LA Philharmonic, Rotterdam Philharmonic and Vienna Symphony. Has made numerous recordings incl. organ music, and works by Hindemith and Gershwin. Artist of Year Award, BBC Music Mag., 1998; ECHO Award, 1998.

**MARSHALL, Sir Woodville (Kemble)**, Kt 2011; PhD; Professor of History, Cave Hill Campus, Barbados, 1977–2000, now Emeritus, and Pro-Vice-Chancellor, 1990–2000, University of the West Indies; *b* Ruby Plantation Tenantry, St Philip, Barbados, 27 March 1935; *s* of Colbert and Eileen Marshall; *m* 1961, Dawn Italia Thompson; one *s* one *d*. *Educ*: Harrison Coll., Barbados; University Coll. of W Indies, Mona, Jamaica (BA 1st Cl. Hons Hist. 1958); Cambridge Univ. (PhD Caribbean Hist. 1964). Asst Lectr, Dept of Hist., Univ. of Ibadan, 1962–63; University of the West Indies: Asst Lectr, then Lectr, Dept of Hist., Mona, Jamaica, 1963–70; Sen. Lectr, 1970–77, Hd, 1976–82, Dept of Hist., Cave Hill, Barbados; Dean, Faculty of Arts and Gen. Studies, 1972–74 and 1985–87. Ed., Jl Caribbean Hist., 1981–90. Rapporteur, Editl Cttee, UNESCO Hist. of Caribbean, 1983–2000. Founding Pres., Assoc. of Caribbean Historians, 1974–77. Vice-President: Assoc. of Caribbean Univs and Res. Insts, 1998–2000; Council, Barbados Mus. *Publications*: The Colthurst Journal, 1997; (ed) I Speak for the People: the memoirs of Wynter Crawford, 2003; (ed) Thoughts on the Objectionable System of Labour for Wages and the Necessity of Substituting a System of Tenancy and Allotment of Staple Cultivation, 2005; Freedom is…: the story of the Rock Hall Village, 2006; The Colthurst Journal 1977 From Plantations to University Campus: the social history of the Cave Hill Campus, Barbados, 2013. *Recreations*: reading (light fiction), watching TV sports (mainly cricket), playing card games, especially poker. *Address*: 11 Paradise Heights, Cave Hill, St Michael, Barbados. *T*: 4251485. *E*: wmarsh@caribsurf.com.

**MARSHALL-ANDREWS, Robert Graham**; QC 1987; a Recorder of the Crown Court, since 1982; *b* 10 April 1944; *s* of late Robin and Eileen Nora Marshall; *m* 1968, Gillian Diana Elliott; one *s* one *d*. *Educ*: Mill Hill Sch.; Univ. of Bristol (LLB; winner, Observer Mace Nat. Debating Competition, 1965). Called to the Bar, Gray's Inn, 1967, Bencher, 1996; Oxford and Midland Circuit. Contested (Lab) Medway, 1992. MP (Lab) Medway, 1997–2010. Founder Mem., Old Testament Prophets, 1996. Dep. Chm., Theatre Council, 1997–2010. Trustee: George Adamson Wildlife Preservation Trust, 1988–; Geffrye Museum, 1990–2011. Chm. of Govs, Grey Court Sch., 1988–94. Hon. DLaws Bristol, 2015. *Publications*: The Palace of Wisdom (novel), 1989; A Man without Guilt (novel), 2002; Off Message, 2011; Camille and the Lost Diaries of Samuel Pepys (novel), 2016; Dump (novel), 2018; contrib. political articles to nat. periodicals. *Recreations*: theatre, reading, Rugby (watching), travelling about. *Address*: Carmelite Chambers, 9 Carmelite Street, EC4Y 0DR. *T*: (020) 7936 6300. *Clubs*: Garrick; Druidstone (Broadhaven, Pembrokeshire).

**MARSHAM**, family name of **Earl of Romney**.

**MARSHAM, Viscount; David Charles Marsham**; *b* 18 April 1977; *s* and *heir* of Earl of Romney, *qv*; *m* 2012, Katherine, *d* of Timothy Phillips; two *s* one *d*. Army Officer; Lt-Col, Coldstream Guards. *Heir*: *s* Hon. James Julian Marsham, *b* 4 Aug. 2014.

**MARSLEN-WILSON, Lorraine Komisarjevsky**; *see* Tyler, L. K.

**MARSLEN-WILSON, Prof. William David**, PhD; FBA 1996; Director of Research, Department of Experimental Psychology, University of Cambridge, 2011; Fellow, Wolfson College, Cambridge, 2000, now Emeritus; *b* Salisbury, Wilts, 5 June 1945; *s* of David William Marslen-Wilson and Pera (née Funk); *m* 1982, Lorraine Komisarjevsky Tyler, *qv*; one *s* one *d*; one *d*. *Educ*: St John's Coll., Oxford (BA 1st cl. Philosophy and Psychology 1967); PhD MIT 1973. Asst Prof., Cttee on Cognition and Communication, Dept of Behavioral Scis, Chicago Univ., 1973–78; Scientific Associate, Max Planck Inst. for Psycholinguistics, Nijmegen, 1977–82; Lectr, Dept of Exptl Psychol., Cambridge Univ., 1982–84; Co-Dir, Max Planck Inst. for Psycholinguistics, 1985–87; Sen. Scientist, MRC Applied Psychol. Unit, Cambridge, 1987–90; Prof. of Psychology, 1990–97, College Fellow, 2000–, Birkbeck Coll., London Univ.; Dir, MRC Applied Psychol. Unit, subseq. MRC Cognition and Brain Scis Unit, Cambridge, 1997–2010. Hon. Prof. of Language and Cognition, Cambridge Univ., 2002–. MAE 1996. DUniv York, 2012. *Publications*: (ed) Lexical Representation and Process, 1989; over 150 contribs to learned jls incl. Science, Nature, Psychological Rev., Jl of Exptl Psychol., Cognition, Lang. and Cognitive Processes. *Recreations*: photography, cooking, gardening. *Address*: Department of Psychology, University of Cambridge, Downing Street, Cambridge CB2 3EB. *T*: (01223) 766975.

**MARSON, Anthony**; Finance Director, C. B. Marketing and Investments Ltd, 1997, retired; *b* 12 Jan. 1938; *m* 1963, Margaret Salmond; three *s*. *Educ*: Bristol Univ. (BA). Finance Dir, Pharmaceutical Div., Beecham Gp, 1968–90; Gp Finance Dir, PSA Services, DoE, 1990–93. *Publications*: Something or Nothing, 2017. *Address*: Bullbeggars House, Church Hill, Woking, Surrey GU21 4QE.

**MARSON, Denise Lynn; Her Honour Judge Marson**; a Circuit Judge, since 2015; *b* Manchester, 30 Jan. 1967; *d* of Eric and Joyce Gresty; *m* 1992, Geoffrey Charles Marson, *qv*; two *s*. *Educ*: Wilmslow Co. High Sch.; Sheffield Univ. (LLB Hons). Called to the Bar, Inner Temple, 1990; pupil and tenant, Sovereign Chambers, Leeds, 1990–2015; a Recorder, 2008–15; Fee-paid Judge of First-tier Tribunal (Health, Educn and Social Care Chamber (Mental Health)), 2011–. *Recreations*: family, dog walking, reading, bee-keeping, cinema. *Address*: Sheffield Family Hearing Centre, The Law Courts, 48 West Bar, Sheffield S3 8PH. *T*: (0114) 201 1140.

**MARSON, Geoffrey Charles**; QC 1997; **His Honour Judge Marson**; a Circuit Judge, since 2005; *b* 30 March 1952; *s* of Charles Marson and Muriel Annie Marson; *m* 1992, Denise Lynn Gresty (*see* D. L. Marson); two *s*. *Educ*: Malton Grammar Sch.; King's Coll. London (LLB Hons). Called to the Bar, Gray's Inn, 1975; Asst Recorder, 1991–95; a Recorder, 1995–2005; Head of Chambers, 1997–2005. Pt-time Pres., Mental Health Review Tribunals (Restricted Panel), 2000–07. *Recreations*: family, wine, cooking, travel. *Address*: Leeds Combined Court Centre, 1 Oxford Row, Leeds LS1 3BG.

**MARSTON, Nicholas Richard; His Honour Judge Marston**; a Circuit Judge, since 2005; a Deputy High Court Judge, since 2007; *b* 24 March 1952; *s* of late Lt Comdr Max Marston, MBE, DSC, RN retd and Iris May Marston; *m* 1985, Suzanne Amanda Lyons; one *s* one *d*. *Educ*: UWIST (LLB Hons). Called to the Bar, Middle Temple, 1975; Asst Recorder, 1998–99; a Recorder, 1999–2005; Designated Family Judge, Hants and IoW, 2008–12; Regl Judge, Bristol and Western Circuit, 2012, Lead Judge, SW Region, 2015–, Court of Protection. *Recreations*: keen historian and traveller, food, wine and friends, cricket, a once misplaced but now largely justified devotion to the Welsh Rugby team. *Address*: The Family Court, Bristol Civil Justice Centre, 2 Redcliff Street, Bristol BS1 6GR.

**MARSTON, Stephen Andrew**; Vice-Chancellor, University of Gloucestershire, since 2011; *b* Pembury, Kent, 7 June 1961; *s* of Charles and Ann Marston; civil partnership 2011, Anthony Broad. *Educ*: Shrewsbury Sch., Shropshire; Magdalene Coll., Cambridge (BA Hons Classics 1982). DES, 1983–91; Econ. Secretariat, Cabinet Office, 1991–94; Divl Manager, DfEE, 1994–98; Dir for Instns, HEFCE, 1998–2002; Dir for Skills, 2002–05, Dir Gen., Lifelong Learning and Skills, 2005–07, DfES; Director General: Further Educn and Skills, DIUS, 2007–09; Univs and Skills, BIS, 2009–11. *Recreations*: cycling, travel, DIY. *Address*: University of Gloucestershire, The Park, Cheltenham, Glos GL50 2RH. *T*: (01242) 714169. *E*: smarston@glos.ac.uk. *Club*: Naval and Military.

**MARTEAU, Dame Theresa (Mary)**, DBE 2017; PhD; FMedSci; Director, Behaviour and Health Research Unit, University of Cambridge, since 2010; Director of Studies in Psychological and Behavioural Sciences, Christ's College, Cambridge, since 2013; *b* London, 7 March 1953; *d* of Pieter Alexandre Marteau and Maureen Patricia Marteau; partner, 1983–98, Dr William Jonathan Boyce; one *s* one *d* and one step *d*. *Educ*: St Michael's Convent Grammar Sch., N Finchley; London Sch. of Econs and Pol Sci. (BSc Social Psychol. 1975); Wolfson Coll., Oxford (MSc Abnormal Psychol. 1977); Univ. of London ext. (PhD Health Psychol. 1985). Lectr in Health Psychol., Royal Free Hosp. Sch. of Medicine, Univ. of London, 1986–93; Sen. Lectr in Health Psychol., Guy's Hosp. Sch. of Medicine, Univ. of London, 1993–95; Prof. of Health Psychol., KCL, 1995–2010. FMedSci 2001; FAcSS (AcSS 2001). Mem., Highbury, Stoke Newington and Islington Book Soc. *Publications*: contribs to scientific jls. *Recreations*: talking while walking or dining, playing my cello at a level somewhat below that which I like to imagine I am playing, Ambridge. *Address*: Christ's College, St Andrew's Street, Cambridge CB2 3BU. *T*: (01223) 334900. *E*: tm388@cam.ac.uk.

**MARTEN, Charlotte Jane**; Headteacher, Rugby High School, 2006–19; *b* Richmond upon Thames, 2 Aug. 1957; *d* of Lewis Brindley Marten and Audrey Marten; *m* 1st, 1979, Gary Couch (marr. diss. 1991); one *s* two *d*; 2nd, 2008, Nigel Biggs. *Educ*: Mount Sch., York; Univ. of Birmingham (BA Hons Eng. Lang. and Lit. 1978); Inst. of Educn, Univ. of London (PGCE 1982); Univ. of Nottingham (MA Educnl Leadership 2004). Teacher, James Allen's Girls' Sch., 1982–94; Hd of English, Brighton and Hove High Sch., 1995–98; Dep. Hd, Northampton High Sch., 1999–2002; Principal, Jersey Coll. for Girls, 2003–06. Chair, Grammar Sch. Heads' Assoc., 2013–15. Trustee, Kidsaid Foundn, 2008–13. Governor: Rugby Sch., 2015–; Stockingford Primary Sch., 2018–. *Publications*: (ed by A. de Waal) The Ins and Outs of Selective Secondary Schools: a debate, 2015. *Recreations*: literature, riding, gardening, theatre. *E*: charlottemarten@hotmail.com.

**MARTEN, Jason Nicholas G.**; *see* Galbraith-Marten, J. N.

**MARTIENSSEN, Prof. Robert Anthony**, PhD; FRS 2006; Professor of Plant Genetics, Cold Spring Harbor Laboratory, since 1995; *b* 21 Dec. 1960. *Educ*: Emmanuel Coll., Cambridge (BA 1982; PhD 1986). Univ. of Calif, Berkeley, 1986–88; Cold Spring Harbor Lab., 1989–. Co-founder and Dir, 2000, now Mem., Scientific Adv. Bd, Orion Genomics. Barbara McClintock Prize for Plant Genetics and Genome Studies, 2018. *Publications*: articles in learned jls. *Address*: Cold Spring Harbor Laboratory, 1 Bungtown Road, Cold Spring Harbor, NY 11724, USA.

**MARTIN, Prof. Alan Douglas**, PhD; FRS 2004; Professor of Theoretical Physics, University of Durham, 1978–2003, now Emeritus and Professorial Fellow, Institute for Particle Physics Phenomenology, since 2003; *b* 4 Dec. 1937; *s* of Frederick Charles Martin and Emily May Martin (née Berkley); *m* 1st, 1964, Rev. Canon Penelope Johnson (marr. diss. 1990); one *s* two *d*; 2nd, 2000, Robin Louise Thodey (*d* 2018). *Educ*: Eltham Coll.; UCL (BSc 1958; PhD 1962). CPhys 1989, FInstP 1989. Res. Associate, Univ. of Illinois, 1962–63; University of Durham: Lectr, 1964–71; Sen. Lectr, 1971–74; Reader, 1974–78; Hd, Dept of Physics, 1989–93; Derman Christopherson Res. Fellow, 1995–96. Res. Associate, CERN, Geneva, 1971–73. Erskine Fellow, Univ. of Canterbury, NZ, 2003; Leverhulme Emeritus Fellow, 2004–06. Max Born Medal and Prize, Inst. of Physics and German Physical Soc., 2007; Chancellor's Medal, Durham Univ., 2015. *Publications*: (with T. D. Spearman) Elementary Particle Theory, 1969; (with F. Halzen) Quarks and Leptons, 1984; (with P. D. B. Collins) Hadron Interactions, 1984; (jtly) Particle Physics and Cosmology, 1989; more than 400 res. papers in scientific jls. *Recreations*: gardening, cycling, listening to music. *Address*: 8 Quarryheads Lane, Durham City DH1 3DY. *T*: (office) (0191) 334 3672, *Fax*: (0191) 334 3658. *E*: A.D.Martin@durham.ac.uk.

**MARTIN, Alastair Gilbert**, FRICS; Secretary and Keeper of the Records, Duchy of Cornwall, since 2013; *b* Reading, 21 Aug. 1960; *s* of Gilbert Martin and Diana Martin (née Hartgill); *m* 1988, Esme Marriott; one *s* one *d*. *Educ*: Royal Agricl Coll., Cirencester. FRICS 1991. Asst, Strutt & Parker, 1982–86; Partner, King Miles, then Mem., Bd of Mgt, Black Horse Agencies Alder King, 1986–91; Dir, Alder King Rural Surveyors, 1991–2001; Partner: Dreweatt Neate, 2001–09; Carter Jonas, 2009–13. Royal Institution of Chartered Surveyors: Pres., Rural Practice Div., 1999–2000; Chairman: Faculties and Forums Bd, 2000–02; Strategy and Resources Bd, 2002–07. *Recreations*: tennis, squash, hunting, shooting. *Address*: Duchy of Cornwall, 10 Buckingham Gate, SW1E 6LA. *T*: (020) 7834 7346. *E*: amartin@duchyofcornwall.org. *Clubs*: Farmers, Boodle's.

**MARTIN, Alexander Gordon, (Sandy)**; MP (Lab) Ipswich, since 2017; *b* 2 May 1957. Member (Lab): Suffolk CC, 1997–2017 (Leader, Lab Gp, 2009–17); Ipswich BC, 2002–14. Shadow Minister for Waste and Recycling, 2018–. Mem., Envmt, Food and Rural Affairs Cttee, 2017–18, Public Admin and Constitutional Affairs Cttee, 2017–18, H of C. *Address*: House of Commons, SW1A 0AA. *E*: sandy.martin.mp@parliament.uk; (office) c/o 33 Silent Street, Ipswich IP1 1TF.

**MARTIN, Prof. Andrew Philip**, DPhil; Professor of Systems Security, University of Oxford, since 2014; Fellow of Kellogg College, Oxford, since 1999; *b* Bath, 1968; *s* of John Martin and Jean Martin. *Educ*: Culverhay Sch., Bath; Pembroke Coll., Oxford (BA Maths and Computation 1989; MA 1994; DPhil Computer Sci. 1995). MBCS 2001, FBCS 2015;

CEng 2002; CITP 2002. Programmer, Praxis Systems plc, 1989–91; Res. Officer, Univ. of Oxford, 1994–95; Res. Fellow, Univ. of Queensland, 1996–98; Lectr in Computer Sci., Univ. of Southampton, 1998–99; Lectr in Software Engrg, Univ. of Oxford, 1999–2014. Vis. Fellow, Macquarie Univ., 2016; Vis. Prof. Univ. of NSW, Canberra, 2016; Adjunct Prof., Griffith Univ., 2017–. Trustee, Bletchley Park Trust, 2016–. Mem. Bd, Cyber Security Body of Knowledge, 2017–. *Publications:* contribs to peer-reviewed jls and academic confs. *Recreations:* oboe, photography, tinkering with smart home gadgets. *Address:* Department of Computer Science, University of Oxford, Wolfson Building, Parks Road, Oxford OX1 3QD. *T:* (01865) 283605. *E:* andrew.martin@cs.ox.ac.uk.

**MARTIN, Anna M.;** *see* Maxwell Martin.

**MARTIN, Barry Robert;** educational consultant, since 2013; Headmaster, Hampton School, 1997–2013; *b* 18 July 1950; *s* of late Robert Martin and Peggy Martin; *m* 1983, Fiona MacLeod; one *s* one *d*. *Educ:* Kingston Grammar Sch.; St Catharine's Coll., Cambridge (MA; Hockey Blue 1973); Inst. of Education, London Univ. (PGCE); Loughborough Univ. (MBA). Cert. Personal Finance Soc. 2009, Dip. Personal Finance Soc. 2013. Asst Master, Kingston GS, 1973–75; Bank of England Overseas Dept, 1975–77; Hd of Econs and Business Studies and Housemaster, Caterham Sch., 1978–83; Hd of Econs, Repton Sch., 1983–85; Housemaster and Dir of Studies, Mill Hill Sch., 1985–92; Principal, Liverpool Coll., 1992–97. Chief Examr, Cambridge A Level Business Studies, 1988–2002. Mem., HMC, 1992–2013 (Hon. Treas., 2007–13); Director: ISC, 2007–08, 2011–13; Ind. Schs Examinations Bd, 2007–13; Forum of Ind. Day Schs, 2011–15. Director: Courtlands Consulting Ltd, 2013–; Clamour Theatre Co. Ltd, 2017–; Sen. Advr, Wild Search, 2014–15. Governor: King's House Sch., 2004–09; Kew Coll., 2008–14; Alleyn's Sch., 2010–15; Mall Sch., 2010–15; Portsmouth Grammar Sch., 2015–18; non-exec. Dir, Radnor House Sevenoaks (Hldgs) Ltd and Radnor House Sch. (Hldgs) Ltd, 2015–. Chm. Trustees, Fitzwygram Foundn, 2019–. FRSA 1994; FCMI (FIMgt 1997). Freeman, Mgt Consultants Co., 2015–. *Publications:* jointly: The Complete A–Z Business Studies Handbook, 1994, 4th edn 2003; The Complete A–Z Economics and Business Studies Handbook, 1996, 3rd edn 2003; Business Studies, 1999, 2nd edn 2003; articles in Business Rev. *Recreation:* Cornwall. *Address:* c/o Hampton School, Hanworth Road, Hampton, Middx TW12 3HD. *T:* (020) 8979 5526. *Clubs:* East India; Hawks (Cambridge).

**MARTIN, Prof. Benjamin Raymond;** Professor of Science and Technology Policy Studies, University of Sussex, since 1996; Associate Fellow, Centre for Science and Policy, University of Cambridge, since 2010; *b* 9 Aug. 1952; *s* of late Adrian Sidney Martin, MBE and of Joan Dorothy (*née* Mingo); *m* 1973, Valerie Ann Bennett; two *s* one *d*. *Educ:* Blundell's Sch.; Churchill Coll., Cambridge (Kitchener Schol.; BA, MA); Univ. of Manchester (MSc). VSO sci. teacher, Nigeria, 1973–75; Science Policy Research Unit, University of Sussex: Fellow, 1978–86; Lectr, 1983–90; Sen. Fellow, 1986–96; Sen. Lectr, 1990–96; Dir, Sci. and Technol. Policy Res., Sci. Policy Res. Unit, 1997–2004. Vis. Lectr, Imperial Coll., London, 1983–84; Vis. Fellow, Max-Planck-Inst. für Gesellschaftsforschung, 1987; Vis. Prof., Centre for Advanced Study, Norwegian Acad. Scis and Letters, 2007–08; Vis. Schol., Faculty of Pol Sci., Univ. of Iceland, 2009–11; Sen. Vis. Fellow, Centre for Business Res., Judge Business Sch., Univ. of Cambridge, 2011–. Specialist Advr, H of L Select Cttee on Sci. and Technol., 2009–10. Chm., Internat. Expert Panel on bibliometric indicators for social scis and humanities, ESF, 2008–09; Member: Steering Gp, UK Technol. Foresight Prog., 1993–2000; Technol Opportunities Panel, EPSRC, 2001–04; BMBF Expert Gp on Demands on Res. Landscapes under Changing Framework Conditions, Berlin, 2007–08; Fruits of Curiosity Adv. Gp on econ. and social value of sci., Royal Soc., 2009–10. Mem. Senate, 1997–2004, and Council, 1997–2002, Univ. of Sussex. Ed., Res. Policy, 2004–. Derek de Solla Price Medal for Sci. Studies, Scientometrics jl, 1997. *Publications:* (with J. Irvine) Foresight in Science, 1984; (with J. Irvine) Research Foresight, 1989; (jtly) Investing in the Future, 1990; (jtly) Equipping Science for the 21st Century, 1997; (jtly) Science in Tomorrow's Europe, 1997; (with P. Nightingale) The Political Economy of Science, Technology and Innovation, 2000; (jtly) Creative Knowledge and Environments, 2004; (jtly) Creativity and Leadership in Science, Technology and Innovation, 2013; (jtly) Innovation Studies: evolution and future challenges, 2013; (jtly) The Triple Challenge for Europe: economic development, climate change and governance, 2015; contrib. papers to learned jls and books. *Recreations:* indoor rowing (10th place, World Indoor Rowing Championships, Boston, 1998), ski-ing, reading, DIY, gardening, family, travelling. *Address:* 16 Longcroft Avenue, Banstead, Surrey SM7 3AE. *T:* (01737) 361163. *E:* B.Martin@sussex.ac.uk.

**MARTIN, Bradley David;** QC 2018; *b* London, 13 March 1966; *s* of Clive Martin and Sonya Martin (*née* Ball, now Landau); *m* 1992, Brinder Bahia; two *s* one *d*. *Educ:* City of London Sch.; Watford Grammar Sch.; Leicester Univ. (LLB Hons 1987). Res. Asst, Faculty of Law, Univ. of Toronto, 1987–88; called to the Bar, Lincoln's Inn, 1990; in practice as barrister, specialising in clinical negligence, 1990–. *Recreations:* guitar, bass, banjo, ukulele, music and film. *Address:* 2 Temple Gardens, EC4Y 9AY. *T:* (020) 7822 1200, *Fax:* (020) 7822 1300. *E:* bmartinqc@2tg.co.uk.

**MARTIN, Campbell;** freelance journalist, since 2007; Member Scotland West, Scottish Parliament, 2003–07 (SNP, 2003–04, Ind, 2004–07); *b* 10 March 1960; *s* of late Campbell Martin and Jeanie, (Bunty), Martin; *m* 1993, Carol Marshall (marr. diss. 2008); one *s* one *d*. *Educ:* Ardrossan Acad.; James Watt Coll., Greenock (HNC Social Scis). Craft apprenticeship, ICI, Ardeer, Ayrshire, 1976–80; various posts, 1980–93; mature student, 1993–94; Buyer, Prestwick, 1995–97; Purchasing Liaison, Manchester, 1997–99, British Aerospace; Parly Asst, Whip's Administrator and Sec. to Shadow Cabinet, SNP Parly Gp, Scottish Parlt, 1999–2003. *Recreation:* reading.

**MARTIN, Dr Catherine Rosemary,** MBE 2013; FRS 2018; Project Leader, John Innes Centre, since 1983; *b* St Albans, 6 April 1955; *d* of Hugh Randolf Martin and Mollie Groombridge Martin; *m* 1992, Gavin Gilliatt. *Educ:* Sir Frederick Osborne High Sch., Welwyn Garden City; Churchill Coll., Cambridge (BA Natural Scis 1977); Robinson Coll., Cambridge (PhD Biochem. 1982). Broadbank Fellow, Univ. of Cambridge, 1981–83. Hon. Prof., UEA, 2000–. Hon. DSc Royal Holloway, London. *Publications:* (contrib.) Plant Biology, 2010; peer-reviewed papers. *Recreations:* Arsenal FC, crime fiction, sudoku. *Address:* John Innes Centre, Norwich Research Park, Norwich NR4 7UH. *T:* (01603) 450275. *E:* cathie.martin@jic.ac.uk.

**MARTIN, Charles David Zelenka;** Senior Partner, Macfarlanes LLP, since 2008; *b* London, 2 Feb. 1961; *s* of John Martin and Joy Martin; *m* 1988, Sarah Wilson; three *s*. *Educ:* Univ. of Bristol (LLB 1982). Admitted solicitor, 1985; Macfarlanes LLP, 1983–, Partner, 1990. Trustee: Pallant House Gall., 2016–; Visitors' Art Foundn, 2016–; Outside In, 2018–. *Recreations:* cooking, art, photography, ski-ing. *Address:* Macfarlanes LLP, 20 Cursitor Street, EC4A 1LP. *T:* (020) 7831 9222. *E:* charles.martin@macfarlanes.com.

**MARTIN, Charles Edmund,** MA; Headmaster, Bristol Grammar School, 1986–99; *b* 19 Sept. 1939; *s* of late Flight Lieut Charles Stuart Martin and of Sheila Martin; *m* 1966, Emily Mary Bozman; one *s* (one *d* decd). *Educ:* Lancing College; Selwyn College, Cambridge (Hons English; MA); Bristol University (PGCE). VSO, Sarawak, 1958–59; Asst Master, Leighton Park School, Reading, 1964–68; Day Housemaster and Hd of Sixth Form,

Sevenoaks School, 1968–71; Head of English Dept and Dep. Headmaster, Pocklington School, 1971–80; Headmaster, King Edward VI Camp Hill Boys' School, Birmingham, 1980–86. Sec., 1992–93, Chm., 1993–94, HMC SW Div.; Divl Rep., HMC Cttee, 1992–94; Member: ISC Assisted Places Cttee, 1997–99; HMC Bridges and Partnership Cttee, 1998–99. Chief Examr, A-level English, UCLES, 1978–83. VSO selector, 1999–. Gov., John Cabot Academy (formerly John Cabot City Technol. Coll.), 2000–11 (Vice Chm., 2007–11). Mem., Sarawak Assoc., 2008–. *Recreations:* travel, hill walking, theatre, ornithology. *Address:* Flat 8 Seawalls, Seawalls Road, Bristol BS9 1PG.

**MARTIN, Christine Jane;** a Judge of the Upper Tribunal (Immigration and Asylum Chamber), and Resident Judge of the First-tier Tribunal (Immigration and Asylum Chamber), Stoke-on-Trent and Nottingham (formerly Resident Senior Immigration Judge, Asylum and Immigration Tribunal, Stoke on Trent and Nottingham), since 2006, and Manchester, since 2011; *b* 20 Jan. 1957; *d* of John Stewart Wreford and Peggy Patricia Wreford (*née* Clark); *m* 1986, Lawford Patrick William Martin; one *s* one *d*. *Educ:* Univ. of Keele (BA Hons 1979); Chester Coll. of Law (Law Soc. Finals 1980). Admitted Solicitor, 1982, then partner in private practice, 1982–2002; Immigration Adjudicator, then Immigration Judge, Manchester, 2003–06. Fee-paid Judge of First-tier Tribunal (Health Educn and Social Care) (formerly Pres. (pt-time), Mental Health Rev. Tribunal), 1996–. *Recreations:* travel, reading, cooking, theatre. *Address:* First-tier Tribunal (Immigration and Asylum Chamber), First Floor, Piccadilly Plaza, Moseley Street, Manchester M1 4AH. *T:* (0161) 234 2073.

**MARTIN, Christopher;** *see* Martin, K.

**MARTIN, Christopher Anthony John;** singer and songwriter; *b* Devon, 1977; *m* 2003, Gwyneth Paltrow, *qv* (marr. diss. 2016); one *s* one *d*. *Educ:* Sherborne Sch.; University Coll. London. Lead singer, Coldplay, 1997–; albums: Parachutes, 2000 (Grammy Award, 2001; BRIT Award, 2001); A Rush of Blood to the Head, 2002 (Grammy Award, 2002; BRIT Award, 2003); X&Y, 2005; Viva la Vida or Death and All His Friends, 2008 (Grammy Award, 2008); Mylo Xyloto, 2011; Ghost Stories, 2014; A Head Full of Dreams, 2015. BRIT Award for best group (jtly), 2001, 2003, 2012, 2016, for best live act (jtly), 2013. *Address:* c/o Parlophone, 5th Floor, EMI House, 43 Brook Green, W6 7EF.

**MARTIN, Christopher George;** management consultant; Director of Personnel, British Broadcasting Corporation, 1981–89, retired; *b* 29 May 1938; *s* of George and Lizbette Martin; *m* 1st, 1960, Moira Hughes (marr. diss. 1975); one *s* one *d*; 2nd, 1981, Elizabeth Buchanan Keith; one *s* decd. *Educ:* Beckenham Sch., Kent. Royal Marines, 1956–62. Group Personnel Manager: Viyella Internat., 1964–70; Great Universal Stores, 1970–74; Personnel Dir, Reed Paper & Board, 1974–76; UK Personnel Dir, Air Products Ltd, 1976–78; Gp Personnel Controller, Rank Organisation Ltd, 1978–81. CCMI (CBIM 1984); FIPM 1984. *Publications:* contrib. Jl of Textile Inst. *Recreations:* music, sailing. *Address:* Barthefere, 81700 Puylaurens, France. *T:* (5) 63705502.

**MARTIN, Christopher Sanford;** Headmaster, Millfield School, 1990–98; *b* 23 Aug. 1938; *s* of late Geoffrey Richard Rex Martin and Hazel Matthews; *m* 1st, 1968, Mary Julia Parry-Evans (marr. diss. 2006); one *s* one *d*; 2nd, 2008, Virginia, Lady Acland (*d* 2019). *Educ:* St Andrews Univ. (MA Mod. Langs; PGCE). Commissioned 2/10 Gurkha Rifles, 1957. Taught at Westminster Sch., 1963–78, at Philips, Exeter Acad., USA, 1966; Head Master, Bristol Cathedral Sch., 1979–90. Member: Privy Council Educnl Panel, 1986–96; Engrg Council Educn Cttee, 1988–96; Adv. Gp on teaching as a profession, Teacher Trng Agency, 1995–98. Chairman: SW Div., HMC, 1987; Choir Schools' Assoc., 1987–89; HMC/SHA Working Party on teacher shortage, 1987–90; Students Partnership Worldwide, 1998–2005; Nat. Rep., HMC Cttee, 1987–89. Founded Textbooks for Africa scheme (ODA), 1988. Chairman: Mental Health Foundn, 2000–04; Hanover Foundn, 2001–08; Bottletop, 2008–12. Pres., Nat. Assoc. for Gifted Children, 2003–15. Governor: City of London Sch., 1998–2019; Springfields Acad., Calne, 2011–15; Red Maids Sch., 2015–19. Gov., Coram Family, 1999–2007; Trustee: Coram, 2008–12; Coram Life Educn, 2010–15; Foundling Mus., 2012–14; Bristol Cathedral Schs Trust, 2016–. *Publications:* Millfield: a school for all seasons, 2007; Head over Heels, 2010. *Recreations:* travel, cycling. *Address:* 28 Caledonia Place, Clifton, Bristol BS8 4DL.

**MARTIN, Ciaran Liam;** Chief Executive, National Cyber Security Centre, Government Communications Headquarters, since 2016; *b* Co. Fermanagh, 19 Sept. 1974; *m*; one *s* one *d*. *Educ:* Hertford Coll., Oxford (BA 1st Cl. Hons Modern Hist. 1996). Datamonitor Ltd, 1996–97; Nat. Audit Office, 1997–99; HM Treasury, 1999–2005; Principal Private Sec. to Cabinet Sec., 2005–08; Security and Intelligence Dir, 2008–11, Constitution Dir, 2011–14, Cabinet Office; Dir Gen., Cyber Security and Communications, GCHQ, 2014–16. *Recreations:* running, football, Gaelic sports. *Address:* National Cyber Security Centre, Nova South, 160 Victoria Street, SW1E 5LB.

**MARTIN, Claire, (Mrs Phillip Jackson),** OBE 2011; jazz singer; Presenter, Jazz Line Up, BBC Radio 3, since 2000; Co-curator, South Coast Jazz Festival, since 2015; *b* 6 Sept. 1967; *d* of David and Carole Godwin; adopted surname Martin as stage name; one *d*; *m* 2008, Phillip Jackson. *Educ:* Carshalton Coll.; Doris Holford Stage Sch. Jazz educator. Has performed with Hallé Orch., Liverpool SO, BBC Big Band, London Jazz Orch., Pete Long Big Band, Laurence Cottle Big Band, HR Big Band (Frankfurt), John Wilson Orch., Rias Big Band (Berlin), Nash Ensemble, Birmingham SO, RTE Orch., Lahti SO (Finland). *Album recordings:* The Waiting Game, 1992; Devil May Care, 1993; Old Boyfriends, 1994; Offbeat, 1995; Make this City Ours, 1997; Take My Heart, 1999; Perfect Alibi, 2000; Every Now and Then, 2001; Too Darn Hot, 2002; Secret Love, 2004; When Lights are Low, 2005; He Never Mentioned Love, 2007; A Modern Art, 2009; (with Sir Richard Rodney Bennett) Witchcraft, 2011; (with Kenny Barron) Too Much in Love to Care, 2012 (Best New Jazz Album, British Jazz Awards, 2013); Time and Place, 2014; (with Ray Gelato) We've Got a World That Swings, 2016; Believin' It, 2019. Best Vocalist, British Jazz Awards, 1996, 1998, 2000, 2002, 2009, 2010, 2018, BBC Jazz Awards, 2003; Gold Badge for services to jazz, BASCA, 2018. *Recreations:* yoga, jazz clubs, basketball. *Address:* 126 Valley Drive, Brighton, Sussex BN1 5FF. *E:* clairemartinjazz@btopenworld.com.

**MARTIN, Dr Claude;** Chancellor, International University in Geneva, since 2006; *b* 20 July 1945; *s* of Julien and Anna Martin-Zellweger; *m* 1985, Judith Füglister; two *s* two *d*. *Educ:* Univ. of Zurich (MSc; PhD Wildlife Ecol.). Field project executant, WWF/IUCN, India, 1971–73; Dir, Bia Nat. Park, Ghana, 1975–78; World Wildlife Fund, subseq. World Wide Fund for Nature: Dir, Switzerland, 1980–90; Dep. Dir Gen. (Prog.), Internat., 1990–93; Dir Gen., WWF Internat., 1993–2005, now Hon. Advr. Comdr, Golden Ark (Netherlands), 2003; Officier, Ordre National (Madagascar), 2004. *Publications:* Die Regenwälder Westafrikas, 1989, trans. as The Rainforests of West Africa, 1991. *Recreations:* mountain climbing, restoration of ancient buildings. *Address:* International University in Geneva, ICC 20, route de Pré-Bois, 1215 Geneva 15, Switzerland.

**MARTIN, Sir Clive (Haydn),** Kt 2001; OBE 1981; TD; FCMA; DL; Chairman: Europa Publications Ltd, 1978–99; MPG Ltd (formerly Staples Printers Ltd), 1978–2009; Lord Mayor of London, 1999–2000; *b* 20 March 1935; *s* of Thomas Stanley Martin and Dorothy Gladys Martin; *m* 1959, Linda Constance Basil Penn; one *s* three *d*. *Educ:* St Albans Sch.;

Haileybury and Imperial Service Coll.; London Sch. of Printing and Graphic Arts; Open Univ. (BEng Hons 2015); University Coll. London (MSc 2018). FCIS 1966; FCMA 1971; MIET 2014. Nat. Service, Germany, commnd RE (Survey), 1956–58. Man. Dir, Staples Printers Ltd, 1972–85. ADC to The Queen, 1982–86. City of London: Alderman, Aldgate Ward, 1985–2005; Sheriff, 1996–97. Master: Stationers' and Newspaper Makers' Co., 1997–98; Chartered Secs' and Administrators' Co., 2004–05. Hon. Artillery Company: CO, 1978–80; Regtl Col, 1981–83; Master Gunner, Tower of London, 1981–83. Vice-Pres., RFCA for Greater London, 2003–12. Hon. Colonel: 135 Ind. Geographic Sqn, RE, 1999–2004; London Regt, 2001–06. Master, Guild of Freemen of City of London, 1995. Trustee, Morden Coll., 1999–2011; Governor: Haileybury, 2001–; City of London Freemen's Sch., 2008–. Hon. DCL City, 1999; Hon. Dr London Inst., 2001. Comdr 1st Degree, Order of Dannebrog (Denmark). *Recreations:* sailing (British Sardinia Cup Team, 1984), cycling, walking. *Address:* Weatherbury, 16 Heath Road, Potters Bar, Herts EN6 1LN. *Clubs:* Oriental, Royal Ocean Racing, East India.

**MARTIN, Dale**; QC 2019; *b* Sheffield, 7 May 1975; *s* of Dennis Martin and Mavis Martin; partner, Christoper Laine; one *d. Educ:* King Edward VII Sch., Sheffield; Univ. of Nottingham (LLB Hons 1st Cl.). Called to the Bar, Inner Temple, 1997; in practice as a barrister, Littleton Chambers, 1998–. Friend, UK Overseas Territories Conservation Forum. *Recreations:* travel, theatre, art, good food, gym, politics, parenting. *Address:* Littleton Chambers, 3 King's Bench Walk North, Temple, EC4Y 7HR. *T:* (020) 7797 8600, *Fax:* (020) 7797 8699. *E:* clerks@littletonchambers.co.uk.

**MARTIN, David Clifford;** Head, Schools Programme, British Council, 2012–14; education and management consultant, since 2014; *b* Plymouth, 20 Dec. 1956; *s* of John Bernard Martin and Elizabeth Alma Martin (*née* Jones); *m* 1988, Sally Elizabeth Bennett; two *s* one *d. Educ:* Chigwell Sch.; Univ. of Durham (BSc Hons Chem. 1978; PGCE 1980). Teacher, Henry Fanshawe Sch., Dronfield, Derbys, 1980–84; Computer-based Learning Co-ordinator for E Midlands Reg., Microelectronics Educn Prog., 1984–86; British Council: Educn Advr, 1988–94; Dep. Dir, Nigeria, 1994–98; Director: Palestinian Territories, 1998–2002; Central Africa, 2002–06; Hungary, 2006–09; Pakistan, 2009–12. *Recreations:* cycling, walking, gardening, singing. *Address:* Maygrove Consulting Ltd, 31 Oathall Road, Haywards Heath RH16 3EG. *T:* 07769 163353. *E:* davidc_martin@yahoo.co.uk.

**MARTIN, David John Pattison;** Partner, A., D., P. & E. Farmers, since 1968; *b* 5 Feb. 1945; *s* of late John Besley Martin, CBE and Muriel Martin; *m* 1977, Basia Dowmunt; one *s* three *d* (and one *d* decd). *Educ:* Norwood Sch., Exeter; Kelly College; Fitzwilliam College, Cambridge (BA Hons 1967). Governor, Dummer Academy, USA, 1963–64; called to the Bar, Inner Temple, 1969; practised until 1976; returned to the Bar, 1998–2014; formerly Dir, family caravan and holiday business. Teignbridge District Councillor (C), 1979–83. Contested Yeovil, 1983. MP (C) Portsmouth South, 1987–97; contested (C) same seat, 1997; PPS to Minister of State, Defence Procurement, 1990, to Sec. of State, Foreign and Commonwealth Affairs, 1990–94. Contested (C): South West Region, EP elecns, 1999; Rugby and Kenilworth, 2001; Bristol W, 2005. *Recreations:* music, golf. *Club:* Hawks (Cambridge).

**MARTIN, (David) Paul;** Chief Executive, Richmond and Wandsworth Borough Councils, since 2016 (Chief Executive, Wandsworth Borough Council, 2010–16); *b* 10 Aug. 1961; *s* of late Leslie John and of Dora Marguerite Martin; *m* (marr. diss.); two *d. Educ:* Ilford Co. High Sch. for Boys; UCW, Aberystwyth (BA Hons); Anglia Business Sch. (MSc). Asst Librarian, Notts CC, 1982–85; Community Services Librarian, Bolton MBC, 1985–87; Area Organiser of Cultural Services, Manchester CC, 1987–91; Hd, Policy and Review, 1991–93, Asst Chief Exec., 1993–97, Cambs CC; Dir, Community Services, 1997–99, Chief Exec., 1999–2002, Peterborough CC; Regl Dir, Govt Office for the SE, 2002–05; Chief Exec., Sutton LBC, 2005–10. *Recreations:* music, theatre, English and American literature, travel, keeping fit. *Address:* The Town Hall, Wandsworth High Street, SW18 2PU. *T:* 07892 401931. *E:* paulmartin_home@msn.com.

**MARTIN, David Weir;** Member (Lab) Scotland, European Parliament, 1999–2019 (Lothians, 1984–99); *b* 26 Aug. 1954; *s* of William Martin and Marion Weir. *Educ:* Liberton High School; Heriot-Watt University (BA Hons Econs); Leicester Univ. (MA 1997). Stockbroker's clerk, 1970–74; animal rights campaigner, 1975–78. Lothian Regional Councillor, 1982–84. European Parliament: Leader, British Lab. Gp, 1987–88; a Vice Pres., 1989–2004. Contested (Lab) Scotland, EP, 2019. Vice-Pres., Internat. Inst. for Democracy; Vice-President: Nat. Playbus Assoc., 1985–; Advocates for Animals (formerly Scottish Soc. for Prevention of Vivisection), 1993–. Dir, St Andrew Animal Fund, 1986–. *Publications:* Europe: an ever closer union, 1991; Fabian pamphlets on the Common Market and on EC enlargement; Wheatley pamphlet on European Union. *Recreations:* soccer, reading.

**MARTIN, Prof. Derek H.;** Professor of Physics, Queen Mary and Westfield College (formerly Queen Mary College), University of London, 1967–94, Emeritus Professor since 1995 (Hon. Fellow, 1996); *b* 18 May 1929; *s* of Alec Gooch Martin and Winifred Martin; *m* 1951, Joyce Sheila Leaper; one *s* one *d. Educ:* Hitchin Boys' Grammar Sch.; Eastbourne Grammar Sch.; Univ. of Nottingham (BSc; PhD). Queen Mary College, London: Lectr, 1954–58, 1962–63; Reader in Experimental Physics, 1963–67; Dean, Faculty of Science, 1968–70; Head of Dept of Physics, 1970–75. DSIR Res. Fellow, 1959–62; Visiting Professor: Univ. of Calif, Berkeley, 1965–66; Univ. of Essex, 1995–97. Member: Astronomy, Space and Radio Bd, SRC, 1975–78; Bd, Athlone Press, 1973–79; Royal Greenwich Observatory Cttee, 1977–80; Senate, Univ. of London, 1981–86; Court, Univ. of Essex, 1986–98. Fellow, Inst. of Physics (Hon. Sec., 1984–94); Mem., Internat. Astronomical Union. NPL Metrology Award, 1983. Editor, Advances in Physics, 1974–84. *Publications:* Magnetism in Solids, 1967; Spectroscopic Techniques, 1967; numerous articles and papers in Proc. Royal Soc., Jl of Physics, etc. *Address:* 14 Avon Mill Place, Pershore, Worcs WR10 1AZ. *T:* (01386) 555301. *Club:* Athenæum.

**MARTIN, Diane Robertson**, CBE 2013; Founder and Director, Dovetail Initiative, since 2012; *b* Dundee, 20 March 1964; *d* of Edward Martin and Margaret Rodgers Martin. *Educ:* Canterbury Girls High Sch., Melbourne; Dundee Coll. of Commerce (Cert. Secretarial Studies, Office Skills and Eng. 1982); Sch. for Urban Mission, Washington, DC (Cert. Urban Studies and Soc. Systems 1994); Counselling and Psychotherapy Central Awarding Body (Cert. Integrative Counselling Skills and Theory 1999); Lambeth Coll., London (Dip. Therapeutic Counselling 2008); Middlesex Univ. (Cert. Gender and Sexual Diversity Therapy 2009). Shop Asst, Top Man, Dundee, 1982–83; care asst, Winged Fellowship Trust, 1985–87; nanny, NY, 1987–93; maternity nurse, London, 1994–97; Founder and Dir, Women's Project, 1998–2012. Lead Gp Prog. Facilitator, Living Proj., 2011–; Pan London Strategic Develt Officer (Prostitution), STRATEtude, 2013–16; Founder and Gp Facilitator, VOICES, 2013–. Trustee, Beyond the Streets, 2003–07, 2013–. *Recreations:* telly, reading in bed, challenging the sex industry and sexual exploitation, carbohydrates, God, the sea, gospel, soul and hip hop music.

**MARTIN, Most Rev. Diarmuid;** *see* Dublin, Archbishop of, and Primate of Ireland, (RC).

**MARTIN, Dòmhnall, (Donald);** Chairman, Acair Ltd, 2008–19; Lord-Lieutenant of Western Isles, since 2016 (Vice Lord-Lieutenant, 2013–16); *b* Bunabhainneadarra, Isle of Harris, 21 March 1947; *s* of late Murdo Martin and Mary Martin (*née* Macleod); *m* 1978, Sandra MacLeay; two *s* one *d. Educ:* Bunabhainneadarra Primary Sch.; Sir E. Scott Sch., Isle of Harris; Inverness High Sch.; Aberdeen Coll. of Commerce (Dip. Public Admin 1990). Civil Service Administrator, DSS, Dept of Agriculture and Fisheries Scotland, MoD and Highlands and Is Develt Bd, 1965–75; Prin. Admin. Asst, 1975–78, Depute Dir of Admin, 1978–97, Comhairle nan Eilean Siar; Dir, Community Develt, 1997–2001, Chief Exec., 2001–07, Comunn na Gàidhlig; Interim Chief Exec., Bòrd na Gàidhlig, 2009–10. Member: Western Isles Children's Panel, 1976–79; Gaelic Broadcasting Cttee, 1997–2003; Harris Tweed Authy Bd, 1997–2013 (Vice Chair, 2002–07; Chair, 2007–13). Member, Board: Attend (UK), 2007–10 (Chair, Attend (Alba), 2007–10); M G Alba, 2008–14; Lews Castle Coll., 2008–14. Sec., Eur. Bureau for Lesser Used Langs (Scottish and UK), 1984–2003. Trustee: Sabhal Mòr Ostaig, 1992–2004; N of Scotland Hydro Electric Community Trust, 2008–; Friends of Nicolson Inst., 2017– (Chm., 2017–); Urras Dileab an t-Siorraidh, 2017– (Vice Chm., 2017–). Clerk, Western Isles Lieutenancy, 1997–2016. DL Western Isles, 2002. Volunteer, Stornoway League of Friends, 1982– (Chair, 1997–2009). Chieftain, Gaelic Soc. of Inverness, 2019–20. *Recreations:* grandparenting, Gaelic culture and broadcasting, local history, genealogy, gardening, watching Hearts FC. *Address:* Druimard, 4 Airigh Ard, Steòrnabhagh, Eilean Leòdhas HS1 2UN. *T:* (01851) 704890. *E:* domhnallm@aol.com.

**MARTIN, Dominic David William**, CVO 2007; HM Diplomatic Service; Vice-President, Statoil, since 2014; *b* 25 Nov. 1964; *s* of Christopher Martin and Felicity Martin (*née* Weston); *m* 1996, Emily Walter; three *d. Educ:* Westminster Sch.; Oriel Coll., Oxford (BA Hons). Joined HM Diplomatic Service, 1987; FCO, 1987–89; Third, later Second Sec., New Delhi, 1989–92; FCO, 1992–96; First Secretary: Buenos Aires, 1996–99; FCO, 1999–2001; Political Counsellor, and Hd, Political Dept, New Delhi, 2001–04; Counsellor (Political, Press and Public Affairs), Washington, 2004–08; UK Perm. Rep. to OECD, Paris, 2008–11; Dir, Prosperity, FCO, 2011–12; Dir, G8 Presidency, Cabinet Office, 2012–14. *Address:* Statoil, 1 Kingdom Street, W2 6BD.

**MARTIN, Donald;** *see* Martin, Dòmhnall.

**MARTIN, Most Rev. Eamon;** *see* Armagh, Archbishop of, (RC).

**MARTIN, Francis James, (Frank);** HM Diplomatic Service, retired; High Commissioner to Botswana, 2005–09; *b* 3 May 1949; *s* of Brian and Elizabeth Martin; *m* 1970, Aileen Margaret Shovlin; two *s* two *d. Educ:* St Ninian's High Sch., Kirkintilloch; Bourne Sch., Kuala Lumpur; St John's, Singapore. Joined FCO, 1968; Third Sec., Reykjavík, 1971–73; Vice Consul (Commercial), Stuttgart, 1973–76; FCO, 1976–78; Vice-Consul (Political/Inf.), Cape Town, 1979–83; Second, later First, Sec. (Instns), UK Representation to EC, Brussels, 1983–88; FCO, 1988; Dep. High Comr, Freetown, 1988–91; FCO, 1991; on secondment to DTI, 1992–95; lang. student, 1995; Dep. Hd of Mission, Luanda, 1995–98; First Sec., and Hd, Commercial Dept, Copenhagen, 1998–2001; FCO, 2001–02; High Comr to Lesotho, 2002–05. *Recreations:* fishing, walking.

**MARTIN, Frank;** Change Manager, Tax Policy Project, HM Treasury, 2003–06; *b* 1 April 1946; *s* of Frank and Sylvia Martin; *m* 1975, Jean Richardson; one *s* one *d. Educ:* Alsop High Sch. for Boys, Liverpool; Sidney Sussex Coll., Cambridge (MA Hist.); LSE (MSc Internat. Relns). COI, 1969–73; DTI, 1973–76; HM Treasury, 1976–2006: Dep. Dir, Central Unit on Purchasing, 1987–89; on secondment as Principal Establishment and Finance Officer, CSO, 1989–93, and TTA, 1999–2001; Second Treasury Officer of Accounts, 1994–98; Dir, Corporate Services, Commonwealth Secretariat, 2001–03 (on secondment). *Recreations:* walking, reading, gardening, listening to music.

**MARTIN, Geoffrey;** *see* Martin, T. G.

**MARTIN, Prof. Geoffrey Almeric Thorndike,** PhD, LittD; FSA; Edwards Professor of Egyptology and Head of Department of Egyptology, University College London, 1988–93, now Emeritus; *b* 28 May 1934; *s* of late Albert Thorndike Martin and Lily Martin (*née* Jackson). *Educ:* Palmer's Sch., Grays Thurrock; University Coll. London (Sir William Meyer Prize, 1961; BA 1963); Corpus Christi Coll., Cambridge; Christ's Coll., Cambridge (MA 1966; PhD 1969; LittD 1994). Chartered Librarian (ALA, 1958–60); FSA 1975. Cataloguer, Brit. Nat. Bibliography, 1957–60; Lady Budge Res. Fellow in Egyptology, Christ's Coll., Cambridge, 1966–70; University College London: Lectr in Egyptology, 1970–78; Reader in Egyptian Archaeology, 1978–87; Prof. (ad hominem) of Egyptology, 1987–88. Wilbour Fellow, Brooklyn Museum, 1969; Rundle Fellow, Aust. Centre for Egyptology, Macquarie Univ., 1985, 1995, 2000; Jane and Morgan Whitney Art Hist. Fellow, Met. Mus. of Art, NY, 1999–2001. Vis. Prof., Collège de France, 1986. Glanville Lectr, Cambridge, 1990. Has lectured extensively in UK and abroad. Assisted at excavations of Egypt Exploration Society at: Buhen, Sudan, 1963; Saqqara, Egypt, 1964–68, 1970–71 (Site Dir, 1971–74; Field Dir, 1975–98); Field Director: Epigraphic Mission, Amarna, Egypt, 1969, 1980; Leiden Excavations, Saqqara, 1999–2000 (Hon. Dir, 2001–); Jt Field Dir, 1998–2001, Field Dir, 2002, Amarna Royal Tombs Project, Valley of the Kings, Thebes; Field Dir, Cambridge Expedn to Valley of the Kings, 2005–; Jt Field Dir, Cambridge Expedn to Valley of the Kings and New Kingdom Res. Foundn, 2014–. Mem. Cttee, Egypt Exploration Soc., 1969–97 (Hon. Vice-Pres., 2012); Rep. for GB, Council of Internat. Assoc. Egyptologists, 1976–82; Mem. Cttee, Bd of Management, Gerald Averay Wainwright Near Eastern Archaeol Fund, Oxford Univ., 1985–89; Christ's College, Cambridge: Hon. Keeper of Muniment Room, 1997–2004; Hon. Keeper of the Silver, 2000–13; Hon. Keeper of the Archives, 2004–; Fellow Commoner (Non-Stipendiary Fellow), 1998–; Sen. Fellow, McDonald Inst. for Archaeological Res., Univ. of Cambridge, 2016–. Patron, Thurrock Local History Soc., 1996–. Corresp. Mem., German Archaeol Inst., 1982. Ed., Egypt in Miniature series (Oxford Expedition to Egypt), 2006–. *Publications:* Egyptian Administrative and Private-Name Seals, 1971; The Royal Tomb at El-Amarna, vol. 1, 1974, vol. 2, 1989; The Tomb of Hetepka, 1979; The Sacred Animal Necropolis at North Saqqara, 1981; (with V. Raisman) Canopic Equipment in the Petrie Collection, 1984; Scarabs, Cylinders and other Ancient Egyptian Seals, 1985; The Tomb Chapels of Paser and Raia, 1985; Corpus of Reliefs of the New Kingdom, vol. 1, 1987; (with A. El-Khouly) Excavations in the Royal Necropolis at El-Amarna, 1987; The Memphite Tomb of Horemheb, 1989; The Hidden Tombs of Memphis, 1991 (German edn 1994); Bibliography of the Amarna Period and its aftermath, 1991; The Tomb of Tia and Tia, 1997; The Tombs of Three Memphite Officials, 2001; Stelae from Egypt and Nubia in the Fitzwilliam Museum, Cambridge, 2005; Private Stelae of the Early Dynastic Period from the Royal Cemetery at Abydos, 2011; The Tomb of Maya and Meryt, I, 2012; Tutankhamun's Regent, 2016; contribs to learned and other jls and to Festschriften; *festschrift:* Another Mouthful of Dust, ed J. van Dijk, 2016. *Recreations:* ancient history, English and European history, bibliography, travel. *Address:* c/o Christ's College, Cambridge CB2 3BU.

**MARTIN, Prof. (George) Steven**, PhD; FRS 1998; Research Virologist, Cancer Research Laboratory, 1983–2016, Professor of Molecular and Cell Biology, 1989–2016, now Emeritus, and Dean, Division of Biological Sciences, 2012–16, University of California at Berkeley; b 19 Sept. 1943; s of Kurt and Hanna Martin; m 1969, Gail Zuckman; one s. Educ: Queens' Coll., Cambridge (MA 1966; PhD 1968). Postdoctoral Fellow, Virus Lab., Univ. of Calif, Berkeley, 1968–71; staff mem., ICRF, London, 1971–75; University of California, Berkeley: Asst Prof., 1975–79, Associate Prof., 1979–83, Prof. of Zoology, 1983–89, Dept of Zool.; Asst Res. Virologist, 1975–79, Associate Res. Virologist, 1979–83, Cancer Res. Lab; Richard and Rhoda Goldman Dist. Prof., Dept of Molecular and Cell Biol., 2002–07; Judy C. Webb Prof. and Chair, Dept of Molecular and Cell Biol., 2007–11. Jane Coffin Childs Meml Fund Fellow, 1968–70; Amer. Cancer Soc. Dernham Fellow, 1970–71; John Simon Guggenheim Meml Foundn Fellow, 1991–92. Scholar Award in Cancer Res., Amer. Cancer Soc., 1991–92. Publications: contribs to Nature, Science, Cell and other scientific jls. Recreations: hiking, reading. Address: University of California at Berkeley, Department of Molecular and Cell Biology, Li Ka Shing Center #3370, Berkeley, CA 94720–3370, USA. T: (510) 6421508.

**MARTIN, Gerard James**; QC 2000; a Recorder, since 2000; b 27 May 1955; m 1980, Deirdre Martin; three s. Educ: St Joseph's Coll., Blackpool; Trinity Hall, Cambridge (BA Law). Called to the Bar, Middle Temple, 1978; Asst Recorder, 1997–2000. Recreations: most sports, good food and wine. Address: Exchange Chambers, One Derby Square, Liverpool L2 9XX.

**MARTIN, Sir Gregory (Michael Gerard)**, Kt 2013; Executive Headteacher, Durand Academy, 2010–15; b Beverley, E Yorks, 2 July 1952; s of George Martin and Thelma Martin; partner, Saffron Elizabeth Rebecca Smith; two s two d. Educ: Norwood Coll., Harrogate; Inst. of Educn, Univ. of London (BEd Hons). Qualified teacher, 1976. Teacher, St Mary's Clapham, 1976–82; Dep. Headteacher, Sudbourne Primary Sch., 1982–86; Headteacher, Durand Jun. Sch., later Durand Primary Sch., 1986–2010, amalgamating Mostyn Gardens Primary Sch., 1999. Recreations: talking, sleeping, arguing (but not always in that order). Club: Manchester United Football.

**MARTIN, Iain James**; author; political commentator, The Times; Editor, Reaction, since 2016; b 2 Oct. 1971; m Fiona; one s. Educ: Castlehead High Sch., Paisley; Univ. of Glasgow (MA 1993). Reporter, Sunday Times Scotland, 1993–97; Political Ed., then Asst Ed., Scotland on Sunday, 1997–2000; Asst Ed. and political commentator, The Scotsman, 2000–01; Dep. Ed., Scotland on Sunday, 2001; Ed., The Scotsman, 2001–04; Ed., Scotland on Sunday, 2004–06; Dep. Ed., Sunday Telegraph, 2006; Gp Exec. Ed., 2007, Head of Comment, 2008–09, Telegraph Media Gp; Dep. Ed., Wall Street Journal Europe, 2009–11. Publications: Making It Happen: Fred Goodwin, RBS and the men who blew up the British economy, 2013; Crash Bang Wallop, 2016.

**MARTIN, Ian**; Senior Visiting Research Fellow, Department of War Studies, King's College London; international consultant; b 10 Aug. 1946; s of Collin and Betty Martin. Educ: Brentwood Sch.; Emmanuel Coll., Cambridge; Harvard Univ. Ford Foundn Representative's Staff, India, 1969–70, Pakistan, 1970–71, Bangladesh, 1972; Community Relations Officer, Redbridge Community Relations Council, 1973–75; Gen. Sec., Jt Council for the Welfare of Immigrants, 1977–82 (Dep. Gen. Sec., 1976–77; Exec. Cttee Mem., 1982–86); Gen. Sec., The Fabian Soc., 1982–85; Sec. Gen., Amnesty Internat., 1986–92 (Hd, Asia Res. Dept, 1985–86). Dir for Human Rights, UN/OAS Internat. Civilian Mission in Haiti, 1993, 1994–95; Chief, UN Human Rights Field Op., Rwanda, 1995–96; Special Advr, UN High Comr for Human Rights, 1998; Dep. High Rep. for Human Rights, Bosnia and Herzegovina, 1998–99; Special Rep. of UN Sec.-Gen., East Timor Popular Consultation, 1999; Dep. Special Rep. of UN Sec.-Gen., UN Mission in Ethiopia and Eritrea, 2000–01; Vice-Pres., Internat. Center for Transitional Justice, NY, 2002–05; Rep. of UN High Comr for Human Rights, Nepal, 2005–06; Special Rep. of UN Sec.-Gen., Nepal, 2007–09; Hd, UN HQ Bd of Inquiry into certain incidents in Gaza Strip, 2009; Special Rep. of UN Sec.-Gen., Libya, 2011–12; Mem., UN Sec.-Gen.'s High Level Ind. Panel on Peace Ops, 2014–15; Exec. Dir, Security Council Report, 2015–18. Sen. Associate, Carnegie Endowment for Internat. Peace, 1993, 1994; Visiting Fellow: Human Rights Centre, Univ. of Essex, 1996–97; Internat. Peace Acad., NY, 2000. Member: Exec. Cttee, NCCL, 1983–85; Redbridge and Waltham Forest AHA, 1977–82; Redbridge HA, 1982–83. Councillor, London Borough of Redbridge, 1978–82. Publications: Immigration Law and Practice (with Larry Grant), 1982; Self-Determination in East Timor, 2001; Nepal's Peace Process at the United Nations, 2010 contributed to: Labour and Equality, Fabian Essays, 1980; Civil Liberties, Cobden Trust Essays, 1984; Hard Choices (ed J. Moore), 1998; Honoring Human Rights (ed A. Henkin), 2000; The United Nations and Regional Security (ed M. Pugh and W. P. S. Sidhu), 2003; Humanitarian Intervention and International Relations (ed J. M. Welsh), 2004; The UN Security Council (ed D. Malone), 2004; Nepal in Transition (ed S. Einsiedel, D. Malone and S. Pradhan), 2012; The Libyan Revolution and its Aftermath (ed P. Cole and B. McQuinn), 2015; The Rôle of Elected Members on the Security Council: key players or lame ducks? (ed N. Schrijver and N. Blokker), 2019. Address: 346 Ben Jonson House, Barbican, EC2Y 8NQ.

**MARTIN, Ian Alexander**; Chairman, SSL International PLC, 2001–05; Executive Chairman, Heath Lambert Holdings Ltd, 2003–05; b 28 Feb. 1935; s of Alexander Martin and Eva (née Gillman); m 1963, Phyllis Mitchell-Bey; one s two d. Educ: Univ. of St Andrews (Medallist in Psychol. 1956–57 and 1957–58; MA). Mem., Inst. of Chartered Accountants, Scotland. Dir, Mine Safety Appliances Co. Ltd, 1969–72; Div. Dir, ITT Europe, 1977–79; Grand Metropolitan: Dir, 1985–94; Gp Man. Dir, 1991–93; Dep. Chm., 1993–94; Chairman: Intercontinental Hotels, 1986–88; Burger King Corp., 1989–93; Pillsbury Co., 1989–93; Internat. Distillers and Vintners, 1992–93; Chm. and Chief Exec., Glenisla Gp Ltd, 1994–97; Chm., 1995–2001, Chief Exec., 2001, Unigate, then Uniq; Chairman: Baxi Gp (formerly Newmond), 1997–2002; Heath Lambert Fenchurch Hldgs (formerly Erycinus), 1997–2005; William Hill, 1999–; 365 Corporation PLC, 1999–2002; Director: St Paul Companies Inc., 1989–96; Grocery Manufacturers of America, 1989–93; Granada Group, 1992–98; House of Fraser, 1994–2000; Nat. Commn on Children, USA, 1990–93. Chm., Europe Cttee, CBI, 1993–94; Mem. Adv. Cttee, Ian Jones & Partners, 1998–. Trustee, Duke of Edinburgh's Award Scheme, 1991–98; Dir, Friends of the Youth Award Inc., 1991–98. Freeman, City of London, 1982. CCMI (CBIM 1986). Recreations: angling, golf, music.

**MARTIN, James Brown**, CBE 2018; Scottish Public Services Ombudsman, 2009–17; b 6 Dec. 1953; s of James and Annie Martin; m 1st, 1975, Anne McNaughton; one s one d; 2nd, 2002, Elaine Smith; one s one d. Educ: Larbert Village and High Schs; Heriot-Watt Univ. (BAEcon); Moray House College of Educn. Teacher, Falkirk High Sch., 1975–79; Field Officer 1979–83, Asst Sec. 1983–88, Gen. Sec., 1988–95, EIS; Dir, Causeway Consulting, 2002–09. Police Complaints Comr for Scotland, 2007–09. Non-exec. Chm., LogicaCMG Scotland, 2002–07. Member: Gen. Council, Scottish TUC, 1987; Exec., ETUCE, 1988; Exec., Education International, 1993; SFC, 2005–09. Mem., Forth Valley Enterprise Bd, 1989. Recreations: Hibernian FC, watching football.

**MARTIN, Janet, (Mrs K. P. Martin)**; Relief Warden (Assisted Independence), Test Valley Housing, 1988–91; b Dorchester, Dorset, 8 Sept. 1927; d of James Wilkinson and Florence Steer; m 1951, Peter Martin, sometime of Southampton HA and Senior Consultant AT&T (ISTEL) Ltd (d 2004); one s one d. Educ: Dorchester Co. Sch. for Girls, Dorset; Weymouth Tech. Coll.; occupational training courses. PA to Group Sec., Herrison HMC, 1949; admin./clerical work, NHS and other, 1956; social research fieldwork, mainly NHS (Wessex mental health care evaluation team), and Social Services (Hants CC and Nat. Inst. for Social Work), 1967–76; residential social worker (children with special needs), Southampton, 1976–78; Social Services Officer, Test Valley, 1978–86; Senior Residential Care Officer (Elderly), Test Valley Social Services, 1986–87. Interviewer, MRC 'National' Survey, 1970–85; Psychosexual Counsellor, Aldermoor Clinic, 1981–84. Mem., Press Council, 1973–78. Recreations: buildings, books.

**MARTIN, Dame Joan Margaret**; see Higgins, Dame J. M.

**MARTIN, Joanna Margaret**; QC 2018; a Recorder, since 2016; b Rustington, 13 Dec. 1967; d of Christopher and Margaret Martin; partner, Mary Galbraith. Educ: Rosemead Sch., Littlehampton; Cambridge Coll. of Arts and Technol. (BA English Lit.); London Univ. (LLB ext.); Bournemouth Univ. (DipLP (Dist.)). Admitted solicitor, 1996; Solicitor, CPS, then Serious Fraud Office, 1996–2003; Solicitor, CPS, Plymouth, 2003–05; called to the Bar, Middle Temple, 2005; in practice as barrister, specialising in criminal law, in particular frauds. Recreations: learning new things, extreme gardening, wild swimming. Address: Devon Chambers, 8 The Crescent, Plymouth PL1 3AB. T: (01752) 661659. E: jo.martin@devonchambers.co.uk.

**MARTIN, His Honour John Alfred Holmes**; QC (NI) 1989; an Upper Tribunal Judge (Administrative Appeals Chamber), 2008–16; b 31 May 1946; s of Very Rev. Dr Alfred Martin and Doris Muriel Martin; m 1983, Barbara Elizabeth Margaret Kyle; one s one d. Educ: Finaghy Primary Sch.; Royal Belfast Academical Instn; Queen's Univ., Belfast (LLB 1969; Dip. Law 1970). Called to the Bar: NI Inn of Court, 1970, Bencher, 2001; Gray's Inn, 1974; King's Inns, 1975; a Dep. Co. Court Judge, 1983–88; a Co. Court Judge, 1990–2011; Crown Court Judge, 1990–97; Recorder of Londonderry, 1993–94; Additional Judge for Co. Court Belfast, 1994–97. Chief Social Security Comr, and Chief Child Support Comr, NI, 1997–2011; Chief Pensions Appeal Comr, NI, 2005–11; Dep. Social Security Comr, 2005–08. Pt-time Chm., 1981–88, Chm., 1988–89, Vice Pres., 1990, Industrial Tribunals, NI; Vice Pres., Fair Employment Tribunal, NI, 1990; Chm. and Pres., Pensions Appeal Tribunals, NI, 2001–11. Member: NI Bar Council, 1983; Council of HM County Court Judges, 1990–2011 (Hon. Sec., 1995–97); Council of HM Judges of the Upper Tribunal Admin. Appeals Chamber (formerly HM Social Security and Child Support Comrs of the UK), 2004–11. Pres., Irish Legal Hist. Soc., 2004–06. Gov., Presbyterian Orphan Soc., 1991–. Vice Pres., Irish Amateur Rowing Assoc., 1978–79; Mem. Jury and Umpire, rowing events, Olympic Games, 1980 and Commonwealth Games, 1986. Recreations: rowing, hill-walking, gardening, reading. Address: Royal Courts of Justice, Chichester Street, Belfast BT1 3JE. T: (028) 9187 0238. Clubs: Ulster Reform; Leander.

**MARTIN, Prof. John Francis**, MD; FRCP; FMedSci; Professor of Cardiovascular Medicine (formerly British Heart Foundation Professor), since 1996, and Leader, Institute of Cardiovascular Science, 2007–09, University College London; Hon. Consultant Physician, University College Hospitals NHS Trust, since 1996; b 8 July 1943; s of Francis Martin and Marie-Antoinette Martin (née Bessler); m 1979, Ide Leddy (marr. diss. 1987); m 1991, Elisabeth Gaillochet (marr. diss. 1995). Educ: English Coll., Valladolid, Spain; Univ. of Sheffield (MB ChB 1973; Gold Medal 1973; MD 1981). FRCP 1989. Lectr in Medicine, Sheffield Univ., 1975–79; Sen. Lectr, Univ. of Melbourne, 1979–81; Hon. Consultant Physician, St Vincent's Hosp., Melbourne, 1979–81; Sen. Lectr, Sheffield Univ., 1981–86; Hon. Consultant Physician, Hallamshire Hosp., 1981–86; Hd, Cardiovascular Res., Wellcome Foundn Res. Labs, 1986–96; Sen. Lectr, 1986–90, BHF Prof. of Cardiovascular Sci., 1990–96, KCL; Hon. Consultant Physician, KCH, 1986–96. Queen Victoria Eugenia Chair, Complutense Univ., Madrid, 2004–05; Adjunct Prof. of Internal Medicine (Cardiology), Yale Univ., 2010–. CSO and Dir, Ark Therapeutics (formerly Eurogene), 2000–12 (Founder, 1997); Chief Scientist and Founder, Magnus Life Science (formerly Magnus), 2009–17. Mem., Animal Procedures Cttee, Home Office, 1998–2006. Pres., Eur. Soc. for Clinical Investigation, 1992–95; Vice Pres., Eur. Soc. Cardiology, 2000–02 (FESC 1995; Mem. Bd, 1998–2006; Chm., European Union Relations Cttee (formerly European Affairs Cttee), 2001–06; Gold Medal, 2008); Founder and Pres., Eur. Critical Care Foundn, 2008–16. Chm., St George Charity, 2017–. Captain, RAMC(V), 1977–83, Major, 1983–86; now RARO (Gurkah Field Force, Hong Kong, 1979; Australian Army Reserve, 1980–81). FMedSci 2000. Hon. DM Kuopio, 2008; DUniv Sheffield Hallam, 2016. Publications: Platelet Heterogeneity, Biology and Pathology, 1990; The Origin of Loneliness: poems and short stories, 2004; contrib. articles to learned jls on cardiovascular biol. and medicine, particularly arteriosclerosis, platelets and acute coronary syndromes and gene therapy. Recreations: poetry, Mediaeval philosophy, language, music. Address: British Heart Foundation Laboratories, Department of Medicine, University College London, 5 University Street, WC1E 6JJ. T: (020) 7679 6339; 21 West Square, SE11 4SN. T: (020) 7735 2212. Club: Athenæum.

**MARTIN, John Howard Sherwell**, FRICS; Senior Partner, Knight Frank, 1996–2004; b 7 Aug. 1945; s of John Robert Henry Martin and Lilian Vera Sherwell; m 1971, Linda Susan Johnson (d 2016); one s two d; m 2019, Susan Intan Wood. Educ: Emanuel Sch. FRICS 1971. Trainee Surveyor, GLC, 1965–71; joined Knight Frank & Rutley, 1971; Partner, 1978–96. Non-exec. Dir, Baltic Exchange, 1993–98. Trustee, St Clement Danes Holborn Estate Charity, 1987–2000. Recreations: travel, antiques, gardening. Address: Rowlands Court, Newchapel Road, Lingfield, Surrey RH7 6BJ. Club: Oriental (Chm., 2017–).

**MARTIN, John Neville**, FREng, FICE, FIStructE; Chairman, Ove Arup Partnership, 1992–95; b 9 April 1932; s of Reginald Martin and Dorothy Sylvia Martin (née Bray); m 1964, Julia Mary Galpin; three s one d. Educ: Royal Grammar Sch., Guildford. FICE 1957; FIStructE 1957; FREng (FEng 1988). Articled pupil with Engr and Surveyor, Woking UDC, 1949–52; Nat. Service, RE, 1952–54; Asst Engr, Sir William Halcrow & Partners, Consulting Engrs, 1954–57; with Ove Arup Partnership, Consulting Engrs, 1957–95. Chm., Ove Arup Foundn, 1996–2000. Chm., Haslemere Dist Scout Council, 1995–2002. Publications: various papers for engrg jls (IStructE). Recreations: Scouting, mountain-walking, music, country dancing.

**MARTIN, John Paul**; consultant; b 6 April 1948; s of Denis Martin and Veronica Martin; m 1972, Jacqueline Davida Gunn; two s one d. Educ: University Coll., Dublin (MA Econ); MPhil Oxford. Res. Asst, Econ. and Social Res. Inst., Dublin, 1970–72; Lectr in Econs, Merton Coll., Oxford, 1974–77; Res. Fellow, Nuffield Coll., Oxford, 1975–77; Lectr in Econs, Univ. of Buckingham, 1975–77; Organisation for Economic Co-operation and Development, Paris: Administrator, 1977–80; Principal Administrator, 1980–83; Hd of Div. and Editor of OECD Employment Outlook, 1983–87; Hd of Div., Econs Dept, 1987–93, and Editor, OECD Economic Outlook, 1992–93; Dep. Dir for Employment, Labour and Social Affairs, 1993–2000; Dir for Educn, Employment, Labour and Social Affairs, 2000–02; Dir for Employment, Labour and Social Affairs, OECD, 2002–13. Pt-time Prof., Institut d'Etudes Politiques de Paris, 1993–; Res. Fellow, Inst. for the Study of Labour, Univ. of Bonn, 2005–; Adjunct Res. Fellow, UCD Geary Inst. for Public Policy, 2014–. Member: Strategic Bd, LIEPP Scis Po, Paris, 2011–; Conseil scientifique d'evaluation de la convention d'Assurance chomage, Unédic, 2015–17; Strategic Adv. Bd, Kiel Centre for Globalisation, 2017–. Member: French Prime Minister's Conseil de l'orientation pour l'emploi, 2005–17; Expert Gp on Future Skills Needs, Irish Govt, 2007–13; Labour Market Council, Irish Govt, 2013–; Council, Econ. and Social Res. Inst., Dublin, 2015–; Nat. Statistics Bd of Ireland, 2017–. Mem., Adv. Bd, World Demographic Assoc., 2006–09. Presidential Dist. Service Award for the Irish Abroad (Ireland), 2013. *Publications:* Trade and Payments Adjustment Under Flexible Exchange Rates, 1977; Youth Unemployment, 1980; The Nature of Youth Unemployment, 1984; many articles in jls such as Economic Jl, Economica, Oxford Economic Papers, Rev. of Econs and Stats, Jl of Internat. Economics, OECD Observer, OECD Economic Studies, Swedish Economic Policy Rev., De Economist, IZA Jl of Labor Policy, Economic and Social Rev., Jl Population Econs. *Recreations:* tennis, golf, reading, wine-tasting.

**MARTIN, John Sharp Buchanan,** FCIHT; non-executive Director, 2010–15, Senior Independent Director, 2012–15, and Vice Chairman, 2015, Lothian Buses Ltd (formerly plc); *b* 7 July 1946; *s* of David Buchanan Martin and Agnes Miller Martin (*née* Craig); *m* 1971, Catriona Susan Stewart Meldrum; one *s* one *d. Educ:* Bell Baxter High Sch., Cupar, Fife; Univ. of St Andrews (BSc). FCIHT (FIHT 2003). Asst Principal, Scottish Educn Dept, 1968–71; Private Sec. to Parly Under-Sec. of State for Scotland, 1971–73; Scottish Office: Principal, 1973–80, seconded to Rayner Scrutinies, 1979–80; Asst Sec., 1980–92; Under-Sec., Sch. Educn and Sport, Educn, subseq. Educn and Industry Dept, 1992–98; Hd of Transport and Planning Gp, then Transport Gp, Scottish Office, later Scottish Exec., 1998–2004; concessionary fares appeals adjudicator for DfT, 2006–10. Mem., SE Scotland Transport Partnership, 2006–18. Public Mem., Network Rail, 2008–10. Member: Adv. Bd, Transport Res. Inst., Edinburgh Napier Univ. (formerly Napier Univ.), 2005–19; Adv. Panel, Rly Heritage Trust, 2010–. *Recreations:* tennis, golf, philately. *Clubs:* Colinton Lawn Tennis, Merchants of Edinburgh Golf.

**MARTIN, John Sinclair,** CBE 1977; farmer, retired; Chairman, Anglian Flood Defence Committee, Environment Agency (formerly National Rivers Authority), 1989–97; *b* 18 Sept. 1931; *s* of Joseph and Claire Martin, Littleport, Ely; *m* 1960, Katharine Elisabeth Barclay, MB, BS; three *s* one *d. Educ:* The Leys Sch., Cambridge; St John's Coll., Cambridge (MA, Dip. in Agriculture). Chairman: Littleport and Downham IDB, 1971–88; JCO Arable Crops and Forage Bd, 1973–76; Eastern Regional Panel, MAFF, 1981–86 (Mem., 1972–78); Great Ouse Local Land Drainage Cttee, AWA, 1983–88; Anglian Drainage Cttee, 1988–89; Member: Eastern Counties Farmers' Management Cttee, 1960–70; ARC, 1968–78; Great Ouse River Authority, 1970–74; Lawes Agricl Trust Cttee, 1982–84; MAFF Priorities Bd, 1984–88; Anglian Water Authority, 1988–89; Vice-Pres., Assoc. of Drainage Authorities, 1986–2010. Chairman: Ely Br., NFU, 1963; Cambs NFU, 1979. High Sheriff, Cambs, 1985–86. *Address:* Denny Abbey, Waterbeach, Cambridge CB25 9PQ. *T:* (01223) 860282. *Club:* Farmers.

**MARTIN, John Vandeleur;** QC 1991; a Judge of the Courts of Appeal of Jersey and Guernsey, 2007–Jan. 2020; a Justice of the Cayman Islands Court of Appeal, since 2013; *b* 17 Jan. 1948; *s* of Col Graham Vandeleur Martin, MC and Margaret Helen (*née* Sherwood); *m* 1974, Stephanie Johnstone Smith; two *s* one *d. Educ:* Malvern Coll.; Pembroke Coll., Cambridge (MA). Called to the Bar, Lincoln's Inn, 1972, Bencher, 1999; Hd of Wilberforce Chambers, 2010–16. Dep. High Court Judge, Chancery Div., 1993–. Liveryman, Drapers' Co., 1973. *Recreations:* almost any opera, swimming in warm water. *Address:* Wilberforce Chambers, 8 New Square, Lincoln's Inn, WC2A 3QP. *T:* (020) 7306 0102.

**MARTIN, Jonathan Arthur,** OBE 1995; former sports broadcasting consultant; Controller, Television Sport, BBC Broadcast, 1996–98; *b* 18 June 1942; *s* of Arthur Martin and Mabel Gladys Martin (*née* Bishop); *m* 1967, Joy Elizabeth Fulker; two *s. Educ:* Gravesend Grammar School; St Edmund Hall, Oxford (BA 1964, English; MA 1992). Joined BBC as general trainee, 1964; producer, Sportsnight, 1969; producer, Match of the Day, 1970; editor, Sportsnight and Match of the Day, 1974; exec. producer, BBC TV Wimbledon tennis coverage, 1979–81; producer, Ski Sunday and Grand Prix, 1978–80; managing editor, Sport, 1980; Head of Sport, 1981–87, Head of Sport and Events, 1987–96, BBC TV. Vice-Pres., EBU Sports Gp, 1984–98; Consultant, Olympic Broadcasting Services, 2000–. *Recreations:* horse-racing, ski-ing, golf, watching sport, especially Watford FC. *Address:* Ty Cerddinen, Penfeidr, Castlemorris, Pembrokeshire SA62 5EN. *Club:* St Davids City Golf.

**MARTIN, Prof. Keith Robert Graham,** DM; FRCOphth; Professor and Head of Ophthalmology, and Director, Centre for Eye Research Australia, University of Melbourne, since 2019; *b* Portadown, NI, 4 April 1969; *s* of Graham and Mabel Martin; *m* 1996, Susan Harden; two *s* one *d. Educ:* Royal Sch., Armagh; St Catharine's Coll., Cambridge (BA Triple 1st Cl. Hons Med. Scis and Neurosci. 1990); Magdalen Coll., Oxford (BM BCh 1993; DM 1999). MRCP 1996; FRCOphth 1998; ALCM 1986. House Officer: in Gen. Medicine, Nuffield Dept of Medicine, John Radcliffe Hosp., Oxford, 1993; in Gen. Surgery, Royal United Hosp., Bath, 1994; Senior House Officer: in Neurol., Nat. Hosp. for Neurol. and Neurosurgery, London, 1994; in Cardiol. and Clin. Pharmacol., Hammersmith Hosp., London, 1995; in Gen. Medicine, John Radcliffe Hosp., Oxford, 1996; in Ophthalmol., Hillingdon Hosp. and Western Eye Hosp., London, 1996; Specialist Registrar in Ophthalmol., E Anglia Rotation, 1997–2000; Res. Fellow, Wilmer Eye Inst., Johns Hopkins Hosp., Baltimore, 2000–02; Clin. and Res. Fellow, Moorfields Eye Hosp. and Inst. of Ophthalmol., 2003–04; University of Cambridge: GSK Clinician Scientist Fellow, Centre for Brain Repair, 2005–10 (Gp Leader, 2005); Lectr in Clin. Neurosci, 2005–10; Prof. of Ophthalmology, 2010–19; Hon. Sen. Res. Fellow, 2019–; Hon. Consultant Ophthalmologist, 2005–19, and Acad. Lead for Ophthalmology, 2010–19, Cambridge Univ. Hosps NHS Foundn Trust. Faculty Mem., NIHR, 2008–. Section Ed., Jl Glaucoma, 2006–. Treas., World Glaucoma Assoc., 2008–15 (Pres., 2018–). Carl Camras Translational Res. Award, Assoc. for Res. in Vision and Ophthalmol., 2010; Sen. Clinician Scientist Award, World Glaucoma Assoc., 2011; Silver Clinical Excellence Award, DoH, 2015. *Publications:* book chapters; contribs to scientific jls and articles on mechanisms of cell death in glaucoma and potential new treatment approaches. *Recreations:* playing the piano, sailing, windsurfing badly, ski-ing, tennis, karate (black belt 2013). *Address:* Centre for Eye Research Australia, 32 Gisborne Street, East Melbourne, Vic 3002, Australia.

**MARTIN, Kevin Joseph;** President, Law Society, 2005–06 (Vice-President, 2004–05); *b* 15 June 1947; *s* of James Arthur Martin and Ivy Lilian Martin; *m* 1971, Maureen McCormack; two *s. Educ:* Sacred Heart Sch., Coventry; Cotton Coll., N Staffs; Coll. of Law, Guildford. Admitted solicitor, 1970. Articled clerk, Tafft & James, Coventry, 1964–70; Solicitor/Partner, Mackintosh & Co., Birmingham, 1970–79; Partner, K. J. Martin & Co., Balsall Common, Solihull, 1979–2001; Consultant, Lodders, Stratford-upon-Avon, 2001–06. Chm., Will Certainty Ltd, 2007–19. Council Mem. for Coventry and Warwickshire, Law Soc., 1996–2013. *Recreations:* golf, ski-ing, classical music, cricket, Rugby. *E:* kevinj_martin@me.com. *Clubs:* Ladbrook Park Golf; Coventry and N Warwickshire Cricket; Law Society Golf (Captain, 2013–14).

**MARTIN, Kit,** CBE 2012; architectural consultant, since 1969; *b* 6 May 1947; *s* of Sir (John) Leslie Martin, RA, and Sadie Speight, architect; *m* 1st, 1970, Julia Margaret Mitchell (marr. diss. 1978); 2nd, 1980, Sally Martha, *d* of late Sqdn Ldr Edwin Brookes; one *d. Educ:* Eton; Jesus Coll., Cambridge (BA 1969; DipArch 1972; MA 1973). Started Martin & Weighton, architectural practice, 1969–76; partner involved in numerous projects to restore and save listed bldgs in UK, France and Italy; Dir, Kit Martin (Historic Houses Rescue) Ltd, 1974–; initiated rescue and conversion of listed bldgs of outstanding architectural interest, including: Dingley Hall, Northants, 1976–79; Gunton Park, Norfolk, 1980–84; Cullen House, Banffshire, 1982–85; Tyninghame House, E Lothian, 1988–92; Burley on the Hill, Rutland, 1993–97; Formakin, Renfrewshire, 1994–99; Maristow, Devon, 1995–99 (several schemes have won local, nat. or European awards); Dir, Historic Bldgs Rescue Ltd, 1993–2002; initiated rescue and conversion of several listed bldgs, including Royal Naval Hosp., Norfolk to housing, and a chapel. Dir, The Prince of Wales's Phoenix Trust (UK Historic Building Preservation Trust), 1997–2001. Projects Consultant, Prince's Regeneration Trust, 2006–. Mem., Historic Bldgs Council for Scotland, 1987–99. Trustee, Save Europe Heritage, 1994–. Hon. FRIBA 2000. *Publications:* The Country House: to be or not to be, 1982; Save Jamaica's Heritage (UNESCO Award), 1990; Silesia: the land of dying country houses, 2009. *Recreations:* ski-ing, squash, private flying with wife, landscape gardening, including restoration of Gunton Park according to historic principles. *Address:* (office) Park Farm, Gunton Park, Hanworth, Norfolk NR11 7HL.

**MARTIN, Sir Laurence (Woodward),** Kt 1994; DL; Senior Adviser, Center for Strategic and International Studies, Washington, 2000–06 (Arleigh Burke Professor of Strategy, 1998–2000); *b* 30 July 1928; *s* of Leonard and Florence Mary Martin; *m* 1951, Betty Parnall (*d* 2005); one *s* (one *d* decd). *Educ:* St Austell Grammar Sch.; Christ's Coll., Cambridge (MA); Yale Univ. (MA, PhD). Flying Officer, RAF, 1948–50; Instr, Yale Univ., 1955–56; Asst Prof., MIT, 1956–61; Rockefeller Fellow for Advanced Study, 1958–59; Associate Prof., Sch. of Advanced Internat. Studies, The Johns Hopkins Univ., 1961–64; Wilson Prof. of Internat. Politics, Univ. of Wales, 1964–68; Prof. of War Studies, King's Coll., Univ. of London, 1968–77, Fellow 1983–; Vice-Chancellor, Univ. of Newcastle upon Tyne, 1978–90, Emeritus Prof., 1991; Dir, RIIA, 1991–96. Research Associate, Washington Center of Foreign Policy Research, 1964–76, 1979–. Barbara Bodichon Fellow, Girton Coll., Cambridge, 2011–. Lees-Knowles Lectr, Cambridge, 1981; BBC Reith Lectr, 1981. Member: SSRC, 1969–76 (Chm. Res. Grants Bd); Internat. Res. Council, Center for Internat. and Strategic Studies (formerly Georgetown Center of Strategic Studies), 1969–77, 1979– (Co-Chm., 1998–); Council, IISS, 1975–83. Consultant, Sandia Labs. DL Tyne and Wear, 1986. Hon. DCL Newcastle, 1991. *Publications:* The Anglo-American Tradition in Foreign Affairs (with Arnold Wolfers), 1956; Peace without Victory, 1958; Neutralism and Non-Alignment, 1962; The Sea in Modern Strategy, 1967; (jtly) America in World Affairs, 1970; Arms and Strategy, 1973; (jtly) Retreat from Empire?, 1973; (jtly) Strategic Thought in the Nuclear Age, 1979; The Two-Edged Sword, 1982; Before the Day After, 1985; The Changing Face of Nuclear Warfare, 1987; (jtly) British Foreign Policy, 1997. *Address:* 35 Witley Court, Coram Street, WC1N 1HD.

**MARTIN, Lewis Vine;** Executive Director, 1995–2002, Chief Executive, Priory of England and Islands, 1999–2002, St John Ambulance; *b* 14 Nov. 1939; *s* of Lewis and Else Martin; *m* 1964, Patricia Mary Thorne; two *d. Educ:* Clarks Coll., Cardiff. Exec. posts in marketing, investment, admin, major projects and gen. management, UK and Europe, Mobil Oil Co. Ltd, 1955–95. *Recreations:* keep fit, swimming, gardening, Rugby (spectator now).

**MARTIN, Dame Louise (Livingstone),** DBE 2019 (CBE 2003); nutritionist; President, Commonwealth Games Federation, since 2015 (Hon. Secretary, 1999–2015); *b* 2 Sept. 1946; *d* of James Stewart Campbell and Minnie Campbell; *m* 1973, Ian Alexander Martin; one *s* one *d. Educ:* Dunfermline High Sch.; Edinburgh Coll. of Domestic Science (Dip. Dom. Sci. Food and Nutrition). Lectr in Nutrition, Edinburgh Coll. of Domestic Science, subseq. Queen Margaret Coll., 1969–72; Head of Department: Glenrothes High Sch., 1972–73; Millburn Acad., Inverness, 1973–75. Tutor, Nat. Coaching Foundn, 1990–2008; Vis. Lectr in Sports Nutrition, Heriot-Watt Univ. and Univ. of Edinburgh, 1994–2001. Board Member: UK Sport, 2002–; Active Stirling, 2006–10; Commonwealth Adv. Bd on Sport, 2009–13 (Chair, 2013–); Chairman: Commonwealth Games Council for Scotland, 1999–2008; sportscotland, 2008–16 (Bd Mem., 1997–2005); Vice Chair, Glasgow 2014 Organising Cttee, 2008–14. Hon. Pres., Scottish Gymnastics, 1999 (Pres., 1993–99). Hon. DArts Abertay, 2007; DUniv: Glasgow Caledonian, 2008; Stirling, 2008; Strathclyde, 2014; Heriot Watt, 2014; West of Scotland, 2017; Edinburgh, 2018. *Recreations:* hill-walking, swimming, reading, travel, classical music.

**MARTIN, Sir Michael C.;** *see* Craig-Martin.

**MARTIN, Micheál;** Member of the Dáil (TD) (FF) Cork South Central, since 1989; President, Fianna Fáil, since 2011; *b* Cork, 1 Aug. 1960; *s* of Paddy and Lana Martin; *m* 1990, Mary O'Shea; two *s* two *d. Educ:* University Coll., Cork (MA Political Hist.). Secondary sch. teacher, St Kieran's Coll., Cork, 1983–89. Minister: for Educn and Sci., 1997–2000; for Health, 2000–04; for Enterprise, Trade and Employment, 2004–08; for Foreign Affairs, 2008–11. Mem., Cork Corp., 1985–99; Alderman, 1991–99; Lord Mayor of Cork, 1992–93. *Publications:* Freedom to Choose, 2009. *Address:* (office) 137 Evergreen Road, Turner's Cross, Cork, Ireland.

**MARTIN, Hon. Paul;** Collector and General Manager, Merchants House of Glasgow, since 2016; *b* 17 March 1967; *s* of Baron Martin of Springburn, PC and of Mary Martin; *m* 1997, Fiona Allen. *Educ:* All Saints Secondary Sch.; Barmulloch Coll., Glasgow. Mem. (Lab) City of Glasgow Council, 1995–99. Mem. (Lab) Glasgow Springburn, 1999–2011, Glasgow Provan, 2011–16, Scottish Parlt; contested (Lab) same seat, 2016. *Address:* Merchants House of Glasgow, 7 West George Street, Glasgow G2 1BA.

**MARTIN, Paul,** CBE 2013; PhD; FIET; adviser and writer, since 2016; Distinguished Fellow, Royal United Services Institute for Defence and Security Studies, since 2016; Hon. Principal Research Fellow, Imperial College London, since 2009; *b* 11 May 1958; *s* of Joseph and Pamela Martin; *m*; two *s* one *d. Educ:* Christ's Coll., Cambridge (MA, PhD). FIET 2017. Harkness Fellow and Postdoctoral Schol., Stanford Univ., 1982–83; Asst Lectr, Cambridge Univ., 1984–86; Fellow, 1985–86 and 2001–04, Sen. Mem., 2004–09, Wolfson Coll., Cambridge; MoD, 1986–2000; Dir of Communication, Cabinet Office, 2000–01; MoD, 2002–13; Dir of Security for Parlt, 2013–16. Mem. Bd, Charity Commn, 2016– (Chm., Public Interest Litigation and High-Risk Cases Cttee, 2019–). *Publications:* (with Patrick Bateson) Measuring Behaviour, 1986, 3rd edn 2007; The Sickening Mind, 1997;

(with Patrick Bateson) Design for a Life, 1999; Counting Sheep, 2002; (with Kristina Murrin) What Worries Parents, 2004; Making Happy People, 2005; Sex, Drugs and Chocolate, 2008; (with Patrick Bateson) Play, Playfulness, Creativity and Innovation, 2013; (with Emma Barrett) Extreme, 2014; The Rules of Security, 2019.

**MARTIN, Paul;** *see* Martin, D. P.

**MARTIN, Rt Hon. Paul (Edgar Philippe),** CC 2011; PC (Canada) 1993; MP (L) for Lasalle-Emard, Quebec, 1988–2008; Prime Minister of Canada, 2003–06; *b* Windsor, Ont, 28 Aug. 1938; *s* of Paul Joseph James Martin and Eleanor Alice Martin; *m* 1965, Sheila Ann Cowan; three *s*. *Educ:* Univ. of Ottawa; Univ. of Toronto (BA Philos. and Hist. 1962); Univ. of Toronto Law Sch. (LLB 1965). Merchant seaman on salvage ops in Arctic; worked in Legal Dept, ECSC, Luxembourg; with Osler, Hoskin & Harcourt, Toronto; called to the Bar, Ontario, 1966; with Power Corp. of Canada; Chm. and Chief Exec. Officer, Canada Steamship Lines; Corporate Dir for several major cos. Critic for: Treasury Bd and Urban Develt, until 1991; Envmt and Associate Finance Critic, 1991–93; Minister responsible for Federal Office of Regl Develt, 1993–97; Finance Minister, Canada, 1993–2002. First Chm., G-20, 1999–2002. Liberal Party of Canada: Co-Chm., Nat. Platform Cttee, 1993; Leader, 2003–06. Mem. Bd, Coalition for Dialogue on Africa, 2009–. Co-Chm., Congo Basin Forest Fund, 2008–; Chm., Capital for Aboriginal Prosperity and Entrepreneurship Fund, 2009–. Pres., Martin Aboriginal Educn Initiative, 2008–. *Address:* (office) 759 Square Victoria, Suite 300, Montreal, QC H2Y 2J7, Canada.

**MARTIN, Paul James, (Paul Merton);** comedian, actor, writer; *b* 9 July 1957; *s* of Albert and Mary Martin; *m* 1991, Caroline Quentin, *qv* (marr. diss. 1999); *m* 2000, Sarah Parkinson (*d* 2003); *m* 2009, Suki Webster. *Educ:* Wimbledon Coll. Civil Servant, Dept of Employment. *Stage:* stand-up comic: London Comedy Store, 1981–; London cabaret circuit, 1982–88; toured England, Scotland and Ireland, 1993; London Palladium, 1994; Live Bed Show, Garrick, 1994; presenter, Paul Merton's Silent Clowns, UK tour, 2007; Paul Merton's Impro Chums, UK tour, 2010, 2019; Out of My Head, UK tour, 2012; actor: Aladdin, Wimbledon Th., 2018; *television* includes: series: Comedy Wavelength, 1987; Whose Line is it Anyway?, 1989–93; Have I Got News For You, 1990–; Paul Merton—the series, 1991, 1993; Paul Merton's Life of Comedy, 1995; Paul Merton's Palladium Story (2 programmes), 1995; Paul Merton in Galton & Simpson, 1996, 1997; The Paul Merton Show, 1996; Room 101, 1999–2007; Paul Merton in China, 2007; Thank God You're Here, 2008; Paul Merton in India, 2008; Paul Merton in Europe, 2010; Paul Merton's Secret Stations, 2016; *films:* An Evening with Gary Lineker, 1994; The Suicidal Dog, 2000 (writer and dir); *radio* series include: Just a Minute, 1988–; I'm Sorry I Haven't a Clue, 1993–; The Masterson Inheritance, 1993–96; Two Priests and a Nun go into a Pub, 2000; Late, 2001; My Obsession, 2019. BAFTA Award, Best Entertainer, 2003. *Publications:* (with Julian Clary) My Life with Fanny the Wonderdog, 1988; Paul Merton's History of the 20th Century, 1993; Have I Got News For You, 1994; My Struggle, 1995; Silent Comedy, 2007; Only When I Laugh (autobiog.), 2014. *Recreations:* tropical fish, walking, film comedy. *Address:* c/o Mandy Ward Artist Management, 4th Floor, 74 Berwick Street, W1F 8TE.

**MARTIN, Prof. Paul William,** CBE 2017; Depute Principal, University of West of Scotland, 2013–18; *b* 12 June 1961; *m* 1980, Jan Lorimer; two *s*. *Educ:* E Glasgow Sch. of Nursing (RN 1982); Ayrshire Central Sch. of Midwifery (RM 1985); Paisley Coll. (RHV (Public Health Nurse) 1987); Glasgow Caledonian Univ. (Dip. Mgt Studies 1992); Napier Univ., Edinburgh (MBA 1998). Health Visitor, 1988–92, Team Leader, Community Nursing Services, 1992–93, Ayrshire and Arran Health Bd; Divl Nurse Business Manager, Moray Health Services, 1993–94; Dir, Nursing, Quality and Community Services, Borders Community Health Services NHS Trust, 1994–99; Exec. Dir, Nursing and Professions Allied to Medicine, 1999–2002; Chief Exec., Highland Primary Care NHS Trust; Interim Chief Exec., NHS Orkney; Chief Nursing Officer, Scotland, and Interim Dir for Health Workforce, 2004–09; University of West of Scotland: Exec. Dean, Faculty of Educn, Health and Social Scis, 2009–12; Vice Principal (Internat.), 2011–12; Interim Depute Principal, 2012–13. Ind. Chair, Child and Adult Protection, S Ayrshire, 2018–. *Publications:* contrib. articles to refereed jls incl. Jl Family Nursing, Ridec; conf. papers.

**MARTIN, Penny Jane;** Editor-in-Chief, The Gentlewoman magazine, since 2009; *b* Glasgow, 28 July 1972; *d* of Douglas Martin and Jennifer Martin (née Marriott, now di Folco); *m* 2006, Barry Kelly. *Educ:* Univ. of Glasgow (MA Hons Hist. of Art); Univ. of Manchester (Postgrad. Dip. Art Gall. and Mus. Studies). Curator: Nat. Mus. of Photography, Film & Television, 1995–98; Fawcett Liby, 1998–2001; Ed.-in-Chief, Showstudio, 2001–08; Prof. of Fashion Imagery, London Coll. of Fashion, UAL, 2008–11. *Recreations:* 18th-century houses, 1960s girl groups, Christmas. *Address:* The Gentlewoman, 1st Floor, 73–75 Mortimer Street, W1W 7SQ. *T:* (020) 7242 8802. *E:* penny@thegentlewoman.com.

**MARTIN, Peter William,** CBE 2006; Managing Director, Journeyman Resolutions, 2007–11; *b* 15 May 1947; *s* of Ronald William Martin and Rosemary Joan Damaris Martin; *m* 1981, Rhonda Mary Craker; two *s* one *d*. *Educ:* King's College Sch., Wimbledon; Goldsmiths', London. Winston Churchill Travelling Fellow, 1986. Regl Dir, Phoenix House, 1978–90; Chief Exec., Addaction, 1990–2005. Non-exec. Dir, Kent and Medway NHS and Social Care Trust, 2007–11. Member: Parole Bd of England and Wales, 1994–2000; Adv. Council for the Misuse of Drugs, 2000–09. Dir and Trustee, Cudham Community Centre Trust, 2009–12. *Recreations:* rambling, field pursuits, meditation, organic gardening, reading and writing, voluntary fundraising for Médecins Sans Frontières. *Address:* Forge Cottage, Cudham TN14 7QB. *Club:* Royal Automobile.

**MARTIN, Prof. Raymond Leslie,** AO 1987; MSc, PhD, ScD, DSc; FRACI, FRSC, FTSE, FAA, FAIM; Professor of Chemistry, Monash University, Melbourne, 1987–92, now Emeritus (Vice-Chancellor, 1977–87); Chairman, Australian Science and Technology Council, 1988–92; *b* 3 Feb. 1926; *s* of Sir Leslie Harold Martin, CBE, FRS, FAA and late Gladys Maude Elaine, *d* of H. J. Bull; *m* 1954, Rena Lillian Laman; three *s* one *d*. *Educ:* Scotch Coll., Melbourne; Univ. of Melbourne (BSc, MSc); Sidney Sussex Coll., Cambridge (PhD, ScD). FRACI 1956; FRSC (FRIC 1974); FTSE (FTS 1989); FAA 1971; FAIM 2003. Resident Tutor in Chemistry, Queen's Coll., Melb., 1947–49 (Fellow, 1979–2004, Sen. Fellow, 2005–); Sidney Sussex Coll., Cambridge: 1851 Exhibn Overseas Scholar, 1949–51; Sen. Scholar, 1952–54; Res. Fellow, 1951–54; Sen. Lectr, Univ. of NSW, 1954–59; Section Leader, 1959–60, and Associate Res. Manager, 1960–62, ICIANZ; Prof. of Inorganic Chem., 1962–72, and Dean of Faculty of Science and Faculty of Music, 1971, Univ. of Melb.; Australian National University, Canberra: Prof. of Inorganic Chem., Inst. of Advanced Studies, 1972–77, Prof. Emeritus 1977; Dean, Res. Sch. of Chem., 1976–77; DSc. Vis. Scientist: Technische Hochschule, Stuttgart, 1953–54; Bell Telephone Labs, NJ, 1967; Vis. Prof., Columbia Univ., NY, 1972. Royal Aust. Chemical Institute: Smith Medal, 1968; Olle Prize, 1974; Inorganic Medal, 1978; Leighton Medal, 1989; Fed. Pres., 1968–69. Chm., Internat. Commn on Atomic Weights and Isotopic Abundances, IUPAC, 1983–87; Mem., Prime Minister's Science Council, 1989–92. Director: Circadian Technologies Ltd, 1986–2002; Heide Park and Art Gall., 1988–92; Winston Churchill Meml Trust, 1983–2006 (Nat. Chm., 1995–2000; Nat. Pres., 2001–06); Chairman: Syngene Ltd, 1996–2008; Optiscan Pty Ltd, 1997–2002; Trustee, Selby Scientific Foundn, 1990–. Council Mem., Victorian Coll. of the Arts, 1984–98 (Dep. Pres., 1991; Pres., 1992–95). Hon. LLD Monash, 1992; Hon. DSc Melbourne, 1996. Queen's Silver Jubilee Medal, 1977; Centenary Medal, Australia, 2003. *Publications:* papers and revs on physical and inorganic chem. mainly in jls of London, Amer. and Aust. Chem. Socs. *Recreations:* ski-ing, golf, lawn tennis (Cambridge Univ. team *v* Oxford, Full Blue; Cambs County Colours). *Address:* PO Box 98, Mount Eliza, Vic 3930, Australia. *Clubs:* Melbourne (Melbourne); Hawks (Cambridge); Frankston Golf (Victoria).

**MARTIN, Rt Rev. Robert David Markland;** Bishop of Marsabit, North Kenya, 2011–16; an Honorary Assistant Bishop, Diocese of Bath and Wells, since 2016; *b* Frimley, 5 May 1949; *s* of Col Alexander Robert Fyers Martin and Alison Mary Martin; *m* 1975, Sue Leney; three *s*. *Educ:* Woodcote House, Windlesham; Bradfield Coll., Berks; Trinity Coll., Cambridge (BA Hons Modern Langs); Trinity Coll., Bristol (BA Hons Theol.). ACA 1974, FCA 1975. Audit Clerk, 1971–74, Sen. Audit Clerk, 1974–77, Peat Marwick Mitchell; Diocesan Accountant, Dio. of Mt Kenya E, 1978–87; ordained deacon, 1991, priest, 1992; Curate, Kingswood Team Ministry, Bristol, 1991–95; Vicar, Holy Trinity, Frome, 1995–2008; Rural Dean, Frome, 2003–08; Suffragan Bishop, All Saints Cathedral, Nairobi, 2008–11. Chm., Provincial Bd of Finance, Kenya, 2013–16. Mission partner, Crosslinks Anglican Mission Agency. Patron, St Philips Community Centre, Mburi, Kenya, 1986–2016. Gov., Trinity First Sch., Frome, 1995–2008. *Recreations:* languages, travelling, birdwatching, reading, mountain trekking. *E:* robandsuemartin@gmail.com. *Club:* Minoans (Cambridge).

**MARTIN, Robert George H.;** *see* Holland-Martin.

**MARTIN, Robin Rupert,** CB 2004; Director, Tax Law Rewrite Project, HM Revenue and Customs (formerly Board of Inland Revenue), 2003–06; *b* 28 Feb. 1946; *s* of late Rupert Claude Martin and Ellen Martin (née Wood); *m* 1972, Jane Elizabeth Mackenzie Smith; three *s*. *Educ:* Harrow Sch.; Worcester Coll., Oxford (MA Hons). VSO: Thailand, 1964–65; India, 1969–70; joined Home Civil Service, 1970: Private Sec. to Chm., Bd of Inland Revenue, 1973–74; Office of Chancellor of Duchy of Lancaster, Cabinet Office, 1976–79; Asst Sec., 1981; Under Sec., 1993; Principal Finance Officer, 1993–2000, Dir, Cross-Cutting Policy, 2000–03, Bd of Inland Revenue. Dir, CS Healthcare, 2003–13. Chair, Shenehom Housing Assoc., 2009–19. Member: Methodology Soc., 2007–; Southwold Sailors' Reading Room Assoc. *Recreations:* infrequent leisurely hill-walking, cricket, second-hand books. *Club:* MCC.

**MARTIN, Roger John Adam;** formerly HM Diplomatic Service; President (formerly Chairman), Population Matters (formerly Optimum Population Trust), since 2009; *b* 21 Jan. 1941; *s* of late Geoffrey (Richard Rex) Martin and of Hazel (née Matthews); *m* 1972, Ann Cornwell (née Sharp) (*d* 2009); one *s*; *m* 2019, Ann Chitty (née Hard). *Educ:* Westminster School; Brasenose College, Oxford (BA). VSO, Northern Rhodesia, 1959–60; Commonwealth Office, 1964–66; Second Sec., Djakarta, 1967, Saigon, 1968–70; First Sec., FCO, 1971–74; Geneva, 1975–79; seconded to Dept of Trade, as Head of Middle East/North Africa Br., 1981–83; Dep. High Comr, Harare, 1983–86; resigned. Vis. Fellow, Univ. of Bath. Mem., Nat. Exec., VSO, 1988–96; Dir, Som Trust for Nature Conservation, subseq. Som Wildlife Trust, 1988–2001 (Vice-Pres., 2001–). Member: Regional Committees: Envmt Agency, 1990–2012; MAFF, 1993–97; Planning Conf., 1996–2000; Heritage Lottery Fund, 2001–06. Founder Mem., SW Regl Assembly, 1998. Mem., Exmoor Nat. Park Authy, 1998–2008; Chm., SW Reg., 2001–06, Trustee, 2003–07, Pres., Som Br., 2006–, CPRE; Pres., Mendip Soc., 2001–09. Hon. DSc UWE, 2001. *Publications:* Southern Africa: the price of apartheid, 1988. *Recreations:* environmental issues, walking, archaeology. *Address:* Barn Cottage, Upper Coxley, near Wells, Somerset BA5 1QS. *T:* (01749) 672180.

**MARTIN, Roland John;** Headmaster, City of London Freemen's School, since 2015; Chief Officer, City of London Corporation, since 2015; *b* Gloucester, 1 March 1971; *s* of late Roland John Martin and of Christine Elizabeth Martin; *Educ:* Rendcomb Coll.; Univ. of York (BA English and Related Lit. 1992); Harvard Grad. Sch. of Educn (Leadership, an Evolving Vision, 2015). Teacher of English, Newcastle-under-Lyme Sch., 1993–98; Teacher of English and Drama, 1998–2011, Housemaster, 2005–11, Eton Coll.; Headmaster, Rendcomb Coll., 2011–15. Inspector, ISI, 2014–. Freeman, City of London, 2017. *Recreations:* educational issues, theatre, reading (especially 18th century novels and modern drama), music (jazz and Mozart), sport (Aston Villa and Gloucester RFC), film, art, cooking, walking, travel. *Address:* City of London Freemen's School, Ashtead Park, Ashtead, Surrey KT21 1ET.

**MARTIN, Prof. Ronald Leonard,** PhD, ScD; FBA 2005; FAcSS; FRGS; Professor of Economic Geography, University of Cambridge, 2000–18, now Emeritus; President, St Catharine's College, Cambridge, 2010–13 (Professorial Fellow, 2002–15, now Emeritus); *b* 17 April 1948; *s* of Bertie Leonard Martin and Joan Gladys Martin (née Claypole); *m* 1974, Lynda Mary Hunt. *Educ:* Gilberd Sch., Colchester; Trinity Coll., Cambridge (BA 1st Cl. Hons Geog.; MA; PhD Geog. 1978; ScD 2014). University of Cambridge: Asst Lectr in Geog., 1974–79; Lectr in Geog., 1979–98; British Acad. Thank-offering to Britain Fellow, 1997–98; Reader in Econ. Geog., 1998–2000; Leverhulme Major Res. Fellowship, 2007–10; Leverhulme Emeritus Fellowship, 2015–17. Roepke Lectr in Econ. Geog., Assoc. American Geographers, 2009; 21st Annual Gregory Lect., Univ. of Southampton, 2013. Fellow, Cambridge-MIT Inst., 2002–08; Associate, Centre for Business Res., Judge Business Sch., Univ. of Cambridge, 2008–. Expert consultant to Cambridge Econometrics, 2010–; Scientific Advr, European Sci. Foundn, 2013–; Mem., Lead Expert Gp, Foresight: Future of Cities, Govt Office for Sci., 2013–16. Chair, Jt Faculty (Law, Criminology and Land Economy) Sen. Promotions Cttee, Univ. of Cambridge, 2014–. FRGS 1992; FAcSS (AcSS 2001). FRSA. Hon. Fellow, Regional Studies Assoc., 2005– (Pres., 2015–). Victoria Medal, RGS, 2016. *Publications:* Towards the Dynamic Analysis of Spatial Systems, 1978; Regional Wage Inflation and Unemployment, 1981; Recollections of a Revolution: geography as spatial science, 1984; The Geography of Deindustrialisation, 1986; Regional Development in the 1990s, 1992; Human Geography: society, space and the social sciences, 1994; Money, Power and Space, 1994; Union Retreat and the Regions, 1996; Money and the Space Economy, 1999; The Reader in Economic Geography, 1999; Geographies of Labour Market Inequality, 2003; Putting Workfare in Place, 2005; Clusters and Regional Development, 2006; The Competitive Advantage of Regions, 2006; (ed) Critical Concepts in Economic Geography, 5 vols, 2007; Economic Geography, 2008; Handbook of Evolutionary Economic Geography, 2010; Handbook of Regional Growth and Innovation, 2011; Handbook of the Geographies of Money and Finance, 2017; Britain's Spatially Unbalanced Economy, 2019; Evolutionary Economic Geography, 2019; contrib. more than 230 articles to various jls, incl. Trans IBG, Envmt and Planning, Jl Econ. Geog., Regl Studies, Econ. Geog., Cambridge Jl Econs, Cambridge Jl of Regions, Economy and Society, Econ. Jl, Jl of Regl Sci., Urban Studies. *Recreations:* politics, Italian opera, classical music, wine, astronomy, garden design, rabbits, reading everything and anything. *Address:* The Vines, Redgate Road, Girton, Cambridge CB3 0PP. *T:* (01223) 277244; St Catharine's College, Cambridge CB2 1RL. *T:* (01223) 338316. *E:* rlm1@cam.ac.uk.

**MARTIN, Ronald Noel**, CB 1998; FRCVS; Chief Veterinary Officer, Department of Agriculture for Northern Ireland, 1990–98; *b* 15 Dec. 1938; *s* of Robert John and Margretta Martin; *m* 1962, Alexandrina Margaret McLeod; two *s*. *Educ*: Royal (Dick) Sch. of Veterinary Studies, Univ. of Edinburgh (BVMS). FRCVS 1995 (MRCVS 1961). Private veterinary practice, 1960–64; Ministry of Agriculture, later Department of Agriculture, for Northern Ireland: Vet. Officer, 1964–69; Divl Vet. Officer, 1969–73; Sen. Principal Vet. Officer, 1973–78; Dep. Chief Vet. Officer, 1978–90. Chm., NI Food Chain Certification Cttee, 2001–10. *Recreations*: gardening, walking, cycling. *Address*: 8 Whiteside, Mountain Road, Newtownards, Co. Down BT23 4UP. *T*: (028) 9181 3962.

**MARTIN, Rosemary**; Headmistress, St Albans High School for Girls, 2009–14; *b* Stourbridge, 29 March 1952; *d* of Leslie and Freda Lay; *m* 1979, Geoffrey Martin; two *s*. *Educ*: Halesowen Grammar Sch.; Liverpool Univ. (BEd); Univ. of E London (MEd); Inst. of Educn, Univ. of London (NPQH 1999). Asst Teacher, then House Mistress, Kirkby Ruffwood Sch., Merseyside, 1974–78; Dep. Hd (Pastoral), Woodside Sch., Newham, 1978–84; Dep. Hd (Curriculum), Loxford Sch., Redbridge, 1984–90; Hd of Girls' Sch., Forest Sch., London, 1990–2000; Headmistress, Combe Bank Sch., Sevenoaks, 2000–09. Gov., St Mary's Sch., Gerrards Cross. *Recreations*: reading, keeping fit, ski-ing, travelling, spending time with my family.

**MARTIN, Rosemary**; General Counsel and Company Secretary, Vodafone Group Plc, since 2010; *b* UK, 12 May 1960; *d* of L. J. and E. V. Martin; *m* 1990, Brian Cooper; two *s* one *d*. *Educ*: Univ. of Sussex (BA Hons 1981); Nottingham Trent Univ. (MBA Legal Practice 1997). Admitted as solicitor, 1985; Solicitor, Rowe & Maw, 1983–97; Gen. Counsel and Co. Sec., Reuters Gp plc, and Dir, Reuters Foundn, 1997–2008; Chief Exec., Practical Law Gp, 2008–09. *Address*: Vodafone Group Plc, One Kingdom Street, Paddington Central, W2 6BY. *E*: rosemary.martin@vodafone.com.

**MARTIN, Simon Charles**, CMG 2013; HM Diplomatic Service; Ambassador to the Kingdom of Bahrain, 2015–19; *b* 15 May 1963; *s* of Nicholas Fearnley Martin and Patricia Margaret Martin (*née* Simpson); *m* 1st, 1988, Sharon Margaret Joel (marr. diss. 2012); one *s* one *d*; 2nd, 2015, Sophie Elisabeth Pike (*née* Bridgford). *Educ*: Cotton Coll., Stoke-on-Trent; King Edward VI Sch., Birmingham; Nottingham Univ. Entered FCO, 1984; lang. trng, 1986; Third, later Second Sec. and Vice-Consul, Rangoon, 1987–90; Second, later First Sec., FCO, 1990–95; lang. trng, 1995; First Secretary: (Commercial), Budapest, 1996–2001; FCO, 2001–03; on secondment to Unilever plc, 2003–05; Counsellor and Dep. Hd of Mission, Prague, 2005–09; Vice-Marshal of Diplomatic Corps, and Dir of Protocol, FCO, 2009–12; Dep. Private Sec. for Foreign and Commonwealth Affairs to the Prince of Wales and the Duchess of Cornwall (on secondment), 2012–15. *Address*: c/o Foreign and Commonwealth Office, King Charles Street, SW1A 2AH.

**MARTIN, Stanley William Frederick**, CVO 1992 (LVO 1981); JP; HM Diplomatic Service, retired; Extra Gentleman Usher to the Queen, since 1993; Protocol Consultant, Foreign and Commonwealth Office, since 1993; *b* 9 Dec. 1934; *s* of Stanley and Winifred Martin; *m* 1960, Hanni Aud Hansen, Copenhagen; one *s* one *d*. *Educ*: Bromley Grammar Sch.; University Coll., Oxford (MA Jurisprudence; Pres., OU Law Soc., 1957); Inner Temple (student Scholar). Nat. Service, 2nd Lieut RASC, 1953–55. Entered CRO, 1958; Asst Private Sec. to Sec. of State, 1959–62; First Secretary: Canberra, 1962–64; Kuala Lumpur, 1964–67; FCO (Planning Staff and Personnel Dept), 1967–70; seconded to CSD (CSSB), 1970–71; HM Asst Marshal of the Diplomatic Corps, 1972–81; First Asst Marshal, 1981–92; Associate Head of Protocol Dept, FCO, 1986–92. Vis. Prof., Diplomatic Acad., Poly. of Central London, subseq. Univ. of Westminster, 1987– (Hon. Fellow, 1998). Diplomatic Consultant: Hyde Park Hotel, then Mandarin Oriental Hyde Park, 1993–99; Grosvenor House, 1999–2002. Member: Cttee, London Diplomatic Assoc., 1972–; Council, Oxford Univ. Soc., 1993–2002; Adv. Council, Spanish Inst. of Protocol Studies, 1997–; Cttee, European-Atlantic Gp, 2003–10. Trustee: Attlee Foundn, 1993–99; Toynbee Hall, 1996–99; Jt Commonwealth Socs Trust, 2005–10; Patron, Apex Trust, 2002– (Vice-Patron, 1995–2002). Adviser: Consular Corps of London, 1993–; London Mayors' Assoc., 2004– (Hon. Mem., 2006). Mem., Commonwealth Observer Gp, Guyana elecns, 1997. Gov., Goodenough Coll. for Overseas Graduates, 2005–10. Freelance lectr, 1993–. Member: Pilgrims; Royal Historical Soc. FRSA 1985. JP Inner London, 1993–2000. Freeman of the City of London, 1988. Companion, Order of Distinguished Service (Brunei), 1992. *Publications*: (jtly) Royal Service: history of the Royal Victorian Order, Medal and Chain, vol. I 1996, vol. II 2001; The Order of Merit: one hundred years of matchless honour, 2006; (contrib.) Diplomatic Handbook, 2nd edn 1977 to 8th edn 2004; (contrib.) Honouring Commonwealth Citizens, 2007; contribs to Jl of Orders and Medals Res. Soc., Jl of Royal Over-Seas League, Bermuda Nat. Mus. Jl, Diplomat mag. *Recreations*: collecting too many books, manuscripts and obituaries, historical research and writing, travelling by train, walking, siestas, watching old films in the afternoon. *Address*: 14 Great Spilmans, Dulwich, SE22 8SZ. *T*: (020) 8693 8181. *Clubs*: Royal Over-Seas League (Mem., Central Council, 1982–2010, Exec. Cttee, 1993–2010); Vice-Chm., 2002–05; Chm., 2005–10; Vice-Pres., 2009–), Oxford and Cambridge, Danish.

**MARTIN, Stephen Frederick**, FRICS; Director General, Institute of Directors, 2017–19; *b* Belfast, 3 Feb. 1966; *s* of Fred and Aillen Martin; *m* 1994, Lisa Cooke; one *s* one *d*. *Educ*: Ulster Univ. (BSc Quantity Surveying 1988); London Business Sch. (MBA 2003). MCIArb 2001; FCIOB 2002; FRICS 2002. Quantity Surveyor, PSA, 1988–92; Commercial Dir, Westinghouse Security Systems, 1992–98; Procurement, Estimating and Quality Control Manager, Kvaerner Metals, 1998–2000; Commercial Dir, Amey Rail, 2000–04; Chief Exec., Barhale Construction, 2004–06; Gp Chief Exec., Clugston Gp, 2006–17. CCMI 2008; FInstD 2011. Mem., Magic Circle. *Recreations*: Business Angel investor, film and television producer, concerts, theatre, travel.

**MARTIN, Stephen Harcourt**; Chief Executive, Higher Education Funding Council for Wales, 2000–03; *b* 4 Sept. 1952; *s* of Robert Harcourt Martin and Joan Winifred Martin (*née* Carpenter); *m* 1988, Amanda Suna Hodges (marr. diss. 2002); one *s* one *d*. *Educ*: Watford GS for Boys; Haywards Heath GS; Hull Univ. (Pol Studies). Nursing Assistant, De La Pole Psych. Hosp., Willerby, 1973–74; Welsh Office: Exec. Officer, Town and Country Planning Div., 1974–77; Admin. Trainee, Health and Industry Depts, 1977–79; Pvte Sec. to successive Perm. Secs, 1979–81; Principal: Health Dept, 1981–85; Housing Div., 1985–87; Asst Sec., Health and Social Services Divs, 1987–92; Under Sec., later Dir, Educn Dept, 1992–97; Prin. Establishments Officer, 1997–99; Sec. and Dir of Policy, Welsh Fourth Channel Authy, 1999–2000; Chief Executive: Further Educn Funding Council for Wales, 2000–01; Nat. Council for Educn and Trng for Wales, 2000–03. *Recreations*: music, literature.

**MARTIN, Prof. Stephen James**, PhD; Professor of Public Policy and Management, Cardiff University, since 2000; Director, Wales Centre for Public Policy (formerly Public Policy Institute for Wales), since 2013; *b* Chatham, 27 Feb. 1961; *s* of James Martin and Marian Martin; *m* 1988, Harriet Hudson; two *d*. *Educ*: Hertford Coll., Oxford (BA 1st Cl. Hons Geog. 1982); Aston Univ. (PhD 1989); Inst d'admin des enterprises, Univ. of Aix-Marseille (Internat. Teaching Prog. 1992). Lectr, Aston Business Sch., 1988–94; Principal Res. Fellow, 1994–99, Reader, 1999–2000, Warwick Business Sch.; Dir, Centre for Local and Regl Govt Res., Cardiff Univ., 2000–13. Member: Bd of Dirs, Local Govt Improvement and Develt (formerly IDeA), 2002–10; Bd, New Local Govt Network, 2007–; Lead Mem., Expert Panel on Local Govt, DCLG, 2009–10. Co-ed., Policy and Politics, 2016–. *Publications*: Public Service Improvement: policies, progress and prospects, 2006; Public Services Inspection in the UK, 2008. *Recreations*: open water diving, watching test cricket, hill walking. *Address*: Wales Centre for Public Policy, 10–12 Museum Place, Cardiff CF10 3BG. *T*: 07773 381107. *E*: steve.martin@wcpp.org.uk.

**MARTIN, Prof. Hon. Stephen Paul**; Chief Executive, Committee for Economic Development of Australia, 2011–17; Chairman, Bank of China (Australia) Ltd, since 2015; *b* 24 June 1948; *s* of Harold and Vera Martin; *m*; one *s* three *d*. *Educ*: ANU (BA); Univ. of Alberta (MA); Sydney Univ. (MTCP); Univ. of NSW (Dip. Ed); PhD Wollongong. High School teacher, 1970–74; Univ. Lectr, 1975–77; Town Planner, NSW Dept of Planning and Environment, 1977–84. MP (Lab) Cunningham, NSW, 1984–2002; Chm., Banking, Finance and Public Administration Cttee, 1987–91; Parly Sec. to Minister for Foreign Affairs and Trade, 1991–93; Speaker, House of Reps, Aust., 1993–96; Shadow Minister: for Sport and Tourism, and for Veterans' Affairs, 1996–97; for Small Business, Customs, Sport and Tourism, 1997–98; for Defence, 1998–2001; for Trade and Tourism, 2001–02. Professorial Fellow, Grad. Sch. of Business and Professional Develt, Univ. of Wollongong, 2002–03; CEO, Univ. of Wollongong in Dubai, 2004–05; Pro Vice-Chancellor (Internat.), Victoria Univ., Melbourne, 2005–08; Dep. Vice-Chancellor (Strategy and Planning), Curtin Univ. of Technol., Perth, 2008; Sen. Consultant, Slade Gp, 2009; Prof. of Business Res., Dir of DBA Prog. and Vice Chancellor's Rep., Gold Coast Campus, Southern Cross Univ., 2010. Dir, Men of League Foundn, 2015–. *Recreations*: swimming, Rugby League, movies. *Address*: 1205/39 Caravel Lane, Docklands, Vic 3008, Australia.

**MARTIN, Steven**; *see* Martin, George S.

**MARTIN, (Thomas) Geoffrey**, OBE 2002; Partner, Johnson Martin Associates, since 2003; *b* 26 July 1940; *s* of Thomas Martin and Saidee Adelaide (*née* Day); *m* 1968, Gay (Madeleine Annesley) Brownrigg; one *s* three *d*. *Educ*: Queen's Univ., Belfast (BSc Hons). President, National Union of Students of England, Wales and Northern Ireland, 1966–68; City of London: Banking, Shipping, 1968–73; Director, Shelter, 1973–74; Diplomatic Staff, Commonwealth Secretariat, 1974–79; Head of EC Office, NI, 1979–85; Head of EC Press and Inf. Services, SE Asia, 1985–87; Hd of External Relations, EC Office, London, 1987–93; Hd of Repn of EC in UK, 1994–2002; Office of Commonwealth Sec.-Gen., 2002–15, Advr, responsible for Strategic Relationships, 2005–15. Vis. Prof., Leeds Univ., 2003–. Hon. DSc Plymouth, 2000. *Address*: 64 Mortlake Road, Kew, Richmond TW9 4AS. *Club*: Travellers.

**MARTIN, Prof. Thomas John**, AO 1996; MD, DSc; FRACP, FRCPA; FRS 2000; FAA; Director, 1988–2002, and John Holt Fellow, since 2003, St Vincent's Institute of Medical Research, University of Melbourne; *b* 24 Jan. 1937; *s* of Thomas Michael and Ellen Agnes Martin; *m* 1964, Christine Mayo Conroy (*d* 1995); two *s* four *d*. *Educ*: Xavier Coll.; Univ. of Melbourne (MB BS 1960; MD 1969; DSc 1979). FRACP 1969; FRCPA 1985; FAA 1996. Registrar and Res. Fellow, RPMS, London, 1965–66; Sen. Res. Fellow, 1967–68, Sen. Lectr, 1968–73, Dept of Medicine, Univ. of Melbourne; Prof. of Chemical Pathology, Univ. of Sheffield, 1974–77; Prof. of Medicine, Univ. of Melbourne, 1977–98, now Emeritus (Chm., Dept of Medicine, 1985–98). Vis. Prof., RPMS, 1973; Vis. Res. Prof. of Medicine, Vanderbilt Univ., Nashville, 2010–18. Hon. MD Sheffield, 1992; DUniv Australian Catholic, 2010; Hon. LLD Melbourne, 2012. *Publications*: more than 600 scientific papers, reviews and book chapters on endocrinology, bone cell biology, cancer and clinical medicine. *Recreations*: music, golf, fly-fishing, travel. *Address*: #23, 27 Barnsbury Road, Deepdene, Vic 3103, Australia. *T*: (61) 415144663. *Club*: Barwon Heads Golf.

**MARTIN, Timothy Randall**; Founder, 1979, and Chairman, since 1983, J. D. Wetherspoon plc; *b* 28 April 1955; *s* of Ray and Olive Martin; *m* Felicity Owen; one *s* three *d*. *Educ*: Nottingham Univ. (LLB). Called to the Bar, 1980. *Address*: J. D. Wetherspoon plc, Wetherspoon House, Central Park, Reeds Crescent, Watford, Herts WD24 4QL. *T*: (01923) 477777. *Club*: Exeter Squash.

**MARTIN, Tom**, OBE 2015; JP; President, since 2006, and non-executive Director, since 1996, ARCO Ltd; Vice Lord-Lieutenant, East Riding of Yorkshire, 2006–11; *b* 22 March 1936; *s* of Thomas Martin and Marjorie Martin; *m* 1960, Anne, *er d* of Thomas W. Boyd, CBE, DSO and Barbara Boyd; one *s* three *d*. *Educ*: Bramcote Sch., Scarborough; Winchester Coll.; Emmanuel Coll., Cambridge (BA Hons Law 1959; MA 1962; Benefactor Bye Fellow 2016). National Service, RNVR (Sub Lt), 1954–56. ARCO Ltd: Dir, 1965–96; Jt Man. Dir, 1969–96; Chm., 1981–2006. Gen. Comr of Income Tax, 1998–2006. Mem. Council, CBI, 1992–99. Mem. (C), Humberside CC, 1977–84. Mem., Magistrates' Adv. Council, 1985–93. Dir, Humber Forum, 2000–10; Founder Chm., E Riding Community Safety Partnership, 1996–2010; Trustee, Humberside Police Tribune Trust, 2001–. Patron, NSPCC, 2004–. Gov., Humberside Univ., 1993–96. JP Hull, 1972; High Sheriff, 1996–97, DL, 1998, ER of Yorks. Hon. Freeman, Beverley, 2015. *Recreations*: a veritable tribe of grandchildren, shooting, travel, antiquarian horology, and in an earlier life rowing, sailing and walking. *Address*: The Chantry, Bourton-on-the-Hill, Moreton-in-Marsh, Glos GL56 9AG. *T*: (01386) 700026. *E*: tom.martin@arco.co.uk. *Clubs*: Naval; Leander; Hawks (Cambridge); Royal Yorks Yacht.

**MARTIN, Prof. Ursula Hilda Mary**, CBE 2012; PhD, FREng; FRSE; Professor of Computer Science, University of Oxford, 2014–18; Senior Research Fellow, Wadham College, Oxford, since 2016; *b* London, 3 Aug. 1953; *d* of late Captain Geoffrey Richard Martin and Anne Louise Martin (*née* Priestman). *Educ*: Abbey Sch., Malvern Wells; Girton Coll., Cambridge (BA 1975); Univ. of Warwick (PhD 1979). Academic roles, univs in London and Manchester, and Univ. of Illinois, Urbana-Champaign, 1979–92; Professor of Computer Science: Royal Holloway, Univ. of London, 1990–92; Univ. of St Andrews, 1992–2002; Prof. of Computer Sci., 2003–14, Vice Principal, Sci. and Engrg, 2005–09, QMUL. FREng 2017; FRSE 2017. *Publications*: Ada Lovelace: the making of a computer scientist, 2018; articles on maths and computer sci. in learned jls. *Address*: Wadham College, Oxford OX1 3PN.

**MARTINDALE, Anu**; *see* Giri, A.

**MARTINEAU, His Honour David Nicholas Nettlefold**; a Circuit Judge, 1994–2013; *b* 27 March 1941; *s* of Frederick Alan Martineau and Vera Ruth Martineau (*née* Naylor); *m* 1968, Elizabeth Mary Allom; one *s* (one *d* deced). *Educ*: Eton; Trinity Coll., Cambridge (MA, LLM). Called to the Bar, Inner Temple, 1964; Asst Recorder, 1982–86; Recorder, 1986–94. Mem., Exec. Cttee, Cystic Fibrosis Trust, 1990–2004. *Recreations*: ski-ing, water ski-ing, wind-surfing, music, wine and food. *Clubs*: MCC; Hawks (Cambridge).

**MARTINEAU, Malcolm John**, OBE 2016; pianist, accompanist; Professor, Royal Academy of Music, since 1987; *b* 3 Feb. 1960; *s* of late George Martineau and Hester Dickson; *m* 2015, Asier Rodriguez Saiz. *Educ*: George Watson's Coll., Edinburgh; St Catharine's Coll., Cambridge (BA 1981); Royal Coll. of Music. Début, Wigmore Hall, 1984; has accompanied many leading singers, incl. Thomas Allen, Dame Janet Baker, Barbara Bonney, Della Jones, Dame Felicity Lott, Ann Murray, Bryn Terfel, Anne Sofie von Otter, Frederica von Stade, and instrumentalists, incl. Emma Johnson; has accompanied master classes, Britten-Pears Sch. Presented song recital series: Debussy and Poulenc, St John's, Smith Square; Britten, Wigmore Hall; Jt Artistic Dir, Liederreise, St John's, Smith Sq., 1998. Recordings incl. complete folk song settings of Beethoven and Britten, instrumental and vocal music incl. Arnold, Brahms, Fauré, Schubert, Schumann, Strauss and song recitals, with various artists. Hon. RAM 1998; Hon. Dr RSAMD, 2004; Hon. Fellow, RWCMD 2017. Accompanist's Prize, Walther Grüner Internat. Lieder Competition, 1983. *Recreations:* theatre-going, cooking. *Address:* c/o Askonas Holt, 15 Fetter Lane, EC4A 1BW. *T:* (020) 7400 1700.

**MARTINEAU-WALKER, Roger Antony;** *see* Walker, Roger A. M.

**MARTINEZ, Odaline de la, (Odaline de la Caridad Martinez Mijares),** FRAM; Cuban American conductor and composer; *b* Matanzas, Cuba, 31 Oct. 1949; *d* of Julian J. Martinez and Odaline M. Martinez. *Educ:* schs in USA; Tulane Univ., New Orleans; Royal Acad. of Music, London; Surrey Univ. FRAM 1990. Jt Founder and Artistic Dir, Lontano (chamber ensemble), 1976–; first woman to conduct an entire Promenade Concert programme, Royal Albert Hall, 1984; Dir, European Women's Orchestra, 1990–; Principal Guest Cond., Camerata of the Americas, 1998. Founder, 1992, and Artistic Dir, Lorelt recording co. Founder Mem., Women in Music, 1985; Founder, London Fest. of American Music, 2006. *Compositions include:* Litanies; Canciones; First String Quartet; *opera includes:* Sister Aimée: an American Legend, 1984; Imoinda, 2008; The Crossing, 2012; Plantation, 2018; *choral works include:* Misa Breve Afro-Cubana; Two American Madrigals; A Las Cinco de la Tarde; Orchestral Scenes from Imoinda. Villa Lobos Medal. *Publications:* (ed) Dame Ethel Smyth: symphonic serenade, 2015. *Address:* c/o Lontano Trust Ltd, Office 44, 219 Walworth Road, SE17 1RL.

**MARTLEW, Eric Anthony;** *b* 3 Jan. 1949; *m* 1970, Elsie Barbara Duggan. *Educ:* Harraby Secondary School, Carlisle; Carlisle Tech. Coll. Nestlé Co. Ltd, 1966–87: joined as lab. technician; later Personnel Manager, Dalston Factory, Carlisle. Member: Carlisle County Borough Council, 1972–74; Cumbria CC, 1973–88 (Chm., 1983–85). Mem., Cumbria Health Authy, later E Cumbria HA, 1977–87 (Chm., 1977–79). MP (Lab) Carlisle, 1987–2010. Opposition spokesman on defence, 1992–95; an Opposition Whip, 1995–97; PPS to Chancellor of Duchy of Lancaster, 1997–98, to Leader of H of L, 1998–2001. Formerly: Chm., All Party Animal Welfare Gp; Joint Chair: W Coast Main Line All Party Gp; All Party Rail Gp; Mem., Chairman's Panel. Vice Chm., Assoc. of Former MPs, 2015–. Trustee: Cumbria Deaf Assoc., 2012–; H of C Members' Fund, 2018–. Hon. Fellow, Univ. of Cumbria, 2016. Hon. Freeman, City of Carlisle, 2016. *Recreations:* photography, fell walking, horse racing.

**MARTONMERE,** 2nd Baron *cr* 1964; **John Stephen Robinson;** *b* 10 July 1963; *s* of Hon. Richard Anthony Gasque Robinson (*d* 1979) and of Wendy Patricia (who *m* subseq. Ronald De Mara), *d* of late James Cecil Blagden; *S* grandfather, 1989; *m* 2001, Marion Elizabeth Wills, *d* of Ian Wills, Toronto; two *s*. *Educ:* Lakefield College School; Senaca College. *Heir: s* Hon. James Ian Robinson, *b* 26 Feb. 2003. *Address:* 67 Donwoods Drive, Toronto, ON M4N 2G6, Canada.

**MARTYN-HEMPHILL,** family name of **Baron Hemphill**.

**MARTYNSKI, Vanessa;** *see* Lloyd, V.

**MARTYR, Peter McCallum;** Partner, since 1985, and Global Chief Executive, since 2013, Norton Rose Fulbright (formerly Norton Rose) LLP; *b* 31 March 1954; *s* of John Walton Martyr and late Jean Wallace Robertson; *m* 1978, Carol Frances Busby; one *s* one *d*. *Educ:* University Coll., Cardiff (LLB Jt Hons). Admitted solicitor, 1979. With Norton Rose, 1977–: Mem., Exec. Cttee, 1997–; Man. Partner, 2002–09; Chief Exec., 2010–13. *Recreations:* rugby (watching), ski-ing, music, classic cars. *Address:* Norton Rose Fulbright LLP, 3 More London Riverside, SE1 2AQ. *T:* (020) 7283 6000, *Fax:* (020) 7283 6500. *E:* peter.martyr@nortonrosefulbright.com.

**MARVEN, Robert;** QC 2018; *b* Chelmsford, 22 March 1970; *s* of Peter and Naomi Marven. *Educ:* Felsted Sch.; Trinity Coll., Cambridge (BA 1993); Inns of Court Sch. of Law (Astbury Schol.). Called to the Bar, Middle Temple, 1994; barrister in private practice, specialising in litigation funding and costs law, 1995–. Ed., Cordery on Legal Services, 2017–. *Recreations:* restaurants, theatre, books. *Address:* 4 New Square, Lincoln's Inn, WC2A 3RJ. *T:* (020) 7822 2000. *E:* r.marven@4newsquare.com.

**MARWICK, George Robert,** CVO 2007; farmer and company director; Lord-Lieutenant of Orkney, 1997–2007 (Vice Lord-Lieutenant, 1995–97); *b* 27 Feb. 1932; *s* of late Robert William Marwick, BSc Hons, MICE, Civil Engr, and Agnes Kemp Marwick (*née* Robson); *m* 1st, 1958, Hanne Jensen (marr. diss. 1989); three *d*; 2nd, 1990, Norma Gerrard (*née* Helm). *Educ:* Port Regis, Dorset; Bryanston Sch., Dorset; Edinburgh Sch. of Agriculture (SDA 1953). Chm. and Man. Dir, Swannay Farms Ltd, 1972–2009; Chairman: Campbeltown Creamery Ltd, 1974–90; Campbeltown Creamery (Hldgs) Ltd, 1974–90; Director: North Eastern Farmers Ltd, 1968–98; Orkney Islands Shipping Co., 1972–87. Chm., N of Scotland Water Bd, 1970–73; Member: Scottish Agricl Cons. Panel (formerly Winter Keep Panel), 1964–98; Countryside Commn for Scotland, 1978–86; Council, NT for Scotland, 1979–84. Ind. Mem., Orkney CC, then Orkney Is Council, 1968–78 (Vice-Convenor, 1970–74; Convenor, 1974–78). JP, 1970–2008, DL, 1976, Orkney. Hon. Sheriff of Grampian, Highlands and Is, 2000. *Recreations:* shooting, motor sport. *Address:* Whitewisp, Orchil Road, Auchterarder, Perthshire PH3 1NB. *T:* (01764) 662381. *Club:* New (Edinburgh).

**MARWICK, Rt Hon. Patricia, (Rt Hon. Tricia);** PC 2012; Member for Mid Fife and Glenrothes, Scottish Parliament, until 2016; Presiding Officer, Scottish Parliament, 2011–16; *b* 5 Nov. 1953; *m* 1975, Frank Marwick; one *s* one *d*. *Educ:* Fife. Former public affairs officer, Shelter. Mem., SNP, 1985– (Mem. NEC, 1997–2000). MSP (SNP) Mid Scotland and Fife, 1999–2007, Fife Central, 2007–11, Mid Fife and Glenrothes, 2011, when elected Presiding Officer. Contested (SNP) Fife Central, 1992, 1997. Chair, NHS Fife, 2017–Dec. 2020.

**MARWOOD, Anthony,** MBE 2018; violinist; *b* 6 July 1965; *s* of late Michael Travers Marwood and Anne (*née* Chevallier). *Educ:* King Edward VI Grammar Sch., Chelmsford; Royal Acad. of Music; Guildhall Sch. of Music and Drama. Internat. engagements as solo violinist with orchestras incl. LA Philharmonic, St Louis Symphony, Boston SO, Acad. of St Martin in the Fields, LPO, Chamber Orch. of Europe, Leipzig Gewandhaus Orch., Mariinsky Orch., Australian Chamber Orch., Sydney SO, Adelaide SO, NZ SO; Mem., Florestan Trio, 1995–2012; Artistic Dir, Irish Chamber Orch., 2006–11; Principal Artistic Partner, Les Violons du Roy, chamber orch., Québec, 2015–; Artistic Partner, Norwegian Chamber Orch., 2016–17; Jt Artistic Dir, Peasmarsh Chamber Music Fest., 1998–; collaborator with dancers and actors. Numerous recordings as soloist and chamber musician. FGS 2013. Instrumentalist Award, Royal Philharmonic Soc., 2006. *Recreations:* theatre, finding myself in Cape Town. *Address:* c/o Hazard Chase, 25 City Road, Cambridge CB1 1DP. *W:* www.anthonymarwood.com.

**MARX, Dame Clare (Lucy), (Mrs A. W. M. Fane),** DBE 2018 (CBE 2007); DL; FRCS; Associate Medical Director, Ipswich Hospital NHS Trust, 2013–18 (Consultant Trauma and Orthopaedic Surgeon, 1993–2014); Chair, General Medical Council, since 2019; *b* Coventry, 15 March 1954; *d* of Francis Marx and Brenda Marx; *m* 1989, Andrew William Mildmay Fane, *qv*. *Educ:* Cheltenham Ladies' Coll.; University Coll. London (MB BS 1977). FRCS 1981; FRCPE 2015. Consultant Orthopaedic Surgeon, St Mary's Hosp. NHS Trust, London, 1990–93; Ipswich Hospital NHS Trust, 1993–: Clin. Dir, Trauma and Orthopaedics, 1994–98; Chm., Med. Staff Cttee, 2003–05. Royal College of Surgeons of England: Mem., Council, 2009–17; Pres., 2014–17; Chairman: Specialist Adv. Cttee in Orthopaedics, Jt Cttee of Higher Surgical Trng, 2005–07; Invited Rev. Mechanism, 2011–. Mem. Council, British Orthopaedic Assoc., 2004– (Pres., 2008–09); Chair, Faculty of Med. Leadership and Mgt, 2017–18 (Founding Sen. Fellow, 2016). FRCSE *ad hominem* 2009; Hon. FRCPSGlas 2015; Hon. FRACS 2017; Hon. FRCSI 2017; Hon. FRCP 2018. Hon DSc Exeter, 2016; Hon. MD Leeds, 2018. Hon. Bencher, Inner Temple, 2017. DL Suffolk, 2008. *Publications:* articles in learned jls on hip and knee arthroplasty and the trauma and orthopaedic curriculum. *Recreations:* walking, gardening, ski-ing. *Address:* General Medical Council, 350 Euston Road, NW1 3JN. *T:* (020) 7189 5092. *E:* chair@gmc-uk.org.

**MARYON DAVIS, Dr Alan Roger,** FRCP; FFPH; FFSEM; Hon. Professor of Public Health, King's College London, since 2007; *b* 21 Jan. 1943; *s* of Cyril Edward Maryon Davis and Hilda May Maryon Davis; *m* 1981, Glynis Anne Davies; two *d*. *Educ:* St Paul's Sch.; St John's Coll., Cambridge (MA 1968; MB BChir 1970); St Thomas's Hosp. Med. Sch. (LRCP, MRCS 1969); London Sch. of Hygiene and Tropical Medicine. MSc (Social Med.) London 1978. MRCP 1972; FFPH (FFCM 1986; MFCM 1978); FRSPH (FRIPHH 1989); FRCP 2005; FFSEM 2007. Early med. career in gen. medicine and rheumatology, later in community medicine; MO, 1977–84, CMO, 1984–87, Health Educn Council; Sen. Med. Advisor, Health Educn Authority, 1987–88; Hon. Consultant, Paddington and N Kensington HA, 1985–88; Hon. Senior Lecturer: in Community Medicine, St Mary's Hosp. Med. Sch., 1985–88; in Public Health, UMDS, then KCL, 1988–2007; Consultant in Public Health Med., W Lambeth, then SE London, subseq. Lambeth, Southwark and Lewisham, HA, 1988–2002; Dir of Public Health, Southwark PCT, 2002–07. Bd Advr, HPA, 2007–10. Vice Chm., Nat. Heart Forum, 2005–13; Chair: RIPH, later RSPH, 2006–09 (Vice Chm., 2002–06); NICE Public Health Prog. Develt Gp (Obesity), 2012–13; NICE Public Health Adv. Cttee, 2013–; Pres., FPH, 2007–10. Mem., Alcohol and Educn Res. Council, 2010–11; Trustee: Medicinema, 2000–18; Drinkaware, 2010–11; Alcohol Change (formerly Alcohol Res.) UK, 2011–19 (Chm., 2014–19); Best Beginnings, 2011–16 (Chm., 2011–16); UK Health Forum, 2013–17 (Vice Chm., 2017–); Medact, 2018– (Internat. Chm., 2019–). Vice Chm., MJA, 2010–11. Writer and broadcaster on health matters, 1975–; BBC radio series include Action Makes the Heart Grow Stronger (Med. Journalists' Assoc. Radio Award), 1983; BBC television series include: Body Matters, 1985–89; Health UK, 1990–91. Editor-in-Chief, Health Education Jl, 1984–88; Med. Advice Columnist, Woman magazine, 1988–2005; Editor, Public Health Today, 2010–18. Hon. FRCGP 2011; Hon. FCMSA 2010. *Publications:* Family Health and Fitness, 1981; Body Facts, 1984; (with J. Thomas) Diet 2000, 1984; (with J. Rogers) How to Save a Life, 1987; PSSST—a Really Useful Guide to Alcohol, 1989; Cholesterol Check, 1991; The Good Health Guide, 1994; Ruby's Health Quest, 1995; The Body-clock Diet, 1996; Feeling Good, 2007; (jtly) Thinking Ahead: why we need to improve children's mental health and wellbeing, 2011; contrib. academic articles to peer-reviewed jls. *Recreations:* eating well, drinking well, singing (not so well) in the humorous group Instant Sunshine. *Address:* Gray Walls, Cuffs Lane, Tisbury, Wilts SP3 6LG. *T:* (01747) 873171.

**MASCHLER, Fay,** MBE 2004; restaurant critic, Evening Standard, since 1972; *b* 15 July 1945; *d* of Mary and Arthur Frederick Coventry; *m* 1970, Thomas Michael Maschler, *qv* (marr. diss. 1987); one *s* two *d*; *m* 1992, Reginald Bernard John Gadney (*d* 2018). *Educ:* Convent of the Sacred Heart, Greenwich, Conn. Copywriter, J. Walter Thompson, 1964; journalist, Radio Times, 1969. *Publications:* Cooking is a Game You Can Eat, 1975; A Child's Book of Manners, 1979; Miserable Aunt Bertha, 1980; Fay Maschler's Guide to Eating Out in London, 1986; Eating In, 1987; Howard & Maschler on Food, 1987; Teach Your Child to Cook, 1988; Evening Standard Restaurant Guides, annually, 1993–. *Address:* 12 Fitzroy Square, W1T 6BU. *Clubs:* Groucho, Car Clamp.

**MASCHLER, Thomas Michael;** Publisher, Jonathan Cape Children's Books, 1991–97; Director, Jonathan Cape Ltd, 1960–97 (Chairman, 1970–91); Founder, Booker Prize for Fiction, 1969; *b* 16 Aug. 1933; *s* of Kurt Leo Maschler and of Rita Masseron (*née* Lechner); *m* 1970, Fay Coventry (*see* Fay Maschler) (marr. diss. 1987); one *s* two *d*; *m* 1988, Regina Kulinicz. *Educ:* Leighton Park School. Production Asst, Andre Deutsch, 1955; Editor, MacGibbon & Kee, 1956–58; Fiction Editor, Penguin Books, 1958–60; Jonathan Cape: Editorial Dir, 1960; Man. Dir, 1966. Associate Producer, The French Lieutenant's Woman (film), 1981. Founder, Book Bus Foundn, 2007. *Publications:* (ed) Declarations, 1957; (ed) New English Dramatists Series, 1959–63; Tom Maschler Publisher (memoirs), 2005.

**MASCIE-TAYLOR, Prof. (Bryan) Hugo,** FRCP, FRCPI; Medical Director, Ernst & Young LLP, since 2016; *b* 21 Aug. 1947; *s* of (Henry) Hugo and (Madeline) Eira Mascie-Taylor; *m* 1st, 1972, Heather Chapman (marr. diss. 1994); one *s*; 2nd, 1994, Louise Thomas; two *s*. *Educ:* Sir Thomas Rich's Sch., Gloucester; Univ. of Leeds; Univ. of California, San Francisco; Ashridge Mgt Coll.; Henley Coll. of Mgt (ADipC 1997). FRCPI 1992; FRCP 1994. Consultant Physician: St James Univ. Hosp., Leeds, 1986–91; (and Clinical Dir), Seacroft Hosp., Leeds, 1991–94; Dir, Strategic Develt, Leeds Community and Mental Health Trust, 1992–94; Med. Dir, 1994–96, Dir, Commng, 1996–98, Leeds HA; Medical Director: Leeds Teaching Hosps NHS Trust, 1998–2009; NHS Confedn, 2009–13; Trust Special Administrator, Mid-Staffs NHS Trust, 2013–14; Med. Dir, Monitor, 2014–16. University of Leeds: Hon. Sen. Clin. Lectr, 1986–2011; Vis. Prof., Sch. of Medicine, 2004–; Vis. Fellow, Univ. of York, 1996–2003. External Examiner: (Masters/Gerontol.), Univ. of Hull, 1996–99; (MBA), Univ. of Durham, 2003–05. Chm., Overseas Partnership and Trng Initiative (OPTIN), 2004–. *Publications:* articles in clinical and mgt jls. *Recreations:* English furniture, ski-ing. *Address:* Ernst & Young LLP, 1 More London Place, SE1 2AF. *T:* 07887 853104. *E:* hugo@mascie-taylor.org.

**MASCORD, Dr David John;** Headmaster, Bristol Grammar School, 1999–2008; *b* 18 Oct. 1950; *s* of George and Evelyn Mascord; *m* 1974, Veronica Mary Chalton Peers; two *s*. *Educ:* York Univ. (BA 1st Cl. Hons Chemistry 1972); St John's Coll., Cambridge (PhD 1976; PGCE with Dist.). Head of Chemistry, Wellington Coll., 1981–86; Sen. Teacher, Aylesbury GS, 1986–89; Asst Hd, 1989–98, Dep. Hd, 1998–99, Bristol GS. *Publications:* (contrib.) The Head Speaks, 2008; contrib. articles in Faraday Discussions of Chem. Soc., Molecular Physics, Jl Chem. Industry. *Recreations:* walking, swimming, personal computing, cooking, reading, particularly Charles Dickens, sketching, painting.

**MASEFIELD, Sir Charles (Beech Gordon),** Kt 1997; CEng, FRAeS, FIMechE; President, BAE SYSTEMS, 2003–07 (Group Marketing Director, 1999–2002, Vice-Chairman, 2002–03); *b* 7 Jan. 1940; *s* of Sir Peter (Gordon) Masefield and Patricia Doreen (*née* Rooney); *m* 1970, Fiona Anne Kessler; two *s*. *Educ:* Eastbourne Coll.; Jesus Coll., Cambridge (MA). CEng 1984; FRAeS 1980; FIMechE 1984. Sales Exec. and Test Pilot, Beagle Aircraft, 1964–70; Hawker Siddeley Aviation: Test Pilot, 1970–76; Dep. Chief Test

Pilot, Manchester, 1976–78; British Aerospace, Manchester: Chief Test Pilot, 1978–80; Project Dir, 1980–81; Prodn Dir, 1981–84; Gen. Manager, 1984–86; Man. Dir, BAe Hatfield, Manchester, Prestwick, 1986–92; Pres., BAe Commercial Aircraft, 1992–93; Sen. Vice-Pres. and Commercial Dir, Airbus Industrie, Toulouse, 1993–94; Hd, Defence Export Services Orgn, 1994–98; Vice-Chm., GEC, 1998–99. Chairman: Microsulis Ltd, 2003–07; Helvetia Wealth Mgt, Switzerland, 2004–15; Zedsen Ltd, 2015–; non-executive Director: Banque Piguet, Switzerland, 2002–04; Qator Foundn, 2003–12; Epicure Berlin, 2012–. Pres., RAeS, 1994–95. FRSA 1999. Hon. FIMechE 2005. *Recreation:* golf. *Address:* Old Hall, Markyate, Herts AL3 8AR. *T:* (01582) 763901.

**MASEFIELD, (John) Thorold,** CMG 1986; HM Diplomatic Service, retired; Governor and Commander-in-Chief of Bermuda, 1997–2001; *b* 1 Oct. 1939; *e s* of late Dr Geoffrey Bussell Masefield, DSc and Mildred Joy Thorold Masefield (*née* Rogers); *m* 1962, Jennifer Mary, MBE (*d* 2019), *d* of late Rev. Dr H. C. Trowell, OBE and late K. M. Trowell, MBE; two *s* one *d* (and one *d* decd). *Educ:* Dragon Sch., Oxford; Repton Sch.; St John's Coll., Cambridge (Scholar) (MA). Joined CRO, 1962; Private Sec. to Permanent Under Sec., 1963–64; Second Secretary: Kuala Lumpur, 1964–65; Warsaw, 1966–67; FCO, 1967–69; First Sec., UK Delegn to Disarmament Conf., 1970–74; Dep. Head, Policy Planning Staff, FCO, 1974–77; Far Eastern Dept, FCO, 1977–79; Counsellor, Head of Chancery and Consul Gen., Islamabad, 1979–82; Head of Personnel Services Dept, FCO, 1982–85; Head, Far Eastern Dept, FCO, 1985–87; Fellow, Center for Internat. Affairs, Harvard Univ., 1987–88; seconded to CSSB, 1988–89; High Comr, Tanzania, 1989–92; Asst Under-Sec. of State, FCO, 1992–94; High Comr, Nigeria, also concurrently Ambassador (non-resident) to the Republics of Benin and of Chad, 1994–97. Dep. Chm., Bermuda Soc., 2006–07. Mem., Brockenhurst Parish Council, 2005–15 (Vice-Chm., 2006–07, 2010–12; Chm., 2007–10). KStJ 1997. *Publications:* article in International Affairs. *Recreation:* fruit and vegetables. *Club:* Brockenhurst Probus.

*See also R. C. Masefield, R. F. Masefield.*

**MASEFIELD, Robin Charles,** CBE 2003; Director General, Northern Ireland Prison Service, 2004–10; *b* Oxford, 16 April 1952; *s* of late Dr Geoffrey Bussell Masefield and Mildred Joy Thorold Masefield (*née* Rogers); *m* 1981, Rosemary Elizabeth Drew; one *s* two *d*. *Educ:* Dragon Sch., Oxford; Marlborough Coll.; St John's Coll., Cambridge (Scholar; BA Social Anthropol. 1973). Joined NI Office, 1973; seconded to Hong Kong Govt, 1980–83, to Immigration and Nationality Dept, Home Office, 1983–86, to HM Prison Service, 1991–94; Hd of Efficiency Scrutiny, Cabinet Office, 1994–95; Dir, Change Mgt, NI Office, 1995–96; Sec., Rev. of Parades and Marches, 1996–97; Dir, Finance and Estate Mgt, 1997–2000; Hd, Patten Action Team, 2000–04. *Publications:* Making the Most of Hong Kong (with Robert Phillips), 1983; Oriental and Other Expresses, 1994; (jtly) Limpsfield, Ancient and Modern, 1997; Twixt Bay and Burn, 2011; (with Desmond Rea) Dealing with the Past: a note to Ambassador Haass, 2013; (with Desmond Rea) Policing in Northern Ireland, Delivering the New Beginning?, 2014; Be Careful, Don't Rush: celebrating 150 years of train travel between Holywood and Bangor, 2015; The History of Palace Barracks (to 1969) and Holywood as a Garrison Town, 2017; Hollywood People, 2018. *Recreations:* gardening, local history and community activism. *Address:* c/o Department of Justice, Stormont, Belfast BT4 3SU.

*See also J. T. Masefield.*

**MASEFIELD, Roger Francis;** QC 2013; *b* Geneva, Switzerland, 24 Dec. 1970; *s* of (John) Thorold Masefield, *qv*; *m* 2001, Catherine Strauss; two *s* one *d*. *Educ:* Dragon Sch., Oxford; Marlborough Coll., Wilts; St John's Coll., Cambridge (Wright Schol.; BA 1st Cl. Law 1993); Magdalen Coll., Oxford (BCL 1st Cl. 1994; Vinerian Schol.). Called to the Bar, Middle Temple, 1994; pupillage, Brick Court Chambers, 1995–96; in practice as barrister, 1996–. *Publications:* (ed) Butterworth's Banking Law Guide, 2006; (contrib.) Paget's Law of Banking, 13th edn, 2007; Banks and Financial Crime, 2008; Competition Litigation, UK Practice and Procedure, 2009. *Recreations:* croquet, snorkelling. *Address:* Brick Court Chambers, 7–8 Essex Street, WC2R 3LD. *T:* (020) 7379 3550, *Fax:* (020) 7379 3558. *Club:* Royal Automobile.

**MASEFIELD, Thorold;** *see* Masefield, J. T.

**MASERI, Attilio,** MD; FRCP; FACC; President, Heart Care Foundation ONLUS, 2008, now Hon. President; *b* 12 Nov. 1935; *s* of Adriano and Antonietta Albini, Italian nobles; *m* 1960, Countess Francesca Maseri Florio di Santo Stefano (*d* 2000); one *s*. *Educ:* Classic Lycée Cividale, Italy; Padua Univ. Med. Sch. Special bds in Cardiology, 1963, in Nuclear Medicine, 1965, Italy. Research fellow: Univ. of Pisa, 1960–65; Columbia Univ., NY, 1965–66; Johns Hopkins Univ., Baltimore, 1966–67; University of Pisa: Asst Prof., 1967–70; Prof. of Internal Medicine, 1970; Prof. of Cardiovascular Pathophysiology, 1972–79; Prof. of Medicine (Locum), 1977–79; Sir John McMichael Prof. of Cardiovascular Medicine, RPMS, Univ. of London, 1979–91; Prof. of Cardiology, and Dir, Inst. of Cardiology, Catholic Univ. of Rome, 1991–2001; Prof. of Cardiology and Dir, Cardiovascular and Thoracic Dept, Vita-Salute San Raffaele Univ., Milan, 2001–08. Lifetime Mem., John Hopkins Soc. of Scholars, 1980. George Von Hevesy Prize for Nuclear Medicine, 1974; King Faisal Prize for Medicine, 1992; Dist. Scientist Award, Amer. Coll. of Cardiology, 1997; Invernizzi Prize for Medicine, Romeo and Enrica Invernizzi Foundn, 1998; Gold Medal Award, Eur. Soc. of Cardiology, 2002; Pres. of Italian Republic's Gold Medal for Culture and Science, 2004; Grand Prix Scientifique, Inst de France, 2004; Gold Medal of Merit, Italian Ministry of Health, 2010. Chevalier d'honneur et devotion, SMO Malta; Knight Grand Cross of Order of Merit (Italy), 2005. *Publications:* Myocardial Blood Flow in Man, 1972; Primary and Secondary Angina, 1977; Perspectives on Coronary Care, 1979; Ischemic Heart Disease: a rational basis for clinical practise and clinical research, 1995; articles in major internat. cardiological and med. jls. *Recreations:* ski-ing, snowboarding, windsurfing, tennis, sailing. *Address:* Heart Care Foundation ONLUS, Via La Marmora 36, 50121 Florence, Italy. *Club:* Queen's.

**MASHAM, Lord; Mark William Philip Cunliffe-Lister;** *b* 15 Sept. 1970; *s* and heir of Earl of Swinton, *qv*, *m* 2000, Felicity Shadbolt; two *s* one *d*. Heir: *s* Hon. William Edward Cunliffe-Lister, *b* 25 May 2004.

**MASHAM OF ILTON,** Baroness *cr* 1970 (Life Peer); **Susan Lilian Primrose Cunliffe-Lister, (Susan, Countess of Swinton);** DL; *b* 14 April 1935; *d* of Sir Ronald Sinclair, 8th Bt and Reba Blair (who *m* 2nd, 1957, Lt-Col H. R. Hildreth, MBE; she *d* 1985), *d* of Anthony Inglis, MD; *m* 1959, Lord Masham (later 2nd Earl of Swinton) (*d* 2006); one *s* one *d* (both adopted). *Educ:* Heathfield School, Ascot; London Polytechnic. Has made career in health and voluntary work. Mem., Peterlee and Newton Aycliffe New Town Corp., 1973–85. Mem., Select Cttee on Sci. and Technol., 1997–. All-Party Parliamentary Groups: Member: British Council Associate Parly Gp, 1999–; Associated Parly Health Gp (formerly Forum), 2001–; Chair: Cancer; Skin; Co-Chair: Antibiotics; Clinical Physiology; Men's Health; Telehealth; HIV/Aids; Autism; Hepatology; Horse; Pro-Life; Tuberculosis; Vice Chairman: Alcohol Misuse; Spinal Cord; Dentistry; Headache Disorders; Heart Disease; Continence Care; Accident Prevention; Animal Welfare; Atrial Fibrillation; Civil Society and Volunteering; First Aid; Muscular Dystrophy; Osteoporosis; Pancreatic Cancer; Stem Cell Transplant; Thrombosis; Vascular Disease; Treasurer: Complex Needs and Dual Diagnosis; Gardening and Horticulture; Primary Care and Public Health; Tranquilizer Addiction; Women's Sport and Fitness; Sec., Malaria and Neglected Tropical Disease. President: N Yorks Red Cross, 1963–88 (Patron, 1989–); Yorks Assoc. for the Disabled, 1963–98; Spinal Injuries Assoc., 1982–; Chartered Soc. of Physiotherapy, 1975–82; Papworth and Enham Village Settlements, 1973–85; Registration Council of Scientists in Health Care, 1991–; Countrywide Workshops Charitable Trust, 1993–97; St Cecilia Orch., Ripon; Vice-President: British Sports Assoc. for the Disabled; Disabled Drivers Assoc.; Assoc. of Occupnl Therapists; Action for Dysphasic Adults; Hosp. Saving Assoc.; Chairman: Bd of Dirs, Phoenix House (Drug Rehabilitation), 1986–92 (Patron, 1992–); Home Office Working Gp on Young People and Alcohol, 1987; Member: Yorks RHA, 1982–90; N Yorks FHSA, 1990–95; Bd of Visitors, Wetherby Young Offenders Instn (formerly Wetherby Youth Custody Centre), 1963–94; Winston Churchill Meml Trust, 1980–2007; Council, London Lighthouse, 1991–98; Trustee, Spinal Res. Trust; Patron many orgns in area of health and disability, including: Disablement Income Gp; Yorks Faculty of GPs; Greenbank Project, Liverpool; Mem. and Governor, Ditchley Foundn, 1980; former Mem., Volunteer Centre. Freedom, Borough of Harrogate, 1989. DL North Yorks, 1991. Hon. FRCGP 1981; Hon. FCSP 1996; Hon. Fellow, Bradford and Ilkley Community Coll., 1988. Hon. MA Open, 1981; DUniv York, 1985; Hon. LLD: Leeds, 1988; Teesside, 1993; Hon. DSc Ulster, 1990; Hon. DLitt Keele, 1993; Hon. DCL UEA, 2001. *Publications:* The World Walks By, 1986. *Recreations:* breeding highland ponies, swimming, table tennis, fishing, flower decoration, gardening. *Address:* Dykes Hill House, Masham, near Ripon, N Yorks HG4 4NS. *T:* (01765) 689241; 46 Westminster Gardens, Marsham Street, SW1P 4JG. *T:* (020) 7834 0700.

**MASHELKAR, Raghunath Anant,** PhD; FRS 1998; National Research Professor, India, since 2011; President, Global Research Alliance, since 2007; *b* 1 Jan. 1943; *s* of late Anant Tukaram Mashelkar and Anjani Anant Mashelkar; *m* 1970, Vaishali R. Mashelkar; one *s* two *d*. *Educ:* Univ. of Bombay (BChemEngrg 1966; PhD 1969). Sen. Scientist, 1976–86, Dir, 1989–95, Nat. Chemical Lab., Pune; Dir Gen., Council of Scientific and Industrial Res., and Sec., Dept of Scientific and Industrial Res., India, 1995–2006; Council of Scientific and Industrial Res. Bhatnagar Fellow, India, 2007–11. Pres., Indian Sci. Congress, 1999–2000. Fellow: Indian Acad. of Scis, 1983 (Vice Pres., 1995–97); Indian Nat. Sci. Acad., 1984 (Viswakarma Medal, 1988); Maharashtra Acad. of Scis, 1985 (Pres., 1991–94); Third World Acad. of Scis, 1994. Hon. DSc: Salford, 1993; Kanpur, 1995; Delhi, 1998; Guwahati Anna (Chennai), Pretoria, 2000; London, 2001; Wisconsin, 2002; Allahabad, 2002; Varanasi, 2002; Baroda, 2003; Kalyani, 2004; Narendra Deva, Faizabad, 2004; Govind Ballabh Pant, Pantnagar, 2004; Maharishi Dayanand, Rohtak, 2005; Guru Nanak Dev, Amritsar, 2005; Mohanlal Sukhadia, Udaipur, 2006; Lucknow, 2006; Hon. DLit Santiniketan, 2006. Herdillia Award, Indian Inst. of Chem. Engrs, 1982; K. G. Naik Gold Medal, 1985; Republic Day Award, NRDC, 1995; Atur Sangtani Award, Atur Foundn, 1998; Lifetime Achievement Award, Indian Analytical Instruments Assoc., 1998; Shanti Sharup Bhatnagar Medal, INSA, 2001; Nat. Award, Lal Bahadur Shastri Inst. of Mgt for Excellence in Public Admin and Mgt Studies, 2002; Medal of Engrg Excellence, WFEO, 2003; New Millennium Innovation Award, Associated Chambers of Commerce and Industry of India, 2003; Lifetime Achievement Award, 2004, Asutosh Mookherjee Meml Award, 2005, Indian Sci. Congress Assoc.; Stars of Asia Award, Business Week, USA, 2005; TWAS Medal, Acad. of Scis for Developing World (TWAS), 2005; Suryadatta Nat. Award, Suryadatta Gp of Insts, 2006. Padmashri, 1991; Padmabhushan, 2000; Padmavibhushan, 2014; Lenovo Sci. Prize, TWAS, 2018. *Publications:* (ed jtly) Advances in Transport Processes, vol. 1, 1980, vol. 2, 1982, vol. 3, 1983, vol. 4, 1986, vol. 8, 1992, vol. 9, 1993; (ed jtly and contrib.) Frontiers in Chemical Reaction Engineering, vols 1 and 2, 1984; (ed jtly) Transport Phenomena in Polymeric Systems, vol. 1, 1987, vol. 2, 1989; (ed jtly) Advances in Transport Phenomena in Fluidizing Systems, 1987; (ed jtly) Recent Trends in Chemical Reaction Engineering, vols 1 and 2, 1987; (ed jtly) Reactions and Reaction Engineering, 1987; (ed jtly and contrib.) Heat Transfer Equipment Design, 1988; (ed jtly) Readings in Solid State Chemistry, 1994; (ed jtly and contrib.) Dynamics of Complex Fluids, 1998; (ed jtly and contrib.) Structure and Dynamics in the Mesoscopic Domain, 1999; (jtly) Intellectual Property and Competitive Strategies in the 21st Century, 2004; Timeless Inspirator: reliving Gandhi, 2010; Reinventing India, 2011; numerous articles in jls and contribs to books. *Address:* 3rd Floor, Adams Court, Above Bank of Baroda, Baner, Pune 411045, India. *T:* 46925703.

**MASKAWA, Prof. Toshihide,** DSc; Special Professor, since 2003, and Director-General, Kobayashi-Maskawa Institute for the Origin of Particles, since 2009, Nagoya University; *b* 7 Feb. 1940. *Educ:* Nagoya Univ. (DSc 1967). Asst Prof., Faculty of Sci., Kyoto Univ., 1970–76; Prof., Yukawa Inst. for Theoretical Physics, 1980–90; Prof., Faculty and Grad. Sch. of Sci., Kyoto Univ., 1990–97; Dir, Yukawa Inst. for Theoretical Physics, 1997–2003, now Prof. Emeritus. Dir, Maskawa Inst. for Sci. and Culture, Kyoto Sangyo Univ. Sakurai Prize, APS, 1985; Japan Acad. Prize, 1985; Asahi Prize, 1994; (jtly) Nobel Prize for Physics, 2008. *Address:* Kobayashi-Maskawa Institute for the Origin of Particles, Nagoya University, Furo-cho, Chikusa-ku, Nagoya, Aichi 464–8602, Japan.

**MASKELL, Prof. Duncan John,** MA, PhD; FMedSci; Vice Chancellor, University of Melbourne, since 2018; *b* 30 May 1961; *s* of Leslie George Maskell and Mary Sheila Horsburgh Maskell; *m* 1992, Dr Sarah Elizabeth Peters; one *s* one *d*. *Educ:* Gonville and Caius Coll., Cambridge (MA, PhD). Res. Scientist, Wellcome Biotech, 1985–88; Res. Fellow, Inst. of Molecular Medicine, John Radcliffe Hosp., Univ. of Oxford, 1988–92; Lectr, Dept of Biochemistry, Imperial Coll., London Univ., 1992–96; University of Cambridge: Marks and Spencer Prof. of Farm Animal Health, Food Sci. and Food Safety, 1996–2018; Hd, Dept of Veterinary Medicine, 2004–13; Hd, Sch. of Biol Scis, 2013–15; Sen. Pro-Vice Chancellor, Planning and Resources, 2015–18; Fellow, Wolfson Coll., Cambridge, 1998–2018. Food Standards Agency: Member: Res. Review Gp, 2000–01; Adv. Cttee on Res., 2002–07; Gen. Adv. Cttee on Sci., 2008–16. Member: Agri-Food Cttee, 1997–2003 (Chm., 2000–03); Strategy Bd, 2000–03, BBSRC; Council, RCVS, 2004–13; Scientific Adv. Bd, Pirbright Inst., 2010–18; Scientific Adv. Bd, Roslin Inst., 2013–18; Internat. Scientific Adv. Bd, Wellcome Trust/Oxford Univ. Clinical Res. Unit, Vietnam, 2012; Internat. Scientific Adv. Bd, WellcomeTrust/Oxford Univ. Clinical Res. Unit, VIZIONS project, 2014; Dist. Vis. Prof. and Mem., 3i Inst. Internat. Scientific Adv. Bd, Univ. of Technol., Sydney, 2011–15. Trustee Bd Mem., BBSRC Inst. of Food Res., 2013–18. Mem., Global Agenda Council on Pandemics, World Econ. Forum, 2008–09. Co-founder: Arrow Therapeutics Ltd, 1998; Discuva Ltd, 2011; Bactevo Ltd, 2013; Polypharmakos Ltd, 2017; non-executive Director: Moredun Res. Inst., 2006–15; Genus plc, 2014–18. FMedSci 2011. Hon. Associate, RCVS, 2017. *Publications:* papers in learned jls on molecular microbiol. and bacterial infectious diseases. *Recreations:* watching cricket, Manchester United, cooking, fine wine, music. *Address:* 9th Floor, Raymond Priestley Building, University of Melbourne, Vic 3010, Australia. *T:* (3) 83446134. *E:* vc@unimelb.edu.au. *Club:* Athenæum.

**MASKELL, Rachael Helen;** MP (Lab) York Central, since 2015; *b* 5 July 1972. *Educ:* Univ. of E Anglia (BSc Physiotherapy 1994). Physiotherapist in hosps incl. Barnet Gen. Hosp.; Hd of Health, Unite, until 2015. Shadow Sec. of State for Envmt and Rural Affairs, 2016–17; Shadow Minister for Transport, 2017–. Mem., Health Select Cttee, 2015–17. *Address:* House of Commons, SW1A 0AA.

**MASKEY, Alexander;** Member (SF) Belfast West, Northern Ireland Assembly, 1998–2003 and since Nov. 2014 (Belfast South, 2003–Nov. 2014); Lord Mayor of Belfast, 2002–03; b 8 Jan. 1952; s of Alexander and Teresa Maskey; m 1976, Elizabeth McKee; two s. Educ: Christian Brothers' Primary Sch.; Donegall Street, Belfast; St Malachy's Coll., Belfast. Mem. (SF), Belfast CC, 1983–2010. Member: Nat. Cttee, Ard Chomhairle, 1994–; NI Forum, 1996–98; NI Policing Bd, 2007–11. Contested (SF) Belfast S, 2001, 2005. Recreations: photography, reading. Address: (office) Connolly House, 147 Andersonstown Road, Belfast BT11 9BW.

**MASKEY, Paul;** MP (SF) Belfast West, since June 2011; b Belfast, 10 June 1967; s of Alexander and Teresa Maskey; m Patricia; two c. Educ: Edmund Rice Coll. Co-ordinator, Fáilte Feirste Thiar; has worked as florist and glass cutter. Mem. (SF) Belfast CC, 2001–09 (Leader, SF Gp, until 2009). Mem. (SF) Belfast W, NI Assembly, 2007–July 2012. Recreations: football, walking. Address: Unit 29, Kennedy Centre, 564–568 Bóthar na bhFál, Béal Feirste BT11 9AE. T: (028) 9620 6402. E: westbelfastmp@sinnfein.ie.

**MASKIN, Prof. Eric Stark,** PhD; Adams University Professor, Harvard University, since 2012; b New York, 12 Dec. 1950; s of Meyer and Bernice Rabkin Maskin; one s one d. Educ: Harvard Univ. (AB Maths 1972; AM Applied Maths 1974; PhD 1976). Res. Fellow, Jesus Coll., Cambridge, 1976–77; Prof., MIT, 1981–84; Prof., 1985–2000, Louis Berkman Prof. of Econs, 1997–2000, Harvard Univ.; Albert O. Hirschman Prof. of Social Sci., Inst. for Advanced Study, Princeton, 2000–11. Guggenheim Fellow, 1980–81; Sloan Res. Fellow, 1983–85. Lectures: Churchill, Cambridge Univ., 1994; Arrow, Stanford Univ., 1998; Schwartz, Northwestern Univ., 2002; Toulouse, Univ. of Toulouse, 2004; Zeuthen, Univ. of Copenhagen, 2004; Marshall, Cambridge Univ., 2007; Klein, Univ. of Penn, 2007. Fellow: Econometric Soc., 1981 (Pres., 2003); Amer. Acad. of Arts and Scis, 1994. Corresp. FBA 2003. Hon. Fellow: St John's Coll., Cambridge, 2004; Jesus Coll., Cambridge, 2009. Mem., NAS, 2008. Hon. MA Cantab, 1977; Hon. DHL Bard Coll., 2008; Dhc Corvinus Univ. of Budapest, 2008; Hon. DSc Cambridge, 2017. Galbraith Teaching Prize, Harvard Univ., 1990, 1992; (jtly) Nobel Prize in Econs, 2007; Erik Kempe Award, Kempe Foundn, 2007; Centennial Medal, Harvard Univ., 2010. Publications: contrib. learned jls incl. Rev. of Econ. Studies, Qly Jl of Econs, Econometrica, Jl of Political Economy. Recreation: music. Address: Department of Economics, Harvard University, Littauer Center, 1805 Cambridge Street, Cambridge, MA 02138, USA. T: (617) 4951746, Fax: (617) 4957730. E: emaskin@fas.harvard.edu.

**MASKREY, Rachel;** see Langdale, R.

**MASLIN, Prof. Mark Andrew,** PhD; FRGS; Professor of Physical Geography, University College London, since 2006 (Director, Environment Institute, 2006–10; Head, Department of Geography, 2007–11); Director, London NERC Doctoral Training Partnership, since 2014; b London, 14 March 1968; s of Christopher Alan and Catherine Anne Maslin; m 1998, Johanna Lucy Andrews; two d. Educ: Univ. of Bristol (BSc 1st Cl. Hons); Darwin Coll., Cambridge (PhD 1993). FRGS 2001. Res. Scientist, Kiel Univ., 1993–95; Lectr in Geog., 1995–2002, Reader in Geog., 2002–06, UCL. Associate Ed., Quarternary Sci. Rev., 2005–; Mem., Editl Bd, Geographical Jl, 2010–. Executive Director: Carbon Auditors Ltd, 2007–12; Rezatec Ltd (formerly Carbon Associates Ltd), 2012–; Global Precious Commodities plc, 2012–13. Science Adviser: CarbonSense Ltd, 2007–; Global Cool Foundn, 2009–. Royal Soc. Wolfson Res. Merit Award for study of early human evolution in E Africa, 2011–16; Royal Soc. Industrial Fellowship, 2012–16. Member: UK Global Forest Monitoring Consortium, 2010–; CSR Adv. Bd, Sopra-Steria Gp (formerly Steria Corporate Responsibility), 2011–. Consultant for TV programmes: Supervolcano, Horizon, Superstorm, Around the World in 60 Minutes, Ice Age Giants, Global Warming Special, Dispatches: Greenwash, Green Britain Week, Timeteam, Wild Brazil, Human Universe, In Our Time, Newsnight, Today Prog., One Strange Rock; contributor: In Our Time: Paleocene-Eocene Thermal Maximum, BBC Radio 4; ITV Weather from Hell, 2018; Briefing Room, Radio 4, 2018; Climate Change: the facts, BBC, 2019. Trustee and co-Dir, TippingPoint: Art and Climate Change, 2006–12. Mem., Adv. Cttee, Cheltenham Sci. Fest., 2009–. Pres., Darwin Coll., Cambridge, 1990–91. Gov., St John's C of E Sch., Stanmore, 2010–15. FRSA 2009. Associate Ed., Quarternary Sci. Rev., 2005–16; Mem., Editl Bd, Global Sustainability, 2017–. Publications: Restless Planet (series): Floods (with Emma Durham), 1999, Storms, 1999, Earthquakes, 1999; Global Warming, 2002, 2nd edn 2007; The Coming Storm, 2002; Stormy Weather, 2002; Etat d'urgence: Le ciel en colère, 2003; Global Warming: a very short introduction, 2004, 2nd edn 2008; The Complete Ice Age, 2009; (ed with S. Randalls) Future Climate Change (4 vols), 2012; Climate: a very short introduction, 2013; (ed with B. McGuire) Climate Forcing of Geological Hazards, 2013; Climate Change: a very short introduction, 2014; The Cradle of Humanity, 2017, 2nd edn 2019; The Human Planet, 2018; over 165 articles in jls incl. Science, Nature, Nature Climate Change, Science Advances, Nature Geoscience, Lancet and Geology. Recreations: reading, theatre, travel, strategy games. Address: Department of Geography, Pearson Building, Gower Street, University College London, WC1E 6BT. T: (020) 7679 2000. E: m.maslin@ucl.ac.uk. Club: Geographical.

**MASOJADA, Bronislaw Edmund, (Bronek);** Chief Executive Officer, Hiscox Ltd, since 2006; b 31 Dec. 1961; s of late Milek Edmund Masojada and of Shirley Mary Masojada (née Johnston); m 1986, Jane Elizabeth Ann Lamont; three s two d. Educ: Univ. of Natal, SA (BSc Civil Engrg 1982; MPhil Mgt Studies 1987); Trinity Coll., Oxford (Rhodes Schol. 1985). Nat. Service, Engrg Corps, S African Army, 1983–84. McKinsey & Co., Sydney, London and Tokyo: Jun. Associate, then Associate, 1989–91; Engagement Manager, 1992–93; Managing Director: Hiscox Gp, 1993–95; Hiscox plc, 1996–2006. Director: Xchanging Insure Services, 2003–06; Pool Re, 2015–. Chm., Insce Intellectual Capital Initiative, 2008–. Dep. Chm. Council, Lloyd's, 2001–07; Lloyd's Underwriting Agents Association: Mem. Cttee, 1999–98; Chm., 2000–01; Mem., Cttee, Lloyd's Mkt Assoc., 2000–01. Dep. Pres., 2003–04, Pres., 2004–05, Insce Inst. of London. Mem. Bd, Assoc. of British Insurers, 2012–. Trustee, Lloyd's Tercentenary Res. Foundn (formerly Lloyd's Tercentenary Fund), 2007–14 (Chm., 2008–14). Master, Insurers' Co., 2013–14 (Liveryman, 2006–12). Recreations: kite surfing, ski-ing, Caterham racing. Address: Hiscox Ltd, 45 Reid Street, Hamilton HM12, Bermuda. T: 2788300, Fax: 2788301. E: bronek.masojada@hiscox.com. Club: Goring Water Sports.

**MASON, Alastair Michael Stuart,** FRCP; Chairman, SSL Ltd, 1996–2003; Partner, Partners in Care, 1996–2003; b 4 March 1944; s of late Adair Stuart and of Rosemary Mason; m 1967 (marr. diss. 2006); two s two d. Educ: Downside Sch.; London Hosp., London Univ. MB BS. MRCP, FRCP 1993; MRCS; FFPH (FFPHM 1991). Hosp. junior appts, 1967–73; Sen. Medical Officer, Dept of Health, 1974–84; Sen. Manager, Arthur Andersen & Co., 1984–88; RMO, S Western RHA, 1988–94. Publications: (ed) Walk don't run, 1985; Information for Action, 1988. Recreations: walking, reading, theatre, opera, racehorse ownership. Address: Bridge House, Bowbridge Lane, Prestbury, Cheltenham, Glos GL52 3BL.

**MASON, Alison Mary;** see Etheridge, A. M.

**MASON, Hon. Sir Anthony (Frank),** AC 1988; KBE 1972 (CBE 1969); Chancellor, University of New South Wales, 1994–99; Chief Justice, High Court of Australia, 1987–95; b Sydney, 21 April 1925; s of F. M. Mason; m 1950, Patricia Mary, d of Dr E. N. McQueen; two s. Educ: Sydney Grammar Sch.; Univ. of Sydney (BA, LLB). RAAF Flying Officer, 1944–45. Admitted to NSW Bar, 1951; QC 1964. Commonwealth Solicitor-General, 1964–69; Judge, Court of Appeal, Supreme Court of NSW, 1969–72; Justice, High Court of Australia, 1972–87; Judge, Supreme Court of Fiji, 1995–2000; Non-permanent Judge, HK Court of Final Appeal, 1997–2015; Pres., Solomon Islands Court of Appeal, 1997–99. Mem., Permanent Court of Arbitration, 1987–99. Mem., Panel of Arbitrators and Advrs, INTELSAT, 1965–69; Presiding Arbitrator, Internat. Centre for Settlement of Investment Disputes (dispute under N Amer. Free Trade Agreement), 1999–2001. Nat. Fellow, Res. Sch. of Social Scis, ANU, 1995–99 (Dist. Vis. Fellow, 2000–); Arthur Goodhart Prof. in Legal Sci., and Vis. Fellow, Gonville and Caius Coll., Cambridge, 1996–97. Vice-Chm., UN Commn on Internat. Trade Law, 1968. Chairman: Nat. Liby of Australia, 1995–98; Adv. Bd, Nat. Inst. for Law, Ethics and Public Affairs, Griffith Univ., 1995–99; Member: Council of Management, British Inst. of Internat. and Comparative Law, 1987–98; Council, ANU, 1969–72; Pro-Chancellor, ANU, 1972–75. Mem., Amer. Law Inst., 1995. FASSA 1989; FRSN 2018; Hon. Fellow, Australian Inst. of Bldg. Hon. Bencher, Lincoln's Inn, 1987. Hon. LLD: ANU, 1980; Sydney, 1988; Melbourne, 1992; Monash, 1995; Griffith, 1995; Deakin, 1995; NSW, 2000; Hong Kong 2005; Hon. DCL Oxford, 1993. Grand Bauhinia Medal (Hong Kong), 2013. Recreations: gardening, swimming. Address: 1 Castlereagh Street, Sydney, NSW 2000, Australia.

**MASON, Benedict;** composer, sound artist and film maker. Educ: King's Coll., Cambridge (schol.; MA); Royal Coll. of Art (MA). Guido d'Arezzo, 1988; John Clementi Collard Fellowship, 1989; Fulbright Fellow, 1990; Deutsche Akademischer Austauschdienst Künstlerprogramm, Berlin, 1994. Compositions include: Hinterstoisser Traverse, 1986; 1st String Quartet, 1987; Lighthouses of England and Wales, 1987 (Britten Prize, 1988); Oil and Petrol Marks on a Wet Road are sometimes held to be Spots where a Rainbow Stood, 1987; Horn Trio, 1987; Six Piano Etudes, 1988; Chaplin Operas, 1989; Sapere Aude for Eighteenth Century Period Instrument Orchestra, 1989; Dreams that do what they're told, 1990; Concerto for the Viola Section accompanied by the Rest of the Orchestra, 1990; Nodding Trilliums and Curve-lined Angles, 1990; Self Referential Songs and Realistic Virelais, 1990; Rilke Songs, 1991; Animals and the Origins of the Dance, 1992; Quantized Quantz, 1992; !, 1992; Colour and Information, 1993; 2nd String Quartet, 1993; Playing Away: an opera about Germany, Opera, Pop Music and Football, 1994. Sound/theatre installations: Ohne Missbrauch der Aufmerksamkeit, 1993; Second Music for a European Concert Hall: Ensemble Modern/Freiburg Barockorchester/Benoît Régent/Mozartsaal, 1994; third music for a european concert hall (espro: eic: i love my life), 1994; Clarinet Concerto, 1995; ASKO/PARADISO: the Fifth Music. Résumé with C. P. E. Bach, 1995; Schumann-Auftrag: Live Hörspiel ohne Worte, 1996; SEVENTH. (for David Alberman and Rolf Hind) PIANO.WITH.VIOLIN.TO.TOUR.ALL.HALLS.MUSIC, 1996; Carré, Nederlands Kamerkoor, Schoenberg Ensemble, Eighth Music for a European Concert Hall (First Music for a Theatre), 1996; Steep Ascent within and away from a Non European Concert Hall: Six Horns, Three Trombones and a Decorated Shed, 1996; Trumpet Concerto, 1997; The Four Slopes of Twice among Gliders of her Gravity (two Steinway model D pianos, two Ampico player pianos and one human being), 1997; Szene für Jean Nouvel (drei Frauenstimmen, drei Spiegelstimmen, Orch., Sampler und Film), 1998; Meld, 2014. Solo exhibn, gastronomic amorous gymnastic etc music, Berlin, 1997. Films: Horn, 1980; Doppler Between, 1983; Resonating Toner, 1985; all stages, 1987; Leading Articles, 1990; Reassurance, 1991; Disclaimer, 1995. Ernst von Siemens Prize, 1992; Paul Fromm Award, 1995; Britten Award, 1996. Publications: outside sight unseen and opened, 2nd edn, 2002. Recreation: litigation.

**MASON, Rt Rev. Beverley Anne;** see Warrington, Bishop Suffragan of.

**MASON, Prof. Christopher,** PhD; FRCS, FRCSI, FRSB; FMedSci; Professor of Cell and Gene Therapy, University College London, since 2017; b Leatherhead, 14 March 1958; s of Keith Reginald James Mason and Daphne Joan Mason (née Lowres); m 2001, Dr Louise. Educ: Imperial Coll. London (BSc 1993); St Thomas's Hosp. Med. Sch. (MB BS 1994); University Coll. London (PhD 2003). FRCS 1999; FRCSI 1999; FRSB (FSB 2010). Prof. of Regenerative Medicine, UCL, 2008–17. CEO, London Regenerative Medicine Network, 2005–; Sen. Scientific Advr, Proteus LLC, 2005–; Co-founder and CSO, AvroBio Inc., 2015–; Co-founder, OriBiotech, 2015. Senior Editor: Regenerative Medicine, 2008–; Cell and Gene Therapy Insights, 2015–. Mem., UK-Israel Sci. Council, 2010–. Trustee, UK Stem Cell Foundn, 2010–16. Recreations: running, cycling. Address: Advanced Centre for Biochemical Engineering, University College London, Bernard Katz Building, Gower Street, WC1E 6BT. E: chris.mason@ucl.ac.uk.

**MASON, Colin Rees,** OBE 2003; TD 1982; Managing Director: Chiltern Broadcast Management (trading name of Aurora World Ltd), since 1997; Capital Radio (SL) Ltd, Freetown, Sierra Leone, since 2005; Chief Executive Officer, Alderney Broadcasting Company Ltd, since 2014; Vice Lord-Lieutenant for Bedfordshire, 2005–18; b 19 Aug. 1943; s of Clifford Harold Mason and Ann Mason (née Jones); m 1968, Grace Angela St Helier Tweney; one s one d. Educ: Gwent Coll., Newport; UCW, Aberystwyth (BA Hons); Magdalene Coll., Cambridge (MPhil); Harvard Grad. Sch. of Business (OPM). Producer, BBC, 1969–74; Prog. Dir, Swansea Sound, 1974–80; Asst Man. Dir, Standard Broadcasting, 1980–82; Man. Dir, Chiltern Radio plc, 1981–95; Dep. Chm., Choice FM, 1995–2004. Dir, Alderney Broadcasting Corp. Ltd, 2003–14. Royal Welsh Regt (formerly Royal Regt of Wales), TA: Lt Col 1984, Col 2000; Pool of Public Information Officers, 1990–93; served Saudi Arabia, Kuwait, 1991; transf. 15 (UK) Psychol Ops Gp, 1997; served Kosovo, 1999–2000, Sierra Leone, Macedonia, 2001, Afghanistan, 2002, Iraq, 2003; Co. Comdt, 2000–04; Hon. Col, 15 (UK) Psychol Ops Gp, 2004–10; Hon. Col, Beds and Herts ACF, 2008–14. High Sheriff, 2002–03, DL 2002, Beds. Recreations: travel, ski-ing. Clubs: Army and Navy, Reform.

**MASON, David Buchanan;** QC 2010; a Recorder, since 2005; b Guildford, 16 Jan. 1963; s of late Donald Mason and of Lynn Mason; one d; partner, Susan Richards. Educ: Cranleigh Sch.; Leicester Univ. (LLB). Called to the Bar, Middle Temple, 1986. Recreations: golf, ski-ing, diving, shooting, singing. Address: No5 Chambers, Fountain Court, Steelhouse Lane, Birmingham B4 6DR. T: 07831 125522. E: dbm@no5.com. Club: Blackwell Golf.

**MASON, Sir David (Kean),** Kt 1992; CBE 1987; BDS, MD; FRCSGlas, FDSRCPS Glas, FDSRCSE, FRCPath; FRSE; Professor of Oral Medicine and Head of the Department of Oral Medicine and Pathology, University of Glasgow Dental School, 1967–92, now Professor Emeritus; Dean of Dental Education, University of Glasgow, 1980–90; b 5 Nov. 1928; s of George Hunter Mason and Margaret Kean; m 1967, Judith Anne Armstrong; two s one d. Educ: Paisley Grammar Sch.; Glasgow Acad.; St Andrews Univ. (LDS 1951, BDS 1952); Glasgow Univ. (MB, ChB 1962, MD (Commendation) 1967). FDSRCSE 1957; FDSRCPS Glas 1967 (Hon. FDSRCPS Glas 1990); FRCSGlas 1973; FRCPath 1976 (MRCPath 1967); FRSE 1999. Served RAF, Dental Br., 1952–54. Registrar in Oral Surgery, Dundee, 1954–56; gen. dental practice, 1956–62; Vis. Dental Surgeon, Glasgow Dental Hosp., 1956–62, Sen. Registrar 1962–64; Sen. Lectr in Dental Surgery and

Pathology, Univ. of Glasgow, 1964–67; Hon. Consultant Dental Surgeon, Glasgow, 1964–67. Chm., National Dental Consultative Cttee, 1976–80 and 1983–87; Member: Medicines Commn, 1976–80; Dental Cttee, MRC, 1973–80; Physiol Systems Bd, MRC, 1976–80; Jt MRC/Health Depts/SERC Dental Cttee, 1984–87; GDC, 1976–94 (Mem., Disciplinary Cttee, 1980–85; Health Cttee, 1985–89; Pres., 1989–94); Dental Cttee, UGC, 1977–87 (Chm., 1983–87); Supervised Trng Gp, UGC, 1984–86; Dental Rev. Wkg Party, UGC, 1986–87; Jt Cttee for Higher Trng in Dentistry, 1977–84; Dental Strategy Rev. Gp, 1980–81; Scientific Prog. Cttee, FDI, 1980–87; Consultant to Commn on Dental Res., FDI, 1973–80. President: W of Scotland Br., BDA, 1983–84; British Soc. for Dental Res. 1984–86; British Soc. for Oral Medicine, 1984–86; GDC, 1989–94; Convener, Dental Council, RCPGlas, 1977–80. Lectures: Charles Tomes, RCS, 1975; Holme, UCH, London, 1977; Caldwell Meml, Univ. of Glasgow, 1983; Evelyn Sprawson, London Hosp. Med. Coll., 1984. Hon. Member: BDA, 1993; Amer. Dental Assoc., 1994; Royal Odonto-Chirurgical Soc. of Scotland, 2010. Hon. FFDRCSI 1988; Hon. FRCSE 1995; Hon. FDSRCS 2002. Hon. DDS Wales, 1991; Hon. LLD Dundee, 1993; Hon. DSc Western Ontario, 1997; DUniv Glasgow, 1998. John Tomes Prize, RCS, 1979; Colyer Medal, RCS, 1992. *Publications*: (jtly) Salivary Glands in Health and Disease, 1975; (jtly) Introduction to Oral Medicine, 1978; (jtly) Self Assessment: Manual I, Oral Surgery, 1978; Manual II, Oral Medicine, 1978; (ed jtly) Oral Manifestations of Systemic Disease, 1980, 2nd edn 1990; (jtly) World Workshop on Oral Medicine, 3 vols, 1988, 1993, 1999. *Recreations:* golf, tennis, gardening, enjoying the pleasures of the countryside. *Address:* Cherry Tree Cottage, Houston Road, Kilmacolm, Renfrewshire PA13 4NY. *Clubs:* Royal & Ancient Golf, Elie Golf House, Kilmacolm Golf.

**MASON, Frances Jane G.;** *see* Gumley-Mason.

**MASON, Jane;** *see* Mason, T. J.

**MASON, Maj. Gen. Jeffrey Sinclair,** MBE 2001; Clerk and Chief Executive Officer, Butchers' Company, since 2014; *b* Glasgow, 19 Nov. 1959; *s* of Alexander David Mason and Irene Elizabeth Mason (*née* Keith); *m* 1981, Lucy Mary Evered; one *s* one *d. Educ:* Glasgow Acad. Joined RM, 1977; DCS, HQ 3 Commando Bde, 1999–2001; CSO Personnel, HQ RM, 2001–02; CO, Commando Logistic Regt, 2002–04; rcds 2004; ACOS, J1/J4, PJHQ, 2004–06; Dir, Defence Supply Chain Ops and Movements, Defence Equipment and Support, 2006–09; rcds 2009; Asst Chief of Defence Staff (Logistic Ops), 2009–11. Man. Dir, Supreme Gp UK, 2011–13; Commercial Dir, Supreme Gp Europe and Commonwealth, 2013–14. Trustee: Falkland Is Chapel, 2005– (Chm., 2012–); Nat. Mus. of Royal Navy, 2015–; Chm. of Trustees, Royal Marines Mus., 2012–18. Chm., E Mersea Parish Council, 2013– (Mem., 2012–). Rep. Col Comdt, RM, 2018–; Hon. Col, RM Reserve, City of London, 2018–. *Recreations:* recent military history, keeping fit (a losing battle), family, renovating house. *Club:* Army and Navy.

**MASON, John Fingland;** Member (SNP) Glasgow Shettleston, Scottish Parliament, since 2011; *b* 1957. CA 1980. Mem. (SNP), Glasgow CC, 1998–2008 (Leader of the Opposition, 1999–2008). MP (SNP) Glasgow E, July 2008–2010; contested (SNP) same seat, 2010. *Recreations:* Easterhouse Baptist Church, hill-walking, camping. *Address:* Scottish Parliament, Edinburgh EH99 1SP.

**MASON, John Kenneth,** CBE 2015; Director for Economic Development (formerly Director for Business), Scottish Government, 2010–16; *b* 26 June 1956; *s* of Kenneth George Mason and Helen Mary Mason (*née* Green); *m* 1990, Alison Margaret Cruickshanks; one *s* one *d. Educ:* Hertford Coll., Oxford (BA Hons Geog. 1978); University Coll. London (MPhil Town Planning 1981). MCIPD 1997. Senior Town Planner: Kent CC, 1980–85; DoE, 1985–87; Principal: DoE, 1988–90; Scottish Office, 1990–94; Dep. Chief Exec., Registers of Scotland, 1994–96; Asst Sec., Enterprise and Industry, Scottish Office, 1996–2000; Scottish Executive: Prin. Private Sec. to First Minister, 2001–02; Under Sec. and Hd, Tourism, Culture and Sport Gp, Educn Dept, 2002–05; Under Sec. and Hd, Envmt Gp, Envmt and Rural Affairs Dept, subseq. Dir, Envmt Gp, 2006–07; Dir for Climate Change, Water Industry and Envmtl Quality, Scottish Exec., later Scottish Govt, 2006–10. Non-executive Director: Scottish Swimming, 2006–18; 2014 Commonwealth Games Organising Cttee, 2011–14; Swimming Trust, 2016–18. Trustee, Linlithgow Burgh Trust, 2017– (Chm., 2018–); Sec., Linlithgow Civic Trust, 2018–. Judge, Beautiful Scotland, 2018–. *Recreations:* bird watching, gardening, walking. *Address:* Linlithgow, W Lothian. *E:* u102526@gmail.com.

**MASON, Rev. Canon Kenneth Staveley;** Canon Theologian, Scottish Episcopal Church, 1995–96; Canon of St Mary's Cathedral, Edinburgh, 1989–96, now Canon Emeritus; *b* 1 Nov. 1931; *s* of Rev. William Peter Mason and Anna Hester (*née* Pildrem); *m* 1958, Barbara Thomson; one *s* one *d. Educ:* Imperial College of Science, London (BSc, ARCS); BD (ext.) London; Wells Theological Coll. Assistant Curate: St Martin, Kingston upon Hull, 1958; Pocklington, 1961; Vicar of Thornton with Allerthorpe and Melbourne, 1963; Sub-Warden and Librarian, KCL, at St Augustine's Coll., Canterbury, 1969; Dir, Canterbury Sch. of Ministry, 1977, Principal, 1981. Examining Chaplain to Archbp of Canterbury, 1979–91; Six Preacher in Canterbury Cath., 1979–84; Hon. Canon of Canterbury, 1984–89; Principal, Edinburgh Theol Coll., later Dir, Theol Inst., Scottish Episcopal Church, 1989–95. *Publications:* George Herbert, Priest and Poet, 1980; Anglicanism, a Canterbury essay, 1987; Priesthood and Society, 1992; Catholic Tradition and the Ordination of Women, 1993; A Great Joy, 2001. *Address:* 2 Williamson Close, Ripon HG4 1AZ. *T:* (01765) 607041.

**MASON, Prof. Malcolm David,** OBE 2017; MD; FRCP, FRCR; FRSB; oncologist; Professor of Cancer Studies (formerly of Clinical Oncology), Cardiff University (formerly University of Wales College of Medicine), since 1997; *b* 31 May 1956; *s* of Seymour and Marion Mason; *m* 1983, Lee-Anne Isaacs; two *d. Educ:* Dulwich Coll. Prep. Sch.; Westminster Sch.; Med. Coll. of St Bartholomew's Hosp. (MB BS 1979; MD 1991). FRCR 1987; FRCP 1997; FRSB (FSB 2011). Lectr in Radiotherapy and Oncol., Inst. of Cancer Res. and Royal Marsden Hosp., 1989–91; Consultant Clinical Oncologist, 1992–96, Hon. Consultant, 1996–, Velindre Hosp., Cardiff. Dir, Wales Cancer Bank, 2004–. Chm., Tenovus Cancer Care, 2018–. Member (pt-time): NRPB, 2000–05; Cttee on Med. Aspects of Radiation in the Envmt, 2003–10. Chairman: Prostate Cancer Clin. Studies Gp, NCRI, 2009–15; UK TNM Evaluation Cttee, UICC, 2009–; Ind. Data Monitoring Cttee, Eur. Orgn for Res. and Treatment of Cancer, 2016–. Chief Investigator, Intergroup NCIC/MRC study est. role of radiotherapy in locally advanced prostate cancer, 1998–. Chm., Tenovus Cancer Care, 2018–. *Publications:* (with L. Mofatt) Prostate Cancer: the facts, 2003, 2nd edn 2010; over 300 contribs to learned jls. *Recreation:* playing the piano music of the great classical masters from Bach to Rachmaninov. *Address:* Velindre Hospital, Whitchurch, Cardiff CF14 2TL. *T:* (029) 2031 6964, *Fax:* (029) 2052 9625. *E:* masonmd@cardiff.ac.uk.

**MASON, Marion Helen;** *see* Smith, M. H.

**MASON, Dame Monica,** DBE 2008 (OBE 2002); Director, Royal Ballet, 2002–12 (Principal Répétiteur, 1991–94), Assistant Director, 1999–2002); *b* 6 Sept. 1941; *d* of Richard Mason and Mrs E. Fabian; *m* 1968, Austin Bennett. *Educ:* Johannesburg, SA; Royal Ballet Sch., London. Joined Royal Ballet in Corps de Ballet, 1958; Sen. Principal until 1989; created role of Chosen Maiden in Rite of Spring, 1962; also created roles in: Diversions, Elite Syncopations, Electra, Manon, Romeo and Juliet, Rituals, Adieu, Isadora, The Four Seasons, The Ropes of Time. Assistant to the Principal Choreographer, Royal Ballet, 1980–84. Chm., Royal Ballet Benevolent Fund, 2014–. Trustee: Cecchetti Soc. Trust; Ashton Foundn; Acting for Others. Hon. FKC, 2013; Hon. Fellow, St Hilda's Coll., Oxford, 2013. DUniv Surrey, 1996. Queen Elizabeth II Coronation Award, RAD, 2011; Special Award, Laurence Olivier Awards, 2012.

**MASON, Paul;** Chairman: Dr Martens Ltd, since 2015; Gaucho Group, since 2017; *b* 14 Feb. 1960; *s* of John and Joan Mason; *m* 1984, Juliet Greenway; three *s. Educ:* Univ. of Manchester (BA 1st Cl. Hons). Various posts, Mars GB Ltd, 1982–90; Buying and Logistics Dir, B&Q plc, 1990–94; Dir, Mgt Bd, Asda plc, 1994–99; Chief Operating Officer, 1999–2000, Pres. and CEO, 2000–01, Asda Walmart UK; CEO, Matalan plc, 2002–04; Pres., Levi Strauss & Co. Europe, 2004–06; CEO, Somerfield Gp, 2006–09; Chairman: Radley & Co. Ltd, 2008–12; Cath Kidson Ltd, 2010–16; Mayborn Gp Ltd, 2011–16; New Look Retailers Ltd, 2014–15.

**MASON, Prof. Paul James,** CB 2003; PhD; FRS 1995; Professor of Meteorology and Director, NCAS Universities Weather and Environment Research Network, University of Reading, 2003–06, now Professor Emeritus; *b* 16 March 1946; *s* of Charles Ernest Edward Mason and Phyllis Mary Mason (*née* Swan); *m* 1968, Elizabeth Mary Slaney; one *s* one *d. Educ:* Univ. of Nottingham (BSc Physics 1967); Univ. of Reading (PhD Geophysics 1972). Meteorological Office: SO, 1967–71; SSO, 1971–74; PSO, 1974–79; Head, Meteorological Res. Unit, Cardington, 1979–85; Asst Dir, Boundary Layer Br., 1985–89; Dep. Dir, Physical Res., 1989–91; Chief Scientist, 1991–2002. Vis. Prof., Univ. of Surrey, 1995–. Chm., Global Climate Observing System Steering Cttee, 2001–04. Member: Editing Cttee, Qly Jl Meteorology, 1983–88; Editl Bd, Boundary Layer Meteorology, 1988–2000. Royal Meteorological Society: Mem. Council, 1989–90; Vice Pres., 1990–92 and 1994–95; Pres., 1992–94. L. G. Groves Prize for Meteorology, MoD, 1980; Buchan Prize, RMetS, 1986. *Publications:* scientific papers in meteorology and fluid dynamics jls. *Recreations:* walking, exploring the countryside. *Address:* Department of Meteorology, University of Reading, PO Box 243, Reading RG6 6BB. *T:* (0118) 931 8954.

**MASON, Rt Rev. Paul James;** RC Bishop of the Forces, since 2018; *b* North Shields, 6 Nov. 1962; *s* of James Mason and Maria Mason (*née* Marchetti). *Educ:* St Anselm's, North Shields; King's Coll. London (MA Medical Law and Ethics); Pontifical Gregorian Univ., Rome (STB; PhL). Asst Priest, Purley, 1998–2001; Sen. Chaplain, Guy's and St Thomas' NHS Trust, 2001–11; Pastoral Dir, Allen Hall Seminary, Chelsea, 2011–13; Episcopal Vicar for Kent, 2014–16; an Auxiliary Bishop, Dio. of Southwark, (RC), 2016–18. *Recreations:* scuba diving, motorcycling, photography, music. *Address:* The Bishop's House, The Hermitage, More Park, West Malling, Kent ME19 6HN.

**MASON, Sir Peter (James),** KBE 2002; FREng; non-executive Chairman, Thames Water, 2006–17; Chief Executive Officer, AMEC plc, 1996–2006; *b* 9 Sept. 1946; *s* of Harvey John Mason and Jenny Mason (*née* Wilson); *m* 1st, 1969, Elizabeth Ann McLaren (marr. diss. 1992); two *s;* 2nd, 1997, Beverly Ann Hunter. *Educ:* Marr Coll., Troon; Univ. of Glasgow (BSc Hons Engrg 1968). Norwest Holst Group Ltd, 1980–92: Man. Dir, Civil Engrg Div., 1980–85; CEO, 1985–92; BICC plc, 1992–96: Dir, 1992–96; CEO, 1992–96; Chm., 1994–96, Balfour Beatty Ltd. Senior Independent Director: BAE Systems plc, 2003–13; Subsea 7 (formerly Acergy), 2011–18 (non-exec. Dir, 2006–09; Chm., 2009–11). Board Mem., UK Trade and Investment (formerly British Trade Internat.), 2000–04; Mem., Olympic Delivery Authy, 2006–09. FREng 2009. *Recreations:* opera, sailing, gardening.

**MASON, Rt Rev. Peter Ralph;** Development Adviser, Wycliffe College, Toronto (Development Director, 2003); *b* 30 April 1943; *s* of late Ralph Victor Mason and of Dorothy Ida Mullin; *m* 1965, Carmen Ruth Ruddock; one *s* two *d. Educ:* McGill Univ. Montreal (BA 1964; BD 1967; MA 1971); Princeton Univ. (DMin 1983). Ordained deacon, 1967, priest, 1968; Asst Curate, St Matthew's, Montreal, 1967–69; Incumbent, parish of Hemmingford, 1969–71; Rector: St Clement's, Montreal, 1971–74; St Peter's, Montreal, 1975–80; St Paul's, Halifax, NS, 1980–85; Principal, Wycliffe Theol Coll., Univ. of Toronto, 1985–92; Bishop of Ontario, 1992–2002. Hon. DD Montreal Diocesan Theol Coll., 1987; Hon. DD: Trinity Coll., Toronto, 1992; Wycliffe Coll., Toronto, 1994. *Recreations:* golf, sailing, ski-ing, opera. *Address:* Wycliffe College, 5 Hoskin Avenue, Toronto, ON M5S 1H7, Canada.

**MASON, Philippa;** *see* Gregory, Philippa.

**MASON, Air Vice-Marshal Richard Anthony, (Tony),** CB 1988; CBE 1981; DSc; Hon. Professor, University of Birmingham, 1996–2012; *b* 22 Oct. 1932; *s* of William and Maud Mason; *m* 1956, Margaret Stewart; one *d. Educ:* Bradford Grammar Sch.; St Andrews Univ. (MA); London Univ. (MA); DSc Birmingham 1997. Commissioned RAF, 1956; Director of Defence Studies, 1977; Director of Personnel (Ground), 1982; Deputy Air Secretary, 1984; Air Sec., 1985–89; Dir, Centre for Studies in Security and Diplomacy, 1988–2001, Leverhulme Emeritus Fellow, 2002–05, Univ. of Birmingham. Leverhulme Airpower Res. Dir, Foundn for Internat. Security, 1989–94. Advr to H of C Defence Cttee, 2001–06. Hon. Freeman, Bor. of Cheltenham, 2001. DL Glos, 2002. Hon. FRAeS 2006. *Publications:* Air Power in the Next Generation (ed), 1978; Readings in Air Power, 1979; (with M. J. Armitage) Air Power in the Nuclear Age, 1981; The RAF Today and Tomorrow, 1982; British Air Power in the 1980s, 1984; The Soviet Air Forces, 1986; War in the Third Dimension, 1986; Air Power and Technology, 1986; To Inherit the Skies, 1990; Air Power: a centennial appraisal, 1994; Air and Space Power: revised roles and technology, 1998; articles in internat. jls on defence policy and strategy. *Recreations:* Rugby, writing, gardening. *Address:* c/o Lloyds Bank, Montpelier Walk, Cheltenham GL50 1SH. *Club:* Royal Air Force.

**MASON, Prof. Sir Ronald,** KCB 1980; FRS 1975; Professor of Chemistry, University of Sussex, 1971–86 (Pro-Vice-Chancellor, 1977); Chairman: British Ceramic Research Ltd, 1990–96; University College Hospitals NHS Trust, 1992–2001; *b* 22 July 1930; *o s* of David John Mason and Olwen Mason (*née* James); *m* 1952, E. Pauline Pattinson; three *d; m* 1979, Elizabeth Rosemary Grey-Edwards (*d* 2009). *Educ:* Univ. of Wales (Fellow, University College Cardiff, 1981); London Univ. (Fellow, UCL, 1996). CChem, FRSC; FIMMM (FIM 1993). Research Assoc., British Empire Cancer Campaign, 1953–61; Lectr, Imperial Coll., 1961–63; Prof. of Inorganic Chemistry, Univ. of Sheffield, 1963–71; Chief Scientific Advr, MoD, 1977–83. Vis. Prof., Univs in Australia, Canada, France, Israel, NZ and US, inc. A. D. Little Prof., MIT, 1970; Univ. of California, Berkeley, 1975; Ohio State Univ., 1976; North Western Univ., 1977; Prof. associé, Univ. de Strasbourg, 1976; Erskine Vis. Prof., Christchurch, NZ, 1977; Prof., Texas, 1982; Vis. Prof. of Internat. Relns, UCW, 1985–95. Schmidt Meml Lectr, Israel, 1977. SRC: Mem., 1971–75; Chm. Chemistry Cttee, 1969–72; Chm. Science Bd, 1972–75; Consultant and Council Mem., RUSI,

1984–88; UK Mem., UN Commn of Disarmament Studies, 1984–92; Chairman: Council for Arms Control, 1986–90; Engrg Technol. Cttee, DTI, 1991–93. Pres., BHRA, 1986–94 (Chm., BHR Gp, 1990–95); Member: ABRC, 1977–83; BBC Adv. Group, 1975–79. Chairman: Hunting Engineering Ltd, 1987 (Dep. Chm., 1985–87); Science Applications Internat. Corp. (UK) Ltd, 1993–96; Xtreamis plc, 1998–2000; Advanced Messaging Ltd, 2004–06; Zone V, 2012–. Pres., Inst. of Materials, 1995–96. Foundation Chm., Stoke Mandeville Burns and Reconstructive Surgery Res. Trust, 1990–94; Chm., UCL Hosps Charities, 2004–07. Hon. FIMechE 1997. Hon. DSc: Wales, 1986; Keele, 1992. Corday-Morgan Medallist, 1965, and Tilden Lectr, 1970, Chemical Society; Medal and Prize for Structural Chem., Chem. Soc., 1973. *Publications:* (ed) Advances in Radiation Biology, 1964, 3rd edn 1969; (ed) Advances in Structure Analysis by Diffraction Methods, 1968, 6th edn 1978; (ed) Physical Processes in Radiation Biology, 1964; many papers in Jl Chem. Soc., Proc. Royal Soc., etc, and on defence issues.

**MASON, Samantha Mary Constance;** *see* Beckett, S. M. C.

**MASON, Susanna Margaret;** Partner, and Middle East Defence Lead, PricewaterhouseCoopers, since 2016; *b* BMH, Rinteln, W Germany, 12 March 1964; *d* of John Fawkes and Margaret June Fawkes (*née* Desjardins); *m* 1991, Ian Paul Mason; two *d* (one *s* decd). *Educ:* Lilley and Stone High Sch. for Girls, Newark; Sunderland Poly. (BA Hons Business Studies); King's Coll. London (MA Internat. Studies); RCDS. ACMA 1991; MCIPS 2010, FCIPS; GCMA. Finance Dir and Co. Sec., Hewitt Associates, 1992–94; Exec. Partner, Coopers & Lybrand, later PricewaterhouseCoopers, then IBM, 1994–2004; Associate Partner, Defence Strategy and Solutions, 2004–08; Dir, Exports and Commercial Strategy, MoD, 2008–12; Dir Gen., Commercial, MoD, 2012–16. *Recreations:* swimming, camping, knitting, church. *Address:* PricewaterhouseCoopers, Al Khatem Tower, Al Maryah Island, Abu Dhabi. *T:* 526504920.

**MASON, (Tania) Jane;** Regional Chairman of Employment Tribunals, London Central Region, 2000–01; *b* 25 Sept. 1936; *d* of late Edward Warner Moeran, sometime MP, and of Pymonie (*née* Fincham); *m* 1961, (James) Stephen Mason, CB (*d* 2012); one *s* two *d*. *Educ:* Frensham Heights Sch. Called to the Bar, Inner Temple, 1961. Law Reporter, Judicial Cttee of Privy Council, 1976–83; Asst Legal Advr, British Council, 1983–86; full-time Chm. of Industrial Tribunals, 1986–92; Regional Chairman: Industrial Tribunals, London S Reg., 1992–97; Industrial, later Employment, Tribunals, London N Reg., 1997–2000. *Recreations:* country life, English novels, art, architecture. *Address:* Amberley House, Church Street, Amberley, West Sussex BN18 9NF. *Club:* Reform.

**MASON, Thomas Gee;** Member (C) North East Scotland, Scottish Parliament, since 2017; *b* Bishops Stortford, Herts, 31 Dec. 1942; *s* of Harold Percy Mason and Mildred Beryl Mason; *m* 1972, Kate Anderson; one *s* two *d*. *Educ:* King's Coll., London (BSc Engrg 1964); Cranfield Sch. of Mgt (MBA 1972). CEng 1966; MICE 1968. Construction Engr, John Laing, 1964–68; Project Engr, Stirling Astaldi (Nigeria) Ltd, 1968–71; Corporate Planner and Dir of Subsidiary, SGB Gp, 1972–74; CEO of Subsidiary, Christian Salvesen Oil Services, 1974–81; Lectr in Business Policy and Mktg, 1983–92, Sen. Lectr, 1992–2010, and Dir, MBA Prog., 1988, Robert Gordon Inst. of Technol., subseq. Robert Gordon Univ. Business Sch. Member (C): Grampian Regl Council, 1993–96; Aberdeen CC, 1996–98, 2017–. MCIM 1989, FCIM 1997, CMktr 1998. MInstD 1981. Mem., RYA. *Recreations:* sailing, PADI Advanced Diver, croquet (Treas., Aberdeen and Crathes Croquet Assoc.). *Address:* Scottish Parliament, Edinburgh EH99 1SP. *T:* (0131) 348 6980. *E:* tom.mason.msp@parliament.scot.

**MASON, Timothy Ian Godson;** arts and heritage consultant; Director, Museums & Galleries Commission, 1995–2000; *b* 11 March 1945; *s* of late Ian Godson Mason and Muriel (*née* Vaile); *m* 1975, Marilyn Ailsa Williams; one *d* one *s*. *Educ:* St Albans Sch., Washington, DC; Bradfield Coll., Berkshire; Christ Church, Oxford (MA). Assistant Manager, Oxford Playhouse, 1966–67; Assistant to Peter Daubeny, World Theatre Season, London, 1967–69; Administrator: Ballet Rambert, 1970–75; Royal Exchange Theatre, Manchester, 1975–77; Director: Western Australian Arts Council, 1977–80; Scottish Arts Council, 1980–90; Consultant on implementation of changes in structure of arts funding, Arts Council of GB, 1990–91; Chief Exec., London Arts Bd, 1991–95. Member: Gen. Adv. Council, BBC, 1990–96; Gen. Council, Commonwealth Assoc. of Museums, 2003–14. Trustee, Civic Trust, 2004–06. Gov., KCH, 2006–11. *Publications:* Care, Diligence & Skill, 1986; Shifting Sands, 2003; Design Reviewed: urban housing, 2004; Designed with Care, 2006. *Recreations:* family, travelling, the arts, museums. *Address:* 82 Farquhar Road, SE19 1LT.

**MASON, Air Vice-Marshal Tony;** *see* Mason, Air Vice-Marshal R. A.

**MASON, William Ernest,** CB 1983; Deputy Secretary (Fisheries and Food), Ministry of Agriculture, Fisheries and Food, 1982–89, retired; *b* 12 Jan. 1929; *s* of Ernest George and Agnes Margaret Mason; *m* 1959, Jean (*née* Bossley); one *s* one *d*. *Educ:* Brockley Grammar Sch.; London Sch. of Economics (BScEcon). RAF, 1947–49; Min. of Food, 1949–54; MAFF, 1954; Principal 1963; Asst Sec. 1970; Under Sec., 1975; Fisheries Sec., 1980. Dir, Food and Agric. Div., NATO Central Supplies Agency (West), 1983–93. Dir, Allied-Lyons, then Allied Domecq, PLC, 1989–98; consultant on food and drink industry, 1989–98. Member: EDC for Distribn Trades, 1975–80; EDC for Food and Drink Manufg Inds, 1976–80; Adv. Bd, Inst. of Food Res., 1993–98. Chm. of Govs, Prendergast Sch. for Girls, 1974–86. FRSA 1989; FIGD 1989; Hon. FIFST 1989. Hon. Keeper of the Quaich, 1989–. *Recreations:* music, reading, modern British painting.

**MASRI, Taher Nashat,** Order of the Renaissance (Jewelled), Jordan, 1991; Order of Al-Kawkab, Jordan, 1974; Order of Al-Nahda, Jordan; Hon. GBE 1988; Member of Senate, Jordan, 1998–2001 and 2005–13; President of Senate, 2009–13 (First Vice President, 2005–09); *b* Nablus, 5 March 1942; *s* of Nashat Masri and Hadiyah Solh; *m* 1968, Samar Bitar; one *s* one *d*. *Educ:* Al-Najah Nat. Coll., Nablus; North Texas State Univ. (BA Business Admin 1965). Central Bank of Jordan, 1965–73; MP Nablus District, Jordan, 1973–74, 1984–88, 1989–97; Minister of State for Occupied Territories Affairs, 1973–74; Ambassador to: Spain, 1975–78; France, 1978–83; Belgium (non-resident), 1979–80; Britain, 1983–84; Perm. Delegate to UNESCO, 1978–83 and to EEC, 1978–80; Foreign Minister, 1984–88 and 1991; Dep. Prime Minister and Minister of State for Economic Affairs, April–Sept. 1989; Chm., Foreign Relations Cttee, 1989–91 and 1992–93; Prime Minister of Jordan and Minister of Defence, June–Nov. 1991; Pres. of Lower House of Parlt, 1993–94. Chm., Foreign Relations Cttee, Jordanian Parlt, 1989–91 and 1992–93. Mem. and Rapporteur, Royal Commn for Drafting of Nat. Charter, 1990; Member and Head of Political Committee: Royal Commn for Drafting Nat. Agenda, 2005; Cttee of All Jordan (Royal Commn), 2006; Mem., Royal Commn to Revise Constitution, 2011. President: Nat. Soc. for Enhancement of Freedom and Democracy, 1993–97; Jordanian Spanish Friends Assoc., 1998–; Nat. Dialogue Cttee, 2011–; Jordan Lebanese Assoc., 2012. Comr for Civil Societies, Arab League, 2002–09; Mem. and Vice Pres., 2006–, Pres., Exec. Cttee, 2009–, Arab Thought Forum. Mem., Adv. Cttee, Anna Lindh Euro-Mediterranean Foundn for Dialogue between Cultures, 2004–06; Chm., 1992–2006, Vice Chm., 2008–, and Vice Pres., Bd of Trustees, 2008–, Princess Haya Cultural Center for Children. Pres., Bd of Trustees, Jordan Univ. for Sci. and Technol., 1998–2010. Pres., Jordan British Soc., 2006–12. Hon. Pres., Arab Student Aid Internat., Jordan, 2012. Grand Cross, Order of Civil Merit, Spain, 1977; Order of Isabel the Catholic, Spain, 1978; Grand Cross, Order of Merit, Germany; Kt Grand Cross, Order of Merit, Italy; Grand Cordon, Ordre Nat. de Cèdre, Lebanon; Grand Decoration with Sash for Services, Austria; Grand Gwanghwa Medal, Order of Diplomatic Service Merit, Rep. of Korea; Grand Officier: Légion d'Honneur, France (Comdr, 1981); Ordre Nat. du Mérite, France. *Address:* PO Box 5550, Amman 11183, Jordan. *T:* (6) 5920600, *Fax:* (6) 4642226.

**MASSENET, Dame Natalie (Sara),** DBE 2016 (MBE 2009); Founder and Executive Chairman, Net-A-Porter Group, 2000–15; Partner, Imaginary Ventures, since 2018; *b* Los Angeles, 13 May 1965; *d* of Bob Rooney and Barbara Rooney; one *s* two *d*. *Educ:* Univ. of Calif, Los Angeles (BA Eng. Lit.). In film business, 1988–90; Moda mag., Italy, 1990–93; W Coast Fashion Ed., WWD and W, 1993–96; Sen. Fashion Ed., Tatler, 1996–99. Chm., British Fashion Council, 2013–17. Non-exec. Co-Chm., Farfetch, 2017. Entrepreneur of the Year, CNBC Eur. Business Leaders Awards, 2008; Innovator of the Year, Harper's Bazaar Awards, 2010; Award for Excellence, Quintessentially Awards, 2010; Creative Leadership Award, Aenne Burda Awards, 2011; British Inspiration Award, 2012.

**MASSER, Prof. David,** PhD; FRS 2005; Professor of Mathematics, University of Basel, 1992–2014, now Emeritus; *b* 8 Nov. 1948; *s* of William and Rose Masser; *m* 1st, 1988, Hedda Freudenschuss (*d* 2009); 2nd, 2015, Hedda Egerer (*d* 2016). *Educ:* Trinity Coll., Cambridge (BA Hons 1970, MA 1974; PhD 1974). University of Nottingham: Lectr, 1973–75 and 1976–79; Reader, 1979–83; Res. Fellow, Trinity Coll., Cambridge, 1975–76; Prof., Univ. of Michigan, Ann Arbor, 1983–92. *Publications:* Elliptic Functions and Transcendence, Lecture Notes in Mathematics, Vol. 437, 1975; Auxiliary Polynomials in Number Theory, 2016; over 110 papers in math. jls. *Address:* Nadelberg 17, 4051 Basel, Switzerland.

**MASSER, Prof. (Francis) Ian,** PhD; LittD; Professor of Urban Planning, International Institute for Aerospace Survey and Earth Sciences, Netherlands, 1998–2002; *b* 14 Sept. 1937; *s* of late Francis Masser and Isabel Masser (*née* Haddaway); *m* 1st, 1962, Alexandra Arnold (*d* 1988); two *d*; 2nd, 1996, Susan Parkin. *Educ:* Malton Grammar Sch.; Univ. of Liverpool (BA, MCD, PhD 1975; LittD 1993). MRTPI 1964. Leverhulme Res. Fellow, UC of Rhodesia and Nyasaland, 1960–61; Associate Planner, Shankland Cox Associates, 1962–64; Lectr, then Sen. Lectr, Univ. of Liverpool, 1964–75; Prof. and Hd of Inst. of Urban and Regional Planning, Univ. of Utrecht, 1975–79; University of Sheffield: Prof. of Town and Regl Planning, 1979–98; Hd, Dept of Town and Regional Planning, 1979–86; Dean, Faculty of Architectural Studies, 1981–84 and 1992–95; Chm., Sheffield Centre for Envmtl Res., 1979–92. Visiting Professor: Hitotsubashi Univ., Tokyo, 1986; Poly. of Turin, 1993–94; Univ. of Utrecht, 1998–2005; UCL, 2003–10; Univ. of Melbourne, 2004–09; Universiti Teknologi Malaysia, 2006. Ed., Papers of Regl Sci. Assoc., 1975–80. Nat. Co-ordinator, ESRC Regl Res. Lab. Initiative, 1986–91; Co-Dir, ESF GISDATA scientific prog., 1991–97. Councillor: Regl Sci. Assoc., 1975–78 (Vice-Pres., 1980–81); Assoc. for Geographic Information, 1991–94, 1999–2003; Chm., Res. Assessment Evaluation Cttee on Geographical and Envmtl Sci., Assoc. of Univs in Netherlands, 1995–96; President: Assoc. of Geographic Information Labs for Europe, 1998–99; European Umbrella Orgn for Geographic Information, 1999–2003; Global Spatial Data Infrastructure Assoc., 2002–04. FRSA 1983; FAcSS 2017. Global Citizen Award, Global Spatial Data Infrastructure Assoc., 2016. *Publications:* Analytical Models for Urban and Regional Planning, 1972; Inter-regional Migration in Tropical Africa, 1975; (ed) Spatial Representation and Spatial Interaction, 1978; (ed) Evaluating Urban Planning Efforts, 1983; (ed) Learning from Other Countries, 1985; (ed) European Geographic Information Infrastructures, 1998; (ed) Handling Geographic Information, 1991; Geography of Europe's Futures, 1992; (ed) Diffusion and Use of Geographic Information Technologies, 1993; (ed) Planning for Cities and Regions in Japan, 1994; Geographical Information Systems and Organisations, 1995; (ed) GIS Diffusion, 1996; Governments and Geographic Information, 1998; GIS Worlds: creating spatial data infrastructures, 2005; Building European SDIs, 2007, 3rd edn 2015; GIS to SDI: a global perspective, 2019. *Recreations:* walking, travel. *Address:* Town End House, Taddington, Buxton, Derbys SK17 9UF. *T:* (01298) 85232.

**MASSEREENE,** 14th Viscount *cr* 1660, **AND FERRARD,** 7th Viscount *cr* 1797; **John David Clotworthy Whyte-Melville Foster Skeffington;** Baron Loughneagh (Ire.), 1660; Baron Oriel (Ire.), 1790; Baron Oriel (UK), 1821; stockbroker with M. D. Barnard & Co.; *b* 3 June 1940; *s* of 13th Viscount and Annabelle Kathleen (*d* 2009), *er d* of H. D. Lewis; *S* father, 1992; *m* 1970, Ann Denise, *er d* of late Norman Rowlandson; two *s* one *d*. *Educ:* St Peter's Court, Millfield; Institute Monte Rosa. Grenadier Guards, 1958–61. Stock Exchange, 1961–64; motor trade, 1964–70; Stock Exchange, 1970–2015; various airships; landowner. *Recreations:* vintage cars, history, shooting. *Heir: s* Hon. Charles John Clotworthy Whyte-Melville Foster Skeffington [*b* 7 Feb. 1973; *m* 2009, Olga, *e d* of Captain Cecil Lewis Dixon-Brown, RM; one *s* one *d*]. *Clubs:* Turf, Pratt's.

**MASSEY,** family name of **Baroness Massey of Darwen.**

**MASSEY OF DARWEN,** Baroness *cr* 1999 (Life Peer), of Darwen in the county of Lancashire; **Doreen Elizabeth Massey;** *b* 5 Sept. 1938; *d* of Mary Ann Hall (*née* Sharrock) and Jack Hall; *m* 1966, Dr Leslie Massey; two *s* one *d*. *Educ:* Darwen Grammar Sch., Lancs; Birmingham Univ. (BA Hons French 1961); DipEd 1962; Inst. of Educn, London Univ. (MA 1985). Graduate service overseas, Gabon, 1962–63; teacher: S Hackney Sch., 1964–67; Springside Sch., Philadelphia, 1967–69; Pre-School Play Group Association, 1973–77; teacher, Walsingham Sch., London, 1977–83 (co-ordinator Health Educn, Head of Year, senior teacher); advisory teacher for personal, social and health educn, ILEA, 1983–85; Manager, Young People's Programme, Health Educn Council, 1985–87; Dir of Educn, 1987–89, Dir, 1989–94, FPA. Chm., Nat. Treatment Agency, 2002–12. Co-Chm., All-Party Parly Gp for Children, 2001–16 (Sec., 2017–); Chair, Sub Cttee for Children, Social Affairs Cttee, H of L, 2017–; Member: Information Cttee, H of L, 2010–15; Affordable Childcare Select Cttee, H of L, 2014–15; Home Affairs Select Cttee, H of L, 2016–; UK Parly Delegn to Council of Europe, 2016– (Rapporteur: on Adolescent Health in Europe, 2017–19; on Violence Against Children within the Sustainable Develt Goals and Coordination of Initiatives on Child Sexual Abuse in Europe). Pres., Brook Adv. Centres; Mem., Nat. Trust; Patron, FPA, 2009–; Trustee, Unicef England, 2010–; Mem., The Lady Taverners, 2004–. FRSA 1992. Hon. Dr (Health Educn) Birmingham, 2014. *Publications:* Sex Education: Why, What and How?, 1988; Sex Education Factpack, 1988; (jtly) Sex Education Training Manual, 1991; (ed) Sex Education Resource Book, 1994; (ed) The Lover's Guide Encyclopedia, 1996; Love on the Road (short stories), 2013; Love and Death in Shanghai (novel), 2018; articles on sex educn, family planning, health educn. *Recreations:* reading, cinema, theatre, opera, art and design, yoga, pilates, sports, vegetarian cookery, travel, gardening. *Address:* House of Lords, SW1A 0PW.

**MASSEY, Vice Adm. Sir Alan (Michael),** KCB 2009; CBE 2003; Chief Executive, Maritime and Coastguard Agency, 2010–18; *b* 9 March 1953; *s* of Harry Massey and Astrid Ellen Irene Massey (*née* Lange); *m* 1987, Julie Samantha Smith; two *s* two *d*. *Educ:* Northgate Grammar Sch., Ipswich; Univ. of Liverpool (BA Hons 1975). Keswick Hall Coll. of Educn (PGCE 1976). HMS: Bulwark, 1979; Norfolk, 1980; Leander, 1981; Brazen, 1984; Ark Royal, 1987; RN staff course, 1989; MoD, London, 1990; NATO, Brussels, 1991; CO,

HMS Newcastle, 1993; MoD, London, 1995; CO, HMS Campbeltown, 1996; rcds, 1998; MoD, London, 1998; NATO SACLANT, 1999; Commanding Officer: HMS Illustrious, 2001; HMS Ark Royal, 2002; PJHQ Northwood, 2003–05; ACNS, MoD, 2005–08; Second Sea Lord and C-in-C Naval Home Comd, 2008–10; Flag ADC to the Queen, 2008–10. Non-exec. Dir, Shoreham Port Authy, 2019–. Younger Brother, Trinity House, 2010. Trustee, Marine Soc. and Sea Cadets, 2011–. Pres., Victory Services Club, 2014–. Hon. Vice-Pres., RN Soccer. Cdre, RNSA, 2008–10. Freeman, City of London, 2014; Mem., Shipwrights' Co., 2011–. Mem., HMS Ark Royal Assoc. *Recreations:* sailing, guitar, languages, family. *Clubs:* Royal Navy of 1765 and 1785; Fleet Air Arm Officers' Assoc.; Royal Naval and Royal Albert Yacht.

**MASSEY, Charles Hamilton;** Chief Executive and Registrar, General Medical Council, since 2016; *b* Southampton, 24 Aug. 1970; *s of* Roger Charles Massey and Catherine Clare Massey (*née* Johnson); *m* 2001, Hilda Anne Hughes; two *s* one *d*. *Educ:* St Catharine's Coll., Cambridge (BA Hist. 1992; MA; MPhil Social Anthropol. and Develt 1993). Policy advr roles, DSS, 1993–2000; Policy Advr, HM Treasury, 2000–01; Deputy Director: Prime Minister's Strategy Unit, 2001–04; Pension Protection, DWP, 2004–05; Exec. Dir for Strategic Develt, Pensions Regulator, 2005–08; Ageing Soc. and State Pensions Dir, DWP, 2008–12; Dir Gen., Ext. Relns, then Strategy and Ext. Relns, then Acute Care and Workfare, DoH, 2012–16. Trustee and Vice Chm., Action on Disability and Develt, 2005–12; Trustee and Chm., Walnut Tree Fund, 2009–. *Address:* General Medical Council, Regent's Place, 350 Euston Road, NW1 3JN. *E:* chiefexecutive@gmc-uk.org.

**MASSEY, Col Hamon Patrick Dunham;** Clerk, Ironmongers' Company, 2005–18; *b* 18 Aug. 1950; *s of* Lt Col Patrick Massey, MC and Bessie Lee Massey; *m* 1988, Cate Campbell; one *s* three *d*. *Educ:* Harrow; RMA Sandhurst; Army Staff Coll., Camberley. Commnd Blues and Royals, 1970; Adjutant, 1977–79; Army Staff Coll., 1982; CO, Household Cavalry Mounted Regt, 1992–94; Defence Attaché, Buenos Aires, 1997–2000; Comdr, Household Cavalry and Silver Stick in Waiting, 2000–05. Trustee: Foundn for Liver Res.; Cothrom. *Recreations:* fishing, gardening, dry stone walls. *Club:* Turf.
*See also* W. G. S. Massey.

**MASSEY, (Robert) Graham;** Managing Director, The Science Archive Ltd, 1996–2001; *b* 28 Sept. 1943; *s of* Robert Albert Massey and Violet Edith Massey (*née* Smith); *m* 1965, Allison Ruth Duerden; one *s* one *d*. *Educ:* Manchester Grammar Sch.; Balliol Coll., Oxford (BA 1st Cl. Hons History). Joined BBC 1965 as general trainee; Producer, Science and Features Dept, 1970; Producer, 1972–81, Editor, 1981–85, Horizon; Series Producer, Making of Mankind (with Richard Leakey), 1979–81; Head, Special Features Unit, BBC Drama, 1985–89; Head, Science and Features Dept, BBC, 1989–91; Dir, Co-productions, 1991–92, Dir, Internat., 1992–94, BBC Enterprises. *Recreations:* theatre, cinema, cooking, restoring Gascony farmhouse. *Address:* 76 The Lexington Apartments, 40 City Road, EC1Y 2AN.

**MASSEY, Roy Cyril,** MBE 1997; Organist and Master of the Choristers, Hereford Cathedral, 1974–2001, Organist Emeritus, 2009; *b* 9 May 1934; *s of* late Cyril Charles Massey and Beatrice May Massey; *m* 1975, Ruth Carol Craddock Grove. *Educ:* Univ. of Birmingham (BMus); privately with David Willcocks. FRCO (CHM); ADCM; ARCM; FRSCM (for distinguished services to church music) 1972. Organist: St Alban's, Conybere Street, Birmingham, 1953–60; St Augustine's, Edgbaston, 1960–65; Croydon Parish Church, 1965–68; Warden, RSCM, 1965–68; Conductor, Croydon Bach Soc., 1966–68; Special Comr of RSCM, 1964–74; Organist to City of Birmingham Choir, 1954–74; Organist and Master of Choristers, Birmingham Cath., 1968–74; Dir of Music, King Edward's Sch., Birmingham, 1968–74. Conductor, Hereford Choral Soc., 1974–2001; Conductor-in-Chief, alternate years Associate Conductor, Three Choirs Festival, 1975–2001; Adviser on organs to dioceses of Birmingham and Hereford, 1974–. Mem. Council and Examiner, RCO, 1970–94 and 1997–2006; Mem., Adv. Council, 1976–78, Council, 1984–98, RSCM; Mem. Council, Friends of Cathedral Music, 1999–2002. President: Birmingham Organists' Assoc., 1970–75; Cathedral Organists' Assoc., 1982–84; IAO, 1991–93; RCO, 2003–05. Fellow, St Michael's Coll., Tenbury, 1976–85. Hon. FGCM 2001. DMus Lambeth, 1990. *Recreations:* motoring, old buildings, walking the dog, theatre. *Address:* 2 King John's Court, Tewkesbury, Glos GL20 6EG. *T:* (01684) 290019. *E:* drroymassey@talktalk.net.

**MASSEY, William Greville Sale;** QC 1996; barrister; *b* 31 Aug. 1953; *s of* late Lt Col Patrick Massey, MC and Bessie Lee Massey (*née* Byrne); *m* 1978, Cecilia D'Oyly Awdry; three *s*. *Educ:* Harrow; Hertford Coll., Oxford (Entrance Schol.; MA). Called to the Bar, Middle Temple, 1977 (Harmsworth Exhibnr), Bencher, 2004. Member: Revenue Bar Assoc., 1978–; Chancery Bar Assoc., 1980–; London Commercial and Common Law Bar Assoc., 1980–. Mem., Tax Cttee, Historic Houses Assoc., 1986–. Governor: Summer Fields Sch., 1996–2013; Harrow Sch., 2000–13. *Recreations:* chess, cricket, opera, gardening, ski-ing. *Address:* Pump Court Tax Chambers, 16 Bedford Row, WC1R 4EF. *T:* (020) 7414 8080, *Fax:* (020) 7414 8099. *E:* clerks@pumptax.com.
*See also* H. P. D. Massey.

**MASSIE, Allan Johnstone,** CBE 2013; FRSL; FRSE; author and journalist; *b* 16 Oct. 1938; *s of* late Alexander Johnstone Massie and Evelyn Jane Wilson Massie (*née* Forbes); *m* 1973, Alison Agnes Graham Langlands; two *s* one *d*. *Educ:* Drumtochty Castle Sch.; Trinity College, Glenalmond; Trinity College, Cambridge (BA). Schoolmaster, Drumtochty Castle Sch., 1960–71; TEFL, Rome, 1972–75; fiction reviewer, The Scotsman, 1976–; Creative Writing Fellow: Edinburgh Univ., 1982–84; Glasgow and Strathclyde Univs, 1985–86; columnist: Glasgow Herald, 1985–88; Sunday Times Scotland, 1987–91; Daily Telegraph, 1991–; The Scotsman, 1992–; Daily Mail, 1994–; Sunday Times Scotland, 1996–2007; Spectator. Mem., Scottish Arts Council, 1989–91. Trustee, Nat. Museums of Scotland, 1995–98. Hon. Pres., Classical Assoc. of Scotland, 2003–05. FRSL 1982; FRSE 2011; Hon. FRIAS 1997. Hon. DLitt Strathclyde. Chevalier, Ordre des Arts et des Lettres. *Publications: fiction:* Change and Decay In All Around I See, 1978; The Last Peacock, 1980; The Death of Men, 1981; One Night in Winter, 1984; Augustus, 1986; A Question of Loyalties, 1989; The Hanging Tree, 1990; Tiberius, 1991; The Sins of the Fathers, 1991; Caesar, 1993; These Enchanted Woods, 1993; The Ragged Lion, 1994; King David: a novel, 1995; Shadows of Empire, 1997; Antony, 1997; Nero's Heirs, 1999; The Evening of the World, 2001; Arthur The King, 2003; Caligula, 2003; Charlemagne and Roland, 2007; Surviving, 2009; Klaus and Other Stories, 2010; Death in Bordeaux, 2011; Cold War in Bordeaux, 2014; End Games in Bordeaux, 2015; *non-fiction:* Muriel Spark, 1979; Ill-Met by Gaslight, 1980; The Caesars, 1983; A Portrait of Scottish Rugby, 1984; Colette, 1986; 101 Great Scots, 1987; Byron's Travels, 1988; Glasgow, 1989; The Novel Today, 1990; Edinburgh, 1994; The Thistle and the Rose, 2005; The Royal Stuarts: a history of the family that shaped Britain, 2010; *plays:* Quintet in October; The Minstrel and the Shirra; First-Class Passengers; Changing Lines. *Recreations:* reading, lunching, watching cricket, Rugby, horse-racing, smoking, walking the dogs. *Address:* Thirladean House, Selkirk TD7 5LU. *T:* (01750) 20393. *E:* allan.massie@btinternet.com. *Clubs:* Academy; Selkirk RFC.

**MASSY,** family name of **Baron Massy**.

**MASSY, 10th Baron** *cr* 1776 (Ire.); **David Hamon Somerset Massy;** *b* 4 March 1947; *s of* 9th Baron Massy and Margaret Elizabeth (*née* Flower); *S* father, 1995. *Educ:* St George's Coll., Weybridge. Late Merchant Navy. *Heir: b* Hon. John Hugh Somerset Massy [*b* 2 Jan. 1950; *m* 1978, Andrea West; one *s*].

**MASTERMAN, His Honour Crispin Grant,** FCIArb; a Circuit Judge, 1995–2012; *b* 1 June 1944; *s of* late Osmond Janson Masterman and Anne Masterman (*née* Bouwens); *m* 1976, Clare Fletcher; one *s* two *d*. *Educ:* St Edward's Sch., Oxford; Univ. of Southampton (BA). FCIArb 1991. Called to the Bar, Middle Temple, 1971; a Recorder, 1988–95; Designated Family Judge, Cardiff and Pontypridd, 2006–12; Court of Protection Judge for Cardiff, 2008–12. Legal Mem., Mental Health Review Tribunal for Wales, 2012–19. Mem., Council, Cardiff Univ., 1995–2004 (Vice-Chair, 1998–2004). Commnd RAFVR, 1966 (Actg Pilot Officer); Asst Instructor, British Gliding Assoc., 1977. *Recreations:* family and friends, walking, golf. *Address:* 28 South Rise, Llanishen, Cardiff CF14 0RH. *T:* (029) 2075 4072.

**MASTERS, Brian Geoffrey John;** author; *b* 25 May 1939; *s of* Geoffrey Howard Masters and Mabel Sophia Charlotte (*née* Ingledew). *Educ:* Wilson's Grammar Sch., London; University Coll., Cardiff (BA 1st cl. Hons 1961); Université de Montpellier. FRSA 1989. *Publications:* Molière, 1969; Sartre, 1969; Saint-Exupéry, 1970; Rabelais, 1971; Camus: a study, 1973; Wynyard Hall and the Londonderry Family, 1974; Dreams about HM The Queen, 1974; The Dukes, 1975; Now Barabbas Was A Rotter: the extraordinary life of Marie Corelli, 1978; The Mistresses of Charles II, 1980; Georgiana, Duchess of Devonshire, 1981; Great Hostesses, 1982; Killing for Company: the case of Dennis Nilsen, 1985 (Gold Dagger Award, CWA); The Swinging Sixties, 1985; The Passion of John Aspinall, 1988; Maharana: the Udaipur Dynasty, 1990; Gary, 1990; The Life of E. F. Benson, 1991; The Shrine of Jeffrey Dahmer, 1993; (ed and trans.) Voltaire's Treatise on Tolerance, 1994; Masters on Murder, 1994; The Evil That Men Do, 1996; She Must Have Known: the trial of Rosemary West, 1996; Thunder in the Air: great actors in great roles, 2000; Getting Personal: a biographer's memoir, 2002; Second Thoughts, 2008; Garrick Collection: the actors, 2010; Six Celebrations on Reaching Seventy, 2013. *Recreations:* etymology, stroking cats. *Address:* 47 Caithness Road, W14 0JD. *T:* (020) 7603 6838; 6 Place E. Granier, 34160 Castries, France. *T:* (4) 67875834. *Clubs:* Garrick (Trustee, 2010–), Beefsteak, Pratt's.

**MASTERS, Dr Christopher,** CBE 2002; Chairman, Energy Assets Group plc, 2012–16; *b* 2 May 1947; *s of* Wilfred and Mary Ann Masters; *m* 1971, Gillian Mary (*née* Hodson); two *d*. *Educ:* Richmond Sch.; King's Coll. London (BSc, AKC); Leeds Univ. (PhD). Research Chemist, Shell Research, Amsterdam, 1971–77; Corporate Planner, Shell Chemicals UK, 1977–79; Business Develt Manager, Christian Salvesen, 1979–81; Dir of Planning, Merchants Refrigerating Co., NY, 1981–82; Managing Director: Christian Salvesen Seafoods, 1983–86; Christian Salvesen Industrial Services, 1984–89; Chief Exec., Christian Salvesen PLC, 1989–97; Exec. Chm., Aggreko plc, 1997–2002; Chairman: Voxar Ltd, 2002–04; Babtie Gp Ltd, 2002–04; SMG plc, 2004–07; Sagentia Gp plc, 2007–10. Non-executive Director: British Assets Trust plc, 1990–2009; Scottish Widows' Fund or Life Assurance Soc., 1992–2000; Wood Gp, 2002–12; Alliance Trust, 2002–12; Crown Agents, 2005–16; Speedy Hire plc, 2011–15; Murgitroyd Gp plc, 2015–17. Chm., Young Enterprise Scotland, 1993–96; Mem., SHEFC, 1995–2005 (Chm., 1998–2005); Mem., Scottish Sci. Adv. Council, 2010–16 (Ind. Co Chair, 2011–16). Mem. Ct, Edinburgh Univ., 2011–17. Chm., Festival City Theatres Trust, 2002–13; Director: Scottish Opera, 1994–99 (Vice Chm., 1996–99); Scottish Chamber Orch., 1995–2012. Master, Merchant Co., City of Edinburgh, 2007–09; Lord Dean, Guild of City of Edinburgh, 2009–11. FRSE 1996. Hon. DBA Strathclyde, 2006; Hon. DLaws St Andrews, 2006; Hon. Dhc Edinburgh 2007; Hon. DEd Abertay Dundee, 2007. *Publications:* Homogeneous Transition—Metal Catalysis, 1981, Russian edn 1983; numerous research papers and patents. *Recreations:* music, wine.

**MASTERS, Guy;** *see* Masters, T. G.

**MASTERS, Robert James;** Headmaster, The Judd School, 2004–17; *b* 14 July 1964; *s of* Thomas Masters and Judith Lindsey Masters (*née* Boothman); *m* 1988, Rachel Clare Pugh; two *s* one *d*. *Educ:* Univ. of Reading (BSc 1st Cl. Hons Maths); Univ. of Bristol (PGCE Maths with Games). Teacher of maths, Gravesend GS for Boys, 1986–97 (Head: of Middle Sch., 1990–93; of Maths, 1993–97); Dep. Headmaster, Torquay Boys' GS, 1997–2004. Additional Mem., HMC, 2007–17. *Recreations:* tennis, cryptic crosswords, narrowboating.

**MASTERS, Sheila Valerie;** *see* Baroness Noakes.

**MASTERS, Prof. (Thomas) Guy,** PhD; FRS 2005; Distinguished Professor, since 2010, and Deputy Director of Research, Scripps Institution of Oceanography, and Associate Vice Chancellor, Marine Sciences, since 2016, University of California, San Diego (Professor of Geophysics, 1985–2010); Director, Institute of Geophysics and Planetary Physics, 2009–16); *b* 5 Oct. 1954; *s of* Thomas James Masters and Joyce Masters; *m* 1982, Virginia Fleming; one *s* one *d*. *Educ:* Victoria Univ. of Manchester (BSc 1st Cl. 1975); King's Coll., Cambridge (PhD 1979). University of California, San Diego: Green Schol., 1979–80, res. geophysicist, 1981–85, IGPP; Dir, Earth Scis, 1999–2002 and 2005–06. Fellow, Amer. Geophysical Union, 1995. Beno Gutenberg Medal, Eur. Geophysical Union, 2011. *Publications:* numerous contribs to leading jls. *Recreations:* horse-riding, ski-ing, gardening. *Address:* Institute of Geophysics and Planetary Physics, Scripps Institution of Oceanography, University of California, San Diego, 9500 Gilman Drive, La Jolla, CA 92093–0225, USA. *T:* (858) 5344122, *Fax:* (858) 5345332. *E:* gmasters@ucsd.edu.

**MASTERSON, Valerie, (Mrs Andrew March),** CBE 1988; opera and concert singer; *d* of Edward Masterson and Rita McGrath; *m* 1965, Andrew March; one *s* one *d*. *Educ:* Holt Hill Convent; studied in London and Milan on scholarship, and with Eduardo Asquez. Début, Landestheater Salzburg; appearances with: D'Oyly Carte Opera, Glyndebourne Festival Opera, ENO, Royal Opera, Covent Garden, etc; appears in principal opera houses in Paris, Aix-en-Provence, Toulouse, Munich, Geneva, Barcelona, Milan, San Francisco, Chile, etc; leading roles in: La Traviata, Le Nozze di Figaro, Manon, Faust, Alcina, Die Entführung aus dem Serail, Così fan tutte, La Bohème, Semele (SWET award, 1983), Die Zauberflöte, Julius Caesar, Rigoletto, Romeo and Juliet, Carmen, Count Ory, Mireille, Louise, Idomeneo, Les Dialogues des Carmélites, The Merry Widow, Xerxes, Orlando, Lucia di Lammermoor. Recordings include: La Traviata; Elisabetta, Regina d'Inghilterra; Der Ring des Nibelungen; The Merry Widow; Julius Caesar; Scipione; several Gilbert and Sullivan operas. Regular broadcasts on radio and TV. Pres., British Youth Opera, 1995–2001 (Vice-Pres., 2001–). Patron, Mousehole Male Voice Choir, 2002. Hon. Pres., Rossini Soc., Paris. FRCM 1992; Hon. RAM 1993. Hon. DLitt South Bank, 1999.

**MASTERTON, Prof. Gordon Grier Thomson,** OBE 2008; DL; FREng; FRSE; Professor of Future Infrastructure, University of Edinburgh, since 2015; Vice President, Jacobs UK Ltd (formerly Babtie Group Ltd, later Jacobs Babtie), 2004–14; *b* 9 June 1954; *s of* late Alexander Bain Masterton and Mary Masterton (*née* Thomson); *m* 1976, Lynda Christine Jeffries; one *s* one *d*. *Educ:* Dunfermline High Sch.; Univ. of Edinburgh (BSc); Open Univ. (BA); Imperial Coll., London (MSc; DIC 1981). CEng 1980; FREng 2006; FICE; FIStructE; FIES; MCIWEM. Joined Babtie Shaw & Morton, 1976; Babtie Group

Ltd: Dir, 1993; Man. Dir of Facilities, 2002–03; Man. Dir, Envmt, 2003–04. Chm., Construction Industry Council, 2010–12 (Chm., Scotland, 2002–04); Mem., Royal Commn on Ancient and Historical Monuments of Scotland, 2003–15 (Vice Chm., 2010–15; Mem., Historic Scotland/RCAHMS Transition Adv. Bd, 2013–15). UK Govt Rep., Crossrail Project, 2009–13; Dir, AWE ML, 2014–15. Chm., Standing Cttee on Structural Safety, 2008–16. Institution of Civil Engineers: Vice-Pres., 2002–05; Pres., 2005–06; Chm., Asia-Pacific Regl Cttee, 2007–13; Chm., Panel for Histl Engrg Works, 2013–; Chm., Disciplinary Bd, 2015–; Vice-Pres., 2008–10, Pres., 2010–12, Instn of Engrs and Shipbuilders in Scotland; Mem. Council, RAEng, 2008–11. Visiting Professor: Univ. of Paisley, 1998–2003; Glasgow Caledonian Univ., 2012–; Univ. of Edinburgh, 2012–15. Buchanan Lectr, ICE/Japan Soc. of Civil Engrs, Tokyo, 2012; MacPherson Lectr, Internat. Council on Systems Engrg, 2017; R. W. Thomson Lectr, IMMM, 2019. Chm., Scottish Lime Centre Trust, 2007–09. Trustee: Royal Soc. of Edinburgh Foundn, 2017–; Macrobert Trust, 2018–; Soc. of Friends of Paisley Abbey, 2018–. Chm., Scottish Engrg Hall of Fame, 2011–. Judge, RAEng MacRobert Award, 2013–16. Pres., Glasgow Grand Opera Soc., 1991–94. Presenter, TV series, Life After People, 2008–10. FRSE 2007. Mem., Incorp. of Hammermen of Glasgow, 2009– (Master, Ct, 2015–; Collector, 2016–17; Deacon, 2018–19); Liveryman, Engineers' Co., 2010– (Mem., Ct of Assts, 2012–; Sen. Warden, 2019–April 2020). DL Renfrewshire, 2018. Hon. DTech Glasgow Caledonian, 2007; Hon. DEng Heriot-Watt, 2012. *Publications:* (ed) Bridges and Retaining Walls—broadening the European horizons, 1994; (jtly) Supreme Sacrifice: a small village and the Great War, 2016; author of 3 technical design guides on concrete foundations and retaining walls, 1995, 1997, 1999; over 40 technical papers. *Recreations:* music, engineering history, genealogy, webmaster for www.themastertons.org and www.engineeringhalloffame.org. *Address:* Corrievreck, Montrose Terrace, Bridge of Weir, Renfrewshire PA11 3DH. *T:* (01505) 613503. *E:* themastertons@btinternet.com. *Club:* Smeatonians.

**MASTERTON, Paul;** MP (C) East Renfrewshire, since 2017; *m*; one *s* one *d*. *Educ:* George Watson's Coll.; Univ. of Dundee (LLB Hons 2007). Trainee solicitor, 2008–10, Solicitor, 2010–12, McGrigors; Solicitor, 2012–14, Associate, 2014–, Pinsent Masons. Mem., Scottish Affairs Cttee, H of C, 2017–. *Address:* House of Commons, SW1A 0AA.

**MASTERTON-SMITH, Cdre Anthony Philip,** RN; CEng; Chairman, Penwood Management Ltd, 2005–13; Chief Executive, Royal College of Physicians, 1998–2005; *b* 2 Aug. 1944; *s* of late Edward Masterton-Smith and Pauline Masterton-Smith (*née* Pilgrim); *m* 1975, Jennifer Sue Sprigings; one *s* one *d*. *Educ:* UCS, Hampstead; BRNC Dartmouth; RNEC Manadon. CEng, MIET (MIEE 1973). Royal Navy, 1962–98: HM Ships Fiskerton, Victorious, Llandaff, Bacchante, Scylla, Southampton; Staff of FO Sea Training, 1978–80; CO, HMS Royal Arthur, 1982–84; jsdc, 1986; Dep. Dir, Naval Recruiting, 1988–91; Defence and Naval Attaché, Tokyo, 1992–95; Cdre, BRNC Dartmouth, 1995–98. Director: RCP Regent's Park Ltd, 2001–05; Vale Health Ltd, 2006–08. Trustee, Princes Risborough Centre Ltd, 2014–. FRSA 2002. Hon. FRCP 2006. *Recreations:* opera, gardening, walking, sport. *Address:* Penwood, Whiteleaf, Bucks HP27 0LU. *Clubs:* Monks Risborough Cricket, Whiteleaf Golf.

**MASUI, Prof. Yoshio,** OC 2003; FRSC 2003; FRS 1998; Professor, University of Toronto, 1978–97, now Emeritus; *b* Kyoto, 6 Oct. 1931; adopted Canadian nationality, 1983; *s* of Fusa-jiro Masui and Toyoko Masui; *m* 1959, Yuriko Suda; one *s* one *d*. *Educ:* Kyoto Univ. (BSc 1953; MSc 1955; PhD 1961). Lectr, 1958–65, Asst Prof., 1965–68, Prof. Emeritus, 1999, Konan Univ., Japan; Staff Biologist, 1966–68, Lectr, 1969, Yale Univ.; Associate Prof. of Zoology, Univ. of Toronto, 1969–78. Hon. DSc Toronto, 1999. Albert Lasker Basic Medical Res. Award (jtly), for pioneering studies of regulation of cell divisions, 1998. *Address:* Department of Cell and System Biology, University of Toronto, 25 Harbord Street, Toronto, ON M5S 3G5, Canada.

**MATANE, Sir Paulias (Nguna),** GCL 2005; GCMG 2005 (CMG 1980); Kt 1986; OBE 1975; writer; Governor-General, Papua New Guinea, 2004–11; *b* Papua New Guinea, 21 Sept. 1931; *s* of Ilias Maila Matane and Elsa Toto; *m* 1957, Kaludia Peril Matane (*d* 2016); two *s* two *d*. *Educ:* Toma Village Higher Sch.; Keravat High Sch.; Sogeri High Sch.; Teacher's College (Dip. Teaching and Education). Asst Teacher, Tauran Primary Sch., PNG, 1957, Headmaster, 1958–61; School Inspector, 1962–66; Dist Sch. Inspector and Dist Educn Officer, 1967–68; Supt, Teacher Educn, 1969; Foundn Mem., Public Service Bd, 1969–70; Dir, Dept of Lands, Surveys and Mines, 1970; Sec., Dept of Business Develt, 1971–75; Ambassador to USA, Mexico and UN, and High Comr to Canada, 1975–80; Sec., Foreign Affairs, PNG, 1980–85. A Vice-Pres., UN Gen. Assembly, 1979. Dep. Dir Gen., Internat. Biographical Center, 2007. Dir and Dep. Chm., PNG Develt Bank, 1971–75; Dir, Nat. Investment and Develt Authy, 1972–75; Dir, Passenger Transport Control Bd, 1971–75. Chairman: Treid Pacific (PNG) Pty Ltd, 1986–90; Newton Pacific (PNG) Pty Ltd, 1995–. Chairman: Review Cttee on Philosophy of Educn, 1986; Cocoa Industry Investigating Cttee, 1987; Foundn for Peoples of South Pacific, PNG, 1989–94; PNG Censorship Bd, 1989–96; Children, Women and Families in PNG: a situation analysis, 1996; Community Consultative Cttee of E New Britain Provincial Govt of Autonomy, 2002–04 (formerly Dep. Chm.); Asia Pacific Leadership Forum, 2003–04. Producer of regular progs for TV, 1990–2004, and radio, 1998–2002. Director, Board of Trustees: Nat. Mus. and Arts Gall., 1995–99 (Pres., 1999–2004); Nat. Libraries and Archives, 1999–2003. Mem. Council, Univ. of PNG, 1982–92. S Pacific Commn Scholarship, 1963; Winston Churchill Scholarship Award, 1967. Paul Harris Fellow, 2007. Hon. DTech Univ. of Technol., Lae, 1985; Hon. PhD Univ. of PNG, 1986; Hon. DLitt Univ. of PNG, 2008. Forsayth Prize, 1952; UN 40th Anniv. Medal, 1985; Man of the Year Award, American Biographical Inst., 2007. KStJ 2005. Contributor, Radio, Daily and Weekly Newspaper, 1980–2005. *Publications:* Kum Tumun of Minj, 1966; A New Guinean Travels through Africa, 1971; My Childhood in New Guinea, 1972; What Good is Business?, 1972; Bai Bisnis I Helpim Yumi Olsem Wanem?, 1973; Exploring South Asia, vol. 1, Two New Guineans Travel through SE Asia, 1974, 2001, vol. 2, 2001; Aimbe the Challenger, 1974; Aimbe the School Dropout, 1974; Aimbe the Magician, 1976; Aimbe the Pastor, 1979; Two Papua New Guineans Discover the Bible Lands, 1987; To Serve with Love, 1989; Chit Chat, vol. 1, 1991, vol. 2, Let's Do It PNG, 1994, vol. 3, 2000; East to West—the longest train trip in the world, 1991; Trekking Through the New Worlds, 1995; Voyage to Antarctica, 1996; Laughter Made in PNG, 1996; Amazing Discoveries in 40 Years of Marriage, 1997; Laughter: its concept and Papua New Guineans, 1997; The Other Side of Port Moresby—in pictures, 1998; A Trip of a Lifetime, 1998; The Word Power, 1998; Waliling United Church: then and now, 1998; Coach Adventures Down Under, 1999; Management Problems in Papua New Guinea: some solutions, 2000; Further Management Problems in Papua New Guinea: their solutions, 2000; Management for Excellence, 2001; Exploring the Holy Lands, 2001; Humour in Papua New Guinea, 2002; Ripples in the South Pacific Ocean, 2002; India: a splendour in cultural diversity, 2004; Papua New Guinea: land of natural beauty and cultural diversity, 2005; The Time Traveller, 2005; Fifty Golden Years: saga of true love in marital and national life, 2006; Travelling Through Australia by Coach, 2007; Cultural Diversity of India, 2007; Education for Integral Human Development, 2008; Aimbe Braves Through Challenges, 2008; Public Addresses to be Privately Addressed, 2008; Christianity: faith and holy days, 2014. *Recreations:* reading, gardening, squash, fishing, writing. *Address:* PO Box 3405, Kokopo, ENB P, Papua New Guinea. *Clubs:* Tamukavar, Tauran Ex Student and Citizens' (Papua New Guinea).

**MATE, Rt Rev. Martin;** Bishop of Eastern Newfoundland and Labrador, 1980–92; *b* 12 Nov. 1929; *s* of John Mate and Hilda Mate (*née* Toope); *m* 1962, Florence Hooper, Registered Nurse; two *s* three *d*. *Educ:* Meml Univ. of Newfoundland; Queen's Coll., St John's, Newfoundland (LTh); Bishop's Univ., Lennoxville, PQ. BA (1st Cl. Hons), MA. Deacon 1952, priest 1953; Curate, Cathedral of St John the Baptist, St John's, Newfoundland, 1952–53; Deacon-in-charge and Rector, Parish of Pushthrough, 1953–58; Incumbent, Mission of St Anthony, 1958–64; Rural Dean, St Barbe, 1958–64; Rector of Cookshire, Quebec, 1964–67; Rector of Catalina, Newfoundland, 1967–72; RD of Bonavista Bay, 1970–72; Rector of Pouch Cove/Torbay, 1972–76; Treasurer, Diocesan Synod of E Newfoundland and Labrador, 1976–80. Hon. DD Queen's Coll., St John's, Newfoundland, 2009. *Publications:* Pentateuchal Criticism, 1967. *Recreations:* carpentry, hunting, fishing, camping. *Address:* 1015–50 Tiffany Court, St John's, NL A1A 0G1, Canada.

**MATEAR, Comr Elizabeth Anne;** Secretary for International Ecumenical Relations, since 2016; *b* 16 Aug. 1952; *d* of Jack and Elizabeth Kowbus; *m* 1978, John Matear; one *s*. *Educ:* Ladybank Primary Sch.; Bell Baxter High Sch.; Jordanhill Coll. (DipSW); Internat. Trng Coll. for Officers, Salvation Army. Social worker: in addiction services, 1973–75, in alcohol assessment, 1977–78; Salvation Army Officer, 1977–; Commanding Officer: Godalming, 1978–80; Reading E, 1980–83; Hove, 1983–85; Chester-le-Street, 1985–87; Divl Youth Work, 1987–90; Church Growth Consultant, 1990–94; CO, Bradford, 1994–95; Dir of Personnel, Yorks Div., 1996–97; Personnel Co-ordinator, UK Territorial HQ, 1997–99; Divl Leader, E Midlands Div., 1999–2001; Caribbean Territorial Leader and Territorial Pres., Women's Ministries, 2001–06; Territorial Leader and Pres., Women's Ministries, UK with Republic of Ireland, 2006–12; Comdg Officer, William Booth Meml Hall, Nottingham, 2012–16. Co-Pres., Churches Together in England, 2007–11; Moderator, Free Church Council, 2007–11. *Recreations:* walking, reading, crossword puzzles, people, Rotarian. *Address:* Salvation Army Territorial Headquarters, 101 Newington Causeway, SE1 6BN. *T:* (020) 7367 4603. *E:* elizabeth.matear@salvationarmy.org.uk.

**MATERLIK, Prof. Gerhard Theodor,** Hon. CBE 2007; FRS 2011; FInstP; Professor of Facilities Science, University College London, 2013–16, now Emeritus Professor of Physics; *b* Marl, Germany, 16 Jan. 1945; *s* of Hans Ptaszynski and Gertrud Marianne Materlik; *m* 1st, 1972, Christa Peters (marr. diss. 2002); two *s*; 2nd, 2008, Sabine Maria Materlik. *Educ:* Univs of Munster and Munich (Dip. Physics 1970); Univ. of Dortmund (Dr rer. nat. 1975). FInstP 2007. Scientific asst, Univ. of Dortmund, 1970–75; Postdoctoral Res. Associate, Cornell Univ., 1975–77; Sen. Res. Associate, Deutsches Elektronen Synchrotron (DESY), 1978–85; Scientific Dir, 1986–93, Associate Dir, and Coordinator for X-ray Free Electron Laser Project, 1994–2001, Hamburg Synchrotron Radiation Lab. at DESY; Scientific Dir, DESY, and Prof. of Physics, Hamburg Univ., 1990–2001; CEO, 2001–13, Principal Diamond Fellow, 2013–14, Diamond Light Source Ltd. Guest Scientist, AT&T Bell Telephone Labs, 1979; Guest Prof. for Academic Industry Cooperation, Stanford Univ. and Stanford Synchrotron Radiation Lab., 1993–94; Visiting Professor: Oxford Univ., 2002–07; Reading Univ., 2003–13; Southampton Univ., 2003–08. Hon. Prof., UCL, 2012–14. Hon. DSc Reading, 2004; Hon Dr Nat. Res. Centre Kurchatov Inst., 2012. *Publications:* (ed jtly) Resonant Anomalous X-Ray Scattering, 1994; over 200 articles in learned jls on application of synchrotron x-rays for studying geometric and electronic structure of atoms and solids, dopants and interfaces/surfaces. *Recreations:* reading, walking, music. *Address:* London Centre for Nanotechnology, University College London, 17–19 Gordon Street, WC1H 0AH. *E:* g.materlik@ucl.ac.uk.

**MATES, James Michael;** Europe Editor, ITN, since 2012; *b* 11 Aug. 1961; *s* of Rt Hon. Michael John Mates, *qv*; *m* 1991, Fiona Margaret Bennett; two *s* one *d*. *Educ:* Marlborough Coll.; Farnham Coll.; Leeds Univ. (BA Hons). Joined Independent Television News, 1983: Tokyo corresp., 1989–91; North of England corresp., 1991–92; Moscow corresp., 1992–94; Diplomatic Ed., 1994–97; Washington corresp., 1997–2002; Sen. Corresp., 2002–11. *Recreations:* bridge, tennis, mountain biking, backgammon. *Address:* c/o Independent TV News, 200 Gray's Inn Road, WC1X 8XZ. *Clubs:* Garrick, Portland.

**MATES, Lt-Col Rt Hon. Michael (John);** PC 2004; *b* 9 June 1934; *s* of Claude John Mates; *m* 1st, 1959, Mary Rosamund Paton (marr. diss. 1980); two *s* two *d*; 2nd, 1982, Rosellen (marr. diss. 1995); one *d*; 3rd, 1998, Christine, *d* of Count and Countess Moltke, Copenhagen. *Educ:* Salisbury Cathedral Sch.; Blundell's Sch.; King's Coll., Cambridge (choral schol.). Joined Army, 1954; 2nd Lieut, RUR, 1955; Queen's Dragoon Guards, RAC, 1961; Major, 1967; Lt-Col, 1973; resigned commn 1974. MP (C) Petersfield, Oct. 1974–1983, E Hampshire, 1983–2010. Minister of State, NI Office, 1992–93. Vice-Chm., Cons. NI Cttee, 1979–81 (Sec., 1974–79); Chairman: Select Cttee on Defence, 1987–92 (Mem., 1979–92); Select Cttee on NI, 2001–05; Cons. Home Affairs Cttee, 1987–88 (Vice-Chm., 1979–87); All-Party Anglo-Irish Gp, 1979–92; Sec., 1922 Cttee, 1987–88, 1997–2010; Mem., Intell. and Security Cttee, 1994–2010; Mem., Butler Review of Intelligence on Weapons of Mass Destruction, 2004; introduced: Farriers Registration Act, 1975; Rent Amendment Act, 1985. Farriers' Co.: Liveryman, 1975–; Asst, 1981; Master, 1986–87. *E:* matesmichael@gmail.com.

*See also* J. M. Mates.

**MATHER, Lt-Col Anthony Charles McClure,** CVO 1998; OBE 1990 (MBE 1965); Secretary, Central Chancery of the Orders of Knighthood and Assistant Comptroller, Lord Chamberlain's Office, 1991–99; Staff Officer to the Earl Marshal, 1999–2014; *b* 21 April 1942; *s* of late Eric James Mather and Stella Mather (*née* McClure); *m* 1966, Gaye, *d* of late Dr Eric Lindsay Dickson and Mrs Louise Tillett; one *s* two *d*. *Educ:* Eton College. Commissioned, Grenadier Guards, 1962; served UK, British Guyana, Germany and Hong Kong; retired 1991. An Extra Equerry to the Queen, 1992–. Freeman, City of London, 1998. *Recreations:* gardening, fishing, music. *Address:* The Horseshoes, Chirton, near Devizes, Wilts SN10 3QR. *T:* (01380) 840261.

**MATHER, Christopher Paul;** a Judge of the Upper Tribunal (Immigration and Asylum Chamber) (formerly a Senior Immigration Judge, Asylum and Immigration Tribunal), 2005–13; a Legal Member, Special Immigration Appeals Commission, 2006–13; a Recorder of the Crown Court, 1996–2013 (Assistant Recorder, 1991–96); a Deputy High Court Judge, 2010–13; *b* 20 June 1947; *s* of Bertrand and Jean Barker Mather; *m* 1970, Pauline Mary Man; twin *s* and *d*. *Educ:* Ellesmere Coll., Shropshire. Admitted solicitor, 1973; Partner and Consultant, Penningtons, 1994–2000. Mem., Hants and IoW Valuation Tribunal, 1988–94; Dep. Dist Judge, 1989–91; Immigration Adjudicator, 2000–03; a Vice Pres., Immigration Appeal Tribunal, 2003–05. Mem., Methodology Soc. *Recreation:* managing and improving a 10 acre estate. *Address:* Little Shootash Farm, Romsey, Hants SO51 6FB. *E:* cpm@candpmather.plus.com. *Club:* Goodwood Road Racing.

**MATHER, Clive;** *see* Mather, H. C.

**MATHER, Graham Christopher Spencer,** CBE 2017; solicitor; President: European Policy Forum, since 1992; European Financial Forum, since 1999; Infrastructure Forum, since 2009; *b* 23 Oct. 1954; *er s* of late Thomas and Doreen Mather; *m* 1st, 1981, Fiona Marion McMillan (marr. diss. 1995), *e d* of Sir Ronald McMillan Bell, QC, MP and of Lady Bell; two *s*; 2nd, 1997, Geneviève, *widow* of James Seton Fairhurst. *Educ:* Hutton Grammar School; New College, Oxford (Burnet Law Scholar); MA Jurisp. Institute of Directors: Asst to Dir Gen., 1980; Head of Policy Unit, 1983; Institute of Economic Affairs: Dep. Dir, 1987; Gen. Dir, 1987–92. MEP (C) Hampshire N and Oxford, 1994–99. Mem., HM Treasury Working Party on Freeports, 1982. Member: Monopolies and Mergers Commission, 1989–94; Competition Appeal Tribunal (formerly Appeal Tribunal, Competition Commn), 2000–11; Ofcom Consumer Panel, 2004–09; Infrastructure Finance Rev. Panel, HM Treasury, 2019; non-executive Director: Ofcom, 2014–; Office of Rail and Road, 2016–. Vis. Fellow, Nuffield Coll., Oxford, 1992–2000. Mem., Westminster City Council, 1982–86; contested (C) Blackburn, 1983. Consultant: Tudor Investment Corp., 1992–2012; Elliott Associates, 2007–; Advr, BIFU, 1997–99; non-exec. Dir, Greenham Trust (formerly Common Community Trust), 2000–. Chm., World Free Zone Convention, 2000–. Vice-Pres., Assoc. of Dist Councils, 1994–97. Trustee: Social Market Foundn, 2008–17; Royal Co. of Berks Churches Trust, 2017–. *Publications:* lectures, papers and contribs to jls; contribs to The Times. *Address:* European Policy Forum, Kings Buildings, 16 Smith Square, SW1P 3HQ. *T:* (020) 7839 7565, *Fax:* (020) 3137 2040. *E:* graham.mather@epfltd.org. *Clubs:* Travellers, Naval.

**MATHER, (Harold) Clive;** Chairman, Matthew 25:35 Trust, since 2007; Director, Emissions Reduction Alberta, since 2016; Chairman: Relational Peacebuilding Initiatives, Geneva, since 2019; Tearfund USA, since 2019; *b* 19 Sept. 1947; *m* 1976, Ann (*née* Mason); one *s* two *d*. *Educ:* Warwick Sch.; Lincoln Coll., Oxford (BA 1969; MA). With Shell, 1969–2007: early career in UK, Brunei and Gabon; Retail Regl Manager, Shell UK, 1984–86; Dir of Personnel and Public Affairs, Shell South Africa, 1986–91; Dir of Human Resources and Admin, Shell UK Ltd, and Dir, Shell Res. Ltd, 1991–95; Chief Inf. Officer, Shell Internat., 1995–97; Dir, Internat., Shell, 1997–99; Chief Exec., Shell Services Internat., 1999–2002; Chm., Shell UK Ltd, and Hd of Global Learning, Shell, 2002–04; Pres. and CEO, Shell Canada, 2004–07; Chairman: Shell Pensions Trust Ltd, 2008–18; UK Shell Pension Plan Trust Ltd, 2013–18; C of E Pensions Bd, 2019–. Chairman: Lensbury Ltd, 1999–2004; Iogen Corpn, 2007–17; Director: Place Dome Inc., 2005–; Badger Explorer ASA, Norway, 2011–13. Mem., Premier of Alberta's Council for Econ. Strategy, 2009–12. Chm., Petroleum Employers' Council, 1994–96. Comr, EOC, 1991–94; Member: Adv. Bd, Relationships Foundn, 1996–; Supervisory Bd, Office of Govt and Commerce, 2002–04; President's Cttee, CBI, 2002–04; British N American Cttee, 2005–; Chairman: Corporate Social Responsibility Acad., 2003–05; IMD Business Council, 2003–04. Chairman: Lambeth Educn Action Zone Forum, 1998–2003; The Garden Tomb (Jerusalem) Assoc., 2008–17; Tearfund, 2008–18; Dep. Chm., Windsor Leadership Trust, 1994–2005. Judge, CCEMC Grand Challenge, 2013–. Trustee, Royal Anniversary Trust, 2003–12. MCIPD 2004; CCMI 2004. FRSA 1992. *Recreations:* sport, good food and good conversation. *Address:* PO Box 1077, Guildford, Surrey GU1 9HQ. *Club:* Lensbury (Teddington).

**MATHER, James Stuart,** CA; Member (SNP) Argyll and Bute, Scottish Parliament, 2007–11 (Highlands and Islands, 2003–07); Chairman, Homes for Scotland, 2016–17; *b* 6 March 1947; *s* of James Stuart Mather and Sarah Morag Mather (*née* MacKenzie); *m* 1980, Maureen Anne (*née* Drysdale); one *s* one *d*. *Educ:* Paisley Grammar Sch.; Greenock High Sch.; Glasgow Univ. Director: Computers for Business (Scotland) Ltd, 1986–96; Business for Scotland, 1997–2004; Scotland in Europe, 2001–03. Opposition spokesman on enterprise and the econ., Scottish Parlt, 2003–07; Minister for Enterprise, Energy and Tourism, 2007–11. Nat. Treas., SNP, 2000–04. Visiting Professor: Univ. of Strathclyde, 2011–18; Heriot-Watt Univ., 2014–. Chm., Gael Ltd, 2011–15. Mem., ICAS, 1971. *Recreations:* cycling, golf, hill-walking, reading. *Address:* 13 Sutherland Avenue, Glasgow G41 4JJ. *Club:* Traigh Golf (Arisaig).

**MATHER, Dr John Cromwell;** Senior Astrophysicist, since 1993, Goddard Fellow, since 1994, Senior Project Scientist, James Webb Space Telescope, since 2005, Goddard Space Flight Center, NASA; *b* Roanoke, Va, 7 Aug. 1946; *s* of Robert E. Mather and Martha Cromwell Mather; *m* 1980, Jane Hauser. *Educ:* Newton High Sch., NJ; Swarthmore Coll., Penn (BA Physics 1968); Univ. of California, Berkeley (PhD Physics 1974). Postdoctoral Fellow, Goddard Inst. for Space Studies, NASA, 1974–76; Study Scientist, 1976–88, Project Scientist, 1988–98, and Principal Investigator, Far Infrared Absolute Spectrophotometer on Cosmic Background Explorer, Goddard Space Flight Center, NASA. (Jtly) Nobel Prize in Physics, 2006. *Publications:* (with J. Boslough) The Very First Light, 1996; articles in jls. *Address:* Astrophysics Science Division, Goddard Space Flight Center, NASA, Code 443, JWST Project, Greenbelt, MD 20771, USA.

**MATHER, John Douglas,** FCILT; Chief Executive, National Freight Consortium plc, 1984–93; *b* 27 Jan. 1936; *s* of John Dollandson and Emma May Mather; *m* 1958, Hilda Patricia (*née* Kirkwood); one *s* (one *d* decd). *Educ:* Manchester Univ. (BACom, MAEcon). Personnel Management: Philips Electrical, 1959–66; Convoys Ltd, 1966–67; Personnel Management, Transport Management, National Freight Company, 1967–93. Chairman: Cranfield Ventures, 2000–06; CIT Hldgs, 2000–06 (Dir, 1994–2006); non-executive Director: Charles Sidney plc (formerly Bletchley Motor Gp), 1993–98; Computer Management Gp, 1993–98; Miller Gp, 1993–2003; St Mary's (Paddington) NHS Trust, 1995–97. Chairman: Bedfordshire TEC, 1991–93; Camden Business Partnership, 1991; London Regeneration Consortium plc, 1993–95. Member: Adv. Bd, Cranfield Sch. of Management, 1992–97; Council, Cranfield Univ., 1993–2006. Trustee, Help The Aged, 1993–2008 (Chm., 1995–2004). Mem., Co. of Carmen. *Recreations:* golf, gardening, travel. *Address:* Roundhale, Love Lane, Kings Langley, Hertfordshire WD4 9HW. *T:* (01923) 263063.

**MATHER, Prof. Tamsin Alice,** PhD; Professor of Earth Sciences, University of Oxford, since 2014; Fellow of University College, Oxford, since 2006; *b* Bristol, 15 Dec. 1976; *d* of William Mather and Felicity Mather; partner, 2004, David Pyle; one *s* one *d*. *Educ:* St John's Coll., Cambridge (MSc Nat. Scis (Chem.) 1999; MPhil Hist. and Philos. of Sci. 2000; PhD Earth Scis 2004). NERC Fellow, Parly Office of Sci. and Technol., 2005; Royal Soc. Dorothy Hodgkin Res. Fellow, Univ. of Cambridge, 2005–06, Univ. of Oxford, 2006–09; Lectr and Academic Fellow, Dept of Earth Scis, Univ. of Oxford, 2006–14. Mem., Sci. Cttee, NERC, 2017–20. Editor, Earth and Planetary Sci. Letters, 2014–19. *Publications:* (ed jtly) Remote-sensing of Volcanoes and Volcanic Processes: integrating observation and modelling, 2013; over 130 articles in internat. jls. *Recreations:* theatre, reading, watersports, hiking, art, family. *Address:* Department of Earth Sciences, University of Oxford, South Parks Road, Oxford OX1 3AN. *T:* (01865) 282125. *E:* Tamsin.Mather@earth.ox.ac.uk.

**MATHER-LEES, Michael Anthony;** QC 2012; *b* Wales; *m* 2007, Lisa; one *s* one *d*. *Educ:* Univ. of London (LLB). Called to the Bar, Inner Temple, 1981. Member: Criminal Bar Assoc.; Eur. Bar Gp; Western Circuit; Wales and Chester Circuit; South Eastern Circuit. *Recreations:* fishing, the arts, Sealyham Terriers, horses. *Address:* Church Court Chambers, Temple, EC4Y 7BL.

**MATHERS, Howard Leslie,** CBE 2008; FREng, FRINA, FCMI; engineering and management consultant (part-time), since 2015; Technical Director, Submarines, Babcock International, 2012–15; *b* Wellington, Som, 21 Feb. 1956; *s* of Leslie Norman Mathers, OBE and Isabelle Josephine Madge Mathers; *m* 1981, Marianne Lischer; two *s* two *d*. *Educ:* Campbell Coll., Belfast; University Coll. London (MSc Naval Architecture); London Business Sch. (MSc (Sloan) Mgt). RCNC 1973; FRINA 2000; FREng 2013. Ministry of Defence: Naval Architect, Frigates and Destroyers, 1979–81; Manager, Submarines Refitting Trades, 1981–83; Civil Asst to Chief Exec. Dockyards, 1983–85; Prog. Manager, Submarine Refits, 1986–88; Sen. Naval Observer, NI, 1988–91; Hd of Naval Architecture, RN Engrg Coll., 1991–94; Design Authy, Submarines, 1995–2000; Dir, In-service Submarines, 2003–07; Chief Engr, Submarines, 2007–09; Dir, Safety and Engrg, 2009–11, Technical Dir, 2012, Defence Equipt and Support, MoD. Chairman: Ship and Envmt Safety Bd, MoD, 2009–12; Defence Nuclear Envmt and Safety Bd, 2009–11; Defence Fuels and Gases Envmt and Safety Bd, 2011. Founding Trustee, Children's Homes in India Trust, 2005–; Trustee, Engrg Develt Trust, 2018–; Chm., Snowhill Gateway Trust, 2014–19. FCMI 2011 (MCMI 1994). *Recreations:* Christian thought, choral singing, golf, DIY. *Address:* Mathers Consulting Ltd, The Lodge, Farringdon, North Petherton, Bridgwater, Som TA6 6PF.

**MATHERS, Peter James,** LVO 1995; HM Diplomatic Service, retired; High Commissioner to Jamaica, 2002–05; *b* 2 April 1946; *s* of Dr James Mathers and Margaret Mathers (*née* Kendrick); *m* 1983, Elisabeth Hoeller; one *s* one *d*. *Educ:* Bradfield Coll., Berks; Open Univ. (BA 1st Cl. Hons 2014). Army SSC, 1968–71. Joined HM Diplomatic Service, 1971: SOAS (Persian), 1972–73; Tehran, 1973–75; Bonn, 1976–78; FCO, 1978–81; Copenhagen, 1981–85; Tehran, 1986–87; FCO, 1987–88; on secondment to UN Office, Vienna, 1988–91; FCO, 1991–95; Dep. High Comr, Barbados and Eastern Caribbean, 1995–98; Counsellor, Commercial and Economic, Stockholm, 1998–2002. *Address:* 2 White Hart Meadows, Ripley, Surrey GU23 6ND.

**MATHESON, Alexander,** CVO 2016; OBE 1990; JP; FRPharmS; Lord-Lieutenant of the Western Isles, 2001–16 (Vice Lord-Lieutenant, 1994–2001); Chairman: Highlands and Islands Airports Ltd, 2001–07; Harris Tweed Authority, 2001–07; *b* 16 Nov. 1941; *s* of Alex Matheson, MB ChB and Catherine Agnes Matheson (*née* Smith), MA; *m* 1965, Irene Mary Davidson, BSc Hons, MSc; two *s* two *d*. *Educ:* Nicolson Inst., Stornoway; Robert Gordon Inst. of Technol., Aberdeen. MRPharmS 1965, FRPharmS 1993. Pharmacist. Man. Dir, 1966–82 and Chm., 1967–, Roderick Smith Ltd. Member: Stornoway Town Council, 1967–75 (Provost, 1971–75); Ross and Cromarty CC, 1967–75. Member: Stornoway Trust Estate, 1967–2009 (Chm., 1971–81); Stornoway Port Authy (formerly Pier and Harbour Commn), 1968–2010 (Chm., 1971–72 and 1991–2001); Western Isles Island Council, 1974–94 (Convener, 1982–90); Western Isles Health Bd, 1974–2001 (Chm., 1993–2001). Pres., Islands Commn of Peripheral Maritime Regions of Europe, 1988–93. Founding Chm., Hebridean Men's Cancer Support Gp, 2007–12. JP Western Is, 1971; Hon. Sheriff, Stornoway, 1972. *Recreations:* genealogy, research and lecturing on local history. *Address:* 33 Newton Street, Stornoway, Isle of Lewis HS1 2RW. *T:* (01851) 704739.

**MATHESON of Matheson, Lt Col Sir Alexander Fergus,** 8th Bt *cr* 1882, of Lochalsh, Co. Ross; 28th Chief of Clan Matheson; LVO 2013; Gentleman Usher to the Queen, since 2015; *b* 26 Aug. 1954; *o s* of Major Sir Fergus John Matheson of Matheson, 7th Bt; *S* father, 2017; *m* 1983, Katharine Davina Mary, *d* of Sir (William Richard) Michael Oswald, *qv*; two *s* one *d*. *Educ:* Eton Coll.; Durham Univ.; RMA Sandhurst; Army Staff Coll. Coldstream Guards, 1973–2001; Temp. Equerry to the Queen, 1982–84; COS, British Forces, Belize, 1992–94; Adjt, RMA Sandhurst, 1995–96; Bde Major, Household Div., 1996–98. CO Oxford Univ. OTC, 1998–2000. Exec. Dir, BSES Expeditions, 2001–05. Sec., Central Chancery, Orders of Knighthood, 2005–14. Extra Equerry to the Queen, 2006–. Mem., Royal Co. of Archers (Queen's Body Guard for Scotland), 2009–. *Recreations:* birds, bicycle, bagpipes. *Heir: s* Andrew William Fergus Matheson of Matheson, yr, *b* 12 March 1985.

**MATHESON, Christian;** MP (Lab) City of Chester, since 2015; *b* Cheshire, 2 Jan. 1968; *m* Katherine; two *d*. *Educ:* London Sch. of Econs and Pol Sci. Formerly Manager in electricity industry; roles with Unite Union. Mem., Culture, Media and Sport, subseq. Digital, Culture, Media and Sport, Select Cttee, 2015–. *Address:* House of Commons, SW1A 0AA.

**MATHESON, His Honour Duncan,** MA, LLM; QC 1989; a Circuit Judge, 2000–11. *Educ:* Rugby Sch.; Trinity Coll., Cambridge. Bencher, Inner Temple, 1994. Jun. Counsel in Legal Aid Matters, Law Soc., 1981–89; a Recorder, 1985–2000. Chairman, Legal Aid Area Committee: London S, 1989–92; London, 1992–95.

**MATHESON, Jamie Graham;** Chairman: Saracen Fund Managers, since 2014; Beatson Cancer Charity, since 2014; Aberdeen Standard Fund Managers Ltd, since 2018; *b* Glasgow, 19 May 1954; *s* of James Monteath Matheson and Marjorie Graham Matheson (*née* Todd); *m* 1990, Angela Douglas Thompson. *Educ:* Loretto Sch. FCSI 2010. Stockbroker, Parsons & Co., later Allied Provincial, 1972–96; Divl Dir, Bell Lawrie, Brewin Dolphin Gp, 1996–2002; Dir, 2002–13, Exec. Chm., 2005–13, Brewin Dolphin Hldgs plc. Director: Scottish Financial Enterprise, 2013–19; McCurrach Gp, 2018–. Non-executive Director: Scottish Radio Hldgs plc, 2000–05; Maven Income and Growth VCT 5 plc (formerly Bluehone AIM VCT2 plc), 2000–13; STV Gp plc, 2007–15; Latchways PLC, 2014–15. Dir, HMS Victory Preservation Co., 2012–. OStJ 1998. *Recreations:* sailing, field sports. *Address:* Hallmoss, Dunlop, Ayrshire KA3 4DT. *T:* (01560) 482002, *Fax:* (01560) 483094. *E:* jamie@hallmoss.com. *Clubs:* Boodle's; Royal Yacht Squadron, Royal Thames Yacht; New (Edinburgh); Western Gailes Golf; Coronado Country (Texas).

**MATHESON, Dame Jilian Norma, (Dame Jil),** DCB 2014; FAcSS; National Statistician and Chief Executive, Office for National Statistics and UK Statistics Authority, 2009–14; *b* Derby, 27 March 1953; *d* of Norman and Margaret Eileen Chambers; *m* 1983, Alan Marsh; one *s* and one step *d*. *Educ:* Ecclesbourne Sch., Duffield, Derbys; Derby Coll. of Further Educn; Univ. of Sussex (BA Hons). Office of Population Censuses and Surveys, later Office for National Statistics: social survey researcher and statistician, 1975–2014; Dep. Dir, 1998; Dir, Population and Demography, Census, 2004–08; Dir Gen. Stats Delivery, 2008–09. Non-exec. Dir, Sports Ground Safety Authy, 2018–. Chair: Cttee on Stats and Statistical Policy, OECD, 2012–14; Statistical Commn, UN, 2014; Impartiality Rev. on Statistics at the BBC, 2015–16; Member: Adv. Cttee on Maths Educn, 2016–; Council, Acad. of Social Sci., 2018–; Dep. Chair, Office for Tackling Injustices, 2019–. Trustee, NatCen, 2015–. FAcSS (AcSS 2001). Hon. DSc: Wolverhampton, 2012; Sussex, 2014; Bath, 2016. *Publications:* (with A. Marsh) Smoking Attitudes and Behaviour, 1983; Voluntary Work, 1990; Participation in Sport, 1991; contrib. articles to learned jls. *Recreations:* cricket, Derby County Football Club, opera, cinema, theatre, novels, walking. *E:* jilmatheson2@gmail.com.

**MATHESON, John Alexander,** CBE 2015; Director, Health Finance, eHealth and Analytics (formerly Health Finance, later Health Finance, eHealth and Pharmaceuticals), Scottish Government, 2008–16; *b* Dingwall, Ross-shire, 23 June 1955; *m* 1979, Sheila Judith Willans; one *s* one *d*. *Educ:* Invergordon Acad.; Heriot Watt Univ. (BA 1976); Univ. of Edinburgh (MBA 1996). Lothian Health Bd, 1979–93; Finance Director: Edinburgh

Healthcare NHS Trust, 1994–99; NHS Lothian, 2000–08. Non-exec. Dir, Telford Coll., Edinburgh, 1998–2007. Pres., CIPFA, 2015–16 (Chm., Scottish Br., 1999; Vice Pres., 2014–15). Mem., Scotch Malt Whisky Soc., 1998–. *Recreations:* golf, hill walking, malt whisky. *T:* 07774 435714. *E:* john@jamatheson.com. *Clubs:* Blackford Golf; Murrayfield Golf.

**MATHESON, Michael;** Member (SNP) Falkirk West, Scottish Parliament, since 2007 (Central Scotland, 1999–2007); Cabinet Secretary for Transport, Infrastructure and Connectivity, since 2018; *b* 8 Sept. 1970; *s* of Edward and Elizabeth Matheson. *Educ:* Queen Margaret Coll., Edinburgh (BSc Occupational Therapy); Open Univ. (BA; Dip.). Health Profession Council State Registered Occupational Therapist. Community Occupational Therapist: Social Work Dept, Highland Regl Council, 1991–93; Central Regl Council, 1993–97; Social Work Services, Stirling Council, 1997–99. SNP dep. spokesperson on health and social policy, 1997–98; Dep. Opposition spokesman for justice and land reform, 1999–2004, Opposition spokesman for culture and sport, 2004–07, Scottish Parlt; Minister for Public Health, 2011–14; Cabinet Sec. for Justice, 2014–18. Scottish Parliament: Member: Cross Party Gp on Sport, 2001; Cross Party Gp on Cuba, 2002; Co-Convenor, Cross Party Gp on Malawi, 2006; Member: Health and Sport Cttee, 2007–11; Eur. and Ext. Relns Cttee, 2010–11; End of Life Assistance (Scotland) Bill Cttee, 2010–11. Member: Ochils Mountain Rescue Team; BSES. *Recreations:* mountaineering, travel, supporting Partick Thistle FC. *Address:* Scottish Parliament, Edinburgh EH99 1SP. *T:* (0131) 348 5671, *Fax:* (0131) 348 6474; (constituency office) 15a East Bridge Street, Falkirk FK1 1YD. *T:* (01324) 629271.

**MATHESON, Stephen Charles Taylor,** CB 1993; Deputy Secretary, 1989–2000, and Deputy Chairman, Inland Revenue, 1993–2000; *b* 27 June 1939; *s* of Robert Matheson and Olive Lovick; *m* 1960, Marna Rutherford Burnett; two *s*. *Educ:* Aberdeen Grammar Sch.; Aberdeen Univ. (MA hons English Lang. and Lit., 1961). HM Inspector of Taxes, 1961–70; Principal, Bd of Inland Revenue, 1970–75; Private Sec. to Paymaster General, 1975–76, to Chancellor of the Exchequer, 1976–77; Board of Inland Revenue, 1977–2000; Project Manager, Computerisation of Pay As You Earn Project; Under Sec., 1984; Dir of IT, 1984; Comr, 1989; Dir Gen. (Management), 1989–94, (Policy and Technical), 1994–2000. CITP; FBCS (Pres., 1991–92); FIPPM (FBIPM 1996). Hon. DBA De Montfort Univ., 1994. *Publications:* Maurice Walsh, Storyteller, 1985; (contrib.) The Listowel Literary Phenomenon, 1994. *Recreations:* Scottish and Irish literature, book collecting, cooking, music.

**MATHEW, Brian Frederick,** MBE 2005; VMH; Editor, Curtis's Botanical Magazine, 1993–2002; *b* 30 Aug. 1936; *s* of Frederick Mathew and Ethel Mathew (*née* Baines); *m* 1966, Helen Margaret Briggs; one *s*. *Educ:* Oxted County Grammar Sch.; RHS Sch. of Horticulture (RHS Dip. in Horticulture (Hons) 1962). Botanist, Royal Botanic Gardens, Kew, 1967–92, Hon. Res. Fellow, 1999. Mem., RHS Horticultural Bd, 2002–04. VMH 1992. *Publications:* Dwarf Bulbs, 1973; The Genus Daphne, 1976; The Larger Bulbs, 1978; A Field Guide to Bulbs of Europe, 1981; The Iris, 1981, 2nd edn 1989; The Crocus, 1982; A Field Guide to the Bulbous Plants of Turkey, 1984; Hellebores, 1989; The Genus Lewisia, 1989; Allium Section Allium, 1996; Growing Bulbs, 1997; Bulbs: the four seasons, 1998; (ed) Genus Cyclamen, 2013. *Recreations:* gardening, photography.

**MATHEW, John Charles;** QC 1977; *b* 3 May 1927; *s* of late Sir Theobald Mathew, KBE, MC, and Lady Mathew; *m* 1952, Jennifer Jane Mathew (*née* Lagden) (*d* 2016); two *d*. *Educ:* Beaumont Coll. Served, Royal Navy, 1945–47. Called to Bar, Lincoln's Inn, 1949; apptd Junior Prosecuting Counsel to the Crown, 1959; First Sen. Prosecuting Counsel to the Crown, 1974–77. Elected a Bencher of Lincoln's Inn, 1970. *Recreations:* golf, shooting, cinema. *Address:* 45 Abingdon Court, 17 Abingdon Villas, W8 6BT. *T:* (020) 7937 7535. *Club:* Garrick.

**MATHEW, Robert Knox, (Robin);** QC 1992; *b* 22 Jan. 1945; *s* of late Robert Mathew, TD, MP and Joan Leslie (*née* Bruce); *m* 1968, Anne Rosella Elliott; one *d*. *Educ:* Eton Coll.; Trinity Coll., Dublin (BA 1967). City and financial journalist, 1968–76. Called to the Bar, Lincoln's Inn, 1974. Asst Parly Boundary Comr, 1992–98. *Recreations:* country pursuits, racing, ski-ing. *Address:* 3 Stone Buildings, Lincoln's Inn, WC2A 3XL; Church Farm, Little Barrington, Burford, Oxon OX18 5TE. *T:* (01451) 844311. *Club:* Boodle's.

**MATHEWS, Vice Adm. Sir Andrew (David Hugh),** KCB 2013 (CB 2008); FREng; Chairman: National Nuclear Laboratory, since 2016 (non-executive Director, since 2014); Babcock Naval Marine, since 2018; *b* Stanford le Hope, Essex, 27 June 1958; *s* of Hugh Leslie Mathews, OBE and Pamela Lorna Mathews (*née* Edwards); *m* 1987, Beverley Yvette Taylor; one *s* one *d*. *Educ:* Newcastle Royal Grammar Sch.; RNEC, Manadon (BSc Hons); RNC, Greenwich (MSc). BRNC, Dartmouth, 1976; nuclear engrg appts at sea and ashore; RN Staff Course, RNC Greenwich, 1989; MEO, HMS Trenchant, 1990–92; MEO, subseq. Captain Sea Trng, 1992–95; Second Sea Lord's Dept, 1995–97; Asst Dir, Nuclear Propulsion Safety, 1997–99; RCDS 2000; Mil. Asst to Chief of Defence Procurement, 2000–02; Naval Base Comdr, Devonport, 2002–05; Dir Gen. Submarines, Defence Equipment and Support, 2005–09; Chief of Materiel (Fleet) and Chief of Fleet Support to Navy Bd, 2009–13. Non-executive Director: Devonport Royal Dockyard Ltd, 2016– (Chm., 2016–); EDF Nuclear New Build Generation Co., 2016– (Special Advr, 2016); Sen. Defence Advr, Atkins, 2016. Pres., Navy Rowing, 2006–13. FREng 2009. *Recreations:* dinghy sailing, cycling, gardening, Cornwall. *Club:* Army and Navy.

**MATHEWS, Harriet Lucy,** CMG 2017; OBE 2005; HM Diplomatic Service; Policy Director, Commonwealth Summit, Cabinet Office, 2017–18; *b* Lilongwe, Malawi, 22 Dec. 1973; *d* of David Laughton Mathews and Julia Mathews; *m* 2018, David George Hamilton Frost, *qv*. *Educ:* S Hampstead High Sch.; Univ. of York (BA Hons Hist.). Entered FCO, 1997; Desk Officer, Central Africa, FCO, 1997–98; Second Sec., Brasilia, 1999–2002; Press Officer, FCO, 2003; Hd, W Africa Section, FCO, 2003–05; First Sec., Tel Aviv, 2005–08; Foreign and Commonwealth Office: Hd, Rule of Law Afghanistan Directorate, 2008–09; Dep. Hd, Climate and Energy Dept, 2009–11; Head: Africa E and W Dept, 2011–14; Ebola Task Force, 2014; Ambassador to Somalia, 2015–16. *Recreations:* cooking (and eating), travel, detective fiction, diving. *Address:* c/o Foreign and Commonwealth Office, King Charles Street, SW1A 2AH. *E:* harriet.mathews@fco.gov.uk.

**MATHEWS, Jeremy Fell,** CMG 1989; Attorney General of Hong Kong, 1988–97; *b* 14 Dec. 1941; *s* of George James and Ivy Priscilla Mathews; *m* 1st, 1968, Sophie Lee (marr. diss. 1992); two *d*; 2nd, 1992, Halima Guterres. *Educ:* Palmer's Grammar Sch., England. Qualified as solicitor, London, 1963; private practice, London, 1963–65; Dep. Dist Registrar in the High Court of Australia, Sydney, 1966–67; Hong Kong Government: Crown Counsel, 1968; Dep. Law Draftsman, 1978; Dep. Crown Solicitor, 1981; Crown Solicitor, 1982. Dep. Dist Chm., Appeals Service, 1998–2003. Chm. Council, Overseas Service Pensioners' Assoc., 2004–13. *Recreations:* reading, gardening, music. *Club:* Hong Kong.

**MATHEWS, Michael Robert;** Partner, Clifford Chance, 1971–2000; President, Law Society of England and Wales, 1998–99; *b* 3 Nov. 1941; *s* of late George Walter Mathews and Betty Mathews (*née* Willcox); *m* 1966, Ann Gieve; two *s* one *d*. *Educ:* Uppingham Sch.; King's Coll., Cambridge (MA). Admitted solicitor, 1966; joined Coward Chance (later Clifford Chance), 1963. Vice Pres. and Chm., City of London Law Soc., 1992–95; Law Society of England and Wales: Mem. Council, 1993–2000; Dep. Vice Pres. and Treas., 1996–97; Vice Pres., 1997–98. Master: City of London Solicitors' Co., 1999–2000; Carpenters' Co., 2007–08. Hon. LLD: City, 1999; Westminster, 2009. *Recreations:* walking, watching good cricket. *Address:* 12 Clare Lawn Avenue, East Sheen, SW14 8BG.

**MATHEWS, Peter Michael,** CMG 2002; Chairman, Black Country Metals Trading Ltd, since 1986; *b* 26 Oct. 1946; *s* of Cyril and Audrey Mathews; *m* 1980, Gillian Anne Hatfield (marr. diss.); one *s* one *d*; *m* 2013, Elizabeth Anne (*née* O'Connell). *Educ:* Ellesmere Coll., Shropshire; Mt Radford Sch., Exeter. UK Trade & Investment (formerly Trade Partners UK): Mem., Bd, 2001–04; Mem., Internat. Trade Develt Adv. Panel, 2001–; Chm., Engrg Sector Adv. Gp, 2006–07; Chm., Advanced Engrg Adv. Bd, 2007–. Pres., Midlands World Trade Forum, 2001–. Mem., Business Forum for Multilingualism, EC, 2007–. Member: Adv. Bd, Bureau of Internat. Recycling, Brussels, 1995–2006; Bd, British Metals Recycling Assoc., 2002–07; Bd, Internat. Reinforcing Bar Assoc., Istanbul; Chm., Convention Cttee, Bureau of Internat. Recycling, 1995–. Nat. Pres., British Metal Fedn, 1997–99. Pres., Dudley Chamber of Commerce, 2002–05; Chm., Black Country Consortium, 2009–; Member: Bd, Black Country Chamber of Commerce, 2002– (Pres., 2007–10); Council, Birmingham Chamber of Commerce, 2002–. Mem., Internat. Adv. Bd, CBI, 2006–10. UKTI Trade Ambassador, West Midlands. Chm., West Midlands Partnership Canal and River Trust, 2012–. Co. Pres., RBL, Staffs, 2013–; Past Pres., Kinver Constitutional Club. MLex 1996; Mem., Inst. of Cast Metal Engrs, 2002; FInstD 1997. FRSA 1990. Hon. Life Mem., Ulster Metals Assoc., 1990. *Recreations:* theatre, golf, snooker, travel. *E:* peter@bcmetals.com.

**MATHEWSON, Sir George (Ross),** Kt 1999; CBE 1985; BSc, PhD, MBA; FRSE, CEng, MIEE; Chairman: Royal Bank of Scotland Group, 2001–06 (Director, 1987–2006; Deputy Chairman, 2000–01); Royal Bank of Scotland, 2001–06 (Director, 1987–2006); National Westminster Bank, 2001–06; Cheviot Asset Management Ltd, since 2006; *b* 14 May 1940; *s* of George Mathewson and Charlotte Gordon (*née* Ross); *m* 1966, Sheila Alexandra Graham (*née* Bennett); two *s*. *Educ:* Perth Academy; St Andrews Univ. (BSc, PhD); Canisius Coll., Buffalo, NY (MBA). Assistant Lecturer, St Andrews Univ., 1964–67; various posts in Research & Development, Avionics Engineering, Bell Aerospace, Buffalo, NY, 1967–72; joined Industrial & Commercial Finance Corp., Edinburgh, 1972; Area Manager, Aberdeen, 1974, and Asst General Manager and Director, 1979; Chief Exec. and Mem., Scottish Develt Agency, 1981–87; Royal Bank of Scotland Group: Dir of Strategic Planning and Develt, 1987–90; Dep. Gp Chief Exec., 1990–92; Gp Chief Exec., 1992–2000. Director: Scottish Investment Trust Ltd, 1981–2009; IIF Inc., 2001–06; Santander Central Hispano, 2001–04; Stagecoach Group plc, 2006–13 (Chm., 2010–13); Chairman: Old Oak (formerly Toscafund) Hldgs Ltd, 1996–; Wood Mackenzie Ltd, 2007–09; Arrow Global Ltd, 2009–15; Shawbrook Bank Ltd, 2010–15. Chm., Council of Econ. Advrs to the Scottish Govt, 2007–10; Mem., Financial Reporting Council, 2004–06. Pres., BBA, 2002–04. Chairman: Glasgow Garden Fest. 1988 Ltd, 1986–87; Bd of Trustees, Royal Botanic Garden, Edinburgh, 2007–11. FCIBS 1994; CCMI (CBIM 1985); FRSE 1988. Hon. LLD: Dundee, 1983; St Andrews, 2000; DUniv Glasgow, 2001; Dr *hc* Edinburgh, 2002. *Publications:* various articles on engineering/finance. *Recreations:* Rugby, tennis, business, hill-walking, ski-ing, cycling. *Address:* Merklands House, Ballintuim, Blairgowrie, Perthshire PH10 7NN. *Club:* New (Edinburgh).

**MATHEWSON, Hew Byrne,** CBE 2010; FDSRCSE; Principal Dental Surgeon, Edinburgh, since 1985; President, 2003–09, Chair, 2009, General Dental Council; Chair, Scottish Dental Practice Board, 2012–19; *b* 18 Nov. 1949; *s* of late Alexander M. Mathewson and Dorothy W. Mathewson; *m* 1971, Lorna A. M. McConnachie; one *s* one *d*. *Educ:* High Sch. of Glasgow; Glasgow Univ. (BDS 1974); Univ. of Wales, Cardiff (LLM 1990). DGDP 1992; FDSRCSE 1995; FDSRCS 2007; Fellow, Internat. Coll. of Dentists, 2017. Associate Dental Surgeon, Wishaw and Canterbury, 1974–77. Asst Dir, Dental Studies, Univ. of Edinburgh, 1987–99; Regl Gen. Practice Vocational Trng Advr, SE Scotland, 1988–96. Chm., Scottish Gen. Dental Services Cttee, 1991–97 and 2010–12; Vice-Chm., UK Gen. Dental Services Cttee, 2000–03; Chm. Interim Bd, Mental Health Tribunal for Scotland Admin, 2008–09. Member: GDC, 1996–2009 (Pres., 2003–09); Council for Healthcare Regulatory Excellence (formerly for Regulation of Health Care Professionals), 2003–08 (Vice-Chm., 2005–06); Council for Registration of Forensic Practitioners, 2006–11; Adv. Council on Misuse of Drugs, 2010–13. Pres., Conf. of Orders and Assimilated Bodies of Dental Practitioners in Europe, 2006–08. Special Advr to Med. and Dental Defence Union of Scotland, 2010–13; Mem. Adv. Bd, Wesleyan Assurance, 2010–. Lay Mem., Appeals Cttee, ICAEW, 2006–12. Chair, Scottish Council, MS Soc., 2012–15. Fellow, British Dental Assoc., 2011–. Mem. Editl Bd, British Dental Jl, 1992–2003. *Recreations:* walking, fishing, travel, carpentry, theatre and cinema, collecting art. *Address:* 176–8 St Johns Road, Edinburgh EH12 8BE.

**MATHEWSON, Iain Arthur Gray,** CMG 2004; HM Diplomatic Service, retired; *b* 16 March 1952; *s* of late John Gray Mathewson and Jane Mathewson (now Murray); *m* 1983, Jennifer Bloch; one *s* one *d*. *Educ:* Downside Sch.; Corpus Christi Coll., Cambridge. HM Customs and Excise, 1974–77; DHSS, 1977–80; FCO, 1980; First Secretary: UK Mission to UN, NY, 1981–84; Warsaw, 1985–88; FCO, 1989–93; Counsellor, Prague, 1993–96; FCO, 1996–2006. Adviser: Citigroup, 2007–09; Detica plc, 2007–09; Candole Partners, 2007–09; Associate Fellow, Internat. Security Prog., Chatham House, 2008–16. Trustee, Alexandra Rose Charities, 2010–16. *Recreations:* golf, music. *Clubs:* Beefsteak; Berkshire Golf, St Enodoc Golf.

**MATHIAS, Prof. Christopher Joseph,** DPhil, DSc; FRCP, FMedSci; Professor of Neurovascular Medicine, University of London, 1991–2013, at Imperial College London (St Mary's Hospital) (formerly Imperial College School of Medicine (St Mary's Hospital), Imperial College of Science, Technology and Medicine), and Institute of Neurology, University College London; Emeritus Professor, UCL Queen Square Institute of Neurology (formerly UCL Institute of Neurology), University College London, since 2014; Consultant Physician: St Mary's Hospital, since 1982; National Hospital for Neurology and Neurosurgery, since 1985; Hospital of St John and St Elizabeth, since 2012; *b* 16 March 1949; *s* of late Lt Elias Mathias, IN and Hilda Mathias (*née* Pereira); *m* 1977, Rosalind (Lindy) Margaret, *d* of late Ambrose Jolleys, Cons. Paediatric Surgeon and of Betty Jolleys; two *s* one *d*. *Educ:* Cathedral and John Connon High Sch., Bombay; St Aloysius Sch., Visakhapatnam; St Joseph's E. H. Sch., Bangalore; St John's Med. Coll., Bangalore Univ. (MB BS 1971); Worcester Coll., Oxford; Wolfson Coll., Oxford (DPhil 1976); Univ. of London (DSc 1995). LRCSE, LRCPSGlas 1974; MRCP 1978, FRCP 1987. Hse Officer, 1971–72, SHO (Medicine), 1972, St Martha's Hosp., Bangalore; Rhodes Schol., Univ. of Oxford, 1972–75; Res. Officer and Hon. Registrar, Dept of Neurology, Churchill Hosp., Oxford, 1972–76; Clinical Asst and Res. Fellow, Nat. Spinal Injuries Centre, Stoke Mandeville Hosp., 1973–76; Sen. Hse Officer, Dept of Medicine, RPMS/Hammersmith Hosp., 1976–77; Registrar in Medicine, St Mary's Hosp., Portsmouth and Dept of Renal

Medicine, Univ. of Southampton, 1977–79; Wellcome Trust Sen. Res. Fellow in Clinical Sci. at St Mary's Hosp. Med. Sch., 1979–84; Wellcome Trust Sen. Lectr in Med. Sci., St Mary's Hosp. Med. Sch. and Inst. of Neurol., 1984–92. Consultant Physician, Western Eye Hosp., 1982–98. Prof. Ruitinga Foundn Award and Vis. Prof., Acad. Med. Centre, Univ. of Amsterdam, 1988; Nimmo Vis. Prof., Univ. of Adelaide, 1996; Visiting Professor: Univ. of Hawaii, 1999; Univ. of Hong Kong, 2008. Dr J. Thomas Meml Oration, St John's Med. Coll., Bangalore Univ., 1988; Lectures: Lord Florey Meml, and Dorothy Mortlock, Royal Adelaide Hosp., Univ. of Adelaide, 1991; BP Regl, RCP, 1992; Thailand Neurological Soc., 1995; Sir Hugh Cairns Meml, Adelaide, 1996; Allan Birch Meml, London, 1997; Sir Gordon Holmes, London, 1998; Abbie Meml, Univ. of Adelaide, 1999; Coll., RCP, 2001; Sir Robert Menzies Meml Foundn, Sydney, 2001; Wahler Meml, London Jewish Med. Soc., 2002; Inaugural, Portuguese Autonomic Soc., Lisbon, 2002; Prof. Dr R. L. Müller Meml, Univ. of Erlangen, 2002; Prof. Athasit Vejajiva, Bangkok, 2003; Sir Roger Bannister, 2004, Chelsea Therapeutics, 2007, Jt Eur. Fedn of Autonomic Socs and Amer. Autonomic Soc.; Prof. Krishnamoorthy, Srinivas, Chennai, 2005; Keynote, 58th Congress of Japanese Neurovegetative Soc., Chiba, 2005; Valsalva, Bologna, 2006; 20th Shri K. Gopalakrishna, Chennai, 2006; Roche, Internal Medicine Assoc. of Aust. and NZ, 2007; Northern Communities Health Foundn, Adelaide, 2007; Swiss Autonomic Soc., Berne, 2008; G. M. Mascarenhas Oration, St John's Medical Coll. N Atlantic Chapter, Florida, 2008; British Peripheral Nerve Soc., London 2008; 19th World Congress of Neurol., Bangkok, 2009; 12th Eur. Fedn of Autonomic Socs, Taormina, 2010; RSocMed, 2013; Plenary, Jt Internat. Soc. of Autonomic Neurosci. and Eur. Fedn of Autonomic Socs, Giessen, 2013; 8th World Congress of Neurorehabilitation, Istanbul, 2014; Plenary, Eur. Fedn of Autonomic Socs, Malaga, 2014; Streeten, Amer. Autonomic Soc., Puerto Rico, 2014; Conclave Lectures, Nat. Inst. of Mental Health and Neuroscis, Bangalore, 2015; 35th T. S. Srinivasan Gold Medal Award and Endowment Oration, Chennai, 2015; Eur. Acad. of Neurol., Berlin, 2015; RCPsych, Birmingham, 2015; 7th British Obesity and Metabolic Surgical Soc. Scientific Meeting, Cardiff, 2016; Internat. Lyme Disease Symposium, London, 2016; Global Neuroscis, Chennai, 2017; Internat. Congress of Parkinson's Disease and Movement Disorders, Vancouver, 2017; 50th Anniv. Congress, Ceylon Coll. of Physicians, Colombo, Sri Lanka, 2017; Neuro-Immunology Symposium, Oxford, 2017; Diabetes UK, London, 2018; Sir Roger Bannister, RSocMed, 2019; Kamla BK Anand Oration, All India Inst. of Med. Scis, New Delhi, 2019. Chairman: Clinical Autonomic Res. Soc., 1987–90 (first Sec., 1982–86); Res. Cttee, World Fedn of Neurol., 1993–97 (Mem., 1989–93); Chm., Scientific Panel, 1994–99, Mem., Task Force, 2004–06, Lead, Task Force on Orthostatic Intolerance, 2008–, European Fedn of Neurol Socs; Pres., Eur. Fedn of Autonomic Socs, 1998–2004; Member: Scientific Cttee, Internat. Spinal Res. Trust, 1996–2008; Bd of Dirs, Amer. Autonomic Soc., 1996–2004; Sec. of State's Hon. Med. Adv. Panel on Driving and Disorders of the Nervous System, 2004–09; Task Force, Amer. Spinal Injury Assoc., 2004–07; Mem. and Chm., MSA-Autonomic Gp, Consensus Conference on MSA, Amer. Acad. of Neurology, Boston, 2007. Consultant, ESA, 1997–2000; Mem., Jt ESA/NASA Neuroscience Rev. Panel, Washington DC, 1997. Non-exec. Dir, W London Mental Health Trust, 2008–10. Mem., NW Thames Regl Adv. Cttee for Distinction Awards, 1999–2001; Chm., Dr P. M. Shankland (Pushpa Chopra) Charitable Trust Prize Fund, 1998–2003; Chair, Autonomic Gp, Ehlers-Danlos Internat. Consortium, Ehlers-Danlos Soc., 2018–. Mem., Bd of Govs, Nat. Soc. for Epilepsy, 2004–08. Patron: Multiple System Atrophy Trust (formerly Autonomic Disorders Assoc. Sarah Matheson Trust), 1997–2018; STARS (Syncope Trust), 2001–; Graham Hughes Internat. Charity for Hughes (Antiphospholipid) Syndrome, 2017–; Founder Trustee, Autonomic Charitable Trust, 2012–; Trustee, Stoke Mandeville Spinal Res., 2017–19. FMedSci 2001. Founder Editor-in-Chief, 1991–95, Co-Editor-in-Chief, 1995–2013, Clinical Autonomic Res.; Member, Editorial Board: Hypertension, 1990–93; Jl of Pharmaceutical Medicine, 1991–95; Functional Neurol., 1990–2003; High Blood Pressure and Cardiovascular Prevention, 1992–2005; Jl of Hypertension, 1994–97; Parkinsonism and Related Disorders, 1995–2005, 2008–11; Internat. Jl of Evidence-Based Healthcare, 2007–12. Dr hc Lisbon, 2007. *Publications:* (ed with Prof. M. Weber) Mild Hypertension: current controversies and new approaches, 1984; (ed with Prof. P. Sever) Concepts in Hypertension: a festschrift for Prof. Sir Stanley Peart, 1989; (ed with Sir Roger Bannister) Autonomic Failure: a textbook of clinical disorders of the autonomic nervous system, 3rd edn 1992, 5th edn 2013; chaps in neurol. and cardiovascular textbooks; papers on nervous system and hormonal control of circulation in neurological, cardiovascular and other medical disorders. *Recreations:* our four grandchildren, gardening, watching cricket and football, observing human (and canine) behaviour. *Address:* Meadowcroft, West End Lane, Stoke Poges, Bucks SL2 4NE. *E:* profmathiasautonomic@gmail.com. *Clubs:* Athenæum, MCC, Royal Society of Medicine; Vincent's (Oxford).

**MATHIAS, Lt Col David Ashley;** Vice Lord-Lieutenant of Dyfed, since 2019; b Llanelli, 11 Oct. 1949; s of William Graham Mathias and Ceinwen Mathias; m 1972, Susan Mary Anthony; two s. *Educ:* Llanelly Boys' Grammar Sch.; BRNC. RN, 1967–80; Regular Army, 1981–91. TA, 1991–2010. DL Dyfed, 2009. Hon. Rotarian, 2014.

**MATHIAS, Surg. Rear-Adm. (D) Frank Russell Bentley;** retired 1985; Director, Naval Dental Services, 1983–85, and Deputy Director of Defence Dental Services (Organisation), Ministry of Defence, 1985; b 27 Dec. 1927; s of Thomas Bentley Mathias and Phebe Ann Mathias; m 1954, Margaret Joyce (née Daniels); one s one d. *Educ:* Narberth Grammar Sch.; Guy's Hosp., London. LDSRCS Eng. 1952. House Surgeon, Sussex County Hosp., Brighton, 1952–53; joined RN, 1953; principal appointments: Staff Dental Surgeon, Flag Officer Malta, 1972; Flotilla Dental Surgeon, Flag Officer Submarines, 1972–74; Comd Dental Surgeon, Flag Officer Naval Air Comd, 1974–76; Dep. Dir, Naval Dental Services, 1976–80; Comd Dental Surgeon to C-in-C Naval Home Comd, 1980–83. QHDS 1982–85. OStJ 1981.
See also Rear Adm. P. B. Mathias.

**MATHIAS, (Jonathan) Glyn,** OBE 2016; Chair, Advisory Committee for Wales, Ofcom, 2017–18 (Member, since 2007); b 19 Feb. 1945; s of late Roland Glyn Mathias and Mary Annie (née Hawes); m 2000, Ann Bowen (née Hughes); one s two d. *Educ:* Llandovery Coll., Carmarthenshire; Jesus Coll., Oxford (MA); Univ. of Southampton (MSc). Reporter, South Wales Echo, 1967–70; News Asst, BBC Southampton, 1970–73; ITN: Political Reporter, London, 1973–81; Political Editor, 1981–86; Asst Editor, 1986–91; Controller, Public Affairs, 1991–93; Chief Political Correspondent, 1993–94; BBC Wales: Political Editor, 1994–99; Manager, Public Affairs, 1999–2000. Sen. Lectr, British Politics, UWIC, 2001–03 (Hon. Fellow, 2004). Mem., Electoral Commn, 2001–08. Mem., Content Bd, Ofcom, 2011–15. Chm., Membership Panel, Dwr Cymru/Welsh Water, 2013–18. Chm., Govs, Ysgol y Bannau, 2010–12. Pres., Brecknock Soc., 2017–. Chm., Editl Bd, New Welsh Rev., 2011–15. *Publications:* (ed) ITN Election Factbook, 1987; (contrib.) Televising Democracies, 1992; Raising an Echo, 2014. *Recreation:* family life. *Address:* Harddfan, Avenue Court, Brecon, Powys LD3 9BE. *T:* (01874) 623368. *E:* glynmathias@btinternet.com. *Club:* Brecon Rugby.

**MATHIAS, Pauline Mary;** Headmistress, More House School, 1974–89; b 4 Oct. 1928; d of Francis and Hilda Donovan; m 1954, Prof. Anthony Peter Mathias; two s. *Educ:* La Retraite High School; Bedford College, London (BA Hons; DipEd). Head of English Dept, London Oratory Sch., 1954–64; Sen. Lectr in English and Admissions Tutor, Coloma Coll. of Education, 1964–74. Mem., ITC, 1991–96. Pres., GSA, 1982–83; Vice-Pres., Women's Careers Foundn, 1985–89; Chairman: ISIS, 1984–86; GBGSA, 1994–98 (Dep. Chm., 1992–94). Governor: Westminster Cathedral Choir Sch., 1978–2003; ESU, 1986–92; St Felix Sch., Southwold, 1986–95 (Chm., 1990–95); London Oratory Sch., 1987–2011 (Dep. Chm., 1994–2000); St Mary's Sch., Ascot, 1995–2002 (Trustee, 2006–17); Godolphin and Latymer Sch., 1995–98. *Address:* 18 Lee Road, Aldeburgh, Suffolk IP15 5HG.

**MATHIAS, Rear Adm. Philip Bentley,** MBE 1991; Partner, Ethos, 2013–14; Director, Better Cities Ltd, since 2014; b Plymouth, 21 May 1958; s of Surg. Rear-Adm. (D) Frank Russell Bentley Mathias, qv; m 1985, Jane Amice Cantan; one s one d. *Educ:* Churcher's Coll., Petersfield; BRNC Dartmouth. Joined BRNC Dartmouth, 1977; CO, HMS Otus (Gulf War), 1988–91; Sen. Trng Officer, BRNC, 1992; CO, HMS Trenchant (Arctic Ops), 1993–94; Staff of Second Sea Lord, 1995–98; Exec. Officer, HMS Invincible (Balkans conflict), 1998–99; RN HQ, MoD, 2000–03; Pres., Admiralty Interview Bd, 2004; Director: Nuclear Policy, MoD, 2006–09; Strategic Defence Rev. (Nuclear), 2010–12. Gov., Duke of York Royal Military Sch., Dover, 2013–16. *Recreations:* keeping unusual tropical fish, big game fishing in Kenya. *E:* philipbmathias@gmail.com.

**MATHIAS, Sean Gerard;** writer and director; b 14 March 1956; s of John Frederick Mathias and Anne Josephine Patricia Mathias (née Harding). *Educ:* Bishop Vaughan Comprehensive Sch., Swansea. Artistic Dir, Haymarket Th., 2009–10. *Writer: plays:* Cowardice, Ambassadors, 1983; A Prayer for Wings, Edinburgh Fest. and Bush Th., 1985; Infidelities, Edinburgh Fest. and Donmar Warehouse, 1985; Poor Nanny, King's Head, Islington, 1989; Swansea Boys, RNT Studio, 1991; *screenplay:* The Lost Language of Cranes, BBC, 1991. *Director: film:* Bent, 1996 (Prix de la Jeunesse, Cannes, 1997); *plays:* Exceptions, New End, 1989; Bent, RNT, transf. Garrick, 1990; Uncle Vanya, RNT, 1992; Ghosts, Sherman Th., Cardiff, 1993; Les Parents Terribles, RNT, 1994; Design for Living, Donmar, transf. Gielgud, 1994; Indiscretions, NY, 1995; A Little Night Music, RNT, 1995; Marlene, Oldham, transf. Lyric, 1996, NY, 1999; Antony and Cleopatra, RNT, 1998; Suddenly Last Summer, Comedy, 1999; Servicemen, NY, 2001; Dance of Death, NY, 2001, Lyric, 2003, Sydney, 2004; The Elephant Man, NY, 2002; Company, Washington, 2002; Antigone, Cape Town, 2004; Aladdin, Old Vic, 2004–05; Shoreditch Madonna, Soho Th., 2005; The Cherry Orchard, LA, 2006; Triptych, Johannesburg, 2007, Southwark Playhouse, 2008; Ring Round the Moon, Playhouse, 2008; Waiting for Godot, UK tour then Th. Royal, Haymarket, 2009–10, Internat. tour, 2010; Breakfast at Tiffany's, Th. Royal, Haymarket, 2009; Heavenly Ivy, The Ivy, 2010; The Syndicate, Chichester Festival Th., UK tour, 2011; Breakfast at Tiffany's, NY, 2013; No Man's Land, Berkeley Rep., 2013, UK tour then Wyndham's, 2016; Waiting for Godot and No Man's Land as Two Plays in Rep, NY, 2013–14; The Unbuilt City, NY, 2015; The Exorcist, Birmingham Rep, 2016, transf. Phoenix, 2017; Gently Down the Stream, NY, 2017, Park Th., 2019; Savage Love, NY, 2018; Ian McKellen on Stage, UK tour, 2019. Dir of the Year, Evening Standard Awards, and Critics' Circle Awards, 1994; Evening Standard Award for Best Revival, 2016. *Publications: plays:* A Prayer for Wings, 1985; Infidelities, 1985; *novella:* Manhattan Mourning, 1989. *Address:* c/o St John Donald, United Agents, 12–26 Lexington Street, W1F 0LE. *T:* (020) 3214 0800.

**MATHIAS, Tania Wyn;** NHS Medical Doctor; d of Roger Wynn Mathias and Vivienne Desiree Mathias. *Educ:* St Paul's Girls' Sch.; St Catherine's Coll. and Christ Church, Oxford (BA, BM, BCh Hons). Refugee Affairs Officer and Health Officer, UNRWA, 1991–93. Mem. (C) Richmond upon Thames LBC, 2010–15. MP (C) Twickenham, 2015–17; contested (C) same seat, 2017. *Recreations:* bird watching, documentary film making.

**MATHIES, Monika W.;** see Wulf-Mathies.

**MATHIESON, Guy Alastair David;** His Honour Judge Mathieson; a Circuit Judge, since 2019; b Bolton, 2 Nov. 1968; s of Robin Edward Alexander Mathieson and Elizabeth Anne Colley; m 1999, Jill; two s. *Educ:* Bolton Sch.; University Coll. of Swansea (Ancient Hist. and Latin); Chester Coll. of Law. Called to the Bar, Middle Temple, 1993; barrister, 1993–2019; a Recorder, 2008–19. *Recreations:* running, cycling, Cub Scout Leader, supporting Rochdale AFC, walking in Lake District. *Address:* Wood Green Crown Court, Woodhall House, Lordship Lane, Wood Green, N22 5LF. *T:* (020) 8826 4100. *E:* hhj.guy.mathieson@ejudiciary.net.

**MATHIESON, Rt Hon. Dame Janet Hilary;** see Smith, Rt Hon. Dame J. H.

**MATHIESON, Katherine Theresa Stewart;** Chief Executive, British Science Association, since 2016; b Durham, 17 Aug. 1975; d of Martin and Susan Mathieson. *Educ:* Selwyn Coll., Cambridge (BSc Hons Natural Scis 1996); Imperial Coll. London (MSc Sci. Communication 1999); City Univ., London (Postgrad. Dip. Information Scis 2003); Cass Business Sch. (Postgrad. Dip. Voluntary Sector Mgt (Dist.) 2011). GP Rep., Merck, Sharp & Dohme, 1996–98; Sci. Information Officer, Sci. Line, 1999–2000; Information Scientist, Forensic Sci. Service, 2000–02; Learning Prog. Manager, 2002–06, Hd, Future Innovators Prog., 2006–09, NESTA; Dir of Educn, 2009–13, Dir of Progs, 2013–16, British Sci. Assoc. Trustee: Royal Commonwealth Soc., 2014–; Enthuse Trust, 2016–. *Recreations:* Guiding, volunteering, travel. *Address:* British Science Association, Wellcome Wolfson Building, 165 Queen's Gate, SW7 5HD. *T:* (020) 7019 4935. *E:* katherine.mathieson@britishscienceassociation.org.

**MATHIESON, Prof. Peter William,** PhD; FRCP, FRCPE, FMedSci; Principal and Vice-Chancellor, University of Edinburgh, since 2018; b Colchester, 18 April 1959; s of William Archibald Mathieson and Elizabeth Alice Mathieson (née Thorn); m 1982, Dr Christina Dowds; one s one d. *Educ:* Humphry Davy Grammar Sch., Penzance (head boy 1977); London Hosp. Med. Coll., Univ. of London (MB BS Hons 1983); Univ. of Cambridge (PhD 1992). MRCP 1986, FRCP 1998; FRCPE 2018. MRC Trng Fellow, 1988–91, MRC Clinician Scientist, 1991–95, Univ. of Cambridge; Dir of Studies, Clin. Medicine, Christ's Coll., Cambridge, 1992–95; University of Bristol: Prof. of Renal Medicine, 1995–2008; Prof. of Medicine, 2008–14; Dean, Faculty of Medicine and Dentistry, 2008–14; Pres., Univ. of Hong Kong, 2014–18. FMedSci 1999. *Publications:* Manual of Nephrology, 2004; 17 chapters in books; over 250 articles in learned jls. *Recreations:* walking, horse riding, spending time with family. *Address:* Principal's Office, University of Edinburgh, Old College, South Bridge, Edinburgh EH8 9YL. *T:* (0131) 650 2150. *E:* principal@ed.ac.uk. *Clubs:* Caledonian; New (Edinburgh).

**MATHRANI, Ranjit;** Chairman, MW Eat Ltd, since 1989; b Bombay, 11 May 1943; s of Kewalram Pribhdas Mathrani, ICS and Kalawati Mathrani; m 1986, Namita Panjabi. *Educ:* Cathedral Sch., Bombay; Sidney Sussex Coll., Cambridge (Mech. Scis); St Stephen's Coll., Univ. of Delhi (BSc Hons 1st Cl.); Univ. of Manchester (Dip. Mgt Scis); Birkbeck Coll., Univ. of London (MSc Econs). Asst Principal, DEA, 1967–69; Asst Principal, Industrial Technol. Div., Ministry of Technol., 1969–71; Principal, ECGD, 1971–72; Department of

Trade and Industry: Principal, Industrial Develt Unit, 1972–73; Dir, Develt. and Sen. Manager, NW Regl Office, 1973–76; Sen. Principal, Industrial Develt Unit, 1976–78; Asst Sec. and Dir, Projects and Export Policy Div., 1978–82; Exec. Dir, Lazard Brothers & Co. Ltd, 1982–87; Man. Dir, Standard Chartered Merchant Bank, subseq. West Merchant Bank Ltd, 1988–94; Chm., Vanguard Capital Ltd, 1994–. Dir, UKHospitality (formerly BHA), 2016–. Trustee, Safer London Foundn, 2010–14. High Sheriff Gtr London, 2010–11. *Recreations:* travel, architecture, mountain walking, music, food and wine, theatre, opera, politics, economics, technology. *Clubs:* Royal Automobile, Home House; Willingdon (Mumbai).

**MATLOCK, Prof. Jack Foust;** American career diplomat; George F. Kennan Professor, Institute for Advanced Study, Princeton, 1996–2001; *b* 1 Oct. 1929; *s* of late Jack F. Matlock and of Nellie Matlock (*née* McSwain); *m* 1949, Rebecca Burrum; four *s* one *d*. *Educ:* Duke Univ. (BA 1950); Columbia Univ. (MA 1952; PhD 2013). Editor and translator on Current Digest of the Soviet Press, 1952–53; Russian language and literature Instructor, Dartmouth Coll., 1953–56; joined US Foreign Service, 1956; served in Moscow, Austria, Ghana, Zanzibar, Tanzania; Vis. Prof. of Political Science, Vanderbilt Univ., 1978–79; Dep. Dir, Foreign Service Inst., 1979–80; Chargé d'Affaires, Moscow, 1981; Ambassador to Czechoslovakia, 1981; Special Asst to President for Nat. Security Affairs and Sen. Dir, European and Soviet Affairs on Nat. Security Council Staff, 1983–86; Ambassador to Soviet Union, 1987–91. Kathryn and Shelby Cullom Davis Prof., Columbia Univ., 1993–96. Vis. Prof. Princeton Univ., 2001–04; Sol Linowitz Prof. of Internat. Relns, Hamilton Coll., 2006; Cyrus Vance Prof., Mount Holyoke Coll., 2007; Rubenstein Fellow and Vis. Scholar, Duke Univ., 2015–17. Masaryk Award, 1983; Superior Honor Award, Dept of State, 1981; Presidential Meritorious Service Award, 1984, 1987. *Publications:* Handbook to Russian edn of Stalin's Works, 1972; Autopsy on an Empire: the American Ambassador's account of the collapse of the Soviet Union, 1995; Reagan and Gorbachev: how the Cold War ended, 2004; Superpower Illusions: how myths and false ideologies led America astray - and how to return to reality, 2010; articles on US-Soviet relations. *Address:* 32 Wagoner Hill Road, Fayetteville, TN 37334, USA. *W:* www.JackMatlock.com. *Club:* Century Association (NY).

**MATOVU, Harold Nsamba;** QC 2010; *b* Mengo, Uganda; *s* of Leonard and Ruth Matovu; *m* 1994, Emma Rose Peto; three *s*. *Educ:* Eton Coll.; Balliol Coll., Oxford (BA Hons Lit.Hum. 1985); Central London Poly. (DipLaw 1986). Called to the Bar, Inner Temple, 1988, Bencher, 2012; in practice as barrister, specialising in commercial law, 1989–; Dep. Counsel to BSE Inquiry, 1998–2000. Member: Professional Conduct Complaints Cttee, 1996–98, Professional Standards Cttee, 2005–06, Bar Council; London Common Law and Commercial Bar Assoc., 1989–; Commercial Bar Assoc., 2000–. *Recreations:* jazz, classical music, theatre, literature, cricket. *Address:* Brick Court Chambers, 7–8 Essex Street, WC2R 3LD. *Club:* Garrick.

**MATSUURA, Koïchiro;** Director-General of UNESCO, 1999–2009; *b* 29 Sept. 1937; *s* of Seichi and Kiyoko Matsuura; *m* 1967, Takako Kirikae; two *s*. *Educ:* Univ. of Tokyo; Haverford Coll., USA (MBA). Counsellor, Embassy of Japan, USA, 1977–80; Consul Gen., Hong Kong, 1985–88; Dir-Gen., Econ. Co-operation Bureau, 1988–90, N American Affairs Bureau, 1990–92, Min. of Foreign Affairs; Dep. Minister for Foreign Affairs (Sherpa for Japan at G-7 Summit), 1992–94; Ambassador of Japan to: Djibouti, 1994–99; France, 1994–99; Andorra, 1996–99. Chm., World Heritage Cttee, UNESCO, 1998–99. Bintang Jasa Utama (Indonesia), 1993; Grand Officer, Nat. Order of Merit (France), 1994; Comdr, Nat. Order of 27 June (Djibouti), 1997. *Publications:* In the Forefront of Economic Co-operation Diplomacy, 1990; History of Japan-United States Relations, 1992; Focusing on the Future: Japan's global role in a changing world, 1993; The G-7 Summit: its history and perspectives, 1994; Development and Perspectives of the Relations between Japan and France, 1995; Japanese Diplomacy at the Dawn of the 21st Century, 1998. *Recreations:* Go, tennis, golf, mountain climbing.

**MATT;** see Pritchett, Matthew.

**MATTAJ, Iain William,** PhD; FRS 1999; FRSE; Director General, European Molecular Biology Laboratory, 2005–18; *b* 5 Oct. 1952; *s* of George Eugeniusz Mattaj and Jane Margaret Mattaj; *m* 1974, Ailsa McCrindle. *Educ:* Edinburgh Univ. (BSc); Leeds Univ. (PhD 1980). Postdoctoral research: Friedrich Miescher Inst., Basel, 1979–82; Biocenter, Basel Univ., 1982–85; Gp Leader, 1985–90, Programme Co-ordinator, 1990–99, Scientific Dir, 1999–2005, EMBL Heidelberg. Exec. Ed., EMBO Jl, 1990–2004. Mem., EMBO, 1989. Pres., Ribonucleic Acid Soc., 1998–2000. FRSE 2000; FMedSci 2016. *Publications:* numerous contribs to scientific jls. *Recreations:* squash, music, literature.

**MATTHEW, Christopher Charles Forrest;** writer and broadcaster; *b* Lewisham, 8 May 1939; *s* of Leonard Douglas and Doris Janet Matthew; *m* 1979, Wendy Mary Mallinson (*née* Whitaker); two *s* and one step *d*. *Educ:* King's Sch., Canterbury (King's Schol.); St Peter's Coll., Oxford (BA 1963; MA 1989). Copywriter, various London advertising agencies, 1964–70; Ed., The Times Travel Guide, 1972–74; columnist, Punch, Vogue, Daily Telegraph, Observer, Daily Mail, Sunday Times, 1976–2006; presenter, programmes for BBC Radio 4, including: Something to Declare, 1977–82; The Travelling Show, 1982–85; Points of Departure, 1980–82; Invaders, 1982–83; Fourth Column, 1990–93; Plain Tales from the Rhododendrons, 1991; Cold Print, 1992; A Nest of Singing Birds, 1996; (with Alan Coren) Freedom Pass, 2003–05; (with Des Lynam) Touchline Tales, 2010–12; (with Terry Waite) Freedom Pass Special, 2012; (with Martin Jarvis) Grey Shorts and Sandals, 2013; The Sage of Cricklewood, 2014; (with Martin Jarvis) Jarvis and Matthew, 2016; contrib. short stories for Original Shorts series, 2005–11; *radio plays:* A Portrait of Richard Hillary, 1980; Madonna's Plumber, 2003; A Nightingale Sang in Fernhurst Road, 2007; *stage play:* Summoned by Betjeman, Yvonne Arnaud Th., Guildford, and tour, 2002; *film:* Three More Men in a Boat, BBC TV, 1993; *television:* The Good Guys, LWT, 1993. *Publications:* A Different World: stories of great hotels, 1974; Diary of a Somebody, 1978; Loosely Engaged, 1980; The Long-Haired Boy, 1980 (adapted for TV as A Perfect Hero, 1991); The Crisp Report, 1981; (with Benny Green) Three Men in a Boat (annotated edn), 1982; The Junket Man, 1983; How to Survive Middle Age, 1983; Family Matters, 1987; The Amber Room, 1995; A Nightingale Sang in Fernhurst Road, 1998; Now We Are Sixty, 1999; Knocking On, 2001; Now We Are Sixty (and a Bit), 2003; Summoned by Balls, 2005; When We Were Fifty, 2007; The Man Who Dropped the Le Creuset on his Toe, 2013; Dog Treats, 2014; A Bus Pass Named Desire, 2016; The Old Man and the Knee, 2017; A Triple-Decker Treat: collected poems for old dogs and young hearts, 2019. *Recreations:* golfing, sailing small waters, lunching with friends, walking in the country with a dog. *Address:* Jonathan Pegg Literary Agency, 67 Wingate Square, SW4 0AF. *Clubs:* Chelsea Arts; Aldeburgh Golf; Slaughden Sailing.

**MATTHEWS, Hon. Lord; Hugh Matthews;** a Senator of the College of Justice in Scotland, since 2007; *b* 4 Dec. 1953; *s* of Hugh Matthews and Maureen Matthews (*née* Rea); *m* 2000, Lindsay M. A. Wilson. *Educ:* St Columba's Primary Sch., Kilmarnock; St Joseph's Acad., Kilmarnock; Glasgow Univ. (LLB Hons). Admitted to Faculty of Advocates, 1979; QC (Scot.) 1992; Standing Jun. Counsel, Dept of Employment, Office in Scotland, 1984–88; Advocate-Depute, 1988–93; temp. Sheriff, 1993–97; Sheriff of Glasgow and Strathkelvin, 1997–2007; temp. Judge, 2004–07. Dep. Chm., Boundary Commn for Scotland, 2016–. *Recreations:* ancient history, golf, football, animal husbandry, astronomy, theatre, music, keeping fit, quizzes. *Clubs:* The Club (Kilmarnock); Scottish Arts (Edinburgh).

**MATTHEWS, Prof. Allan,** PhD; FREng, CEng, FIMechE, FIET, FIMMM, FIMF; Professor of Surface Engineering and Tribology, since 2016, and Director, BP International Centre for Advanced Materials, since 2017, University of Manchester (Deputy Director, 2016–17); *b* Wigan, 28 June 1952; *s* of Thomas Matthews and Elizabeth, (Lily), Matthews (*née* Halton); *m* 1975, Helen Irene Gregson; one *s* one *d*. *Educ:* All Saints Sch., Appley Bridge; Shevington Jun. Sch.; Upholland Grammar Sch.; Univ. of Salford (BSc Mech. Engrg 1974; PhD 1980); Manchester Poly. (Dip. Mgt Studies 1976). Technologist apprenticeship, Hawker Siddeley Dynamics, 1970–74; Graduate Technologist, Proj. Mgt Dept, British Aerospace, 1974–76; Res. Asst, 1976–88, Res. Fellow, 1977–82, Univ. of Salford; University of Hull: Lectr, 1982–86; Sen. Lectr, 1986–87; Reader, 1987–89; Prof., 1989–2002; Dir, Res. Centre in Surface Engrg, subseq. at Univ. of Sheffield, then at Univ. of Manchester, 1991–; University of Sheffield: Prof. of Surface Engrg, 2003–16; Hd, Dept of Materials Sci. and Engrg, 2007–11; Exec. Dir, Leonardo Centre for Tribology and Surface Technol., 2012–16. Chm., British Vacuum Council, 2004–05. Dir, Ion Coat Ltd, 1982–. Mem., EPSRC Strategic Adv. Network, 2014–. Mem., Exec. Cttee, Advanced Surface Engrg Div., American Vacuum Soc., 2000–04 (Chm., 2003); Mem. Bd, Soc. of Vacuum Coaters, 2008–15. FIMechE 1996; FIET (FIEE 1996); FIMMM 1997; FIMF 1997; FREng 2012. Gold Medal, IMMM, 2011; RF Bunshah Award, Advanced Surface Engrg Div., Amer. Vacuum Soc., 2018. Editor, 1987–2013, Editor-in-Chief, 2013–, Surface and Coatings Technol. *Publications:* (ed jtly) Advanced Surface Coatings: a handbook of surface engineering, 1991; (jtly) The UK Engineering Coatings Industry in 2005, 1992; Coatings Tribology: properties, mechanisms, techniques and applications in surface engineering (with K. Holmberg), 1994, 2nd edn 2009; 2005 Revisited: the UK engineering coatings industry to 2010, 1998; The UK Surface Engineering Industry, 2010; (jtly) Surface Engineering Processes in Design and Manufacture: an introductory guide, 2011; over 350 papers in jls; fifteen patents. *Recreations:* walking, music, football, golf, Rugby. *Address:* School of Materials, BP International Centre for Advanced Materials, Pariser Building, University of Manchester, Manchester M1 3BB. *T:* (0161) 306 4284, *Fax:* (0161) 275 4865. *E:* Allan.Matthews@manchester.ac.uk.

**MATTHEWS, Rt Rev. Anthony Francis Berners H.;** see Hall-Matthews.

**MATTHEWS, Colin,** OBE 2011; DPhil; FRNCM, FRCM; composer; Prince Consort Professor of Composition, Royal College of Music, since 2001; *b* 13 Feb. 1946; *s* of Herbert and Elsie Matthews; *m* 1977, Belinda Lloyd; one *s* two *d*. *Educ:* Univ. of Nottingham (BA Classics, MPhil Composition); Univ. of Sussex (DPhil). Studied composition with Arnold Whittall and Nicholas Maw, 1967–70; collaborated with Deryck Cooke on performing version of Mahler's Tenth Symphony, 1964–74; asst to Benjamin Britten, 1971–76; worked with Imogen Holst, 1972–84; taught at Univ. of Sussex, 1971–72, 1976–77. Associate Composer: LSO, 1990–99; Hallé Orch., 2001–11 (Composer Emeritus, 2011–). Distinguished Vis. Fellow, Univ. of Manchester, 2001–; Special Prof. of Music, Univ. of Nottingham, 2007–. Dir, Holst Estate and Holst Foundn, 1973–; Trustee, Britten-Pears Foundn, 1983– (Music Dir, 2008–); Dir, Britten Estate, 1983– (Chm., 2000–); Mem. Council and Exec. Cttee, SPNM, 1981–93, 1994–99; Exec. Mem. Council, Aldeburgh Foundn, 1984–93; Mem., Music Panel, Radcliffe Trust, 1985–; Dir, PRS, 1992–95; Trustee (formerly Mem. Council), RPS, 2005–. Founder, NMC Recordings Ltd, 1988. Dir, LSO Panufnik Young Composers Scheme, 2005–. Gov., RNCM, 2000–08. Patron, Musicians against Nuclear Arms, 1985–. FRNCM 2003; FRCM 2007. Hon. RAM 2010. Hon. DMus Nottingham, 1998. Scottish National Orch. Ian Whyte Award, 1975; Park Lane Group Composer Award, 1983; Royal Philharmonic Soc. Award, 1996; British Composer Award, BASCA, 2012, 2013. *Principal works:* Fourth Sonata, 1974; Night Music, 1976; Sonata no 5 'Landscape', 1977–81; String Quartet no 1, 1979; Oboe Quartet, 1981; The Great Journey, 1981–88; Divertimento for Double String Quartet, 1982; Toccata Meccanica, 1984; Night's Mask, 1984; Cello Concerto, 1984; Suns Dance, 1985; Five Duos, 1985; Three Enigmas, 1985; String Quartet no 2, 1985; Pursuit (ballet), 1986; Monody, 1986–87; Eleven Studies in Velocity, 1987; Two Part Invention, 1987; Cortège, 1988; Hidden Variables, 1989; Quatrain, 1989; Second Oboe Quartet, 1990; Five Concertinos, 1990; Chiaroscuro, 1990; Machines and Dreams, 1990; Broken Symmetry, 1990–91; Renewal, 1990–96; Contraflow, 1992; Memorial, 1992; String Quartet no 3, 1994; …through the glass, 1994; 23 Frames, 1995; Cello Concerto no 2, 1996; Renewal, 1996; My Life So Far (film score), 1998; Two Tributes, 1999; Aftertones, 2000; Pluto, 2000; Continuum, 2000; Horn Concerto, 2001; Debussy Preludes, 2001–07; Reflected Images, 2003; A Voice to Wake, 2005; Berceuse for Dresden, 2005; Turning Point, 2006; Alphabicycle Order, 2007; The Island, 2008; Violin Concerto, 2009; Crossing the Alps, 2010; Night Rides, 2011; No Man's Land, 2011; Grand Barcarolle, 2011; String Quartet no 4, 2012; Nowhere to Hide, 2013; Traces Remain, 2014; The Pied Piper of Hamelin, 2015; String Quartet no 5, 2015; Voices of the Air, 2016; A Land of Rain, 2017; As Time Returns, 2018; Postludes, 2019. *Publications:* contribs to Musical Times, Tempo, TLS, etc. *Recreations:* wine, very amateur astrophysics. *Address:* c/o Faber Music Ltd, Bloomsbury House, 74–77 Great Russell Street, WC1B 3DA. *T:* (020) 7908 5310, *Fax:* (020) 7908 5339. *E:* information@fabermusic.com. *Club:* Leyton Orient Supporters'.
*See also* D. J. Matthews.

**MATTHEWS, Brother Daniel (Fairbairn),** SSF; Minister General, Society of Saint Francis, 1997–2007; *b* 7 Sept. 1936; *s* of Maxwell and Mary Matthews. *Educ:* S Shields Marine Coll. (1st Cl. Marine Engrg); Bishop Patteson Theological Coll., Kohimarama, Solomon Is (DipTh). Chief Engr (Marine), 1957–63; joined Society of St Francis, 1964: Guardian, Solomon Is, 1975–81; Minister Provincial, Australia and NZ, 1981–97. *Recreations:* walking, reading. *Address:* Society of Saint Francis, c/o The Friary, 115 Cornwall Street, Annerley, Qld 4103, Australia.

**MATTHEWS, David;** see Matthews, His Honour William D.

**MATTHEWS, David John;** composer; *b* 9 March 1943; *s* of Herbert and Elsie Matthews; *m* 1st, 1995, Jean Hasse (marr. diss. 2002); 2nd, 2005, Jenifer Wakelyn. *Educ:* Bancroft's Sch., Woodford; Univ. of Nottingham (BA Classics). Studied composition with Anthony Milner, 1967–69; Asst to Benjamin Britten, 1966–70. Musical Dir, Deal Fest., 1989–2003; Composer in Association, Britten Sinfonia, 1997–2001. Collaborated with Deryck Cooke on performing version of Mahler's Tenth Symphony, 1964–74. Hon. DMus Nottingham, 1997. *Compositions include:* 3 songs for soprano and orchestra, 1968; String Quartet No 1, 1970; Symphony No 1, 1975; String Quartet No 2, 1976; Symphony No 2, 1977; String Quartet No 3, 1977; September Music, for small orch., 1979; Ehmals und Jetzt, 6 songs for soprano and piano, 1979; The Company of Lovers, 5 choral songs, 1980; String Quartet No 4, 1981; Serenade, for chamber orch., 1982; Violin Concerto No 1, 1982; The Golden Kingdom, 9 songs for high voice and piano, 1983; Piano Trio No 1, 1983; Clarinet Quartet, 1984; Symphony No 3, 1985; In the Dark Time, for orch., 1985; Variations for strings, 1986; The Flaying of Marsyas, for oboe and string quartet, 1987; Chaconne, for orch., 1987; Cantiga, for soprano and chamber orch., 1988; The Ship of Death, for chorus, 1989; Piano

Sonata, 1989; String Trio, 1989; Romanza, for 'cello and small orch., 1990; The Music of Dawn, for orch., 1990; Symphony No 4, 1990; Capriccio, for 2 horns and strings, 1991; String Quartet No 6, 1991; Oboe Concerto, 1992; The Sleeping Lord, for sop. and ensemble, 1992; A Vision and a Journey, for orch., 1993; Piano Trio No 2, 1993; A Congress of Passions, for voice, oboe and piano, 1994; Vespers, for soli, chorus and orch., 1994; Skies now are Skies, for tenor and string quartet, 1994; A Song and Dance Sketchbook, for piano quartet, 1995; Sinfonia, for orch., 1995; Moments of Vision, for chorus, 1995; Two Pieces for Strings: Little Chaconne, 1996, Fall Dances, 1999; Hurrahing in Harvest, for chorus, 1997; Variations, for piano, 1997; Burnham Wick, for small orch., 1997; Violin Concerto No 2, 1998; String Quartet No 8, 1998; Symphony No 5, 1999; String Quartet No 9, 2000; Aubade, for chamber orch., 2001; String Quartet No 10, 2001; After Sunrise, for chamber orch., 2001; Cello Concerto, 2002; Fifteen Fugues for solo violin, 2002; String Trio No 2, 2003; L'Invitation au voyage, for voice and piano quartet, 2003; Aequam memento, for chorus, 2004; Piano Quintet, 2004; Journeying Songs, for 'cello, 2004; Piano Trio No 3, 2005; Movement of Autumn, for sop. and chamber orch., 2005; Fanfares and Flowers, for symphonic wind band, 2006; Terrible Beauty, for voice and ensemble, 2007; Symphony No 6, 2007; Adonis, for violin and piano, 2007; One Foot in Eden, for tenor and piano quintet, 2008; String Quartet No 11, 2008; Symphony No 7, 2009; Piano Concerto, 2009; Dark Pastoral, for orch., 2009; Actaeon, for narrator and ensemble, 2010; String Quartet No 12, 2010; Horn Quintet, 2010; Toward Sunrise, for orch., 2011; Romanza, for violin and strings, 2012; Fortune's Wheel, for chorus and strings, 2012; A Blackbird Sang, for flute and string trio, 2013; Double Concerto, for violin, viola and strings, 2013; Four Portraits, for piano, 2013; A Vision of the Sea, for orch., 2013; Sonatina, for violin and piano, 2013; Symphony No 8, 2014; To What God shall we chant our songs of battle?, for chorus, 2014; Fifteen Preludes for solo violin, 2014; Nachtgesang, for orch., 2015; String Quartet No 13, 2015; Norfolk March, for orch., 2015; Symphony No 9, 2016; Variations on a Theme of Haydn, for piano four hands, 2016; String Quartet No 14, 2016; Le lac, for soprano and chamber orch., 2017; New Fire, for orch., 2017; White Flame, for voice and ensemble, 2018; Concerto for Orch., 2018; Recessional and National Anthem, for chorus and orch., 2018. *Publications*: Michael Tippett, 1980; Landscape into Sound, 1992; Britten, 2003; David Matthews: essays, tributes and criticism, 2014; contribs to Musical Times, Tempo, TLS. *Recreations*: walking, sketching, birdwatching, wine. *Address*: c/o Faber Music Ltd, Bloomsbury House, 74–77 Great Russell Street, WC1B 3DA.
See also C. Matthews.

**MATTHEWS, Prof. David Richard,** DPhil; FRCP; Professor of Diabetes Medicine, University of Oxford, 2002–18, now Emeritus; Fellow, 1998–2018, Medical Tutor, 1998–2018, and Dean, 2015–18, Harris Manchester College, Oxford, now Emeritus Fellow (Vice Principal, 2012–15); Founder Chairman, Oxford Centre for Diabetes, Endocrinology and Metabolism, 2000–10, now Emeritus; b 22 Sept. 1947; s of William John Matthews and Ena Matthews (née Brading); m 1970, Clare Tegla; one s two d. *Educ*: Chigwell Sch.; Corpus Christi Coll., Oxford (Sen. Schol. 1970; MA, DPhil 1973; BM BCh 1975). FRCP 1994. Oxford University: Nuffield Jun. Res. Fellow, Balliol Coll., 1981–84; Joan and Richard Doll Sen. Res. Fellow, Green Coll., 1984–88; Hon. Consultant Physician, Diabetes Res. Labs, 1988–92; Consultant Physician, Oxford Radcliffe Hosps NHS Trust, 1992–2010; Co-dir, UK Diabetes Res. Network, 2007–14. Sen. Investigator, NIHR, 2009–12. Pres., Eur. Assoc. Study of Diabetes, 2019–. Mem., Assoc. of Physicians. FRSocMed. Methodist lay preacher, 1977–; Member: Methodist Council, 2014–16; Strategy and Resources Cttee, Methodist Ch, 2018–; Trustee, 2005–08, Chm., 2008–11, Methodist Relief and Develt Fund. *Publications*: over 300 peer-reviewed papers in field of diabetes. *Recreations*: science and religion, gardening, playing the piano badly, keeping cheerful. *Address*: 18 Norreys Road, Cumnor, Oxford OX2 9PT. *E*: david.matthews@ocdem.ox.ac.uk.

**MATTHEWS, Douglas,** MBE 2013; FRSL; book indexer, since 1957; Librarian, The London Library, 1980–93; b 23 Aug. 1927; s of Benjamin Matthews and Mary (née Pearson); m 1968, Sarah Maria Williams (marr. diss. 1991); two d. *Educ*: Acklam Hall Sch., Middlesbrough; Durham Univ. (BA). FRSL 1999. Assistant: India Office Library, 1952–62; Kungl. Bibliotekt, Stockholm, 1956–57; Librarian, Home Office, 1962–64; Dep. Librarian, London Library, 1965–80. Trustee, Royal Literary Fund, 1993–2014 (Registrar, 2004–14). Mem. Court, Univ. of Sussex, 1983–94. *Address*: 1 Priory Terrace, Mountfield Road, Lewes, Sussex BN7 2UT. *T*: (01273) 475635. *Club*: Garrick.

**MATTHEWS, Duncan Henry Rowland;** QC 2002; b 1 Sept. 1961; m 1st, 1991, Hon. Emma Elizabeth, d of Baron Griffiths, MC, PC (marr. diss. 2015); one s one d; 2nd, 2016, Heloise Elizabeth Mary Revel; two s. *Educ*: Westminster Sch. (Queen's Schol.); Dante Alighieri Sch., Florence (Dip. Italian); Magdalen Coll., Oxford (BA Modern Hist., 1984; MA 1996); City Univ. (Dip. Law); Inns of Court Sch. of Law. Called to the Bar, Gray's Inn, 1986, Bencher, 2006. Pupil barrister, 1986–87, barrister, 1987–, Hd of Chambers, 2014–, 3, later 20 Essex Street Chambers. Dir, London Court of Internat. Arbitration, 2019. Chairman: Bar Council Educn and Trng Cttee, 2004–05; Bar Council Trng for Bar Cttee, 2006–07; Supporting Mems Liaison Cttee, London Maritime Arbitrators Assoc., 2006–. Mem., Gen. Council, Bar Neuberger Adv. Cttee, 2006–07 (Chm., Monitoring and Implementation Gp, 2008–09). Bar Council Trustee, Inns of Court and Bar Educnl Trust, 2006–18; Trustee, Council of Inns of Court, 2015–; Mem., Gray's Inn Mgt Cttee, 2015–. Mem., Ext. Adv. Panel, Mod. Hist. Faculty, Univ. of Oxford, 2011–. *Recreations*: Real tennis, tennis, bridge, theatre, reading, history. *Address*: (chambers) 20 Essex Street, WC2R 3AL. *T*: (020) 7842 1200, *Fax*: (020) 7842 1270. *E*: clerks@20essexst.com. *Clubs*: Garrick, Hurlingham, 5 Hertford Street, Soho House.

**MATTHEWS, Elleke Deirdre;** see Boehmer, E. D.

**MATTHEWS, Gillian;** QC 2009; **Her Honour Judge Gillian Matthews;** a Circuit Judge, since 2010; Designated Family Judge for Cleveland and South Durham, since 2015 (Designated Civil Judge, 2013–15); b Middlesbrough, 22 June 1963; d of Ivor Matthews and Jean Matthews (née Agar); m 1993, John Cowie Elvidge, qv; two d. *Educ*: Univ. of Hull (LLB). Called to the Bar, Inner Temple, 1985, Bencher, 2016; Recorder, 2005–10. Hon. DLaws Teesside, 2014. *Recreations*: singing in jazz bands, running, tennis, golf. *Address*: Teesside Combined Court Centre, Russell Street, Middlesbrough TS1 2AE.

**MATTHEWS, Graham George;** Partner, Peterkins, Aberdeen, since 1988; President, Law Society of Scotland, 2017–18; b Huntly, 8 June 1956; s of John Gray Matthews and Christina Matthews; m 2012, Vanya-Louise Culley; two d by previous marriage. *Educ*: Badenscoth Primary Sch.; Inverurie Acad.; Aberdeen Univ. (LLB 1977). Admitted solicitor, 1979; apprentice, 1977–79, Solicitor, 1979–81, John Malone & Co., Edinburgh; Solicitor, 1981–83, Partner, 1983–88, Milne & Mackinnon, Aberdeen. *Recreations*: horse riding and breeding, gardening, motoring, arrhythmic guitar playing. *Address*: 60 Market Place, Inverurie, Aberdeenshire AB51 3XN. *T*: (01467) 672800, *Fax*: (01467) 672819. *E*: ggm@peterkins.com.

**MATTHEWS, Hugh;** see Matthews, Hon. Lord.

**MATTHEWS, Jeffery Edward,** MBE 2004; FCSD; freelance graphic designer and consultant, since 1952; b 3 April 1928; s of Henry Edward Matthews and Sybil Frances (née Cooke); m 1953, (Sylvia Lilian) Christine (née Hoar) (d 1994); one s one d. *Educ*: Alleyn's; Brixton Sch. of Building (Interior Design; NDD). AIBD 1951; FCSD (FSIAD 1978). Graphic designer with J. Edward Sander, 1949–52; part-time tutor, 1952–55. Lettering and calligraphy assessor for SIAD, 1970–. Designs for Post Office: decimal to pay labels, 1971; fount of numerals for definitive stamps, 1981; stamps: United Nations, 1965; British bridges, 1968; definitives for Scotland, Wales, NI and IOM, 1971; Royal Silver Wedding, 1972; 25th Anniversary of the Coronation, 1978; London, 1980; 80th birthday of the Queen Mother, 1980; Christmas, 1980; Wedding of Prince Charles and Lady Diana Spencer, 1981; Quincentenary of College of Arms, 1984; 60th birthday of the Queen, 1986; Wedding of Prince Andrew and Sarah Ferguson, 1986; Order of the Thistle Tercentenary of Revival, 1987; 150th Anniversary of the Penny Black, 1990; self-adhesive definitives, 1993; The Queen's Beasts, 1998; Jeffery Matthews miniature sheet, 2000; End of War miniature sheet, 2005; Machin definitives 40th Anniversary miniature sheet, 2007; also first-day covers, postmarks, presentation packs, souvenir books and posters; one of three stamp designers featured in PO film, Picture to Post, 1969. Other design work includes: title banner lettering and coat of arms, Sunday Times, 1968; cover design and lettering for official prog., Royal Wedding, 1981; The Royal Mint, commemorative medal, Order of the Thistle, 1987; Millennium commemorative crown piece, 1999; End of War commemorative medal, 2005; stained glass window for Forest Hill Methodist Ch and accompanying film (Light Through Geometry), 2007; official heraldry and symbols, HMSO; hand-drawn lettering, COI; calligraphy, packaging, promotion and bookbinding designs, logotypes, brand images and hand-drawn lettering, for various firms including Unicover Corp., USA, Harrison & Sons Ltd, Metal Box Co., John Dickinson, Reader's Digest Assoc. Ltd, Encyc. Britannica Internat. Ltd, ICI and H. R. Higgins (Coffee-man) Ltd. Work exhibited in A History of Bookplates in Britain, V&A Mus., 1979; contrib. Oral History of the Post Office collection, British Liby, 2001. Citizen and Goldsmith of London (Freedom by Patrimony), 1949. FRSA 1987. Rowland Hill Award for Outstanding Contribution, 2004, Phillips Gold Medal for Stamp Design, 2005, Royal Mail. *Publications*: (contrib.) Designers in Britain, 1964, 1971; (contrib.) 45 Wood-engravers, 1982; (contrib.) Royal Mail Year Book, 1984, 1986, 1987, 1998; (contrib.) Queen Elizabeth II: a Jubilee portrait in stamps, 2002. *Recreations*: furniture restoration, playing the guitar, gardening, DIY.

**MATTHEWS, John,** CBE 1990; FRAgS; Director, Institute of Engineering Research, Agricultural and Food Research Council (formerly National Institute of Agricultural Engineering), 1984–90; b 4 July 1930; s of John Frederick Matthews and Catherine Edith Matthews (née Terry); m 1982 (marr. diss. 1993); two d; m 2000, June Robinson. *Educ*: Royal Latin School, Buckingham. BSc (Physics) London. CPhys, FInstP; CEng; FIAgrE 1970 (Hon. FIAgrE 1994). Scientist, GEC Res. Labs, 1951–59; National Institute of Agricultural Engineering: joined 1959; Head of Tractor Performance Dept, 1967–73; Head of Tractor and Cultivation Div., 1973–83; Asst Dir, 1983–84; Dir, 1984–90. Vis. Prof., Cranfield Inst. of Technology, 1987. Vice Chm., Ceredigion and Mid-Wales NHS Trust, 2000–03 (Dir, 1992–2003). Mem., Bd of Management, AFRC, 1986–90. Formerly Chm., Technical Cttees, Internat. Standards Orgn and OECD; Pres., Inst. of Agricl Engineers, 1986–88. Pro-Chancellor, Univ. of Luton, 1993–98 (Univ. of Govs, Luton Coll. of Higher Educn, 1989–93). Fellow: Ergonomics Soc.; Academie Georgofili, Italy, 1991. Mem., RAFA; Chm., Teifiside Probus Club, 2002–06. Research Medal, RASE, 1983. Max Eyth Medallion (Germany), 1990; Chevalier de Merite Agricole (France), 1992. *Publications*: (contrib.) Fream's Elements of Agriculture, 1984; (ed) Progress in Agricultural Physics and Engineering, 1991; contribs to other books and jls on agricultural engineering and ergonomics. *Recreations*: gardening, travel. *Address*: Carron, Aberporth, Cardigan, Ceredigion SA43 2DA.

**MATTHEWS, Prof. John Burr Lumley, (Jack),** FRSE; Director, 1988–96 and Secretary, 1988–99, Scottish Association for Marine Science (formerly Scottish Marine Biological Association) (Hon. Fellow, 1999); b 23 April 1935; s of Dr John Lumley Matthews and Susan Agnes Matthews; m 1962, Jane Rosemary Goldsmith; one s two d. *Educ*: Warwick Sch.; St John's Coll., Oxford (MA, DPhil). FRSE 1988. Res. Scientist, Oceanographic Lab., Edinburgh, 1961–67; University of Bergen: Lectr, Sen. Lectr, Marine Biology, 1967–78; Prof., Marine Biology, 1978–84; Dep. Dir, Scottish Marine Biol Assoc., 1984–88; Dir, Dunstaffnage Marine Lab., NERC, 1988–94. Vis. Prof., Oceanography, Univ. of British Columbia, 1977–78; Hon. Prof., Biology, Univ. of Stirling, 1984–. Member: Cttee for Scotland, Nature Conservancy Council, 1989–91; SW Regl Bd, Scottish Natural Heritage, 1992–97 (Dep. Chm., 1994–97). Sec., Internat. Assoc. of Biol Oceanography, 1994–2002. Mem., Bd and Acad. Council, Univ. of the Highlands and Islands Ltd, 1993–96. Trustee: Internat. Sch., Bergen, 1980–84; Oban Hospice, 1999–2005; Hebridean Whale & Dolphin Trust, 2000–08 (Chm., 2001–08; Patron, 2009–); Nadair Trust, 2003–07. Founding Fellow, Inst. for Contemp. Scotland, 2000; FRSA 1989. *Publications*: (ed jtly) Freshwater on the Sea, 1976; Aquatic Life Cycle Strategies, 1999; (ed jtly and contrib.) Achievements of the Continuous Plankton Recorder Survey and a Vision for its Future, 2003; contribs to marine sci. jls. *Recreations*: gardening, pethau cymreig. *Address*: The Well, 18 Manse Road, Milnathort, Kinross KY13 9YQ. *T*: (01577) 861066.

**MATTHEWS, Prof. John Frederick,** DPhil; FRHistS; FSA; FBA 1990; Professor of Roman History, Departments of Classics and History, since 1996, and John M. Schiff Professor of Classics and History, 2001–14, now Emeritus, Yale University (Chair of Classics, 1998–2005 and 2008–09); b 15 Feb. 1940; s of Jack and Mary Matthews; m 1st, 1965, Elaine Jackson (marr. diss. 1995); two d; 2nd, 1995, Veronika Grimm. *Educ*: Wyggeston Boys' Sch., Leicester; Queen's Coll., Oxford (MA 1965; DPhil 1970). FRHistS 1986; FSA 1993. Oxford University: Dyson Jun. Res. Fellow in Greek Culture, Balliol Coll., 1965–69; Conington Prize, 1971; Univ. Lectr in Middle and Late Roman Empire, 1969–90; Reader, 1990–92; Prof. of Middle and Later Roman History, 1992–96; Official Fellow, Corpus Christi Coll., 1969–76; Fellow, and Praelector in Ancient History, Queen's College, Oxford, 1976–96. Inst. for Advanced Study, Princeton, 1980–81; British Acad. Reader in Humanities, 1988–90; Fellow, Nat. Humanities Center, N Carolina, 1995–96. Vis. Prof., Sch. of Archaeology and Ancient History, Univ. of Leicester, 2006–. Chm. of Govs, Cheney Sch., Oxford, 1986–91. Hon. DLitt Leicester, 2003. *Publications*: Western Aristocracies and Imperial Court AD 364–425, 1975; (with T. J. Cornell) Atlas of the Roman World, 1982; Political Life and Culture in late Roman Society, 1985; The Roman Empire of Ammianus, 1989; (with Peter Heather) The Goths in the Fourth Century, 1991; Laying Down the Law: a study of the Theodosian Code, 2000; The Journey of Theophanes: travel, business and daily life in the Roman East, 2006 (James Henry Breasted Prize, American Historical Assoc., 2007); Roman Perspectives: studies in the social, political and cultural history of the first to fifth centuries, 2010. *Recreations*: playing the piano, listening to music, suburban gardening. *Address*: 160 McKinley Avenue, New Haven, CT 06515, USA. *T*: (203) 3898137.

**MATTHEWS, John Waylett;** Chairman, Regus plc, 2002–10; b 22 Sept. 1944; s of late Percy Victor Matthews and Phyllis Edith Matthews (née Waylett); m 1972, Lesley Marjorie Halliday; two s one d. *Educ*: Forest Sch. FCA 1967. Dixon Wilson & Co., 1961–69; N. M. Rothschild & Sons, 1969–71; County Natwest, 1971–88 (Sen. Dir, 1984–88); Dep. Chm./

CEO, Beazer plc, 1988–91; CEO, Indosuez Capital, 1991–94; Chm., Crest Nicholson plc, 1996–2007. Non-executive Director: Rotork plc, 1998–2008; SDL plc, 2001–; Diploma plc, 2003–13; Center Parcs plc, 2003–06; Minerva plc, 2007–11; Aurelian Oil and Gas plc, 2010–13. Gov., Forest Sch., 1998–2016 (Chm., 2001–16). *Recreations:* golf, shooting, skiing. *E:* johnwaymatthews@gmail.com. *Clubs:* City of London, Royal Automobile, MCC.

**MATTHEWS, Kathryn Ann;** Member, Council of Duchy of Lancaster, since 2015; Chairman, Barclays Investment Solutions Ltd, since 2018; *b* Sheffield, 22 Dec. 1959; *d* of late Gordon Board Matthews and of Ann Clarke Matthews (née Micklethwaite, now Graham); *m* 1989, Rupert Wills; two *s* one *d*. *Educ:* Benenden Sch.; Stowe Sch.; Bristol Univ. (BSc Hons Econs). Dir, Baring Asset Mgt, 1995–97; Jt Chief Exec., Santander Global Advrs, 1998–2001; Eur. Partner, Mercer Manager Advrs, 2001–03; Chief Investment Officer, Asia and Japan Equities, Fidelity Internat. (Hong Kong), 2005–09; Dir, 2010–17, Chm., 2013–17, Montanaro UK Smaller Cos Investment Trust plc. Non-executive Director: Hermes Fund Managers, 2009–17; Rathbone Brothers plc, 2010–19; Aperam plc, 2010–; J O Hambro Capital Mgt Hldgs, 2017–; Barclays Bank UK, 2018–; Pender Gp. Mem., Bd of Trustees, Nuffield Trust, 2013–. *Recreations:* ski-ing, theatre, opera, family.

**MATTHEWS, Lynne Teresa;** a District Judge (Magistrates' Courts), since 2011; *b* Stoke-on-Trent, 7 July 1965; *d* of John Sproston and Janet Sproston (now Oakley); *m* 2005, Christopher Austins; two *s* two *d*. *Educ:* Moorside High Sch.; Nottingham Univ. (LLB). Called to the Bar, Inner Temple, 1987; in practice at the Bar, specialising in criminal law, 1987–2011. Gov., Chew Valley Sch., 2007–. *Recreations:* opera, theatre, gardening, hill walking. *Address:* Bristol Magistrates' Court, Marlborough Street, Bristol BS1 3NU.

**MATTHEWS, Margaret;** *see* Gilmore, M.

**MATTHEWS, Mark;** HM Diplomatic Service; Foreign and Commonwealth Office, since 2017; *b* England, 1968; *s* of Canon Medwyn Matthews and June Matthews; *m* 1997, Dr Shauna Rudge; one *s* one *d*. *Educ:* St Brendan's Sixth Form Coll., Bristol; St Edmund Hall, Oxford (MA Modern Langs). Entered FCO, 1990; Political and Press Officer, Abu Dhabi, 1997–2000; Spokesperson for ME and N Africa, FCO, 2000–03; Alt. Perm. Rep. to Orgn for Prohibition of Chem. Weapons, The Hague, 2003–07; Dep. Hd of Mission and Consul-Gen., Libya, 2007–10; Dep. Special Rep., Nat. Transitional Council, Libya, 2011; Ambassador and Dep. Perm. Rep. to UN and other internat. orgns, Geneva, 2013–17. *Recreations:* improving my Arabic, reading, walking. *Address:* c/o Foreign and Commonwealth Office, King Charles Street, SW1A 2AH. *E:* mark.matthews@fco.gov.uk.

**MATTHEWS, Moira;** *see* Doherty, M.

**MATTHEWS, Paul Bernard,** LLD; **His Honour Judge Paul Matthews;** a Specialist Civil Circuit Judge, since 2017; *b* 21 Aug. 1955; *s* of Leonard William Matthews, KSG and late Noreen Elizabeth Matthews; *m* 1986, Katie Bradford. *Educ:* St Peter's Sch., Bournemouth; UCL (Charlotte Ashby Prize, Andrews Prize, 1976; LLB 1977); St Edmund Hall, Oxford (BCL 1979); Univ. of London (LLD 1995); Inns of Court Sch. of Law (Exam. Prize, Council of Legal Educn, 1981). Called to the Bar, Gray's Inn, 1981; admitted Solicitor: England and Wales, 1987; Ireland, 1997; Solicitor-Advocate (Higher Courts: Civil), 2001. In private practice as barrister, 1982–84; Hopkins & Wood, London: Legal Asst, 1984–87; Partner, 1987–92; Consultant Solicitor, 1992–96; Consultant Solicitor, Withers LLP, 1996–2015; Deputy Coroner: City of London, 1994–2002; Royal Household, 2002–06; (*ad hoc*) N London, 2004–07; HM Sen. Coroner (formerly HM Coroner), City of London, 2002–16; Dep. Master, 2008–15, Master, 2015–17, High Court of Justice, Chancery Div.; a Recorder, 2010–17. Judge (pt-time), Court of Trusts and Fiduciary Relns, Rep. of San Marino, 2014–. Tutor (pt-time), 1978–79, Lectr in Law, 1979–83, UCL; Tutor (pt-time), St Edmund Hall, Oxford, 1979–80. Visiting Lecturer: City Univ., 1981–84; UCL, 1985–86; Inst. de Droit des Affaires, Univ. d'Aix-Marseille, 1991–99; Vis. Sen. Lectr, KCL, 1991–94; Visiting Professor: KCL, 1995–2004, 2015– (Hon. Prof., 2004–15); Jersey Inst. of Law, 2009–12; Referent, Univ. of Liechtenstein, 2010–15. Mem., Common Core of Eur. Private Law Project, Univ. of Trento, 2001–15. Dep. Chm., Trust Law Cttee, 2005– (Mem., Wkg Parties on Trustees' Exoneration and Trustees' Indemnity, 1997–99); Member: Guernsey Trust Law Review Cttee, 2000–15; Wkg Party on Coroners and Inquests, Law Soc., 2003–15; EC Gp of Experts on property consequences of marriage and on wills and succession in EU, 2005–08; Specialist Advr, H of C Constitutional Affairs Cttee, 2006–08; Coroner Mem., Review Bodies, 2006–. Member: Soc. of Legal Scholars, 1979–; British Inst. of Internat. and Comparative Law, 1989–; Coroners' Soc. of England and Wales, 1994–; Soc. of Trust and Estate Practitioners, 1996–; Internat. Acad. of Estate and Trust Lawyers, 2004–. Member: Selden Soc., 2002–; Stair Soc., 2003–. FRSocMed 2005. FRSA 1994. Fellow, Eur. Law Inst., 2015. Liveryman, City of London Solicitors' Co., 1992–. Trustee, David Isaacs Fund, 2002–16. Jt Ed., Trust Law Internat., 2005–11 (Asst Ed., 1995–2004); Mem. Editl Bd, Jersey Law Review, 1997–. *Publications:* (ed with K. Bradford) Butterworths Business Landlord and Tenant Handbook, 1996, 6th edn 2012; Jervis on Coroners, 10th edn 1986 to 13th edn 2014 (10th and 11th edns with J. C. Foreman); (with T. Sowden) The Jersey Law of Trusts, 1988, 3rd edn 1994; (with S. C. Nicolle) The Jersey Law of Property, 1991; (with H. M. Malek) Discovery, 1992, 2nd edn as Disclosure, 2000, 5th edn 2017; (with D. Millichap) A Guide to the Leasehold Reform, Housing and Urban Development Act 1993, 1993; (with H. Barraclough) A Practitioner's Guide to the Trusts of Land and Appointment of Trustees Act 1996, 1996; Trusts: migration and change of proper law, 1997; Trust and Estate Disputes, 1999; (ed with D. Hayton and C. Mitchell) Underhill & Hayton's Law of Trusts and Trustees, 17th edn 2006 to 19th edn 2016; Jersey Trusts Law Study Guide, 2009, 4th edn 2012; contrib. Halsbury's Laws of England, 4th edn reissue and 5th edn; articles, notes and reviews in learned jls. *Recreations:* reading, music, local history, cinema, languages. *Address:* Bristol Civil and Family Justice Centre, 2 Redcliff Street, Bristol BS1 6GR; School of Law, King's College, Strand, WC2R 2LS. *E:* paul.matthews@kcl.ac.uk. *Club:* Athenæum.

**MATTHEWS, Prof. Paul McMahan,** OBE 2008; DPhil, MD; FRCP, FRCPC, FMedSci; Edmond and Lily Safra Professor of Translational Neuroscience and Therapeutics, since 2014, Head, Division of Brain Sciences, since 2012, and Professor of Clinical Neuroscience, since 2006, Imperial College London; Associate Director, UK Dementia Research Institute, since 2017; *b* Chicago, 30 June 1956; *s* of Charles Vaughn Matthews and Bernice Mary Matthews; *m* 1982, Catherine Comfort; one *s* one *d*. *Educ:* Carbondale Community High Sch., Ill; St Edmund Hall, Oxford (BA Hons 1977; DPhil 1982); Sch. of Medicine, Stanford Univ. (MD 1986). FRCPC 1990; FRCP 2000. Postdoctoral Fellow: Radcliffe Infirmary, Univ. of Oxford, 1982–83; Stanford Univ., 1983–86; intern (Medicine) Stanford Univ. Med. Centre, 1986–87; McGill University, Montreal: Resident in Neurol., 1987–90, Chief Resident, 1989; Clin. Res. Fellow (Neurogenetics), Montreal Neurol Inst., 1989–90; University of Oxford: MRC (Canada) Clinician-Scientist, Genetics Lab., Dept of Biochem., 1990–93; Hon. Sen. Registrar and Actg Clin. Lectr, Dept of Clin. Neurol., 1991–93; Asst Prof. of Neurol., McGill Univ., Montreal, 1993–95; University of Oxford: MRC Clin. Res. Reader, 1995–2000, MRC Clin. Res. Prof., 2000–08, Dept of Neurol.; Dir, Centre for Functional Magnetic Resonance Imaging of the Brain, 1995–2005; Fellow, St Edmund Hall, Oxford, 1997–. GlaxoSmithKline: Vice Pres., Pharmaceuticals, 2005–14; Hd, GSK Clin. Imaging Centre, 2005–11; Hd, Global Imaging Unit, 2011–12. NIHR Sen. Investigator, 2015–. Hon. Prof., Sch. of Med. and Vet. Scis, Univ. of Edinburgh, 2014–; Vis. Prof., Lee Kong Chian Sch. of Medicine, Singapore, 2015–. MAE 2015. FMedSci 2014. *Publications:* (ed jtly) Functional Magnetic Resonance Imaging, 2001; (with J. McQuain) The Bard on the Brain, 2003; (ed jtly) The Memory Process, 2010; over 350 academic papers and chapters. *Recreations:* Japanese woodblock print collection, art, reading, walking. *Address:* Imperial College London, Burlington Danes, Hammersmith Hospital, Du Cane Road, W12 0NN. *E:* p.matthews@imperial.ac.uk. *Club:* Athenæum.

**MATTHEWS, Prof. Peter Bryan Conrad,** FRS 1973; MD, DSc; Professor of Sensorimotor Physiology, 1987–96, now Emeritus and Student of Christ Church, 1958–96, now Emeritus, University of Oxford; *b* 23 Dec. 1928; *s* of Prof. Sir Bryan Matthews, CBE, FRS; *m* 1956, Margaret Rosemary Blears; one *s* one *d*. *Educ:* Marlborough Coll.; King's Coll., Cambridge; Oxford Univ. Clinical School. Oxford University: Univ. Lectr in Physiology, 1961–77; Reader, 1978–86; Tutor, Christ Church, 1958–86. Sir Lionel Whitby Medal, Cambridge Univ., 1959; Robert Bing Prize, Swiss Acad. of Med. Science, 1971. *Publications:* Mammalian Muscle Receptors and their Central Actions, 1972; papers on neurophysiology in various scientific jls. *Address:* The Hurst, 43 Bentley Drive, Oswestry SY11 1TQ. *T:* (01691) 659633.

**MATTHEWS, Prof. Peter Hugoe,** LittD; FBA 1985; Professor of Linguistics, University of Cambridge, 1980–2001, now Emeritus (Head of Department of Linguistics, 1980–96); Fellow, since 1980, Praelector, 1987–2001, St John's College, Cambridge; *b* 10 March 1934; *s* of John Hugo and Cecily Eileen Emsley Matthews; *m* 1984, Lucienne Marie Jeanne Schleich; one step *s* one step *d*. *Educ:* Montpellier Sch., Paignton; Clifton Coll.; St John's Coll., Cambridge (MA 1960; LittD 1988). Lectr in Linguistics, UCNW, 1961–65 (on leave Indiana Univ., Bloomington, 1963–64); University of Reading: Lectr in Linguistic Science, 1965–69; Reader, 1969–75; Prof., 1975–80 (on leave as Fellow, King's Coll., Cambridge, 1970–71, and as Fellow, Netherlands Inst. of Advanced Study, Wassenaar, 1977–78). Pres., Philological Soc., 1992–96 (Vice-Pres., 1996–). Hon. Mem., Linguistic Soc. of America, 1994–. An Editor, Jl of Linguistics, 1970–79. *Publications:* Inflectional Morphology, 1972; Morphology, 1974, 2nd edn 1991; Generative Grammar and Linguistic Competence, 1979; Syntax, 1981; Grammatical Theory in the United States from Bloomfield to Chomsky, 1993; The Concise Oxford Dictionary of Linguistics, 1997, 3rd edn 2014; A Short History of Structural Linguistics, 2001; Linguistics: a very short introduction, 2003; Syntactic Relations, 2007; The Positions of Adjectives in English, 2014; What Graeco-Roman Grammar Was About, 2019; articles and book chapters. *Recreations:* cycling, gardening. *Address:* 10 Fendon Close, Cambridge CB1 7RU. *T:* (01223) 247553.

**MATTHEWS, Peter John,** CBE 2016 (OBE 2007); PhD; Chairman, Natural Resources Wales, 2012–15; *b* Croydon, 11 Jan. 1943; *s* of Charles George Peter Matthews and Millicent Ethel Matthews; *m* 1965, Elisabeth Mitchell; one *s* one *d*. *Educ:* Harvey Grammar Sch., Folkestone; Medway and Maidstone Coll. of Technol.; Thames Poly.; CNAA (PhD 1973). CChem 1975; MRIC 1967, FRSC 1975; CWEM 1987; CEnv 2006. Anglian Water, 1974–99, latterly Dep. Man. Dir, Anglian Water Internat. Member, Board: EA, 2000–06; Port of London Authy, 2006–12; Mem., Lighthouse Bd, Trinity House, 2012–; Chairman: Sustainable Organic Resources Partnership, 2004–13; NI Utility Regulator, 2006–12; Mem., Royal Commn on Envmtl Pollution, 2008–11. Trustee, 1994–2012, Pres., 1998–99, CIWEM; Mem. Bd, 1982–2011, Pres., 1997–98, Eur. Water Assoc. (Hon. Mem., 2011); Dir, Soc. for Envmt, 2003– (Chm., 2005–06, 2015–; Hon. Fellow, 2009). Visiting Professor: Imperial Coll. London, 1991–2004; Anglia Ruskin Univ., 2006–19 (Gov., 1998–2007). William Pitt Fellow, Pembroke Coll., Cambridge, 1999. Freeman, City of London, 1999; Mem., Water Conservators' Co., 1994 (Master, 2012–13). Fellow, Inst. of Water (Fellow, Instn of Water Officers, 1988). Hon. Fellow, Chartered Instn of Wastes Mgt, 2003. Hon. Fellow, Massey Univ., NZ, 1999. Hon. DSc Anglia Ruskin, 1995. William Lockett Award, IWPC, 1967; Res. Prize, Thames Poly., 1973; Carey Premium Award, IWES, 1976; William Hatfield Award, Water Envmt Fedn/CIWEM, 1993; Ehrennadel Award, Abwasser Technische Vereinigung, Germany, 2003; President's Award, CIWEM, 2007; William Dunbar Medal, Eur. Water Assoc., 2010. *Publications:* contribs to books and articles on water sci. and engrg, gen. envmt mgt, innovation, knowledge and wisdom mgt, learning orgns, ethics, gen. orgnl mgt, professional bodies. *Recreations:* sketching and painting, photography, travel, gardening, collecting vintage, antiques (especially model soldiers), writing, publishing. *Address:* Slepey House, 23 Honey Hill, Fenstanton, Cambs PE28 9JP.

**MATTHEWS, Philip Rodway B.;** *see* Bushill-Matthews.

**MATTHEWS, His Honour Phillip Rowland;** a Circuit Judge, 2009–18; *b* Port Talbot, Wales, 18 Nov. 1947; *s* of Abraham and Phyllis Matthews; *m* 1979, Barbara Christine; one *s* two *d*. *Educ:* Marlborough Coll.; St Catharine's Coll., Cambridge (BA 1969). Called to the Bar, Inner Temple, 1974; Asst Recorder, 1990–93, Recorder, 1993–2009; Hd of Chambers, Francis Taylor Bldg, 1991–96. *Recreations:* golf, watching Wales Rugby, music. *E:* phillipmatthews@blueyonder.co.uk. *Club:* Hawks (Cambridge).

**MATTHEWS, Richard Andrew;** QC 2010; *b* Maidstone, 5 April 1966; *s* of Stanley Matthews and Shirley Matthews; *m* 1994, Valérie Carnis; one *s* one *d*. *Educ:* Christ's Coll., Finchley; Girton Coll., Cambridge (BA 1987; MA 1991). Called to the Bar, Inner Temple, 1989; in practice as barrister, specialising in criminal and health and safety law. *Publications:* Health and Safety Enforcement: law and practice, 2003, 3rd edn 2010; Blackstone's Guide to the Corporate Manslaughter and Corporate Homicide Act 2007, 2008. *Recreations:* family, reading, opera. *Address:* 2 Bedford Row, WC1R 4BU. *T:* (020) 7440 8888. *E:* rmatthews@2bedfordrow.co.uk.

**MATTHEWS, Prof. Roger John,** PhD; Professor of Near Eastern Archaeology, University of Reading, since 2011; *b* Cardiff, 21 Aug. 1954; *s* of Bryan and Joyce Matthews; *m* 1988, Dr Wendy Knight. *Educ:* Wilmslow Grammar Sch.; Manchester Univ. (BA 1983); St John's Coll., Cambridge (MPhil 1984; PhD 1990). Director: British Sch. of Archaeol. in Iraq, 1988–95; British Inst. at Ankara, 1995–2001; Lectr, 2001–03, Reader, 2003–07, Prof. of Near Eastern Archaeol., 2007–11, Inst. of Archaeol., UCL. *Publications:* Early Prehistory of Mesopotamia, 2000; Archaeology of Mesopotamia, 2003; At Empires' Edge, 2009; (ed with R. Matthews) Proceedings of the 7th International Congress on the Archaeology of the Ancient Near East, 3 vols, 2012. *Recreations:* gardening, guitar-playing. *Address:* Department of Archaeology, University of Reading, Whiteknights Box 227, Reading, Berks RG6 6AB. *T:* (0118) 378 7564. *E:* r.j.matthews@reading.ac.uk.

**MATTHEWS, Rupert;** Member (C) East Midlands Region, European Parliament, 2017–19; *b* Dorking, 5 Dec. 1961; *m* 2001, Joanna; two *d*. *Educ:* Esher Grammar Sch. Freelance writer and editor, 1988–; Editl Dir, Bretwalda Books, 2011–. Nat. Campaigns Manager, Better Off Out, 2015–16. Lectr, Internat. Metaphysical Univ. Contested (C) E Midlands, EP, 2009, 2014, 2019. *Publications:* Germany: land of many dreams, 1986; Italy: land of many dreams, 1986; Natural Wonders of America: the making of a mighty continent, 1986; Julius Caesar, 1988; Let's Look at Castles, 1988; Amazing Scoundrels and Villains, 1988; Amazing UFOs and Aliens, 1988; Atlas of Natural Wonders, 1988; Monster Mysteries, 1988; Scoundrels and Villains, 1988; Spine Chilling Book of Horror, 1988; Spine Chilling Book of Monsters, 1988; The Eruption of Krakatoa, 1988; The Fire of London,

1988; Winston Churchill, 1988; The Power Brokers: kingmakers and usurpers throughout history, 1989; The Race to the South Pole, 1989; The Voyage of Columbus, 1989; The Supernatural, 1989; The Age of Mammals, 1989; The Attack on the Lusitania, 1989; The Dinosaur Age, 1989; How Life Began, 1989; Prehistoric Life, 1989; Ice Age Animals, 1989; Africa: the land and the people, 1989; Tropical Rainforests of the World, 1990; The First People, 1990; The First Settlements, 1990; Castles, 1990; Crazy Crimes, 1990; Dictionary of Dinosaurs, 1990; Eyewitness to the 80's, 1990; Siege, 1990; How They Live: sharks, 1990; How They Live: tigers, 1990; Let's Look at Ships and Boats, 1990; Living in a Castle, 1990; Majesty of the Horse, 1990; Viking Explorers, 1990; Maneaters, 1990; Record Breakers of the Air, 1990; Record Breakers of the Land, 1990; Record Breakers of the Sea, 1990; Roman Soldiers, 1990; France: a photographic journey, 1991; Italy: a photographic journey, 1991; Industry, 1991; Landscapes of Britain, 1992; Landscapes of Ireland, 1992; Communicating by Signs, 1992; Illustrated History of the 20th Century, 1993; Africa: the mighty continent, 1993; Dinosaurs: a picture dictionary, 1993; Haunted Edinburgh, 1993; Haunted London, 1993; Haunted Oxford, 1993; The Illustrated Encyclopedia of Prehistoric Life, 1994; Haunted Bath, 1994; Dinosaurs, 1995; Cars and Trucks, 1995; Dangerous and Deadly, 1995; Amazing History Facts, 1997; Amazing Animal Facts: amazing facts at your fingertips, 1997; Ancient Egyptians, 1998; Elvis, 1998; UFOs, 1999; Cooking a Meal, 2000; Going to School, 2000; Telling the Time, 2000; The Renaissance, 2000; Myths and Civilizations of the Ancient Chinese, 2001; Frederic Remington, 2001; Board Game Media, 2002; Cretaceous Dinosaurs, 2002; Everything You Need to Know About the British: 200 insights into our way of life, 2002; Raiders and Invaders, 2003; Let's Explore Dinosaurs, 2003; Gone Forever dinosaur series, 2003, 2004; The Age of the Gladiators: savagery and spectacle in Ancient Rome, 2004; Dinosaur Dictionary: an A to Z of dinosaurs and prehistoric reptiles, 2004; Haunted Places of Devon, 2004; Haunted Places of Bedfordshire and Buckinghamshire, 2004; Haunted Places of Kent, 2004; Haunted Places of Wiltshire, 2004; Ghost Hunter Walks in Dorset, 2004; Heroes of Bomber Command: Lincolnshire, 2005; Ghost Hunter Walks in Kent, 2005; Haunted Places of Nottinghamshire, 2005; Haunted Places of Shropshire, 2005; Haunted Places of Warwickshire, 2005; Haunted Places of Dorset, 2006; Ghosthunter's Guide to England, 2006; Winter Celebrations, 2006; World War I (1000 Facts), 2006; Heroes of Bomber Command: Norfolk, 2006; Prophets and Gods, 2006; Battle of Thermopylae: campaign in context, 2006; Lost Railways of Berkshire, 2006; 100 Things You Should Know About Explorers, 2006; Elvis: the king of rock and roll, 2006; Everyday Celebrations, 2006; The Battle of Crecy: a campaign in context, 2007; 100 Things You Should Know About Gladiators, 2007; 100 Things You Should Know About Arms and Armour, 2007; You Wouldn't Want to be a Mayan Soothsayer!, 2007; You Wouldn't Want to be an Assyrian Soldier!, 2007; Avoid Being a Sumerian Slave, 2007; Avoid Being a Mayan Soothsayer, 2007; Avoid Being an Assyrian Soldier, 2007; Alien Encounters: true-life stories of aliens, UFOs and other extra-terrestrial phenomena, 2007; The Natural World, 2007; The World Wars, 2007; What About Dinosaurs?, 2007; Heroes of Fighter Command: Sussex, 2007; Heroes of Fighter Command: Surrey, 2008; Unseen World: the science, theories and phenomena behind events paranormal, 2008; Victorian Britain, 2008; Bigfoot and Other Mysterious Creatures, 2008; Susquatch, 2008; Illustrated Encyclopedia of Mammals, 2008; History Timelines, 2008; Heroes, Rascals and Rogues, 2008; Battlefield Walks Devon, 2008; Battlefield Walks Kent and Sussex, 2008; Battlefield Walks Northumberland, 2008; Alexander the Great at the Battle of Granicus, 2008; 1000 Facts: Ancient Greece, 2008; 1000 Facts: Ancient Rome, 2008; Dinosaur Families, 2008; Dinosaur Food, 2008; 100 Facts on Prehistoric Life, 2008; Action File Egypt, 2008; Action Files Gladiators, 2008; The Great Big Book of Dinosaurs, 2008; 100 Things You Should Know About Penguins, 2008; Haunted Gloucestershire, 2008; Haunted Herefordshire, 2008; Haunted Sunderland, 2008; Haunted Hampshire, 2009; Haunted York, 2009; Roswell, 2009; Weapons of War, 2009; Conquerors, 2009; The Spanish Armada, 2009; Dinosaur Combat, 2009; Dinosaurs in Action, 2009; Encyclopedia of the Paranormal, 2009; Poltergeists and Other Hauntings, 2009; UFOs: a history of alien activity from sightings to abductions to global threat, 2009; Leicestershire's Food and Drink, 2009; 100 Facts on Arms and Armour, 2009; 100 Things You Should Know About Prehistoric Life, 2010; Paranormal Surrey, 2010; On the Trail of the Real St George, 2010; A Little Book of Surrey, 2010; Wales, A Very Peculiar History, 2010; Ripley Twists: dinosaurs, 2010; RAF Bomber Command at War, 2010; Hitler's Forgotten Secret Weapon, 2010; Avoid Being a 1920s Gangster, 2010; Ancient World, 2010; Danger Zone, 2010; Battle Honours of the Royal Hampshire Regiment, 2011; Hampshire Past and Present, 2011; Haunted Surrey, 2011; Ancient Mysteries: ankylosaurus, 2011; Ancient Mysteries: apatosaurus, 2011; How the Steam Railways Came to Surrey, 2011; Unexplained Disappearances, 2011; Unexplained Ghosts and Spirits, 2011; Unexplained Strange Animals, 2011; Unexplained Ancient Mysteries, 2011; A Little Book of the Paranormal, 2011; How to be a Successful Election Candidate, 2011; Heroes of the RAF: No 50 Squadron, 2012; Eyewitness Explorer, 2012; Ceawlin: the man who created England, 2012; The Jacobite Wars, 2012; Titanic, 2012; Mysterious Yorkshire, 2012; Mad About Pirates, 2012; Extreme Dinosaurs series, 2012, 2013; Bretwalda Battles series, 2012, 2013; Hide-and-Ghost Seek, 2013; Dinosaur Handbook, 2013; On the Trail of the Real Robin Hood, 2013; Jack the Ripper's Streets of Terror, 2013; World War II (100 Facts), 2013; Mysterious Cornwall, 2013; Mysterious Northumberland, 2013; England Versus Scotland: great British battles, 2013; Hitler: military commander, 2013; The Popes, 2014; Illustrated Encyclopedia of Small Arms, 2014; Dinopedia, 2014; Battle in the Air, 2014; Battle at the Castle, 2014; Stalingrad, 2015; Kursk, 2015; The Battle of Waterloo, 2015; Conquistadors, 2015; Knights and Castles, 2016; 50 Things You Should Know About the Tudors, 2016; Pub and Teashop Drives in Kent, 2016; Spartans, 2016; Samurai, 2016; Ghosts and Poltergeists, 2016; Ninjas (Fearless Warriors), 2016; Mongols (Fearless Warriors), 2016; Winter God: the authorised biography of Father Christmas, 2016; A History of Christmas Foods, 2016; Ernest Shackleton, 2017; 100 Facts: Vikings, 2017; The Little History of Buttons, 2017; The Coronations of Henry VIII, 2017; Dick Whittington's London, 2017; Jane Austen and the Military, 2017; The Great British Cream Tea, 2017.

**MATTHEWS, Her Honour Suzan Patricia, (Mrs A. R. Matthews);** QC 1993; a Circuit Judge, 2003–14; a Deputy Circuit Judge, since 2014; *b* 5 Dec. 1947; *y c* of late Sidney Herbert Clark and Susan Hadnett Clark (*née* Mathews); *m* 1970, Anthony Robert Matthews; one *s*. *Educ*: Univ. of Bradford (BSc Hons Business Admin 1972). Called to the Bar, Middle Temple, 1974. Asst Recorder, 1991–95; a Recorder, 1995–2003. Asst Boundary Comr, 1992–2003. Councillor, SE Region, Gas Consumers' Council, 1987–96. Member: Criminal Injuries Compensation Appeals Panel, 1996–2003; Adv. Bd on Family Law, 1997–2002; Criminal Injuries Compensation Bd, 1999–2000; Mental Health Rev. Tribunal (Restricted Patients) Panel, 1999–2003; Dep. Chm., Criminal Injuries Compensation Appeals Panel, 2000–03. Chm., Inquiry into Richard Neale for Sec. of State for Health, 2002–04. Chair, Disciplinary Cttee, ACCA, 2016–. Pres., The Valley Trust, 2000–08. *Recreations*: historical research, music, gardening. *Address*: c/o Guildford Crown Court, Bedford Road, Guildford GU1 4ST. *T*: (01483) 468500.

**MATTHEWS, Sir Terence (Hedley),** Kt 2001; OBE 1994; OC 2017; FREng, FIET; Chairman: Mitel Networks, since 2001; March Networks Corporation, since 2004 (Chief Executive Officer, 2000–04); *b* 6 June 1943. *Educ*: Univ. of Wales, Swansea (BSc). Co-founder, Mitel Corp., 1972–85; Founder, Chm. and Pres., Newbridge Networks Corp., 1986–2000. Founder and Investor, Celtic House Internat., 1994–; founder and Chm., Wesley Clover International Corp.; Chairman: Covendia Corp.; DragonWave; Tundra Semiconductor Corp.; Celtic Manor Resort, Wales. FREng (FEng 1998). *Address*: Mitel Networks, 350 Legget Drive, Kanata, ON K2K 2W7, Canada.

**MATTHEWS, Timothy John;** Chief Executive, Remploy Ltd, 2008–13; Chair, Pursuing Independent Paths, since 2015; *b* 24 June 1951; *s* of Kenneth James Matthews and Vera Joan Matthews (*née* Fittall); *m* 1984, Sally Vivien Davies; two *s*. *Educ*: Peterhouse, Cambridge (BA Hons History). Admin. Trainee, DHSS, 1974; Private Sec. to Perm. Sec., DHSS, 1978–79; Dist Gen. Administrator, Bloomsbury HA, 1984; Gen. Manager, Middlesex Hosp., 1985; Dist Gen. Manager, Maidstone HA, 1988; Chief Executive: St Thomas' Hosp., 1991; Guy's and St Thomas' Hosp. Trust, 1993–2000; Chief Exec., Highways Agency, 2000–03; Man. Dir, Parsons Brinckerhoff Ltd, 2003–08. Dir, J. Laing plc, 2004–07. Director: S Bank Careers, 1996–2000; Focus Central London TEC, 1997–2001; S Bank Employers' Gp, 1998–2000; Geoffrey Osborne Ltd, 2011–. Trustee, Kent Community Housing Trust, 1991–94. Gov., Univ. of Coventry, 2010–18. *Recreations*: opera, long distance walking, watching cricket, collecting wine. *Club*: Surrey CC.

**MATTHEWS, Trevor John;** Chairman: 1stAvailable Ltd, since 2015; State Insurance Regulatory Authority, since 2015; *b* Sydney, 25 March 1952; *s* of Jack and Vinda Latham Matthews; *m* 1999, Michele; two *s*; one *s* from previous marriage. *Educ*: Macquarie Univ., Sydney (MA 1978). FIA 1975. Legal & General Assce Hldgs Australia, 1972–89, Man. Dir, 1989–96; Gen. Manager, Personal Financial Services, National Australia Bank, 1996–98; Exec. Gen. Manager, Canadian Ops, Manulife, 1998–2001; Pres. and CEO, Manulife Japan, 2001–04; Chief Executive: UK Financial Services, Standard Life, 2004–08; Friends Provident, 2008–11; Chief Exec., 2011–12, Chm., 2012–13, Aviva UK; Exec. Dir and Chm., Developed Markets, Aviva plc, 2012–13. Non-executive Director: FNZ Australia Pty Ltd, 2013–; Cover-More Insce, 2013–; Bupa Australia, 2014–; AMP, 2014–. Chm., Financial Skills Partnership (formerly Financial Services Skills Council), 2010–13; Mem., UK Commn for Employment and Skills, 2011–13. *Recreations*: travel, reading, family. *Clubs*: Union, University and Schools of Sydney; Royal Sydney Yacht Squadron.

**MATTHEWS, Rt Rev. Victoria;** Bishop of Christchurch, 2008–18; *b* 1954; *d* of late Beverley Matthews and Pauline Ritchie Matthews. *Educ*: Trinity Coll., Univ. of Toronto (BA (Hons) 1976; ThM 1987); Yale Univ. Divinity Sch. (MDiv 1979). Ordained deacon, 1979, priest, 1980; Asst Curate, St Andrew, Scarborough, 1979–83; Incumbent: Parish of Georgina, York-Simcoe, 1983–87; All Souls, Lansing, York-Scarborough, 1987–94; Suffragan Bishop of Toronto (Bishop of the Credit Valley), 1994–97; Bishop of Edmonton (Alberta), 1997–2007; Bishop-in-residence, Wycliffe Coll., Toronto, 2008. N Amer. Theol Fellow, 1976–79. Mem., Inter-Anglican Standing Commn on Unity Faith and Order, 2008–. *Recreations*: reading, hiking, swimming, travel.

**MATTHEWS, His Honour (William) David;** a Circuit Judge, 1992–2008; *b* 19 Nov. 1940; *s* of Edwin Kenneth William Matthews and Bessie Matthews; *m* 1965, Pauline Georgina May Lewis; two *s*. *Educ*: Wycliffe Coll. Admitted Solicitor, 1964; Partner, T. A. Matthews & Co., 1965–92; a Recorder, 1990–92. Tribunal Judge, First-tier Tribunal (Health, Educn and Social Care Chamber) (formerly Mem., Mental Health Review Tribunal), 2001–11. Chm., W Mercia Criminal Justice Strategy Cttee, 2000–03. Pres., Herefordshire, Breconshire and Radnorshire Incorp. Law Soc., 1988–89. Mem. Council, Three Counties Agricl Soc., 1978–2001. Gov., Wycliffe Coll., 1985–90. *Recreations*: cricket, boats, National Hunt racing.

**MATTHIAS, David Huw;** QC 2006; FCIArb; *b* Cardiff, 13 Feb. 1954; *s* of David and Joan Matthias; *m* 1981, Sarah Widdows; three *s* one *d*. Lieut, RTR, 1973–76. Called to the Bar, Inner Temple, 1980; in practice as barrister, specialising in commercial litigation and arbitration, judicial review. FCIArb 1999. *Recreations*: supporting Welsh Rugby, sailing, running and walking with my dogs, cooking and eating out, theatre-going. *Address*: Francis Taylor Building, Inner Temple, EC4Y 7BY. *T*: (020) 7353 8415, *Fax*: (020) 7353 7622. *E*: david.matthias@ftb.eu.com.

**MATTHIAS, David Richard E.;** *see* Everitt-Matthias.

**MATTILA, Karita Marjatta;** opera singer, soprano; *b* 5 Sept. 1960; *d* of Erkki and Arja Mattila; *m* 1992, Tapio Kuneinen. *Educ*: Sibelius Acad., Helsinki; private studies in London. Début: Finnish Nat. Opera, 1983; Royal Opera House, Covent Garden, 1986; Metropolitan Opera, NY, 1990; has performed in opera houses worldwide; major rôles include: Donna Elvira, Don Giovanni, Vienna State Opera and Metropolitan Opera, 1990; Amelia in Simon Boccanegra, Teatro Colon, 1995, Florence, 2002; title rôle, Manon Lescaut, Tampere Opera, Finland, 1999, Metropolitan Opera, NY, 2008; title rôle, Salome, Paris Opera, 2003, Metropolitan Opera, 2004, 2008; title rôle, Tosca, Metropolitan Opera, 2009, Munich Opera Fest., 2010; created rôle of Emilie in Emilie de Châtelet, Opera Nat. de Lyon, 2010; Marie in Wozzeck, ROH, 2013; title rôle in Ariadne auf Naxos, ROH, 2014; Madame de Croissy in Dialogues des Carmélites, Metropolitan Opera, 2019; has performed with conductors incl. Abbado, Haitink, Mehta and Solti; has worked with theatre directors incl. Luc Bondy and Lev Dodin; concert and recital performances. Has made numerous recordings. Outstanding Perf. Award, Evening Standard, 1997; François Reichenbech Prize, Académie du Disque Lyrique, 1997; Grammy Awards, 1998, 2004; Musician of Year Award, Musical America, 2005. Hon. RAM 2011. Chevalier des Arts et des Lettres (France), 2003. *Address*: c/o HarrisonParrott, The Ark, 201 Talgarth Road, W6 8BJ.

**MATTINGLEY, Brig. Colin Grierson,** CBE 1985 (OBE 1980); Clerk to the Grocers' Company, 1988–98; *b* 12 Oct. 1938; *s* of Lt-Col Wallace Grierson Mattingley, KOSB and Jeanette McLaren Mattingley (*née* Service); *m* 1964, Margaretta Eli Kühle; two *d*. *Educ*: Wellington Coll.; RMA Sandhurst. rcds, ndc, psc. Commnd KOSB, 1958; sc 1971; comd 1st Bn KOSB, 1979–81; Jun. Directing Staff, RCDS, 1981–82; Comdr, 8 Inf. Bde, 1982–84; Dir, Army Service Conditions, 1985–87; retd 1988. Col, KOSB, 1990–95. *Recreations*: sketching, walking, landscape gardening, sculpting. *Address*: 51 Coxwell Street, Cirencester, Glos GL7 2BQ. *Clubs*: Army and Navy, Victory Services.

**MATTINGLY, Prof. David John,** PhD; FSA; FBA 2003; Professor of Roman Archaeology, since 1998, and Head, School of Archaeology and Ancient History, 2015–19, University of Leicester; *b* 18 May 1958; *s* of Harold B. Mattingly and Erica R. Mattingly (*née* Stuart); *m* 1981, Jennifer Warrell-Bowring; one *s* two *d*. *Educ*: Univ. of Manchester (BA 1st Cl. Hons History 1980; PhD 1984). British Acad. Postdoctoral Fellow, Inst. of Archaeol., Univ. of Oxford, 1986–89; Asst Prof., Dept of Classical Studies, Univ. of Michigan, 1989–91; University of Leicester: Lectr, 1991–95, Reader, 1995–98, Acting Hd, 1998–99, 2002, 2013–14, Sch. of Archaeol. and Ancient Hist.; Dir of Res., Coll. of Arts, Humanities and Law, 2009–12; Site Dir for Univ. of Leicester, Midlands3Cities PhD consortium, 2013–16. British Acad. Res. Reader, 1999–2001. Chm., Soc. for Libyan Studies, 1996–2001. Eur. Res. Council grant assessor, 2009, 2011, 2013; Panel Mem., RAE 2008 (Archaeol. and Classics), REF 2014 (Archaeol.), Sub-Panel Chair, REF 2021 (Archaeol.). Lectures: Miriam Balmuth, Tufts Univ., 2006; T. S. Jerome, Rome and Univ. of Michigan, 2013. FSA 1993. MAE 2013. *Publications*: (ed jtly) Town and Country in

Roman Tripolitania, 1985; (ed jtly) Libya: research in archaeology, environment, history and society, 1989; (with B. Jones) An Atlas of Roman Britain, 1990, rev. edn 1993; (ed jtly) Leptiminus (Lamta): a Roman port city in Tunisia, Report No 1, 1992; Tripolitania, 1995; (ed jtly) Farming the Desert: the UNESCO Libyan Valleys Archaeological Survey, Vols 1 and 2, 1996 (J. Wiseman Book Award); (ed) Dialogues in Roman Imperialism: power, discourse and discrepant experience in the Roman Empire, 1997; (ed jtly) Life, Death and Entertainment in Ancient Rome, 1999; (ed jtly) Geographical Information Systems and Landscape Archaeology, 1999; (series ed.) Archaeology of Mediterranean Landscapes, 5 vols, 1999–2000; (ed jtly) Economies Beyond Agriculture in the Classical World, 2001; (jtly) Leptiminus (Lamta): a Roman port city in Tunisia: the east baths, cemeteries, kilns, Venus mosaic, site museum and other studies, Report No 2, 2001, the urban survey, Report No 3, 2011; (jtly) The Archaeology of Fazzan, Vol. 1, Synthesis, 2003, Vol. 2, Gazetteer, Pottery and Other Finds, 2007, Vol. 3, Excavations by C. M. Daniels, 2010, Vol. 4, Survey and Excavations at Old Jarma, 2013; (ed jtly) The Libyan Desert: natural resources and cultural heritage, 2006; An Imperial Possession: Britain in the Roman Empire, 2006; (ed jtly) Cambridge Dictionary of Classical Civilization, 2006; (ed jtly) Archaeology and Desertification: the Wadi Faynan landscape survey, southern Jordan, 2007; (ed jtly) From Present to Past through Landscape, 2009; Imperialism, Power and Identity Experiencing the Roman Empire, 2011; (jtly) Trade in the Ancient Sahara and Beyond, 2017; (jtly) Burials, Migration and Identity in the Ancient Sahara and Beyond, 2019; (jtly) Urbanisation and State Formation in the Ancient Sahara and Beyond, 2019; 275 articles and papers. *Recreations:* family, book group. *Address:* School of Archaeology and Ancient History, University of Leicester, Leicester LE1 7RH. *T:* (0116) 252 2610, *Fax:* (0116) 252 5005. *E:* djm7@le.ac.uk.

**MATTINSON, Deborah Susan;** Founder Director, BritainThinks, and WorldThinks, since 2010; *b* 17 Sept. 1956; *d* of late R. R. and J. M. Mattinson; *m* 1989, David Arnold Pelly; two *s* one *d. Educ:* Bristol Univ. (LLB). Account Manager, McCann Erickson, 1978–83; Account Dir, Ayer Barker, 1983–85; Co-founder, Gould Mattinson, 1985–90; Founder, GMA Monitor, 1990–92; Jt CEO, Opinion Leader Res., 1992–2007; Jt Chm., Chime Res. and Engagement Div., 2000–10. Comr, EOC, 2002–07. Chair, Young Women's Trust (formerly YWCA), 2012–. Trustee: Green Alliance, 2004–09; Dance Umbrella, 2008–14; Theatre Royal Stratford East, 2016–. *Publications:* Talking to a Brick Wall: how New Labour stopped listening to the voter and why we need a new politics, 2010. *Recreations:* family, reading, walking, theatre.

**MATTMANN, Sara Binzer;** *see* Hobolt, S. B.

**MATUSSEK, Thomas;** Senior Adviser, Flint Global, since 2016; *b* 18 Sept. 1947; *m* 1975, Ursula Schütten; one *s* two *d. Educ:* Sorbonne, Paris; Univ. of Bonn. Judge's Asst and Asst Lectr, Univ. of Bonn, 1973–75; entered German Foreign Service, 1975; Foreign Office, Bonn, 1975–77; London, 1977–80; Federal Chancellery, European Affairs, Bonn, 1980–83; New Delhi, 1983–86; Lisbon, 1986–88; Foreign Office, Bonn, 1988–92; Chief of Staff and Hd of Foreign Minister's Private Office, Bonn, 1992–94; Dep. Chief of Mission, Washington, 1994–99; Dir Gen., Political Affairs, Foreign Office, 1999–2002; Ambassador to UK, 2002–06; Permanent Representative of Germany to the UN, 2006–09; Ambassador of Germany to India, 2009–11. Head of Public Affairs, Deutsche Bank AG, 2011–13; Man. Dir, Alfred Herrhausen Soc., 2013–16. *Recreations:* mountaineering, ski-ing. *Clubs:* Athenæum, Royal Automobile, Naval and Military, Travellers.

**MATUTES JUAN, Abel;** President, Palladium Hotel Group (formerly Fiesta Hotel Group S.L.), since 2005; Chairman, Grupo de Empresas Matutes; *b* 31 Oct. 1941; *s* of Antonio Matutes and Carmen Juan; *m* Nieves Prats Prats; one *s* three *d. Educ:* University of Barcelona (Law and Economic Sciences). Prof., Barcelona Univ., 1963; Vice-Pres., Employers Organization for Tourism, Ibiza-Formentera, 1964–79; Mayor of Ibiza, 1970–71; Senator, Ibiza and Formentera in Alianza Popular (opposition party), 1977–82; Vice-Pres., Partido Popular (formerly Alianza Popular), 1979– (Pres., Economy Cttee); Mem., EEC, 1986–94; MEP for Spain, 1994–96; Pres., Commn for External Relations and Security, EP, 1994–96; Minister for Foreign Affairs, Spain, 1996–2000. Pres., Nat. Electoral Cttee; Spokesman for Economy and Finance, Grupo Popular in Congress (Parlt). Member: Bd, Banco Santander, 2002–; Adv. Bd, TUI. *Recreation:* tennis. *Address:* POB 416, Ibiza. *Clubs:* Golf Rocalliza (Ibiza); de Campo Tennis (Ibiza).

**MAUCERI, John Francis;** conductor, educator, writer and producer; Founding Director, Hollywood Bowl Orchestra, since 2006 (Director, 1991–97; Principal Conductor, 1997–2006); *b* 12 Sept. 1945; *s* of Gene B. Mauceri and Mary Elizabeth (*née* Marino); *m* 1968, Betty Ann Weiss; one *s. Educ:* Yale Univ. (BA, MPhil). Music Dir, Yale Symphony Orch., 1968–74; Associate Prof., Yale Univ., 1974–84; Music Director: Washington Opera, 1979–82; Orchestras, Kennedy Center, 1979–91; Amer. Symphony Orch., NYC, 1985–87; Scottish Opera, 1987–93; Teatro Regio, Torino, 1994–98; Pittsburgh Opera, 2001–06; Leonard Bernstein Fest., LSO, 1986; Conductor, Amer. Nat. Tour, Boston Pops Orch., 1987; Musical Dir, Candide, NY, 1973; co-Producer, musical play, On Your Toes, 1983; Musical Supervisor, Song and Dance, Broadway, 1985; Guest Conductor major orchestras, incl. NY Philharmonic, Chicago SO, LSO, ORF, LA Philharmonic, LPO, NY Philharmonic and opera houses, incl. La Scala, Royal Opera House, ENO, Metropolitan, NY, Deutsche Oper, Berlin, San Francisco Opera, Chicago Lyric; Conductor/arranger, Grammy Awards 50th Anniv., 2008; Creative Consultant, Walt Disney Educnl Prodns, 2009. Vis. Prof., Yale Univ., 2001. Dir, Charles Ives Soc., 1986–91 (Mem., 1986–); Mem., Adv. Bd, Amer. Inst. for Verdi Studies, 1986–; Consultant: for Music Theater, Kennedy Center for Performing Arts, Washington, 1982–91; Leonard Bernstein Orgn, 2006–; Trustee, Nat. Inst. for Music Theater, 1986–91. Member Advisory Board: Kurt Weill Edn, 1996–; Leonard Bernstein Center for Learning, 2006–; Film Music Soc., 2006–. Chancellor, Univ. of N Carolina Sch. of the Arts (formerly N Carolina Sch. of the Arts), 2006–13. Fellow, Amer. Acad. Berlin, 1999. Television appearances; numerous recordings, incl. first recording of Blitzstein's The Cradle Will Rock, 2018 (Grammy award for Candide recording, 1987; Edison Klassiek Award, 1991; Deutsche Schallplatten Prize, 1991, 1992, 1993, 1994; ECHO Award for Das Wunder der Heliane, 1994; Cannes Classical Award for Kurt Weill's Der Protagonist, 2003); soundtrack to film Evita, 1996; contrib. to film score DVD commentary, incl. El Cid, The Fall of the Roman Empire, The Adventures of Robin Hood, Bambi, Sunset Blvd, The Sea, Hawk, West Side Story. Antoinette Perry Award, League of NY Theatres and Producers, 1983; Drama Desk Award, 1983; Outer Critics Circle Award, 1983; Arts award, Yale Univ., 1985; Olivier award for Best Musical for Candide, adaptation for Scottish Opera/Old Vic prodn, 1988; Wavenden All Music Award for Conductor of the Year, 1989; Emmy Award, 1994, 1998, 2014; Soc. for Preservation of Film Music Award, 1995; Diapason d'Or, 1997 and 2007; Treasures of LA Award, 2007; Nat. Educnl Telecommunications Award, 2012; Oliver Ditson Conducting Award, Columbia Univ., 2015. Contrib., Huffington Post blogs, 2012–. *Publications:* (contrib.) Sennets and Tuckets: a Bernstein celebration (ed Ledbetter), 1988; (contrib.) Atti di Convegno Internazionale: Verdi 2001, 2003; Celebrating West Side Story, 2007; Maestros and Their Music: the art and alchemy of conducting, 2017; For the Love of Music: a conductor's guide to the art of listening, 2019; musical editor of many works; various articles for Scottish Opera programmes, newspapers, magazines and jls. *Address:* c/o Columbia Artists Management, 1790 Broadway, New York, NY 10019-1412, USA. *W:* www.johnmauceri.com.

**MAUDE,** family name of **Viscount Hawarden** and **Baron Maude of Horsham**.

**MAUDE OF HORSHAM,** Baron *cr* 2015 (Life Peer), of Shipley in the County of West Sussex; **Francis Anthony Aylmer Maude;** PC 1992; *b* 4 July 1953; *s* of Baron Maude of Stratford-upon-Avon, TD, PC; *m* 1984, Christina Jane, *yr d* of late Peter Hadfield, Shrewsbury; two *s* three *d. Educ:* Abingdon Sch.; Corpus Christi Coll., Cambridge (MA (Hons) History; Avory Studentship; Halse Prize). Called to Bar, Inner Temple, 1977 (scholar; Forster Boulton Prize), Bencher, 2011. Councillor, Westminster CC, 1978–84. MP (C) Warwicks N, 1983–92; contested (C) Warwicks N, 1992; MP (C) Horsham, 1997–2015. PPS to Minister of State for Employment, 1984–85; an Asst Government Whip, 1985–87; Parly Under Sec. of State, DTI, 1987–89; Minister of State, FCO, 1989–90; Financial Sec. to HM Treasury, 1990–92; Shadow Chancellor, 1998–2000; Shadow Foreign Sec., 2000–01; Chm., Conservative Party, 2005–07; Shadow Minister for the Cabinet Office and Shadow Chancellor of the Duchy of Lancaster, 2007–10; Minister for the Cabinet Office and Paymaster Gen., 2010–15; Minister of State (Minister for Trade and Investment), BIS and FCO, 2015–16. Chm., Govt's Deregulation Task Force, 1994–97. Director: Salomon Brothers, 1992–93; Asda Gp, 1992–99; Man. Dir, 1993–97, Adv. Dir, 1997–98, Morgan Stanley & Co.; Dep. Chm., Benfield Gp, 2003–08; Chairman: Incepta Gp, 2004–06; Mission Marketing Gp, 2006–09. Partner, Francis Maude Associates, 2016–; Sen. Advr, Covington & Burling LLP, 2016–; Chm., Cogent Elliot Gp Ltd, 2016–. *Recreations:* ski-ing, cricket, reading, music. *Address:* House of Lords, SW1A 0PW.

**MAUDSLAY, Richard Henry,** CBE 2006; FREng; FIET; Chairman, Advisory Board, Perseus Global Ltd, 2009–18; Adviser: Geothermic Solutions LLC, since 2013; Marble Arch Partners LLC, since 2018; *b* 19 Nov. 1946; *s* of Cecil Winton Maudslay and Charity Magdalen (*née* Johnston); *m* 1968, Rosalind Elizabeth Seville; two *d. Educ:* Christ's Hosp., Horsham; Edinburgh Univ. (BSc Electrical Engrg). CEng 1977; FIET (FIEE 1985); FREng 1994. Grad. trainee, Scottish Electrical Trng Scheme, 1968–69; Systems Analyst, Parsons Peebles, 1969–71; Systems Manager: Reyrolle Belmos, 1971–72; and Corporate Planner, Parsons Peebles, 1972–74; Prodn Manager, Parsons Peebles Power Transformers, 1974–78; Gen. Manager, Transformadores Parsons Peebles de Mexico, 1978–85; Managing Director: NEI Parsons, 1985–92; Rolls-Royce Industrial Power Gp, 1992–97 (Mem. Bd, Rolls-Royce Plc, 1994–97). Chm., Hardy & Greys Ltd, 1999–2013; Dep. Chm., Port of Blyth, 2004–14; non-executive Director: dominick hunter Gp plc, 2000–05; N G Bailey Gp Ltd, 2001–10; Reece Gp Ltd, 2014–16. Mem. Bd, One NorthEast (RDA), 1999–2004 (Dep. Chm., 2002–04). Chairman: N E Sci. and Industry Council, 2004–08; Defence Sci. and Technol. Lab., MoD, 2005–08; Nat. Nuclear Lab., 2009–15. Mem., Business Chamber, Enterprise Policy Gp, EC, 2007–12. Pres., BEAMA, 1996–98. Chm., British Mexican Soc., 2008–. *Recreations:* music, restoring and building houses, travel in Mexico. *Address:* High Ecclestoun, Rothbury, Morpeth, Northumberland NE65 7YJ.

**MAUGER-THOMPSON, Anita Joy, (Annie);** Director, Mauger-Thompson-Solo Ltd, since 2018; *b* Jersey, 19 March 1963; *m* 2018, James E. Thompson. *Educ:* Exeter Univ. (BA Hons Hist. 1984); Coll. of Librarianship, Wales (Postgrad. DipLib 1985); Leeds Metropolitan Univ. (MBA 2002). MCLIP 2004. Asst Librarian, Beds CC, 1986–87; Branch Librarian, E Lothian Council, 1987–88; various library roles, City of Edinburgh Council, 1988–95; Principal Librarian, Midlothian Council, 1995–99; Hd, Libraries and Heritage, City of York, 2000–03; Chief Exec., Yorks MLA, 2003–08; Acting CEO, Bradford Action for Refugees, 2009–10; management consultant, 2009–10; Chief Exec., CILIP, 2010–14; Exec. Dir, Devolved Nations (formerly Dir, Nat. Business Units), Chartered Inst. of Housing, 2014–18. *Address:* Musselburgh, East Lothian.

**MAUGHAM, Jolyon Toby Dennis;** QC 2015; *b* London, 1 July 1971; *s* of David Henry Benedictus, *qv* and Lynne Joyce Maugham and adopted *s* of Alan Barker; *m* 2007, Claire Elizabeth Prihartini; three *d. Educ:* Wellington High Sch., New Zealand; Durham Univ. (LLB); Katholieke Universiteit Leuven; Birkbeck Coll., Univ. of London (MA). BVC. Called to the Bar, Middle Temple, 1997; in practice as a barrister, 1997–. Praeses Elit, 2018. *Recreations:* windmilling, reading Beckett, tax policy, child rearing. *Address:* Devereux Chambers, 3 Devereux Court, WC2R 3JH. *T:* (020) 7353 7534. *E:* maugham@devchambers.co.uk.

**MAUGHAN, Sir Deryck C.,** Kt 2002; Senior Advisor, Kohlberg Kravis Roberts & Company, 2013–14 (Partner, 2005–13); *b* 20 Dec. 1947; *s* of Renwick Maughan and Muriel Maughan; *m* 1981, Va; one *d. Educ:* King's Coll., London (BA Hons 1969); Stanford Univ. (MS 1978). HM Treasury, 1969–79; Chief Exec., Salomon Bros, 1992–97; Vice Chm., Citigroup Inc., 1998–2004. Vice-Chm., NY Stock Exchange, 1996–2000. Harkness Fellow, 1977–78. Trustee, British Mus., 2013–. *Club:* Metropolitan (New York).

**MAULEVERER, (Peter) Bruce;** QC 1985; FCIArb 1997; a Recorder, 1985–2004; a Deputy High Court Judge, 1992–2004; *b* 22 Nov. 1946; *s* of late Major Algernon Arthur Mauleverer and Hazel Mary Mauleverer; *m* 1971, Sara (*née* Hudson-Evans); two *s* two *d. Educ:* Sherborne School; University College, Univ. of Durham (BA 1968); Birkbeck Coll., Univ. of London (MA Philos. 2007); Univ. of Buckingham (MA Mil. Hist. 2012). Called to the Bar, Inner Temple, 1969, Bencher 1993; Hd of Chambers, 4 Pump Ct, 1992–2000. Patron, Internat. Law Assoc., 2014– (Hon. Sec.-Gen., 1986–93; Vice-Chm., 1993–2014; Patron, 2014–). Vice-Pres., International. Social Sci. Council, UNESCO, 1998–2000. Trustee: UNICEF UK, 2002–08; Tavistock Centre for Couple Relationships, 2005–16; Jubilee Sailing Trust, 2006–13 (Chm., 2009–13); MapAction, 2010–13; The Listen Charity, 2014– (Chm., 2016–); Northwick Park Inst. for Medical Res., 2015–. Mem., Knights of the Round Table, 2015–. *Recreations:* sailing, ski-ing, travel, opera. *Address:* Eliot Vale House, 8 Eliot Vale, Blackheath, SE3 0UW. *T:* (020) 8852 2070. *Clubs:* Garrick, Royal Ocean Racing, Royal Yacht Squadron, Royal Cruising, Pilgrims.

**MAUNSELL, (Caroline) Harriet,** OBE 1994; *b* 22 Aug. 1943; *d* of Dr Geoffrey Sharman Dawes and Margaret Joan (*née* Monk); *m* 1986, Michael Brooke Maunsell, *qv. Educ:* Somerville Coll., Oxford (MA 1965). Called to the Bar, Middle Temple, 1973; Solicitor, 1978. Courtaulds Ltd, 1965–77; Lovell White & King, subseq. Lovells, 1977–97, Partner, 1980–97. Member: Occupational Pensions Bd, 1987–97 (Dep. Chm., 1992–97; Chm., 1993); Council, Occupational Pensions Adv. Service, 1990–93; OPRA, 1997–2005 (Chm., 2001–05). Co-founder and first Chm., Assoc. of Pension Lawyers, 1984–85 (Mem. cttees, 1984–97). Non-executive Director: Serious Fraud Office, 2004–09; Pension Insurance Corp., 2012–16; Mem., With-Profits Cttee, Aviva (formerly Norwich Union), 2007–11. Dir, Ambache Chamber Orchestra, 1996–2002; Council Mem., Cheltenham Ladies' Coll., 1998–2001; Mem., Somerville Develt Bd, 2004–10 (Chm., 2005–10). *Publications:* (with Jane Samsworth) Guide to the Pensions Act 1995, 1995. *Recreations:* reading, music, travel. *Address:* 21 Edward's Cottages, N1 2XL.

**MAUNSELL, Michael Brooke;** b 29 Jan. 1942; s of Captain Terence Augustus Ker Maunsell, RN and Elizabeth (née Brooke); m 1st, 1965, Susan Pamela Smith (marr. diss. 1986; she d 2015); 2nd, 1986, (Caroline) Harriet Dawes (see C. H. Maunsell). Educ: Monkton Combe Sch.; Gonville and Caius Coll., Cambridge (MA, LLB); Rose Bruford Coll. (BA Opera Studies). Admitted Solicitor, 1967; with Lovell White & King (Solicitors), 1967–88: Partner, 1971–88; Admin. Partner, 1978–83; Partner, 1988–97, Managing Partner, 1993–97, Lovell White Durrant; Sen. Fellow, British Inst. of Internat. and Comparative Law, 1998–2000. Mem., Determinations Panel, Pensions Regulator, 2005–12. Dir, J. M. Jones & Sons (Holdings) Ltd, 1981–91. Chm., Educn and Trng Cttee, City of London Law Soc., 1978–91; Mem., London (No 13) Local, then Area, Legal Aid Cttee, 1971–89. Adminr, City Solicitors Educnl Trust, 2000–08. Trustee: Highgate Cemetery Charity, 1988–95; Kings Corner Project (Islington), 1997–2008; Richard Cloudesley's Charity, 2010– (Vice-Chair, 2013–18); Dulwich Almshouse Charity, 2010–17; Dulwich Estate, 2012–17. Governor: Grey Coat Hosp., Westminster, 1997–2005; Bishopsgate Foundn, 2002–12 (Dep. Chm., 2007–08; Chm., 2008–11). Liveryman, City of London Solicitors' Co., 1973–. Recreations: opera, theatre, travel, good living. Address: 21 Edward's Cottages, N1 2XL.

**MAUREY, Catherine Ésöhé, (Kiki),** OBE 2013; executive coach-mentor-speaker, since 2009; Director, Kiki Maurey Consultancy Ltd, since 2007; b Parkstone, Poole, 11 June 1952; d of Ernest Danson Omoregie and Barbara Vivienne Maurey (née Blewett). Educ: Univ. of Southampton (BSc Jt Hons Politics and Sociol. 1989); Univ. of Warwick Business Sch. (MBA 1991); Oxford Sch. of Coaching and Mentoring (Adv. Dip. (Dist.), Professional Coach-Mentoring 2009). Child minder and cleaning lady, 1972–81; admin posts commencing with temp. clerk typist, Health and Housing, New Forest DC, 1982–86; Econ. Develt Unit, Southampton CC, 1989–90; various pt-time roles, 1990–92, incl. Sen. Lectr, Univ. of Bournemouth, trng consultant to Exxon Chemicals Ltd; Dir, Business Ops and Mktg, Focus Consultancy Ltd, 1992–95; various sen. freelance contracts, 1995–97; Sen. Prog. Dir (pt-time), Southampton, Common Purpose, 1997–2000; various sen. freelance policy and prog. contracts, 2000–02, incl. Policy Innovation Unit, DfES and DoH; Sen. Fellow (pt-time), OPM, 2002–03; Women's Enterprise Champion and Consultant (pt-time), Small Business Service, DTI, 2003–06; Associate Dir, Strategy (pt-time), Prowess, 2004–05; various sen. freelance mgt and policy contracts, public, not-for-profit and private sectors, 2003–07. Non-executive Director: Southampton and SW Hampshire HA (Chm., Audit Cttee), 1997–2002; Learning and Skills Develt Agency, 2002–04; Mem. Bd, Nat. Ethnic Minority Business Task Force, 2007–09; Chm., S Central Connexions Partnership, 2002–05. Recreations: maximising purpose and enjoyment in my professional and personal life; lover of books, gardening, birdwatching and my horses; regular contributor and author on life and leadership, etc. Address: Holly House, 31 Queens Road, Lyndhurst, Hants SO43 7BR. T: 07760 270392. E: kiki@kikimaurey.com.

**MAURICE, Clare;** Founder Partner, Maurice Turnor Gardner LLP, since 2009; b Frimley, Surrey, 25 Feb. 1954; d of Antony Colin Deans Rankin and Barbara Rankin (née Vernon); m 1980, Ian Maurice; two d. Educ: Sherborne Sch. for Girls; Univ. of Birmingham (LLB Hons). Admitted Solicitor, 1978; Partner, Allen & Overy LLP, 1985–2009. Dir, Symm Gp Ltd, 2009–15. Chairman: Barts and the London Charity, 2001–09; SafeLives (formerly Coordinated Action Against Domestic Abuse), 2011–17. Trustee, The London Clinic, 2015–17. Recreations: theatre, the turf, travel, champagne. Address: 33 Norland Square, W11 4PU. T: (020) 7221 0962. E: clare.maurice@mtgllp.com. Club: Reform.

**MAURICE, Rt Rev. Peter David;** Bishop Suffragan of Taunton, 2006–15; b 16 April 1951; s of Eric and Pamela Maurice; m 1977, Elizabeth Maun; two s one d. Educ: Durham Univ. (BA 1972); Coll. of the Resurrection, Mirfield. Ordained deacon, 1975, priest, 1976; Curate, St Paul, Wandsworth, 1975–79; Team Vicar, Mortlake with E Sheen, 1979–85; Vicar, Holy Trinity, Rotherhithe, 1985–96; RD, Bermondsey, 1991–96; Vicar, All Saints, Tooting, 1996–2003; Archdeacon of Wells, 2003–06. Recreations: avid sports fan, enjoying holidays, birdwatching. Address: 14 Saltwood Road, Maidstone ME15 6UY.

**MAURICE, Dr Rita Joy;** Director of Statistics, Home Office, 1977–89; b 10 May 1929; d of A. N. Maurice and F. A. Maurice (née Dean). Educ: East Grinstead County Sch.; University Coll., London. BSc (Econ) 1951; PhD 1958. Asst Lectr, subseq. Lectr in Economic Statistics, University Coll., London, 1951–58; Statistician, Min. of Health, 1959–62; Statistician, subseq. Chief Statistician, Central Statistical Office, 1962–72; Head of Economics and Statistics Div. 6, Depts of Industry, Trade and Prices and Consumer Protection, 1972–77. Member: Council, Royal Statistical Soc., 1978–82; Parole Bd, 1991–94; Retail Prices Index Adv. Cttee, 1992–94. Publications: (ed) National Accounts Statistics: sources and methods, 1968; articles in statistical jls. Address: 10 Fairfax Place, Swiss Cottage, NW6 4EH.

**MAVOR, Prof. John,** FREng; FRSE; Vice-President (Physical Science and Engineering), Royal Society of Edinburgh, 2004–07; Principal and Vice-Chancellor, Napier University, 1994–2002; b 18 July 1942; s of Gordon Hattersley Mavor and Wilhelmina Baillie McAllister; m 1968, Susan Christina Colton; two d. Educ: City Univ., London; London Univ. (BSc, PhD, DSc(Eng)); Edinburgh Univ. (MPhil 2007). FInstP; FIEEE; FIET. AEI Res. Labs, London, 1964–65; Texas Instruments Ltd, Bedford, 1968–70; Emihus Microcomponents, Glenrothes, 1970–71; University of Edinburgh: Lectr, 1971; Reader, 1979; Lothian Chair of Microelectronics, 1980; Head of Dept of Electrical Engrg, 1984–89; Prof. of Electrical Engrg, 1986–94; Dean, 1989–94, and Provost, 1992–94, Faculty of Sci. and Engrg. Hon. DSc: Greenwich, 1998; City, 1998. Publications: MOST Integrated Circuit Engineering, 1973; Introduction to MOS LSI Design, 1983; over 150 technical papers in professional electronics jls. Recreations: gardening, walking, steam railways.

**MAVOR, Katherine Lyndsay;** Chief Executive, English Heritage, since 2015; b London, 30 March 1962; d of John Mavor and Jennifer Mavor; m 1989, Andrew Williams; two s. Educ: Westbourne Sch. for Girls, Glasgow; Trinity Coll., Oxford (MA Mod. Langs 1984); Hon. Fellow 2015). Poly of Central London (Postgrad. Dip. Mktg). Graduate trainee, Thomson Books, 1984–85; Product Manager, Macmillan Press, 1985–86; Publicity Manager, Unwin Hyman, 1987–88; Mktg Manager, Kogan Page, 1988–90; Mktg Dir, Regent Schs of English, 1990–94; Man. Dir, Anglo-Polish Interchange, 1994–97; Chief Executive: Language Line, 1998–2004; Project Scotland, 2005–09; Nat. Trust for Scotland, 2009–15. Trustee: Nat. Youth Th., 2012–18; Saltire Endowment Trust, 2014–16. DUniv Heriot-Watt, 2014. Recreations: hill walking, history, classical music, art, cinema, theatre, fiction, visiting heritage sites. Address: English Heritage, 100 Wood Street, EC2V 7AN. T: (020) 7973 3386. E: Kate.Mavor@english-heritage.org.uk.

**MAWBY, Colin (John Beverley);** conductor and composer; Conductor, National Irish Chamber Choir, 1996–2001; b 9 May 1936; e s of Bernard Mawby and Enid Mawby (née Vaux); m 1987, Beverley Courtney; two s. Educ: St Swithun's Primary Sch., Portsmouth; Westminster Cathedral Choir Sch.; Royal Coll. of Music. Organist and Choirmaster of Our Lady's Church, Warwick St, W1, 1953; Choirmaster of Plymouth Cath., 1955; Organist and Choirmaster of St Anne's, Vauxhall, 1957; Asst Master of Music, Westminster Cath., 1959; Master of Music, 1961–75; Dir of Music, Sacred Heart, Wimbledon, 1978–81; Choral Dir, Radio Telefis Eireann, 1981–95. Conductor: Westminster Chamber Choir, 1971–78; Westminster Cathedral String Orchestra, 1971–78; New Westminster Chorus, 1972–80; Horniman Singers, 1979–80. Prof. of Harmony, Trinity Coll. of Music, 1975–81. Director (Catholic) Publisher, L. J. Cary & Co., 1963; Vice-Pres., Brit. Fedn of Pueri Cantores, 1966; Member: Council, Latin Liturgical Assoc., 1969; Adv. Panel, Royal Sch. of Church Music, 1974; Music Sub-Cttee, Westminster Arts Council, 1974. Hon. FGCM 1988. Broadcaster and recording artist; freelance journalism. KSG 2006. Publications: Church music including fifty Masses, anthems, motets, two children's operas and Holy Week music. Recreation: wine drinking. Address: 29b Lawrence Road, East Ham, E6 1JN. E: colinmawby@btinternet.com.

**MAWBY, Peter John;** lecturer and ornithologist; Headmaster, Lancaster Royal Grammar School, 1983–2001; b 17 Aug. 1941; s of Norman James Mawby and May Mawby (née Huse); m 1968, Gillian Fay Moore; one s one d. Educ: Sedbergh Sch.; Queens' Coll., Cambridge (DipEd 1964; MA 1966). Assistant Teacher: Shrewsbury Sch., 1964–65; St John's Sch., Leatherhead, 1965–68; Head of Biology, Edinburgh Acad., 1968–79; Head of Science, Cheltenham Coll., 1979–83. Member: Council, Brathay Exploration Gp, 1989–95; Court, Lancaster Univ., 1989–2001; Headteacher Mentoring Exec. Cttee, Grant-Maintained Schs' Centre, 1992–99. Consultant, Rydal Hall, Dio. of Carlisle, 2003–05. Chm., Lancs br., Cambridge Soc., 2006–18; Pres., Old Lancastrian Club, 2006–07. Publications: (with M. B. V. Roberts) Biology 11–13, 1983; Biology Questions, 1985; Longman Science 11–14: Biology, 1991, 3rd edn 1996. Recreation: playing the 'cello. Address: Lowhill, Haverbreaks Road, Lancaster LA1 5BJ.

**MAWDSLEY, Harry Paul,** OBE 2003; JP; DL; Chairman, Magistrates' Association, 1999–2002; b 21 July 1939; s of Harry and Jessie Mawdsley; m 1970, Anne Horton Rigby (d 2014); two s. Educ: Univ. of Massachusetts (MSc 1969); Univ. of Manchester (MEd 1974). Teacher, Birmingham schs, 1961–66; Lectr, Alsager Trng Coll., Cheshire, 1966–85; Principal Lectr and Hd, Dept of Sport Sci., Crewe and Alsager Coll. of Higher Educn, 1985–88; Hd, Admissions and Mktg, Manchester Metropolitan Univ., 1988–99. Vice-Pres., British Univs Sports Assoc., 2000–. JP South Cheshire, 1975; DL Cheshire 2003. Recreations: jogging, gardening, foreign travel. Club: Army and Navy.

**MAWER, Sir Philip (John Courtney),** Kt 2002; Prime Minister's Independent Adviser on Ministerial Interests, 2008–11; b 30 July 1947; s of Eric Douglas and Thora Constance Mawer; m 1972, Mary Ann Moxon; one s two d. Educ: Hull Grammar Sch.; Edinburgh Univ. (MA Hons Politics 1971); DPA (London Univ. External) 1973. Senior Pres., Student Representative Council, 1969–70. Home Office, 1971; Private Sec. to Minister of State, 1974–76; Nuffield and Leverhulme Travelling Fellowship, 1978–79; Sec., Lord Scarman's Inquiry into Brixton disturbances, 1981; Asst Sec., Head of Industrial Relations, Prison Dept, 1984–87; Principal Private Sec. to Home Sec. (Rt Hon. Douglas Hurd), 1987–89; Under-Secretary, Cabinet Office, 1989–90; Secretary-General: Gen. Synod of C of E, 1990–2002; Archbishops' Council, 1999–2002; Parly Comr for Standards, 2002–07. Chm., Professional Regulation Exec. Cttee of Actuarial Profession, 2009–13; Member: Adv. Bd, Notarial Profession in Eng. and Wales, 2013–16; Business Cttee, Gen. Council, Univ. of Edinburgh, 2014–18. Dir, Ecclesiastical Insce Gp, 1996–2002, 2008–13 (Dep. Chm., 2010–13), Ind. Reviewer, Women Bishops Legislation, 2014–18. Mem., All Churches Trust, 1992– (Dir, 2010–; Dep. Chm., 2013; Chm., 2013–); Trustee, Foundn for Church Leadership, 2003–10; Mem. Governing Body, SPCK, 1994–2002. Patron: Church Homeless (formerly Housing) Trust, 1996–2019; Isabel Hospice, 2004–12. Hon. Lay Canon, St Alban's Cathedral, 2003–12; Provincial Canon, York Minster, 2015–. FRSA 1991–2007. Hon. FIA 2014. Hon. DLitt Hull, 2006; Hon. LLD Hertfordshire, 2007. Recreation: family and friends.

**MAWHINNEY,** family name of **Baron Mawhinney.**

**MAWHINNEY,** Baron cr 2005 (Life Peer), of Peterborough, in the county of Cambridgeshire; **Brian Stanley Mawhinney,** Kt 1997; PC 1994; b 26 July 1940; s of Frederick Stanley Arnot Mawhinney and Coralie Jean Mawhinney; m 1965, Betty Louise Oja; two s one d. Educ: Royal Belfast Academical Instn; Queen's Univ., Belfast (BSc); Univ. of Michigan, USA (MSc); Univ. of London (PhD). Asst Prof. of Radiation Research, Univ. of Iowa, USA, 1968–70; Lectr, subsequently Sen. Lectr, Royal Free Hospital School of Medicine, 1970–84. Mem., MRC, 1980–83. Mem., Gen. Synod of C of E, 1985–90. MP (C): Peterborough, 1979–97; Cambs NW, 1997–2005. PPS to Ministers in HM Treasury, Employment and NI, 1982–86; Under Sec. of State for NI, 1986–90; Minister of State: NI Office, 1990–92; DoH, 1992–94; Sec. of State for Transport, 1994–95; Minister without Portfolio, 1995–97; Opposition front bench spokesman on home affairs, 1997–98. Pres., Cons. Trade Unionists, 1987–90 (Vice-Pres., 1984–87); Chm. of Cons. Party, 1995–97. Mem., AUT. Contested (C) Stockton on Tees, Oct. 1974. Non-exec. dir of cos in England; Chm., Football League, 2003–10 (Hon. Pres., 2010–13); Jt Dep. Chm., England 2018 World Cup Bid, 2008–. Freedom, City of Peterborough, 2008. Hon. LLD QUB, 2008. Publications: (jtly) Conflict and Christianity in Northern Ireland, 1976; In the Firing Line, 1999; Just a Simple Belfast Boy (memoir), 2013. Recreations: sport, reading. Address: House of Lords, SW1A 0PW.

**MAWHOOD, Caroline Gillian, (Mrs J. P. Nettel);** Assistant Auditor General, National Audit Office, 1996–2009; b 17 July 1953; d of John Lennox Mawhood and Joan Constance Dick; m 1980, Julian Philip Nettel, qv; two s. Educ: Queen Anne's Sch., Caversham; Bristol Univ. (BScSoc Geography). CIPFA. Joined Exchequer and Audit Dept, 1976, Dep. Dir, 1989–92; Office of the Auditor General, Canada, 1992–93; Dir of Corporate Policy, Nat. Audit Office, 1993–95. Pres., CIPFA, 2008–09. Independent Member: Audit Cttee, DECC, 2010–16; Debt Mgt Office, 2010–19; Corp. of London, 2010–; Audit Progress Cttee, EC, 2011–19; Food Standards Agency, 2013–14. Member: Exec. Cttee, IFS; Bd, Kingston Univ. Trustee, 2007–15, Hon. Treas., 2009–15, Breast Cancer Now (formerly Breakthrough Breast Cancer); Trustee, Wimbledon Guild Charity, 2012–. Publications: (contrib.) State Audit in the European Union, 1996; (contrib.) Protecting the Public Purse, 2015. Recreations: golf, tennis, swimming, bridge. Clubs: Roehampton, Wimbledon Park Golf, Royal Thames Yacht.

**MAWREY, Richard Brooks;** QC 1986; a Recorder of the Crown Court, 1986–2015; a Deputy High Court Judge, 1995–2015; b 20 Aug. 1942; s of Philip Stephen Mawrey and Alice Brooks Mawrey; m 1965, Gillian Margaret Butt, d of Francis Butt and Alice Margaret Butt; one d. Educ: Rossall School; Magdalen College, Oxford (BA, 1st class Hons Law, 1963; Eldon Law Scholar, 1964; MA 1967). Albion Richardson Scholar, Gray's Inn, 1964; called to the Bar, Gray's Inn, 1964, Bencher, 2004; Lectr in Law, Magdalen College, Oxford, 1964–65, Trinity College, Oxford, 1965–69. An Election Comr, 1995–2015. Co-Founder and Trustee, Historic Gardens Foundn, 1995–; Chm., Oxfordshire Gardens Trust, 2002–06. Hon. DLaws Buckingham, 2018. Publications: Computers and the Law, 1988; specialist editor: Consumer Credit Legislation, 1983; Butterworths County Court Precedents, 1985; Bullen & Leake & Jacob's Precedents of Pleadings, 13th edn 1990, 17th edn 2012; Butterworths Civil Court Pleadings, 1999–; Butterworths Commercial and Consumer Law Handbook, 2005–; Goode: Consumer Credit Law and Practice, 2006; Blackstone's Guide to the Consumer Credit Act 2006, 2006; Encyclopaedia of Banking Laws, 2011–. Recreations: history, opera, cooking. Address: 2 Harcourt Buildings, Temple, EC4Y 9DB. T: (020) 7583 9020.

**MAWSON**, family name of **Baron Mawson**.

**MAWSON**, Baron *cr* 2007 (Life Peer), of Bromley-by-Bow, in the London Borough of Tower Hamlets; **Andrew Mawson**, OBE 2000; *b* 8 Nov. 1954; *s* of Jack and Mary Mawson; *m* 1975, Susan Barnes; two *s* one *d*. *Educ:* Manchester Univ. (BA 1979; MPhil 1987). Church Minister, United Reformed Church, 1984–. Founder, 1984, Chief Exec., 1984–96, now Pres., Bromley-by-Bow Centre; Co-Founder, 1998, Exec. Dir, 1998–2004, now Pres., Community Action Network. Founder Chm., 1996, now Pres., Stanton Guildhouse, Glos. Founder, 2006, Chm., 2012–, Water City CIC (formerly Water City Gp). Dir, Andrew Mawson Partnerships, St Paul's Way Transformation Project, 2007–; non-exec. Dir, Olympic Park Legacy Co., later London Legacy Develt Corp., 2009–18; Chairman: Well North, 2015–19; Well North Enterprises, 2018–. Chairman, Trustees: Legacy List, 2010–15; SS Robin Trust, 2015–17. Chm., Blackheath Conservatoire, 2012–15. *Publications:* (jtly) Church and the City, 1975; (jtly) People before Structures, 1999; The Social Entrepreneur, 2008; The St Paul's Way Transformation Project: building the road as we walk it, 2012. *Recreation:* music. *Address:* House of Lords, SW1A 0PW. *T:* (020) 7620 6000. *E:* andrew@amawsonpartnerships.com.

**MAXTON**, family name of **Baron Maxton**.

**MAXTON**, Baron *cr* 2004 (Life Peer), of Blackwaterfoot in Ayrshire and Arran; **John Alston Maxton**; *b* 5 May 1936; *s* of late John Maxton, agr. economist, and Jenny Maxton; *m* 1970, Christine Maxton; three *s*. *Educ:* Lord Williams' Grammar Sch., Thame; Oxford Univ. Lectr in Social Studies, Hamilton Coll. Chm., Assoc. of Lectrs in Colls of Educn, Scotland; Member: Educnl Inst. of Scotland; Socialist Educnl Assoc.; MSF. Joined Lab. Party, 1970. MP (Lab) Glasgow, Cathcart, 1979–2001. Opposition spokesman on health, local govt, and housing in Scotland, 1985–87, on Scotland, 1987–92; Scottish and Treasury Whip, 1984–85. Member: Scottish Select Cttee, 1981–83; Public Accounts Cttee, 1983–84; Culture, Media and Sport (formerly Nat. Heritage) Select Cttee, 1992–2001; Speaker's Panel of Chairmen, 1994–2001. *Recreations:* family, listening to jazz, gym and fitness, new technology.

**MAXTON, Julie Katharine**, CBE 2017; PhD; Executive Director, Royal Society, since 2011; Visiting Fellow, University College, Oxford, since 2011; *b* Edinburgh, 31 Aug. 1955; *d* of Col Kenneth Maxton and Katriona Justine Maxton; *m* 1984, Major James Donald Carson, MBE, FTCL (*d* 2008); one *s*. *Educ:* St George's Sch., Edinburgh; University Coll. London (LLB Hons 1976); Univ. of Canterbury (LLM Hons); MA Oxon; Univ. of Auckland (PhD 1990). Called to the Bar, Middle Temple, 1978, Bencher, 2012; admitted to Bar of NZ, 1982; in practice as a barrister, 1982–2006, Mem., 4 New Sq., 2012–; Lectr in Law, Univ. of Canterbury, 1978–85; University of Auckland: Sen. Lectr in Law, 1986–91; Associate Prof. of Law, 1992; Prof. of Law, 1993–2006; Dean, Faculty of Law, 2001–06; Dep. Vice Chancellor, 2003–04; Registrar, 2006–11, Mem., Law Faculty, 2006–11, Univ. of Oxford; Fellow, University Coll., Oxford, 2006–11. Member, Board: Engrg UK, 2012–18; Sense about Science, 2017–; Trustees, Alan Turing Inst., 2017–; Trustees, Faraday Instn, 2018–. Member: Internat. Adv. Panel, National Univ. of Singapore, 2008–18; Internat. Adv. Bd, Blavatnik Sch. of Govt, Oxford, 2012–18. Mem. Bd, Charities Aid Foundn, 2015–18. Gov., Haberdashers' Aske's Sch., 2012–18. Freeman, Goldsmiths' Co., 2015–. DUniv Huddersfield, 2016; Hon. LLD: Canterbury, 2017; Warwick, 2018; Hull, 2019; Bristol, 2019. *Publications:* articles in legal jls concerned with equity, trusts, commercial law, damages. *Recreations:* reading, music, sport, theatre. *Address:* Royal Society, 6–9 Carlton House Terrace, SW1Y 5AG. *T:* (020) 7451 2500, *Fax:* (020) 7930 2170. *E:* julie.maxton@royalsociety.org.

**MAXWELL**, family name of **Barons de Ros** and **Farnham**.

**MAXWELL, Clive Andrew**, CBE 2009; FRGS; Director General, High Speed and Major Rail Projects, Department for Transport, since 2017; *b* Maidstone, Kent, 19 June 1971; *s* of Norman and Gillian Maxwell; *m* 2003, Alissa Bell; two *s*. *Educ:* King Edward VI Grammar Sch., Chelmsford; St Catherine's Coll., Oxford (BA Hons Geog. 1992). HM Treasury: various roles, 1992–2004; Director: Financial Services, 2004–07; Financial Stability, 2007–09; Sen. Dir, 2009–10, Exec. Dir, 2010–12, Chief Exec., 2012–14, OFT; Dir Gen., Energy Transformation, BEIS, 2014–17. Trustee: Kent Wildlife Trust, 2011–; Crystal Palace Park Trust, 2018–. FRGS 2000.

**MAXWELL, Prof. David James**, DPhil; Dixie Professor of Ecclesiastical History, University of Cambridge, since 2011; Fellow, Emmanuel College, Cambridge, since 2011; *b* Bushey, Herts, 8 Dec. 1963; *s* of John Maxwell and Teresa Maxwell (*née* Lucas); *m* 2002, Mandy Ridgway; two *s*. *Educ:* Watford Grammar Sch. for Boys; Univ. of Manchester (BA Hist. 1986); St Antony's Coll., Oxford (DPhil Hist. 1994). Hd of Hist. and House Master, Emmanuel Secondary Sch., Zimbabwe, 1987–90; Res. Fellow, Dept of Social Anthropol., Univ. of Manchester, 1994; University of Keele: Lectr in Internat. Hist., 1994–2001; Sen. Lectr in Hist., 2001–07; Prof. of African Hist., 2007–11. Ed., Jl of Religion in Africa, 1998–2005. Vice-Chm., Britain-Zimbabwe Soc., 1997–2000; Pres., African Studies Assoc. UK, 2014–16 (Vice-Pres., 2012–14). Trustee: Domboshawa House Theol Coll., Harare, 2000–; Southern African Book Develt Educn Trust, UK, 2002–08. *Publications:* Christians and Chiefs in Zimbabwe: a social history of the Hwesa people *c* 1870s–1990s, 1999; (ed with Ingrid Lawrie) Christianity and the African Imagination: essays in honour of Adrian Hastings, 2002; African Gifts of the Spirit: Pentecostalism and the rise of a Zimbabwean transnational religious movement, 2006; (ed with Patrick Harries) The Spiritual in the Secular: missionaries and knowledge about Africa, 2012; (ed jtly) Relocating World Christianity: interdisciplinary studies in universal and local expressions of the Christian faith, 2017. *Recreations:* walking, gardening, theatre, cinema, photography, family. *Address:* Emmanuel College, St Andrew's Street, Cambridge CB2 3AP. *T:* (01223) 334200.

**MAXWELL, Dominic;** *see* Maxwell-Scott, Sir D. J.

**MAXWELL, Ian Robert Charles;** company director; *b* 15 June 1956; *s* of late (Ian) Robert Maxwell, MC; *m* 1st, 1991, Laura Plumb (marr. diss. 1998); 2nd, 1999, Tara Dudley Smith (marr. diss. 2010); one *s*. *Educ:* Marlborough; Balliol Coll., Oxford (MA). Pergamon Press, 1978–83; Prince's Charitable Trust, 1983–84; British Printing & Communication Corporation, later Maxwell Communication Corporation, 1985–91 (Jt Man. Dir, 1988–91); Chm., Agence Centrale de Presse, 1986–89; Chairman and Publisher: Mirror Gp Newspapers, 1991 (Dir, 1987–91); The European Newspaper, 1991 (Dir, 1990–91); Publisher, 1995–98, Editl Consultant, 1998–2015, Maximov Publications. Dir, COJIT, 2018–. Mem., Nat. Theatre Develt Council, 1986–91; Pres., Club d'Investissement Media, 1988–91. Vice Pres., Derby County Football Club, 1987–91 (Chm., 1984–87). *Recreations:* music, ski-ing, water ski-ing, football.
 *See also* K. F. H. Maxwell.

**MAXWELL, Prof. James Rankin**, PhD, DSc; FRS 1997; Senior Research Fellow, University of Bristol, 1999–2010 (Professor of Organic Geochemistry, 1990–99, now Emeritus); *b* 20 April 1941; *s* of John J. and Helen M. T. Maxwell; *m* 1964, Joy Millar Hunter; one *d* (one *s* decd). *Educ:* Univ. of Glasgow (BSc; PhD 1967); DSc Bristol 1982. Research Asst, Univ. of Glasgow, 1967; Postdoctoral Res. Chemist, Univ. of Calif, Berkeley, 1967–68; University of Bristol: Postdoctoral Fellow, 1968–69; Res. Associate, 1969–72; Lectr, 1972–78; Reader, 1978–90; Hd, Envmtl and Analytical Chem. Section, 1991–99. Geochemistry Fellow, Geochem. Soc., USA and European Assoc. Geochem., 1996. J. Clarence Karcher Medal, Univ. of Oklahoma, 1979; Treibs Medal, Geochem. Soc., USA, 1989. *Publications:* numerous papers in learned jls. *Recreations:* walking, gardening, cooking. *Address:* School of Chemistry, University of Bristol, Cantock's Close, Bristol BS8 1TS. *T:* (0117) 331 7554.

**MAXWELL, His Honour John Frederick Michael;** a Circuit Judge, 2005–13; *b* 20 May 1943; *s* of Frederic Michael and Mabel Doreen Maxwell; *m* 1986, Jayne Elizabeth Hunter; one *s* one *d*, and two step *s*. *Educ:* Dover Coll.; New Coll., Oxford (MA Juris.). Called to the Bar, Inner Temple, 1965; a Dep. Stipendiary Magistrate, 1978–90; Asst Recorder, 1990–95; a Recorder, 1995–2005. Standing Counsel to: HM Customs and Excise, 1995–2005; Revenue and Customs Prosecutions Office, 2005. Chm., Birmingham Karma Ling, 1991–2017; Trustee: Rokpa Trust, 1996–; Tara Trust, 2008– (Chm., 2016–); Solihull SO, 2014–. Mem., RYA. *Recreations:* music, yachting. *E:* john@maxwell100.plus.com. *Clubs:* Old Gaffers Assoc.; Cardiff Bay Yacht.

**MAXWELL, John Hunter;** Chairman, DX Services plc, 2004–06; *b* 25 Sept. 1944; *s* of late John Hunter Maxwell, OBE and of Susan Elizabeth Una Smith; *m* 1967, Janet Margaret Frew (marr. diss. 2010); three *s*. *Educ:* Melville Coll., Edinburgh; Dumfries Acad.; Edinburgh Univ. CA 1967. T. Hunter Thompson & Co., CA, Edinburgh, 1962–67; Regl Dir, Far East, Rank Xerox Ltd, 1967–83; Gp Financial Controller, Grand Metropolitan plc, 1983–86; Chief Executive: Provincial Gp, 1986–92; BPB Industries plc, 1992–93; non-exec. Dir, Alliance & Leicester, 1993–94; Corporate Develt Dir, Prudential Corp. plc, 1994–96; Dir Gen., AA, 1996–2000; Chm., Wellington Underwriting plc, 2000–03. Non-executive Director: RAC, 2000–10; Provident Financial, 2000–09; The Big Food Gp plc, 2001–05; Parity Gp plc, 2002–05; Royal & Sun Alliance plc, 2003–13; Homeserve plc, 2004–09; MSA, 2007–10; First Assist Ltd, 2009–11. Chm., IAM, 2002–07 (Mem. Council, 1997–2007). CCMI (CIMgt 1992); FIMI 1997; FRSA 1997. Trustee, RAF Benevolent Fund, 2004–07. Gov., Royal Ballet Sch., 2000–06. Hon. Treas., Cruising Assoc., 1973–74. Freeman, City of London, 1998; Liveryman, Coachmakers' and Coach Harness Makers' Co., 1998–2006. *Recreations:* sailing, classic cars, travel, arts. *Address:* 2 Pavilion Court, 15 Gatliff Road, SW1W 8QT. *Clubs:* Royal Automobile (Mem. Cttee, 2004–10), Royal Thames Yacht (Mem. Cttee, 2010–13).

**MAXWELL, Kevin Francis Herbert;** Chairman, Avenue Partners Ltd, since 2009; *b* 20 Feb. 1959; *s* of late (Ian) Robert Maxwell, MC; *m* 1984, Pandora Deborah Karen Warnford-Davis (marr. diss. 2012); two *s* five *d*. *Educ:* Marlborough Coll.; Balliol Coll., Oxford (MA Hons). Chairman: Maxwell Communication Corporation, 1991 (Dir, 1986–91); Macmillan Inc., 1991 (Dir, 1988–91); Telemonde Inc., 1999–2002; Corunna Gp, 2007–09; Dir, Guinness Mahon Hldgs, 1989–92. Chm., Oxford United FC, 1987–92. Trustee, New Sch. for Social Research, NYC, 1989–92. *Recreations:* books, cooking, football.
 *See also* I. R. C. Maxwell.

**MAXWELL, Liam;** Director, Government Transformation, Amazon Web Services, since 2018; *b* Kenya, June 1968; *s* of Derek Cullen Maxwell and Margaret Maxwell; *m* 2001, Victoria Wakely; two *s* one *d*. *Educ:* Christ's Hospital, Horsham; New Coll., Oxford (BA Human Scis). IT Manager, Office Angels, 1994–97; Eur. Technol. Manager, Adecco, 1997–2000; Hd, IT, Capita Resourcing, 2001–04; Hd, Computing, Eton Coll., 2004–12; Chief Technol. Officer, 2012–16, Nat. Technol. Advr, 2016–18, HM Govt. Mem. (C), Royal Bor. of Windsor and Maidenhead Council, 2007–11 (Mem., Cabinet, 2009–11). *Recreations:* cycling, listening to choral music. *Address:* Amazon Web Services, 60 Holborn Viaduct, EC1A 2FD. *W:* www.twitter.com/liammax.

**MAXWELL, Sir Michael (Eustace George),** 9th Bt *cr* 1681 (NS), of Monreith, Wigtownshire; MRICS; *b* 28 Aug. 1943; *s* of Major Eustace Maxwell (*d* 1971) and late Dorothy Vivien, *d* of Captain George Bellville; S uncle, 1987. *Educ:* Eton; College of Estate Management. *Recreations:* microlights, curling, tennis, ski-ing. *Address:* 56 Queensmill Road, SW6 6JS. *Clubs:* Stranraer Rugby; Port William Tennis.

**MAXWELL, Sir Nigel Mellor H.;** *see* Heron-Maxwell.

**MAXWELL, Prof. Patrick Henry**, DPhil; FRCP, FMedSci; Regius Professor of Physic, University of Cambridge, since 2012; Fellow, Trinity College, Cambridge, since 2012; *b* 12 March 1962; *s* of Robert James Maxwell, *qv*; *m* 1989, Margaret Jane Hughes; two *s* one *d*. *Educ:* Eton (King's Schol.); Corpus Christi Coll., Oxford (BA Physiol Scis 1983; DPhil 1994; Hon. Fellow 2012); St Thomas's Hosp. Med. Sch., London (MB BS Distn 1986). MRCP 1989, FRCP 1995. House Officer, St Thomas' Hosp. and Worthing Hosp., 1986–87; Sen. House Officer, Hammersmith Hosp. Renal Unit, St Thomas' Hosp., Nat. Heart Hosp. and Nat. Hosp. for Neurology and Neurosurgery, 1987–89; Registrar, Lewisham Hosp. and Guy's Hosp., 1989–91; University of Oxford: MRC Trng Fellow, Inst. of Molecular Medicine, 1991–94; Clinical Lectr, 1994–96; Univ. Lectr, and Hon. Consultant Nephrologist, 1996–2000; Reader in Nephrology, 2000–02; Prof. of Nephrology, Imperial Coll., London, 2002–08; Hon. Consultant Physician, Imperial Coll. Healthcare NHS Trust (formerly Hammersmith Hosps), 2002–08; University College London: Prof. of Medicine, 2008–12; Hd, Div. of Medicine, 2008–11; Vice Dean for Experimental Medicine, 2009–11; Dean, Faculty of Med. Scis, 2011–12; Hon. Consultant Physician, Royal Free Hosp., 2008–12. Registrar, Acad. of Medical Scis, 2006–12. Sen. Investigator, NIHR, 2007–12 and 2015–18; Exec., Francis Crick Inst., 2011–12. Director: Global Medical Excellence Cluster Ltd, 2009–; Imanova Ltd, 2011–12; Cambridge Univ. Health Partners, 2012–; Scottish Mortgage Investment Trust, 2016–; non-exec. Dir, Cambridge Univ. Hosps NHS Foundn Trust, 2012–. Chairman: Physiological Scis Funding Cttee, Wellcome Trust, 2008–11; Scientific Advisory Board: Rosetrees Trust, 2010–; Lister Inst., 2013–18; Chair, Molecular and Cellular Medical Bd, MRC, 2014–17. Member: Renal Assoc.; Assoc. of Physicians of GB and Ire. Fellow, Faculty of Medicine, Imperial Coll. London, 2013–17. FMedSci 2005. Mem., Editl Adv. Bd, BMA, 2013–17. *Publications:* Medical Masterclass: nephrology, 2001, 2nd edn 2008; articles in learned jls on erythropoietin, HIF-1 and oxygen sensing. *Recreations:* sailing, losing to my children at chess. *Address:* School of Clinical Medicine, University of Cambridge, Box 111, Cambridge Biomedical Campus, Hills Road, Cambridge CB2 0SP. *T:* (01223) 336738. *E:* regius@medschl.cam.ac.uk.

**MAXWELL, Richard;** QC 1988; a Recorder, 1992–2016; a Deputy High Court Judge, 1998–2016; *b* 21 Dec. 1943; *s* of Thomas and Kathleen Marjorie Maxwell; *m* 1966, Judith Ann Maxwell; two *s* two *d*. *Educ:* Nottingham High Sch.; Hertford College, Oxford (MA). Lectr in Law, 1966–68; called to the Bar, Inner Temple, 1968; in practice as a barrister, 1968–2009; Asst Recorder, 1989–92. *Recreations:* salt and freshwater fly fishing, golf, wine, single malt whisky, learning modern Greek, bowls. *Clubs:* Darley Dale Flyfishers' (Chm., 2007–16); Beeston Fields Golf; Queen Anne's Bowling Green; Peak Forest Angling, Derwent Fly Fishing.

**MAXWELL, Robert James**, CVO 1998; CBE 1993; FRCPE; Chairman, The Gloucestershire Partnership NHS Trust, 2002–08; *b* 26 June 1934; *s* of Dr George B. Maxwell, MC and Cathleen Maxwell; *m* 1960, Jane FitzGibbon (*d* 2015); three *s* two *d*. *Educ:* Leighton Park Sch.; New Coll., Oxford (BA 1st Cl. Hons, MA; Newdigate Prize for Poetry); Univ. of Pennsylvania (MA); LSE (PhD); Univ. of Tromsø (Dip. in Health Econs). CGMA 2012. FCMA; FRCPE 1997; 2nd Lieut, Cameronians (Scottish Rifles), 1952–54. Union Corp., 1958–66; McKinsey & Co., 1966–75; Administrator to Special Trustees, St Thomas' Hosp., 1975–80; Sec. and Chief Exec., The King's Fund, 1980–97. Pres., European Healthcare Management Assoc., 1985–87; Pres., Open Section, RSocMed, 1986–88; Chm. Council, Foundn for Integrated Medicine, 1998–2001. Chm., Court, LSHTM, 1985–95; Mem. Council, London Univ., 2004–08; Governor: NISW, 1981–98; UMDS, 1989–98; Director: Guy's and Lewisham Trust, 1990–93; Lewisham NHS Trust, 1993–98; Severn NHS Trust, 1998–2002; Mem., Bd of Management, Med. Defence Union, 1990–98 (Hon. Fellow, 1998). Chm., Leighton Park Sch., 1981–2001. FRSA 1995. Hon. FRCGP 1994; Hon. MRCP 1987; Hon. Mem., Assoc. of Anaesthetists, 1990. Trustee: Joseph Rowntree Foundn, 1994–2009; Thrive (formerly Horticultural Therapy), 1998–2009; Pharmacy Practice Res. Trust, 1999–2005. JP Inner London Youth and Family Courts (Chm.), 1971–98; JP S Glos, 1999–2004. DUniv Brunel, 1993; Hon. DLitt West of England, 1993. *Publications:* Health Care: the growing dilemma, 1974; Health and Wealth, 1981; Reshaping the National Health Service, 1988; Spotlight on the Cities, 1989; An Unplayable Hand?: BSE, CJD and British Government, 1997; (with B. Wannell) Persian Poems, 2012; Naming the Animals and other poems, 2017. *Recreations:* poetry, walking, stained glass, not quite catching up with correspondence. *Address:* Pitt Court Manor, North Nibley, Dursley, Glos GL11 6EL. *Club:* Brooks's.
*See also* P. H. Maxwell.

**MAXWELL, Simon Jeffrey**, CBE 2007; Senior Research Associate, Overseas Development Institute, since 2009 (Director, 1997–2009); Emeritus Fellow, Institute of Development Studies, University of Sussex, 2015 (Fellow, 1981–97); Director, Simon Maxwell Ltd, since 2010; *b* 1 May 1948; *s* of Frederick Norman Maxwell and Ruth Maxwell (*née* Salinsky); *m* 1973, Catherine Elizabeth Pelly; three *s*. *Educ:* Lycée d'Anvers; Solihull Sch.; St Edmund Hall, Oxford (BA PPE 1970); Univ. of Sussex (MA Develt Econs 1973). United Nations Development Programme: Jun. Professional Officer, Nairobi, 1970–72; Asst Res. Rep., New Delhi, 1973–77; Agricl Economist, ODA, Santa Cruz, Bolivia, 1978–81. World Economic Forum: Dep. Chm., Global Agenda Council on Humanitarian Affairs, 2010–11 (Chm., 2008–10); Mem., Global Agenda Council on Poverty and Econ. Develt, 2011–14. Mem., Scientific Adv. Bd, EU Develt Corp., 2012–14. Mem., Adv. Gp, IPPR, 2009–; Specialist Advr, H of C Select Cttee on Internat. Develt, 2010–. Member: Oxfam Field Cttee for Latin America, 1981–84; Ind. Gp on British Aid, 1982–; UN Adv. Gp on Nutrition, 1990–96; Program Adv. Panel, Foundn for Develt Co-operation, 1997–2009; Bd, Fair Trade Foundn, 2008–14; Bd, Fundación para las Relaciones Internacionales y el Diálogo Exterior, 2011–15; Bd, Internat. Food Policy Res. Inst., 2013–18. Chm., European Think Tanks Gp, 2015–19. External Examiner, Wye Coll., Univ. of London, 1995–98; Gov., Inst. of Develt Studies, 1996–97. Mem. Council, Develt Studies Assoc. of UK and Ireland, 1998–2005 (Pres., 2001–05). Trustee, Action for Conservation through Tourism, 1998–2004; Patron, One World Media (formerly Broadcasting Trust), 1998–; Mem., Adv. Cttee, Charter 99, 1999–2002. Fellow, World Econ. Forum, 2003–10; Hon. Fellow, Foreign Policy Assoc., NY, 2003–. *Publications:* numerous pubns on poverty, food security, aid and agricl develt. *Address:* 20 West Drive, Brighton, E Sussex BN2 0GD. *W:* www.simonmaxwell.eu.

**MAXWELL, Stewart;** *see* Maxwell, W. S.

**MAXWELL, William**, PhD; CPsychol; Chief Executive, Education Scotland, 2012–17 (Interim Chief Executive, 2011); *b* Edinburgh, 14 Nov. 1957; *s* of Joseph Maxwell and Christine Maxwell; *m* Margaret; two *d*. *Educ:* High Sch. of Dundee; University Coll., Oxford (BA); Univ. of Glasgow (MAppSci); Univ. of Edinburgh (PhD). Area Principal Psychologist, Grampian Council, 1992–94; HM Inspectorate of Education: Inspector of Schs, 1994–2002; Chief Inspector of Educn, 2002–06; Hd, Educn, Information and Analytical Services, Scottish Exec., subseq. Scottish Govt, 2006–08; Chief Inspector of Educn and Trng Wales, HM Inspectorate for Educn and Trng in Wales, 2008–10; Sen. Chief Inspector of Educn, HM Inspectorate of Educn, 2010–11. FRSA. *Recreations:* climbing and mountaineering, cycling, the arts.

**MAXWELL, (William) Stewart;** Special Adviser (Business, Economy, Skills and Fair Work) to First Minister of Scotland, since 2017; *b* 24 Dec. 1963; *s* of William Maxwell and Margaret Maxwell; *m* 1995, Mary Stevenson; one *d*. *Educ:* Glasgow Coll. of Technol. (BA Hons Soc. Sci.). Wilmax Ltd (family business), 1986–88, 1991–93; Admin. Officer, Scottish Training Foundn, 1988–91; Strathclyde Fire Brigade: Industrial Trng Manager, 1993–94; Sen. Admin. Officer, 1994–2001; Mgt Inf. System Project Manager, 2001–03. Scottish Parliament: Mem. (SNP) Scotland W, 2003–16; contested (SNP) Eastwood, 2016; Shadow Dep. Minister for Health, 2004–06; Shadow Minister for Sport, Culture and Media, 2006–07; Minister for Communities and Sport, 2007–09; Dep. Convener, Justice 1 Cttee, 2003–04; Member: Subordinate Legislation Cttee, 2003–07; Justice 2 Cttee, 2004–06; Enterprise and Culture Cttee, 2006–07; Justice Cttee, 2009–11; EU Cttee of the Regions, 2009–16; Referendum (Scotland) Bill Cttee, 2013–14; Devolution (Further Powers) Cttee, 2014–16; Convener, Educn and Culture Cttee, 2011–16; Vice Pres., Eur. Alliance Gp, 2012–16. Vice Convener, Publicity, 2003–04, Mem., NEC, 2003–04, SNP. Hon. Vice-Pres., Royal Envmtl Health Inst. of Scot., 2006–. *Recreations:* cinema, theatre, Rugby (debenture holder at Murrayfield), swimming, golf, reading, eating out, photography, scuba diving.

**MAXWELL MACDONALD, Sir John (Ronald),** 12th Bt *cr* 1682 (NS), of Pollok, Renfrewshire; *b* Edinburgh, 22 May 1936; *er s* of late John Maxwell Macdonald and Dame Anne Maxwell Macdonald, Btss (11th in line); *S* mother, 2011; *m* 1964, Eleanor Ruth Laird; two *s* one *d*. *Educ:* Winchester. Retired from land management. *Recreations:* fishing, sailing. *Heir: er s* John Ranald Maxwell Macdonald [*b* 16 Sept. 1965; *m* 1998, Emma Katherine Logie; one *s* two *d*]. *Address:* Gortinanane House, Tayinloan, Tarbert, Argyll PA29 6XG. *T:* (01583) 441223.

**MAXWELL MARTIN, Anna;** actor; *b* Beverley, E Yorks; *m* 2010, Roger Harry Michell, *qv*; two *d*. *Educ:* Beverley High Sch.; Liverpool Univ. (BA Hons Hist.). Theatre includes: Little Foxes, Donmar, 2001; National Theatre: Coast of Utopia, 2002; Honour, The Three Sisters, 2003; His Dark Materials, 2003–04; King Lear, 2014; Dumbshow, 2004, The Entertainer, 2006, Royal Court; Other Hands, Soho, 2006; Cabaret, Lyric, 2006; Measure for Measure, Almeida, 2010; Di and Viv and Rose, Hampstead, 2013; Macbeth, Young Vic, 2015; Consent, NT, 2017; *films* include: The Hours, 2003; Enduring Love, 2004; Becoming Jane, 2007; *television* includes: North and South, 2004; Bleak House, 2005 (Best Actress, BAFTA, 2006); White Girl, 2008; Poppy Shakespeare, 2008 (Best Actress, BAFTA, 2009); Moonshot, 2009; On Expenses, 2010; South Riding, 2011; The Night Watch, 2011; Accused, 2012; The Bletchley Circle, 2012; Death Comes to Pemberley, 2013; Birthday, 2015; Midwinter of the Spirit, 2015; And Then There Were None, 2015; The Frankenstein Chronicles, 2015; Reg, 2016; Motherland, 2016, 2017, 2018; Line of Duty, 2019. *Address:* c/o Troika Talent, 180 Great Portland Street, W1W 5QZ.

**MAXWELL SCOTT, Sir Dominic James,** 14th Bt *cr* 1642, of Haggerston, Northumberland; journalist (as Dominic Maxwell); chief theatre critic, The Times, 2013–15; *b* 22 July 1968; *s* of Sir Michael Fergus Maxwell Scott, 13th Bt and of Deirdre Moira, *d* of late Alexander McKechnie; *S* father, 1989; *m* 2004, Emma Jane, *d* of late Keith Perry; two *d*. *Educ:* Eton; Sussex Univ. Dir, Abbotsford Trust, 2008–11. *Heir: b* Matthew Joseph Maxwell Scott [*b* 27 Aug. 1976; *m* 2010, Melanie Louise, *d* of late Alan Greenall; two *s*].

**MAXWELL-SCOTT, James Herbert;** QC 2016; a Recorder, since 2018; *b* Wimbledon, 1971; *s* of David and Isabel Maxwell Scott; *m* 2003, Anoushka Lutikov; two *s*. *Educ:* Worth Sch.; Christ's Coll., Cambridge (BA 1993); Christ Church, Oxford (BCL). Called to the Bar, Gray's Inn, 1995. *Recreations:* theatre, opera, ski-ing, golf, cricket, wine, whisky. *Address:* Crown Office Chambers, 2 Crown Office Row, Temple, EC4Y 7HJ. *Clubs:* Royal Wimbledon Golf, Nairn Golf.

**MAXWELL-TIMMINS, Nicholas James;** *see* Timmins.

**MAY,** family name of **Barons May** and **May of Oxford**.

**MAY,** 4th Baron *cr* 1935, of Weybridge, co. Surrey; **Jasper Bertram St John May;** Bt 1931; *b* 24 Oct. 1965; *o s* of 3rd Baron May and of Jillian Mary (*née* Shipton); *S* father, 2006; *m* 2012, John Peter Daly. *Educ:* Harrow.

**MAY OF OXFORD,** Baron *cr* 2001 (Life Peer), of Oxford in the County of Oxfordshire; **Robert McCredie May,** OM 2002; AC 1998; Kt 1996; FRS 1979; Royal Society Research Professor, Department of Zoology, Oxford University, 1988–2002, now Emeritus; Fellow of Merton College, Oxford, 1988–2001, now Emeritus; President, Royal Society, 2000–05; *b* 8 Jan. 1936; *s* of Henry W. May and Kathleen M. May; *m* 1962, Judith (*née* Feiner); one *d*. *Educ:* Sydney Boys' High Sch.; Sydney Univ. BSc 1956, PhD (Theoretical Physics) 1959. Gordon Mackay Lectr in Applied Maths, Harvard Univ., 1959–61; Sydney Univ.: Sen. Lectr in Theoretical Physics, 1962–64; Reader, 1964–69; Personal Chair, 1969–73; Princeton University: Prof. of Biology, 1973–88; Class of 1877 Prof. of Zoology, 1975–88; Chm., Univ. Res. Bd, 1977–88; Chief Scientific Advr to the UK Govt and Hd of the OST, 1995–2000. Vis. Prof., Imperial Coll., 1975–88; visiting appointments at: Harvard, 1966; California Inst. of Technology, 1967; UKAEA Culham Lab., 1971; Magdalen Coll., Oxford, 1971; Inst. for Advanced Study, Princeton, 1972; King's Coll., Cambridge, 1976. Chm., Natural History Mus., 1994–98 (Trustee, 1991–93); Trustee: WWF (UK), 1990–94; Royal Botanic Gardens, Kew, 1991–96; Nuffield Foundn, 1993–2005. Non-exec. Dir, Dstl, 2005–13. Mem., H of L, 2001–17. Member: Smithsonian Council, USA, 1988–91; Jt Nature Conservation Council, 1989–95; Bd of Trustees, British Council, 2001–06; UK Climate Change Cttee, 2008–15. Founder FMedSci 1998. Hon. Fellow: Amer. Soc. for Biochemistry, 1993; British Ecol Soc., 1995 (Pres., 1992–93); Australian Acad. of Technol Scis and Engrg, 2001; Linnean Soc., 2008; Hon. FInstP 2002; Hon. FREng 2005; Hon. FIBiol 2006. Overseas Mem., Australian Acad. of Sci., 1991; For. Associate, US Nat. Acad. of Scis, 1992. Honorary degrees from Uppsala, ETH Zürich, Yale, Princeton, Sydney, Oxford, Harvard and many other UK universities. Linnean Medal, 1991; Crafoord Prize, Royal Swedish Acad. of Scis, 1996; Swiss-Italian Balzan Prize, 1998; Japanese Blue Planet Prize, 2001; Copley Medal, Royal Soc., 2007. *Publications:* Stability and Complexity in Model Ecosystems, 1973, 2nd edn 1974; Theoretical Ecology: Principles and Applications, 1976, 3rd edn 2007; Population Biology of Infectious Diseases, 1982; Exploitation of Marine Communities, 1984; Perspectives in Ecological Theory, 1989; Infectious Diseases of Humans: dynamics and control, 1991; Extinction Rates, 1994; Evolution of Biological Diversity, 1999; Virus Dynamics, 2000; articles in mathematical, biol and physics jls. *Recreations:* tennis, running, bridge.

**MAY, Prof. Anthony Dormer,** OBE 2004; FREng; Professor of Transport Engineering, University of Leeds, 1977–2009, now Emeritus; *b* 29 Feb. 1944; *s* of Albert James Gooding May and Beatrice Mary May; *m* 1968, Jennifer Margaret Caroline Hesketh. *Educ:* Bedford Sch.; Pembroke Coll., Cambridge (BA 1st cl. Hons (Mech. Scis) 1966, MA 1969); Yale Univ. 1967. CEng 1972; FICE 1993. Gp Planner Roads, GLC, 1967–77. Dir, MVA Ltd, 1985–2001. FREng 1995. *Publications:* over 80 papers in academic jls. *Recreations:* choral singing, canals, gardening, travel. *Address:* 10 Newton Terrace, York YO1 6HE. *T:* (01904) 621796.

**MAY, Rt Hon. Sir Anthony (Tristram Kenneth),** Kt 1991; PC 1998; Interception of Communications Commissioner, 2013–15; President, Queen's Bench Division, High Court of Justice, 2008–11 (Vice-President, 2002–08); *b* 9 Sept. 1940; *s* of late Kenneth Sibley May and Joan Marguérite (*née* Oldaker); *m* 1968, Stella Gay Pattisson; one *s* two *d*. *Educ:* Bradfield Coll.; Worcester Coll., Oxford (Trevelyan Scholar 1960, Hon. Scholar 1962; MA; Hon. Fellow, 1999). Called to the Bar, Inner Temple, 1967 (Scholar, 1965; Bencher, 1985; Reader, 2007; Treas., 2008); QC 1979; a Recorder, 1985–91; a Judge of the High Court of Justice, QBD, 1991–97; a Lord Justice of Appeal, 1997–2008; Dep. Hd of Civil Justice, 2000–03. Jun. Counsel to DoE for Land Commn Act Matters, 1972–75; Chm., Commn of Inquiry, Savings and Investment Bank Ltd, IoM, 1990. A Judge, Employment Appeal Tribunal, 1993–97; Judge in Charge, Non-Jury List, 1995–97. Chm., Security Vetting Appeals Panel, 1997–2000. Vice-Chm., Official Referees Bar Assoc., 1987–91. Mem., Civil Procedure Rule Cttee, 1997–2003. President: Technol. and Construction Bar Assoc., 2002–13; Soc. of Construction Law, 2004–12. Vice-Pres., Guildford Choral Soc., 1991– (Chm., 1980–91). Mem. Council, Wycombe Abbey Sch., 1997–2014. *Publications:* (ed) Keating on Building Contracts, 5th edn 1991, 6th edn 1995. *Recreations:* gardening, music, books, bonfires. *Club:* Garrick.

**MAY, Dr Brian Harold,** CBE 2005; guitarist, songwriter and producer; Owner, London Stereoscopic Company, since 2008; *b* Hampton, Middx, 19 July 1947; *s* of Harold and Ruth May; *m* 1st, 1976, Christine Mullen (marr. diss. 1988); one *s* two *d*; 2nd, 2000, Anita Dobson. *Educ:* Hampton Grammar Sch.; Imperial Coll. London (BSc 1974; PhD Astrophysics 2007). Founding Mem., Queen, 1970–; albums: Queen, 1973; Queen II, 1974; Sheer Heart Attack, 1974; A Night at the Opera, 1975; A Day at the Races, 1976; News of the World, 1977; Jazz, 1978; Live Killers, 1979; The Game, 1980; Flash Gordon Original Soundtrack, 1980; Hot Space, 1982; The Works, 1984; A Kind of Magic, 1986; The Miracle, 1989; Innuendo, 1991; Made in Heaven, 1995; (with Paul Rodgers) The Cosmos Rocks, 2008; solo albums: Back to the Light, 1993; Another World, 1998. Writer of music, Macbeth, for Red and Gold Th. Co., 1987; Prod. and Music Dir, We Will Rock You, Dominion Th., 2002 and worldwide. Trustee, Mercury Phoenix Trust, 1992–. Chancellor, Liverpool John Moores Univ., 2008–13 (Hon. Fellow, 2007). Vice-Pres., RSPCA, 2012–. Hon. DSc: Herts, 2002; Exeter, 2007. *Publications:* (jtly) Bang! The Complete History of the Universe, 2006; A Survey of Radical Velocities in the Zodiacal

Dust Cloud, 2008; (with E. Vidal) A Village Lost and Found, 2009; (jtly) Cosmic Tourist, 2012; (jtly) Diableries: stereoscopic adventures in Hell, 2013; (jtly) The Poor Man's Picture Gallery, 2014. *Address:* Duck Productions Ltd, PO Box 141, Windlesham, Surrey GU20 6YW.

MAY, Catherine Jean; Corporate Affairs Director, SABMiller plc, 2012–14; *b* Shoreham-by-Sea, W Sussex, 14 Dec. 1964; *d* of Robert and Jean May; *m* 1999, Matthew Guarente; two *s*. *Educ:* King's Manor Sch.; Univ. of London (BA English). Partner, Luther Pendragon, 1997–2000; Corporate Relns Dir, Reed Elsevier plc, 2000–06; Corporate Affairs Dir, Centrica plc, 2006–12. Trustee: ENO, 2011– (Sen. Ind. Dir, 2016–); Nat. Funding Scheme, 2012–16. *Recreations:* opera, cookery, ski-ing, family.

MAY, Charlotte Louisa, (Mrs Yemi Pearse); QC 2014; *b* Reading; *d* of Anthony and Catherine May; *m* 2000, Yemi Pearse; two *d*. *Educ:* Abbey Sch., Reading; Brasenose Coll., Oxford (BA Biochem.); City Univ. (DipLaw (Commendation)). Called to the Bar, Inner Temple, 1995; in practice as barrister, specialising in intellectual property. *Publications:* (contrib.) The Modern Law of Copyright and Designs, 4th edn 2011, 5th edn as The Modern Law of Copyright, 2018. *Recreations:* running, tennis. *Address:* 8 New Square, Lincoln's Inn, WC2A 3QP. *T:* (020) 7405 4321. *E:* charlotte.may@8newsquare.co.uk. *Club:* Roehampton.

MAY, David; *see* May, M. D.

MAY, Douglas James; QC (Scot) 1989; FRPS; an Upper Tribunal Judge (Administrative Appeals Chamber) (formerly a Social Security Commissioner and a Child Support Commissioner), 1993–2015, (fee-paid), since 2015; *b* 7 May 1946; *s* of Thomas May and Violet Mary Brough Boyd or May. *Educ:* George Heriot's Sch., Edinburgh; Edinburgh Univ. Advocate 1971. Temporary Sheriff, 1990–99. Mem., Tribunal Procedure Cttee, 2008–15. Contested (C): Edinburgh E, Feb. 1974; Glasgow Cathcart, 1983. Pres., Edinburgh Photographic Soc., 1996–99; Chm., Conceptual and Contemporary Distinctions Panel, RPS, 2010–17. FRPS 2002. *Recreations:* golf, photography, travel, concert going. *Address:* Upper Tribunal (Administrative Appeals Chamber), George House, 126 George Street, Edinburgh EH2 4HH. *Clubs:* Merchants of Edinburgh Golf (Captain, 1997–99), Luffness New Golf.

MAY, James Nicholas Welby; Director-General, UK Offshore Operators Association, 1997–2003; *b* 21 Feb. 1949; *s* of late Richard Percy May and Caroline Rosemary Welby May (*née* Jack); *m* 1979, Diana Mary Tamplin; two *s*. *Educ:* Sherborne Sch., Dorset; Southampton Univ. (BSc 1970); College of Law. Called to the Bar, Lincoln's Inn, 1974. Programme Officer, UNEP, 1976–77; Project Officer, IUCN, 1977–78; Legal Officer, Friends of the Earth, 1978–79; Legal Adviser, NFU, 1980–89; Dir-Gen., British Retail Consortium, 1989–97. Sec., Footwear Distributors' Fedn, 1989–97; Member: Countryside Commn Common Land Forum, 1984–86; Nat. Retail Trng Council, 1989–97; Distributive Occupational Standards Council, 1993–97; Council, 1996–2003, Trade Assoc. Council, 1998–2003, CBI; Meteorological Cttee, 1997–99; HSE Open Govt Complaints Panel, 2003–05. Non-executive Director: Meteorological Office, 2000–07; Roehampton Club Members Ltd, 2011–16; non-exec. Chm., Common Data Access Ltd, 2000–03; non-executive Member: Land Command Bd, 2004–07 (Chm., Audit Cttee, 2004–07); Defence Audit Cttee, 2005–07. Trustee: Sherborne Sch. Foundn, 1999–2004; Friends of Barnes Common, 2015–. *Recreations:* travel, tennis, ski-ing, golf. *E:* james.diana@blueyonder.co.uk. *Club:* Roehampton (Hon. Co. Sec., 2010–16).

MAY, Jill Miranda; External Member, Prudential Regulation Authority Committee, since 2018; *b* London, 5 June 1961; *d* of John Langham and Irene Langham; *m* 1988, Mick May; two *s* four *d*. *Educ:* Benenden Sch.; Durham Univ. (BA Econs 1982). Corporate Finance, S. G. Warburg & Co. Ltd, 1982–95; Man. Dir, UBS AG, 2001–12. Dir, Langham Industries, 1996–. Non-executive Director: ICAEW, 2015–19; JPMorgan Claverhouse, 2017–; Ruffer Investment Co., 2017–; Sirius Real Estate, 2017–; Standard Life Investments Property Income Trust, 2019–. Panel Member: Competition Commn, 2013–14; Competition and Markets Authy, 2013–18 (Panel Mem. non-exec. Dir, 2013–16); Mem. Complaints Cttee, IPSO, 2014–17. Member: Council, Nat. Trust, 2011–14; Council, Durham Univ., 2012–18; Cancer Research UK, 2015–. Gov., Wellington Coll., 2015–. *Recreations:* travel, long-distance running, alpine walking, ski-ing. *Address:* 29 Palace Gardens Terrace, W8 4SB. *T:* (020) 7221 5779. *E:* jill.may50@gmail.com. *Clubs:* Hurlingham, 5 Hertford Street.

MAY, Air Vice-Marshal John Anthony Gerard, CB 1995; CBE 1993; Air Officer Training and Air Officer Commanding Training Group, Headquarters Personnel and Training Command, and Chief Executive, Training Group Defence Agency, 1994–97; *b* 12 Nov. 1941; *s* of late Anthony Frederick May and Beatrice Mary (*née* Niblett); *m* 1964, Margaret Anne Chester; two *s*. *Educ:* City of London Sch. Joined RAF 1961; flying trng, then Qualified Flying Instr, Linton-on-Ouse; Lightning aircraft, 1966; served with Nos 56, 5 and 19 Sqns; Staff Coll., Camberley, 1977; Chief Flying Instr, RAF Cranwell, 1979; Stn Comdr, Binbrook, 1985; Dep. Dir of Air Defence, MoD, 1987; Air Cdre Policy and Plans, RAF Support Comd, 1989; AOC No 38 Gp, and SASO, HQ Strike Comd, 1993–94. RAFVR(T) Qualified Flying Instructor (Tutor aircraft), No 5 Air Experience Flight, 1999–, Dep. Flight Comdr, 2015–. Vice-Chm. (Air), E Anglia RFCA, 2003–10. QCVSA 1971. *Recreations:* alpine ski-ing, classic cars. *Address:* 157 Sapley Road, Hartford, Huntingdon, Cambs PE29 1YT.

MAY, John Clive Cecil; DL; Secretary General, Duke of Edinburgh's International Award Foundation, since 2011; *b* London, 17 Aug. 1964; *s* of John and Jennifer May. *Educ:* Wycliffe Coll.; Bristol Univ. (BA Jt Hons Drama and English 1985); Westminster Coll., Oxford (PGCE 1986); Open Univ. (MA Educn 1991). Teacher, Chadsmead Sch., Staffs, 1986–90; Dep. Hd, Scaynes Hill Sch., W Sussex, 1990–93; Hd, Handcross Sch., W Sussex, 1993–96; Hd, Manor Farm Sch., Bucks, 1996–99; Educn Dir, BITC, 1999–2003; Chief Executive Officer: Career Academies UK, 2003–09; Young Enterprise, 2009–11. Founding Dir and Mem., Adv. Bd, Teach First, 2002–14. Vice Chm., World Orgn of Scout Movement, 2008–14. Mem., Nat. Bd, UNICEF UK, 1992–98. Trustee: Scout Assoc., UK, 1982–2005; Marine Soc. and Sea Cadets, 2015–. FRSA. DL Oxfordshire, 2018. Queen's Award for Enterprise Promotion, 2008. *Recreations:* long distance running, hill walking, travel, theatre, Scouting. *Address:* Award House, 7–11 St Matthew's Road, SW1P 2JT. *T:* (020) 7222 4242. *E:* john.may@intaward.org. *Club:* Lansdowne.

MAY, Jonathan James Seaburne B.; *see* Bourne-May.

MAY, Hon. Dame Juliet Mary, DBE 2015; Hon. Mrs Justice May; a Judge of the High Court, Queen's Bench Division, since 2015; *b* London; *d* of Rt Hon. Sir John Douglas May, PC and Mary May; *m* 1988, (Jonathan) James (O'Grady) Cameron, *qv*; three *d*. *Educ:* Wadham Coll., Oxford (BA Psychol., Phil. and Physiol.); Inst. of Psychiatry (MPhil Clin. Psychol.); City Univ. (DipLaw); Inns of Court Sch. of Law (BVC). Sen. Clin. Psychologist, 1983–86; called to the Bar, Inner Temple, 1988, Bencher, 2010; in practice as barrister, specialising in commercial law, 1988–2008; QC 2008; a Circuit Judge, 2008–15. *Address:* Royal Courts of Justice, Strand, WC2A 2LL.

MAY, Prof. (Michael) David, DSc; FRS 1991; FREng; Professor, Department of Computer Science, Bristol University; *b* Holmfirth, 24 Feb. 1951; *s* of Douglas May. *Educ:* Queen Elizabeth's GS, Wakefield; King's Coll., Cambridge (BA 1972; MA 1976); DSc Southampton. Lectr, Dept of Computer Sci., Warwick Univ.; Technology Manager (Computer Architecture), Inmos Ltd, Bristol; co-founder and Chief Tech. Officer, XMOS Ltd. Vis. Prof. of Engrg Design, Oxford Univ., 1991. FREng 2010. *Publications:* (ed jtly) Networks, Routers and Transputers: function, performance and application, 1993. *Address:* Department of Computer Science, University of Bristol, Merchant Venturers' Building, Woodland Road, Bristol BS8 1UB. *T:* (0117) 954 5134; 9 Eaton Crescent, Clifton, Bristol BS8 2EJ. *T:* (0117) 974 2586.

MAY, Prof. Stephen Anthony, PhD; FRCVS; Professor of Education and Senior Vice Principal, Royal Veterinary College, University of London, since 2017; President, Royal College of Veterinary Surgeons, 2017–18 (Senior Vice President, 2018–19); *b* Leeds, 7 Dec. 1955; *s* of Roderick Reginald and Sheila Mollie May; *m* 1983, Hilary Clare West; two *s* one *d*. *Educ:* Manchester Grammar Sch.; St Catharine's Coll., Cambridge (BA Pathol. 1977; VetMB 1980; MA 1981); Royal Veterinary Coll. (PhD 1989). MRCVS 1980, FRCVS 2002; Dip. Radiol. 1984, Dip. Equine Orthopaedics 1992, RCVS; Dip. Eur. Coll. Veterinary Surgeons 1993. University of Liverpool: Large Animal HO, 1980–81; Resident, 1982–85; Lectr, then Sen. Lectr, 1988–92; Prof. of Equine Medicine and Surgery, 1993–2017, Vice Principal for Teaching, 2000–13, Dep. Principal, 2004–17, RVC. President: Eur. Coll. of Vet. Surgeons, 2008–09; Eur. Bd of Vet. Specialisation, 2014–16. *Publications:* contrib. peer-reviewed papers and textbook chapters on equine orthopaedics and rheumatol., diagnostic imaging, and professional ethics and educn. *Recreations:* violin repair, house renovation, garden, family, theatre. *Address:* Royal Veterinary College, Hawkshead Lane, North Mymms, Hatfield, Herts AL9 7TA. *T:* (01707) 666270. *E:* smay@rvc.ac.uk; Royal College of Veterinary Surgeons, Belgravia House, 62–64 Horseferry Road, SW1P 2AF. *T:* (020) 7222 2001.

MAY, Rt Hon. Theresa Mary; PC 2003; MP (C) Maidenhead, since 1997; Prime Minister and First Lord of the Treasury, 2016–19; *b* 1 Oct. 1956; *d* of Rev. Hubert Brasier and Zaidee Brasier (*née* Barnes); *m* 1980, Philip John May. *Educ:* St Hugh's Coll., Oxford (MA). Bank of England, 1977–83; Inter-Bank Res. Orgn, 1983–85; Assoc. for Payment Clearing Services, 1985–97 (Hd of European Affairs Unit, 1989–96). Mem. (C), Merton LBC, 1986–94. Contested (C): Durham NW, 1992; Barking, June 1994. Opposition frontbench spokesman on educn and employment, 1998–99; Shadow Secretary of State: for Educn and Employment, 1999–2001; for Transport, Local Govt and the Regions, 2001–02; for Transport, 2002; for Envmt and Transport, 2003–04; for the Family, 2004–05, also for Culture, Media and Sport, 2005; Chm., Cons. Party, 2002–03; Shadow Leader, H of C, 2005–09; Shadow Minister for Women, 2007–10; Shadow Sec. of State for Work and Pensions, 2009–10; Sec. of State for the Home Dept, 2010–16; Minister for Women and for Equalities, 2010–12. *Recreations:* walking, cooking. *Address:* House of Commons, SW1A 0AA. *Clubs:* Carlton; Maidenhead Conservative; Leander.

MAYALL, Prof. James Bardsley Lawson, FBA 2001; Sir Patrick Sheehy Professor of International Relations, University of Cambridge, 1998–2004; Fellow, 1998–2004, now Emeritus, Vice-Master, 2003–04, and Director of Studies in Human, Political and Social Science, since 2004, Sidney Sussex College, Cambridge; *b* 14 April 1937; *s* of Robert Cecil Mayall and Rhoda Anne (*née* Stote); *m* 1st, 1964, Margaret Berry (marr. diss. 1990); one *d*; 2nd, 1991, Avril Doris Whalley. *Educ:* Shrewsbury Sch.; Sidney Sussex Coll., Cambridge (BA Hist. Tripos 1960; MA 1998). Sir John Dill Fellow, Princeton Univ., NJ, 1960–61; BoT, 1961–64; British High Commn, New Delhi, 1964–65; London School of Economics: Dept of Internat. Relns, 1966–98; Prof. of Internat. Relns, 1991–98, Prof. Emeritus, 1998–; Chm., Steering Cttee, Centre for Internat. Studies, 1991–98. Mem. Council, RIIA, 1992–98 (Associate Editor, Survey and Documents of Internat. Affairs, 1967–71). Chm., Adv. Bd, Inst. of Commonwealth Studies, Univ. of London, 2006–14; Academic Advr, RCDS, 2008–13; Hd of Internat. Relns, William Grosvenor Partnership, 2014–19; Special Advr, WGP Global, 2019–. *Publications:* Africa and the Cold War, 1971; (Associate Ed.) Survey of International Affairs 1963, 1977; (ed jtly) A New International Commodity Regime, 1979; (ed jtly) The End of the Post-War Era: documents on Great Power relns 1968–75, 1980; (ed) The Community of States: a study in international political theory, 1982; Nationalism and International Society, 1990; (ed jtly) The Fallacies of Hope: the post Colonial record of the Commonwealth Third World, 1991; (ed) The New Interventionism 1991–94: United Nations experience in Cambodia, Former Yugoslavia and Somalia, 1996; World Politics: progress and its limits, 2000; (ed jtly) International Human Rights in the 21st Century: protecting the rights of groups, 2003; (with K. Srinivasan) Towards the New Horizons: world order in the Twenty First Century, 2009; (ed) The Contemporary Commonwealth, 1965–2009: essays to mark the centenary of the publication of The Round Table, 2009; (ed jtly) The New Protectorates: international tutelage and the making of liberal states, 2011; (ed jtly) Values in Foreign Policy: investigating ideals and interests, 2019. *Recreations:* cooking, gardening, watching cricket, walking the dog. *Address:* Sidney Sussex College, Sidney Street, Cambridge CB2 3HU. *T:* (01223) 767228. *Clubs:* MCC, Travellers; Indian Internat. Centre (Delhi).

MAYALL, Lt Gen. Sir Simon (Vincent), KBE 2014; CB 2010; Senior Adviser, Greenhill, since 2015; *b* London, 7 March 1956; *s* of Air Cdre Paul Vincent Mayall and Alexis Leonora Mayall. *Educ:* St George's Coll., Weybridge; Balliol Coll., Oxford (MA Hons Modern Hist.); King's Coll. London (MA Internat. Relns). Commnd 15th/19th King's Royal Hussars, 1979; served Sultan's Armed Forces, Oman, 1985–87; Staff Coll., then MoD, later Regtl Duty, 1987–93; MA to Dep. SACEUR, 1993–95; Defence Fellow, St Antony's Coll., Oxford, 1995–97; CO, 1st Queen's Dragoon Guards, 1997–99; Col, Army Plans, MoD, 1999–2001; Comdr, 1st Mechanised Bde, 2001–02; rcds, 2003; Dir, Army Plans, 2004–06; Dep. Comdr, Multi-Nat. Corps - Iraq, 2006–07; ACGS, 2007–09; DCDS (Ops), 2009–11; Defence Sen. Advr to the Middle East, 2011–14; Prime Minister's Security Envoy to Iraq, 2014–15. Lieut, Tower of London, 2015–. Regtl Col, Queen's Dragoon Guards, 2008–19; Dep. Col Comdt, AGC (Army Legal Services), 2009–15. Hon. Col, Univ. of London OTC, 2009–15. QCVS 2003. Officer, Legion of Merit (USA), 2007. *Publications:* Turkey, Thwarted Ambition, 1997, 2nd edn 2005. *Recreations:* theatre, history, travel, shooting, ski-ing, tennis. *Address:* 14 Earl's Court Square, SW5 9DN. *Clubs:* Garrick, Beefsteak, Cavalry and Guards, Chelsea Arts.

MAYER, Alex; Member (Lab) Eastern, European Parliament, Nov. 2016–2019; *b* High Wycombe, 2 June 1981; *d* of Ralph and Louise Mayer. *Educ:* Exeter Univ. (BA Hist.); Leeds Univ. (MA Politics and Parly Studies). Campaign organiser, Cambridge Labour Party, 2003–07; constituency asst to Anne Campbell, MP, 2003–05; Regl Organiser, E of England Labour Party, 2007–10; Press Officer, Richard Howitt, MEP, 2010–11; Regl Fundraising Manager, E Anglia, BHF, 2011–14; Nat. Co-ordinator, Socialist Envmt and Resources Assoc., 2014–15; Sen. Parly Advr to Daniel Zeichner, MP, 2015–16. Contested (Lab) Eastern, EP, 2019. *Recreations:* love campaigning and chocolate, life member of English Heritage and National Trust.

MAYER, Anthony; *see* Mayer, R. A. J.

**MAYER, (Anthony) David**, FRCS; Consultant Hepatobiliary and Liver Transplant Surgeon, Queen Elizabeth Hospital, Birmingham, and Honorary Consultant Liver Transplant Surgeon, Birmingham Children's Hospital, 1990; Clinical Lead for Organ Retrieval, NHS Blood and Transplant, 2008; *b* 11 Jan. 1950; *s* of John Mayer and Sheila Mayer (*née* Lesser); *m* 1977, Helen Rastall; three *d*. *Educ*: Tonbridge Sch.; Univ. of Sussex (BSc 1971); Guy's Hosp., Univ. of London (MB BS 1976; MS 1986). FRCS 1980. House Officer, 1976–77, SHO, 1977, Guy's Hosp.; SHO, Brighton Gen. Hosp. and Royal Sussex Co. Hosp., 1978–80; Registrar, Scarborough Hosp., 1980–81; Res. Fellow, Leeds Gen. Infirmary, 1982–84; Registrar, Walsgrave Hosp., Coventry, 1985–86; Sen. Registrar, Queen Elizabeth Hosp., Birmingham, 1986–88; Vis. Fellow, UCSD, 1988–89. Hon. Sen. Lectr, Univ. of Birmingham, 1990. Chm., Liver Adv. Gp to UK Transplant, 2003–08; Pres., Transplantation Section, RSM, 2003–09. *Publications*: various articles on transplantation and surgery in med. jls, inc. Lancet, BMJ, New England Jl of Medicine and British Jl of Surgery. *Recreations*: cycling, music, literature, theatre. *Club*: Royal Society of Medicine.

**MAYER, Catherine**; author and journalist; Co-Founder and President, Women's Equality Party, since 2015; *b* USA, 1961; *d* of Prof. David Mayer and Anne Mayer Bird; *m* Andy Gill. *Educ*: Manchester High Sch. for Girls; Sussex Univ. (BA Hons); Albert-Ludwig Univ., Freiburg. Mktg Exec., 1983–84, writer, 1984–87, Economist; Deputy Editor: Business Traveller, 1988–90; Internat. Mgt, 1990–93; London corresp., Focus, 1993–2004; Time: Sen. Ed., 2004–06; London Bureau Chief, 2006–11; Europe Ed., 2011–13; Ed.-at-Large, 2013–15. Exec. Dir, Datum Future, 2018–. Pres., Foreign Press Assoc., 2003–05. Mem., Founding Cttee, WOW—Women of the World Fest., 2010–; Co-founder, Primadonna Fest., 2019–. Judge, Women's Prize for Fiction, 2018. *Publications*: Amortality: the pleasures and perils of living agelessly, 2011; Charles: the heart of a king, 2015; Attack of the 50ft Women: how gender equality can save the world, 2017. *Recreations*: cooking and stirring. *W*: www.catherinemayer.co.uk.

**MAYER, Prof. Colin Peter**, CBE 2017; FBA 2013; Peter Moores Professor of Management Studies, Saïd Business School (formerly School of Management Studies), University of Oxford, since 1994 (Peter Moores Dean, 2006–11); Fellow, Wadham College, Oxford, 1994–2006 and since 2011; *b* 12 May 1953; *s* of late Harold Charles Mayer and Anne Louise Mayer; *m* 1979, Annette Patricia Haynes; two *d*. *Educ*: St Paul's Sch.; Oriel College, Oxford (Hon. Fellow, 2006); Wolfson College, Oxford (MA, BPhil, DPhil); Harvard Univ. HM Treasury, 1976–78; Harkness Fellow, Harvard, 1979–80; Fellow in Economics, St Anne's College, Oxford, 1980–86 (Hon. Fellow, 1993); Price Waterhouse Prof. of Corporate Finance, City Univ. Business Sch., 1987–92; Prof. of Econs and Finance, Univ. of Warwick, 1992–94; Fellow, St Edmund Hall, Oxford, 2006–11. Chairman: ESF Network in Financial Markets, 1989–94; Oxford Economic Research Associates, subseq. OXERA Hldgs, Ltd, 1987–2010; Humanities and Social Scis Res. Ethics Cttee, Oxford Univ., 2014–19; Chm., Mgt and Business Studies Gp, 2017–19, Lead Academic, Future of Corporation Prog., 2017–, British Acad.; non-exec. Dir, Aurora Energy Res., 2013–; Dir, Oxford Financial Res. Centre, 1998–2006; Mem., Internat. Adv. Bd, Securities and Exchange Bd of India, 2015–17. Delegate, OUP, 1996–2006 (Chm., Audit Cttee, 2002–06). Member: Competition Appeal Tribunal, 2011–18; Natural Capital Cttee, DEFRA, 2012–; Internat. Adv. Bd, Safra Center, Tel Aviv Univ., 2018–; Adv. Council, Embankment Project or Inclusive Capital, 2018–; High Level Adv. Gp, World Business Council for Sustainable Develt, 2019–. Mem. Exec. Cttee, REconS, 2002–06. Inaugural Fellow, European Corporate Governance Inst., 2002–. Gov., St Paul's Sch., London, 2002–11. Trustee, Oxford Playhouse, 2015–. Associate Editor: Jl of Internat. Financial Management; Jl of European Financial Management; Oxford Review of Economic Policy. *Publications*: (with J. Kay and J. Edwards) Economic Analysis of Accounting Profitability, 1986; (with J. Franks) Risk, Regulation and Investor Protection, 1989; (with A. Giovannini) European Financial Integration, 1991; (with X. Vives) Capital Markets and Financial Intermediation, 1993; (with T. Jenkinson) Hostile Takeovers, 1994; (with J. Franks and L. C. da Silva) Asset Management and Investor Protection, 2002; (with X. Freixas and P. Hartmann) Handbook of European Financial Markets and Institutions, 2008; Firm Commitment: why the corporation is failing us and how to restore trust in it, 2013; (jtly) Principles of Financial Regulation, 2016; (jtly) Finance and Investment: the case of Europe, 2018; Prosperity: better business makes the greater good, 2018; articles in economic and finance jls. *Recreations*: piano, jogging, reading philosophy and science. *Address*: Saïd Business School, University of Oxford, Park End Street, Oxford OX1 1HP. *T*: (01865) 288811.

**MAYER, David**; see Mayer, A. D.

**MAYER, John**; see Mayer, R. J.

**MAYER, (Ralph) Anthony (Jeffrey)**, CBE 2000; Chairman, One Housing Group, 2012–18; *b* 24 Feb. 1946; *s* of George Mayer and Margaret (*née* Jones); *m* 1971, Ann Gowen; one *s* one *d*. *Educ*: City of Bath Boys' Sch.; Lycée Michelet, Paris; St Edmund Hall, Oxford (BA Hons PPE). Ministry of Housing and Local Government, subseq. Department of the Environment, 1967–85: Asst Principal, 1967–72; seconded as Pvte Sec. to Parly Sec., CSD, 1971–72; Principal, 1972–81; seconded as Mem., CPRS, 1974–76, and as Prin. Pvte Sec. to Sec. of State for Transport, 1980–82; Asst Sec., 1981–85; Asst Dir, N. M. Rothschild and Sons, 1985–87; Man. Dir (Finance and Admin), Rothschild Asset Management, 1987–91; Chief Exec., Housing Corp., 1991–2000; Actg Chief Exec., Transport for London, 2000; Chief Exec., GLA, 2000–08; Chairman: Tenant Services Authy, 2008–12; London Pensions Fund Authy, 2009–12. *Recreations*: bridge, travel, writing novels. *Address*: 37 Copthall Gardens, Twickenham, Middlesex TW1 4HH.

**MAYER, Prof. Roland George**, PhD; Professor of Classics, King's College London, 1996–2015, Emeritus Professor, 2016; *b* Annapolis, Md, 24 July 1947; *s* of Roland George Mayer, Jr and Mary Clare Devine; civil partnership 2014, David Munro. *Educ*: Univ. of Calif at Berkeley (BA 1967); Peterhouse, Cambridge (BA 1972; PhD 1977). Res. Fellow, Bedford Coll., Univ. of London, 1976–79; Lectr, 1979–88, Sen. Lectr, 1988–89, Birkbeck Coll., Univ. of London; Sen. Lectr, KCL, 1989–96. Hon. Sec., Soc. for Promotion of Roman Studies, 2017–. Editor, Classical Review, 1994–2001. *Publications*: Seneca: Phaedra, 2002; *edited*: Lucan, Civil War 8, 1982; Horace, Epistles 1, 1994; Tacitus, Dialogus, 2001; (with M. Coffey) Seneca, Phaedra, 1990; Horace, Odes Book I, 2012. *Recreations*: opera, South German Baroque churches. *Address*: Flat 9, 18–21 Wilmington Square, WC1X 0ER. *T*: (020) 7833 1845.

**MAYER, Prof. (Roland) John**, FRCPath; Professor of Molecular Cell Biology, 1986, now Emeritus, and Head of Molecular Cell Biology, School of Biomedical Sciences, 1997, University of Nottingham; *b* 30 April 1943; *s* of George and Ethel Mayer; *m* 1967, Elaine Ing; two *s*. *Educ*: Univ. of Birmingham (BSc 1st Cl., 1965; PhD 1968); DSc Nottingham 1980. Lectr, Sen. Lectr and Reader, Univ. of Nottingham, 1970–86. *Publications*: (with J. H. Walker) Immunochemical Methods in the Biological Sciences: enzymes and proteins, 1980; (with J. H. Walker) Immunochemical Methods in Cell and Molecular Biology, 1987; (with F. J. Doherty) Intracellular Protein Degradation, 1992; contribs to learned jls. *Recreation*: golf. *Address*: School of Molecular Medical Sciences, University of Nottingham Medical School, Queen's Medical Centre, Nottingham NG7 2UH. *T*: (0115) 970 9369.

**MAYER, Thomas**, CBE 1985; FREng; Chairman, Eldonray Ltd, 1990–2004; *b* 17 Dec. 1928; *s* of Hans and Jeanette Mayer; *m* 1st, 1956 (marr. diss. 1975); one *s* one *d*; 2nd, 1975, Jean Patricia Burrows. *Educ*: King's Sch., Harrow; Regent Street Polytechnic (BScEng 1948). FIET (FIEE 1964); FRTS 1968; FREng (FEng 1987); CRAeS 1990. Broadcasting Div., Marconi Co. Ltd, 1948–68; Man. Dir, Marconi Elliott Micro-Electronics Ltd, 1968–69; Man. Dir, Marconi Communication Systems Ltd, 1969–81; Man. Dir, 1981–86, Chm., 1981–90, THORN EMI Electronics Ltd; Chief Exec., THORN EMI Technology Gp, 1986–88; Exec. Dir, THORN EMI plc, 1987–90. Chairman: THORN EMI Varian Ltd, 1981–89; Holmes Protection Gp, 1990–97; ITT Defence Ltd, 1993–97; Director: Thorn Ericsson, 1981–88; Systron Donner Corp., 1983–90; Inmos Corp., 1985–88; Babcock Thorn Ltd, 1985–90; THORN EMI Australia, 1987–88; non-executive Director: Devonport Management Ltd, 1990–97; Eurodis Electron (formerly Electron House) plc, 1991–2002. Chm., UK Nat. Widescreen Television Forum, DTI, 1991–97. Member: Council, IEE, 1971–74; Council, Electronic Engrg Assoc., 1974–75, 1981–87 (Pres., 1982–83); Nat. Electronics Council, 1983–98; SBAC, 1984–90 (Pres., 1987–88). Liveryman, Worshipful Co. of Engineers, 1984–. *Recreations*: golf, swimming, theatre. *Address*: Rosewood Cottage, The Butts, Church Street, Princes Risborough, Bucks HP27 9AN. *T*: (01844) 344194. *Club*: Ellesborough Golf.

**MAYER, Her Honour Vera**; a Circuit Judge, 2002–18; *b* 11 June 1948; *d* of Milan and Suzanna Mayer; two *d*. *Educ*: Bar-Ilan Univ., Israel (BA Psychol.); Inst. of Educn, Univ. of London (MSc Child Develt). Called to the Bar, Gray's Inn, 1978; Asst Recorder, 1998–2000; Recorder, 2000–02. Mem., Professional Conduct Cttee, Bar Council, 2000–02. *Recreations*: action-packed travel, photography, music, theatre.

**MAYER-SCHÖNBERGER, Prof. Viktor**, Dr jur; Professor of Internet Governance and Regulation, since 2010, and Director of Advancement, Oxford Internet Institute, 2012–13, University of Oxford; Fellow, Keble College, Oxford, since 2010; *b* Austria. *Educ*: Harvard Law Sch. (LLM 1989); Law Sch., Salzburg (Dr jur 1991); London Sch. of Econs and Pol Sci. (MSc Internat. Relns 1992). Founder, Ikarus Software, 1986–92; Asst Prof., 1999–2003, Associate Prof., 2003–08, Harvard Univ.; Associate Prof., Lee Kuan Yew Sch. of Public Policy, and Dir, Information and Innovation Policy Res. Centre, Nat. Univ. of Singapore, 2008–10. Advr to Minister of Finance, Austria, 2009–. Mem., Global Adv. Council, World Econ. Forum, 2010–. Mem., Trustworthy Computing Academic Adv. Bd, 2005–. *Publications*: Governance and Information Technology, 2007; Delete: the virtue of forgetting in the digital age, 2009; (with K. Cukier) Big Data: a revolution that will transform how we live, work and think, 2013; (with T. Ramge) Reinventing Capitalism in the Age of Big Data, 2018. *Address*: Oxford Internet Institute, 1 St Giles, Oxford OX1 3JS. *E*: vms@acm.org.

**MAYES, Maj.-Gen. Frederick Brian**, CB 1995; FRCS; Director General, Army Medical Services, 1993–96; *b* 24 Aug. 1934; *s* of late Harry Frederick and Constance Enid Mayes; *m* 1962, Mary Anna Georgina Roche; one *s* two *d* (and one *s* decd). *Educ*: Wyggeston Grammar Sch., Leicester; St Mary's Hosp. Med. Sch. (MB BS London 1958). Commissioned Lieut RAMC, 1960; served Aden, E Africa, BAOR, UK; Consultant in Surgery, 1972; CO, BMH Hannover, 1984–87; CO, Cambridge Mil. Hosp., Aldershot, 1987–88; Consultant Surgeon, HQ BAOR, 1988–90; Comdr Med., HQ BAOR, 1990–93. QHS, 1991–96. Pres., St John's Ambulance, Germany, 1990. CStJ 1993. *Recreations*: off-shore sailing, bridge, mountaineering. *Address*: Mornington, 9 Searle Road, Farnham, Surrey GU9 8LJ. *T*: (01252) 715453.

**MAYES, Ian**; QC 1993; *b* 11 Sept. 1951; marr. diss.; two *s*. *Educ*: Highgate Sch. (Foundation Schol.); Trinity Coll., Cambridge (Hooper Prizeman). Called to the Bar, Middle Temple, 1974 (Harmsworth Schol.); Bencher, 2001); a Recorder, 2000–10. Dept of Trade Inspection, London Capital Group Ltd, 1975–77; Standing Counsel to Inland Revenue, 1983–93. Chm., Disciplinary Tribunal, Lloyd's of London. Mem., Justice Cttee on Fraud Trials. Chairman: Art First; Kettle's Yard Develt Appeal. Master, Security Professionals' Co., 2016–17. *Recreation*: collecting. *Address*: Enterprise Chambers, 9 Old Square, Lincoln's Inn, WC2A 3SR. *T*: (020) 7405 9471. *Clubs*: Garrick, Chelsea Arts.

**MAYES, Rt Rev. Michael Hugh Gunton**; Bishop of Limerick and Killaloe, 2000–08; *b* 31 Aug. 1941; *s* of Thomas David Dougan Mayes and Hilary Gunton; *m* 1966, Elizabeth Annie Eleanor Irwin; one *s* two *d*. *Educ*: The Royal Sch., Armagh; Trinity Coll., Dublin (BA); Univ. of London (BD). Ordained, 1964; Assistant Curate: St Mark's, Portadown, 1964–67; St Columba's, Portadown, 1967–68; Missionary, Japan, 1968–74; Incumbent: St Michael's, Cork, 1975–86; Moviddy, Cork, 1986–88; Rathcooney, Cork, 1988–93; Archdeacon of Cork, Cloyne and Ross, 1986–93; Bishop of Kilmore, Elphin and Ardagh, 1993–2000. *Recreations*: reading, music, photography, walking. *Address*: 5 The Crescent, Rockfield, Church Road, Blackrock, Cork T12 R9X3, Ireland. *T*: (21) 4967688. *E*: mhg.mayes@gmail.com.

**MAYFIELD, Sir Andrew Charles, (Sir Charlie)**, Kt 2013; Chairman, John Lewis Partnership, 2007–20; *b* Hants, 25 Dec. 1966; *s* of Richard and Rosemary Mayfield; *m* 1993, Elizabeth Paton; one *s* two *d*. *Educ*: Radley Coll.; RMA, Sandhurst (Sword of Honour); Cranfield Sch. of Mgt (MBA). Captain, Scots Guards, 1986–91. Asst Product Manager, SmithKline Beecham, 1992–96; Consultant, McKinsey & Co., 1996–2000; John Lewis Partnership: Hd, Business Develt, 2000–01; Develt Dir, 2001–05; Man. Dir, 2005–07. Mem., UK Commn for Employment and Skills, 2007– (Chair, 2010–); Chm., British Retail Consortium, 2014–16. Dir, Central Surrey Health Trustee Ltd, 2013–; Chm., QA Gp, 2017–. Pres., Employee Ownership Assoc., 2011–. Mem. Council, Radley Coll., 2010–. Trustee: Scots Guards Charitable Fund, 2007–; British Mus., 2018–. Hon. Fellow, Univ. of Central Lancs, 2007. DUniv Loughborough, 2013; Hon. DBus London, 2013. *Recreations*: walking, ski-ing, sailing. *Address*: John Lewis Partnership, Partnership House, Carlisle Place, SW1P 1BX. *T*: (020) 7828 1000.

**MAYFIELD, Rt Rev. Christopher John**; Bishop of Manchester, 1993–2002; Hon. Assistant Bishop, Diocese of Worcester, since 2002; *b* 18 Dec. 1935; *s* of Dr Roger Bolton Mayfield and Muriel Eileen Mayfield; *m* 1962, Caroline Ann Roberts; two *s* one *d*. *Educ*: Sedbergh School; Gonville and Caius Coll., Cambridge (MA 1961); Linacre House, Oxford (Dip. Theology); MSc Cranfield Univ. 1984. Deacon 1963, priest 1964, Birmingham; Curate of St Martin in the Bull Ring, Birmingham, 1963–67; Lecturer at St Martin's, Birmingham, 1967–71; Chaplain at Children's Hospital, Birmingham, 1967–71; Vicar of Luton, 1971–80 (with East Hyde, 1971–76); RD of Luton, 1974–79; Archdeacon of Bedford, 1979–85; Bishop Suffragan of Wolverhampton, 1985–93. Dean of Retired Clergy, Dio. of Worcester, 2010–15. Mem., H of L, 1998–2002. Treas., Worcester Civic Soc., 2009–11. *Recreations*: family, gardening, walking. *Address*: 23 Petunia Close, St Peter's, Worcester WR5 3RT.

**MAYHEW, (Brian Arthur) Charles**, MBE 2006; FRGS; Chief Executive, Tusk Trust, since 2001; *b* London, 1 Feb. 1961; *s* of Brian and Patricia Mayhew; *m* 1993, Caroline Farrer; one *s* three *d*. *Educ*: Wellington Coll., Berks. Marine broker, Willis Faber & Dumas, 1980–85; leader of expedition, Young Europe Africa, 1985–86; Independent Financial Adviser: Bentley Leek McMullen, 1986–88; MM Ltd, 1988–2001. Pres., Tusk USA, 2003–18; *ex officio* Trustee, Tusk USA Inc., 2011–18; Trustee, Ernest Kleinwort Charitable

Trust, 2013–. Co-producer, feature film, Lost in Africa, 1992. FRGS 1989. *Recreations:* motor-racing, ski-ing, walking, gardening, safari wildlife conservation. *Address:* Tusk Trust, Cheapside House, High Street, Gillingham, Dorset SP8 4AA. *T:* (01747) 831005. *E:* info@tusk.org.

**MAYHEW, David Lionel,** CBE 2011; Chairman: Cazenove Capital Holdings Ltd, 2005–13; JPMorgan Cazenove, 2010–11; Vice Chairman, JPMorgan, since 2010; *b* 20 May 1940; *s* of Lionel Geoffrey Mayhew and Biddy Vowe Mayhew; *m* 1966, Virginia Ann Wonnacott; two *s* one *d. Educ:* Eton Coll. With Panmure Gordon, 1961–69; Cazenove & Co., subseq. JPMorgan Cazenove Ltd, 1969–2011, Partner, 1971–2001; Chairman: Cazenove Gp, 2001–10; JPMorgan Cazenove Hldgs, 2005–10. Non-exec. Dir, Rio Tinto plc, 2000–10. Trustee: Royal Anniversary Trust, 2005–14; Game and Wildlife Conservation Trust, 2012–; Chm., Trustees, Alzheimer's Res. UK, 2012–. UK Dementia Envoy, 2016–. *Recreations:* farming, country pursuits. *Address:* c/o J.P. Morgan Cazenove, 25 Bank Street, E14 5JP. *Clubs:* Boodle's; Swinley Golf; New Zealand Golf.

**MAYHEW, Air Marshal Gerard Michael David,** CBE 2015; Deputy Commander Operations, Headquarters Air Command, since 2019; Air Member for Operations, since 2019; *b* Sutton Coldfield, 15 Feb. 1969; *m* 1996, Susan Meredith Whittaker. *Educ:* St Benedict's, Alcester; Alcester Grammar Sch. Commnd RAF, 1988; Air Traffic Control Officer, 1988–90; Jaguar pilot and qwi, 1990–96; operational exchange tour, F16, USAF, 1996–2000; 41 (F) Sqdn Flight Comdr, Jaguar, 2000–03; Personnel Mgt Agency, 2003–05; Advanced Command and Staff Coll., 2005; Concepts Team, Defence Concepts and Doctrine Centre, 2005–07; OC XIII Sqdn, Tornado GR4, 2007–09; Sen. Appts Team leader, MoD, 2009–11; Asst Dir Jt Strike, Directorate of Jt Capability, MoD, 2011; Dep. PSO to CDS, 2011–12; AO Scotland and Station Comdr RAF Leuchars, 2013–15; HCSC 2015; Dep. Dir for Defence and Homeland Security, Strategic Defence and Security Rev., 2015; AOC No 1 Gp, 2016–18; Asst Chief of the Air Staff, 2018–19. *Address:* Air Command, RAF High Wycombe, Bucks HP14 4UE. *Club:* Royal Air Force.

**MAYHEW, Jeremy Paul;** Chairman, Finance Committee, City of London Corporation, since 2016 (Chairman: Audit and Risk Management Committee, 2011–14; City Bridge Trust Committee, 2014–16; Deputy Chairman, Policy and Resources Committee, 2013–16); *b* Bristol, 1 Feb. 1959; *s* of late Yon Richard Mayhew and Cora Angela Mayhew (*née* Lamboll). *Educ:* Clifton Coll., Bristol; Western Reserve Acad., Ohio (ESU Schol.); Balliol Coll., Oxford (MA PPE; scholar); Harvard Business Sch. (MBA High Dist. 1989). BBC Television: trainee asst producer, 1980–82; Asst Producer, Current Affairs, 1982–84; independent prod./dir, documentary and current affairs for Channel 4, 1984–87; Strategy Consultant, Booz Allen & Hamilton, 1989–90; Special Advr to Sec. of State for Trade and Industry, then for Social Security, 1990–93; Hd, Strategy Devpt, BBC, 1993–95; Dir, New Media, 1995–99, Dir, New Ventures and Strategy, 1999–2001, Dir, Bd, 1997–2001, BBC Worldwide Ltd; Dir and Hd, Strategy Practice, Human Capital consultancy, 2001–02; Sen. Advr, 2002–03 and 2008–09, Partner, 2003–08, Spectrum Strategy Consultants, later Spectrum Value Partners; Chm., 2008–11, Dep. Chm., 2011–12, Bd, Barbican Centre. Sen. Advr, Oliver & Ohlbaum Associates, 2010–11; Sen. Advr, PwC Consultancy, 2012–. Non-executive Director: Learning and Skills Devlt Agency, 1999–2002; Strategic Rail Authy, 2000–06; London Devlt Agency, 2008–12. Mem. (Public Rep.), Evaluation Cttee, ESRC, 2011–14; non-exec. Advr, Commissioning and Procurement, Mayor of London's Office for Policing and Crime, 2012–14; Member: UK Govt's Regulatory Policy Cttee, 2012–; Legal Services Bd, 2016–19; British Transport Police Authy, 2017–. Mem., Ct of Common Council, City of London, 1996– (Chm., Educn Cttee, 2005–06). Mem. Council, London Chamber of Commerce and Industry, 1998–. Trustee: Hammersmith United Charities, 1991–96; British Friends of Harvard Business Sch., 1993–; City Arts Trust, 2001–; Thames Fest. Trust, 2004–08; Crossrail Art Foundn, 2014–; Mem., City of London Academies Trust, 2016–18. Governor: Sacred Heart Jun. Sch., 1990–96; City Literary Inst., 1998–2002; Clifton Coll., 2000–; London Guildhall Univ., 2000–02; London Metropolitan Univ., 2002–10; Prior Weston Primary Sch., Islington, 2014–; Homerton Univ. Hosp., 2018–; Mem. Court, City Univ., 1996–; Donation Gov., Christ's Hosp., 1998–. Constit. Officer, Hammersmith Cons. Assoc., 1990–93; Mem., Council, Bow Gp, 1990–93. Pres., Harvard Business Sch. Club of London, 1997, 1998. Sec. and Treas., Oxford Union Soc., 1979. Freeman, City of London, 1994; Liveryman, Loriners' Co., 1995– (Mem. Court, 2012–). *Recreations:* collecting political caricatures, theatre, cinema, art galleries, arguing. *Address:* City of London Corporation, PO Box 270, Guildhall, EC2P 2EJ. *T:* (020) 7600 4070, 07718 653215. *E:* jeremymayhew@btinternet.com. *Clubs:* Reform, Guildhall.

**MAYHEW, Dame Judith;** *see* Mayhew Jonas, Dame J.

**MAYHEW, Kenneth;** Professor of Education and Economic Performance, University of Oxford, 2008–14, now Emeritus (Reader in Economics, 1996–2008); Fellow and Tutor in Economics, Pembroke College, Oxford, 1976–2014, now Emeritus Fellow (Vicegerent, 2000–03); Extraordinary Professor, Maastricht University, since 2014; *b* 1 Sept. 1947; *s* of late Albert Chadwick Mayhew and Alice Mayhew (*née* Leigh). *Educ:* Manchester Grammar Sch.; Worcester Coll., Oxford (MA); London School of Economics (MScEcon). Economic Asst, HM Treasury, 1970–72; Res. Officer, Queen Elizabeth House, Oxford, 1972; Asst Res. Officer, then Res. Officer, Inst. of Economics and Statistics, Oxford, 1972–81; Economic Dir, NEDO, 1989–91; Dir, ESRC Centre on Skills, Knowledge and Orgnl Perf., subseq. Centre on Skills, Knowledge and Orgnl Perf., 1998–2014. Vis. Associate Prof., Cornell Univ., 1981. Advr, CBI, 1983. Mem., Armed Forces Pay Review Body, 2014–. Editor, Oxford Bull. of Econs and Stats, 1976–88; Associate Editor: Oxford Review of Economic Policy, 1984–; Oxford Economic Papers, 1997–; Mem., Editl Bd, Oxford Rev. of Educn, 2009–19. *Publications:* Trade Unions and the Labour Market, 1983; (ed with D. Robinson) Pay Policies for the Future, 1983; (ed with A. Bowen) Improving Incentives for the Low Paid, 1990; (ed with A. Bowen) Reducing Regional Inequalities, 1991; (ed jtly) Providing Health Care, 1991; (ed jtly) Britain's Training Deficit, 1994; (ed jtly) The Economics of Skills Obsolescence, 2002; (ed jtly) Low Wage Work in the UK, 2008; (ed jtly) The Oxford Handbook of Skills and Training, 2017; reports and numerous articles on labour econs and industrial relns in learned jls. *Recreations:* travel, literature. *Address:* 3 Bitterell, Eynsham, Oxon OX29 4JL. *T:* (01865) 883547. *Club:* Reform.

**MAYHEW, Prof. Leslie Dennis,** PhD; Professor of Statistics, Cass Business School, City, University of London (formerly City University Business School, then Cass Business School, City University), since 2002; Managing Director, Mayhew Harper Associates Ltd (formerly Mayhew Associates Ltd), since 2001; *b* 7 Nov. 1947; *s* of Charles and Violet Mayhew; *m* 1984, Karin Sigmund; two *s* one *d. Educ:* Birkbeck Coll., London (BSc Hons (1st class); PhD 1979). Dir of OR, later Business Devlt Manager, Benefits Agency, and sen. post in Finance/Planning, DHSS, then DSS, 1979–93; Dir of Central Services and Prin. Estabts and Finance Officer, GCS, 1993–96; Gp Dir for Admin. Services and Registration, ONS, 1996–98; Prof. of Geography, Birkbeck Coll., London Univ., 1998–2001. Res. Schol., Internat. Inst. for Applied Systems Analysis, Vienna, 1980–82 and 1999–; Vis. Prof., Birkbeck Coll., London Univ., 1995–98. Mem., REconS, 2009. Hon. FIA 200. *Publications:* Urban Hospital Location, 1986, repubd 2019; (jtly) The Economic Impacts of Population Ageing in Japan, 2004; (jtly) Unlocking the Potential, 2014; contrib. learned jls and periodicals in health, transport, geography and operational res. (current research: ageing, pensions, disability, inequalities, demography, use of administrative data, health and social care). *Recreations:* tennis, music, travelling, walking. *Address:* Faculty of Actuarial Science and Insurance, Cass Business School, 106 Bunhill Row, EC1Y 8TZ. *E:* lesmayhew@googlemail.com.

**MAYHEW JONAS, Dame Judith,** DBE 2002; Commissioner, Commonwealth War Graves Commission, since 2019; *b* 18 Oct. 1948; *m* 1st, 1976 (marr. diss. 1986); 2nd, 2003, Christopher William Jonas, *qv. Educ:* Univ. of Otago, NZ (LLM 1973). Barrister and Solicitor, NZ, 1973; admitted Solicitor, England and Wales, 1993. Lectr in Law, Univ. of Otago, 1970–73; Lecturer in Law and Sub Dean: Univ. of Southampton, 1973–76; King's Coll., London, 1976–89; Dir, Anglo French law degree, Sorbonne, Paris, 1976–89; Dir of Training and Employment Law, Titmuss Sainer Dechert, 1989–94; Dir of Educn and Trng, Wilde Sapte, 1994–99; Provost, King's Coll., Cambridge, 2003–06; Chancellor (formerly Provost), Bishop Grosseteste Univ. Coll., later Bishop Grosseteste Univ., 2008–. Chm., Private Investment Commn, 2000–06. Non-exec. Dir, Merrill Lynch & Co. Inc., USA, 2006–08 (Advr, 2003–06); Special Advisor: to Chm., Clifford Chance, 2000–03; City and Business Advr to Mayor of London, 2000–04; Tishman Speyer, 2013–19. Mem., Adv. Cttee, Barclays Wealth UK Private Bank, 2012–13. Corporation of London: Mem., Court of Common Council, 1986–2004; Chm., Educn Cttee, 1989–95; Chm., 1997–2003, Dep. Chm., 2003–04, Policy and Resources Cttee. Director: Gresham Coll., 1990–2009; ESU, 1993–99; Geffrye Mus., 1995–99; Internat. Financial Services London (formerly British Invisibles), 1996–2004; City Disputes Panel, 1996–99; London First Centre, 1996–2002; London First, 1997–2003; 4Ps, 1997–2004; London Development Partnership, 1998–2000; London Develt Agency, 2000–04; Tower Hamlets Educn Business Partnership, 2001–03; Chairman: New West End Co., 2008–13; London & Partners, 2011–13. Chairman: London-NY Dialogues, 1997–; Apeldoorn: British-Dutch Dialogues, 2010–. Trustee: Natural History Mus., 1998–2006; Imperial War Mus., 2008–17; Commonwealth War Graves Foundn, 2017–; Imperial War Mus. Devlt Trust, 2017–; Global Trustee, Urban Land Inst., 2013–; Mem. Council, BM Devlt Trust, 2001–02; non-exec. Dir, Housing Finance Inst., 2015–. Chairman: Royal Opera House, 2003–08; Ind. Schs Council, 2008–11; Sen. Advr, Chatham House, 2010–. Governor: London Guildhall Univ., 1992–99, 2000–03; Birkbeck Coll., London Univ., 1993–2004 (Chm., 1999–2003; Fellow, 2003); Imperial Coll., London Univ., 2001–04. Fellow, London Business Sch., 2003; FCGI 2004; Hon. FICPD 2004. Hon. DLaws: Otago, 1998; City, 1999; London Metropolitan, 2003. Officer, Order of Orange-Nassau (Netherlands), 2018. *Recreations:* opera, ballet, gardening, tennis. *Address:* 25 Victoria Square, SW1W 0RB. *Club:* Guildhall.

**MAYLAND, Rev. Canon Ralph,** VRD 1962 and bar 1972; non-stipendiary Priest-in-Charge, Brancepeth, 1994–96; 31 March; *s* of James Henry and Lucy Mayland; *m* 1959, Rev. Jean Mary Goldstraw; one *d* and one adopted *d. Educ:* Cockburn High Sch., Leeds; Leeds City Training Coll.; Westminster Coll., London Univ.; Ripon Hall, Oxford. Schoolteacher, 1945–46; RN, 1946–51; perm. commn, RNR, 1952, Chaplain, 1961–82; 3rd yr student, 1951–52; schoolteacher, 1952–57; theol student, 1957–59. Curate of Lambeth, 1959–62; Priest-in-charge, St Paul's, Manton, Worksop, 1962–67; Vicar, St Margaret's, Brightside, 1968–72; Chaplain, Sheffield Industrial Mission, 1968–75; Vicar, St Mary's, Ecclesfield, 1972–82; Chaplain to Master Cutler, 1979–80; Canon and Treasurer, York Minster, 1982–94, Canon Emeritus, 1994–. Hon. Chaplain, HMS York, 1989–2011; Chaplain, 8th Destroyer Assoc., 2000–12. Life Mem., Royal Naval Assoc. *Recreation:* collecting Victorian children's literature. *Address:* 5 Hackwood Glade, Hexham, Northumberland NE46 1AL.

**MAYNARD, Dr Alice Mary,** CBE 2015; Director, Future Inclusion Ltd, since 2003; *b* Chalfont St Giles, 28 Nov. 1957; *d* of Rupert Maynard and Mary Maynard (*née* Hunt). *Educ:* Univ. of York (BA Hons 1980); Ashridge Business Sch. (MBA 1991); Cranfield Univ. (DBA 2008). CDir 2011. Sen. Programmer, Software Scis, 1980–84; Prog. Manager, Lotus Devlt, 1984–88; Software Manager, Ashton-Tate Europe, 1988–90; Dir, Equal Ability Ltd, 1992–96; Sen. Consultant, Churchill & Friend, 1997–98; Hd, Disability Strategy, Network Rail, 1998–2003; Social Inclusion Advr, TfL, 2001–02; HR Consultant, London Underground, 2001. Associate, Business Disability Internat., 2015–. Non-executive Director: HMRC, 2016–; TfL, 2016–. Member: Human Genetics Commn, 2006–12; Cttee on Fuel Poverty, 2016–18. Mem., Eastern Area Cttee, Jephson Housing Assoc., 2003–08. Trustee, Nat. Information Forum, 2000–02; Trustee and Chair, Milton Keynes Racial Equality Council, 2004–07; Trustee/Director: Swanswell Charitable Trust, 2015–16; Cross and Stable Charities, 2015–; Milton Keynes Community Foundn, 2017–. FRSA 2011. DUniv York, 2014. *Publications:* (contrib.) Disabling Barriers, Enabling Environments, 1993, 3rd edn 2013; contrib. articles to Jl Transportation and Land Use, Transed 2007 conf. papers. *Recreations:* choral and a capella singing, entertaining, reading. *T:* (01908) 665850. *E:* am@alicemaynard.co.uk.

**MAYNARD, Paul Christopher;** MP (C) Blackpool North and Cleveleys, since 2010; Parliamentary Under-Secretary of State, Department for Transport, since 2019; *b* Crewe, 16 Dec. 1975; *s* of Brian and Rosemary Maynard. *Educ:* University Coll., Oxford (BA Hons Modern Hist.). Special Advr to Dr Liam Fox, MP, 1999–2007. Contested (C) Twickenham, 2005. Parly Under-Sec. of State, DfT, 2016–18; a Lord Commissioner of HM Treasury (Govt Whip), 2018–19; Parly Under-Sec. of State, MoJ, 2019. *Address:* House of Commons, SW1A 0AA.

**MAYNARD, Roger Paul;** Consultant, International Airlines Group, since 2011; Director of Investment and Alliances (formerly Investment and Joint Ventures), British Airways, 1996–2011; *b* 10 Feb. 1943; *s* of Leonard John Maynard and May Gertrude Blake; *m* 1st, 1966 (marr. diss. 2004); three *s* (including twin *s*); 2nd, 2011, Judith Lane. *Educ:* Purley Grammar Sch., Surrey; Queens' Coll., Cambridge (MA Hons Economics). Asst Principal, Bd of Trade, 1965; Second Secretary, UK Mission to UN and Internat. Organisations, Geneva, 1968; Principal: Dept of Industry, Shipbuilding Division, 1972; Dept of Trade, Airports Policy, 1975; Asst Sec., Dept of Industry, Air Division, 1978; Counsellor, Aviation and Shipping, British Embassy, Washington, 1982; British Airways: Vice Pres., Commercial Affairs, N America, 1987–89; Exec. Vice Pres., N America, 1989; Dir, Investor Relations and Marketplace Performance, 1989–91; Dir, Corporate Strategy, 1991–96. Chairman: British Airways Pension Investment Mgt Ltd, 2005–09; British Airways Pension Scheme, 2018–. Non-executive Director: US Air, 1993–96; Qantas, 1993–2004; Iberia, 2000–11; AJW Aviation, 2011–14. Senior Advisor: L.E.K. Consulting, 2014–; ICF Consultancy, 2017–. *Recreations:* cricket, golf, music. *Address:* 43 Rosebank, Holyport Road, Fulham, SW6 6LQ.

**MAYNE, Prof. David Quinn,** FRS 1985; FREng; Professor of Electrical and Computer Engineering, University of California, Davis, 1989–96, now Professor Emeritus; Senior Research Investigator, Department of Electrical and Electronic Engineering, Imperial College London, since 1996; *b* 23 April 1930; *s* of Leslie Harper Mayne and Jane Quin; *m* 1954, Josephine Mary Hess; three *d. Educ:* Univ. of the Witwatersrand, Johannesburg (BSc (Eng), MSc); Imperial Coll. London (DIC, PhD, DSc). FIET, FIEEE; FREng (FEng 1987). Lectr, Univ. of Witwatersrand, 1950–54, 1956–59; R&D Engineer, British Thomson Houston Co., Rugby, 1955–56; Imperial College: Lectr, 1959–67, Reader, 1967–71; Prof. of Control Theory, 1971–89, now Prof. Emeritus; Sen. Sci. Res. Fellow, 1979–80; Hd of

Dept of Electrical Engrg, 1984–88. Research Consultant, 1974–, at Univs of California (Berkeley, and Santa Barbara), Lund, Newcastle NSW, and Wisconsin. Res. Fellow, Harvard Univ., 1970; Vis. Prof., Academia Sinica, Beijing, Shanghai and Guangzhou, 1981; Hon. Prof., Beihang Univ., Beijing, 2006. Corresp. Mem., Nacional Acad. de Ingenieria, Mexico, 1983. FIC 2000; Fellow, IFAC, 2006. Hon. DEng Lund Univ., 1995. Heaviside Premium, IEE, 1981, 1985; Sir Harold Hartley Medal, Inst. of Measurement and Control, 1986; Control Systems Award, IEEE, 2009; High Impact Paper Award, 2011, Quazza Medal, 2014, IFAC. *Publications*: Differential Dynamic Programming, vol. 24 in Modern Analytic and Computational Methods in Science and Mathematics (with D. H. Jacobson, ed R. Bellman), 1970; Geometric Methods in System Theory, proc. NATO Advanced Study Inst., (ed. with R. W. Brockett), 1973; (with J. B. Rawlings) Model Predictive Control: theory and design, 2009; (with J. B. Rawlings and M. Diehl) Model Predictive Control: theory, computation and design, 2017; contribs to learned jls. *Recreations*: walking, cross-country ski-ing. *Address*: Department of Electrical and Electronic Engineering, Imperial College London, SW7 2BT.

**MAYO**, 11th Earl of, *cr* 1785; **Charles Diarmuidh John Bourke**; Baron Naas, 1776; Viscount Mayo, 1781; *b* 11 June 1953; *e s* of 10th Earl of Mayo and his 1st wife, Margaret Jane Robinson Harrison; S father, 2006; *m* 1st, 1975, Marie Antoinette Cronnelly (marr. diss. 1979); one *d*; 2nd, 1985, Marie Veronica Mannion; two *s*. *Educ*: St Aubyn's, Rottingdean; Portora Royal Sch., Enniskillen; QUB; Bolton Street Coll. of Technology, Dublin. *Heir*: *s* Lord Naas, *qv*. *Address*: Derryinver, Beach Road, Clifden, Co. Galway, Eire.

**MAYO, Col (Edward) John**, OBE 1976; Director General, Help the Aged, 1983–96; *b* 24 May 1931; *s* of late Rev. Thomas Edward Mayo, JP, and Constance Muriel Mayo; *m* 1st, 1961, Jacqueline Margaret Anne Armstrong, MBE 1985, Lieut WRAC (*d* 1993), *d* of late Brig. C. D. Armstrong, CBE, DSO, MC; one *s*; 2nd, 1998, Pamela Joyce Shimwell (MBE 2014). *Educ*: King's Coll., Taunton. Commissioned into Royal Regt of Artillery, 1951; served Malta and N Africa 36 HAA Regt, 1951–55; ADC to Governor of Malta, 1953–54; 2nd Regt RHA, BAOR, 1955–58; ADC to C-in-C BAOR/Comdr Northern Army Gp, 1958–60; 20 Field Regt, RA UK, 1960–61; Adjt 20 Field Regt, RA Malaya, 1961–63; Adjt 254 (City of London) Regt RA(TA), 1963–64; Instr RMA, Sandhurst, 1964–66; GSO3 Mil. Operations, MoD, 1966–68; Second in Comd 20 Heavy Regt, RA BAOR, 1968–70; GSO2 Instr Staff Coll., 1970–72; commanded 17 Trng Regt and Depot RA, 1972–74, and The Depot Regt RA, 1974–75; GSO1 Public Relations MoD, 1976–79; Col GS; Public Information BAOR, 1979–83; retired 1983. Dir, Executive Communication Consultants (IOM) Ltd, 1999–2008. Chm. Comrs, Jurby, IOM, 2002–04, 2008–09. Mem. Bd, HelpAge Sri Lanka, 1985–; Trustee: HelpAge Kenya, 1984–; HelpAge India, 1985–99; Global Cancer, 1998–2004; Combat Stress, 1993–2005. Patron: The Homeless Fund, 1996–2001; Gesture, 2002–03; Employers Retirement Assoc., 2003–. MCIPR (MIPR 1981). FRSA 1987. *Publications*: miscellaneous articles on military matters. *Recreations*: fishing, gardening, sailing, travelling, collecting and restoring antiques. *Address*: Ballamoar Castle, Sandygate, Isle of Man IM7 3AJ. *T*: (01624) 897504. *E*: mayo@manx.net. *Clubs*: Army and Navy, Special Forces, Woodroffe's, MCC.

**MAYO, Rupert Charles; His Honour Judge Mayo**; a Circuit Judge, since 2009; Resident Judge, Northampton Crown Court, since 2011; Justice of the Court of Appeal of St Helena, Ascension Island and Tristan da Cunha, since 2016; *b* Hemel Hempstead, 5 March 1963; *s* of late Philip Arthur Mayo and Jill Mary Mayo (*née* Jenkins); *m* 1st, 1990 (marr. diss. 2008); one *s* two *d*; 2nd, 2013, Vanessa Juliette Marshall, *qv*; one *s*. *Educ*: Bedford Sch.; Durham Univ. (BA Hons Law and Politics). Called to the Bar, Gray's Inn, 1987; in practice in London and on Midland Circuit, principally in crime (fraud and serious offences) and regulatory work, London, 1987–2009; a Recorder, 2005–09. Hon. Recorder, Bor. of Northampton, 2018–. Trustee, Rutland Agricl Soc., 2006–. Chm., Cottesmore Hunt, 2004–06. Ed., Hong Kong Current Law, 1985–86. *Recreations*: sailing, cookery, shooting, keeping pigs and poultry, cycling. *Address*: Northampton Crown Court, 85–87 Lady's Lane, Northampton NN1 3HQ.

**MAYO, Simon Andrew Hicks**; Presenter: Kermode and Mayo's Film Review, BBC Radio Five Live, since 2001; Scala Radio, since 2019; *b* 21 Sept. 1958; *s* of Derek Leslie Mayo and Gillian Mary Mayo; *m* 1986, Hilary Mary Bird; two *s* one *d*. *Educ*: Solihull Sch.; Worthing Grammar Sch.; Warwick Univ. (BA Hons). Presenter: Breakfast Show, 1988–93, Morning Show, 1993–2001, Radio 1; Album Chart Show, Radio 2, 2001–07; Radio 5 Live Afternoon Show, 2001–09; Drivetime Show, Radio 2, 2010–18; Jo Whiley & Simon Mayo Show, Radio 2, 2018; television: Scruples, 1988; Best of Magic, 1989; Confessions, 1994, 1995, 1996, 1997; The Big End, 1999; Winning Lines, 1998–2000; Dig!, 2005. Hon. Vice-Pres., Melchester Rovers, 1989. Hon. DLitt Warwick, 2005. *Publications*: (with S. Jenkins) Breakfast in the Holy Land, 1988; Confessions, 1991; Further Confessions, 1992; (with M. Wroe) Snogging, 1992; (with M. Wroe) The Big Match, 1993; Very Worst of Confessions, 1993; Classic Confessions, 1994; *novels*: for children: Itch, 2012; Itch Rocks, 2013; Itchcraft, 2014; Blame, 2016; for adults: Mad Blood Stirring, 2018. *Recreations*: etymology, astronomy, the school run, walking in bad weather, thinking up quizzes. *Address*: c/o PBJ Management, 22 Rathbone Street, W1T 1LG.

**MAYO, Simon Herbert**; Vice President, Court of Appeal of the High Court, Hong Kong, 2000–03; *b* 15 Nov. 1937; *s* of late Herbert and Marjorie Mayo; *m* 1966, Catherine Yin Ying Young; one *s* one *d*. *Educ*: Harrow Sch. Admitted a solicitor, England and Wales, 1961, Hong Kong, 1963; called as barrister and solicitor, W Australia, 1967. Asst Legal Advr, GEC, 1961; Asst Solicitor, Deacons, Solicitors, Hong Kong, 1963; in private practice, WA, 1967; Asst Registrar, 1968, Registrar, 1976, Supreme Court of Hong Kong; a Judge of the High Court, Hong Kong, 1980–95; Justice of Appeal, Court of Appeal of Supreme, then High, Court, Hong Kong, 1995–2000. *Recreations*: golf, music, literature, walking. *Clubs*: Hong Kong, Sheko Country (Hong Kong).

**MAYO, Simon Peter**; QC 2008; a Recorder, since 2009; *b* London, 23 Sept. 1961; *s* of Peter and Anita Mayo. Called to the Bar, Inner Temple, 1985; in practice as barrister specialising in criminal law, 1985–. *Recreations*: Rugby, motorsport, running, cycling, swimming, travel. *Address*: 187 Fleet Street, EC4A 2AT. *T*: (020) 7430 7430.

**MAYO, Vanessa Juliette**; *see* Marshall, V. J.

**MAYOR ZARAGOZA, Federico**; President, Fundación Cultura de Paz, Madrid, since 1999; *b* Barcelona, 27 Jan. 1934; *s* of Federico Mayor and Juana Zaragoza; *m* 1956, Maria Angeles Menéndez; two *s* one *d*. *Educ*: Madrid Complutense Univ. Granada University: Prof. of Biochemistry, 1963–73; Rector, 1968–72; Prof. of Biochemistry, Univ. Autónoma, Madrid, 1973. Dir, 1974–78, Scientific Chm., 1983–87, Molecular Biology Centre, Higher Council for Scientific Research. Under-Sec., Min. for Educn and Science, 1974–75; Pres., Commn for Study of Special Set of Rules for the four Catalan Provinces, 1976; Mem., Cortes (Parliament) for Granada, 1977–78; Dep. Dir-Gen., UNESCO, 1978–81; Minister for Educn and Science, Spain, 1981–82; Special Advr to Dir-Gen., UNESCO, 1982; Dir, Inst. of Sciences of Man, Madrid, 1983–87; Dir-Gen., UNESCO, 1987–99. Mem., European Parlt, 1987. Chair, Expert Gp, European Res. Council, 2003; Co-Chair, Alliance of Civilizations, UN, 2005–06. President: Initiative for Sci. in Europe, 2007–11; Internat. Commn Against the Death Penalty, 2010–18; Co-Pres., Inst. of Human Rights, Democracy and Culture of Peace, Autonomous Univ. of Madrid, 2016–. *Address*: Mar Caribe, 15 Interland, Majadahonda, 28220 Madrid, Spain.

**MAYOU, Prof. Richard Anthony**, FRCP, FRCPsych; Professor of Psychiatry, University of Oxford, 1997–2004 and Fellow, Nuffield College, Oxford, 1976–2005, now Emeritus; *b* 23 Nov. 1940; *s* of Cecil Richard Mayou and Kathleen (*née* Batt); *m* 1981, Ann Foster (*née* Bowler) (*d* 2011); one step *s* one step *d*. *Educ*: King Edward's Sch., Birmingham; St John's Coll., Oxford (open scholar; BM, MSc, MA); Inst. of Psychiatry, London Univ. (MPhil). FRCPsych 1979; FRCP 1985. House Officer, Queen Elizabeth Hosp., Birmingham, 1966–67; House Physician, Hammersmith and Brompton Hosps, London, 1967–68; Registrar, then Sen. Registrar, Maudsley & Bethlem Royal Hosps, London, 1968–72; Lectr and Clinical Reader in Psychiatry, Oxford, 1973–97. Chm., Friends of Oxford Univ. Botanic Garden, 2004–17. *Publications*: Shorter Oxford Textbook of Psychiatry, 1983, 4th edn 2001; Psychiatry Core Text, 1994, 3rd edn 2004; contribs to learned jls on psychological aspects of medical symptoms and disorders. *Recreations*: countryside, gardening, architecture, the arts. *Address*: 9 Beaumont Buildings, Oxford OX1 2LL. *T*: (01865) 423131. *E*: richard.mayou@nuffield.ox.ac.uk. *Club*: Athenæum.

**MAYR-HARTING, Prof. Henry Maria Robert Egmont**, DPhil, DD; FBA 1992; Regius Professor of Ecclesiastical History, University of Oxford, 1997–2003, now Emeritus; Co-Censor of Degrees, Christ Church, Oxford, 2004–16 (Lay Canon, 1997–2003; Emeritus Canon, 2013); *b* 6 April 1936; *s* of Herbert Mayr-Harting and Anna Mayr-Harting (*née* Münzer), Prague; *m* 1968, Caroline Henry; one *s* one *d*. *Educ*: Douai School; Merton Coll., Oxford (BA Mod. Hist. 1957; MA; DPhil 1961; DD 2010). Asst Lectr and Lectr in Medieval History, Univ. of Liverpool, 1960–68; Fellow, and Tutor in Medieval History, 1968–97, Emeritus Fellow, 1997, St Peter's Coll., Oxford; Lectr in Medieval History, Merton Coll., Oxford, 1976–96; Reader in Medieval History, Oxford Univ., 1993–97. Vis. Fellow, Peterhouse, Cambridge, 1983; Slade Prof. of Fine Art, Oxford Univ., 1987–88; Brown Foundn Fellow, Univ. of the South, Tennessee, 1992. Warburton Lect., Lincoln's Inn, 2008. Corresp. Mem., Austrian Acad. of Scis, 2001. Pres., Henry Bradshaw Soc., 2019. Confrater, Douai Abbey, 2003. Hon. DLitt: Lawrence Univ., Wisconsin, 1998; Univ. of the South, Tennessee, 1999; UEA, 2009. *Publications*: The Acta of the Bishops of Chichester 1075–1207, 1965; The Coming of Christianity to Anglo-Saxon England, 1972, 3rd edn 1991; What to do in the Penwith Peninsula, Cornwall, in less than perfect weather, 1987, 2nd edn 1988; Ottonian Book Illumination: an historical study, 2 vols, 1991 (trans. German 1991), 2nd edn 1999; Two Conversions to Christianity: the Bulgarians and the Anglo-Saxons (Stenton Lecture), 1994; Perceptions of Angels in History (inaugural lecture), 1998; (ed with Richard Harries) Christianity: two thousand years, 2001; Church and Cosmos in Early Ottonian Germany: the view from Cologne, 2007; Religion and Society in the Medieval West 600–1200: selected papers, 2010; Religion, Politics and Society in Britain 1066–1272, 2011; articles in learned jls, conference and symposia collections, Libelli Rhenani and Festschriften. *Recreations*: music, especially playing keyboard instruments; watching cricket. *Address*: St Peter's College, Oxford OX1 2DL; 29 Portland Road, Oxford OX2 7EZ. *Clubs*: Athenæum; Worcestershire County Cricket.

**MAZANKOWSKI, Rt Hon. Donald (Frank)**; PC (Can.) 1979; CC 2013 (OC 2000); AOE 2003; Deputy Prime Minister of Canada, 1986–93; Minister of Finance, 1991–93; *b* 27 July 1935; *s* of late Frank Mazankowski and Dora (*née* Lonowski); *m* 1958, Lorraine Poleschuk; three *s*. *Educ*: High Sch., Viking, Alberta. MP (Progressive Conservative), Vegreville, 1968–93; Minister for Transport and Minister responsible for Canadian Wheat Bd, 1979–80; Minister of Transport, 1984–86; Pres. of Queen's Privy Council for Canada, 1986–91; Minister of Agriculture, 1988–91; Minister responsible for Privatization, 1988; Govt House Leader and Pres. of Privy Council, 1986–91. Director: Shaw Communications Inc., 1993–2009; IMG Financial (formerly Investors Group) Inc., 1994–2010; Great West Life Assce Co., 1994–2010; Power Corp. of Canada, 1996; Weyerhaeuser Co., 1997–2009; ATCO Gp, 1999; Canadian Oilsands Trust, 2002–10; Dir and Trustee, Yellow Pages Gp, 2003–10. Chairman: Canadian Genetics Diseases Network, 1998–2004; Premier's Adv. Council on Health, Alberta, 2000–02. Hon. DEng Technical Univ. of Nova Scotia, 1987; Hon. LLD Alberta, 1993. *Address*: 80 Nottingham Inlet, Sherwood Park, AB T8A 6N2, Canada. *E*: donmaz@shaw.ca.

**MBEKI, Thabo Mvuyelwa**, Hon. GCMG 2000; President of South Africa, 1999–2008 (Deputy President, 1994–99); President, African National Congress, 1997–2007 (Deputy President, 1994–97); *b* 18 June 1942; *s* of late Govan and of Epainette Mbeki; *m* 1974, Zanele Dlamini. *Educ*: St John's High Sch., Umtata; Lovedale Inst.; Sussex Univ. (MA Econs; Hon. LLD 1995). Youth organiser, ANC, Johannesburg, 1961–62; left S Africa, 1962; worked in ANC Offices, London, 1967–70; mil. training, USSR, 1970; African National Congress: Asst Sec., Revolutionary Council, 1971–72; Mem., NEC, 1975–2007; Acting Rep., Swaziland, 1975–76; Rep. Nigeria, 1976–78; Political Sec., President's Office, 1978; Dir, Information and Publicity, 1984–89; Hd, Dept of Internat. Affairs, 1989–94 (Hd, delegn talks with S African Govt which led to unbanning of ANC and release of political prisoners, 1989; Mem., delegn concerning talks with S African Govt, 1990); Chm., 1993. Est. Thabo Mbeki Foundn, 2008.

**M'BOW, Amadou-Mahtar**; Director-General of Unesco, 1974–87; *b* 20 March 1921; *s* of Fara-N'Diaye M'Bow and N'Goné Casset, Senegal; *m* 1951, Raymonde Sylvain; one *s* two *d*. *Educ*: Univ. of Paris. Teacher, Rosso Coll., Mauritania, 1951–53; Dir, Service of Fundamental and Community Educn, Senegal, 1953–57; Min. of Education and Culture, 1957–58; Teacher at Lycée Faidherbe, St-Louis, Senegal, 1958–64; Prof., Ecole Normale Supérieure, Dakar, 1964–66; Minister of Educn, 1966–68; Mem. Nat. Assembly, Senegal, 1968–70; Minister of Culture, Youth and Sports 1968–70; Asst Dir-Gen. for Educn, UNESCO, 1970–74. Pres., Assises Nationales du Sénégale, 2008–09. Member: Acad. des Sciences d'Outre-Mer, 1977; Acad. of Kingdom of Morocco, 1981; Hon. Mem., Royal Acad. Fine Arts, San Temo, Spain, 1977; For. Mem., Acad. of Athens, 1983. Hon. Professor: Ecole normale supérieure, Dakar, 1979; Ind. Univ. of Santo Domingo, 1978; Nat. Ind. Univ. of Mexico, 1979. Hon. Dr: Buenos Aires, 1974; Granada (Lit. and Phil.), Sherbrooke (Educn), West Indies (Laws), 1975; Open, Kliment Ohridski, Sofia, Nairobi (Lit.), 1976; Malaya (Lit.), Philippines (Laws), Venice (Geog.), Uppsala (Soc. Scis), Moscow (Soc. Scis), Paris I, 1977; Andes (Philos.), Peru (Educn Scis), Haiti, Tribhunvan Univ., Nepal (Lit.), State Univ., Mongolia, Khartoum (Law), Sri Lanka, 1978; Charles Univ., Prague (Phil.), Tashkent, Québec, 1979; Nat. Univ. of Zaïre, Madras, Belgrade, Ivory Coast, Sierra Leone, 1980; Univ. Gama Filho, Brazil, 1981; Nat. Univ. of Lesotho, 1981; Univ. of Benin, 1981; Technical Univ. of Middle East, Ankara, 1981; Univ. of Ankara, 1981, Univ. of Gand, Belgium, 1982; Nat. Univ. of Seoul, 1982; State Univ. of Kiev, 1982; Laval Univ., Quebec, 1982; Quaid-i-Azam Univ., Islamabad, 1983; Jawaharlal Nehru Univ., New Delhi, 1983; Aix-Marseilles Univ., 1983; Beijing Univ., China, 1983; Kim Il Sung Univ., PDR of Korea (Pedagogy), 1983; Lucknow Univ., India (Lit.), 1983; Chulalongkorn Univ., Thailand (Pedagogy), 1983; Sokoto Univ., Nigeria (Lit.), 1984; Malta Univ., 1986; Polytechnic Univ. of Catalonia, Cauca Univ. Popayan (Colombia), Univ. of Mayor, Real y Pontificia de San Francisco Xavier de Chuquisaca, Sucre (Bolivia),

1987; Grand Tribute, Univ. Candido Mendes, Brazil, 1981. Order of Merit, Senegal; Grand Cross: Order of the Liberator, Order of Andres Bello and Order of Francisco de Miranda, Venezuela; Order of Merit and Juan Montalvo National Order of Merit (Educn), Ecuador; Order of Miguel Antonio Caro y Rufino José Cuervo, Colombia; Order of Stara Planina, Bulgaria; Order of the Sun, Peru; Order of Merit of Duarte, Sanchez and Mella, Dominican Republic; National Order of the Lion, Senegal; Order of Alphonso X the Sabio, Spain; Order of the Southern Cross and Order of Merit of Guararapes, Brazil; Order of Distinguished Diplomatic Service Merit, Republic of Korea; Order of Sikatuna, Philippines; Order of Merit, Indonesia; Order of Merit, Syrian Arab Republic; Order of Merit, Jordan; Order of the Arab Republic of Egypt; Order of Felix Varela, Cuba; Grand Cross: Order of Nat. Flag (PDR of Korea); Order of Meritorious Action (Libya); Nat. Order of Andean Condor (Bolivia); Grand Order of Education (Bolivia); Grand Officer: National Order of Ivory Coast; National Order of Guinea; Order of Merit, Cameroon; National Order of Merit, Mauritania; Order of Independence, Tunisia; Commander: Order of Academic Palms; National Order of Upper Volta; Order of the Gabonese Merit; Order of Arts and Letters, France; Grand Medal, Order of the Inconfidência, State of Minas Gerais, Brazil; Medal: Order of Merit of Caetés, Olinda, Brazil; Order of Manual José Hurtado, Panama; Superior Decoration for Education, Jordan. Man and his World Peace Prize, Canada, 1978; Gold Medal of Olympic Order, 1981; Gold Medal of ALECSO (Arab Educnl, Cultural and Scientific Orgn), 1981; Internat. Dimitrov Prize, 1982; Gold Medal: Champion of Africa, 1986, of Andalucia, 1987. *Publications:* Le temps des peuples, ed R. Laffont, 1982; Where the Future Begins, 1982; Hope for the Future, 1984; Unesco: universality and international intellectual co-operation, 1985; numerous monographs, articles in educnl jls, textbooks, etc.

**MBUBAEGBU, Stella Ngozi**, CBE 2008; Principal and Chief Executive, Highbury College, Portsmouth, since 2001; *b* Obinagu, Nigeria, 27 Oct. 1955; *d* of Isaac and Patience Ene; *m* 1982, Chima Mbubaegbu; three *d*. *Educ:* Univ. of Benin (BA Hons English; MA); Univ. of Greenwich (PGCE); Univ. of Sheffield (MEd Dist.). Asst Registrar, W African Exams Council, 1983–89; Lectr, Sen. Lectr of Quality, then Manager, Southwark Coll., 1989–98; Dir, Planning and Quality, 1998–2000, Vice Principal, 2000–01, Croydon Coll. Mem. Bd, Learning and Skills Improvement Service, 2008; Chm., Further Educn Constituency Panel, Lifelong Learning UK, 2009. Chm., Black Leadership Initiative, 2002. Pres., Assoc. of Coll. Mgt, 2009. Fellow, Inst. for Learning, 2008; FRSA 2002. MInstD 2007. *Recreations:* reading, travel. *Address:* Highbury College, Tudor Crescent, Portsmouth, Hants PO6 2SA. *T:* (023) 9231 3215. *E:* stella.mbubaegbu@highbury.ac.uk.

**MEACHER**, family name of **Baroness Meacher**.

**MEACHER**, Baroness *cr* 2006 (Life Peer), of Spitalfields in the London Borough of Tower Hamlets; **Molly Christine Meacher;** Chairman, All Party Parliamentary Group for Drug Policy Reform, since 2011; *b* 15 May 1940; *d* of William F. and Lucy M. Reid; *m* 1991, Peter Richard Grenville Layard (*see* Baron Layard); two *s* two *d* by a former *m*. *Educ:* Berkhamsted Sch. for Girls; York Univ. (BScEcon); Univ. of London (DipSoc; CQSW). Campaign Dir and Res. Officer, CPAG, 1970–72; Projects Officer, Mental Health Foundn, 1973–78; Approved Social Worker, 1980–82; Mgr, Nat. Assoc. of CABx, 1982–84; Parly Officer, BASW, 1984–87; CEO, Campaign for Work, 1987–92; Advr to Russian Govt, 1991–94; Mem., later Dep. then Acting Chm., Police Complaints Authy, 1994–2002; Chairman: Security Industry Authy, 2002–04; E London NHS Foundn Trust (formerly E London and The City Mental Health NHS Trust), 2004–12; non-exec. Dir, Tower Hamlets Healthcare NHS Trust, 1994–98. Mental Health Act Comr, 1987–92; Comr, Marmot Commn on Inequalities in Health, 2008–10. Pres., Haemophilia Soc., 2014–; Chair, Dignity in Dying, 2016–. Trustee, Russian European Trust, 1998–2010. *Publications:* Scrounging on the Welfare, 1970; (jtly) To Him Who Hath, 1971; New Methods of Mental Health Care, 1979; (contrib.) The Mentally Disordered Offender, 1991. *Recreations:* music, golf, bridge, grandchildren. *Address:* House of Lords, SW1A 0PW. *E:* meachermc@parliament.uk.

**MEACHIN, Andrew Philip;** a District Judge (Magistrates' Courts), since 2012; *b* Nantwich, 12 July 1953; *s* of Jack Meachin and Brenda Meachin; *m* (marr. diss.); three *s* one *d*. *Educ:* King's Sch., Macclesfield; Coll. of Commerce, Aston Univ. Articled Clerk, Howarth Maitland & Son, Bury, Lancs, 1972–77; admitted solicitor, 1977; Solicitor and Partner, Wains (formerly Wain, Langstaff, Payne and Goalen), 1978–2012; Acting Stipendiary Magistrate, subseq. Dep. District Judge, 1999–2012. *Recreations:* cycling, walking, golf, theatre. *Address:* Derby Justice Centre, St Mary's Gate, Derby DE1 3JR. *T:* (01332) 362000. *E:* apmeach@icloud.com.

**MEAD, Deryk,** CBE 2003; Chief Executive, NCH (formerly NCH Action for Children), 1996–2004; *b* 3 July 1945; *s* of Joe and Ruth Mead; *m* 1967, Susan Margaret Kay; two *s*. *Educ:* Univ. of Manchester (BSc, MSc); Univ. of Leeds (DipPSW); CQSW. Approved Sch. Officer, Burnley, 1969–74; Principal Officer, Social Services, Lancs, 1974–79; Deputy Director of Social Services: Rochdale, 1979–87; Cumbria, 1987–91; Dir of Social Services, Gloucestershire, 1991–96. Member: Meat Hygiene Bd, 2005–07; Bd, Passenger Focus, 2005; Bd, NHS Midlands and East (formerly W Midlands Strategic HA), 2007–; Public Mem., Network Rail, 2007. *Publications:* contrib. to numerous publications. *Recreations:* fell running, rock and ice climbing, sea kayaking.

**MEAD, Dr Keith Owen,** CB 2000; CEng, FIET; CMath, FIMA; Director of Technology and Engineering, Government Communications Headquarters, 1994–2000; *b* 14 Oct. 1945; *s* of Kenneth Stanley Mead and Constance Louise Mead; *m* 1971, Fiona McDonald McCall (*d* 2018); one *s* one *d*. *Educ:* Southend High Sch. for Boys; Sussex Univ. (BSc); Liverpool Univ. (PhD 1971). CEng 1996, FIET (FIEE 1996); CMath 1996, FIMA 1996; ATCL (MusEd) 2001. Joined GCHQ, 1970; PSO, 1975; Asst Sec., 1987; RCDS 1990; Under Sec., 1994. Mem. Council, IMA, 1999–2002. *Publications:* maths res. papers in learned jls. *Recreations:* playing the piano, teaching and arranging music, walking. *E:* me@keithmead.name.

**MEAD, Dr Timothy John;** Registrary, University of Cambridge, 1997–2007, now Emeritus; Fellow, Wolfson College, Cambridge, 1997–2010, now Emeritus; Secretary, Cambridge Commonwealth and Overseas Trusts, 2008–10; Honorary Director, Cambridge European Trust, 2008–10; *b* 31 May 1947; *s* of Ernest Arthur Mead and Catherine Beryl Louisa Mead (*née* Midlane); *m* 1971, Anne Frances Glasson; one *s* one *d*. *Educ:* Queen Mary Coll., Univ. of London (BSc Hons 1969); Churchill Coll., Cambridge (PhD 1972). Admin. Asst, Univ. of Sheffield, 1972–75; University of Southampton: Asst Registrar, 1976–79; Asst Sec., 1979–82; Sen. Asst Registrar, 1982–86; Dep. Registrar and Academic Sec., Univ. of Nottingham, 1986–91; Registrar, 1991–97, and Sec., 1996–97, Univ. of Kent at Canterbury. Dir, Univs and Colls Staff Develt Agency, 1996–2004. Mem., Panel of Ind. Persons, Glos CC, 2013–17. Treasurer: Mickleton Methodist Church, 2012–; Mickleton Soc., 2013–17. Governor: Hills Rd Sixth Form Coll., Cambridge, 2001–08 (Chm., 2003–08); Addenbrooke's Hosp. NHS Foundn Trust, 2004–07. *Publications:* articles in Jl of Chemical Soc. *Recreations:* music, natural history. *Address:* 12 Sovereign Fields, Mickleton, Chipping Campden GL55 6RG. *E:* timothymead05@gmail.com. *Club:* Oxford and Cambridge.

**MEADE**, family name of **Earl of Clanwilliam**.

**MEADE, Richard David;** QC 2008; a Recorder, since 2010; a Deputy High Court Judge, since 2012; *b* London, 14 Nov. 1966; *s* of Prof. Thomas Wilson Meade, *qv*; *m* 2003, Sara Louise Payne; one *s* two *d*. *Educ:* William Ellis Sch., London; University Coll., Oxford (BA Juris.). Called to the Bar, Lincoln's Inn, 1991; in practice as barrister specialising in intellectual property, 1991–. *Publications:* (ed jtly) Kerly's Law of Trade Marks and Trade Names, 13th edn 2001, 14th edn 2005. *Recreations:* poker, family. *Address:* 8 New Square, Lincoln's Inn, WC2A 3QP. *Clubs:* Barracuda, Victoria Sporting.

**MEADE, Prof. Thomas Wilson,** DM; FRCP, FMedSci; FRS 1996; Emeritus Professor of Epidemiology, Department of Epidemiology and Population Health, London School of Hygiene and Tropical Medicine, since 2001; *b* 21 Jan. 1936; *s* of James Edward Meade, CB, FBA, and Elizabeth Margaret (*née* Wilson); *m* 1962, Helen Elizabeth Perks; one *s* two *d*. *Educ:* Westminster Sch.; Christ Church, Oxford; St Bartholomew's Hosp. Sen. Lectr, Dept of Public Health, LSHTM, 1968–70 (on secondment to Schieffelin Leprosy Research Sanatorium, S India, 1969–70); Dir, MRC Epidemiol. and Med. Care Unit, Northwick Park Hosp., then Wolfson Inst. of Preventive Medicine, 1970–2001, and Prof. of Epidemiol., Bart's and The Royal London Hosp. Sch. of Medicine and Dentistry, 1992–2001, QMW, later QMUL. Member: MRC Physiological Systems and Disorders Bd, 1974–78; MRC Health Services Res. Panel and Cttee, 1981–90; Wellcome Trust Physiology and Pharmacology Panel, 1990–95; Council, Royal Soc., 1998–99. Founder FMedSci 1998. Hon. DSc QMUL, 2010. Internat. Balzan Prize, Fondazione Internazionale Premio E. Balzan, 1997; MRC Millennium Medal, 2002. *Publications:* papers on thrombosis and arterial disease. *Recreations:* allotment, drawing, music. *Address:* 45 Cholmeley Lodge, Cholmeley Park, N6 5EN. *T:* (020) 8340 6260. *Club:* Leander (Henley-on-Thames).
*See also* R. D. Meade.

**MEADES, Jonathan Turner,** FRSL; journalist, writer and television performer; *b* 21 Jan. 1947; *s* of late John William Meades and Margery Agnes Meades (*née* Hogg); *m* 1st, 1980, Sally Dorothy Renée (marr. diss. 1986), *d* of Raymond Brown; twin *d*, 2nd, 1988, Frances Anne (marr. diss. 1997), *d* of Sir William Bentley, KCMG; two *d*; 3rd, 2003, Colette Claudine Elizabeth, *d* of Michael Forder. *Educ:* King's Coll., Taunton; RADA. Editor, Event, 1981–82; Features Editor, Tatler, 1982–85; Restaurant Critic, The Times, 1986–2001. Columnist, The Times, 2001–05; contributor to magazines and newspapers, 1971–, including: Books and Bookmen, Time Out, Observer, Architects Jl, Sunday Times, Harpers and Queen, Vogue, Literary Review, Tatler, A La Carte, Independent, Sunday Correspondent, Mail on Sunday, Evening Standard. *Television: series:* The Victorian House, 1987; Abroad in Britain, 1991; Further Abroad, 1994; Even Further Abroad, 1997; Meades Eats, 2003; Abroad Again in Britain, 2006; Jonathan Meades: Abroad Again, 2007; Magnetic North, 2008; Jonathan Meades: Off Kilter, 2009; Jonathan Meades on France, 2012; Jonathan Meades: the Joy of Essex, 2013; Bunkers, Brutalism, Bloodymindedness: Concrete Poetry, 2014; Mussolini, Monuments and Modernism, 2016; Jonathan Meades on Jargon, 2018; *films:* Jerry Building, 1994; Heart Bypass, 1998; Travels with Pevsner: Worcestershire, 1998; Victoria Died in 1901 and is Still Alive Today, 2001; tvSSFBM EHKL, 2001; Joebuilding, 2006; Benbuilding, 2016; Franco Building, 2019; *film script:* L'Atlantide, 1991; *exhibition:* Ape Forgets Medication: treyfs and artnacks, Londonewcastle Project, Shoreditch, 2016. FRSL 2019. Hon. FRIBA 2013; Hon. Fellow, Nat. Secular Soc., 1996. Hon. Patron, Internat. Anthony Burgess Foundn, 2012. *Publications:* This is Their Life, 1979; An Illustrated Atlas of the World's Great Buildings, 1980; Filthy English (short stories), 1984; Peter Knows what Dick Likes, 1989; Pompey (novel), 1993; The Fowler Family Business (novel), 2002; Incest and Morris Dancing, 2002; Museum Without Walls, 2012; Pidgin Snaps, 2013; An Encyclopaedia of Myself, 2014 (Spear's Non-fiction Award, 2015); The Plagiarist In The Kitchen, 2016. *Recreations:* buildings, mushrooms, woods. *Address:* c/o Anita Land Ltd, 10 Wyndham Place, W1H 2PU. *E:* anita@anitaland.com. *Club:* Academy.

**MEADOW, Sir (Samuel) Roy,** Kt 1997; FRCP, FRCPE, FRCPCH; Professor and Head of Department of Paediatrics and Child Health, University of Leeds, 1980–98, now Emeritus Professor; *b* 9 June 1933; *m* 1st, 1962, Gillian Margaret Maclennan; one *s* one *d*; 2nd, 1978, Marianne Jane Harvey; 3rd, 2009, Donna Andrea Rosenberg. *Educ:* Wigan Grammar Sch.; Bromsgrove Sch.; Worcester Coll., Oxford (BA Hons Physiol. 1957; MA, BM BCh 1960); Guys Hosp. Med. Sch. DRCOG 1962; DCH 1963; MRCP 1964, FRCP 1974; FRCPE 1996; FRCPCH 1997. Partner GP, Banbury, 1962–64; junior appts at Guy's Hosp., Evelina Children's Hosp., Hosp. for Sick Children, London and Royal Alexandra Hosp., Brighton, 1964–67; MRC Sen. Res. Fellow, Birmingham Univ., 1967–68; Sen. Lectr and Consultant Paediatrician, Leeds Univ., 1970–80. Consultant Advr to CMO, DoH, 1997–2000. Blackwell Vis. Prof., NZ Paediatric Assoc., 1989; Kildorrery Lectr, Irish Paed. Assoc., 1987; Charles West Lectr, RCP, 1993. Chairman: Assoc. for Child Psychology and Psychiatry, 1983–84; Enuresis Resource and Inf. Centre, 1996–2004. President: BPA, 1994–96 (Chm., Acad. Bd, 1990–94); (Inaugural), RCPCH, 1996–97. Editor, Archives of Diseases in Childhood, 1979–87. Dawson Williams Prize, BMA, 1994; James Spence Medal, RCPCH, 1999. *Publications:* Lecture Notes on Paediatrics, 1973, 7th edn 2001; Bladder Control and Enuresis, 1973; The Child and His Symptoms, 1978; ABC of Child Abuse, 1989, 4th edn as ABC of Child Protection, 2007; Paediatric Kidney Disease, 1992; reports and papers on teratogenicity of anticonvulsant drugs, Munchausen Syndrome by proxy child abuse, childhood renal and urinary tract disorders and child abuse.

**MEADOWCROFT, Michael James;** politician, writer and public affairs consultant; *b* 6 March 1942; marr. diss.; one *s* one *d*; *m* 2nd, 1987, Elizabeth Bee. *Educ:* King George V Sch., Southport; Bradford Univ. (MPhil 1978). Chm., Merseyside Regl Young Liberal Orgn, 1961; Liberal Party Local Govt Officer, 1962–67; Sec., Yorks Liberal Fedn, 1967–70; Asst Sec., Joseph Rowntree Social Service Trust, 1970–78; Gen. Sec., Bradford Metropolitan Council for Voluntary Service, 1978–83. Senior Vis. Fellow, PSI, 1989. Dir, Electoral Reform Consultancy Services, 1992–94. Columnist: The Times, 1986–87; Yorkshire Post, 2004–07; Clarinet and Saxophone Mag., 2007–09. Member: Leeds City Council, 1968–83; W Yorks MCC, 1973–76, 1981–83. Dir, Leeds Grand Theatre and Opera House, 1971–83; Chm., Leeds Library, 2008–16. Chm., Liberal Party Assembly Cttee, 1977–81; Pres. Elect, 1987–88, Pres., 1993–2002, Liberal Party; Chair, Leeds Liberal Democrats, 2010–11; Mem., Yorks and Humber Regl Exec., Liberal Democrats, 2017–. Contested (L) Leeds W, Feb. and Oct. 1974, 1987, 1992. MP (L) Leeds W, 1983–87. Chm., Electoral Reform Soc., 1989–93. Has undertaken 56 missions to 36 new and emerging democracies; Co-ordinator: UN Electoral Assistance Secretariat, Malawi, 1994; OSCE Internat. Observer Mission, Russian Presidential elecn, 1996, Bulgaria, 1996, Bosnia Refugee Vote, 1996; EU Observation Unit, Suriname Nat. Assembly elecns, 2000; EU Chief Observer, Zambian Presidential elecns, 2001; Advr on Jerusalem, EU Electoral Unit, Palestinian Assembly elecns, 1995–96; Consultant, Cttee for Free and Fair Elections, Cambodia, 1997; European Co-Dir, EC Support to Democratic Electoral Process in Cambodia, 1998; Post-Electoral Advr, Indonesian Assembly elecns, 1999; Consultant to: EC's TACIS project in Uzbekistan, 2002; Ind. Electoral Commn, Dem. Rep. of Congo, 2004–05; Electoral Commn, Benin, 2006; Nat. Democratic Inst. project, Bangladesh, 2008–12; IPU mission to Parliament of Oman, 2014, to Parliament of Egypt, 2016. Trustee, Parly Outreach Trust, 2015–. Hon. Alderman, City of Leeds, 2002. Chevalier,

Commanderie de Faugères, 1998. *Publications:* Liberal Party Local Government Handbook (with Pratap Chitnis), 1963; Success in Local Government, 1971; Liberals and a Popular Front, 1974; Local Government Finance, 1975; A Manifesto for Local Government, 1975; The Bluffer's Guide to Politics, 1976; Liberal Values for a New Decade, 1980; Social Democracy—Barrier or Bridge?, 1981; Liberalism and the Left, 1982; Liberalism and the Right, 1983; Liberalism Today and Tomorrow, 1989; The Politics of Electoral Reform, 1991; Diversity in Danger, 1992; The Case for the Liberal Party, 1992; (with E. Bee) Faugères: a guide to the Appellation, 1996, 3rd edn 2005 (French edn 2006); Focus on Freedom, 1997, 3rd edn 2001; (jtly) Philatelic Fiction: a bibliography, 2010; (ed) Freedom, Liberty and Fairness, 2011; Guide to the Artworks of the National Liberal Club, 2011; (ed jtly) The Leeds Yellow Book, 2015, vol. 2, 2018; (contrib.) Leeds and its Jewish Community, 2019. *Recreations:* music (including jazz; Leader, Granny Lee Jazz Band), French philately, Leeds political history. *Address:* Waterloo Lodge, 72 Waterloo Lane, Bramley, Leeds LS13 2JF. *T:* (0113) 257 6232. *E:* meadowcroft@bramley.demon.co.uk. *W:* www.bramley.demon.co.uk. *Clubs:* National Liberal (Mem., Gen. Cttee, 1989–; Archivist, 2009–19); Armley Liberal, Upper and Lower Wortley Liberal (Leeds).

**MEADOWS, Graham David;** Chief Executive, MC+TS-Europe sprl, since 2007; Special Adviser to European Commissioner for Social Policy, 2007–09, to Commissioner for Employment, Social Affairs and Inclusion, 2009–14, to Commissioner for Agriculture and Rural Affairs, since 2015; *b* 17 Dec. 1941; *s* of late Albert Edward Meadows and Jessica Maude Titmus; two *d*; *m* 1995, Ruth Ringer. *Educ:* Edinburgh Univ. MA Hons Political Economy. Journalist, 1958–69, specialising latterly in agric. affairs; European corresp., Farmers' Weekly (based in Brussels), 1973–75; EC 1975–2006; Mem., agric. policy unit; adviser on agricl, fisheries and envmt policy, Office of Pres. of EEC (Gaston E. Thorn), 1981–84; Chef de Cabinet of Stanley Clinton Davis, Mem. of EEC responsible for transport, envmt and nuclear safety, 1985–89; Dir, 1989–2003, Acting Dir Gen., 2003–04, Dir-Gen., Regl Policy, 2004–06, Commn of European Communities. Hon. Prof., Sch. of City and Regional Planning, Cardiff Univ., 2007–12. DUniv Strathclyde, 2006. Emperor Maximilian Prize for Service to Eur. Regl Politics, CLRAE, 2007. *Recreations:* mountain walking, reading in the history of economic thought.

**MEADOWS, Pamela Catherine, (Mrs P. A. Ormerod);** Visiting Fellow, National Institute of Economic and Social Research, 1998–2016; Chairman, Synergy Research and Consulting, 2004–13; *b* 9 Jan. 1949; *d* of late Sidney James Meadows, OBE and of Hilda Catherine (née Farley); *m* 1975, Paul Andrew Ormerod; one *s. Educ:* Kenya High Sch., Nairobi; Penrhos Coll., Colwyn Bay; Univ. of Durham (BA Econs 1970); Birkbeck Coll., Univ. of London (MSc Econs 1978). Research Officer, NIESR, 1970–74; Sen. Econ. Asst, then Econ. Advr, Home Office, 1974–78; Department of Employment: Econ. Advr, 1978–88; Grade 5, 1988–92; Chief Economic Advr, and Hd of Econs, Res. and Evaluation Div., 1992–93; Dir, PSI, 1993–98. Vis. Prof., Arbetslivsinstitutet, Stockholm, 1998–2000. Member: Better Regulation Task Force, 1997–2000; Financial Services Consumer Panel, 2011–. Trustee, Employment Policy Inst., 1995–2000; Mem. Exec. Cttee, Public Mgt and Policy Assoc., 1998–2001. Gov., Birkbeck Coll., 1997–2001.

**MEADWAY, (Richard) John,** PhD; Under Secretary, Department of Trade and Industry, 1989–96; *b* 30 Dec. 1944; *s* of late Norman Pardey Meadway and Constance Meadway (later Kellaway); *m* 1968, Rev. Dr Jeanette Valerie (née Partis); two *d. Educ:* Collyer's Sch., Horsham; Peterhouse, Cambridge (MA NatScis); Edinburgh Univ. (PhD); Oxford Univ. (MA). Asst Principal, Min. of Technology, 1970; Private Secretary: to Minister for Trade and Consumer Affairs, 1973; to Sec. of State for Prices and Consumer Protection, 1974; to the Prime Minister, 1976–78; Asst Sec., Dept of Trade, later DTI, 1979–89; Hd of Overseas Trade Div. 2, 1989–94, Hd of Export Control and Non-Proliferation Div., 1994–96, DTI. UK Gov., IAEA, 1994–96. Dir of Fitness to Practise, GMC, 1997–98. Chm., Newham Mind, 1998–2003. Trustee, Refugee Legal Centre, 1999–2006. FRSA 1995. *Publications:* papers on the amino-acid sequences of proteins. *Recreations:* reading, travel. *Address:* 4 Glebe Avenue, Woodford Green, Essex IG8 9HB. *T:* (020) 8504 1958. *Club:* Reform.

**MEAGER, Michael Anthony;** Director of Estates, Department of Health, 1989–91; *b* 15 Feb. 1931; *s* of Arthur Pattison Meager and Dora Edith Meager (née Greeves); *m* 1954, Val Cranmer Benson (*d* 2013); two *s* one *d. Educ:* Royal Naval Coll., Dartmouth; Clacton County High Sch.; Architectural Assoc. Sch. of Architecture. ARIBA 1955; AADip 1956. National Service, RE, 1955–57: commnd 1956, served Cyprus, 1956–57. HMOCS, Kenya, 1958–63; architect in private practice, 1964–66; Department of Health (formerly MoH and DHSS), 1966–91: Chief Archt, 1986–88; Dir of Health Building, 1988–89. *Club:* Royal Over-Seas League.

**MEAGHER, Prof. Thomas Robert,** PhD; Professor of Plant Biology, University of St Andrews, since 1999; *b* Oakland, Calif, 23 Nov. 1952; *s* of William Richard Meagher and Martha Meagher (née Bischoff); *m* 1977, Dr Laura Reinertsen. *Educ:* Univ. of S Florida (BA Hons Botany 1973); Duke Univ., N Carolina (PhD 1978). Duke University: teaching asst, Botany Dept, 1973–74; NIH Grad. traineeship, Univ. Prog. in Genetics, 1974–78; Res. Associate, 1978–82, Res. Scientist, 1983, Botany Dept; Temp. Instructor, Zool. Dept, 1984; Res. Scientist, Botany Dept, 1984–87; Asst Prof., 1987–90, Associate Prof., 1990–98, Prof., 1998–99, Rutgers Univ.; Dir, Centre for Evolution, Genes and Genomics, Univ. of St Andrews, 2004–12. Fulbright Schol., Dept of Pure Maths and Math. Stats, Univ. of Cambridge, 1982–83. Vis. Scientist, Univ. of Edinburgh, Royal Botanic Gdn, 1995–96; Hon. Prof., Scottish Crop Res. Inst., 2003–. Member: Sci. Adv. Council, 2004–09, Tree Health and Plant Biosecurity Task Force, 2012, DEFRA. Natural Environment Research Council: Mem., 2007–13; Chairman: Neomics Expert Wkg Gp, 2010; Adv. and Implementation Gp, Envmtl Omics Synthesis Centre, 2012–. Mem. Council, 2010–16, Chair, Educn and Outreach Cttee, 2010–16, Soc. for Study of Evolution. Trustee: Royal Botanic Gdn Edinburgh, 2013–; St Andrews Botanic Gdn, 2014–. Member, Editorial Board: Evolution, 1988–93, 2007–17; Amer. Naturalist, 1990–93; Molecular Ecology, 1992–99; Jl of Evolutionary Biology, 1993–96; Heredity, 2000–17; Ecology Letters, 2001–04. *Publications:* contributor: Plant Reproductive Ecology: patterns and strategies, 1988; Sexual Dimorphism in Plants, 1999; (with C. Vassiliadis) Genes in the Environment, 2003; contrib. learned jls incl. Amer. Naturalist, Amer. Jl of Botany, Annals of Botany, Biological Conservation, Biological Jl Linnean Soc., Biometrics, BioScience, California Jl of Sci. Educn, Conservation Letters, Crop Sci., Ecology, Ecol. Applications, Evolution, Evolutionary Ecology Res., Genetics, Genetic Res., Heredity, Jl of Evolutionary Biology, New Phytologist, Phil Transactions of Royal Soc., Proc. of Royal Soc., Theoretical and Applied Genetics, Theoretical Population Biology. *Recreation:* French horn (Mem., Scottish Vienna Horn Soc.). *Address:* School of Biology, University of St Andrews, St Andrews, Fife KY16 9TH. *T:* (01334) 463364, *Fax:* (01334) 463366. *E:* trm3@st-and.ac.uk.

**MEAKINS, Prof. Jonathan Larmonth,** OC 2000; MD; DSc; Nuffield Professor of Surgery, University of Oxford, 2002–08, now Emeritus; Fellow, Balliol College, Oxford, 2002; *b* 8 Jan. 1941; *s* of Jonathan Fayette Meakins and Mildred Dawson Meakins (née Larmonth); *m* 1972, Dr Jacqueline McClaran. *Educ:* McGill Univ. (BSc 1962); Univ. of Western Ontario (MD 1966); Univ. of Cincinnati (DSc 1972). Royal Victoria Hospital, Montreal: Consultant Surgeon, 1974–2002; Surgeon in Chief, 1988–98; McGill University: Asst Prof. of Surgery and Microbiol., 1974–79; Associate Prof., 1979–81; Prof. of Surgery and Microbiol., 1981–2002; Prof. and Chair of Surgery, 1988–93 and 1998–2002; Surgeon in Chief, McGill Univ. Health Centre, 1998–2002. Regent, 1993–2002, Vice Chair, 2000–02, Amer. Coll. of Surgeons. KM 1993. Hon. DSc: McGill, 2015; Western, 2018. *Publications:* Surgical Infection in Critical Care Medicine, 1985; (with J. C. McClaran) Surgical Care of the Elderly, 1988; (jtly) ACS Surgery: principles and practice, 1988, 5th edn 2003; (jtly) Host Defence Dysfunction in Trauma, Shock and Sepsis: mechanisms and therapeutic approaches, 1993; Surgical Infections: diagnosis and treatment, 1994. *Recreations:* tennis, golf, gardening, cooking, art history. *Clubs:* University (Montreal); Royal Montreal Golf, Montreal Indoor Tennis.

**MEALE, Sir (Joseph) Alan,** Kt 2011; *b* 31 July 1949; *s* of late Albert Henry and Elizabeth Meale; *m* 1983, Diana Gilhespy; one *s* one *d. Educ:* St Joseph's RC School; Ruskin College, Oxford; Sheffield Hallam Univ. (MA 1997). Seaman, British Merchant Navy, 1964–68; engineering worker, 1968–75; Nat. Employment Develt Officer, NACRO, 1977–80; Asst to Gen. Sec., ASLEF, 1980–83; Political Advr to Rt Hon. Barbara Castle, MP, 1977–79, to Rt Hon. Tony Benn, MP, 1980–86; Parly and Political Advr to Michael Meacher, MP, 1983–87; Sec., Socialist Campaign Gp of Labour MPs, 1981–87. MP (Lab) Mansfield, 1987–2017; contested (Lab) same seat, 2017. An Opposition Whip, 1992–94; PPS to Dep. Leader of Lab. Party, 1994–97, to Dep. Prime Minister, 1997–98; Parly Under-Sec. of State, DETR, 1998–99. Mem., Select Cttee on European Legislation, 1987–89, on Home Affairs, 1989–92, on Finance, 2015–17; Chair, Cross Rail Select Cttee, 2005–08; Treas., Parly All Party Football Gp, 1989; Chairman: All Party Racing and Bloodstocks Cttee, 2005–17; Parly All Party Greece Gp, 2015–17; Chairman: British Cyprus Cttee, 1992–2017; British Section, CPA Cyprus Gp, 2007–17; Member: Parly Court of Referees, 1997–2017; Speaker's Panel, H of C, 2010–17. Council of Europe: Mem., 2000–17; First Vice-Pres., 2002–17; Chair, Sustainable Democracy, 2011–04; President: Envmt, Agric., Local and Regl Democracy Cttee, 2008–17; Eur. Prize Cttee, 2011–17; Chief Whip, Council of Europe and Western EU British Delegn, 2007–17; Mem., Socialist Bureau, 2011–17; Leader, Labour Gp, 2012–17; Mem., Eur. Interim Security and Defence Cttee, Western EU, 2012–17. Mem., British-Irish Assembly, 2014–17. Fellow and Postgrad. Fellow, Industry and Parly Trust, 1989; Fellow, Armed Forces Parly Scheme (ranked Major). UK Parly Rep., Retired Mems Assoc., 2011–17; Pres., Retired Miners Assoc., 2013–. Hon. Mem., Notts Br., NUM. Vice-Pres., Executive, Portland Coll. Trust, 1988–2011; Trustee, Parly Trust Fund, 2015–. Member: Exec., SSAFA, 1989–97; War Pensions Bd, 1989–97. Comr, Commonwealth War Graves Commn, 2002–10. Pres., Mansfield Town AFC, 2004–09. *Recreations:* reading, owner and breeder of thoroughbred horses, writing.

**MEAR, Stephen;** choreographer and director; Associate Choreographer, Chichester Festival Theatre, 2009–16; President, Bird College, since 2018; *b* 19 Feb. 1964; *s* of Albert Heathcote and Zena Fay Mear; partner, Mark Smith. *Educ:* London Studio Centre. Dancer, later dance captain, in West End musicals, incl. 42nd Street, Cats, Follies, Some Like It Hot, Anything Goes, Evita, Crazy for You, 1984–90; choreographer: Of Thee I Sing, Bridewell, 1999; A Little Night Music, Japan; Bouncers, Woman in Love, Derby Playhouse; Grapevine (world première), later retitled Soul Train; Shakers, Northampton Th. Royal; Love Off the Shelf, Harrogate Th.; Snoopy, Watermill Th., Newbury; Grease, Athens; Ruthie Henshall in Concert, RFH and tour; She Loves Me, Canada; Gary Wilmot's Showstoppers Tour; Whitelight Tradeshow; Singin' in the Rain, W Yorks Playhouse, NT and tour, 2000 (What's On Stage award); Stepping Out, Smoking with Lou Lou, Half a Sixpence, W Yorks Playhouse, 2000; (with Bob Avian) The Witches of Eastwick, Th. Royal, Drury Lane, 2001, Australian tour; Don Giovanni, Royal Opera House, 2002; Honk!, Japan and Singapore; The Three Musketeers, Rotterdam, 2003; Anything Goes, NT and Th. Royal, Drury Lane, 2003–04; Tonight's the Night, Victoria Palace, 2004; Acorn Antiques, Th. Royal, Haymarket and UK tour, 2005; On the Town, ENO, 2005; (with Matthew Bourne) Mary Poppins, Prince Edward, 2005, NY, UK and US tour, Netherlands and Australia (Olivier Award for Best Choreography; LA Drama Critics Award for Best Choreography, 2010; Helpmann Award for Best Choreography, Australia, 2011); Vienna and UK tour, 2015, UK tour, 2016, Zurich and Dubai, 2017, Hamburg and Tokyo, 2018; Sinatra at the Palladium, 2006; The Little Mermaid, NY, 2007; Gigi, 2009, Hello Dolly, 2009 (Olivier Award for Best Choreography, 2010), Regents Park Open Air Th.; Sweet Charity, Menier Chocolate Factory Th., 2009–10, Th. Royal, Haymarket, 2010; Shoes (also dir), Sadler's Wells Th., 2010; Betty Blue Eyes, Novello Th., 2011; Crazy For You, Regents Park Open Air Th., Novello, 2011; Me and My Girl, Crucible, Sheffield, 2010; Stephen Ward, Aldwych Th., 2013; Ragtime, Milwaukee Repertory Th., 2013; Die Fledermaus, Metropolitan Opera, NY, 2013–14; City of Angels, Donmar Th., 2014; The Vote, Donmar Th., 2015; Dreamgirls, Milwaukee Repertory Th., 2015; Singin' in the Rain, Th. Du Châtelet, 2015–16, Grand Palais, Paris, 2017; Chitty Chitty Bang Bang, W Yorkshire Playhouse, 2015, UK tour, 2016; Sunset Boulevard, ENO, 2016, NY, 2017; The Girls, Lowry Th., 2016; 42nd Street, Châtelet Th., Paris (and dir), 2016; Thoroughly Modern Millie, Kilworth House Th. (and dir), 2016; The Resistible Rise of Arturo Ui (Movement Dir), Donmar Warehouse, 2017; Top Hat, Kilworth House Th. (and dir), 2017; Guys and Dolls, Milwaukee Repertory Th., 2017, (and dir) Albert Hall, concert version, 2018; Scrooge the Musical, Leicester Curve Th., 2017; Chess, ENO, 2018; White Christmas, Leicester Curve Th., 2018, Dominion Th., 2019; Funny Girl, Guys and Dolls, Th. Marigny, Paris, 2019; (dir) Little Shop of Horrors, Storyhouse, Chester, 2019; Mary Poppins, Prince Edward Th., 2019; Chichester Festival Theatre: Putting It Together, 2001; Just So, 2004 (also N Shore Music Th., Mass, USA); How to Succeed in Business Without Really Trying, 2005; Music Man, Funny Girl, 2008; The Grapes of Wrath, 2009; She Loves Me (also dir), 2011; Kiss Me, Kate, 2012; The Pajama Game, 2013 (also Shaftesbury Th., 2014); Gypsy, 2014 (also Savoy Th., 2015, live TV broadcast, 2015); Amadeus, 2014; Mack and Mabel, 2015 (also UK tour). Choreographer for TV: Victoria Wood's Christmas Special, BBC, 2009; So You Think You Can Dance, BBC, 2010; Psychobitches, Sky Arts, 2012, Tracey Ullman's Show, BBC, 2016, and of several television adverts and music videos incl. Goldfrapp and Oasis. Hon. DArts Greenwich, 2019. Carl Alan Award, Internat. Dance Teachers' Assoc., 2007 and 2015; Dance Companion Award, Liverpool Inst. for Performing Arts, 2013. *Recreations:* theatre, film, music. *Address:* Judy Daish Associates Ltd, 2 Saint Charles Place, W10 6EG. *T:* (020) 8964 8811. *E:* judy@judydaish.com, mearstephen@hotmail.com.

**MEARA, Ven. David Gwynne;** Rector, St Bride's Church, Fleet Street, 2000–14; Archdeacon of London, 2009–14, now Archdeacon Emeritus; *b* 30 June 1947; *s* of Gwynne and Winifred Meara; *m* 1973, Rosemary Anne, *d* of John and Audrey Alexander; two *s* two *d. Educ:* Merchant Taylors' Sch., Northwood; Oriel Coll., Oxford (BA Lit. Hum. 1970; BA Theol. 1972; MA 1973); Cuddesdon Theol Coll., Oxford. Lambeth Dip. 1975. Ordained deacon, 1973, priest, 1974; Curate, Christchurch, Reading, 1973–77; Chaplain, Univ. of Reading, 1977–82; Vicar, Basildon, Aldworth and Ashampstead, 1982–94; RD, Bradfield, 1990–94; Rector, 1994–2000, Area Dean, 1996–2000, Buckingham; Priest-in-charge, London Guild Church of St Mary Aldermary, 2010–12. Sec., 1980–2000, Chm., 1990–2000, Oxford Diocesan Adv. Gp on Mission; Mem., Oxford DAC, 1998–2000. Hon. Canon, 1997–, Hon. Chaplain, 2015–, Christ Church Cathedral, Oxford; Acting Chaplain: Canary Wharf Multi-Faith Chaplaincy, 2014; Oriel Coll., Oxford, 2016, 2017 (Mem., Sen. Common Room). Chaplain, Co. of Spectacle Makers, 2006–07. Liveryman:

Turners' Co., 2012–; Co. of Stationers and Newspaper Makers, 2014–; Co. of Marketors, 2014–. Pres., Monumental Brass Soc., 2002–11. FSA 1994. Fellow, Soc. of Editors, 2014. Special Award, British Press Association 2010. *Publications:* The Foundation of St Augustine at Reading, 1982; Victorian Memorial Brasses, 1983; A. W. N. Pugin and the Revival of Memorial Brasses, 1991; Modern Memorial Brasses, 2008; Remembered Lives, 2013; The Kindersley Workshop in Oxfordshire, 2017; Anglo-Scottish Sleepers, 2018; The Great Scuttle 1919, 2019; Betjeman's Favourite Buildings, 2020; *contributions to:* Blue Guide to English Parish Churches, (Berkshire), 1985; Catalogue of Pugin Exhibition, V & A Mus., 1994; Catalogue of Pugin Exhibition, NY, 1995; Monumental Brasses as Art and History, 1996. *Recreations:* church-crawling, opera, art galleries. *Address:* Stonewalls Barn, 10 The Closes, Kidlington, Oxon OX5 2DP. *Club:* Athenæum.

**MEARNS, Ian;** MP (Lab) Gateshead, since 2010; *b* Newcastle upon Tyne, April 1957. *Educ:* St Mary's RC Primary Sch., Forest Hall; St Mary's RC Tech. Sch., Newcastle upon Tyne. With Northern Gas, 1974–85. Chair: Educn Comm, UNESCO, 1993–2000; Scrutiny Policy Rev. Gp, NE Assembly. Council Rep., LGA (Vice-Pres., 2010–11; Vice-Chair: Envmt Bd; Culture Tourism and Sport Bd; Mem., Educn Exec.). Mem. (Lab) Gateshead Council, 1983–2010 (Dep. Leader, 2002–10). Mem., Educn Select Cttee, 2010–; Chair, Backbench Business Cttee, 2015–. *Address:* House of Commons, SW1A 0AA.

**MEARS, Dr Adrian Leonard,** CBE 2005; FInstP; Director, Scienogy Ltd, 2005–13; *b* 27 May 1944; *s* of Leonard Mears and Marjorie (*née* Isaac); *m* 1969, Barbara Bayne; two *s. Educ:* Highgate Sch.; Christ Church, Oxford (DPhil, MA). Res. Associate, Univ. of Md, USA, 1969–71; joined RRE (later Royal Signals and Radar Establishment), 1971: worked on display technology, optoelectronics and lasers, 1971–81; Hd, Signal Processing, 1981–86; Dir of Science (Comd, Control, Communications and Inf. Systems), MoD, 1987–89; Dep. Dir and Commercial Dir, RSRE, 1990–91; Tech. and Quality Dir, DRA, 1991–95; Tech. Dir, 1995–2001, Chief Knowledge Officer, 1998–2000, DERA; Tech. Dir, QinetiQ, 2001–05. *Recreations:* walking, theatre, music, local councillor. *Address:* 21 Collum End Rise, Leckhampton, Glos GL53 0PA. *T:* (01242) 521050.

**MEARS, Martin John Patrick;** solicitor in private practice; President of the Law Society, 1995–96; *b* 12 Feb. 1940; *s* of J. F. Mears and E. Mears; seven *c. Educ:* St Illtyd's College, Cardiff; Wadham Coll., Oxford (MA, BCL). Solicitor, 1966. Editor, legal satirical jl, Caterpillar. *Publications:* numerous articles in national, regional and legal press. *Recreations:* Law Society, journalism, travel, reading. *Address:* Mears Hobbs & Durrant, 92 High Street, Gorleston, Great Yarmouth, Norfolk NR31 6RH; Old Rectory, Haddiscoe, Norwich NR14 6PG. *Clubs:* Oxford and Cambridge; Norfolk (Norwich).

**MEARS, Oliver;** Director of Opera, Royal Opera House, since 2017; *b* Norwich, 5 Feb. 1979; *s* of Martin Mears and Elisabeth Juen. *Educ:* Norwich Sch.; Lincoln Coll., Oxford (BA English and Hist. 2000). Artistic Director: Second Movement, 2004–; NI Opera, 2010–17. *Productions include:* for Northern Ireland Opera: Tosca, 2011; Noye's Fludde, 2012; The Flying Dutchman, 2013; Salome, 2015; Don Giovanni, Bergen Nat. Opera, 2015; Macbeth, WNO, 2016. *Recreations:* travel, food, theatre, cinema, family. *Address:* Royal Opera House, Bow Street, Covent Garden, WC2E 9DD.

**MEARS, Patrick Michael,** OBE 2019; tax adviser, since 1982; *b* London, 19 Jan. 1958; *s* of Alex Benjamin Albert Mears and Moira Mears; *m* 1st, 1983, Carol Anders (*d* 1987); one *d*; 2nd, 1995, Rachel Anderson; one *s. Educ:* Henley Grammar Sch.; London Sch. of Econs and Pol Sci. (LLB Hons 1979). Admitted solicitor, 1982; Allen & Overy: joined, 1980; Tax Partner, 1988–2011; Consultant, 2011–12. Chm., Adv. Panel, General Anti-Abuse Rule, HMRC, 2013–. Chm., LSE Alumni Assoc., 2013–. Trustee, Gingerbread, 2012–18 (Hon. Vice Pres., 2018–). *Recreations:* theatre, fine art, tennis, bridge. *Address:* 15 Burbage Road, SE24 9HJ. *E:* patrick@mears.eu. *Clubs:* Dulwich Lawn Tennis; Surrey County Cricket.

**MEATH, 15th Earl of,** *cr* 1627; **John Anthony Brabazon;** Baron Ardee (Ire.) 1616; Baron Chaworth (UK) 1831; *b* 11 May 1941; *er s* of 14th Earl of Meath, and Elizabeth Mary (*née* Bowlby); *S* father, 1998; *m* 1973, Xenia Goudime; one *s* two *d. Educ:* Harrow. Page of Honour to the Queen, 1956–58. Served Grenadier Guards, 1960–63. *Heir: s* Lord Ardee, *qv. Address:* Killruddery, Bray, Co. Wicklow, Ireland.

**MEATH, Bishop of, (RC),** since 1990; **Most Rev. Michael Smith;** *b* 6 June 1940; *s* of John Smith and Bridget Fagan. *Educ:* Gilson Endowed Sch., Oldcastle; St Finian's Coll., Mullingar; Lateran Univ., Rome (DCL 1966). Ordained priest, 1963; Curate, Clonmellon, 1967–68; Chaplain: St Loman's Hosp., 1968–74; Sacred Heart Hosp., 1975–84; Auxiliary Bp of Meath, 1984–88; Coadjutor Bp of Meath, 1988–90. Diocesan Sec., dio. of Meath, 1968–84; Sec., Irish Bishops' Conf., 1984–98 (Exec. Sec., 1970–84). *Recreations:* golf, walking. *Address:* The Bishop's House, Dublin Road, Mullingar, Co. Westmeath, Ireland. *T:* (44) 9348841, 9342039, *Fax:* (44) 9343020. *E:* bishop@dioceseofmeath.ie.

**MEATH AND KILDARE, Bishop of,** since 2013; **Most Rev. Patricia Storey;** *b* Northern Ireland, 30 March 1960; *d* of Norman and Eleanor Shaw; *m* 1983, Earl Storey; one *s* one *d. Educ:* Methodist Coll., Belfast; Trinity Coll., Dublin (MA Hons 1983; BTh 1994). Ordained deacon, 1997, priest, 1998; Curate, Ballymena, 1997–2000; Team Vicar, Glenavy, 2000–04; Rector, St Augustine's, Londonderry, 2004–13. Youth Worker Co-ord., C of I Youth Dept, 2000–04. *Recreations:* reading, dog-walking, book club, swimming, creative writing, eating out. *Address:* The Bishop's House, Moyglare, Maynooth, Co. Kildare, Ireland. *T:* (1) 6289825. *E:* bishop@meath.anglican.org.

**MEATH BAKER, (William John) Clovis,** CMG 2013; OBE 2002; HM Diplomatic Service, retired; Director, Foreign and Commonwealth Office, 2013; *b* 11 May 1959; *s* of late William Gregory Francis Meath Baker and of Priscilla Ann Meath Baker (*née* Gurney); *m* 1985, Elizabeth Diana Woodham-Smith; four *d. Educ:* Eton (King's Schol.); Magdalen Coll., Oxford (MA). Short Service Commn, 2nd Goorkhas (Sirmoor Rifles), 1981–84. Entered FCO, 1985; Second, later First Sec. (Chancery and Inf.), and Consul, Kabul, 1988–89; FCO, 1989; First Secretary and Consul, Prague, 1989–93; FCO, 1993–97; Consul (Pol) Istanbul, 1997–2000; First Sec., FCO, 2000–02; Counsellor: (Pol), Kabul, 2002; FCO, 2003; hcsc 2006; Dir, Intelligence Prodn, GCHQ, 2010–13. Deployable Civilian Expert, Stabilisation Unit, 2014–; Prime Minister's Counter-Terrorism Capability Envoy to Pakistan, 2014–. Advr, HSBC, 2016–18. Chm., Walsingham Estate Co., 2006–. Associate Fellow, RUSI. *Clubs:* Athenæum, Beefsteak.

**MEDCROFT, Nicholas Julian;** QC 2019; a Recorder, since 2018; *b* 28 Feb. 1975; *s* of Graham Medcroft and late Pamela Medcroft; *m* 2006, Jacqueline; two *s* (and one *s* decd). *Educ:* Felsted Sch.; Durham Univ. (LLB Hons 1997). Called to the Bar, Lincoln's Inn, 1998; in practice as a barrister, specialising in commercial law. *Address:* Fountain Court Chambers, Fountain Court, Temple, EC4Y 9DH. *T:* (020) 7583 3335. *E:* njm@fountaincourt.co.uk.

**MEDDINGS, Richard Henry;** Chairman, TSB Bank plc, since 2018 (non-executive Director, since 2017); *b* Wolverhampton, 12 March 1958; *s* of late Ronald Jack Meddings and Brenda Meddings; *m* Henrietta Took; two *s* one *d. Educ:* Wolverhampton Grammar Sch.; Exeter Coll., Oxford (BA Hons Modern Hist.). ACA. Price Waterhouse, 1980–84; Hill Samuel Bank, 1984–96; BZW, later CSFB, 1996–99; Gp Finance Dir, Woolwich plc, 1999–2000; Gp Financial Controller and Chief Operating Officer, Wealth Mgt, Barclays plc, 2000–02; Gp Exec. Dir, 2002–14, Gp Finance Dir, 2006–14, Standard Chartered plc. Non-executive Director: 3i plc, 2008–14; Legal & General, 2014–17; HM Treasury, 2014–; Deutsche Bank, 2015–; Jardine Lloyd Thompson Gp plc, 2017–19. Mem. Bd, ICC UK, 2008–. Mem. Bd, Seeing is Believing, 2003–14 (Chm., 2004–14). Trustee, Teach First, 2016–. *Recreations:* fishing, golf, equestrian, football, cricket, medieval history.

**MEDHURST, Brian,** BEM 2017; Managing Director (International Division), Prudential Corporation plc, 1985–94; *b* 18 March 1935; *s* of late Eric Gilbert Medhurst and Bertha May (*née* Kinggett); *m* 1960, Patricia Anne Beer; two *s* one *d. Educ:* Godalming Grammar Sch.; Trinity Coll., Cambridge (MA). FIA 1962 (Mem. Council, 1982–87). Joined Prudential Assurance Co. Ltd, 1958; Deputy Investment Manager, 1972; Investment Manager, 1975; Jt Chief Investment Manager, 1981; Gen. Manager, 1982. *Recreations:* chess, bridge, golf, tree felling. *Address:* Woodcroft, Yelverton, Devon PL20 6HY. *T:* (01822) 853337. *Club:* Yelverton Golf.

**MEDINA, Earl of; Henry David Louis Mountbatten;** *b* 19 Oct. 1991; *s* and *heir* of Marquess of Milford Haven, *qv. Educ:* Millfield.

**MEDINA-MORA ICAZA, Eduardo;** a Justice of the Supreme Court of Mexico, since 2015; *b* Mexico City, 30 Jan. 1957; *m* Laura; three *c. Educ:* National Autonomous Univ. of Mexico. Corporate Dir, Strategic Planning and Dep. Dir Gen., DESC Gp, 1991–2000; Dir Gen., Centre for Investigation and Nat. Security, 2000–05; Mem., Nat. Security Council, 2000–09; Minister (Sec.) of Public Security, 2005–06; Pres., Nat. Public Security Council, 2005–06; Attorney-Gen., 2006–09; Ambassador of Mexico to the Court of St James's, 2010–13. Chief Negotiator for Border Security Agreement Mexico-US, 2002; Chief Security Negotiator for Alliance for Prosperity and Security in N America, 2004–05; Ambassador of Mexico to USA, 2013–15; Member: High Level Gp on Border Security with Guatemala and Belize; Mexican security delegns in bilateral meetings with US, Canada, Colombia and Guatemala. Coordinator, legal adv. gp to Mexican Govt during N American Free Trade Agreement negotiations. Member: Mexican Barrister Assoc.; Amer. Bar Assoc.; Chatham House. *Publications:* Fisheries in the Exclusive Economic Zone, 1989; (jtly) Legitimate Use of Force, 2008. *Address:* Supreme Court, Pino Suárez 2, Colonia Centro, Delegación Cuauhtémoc, C.P. 06065, Mexico.

**MEDLAND, Simon Edward;** QC 2011; **His Honour Judge Medland;** a Circuit Judge, since 2018; *b* 1965; *s* of W. J. Medland and B. M. R. Medland; *m* 2000, Teejay, *d* of M. Fairey, Pouzolles, France; one *s* one *d. Educ:* Mostyn Hse Sch., Parkgate; Wrekin Coll., Wellington; Univ. of Hull (BA); City Univ. (DipLaw); Inns of Court Sch. of Law. Called to the Bar, Middle Temple, 1991 (Ede and Ravenscroft Prize; Gottlieb Award), Bencher, 2018; a Recorder, 2005–18; Circuit Jun., Chester, 2008–10. *Recreations:* playing the organ and the piano, ski-ing, historical research, shooting, supporting Tranmere Rovers FC. *Address:* Preston Crown Court, Ring Way, Preston PR1 2LL. *Club:* City (Chester).

**MEDLEY, George Julius,** OBE 1989; Director, WWF-UK (World Wide Fund for Nature) (formerly World Wildlife Fund (UK)), 1978–93; *b* 2 Aug. 1930; *s* of late Brig. Edgar Julius Medley, DSO, OBE, MC and Norah Medley (*née* Templer); *m* 1952, Vera Frances Brand; one *s* one *d. Educ:* Winchester College; Wye College, Univ. of London. BSc (Hort.); London Business Sch. (Sen. Exec. Prog., 1968). Fruit farmer, 1952–56; Manager, Chemical Dept, Harrisons & Crosfield, Colombo, 1957–63; Dir, Fisons (Ceylon), 1960–63; Tech. Develt Manager, Tata Fison, Bangalore, 1963–64; Gen. Manager Pesticides Div., Tata Fison Industries, Bombay, 1964–68; Sales Manager, Western Hemisphere, Agrochemicals, Fisons Internat. Div., 1968–69; Overseas Manager, Fisons Agrochemical Div., 1970–71; Dep. Managing Dir, Glaxo Labs, India, 1972–73, Managing Dir, 1973–77. Chm., Alexis Productions Ltd, 1994–98; Director: Edward Jewson Services to Charities Ltd, 1993–2001; Tisbury Halls, 2006–11. Member: Radioactive Waste Management Adv. Cttee, 1991–98; UK Ecolabelling Bd, 1995–99. Vice-Pres., Organisation of Pharmaceutical Producers of India, 1974–77; Founder Mem. and Vice-Chm., Inst. of Charity Fundraising Managers, 1983 (Chm., 1984–85); Treasurer: Wilts Country Markets Ltd (formerly Wilts WI Market Soc.), 1993–99, 2004–07; Wilts Wildlife Trust, 1994–99 (Pres., 1999–2003); Trustee: Farming and Wildlife Adv. Gp, 1984–93; Internat. Inst. for Envmt and Develt, 1989–93; Falkland Islands Foundn, 1985–92. Member: Tisbury Parish Council, 2001–07 (Vice-Chm., 2002–07); Exec. Cttee, Wilts Village Halls Assoc., 2006–11. FCMI; FICFM 1988. Officer, Order of Golden Ark (Netherlands), 1993. *Publications:* contrib. to Strategic Planning Soc. Jl. *Recreations:* gardening, DIY. *Address:* Tyntes Place, Lady Down View, Tisbury, Wilts SP3 6LL. *T:* (01747) 870047.

**MEDLICOTT, Michael Geoffrey;** Chief Executive (formerly Managing Director), Servus (formerly Opus) Holdings plc, 1997–2001; *b* 2 June 1943; *s* of Geoffrey Henry Medlicott and Beryl Ann Medlicott (*née* Burchell); *m* 1st, 1973, Diana Grace Fallaw (marr. diss. 1998); one *s* three *d*; 2nd, 1999, Susan Caroline Whittall. *Educ:* Downside School; Lincoln College, Oxford (Scholar; MA). Management Trainee, P&O-Orient Lines, 1965–66; Shipping Asst, Mackinnon, Mackenzie & Co., Bombay, 1966–68, Tokyo, 1968–69; Asst to Management, P&O-Orient Lines, 1969–71; P&O Cruises: Develt Analyst, 1971–73; Asst Fleet Manager, 1973–75; Gen. Manager, Fleet, 1975–80; Gen. Manager, Europe, 1980–83; Dir, Europe, 1983–86; Man. Dir, Swan Hellenic, 1983–86; Man. Dir, P&O Air Holidays, 1980–86; Dir, P&O Travel, 1980–84; Chief Exec., BTA, 1986–93; Vice Pres., Europe, 1993–96, Europe and Asia, 1996–97, Delta Airlines Inc. Chairman: Delta Aeroflot Travel Enterprises (Moscow), 1996–97; Servus Facilities Mgt Ltd, 1998–2001; Servus b2b Ltd, 2000–01; Transaction Dir, Nomura Internat. Principal Finance Gp, 1997–2000; Director: Deltair UK Investments, 1995–96; Lesteris Ltd, 1995–96; Gatwick Handling Internat. Ltd, 1995–96; Grand Facilities Mgt Holdings Ltd, 1998–2000; Member, Board: Manchester Airport plc, 2002–04; Manchester Airports Gp plc, 2004–10; John Laing plc, 2004–06; Laing Rail Ltd, 2006–08; M40 Trains Ltd, 2006–08; OCS Gp Ltd, 2006–15 (Chm., Audit Cttee, 2008–12, 2013–15; Mem., Audit, Nominations and Remuneration Cttees, 2008–15); Myriad Healthcare Ltd (formerly Caring Homes Gp), 2010–15 (Chm., 2008–10, 2013–15; Mem., Audit Cttee, 2008–13; Chairman: Risk Cttee, 2012–15; Audit and Remuneration Cttees, 2013–15); Chm., MHL (formerly Myriad Healthcare) Holdco Ltd, 2015–; Dir, Caring Homes Healthcare Gp Ltd; Chm., Investors Cttee, ING REIM Ltd Infrastructure Fund, 2007–09. Chm., European Travel Commn, 1992–93 (Chm., Planning Cttee, 1990–92). Member: Council of Management: Passenger Shipping Assoc., 1983–86; Heritage of London Trust, 1987–2008; London Tourist Bd, 1992–93; Council, Visit Britain Gp, 1988–2008; Bd, British-Amer. Chamber of Commerce, 1996–97; Bd, Nat. Savings & Investments, HM Treasury, 2003–09 (Chm., Audit Cttee, 2005–07; Appts and Remuneration Cttee, 2007–09); Bd, CAA, 2010– (Member: Remuneration Cttee, 2010–; Audit Cttee, 2014–); Bd, CAA Internat., 2010–; Chm., Air Travel Trust, 2013–; Bd, Virgin Healthcare Hldgs Ltd, 2015– (Chm., Quality Cttee, 2015–; Mem., Audit Cttee, 2015–). Member: Adv. Panel, Languages Lead Body, Dept of Employment, 1990–93; Adv. Council, Univ. of Surrey Tourism Dept, 1991–93; Hon. Bd, Univ. Center of Hellenic and European Studies, Piraeus, 1994–. Trustee, British Travel & Educnl Trust, 1986–93. LEA Gov., Ecchinswell and Sydmonton C of E Primary Sch., 1999–2003. Mem., Royal Philatelic Soc. (Fellow, Gold Plaquette, 2016). FRSA 1986. CRAeS 1994. Queen Mother's Birthday Award for Envmtl Improvement, 1993, 1995. *Publications:* (contrib.) Facility Management: risks and opportunities, 2000; (with Sir J. Marriott and R. A. Ramkissoon)

Trinidad: a philatelic history to 1913, 2010 (4 Internat. Gold Medals, 2010, 2011 and 2012; Charles J. Peterson Literature Grand Award and Gold Medal, Nat. Philatelic Exhibns, 2011; contribs to British West Indies Study Circle Bulletin, 1970–. *Recreations:* philately, opera, travelling in perfect company. *Club:* Oxford and Cambridge.

**MEDLYCOTT, Sir Mervyn (Tregonwell),** 9th Bt *cr* 1808, of Ven House, Somerset; *b* 20 Feb. 1947; *s* of Thomas Anthony Hutchings Medlycott (*d* 1970) (2nd *s* of 7th Bt) and Cecilia Mary Medlycott, *d* of late Major Cecil Harold Eden; *S* uncle, 1986. Genealogist; FSG 1990; Vice Pres., Soc. of Genealogists, 2015–; Pres., Somerset and Dorset Family History Soc., 1986– (Founder and Hon. Sec., 1975–77; Chm., 1977–84; Vice-Pres., 1984–86). *Heir:* none. *Address:* The Manor House, Sandford Orcas, Sherborne, Dorset DT9 4SB. *T:* (01963) 220206.

**MEDVEDEV, Dmitry Anatolyevich,** PhD; Prime Minister of Russia, since 2012; Chairman, United Russia Party, since 2012; *b* Leningrad, 14 Sept. 1965; *m* 1993, Svetlana Vladimirovna; one *s*. *Educ:* Leningrad State Univ. (PhD Law 1990). Lectr, St Petersburg State Univ., 1990–99; Advr to Chm., Leningrad CC, 1990–95; Expert Consultant to Cttee for Ext. Affairs, St Petersburg City Hall, 1990–95; Dep. Govt COS, 1999; Dep. COS, 1999–2000, First Dep. COS, 2000–03, COS, 2003–05, Presidential Exec. Office; First Dep. Prime Minister, 2005–08; President of Russia, 2008–12. Chm., 2000–01 and 2002–08, Dep. Chm., 2001–02, Bd of Dirs, OAO Gazprom. *Address:* Office of the Prime Minister, White House, 2 Krasnopresnenskaya Naberezhnaya, Moscow 103274, Russia.

**MEDWAY, Lord; John Jason Gathorne-Hardy;** *b* 26 Oct. 1968; *s* and *heir* of 5th Earl of Cranbrook, *qv*.

**MEDWAY, Susan Clare;** Director, Chelsea Physic Garden, since 2014; *b* Essex, June 1965; *d* of Richard and Anne Whybrow; *m* 1997, John Medway. Hse steward, Uppark House, NT, 1994–97; Hse Manager, Chartwell, NT, 1997–2001; Property Manager, Sheffield Park Gdn and Estate, 2001–09; on secondment as Property Manager, Stowe Landscape Gdn, 2006–07; Gen. Manager, Sissinghurst Castle portfolio, 2009–11; Commercial and Ops Dir, Design Mus., 2011–14. Mem. Cttee, London Gardens Network, 2015–. Trustee, London Gardens Soc., 2016–. Freeman, City of London, 2018; Liveryman, Gardeners' Co., 2018. *Recreations:* travel, gardening, museums, galleries, historic properties, sailing. *Address:* Chelsea Physic Garden, 66 Royal Hospital Road, SW3 4HS. *T:* (020) 7352 5646. *E:* smedway@chelseaphysicgarden.co.uk.

**MEEK, Elizabeth Jane,** CBE 2000; Chair, Twining Enterprise, since 2017; *b* 5 Sept. 1950; *d* of Patrick and Gladys Cox; *m* 1975, Innes Meek; three *d*. *Educ:* John Port Sch., Etwall, Derbyshire; Univ. of Exeter (BA Hons English). Joined Civil Service (fast stream entry), 1972; Department of the Environment, then of Environment, Transport and the Regions, subseq. for Transport, Local Government and the Regions: Asst Private Sec. to Sec. of State, DoE, 1978–79; First Sec., British High Commn, Lagos, 1979–81 (on secondment); Govt link with Manchester Olympic Bid, 1991–93; Hd, London Policy Unit, 1993–94; Hd, Strategy and Co-ordination Unit, 1994–97, Dir, GLA Div. (setting up Mayor and Assembly of London), 1997–2000, Govt Office for London; Interim Dir Communications and Public Affairs, Transport for London, 2000–01 (on secondment); Regional Director: Govt Office for London, 2001–08; Govt Office for NW, 2008–11. Mem., Schizophrenia Commn, 2011–12; Trustee, McPin Foundn, 2013–16. Non-exec. Dir, Sanctuary Housing, 2011–17. Mem. Bd, Film London, 2011–18. Gov., Birkbeck, Univ. of London, 2011– (Vice Chair, 2016–). *Publications:* Survive Lagos, 1982. *Recreations:* mountain walking, ski-ing. *E:* zilkeem@gmail.com.

**MEEK, Kingsley John Neville, (Kip);** Inquiry Chairman, Competition and Markets Authority, since 2018; *b* Arusha, Tanzania, 18 April 1955; *s* of Charles Innes Meek and Nona Corry Meek (*née* Hurford); *m* 1986, Marian O'Connor; two *s* two *d*. *Educ:* Magdalen Coll., Oxford (BA 1st Cl. Hons Modern Hist.); London Business Sch. (MSc with Dist.). Boston Consulting Gp, 1977–79; McKinsey & Co., 1981–83; Dep. Dir, BT, 1983–85; Partner, Coopers & Lybrand, 1985–93; Man. Dir, Spectrum Strategy Consultants, 1993–2003. Chairman: Broadband Stakeholder Gp, 2007–10; South West Screen, 2010–12; Enders Analysis, 2015–16; Ascension Ventures, 2018–; A Million Ads, 2018–. Mem. Bd, Radiocentre, 2007–18 (Chm., 2013–18). Mem. Bd, Ofcom, 2004–07. Chm., Eur. Regulators Gp, 2007; Ind. Spectrum Broker, Govt Spectrum Modernisation Prog., 2009–10. *Publications:* (with R. Foster) Public Service Broadcasting in the United Kingdom, 2008; Report of the Independent Spectrum Broker, 2009. *Recreations:* tennis, bridge, Chelsea Football Club. *Address:* 51 Onslow Gardens, N10 3JY. *T:* (020) 8444 2032.

**MEEK, Stephen Donald Andrew;** Director, Qatar Academy, Doha, Qatar, since 2019; *b* 27 Nov. 1952; *s* of George Edward Meek and Joan Meek; *m* 1987, Christine Sanders; two *s*. *Educ:* St John's Sch., Leatherhead; St Andrews Univ. (MA 1st Cl. Hons Mediaeval and Modern Hist.); Worcester Coll., Oxford (PGCE). History teacher, Dulwich Coll., 1978–85; Sherborne School, 1985–95: Hd of Hist., 1985–90; Housemaster, School House, 1990–95; Headmaster, Hurstpierpoint Coll., 1995–2004; Principal, Geelong Grammar Sch., Australia, 2004–18. Director: World's Leading Schs Assoc., 2011–18; Positive Educn Schs Assoc., 2012–15; Chair, Associated Public Sch. Heads, 2016–18. Mem., Steering Cttee, Internat. Positive Educn Network, 2016–. Pres., Victorian Schs RU, 2008–18. *Recreations:* house in France, golf, bridge. *Address:* PO Box 588, East Melbourne, Vic 8002, Australia. *E:* sdameek@gmail.com.

**MEEK, Stephen Graham;** Director, Institute for Policy and Engagement, University of Nottingham, since 2018; *b* 4 Aug. 1965; *s* of Gerald Arthur Meek and Judith Ann Meek; *m* 1994, Juliet Louise Greer; one *s* (and one *s* decd). *Educ:* Rugby Sch.; Univ. of Edinburgh (MA Hons Pols and Hist. 1988); Univ. of Essex (MA Philos. 1989). HM Treasury, 1992–2005: Private Sec. to Economic Sec., 1994–95; Policy Advr, Social Security Team, 1997–2000; Hd, Home Financial Services Team, 2001–03; Hd, Educn, Trng and Culture Team, 2003–05; Prog. Dir for Children and Young People, LGA, 2005–06; Dir of Strategy, DFES, later DCSF, 2006–08; Dir, Young People: Qualifications Strategy and Reform, DCSF, later DFE, 2008–11; Acting Dir Gen., Educn Standards, DFE, 2012–13; Dir of Strategy, Communications and Private Office, DCLG, 2015–17. *Address:* Institute for Policy and Engagement, University of Nottingham, University Park, Nottingham, NG7 2RD.

**MEEKE, (Robert) Martin (James);** QC 2000; a Recorder, 1995; *b* 25 Dec. 1950; *s* of James Alexander Meeke and Mildred Alverta Meeke; *m* 1973, Beverley Ann Evans; one *s* one *d*. *Educ:* Allhallows Sch., Devon; Bristol Univ. (LLB Hons). Called to the Bar, Gray's Inn, 1973. *Address:* Colleton Chambers, Colleton Crescent, Exeter EX2 4DG. *T:* (01392) 274898.

**MEESE, Edwin,** III; lawyer; Ronald Reagan Distinguished Fellow in Public Policy, 1988, now Emeritus Fellow, and Chairman, Center for Legal and Judicial Studies, 2001–13, Heritage Foundation, Washington (Trustee, since 2017); Distinguished Visiting Fellow, Hoover Institution, Stanford University, California, 1988; *b* Oakland, Calif, 2 Dec. 1931; *s* of Edwin Meese Jr and Leone Meese; *m* 1958, Ursula Herrick; one *s* one *d* (and one *s* decd). *Educ:* Oakland High Sch.; Yale Univ. (BA 1953); Univ. of Calif at Berkeley (JD 1958). Dep. Dist Attorney, Alameda County, 1959–67; Sec. of Legal Affairs to Gov. of Calif, Ronald Reagan, 1967–69; Exec. Assistant and C of S to Gov. of Calif, 1969–75; Vice-Pres., Rohr Industries, 1975–76; Attorney at Law, 1976–80; Dir, Center for Criminal Justice Policy and Management, Univ. of San Diego, 1977–81; Prof. of Law, Univ. of San Diego Law Sch., 1978–81; Counsellor to Pres. of USA, 1981–85; Attorney Gen. of USA, 1985–88. Hon. LLD: Delaware Law Sch.; Widener Univ.; Univ. of San Diego; Valparaiso Univ.; California Lutheran Coll.; Universidad Francisco Marroquin, Guatemala. *Publications:* With Reagan: the inside story, 1992; (jtly) Leadership, Ethics and Policing: challenges for the 21st century, 2003, 2nd edn 2009; contribs to professional jls. *Address:* The Heritage Foundation, 214 Massachusetts Avenue, NE, Washington, DC 20002–4999, USA.

**MEESON, Nigel Keith;** QC 2002; Head of Asia Disputes and Restructuring, Conyers Dill & Pearman, Hong Kong, since 2015; *b* 10 Feb. 1959; *s* of Arthur Edward Meeson and Beryl Grace Meeson; *m* 1st, 1982, Beverley Christine Frank (marr. diss. 2006); two *d*; 2nd, 2007, Gaylene Brereton; one *d*. *Educ:* St Albans Sch., Herts; Magdalen Coll., Oxford (BA Hons Juris., MA). Called to the Bar, Middle Temple, 1982; Attorney, State Bar of Calif, 1990; Accredited Mediator, CEDR, 1993; FCIArb 2006; in practice as Barrister, 1983–2007; a Recorder, 2004–13; admitted to the Bar: of Cayman Is, 2007; of BVI, 2008; Hd of Litigation, Conyers Dill & Pearman, Cayman Islands, 2007–15; acting Judge of Grand Court, Cayman Islands, 2007–15. Member, Panel of Arbitrators: HK Internat. Arbitration Centre, 2015–; Singapore Internat. Commercial Court, 2016–. Vis. Lectr, UCL, 1994–2005. *Publications:* The Practice and Procedure of the Admiralty Court, 1986; Ship and Aircraft Mortgages, 1989; Admiralty Jurisdiction and Practice, 1993, 5th edn 2018; (contrib.) Ship Sale and Purchase, 2nd edn 1993, 3rd edn 1998; (contrib.) International Commercial Dispute Resolution, 2009; (contrib.) Cross Border Judicial Co-operation in Offshore Litigation, 2009, 2nd edn 2016; (contrib.) International Civil Fraud, 2014; (contrib.) Cayman Islands Company & Commercial Law, 2015. *Recreations:* sailing, ski-ing, golf. *Address:* Conyers Dill & Pearman, 29th Floor, One Exchange Square, 8 Connaught Place, Central, Hong Kong SAR. *T:* 25247106, *Fax:* 28459268. *E:* nigel.meeson@conyersdill.com.

**MEEUWISSEN, Anthony,** RDI 2013; freelance designer and illustrator, since 1967; *b* London, 26 June 1938; *s* of Henricus and Olive Meeuwissen; two *d*; *m* 2013, Marie-Beatrice Gwynn. *Educ:* Strode's Grammar Sch., Egham. Has undertaken commns from Penguin Books, Radio Times, Sunday Times Mag., Royal Mail, Pentagram Design. Collection of work, Dept of Prints and Drawings, V&A Mus., 1976; retrospective exhibn, Stroud Mus., 2009; exhibn, Corinium Mus., Cirencester, 2010. One Gold, Two Silver Awards, D&AD, 1972; Francobollo d'Oro award for world's most beautiful stamp (for Royal Mail 20½ p Christmas stamp, 1983), La XXXVI Fiera del Francobollo a Riccione, 1984. FRSA. *Publications:* (illustrator) The Witch's Hat, by Irwin Dermer, 1975; The Key of the Kingdom, 1992 (D&AD Gold Award, WH Smith Illustration Award, 1993); Remarkable Animals, 1997, miniature edn 2009. *Recreations:* country walks, reading, listening to music, visiting art galleries. *Address:* The Old House, St Chloe, Amberley, Stroud, Glos GL5 5AP. *T:* (01453) 873276. *E:* tonymeeuwissen@live.co.uk.

**MEGAHEY, Leslie;** writer and director, film, television and theatre; *b* 22 Dec. 1944; *s* of Rev. Thomas and Beatrice Megahey. *Educ:* King Edward VI Grammar Sch., Lichfield; Pembroke Coll., Oxford. BBC general trainee, 1965; radio drama, script editor, producer, 1967; director, producer, TV arts series, 1968–; Exec. Producer, Arena, 1978–79; Editor, Omnibus, 1979–81, Co-Editor, 1985–87; Head of Music and Arts, BBC TV, 1988–91; other *television:* The Orson Welles Story, 1982; Artists and Models, 1986; The RKO Story, 1987; Leonardo, 2003; numerous drama-documentaries; *films:* Schalcken the Painter, 1979; Cariani and the Courtesans, 1987; Duke Bluebeard's Castle (filmed opera), 1988; The Hour of the Pig, 1993; Earth (co-writer, narration script), 2007; *theatre:* (dir and co-author) Jack—a night on the town, Criterion, 1994, NY, 1996. Mem., Arts Council Adv. Panel, Film and TV, 1985–89. Awards: BAFTA, 1980; Prague, 1975; Asolo, 1985; NY, 1987; Banff, 1987; Royal Philharmonic, 1989; Prix Italia, 1989; Argentine Film Critics', 1999; Lifetime Achievement, Montréal FIFA Fest., 2001. *Publications:* (jtly) Akira Kurosawa: a life in film, 2018. *Address:* c/o The Agency, 24 Pottery Lane, W11 4LZ.

**MEGAINEY, Zina Ruth;** *see* Etheridge, Z. R.

**MEGARRY, Helen Mary;** Adjudicator, HM Revenue and Customs and Valuation Office Agency, since 2016; *b* Portsmouth; *d* of Alan and Angela Megarry; *m* 1995, John Greenwood; two *s*. *Educ:* Portsmouth High Sch.; University Coll. London (LLB); Guildford Law Sch. Housing Ombudsman Service: Dir of Casework, 2006–12; Dep. Ombudsman and Chief Operating Officer, 2013–16; Interim Housing Ombudsman, 2015. Mem., Exec. Cttee, Ombudsman Assoc., 2016–. *Address:* Adjudicator's Office, PO Box 10280, Nottingham NG2 9PF. *T:* 0300 057 1111, *Fax:* 0300 059 4513. *E:* helen.megarry@adjudicatorsoffice.gsi.gov.uk.

**MEGGS, Anthony Jan Michael,** CB 2019; Chairman, Crossrail Ltd, since 2019; *b* London, 23 Sept. 1952; *s* of Mick and Bep Meggs; *m* 2013, Victoria Preston; two *c*. *Educ:* Fitzwilliam Coll., Cambridge (BA Natural Scis 1973); Imperial Coll., London (MSc Petroleum Engrg); Stanford Univ. (MSc Mgt). Hd, Gp Technol., BP, 2001–08; Vis. Scientist, MIT, 2008–10; Exec. Vice Pres., Talisman, 2011–13; CEO, Infrastructure and Projects Authy, 2015–18. *Recreations:* music, reading, cinema. *Address:* Crossrail Ltd, 5 Endeavour Square, E20 1JN. *T:* (020) 7918 2908. *E:* tonymeggs@crossrail.tfl.gov.uk. *Club:* Athenæum.

**MEGHIR, Prof. Konstantinos Ektor Dimitrios, (Costas),** PhD; FBA 2005; Douglas A. Warner III Professor of Economics, Yale University, since 2010; *b* 13 Feb. 1959; *s* of John and Marie-Jose Meghir; *m* 1987, Sofia Skalistiri; one *s* one *d*. *Educ:* Univ. of Manchester (BA Econs, MA Econs; PhD 1985). Res. Schol., Internat. Inst. for Applied Systems Analysis, Vienna, 1982–83; Temp. Lectr, Univ. of Manchester, 1983–84; University College London: Res. Officer, 1984–85; Lectr, 1985–91; Reader, 1991–92; Prof. of Econs, 1992–2011; Hd, Dept of Econs, 2005–08. Dep. Res. Dir, 1991–2005, Co-Dir, 2005–11, ESRC Centre, Inst. of Fiscal Studies. Member, Council: REconS, 2007–12 (Mem. Exec., 2008–12); Econometric Soc., 2011– (Fellow, 2000). Bodossaki Foundn Prize, 1997; Frisch Prize, Econometric Soc., 2000. Jt Man. Ed., Econ. Jl, 1996–2001; Co-ed., Econometrica, 2001–06. *Publications:* contribs to learned jls. *Recreations:* sailing, ski-ing, photography. *Address:* Department of Economics, Yale University, 37 Hillhouse Avenue, CT 06511, USA. *T:* (203) 4323558, *Fax:* (203) 4326323. *E:* c.meghir@yale.edu.

**MEHAFFEY, Rt Rev. James;** Bishop of Derry and Raphoe, 1980–2002; *b* 29 March 1931; *s* of John and Sarah Mehaffey; *m* 1956, Thelma P. L. Jackson; two *s* one *d*. *Educ:* Trinity College, Dublin (MA, BD); Queen's University, Belfast (PhD). Curate Assistant: St Patrick's, Belfast, 1954–56; St John's, Deptford, London, 1956–58; Minor Canon, Down Cathedral, 1958–60; Bishop's Curate, St Christopher's, Belfast, 1960–62; Incumbent: Kilkeel, Diocese of Dromore, 1962–66; Cregagh, Diocese of Down, 1966–80. Freeman: City of London, 2002; City of Derry, 2015. Hon. DLitt Ulster, 1999. *Address:* 10 Clearwater, Londonderry BT47 6BE. *T:* (028) 7134 2624. *E:* james.mehaffey@btinternet.com.

**MEHMET, Alper,** MVO 1990; HM Diplomatic Service, retired; Ambassador to Iceland, 2004–08; *b* Cyprus, 28 Aug. 1948; *s* of late Bekir Mehmet and of Leman Mehmet; *m* 1968, Elaine Susan Tarrant; two *d*. *Educ:* Parmiter's Grammar Sch.; Bristol Poly. Entered Home Office, 1970; Immigration Service, 1970–79; Lagos, 1979–83; transf. to HM Diplomatic Service (first immigrant Mem. and Muslim to reach Ambassador rank); Asst Pvte Sec. to Parly Under-Sec. of State, FCO, 1983–85; Second Sec., Bucharest, 1986–89; Dep. Hd of Mission, Reykjavík, 1989–93; FCO, 1993–98; First Sec., Bonn, 1999, Berlin, 1999–2003. Special Advr on Iceland, FIPRA Internat., 2009–. Consultant, Stabilisation Unit (jt FCO, MoD and DFID), 2009–. UK Dir, Aqua Omnis Water Co., 2011–. Mem. Adv. Council and spokesman, Migration Watch UK, 2010– (Vice Chm., 2010–). Mem. Bd, FCO Assoc., 2013–. Trustee and Treas., City and Hackney Alcohol Service, 2010–12. Foundn Gov., 1995–, Foundn Trustee, 1997–, Chm. Bd, 2015–, Parmiter's Sch. (Mem., Academy Bd, 2012–); Chm., Old Parmiter's Soc., 2014–16. Public speaker, TV and radio commentator, and writer on immigration, social issues and Cyprus. *Recreation:* amateur dramatics (Mem., Chingford Amateur Dramatic and Operatic Soc.). *E:* alp.mehmet@me.com.

**MEHTA, Bharat,** CBE 2016 (OBE 2000); Chief Executive (formerly Clerk to the Trustees), Trust for London (formerly City Parochial Foundation), since 1998; *b* 5 March 1956; *s* of Maganlal Jinabhai Mehta and Rattanben Mehta; *m* 1990, Sally Anne Chambers; two *d*. *Educ:* Plymouth Poly. (BA Hons Psychology 1979); UCL (MSc Ergonomics 1981). Researcher, MRC, 1979–80; Community Develt Worker, Pensioners Link, 1981–84; Policy Officer, NCVO, 1984–86; Principal Officer, Waltham Forest LBC, 1987–89; Dir of Develt, 1989–93, CEO, 1993–98, Nat. Schizophrenia Fellowship. Chm., Active Community Unit Adv. Gp, Home Office, 2003–04. Dir, Social Justice and Human Rights Centre Ltd, 2011–. Member: HM Treasury and Cabinet Office spending review of future role of third sector in econ. and social regeneration, 2006–07; Mental Health Foundn Commn on Ageing, 2011–13. Non-exec. Dir, N Middlesex Univ. Hosp. NHS Trust, 2005–09 (Vice Chm., 2008–09). Chm., Resource for London, 2011–16. Patron, Revolving Doors Agency, 1998–. Member, Board: Joseph Rowntree Foundn, 2003–13; Social Justice and Human Rights Centre Ltd, 2011–; Home Gp, 2014–; London Emergencies Trust, 2016–; Park Th., 2018–. Chair, Young Londoners Fund, 2009–10; Mem., Exec. Cttee, London Funders, 2011–. Chm., Governing Body, Bowes Primary Sch., 2000–05. Judge, Charity Awards, 2005–09. Fellow, British American Proj., 1996. FRSA 2003. Hon. DPhil LMU, 2017. *Publications:* contrib. British Jl of Psychology. *Recreations:* field hockey, swimming, history. *Address:* Trust for London, 4 Chiswell Street, EC1Y 4UP. *Clubs:* Southgate Adelaide Hockey (Vice Pres., 2002–; Captain, 2008–), Griffins Hockey.

**MEHTA, Prof. Goverdhan,** Padma Shri 2000; PhD; FRS 2005; FNA; National Research Professor, since 2009, and Lily Grantee and Jubilant Bhartia Chair, University of Hyderabad; *b* 1943. *Educ:* Univ. of Rajasthan (MSc); Univ. of Pune (PhD). Res. Associate, Michigan State and Ohio State Univs, 1967–69; Lectr, then Asst Prof., Indian Inst. of Technol., 1969–77; Prof. of Chemistry, 1977–98, Founder Dean, 1977–86, Vice-Chancellor, 1994–98, Univ. of Hyderabad; Prof. of Chemistry and Dir, 1998–2005, CSIR Bhatnagar Fellow, Dept of Organic Chemistry, 2005–10, Indian Inst. of Science. President: INSA, 1999–2001; ICSU, 2005–08. Chevalier, Légion d'Honneur (France), 2004; Cross, Order of Merit (Germany), 2016. *Address:* School of Chemistry, Central University, Hyderabad 500 046, India.

**MEHTA, Ved (Parkash),** FRSL; writer; *b* Lahore, 21 March 1934; 2nd *s* of late Dr Amolak Ram Mehta (former Dep. Director General of Health Services, Govt of India), and Shanti Devi Mehta (née Mehra); naturalized citizen of USA, 1975; *m* 1983, Linn Fenimore Cooper Cary, *d* of late William L. Cary and of Katherine Cary; two *d*. *Educ:* Arkansas Sch. for the Blind; Pomona Coll. (BA 1956); Balliol Coll., Oxford (Hazen Fellow, 1956–59; BA Hons Mod. Hist. Oxon, 1959; MA 1962; Hon. Fellow, 1999); Harvard Univ. (MA 1961). Phi Beta Kappa, 1955. Harvard Prize Fellow, 1959–60; Residential Fellow, Eliot House, Harvard Univ., 1959–61; Guggenheim Fellow, 1971–72, 1977–78; Ford Foundn Travel and Study Grantee, 1971–76, Public Policy Grantee, 1979–82; MacArthur Prize Fellow, 1982–87. Staff writer, The New Yorker, 1961–94. Yale University: Rosenkranz Chair in Writing, 1990–93; Lectr in History, 1990, 1991, 1992; Lectr in English, 1991–93; Residential Fellow, 1990–93, Fellow, 1993–, Berkeley Coll. Vis. Schol., Case Western Reserve Univ., 1974; Beatty Lectr, McGill Univ., 1979; Vis. Prof. of Literature, Bard Coll., 1985, 1986; Noble Foundn Vis. Prof. of Art and Cultural History, Sarah Lawrence Coll., 1988; Vis. Fellow (Literature), Balliol Coll., 1988–89; Vis. Prof. of English, NY Univ., 1989–90; Arnold Bernhard Vis. Prof. of English and History, Williams Coll., 1994; Randolph Distinguished Vis. Prof. of English and History, Vassar Coll., 1994–96; Sen. Fellow, Freedom Forum, Media Studies Center, 1996–97; Fellow, Center for Advanced Study in Behavioral Scis, 1997–98. Mem. Council on Foreign Relations, 1979–. Member: Usage Panel, Amer. Heritage Dictionary, 1982; Johnsonians, 2006. Fellow, NY Inst. for Humanities, 1988–92. FRSL 2009. Official delegate, Jaipur Literature Fest., 2014. Hon. DLit: Pomona, 1972; Bard, 1982; Williams 1986; Stirling, 1988; Bowdoin, 1995; Panjab Univ., Chandigarh, 2009. Assoc. of Indians in America Award, 1978; Silver Medal, Signet Soc., Harvard, 1983; Distinguished Service Award, Asian/Pacific Americans Liby Assoc., 1986; NYC Mayor's Liberty Medal, 1986; Centenary Barrows Award, Pomona Coll., 1987; Literary Lion Medal, 1990, Literary Lion Centennial Award, 1996, NY Public Liby; NY State Asian-American Heritage Month Award, 1991; Arkansas Traveler Award, Univ. of Arkansas, 2006. *Publications:* Face to Face, 1957 (Secondary Educn Annual Book Award, 1958; serial reading on BBC Light prog., 1958, dramatization on Home prog., 1959; reissued 1967, 1978); Walking the Indian Streets, 1960, rev. edn 1971; Fly and the Fly-Bottle, 1963, 2nd edn 1983 introd. Jasper Griffin; The New Theologian, 1966; Delinquent Chacha (fiction), 1967; Portrait of India, 1970, 2nd edn 1993; John Is Easy to Please, 1971; Mahatma Gandhi and His Apostles, 1977, reissued 1993; The New India, 1978; Photographs of Chachaji, 1980; A Family Affair: India under three Prime Ministers, 1982; Three Stories of the Raj (fiction), 1986; Rajiv Gandhi and Rama's Kingdom, 1995; A Ved Mehta Reader: the craft of the essay, 1998; Continents of Exile (autobiography): Daddyji, 1972; Mamaji, 1979; Vedi, 1982; The Ledge Between the Streams, 1984; Sound-Shadows of the New World, 1986; The Stolen Light, 1989; Up at Oxford, 1993; Remembering Mr Shawn's New Yorker: the invisible art of editing, 1998; All For Love, 2001; Dark Harbor, 2003; The Red Letters, 2004; Veritas, 2011; The Essential Ved Mehta, 2013; numerous translations, 1957–. Writer and commentator of TV documentary film Chachaji: My Poor Relation, PBS, 1978, BBC, 1980 (DuPont Columbia Award for Excellence in Broadcast Journalism, 1977–78). *Recreation:* listening to Indian and Western music. *Address:* 139 East 79th Street, New York, NY 10075, USA. *T:* (212) 7377487, *Fax:* (212) 4727220. *Clubs:* Century Association (NY) (Trustee, 1973–75; Mem. Wine Cttee, 2000–04); Tarratine (Dark Harbor, Maine).

**MEHTA, Zubin;** Music Director for life, Israel Philharmonic Orchestra, 1981–2019 (Musical Adviser, 1962–77; Music Director, 1977–81); Artistic Director, Maggio Musicale Fiorentino, 1986–2016, now Hon. Life Director; General Music Director, Bavarian State Opera, 1998–2006; *b* 29 April 1936; *s* of Mehli Mehta; *m* 1st, 1958, Carmen Lasky (marr. diss. 1964); one *s* one *d*; 2nd, 1969, Nancy Kovack. *Educ:* St Xavier's Coll., Bombay; Musikakademie, Vienna. First Concert, Vienna, 1958; first prize internat. comp., Liverpool, 1958; US debut, Philadelphia Orch., 1960; debut with Israel and Vienna Philharmonic Orchs, 1961; Music Director, Montreal Symphony Orch., 1961–67; European tour with this orch., 1962; guest conducting, major European Orchs, 1962; Music Director: Los Angeles Philharmonic Orch., 1962–78 (Hon. Conductor, 2006); New York Philharmonic, 1978–91. Opera debut, Montreal, Tosca, 1964; debut Metropolitan Opera, Aida, 1965; operas at Metropolitan incl.: Tosca, Turandot, Otello, Carmen, Mourning becomes Elektra (world première), Trovatore, etc. Toured regularly with Israel Philharmonic Orchs and occasionally with Vienna Phil. Orch.; regular guest conducting with Vienna Phil., Berlin Phil., Orch. de Paris. Hon. Doctorates: Colgate Univ.; Brooklyn Coll.; Westminster Coll.; Occidental Coll.; Sir George Williams Univ., Canada; Weizmann Inst. of Science, Israel; Tel-Aviv Univ. Holds numerous awards; Israel Wolf Foundn Prize, 1996; Praemium Imperiale, Japan Art Assoc., 2008. Padma Bhushan (India), 1967; Commendatore of Italy; Médaille d'Or Verneil, City of Paris, 1984; Presidential Medal of Distinction (Israel), 2012. *Publications:* The Score of My Life (memoir), 2008. *Address:* 27 Oakmont Drive, Los Angeles, CA 90049–1901, USA. *T:* (310) 4443111.

**MEIER, Maj.-Gen. Anthony Leslie,** CB 1995; OBE 1981; Director-General, Management and Support of Intelligence, Ministry of Defence, 1991–94; *b* 3 Sept. 1937; *s* of late Eric Leslie Francis Meier and Vera Madge Meier (née Terry); *m* 1973, Susanne Jennifer Manley; two *s* one *d*. *Educ:* Latymer Upper Sch.; RMA Sandhurst. Commissioned RASC, 1957, later RCT; regtl appts, Germany and on secondment to Brigade of Gurkhas, Far East, 1958–68; Staff Coll., 1969; MoD, 31 Sqn GTR, NDC, HQ BAOR, CO 8 Regt RCT, to 1981; Col GS Coord (COS), Staff Coll., 1981–84; NATO Defence Coll., Rome, 1984–85; HQ AFCENT, 1985–87; Dir of Intell. (Warsaw Pact), MoD, 1988–90. Dir, Macmillan Appeal for Brighton and Hove Hospice, 1994–96; non-exec. Dir, Eastbourne Hosps NHS Trust, 1994–2002. Adjudicator, Criminal Injuries Compensation Appeals Panel, 1997–2007. Chm., Bd of Govs, St Bede's Prep. Sch., Eastbourne, 1994–99; Dep. Chm., 1999–2008, Chm., 2008–18, Bd of Govs, St Bede's Sch., Sussex; Special Comr, Duke of York's Royal Mil. Sch., 1998–2008 (Chm., 2003–08). *Publications:* Notes on the Soviet Ground Forces, 1972; articles in Internat. Defense Review. *Recreation:* sport. *Address:* c/o National Westminster Bank, 96 Terminus Road, Eastbourne, E Sussex BN21 3LX.

**MEIER, His Honour David Benjamin;** a Circuit Judge, 1993–2003; Designated Care Judge for Buckinghamshire, 2001–03; *b* 8 Oct. 1938; *s* of Arnold Meier, PhD and Irma Meier; *m* 1964, Kathleen Lesly Wilton; one *d*. *Educ:* Bury Grammar Sch.; King's College London (LLB). Admitted Law Society, 1964; Solicitor. Metropolitan Stipendiary Magistrate, 1985–93; a Recorder, 1991–93. Pres., Mental Health Tribunals, 1988–2000; Chairman: Juvenile Court, 1988–93; Family Panel, 1991–93. Pres., N Middx Law Soc., 1984–85. *Recreations:* golf, playing trombone.

**MEIER, Richard Alan;** principal architect, Richard Meier & Partners Architects (formerly Richard Meier & Associates, New York), 1963–2018; *b* Newark, NJ, 12 Oct. 1934; *s* of Jerome Meier and Carolyn Meier (née Kaltenbacher); *m* 1978, Katherine Gormley (marr. diss. 1987); one *s* one *d*. *Educ:* Cornell Univ. (BAArch 1957). FAIA. Architect with: Frank Grad & Sons, NJ, 1957; Davis Brody & Wisniewski, NY, 1958–59; Skidmore, Owings & Merrill, 1959–60; Marcel Breuer & Associates, 1960–63. Adjunct Prof. of Architecture, Cooper Union, 1963–73; Visiting Professor: Yale Univ., 1975, 1977, 2008; Harvard Univ., 1977; UCLA, 1987, 1998. *Major works* include: Smith House, Darien, Conn, 1967, and houses in Harbor Springs, E Hampton, Malibu, Dallas, New York, Florida, Pittsburgh and Naples; Bronx Developmental Center, NY, 1977; Atheneum, New Harmony, 1979; High Mus. of Art, Atlanta, 1983; Mus. für Angewandte Kunst (formerly Kunsthandwerk), Frankfurt, 1984; Canal Plus HQ, Paris, 1992; City Hall and Central Liby, The Hague, 1995; Mus. of Contemp. Art, Barcelona, 1995; Getty Center, LA, 1997; 173/176 Perry St, NY, 2002; 66 Restaurant, NY, 2003; Center for Possibility Thinking, California, 2003; Jubilee Church, Rome, 2003; Burda Collection Mus., Baden-Baden, 2004; San Jose City Hall, 2005; 165 Charles St, NY, 2006; Ara Pacis Mus., Rome, 2006; Arp Museum, Rolandseck, Germany, 2007; Weill Hall, Ithaca, NY, 2008; On Prospect Park, NY, 2008; Saint-Denis, France, 2009; Italcementi i.Lab, Bergamo, 2012 (Greenbuilding Plus Award: Best New Building, 2010); OCT Shenzhen Clubhouse, Shenzhen, China, 2012; Seamarq Hotel, Gangneung, South Korea, 2016; Cittadella Bridge, Alessandria, Italy, 2017. *Exhibitions* include: XV Triennale, Milan, 1973; Mus. of Modern Art, NY, 1975, 1981; Princeton Univ., 1976; Cooper-Hewitt Mus., NY, 1976–77, 2009; Athens, 1982–83; Tokyo, 1988; Naples, 1991; Rome, 1993; Nagoya, 1996; Paris, 1999; London, 2007; Guggenheim, NY, 2010; Mumbai, 2010. 5 Architectural Record awards, 1964–77; 99 AIA Awards, 1968–2008; Pritzker Prize for Architecture, 1984; RIBA Gold Medal, 1988; 5 Progressive Architecture awards, 1979–95; AIA Gold Medal, 1997; Praemium Imperiale, Japan, 1997; Gold Medal for Architecture, AAAL, 2008; President's Medal, Architectural League of NY, 2009. Comdr, Ordre des Arts et Lettres (France), 1992 (Officier, 1984). *Publications:* On Architecture, 1982; Richard Meier, Architect, vol. 1 1984, vol. 2 1991, vol. 3 1999; vol. 4 2004; vol. 5 2009; Richard Meier Museums, 2006; Richard Meier Houses and Apartments, 2008; Richard Meier & Partners Complete Works: 1963–2008, 2008; contribs to professional jls. *Address:* c/o 475 Tenth Avenue, Floor 6, New York, NY 10018–1120, USA.

**MEIKLEJOHN, Dominic Francis,** OBE 2007; HM Diplomatic Service; Head, Overseas Business Network Initiative, Department for International Trade (formerly UK Trade and Investment), since 2015; *b* London, 14 Nov. 1967; *s* of David Meiklejohn and Eileen Meiklejohn; *m* 2008, Joanne Farrand; one *d*. *Educ:* Taunton Sch.; Merton Coll., Oxford (BA PPE). HM Customs and Excise; joined FCO, 1990; EC Dept, 1990–92; Hd, British Know-How Fund, British Embassy, Warsaw, 1993–96; OSCE Mission, Tirana, 1997; Hd, India Team, FCO, 1998–99; First Sec., Warsaw, 2000–03; Dep. Hd, Envmt Policy Dept, FCO, 2004; Deputy Consul-General: Basra, 2006–07; New York, 2008–12; High Comr to Solomon Is, Vanuatu and Nauru, 2012–15. *Recreations:* football, cricket, golf. *Address:* Department for International Trade, King Charles Street, SW1A 2AH.

**MEIN, Very Rev. James Adlington;** Dean of the Episcopal Church, Diocese of Edinburgh, 2001–04, now Dean Emeritus; Rector of Christ Church, Morningside, 1990–2004; *b* 29 Dec. 1938; *s* of James Helliwell Mein and Kathleen Elsie Mein (née Dawson); *m* 1966, Helen Shaw (née Forrester-Paton); one *s* one *d*. *Educ:* Nottingham Univ. (BA Hons Theol. 1960); Westcott House, Cambridge. Ordained deacon, 1963, priest, 1964; Curate, St Columba, Edinburgh, 1963–67; Chaplain to Bp of Edinburgh, 1965–67; Sec., Christian Service Cttee, Malawi, 1967–72; Rector, St Mary, Grangemouth, 1972–82, with Bo'ness, 1976–82; Team Priest, Livingston, 1982–90; Canon, St Mary's Cathedral, Edinburgh, 1990–2001. *Recreations:* walking, golf, reading, television. *Address:* Cardhu, Bridgend, Linlithgow EH49 6NH. *T:* (01506) 834317. *E:* jim@meins.plus.com.

**MEIRION-JONES, Prof. Gwyn Idris,** FSA 1981; author and consultant on historic buildings; Professor Emeritus, London Metropolitan University; *b* 24 Dec. 1933; *e s* of late Maelgwyn Meirion-Jones and Enid Roberts, Manchester; *m* 1961, Monica (*d* 2003), *e d* of late George and Marion Havard, Winchester. *Educ:* North Manchester Grammar School; King's College London (BSc, MPhil, PhD). National Service, RAF Mountain Rescue, 1954–56. Schoolmaster, 1959–68; Lectr in Geography, Kingston Coll. of Technology, 1968; Sir John Cass College, later City of London Polytechnic: Sen. Lectr i/c Geography,

1969; Principal Lectr i/c, 1970; Head of Geography, 1970–89; Personal Chair, 1983–89, then Prof. Emeritus; Hon. Research Fellow, 1989–. Leverhulme Research Fellow, 1985–87; Vis. Prof. of Archaeol., Univ. of Reading, 1995–2007. Dir, Soc. of Antiquaries, 2001–02. British Assoc. for the Advancement of Science: Sec., 1973–78, Recorder, 1978–83, Pres., 1992–93, Section H (Anthropology and Archaeology); Mem. Council, 1977–80; Mem. Gen. Cttee, 1977–83; Ancient Monuments Society: Mem. Council, 1974–79 and 1983–94; Hon. Sec., 1976–79; Vice-Pres., 1979–; Editor, 1985–94; Pres., Cambrian Archaeol Assoc., 2011–12. Member: Royal Commn on Historical Monuments of England, 1985–97; Adv. Cttee on Bldgs and Domestic Life, Welsh Folk Mus., 1991–95. Hon. Pres., Domestic Buildings Res. Gp (Surrey), 1991– (Pres., 1986–91). Editor, Medieval Village Res. Gp, 1978–86. Liveryman, Livery Co. of Wales (formerly Welsh Livery Guild), 2007–. Hon. Corresp. Mem., Soc. Jersiaise, 1980–90 and 1990–; Corresponding Member: Cie des Architectes en Chef des Monuments Historiques, 1989–; Soc. d'Histoire et d'Archéol. de Bretagne, 1997–. Exhibitions: vernacular architecture of Brittany, on tour 1982–89; Architecture vernaculaire en Bretagne (15e–20e siècles), Rennes and tour, 1984–89. *Publications:* La Maison traditionnelle (bibliog.), 1978; The Vernacular Architecture of Brittany, 1982; (with Michael Jones) Aimer les Châteaux de Bretagne, 1991 (trans. English and German); (with Michael Jones) Les Châteaux de Bretagne, 1992; (jtly) Manorial Domestic Buildings in England and Northern France, 1993; (jtly) La Ville de Cluny et ses Maisons XI$^e$–XV$^e$ siècles, 1997; (jtly) The Seigneurial Residence in Western Europe AD c 800–1600, 2002; (dir, ed and contrib.) La Demeure Seigneuriale dans l'Espace Plantagenêt, XIe–XVIe siècles: salles, chambres et tours, Rennes, 2012; papers in sci., archaeol and ethnol jls. *Recreations:* food, wine, music, walking, fly-fishing. *Address:* 11 Avondale Road, Fleet, Hants GU51 3BH. *T:* (01252) 614300. *E:* gwynmj@orange.fr. *Clubs:* Athenæum; Royal Scots (Edinburgh).

**MEISEL, Prof. John**, CC 1999 (OC 1989); PhD; FRSC; President, Royal Society of Canada, 1992–95; Sir Edward Peacock Professor of Political Science, Queen's University, Canada, 1983–94, now Emeritus; Co-Editor (formerly Editor), International Political Science Review, 1979–95; *b* 23 Oct. 1923; *s* of Fryda S. Meisel and Anne Meisel (*née* Heller); *m* 1949, Murie A. Kelly (decd). *Educ:* Pickering Coll.; Univ. of Toronto (BA, MA); LSE (PhD). FRSC 1974. Political scientist; Queen's University, Canada: Instructor to Prof., 1949–79; Hardy Prof. of Political Science, 1963–79. Vis. Prof., Yale, 1976–77; Commonwealth Dist. Vis. Prof., UK, 1978. Chm., Canadian Radio-TV and Telecommunications Commn, 1980–83. President: Canadian Pol Sci. Assoc., 1973–74; Social Sci. Fedn of Canada, 1975–76. Hon. LLD: Brock; Calgary; Carleton; Queen's; Guelph; Toronto; Regina; DU Ottawa; Hon. DLitt Waterloo; Hon. DSS Laval. Canada Medals: Confedn Centennial, 1967; 125th Anniv. Confedn, 1992; Silver Jubilee Medal, 1977. *Publications:* The Canadian General Election of 1957, 1962; Papers on the 1962 Election, 1964; Working Papers on Canadian Politics, 1972; (with Vincent Lemieux) Ethnic Relations in Canadian Voluntary Associations, 1972; Cleavages, Parties and Values in Canada, 1974; (with Jean Laponce) Debating the Constitution, 1994; A Life of Learning and Other Pleasures: John Meisel's tale, 2012; numerous articles in acad. jls. *Recreations:* visual and performing arts, hiking, bird watching, flower admiring, indoor gardening, printed word. *Address:* St Lawrence Place, Apt 615, 181 Ontario Street, Kingston, ON K7L 5M1, Canada. *E:* meiselj@queensu.ca.

**MEIXNER, Helen Ann Elizabeth, (Mrs Helen Thornton)**, CMG 2001; Regional Director, South-East Europe and Director, Romania, 1997–2001, British Council; *b* 26 May 1941; *d* of Henry Gerard and Valerie Meixner; *m* Jack Edward Clive Thornton, CB, OBE (d 1996). *Educ:* Sydney C of E Grammar Sch. for Girls, Darlinghurst; Univ. of Queensland (BA 1961); Sch. of Slavonic and East European Studies, UCL (MA 2004). Teacher, Abbotsleigh Girls' Sch., Wahroonga, 1962; Educn Asst, ABC, 1963–64; joined British Council, 1966; Recruitment Unit, Zagreb Office, Exchanges, Courses, Staff Recruitment, Dir-Gen.'s and Personnel Depts; Head, Design, Production and Publishing Dept, 1984–86; Dep. Dir, Personnel and Head, Personnel Dept, 1986–91; Dir of Libraries, Books and Information Div., 1991–94; Dep. Dir, Professional Services and Head, Consultancy Gp, 1994–96; Dir, Central Europe, 1996–97. Member: Council, Ranfurly Liby Service, 1991–94; Exec. Cttee, VSO, 1995–97; Council, Book Aid Internat., 2001–08; Bd Mem., Sir John Cass's Foundn, 2009–16 (Chm. Grants Cttee, 2016). Dir, Cornerhouse, Manchester, 1993–95. Trustee, Anglo-Romanian Educnl Trust, 2002–09. Governor: Langford Primary Sch., Fulham, 2002–12 (Chm., 2008–11); Sir John Cass's Foundn and Redcoat Secondary Sch., 2010–16; Anglia Ruskin Univ., 2013–16. JP Inner London, 1988–98. *Recreations:* music, reading, walking, travel. *Address:* 131 Dalling Road, W6 0ET. *T:* (020) 8748 7692.

**MELBOURNE, Archbishop of**, since 2006, and Primate of Australia, since 2014; **Most Rev. Philip Leslie Freier**, PhD; *b* 9 Feb. 1955; *m* 1976, Joy Launder; two *s. Educ:* Qld Inst. of Technol. (BAppSc 1975); Univ. of Qld (DipEd 1976); St John's Coll., Morpeth (Associate Dip. in Theol 1984); Melbourne Coll. of Divinity (BD 1984); Univ. of Newcastle (MEdSt 1984); James Cook Univ., Townsville (PhD 2000). Teacher, Qld Educn Dept, 1976–81. Ordained deacon, 1983, priest, 1984; Deacon in Charge, Ch of the Ascension, Kowanyama, 1983–84; Priest in Charge, 1984–88; Rector: St Oswald, Banyo, 1988–93; Christ Ch, Bundaberg, 1989–92; Bishop of Northern Territory, 1999–2006. Area Dean: Brisbane N, 1992–93; the Burnett, 1995–98; Examining Chaplain to Archbp of Brisbane, 1993–99. Member: Diocesan Council, Dio. Carpentaria, 1986–88; Gen. Synod, 1987–98 (Mem., Missionary and Ecumenical Commn, 1995–98); Provincial Synod, 1987–98 (Mem., Standing Cttee, 1988–); Diocesan Council, Dio. Brisbane, 1991–94. *Publications:* Thaw Pathn a Palal Nguwl, 1978; (with E. J. Freier) Kupmari, A Picture Book, 1978; Science Program for Aboriginal Community Schools, 1980; (jtly) Mathematical Program for Schools in Aboriginal and Torres Strait Islander Communities, 1983; articles in jls. *Address:* The Anglican Centre, 209 Flinders Lane, Melbourne, Vic 3000, Australia.

**MELBOURNE, Dean of;** *see* Loewe, Very Rev. A.

**MELDING, David Robert Michael**, CBE 2018; Member (C) South Wales Central, National Assembly for Wales, since 1999; *b* 28 Aug. 1962; *s* of late David Graham Melding and of Edwina Margaret Melding (*née* King). *Educ:* Dwr-y-Felin Comprehensive Sch., Neath; UC Cardiff (BScEcon); Coll. of William and Mary, Virginia (MA). Cons. Res. Dept, 1986–89; Dep. Dir, Welsh Centre for Internat. Affairs, 1989–96; Manager, Carers Nat. Assoc. in Wales, 1996–99. Dep. Presiding Officer, Nat. Assembly for Wales, 2011–16. OStJ 2016. *Publications:* Will Britain Survive Beyond 2020?, 2009; The Reformed Union: the UK as a federation, 2013. *Recreations:* swimming, reading, walking, sipping Monnet Cognac while lamenting Brexit. *Address:* National Assembly for Wales, Cardiff Bay, Cardiff CF99 1NA. *T:* 0300 200 7222. *E:* david.melding@assembly.wales.

**MELDRUM, Sir Graham**, Kt 2002; CBE 1994; QFSM 1989; FIFireE; Chairman, West Midlands Ambulance Service NHS Trust, since 2007; *b* 23 Oct. 1945; *s* of George Meldrum and Agnes (*née* Gordon); *m* 1964, Catherine Meier; one *s* one *d. Educ:* Inverurie Acad., Aberdeenshire. FIFireE 1995. Fireman to Station Officer, London Fire Bde, 1963–73; Instructor, in the rank of Asst Divl Officer, Fire Service Coll., 1973–74; Divl Officer III, Hants Fire Service, 1974–76; Tyne and Wear: Divl Officer II, 1976–79; Divl Officer I, 1979–80; Sen. Divl Officer, 1980–83; West Midlands: Asst Chief Officer, 1983–84; Dep. Chief Fire Officer, 1984–90; Chief Fire Officer, 1990–97; HM Chief Inspector of Fire Services, 1998–2007. Pres., Chief and Asst Chief Fire Officers' Assoc., 1994–95; Chairman: Fire Services Nat. Benevolent Fund, 1994; CACFOA (Research) Ltd, 1988–; CACFOA (Services) Ltd, 1988–. DUniv 1997. OStJ 1998. *Publications:* papers on fire engrg in jls. *Recreations:* computers, motor-cycling, railways, industrial archaeology, community work. *Address:* St Francis Chapel, Bridge Street, Kineton, Warwicks CV35 0JR.

**MELDRUM, Hamish Robin Peter**, FRCGP; FRCPE; Chairman of Council, British Medical Association, 2007–12 (Member, 2000–12); Deputy Chairman, BMJ Publishing Group, since 2014; *b* Edinburgh, 14 April 1948; *s* of James S. Meldrum and Mary I. Meldrum (*née* MacGregor); *m* 1974, Mhairi M. K.; two *s* one *d. Educ:* Stirling High Sch.; Edinburgh Univ. (BSc Med. Sci. 1969; MB ChB 1972). DRCOG 1977; FRCGP 2001; FRCPE. Hse physician, Edinburgh Royal Infirmary, 1972–73; Med. SHO, then Registrar, Torbay Hosp., Devon, 1973–76; GP trainee, Harrogate, 1976–78; Principal in Gen. Practice, Bridlington, E Yorks, 1978–2011. Mem., GPs Cttee, BMA, 1991–2012 (Chm., 2004–07). *Publications:* contrib. med. jls incl. BMJ. *Recreations:* sport (watching most, playing tennis, running, golf and keep fit), hill walking, music (varied), wine appreciation, good company and discussion. *Address:* Ardbeg, 4 Kinnear Road, Edinburgh EH3 5PE. *T:* (0131) 552 4191.

**MELDRUM, James;** Keeper, Registers of Scotland, 2003–09; *b* 9 Aug. 1952; *s* of late George and Marion Meldrum. *Educ:* Lenzie Academy; Glasgow Univ. (MA Hons). Joined Scottish Office 1973; Principal, 1979–86; Dep. Dir, Scottish Courts Admin, 1986–91; Head, Investment Assistance Div., Scottish Office Industry Dept, 1991–94; Registrar General for Scotland, 1994–99; Dir, Admin. Services, Scottish Exec., 1999–2002; Dir of Business Mgt and Area Business Manager, Glasgow, Crown Office and Procurator Fiscal Service, 2002–03. FRSA 2008. *Recreations:* reading, music, gardening. *Address:* 5 Roman Road, Kirkintilloch, Glasgow G66 1EE. *T:* (0141) 776 7071.

**MELDRUM, Keith Cameron**, CB 1995; Chief Veterinary Officer, Ministry of Agriculture, Fisheries and Food, 1988–97; *b* 19 April 1937; *s* of Dr Walter James Meldrum and Mrs Eileen Lydia Meldrum; *m* 1st, 1962, Rosemary Ann (*née* Crawford) (marr. diss. 1980); two *s* one *d*; 2nd, 1982, Vivien Mary (*née* Fisher). *Educ:* Uppingham; Edinburgh Univ. Qualified as veterinary surgeon, 1961; general practice, Scunthorpe, 1961–63; joined MAFF, Oxford, 1963; Divl Vet. Officer, Tolworth, 1972, Leamington Spa, 1975; Dep. Regional Vet. Officer, Nottingham, 1978; Regional Vet. Officer, Tolworth, 1980; Asst Chief Vet. Officer, Tolworth, 1983; Dir of Vet. Field Service, 1986. UK Deleg., Office Internat. des Epizooties, 1988–97. Mem. Council, RCVS, 1988–97. Gov., Inst. of Animal Health, 1988–97. Trustee, Animal Health Trust, 2002–07. Hon. FRSPH (Hon. FRSH 2000). Bledisloe Vet. Award, RASE, 1995; Equine Veterinary Award, BEVA, 2012. *Recreation:* outdoor activities. *Address:* The Orchard, Swaynes Lane, Merrow, Guildford, Surrey GU1 2XX. *Club:* Farmers.

**MELGUND, Viscount; Gilbert Francis Elliot-Murray-Kynynmound;** *b* 15 Aug. 1984; *s* and *heir* of Earl of Minto, *qv. Educ:* Marlborough Coll.

**MELHUISH, Prof. Edward Charles**, OBE 2016; PhD; Professor of Human Development (formerly Research Professor), and Academic Research Leader, Department of Education, University of Oxford, since 2012; *b* 3 April 1950; *s* of Robert Hector Melhuish and Elsie Beatrice Melhuish; one *s* four *d. Educ:* Univ. of Bristol (BSc); Univ. of London (PhD 1980). Researcher, Univ. of London, 1981–86; Lectr, UCNW, Bangor, 1987–94; Prof., Cardiff Univ., 1994–2000; Prof. of Human Develt (formerly Psychology), Birkbeck, 2001–, and Dir, Inst. for the Study of Children, Families and Social Issues, 2010–12, Univ. of London. Vis. Prof., Univ. of Wollongong, 2014–18. Consultant: OECD, WHO, EU. Exec. Dir, Nat. Evaluation of Sure Start, 2001–12. Trustee: WAVE Trust, 2013–18; Foundn Years Trust, 2013–; Advr, Save the Children Fund, 2014–. FBPsS 2000; FAcSS 2012; FAPS 2018. *Publications:* Day Care for Young Children: international perspectives, 1991; Early Childhood Care and Education, 2006; The National Evaluation of Sure Start: does area-based early intervention work?, 2007; Early Childhood Matters, 2010; (jtly) Effective Teachers in Primary Schools: key research on pedagogy and children's learning, 2014, 2019; (jtly) Assessing Quality in Early Childhood Education and Care, 2015. *Recreations:* reading, music, film, sailing, Rugby, travel, five grandchildren.

**MELHUISH, Sir (Michael) Ramsay**, KBE 1993; CMG 1982; HM Diplomatic Service, retired; *b* 17 March 1932; *s* of late Henry Whitfield Melhuish and Jeanette Ramsay Pender Melhuish; *m* 1961, Stella Phillips; two *s* two *d. Educ:* Royal Masonic Sch., Bushey; St John's Coll., Oxford (BA). FO, 1955; MECAS, 1956; Third Sec., Bahrain, 1957; FO, 1959; Second Sec., Singapore, 1961; First Sec. (Commercial) and Consul, Prague, 1963; First Sec. and Head of Chancery, Bahrain, 1966; DSAO (later FCO), 1968; First Sec., Washington, 1970; Counsellor, Amman, 1973; Head of N America Dept, FCO, 1976; Counsellor (Commercial), Warsaw, 1979–82; Ambassador, Kuwait, 1982–85; High Comr, Zimbabwe, 1985–89; Ambassador, Thailand, 1989–92. Head, EC Monitor Mission, Zagreb, July–Dec. 1992. *Recreations:* tennis, golf. *Address:* Longwood Lodge, Leatherhead Road, Oxshott, Surrey KT22 0ET.

**MELIA, Christine Hilary;** Director, Italy, British Council, 2009–14; *b* Wirral, Cheshire, 24 March 1954; *d* of Peter Melia and Alice Shone; partner, Prof. Barrie Walsham Bycroft, *qv. Educ:* W Kirby Grammar Sch., Wirral; Nottingham Univ. (BA Jt Hons Geog. and Archaeol.). Joined British Council, 1979; London, 1979–85; Romania, 1985–88; London, 1988–90; Brazil, 1990–94; Caribbean, 1995; London, 1996–99; Spain, 1999–2004; Oxford, 2004–08. *Recreations:* travel, archaeology, food, wine, beekeeping, relaxing anywhere near the sea. *Address:* 4 Merrivale Square, Oxford OX2 6QX. *E:* christine.melia1@gmail.com. *Club:* Lansdowne.

**MELIA, Dr Terence Patrick**, CBE 1993; Chairman, Learning and Skills Development Agency, 2000–03; *b* 17 Dec. 1934; *s* of John and Kathleen Melia (*née* Traynor); *m* 1976, Madeline (*née* Carney); one *d. Educ:* Sir John Deane's Grammar Sch., Northwich; Leeds Univ. (PhD); J. B. Cohen Prize, 1961). CChem, FRSC. Technical Officer, ICI, 1961–64; Lectr, then Sen. Lectr, Salford Univ., 1964–70; Principal, North Lindsey Coll. of Technology, 1970–74; HM Inspector of Schools, 1974–92: Regional Staff Inspector, 1982–84; Chief Inspector, Further and Higher Educn, 1985–86; Chief Inspector, Higher Educn, 1985–91; Sen. Chief Inspector, HM Inspectorate of Schs, 1991–92; Chief Inspector, FEFC, 1993–96. Carried out, on behalf of Further Education Funding Council, subseq., Learning and Skills Council: official enquiries into: Bilston Coll., Melton Mowbray Coll., 1999; Sheffield Coll., 2000; Manchester Coll. of Arts and Technol., W Herts Coll., 2004; Strategic Area Reviews of Post-16 Educn, 2001–04. Vis. Prof., Leeds Metropolitan Univ., 1993–96. Chairman: Further Educn Staff Develt Forum, 1996–99; Further Educn Develt Agency, 1997–2000; Further Educn NTO, 1999–2001; Educn Policy Cttee, RSA Exams, 1996–99. Gov., Hills Road Sixth Form Coll., Cambridge, 2001–04. Hon. DSc Salford, 1998; Hon. DEd: Bradford, 2005; Plymouth, 2006. Plastics and Polymer Gp Prize, Soc. of Chemical Industry, 1964. *Publications:* Masers and Lasers, 1967; reports on official enquiries and strategic area reviews; papers on thermodynamics of polymerisation, thermal properties of polymers, effects of ionizing radiation, chemical thermodynamics, nucleation kinetics, thermal properties of transition metal compounds and gas kinetics. *Recreations:* golf, gardening.

**MELLANBY, Carolyn Ann Fitzherbert; Her Honour Judge Mellanby;** a Circuit Judge, since 2018; *b* Shrewsbury, 30 April 1952; *d* of late Christopher Fitzherbert Jones and Eileen Eunice Jones (*née* Newport); *m* 1973, Alexander Robert Mellanby; one *s* one *d*. *Educ:* Hinchley Wood Co. Secondary Sch., Surrey; King's Coll., London (LLB 1973; AKC). Higher Rights of Audience (Criminal), 1994. Called to the Bar, Gray's Inn, 1975; Dep. Chief Clerk, Camberwell Green Magistrates' Court, 1977; Magistrates' Court Clerk, Hertford, 1977–78; Magistrate, Seychelles, 1982–85; Crown Prosecutor, Devon, 1986–89; admitted as solicitor, 1990; Partner, Ford Simey Solicitors, Exeter, 1990–2002; Solicitor and Hd, Family Dept, Christian Khan Solicitors, London, 2003–04; Consultant, Steel and Shamash Solicitors, London, 2004–09; Dep. Stipendiary Magistrate, later Dep. Dist Judge, 2000–09; Dist Judge (Magistrates' Courts), 2009–18. Mem. and Examr, Children Panel, Law Soc., 1992–2009. *Recreations:* family, gardening, travel. *Address:* Watford County Court, 3rd Floor, Cassiobury House, 11–19 Station Road, Watford, Herts WD17 1EZ.

**MELLARS, Sir Paul Anthony,** Kt 2010; ScD; FBA 1990; Fellow, Corpus Christi College, Cambridge, since 1981 (President, 1992–2000); Professor of Prehistory and Human Evolution, Cambridge University, 1997–2007, now Emeritus; *b* 29 Oct. 1939; *s* of Herbert and Elaine Mellars; *m* 1969, Anny Chanut. *Educ:* Woodhouse Grammar Sch., Sheffield; Fitzwilliam Coll., Cambridge (Exhibnr; BA 1st Cl. Hons Archaeol. and Anthropol. 1962; MA 1965; PhD 1967; ScD 1988). FSA 1977. Sir James Knott Res. Fellow, Univ. of Newcastle upon Tyne, 1968–70; University of Sheffield: Lectr in Prehistory and Archaeol., 1970–75; Sen. Lectr, 1975–80; Reader, 1980–81; University of Cambridge: Lect, 1981–91; Reader in Archaeology, 1991–97. British Academy: Res. Reader, 1989–91; Reckitt Archaeol. Lectr, 1991; Vis. Prof., SUNY (Binghamton), 1974; Vis. Fellow, ANU, 1981; Danish Res. Council Vis. Lectr, Copenhagen and Aarhus Univs, 1985. President: Hunter Archaeol. Soc., 1975–80; Prehistoric Soc., 1998–2000 (Vice Pres., 1992–95); Chm., Archaeol. Sci. Cttee, Council for British Archaeol., 1980–87; Mem. Council, British Acad., 1994–97 (Chm., Archaeol. Sect., 1995). MAE 1999. Hon. Mem., Italian Inst. of Prehistoric & Proto-historic Sciences, 1997. *Publications:* (ed) The Early Postglacial Settlement of Northern Europe, 1976; Excavations of Oronsay, 1987; (ed) Research Priorities of Archaeological Science, 1987; (ed) The Human Revolution, 1989; (ed) The Emergence of Modern Humans, 1990; The Middle Palaeolithic: adaptation, behaviour & variability, 1991; (ed) The Origin of Modern Humans and the Impact of Science-based Dating, 1992; The Neanderthal Legacy, 1996; (ed) Modelling the Early Human Mind, 1996; Star Carr in Context, 1998; articles in archaeol. jls. *Recreations:* music, foreign travel. *Address:* Long Gable, Elsworth, Cambs CB23 4HX. *T:* (01954) 267275; Department of Archaeology, University of Cambridge, Downing Street, Cambridge CB2 3DZ. *T:* (01223) 333520.

**MELLENEY, Clare Patricia;** *see* Montgomery, C. P.

**MELLING, Dr Jack;** consultant and contractor, US Government Accountability Office, Washington, since 1998; *b* 8 Feb. 1940; *s* of John Melling and Mary (*née* Marsden); *m* 1967, Susan Ewart. *Educ:* Rivington and Blackrod Grammar Sch.; Manchester Univ. (BSc, MSc); Bath Univ. (PhD). FRPharmS 1977; FRSB (FIBiol 1979); FRCPath 1996; FRSC 2012. Res. Asst, Bath Univ., 1965–68; Lectr, Heriot-Watt Univ., 1968–69; SSO, then PSO, MoD, 1969–79; Dir, Vaccine Res. and Prodn Lab., PHLS, 1979–87; Dep. Dir, 1987–93, Dir, 1993–96, Centre for Applied Microbiology and Res., Porton Down; Dir, Biologicals Develt Center, Salk Inst. for Biol Studies, USA, 1996–2001; Dir (part-time), Karl Landsteiner Inst., Vienna, 2001–03; Sen. Project Manager (part-time), Battelle Meml Inst., Columbus, Ohio, 2001–05; Sen. Sci. Fellow, Center for Arms Control and Non-Proliferation, Washington, 2004–09. Visiting Professor: Rutgers Univ., 1979–84; Aston Univ., 1981–96; Westminster Univ., 1995–2005; Gastprofessor, Inst. for Social and Preventive Medicine, Univ. of Zürich, 1999–2006. Society of Chemical Industry: Mem. Council, 1983–86, 1998–2001; Sec., 1975–81, Chm., 1981–83, Biotechnology Gp; Chm. Pubns Cttee, 1999–2004; Hon. Treas., 2004–09; Chm., Bd of Trustees, 2009–15. Member: British Nat. Cttee for Microbiol., 1978–84; MRC Cttee on Develt of Vaccines and Immunol Products, 1979–96; Cttee on Safety of Medicines Biologicals Subcttee, 1982–99; Ind. Register Defence Scientific Adv. Council, 1994–98; Res. Adv. Cttee on Gulf War Veterans' Illnesses, US Dept of Veterans' Affairs, 2002–13. Sec., British Co-ordinating Cttee for Biotechnol., 1981–85; Sen. Scientific Advr, Internat. AIDS Vaccine Initiative, 1999–2006. Editor, Jl of Chem. Technol. and Biotechnol., 1985–2017, now Emeritus Editor; Mem. Editl Bd, Vaccine, 1983–. Lampitt Medal, SCI, 1993. *Publications:* Continuous Culture Applications and New Fields, 1977; Adhesion of Micro-organisms to Surfaces, 1979; The Microbial Cell Surface and Adhesion, 1981; Biosafety in Industrial Technology, 1994; papers in scientific jls. *Recreation:* walking. *Address:* US Government Accountability Office, 441 G Street NW, Washington, DC20548, USA. *E:* mellingj@gao.gov. *Clubs:* Athenæum, Royal Society of Medicine.

**MELLITT, Prof. Brian,** FREng; Chairman, Building Research Establishment, 1998–2010; *b* 29 May 1940; *s* of John and Nellie Mellitt; *m* 1961, Lyn Waring; one *s* one *d*. *Educ:* Loughborough Univ.; Imperial College, London Univ. (BTechEng, DIC). FIET, FIMechE, FIRSE, FREng (FEng 1990). Student apprentice, 1956, Junior Engineer, 1962, R&D Engineer, 1964, English Electric Co.; Lectr and Sen. Lectr, Huddersfield Polytechnic, 1966–67; Research Dept, British Rlys Bd, 1968–70; University of Birmingham: Lectr, 1971; Sen. Lectr, 1979; Prof., 1982; Head of Dept of Electronic and Electrical Engrg, 1986; Dean, Faculty of Engrg, 1987–88; Hon. Prof. of Electronic Engrg, 1989; Dir Engrg, London Underground Ltd, 1989–95; Dir, Metro Power, 1990–95; Dir of Engrg and Prodn, Railtrack PLC, 1995–99; Engrg Advr, Railtrack (UK), 1999–2000. Consultant Engineer, railway related organisations, 1972–. Chairman: BMCONSULT Ltd, 1999–; Metro-Consulting Ltd, 2000–02; SIRA Ltd, 2001–06; Director: Railway College Ltd, then Catalis Rail Trng, 1998–2000; Jarvis plc, 2002–09; Rail Advr, NM Rothschild, 1999–2003. President: Welding Inst., 2000–01; IEE, 2001–02 (Vice Pres., 1996–99; Dep. Pres., 1999–2001). Editor, IEE Procs (B), 1978–2013. Hon. Fellow, Assoc. of Project Managers, 1998. Hon. DTech Loughborough, 1991; Hon. DSc Huddersfield, 1998; Hon. DEng Birmingham, 1999. Leonardo da Vinci Award, Italian Assoc. for Industrial Design, 1989. *Publications:* contribs on electric railway topics to learned jls. *Recreation:* bridge. *Address:* The Priory, 36 Church Street, Stilton, Cambs PE7 3RF. *T:* (01733) 240573. *Club:* Athenæum.

**MELLO, Prof. Craig C.,** PhD; Distinguished Professor, Program in Molecular Medicine, University of Massachusetts; Investigator, Howard Hughes Medical Institute, since 2000; *b* New Haven, Conn, 18 Oct. 1960; *s* of James and Sally Mello; *m* Margaret Hunter (marr. diss.); one *d*; *m* 1998, Edit Kiss; one *d*, and one step *s* one step *d*. *Educ:* Fairfax High Sch., Va; Brown Univ. (BS); Univ. of Colorado at Boulder; Harvard Univ. (PhD). Postdoctoral Fellow, Fred Hutchinson Cancer Res. Center, Seattle, 1990–94; joined Univ. of Massachusetts Medical Sch., 1994, Blais Univ. Chair in Molecular Medicine, 2003. (Jtly) Nobel Prize in Medicine, 2006. *Address:* Program in Molecular Medicine, University of Massachusetts Medical School, 373 Plantation Street, Worcester, MA 01605, USA.

**MELLON, Sir James,** KCMG 1988 (CMG 1979); HM Diplomatic Service, retired; Chairman, Charlemagne Capital (UK) Ltd (formerly Regent Europe Asset Management), 2000–17; *b* 25 Jan. 1929; *s* of James Mellon and Margaret Traynor; *m* 1st, 1956, Frances Murray (*d* 1976); one *s* three *d*; 2nd, 1979, Mrs Philippa Shuttleworth (*née* Hartley); three step *s* one step *d*. *Educ:* Glasgow Univ. (MA). Dept of Agriculture for Scotland, 1953–60; Agricultural Attaché, Copenhagen and The Hague, 1960–63; FO, 1963–64; Head of Chancery, Dakar, 1964–66; UK Delegn to European Communities, 1967–72; Counsellor, 1970; Hd of Sci. and Technol. Dept, FCO, 1973–75; Commercial Counsellor, East Berlin, 1975–76; Head of Trade Relations and Export Dept, FCO, 1976–78; High Comr in Ghana and Ambassador to Togo, 1978–83; Ambassador to Denmark, 1983–86; Dir-Gen. for Trade and Investment, USA, and Consul-Gen., New York, 1986–88. Chairman: Scottish Homes, 1989–96; Thamesmead Town, 1993–96; Regent Pacific Corp. Finance, 1999–2001; Dir, Webis Hldgs plc, 2012–. Res. Associate, Sainsbury Res. Unit, UEA, 2014–15. Fellow, Royal Anthropological Inst., 2017. *Publications:* A Danish Gospel, 1986; Og Gamle Danmark, 1992; (ed and trans.) Per Federspiel, 2005; The Great African Bangle Culture, 2018. *Address:* 6 Leydon Close, SE16 5PF. *Club:* New (Edinburgh).

**MELLOR, Prof. David Hugh;** Pro-Vice-Chancellor, University of Cambridge, 2000–01; Professor of Philosophy, University of Cambridge, 1986–99; Fellow, Darwin College, Cambridge, 1971–2005 (Vice-Master, 1983–87); *b* 10 July 1938; *s* of Sydney David Mellor and Ethel Naomi Mellor (*née* Hughes). *Educ:* Manchester Grammar School; Pembroke College, Cambridge (BA Nat. Scis and Chem. Eng. 1960; MA; PhD 1968; ScD 1990; MEng 1992); Univ. of Minnesota (Harkness Fellowship; MSc Chem. Eng. 1962). Technical Officer, ICI Central Instruments Lab., 1962–63; Cambridge University: Research Student in Philosophy, Pembroke Coll., 1963–68; Fellow, Pembroke Coll., 1964–68; Univ. Asst Lectr in Philosophy, 1965–70; Univ. Lectr in Philosophy, 1970–83; Univ. Reader in Metaphysics, 1983–85. Vis. Fellow in Philosophy, ANU, 1975; Radcliffe Trust Fellow in Philosophy, 1978–80. Hon. Prof. of Philosophy, Univ. of Keele, 1989–92. President: British Soc. for the Philos. of Science, 1985–87; Aristotelian Soc., 1992–93. Chm., Analysis Trust, 2000–08. Editor: British Journal for the Philosophy of Science, 1968–70; Cambridge Studies in Philosophy, 1978–82. FBA 1983–2008. Hon. FAHA 2003. Hon. PhD Lund, 1997. *Publications:* The Matter of Chance, 1971; Real Time, 1981; Matters of Metaphysics, 1991; The Facts of Causation, 1995; Real Time II, 1998; Probability: a philosophical introduction, 2005; Mind, Meaning, and Reality, 2012; articles in Mind, Analysis, Philosophy of Science, Philosophy, Philosophical Review, Ratio, Isis, British Jl for Philosophy of Science, Jl of Philosophy. *Recreation:* theatre. *Address:* 25 Orchard Street, Cambridge CB1 1JS.

**MELLOR, Rt Hon. David John;** PC 1990; QC 1987; broadcaster, journalist and international business adviser; *b* 12 March 1949; *s* of late Mr and Mrs Douglas H. Mellor; *m* 1974, Judith Mary Hall (marr. diss. 1995); two *s*. *Educ:* Swanage Grammar Sch.; Christ's Coll., Cambridge (BA Hons 1970). FZS 1981. Called to the Bar, Inner Temple, 1972; in practice thereafter. Chm., Cambridge Univ. Conservative Assoc., 1970; contested West Bromwich E, Oct. 1974; MP (C) Putney, 1979–97; contested (C) same seat, 1997. PPS to Leader of Commons and Chancellor of the Duchy of Lancaster, 1981; Parly Under-Sec. of State, Dept of Energy, 1981–83, Home Office, 1983–86; Minister of State: Home Office, 1986–87; Foreign and Commonwealth Office, 1987–88; Dept of Health, 1988–89; Home Office, 1989–90; Privy Council Office (Minister for the Arts), 1990; Chief Sec. to the Treasury, 1990–92; Sec. of State for Nat. Heritage, 1992. Sec., Cons. Parly Legal Cttee, 1979–81; Vice-Chm., Greater London Cons. Members Cttee, 1980–81. Chairman: Sports Aid Foundn, 1993–97; Football Task Force, 1997–99. Special Trustee, Westminster Hosp., 1980–87; Trustee, Fund for the Replacement of Animals in Medical Experiments, 2004– (Co-Patron, 2005–). Mem. Council, NYO, 1981–; Mem. Bd, ENO, 1993–95; Pres., Bournemouth SO, 2000–09. Presenter: 6.06, 1993–99, Mellor, 1999–2001, BBC Radio 5; Vintage Years (series), BBC Radio 3, 1993–2000; The Midnight Hour, BBC2, 1997–99; New CD Show and David Mellor on Classic FM; David Mellor and Ken Livingstone Show, LBC, 2010–16. Music Critic, Mail on Sunday, 2000–; columnist: The Guardian, 1992–94; The People, 1998–2003; sports columnist, Evening Standard, 1997–2009. BBC Radio Personality of the Year, Variety Club of GB, 1995. Hon. Associate, BVA, 1986. *Recreations:* classical music, reading, football.

**MELLOR, Derrick,** CBE 1984; HM Diplomatic Service, retired; re-employed at Foreign and Commonwealth Office, since 1984; Occasional Lecturer, School of Oriental and African Studies, since 1987; *b* 11 Jan. 1926; *s* of William Mellor and Alice (*née* Hurst); *m* 1954, Kathleen (*née* Hodgson); two *s* one *d*. Served Army, 1945–49. Board of Trade, 1950–57; Trade Commission Service, 1958–64: served Kuala Lumpur and Sydney; HM Diplomatic Service, 1964–: served Copenhagen, Caracas, Asunción (Ambassador, 1979–84) and London; Trng Consultant, FCO, 1987–. Project Dir for S Amer., GAP Activity Projects (GAP) Ltd, 1993–. Treasurer: Lord De La Warr Almshouses, 1995–2005; Wealden Cons. Party, 2000–. *Recreations:* tennis, golf, ski-ing. *Address:* Summerford Farmhouse, Withyham, E Sussex TN7 4DA. *T:* (01892) 770707. *Club:* Army and Navy.

**MELLOR, Fiona;** *see* MacCarthy, F.

**MELLOR, Dame Julie (Thérèse),** DBE 2006; Chair: Demos, since 2018; Federation for Industry Sector Skills and Standards, since 2018; *b* 29 Jan. 1957; *d* of Gp Capt. Edward Vernon Mellor and late Patricia Ann Mellor; *m* 1990, Nick Reed; one *s* one *d*. *Educ:* Winchester Co. High Sch. for Girls; Brasenose Coll., Oxford (BA Hons Exptl Psychol.; Hon. Fellow, 2003). Eleanor Emerson Fellow in Labour Educn, Cornell Univ., NY and teacher, Inst. for Educn Res. on Women and Work, 1979–81; Employee Relns Advr, Shell UK, 1981–83; Econ. Develt Officer, London Borough of Islington, 1983–84; Sen. Employment Policy Advr and Dep. Hd, Contract Compliance, Equal Opportunities Unit, ILEA, 1984–89; Equal Opportunities Manager, TSB Gp, 1989–91; Corporate Human Resources Dir, British Gas, 1992–96; owner and principal consultant, Julie Mellor Consultants, 1996–99; Chair, EOC, 1999–2005; Partner, PricewaterhouseCoopers, 2005–11; Parly and Health Service Ombudsman, 2012–17. Mem., CRE, 1995–2002. Member: Minister's Nat. Adv. Council on Employment of Disabled People, 1993–95; Bd, Employers' Forum on Disability, 2001–09; Bd, NCC, 2001–07; Bd, DIUS, later BIS, 2008–11. Trustee: Green Alliance, 2007–10; NESTA, 2012–17; Clore Social Leadership, 2017–18; Involve, 2017–. Chair: Fatherhood Inst. (formerly Fathers Direct), 2005–08; Young Foundn, 2016–. FCGI 2003. Hon. DPhil Anglia, 2003. *Recreations:* theatre, travel, food, family.

**MELLOR, Very Rev. (Kenneth) Paul;** Dean of Guernsey, Rector of St Peter Port and Priest-in-Charge of Sark, 2003–14; *b* 11 Aug. 1949; *s* of William Lewis and Frances Emma, (Peggy), Mellor; *m* 1972, Lindsey Helen Vinall; three *s*. *Educ:* Ashfield Sch., Kirkby-in-Ashfield; Southampton Univ. (BA Theol. 1971); Leeds Univ. (MA Theol. 1972); Cuddesdon Coll. Ordained deacon, 1973, priest, 1974; Curate: St Mary the Virgin, Cottingham, 1973–76; All Saints, Ascot, 1976–80; Vicar: St Mary Magdalen, Tilehurst, 1980–85; St Lalluwy, Menheniot, 1985–94; Canon Treasurer and Canon Residentiary, Truro Cathedral, 1994–2003 (Hon. Canon, 1990–94). RD, W Wivelshire, 1990–94; Chm., Truro Diocesan Bd for Mission and Unity, 1990–95. Member: Gen. Synod, 1994–;

Cathedral Fabric Commn for England, 1995–2000. Hon. Canon, Winchester Cathedral, 2003–14, now Canon Emeritus. *Recreations:* walking, reading (esp. modern fiction), theatre, travel. *Address:* The Master's House, St Nicholas Hospital, St Nicholas Road, Salisbury, Wilts SP1 2SW. *E:* kpaulmellor@cwgsy.net.

**MELLOR, Ronald William**, CBE 1984; FREng, FIMechE; Secretary, Institution of Mechanical Engineers, 1987–93; *b* 8 Dec. 1930; *s* of William and Helen Edna Mellor; *m* 1st, 1956, Jean Sephton (*d* 2010); one *s* one *d*; 2nd, 2012, Alison Rice. *Educ:* Highgate School; King's College London (BSc Eng). FIMechE 1980; FREng (FEng 1983). Commnd RA, 1950. Ford Motor Co.: Manager Cortina Product Planning, 1964; Manager Truck Product Planning, 1965; Chief Research Engineer, 1969; Chief Engine Engineer, 1970; Chief Body Engineer, Ford Werke AG, W Germany, 1974; Vice Pres. Car Engineering, Ford of Europe Inc., 1975–87; Dir, Ford Motor Co. Ltd, 1983–87. Mem., Bd of Govs, Anglia Polytechnic Univ., 1993–2002 (Hon. Fellow, 2004). Liveryman, Co. of Carmen, 1990–. Thomas Hawksley Lectr, IMechE, 1983. *Recreations:* yachting, dinghy sailing.

**MELLOWS, Heather Jean, (Mrs A. Johnson),** OBE 2011; FRCOG; Consultant Obstetrician and Gynaecologist, Doncaster and Bassetlaw Hospitals NHS Foundation Trust, 1988–2011; Professional Adviser, Obstetrics and Gynaecology, Department of Health (on secondment), 2008–11 (Part-time Adviser, 2006–08 and 2011–12); *b* 13 March 1951; *d* of late A. Paul Mellows, DFC, MA, LLB and of Jean Mellows (*née* Wells); *m* 1982, Anthony Johnson (*d* 2012); two step *s*. *Educ:* Royal Free Hosp. Sch. of Medicine (MB BS 1974). FRCOG 1993; FFFP 2007. Regl Assessor in Obstetrics, Confidential Enquiry into Maternal Deaths, 1993–2008; Mem. Panel, Sec. of State's Inquiry into Quality and Practice within the NHS, arising from the actions of Rodney Ledward, 1999–2000 (reported, 2000). Co-Chm., Maternity Module, Children's Nat. Service Framework, 2002–04. Royal College of Obstetricians and Gynaecologists: Mem. Council, 1986–92, 1994–96 and 1999–2001; Chm., Hosp. Recognition Cttee, 1994–96; Jun. Vice Pres., 2001–04. *Address:* 8 Bedford Close, W4 2UE.

**MELLY, Kama Louise;** QC 2016; a Recorder, since 2018; *b* London, 15 Feb. 1973; *d* of Manu Melly and Maureen Coffey; *m* 2002, Michael Collins; one *s* one *d*. *Educ:* Leeds Univ. (LLB); Inns of Court Sch. of Law. Called to the Bar, Middle Temple, 1997, Bencher, 2018. Mem., Bar Council; Chm., Bar Conf., 2015. *Recreations:* walking, cooking, reading. *Address:* Park Square Barristers, 6 Park Square East, Leeds LS1 2LW. *T:* (0113) 245 9763. *E:* mellyqc@psqb.co.uk.

**MELLY, Rear Adm. Richard Graham, (Dick);** Clerk, Goldsmiths' Company, 2005–16; *b* 31 Dec. 1953; *s* of Peter Emerson Melly and Shirley Julia Melly (*née* Higham); *m* 1987, Lynne Griffiths; two *d*. *Educ:* Winchester House Sch.; Stowe Sch.; Univ. of Manchester (BSc (Mech. Engrg) 1974); RNEC (MSc (Marine Engrg) 1980). CEng 1987–2007. Her Majesty's Ships: Devonshire, 1976–78; Hermes, 1980–82; Nottingham, 1988–90; staffing duties, MoD, 1993–95; Superintendent Ships, Portsmouth, 1995–98; rcds 2000; Dir, Naval Manning, 2001–03; COS to Second Sea Lord and C-in-C, Naval Home Comd, 2003–05. Trustee, Falkland Is Meml Chapel Trust, 2003–. Member: British Hallmarking Council, 2005–16; Council, Goldsmiths Coll., 2005–16. Trustee: Goldsmiths' Centre, 2007–16; Tall Ships Youth Trust, 2017–. Pres., Hermes Assoc., 2012–. Gov., Wickham C of E Primary Sch., 2016–. *Recreations:* travel, computing, DIY. *Address:* 120 Rowner Road, Gosport, Hants PO13 9RG.

**MELMOTH, Sir Graham (John),** Kt 2002; Chief Executive, Co-operative Group Ltd (formerly Co-operative Wholesale Society), 1996–2002; *b* 18 March 1938; *s* of Harry James Melmoth and Marjorie Doris Melmoth (*née* Isitt); *m* 1967, Jennifer Mary Banning; two *s*. *Educ:* City of London Sch. FCIS 1972. National Service, 1957–59 (Lieut), RA. Asst Sec., Chartered Inst. of Patent Agents, 1961–65; Sec., BOC-AIRCO, 1965–69; Dep. Sec., Fisons, 1969–72; Sec., Letraset, 1972–75; CWS, then Co-operative Group Ltd: Sec., 1975–95; Director: Co-operative Bank plc, 1992–2003; Co-operative Press Ltd, 1994–98; Co-operative Insurance Soc. Ltd, 1996–2003. Chm., Ringway Developments plc, 1995–2002 (Dir, 1988–2002); Dir, Unity Trust Bank plc, 1992–98. Chairman: Manchester TEC Ltd, 1999–2001 (Dir, 1997–2001); Manchester Enterprises Ltd, 2001–03. Chm., NCVO, 2004–10; Pres., Gtr Manchester Centre for Vol. Orgns, 2011–13. Mem. Council, NACRO, 1998–2004. Trustee: New Lanark Conservation Trust, 1987–2004; Nat. Mus. of Labour History, 1995–2001; Charities Aid Foundn, 2004–10; CVS Cheshire East, 2013–16. Pres., Internat. Co-operative Alliance, Geneva, 1995–97. CCMI (CIMgt 1997). FIGD 1996; FRSA 1996. *Recreations:* opera, theatre, Co-operative history. *Address:* Greengarth, Dockray, Cumbria CA11 0LS. *Club:* Reform.

**MELROSE, Dianna Patricia;** HM Diplomatic Service, retired; High Commissioner to Tanzania, 2013–16; Associate, Ambassador Partnership, since 2017; *b* Bulawayo, S Rhodesia, 24 June 1952; *d* of late Gp Captain James F. C. Melrose and Audrey Melrose (*née* Macqueen); *m* 1987, Chris Dammers (marr. diss.); two *s*. *Educ:* St Catherine's Sch., Bramley, Surrey; King's Coll. London (BA Hons Spanish and French); Inst. of Latin American Studies, Univ. of London (MA). Latin America Section, Noram Investment Services, 1973–74; C. E. Heath & Co., 1975–78; Specialist Tours Officer (Latin America), British Council, 1978–79; Oxfam: Policy Advr, 1980–84; Hd, Public Affairs Unit, 1984–92; Public Policy Dir, Oxfam UK, 1992–93; Policy Dir, Oxfam GB, 1993–99; Dep. Hd, 1999–2000, Hd, 2000–03, Policy Planning Staff, FCO; Hd, Extractive Industries Unit, 2003, Internat. Trade Dept, 2003–06, DFID; Hd, Enlargement and SE Europe Gp, FCO, 2006–08; Ambassador to Cuba, 2008–12. Trustee: ODI, 2016–; Save the Children UK, 2017–. *Publications:* Bitter Pills: medicines and the third world poor, 1982; Nicaragua: the threat of a good example, 1985. *Recreations:* travel, reading, swimming, Pilates and Zumba. *Address:* 26 Victoria Road, Oxford OX2 7QD. *E:* diannamelrose.DM@gmail.com.

**MELROSE, Sarah Jane;** *see* Tynan, S. J.

**MELTON, Christopher;** QC 2001; a Recorder, since 2005; *b* 15 Nov. 1958; *s* of Derek Edward and Margaret Melton; *m* 1990, Karen Jacqueline Holder; two *s* two *d*. *Educ:* Manchester Grammar Sch.; Bristol Univ. Called to the Bar, Gray's Inn, 1982; in practice, specialising in medical law. *Recreations:* running, golf, ski-ing, Francophile. *Address:* (chambers) 12 Byrom Street, Manchester M3 4PP. *Clubs:* Bowdon Lawn Tennis; Dunham Forest Golf.

**MELVILL JONES, Prof. Geoffrey,** FRS 1979; FRSC 1979; FCASI; FRAeS; Emeritus Professor, McGill University, since 1992; Adjunct Professor, since 1992, Research Professor, since 2001, University of Calgary; *b* 14 Jan. 1923; *s* of Sir Bennett Melvill Jones, CBE, AFC, FRS and Dorothy Laxton Jotham; *m* 1953, Jenny Marigold Burnaby; two *s* two *d*. *Educ:* King's Choir Sch.; Dauntsey's Sch.; Cambridge Univ. (BA, MA, MB, BCh). Appointments in UK, 1950–61: House Surgeon, Middlesex Hosp., 1950; Sen. Ho. Surg., Otolaryngology, Addenbrooke's Hosp., Cambridge, 1950–51; Scientific Flying Personnel MO, RAF, 1951; Scientific MO, RAF Inst. of Aviation Medicine, Farnborough, Hants, 1951–55; Scientific Officer (external staff), Medical Research Council of Gt Britain, 1955–61; McGill University: Dir, Aviation, later Aerospace Med. Res. Unit, 1961–88; Associate Prof., 1961–68; Full Prof., 1968–91; Hosmer Res. Prof. of Physiol., 1978–91. Vis. Prof., Collège de France, 1979. Fellow, Aerospace Medical Assoc., 1969; FCASI 1965; FRAeS 1981. Skylab Achievement Award, 1974; first recipient, Dohlman Medal for research in the field of orientation and postural control, 1986; Robert Bárány Jubilee Gold Medal for most significant research on vestibular function during past 5 years, Bárány Soc., 1988; Ashton Graybiel Lectureship Award, US Navy, 1989; Stewart Meml Lectureship Award, RAeS, 1989; Buchanan-Barbour Award, RAeS, 1990; McLaughlan Medal, RSCan, 1991. *Publications:* Mammalian Vestibular Physiology, 1979 (NY); Adaptive Mechanisms in Gaze Control, 1985; 159 research papers in physiological jls, and book chapters. *Recreations:* outdoor activities, music, drawing and painting, gliding. *Address:* Department of Clinical Neurosciences, Faculty of Medicine, University of Calgary, 3330 Hospital Drive NW, Calgary, AB T2N 4N1, Canada. *T:* (403) 220 8764.

**MELVILLE;** *see* Leslie Melville, family name of Earl of Leven and Melville.

**MELVILLE,** 10th Viscount *cr* 1802; **Robert Henry Kirkpatrick Dundas;** Baron Duneira 1802; *b* 23 April 1984; *er s* of 9th Viscount Melville and of Fiona Margaret (*née* Stilgoe); *S* father, 2011; *m* 2016, Lucinda Lowe; one *s*. *Educ:* Marlborough. *Heir:* *s* Hon. Max David Henry Dundas, *b* 2018.

**MELVILLE, Anthony Edwin;** Headmaster, The Perse School, Cambridge, 1969–87; *b* 28 April 1929; *yr s* of Sir Leslie Galfreid Melville, KBE; *m* 1964, Pauline Marianne Surtees Simpson, *d* of Major A. F. Simpson, Indian Army; two *d*. *Educ:* Sydney Church of England Grammar Sch.; Univ. of Sydney (BA); King's Coll., Cambridge (MA). Sydney Univ. Medal in English, 1950; Pt II History Tripos, 1st cl. with dist., 1952; Lightfoot Schol. in Eccles. History, 1954. Asst Master, Haileybury Coll., 1953. *Recreations:* reading, gardening, music. *Address:* 4 Field Way, Cambridge CB1 8RW. *Club:* East India.

**MELVILLE, Sir David,** Kt 2007; CBE 2001; PhD; CPhys, FInstP; Vice-Chancellor, University of Kent, 2001–07; Chairman, Pearson Education Ltd, since 2012 (Board Member, since 2011); *b* 4 April 1944; *s* of late Frederick George Melville and Mary Melville; *m* (marr. diss.); one *s* two *d*; *m* 2012, Hilary Anne Edridge. *Educ:* Clitheroe Royal Grammar Sch.; Sheffield Univ. (BSc 1st Cl. Hons 1965; PhD 1969); Columbia Univ. CPhys, FInstP 1978. Southampton University: Lectr in Physics, 1968–78; Sen. Lectr, 1978–84; Lancashire Polytechnic: Prof. of Physics and Head, Sch. of Physics and Astronomy, 1985–86; Asst Dir, 1986–89; Vice-Rector, 1989–91; Dir, Middlesex Polytechnic, 1991–92; Vice-Chancellor, Middlesex Univ., 1992–96; Chief Exec., FEFC, 1996–2001. ICI Res. Fellow, 1968; Visiting Professor: Univ. of Parma, Italy, 1974–80; Oporto Univ., Portugal, 1983; Univ. of Warwick, 1997–2003; Visiting Scientist: ICI Corporate Lab., Runcorn, 1975; Consiglio Nazionale delle Ricerche, Italy, 1976–80; Thames Gateway: Member: Further and Higher Educn Advrs Gp, 2002–10 (Co-Chm., 2008–10); Strategic Partnership, DCLG, 2006–10; Strategic Exec., 2009–10; Skills Envoy, 2008–11; Skills Commn, 2010–13; Higher Educn Commn, 2012–. Mem. Bd, British Non-Ferrous Metals Ltd, 1987–92. Vice-Chm., CVCP, 1995–96. Member: Council, BNF Metals Technol. Centre, 1986–92; SERC Materials Commn, 1988–92; SERC Condensed Matter Sub-Cttee, 1986–88; SERC Physics Cttee, 1988–92; SERC Metals and Magnetic Materials Cttee, 1988–92; Council for Industry and Higher Educn, 1994–96, 2001–07; Council, Inst. of Employment Studies, 1998–2001; Jt DfEE/DCMS Educn and Libraries Task Gp, 1999–2000; Bd, Higher Educn Stats Agency, 2002–07 (Chm., 2003–07); Bd, The Place, 2002–08; Kent Ambassadors, 2002–09; Bd, Higher Educn Prospects, 2002–07; DfES 14–19 Curriculum and Qualifications Adv. Cttee, 2003–04; DfES Foundn Degree Task Force, 2003–04; Kent Strategic Partnership, 2003–07; SE England Regl Assembly, 2003–06; SE England Sci., Engrg and Technol. Adv. Council, 2003–06; Bd, Lifelong Learning UK, 2004–10 (Chm., 2006–10); QCDA (formerly QCA) Quals and Skills Adv. Gp, 2004–10; DfES Rev. of Further Educn Colls, 2005–06; Bd, Medway Renaissance Partnership, 2005–07; Bd, Edexcel, 2005–11; Bd, ifs Sch. of Finance (formerly Inst. of Financial Services), 2005–11; DIUS Higher Educn Project Bd, 2006–08; BIS (formerly DIUS) Sci., Technol., Engrg and Math. High Level Strategy Gp, 2007–10; Adv. Bd, Black Leadership Initiative, 2007–10; Bd, Network for Black Professionals, 2010–16; Bd, Policy Connect, 2018–. Chairman: SERC Magnetism and Magnetic Materials Initiative, 1989–91; UK and Republic of Ireland Chapter, Magnetics Soc., IEEE, 1988–93; Internat. Congress on Magnetism, Edinburgh, 1991; Health and Safety Cttee, Univs and Colleges Employers Assoc., 2003–07; Univs Race Equality Consultation Project, 2003–05; Univ. Vocational Awards Council, 2003–08; Higher Educn SE, 2003–06; Kent and Medway LSC, 2006–08; Cttee of Inquiry into Changing Learner Experience, 2008–09; Bd, Kent, Surrey and Sussex NHS Postgrad. Deanery, 2011–12; Bd, Health Educn Kent, Surrey and Sussex, 2012–13; Vice-Chm., Kent Public Service Bd, 2004–07. Member, Board: K Coll. (formerly W Kent Coll.), 2008–12; London S Bank Univ., 2009–12; Manchester Metropolitan Univ., 2011–17; Policy Connect, 2018–. Hon. Pres., Co. of Middx Trust, 1992–; Trustee: Learning from Experience Trust, 2001–09; Faversham Soc., 2018–; Vice-Chm., Trustees, Marlowe and Folkestone Academies, 2005–09; Patron: 157 Gp of FE Colls, 2007–17; Comprehensive Future, 2008–; N Kent Thames Gateway Young Chamber, 2009–; Faversham Fest., 2010–13; Faversham Creek Trust, 2012–; Chm., Faversham and Oare Heritage Harbour; Vice-Patron, Disabled Sailors Assoc., 2010–. DUniv: Middlesex, 1997; Derby, 2000; Hon. DSc: Sheffield, 1997; Southampton, 2001; Manchester Metropolitan, 2018; Hon. DCL Kent 2008. *Publications:* articles on magnetism, magnetic materials and biophysics in scientific and engrg jls; articles on educn and skills in nat. press. *Recreations:* sailing, golf.

**MELVILLE, (Richard) David;** QC 2002; **His Honour Judge Melville;** a Circuit Judge, since 2015; *b* 22 April 1953; *s* of late Col Robert Melville and Joan Emerton Melville (*née* Hawkins); *m* 1981, Catharine Mary Wingate; one *s* one *d*. *Educ:* Wellington Coll.; Pembroke Coll., Cambridge (BA 1974, MA 1978). Called to the Bar, Inner Temple, 1975, Bencher, 2007; Recorder, 2007–15. *Recreations:* sailing, painting, piano. *Address:* Portsmouth Combined Court Centre, Winston Churchill Avenue, Portsmouth PO1 2EB. *Clubs:* Garrick; Bar Yacht; Royal Corinthian Yacht; Itchenor Sailing; West Wittering Sailing.

**MELVILLE-ROSS, (Irene) Ruth, (Lady Melville-Ross);** *see* Spellman, (Irene) Ruth.

**MELVILLE-ROSS, Sir Timothy David, (Sir Tim),** Kt 2018; CBE 2005; Chairman, Homerton University Hospital NHS Foundation Trust, 2013–19; *b* 3 Oct. 1944; *s* of late Antony Stuart Melville-Ross and Anne Barclay Fane; *m* 1967, Camilla Mary Harlackenden (marr. diss. 2013); two *s* one *d*; *m* 2014, (Irene) Ruth Spellman, *qv*. *Educ:* Uppingham School; Portsmouth College of Technology (Dip Business Studies). British Petroleum, 1963–73; Rowe, Swann & Co., stockbrokers, 1973–74; joined Nationwide Building Soc., 1974: Dir and Chief Gen. Man., 1985–87; Dir and Chief Exec., 1987–94; Dir Gen., Inst. of Dirs, 1994–99; Chm., Investors in People UK, 1999–2006. Dep. Chm., Monument Oil and Gas plc, 1997–99 (Dir, 1992–99); Chairman: NewsCast Ltd, 2000–04; Bank Insinger de Beaufort NV, 2000–05; DTZ Hldgs plc, 2000–11; Manganese Bronze plc, 2003–12 (Dir, 2000–12); Royal London Mutual Insce Ltd, 2005–13 (Dir, 1999–2013; Dep. Chm., 2002–05); Bovis Homes Gp plc, 2005–08 (Dir, 1998–2008); HEFCE, 2008–18; Salad Finance Ltd, 2018–; Dir, HEP-UK Ltd, 2018–. Member Council: Industrial Soc., 1986–95;

**MENARY, Andrew Gwyn;** QC 2003; **His Honour Judge Menary;** a Circuit Judge, since 2013; a Senior Circuit Judge, since 2019; Resident Judge, Liverpool Crown Court, since 2019; *b* 29 March 1959; *m* 1st (marr. diss); one *s* one *d*; 2nd, 2010, Josephine Ann; two step *s*. *Educ:* BA Hons Law. Called to the Bar, Inner Temple, 1982; in practice as barrister, Liverpool, 1982–2013; a Recorder, 2002–13. Hon. Recorder of Liverpool, 2019–. *Recreations:* walking in the Lake District, supporting Manchester United. *Address:* Queen Elizabeth II Law Courts, Derby Square, Liverpool L2 1XA.

**MENCHÚ, Rigoberta;** human rights activist; Goodwill Ambassador, UNESCO, since 1996; *b* 9 Jan. 1959; *d* of late Vicente Menchú, Mayan resistance leader and founder, Cttee of Peasant Unity (CUC), Guatemala, and Juana Menchú; *m* 1995, Angel Canil. Works for indigenous peoples' rights; founded Rigoberta Menchú Tum Foundn, Guatemala City; Member: CUC; United Representation of Guatemalan Opposition; Five Hundred Years of Resistance Campaign; UN Working Group on Indigenous Populations; UN Internat. Indian Treaty Council. Pres., Indigenous Initiative for Peace, UN, 1999. Contested (Frento Amplio) Presidential elections, Guatemala, 2007 and 2011. Nobel Peace Prize, 1992. *Publications:* (with Elisabeth Burgos-Debray) I, Rigoberta Menchú, 1983 (trans. English 1984; in 12 other langs); (with Gianni Minà y Dante Liano) Rigoberta: grandchild of the Mayas, 1998 (trans. Italian and English).

**MENDELSOHN,** family name of **Baron Mendelsohn**.

**MENDELSOHN, Baron** *cr* 2013 (Life Peer), of Finchley in the London Borough of Barnet; **Jonathan Neil, (Jon), Mendelsohn;** Partner, Oakvale Capital LLP, since 2011; *b* London, 1966; *s* of Jeffrey and Evelyn Mendelsohn; *m* 1994, Nicola Clyne (see N. Mendelsohn); three *s* one *d*. *Educ:* Leeds Univ. (BA). Asst to Leader of the Opposition, 1995–97; Labour Party: Dir, Gen. Election Resources, 2007–10; Asst Treas., 2009–10. House of Lords: an Opposition Whip, H of L, 2014–15; Shadow spokesman on Business, 2015–18, on Internat. Trade, 2016–18, on Sci., Res. and Innovation, 2016–18. *Address:* House of Lords, SW1A 0PW. *T:* (020) 7219 3199.

**MENDELSOHN, Nicola, (Lady Mendelsohn),** CBE 2015; Vice-President of Europe, Middle East and Africa, Facebook, since 2013; *b* Manchester, 29 Aug. 1971; *d* of Barry Clyne and Celia Clyne; *m* 1994, Jonathan Mendelsohn (see Baron Mendelsohn); three *s* one *d*. *Educ:* Manchester High Sch. for Girls; Univ. of Leeds (BA Hons Eng. and Theatre Studies 1992). Account Manager, 1992–98, Business Develt Dir, 1998–2004, Bartle Bogle Hegarty; Dep. Chm., Grey London, 2004–08; Exec. Chm., Karmarama, 2008–13. Non-exec. Dir, Diageo, 2014–. Dir, Fragrance Foundn, 2001–11. Mem. Bd, Cosmetic Exec. Women, 2003–11; Chm., Corporate Bd, Women's Aid, 2007–13; Trustee, White Ribbon Alliance, 2011–13; Co-Chm., Creative Industries Council, 2012–18. Dir, Baileys Women's Prize for Fiction (formerly Orange Prize for Fiction, then Women's Prize for Fiction), 2012–18. Pres., Inst. of Practitioners in Advertising, 2011–13. Mem., Marketing Soc. Founder, Follicular Lymphoma Foundn, 2019–. *Recreations:* theatre, cinema, family, travel, charity work, feminism. *E:* nicola@redcapital.eu. *Clubs:* 30, Women in Advertising and Communications, London (Pres., 2008–09); Marketing Group of Great Britain.

**MENDELSOHN, Robert Victor,** JD; private investor and advisor to international businesses, since 2003; Chairman, Navigators Group, Inc., since 2013 (Director, since 2010); *b* NYC, 1946; *m* 1968, Patricia Fielding; one *s* one *d*. *Educ:* Georgetown Univ. (AB 1968); Harvard Univ. (JD 1971). Called to the Bar, NY, 1971; Attorney, Willkie Farr & Gallagher, NYC, 1971–74; Pres. and Dir, W. R. Berkley Corp., Greenwich, Conn, 1974–93; Chief Exec., 1994–97, Chm., 1997–2002, Royal & Sun Alliance USA, Inc., Charlotte, NC; Gp Chief Exec. and Dir, Royal & Sun Alliance Insce Gp plc, 1997–2002. Director: Amer. Insce Assoc., 1994–2003 (Chm., 1999–2000); Internat. Insce Soc., 1999–2005; Inspirica, Inc., 2011–. Comr. Auth Council, Insce Co. Execs, 1998–2000. Mem., UK-China Forum, 1999. Mem., Bd of Regents, Georgetown Univ., Washington, 1999–2005; Dir, Georgetown Univ. Library, 2006–; Mem. Adv. Bd, Harvard Prog. on Corp. Governance, 2006–12. *Recreations:* golf, walking, ski-ing, sailing.

**MENDELSON, Charlotte Jane,** FRSL; novelist, since 2001; *b* London, 1 Nov. 1972; *d* of Prof. Maurice Harvey Mendelson, *qv*; *m*; one *s* one *d*. *Educ:* Oxford High Sch.; New Coll., Oxford (BA Ancient and Modern Hist.). Editor: Jonathan Cape, 1996–97; Headline Rev., 1998–2014. Vis. Prof. of Creative Writing, Royal Holloway, Univ. of London, 2015–; Gardening Correspondent, New Yorker, 2017–. FRSL 2018. *Publications:* Love in Idleness, 2001; Daughters of Jerusalem, 2003 (John Llewellyn Rhys Prize, Booktrust, 2003; K. Blundell Trust Award, 2003; Somerset Maugham Award, Soc. of Authors, 2004); When We Were Bad, 2007; Almost English, 2013; Rhapsody in Green, 2016. *Recreations:* eating, buying books, gardening, reading in the bath. *Address:* c/o Rogers, Coleridge & White, 20 Powis Mews, W11 1JN. *W:* www.charlottemendelson.com.

**MENDELSON, Prof. Maurice Harvey;** QC 1992; DPhil; barrister and arbitrator; Professor of International Law, University of London at University College London, 1987–2001, now Emeritus; *b* 27 Aug. 1943; *s* of William Maizel Mendelson and Anne (née Aaronson); *m* 1968, Katharine Julia Olga Kertesz; two *d*. *Educ:* St Marylebone Grammar Sch.; New Coll., Oxford (BA 1st Cl. Hons Jurisprudence 1964; MA; DPhil 1971). Called to the Bar, Lincoln's Inn, 1965 (Bencher, 2000); Internat. Law Fund School., 1966; Leverhulme European Res. Schol., 1966–67; Lectr in Laws, KCL, 1968–74; Kennedy Law Schol., Lincoln's Inn, 1970–73; Official Fellow and Tutor in Law, St John's Coll., Oxford, and Univ. Lectr in Law, Oxford, 1975–86. Fulbright Vis. Schol., Harvard Law Sch., 1977; Visiting Professor: Univ. of N Carolina, 1982; Univ. of Pennsylvania, 1986; Univ. of Paris II, 1993; Univ. of NSW, 1999; Univ. of Paris X, 2002–03. Mem., Bd of Editors, British Yearbook of Internat. Law, 1995–. Mem., Amer. Law Inst., 2000. FRGS 1995. Officier, Ordre de la Valeur (Cameroon), 2003. *Publications:* articles in internat. law jls, etc; reports to Internat. Law Assoc. *Recreations:* the arts, painting, swimming, tennis (Real and lawn). *Address:* Blackstone Chambers, Blackstone House, Temple, EC4Y 9BW. *T:* (020) 7583 1770. *E:* clerks@blackstonechambers.com. *Club:* Athenæum.
See also C. J. Mendelson.

**MENDES, Alison Louise;** see Balsom, A. L.

**MENDES, Samuel Alexander,** CBE 2000; Co-Founder, and Director, Neal Street Productions, since 2003; *b* 1 Aug. 1965; *s* of Valerie Hélène Mendes (née Barnett) and James Peter Mendes; *m* 2003, Kate Elizabeth Winslet, *qv* (marr. diss. 2010); one *s*; *m* 2017, Alison Louise Balsom, *qv*; one *s*. *Educ:* Magdalen Coll. Sch., Oxford; Peterhouse, Cambridge (BA English, 1st Cl. Hons). Asst Dir, Chichester Festival, 1987–88, Artistic Director, Minerva Studio Theatre, 1989: productions included: Summerfolk, 1989; Love's Labour's Lost, 1989; Artistic Dir, Donmar Warehouse Th., 1992–2002; productions at *Donmar Warehouse* include: Assassins, 1992; Translations, 1993; Cabaret, 1993, NY (Tony Award for Best Revival of Musical), 1998, 2014; Glengarry Glen Ross, 1994; The Glass Menagerie (Olivier Award), 1995; Company (Olivier Award), 1995; Habeas Corpus, 1996; The Fix, 1997; The Front Page, 1997; The Blue Room, 1998, NY, 1999; To the Green Fields and Beyond, 2000; Twelfth Night, 2002, NY, 2003; Uncle Vanya, 2002, NY, 2003; productions as freelance director: *Royal Shakespeare Co.:* Troilus and Cressida, 1990; The Alchemist, 1991; Richard III, 1992; The Tempest, 1993; *Royal National Theatre:* The Sea, 1991; The Rise and Fall of Little Voice, 1992; The Birthday Party, 1994; Othello, 1997; King Lear, 2014; The Lehman Trilogy, 2018, transf. Piccadilly Th., 2019; The Cherry Orchard, Aldwych, 1989; London Assurance, Haymarket, 1989; Kean, Old Vic, 1990; The Plough and the Stars, Young Vic, 1991; Oliver!, Palladium, 1994; Gypsy, NY, 2003; The Vertical Hour, NY, 2006; The Winter's Tale, The Cherry Orchard, Old Vic, 2009; The Tempest, As You Like It, Old Vic, 2010; Richard III, Old Vic, 2011; Charlie and the Chocolate Factory, Th. Royal, 2013; The Ferryman, Royal Court Th., 2017 (Best Dir, Evening Standard Th. Awards, 2017, Olivier Awards, 2018, Tony Awards, 2019). *Films:* American Beauty, 1999 (Academy Award for Best Dir, 2000); Road to Perdition, 2002; Jarhead, 2006; Revolutionary Road, Away We Go, 2009; Skyfall, 2012 (Empire Award for Best Dir); Spectre, 2015; television, The Hollow Crown, 2012. Numerous other awards.

**MENDONÇA, Nicola;** Global President, Accenture Interactive Operations, since 2018; *b* UK, 3 Dec. 1969; *d* of Dennis and Lorna Mendonça. *Educ:* Univ. of Wales Coll., Cardiff (BA Hons English and Spanish); Harvard Business Sch.; Stanford Univ. Grad. Sch. of Business. Media Manager, CIA Media Network UK, 1992–95; Gp Media Dir, Leo Burnett, 1995–98; Strategic Mktg Dir, Capital Radio, 1998–2002; Mktg and New Business Dir, OMD, EMEA, 2002–05; Business Develt Dir, Omnicom Media Gp EMEA, 2005–07; Pres., OMD, EMEA, 2007–17. Mem. Bd, Internet Advertising Bureau Europe, 2015–18. *Recreations:* travel, tennis. *E:* nikki.mendonca@accenture.com.

**MENDOZA, June Yvonne,** AO 1989; OBE 2004; RP; ROI; artist; *d* of John Morton and Dot (née Mendoza), musicians; *m* 1960, Keith Ashley Victor Mackrell, *qv*; one *s* three *d*. *Educ:* Lauriston Girls' Sch., Melbourne; St Martin's Sch. of Art. Member: RP 1970; ROI 1968. Portraits for govt, regts, industry and commerce, academia, medicine, theatre, sport (e.g. Chris Evert for Wimbledon Mus.), and in public and private collections internationally. These include: Queen Elizabeth II; Queen Elizabeth the Queen Mother; Prince and Princess of Wales; Margaret Thatcher; John Major; Prime Minister of Australia, Sir John Gorton; Prime Minister of Fiji, Ratu Sir Kamisese Mara; Prime Minister of Singapore, Goh Chok Tong; former Prime Minister of Singapore, Lee Kuan Yew; Pres. of Iceland, Vigdis Finnbogadottir; Pres. of Philippines, Corazón Aquino; Donald Coggan, Robert Runcie, and George Carey, severally, while Archbishop of Canterbury; large group paintings include: The House of Commons in Session, 1986; House of Representatives, for new Parliament building in Canberra; private series of musicians include: Sir Yehudi Menuhin; Sir Georg Solti; Dame Joan Sutherland; Sir Colin Davis; Sir Charles Mackerras; Sir Michael Tippett. Lectures internationally; appearances on art programmes, TV and radio. Hon. Freeman, City of London; Hon. Mem., Barbers' Co. Hon. Mem., Soc. of Women Artists, 1986. Hon. DLitt: Bath, 1986; Loughborough, 1994; DUniv Open, 2003. *Address:* 34 Inner Park Road, SW19 6DD.

**MENDOZA, Neil Francis Jeremy;** Provost, Oriel College, Oxford, since 2018; *b* London, 2 Nov. 1959; *s* of Martin Mendoza and Dianne Mendoza; *m* 1993, Amelia Wallace; one *s* one *d*. *Educ:* Haberdashers' Aske's Sch.; Oriel Coll., Oxford (BA Geog. 1981; MA). Banking Exec., Morgan Guaranty Trust Co. of New York, 1981–83; Dir, Albion Films, 1983–87; Co-Founder and Chief Exec., Forward Ltd, 1987–2001; Director: Hammer Films, 1998–2002; Cross Asset Mgt, 1998–2005; Golden Square Ltd, 2005–; Pencil Agency, 2011–; MeiraGTx Ltd, 2015–; Chm., Victoria Private Investment Office, 2010–18. Non-exec. Bd Mem., DCMS, 2016–. Member: Adv. Council and Steering Cttee, New Europe, 1999–2002; Steering Gp, No Campaign, 2000–02. Govt Reviewer, Mendoza Rev. of Mus in England, 2016–18; Panel Mem., Govt Rev. into English Churches and Cathedrals, DCMS, 2016–. Comr, Historic England, 2016–. Chairman: Landmark Trust, 2012–; Prince's Foundn for Children and the Arts, 2013–17; Illuminated River Foundn, 2018–; Trustee: Forward Arts Foundn, 1994–2013; Shakespeare Schs Fest., 2010–15; Vice Chm., Soho Th., 2007–18. Judge, Olivier Th. Awards, 2010–11. *Recreations:* Shakespeare, bridge, running. *Address:* 50 Albemarle Street, W1S 4BD. *T:* (020) 7493 4361. *E:* mendoza.neil@gmail.com. *Clubs:* Academy, Portland, Army and Navy, Oxford and Cambridge.

**MENDUS, Prof. Susan Lesley,** CBE 2013; FBA 2004; FLSW; Professor of Political Philosophy, University of York, 1996–2012, now Morrell Professor Emerita; *b* 25 Aug. 1951; *d* of John and Beryl Coker; *m* 1977, Andrew Mendus. *Educ:* UC of Wales, Aberystwyth (BA); Lady Margaret Hall, Oxford (BPhil). University of York: Lectr in Philos., 1975–90; Sen. Lectr in Political Philos., 1990–95; Dir, Morrell Studies in Toleration Prog., 1995–2000. FLSW 2010. *Publications:* Toleration and the Limits of Liberalism, 1989; Impartiality in Moral and Political Philosophy, 2002; Politics and Morality, 2009. *Recreations:* theatre, swimming, birdwatching. *Address:* 117 Osbaldwick Lane, York YO10 3AY. *T:* (01904) 413831. *E:* sue.mendus@york.ac.uk.

**MENEM, Carlos Saúl;** President of Argentina, 1989–99; *b* 2 July 1935; *s* of Saúl Menem and Mohibe Akil; *m* 1966, Zulema Fátima Yoma (marr. diss.); one *d* (one *s* decd); *m* 2001, Cecilia Bolloco (marr. diss. 2008); one *s*. *Educ:* Córdoba Univ. Legal Advr, Confederación General del Trabajo, La Rioja, 1955–70; lawyer, La Rioja, 1958; Gov., La Rioja, 1973–76, 1983–89; imprisoned, 1976–81. Pres., Partido Justicialista, La Rioja, 1963–. Vice Pres., Confedn of Latin American Popular Parties, 1990–. Founder, Juventud Peronista (Peronist youth gp), 1955. *Publications:* Argentina, Now or Never; Argentina Year 2000; (jtly) The Productive Revolution.

**MENEVIA, Bishop of, (RC),** since 2008; **Rt Rev. Thomas Matthew Burns,** SM; *b* Belfast, 3 June 1944; *s* of late William James Burns and Louisa Mary Burns (née McGarry). *Educ:* St Mary's Coll., Blackburn; Heythrop Coll., London Univ. (BD Hons 1973); Open Univ. (BA 1984). Joined SM, 1965; ordained, 1971; Curate, St Anne's, Whitechapel, 1973–74; Head of Econs, St Mary's GS, Sidcup, 1974–78; Head of Econs and Social Scis, St Mary's Sixth-Form Coll., Blackburn, 1979–86; Chaplain, RN, 1986–92; Bursar General, Marist Fathers, Rome, 1992–94; Chaplain, RN, 1994–98; VG 1998–2002; Princ. RC Chaplain, RN, and Dir, Trng and Progs, then Dir, Manning, Naval Chaplaincy Service, MoD, 1998–2002; RC Bishop of the Forces, 2002–08. Bishop Promoter and Trustee of the Apostleship of the Sea, 2003–17; Bd Mem. and Trustee, St Luke's Centre, Manchester, 2005–. *Publications:* pamphlet, Index to the Laws of Rugby Football, 1997. *Recreations:* Rugby (advisor to referees), action novels, film-going. *Address:* Curial Office, 27 Convent Street, Greenhill, Swansea SA1 2BX. *T:* (01792) 644017.

**MENIN, Rt Rev. Malcolm James;** Bishop Suffragan of Knaresborough, 1986–97; an Hon. Assistant Bishop, Diocese of Norwich, since 2000; *b* 26 Sept. 1932; *s* of Rev. James Nicholas Menin and Doreen Menin; *m* 1958, Jennifer Mary Cullen; one *s* three *d*. *Educ:* Dragon School; St Edward's School; University Coll., Oxford (MA); Cuddesdon Coll. Curate: Holy Spirit, Southsea, 1957–59; St Peter and St Paul, Fareham, 1959–62; Vicar of St James, Norwich, later St Mary Magdalene with St James, Norwich, 1962–86; RD Norwich East, 1981–86; Hon. Canon, Norwich Cathedral, 1982–86. *Recreations:* walking, photography, carpentry. *Address:* 32c Bracondale, Norwich NR1 2AN. *T:* (01603) 627987.

**MENKES, Suzy Peta, (Mrs S. P. Menkes-Spanier),** OBE 2005; Editor, Vogue International, Condé Nast International, since 2014; *b* 24 Dec. 1943; *d* of late Edouard Gerald Lionel Menkès and Betty Curtis Lightfoot; *m* 1969, David Graham Spanier (*d* 2000); three *s* (one *d* decd). *Educ:* Univ. of Cambridge (MA). Editor, Varsity newspaper, Cambridge, 1966; Jun. Reporter, The Times, 1966–69; Fashion Editor, Evening Standard, 1969–77; Women's Editor, Daily Express, 1977–80; Fashion Editor: The Times, 1980–87; The Independent, 1987–88; Internat. Herald Tribune, later Internat. New York Times, 1988–2014. Freeman: City of Milan, 1986; City of London, 1987. Chevalier, Légion d'Honneur (France), 2005. British Press Awards Commendations, 1983 and 1984; Eugenia Sheppard Award for Fashion Journalism, Council of Fashion Designers of America, 1995; Special Recognition Award, British Fashion Awards, 2013; Fiorino d'Oro, City of Florence, 2013. *Publications:* The Knitwear Revolution, 1983; The Royal Jewels, 1985, 3rd edn 1988; The Windsor Style, 1987; Queen and Country, 1992. *Recreations:* family life, reading, opera, Royal history. *Address:* c/o Condé Nast International, The Adelphi, 1–11 John Adam Street, WC2N 6HJ.

**MENNELL, Prof. Julie,** PhD; Vice-Chancellor, University of Cumbria, since 2016; *b* Middlesbrough, 4 Feb. 1970; *d* of Richard Agars Sowerby and Linda Ann Sowerby (*née* Marsden, now Hobson); *m* 1992, John Richard Mennell; two *s* one *d*. *Educ:* Univ. of Leeds (BSc Maths and Physics 1992); Teesside Univ. (Postgrad. Cert. Learning and Teaching in Higher Educn; PhD Applied Physics 1997). Joined Lancs Police Force, 1992; worked with police forces incl. Metropolitan Police, Gtr Manchester Police, Algerian Gendarmerie and Botswana Police Service. Teesside University: Res. and Teaching Fellow, 1995–97; Lectr, 1997–98, Sen. Lectr, 1998–2001, in Measurement Sci.; Principal Lectr, and Learning and Teaching Co-ordinator, 2001–02; Subject Gp Leader, Professional Applications of Sci., 2002–04, Asst Dean, and Dir, Centre for Forensic Investigation, Sch. of Sci. and Technol., 2002–06; Prof. and Dean, Sch. of Applied Scis, Northumbria Univ., 2006–10; Dep. Vice Chancellor (Academic), Univ. of Sunderland, 2010–16. Hon. Mem., NE Assoc. of Sci. Educn, 2012– (Pres., 2010–12). FHEA 2006; FCSFS 2006; Fellow, Inst. of Measurement and Control, 2007. FRSA 2006. *Publications:* (contrib.) Clinical Forensic Medicine, 3rd edn, 2009; contrib. articles on flow measurement, radiometric techniques and forensics to jls. *Recreations:* spending time with family and friends, Lake District, walking, sport. *Address:* Vice Chancellor's Office, University of Cumbria, Fusehill Street, Carlisle CA1 2HH. *T:* (01228) 634700. *E:* julie.mennell@cumbria.ac.uk.

**MENNELL, Stuart Leslie;** Clerk, Hawkwell Parish Council, 2002–12; *b* 17 Oct. 1948; *s* of Albert Edward Mennell and Iris Mennell (*née* Jackson); *m* 1st, 1970, Margaret Hirst (*d* 2000); three *d*; 2nd, 2009, Tricia Stanford. *Educ:* Barlby High Sch., E Yorks. Ministry of Social Security, 1968–72; HM Customs & Excise: Preventive Duties, 1972–75; VAT, 1975–78; Regl Personnel Officer, 1978–82; Statistical Office, 1982–84; HQ Personnel Manager, 1984–86; Estate Manager, 1986–88; National Maritime Museum: Estabt Officer, 1988–89; Personnel & Corporate Planning Manager, 1989–93; Dir, Collections and Mus. Services Div., 1993–2001; Dir, Strategic Develts, 2001. MIPD 1989. *Recreations:* classic motorcycles, motorcycling, walking. *Address:* Chadwell, Lambourne Hall Road, Canewdon, Essex SS4 3PG. *T:* (01702) 257179. *E:* stuart.mennell@btinternet.com.

**MENNINI, Most Rev. Antonio;** Official of the Secretariat of State, since 2017; *b* Rome, 2 Sept. 1947. *Educ:* Pontifical Univ. (DTh). Ordained priest, Rome, 1974; entered Diplomatic Service of the Holy See, 1981; served in Uganda and Turkey; Italian and S African Desk, Section for Relns with States of the Secretariat of State, 1986–2000; Apostolic Nuncio to Bulgaria, 2000–02; apptd Titular Archbishop of Ferento, 2000; Representative of the Holy See to the Russian Fedn, 2002–11; Apostolic Nuncio to: Russian Fedn, 2002–08; Uzbekistan, 2008–10; Court of St James's, 2010–17. *Address:* c/o Secretariat of State, Palazzo Apostolico Vaticano, 00120 Vatican City State.

**MENON, Prof. David Krishna,** MD; PhD; FRCP, FRCA, FFICM, FMedSci; Professor of Anaesthesia, University of Cambridge, since 2000; Fellow, Queens' College, Cambridge, since 2002; *b* 21 Aug. 1956; *s* of Parakat Govindan Kutty Menon and Violet Rebecca Menon; *m* 1988, Wendy Humphreys; one *s*. *Educ:* Univ. of Madras (MB BS, MD 1992); RPMS, Univ. of London (PhD 1995). FRCA 1988; FRCP 1999. Residency in Internal Medicine, Jawaharlal Inst., Pondicherry, India, 1978–83; Registrar: in Medicine, Professorial Med. Unit, Leeds Gen. Infirmary, 1984–86; in Anaesthetics, Royal Free Hosp., London, 1987–88; MRC Res. Fellow, Robert Steiner Magnetic Resonance Unit, Hammersmith Hosp., 1989–91; Clinical Lectr, 1992–93, Lectr in Anaesthesia, 1993–2000, Univ. of Cambridge; Lead Consultant and Dir, Neurocritical Care, Addenbrooke's Hosp., 1997–2001. Sen. Investigator, NIHR, 2009–. Chair, Eur. Brain Injury Consortium, 2014– (Co-Chair, 2007–14). Member: Council, Intensive Care Soc., 2002–09; Founding Bd, Faculty of Intensive Care Medicine, 2010–16. Founder FMedSci 1998; FFICM 2011. Hon. Fellow, Neurocritical Care Soc., 2016. *Publications:* Textbook of Neuroanaesthesia and Critical Care, 1998; contrib. to several textbooks, incl. Oxford Textbook of Critical Care, 1999, and Oxford Textbook of Medicine, 2001, 2015; contribs to various jls on topics of critical care and neuroscis. *Recreations:* basketball, science fiction, cooking. *Address:* University Department of Anaesthesia, Box 93, Addenbrooke's Hospital, Hills Road, Cambridge CB2 0QQ. *T:* (01223) 217889. *Club:* Royal Society of Medicine.

**MENON, Girish;** Chief Executive, ActionAid UK, since 2015. *Educ:* Gujarat Univ. (BCom Accountancy and Audit 1983); Inst. of Rural Mgt Anand (Postgrad. Dip. Rural Mgt 1985); Univ. of Exeter (Postgrad. Cert. Professional Develt in Mgt Leadership 2010). Mktg Exec., Gujarat Co-op. Oilseeds Mktg Fedn, 1985; Prog. Co-ordinator, Surendranagar Dist Team, Aga Khan Rural Support Prog., India, 1985–88; ActionAid: Asst Dir, 1988–93; Prog. Manager, Delhi Regl Officer, 1993–94; Regl Manager, Bhopal, 1994–97; Man. Dir, Action Enterprise, India, 1997–98; Regl Manager, Bangalore, 1997–2000, Dir (India Chapter), 2000–02, Plan Internat.; Social Develt Advr, DFID, India, 2002–04; Dir, Internat. Progs, and Dep. Chief Exec., WaterAid, London, 2005–15. *Recreations:* social, media, writing, singing, reading, Bollywood. *Address:* ActionAid UK, 33–39 Bowling Green Lane, EC1R 0BJ. *T:* 07710 390067.

**MENON, Rajiv;** QC 2011; *b* Newport, Wales, 19 April 1964; *s* of Dr Gopinath Menon and Dr Marioula Menon; *m* 1996, Anita Kirpal; two *c*. *Educ:* Dartmouth Coll. (BA 1987); London Sch. of Econs and Pol Sci. (MSc 1988); Coll. of Law (CPE 1992); Inns of Court Sch. of Law (BVC 1993). Called to the Bar, Middle Temple, 1993. *Address:* Garden Court Chambers, 57–60 Lincoln's Inn Fields, WC2A 3LS. *T:* (020) 7993 7803, *Fax:* (020) 7269 5669. *E:* rajivm@gclaw.co.uk.

**MENSAH, Barbara; Her Honour Judge Mensah;** a Circuit Judge, since 2005; a Judge of the Upper Tribunal (Immigration and Asylum Chamber) (formerly a Vice President, Immigration Appeal Tribunal, later a Senior Immigration Judge, Asylum and Immigration Tribunal), since 2003; *b* 4 March 1959; *d* of Benjamin Amponsah Mensah and Victoria (*née* Apomasu). *Educ:* Wadhurst Coll., Kent; Millfield Sch.; UC of Swansea (BSc Philos.); City Univ. (Dip Law); Council of Legal Educn (Bar Finals); Queen Mary and Westfield Coll., London (LLM). Called to the Bar, Lincoln's Inn, 1984, Bencher, 2005. Lawyer, International Tobacco (Ghana) Ltd, 1987–89; pt-time Sen. Lectr, Inns of Court Sch. of Law, 1990–2000; Immigration Adjudicator, 1995; Dep. District Judge (Magistrates' Courts), 1998; a Recorder, 2003–05. Member: Adv. Bd on Restricted Patients, 1999–2002; Legal Services Consultative Panel, 2000–02. Mem., Disciplinary Panel, Bar Council, 2001. Mem. (pt-time), Mental Health Tribunal, 2011–. ACIArb, 1994–2000. Hon. LLD City, 2016. *Publications:* The Prison Guide (with Andrew Goodman), 1999; European Human Rights Case Locator 1960–2000, 2000; European Human Rights Case Summaries, 2001; contrib. to Inns of Court Sch. of Law Bar Manuals. *Recreations:* swimming, reading, music. *Address:* Luton Crown Court, 7 George Street, Luton, Beds LU1 2AA.

**MENSAH, Evelyn Justina A.;** *see* Asante-Mensah.

**MENSCH, Louise;** *b* London, 1971; *d* of Nicholas Bagshawe and Daphne Bagshawe (*née* Triggs); *m* Anthony LoCicero (marr. diss.); two *s* one *d*; *m* 2011, Peter Mensch. *Educ:* Sacred Heart Sch., Tunbridge Wells; Woldingham Sch., Surrey; Christ Church, Oxford (BA English). PR and Mktg Manager, EMI Classics and Sony Music, 1992–93; novelist, 1994–. MP (C) Corby, 2010–Aug. 2012. *Publications:* (as Louise Bagshawe): Career Girls, 1995; The Movie, 1996; Tall Poppies, 1997; Venus Envy, 1998; A Kept Woman, 2000; When She Was Bad, 2001; The Devil You Know, 2003; Monday's Child, 2004; Tuesday's Child, 2005; Sparkles, 2006; Glamour, 2007; Glitz, 2008; Passion, 2009; Desire, 2010; Destiny, 2011; (as Louise Mensch): Beauty, 2014; Career Game, 2015. *Recreations:* reading, travel, music. *Club:* Groucho.

**MENTETH, Sir Charles S.;** *see* Stuart-Menteth.

**MENZIES, Rt Hon. Lord; Duncan Adam Young Menzies;** PC 2012; a Senator of the College of Justice in Scotland, since 2001; *b* 28 Aug. 1953; *s* of late Douglas William Livingstone Menzies and Margaret Adam (*née* Young); *m* 1979, Hilary Elizabeth McLauchlan Weston; two *s*. *Educ:* Cargilfield; Glenalmond (schol.); Wadham Coll., Oxford (schol.; MA); Edinburgh Univ. (LLB). Admitted Advocate, 1978; Standing Junior Counsel to Admiralty, 1984–91; QC (Scot.) 1991; Temp. Sheriff, 1996–97; Home Advocate Depute, 1998–2000. Chm., Scottish Planning, Local Govt and Envmtl Bar Gp, 1997–2001. Dep. Chm., Scottish Civil Justice Council, 2013–19. Contested (C): Midlothian, 1983; Edinburgh Leith, 1987. Mem., von Poser Soc. of Scotland, 1996–. Founder, Scottish Wine Soc., 1976; Maître, Commanderie de Bordeaux à Edimbourg, 2012. *Recreations:* shooting, golf, wine. *Address:* Court of Session, Parliament House, Parliament Square, Edinburgh EH1 1RQ. *Clubs:* Saintsbury; New (Edinburgh); Honourable Company of Edinburgh Golfers.

**MENZIES, Duncan Adam Young;** *see* Menzies, Rt Hon. Lord.

**MENZIES, Mark;** MP (C) Fylde, since 2010; *b* Irvine, 18 May 1971; *s* of Andrew Menzies and Mary Isobel Menzies. *Educ:* Keil Sch., Dumbarton; Univ. of Glasgow (MA Hons Econ. and Social Hist.). With Marks & Spencer plc, 1994–95; Mktg Manager, Asda Stores Ltd, 1995–2007; Hd, Local Mktg, Wm Morrison Supermarkets plc, 2008–10. Contested (C): Glasgow Govan, 2001; Selby, 2005. PPS to Minister for Energy, 2010–12, to Minister for Housing, 2012–13, to Minister for Internat. Develt, 2013–14; Prime Minister's Trade Envoy to Chile, Colombia and Peru, 2017–, to Argentina, 2018–. Member: Transport Select Cttee, 2015–17; Internat. Develt Select Cttee, 2018–. *Recreations:* ski-ing, walking, cinema. *Address:* House of Commons, SW1A 0AA. *T:* (020) 7219 7073, *Fax:* (020) 7219 2235. *E:* mark.menzies.mp@parliament.uk.

**MENZIES, Lt-Gen. Robert Clark,** CB 2002; OBE 1989; Surgeon General to the Armed Forces, 2000–02; *b* 1 June 1944; *s* of late Flt Lieut Robert Clark Menzies and Jane, (Jean), Reid Menzies; *m* 1st, 1967, Dr Joanna, (Joan), Letitia Lindsay Dunning (marr. diss. 2006); one *s* one *d*; 2nd, 2006, Dr Hansa Thakkar. *Educ:* Kilmarnock Acad.; Glasgow Univ. (MB ChB 1967). DMJ (Pathology) 1976; MRCPath 1980, FRCPath 1992; FFPH (FFPHM 1999); FRCPE 2000. OC, Med. Reception Stn, Warminster, 1969; Trainee Pathologist, Leishman Lab., Cambridge Mil. Hosp., 1971–72; Pathologist, BMH, Rinteln, 1973–75; Registrar in Pathology, Queen Alexandra Mil. Hosp., 1975–76; British Army Exchange Pathologist, Armed Forces Inst. of Pathology, Washington, 1976–78 (Chief, Missile Trauma Pathology Br. and Hon. Professional Lectr, George Washington Univ.); Sen. Registrar in Pathology, Leishman Lab., Cambridge Mil. Hosp., 1978–81; Lectr in Forensic Medicine, Charing Cross Hosp. Med. Sch., 1981–83; Consultant Pathologist, Leishman Lab., 1983–85; Prof. of Mil. Pathology, Royal Army Med. Coll. and RCPath, 1985–89; CO, BMH Rinteln, 1989–92; Dir of Army Pathology, 1992–94; CO, 217 (London) Gen. Hosp. RAMC(V), 1994–95; Commander Medical: HQ London Dist, 1995–96; HQ Land Comd, 1996–99; Dir Gen., AMS, 1999–2000. QHS 1996–2003. Chief Med. Officer, 2003–05, Actg Chief Comdr, 2005–06, St John Ambulance. Pres., Stapleford & Berwick St James Br., 2003–06, Heyford and District Br., 2012–, RBL; Army Benevolent Fund Oxfordshire Cttee, 2018–. Chm., Upper Heyford Parish Council, 2011–14. Freeman, City of London, 1995. CStJ 2006 (Trustee and Dir, Priory of England and the Islands, Order of St John, 2004–06). *Publications:* articles on pathology, particularly forensic pathology, in jls. *Recreations:* walking, travelling, photography, reading, poetry, music, Bentley motor car. *Clubs:* Army and Navy, Victory Services.

**MEON, Archdeacon of The;** *see* Collins, Ven. G. A.

**MER, Francis Paul;** Honorary Chairman, Board of Directors, Safran, since 2013 (Chairman, Supervisory Board, 2007–11; Vice Chairman, Board of Directors, 2011–13); Minister of Economy, Finance and Industry, France, 2002–04; *b* 25 May 1939; *s* of René Mer and Yvonne Casalta; *m* 1964, Catherine Bonfils; three *d*. *Educ:* Ecole Nationale Supérieure des Mines, Paris; Ecole Polytechnique. Mining engr, Ministry of Industry, 1966; tech. advr, Abidjan, 1967–68; joined St-Gobain Pont-à-Mousson Gp, 1970: St-Gobain Industries: Dir of Planning, 1971–73; Dir-Gen. Planning, 1973; Manager, 1974–78; St-Gobain Pont-à-Mousson: Dir of Planning, 1973; Asst Dir-Gen., 1978–82; Pres. Dir-Gen., Pont-à-Mousson SA, 1982–86; Pres. Dir-Gen., Usinor-Sacilor, 1986–2002; Chm., Usinor Gp, 2001–02; Co-Chm., Arcelor, 2002. Director: Credit Lyonnais, 1997–2002; Electricité de France, 1997; Air France, 1997–2002; Rhodia, 2004–11; Adecco, 2004–11. Chairman: Eurofer, 1990–97; IISI, 1997–98. President: French Steel Fedn, 1988–2002; Nat. Tech. Res. Assoc., 1991–2002; formerly President: Entreprise pour l'environnement; Cercle de l'industrie. Commandeur: Légion d'Honneur (France); Ordre Nat. du Mérite (France).

**MERCADO, Anthony Raymond,** CEng, FIET; Senior Associate, First Class Partnerships, since 2014; Director, MERCT Consulting Ltd, since 2014; *b* Johannesburg, 20 May 1951. *Educ:* Univ. of Witwatersrand (BSc Electrical Engrg). CEng 2002; FIET 2002. South African Rlys, 1974–88; Engrg Dir, GEC Traction, 1988–96; Operations Dir, Alstom Transport Systems, 1996–2000; Engrg Dir, Alstom Transport, 2000–04; Man. Dir, Alstom W Coast Train Care, 2005–08; Dir, Rail Technical and Professional, DfT, 2008–11; Customer Dir, 2011–14, Dir of Rail Develt Policy, 2013–14, Alstom Transport UK. Ind. non-exec. Dir, Willow Topco Ltd, 2016–; non-exec. Dir, PSP Investments, 2016–. *T:* 07801 772446. *E:* armercado51@gmail.com.

**MERCER, (Christine) Ruth;** Headmistress, Godolphin and Latymer School, 2009–17; *b* Preston, 19 June 1962; *d* of George Mercer and Joan Evelyn Mercer (*née* Stopforth); *m* 1988, Colin B. Horsley; one *s* one *d*. *Educ:* Bedford Coll., London (BA Hons Hist. 1983); St Catherine's Coll., Oxford (PGCE 1984); Dept of Contg Educn, Univ. of Oxford (Adv.

**MERCER,** Dip. Local Hist. 2006). Hd of Hist. and Politics, Notting Hill and Ealing High Sch., 1992–98; Dep. Headmistress, Godolphin and Latymer Sch., 1998–2002; Headmistress, Northwood Coll., 2002–08. *Recreations:* travel, fell walking, genealogy, reading, history, swimming.

**MERCER, His Honour Geoffrey Dallas;** a Circuit Judge, South Eastern Circuit, 1991–2005; *b* 17 Dec. 1935; *s* of Leon Dallas Mercer, FRCS and Veronica Kathleen Mary Lillian Mercer (née Pitt-Lancaster). *Educ:* Clifton Coll., Bristol; St John's Coll., Cambridge (MA, LLM). Called to the Bar, Gray's Inn, 1960; practised at the Bar, 1961–91; Hd of Chambers, 1985–91; an Asst Recorder, 1986; a Recorder, 1990. Former English Youth International and Cheshire County golfer. *Recreations:* golf, music. *Clubs:* Royal Automobile; Burhill Golf; Worplesdon Golf.

**MERCER, Giles;** *see* Mercer, R. G. G.

**MERCER, Hugh Charles;** QC 2008; barrister; a Deputy High Court Judge, since 2018; *b* Barnard Castle, Co. Durham; *s* of Keith and Gabrielle Mercer; *m* 1995, Isabelle Corbeel; two *s* (one *d* decd). *Educ:* Downing Coll., Cambridge (BA 1984); Université Libre de Bruxelles (Licence spéciale en droit européen). Called to the Bar, Middle Temple, 1985, Bencher, 2012; in practice as barrister specialising in EU and internat. law; Chambers of Mark Littman, QC, 1987–95; Essex Court Chambers, 1995–; Eur. Circuit, Bar of England and Wales, 2001–. Hd, UK Delegn to Council of Bars and Law Socs of Europe, 2007–10; Chairman: CCBE Perm. Delegn to Court of Justice of the UK, 2010–16; CCBE EU Lawyers Cttee, 2016–. *Publications:* Commercial Debt in Europe: recovery and remedies, 1991; European Civil Practice, 2004. *Recreations:* squash, mountain walking, gardening, scout leader. *Address:* Essex Court Chambers, 24 Lincoln's Inn Fields, WC2A 3EG. *T:* (020) 7813 8000, *Fax:* (020) 7813 8080. *Clubs:* Royal Automobile; Achille Ratti Climbing.

**MERCER, Johnny;** MP (C) Plymouth Moor View, since 2015; Parliamentary Under-Secretary of State (Minister for Defence People and Veterans), Ministry of Defence and Cabinet Office, since 2019; *b* Dartford, Kent, 17 Aug. 1981; *s* of Andrew Mercer and Margaret Mercer; *m* Felicity Cornelius; two *d*. *Educ:* Eastbourne Coll.; Royal Mil. Acad. Sandhurst. Intern, City of London, 2000–02; Officer, Army, 2002–14. Member: Defence Cttee, 2015–; Health and Social Care (formerly Health) Select Cttee, 2017–. *Publications:* We Were Warriors, 2017. *Address:* House of Commons, SW1A 0AA. *E:* johnny.mercer.mp@parliament.uk.

**MERCER, Lesley;** Director, Employment Relations and Union Services, Chartered Society of Physiotherapy, 2005–14; *b* Clitheroe, Lancs, 6 Aug. 1954; *d* of Sqdn Ldr Donald Mercer and Jean Mercer; partner, 1980, *m* 2016, Graham Taylor. *Educ:* Accrington High Sch.; Univ. of Nottingham (BA (Hons) Politics 1975). Asst Res. Officer, Merchant Navy and Airline Officers Assoc., 1977–79; Exec. Asst, 1979–85, Negotiations Officer, 1985–95, Soc. of Civil and Public Servants, subseq. Nat. Union of Civil and Public Servants; Sen. Negotiating Officer, 1995–2000, Asst Dir, 2000–05, CSP. Member: Industrial Tribunal Panel, 1989–2002; Central Arbitration Cttee, 2002–19; Ind. Lay Chm., NHS Complaints Procedure, 1998–2002; ACAS Panel of Ind. Arbitrators, 2015–19; Armed Forces Pay Review Body, 2016–. Pres., 2012–13, Vice-Pres., 2013–14, TUC. Trustee Dir, Nautilus Internat., 2015–. Hon. FCSP 2012. DUniv Keele, 2015. *Recreations:* stained glass restoration, cycling, walking, gardening.

**MERCER, Patrick John,** OBE 1997 (MBE 1992); *b* 26 June 1956; *s* of late Rt Rev. Eric Arthur John Mercer and of Rosemary Wilma (née Denby); *m* 1990, Catriona Jane Beaton; one *s*. *Educ:* King's Sch., Chester; Exeter Coll., Oxford (MA Mod. Hist. 1980). Commnd 1st Bn Worcs and Sherwood Foresters, 1975: served NI, 1975–77; Captain: BAOR and W Belfast, 1980–83 (despatches); Instructor, Brecon, 1984–86; Major: Chief Instructor, Ugandan Sch. of Inf., 1986; Jun. Inf. Bn, Shorncliffe, 1986–88; sc, Camberley, 1988; Co. Comdr, Omagh, NI, 1989–90 (GOC's Commendation); SO2 G3 (Ops), HQ NI, 1991–92; Chief Instructor, Platoon Comdr's Course, 1993; Lieut Col, SO1 Instructor, Staff Coll., Camberley, 1994–95; CO, Tidworth, Bosnia, Canada, 1995–97; Col, Hd of Strategy, Army Trng and Recruitment Agency, 1997–99; Defence Corresp., Today prog., BBC Radio 4, 1999. Mem., KCL team tasked with writing defence policy for E Timor, 2000. MP for Newark, 2001–April 2014 (C, 2001–13, Ind, 2013–April 2014). Opposition front bench spokesman on home, constitutional and legal affairs, 2003–07, on homeland security, 2004–07; Chm., Counter-Terrorist Sub-Cttee, 2009–10. Company Dir, Military History Live Ltd, 2016–. Hon. Col, Notts ACF, 2007–11. *Publications:* Inkermann: the soldiers' battle, 1997; Give Them a Volley and Charge, 1997; To Do and Die, 2009; Dust and Steel, 2010; Red Runs the Helmand, 2011; Doctor Watson's War, 2015; Doctor Watson's Charge, 2015; Doctor Watson's Bout, 2015; Doctor Watson's Terror, 2016; Doctor Watson's Mess, 2016; contrib. jls and newspapers. *Recreations:* water-colour painting, history, bird watching, country sports. *Club:* Newark Working Men's.

**MERCER, Dr (Robert) Giles (Graham);** Headmaster, Prior Park College, 1996–2009; *b* 30 May 1949; *s* of late Leonard and Florence Elizabeth Mercer; *m* 1974, Caroline Mary Brougham; one *s*. *Educ:* Austin Friars School, Carlisle; Churchill College, Cambridge (Scholar; 1st cl. Hist. Tripos, Pts I and II; MA); St John's College, Oxford (Sen. Schol., DPhil). Giorgio Cini Foundn Schol., Venice, 1973. Head of History, Charterhouse, 1974–76; Asst Principal, MoD, 1976–78; Dir of Studies and Head of History, Sherborne School, 1979–85; Headmaster, Stonyhurst Coll., 1985–96. Life Mem., Catholic Union, 1985; Mem., Catholic Record Soc., 2009–; Cttee, Assoc. of Papal Orders in GB, 2010–13. Chm., 2000–04, Vice-Pres., 2006–, Catholic Ind. Schs Conf.; Trustee: Bloxham Conf., 2008–10; Bath Preservation Trust, 2009–14; Clifton Dio., 2009–16. Friend of Downside Abbey, 2010–. Governor: All Hallows Prep. Sch., Shepton Mallett, 1999–2009; St Mary's Sch., Shaftesbury, 2005–07; St John's Catholic Primary Sch., Bath, 2012– (Chm., Curriculum Cttee, 2012–14; Chm. of Govs, 2014–); Downside Sch., 2015–16 (Vice-Chm., 2015–16). Hon. Fellow, Rank Foundn, 2009, KSG 2004. *Publications:* The Teaching of Gasparino Barzizza, 1979; Convert, Scholar, Bishop: William Brownlow 1830–1901, 2016. *Recreations:* art, music, travel, tennis, theatre. *Address:* Inglewood, 84 Bloomfield Avenue, Bath BA2 3AD. *E:* giles.mercer530@gmail.com.

**MERCER, Rev. Mgr Robert William Stanley,** CR; Diocesan Bishop, Anglican Catholic Church of Canada, 1989–2005 (Assistant Bishop, 1988–89); *b* 10 Jan. 1935; *s* of Harold Windrum Mercer and Kathleen Frampton. *Educ:* Grey School, Port Elizabeth, S Africa; St Paul's Theological Coll., Grahamstown, SA (LTh). Deacon 1959, priest 1960, Matabeleland; Asst Curate, Hillside, Bulawayo, 1959–63; Novice, CR, 1963; professed, 1965; at Mirfield, 1963–66; at St Teilo's Priory, Cardiff, 1966–68; Prior and Rector of Stellenbosch, S Africa, 1968–70; deported from SA, 1970; Chaplain, St Augustine's School, Penhalonga, Rhodesia, 1971–72; Rector of Borrowdale, Salisbury, Rhodesia, 1972–77; Bishop of Matabeleland, 1977–87. Ordained deacon and priest, Personal Ordinariate of Our Lady of Walsingham (RC), 2012. Sub-Prelate, Order of St John of Jerusalem, 1981. *Address:* 3 The Limes, St Botolph's Road, Worthing, W Sussex BN11 4HY.

**MERCER, Ruth;** *see* Mercer, C. R.

**MERCHANT, Eileen;** Headmistress, Putney High School (GDST), 1991–2002; *b* 20 Feb. 1944; *d* of Jeremiah and Ellen McGill; *m* 1966, John Richard Merchant, *qv*; two *s*. *Educ:* Sheffield Univ. (BSc 1st Cl. Chem.). Dir of Studies, Bedford High Sch., 1974–86; Dep. Hd, Latymer Sch., Edmonton, 1986–91. JP Wimbledon, 1999–2003, Sussex, 2005–14. *Recreations:* birdwatching, reading, walking.

**MERCHANT, John Richard;** Director of Resources, Voluntary Service Overseas, 1995–2003; *b* 4 June 1945; *s* of William Henry Merchant and Eileen Merchant; *m* 1966, Eileen McGill (*see* E. Merchant); two *s*. *Educ:* Gravesend Grammar Sch.; Sheffield Univ. (BSc); Cranfield Inst. of Technol. (MSc); Open Univ. (BSc). Lyons Bakery Ltd, 1966–69; Lectr, Cranfield Inst. of Technol., 1969–75; Statistician, MoD, 1975–79; Chief Statistician, CS Coll., 1979–82; Asst Sec., Cabinet Office (MPO), 1982–84; Principal Finance and Estabt Officer, DPP, 1984–86; Crown Prosecution Service, 1986–88; Under Sec., 1985; Sec. and Dir, Council Policy and Admin, SERC, 1988–94; Grade 3, Office of Public Service and Science, 1994. *Recreations:* Nigerian postal history, birdwatching.

**MEREDITH, Most Rev. Bevan;** Archbishop of Papua New Guinea, Primate of the Province of Papua New Guinea, 1991–95; Bishop of New Guinea Islands, 1977–95; licensed to officiate, diocese of Brisbane, since 1995; Hon. Assistant, St Faith's Parish, Strathpine, since 1995; *b* Alstonville, NSW, 14 Aug. 1927; 3rd *c* of Stanley Meredith and Edith Meredith (née Witchard). *Educ:* Univ. of Queensland; St Francis Theol Coll., Brisbane. Teacher, Slade Sch., Warwick, Qld and Housemaster, Highfields House, 1948–53; Staff, Martyrs' Meml Sch., PNG, 1954–58; deacon 1961, priest 1962, St Thomas, Toowong; Priest-in-charge, Managalas, PNG, 1963–67; Asst Bp of New Guinea, 1967–77. *Recreations:* music, photography, philately.

**MEREDITH, David Michael;** District Judge (Magistrates' Courts) (formerly Stipendiary Magistrate), Leicestershire, 1995–2011; *b* 2 May 1945; *s* of George and Phyllis Maude Meredith; one *s*; *m* 2008, Anne Marsden (née Middlebrook). *Educ:* King Edward VII Sch., Sheffield; St Edmund Hall, Oxford (BA, DipEd). Asst Teacher, Chorlton High Sch., 1969–70, and King Edward VII Sch., Sheffield, 1970–74; admitted solicitor, 1977; Articled Clerk and Asst Solicitor, 1975–81, Partner, 1981–95, Graysons, Sheffield. *Recreations:* football, bad golf, theatre, travel. *Clubs:* Vincent's (Oxford); Charnwood Forest Golf.

**MEREDITH, Richard Alban Creed,** MA; Head Master, Monkton Combe School, 1978–90; *b* 1 Feb. 1935; *s* of late Canon R. Creed Meredith; *m* 1968, Hazel Eveline Mercia Parry; one *s* one *d*. *Educ:* Stowe Sch.; Jesus Coll., Cambridge. Asst Master (Modern Langs), 1957–70, Housemaster, 1962–70, King's Sch., Canterbury; Headmaster, Giggleswick Sch., 1970–78. CMS Area Sec., dios of Derby, Leicester and Southwell, 1990–98. Reader, Church of England, 1957–. *Recreations:* walking, foreign travel, music, gardening. *Address:* Beacon Knoll, 334 Beacon Road, Loughborough LE11 2RD. *T:* (01509) 212008.

**MERES, Lisa Moreen;** *see* Opie, L. M.

**MERIFIELD, Sir Anthony (James),** KCVO 2000; CB 1994; The Ceremonial Officer, Cabinet Office, 1994–2000; *b* 5 March 1934; *s* of late Francis Bertram Merifield and Richardina (née Parker); *m* 1980, Pamela Pratt. *Educ:* Chesterfield Sch.; Shrewsbury Sch.; Wadham Coll., Oxford (MA). National Service, 1952–54, Royal Tank Regt. HM Overseas Civil Service, Kenya, 1958–65; Department of Health and Social Security: Principal, 1965–71; Asst Sec., 1971–77; Under Secretary, 1978–82; Under Sec., NI Office, 1982–85; Dir of Regl Liaison, NHS Management Bd, DHSS, subseq. NHS Management Exec., DoH, 1986–91; Head of Sen. and Public Appts Gp, Cabinet Office, 1991–94. Chm., KCH Charity (formerly Charitable Trust), 2004–12. *Address:* 49 Carson Road, SE21 8HT. *T:* (020) 8670 1546. *Clubs:* Athenæum; Achilles; Dulwich and Sydenham Hill Golf.

**MERKEL, Dr Angela Dorothea;** Member, Bundestag, since 1990; Chancellor, Federal Republic of Germany, since 2005; Chairman, Christian Democratic Union, 2000–18; *b* Hamburg, 17 July 1954; *d* of Horst Kasner and Herlinde Kasner; *m* 1998, Prof. Dr Joachim Sauer. *Educ:* Univ. of Leipzig; Zentralinstitut für physikalische Chemie, East Berlin (Dr rer. nat. Physics 1986). Res. Associate in Quantum Chemistry, Zentralinstitut für Physikalische Chemie, East Berlin, 1978–90; joined Demokratischer Aufbruch, 1989, Press Spokesperson, 1990, Dep. Spokesperson for Govt of Lothar de Maizière, March–Oct. 1990; joined CDU, 1990; Dep. Federal Chm., 1991–98; Chm., CDU, Fed. State of Mecklenburg-Vorpommern, 1993–2000; Gen. Sec., CDU, 1998–2000; Chm., CDU/CSU Parly Gp, Bundestag, 2002–05. Federal Minister: for Women and Young People, 1991–94; for Environment, Nature Conservation and Nuclear Safety, 1994–98. Hon. DLaws Harvard, 2019. *Publications:* Der Preis des Überlebens: Gedanken und Gespräche über zukünftige Aufgaben der Umweltpolitik, 1997; Europa und die deutsche Einheit: Zehn Jahre Wiedervereinigung: Bilanz und Ausblick, 2000; (with Hugo Müller-Vogg) Mein Weg: ein Gespräch mit Hugo Müller-Vogg, 2005; Daran Glaube Ich: Christliche Standpunkte, 2013. *Recreations:* reading, hiking, gardening. *Address:* c/o Bundeskanzleramt, Willy Brandt Strasse 1, 10557 Berlin, Germany. *T:* (30) 1840000, *Fax:* (30) 1840002357. *E:* internetpost@bundeskanzlerin.de.

**MERRICK, Benjamin Robert;** HM Diplomatic Service; Director, Overseas Territories, Foreign and Commonwealth Office, since 2017; Commissioner: of the British Antarctic Territory, since 2017; of the British Indian Ocean Territory, since 2017; *m*; one *s* one *d*. *Educ:* Exeter Coll., Oxford (BA 1997); London Sch. of Econs and Political Sci. (MSc 2014). MoD, 1997–2002; Implementation Team Leader, Social Exclusion Unit, ODPM, 2002–05; Ministry of Defence: Asst Hd, Ops, 2005–07; Dep. Hd, Equipment Approvals, 2007–09; Head: Acquisition Reform, 2009–11; Arms Control and Counter Proliferation, 2012–15; Dep. Dir, Overseas Territories, FCO, 2015–17. *Recreations:* reading, travel, long walks, cooking. *Address:* c/o Foreign and Commonwealth Office, King Charles Street, SW1A 2AH.

**MERRICK, Caragh;** Member of Council, since 2006, and Treasurer, since 2014, Royal College of Art; Member of Council, since 2013, and Treasurer, since 2014, University of Birmingham; *b* Belfast, 15 Nov. 1955; *d* of Robert Hagan Maginess and Daphne Anne Maginess (née Ferris); *m* 1983, John Edward Merrick. *Educ:* Belfast Royal Acad.; Univ. of St Andrews (MA). FCA 1982. Deloitte Haskins & Sells: Accountant, 1981–84; Manager, 1984–88; Sen. Manager, 1988–89; Audit Partner, Coopers & Lybrand Deloitte, then Coopers & Lybrand, later PricewaterhouseCoopers, 1990–2002; independent consultant, 2002–08. Chm., Worcs Acute Hosps NHS Trust, 2016–18. Trustee: RNT, 2002–08; RNT Foundn, 2009–13; Nat. Foundn for Youth Music, 2008–12 (Chm., Finance and Audit Cttee, 2008–12); Musicians' Benevolent Fund, later Help Musicians UK, 2010–16 (Hon. Treas., 2013–15); UCAS, 2011–16 (Chm., Finance Cttee, 2012–16). FRSA. DUniv Birmingham 2018. *Recreations:* theatre, ballet, music.

**MERRICK, Prof. Linda,** PhD; Principal, Royal Northern College of Music, since 2013; *b* Bristol, 11 May 1963; *d* of Dennis Francis Merrick and Joyce Grace Merrick; *m* 2002, Dr Martin Ellerby, composer. *Educ:* Hengrove Sch., Bristol; Royal Acad. of Music (GRSM Hons 1984; LRAM 1982; ARAM 1998); Univ. of Reading (MMus 1995); Birmingham Conservatoire, Univ. of Central England (PhD 2004). Hd, Music, LCM, 1997–2001; Royal Northern College of Music: Dir, Performance Studies and Sen. Tutor in Clarinet, 2001–02; Hd, Professional Performance Studies, 2002–04; Dep. Vice-Principal and Dir,

Centre for Excellence in Teaching and Learning, 2004–06; Vice-Principal, 2006–12. Chair, Conservatoires UK, 2017–. Recordings include 30 CDs. FHEA 2004; FRNCM 2007; FLCM; FRSA. Hon. VCM 1984. *Publications:* Collaboration between Composer and Performers: British clarinet concertos 1990–2004, 2009. *Recreations:* travel, French literature, films and film music, walking, swimming, cooking. *Address:* Royal Northern College of Music, 124 Oxford Road, Manchester M13 9RD. *T:* (0161) 907 5273, 5382. *E:* linda.merrick@rncm.ac.uk.

**MERRICKS, Walter Hugh,** CBE 2007; Chairman, IMPRESS: The Independent Monitor for the Press, since 2015; *b* 4 June 1945; 2nd *s* of late Dick and Phoebe Merricks, Icklesham, Sussex; *m* 1982, Olivia Montuschi; one *s* one *d,* and one step *s. Educ:* Bradfield College, Berks; Trinity College, Oxford. MA Hons (Jurisp). Articled Clerk with Batt, Holden, 1968–70; admitted Solicitor, 1970; Hubbard Travelling Scholar, Montreal, 1971; Dir, Camden Community Law Centre, 1972–76; Lectr in Law, Brunel Univ., 1976–81; legal affairs writer, New Law Journal, 1982–85; Law Society: Sec., Professional and Public Relations, 1985–87; Asst Sec.-Gen. (Communications), 1987–95; Dir, Professional and Legal Policy, 1995–96; Insurance Ombudsman, 1996–99; Chief Ombudsman, Financial Ombudsman Service, 1999–2009; Chm., Office of Health Professions Adjudicator, 2009–12; Service Complaint Adjudicator, Legal Ombudsman, 2011–15; Service Complaint Reviewer, RICS, 2012–; a Gambling Comr, 2012–17; Ind. Code Reviewer, British Copyright Council, 2013–14; Sen. Associate, Verita, 2013–; Ind. Complaint Reviewer, FRC, 2019–; Class rep., Competition Tribunal consumer action against Mastercard, 2016–. Member: Royal Commn on Criminal Procedure, 1978–81; Fraud Trials (Roskill) Cttee, 1984–86; Victim Support Wkg Party on Financial Compensation, 1992–93. Pres., British Insce Law Assoc., 2006–08; Chairman: British and Irish Ombudsman Assoc., 2001–04; Nat. Gamete Donation Trust, 2000–01; Internat. Network of Financial Ombudsman Schemes, 2007–09; Donor Conception Network, 2007–17; Trustees, Acad. of Med. Royal Colleges, 2011–16; Member: HFEA, 2002– (Chm., 2007–08); Bd (formerly Council), Ombudsman Service Ltd, 2010–15; CAA Consumer Panel, 2018–. Mem. Council, Justice, 2004– (Mem. Exec. Cttee, 2008–; Chm., Bd (formerly Exec. Bd), 2016–); Hon. FCII 2004. Hon. LLD London Guildhall, 2001. Achievement Award, British Insce Awards, 2004.

**MERRIDALE, Prof. Catherine Anne,** PhD; FBA 2016; writer and historian; Professor of Contemporary History, Queen Mary, University of London, 2004–14; *b* 12 Oct. 1959; *d* of Philip Merridale and Anne Merridale; *m* 2004, Frank Philip Payne. *Educ:* Andover Grammar Sch.; Cricklade Coll., Andover; King's Coll., Cambridge (BA 1st Cl. Hons Hist. 1982); Centre for Russian and East European Studies, Univ. of Birmingham (PhD 1987). British Council Postgrad. Exchange, Moscow State Univ., 1986; Res. Fellow, 1987–91, Sen. Res. Fellow, 1991–93, King's Coll., Cambridge; Lectr, Sen. Lectr, then Reader in Europ. Hist., Univ. of Bristol, 1993–2004. Res. Fellow, Robinson Coll., Cambridge, Centre for Hist. and Econs, King's Coll., Cambridge and Cambridge Gp for Hist. of Popn and Social Structure, 1996–98; Sen. Res. Fellow, Inst. of Histl Res., Univ. of London, 2014–; Sen. Res. Associate, Centre for Hist. and Econs, Univ. of Cambridge, 2014–). *Publications:* Moscow Politics and the Rise of Stalin, 1990; (ed jtly and contrib.) Perestroika: the historical perspective, 1991; Night of Stone: death and memory in Russia, 2000 (Heinemann Prize for Lit., 2001); Ivan's War: the Red Army 1939–45, 2005; Red Fortress: the secret heart of Russia's history, 2013 (Wolfson Hist. Prize, Pushkin House Russian Book Prize, 2014); Lenin on the Train, 2016. *Recreation:* searching for Eden. *Address:* c/o Rogers, Coleridge and White Ltd, 20 Powis Mews, W11 1JN.

**MERRILL, Alastair James Stuart;** Vice Principal, University of St Andrews, since 2015; *b* Blackpool, 17 Jan. 1963; *s* of Howard Merrill and Catherine Merrill; *m* 1994, Janet Noakes; three *s. Educ:* Arnold Sch., Blackpool; Pembroke Coll., Cambridge (BA Hons Hist. 1985). FCIPS 2013. Fast stream, MoD, 1986–89; Second Sec., UK Delegn to NATO, 1989–91; Policy Officer, MoD, 1991–94; Civil Sec., UN Protection Forces, 1995; Dep. Dir of Private Office, HQ NATO, 1996–2001; Scottish Executive, later Scottish Government: Hd, Analytical Services, Educn Dept, 2001–03; Hd, Changing to Deliver, 2003–05; Hd, Police Div., 2005–08; Dir, Corporate Services, Scottish Prison Service, 2008–09; Commercial Dir and Chief Procurement Officer, 2009–15. *Recreations:* family, Boys' Brigade, sailing, motorcycling, choral singing. *Address:* University of St Andrews, College Gate, North Street, St Andrews, Fife KY16 9AJ. *T:* (01334) 462460. *E:* vpgov@st-andrews.ac.uk. *Club:* St Mary's Loch Sailing.

**MERRILL, Dame Fiona Claire;** *see* Reynolds, Dame F. C.

**MERRIMAN, Air Vice-Marshal (Henry) Alan,** CB 1985; CBE 1973; AFC 1957, and Bar 1961; DL; defence and aerospace consultant; *b* 17 May 1929; *s* of Henry Victor Merriman and Winifred Ellen Merriman; *m* 1965, Mary Brenda Stephenson; three *d. Educ:* Hertford Grammar Sch.; RAF Coll., Cranwell. Graduate, Empire Test Pilots Sch. FRAeS 1977. Commnd, 1951; Qual. Flying Instr, 263 F Sqdn, Empire Test Pilots Sch., Fighter Test Sqdn, A&AEE, Central Fighter Estabt, and RAF Staff Coll., 1952–63; Personal Air Sec. to Minister of Defence for RAF, 1964–66; Jt Services Staff Coll., 1966; OC Fighter Test Sqdn, A&AEE, 1966–69; HQ 38 Gp, 1969–70; Stn Comdr, RAF Wittering, 1970–72; RCDS, 1973; CO Empire Test Pilots Sch., 1974–75; Comdt, A&AEE, 1975–77; Dir, Operational Requirements (1), 1977–81; Mil. Dep. to Head of Defence Sales, 1981–84. Pres., Cambridge Br., RAFA, 2010–17. Queen's Commendation for Valuable Services in the Air, 1956. DL Herts, 1995. *Recreations:* classic cars and aircraft, gardening. *Club:* Royal Air Force.

**MERRIMAN, Huw William;** MP (C) Bexhill and Battle, since 2015; *b* Brackley, Northants, 13 July 1973; *s* of Richard and Ann Merriman. *Educ:* Buckingham Co. Secondary Sch.; Aylesbury Coll. of Further Educn; Durham Univ. (BA Hons Law); Inns of Court Sch. of Law. Called to the Bar, Inner Temple, 1996; in practice as barrister, 1997; Man. Dir, Lehman Bros in Admin, 2008–15. Mem. (C), Wealden DC, 2007–15. Contested (C) NE Derbys, 2010. *Recreations:* cooking, gardening, beekeeping. *Address:* House of Commons, SW1A 0AA. *T:* (020) 7219 8712. *E:* huw.merriman.mp@parliament.uk. *Clubs:* Farmers; Bexhill Conservative.

**MERRIMAN, Nicholas John,** PhD; Director, Horniman Museum and Gardens, since 2018; *b* 6 June 1960; *s* of Michael and Pamela Merriman; *m* 1st (marr. diss.); two *s*; 2nd, 2010, Maria Balshaw; one step *s* one step *d. Educ:* King Edward's Sch., Birmingham; St John's Coll., Cambridge (BA Archaeol. 1982; PhD 1989); Univ. of Leicester (Cert. Mus. Studies). AMA; FSA. Museum of London: Asst Keeper, Prehistory, 1986–91; Hd, Dept of Early London Hist. and Collections, 1991–97; University College London: Sen. Lectr, then Reader, in Mus. Studies, Inst. of Archaeol., 1997–2006; Curator, 1998–2006, Dir, 2006 Mus and Collections; Dir, Manchester Mus., Univ. of Manchester, 2006–18. Pres., Council for British Archaeol., 2005–08. Chm., Univ. Museums Gp, 2008–13. Chair: Collections Trust, 2014–17; Rothesay Pavilion Trust, 2014–; Wellcome Trust Inspiring Science, 2017–. *Publications:* Beyond the Glass Case: the past, the heritage and the public in Britain, 1991; The Peopling of London, 1993; Making Early Histories in Museums, 1999; Public Archaeology, 2004. *Recreations:* running, family. *Address:* Horniman Museum and Gardens, 100 London Road, Forest Hill, SE23 3PQ. *T:* (020) 8699 1872. *E:* nmerriman@horniman.ac.uk.

**MERRITT, Prof. John Edward;** Emeritus Professor, The Open University, since 1987; *b* 13 June 1926; *s* of Leonard Merritt and Janet (*née* Hartford); *m* 1948, Denise Edmondson (*d* 2017); two *s. Educ:* Univ. of Durham (BA); Univ. of London (DipEdPsychol). AFBPsS; FRSA. Sandhurst, 1945–46; Trng Officer, Border Regt, 1946–48. Educnl Psychologist, Lancs LEA, 1957–59; Sen. Educnl Psychologist, Hull LEA, 1959–63; Lectr, Inst. of Educn, Univ. of Durham, 1964–71; Prof. of Teacher Educn, Open Univ., 1971–85, retd. Hon. Res. Fellow, Charlotte Mason Coll., Ambleside, 1986–88. Pres., UK Reading Assoc., 1969–70; Chm., 5th World Congress on Reading, Vienna, 1974; Mem., Nat. Cttee of Inquiry into Reading and Use of English (Bullock Cttee), 1973–75. Hon. FCP 1994. *Publications:* Reading and the Curriculum (ed), 1971; A Framework for Curriculum Design, 1972; (ed jtly) Reading Today and Tomorrow, 1972; (ed jtly) The Reading Curriculum, 1972; Perspectives on Reading, 1973; What Shall We Teach, 1974; Make Democracy Work, 2010; Installing Proactive Democracy: a guide for the not so dumb, 2011; The Republic of Soccon: the birth, decline and painful rebirth of democracy, 2011; Democracy-in-Action; numerous papers in educnl jls. *Recreations:* fell walking, orienteering, climbing, ski-ing, theatre. *Address:* Highfield, 5 Cross Street, Keswick, Cumbria CA12 4DE. *T:* (01768) 774875.

**MERRIVALE,** 4th Baron *cr* 1925, of Walkhampton, Co. Devon; **Derek John Philip Duke;** *b* 16 March 1948; *s* of 3rd Baron Merrivale and of Colette, *d* of John Douglas Wise, Bordeaux, France; *S* father, 2007; *m* 1976, Guillemette Daras; one *s* three *d* (of whom one *s* one *d* are twins). *Heir: s* Hon. Thomas Duke [*b* 25 March 1980; *m* 2007, Diane Castel].

**MERRON, Gillian Joanna;** Chief Executive, Board of Deputies of British Jews, since 2014; *b* 12 April 1959. *Educ:* Wanstead High Sch.; Univ. of Lancaster (BSc Hons (Mgt Scis) 1981). Community Develt and Small Business Advr, 1982–87; Sen. Regl Union Officer, E Midlands, 1987–97. MP (Lab) Lincoln, 1997–2010; contested (Lab) same seat, 2010. PPS to Minister of State for the Armed Forces, 1998–99, to Minister of State for Defence Procurement, 1999–2001, to Sec. of State for NI, 2001–02; an Asst Govt Whip, 2002–04; a Lord Comr of HM Treasury (Govt Whip), 2004–06; Parly Under-Sec. of State, DfT, 2006–07; a Parly Sec., Cabinet Office, and Minister for the E Midlands, 2007–08; Parly Under-Sec. of State, DFID, 2008, FCO, 2008–09; Minister of State (Minister for Public Health), DoH, 2009–10. Mem., Select Cttee on Trade and Industry, 1997–98. Vice-Chm., PLP Back bench Cttee on Foreign and Commonwealth Affairs, 1997–98; Chm., E Midlands Gp of Lab. MPs, 1999–2002. Mem. Bd, Westminster Foundn for Democracy, 1998–2001. Grad., Armed Forces Parly Scheme (RAF), 1997–98; Fellow, Industry and Parlt Trust, 2002–; VSO placement, Guyana, 2005. Divl Dir, Cool Milk Gp, 2010–14. Dir (unpaid), E Midlands Sport, 2000–03. European Rep., Weightwatchers Internat. 2011–14. Chm., Bus Users UK, 2011–14. Volunteer, Smart Works, 2010–15. Nat. Officer and Trustee, Liberal Judaism. Patron, Transport Benevolent Fund. Mentor, The Prince's Trust. *Recreations:* running, theatre, films. *Address:* Board of Deputies of British Jews, 1 Torriano Mews, NW5 2RZ. *E:* gillian.merron@bod.org.uk.

**MERRY, David Byron,** CMG 2000; HM Diplomatic Service, retired; High Commissioner, Gaborone, 2001–05; *b* 16 Sept. 1945; *s* of late Colin Merry and Audrey Merry (*née* Handley); *m* 1967, Patricia Ann Ellis; one *s* two *d. Educ:* King Edward VII Sch., Sheffield; Ecclesfield Grammar Sch. Min. of Aviation, 1961–65; entered HM Diplomatic Service, 1965; Bangkok, 1969–73; Budapest, 1974–77; FCO, 1977–81; First Sec. (Econ.) and Civil Air Attaché, Bonn, 1981–85; Head of Chancery, E Berlin, 1985–88; FCO, 1989–93; Counsellor and Dep. Head of Mission, Manila, 1993–97; Dep. High Comr, Karachi, 1997–2000; FCO, 2000–01. *Recreations:* swimming, walking. *Address:* 22 Orchard Close, Hawley, Camberley, Surrey GU17 9EX.

**MERRYLEES, Prof. Andrew,** RSA 1991; RIBA; FRIAS, FCSD; architect, artist and planner; *b* 13 Oct. 1933; *s* of Andrew Merrylees and Mary McGowan Craig; *m* 1959, Maie Crawford; two *s* one *d. Educ:* Glasgow Sch. of Architecture (BArch 1956; DipTP 1957). RIBA 1958; FRIAS 1977; FCSD 1978. Joined Sir Basil Spence, Glover & Ferguson, 1952: student, 1952–57; architect, 1957–68; Associate, 1968; Partner, 1972–85; Principal, Andrew Merrylees Associates, then Andrew Merrylees Grierson & Robertson, subseq. Merrylees & Robertson, 1985–2000, merged with Hypostyle, 2001; consultant in private architectural practice, Hypostyle Architects, 2001–10. Consultant Architect: SCONUL, 1964–79; UC Dublin, 1973–91. Hon. Prof. of Architecture, Univ. of Dundee, 1998–. Member: Adv. Council for Arts in Scotland, 1989–97; Council, RIAS, 1991–94. Mem., Edinburgh Fest. Soc., 1979–. Trustee, RSA Foundn, 2012–. *Major projects include:* university buildings at Edinburgh (Civic Trust Award, for Univ. Liby, 1969; later listed by Historic Scotland), Heriot-Watt, Dublin, Liverpool, Newcastle and Aston in Birmingham; Scottish HQ for AA; Sorting Office for PO, Edinburgh (Art in Architecture Award, Saltire Soc., 1983); Nat. Liby of Scotland (SCONUL Award, 1996); British Golf Mus., St Andrews; Motherwell Heritage Centre. FRSA 1993. Winner, numerous design competitions, including: UC Dublin Liby; Liverpool Univ. Arts Liby; Conf. Centre, Heriot-Watt Univ.; John Logie Baird Visions Centre, Glasgow; Dundee Sci. Centre. Numerous awards, including: Bronze Medal, RIBA, 1968; Gold Medal, Royal Scottish Acad., 1984; Lifetime Achievement Award, RIAS, 2013. *Recreations:* interested in all art forms, drawing and painting has been life-long pursuit running in parallel with and informing design, exhibiting at Royal Scottish Academy, Scottish Arts Council, London, Warsaw, Paris and St Raphael. *W:* www.andrewmerrylees.com. *Club:* Scottish Arts (Edinburgh).

**MERSEY,** 5th Viscount *cr* 1916, of Toxteth; **Edward John Hallam Bigham;** Lord Nairne 1681; Baron Mersey 1910; *b* 23 May 1966; *s* of 4th Viscount Mersey and of Joanna (*née* Murray); *S* father, 2006; *m* 1st, 1994, Claire Haigh (marr. diss. 1996); 2nd, 2001, Clare, *d* of Robert Schaw Miller; two *d. Educ:* Eton; Balliol Coll., Oxford; Trinity Coll. of Music, London; Ludwig-Maximilians Univ., Munich. Composer of works incl. The Nairne Ballads, Glenfinglas, Portsonachan, An Caisteal, Culebra, Staffa. Recordings with Royal Scottish Nat. Orch., Scottish Ensemble and Polish Nat. Radio SO. *Heir: uncle* Hon. David Edward Hugh Bigham [*b* 14 April 1938; *m* 1965, Anthea Rosemary Seymour; three *s* one *d*]. *W:* www.nedbigham.com.

**MERTHYR,** 5th Baron *cr* 1911, of Senghenydd, co. Glamorgan; **David Trevor Lewis;** Bt 1896; *b* 21 Feb. 1977; *o s* of Trevor Oswin Lewis, CBE (disclaimed his peerage for life and did not use his title of baronet) and of Susan Jane Lewis (*née* Birt-Llewellin); *S* father, 2015; *m* 2002, Elizabeth Jane Widdows; two *d. Heir: uncle* Hon. Peter Herbert Lewis [*b* 25 March 1937; *m* 1974, Caroline Monica Cadogan; one *d*].

**MERTON, Viscount; Thomas John Horatio Nelson;** *b* 27 April 2010; *s* and *heir* of Earl Nelson, *qv*.

**MERTON, Paul;** *see* Martin, P. J.

**MERTON, Prof. Robert C.,** PhD; School of Management Distinguished Professor of Finance, Sloan School of Management, Massachusetts Institute of Technology, since 2010; Resident Scientist, Dimensional Holdings Inc., since 2009; *b* 31 July 1944; *s* of late Robert K. Merton and Suzanne C. Merton; *m* 1966, June Rose (separated 1996); two *s* one *d. Educ:* Columbia Univ. (BS Engrg Math. 1966); California Inst. of Technology (MS Applied

Math. 1967); MIT (PhD Econs 1970). Massachusetts Institute of Technology: Asst Prof., 1970–73, Associate Prof., 1973–74, Prof., 1974–80, of Finance; J. C. Penney Prof. of Management, 1980–88; George Fisher Baker Prof. of Business Admin, 1988–98, John and Natty McArthur University Prof., 1998–2010, now Univ. Prof. Emeritus, Harvard Univ.; S. Donald Sussman Fellow, 2016–17. Member: NAS, 1993; Amer. Assoc. for Cancer Res., 2014–. Fellow: Amer. Acad. of Arts and Scis; Econometric Soc.; Internat. Assoc. of Financial Engrs; Inst. for Quantitative Res. in Finance; Financial Mgt Assoc.; Amer. Finance Assoc. Hon. Professor: Hautes Etudes Commerciales, France, 1995; St Petersburg Univ. of Mgt and Econs, Russia, 2011; Univ. of Electronic Sci. and Technol. of China, 2017; Sichuan Univ., 2017. Hamilton Lect., RIA, 2010. Dist. Fellow, Center for Financial Studies, Goethe Univ., Frankfurt, 2014–. Hon. LLD Chicago, 1991; Hon. DEconSc Lausanne, 1996; Dr hc Paris Dauphine, 1997; Nacional Mayor de San Marcos, Peru, 2004; Universidad Católica de Chile, Santiago, 2014; Instituto Politécnico Nacional, Mexico, 2016; Universidad Michoacana de San Nicolás de Hidalgo, Morelia, 2017; Hon. Dr Mgt Sci., Nat. Sun Yat-sen Univ., Taiwan, 1998; Hon. DSc: Athens Univ. of Econs and Business, 2003; Claremont Graduate Univ., 2008; Chinese Univ. of Hong Kong, 2014; Hon. DPhil Nacional Federico Villarreal, Peru, 2004; Hon. DBA Macau, 2014. Leo Melamed Prize, Univ. of Chicago, 1983; Financial Engr of the Year Award, Internat. Assoc. of Financial Engrs, 1993; Internat. Prize, Accademia Nazionale dei Lincei, 1993; FORCE Award for Financial Innovation, Fuqua Sch. of Business, Duke Univ., 1993; Nobel Prize for Economics, 1997; Michael I. Pupin Medal for Service to the Nation, Columbia Univ., 1998; Distinguished Alumni Award, CIT, 1999; Nicholas Molodovsky Award, Assoc. for Investment Mgt and Res., 2003; Higher Standard Award, Professional Risk Managers' Internat. Assoc., 2006; Hall of Fame, Fixed Income Analysts Soc., 2007; Dist. Finance Educator Award, Financial Educn Assoc., 2008; Award for Foundational Contribs to Finance, Owen Sch. of Mgt, Vanderbilt Univ., 2008; Robert A. Muh Award in Humanities, Arts and Social Scis, MIT, 2009; Tjailing C. Koopmans Asset Award, Tilburg Univ., 2009; Award for Outstanding Contribs to Financial Econs, LECG, 2010; Kolmogorov Medal, Univ. of London, 2010; Melamed-Arditti Innovation Award, CME Gp, 2011; WFE Award for Excellence, World Fedn of Exchanges, 2013; Lifetime Achievement Award, Financial Intermediation Res. Soc., 2014. *Publications:* Continuous-Time Finance, 1990, rev. edn 1992; (jtly) Casebook in Financial Engineering: applied studies of financial innovation, 1995; (jtly) The Global Financial System: a functional perspective, 1995; (jtly) Finance, 2000; (jtly) Risk Management and International Financial Fragility, 2003; (jtly) The Derivatives Sourcebook: foundations and trends in finance, 2006; Financial Economics, 2nd edn 2009; contribs to scientific jls. *Address:* Sloan School of Management, Massachusetts Institute of Technology, 77 Massachusetts Avenue, E62–634, Cambridge, MA 02139, USA.

**MERZ, (Joachim) Friedrich;** Partner, Mayer Brown LLP, since 2005; *b* 11 Nov. 1955; *m* 1981, Charlotte Gass; one *s* two *d. Educ:* Univ. of Bonn. Mil. service, 1975–76. Practical trng in judicial and other legal work, Saarbrücken and Johannesburg, SA, 1982–85; magistrate, Saarbrücken, 1985–86; lawyer, 1986–: German Chemical Industry Assoc., Bonn, Frankfurt, 1986–89. Chm., Atlantik-Brücke e.V., 2009–. MEP (CDU/CSU) S Westfalia, 1989–94; Mem. (CDU/CSU) Bundestag, 1994–2009. Mem., Finance Cttee and Cttee for Eur. Affairs, Bundestag, 1994–2009. CDU/CSU Parliamentary Group: co-ordinator, on Finance Cttee, 1996–98; Dep. Chm., 1998–2000, 2002–04; Chm., 2000–02; Member: Bd, CDU Nordrhein-Westfalen, 1997–; Fed. Bd, 1998–2000, Presidium, 2002–04, CDU party.

**MESHER, John;** an Upper Tribunal Judge (Administrative Appeals Chamber) (formerly a Social Security Commissioner and Child Support Commissioner), 1993–2019; *b* 25 June 1947; *s* of late Percy Charles Mesher and Dorothy Mesher; *m* 1973, Hilary Anne Wilkens; one *s* one *d* (and one *d* decd). *Educ:* Bancroft's Sch.; University Coll., Oxford (BA Jurisp, BCL); Yale Law Sch. (LLM). Called to the Bar, Gray's Inn, 1970; Lectr in Laws, QMC, 1969–76; University of Sheffield: Lectr in Law, Sen. Lectr and Reader, 1976–93; Simmons & Simmons Res. Fellow in Pensions Law, 1988–93; Prof. Associate, 1993–. Part-time Chm. of Social Security, Medical, and Disability Appeals Tribunals, 1981–93, Pensions Appeal Tribunals, 1995–2004; Dep. Social Security Comr, 1991–93. Editor, Occupational Pensions Law Reports, 1992–97; Section Editor, Encyclopedia of Employment Law, 1991–97. *Publications:* Compensation for Unemployment, 1976; CPAG's Supplementary Benefit Legislation Annotated, 1983, 10th edn, as Income-Related Benefits: the Legislation, 1993; (contrib.) Rayden and Jackson on Divorce and Family Matters, 17th edn 1997; (contrib.) Social Security Legislation, vol. II, Income Support, Jobseeker's Allowance, State Pension Credit and the Social Fund, vol. v, Universal Credit, 2014–; contribs to learned jls.

**MESHOULAM, Melanie;** *see* Clore, M.

**MESIĆ, Stjepan,** Hon. GCMG 2001; President, Republic of Croatia, 2000–10; *b* 24 Dec. 1934; *s* of Josip and Mandica Mesić; *m* 1961, Milka; two *d. Educ:* Univ. of Zagreb (LLB). Mayor, Orahovica, Croatia, 1967–71; MP Socialist Republic of Croatia, 1965–71; involved in Croatian Spring movt and served one-year jail sentence; Sec., 1990, Hd, Exec. Cttee, 1992, Croatian Democratic Union; Prime Minister, Socialist Republic of Croatia, May–Aug. 1990; last Pres., Yugoslavia, May–Dec. 1991; Speaker, Parlt of Republic of Croatia, 1992–94; Founder, Croatian Ind. Democrats Party (HND), 1994; Mem., Croatian Nat. Party (HNS), 1997–2000 (Exec. Vice-Pres. and Pres., Zagreb Br.). Charles Univ. Medal, 2001. Homeland War Meml Medal (Croatia), 1993; State Order of Star of Romania, 2000; Grand Star, Decoration of Honour for Merit (Austria), 2001; Golden Order, Gjergj Kastrioti Skënderbeu (Albania), 2001; Grand Cross, Order of Saviour (Greece), 2001; Order of White Double Cross, 1st class (Slovakia), 2001; Knight Grand Cross, Order of Merit with Grand Cordon (Italy), 2001; Grand Cross with Collar, Order of the Republic (Hungary), 2002; Dostyk Order, 1st degree (Kazakhstan), 2002; Order of the Crown (Malaysia), 2002; Grand Order of King Tomislav with Sash and Grand Star (Croatia), 2005; Order of Merit (Chile), 2008. *Publications:* The Break-up of Yugoslavia: political memoirs, 1992, 2nd edn 1994. *Recreations:* Nanbudo, swimming. *Address:* c/o Office of the President of the Republic of Croatia, Pantovčak 241, 10 000 Zagreb, Croatia.

**MESSENGER, Gen. Sir Gordon (Kenneth),** KCB 2016 (CB 2015); DSO 2003 (Bar 2009); OBE 2000; Vice Chief of Defence Staff, 2016–19; Aide-de-Camp General to the Queen, 2016–19; *b* Dundee, 15 April 1962; *s* of Angus Messenger and Elinor Messenger; *m* 1988, Sarah Louise Middleton; one *s* two *d. Educ:* King Edward VI Sch., Southampton; Univ. of Leicester (BSc Geog. 1983). Joined Royal Marines, 1983; CO 40 Cdo, 2001–03; Comdr 3 Cdo Bde, 2008–09; COS (Ops) Perm. Jt HQ, 2010–12; Dep. Comdr, Allied Land Comd, 2013–14; DCDS (Mil. Strategy and Ops), 2014–16. *Recreations:* golf, gardening, getting fit.

**MESSERVY-WHITING, Maj.-Gen. Graham Gerald,** CBE 2003 (MBE 1980); Member, War Pensions and Armed Forces Compensation Chambers, First-tier Tribunal (formerly Pensions Appeal Tribunal), since 2005; *b* 20 Oct. 1946; *s* of late Gerald and Kathleen Messervy-Whiting; *m* 1969, Shirley Hitchinson (*d* 2019); one *s. Educ:* Lycée Français de Londres; Army Staff Coll.; RAF Staff Coll. Commnd Intelligence Corps, 1967; Regtl duty, 1 KOSB, Germany, Libya, Cyprus, Hong Kong, 1968–82; jsdc 1984; Secretariat Chiefs of Staff, 1984–86; CO, Intelligence and Security Gp, Germany, 1986–88;
Briefing Officer, SACEUR, 1988–91; rcds 1992; Mil. Advr to Lord Owen, 1992–93; Res. Fellow, KCL, 1993; Dir, Defence Commitments Staff, 1994–95; COS, WEU, 1995–98; Asst Dir, Ops, GCHQ, 1998–2000; C of S, EU Mil. Staff, 2000–03. Dep. Dir, Centre for Studies in Security and Diplomacy, Univ. of Birmingham, 2003–10. FRUSI 1996. Associate Fellow, Chatham House, 2003–07. *Publications:* contribs to academic pubns on Eur. security and defence issues. *Recreations:* travel, bridge, natural history. *E:* ggmw3@btinternet.com. *Club:* Army and Navy.

**MESSITER, Malcolm Cassan;** oboist; Founder and Managing Director: Messiter Software, since 1985; Trans-Send International Ltd, since 1992; *b* 1 April 1949; *s* of late Ian and Enid Messiter; *m* 1st, 1972, Christine (marr. diss. 1998); one *d*; 2nd, 2016, Rachel Sanders-Hewett. *Educ:* Bryanston Sch.; Paris Conservatoire; Royal Coll. of Music (ARCM Hons 1971). First Oboe: BBC Concert Orchestra, 1971–77; London Mozart Players, 1977–83; London Festival Orchestra, 1985–; many solo concerts. Several recordings. Founder: Virtual Orchestra Co. Ltd, 1999; Barnet Chamber Music Club, 2010. Owner, Just a Minute, BBC Radio 4, 2001–. *Publications:* personal computer software and manuals, guides to remote controlled model helicopters and aeroplanes. *Recreations:* wine, chamber music, model helicopters, oboe playing, automated harpsichords. *Address:* 47 Sutton Crescent, Barnet, Herts EN5 2SW.

**MESTON,** family name of **Baron Meston**.

**MESTON, 3rd Baron** *cr* 1919, of Agra and Dunottar; **James Meston;** QC 1996; **His Honour Judge Meston;** a Circuit Judge, since 1999; *b* 10 Feb. 1950; *s* of 2nd Baron Meston and Diana Mary Came, *d* of Capt. O. S. Doll; *S* father, 1984; *m* 1974, Jean Rebecca Anne, *d* of John Carder; one *s* two *d. Educ:* Wellington College; St Catharine's Coll., Cambridge (MA); Leicester Univ. (LLM). Barrister, Middle Temple, 1973; Jun. Counsel to Queen's Proctor, 1992–96; a Recorder, 1997–99; Designated Family Judge, Dorset, 2015–18. Legal Assessor, 1991–99, Sen. Legal Assessor, 1999, UKCC. Appeal Steward, BBB of C, 1993–2001. Pres., British Soc. of Commerce, 1984–92. Vice Pres., Family Mediators Assoc., 1999–. *Heir: s* Hon. Thomas James Dougall Meston [*b* 21 Oct. 1977; *m* 2009, Anna Ching; two *s*]. *Address:* Queen Elizabeth Building, Temple, EC4Y 9BS. *Club:* Hawks (Cambridge).

**METCALF, His Honour Christopher Sherwood John;** a Circuit Judge, 2001–11; *b* 18 May 1945; *s* of Bernard Metcalf and Margaret Metcalf; *m* 1977, Pamela Falconer; two *s* two *d. Educ:* The Leys Sch., Cambridge; W Georgia Coll., USA (Rotary Internat. Schol. 1963). Called to the Bar, Middle Temple, 1972; in practice on Midland and Oxford Circuit, 1972–2001; Asst Recorder, 1991–95; Recorder, 1995–2001. Member: Mental Health Rev. Tribunal, 2001–15; Parole Bd, 2002–17. *Recreations:* foreign travel, church architecture, private enterprise, games, choral music, painting, golf.

**METCALF, Sir David (Harry),** Kt 2013; CBE 2008; PhD; Professor of Industrial Relations, London School of Economics, 1985–2009, now Emeritus Professor, Centre for Economic Performance; *b* 15 May 1942; *s* of Dorothy and Dorothy Metcalf; *m* 1968, Helen Pitt (Dame Helen Metcalf, DBE, *d* 2003); one *s. Educ:* Manchester Univ. (BA Econ 1964; MA 1966); London Univ. (PhD 1971). Apprentice welder, English Electric, 1959–61; Lectr in Econs, LSE, 1967–75; Special Advr to Minister for Social Security, 1976–79; Prof. of Econs, Kent Univ., 1978–85. Comr, Low Pay Commn, 1997–2007; Director: Starting Price Regulatory Commn, 2005–; Labour Market Enforcement, 2017–19; Mem., Rev. Body on Sen. Salaries, 2009–15. Chm., Home Office Migration Adv. Cttee, 2007–16. Editor, British Jl Industrial Relns, 1990–95. *Publications:* Low Pay, Occupational Mobility and Minimum Wage Policy in Britain, 1983; New Perspectives on Industrial Disputes, 1993; Trade Unions: resurgence or demise?, 2005; articles in Econ. Jl, Industrial and Labor Relns Rev., etc. *Recreations:* horse-racing (owner and investor), watching Tottenham Hotspur FC. *Address:* 18 St Georges Avenue, N7 0HD. *T:* (020) 7607 5902. *E:* d.metcalf@lse.ac.uk. *Club:* MCC.

**METCALFE, Adrian Peter,** OBE 2001; international sport and media consultant; *b* 2 March 1942; *s* of Hylton and Cora Metcalfe; *m* Catherine, Baroness von Delvig; one *s* one *d* by former marriage. *Educ:* Roundhay Sch., Leeds; Magdalen Coll., Oxford. Reporter, Sunday Express, 1964; Dep. Editor, World of Sport, ABC TV, 1965; Producer, Sports Arena, LWT, 1968; Presenter, CBS Sports Spectacular, 1972–76; Man. Dir, AMO Productions, 1976; Sen. Commissioning Editor, Sport and Features, Channel 4 TV, 1981; Commentator, ITV, 1966–87; Director of Programmes: Eurosport, 1989–91; Tyne Tees Television Ltd, 1991–92; Dir, Venue Production, Atlantic Olympic Games, 1994–96; Chm., API Television, 1996–98; Exec. Publr, worldsport.com, 1998–2000; Chm., AMDM Agency, 2003; Dir, World Professional Billiards and Snooker Assoc., 2004. GB Record, 400m, 45·7, ranked No 1 in the world at 400m, 1961; Gold Medal, 400m and 4×400m, World Student Games, 1963; Silver Medal, 4×400m, Tokyo Olympics, 1964; 7 British Records, 4 European Records, 1961–64. Pres., OUAC, 1962–63. Mem., UK Sport, 1998 (Chm., Major Events Steering Gp, 1999–2003); Life Vice-Pres. and Trustee, SportsAid (formerly Sports Aid Foundn), 1990. *Recreations:* still running, Russian culture.

**METCALFE, Charles;** wine and food presenter, writer and entertainer; *b* London, 15 April 1949; *s* of John Alan and Ann Monck Mason Metcalfe; *m* 1986, Kathryn McWhirter; one *s* two *d. Educ:* Eton Coll.; Christ Church, Oxford (MA Hons English Lang. and Lit.). Investment analyst, London Wall Gp, 1973–75; opera singer, tour guide and cook, 1975–83; Associate Ed., Wine Internat. mag., 1983–2005; Co-Chm., Internat. Wine Challenge, 1983–. TV presenter, 1987–; progs incl. This Morning, Great British Food, Simply Greek, Taste Today, Great Food Live. Hon. Pres., Assoc. of Wine Educators, 2002–; Chm. of Judges, Acad. of Chocolate Awards, 2015. Chm., Balcombe Parish Council, 2015–. Gran Orden de Caballeros del Vino, 1997; Comendador, Ordem do Mérito Empresarial (Classe do Mérito Agrícola) (Portugal), 2012. *Publications:* with Kathryn McWhirter: The Wines of Spain and Portugal, 1988; Sainsbury's The Wines of Spain and Portugal, 1991; Sainsbury's Pocket Food and Wine Guide, 1995; The Wine and Food Lover's Guide to Portugal, 2007. *Recreations:* cooking, singing, environmental campaigning. *Address:* Old Inn House, London Road, Balcombe RH17 6JQ. *T:* (01444) 811682. *E:* charlesmetcalfe@btopenworld.com.

**METCALFE, Prof. Ian Saxley,** PhD; FREng; CEng, FIChemE; CChem, FRSC; Professor of Chemical Engineering, Newcastle University, since 2005; *b* Stockton-on-Tees, 7 Aug. 1961; *s* of Saxley Metcalfe and Margaret Metcalfe; *m* 2004, Maria Isabel Yorquez Ramirez; two *d. Educ:* Imperial Coll., London (BScEng 1982); Princeton Univ. (MA Chem. Engrg 1984; PhD Chem. Engrg 1987). CEng 1991; MIChemE 1991, FIChemE 2004; CChem 1992; MRSC 1992, FRSC 2012. Lectr, 1987–96, Sen. Lectr, 1996–97, Dept of Chem. Engrg, Imperial Coll., London; Prof. of Chemical Engrg, Univ. of Edinburgh, 1997–2001; Prof. of Chemical Engrg, UMIST, subseq. Univ. of Manchester, 2001–04, Vis. Prof., 2005–. FREng 2012. Exec. Editor, Chemical Engineering Science, 2001–13. *Publications:* Chemical Reaction Engineering: a first course, 1997. *Recreation:* dreaming of Buachaille Etive Mor on a sunny day. *Address:* School of Chemical Engineering and Advanced Materials, Merz Court, Newcastle University, Newcastle upon Tyne NE1 7RU. *T:* (0191) 222 5279. *E:* i.metcalfe@ncl.ac.uk.

**METCALFE, Prof. James Charles,** PhD; Professor of Mammalian Cell Biochemistry, University of Cambridge, 1996–2007, now Emeritus; Fellow, Darwin College, Cambridge, 1975–2000; *b* 20 July 1939; *s* of Cyril Tom Metcalfe and Olive Kate (*née* Ayling); *m* 1st, 1969, Susan Milner (marr. diss.); one *s* one *d*; 2nd, 1983, Aviva Miriam Tolkovsky. *Educ:* St Paul's Sch.; Sidney Sussex Coll., Cambridge (MA; PhD 1965). Research Fellow, Dept of Pharmacology, Cambridge Univ. and Dept of Pharmacology, Harvard Med. Sch., 1965–67; Mem. Scientific Staff, MRC Molecular Pharmacology Unit, Dept of Pharmacology, Cambridge, 1967–72; Res. Fellow, Dept of Chemistry, Stanford Univ., 1968; Perm. MRC appt, 1970; Div. of Molecular Pharmacology, NIMR, 1972–73; Univ. Lectr, Dept of Pharmacology, Cambridge, 1974; Sir William Dunn Reader, Dept of Biochem., Cambridge, 1974–96. Chm., Scientific Cttee, CRC, 1995–2000; Trustee and Chm., Scientific Cttee, EMF Biol Res. Trust, 2005–. Mem., EMBO, 1981. Fogarty Internat. Schol., NIH, 1979. Colworth Medal, Biochem. Soc., 1973. *Publications:* papers in scientific jls. *Recreations:* walking in France, reading, ski-ing. *Address:* Sanger Building, Department of Biochemistry, University of Cambridge, 80 Tennis Court Road, Old Addenbrookes Site, Cambridge CB2 1GA. *T:* (01223) 333633.

**METCALFE, Prof. (John) Stanley,** CBE 1993; Stanley Jevons Professor of Political Economy and Cobden Lecturer, School of Economic Studies, 1992–2008, now Professor Emeritus, Director, Policy Research in Engineering, Science and Technology, 1984–2008, and Co-executive Director, ESRC Centre for Research on Innovation and Competition, 1997–2006 (Executive Director, 1997), University of Manchester; *b* 20 March 1946; *m* 1967, Joan Shrouder; one *s* one *d*. *Educ:* Liverpool Collegiate High Sch.; Univ. of Manchester (BA 1967; MSc 1968). Lectr in Econs, Univ. of Manchester, 1967–74; Lectr, then Sen. Lectr in Econs, Univ. of Liverpool, 1974–80; University of Manchester: Prof. of Econs, 1980–2008, now Emeritus; Hd, Dept of Econs, 1986–89; Dean of Social Sci. Faculty, 1992–95; Mem. Court, 1992–2004 (Mem., Finance Cttee, 1977–2004); Interim Dean, Faculty of Med. and Human Scis, 2003–04. Vis. Prof. in Econs, Univ. of Queensland, 1996–; Adjunct Prof. of Econs, Curtin Univ. of Technol., 2008–. Vis. Fellow, Centre for Business Res., Cambridge Univ., 2007–. Member: ACARD, 1983–87; ACOST, 1987–92; MMC, 1991–97. President: Manchester Statistical Soc., 1992–94; Internat. J. A. Schumpeter Soc., 1999–2000. AcSS 2003. FRSA. *Publications:* (contrib.) The UK Economy, 1975; (jtly) Post Innovation Performance, 1986; (jtly) New Electronic Information: the UK database industry in its international context, 1987; (ed jtly) Barriers to Growth in Small Firms, 1989; The Enterprise Challenge: overcoming barriers to growth in small firms, 1990; (ed jtly) Evolutionary Theories of Economic and Technological Change, 1991; (ed jtly) Wealth from Diversity, 1996; Evolutionary Economics and Creative Destruction, 1998. *Address:* Manchester Institute of Innovation Research, University of Manchester, Harold Hankins Building, Booth Street West, Manchester M13 9QH.

**METCALFE, Julian Edward,** OBE 2014 (MBE 2000); Founder, 1986, Creative Director, 2003–08, Pret a Manger; Founder and Creative Director, Metcalfe's Food Company, since 2008; *b* 14 Dec. 1959; *s* of David Metcalfe and Alexa (*née* Boycun); one *d*; *m* 1st, 1993, Melanie Willson (marr. diss.); two *s*; 2nd, 2011, Brooke de Ocampo. *Educ:* Harrow; Central London Poly. (BSc). Founder, Itsu, 1997. *Recreation:* eating. *Address:* (office) 3rd Floor, 53 Parker Street, WC2B 5PT. *Club:* White's.

**METCALFE, Julian Ross;** HM Diplomatic Service, retired; Director of Advocacy, International Agency for Prevention of Blindness, 2010–12; *b* 24 Feb. 1956; *s* of late Patrick Ross Metcalfe and Marjory Gillian Metcalfe (*née* Gaze); *m* 1983, Rachel Mai Jones; one *d*. *Educ:* Horris Hill Sch.; Cheltenham Coll.; Univ. of Bristol (BSc Pols and Econs 1978); Univ. of Sussex (MA Econs 1981). Project Trust Volunteer, mentally handicapped children, S Africa, 1975; ODI Fellow serving as Health Planning Officer, Govt of Malawi, 1978–81; consultant, Commodities Res. Unit, 1982–83; FCO Econ. Advr, 1983–87; First Sec., Cairo, 1987–91; Southern Africa Dept, 1991–93, Eastern Adriatic Dept, 1993–95, FCO; Hd, UK Delegn, EC Monitoring Mission to Former Yugoslavia, 1995; Dep. Hd of Mission, Zagreb, 1995–97; Jt Hd, Eastern Adriatic Dept (dealing with Balkans), FCO, 1997–2000; Hd, Estate Strategy Unit, FCO, 2000–04; Dep. Perm. Rep. to the UN, Geneva, 2005–09. *Recreations:* camping, helping in garden. *E:* Julianmetcalfe@yahoo.com. *Club:* Royal Over-Seas League.

**METCALFE, Stanley;** *see* Metcalfe, J. S.

**METCALFE, Stephen James;** MP (C) South Basildon and East Thurrock, since 2010; *b* Walthamstow, 9 Jan. 1966; *s* of David John and Valerie Metcalfe; *m* 1988, Angela Claire Giblett; one *s* one *d*. *Educ:* Loughton Sch.; Buckhurst Hill Co. High Sch. Order Clerk, Burrup Matthieson, 1985–86; Metloc Printers Ltd: Sales Exec., 1986–87; Studio Manager, 1987–92; Dir, 1992–2011. Mem. (C Epping Forest DC, 2003–07. Contested (C) Ilford S, 2005. PPS to Sec. of State for Justice, 2014–15, to Minister of State for Schs and Minister of State for Vulnerable Children and Families, 2015–16. Government Envoy, Year of Engineering, 2018. Mem., Sci. and Technol. Select Cttee, 2010–15, 2017– (Chm., 2016–17); Chm., Parly Scientific Cttee, 2015– (Dep. Chm., 2014–15). *Publications:* wine appreciation, theatre, Rugby, football. *Address:* House of Commons, SW1A 0AA. *T:* (020) 7219 7009. *E:* stephen.metcalfe.mp@parliament.uk.

**METGE, Dame (Alice) Joan,** DBE 1987; research anthropologist and writer; *b* 21 Feb. 1930; *d* of Cedric Leslie Metge and Alice May (*née* Rigg). *Educ:* Auckland Univ. (MA); London School of Economics (PhD). Jun. Lectr, Geography Dept, Auckland Univ., 1952; research and doctoral study, 1953–61; Lectr, Univ. Extension, Auckland Univ., 1961–64; University of Wellington: Sen. Lectr, Anthropology Dept, 1965–67, Associate Prof., 1968–88. Fifth Captain James Cook Res. Fellow, 1981–83. Hon. DLitt Auckland, 2001. Hutchinson Medal, LSE, 1958; Elsdon Best Meml Medal, Polynesian Soc., 1987; Te Rangi Hiroa Medal, Royal Soc. of NZ, 1997; Asia-Pacific Mediation Forum Peace Prize, 2006; Prime Minister's Award for Literary Achievement in Non-Fiction, 2015. *Publications:* A New Maori Migration, 1964; The Maoris of New Zealand, 1967, rev. edn 1976; (with Patricia Kinloch) Talking Past Each Other, 1978; In and Out of Touch, 1986; Te Kohao o Te Ngira, 1990; New Growth From Old, 1995; Korero Tahi-Talking Together, 2001; Tuamaka: the challenge of difference in Aotearoa New Zealand, 2010; Tauira: Maori methods of learning and teaching, 2015. *Recreations:* theatre, music, reading, gardening. *Address:* 3 Mariri Road, Onehunga, Auckland 1061, New Zealand. *T:* (9) 6345757.

**METHAM, Patricia;** education consultant, since 2014; National Lead for English, Office for Standards in Education, Children's Services and Skills, since 2013; *b* Cairo, 1 March 1945; *d* of John (Jack) Andrews and Jane Starrett Andrews; *m* 1st, 1966, Nicholas Hern (marr. diss.); two *d*; 2nd, 1986, Dr Tim Metham. *Educ:* Upper Chine Sch., Isle of Wight; Bristol Univ. (BA English and Drama). English and Drama Teacher: Dartford Girls' Grammar Sch., 1966–67; Sir Leo Schultz High Sch., Hull, 1967; Newland High Sch., Hull, 1967–72; Wimbledon High Sch., 1975–82 (School-Teacher Fellow, Merton Coll., Oxford, 1981); Head of English and Sixth Form, Francis Holland Sch., London, 1982–87; Head: Farlington Sch., Horsham, 1987–92; Ashford, Sch., 1992–97; Roedean Sch., 1997–2002; Principal, Internat. Regent's Sch., Thailand, 2003–05. HM Inspector of Schs, 2006–14. Vice Chm., Ind. Schs Exams Bd, 1999. JP, Horsham, then Ashford, 1991–97. *Publications:* editor of seven critical play texts. *Recreations:* theatre, choral singing, travel to centres of archaeological and cultural interest (in Europe, particularly), good food and good wine.

**METHUEN, 8th Baron** *cr* 1838; **James Paul Archibald Methuen-Campbell;** *b* Ludlow, 25 Oct. 1952; *s* of Christopher Paul Mansel Campbell Methuen-Campbell and Oona Methuen-Campbell (*née* Treherne); *S* cousin, 2014. *Educ:* Stowe Sch. Music critic, musicologist and author. *Publications:* Chopin Playing, 1981; (contrib.) Cambridge Companion to Chopin, 1992; Denton Welch: writer and artist, 2002; Claughton Pellew, 2019; past regular contribs to Records and Recording, Gramophone, The Times. *Recreations:* playing piano, photography. *Heir:* half-*b* Thomas Rice Mansel Methuen-Campbell, *b* 4 March 1977. *Address:* Corsham Court, Corsham, Wilts SN13 0BZ. *E:* jamesmethc@gmail.com.

**METHUEN, Richard St Barbe;** QC 1997; a Recorder, since 2002; *b* 22 Aug. 1950; *s* of John Methuen and Rosemary Methuen; *m* 1974, Mary Catherine Griffiths, LLB, MA, *d* of David Howard Griffiths, OBE; one *s* two *d*. *Educ:* Marlborough College; Inns of Court Sch. of Law. Called to the Bar, Lincoln's Inn, 1972. Head of Chambers, 2000–05. Mediator in personal injury work. *Address:* 12 King's Bench Walk, Temple, EC4Y 7EL. *E:* methuen@12kbw.co.uk.

**METHUEN-CAMPBELL,** family name of **Baron Methuen**.

**METHVEN, Rear Adm. Paul,** CB 2019; CEng; Director, Submarines Acquisition, since 2017; *b* Inverness, 14 April 1969; *s* of Leonard and Margaret Methven; *m* 1993, Gillian Leech; one *s* one *d*. *Educ:* Portree High Sch.; Glenalmond Coll.; Royal Naval Engrg Coll. (BEng 1991); University Coll. London (MSc 1998); Bath Univ. (MBA 2004). CEng, MIMarEST 1998. Joined RN, 1988; Marine Engr Officer, HMS Triumph, 2002–04; Ministry of Defence: MA to Dir Gen. Nuclear, 2004–06; Astute 4–7 Nuclear Propulsion Manager, 2006–08; Asst Hd, Strategy Mgt, 2008–10; Superintendent Submarines, 2010–14; Head: Type 26 Global Combat Ship, 2014–16; Nat. Shipbuilding Strategy, Defence Equipment and Support, 2016–17. *Recreations:* sailing, ski-ing, squash, bagpipes. *Clubs:* Royal Naval Sailing Association; Royal Torbay Yacht.

**METTERS, Dr Jeremy Stanley,** CB 1994; FRCOG; Deputy Chief Medical Officer, Department of Health, 1989–99; HM Inspector of Anatomy, 1999–2005; *b* 6 June 1939; *s* of late Thomas Lee Metters and Henrietta Currey; *m* 1962, Margaret Howell; two *s* one *d*. *Educ:* Eton; Magdalene College, Cambridge; St Thomas' Hosp. (MB BChir 1963, MA 1965). MRCOG 1970, FRCOG 1982. House officer posts, St Thomas' Hosp. and Reading, 1963–66; Lectr in Obst. and Gyn., St Thomas' Hosp., 1968–70; Registrar in Radiotherapy, 1970–72; DHSS 1972; SPMO (Under Sec.), 1984; Dep. Chief Scientist, DHSS, later Dept of Health, 1986–89. Member: Council of Europe Cttee on Bioethics (formerly Ethical and Legal Problems relating to Human Genetics), 1983–89; ESRC, 1986–88. *Publications:* papers in med. and sci. jls. *Recreations:* DIY, steam preservation.

**METTYEAR, His Honour Michael King;** DL; a Circuit Judge, 1992–2015; *b* 22 Sept. 1946; *s* of Charles Frank Henry King and Vera May (*née* Moore); *m* 1984, Gail Stafford; one *s* one *d*. *Educ:* LLB London (external). Called to the Bar, Middle Temple, 1971; a Recorder, 1990–92; Hon. Recorder, Kingston upon Hull and ER of Yorks, 2003–14; a pt-time Justice of Grand Ct of Cayman Islands, 2012–16. Member: Sentencing Adv. Panel, 1999–2004; Sentencing Guidelines Council, 2004–10. DL E Yorks, 2014. *Recreations:* tennis, travel, ski-ing.

**METZ, David Henry,** PhD; Honorary Professor, Centre for Transport Studies, University College London, since 2015 (Visiting Professor, 2005–15); *b* 11 March 1941; *s* of Lewis and Esther Metz; *m* 1st, 1966, Marilyn Ann Yeatman (marr. diss. 1980); one *s*; 2nd, 1994, Monica Mary Threlfall. *Educ:* City of London Sch.; University Coll. London (BSc Chem., MSc Biochem.); King's Coll. London (PhD Biophysics). Virology Division, National Institute for Medical Research, 1967–76: Fellow, Helen Hay Whitney Foundn, 1967–69; Mem., MRC Scientific Staff, 1969–76; Res. Fellow, Dept of Microbiol., Harvard Med. Sch., and Children's Hosp. Med. Center, Boston, 1972–73; Dept of Energy, 1976–86; Dep. Dir-Gen., Office of Gas Supply, 1986–89; Dept of Energy, 1989–92; Chief Scientist, Dept of Transport, 1992–97; Dir, AgeNet, Wolfson Inst. of Preventive Medicine, 1997–2000. Vis. Prof., Centre for Ageing and Public Health, LSHTM, 2000–06. Non-executive Director: Camden and Islington Community Health Services NHS Trust, 2001–02; Camden PCT, 2002–11. Member: Mgt Bd, TRRL, 1993–96; Res. and Technol. Cttee, BR, 1994–96; Res. Adv. Council, NATS, 1997–99; Financial Services Consumer Panel, 2005–11. Mem. Mgt Bd, Oxford Dementia Centre, 1999–2001. *Publications:* Older, Richer, Fitter (with M. Underwood), 2005; The Limits to Travel, 2008; Peak Car: the future of travel, 2014; Travel Fast or Smart?, 2016; Driving Change: travel in the twenty-first century, 2019; papers in sci. jls. *Address:* 32 Laurier Road, NW5 1SJ.

**METZER, Anthony David Erwin;** QC 2013; a Deputy High Court Judge, since 2018; a Judge of Upper Tribunal (Asylum and Immigration Chamber), since 2018; *b* Edgware, Middx, 19 July 1963; *s* of Kurt Metzer and Louise Taylor; *m* 1988, Prof. Louise Sylvester; one *s* two *d*. *Educ:* Edgware Jun. Sch.; Haberdashers' Aske's Sch. for Boys; Wadham Coll., Oxford (BA Juris.); Inns of Court Sch. of Law. Called to the Bar, Middle Temple, 1987; in practice as a barrister, specialising in crime, civil incl. actions against the police and inquests, and immigration; Dr Johnson's Bldgs, 1988–90; Doughty St Chambers, 1990–2007; 23 Essex St, 2007–11; Argent Chambers, 2011–14; Hd of Chambers, Goldsmith Chambers, 2014–; Door Tenant, Exchange Chambers, 2014–; First-tier Immigration Judge, 2002–19; First-tier War Pensions and Armed Forces Compensation Tribunal, 2018–. *Publications:* (with Julian Weinberg) Criminal Litigation: first steps to survival, 1999. *Recreations:* theatre, music, football, cricket, meteorology. *Address:* Goldsmith Chambers, Goldsmith Building, Temple, EC4Y 7BL. *T:* (020) 7353 6802, *Fax:* (020) 7583 5255. *E:* a.metzer@goldsmithchambers.com.

**MEWIES, Sandra Elaine, (Sandy);** Member (Lab) Delyn, 2003–16, and Commissioner, 2011–16, National Assembly for Wales; *b* 16 Feb. 1950; *d* of Tom Oldland and Margaret Owens; *m* 1976, Paul Mewies; one *s*. *Educ:* Grove Park Girls' Grammar Sch.; Open Univ. (BA Hons). Journalist, 1967–87; marketing/PR, 1988–90; Community Care Co-ordinator, Clwyd, 1991–93; Lay Inspector of Schs, 1993–2002. Mem., Wrexham CBC, 1988–2004 (Mayor, 2000–01). Dir, Wales European Centre, 1997–2003; Bd Mem., N Wales Probation, 2000–03. Chm., Eur. and Ext. Affairs Cttee, 2003–10, Community and Culture Cttee, 2010–11, Nat. Assembly for Wales. Non-exec. Dir, Clwyd Alyn Housing, 2017–. Hon. Fellow, NE Wales Inst., later Glyndŵr Univ., 2002–. *Recreations:* reading, cooking.

**MEXBOROUGH, 8th Earl of,** *cr* 1766; **John Christopher George Savile;** Baron Pollington, 1753; Viscount Pollington, 1766; *b* 16 May 1931; *s* of 7th Earl of Mexborough, and Josephine Bertha Emily (*d* 1992), *d* of late Captain Andrew Mansel Talbot Fletcher; *S* father, 1980; *m* 1st, 1958, Lady Elizabeth Hariot (marr. diss. 1972; she *d* 1987), *d* of 6th Earl of Verulam; one *s* (one *d* decd); 2nd, 1972, Mrs Catherine Joyce Vivian, *d* of late J. K. Hope, CBE, DL; one *s* one *d*. *Educ:* MIMI. *Heir: s* Viscount Pollington, *qv*. *Address:* Old Manor House, Helmsley, York YO62 5AB. *T:* (01439) 771387. *Clubs:* White's; All England Lawn Tennis and Croquet; Royal Air Squadron.

**MEYER,** Baroness *cr* 2018 (Life Peer), of Nine Elms in the London Borough of Wandsworth; **Catherine Irene Jacqueline Meyer,** CBE 2012; Founder, 1999, and President, since 2017, Action Against Abduction (formerly Parents and Abducted Children Together) (Chief Executive, 1999–2017); *b* Baden-Baden, 26 Jan. 1953; *d* of late Maurice Laylle and of Olga Laylle (*née* Iliyna-Voejkov); *m* 1997, Sir Christopher John Rome Meyer, *qv*; two step *s*, and two *s* by a previous marriage. *Educ:* Lycée Charles de Gaulle, London (Baccalauréat); Sch. of Slavonic and E European Studies, Univ. of London (BA Hons). Account Executive: Merrill Lynch Inc., 1976–79; Dean Witter Ltd, 1979–80; E. F. Hutton and Co., 1980–85; Interdealer Broker, Tradition, 1992–93; Account Exec., Deutsche Bank, 1993–94; Sen. Account Exec., San Paulo Bank, 1994–96. Co-Founder, Internat. Centre for Missing and Exploited Children, 1998. Non-executive Director: LIFFE, 2003–08; London Inst. for Math. Scis, 2013–14. Nat. Treas., Cons. Party, 2010–15. Sen. Advr, Pagefield Communications, 2016–18. *Publications:* Handbook on the Mechanism of the L.M.E. Option Market, 1982; Two Children Behind a Wall, 1997; They Are My Children Too, 1999. *Recreations:* politics, interior decorating, ski-ing. *Address:* House of Lords, SW1A 0PW. *E:* Catmeyer18@mac.com, MeyerC@parliament.uk. *Clubs:* Walbrook, Ivy.

**MEYER, Sir (Anthony) Ashley (Frank),** 4th Bt *cr* 1910, of Shortgrove, Newport, Essex; *b* 23 Aug. 1944; *s* of Sir Anthony Meyer, 3rd Bt and Barbadee Violet Meyer (*née* Knight); *S* father, 2004, but his name does not appear on the Official Roll of the Baronetage; *m* 1966, Susan Mathilda (marr. diss. 1980), *d* of Charles Freestone; one *d*. *Educ:* Goldsmiths' Coll., London Univ. *Heir:* none.

**MEYER, Sir Christopher (John Rome),** KCMG 1998 (CMG 1988); HM Diplomatic Service, retired; company director, consultant, writer and television documentary presenter; *b* 22 Feb. 1944; *s* of Flight Lieut R. H. R. Meyer (killed in action 1944) and late Mrs E. P. L. Meyer (subseq. Mrs A. B. Landells); *m* 1976, Françoise Elizabeth Hedges (marr. diss.), *d* of Air Cdre Sir Archibald Winskill, KCVO, CBE, DFC, AE; two *s*, and one step *s*; *m* 1997, Catherine Irene Jacqueline Laylle (*see* Baroness Meyer); two step *s*. *Educ:* Lancing College; Lycée Henri IV, Paris; Peterhouse, Cambridge (MA History; Hon. Fellow, 2002); Johns Hopkins Sch. of Advanced Internat. Studies, Bologna. Third Sec., FO, 1966–67; Army Sch. of Education, 1967–68; Third, later Second, Sec., Moscow, 1968–70; Second Sec., Madrid, 1970–73; First Sec., FCO, 1973–78; First Sec., UK Perm. Rep. to European Communities, 1978–82; Counsellor and Hd of Chancery, Moscow, 1982–84; Head of News Dept, FCO, 1984–88; Fellow, Center for Internat. Affairs, Harvard, 1988–89; Minister (Commercial), 1989–92, Minister and Dep. Hd of Mission, 1992–93, Washington; Press Sec. to Prime Minister (on secondment to Cabinet Office), 1994–96; Ambassador: to Germany, 1997; to USA, 1997–2003. Chm., Press Complaints Commn, 2003–09. Non-executive Director: GKN, 2003–10; Arbuthnot Banking Gp, 2007–; Member, International Advisory Board: British-American Business Inc., 2003–; Fleishman-Hillard, 2008–11; Chm., 2011–19, Mem., 2019–, Adv. Bd, Pagefield. Sen. Associate Fellow, 2013–18, Dist. Fellow, 2018–, RUSI. Morehead-Cain Vis. Prof., Univ. of N Carolina, 2010. Documentary presenter: Mortgaged to the Yanks, 2006, Getting Our Way, 2010, World War 3: Inside the War Room, 2016, BBC TV; Lying Abroad, 2006, How to Succeed at Summits, 2006, Corridors of Power, 2007, The Watchdog and the Feral Beast, 2009, BBC Radio 4; Networks of Power, Sky Atlantic, 2012. Gov., ESU, 2006–10. Pres., Printing Charity, 2011. Mem., Exec. Cttee, Pilgrims Soc., 2005–11. Trustee, Parents and Abducted Children Together, 2010–15. Mem., Stationers' and Newspaper Makers' Co., 2009–; Freeman, City of London, 2009. *Publications:* DC Confidential, 2005; Getting Our Way, 2009; Only Child, 2013. *Clubs:* Ivy, Walbrook.

**MEYER, Rabbi David;** Executive Director, Partnerships for Jewish Schools, since 2015; Chief Executive Officer, Jewish Schools Network, since 2016; *b* London, 23 June 1966; *s* of Benjamin Meyer and Maisie Meyer; *m* 1994, Meira K. Azose; three *s* two *d*. *Educ:* Hasmonean High Sch.; Kerem B'Yavneh Coll.; Jews' Coll. (BA Hons Jewish Studies 1989); Inst. of Educn, Univ. of London (PGCE 1990); City Univ. (MBA Mktg 1991); Kollel Pischei Teshuva (Rabbinical Ordination); Nat. Coll. for Sch. Leadership (NPQH 2007; Exec. Headteacher Cert. 2009). Ordained Rabbi, 1996; Exec. Dir, Jewish Assoc. for Business Ethics, 1996–97, Rabbinical Dir, 1997–2012; Hasmonean High School: Informal Educator and Dep. Headteacher, 1997–2005; Headteacher, 2005–09; Exec. Headteacher, 2009–15. Educnl consultant and lectr, 1994–; Educnl Programming, Yad Vashem, 1994–95; Sen. Lectr, Aish Hatorah, 1996–2000. *Recreations:* family, Daf Yomi, hiking, cycling, reading, trouble shooting, annoying his sister and brother, looking on the bright side of life. *Address:* Partnerships for Jewish Schools, Beit Meir, 44a Albert Road, NW4 2SJ.

**MEYER, David Patrick;** Chairman, Digital Mobile Spectrum Ltd, since 2017; *b* Liverpool, 15 Nov. 1959; *s* of Denis Meyer and Joyce Meyer (*née* Harrison); *m* 1985, Emma Alden (marr. diss. 1993); one *d* (and one *d* decd). *Educ:* Brighton, Hove and Sussex Grammar Sch.; RMA Sandhurst; Army Staff Coll.; King's Coll. London (MA Internat. Studies 2006). FBCS 2006; CITP 2006. Royal Signals Officer, 1979–2010; CO 14th Signal Regt (Electronic Warfare), 1999–2001; Comdr, 11th Signal Bde, 2003–05; rcds 2006; Dep. Chief Inf. Officer, MoD, 2008–10; Chief Inf. Officer, FCO, 2010–13. Strategy Consultant, Beacon Technol. Services, 2013–. Chm., Spectrum Policy Forum, techUK, 2015–. MInstD. *Recreations:* reading, politics, current affairs, technology. *E:* david@btsl.co.uk.

**MEYER, Julie Marie,** Hon. MBE 2012; Founder and Chief Executive Officer, Ariadne Capital, 2000–12; Founder, Entrepreneur Country, since 2009; Managing Partner, Ariadne Capital Entrepreneurs Fund, since 2011; *b* 28 Aug. 1966. *Educ:* Valparaiso Univ. (BA Dist. 1988); INSEAD (MBA 1997). Consultant: AC3, Paris, 1989–91; Meyer Gp, Paris, 1992–93; Account Manager, Cunningham Communication, 1994–97; Associate, Roland Berger & Partner, Paris, 1997; Co-Founder and Chief Marketing Officer, First Tuesday, 1998–2000; Asst Dir, NewMedia Investors, 1998–99. Member, Board of Directors: INSEAD, 2009–; Vestergaard Frandsen, 2010–; Group Silverline, 2012–; Quill Content Ltd, 2013–; Taggstar UK Ltd, 2014–. *Publications:* Welcome to Entrepreneur Country, 2012. *Recreations:* Pastis and Amaretto, any kind of sport, taking weekend trips, genealogy, carrying on family traditions, finding John Galt, building Entrepreneur Country. *Address:* Ariadne Capital, 17–19 Cockspur Street, SW1Y 5BL.

**MEYER, Prof. Julienne Elizabeth,** CBE 2015; PhD; Professor of Nursing Care for Older People, City, University of London (formerly City University London), since 1999; Executive Director, My Home Life, since 2007; *b* Manchester, 31 Aug. 1956; *d* of Neil Meyer and Margaret Meyer; *m* 1979, Martin Davies; one *s*. *Educ:* Broad Oak Primary Sch.; Fallowfield C of E High Sch.; Leeds Poly. (BSc Nursing; RN); Garnett Coll., Roehampton (Cert Ed (FE); RNT); King's Coll. London (MSc Nursing; PhD Nursing 1995). Clin. nurse, Charing Cross Hosp., London, 1978–84; Nurse Tutor, West Thames Sch. of Nursing, 1984–87; Res. Fellow, 1987–90, Lectr in Nursing, 1990–96, KCL; Reader in Adult Nursing, City Univ. London, 1996–99. Adjunct Professor: Univ. of South Australia, 2003–10, 2013–; Griffith Univ., 2010–15, 2017–; Federation Univ. Australia, 2014–17; Vis. Prof., Univ. of Wisconsin-Madison, 2011–14. Associate, King's Fund, 2018–. *Publications:* Lay Participation in Care in a Hospital Setting: an action research study, 2001; (ed jtly) Understanding Care Homes: a research and development perspective, 2008; articles in acad. and professional jls, 1998–. *Recreations:* family life, book club, film club, supper club. *Address:* Nursing Division, School of Health Sciences, City, University of London, Northampton Square, EC1V 0HB. *T:* (020) 7040 5791/5776. *E:* j.meyer@city.ac.uk.

**MEYER, Michael Siegfried;** Chairman, SAPO PLC, since 2018; General Partner, EMESS Capital LLP, since 2006; *b* 2 May 1950; *s* of late Ernest Meyer and Gretta Gillis and step *s* of late Leo Gillis; *m* 1st, 1984, Jill Benedict (marr. diss. 1990); one *d*; 2nd, 1994, Livia Hannah, *o d* of Maj.-Gen. Monty Green. *Educ:* South African College School, Cape Town. FCIS. Company Secretary, Heenan Beddow International, 1973–75; Director, 1976–79, Chief Exec., 1980–82, Chm. and Chief Exec., 1983–2000, EMESS plc; Man. Dir, Brilliant Hldgs GmbH, Germany, 1987–2000; Pres., Alsy Lighting Inc., 1988–2000; Chm., Supervisory Bd, Eclatec SA, France, 1989–2000; Chm. and CEO, Direct Message plc, 2002–05; Chairman: Remote Controlled Lighting, 2001–13; Windmill Ltd, 2002–18; Domes of Silence Gp Ltd, 2005–16; Ohlsson Ltd, 2014–18; Director: Meyer Leclerc & Co., 1982–2010; Design Trust, 1994–2001; Aluminium Shapes Ltd, 2002–16; Construct London, 2005–07; Partner, EMESS Capital 202 LLP, 2007–; non-executive Director: Royal Sovereign Group, 1986–90; Henderson Smaller Cos Investment Trust, 1990–2002; Walker Greenbank, 1991–97. FRSA. *Recreations:* cricket, Rugby, cinema, theatre. *Address:* WeWork, Emess Capital LLP, Hermannstrasse 13, 20095 Hamburg, Germany. *Clubs:* Naval and Military, MCC, Lansdowne; Western Province Cricket (Cape Town).

**MEYER, Stephen Richard;** Chief Inspector, Marine Accident Investigation Branch, Department for Transport (formerly Department for Transport, Local Government and the Regions), 2002–10; *b* 28 Aug. 1950; *s* of Ernest Frederick Meyer and Rita Agnes Meyer (*née* Humphreys); *m* 1977, Erica Michelle Diana, *d* of late Captain N. Hall, Jersey; two *d*. *Educ:* Merchant Taylors' Sch., Crosby; BRNC, Dartmouth. Joined RN, 1968; served HMS Tenby, Charybdis, Beachampton, Apollo, and USS Raleigh, 1969–74; loaned Sultan of Oman's Navy, i/c Sultan's Naval Vessel Al Mansur, 1975; comd HMS Bildeston, 1975–77; Flag Lieut to Adm. Sir Henry Leach, 1977–79; qualified principal warfare officer, 1980; served HM ships Coventry and Broadsword, 1980–83; commanded: HMS Galatea, 1985–86; HMS Liverpool, 1986–88; HMS Fearless, 1990–91; Head of Maritime Intelligence, 1992–93; Dir of Navy Plans, 1994–97; comd, HMS Illustrious, 1997–98; Head of Jt Force 2000 Study Team, 1998; Military Advr to High Representative, Sarajevo, 1999–2000; Comdr UK Task Gp, UK Maritime Forces, and Comdr Anti Submarine Warfare Striking Force, 2000–01; Chief of Staff, Permt Jt HQ, 2001–02; retd in rank of Rear-Adm. Mem., Safety Panel of Experts, Cruise Lines Internat. Assoc., 2012–. Trustee: CHIRP Charitable Trust, 2003–10; Blind Veterans UK, 2012–15; Southampton Solent Univ. Res. Funds, 2016–. *Recreations:* family, home, friends. *Address:* c/o Naval Secretary, Leach Building, Whale Island, Portsmouth PO2 8BY.

**MEYLER, John William F.;** *see* Forbes-Meyler.

**MEYRIC HUGHES, Henry Andrew Carne;** independent curator and consultant; President, International Foundation Manifesta (formerly European Visual Arts Manifestation), 1995–2007 (Founding Board Member, since 1993; Chairman, 1995–2006); Chair, International Awards for Art Criticism, Shanghai/London, since 2014; *b* 1 April 1942; *s* of late Reginald Richard Meyric Hughes and of Jean Mary Carne Meyric Hughes (*née* Pratt); *m* 1968, Alison Hamilton Faulds; one *s* one *d*. *Educ:* Shrewsbury Sch.; Univs of Rennes and Munich; University Coll., Oxford (BA Hons); Univ. of Sussex (MA). British Council, 1968–92: Berlin, Lima, Paris, Milan, London; Dir, Fine Arts Dept, later Visual Arts Dept, 1986–92; Dir of Exhibns, South Bank Centre (Hayward Gall., Nat. Touring Exhibns, Arts Council Collection), 1992–96. British Comr, Venice Biennale and São Paulo Bienal, 1986–92; Official Comr, XXXIII Council of Europe exhibn, London, Barcelona and Berlin, 1995–96; Curator, Cypriot Pavilion, Venice Biennale, 2003; Co-curator: The Romantic Spirit in German Art, 1790–1990, Edinburgh, London, Munich, 1994; Blast to Freeze: British Art in the Twentieth Century, Wolfsburg and Toulouse, 2002–03; The Desire for Freedom: art in Europe since 1945, XXXth Council of Europe exhibn, Berlin, Milan, Tallinn, Krakow, Thessaloniki, Prague, Brussels and accompanying progs, 2012–15; Associate Curator, The Age of Modernism, Berlin, 1997. Dir, Riverside Trust, 1986–95; Mem. Court, RCA, 1986–92; Mem., Faculty of Fine Arts, British Sch. at Rome, 1988–94. Board Member: Internat. Assoc. of Curators of Contemp. Art, 1992–97; Konsthallen, Göteborg, 1995–2000; Inst. of Internat. Visual Arts, 1996–2016; Pres., British Sect., 1988–91, Internat. Pres., 2002–08, Mem., Adv. Bd, 2012–, AICA. Special Advr, Council of Europe exhibns, 2008–14 (Mem., Gp of Consultants, 2006–10). Pres. of Jury, Diploma examinations, École Nationale Supérieure des Beaux-Arts, Paris, 2004; Ext. Examiner, MA Curating Contemp. Art prog., RCA, 2011–13. Member: Cttee of Mgt, Matt's Gall., London, 1993–; Scientific Committee: Museum Moderner Kunst Stiftung Ludwig Wien, 2001–02; Galleria d'Arte Moderna, Bologna, 2001–05; Archives de la Critique d'Art, Rennes, 2002– (Mem., Adv. Bd, 2002–), and Critique d'Art, 2010–; Dox Centre for Contemporary Art, Prague, 2004–. Trustee, Arnolfini Gall., Bristol, 2006–13. Chm., UK-China John Moores Critics Awards, 2012–13. Hon. Pres., Internat. Assoc. of Art Critics, Paris, 2008– (Pres., 2002–08). Member, Jury: Turner Prize, 1988; Biennale de Cetinje, 2002; Caribbean Biennial, 2003; Gwangju Biennale, 2004 (Chm.); Premio Furla, Bologna, 2005; Dakar Biennial, 2006. Silver Medal, Czech Soc. for Internat. Cultural Relations, 1986. Officier, l'Ordre Nat. des Arts et des Lettres (France), 1997; Bundesverdienstkreuz (Germany), 2002. *Publications:* (contrib.) Il Dono/The Gift: generous offerings threatening hospitality in art, 2001; (ed jtly) From Art School to Professional Practice, 2008; (contrib.) Curare l'arte, 2008; (contrib.) Le Demi-siècle de Pierre Restany, 2009; (contrib.) Different Avant-Gardes in Central and East Europe after World War II, 2009; (ed jtly) AICA in the Age of Globalisation, 2010; (ed jtly) African Contemporary Art: critical concerns, 2011; (ed) The European Idea in Art and Art History, 2015; Lee Yil: dynamics of expansion and reduction, 2018; articles on visual arts and cultural relations, UK and overseas, 1966–, incl. contrib. to Burlington Mag., Critique d'Art, Manifesta Jl, THES. *Recreations:* music, Europe. *Address:* 13 Ashchurch Grove, W12 9BT. *T:* and *Fax:* (020) 8749 4098. *E:* henry.meyrichughes@tiscali.co.uk.

**MEYRICK, Sir George (Christopher Cadafael Tapps Gervis),** 7th Bt *cr* 1791, of Hinton Admiral; *b* 10 March 1941; *s* of Sir George David Eliott Tapps Gervis Meyrick, 6th Bt, MC and Ann, *d* of late Clive Miller; *S* father, 1988; *m* 1968, Jean Louise, *d* of late Lord William Montagu Douglas Scott and Lady William Montagu Douglas Scott; two *s* one *d*. *Educ:* Eton; Trinity College, Cambridge (MA). FRICS. *Heir: s* George William Owen Tapps Gervis Meyrick [*b* 3 April 1970; *m* 2006, Candida Clark; one *s* two *d*]. *Address:* Hinton Admiral, Christchurch, Dorset BH23 7DY; Bodorgan, Isle of Anglesey LL62 5LW. *Club:* Boodle's.

**MEYRICK, Rt Rev. Jonathan;** *see* Lynn, Bishop Suffragan of.

**MEYRICK, (Sir) Timothy (Thomas Charlton),** (5th Bt *cr* 1880, of Bush, Pembrokeshire, but does not use the title); *b* 5 Nov. 1963; *s* of Sir David John Charlton Meyrick, 4th Bt and of Penelope Anne (*née* Marsden-Smedley); *S* father, 2004, but his name does not appear on the Official Roll of the Baronetage; *m* 2003, Natasha Domenica Bernabei. *Educ:* Eton; Bristol Univ. *Heir: b* Simon Edward Meyrick [*b* 20 Sept. 1965; *m* 1989, Jennifer Amanda Irvine; one *s* one *d*].

**MIAN, (Nighat) Mehmuda;** Associate Director and Clerk to Trustees, Lokahi Foundation, since 2007; *b* 30 July 1962; *d* of Manzoor Alam and Naziran Mian. *Educ:* Teesside High Sch. for Girls; Univ. of Birmingham (LLB Hons Law with French 1994); Coll. of Law, Chester. Admitted solicitor, 1989; articled clerk, then solicitor, Edge & Ellison, 1985–91; solicitor, Wansbroughs Willey Hargrave, 1991–94; Office for the Supervision of Solicitors, Law Soc., 1994–98. Member: Police Complaints Authy, 1998–2004; Ind. Police Complaints Commn, 2004–09; Ind. Safeguarding Authy, 2008–12; Disciplinary Cttee, RCVS, 2015–. Non-executive Director: Berks Health Foundn Trust, 2015–; IPSO, 2015–. Trustee, BBC Trust, 2006–12. *Recreations:* reading, trekking, travelling, charity fund raising, spending time with family and friends, trying to keep fit.

**MICHAEL, Rt Hon. Alun (Edward);** PC 1998; JP; Police and Crime Commissioner (Lab) for South Wales, since 2012; *b* 22 Aug. 1943; *m* 1966, Mary Crawley; two *s* three *d*. *Educ:* Colwyn Bay GS; Keele Univ. (BA Hons English and Phil.). Journalist, South Wales Echo, 1966–71; Youth and Community Worker, Cardiff, 1972–84; Area Community Education Officer, Grangetown and Butetown, 1984–87. Mem., Cardiff City Council, 1973–89 (sometime Chm., Finance, Planning, Performance Review, and Econ. Develt, and Chief Whip, Labour Gp). Dir, Cardiff and Vale Enterprise. Mem. (Lab and Co-op) Wales Mid and West, and First Sec. for Wales, Nat. Assembly for Wales, 1999–2000. MP (Lab and Co-op) Cardiff S and Penarth, 1987–Oct. 2012. An Opposition Whip, 1987–88; Opposition frontbench spokesman: on Welsh Affairs, 1988–92; on Home Affairs and the voluntary sector, 1992–97; Minister of State, Home Office, 1997–98; Sec. of State for Wales, 1998–99; Minister of State (Minister for Rural Affairs and Local Envmtl Quality, DEFRA, 2001–05; Minister of State, DTI, 2005–06. Chairman: Co-operative Parly Gp, 1988–92; Parly Friends of Co-operative Ideal, 1988–92; Member: Nat. Exec., Co-op. Party, 1988–92; Parly Cttee, Co-op. Union, 1988–94. Chairman: All-Party Gp on Alcohol Misuse, 1991–93, 1998–; All-Party, Penal Affairs Gp; Parly Friends of WNO, 1991–97; Jt Chm., All-Party Gp on Somalia, 1989–97; Vice-Chm., All-Party Penal Affairs Gp, 1991–97; Jt Sec., All-Party Gp for Further and Tertiary Educn, 1990–97; Sec., All-Party Panel for Personal Social Services, 1990–93. Formerly: Mem. Bd, Crime Concern; Vice-Pres., YHA; Mem. Exec., Nat. Youth Bureau. Formerly Vice-Pres., Bldg Socs Assoc. Dep. Chm., Cardiff Bay Opera House Trust, 1994–96; Mem. Bd, Cardiff and Vale Enterprise, 1982–93; plays leading role locally in community develt projects. FRSA 2003. JP Cardiff, 1972 (Chm., Cardiff Juvenile Bench, 1986–87; formerly Mem., S Glam Probation Cttee). *Recreations:* long-distance running, mountain walking, opera, listening to classical music, reading. *Clubs:* Penarth Labour; Grange Stars; Earlswood.

**MICHAEL, Sir Duncan,** Kt 2001; PhD; FREng; Chairman, Ove Arup Partnership, 1995–2000 (Director, 1977–2002); Trustee, 1977–2006; Chairman of Trustees, 1995–2004); Trustee, Ove Arup Foundation, 1995–2016, now Advisor; *b* 26 May 1937; *s* of Donald Michael and Lydia Cameron MacKenzie; *m* 1960, Joan Clay; two *s* one *d*. *Educ:* Beauly Public School; Inverness Royal Academy. BSc Edinburgh; PhD Leeds. FICE 1975; FIStructE 1975; FREng (FEng 1981); FHKIE 1981; FRSE 2005. Engr, Dunoan Logan Contractors, 1955–58; Lectr, Leeds Univ., 1961; Engr, Ove Arup Partnership, 1962; Chm., Arup China/Hong Kong, 1978–88. Member: Council, IStructE, 1977–80, 1983–89; Jt Bd of Moderators of Engrg Instns, 1985–92; SE Asia Trade Adv. Group, BOTB, 1982–85; Civil Engineering Cttee, SERC, 1980–83; Council, Royal Acad. Engrg, 1994–2005 (Chm., Awards Cttee, 1995–99; Vice Pres., 1999–2005; new HQ project bd, 2004–12); Membership Cttee Panel, RSE, 2006–09; Vice-Chm., Council of Tall Buildings & Urban Habitat, 1980–96; Member: Educn and Trng Affairs Cttee, CBI, 1997–2003; State of the Nation Assessment Panel, ICE, 2000–03; Adv. Bd, Master of Research, Univ. of Dundee, 2000–07 (Chm., 2000–04); Supervisor, Arup/RAE Chair in Fire Safety, 2007–17, Arup/RAE Res. Fellowship in Sociology of Fire Safety, 2011–, Edinburgh Univ.; Chm., Engrg Adv. Bd, Aberdeen Univ., 1998–2012; Mentor: Professors of Design for Sustainable Engrg, Univ. of Cambridge, 2000–05; Imperial Coll., London, 2001–09; Member: Industrial Adv. Cttee, Churchill Coll., Cambridge, 2000–05; Academic Adv. Bd, Univ. of Highlands and Islands proj., 1999–2001; Bd, Housing Corp., 2000–08 (Chairman: Investment Cttee, 2002–08; Gold Awards Judging Panel, 2005–08); Mgt Bd, Scottish Res. Partnership in Engrg, 2007–11; Dir, GB Social Housing plc, 2010–; land assets advr to Chm., UCL Health Trust, 2005–08; Design Advr, Planning Cttee, London Bor. of Merton, 2007–19. Fellowship of Engrg Vis. Prof., Aberdeen Univ., 1989–94; Vis. Prof., Leeds Univ., 1990–94. Trustee: Lydia Michael Trust, 2000–; Useful Simple Trust, 2009–. Pres., NW Wimbledon Residents' Assoc., 2010–15. Fellow, Inst. of Scottish Shipbldrs and Engrs, 2000; Mem., Smeatonian Soc. of Civil Engrs, 2001. Hon. FRIBA 2009. Hon. DEng: Abertay Dundee, 1997; UMIST, 1999; Hon. DSc: Aberdeen, 2001; Robert Gordon, 2003; Strathclyde, 2005; Edinburgh, 2007. Gold Medal, IStructE, 2000. Jt Ed., Engrg and Philosophy Monist, 2006–09; Mem., Editl Adv. Bd, Philosophy of Engrg, 2009–. *Publications:* Skyscrapers, 1987; lectures and engineering papers in technical jls. *Recreations:* garden, lecturing, Scottish archaeology, opera. *Address:* Teanacoil, 121 Alwoodley Lane, Leeds LS17 7PN. *Clubs:* Caledonian, London Scottish Wimbledon.

**MICHAEL, Prof. Ian David Lewis;** King Alfonso XIII Professor of Spanish Studies, University of Oxford, 1982–2003, now Emeritus; Fellow, Exeter College, Oxford, 1982–2003, now Emeritus; *b* 26 May 1936; *o s* of late Cyril George Michael and Glenys Morwen (*née* Lewis). *Educ:* Neath Grammar Sch.; King's Coll., London (BA First Class Hons Spanish 1957; FKC 2002); PhD Manchester 1967. University of Manchester: Asst Lectr in Spanish, 1957–60; Lectr in Spanish, 1960–69; Sen. Lectr in Spanish, 1969–70; University of Southampton: Prof. of Spanish and Hd of Spanish Dept, 1971–82; Dep. Dean, Faculty of Arts, 1975–77, 1980–82; Sen. Curator and Chm., Univ. Library Cttee, 1980–82; Oxford University: Curator, Taylor Instn, 1994–2000; Chm., Faculty Bd of Mod. Langs, 1999–2000. Leverhulme Faculty Fellow in European Studies (at Madrid), 1977–78; first British-Spanish Foundn Vis. Prof., Complutensian Univ., Madrid, 1993–94. Member: Gp of Three for Spain (Humanities research review), Eur. Science Foundn, 1987; Welsh Acad. (Eng. Lang. Section), 1995–; Corresp. Mem., Royal Spanish Acad., 2009. Pres., Assoc. of Hispanists of GB and Ire., 1990–92; Pres., Oxford Medieval Soc., 2002–03; Mem., Oxford Soc., Madrid, 2004–; Trustee, Nat. Library of Spain, 2009–14. Comdr, Order of Isabel la Católica (Spain), 1986. *Publications:* The Treatment of Classical Material in the Libro de Alexandre, 1970; Spanish Literature and Learning to 1474, in, Spain: a Companion to Spanish studies, 1973, 3rd edn 1977; The Poem of the Cid, 1975, new edn 1984; Poema de Mio Cid, 1976, 2nd edn 1979; Gwyn Thomas, 1977; chapter on Poem of My Cid in New Pelican Guide to English Literature. I ii, 1983; (ed) Sound on Vision: studies on Spanish cinema, 1999; (ed) Context, Meaning and Reception of Celestina, 2000; Gonzalo de Berceo, Miracles of Our Lady, 2006; (with J. C. Bayo) Cantar de Mio Cid, 2008; articles in various learned jls and Festschriften; *as David Serafín:* Saturday of Glory, 1979 (John Creasey Meml Award, CWA, 1980); Madrid Underground, 1982; Christmas Rising, 1982; The Body in Cadiz Bay, 1985; Port of Light, 1987; The Angel of Torremolinos, 1988. *Recreations:* writing pseudonymous fiction; opera. *Address:* Calle Goya, 57 (buzón 10), 28001 Madrid, Spain. *T:* (91) 5769218. *E:* iandavidlm@gmail.com.

**MICHAEL, Sir Jonathan,** Kt 2005; FRCP; independent healthcare consultant; Chief Executive, Oxford University Hospitals (formerly Oxford Radcliffe Hospitals) NHS Trust, 2010–15; *b* 21 May 1945; *s* of late Ian Lockie Michael, CBE; *m* 1st, 1975, Jacqueline Deluz (marr. diss. 1992); one *s* three *d*; 2nd, 2005, Karen E. Young. *Educ:* Bristol Grammar Sch.; St Thomas's Hosp. Med. Sch., London Univ. (MB BS 1970). MRCS 1970; MRCP 1973, FRCP 1985. Consultant Physician and Nephrologist, Queen Elizabeth Hosp., Birmingham, 1980–2000; Med. Dir, 1994–97, Chief Exec., 1997–2000, University Hosp. Birmingham NHS Trust; Chief Exec., Guy's and St Thomas' Hosp. NHS Trust, then NHS Foundn Trust, 2000–07; Man. Dir, BT Health, BT Global Services, 2007–10. Chm., Inquiry into access to healthcare for people with learning disabilities, 2007 (report, Healthcare for All, 2008). Chairman: Assoc. UK Univ. Hosps, 2004–07; Bd of NHS Foundn Trust Network, 2006–07. Trustee, King's Fund, 2012–. Gov., Edgbaston High Sch. for Girls, Birmingham, 1988–2000 (Chm. Govs, 1997–2000; Vice-Pres., 2000–05). FKC 2005. *Publications:* contrib. articles on nephrology and medical science. *E:* jonathan@beechlawnconsulting.com.

**MICHAEL, Peter Anthony,** CBE 1998; Director, Central Policy, HM Revenue and Customs, 2008–11; *b* 2 July 1954; *s* of Taxis Michael and Helen Marie Teresa Michael; *m* 1989, Joanne Elizabeth Angel; two *d*. *Educ:* Pierrepont Sch.; City of London Univ. (Dip. English Law 1976). HM Treasury: Policy Advr, Industrial Policy Div., 1978–79; Private Secretary: to Minister of State (Lords), 1981; to Minister of State (Commons), 1982; Board of Inland Revenue, later HM Revenue and Customs: Policy Adviser: Capital Taxes Div., 1985–89; Internat. Div., 1989–90; Asst Dir, EC Unit, Internat. Div., 1990–98; Director: EU Div., 1998–2000; EU Coordination and Strategy, Internat., 2000–01; Tax Law Rewrite Project, 2001–03; Revenue Policy: Strategy and Co-ordination, 2003–05; Dep. Dir (formerly Dir, Policy Improvement and Professionalism), Central Policy, 2005–08. *Recreations:* playing the piano, fly-fishing.

**MICHAEL, Sir Peter (Colin),** Kt 1989; CBE 1983; Chairman: Classic FM, 1993–2008 (Director, 1991–2008); Pilot Investment Trust, 1993–97; *b* 17 June 1938; *s* of Albert and Enid Michael; *m* 1962, Margaret Baldwin; two *s*. *Educ:* Whitgift Sch., Croydon; Queen Mary Coll., Univ. of London (BSc Elec. Engrg; Fellow, 1983). Chairman: Micro Consultants Group, 1969–85; Quantel Ltd, 1974–89; Databasix Ltd, 1986–88; UEI plc, 1986–89 (Dep. Chm., 1981–85); Cray Electronics, 1989–93. Dir, Rutherford Asset Management, 1995–97; non-executive Director: GWR Gp plc, 1996–2005; Neverfail Holdings Ltd, 2001–14; GCap Media plc, 2005–08. Chairman: Peter Michael Winery, Calif., 1982–; Donnington Valley Hotel, 1991–; The Vineyard at Stockcross, 1997–; Pelican Cancer Centre, 1999–2018; Virtual Music Stores Ltd, 2000–08. Member: Adv. Council for Applied R&D, 1982–85; NCB, 1983–86; ACARD Sub-Gp on Annual Review of Govt Funded R&D, 1985–86; Technol. Requirements Bd, DTI, 1986–88; Adv. Cttee, Royal Mint, 1999–2007; Modern Collection Cttee, 2006–09, Wine Sub-cttee, 2006–09, Goldsmiths' Co. Paper on City financing of electronics companies to PITCOM, 1988. Chairman: Royal Soc. of British Sculptors Appeal, 1992; Chelsea Harbour '93 Internat. Sculpture Exhibn Appeal; The Sculpture Company, 1995–99. Mem. Council, RCA, 2012–15. Chm., Greenham Trust (formerly Greenham Common Community Trust), 1996–2018. Humphrey Davies Lecture, QMC, 1984. Freeman, City of London, 1984; Liveryman, Goldsmiths' Co., 1988 (Freeman, 1984). CCMI (CBIM 1982). FRSA 1984. Hon. FBKSTS 1981. Hon. LLD Reading, 2004. The Guardian Young Businessman of the Year, 1982. *Recreations:* opera, classical music, wine, sculpture, writing rhyme. *Address:* (office) Buckingham House, West Street, Newbury, Berks RG14 1BE. *T:* (01635) 552502.

**MICHAELS, Adrian Robert;** Director, FirstWord Media Ltd, since 2014; *b* London, 8 Sept. 1969; *s* of Barry and Naomi Michaels; *m* 2000, Elena Lugli; two *d*. *Educ:* University Coll. Sch., Hampstead; Trinity Coll., Oxford (BA PPE). With Financial Times, 1993–2008: Americas Page Ed., 1997–99; NY corresp., 1999–2004; Milan corresp., 2004–08; Telegraph Media Group: Gp Foreign Ed., 2008–11; Editl Dir, Commercial, 2011–14. *Recreations:* golf, cheese. *Address:* FirstWord Media Ltd, 7 Henrietta Street, WC2E 8PS. *E:* info@firstword.co.uk. *Clubs:* MCC (Associate Mem.); Hindhead Golf.

**MICHAELS-MOORE, Anthony;** *see* Moore.

**MICHALOS, Christina Antigone Diana;** QC 2019; *d* of Dr Milton Michalos and Dr Sandra Lloyd. *Educ:* LLB; MA Med. Law and Ethics; Postgrad. Dip. Internat. and Comparative Copyright Law; Postgrad. Cert. Sports Law; Inst. of Fundraising (Dip. Fundraising). Called to the Bar, Gray's Inn, 1994, Bencher, 2015. Mem., Leadership Commn, W Midlands Combined Authy, 2017–18. Mem., Bar Council, 2008–14, 2019–; Chm., Bar Council/Inns of Court Neuberger Diversity Film Project Gp, 2009–11. Trustee, Birmingham Women's and Children's Hosp., 2013– (Chm., Fundraising Cttee, 2014–19). *Publications:* The Law of Photography and Digital Images, 2004; (contrib.) The Trials of Art, 2007. *Recreations:* theatre, heraldic art, calligraphy and illumination, cricket. *Address:* 5RB, 5 Gray's Inn Square, WC1R 5AH. *T:* (020) 7242 2902. *E:* clerks@5rb.com.

**MICHEL, Caroline Jayne, (Lady Evans of Temple Guiting);** Chief Executive Officer, Peters Fraser & Dunlop, since 2007; *b* Harrogate, 4 April 1959; *d* of Wolfgang Michel and Valerie Michel (*née* Cryer); *m* 1991, Matthew Evans (later Baron Evans of Temple Guiting, CBE) (*d* 2016); two *s* one *d*. *Educ:* Oakdene Sch.; Univ. of Edinburgh (BA Sanskrit 1980) MA). Chatto & Windus; Jonathan Cape; Bloomsbury Publishing; Granta; Orion; Publisher: Vintage, 1993–2003; Harper Press, 2003–05; CEO William Morris Agency, 2005–07. Chair: BFI Trust, 2011– (Gov., BFI, 2003–09); Hay Literary Festivals, 2015–. Member: Adv. Cttee, Booker Prize Foundn, 1994–2001; Veuve Clicquot Business Woman Award Panel, 2011–; Govt Adv. Panel on public library service in England, 2014–15. Trustee, Somerset House, 2013–. Vice Pres., London Liby, 2016–. FRSA. *Recreation:* reading. *Address:* Peters Fraser & Dunlop, 55 New Oxford Street, WC2A 1BS. *T:* (020) 7344 1055. *E:* cmichel@pfd.co.uk. *Clubs:* Groucho, Hurlingham, Ivy, 5 Hertford Street.

**MICHEL, Prof. (Christopher) Charles,** DPhil; FRCP; Professor of Physiology, Imperial College School of Medicine (formerly St Mary's Hospital Medical School), 1984–2000, now Emeritus Professor of Physiology and Bioengineering; *b* 23 March 1938; *s* of late Maurice and May Michel; *m* 1965, Rosalind McCrink; one *s* one *d*. *Educ:* Leeds Grammar Sch.; Queen's Coll., Oxford (BA 1959, 1st cl. Physiol.; MA, DPhil 1962; BM BCh 1965). MRCP 1986, FRCP 1996. US Public Health Postdoctoral Res. Fellow, 1962; Oxford University: Deptl Demonstrator in Physiol., 1964–67; Univ. Lectr in Physiol., 1967–84; Fellow and Praelector in Physiol., Queen's Coll., 1966–84. Lectures: Oliver-Sharpey, RCP, 1985; Annual Prize Review, Physiol. Soc., 1987; Starling Centenary, World Congress for Microcirculation, 1996; Haliburton, KCL, 2000; Zweifach Meml, UCSD, 2001. Sec., Physiol Soc., 1980–83; Chm., RN Personnel Res. Cttee, 1991–96, Army Personnel Res. Cttee, 1993–94, MRC. Hon. Member: Amer. Physiol. Soc., 1993; Brit. Microcirculation Soc., 2001; Physiol Soc., 2001. Malpighi Prize, Eur. Soc. for Microcirculation, 1984; Nishimaru-Tsuchiya Internat. Award, Japanese Soc. for Microcirculation, 2010. *Publications:* (ed with E. M. Renkin) American Handbook of Physiology: the microcirculation, 1984; articles in learned jls. *Recreations:* walking, ornithology, reading. *Address:* Sundial House, High Street, Alderney, Channel Islands GY9 3UG.

**MICHEL, Prof. Dr Hartmut;** Director, Max Planck Institute of Biophysics, Frankfurt am Main, since 1987; *b* Ludwigsburg, W Germany, 18 July 1948; *s* of Karl Michel and Frieda Michel; *m* (marr. diss.); one *s* two *d.* *Educ:* Universities of: Tübingen (Dip. in biochem.); Würzburg (PhD); Munich (habilitation for biochemistry, 1986). Res. associate with D. Oesterhelt, Univ. of Würzburg, 1977–79; group leader in D. Oesterhelt's dept, Max-Planck-Inst. of Biochemistry, Martinsried, until 1987. Mem., German Sci. Council, 2004–10. For. Mem., Royal Soc., 2005. Various prizes, including: Biophysics Prize of Amer. Phys. Soc., 1986; Otto Klung Prize for Chemistry, 1986; (jtly) Otto Bayer Prize, 1988; (jtly) Nobel Prize for Chemistry, 1988; Keilin Medal, Biochemical Soc., 2008. *Publications:* (ed) Crystallization of Membrane Proteins, 1990. *Recreations:* nature, wild life, physical exercise, readings on history and travel. *Address:* Max Planck Institut für Biophysik, Max von Laue Strasse 3, 60438 Frankfurt am Main, Germany. *T:* (69) 63031001, *Fax:* (69) 63031002.

**MICHEL, Louis;** Member (Mouvement Réformateur), European Parliament, 2009–19; *b* 2 Sept. 1947; *m*; two *c.* German lang. teacher, 1968; Lectr, Inst. Supérieur de Commerce, St Louis; Prof. of Dutch, English and German Lit., Ecole Normale Provinciale, Jodoigne, 1968–78. MHR (PRL), Belgium, 1978–99; Mem., parly commns on Finance, Budget, Instnl Reforms, and Commn on supervising electoral expenditures; elected to Senate, 1999, 2003, 2004; Dep. Prime Minister and Minister of Foreign Affairs, Belgium, 1999–2004; Mem., European Commn, 2004–09. Mem., Benelux Interparly Consultative Council. Dep. Pres., Liberal Internat. Mem. Bd, ELDR. Liberal Reform Party (PRL): Sec.-Gen., 1980–82; Pres., 1982–90 and 1995–99; Pres., Parly Gp in Council of Walloon Reg., 1991–92; Parly Gp in House of Reps, 1992–95. Alderman, 1977–82, Mayor, 1983–2004, Jodoigne. Comdr, Order of Leopold (Belgium), 1995; Grand-Croix: Order of Infante Dom Henrique (Portugal), 1999; Ordre of Orange-Nassau (Netherlands), 2000; Order of Isabel la Católica (Spain), 2000; Ordre Royal de l'Etoile Polaire (Sweden), 2001; Grand Officier, Légion d'Honneur, 2003. *Publications:* (with D. Ducarme) Le défi vert, 1980; (with P. Monfils) L'enfant, 1984; Libres et forts-projet éducatif pour réussir le futur, 1986; Wallons et optimistes, 1997; De echte Walen, 1997; Rendre Confiance, 1998; Objectif 100 La Wallonnie j'y crois!, 1998; Lettre aux citoyens de mon pays, 1999; L'axe du Bien, 2003; Horizons, 2004; L'Europe-Afrique: indispensable alliance; L'appui budgétaire; Jean Ray: une conscience; Les 100 raisons d'aimer l'Europe.

**MICHEL, Roger Lee, Jr;** Executive Director, Institute for Digital Archaeology, since 2012; *b* Baltimore, 8 Jan. 1962; *s* of Roger Lee Michel, Sr and Mary Carll Michel; one *d.* *Educ:* Williams Coll. (BA Hons 1984); Trinity Coll., Oxford (MLitt 1988); Harvard Law Sch. (JD Hons 1989). Associate, Hill & Barlow, 1989–91; Asst Dist Attorney, Suffolk Dist, USA, 1991–94; Sen. Counsel, Mass Appeals Court, USA, 1994–2008; Mem., Mass Parole Bd, 2008–12; Asst Dist Attorney, Bristol Dist, USA, 2012–18. Lectr, Boston Univ., 1993–2017. Sir Thomas Pope Fellow, Trinity Coll., Oxford, 2018–. Publisher, Arion Mag., 2016–. *Publications:* articles in Massachusetts Law Rev. and Boston Bar Jl. *Recreations:* antiquarian books, horology, shooting, horseback riding, croquet. *Address:* Trinity College, Oxford OX1 3BH. *T:* (office) (USA) (617) 4179488. *E:* director@digitalarchaeology.org.uk. *Clubs:* Union, Club of Odd Volumes (Boston); Greenspring Valley Hunt (Baltimore).

**MICHELL, Michael John;** Head, Oil and Gas Division, Department of Trade and Industry, 1993–98; *b* 12 Dec. 1942; *s* of late John Martin Michell and of Pamela Mary Michell; *m* 1st, 1965, Pamela Marianne Tombs (marr. diss. 1978); two *s* (one *d* decd); 2nd, 1978, Alison Mary Macfarlane (marr. diss. 2005; she *d* 2013); two *s*; 3rd, 2005, Janice Margaret Bintcliffe. *Educ:* Marlborough College; Corpus Christi College, Cambridge (BA 1964). Min. of Aviation, 1964; Private Sec. to Sir Conrad Melville, 1968–69; Concorde Div., 1969–73; Sec. to Sandilands Cttee on inflation accounting, 1973–75; Private Sec. to Sec. of State for Industry, 1975–77; HM Treasury, 1977–80; Industrial Policy Div., Dept of Industry, 1980–82; RCDS 1983; Department of Trade and Industry: Head, Air Div., 1984–88; Chief Exec., Radio Div., subseq. Radiocommunications Agency, 1988–93. Director: Prestbury Enterprises Ltd, 1998–2011; Eni UK Ltd, 1999–2010.

**MICHELL, Prof. Robert Hall,** FRS 1986; FMedSci; FRSB; Royal Society Research Professor at the University of Birmingham, 1987–2006, now Emeritus; *b* 16 April 1941; *s* of Rowland Charles Michell and Elsie Lorna Michell; two *s* one *d.* *Educ:* Crewkerne School, Somerset; Univ. of Birmingham (BSc Med. Biochem. and Pharmacol. 1962; PhD Med. Biochem. 1965; DSc 1978). Research Fellow, Birmingham, 1965–66, 1968–70, Harvard Med. Sch., 1966–68; Birmingham University: Lectr in Biochemistry, 1970–81; Sen. Lectr, 1981–84; Reader, 1984–86; Prof. of Biochemistry, 1986–87. Mem., Physiol. Systems and Disorders Bd, 1985–90, Chm., Grants Cttee B, 1988–90, MRC; Member: Fellowships Cttee, BHF, 1992–97; Fellowships Selection Panel, Lister Inst. of Preventive Medicine, 1999–2005; Fellowship Review Panel, Human Frontiers Sci. Prog., 1999–2001. Mem., Biochem. Panel, 1996 RAE, Biol Scis Panel, 2001 and 2008 RAEs, HEFCE. Member: Adv. Bd, Beit Meml Trust, 1993–2006; Council, Royal Soc., 1996–97; Adv. Bd, EMF Res. Trust, 2000–10. Pres., Med. Scis Sect., BAAS, 1993–94. Mem., EMBO, 1991. Morton Lectr, 2002, Hon. Mem., 2010, Biochem. Soc. Member, Editorial Boards: Jl Neurochem., 1974–80; Cell Calcium, 1979–89; Biochem. Jl, 1983–88; Current Opinion in Cell Biology, 1988–; Procs Royal Soc. B, 1989–97; Jl of Molecular Endocrinology, 1992–99; Molecular Membrane Biology, 1993–2007. FMedSci 2002; FRSB 2013. Chm. Govs, Cadbury Sixth Form Coll., 2010–15. CIBA Medal, Biochemical Soc., 1988. *Publications:* (with J. B. Finean and R. Coleman) Membranes and their Cellular Functions, 1974, 3rd edn 1984; (ed with J. B. Finean) Membrane Structure, vol. 1 of New Comprehensive Biochemistry, 1981; (ed with J. W. Putney, Jr) Inositol Lipids in Cellular Signalling, 1987; (ed with M. J. Berridge) Inositol Lipids and Transmembrane Signalling, 1988; (ed jtly) Inositol Lipids and Cellular Signalling, 1989; (jtly) Lipids: biochemistry, biotechnology and health, 6th edn 2016; contribs to Nature, Biochem. Jl and sci. jls. *Recreations:* birdwatching, wilderness, pottery. *Address:* 59 Weoley Park Road, Birmingham B29 6QZ. *T:* (0121) 472 1356.

**MICHELL, Roger Harry;** director; *b* 5 June 1956; *s* of H. D. Michell, DFC, and Jillian Green; *m* 1st, 1992, Kate Buffery (marr. diss. 2002); one *s* one *d*; 2nd, 2010, Anna Maxwell Martin, *qv*; two *d.* *Educ:* Clifton Coll., Bristol; Queens' Coll., Cambridge (BA Hons). With Royal Court Th., 1978–80, Royal Shakespeare Th., 1985–91. Judith E. Wilson Sen. Fellow, Cambridge Univ., 1990. *Plays* include: Private Dick, Edinburgh and Whitehall, 1980; The Catch, Royal Court, 1981; White Glove, Lyric, Hammersmith, 1982; Marya, Old Vic., 1990; My Night with Reg, Royal Court and Criterion, 1995; Some Sunny Day, Hampstead, 1996; Old Times, 2004, Betrayal, 2007, Donmar Warehouse; The Female of the Species, Vaudeville, 2008; Rope, Almeida, 2009; Tribes, Royal Court, 2010; Farewell to the Theatre, Hampstead, 2012; Birthday, Royal Court, 2012; Waste, Nat. Th., 2015; Mood Music, Old Vic, 2018; Royal Shakespeare Company: Merchant of Venice, 1986; Dead Monkey, 1986; Hamlet, 1987; Temptation, 1987; Conversation, 1987; Constant Couple, 1988; Restoration, 1988; Some Americans Abroad, 1989; Redevelopment, 1989; Two Shakespearean Actors, 1990; Royal National Theatre: The Coup, 1991; Under Milk Wood, 1995; The Homecoming, 1997; Blue/Orange, 2000; Honour, 2003; Landscape with Weapon, 2007; Consent, 2017, transf. Harold Pinter Th., 2018; *television* includes: Buddha of Suburbia, 1994; Ready When You Are, Mr Patel, 1995; My Night with Reg, 1997; Michael Redgrave, My Father, 1998; The Lost Honour of Christopher Jefferies, 2014; Birthday, 2015; *films*: Persuasion, 1995; Titanic Town, 1999; Notting Hill, 1999; Changing Lanes, 2002; The Mother, 2003; Enduring Love, 2004; Venus, 2007; Morning Glory, 2010; Hyde Park on Hudson, 2013; Le Week-End, 2013; My Cousin Rachel, 2017; Nothing Like a Dame, 2018; Blackbird, 2019. *Address:* c/o Independent Talent Group Ltd, 40 Whitfield Street, W1T 2RH.

**MICHELS, Sir David (Michael Charles),** Kt 2006; Chairman, Michels&Taylor, since 2007; President, Institute of Hospitality, 2012–16; *b* 8 Dec. 1946; *s* of Klaus Peter and Thelma Sadie Michels; *m* 1973, Michele Ann Arnold; one *s* one *d.* *Educ:* Hendon Coll. FIH. Grand Metropolitan, 1966–81; Ladbrokes: Sales and Marketing Dir, Hotels, 1981–83; Man. Dir, Leisure Div., 1983–85; Man. Dir, Ladbroke Hotels, 1985–87; Hilton International: Sen. Vice-Pres., Sales and Marketing, 1987–89; Dep. Chm., Hilton UK and Exec. Vice-Pres., Hilton Worldwide, 1989–91; Chief Exec., Stakis plc, 1991–99; Chief Executive: Hilton Internat. Hotels, 1999–2000; Hilton Gp plc, 2000–06. Sen. Eur. Strategist, Strategic Hotels & Resorts, 2007–. Dep. Chm., Marks and Spencer Gp plc, 2008–12; non-exec. Dir, British Land Co. plc, 2003–08; Sen. Ind. Dir, easyJet plc, 2006–11; Dep. Chm., Reach4entertainment Enterprises, 2018–. Trustee, Anne Frank Trust. Hon. DLitt Glasgow Caledonian, 1993. *Recreations:* tennis, poker, reading.

**MICHIE, Prof. Jonathan,** DPhil; FAcSS; Professor of Innovation and Knowledge Exchange, and Director, Department for Continuing Education, University of Oxford, since 2008; President, Kellogg College, Oxford, since 2008; *b* 25 March 1957; *s* of late Prof. Donald Michie and (Dame) Dr Anne Laura McLaren, DBE, FRS; *m* 1988, Carolyn Grace Downs, *qv*; two *s.* *Educ:* Balliol Coll., Oxford (BA 1st Cl. Hons PPE); Queen Mary Coll., London (MSc Econ (Dist.)); DPhil Econ Oxon 1985. Lectr, Univ. of Oxford, 1983; Res. Officer, Econ. Dept, TUC, 1983–88; Expert to EC, Brussels, 1988–90; Fellow in Econs, St Catharine's Coll., Cambridge, 1990–92; Lectr in Accounting and Finance, Judge Business Sch., Univ. of Cambridge, 1992–97; Dir, Contracts and Competition Prog., ESRC, 1992–97; Sainsbury Prof. of Mgt, Birkbeck Coll., Univ. of London, 1997–2004; Prof. of Mgt and Dir, Business Sch., Univ. of Birmingham, 2004–08. Vis. Prof., European Univ. Inst., 2016–; Sen. Fellow, Rutgers Univ., 2017–. Hon. Prof., Univ. of Witwatersrand, 2017–. Member: Enterprise and Skills Strategic Adv. Cttee, HEFCE, 2009–13; Econ. Adv. Panel, DEFRA, 2012–. Non-exec. Dir, Sandwell and W Birmingham Hosps NHS Trust, 2006–08 (Chm., Audit Cttee, 2006–08). Mem. Council, ACAS, 2007–14 (Chm., Audit Cttee, 2007–10). Member: Council, Univ. of Birmingham, 2005–08 (Mem., Investments Cttee, 2005–08); Nat. Exec. Cttee, Assoc. of Business Schs, 2005–08 (Treas., 2005–08); Bd, Oxford Univ. Soc., 2010–18 (Treas., 2010–18); Finance Cttee, Univ. of Oxford, 2012–19; Mem., Finance Cttee, 2013–16, Pensions Trustee, 2013–16, UCAS; Chm., Bd of Govs, UWC Atlantic Coll., 2015– (Mem. Council, 2015–, Chairs Cttee, 2015–, UWC). Panel Mem. for Mgt and Business, REF 2021, 2018–. Chair, Oxford Ltd, 2018–. Co-Sec., Centenary Commn on Adult Educn, 2019. FAcSS (AcSS 2010) (Mem. Council, 2011–17; Chm., Audit and Risk Mgt Cttee, 2011–17). Ed., Internat. Rev. of Applied Economics, 2017–. *Publications:* Wages in the Business Cycle, 1987; (jtly) The Political Economy of Competitiveness, 2000; (ed) A Reader's Guide to Social Science, 2001; (ed jtly) Systems of Production, 2002; (ed) The Handbook of Globalisation, 2003, 3rd edn 2019; (ed jtly) The Political Economy of the Environment, 2011; (ed jtly) Why the Social Sciences Matter, 2015; (ed jtly) The Oxford Handbook of Mutual, Co-operative and Co-owned Business, 2017; (ed) Globalisation and Governance, 3 vols, 2017; An Advanced Introduction to Globalisation, 2017. *Recreations:* supporting Manchester United and FC United of Manchester, campaigning for supporter control of football clubs. *Address:* Kellogg College, Oxford OX2 6PN. *T:* (01865) 612003, *Fax:* (01865) 612001. *E:* jonathan.michie@kellogg.ox.ac.uk.
See also S. F. D. Michie.

**MICHIE, Prof. Susan Fiona Dorinthea,** DPhil; FBPsS, FAcSS, FMedSci; Director, Centre for Behaviour Change, since 2014, and Professor of Health Psychology, since 2005, University College London; *b* London, 19 June 1955; *d* of late Prof. Donald Michie and (Dame) Anne Laura Dorinthea McLaren, DBE, FRS; *m* 2009, Prof. Robert West; one *s* two *d.* *Educ:* St Anne's Coll., Oxford (BA Exptl Psychol. 1976); Inst. of Psychiatry, Univ. of London (MPhil Clin. Psychol. 1978); Wadham Coll., Oxford (DPhil Develtl Psychol. 1982). Chartered Clin. Psychologist 1978; Chartered Health Psychologist 1993. Royal Free Hospital School of Medicine: Clinical Psychologist and Hon. Lectr in Develtl Psychol., 1984–91; Sen. Clinical Psychologist and Hon. Sen. Lectr in Health Psychol., 1991–2002; Sen. Res. Fellow in Clin. Health Psychol., Royal Free and UC Med. Sch., 1989–2002; King's College London: Dep. Dir, Psychol. and Genetics Res. Gp, 1993–2002; Res. Fellow, 1993–96; Sen. Res. Fellow, 1996–2001; Reader in Health Psychol., 2001–02; University College London: Reader in Health Psychol., 2002–05; Co-Director, Centre for Outcomes Research and Effectiveness, 2002–; Dir, Health Psychology Res. Gp, 2002–; Dir, Health Psychol. Res., 2002–12, Hon. Consultant Clin. Psychologist, 2002–, Camden and Islington Mental Health and Social Care Trust, Camden and Islington PCTs; Sen. Scientist, MRC Health Services Res. Collaboration, Univ. of Bristol (part-time secondment), 2006–09; Co-Dir, 2009–15, Scientific Advr, 2015–, Nat. Centre for Smoking Cessation and Trng UK. FBPsS 2001; Fellow, Eur. Health Psychol. Soc., 2007; FAcSS 2012; FMedSci 2017. *Publications:* (jtly) Preventive Medicine for Total Health, 1998; (jtly) The Psychological Care of Medical Patients: a practical guide, 2nd edn 2003; (ed jtly) Health Psychology in Practice, 2004; (jtly) Improving Health: changing behaviour, 2007; (jtly) The Behaviour Change Wheel: a guide to designing interventions, 2014; (jtly) An ABC of Behaviour Change Theories, 2014; (jtly) Thinking About Behaviour Change: an interdisciplinary dialogue, 2015; (jtly) A Guide to Development and Evaluation of Digital Behaviour Change Interventions in Healthcare, 2015; over 400 jl articles, 35 books and book chapters, 400 conference abstracts. *Address:* Department of Clinical, Educational and Health Psychology, University College London, 1–19 Torrington Place, WC1E 7HB. *T:* (020) 7679 5930, *Fax:* (020) 7916 8511. *E:* s.michie@ucl.ac.uk. *W:* www.twitter.com/susanmichie.
See also J. Michie.

**MICKELSON, Philip Alfred;** golfer; *b* San Diego, 16 June 1970; *s* of Philip Mickelson and Mary Mickelson; *m* Amy McBride; one *s* two *d.* *Educ:* Arizona State Univ. Winner, Northern Telecom Open (as amateur), 1991; professional golfer, 1992–; wins include: Buick Invitational, 1993, 2000, 2001; Mercedes Championship, 1994, 1998; Northern Telecom Open, 1995; NEC World Series Golf, 1996; AT&T Pebble Beach Nat. Pro-Am, 1998, 2005; BellSouth Classic, 2000, 2005; PGA Tour Championship, 2000; US Masters Tournament, 2004, 2006, 2010; PGA Championship, 2005; Open, 2013; Member: US Ryder Cup Team, 1995, 1997, 1999 (winners), 2002, 2004, 2010, 2012, 2014, 2018; President's Cup Team, 1994 (winners), 1996 (winners), 1998, 2000 (winners), 2003. *Address:* c/o Lagardère, 488 Madison Avenue, 16th floor, New York, NY 10022, USA; c/o PGA Tour, 112 PGA Tour Boulevard, Ponte Vedra Beach, FL 32082, USA.

**MICKLETHWAIT, (Richard) John,** CBE 2016; Editor-in-Chief, Bloomberg News, since 2015; *b* 11 Aug. 1962; *s* of late Richard Miles Micklethwait and of Jane Evelyn Micklethwait (*née* Codrington); *m* 1992, Fevronia Read; three *s. Educ*: Ampleforth Coll., York; Magdalen Coll., Oxford (BA Modern Hist.). The Economist: Finance corresp., 1987–90; W Coast Bureau Chief, 1990–93; Business ed., 1993–97; NY Bureau Chief, 1997–2000; US ed., 2000–06; Ed., 2006–15. Trustee, British Mus., 2011–. *Publications*: with Adrian Wooldridge: The Witch Doctors, 1996; A Future Perfect, 2000; The Company, 2003; The Right Nation, 2004; God is Back: how the global rise of faith is changing the world, 2009; The Fourth Revolution: the global race to reinvent the state, 2014. *Recreations*: sport, dog walking. *Address*: Bloomberg News, 731 Lexington Avenue, New York, NY 10022, USA. *Club*: Royal Automobile.

**MICKLEWHITE, Sir Michael;** *see* Caine, Sir Michael.

**MIDDLE, Anne Hilary;** Headteacher, Parkstone Grammar School, Poole, 2001–13; *b* 21 March 1952; *d* of late Louis Shinwell and of Sylvia Shinwell; *m* 2002, Keith Middle; one step *s* one step *d. Educ*: Univ. of Glasgow (MA; PGCE). John Kelly Girls' School, Brent, London: Teacher of Hist., 1973–80; responsible for teaching Econs, 1975–86; Hd of Careers, 1980–86; Dep. Dir, Sixth Form, 1983–86; Tiffin Girls' School, Kingston, London: Sen. Teacher, 1986–88; Hd, Middle Sch. and Careers, 1986–88; Dep. Headteacher, 1988–95; Headteacher, Queen Elizabeth Girls' Sch., Barnet, London, 1995–2001. Pres., Assoc. of Maintained Girls' Schs, 2004–05; Mem., GSHA, 2008–13. Chm., Delta Educn Trust, 2014–. *Recreations*: golf, reading, travel, antiques. *Address*: 31 Deverel Road, Charlton Down, Dorchester, Dorset DT2 9UD. *E*: annemiddle31@yahoo.co.uk. *Club*: Dorset Golf and Country (Bere Regis).

**MIDDLE, Dr Jonathan Guy;** Chairman, Association for Quality Management in Laboratory Medicine, since 2009; *b* Weston-super-Mare, 4 March 1949; *s* of Lionel Guy Middle and Joan Middle (*née* Bennett); *m* 1978, Fiona Anne Mulligan; two *d. Educ*: Weston-super-Mare Grammar Sch. for Boys; Fitzwilliam Coll., Cambridge (BA Hons Nat. Scis 1970); Univ. of Newcastle upon Tyne (PhD 1979); Univ. of West London (ALCM Jazz Saxophone Performance 2013). Res. Associate, CRC Labs, Univ. of Newcastle upon Tyne, 1973–76; Res. Officer, CRC Labs, Univ. of Nottingham, 1976–80; Basic Grade Clin. Biochemist, 1980–84, Sen. Grade Clin. Biochemist, 1984–87, Dept of Chemical Pathol., Royal Liverpool Hosp.; Principal Biochemist and Organiser UK Nat. External Quality Assessment Service for Steroid Hormones, Univ. Hosp. of Wales, Cardiff, 1987–96; Dep. Dir UK Nat. External Quality Assessment Service for Clin. Chemistry, Univ. Hosp. Birmingham, 1996–2010; Hon. Sen. Res. Fellow, Dept of Medicine, Univ. of Birmingham, 1996–2010. Member: BSI CH212, 2012–; ISO TC212 Wkg Gp 2, 2014–. STEM Ambassador for Sci., Sci., Technol., Engrg and Maths Network, 2011–. Fellow, Assoc. of Clin. Biochem., 2012. Top 100 UK Practising Scientists Award, Science Council, 2014. *Publications*: (contrib. chapter) Steroid Analysis, 1995, 2nd edn 2010; articles mainly in Annals of Clin. Biochem. *Recreations*: leading 'Second City Sax' saxophone quartet, playing saxophone in Birmingham University Music Society Saxophone Ensemble and Wind Band, playing keyboards in 'Earlswood' trio and other local bands. *Address*: Association for Quality Management in Laboratory Medicine, PO Box 15252, Birmingham B16 6HD. *E*: mail@aqmlm.org.uk.

**MIDDLEBROOK, Ven. David John;** Archdeacon of Bedford, since 2019; *b* Ipswich, 13 Dec. 1961; *s* of Bryan and Dulcie Middlebrook; *m* 1987, Anne Green; one *s* one *d. Educ*: Newcastle Univ. (BSc Geog. and Geol. 1983); Cranfield Inst. of Technol. (MSc Distribn Technol. and Mgt 1985); Trinity Coll., Bristol (BA Theol. 1998). Exel Logistics (Nat. Freight), 1985–93; Area Organiser, Leprosy Mission, 1993–96; ordained deacon, 1998, priest, 1999; Asst Curate, Christ Church, Chorleywood, 1998–2002; Team Vicar, St Barnabas, Hemel Hempstead, 2002–08; Vicar, St Luke's, Watford, 2008–19; Rural Dean, Watford, 2009–14. Hon. Canon, St Albans Cathedral, 2013–. *Recreations*: running, walking, gardening, reading. *Address*: 17 Lansdowne Road, Luton LU3 1EE. *T*: (01727) 818167. *E*: archdbed@stalbans.anglican.org.

**MIDDLEBURGH, Rabbi Dr Charles Hadley;** Rabbi: Dublin Jewish Progressive Congregation, 2002–11, Rabbi Emeritus, since 2015; Cardiff Reform Synagogue, 2004–14; Director of Jewish Studies, since 2011, Dean, since 2014, and Reader in Bible and Liturgy, since 2015, Leo Baeck College; Lecturer, Irish School of Ecumenics, Trinity College, Dublin, 2002–09; *b* 2 Oct. 1956; *s* of late Hyman Middleburgh and Elizabeth Middleburgh; *m* 1984, Gilly Blyth. *Educ*: Brighton Coll.; University Coll. London (BA Hons, PhD 1982); Leo Baeck Coll. Lay reader, Brighton and Hove Progressive Synagogue, 1975–77; Minister, Kingston Liberal Synagogue, 1977–83; ordained 1986; Rabbi, Harrow and Wembley Progressive Synagogue, 1983–97; Exec. Dir, ULPS, 1997–2002; Rabbi, Progressive Judaism in Denmark, 2002–05. Leo Baeck College: Lectr in Bible, Aramaic, Rabbinic Practice, 1985–2002; Sen. Lectr in Rabbinics, 2003–15; Interim Dir of Rabbinic Studies, 2005–06; Hon. Dir of Studies, 2008–11. Patron, Dignity in Dying, 2004–. Occasional broadcaster, BBC Radio 4 and World Service, 1997–, RTE, Radio Eireann. FZS 1997; FRSA 2017. *Publications*: (Associate Ed.) Union of Liberal and Progressive Synagogues Daily, Sabbath and Festival Prayer Book, 1995; (ed jtly) Union of Liberal and Progressive Synagogues High Holy Days Prayerbook, 2003; (ed jtly) High and Holy Days: a book of Jewish wisdom, 2010; (ed jtly) A Jewish Book of Comfort, 2014; Bright and Beautiful: poems inspired by the natural world, 2015; The Prophets: a sideways view, 2017; Great and Small: more poems inspired by the natural world, 2017; Stumbling on the Mountains of Twilight: a rabbi's view of the world 1992–2019. *Recreations*: animal photography, writing poetry, reading obsessively, playing with my grandchildren. *E*: charles.middleburgh@lbc.ac.uk.

**MIDDLEHURST, Tom;** Member (Lab) Alyn and Deeside, National Assembly for Wales, 1999–2003; *b* 25 June 1936; *s* of late James Middlehurst and Agnes Middlehurst; *m* 1986, Patricia Mary; one *s* one *d* from a previous marriage. *Educ*: Ormskirk Grammar Sch.; Wigan Tech. Coll.; Liverpool Poly. Engrg apprentice, 1952–57; Underground Engr, NCB, 1957–63; engr, 1963–71; Local Govt Officer, Flintshire, later Clwyd, CC, 1971–93. Mem. (Lab), Alyn and Deeside DC, 1986–95; Mem. (Lab), Clwyd CC, 1993–95 (Chm., Housing Cttee; Chm., Personnel Cttee); Leader (Lab), Flintshire CC, 1995–99. Chm., Welsh Local Govt Assoc., 1997–99. National Assembly for Wales: Sec. for Post-16 Educn and Training, 1999–2000; Member: N Wales Cttee, 1999–2003; European Affairs Cttee, 2000–03; Local Govt and Housing Cttee, 2000–03; Envmt, Planning and Transport Cttee, 2000–03. Mem., Labour Party, 1961–; Mem. Bd of Dirs, Wales European Centre. Chairman: Welsh Crown Green Bowling Assoc., 2005–11; Flintshire Sports Council, 2005–11. Chm. Govs, Clwyd Theatr Cymru, 1995–99.

**MIDDLESBROUGH, Bishop of, (RC),** since 2008; **Rt Rev. Terence Patrick Drainey;** *b* Manchester, 1 Aug. 1949; *s* of Joseph Patrick Drainey and Mary Elizabeth Drainey (*née* Roebuck). *Educ*: Augustinian Theol Studium, Pontifical Univ. of Comillas, Valladolid (STB). Ordained priest, 1975; St Wulstan, Great Harwood, 1975–80; St Thomas of Canterbury, Higher Broughton, Salford, 1980–85; Immaculate Conception and St Philip Neri, Radcliffe, 1985–86; Priest (*fidei donum*), Archdiocese of Kisumu, Western Kenya, 1986–91; Parish Priest: Holy Cross, Patricroft, 1991–94; St Bernadette's, Whitefield, 1994–97; Spiritual Dir, 1997–2003, Dir of the Propaedeutic Prog., 1998–2003, Royal English Coll. of St Albans, Valladolid; Pres., St Cuthbert's Coll., Ushaw, 2003–07. Mem., Bishops' Conference Dept of Catholic Educn and Formation, 2008–; Bishops' Conference Liaison with: Seminary Rectors of Seminaries of England and Wales; National Conference of Vocation. Chairman: Nat. Office for Vocations; Caritas Social Action Network, 2014–. Appointed Papal Chaplain by His Holiness Pope Benedict XVI, 2006. *Recreations*: music, especially choral, walking, gardening. *Address*: (residence) Bishop's House, 16 Cambridge Road, Middlesbrough TS5 5NN. *T*: (01642) 818253; (office) Curial Office, 50a The Avenue, Linthorpe, Middlesbrough TS5 6QT. *T*: (01642) 850505.

**MIDDLESEX, Archdeacon of;** *no new appointment at time of going to press*.

**MIDDLETON,** 13th Baron *cr* 1711; **Michael Charles James Willoughby;** DL; Bt 1677; *b* London, 14 July 1948; *s* of 12th Baron Middleton, MC and Janet (*née* Marshall-Cornwall); *S* father, 2011; *m* 1974, Hon. Lucy Corinna Agneta Sidney, *y d* of 1st Viscount De L'Isle, VC, KG, KCMG, GCVO, PC; two *s* three *d. Educ*: Eton Coll.; Mons OCS; E Riding Coll. of Agriculture. Lieut, Coldstream Guards, 1967–71, QOY, 1971–75. Vice Pres., Europe, CLA, 2005–10. Jt Master, Middleton Hunt, 2009–13. Pres., Yorks Agricl Soc., 2016–17. DL ER Yorks, 2004. *Heir*: *s* Hon. James William Michael Willoughby [*b* 8 March 1976; *m* 2005, Lady Cara Mary Cecilia Boyle, *er d* of Earl of Cork and Orrery, *qv*; two *s* one *d*]. *Address*: North Grimston House, Malton, N Yorks YO17 8AX. *T*: (01944) 768204. *Clubs*: Cavalry and Guards, Pratt's.

**MIDDLETON, Bishop Suffragan of,** since 2008; **Rt Rev. Mark Davies;** *b* 12 May 1962; *s* of late Cyril and of Gwen Davies. *Educ*: UC of Ripon and York St John (BA Hons Leeds 1985); Coll. of the Resurrection, Mirfield (Cert. Pastoral Theol. 1986). Ordained deacon, 1989, priest, 1990; Asst Curate, Barnsley St Mary, 1989–92; Priest-in-charge, Barnsley St Paul, 1992–95; Rector of Hemsworth, 1995–2006; Asst Diocesan Dir of Ordinands, Wakefield, 1998–2006; RD, Pontefract, 2000–06; Archdeacon of Rochdale, 2006–08. Proctor in Convocation, 2000–06; Hon. Canon, Wakefield Cathedral, 2002–06. *Recreations*: music, food, walking. *Address*: The Hollies, Manchester Road, Rochdale OL11 3QY. *T*: (01706) 358550. *E*: bishopmark@manchester.anglican.org.

**MIDDLETON, Prof. Campbell Ross,** PhD; Laing O'Rourke Professor of Construction Engineering, University of Cambridge, since 2011; *b* Sydney, 1959. *Educ*: Hutchins Sch., Hobart; Univ. of Tasmania (BE Hons 1981); Imperial Coll. London (MSc 1985; DIC); King's Coll., Cambridge (PhD 1993). FICE; FIE(Aust); CEng; CPEng. Dept of Main Roads, Tasmania, 1981–87; Engr, Ove Arup & Partners, London, 1987–88; University of Cambridge: Res. Asst, 1989–93; Sen. Res. Associate, 1993–94; Asst Dir of Res., 1995–99; Lectr, 1999–2000; Sen. Lectr, 2000–11. *Address*: Department of Engineering, Trumpington Street, Cambridge CB2 1PZ. *T*: (01223) 332726. *E*: prof@construction.cam.ac.uk.

**MIDDLETON, David Fraser,** CBE 2015; Chairman, Scottish Qualifications Authority, since 2017; *b* 23 June 1956; *s* of late Fraser Middleton and Margaret Middleton; *m* 1992, Diane Lamberton; one *d. Educ*: Univ. of Glasgow (MA Hons (Modern Hist. and Political Econ.)). Joined Scottish Office, as administrative trainee, 1978: Private Sec. to successive Ministers of State, 1982–84; on secondment to Cabinet Office, 1984; Br. Hd, Finance Gp (Housing and Educn), 1984–89; Head, Whitfield Urban Partnership, Dundee, 1989–91; Hd of Div., Scottish Develt Dept, 1991–96; Hd Policy, Finance and Strategy Div., Roads Directorate, 1996–97; Hd, Personnel, 1997–99; Dir of Implementation, Scottish Exec., Jan.–June 1999; Head: Local Govt Gp, 1999–2001; Local Govt and External Relns, 2001–02; Rural Gp, Scottish Exec. Envmt and Rural Affairs Dept, 2002–06; Dir of Special Projects, UHI (on attachment), 2006–07; Deputy Chief Exec. and Dir of Corporate Services, Crown Office and Procurator Fiscal Service, Scottish Exec., then Scottish Govt, 2007; Hd, Scotland Office, 2007–09; Chief Executive: Transport Scotland, 2009–15; Historic Envmt Scotland, 2015–16. *Recreations*: golf, gardening. *Address*: Scottish Qualifications Authority, Optima Building, 58 Robertson Street, Glasgow G2 8DQ. *Club*: Royal Musselburgh Golf.

**MIDDLETON, (David) Miles,** CBE 1992; Vice Chairman, Community Action Northumberland, since 2018 (Director, since 2015); Partner, Middleton Associates, since 1993; *b* 15 June 1938; *s* of Harry Middleton and of Dorothy Hannah Middleton (*née* Nisbet); *m* 1st, 1962, Mary Gale (marr. diss. 1979); one *s* one *d*; 2nd, 1980, Elizabeth, (Bobbie), Lancaster; two step *s* two step *d. Educ*: Sedbergh Sch. ACA 1962, FCA 1972. Articled Clerk, Strachan & Co., 1956–61; Audit Sen., Coopers Brothers & Co., 1962–64; Coopers & Lybrand: Manager, Zürich, 1964–68; Newcastle upon Tyne office, 1968–71, 1986–90; Middlesbrough office, 1971–86; Partner, 1974; Sen. Partner, NE Practice, 1990–93. Chairman: Northern Enterprise Ltd, 1988–99; Hadrian's Wall Tourism Partnership, 2000–05; Isos Housing Gp, 2005–11. Member Board: Rural Develt Commn, 1992–99 (Chm., 1997–99); NE Regl Develt Agency, 1999–2001; Countryside Agency, 1999–2000; Milecastle Housing (formerly Tynedale Housing), 2000–05 (Chm., 2003–05). Chm., Tees Valley Learning and Skills Council, 2000–04. Pres., British Chamber of Commerce, 1990–92. *Address*: Stanegate, St Helen's Lane, Corbridge, Northumberland NE45 5JD. *T*: (01434) 633545. *Club*: Northern Counties (Newcastle upon Tyne).

**MIDDLETON, Dianne, (Di);** QC 2017; *b* Bristol, 24 Nov. 1965; *d* of William Middleton and Margaret Middleton; partner, NSR Khan; two *s. Educ*: Manchester Poly. (BA Hons 1988); St Hilda's Coll., Oxford (PGCE 1989); BPP Law Sch. (DipLaw 1996); Inns of Court Sch. of Law. Teacher, Hackney Sixth Form Centre, 1990–95; called to the Bar, Inner Temple, 1997; in practice as a barrister, specialising in criminal defence, Goldsmith Chambers, 1997–2001, 1 Pump Court Chambers, 2001–04, Tooks Chambers, 2004–13. *Recreations*: stand-up paddle boarding, receiving unbridled canine affection, gazing lovingly at municipal architecture, drinking wine. *Address*: Garden Court Chambers, 57–60 Lincoln's Inn Fields, WC2A 3LJ. *T*: (020) 7993 6100. *E*: info@gclaw.co.uk.

**MIDDLETON, Edward Bernard;** Partner, PKF (UK) LLP, Chartered Accountants, 1979–2008; Director, London Cremation Company plc, since 2011; *b* 5 July 1948; *s* of Bernard and Bettie Middleton; *m* 1971, Rosemary Spence Brown; three *s. Educ*: Aldenham Sch., Elstree; Chartered Accountant, 1970. Joined London office of Pannell Kerr Forster, 1971; Nairobi office, 1973; Audit Manager, London office, 1975; seconded to DTI as Dir, Industrial Develt Unit, 1984–86. Dir, PKF Hotel Consultancy Services, 1996–2008. Mem. sub-cttee, Consultative Cttee of Accountancy Bodies, 1980–84. Hon. Treas., Hospitality Action (formerly Hotel and Catering Benevolent Assoc.), 1992–2009; Mem. Council, British Assoc. of Hospitality Accountants, 1997–2007. Trustee, ResCU, 2010–. Liveryman, 2004, Mem. of Ct, 2008–17, Spectacle Makers' Co. (Master, 2015–16). Trustee: Spectacle Makers Charity, 2009–12; Educn Trust, 2010–). *Recreations*: sailing, photography. *Address*: Barrans, Bury Green, Little Hadham, Ware, Herts SG11 2ES. *T*: (01279) 658684. *Clubs*: Reform; Yealm Yacht.

**MIDDLETON, Jeremy Peter,** CBE 2012; Managing Director, Middleton Enterprises Ltd, since 1990; *b* Burton on Trent, 19 Nov. 1960; *s* of Dennis Middleton and Vivienne Middleton; *m* 1988, Catherine Smith; one *s* two *d. Educ*: Univ. of Kent (BA Hons Hist.). Brand Manager, Procter and Gamble, 1984–88; Supervising Consultant, Price Waterhouse, 1988–90; Co-Founder, 1990, Mem., Exec. Cttee, 1992–, Homeserve. Chm., Conviction Investment Partners, 2018–. Mem. Bd, N Eastern LEP, 2012–16. Founder, Charity

Escapes, 2017–. Contested (C): Newcastle upon Tyne East and Wallsend, 1997; Hartlepool, Sept. 2004. Pres., 2008–09, Chm., 2009–12, Conservative Nat. Convention; Dep. Chm., Conservative Party, 2009–12. *Recreations:* ski-ing, trekking, cinema, tolerance. *E:* jeremy@middletonenterprises.com.

**MIDDLETON, Rear-Adm. (John) Patrick (Windsor),** CB 1992; Secretary, Royal Commission for the Exhibition of 1851, 1995–2002; *b* 15 March 1938; *s* of late Comdr John Henry Dudley Middleton, RN and Norna Mary Tessimond (*née* Hitchings); *m* 1962, Jane Rodwell Gibbs; one *s* one *d*. *Educ:* Cheltenham College; BRNC Dartmouth; RNEC Manadon. CEng, MIMechE, MIMarEST. Entered Royal Navy 1954; CSO(E) to Flag Officer Submarines, 1981; CSO(E) Falkland Islands, 1983; Captain Naval Drafting, 1984; Dir, In Service Submarines, 1987; CSO (Engrg), later (Support), to C-in-C Fleet, 1989–92, retd. Trustee, CARE for People with Learning Disabilities, 1993–2007 (Chm. Trustees, 1998–2007). Liveryman: Armourers and Brasiers' Co., 1971– (Mem. Ct of Assts, 1995–2015; Master, 2001–02). Gov., Chilmark and Fonthill Bishop Primary Sch., 2003–07 and 2016–18. *Publications:* Admiral Clanky Entertains, 2010. *Recreations:* sailing, walking, gardening, writing. *Address:* Manora, Chilmark, Wilts SP3 5AH. *T:* (01722) 716231. *E:* mimanora@aol.com.

**MIDDLETON, Julia;** Founder, 1989 and Innovation Officer, since 2019, Common Purpose Charitable Trust (Chief Executive, 1989–2018); *b* London, 21 April 1958; *d* of Eric Morland and Agnes Morland; *m* 1984, Rupert Middleton; two *s* three *d*. *Educ:* Lycée Français de New York; Lycée Ferney Voltaire, London; Lycée Français Charles de Gaulle, London; London Sch. of Econs and Political Sci. (BSc Econs). Industrial Soc., 1980–88. Trustee: Alfanar, 2005–; Media Standards Trust; Impetus Trust. Mem., Internat. Adv. Council, Fundação Dom Cabral, 2012–. *Publications:* Beyond Authority: leadership in a changing world, 2007; Cultural Intelligence - CQ: the competitive edge for leaders crossing borders, 2014. *Address:* Common Purpose Charitable Trust, 38 Artillery Lane, E1 7LS. *T:* (020) 7608 8100. *E:* julia.middleton@commonpurpose.org.

**MIDDLETON, Lawrence John,** CMG 1985; PhD; HM Diplomatic Service; Ambassador to the Republic of Korea, 1986–90, retired; *b* 27 March 1930; *s* of John James Middleton and Mary (*née* Horgan); *m* 1963, Sheila Elizabeth Hoey; two *s* one *d*. *Educ:* Finchley Catholic Grammar Sch.; Regent Street Poly. (BSc (ext.) 1949); King's Coll., London (BSc Special Hons 1951, PhD 1954). Scientific Officer, ARC, 1954–60 and 1962–63; Asst Specialist, Univ. of Calif, Berkeley, 1959–60; on secondment as Cons. to FAO and to UN Cttee on Effects of Atomic Radiation, 1960–62 and to CENTO Inst. of Nuclear Science, 1963–65; Principal, Min. of Agriculture, 1966–68; First Sec., FO, 1968; Washington, 1969–71; Kuala Lumpur, 1971–74; Counsellor (Commercial), Belgrade, 1974–78; Dir of Research, FCO, 1978–80; Cabinet Office, 1980–82; Counsellor, UK Delegn to Conf. on Disarmament, Geneva, 1982–84; Sen. DS, RCDS, 1984–86. Mem. Council, 1994–2001, Vice-Pres., 1998–2001, Royal Asiatic Soc. (FRAS 1992); Chm., Anglo-Korean Soc., 1995–2002. Chm., N Oxford Defence Assoc., 1995–2000. *Address:* 12 Polstead Road, Oxford OX2 6TN.

**MIDDLETON, Marc William;** Partner, EY, since 2013; *b* London, 18 July 1961; *s* of William Middleton and Catherine Middleton; *m* 1990, Marcia Jenkins; three *s* one *d*. *Educ:* Haberdashers' Aske's Hatcham Sch.; Univ. of Manchester (BA Hons Mod. Langs). Partner and Man. Dir, N. M. Rothschild & Sons Ltd, 1984–2008; Man. Dir, Shareholder Executive, BIS, 2008–10; Vice-Chm., Macquarie Capital, 2010–12. *Recreations:* Rugby, boxing, cycling, running, ski-ing, theatre. *Clubs:* Barnes Rugby Football, Olympic Barnes.

**MIDDLETON, Rev. Canon Michael John;** Canon of Westminster, 1997–2004, now Canon Emeritus; Treasurer, 1997–2004, and Almoner, 2000–04, Westminster Abbey; *b* 21 July 1940; *s* of Bernard and Gladys Middleton; *m* 1965, Anne Elisabeth Parker; two *s* one *d*. *Educ:* Weymouth Grammar Sch.; St Cuthbert's Soc., Durham (BSc); Fitzwilliam Coll., Cambridge (MA); Westcott House, Cambridge. Ordained: deacon, 1966; priest, 1967; Curate, St George's Jesmond, Newcastle, 1966–69; Chaplain: St George's Grammar Sch., Cape Town, 1969–72; King's School, Tynemouth, 1972–77; Vicar, St George's, Jesmond, Newcastle, 1977–85; Rector of Hexham, 1985–92; Archdeacon of Swindon, 1992–97. Acting Archdeacon of Westmorland and Furness, 2012. Hon. Canon of Newcastle, 1990. Proctor in Convocation, 1980–92. *Recreations:* walking, Westerns. *Address:* 2 Cleveland Mews, Cleveland Road, Chichester PO19 7AD. *T:* (01243) 530580.

**MIDDLETON, Miles;** *see* Middleton, D. M.

**MIDDLETON, Rear-Adm. Patrick;** *see* Middleton, Rear-Adm. J. P. W.

**MIDDLETON, Sir Peter (Edward),** GCB 1989 (KCB 1984); Director, 1991–2004, Chief Executive Officer, 1998–99, and Chairman, 1999–2004, Barclays Bank (Deputy Chairman, 1991–98; Chairman, BZW Banking Division, 1991–98); Chairman: Marsh Ltd, 2005–13; Burford Capital Ltd, since 2009; UK Chairman, Marsh & McLennan Companies, 2007–14 (Member, International Advisory Board, 2005–09); *b* 2 April 1934; *m* 1st, 1964, Valerie Ann Lindup (*d* 1987); one *d* (one *s* decd); 2nd, 1990, Constance Owen. *Educ:* Sheffield City Grammar Sch.; Sheffield Univ. (BA; Hon. DLitt 1984); Bristol Univ. Served RAPC, 1958–60. HM Treasury: Senior Information Officer, 1962; Principal, 1964; Asst Director, Centre for Administrative Studies, 1967–69; Private Sec. to Chancellor of the Exchequer, 1969–72; Treasury Press Secretary, 1972–75; Head of Monetary Policy Div., 1975; Under Secretary, 1976; Dep. Sec., 1980–83; Permanent Sec., 1983–91. Director: Bass PLC, 1992–2001; General Accident Fire & Life Assurance Corp. plc, later CGU plc, 1992–98; United Utilities PLC (formerly NW Water Gp), 1994–2007 (Vice-Chm., 1998–99; Chm., 1999–2000; Dep. Chm., 2000–07); MTS OJSC, 2005–07; Chairman: Camelot Gp plc, 2004–10; Barclays Asia Pacific Adv. Cttee, 2004–12; Three Delta Adv. Bd, 2006–11; Adv. Bd, Burford Advrs LLP, 2007–09; Mercer Ltd, 2009–14; Hamilton Ventures, 2009–; Hume Capital Securities plc, 2014–15; XCAP Securities plc, 2012–14; Burford Capital Hldgs (UK) Ltd (formerly Firstassist Legal Gp Hldgs Ltd), 2012–; Resort Gp, 2015–18; Directa UK Plus Ltd, 2015–. Mem., Adv. Bd, Financial Dynamics, 2004–09; Sen. Advr, Fenchurch Adv. Partners, 2005–12; Mem., Adv. Bd, ST Telemedia, 2010–12. Chairman: Sheffield Urban Regeneration Co. Ltd (Sheffield 1), 2000–05; Creative Sheffield, 2006–11. Chm., CEDR, 2004–11. Dir, Internat. Monetary Conf., 2001–03; Mem. Adv. Council, Monetary Authy of Singapore, 2001–05. Member: Adv. Bd, Nat. Econ. Res. Associates 1991; Exec. Cttee, Centre for Econ. Policy Res. Pres., British Bankers' Assoc., 2004–06. Trustee, InterMedia Res. and Consulting Europe, 2011–14. Vis. Fellow, Nuffield Coll., Oxford, 1981–89. Dir, Inst. of Contemporary British History, 2001–03 (Chm., 1992–2001). Mem. Council, 1991–, Chancellor, 1999–2015, now Emeritus, Univ. of Sheffield (Pro-Chancellor, 1997–99; Hon. Prof., Mgt Sch., 2011–); Mem. Council, Manchester Business Sch., 1985–92; Governor: London Business Sch., 1984–90; Ditchley Foundn, 1985–; NIESR, 1991–2007. Dir, English Chamber Orch. and Music Soc., 1992–2003. Trustee, Philharmonia Trust Ltd, 2012–. Cdre, Civil Service Sailing Assoc., 1984–92. *Recreations:* hill walking, music, outdoor sports. *Address:* c/o Gill Herbert, Marsh & McLennan Companies, Tower Place East, Tower Place, EC3R 5BU. *Club:* Reform.

**MIDDLETON, Prof. Richard,** DPhil; FBA 2004; Professor of Music, University of Newcastle upon Tyne, 1998–2005, now Emeritus; *b* 4 Feb. 1945; *s* of Harold and Joan Middleton; *m* 1969, Jane Pescod Harding; three *d*. *Educ:* Clare Coll., Cambridge (BA 1966); Univ. of York (DPhil 1970). Staff Tutor in Music, Dept of Extramural Studies, Univ. of Birmingham, 1970–72; Open University: Lectr, 1972–79; Sen. Lectr, 1979–95; Reader in Music and Cultural Studies, 1995–97. Corresp. Mem., Amer. Musicological Soc., 2008. Hon. DHL Chicago, 2006. *Publications:* Pop Music and the Blues, 1972; Studying Popular Music, 1990; (ed) Reading Pop, 2000; (ed jtly) The Cultural Study of Music: a critical introduction, 2003, rev. edn 2011; Voicing the Popular, 2006; Musical Belongings, 2009. *Recreation:* farming. *Address:* Lochhill Farm, Crossmichael, Castle Douglas DG7 3BE.

**MIDDLETON, Richard Harry;** Chair, Commonwealth Scholarship Commission, since 2015 (Member, 2009–15); *b* Cheltenham, 27 March 1955; *s* of Harry and Beryl Middleton; partner, 1989, Heather McAteer; one *s* one *d*. *Educ:* Cheltenham Grammar Sch.; Univ. of York (BA 1977); Univ. of London (MA 1979); Open Univ. (MBA 2000). Field Worker, CHAR, 1980–85; Housing Officer, GLC, 1985–86; Dir, Housing Advice Switchboard and Housing Services Agency, 1987–94; Gen. Manager, Health and Personal Social Services NI, 1994–97; Ops Dir, MRC, 1997–2002; Directorate Manager, Univ. Hosps of Leicester NHS Trust, 2002–07; Chief Operating Officer, Aston Univ., 2007–10; Interim Hd of Resources and Planning, Kingston Univ., 2011–13; Registrar, City Univ. London, 2013; Interim Acad. Registrar, Univ. of Beds, 2013–14; Prog. Manager, Student Educn Service, Univ. of Leeds, 2014–15; Interim Dep. Vice Chancellor, Middlesex Univ., 2015–16; Interim Registrar and Sec., Univ. of Plymouth, 2017; Interim Academic Registrar, Univ. of Wolverhampton, 2018; Interim Academic Registrar, Univ. of Derby, 2019. Consultant, Develt for Res. Up-take in Sub-Saharan Africa prog., 2012–17. FRSA. *Publications:* Who's to Benefit?, 1985. *Recreations:* cycling, walking and talking in good company. *Address:* Commonwealth Scholarship Commission, c/o Association of Commonwealth Universities, Woburn House, Tavistock Square, WC1H 9HF. *E:* richard.middleton@cscuk.org.uk.

**MIDDLETON, Timothy John;** Director in the Legal Service, Council of the European Union, 2003–18; *b* 15 Sept. 1953; *s* of William Smith Middleton and Brenda Mary Middleton; *m* 1983, Janet Kathleen Elliott; one *s* two *d*. *Educ:* King Edward VII Grammar Sch., Coalville, Leics; Balliol Coll., Oxford (MA Jurisprudence); Coll. of Law. Called to the Bar, Gray's Inn, 1977; Legal Asst, 1979–83, Sen. Legal Asst, 1983–85, MAFF; on secondment to Directorate Gen. VI (Agriculture), CEC, 1985–87; Lawyer: MAFF, 1987–89; Legal Secretariat to Law Officers, 1989–92; Legal Dir, Intervention Bd, 1992–94; Hd of a Legal Div., MAFF, 1994–97; Dep. Legal Advr, Home Office, 1997–2001; Solicitor to Equitable Life Inquiry, 2001–03. Governor: Broadwater Sch., Godalming, 1999–2003; Green Lane Infants Sch., Godalming, 1996–2000. Churchwarden, St John the Evangelist, Farncombe, 2000–03. *Recreations:* modern literature, theatre, cooking.

**MIDGLEY, Darrell;** Director, D&CM Consulting Ltd, since 2018; Director, Projects, Department for Business, Energy and Industrial Strategy, 2017; *b* Portsmouth, 13 March 1957; *s* of Norman Tomlinson Midgley and Joan Midgley; *m* 1981, Carole Patricia; one *s* one *d*. *Educ:* Portsmouth Northern Grammar Sch.; Bath Technical Coll. (HNC Engrg 1979); Kingston Poly. (MSc (Dist.) Adv. Manufg 1989). Ministry of Defence: Defence Fixed Networks Team Leader, 2002–06; Armoured Vehicle Pathfinder Team Leader, 2006; Satellite Team Leader, 2007–09; Hd, Networks, 2009–12; Chief Inf. Officer, BIS, 2012–15; Prog. Dir, NATO, 2015–17. *Recreations:* sport, military history, family, gardening.

**MIDGLEY, Prof. Paul Anthony,** PhD; FRS 2014; Professor of Materials Science, since 2008 and Head, Department of Materials Science and Metallurgy, since 2018, University of Cambridge; Fellow, Peterhouse, Cambridge, since 2000; *b* Welwyn Garden City, 22 March 1966; *s* of John Barry Midgley and Hazel Malvene Midgley; *m* 2015, Caroline Louise Harbord. *Educ:* Univ. of Bristol (BSc 1987; MSc 1988; PhD 1991). Royal Exhibn of 1851 Res. Fellow, 1991–93, Royal Soc. Univ. Res. Fellow, 1994–97, Univ. of Bristol; University of Cambridge: Asst Dir of Res., 1997–2000; Lectr, 2000–01; Sen. Lectr, 2001–03; Reader in Electron Microscopy, 2003–08; Lectr, Peterhouse, Cambridge, 2000–08. Pres., Eur. Microscopy Soc., 2008–12. Hon. FRMS 2016. *Publications:* contrib. papers to learned jls on electron microscopy and its application. *Recreations:* walking, cricket, cinema, badminton, art. *Address:* Department of Materials Science and Metallurgy, University of Cambridge, 27 Charles Babbage Road, Cambridge CB3 0FS. *T:* (01223) 334561, *Fax:* (01223) 334567. *E:* pam33@cam.ac.uk.

**MIDHA, Dr Arun Daniel;** Lay Member, Committee on Standards, House of Commons, since 2016; *b* Swansea, 24 April 1964; *s* of Dr Rajendra Nath Midha, JP, FRCP and Olive Marion Midha, MBE, JP; *m* 1991, Susan Margaret Williams; one *s* one *d*. *Educ:* Gowerton Comprehensive Sch.; Swansea Univ. (BSc Econ.; PhD 1996); Cardiff Univ. (MBA 1990); Exeter Coll., Oxford (Dip. Social Studies 1989). Grad. trainee, Lloyds Bank, 1989–90; Commerce and Industry Advr, Health Promotion Authy for Wales, 1990–94; Asst Dir, Welsh Combined Centres for Public Health, 1994–2001; Associate Dir, Business Planning, then Dir of Strategy and Resources, Sch. of Postgrad. Med. and Dental Educn, Cardiff Univ., 2001–09. Case Examr, RCVS (Vet. Surgeons, then Vet. Nurses), 2012–. Ind. Chair: Retrospective Contg Health Care Reviews, NHS Wales, 2010–; Retrospective Contg Health Care Reviews, NHS England, 2019; Chair: Renal Adv. Bd, Nat. Assembly for Wales, 2005–08; Natural Resources Corporate Governance Cttee, Welsh Govt, 2010–14; Ind. Mem., Nat. Adv. Bd (NHS Wales), Welsh Govt, 2010–12; Mem., Resources Cttee, Welsh Audit Office, 2011–13. Mem., Welsh Lang. Bd, 2000–10. Lay Member: GMC, 2000–09 (Mem., Educn and Resources Cttee, 2000–08; Treas., 2003–09); Health Professions Council, 2008–13; Professional Conduct Cttee, Bar Standards Bd, 2009–18; Appeals and Malpractice Panel, Welsh Jt Educn Cttee, 2015–17; Gen. Pharmaceutical Council, 2016–. Chair, Code of Conduct Panel, Royal Pharmaceutical Soc. for GB, 2005–11; Ind. Mem., Audit, Risk and Assce Cttee, NMC, 2006–10. Lay Mem., PMETB, 2007–10 (Mem., Audit Cttee, 2007–10). Lay Mem., Cttee on Clin. Excellence Awards in Wales, 2008–14. Member: Broadcasting Council for Wales, 2005–10; Glas Cymru/Welsh Water, 2014–16; HEFCW, 2015–18; Bd, Qualifications Wales, 2017–. Mem. Council, Swansea Univ., 2011–12. Assessor, Queen's Anniversary Prizes for Further and Higher Educn, 2008–. Trustee and Mem. Bd, Acad. Med. Royal Colls, 2008–09; Trustee and Hon. Sec., Welsh Rugby Charitable Trust, 2015–19. Gov., Ysgol Plasmawr Secondary Sch., 2009–. Welsh Rugby Union referee, 1984–98. JP Cardiff, 1994–2004; High Sheriff, S Glamorgan, 2012–13. *Recreations:* Rugby, football (Swansea City FC), theatre, opera, family.

**MIDLETON, 12th Viscount** *cr* 1717 (Ire.); **Alan Henry Brodrick;** Baron Brodrick of Midleton, Co. Cork 1715; Baron Brodrick of Peper Harow 1796; President, British Horological Institute, since 2015 (Chairman, 1999–2000; Curator, 2001–14); *b* 4 Aug. 1949; *s* of Alan Rupert Brodrick (*d* 1972) (*egs* of 7th Viscount) and of Alice Elizabeth, *d* of G. R. Roberts; *S* uncle, 1989; *m* 1st, 1978, Julia Helen (marr. diss. 2002), *d* of Michael Pitt; two *s* one *d*; 2nd, 2002, Maureen Susan, *d* of Joseph Sime. *Educ:* St Edmund's School,

Canterbury. Keeper of Horology, John Gershom Parkington Collection of Time Measurement Instruments, Bury St Edmunds, 1986–2002. British Horological Institute: FBHI; Mem. Council, 1993; Chm. Museum and Liby Cttee, 1994; Chm., Mus. Trust, 1995. *Recreation:* bicycling. *Heir: s* Hon. Ashley Rupert Brodrick, *b* 25 Nov. 1980.

**MIDORI;** *see* Goto, Mi Dori.

**MIDWINTER, Eric Clare,** OBE 1992; MA, DPhil; writer; *b* 11 Feb. 1932; *m*; two *s* one *d*. *Educ:* St Catharine's Coll., Cambridge (BA Hons History); Univs of Liverpool (MA Educn) and York (DPhil). Educational posts, incl. Dir of Liverpool Educn Priority Area Project, 1955–75; Head, Public Affairs Unit, Nat. Consumer Council, 1975–80; Dir, Centre for Policy on Ageing, 1980–91, Chm., 2002–10. Chairman: Council, Adv. Centre for Educn, 1976–84; London Transport Users Consultative Cttee, 1977–84; London Regl Passengers' Cttee, 1984–96; Community Educn Develt Centre, 1995–2001. Mem., POW Adv. Cttee on Disability, 1990–95. Vis. Prof. of Educn, Univ. of Exeter, 1993–2002. Pres., Assoc. of Cricket Statisticians and Historians, 1997–2004. Chm., Cricket Soc. Book of the Year Award, 2002–09. DUniv Open, 1989. *Publications:* Victorian Social Reform, 1968; Law and Order in Victorian Lancashire, 1968; Social Administration in Lancashire, 1969; Nineteenth Century Education, 1970; Old Liverpool, 1971; Projections: an education priority project at work, 1972; Social Environment and the Urban School, 1972; Priority Education, 1972; Patterns of Community Education, 1973; (ed) Teaching in the Urban Community School, 1973; (ed) Pre-School Priorities, 1974; Education and the Community, 1975; Education for Sale, 1977; Make 'Em Laugh: famous comedians and their world, 1978; Schools and Society, 1980; W. G. Grace: his life and times, 1981; Age is Opportunity: education and older people, 1982; (ed) Mutual Aid Universities, 1984; The Wage of Retirement: the case for a new pensions policy, 1985; Fair Game: myth and reality in sport, 1986; Caring for Cash: the issue of private domiciliary care, 1986; Redefining Old Age, 1987; The Lost Seasons: wartime cricket 1939–1945, 1987; (ed) Retired Leisure, 1987; Polls Apart? Older Voters and the 1987 General Election, 1987; New Design for Old, Function, Style and Older People, 1988; Red Roses Crest the Caps: a history of Lancashire cricket, 1989; Creating Chances: arts by older people, 1990; Old Order: crime and older people, 1990; Out of Focus: old age, the press and broadcasting, 1991; Brylcreem summer: the 1947 cricket season, 1991; An Illustrated History of County Cricket, 1992; Lifelines, 1994; The Development of Social Welfare in Britain, 1994; First Knock: cricket's opening pairs, 1994; European Year '93, 1995; 150 Years: a celebration: Surrey CCC, 1995; Thriving People: the growth and prospects of the U3A in the UK, 1995; Darling Old Oval: history of Surrey County Cricket Club, 1995; State Educator: the life and enduring influence of W. E. Forster, 1996; Pensioned Off: retirement and income examined, 1997; Yesterdays: the way we were, 1998; The Billy Bunter Syndrome: or why Britain failed to create a relevant secondary school system, 1998; (ed) MCC Yearbook, 1998, 1999, MCC Annual, 2000–06; From Meadowland to Multinational: a review of cricket's social history, 2000; Yesterdays: our finest hours, 2001; Quill on Willow: cricket in literature, 2001; Best-remembered: a hundred stars of yesteryear, 2002; As One Stage Door Closes: the story of John Wade, jobbing conjuror, 2002; Novel Approaches: a guide to the popular classic novel, 2003; 500 Beacons: the USA story, 2004; Red Shirts and Roses: the story of the two Old Traffords, 2005; The People's Jesters: Twentieth Century British comedians, 2006; Lord Salisbury, 2006; Parish to Planet: how football came to rule the world, 2007; George Duckworth, Warrington's Ambassador at Large, 2007; An Outline of Political Thought and Practice, 2008; I Say, I Say, I Say: the double act story, 2009; The Cricketer's Progress: Meadowland to Mumbai, 2010; Best-remembered II: cinema and radio, 2013; Guide to Cricket Lore, 2014; The Collective Age: 1850–1950: the rise and fall of a fairer society, 2017; Class Peace: an analysis of social status and cricket 1846–1962, 2017; Labour's Prize Band: Attlee's ministry analysed, 2018; *relevant publication:* Variety is the Spice of Life: the worlds of Eric Midwinter, by Jeremy Hardie, 2015. *Recreations:* sport, comedy. *Clubs:* Savage, MCC; Lancashire CC.

**MIDWINTER, Prof. John Edwin,** OBE 1984; PhD; FRS 1985; FREng; Pender Professor of Electronic Engineering, University College London, 1991–2004, now Professor Emeritus; *b* 8 March 1938; *s* of Henry C. and Vera J. Midwinter; *m* 1961, Maureen Anne Holt; two *s* two *d*. *Educ:* St Bartholomew's Grammar Sch., Newbury, Berks; King's Coll., Univ. of London (BSc Physics, 1961; AKC 1961). PhD Physics, London (ext.), 1968. MInstP 1973; FIET (FIEE 1980); Hon. Fellow 2009); FIEEE 1983; FREng (FEng 1984). Joined RRE, Malvern, as Scientific Officer, 1961 (research on lasers and non-linear optics); Sen. Scientific Officer, 1964–68; Perkin Elmer Corp., Norwalk, Conn, USA, 1968–70; Res. Center, Materials Research Center, Allied Chemical Corp., Morristown, NJ, USA, 1970–71; Head of Optical Fibre Develt, PO Res. Centre, Martlesham, 1971–77; Head, Optical Communications Technol., British Telecom Res. Labs, 1977–84; University College London: BT Prof. of Optoelectronics, 1984–91; Head, Dept of Electronic Engrg, later of Electronic and Electrical Engrg, 1988–98; Vice Provost, 1994–99. Pres., IEE, 2000–01 (Vice Pres., 1994; Dep. Pres., 1998–2000; Chm., Electronics Div., 1991–92). Lectures: Bruce Preller, RSE, 1983; Clifford Patterson, Royal Soc., 1983; Cantor, RSA, 1984; lectures on climate change and low carbon living, 2006–. Hon. DSc: Nottingham, 2000; Loughborough, 2001; QUB, 2004. Electronics Div. Premium, 1981, J. J. Thompson Medal, 1987, Faraday Medal, 1997, IEE; Eric Sumner Award and Medal, IEEE, 2002. *Publications:* Applied Non-Linear Optics, 1972; Optical Fibers for Transmission, 1979 (Best Book in Technol. Award, Amer. Publishers' Assoc., 1980); over 200 papers on lasers, non-linear optics and optical communications. *Recreations:* country and mountain walking, ski-ing, public and schools lectures on climate change and renewable energy. *E:* john.midwinter@btopenworld.com.

**MIELE, Claire Lizbeth;** *see* Johnston, C. L.

**MIERS, Sir (Henry) David (Alastair Capel),** KBE 1985; CMG 1979; HM Diplomatic Service, retired; Chairman, Society of Pension Consultants, 1998–2006; *b* 10 Jan. 1937; *s* of late Col R. D. M. C. Miers, DSO, QO Cameron Highlanders, and Honor (*née* Bucknill); *m* 1966, Imelda Maria Emilia, *d* of Jean-Baptiste Wouters, Huizingen, Belgium; two *s* one *d*. *Educ:* Winchester; University Coll., Oxford. Tokyo, 1963; Vientiane, 1966; Private Sec. to Minister of State, FO, 1968; Paris, 1972; Counsellor, Tehran, 1977–79; Hd, Middle Eastern Dept, FCO, 1980–83; Ambassador to Lebanon, 1983–85; Asst Under-Sec. of State, FCO, 1986–89; Ambassador to Greece, 1989–93; to Netherlands, 1993–96. Chairman: British-Lebanese Assoc., 1998–2012; Anglo-Hellenic League, 1999–2007.

**MIERS, Thomasina Jean,** OBE 2019; chef and food writer; Co-founder and Director, Wahaca (Oaxaca Ltd), since 2006; *b* Cheltenham, 5 Feb. 1976; *d* of Probyn and Niki Miers; *m* 2011; Mark Williams; three *d*. *Educ:* St Paul's Girls' Sch.; Edinburgh Univ. (MA Econs and Modern Langs). VAT consultant, Arthur Andersen, 1995; Digital Strategist, EHS Real Time, 2000–02. Columnist: Sunday Times, 2006–09; Guardian. Trustee, Chefs in Sch. *Publications:* (ed jtly) Soup Kitchen, 2005; Cook, 2006; Wild Gourmets, 2007; Mexican Food Made Simple, 2010; Wahaca: Mexican food at home, 2012; Chilli Notes, 2014; Home Cook, 2017. *Recreations:* creating school gardens, improving school food, tennis, cycling, reading, family, dancing, eating, walking, opera, travel. *Address:* c/o Greene & Heaton, 37 Goldhawk Road, W12 8QQ. *T:* (020) 8749 0315. *E:* hfaulks@greeneheaton.co.uk.

**MIESENBÖCK, Prof. Gero,** MD; FRS 2015; Waynflete Professor of Physiology, since 2007, and Director, Centre for Neural Circuits and Behaviour, since 2011, University of Oxford; *b* 15 July 1965; *s* of Dr Gottfried and Hannelore Miesenböck; *m* 1997, Barrie Dolnick; one *d*. *Educ:* Univ. of Innsbruck (MD 1993); Umeå Univ., Sweden. Postdoctoral Fellow, 1992–98, Asst Mem. and Hd, Lab. of Neural Systems, 1999–2004, Meml Sloan-Kettering Cancer Center, NY; Asst Prof. of Cell Biol., Genetics and Neurosci., Weill Med. Coll. of Cornell Univ., NY, 1999–2004; Associate Prof. of Cell Biol. and Molecular Physiol., Yale Univ. Sch. of Medicine, 2004–07. Member: EMBO, 2008; Austrian Acad. of Sci., 2014; German Acad. of Sci. Leopoldina, 2016. FMedSci 2012. Hon. Dr TCD, 2017. InBev-Baillet Latour Internat. Health Prize, 2012; Brain Prize, Grete Lundbeck Eur. Brain Res. Foundn, 2013; Gabbay Award, Rosenstiel Center, Brandeis Univ., 2013; Heinrich Wieland Prize, 2015; BBVA Foundn Frontiers of Knowledge Award, 2015; Massry Prize, USC, 2016. *Publications:* contribs to learned jls. *Recreations:* literature, travel, hiking, ski-ing, history of science. *Address:* Centre for Neural Circuits and Behaviour, University of Oxford, Tinsley Building, Mansfield Road, Oxford OX1 3SR.

**MIFFLIN, Helen; Her Honour Judge Mifflin;** a Circuit Judge, since 2008; *b* Blaina, Blaenau, Gwent, 29 April 1960; *d* of Thomas George Mifflin and Sarah Elizabeth Mifflin; *m* 1986, Leslie Adrian Blohm, *qv*; two *d*. *Educ:* Univ. of Leicester (LLB Hons 1981); Inns of Court Sch. of Law. Called to the Bar, Lincoln's Inn, 1982; in practice as barrister specialising in family law (care proceedings and ancillary relief); Recorder, 2000–08. *Recreations:* musical theatre, reading, cooking. *Address:* Swansea Civil Justice Centre, Caravella House, Quay West, Quay Street, Swansea SA1 1SP. *T:* (01792) 485800.

**MIFLIN, Dr Benjamin John,** PhD; Chairman, Crop Evaluation Ltd, 2000–09; Director, 1994–99, Lawes Trust Fellow, 1999–2012, Rothamsted Research (formerly Institute of Arable Crops Research Rothamsted); *b* 7 Jan. 1939; *s* of late Stanley Miflin and Kathleen (*née* Davies); *m* 1964, Hilary Newman; three *d*. *Educ:* Univ. of Nottingham (BSc); Univ. of Illinois (MS); QMC and Imperial Coll., London (PhD 1965). FRAgS 1988; FRSB (FIBiol 1997). Lectr in Plant Scis (Plant Biochem.), Sch. of Agric., Univ. of Newcastle upon Tyne, 1965–73; Hd, Biochem. Dept, 1973–85, and Dir of Molecular Scis, 1985–85, Rothamsted Exptl Stn, Harpenden; Hd, Internat. R & D, Ciba-Geigy Seeds, Basle, 1986–93. Vis. Prof., Univ. of Nottingham, 1981–85 and 1994–2000. Mem., Adv. Cttee on Novel Foods and Processes, 1995–98. Corresp. Mem., Amer. Soc. of Plant Physiologists, 1986. *Publications:* (ed) The Biochemistry of Plants, Vol. 5, 1980, (ed with P. J. Lea) Vol. 16, 1990; (ed) Oxford Surveys of Plant Cell and Molecular Biology, Vols 1–7, 1984–91; numerous papers in field of plant biochem. and related subjects. *Recreations:* ski-ing, gardening, photography. *Address:* St Martin's, 51 Steyne Road, Seaford, E Sussex BN25 1HU.

**MIFSUD BONNICI, Dr Carmelo,** BA, LLD; Prime Minister of Malta, 1984–87; *b* 17 July 1933; *s* of Dr Lorenzo Mifsud Bonnici, and Catherine (*née* Buttigieg). *Educ:* Govt sch. and Lyceum, Malta; Univ. of Malta (BA, LLD); University Coll. London. Lectr in Industrial and Fiscal Law, Univ. of Malta, 1969–86. Legal Consultant, General Workers' Union, 1969–83; Dep. Leader, Labour Party, responsible for Party affairs, 1980–82; Designate Leader of the Labour Movement, 1982; co-opted to Parlt, 1983, Minister of Labour and Social Services, 1983; Sen. Dep. Prime Minister, 1983–84; Leader, Labour Party, 1984–92; MP First District, 1987–96. *Recreation:* reading. *Address:* Hamrun, Malta.

**MIFSUD BONNICI, Dr Ugo;** President of Malta, 1994–99; *b* 8 Nov. 1932; *m* 1959, Gemma Bianco; two *s* one *d*. *Educ:* Lyceum, Malta; Univ. of Malta (BA 1952; LLD 1955). Elected MP, 2nd Electoral Div., 1966–94; Shadow Minister of Educn, 1971–87; President: General Council, 1976; Admin. Council, 1976; Minister of: Educn, 1987–90; Educn and the Interior, 1990–92; Educn and Human Resources, 1992–94. Mem., Venice Commn, 2001–13. Companion of Honour, Nat. Order of Merit (Malta). *Publications:* Biex il-Futur Jerga' Jibda, 1976; Il-Linja t-Tajba, 1980; Biex il-Futur Rega' Beda, 1992; Il-Manwal tal-President, 1997; Kif Sirna Republika, 1999; An Introduction to Comparative Law, 2004; An Introduction to Cultural Heritage Law, 2008; An Introduction to the Law of Education, 2014; Konvinzjoni u Esperjenza, 2015. *Recreations:* reading, writing, listening to music. *Address:* 18 Triq Erin Serracino Inglott, Cospicua, BML 1305, Malta. *Club:* Casino Maltese.

**MILAŠINOVIĆ MARTINOVIĆ, Tanja,** PhD; Head, Department for Economic Diplomacy, Ministry of Foreign Affairs, Bosnia and Herzegovina, since 2016; *b* 28 June 1962; *d* of Rade and Radosava Milašinović. *Educ:* Univ. of Zagreb (MSc 1988); Univ. of Ljubljana (PhD 1992). Asst, Fac. of Mining, Geol. and Petroleum, Univ. of Zagreb, 1986–87; res. work, 1987–91, Asst, 1989–91, Inst. of Experimental Physics, Ludwig Maximilians Univ., Munich; Asst Prof., Faculties of Agric. and of Forestry, Univ. of Belgrade, 1992–98; Asst Minister, Min. of Foreign Econ. Affairs, Rep. of Srpska Govt, 1998–2001; Minister Counsellor and Chargé d'Affaires, Mission of Bosnia and Herzegovina to EU, Min. of Foreign Affairs, 2001–05; Ambassador of Bosnia and Herzegovina to the Court of St James's, 2005–08; Hd, Dept. for Western Europe, Min. of Foreign Affairs of Bosnia and Herzegovina, 2008–11; Ambassador to Austria, 2012–15. *Publications:* articles in learned jls. *Recreation:* tennis. *Address:* Ministry of Foreign Affairs, Musala 2, Sarajevo 71000, Bosnia and Herzegovina.

**MILBANK, Prof. (Alasdair) John,** PhD, DD; Research Professor of Religion, Politics and Ethics, 2004–16, now Professor Emeritus, and Director, Centre of Theology and Philosophy, 2004–16, now President, University of Nottingham; *b* 23 Oct. 1952; *s* of John Douglas Milbank and Jean Hyslop Milbank; *m* 1978, Alison Grant Legg; one *s* one *d*. *Educ:* Queen's Coll., Oxford (MA); PhD Birmingham 1986; DD Cantab 1998. Christendom Trust Teaching Fellow, Lancaster Univ., 1983–91; University of Cambridge: Lectr in Theol., 1991–96; Reader in Philosophical Theol., 1996–98; Fellow, Peterhouse, 1993–98; Frances Myers Ball Prof. of Philosophical Theol., Univ. of Virginia, 1999–2004. *Publications:* Theology and Social Theory, 1990, 2nd edn 2006; The Religious Dimension in Vico's Thought, Part I 1991, Part II 1992; The Word Made Strange: theology, language, culture, 1996; The Mercurial Wood (poems), 1997; (ed jtly) Radical Orthodoxy: a new theology, 1998; (with C. Pickstock) Truth in Aquinas, 2001; Being Reconciled: ontology and pardon, 2002; The Suspended Middle, 2005; The Legend of Death (poems), 2008; The Monstrosity of Christ, 2009; The Future of Love: essays in political theology, 2009; Paul's New Moment, 2010; Beyond Secular Order, 2013; The Dances of Albion (poems), 2015; (with A. Pabst) The Politics of Virtue, 2017. *Recreations:* walking, poetry, photography, cinema, reading fiction, early music, archaeology. *Address:* Burgage Hill Cottage, Burgage, Southwell, Notts NG25 0EP. *T:* (01636) 819224. *E:* john.milbank@nottingham.ac.uk. *Club:* Travellers.

**MILBANK, Sir Edward (Mark Somerset),** 6th Bt *cr* 1882, of Well, co. York and of Hart, Co. Durham; owner, Barningham Estate; *b* Colchester, Essex, 9 April 1973; *er s* of Sir Anthony Frederick Milbank, 5th Bt and of Belinda Beatrice Milbank (*née* Gore); *S* father, 2016; *m* 2008, Natalie Ann Hicks-Löbbecke; two *s* one *d*. *Educ:* Aysgarth Sch.; Eton Coll.; Newcastle Univ. (BA Hons). With Quintus Gp, 1999–2005; Founder and Dir, Montenegro Property Fund, 2005–10; Trustee, Barningham Estate, 2010–; Founder and Dir, Pennine Biomass, 2013–. *Recreations:* ski-ing, most sports. *Heir: s* Harry Frederick Somerset Milbank, *b* 29 Nov. 2009. *Address:* Barningham Park, Richmond, N Yorks DL11 7DW. *T:* (01833) 621343. *E:* milbank@barninghamestate.com.

**MILBANK, John;** *see* Milbank, A. J.

**MILBERG, Dr Joachim;** Chairman, Supervisory Board, BMW AG, 2004–15 (Member, 2002–04); *b* Verl, Westfalia, 10 April 1943. *Educ:* Bielefeld State Engrg Coll.; Berlin Tech. Univ. (Dr ing 1971). Apprentice machine fitter, 1959–62; Res. Asst, Inst. Machine Tool and Prodn Technol., Berlin Tech. Univ., 1970–72; Exec. Manager, 1972–78, Hd, Automatic Turning Machines Div., 1978–81, Werkzeugmaschinenfabrik Gildemeister AG; Prof. of Machine Tools and Mgt Sci., Munich Tech. Univ., 1981–93; BMW AG: Member Board of Management: Prodn, 1993–98; Engrg and Prodn, 1998–99; Chm., Bd of Mgt, 1999–2002. Dir, Deere & Co., 2003; Vice Chm., Supervisory Bd, Bertelsmann.

**MILBORNE-SWINNERTON-PILKINGTON, Sir Thomas Henry;** *see* Pilkington.

**MILBOURN, Dr Graham Maurice;** Director, National Institute of Agricultural Botany, Cambridge, 1981–90, retired; *b* 4 Sept. 1930; *s* of late Frank Milbourn, BSc and Winifred Milbourn; *m* 1956, Louise Lawson, BSc Hons; three *s. Educ:* Reading Univ. (BSc, MSc, PhD). Served RN, 1948–50. Asst Lectr, Reading Univ., 1953–56; SO, ARC Radiobiological Lab., 1956–61; Sen. Lectr, Crop Production, Wye Coll., London Univ., 1961–77; Prof. of Crop Production, Sch. of Agric., Edinburgh Univ., 1977–81. Vis. Prof., Silsoe Coll., Cranfield Univ. (formerly Inst. of Technology), 1991–2003. President: Assoc. Applied Biologists, 1991; Assoc. Ind. Crop Consultants, 1993. *Publications:* papers on physiology of cereals (particularly maize) and vegetables for processing, uptake of radio-nucleides by crops. *Recreation:* sailing.

**MILBURN, Rt Hon. Alan;** PC 1998; Chairman, Social Mobility Commission (formerly Social Mobility and Child Poverty Commission), 2012–17; *b* 27 Jan. 1958; *m* 2007, Dr Ruth Briel; two *s. Educ:* Stokesley Comprehensive Sch.; Lancaster Univ. (BA). Co-ordinator, Trade Union Studies Information Unit, Newcastle, 1984–90; Sen. Business Development Officer, N Tyneside MBC, 1990–92. MP (Lab) Darlington, 1992–2010. Opposition front bench spokesman on health, 1995–96, on Treasury and econ. affairs, 1996–97; Minister of State, DoH, 1997–98; Chief Sec. to HM Treasury, 1998–99; Sec. of State for Health, 1999–2003; Chancellor, Duchy of Lancaster, 2004–05. Mem., Public Accounts Cttee, 1994–95; Chair, PLP Treasury Cttee, 1992–95. Govt's Ind. Reviewer on Social Mobility, 2010–12, and on Child Poverty, 2011–12. Chancellor, Lancaster Univ., 2015–.

**MILBURN, Sir Anthony (Rupert),** 5th Bt *cr* 1905; landowner; *b* 17 April 1947; *s* of Major Rupert Leonard Eversley Milburn (*yr s* of 3rd Bt) (*d* 1974) and of Anne Mary, *d* of late Major Austin Scott Murray, MC; *S* uncle, 1985; *m* 1977, Olivia Shirley, *y d* of Captain Thomas Noel Catlow, CBE, DL, RN; two *s* one *d. Educ:* Hawtreys, Savernake Forest; Eton College; Cirencester Agricultural Coll. MRICS. *Recreation:* sporting and rural pursuits. *Heir: s* Patrick Thomas Milburn [*b* 4 Dec. 1980; *m* 2009, Marina Louise, *o d* of Sir David Ralli, Bt, *qv*; one *s*]. *Address:* Bog House, Matfen, Newcastle upon Tyne NE20 0RF. *Club:* New (Edinburgh).

**MILDMAY, Sir Walter John Hugh St J.;** *see* St John-Mildmay.

**MILDON, David Wallis;** QC 2000; *b* 19 Sept. 1955; *s* of His Honour Arthur Leonard Mildon; *m* 1st, 1983, Lesley Mary Richardson (*d* 2013); one *s* one *d*; 2nd, 2016, Sue Macdiarmid. *Educ:* Emmanuel Coll., Cambridge (LLB; MA). Called to the Bar, Middle Temple, 1980, Bencher, 2019; in practice at the Bar, 1980–. *Recreations:* music, sailing. *Address:* Essex Court Chambers, 24 Lincoln's Inn Fields, WC2A 3EG. *T:* (020) 7813 8000.

**MILDON, Russell;** occasional speaker and consultant; Director, Common Market Organisations, European Commission, 2005–09; *b* 22 Aug. 1949; *s* of R. F. Mildon and J. Mildon (*née* Kröpfl); *m* 1973, Micheline Williams; two *s* one *d. Educ:* Royal Holloway Coll., London Univ. (Open Schol.; BSc Hons); Brunel Univ. (MTech). HSO, UK Civil Service, 1970–74; with Commission of the European Communities, 1974–2009: Statistics, studies and reports (Agricl), 1974–81; Gen. Affairs Gp, 1981–83; Private Sec. to Dep. Dir Gen., Agricl Markets, 1983–86; Advr to Vice-Pres., 1986–89; Head: Unit for Analysis of Situation of Agricl Holdings, 1989; Unit for Oilseeds and Protein Crops, 1989–93; Director: Internat. affairs relating to agric., 1993–96; orgn of markets in specialised crops, 1996–2001; Audit of Agricl Expenditure, Personnel and Admin, 2001–02; orgn of markets in crops, 2002–05. Occasional speaker and consultant. President's Medal (Austria), 1996; Chevalier, Ordre nationale du Mérite (France). *Recreations:* wine and spirits, chess, travel.

**MILEHAM, Peter,** OBE 2016; DL; National President, British Chambers of Commerce, 2006–08 (Director, 2002–08); *b* 31 March 1943; *s* of William John Mileham and Mary Margaret, (Mayda), Mileham (*née* Kerrigan); *m* 1973, Shelagh Frances Preston (*d* 2015); two *d. Educ:* Scarborough Tech. Coll. (HND Bldg 1965); Hull and York Tech. Colls. MIOB. Dir, Liquid Plastics Ltd, Preston, 1973–2008. Chm., Preston and NW, Yorkshire Bank, 2005–12. Mem., Parly All Party Corporate Governance Gp, 2007–; Chm., Cons. Northern Transport Commn, 2009–. Director: NW Lancs Chamber of Commerce, 1992–2011; Creative Lancashire, 2013–. Vice Pres., Eurochambres Brussels, 2006–09. Dir, UK India Business Council, 2006–09. Chm., British Venezuelan Chamber of Commerce, 2004–10. Mem. Council: Duchy of Lancaster Benevolent Fund, 2006–12; St John Ambulance, 2008–12. Dir, Bd of Trustees, Blackburn Cathedral, 2012–. Chm., Rosemere Cancer Care Foundn, Lancs and S Cumbria, 2018– (Ambassador, 1980–2018); Citizens in Policing Ambassador, Lancs Constabulary, 2013–. Advr, Lionheart Trust, Glasgow, 2009–. Hon. Fellow, Univ. of Central Lancashire, 2009–. DL 2004, High Sheriff 2011–12, Lancs. Prestonian of the Year, Preston Guild, 2012. *Publications:* various papers and articles in leading construction industry press. *Recreations:* gardening, arts, classical music. *Address:* Buckleyhow, 46 Lightfoot Lane, Fulwood, Preston PR2 3LR. *T:* (01772) 862220. *E:* mr.peter.mileham@gmail.com.

**MILES, Barry;** author; *b* Cheltenham, Glos, 21 Feb. 1943; *s* of Albert Miles and May Miles; *m* 1994, Rosemary Bailey; one *s. Educ:* Cirencester Grammar Sch.; Gloucestershire Coll. of Art (NDD 1963); Univ. of London (ATD 1964). Manager, Better Books, 1965; co-owner and Manager, Indica Books and Gall., 1965–70; co-Founder, publisher, editor, Mem. Editl Bd, International Times, 1966–74; audio archivist to Allen Ginsberg, 1970–72; archivist to William Burroughs, 1972; Editor, Time Out, 1978–79. Vis. Fellow, Liverpool John Moores Univ., 2007–. *Publications:* A Catalogue of the William S. Burroughs Archive, 1973; (with Joe Maynard) William S. Burroughs: a bibliography 1953–73, 1978; Ginsberg: a biography, 1989, 2nd edn 2002; William Burroughs: el hombre invisible, 1993; Paul McCartney: many years from now, 1997; (with Charles Perry) I Want to Take You Higher: the psychedelic era 1965–69, 1998; The Beatles: a diary, 1998; Jack Kerouac, King of the Beats: a portrait, 1998; The Beat Hotel: Ginsberg, Burroughs, and Corso in Paris, 1957–1963, 2000; In the Sixties, 2002; Hippie, 2003; Frank Zappa, 2004; Bukowski, 2005; Pink Floyd: the early years, 2006; Peace: 50 years of protest 1958–2008, 2008; The British Invasion, 2009; London Calling: a countercultural history of London since 1945, 2009; In the Seventies, 2011; William S. Burroughs: a life, 2014; The Zapple Diaries, 2019. *Recreations:* visiting art openings, drinking with friends in Soho. *Address:* c/o Antony Harwood Literary Agency, 103 Walton Street, Oxford OX2 6EB. *T:* (01865) 559615. *E:* james@antonyharwood.com. *W:* barrymiles.co.uk. *Club:* Groucho.

**MILES, Brian,** CBE 1994; RD 1970; FNI; RNR (retired); Director, Royal National Lifeboat Institution, 1988–98; *b* 23 Feb. 1937; *s* of Terence Clifford Miles and Muriel Irene Terry; *m* 1964, Elizabeth Anne Scott; one *s* two *d. Educ:* Reed's School, Cobham; HMS Conway; Merchant Navy Cadet School. Master Mariner (Foreign Going) Cert. P&O Orient Lines: Cadet, 1954–57; Deck Officer, 1958–64; RNLI: Divl Inspector, 1964–73; Asst to Director, 1974–79; Ops Staff Officer, 1979–81; Dep. Dir, 1982–87. Chairman: Friends of Dolphin Trust, 1989–2017; Poole Arts Trust, 1996–2003; Member Council: Royal Nat. Mission to Deep Sea Fishermen, 1999–2012 (Dep. Chm., 2001–05, Chm., 2005–09); Dorset Br., BRCS, 2000–03. FNI 1989; CCMI (CIMgt 1994). Freeman, City of London, 1993; Mem., Master Mariners' Co., 1994–. Younger Brother, Trinity House, 1994. Comdr, Order of Lion (Finland), 1997. *Address:* 8 Longfield Drive, West Parley, Ferndown, Dorset BH22 8TY. *T:* (01202) 571739.

**MILES, Caroline Valerie;** *see* Pidgeon, C. V.

**MILES, Prof. Christopher John;** film director and producer; *b* 19 April 1939; *s* of late John Miles, MC and Clarice Baskerville (*née* Remnant); *m* 1967, Susan Helen Howard Armstrong; one *d. Educ:* Winchester Coll.; Institut des Hautes Etudes Cinématographiques, Paris. Dir, Milesian Film Productions, 1962–; *films include:* Six Sided Triangle, 1963; The Virgin and the Gypsy, 1970 (Best Film Award, US and UK Critics, 1970); Time for Loving, 1972; The Maids, 1974; That Lucky Touch, 1976; Alternative Three, 1977; Priest of Love: life of D. H. Lawrence, 1981; Lord Elgin and some stones of no value, 1985; Cyclone Warning Class 4, 1994; The Clandestine Marriage, 1999; *theatre:* Skin of our Teeth, Chicago, 1973; The Two Symposiums (Il Simposio antico e moderno), Italy, 2013; *television:* Zinotchka, 1973; Neck, 1978; Love in the Ancient World, 1996; Fire from Olympia, 2004. Prof. of Film and Television, RCA, 1989–93. Lecture tours: India, for British Council, 1985; USA, 1986. FRCA 1989. Patron, Marlowe Soc., 1995–. *Publications:* Alternative Three, 1977 (trans. 5 langs); (with John Julius Norwich) Love in the Ancient World, 1996; (contrib.) H of C Report on Film, 1982; contrib. Image et Son, D. H. Lawrence Soc. Jl. *Recreations:* film-making, long walks and sketching in Arcadia. *Address:* 4 Lansdowne Grove, Devizes, Wilts SN10 1NZ. *Club:* Garrick.

**MILES, David,** FSA; Chief Archaeological Advisor, English Heritage, 2005–08 (Chief Archaeologist, 1999–2005); *b* 6 Dec. 1947; *s* of Tom and Norah Miles; *m* 1969, Gwyn Morgan (*see* Gwyn Miles); one *s* one *d. Educ:* St Gregory's Grammar Sch., Huddersfield; King Edward VI Grammar Sch., Nuneaton; Birmingham Univ. (BA Hons). Dir of Excavations, M5 Excavation Cttee, 1970–71; Res. Asst, Bristol Univ., 1971–72; Director of Excavations: Abingdon Excavation Cttee, 1972–73; Upper Thames Excavation Cttee, 1973–74; Dep. Dir, 1974–87, Dir, 1987–99, Oxford Archaeological Unit. FSA 1984; FSAScot 2000. MCIfA (MIFA 1988). *Publications:* (with D. Benson) The Upper Thames Valley, 1974; An Introduction to Archaeology, 1977; (ed) The Romano-British Countryside, 1982; (ed with B. Cunliffe) Aspects of the Iron Age in Central Southern Britain, 1984; (ed with K. Branigan) The Economies of Romano-British Villas, 1987; (jtly) Two Oxfordshire Anglo-Saxon Cemeteries: Berinsfield and Didcot, 1995; (jtly) The Anglo-Saxon Cemetery at Butler's Field, Lechlade, Gloucestershire, 1998; (jtly) Uffington White Horse and its Landscape, 2003; The Tribes of Britain, 2005; (jtly) Iron Age and Roman Settlement in the Thames Valley, 2007; The Tale of the Axe: how the Neolithic revolution transformed Britain, 2016; contrib. to learned jls, newspapers and magazines. *Recreations:* reading, gardening, arts. *Address:* Whornes Place, Rochester Road, Cuxton, Rochester, Kent ME2 1AE; Pailler de la Devezette, 30460 Lasalle, France. *E:* david.miles66@btinternet.com.

**MILES, Prof. David Kenneth,** CBE 2016; PhD; Professor of Financial Economics, Imperial College London, since 2015; *b* 6 Oct. 1959; *s* of Kenneth Douglas Miles and Rebecca Owen; *m* 1997, Faye Dimdore; one *s* two *d. Educ:* Bishop Gore Sch., Swansea; University Coll., Oxford (BA PPE 1981); Nuffield Coll., Oxford (MPhil Econs 1983); Birkbeck Coll., London (PhD Econs 1993). Economist, Bank of England, 1983–89; Lectr, then Reader, Birkbeck Coll., London, 1989–93; Econ. Advr, Bank of England, 1993–94; Chief UK Economist, Merrill Lynch, 1994–96; Prof. of Financial Econs, 1996–2004, Vis. Prof., 2004–15, Imperial Coll. London; Man. Dir in Econ. Res. and Chief UK Economist, Morgan Stanley, 2004–09. Mem., MPC, Bank of England, 2009–15. Non-exec. Dir, FSA, 2004–09; Specialist Advr, Treasury Select Cttee, 1999–. Fellow, Centre for Econ. Policy Res., 1992–; Member, Council: NIESR, 2004–; REconS, 2010–. Gov., Pensions Inst., 2002–; Trustee, IFS, 2010–. Ed., Fiscal Studies, 1997–2004. *Publications:* Housing, Financial Markets and the Wider Economy, 1994; (with A. Scott) Macroeconomics: understanding the wealth of nations, 2001, 2nd edn 2004; (ed jtly) The Economics of Public Spending, 2003; The Miles Review of the UK Mortgage Market, 2004; (with A. Scott and F. Breedon) Macroeconomics: understanding the global economy, 2012; articles in econs jls and chapters in books. *Recreations:* cinema, squash, Rugby, children. *Address:* Imperial College Business School, Imperial College London, South Kensington Campus, SW7 2AZ.

**MILES, Gwyn;** Director, Somerset House Trust, 2006–14; *b* 17 Nov. 1947; *d* of Sir Morien Morgan, CB, FRS and of Lady Morgan (*née* Axford); *m* 1969, David Miles, *qv*; one *s* one *d. Educ:* Bristol Univ. (BSc Physiol.); Bath Univ. (DipEd); Museums Assoc. (Cert. in Conservation). Research Assistant: McGill Univ., Montreal, 1969; Bristol Univ., 1969–70; Science Teacher, St Mary Redcliffe and Temple Sch., Bristol, 1971; Department of Antiquities, Ashmolean Museum, Oxford: Conservator, 1972–82; Head of Conservation, 1982–85; Victoria and Albert Museum: Dep. Keeper of Conservation, 1985–89; Surveyor of Collections, 1989–95; Dir of Major Projects, 1995–2002; Dir, Projects and Estate, 2002–05. Trustee: The Making, 2004–12; Sainsbury Centre for the Visual Arts, 2011–16. Hon. FRIBA 2011. *Publications:* Traditional Knitting in the British Isles, 1979; articles on conservation, collections management and gardening. *Recreations:* gardening, birdwatching, arts. *Address:* Whornes Place, 97 Rochester Road, Cuxton, Rochester, Kent ME2 1AE. *T:* (01634) 939639; Le Pailler de la Devezette, 30460 Lasalle, France.

**MILES, (Henry) Michael (Pearson),** OBE 1989; Chairman: Schroders, 2003–12; Johnson Matthey PLC, 1998–2006 (Director, 1990–2006); London Mining plc, 2013–14; *b* 19 April 1936; *s* of Brig. H. G. P. Miles and Margaret Miles; *m* 1967, Carol Jane Berg; two *s* one *d. Educ:* Wellington Coll. National Service, Duke of Wellington's Regt, 1955–57. Joined John Swire & Sons, 1958; Dir, John Swire & Sons (HK) Ltd, 1970–99 (Chm., 1984–88); Managing Director: John Swire & Sons (Japan) Ltd, 1973–76; Cathay Pacific Airways Ltd, 1978–84 (Chm., 1984–88); Chm., Swire Pacific, 1984–88; Exec. Dir, 1988–99, Advr to Board, 1999–2009, John Swire & Sons Ltd. Director: Baring PLC, 1989–95 (Jt Dep. Chm., 1994–95); Portals Holdings, 1990–95; BP, 1994–2006; ING Baring Hldgs Co., 1995–2002; BICC, 1996–2002. Chm., Hong Kong Tourist Assoc., 1984–88. Vice Pres., China Britain Business Gp, 1995–2000. Gov., Wellington Coll., 1988–2005. *Recreations:* golf, tennis. *Address:* 33 St Leonard's Terrace, SW3 4QQ. *Clubs:* White's; Royal and Ancient Golf; Berkshire Golf; Sunningdale Golf.

**MILES, Jenefer Mary;** *see* Blackwell, J. M.

**MILES, Prof. John Richard**; Professor of Fashion and Textiles, Bath Spa University (formerly Bath Spa University College), 2002–13, now Emeritus; *b* 22 June 1944; *s* of Thomas William Miles and Hilda Mary Miles (*née* Davis); *m* 1st, 1963, Judith Bud (marr. diss.); 2nd, 2016, Philip Clark-Coates. *Educ*: Croydon Coll. of Art; Royal Coll. of Art (MDes). Set up design studio, Miles Calver and Pound (now Calver and Pound), 1973–78 (Director); Founder Dir, Peppermint Prints, 1978–82; founded John Miles Partnership, 1996. Head, Textiles and Fashion, Brighton Polytechnic, 1979–85; Design Dir, Courtaulds, 1985–87; Gen. Manager, Next, 1987–89; Prof. of Fashion and Textiles, RCA, 1989–97; Dir of Product Mkting, DMC, France, 1997–2000; Prof. of Design, Southampton Univ., 2001–02. Visiting Professor: Huddersfield Univ., 2010–; Univ. of Derby, 2014–. External examr to various univs, incl. Chief Ext. Examr, Staffs Univ., 2013–, and Wolverhampton Univ., 2015–. Advr, Goldsmiths, Univ. of London, 2013–14. Consultant, Studio Claire and Lyn; Dir, Miles Whiston and Wright, 1989–96. Chm., Textile and Fashion Panel, CNAA, 1983–96; Mem., Industrial Lead Body, 1991–95. Governor, Winchester Sch. of Art, 1989–94. Trustee, Royal Sch. of Needlework, 2016–. Hon. Dr of Design, Southampton, 1998. *Recreations*: gardening, films, cooking, reading, collecting. *Address*: The Old School House, 54 Main Street, South Rauceby, Sleaford, Lincs NG34 8QQ.

**MILES, John Seeley**, FCSD, FSTD; typographer and graphic designer; *b* 11 Feb. 1931; *s* of Thomas William Miles and Winifred (*née* Seeley); *m* 1955, Louise Wilson; one *s* two *d*. *Educ*: Beckenham and Penge Grammar Sch.; Beckenham School of Art. FCSD (FSIAD 1973); FSTD 1974 (Hon. FSTD 2016). UN travelling schol. to Netherlands to practise typography and punch cutting under Jan van Krimpen and S. L. Hartz, 1954–55; Assistant to Hans Schmoller at Penguin Books, 1955–58; joined Colin Banks to form design partnership, Banks and Miles, 1958, Partner, 1958–96; Dir, Parsimony Press, 1999–2003. Consultant to: Zoological Soc., Regent's Park and Whipsnade, 1958–82; Expanded Metal Co., 1960–83; Consumers' Assoc., 1964–93; British Council, 1968–83; The Post Office, 1972–83; E Midlands Arts Assoc., 1974–79; Curwen Press, 1970–72; Basilisk Press, 1976–79; Enscheded en Zn, Netherlands, 1980–94; British Telecom, 1980–89; BAA, 1983–87; typographic advisor, HMSO, 1985–96; design advisor: Agricl Inf. Workshop, Udaipur, India, 1973; Monotype Corp., 1985–92; hon. design advisor: UEA, 1990–97; UNHCR, Geneva, 1994–99; Internat. Assoc. Univs, Paris, 2000–03; Aston-Mansfield Charities, 2001–03; Memorial Arts Charity, 2005–14; Southwell Minster, 2008–14. Designed banknote series Netherlands Antilles, 1987. Member: PO Design Adv. Cttee, 1972–76; Icograda Internat. Archive Cttee, 1993–2003. American Heritage Lectr, New York, 1960; held seminar, Graphic Inst., Stockholm, 1977 and 1986. Chairman: Wynkyn de Worde Soc., 1973–74; Arbitration Cttee, Assoc. Typographique Internationale, 1984–2002; Mem., Soc. Roy. des Bibliophiles et Iconophiles de Belgique, 1991–94. Governor, Central School of Arts and Crafts, 1978–85; External examiner: London Coll. of Printing, 1984–88; Technische Hoogschool Delft, 1986–87; Reading Univ., 1990–93; De Montfort Univ., 1994–99; Plymouth Univ., 2004–07. Mem. CGLI, 1986. Exhibitions: London, 1971, 1978; Amsterdam and Brussels, 1977; Hamburg, 1991. FRSA 1988. (With Colin Banks) Green Product Award, 1989; BBC Envmtl Award, 1990. *Publications*: The Puffin Noah's Ark, 1958; Design for Desktop Publishing, 1987; articles and reviews in professional jls. *Recreations*: gardening, painting, reading aloud. *Address*: Pit Cottage, Tunstall Common, Woodbridge, Suffolk IP12 2JR. *T*: (01728) 688889. *Club*: Double Crown.

**MILES, Prof. Mervyn John**, PhD; FRS 2011; CPhys, FInstP; Professor of Physics, since 1999, and Director, Centre for Nanoscience and Quantum Information, 2011–14, University of Bristol; *b* Worcester, 24 Nov. 1948; *s* of Edward John Miles and Olive Booth Miles (*née* Hockett); *m* 1973, Elizabeth Ann Callahan; two *s*. *Educ*: Worcester Royal Grammar Sch.; Univ. of Birmingham (BSc Hons; MSc Physics of Solids; PhD 1974). CPhys 1980; FInstP 2003. Alexander von Humboldt Fellow, Saarbrücken Univ., 1975–77; Res. Associate, Case Western Reserve Univ., 1977–78; Res. Asst, Physics Dept, Univ. of Bristol, 1978–81; SSO, 1981–86, PSO, 1986–89, BBSRC Inst. of Food Res., Norwich; Lectr, then Reader, Bristol Univ., 1989–99. Chief Scientific Advr, IOP Publishing, 2012–. *Publications*: contribs to scientific jls and chapters in books. *Recreations*: music, listening and playing (classical, jazz, rock, avant garde), half-marathon running, architectural studies. *Address*: H. H. Wills Physics Laboratory, University of Bristol, Tyndall Avenue, Bristol BS8 1TL. *T*: (0117) 928 8707, *Fax*: (0117) 925 5624. *E*: m.j.miles@bristol.ac.uk.

**MILES, Michael**; *see* Miles, H. M. P.

**MILES, Oliver**; *see* Miles, R. O.

**MILES, Sir Philip John**, 7th Bt *cr* 1859, of Leigh Court, Somersetshire; *b* 10 Aug. 1953; *o s* of Sir William Napier Maurice Miles, 6th Bt and Pamela (*née* Dillon); *S* father, 2010, but his name does not appear on the Official Roll of the Baronetage. *Educ*: Northease Manor, Lewes. High Sheriff, Wilts, 1999. *Heir*: none.

**MILES, (Richard) Oliver**, CMG 1984; HM Diplomatic Service, retired; Senior Consultant, Al Shafie Miles Ltd, since 2011; Founder Editor, Arab Digest newsletter, since 2015; *b* 6 March 1936; *s* of George Miles and Olive (*née* Clapham); *m* 1968, Julia, *d* of late Prof. J. S. Weiner; three *s* one *d*. *Educ*: Ampleforth Coll.; Merton Coll., Oxford (Oriental Studies). Entered Diplomatic Service, 1960; served in Abu Dhabi, Amman, Aden, Mukalla, Nicosia, Jedda; Counsellor, Athens, 1977–80; Head of Near East and N Africa Dept, FCO, 1980–83; Ambassador to: Libya, 1984; Luxembourg, 1985–88; Under-Sec. on loan to NI Office, Belfast, 1988–90; Asst Under Sec. of State (Economic), FCO, 1990–91; Dir Gen. of Jt Directorate, Overseas Trade Services, FCO/DTI, 1991–93; Ambassador to Greece, 1993–96. Dir and Sen. Consultant, 1997–2012, Chm., 2000–09, MEC Internat. Ltd. Non-exec. Dir, Vickers Defence Systems, 1990–93. Dep. Chm., Libyan British Business Council, 2004–. Chm., Host (Hosting for Overseas Students), 1998–2004; Pres., Soc. for Libyan Studies, 1998–2005. Dist. Vis. Prof., Amer. Univ., Cairo, 2005. *Recreations*: bird-watching, reading poetry, playing the flute. *Club*: Travellers.

**MILES, Robert John**; QC 2002; Attorney General, Duchy of Lancaster, since 2012; *b* 29 Nov. 1962; *s* of David and Marion Miles; *m* 1999, Lisabel Mary Macdonald. *Educ*: Christ Church, Oxford (MA, BCL). Called to the Bar, Lincoln's Inn, 1987, Bencher, 2007; in practice, specialising in company and commercial law. *Address*: 4 Stone Buildings, Lincoln's Inn, WC2A 3XT. *T*: (020) 7242 5524. *Club*: Garrick.

**MILES, Roger Steele**, PhD, DSc; Head, Department of Public Services, The Natural History Museum (formerly British Museum (Natural History)), 1975–94; *b* 31 Aug. 1937; *s* of John Edward Miles and Dorothy Mildred (*née* Steele); *m* 1960, Ann Blake; one *s* one *d*. *Educ*: Malet Lambert High Sch., Hull; King's Coll., Univ. of Durham (BSc, PhD, DSc). Sen. Res. Award, DSIR, 1962–64; Sen. Res. Fellow, Royal Scottish Museum, 1964–66, Sen. Scientific Officer, 1966–68; Sen. Sci. Officer, BM (Nat. Hist.), 1968–71, Principal Sci. Officer, 1971–74. Hon. Fellow, Columbia Pacific Univ., 1983. *Publications*: Palaeozoic Fishes, 2nd edn, 1971 (1st edn, J. A. Moy-Thomas, 1939); (ed, with P. H. Greenwood and C. Patterson) Interrelationships of Fishes, 1973; (ed, with S. M. Andrews and A. D. Walker) Problems in Vertebrate Evolution, 1977; (with others) The Design of Educational Exhibits, 1982, 2nd edn 1988; (ed with L. Zavala) Towards the Museum of the Future, 1994 (trans. Spanish and revised, 1995); papers and monographs on anatomy and palaeontology of fishes, articles on museums, in jls. *Recreations*: music, twentieth century art and architecture. *Address*: 3 Eagle Lane, Snaresbrook, E11 1PF. *T*: (020) 8989 5684.

**MILES, Wendy Ann**; *see* Henry, W. A.

**MILES, Wendy Jane**; QC 2015; Partner, Debevoise & Plimpton, since 2017; *b* Te Aroha, NZ, 21 Oct. 1970; *d* of William John Miles and Barbara Mary Miles; *m* 2000, Kym Vincent McConnell; two *s*. *Educ*: Univ. of Canterbury, NZ (BA LLB 1994; LLM Hons 1998). Admitted solicitor, NZ and England, 1994; Associate, Russell McVeagh, Wellington, 1996–98; Associate, 1999–2004, Partner, 2005–14, Wilmer Hale; Partner, Boies, Schiller and Flexner LLP, 2014–17. Vice-Pres., ICC Court of Internat. Arbitration, 2015–. Chair, Bd of Trustees, CIArb, 2014–; Vice-Chm., Arbitration Cttee, IBA, 2015– (Sec., 2014–15). *Recreations*: travel, reading, music, cycling. *Address*: c/o Debevoise & Plimpton, 65 Gresham Street, EC2V 7NQ.

**MILES, William**; Chief Executive, West Yorkshire County Council, and Clerk to the Lieutenancy, West Yorkshire, 1984–86; *b* 26 Sept. 1933; *s* of William and Gladys Miles; *m* 1961, Jillian Anne Wilson; three *s*. *Educ*: Wyggeston School, Leicester; Trinity Hall, Cambridge (MA, LLM). Solicitor. Asst Solicitor, Leicester, Doncaster and Exeter County Boroughs, 1960–66; Asst Town Clerk, Leicester Co. Borough, 1966–69; Dep. Town Clerk, Blackpool Co. Borough, 1969–73; City Legal Adviser, Newcastle upon Tyne, 1973–74; Chief Exec., Gateshead Borough Council, 1974–84. Mem., Local Govt Residuary Body (England), 1995–99. *Recreations*: bridge, hill walking, sport. *Address*: 3 St Stephen's Manor, Cheltenham GL51 3GF. *T*: (01242) 575840.

**MILFORD**, 4th Baron *cr* 1939, of Llanstephan, co. Radnor; **Guy Wogan Philipps**; QC 2002; Bt 1919; *b* 25 July 1961; *e s* of 3rd Baron Milford and Hon. Mary Makins (now Viscountess Norwich), *e d* of 1st Baron Sherfield, GCB, GCMG, FRS; *S* father, 1999; *m* 1996, Alice Sherwood; two *s*. *Educ*: Eton Coll.; Magdalen Coll., Oxford (MA); City Univ. (DipLaw); Regent's Park Coll., Oxford (MSt). Called to the Bar, Inner Temple, 1986. *Publications*: Bad Behaviour, 1988. *Heir*: *s* Hon. Archie Sherwood Philipps, *b* 12 March 1997. *Address*: Llanstephan House, Llanstephan, Brecon, Powys LD3 0YR. *T*: (01982) 560693. *E*: gmilford@outlook.com.

**MILFORD, His Honour John Tillman**; QC 1989; a Circuit Judge, 2002–16; *b* 4 Feb. 1946; *s* of late Dr Roy Douglas Milford, Strathtay, Perthshire, and Jessie Milford (*née* Rhind), JP; *m* 1975, Mary Alice, *d* of late Dr E. A. Spriggs of Wylam, Northumberland; three *d*. *Educ*: The Cathedral School, Salisbury; Hurstpierpoint; Exeter Univ. (LLB). Called to the Bar, Inner Temple, 1969, Bencher, 1998; in practice on NE Circuit, 1970–2002. Head, Trinity Chambers, Newcastle upon Tyne, 1985–99; a Recorder, 1985–2002; a Dep. High Court Judge, 1994–2002; Liaison Judge to Northumberland and N Tyneside Justices, 2003–11. Chm., Northumbria Area Judicial Forum, 2005–11. County Chairman: British Field Sports Soc. for South Northumberland, 1996–98; Countryside Alliance for South Northumberland, 1998–99; Regl Chm., Countryside Alliance for NE England, 1999–2002. Chairman: River Tyne Fishing Festival, 1997; Bywell Country Fair, 1999, 2000; Vice-Chm., Newcastle and Dist Beagles, 1999–2005. Trustee, Get Hooked on Fishing, 2003–13 (Chm., 2005–13). *Recreations*: fishing, shooting, gardening, ballet. *Club*: Northern Counties (Newcastle upon Tyne) (Chm., 2003–07).

**MILFORD HAVEN**, 4th Marquess of, *cr* 1917; **George Ivar Louis Mountbatten**; Earl of Medina, 1917; Viscount Alderney, 1917; *b* 6 June 1961; *s* of 3rd Marquess of Milford Haven, OBE, DSC, and of Janet Mercedes, *d* of late Major Francis Bryce, OBE; *S* father, 1970; *m* 1989, Sarah Georgina (marr. diss. 1996), *d* of late George Alfred Walker; one *s* one *d*; *m* 1997, Clare Wentworth-Stanley. *Heir*: *s* Earl of Medina, *qv*.

**MILIBAND, Rt Hon. David (Wright)**; PC 2005; President and Chief Executive, International Rescue Committee, since 2013; *b* 15 July 1965; *s* of late Ralph Miliband and of Marion Miliband (*née* Kozak); *m* 1998, Louise Shackelton; two adopted *s*. *Educ*: Corpus Christi Coll., Oxford (BA 1st Cl. Hons PPE); Massachusetts Inst. of Technol. (Kennedy Schol.; MSc Political Sci.). Res. Fellow, Inst. of Public Policy Res., 1989–94; Head of Policy, Office of Leader of the Opposition, 1994–97; Dir of Policy, 1997, Head, 1998–2001, Prime Minister's Policy Unit. MP (Lab) South Shields, 2001–April 2013. Minister of State: DfES, 2002–04; Cabinet Office, 2004–05; Minister of State (Minister for Communities and Local Govt), ODPM, 2005–06; Sec. of State for Envmt, Food and Rural Affairs, 2006–07, for Foreign and Commonwealth Affairs, 2007–10. Sec., Commn on Social Justice, 1992–94. Vice Chm., Sunderland AFC, 2011–13. *Publications*: (ed) Re-inventing the Left, 1994; (ed jtly) Paying for Inequality: the economic cost of social injustice, 1994; Rescue: refugees and the crisis of our time, 2017. *Recreation*: raising two sons. *Address*: International Rescue Committee, 122 East 42nd Street, New York, NY 10168, USA. *Clubs*: Whitelaws Social, Cleadon Social.
*See also* Rt Hon. E. Miliband.

**MILIBAND, Rt Hon. Edward**; PC 2007; MP (Lab) Doncaster North, since 2005; *b* 24 Dec. 1969; *s* of late Ralph Miliband and of Marion Miliband (*née* Kozak); *m* 2011, Justine Thornton; two *s*. *Educ*: Corpus Christi Coll., Oxford (BA); London Sch. of Economics (MSc (Econ)). TV journalist; speechwriter and researcher for Harriet Harman, MP, 1993, for Rt Hon. Gordon Brown, MP, 1994–97; Special Advr to Chancellor of the Exchequer, 1997–2002; Lectr in Govt, Harvard Univ., 2002–04; Chm., Council of Econ. Advrs, HM Treasury, 2004–05. Parly Sec., Cabinet Office, 2006–07; Chancellor of the Duchy of Lancaster and Minister for the Cabinet Office, 2007–08; Sec. of State for Energy and Climate Change, 2008–10; Shadow Sec. of State for Energy and Climate Change, 2010; Leader of the Labour Party and Leader of the Opposition, 2010–15. *Address*: House of Commons, SW1A 0AA.
*See also* Rt Hon. D. W. Miliband.

**MILINGO, Emmanuel**; Former Archbishop of Lusaka (Archbishop, (RC), 1969–83); *b* 13 June 1930; *s* of Yakobe Milingo Chilumbu and Tomaide Lumbiwe Miti; *m* 2001, Maria Sung. *Educ*: Kachebere Seminary, Malawi; Pastoral Inst., Rome; University Coll., Dublin. Ordained priest, 1958; Curate: Minga Parish, Chipata Dio., 1958–60; St Mary's Parish, 1960–61; Chipata Cathedral, 1963–64; Parish Priest, Chipata Cathedral, 1964–65; Sec. for Communications at Catholic Secretariat, Lusaka, 1966–69. Founder, The Daughters of the Redeemer, Congregation for young ladies, 1971. Dep. Hd, Pontifical Council for Pastoral Care of Migrants and Itinerant Peoples, 1983–99. Laicized 2009. *Publications*: Amake-Joni, 1972; To Die to Give Life, 1975; Summer Lectures for the Daughters of the Redeemer, 1976; The Way to Daughterhood; My God is a Living God, 1981; Lord Jesus, My Lord and Saviour, 1982; Demarcations, 1982; The Flower Garden of Jesus the Redeemer; My Prayers Are Not Heard; Precautions in the Ministry of Deliverance. *Recreation*: music.

**MILL, Douglas Russell**; Principal, Douglas Mill Consulting, since 2008; Director, Professional Legal Practice, University of Glasgow, 2009–13; *b* 3 Jan. 1957; *s* of Alan M. L. Mill and Anna B. Mill (*née* Russell); *m* 1982, Christine Rankin (marr. diss. 2017); two *s* one *d*. *Educ*: Paisley Grammar Sch.; Glasgow Univ. (LLB, BA, MBA). Apprentice, Wright & Crawford, 1978–80; Partner: Cameron Pinkerton Haggarty, 1980–85; MacFarlane Young

**MILL, Ian Alexander;** QC 1999; b 9 April 1958; s of Ronald MacLauchlan Mill and Thelma Anita Mill; m 1987, Mary Emma Clayden; three s. Educ: Epsom Coll.; Trinity Hall, Cambridge (MA Classics and Law). Called to the Bar, Middle Temple, 1981; in practice at the Bar, 1982–. Recreations: cricket, golf, film, theatre, good food and wine. Address: Blackstone House, Temple, EC4Y 9BW. T: (020) 7583 1770. Club: MCC.

**MILLAIS, Sir Geoffroy Richard Everett,** 6th Bt cr 1885, of Palace Gate, Kensington and Saint Ouen, Jersey; b 27 Dec. 1941; s of Sir Ralph Regnault Millais, 5th Bt and his 1st wife, Felicity Caroline Mary Ward (née Warner) (d 1994), d of Brig.-Gen. W. W. Warner, CMG; S father, 1992. Heir: cousin John Frederic Millais [b 17 Sept. 1949; m 1991, Susan Clayton; two d].

**MILLAR,** family name of **Baron Inchyra**.

**MILLAR, Alison;** see Millar, H. R. A.

**MILLAR, Amanda;** Partner, McCash & Hunter LLP, since 2015; Vice President, 2019–May 2020, President, from June 2020, Law Society of Scotland; b Irvine, 24 Aug. 1971; d of Andrew Coulter McCrindle and Dorothy Kerr and step d of Alistair Millar; civil partnership 2012, m 2016, Joyce Anne Buchanan. Educ: Marr Coll.; Univ. of Strathclyde (LLB Hons; DipLP). Lectr, Glasgow Caledonian Univ., 1994–96; trainee solicitor, 1997–99; admitted solicitor, 1999; Solicitor: Johnston & Herron, 1999–2000; Blackadders, 2000–02; Miller Hendry, 2002–06; McCash & Hunter, 2006–. Chair, Mindspace (formerly Perth Assoc. for Mental Health) Ltd, 2009–16; Mem., Expert Adv. Gp, Centre for Mental Health and Capacity Law, Edinburgh Napier Univ., 2015–. Non-exec. Chair, Changing the Chemistry, 2016–19. Address: Law Society of Scotland, Atria One, 144 Morrison Street, Edinburgh EH3 8BR. E: VicePresident@lawscot.org.uk.

**MILLAR, Prof. Andrew John McWalter,** PhD; FRS 2012; FRSE; Professor of Systems Biology, since 2004, and Associate Director, SynthSys, since 2012, University of Edinburgh; b London, 12 Oct. 1966; s of David McW. Millar and H. Josephine Millar; m 1998, Prof. Karen J. Halliday; one s one d. Educ: Eur. Sch. of Luxembourg; Gonville and Caius Coll., Cambridge (BA 1st Cl. Hons Genetics 1988); Rockefeller Univ. (PhD 1994). Life Scis Res. Foundn post-doctoral Fellow, NSF Center for Biol Timing, Univ. of Virginia, 1994–95; Lectr, 1996–99, Reader, 1999–2002, Prof., 2002–04, Dept of Biol Scis, Univ. of Warwick; Founding Dir, Centre for Systems Biol., Univ. of Edinburgh, 2007–11. Theme Dir for Systems Biol., Scottish Univs Life Scis Alliance, 2007–09. Chief Scientific Advr on Envmt, Natural Resources and Agric. for Scottish Govt, 2018–. Non-exec. dir, James Hutton Inst., 2017–18. Member: EMBO, 2011–; UKRI-BBSRC, 2018–. FRSE 2013. Publications: (with P. J. Lumsden) Biological Rhythms and Photoperiodism in Plants, 1998; contrib. over 100 res. articles on biol rhythms and systems biol. Recreations: ski-ing, ice skating, travel. Address: SynthSys, University of Edinburgh, C. H. Waddington Building, King's Buildings, Edinburgh EH9 3BF. T: (0131) 651 3325, Fax: (0131) 651 9068. E: andrew.millar@ed.ac.uk.

**MILLAR, Anthony Bruce;** Chairman, Canadian Zinc (formerly San Andreas Resources) Corporation, 1994–2000; b 5 Oct. 1941; s of late James Desmond Millar and Josephine Georgina Millar (née Brice); m 1964, Judith Anne (née Jester); two d. Educ: Haileybury and Imperial Service College. FCA 1974 (ACA 1964). Asst to Group Management Accountant and Group Treasurer, Viyella Internat. Fedn, 1964–67; United Transport Overseas Ltd, Nairobi, and London (Dep. Group Financial Controller), 1967–72; Finance Dir, Fairfield Property Co. Ltd, 1972–75; Consultant, 1975–77; Managing Dir, Provincial Laundries Ltd, 1977–81; Dep. Chm., Hawley Group, 1981–82; Chm., 1982–92, Hon. Pres., 1992–2000, The Albert Fisher Gp. Freeman, City of London, 1993–; Liveryman, Fruiterers' Co., 1993– (Hon. Asst, Ct, 2001–03). Recreations: swimming, walking, bridge, travel. Club: Mark's.

**MILLAR, Douglas George,** CB 2007; Clerk Assistant, 2003–09, and Director General, Chamber and Committee Services, 2008–09, House of Commons; occasional consultant on parliamentary organisation, since 2009; b 15 Feb. 1946; s of late George Millar and Doris Mary Millar (née Morris); m 1st, 1967, Susan Mary Farrow (marr. diss. 1986); one s one d; 2nd, 1987, (Jane) Victoria Howard Smith; one s one d. Educ: City of Norwich Sch.; Bristol Univ. (BA Hons History 1967); Reading Univ. (MA Politics 1968). A Clerk, H of C, 1968–2009; Clerk of Defence Cttee, 1979–83; Clerk i/c Private Members' Bills and Divs, 1983–87; Clerk of Home Affairs Cttee, 1987–89; Principal Clerk and Clerk of Financial Cttees and Treasury and Civil Service Cttee, 1989–91; Sec. to Public Accounts Commn, 1989–91; Second Clerk, Select Cttees, 1991–94; Clerk of Select Cttees, 1994–97; Departmental Finance Officer, 1994–2003; Prin. Clerk, Table Office, 1998–2001; Clerk of Legislation, 2001–02. Jt Sec., Assoc. of Secs Gen. of Parlts, 1971–77. Publications: (ed jtly) Erskine May Parliamentary Practice, 2011; articles and reviews in parly and political jls. Recreations: watching Norwich City, family, golf, walking on the Norfolk coast, travelling. Club: Roehampton.

**MILLAR, Fiona;** writer, journalist, Education Guardian, since 2003; b London, 2 Jan. 1958; d of Robert Millar and Audrey Millar; partner, Alastair John Campbell, qv; two s one d. Educ: Camden Sch. for Girls; University Coll. London (BSc Econs and Econ. Hist.). Graduate trng scheme, Mirror Gp, 1980–82; Daily Express, 1982–88; freelance journalist, 1988–94; Office of the Leader of the Opposition, 1995–97; Special Advr to the Prime Minister, 1997–2003. Television programmes: writer and presenter, The Best for My Child, 2004; presenter: Involving Parents, 2005; The Parents' Guide, 2006; Admissions Code, 2007; The School Report, 2009. Chm., Comprehensive Future, 2008–12. Co-founder, Local Schs Network, 2010–. Mem., Ministerial Adv. Gp for Educn and Skills, Welsh Govt, 2010–13. Chairman: Trustees, Family and Parenting Inst., 2004–10; Nat. Youth Arts Trust, 2013–17; Young Camden Foundn, 2017–. Chairman of Governors: Gospel Oak Prim. Sch., 2000–10; William Ellis Sch., 2008–; Gov., Parliament Hill Sch., 2012–. Publications: (with Glenys Kinnock) By Faith and Daring, 1993; (with Melissa Benn) A Comprehensive Future, 2006; The Secret World of the Working Mother, 2009; A New Conversation with Parents, 2011; The Best for My Child, 2018. Recreations: swimming, reading, my children and friends, learning French. Address: 13 Estelle Road, NW3 2JX.
See also G. J. Millar.

**MILLAR, Gavin James;** QC 2000; a Recorder, since 2003; b 10 July 1959; s of Robert and Audrey Millar; partner, Carmel Mary Elizabeth Fitzsimons; one s three d. Educ: St Peter's Coll., Oxford (BA Jurisprudence). Called to the Bar: Lincoln's Inn, 1981; NI, 2010. Founder Mem., Doughty St Chambers, 1990. Council of Europe Expert on Freedom of Expression, 2002–. Chair, Centre for Investigative Journalism, 2013–15. Mem., Public Affairs Cttee, Bar Council, 1995–97; Vice-Chm., Soc. of Labour Lawyers, 1999–2001. Mem. (Lab) Westminster CC, 1985–94. Publications: (jtly) Media Law and Human Rights, 2001, 2nd edn 2009; (jtly) Newsgathering: law, regulation and the public interest, 2016. Recreations: family, football, painting. Address: Matrix Chambers, Griffin Building, Gray's Inn, WC1R 5LN. Club: Manchester United Football.
See also F. Millar.

**MILLAR, Graeme Stewart,** CBE 2006; FRPharmS; Director, Graeme Millar Ltd, since 1982; Chairman: Fletcher Jones Ltd, since 2000; Teko LLC, since 2011; b 20 Feb. 1955; s of Stewart and Louise Millar; m 1978, Fay Cooper Kennedy; three s. Educ: Heriot-Watt Univ. (BSc Hons Pharmacy). FRPharmS 1999. Director: Dunfermline Bldg Soc., 2001–09 (Vice Chm., 2007–09); Essentia Gp Ltd, 2003–08; Lomax Mobility Ltd, 2005–07. Dir, NCC, and Chm., Scottish Consumer Council, 2000–06; Chairman: Scottish Construction Forum, 2004–08; Scottish Food Adv. Cttee, 2006–11; Dir, Food Standards Agency, 2005–11. Non-exec. Dir, Scottish Rugby Union, 2006–08. Chairman: Sick Kids Friends Foundn, 2000–08; Lomond Centre, 2012. Mem. Adv. Bd, Reform Scotland, 2012–16. Hon. Prof. of Pharmacy, Robert Gordon's Univ., Aberdeen, 2006–. Recreations: Rugby (spectator), golf, family and friends, good food and wine. Address: 2 Campbell Avenue, Edinburgh EH12 6DS. T: 07768 924790, T: and Fax: (0131) 337 0608. E: millargraeme@yahoo.co.uk. Clubs: New (Edinburgh); Royal Burgess Golfing Society (Edinburgh); Golf House (Elie, Fife).

**MILLAR, (Helen Rosemary) Alison;** Lord-Lieutenant of County Londonderry, since 2018; b Banbridge, Co. Down, 1952; d of Robert Lindsay Kennedy and Eliza Jane Kennedy; m Alan Patrick Millar; one s one d. Educ: Omagh Acad.; Queen's Univ. of Belfast (LLB). Admitted solicitor, 1977; Solicitor, 1977–81, Partner, 1981–2017, Wray & Baxter, then Macaulay Wray Solicitors; Chm. (pt-time), Appeals Service, NI, 1981–. Ordinary Member: Turf Club, Ireland, 2017–; Irish Nat. Hunt Steeplechase Cttee, 2017–; Licensing Cttee, Irish Horseracing Regulatory Bd, 2019–. DL Londonderry, 2009. Recreations: National Hunt racing, hunting (former Master of Route Hunt), golfing. Address: Crossmakeever Cottage, 81 Kinnyglass Road, Coleraine, Co. Londonderry BT51 4NP. E: hramillar@gmail.com. Club: Royal Portrush Golf.

**MILLAR, Prof. Jane Isobel,** OBE 2001; DPhil; FBA 2014; FAcSS; Professor of Social Policy, University of Bath, since 1994; b Tynemouth, 7 July 1953; d of Robert Coulson Millar and Margaret Elizabeth Millar; m 2008, Jeremy Andrew Toop Cooper. Educ: Univ. of Sussex (BA 1974); Brunel Univ. (MA 1980); Univ. of York (DPhil 1987). Res. Officer, DHSS, 1980–83; Res. Fellow, Social Policy Res. Unit, Univ. of York, 1983–85; Lectr in Social Policy, Univ. of Ulster, 1985–88; Lectr, 1988–91, Reader, 1991–94, Pro-Vice Chancellor, 2006–15, Univ. of Bath. FAcSS (AcSS 2002). Publications: (with C. Glendinning) Women and Poverty in Britain, 1987, 2nd edn 1992; Poverty and the Lone-Parent Family: the challenge to social policy, 1989; Understanding Social Security, 2003, 3rd edn 2018; contrib. articles to learned jls incl. Jl Social Policy, Social Policy and Admin, Social Policy and Society. Address: Institute for Policy Research, University of Bath, Bath BA2 7AY. T: (01225) 386711. E: j.i.millar@bath.ac.uk.

**MILLAR, Rt Rev. Preb. John Alexander Kirkpatrick, (Sandy);** Bishop, Church of Uganda, since 2005; an Honorary Assistant Bishop: (Bishop in Mission), Diocese of London, since 2006; Diocese of St Edmundsbury and Ipswich, since 2012; b 13 Nov. 1939; s of Maj.-Gen. Robert Kirkpatrick Millar of Orton, CB, DSO and Frances (née Beyts); m 1971, Annette Fisher; one s three d. Educ: Eton; Trinity Coll., Cambridge (BA 1962; MA 1966); Univ. of Durham (DipTh). Deacon 1976; priest 1977; Curate, 1976–85, Vicar, 1985–2005, Holy Trinity Brompton, with St Paul, Onslow Square; Area Dean, Chelsea, 1989–94; Prebendary, St Paul's Cathedral, 1997–2010; Priest-in-charge, St Mark's, Tollington Park, 2003–11. Address: Fairlawn, 37 Alde Lane, Aldeburgh IP15 5DZ. T: (01728) 452926.

**MILLAR, Air Vice-Marshal Peter,** CB 1998; Director of Administration, Magna Medica-Medical City Ltd, since 2014; Chief Operating Officer, Therabeam Ltd, since 2015; b 20 June 1942; s of Air Cdre John Christopher Millar, RAF and Patricia Millar (née Allen); m 1966, Annette McMillan; one s two d. Educ: Malvern Coll.; RAF Coll., Cranwell. Served RAF: No 20 Sqn, Singapore, 1964–66; No 4 FTS, RAF Valley, 1967–69; Central Flying Sch., RAF Kemble, 1969–71; 560 Trng Sqn, Randolph AFB, Texas, 1971–74; RAF Staff Coll., 1974; Flight Commander: No 20 Sqn, Wildenrath, 1975–77; No 4 Sqn, Gutersloh, 1977–78; MoD, 1978–79; Sqn Comdr, No 233 OCU, RAF Wittering, 1979–82; USAF Air Warfare Coll., Maxwell AFB, Alabama, 1982–83; Brit. Defence Staff, Washington, 1983–84; Stn Comdr, RAF Wittering, 1985–86; RCDS 1987; on staff, UK Mil. Rep., NATO HQ, 1988–90; Dir NATO, MoD, 1990–93; HQ AAFCE, Ramstein AFB, Germany, 1993–95; Adminr, Sovereign Base Areas and Comdr, British Forces Cyprus, 1995–98; retd 1998. Dir of Security, Medical World Inc., and Dir, Internat. Admin, Medical Mall Ltd, 1998–99. Mem. Adv. Bd, World Challenge Expeditions Ltd, 2000–04; Dir, Ops, Intellectual Property Rights Protection Ltd, 2003–06. Chairman: Biotrans Consortium, 2004–08; Terrafuels Ltd, 2006–08; C-Green Fuels Ltd, 2006–12; Dir, Carbon Trading, 2005–08, Dir, Energy Sector, 2008–09, C-Questor Ltd; Sen. Vice Pres., Bio-Energy GHG Corp., 2010–12. Gov., Queen Alexandra's Hosp. Home, 2005–14. FRAeS 1997. Recreations: ski-ing, golf, off-shore sailing. Club: Royal Air Force.

**MILLAR, Peter Carmichael,** OBE 1978; Deputy Keeper of HM Signet, 1983–91; b 19 Feb. 1927; s of late Rev. Peter Carmichael Millar, OBE, DD and of Ailsa Ross Brown Campbell or Millar; m 1953, Kirsteen Lindsay Carnegie, d of late Col David Carnegie, CB, OBE, TD, DL, Dep. Gen. Manager, Clydesdale Bank; two s two d. Educ: Aberdeen Grammar Sch.; Glasgow Univ.; St Andrews Univ.; Edinburgh Univ. MA, LLB; WS. Served RN, 1944–47. Partner in law firms, Messrs W. & T. P. Manuel, WS, 1954–62; Aitken, Kinnear & Co., WS, 1963–87; Aitken Nairn, WS, 1987–92. Clerk to Soc. of Writers to HM Signet, 1964–83. Chairman: Church of Scotland Gen. Trustees, 1973–85; Mental Welfare Commn for Scotland, 1983–91; (part-time) Medical Appeal Tribunals, 1991–99; Pension Appeal Tribunals, 1992–99. Convener, Scottish Child and Family Alliance, later Children in Scotland, 1992–95. Recreations: golf, hill-walking, music. Clubs: New (Edinburgh); Hon. Co. of Edinburgh Golfers, Bruntsfield Links Golfing Society.

**MILLAR, Robert Brandon,** CA; Director, Ediston Homes Ltd, since 2013; b 30 March 1950; m 1975, Sandra Falconer; one s one d. Educ: George Heriot's Sch.; Edinburgh Univ. (MA Hons Econs). Gen. Mgt, BT, 1972–74; CA apprenticeship, Touche Ross & Co., 1974–78; Accountant, Bredero UK, 1978–79; Financial Controller, Castle Rock HA, 1979–83; Manager Registration, Housing Corp., 1983–89; Dir of Strategy, Scottish Homes, 1989–97; Finance Dir, Miller Homes, 1997–99; Chief Exec., Scottish Homes, subseq. Communities Scotland, 2000–03; Chief Exec., 2004–08, Develt Dir, 2008–12, New City Vision. Recreation: various sports. Club: Merchants of Edinburgh Golf.

**MILLAR, Prof. Robert Hamilton, (Robin),** OBE 2015; PhD; Salters' Professor of Science Education, University of York, 2006–14, now Emeritus; b Ballymena, NI, 7 July 1948; s of Robert and Margaret Millar; m 1973, Elizabeth Mackenzie; one s one d. Educ: Ballymena Acad.; Clare Coll., Cambridge (BA Natural Scis 1970); Univ. of Edinburgh (PhD Med. Physics 1973; DipEd 1974; MPhil 1981). MInstP 1984, FInstP 2013, Hon. FInstP 2017. School teacher, Lothian Regl Council, 1974–82; University of York: Lectr in Educn, 1982–90; Sen. Lectr, 1990–96; Prof. of Sci. Educn, 1996–2006. President: Eur. Sci.

Educn Res. Assoc., 1999–2003; ASE, 2012. *Publications:* Doing Science: images of science in science education, 1989, 2011; Understanding Physics, 1989; (jtly) Young People's Images of Science, 1996; (jtly) Beyond 2000: science education for the future, 1998; (jtly) Science for Public Understanding, 2000; (ed jtly) Improving Science Education: the contribution of research, 2000; (ed jtly) Making a Difference: evaluation as a tool for improving science education, 2005; (jtly) Improving Subject Teaching: lessons from research in science education, 2006; Analysing Practical Science Activities to Assess and Improve their Effectiveness, 2010; contribs to learned jls in field of sci. educn. *Recreations:* hill-walking, choral singing, reading, photography. *Address:* Department of Education, University of York, Heslington, York YO10 5DD. *T:* (01904) 323469, *Fax:* (01904) 322605. *E:* robin.millar@york.ac.uk.

**MILLAR, Robin John Christian**, CBE 2010; musician and record producer; *b* London, 18 Dec. 1951; *s* of Dr Bruce Millar and Anne Millar; one *s* one *d*; partner, Shelley Davies. *Educ:* Enfield Grammar Sch.; Queens' Coll., Cambridge (BA 1973; MA 1976). Chm., Scarlett Gp plc, 1982–90; Chm. and CEO, Whitfield Street Studios Ltd, 2004–07; Chm., Blue Raincoat Chrysalis Gp Ltd, 2013–. Produced 44 No. 1 records and 150 gold and platinum records, incl. Diamond Life, by Sade; produced 1996 Olympic Games opening ceremony. Vis. Prof. and Lectr in commercial music, RAM, LCM, Surrey Univ. and Univ. of Modena. Hon. Prof., LCM, 2007–. Member, Board: Nat. Skills Acad. for Creative and Cultural, 2009–16; Inst. for Apprenticeships and Tech. Educn (formerly Inst. for Apprenticeships), 2017–. Trustee, Creative and Cultural Skills UK, 2009–16. Global Ambassador, Leonard Cheshire, 2018–. Hon. Patron, Music Producers Guild, 2000. Fellow, Assoc. of Professional Recording Services, 2009. *Recreations:* adventure, reading, sport. *W:* www.robinmillar.org.uk. *Clubs:* Groucho (Hon. Life Mem.), Conduit (Founding Mem.).

**MILLAR, Samira;** *see* Ahmed, Samira.

**MILLAR, Rt Rev. Preb. Sandy;** *see* Millar, Rt Rev. Preb. J. A. K.

**MILLAR, Stephen Samuel Alexander;** Managing Partner, CMS Cameron McKenna Nabarro Olswang LLP, since 2016; *b* Ballymena, NI, 22 Nov. 1972; *s* of William and Josephine Millar; *m* 1997, Pauline Cardy; two *s* one *d*. *Educ:* Dalbeattie High Sch.; Univ. of Dundee (LLB Hons Mineral Law and Policy; LLM). Trainee, lawyer, Associate, then Partner, Paull & Williamsons, Aberdeen, 1994–2003; Partner, CMS, 2003–. *Address:* CMS Cameron McKenna Nabarro Olswang LLP, Cannon Place, 78 Cannon Street, EC4N 6AF. *T:* (020) 7367 3078. *E:* stephen.millar@cms-cmno.com.

**MILLARD, Anthony Paul;** Founder and Chairman, Anthony Millard Consulting, since 2004; *b* 21 Sept. 1948; *s* of Leonard William Millard and Marjorie Ethel Millard (*née* Manley); *m* 1971, Lesley Margaret Baker; one *s* three *d*. *Educ:* Solihull Sch.; LSE (BSc Econ); Balliol Coll., Oxford (PGCE). Teaching in Zambia, 1971–74; Stagiaire (specialist trainee) with EC, 1974–75; Wells Cathedral School: Asst Master, 1975–77; Housemaster, 1977–86; Dep. Headmaster, 1982–86; Headmaster: Wycliffe Coll., Glos, 1987–93; Giggleswick Sch., 1993–2001. Man. Dir, Schools Div., Nord Anglia plc, 2002–03. Chairman: ISIS (Central), 1990–92; Services Cttee, HMC, 1995–2001; Boarding Schs Assoc., 1999–2000 (Mem. Exec. Cttee, 1995–2001); Vice Chm., Bloxham Project Cttee, 1991–96; Mem. Council, ISCO, 1995–98. Contested (C) Wirral South, 2001. Chm., Internat. British Schs, 2011–16 (Chm. Govs, British Internat. Sch., NY, 2006–16); Governor: Geneva English Sch., 2011–15; Greensteds Sch., Nakuru, Kenya, 2015–. FRSA 1986. *Recreations:* history, Shakespeare, mountains. *Address:* Brookside Cottage, Ewen, Cirencester, Glos GL7 6BU. *T:* (01285) 770365. *E:* anthony@ewenelite.com. *Club:* East India, Devonshire, Sports and Public Schools.

**MILLARD, Dennis Henry;** Chairman, Halfords Group plc, since 2009; *b* New York, 28 Feb. 1949; *s* of Harry and Edna Millard; *m* 1972, Paula; two *s* one *d*. *Educ:* Univ. of Natal, SA; Univ. of Cape Town Grad. Sch. of Business (MBA). CTA; CA (SA). Dir, Finance and Planning, Plate Glass Gp (SA), 1980–93; Finance Director: Medeva plc, 1994–96; Cookson Gp plc, 1996–2005. Chm., Connect (formerly Smiths News plc), 2006–15; non-executive Director: Exel plc, 2003–05; Xchanging plc, 2005–12; Debenhams plc, 2006–17; Premier Farnell plc, 2007–15; Sen. Ind. Dir and Dep. Chm., Pets at Home Gp plc, 2014–. *Recreations:* surfing, golf, cycling. *Address:* Kingscote, Binfield Road, Wokingham, Berks RG40 5PP. *T:* (01344) 451216. *E:* dennis.millard@btinternet.com. *Clubs:* Sunningdale Golf; Durban Country (SA).

**MILLARD, Keith Haverland;** senior executive mentor and coach, since 2000; Group Chairman, Surrey, Vistage, 2000–14; President, Institution of Mechanical Engineers, 2009–10; *b* Enfield, 20 Nov. 1942; *s* of Harold Millard and Kathleen Millard (*née* Hill); *m* 1966, Anne Sherrington; two *s*. *Educ:* Latymer Sch., Edmonton; Hendon Coll. of Technol.; Peterborough Tech. Coll. (HNC Mech. Engrg). CEng 1972; FIMechE 1977. Consulting engr, 1970–83; Man. Dir, Gilbert Associates, 1983–94; Business Develt Dir, Balfour Beatty Internat., 1994–96; Vice Pres., Parsons Corp., 1996–98. Institution of Mechanical Engineers: Trustee, 2004–09; Dep. Pres., 2007–09; Trustee, IMechE Pension Fund, 2010–17 (Chm., 2013–17). FInstD. Freeman, City of London, 2008; Liveryman, Engineers' Co., 2008. Paul Harris Fellow, Rotary Internat., 2008. *Recreations:* music, theatre, keeping fit. *Club:* Rotary (Pres., Woking District, 1991–92).

**MILLARD, Moira Sarah;** *see* Sinclair, M. S.

**MILLARD, Rosemary Harriet**, OBE 2018; Chair, Children in Need, since 2018; *b* London, 17 April 1965; *d* of John and Rosemary Millard; two *s* two *d*; partner, Alexander Graham, *qv*. *Educ:* Wimbledon High Sch., GDST; Hull Univ. (BA Hons English and Drama 1987); London Coll. of Communications; Courtauld Inst. Researcher: Tyne Tees TV, 1988–90; Granada TV, 1990–92; Presenter, Meridian TV, 1992–95; Arts corresp., BBC, 1995–2004; Arts Ed., New Statesman, 2004–06; feature writer: Sunday Times, 2004–09; Daily Telegraph, 2009–11; columnist, Independent, 2011–14; Chair, Hull City of Culture, 2014–18. Chair, Bd of Trustees, Firstsite, 2017–; Trustee, Opera North, 2017– (Dep. Chair, 2019–). Hon. DLitt Hull, 2017. *Publications:* The Tastemakers: UK art now, 2001, 2nd edn 2002; Bonnes Vacances!, 2011; The Square (novel), 2015; The Brazilian (novel), 2017. *Recreations:* marathon running (especially all the Marathon Majors), the Humber Bridge, visiting roads named after General Charles de Gaulle. *T:* 07889 021466. *E:* rosie.millard@virgin.net.

**MILLEDGE, Peter Neil**, CB 2017; Counsel to the Chairman of Committees, House of Lords, 2013–16 (Deputy Counsel, 2005–13); *b* 4 March 1955; *s* of late Frederick Milledge and Mary Kirkwood Milledge (*née* Cree); *m* 1979, Jennifer Miriam Greenall; two *s*. *Educ:* Newport (Essex) Grammar Sch.; King's Coll. London (LLB 1976). Called to the Bar, Middle Temple, 1977; joined Govt Legal Service, 1979; Legal Asst, 1979–82, Sen. Legal Asst, 1982–85, Asst Solicitor, 1985, DHSS; seconded to Law Officers' Dept, 1987–89; Asst Dir, Legal Services, DSS, subseq. DWP, 1989–2005. Governor: Newport Free GS, Saffron Walden, 2008–14; Joyce Frankland Acad., Newport, 2014–16. *Publications:* (contrib.) Tribunals: practice and procedure, 1986; contribs to legal jls. *Recreations:* walking, gardening, local history. *T:* (01799) 550723.

**MILLER,** family name of **Baroness Miller of Chilthorne Domer**.

**MILLER OF CHILTHORNE DOMER**, Baroness *cr* 1998 (Life Peer), of Chilthorne Domer in the co. of Somerset; **Susan Elizabeth Miller;** *b* 1 Jan. 1954; *d* of Frederick Oliver Meddows Taylor and Norah Langham; *m* 1st, 1980, John Miller (marr. diss. 1998); one *d* (and one *d* decd); 2nd, 1999, Humphrey Temperley. *Educ:* Sidcot Sch.; Oxford Poly. David & Charles, Publishers, 1975–77; Weidenfeld & Nicholson, 1977; Penguin Books, 1977–79; bookshop owner, Sherborne and Yeovil, 1979–89. Lib Dem spokesman on envmt, food and rural affairs, H of L, 1999–2007, on home affairs, 2007–09; All Party Parliamentary Groups: Chairman: Street Children; Agroecology; Food and Health; Conservation and Wildlife. Member (Lib Dem): S Somerset DC, 1991–98 (Leader, 1996–98); Somerset CC, 1997–2005. Parish Councillor, Chilthorne Domer, 1987–. *Recreations:* horse riding, gardening, viniculture, reading, friends. *Address:* House of Lords, SW1A 0PW.

**MILLER, Amelia, (Mrs Michael Miller);** *see* Freedman, A.

**MILLER, Prof. Andrew**, CBE 1999; PhD; FRSE; Principal and Vice-Chancellor, Stirling University, 1994–2001, Professor Emeritus, since 2001; Secretary and Treasurer, Carnegie Trust for the Universities of Scotland, 2004–13; *b* 15 Feb. 1936; *s* of William Hamilton Miller and Susan Anderson (*née* Auld); *m* 1962, Rosemary Singleton Hannah Fyvie; one *s* one *d*. *Educ:* Beath High Sch.; Edinburgh Univ. (BSc Hons 1958; PhD 1962); Wolfson Coll., Oxford (MA 1967; Hon. Fellow, 1995). Postdoctoral Fellow, CSIRO, Melbourne, 1962–65; Tutor in Chemistry, Ormond Coll., Melbourne Univ., 1963–65; Staff Scientist, MRC Lab. of Molecular Biol., Cambridge, 1965–66; Lectr in Molecular Biophysics, Oxford Univ., 1966–83; Fellow, Wolfson Coll., Oxford, 1967–83; on secondment as Hd, EMBL, Grenoble, 1975–80; Edinburgh University: Prof. of Biochem., 1984–94; on secondment as Dir of Res., European Synchrotron Radiation Facility, Grenoble, 1986–91; Vice-Dean of Medicine, 1991–93; Vice-Provost of Medicine and Veterinary Medicine, 1992–93; Vice-Principal, 1993–94; Mem., Business Cttee, Gen. Council, 2017–. Gen. Sec., RSE, 2001–05, 2007; Chm., RSE Scotland Foundn, 2007–09; Interim Chief Exec., Cancer Research UK, 2001–02. Chm., Internat. Centre for Math. Scis, Edinburgh, 2001–05. Leverhulme Emeritus Fellowship, 2001–03. Member: Action Gp on Standards in Scottish Schs, DFEE, 1997–99; Scottish Exec. Sci. Strategy Gp, 1999–2001; Bd, Food Standards Agency, 2003–05; Dep. Chm., Scottish Food Adv. Cttee, 2003–05. Dir, Scottish Knowledge plc, 1997–2002. Advr, Wellcome Trust, on UK-Wellcome-French-Synchrotron, 1999–2000. Mem. Council, Open Univ., 2001–05. FRSE 1986 (Mem. Council, 1997–2009). DUniv: Stirling, 2002; Open, 2007. Bicentennial Medal, RSE, 2007. *Publications:* (ed jtly) Minerals in Biology, 1984; 180 papers on collagen and muscle in scientific jls incl. Nature, Jl Molecular Biol. *Recreations:* music, walking, reading, wondering. *Address:* 5 Blackford Hill Grove, Edinburgh EH9 3HA.

**MILLER, Andrew;** QC 2014; barrister, arbitrator and mediator; *b* London, 11 Dec. 1962; *s* of late Michael Irvine and of Josephine Miller; *m* 1994, Laura Rodriguez Garcia (marr. diss. 2016); one *s* (and one *s* decd); partner, Esther Yael Marlow. *Educ:* Preston Manor High Sch., Wembley; Univ. of Southampton (LLB); Council of Legal Educn. FCIArb 1999. Called to the Bar, Inner Temple, 1989; in practice as a barrister, specialising in commercial, construction and insurance disputes, 1989–; arbitrator, 1999–; mediator, 2014–. Co. Sec. and Trustee, Compassionate Friends. *Recreations:* travelling, yoga theatre, diving, walking, cycling, ski-ing, gym and spinning. *Address:* 2 Temple Gardens, Temple, EC4Y 9AY. *T:* (020) 7822 1200, *Fax:* (020) 7822 1300. *E:* amiller@2tg.co.uk.

**MILLER, Andrew Arthur;** Partner, Terra Firma Capital Partners, since 2016; *b* 10 July 1966; *s* of Sir Ronald Andrew Baird Miller, *qv*; *m* 1991, Helen Connolly; two *s* one *d*. *Educ:* Dollar Acad.; Univ. of Edinburgh (LLB Hons). CA 1991. CA trainee, Price Waterhouse, 1988–91; Costing Systems Manager, 1991–92, Factory Finance Manager and Brand Analyst, Detergents, 1992–94; Procter & Gamble; Corporate Finance Manager, Holiday Inn/Britvic Soft Drinks, Bass plc, 1994–95; Commercial Planning Manager, Walkers Snack Foods UK, 1996–97, Dir of Finance, Frito Lay Europe Ops, 1997–2000, Pepsico Gp; Man. Dir, Postanywhere, 2000–02; Gp Financial Controller, 2002–04, Chief Financial Officer, 2004–09, Trader Media Gp; Chief Financial Officer, 2009–10, CEO, 2010–15, Guardian Media Gp plc. Non-executive Director: Automobile Assoc., 2014–18; Ocean Outdoors, 2018–; Director: Consolidated Pastoral Co., Australia, 2016–; Welcome Hotels, Germany, 2017–; Chair, Food Folk, Norway, 2017–. Advr, Their World, 2017–. Gov., Benjamin Franklin House, 2014–. *Recreations:* family, sport, the arts. *Club:* Caledonian.

**MILLER, Dr Andrew Brooke**, FRSL; author; *b* Bristol, 1960; *s* of Kieth Wyndham Miller and Molly Anne Collard; one *d*. *Educ:* Middlesex Poly. (BA); Univ. of East Anglia (MA Creative Writing 1991); Lancaster Univ. (PhD Critical and Creative Writing 1995). FRSL 2012. *Publications:* Ingenious Pain, 1997 (James Tait Black Meml Prize, Premio Grinzane Cavour, Italy, Internat. IMPAC Dublin Literary Award); Casanova, 1998; Oxygen, 2001; The Optimists, 2005; One Morning Like a Bird, 2008; Pure, 2011 (Costa Novel Award and Costa Book of Year, 2012); The Crossing, 2015; Now We Shall Be Entirely Free, 2018. *Recreations:* aikido (Japanese martial art), playing the mandolin in a folk band, keeping chickens.

**MILLER, Andrew James;** arts consultant and broadcaster; UK Government Disability Champion, Arts and Culture, since 2018; *b* Glasgow, 31 Oct. 1966; *s* of Norman Charles Anderson Miller and Anne Jean McCaig Miller; *m* 2006, Timothy Meacock. *Educ:* High Sch. of Glasgow; Univ. of Stirling (BA HIst.). Broadcaster, 1986–2003: one of the first disabled presenters on mainstream British network television; series incl. Boom!, Advice Shop, Q&A, Eikon, On the Road; progs as producer/director incl. VE-50 and VJ-50, Tune Team; documentary subjects incl. Billy Mackenzie, Gerry Rafferty, Anthony Gormley, Bill Viola, William McGonagall and Skibo Castle. Music Officer, Sen. Manager, then Hd, Performing Arts, Arts Council England, 2003–10; Hd, Creative Programming, RWCMD, 2011–16; estabd new arts centre in Cardiff; Creator and Exec. Producer, Russia 17 Season, Wales, 2017. Exec. Associate, Royal & Derngate Northampton, 2017. Member: Council, Arts Council of Wales, 2012–; Bd, The Space, 2016–19; Council, Arts Council England, 2017–; Bd, WNO, 2019–. Arts consultant and advisor to Univ. of Oxford, Paul Hamlyn Foundn, British Council, Unlimited and BFI, 2018–19. Dir, Scottish Student Drama Fest., 1987. Judge, TMA Theatre Awards, 2001–03. *Recreations:* disco, 20th century and contemporary art, visiting European palaces and mausoleums, smoking. *Address:* c/o Governance Team, Arts Council England, 21 Bloomsbury Street, Fitzrovia, WC1B 3HF. *E:* andrew.milleracsc@gmail.com. *W:* www.twitter.com/AndrewM_Arts, www.linkedin.com/andrew-miller-arts. *Club:* Groucho.

**MILLER, Andrew Peter;** science policy advisor, since 2015; *b* 23 March 1949; *s* of late Ernest William Thomas Miller and of Daphne May Miller; *m* Frances Ewan; two *s* one *d*. *Educ:* Hayling Island Secondary Sch.; LSE (Mature Student; Dip. Indust. Relations 1976). Lab. Technician, Dept of Geology, Portsmouth Poly., specialising in X-RF and X-RD analysis, 1967–76; Divl Officer, ASTMS, subseq. MSF, 1977–92. MP (Lab) Ellesmere Port and Neston, 1992–2015. PPS, DTI, 2001–05. Chairman: Regulatory Reform Select Cttee, 2005–10; Science and Technol. Select Cttee, 2010–15 (Mem., 1992–97); Parly and Scientific Cttee, 2010–15; Chm., 2005–10, Vice Chm., 2010–15, PITCOM, subseq.

PICTFOR; Vice Chm., PLP Cttee on Science and Technol., 1993–97; Treas., 1997–2000, Vice Pres., 2000–03, Parlt and Sci. Cttee. Ldr, PLP Leadership Campaign Team, 1997–98. Dir, Eur. Informatics Market, 1996–98. Chairman: Adv. Bd, Thornton Sci. Park, 2012–16; Ext. Engagement Bd, Grantham Centre for Sustainable Futures, Univ. of Sheffield, 2015–18; Dir, Thornton Res. Properties Ltd, 2014–. Mem., Royal Soc. Sci. Policy Adv. Gp, 2015–18. Pres., Computing for Labour, 1993–2015. Trustee: Newton's Apple, 2010–; UK Res. Integrity Office, 2017–. Mem. Council, Univ. of Chester, 2019–. *Publications:* (jtly) North West Economic Strategy, 1987. *Recreations:* walking, photography. *Address:* Hollytree Cottage, Commonside, Alvanley, Cheshire WA6 9HB. *T:* (01928) 722642.

**MILLER, Sir Anthony Thomas,** 13th Bt *cr* 1705, of Chichester, Sussex; *b* 4 May 1955; *o s* of Sir Harry Miller, 12th Bt, and of Gwynedd Margaret Miller (*née* Sheriff); *S* father, 2007; *m* 1990, Barbara Battersby (*née* Kensington); two *s*, and two step *s* one step *d*. *Heir: s* Thomas Kensington Miller, *b* 26 Feb. 1994.

**MILLER, Hon. (Arthur) Daniel;** consultant; Premier, British Columbia, 1999–2000; *b* 24 Dec. 1944; *s* of Arthur William Miller and Evelyn Estelle Miller (*née* Lewis); *m* 1987, Beverly Gayle Ballard (*née* Bartram) (*d* 2015); three *s* two *d*. *Educ:* N Vancouver Secondary Sch. Millwright. Former Mem. Council, Prince Rupert City. Government of British Columbia: MLA (NDP) North Coast, 1986–2001; Minister of: Forests, 1991–93; Skills, Training and Labour, 1993–96; Municipal Affairs, 1996–97; Dep. Premier, 1996–99; Minister: of Employment and Investment, 1997–98; of Energy and Mines, and resp. for Northern Develt, 1998–2001. *Address:* 1234 Richardson Street, Victoria, BC V8V 3E1, Canada.

**MILLER, Bill;** *b* 22 July 1954; *s* of George and Janet Miller; one *s* one *d*. *Educ:* Paisley Coll.; Kingston Poly. (BSc Land Econs). DipTP; MRICS. Surveyor, Glasgow DC, 1978–94. Councillor (Lab) Strathclyde, 1986–94. MEP (Lab) Glasgow, 1994–99, Scotland, 1999–2004. *Recreations:* record collecting, Kilmarnock Football Club, golf. *Club:* Castlemilk Labour (Glasgow).

**MILLER, Carolyn,** CBE 2013; consultant on international development management, since 2013; Chair, INTRAC, since 2015; *b* 20 Nov. 1951; *d* of Norman and Irene Miller. *Educ:* Southampton Univ. (BSc); City Univ., London (DipTP). Local govt, 1973–84; Sen. Advr to Ministry of Planning, Nicaragua, 1984–87; Save the Children: Prog. Dir, Mozambique/Angola, 1987–89; Hd, Southern Africa Regl Office, 1989–91; Dir, Asia, Latin America and Caribbean, ME, 1991–96; Dir of Progs, 1996–2001; Dir, Eastern Europe and the Western Hemisphere, subseq. Europe, ME and Americas, DFID, 2001–04; Chief Exec., Merlin, 2005–13. Non-exec. Dir, Oxford Policy Mgt, 2015–. *Recreations:* walking, arts. *E:* carolyn.millerpersonal@gmail.com.

**MILLER, Cheryl;** *see* Miller, D. C.

**MILLER, Christopher;** *see* Miller, J. C.

**MILLER, Colin Brown;** Sheriff for South Strathclyde, Dumfries and Galloway, 1991–2010, recommissioned Sheriff, 2010–16, Hon. Sheriff, 2017; *b* 4 Oct. 1946; *s* of late James Miller and Isabella Brown or Miller; *m* 1972, Joan Elizabeth Blyth; three *s*. *Educ:* Paisley Grammar Sch.; Glasgow Univ. (LLB 1967). Solicitor in private practice, 1969–91. Mem. Council, Law Soc. of Scotland, and Convener of various cttees, 1983–91. Dean, Faculty of Procurators in Paisley, 1991. *Recreations:* walking, family, railways, ships, motor vehicles, photography, visiting Australia. *Address:* Sheriffs' Chambers, Wellington Square, Ayr KA7 1EE. *T:* (01292) 268474.

**MILLER, Hon. Daniel;** *see* Miller, Hon. A. D.

**MILLER, Prof. Daniel Malcolm Stuart,** PhD; FBA 2008; Professor of Anthropology, University College London, since 1995; *b* 1954; *m* Rickie Burman; one *s* one *d*. *Educ:* St John's Coll., Cambridge (BA 1976; PhD Anthropol. and Archaeol. 1984). Lectr, 1981–90, Reader, 1990–95, UCL. *Publications:* (ed with C. Tilley) Ideology, Power and Prehistory, 1984; Artefacts as Categories, 1985; Material Culture and Mass Consumption, 1987; (ed jtly) Domination and Resistance, 1989; (ed) Unwrapping Christmas, 1993; Modernity: an ethnographic approach, 1994; Acknowledging Consumption, 1995; (ed) Worlds Apart: modernity through the prism of the local, 1995; Capitalism: an ethnographic approach, 1997; A Theory of Shopping, 1998; (ed) Material Cultures, 1998; (with J. Carrier) Virtualism: a new political economy, 1998; (jtly) Shopping Place and Identity, 1998; (jtly) Commercial Cultures, 2000; (with D. Slater) The Internet: an ethnographic approach, 2000; The Dialectics of Shopping, 2001; (ed) Car Cultures, 2001; (ed) Consumption, 4 vols, 2001; Home Possessions, 2001; (with M. Bannerjee) The Sari, 2003; (ed with S. Küchler) Clothing as Material Culture, 2005; Materiality, 2005; (with H. Horst) The Cell Phone: an anthropology of communication, 2006; The Comfort of Things, 2008; Anthropology and the Individual, 2009; Stuff, 2009; (with Z. Búriková) Au Pair, 2010; (ed with S. Woodward) Global Denim, 2010; Tales from Facebook, 2011; Weinachten: das globale Fest, 2011; (with S. Woodward) Blue Jeans: the art of the ordinary, 2012; (with M. Madianou) Migration and New Media: transnational families, 2012; Consumption and its Consequences, 2012; (ed with H. Horst) Digital Anthropology, 2012; (with J. Sinanan) Webcam, 2014; Social Media in an English Village, 2016; (jtly) How The World Changed Social Media, 2016; (with J. Sinanan) Visualising Facebook, 2017; The Comfort of People, 2017. *Address:* Department of Anthropology, University College London, 14 Taviton Street, WC1H 0BW.

**MILLER, Ven. Darren Noel;** Archdeacon of Ashford, since 2018; *b* Colchester, 27 Oct. 1967; *m* 2005, Susan; one *s* one *d*. *Educ:* Birmingham Univ. (BSocSc 1989); Coll. of the Resurrection, Mirfield; Chichester Theol Coll. (BTh 1995). Ordained deacon, 1995, priest, 1996; Curate: St Gabriel, Weoley Castle, 1995–98; All Saints, Shard End, 1998–2000; Vicar, St Cuthbert of Lindisfarne, Castle Vale, 2000–06; Area Dean, Sutton Coldfield, 2004–06; Team Rector, Cheam, 2006–18; Area Dean, Sutton, 2013–18. Hon. Canon, Southwark Cathedral, 2016–18. *Recreations:* family time, walking, watching sport especially American Football. *Address:* The Archdeaconry, Pett Lane, Charing, Ashford, Kent TN27 0DL.

**MILLER, David;** journalist and author; columnist: Daily Telegraph, 1997–2009; Daily Express, 2010–12; Sport Intern, since 2012; Chief Sports Correspondent, The Times, 1983–97; *b* 1 March 1935; *er s* of Wilfred Miller and Everilda Miller (*née* Milne-Redhead); *m* 1957, Marita Marjorie Malyon; one *s* one *d*. *Educ:* Charterhouse; Peterhouse, Cambridge (Nat. Sci. Tripos; CUAFC *v* Oxford, 1954–55). Sub-editor, The Times, 1956–59; Sports Correspondent: Daily Telegraph, 1960–73; Sunday Telegraph, 1961–73; Chief Sports Corresp., Daily Express, 1973–82. Has covered 25 Summer and Winter Olympic Games and 14 Football World Cups, attended 62 FA Cup Finals, 450 England football internationals and 51 Wimbledon Championships. Member: Press Commn of IAAF, 1988–2004; FIFA Press Commn, 1993–97. Chm., Sports Writers' Assoc. of GB, 1981–84; Mem., Internat. Soc. of Olympic Historians, 1993–. Sports Writer of Year Award, What the Papers Say, 1986; Doug Gardner Services to Journalism Award, Sports Writers' Assoc., 2001; FIFA Centenary Jules Rimet Award, 2004; Vikelas Award, Internat. Soc. of Olympic Historians, 2015; Hall of Fame, Olympic Journalists Assoc., 2015. *Publications:* Father of Football: biography of Sir Matt Busby, 1970; World Cup, 1970; World Cup, 1974; The Argentina Story, 1978; Cup Magic, 1981; (with Sebastian Coe) Running Free, 1981; The World to Play For, 1982; Coming Back, 1984; England's Last Glory, 1986, updated 1996, 2006, 2014; Sports Writers' Eye (anthology), 1989; Stanley Matthews, 1990; Born to Run, 1992; (jtly) History of IAAF, 1992; Olympic Revolution: biography of Juan Antonio Samaranch, 1992 (trans. 8 langs); Our Sporting Times, 1996; (co-author) Opus: a history of Arsenal FC, 2007; (jtly) Olympic Guardians (1896–2010): biography of eight IOC presidents, 2010 (trans. French); (jtly) Centenary History, IAAF, 2012; (jtly) World History of Relays, IAAF, 2014; Korean Olympic Icon: Kim Un Yong's resilient odyssey, 2019; Official IOC books: Seoul '88; Albertville '92; Lillehammer '94; Atlanta '96; Nagano '98; Athens to Athens: official history, 1894–2004, of the International Olympic Committee and the Olympic Games, 2003, 6th edn as Athens to Pyeongchang, 1894–2018, 2018. *Recreations:* sailing, reading. *E:* dmiller2@btconnect.com. *Clubs:* Royal Thames Yacht; Hawks (Cambridge); Achilles; Corinthian Casuals Football; Pegasus Football (Oxford).

**MILLER, Prof. David Andrew Barclay,** FRS 1995; W. M. Keck Foundation Professor of Electrical Engineering, since 1997 (Professor of Electrical Engineering, since 1996), and Co-Director, Stanford Photonics Research Centre, since 1999, Stanford University; *b* 19 Feb. 1954; *s* of Matthew Barclay Miller and Martha Sanders Miller (*née* Dalling); *m* 1976, Patricia Elizabeth Gillies; one *s* one *d*. *Educ:* St Andrews Univ. (BSc Hons 1976); Heriot-Watt Univ. (PhD Phys 1979). FIEEE 1995. Res. Associate, 1979, Lectr, 1980–81, Heriot-Watt Univ.; Technical Staff, 1981–87, Head of Advanced Photonic Res. Dept, 1987–96, AT&T Bell subseq. Bell, Laboratories, Holmdel, NJ; Dir, E. L. Ginzton Lab., 1997–2006, Dir, Solid State and Photonics Lab., 1997–2009, Stanford Univ. Pres., IEEE Lasers and Electro-Optics Soc., 1995. Fellow: Amer. Phys. Soc.; Optical Soc. of America (Adolph Lomb Medal, 1986; R. W. Wood Prize, 1988); Corresp. FRSE 2002. MNAS 2008; Mem., NAE, 2010. Internat. Prize in Optics, Internat. Commn for Optics, 1991; Third Millennium Medal, IEEE, 2000. Hon. Dr Natural and Applied Scis, Free Univ. Brussels, 1997; Hon. DEng Heriot-Watt, 2003. *Publications:* Quantum Mechanics for Scientists and Engineers, 2009; numerous papers in learned jls. *Recreation:* clarinet and saxophone playing. *Address:* Ginzton Laboratory, 348 Via Pueblo Mall, Stanford University, Stanford, CA 94305–4088, USA. *T:* (650) 7230111; 815 San Francisco Court, Stanford, CA 94305, USA.

**MILLER, Prof. David Leslie,** DPhil; FBA 2002; Professor of Political Theory, University of Oxford, since 2002; Fellow in Social and Political Theory, Nuffield College, Oxford, since 1979; *b* 8 March 1946; *s* of Leslie Miller and Alice (*née* Renfrew); *m* 1982, Susan Deborah Hersh (marr. diss. 2009); two *s* one *d*. *Educ:* Canford Sch.; Selwyn Coll., Cambridge (BA, MA); Balliol Coll., Oxford (BPhil, DPhil 1974). Lecturer in Politics: Univ. of Lancaster, 1969–76; UEA, 1976–79; Jun. Proctor, Univ. of Oxford, 1988–89. Vis. Prof. of Law and Philosophy, Queen's Univ., Ont, 2016–. *Publications:* Social Justice, 1976; Philosophy and Ideology in Hume's Political Thought, 1981; (with L. Siedentop) The Nature of Political Theory, 1983; Anarchism, 1984; (jtly) The Blackwell Encyclopaedia of Political Thought, 1986; Market, State and Community: theoretical foundations of market socialism, 1989; Liberty, 1991; (with M. Walzer) Pluralism, Justice and Equality, 1995; On Nationality, 1995; Principles of Social Justice, 1999; Citizenship and National Identity, 2000; (with S. Hashmi) Boundaries and Justice: diverse ethical perspectives, 2001; Political Philosophy: a very short introduction, 2003; National Responsibility and Global Justice, 2007; Justice for Earthlings, 2013; Strangers in Our Midst: the political philosophy of immigration, 2016. *Recreations:* tennis, hiking, theatre, music. *Address:* Nuffield College, Oxford OX1 1NF. *T:* (01865) 278569, *Fax:* (01865) 278621. *E:* david.miller@nuffield.ox.ac.uk.

**MILLER, Prof. David Louis,** MD; FRCP, FFPH; Professor of Public Health Medicine, St Mary's Hospital Medical School, University of London, 1983–95, now Emeritus Professor; *b* 16 Sept. 1930; *s* of John Henry Charles Miller and Muriel (*née* Rogers); *m* 1955, Wendy Joy Clark; three *s* one *d*. *Educ:* The Leys, Cambridge (Exhibnr); Peddie Sch., Hightstown, NJ, USA (Schol.); Clare Coll., Cambridge (BA 1952, MA 1955; MB, BChir 1955; MD 1965); St Thomas's Hosp. Med. Sch. (Scholar). DPH 1964; FRCP 1978 (MRCP 1973); FFPH (FFCM 1972). House Officer, St Thomas' Hosp., 1956–57; MO, RAF, 1957–60; Research Asst, RPMS, 1960–62; Epidemiologist, PHLS, 1962–71; US Public Health Service Internat. Res. Fellow, Johns Hopkins Sch. of Hygiene and Public Health, Md, 1965–66; Prof. of Community Medicine, Middlesex Hosp. Med. Sch., 1972–82. Hon. Sen. Res. Fellow, UMDS of Guy's and St Thomas' Hosp., then GKT, 1995–2002. Aneurin Bevan Meml Fellowship, Govt of India, 1981. Pres., Sect. Epidemiology, RSocMed, 1986–88; Acad. Registrar, FPHM, RCP, 1989–94. Life Mem., Soc. of Scholars, Johns Hopkins Univ., 1983. President: Central YMCA, 1986–2002 (Chm., 1977–99); Metropolitan Region of YMCAs, 2001–09. Gold Order Red Triangle, YMCA, 2013. *Publications:* (jtly) Lecture Notes on Epidemiology and Public Health Medicine, 1975, 5th edn 2004; Epidemiology of Diseases, 1982; pubns on epidemiology, esp. respiratory infections, vaccines, HIV and health services. *Recreations:* walking, music, youth and community. *Club:* Royal Society of Medicine.

*See also* R. C. W. Miller.

**MILLER, David Nathan; His Honour Judge David Miller;** a Circuit Judge, since 2017; *b* London, 22 May 1961; *s* of Mathew and Phyliss Miller; *m* 1989, Elizabeth Anne Strutt; two *s*. *Educ:* Hasmonean Sch., Hendon; King's Coll. London (LLB Hons 1983); Inns of Court Sch. of Law; Coll. of Law. Called to the Bar, Middle Temple, 1984; admitted as solicitor, 1988; a Dep. Dist Judge (Magistrates' Courts), 2006–17; a Recorder, Wales Circuit, 2009–17. *Recreations:* music festivals, concerts, running, walking, travel. *Address:* Woolwich Crown Court, 2 Belmarsh Road, SE28 0EY. *T:* (020) 8312 7000.

**MILLER, His Honour David Quentin;** a Circuit Judge, 1987–2000; *b* 22 Oct. 1936; *s* of Alfred Bowen Badger and Mair Angharad Evans. *Educ:* Ellesmere Coll., Shropshire; London Sch. of Econs and Pol Science, London Univ. (LLB Hons 1956). Called to the Bar, Middle Temple, 1958; admitted Barrister and Solicitor of the Supreme Court of NZ, 1959. In practice, SE Circuit, 1960–82; Metropolitan Stipendiary Magistrate, 1982–87; a Recorder, 1986–87. *Recreations:* history, walking, gardening, art, music, Trollope Society. *Address:* Highfields, Bullinghope, Hereford HR2 8EB. *T:* (01432) 273995.

**MILLER, Sir Donald (John),** Kt 1990; FRSE, FREng, FIMechE, FIET; Chairman, ScottishPower (formerly South of Scotland Electricity Board), 1982–92; *b* 9 Feb. 1927; *s* of John Miller and Maud (*née* White); *m* 1973, Fay Glendinning Herriot; one *s* two *d*. *Educ:* Banchory Academy; Univ. of Aberdeen (BScEng). FEng 1981. Metropolitan Vickers, 1947–53; British Electricity Authority, 1953–55; Preece, Cardew and Rider (Consulting Engrs), 1955–66; Chief Engr, North of Scotland Hydro-Electric Bd, 1966–74; Dir of Engrg, then Dep. Chm., SSEB, 1974–82. Chairman: Premium Trust, 1993–98; Nat. Cycle Network Steering Cttee, 1995–2001. Chm., Power Div., IEE, 1979. Hon. Mem., British Nuclear Energy Soc., 1989. Hon. MIES 2015. DUniv Strathclyde, 1992; Hon. DSc Aberdeen, 1997. *Publications:* papers to IEE. *Recreations:* reading, gardening, sailing.

**MILLER, (Dorothy) Cheryl,** CBE 2002; Chief Executive (formerly Head of Paid Service), East Sussex County Council, 1994–2010; Managing Director, Cheryl Miller Associates Ltd, since 2011; *b* 31 Aug. 1954; *d* of Sidney Radcliffe and Dorothy (*née* Ainsworth); *m* 1976, Graham Edwin Miller; one *s* one *d*. *Educ:* Preston Park Sch., Lancs; Preston Sixth Form

Coll.; Manchester Univ. (BA Hons). Admin. Trainee, CSD, 1975–77; HEO(D) and Asst Private Sec. to Lord Privy Seal and Leader of House of Lords, 1977–78; Personnel Policy Br., CSD, 1979–80; Mem., PM's Advr on Efficiency (Lord Rayner) Scrutiny Team, 1980; Cabinet Office: Head, CS Policy on Retirement and Redundancy Conduct and Discipline Br., 1980–84; Head, Constitutional Br., Machinery of Govt Div., 1984–85; Asst Dir, then Dep. Dir, then Hd, CSSB, 1986–90; Head, Staff Develt, DTI, 1991; County Personnel Officer, 1991–93 and Head, Exec. Office, 1992–93, E Sussex CC. Member: Royal Commn on Envmtl Pollution, 2000–03; Stakeholder Gp, Foresight Flood and Coastal Defence Project, OST, 2003–04; Geographic Inf. Panel, ODPM, later DCLG, 2005–08. Non-executive Director: Sussex Enterprise, 1994–2002; Wired Sussex, 1999–2002. Mem., SEEDA Adv. Council, 1998–2004. Chm., ACCE, 2000–01; Pres., SOLACE, 2004–05 (Vice-Pres., 2002–04). Chairman: E Sussex Youth Offending Bd, 2000–10; E Sussex Drug and Alcohol Action Team, 2000–06; Wokingham Improvement Bd, 2009–10; Slough Improvement Bd, 2011–14; Board Member: E Sussex Economic Partnership, 1996–2005; E Sussex Strategic Partnership, 2001–06; Brighton Univ., 2010–16 (Chairman: Staff Appeals Cttee, 2012–16; Audit Cttee, 2014–15; Finance and Infrastructure Cttee, 2015–16; Remuneration Cttee, 2015–16; Dep. Chm., Bd of Govs, 2015–16). Trustee and Dir, Hastings Academies Trust, 2011–16 (Chairman: Audit Cttee, 2014–15; Remuneration Cttee, 2015–16); Mem., SE Council, Prince's Trust, 2011–13. *Recreations:* theatre, music, literature, women's equality issues.

**MILLER, Very Rev. Geoffrey Vincent;** Dean of Newcastle, since 2018; *b* 26 Jan. 1956; *s* of late Harold and Vera Miller; *m* 1993, Elaine; one *s*. *Educ:* Sharston High Sch., Manchester; Durham Univ. (BEd 1978); St John's Coll., Nottingham (DPS 1983); Newcastle Univ. (MA with distinction 1994). Ordained deacon, 1983, priest, 1984; Curate, Jarrow, 1983–86; Team Vicar, St Aidan and St Luke, Billingham, 1986–92; Diocesan Urban Develt Officer, Dio. Durham, 1991–99; Community Chaplain, Stockton-on-Tees, 1992–94; Priest-in-charge, 1994–96, Vicar, 1996–99, St Cuthbert, Darlington; Diocesan Urban Officer and Residentiary Canon, St Nicholas Cathedral, Newcastle upon Tyne, 1999–2005; Archdeacon of Northumberland, 2005–18. Chm., British Cttee, French Protestant Industrial Mission, 2000–. *Recreation:* looking on the brighter side. *Address:* 26 Mitchell Avenue, Newcastle upon Tyne NE2 3LA. *T:* (0191) 273 8245, *Fax:* (0191) 226 0286. *E:* g.miller@newcastle.anglican.org.

**MILLER, Rt Rev. Harold Creeth;** Bishop of Down and Dromore, 1997–2019; *b* 23 Feb. 1950; *s* of Harold Miller and Violet (*née* McGinley); *m* 1978, Elizabeth Adelaide Harper; two *s* two *d*. *Educ:* Trinity Coll., Dublin (MA); Nottingham Univ. (BA Hons Theol.); St John's Theol Coll., Nottingham (DPS). Ordained deacon, 1976, priest, 1977; Asst Curate, St Nicholas, Carrickfergus, 1976–79; Dir of Extension Studies and Chaplain, St John's Coll., Nottingham, 1979–84; Chaplain, QUB, 1984–89; Rector of Carrigrohane Union of Parishes, Cork, 1989–97. Hon. DD Nashotah Hse Theol Seminary, Wisconsin, 2016. *Publications:* Anglican Worship Today, 1980; Whose Office? daily prayer for the people of God, 1982; Finding a Personal Rule of Life, 1984, 2nd edn 1987; New Ways in Worship, 1986; Making an Occasion of It, 1994; Outreach in the Local Church, 2000; The Desire of our Soul, 2004; (contrib.) The Oxford Guide to the Book of Common Prayer, 2006; Week of All Weeks, 2015; (ed) Thanks and Praise, 2015; articles in Search. *Recreations:* music, travel, phillumeny.

**MILLER, Iain George;** Partner, Kingsley Napley LLP, since 2016; *b* Sunderland, 16 March 1963; *s* of late George Miller and of Margaret Miller; *m* 1990, Maria Frances Lewis (*see* Rt Hon. M. F. L. Miller); two *s* one *d*. *Educ:* Earl Haig Secondary Sch., Toronto; Loughborough Grammar Sch.; London Sch. of Econs and Pol Sci. (LLB Hons). Admitted as solicitor, 1988; articled clerk, 1986–88, Asst Solicitor, 1988–91, Stephenson Harwood; Asst Solicitor, Jaques & Lewis, 1991–94; Asst Solicitor, 1994–95, Partner, 1995–2006, Wright Son & Pepper; Partner, Bevan Brittan LLP, 2006–16. Chair, Assoc. of Regulatory and Disciplinary Lawyers, 2018– (Vice-Chair, 2016–18). *Publications:* Gen. Ed. (with A. Hopper, QC), Cordery on Legal Services, looseleaf, 2011–16, sole Gen. Ed., 2016–; Butterworths Guide to the Legal Services Act 2007, 2009; (jtly) Alternative Business Structures, 2012. *Recreations:* children, wife, Sunderland AFC and managing the stress caused by each of them. *Address:* Kingsley Napley LLP, Knights Quarter, 14 St John's Lane, EC1M 4AJ. *T:* (020) 7566 5273. *E:* imiller@kingsleynapley.co.uk.

**MILLER, Ian Harper Lawson;** Sheriff of Glasgow and Strathkelvin at Glasgow, since 2001; *b* 16 Jan. 1954; *s* of late Henry Young Miller and Jean Watson Harper Miller (*née* Lyall); *m* 1987, Sheila Matthews Howie; one *s* three *d*. *Educ:* Robert Gordon's Coll., Aberdeen; Univ. of Aberdeen (MA Hons Hist. 1976; LLB 1978). Solicitor, 1980–91; Partner, Burnett & Reid, Solicitors, Aberdeen, 1986–91; called to the Scottish Bar, 1992; Temp. Sheriff, 1998; Sheriff of Grampian Highland and Islands at Aberdeen, 1998–2001. Pt-time Tutor, Dept of Scots Law, Univ. of Aberdeen, 1981–91. Mem., Sheriff Court Rules Council, 1987–91. A Convener, Presbyterian Commn, Ch of Scot., 2013–. Mem. Council, St George's Sch. for Girls, Edinburgh, 2015–. *Recreations:* reading, music, family life, golf. *Address:* Sheriff's Chambers, Glasgow Sheriff Court, 1 Carlton Place, Glasgow G5 9DA. *T:* (0141) 429 8888; 25 Wester Coates Avenue, Edinburgh EH12 5LS. *T:* (0131) 346 1853. *Clubs:* Royal Northern and University (Aberdeen); Royal Aberdeen Golf.

**MILLER, Dr Jacques Francis Albert Pierre,** AC 2003 (AO 1981); FRS 1970; FAA 1970; Head of Experimental Pathology Unit, Walter and Eliza Hall Institute of Medical Research, 1966–96; Professor of Experimental Immunology, University of Melbourne, 1990–97, now Emeritus; *b* 2 April 1931; French parents; *m* 1956, Margaret Denise Houen. *Educ:* St Aloysius' Coll., Sydney. BSc (Med.) 1953, MB, BS 1955, Sydney; PhD 1960, DSc 1965, London; BA Melbourne 1985. Sen. Scientist, Chester Beatty Res. Inst., London, 1960–66; Reader, Exper. Pathology, Univ. of London, 1965–66. Croonian Lectr, Royal Soc., 1992. For. Mem., Académie Royale de Médecine de Belgique, 1969; For. Associate, US Nat. Acad. Scis, 1982. Hon. MD Sydney, 1986. Langer-Teplitz Cancer Research Award (USA), 1965; Gairdner Foundn Award (Canada), 1966; Encyclopaedia Britannica (Australia) Award, 1966; Scientific Medal of Zoological Soc. of London, 1966; Burnet Medal, Austr. Acad. of Scis, 1971; Paul Ehrlich Award, Germany, 1974; Rabbi Shai Shacknai Meml Prize, Hadassah Med. Sch., Jerusalem, 1978; Saint-Vincent Internat. Prize for Med. Res., Italy, 1983; first Sandoz Immunology Prize, 1990; first Medawar Prize, Transplantation Soc., 1990; J. Allyn Taylor Internat. Prize for Medicine, John Robarts Res. Inst., 1995; Florey-Faulding Medal and Prize, Australian Inst. of Pol Sci., 2000; Copley Medal, Royal Soc., 2001; PM's Prize for Science, Australia, 2003; Japan Prize for Medicine and Medicinal Sci., 2018. *Publications:* over 400 papers in scientific jls and several chapters in books, mainly dealing with thymus and immunity. *Recreations:* music, photography, art, literature. *Address:* Walter and Eliza Hall Institute of Medical Research, 1G Royal Parade, Parkville, Victoria 3050, Australia. *T:* (3) 93452555.

**MILLER, James,** CBE 1986; Chairman, Miller Group Ltd (formerly James Miller & Partners), 1970–99; *b* 1 Sept. 1934; *s* of Sir James Miller, GBE, and Lady Ella Jane Miller; *m* 1st, 1959, Kathleen Dewar; one *s* two *d*; 2nd, 1969, Iris Lloyd-Webb; one *d*. *Educ:* Edinburgh Acad.; Harrow Sch.; Balliol Coll., Oxford (MA Engrg Sci.). Joined James Miller & Partners, 1958; Board Mem., 1960; Man. Dir, 1970–91. Director: Life Assoc. of Scotland, 1981–93; British Linen Bank, 1983–99 (Chm., 1997–99); Britoil, 1988–90; Bank of Scotland, 1993–2000; Mem., Scottish Adv. Bd, British Petroleum, 1990–2001. Pres., FCEC, 1990–93 (Chm., 1985–86). Dir, Royal Scottish Nat. Orchestra, 1996–2002 (Chm., 1997–2002). Chm., Court, Heriot-Watt Univ., 1990–96. Hon. Consul for Austria, 1994–2003; Dean, Consular Corps in Edinburgh, Leith, 1999–2001. *Recreation:* shooting. *Address:* Flat 71, 1 Donaldson Drive, Edinburgh EH12 5FA. *T:* (0131) 337 2289. *Club:* City Livery.

**MILLER, (James) Christopher,** FCA; Executive Vice-Chairman, Melrose plc, since 2019 (Chairman, 2003–19); *b* Birmingham, 25 Sept. 1951; *s* of James and Florence Miller; *m* 1974, Monica Stump; one *s* two *d*. *Educ:* Downside Sch.; Brasenose Coll., Oxford (MA Hons PPE). FCA 1977. Coopers & Lybrand, 1973–82; Associate Dir, Hanson plc, 1982–88; Chief Exec., Wassall plc, 1988–2000. *Recreations:* fishing, golf, ski-ing, shooting. *Address:* Melrose plc, Leconfield House, Curzon Street, W1J 5JA. *Clubs:* Boodle's; Sunningdale Golf, Royal St George's Golf, Royal Wimbledon Golf.

**MILLER, James Francis Xavier;** Headmaster, Royal Grammar School, Newcastle upon Tyne, 1994–2008; *b* 3 March 1950; *yr s* of late Lt-Col John Francis Miller and Barbara Mary Miller (*née* Cooke); *m* 1976, Ruth Ellen Rowland (*née* Macbeth); two *s*. *Educ:* Douai Sch.; Merton Coll., Oxford (BA Classical Mods and PPE; MA). Winchester College: Asst Master, 1972–89; Hd of Econs, 1978–82; Housemaster, 1982–89; Headmaster, Framlingham Coll., 1989–94. Chm., Amazing Grades Ltd (formerly study-links.com), 2000–09. Councillor, Winchester CC, 1976–83 (Chm., Health and Works Cttee, 1979–82). Governor: Hereford Sixth Form Coll., 2009– (Chm., 2019–); King Edward's Sch. and King Edward's High Sch., Birmingham, 2009–12. Member: Eardisland Parish Council, 2011–14; Cttee, Hereford Historic Churches Trust, 2009–13. Trustee, Hereford Music Pool, 2014– (Chm., 2017–). FRSA 1994. *Recreations:* opera, crosswords, theatre, trying to play the sax less badly, malt whisky, bridge, photographing Herefordshire's historic churches. *Address:* Orchard Cottage, Eardisland, Leominster, Herefordshire HR6 9BJ. *T:* (01544) 388454.

**MILLER, Jane Elizabeth Mackay;** QC 2000; **Her Honour Judge Miller;** a Circuit Judge, since 2010; *b* Rochester, Kent, 7 March 1956; *d* of Keith Mackay Miller and Edna Miller (*née* Rawlings); *m* 1982; three *s*. *Educ:* Maidstone Grammar Sch. for Girls; Univ. of Bristol (LLB). Called to the Bar, Inner Temple, 1979; Recorder, 1998–2010; Jt Hd of Chambers, 3 Pump Court, Temple, 2005–10. *Recreations:* gardening, cooking, violin playing, tennis, ski-ing. *Address:* Winchester Combined Court Centre, The Law Courts, Winchester, Hants SO23 9DL. *T:* (01962) 814100.

**MILLER, Very Rev. John Dunlop;** Minister, Castlemilk East Parish Church, Glasgow, 1971–2007; Moderator of the General Assembly of the Church of Scotland, 2001–02; *b* 11 Nov. 1941; *s* of Rev. Ian Robert Newton Miller and Dr Jessie Sinclair Miller (*née* Dunlop); *m* 1968, Mary Glen Robertson; one *s* two *d*. *Educ:* Kilmarnock Acad.; Merchant Taylors' Sch.; Corpus Christi Coll., Oxford (BA 1964); New Coll., Edinburgh (BD 1967); Union Theol Seminary, NY (STM 1970). Ordained 1971. Hon. DD Glasgow, 2001. *Publications:* Ministry and Mission in Working Class Areas, 1976; Buildings and Mission in Working Class Areas, 1986; Reflections on the Beatitudes, 2002; Silent Heroes, 2004; A Simple Life, 2014. *Recreation:* cycling. *Address:* 98 Kirkcaldy Road, Glasgow G41 4LD.

**MILLER, John Harmsworth,** CBE 2006; architect in private practice; *b* 18 Aug. 1930; *s* of Charles Miller and Brenda Miller (*née* Borrett); *m* 1st, 1957, Patricia Rhodes (marr. diss. 1975; she *d* 2015); two *d*; 2nd, 1985, Su Rogers. *Educ:* Charterhouse; Architectural Assoc. Sch. of Architecture (AA Dip. Hons 1957). ARIBA 1959. Private practice, Colquhoun and Miller, 1961–90, John Miller and Partners, 1990–; works include: Forest Gate High Sch., West Ham (Newham), 1965; Chemistry Labs, Royal Holloway Coll., London Univ., 1970; Melrose Activity Centre, Milton Keynes Develt Corp. (Commendation, Steel Awards, 1975); Pillwood House, Feock, Cornwall (RIBA Regional Award, 1975; Listed Grade II*, 2017); housing, Caversham Road/Gaisford Street, Camden, 1978; single person flats, Hornsey Lane, Haringey, 1980; Oldbrook, Milton Keynes (Silver Award, Architectural Design, 1987; Highly Commended, Housing Design and Civic Trust Awards); Whitechapel Art Gall. extension, 1985 (RIBA Regl Award, 1988; Civic Trust Award, 1988); Gulbenkian Gall. for RCA, 1989; Stevens Bldg for RCA, and Nomura Gall. and bookshop for Tate Gall., 1991; Queen's building, UEA (RIBA Nat. Award) and new 20th century galls for Nat. Portrait Gall., 1993; Elizabeth Fry building, UEA, 1995 (RIBA Regl Award); Ramphal building, Warwick Univ., 1996; Serpentine Gall., 1998; Shackleton Meml Library, Scott Polar Res. Inst., Cambridge Univ., 1999 (RIBA Regl Award); Tate Gall. Centenary Develt for Tate Britain, 2001 (RIBA Nat. Award); Library, Newnham Coll., Cambridge, and Courtyard Develt, Fitzwilliam Mus., Cambridge, 2004 (RIBA Nat. Award, 2005); Playfair Project, Nat. Galls of Scotland, 2004; Brindley Arts Centre, 2005 (RIBA Nat. Award; Civic Trust Award); Business Sch., Warwick Univ., 2008. Exhibition Designs: Dada and Surrealism Reviewed, 1978; Ten Modern Houses, 1980; Picasso's Picassos, 1981; Adolf Loos, 1985; Matisse Picasso, 2002; Anthony Caro, 2006. Tutor: RCA and AA, 1961–73; Cambridge Sch. of Arch., 1969–70; Prof. of Environmental Design, RCA, 1975–85, Fellow 1976, Hon. Fellow, 1985. FRSA 1985. Vis. Prof., Sch. of Arch., UC Dublin, 1985. Visiting Critic: Cornell Univ. Sch. of Arch., Ithaca, 1966, 1968 and 1971; Princeton Univ. Sch. of Arch., NJ, 1970; Dublin Univ. Sch. of Arch., 1972–73; Univ. of Toronto, 1985. Trustee, De La Warr Pavilion, Bexhill, 2002–08. European Prize for Architecture, 1988. *Publications:* Custom and Innovation, 2009; contribs to architect. jls. *Address:* Apt 10, The Beauchamp Building, Brookes Market, EC1N 7SX. *T:* (020) 7242 2404.

**MILLER, Most Rev. John Michael;** *see* Vancouver, Archbishop of, (RC).

**MILLER, Jonathan;** Foreign Affairs Correspondent, Bangkok, Channel 4 News, since 2018; *b* 21 Oct. 1962; *s* of John Miller and Sheila Rankin; *m* 1994, Cornelia Dobb; one *d*. *Educ:* Monkton Combe Sch., Bath; Durham Univ. (BA Hons Geog.). Journalist, South mag., 1986–89; freelance journalist, SE Asia, 1989–92; journalist, BBC World Service, 1992–94; Indochina Corresp., 1994–95, Bangkok Corresp., 1995–97, BBC; ind. film-maker, 1997–2003; Foreign Affairs Corresp., 2003–15, Asia Corresp., 2015–18, Channel 4 News. Specialist Journalist of the Year, 2006, Internat. News Award, 2006, RTS; TV News Award, Amnesty Internat., 2006 and 2009; Internat. News Coverage Award (Lebanon), 2007, (Congo) 2009, RTS; Broadcast Journalist of the Year Award, One World, 2009. *Publications:* Duterte Harry: fire and fury in the Philippines, 2018. *Recreations:* travelling, photography, cooking curry, mountain walking. *Address:* Channel 4 News, ITN, 200 Gray's Inn Road, WC1X 8XZ. *T:* (020) 7430 4606. *E:* jonathan.miller@itn.co.uk.

**MILLER, Sir Jonathan (Wolfe),** Kt 2002; CBE 1983; stage director, writer and broadcaster; *b* 21 July 1934; *s* of late Emanuel Miller, DPM, FRCP; *m* 1956, Helen Rachel Collet; two *s* one *d*. *Educ:* St Paul's Sch.; St John's Coll., Cambridge (MB, BCh 1959). Hon. Fellow 1982. FRCP 1997; FRCPE 1998. Research Fellow: in Hist. of Med., UCL, 1970–73; in Neuropsychol., Univ. of Sussex. Associate Director, Nat. Theatre, 1973–75; Artistic Dir, Old Vic, 1988–90. Mem., Arts Council, 1975–76. Vis. Prof. in Drama, Westfield Coll., London, 1977; Fellow, UCL, 1981–. Co-author and appeared in Beyond the Fringe, 1961–64; stage directing in London and NY, 1965–67; *television:* Editor, BBC Monitor, 1965; directed films for BBC TV (incl. Alice in Wonderland), 1966; Exec. Producer, BBC Shakespeare series, 1979–81; writer and presenter, TV series, including:

The Body in Question, 1978; Madness, 1991; Opera Works, 1997; Jonathan Miller's Brief History of Disbelief, 2004; *radio*: Self-Made Things (series), Radio 4, 2005; *stage*: School for Scandal, 1968, The Seagull, 1969, The Malcontent, 1973, Nottingham Playhouse; King Lear, The Merchant of Venice, Old Vic, 1970; The Tempest, Mermaid, 1970; Hamlet, Arts Theatre, Cambridge, 1970; Danton's Death, 1971, School for Scandal, 1972, Measure for Measure, 1974, Marriage of Figaro, 1974, The Freeway, 1974, Nat. Theatre; The Taming of the Shrew, 1972, The Seagull, 1973, Chichester; Family Romances, 1974, The Importance of Being Earnest, 1975, All's Well That Ends Well, 1975, Greenwich; Three Sisters, Cambridge, 1976; She Would If She Could, Greenwich, 1979; Long Day's Journey Into Night, Haymarket, 1986; The Taming of the Shrew, RSC, Stratford, 1987, Barbican, 1988; (jtly adapted and directed) The Emperor, Royal Court, 1987 (televised, 1988); Andromache, One Way Pendulum, Bussy D'Ambois, The Tempest, Candide, Old Vic, 1988; King Lear, The Liar, Old Vic, 1989; The Way of the World, Gate Theatre, Dublin, 1992; A Midsummer Night's Dream, Almeida, 1996; As You Like It, Gate Theatre, Dublin, 2000; The Cherry Orchard, Crucible, Sheffield, 2007; Hamlet, Tobacco Factory, Bristol, 2008; Rutherford & Son, nat. tour, 2013; King Lear, Viaduct, Halifax, 2015; *film*: Take a Girl Like You, 1970; *operas*: Arden Must Die, Sadler's Wells Theatre, 1974; The Cunning Little Vixen, Glyndebourne, 1975 and 1977; English National Opera: The Marriage of Figaro, 1978; The Turn of the Screw, 1979, 1991; Arabella, 1980; Otello, 1981; Rigoletto, 1982, 1985, 1995, 2017; Don Giovanni, 1985; The Magic Flute, 1986; Tosca, 1986; The Mikado, 1986, 1988, 1993, 2004, 2006; The Barber of Seville, 1987, 2006, 2013, 2015, 2017; Der Rosenkavalier, 1994; Carmen, 1995; La Traviata, 1996; The Elixir of Love, 2010, 2011; La Bohème, 2013; Kent Opera: Così Fan Tutte, 1975; Rigoletto, 1975; Orfeo, 1976; Eugene Onegin, 1977; La Traviata, 1979; Falstaff, 1980, 1981; Fidelio, 1982, 1983, 1988; La Scala: La Fanciulla del West, 1991; Manon Lescaut, 1992; Maggio Musicale, Florence: Don Giovanni, 1990; Così fan Tutte, Tosca, 1991; Marriage of Figaro, 1992; Idomeneo, 1996; Metropolitan Opera, New York: Katya Kabanova, 1991; Pelléas et Mélisande, 1995; Marriage of Figaro, Vienna State Opera, 1991; Roberto Devereux, Monte Carlo, 1992; Die Gezeichneten, Zürich, 1992; Maria Stuarda, Monte Carlo, 1993; The Secret Marriage, Opera North, 1993; Falstaff, Zürich, 1993; L'Incoronazione di Poppea, Glimmerglass Opera, 1994; Così fan tutti, Royal Opera House, and Rome, 1995; The Beggar's Opera, Wilton's Music Hall, 1999; Don Pasquale, Royal Opera House, 2004 and 2010; La Clemenza di Tito, Zürich, 2005; St Matthew Passion, Brooklyn Acad. of Music, 2006; *exhibitions*: Mirror Image: Jonathan Miller on reflection, Nat. Gall., 1998; Metal, wood and paper constructions, Boundary Gall., 2003; Jonathan Miller Works from 1962–2013, Cross Street Gall., 2013. Hon. Fellow, RA, 1991; Hon. DLitt: Leicester, 1981; Cambridge, 1996. Silver Medal, Royal TV Soc., 1981; Albert Medal, RSA, 1990. *Publications*: McLuhan, 1971; (ed) Freud: the man, his world, his influence, 1972; The Body in Question, 1978; Subsequent Performances, 1986; (ed) The Don Giovanni Book: myths of seduction and betrayal, 1990; On Reflection, 1998. *Recreation*: deep sleep. *E*: jwmiller@btinternet.com.

**MILLER, Judith Henderson**; author and publishing consultant; *b* 16 Sept. 1951; *d* of Andrew and Bertha Cairns; *m* 1978, Martin John Miller (marr. diss. 1992; he *d* 2013); two *d*. *Educ*: Galashiels Acad.; Edinburgh Univ. (MA Hons English, 1973). Copywriter, WHT Advertising, Auckland, NZ, 1973–74; Editor, Lyle Publications, Galashiels, 1974–75; Occupational Guidance Officer, Dept of Employment, 1975–79; Man. Dir and Editor, Miller Publications, 1979–98; with Martin Miller opened Chilston Park Hotel, 1985; Man. Dir, MJM Publishing Projects, 1985–92; Co-Founder, Miller's Magazine, 1991. Television appearances include The House Detectives, The Art and Antiques Hour, The Antiques Trail, The Martha Stewart Show, Antiques Roadshow. *Publications*: Miller's Antiques and Collectables: the facts at your fingertips, 1993; Miller's Classic Motorcycles Price Guide, annually, 1993–98; Miller's Art Nouveau and Art Deco Buyer's Guide, 1995; Miller's Pine and Country Furniture Buyer's Guide, 1995; Period Kitchens, 1995; Period Fireplaces, 1995; How to Make Money out of Antiques, 1995; Period Soft Furnishings, 1996; Country Finishes and Effects, 1997; Miller's Clocks and Barometers Buyer's Guide, 1997; Wooden Houses, 1997; Care and Repair of Antiques and Collectables, 1997; The Style Sourcebook, 1998; Classic Style, 1998; Miller's Antiques Encyclopaedia, 1998; Period Details Sourcebook, 1999; A Closer Look at Antiques, 2000; Colour, 2000; Dorling Kindersley Antiques Price Guide, annually, 2003–; Collectables Price Guide, annually, 2003–; (with John Wainwright) Dorling Kindersley Collectors Guide to Costume Jewellery, 2003; Art Nouveau, 2004; Twentieth Century Glass, 2004; Arts and Crafts, 2005; Art Deco, 2005; Dorling Kindersley Furniture, 2005; Twentieth Century Roadshow, 2005; Buy, Keep or Sell, 2005; Tribal Art, 2006; Handbags, 2006; Perfume Bottles, 2006; Sixties Style, 2006; Metal Toys, 2006; Decorative Arts, 2006; Antiques Detective, 2007; with Martin Miller: Miller's Antiques Price Guide, annually 1979–98; The Antiques Directory—Furniture, 1985; Period Details, 1987; Miller's Pocket Antiques Fact File, 1988; Period Style, 1989; Understanding Antiques, 1989; Miller's Collectables Price Guide, annually 1989–98; Country Style, 1990; Miller's Collectors Cars Price Guide, annually 1991–98; Miller's Art Deco Checklist, 1991; Furniture Checklist, 1991; Period Finishes and Effects, 1992; Victorian Style, 1993. *Recreations*: antiques!, bridge. *Club*: Groucho.

**MILLER, Julian Alexander**, CB 2003; Staff Counsellor, intelligence and security agencies, since 2016; Deputy National Security Adviser, Cabinet Office, 2010–15; *b* 14 July 1955; *s* of Allan Douglas Stewart Miller and Mavis Jean Miller; *m* 1986, Roslin Mair; one *s* one *d*. *Educ*: Farnham Grammar Sch.; Sussex Univ. (BSc); Leeds Univ. (PhD 1980). Joined MoD, 1980: on loan to CSD, 1988; Private Sec. to Armed Forces Minister, 1990–92; on loan to FCO as First Sec., then Counsellor, UK Delegn to NATO, 1992–96; Hd, Resources and Programmes, Army, then Prog. Develt, 1996–99; Private Sec. to Defence Sec., 1999–2001; on loan to Cabinet Office as Chief, Assessments Staff, 2001–03; Dir Gen., Service Personnel Policy, 2003–06, Dir (formerly Dir Gen.), Resources and Plans, 2006–09, MoD; Dir, Foreign and Defence Policy, Cabinet Office, 2009–10. *Recreations*: reading, photography.

**MILLER, Kenneth William**, FCA; non-executive Director, Colt Group, since 1999 (Chairman, 2000–14); *b* 4 Feb. 1939; *s* of Albert William Miller and Winifred (*née* Ashworth); *m* 1st, 1964, Carol Susan Hislop (marr. diss. 1987); one *s* one *d*; 2nd, 1988, Jean Helen McPhail McInnes. *Educ*: Surbiton County Grammar Sch. FCA 1961. Company Sec., Hunting Associated Industries, 1965–73; Asst Finance Dir, Hunting Gp, 1969–73; Commercial Dir, E. A. Gibson & Co. Ltd, 1973–78; Hunting Petroleum Services plc: Dir, 1978–87; Man. Dir, 1987–89; Chief Exec., Hunting plc, 1989–2000. *Recreations*: reading, sport, music. *Address*: Colt Group, Unit 12, The Briars, Waterberry Lane, Waterlooville, Hants PO7 7YH. *T*: (023) 9245 1111. *Club*: Royal Automobile.

**MILLER, Leszek**; Deputy (Dem. Left Alliance) for Łódź, 1991–2005; Prime Minister of Poland, 2001–04; *b* Zyrardów, 3 July 1946; *m* 1969, Aleksandra Borowiec; one *s*. *Educ*: Higher Sch. of Social Scis, Warsaw (MPolSci.). Electrician, Enterprise of Linen industry, Zyrardów, 1963–70; became social and trade union activist, 1970; Polish United Workers' Party (PUWP): Youth Div., 1977–84; staff mem., 1988–99, Central Cttee; First Sec., Voivodeship's Cttee, 1985–88; Mem., Politburo Central Cttee, 1989–90. Minister: of Labour and Social Policy, 1993–96; and Hd, Council of Ministers' Office, 1996; of Internal Affairs and Admin, 1997. Socialdemocracy party, now Democratic Left Alliance: Gen. Sec., 1990–93; Vice-Chm., 1993–97; Chm., 1997–2001. Goodwill Ambassador, Polish Cttee, UNICEF, 2000–. Golden Cross of Merit, 1979; Kt's Cross, Polonia Restituta (Poland), 1984. *Recreations*: angling, literature.

**MILLER, Ven. Luke Jonathan**; Archdeacon of London, since 2016; Rector, St Andrew-by-the-Wardrobe with St Ann, Blackfriars, since 2016 (Priest-in-charge, 2015–16); Priest-in-charge, St Botolph Bishopsgate, 2016–18; London Area Chaplain to the Sea Cadets, since 2016; *b* Scunthorpe, 27 June 1966; *s* of Paul Richard Miller and Hilary Jane Miller; *m* 1995, Jacqueline Ann Blunden; three *s*. *Educ*: Haileybury; Sidney Sussex Coll., Cambridge (Barcroft Exhibn; Taylor Scholarship; BA 1987, MA 1991 (History Tripos)); St Stephen's House, Oxford Honour Sch. of Theol. (BA 1990, MA 1993). Ordained deacon, 1991, priest, 1992; Asst Curate, St Matthew, Oxhey, 1991–94; Asst Curate, 1994–95, Vicar, 1995–2011, St Mary the Virgin, Tottenham; Area Dean, East Haringey, 2005–11; Priest-in-charge, Holy Trinity, Winchmore Hill, 2011–12; Archdeacon of Hampstead, 2011–15. Local Vicar, Soc. of the Holy Cross, Chapter of Christ the King, 2003–12. Mem., Gen. Synod, 2015–. Chm., Faith Sector, London Resilience Forum, 2013–. Chm., Exec. Cttee, 2018–, Sec., 2018–, London Church Leaders. Member, Council: St Stephen's House, 2008– (Chm., Finance and Gen. Purposes, 2008–16); Haileybury, 2006–18. Chm., London Diocesan Bd for Schools, 2016–. Trustee: Bishopsgate Inst., 2016– (Chm., 2019); C of E Stipends Trust, 2017–; Stationers' Hall Charity, 2017–. Gov., Mulberry Primary Sch., 1996–2011 (Chair, 2001–11). Pres., Haileybury Soc., 2011. *Publications*: The Sorrow of Nature: the Way of the Cross with George Congreve and St Thérèse of Lisieux, 2014. *Recreations*: painting, reading, gardening. *Address*: The Rectory, St Andrew's House, 35 St Andrew's Hill, EC4V 5DE. *T*: (office) (020) 3837 5201. *E*: luke.miller7@btinternet.com.

**MILLER, Prof. Marcus Hay**, PhD; Professor of Economics, since 1974, and Research Associate, ESRC Centre for Competitive Advantage in the Global Economy, University of Warwick; *b* 9 Sept. 1941; *s* of J. Irvine Miller and Rose H. (*née* Moir); *m* 1967, Margaret Ellen Hummel (marr. diss.; she *d* 2001); two *d*. *Educ*: Price's Sch., Fareham, Hants; University Coll., Oxford (BA 1st Cl. PPE); Yale Univ. (Henry Fellowship, MA, PhD Econ). Lecturer, London School of Economics, 1967–76; Prof. of Economics, Univ. of Manchester, 1976–78. Economist, 1972–73, Houblon-Norman Fellow, 1981–82, Bank of England; Vis. Associate Prof. of Internat. Finance, Univ. of Chicago, 1976; Vis. Prof. of Public and Internat. Affairs, Princeton Univ., 1983; Res. Fellow, Centre for Economic Policy Res., 1983 (Co-Dir, Internat. Macroeconomics Prog., 1986–91); Vis. Fellow, Inst. for Internat. Econs, Washington, 1986. Member, Academic Panel, HM Treasury, 1976 (Chm., 1979–80); Adviser, House of Commons Select Cttee on the Treasury and Civil Service, 1980–81. Mem. Management Cttee, NIESR, 1980–91. *Publications*: joint editor: Monetary Policy and Economic Activity in West Germany, 1977; Essays on Fiscal and Monetary Policy, 1981; Targets and Indicators: a blueprint for the international co-ordination of economic policy, 1993; Exchange Rate Targets and Currency Bands 1992; The Asian Financial Crisis, 1999; articles in professional jls, mainly on domestic and internat. macroecons. *Recreations*: sailboarding, contemporary dance. *Address*: Department of Economics, University of Warwick, Coventry CV4 7AL. *E*: marcus.miller@warwick.ac.uk. *Club*: Reform.

**MILLER, Rt Hon. Maria (Frances Lewis)**; PC 2012; MP (C) Basingstoke, since 2005; *b* 26 March 1964; *d* of John and June Lewis; *m* 1990, Iain George Miller, *qv*; two *s* one *d*. *Educ*: London Sch. of Econs (BSc Hons Econs 1985). Advertising Exec., Grey Advertising, 1985–90; Advertising and Mktg Manager, Texaco, 1990–95; Director: Grey Advertising, 1995–2000; Rowland Co., then PR21, 2000–02. Shadow Minister: for Education, 2005–06; for Family Welfare incl. CSA, 2006–07; for Family, 2007–10; Parly Under-Sec. of State, DWP, 2010–12; Sec. of State for Culture, Media and Sport and Minister for Women and for Equalities, 2012–14. Chm., Women and Equalities Select Cttee, 2015–. Pres., Wolverhampton NE Cons. Assoc., 2001–05; Chm., Wimbledon Cons. Assoc., 2002–03; Dir and Trustee, CPA, 2017–. Trustee, Belarus Free Theatre, 2015–. *Recreations*: growing vegetables, my family, my dog. *Address*: House of Commons, SW1A 0AA. *T*: (020) 7219 3000. *E*: maria.miller.mp@parliament.uk.

**MILLER, Rev. Canon Paul**; Chaplain to the Queen, 2005–19; *b* 24 Feb. 1949; *s* of late Sidney George Miller and Florence Lilian Miller; *m* 1976, Lynette Jane Warren; three *s*. *Educ*: Cannock Sch., Chelsfield; Bromley Grammar Sch. for Boys; Oak Hill Theol Coll. Ordained deacon 1974, priest 1975; Assistant Curate: Upton, dio. Exeter, 1974–77; Farnborough, dio. Guildford, 1977–78; Vicar: St Luke, Torquay, 1978–86; Green Street Green and Pratts Bottom, 1986–2001; Rural Dean of Orpington, 1996–2001; Vicar of Shortlands, Bromley, 2001–12; Area Dean of Beckenham, 2009–12; Chaplain of the Isles of Scilly, 2012–15; Permission to Officiate: Dio. Canterbury, 2016–; Dio. Rochester, 2016–. Hon. Canon, Rochester, 2000–12, now Canon Emeritus; Anglican Ecumenical Borough Dean, Bromley, 2006–12. SBStJ 1984. *Recreations*: cricket, golf, football, travel, philately. *Address*: 11 Bishopswood, Kingsnorth, Ashford, Kent TN23 3RD. *T*: (01233) 365176. *E*: paulmiller@roundisland.net.

**MILLER, Air Cdre Richard Albert**, OBE 1976; FRAeS; Chairman, DGB Sterling (formerly Dinol GB) Ltd, 1998–2006; *b* 12 July 1936; *s* of Albert and Emily Kate Miller; *m* 1959, Beryl Marjorie Thompson (*d* 2010); one *s* one *d*. *Educ*: Northampton Grammar Sch.; Coll. of Art, Nottingham; Open Univ. (DipEd, BA Hons); Poly. of E London (MA, MSc). Royal Air Force, 1956–82, Pilot; Flying Duties, 1957–70; RAF Advanced Staff Course, 1970; MoD, 1971–72; OC 36 Sqn, RAF Lyneham, 1973–75; Station Comdr, RAF Benson and Dep. Captain of Queen's Flight, 1976–78; ADC to the Queen, 1976–78; RAF Diamond Jubilee Fellow, Univ. of S Calif and Fitzwilliam Coll., Cambridge, 1979; Dir, Dept of Air Warfare, RAF Coll., 1980; Dir, Air Staff Briefing, MoD, 1981–82; Dir, PR (RAF), MoD, 1982–84; retired (Air Cdre). Executive Air Weapons, BAe Inc., USA, 1985–86; Dir, Defence Procurement Management Gp, 1986–88, Dean, Continuing Educn, 1987–89, Dir, Sch. of Defence Management, 1988–95, RMCS; Dir of Strategic Mgt, Sch. of Defence Mgt, RMCS, Cranfield Univ., 1995–97. Visiting Professor: Cranfield Univ., 1997–2006; Bath Univ., 1999–2010. FCMI 1981. Freedom, City of London, 1982. QCVSA 1965, 1970. *Recreations*: French cultural and language studies, computing. *Address*: 32 Adam Court, Ravenscroft Road, Henley-on-Thames, Oxfordshire RG9 2BJ. *T*: (01491) 578281. *Clubs*: Royal Air Force; Phyllis Court (Henley-on-Thames).

**MILLER, Richard Charles William**; Chief Executive, Sentebale, since 2019; *b* 5 March 1962; *s* of Prof. David Louis Miller, *qv*; *m* 1990, Sally Gardner; three *s*. *Educ*: Leys Sch., Cambridge; Univ. of Bristol (BSc Hons Soc. Admin and Pols 1984). Catholic Agency for Overseas Development: Africa Progs Officer, 1986–92; Dep. Dir, 1992–98; S Africa Regl Rep., 1998–2003; Exec. Dir, ActionAid UK, 2004–15; Humanitarian Dir, ActionAid Internat., 2015–19. Mem., Adv. Bd, Traidcraft Exchange, 1986–89. Trustee: IVS, 1984–87; Disasters Emergency Cttee, 2004–15; ActionAid Netherlands (formerly ActionAid Inst. for Southern Africa), 2008–14; ActionAid USA, 2012–18. Gov., Downlands Sch., Hassocks, 2009–15. *Recreations*: travel, music, season ticket holder Brighton and Hove Albion FC, spending time with family, reading, tennis. *Address*: Sentebale, 17 Gresse Street, 6 Evelyn Yard Entrance, W1T 1QL. *T*: (020) 7730 0226. *E*: richard.miller@sentebale.org.

**MILLER, Richard Hugh**; QC 1995; b 1 Feb. 1953; s of Sir Stephen James Hamilton Miller, KCVO, FRCS and Lady (Heather) Miller. *Educ:* Charterhouse; Univ. of Sussex (BSc Chem. Physics). Called to the Bar, Middle Temple, 1976, Bencher, 2007 (Chm., Finance Cttee and Mem., Exec. Cttee, 2012–15); in practice at the Bar, specialising in patent matters; Hd of Chambers, Three New Square Intellectual Property, 2012–18. Chm., Intellectual Property Bar Assoc., 2005–11 (Vice-Chm., 2004–05); Member: Bar Council, 2006–11 (Member: European Cttee, 2005–11 (Co-Chm., 2009–11); Professional Practice and Ethics Cttee, 2008–; Access to the Bar Cttee, 2009–10); Patents Sub-Gp, Council of Bars and Law Socs of Europe, 2008–; Working Gp for reform of Patents County Court, 2009; Observer Mem. Council, UK Gp, Internat. Assoc. for Protection of Intellectual Property, 2006–. *Publications:* (ed jtly) Terrell on the Law of Patents, 14th edn 1994 to 17th edn 2011. *Recreations:* travel, films. *Address:* Three New Square Intellectual Property, Lincoln's Inn, WC2A 3RS. *T:* (020) 7405 1111.

**MILLER, Robert Alexander Gavin D.**; *see* Douglas Miller.

**MILLER, Robin Anthony**; a Recorder of the Crown Court, 1978–2003; b 15 Sept. 1937; s of William Alexander Miller, CBE, BEM, and Winifred Miller; m 1962, Irene Joanna Kennedy; two s one d. *Educ:* Devonport High Sch., Plymouth; Wadham Coll., Oxford (MA). Called to the Bar, Middle Temple, 1960. *Address:* Flat 6, 1 Walker Terrace, West Hoe, Plymouth, Devon PL1 3BN. *T:* (01752) 604487.

**MILLER, Sir Robin (Robert William)**, Kt 2003; Chairman: Edge Performance VCT, since 2005; Rightster, since 2015; Digitalbox Group, since 2015; Director, Robin Miller Consultants Ltd. Joined East Midlands Allied Press as jun. reporter, Motor Cycle News, 1965; various sen. editl roles; Man. Dir, Mag. Div., 1974; Mem. Bd, 1976–2003; Chief Exec., 1985–98 and 2001–03, non-exec. Chm., 1998–2001, Emap plc. Chairman: Entertainment Rights plc, 2008–09; Setanta, 2009; Butler, Tanner & Dennis, 2010–14. Non-executive Chairman: HMV Gp, 2004–05; Boosey & Hawkes Music Publishers Ltd; GetMeMedia, 2009–12; non-executive Director: Moss Bros plc, 1998–2001; Channel 4 TV, 1999–2006; Mecom Gp plc, 2005–09; Racing Post; former non-exec. Dir, Horserace Totalisator Bd. Chm., E Regl Sports Bd, Sport England, 2003–05; Mem. Panel, UK Sports Inst., 2000–. Trustee: Golf Foundation; Riders for Health. *Address:* (office) 3rd Floor, Albemarle House, Albemarle Street, W1S 4HA.

**MILLER, Sir Ronald (Andrew Baird)**, Kt 1993; CBE 1985; CA; b 13 May 1937; m 1965, Elizabeth Ann Gordon; one s one d. *Educ:* Daniel Stewart's Coll.; Univ. of Edinburgh (BSc). With Dawson Internat., 1968–95: Dir, 1976; Chm. and Chief Exec., 1982–91; Exec. Chm., 1991–95. Director: Securities Trust of Scotland, 1983–2001; Christian Salvesen, 1987–97; Aggreko, 1997–2002; Mem. Bd, Scottish Amicable, 1997–2003 (Dir, Scottish Amicable Life Assce Soc., 1987–97, Dep. Chm., 1994–97). Chairman: British Knitting and Clothing Export Council (later British Fashion Exports), 1993–97 (Mem., 1987–98; Vice Pres., 1997–); Scottish Textile Assoc., 1992–95 (Mem., 1992–98); Cttee of Chairmen of Scottish Higher Educn Instns, 1999–2001; Member: N Amer. Adv. Gp, DTI, 1986–96; ScotBIC, 1990–95; Quality Scotland, 1991–95; Scottish Council, CBI, 1992–95; British Apparel and Textile Confedn, 1993–95; SHEFC, 1992–95; Quality Assurance Agency for Higher Educn, 1997–2003 (Chm., Scottish Cttee, 1998–2003); Walpole Cttee, 1992–95; SCOTrust, 1994–99. Mem. Court, Edinburgh Napier (formerly Napier) Univ., 1992–2001 (Chm. Court, 1998–2001; Chm., Develt Trust, 2001–17). Liveryman, Woolmen's Co., 1992–. FRSA; CCMI. DSc *hc* Heriot-Watt, 1992; DUniv Napier, 2001. *Club:* Caledonian.
*See also* A. A. Miller.

**MILLER, Ronald Kinsman**, CB 1989; Solicitor of Inland Revenue, 1986–90, retired; part-time Chairman, VAT and Duties Tribunals, 1991–2002; b 12 Nov. 1929; s of William Miller and Elsie May Kinsman; m 1952, Doris Alice Dew (d 2009); one s one d. *Educ:* Colchester Royal Grammar Sch. Served RN, 1948–50. Called to the Bar, Gray's Inn, 1953. Joined Inland Revenue, 1950; Asst Solicitor, 1971; Law Officers' Dept, 1977–79; Principal Asst Solicitor, 1981–86. *Recreations:* gardening, reading, music. *Address:* 4 Liskeard Close, Chislehurst, Kent BR7 6RT. *T:* (020) 8467 8041. *Club:* Athenæum.

**MILLER, Dr Roy Frank**; Vice-Principal, 1985–98, Hon. Research Fellow in Physics, since 1998, Royal Holloway and Bedford New College, University of London; b 20 Sept. 1935; s of Thomas R. Miller and Margaret Ann Tattum; m 1961, Ruth Naomi Kenchington; one s. *Educ:* Wembley County Grammar Sch.; University Coll. SW England, Exeter; Royal Holloway Coll. BSc, PhD, FInstP. Teacher, Halbutt Secondary Modern Sch., 1957; Royal Holloway College: Demonstrator, 1957, Asst Lectr, 1960, Lectr, 1963, Sen. Lectr, 1973, Physics Dept; Vice-Principal, 1978–81; Acting Principal, 1981–82; Principal, 1982–85; Hon. Fellow, 2000. Research Associate and Teaching Fellow, Case Western Reserve Univ., Ohio, USA, 1967–68. Mem. Senate, Univ. of London, 1981–85; Chm., Bd, Inst. of Classical Studies, Univ. of London, 1983–2001; Trustee, 1982–, Governor, 1982–2017, Strode's Foundn, Strode's Coll., Egham. MRI. *Publications:* articles in Jl Phys C, Phil. Mag., Vacuum, Proc. Royal Soc. A. *Recreations:* mountaineering, squash, music. *Club:* Athenæum.

**MILLER, Sidney James**, MA; Citizens' Advice Bureau Adviser, Bedford, 1996–2015; b 25 Jan. 1943; s of Sidney Tomsett Miller and Mary Ada Miller (née Marshall); m 1971, Judith Branney (née Passingham); three s one d. *Educ:* Clifton Coll., Bristol; Jesus Coll., Cambridge (MA). Harvard Univ.; De Montfort Univ. VIth Form Classical Master and House Tutor, Clifton Coll., Bristol, 1965–68; Asst Master and Classical Tutor, Eton Coll., 1968–73, Head of Classical Dept, 1971–73; Dep. Headmaster (Organisation), Bridgewater Hall, Stantonbury Campus, Milton Keynes, 1974–77; Headmaster, Kingston Grammar Sch., Kingston upon Thames, 1977–86; Head Master, Bedford Sch., 1986–88; Professional Officer, Sch. Exams and Assessment Council, 1988–89; HEO, DES, later DFE, 1989–95. Mem., Gen. Synod of C of E, 1994–95. Dir, Bedford Concern for the Homeless and Rootless, 1996–2008 (Chm., 2005–08); Member: Community Resettlement Support Project, 2009–15; Friends For Life, 2009–13. Official Prison Visitor, 2009–; Ind. Custody Visitor, 2009–13; volunteer Lay Mem., Bedford Prison Chaplaincy, 2016–. Mem., Gideon Assoc., 1992–; Founder Mem., Bedford Millennium Probus Club, 1999– (Chm., 2007–08). Mem., Walk Uganda Christian mission gp, 2002–18. *Publications:* (ed jtly) Greek Unprepared Translation, 1968; (ed jtly) Inscriptions of the Roman Empire AD14–117, 1971; article in Didaskalos, 1972. *Recreations:* watching sports, learning languages, exercising at gym. *Address:* 33A Bushmead Avenue, Bedford MK40 3QH. *Clubs:* MCC; Achilles; Bedford Rugby.

**MILLER of Glenlee, Sir Stephen (William Macdonald)**, 8th Bt *cr* 1788, of Glenlee, Kirkcudbrightshire; FRCGP; General Practitioner, since 1986; b 20 June 1953; s of Sir Macdonald Miller of Glenlee, 7th Bt and Marion Jane Audrey Pettit, (Audrey, Lady Miller of Glenlee); S father, 1991; m 1st, 1978, Mary (d 1989), d of G. B. Owens; one s one d; 2nd, 1990, Caroline Clark (née Chasemore); one step s one step d. *Educ:* Rugby Sch.; St Bartholomew's Hosp. MB; FRCS 1981; MRCGP 1986, FRCGP 1995. Surgical Registrar, Sheffield, 1979–81; Orthopaedic Registrar, Newcastle, 1982–84. Vice-Chm., Northern Locality, Devon CCG, 2014–17. *Publications:* various papers in med. jls. *Recreations:* gardening, fishing. *Heir:* s James Stephen Macdonald Miller, b 25 July 1981. *Address:* Burrowland, Sandford, Crediton, Devon EX17 4EL.

**MILLER, Prof. William Lockley**, PhD; FBA 1994; FRSE; Edward Caird Professor of Politics, Glasgow University, 1985–2009, now Emeritus; b 12 Aug. 1943; s of William Lockley Miller and Florence Ratcliffe; m 1967, Fiona Thomson; two s one d. *Educ:* Edinburgh Univ. (MA 1st Cl. Maths and Nat. Phil. 1965); Newcastle Univ. (PhD Computing 1970). Lectr in Politics, Sen. Lectr and Prof., Strathclyde Univ., 1968–85. Vis. Prof. in Politics, Virginia Tech., Blacksburg, 1983–84. FRSE 1999. *Publications:* Electoral Dynamics, 1977; The End of British Politics?, 1981; The Survey Method, 1983; (with Martin Harrop) Elections and Voters, 1987; Irrelevant Elections?, 1988; (jtly) How Voters Change, 1990; Media and Voters, 1991; (jtly) Alternatives to Freedom, 1995; (jtly) Political Culture in Contemporary Britain, 1996; (jtly) Values and Political Change in Postcommunist Europe, 1998; (jtly) Models of Local Governance, 2000; (jtly) A Culture of Corruption?, 2001 (Ukrainian edn, 2004); (ed) Anglo-Scottish Relations from 1900 to Devolution and Beyond, 2005; (jtly) Multicultural Nationalism: Islamophobia, Anglophobia and devolution, 2006; (jtly) The Open Economy and its Enemies: public attitudes in east Asia and eastern Europe, 2006. *Recreation:* hill walking. *Address:* School of Social and Political Sciences, Adam Smith Building, Bute Gardens, The University, Glasgow G12 8RT. *T:* (0141) 339 8855.

**MILLER SMITH, Charles**; Chairman: Edge International Management Ltd, since 2014; Pollen + Grace, since 2016; b 7 Nov. 1939; s of William Smith and Margaret Pettigrew Brownlie Wardrope; adopted grandfather's surname, Miller Smith, 1963; m 1st, 1964, Dorothy Agnes Wilson Adams (d 1999); one s two d; 2nd, 2004, Debjani Jash (marr. diss. 2010). *Educ:* Glasgow Acad.; St Andrews Univ. (MA). ACCA. Unilever: Financial Dir, Vinyl Products, 1970–73; Head of Planning, 1974; Finance Dir, Walls Meat Co., 1976; Vice-Chm., Hindustan Lever, 1979–81; Speciality Chemicals Group, 1981; Chief Executive: PPF Internat., 1983; Quest Internat., 1986; Financial Dir, Unilever Board, 1989; Exec., Unilever Foods, 1993–94; Imperial Chemical Industries: Dir, 1994–2001; Chief Exec., 1995–99; Chm., 1999–2001; Dep. Chm., 1999–2000, Chm., 2000–07, Chm., Adv. Bd, 2007–09, Scottish Power plc. Chm., Firstsource Solutions UK Ltd, 2008–19 (non-exec. Dir, 2001–19); non-executive Director: Midland Bank, 1994–96; HSBC Hldgs plc, 1996–2001; Premier Foods plc, 2009–15; Senior Adviser: Goldman Sachs, 2001–05; Warburg Pincus, 2005–14; Deutsche Bank (RREEF Infrastructure), 2007–11. Mem. Mgt Bd, MoD, 2002–07. Hon. LLD St Andrews, 1995. *Recreations:* reading, walking. *Address:* 8 Stack House, Cundy Street, SW1W 9JS. *Club:* National.

**MILLETT**, family name of **Baron Millett**.

**MILLETT, Baron** *cr* 1998 (Life Peer), of St Marylebone in the City of Westminster; **Peter Julian Millett**, Kt 1986; PC 1994; a Lord of Appeal in Ordinary, 1998–2004; a non-permanent Judge, Court of Final Appeal, Hong Kong, 2000–17; b 23 June 1932; s of late Denis Millett and Adele Millett; m 1959, Ann Mireille, d of late David Harris; two s (and one s decd). *Educ:* Harrow; Trinity Hall, Cambridge (Schol.; MA; Hon. Fellow, 1994). Nat. Service, RAF, 1955–57 (Flying Officer). Called to Bar, Middle Temple, 1955, *ad eundem* Lincoln's Inn, 1959 (Bencher, 1980, Treas., 2004), Singapore, 1976, Hong Kong, 1979; at Chancery Bar, 1958–86; QC 1973; a Judge of the High Court of Justice, Chancery Div., 1986–94; a Lord Justice of Appeal, 1994–98. Mem., H of L, 1998–2017. Examr and Lectr in Practical Conveyancing, Council of Legal Educn, 1962–76. Junior Counsel to Dept of Trade and Industry in Chancery matters, 1967–73. Mem., General Council of the Bar, 1971–75. Outside Mem., Law Commn on working party on co-ownership of matrimonial home, 1972–73; Mem., Dept of Trade Insolvency Law Review Cttee, 1977–82. Pres., West London Synagogue of British Jews, 1991–95. Editor-in-Chief, Encyc. of Forms and Precedents, 1988–. Hon. Fellow, QMUL, 2012. Hon. LLD London, 2000. Gold Bauhinia Star (Hong Kong), 2015. *Publications:* contrib. to Halsbury's Laws of England; articles in legal jls. *Recreations:* philately, bridge, The Times crossword. *Address:* 18 Portman Close, W1H 6BR. *T:* (020) 7935 1152; St Andrews, 38 Kewhurst Avenue, Cooden, Bexhill-on-Sea, East Sussex TN39 3BH.
*See also* Hon. R. L. Millett.

**MILLETT, Alexandra**; *see* Healy, A.

**MILLETT, Anthea Christine**, CBE 2000; Commissioner, Civil Service Commission, 2007–12; b 2 Nov. 1941; d of Rupert Millett and Lucy Millett. *Educ:* Erdington Grammar School for Girls, Birmingham; Bedford Coll., Univ. of London (BA Hons). Teacher: Channing School, Highgate, 1963–65; Bournville Grammar Tech. Sch., Birmingham, 1965–67; Solihull High Sch., 1967–71 (Head of Dept); Dep. Head, Tile Hill Comprehensive Sch., Coventry, 1972–77. HM Inspectorate of Schools, subseq. OFSTED, 1978–95: Chief Inspector, 1987–92; Dir of Inspection, 1993–95; Chief Exec., TTA, 1995–99. Chairman: Wilts HA, 2000–02; Avon, Glos and Wilts Strategic HA, 2002–06. Mem., Cttee of Enquiry, Mgt and Govt of Schools, 1975–77. FRGS; FRSA. *Recreations:* travel, walking, gardening, DIY.

**MILLETT, Prof. Martin John**, DPhil; FSA; FBA 2006; Laurence Professor of Classical Archaeology, University of Cambridge, since 2001 (Head of School of Arts and Humanities, 2014–18); Fellow, Fitzwilliam College, Cambridge, since 2001; b 30 Sept. 1955; s of John Millett and Sybil Vera Millett (née Paine); m 2005, Joanna Story; one s one d. *Educ:* Inst. of Archaeology, Univ. of London (BA 1977); Merton Coll., Oxford (DPhil 1983). FSA 1984. Asst Keeper of Archaeol., Hants Co. Mus. Service, 1980–81; University of Durham: Lectr, 1981–91; Sen. Lectr, 1991–95; Prof. of Archaeol., 1995–98; Prof. of Classical Archaeol., Univ. of Southampton, 1999–2001. Vice-Pres., British Acad., 2010–14. Dir, 2001–07, Treas., 2007–11, Soc. of Antiquaries. Asst Ed., 1986–89, Ed., 1989–94, Archaeological Jl. *Publications:* The Romanization of Britain, 1990; Roman Britain, 1995; ed monographs and papers on Roman archaeology; contrib. numerous articles to learned jls. *Recreations:* food, wine, house restoration, the outdoors. *Address:* Faculty of Classics, University of Cambridge, Sidgwick Avenue, Cambridge CB3 9DA. *T:* (01223) 335161, *Fax:* (01223) 335409. *E:* mjm62@cam.ac.uk.

**MILLETT, Peter Joseph**, CMG 2013; HM Diplomatic Service, retired; Ambassador to Libya, 2015–18; b 23 Jan. 1955; m 1981, June Harnett; three d. Entered FCO, 1974; Vice Consul, Caracas, 1978–80; Second Sec., Doha, 1981–85; FCO, 1986–89; First Sec., UK Repn to EU, Brussels, 1989–93; Hd, Personnel Policy, FCO, 1993–96; Dep. Hd of Mission, Athens, 1997–2001; Dir, Security, FCO, 2002–05; High Comr to Cyprus, 2005–10; Ambassador to Jordan, 2011–15. *E:* pjmillett@hotmail.co.uk.

**MILLETT, Hon. Richard (Lester)**; QC 2003; a Recorder, since 2010; a Deputy High Court Judge (Chancery Division), since 2013; b 29 Sept. 1961; s of Baron Millett, *qv*; m 1988, Patricia Mary Natalie Spencer; one s two d. *Educ:* Harrow Sch.; Trinity Hall, Cambridge (BA Hons Classical Tripos Pt 1, Law Tripos Pt 2; lightweight rowing blue, 1983). Called to the Bar, Lincoln's Inn, 1985 (Megarry Prize for Landlord and Tenant Law), Bencher, 2013; Standing Jun. Counsel to the Crown (Treasury A Panel), 2001–03; Leading Counsel to Grenfell Tower Inquiry, 2017. *Publications:* (with G. Andrews) The Law of Guarantees, 1992, 7th edn 2015; Atkin's Court Forms, vol. 21, Guarantee and Indemnity, 2015; contrib. Law Qly Rev., Halsbury's Laws of England, Jl of Internat. Business and Law.

*Recreations:* Alpinism, gastronomy, fishing, shooting, music. *Address:* 53 Gloucester Avenue, NW1 7BA. *T:* (020) 7267 9804; Slivericks House, Ashburnham, Battle, E Sussex TN33 9PE; Essex Court Chambers, 24 Lincoln's Inn Fields, WC2A 3EG. *Clubs:* Royal Automobile; Leander (Henley-on-Thames).

**MILLGATE, Prof. Michael Henry,** PhD; FRSC; FRSL; University Professor of English, Emeritus, Toronto University, since 1994; *b* 19 July 1929; *s* of Stanley Millgate and Marjorie Louisa (*née* Norris); *m* 1960, Jane, *d* of Maurice and Marie Barr. *Educ:* St Catharine's Coll., Cambridge (MA); Michigan Univ.; Leeds Univ. (PhD). Tutor-Organizer, WEA, E Lindsey, 1953–56; Lectr in English Lit., Leeds Univ., 1958–64; Prof. of English and Chm. of the Dept, York Univ., Ont, 1964–67; Prof. of English, Toronto Univ., 1967–94 (University Prof., 1987–94). Killam Sen. Res. Schol., 1974–75; Killam Res. Fellow, 1986–88; John Simon Guggenheim Meml Fellow, 1977–78. FRSC 1982; FRSL 1984. Pierre Chauveau Medal, RSC, 1999. *Publications:* William Faulkner, 1961; (ed) Tennyson: Selected Poems, 1963; American Social Fiction, 1964; (ed jtly) Transatlantic Dialogue, 1966; The Achievement of William Faulkner, 1966; (ed jtly) Lion in the Garden, 1968; Thomas Hardy: his career as a novelist, 1971; (ed jtly) The Collected Letters of Thomas Hardy, vols I–VIII, 1978–2012; Thomas Hardy: a biography, 1982, rev. and expanded edn as Thomas Hardy: a biography revisited, 2004; (ed) The Life and Work of Thomas Hardy, 1985; (ed) William Faulkner Manuscripts 20, 21, 22 and 23, 1987; (ed) New Essays on Light in August, 1987; (ed) Thomas Hardy: selected letters, 1990; Testamentary Acts: Browning, Tennyson, James, Hardy, 1992; (ed jtly) Thomas Hardy's 'Studies, Specimens &c' Notebook, 1994; (ed) Letters of Emma and Florence Hardy, 1996; Faulkner's Place, 1997; (ed) Thomas Hardy's Public Voice, 2001; (ed jtly) Thomas Hardy's Poetical Matter Notebook, 2009.

**MILLICHIP, Jane Helen;** Managing Director, Sky Vision, since 2013; *b* Bewdley, Worcs, 17 Aug. 1965; *d* of Brian William Millichip and Kathleen Emily Lloyd; *m* Paul Freedman; two *s. Educ:* Bewdley High Sch.; Sheffield Hallam Univ. (BA Hons Mod. Langs and Political Sci.). Journalist, Haymarket Publishing, 1989–92; Editor, TV World, 1992–97; Sen. Commng Editor, Living TV, 2000–04; Managing Director: South Pacific Pictures, NZ, 2004–07; RDF Rights, 2007–10; Zodiak Rights, 2010–13. Director: Love Prodns Ltd, 2014–; Blast Films Ltd, 2015–; Sugar Films Ltd, 2016–; Uncle Bert Ltd, 2016–; True North Prodns Ltd, 2017–; Avanti Media Gp Ltd, 2017–; Jupiter Entertainment; Znak and Co.; Talos Films; Darbyshire Ltd. Director: Edinburgh Internat. Television Festival Ltd, 2018–; Edinburgh Television Festival Council, 2018–. *Recreations:* learning to fly (private pilots licence), mixology, surfing, scuba diving, keeping pigs and sheep, walking the dog, exercise. *Address:* Sky, Central, Grant Way, Isleworth TW7 5QD. *E:* jane.millichip@sky.uk.

**MILLIDGE, Jonathan Varley,** MBE 2016; Group Human Resources Director, Royal Mail Group, since 2014; *b* Birmingham, 16 March 1964; *s* of Christopher and Kathleen Millidge; *m* 1989, Judith Stillwell; one *s* one *d. Educ:* Oakham Sch.; Royal Holloway Coll., Univ. of London (BA Hons). Dir, Resources, SSL, 1997–98; Gen. Manager West, Post Office Ltd, 1998–2000; HR Dir, Parcel Force, 2000–03; Royal Mail Group: Dir, Employee Relns, 2003–07; HR Dir, 2007–10; Company Sec., 2010–14. Chm., Nat. Design Consultancy, 2001–14. Chm., Angard Ltd, 2014–. Trustee, Royal Mail Defined Contribution Plan, 2008–. FCMA 1995; FCIPD 2010. *Recreations:* travel, woodland management. *Address:* (office) 100 Victoria Embankment, EC4Y 0HQ. *T:* (020) 7449 8112, *Fax:* (020) 7530 7104. *E:* jon.millidge@royalmail.com.

**MILLIGAN, Andrew,** OBE 2015; Head, Global Strategy, Aberdeen Standard (formerly Standard Life) Investments, since 2000; *b* London, Nov. 1956; *s* of Owen and Bunty Milligan; *m* 1984, Rosemary; two *s. Educ:* Finchley Catholic Grammar Sch.; Bristol Univ. (BSc Econs and Econ. Hist. 1979). HM Treasury, incl. roles in social security, North Sea oil and gas, and IMF/World Bank divs, 1979–86; Econ. Advr, Lloyds Bank, 1986–91; Internat. Economist, Smith New Court, 1991–94; Chief Economist, New Japan Securities Europe, 1994–96; Dir, Econ. Res., Aviva/Morley Fund Mgt, 1996–2000. Mem., Governing Bd, Technol. Strategy Bd, 2007–14. Member: Court, Heriot-Watt Univ., 2011–; Bd, Edinburgh Business Sch., 2015–17. Mem. Bd, Work Place Chaplaincy Scotland, 2011– (Chm., 2016–18). Mem. Council, Soc. of Business Economists, 1990–2018 (Fellow, 2008). *Recreations:* croquet in the summer, Rugby in the winter. *Address:* Aberdeen Standard Investments, 6 St Andrew Square, Edinburgh EH2 2AH. *T:* (0131) 245 8394. *E:* Andrew.milligan@aberdeenstandard.com.

**MILLIGAN, Eric;** JP; Member (Lab), City of Edinburgh Council, 1995–2017; Convener, Lothian and Borders Police Board, 2003–07; *b* 27 Jan. 1951; *m* Janis. *Educ:* Tynecastle High Sch.; Napier Coll. Former printer. Member (Lab): Edinburgh DC, 1974–78; Lothian Regl Council, 1978–96 (Chm., Finance Cttee, 1980–82, 1986–90; Convener, 1990–96); Convener, Edinburgh City Council, 1995–96; Lord Provost and Lord-Lieutenant of Edinburgh, 1996–2003. Mem., COSLA, 1980–82, 1986–96 (Pres., 1988–90). Convener, Edinburgh Licensing Bd, 2012–17. Dir, Edinburgh Fest. Soc., 1996–2003; Chm., Edinburgh Military Tattoo Ltd, 1996–2003. Trustee, Royal Yacht Britannia, 2000–16. JP Edinburgh, 1996. Hon. FRCSE 2000. Hon. DBA Napier, 1999; DUniv Heriot-Watt, 2004. Chevalier, Ordre Nat. du Mérite (France), 1996; Gold Medal, Mayor of Paris, 2015. *Recreations:* watching football and Rugby as played by Heart of Midlothian FC and Boroughmuir RFC, listening to music. *Clubs:* New, Royal Scots (Edinburgh); Boroughmuir Rugby Football.

**MILLIGAN, Iain Anstruther;** QC 1991; *b* 21 April 1950; *s* of late Wyndham Macbeth Moir Milligan, MBE, TD; *m* 1979, Zara Ann Louise Spearman; one *s* two *d. Educ:* Eton; Magdalene College, Cambridge (MA); College of Law. Called to the Bar, Inner Temple, 1973, Bencher, 2002. Head of Chambers, 1999–2014. *Recreations:* farming, forestry, walking. *Address:* 20 Essex Street, WC2R 3AL. *T:* (020) 7842 1200; Dunesslin, Dunscore, Dumfries DG2 0UR. *T:* (01387) 820345.

**MILLIGAN, June Elizabeth,** PhD; Director General, Local Government and Communities (formerly Public Services and Local Government Delivery), Welsh Government (formerly Welsh Assembly Government), 2010–15; a Civil Service Commissioner, since 2017; *b* Glasgow, 23 June 1959; *d* of Thomas Edward Cole and Enid Charlton Cole; *m* 1980, Brian Milligan; one *s* one *d. Educ:* Univ. of Glasgow (MA 1st Cl. Hons 1979; PhD 1982; BD 2008). Asst Prison Gov., 1983–85, Prison Gov. Grade V, 1985–89, Home Office; joined Welsh Office, 1989; First Sec., UK Repn to EU, Brussels, FCO, 1993–96; Principal Private Sec. to Sec. of State for Wales, 1996–99; Hd of Devolved Admins Dept, FCO, 2000; Welsh Assembly Government: Hd, Envmt, 2000–06; Business Develt Dir, 2006–09; Dir, Social Justice and Local Govt Dept, 2010. Wales Comr, Equality and Human Rights Commn, 2016–. Mem. Ct, Univ. of Glasgow, 2015–. Trustee, Young Foundn, 2016–17. *Recreations:* celebrating life and love, constantly learning.

**MILLIGAN, Scott Gregor;** Director of Legal Services and Chief Legal Adviser, Department of Energy and Climate Change, 2008–13; *b* 28 Oct. 1951; *s* of late Gregor Stormont Milligan and Marylla Milligan (*née* Jolles); *m* 1984, Elizabeth Mary Cliff; one *s* two *d. Educ:* Christ's Hosp. Sch.; Mansfield Coll., Oxford (BA Modern Hist. 1973). Called to the Bar, Middle Temple, 1975; joined Govt Legal Service, 1977; Legal Asst, 1977–81, Sen. Legal Asst, 1981–85, Dept of Employment; Asst Solicitor, advising Dept of Employment, Treasury Solicitor's Dept and Dept of Energy, 1985–92; Asst Solicitor, DTI, 1992–2001; Dir, Legal Services Gp, DTI, then BERR, 2001–08. Chm., Whitehall Prosecutors' Gp, 2001–04. Trustee, Kingston Friends' Trusts, 2001–. *Recreations:* cycling, singing, Spring Grove Fringe theatre.

**MILLIGAN, His Honour Timothy James;** a Circuit Judge, 1991–2008; *b* 16 March 1940; *s* of Dr Peter James Wyatt Milligan and Rosemary Elizabeth Ann (*née* Dutton); *m* 1976, Sally Marcella (*née* Priest) (marr. diss. 1999); two step *s. Educ:* Frilsham House Prep. School; Winchester Coll.; Grenoble Univ. (1st and 2nd Foreigner's Degrees). Articled Clerk, Taylor Garrett, 1960–65; admitted Solicitor, 1967; Asst Solicitor, Leeds Smith, Beds, 1967–69; Asst Solicitor, then Partner, Triggs Turner, Guildford, 1969–73; Solicitor, then Partner, Warner & Richardson, Winchester, 1973–91; HM Coroner, Central Hants, 1982–91; a Recorder of the Crown Court, 1988–91. Hon. Mem., Coroners Soc. of GB, 1991; Mem. of various Old Wykehamist clubs and assocs. Chm. Disciplinary Cttee of Rackets Cttee, Tennis and Rackets Assoc., 1998–. Gov., St Columba C of E Primary Acad., 2004–. *Recreations:* rackets, cricket, football, reading, music, theatre, cinema. *Clubs:* MCC; Hampshire CC (Mem. Cttee, 1993–); Jesters; Tennis and Rackets Association (Mem., Rackets Cttee, 1988–98).

**MILLIKEN, Rt Hon. Peter (Andrew Stewart),** OC 2014; PC (Can.) 2012; Distinguished Fellow, School of Policy Studies, Queen's University, Kingston, Ont, since 2011; Speaker, House of Commons, Canada, 2001–11; *b* Kingston, Ont, 12 Nov. 1946; *s* of John Andrew Milliken and Catherine Margaret (*née* McCuaig). *Educ:* Queen's Univ. (BA Hons 1968); Wadham Coll., Oxford (BA 1970, MA 1978); Dalhousie Univ. (LLB 1971). Called to the Bar, Ont., and Solicitor, Supreme Court of Ont., 1973; in practice with Cunningham Swan, Carty, Little & Bonham, 1973–88. MP (L) Kingston and the Islands, 1988–2011. Parly Sec. to Govt House Leader, 1993–96; Dep. Chm., Cttees of Whole House, 1996–97; Dep. Speaker and Chm., Cttees of Whole House, 1997–2001. Special Advr, Cunningham Swan, Carty, Little & Bonham, 2011–15. Mem., Coroners' Council, Ont., 1985–88. *Address:* 2626 Leeman Road, Elginburg, ON K0H 1M0, Canada.

**MILLIKEN-SMITH, Mark Gordon;** QC 2006; a Recorder of the Crown Court, since 2004; *b* 4 July 1963; *s* of John Michael Milliken-Smith and Gillian Frances Milliken-Smith (*née* Woods, now Bird); *m* 1991, Sybella Anne Wilson; one *s* one *d. Educ:* Wellington Coll.; Univ. of Bristol (LLB Hons 1985). Called to the Bar, Gray's Inn, 1986; in practice, specialising in criminal law, fraud, sports law and professional discipline. *Recreations:* family, and enjoying watching as much sport, especially cricket and Rugby, as possible. *Address:* 2 Bedford Row, WC1R 4BU. *T:* (020) 7440 8888, *Fax:* (020) 7242 1738. *E:* mmilliken-smith@2bedfordrow.co.uk. *Clubs:* MCC; Hankley Common.

**MILLING, Amanda Anne;** MP (C) Cannock Chase, since 2015; Treasurer of HM Household (Deputy Chief Whip), since 2019; *b* Burton upon Trent, 12 March 1975; *d* of Humphrey and Patricia Milling. *Educ:* Moreton Hall Sch.; University Coll. London (BSc Hons Econs). Researcher, SW1 Res., 1997–99; Quaestor Research and Marketing Strategists: Sen. Res. Exec., 1999–2000; Res. Manager, 2000–03; Associate Dir, 2003–06; Res. Dir, 2006–10; Dir, Optimisa Res., 2010–14. An Asst Govt Whip, 2018–19. *Recreation:* running. *Address:* House of Commons, SW1A 0AA. *T:* (020) 7219 8356. *E:* amanda.milling.mp@parliament.uk.

**MILLINGTON, Anthony Nigel Raymond,** OBE 2011; Director General, Tokyo Office, European Automobile Manufacturers Association, 1995–2016; *b* 29 Jan. 1945; *m* 1969, Susan Carolyn (*née* Steilberg) (*d* 2016); two *s. Educ:* Ipswich School; Univ. of Grenoble; Trinity College, Cambridge (BA); Univ. of Chicago. HM Diplomatic Service, 1968–94: FCO, 1968; Tokyo, 1969–76; FCO, 1976–80; Paris, 1980–84; Japanese National Defence College, 1984–85; Head of Chancery, Tokyo, 1985–88; Head of Far Eastern Dept, FCO, 1989–90; Rolls-Royce PLC, 1990; Pres., Rolls-Royce (Far East) Ltd, 1990–94 (on leave of absence); FCO, 1994. Mem., Japanese Prime Minister's Regulatory Reform Commn, 1998–2002. Advr to Bd of Dirs, Japan Automobile Importers' Assoc., 2001–16. Chm., Automobile Cttee, Eur. Business Council in Japan, 2010–16. Chm Bd of Trustees, British Sch. in Tokyo, 2004–10; Mem. Council, Japan-British Soc., 2010–16 (Exec. Dir, 2013–16); Dir, ESU, Japan, 2012–16. *Recreations:* tennis, walking in the countryside. *Address:* 19 Hillside, Wimbledon Village, SW19 4NL. *T:* 07955 266446; 8 Smith Road, Hanover, NH 03755, USA. *T:* (603) 3066203. *E:* anrm@gol.com. *Clubs:* Royal Automobile; Wimbledon (Mem., Tennis Cttee, 2018–).

**MILLINGTON, Christopher John;** QC 2001; a Recorder, since 1995; *b* 31 Oct. 1951; *s* of Dennis Millington and Christine Millington; *m* 1976, Jane Elisabeth Bucknell; one *s* one *d. Educ:* Birmingham Univ. (LLB, LLM). Called to the Bar, Gray's Inn, 1976; in chambers, Birmingham, 1976–. *Recreations:* tennis, golf, travel, music, especially rock guitar. *Address:* St Philip's Chambers, 55 Temple Row, Birmingham B2 5LS. *T:* (0121) 246 7000. *Clubs:* Edgbaston Priory Tennis, Blackwell Golf.

**MILLINGTON, Tamara;** *see* Ingram, T.

**MILLION, His Honour Clive Ernest;** a Circuit Judge, 2009–16; *b* 7 Sept. 1946; *s* of Arthur Ernest Million and Phyllis May Million; *m* 1st, 1975, Pauline Margaret Lock (*d* 2011); three *s*, 2nd, 2012, Linda June Bone; one step *s* two step *d. Educ:* St Dunstan's Coll.; Birmingham Coll. of Art and Design (BA Hons Industrial Design (Engrg) 1969). Called to the Bar, Middle Temple, 1975; District Judge, Principal Registry, Family Div., 1993–2009; Asst Recorder, 1995–99; Recorder, 1999–2009. Mem., Parole Bd of England and Wales, 2010–. *Publications:* Family Law: tips & traps, 2009. *Recreations:* anything legal, but non-legal.

**MILLON, Charles;** Ambassador of France to UN Food and Agriculture Organization, 2003–07; *b* Belley, Ain, 12 Nov. 1945; *s* of Gabriel Millon and Suzanne Millon (*née* Gunet); *m* 1970, Chantal Delsol; six *c. Educ:* Lamartine Instn, Belley; Saint-Marie Sch., Lyon. Asst Lectr, 1969; legal and fiscal consultant, 1969–. Deputy (UDF-PR) for Belley-Gex, elected 1978, 1981, 1986, 1988, 1993, 1995, 1997; Mem., Regl Council for Rhône-Alpes, elected 1981, 1986 (Pres., 1988–98); Mem., Gen. Council of the Ain (Canton of Belley), 1985–88; French National Assembly: Vice-Pres., 1986–88; Mem., Foreign Cttee, 1988; Pres., Parly Gp of UDF, 1989–95; Minister of Defence, 1995–97. Pres., Departmental Fedn, PR and UDF, 1983–85; Mem., Pol Bd, PR, 1984–95. Founder, 1998, Pres., 1998–99, Leader, 1999–2003, Droite Libérale Chrétienne. Mayor of Belley, 1977–2001; Municipal Councillor and Urban Community Councillor, Lyon, 2001–08. Associate: Intelstrat, Paris; Cross Invest, London; Founding Mem., Conseil d'admin, Institut Thomas More. *Publications:* L'extravagante histoire des nationalisations, 1984; L'alternance-Vérité, 1986; La tentation du conservatisme, 1995; La Paix Civile, 1998; Lettre d'un ami impertinent à Jacques Chirac, 2002.

**MILLS;** *see* Platts-Mills.

**MILLS,** family name of **Viscount Mills**.

**MILLS**, 3rd Viscount *cr* 1962; **Christopher Philip Roger Mills**; Bt 1953; Baron 1957; Regional Director, Environment Agency Wales, 2006–13; *b* 20 May 1956; *s* of 2nd Viscount Mills and Joan Dorothy (*d* 1998), *d* of James Shirreff; *S* father, 1988; *m* 1980, Lesley Alison, *er d* of Alan Bailey. *Educ*: Oundle School; Univ. of London (BSc Hons Biol Scis; MSc Applied Fish Biology); Plymouth Poly. Biologist at Salmon Research Trust of Ireland, 1980–89; National Rivers Authority: Technical Asst, 1989–91; Area Fisheries, Recreation and Ecology Manager, NW Region, 1991–95; Area Manager, Thames Reg., 1995–96; Area Manager, Thames Reg., Envmt Agency, 1996. Member Council: Inst. of Fisheries Mgt, 1993; RSPB, 1995–2000. *Publications*: papers in Aquaculture, Aquaculture and Fisheries Management, Fish Biology. *Recreations*: flyfishing, fine wines.

**MILLS, Dame Anne (Jane)**, DCMG 2015; CBE 2007; PhD; FRS 2013; FMedSci; Professor of Health Economics and Policy, since 1995, and Deputy Director and Provost (formerly Vice-Director), since 2011, London School of Hygiene and Tropical Medicine; *b* 26 Jan. 1951; *d* of Maurice and Anthea Mills; *m* 1979, Patrick Corran; two *s*. *Educ*: Aston Clinton Primary Sch.; Aylesbury High Sch.; Oxford High Sch.; St Hilda's Coll., Oxford (MA Hist. and Econs 1973); Leeds Univ. (Dip. Health Services Studies 1976); PhD Health Econs London Univ. 1990. Fellow, ODI, 1973–75; Res. Officer, Nuffield Inst. for Health Services Studies, 1976–79; London School of Hygiene and Tropical Medicine: Lectr, 1979–86, Sen. Lectr, 1986–92, Reader, 1992–95, in Health Econs; Hd, Faculty of Public Health and Policy, 2006–11. Co-Chm., Wkg Gp 5, Commn on Macroecons and Health, 2000–02. Foreign Associate, Inst. of Medicine, 2006–. Pres., Internat. Health Econs Assoc., 2012–13. FMedSci 2009. Prince Mahidol Award for Medicine, 2009; Lifetime Service to field of HPSR Award, Health Systems Global, 2016; Galen Medal for Therapeutics, Apothecaries' Soc., 2017. *Publications*: (with K. Lee) Policy Making and Planning in the Health Sector, 1982; (ed with K. Lee) The Economics of Health in Developing Countries, 1983; (ed jtly) Health System Decentralization Concepts, Issues and Country Experience, 1990; (ed with K. Lee) Health Economics Research in Developing Countries, 1993; (ed jtly) Private Health Providers in Developing Countries: serving the public interest?, 1997; (ed) Reforming Health Sectors, 2000; (jtly) The Challenge of Health Sector Reform: what must governments do?, 2001; (ed jtly) International Public Health, 2001, 4th edn as Global Health: diseases, programs, systems and policies, 2018; (ed jtly) Priorities in Health, 2006; (ed jtly) Disease Control Priorities in Developing Countries, 2nd edn 2006; (ed jtly) Health, Economic Development and Household Poverty: from understanding to action, 2007; (ed jtly) Good Health at Low Cost: 25 years on, 2011. *Recreations*: music, walking, cooking. *Address*: London School of Hygiene and Tropical Medicine, Keppel Street, WC1E 7HT. *T*: (020) 7927 2354, *Fax*: (020) 7636 7679. *E*: anne.mills@lshtm.ac.uk.

**MILLS, Carole Denise**; Chief Executive, Derby City Council, since 2018; *b* Coventry, 7 Dec. 1963; *d* of Peter and Pauline Mills; *m* (marr. diss.); one *s*; *m* 2011, Paul Humphrey; two step *s*. *Educ*: Wolverhampton Poly. CPFA 1992, FCPFA 2016. Coventry HA, 1983–86; Coventry CC, 1986–88; Walsall Metropolitan Borough Council: various posts, 1988–2002; Actg Chief Financial Officer, 2002–03; Exec. Dir, Corporate Services, 2003–07. Chartered Institute of Public Finance and Accountancy: Mem. Council, 2007–08, 2009–10, 2012–15; Vice Pres., 2005–07, Pres., 2007–09, Midlands. Chm., Finance Adv. Gp, W Midlands, LGA, 2004–07; Nottingham City Council: Corporate Dir of Resources, 2007–08; Dep. Chief Exec., Corporate Dir of Resources and Chief Finance Officer, 2008–14; Actg Chief Exec., 2012; Chief Exec., Milton Keynes Council, 2014–18. Accredited peer, LGA (formerly IDeA), 2005–. Non-exec. Dir, Midland Heart (Housing Assoc.), 2017– (Chair, Operations Cttee, 2018–). Governor: Victoria Infant Sch., Sandwell, 1996–99 (Vice Chm., 1998–99); Bishop Vesey Grammar Sch., 2003–07 (Chm., Finance and Estates Cttee, 2005–07). *E*: caroledmills@icloud.com.

**MILLS, David John**; Chief Executive, Post Office Ltd, 2002–05; Senior Independent Director, One Savings Bank plc, 2011–14; *b* 9 Feb. 1944; *s* of John Henry Mills and Violet Germaine Mills; *m* 1967, Lesley Jacqueline Wand; one *s* two *d*. *Educ*: London Business Sch. (Dist. Sloan Fellow). Joined Midland Bank, later HSBC, 1962; Gen. Manager, HSBC, 1989–2002; Dir, Royal Mail Gp Hldgs, 2002–05. Chm., My Home Move Ltd, 2006–11; Director: Camelot Gp plc, 2003–06; Cardpoint plc, 2007–08; Payzone plc, 2007–10. Dir, PIA, 1995–2000. Chm., Employers' Forum on Disability Ltd, 2004–07; Mem., Nat. Disability Council, 1993–95. Trustee, RADAR, 2004–09; Vice Pres., Vitalise, 2005–15. *Recreations*: family, wine, fishing, motorsport. *E*: david@davidjmills.com. *Club*: Royal Automobile.

**MILLS, Geoffrey Thomas**; Headmaster, Latymer School, 1983–98; *b* 13 Nov. 1935; *s* of Thomas Henry Mills and Margaret Jane (*née* Lewington); *m* 1970, Dorothy Anne Williams; one *s* three *d*. *Educ*: Enfield Grammar Sch.; Clare Coll., Cambridge (MA). Nat. Service, Corporal Clerk, RASC, 1954–56. Foreign lang. asst, Lyons, France, 1960–61; teacher of French and Spanish, Guthlaxton Grammar Sch., Leicester, 1961–62; Hd of Spanish, Sweyne Grammar Tech. Sch., Rayleigh, Essex, 1962–65; Head of Modern Languages: Coborn Sch. for Girls, Bow, 1965–69; Woodhouse Grammar Sch., Finchley, 1969–73; Dir of Studies, Longdean Sch., Hemel Hempstead, 1973–78; Headmaster, Manhood High Sch. and Community Centre, Selsey, W Sussex, 1978–83. Ind. Chm., Standards Cttee, London Borough of Enfield, 1999–2010. Freeman, London Bor. of Enfield, 2012. *Recreations*: golf (Blue, 1958), bridge, crosswords, reading. *Address*: 59 Wades Hill, Winchmore Hill, N21 1BD. *T*: (020) 8360 7335. *Club*: Mid Herts Golf (Wheathampstead).

**MILLS, Sir (George) Ian**, Kt 2001; FCA, FIC, CMC, FIHM; Commissioner, London Region, NHS Executive, Department of Health, 2001–03; Member, NHS Appointments Commission, 2001–03; *b* 19 Nov. 1935; *s* of George Haxton Mills and Evelyn Mary (*née* Owen); *m* 1968, Margaret Elizabeth Dunstan; one *s* one *d* (and one *s* decd). *Educ*: Taunton's Grammar Sch., Southampton. FCA 1960; FIC (FIMC 1964); LHSM 1985; FIHM 1990; CMC 2000. Articled to Beal, Young & Booth, Southampton, 1954–60; Price Waterhouse, London, 1960–65; seconded to World Bank team assisting Govt of Pakistan Treasury, 1962; Chief Accountant, Univ. of Ibadan, Nigeria, 1965–68; rejoined Price Waterhouse, 1968; London Office, 1968–70; Newcastle upon Tyne Office, as Manager i/c Northern and Scottish Management Consultancy Ops, 1970–73; Partner, 1973; London Office, 1973–85; i/c Africa Management Consultancy Services, 1975–83; Nat. Dir, Central Govt Services, 1983–85; Nation Health Service Management Board, 1985–89: Dir of Financial Management, 1985–88; Dir of Resource Management, 1988–89; rejoined Price Waterhouse, 1989; Sen. Partner, Business Development Europe, 1989–91. Chairman: Lewisham and N Southwark HA, 1991–93; SE London HA, 1993–96; SE London Commissioning Agency, 1991–93; Lambeth, Southwark and Lewisham Health Commn, then HA, 1993–96; N Thames, then London, Reg., NHS Exec., DOH, 1996–2001. Mem., NHS Policy Bd, then Sec. of State for Health's Regl Chairmen's Adv. Cttee, 1996–2001. Mem., Ind. Remuneration Panel, London Borough of Lewisham, 2001–10 (Chm., 2001–10). Member: Blackheath Preservation Trust Ltd, 1991–2004; Bd of Govs, UMDS of Guy's and St Thomas' Hosps, 1991–96; IHSM Consultants, 1992–96; Bd of Govs, St Christopher's Hospice, 1993–2003 (Chm., 2000–03); Delegacy, KCH Med. Sch., 1993–96; Bd of Trustees, Blackheath Historic Bldgs Trust, 2003–11 (Chm., 2003–11); Bd of Trustees, Age Exchange Theatre Trust, 2008–14 (Chm., 2008–14). Trustee, SE London Community Foundn, 1995–2000; Pres. and Trustee, Talk About Art Trust, 2014– (Chm., 2014–16); Chm. and Trustee, Youth First Mutual Lewisham, 2016–. Freeman, London Borough of Lewisham, 2018. FRSA. Member: Editl Adv. Bd, Health Services Jl, 1992–96; Editl Bd, British Jl of Health Care Mgt, 1996–2003. *Publications*: St Margaret, Lee: a new guide, 1996, updated 2016; Rebirth of a Building, 2000; Craftsmen of St Margaret, 2006; articles in financial, educnl and med. jls. *Recreations*: classical music, photography, travel, heritage. *Address*: 60 Belmont Hill, SE13 5DN. *T*: (020) 8852 2457. *Club*: Royal Society of Arts.

**MILLS, Gloria Helenly**, CBE 2005 (MBE 1999); National Secretary, UNISON, since 2006; *b* 1958; *d* of James and Olga Mills. *Educ*: Open Univ. (Prof. Cert. Mgt 2003; Prof. Dip. Mgt 2004; MBA 2007). MCIPD 2004. NUPE: Regl Area Officer, 1985; Sen. Nat. Officer, Equal Rights, 1987; UNISON: Dir of Equal Opportunities, then of Equalities, 1993–2006; Nat. Organiser (Equalities), 1999–2006; Mem., Sen. Mgt Gp, 2004–. Trades Union Congress: Member: Women's Cttee, 1989–; General Council, 1994–; Exec. Cttee, 2000–; Pres., 2005–06; Chairman: Race Relns Cttee, 1995, 2000–; Women's Conf., 1999; Mem., Gen. Council, ITUC, 2006–. Member: Race Relns Forum, 1998–2003, Race Equality Adv. Panel, 2003–, Home Office; Race, Employment and Educn Forum, DFEE, 1998–2001; Employment Appeal Tribunal, 2000–; Commn for Racial Equality, 2002–07; Adv. Cttee on Equal Opportunities, EC, 2011–. Member: Race Equality Adv. Gp, FA, 2007; Adv. Council, Involvement and Partnership Assoc., 2015–. Public Services International: Exec. Bd, 2002–; Vice-Chm., World Women's Cttee, 2004; President: Women and Gender Equality Cttee, Eur. Public Services Confedn, 2010–; ETUC Women's Cttee, 2015– (Chm., 2003; Vice Pres. 2010–15). Mem., Mgt Cttee, European Trade Union Inst., 2015–. Mother of Chapel: NATSOPA, 1980–85; SOGAT, 1982–85. FRSA 1998. MCMI 2008. Hon. LLD Staffordshire, 2006. *Publications*: various articles on race equality and gender inc. article on combating institutional racism in Industrial Law Jl. *Recreations*: reading, cricket, football, Arsenal. *Address*: UNISON, 130 Euston Road, NW1 2AY. *T*: (020) 7121 5409. *E*: glormlls@aol.com, g.mills@unison.co.uk.

**MILLS, Harold Hernshaw**, CB 1995; Chairman, Caledonian MacBrayne Ltd, 1999–2006; *b* 2 March 1938; *s* of late Harold and Margaret Mills; *m* 1973, Marion Elizabeth Beattie, MA. *Educ*: Greenock High Sch.; Univ. of Glasgow (BSc, PhD). Cancer Research Scientist, Roswell Park Memorial Inst., Buffalo, NY, 1962–64; Lectr, Glasgow Univ., 1964–69; Principal, Scottish Home and Health Dept, 1970–76; Asst Secretary: Scottish Office, 1976–81; Privy Council Office, 1981–83; Scottish Development Dept, 1983–84; Under Sec., Scottish Develt Dept, 1984–88; Prin. Finance Officer, Scottish Office, 1988–92; Sec., Scottish Office Envmt Dept, 1992–95; Sec. and Hd of Dept, Scottish Office Develt Dept, 1995–98. Mem., Greenock Town Council, 1965–69 (Hon. Treas., 1967–69). Mem. Bd, Home in Scotland, 1998–2004 (Chm., 2000–04). Director: Northlink Orkney and Shetland Ferries Ltd, 2000–09; Edinburgh City Centre Partnership, 2002–06; Northlink Ferries Ltd, 2006–09. Chairman: LandTrust, 1998–2014 (Mem. Bd, 1998–2015); Edinburgh World Heritage Trust, 1999–2006; Trustee: Scottish Maritime Mus., 1998–2016; Edinburgh Old Town and South Side Trust, 1999–2006; Scottish Maritime (formerly City of Adelaide Charitable) Trust, 2005–16; Viewpoint Trust, 2008–; Scottish Waterways Trust, 2012–14. Gov., Queen Margaret UC, Edinburgh, 1998–2004. *Publications*: scientific papers in jls of learned socs on the crystal structure of chemical compounds. *Address*: 21 Hatton Place, Edinburgh EH9 1UB. *T*: (0131) 667 7910.

**MILLS, Helena**, CBE 2017; Chief Executive Officer, Burnt Mill Academy Trust, since 2013 (Head Teacher, Burnt Mill School, 2010–13); *b* 24 Nov. 1967; *d* of Malcolm Mills and Barbara Mills (*née* Scahill); *m* 1991, Mark Wade; two *s* one *d*. *Educ*: Broughton High Sch.; Royal Holloway and Bedford Coll., Univ. of London (BA (Hons) Hist. 1989); Inst. of Educn (PGCE 1990; NPQH 2004). Teacher of History, Brampton Manor Comp. Sch., 1990; Hd of History, Bonus Pastor Comp. Sch., 1993–95; Hd of Humanities, 1995–2000, Asst Hd, 2000–02, Brampton Manor Comp. Sch.; Deputy Head: St Catherine's Comp. Sch. for Girls, 2002–05; St Bonaventure Comp. Sch. for Boys, 2005–10. *Publications*: (contrib.) Self-Improving Schools, 2015. *Recreations*: cycling, running, literature. *Address*: Burnt Mill Academy Trust, First Avenue, Harlow CM20 2NR. *T*: 07917 700354. *E*: millsh@bmatrust.org.uk.

**MILLS, Sir Ian**; *see* Mills, Sir G. I.

**MILLS, Prof. Ian Mark**, OBE 2015; FRS 1996; Professor of Chemical Spectroscopy, University of Reading, 1966–95, now Emeritus; *b* 9 June 1930; *s* of John Mills, MD and Margheurita Alice Gertrude Mills (*née* Gooding); *m* 1957, Margaret Mary Maynard; one *s* one *d*. *Educ*: Leighton Park Sch.; Univ. of Reading (BSc); St John's Coll., Oxford (DPhil). Res. Fellow, Univ. of Minnesota, 1954–56; Res. Fellow in Theoretical Chem., Corpus Christi Coll., Cambridge, 1956–57; University of Reading: Lectr in Chemistry, 1957–64; Reader, 1964–66; Leverhulme Emeritus Res. Fellow, 1996–98. Mem. and Chm. of various cttees, IUPAC, 1985–2000; Royal Society of Chemistry: Vice-Pres., Faraday Div., 1984–86; Mem., British Nat. Cttee for IUPAC, 1992–2000 (Chm., 1998–2000); Mem. Council, Royal Instn, 2000–03. Pres., Consultative Cttee on Units, Bureau Internat. des Poids et Mesures, 1995–2014 (Hon. Mem., 2014); Chm., Cttee on Symbols and Units, BSI, 1996–2003. Hon. DSc Reading, 2015. Lomb Medal 1960, Fellow 1974, Lippincott Medal 1982, Optical Soc. of America; Spectroscopy Award, RSC, 1990. Editor, Molecular Physics, 1972–77 and 1995–2004. *Publications*: (ed jtly) Quantities, Units and Symbols in Physical Chemistry, 1988, 3rd edn 2006; papers in learned jls. *Recreations*: walking, sailing, socialising and arguing in company with family, children and grandchildren, and Cathie Deeley and others. *Address*: 57 Christchurch Road, Reading RG2 7BD. *T*: (0118) 987 2335. *E*: i.m.mills@reading.ac.uk; mills704ian@gmail.com; School of Chemistry, University of Reading RG6 6AD. *T*: 07770 227678.

**MILLS, John Frederick**, CBE 2008; Director, Rural Policy, Department for Environment, Food and Rural Affairs, 2003–07; *b* 6 Sept. 1950; *s* of Henry Alfred Mills and Jean Margaret Aitchison; *m* 1st, 1974, Jean Marie Correia (*d* 1999); one *s* three *d*; 2nd, 2003, Imogen Stephanie Nicholls. *Educ*: Highgate Sch.; The Queen's Coll., Oxford (MA, BLitt (Mod. Hist.)); Merton Coll., Oxford (Domus Sen. Schol.). Department of Trade and Industry, 1974–92: Private Sec. to Minister of State for Industry, 1976–78; seconded to Govt of Hong Kong, 1981–85; Hd of Internat. Telecommunications Policy, 1986–89; Mem., Prime Minister's Policy Unit, 1989–92; Dir of Consumer Affairs, OFT, 1992–95; Chief Executive: Cornwall CC, 1995–99; Policy and Resources Dept, States of Jersey, 1999–2003. Income Tax Comr of Appeal, Jersey, 2009–17. Non-executive Director: Royal Cornwall Hosps NHS Trust, 2007–09; Port of London Authy, 2008–14 (Vice Chm., 2009–14); Dir, Ports of Jersey Ltd (formerly Jersey Harbours and Airport Shadow Bd), 2010– (Dep. Chm., 2015–). Member: Commn for Rural Communities, 2009–13; Jersey Financial Services Commn, 2009–14; Office of Channel Is Financial Services Ombudsman, 2014–; Jersey Charity Comr, 2017–. Mem., OFT Adv. Panel, 2001–03. Gov., Highgate Sch., 1993–2017 (Treasurer and Chm., 1999–2017). *Address*: Le Picachon, Les Varines, Jersey JE2 7SB. *T*: (01534) 732374.

**MILLS, Sir Jonathan Edward Harland**, Kt 2013; AO 2011; FRSE; Programme Director, Edinburgh International Culture Summit, since 2014; *b* 21 March 1963; *s* of Dr Frank Mills, AO and Elayne Mary Mills. *Educ*: Univ. of Sydney (BMus Composition); RMIT Univ. (MArch Acoustic Design); studied composition with Peter Sculthorpe, Sydney, and piano and composition with Lidia Arcuri-Baldecchi and Bruno Bettinelli, Italy. FRSE 2010.

Artistic Dir, Blue Mountains Fest., 1988–90; Composer-in-Residence and Res. Fellow in Envmtl Acoustics, RMIT Univ., 1992–97; Artistic Advr, Brisbane Biennial Internat. Music Fest., 1995–97; Artistic Dir, Melbourne Fest. (incl. Dir, Melbourne's Millennium Eve celebrations, 31 Dec. 1999 and Federation Fest., 2001), 2000–01; Composer-in-Residence, Bundanon Trust, 2002; Dir, Alfred Deakin Innovation Lects, 2003–05; Artistic Advr, Recital Centre and Elisabeth Murdoch Hall, Melbourne, 2005–06; Dir, Edinburgh Internat. Fest., 2007–14; Inaugural Artistic Curator, Lincoln Center Global Exchange, NY, 2015. Adjunct Professor: Envmtl Acoustics, RMIT Univ., 1998–2003; La Trobe Univ., 2004–07; Vice Chancellor's Fellow, Univ. of Melbourne, 2006 and 2015–17; Vis. Prof., Edinburgh Napier Univ., 2008–14; Vis. Prof., 2008–17, Hon. Prof., 2018–, Edinburgh Univ.; Melbourne Enterprise Prof., Univ. of Melbourne, 2017–; Trumbull Fellow and Vis. Prof., Yale Sch. of Music, 2017–; Vis. Prof., IEDC - Bled Sch. of Mgt, Slovenia. Member: Australian Internat. Cultural Council, 1998–2003; Australian Heritage Commn, 2002–04; New Media Arts Bd, 2003–05, Maj. Performing Arts Bd, 2005, Australia Council; Australian Heritage Council, 2004–06; Board Member: Synergy Percussion, 2001–06; Melbourne Recital Hall, 2004–05; Art Exhibns Australia, 2005; Chairman: Commonwealth Govt Review into Australian Youth Orch. and Australian Nat. Acad. of Music, 2004–05; Review of Opera for Victoria Govt, 2005; Arts and Creative Economy Adv. Gp, British Council, 2012–15. Gov., Royal Conservatoire of Scotland, 2017–. Member Jury: Pratt Prize for Music Th., 2002–12; Ian Potter Foundn Music Commns, 2003–05; Gustav Mahler Internat. Conducting Competition, Bamberg, 2010; Chair, internat. jury, Europe for Festivals, Festivals for Europe (EU initiative), 2017–20. Patron, Leigh Warren & Dancers, 2001–. Andrew Carnegie Lect., Univ. of St Andrews, 2018. Works and performances include: Ethereal Eye (electro-acoustic dance opera), 1996; The Ghost Wife (chamber opera, libretto by Dorothy Porter), 1999; Sandakan Threnody (for solo tenor, chorus and orch.), 2001, theatrical version, 2004; The Eternity Man (chamber opera, libretto by Dorothy Porter), 2003; Eucalyptus (opera based on Murray Bail novel, libretto by Meredith Oakes), 2018; various other works for radio, film, theatre and concert perf. Cultural Fellow, KCL, 2016–. FRSA. DUniv: Stirling, 2008; Queen Margaret Univ., 2009; Dr *hc* Edinburgh, 2012; Hon. DLitt St Andrews, 2013; Hon. DArts RMIT, 2013; Hon. DMus Sydney, 2015. Centenary Medal, Australia, 2002; Prix Italia, 2005; Gloria Artis Medal (Poland), 2013. Chevalier, Ordre des Arts et des Lettres (France), 2014. *Address:* c/o Edinburgh International Culture Summit, 48 Queen Street, Edinburgh EH2 3NR.

**MILLS, Sir Keith (Edward),** GBE 2013; Kt 2006; DL; Deputy Chairman, London Organising Committee, 2012 Olympic Games, 2005–13; Chairman: KEM Management Ltd, since 2000; ORIGIN Sports Group, since 2016; *b* 15 May 1950; *s* of Edward James Mills and Margaret Katherine Mills; *m* 1974, Maureen Elizabeth Simmons; one *s* one *d*. *Educ:* St Martin's, Brentwood. Mktg Exec., Economist newspaper, 1969–74; Mktg Manager, Financial Times, 1974–77; Account Dir, Newton & Godin Advertising, 1977–80; Man. Dir, Nadler & Larimer Advertising, 1980–84; Chm. and CEO, Mills Smith & Partners, 1984–89; CEO, Air Miles UK Ltd, 1988–92; Chairman: Loyalty Management Gp, 1992–2007; Loyalty Management UK Ltd, 2001. Internat. Pres. and CEO, London 2012 Ltd, 2003–06. Dir, AT Racing Ltd, 2006–; non-exec. Dir, Tottenham Hotspur plc, 2007–16. Chairman: Trustees, Sported Foundn (formerly Inspired By Sport Foundn), 2008–18; Invictus Games Foundn, 2014; Trustees, Royal Foundn of The Duke and Duchess of Cambridge (formerly of The Duke and Duchess of Cambridge and Prince Harry, then the Duke and Duchess of Sussex), 2016–; Trustee, RA, 2013–16. DL Kent, 2008. Hon. PhD: Loughborough, 2006; Bath, 2011; Anglia Ruskin, 2011; Essex, 2013; Canterbury Christ Ch, 2014. *Recreations:* sailing, music, travelling. *Address:* 34 Hans Place, SW1X 0JZ. *T:* (office) (020) 7389 1900. *E:* k.mills@kemmanagement.co.uk. *Clubs:* Royal Thames Yacht, Royal Yacht Squadron; New York Yacht.

**MILLS, Leif Anthony,** CBE 1995; General Secretary, Banking, Insurance and Finance Union (formerly National Union of Bank Employees), 1972–96; Chairman, Covent Garden Market Authority, 1998–2005; *b* 25 March 1936; *s* of English father and Norwegian mother; *m* 1958, Gillian Margaret Smith (*d* 2003); two *s* two *d*. *Educ:* Balliol Coll., Oxford. MA Hons PPE. Commnd in Royal Military Police, 1957–59. Trade Union Official, Nat. Union of Bank Employees, 1960–96: Research Officer, 1960; Asst Gen. Sec., 1962; Dep. Gen. Sec., 1968. Mem. various arbitration tribunals; Member: TUC Non-Manual Workers Adv. Cttee, 1967–72; TUC Gen. Council, 1983–96 (Pres., 1994–95); Office of Manpower Economics Adv. Cttee on Equal Pay, 1971; Cttee to Review the Functioning of Financial Instns, 1977–80; CS Pay Res. Unit Bd, 1978–81; Armed Forces Pay Review Body, 1980–87; Monopolies and Mergers Commn, 1982–91; Financial Reporting Council, 1990–96; Ind. Review Cttee on Higher Educn Pay & Conditions, 1998–99; Chairman: TUC Financial Services Cttee, 1983–96; TUC Educn and Training Cttee, 1989–94. Member: BBC Consultative Gp on Social Effects of Television, 1978–80; Council, NCVQ, 1992–96; Bd, Investors in People, 1992–96; PIA Ombudsman Council, 1994–2000 (Dep. Chm., 1997–2000); Bd, Employment Tribunal Service, 1996–2001; Council, Consumers' Assoc., 1996–2002. Contested (Lab) Salisbury, 1964, 1965 (by-elecn). Mem. Governing Body, London Business Sch., 1988–92. Trustee, Civic Trust, 1988–96. FRGS 1992. *Publications:* biography (unpublished), Cook: A History of the Life and Explorations of Dr Frederick Albert Cook, SPRI ms 883, Cambridge, 1970; (published) Frank Wild, Antarctic explorer, 1999; Men of Ice: two polar biographies, 2008; The Redoubtable Mrs Smith: a trade union novel, 2010; The Adventures of Mrs Smith: some trade union stories, 2011. *Recreations:* rowing, chess. *Address:* 1 Orchard View, High Street, Cuddesdon, Oxford OX44 9HP. *T:* (01865) 872022. *Clubs:* Oxford and Cambridge; Oxford University Boat, Weybridge Rowing (Pres., 2008–18).

**MILLS, Rt Rev. Murray John;** Bishop of Waiapu, 1991–2002; Waiapu Diocesan Archivist, since 2008; *b* 29 May 1936; *s* of Robert Claude Mills and Mabel Winifred Mills; *m* 1961, Judith Anne Cotton; two *s* three *d*. *Educ:* Auckland Univ. (BA, MA); St John's Theol Coll. (LTh (First Cl. Hons)). Ordained: Deacon, 1960; Priest, 1961 (dio. of Auckland); Assistant Curate: Papakura, 1960–63; Whangarei, 1963–65; Vicar: Bay of Islands, 1965–70; Matamata, 1970–75; Archdeacon of Waikato, 1976–81; Vicar-Gen., dio. of Waikato, 1978–84; Vicar: Tokoroa, 1981–84; St John's Cathedral, Napier (dio. of Waiapu) and Dean of Waiapu, 1984–91. Examining Chaplain to Bishop of Waikato, 1974–84; Advr in Christian Educn, 1976–81. Liaison Bp, Oceania Mission to Seafarers, 1998–2002; Pres., Conf. of Churches in Aotearoa, NZ, 2000–03. Mem., Assoc. of Christian Spiritual Dirs, 2003–. *Publications:* History of Christ Church, Papakura, 1961. *Recreations:* tramping, gardening, drama, politics, music, reading. *Address:* 12 Clyde Road, Napier 4110, New Zealand. *T:* (6) 8350884.

**MILLS, Nigel John;** MP (C) Amber Valley, since 2010; *b* Jacksdale, 1974; *s* of John and Rosemary Mills; *m* 2013, Alice Elizabeth Ward. *Educ:* Univ. of Newcastle upon Tyne (BA Classics). ACA 2000. Tax Advisor: PricewaterhouseCoopers, 1998–2010; Deloitte, 2010. Mem. (C) Amber Valley BC, 2004–11; Heanor and Loscoe Town Council, 2007–11. Member, Select Committee: on Admin, 2010–17; on NI Affairs, 2011–; on Work and Pensions, 2012–15; Public Accounts, 2015–. *Address:* House of Commons, SW1A 0AA.

**MILLS, Nigel John,** CBE 2018; Co-Founder and Chief Executive Officer, The Lakes Distillery Co. Ltd, since 2012; *b* Newcastle upon Tyne, 30 Sept. 1958; *s* of John Richardson Mills and Rita Leona Mills; *m* 1987, Susan; one *s* one *d*. *Educ:* King's Sch., Tynemouth; Lancaster Univ. (BA(Econ) Hons 1980). ACA 1984. Price Waterhouse, 1980–86; CEO, Mills Gp plc, 1986–2011. Non-executive Director: Closewalk Ltd, 1975–; Trout Hotel Ltd, 1989–. Board Member: Assoc. of Convenience Stores, 2005–11; Entrepreneurs Forum, 2008– (Chm., 2012–18). *Recreations:* golf, tennis, gym. *Address:* Newcastle upon Tyne NE3 2EA. *T:* 07860 72026. *E:* nigel.mills@closewalk.co.uk. *Clubs:* Northumberland Golf, Gosforth Close House Golf.

**MILLS, Oliver Arthur Seymour;** care and health improvement adviser, 2014–17; independent consultant, 2011–17; National Programme Director, Towards Excellence in Adult Social Care, 2011–14; *b* 11 Oct. 1951; *s* of Seymour Herbert Hatten Mills and Mary Patricia Mills; *m* 1990, Janice Reay; two *s*, and one step *d*. *Educ:* Tonbridge Sch.; Univ. of Warwick (BA Hons Hist. 1973); Wadham Coll., Oxford (MSc Applied Soc. Studies 1979; CQSW 1979). Social worker, London Bor. of Camden, 1980–84; Team Leader, London Bor. of Lewisham, 1984–87; Kent County Council, 1987–2011: Social Services Directorate: Asst Dir, 1992–98; Dir, Ops, 1998–2005; Strategic Dir, Social Services, 2005–06; Man. Dir, Adult Social Services, 2006–11. Chm., SE Region, ADASS, 2007–11. Trustee: Football Beyond Borders, 2014– (Chm., 2014–17); Choice Support (formerly mcch (Maidstone Community Care Housing)), 2016– (Chm., 2016–); Partnership Support Gp, 2017– (Chm., 2017–). *Recreations:* playing tennis, music. *Address:* 8 Grove Hill Gardens, Tunbridge Wells, Kent TN1 1SS. *E:* oasmills@btinternet.com.

**MILLS, Sir Peter (Frederick Leighton),** 3rd Bt *cr* 1921; *b* 9 July 1924; *s* of Major Sir Frederick Leighton Victor Mills, 2nd Bt, MC, RA, MICE, and Doris (*née* Armitage); S father, 1955; *m* 1954, Pauline Mary, *d* of L. R. Allen, Calverton, Notts; one *s* (one adopted *d* decd). *Educ:* Eastbourne Coll.; Cedara Coll. of Agriculture, University of Natal (BSc Agric.). Served HM Forces, 1943–47. CS, Fedn Rhodesia and Nyasaland, 1953; with Rhodesia Min. of Agric., 1964, Zimbabwe Min. of Agric., 1980–90. *Heir: s* Michael Victor Leighton Mills [*b* 30 Aug. 1957; *m* 1981, Susan, *d* of J. Doig, Harare, Zimbabwe].

**MILLS, Rev. Peter Watson,** CB 2010; Minister, Largoward with St Monans, 2013–18; *b* 9 Feb. 1955; *s* of late Peter Watson Mills and of Janet (*née* Lonsdale); *m* 1979, Sheila Anderson; two *d*. *Educ:* Arbroath High Sch.; Christ's Coll., Univ. of Aberdeen (BD 1983, CPS 1983). Police Constable, Grampian Police, 1974–78. Licensed 1983, ordained, 1984; Asst Minister, Montrose, 1983–84; RAF Chaplain, 1984–2009; Principal Chaplain, C of S and Free Churches, 2001–06; Chaplain-in-Chief and Dir Gen. Chaplaincy Services, 2006–09; Minister, St Andrew's, Corby, 2009–13. Clerk, Presbytery of England, 2010–13; Chair, Churches Together, Corby District, 2010–13; Moderator, Presbytery of St Andrews, 2017–18. QHC 2001–10. Hon. DD Aberdeen, 2009. *Recreations:* reading, music, electric guitar. *Address:* 16 Pearce Drive, Lawley, Telford TF3 5JQ. *Club:* Royal Air Force.

**MILLS, Peter William;** QC (Can.) 1985; company director and business consultant, 1999–2013; *b* 22 July 1942; *s* of Joseph Roger Mills and Jane Evelyn (*née* Roscoe); *m* 1967, Eveline Jane (*née* Black); two *s*. *Educ:* Dalhousie Univ. Law Sch. (JD (LLB 1967)); Dalhousie Univ. (BComm). ICD.D 2005. Barrister and solicitor, Ont, Canada; with McInnes, Cooper and Robertson, Halifax, 1967; Solicitor, Canadian Pacific Ltd, Montreal and Toronto, 1967–71; Dir, Cammell Laird Shipbuilders Ltd, 1971–76; Mem., Org Cttee for British Shipbuilders, 1976–77; Manager, Currie, Coopers & Lybrand Ltd, Toronto, 1977–79; The Woodbridge Co. Ltd: Gen. Counsel, 1980–98; Vice-Pres., 1980–87; Dir, 1982–98; Sen. Vice-Pres., 1988–98. Director: Corporate Develt, FP Publications Ltd, 1979–80; Augusta Newsprint Co., 1981–2011; Hudson's Bay Co., 1985–2006; Markborough Properties Inc., 1986–97; Cambridge Shopping Centres Ltd, 1997–2001; Cadillac Fairview Corp. Ltd, 2001–12; Torstar Corp., 2004–06; Jacques Whitford Ltd, 2007–09. Occasional Exec. in Residence, Rotman Sch. of Business, Univ. of Toronto. Examr for Certification in Dirs' Educn Prog., Inst. of Corporate Dirs. Dir, St John's Rehabilitation Hosp. Foundn, 2002–03; Chm., Hudson's Bay Co. History Foundn, 2005–06. Dir, Canadian Inst. of Chartered Accts, 2004–10. Occasional panelist on governance, business and legal subjects. *Recreations:* golf, sailing, travel, reading. *Address:* 390 Glencairn Avenue, Toronto, ON M5N 1V1, Canada. *E:* pwmills@sympatico.ca. *Club:* York Downs Golf and Country (Toronto).

**MILLS, Richard Michael;** Chairman and Chief Executive, Delfont Mackintosh Theatres Ltd, 1991–96; *b* 26 June 1931; *s* of Richard Henry Mills and Catherine Keeley; *m* 1st, 1960, Lynda Taylor (marr. diss. 1967); one *d*, 2nd, 1983, Sheila White (*d* 2018); two *s*. Commenced working in the theatre as an Assistant Stage Manager in 1948, and worked in every capacity, including acting and stage management. Joined Bernard Delfont Ltd, 1962; Dir, 1967; Dep. Chm., 1970–79; Chm., 1979–91; Chief Exec., 1970–91; Managing Director: Prince of Wales Theatre, 1970–96; Prince Edward Theatre, 1978–96. Director: EMI Film & Theatre Corp., 1970–81; Trust House Forte Leisure, 1980–83; First Leisure Corp., 1983–93. Member: Nat. Theatre Bd, 1976–91; Finance and Gen. Purposes Cttee, NT, 1976–91; Drama Panel, Arts Council of GB, 1976–77; English Tourist Bd, 1982–85. Pres., Stage Golfing Soc., 2004–05. Shows worked on in the West End, 1948–62, include: I Remember Mama, Tuppence Coloured, Medea, Adventure Story, Anne Veronica, The Devil's General, I Capture the Castle, No Escape, Misery Me, Three Times a Day, The Sun of York, To my Love, Be my Guest, Hunter's Moon, The Iceman Cometh, Brouhaha, Detour after Dark, The Ginger Man, Sound of Murder, Will You Walk a Little Faster, Pool's Paradise, Belle, Come Blow your Horn. Whilst Gen. Manager and Dir with Bernard Delfont Ltd: Never Too Late, Pickwick, 1962; Caligula, Maggie May, Little Me, Our Man Crichton, 1963; The Roar of the Greasepaint (NY), Pickwick (NY), Twang, Barefoot in the Park, 1964; The Owl and the Pussycat, The Matchgirls, Funny Girl, Joey Joey, The Odd Couple, 1965; Queenie, Sweet Charity, The Four Musketeers, 1966; Golden Boy, Look Back in Anger (revival), Mame, Cat Among the Pigeons, 1968; Carol Channing, Danny La Rue at the Palace, 1969; Kean, Lulu, 1970; Applause, The Unknown Soldier and his Wife, 1971. With Lord Delfont presented in the West End: The Good Old Bad Old Days, Mardi Gras, Brief Lives, Queen Daniella, Cinderella, Henry IV, Harvey, Sammy Cahn's Songbook, Streetcar Named Desire, Good Companions, It's All Right if I Do It, Charley's Aunt, An Evening with Tommy Steele, Gomes, The Wolf, Danny La Rue Show, Beyond the Rainbow, Dad's Army, Plumber's Progress, Paul Daniels Magic Show, Underneath the Arches, Little Me, The Best Little Whorehouse in Texas, and over 200 pantomimes and summer season shows. *Recreations:* golf, poker. *Clubs:* Royal Automobile; Richmond Golf.

**MILLS, Robert Ferris;** Under Secretary, Department of Finance and Personnel, Northern Ireland, 1990–96, retired; *b* 21 Sept. 1939; *s* of Robert and Rachel Mills; *m* 1st, 1968, Irene Sandra Miskelly (marr. diss. 1978); one *s* one *d*; 2nd, 1984, Frances Elizabeth Gillies; two step *d*. *Educ:* Sullivan Upper School, Holywood, Co. Down; Queen's Univ., Belfast (BA Hons). Inland Revenue, 1961–64; Min. of Commerce, NI, 1964–68; Dept of Housing and Local Govt, 1968–71; Dept of the Environment, NI, 1971–75; Asst Sec., 1975–83, Under Sec., 1983–90, Dept of Health and Social Services, NI. *Recreations:* golf, tennis, travel, the arts.

**MILLS, Simon Yarnton**; Herbal Strategist, Pukka Herbs, since 2016; *b* Lyons, France, 2 Nov. 1949; *s* of Hamilton and Vlasta Mills; partner, 1988, Rachel Charlesworth (now Mills); one *s* one *d* and two step *d. Educ:* Sacred Heart Coll., Auckland, NZ; Churchill Coll., Cambridge (BA Med. Scis Tripos 1970). Nurseryman and horticultural consultant, 1970–77; herbal practitioner, 1977–; Pres., Nat. Inst. of Medical Herbalists, 1983–88; Founder Chm., Council for Complementary and Alternative Medicine, 1985–89; Founder Director: Centre for Complementary Health Studies, Univ. of Exeter, 1987–2000; MSc Prog. in Herbal Medicine, Maryland Univ. of Integrative Health (formerly Tai Sophia Inst., Md), 2000–14; Sen. Teaching Fellow, Peninsula Med. Sch., Exeter, 2003–08; Project Lead, Integrated Self Care in Family Practice prog., DoH, 2008–11; Man. Dir, Sustaincare CIC, 2008–16. Specialist Advr, H of L Select Cttee on Complementary and Alternative Medicine, 1999–2000. Professional Mem., Herbal Medicine Adv. Cttee, 2005–09. Chm., British Herbal Medicine Assoc., 1999–2004. *Publications:* Alternatives in Healing, 1988; Out of the Earth, 1991; (with K. Bone) Principles and Practice of Phytotherapy, 2000, 2nd edn 2013; (with K. Bone) The Essential Guide to Herbal Safety, 2005. *Recreations:* gardening, walking, finding good country pubs, fly fishing. *Address:* Notaries House, Chapel Street, Exeter EX1 1AJ. *T:* (01392) 423210, *Fax:* (01392) 424864. *E:* symills@gmail.com. *Club:* Royal Society of Medicine.

**MILLS, (William) Stratton**; Senior Partner, 1974–2000, Consultant, 2000–05, Mills, Selig, Solicitors, Belfast (Partner, 1959–74); company director; Chairman, Hampden Group PLC (formerly Hampden Homecare plc), 1992–99; *b* 1 July 1932; *o s* of late Dr J. V. S. Mills, CBE, Resident Magistrate for City of Belfast, and Margaret Florence (*née* Byford); *m* 1959, Merriel E. R. Whitla, *o d* of late Mr and Mrs R. J. Whitla, Belfast; three *s. Educ:* Campbell Coll., Belfast; Queen's Univ., Belfast (LLB). Vice-Chm., Federation of University Conservative and Unionist Assocs, 1952–53 and 1954–55; admitted a Solicitor, 1958. MP (UU) Belfast N, Oct. 1959–Dec. 1972; MP (Alliance) Belfast N, April 1973–Feb. 1974; PPS to Parly Sec., Ministry of Transport, 1961–64; Member: Estimates Cttee, 1964–70; Exec. Cttee, 1922 Cttee, 1967–70, 1973; Hon. Sec. Conservative Broadcasting Cttee, 1963–70, Chm., 1970–73; Mem., Mr Speaker's Conference on Electoral Law, 1967. Mem., One Nation Gp, 1972–73. Member: Adv. Bd, Public Records Office, NI, 1996–2008; Bd, Historic Bldgs Council for NI, 2004–10. Chm., Ulster Orchestra Soc. Ltd, 1980–90; Mem. Bd, Castleward Opera, 1988–98; Dir, Opera Rara, 1998–2015. Mem. Council, Winston Churchill Meml Trust, 1990–95. Arnold Goodman Award, for encouragement of business sponsorship of the arts, 1990. *Address:* 17 Malone Park, Belfast BT9 6NJ. *Clubs:* Carlton, MCC; Reform (Belfast); Royal County Down Golf.

**MILLS-EVANS, Carole Denise;** *see* Mills, C. D.

**MILLSON, Tony;** HM Diplomatic Service, retired; Counsellor, Foreign and Commonwealth Office, 2001–03; *b* 25 Nov. 1951; *s* of Donald Millson and Joan (*née* Whittle); civil partnership 2019, Anthony James Davis. *Educ:* Grimsby Wintringham Grammar Sch. Entered HM Diplomatic Service, 1970; MECAS, 1973; Third Sec. (Commercial), Tripoli, 1974–76; Third, later Second Sec. (Develt), Amman, 1976–80; FCO, 1980–83; Second Sec., BMG Berlin, 1983–86; First Sec., FCO, 1986–88; Hd of Chancery, Kuwait, 1988–90; FCO, 1991–93; Ambassador to Macedonia, 1993–97; Counsellor, FCO, 1997–98; High Comr, The Gambia, 1998–2000; Dep. High Comr, Abuja, 2000–01. JP London, 2004–16; Chm., Balham Youth Court, 2011. *Recreations:* reading, listening to music, surfing the web, long walks, eating out, volunteering at Southwark Playhouse. *Address:* 7 George Mathers Road, Kennington, SE11 4RU. *T:* (020) 3524 6719.

**MILLWARD, Michael Timothy Lawrence;** international adviser, since 2016; Director, Rabat Office, and Representative to Morocco, Algeria, Mauritania and Tunisia, UNESCO, 2014–16; *b* Bath, 5 July 1954; *s* of Lawrence Millward and Alison Millward (*née* Griffiths); *m* 1979, Michelle Rey; one *s. Educ:* Wallington High Sch. for Boys; Salford Univ. (BSc Hons Mod. Langs 1976). FTCL 1972. Teacher, English to foreigners, 1976–78; translator, 1978–84; Language Reviser, UNESCO, 1985–89; Asst Exec. Dir, ICSU, 1989–93; UNESCO: Liaison Officer, NGOs, External Relns, 1994–99; Sen. Liaison Officer, Office of Dir-Gen., 1999–2003; Dir, Exec. Office, Science Sector, 2003–05; Interim Dir, UNESCO Inst. for Stats, then Interim Dir, UNESCO Office, Venice, 2005–06; Sec., Gen. Conference of UNESCO, 2006–08; Dep. Dir, 2008–09, Dir, 2009–13, Governing Bodies Secretariat, and Sec., Gen. Conf. and Exec. Bd, 2009–13, UNESCO. Mem., Les Musicales du Luberon. *Recreations:* music, literature, theatre, travel, cuisine.

**MILMAN, Andrée, (Mrs David Milman);** *see* Grenfell, A.

**MILMAN, Sir David (Patrick),** 10th Bt *cr* 1800, of Levaton-in-Woodland, Devonshire; educational consultant, since 1999; *b* 24 Aug. 1945; *er s* of Lt-Col Sir Derek Milman, 9th Bt and Christine Margaret Milman (*née* Whitehouse); *S* father, 1999; *m* 1969, Christina Hunt; one *s* one *d. Educ:* London Univ. (Teacher's Cert. 1st cl. 1968; BEd (Hons) 1969) MA 1976). Headteacher, 1981–89; Headteacher Trng Co-ordinator, ILEA, 1988–89; Asst Dir, Sch. Mgt South, 1989–91; Area Advr, 1991–93, Sen. Area Advr, 1993–98, NW Kent; District Adv. Officer, Dartford, 1998–99. *Publications:* Teachers' Guidelines to Take Part Readers Series, 1973; Take a Look Series, 1974; What do you think?, 1976; Senior Manager's Personal Profile, 1991. *Recreations:* ornithology, painting, philosophy. *Heir: s* Thomas Hart Milman, *b* 7 Oct. 1976. *Address:* 71 Camden Road, Sevenoaks, Kent TN13 3LU. *T:* (01732) 459089.

**MILMO, His Honour John Boyle Martin;** QC 1984; a Circuit Judge, 2004–13; *b* 19 Jan. 1943; *s* of late Dermod Hubert Francis Milmo, MB BCh and Eileen Clare Milmo (*née* White). *Educ:* Downside Sch.; Trinity Coll., Dublin (MA, LLB). Called to the Bar, Lincoln's Inn, 1966, Bencher, 1992; a Recorder, 1982–2004; a Dep. High Ct Judge, 1993–2004. Mem., Parole Bd, 2005–16. Mem., Bar Council, 1992–2002 (Chm., Legal Aid and Fees Cttee, 1996–97). Chm., Adv. Bd, Criminal Justice Res. Centre, Nottingham Univ., 2014–18. Trustee, Historic Singers Trust, 2004–. *Recreations:* opera, discography. *Club:* United Services (Nottingham).

**MILMO, Patrick Helenus;** QC 1985; *b* 11 May 1938; *s* of Sir Helenus Milmo; *m* 1968, Marina, *d* of late Alexis Schiray and Xenia Schiray; one *s* one *d. Educ:* Downside; Trinity Coll., Cambridge (BA 1961; MA 1997). Harmsworth Scholar; called to the Bar, Middle Temple, 1962 (Bencher, 1994; Reader, 2005). Part-time employment judge, 1998–2010. Asst Comr, Parly Boundary Commn, 2000–08. Dep. Chm., Disciplinary Cttee, RPSGB, 2008–10; Chm., Fitness to Practise Cttee, Gen. Pharmaceutical Council, 2010–16; Mem., Disciplinary Panel, British Horseracing Authy, 2016–. *Publications:* (ed jtly) Gatley on Libel and Slander, 9th edn 1998 to 11th edn 2009. *Recreations:* wine, horse-racing, cinema. *Address:* 5 Gray's Inn Square, Gray's Inn, WC1R 5AH; 7 Baalbec Road, N5 1QN.

**MILNE,** family name of **Baron Milne**.

**MILNE, 3rd Baron** *cr* 1933, of Salonika and of Rubislaw, co. Aberdeen; **George Alexander Milne;** self-employed chair caner (Abelcaner); *b* 1 April 1941; *s* of 2nd Baron Milne, TD and of Cicely Abigail Milne (*née* Leslie); *S* father, 2005. *Educ:* Winchester. Liveryman, Grocers' Co. *Recreations:* sailing, bicycling, golf. *Heir: b* Hon. Iain Charles Luis Milne [*b* 16 Sept. 1949; *m* 1987, Berta Guerrero; two *s*]. *T:* (020) 8977 9761. *E:* george.milne2@btinternet.com. *Club:* Pilgrims.

**MILNE, Alexander Hugh;** QC 2010; **His Honour Judge Milne;** a Circuit Judge, since 2018; *b* Hull, 20 April 1959; *s* of late Michael Oliver Milne and of Maureen Milne; *m* 1993, Sian Elizabeth Fleet (*née* Brewis); one step *s* one step *d. Educ:* Nottingham Univ. (BA Hons Law 1980). Called to the Bar, Gray's Inn, 1981, Bencher, 2015; Claims Corresp., W of England Protection and Indemnity Club, 1982–86; Campaigns Officer, British Section, Amnesty Internat., 1986; Blick & Co., Solicitors, 1986–87; barrister in private practice, specialising in criminal, regulatory and disciplinary law and public enquiries, 1987–2018; a Recorder, 2007–18. Sen. Trial Counsel to Office of Prosecutor, Special Tribunal for Lebanon, 2013–18. Alternate Comr, Disciplinary Bd for Counsel, Internat. Criminal Ct, 2015–19. Associate MCIArb 2011; Supporting Mem., London Maritime Arbitrators Assoc., 2012–. *Publications:* (Contrib. Ed.) Arlidge and Parry on Fraud. *Recreations:* golf (in warmer climes), dog-walking. *Address:* Blackfriars Crown Court, 1–15 Pocock Street, SE1 0BT. *T:* (020) 7922 5800.

**MILNE, David Calder;** QC 1987; a Recorder, 1994–2006 (Assistant Recorder, 1989–94); *b* 22 Sept. 1945; *s* of late Ernest and Helena Milne; *m* 1st, 1978, Rosemary Bond (marr. diss. 1999); one *d;* 2nd, 2013, Amanda Robin Shepherd (*née* Clezy). *Educ:* Harrow Sch.; Oxford Univ. (MA). ACA 1969; FCA 1974. Articled to Whinney Murray & Co., chartered accountants, 1966–69; called to the Bar, Lincoln's Inn, 1970, Bencher, 1996. Trustee: Wildfowl and Wetlands Trust, 2002–11; British Trust for Ornithology, 2009–12. Hon. Fellow, Chartered Inst. of Taxation, 2009. *Recreations:* natural history, music, golf, Rugby. *Address:* (chambers) 16 Bedford Row, WC1R 4EF. *T:* (020) 7414 8080. *E:* dmilne@pumptax.com. *Clubs:* Garrick, Gnomes; Walton Heath Golf.

**MILNE, Maj. Gen. John,** CB 2000; Regimental Controller, Royal Artillery, 2009–16; *b* 13 Oct. 1946; *s* of Donald William Milne and Evelyn (*née* Ayrer); *m* 1970, Cherrill Rosemary Tookey; two *s* one *d. Educ:* Lowestoft Grammar Sch.; Royal Coll. of Defence Studies. Commnd, Royal Artillery, 1966: helicopter pilot, 1970–74; Mil. Asst, COS Northern Army Gp, 1980–82; Comdr, 2 Field Regt, 1986–88; Dep. Comdr, 7 Armd Bde, Saudi Arabia, 1990; Comdr, 1 Artillery Bde, 1992–93; Dir, Army Recruiting, 1994–97; Dep. Comdr for Logistics, Stabilisation Force, Bosnia Herzogovina, 1997; Dir for Support, Allied Land Forces, Central Europe, 1998–99; COS Kosovo Force, Pristina, 1999–2000. Col Comdt, RA, 2001–07. Registrar, St Paul's Cathedral, 2001–08. Trustee: Haig Homes, 2010–18; Mus. of Army Chaplaincy, 2018–. Freeman, City of London, 2001; Liveryman, Masons' Co., 2002–. Bronze Star (US), 1991. *Recreations:* tennis, golf, bridge. *Address:* Lloyds Bank, 174 Fleet Road, Fleet, Hants GU51 4DD.

**MILNE, Judith Frances;** *see* English, J. F.

**MILNE, Nanette Lilian Margaret,** OBE 1994; Member (C) Scotland North East, Scottish Parliament, 2003–16; *b* 27 April 1942; *d* of Harold G. Gordon and Hannah L. C. Gordon (*née* Stephen); *m* 1965, Alan Ducat Milne; one *s* one *d. Educ:* Aberdeen High Sch. for Girls; Univ. of Aberdeen (MB ChB 1965). FFARCS 1969. Medical Officer, Grampian Health Board, later Aberdeen Royal Hospitals NHS Trust: anaesthetics, 1966–73; oncology research, 1980–92. Mem. (C), City of Aberdeen DC, 1988–96, Aberdeen CC, 1995–99. Vice-Chm., Scottish Cons. and Unionist Party, 1989–93. JP Aberdeen, 1993–2007. Hon. Dr Aberdeen, 2016. *Publications:* contrib. to BMJ on cardiovascular effects of laparoscopy and on colorectal cancer. *Recreations:* gardening, sports.

**MILNE, Nikola Caroline;** *see* Stewart, N. C.

**MILNE, Ronald Robert,** FRSE; FCLIP; Dean, Educational Resources and Technology, Yale-NUS College, Singapore, since 2016; *b* 14 Feb. 1957; *s* of Robert Hally Milne and Joyce (*née* McRobbie). *Educ:* Perth Acad.; Berwickshire High Sch.; Univ. of Edinburgh (MA 1979); University Coll. London (MA 1984); MA Oxon 2003. FCLIP (FLA 2001). SCONUL trainee, Cambridge Univ. Liby, 1981–82; Sen. Liby Asst, Univ. of London Liby Resources Co-ordinating Cttee, 1983–85; Asst Librarian, Glasgow Univ. Liby, 1985–90; Sub-Librarian, Trinity Coll., Cambridge, 1990–94; Asst Dir of Liby Services, KCL, 1994–98; Dir, Res. Support Libraries Prog., 1998–2002; Dep. to Dir, Univ. Liby Services and to Bodley's Librarian, 2002–04; Acting Dir and Bodley's Librarian, 2004–07, Oxford Univ.; Fellow, Wolfson Coll., Oxford, 2003–07; Dir of Scholarship and Collections, British Liby, 2007–09; Associate Chief Librarian (Research Collections), Alexander Turnbull Liby, Nat. Liby of NZ, 2009–11; Dep. Chief Exec. and Heritage Services Br. Manager, 2011–13, Dir, Heritage Projects, 2013–14, Min. for Culture and Heritage, NZ; George Lyndon Hicks Fellow, Nat. Liby of Singapore, 2016. FRSA 2000; FRSE 2006. *Publications:* contribs to professional jls and books. *Recreations:* travel, hiking, listening to music, photography. *Address:* Yale-NUS College, 20 College Avenue West, Singapore 138529. *E:* ronald.milne@yale-nus.edu.sg. *Clubs:* Reform; New Zealand Alpine.

**MILNE, Lt Col Simon Stephen,** MBE 1996; FRGS; Regius Keeper, Royal Botanic Garden Edinburgh, since 2014; *b* Dundee, 30 Jan. 1959; *s* of Stephen Milne and Susan Milne (*née* Cox); *m* 1993, Françoise Sevaux; one *s* two *d. Educ:* Univ. of St Andrews (BSc 1979); RNC Greenwich. Royal Marines, 1976–2000: 2nd Lt 1976; served: 41 and 45 Commandos; Comacchio Gp; HQ 3 Cdo Bde; HQ Cdo Forces; Dept of Comdt Gen.; Directorate of Navy Plans, MoD; Rapid Response Force Operational Staff, Bosnia; HQ NI. Dir, Sir Harold Hillier Gardens and Arboretum, 2000–04; Chief Exec., Scottish Wildlife Trust, 2004–14. Hon. Prof., Univ. of Edinburgh, 2016–18. Trustee: Sibbald Trust, 2014–; Younger Benmore Trust, 2014–; Macintyre Begonia Trust, 2015–; Crawick Multiverse Trust, 2016–. Hon. Vice Pres., Royal Caledonian Horticultural Soc., 2014. Mem., HM Bodyguard, Hon. Corps of Gentlemen at Arms, 2012–. FRGS 1990. *Publications:* articles on conservation and biodiversity. *Recreations:* ski-ing, country pursuits, gardening, ornithology. *Address:* Royal Botanic Garden Edinburgh, 20A Inverleith Row, Edinburgh EH3 5LR. *Club:* Army and Navy.

**MILNE, Prof. William Ireland,** PhD; FREng, FIET, FIMMM; Professor of Electrical Engineering, 1996–2015, now Emeritus, and Director, Centre for Advanced Photonics and Electronics, 2005–15, University of Cambridge; Fellow, Churchill College, Cambridge, since 1977; *b* 15 Feb. 1948; *s* of William Ireland Milne and Jenelia Foy Kelso Milne (*née* Reid); *m* 1st, 1971, Jennifer Stovell (marr. diss. 1991); one *s* one *d;* 2nd, 1992, Catharina Jacqueline Ann Baker; one step *s* one step *d. Educ:* Forfar Acad.; St Andrews Univ. (BSc Hons 1970); Imperial Coll., London DIC, PhD 1973). FIET (FIEE 1989); FIMMM (FIM 1999). Sen. Scientist, then Principal Scientist, Plessey Res. Centre, Caswell, 1973–76; Engineering Department, University of Cambridge: Asst Lectr, 1976–80; Lectr, 1980–90; Reader, 1990–96; Hd, Electrical Div., 1999–2014. Visiting Professor: Tokyo Inst. of Technol., 1985 (Dist. Vis. Prof., 2014–16); Nanyang Technol Univ., Singapore, 1993; Gifu Univ., Japan, 2001; South East Univ., Nanying, 2007–; Shizuoka Univ., 2010–; Hong

Kong Poly. Univ., 2014; Dist. Vis. Prof., Nat. Univ. of Singapore, 2008; Hon. Prof., Coll. of Sci. and Technol. of Huazhang Normal Univ., 2007–; Dist. Vis. Scientist, Changchun Univ. of Sci. and Technol., China, 2017–; Dist. Vis. Scholar, Kyung Hee Univ. Seoul, 2009–16; Erskine Fellow, Univ. of Christchurch, NZ, 2015; 1000 Talents Chair, Zhejiang Univ., China, 2016. FREng 2006. Hon. DEng Univ. of Waterloo, Toronto, 2003. J. J. Thomson Medal, IET, 2008; NANOSMAT Prize, 2010. *Recreations:* golf, tennis, travel. *Address:* Electrical Division Building, Engineering Department, Cambridge University, 9 J. J. Thomson Avenue, Cambridge CB3 0FA.

**MILNE-WATSON, Sir Andrew (Michael),** 4th Bt *cr* 1937, of Ashley, Longbredy, co. Dorset; Partner, GM-W Fabrics, since 2009; *b* 10 Nov. 1944; *o s* of Sir Michael Milne-Watson, 3rd Bt, CBE and Mary Lisette Gunion Milne-Watson (*née* Bagnall); *S* father, 1999; *m* 1st, 1970, Beverley Jane Gabrielle Cotton (marr. diss. 1981); one *s* one *d*; 2nd, 1983, Gisella Stafford (*née* Tisdall); one *s*. *Educ:* Eton. Sales and Mgt Trainee, Sidney Flavel & Co. Ltd, 1965–68; Mgt Trainee, E Midlands Gas Bd, 1968–69; Ogilvy & Mather (UK): Trainee, 1969; Account Mgr, 1970; Account Dir, 1973–79; Managing and Client Service Director: Mathers Advertising Ltd, 1979–82; Phoenix Advertising Ltd, 1982–84; Dep. Chm., Lewis Broadbent Advertising Ltd, 1984–87; founded: Minerva Publications Ltd, 1987–89; MW Communications Ltd, 1989–90; Dir of Advertising and Mktg, Inc. Publications, 1990–93; Proprietor, A. D. R. Associates Ltd, 1993–2009. Liveryman, Grocers' Co. *Recreations:* cooking, gardening, building renovation. *Heir: s* David Alastair Milne-Watson [*b* 24 Aug. 1971; *m* 2000, Sandra M. Geraldi, Campinas, Brazil]. *Address:* 164 Rivermead Court, SW6 3SF. *T:* 07768 514310. *Club:* Garrick.

**MILNER,** family name of **Baron Milner of Leeds**.

**MILNER OF LEEDS,** 3rd Baron *cr* 1951; **Richard James Milner;** *b* 16 May 1959; *s* of 2nd Baron Milner of Leeds, AE and Sheila Margaret (*née* Hartley); *S* father, 2003; *m* 1988, Margaret, *y d* of G. F. Voisin; two *d*. *Educ:* Charterhouse; Surrey Univ. (BSc). Freeman, City of London, 1988; Liveryman, Clothworkers' Co., 1988. Mem., Vins Sans Frontières, Jersey. *Heir:* none.

**MILNER, Prof. (Arthur) David,** PhD; FRS 2011; FRSE; Professor of Cognitive Neuroscience, University of Durham, 2000–08, now Emeritus; *b* 16 July 1943; *s* of Arthur Milner and Sarah Ellen Milner (*née* Gaunt); *m* 1965, Christine Armitage; two *s*. *Educ:* Bradford Grammar Sch.; Lincoln Coll., Oxford (Open Schol.; BA 1965; MA 1970); Inst. of Psychiatry, London (DipPsych 1966; PhD 1971). Res. Asst, Inst. of Psychiatry, London, 1966–70; University of St Andrews: Lectr, 1970–82, Sen. Lectr, 1982–85, in Psychology; Reader in Neuropsychology, 1985–90; Prof. of Neuropsychology, 1990–2000; Chm., Dept of Psychology, 1983–88; Dean, Faculty of Science, 1992–94; Head, Sch. of Psychology, 1994–97. Hon. Prof., Univ. of Edinburgh, 2015–. FRSE 1992. *Publications:* The Neuropsychology of Consciousness, 1992; (with M. A. Goodale) The Visual Brain in Action, 1995, 2nd edn 2006; Comparative Neuropsychology, 1998; Cognitive and Neural Bases of Spatial Neglect, 2002; (with M. A. Goodale) Sight Unseen, 2004 (BPsS Book Award, 2005), 2nd edn 2013; The Roots of Visual Awareness, 2004; sci. articles in learned jls and books, mainly on brain mechanisms underlying visual perception, visual guidance of movement, and visual attention. *Recreations:* walking, cinema, jazz.

**MILNER, Prof. Brenda (Atkinson),** CC 2004 (OC 1984); GOQ 2009 (OQ 1985); FRS 1979; FRSC 1976; Professor, Department of Neurology and Neurosurgery, McGill University, since 1970; Dorothy J. Killam Professor, Montreal Neurological Institute, since 1993 (Head of Neuropsychology Research Unit, 1970–91); *b* 15 July 1918; *d* of Samuel Langford and Clarice Frances Leslie (*née* Doig). *Educ:* Univ. of Cambridge (BA, MA, ScD); McGill Univ. (PhD). Experimental Officer, Min. of Supply, 1941–44; Professeur Agrégé, Inst. de Psychologie, Univ. de Montréal, 1944–52; Res. Associate, Psychology Dept, McGill Univ., 1952–53; Lectr, 1953–60, Asst Prof., 1960–64, Associate Prof., 1964–70, Dept of Neurology and Neurosurgery, McGill Univ. Hon. LLD: Queen's Univ., Kingston, Ont, 1980; Cambridge, 2000; Hon. DSc: Manitoba, 1982; Lethbridge, 1986; Mount Holyoke, 1986; Toronto, 1987; McGill, 1991; Wesleyan, 1991; Acadia, 1991; St Andrews, 1992; Hartford, 1997; McMaster, 1999; Memorial, 2002; Columbia, 2002; Ryerson, 2008; Hon. DSocSc Laval, 1987; Hon. Dr Montreal, 1988; Hon. DHumLit Mount St Vincent, 1988; DU Ottawa, 2004. Izaak Walton Killam Prize, Canada Council, 1983; Hermann von Helmholtz Prize, Inst. for Cognitive Neuroscience, USA, 1984; Ralph W. Gerard Prize, Soc. for Neuroscience, 1987; Wilder Penfield Prize, PQ, 1993; Metropolitan Life Foundn award, 1996; John. P. McGovern Award, AAAS, 2001; D. O. Hebb Award, Canadian Soc. for Brain, Behaviour and Cognitive Sci., 2001; Neurosci. Award, NAS, 2004; Gairder Foundn Award in Health Res., 2005; Pearl Meister Greengard Prize, 2011; Balzan Prize, Internat. Balzan Prize Foundn, 2012; Dan David Prize, Dan David Foundn, 2014; Kavli Prize in Neurosci., 2014. Grand Dame of Merit, Order of Malta, 1985. *Publications:* mainly articles in neurological and psychological jls. *Address:* Montreal Neurological Institute, 3801 University Street, Montreal, QC H3A 2B4, Canada. *T:* (514) 3988503, *Fax:* (514) 3988540.

**MILNER, David;** *see* Milner, A. D.

**MILNER, Eileen Maria;** Chief Executive, Education and Skills Funding Agency, since 2017; *b* Brighton, 26 Oct. 1963; *d* of Richard and Margaret Milner; *m* 1989, Richard Atkinson; one *d*. *Educ:* Bodmin Sch., Cornwall; Univ. of Wales, Aberystwyth (BA English; Postgrad. Dip. Mktg). Executive Director: Northgate Public Services, 2010–13; Care Quality Commn, 2013–17. Trustee, Bell Educnl Trust, 2009–15. *Publications:* Managing Information and Knowledge in the Public Sector, 1999; Delivering the Vision, 2000; Lesson in Leadership, 2004. *Recreations:* travel, gardening, family. *Address:* Education and Skills Funding Agency, 4th Floor, Sanctuary Buildings, Great Smith Street, SW1P 3BT. *T:* 07795 454394, 07384 456757. *E:* Eileen.milner@education.gov.uk. *Club:* Royal Over-Seas League.

**MILNER, Rt Rev. Ronald James;** Bishop Suffragan of Burnley, 1988–93; Hon. Assistant Bishop, diocese of Southwell and Nottingham (formerly diocese of Southwell), since 1994; *b* 16 May 1927; *s* of Maurice and Muriel Milner; *m* 1950, Audrey Cynthia Howard (*d* 2017); two *s* two *d* (and one *d* decd). *Educ:* Hull Grammar School; Pembroke Coll., Cambridge (MA); Wycliffe Hall, Oxford. Ordained deacon, 1953, priest, 1954; Succentor, Sheffield Cathedral, 1953–58; Vicar: Westwood, Coventry, 1958–64; St James, Fletchamstead, Coventry, 1964–70; Rector of St Mary's, Southampton, 1970–73; Rector of the Southampton Team Ministry, 1973–83; Archdeacon of Lincoln, 1983–88. *Recreations:* ornithology, walking, music. *Address:* 7 Crafts Way, Southwell, Notts NG25 0BL.

**MILNER, Dr Simon Trevor;** Vice President, Public Policy, Asia and Pacific, Facebook, since 2018; *b* 23 April 1967; *s* of Trevor Winston Milner and Christine Mary Milner; *m* 1991, Sarah Wells; two *s* one *d*. *Educ:* Bradford Grammar Sch.; Wadham Coll., Oxford (BA Hons Hist. and Econs); London Sch. of Econs (MSc Industrial Relns, PhD Industrial Relns 1993). London School of Economics: Res. Officer, Centre for Econ. Performance, 1990–94; Lectr, Dept of Industrial Relns, 1994–95; Sec., Commn on Public Policy and British Business, IPPR, 1995–97; Sen. Advr, Policy and Planning, 1997–99, Secretary, 2000–05, BBC; BT plc: Hd, Ext. Relns, Equality of Access Office, 2005–08; Dir, Media and Convergence Policy, 2008–09; Dir, Gp Industry Policy, 2009–11; Dir of Policy, UK and Ireland, 2012–14, UK, Middle East and Africa, 2014–18, Facebook. *Publications:* New Perspectives on Industrial Disputes, 1993. *Recreations:* children, football, camping, festivals.

**MILNER, Sir Timothy William Lycett, (Sir Tim),** 10th Bt *cr* 1717, of Nun Appleton Hall, Yorkshire; *b* 11 Oct. 1936; *er s* of Sir (George Edward) Mordaunt Milner, 9th Bt and Barbara Audrey (*d* 1951), *d* of Henry Noel Belsham; *S* father, 1995. *Heir: nephew* Marcus Charles Mordaunt Milner [*b* 6 Jan. 1968; *m* 1998, Catherine Anne Lane; two *s*]. *Address:* c/o Natte Valleij, Box 4, Klapmuts 7625, South Africa.

**MILNER-GULLAND, Prof. Eleanor Jane,** PhD; Tasso Leventis Professor of Biodiversity, Department of Zoology, University of Oxford, since 2015; Fellow of Merton College, Oxford, since 2015; *b* Cuckfield, 3 June 1967; *d* of Prof. Robert Rainsford Milner-Gulland, *qv*; *m* 1993, Prof. Martin Stewart Williams; one *s*. *Educ:* Steyning Grammar Sch.; New Coll., Oxford (BA Pure and Applied Biol. 1988); Imperial Coll. London (PhD Natural Resource Mgt). Jun. Res. Fellow, New Coll., Oxford, 1990–93; Res. Fellow, Univ. of British Columbia, 1993; Lectr in Mathematical Ecol., Univ. of Warwick, 1994–98; Imperial College London: Lectr in Resource Econs, 1999–2002; Reader in Resource Econs, 2002–07; Prof. in Conservation Sci., 2007–15. Scientific Fellow, Zool Soc. of London, 1997–2007; Hon. Res. Fellow, Inst. of Zoology, 2007–. Hon. Dr Applied Ecol., Hedmark University Coll., 2014; Hon. Dr, Swedish Univ. of Agricl Scis, 2018. Dist. Service Award, Soc. for Conservation Biol., 2019. *Publications:* Conservation of Biological Resources, 1998; Wildlife Conservation and Sustainable Use: a handbook of techniques, 2007; Animal Migration: a synthesis, 2011; Conservation Decisions in a Complex World: from models to implementation, 2017; over 200 articles in peer-reviewed jls. *Recreations:* horse riding, dog walking, languages, travel. *Address:* Department of Zoology, University of Oxford, South Parks Road, Oxford OX1 3PS. *T:* (01865) 271260. *E:* ej.milner-gulland@zoo.ox.ac.uk.

**MILNER-GULLAND, Prof. Robert Rainsford, (Robin),** FBA 2002; FSA; Professor of Russian and East European Studies, 1993–2001, Research Professor in Russian, 2001–09, School of Humanities (formerly School of European Studies), University of Sussex, now Professor Emeritus (50th Anniversary Fellow, 2011); *b* 24 Feb. 1936; *s* of late Laurence Harry Milner-Gulland and Ruth (Nancy) Milner-Gulland (*née* Bavin); *m* 1966, Alison Margaret Taylor; one *s* two *d*. *Educ:* Westminster Sch.; New Coll., Oxford (Schol., then Sen. Schol.; BA Modern Langs, MA); Moscow Univ. University of Sussex: Asst Lectr, then Lectr, Sch. of Eur. Studies, 1962–74; Reader in Russian and E Eur. Studies, 1974–93. Member: Cttee, British Univs Assoc. of Slavists, 1970–78; Sussex Historic Churches Trust, 2002–; Res. Cttee, Sussex Archaeological Soc., 2005–. FSA 1988. Coronation Medal, 1953. Ed., South Downs book series, 2012–. *Publications:* Soviet Russian Verse: an anthology, 1964; (with M. Dewhirst) Russian Writing Today, 1974; (with J. Bowlt) An Introduction to Russian Art and Architecture, 1980; Cultural Atlas of Russia, 1989, 2nd edn 1998; (ed and trans.) The Life of Zabolotsky, 1994; The Russians, 1997, 2nd edn 1999; (ed and trans.) Icon and Devotion, by O. Tarasov, 2002; (ed and trans.) Framing Russian Art, by O. Tarasov, 2011; (with D. Parsons) Churches and Chapels of the South Downs National Park, 2017; contrib. articles to learned jls on many aspects of Russian studies and on Romanesque art of Sussex. *Recreations:* walking, archaeology. *Address:* Arts Building, University of Sussex, Falmer, Brighton, Sussex BN1 9QN. *T:* (home) (01903) 892602. *E:* r.r.milner-gulland@sussex.ac.uk.

*See also* E. J. Milner-Gulland.

**MILNES COATES, Prof. Sir Anthony (Robert),** 4th Bt *cr* 1911; BSc, MB BS, MD; FRCPath, FRCP; Professor of Medical Microbiology, St George's, University of London (formerly St George's Hospital Medical School), since 1989; *b* 8 Dec. 1948; *s* of Sir Robert Edward James Clive Milnes Coates, 3rd Bt, DSO, and Lady Patricia Ethel, *d* of 4th Earl of Listowel; *S* father, 1982; *m* 1978, Harriet Ann Burton; one *s* two *d*. *Educ:* Eton; BSc London 1970; St Thomas's Hospital, London Univ. (MB BS 1973; MD 1984). MRCS 1973; MRCP 1978, FRCP 1998; FRCPath 1999. MRC Trng Res. Fellow, Dept of Bacteriology, RPMS, 1979–82; Sen. Registrar in Bacteriology, RPMS, 1982–84; Sen. Lectr (Hon. Consultant), Dept of Medical Microbiology, London Hosp. Medical Coll., 1984–90. Councillor, 1980–2018, Mayor, 2002–03, Royal Borough of Kensington and Chelsea. *Heir: s* Thomas Anthony Milnes Coates, *b* 19 Nov. 1986. *Address:* Hereford Cottage, 135 Gloucester Road, SW7 4TH. *Club:* Brooks's.

**MILNOR, (Margaret) Dusa;** *see* McDuff, M. D.

**MILROY, Prof. (Ann) Lesley,** PhD; Fellow, Faculty of Linguistics and Philology (formerly Centre for Linguistics and Philology), University of Oxford, since 2005; Hans Kurath Collegiate Professor of Linguistics, University of Michigan, 2000–05, now Professor Emerita; *b* 5 March 1944; *d* of Thomas Keddy Cross and Janet Elizabeth Cross; *m* 1965, Prof. James R. D. Milroy; three *s*. *Educ:* Univ. of Manchester (BA 1st Cl. Hons English 1965; MA 1967); Queen's Univ. Belfast (PhD 1979). Various lecturing posts, Ulster Poly., 1972–82; Sen. Simon Research Fellow, Univ. of Manchester, 1982–83; University of Newcastle upon Tyne: Lectr in Linguistics, 1983–85; Sen. Lectr, 1985–88; Prof. of Sociolinguistics, 1988–98 (on leave of absence, 1994–98); Prof. of Linguistics, Univ. of Michigan, 1994–2000. Vis. Fellow, Univ. of Canterbury, Christchurch, NZ, 1992; Hon. Vis. Prof., Univ. of York. Hon. FRCSLT 2016. *Publications:* Language and Social Networks, 1980, 2nd edn 1987; Observing and Analysing Natural Language, 1987; (with J. Milroy) Authority in Language: investigating language prescription and standardisation, 1987, 4th edn 2012; (with R. Lesser) Linguistics and Aphasia: psycholinguistic and pragmatic aspects of intervention, 1993; (ed with J. Milroy) Real English: the grammar of English dialects in the British Isles, 1993; (ed with P. Muysken) One Speaker, Two Languages: cross-disciplinary perspectives on codeswitching, 1995; (with M. Gordon) Sociolinguistics: method and interpretation, 2003; contrib. articles to learned jls. *Recreations:* swimming, walking, reading. *Address:* Stable Cottage, Hempton Road, Deddington, Oxon OX15 0TL.

**MILROY, Hugh;** *see* Milroy, W. H.

**MILROY, Lesley;** *see* Milroy, A. L.

**MILROY, Lisa Katharine,** RA 2005; painter; Head of Graduate Painting, Slade Sch. of Fine Art, University College London, since 2009; *b* Vancouver, 16 Jan. 1959; *d* of Reginald Charles Milroy and Leona Vera Milroy (*née* Demchuk); *m* 2011, Lewis Biggs, *qv*. *Educ:* St Martin's Sch. of Art; Goldsmiths' Coll., Univ. of London (BA 1st Cl. Hons Fine Arts 1982). *Solo exhibitions* include: Nicola Jacobs Gall., London, 1984, 1986, 1988; John Berggruen Gall., San Francisco, 1989, 1992; Kunsthalle Bern, 1990; Galerie Luis Campaña, Frankfurt, 1991, Cologne, 1993, 1997, 2003; Waddington Galls, London, 1993, 1998; Galerie Jennifer Flay, Paris, 1993, 1996, 1999; Gall. Shoko Nagai, Tokyo, 1994; Travel Paintings, Chisenhale Gall., London, Ikon Gall., Birmingham, Fruitmarket, Edinburgh, 1995–96; Alan Cristea Gall., London, 1998, 2000, 2003, 2005, 2009; Tate, Liverpool, 2001; Galerie Xippas, Paris, 2005, 2007; New Art Centre Sculpture Park and Gall., Roche Court, Wilts, Galerie Lelong, Zürich, 2006, 2009; Ikon Gall., Birmingham, 2007; Mansun Farm, The

Retreat, Ahmedabad, 2016; Here & There: Paintings by Lisa Milroy, Parasol unit foundn for contemporary art, London, 2018; Contemp. Art Gall., Nairobi, 2018; *group exhibitions* include: Sydney Biennale, 1986, 1998; John Moores Liverpool Exhibns, Walker Art Gall., Liverpool, 1985, 1987, 1989, 2002, 2004; Carnegie Internat., 1991; Tate Gall., 1992, 1995, 2004, 2012; Calouste Gulbenkian Foundn, Lisbon, 1992, 1997; Tate Gall., Liverpool, 1996, 1998; Today Mus., Beijing, 2009; Grosse Geister: Artist's Room, Kunstmuseum, Bonn, 2014; Modern Art Revisited, Tottori Prefectural Mus. (touring), 2018; *work in public collections* including: Arts Council Collection; British Council; Calouste Gulbenkian Foundn, Lisbon; Contemporary Art Soc.; FRAC Occitanie Montpellier; Fukuoka Art Mus., Japan; Metropolitan Mus. of Art, NY; Tate, London; Tokyo Metropolitan Art Collection. Advr, Rijksakademie Van Beeldende Kunsten, Amsterdam, 1995–. Artist Trustee, Tate Gall., 2013–17; Liaison Trustee, Nat. Gall., 2015–17. 1st prize, John Moores Prize, 1989; D&AD Silver Award for Royal Mail Millennium Stamp, 2000. *Recreation:* hiking. *Address:* c/o Royal Academy of Arts, Burlington House, Piccadilly, W1J 0BD.

**MILROY, (William) Hugh,** OBE 2011; PhD; Chief Executive Officer, Veterans Aid, since 2005; *b* Kilmarnock, 8 Feb. 1956; *s* of late William Milroy and of Mary Milroy; *m* 1987, Lorraine Ann Coombes; two *d. Educ:* Univ. of Southampton (BTh 1986); Univ. of East Anglia (MA 1996; PhD 2001). Inspector, Royal HK Police, 1977–81; contract security advr, oil industry, 1981–83; Officer, RAF, 1986–2003, retd as Wing Comdr. Team Member: Howard League for Penal Reform Inq. into veterans in prison, 2009; Rev. into Former Members of Armed Forces and Criminal Justice System by Stephen Phillips, QC, MP, 2014. Advr, Office of Veterans Ombudsman, Canada, 2011–18. Dir, Forces in Mind Trust, 2012–13. Sen. Vis. Res. Fellow, 2010–13, Guest Lectr, MSc in War Studies and Psychiatry, 2010–, KCL; Hon. Vis. Fellow, Sch. of Social Work, UEA, 2016–. Hon. DCL UEA, 2016. Freeman, City of London, 2011. *Publications:* (contrib.) Pathways of Human Development, 2009; (contrib.) Defense and Security Analysis. *Recreations:* fishing, country pursuits. *Address:* Veterans Aid, 27 Victoria Square, SW1W 0RB. *T:* (020) 7828 2468. *E:* ceo@veterans-aid.net. *Clubs:* Royal Air Force, Army and Navy.

**MILTON, Rt Hon. Anne (Frances);** PC 2015; MP for Guildford, since 2005 (C, 2005–19; Ind, since 2019); *b* 3 Nov. 1955; *d* of late Patrick Turner and Nesta Turner; *m* Dr Graham Henderson; three *s* one *d. Educ:* Haywards Heath Grammar Sch.; St Bartholomew's Hospital Sch. of Nursing (RGN 1977). Staff Nurse, 1977–78, Research Nurse, 1978–81, St Bartholomew's Hosp.; District Nursing Sister: City and Hackney HA, 1981–83; St Thomas' Hosp., London, 1983–85; Med. Advr on Housing for E London and City HA, 1985–2000; self-employed med. advr to social housing providers, 2000–05. Parly Under-Sec. of State, DoH, 2010–12; a Lord Comr of HM Treasury (Govt Whip), 2012–14; Vice-Chamberlain of HM Household (Govt Whip), 2014–15; Treasurer of HM Household (Dep. Chief Whip), 2015–17; Minister of State, DfE, 2017–19. *Address:* House of Commons, SW1A 0AA. *T:* (020) 7219 8392. *E:* anne.milton.mp@parliament.uk.

**MILTON, Maj.-Gen. Anthony Arthur,** CB 2002; OBE 1995; Commandant General Royal Marines, and Commander United Kingdom Amphibious Forces, 2002–04; *b* 19 Aug. 1949; *s* of W. W. Milton; *m* 1972, Nova Mary Biscombe; three *d. Educ:* King Edward VI Sch., Chelmsford; St John's Coll., Cambridge (MPhil Internat. Relns; Fellow Commoner, 2007). Commnd Royal Marines, 1967; Subaltern, 42, 45 and 40 Commando, serving in Far East, Norway, Caribbean, Cyprus and NI, 1970–76; exchange tour with USMC, 1976–78; CTC, Lympstone, 1978–81; Army Staff Coll., 1982; MoD, 1983–84; Equerry to the Duke of Edinburgh, 1983–84; Co. Comdr, 42 Commando, 1985–86; COS, 3 Commando Bde, 1987–89; MoD, 1991–92; CO, 40 Commando, Norway and NI, 1992–94; rcds 1995; Comdr, 3 Commando Bde, 1995–97; Dir, N Atlantic and Western Europe, 1997–98; ADC to the Queen, 1997–99; Dir Gen., Jt Doctrine and Concepts, MoD, 1999–2002. SW Regl Chm., Campaign to Protect Rural England, 2009–15. Vis. Fellow, Cambridge Univ., 2007. FRGS 1992. Freeman, City of London, 2004. Liveryman, Plaisterers' Co., 2004. *Publications:* academic articles. *Recreations:* travel, music, mountains. *Club:* Army and Navy.

**MILTON, Derek Francis,** CMG 1990; HM Diplomatic Service, retired; student of Polish and German; *b* 11 Nov. 1935; *s* of Francis Henry Milton and Florence Elizabeth Maud Kirby; *m* 1st, 1960, Helge Kahle; two *s*; 2nd, 1977, Catherine Walmsley. *Educ:* Preston Manor County Grammar Sch., Wembley; Manchester Univ. (BA Hons Politics and Modern History, 1959). RAF, 1954–56. Colonial Office, 1959–63; Asst Private Sec. to Commonwealth and Colonial Sec., 1962–64; Commonwealth Prime Ministers' Meeting Secretariat, 1964; First Secretary: CRO (later FO), 1964–67; UK Mission to UN, New York, 1967–71; Rome, 1972–75; FCO, 1975–77; Counsellor: Civil Service Res. Fellow, Glasgow Univ., 1977–78; Caracas, 1978–79; Dept of Trade, 1980–82; Overseas Inspectorate, 1982–84; Minister-Counsellor, Mexico City, 1984–87; RCDS, 1988; High Comr, Kingston, Jamaica, and non-resident Ambassador to Haiti, 1989–95. Americas Res. Gp, Res. Analysts, FCO, 1995–99 (on contract). *Recreations:* QPR Football Club, travel, writing. *Address:* 31 Park Road, Beckenham BR3 1QG.

**MILVERTON,** 2nd Baron *cr* 1947, of Lagos and of Clifton; **Rev. Fraser Arthur Richard Richards;** Rector of Christian Malford with Sutton Benger and Tytherton Kellaways, 1967–93; *b* 21 July 1930; *s* of 1st Baron Milverton, GCMG, and Noelle Benda, *d* of Charles Basil Whitehead; *S* father, 1978; *m* 1957, Mary Dorothy, BD, *d* of late Leslie Fly, ARCM, Corsham, Wilts; two *d. Educ:* De Carteret Prep. Sch., Jamaica; Ridley Coll., Ontario; Clifton Coll.; Egerton Agric. Coll., Kenya; Bishops' Coll., Cheshunt. Royal Signals, 1949–50; Kenya Police, 1952–53. Deacon 1957, priest 1958, dio. Rochester; Curate: Beckenham, 1957–59; St John Baptist, Sevenoaks, 1959–60; Great Bookham, 1960–63; Vicar of Okewood with Forest Green, 1963–67. Chaplain, Wilts ACF, 1968–81. Trustee and Dir, Voice (UK) Ltd. Former Gov., Clifton Coll. *Recreations:* family, reading, current affairs and history; enjoys music and walking; interested in tennis, swimming, cricket and Rugby Union. *Heir: b* Hon. Michael Hugh Richards [*b* 1 Aug. 1936; *m* 1st, 1960, Edna Leonie (*d* 2001), *y d* of Col Leo Steveni, OBE, MC; one *s*; 2nd, 2006, Janet Street].

**MILWARD, Timothy Michael,** FRCS; Consultant Plastic Surgeon to Leicester Royal Infirmary, Pilgrim Hospital, Boston, and Lincoln County Hospital, 1976–2002, now Emeritus; *b* 24 March 1937; *s* of Francis John and Rosemary Gwendoline Milward; *m* 1970, Susan Isabel; four *d* (incl. twins). *Educ:* Rugby Sch.; Clare Coll., Cambridge (MB, BCh, MA); St Thomas' Hosp. President: British Assoc. of Aesthetic Plastic Surgeons, 1987–88; BAPS, 1996; Mem., Senate of Surgery of GB and Ireland, 1995–98. Fellow, Acad. of Experts. *Publications:* contrib. British Jl of Plastic Surgery. *Recreations:* squash, tennis, walking with friends, silversmith.

**MIMICA, Neven;** Member, European Commission, 2013–19; *m*; two *c. Educ:* Univ. of Zagreb (MA Econs 1987). Import-export clerk, Astra, 1977–78; Yugoslavian State Committee for Foreign Relations: staff mem., 1978–80, Advr, 1980–83; Asst Chm., 1983–87; served Diplomatic Service of Yugoslavia, 1987–91, Croatia, 1991–97; Asst Minister, then Dep. Minister of the Economy, Chief Negotiator for Stabilisation and Association Agreement and WTO accession of Croatia, 1997–2001; Minister for Eur. Integration, 2001–03; MP (SDP), 2004–08; Dep. Speaker and Chm., Eur. Integration Cttee, Croatian Parlt, 2008–11; Dep. Prime Minister for Internal, Foreign and Eur. Policy, 2011–13.

**MIMPRISS, Peter Hugh Trevor,** CVO 2001; Charities Adviser to HRH the Prince of Wales, 2004–06; *b* 22 Aug. 1943; *s* of Hugh Trevor Baber Mimpriss and Gwyneth Mary Mimpriss (*née* Bartley); *m* 1st, 1971, Hilary Ann Reed (marr. diss. 1992); two *d*; 2nd, 1992, Elisabeth Lesley Molle. *Educ:* Sherborne Sch. Admitted solicitor, 1967. Joined Allen & Overy, 1968; Partner, 1972–2002; univ. solicitor, Univ. of London, 1995–2002; Dir, Edmond J. Safra Philanthropic Foundn, 2002–04. Chairman: Charity Law Assoc., 1992–97; Chariguard Gp of Common Investment Funds, 1994–2000. Director: Leeds Castle Foundn, 1980–2006; Chatham Historic Dockyard Trust, 1986–2000; Weston Park Foundn, 1986–2001; Lawcare (formerly Solcare), 1997–2002; PYBT, 1997–99; Prince's Regeneration Trust, 2002–08; Member, Council: Prince's Trust, 1998–2007; King George Jubilee Trust, 2000–06; Queen's Trust (formerly Queen's Silver Jubilee Trust), 2000–; Trustee: Inst. of Philanthropy, 2000–07; World Trade Centre Disaster Fund, 2001–06; Prince of Wales Arts and Kids Foundn, later Prince's Foundn for Children and the Arts, 2004–08; Prince's Sch. of Traditional Arts, 2005–08; Autism Speaks (formerly Nat. Alliance of Autism Res.), 2005–08 (Dep. Chm., 2005–08); Sir Edward Heath Charitable Foundn, 2005–10; Jewish Mus., 2006–11; Edwina Mountbatten and Leonora Children's Foundn, 2009–; John Ellerman Foundn, 2009–13; St Helena's Hospice, 2012–15; Medical Detection Dogs, 2015–18. Pres., LOOK-UK, 2016–. Hon. DCL Durham, 2003. *Recreations:* walking, maritime history, vintage cars, collecting books. *Clubs:* Athenæum, Garrick.

**MIMS, Prof. Cedric Arthur,** MD, FRCPath; Professor of Microbiology, Guy's Hospital Medical School, London, 1972–90; *b* 9 Dec. 1924; *s* of A. H. and Irene Mims; *m* 1952, Valerie Vickery; two *s* two *d. Educ:* Mill Hill Sch.; University Coll. London (BSc (Zool)); Middlesex Hosp. Med. Sch. (MB, BS, MD). Medical Research Officer, East African Virus Research Inst., Entebbe, Uganda, 1953–56; Research Fellow and Professorial Fellow, John Curtin Sch. of Med. Research, Australian Nat. Univ., Canberra, 1957–72; Rockefeller Foundn Fellow, Children's Hosp. Med. Centre, Boston, USA, 1963–64; Visiting Fellow, Wistar Inst., Philadelphia, USA, 1969–70. *Publications:* (jtly) The Biology of Animal Viruses, 1974; Mims' Pathogenesis of Infectious Disease, 1976, 5th edn 2000; (with D. O. White) Viral Pathogenesis and Immunology, 1984; (jtly) Medical Microbiology, 1993, 4th edn 2008; When We Die, 1998; The War Within Us, 2000; Love and Old Age, 2003; Fouling the Nest, 2006; The Story of Food, 2008; The Story of Childbirth, 2009; Celebrating the Human Hand, 2010; Lying, Walking, Running, 2014; Mightier Than the Sword: the story of the penis, 2014; The Enchanting World of Smell, 2014; The Tyranny of Gravity, 2015; Imagination, 2016; The Magic of Feathers, 2018; numerous papers on the pathogenesis of virus infections. *Address:* 1/10 Murray Crescent, Griffith, ACT 2603, Australia.

**MINA, Denise;** writer, since 1998; *b* East Kilbride, 21 Aug. 1966; *d* of Edith Toner; *m* 2005, Stephen Evans; one *s* (and one *s* decd). *Educ:* Univ. of Glasgow (LLB 1991); Univ. of Strathclyde. Chair, Glasgow Film Th., 2016–. Regular presenter and contrib. to radio and TV. *Plays:* Ida Tamson, 2006; A Drunk Woman Looks at the Thistle, 2007; Meet Me, 2013; *radio plays:* Hurtle, BBC Radio 4, 2003; The Meek, BBC Radio 3, 2009. Hon. DLitt Glasgow, 2008. Gilbert Forbes Medal for Forensic Medicine and Sci., Univ. of Glasgow, 1991. *Publications: novels:* Garnethill trilogy: Garnethill, 1998 (John Creasy Dagger for Best First Crime Novel, Crime Writer Assoc., Scotland on Sunday/Glenfiddich Spirit of Scotland Award, 1998); Exile, 2000; Resolution, 2001; Patricia 'Paddy' Meehan series: The Field of Blood, 2005; The Dead Hour, 2006; The Last Breath, 2007; Alex Morrow series: Still Midnight, 2009; The End of the Wasp Season, 2010 (Martin Beck Award, Swedish Crime Writers' Acad., 2011; Theakston's Old Peculier Crime Novel of the Year, 2012); Gods and Beasts, 2012 (Theakston's Old Peculier Crime Novel of the Year, 2013); The Red Road, 2013; Blood, Salt, Water, 2014; other novels: Sanctum, 2003; The Long Drop, 2017 (McIlvanney Prize for Scottish Crime Book of the Year, Gordon Burn Prize, 2017); Conviction, 2019; *comic collections and graphic novels:* Hellblazer: Empathy is the Enemy, 2006, The Red Right Hand, 2007; A Sickness in the Family, 2010; (adapted) The Girl with the Dragon Tattoo, Book 1, 2012, Book 2, 2013; writings for Glasgow Herald, The Guardian, New York Times, La Libération. *Recreation:* cycling. *Address:* (literary agent) c/o Jon Wood, Rogers Coleridge and White, 20 Powis Mews, W11 1JN; (film, TV and theatre agent) c/o Mark Casarotto, Casarotto Ramsay and Associates, 3rd Floor, 7 Savoy Court, Strand, WC2R 0EX.

**MINA, Jacqueline Kathleen,** OBE 2012; goldsmith and jewellery designer; *b* 5 Feb. 1942; *d* of John Frederick Bartlett and Kay Crome and step *d* of Emanuel Hurwitz; one *s*; *m* 1966, Michael Christou Minas; one *d. Educ:* Hornsey Coll. of Art and Crafts; Royal Coll. of Art (DesRCA 1965). Has worked from own studio/workshop, 1965–. Part-time teaching posts include: Harrow Sch. of Art, 1965–70; Farnham Sch. of Art and Design, 1965–75; RCA, 1972–94; Leicester Coll. of Art, 1975–84. External examiner: Edinburgh Coll. of Art, 1989–91; Glasgow Sch. of Art, 1992–96; Bucks UC, 1997–2000. Member: Jury, Jerwood Prize for Applied Arts (Jewellery), 2007; Selection Panel, Contemp. Applied Arts, 2015–. Mem., Assoc. for Contemporary Jewellery, 1997. FRSA 1999–2016. Freeman, 1985, Lady Liveryman, 1995, Co. of Goldsmiths. Trustee, Bishopsland Educnl Trust, 2001–15. Work in exhibitions in UK, Europe and USA, including: Oxford Gall., 1980; Byzantium, NY, 1985; V&A Mus., 1985; Goldsmiths' Hall, London, 1997; Crafts Council Shop at V&A, 2000; World Craft Forum, Kanazawa, Japan, 2003; Collect, annually, V&A Mus., 2004–08, Saatchi Gall., London, 2008–18; Orgold, Flow Gall., 2004, Scottish Gall., Ruthin Crafts Centre, Wales, 2005; L'or, Bijoux d'Europe, France, 2005; The Goldmark, Thomas Goode, London, 2006; Diamonds, Contemp. Applied Arts, London, 2008, 2010; Kath Libbert Jewellery Gall., Salts Mill, 2009; Cox & Power, London, 2009; V&A Mus., 2009; Dovecot Gall., Edinburgh, 2010; Goldsmiths' Hall (retrospective), 2011; Contemp. Applied Arts, Scottish Gall., Ruthin Craft Centre (solo touring exhibn), 2011; Touching Gold, Scottish Gall., 2012; Lesley Craze Gall., London, 2014; Out of Sight, Contemp. Applied Arts, London, 2014; Masters of Modern Jewellery, Beetles+Huxley Gall., London, 2014; Modern Masters, Scottish Gall., Edinburgh, 2015; A Sense of Jewellery, Goldsmiths' Centre, London, 2015; Jacqueline Mina at 75, Scottish Gall., 2017; Hand Head Heart, Court Barn Mus., Chipping Camden, 2018; group exhibitions: Silver, Savile Club, 2013; Contemp. Silver, Drapers' Hall, 2014; Goldsmiths' Fair, 2014; 30 Years in the Making, Lesley Craze Gall., London, 2014; A Showcase of New Work, Scottish Gall., Edinburgh, 2015; Ringing the Changes, Victoria Sewart Gall., Plymouth, 2015; Premio Internazionale Mario Pinton, Oratorio di San Rocco, Padua, Italy, 2015; 175th Anniv. exhibn, Scottish Gall., 2017; 20:20 Visions, Assoc. for Contemp. Jewellery, Nat. Centre for Craft and Design and tour, 2017; Colour Theory, Contemp. Applied Arts, 2018; 25th Anniv. Exhibn, Bishopsland, 2018; Oxford Pioneers, Oxford Ceramics Gall., 2018; work in public collections in UK and USA, including: Cooper Hewitt Mus., NY; Goldsmiths' Hall; Nat. Mus. of Scotland, Edinburgh; V&A Mus.; Crafts Council, London; Cleveland Contemp. Jewellery Collection, Middlesbrough Inst. of Modern Art; Mus. of Art & Design, NY City. Jerwood Prize for Applied Arts (Jewellery), Jerwood Foundn, 2000. *Publications:* (contrib.) V&A 150th Anniversary Album, 2007; contrib. articles to jls incl. Crafts mag., Jewellery Studies, Findings. *Recreations:* music (appreciation), contemporary dance (appreciation), choral singing, gardening, cooking, swimming, grannying. *Address:* c/o The Goldsmiths' Company, Goldsmiths' Hall, Foster Lane, EC2V 6BN. *T:* (020) 7606 7010, *Fax:* (020) 7606 1511.

**MINCHIN, Timothy David**; musician, composer, songwriter, actor and comedian; b Northampton, 7 Oct. 1975; s of Dr David Minchin and Ros Minchin; m 2002, Sarah Gardiner; one s one d. Educ: Univ. of Western Australia (BA Eng. and Theatre 1995); Western Australia Acad. of Performing Arts (Dip. Contemporary Music 1998). Comedy shows include: Dark Side, Melbourne Internat. Comedy Festival, Edinburgh Fringe Fest. (Perrier Award for Best Newcomer), 2005; Ready For This?, Edinburgh Fringe Fest., 2008, UK tour, 2008–09, Australia and NZ tour, 2009; Tim Minchin and the Heritage Orchestra, UK tour, 2010–11, Australia tour, 2011; Tim Minchin vs the Orchestra, Australia tour, 2012; Back, Australia, NZ and UK tour, 2019; appearances on major UK, Australian and US TV shows. Composer of music and lyrics for Matilda The Musical, RSC, 2010, transf. West End, 2011, NY, 2013, Sydney, 2016, UK and Ireland tour, 2018; Groundhog Day, Old Vic, 2016. Performer: (as Judas Iscariot), Jesus Christ Superstar, O2 Arena, 2012, Australian tour, 2013; Rosencrantz and Guildenstern are Dead, Sydney Th. Co., 2013. Actor in film, Robin Hood, 2018. Publications: (with D. C. Turner and T. King) Storm, 2014; (with Steve Antony) When I Grow Up, 2017. Address: c/o Caroline Chignell, PBJ Management, 22 Rathbone Street, W1T 1LG. T: (020) 7287 1112.

**MINDHAM, Prof. Richard Hugh Shiels**, MD; DSc; FRCP, FRCPsych; Nuffield Professor of Psychiatry, 1977–2000, now Emeritus, and Dean, Faculty of Medicine, Dentistry and Health, 1996–97, University of Leeds; b 25 March 1935; s of Thomas Raper Mindham and Winifred Gertrude Mindham; m 1971, Barbara Harris Reid; one s one d. Educ: Guy's Hosp. Medical Sch. (MB BS 1959); Inst. of Psychiatry, Univ. of London (MD 1974); Univ. of Leeds (MA Hist. and Theory of Architecture 2004); King's Coll. London (DSc 2016). FRCPsych 1977; FRCPE 1978; FRCP 2000. Nottingham University Medical School: Sen. Lectr in Psychiatry, 1972–76; Reader, 1976–77; Dean of Postgrad. Studies, Univ. of Leeds, 1994–96. Vis. Prof., Johns Hopkins Univ., 1982. Chief Examr, RCPsych, 1995–98. Publications: papers on psychiatry, psychopharmacology, Parkinson's disease, med. educn and architecture of psychiatric hosps. Recreations: music, architecture, walking. E: r.h.s.mindham@gmail.com. Clubs: Royal Society of Medicine; Western (Glasgow).

**MINFORD, Prof. (Anthony) Patrick (Leslie)**, CBE 1996; Professor of Applied Economics, Cardiff Business School, Cardiff University, since 1997; b 17 May 1943; s of Leslie Mackay Minford and Patricia Mary (née Sale); m 1970, Rosemary Irene Allcorn; two s one d. Educ: Horris Hill; Winchester Coll. (scholar); Balliol Coll., Oxford (schol.; BA); London Sch. of Economics (grad. studies; MScEcon, PhD). Economic Asst, Min. of Overseas Development, London, 1966; Economist, Min. of Finance, Malawi, 1967–69; Economic Adviser: Director's Staff, Courtaulds Ltd, 1970–71; HM Treasury, 1971–73, and HM Treasury Delegn in Washington, 1973–74; Visiting Hallsworth Fellow, Manchester Univ., 1974–75; Editor, NIESR Review, 1975–76; Edward Gonner Prof. of Applied Econs, Liverpool Univ., 1976–97. Vis. Prof., Cardiff Business Sch., 1993–97. Dir, Merseyside Develt Corp., 1988–89. Mem., Monopolies and Mergers Commn, 1990–96. Mem., HM Treasury's Panel of Economic Forecasters, 1993–96. Mem. Bd, WNO, 1993–98. Contrarian Prize, 2017. Publications: Substitution Effects, Speculation and Exchange Rate Stability, 1978; (jtly) Unemployment—Cause and Cure, 1983, 2nd edn 1985; (jtly) Rational Expectations and the New Macroeconomics, 1983; (jtly) The Housing Morass, 1987; The Supply Side Revolution in Britain, 1991; (jtly) The Cost of Europe, 1992; Rational Expectations Macroeconomics, 1992; Markets Not Stakes, 1998; (jtly) Britain and Europe: choices for change, 1999; (jtly) Advanced Macroeconomics: a primer, 2002, 2nd edn 2019; (jtly) Money Matters: essays in honour of Alan Walters, 2004; (jtly) Should Britain Leave the EU?: an economic analysis of a troubled relationship, 2005, 2nd edn 2015; An Agenda for Tax Reform, 2006; articles in learned jls on monetary and internat. economics. Address: Cardiff Business School, Cardiff University, Cardiff CF10 3EU.

**MINGAY, (Frederick) Ray**, CMG 1992; Chief Executive, Trade Development Services, since 1997; consultant to various companies and other organisations; b 7 July 1938; s of Cecil Stanley and Madge Elizabeth Mingay; m 1963, Joan Heather Roberts (d 2001); three s one d. Educ: Tottenham Grammar Sch.; St Catharine's Coll., Cambridge (Open Exhibnr; MA); London Univ. (Postgrad. Dip. Pub. Admin.); Min. of Educn Cert. of Teaching Competence. Nat. Service, 1959–61: 2nd Lieut RAEC; attached RIF, Kenya. Administration, St Thomas' Hosp., 1961; schoolmaster, 1961–62; Min. of Transport, 1962–64; BoT, 1964; Chrysler (UK) Ltd, 1968–70; Consul (Commercial), Milan, 1970–73; Asst Sec., Dept of Trade, 1973–78; Counsellor (Commercial), Washington, 1978–83; Under Secretary: Mechanical and Electrical Engrg Div., DTI, 1983–86; Regl Investment and Develt Div., DTI, 1986–88; Consul-Gen., Chicago, 1988–92; Head of Overseas Trade Div. DTI, 1992–93; Dir-Gen., Export Promotion, DTI, 1993–97 (concurrently Asst Under Sec. of State, FCO (Jt Export Promotion Directorate), 1993–96). Mem., Business Appts Panel, later Public Appts Assessor, DTI, subseq. BERR, then BIS, 2002–12; Ind. Mediator, 2006–; OCPA Accredited Ind. Public Appts Assessor, 2012–18. Dir, Cove Holidays Ltd, 1977–80; non-executive Director: Aalco, 1983–87; Amari World Steel, 1987–88. Mem., BOTB, 1993–97. Mem., Mid-West Marshall Scholar Selection Cttee, 1988–92. Churchill Fellow, Westminster Coll., Fulton, Mo, 1991. Trustee, St Andrew's Youth Club (1866), Westminster, 2008 (Vice Pres., 2017–). FCMI; FRSA. Hon. Citizen, Minneapolis, 1990. Club: Reform.

**MINGHELLA, Loretta Caroline Rose**, OBE 2010; First Church Estates Commissioner, since 2017; b Isle of Wight, 4 March 1962; d of Edward Minghella and late Gloria Alberta Minghella, MBE; m 1992, Christopher Parsons; one s one d. Educ: Medina High Sch.; Clare Coll., Cambridge (BA Hons Law 1984); Coll. of Law. Admitted solicitor, 1987. Articled clerk, then solicitor, Kingsley Napley, 1985–89; Legal Advr, DTI, 1989–90; Securities and Investments Board, later Financial Services Authority: Asst Dir, 1990–93; Hd, Enforcement Law and Policy, 1993–98; Hd, Enforcement Law, Policy and Internat. Co-operation, 1998–2004; Chief Exec., Financial Services Compensation Scheme, 2004–10; Chief Exec. (formerly Dir), Christian Aid, 2010–17. Chm., Enforcement Cttee, IOSCO, 2003–04. Trustee: Disasters Emergency Cttee, 2010–; St George's House Trust, Windsor Castle, 2015–. Sarum Canon, Salisbury Cathedral, 2016–. Publications: (jtly) Blackstone's Guide to the Financial Services and Markets Act 2000, 2001. Recreations: singing, theatre, ice cream tasting. Address: Church Commissioners, Church House, Great Smith Street, SW1P 3AZ.

**MINGINISH, Hon. Lord; Roderick John MacLeod**; Chairman, Scottish Land Court, and President, Lands Tribunal for Scotland, since 2014; b Uig, Isle of Skye, 7 Dec. 1952; s of Roderick MacLeod and Chirsty Mary MacLeod (née Morrison); m 1980, Lorna Jane Robertson; one s. Educ: Portnalong Junior Secondary Sch.; Portree High Sch.; Univ. of Edinburgh (LLB Hons 1975). Admitted Solicitor, 1979, Advocate, 1994; Sheriff, 2000; Dep. Chm., Scottish Land Court, 2006–14; QC (Scot.) 2013. Chm., Bd of Dirs, Sabhal Mòr Ostaig, 2005–15. Recreations: walking, cycling, bird watching. Address: Scottish Land Court, George House, 126 George Street, Edinburgh EH2 4HH. T: (0131) 271 4357.

**MINGOS, Prof. (David) Michael (Patrick)**, DPhil; FRS 1992; CChem, FRSC; Principal, St Edmund Hall, Oxford, 1999–2009; Professor of Chemistry, University of Oxford, 2000–09, now Emeritus; b 6 Aug. 1944; s of Vasso Mingos and Rose Enid Billie Hayes (née Griffiths); m 1967, Stacey Mary Hosken; one s one d. Educ: Univ. of Manchester (BSc); Univ. of Sussex (DPhil). CChem 1983; FRSC 1983. Fulbright Fellow, Northwestern Univ., 1968–70; ICI Fellow, Sussex Univ., 1970–71; Lectr, QMC, 1971–76; University of Oxford: Lectr, 1976–90; Reader, 1990–92; Fellow, Keble Coll., 1976–92 and by special election, 1993 (Hon. Fellow, 1999); Univ. Assessor, 1991–92; Sir Edward Frankland BP Prof. of Inorganic Chemistry, Imperial Coll., Univ. of London, 1992–99; Dean, Royal Coll. of Sci., 1996–99. Dist. Prof., Xi'an Petroleum Inst., China, 1994–; Wilhelm Manchot Res. Prof. and prize, Munich, 1995; Vis. Prof., Imperial Coll., London, 1999–2002; Croucher Foundn Dist. Vis. Prof. for Hong Kong, 2016; Univ. of Auckland Foundn Visitor, 2000. Univ. of Sussex 50th Anniv. Fellow, 2012; Fellow, Eur. Acad. of Scis, 2017. Lee Meml Lecture, Univ. of Chicago, 1997. Vice Pres., Dalton Div., RSC, 1993–96. Gov., Harrow Sch., 1994–2004. Hon. DSc: UMIST, 2000; Sussex, 2001. Corday Morgan Medal, 1980, Tilden Medal, 1988, Chemistry of Noble Metals Award, 1983, RSC; M. J. Collins Prize, for innovation in microwave chemistry, CEM Corp., 1996; Alexander von Humboldt Stiftung Forschungspreis, 1999. Regl Editor, Jl of Organometallic Chem., 1996–2006; Member, Editorial Board: Transition Metal Chem., 1975–2006; Structure and Bonding, 1983– (Man. Ed., 2002–); New Jl of Chem., 1986–96; Jl of Organometallic Chem., 1991–; Chemical Soc. Rev., 1992–97; Advances in Inorganic Chem., 1992–2000; Inorganic Chemistry, 1997–99. Blaise Pascal Medal for Chem., Eur. Acad. of Scis, 2017. Publications: Introduction to Cluster Chemistry, 1990; Essentials of Inorganic Chemistry 1, 1995; Essential Trends in Inorganic Chemistry, 1997; (ed) Structural and Electronic Paradigms in Cluster Chemistry, 1997; Essentials of Inorganic Chemistry 2, 1998; (ed) Liquid Crystals, Vols 1 and 2, 1999; (ed) Supramolecular Assembly via Hydrogen Bonds, Vols 1 and 2, 2004; (Ed.-in-Chief) Comprehensive Organo-metallic Chemistry III, Vols 1–13, 2007; (ed and contrib.) Nitrosyl Complexes in Inorganic Chemistry, Biochemistry and Medicine, vols 1 and 2, 2014; (ed and contrib.) Gold Clusters, Colloids and Nano-particles, vols 1 and 2, 2014; (ed and contrib.) 50 Years of Structure and Bonding: the anniversary volume, 2016; The Chemical Bond: 100 years old and getting stronger, vols 1, 2 and 3, 2016; contribs to jls of learned socs. Recreations: cricket, tennis, walking. Address: Inorganic Chemistry Laboratory, University of Oxford, South Parks Road, Oxford OX1 3QR. T: (01865) 272631. E: michael.mingos@seh.ox.ac.uk.

**MINKOWSKI, Prof. Christopher Zand**, PhD; Boden Professor of Sanskrit, University of Oxford, since 2005; Fellow of Balliol College, Oxford, since 2005; b 13 May 1953; s of late Prof. Jan M. Minkowski and Anne Shreve Minkowski. Educ: Gilman Sch., Baltimore; Harvard Coll. (AB English 1975; Harvard Nat. Schol.; Editl Bd, Lampoon, Advocate); Univ. of Delhi (Dip. Hindi 1976); Harvard Univ. (AM 1980; PhD Sanskrit and Indian Studies 1986). Vis. Asst Prof. of Asian Langs and Lits, Univ. of Iowa, 1984–85; Instructor in Sanskrit, Brown Univ., 1985–87; Jun. Res. Fellow in Indology, Wolfson Coll., Oxford, 1988–89; Asst Prof., then Associate Prof., subseq. Prof., of Asian Studies and Classics, Cornell Univ., 1989–2006. Fulbright Res. Schol., Poona Univ., 1996–97; Mem., Sch. of Historical Studies, Inst. for Advanced Study, Princeton, 2010; Dir d'études invité, École des hautes études en sciences sociales, Paris, 2011; Gastwissenschaftler, Max-Planck-Institut für Wissenschaftsgeschichte, Berlin, 2012; Kosmos Fellow, Humboldt Univ., Berlin, 2015; Vis. Fellow, Centre for Study of Developing Societies, Delhi, 2016. Publications: Priesthood in Ancient India, 1991; numerous articles in learned jls on Vedic ritual, religion and literature, Sanskrit epics, hist. of astronomy and cosmology, and intellectual hist. of early Mod. S Asia. Recreations: walking, gardening, further adventures in the improbable. Address: Balliol College, Oxford OX1 3BJ.

**MINN, U Kyaw Zwar**; Ambassador of the Republic of the Union of Myanmar to the Court of St James's, since 2013, and (non-resident) to Ireland and Sweden, since 2014, and to Denmark, since 2015; b Yangon, 2 June 1958; s of U Kyaw Min and Daw Ye Ye; m 1985, Aye Minn Myat; one s. Educ: Defence Studies Acad. (BSc); Nat. Defence Coll., Myanmar (MA Defence Studies); Lockland Airforce Base, Texas (Dip. Amer. Eng. Lang.); Fort Lec, Va (Dip. Aerial Delivery and Material Officer Course). Served in Defence Service (Myanmar Army) up to rank of Col, 1977–2008; Minister Counsellor, Min. of Foreign Affairs, 2008–10; Ambassador: to Myanmar Mission, NY, 2010–11; to France, 2011–13, and (non resident) to Andorra, Spain and Swiss Confederation, 2012–13. Dist. Service Medal; Gen. Service Medal; People's War Medal; State Peace and Tranquility Medal; Maing Yan/Me Tha Waw Battle Star; Conquest over Threat Medal; Service Medal; Campaign Star. Recreations: painting, golf, socialising. Address: Embassy of the Republic of the Union of Myanmar, 19A Charles Street, W1J 5DX. T: (020) 7148 0749, Fax: (020) 7409 7043. E: ambassadoroffice@londonmyanmarembassy.com. Clubs: Travellers; Brocket Hall Golf.

**MINOGUE, (Elizabeth) Ann, (Lady Stevenson of Balmacara)**; Senior Consultant, Macfarlanes LLP, since 2016 (Partner, 2013–16); b Harrogate, 17 Oct. 1955; d of John Minogue and Jean Minogue; m 1991, Robert Wilfrid, (Wilf), Stevenson (see Baron Stevenson of Balmacara); one s two d. Educ: Aylesbury High Sch.; Clare Coll., Cambridge (BA 1977). Admitted solicitor, 1980; Partner: McKenna & Co., then Cameron McKenna, 1985–2001; Linklaters LLP, 2001–09; Ashurst LLP, 2009–13. President: British Council for Offices, 2005–06; City Property Assoc., 2012–14. Governor: London Contemporary Dance Trust, 1998–2004; City Univ., London, 2000–09; London Metropolitan Univ., 2009–18 (Vice Chair, 2014–18). Member: Risk and Adv. Bd, East Bank project, Queen Elizabeth Olympic Park; Develt Adv. Bd, Guy's and St Thomas' Hosps. Publications: (ed jtly) Construction Law Handbook, subseq. ICE Manual of Construction Law, 2010. Recreations: Irish history, Russian, family. Address: Macfarlanes LLP, 20 Cursitor Street, EC4A 1LT. T: (020) 7849 2912. E: ann.minogue@macfarlanes.com.

**MINSON, Prof. Anthony Charles**, PhD; Professor of Virology, University of Cambridge, 1991–2010, now Emeritus; Fellow of Wolfson College, Cambridge, since 1982; Chairman, Cambridge University Press, 2010–12; b 8 Feb. 1944; s of Charles Minson and Esney Minson (née Lewis); m 1976, Jennifer Mary Phillips; one s one d. Educ: Ilford High Sch.; Birmingham Univ. (BSc); Australian Nat. Univ. (PhD 1969). Lectr, Univ. of Birmingham, 1974–76; Res. Fellow, 1976–82, Lectr, 1982–91, Pro-Vice-Chancellor, 2003–09, Univ. of Cambridge. Mem. Council, Soc. of Gen. Microbiol., 1990–93, 2003–06. Mem., Governing Body, Inst. of Animal Health, 1997–2003. Trustee: Animal Health Trust, 2007–18; Lister Inst., 2010–15. FMedSci 2002. Publications: scientific papers on biology and pathogenesis of animal and plant viruses. Recreation: sailing. Address: 113 Cambridge Road, Great Shelford, Cambridge CB22 5JJ. T: 07969 675544. E: acm8@cam.ac.uk.

**MINTER, Graham Leslie**, LVO 1983; HM Diplomatic Service, retired; Associate, Day Associates, since 2011; South America Regional coordinator (formerly South America country coordinator), Amnesty International, since 2012; b 4 Jan. 1950; s of Norman Leslie Minter and Beryl Winifred Minter; m 1975, Peter Anne Scott; one s two d. Educ: Orange Hill County Grammar Sch. HM Diplomatic Service, 1968–2005: FCO, 1968–71; Anguilla, 1971–72; Latin American Floater, 1973–75; Asunción, 1975–78; FCO, 1978–79; First Secretary: (Econ.), Mexico City, 1979–84; FCO, 1984–90; Canberra, 1990–94; FCO, 1994–98; Ambassador to Bolivia, 1998–2001; Dep. Hd, Economic Policy Dept, FCO, 2002–04; Gp Hd, Global Business Gp, FCO, 2004–05. Sen. Consultant, Internat. Business Leaders' Forum, 2005–11. Recreations: travel, music, walking, reading, genealogy, birdwatching, table tennis, tennis, football. Address: Ringlestone, Goudhurst Road, Marden, Kent TN12 9JY.

**MINTER, Susan Anne,** FCIHort, CHort; horticultural consultant, since 2005; *b* Hammersmith, 6 April 1949; *d* of Harry and Norah Minter; civil partnership 2006, Penelope Ruth Hammond. *Educ:* N London Collegiate Sch.; Girton Coll., Cambridge (BA Hons Hist. 1971); Univ. of Calif, Berkeley (Fulbright Travel Schol.). FCIHort (FIHort 2003); CHort 2017. Editor of encyclopaedias, Fabbri & Partners, then freelance, 1972–82; Supervisor, Palm House, Royal Botanic Gdns, Kew, 1985–91; Curator, Chelsea Physic Gdn, 1991–2001; Horticultural Dir, Eden Project, 2001–05. Hon. Sec., Chartered Inst. of Horticulture (formerly Inst. of Horticulture), 2007– (Pres., 2010–12). Chair, Herb Soc., 2008–13; Mem., Tender and Ornamental Plants Cttee, RHS, 1992–2012. Mem. SW Cttee, HLF, 2016–19. Trustee: Horniman Mus. and Gdns, 1999–2009 (Mem., Gdns Cttee, 2009–12); Xplore, 2015–. Govt Ambassador for Diversity in Public Appts, 2009–. Devon NHS Health Champion, 2015–16. FLS 1991–2017. Veitch Meml Medal, RHS, 2013. *Publications:* The Greatest Glasshouse: the rainforests recreated, 1990; The Healing Garden, 1993, rev. edn 2004; The Apothecaries Garden: a history of Chelsea Physic Garden, 2000; The Well-Connected Gardener, 2010. *Recreations:* travel, photography, films/exhibitions, body-boarding, cliff walking, gardening, taking specialist gardening tours in UK and Europe, Spectrum (LGBT choir). *Address:* c/o Chartered Institute of Horticulture, BGA House, Nottingham Road, Louth, Lincs LN11 0WB. *E:* cih@horticulture.org.uk.

**MINTO, 7th Earl of,** *cr* 1813; **Gilbert Timothy George Lariston Elliot-Murray-Kynynmound;** Bt 1700; Baron Minto, 1797; Viscount Melgund, 1813; Deputy Chairman, Paperchase, since 2018 (Chief Executive Officer, 1996–2018); *b* 1 Dec. 1953; *s* of 6th Earl of Minto, OBE and Lady Caroline, *d* of 9th Earl of Jersey; *S* father, 2005; *m* 1983, Diana, *yr d* of Brian Trafford; two *s* one *d* (and one *s* decd). *Educ:* Eton; North East London Polytechnic (BSc Hons 1983). MRICS. Lieut, Scots Guards, 1972–76. Mem., Royal Co. of Archers, Queen's Body Guard for Scotland, 1983–. *Heir:* s Viscount Melgund, *qv. Clubs:* White's, Shikar.

**MINTO, Dr Alfred,** FRCPsych; Consultant Psychiatrist (Rehabilitation), Southern Derbyshire Health Authority, 1988–90, retired 1991; *b* 23 Sept. 1928; *s* of Alfred Minto and Marjorie Mavor Goudie Leask; *m* 1949, Frances Oliver Bradbrook; two *s* two *d. Educ:* Aberdeen Central Sch.; Aberdeen Univ. (MB ChB 1951); MA History, Univ. of Nottingham, 1996. DPM RCS&P London 1961; MRCPsych 1972, FRCPsych 1974. House Physician, Huddersfield Royal Inf., 1952; Sen. House Officer/Jun. Hosp. Med. Officer, Fairmile Hosp., Wallingford, 1952–56; Sen. Registrar, St Luke's Hosp., Middlesbrough, 1956–59; Sen. Hosp. Med. Officer, 1959–63, Conslt Psychiatrist, 1963, Mapperley Hosp., Nottingham; Conslt Psychiatrist i/c, Alcoholism and Drug Addiction Service, Sheffield RHB, 1963–68; Conslt Psychiatrist, St Ann's and Mapperley Hosps, 1968–81; Med. Dir, Rampton Hosp., 1981–85; Associate Prof. of Psychiatry, Univ. of Calgary, and Clinical Dir of Forensic Psychiatry, Calgary Gen. Hosp., Alberta, 1986–87. Clinical Teacher, Nottingham Univ. Med. Sch., 1971–85; Special Lectr in Forensic Psych., Nottingham Univ., 1982–85. Conslt Psychiatrist, CS Comrs, 1964–85. *Publications:* Key Issues in Mental Health, 1982; papers on alcoholism, community care, toxoplasmosis. *Recreations:* books, people. *Address:* 76 Walsingham Road, Nottingham NG5 4NR.

**MINTON, Yvonne Fay,** CBE 1980; mezzo-soprano; *er d* of R. T. Minton, Sydney; *m* 1965, William Barclay; one *s* one *d. Educ:* Sydney Conservatorium of Music. Elsa Stralia Scholar, Sydney, 1957–60; won Canberra Operatic Aria Competition, 1960; won Kathleen Ferrier Prize at s'Hertogenbosch Vocal Competition, 1961. Joined Royal Opera House as a Principal Mezzo-Soprano, 1965. Major roles include: Octavian in Der Rosenkavalier; Dorabella in Così fan Tutte; Marina in Boris Godunov; Helen in King Priam; Cherubino in Marriage of Figaro; Orfeo in Gluck's Orfeo; Sextus in La clemenza di Tito; Dido in The Trojans at Carthage; Kundry in Parsifal; Charlotte in Werther; Countess Geschwitz in Lulu. Recordings include Octavian in Der Rosenkavalier, Mozart Requiem, Elgar's The Kingdom, etc. Guest Artist with Cologne Opera Company, Oct. 1969–. Hon. RAM 1975. *Recreations:* reading, gardening.

**MINZLY, Angela Christine Mary;** *see* Heylin, A. C. M.

**MIODOWNIK, Prof. Mark Andrew,** MBE 2018; PhD; Professor of Materials and Society, and Director, Institute of Making, University College London, since 2012; *b* London, 25 April 1969; *s* of late Peter Miodownik and Kathleen Miodownik; *m* Ruby Wright; one *s. Educ:* St Catherine's Coll., Oxford (BA 1st Cl. 1992; PhD Turbine Jet Engine Alloys 1996). Worked in engrg res. instns, USA, Ireland and UK; former Hd, Materials Res. Gp, KCL. Has made radio progs for BBC Radio 4; television series: materials sci. consultant, Wonderstuff, 2011; presenter: How It Works, 2012; Everyday Miracles, 2014; Chef vs Science: the ultimate kitchen challenge, 2016. Writer on materials sci. and engrg issues. Mem., Editl Bd, Interdisciplinary Sci. Reviews. *Publications:* (jtly) Computational Materials Engineering, 2007; Stuff Matters: the strange stories of the marvellous materials that shape our man-made world, 2013; Liquid: the delightful and dangerous substances that flow through our lives, 2018. *Address:* Mechanical Engineering Department, University College London, Gower Street, WC1E 6BT. *Club:* Royal Automobile.

**MIQUEL, Raymond Clive,** CBE 1981; Chairman and Managing Director, Lees Foods plc (formerly Lees Group Ltd), 1992–2009; Chairman, Scottish Sports Council, 1987–91; Member, Sports Council, 1988–91; *b* 28 May 1931; *m* 1958; one *s* two *d. Educ:* Allan Glen's Sch., Glasgow; Glasgow Technical Coll. Joined Arthur Bell & Sons Ltd as Works Study Engineer, 1956; Production Controller, 1958; Production Director, 1962; Dep. Man. Dir, 1965; Man. Dir, 1968–85; Dep. Chm., 1972; Chm., 1973–85. Chairman: Towmaster Transport Co. Ltd, 1974–86; Canning Town Glass Ltd, 1974–86; Wellington Importers Ltd, USA, 1984–86; Gleneagles Hotels PLC, 1984–86; Chm. and Chief Exec., Belhaven plc, 1986–88. Dir, Golf Fund Plc, 1989–94. Hon. Prof. in Business Develt, Glasgow Univ., 1985–. Member: British Internat. Sports Cttee, 1987–91; Sport and Recreation Alliance (formerly CCPR), 1984–. Governor, Sports Aid Foundn, 1979–2000. Sponsor: Raymond Miquel Teaching Fellowship in Entrepreneurial Mgt, Glasgow Univ. Business Sch., 2010; Professor Raymond Miquel Enterprise Initiative, Adam Smith Business Sch., Univ. of Glasgow, 2013. CCMI (CBIM 1981). *Publications:* Business as Usual: the Miquel way (autobiog.), 2000, 2nd edn 2012. *Address:* Whitedene, Caledonian Crescent, Gleneagles, Perthshire, Scotland PH3 1NG.

**MIRCHANDANI, Siân;** QC 2019; *b* Swansea, 24 March 1967; *d* of Narain Mirchandani and Phyllis Mirchandani (*née* Davies); *m* 2003 (marr. diss. 2013); two *d. Educ:* Olchfa Comprehensive Sch., Cambridge; Emmanuel Coll., Cambridge (BA 1989; MB Vet. Medicine 1992); City Univ. (DipLaw 1996). Inns of Court Sch. of Law. Resident veterinary surgeon and Jun. Fellow, Bristol Vet. Sch., 1993–95; called to the Bar, Inner Temple, 1997; in practice as barrister, specialising in commercial, professional negligence and construction law, 1998–. *Recreations:* yoga, family, body boarding, surfing, beach walking, art collecting. *Address:* 4 New Square, Lincoln's Inn, WC2A 3RJ. *T:* (020) 7822 2005. *E:* s.mirchandani@4newsquare.com. *Club:* House of St Barnabas.

**MIRESKANDARI, Razi;** Managing Partner, Simons Muirhead & Burton Solicitors, since 2010; *b* Tehran, 22 Aug. 1957; *s* of Taghi and Parichehreh Mireskandari; one *s* two *d. Educ:* Sir Walter St John's Grammar Sch., Battersea; Univ. of Sussex (BA Internat. Relns); Keele Univ. (MA Law of the Sea); Guildford Coll. of Law (Law Soc. Finals); Manchester Univ. (Post Grad. Cert. Legal Practice Mgt). Admitted solicitor, 1986; Partner, Simons Muirhead & Burton Solicitors, 1989–. Dir, Death Penalty Project, 2005–. *Recreations:* squash, poker, all the arts London has to offer. *Address:* c/o Simons Muirhead & Burton LLP, 87–91 Newman Street, W1T 3EY. *T:* 07973 832580. *E:* razi@smab.co.uk. *Clubs:* Groucho; Dulwich Squash.

**MIRMAN, Sophie, (Mrs R. P. Ross);** Joint Managing Director, Trotters Childrenswear and Accessories, since 1990; *b* 28 Oct. 1956; *d* of late Simone and Serge Mirman; *m* 1984, Richard Philip Ross; one *s* two *d. Educ:* French Lycée, London. Marks & Spencer, 1974–81; Gen. Manager, 1981–82, Man. Dir, 1982–83, Tie Rack; Co-Founder, Sock Shop International, 1983; Chm. and Joint Man. Dir, Sock Shop International plc, 1983–90. *Recreations:* family, sport. *Address:* (office) 3 Gorst Road, NW10 6LA.

**MIRO, Victoria,** OBE 2018; Founder, and Director, Victoria Miro Gallery, since 1985; *b* 1 July 1945; *d* of Montagu and Jane Cooper; *m* 1970, Warren Miro; one *s* one *d. Educ:* Slade Sch. of Fine Art. Represents artists, including Chris Ofili, Peter Doig, Isaac Julien, Doug Aitken, Yayoi Kusama, Grayson Perry, Ian Hamilton Finlay. *Recreations:* food, fashion. *Address:* Victoria Miro Gallery, 16 Wharf Road, N1 7RW. *T:* (020) 7336 8109, *Fax:* (020) 7251 5596. *E:* victoria@victoria-miro.com.

**MIRON, Stephen Gabriel;** Group Chief Executive, Global Media & Entertainment (formerly Global Radio), since 2008; *b* Kingston upon Thames, 8 May 1965; *s* of Roger Miron and Josephine Miron (now Kaye); *m* 2005, Suzanne Grover; two *d. Educ:* Hampton Sch. Advertising Exec., Independent Television Pubns, 1985–88; Advertising Manager, Mail on Sunday, 1988–98; Commercial Dir, Independent Newspapers, 1998–2001; Managing Director: Associated New Ventures, 2002–03; Mail on Sunday and Mail Digital, 2003–08. Mem., Adv. Bd, Bartle Bogle Hegarty, 2013–. Member: Marketing Gp of GB; 30 Club (Past Pres.). *Recreations:* golf, family, gym, cars, gadgets, Twitter, Facebook. *Address:* Global Media & Entertainment, 30 Leicester Square, WC2H 7LA. *T:* (020) 7766 6077. *E:* stephen@global.com. *Clubs:* Soho House, Arts, George, Ivy; Wisley Golf, Beaverbrook Golf.

**MIRRÉ, Federico;** Ambassador of the Argentine Republic to the Court of St James's, 2003–08; Permanent Representative to International Maritime Organisation, 2003–08; *b* 7 Aug. 1938; *s* of Emilio Juan Mirré and Marie Teresa (*née* Gavaldá-Lavin); *m* 1966; two *d; m* 2002, Cecilia Duhau. *Educ:* Manuel Belgrano Sch. of Marist Brothers; Univ. of Buenos Aires (LLB); Inst. of Foreign Service, Buenos Aires. Asst Prof. of Public Internat. Law, Univ. of Buenos Aires, 1977–79; Counsellor, Delegn to Papal Mediation, Vatican, 1979–81; Southern Patagonia Diplomatic Liaison Officer with Internat. Red Cross, 1982; Mem., Delegn to British-Argentine Negotiations on Malvinas, Berne, 1984; Minister, Paris, 1985–88; Ambassador to Ivory Coast, Burkina Fasso and Niger, 1988–91; Agent for Argentina on Laguna del Desierto boundary case with Chile, 1991–94; Ambassador to Norway and Iceland, 1994–99; Legal Advr, Min. of Foreign Affairs, 1999; Dir, Internat. Security, Min. of Labour, 2000–02; Hd, Dept of Western Europe, Min. of Foreign Affairs, 2002–03. Dir, Fundación Andina, 1991–94. Pres., Professional Assoc. of Foreign Service, 1992–94. Ed., Perspectiva Internacional, 1991–94. *Recreations:* photography, golf, sailing. *E:* femirre@gmail.com. *Club:* White's.

**MIRREN, Dame Helen,** DBE 2003; actress; *b* 26 July 1945; *m* 1997, Taylor Hackford. *Theatre includes: RSC:* Troilus and Cressida, Much Ado About Nothing, 1968; Richard III, Hamlet, The Two Gentlemen of Verona, 1970; Miss Julie, 1971; Macbeth, 1974; Henry VI parts I, II and III, 1977; Antony and Cleopatra, The Roaring Girl, 1983; *other:* Teeth 'n' Smiles, Royal Court, 1974; The Bed Before Yesterday, Lyric, 1976; Measure for Measure, Riverside, 1979; The Duchess of Malfi, Manchester Royal Exchange, 1980; Faith Healer, Royal Court, 1981; Extremities, Duchess, 1984; Two Way Mirror, Young Vic, 1988; Sex Please, We're Italian, Young Vic, 1991; A Month in the Country, Albery, and Roundabout, Broadway, 1994; Antony and Cleopatra, RNT, 1998; Collected Stories, Haymarket, 1999; Orpheus Descending, Donmar, 2000; Dance of Death, NY, 2001; Mourning Becomes Electra, NT, 2003; Phèdre, NT, 2009; The Audience, Gielgud Th., 2013 (Olivier Award for Best Actress), NY, 2015 (Tony Award for Best Actress in a Leading Role). *Films include:* Age of Consent, 1969; Savage Messiah, 1971; O Lucky Man, 1973; Caligula, 1977; The Long Good Friday, 1980; Excalibur, 1981; Cal, 1984; 2010, 1985; White Nights, Heavenly Pursuits, 1986; The Mosquito Coast, 1987; Pascali's Island, When the Whales Came, 1988; Bethune: The Making of a Hero, 1989; The Cook, The Thief, his Wife and her Lover, 1989; The Comfort of Strangers, 1989; Where Angels Fear to Tread, 1990; The Madness of King George, 1994; Some Mother's Son, 1996; Teaching Mrs Tingle, 1998; Greenfingers, The Pledge, 2001; Last Orders, Gosford Park, 2002; Calendar Girls, 2003; The Clearing, 2004; The Queen, 2006 (Best Actress, Oscar award, 2007); Inkheart, 2008; State of Play, 2009; The Last Station, Red, 2010; Brighton Rock, The Tempest, Arthur, The Debt, 2011; Hitchcock, Red 2, 2013; The Hundred-Foot Journey, 2014; Woman in Gold, Trumbo, 2015; Eye in the Sky, Collateral Beauty, 2016; Fast & Furious 8, 2017; Winchester, The Leisure Seeker, The Nutcracker and the Four Realms, 2018; Fast & Furious Presents: Hobbs & Shaw, The Good Liar, 2019. *TV includes:* Prime Suspect (7 series), 1991–96, 2003, 2006 (Emmy Award, 2007); Painted Lady, 1997; Ayn Rand, 1998; Losing Chase; The Roman Spring of Mrs Stone; Elizabeth I; (dir) Happy Birthday (USA); Phil Spector, 2013 (Screen Actors Guild Award, 2014); Catherine the Great, 2019. Fellow, BAFTA, 2014. *Publications:* In the Frame: my life in words and pictures, 2007. *Address:* c/o PO Box 71253, SW11 9FX.

**MIRSKY, Prof. Rhona Mary,** PhD; Professor of Developmental Neurobiology, University College London, 1990–2004, now Emeritus; *b* 29 May 1939; *d* of Thomas Gibson Pearson and Lynda Pearson (*née* Williams); *m* 1963, Jonathan Mirsky (marr. diss. 1985); *m* 2006, Kristján R. Jessen. *Educ:* New Hall, Cambridge (BA 1961; PhD 1964). Biochemistry Department, Dartmouth Medical School, USA: Instr, 1966–69; Asst Prof., 1969–73; Res. Associate (Asst Prof.), 1973–75; University College London: Vis. Scientist, 1974, Associate Res. Fellow, 1975–81, MRC Neuroimmunology Project, Dept of Zoology; Lectr, 1981–85, Reader, 1985–90, Dept of Anatomy and Develtl Biology. Mem. Council, MRC, 1998–2001. FMedSci 2001. *Publications:* numerous papers in scientific jls. *Address:* Department of Cell and Developmental Biology, University College London, Gower Street, WC1E 6BT. *T:* (020) 7679 3380.

**MIRVIS, Chief Rabbi Ephraim;** Chief Rabbi of the United Hebrew Congregations of the Commonwealth, since 2013; *b* Johannesburg, 1956; *s* of Rabbi Dr Lionel Mirvis and late Freida Mirvis; *m* Valerie; four *s* (one *d* decd). *Educ:* Herzlia High Sch., Cape Town; Yeshivat Kerem BeYavne, Israel; Yeshivat Har Etzion, Israel; Univ. of South Africa (BA Educn and Classical Hebrew); Yaacov Herzog Teachers Coll., Israel. Rabbinic ordination, Machon Ariel, Jerusalem, 1978–80; Chief Rabbi of Ireland, 1984–92; Rabbi, Western Marble Arch Synagogue, 1992–96; Sen. Rabbi, Finchley Utd Synagogue (Kinloss), 1996–2013. Associate Pres., Conf. of European Rabbis (Mem., Steering Cttee), 2013–.

Chm., Irish Nat. Council for Soviet Jewry, 1984–92; Pres., Irish Council of Christians and Jews, 1985–92; Chm., Rabbinical Council of Utd Synagogue, 1999–2002. DHumLit Touro Coll., NY, 2016. *Address*: Office of the Chief Rabbi, 305 Ballards Lane, N12 8GB. *T*: (020) 8343 6301.

**MIRZOEFF, Edward,** CVO 1993; CBE 1997; television director, executive producer and consultant; *b* 11 April 1936; *s* of late Eliachar Mirzoeff and Penina (*née* Asherov); *m* 1961, Judith Topper; three *s*. *Educ*: Hasmonean Grammar Sch.; Queen's Coll., Oxford (Open Scholarship in Mod. History; MA). Market Researcher, Social Surveys (Gallup Poll) Ltd, 1958–59; Public Relns Exec., Duncan McLeish & Associates, 1960–61; Asst Editor, Shoppers' Guide, 1961–63; with BBC Television, 1963–2000: director and producer of film documentaries incl. (with Sir John Betjeman) Metro-land, 1973, A Passion for Churches, 1974, and The Queen's Realm, 1977; Target Tirpitz, 1973; Police - Harrow Road, 1975; The Regiment, 1977; The Front Garden, 1979; The Ritz (BAFTA Award for Best Documentary), 1981; The Englishwoman and The Horse, 1981; The Venetian Dance Master, 1984; Elizabeth R (British Video Award), 1992; Torvill and Dean: facing the music, 1994; Treasures in Trust, 1995; John Betjeman – the last laugh, 2001; Series Editor: Bird's-Eye View, 1969–71; Year of the French, 1982–83; In At The Deep End, 1983–84; Just Another Day, 1983–85; Real Lives, 1985; Editor, 40 Minutes, 1985–89 (BAFTA Awards for Best Factual Series, 1985, 1989; Samuelson Award, Birmingham Fest., 1988); Executive Producer: Fire in the Blood, Pandora's Box, 1992; The Ark, 1993; True Brits, 1994; Situation Vacant, 1995; The House, 1996 (Royal Philharmonic Soc. Music Award for Radio, TV and Video, 1996; BPG Award for Best Documentary Series, 1996; Internat. Emmy, 1996); Full Circle with Michael Palin, 1997; The 50 Years War: Israel and the Arabs, 1998; Children's Hospital, 1998–2000; Michael Palin's Hemingway Adventure, 1999; Queen Elizabeth the Queen Mother, 2002; The Lord's Tale, 2002; A Very English Village, 2005. Chm., BAFTA, 1995–97 (Trustee, 1999–2006; Vice-Chm., TV, 1991–95); Trustee, David Lean BAFTA Foundn, 2006–11. Chm., Grierson (formerly Grierson Meml) Trust, 2002–06 (Trustee, 1999–2009; Vice-Chm., 2000–02; Patron, 2010–15). Mem., Salisbury Cathedral Council, 2002–10. Dir, Dirs' and Producers' Rights Soc., 1999–2007. Vice-Pres., Betjeman Soc., 2006– (Betjeman Lect., 2014). BFI TV Award, 1988; Alan Clarke Award for Outstanding Creative Contribn to Television, BAFTA, 1995. *Publications*: articles for The Oldie, Standpoint. *Recreations*: opera, literature, lunching with friends. *Address*: 9 Westmoreland Road, SW13 9RZ. *T*: (020) 8748 9247. *Club*: Garrick.

**MISCAMPBELL, Gillian Margaret Mary,** OBE 1982; DL; Chairman, Stoke Mandeville Hospital NHS Trust, 1995–2001; *b* 31 Dec. 1935; *d* of late Brig. Francis William Gibb and Agnes Winifred Gibb; *m* 1958, Alexander Malcolm Miscampbell (*d* 2010); three *s*. *Educ*: St Leonard's Sch. Member: Area Manpower Bd, 1985–88; Milton Keynes Develt Corp. Bd, 1990–92. Chm., Aylesbury Vale HA, 1981–93; Mem., Bucks HA, 1993–95. Mem. (C), Bucks CC, 1977–93 (Chm., 1989–93; Chm., Educn Cttee, 1985–89). Chm., Aylesbury Cons. Assoc., 1975–78; Vice Chm., Nat. Women's Adv. Cttee, Cons. Party, 1979–80. University of Buckingham: Mem. Council, 1985–2005 (Vice Chm., 1994–2005); Chm., F and GP Cttee, 1993–98. Chm., Cancer Care and Haematol. Fund, Stoke Mandeville Hosp., 2004–09. Dir, Buckinghamshire Foundn, 1999–2006; Chm., Aylesbury Grammar Sch. Foundn, 2005–14. DL Bucks, 1993. DUniv Buckingham, 1998. *Address*: Rosemount, 15 Upper Street, Quainton, Aylesbury, Bucks HP22 4AY. *T*: (01296) 655318.

**MISKA, Prof. Eric Alexander,** PhD; Herchel Smith Professor of Molecular Genetics, University of Cambridge, since 2013; *b* Bitburg, Germany, 29 June 1971; *s* of Siegfried Miska and Erica (*née* Steindorf); *m* 2000, Ines Alvarez Garcia; one *s* one *d*. *Educ*: St Wiliborod Gymnasium, Bitburg; Trinity Coll., Dublin (BA Biochem. 1996); King's Coll., Cambridge (PhD Pathol. 2000). Wellcome Trust Prize Fellow, Bob Horvitz Lab., 2000–03; Howard Hughes Med. Inst. Res. Associate, 2003–04; MIT; Gp Leader, Wellcome Trust/Cancer Res. UK Gurdon Inst., Univ. of Cambridge, 2005–; Fellow, Pembroke Coll., Cambridge, 2006–13. *Publications*: many res. papers and review articles in leading scientific jls, particularly in areas of non-coding RNA. *Recreations*: running, hiking, cycling, opera. *Address*: Wellcome/Cancer Research UK Gurdon Institute, University of Cambridge, Tennis Court Road, Cambridge CB2 1QN. *T*: (01223) 767220. *E*: eric.miska@gurdon.cam.ac.uk. *W*: www.ericmiskalab.org.

**MISKIN, Charles James Monckton;** QC 1998; a Recorder, since 1998; *b* 29 Nov. 1952; *s* of late Nigel Monckton Miskin and Hilda Meryl Miskin (*née* Knight); *m* 1st, 1982, Karen Elizabeth Booth (marr. diss. 1995); one *s* three *d*; 2nd, 2005, Angharad Jocelyn Start; one *s* two *d*. *Educ*: Charterhouse Sch. (Sutton Pakyenner); Worcester Coll., Oxford (Open Exhibnr; BA Hons Juris. 1974; MA 1978). Called to the Bar, Gray's Inn, 1975, Bencher, 2005; in practice as barrister, 1975–, Hd of Chambers, 2003–06; Mem., S Eastern Circuit; Asst Recorder, 1992–98; Standing Counsel to Inland Revenue, 1993–98. Mem., Criminal Bar Assoc., 1977–. Chm., Bar Theatrical Soc., 1986–. Liveryman: Wax Chandlers' Co., 1975–; Armourers' and Brasiers' Co., 1986–. *Recreations*: travel, opera, history, the children, laughter. *Address*: 23 Essex Street, WC2R 3AA. *T*: (020) 7413 0353. *Clubs*: Travellers, Hurlingham.

**MISTRY, Cyrus Pallonji,** FICE; Chairman, Tata Sons Ltd, 2012–16 (Director, since 2006); *b* Mumbai, India, 4 July 1968; *s* of Pallonji S. Mistry and Patsy P. Mistry; *m* Rohiqa C.; two *s*. *Educ*: Cathedral and John Connon Sch., Mumbai; Imperial Coll. London (BSc Civil Engrg 1990); London Business Sch. (MSc Mgt 1997). Dir, Shapoorji Pallonji & Co. Ltd, 1991; Man. Dir, Shapoorji Pallonji Gp, 1994; Chairman: Tata Steel; Tata Motors; Tata Consultancy Services; Tata Power; Indian Hotels Co.; Tata Global Beverages; Tata Chemicals. *Recreation*: playing golf occasionally.

**MISTRY, Dhruva,** Hon. CBE 2001; RA 1991; FRSS; sculptor, painter and printmaker; *b* Kanjari, Gujarat, 1 Jan. 1957; *s* of Pramodray and Kantaben Mistry. *Educ*: Maharaja Sayajirao Univ. of Baroda (MA 1981); RCA (British Council schol.; MA 1983). Freelance Sculptor Agent, Nigel Greenwood Gall., London, 1983–97; Artist-in-residence, Kettle's Yard, and Fellow of Churchill Coll., Cambridge, 1984–85; Sculptor-in-residence, V&A Mus., 1988; Prof., Hd of Sculpture and Dean, Faculty of Fine Arts, MS Univ. of Baroda, 1999–2002. Solo exhibitions include: Art Heritage, New Delhi, 1981, transf. to Jehangir Art Gall., Bombay, 1982, 2005; Contemp. Art Gall., Amdavad, 1983; Kettle's Yard Gall., Cambridge, 1985; Walker Art Gall., Liverpool, 1986; Nigel Greenwood Gall., London, 1987, 1990; Collins Gall., Glasgow, 1988; Laing Art Gall., Newcastle-upon-Tyne, 1989; Modern Art Gall., Fukuoka Art Mus., Fukuoka, 1994; Royal Acad., Friends Room, 1995; Meghraj Gall., London, 1996; Bothy Gall., Yorks Sculpture Park, W Bretton 1997; Nazar Gall., Vadodara, 1998; Gall. Espace, New Delhi, 1999; Limerick City Gall. of Art, Limerick, 2000; Sakshi Gall., Mumbai, 2001, 2005; Queen's Gall., British Council, New Delhi 2001; Rabindra Bhavan, Lalit Kala Akademi, New Delhi, 2005; Bodhi Art, Travancore Palace and Art Pilgrim, New Delhi, 2007; Harmony Art Foundn, Mumbai, 2008; Hatheesing Centre, Ahmedabad, 2010; Grosvenor Vadehra Art Gall., London, 2011; group exhibitions include: Royal Acad., London, 1982, 1996; Hayward Gall., London, Twinning Gall., NY, 1985; Kettle's Yard, Cambridge, 1987; Business Design Centre, London, 1995; Sakshi Gall., Mumbai, 2000; Lalit Kal Akademi, Delhi, 2001; Grosvenor Gall., London, 2005, 2007, 2009; Royal Acad. Summer Exhibns: 1988, 2008, 2010. Rep. Britain at 3rd Rodin Grand Prize Exhibn, Japan, 1990. Works in public collections including: Lalit Kala Akademi, New Delhi; Tate Gall., Arts Council, British Council and V&A Mus., British Liby, British Mus., London; Nat. Mus. of Wales, Cardiff; Fukuoka Asian Art Mus., Japan; open air collections include sculptures at Goodwood, Yorks Sculpture Park and Hakone Open Air Mus., Japan; works of art for: Victoria Square, Birmingham, commnd by Birmingham CC, 1992; Tamano City Project, Uno, Japan, 2002; LNG Petronet, Dahej, 2003; Delhi Univ., 2005. FRSS (FRBS 1993). DUniv UCE, 2007. Madame Tussaud's Award for Art at RCA, 1983; Jack Goldhill Award, Royal Acad. of Arts, 1991; Award for Design of Humanities Prize Medal, 1994; Design and Pres.'s Award for Victoria Square Sculptures, 1995; Landscape Inst. and Marsh Fountain of the Year Award, 1995; Award of Excellence, Gujarat Gaurav Samiti, 2006; Triveni Award, Vadodora, 2014. *Recreations*: photography, reading, walking. *Address*: (office) 76 Anu Shakti Nagar, Sama, Vadodara-390024, Gujarat, India. *T*: (265) 2712949, (mobile) (91) 9376214606. *E*: dhruva@dhruvamistry.com. *W*: www.dhruvamistry.com.

**MISTRY, Rohinton,** CM 2015; FRSL; author; *b* Bombay, 1952; *m* 1975, Freny Elavia. *Educ*: Villa Theresa Prim. Sch., Bombay; St Xavier's High Sch., Bombay; Bombay Univ. (BSc Maths and Econs 1973); Univ. of Toronto (BA Eng. and Philos. 1983). Bank clerk, Toronto, 1975–85. FRSL 2009. DUniv Ottawa, 1996; Hon. DLitt: Toronto, 1999; York, 2003; Ryerson, 2012. Canada-Australia Literary Award, 1995; Trudeau Fellowship, Trudeau Foundn, 2004; Guggenheim Fellowship, 2005; Neustadt Internat. Prize for Literature, 2012. *Publications*: Tales From Firozsha Baag (short stories), 1987; novels: Such a Long Journey, 1991 (Gov. Gen.'s Award for Fiction, Canada, 1991; Commonwealth Writers' Prize for Best Book, 1992); A Fine Balance, 1995 (Giller Prize, Canada, 1995; Commonwealth Writers' Prize for Best Book, 1996; Winnifred Holtby Award, RSL, 1997; LA Times Fiction Prize, 1997); Family Matters (Kiriyama Pacific Rim Book Prize for Fiction), 2002; short stories and travel essays in literary periodicals and anthologies; works translated into 33 langs. *Address*: c/o Westwood Creative Artists Ltd, 386 Huron Street, Toronto, ON M5S 2G6, Canada. *E*: bruce@wcaltd.com.

**MITCALFE, (Joan) Kirsteen,** MBE 2017; Vice Lord-Lieutenant of Moray, 2005–11; *b* 23 July 1936; *d* of Douglas and Jenny Mackessack; *m* 1959, Hugh Mitcalfe (*d* 2019); four *d*. *Educ*: Oxenfoord Castle Sch., Midlothian; Open Univ. (BA Hons). Secretary: Moray and Nairn Br., Pony Club, 1971–96; Forres Br., Riding for the Disabled, 1972–90; Burgie Internat. Horse Trials, 1988–2003. Chm. Trustees, Kinloss Abbey, 2013–. Gov., Gordonstoun Sch., 1981–94. Voluntary work with hospice movt, WRVS and as church sec. *Recreations*: ski-ing, fishing, travelling, music. *Address*: Thunderton Cottage, 79 Findhorn, Moray IV36 3YF. *T*: (01309) 690775. *E*: k.mitcalfe@btinternet.com.

**MITCHARD, (Gerald Steven) Paul;** QC 2008; Director, Career Planning and Professionalism, Faculty of Law, Chinese University of Hong Kong, since 2014; *b* Paulton, 2 Jan. 1952; *s* of Gerald Mitchard and Janet Mitchard; *m* 1987, Dorothy Grant; two *s*. *Educ*: Lincoln Coll., Oxford (MA Juris. 1974). Slaughter and May, 1977–84; Simmons & Simmons: Partner, 1984–99; Head of Litigation, 1993–99; Partner, Wilmer, Cutler & Pickering, 1999–2001; Head, Eur. Arbitration and Litigation, 2001–09, Global Co-head and Head of Asia, Internat. Arbitration and Litigation Gp, 2009–14, Skadden, Arps, Slate, Meagher & Flom (UK) LLP. Vis. Prof. of Law, China Univ. of Politics and Law, Beijing, 2012–15. *Recreations*: hiking, reading, scuba diving. *Address*: Faculty of Law, Chinese University of Hong Kong, Shatin, New Territories, Hong Kong. *Club*: Vincent's (Oxford).

**MITCHELL,** family name of **Baron Mitchell**.

**MITCHELL,** Baron *cr* 2000 (Life Peer), of Hampstead in the London Borough of Camden; **Parry Andrew Mitchell;** *b* 6 May 1943; *s* of Leon and Rose Mitchell; *m* 1st, 1972, Doreen Hargreaves (marr. diss.); one *d*; 2nd, 1988, Hannah Ruth Lowy; two *s* (twins). *Educ*: Christ's Coll., Finchley; Univ. of London (BSc ext.); Columbia Univ. NY (MBA). Chm., United Leasing plc, 1976–87. Opposition spokesperson, BIS, 2012–13. Member: H of L Select Cttee on Sci. and Technol., 2003–07, on EU, Sub-Cttee B, Internal Market, 2007–09; Jt Cttee on Nat. Security Strategy. Enterprise Advr to Labour Party, 2013–; Chm., Lab. Digital, 2013–15. Chairman: Syscap plc, 1992–2006; Weizmann UK, 2005–09; Instant Impact Ltd, 2014–. Chairman: eLearning Foundn, 2006–10; Coexistence Trust, 2008–12; Founder Trustee, Lowy Mitchell Foundn. *Recreations*: gym obsessive, cyclist in the hills of Umbria, jazz night and day, opera, theatre and the cinema. *Address*: House of Lords, SW1A 0PW. *T*: 07515 339792. *E*: parrym@mac.com.

**MITCHELL, Alison Janet; Her Honour Judge Mitchell;** a Circuit Judge, since 2016; *b* Sedgefield, Co. Durham, 24 May 1963; *d* of Derek Hunt and Sheila Hunt; *m* 1992, Nick Mitchell; one *s* one *d*. *Educ*: Wolsingham Comp. Sch.; Fitzwilliam Coll., Cambridge (BA Hons Law 1985). Called to the Bar, Gray's Inn, 1986; a Recorder, 2009–16. *Recreations*: going to book group without having read the book, obsessively tending my compost bin, collecting 'vintage' crockery and rescuing it from dishwasher, changing my forgotten passwords. *Address*: The Family Court, Sessions House, Lancaster Road, Preston PR1 2PD. *T*: (01772) 272845.

**MITCHELL, Rt Hon. Andrew (John Bower);** PC 2010; MP (C) Sutton Coldfield, since 2001; *b* 23 March 1956; *s* of Sir David Bower Mitchell and Pamela Elaine (*née* Haward); *m* 1985, Sharon Denise (*née* Bennett); two *d*. *Educ*: Rugby; Jesus Coll., Cambridge (MA History). 1st RTR (Short Service (Limited) Commission), 1975; served with UNFICYP. Pres., Cambridge Union, 1978; Chm., Cambridge Univ. Conservatives, 1977; rep. GB in E-SU American debating tour, 1978. Internat. and Corp. business, Lazard Brothers & Co., 1979–87, Consultant, 1987–92; Dir, Lazard Gp Cos, 1997–2009. Senior Strategy Adviser: Boots Co., 1997–2001; Accenture (formerly Andersen Consulting), 1997–2009; Investec, 2013–; Ernst & Young, 2016–. Director: Miller Insce Gp, 1997–2001; Commer Gp, 1998–2002; Financial Dynamics Holdings, 1998–2002. Advr to Bd, Hakluyt, 1998–2001. Contested (C) Sunderland South, 1983. MP (C) Gedling, 1987–97; contested (C) same seat, 1997. A Vice-Chm., Cons. Party, with special responsibility for candidates, 1992–93; An Asst Govt Whip, 1992–94; a Lord Comr of HM Treasury (Govt Whip), 1994–95; Parly Under Sec. of State, DSS, 1995–97; Opposition front bench spokesman: economic affairs, 2003–04; police and home affairs, 2004–05; Shadow Sec. of State for internat. develt, 2005–10; Sec. of State for Internat. Develt, 2010–12; Parly Sec. to HM Treasury (Govt Chief Whip), 2012. Sen. Res. Associate, Jesus Coll., Cambridge, 2018–. Sec., One Nation Gp of Conservative MPs, 1989–92, 2005–. Chm., Coningsby Club, 1983; President: Islington North Conservatives, 1996–2006 (Chm., 1983–85); Gedling Cons. Assoc., 2004–. Vice-Chm., 1998–2010, Trustee, 2010–15, Alexandra Rose Charity. Member Council: SOS Sahel, 1991–2010; GAP, 2000–05. Fellow, Centre for Rising Powers, Cambridge Univ., 2016; Vis. Fellow, Harvard Univ., 2016–. *Recreations*: ski-ing, music, travel, wine. *Address*: 30 Gibson Square, N1 0RD. *T*: (020) 7226 5519; 8 Tudor Road, Sutton Coldfield B73 6BA. *T*: (0121) 355 5519. *Clubs*: Cambridge Union Society (Cambridge); Carlton and District Constitutional (Gedling); Sutton Coldfield Conservative.

**MITCHELL, Andrew Jonathan,** CMG 2013; HM Trade Commissioner for Europe, since 2018; *b* 7 March 1967; *s* of Michael John Mitchell and Patricia Anne Mitchell; *m* 1996, Helen Sarah Anne Magee; two *s* one *d*. *Educ*: St Mary's Coll., Crosby, Liverpool; Queen's Coll., Oxford (BA 1st Cl. Hons Mod. Langs 1990; Laming Scholar, Queen's Coll. Bursary, Markham Prize for French). Joined FCO, 1991; Second Sec., Bonn, 1993; First Sec., FCO,

1996; Dep. Hd of Mission, Kathmandu, 1999; Counsellor, FCO, 2002–07; Ambassador to Sweden, 2007–11; FCO Dir for 2012 Olympic and Paralympic Games, London, FCO, 2011–12; Dir, Prosperity, FCO, 2012–14; Dir, M-is plc, 2015–18. *Recreations:* enjoy cricket, Rugby and soccer, keen walker, reader of history, sciences, politics and current affairs. *Clubs:* MCC, Army and Navy, Soho House; Vincent's (Oxford).

**MITCHELL, Andrew Robert;** QC 1998; a Recorder, since 1999; *b* 6 Aug. 1954; *s* of late Malcolm Mitchell and of Edna Audrey Mitchell; *m* 1st, 1982, Patricia Ann Fairbairn (marr. diss. 1991); 2nd, 1992, Carolyn Ann Blore; one *s* one *d. Educ:* Haberdashers' Aske's Sch.; Council of Legal Educn. Called to the Bar, Gray's Inn, 1976, Bencher, 2005; in practice at the Bar, 1976–; Asst Recorder, 1995–99. Head: Furnival Chambers, 1990–2008; Chambers of Andrew Mitchell QC, 2008–19. Mem., Gen. Council of Bar, 2003–11 (Treas., 2008–11). Mem. (C) Haringey LBC, 1984–94 (Leader of the Opposition, 1989–91). Contested (C) Islington S and Finsbury, 1987. Gov., Highgate Primary Sch., 1984–99 (Chm. of Govs, 1997–98). *Publications:* Confiscation and Proceeds of Crime, 1993, 3rd edn (ed jtly) 2002–; Concise Guide to Criminal Procedure Investigations Act 1996, 1997; (contrib.) Administrative Court: practice *v* procedure, 2006. *Recreations:* watching football and cricket, trying to keep fit. *Address:* 33 Chancery Lane, WC2A 1EN. *T:* (020) 7440 9950. *E:* arm@33cllaw.com. *Clubs:* Royal Automobile, MCC.

**MITCHELL, His Honour Anthony Paul;** a Circuit Judge, 2000–12; *b* 9 Aug. 1941; *s* of Arthur Leslie Mitchell and Ivy Muriel Mitchell (*née* Simpson); *m* 1st, 1972, Shirley Ann Donovan (marr. diss. 1985); one *s* one *d*, and one step *s* one step *d*; 2nd, 1989, Julia Fryer (*d* 2000); one step *s* one step *d*; 3rd, 2003, Bethan Henderson; one step *s* one step *d. Educ:* Whitgift Sch., Croydon; Coll. of Law, London. Articled, Routh Stacey & Co.; qualified, 1965; admitted Solicitor, 1966; Partner, Toller Hales Collcutt, 1969–2000; Dep. Dist Judge, 1982–2000; Asst Recorder, 1991–95; Recorder, 1995–2000. *Recreations:* time with family and friends, theatre, opera, cinema, walking, watching sport, keeping fit; Christianity and supporting my church and its musical tradition; Southern Burgundy, its wines and its weather, supporting National Youth Advocacy Service and its work with young people and vulnerable young adults, and still things spiritual with a small 's'. *Club:* Lansdowne.

**MITCHELL, Austin Vernon,** DPhil; *b* 19 Sept. 1934; *s* of Richard Vernon Mitchell and Ethel Mary Mitchell; *m* 1st, Patricia Dorothea Jackson (marr. diss.); two *d*; 2nd, Linda Mary McDougall; one *s* one *d. Educ:* Woodbottom Council Sch.; Bingley Grammar Sch.; Manchester Univ. (BA, MA); Nuffield Coll., Oxford (DPhil). Lectr in History, Univ. of Otago, Dunedin, NZ, 1959–63; Sen. Lectr in Politics, Univ. of Canterbury, Christchurch, NZ, 1963–67; Official Fellow, Nuffield Coll., Oxford, 1967–69; Journalist, Yorkshire Television, 1969–71; Presenter, BBC Current Affairs Gp, 1972–73; Journalist, Yorkshire TV, 1973–77; Co-presenter, Target, Sky TV, 1989–98. MP (Lab) Grimsby, April 1977–1983, Great Grimsby, 1983–2015. PPS to Minister of State for Prices and Consumer Protection, 1977–79; Opposition front bench spokesman on trade and industry, 1987–89. Member, Select Committee: on Treasury and Civil Service, 1983–87; on agric., 1997–2001; on envmt, food and rural affairs, 2001–05; Public Accounts, 2006–15. Mem., Public Accounts Commn, 1997–2015. Chair, Yorks and Humber Seafood Gp, Yorks Forward, 2007–11. Lectr, Summer Sch., Univ. of Canterbury, NZ, 2015–16. Mem., OT Prophets. Associate Ed., House Magazine. ONZM 2001. High Steward, NE Lincs, 2015. Order of the Falcon (Iceland), 2015. *Publications:* New Zealand Politics In Action, 1962; Government By Party, 1966; The Whigs in Opposition 1815–1830, 1969; Politics and People in New Zealand, 1970; Yorkshire Jokes, 1971; The Half-Gallon Quarter-Acre Pavlova Paradise, 1974; Can Labour Win Again, 1979; Westminster Man, 1982; The Case for Labour, 1983; Four Years in the Death of the Labour Party, 1983; Yorkshire Jokes, 1988; Teach Thissen Tyke, 1988; Britain: beyond the blue horizon, 1989; Competitive Socialism, 1989; Accounting for Change, 1993; Election '45, 1995; Corporate Governance Matters, 1996; The Common Fisheries Policy: end or mend?, 1996; (with David Wienir) Last Time: Labour's lessons from the sixties, 1997; (with Anne Tate) Fishermen: the rise and fall of deep water trawling, 1997; Parliament in Pictures, 1999; Farewell My Lords, 1999; Austin Mitchell's Yorksher, 2002; Pavlova Paradise Revisited, 2002; Austin Mitchell's Yorkshire Sayings, 2004; Taming the Corporations, 2005; The Pensions Scandal, 2007; Grand Book of Yorkshire Humour, 2009; Calendar Boy, 2014; Revenge of the Rich, 2017; Confessions of a Political Maverick, 2018. *Recreation:* worriting (*sic*). *Address:* Longfield, Dean Lane, Sowerby Bridge, W Yorks HX6 1HE. *E:* austinmitchellxmp@gmail.com.

**MITCHELL, Bryan James,** CB 2006; Director, Business and Information Management Directorate, Welsh Assembly Government, 2003–05; *b* 1 March 1945; *s* of Herbert Mitchell and Hilda (*née* Grant); *m*; four *d. Educ:* Robert Clack Technical Sch., Dagenham; Open Univ. (BA). MoT, 1967–74; CSD, 1974–76; DoE, 1976–78; Welsh Office, 1978–99; Dep. Clerk to Nat. Assembly for Wales, 1999–2000; Welsh Assembly Govt, 2000–05. Mem. Bd, Habinteg Housing Assoc., Ulster, 2012–17. Associate Consultant, Siemens Business Services. Assessor, Welsh LGA Excellence Prog., 2006–08.

**MITCHELL, Prof. Catherine Hilary Claire,** PhD; Professor of Energy Policy, University of Exeter, since 2007; *b* Plymouth, 4 March 1956; *d* of Prof. Duncan Mitchell and Dr Margaret Mitchell. *Educ:* Maynard Sch., Exeter; Univ. of London (BA Hist. 1981); Boston Univ. (MA Energy and Envmtl Studies 1989); Sussex Univ. (PhD Technol. and Innovation Policy 1994). Res. Fellow, Univ. of Sussex, 1993–2000; Principal Res. Fellow, Warwick Business Sch., Univ. of Warwick, 2000–07. Mem., Policy Adv. Council, IPPR. *Publications:* The Political Economy of Sustainable Energy, 2008, 2nd edn 2010. *Recreations:* modern art, gardening, walking, theatre, film. *Address:* Energy Policy Group, University of Exeter, Penryn, Cornwall TR10 9FE. *T:* (01326) 253788. *E:* catherine.mitchell@exeter.ac.uk. *Club:* Reform.

**MITCHELL, Prof. Charles,** PhD; FBA 2017; Professor of Law, University College London, since 2010; *b* London, 13 May 1965; *s* of James Mitchell and Janice Mitchell (*née* Davison); *m* 1994, Charlotte Lennox-Boyd; two *s* one *d. Educ:* Magdalen Coll., Oxford (BA Modern Hist. 1987); City Univ. (DipLaw 1988); University Coll. London (LLM 1989; PhD Law 1993). King's College London: Lectr in Law, 1996–2002; Reader in Law, 2002–04; Prof. of Law, 2004–09; Prof. of Law, Univ. of Oxford, 2009–10; Fellow in Law, Jesus Coll., Oxford, 2009–10. Hon. QC 2019. *Publications:* The Law of Contribution and Reimbursement, 2003; Subrogation: law and practice, 2007; (jtly) Goff & Jones: The Law of Unjust Enrichment, 9th edn, 2016; (jtly) Underhill & Hayton: Law Relating to Trusts and Trustees, 19th edn, 2016; (jtly) Law and Society in England, 1750–1950, 2nd edn 2019. *Address:* Faculty of Laws, University College London, Bentham House, Endsleigh Gardens, WC1H 0EG. *E:* charles.mitchell@ucl.ac.uk.

**MITCHELL, Charles Julian Humphrey;** *see* Mitchell, Julian.

**MITCHELL, Charlotte Isabel;** *b* 3 May 1953; *d* of (John) Angus (Macbeth) Mitchell, CB, CVO, MC and of Ann Katharine (*née* Williamson), MA, MPhil, author; *m* 1st, 1972 (marr. diss. 2000); one *s* one *d*; 2nd, 2002, Paul Southall. *Educ:* St George's Sch. for Girls, Edinburgh; Birmingham Coll. of Art (DipAD 1974); Dip Wine and Spirits 1991. Exhibn organiser, Scottish Craft Centre, 1974–76; Director: Real Foods Ltd, 1976–97; Go Organic Ltd, 1998–2003; organic food consultant, Waitrose plc, 1998–2002. Trustee, 1987–2005, Dir, 1990–92, Chm., 1990–97, Hon. Vice-Pres., 2006–, Soil Assoc. Trustee, Knockando Wool Mill, Speyside, 2004–12. Hon. Mem., BBC Scotland Adv. Council for Rural and Agricl Affairs, 1994–98. Regular contrib., New Pathways mag. *Publications:* The Organic Wine Guide, 1987. *Recreations:* food, wine, music, books, gardening.
*See also* J. J. Mitchell.

**MITCHELL, His Honour Christopher Richard;** a Circuit Judge, 2003–12; Resident Judge, Basildon Combined Court Centre, 2007–11; *b* 16 Sept. 1942; *e s* of late Anthony Geoffrey Fulton Mitchell and of Cynthia Grace Mitchell (*née* Charlton); *m* 1980, Elisabeth Jeanne Antonine Pineau, *e d* of late Jean Pineau; one *d. Educ:* St Dunstan's Coll.; King's Coll. London (LLB 1964). Treasury Solicitor's Dept, 1965–69; called to the Bar, Gray's Inn, 1968; in practice at the Bar, London and S Eastern Circuit (crime), 1969–2003; Asst Recorder, 1987–91, Recorder, 1991–2003; Immigration Appeal Adjudicator, 1998–2003. Asst Comr, Parly Boundary Commn, 1993–94. *Recreations:* hill-walking, books, European railways, cycling, wooding. *Address:* c/o Amber Mercele, Hollis Whiteman Chambers, Lawrence Pountney Hill, EC4R 0EU. *T:* (020) 7933 8855.

**MITCHELL, His Honour David Charles;** a Circuit Judge, South Eastern Circuit, 2001–16; Designated Civil Judge, London, 2007–16; a Senior Circuit Judge, 2010–16; Senior Resident Judge, Central London Civil Justice Centre, 2011–16; *b* 4 May 1950; *s* of Charles and Eileen Mitchell; *m* 1973, Susan Cawthera; one *s* one *d. Educ:* state schs; St Catherine's Coll., Oxford (MA Juris.). Called to the Bar, Inner Temple, 1972, Bencher, 2014; barrister-at-law, Bradford Chambers, 1972–99, Pump Court, Temple, 1999–2001; specialised in civil and family law, crime and personal injury; Asst Recorder, 1989–93; a Recorder, 1993–2001; Chm., Mental Health Rev. Tribunal (Restricted Panel), 2003–05; Designated Civil Judge: Kent, 2003–07. Course Dir, Judicial Studies Bd Civil Refresher Course, 2008–11. *Recreations:* hill-walking, ski-ing, the theatre, listening to classical music, anything connected with France.

**MITCHELL, David James Stuart;** freelance comedy actor and writer, since 1996; *b* Salisbury, 14 July 1974; *s* of Ian Douglas Mitchell and Kathryn Grey Mitchell (*née* Hughes); *m* 2012, Victoria, *d* of late Alan Coren and of Anne Coren; one *d. Educ:* Abingdon Sch.; Peterhouse, Cambridge (BA Hons 1996). *Television* includes: as actor and writer: Blunder, 2006; with Robert Webb: Bruiser, 2000; The Mitchell and Webb Situation, 2001; Peep Show, 2003–15 (Best Comedy Performance, BAFTA, 2008); That Mitchell and Webb Look, 2006–; Would I Lie to You?, 2007–; The Bubble, 2010; 10 O'Clock Live, 2011–13; Back, 2017–; as actor: Jam & Jerusalem, 2006–09; Ambassadors, 2013; The Incredible Adventures of Professor Branestawm, 2014–15; host, Was It Something I Said?, 2013; Upstart Crow, 2016, 2017, 2018; *radio:* (with Robert Webb) That Mitchell and Webb Sound, 2003–; The Unbelievable Truth, 2007–; Behaving Ourselves: Mitchell on manners, 2016; *films:* Magicians, 2007; Greed, 2019. UK tour, Brydon, Mack and Mitchell: town to town, 2019. Columnist, The Observer, 2008–. *Publications:* (with R. Webb) This Mitchell and Webb Book, 2009; Back Story, 2012; Thinking About It Only Makes It Worse, 2014; Dishonesty is the Second-Best Policy: and other rules to live by, 2019. *Recreations:* walking, talking. *Address:* c/o Michele Milburn, Milburn Browning Associates, The Old Truman Brewery, 91 Brick Lane, E1 6QL. *T:* (020) 3582 9370, *Fax:* (020) 3582 9377. *E:* Michele@milburnbrowning.com.
*See also* G. R. P. Coren.

**MITCHELL, David McKenzie,** MD; FRCP; Consultant Physician, St Mary's Hospital, Paddington, 1987–2014, and Medical Director, Imperial College Healthcare NHS Trust (formerly St Mary's NHS Trust), 1998–2014; Medical Director, Hospital of St John and St Elizabeth, since 2015; *b* 27 July 1948; *s* of John Bernard Mitchell and Elizabeth Mitchell; *m* 1st, 1977, Elizabeth Gaminara (marr. diss. 2005); one *s* one *d*; 2nd, 2009, Jennifer Leigh Hardyment. *Educ:* Mostyn House Sch.; Oundle Sch.; Gonville and Caius Coll., Cambridge (MB BChir 1974; MD 1983); Middlesex Hosp.; London Univ. (BA (Philos.) 1983, ext.); Keele Univ. (MBA 1998). FRCP 1991. Trng posts in gen. and respiratory medicine, Hammersmith Hosp., Brompton Hosp., UCH, London Chest Hosp., 1973–87; Res. Fellow in Immunology, ICRF, 1980–82. Trustee, Royal Hosp. for Neuro-disability, 2015–. Liveryman, Musicians' Co., 2005. *Publications:* Respiratory Medicine Revision, 1986; AIDS and the Lung, 1990; Recent Advances in Respiratory Medicine, 1991; papers on various aspects of respiratory medicine. *Recreations:* playing jazz saxophone, classical music, opera, philosophy, travel. *Address:* Hospital of St John and St Elizabeth, Grove End Road, NW8 9NH. *T:* (020) 7806 4000. *E:* david.mitchell@hje.org.uk. *Club:* Athenæum.

**MITCHELL, David William,** CBE 1983; Chairman, 2001–04, Hon. President, 2005–10, Scottish Conservative and Unionist Party; *b* 4 Jan. 1933; *m* 1965, Lynda Katherine Marion Guy; one *d. Educ:* Merchiston Castle School, Edinburgh. Nat. Service, 1950–52 (commnd RSF); seconded to 4th Nigerian Regt, RWAFF). Western RHB, 1968–75; Director: Mallinson, Denny (Scotland), 1975–89; Hunter Timber (Scotland), 1989–92; Jt Man. Dir, M & N Norman (Timber) Ltd, 1992–96. Chm., Cumbernauld New Town Develt Corp., 1987–97. Member: Exec. Cttee, Scottish Council Develt and Industry, 1979–95; Scottish Council, CBI, 1980–85; Scottish Exec. Cttee, Inst. of Directors, 1984–91. President: Timber Trade Benevolent Soc., 1974; Scottish Timber Trade Assoc., 1984. Pres., Scottish Cons. and Unionist Assoc., 1980–82; Treasurer, Scottish Cons. Party, 1990–93, 1998–2001. Gov., Craighalbert Centre for Children with Motor Neurone Disease, 1992–95. *Recreations:* golf, shooting, fishing. *Address:* The Old Mill House, Symington, Ayrshire KA1 5QL. *T:* (01563) 830851. *Clubs:* Western (Glasgow); Royal and Ancient Golf, Prestwick Golf; Queen's Park Football.

**MITCHELL, His Honour Fergus Irvine;** a Circuit Judge, 1996–2014; *b* 30 March 1947; *s* of Sir George Irvine Mitchell, CB, QC (Scot.) and Elizabeth Mitchell (*née* Leigh Pemberton), JP; *m* 1972, Sally Maureen, *yr d* of Sir Derrick Capper, QPM and Muriel Capper; one *s* one *d. Educ:* Tiffin Boys' Sch., Kingston-upon-Thames. Called to the Bar, Gray's Inn, 1971; Asst Recorder, 1989; Recorder, 1993. Member: Gen. Council of the Bar, 1992–95; Professional Conduct Cttee, 1993–95; Bar Race Relations Cttee, 1994–95. Chm., Lord Chancellor's Adv. Cttee, SW London, 2000–11; Magistrates' Liaison Judge, SW London, 2000–13. Mem., Mental Health Tribunal Restricted Patients Panel, 2000–. *Recreations:* France, opera.

**MITCHELL, George Edward,** CBE 2006; Chairman, The Malcolm Group, since 2006; *b* 7 April 1950; *m* 1971, Agnes Rutherford; three *d. Educ:* Forrester High Sch., Edinburgh. Joined Bank of Scotland, 1966: held a wide range of posts, incl. periods in Hong Kong, NY and London; Chief Exec., Bank of Scotland Retail Bank, 1999–2000; Chief Exec., Corporate, HBOS, 2001–05, Gov., 2003–05, Bank of Scotland. Director: Intrinsic Financial Services, 2006–; BUPA, 2007–. *Recreations:* football, tennis.

**MITCHELL, Hon. George John,** Hon. GBE 1999; lawyer; Partner, DLA Piper LLP, since 2005 (Chairman, 2005–08, now Emeritus); *b* 20 Aug. 1933; *s* of George and Mary Mitchell; *m* 1959, Sally L. Heath (marr. diss.); one *d*; *m* 1994, Heather MacLachlan; one *s* one *d. Educ:* Bowdoin Coll. (BA 1954); Georgetown Univ. (LLB 1960). Served US Army, 1954–56 (1st Lieut). Admitted to Bar of Maine and of Washington, 1960, to DC Bar, 1960; Trial Attorney, Anti-Trust Div., Dept of Justice, Washington, 1960–62; Exec. Asst to Senator Edmund Muskie, 1962–65; Partner, Jensen, Baird, Gardner, Donovan & Henry, Portland, 1965–77; US Attorney, Maine, 1977–79; US Dist Judge, N Maine, 1979–80; US Senator

(Democrat) from Maine, 1980–95; Majority Leader, US Senate, 1988–95. Chm., Irish Peace Talks, 1995–98; Special US Envoy to the Middle East, 2009–11. Chm., Walt Disney Co., 2004. Chancellor, QUB, 1999–2009. Hd, Internat. Adv. Council, Thames Water, 1999–. Hon. LLD: QUB, 1997; Cambridge, 2010. Presidential Medal of Freedom (USA), 1999. *Publications:* (jtly) Men of Zeal: a candid inside story of the Iran-Contra Hearings, 1988; World on Fire, 1990; Not For America Alone: the triumph of democracy and the fall of communism, 1997; Making Peace, 1999; The Negotiator, 2015; A Path to Peace, 2016. *Address:* DLA Piper LLP, 1251 Avenue of the Americas, New York, NY 10020–1104, USA.

**MITCHELL, Gordon Scotland;** Director, Starburst Consulting Ltd, since 2006; *b* 30 Dec. 1956. *Educ:* Univ. of Edinburgh (MA Hons); Univ. of Newcastle upon Tyne (BPhil); Bristol Business Sch., UWE (MBA 1997). Posts in nat. voluntary sector, 1982–92; Hd, Policy and Corporate Relns, Newport CBC, 1992–97; Chief Executive: Bracknell Forest BC, 1998–2003; Nottingham CC, 2003–06. Non-exec. Dir, Glos Hosps NHS Foundn Trust, 2009–16 (Vice Chm., 2012–16). Prog. Dir, Solace-Macmillan Partnership, 2016–. Governor: Nottingham Trent Univ., 2004–09; Glos Coll., 2008. *Recreations:* good food and wine, lying in the sun. *Address:* 36 William Bancroft Building, Roden Street, Nottingham NG3 1GH.

**MITCHELL, Gregory Charles Mathew;** QC 1997; PhD; a Recorder, since 2000; *b* 27 July 1954; *s* of late John Matthew Mitchell, CBE and of Eva Maria Mitchell; three *s* one *d*. *Educ:* King's Coll., London (BA Hons); PhD); City Univ. (Dip. Law). Called to the Bar, Gray's Inn, 1979, Bencher, 2005. *Recreations:* ski-ing, scuba diving, tennis. *Address:* 3 Verulam Buildings, Gray's Inn, WC1R 5NT. *T:* (020) 7831 8441.

**MITCHELL, Harry;** QC 1987; Company Secretary, The Wellcome Foundation Ltd, 1976–92, and Wellcome plc, 1985–92; *b* 27 Oct. 1930; *s* of Harry and Lily Mitchell; *m* 1960, Mrs Megan Knill (*née* Watkins); one step *s* one step *d*. *Educ:* Bolton School; Corpus Christi College, Cambridge (BA). FCIS. Called to the Bar, Gray's Inn, 1968. Asst District Comr, Colonial Service, Sierra Leone, 1954–59; Company Sec., Asbestos Cement, Bombay, 1960–64; Asst Company Sec., British Aluminium Co., 1964–66; Legal Manager/Exec. Dir Legal, Hawker Siddeley Aviation, 1966–76. Chm., Bar Assoc. for Commerce, Finance and Industry, 1984–85 (Vice-Pres., 1986–); Mem. Senate of Inns of Court and Bar and Bar Council, 1978–81, 1983–86; Part-time Immigration Adjudicator, 1992–2002. Director: Berkeley Square Pension Trustee Co. Ltd, 2004–08; Berkeley Square Common Investment Fund Ltd, 2005–08. Mem., Adv. Council and Hon. Legal Advr, Migrationwatch UK, 2003–. Mem., CBI London Regional Council, 1990–92. Board Member: Sarsen Housing Assoc., Devizes, 1994–2006 (Chm., 1995–2001); Silbury Gp Ltd, 2003–05; Ridgeway Community Housing Assoc., 2003–04. Trustee, Migraine Trust, 1995–2005. *Publications:* Remote Corners: a Sierra Leone memoir, 2002; Confessions of a Briefless Barrister (autobiog.), 2016; articles in New Law Jl, Business Law Review and Jl of Immigration, Asylum and Nationality Law; numerous legal briefing papers on immigration and asylum law. *Recreations:* playing piano, opera, reading, travel. *Address:* The Mount, Brook Street, Great Bedwyn, Marlborough, Wilts SN8 3LZ. *T:* (01672) 870898. *E:* harrymitchellqc@gmail.com.

**MITCHELL, Iain Grant;** QC (Scot.) 1992; barrister; *b* 15 Nov. 1951; *s* of late John Grant Mitchell and Isobel (*née* Gilhespie). *Educ:* Perth Acad.; Edinburgh Univ. (LLB Hons 1973). Called to the Scottish Bar, 1976; Temp. Sheriff, 1992–97; called to the Bar, Middle Temple, 2012. Vice-Chm., 2001–07, Chm., 2007–, Scottish Soc. for Computers and Law. Mem., IT Cttee, Bar Council, 2011–; UK Rep., IT Cttee, 2011–, Chm., Wkg Pty on Surveillance, 2015–, CCBE. Exec. Ed., Scottish Parlt Law Rev., 1999–2003; Joint Editor: E-Law Rev., 2001–04; Internat. Free and Open Source Law Rev., 2009–. Cons. local govt cand. on various occasions, 1973–82; contested (C): Falkirk W, 1983; Kirkcaldy, 1987; Cumbernauld and Kilsyth, 1992; Dunfermline East, 1997; Dundee E, Scottish Parlt, 1999; Scotland, EP elecns, 1999; Edinburgh North & Leith, 2001; Falkirk W, Scottish Parlt, 2003. Hon. Secretary: Scottish Cons. & Unionist Assoc., 1993–98; Scottish Cons. & Unionist Party, 1998–2001; Chm., Edinburgh Central Cons. Assoc., 2003–05. Chairman: N Queensferry Community Council, 2007–10 and 2012–; N Queensferry Community Trust, 2012–. Mem., Exec. Cttee, Scottish Council, European Movement, 1992–. Director: Scottish Baroque Ensemble Ltd, 1985–2003 (Chm., 1999–2003); Cappella Nova, 2007–; Chairman: Trust for an Internat. Opera Theatre of Scotland, 1984–; N Queensferry Railway Station Preservation Trust, 2006–; Perthshire Public Arts Trust, 2007– (Trustee, 2000–07). Vis. Lectr, Inst. for Information, Telecommunications and Media Law, Westfälische Wilhelms-Univ., Germany. Reader, 2005–, Mem., Ch and Society Council, 2009–, Ch of Scotland. FSA (Scot) 1974; FRSA 1988. Freeman, City of London, 2010–; Liveryman, Information Technologists' Co., 2010– (Freeman, 2008–09); Mem., Merchant Co. of Edinburgh, 2006–. *Publications:* (contrib.) Electronic Evidence, 2nd edn 2010, 3rd edn 2012; (contrib.) FOSS Law Book, 2011; (contrib.) Open Source Software: law, policy and practice, 2013; (contrib.) Innovation and Future of the Legal Profession in Europe, 2017. *Recreations:* music and the arts, photography, cinema, walking, travel, finding enough hours in the day. *Address:* Advocates' Library, Parliament House, High Street, Edinburgh EH1 1RF. *T:* (0131) 226 5071. *Club:* Scottish Arts (Edinburgh).

**MITCHELL, James;** Social Security Commissioner, 1980–95; a Child Support Commissioner, 1993–95; *b* 11 June 1926; *s* of James Hill Mitchell and Marjorie Kate Mitchell (*née* Williams); *m* 1957, Diane Iris Mackintosh (*d* 2012); two *d*. *Educ:* Merchiston Castle Sch., Edinburgh; Brasenose Coll., Oxford, 1944–45 and 1948–51 (Open Exhibnr, BCL, MA). Served RAFVR, 1945–48. Assistant Master, Edge Grove Preparatory Sch., Herts, 1952–55; called to the Bar, Middle Temple, 1954; private practice as barrister/solicitor, Gold Coast/Ghana, 1956–58; practice as barrister, London, 1958–80. Most Hon. Order of Crown of Brunei, 3rd Cl. 1959, 2nd Cl. 1972. *Recreations:* walking, railways, the Jacobites.

**MITCHELL, Rt Hon. Sir James (Fitz Allen),** KCMG 1995; PC 1985; Prime Minister of St Vincent and the Grenadines, 1984–2000; *b* 15 May 1931; *s* of Reginald and Lois Mitchell; *m* (marr. diss.); four *d*. *Educ:* Imperial College of Tropical Agriculture (DICTA); University of British Columbia (BSA). MRSB (MIBiol 1965); CBiol 1973. Agronomist, 1958–65; owner, Hotel Frangipani, Bequia, 1966–, and other cos; Mem., Bd of Dirs, Mustique Co., 1968–74 and 1984–2001. MP for Grenadines, 1966–2001; Minister of Trade, Agriculture and Tourism, 1967–72; Premier, 1972–74; Minister of Foreign Affairs, 1984–92; Minister of Finance, 1984–98. Founder and Pres., New Democratic Party, 1975–2000; Chm., Caribbean Democrat Union, 1991–; Vice-Chm., Internat. Democrat Union, 1992– (Co-Chair, Nicaragua Observer Team and Hungary Observer Team, 1990); Chm., Caribbean Community, 2000. Chm., Commonwealth Observer Gp, Lesotho Gen. Election, 2002. Mem., Inter Action Council, 2008–. Patron, Friends of Bequia Hosp., 2016–. Alumni Award of Distinction, 1988, Centenary Award, 2008, Univ. of BC. Chevalier d'honneur, Chaîne des Rôtisseurs, 1995. Order of the Liberator (Venezuela), 1972; Order of Propitious Clouds (Taiwan), 1995; Gran Cruz, Order of Infante Dom Henrique (Portugal), 1997; Grand Cross, Order of Knights of Malta, 1998. *Publications:* World Fungicide Usage, 1967; Caribbean Crusade, 1989; Guiding Change in the Islands, 1996; A Season of Light, 2001; Beyond the Islands (autobiog.), 2006. *Recreation:* planting trees. *Address:* Bequia, St Vincent, West Indies. *T:* 4583255. *Clubs:* St Vincent Nat. Trust; Bequia Sailing (Founder, 1976).

**MITCHELL, (Janet) Margaret;** JP; Member (C) Scotland Central, Scottish Parliament, since 2003; *b* 15 Nov. 1952; *d* of late John Aitken Fleming and Margaret McRae Fleming (*née* Anderson); *m* 1978, Henry Thomson Mitchell. *Educ:* Coatbridge High Sch.; Hamilton Teacher Training Coll. (DipEd); Open Univ. (BA); Strathclyde Univ. (LLB; DipLLP); Jordanhill Coll. (Dip Media Studies). Primary school teacher, Airdrie and Bothwell, 1974–93. Mem. and Cons. Gp Leader, Hamilton DC, 1988–96. Non-exec. Dir, Stonehouse and Hairmyres NHS Trust, 1993–97; Special Advr to David McLetchie, MSP and James Douglas Hamilton, MSP, 1999–2002. Scottish Cons. justice spokesman, 2003–07 and 2013–16; Scottish Parliament: Convener: Dyslexia Cross Party Cttee, 2007–; Equal Opportunities Cttee, 2007–11; Cross Party Gp on Adult Survivors of Childhood Sexual Abuse, 2011–18 (Mem.); Caribbean Cross Party Gp, 2011–16; Justice Cttee, 2016– (Mem., 2013–); Co-Convener, Taiwan Cross Party Gp, 2011– (Mem., 2009–11); Dep. Convener, Cttee on Scottish Govt Handling of Harassment Complaints, 2019–. Mem., Scottish Cons. Party Exec., 2002–03. JP South Lanarks, 1990. *Recreations:* music, cycling, photography. *Address:* Huntly Lodge, Fairfield Place, Bothwell G71 8RP; Scottish Parliament, Edinburgh EH99 1SP. *E:* Margaret.Mitchell.msp@parliament.scot. *Club:* New (Edinburgh).

**MITCHELL, Jeremy George Swale Hamilton;** consumer policy adviser; *b* 25 May 1929; *s* of late George Oswald Mitchell and late Agnes Josephine Mitchell; *m* 1st, 1956, Margaret Mary Ayres (marr. diss. 1988); three *s* one *d*; 2nd, 1989, Janet Rosemary Powney. *Educ:* Ampleforth; Brasenose and Nuffield Colls, Oxford (MA). 2nd Lt, RA, 1948–49. Dep. Research Dir, then Dir of Information, Consumers' Assoc. (Which?), 1958–65; Asst Sec., Nat. Econ. Develt Office, 1965–66; Scientific Sec., then Sec., SSRC, 1966–74; Under Sec., and Dir of Consumer Affairs, Office of Fair Trading, 1974–77; Under Sec. and Dir, Nat. Consumer Council, 1977–86. Member: Economic Develt Cttee for the Distributive Trades, 1981–86; Independent Cttee for Supervision of Telephone Information Services, 1989–97; Direct Mail Services Standards Bd, 1990–95; Bd, PIA, 1994–2000; Scottish Consumer Council, 1995–2000; Telecoms Ombudsman Service Council, 2002–06; Scottish Solicitors' Discipline Tribunal, 2004–08; Consumer Panel, OFCOM, 2006–08; Chm., Scottish Adv. Cttee on Telecommunications, 1998–2003; Comr for Scotland, Broadcasting Standards Commn, 1999–2000. *Publications:* (ed) SSRC Reviews of Research, series, 1968–73; (ed jtly) Social Science Research and Industry, 1971; Betting, 1972; (ed) Marketing and the Consumer Movement, 1978; (ed jtly) The Information Society, 1985; (ed) Money and the Consumer, 1988; Electronic Banking and the Consumer, 1988; The Consumer and Financial Services, 1990; Banker's Racket or Consumer Benefit?, 1991; (ed jtly) Television and the Viewer Interest, 1994; Shrapnel and Whizzbangs, 2008. *Recreations:* Swinburne, racing. *Address:* 19 Eglinton Crescent, Edinburgh EH12 5BY.

**MITCHELL, John;** *see* Mitchell, R. J.

**MITCHELL, Dr John Francis Brake,** OBE 2001; FRS 2004; FRMetS; FIMA; Research Fellow, Meteorological Office, since 2018; *b* 7 Oct. 1948; *s* of Norman Brake Mitchell and Edith Alexandra Mitchell (*née* Reside); *m* 1973, Catriona Rogers; one *s* two *d*. *Educ:* Down High Sch., Downpatrick; Queen's Univ., Belfast (BSc Applied Maths 1970; PhD Theoretical Physics 1973). FRMetS 1973. Joined Meteorological Office, 1973: HSO, 1973–75; SSO, 1975–78; PSO, 1978–88; Grade 6, 1988–2002; Chief Scientist, 2002–07; Dir, Climate Sci., 2007–10; Principal Res. Fellow, 2010–18. Vis. Prof., Sch. of Maths, Meteorol. and Physics, Univ. of Reading, 2004–; Hon. Prof. of Envmtl Scis, UEA, 2003–; Hon. Vis. Prof., Sch. of Engrg, Univ. of Exeter, 2007–12. Symons Meml Lectr, RMetS, 2003. Mem., NERC, 2007–09. Member, Editorial Board: Climate Dynamics, 1994–; Proc. Royal Soc. A, 2013–. MAE 1998; FIMA 2003. L. G. Groves Meml Prize for Meteorol., 1984; (jtly) Mumm Gerbier Award, 1997 and 1998; Hans Oeschger Medal, European Geophysical Soc., 2004; Symons Gold Medal, RMetS, 2011. *Publications:* contrib. scientific papers on climate and climate change. *Recreations:* sport, outdoor pursuits, photography. *Address:* Meteorological Office, Fitzroy Road, Exeter EX1 3PB. *T:* (01392) 885167, *Fax:* 0845 300 1300. *E:* john.f.mitchell@metoffice.gov.uk.

**MITCHELL, John Gall;** QC (Scot.) 1970; a Deputy Social Security Commissioner and a Deputy Child Support Commissioner, 1999–2001 (a Social Security (formerly National Insurance) Commissioner, 1979–99; a Child Support Commissioner, 1993–99); *b* 5 May 1931; *s* of late Rev. William G. Mitchell, MA; *m* 1st, 1959, Anne Bertram Jardine (*d* 1986); three *s* one *d*; 2nd, 1988, Margaret, *d* of late J. W. Galbraith. *Educ:* Royal High Sch., Edinburgh; Edinburgh Univ. (MA, LLB). Commn, HM Forces, 1954–56 (Nat. Service). Advocate 1957. Standing Junior Counsel, Customs and Excise, Scotland, 1964–70; Chairman: Industrial Tribunals, Scotland, 1966–80; Legal Aid Supreme Court Cttee, Scotland, 1974–79; Pensions Appeals Tribunal, Scotland, 1974–80. Hon. Sheriff: of Lanarkshire, 1970–74; of S Strathclyde, 1975–79. *Address:* Rosemount, Park Road, Dalkeith, Midlothian EH22 3DH.

**MITCHELL, John Logan;** QC (Scot.) 1987; *b* 23 June 1947; *s* of Robert Mitchell and Dorothy Mitchell; *m* 1973, Christine Brownlee Thomson; one *s* one *d*. *Educ:* Royal High School, Edinburgh (Past Pres., Former Pupils' Club); Edinburgh Univ. (LLB Hons). Called to the Bar, 1974; Standing Junior Counsel: to Dept of Agriculture and Fisheries for Scotland, 1979; Forestry Commission for Scotland, 1979; Advocate Depute, 1981–85. *Recreation:* golf. *Address:* 17 Braid Farm Road, Edinburgh EH10 6LE. *T:* (0131) 447 8099. *Clubs:* Mortonhall Golf, Craigielaw Golf, Luffness New Golf.

**MITCHELL, Jonathan James;** QC (Scot.) 1992; *b* 4 Aug. 1951; *s* of (John) Angus (Macbeth) Mitchell, CB, CVO, MC and of Ann Katharine (*née* Williamson); *m* 1987, Melinda McGarry (marr. diss. 2016); one *s* one *d*. *Educ:* Marlborough Coll.; New Coll., Oxford (BA); Edinburgh Univ. (LLB). Advocate, 1979; Temp. Sheriff, 1988–95. Dep. Social Security Comr, 1994–2002. *Publications:* Eviction and Rent Arrears, 1994. *T:* 07739 639343, *Fax:* (0131) 220 2654. *E:* jonathanmitchell@mac.com. *W:* www.jonathanmitchell.info.
*See also* C. I. Mitchell.

**MITCHELL, Julian,** FSA, FRSL; writer; *b* 1 May 1935; *s* of late William Moncur Mitchell and of Christine Mary (*née* Browne). *Educ:* Winchester; Wadham Coll., Oxford. Nat. Service in Submarines, 1953–55; Temp. Acting Sub-Lieut, RNVR. Member: Literature Panel, Arts Council, 1966–69; Welsh Arts Council, 1988–92 (Chm. Drama Cttee, 1989–92). Curator: Joshua Gosselin exhibn, Chepstow, 2003; Wye Tour and its Artists, Chepstow, 2010. Wolfson Lecture, Oxford, 2003. John Llewellyn Rhys Prize, 1965; Somerset Maugham Award, 1966. Television plays include: Shadow in the Sun; A Question of Degree; Rust; Abide With Me (Internat. Critics Prize, Monte Carlo, 1977); Survival of the Fittest; Consenting Adults (Scottish BAFTA 2007); adaptations of: Persuasion; The Alien Corn; Staying On; The Good Soldier; The Mysterious Stranger; The Weather in the Streets; Inspector Morse; series, Jennie, Lady Randolph Churchill, 1974; television documentary: All the Waters of Wye, 1990. Films: Arabesque, 1965; Vincent and Theo, 1990; Wilde, 1997. FRSL 1985; FSA 2010. *Publications: novels:* Imaginary Toys, 1961; A

Disturbing Influence, 1962; As Far As You Can Go, 1963; The White Father, 1964; A Circle of Friends, 1966; The Undiscovered Country, 1968; *biography*: (with Peregrine Churchill) Jennie: Lady Randolph Churchill, 1974; *autobiography*: A Disgraceful Anomaly, 2003; *translation*: Henry IV (Pirandello), 1979 (John Florio Prize, 1980); *plays*: Half-Life, 1977; The Enemy Within, 1980; Another Country, 1981 (SWET play of the year, 1982; filmed, 1984); Francis, 1983; After Aida (or Verdi's Messiah), 1986; Adelina Patti, 1987; Falling Over England, 1994; August, 1994 (adapted from Chekhov's Uncle Vanya; filmed, 1996); The Good Soldier (adapted from Ford Madox Ford), 2010; Family Business, 2011; The Welsh Boy (adapted from James Parry's The True Anti-Pamela), 2012; *screenplay*: Wilde, 1997; (adapted from Ivy Compton-Burnett): A Heritage and Its History, 1965; A Family and a Fortune, 1975; (contrib.) History and Fiction, ed by R. L. O. Tomlin, 2005; contribs to: Welsh History Review, The Monmouthshire Antiquary; Gwent County History. *Recreation*: local history. *Address*: 35 Abingdon Court, W8 6BT. *E*: julian.mitchell606@btinternet.com.

**MITCHELL, Prof. Juliet Constance Wyatt, (Lady Goody),** FBA 2010; writer, since 1962; psychoanalyst, since 1978; Professorial Research Fellow, Expanded Doctoral School in Psychoanalytic Studies, Psychoanalysis Unit, since 2012, University College London (Director, 2010–12); *b* Christchurch, NZ, 4 Oct. 1940; *d* of Leonard Huskins and Marjorie Editha Mitchell; *m* 1962, Frances Rory Peregrine Anderson; *m* 1977, Dr Martin Rossdale; one *d*; *m* 2000, Sir John Rankine, (Sir Jack), Goody, FBA (*d* 2015); one step *s* four step *d*. *Educ*: King Alfred Sch., London; St Anne's Coll., Oxford (MA). University of Cambridge: Lectr of Gender Studies, 1996–2000; Prof. of Psychoanalysis and Gender Studies, 2000–09, now Emeritus; Founder Dir, Centre for Gender Studies, 2008 (now Hon.); Fellow, Jesus Coll., Cambridge, 1996–2008, now Emeritus. Andrew Mellon Vis. Prof., Courtauld Inst. of Fine Art, 2011–12. Emeritus Leverhulme Scholar, 2011–14. Fellow: British Psychoanalytical Soc., 1978; Internat. Psychoanalytical Assoc., 1978. *Publications*: Women's Estate, 1972; Psychoanalysis and Feminism, 1974, 2nd edn 2000; (with A. Oakley) The Rights and Wrongs of Women, 1976; Women: the longest revolution, 1984; (with J. Rose) Lacan and the école freudienne, 1984; Selected Melanie Klein, 1986; (with A. Oakley) What is Feminism?, 1986; Before I Was I: essays of Enid Balint, 1993; (with A. Oakley) Who's Afraid of Feminism?, 1997; Mad Men and Medusas, 2000, 2nd edn 2010; Siblings: sex and violence, 2003, 2nd edn 2010; contribs to learned jls. *Recreations*: reading, swimming, theatre. *Address*: Jesus College, Cambridge CB5 8BL. *T*: (01223) 305271. *E*: jcwm2@cam.ac.uk.

**MITCHELL, Katrina Jane, (Katie),** OBE 2009; freelance director; Associate Director, Royal National Theatre, 2003; *b* 23 Sept. 1964; *d* of Michael and Sally Mitchell. *Educ*: Magdalen Coll., Oxford (MA Eng. Lit. and Lang.). Asst Dir, 1989–90, Associate Dir, 1996–98, RSC; Associate Dir, Royal Court Th., 2001–04. Productions directed: Gate Theatre, Notting Hill: Vassa Zheleznova, 1991; Women of Troy, 1991; The House of Bernarda Alba, 1992; Royal Shakespeare Company: The Dybbuk, 1992; Ghosts, 1993; Henry VI, 1995; Easter, 1995; The Phoenician Women, 1996; Beckett Shorts, 1997; Uncle Vanya, 1998; Royal Court: Live Like Pigs, 1993; The Country, 2000; Mountain Language, Ashes to Ashes, 2001; Nightsongs, Face to the Wall, 2002; Forty Winks, 2004; The City, 2008; 2071, 2014, transf. Deutsches Schauspielhaus, Hamburg, 2014; Ophelias Zimmer, 2016; Anatomy of a Suicide, 2017; Abbey Theatre, Dublin: The Last Ones, 1993; Iphigenia at Aulis, 2001; National Theatre: Rutherford and Son, 1994; Machine Wreckers, 1995; The Oresteia, 1999; Ivanov, 2002; Three Sisters, 2003; Iphigenia at Aulis, 2004; A Dream Play, 2005; The Seagull, Waves, 2006; Women of Troy, 2007; Some Trace of Her…, 2008; Pains of Youth, 2009; Cat in the Hat, 2009; Cleansed, 2016; When We Have Sufficiently Tortured Each Other, 2019; Welsh National Opera: Don Giovanni, 1996; Jenufa, 1998; Katya Kabanova, 2001; Jephtha, 2003, restaged, ENO, 2005; The Sacrifice, 2007; Endgame, 1996, Four Quartets, 2009, Donmar Warehouse; The Maids, 1999, The Cherry Orchard, 2014, The Way Back Home, 2014, Young Vic; Easter, 2001, Krapp's Last Tape, 2004, The Maids, 2008, Royal Dramatic Th., Stockholm; Request Programme, Schauspielhaus, Cologne, 2008; After Dido, ENO/Young Vic, 2009; Parthenogenesis, ROH, 2009; Al Gran Sole Carico D'Amore, Salzburg Fest., 2009; Idomeneo, ENO, 2010; The Trial of Ubu, Hampstead Th., 2012; Written on Skin, Aix-en-Provence Fest., 2012, ROH, 2013; Hansel and Gretel, RNT, 2012; Fräulein Julie, Barbican, 2013; Lucia di Lammermoor, ROH, 2016; The Forbidden Zone, Barbican, 2016; Lucia di Lammermoor, ROH, 2017; Lessons in Love and Violence, ROH, 2018; Norma Jeane Baker of Troy, The Shed, NY, 2019; television: Widowing of Mrs Holroyd, 1995; Turn of the Screw, 2004. *Address*: c/o Julia Kreitman, The Agency, 24 Pottery Lane, W11 4LZ.

**MITCHELL, Madeleine Louise;** solo concert violinist; chamber musician; Professor, Royal College of Music, since 1994; Director: London Chamber Ensemble, since 1994; Red Violin Ltd, since 1997 (Artistic Director, Red Violin Festival, 1997, 2007); *b* 2 March 1957; *d* of Desmond Mitchell and Evelyn Mitchell (*née* Jones); one *d*. *Educ*: Hornchurch Grammar Sch.; Royal Coll. of Music (Jun. Exhibnr; Open Foundn Scholar; GRSM (1st Cl. Hons); ARCM (Performance Hons), ARCM (Teacher Hons)); Eastman Sch. of Music, NY (Fulbright/ITT Fellow); Univ. of Rochester (MMus Performance and Lit.). Violinist and violist, Sir Peter Maxwell Davies' The Fires of London, 1985–87; Leader, Bridge String Quartet, 2000–07. Performed as soloist in over 50 countries in recitals and concertos with Royal Philharmonic, BBC Ulster, St Petersburg Philharmonic, Polish Radio Symphony, Württemberg Chamber, Czech Radio, Munich Chamber, Academy of London, Orch. of the Swan, Orch. de Bahia Brazil, Welsh Chamber Orch., BBC Nat. Orch. of Wales, South Arizona Symphony, Samara Philharmonic of Russia. Numerous internat. festivals and venues incl. BBC Proms, Wigmore Hall, Moscow Conservatoire, Vienna Schönberg Centre, Singapore Victoria Hall, Lincoln Center, NY, Sydney Opera House, Seoul Centre for the Arts, Barbican, South Bank; Artist-in-Residence, Canberra Music Fest., 2013. TV and radio broadcasts. Recordings, including: Messiaen Quatuor pour la fin du temps; In Sunlight: pieces for Madeleine Mitchell; Violin Muse; Fiddlesticks. Vice-Pres., Kensington and Chelsea Music Soc., 2001–. Mem., Council, RCM, 2013–16. FRSA 2000. Tagore Gold Medal, RCM, 1978. *Recreations*: art galleries, opera, gardens, the sea, cycling. *E*: info@madeleinemitchell.com. *W*: www.madeleinemitchell.com.

**MITCHELL, Margaret;** *see* Mitchell, Jane M.

**MITCHELL, Michael James Ross,** PhD; Director General, National Networks (formerly Rail, then Rail and National Networks), Department for Transport, 2005–11; *b* 22 Feb. 1948; *s* of James and Margaret Mitchell; *m* 1971, Jillian Mary Tomory; two *s*. *Educ*: Univ. of Aberdeen (MA Hons 1970; PhD 1993); Univ. of Edinburgh (MBA 1987). CMILT (MCIT 1977). With BR, 1970–86 (Area Manager, Coventry, 1978–80); Eastern Scottish Omnibuses Ltd, 1986–94 (Ops Dir, 1990–94); Man. Dir, Grampian Regl Transport, later FirstBus plc, 1994–97; FirstGroup plc: Divl Dir, 1997; Man. Dir, First Great Western, 1998; Dir, Rail, 1999; Chief Operating Officer, 2001–04; Business Develt Dir, 2004–05. *Publications*: Aberdeen Suburban Tramways, 1980, revd edn 1981; Aberdeen District Tramways, 1983; Fae Dee to Don and Back Again: 100 years of Aberdeen transport, 1998; Aberdeenshire Tramways, 2013; Montrose and Bervie Railway, 2015; Great North of Scotland Railway Buses, 2017. *Recreations*: vintage bus restoration, photography, travel.

**MITCHELL, Michelle Elizabeth,** OBE 2016; Chief Executive Officer, Cancer Research UK, since 2018; *b* Ellesmere Port, 13 March 1972; *d* of James Alexander Graham Mitchell and Elizabeth Mitchell; partner, Sean McKee; one *s* one *d*. *Educ*: Sutton High Sch.; Univ. of Manchester (BA Hons Econs 1994); University Coll. London (MSc Pols and Public Admin 1997); INSEAD (Internat. Exec. Prog.); Harvard Univ. (Innovations in Govt). Political advr roles, UK Parlt, 1994–97; Hd, Parly Unit, Charter 88, 1997–2000; Govt Affairs Advr, NSPCC UK, 2000–02; Age Concern, later Age UK: Hd, Public Affairs, 2002–07; Communications Dir, 2007–10; Charity Dir, 2010–12; Charity Dir Gen., 2012–13; CEO, Multiple Sclerosis Soc., 2013–18. Non-exec. Dir, NHS England, 2016–. Chm., Trustees, Fawcett Soc., 2005–08; Trustee: Young Women's Trust, 2013–; King's Fund, 2014–; Dir, Power to Change Trust, 2014–. Nat. Commng Support, 2013–; Mem., Multiple Sclerosis Internat. Fedn, 2013–. MCIPR. *Recreations*: yoga, cooking. *Address*: Cancer Research UK, Angel Building, 407 St John Street, EC1V 4AD.

**MITCHELL, Very Rev. Patrick Reynolds,** KCVO 1998; Dean of Windsor, 1989–98; Register, Order of the Garter, 1989–98; Domestic Chaplain to the Queen, 1989–98; *b* 17 March 1930; *s* of late Lt-Col Percy Reynolds Mitchell, DSO; *m* 1st, 1959, Mary Evelyn (*née* Phillips) (*d* 1986); three *s* one *d*; 2nd, 1988, Pamela (*d* 2016), *d* of late A. G. Le Marchant and *widow* of Henry Douglas-Pennant; one step *s* one step *d* (and two step *s* decd). *Educ*: Eton Coll.; Merton Coll., Oxford (MA Theol); Wells Theol Coll. Officer in Welsh Guards (National Service), 1948–49. Deacon, 1954; priest, 1955; Curate at St Mark's, Mansfield, 1954–57; Priest-Vicar of Wells Cathedral and Chaplain of Wells Theological Coll., 1957–60; Vicar of St James', Milton, Portsmouth, 1961–67; Vicar of Frome Selwood, Somerset, 1967–73; Dean of Wells, 1973–89; Director of Ordination Candidates for Bath and Wells, 1971–74. Res. Fellow, Merton Coll., Oxford, 1984. Chm., Cathedral Libraries and Archives Assoc., 1997–2001. Member: Adv. Bd for Redundant Churches, 1978–92; Cathedrals Adv. Commn for England, 1981–91. Governor, Wellington Coll., 1994–98. Hon. Freeman, City of Wells, 1986. FSA 1981.

**MITCHELL, Paul; His Honour Judge Paul Mitchell;** a Circuit Judge, since 2018; *b* Redruth, Cornwall, 5 Oct. 1963; *s* of late Fernleigh and Zelda Mitchell; *m* 2014, Shelagh Callaghan; two *d* and two step *s* two step *d*. *Educ*: Redruth Comprehensive Sch.; Univ. of London (LLB Hons). Admitted as solicitor, 1991; Partner, Hancock and Lawrence, then Hancock Caffin, 1992–2003; Dep. Dist Judge, 1999–2003; Dist Judge, 2003–18; a Recorder, 2010–18. *Recreations*: reading, history, all ball sports, walking the Cornish coastal paths. *Address*: Plymouth Combined Court, The Law Courts, Armada Way, Plymouth, Devon PL1 2ER. *Club*: Sloan.

**MITCHELL, Paul England;** Consultant, Taylor Wessing LLP, 2011–17; *b* St Albans, 2 Nov. 1951; *s* of late Ronald England Mitchell and Katia Patricia Mitchell; *m* 1984, Catherine Anne Ros-Jones (marr. diss. 2002); one *s* one *d*. *Educ*: Canford Sch.; Bristol Univ. (LLB Hons). Admitted as solicitor, 1976. Joynson-Hicks & Co., subseq. Taylor Joynson Garrett, then Taylor Wessing LLP: articled clerk, 1974–76; Asst Solicitor, 1976–78; Partner, 1978–2011. Chm., British Copyright Council, 2005–13; Trustee, Copyright Soc. of USA, 2009–12. Director: Rambert Dance Co., 2002–13; Dancers Career Develt, 2008–; Roald Dahl Mus. and Story Centre, 2010– (Chm., 2014–); PRS for Music, 2015–18. Trustee, Royal Ballet Benevolent Fund, 2014–. Freeman: City of London, 1993; Fishmongers' Co., 1993. FRSA. *Publications*: (with D. Lester) Joynson-Hicks on UK Copyright, 1989. *Recreations*: family, walking, reading, food and wine, contemporary dance, sailing. *Address*: 74 Palace Road, SW2 3JX. *T*: (020) 8671 1564. *E*: paulm75@hotmail.com. *Club*: Garrick.

**MITCHELL, Paul Stuart,** PhD; QC 2016; *b* Sidcup, Kent, 15 May 1968; *s* of Ian Stuart Mitchell and Alethea Rosemary Mitchell (*née* Howell); *m* 2003, Lucia Mahdjoubian; two *d*. *Educ*: Sevenoaks Sch.; King's Coll., Cambridge (BA Oriental Studies 1990; PhD Oriental Studies 1997); Sch. of Oriental and African Studies, Univ. of London (MA 1993). Called to the Bar, Lincoln's Inn, 1999; in practice as a barrister, specialising in professional negligence, 1999–. *Publications*: (contrib.) Flenley and Leech on Solicitor's Negligence and Liability, 2nd edn 2008, 3rd edn 2012; (ed) Stone in a Landslide, by Maria Barbal, 2010. *Recreations*: playing, learning new languages, reading, music, dining, chatting, running, cycling. *Address*: 4 New Square, Lincoln's Inn, WC2A 3RJ. *E*: p.mitchell@4newsquare.com.

**MITCHELL, His Honour (Richard) John;** a Circuit Judge, 2005–17; *b* 28 Oct. 1948; *s* of Kenneth Frank Mitchell and Edith Mitchell; *m* 1977, Marlene Le Saint; two *s*. *Educ*: Brentwood Sch.; Peterhouse, Cambridge (MA 1980). Called to the Bar, Middle Temple, 1972, Bencher, 2012; a District Judge, 1999–2005. Foundn Gov., Addey and Stanhope Sch., 2010–17. *Publications*: Children Act Private Law Proceedings: a handbook, 2003, 3rd edn 2012; Adoption and Special Guardianship, 2009. *Recreations*: walking, theatre, historical research. *Address*: The Treasury Office, Ashley Building, Middle Temple Lane, Temple, EC4Y 9BT.

**MITCHELL, Sarah Jane;** Director, Mitchell Clow Ltd Management Consulting, since 2016; *b* St Margaret's Bay, Dover, 30 Sept. 1960; *d* of John Mitchell (Master Mariner) and Hilda Mitchell, QARANC; *m* 2007, Adam Clow; two *s*. *Educ*: Univ. of Essex (BA Hons Sociol. 1982); Univ. of Southampton (CQSW; DASS 1984); Portsmouth Univ. (MBA 1993). Hampshire County Council Social Services: Social Worker, 1984–87; Project Manager, 1987–88; Team Manager, 1988–91; Service Manager, 1990–93; Prin. Advr, Mental Health, 1993–94; Care Mgt Co-ordinator, 1994–96; Inspector, Social Services Inspectorate, 1996–97, Hd of Policy, NHS Exec., 1997–98, DoH; Asst Dir, Older People, Portsmouth CC, 1999–2004; Owner, SJM Consulting, 2004–06; Dir, Community Services, IoW Council, 2006–09; Strategic Dir, Adult Social Care, Surrey CC, 2009–13; Dir, LGA, 2014–16. *Recreations*: raising two wonderful young men, scuba diving, riding, camping, travelling, loving living in Southsea.

**MITCHELL, Prof. Stephen,** DPhil; FBA 2002; Leverhulme Professor of Hellenistic Culture, University of Exeter, 2002–11, now Emeritus Professor; *b* 26 May 1948; *s* of David and Barbara Mitchell; *m* 1974, Matina Weinstein; three *s*. *Educ*: St John's Coll., Oxford (BA 1970; MA, DPhil 1975; Hon. Fellow 2018). Lectr, 1976, Sen. Lectr, 1984, Reader, 1989, Prof., 1993–2001, UC of Swansea, subseq. Univ. of Wales, Swansea; Dir, Exeter Turkish Studies, Univ. of Exeter, 2009–11. Vis. Fellow, Inst. of Advanced Study, Princeton, 1983–84; British Acad. Res. Reader, 1990–92. Chm., British Inst. at Ankara, 2016–. Hon. DTheol Humboldt, Berlin, 2006. *Publications*: Anatolia: land, men and gods in Asia Minor, 1993; Cremna in Pisidia: an ancient city in peace and in war, 1995; Pisidian Antioch: the site and its monuments, 1998; A History of the Later Roman Empire 284–641, 2007, 2nd edn 2015; One God: Pagan monotheism in the Roman Empire, 2010; The Greek and Latin Inscriptions of Ankara, 2012. *Recreations*: walking, travel, wine. *Address*: British Institute at Ankara, c/o British Academy, 10 Carlton House Terrace, SW1Y 5AH. *E*: mitchank@gmail.com.

**MITCHELL, Hon. Sir Stephen (George),** Kt 1993; a Judge of the High Court of Justice, Queen's Bench Division, 1993–2003; President, National Security Appeals Panel, Information Tribunal, 2004–07; *b* 19 Sept. 1941; *s* of Sydney Mitchell and Joan Mitchell (*née* Dick); *m* 1978, Alison Clare (*née* Roseveare) (*d* 1998); two *d*. *Educ*: Bedford Sch.; Hertford Coll., Oxford (MA). Called to the Bar, Middle Temple, 1964, Bencher, 1993;

Second Prosecuting Counsel to the Crown, Inner London Crown Court, 1975; Central Criminal Court: a Junior Prosecuting Counsel to the Crown, 1977; a Senior Prosecuting Counsel to the Crown, 1981–86; QC 1986; a Recorder, 1985–89; a Circuit Judge, 1989–93. Dep. Chm., Security Vetting Appeals Panel, 2001–04. Mem., Judicial Studies Bd, 1991–93. DUniv Derby, 2016. *Publications:* (ed) Phipson on Evidence, 11th edn, 1970; (ed) Archbold's Criminal Pleading Evidence and Practice, 1971–88; The Marks on Chelsea-Derby and Early Crossed-Batons Useful Wares 1770–c1790, 2007, 1st Supplement, 2009. *Address:* Royal Courts of Justice, Strand, WC2A 2LL.

**MITCHELL, Stephen Graham;** Director, Parkfield House Communication Services Ltd, 2014–18; *b* 14 July 1949; *s* of Derek Mitchell and Phyllis Mitchell (*née* Rigden); *m* 1977, Barbara Gilder (*d* 2019); one *s* one *d*. *Educ:* Loughborough Grammar Sch.; Manchester Univ. (BA Hons). Reporter, Thompson Newspapers, Newcastle Jl, S Wales Echo, The Times, 1971–74; BBC: producer, reporter, Radio Newsroom, and Duty Editor, Today prog., 1974–84; Dep. Foreign News Ed., 1985; Ed., Parly Output, 1986–88; Ed., then Man. Ed., Radio Newsroom, 1988–93; Ed., Radio News Progs, 1993–97; Dep. Hd, News Progs (Bimedia), 1997–99; Hd, Radio News, 2000–07; Hd of News Progs, BBC, 2007–13; Dep. Dir, BBC News, 2008–13. Dir, NCTJ, 2012–17. Trustee, Services Sound and Vision Corp., 2017–18. *Recreations:* theatre, opera, reading. *Address:* 30 Amenbury Lane, Harpenden, Herts AL5 2DF.

**MITCHELL, Stuart Robert;** Chief Executive, SIG plc, 2013–16; *b* Watford, 22 Dec. 1960; *s* of Arthur Robert Mitchell and Margaret Patricia Mitchell; *m* 1987, Tracey Victoria Webb; one *s* one *d*. *Educ:* Tadcaster Grammar Sch.; Univ. of Manchester Inst. of Sci. and Technol. (BSc Mgt Scis). J. Sainsbury plc: joined as graduate trainee, 1981; Trading Dir, 2000–03; Man. Dir, 2003–04; Man. Dir, A. S. Watson, Taiwan, 2005–06; CEO, Wilkinsons Hardware Stores Ltd, 2006–12. Non-exec. Dir, Enactus (formerly SIFE), 2011–. Chm., The Writer, 2017–. *Recreations:* ski-ing, golf, travel, sailing, cookery. *Address:* The Oaks, Oaks Road, Reigate, Surrey RH2 0LE. *E:* sr.mitchell@hotmail.co.uk. *Clubs:* Royal Automobile; Dorking Rugby (Dir, 2014–).

**MITCHELL, Valerie Joy,** OBE 2001; Chairman, Cultural Affairs Committee, English-Speaking Union of the Commonwealth, since 2009 (Director-General, 1994–2009); *b* 2 March 1941; *d* of Henry Frederick Twidale and Dorothy Mary (*née* Pierce), MBE; *m* 1st, 1962, Henri Pierre Eschauzier (marr. diss. 1970); two *s*, 2nd, 1972, Graham Rangeley Mitchell (*d* 2017); one *d*. *Educ:* Beaufront Sch., Camberley; McGill Univ., Montreal (BA Hons). PA to Asst Dean of Arts and Sci., McGill Univ., Montreal, 1962–64; PR Consultant to Mayer-Lismann Opera Workshop, 1970–80; English-Speaking Union: Asst, Educn Dept, 1980–83; Dir of Branches and Cultural Affairs, 1983–94; Dep. Dir-Gen., 1989–94; Sec.-Gen., Internat. Council of ESU Worldwide, 1994–2009. Member: Internat. Cttee, Shakespeare Globe Centre, 2000–05 and 2014–; Exec. Cttee, European Atlantic Gp, 2001–; Pilgrims Soc., 2003–11; Council, Shakespeare's Globe, 2014–; Trustee: Shakespeare Globe Trust, 2006–14; Longborough Fest. Opera, 2006–; Harvard House Meml Trust, 2008–. FRSA 1987. *Recreations:* music, theatre, tennis, walking. *Address:* 2 Glenside Gardens, Shady Bower, Salisbury SP1 2RF.
*See also S. A. Price.*

**MITCHELL COTTS, Sir Richard Crichton;** *see* Cotts.

**MITCHELL-INNES, Alistair Campbell;** Chairman, Next Pension Trustees Ltd, 1991–2005; *b* 1 March 1934; *s* of Peter Mitchell-Innes; *m* 1957, Penelope Ann Hill; one *s* two *d*. *Educ:* Charterhouse; Stanford Business Sch. (Executive Program). Nat. Service, Lieut, Parachute Regt, 1953–54. Dir, Brooke Bond Gp plc, 1979–84; Chief Exec., Nabisco Gp Ltd, 1985–88; Chief Exec., Isosceles plc, 1991–93; Dep. Chm., H. P. Bulmer (Holdings) plc, 1990–2001; Chairman: Sidney C. Banks plc, 1994–2000; Anglo & Overseas Trust PLC, 1996–2004. Non-exec. Dir, 1989–2004, Dep. Chm., 2002–04, Next plc. TA, 1954–63. *Recreations:* golf, cricket, military history. *Address:* 9 Market Street, Rye, E Sussex TN31 7LA. *Clubs:* Caledonian, MCC (Life Mem.); Berkshire Golf; Rye Golf.

**MITCHELL KILPATRICK, Reginald;** Director, Local Government Department, Welsh Government, since 2011; *b* London, 1963; *s* of Thomas and Mary Kilpatrick; *m* 1994, Joanna Clare Mitchell; one *s* one *d*. *Educ:* Oathall Comprehensive Sch., Haywards Heath; Univ. of Glamorgan (BSc Behavioural Sci. 1987); Sheffield Hallam Univ. (Postgrad. Dip. Applied Stats 1991); Cardiff Business Sch. (MPA 2011). Asst Statistician, Local Govt, Educn and Demography, 1988–91, Hd of Educn Statistics, 1991–94, Welsh Office; Dir, Wales Cancer Registry, 1994–96; Welsh Government: Head: of Health Financial Mgt, 1996–99; of Museums Policy, Wales Millennium Centre Project Lead, 1999–2002; Sponsorship Br., Welsh Develt Agency, 2002–03; Deputy Director: Assembly Budget Planning and Mgt, 2003–07; Local Govt Policy, 2007–11. *Recreations:* modern literature, contemporary music, learning the guitar, creating stained glass. *Address:* Welsh Government, Cathays Park, Cardiff CF10 3NQ. *T:* (029) 2082 5913. *E:* reg.kilpatrick@wales.gov.wales.

**MITCHELL-THOMSON,** family name of **Baron Selsdon**.

**MITCHESON, Thomas George Moseley;** QC 2014; *b* London, 6 June 1972; *s* of late George Anthony Mitcheson and of Lavinia Anne Mitcheson (*née* Moseley); *m* 2003, Elizabeth Adair Peltzer Dunn; one *s* one *d*. *Educ:* Eton Coll.; Trinity Coll., Cambridge (BA 1st Cl. Hons Natural Scis 1994); City Univ. (DipLaw 1995); Inns of Court Sch. of Law. Called to the Bar, Inner Temple, 1996, Bencher, 2017; in practice at Intellectual Property Bar; Standing Counsel to Comptroller Gen. of Patents, 2009–14; appointed to hear Trade Mark Appeals, 2016–. Dir, Old Etonian Housing Assoc., 2004– (Chm., 2010–16). *Publications:* (ed jtly) Terrell on the Law of Patents, 18th edn 2016. *Recreations:* family, singing (London Oriana Choir Mem., 1998–), the beaches of North Norfolk, golf. *Address:* Three New Square, Lincoln's Inn, WC2A 3RS. *T:* (020) 7405 1111. *E:* clerks@3newsquare.co.uk.

**MITCHINER, Dr John Edward;** HM Diplomatic Service, retired; High Commissioner to Sierra Leone, and Ambassador (non-resident) to Liberia, 2003–06; *b* 12 Sept. 1951; *s* of late Geoffrey Morford Mitchiner and Ursula Angela Mitchiner (*née* Adolph); *m* 1983, Elizabeth Mary Ford, MA, MNIMH. *Educ:* John Fisher Sch., Purley; Beaumont Coll., Old Windsor; Bristol Univ. (BA 1972); Sch. of Oriental and African Studies, London Univ. (MA 1973; PhD 1977). ACU Res. Fellow, Visva-Bharati Univ., Santiniketan, 1977–78; Bipradas Palchaudhuri Fellow, Calcutta Univ., 1978–79; joined FCO, 1980; Third, later Second Sec. (Information), Istanbul, 1982–85; FCO, 1985–87; Second Sec. (Develt), New Delhi, 1987–91; Second, later First Sec. (Political), Berne, 1991–95; Head, Japan Section, FCO, 1995–96; Ambassador to Armenia, 1997–99; Dep. High Comr, Kolkata, India, 2000–03. MRAS. *Publications:* Studies in the Indus Valley Inscriptions, 1978; Traditions of the Seven Rsis, 1982, 2nd edn 2000; The Yuga Purana, 1986, 2nd edn 2002; Guru: the search for enlightenment, 1992; contribs to learned jls. *Recreations:* sheep farming, bridge, tennis, family history. *Address:* Bower Farm, Whitland SA34 0QX.

**MITCHISON, Avrion;** *see* Mitchison, N. A.

**MITCHISON, Prof. (Nicholas) Avrion,** FRS 1967; Jodrell Professor of Zoology and Comparative Anatomy, University College London, 1970–89, Emeritus Professor, 1990 and Hon. Senior Fellow, Institute of Ophthalmology, 1998–2010 (Hon. Fellow, 1993; Senior Fellow, Department of Immunology, 1996–98); *b* 5 May 1928; 3rd *s* of Baron Mitchison, CBE, QC, and late Naomi Margaret Mitchison, CBE, writer; *m* 1957, Lorna Margaret, *d* of Maj.-Gen. J. S. S. Martin, CSI; two *s* three *d*. *Educ:* Leighton Park Sch.; New Coll., Oxford (MA 1949). Fellow of Magdalen College, 1950–52; Commonwealth Fund Fellow, 1952–54; Lecturer, Edinburgh Univ., 1954–61; Reader, Edinburgh Univ., 1961–62; Head of Div. of Experimental Biology, Nat. Inst. for Med. Research, 1962–71; Scientific Dir, Deutsches Rheuma-Forschungszentrum Berlin, 1990–96. Hon. Member: German Soc. of Immunol., 1996; German Soc. of Rheumatol.; Foreign Hon. Mem., American Acad. of Arts and Scis, 1987; Foreign Associate, NAS, 1990; Foreign Mem., Polish Acad. Arts and Scis, 1998. Hon. MD Edinburgh, 1977; Hon. PhD Weizmann Inst., 1994. Scientific Medal, ZSL, 1962; Paul Ehrlich and Ludwig Darmstaedter Prize, 1975; Sandoz Prize in Basic Immunol., Novartis, 1995; Robert Koch Gold Medal, 2001. *Publications:* articles in scientific journals and over 200 articles cited in PubMed. *Address:* 13 Framfield Road, N5 1UU. *T:* (020) 7359 5344. *E:* n.mitchison@ucl.ac.uk.

**MITFORD,** family name of **Baron Redesdale**.

**MITFORD-SLADE, Patrick Buxton,** OBE 2000; Partner, Cazenove & Co., 1972–96; *b* 7 Sept. 1936; *s* of late Col Cecil Townley Mitford-Slade and Phyllis, *d* of E. G. Buxton; *m* 1964, Anne Catharine Stanton (separated 2000), *d* of late Major Arthur Holbrow Stanton, MBE; one *s* two *d*. *Educ:* Eton Coll.; RMA Sandhurst. Commissioned 60th Rifles, 1955, Captain; served Libya, NI, Berlin and British Guyana; Adjt, 2nd Green Jackets, KRRC, 1962–65; Instructor, RMA Sandhurst, 1965–67. Stockbroker, Cazenove & Co., 1968–96; Man. Dir, Cazenove Money Brokers, 1986–96. Non-executive Director: Clive Securities Group Ltd, 1996–99; John Govett Holdings Ltd, 1996–97; Clive Discount Co. Ltd, 1996–98; Investec Bank (UK) Ltd, 1996–98; AIB Asset Management Hldgs Ltd, 1997–98; SG Hambros Bank (formerly SG Hambros Bank & Trust Co.) Ltd, 2001–08. Asst Sec., Panel on Takeovers and Mergers, 1970–72; Mem., Stock Exchange, 1972–86, Internat. Stock Exchange, 1986–92 (Mem. Council, 1976–91; Dep. Chm., 1982–85); Chairman: City Telecommunications Cttee, 1983–92; Securities Industry Steering Cttee on Taurus, 1988–90; Money Brokers Assoc., 1990–96; Dep. Chm., Stock Borrowing and Lending Cttee, 1996–98. Vice Pres., St Luke's Healthcare for the Clergy (formerly St Luke's Hosp. for the Clergy), 2012– (Hon. Treas., 1994–2001; Chm., 2001–11). Vice Pres., Officers' Assoc., 1985– (Chm., 1985–2000); Mem., Benevolent and Strategy Cttee, RBL, 1998–2005; Vice Pres., Royal (formerly British) Commonwealth Ex-Services League, 2016– (Mem. Council, 1985–; Hon. Treas., 1993–2005; Hon. Recorder, 2005–16). Chairman: Royal Green Jackets Administrative Trustees, 2005–08 (Trustee, 1996–2008); The Rifles Regtl Trustees, 2007–13. Jt Pres., Reed's Sch., 2009– (Gov., 2001–08; Chm., 2002–08). *Recreations:* shooting, fishing. *Address:* The White House, Wivelrod, Alton, Hants GU34 4AR. *Club:* Army and Navy.

**MITHANI, Abbas; His Honour Judge Mithani;** a Circuit Judge, since 2006; Designated Civil Judge for Warwick and West Midlands, since 2019; *b* 27 Feb. 1958; *s* of late Hussein Mithani and of Lailabanu Mithani; *m* 1982, Sajeda Nurmohomed; two *s* one *d*. *Educ:* Univ. of Newcastle upon Tyne (LLB Hons); Univ. of Keele (LLM). Admitted solicitor (with Hons), 1981; Licensed Insolvency Practitioner, 1987; Civil Higher Court Advocate, 1994; Dep. Bankruptcy Registrar, 1994. Dep. Dist Judge, 1993–99; Dist Judge, 1999–2006; a Recorder, 2000–06. Hon. Prof. of Law, Univ. of Birmingham, 2000–07 and 2009–15; Visiting Professor of Law: Newcastle Univ., 2008–; Kingston Univ., 2009–. Mem. Court, Newcastle Univ., 2005–11. Hon. QC 2009. Hon. LLD Kingston, 2015. Asian Jewel Award for Legal Excellence for Central Britain, Inst. of Asian Professionals, 2003; Lifetime Achievement Award, Soc. of Asian Lawyers, 2009. *Publications:* Islamic Wills, 1994; Mithani and Wheeler, 1995, 2nd edn as Mithani: Directors' Disqualification, 1998; *contributor:* Encyclopaedia of Forms and Precedents, 5th edn; Atkin's Court Forms, 2nd edn; Civil Court Service, 2000–18; Kelly's Draftsman, 18th edn 2002; numerous contribs to Law Soc.'s Gazette, Insolvency Law and Practice and other jls on commercial litigation, insolvency and directors' duties. *Recreations:* keen interest in history and literature, watching all kinds of sports.

**MITHEN, Prof. Steven John,** PhD; FBA 2004; FSA, FSAScot; Professor of Early Prehistory, University of Reading, since 2000 (Deputy Vice Chancellor, 2014–18); *b* 16 Oct. 1960; *s* of William Mithen and Patricia Mithen; *m* 1985, Susan Orton; one *s* two *d*. *Educ:* Slade Sch. of Fine Art; Univ. of Sheffield (BA 1st cl. Hons (Prehist. and Archaeol.) 1983); Univ. of York (MSc (Biol Computation) 1984); Univ. of Cambridge (PhD (Archaeol.) 1987). University of Cambridge: Res. Fellow in Archaeol., Trinity Hall, 1987–90; Lectr in Archaeol. (temp.), 1989–91; Res. Associate in Archaeol., McDonald Inst., 1991–92; University of Reading: Lectr, 1992–96, Sen. Lectr, 1996–98, in Archaeol.; Reader in Early Prehistory, 1998–2000; Hd, Sch. of Human and Envmtl Scis, 2003–08; Dean, Faculty of Sci., 2008–10; Pro Vice Chancellor, 2010–14. FSAScot 1993; FSA 1998. *Publications:* Thoughtful Foragers: a study of prehistoric decision making, 1990; The Prehistory of the Mind: a search for the origins of art, science and religion, 1996; (ed) Creativity in Human Evolution and Prehistory, 1998; (ed) Hunter-Gatherer Landscape Archaeology: the Southern Hebrides Mesolithic Project 1988–1998, 2 vols, 2001; After the Ice: a global human history 20,000–5,000 BC, 2003; The Singing Neanderthals, 2005; The Early Prehistory of Wadi Faynan, 2007; To The Islands, 2010; (ed) Water, Life and Civilization, 2011; Thirst: water and power in the ancient world, 2012; articles in jls incl. Antiquity, Jl of Archaeol Sci., Jl of Human Evolution, Current Anthropol. and Levant. *Recreation:* family. *Address:* University of Reading, PO Box 217, Reading RG6 6AH. *T:* (0118) 987 5123, *Fax:* (0118) 931 4404. *E:* s.j.mithen@reading.ac.uk.

**MITRA, Prof. Sugata,** PhD; Professor of Educational Technology and Principal Research Investigator, Newcastle University, since 2006; *b* Calcutta, 12 Feb. 1952; *s* of Shib Kumar Mitra and Sati Mitra; *m* 1978, Sushmita Ghosh; one *s*. *Educ:* Jadavpur Univ., Calcutta (BSc Physics); Indian Inst. of Technol., New Delhi (MSc Physics; PhD Physics 1978). Dir, Publishing Systems, Unite India Periodicals, New Delhi, 1982–90; Chief Scientist, NIIT Ltd, India, 1990–2006. Vis. Prof., MIT Medialab, Cambridge, Mass, 2011–12. Mem., India Habitat Centre. Hon. Dr: Tech. Univ. of Delft, 2011; Open Univ., 2015; Universidad Siglo 21, Argentina, 2016. TED Award, 2013; Dewang Mehta Award, Dewang Mehta Foundn, India, 2005. *Publications:* Introduction to Multi-Media Systems, 2002; The Hole in the Wall, 2006; Beyond the Hole in the Wall, 2012. *Recreation:* research. *Address:* 8 Burlison Gardens, Gateshead NE10 0EE. *T:* 07949 117557. *E:* sugata.mitra@gmail.com; CL 211 Salt Lake City, Calcutta 700091, India. *T:* 8017033887. *Club:* Press (India).

**MITSAKIS, Prof. Kariofilis;** Professor of Modern Greek Literature, University of Athens, 1978–99, now Emeritus; *b* 12 May 1932; *s* of Christos and Crystalli Mitsakis; *m* 1966, Anthoula Chalkia; two *s*. *Educ:* Univs of Thessaloniki (BA, PhD), Oxford (MA, DPhil) and Munich. Scientific Collaborator, National Research Foundn of Greece, 1959–62; Associate Prof. of Byzantine and Modern Greek Literature, Univ. of Maryland, 1966–68; Chm. of Dept of Comparative Literature, Univ. of Maryland, 1967–68; Sotheby and Bywater Prof. of Byzantine and Modern Greek Language and Literature, Univ. of Oxford, 1968–72; Prof.

of Modern Greek Lit., Univ. of Thessaloniki, 1972–75; Dir, Inst. for Balkan Studies, Thessaloniki, 1972–80. Hon. DLitt and Ph Johannesburg, 2001. Gottfried Herder Prize, Vienna Univ., 2000. *Publications:* Problems Concerning the Text, the Sources and the Dating of the Achilleid, 1962 (in Greek); The Greek Sonnet, 1962 (in Greek); The Language of Romanos the Melodist, 1967 (in English); The Byzantine Alexanderromance from the Cod. Vindob. theol. gr. 244, 1967 (in German); Byzantine Hymnography, 1971 (in Greek); Petrarchism in Greece, 1973 (in Greek); Introduction to Modern Greek Literature, 1973 (in Greek); Homer in Modern Greek Literature, 1976 (in Greek); George Viziynos, 1977 (in Greek); Modern Greek Prose: the Generation of the '30s, 1978 (in Greek); Modern Greek Music and Poetry, 1979 (in Greek and English); March Through the Time, 1982; The Living Water, 1983; Points of Reference, 1987 (in Greek); The Cycles with their trails that rise and fall, 1991 (in Greek); The Boston Essays, 1993 (in Greek); The Oxford Essays, 1995 (in Greek); The Alexanderromance, 2001 (in Greek); Modern Greek Miscellany, 2001 (in Greek); In Imagination and in Word: studies on the poet C. P. Cavafy, 2001 (in Greek); Pan the Great: studies on the poet A. Sikelianos, 2001 (in Greek); contribs to Balkan Studies, Byzantinisch-Neugriechische Jahrbücher, Byzantinische Zeitschrift, Comparative Literature Studies, Diptycha, Etudes Byzantines-Byzantine Studies, Glotta, Hellenika, Jahrbuch der Oesterreichischen Byzantinischen Gesellschaft, Nea Hestia, etc. *Recreations:* music, travelling. *Address:* 25 Troados Street, Aghia Paraskevi, 153 42 Athens, Greece.

**MITTAL, Lakshmi Niwas;** President and Chief Executive Officer, ArcelorMittal, since 2006 (Chairman and Chief Executive Officer, Mittal Steel Company Ltd, 2004–06); *b* 15 June 1950; *s* of Mohan Lal and Guta Mittal; *m* 1971, Usha; one *s* one *d*. *Educ:* St Xavier's Coll., Calcutta (BCom). Founded The LNM Group, Indonesia, 1976 (Chm.); subseq. expanded operations into Trinidad and Tobago, Mexico, Canada, Germany, Kazakhstan, USA, France, Algeria, Romania, S Africa and Czech Repub.; former Chm. and CEO, Ispat Internat. NV and LNM Holdings NV; Chm. and CEO of many group mem. cos. Has championed development of integrated mini-mills and use of direct reduced iron (DRI) as scrap substitute for steelmaking. Founder, LNM Foundn for charitable progs in India. Steelmaker of the Year, New Steel Magazine, 1996; Willy Korf Steel Vision Award, American Metal Market/World Steel Dynamics, 1998. *Recreations:* yoga, swimming. *Address:* ArcelorMittal, 7th Floor, Berkeley Square House, Berkeley Square, W1J 6DA.

**MITTER, Prof. Rana Shantashil Rajyeswar,** OBE 2019; PhD; FBA 2015; Professor of History and Politics of Modern China, since 2008, and Director, China Centre, since 2013, University of Oxford; Fellow, St Cross College, Oxford, since 2001; *b* Cambridge, 11 Aug. 1969; *s* of Partha and late Swasti Mitter; *m* 2004, Katharine Wilson; one *d*. *Educ:* King's Coll., Cambridge (BA 1992; PhD 1996; Pres., Cambridge Union, 1991); Harvard Univ. (Kennedy Schol.). Jun. Lectr, Univ. of Oxford and Jun. Res. Fellow, Wolfson Coll., Oxford, 1996–99; Lectr in Hist., Warwick Univ., 1999–2001; Lectr in Hist. and Politics of Modern China, Univ. of Oxford, 2001–08. Presenter, Night Waves, and Free Thinking, BBC Radio 3, 2007–; Chinese Characters, BBC Radio 4, 2018. *Publications:* The Manchurian Myth: nationalism, resistance and collaboration in modern China, 2000; A Bitter Revolution: China's struggle with the modern world, 2004 (THES Young Acad. Author of Year, 2005); Modern China: a very short introduction, 2008, 2nd edn 2016; China's War with Japan, 1937–45: the struggle for survival, 2013 (RUSI/Duke of Westminster's Medal for Mil. Lit., 2014; US edn as Forgotten Ally, 2013). *Recreations:* biographies of long-forgotten 1970s politicians, reminiscences of best-forgotten 1970s television programmes. *Address:* China Centre, University of Oxford, Dickson Poon Building, Canterbury Road, Oxford OX2 6LU. *E:* rana.mitter@orinst.ox.ac.uk.

**MITTING, Hon. Sir John Edward,** Kt 2001; a Judge of the High Court of Justice, Queen's Bench Division, 2001–17; *b* 8 Oct. 1947; *s* of late Alison Kennard Mitting and Eleanor Mary Mitting; *m* 1977, Judith Clare (*née* Hampson); three *s*. *Educ:* Downside Sch.; Trinity Hall, Cambridge (BA, LLB). Called to the Bar, Gray's Inn, 1970, Bencher, 1996; QC 1987; a Recorder, 1988–2001; Chm., Special Immigration Appeal Commn, 2007–12; Vice-Pres., Investigatory Powers Tribunal, 2015–17; Chm., Undercover Policing Inquiry, 2017–. *Recreations:* wine, food, bridge. *Club:* Garrick.

**MITTLER, Prof. Peter Joseph,** CBE 1981; MA, PhD, MEd; CPsychol; FBPsS, FIASSID; Professor of Special Education, University of Manchester, 1973–95, now Emeritus (Dean, Faculty of Education and Director, School of Education, 1991–94; Hon. Research Fellow, since 2009); human rights consultant on Alzheimer's and dementias; *b* 2 April 1930; *s* of Dr Gustav Mittler and Gertrude Mittler; *m* 1st, 1955, Helle Katscher (marr. diss. 1997); three *s*; 2nd, 1997, Penelope Anastasia Platt. *Educ:* Merchant Taylors' Sch., Crosby; Pembroke Coll., Cambridge (MA); PhD London; MEd Manchester. Clinical Psychologist, Warneford and Park Hosps, Oxford, 1954–58; Principal Psychologist, Reading Area Psychiatric Services, 1958–63; Lectr in Psychology, Birkbeck Coll., Univ. of London, 1963–68; Manchester University: Dir, Hester Adrian Res. Centre, 1968–82; Dir, Centre for Educnl Guidance and Special Needs, Dept of Educn, 1977–91; Dep. Dir, Sch. of Educn, 1989–91. Vis. Prof., Manchester Metropolitan Univ., 1996–97; Distinguished Vis. Prof., Univ. of Hong Kong, 1997–98; Fellow, Centre for Policy Studies, Dartington, 1995–. Chm., Nat. Develt Gp for Mentally Handicapped, 1975–80; Mem., Schs Exams and Assessment Council, 1988–90. Pres., Internat. League of Socs for Persons with Mental Handicap, 1982–86 (Vice-Pres., 1978–82); Mem., Prince of Wales Adv. Gp on Disability, 1984–90; Chm. Trustees and Council, British Inst. of Learning Disabilities, 1995–97; Human Rights Advr, Dementia Alliance Internat., 2015–17; Human Rights Ambassador, Dementia Alliance Internat. and Alzheimer's Disease Internat., 2017; Advr on disability to UN, UNESCO, WHO, ILO, UNICEF. FRSA 2018. *Publications:* ed, Psychological Assessment of Mental and Physical Handicaps, 1970; The Study of Twins, 1971; ed, Assessment for Learning in the Mentally Handicapped, 1973; ed, Research to Practice in Mental Retardation (3 vols), 1977; People not Patients, 1979; (jtly) Teaching Language and Communication to the Mentally Handicapped, (Schools Council), 1979; (ed jtly) Advances in Mental Handicap Research, 1980; (ed) Frontiers of Knowledge in Mental Retardation (2 vols), 1981; (ed jtly) Approaches to Partnership: professionals and parents of mentally handicapped people, 1983; (ed jtly) Aspects of Competence in Mentally Handicapped People, 1983; (ed jtly) Staff Training in Mental Handicap, 1987; (jtly) Inset and Special Educational Needs: running short, school-focused inservice courses, 1988; (ed jtly) Special Needs Education (World Yearbook of Education), 1993; Teacher Education for Special Educational Needs, 1993; (jtly) Innovations in Family Support for People with Learning Difficulties, 1994; (ed jtly) Teacher Education for Special Needs in Europe, 1995; (ed) Changing Policy and Practice for People with Learning Disabilities, 1995; (jtly) Disability and the Family, 1995; Working Towards Inclusive Education: social contexts, 2000; (jtly) Promoting the Human Rights of Children with Disabilities, 2007; Thinking Globally Acting Locally: a personal journey, 2010; Overcoming Exclusion: social justice through education, 2013; papers in psychol and educnl jls. *Recreations:* music, Italy. *Address:* 8 Drayton Manor, Parrs Wood Road, Manchester M20 5GJ. *E:* Peter.Mittler@manchester.ac.uk.

**MIURIN, Fields W.;** *see* Wicker-Miurin.

**MIYAKE, Kazunaru, (Issey);** fashion designer; *b* 22 April 1938. *Educ:* Tama Art Univ., Tokyo; Chambre Syndicale de la Couture, Paris. Assistant Designer: Guy Laroche, Paris, 1966–68; Hubert de Givenchy, Paris, 1968–69; Designer, Geoffrey Beene, NY, 1969–70; established Miyake Design Studio, Tokyo, 1970; first Paris fashion show, 1973; Founder: Pleats Please, 1993; A-POC, 1999. Co-Dir, 21_21 Design Sight, Tokyo, 2012–. *Exhibitions:* Bodyworks - Fashion Without Taboos, Tokyo, San Francisco, LA, London, 1985; Musée des Arts Décoratifs, Paris, 1988; Issey Miyake Making Things, Paris, 1998, NY, 1999, Tokyo, 2000; The Work of Miyake Issey, Nat. Art Centre, Tokyo, 2016. Numerous awards. Hon. Dr: RCA, 1993; Lyon, 1999. Bunka Korosha (Japan), 1998; Order of Culture (Japan), 2010; Comdr, Légion d'honneur (France), 2016 (Chevalier, 1993). *Publications:* East Meets West, 1978; Issey Miyake Bodyworks, 1983. *Address:* Issey Miyake Inc., 1–12–10 Tomigaya Shibuya-ku, Tokyo 151–8554, Japan.

**MKAPA, Benjamin William;** President, United Republic of Tanzania, 1995–2005; *b* 12 Nov. 1938; *s* of William Matwani and Stephania Nambanga; *m* 1966, Anna Joseph Maro; two *s*. *Educ:* Lupaso Primary Sch.; Ndanda Secondary Sch.; Kigonsera Seminary; St Francis Coll., Pugu (Cambridge Sch. Cert.); Makerere UC (BA Hons 1962); Sch. of Internat. Affairs, Columbia Univ. Admin. Officer, subseq. Dist Officer, then Foreign Service Officer, Dodoma, 1962; Managing Editor: The Nationalist and Uhuru, 1966–72; The Daily News, and The Sunday News, 1972–74; Press Sec. to President, 1974–76; Founding Dir, Tanzania News Agency, 1976; High Comr to Nigeria, 1976–77; nominated MP, 1977–82, 1984–85; elected MP for Nanyumbu, 1985, re-elected 1990; Minister for Foreign Affairs, 1977–82, 1984–90; Minister for Information and Culture, 1980–82; High Comr to Canada, 1982–83; Ambassador to USA, 1983–84; Minister for Information and Broadcasting, 1990–92; Minister for Science, Tech. and Higher Educn, 1992–95. Chm., 1996–2006, Mem., 1977–, Chama cha Mapinduzi (Revolutionary Party). Co-Chm., World Commn on Social Dimension of Globalisation, 2002; Chm., Southern African Develt Community, 2003–04; Member: Commn for Africa, 2004; UN Commn on Legal Empowerment of the Poor, 2006–08; African Union Panel of Eminent Persons, 2008. Chm., South Centre, Geneva; Co-Chairman: Investment Climate Facility for Africa; Africa Emerging Markets Forum. Member, Bd of Trustees: African Wildlife Foundn; Aga Khan Univ. Member: Club of Madrid; InterAction Council; Africa Forum. Global Leadership Award, Jane Goodall Inst., 2007. *Address:* PO Box 7652, Charambe Street No 22, Upanga, Dar es Salaam, Tanzania.

**MLINARIC, David,** CBE 2009; interior decorator and designer, 1964–2004; founded David Mlinaric Ltd, 1964, became Mlinaric, Henry and Zervudachi Ltd, 1989; *b* 12 March 1939; *s* of Franjo and Mabel Mlinaric; *m* 1969, Martha Laycock; one *s* two *d*. *Educ:* Downside Sch.; Bartlett Sch. of Architecture; University Coll. London. Private and commercial interior designing and decorating, often in historic bldgs. Work includes: British Embassies in Washington, 1982, Paris, 1983; rooms in Nat. Gall. and NPG, London, 1986; Spencer House, London, 1990; Royal Opera House, Covent Garden; British Galls, V&A Mus.; Waddesdon Manor, 2000; Chatsworth House, 2006; Wilton House, 2008; Broadlands, 2009 and 2019; Admiralty Arch, 2015. Fellow, BIDA. Hon. Fellow, RCA, 1987. *Publications:* (with M. Cecil) Mlinaric on Decorating, 2008; (with Derry Moore) Great English Interiors, 2018. *Recreations:* gardening, sightseeing. *Address:* Manor House, Spargrove, Evercreech, Shepton Mallet, Somerset BA4 6HQ.

**MO, Timothy Peter;** writer; *b* 30 Dec. 1950; *s* of Peter Mo Wan Lung and Barbara Helena Falkingham. *Educ:* Convent of the Precious Blood, Hong Kong; Mill Hill School; St John's Coll., Oxford (BA; Gibbs Prize 1971). *Publications:* The Monkey King, 1978 (Geoffrey Faber Meml Prize, 1979); Sour Sweet, 1982 (Hawthornden Prize, 1983; filmed, 1989); An Insular Possession, 1986; The Redundancy of Courage, 1991 (E. M. Forster Award, Amer. Acad. and Inst. of Arts and Letters, 1992); Brownout on Breadfruit Boulevard, 1995; Renegade or Halo[2] (James Tait Black Meml Prize), 1999; Pure, 2012. *Recreations:* scuba diving, weight training, gourmandising. *E:* timothymo7@hotmail.com.

**MOBARIK,** Baroness *cr* 2014 (Life Peer), of Mearns in the County of Renfrewshire; **Nosheena Shaheen Mobarik,** CBE 2014 (OBE 2004); Member (C) Scotland, European Parliament, since 2017; *b* Pakistan, 1957; *d* of Muhammed Tufail Shaheen; *m* Iqbal Mobarik; one *s* one *d*. *Educ:* Strathclyde Univ. Co-founder and Dir, M Computer Technologies, 1997–2013. Founder and Convenor, Scotland Pakistan Network; Chm., Pakistan Britain Trade Investment Forum; Chm., CBI Scotland, 2011–13. A Baroness in Waiting (Govt Whip), 2016–17. *Address:* European Parliament, Rue Wiertz 60, 1047 Brussels, Belgium.

**MOBED, Rohinton;** Chief Executive Officer, Elsevier, 2012–19; *b* London, 29 May 1959; *s* of Yazdi Mobed and Goolcher Mobed; *m* 1990, Suzanne Taylor; two *d*. *Educ:* Trinity Coll., Cambridge (BA Engrg 1980); Imperial Coll. London (MSc Petroleum Engrg 1987). Schlumberger, 1980–2004: Vice Pres., Asia, GeoQuest, 1997–98; Mktg Manager, Asia, 1998–99; Vice Pres., Data Mgt, 2000–01; IHS: Pres., IHS Energy, 2004–07; Co-Pres. and Chief Operating Officer Energy, 2007–08; Co-Chm., 2008–09; Pres., Academic, Cengage Learning, 2009–10; Hd, sci. and technol. businesses, Elsevier, 2011–12. Non-exec. Dir, Aveva plc, 2017–. *E:* ronmobed@live.com. *Club:* Oxford and Cambridge.

**MOBERLY, Nicholas Hamilton;** Chief Executive, Multiple Sclerosis Society, since 2019; *b* Athens, Greece, 11 May 1963; *s* of Sir John Campbell Moberly, KBE, CMG and Patience Moberly; *m* 1991, Prof. Margaret Callan; one *s* two *d*. *Educ:* Dragon Sch., Oxford; Winchester Coll., Winchester; Queen's Coll., Cambridge (BA Hons English Lit. 1984). Asst Manager, Samuel Montagu & Co. Ltd, 1984–87; First Sec., FCO, 1987–93; Sen. Engagement Manager, McKinsey & Co. Inc., 1994–99; Dir, Global Ops, Netdecisions Ltd, 2000–02; ind. consultant, 2002; Dir, Strategic Develt, KCH NHS Trust, 2003–06; CEO, Royal Surrey Co. Hosp. NHS Foundn Trust, 2006–15; CEO, King's Coll. Hosp. NHS Foundn Trust, 2015–18. *Recreations:* running, ski-ing, kite surfing, hill walking. *Address:* 19 Cloncurry Street, SW6 6DR. *E:* nicmo11@hotmail.co.uk.

**MOBERLY, Sir Patrick (Hamilton),** KCMG 1986 (CMG 1978); HM Diplomatic Service, retired; Ambassador to South Africa, 1984–87; *b* 2 Sept. 1928; *yr s* of G. H. Moberly; *m* 1955, Mary Penfold (*d* 2019); two *s* one *d*. *Educ:* Winchester; Trinity Coll., Oxford (MA). HM Diplomatic Service, 1951–88; diplomatic posts in: Baghdad, 1953; Prague, 1957; Foreign Office, 1959; Dakar, 1962; Min. of Defence, 1965; Commonwealth Office, 1967; Canada, 1969; Israel, 1970; FCO, 1974; Asst Under-Sec. of State, 1976–81; Ambassador to Israel, 1981–84. *Recreations:* opera, seeing family and friends. *Address:* 38 Lingfield Road, SW19 4PZ.

**MOCATTA, Jane;** *see* Bewsey, J.

**MOCHAN, Charles Francis;** HM Diplomatic Service, retired; High Commissioner to Fiji, and also (non-resident) to Kiribati, Tuvalu and Nauru, 2002–06; *b* 6 Aug. 1948; *s* of Charles Mochan and Margaret Mochan (*née* Love); *m* 1970, Ilse Sybilla Carleon Cruttwell; one *s* one *d*. *Educ:* St Patrick's High Sch., Dumbarton. MoD (Navy), 1966; joined FCO 1967; Port Elizabeth, S Africa, 1970–72; Kingston, Jamaica, 1972–74; FCO, 1974–77; Seoul,

1977–80; Second, later First Sec., Helsinki, 1981–84; FCO, 1984–87; Dep. High Comr, Mauritius, 1988–91; FCO, 1991–95; Consul-Gen., Casablanca, 1995–98; Ambassador to Republic of Madagascar, 1999–2002, and concurrently to Federal Islamic Republic of Comoros, 2001–02. *Recreations:* soccer, ornithology, music, walking, golf.

**MODARRESSI, Anne, (Mrs T. M. Modarressi);** *see* Tyler, A.

**MODI, Prof. Neena,** MD; FRCP, FRCPCH; Professor of Neonatal Medicine, Imperial College London, since 2003; Honorary Consultant, Chelsea and Westminster NHS Foundation Trust, since 2003; *b* Durban, S Africa; *d* of Krishnalal Jivanlal Modi and Kusum Modi (*née* Mehta); *m* 1979, Robert Carr; one *s* one *d*. *Educ:* Dr Ribeiro Goan Sch., Nairobi; Duke of Gloucester High Sch., Nairobi; Univ. of Edinburgh Med. Sch. (MB ChB 1976; MD 1991). MRCP 1979, FRCP 1994; FRCPCH 1997, Hon. FRCPCH 2019. House Officer in Gen. Surgery, 1976–77, in Gen. Medicine, 1977, Royal Infirmary, Edinburgh; Senior House Officer: in Paediatrics, Royal Hosp. for Sick Children, Edinburgh, 1977–78; in Infectious Diseases, City Hosp., Edinburgh, 1978–79; Registrar in Gen. Paediatrics, Western Gen. Hosp., Edinburgh, 1980–82; Lectr in Neonatal Paediatrics and Bliss Fellow, UCL, 1982–83; University of Liverpool: Alder Hey Children's Res. Fellow in Paediatric Nephrol., 1984; Lectr and Hon. Sen. Registrar in Paediatrics, 1984–87; Sen. Lectr, 1987–2003, Dir, Neonatal Data Analysis Unit, 2007–, Imperial College London; Hon. Consultant, Hammersmith Hosp., 1987–2003. Dir, Neonatal Update: the Science of Newborn Care, 2001–. Chair, Ethics Cttee, BMJ, 2010–15. President: Neonatal Soc., 2012–15; Academic Paediatrics Assoc. of GB and Ireland, 2014–15; RCPCH, 2015–18 (Sci. and Res. Vice Pres., 2009–14); Medical Women's Fedn, May 2020–. Hon. Fellow: British Assoc. of Perinatal Medicine, 2015; Turkish Neonatal Soc., 2016; Hon. FFPM 2017. *Publications:* 30 chapters in books; approx. 200 articles in jls. *Recreations:* mountain walking, cooking, science fiction, fast cars. *Address:* Imperial College London, Chelsea and Westminster NHS Foundation Trust, 369 Fulham Road, SW10 9NH. *T:* (020) 3315 5101, *Fax:* (020) 3315 8050. *E:* n.modi@imperial.ac.uk. *Clubs:* College, 1942.

**MODIANO, Patrick;** writer; *b* Boulogne-Billancourt, France, 30 July 1945; *s* of late Albert Modiano and Luisa Modiano (*née* Colpeyn); *m* 1970, Dominique Zehrfuss; two *d*. *Educ:* Lycée Henri-IV, Paris. Writer, 1967–. Screenplay (with Louis Malle), Lacombe Lucien, 1974. Prix mondial Cino Del Duca for lifetime achievement, Institut de France, 2010; Austrian State Prize for Eur. Lit., 2012; Nobel Prize in Literature, 2014. *Publications:* La place de l'étoile, 1968; La ronde de nuit, 1969 (Night Rounds, 1971); Les boulevards de ceinture (Grand Prix du Roman, Académie française), 1972 (Ring Roads, 1974); Villa Triste, 1975 (Villa Triste, 1977) (filmed as Le parfum d'Yvonne, 1994); Emmanuel Berl: Interrogatoire, 1976; Livret de famille, 1977; Rue des boutiques obscures (Prix Goncourt), 1978 (Missing Person, 1980); Une jeunesse, 1981 (filmed, 1983); Memory Lane, 1981; De si braves garçons, 1982 (filmed as Charell, 2006); Poupée blonde de Pierre Michel Wals, 1983; Quartier perdu, 1985 (A Trace of Malice, 1988); (with Dominique Zehrfuss) Une aventure de Choura, 1986; Dimanches d'août, 1986 (filmed as Te quiero, 2001); (with Dominique Zehrfuss) Une fiancée pour Choura, 1987; Remise de peine, 1988; Catherine Certitude, 1988; Vestiaire de l'enfance, 1989; Voyage de noces, 1990 (Honeymoon, 1992); Paris tendresse, 1990; Fleurs de ruine, 1991; Un cirque passe, 1992 (After the Circus, 2015) (filmed as Des gens qui passent, 2009); Chien de printemps, 1993; (with Zina Modiano) Les Chiens de la rue du Soleil, 1994; Du plus loin de l'oubli, 1995 (Out of the Dark, 1998); (with Catherine Deneuve) Elle s'appelait Françoise, 1996; Dora Bruder, 1997 (Dora Bruder, 1999); Aux jours anciens, 1998; Des inconnues, 1999; La Petite Bijou, 2001; Éphéméride, 2001; Accident nocturne, 2003; Dieu prend-il soin des bœufs?, 2003; Un pedigree, 2005 (Pedigree: a memoir, 2015); (with Dominique Zehrfuss) 28 Paradis, 2005; Dans le café de la jeunesse perdue, 2007; L'horizon, 2010; L'herbe des nuits, 2012; (with Dominique Zehrfuss and Marie Modiano) 28 Paradis, 28 Enfers, 2012; Romans, 2013; Pour que tu ne te perdes pas dans le quartier, 2014; Suspended Sentences: three novellas, 2014. *Address:* c/o Éditions Gallimard, 5 rue Gaston Gallimard, 75328 Paris cedex 07, Paris.

**MODOOD, Prof. Tariq,** MBE 2001; PhD; FBA 2017; FAcSS; Professor of Sociology, Politics and Public Policy, since 1997 and Director, Centre for the Study of Ethnicity and Citizenship, since 1999, University of Bristol; *b* Karachi, 4 Oct. 1952; *s* of Mirza Sabhuddin Modood and Nafeesa Modood; *m* 1979, Glynthea Thompson; two *d*. *Educ:* Univ. of Durham (BA Hons Philos. and Pol 1974, MA Politics 1975); University Coll., Swansea (PhD Philos. 1984). Temp. Lectr in Politics, Univ. of Bristol, 1980–81; Temp. Lectr in Social Philos., QUB, 1981–82; HM Inspector of Taxes, Oxford, 1982–83; Temp. Lectr in Politics, University Coll., Swansea, 1984–85; Equal Opportunities Officer, London Bor. of Hillingdon, 1987–89; Principal Employment Officer, Commn for Racial Equality, 1989–91; Gwilym Gibbon Res. Fellow, Nuffield Coll., Oxford, 1991–92; Hallsworth Res. Fellow, Univ. of Manchester, 1992–94; Prog. Dir, PSI, London, 1993–97. FAcSS (AcSS 2004); FRSA. *Publications:* Not Easy Being British: colour, culture and citizenship, 1992; (jtly) Ethnic Minorities in Britain: diversity and disadvantage—the fourth national survey of ethnic minorities, 1997; Multicultural Politics: racism, ethnicity and Muslims in Britain, 2005; (ed jtly) Ethnicity, Social Mobility and Public Policy in the US and UK, 2005; Multiculturalism: a civic idea, 2007, 2nd edn 2013; (ed with Geoffrey Levey) Secularism, Religion and Multicultural Citizenship, 2009; Still Not Easy Being British: struggles for a multicultural citizenship, 2010; (ed with John Salt) Global Migration, Ethnicity and Britishness, 2011; (ed jtly) European Multiculturalisms: cultural, religious and ethnic challenges, 2012; (ed jtly) Multiculturalism Rethought, 2015; (ed jtly) Multiculturalism and Interculturalism, 2016; (ed jtly) The Problems of Religious Diversity: European challenges, Asian approaches, 2017; Essays on Secularism and Multiculturalism, 2019. *Recreations:* cycling, swimming, films, novels, opera, theatre. *E:* t.modood@bristol.ac.uk.

**MODRICH, Prof. Paul Lawrence,** PhD; James B. Duke Professor of Biochemistry and Chemistry, Duke University, since 2015 (James B. Duke Professor of Biochemistry, 1988–2015); Investigator, Howard Hughes Institute, since 1994; *b* Raton, New Mexico, 13 June 1946; *s* of Laurence G. and Margaret E. Mogrich. *Educ:* Massachusetts Inst. of Technol. (BS Biol. 1968); Stanford Univ. (PhD 1973). Postdoctoral study in biol. chem., Harvard Univ., 1973–74; Asst Prof. of Chemistry, Univ. of Calif, Berkeley, 1974–76; Duke University: Asst Prof. of Biochem., 1976–80; Associate Prof. of Biochem., 1980–84; Prof. of Biochem., 1984–88; Dir, Duke Univ. Prog. in Genetics, 1989–92. Associate Ed., Biochem., 1992–94; Member: Editorial Board: Nucleic Acids Res., 1980–82; Jl Biol Chem., 1982–83; Proc. NAS, 2000–08; DNA Repair, 2003–08; Editl Adv. Bd, Biochem., 1986–91, 1995–2003; Editl Cttee, Annual Rev. of Biochem., 2004–. National Institute of Environmental Health Sciences: Member: Bd of Scientific Counselors, 1995–2000; Ext. Rev. Gp, 1996–97; Dir, Rev. Panel, 2001. Member: NAS, 1993; Nat. Acad. Medicine (formerly Inst. Medicine), 2003. FAAAS 1998; Fellow: Amer. Acad. Microbiol., 2003; Amer. Acad. Arts and Scis, 2004; Hon. FRSC 2016. Pfizer Award in Enzyme Chem., Amer. Chem. Soc., 1983; Gen. Motors Mott Prize in Cancer Res., 1996; Robert J. and Claire Pasarow Foundn Award in Cancer Res., 1999; Medal of Honor, Amer. Cancer Soc., 2005; (jtly) Nobel Prize in Chemistry, 2015; Arthur Kornberg and Paul Berg Lifetime Achievement Award in Biomed. Scis, Stanford Medicine Alumni Assoc., 2016. *Publications:* contribs to scientific jls incl. Jl Biol Chem., Jl Molecular Biol., Biochem., Proc. NAS USA, Nucleic Acids Res., Science, EMBO Jl, Oncogene, Cell. *Address:* Department of Biochemistry, Box 3711, Duke University Medical Center, Durham, NC 27710, USA.

**MOELLER, Prof. Scott David;** Professor in the Practice of Finance, since 2010, and Director, Mergers and Acquisitions Research Centre, since 2008, Cass Business School, City, University of London (formerly City University London); *b* NJ, USA, 22 March 1954; *s* of Paul and Dorothy Moeller; *m* 2001, Dr Daniela Schwartz; two *s* two *d*. *Educ:* Yale Univ. (BA 1976; MA 1976; MBA 1978). Associate, then Sen. Associate, Booz Allen Hamilton, 1977, 1978–84; Morgan Stanley, 1984–96: Sen. Associate, then Vice Pres., NY; Exec. Dir, Tokyo; Geschäftsführer, Frankfurt; Man. Dir, Deutsche Bank, London, 1996–2001; Chief Exec., Executive Educn, Cass Business Sch., City Univ. London, 2002–10. *Publications:* (with C. Brady) Intelligent M & A: navigating the mergers and acquisitions minefield, 2007; Surviving M & A: make the most of your company being acquired, 2009; (ed) Finance Essentials: the practitioner's guide, 2012; (ed) The M&A Collection: themes in best practice, 2014; (jtly) Why Deals Fail, and How to Rescue Them, 2016. *Address:* Cass Business School, City, University of London, 106 Bunhill Row, EC1Y 8TZ. *E:* scott.moeller@city.ac.uk.

**MOELWYN-HUGHES, Louise Joanne;** Master, Marlborough College, since 2018; *b* Dublin, 2 Nov. 1970; *d* of Thomas Nigel Playfair and Joan Margaret Playfair; *m* 2009, Owen Tudor Moelwyn-Hughes; two *s* one *d*. *Educ:* Methodist Coll., Belfast; Magdalene Coll., Cambridge (MA); Open Univ. (MEd). Asst Master (Classics and Arabic), 1992–2005, Housemistress, 2003–05, Marlborough Coll.; Sen. Dep. Hd, Perse Sch., Cambridge, 2005–11; Head, St Edmund's Sch., Canterbury, 2011–18. *Recreations:* sport, music, South Africa. *Address:* The Master's Lodge, Marlborough College, Marlborough, Wilts SN8 1PA. *Clubs:* East India, Lansdowne.

**MOERAN, Fenner Orlando;** QC 2014; *b* London, 14 Aug. 1972; *s* of Edward and Jacky Moeran; *m* 2002, Emma Judge; one *s* one *d*. *Educ:* University Coll. Sch.; Univ. of Bristol (BSc Politics and Philosophy); City Univ. (DipLaw). Called to the Bar, Lincoln's Inn, 1996. *Recreations:* family, walking. *Address:* Wilberforce Chambers, 8 New Square, Lincoln's Inn, WC2A 3QP.

**MOFFAT, Captain (Alexander) Iain (Black),** RD 1980 (and Bar 1988); CEng, MICE; RNR retired; Vice Lord-Lieutenant for Northumberland, 2002–13 (Acting Lord-Lieutenant, 2009); Professorial Fellow in Dam Engineering, University of Newcastle upon Tyne, since 2004 (Visiting Fellow, 2000–04); *b* 29 March 1938; *s* of late Alexander Moffat and Margaret D. H. Moffat (*née* Black); *m* 1963, Madeline Wright; one *s* one *d*. *Educ:* Edinburgh Acad.; Univ. of Edinburgh (BSc). CEng, MICE 1970; FGS 1987. Civil Engr posts, 1962–66; University of Newcastle upon Tyne: Lectr, 1966–74; Sen. Lectr, 1974–2000; Dep. Head, Dept of Civil Engrg, 1991–98. Vis. Sen. Lectr, Univ. of Durham, 1998–2001. Pro-Chm., Northumbrian Univs Mil. Educn Cttee, 2003–12; Mem., ICE Panel for Historic Engrg Works, 2005–10. ICE Smeaton Lect., 2010. Vice-Chm. (RN and RM), RFCA for N of England, 1996–2003. Trustee, HMS Trincomalee Trust, 2008–17. CO, Tyne Div., RNR, HMS Calliope, 1982–86. DL Northumberland, 1990. *Publications:* (jtly) Hydraulic Structures, 1990, 4th edn 2007; numerous contribs/papers to professional jls and conf. proc. on issues in dam engrg, geotechnics, etc. *Recreations:* walking, history (technology (development of the submarine), naval, military, social (19th and 20th Century)), travel, reading. *Address:* 43 Bishops Hill, Acomb, Hexham, Northumberland NE46 4NH. *T:* (01434) 605243. *E:* aibmoffat@hotmail.com.

**MOFFAT, Alistair Murray;** author and broadcaster; *b* 16 June 1950; *s* of John and Ellen Moffat; *m* 1976, Lindsay Anne Reid Thomas; one *s* two *d*. *Educ:* Kelso High Sch.; St Andrews Univ. (MA Hons); Edinburgh Univ. (CertEd); London Univ. (MPhil). Administrator, Edinburgh Festival Fringe, 1976–81; Scottish Television, subseq. Scottish Media Group: Arts Corresp., 1981–86; Controller of Features, 1987–90; Dir of Progs, 1990–93; Chief Exec., then Man. Dir, Scottish Television Enterprises, 1993–99. Chm., Scottish TV Regl Bd, 1999–2003. Dir, Borders Book Fest., 2015–. Chm., Great Tapestry of Scotland, 2011–. Rector, St Andrews Univ., 2011–14. FRSA. *Publications:* The Edinburgh Fringe, 1978; Kelsae: a history from earliest times, 1985; Remembering Charles Rennie Mackintosh, 1989; Arthur and the Lost Kingdoms, 1999; The Sea Kingdoms, 2001; The Borders, 2002; Homing, 2003; Heartland, 2004; Before Scotland, 2005; Tyneside, 2005; East Lothian, 2006; The Reivers, 2007; Fife: a history, 2007; The Wall, 2008; Edinburgh, a History, 2008; Tuscany: a history, 2009; The Faded Map, 2010; The Highland Clans, 2010; The Scots: a genetic journey, 2011; Britain's Last Frontier, 2012; The British: a genetic journey, 2013; Hawick: a history from earliest times, 2014; Bannockburn: the battle for a nation, 2014; The Great Tapestry of Scotland, 2014; The Making of the Great Tapestry of Scotland, 2014; Scotland: a history from earliest times, 2015; (jtly) Who Built Scotland, 2017; The Hidden Ways, 2017; To the Island of Tides: a journey to Lindisfarne, 2019. *Recreation:* apprentice groom. *Address:* The Henhouse, Selkirk TD7 5EY.

**MOFFAT, Anne;** *b* 30 March 1958; *d* of Francis Hunter Moffat and late Wilma Haxton Moffat; *m* 1984, David Adair Harold Picking (marr. diss. 2003); one *s*; *m* 2009, Lawrence Mulligan McCran. *Educ:* Woodmill High Comprehensive Sch. Nurse: Fife Health Bd, 1975–80; NI Eastern Health and Social Service, 1980–83 (staff nurse, 1982–83); staff nurse, then nursing sister, E Kent Community Health Care NHS Trust, 1984–2001. MP (Lab) E Lothian, 2001–10. Mem., NEC, COHSE, 1990; Mem., NEC, 1993–2001, Nat. Pres., 1999–2000, UNISON. Mem. (Lab), Ashford BC, 1994–98.

**MOFFAT, David Andrew,** PhD; FRCS; Consultant Neurotologist and Skull Base Surgeon, Addenbrooke's Hospital, Cambridge, 1981–2012, now Hon. Emeritus Consultant; Associate Lecturer, University of Cambridge, since 1981 (Lecturer, 1981); *b* 27 June 1947; *s* of late Graham and Myra Moffat; *m* 1970, Jane Elizabeth; two *s* one *d*. *Educ:* St Nicholas Sch., Northwood; London Hospital Med. Coll. (BSc Hons 1968; MB BS 1971); Hon. MA Cantab 1984; Radboud Univ., Nijmegen (PhD 2012). MRCS 1971, FRCS 1977; LRCP 1971. Consultant Surgeon, Westminster Hosp., 1979–80. Chm., Intercollegiate Specialty Bd and Panel of Examiners, 1998–2001; Mem., Specialist Adv. Cttee in Otolaryngology, 2001–06. Hunterian Prof. of Surgery, RCS, 2009–11. Master, British Academic Conf. in Otolaryngology, 2006–09. Pres., Section of Otology, RSocMed, 2003–04 (Hon. Mem., 2018); Hon. Mem., German ENT Soc. Gold Medal, Internat. Fedn of Oto-rhino-laryngol Socs, 2013; House-Hirselberger Lifetime Achievement Award, Amer. Neurol Soc., 2016. *Publications:* (ed jtly) Recent Advances in Otolaryngology, 7, 1995, 8, 2007; Clinical Aspects and Outcomes of Lateral Skull Base Surgery, 2012; 33 chapters in textbooks; 188 papers in learned jls on neurology and skull base surgery including acoustic neuroma, meningioma, glomus jugulare tumours, squamous cell carcinomas of temporal bone, Ménière's disease, electrophysiology. *Recreations:* theatre, ballet, opera, motoring, golf, ski-ing. *Address:* Department of Neuro-otology and Skull Base Surgery, Box 48, Addenbrooke's Hospital, Cambridge University Hospitals NHS Foundation Trust, Hills Road, Cambridge CB2 0QQ. *T:* and *Fax:* (01223) 364114. *E:* moffatd@me.com. *Club:* Royal Worlington and Newmarket Golf.

**MOFFAT, Rev. Canon George;** Rector, Priory Church of St Mary and St Cuthbert, Bolton Abbey, 2007–12; Hon. Chaplain to the Queen, 2000–16; *b* 31 July 1946; *s* of George and Mary Moffat; *m* 1975, Peta Ollen; two *d*. *Educ:* Edinburgh Theol Coll.; New Coll., Edinburgh (BD 1977); Open Univ. (BA Hons 1987); Bradford Univ. (MA 2004). Ordained deacon, 1972, priest, 1973; Curate: Christ Church, Falkirk, 1973–76; St Peter, Lutton Place, Edinburgh, 1976–81; Anglican Chaplain, Edinburgh Univ., 1977–81;

Curate, St Leonard and All Saints, Heston, 1981–84; Vicar, St Mary the Virgin, S Emsall, 1984–93; Team Rector, Manningham, 1993–2007. Hon. Canon, Bradford Cathedral, 2002–12, now Emeritus. Non-exec. Dir, Bradford City Teaching PCT, 2003–06. *Recreations:* country walking, supporting creative modern dance, managing rough woodland and establishing a cider and perry orchard. *Address:* Fir Cottage, The Stenders, Mitcheldean GL17 0JE. *T:* (01594) 543668. *E:* rev.g.moffat@gmail.com.

**MOFFAT, Captain Iain;** *see* Moffat, Captain A. I. B.

**MOFFATT, Prof. (Henry) Keith,** ScD; FRS 1986; FRSE; Professor of Mathematical Physics, University of Cambridge, 1980–2002, now Professor Emeritus (Head of Department of Applied Mathematics and Theoretical Physics, 1983–91); Fellow, Trinity College, Cambridge, 1961–76, and since 1980; *b* 12 April 1935; *s* of late Frederick Henry Moffatt and Emmeline Marchant Fleming; *m* 1960, Katharine, (Linty), Stiven, *d* of late Rev. D. S. Stiven, MC, DD; one *s* two *d* (and one *s* decd). *Educ:* George Watson's Coll., Edinburgh; Edinburgh Univ. (BSc); Cambridge Univ. (BA, PhD, ScD). Lectr in Maths, Cambridge Univ., and Dir of Studies in Maths, Trinity Coll., 1961–76 (Tutor, 1971–75, Sen. Tutor, 1975); Prof. of Applied Maths, Bristol Univ., 1977–80; Dir, Isaac Newton Inst. for Mathematical Scis, Cambridge Univ., 1996–2001. Visiting appts, Stanford Univ. and Johns Hopkins Univ., 1965, Univ. of Paris VI, 1975–76, Institut de Mécanique, Grenoble, 1986, Univ. of California, San Diego, 1987, Santa Barbara, 1991, Ecole Polytechnique Palaiseau, 1992–99, Kyoto Univ., 1993; Blaise Pascal Internat. Chair, Ecole Normale Supérieure, Paris, 2001–03. Pres., IUTAM, 2000–04. Mem. Council and Trustee, African Inst. for Math. Scis, 2003–12; Member: Scientific Adv. Bd, Inst. for Math. Scis, Singapore, 2002–10; Council, Internat. Centre for Mech. Scis, 2002–10; Information, Communication and Emergent Technologies Panel, Science Foundn Ireland, 2008–11; Bd, African Inst. for Math. Scis—Next Einstein Initiative, 2009–15; Conseil d'Enseignement et Recherche, Ecole Polytechnique, 2009–13. Co-editor, Journal of Fluid Mechanics, 1966–83. Foreign Mem., Royal Netherlands Acad. of Arts and Scis, 1991; Associé Etranger, Acad. des Sciences, Paris, 1998; Socio Straniero, Acad. Nazionale dei Lincei, Rome, 2001; Foreign Member: Nat. Acad. of Scis, USA, 2008; Acad. of Scis, Lisbon, 2010. MAE 1974. FRSE 1988; Fellow, APS, 2003. Hon. FIMA 2007. D*hc* Inst. Nat Polytechnique de Grenoble, 1987; Hon. DSc: SUNY, 1990; Edinburgh, 2001; Eindhoven Tech. Univ., 2006; Glasgow, 2007. Panetti-Ferrari Prize and Gold Medal, 2001; Euromech Fluid Mechanics Prize, 2003; Sen. Whitehead Prize, LMS, 2005; Hughes Medal, Royal Soc., 2005; David Crighton Medal, LMS/IMA, 2010; Fluid Dynamics Prize and Otto LaPorte Lect., APS, 2018. Officier des Palmes Académiques, 1998. *Publications:* Magnetic Field Generation in Electrically Conducting Fluids, 1978; (ed jtly) Topological Fluid Mechanics, 1990; (ed jtly) Topological Aspects of the Dynamics of Fluids and Plasmas, 1992; (ed jtly) Tubes, Sheets and Singularities in Fluid Dynamics, 2003; (ed jtly) A Voyage Through Turbulence, 2011; (ed jtly) Environmental Hazards: the fluid dynamics and geophysics of extreme events, 2011; (ed jtly) Fundamental Problems of Turbulence, 2014; (with E. Dormy) Self-Exciting Fluid Dynamos, 2019; papers in fluid mechanics and dynamo theory in Jl Fluid Mech. and other jls. *Recreations:* baking bread, poetry. *Address:* Trinity College, Cambridge CB2 1TQ.

**MOFFATT, Laura Jean;** *b* 9 April 1954; *d* of Stanley and Barbara Field; *m* 1975, Colin Moffatt; three *s*. *Educ:* Hazelwick Comprehensive Sch., Crawley; Crawley Coll. of Technology. SRN, 1975–97. Mem. (Lab), Crawley BC, 1984–97 (Mayor, 1989–90). Contested (Lab) Crawley, 1992. MP (Lab) Crawley, 1997–2010. Parliamentary Private Secretary: to Lord Chancellor, 2001–04; to Sec. of State, DWP, 2005–06; to Minister of State, DfES, 2006; to Sec. of State, DfES, 2006–07; to Sec. of State, DoH, 2007–09; Asst Regl Minister for the SE, 2009–10. *Recreations:* pets, walking, holidays with family.

**MOFFETT, David Leslie;** Director, Commercial and Experience, International Rugby Academy, New Zealand, since 2017; *b* 17 May 1947; *s* of Henry Albert Moffett and Barbara Moffett, later Pinkney; *m* 1970, Lauren Jacqueline Dartnell; one *s* one *d*; *m* 2008, Kerri-Ann Brooks. *Educ:* Nairobi Primary Sch.; Prince of Wales Sch., Nairobi; Brisbane Boys' Coll. Man. Dir, Pacific Waste Management, Sydney, 1981–86; Exec. Dir, NSW Rugby, 1992–95; Chief Executive Officer: SANZAR, 1995–96; NZ RFU, 1996–99; Nat. Rugby League, Australia, 1999–2001; Sport England, 2002; Welsh Rugby Union, 2002–05; owner, Matrix Sports, NZ, 2005; Man. Dir, Moffett Partnership, 2013. *Recreations:* walking, reading, cycling, photography.

**MOFFETT, Jonathan Keith;** QC 2017; *b* Belfast, 2 Oct. 1971; *s* of Jack and Mildred Moffett; *m* 2011, Sarah Irene Tyler. *Educ:* Girton Coll., Cambridge (BA Hons 1993; LLM 1994). Called to the Bar, Inner Temple, 1996; in practice as barrister, specialising in public law and human rights. *Publications:* (jtly) Judicial Review: principles and procedure, 2013. *Recreations:* Rugby Union, cycling, modern literature, cinema, music. *Address:* 11KBW, 11 King's Bench Walk, Temple, EC4Y 7EQ. *T:* (020) 7632 8500, *Fax:* (020) 7583 9123. *E:* Jonathan.Moffett@11kbw.com. *Clubs:* Oldmads (Rosslyn Park); Rosslyn Park Football (RFU).

**MOFFETT, Peter;** actor (stage name Peter Davison); *b* 13 April 1951; *s* of Claude and late Sheila Moffett; *m* 2003, Elizabeth Heery; two *s*, and one *d* from previous marriage. *Educ:* Winston Churchill Comprehensive Sch., Woking; Central Sch. of Speech and Drama (Acting Dip.). *Television* series: All Creatures Great and Small, 1978; Dr Who, 1981–84; A Very Peculiar Practice, 1986–87; Campion, 1989; Ain't Misbehavin', 1993; At Home with the Braithwaites, 2000; Last Detective, 2003; Too Good to be True, 2003; Distant Shores, 2005; The Complete Guide to Parenting, 2006; Fear, Stress and Anger, 2007 (Best Comedy Actor, Monte Carlo TV Fest., 2007); Unforgiven, 2009; Law and Order: UK, 2011–14; Pat and Cabbage, 2013; writer and dir, The Five(ish) Doctors (for BBC Dr Who 50th anniv.), 2013; *stage:* King Arthur in Spamalot, Palace Th., 2007; Legally Blonde, Savoy, 2010; The Vertical Hour, Park Th., 2014; Gypsy, Savoy Th., 2015. Top Man of Year Award, Multi-coloured Swap Shop, 1982. *Recreation:* sailing down the Thames.

**MOFFITT, Prof. Terrie Edith,** PhD; FBA 2004; FMedSci; Knut Schmidt Nielsen Professor of Psychology and Neuroscience, since 2008, and Nannerl O. Keohane University Professor, since 2013, Duke University; *b* 9 March 1955; *d* of Terry W. Moffitt and Glenda Macon Moffitt; *m* 1990, Prof. Avshalom Caspi, *qv*. *Educ:* Univ. of NC, Chapel Hill (BA 1977); USC (PhD 1984). Postdoctoral Fellow, UCLA, 1984; Res. Asst Prof., USC and Vis. Scholar, Univ. of Otago, NZ, 1985–86; Prof., Dept of Psychol., Univ. of Wisconsin, Madison, 1987–2007; Associate Dir, Dunedin Multidisciplinary Health and Develt Study, Dunedin Sch. of Medicine, Univ. of Otago, 1991–; Prof. of Social Behaviour and Develt, Inst. of Psychiatry, KCL, 1997–; Prof., Dept of Psychol. and Neurosci., Duke Univ., 2007–08. Trustee, Nuffield Foundn, 2011–. MAE 2005; FMedSci 1999; Fellow: Amer. Soc. of Criminology, 2003; Amer. Psychopathol Assoc., 2005; Amer. Acad. of Pol and Social Sci., 2008; Assoc. for Psychol Sci., 2009; US Nat. Acad. of Medicine; FKC 2010. Early Career Contribn Award, 1993, Dist. Career Award in Clin. Child Psychol., 2006, Dist. Career Award, 2016, Amer. Psychol Assoc.; Stockholm Prize in Criminology, 2007; Klaus-Grawe Prize in Clin. Psychol., Klaus Grawe Foundn, 2009; NARSAD Ruane Prize, Brain and Behaviour Res. Foundn, 2010; Klaus J. Jacobs Prize, Jacobs Foundn, 2010. *Publications:* Sex Differences in Antisocial Behaviours, 2001; over 300 articles in jls incl. Science, Lancet, JAMA, Proc. NAS, Archives of General Psychiatry, etc. *Recreations:* trekking and camping in the world's 'orange' countries on a scale from 'blue' (Scandinavia) to 'red' (Angola and Iran), working on her 250-acre farm in North Carolina. *Address:* Duke University, Box 104410, Suite 201 Grey House, 2020 Main Street, Durham, NC 27708, USA. *E:* terrie.moffitt@duke.edu. *W:* www.moffittcaspi.com.

**MOGER, Christopher Richard Derwent;** QC 1992; a Recorder, since 1993 (an Assistant Recorder, 1990–93); a Deputy High Court Judge, since 1999; international commercial arbitrator; *b* 28 July 1949; *s* of late Richard Vernon Derwent Moger and Cecile Eva Rosales Moger (*née* Power); *m* 1st, 1974, Victoria Trollope (marr. diss. 1991); three *s*; 2nd, 1991, Prudence Da Cunha. *Educ:* Sherborne School; Bristol Univ. (LLB Hons). FCIArb 1997. Called to the Bar, Inner Temple, 1972, Bencher, 2001; in practice as barrister, 1972–2017. Independent Arbitrator and Panel Member: Hong Kong Internat. Arbitration Centre; China Internat. Econ. and Trade Arbitration Commn, 2014–; Singapore Internat. Arbitration Centre, 2017–; KCAB Internat. (Korea); Asian Internat. Arbitration Centre (Kuala Lumpur). *Recreations:* fishing, walking. *Address:* 4 Pump Court, Temple, EC4Y 7AN. *T:* (020) 7842 5555. *Club:* Garrick.

**MOGFORD, Jeremy Lewis;** Managing Director: Mogford Ltd, since 1998; Mogford Hotels Ltd, since 1998; *b* 9 Oct. 1947; *s* of Peter Charles Mogford and Pamela Margaret Mogford (*née* Bennett); *m* 1971, Hilary Jane Raymond; one *s* one *d*. *Educ:* Canford Sch.; Royal Grammar Sch., High Wycombe; Univ. of Surrey (BSc Hotel and Catering Admin). MIH (MHCIMA 1971). Founder, owner and Man. Dir, 1973–97, Consultant, 1997–, Browns Restaurants Ltd; Director: Peachey Productions, 1998–2000; Ruso Ltd, 2001–17; RTLS (formerly RFTRAQ) Ltd, 2007– (Chm., 2014–); Backyard Chicken Co. Ltd, 2019–. Mem. Exec. Cttee, Restaurant Assoc. of GB, 1998–2003. Dir and Sponsor, Discerning Eye Art Exhibn, 1995–97; Sponsor, Oxford Lit. Fest., 1995; Jt Chm., ROX (Backing Oxford Business), 1999–; Chm., Oxford High St Assoc., 2008–. Trustee, Photo Oxford, 2015–. Sponsor, annual short story competition, Jeremy Mogford Prize for Food and Drink Writing, 2013–. DUniv Oxford Brookes, 2001. Independent Gp Restaurateur of the Year, Caterer and Hotelkeeper mag., 1997. *Recreations:* topiary, fly fishing, 20th century British art. *Address:* c/o Mogford Ltd, 36 St Giles, Oxford OX1 3LD. *Clubs:* Garrick, Groucho, Soho House, 5 Hertford Street.

**MOGG,** family name of **Baron Mogg**.

**MOGG,** Baron *cr* 2008 (Life Peer), of Queen's Park in the County of East Sussex; **John Frederick Mogg,** KCMG 2003; European Adviser to Gas and Electricity Markets Authority, since 2013 (non-executive Chairman and Member, 2003–13); *b* 5 Oct. 1943; *s* of Thomas W. Mogg and Cora M. Mogg; *m* 1967, Anne Smith; one *d* one *s*. *Educ:* Bishop Vesey's Grammar Sch., Sutton Coldfield; Birmingham Univ. (BA Hons). Rediffusion Ltd, 1965–74; Principal: Office of Fair Trading, 1974–76; Dept of Trade (Insurance Div.), 1976–79; First Sec., UK Perm. Representation, Brussels, 1979–82; Department of Trade and Industry: Asst Sec., Minerals and Metals Div., 1982–85; PPS to Sec. of State for Trade and Industry, 1985–86; Under Secretary: European Policy Div., 1986–87; Industrial Materials Market Div., 1987–89; Dep. Hd, European Secretariat, Cabinet Office, 1989–90; Dep. Dir Gen., DGIII, EC, 1990–93; Dir Gen., DGXV, subseq. DG Internal Mkt, EC, 1993–2003. Mem., H of L, 2008–19. Chairman: Eur. Regulators' Gp for Electricity and Gas, 2005–11; Internat. Confedn of Energy Regulators, 2009–15; Bd of Regulators, Agency for Co-operation of Regulators, 2010–17; Adv. Bd, EU Observatory on IP Infringements, 2012–16; Mem., Internat. Adv. Panel, Singapore, 2006–16; Mem. Adv. Council, 2012–16, Mem. Bd, 2016–, Electric Power Res. Inst. Pres., Council of Eur. Energy Regulators, 2005–17. Special Advr to Pres., Office for Harmonization in Internal Market, 2009–17. Chm., Govs, Univ. of Brighton, 2006–15; Gov., Brighton Coll., 2016– (Chm., 2017–). Trustee, Brighton Philharmonic Orch., 2006–12.

**MOGG, Rt Hon. Jacob William R.;** *see* Rees-Mogg.

**MOGGACH, Deborah,** OBE 2018; novelist, journalist and script-writer; *b* 28 June 1948; *d* of late Richard Alexander Hough, writer and of Helen Charlotte (*née* Woodyatt); *m* 1971, Anthony Austin Moggach (marr. diss. 1988); one *s* one *d*. *Educ:* Camden Sch. for Girls; Bristol Univ. (BA Hons English); Inst. of Educn, Univ. of London (BEd English). Mem., Exec. Cttee, English PEN, 1992–95; Chm., Soc. of Authors, 1999–2001 (Mem., Broadcasting Cttee, 1995–97, Mgt Cttee, 1998–2000). Television includes: Crown Court, 1983; To Have and to Hold, 1986; Stolen, 1990; Goggle Eyes (adaptation; Writers' Guild Award for Best Adapted Serial), 1993; Seesaw, 1998; Close Relations, 1998; Love in a Cold Climate (adaptation), 2001; Final Demand, 2003; Diary of Anne Frank, 2009; stage play, Double Take, Liverpool Playhouse, 1990, Chichester Fest. Theatre, 1993; film script, Pride and Prejudice (adaptation), 2005; screenplay, Tulip Fever, 2017. Young Journalist of the Year, Westminster Arts Council, 1975. FRSL 1998. Hon. DLitt Bristol, 2005. *Publications:* You Must Be Sisters, 1978; Close to Home, 1979; A Quiet Drink, 1980; Hot Water Man, 1982; Porky, 1983; To Have and To Hold, 1986; Smile and other stories, 1987; Driving in the Dark, 1988; Stolen, 1990; The Stand-In, 1991; The Ex-Wives, 1993; Changing Babies, 1995; Seesaw, 1996; Close Relations, 1997; Tulip Fever, 1999 (filmed, 2018); Final Demand, 2001; These Foolish Things, 2004 (filmed as The Best Exotic Marigold Hotel, 2012); In The Dark, 2007; Heartbreak Hotel, 2013; Something to Hide, 2015; The Carer, 2019. *Recreation:* walking around London looking into people's windows. *Address:* c/o Curtis Brown, 28–29 Haymarket, SW1Y 4SP. *T:* (020) 7396 6600.

**MOGGRIDGE, Harry Traherne, (Hal),** OBE 1986; PPLI; FCIHort; RIBA; Consultant, Colvin and Moggridge, Landscape Consultants (established 1922), since 1997 (Partner, 1969–97; Senior Partner, 1981–97); *b* London, 2 Feb. 1936; *s* of late Lt-Col Harry Weston Moggridge, CMG, and Helen Mary Ferrier Taylor; *m* 1963, Hon. Catherine Greville Herbert, *yr d* of 2nd Baron Hemingford; two *s* one *d*. *Educ:* Tonbridge Sch.; Architectural Assoc. (Dip.); evening lectures in landscape design under Prof. P. Youngman. RIBA 1962. Notts CC, 1960; Asst to Geoffrey Jellicoe, 1961–63; Site architect for Sir Wm Halcrow & Ptrs, Tema Harbour, Ghana, 1964–65; Landscape asst, GLC, 1966–67; own practice; entered into partnership with late Brenda Colvin, CBE, PPILA, 1969, continuing in partnership with Christopher Carter, ALI, and staff of fifteen. Prof. of Landscape Architecture, Univ. of Sheffield, 1984–86. Member: Royal Fine Art Commn, 1988–99; Nat. Trust Architectural Panel, 1991–2009. Mem., Landscape Inst., 1967 (Mem. Council, 1970–83; Hon. Sec., Vice Pres., Pres. 1979–81) and 1987–93 (Deleg. to Internat. Fedn of Landscape Architects, 1980–90 and 2002–06; Chm., Internat. Cttee, 1986–92); Chm., Landscape Foundn, 1995–99. Mem., ICOMOS-IFLA Internat. Cttee on Cultural Landscapes, 2000–; Mem., ICOMOS-UK Cultural Landscapes and Historic Gdns Cttee, 2003–; IFLA Rep., UNESCO Historic Urban Landscape Wkg Gp, 2006–09. Chm., Penllergare Trust, 2000–12. Landscape works include: Brenig Reservoir, Clwyd; White Horse Hill, a new car park and restoration of grass downland; Gale Common Hill, Yorkshire, woods and fields over 100 million cubic metres of waste ash and shale built over 60 years; quarries; countryside studies; reclamation; public and private gardens; restoration of historic parks (e.g. Blenheim, Knole, Castle Hill, Dinefwr, Aberglasney garden), creation of new parks and consultancy for Inner Royal Parks of London; master plans for RHS Wisley Gdns and for Welsh Nat. Botanic Gdns. FRSA. VMH 2000; President's Medal, Landscape Inst., 2002; Europa Nostra Medal, 2003. *Publications:* Slow Growth: on the art of landscape architecture, 2017; numerous articles and chapters of books describing works or

technical subjects. *Recreations:* looking at pictures, gardens, buildings, towns, landscapes and people in these places; walking, theatre, grandchildren. *Address:* Filkins, Lechlade, Glos GL7 3JQ. *T:* (01367) 860225. *Club:* Farmers.
*See also Lady Goodhart.*

**MOGRA, Shaykh Ibrahim;** Imam, Leicester, since 1990; Member, National Council, Muslim Council of Britain, since 2002; *b* Malawi, 9 Oct. 1965; *s* of Umar Mogra and Zubaydah Ibrahim; *m* 1990, Rayhanah Sulayman; four *s. Educ:* Darul-Ulum, Holcombe (Al-Alimiyyah 1990); Al-Azhar Univ., Cairo (Licentiate 1992); Sch. of Oriental and African Studies, Univ. of London (MA 1998). Dir and Principal, Khazinat al-Ilm, Madaris of Arabic and Muslim Life Studies, Leicester, 1994–. Mem., Religions for Peace UK, 2009– (Chm., 2009–15); Co-Chm., Christian Muslim Forum, 2011–; Member: Eur. Council of Religious Leaders, 2005–; Imams and Rabbis for Peace, 2005–; Niwano Peace Prize Cttee, Japan, 2008–15; World Faiths Adv. Gp, Univ. Leicester, 2010–. Faculty Mem., St George's Coll., Jerusalem, 2015–. Chaplain, Canary Wharf, 2013–; Chaplain and Mentor, Cambridge Muslim Coll., 2017–. Hon. DLitt De Montfort, 2016. *Recreations:* football, cricket, swimming, DIY, keeps tropical fish. *E:* ibrahimmogra@hotmail.com. *W:* www.twitter.com/IbrahimMogra.

**MOGREN, Dr Håkan Lars;** Deputy Chairman, AstraZeneca PLC, 1999–2009; *b* 17 Sept. 1944; *s* of late Ivan and Märta Mogren; *m* 1975, Anne Marie (*née* Hermansson); two *s. Educ:* Royal Inst. of Technol., Stockholm (DSc Biotechnol. 1969). President and Chief Executive Officer: AB Marabou (Sweden), 1977–88; Astra AB (Sweden), 1988–99. Chairman: Reckitt Benckiser plc, 2001–03; Affibody AB, 2002–05; Vice Chm., Gambro AB, 1996–2006; Director: Investor AB, 1990–2010; Norsk Hydro ASA, 2001–07; Groupe Danone SA, 2003; Mem. Supervisory Bd, Rémy-Cointreau SA, 2003–08. Chairman: Res. Inst. of Industrial Econs, Sweden, 1993–2003; Sweden-Japan Foundn, Sweden, 1998–2003 (Dir, 1991–); Sweden-America Foundn, Sweden, 2000–; British-Swedish Chamber of Commerce, Sweden, 2001–03; Dir, Marianne and Marcus Wallenberg Foundn, 1999–. Member: Swedish Gastronomic Acad., 1985–; Royal Swedish Acad. of Engrg Scis, 1988–. Hon. DSc Leicester, 1998. King's Medal with Ribbon, Order of Seraphims (Sweden), 1998; Chevalier, Légion d'Honneur (France), 1995; Order of Rising Sun (Japan), 2007.

**MOHAN, Dominic James;** Founder and Chief Executive Officer, Dominic Mohan Media, since 2018; *b* Bath, 26 May 1969; *s* of Michael and Deborah Mohan; *m* 1998, Michelle Knee; two *s* two *d. Educ:* Neale-Wade Sch., March; Univ. of Southampton (BA); Rutgers Univ., NJ. Reporter: Sunday Mirror, 1992–94; News of the World, 1994–95; The Sun: showbiz reporter, 1996–97; Dep. Ed., 1997–98, Ed., 1998–2003, showbiz; Asst Ed. and columnist, 2003–04; Associate Ed. (Features), 2004–07; Dep. Ed., 2007–09; Ed., 2009–13; Ed., The Sun on Sunday, 2012–13; Advr to Chief Exec., News Corp., 2013–15; Chief Exec., Outside Orgn, 2015–18; columnist, Bizarre, 1998–2003. DJ, Virgin Radio, 2002–04 (Sony Gold Radio Award, 2003). Hugh Cudlipp Award, BPA, 2005. *Recreations:* my four beautiful children, music, film, sport, Bristol City and Arsenal FC. *E:* dominicmohan@dominicmohanmedia.com. *Clubs:* Groucho, Soho House, Ten Trinity Square.

**MOHYEDDIN, Zia;** actor; President and Chief Executive Officer, National Academy of Performing Arts, Pakistan (Chairman, 2004); *b* 20 June 1931. *Educ:* Punjab University (BA Hons). Freelance directing for Aust. broadcasting, 1951–52; RADA, 1953–54; Pakistan stage appearances, 1956–59; UK stage, 1959–71; Dir Gen., Pakistan Nat. Performing Ensemble, to 1977; producer and dir, Central TV, 1980–94; *stage:* appearances include: A Passage to India, 1960; The Alchemist, 1964; The Merchant of Venice, 1966; Volpone, 1967; The Guide, 1968; On The Rocks, 1969; Measure for Measure, 1981; Film, Film, Film, 1986; *films:* Lawrence of Arabia, 1961; Sammy Going South, 1963; The Sailor from Gibraltar; Khartoum, 1965; Ashanti, 1982; Assam Garden, 1985; Immaculate Conception, 1992; The Odyssey; Doomsday Gun, 1993; L'Enfant des Rues, 1994; *television series:* The Hidden Truth, 1964; Gangsters, 1979; Jewel in the Crown, 1983; King of the Ghetto, 1986; Mountbatten, 1988; Shalom Salaam, 1989; creator, Family Pride, Channel Four, 1990. *Recreations:* reading, bridge, watching cricket. *Address:* c/o National Academy of Performing Arts, Old Hindu Gymkhana Building, M. R. Kiyani Road, Karachi, Pakistan. *Club:* Savile.

**MOHYUDDIN, David Niaz;** QC 2016; a Recorder, since 2019; *b* Lahore, 18 Sept. 1975; *s* of Iftikhar and Anne Mohyuddin; *m* 2013, Jane Ahern. *Educ:* Bolton Sch. (Boys' Div.); Univ. of Birmingham (LLB 1997); Inns of Court Sch. of Law. Called to the Bar, Lincoln's Inn, 1999; in practice as barrister, specialising in commercial law, Manchester, 2000–, London, 2009–; Mem., Attorney Gen.'s Panel of Jun. Counsel, 2007–16. Lead Advocacy Tutor, Lincoln's Inn, 2011–. Gov., Bolton Sch., 2012– (Vice-Chm., 2015–). *Recreations:* being outdoors, eating and drinking, taking photographs. *Address:* Exchange Chambers, 5th Floor, 201 Deansgate, Manchester M3 3NW. *T:* (0161) 833 2722. *E:* mohyuddinqc@exchangechambers.co.uk; Three Stone, 3 Stone Buildings, Lincoln's Inn, WC2A 3XL. *T:* (020) 7831 4445. *E:* dmohyuddin@threestone.law. *Club:* Manchester Tennis and Racquets.

**MOI, Daniel arap;** President of Kenya, 1978–2002; Minister of Defence, 1979–2002; *b* Rift Valley Province, 2 Sept. 1924. *Educ:* African Inland Mission Sch., Kabartonjo; Govt African Sch., Kapsabet. Teacher, 1946–56. MLC, 1957; Mem. for Baringo, House of Representatives, 1963–78; Minister for Educn, 1961; Minister for Local Govt, 1962–64; Minister for Home Affairs, 1964–67; Vice-Pres. of Kenya, 1967–78. Chm., Kenya African Democratic Union (KADU), 1960; Pres., Kenya African Nat. Union (KANU) for Rift Valley Province, 1966; Pres. of KANU, 1978–2003. Chm., Rift Valley Provincial Council. Former Member: Rift Valley Educn Bd; Kalenjin Language Cttee; Commonwealth Higher Educn Cttee; Kenya Meat Commn; Bd of Governors, African Girls' High Sch., Kikuyu. EGH, EBS. *Address:* c/o State House, PO Box 40530, Nairobi, Kenya.

**MOIR, Arthur Hastings;** Clerk to the Northern Ireland Assembly, 2001–07; *b* 18 Oct. 1948; *s* of Arthur Moir and Kathleen Moir (*née* Hastings); *m* 1987, Catherine Quinn; three *d. Educ:* Belfast Royal Acad.; Queen's Univ., Belfast (LLB Hons 1971). Admitted solicitor, 1974; Partner: Alex Stewart & Son Solicitors, 1978–84; McConnell and Moir Solicitors, 1984–88; Legal Advr, Land Registry of NI, 1988–93; Registrar of Titles and Land Purchase Trustee, 1993–2001; Chief Exec., Land Registers of NI, 1995–2001. Part-time legal consultant and expert witness, 2007–. Mem., Soc. of Expert Witnesses, 2009–. Chm., N Down CAB, 2011–14 (Vice Chair, 2016–19). *Publications:* The Land Registration Manual, 1994, 2nd edn 2005; Moir on Land Registration, 2011. *Recreations:* reading, writing, playing bridge, losing golf balls. *Address:* Lincoln Building, Great Victoria Street, Belfast BT2 7SL.

**MOIR, Sir Christopher Ernest,** 4th Bt *cr* 1916, of Whitehanger, Fernhurst, co. Sussex; *b* 22 May 1955; *e s* of Sir Ernest Ian Royds Moir, 3rd Bt and of Margaret Hanham, *d* of George Eric Carter; *S* father, 1998; *m* 1983, Mrs Vanessa Kirtikar, *yr d* of V. A. Crosby; twin *s,* and one step *d. Educ:* King's College Sch., Wimbledon. FCA 1976. *Heir: er s* Oliver Royds Moir, *b* 9 Oct. 1984. *Address:* Three Gates, 174 Coombe Lane West, Kingston upon Thames, Surrey KT2 7DE.

**MOIR, Dorothy Carnegie,** CBE 2003; MD; FRCP, FFPH; Hon. Clinical Senior Lecturer in Public Health, Aberdeen University, 2008–17; *b* 27 March 1942; *d* of Charles Carnegie Coull and Jessie Coull (*née* Ritchie); *m* 1970, Alexander David Moir; three *s. Educ:* Albyn Sch. for Girls, Aberdeen; Aberdeen Univ. (MB ChB 1965; MD 1970); Open Univ. (MBA 2000). FFPH (FFPHM 1988); FRCP 1996; FICS 2001. Resident Med. House Officer, Aberdeen Royal Infirmary, 1965–66; Resident Surg. House Officer, Royal Aberdeen Children's Hosp., 1966; Res. Fellow in Therapeutics, 1966–69, Lectr in Community Medicine, 1970–79, Univ. of Aberdeen; Community Medicine Specialist, Grampian Health Bd, 1979–88; Unit MO, Acute Services, Aberdeen Royal Infirmary, 1984–88; Director of Public Health and Chief Administrative Medical Officer: Forth Valley Health Bd, 1988–94; Lanarkshire Health Bd, 1994–2008; Hon. Consultant in Public Health Medicine, Grampian Health Bd, Aberdeen, 2008–13. Student of law, North East Scotland Coll., Aberdeen. *Publications:* (jtly) The Prescription and Administration of Drugs in Hospital: a programmed learning text, 1970, 3rd edn 1988; many articles in med. and pharmaceut. jls. *Address:* Medical School, Aberdeen University, Polwarth Building, Foresterhill, Aberdeen AB25 2ZD.

**MOIR, James William Charles,** CBE 2003; LVO 2002; Controller, BBC Radio 2, 1995–2003; *b* 5 Nov. 1941; *s* of William Charles Moir and Mary Margaret Moir (*née* Daly); *m* 1966, Julia (*née* Smalley); two *s* one *d. Educ:* Gunnersbury Catholic Grammar Sch.; Univ. of Nottingham (BA). Joined BBC TV Light Entertainment Group, 1963; Producer, Light Entertainment, 1970, Exec. Producer, 1979; Head of Variety, 1982–87; Head of Gp, 1987–93; Dep. Dir, Corporate Affairs, BBC, 1993–95. BBC Royal Liaison, 1992–2003. Chm., EBU Working Pty on Light Entertainment, 1992–94. Mem., Internat. Media Centre, Univ. of Salford, 2001–03. Trustee: Symphony Hall, Birmingham, 1996–2014; British Forces Foundn, 2014–. Hon. Mem. Council, NSPCC, 1990–. Hon. Pres., Students' Union, Univ. of Nottingham, 2002–05. FRTS 1990; Fellow, Radio Acad., 1998 (Outstanding Contrib. to Music Radio, 2001). Hon. DLitt Nottingham, 2004. Gold Badge of Merit, British Acad. Composers & Songwriters, 1993; Outstanding Contrib. to Broadcasting, BPG, 2002; Sandford St Martin Trust Radio Award for services to religious broadcasting, 2002. KSG 2004. *Address:* The Lawn, Elm Park Road, Pinner, Middx HA5 3LE. *Clubs:* Reform, Garrick.

**MOIR, Judith Patricia; Her Honour Judge Moir;** a Circuit Judge, since 1999; *b* 2 Dec. 1954; *d* of Norman and Stephanie Edwardson; *m* 1977, Charles Geoffrey Moir (marr. diss. 2002); two *s* one *d. Educ:* Central Newcastle High Sch.; Somerville Coll., Oxford (BA Jurisp.). Called to the Bar, Gray's Inn, 1978; in practice at the Bar, NE Circuit, 1978–99; Designated Family Judge, Northumbria and N Durham, 2000–14. *Recreation:* family. *Address:* Newcastle Combined Court Centre, Quayside, Newcastle upon Tyne NE1 3LA.

**MOIR, Rosalind Claire;** *see* Love, R. C.

**MOIR, Stephen Smeaton;** Executive Director of Resources, City of Edinburgh Council, since 2017; *b* Edinburgh, 27 Sept. 1973; *s* of Alexander Moir and Athene Moir; *m* 2016, Roy David McLennan. *Educ:* Edinburgh Napier Univ. (BSc Hons Biol Scis 1995); Heriot-Watt Univ. (MSc Personnel Mgt with IT 1996). FCIPD 2009; FCMI 2009. Personnel Asst, Lothian and Borders Police, 1996–98; Employee Resourcing Asst, Midlothian Council, 1998–99; Personnel Officer, Cambs Police, 1999–2000; Human Resources Manager, Lancashire Constabulary, 2000–03; Hd, Human Resources, South Tyneside Council, 2003–05; Corporate Dir, People, Policy and Law, Cambs CC, 2005–11; Dep. Chief Exec., Yorks Ambulance Service NHS Trust, 2011–13; Chief People Officer, NHS England, 2013–17. Lay Mem., Court, Edinburgh Napier Univ., 2018–. FRSA 2009. Hon. DPhil Middlesex, 2016. *Recreations:* reading, cinema, walking, family. *Address:* City of Edinburgh Council, 2.6 Business Centre, Waverley Court, 4 East Market Street, Edinburgh EH8 8BG. *T:* (0131) 529 4822. *E:* stephen.moir@edinburgh.gov.uk.

**MOIZER, Prof. Peter,** PhD; FCA; Professor of Accounting, since 1989, and Executive Dean, Business School, since 2008, University of Leeds; *b* Blackburn, 6 Oct. 1951; *s* of Albert and Kathleen Moizer; *m* 1989, Susan Hatch; two *s* one *d. Educ:* Queen Elizabeth Grammar Sch., Blackburn; Merton Coll., Oxford (MA); Univ. of Manchester (MA (Econ); PhD 2003). FCA 1979. Auditor, Price Waterhouse & Co., 1974–79; Lectr, 1979–88, Sen. Lectr, 1988–89, Manchester Univ. Reporting Mem., Competition Commn, 2001–09. Advr, Gtr Manchester Pension Fund, 1987–. Mem. Council, 2000–04, Sen. Moderator, 2003–, ICAEW. CCMI 2015. *Publications:* Governance and Auditing, 2005; contribs to jls. *Recreations:* ballet, opera, theatre, viola. *Address:* Leeds University Business School, University of Leeds, Leeds LS2 9JT. *T:* (0113) 343 4499. *E:* pm@lubs.leeds.ac.uk. *Club:* Penn.

**MOLE, Christopher David;** Chief Executive Officer, Eastern Savings and Loans Credit Union (formerly General Manager, Ipswich and Suffolk Credit Union), since 2011; *b* 16 March 1958; *m* 1996, Shona Gibb; two *s. Educ:* Dulwich Coll.; Univ. of Kent (BSc 1979). Technologist, Plessey Res., 1979–81; Res. Manager, BT Labs, Martlesham, 1981–98. Mem. (Lab) Suffolk CC, 1985–2001 (Leader of Council, 1993–2001); Mem., Gen. Assembly, LGA. Dep. Chm., E of England Develt Agency, 1998–2001. MP (Lab) Ipswich, Nov. 2001–2010; contested (Lab) same seat, 2010. PPS to Minister for Local Govt, 2005–06, 2007–08; an Asst Govt Whip, 2008–09; Parly Under-Sec. of State, DfT, 2009–10. Mem., Select Cttee, ODPM, 2003–05, on Sci. and Technol., 2007.

**MOLE, His Honour David Richard Penton;** QC 1990; a Circuit Judge, 2002–13; *b* 1 April 1943; *s* of late Rev. Arthur Penton Mole and Margaret Isobel Mole; *m* 1969, Anu-Reet (*née* Nigol); three *s* one *d. Educ:* St John's School, Leatherhead; Trinity College, Dublin (MA); LSE (LLM). City of London College, 1967–74 (Sen. Lectr, 1971); called to the Bar, Inner Temple, 1970; Standing Junior Counsel to Inland Revenue in rating valuation matters, 1984; a Recorder, 1995–2002; Jt Hd of Chambers, 2000–02; authorised to act as High Ct Judge in Admin Ct, 2004. Legal Mem., Lands Tribunal, 2006–09; a Judge of the Upper Tribunal (Lands Chamber), 2009–13, Dep. Judge of the Upper Tribunal, 2013–15; Mem., Parole Bd, 2003–13. Dir, Light Aircraft Assoc., 2016– (Co. Sec., 2017–; Vice-Chm., 2018–). Part-time cartoonist, 1979–83. *Publications:* contribs to Jl of Planning Law. *Recreations:* walking, drawing, painting, flying.
*See also S. G. Mole.*

**MOLE, Stuart Gordon,** CVO 2009; OBE 1984; Director-General, Royal Commonwealth Society, 2000–09; Senior Associate, Sarlsdown Associates, since 2009; *b* 15 Jan. 1949; *s* of late Rev. Arthur Penton Mole and Margaret Isobel Mole; *m* 1st, 1971 (marr. diss. 1977); 2nd, 1982, Katherine Madeleine Anthea Little (marr. diss. 1996); two *s,* partner, Helen Catherine Vines; one *d. Educ:* St Paul's Cathedral Choir Sch.; St John's Sch., Leatherhead (music schol.); Univ. of Nottingham (BA 1970); Hertford Coll., Oxford (PGCE 1971); Birkbeck Coll., Univ. of London (MSc 1974). Lectr, Chelmsford Coll., 1971–75; Parly Press Officer, Liberal Party, 1975–77; Dir, OUTSET youth and disability charity, 1977–80; Hd, Office of Leader of Liberal Party, 1980–83; political lobbyist and speechwriter, 1983–84; Commonwealth Secretariat: Special Asst to Sec.-Gen., 1984–90; Dir, Sec.-Gen's Office, 1990–2000. Sen. Res. Fellow, Inst. of Commonwealth Studies, Univ. of London, 2010–16 (Mem. Adv. Council, 2013–15). Mem. (Lib Dem), Chelmsford BC, 1972–87 (Chm., P & R Cttee, 1983–87). Contested: (L) Chelmsford, Feb. and Oct. 1974, 1979,

1983, 1987; (Lib Dem) N Essex and S Suffolk, European Parlt, 1994; (Lib Dem) E Devon, 2015. Hd, Leader's Gen. Election Campaign Tour, 1993. Dir and Mem. Editl Bd, The Round Table: Commonwealth Jl of Internat. Affairs, 1994– (Chm., 2011–17). Pres., Bath and Dist Royal Commonwealth Soc., 2009–. Hon. Fellow in Politics, 2009–12, doctoral res. student (pt-time), 2013–, Univ. of Exeter. Patron, Commonwealth Resounds, 2009–. *Recreations:* choral music, singing. *Address:* c/o Sarlsdown Associates, 5a Sarlsdown Road, Exmouth, Devon EX8 2HY. *Clubs:* Royal Over-Seas League; Bristol Commonwealth Society.
See also D. R. P. Mole.

**MOLESWORTH**, family name of Viscount Molesworth.

**MOLESWORTH**, 12th Viscount cr 1716 (Ire.); **Robert Bysse Kelham Molesworth**; Baron Philipstown 1716; businessman; *b* 4 June 1959; *s* of 11th Viscount Molesworth and Anne Florence (*née* Cohen; *d* 1983); S father, 1997. *Educ:* Cheltenham; Sussex Univ. (BA Philosophy). *Recreations:* ballroom dancing, travel, carpentry. *Heir: b* Hon. William John Charles Molesworth [*b* 20 Oct. 1960; *m* 2008, Natalia, *o d* of Vladimir Androsov; one *s* two *d*].

**MOLESWORTH, Allen Henry Neville;** management consultant; *b* 20 Aug. 1931; *s* of late Roger Bevil Molesworth (Colonel RA), and of Iris Alice Molesworth (*née* Kennion); *m* 1970, Gail Cheng Kwai Chan. *Educ:* Wellington Coll., Berks; Trinity Coll., Cambridge (MA). FCA. 2nd Lt, 4th Queen's Own Hussars, Malaya, 1950. Project Accounts, John Laing & Sons (Canada) Ltd, 1954–58; Singleton Fabian & Co., Chartered Accountants, 1959–63; Consultant: Standard Telephones & Cables Ltd, 1963–67; Coopers & Lybrand Associates Ltd, 1967–76: India, 1970; Kuwait, 1971; France, 1972; New Hebrides, 1972; Laos, 1974; Tonga, 1975; Financial and Admin. Controller, Crown Agents, 1976–84; Chief Accountant, British Telecom Property, 1984–90. *Recreations:* shooting, ski-ing, music, restoring antiques. *Address:* c/o Lloyds, PO Box 99 BX1 1LT. *Clubs:* 1900, Coningsby.

**MOLESWORTH-ST AUBYN, Sir William**, 16th Bt cr 1689, of Pencarrow, Cornwall; *b* 23 Nov. 1958; *s* of Sir Arscott Molesworth-St Aubyn, 15th Bt, MBE and of Iona Audrey Armatrude, *d* of Adm. Sir Francis Loftus Tottenham, KCB, CBE; S father, 1998; *m* 1988, Carolyn, *er d* of William Tozier; two *s* one *d*. *Educ:* Harrow. Late Captain, The Royal Green Jackets. *Heir: s* Archie Hender Molesworth-St Aubyn, *b* 27 March 1997.

**MOLINA, Prof. Mario Jose**, PhD; Professor, Department of Chemistry and Biochemistry, University of California, San Diego, since 2004; President, Mario Molina Center, Mexico City, since 2004; *b* 19 March 1943; *s* of Roberto Molina-Pasquel and Leonor Henriquez de Molina; *m* 2006, Guadalupe Alvarez. *Educ:* Univ. Nacional Autónoma de México (Ingeniero Químico 1965); Univ. of Calif, Berkeley (PhD 1972). Asst Prof., Univ. Nacional Autónoma de México, 1967–68; Res. Associate, Univ. of Calif, Berkeley, 1972–73; Res. Associate, 1973–74, Asst Prof., 1975–79, Associate Prof., 1979–82, Univ. of Calif, Irvine; Sen. Res. Scientist, Jet Propulsion Lab., Calif, 1983–89; Prof., Dept of Earth, Atmospheric and Planetary Scis and Dept of Chemistry, MIT, 1989–2004. Mem., US Nat. Acad. of Scis, 1993. Tyler Ecology and Energy Prize, USA, 1983; (jtly) Nobel Prize for Chemistry, 1995. *Publications:* articles in jls and chapters in books. *Recreations:* music, tennis. *Address:* Department of Chemistry and Biochemistry, University of California, San Diego, 9500 Gilman Drive MC 0356, La Jolla, CA 92093, USA.

**MØLLER, Dr Per Stig;** Commander, First Class, Order of Dannebrog (Denmark), 2002; MP (C) Gentofte, 1983–87, Frederiksberg, 1987–2015, Denmark; *b* 27 Aug. 1942; *s* of Poul and Lis Møller. *Educ:* Univ. of Copenhagen (MA Comparative Lit. 1967, PhD 1973). Cultural Ed., Radio Denmark, 1973–74; Lectr, Sorbonne, Paris, 1974–76; Dep. Hd, Culture and Society Dept, 1974 and 1976–79, Chief of Progs for Dir of Progs, 1979–84, Radio Denmark; Vice-Chm., 1985–86, Chm., 1986–87, Radio Council. Commentator, Berlingske Tidende, 1984–2001. Minister for the Envmt, 1990–93; Mem., Foreign Policy Cttee, 1994–2001; Chm., Security Policy Cttee, 1994–96; foreign policy spokesman, 1998–2001; Minister for Foreign Affairs, 2001–10; Minister for Culture, 2010–11. Mem., Council of Europe, 1987–90, 1994–97 and 1998–2001. Danish Conservative Party: Mem., Exec. Cttee, 1985–89 and 1993–98; Chm., 1997–98; Political Leader, Parly Party, 1997–98. Chm., Popular Educn Assoc., 1983–89. Georg Brandes Award, Soc. of Danish Lit. Critics, 1996; Einar Hansen Res. Fund Award, 1997; Cultural Award, Popular Educn Assoc., 1998; Raoul Wallenberg Medal, 1998; Kaj Munk Award, 2001; Rosenkjær Award, 2001; Robert Schuman Medal, 2003. Chevalier, Ordre National du Lion (Senegal), 1975; Grosskreuz des Verdienstordens (Germany), 2002; Comdr, Ordre National (Benin), 2003; Grand Cross, Order of Crown of Oak (Luxembourg), 2003; Gold Nersornaat (Greenland), 2005; Order of Stara Planina, 1st Cl. (Bulgaria), 2006; Comdr Grand Cross, Order of Polar Star (Sweden), 2007; Grand Cross, Order of South Cross (Brazil), 2007; Grand Cross of Comdr, Order for Merits to Lithuania, 2007. *Publications:* La Critique dramatique et littéraire de Malte-Brun, 1971; Malte-Bruns litterære Kritik og dens Plads i Transformationsprocessen, 1973; Erotismen, 1973; København-Paris t/r, 1973; På Sporet af det forsvundne Menneske, 1976; Livet i Gøgereden, 1978; Fra Tid til Anden, 1979; Tro, Håb og Fællesskab, 1980; Midt i Redeligheden, 1981; Orwells Håb og Frygt, 1983; Nat uden Daggry, 1985; (jtly) Mulighedernes Samfund, 1985; Stemmer fra Øst, 1987; Historien om Estland, Letland og Litauen, 1990; Kurs mod Katastrofer?, 1993; Miljøproblemer, 1995; Den naturlige Orden - Tolv år der flyttede Verden, 1996; Spor. Udvalgte Skrifter om det åbne Samfund og dets Værdier, 1997; Magt og Afmagt, 1999; Munk, 2000; Mere Munk, 2003; Samtale fremme forståelsen, 2010; Udenrigsminister - Erindringer, 2017.

**MOLLET, Richard James;** Head of European Government Affairs, RELX Group, since 2016; *b* Swansea, 9 Jan. 1970; *s* of Keith Mollet and Helen Mollet; *m* 2000, Nicola Laffan; three *s*. *Educ:* Olchfa Comp. Sch., Swansea; Worcester Coll., Oxford (BA Hons PPE 1992). Officer, RN, 1988–96; Account Dir, Ludgate Communications, 1996–2000; Dir, PPS Ltd, 2000–02; Associate Director: Fleishman-Hillard, 2002–05; Edelman, 2005–06; Dir, Public Affairs, BPI, 2006–10; Chief Exec., Publishers Assoc., 2010–16. Chair, Alliance for IP (formerly Alliance Against IP Theft), 2010–16 (Vice Chm., 2010–12). Member, Board: Book Industry Communications Ltd, 2010–16; Publishers' Licensing Soc., 2014–16; Copyright Licensing Agency., 2014–16. Chm. Trustees, World Book Day Ltd, 2011–16. Contested (Lab) Surrey SW, 2010. *Recreations:* song writing, performing music, football (playing and watching), snowboarding, tennis, chess, reading, literature, film, theatre. *Address:* Talbot Mead, Ballsdown, Chiddingfold, Surrey GU8 4XJ. *T:* 07778 660304. *E:* mollets@btinternet.com.

**MOLLON, Prof. John Dixon**, DSc; FRS 1999; Professor of Visual Neuroscience, University of Cambridge, 1998–2011; Fellow, since 1996, Director of Studies, Psychological and Behavioural Sciences, since 2013, and President, since 2013, Gonville and Caius College, Cambridge; *b* 12 Sept. 1944; *s* of Arthur Greenwood Mollon and Joyce Dorothy Mollon; *m* 2017, Dr Marina Danilova. *Educ:* Scarborough High Sch.; Hertford Coll., Oxford (BA 1966; DPhil 1970). Sen. Schol., Wadham Coll., Oxford, 1967–69; Postdoctoral Fellow, Bell Telephone Labs, NJ, 1970; Lectr in Psychology, Corpus Christi Coll., Oxford, 1971–72; University of Cambridge: Univ. Demonstrator, 1972–76; Lectr, 1976–93, Reader, 1993–98, in Exptl Psychology. Hon. Sec., Experimental Psychology Soc., 1974–78. President: Cambridge Philosophical Soc., 2012–13; International Colour Vision Soc., 2011–. Fellow, Optical Soc. of America, 1984. *Publications:* (with H. B. Barlow) The Senses, 1982; (with L. T. Sharpe) Colour Vision: physiology and psychophysics, 1983; (with J. Pokorny and K. Knoblauch) Normal and Defective Colour Vision, 2003. *Recreations:* collecting antiquarian books and oak and walnut furniture, historical research. *Address:* Gonville and Caius College, Cambridge CB2 1TA.

**MOLLOY, Francie;** MP (SF) Mid Ulster, since March 2013; *b* Derrymagowan, Co. Tyrone, 16 Dec. 1950; *m;* two *s* two *d*. *Educ:* St Patrick's Intermediate Sch., Dungannon; Newry Further Educn Coll. Apprentice fitter/welder, Felden Govt Trng Centre, Belfast; fitter/welder, Planet/Powerscreen, Ulster; full-time political activist, 1980; Dir of Elections for Bobby Sands, 1981. Mem. (SF) Dungannon and S Tyrone BC, 1985–89 and 1993 (Mayor, 2001–02 and 2005–06; Dep. Mayor, 2003–04). Mem. (SF) NI Assembly, 1998–2013. Chm., Finance and Personnel Cttee, 1999–2003, Dep. Speaker, 2006–07 and 2007–11, Principal Dep. Speaker, 2011–13, NI Assembly. Contested (SF) NI, EP, 1994. *Address:* c/o Sinn Féin, 55 Falls Road, Belfast BT12 4PD.

**MOLLOY, Michael John;** writer; *b* 22 Dec. 1940; *s* of John George and Margaret Ellen Molloy; *m* 1964, Sandra June Foley; three *d*. *Educ:* Ealing School of Art. Sunday Pictorial, 1956; Daily Sketch, 1960; Daily Mirror, 1962–85: Editor, Mirror Magazine, 1969; Asst Editor, 1970; Dep. Editor, 1975; Editor, Dec. 1975–1985; Editor, Sunday Mirror, 1986–88; Mirror Group Newspapers: Director, 1976–90; Editor in Chief, 1985–90. Exhibitions of paintings: Galerie Aalders, S France, 2001; Walton Gall., London, 2003. *Publications:* The Black Dwarf, 1985; The Kid from Riga, 1987; The Harlot of Jericho, 1989; The Century, 1990; The Gallery, 1991; Sweet Sixteen, 1992; Cat's Paw, 1993; Home Before Dark, 1994; Dogsbody, 1995; The Witch Trade, 2001; The Time Witches, 2002; Wild West Witches, 2003; The House on Falling Star Hill, 2004; Peter Raven Under Fire, 2005; Peter Raven and the Pirate Raid, 2015; The Happy Hack (memoir), 2016. *Recreations:* reading, writing, painting. *Club:* Savile.

**MOLONEY, His Honour Patrick Martin Joseph;** QC 1998; a Circuit Judge, 2007–18; Designated Civil Judge, East Anglia, 2009–18; *b* 2 July 1953; *s* of late Dr Eamon Moloney and Jean Moloney (*née* Handley); *m* 2003, Sarah Harrison; one step *s* two step *d*. *Educ:* Prior Park Coll., Bath; St Catherine's Coll., Oxford (Open Schol.; BA Hons Jurisp. 1973; BCL 1974). Vis. Asst Prof., Univ. of British Columbia, 1974–75; called to the Bar, Middle Temple, 1976 (Harmsworth Schol.; Bencher, 2006); in practice at the Bar, specialising in libel law, 1978–2007; a Recorder, 2000–07. Mem. Bar, NI, 1999. FRGS 2003. *Publications:* (contrib. jtly) Halsbury's Laws of England, 1997. *Recreation:* independent travel. *Club:* Reform.

**MOLONEY, Dr Timothy John;** QC 2010; *b* Ashton-under-Lyne, 10 Aug. 1965; *s* of James Moloney and Marie Moloney; *m* 1994, Tanya Burgess; one *s* one *d*. *Educ:* Loreto Sixth Form Coll., Manchester; Univ. of Birmingham (LLB Law and Politics 1987; PhD Law 1990). Lectr in Law, Univ. of Birmingham, 1990–92. Called to the Bar, Middle Temple, 1993; in practice as a barrister, 1994–. *Publications:* Rook and Ward on Sexual Offences, 3rd edn 2004, 4th edn 2010; (jtly) Blackstone's Guide to the Criminal Procedure Rules 2005, 2005, 2nd edn 2010; (contrib.) Blackstone's Criminal Practice, 2007–. *Recreations:* country walks, Benjamin Britten, Patrick Heron, The Fall, watching sport. *Address:* 54 Doughty Street, WC1N 2LS. *T:* (020) 7404 1313. *E:* t.moloney@doughtystreet.co.uk.

**MOLONY, Sir Peter John**, 4th Bt cr 1925, of the City of Dublin; *b* 17 Aug. 1937; *s* of Sir Joseph Molony, KCVO, QC and Carmen Mary Molony (*née* Dent, later Slay); S cousin, 2014; *m* 1964, Elizabeth Mary Chaytor; three *s* one *d* (and one *s* decd). *Heir: s* John Benjamin Molony [*b* 19 Oct. 1966; *m* 2002, Rosemary McGrath; one *s* one *d*].

**MOLYNEUX, Anne**, MBE 2015; **Her Honour Judge Molyneux;** a Circuit Judge, since 2007; *b* Southport, 12 Jan. 1959; *d* of Robert Molyneux and Audrey Molyneux (*née* Young); *m* 2006, George Jonathan Morris; one *s* one *d* by a previous marriage. *Educ:* Univ. of Sheffield (LLB Hons 1979); Chester Coll. of Law. Admitted solicitor, 1983; Recorder, 2000–07. Mem., 2003–07, Judicial Mem., 2010–, Parole Bd. Mem., Law Soc. *Recreations:* walking, reading (Mem., Ealing and Fulham Book Club), family. *Address:* Central Criminal Court, Old Bailey, EC4M 7EH. *E:* hhj.anne.molyneux@ejudiciary.net.

**MOLYNEUX, Prof. David Hurst**, DSc; Professor of Tropical Health Sciences, University of Liverpool, 1991–2008, now Emeritus, and Senior Professorial Fellow, 2008–16 (Director, Liverpool School of Tropical Medicine, 1991–2000, Hon. Professor, 2018); *b* 9 April 1943; *s* of Reginald Frank Molyneux and Monica Foden Molyneux; *m* 1969, Anita Elisabeth Bateson; one *s* one *d*. *Educ:* Denstone Coll.; Emmanuel Coll., Cambridge (BA 1965; PhD 1969; MA 1969; DSc 1992). FRSB (FIBiol 1984). Lectr, Dept of Parasitology, Liverpool Sch. of Tropical Medicine, 1968–77; seconded as Research Officer to Nigerian Inst. for Trypanosomiasis, Kaduna, 1970–72, as Project Manager to UNDP/WHO, Bobo Dioulasso, Burkina Faso, 1975–77; Prof. of Biology, Univ. of Salford, 1977–91. Dir, DFID/Glaxo SmithKline Lymphatic Filariasis Support Centre, 2000–08. Member: WHO Cttees incl. Onchocerciasis, Guinea worm, Parasitic Diseases; Internat. Commn on Disease Eradication, 2001–. Mem., Bd of Trustees, 1999–2008, Chm. Bd, 2005–08, Pres., 2005–07, JRS Biodiversity Foundn (formerly Biosis, subseq. JRS Foundn), Philadelphia. Trustee, Nat. Museums and Galls on Merseyside, 1995–2000. President: British Soc. of Parasitology, 1992; RSTM&H, 2007–09. Mem., Governing Body, Inst. of Animal Health, 2001–09. Hon. FRCP 2006. Hon. Fellow, Liverpool John Moores Univ., 2010. Hon. Internat. Fellow, American Soc. of Tropical Med., 2014. Hon. DSc: Georgetown, Washington, 2010; Health and Allied Scis, Ho, Ghana, 2019. Chalmers Medal, 1987, Manson Medal, 2013, RSTM&H; Wright Medal, British Soc. of Parasitology, 1989; McKay Medal, Amer. Soc. of Tropical Medicine, 2007; Kyelem Medal, Task Force for Global Health, 2017; Mary Kingsley Medal, Liverpool Sch. of Tropical Medicine, 2018. *Publications:* The Biology of Trypanosoma and Leishmania: parasites of man and domestic animals (with R. W. Ashford), 1983; (ed) Control of Human Parasitic Diseases, 2006; numerous contribs to professional jls. *Recreations:* golf, music, travel, primitive art. *Address:* Liverpool School of Tropical Medicine, Pembroke Place, Liverpool L3 5QA. *T:* (0151) 705 3291; Kingsley Cottage, Town Well, Kingsley, Cheshire WA6 8EZ. *T:* (01928) 788397. *Club:* Delamere Forest Golf (Captain, 2007–08).

**MOLYNEUX, Helena;** Chair, Practical Action, since 2013 (Trustee, since 2008); *b* 17 Aug. 1948; *d* of Joseph and Mary Molyneux. *Educ:* Manchester Univ. (BSc); Cranfield Inst. of Technol. (MBA). FCIPD (FIPD 1994). United Biscuits, 1969–73; Univ. of Sierra Leone, 1973–76; Bank of America: Personnel Manager, Bank of Amer. Internat., 1979–80; Divl Personnel Manager, NT & SA, San Francisco, 1980–82; Head, Employee Relns and Personnel Planning, Eur., ME and Africa Div., 1982–87; Bankers Trust Co.: Head, Employee Relns and Staffing, Eur., 1987–89; Dir, Corporate Personnel, Eur., 1989–93; Dir of Personnel, British Council, 1993–2000; Consultant: HelenaMolyneux Consulting, 2000–04; Telos Partners Ltd, 2004–12. Vice-Chm., 1997–2001, Chm., 2001–08, Progressio (formerly Catholic Inst. for Internat. Relations). *Recreations:* Dorset, international development.

**MOLYNEUX, Prof. Maxine Deirdre**, PhD; Professor of Sociology, University College London, since 2012 (Founding Director, Institute of the Americas, 2012–14); *b* Pakistan, 24 May 1948; *d* of Cyril James Molyneux and Sarah Jane Jamieson; *m* 1979, Prof. Fred Halliday, FBA (*d* 2010); one *s*. *Educ*: Walsingham House Sch., India; Northlands, Argentina; British Sch., Uruguay; Univ. of Essex (BA Hons Sociol. 1975; PhD Sociol. 1983). AIL 1967. Lectr in Sociol., Univ. of Essex, 1976–92; Lectr in Political Sociol., Birkbeck Coll., Univ. of London, 1992–94; School of Advanced Study, University of London: Lectr, 1994–96, Sen. Lectr, 1996–99, Prof. of Sociol., 2000–12, Inst. of Latin Amer. Studies, subseq. Inst. for the Study of the Americas; Dir, Inst. for the Study of the Americas, 2008–12. Member: HEFCE RAE Americas Panel, 2001; LAC Areas Panel, British Acad., 2008–; Scientific Council, GIS Institut des Amériques, Paris, 2010–; Adv. Panel, DFID-funded res. project on Social Accountability in Social Protection investigating five countries in Africa and Asia under contract to Development Pathways, 2016–; Chair: Standing Conf. UK Latin America and Caribbean Centres, 2008–16; Internat. Develt Policy Rev. Taskforce on Inequality Between and Within Countries, Labour Party, 2011–12; UK Res. Council Awards Panel, Newton-Picarte Fund, 2015. Member: Exec. Cttee, World Univ. Service, 1981–84; Exec. Cttee, Soc. of Latin American Studies, 2008–11; Exec. Cttee, Latin Amer. Studies Assoc., 2010–13; Adv. Cttee, Simon Bolivar Professorship in Latin American Studies, Cambridge Univ., 2013–16. Res. Dir, Transforming Cash Transfers project, DFID/ODI 5, 2012–13. Mem., Bd of Trustees, Canning House, 2008–14 (Associate Fellow, 2019–). Series Ed. and Man. Ed., Palgrave Studies of the Americas, 2008–; Founding Ed., UCL Press series, Modern Americas, 2018–. *Publications*: La Voz de la Mujer: Periódico Comunista-Anárquico, 1997, 2nd edn 2019; State Policies and the Position of Women in Democratic Yemen, 1982; (with Fred Halliday) The Ethiopian Revolution, 1982; (ed with E. Dore) The Hidden Histories of Gender and the State in Latin America, 2000; (ed with N. Craske) Gender and the Politics of Rights and Democracy in Latin America, 2002; Women's Movements in International Perspective, 2000 (Movimientos de Mujeres en América Latina: Estudio Comparativa y Teórico, 2003); (with Sian Lazar) Doing the Rights Thing: rights-based development and Latin American NGOs in Latin America, 2003; (ed with S. Razavi) Gender Justice, Development and Rights, 2003; (ed with Andrea Cornwall) The Politics of Rights: dilemmas for feminist praxis, 2007; (ed with N. Jones and F. Samuels) Can Cash Transfers Have Transformative Effects?, 2017. *Recreations*: music, art, travel, good food. *Address*: 17 Onslow Gardens, N10 3JT.

**MOLYNEUX, Peter Douglas**, OBE 2005; designer, producer and programmer of computer games; Creative Director, 22 Cans Ltd, since 2012; *b* 5 May 1959; *s* of George and Myrna Molyneux; *m* 2007, Emma Margaret Douglas; one *s*. *Educ*: Bearwood Coll., Wokingham; Farnborough Tech. Coll.; Southampton Univ. (BSc Computer Scis). Co-founder, Bullfrog Prodns, Guildford, 1987; Co-founder and Man. Dir, Lionhead Studios, 1997–2012; designer and programmer: Populous, 1989; Powermonger, 1990; Populous 2, 1991; Black & White, 2001; designer and producer: Syndicate, 1993; (and programmer) Theme Park, 1994; Magic Carpet, 1994; (and programmer) Dungeon Keeper, 1997; designer: Fable, 2004; Fable: The Lost Chapters, 2005; Black & White 2, 2005; The Movies, 2005; Black & White: Battle of the Gods, 2006; Fable 2, 2008; Fable 3, 2010; Curiosity, 2012; Godus, 2013. Fellow, BAFTA, 2011. Hon. DTech: Abertay Dundee, 2003; Bournemouth, 2005; Southampton, 2007; DUniv Surrey, 2007. Chevalier, Order of Arts and Letters (France), 2007. *Recreation*: playing poker and board games. *Address*: 22 Cans, 6 Stirling House, Stirling Road, Surrey Research Park, Guildford GU2 7RF. *T*: (01483) 484962. *E*: pmolyneux@22cans.com. *W*: www.twitter.com/pmolyneux.

**MOMTAZ, Sam**; QC 2017; *b* Tehran, 1 Dec. 1971; *s* of Tofigh Momtaz and Parvaneh Emami. *Educ*: Hendon Sch.; Queen Mary and Westfield Coll., Univ. of London (LLB Hons). Called to the Bar, Lincoln's Inn, 1995; in practice as barrister, specialising in family law, esp. children's cases. *Recreations*: football, supporter of Liverpool FC. *Address*: 1GC | Family Law, 10 Lincoln's Inn Fields, WC2A 3BP. *T*: (020) 7797 7900, *Fax*: (020) 7797 7929. *E*: momtaz@1gc.com.

**MONAGHAN, Carol**; MP (SNP) Glasgow North West, since 2015; *b* Glasgow, 2 Aug. 1972; *d* of Robert Monaghan and Margaret Monaghan (*née* Monaghan); *m* 2006, Feargal Dalton; one *s* two *d*. *Educ*: Univ. of Strathclyde (BSc Hons Laser Physics and Optoelectronics 1993); St Andrew's Coll. of Educn (PGCE Physics and Maths). Teacher, Glasgow schs; Hd of Physics, Hyndland Secondary Sch., 2000–04; Lectr in Educn, Univ. of Glasgow, 2004–06; Hd of Sci., Hyndland Secondary Sch., 2006–14. Consultant, Scottish Qualifications Authy, 2010–14. Mem., Sci. and Technol. Select Cttee, 2015–. *Address*: House of Commons, SW1A 0AA.

**MONAGHAN, Charles Edward**, CA; Chairman, Aegon UK, 1999–2005; President, Institute of Chartered Accountants of Scotland, 1999–2000; *b* 20 June 1940; *s* of Charles Monaghan and Elspeth Margaret Monaghan; *m* 1971, Dorothy Evelyn Hince; one *s*. *Educ*: Loretto Sch.; Edinburgh Univ. (BSc). CA 1965. Unilever, 1965–98: Ops Mem., E Asia Pacific, 1991–95; Head, Exec. Cttee Secretariat, 1996–98; Dir, Scottish Equitable, 1995. *Recreations*: tennis, golf, gardening. *Address*: 10 Wool Road, Wimbledon, SW20 0HW. *T*: (020) 8946 8825. *Clubs*: Caledonian, Wimbledon; Royal Wimbledon Golf.

**MONAGHAN, Emma Victoria**; *see* Morgan, E. V.

**MONAGHAN, Karon**; QC 2008; *b* London, 21 June 1963. *Educ*: Ealing Coll. of Higher Educn (LLB). Called to the Bar, Inner Temple, 1989; in practice as barrister specialising in equality law. *Publications*: Equality Law, 2007, 2nd edn 2013. *Address*: Matrix Chambers, Griffin Building, Gray's Inn, WC1R 5LN.

**MONAGHAN, Dr Paul William**; *b* Montrose, 1965; *s* of William Monaghan and Margaret Monaghan (*née* Innes); partner, Stephanie Anderson; one *d*. *Educ*: Inverness Royal Acad.; Univ. of Stirling (BA Hons 1st Psychol. and Sociol.; PhD Social Policy 2004). MBPsS 1999. Hd, Planning and Develt, Northern Constabulary, 2003–08; Dir and Gen. Manager, Highland Homeless Trust, 2008–15. MP (SNP) Caithness, Sutherland and Easter Ross, 2015–17; contested (SNP) same seat, 2017. Mem., Select Cttee on Envmt, Food and Rural Affairs, 2015–17, on Eur. Scrutiny, 2016–17. FInstLM 2007. *Recreations*: travel, cycling.

**MONAHAN, Erwin James, (Erwin James)**; author; columnist and contributor, Guardian, since 1998; Editor-in-Chief, Inside Time, since 2016; *b* Clevedon, 18 April 1957; *s* of Erwin James Monahan and Jeanie Monahan; two *d*. *Educ*: Ilkley Grammar Sch.; Open Univ. (Dip. Eur. Hum.; BA; MUniv). Drifter, criminal, 1972–82; fugitive in French Foreign Legion, 1982–84; life prisoner, 1984–2004. Develt Manager, Prisoners' Advice Service, 2004–06. Mem., Bd, Unlocked, 2017–. Trustee: Prison Reform Trust, 2005–19; Alternatives to Violence Project Britain, 2009–11; Turnkey Trust, 2012–13; Koestler Trust, 2017–18. Patron: Create, 2007–; Blue Sky, 2008–; Reader Orgn, 2012–; Writers in Prison Foundn, 2012–; Human Writes, 2014–; Prison Phoenix Trust, 2015–. FRSA. *Publications*: (as Erwin James) A Life Inside: a prisoner's notebook, 2003; The Home Stretch: from prison to parole, 2005; (contrib.) Humane Prisons, 2006; Redeemable: a memoir of darkness and hope, 2016. *Address*: c/o DGA, 55 Monmouth Street, WC2H 9DG. *T*: 07828 421707. *E*: erwin.james@theguardian.com.

**MONBIOT, George Joshua**; freelance author and journalist, since 1987; columnist, The Guardian, since 1995; Founder, Rewilding Britain, 2015; *b* 27 Jan. 1963; *s* of Raymond Geoffrey Monbiot, *qv*. *Educ*: Brasenose Coll., Oxford (BA, MA Zool.). BBC radio producer, 1985–87. Vis. Fellow, Green Coll., Oxford, 1993–95; Visiting Professor: Univ. of E London, 1997–99; Univ. of Bristol, 1999; Hon. Professor: Univ. of Keele, 1999–2000; Oxford Brookes Univ., 2003–. Hon. Fellow, Univ. of Cardiff, 2007. DU Essex, 2007. Sony Award for Radio Production, 1987; Lloyds Nat. Screenwriters Award, 1987; Sir Peter Kent Award, 1991; UN Global 500 Award, 1995; OneWorld Trust Media Award, 1996; Thomson Reuters Zoological Record Award, ZSL, 2013. Writer (with Ewan McLennan), album, Breaking the Spell of Loneliness, 2016. *Publications*: Poisoned Arrows, 1989, 2nd edn 2003; Amazon Watershed, 1991; No Man's Land, 1994, 2nd edn 2003; Captive State, 2000, 2nd edn 2001; The Age of Consent, 2003, 2nd edn 2004; Heat, 2006; Bring on the Apocalypse: six arguments for global justice, 2008; Feral: searching for enchantment on the frontiers of rewilding, 2013 (Best Gen. Biology Book, Soc. of Biol. Book Awards, 2014; Nonfiction Award, Orion Book Awards, 2015); Out of the Wreckage: a new politics for an age of crisis, 2017. *Recreations*: natural history, kayaking, ultimate frisbee, apple growing, gardening, cooking, conversation. *Address*: Y Goeden Eirin, Newtown Road, Machynlleth SY20 8EY. *T*: (01654) 702758. *E*: george@monbiot.com.

**MONBIOT, Raymond Geoffrey**, CBE 1994 (MBE 1981); Deputy Chairman, Conservative Party, 2003–06; Chairman, Rotherfield Management Ltd, 1988–2011; *b* 1 Sept. 1937; *s* of Maurice and Ruth Monbiot; *m* 1961, Rosalie Vivien Gresham (*née* Cooke), OBE; one *s* one *d* (and one *d* decd). *Educ*: Westminster Sch.; London Business Sch. From pastry chef to Man. Dir of three subsids, J. Lyons & Co. Ltd, 1956–78; Man. Dir, Associated Biscuits, 1978–82; Chm., Campbell's Soups UK, 1982–88. Chm., Nat. Cons. Convention, 2003–06; Chm., Finance Cttee, 2004–06, Treas., Regl Develt, 2007–11, Cons. Party. Chm., Northants and Berks, Duke of Edinburgh Award Industrial Projects, 1976–86. Fellow, Mktg Soc. Freeman, City of London; Liveryman, Butchers' Co. David Ogilvy Award for Mktg, Campbell's Soups UK, 1985. *Publications*: How to Manage Your Boss, 1981; The Burnhams Book of Characters, 2002; The Characters of North Norfolk, 2003; More Characters of North Norfolk, 2006; Retirement is for Younger People, 2012; Characters of Fakenham, 2016; More Characters of Fakenham, 2016. *Recreations*: gardening, cooking, writing, growing heritage apples. *Address*: Eastgate House, Burnham Market, Norfolk PE31 8HH. *T*: (01328) 730928. *E*: rotherfieldmgmnt@btconnect.com. *Club*: Farmers.

*See also* G. J. Monbiot.

**MONCADA, Sir Salvador**, Kt 2010; FRCP, FMedSci; FRS 1988; Professor of Cancer Sciences and Research Domain Director, Cancer, University of Manchester, since 2016; Director, 1996–2011, and Professor Emeritus of Experimental Biology and Therapeutics, 2013, Wolfson Institute for Biomedical Research (formerly Institute for Strategic Medical Research (Cruciform Project)), University College London; *b* 3 Dec. 1944; *s* of Dr Salvador Eduardo Moncada and Jenny Seidner; *m* 1st, 1966; one *d*; 2nd, 1998, HRH Princess Esmeralda of Belgium; one *s* one *d*. *Educ*: Univ. of El Salvador (DMS 1970); London Univ. (DPhil 1973; DSc 1983). FRCP 1994. GP, Social Service of El Salvador, 1969; Associate Prof. of Pharmacol. and Physiol., Univ. of Honduras, 1974–75; Wellcome Research Laboratories, 1971–73 and 1975–95: Sen. Scientist, 1975–77; Hd of Dept of Prostaglandin Res., 1977–85; Dir, Therapeutic Res. Div., 1984–86; Dir of Res., Wellcome Foundn, 1986–95. University of Manchester: Prof. of Translational Medicine and Strategic Advr, Centre for Cellular Metabolism, Inst. of Human Develt, 2013; Dir, Inst. of Cancer Scis. Croonian Lect., Royal Soc., 2005. Mem., British Pharmacol Soc., 1974 (Hon. Fellow, 2012). Founder FMedSci 1998. Associate Fellow, Third World Acad. of Sciences, 1988; For. Associate, Nat. Acad. of Scis, USA, 1994. Dr *hc*: Univ. of Complutense de Madrid, 1986; Univ. of Honduras, 1987; Univ. of Cantabria, 1988; Hon. DSc: Sussex, 1994; Mt Sinai Sch. of Medicine, NY, 1995; Nottingham, 1995; Univ. Pierre & Marie Curie, Paris, 1997. Peter Debeye Prize (jtly), Limburg Univ., 1980; Prince of Asturias Prize for Science and Technology, 1990; Royal Medal, Royal Soc., 1994; Amsterdam Prize for Medicine, 1997; Ernst Jung Gold Medal for Medicine, Jung Foundn for Sci. and Res., Germany, 2013. *Publications*: (Scientific Ed.) British Medical Bulletin, 39 pt 3: Prostacyclin, Thromboxane and Leukotrienes, 1983; Nitric oxide from L-arginine: a bioregulatory system, 1990; (ed jtly) The Biology of Nitric Oxide, pts 3 and 4, 1994, pt 5, 1996, pt 6, 1998, pt 7, 2000; (ed jtly) Nitric Oxide and the Vascular Endothelium, 2006. *Recreations*: music, literature, theatre. *Address*: Manchester Cancer Research Centre, University of Manchester, Wilmslow Road, Manchester M20 4QL.

**MONCASTER, John Anthony**; Master of the Senior (formerly Supreme) Court, Chancery Division, 1992–2011; *b* Louth, Lincs, 15 Oct. 1939; *oc* of Jack Moncaster and Muriel (*née* Butterick); *m* 1966, Gillian Ann, *o d* of Rev. Royston York; two *s* two *d*. Called to the Bar, Gray's Inn, 1961; practised at Chancery Bar. *Recreation*: books. *Address*: 24 Minster Yard, Lincoln LN2 1PY.

**MONCK**, family name of **Viscount Monck**.

**MONCK, 7th Viscount** *cr* 1801; **Charles Stanley Monck**; *S* father, 1982 but does not use the title. *Heir*: *b* Hon. George Stanley Monck.

**MONCK, Elizabeth Mary, (Lady Monck)**, PhD; Senior Research Officer, Thomas Coram Research Unit, Institute of Education, 1997–2008; *b* 7 Aug. 1934; *d* of Geoffrey Dugdale Kirwan and Molly Kirwan (*née* Morrow); *m* 1960, Sir Nicholas Jeremy Monck, KCB (*d* 2013); three *s*. *Educ*: Godolphin Sch., Salisbury; Newnham Coll., Cambridge (MA); UCL (PhD 1996). MRC Social Psychiatry Res. Unit, Inst. Psychiatry, 1957–62; EIU, 1969–73; Research Officer: Centre for Envmtl Studies, 1974–80; Acad. Dept Child Psychiatry, Inst. Child Health, 1980–95; Associate, Newnham Coll., Cambridge, 1997–2003; Hon. Associate, 2011. Mem., ILEA, 1986–90. Mem., 1990–93, Chm., 1993–97, Regl Customer Service Cttee (Thames), OFWAT; Ind. Mem., Cttee on Chemicals and Materials in Public Water Supply, Drinking Water Inspectorate, 1998–2001; Reporting Mem., Competition Commn, 1999–2004. Trustee: National Gall., 1993–99; Family Rights Group, 2005–15; National Gall. Trust, 2009–. *Publications*: books include: (with R. Dobbs) The Great Ormond Street Adolescent Life Events Dictionary of Contextual Threat Ratings, 1985; (ed and contrib.) Emotional and Behavioural Problems in Adolescents: a multi-disciplinary approach to identification and management, 1988; (with A. Kelly) Managing Effective Schools, 1992; (with V. Wigfall and J. Reynolds) The Role of Concurrent Planning: making permanent placements for young children; (with A. Rushton) Enhancing Adoptive Parenting: a test of effectiveness. *Recreations*: walking, gardening, listening to music, painting, travel.

**MONCKTON**, family name of **Viscounts Galway** and **Monckton of Brenchley**.

**MONCKTON OF BRENCHLEY, 3rd Viscount** *cr* 1957; **Christopher Walter Monckton**; Director: Christopher Monckton Ltd, consultants, 1987–2006; Monckton Enterprises Ltd, since 2009; *b* 14 Feb. 1952; *s* of 2nd Viscount Monckton of Brenchley, CB, OBE, MC and Marianna Laetitia (*née* Bower); *S* father, 2006; *m* 1990, Juliet Mary Anne, *y d* of Jørgen Malherbe Jensen. *Educ*: Harrow; Churchill Coll., Cambridge (BA 1973, MA 1977); University Coll., Cardiff; Dip. Journalism Studies (Wales), 1974. Standing Cttee,

Cambridge Union Soc., 1973; Treas., Cambridge Univ. Conservative Assoc., 1973. Reporter, Yorkshire Post, 1974–75, Leader-Writer, 1975–77; Press Officer, Conservative Central Office, 1977–78; Editor-designate, The Universe, 1978, Editor, 1979–81; Managing Editor, Telegraph Sunday Magazine, 1981–82; Leader-Writer, The Standard, 1982; Special Advr to Prime Minister's Policy Unit, 1982–86; Asst Editor, Today, 1986–87; Consulting Editor, 1987–92, Chief Leader-Writer, 1990–92, Evening Standard. Chief Policy Advr, Sci. and Public Policy Inst., Washington DC, 2007–. Dep. Leader, 2010, Hd of Policy, 2011, Leader, Scotland, 2012–13, UKIP. Freeman, City of London, and Liveryman, Worshipful Co. of Broderers, 1973–. Member: Internat. MENSA Ltd, 1975–; St John Amb. Brigade (Wetherby Div.), 1976–77; Hon. Soc. of the Middle Temple, 1979–; RC Mass Media Commn, 1979–; Sec. to Econ., Forward Strategy, Health, and Employment Study Gps, Centre For Policy Studies, 1980–82. Visiting Lecturer: in Business Studies, Columbia Univ., NY, 1980; St Andrews Univ., 1996; Hartford Univ., 2008, 2012; Rochester Univ., 2008; Prague Sch. of Econs, 2011; Princeton Univ., 2012; Nerenberg Lectr in Math., Univ. of W Ontario, 2012. Expert Reviewer, Intergovtl Panel on Climate Change, 2013; Non-Intergovtl Panel on Climate Change, 2014. Trustee, Hales Trophy for Blue Riband of Atlantic, 1986–. Gov., London Oratory Sch., 1991–96. Editor, Not the Church Times, 1982. Kt SMO, Malta, 1973; OStJ 1973. DL Greater London, 1988–96. Intelligence Medal, Army of Colombia, 2013. *Publications:* The Laker Story (with Ivan Fallon), 1982; Anglican Orders: null and void?, 1986; The Aids Report, 1987; Sudoku X, 2005; Sudoku X-mas, 2005; Sudoku Xpert, 2005; Junior Sudoku X, 2005; Sudoku Xtreme, 2005; (contrib.) Evidence-Based Climate Science, 2011; contrib. articles in Physics and Society, Jl of Chartered Insce Inst. of London, Annual Procs of Seminars on Planetary Emergencies, Energy & Envmt, Coordinates Jl of Marine Navigation, Chinese Sci. Bulletin. *Recreation:* romance. *Heir: b* Hon. Timothy David Robert Monckton [*b* 15 Aug. 1955; *m* 1984, Jennifer Carmody; three *s*]. *T:* 07814 556423. *E:* monckton@mail.com. *Clubs:* Brooks's, Beefsteak, Pratt's.
*See also* Hon. R. M. *Monckton.*

**MONCKTON, Hon. Rosa(mond) Mary, (Hon. Mrs Dominic Lawson),** MBE 2017; Chairman, Asprey & Garrard UK Ltd, 2002–05 (Chief Executive, 2000–02); Co-Founder, Campaign for Learning Disabled, 2014; Founder and Trustee, since 2016, and Chairman, since 2017, Team Domenica; *b* 26 Oct. 1953; *d* of 2nd Viscount Monckton of Brenchley, CB, OBE, MC; *m* 1991, Hon. Dominic Ralph Campden Lawson, *qv*; two *d. Educ:* Ursuline Convent, Tildonk, Belgium. Asst Man. Dir, Cartier, London, 1979; Sales and Exhibn Manager, Tabbah Jewellers, Monte Carlo, 1980; Promotions Manager, Asprey, 1982–85; Man. Dir, 1986–97, Pres., 1997–2000, Tiffany, London. Non-exec. Dir, Watches of Switzerland Gp (formerly Aurum Hldgs Ltd), 2014–. Chm., KIDS, 1999–2004 (Pres., 2004–); Mem., Diana, Princess of Wales Meml Cttee, 1997–2004 (Chm., Fountain Design Cttee, 2001–02). Presenter of TV documentaries including: When a Mother's Love is not Enough, 2008; Tormented Lives, 2010; Letting Go, 2012. Liveryman, Goldsmiths' Co., 2000–. *Address:* Cox's Mill, Dallington, Heathfield, E Sussex TN21 9JG.

**MONCREIFF,** family name of **Baron Moncreiff.**

**MONCREIFF,** 6th Baron *cr* 1873, of Tulliebole, co. Kinross; **Rhoderick Harry Wellwood Moncreiff**; Bt (NS) 1626, (UK) 1871; *b* 22 March 1954; *o s* of 5th Baron Moncreiff and Enid Marion Watson (*née* Locke); *S* father, 2002; *m* 1982, Alison Elizabeth Anne, *d* of J. D. A. Ross; two *s*. *Heir: s* Hon. Harry James Wellwood Moncreiff, *b* 12 Aug. 1986.

**MONCREIFFE of that Ilk, Hon. Peregrine David Euan Malcolm;** *b* 16 Feb. 1951; *s* of Sir Iain Moncreiffe of that Ilk, 11th Bt, CVO, DL, QC (Scot.) and Countess of Erroll, 23rd in line; *m* 1988, Miranda Fox-Pitt; two *s* four *d*. *Educ:* Eton; Christ Church, Oxford (MA Modern Hist.). Lieut, Atholl Highlanders, 1978. Investment banker: with White Weld & Co. Ltd/Credit Suisse First Boston Ltd, 1972–82; Lehman Brothers Kuhn Loeb/ Shearson Lehman, 1982–86; E. F. Hutton & Co., 1986–88; Chief Exec., Buchanan Partners Ltd, 1990–99. Mem., Royal Commn on Ancient and Historical Monuments of Scotland, 1989–94. Chm., Scottish Ballet, 1988–90. Trustee, Save the Rhino, 1991–2000. Mem., Royal Co. of Archers (Queen's Body Guard for Scotland), 1979–. Freeman, City of London; Liveryman, Co. of Fishmongers, 1987–. Knight of Honour and Devotion, Sovereign Order of St John of Jerusalem, 2001. *Address:* Highfield Place, La Pouqelaye, St Helier, Jersey JE2 3GG. *Clubs:* White's, Turf, Pratt's; New (Edinburgh); Leander (Henley); Brook (New York).
*See also* Earl of *Erroll.*

**MONCRIEFF, Rear Adm. Ian,** CBE 2010; DL; Chief Executive, United Kingdom Hydrographic Office, 2011–15 (National Hydrographer, 2006–10; Chief Operating Officer, 2010–11); *b* 5 Jan. 1955; *s* of Donald and Ellen Moncrieff; *m* 1986, Marion McLennan; two *s. Educ:* Kirkham High Sch.; Preston VI Form Coll.; Univ. of Keele (BA Hons Geog. and Geol. 1977); BRNC Dartmouth. Served in HM Ships Sheffield, Arrow, Yarnton and Nottingham, 1978–85; qualified as Principal Warfare Officer and specialist in communications, 1985; Principal Warfare Officer, HMS Glasgow, 1986; i/c new entry radio operator trng, HMS Mercury, 1986–88; Royal Cypher Officer and Flag Lieut, HMY Britannia, 1988–90; Desk Officer, Directorate of Naval Plans and Progs, MoD, 1990–92; CO, HMS Nottingham, 1992–94; DACOS Policy and Progs to C-in-C Fleet, 1994–97; Comdr, HMS Invincible, 1997–98; Captain 1998; CSO Plans and Policy to CGRM, 1998–2001; CO, HMS Endurance, 2001–03; Cdre 2003; Dir, Navy Communications and Inf. Systems, 2003–04; hcsc 2005; Comdr British Forces South Atlantic, 2005–06; Rear Adm., 2006; retd 2010. Non-exec. Dir and Marine Mem. Bd, PLA, 2015–. Mem., British Antarctic Survey/NERC Operational and Safety Advice Panel, 2016–. Mem. Council, RNLI, 2007–13. Mem., Hon. Co. of Master Mariners, 2000–. Younger Brother, Trinity House, 2007–. MInstD 1996. Cert. Co. Direction, IoD, 2011. Trustee, Falklands Conservation, 2010–. Gov., Taunton Sch., 2016–. DL Somerset, 2014. *Recreations:* wildlife photography, fly fishing. *Address:* Port of London Authority, London River House, Royal Pier Road, Gravesend, Kent DA12 2BG. *Clubs:* Naval and Military, Antarctic.

**MONCRIEFF, Lucy Ann S.;** *see* Scott-Moncrieff.

**MONCRIEFF, Dame Suzanne Elizabeth, (Dame Suzie),** DNZM 2012 (ONZM 1998); sculptor; Founder and Director, World of WearableArt Ltd, since 1987; *b* Ashburton, NZ, 7 June 1949; *d* of John Dick and Dorothy Dick; one *d. Educ:* Waimea Coll. (Sch. Cert.); Univ. Entrance English. Hon. DFA Massey, NZ, 2014. *Address:* World of WearableArt Ltd, 95 Quarantine Road, Annesbrook, Nelson 7011, New Zealand.

**MONDALE, Walter Frederick;** American Ambassador to Japan, 1993–96; *b* Ceylon, Minnesota, 5 Jan. 1928; *s* of Rev. Theodore Sigvaard Mondale and Claribel Hope (*née* Cowan); *m* 1955, Joan Adams (*d* 2014); two *s* (one *d* decd). *Educ:* public schs, Minnesota; Macalester Coll., Univ. of Minnesota (BA *cum laude*); Univ. of Minnesota Law Sch. (LLB). Served with Army, 1951–53. Admitted to Minn. Bar, 1956; private law practice, Minneapolis, 1956–60; Attorney-Gen., Minnesota, 1960–65; Senator from Minnesota, 1965–76; Vice-Pres., USA, 1977–81; Counsel with Winston & Strawn, 1981–87; Partner with Dorsey & Whitney, 1987–93. Democratic Candidate for Vice-Pres., USA, 1976, 1980; Democratic Candidate for Pres., USA, 1984. Chm., Nat. Democratic Inst. for Internat. Affairs, 1987–93. Mem., Democratic Farm Labor Party. *Publications:* The Accountability of Power, 1975; The Good Fight: a life in liberal politics, 2010. *Address:* c/o Dorsey & Whitney LLP, # 1500, 50 South 6th Street, Minneapolis, MN 55402–1498, USA.

**MONDS, Prof. Fabian Charles,** CBE 1997; PhD; Professor of Information Systems, 1987–2000, now Emeritus, and Pro-Vice-Chancellor (Planning), 1993–2000, University of Ulster; Chairman, Northern Ireland Centre for Trauma and Transformation, 2002–15; *b* 1 Nov. 1940; *s* of Edward James Monds and Mary Brigid (*née* McPoland); *m* 1967, Eileen Joan Graham; two *d. Educ:* Queen's Univ., Belfast (BSc; PhD). CEng, MIET, MBCS. Vis. Asst Prof., Purdue Univ., USA, 1965, 1966; Lectr, 1967–77, Sen. Lectr, 1977–78, Reader, 1978–86, QUB; Dean, Faculty of Informatics, 1989–93, Provost, Magee Coll., Londonderry, 1995–2000, Univ. of Ulster. Gov. for NI, BBC, 1999–2006; Chairman: NI Inf. Age Initiative, 1999–2002; Univ. of Ulster Sci. Res. Parks Ltd, 1999–2002; NI Industrial Res. and Technol. Unit, 2000–01; Omagh 2010 Task Force, 2001–02; Invest Northern Ireland, 2002–05; Omagh Enterprise Co., 2008–14; Co-Chm., US-Ireland R&D Partnership, 2005–14; Vice-Chm., North West Regl Coll., 2008–15. Trustee, UK Teaching Awards Trust, 1999–2006. CCMI. *Publications:* Minicomputer Systems, 1979; (with R. McLaughlin) An Introduction to Mini and Micro Computers, 1981, 2nd edn 1984; The Business of Electronic Product Development, 1984; two patents; contrib. learned jls. *Recreation:* motorhoming.

**MONE,** family name of **Baroness Mone**.

**MONE,** Baroness *cr* 2015 (Life Peer), of Mayfair in the City of Westminster; **Michelle Georgina Mone,** OBE 2010; *b* Glasgow, 8 Oct. 1971; *née* Allan; *m* Michael Mone (marr. diss. 2011); one *s* two *d*. Work as a model; office junior to Hd, Sales and Mktg for Scotland, Labatt Brewers, until 1995; Founder and Mem. Bd, Ultimo, 1996–2015; co-owner, Ultimo Brands Internat., until 2016; global inspirational speaker, 2005–. Chair, Mone Review (to encourage business start-ups in disadvantaged areas), 2015–. Mem., Bd of Dirs, Prince's Scottish Youth Business Trust, 2001–. *Publications:* My Fight to the Top (autobiog.), 2015. *Address:* House of Lords, SW1A 0PW.

**MONEO VALLÉS, Prof. José Rafael, (Prof. Rafael Moneo);** architect; Josep Lluis Sert Professor of Architecture, Graduate School of Design, Harvard University, since 1991; *b* Tudela, Spain, 9 May 1937; *s* of Rafael Moneo and Teresa Vallés; *m* 1963, Belén Feduchi; three *d. Educ:* Tech. Sch. of Madrid (degree in arch., 1961). Fellow, Spanish Acad., Rome, 1963–65; Asst Prof., Technical Sch. of Architecture, Madrid, 1966–70; Prof. of Architectural Theory, Technical School of Architecture, Barcelona, 1970–80; Prof. of Composition, Tech. Sch. of Madrid, 1980–85; Chm., Dept of Architecture, Harvard Univ., 1985–90. Projects include: Diestre Factory, Zaragoza, 1967; Pamplona Bull Ring, 1967; Urumea Residential Building, San Sebastián, 1971; (with Ramón Bescós) Bankinter Bank, Madrid, 1976; Logroño Town Hall, 1976; Nat. Mus. of Roman Art, Mérida, 1986; Previsión Española Insurance Co., Seville, 1987; Bank of Spain, Jaén, 1988; San Pablo Airport, Seville, 1992; Architectural Assoc. of Tarragona, 1992; Atocha Railway Stn, Madrid, 1992; Thyssen-Bornemisza Mus., Madrid, 1992; Pilar and Joan Miró Foundn, Palma de Mallorca, 1992; Davis Art Mus., Wellesley Coll., Mass, 1993; (with Manuel de Solá-Morales) Diagonal Buildings, Barcelona, 1993; Don Benito Cultural Centre, Badajoz, 1997; Museums of Modern Art and Architecture, Stockholm, 1998; Town Hall extension, Murcia, 1998; Barcelona Concert Hall, 1999; Kursaal Auditorium and Congress Centre, San Sebastián, 1999; Potsdamer Platz Hotel and office building, Berlin; Audrey Jones Beck Building, Mus. of Fine Arts, Houston, 2000; Cathedral of Our Lady of the Angels, Los Angeles, 2002; (with Belén Moneo) new studios, Cranbrook Acad. of Art, 2002; Arenberg Campus Liby, Catholic Univ. Leuven, 2002; Chivite Winery, Arinzano, Navarra, 2002; Gregorio Marañón Mother's and Children's Hosp., Madrid, 2003; Gen. and Royal Archive of Navarra, Pamplona, 2003; Art and Nature Centre, Beulas Foundn, Huesca, 2004; (with José Antonio Martínez Lapeña and Elías Torres) apts, Sabadell, 2005; (with Alberto Nicolau) apts, La Haya, 2006; extension, Bank of Spain, Madrid, 2006; extension, Prado Mus., Madrid, 2007; Lab. for Integrated Sci. and Engrg, Harvard Univ., 2007; Mus. of Roman Th., Cartagena, 2008; Aragonia commercial center, apts, hotel and offices, 2008; Panticosa Resort Hotels, 2008; Novartis Lab., Basel, 2008; Chace Center, RI Sch. of Design, 2008; Liby, Univ. of Deusto, Bilbao, 2009; (with Moneo/Brock Architects) NW Sci. Bldg, Columbia Univ., 2010; extension to Atocha Rlwy Stn, Madrid, 2010; parish ch, Riberas de Loiola, San Sebastian, 2011. Gold Medal for Achievement in Fine Arts (Spain), 1992; Gold Medal: French Acad. of Architecture, 1996; Internat. Union of Architects, 1996; Pritzker Prize, 1996; Royal Gold Medal, RIBA, 2003. *Publications:* (jtly) Grand Hyatt Berlin, 2000; (jtly) Theoretical Anxiety and Design Strategies in the Work of Eight Contemporary Architects, 2004; Rafael Moneo: remarks on 21 works, 2010; articles in learned jls. *Address:* Calle Cinca 5, Madrid 28002, Spain; Department of Architecture, Harvard Graduate School of Design, 48 Quincy Street, Cambridge, MA 02138, USA.

**MONEY-COUTTS,** family name of **Baron Latymer**.

**MONHEMIUS, Prof. (Andrew) John,** PhD; CEng; Roy Wright Professor of Mineral and Environmental Engineering, 1996–2004, now Professor Emeritus, and Dean, Royal School of Mines, 2000–04, Imperial College of Science, Technology and Medicine, London University; Director, Anglo Asian Mining plc, since 2009; *b* 3 Oct. 1942; *s* of Frank Andre Monhemius and Edna Rowlands Monhemius; *m* 1966, Johanna Werson; one *s* one *d. Educ:* Univ. of Birmingham (BSc); Univ. of British Columbia (MASc); Imperial Coll., Univ. of London (PhD; DIC). CEng. Royal School of Mines, Imperial College: Lectr, 1966–86; Reader, 1986–96. Vis. Prof. of Extractive Metallurgy, Federal Univ. of Rio de Janeiro, 1973–75. FIMMM (FIMM 1984). Mem., Chaps Club. *Publications:* (ed with J. E. Dutrizac) Iron Control in Hydrometallurgy, 1986; more than 130 papers in scientific and tech. jls and conf. procs. *Club:* Twickenham Yacht.

**MONK, (David) Alec (George);** Chairman, Charles Wells Ltd, 1998–2003 (Director, 1989–2003); *b* 13 Dec. 1942; *s* of Philip Aylmer and Elizabeth Jane Monk; *m* 1965, Jean Ann Searle; two *s* two *d. Educ:* Jesus College, Oxford (MA (PPE); Hon. Fellow, 1999). Research Staff, Corporate Finance and Taxation, Sheffield Univ., 1966 and London Business Sch., 1967; Senior Financial Asst, Treasurer's Dept, Esso Petroleum Co., 1968; various positions with The Rio Tinto-Zinc Corp., 1968–77, Dir, 1974–77; Vice-Pres. and Dir, AEA Investors Inc., 1977–81; Chm. and Chief Exec., The Gateway Corp. (formerly Dee Corp.) PLC, 1981–89; CEO, Tri-Delta Corp. Ltd, 1990–93. Dir, Scottish Eastern Investment Trust, 1985–98. Mem., NEDC, 1986–90. Pres., Inst. of Grocery Distribution, 1987–89. Poole Harbour Comr, 2009–12. Vis. Indust. Fellow, Manchester Business Sch., 1984. Hon. Fellow, St Hugh's Coll., Oxford, 1985; Foundn Fellow, New Hall, Cambridge, 2001. Hon. LLD Sheffield, 1988. *Publications:* (with A. J. Merrett) Inflation, Taxation and Executive Remuneration, 1967. *Recreations:* sports, reading.

**MONK, Fiona Beverley;** Regional Employment Judge, Birmingham, since 2011; *b* London, 8 Sept. 1963; *d* of Ian and Beverley Monk; *m* 2009; two *d*; one step *s. Educ:* Chelmsford Co. High Sch. for Girls; Warwick Univ. (LLB Hons); Brunel Univ. (MA Law and Discrimination). Admitted solicitor, 1988; solicitor, Coventry Law Centre, 1989–97; Employment Judge, pt-time, 2000–07, full-time, 2007–11; Diversity and Community

Relns Judge, 2013; role model and mentor Judge, 2014; Sen. Resident Judge, First-tier Tribunal (War Pensions and Armed Forces Compensation Chamber), 2016– (Actg Pres., 2018); Principal Judge for Strategy and Implementation, 2018–. Comr, Judicial Appts Commn, 2017–. Adjudicator (pt-time), Law Soc., 2005–07. *Recreations:* running, cooking, reading, family, theatre, holidays.

**MONK, Heath Jon;** Executive Director: Foundation of the Schools of King Edward VI in Birmingham, since 2016; King Edward VI Academy Trust Birmingham, since 2017; *b* Hastings, E Sussex, 22 July 1970; *s of* Michael Monk and Molly Monk; *m* 1996, Lucy Katharine Knowling; two *s* one *d* (incl. twin *s*). *Educ:* Christ's Hospital Sch.; Queen's Coll., Oxford (BA Hons 1st Cl. Eng. Lang. and Lit. 1992); Univ. of Sheffield (PGCE 1994). Teacher of English and Drama, Bennett Meml Diocesan Sch., 1994–96; Asst Housemaster, Sevenoaks Sch., 1996–2000; Dep. Dir, DFEE, subseq. DFES, later DCFS, 2000–07; Chief Exec., Future Leaders Trust, 2007–16. Advr, Place2Be, 2017–. Trustee: Teaching Leaders, 2011–16; Learning Trust for Excellence, 2017–; Birmingham Educn Partnership, 2018–; Windsor Academy Trust, 2018–. *Recreations:* sport, cricket, golf, football (West Ham United), baseball (Seattle Mariners), cooking, theatre. *Address:* Foundation Office, Edgbaston Park Road, Birmingham B15 2UD. *T:* (0121) 472 1147. *E:* office@ske.uk.net. *Club:* Moseley Golf.

**MONK, Joanne Elizabeth;** *see* Wheeler, J. E.

**MONK, Richard Gordon,** CMG 2009; OBE 2000; QPM 1995; international police commissioner and foreign states' police adviser, 1996–2012; *b* Barnet, Herts, 4 July 1944; *s of* Ernest and Thelma Monk; *m* 1988, Barbara Marshall; four *s* one *d. Educ:* E Barnet Grammar Sch.; Metropolitan Police Cadet Corps; Univ. of Durham (BA Hons Politics). Joined Metropolitan Police, 1963; Chief Superintendent, Brixton, 1986–88; Comdr, Metropolitan Police, 1988–91; Asst Chief Constable, Devon and Cornwall Constabulary, 1991–94; Asst Inspector, HM Inspectorate of Constabulary, 1994–98; Police Advr, Administrator of Sovereign Base Area, Cyprus, 1996–98; Police Comr, UN Internat. Police Task Force in Bosnia, 1998–99; Mem., UN Sec. Gen.'s Panel on Peace Ops, 2000; Dir and Sen. Police Advr to Sec. Gen., OSCE, 2002–06; Advr, US Inst. for Peace in Nepal, 2007; Police Comr, nat. and UN internat. police in Kosovo, 2007–08. Hon. Prof., Kyrgyzstan Nat. Police Acad., 2003–; Mem. Adv. Council, Internat. Network to Promote the Rule of Law, US Inst. of Peace, 2005–; Mem., Strategic Develt Bd, Durham Global Security Inst., Durham Univ., 2010–. Member: Council, NACRO, 1988–94; Funding Panel, Nat. Assoc. of Victim Support Schemes, 1988–94. Trustee, then Chm., Lucy Faithfull Foundn, 1993–98 (Patron, 1998–); Trustee, Suzy Lamplugh Trust, 1999–2005. Freeman, City of London, 2000. Liveryman, Co. of Security Professionals, 2008– (Principal Founder and Mem., Ct of Assts, 1999–; Chm., Bd of Trustees, 1999–2002 and 2008–12). Graduate, FBI Nat. Acad., 1985; Chm., FBI European Chapter, 1996. Hon. DCL Durham, 2009. UN Medals, Bosnia, 1998, Kosovo 2007. Presidential Order of Merit (Kosovo), 2016. *Publications:* Study on Policing in the Former Republic of Yugoslavia, 2001; Trends in Policing: interviews with police leaders across the globe, 2010. *Recreations:* grandchildren, classic cars and motor cycles, fitness training, attending senior common room, St Chad's College, Durham University. *Address:* 19 Rivermead, East Molesey, Surrey KT8 9AZ. *T:* (020) 8941 9600. *E:* richard.monk@virgin.net. *Club:* Reform.

**MONK, Dame Susan Catherine Hampsher-;** *see* Leather, Dame S. C.

**MONK BRETTON,** 3rd Baron *cr* 1884; **John Charles Dodson;** DL; *b* 17 July 1924; *o s of* 2nd Baron and Ruth (*d* 1967), 2nd *d of* late Hon. Charles Brand; *S* father, 1933; *m* 1958, Zoë Diana Scott; two *s. Educ:* Westminster Sch.; New Coll., Oxford (MA Agric.). DL E Sussex, 1983. *Heir: s* Hon. Christopher Mark Dodson [*b* 2 Aug. 1958; *m* 1988, Karen, *o d of* B. J. McKelvain, Fairfield, Conn; two *s* one *d*]. *Address:* Chemin de la Becque 24, 1814 La Tour de Peilz, Switzerland. *T:* (21) 9442912.

**MONKHOUSE, Richard Graham;** JP; Chairman, Why me?, since 2016; Witness Support volunteer, Manchester Crown Court, since 2017; *b* Carlisle, 30 July 1946; *s of* Philip Monkhouse and Margaret Monkhouse; *m* 1979, Jayne Pittilla, OBE. *Educ:* Altrincham Grammar Sch.; Bradford Univ.; Newcastle Poly. (DMS 1974). Actuarial student, NEL, 1968–71; Actuarial Asst, MPA, 1971–72; PA to Gen. Manager, Slater Walker Insurance, 1972–73; Gp Product Manager, United Africa Co., 1974–84; Mktg Manager, Elcometer Instruments, 1984–94; self-employed Statistical Process Control consultant, 1994–. Magistrates' Association: Trustee, 2008–15; Dep. Chm., 2011–13; Chm., 2013–15. JP Trafford, 1997 (Bench Chm., 2005–07). Ind. Complaints and Appeals Examiner, Restorative Justice Council, 2016–. *Recreations:* sports, football (Man Utd), Rugby League (Wigan), music (choral, opera, classical), reading, cooking. *T:* 07761 211466. *E:* rgm2@btinternet.com.

**MONKS,** family name of **Baron Monks.**

**MONKS,** Baron *cr* 2010 (Life Peer), of Blackley in the County of Greater Manchester; **John Stephen Monks;** General Secretary, European Trades Union Confederation, 2003–11; *b* 5 Aug. 1945; *s of* Charles Edward Monks and Bessie Evelyn Monks; *m* 1970, Francine Jacqueline Schenk; two *s* one *d. Educ:* Ducie Technical High Sch., Manchester; Nottingham Univ. (BA Econ). Joined TUC, 1969; Hd of Orgn and Industrial Relns Dept, 1977–87; Dep. Gen. Sec., 1987–93; Gen. Sec., 1993–2003. Member: Council, ACAS, 1979–95; ESRC, 1988–91; Takeover Panel, 2018–. Vice-Chm., Learning and Skills Council, 2001–04. Trustee, People's History Museum (formerly Nat. Museum of Labour History), 1988–2017 (Chm. of Trustees, 2004–17). Vis. Prof., Manchester Business Sch., Univ. of Manchester (formerly at UMIST, then at Sch. of Mgt, Univ. of Manchester), 1996–2016. Pres., BALPA, 2011–. Non-exec. Dir, Thompsons' Solicitors, 2010–19; Trustee Dir, NOW: Pensions, 2011–17. *Recreations:* hiking, music, cycling. *Address:* House of Lords, SW1A 0PW.

**MONKS, Prof. Paul Steven,** DPhil; Professor of Atmospheric Chemistry and Earth Observation Science, since 2007, Pro Vice Chancellor and Head, College of Science and Engineering, since 2016, University of Leicester; *b* St Helens, Lancs, 25 May 1967; *s of* Ken Monks and Barbara Monks; *m* 2002, Alison Riding; two *d. Educ:* Cowley High Sch., St Helens; Univ. of Warwick (BSc Hons 1988); Univ. of Oxford (DPhil 1992). NAS/Nat. Res. Council Resident Res. Associate, NASA, Goddard Space Flight Centre, Greenbelt, 1992–94; Sen. Res. Associate, Sch. of Envmtl Scis, UEA, 1994–96; Lectr, 1996–2002, Reader, 2002–07, Dept of Chem., Univ. of Leicester. Chm., Air Quality Expert Gp, DEFRA, 2009–; Member: Space Leadership Council, 2010–16; Council, NERC, 2011–15; Envmtl Pollution and Atmospheric Chem. Scientific Steering Cttee, 2014–; Sci. Adv. Council, DEFRA, 2015–. Co-Chm., Internat. Geosphere-Biosphere Prog.-Internat. Global Atmospheric Chem. proj., 2008–14. FRMetS 2004; FRSC 2004. *Publications:* over 200 articles in learned jls on physical chem., air pollution, breathomics and atmospheric sci. *Recreations:* tennis, family, wine tasting (rare varieties), heritage steam, musicals, Italy. *Address:* Department of Chemistry, University of Leicester, Leicester LE1 7RH. *T:* (0116) 252 2141, 07554 333020, (Secretary) (0116) 252 3497, *Fax:* (0116) 252 3789.

**MONKSWELL,** 5th Baron *cr* 1885; **Gerard Collier;** *b* 28 Jan. 1947; *s of* William Adrian Larry Collier and Helen (*née* Dunbar); *S* to disclaimed barony of father, 1984; *m* 1974, Ann Valerie Collins; two *s* one *d. Educ:* Portsmouth Polytechnic (BSc Mech. Eng, 1971); Slough Polytechnic (Cert. in Works Management 1972). Massey Ferguson Manufg Co. Ltd: Product Quality Engineer, 1972; Service Administration Manager, 1984–89; Customer Advr, B&Q, 2001–06; self-employed, 2006–. Mem. (Lab), Manchester City Council, 1989–94. Mem., H of L, 1985–99. *Recreations:* politics, swimming, movies. *Heir: s* Hon. James Adrian Collier, *b* 29 March 1977. *Address:* 183 Egerton Road South, Manchester M21 0XD.

**MONMOUTH, Bishop of;** *no new appointment at time of going to press.*

**MONRO, (Andrew) Hugh;** educational consultant, since 2005; Head, Bristol Cathedral School, 2007–08; Founding Principal, Bristol Cathedral Choir Academy, 2008–09; *b* 2 March 1950; *s of* late Andrew Killey Monro, FRCS and Diana Louise (*née* Rhys); *m* 1974, Elizabeth Clare Rust; one *s* one *d. Educ:* Rugby School; Pembroke College, Cambridge (MA; PGCE). Graduate trainee, Metal Box, 1973; Haileybury College, 1974–79; Noble & Greenough School, Boston, Mass, 1977–78; Loretto School, 1979–86; Headmaster: Worksop College, 1986–90; Clifton College, 1990–2000; Master, Wellington College, 2000–05. *Recreations:* American literature, Cornish churches, Scottish Rugby. *Club:* Hawks (Cambridge).

**MONRO, Maj.-Gen. Hon. Seymour Hector Russell Hale,** CBE 1996; LVO 2010; DL; Executive Chairman and Director, Highland Military Tattoo, since 2013; *b* 7 May 1950; *s of* Rt Hon. Lord Monro of Langholm, AE, PC, DL and (Elizabeth) Anne (*née* Welch); *m* 1977, Angela Sandeman; three *s. Educ:* Cargilfield Sch.; Glenalmond Coll.; RMA, Sandhurst. MA to Comdr 1st Br. Corps, 1982–84; Co. Comdr, 1st Bn Queen's Own Highlanders, 1984–86; Instr, All Arms Tactics, Warminster, 1986–87; Directing Staff, Army Staff Coll., 1987–89; CO, 1st Bn, Queen's Own Highlanders, 1989–91; Col, Gen. Staff, MoD, 1991–94; Comdr, 39 Inf. Bde, 1994–95; Pres., Regular Commns Bd, 1996–97; Dep. Chief, Jt Ops, HQ SFOR, 1997; Dir, Infantry, 1998–2001; Dep. Comdr, NATO Rapid Deployable Corps (Italy), 2001–03. ADC to the Queen, 1998–2001. Adjutant, Queen's Body Guard for Scotland, 2001–09. Dir, CairnGorm Mountain Ltd, 2009–14. Dir, Atlantic Salmon Trust, 2004–08; Pres., Forres Br., RBL Scotland, 2018–. Chairman: Highlands and Islands Bd, Prince's Trust, 2004–07; Highlanders' Mus., 2004–13; Highland Heritage Appeal, 2007–13; Findhorn, Nairn and Lossie Fisheries Trust, 2008–15; Pres., Brisbane Observatory Trust, 2012–. Mem. Council, Glenalmond Coll., 1993–2003. Pres., Forres and Dist Pipe Band, 2012–; Convenor, Northern Meeting Piping Trust, 2012–; Chieftain, European Pipe Band Championships, 2017. Hon. Air Cdre, No 2622 (Highland) Sqdn, RAuxAF, 2008–19. DL Moray, 2011. *Recreations:* shooting, fishing, golf, photography, conservation, travel, vintage cars. *Address:* Kirkton, Dallas, Moray IV36 2RZ. *Club:* New (Edinburgh).

**MONRO, Stuart Kinnaird,** OBE 2007; PhD; FRSE; Scientific Director: Our Dynamic Earth, Edinburgh, 2004–14; Scottish (formerly Edinburgh) Consortium for Rural Research, 2008–18; *b* 3 March 1947; *s of* William Kinnaird Monro and Williamena Milne Monro; *m* 1971, Shiela Dowie Wallace; three *s* one *d. Educ:* Aberdeen Acad.; Univ. of Aberdeen (BSc 1970); Univ. of Edinburgh (PhD 1982; Hon. Fellow 2005). FGS 1990; CGeol 1991; FHEA 2007 (ILTM 2001). Principal Geologist, British Geol Survey, 1970–2004; Tutor in Earth Scis (pt-time), Open Univ., 1982–2009. Vis. Prof., 2008–14, Hon. Prof., 2014–, Sch. of Geoscis, Univ. of Edinburgh. Sec., Standing Gp on Envmtl Geol., Dirs of Western Geol Surveys, 1984–88; Member: Scottish Sci. Adv. Council (formerly Adv. Cttee), 2003–09 (Ind. Co.-Chm., 2007–09); Young People's Cttee, RSE, 2005–08 (Convenor, 2016–); non-exec. Dir, Edinburgh Internat. Sci. Fest., 2004–19; Trustee, Nat. Mus Scotland (formerly Nat. Mus of Scotland), 2005–13. Member: Council, Open Univ., 1994–2002; Court, Univ. of Edinburgh, 2007–14 (Vice-Convener, 2011–14); Court, Univ. of St Andrews, 2014– (Mem., Audit and Risk Cttee, 2014–19; Convener, Governance and Nominations Cttee, 2018–; Dep. Chair, 2018–). President: Westmorland Geol Soc., 1994–2005; Edinburgh Geol Soc., 2006–07, 2016–18; Mem. Council, Geol Soc. of London, 2009–12. Hon. Geol Advr, John Muir Trust, 2005–. FRSSA 1998 (Pres., 2002–05, 2015–18); FRSE 2010 (Convener, Young People's Cttee, 2016–); FSAScot 2011; FRSGS 2014. DUniv Open, 2011; Hon. DSc: Heriot-Watt, 2014; Edinburgh, 2014. Dist. Service Award, Geol Soc. of London, 2009; Silver Medal, Royal Scottish Soc. for Arts, 2018. *Publications:* Geology of the Irvine District, 1999; various scientific papers and reports. *Recreations:* theatre, travel, the great outdoors—especially the rocks! *Address:* 34 Swanston Grove, Edinburgh EH10 7BW. *T:* (0131) 477 1124. *E:* stuart.monro@blueyonder.co.uk. *Clubs:* Rotary, Twenty (Edinburgh).

**MONRO DAVIES, His Honour William Llewellyn;** QC 1974; a Circuit Judge, 1976–99; *b* 12 Feb. 1927; *s of* Thomas Llewellyn Davies and Emily Constance Davies; *m* 1956, Jean (*d* 2014), *d of* late E. G. Innes; one *s* one *d. Educ:* Christ Coll., Brecon; Trinity Coll., Oxford (MA, LitHum). Served in RNVR, 1945–48 (Sub-Lt). Called to the Bar, Inner Temple, 1954. Mem., Gen. Council of the Bar, 1971–75. A Recorder of the Crown Court, 1972–76. *Recreations:* the theatre and cinema; watching Rugby football.
*See also* N. A. Stewart.

**MONROE, Dame Barbara,** DBE 2010; Chief Executive, St Christopher's Hospice, London, 2000–14; *b* Cowley, 6 April 1951; *d of* Robert Jones and Phyllis Jones; *m* 1975, Jeremy Monroe; one *s* one *d. Educ:* Oxford High Sch. GPDST; St Anne's Coll., Oxford (BA Hons 1973); Univ. of Exeter (BPhil, CQSW 1975). Probation Officer, Inner London Probation Service, 1974–76; Social Worker: Avon Social Services, 1976–80; Atkinson Morley's Hosp., 1982–87; St Christopher's Hospice: Principal Social Worker, 1987–89; Dir, Social Work, 1989–97; Dir, Patient and Family Services, 1997–2000. Hon. Prof., Internat. Observatory on End of Life Care, Lancaster Univ., 2009–14; Hon. Sen. Lectr, Faculty of Medicine and Health Scis, Univ. of Auckland, 2006–14. Ind. Mem., Community, Voluntary and Local Services Honours Cttee, 2013–18; Interim Chair, Public Services Honours Cttee, 2018–. Chm., Childhood Bereavement Network, 2000–09; Vice Chm., Commn on Future of Hospice Care, 2011–13; Mem., Internat. Work Gp on Death, Dying and Bereavement, 1997–2014. Special Comr, Royal Hosp. Chelsea, 2013– (Dep. Chair, 2019–). Trustee, Marie Curie (formerly Marie Curie Cancer Care), 2014– (Sen. Ind. Trustee, 2019–); Chair, Compassion in Dying, 2019– (Trustee, 2017–19). FRSA. Hon. DSc Lancaster, 2017. Lifetime Achievement Award, Assoc. Death Educn and Counselling, 2017. *Publications:* (jtly) Good Practices in Palliative Care: a psychosocial perspective, 1998; (ed with D. Oliviere) Patient Participation in Palliative Care: a voice for the voiceless, 2003; (ed with D. Oliviere) Death, Dying and Social Differences, 2004, 2nd edn (ed with D. Oliviere and S. Payne) 2011; (ed with F. Kraus) Brief Interventions with Bereaved Children, 2004, 2nd edn 2010; (ed with D. Oliviere) Resilience in Palliative Care: achievement in adversity, 2007. *Recreations:* my family, theatre, walking, books, wine and the maintenance always of a half full glass.

**MONSON,** family name of **Baron Monson.**

**MONSON**, 12th Baron cr 1728; **Nicholas John Monson**; Bt 1611; writer and journalist, since 1978; investor relations consultant, since 2007; b London, 19 Oct. 1955; e s of 11th Baron Monson and of Emma, o d of late Anthony Devas, ARA, RP; S father, 2011; m 1st, 1981, Hilary Martin (marr. diss. 1996); one d (one s decd); 2nd, 2002, La Ilustrisima Maria Victoria Nicklin Perez; 3rd, 2010, Silvana Fernandes, widow of Nicholas Jessen. Educ: Eton Coll.; Kingston Poly. PR Dir, 1986; Chairman: Sinovation plc, 2003–06; Grenfell Consulting Ltd, 2010–16. Campaigner for reform of drug laws, 2017–. Publications: (with Debra Scott) The Nouveaux Pauvres, 1984; (with Sarah Goodall) The Palace Diaries, 2006. Recreations: reading, disco dancing. Heir: b Hon. Andrew Anthony John Monson [b 12 May 1959; m 1993, Emily Wheeler-Bennett; two d]. Address: Victoria Spa Lodge, Bishopton Lane, Stratford upon Avon CV37 9QY. E: lordmonson@gmail.com. Club: Travellers.

**MONSON**, (John) Guy (Elmhirst); Chief Investment Officer, since 2008, and Senior Partner, since 2016, Sarasin & Partners LLP (Managing Partner, 2008–16); b London, 11 Sept. 1962; s of Hon. Jeremy David Alfonso John Monson and Patricia Mary, yr d of late Maj. George Barker, MFH; m 1995, Lady Olivia Rose Mildred FitzRoy, y d of 11th Duke of Grafton, KG; two d. Educ: Eton Coll.; Lady Margaret Hall, Oxford (BA PPE 1984). Joined Sarasin Investment Management Ltd, 1984; Dir, 1989–; Chief Investment Officer, 1993–2007; CEO, 2007; Chief Investment Officer, Bank Sarasin Gp, 1997–2007; Partner, Bank Sarasin & Co., 2001–02. Mem., Ideas Adv. Bd, LSE, 2009–. Trustee: Chatsworth House Trust, 2009–; Invictus Games Foundn, 2015–. Recreation: steam engines. Address: Sarasin & Partners LLP, Juxon House, 100 St Paul's Churchyard, EC4M 8BU. T: (020) 7038 7000. Clubs: White's, Pratt's.

**MONSON**, Prof. John Rowat Telford, MD; FRCS, FRCSI, FACS; Professor of Surgery, University of Central Florida, since 2016; Executive Director, Colorectal Surgery, Florida Hospital System, since 2016; Clinical Director, Surgical Health Outcomes Consortium, since 2016, and Chairman, Digestive Health and Surgery Institute, since 2018, Florida Hospital; b 14 Jan. 1956; s of Desmond Monson and Ann Monson; m 1980, Aideen White, MB; two s one d. Educ: Sandford Park Secondary Sch., Dublin; Trinity Coll. Dublin (MB BCh, BAO 1977; MD 1987). FRCSI 1983; FRCS 1987; FACS 1992; FRCSE (ad hominem) 2004. Pre-registration house officer, Royal City of Dublin Hosp., 1979; pre-Fellowship surgical trng, Dublin, 1980–83; post Fellowship surgical trng, Leeds, 1983–84; Res. Fellow, Univ. of Leeds, 1985–86; Sen. Registrar, Surgical Trng, Dublin, 1986–89; Fellow in Surgical Oncology, Mayo Clinic, USA, 1989–90; Asst Dir and Sen. Lectr in Surgery, St Mary's Hosp. Med. Sch., London, 1990–93; Prof. of Surgery and Hd of Dept, Academic Surgical Unit, 1993–2008, Hon. Prof., 2008–, Univ. of Hull; and University of Rochester Medical Center, New York: Chief, Div. of Colorectal Surgery, and Vice-Chm. of Surgery, 2008–16; Vice-Chm., Quality and Surgical Outcomes, 2011–16; Dir, Surgical Health Outcomes and Res. Enterprise, 2012–16; Adjunct Prof. of Surgery, 2016–18. Surgical Res. Soc. Internat. Travelling Fellow, 1986; Edward Halloran Bennett Travelling Fellow in Surgery, 1989; James IV Assoc. Internat. Fellow, 1996. Visiting Professor: UCLA; Univ. of Texas; Monash Univ.; Australasian Coll. of Surgeons, 2009; Sir Edwin Tooth Vis. Prof., Univ. of Queensland, 2003. Mem. Council, British Jl of Surgery, 1997–2004. Vice-Pres., British Assoc. of Surgical Oncology, 1997; Hon. Sec., Surgical Res. Soc. of GB and Ireland, 1998–2004; Member: James IV Assoc. of Surgeons, 1999– (Dir, 2000–); Exec. Council, Amer. Soc. of Colon and Rectal Surgeons, 2014– (Chm., Res. Cttee, 2012–); Pres., Multidisciplinary Internat. Rectal Cancer Soc., 2012–13; Vice Pres., Optimizing Surgical Treatment of Rectal Cancer Internat. Collaborative, 2012–. Member: Special Adv. Cttee for Gen. Surgery in UK, 2000–06; Health Innovation Council, 2007–; Commn on Cancer, 2015–; Advr, NHS Modernisation Agency, 2002–; Bd Mem., BUPA Foundn, 2006–09; Nat. Co-ordinator, Laparoscopic Colorectal Trng Prog., DoH, 2008–09. Examiner, Intercollegiate Bd in Gen. Surgery, 2000–; Ext. Examiner, Univ. of Malaysia, 2001. 14th Millin Lectr, RCSI, 1990; Robert Smith Lectr, RCSI, 2006; Johnson and Johnson Lectr, RCSI, 2010; Gerhard Buess Lectr, 2012. Fellow, Amer. Soc. of Colon and Rectal Surgeons, 1995. Hon. FRCSGlas, 1998; Hon. Fellow: Soc. of Univ. Surgeons, USA, 2002; Assoc. of Surgeons of GB and Ireland, 2011. Section Ed., Media, Book Revs and For Debate, Diseases of Colon and Rectum, 2010–16 (Media Ed., 2008–16); Mem., Editl Bd, Annals of Surgery, 2014–; Co-Ed., Diseases of Colon and Rectal Surgery, 2016– (Asst Ed., 2014–16). Publications: (ed with A. Darzi) Laparoscopic Inguinal Hernia Repair, 1994; (ed jtly) Atlas of Surgical Oncology, 1994; (with A. Darzi) Laparoscopic Colorectal Surgery, 1995; (ed jtly) Surgical Emergencies, 1999; (ed jtly) Keighley and Williams' Surgery of the Anus, Rectum and Colon, 4th edn, 2018; 370 contribs on subjects of colorectal surgery, tumour immunology and laparoscopic surgery in jls incl. Lancet, Brit. Jl Surgery, Brit. Jl Cancer and Annals of Surgery. Recreations: wine, classic cars, historic motor racing, armchair sport, bad golf. Address: Surgical Health Outcomes Consortium, 2415 N Orange Avenue, Suite 102, Orlando, FL 32804, USA.

**MONTAGNIER**, Prof. Luc; Professor, Pasteur Institute, Paris, 1985–2000, now Emeritus (Head of Viral Oncology Unit, 1972–2000); Director of Research, Centre national de la recherche scientifique, 1974–2001; University Chair Professor, Shanghai Jiao Tong University, 2010; b 18 Aug. 1932; s of Antoine Montagnier and Marianne (née Rousselet); m 1961, Dorothea Ackermann; one s two d. Educ: Collège de Châtellerault; Univ. de Poitiers; Univ. de Paris. Asst, 1955–60, Attaché, 1960, Head, 1963, Head of Research, 1967, Faculty of Science, Paris; Head of Lab., Inst. of Radium, 1965–71. Dist. Prof. and Dir, B. and G. Salick Center for Molecular and Cellular Biol., Queens Coll., CUNY, 1997–2001. Co-discoverer of AIDS virus, 1983. Nobel Prize in Physiology or Medicine, 2008. Grand Officier, Légion d'honneur (France); Commandeur, Ordre national du Mérite (France). Publications: Vaincre le Sida, 1986; Des virus et des hommes, 1994; Virus, 2000; Les Combats de la vie, 2008; Le Nobel et Le Moine, 2009; scientific papers on research into AIDS, molecular biology, virology, etc.

**MONTAGU**; see Douglas-Scott-Montagu.

**MONTAGU**, family name of **Duke of Manchester**, **Earl of Sandwich**, and **Baron Swaythling**.

**MONTAGU OF BEAULIEU**, 4th Baron cr 1885; **Ralph Douglas-Scott-Montagu**; b 13 March 1961; s of 3rd Baron Montagu of Beaulieu and Elizabeth Belinda Douglas-Scott-Montagu (née Crossley); S father, 2015; m 2005, Ailsa Camm. Heir: half-b Hon. Jonathan Deane Douglas-Scott-Montagu, b 11 Oct. 1975.

**MONTAGU**, Jennifer Iris Rachel, CBE 2012; LVO 2006; PhD; FBA 1986; FSA; Curator of the Photograph Collection, Warburg Institute, 1971–91, now Hon. Fellow; b 20 March 1931; d of late Hon. Ewen Edward Samuel Montagu, CBE, QC. Educ: Brearley Sch., New York; Benenden Sch., Kent; Lady Margaret Hall, Oxford (BA; Hon. Fellow 1985); Warburg Inst., London (PhD). FSA 2008. Assistant Regional Director, Arts Council of Gt Britain, North West Region, 1953–54; Lecturer in the History of Art, Reading Univ., 1958–64; Asst Curator of the Photograph Collection, Warburg Inst., 1964–71. Slade Prof. and Fellow of Jesus Coll., Cambridge, 1980–81; Andrew W. Mellon Lectr, Nat. Gall. of Art, Washington, 1991; Invited Prof., Collège de France, 1994. Member: Academic Awards Cttee, British Fedn of University Women, 1963–89; Executive Cttee, National Art-Collections Fund, 1973–2005; Consultative Cttee, Burlington Magazine, 1975–; Cttee, The Jewish Museum, 1983–; Reviewing Cttee on Export of Works of Art, 1987–96. Trustee: Wallace Collection, 1989–2001; BM, 1994–2001. Hon. Academician, Accademia Clementina, Bologna, 1988. Serena Medal for Italian Studies, British Acad., 1992; Accademica Cultora, Accademia di San Luca, Rome, 2000; Premio Cultori di Roma, 2001; Premio Daria Borghese, 2001; Socio Onorario dell'Università e Nobil Collegio degli Orefici Gioiellieri Argentieri dell'Alma, Città di Roma, 2003; Premio Galilei, Storia dell'Arte Italiana, 2015. Chevalier de la Légion d'honneur (France), 1999; Ufficiale dell'Ordine al Merito (Italy), 2003; Comdr, Ordre des Arts et des Lettres (France), 2013 (Officier, 1991). Publications: Bronzes, 1963; (with Jacques Thuillier) Catalogue of exhibn Charles Le Brun, 1963; Alessandro Algardi, 1985 (special Mitchell Prize); Roman Baroque Sculpture: the industry of art, 1989; The Expression of the Passions, 1994; Gold, Silver and Bronze: metal sculpture of the Roman Baroque, 1996; (ed and contrib.) Algardi: l'altra faccia del Barocco, 1999; (ed and contrib.) Ori e argenti: Capolavori del '700 da Arrighi a Valadier, 2007; Antonio Arrighi: a silversmith and bronze founder in Baroque Rome, 2009; articles in learned periodicals. Address: 10 Roland Way, SW7 3RE. T: (020) 7373 6691; Warburg Institute, Woburn Square, WC1H 0AB.

**MONTAGU**, Sir Nicholas (Lionel John), KCB 2001 (CB 1993); Chairman, Financial Ombudsman Service, 2012–19; b 12 March 1944; s of late John Eric Montagu and Barbara Joyce Montagu, OBE; m 1974, Jennian Ford Geddes, o d of late Ford Irvine Geddes, MBE; two d. Educ: Rugby Sch.; New Coll., Oxford (MA). Asst Lectr 1966–69, Lectr 1969–74, in Philosophy, Univ. of Reading; Department of Social Security (formerly Department of Health and Social Security): Principal, 1974–81 (seconded to Cabinet Office, 1978–80); Asst Sec., 1981–86; Under Sec., 1986–90; Deputy Secretary, 1990 (seconded to Dept of Transport, 1992–97): Public Transport, 1992–94; Infrastructure, 1994–95; Railways, 1995–97; Hd, Econ. and Domestic Secretariat, Cabinet Office, 1997. Chm., Board of Inland Revenue, 1997–2004. Chm., NCVO Charity Tax Commn, 2017–. Adviser: IDDAS, 2005–11; Equiniti, 2010–12; Dir, Xafinity, 2005–10; Mem., Adv. Bd, PricewaterhouseCoopers, 2009–11; non-exec. Dir, PIC Hldgs, 2006–11; Chairman: With-Profits Cttee, Aviva UK Life (formerly Norwich Union), 2007–11. Chairman: Council, QMUL, 2009–17; Cttee of Univ. Chairs, 2011–14. Hon. Freeman, Drapers' Co., 2017. DUniv: Middlesex, 2001; Bradford, 2003; Hon. DLitt Reading, 2012; Hon. MSc London Inst. of Banking and Finance, 2018. Publications: Brought to Account (report of Rayner Scrutiny on National Insurance Contributions), 1981; The Pale Yellow Amoeba (report of peer review of DCMS), 2000; articles in newspapers and magazines. Recreations: cooking, walking, shopping.

**MONTAGU DOUGLAS SCOTT**, family name of **Duke of Buccleuch**.

**MONTAGU-POLLOCK**, Sir Guy Maximilian; see Pollock, Sir G. M. M.

**MONTAGU STUART WORTLEY**, family name of **Earl of Wharncliffe**.

**MONTAGUE**, family name of **Baron Amwell**.

**MONTAGUE**, Sir Adrian (Alastair), Kt 2006; CBE 2001; Chairman, Aviva, since 2015 (Senior Independent Director, since 2013); b 28 Feb. 1948; s of late Charles Edward Montague and Olive Montague (née Jones); m 1st, 1970, Pamela Evans (marr. diss. 1982; she d 2000); one s two d; 2nd, 1986, Penelope Webb (marr. diss. 2009); one s; 3rd, 2015, Innes Daubeney. Educ: Trinity Hall, Cambridge (MA). Admitted Solicitor, 1973; with Linklaters & Paines, Solicitors, 1971–94 (Partner, 1979); Dir, Kleinwort Benson, subseq. Dresdner Kleinwort Benson, 1994–97; Chief Exec., Private Finance Initiative Task Force, HM Treasury, 1997–2000; Deputy Chairman: Partnerships UK, 2000–01; Network Rail, 2001–04; Chairman: British Energy Gp plc, 2002–09; Michael Page Internat., 2002–11; Cross London Rail Links Ltd, 2004–05; Friends Provident plc, later Friends Provident Gp plc, 2005–09 (Ind. Dir, 2004–09); Infrastructure Investors Ltd, 2005–09; London First, 2009–11 (non-exec. Dir, 2007–11); Anglian Water Gp, 2009–15; 3i Gp plc, 2010–15; Hurricane Exploration, 2011–13; Adv. Gp, Green Investment Bank, 2011–12 (Dep. Chair, 2012–13; Sen. Ind. Dir, 2012–13); Manchester Airports Gp, 2014–; Cadent Gas Ltd, 2017–. Non-executive Director: CellMark AB, 2000–18; Skanska AB, 2007–15. Mem., Strategic Rail Authy, 2000–01. Chm., Adv. Bd, Reform, 2010–12. Trustee: Historic Royal Palaces, 2007–13; Commonwealth War Graves Foundn, 2017–; Chm., Bd of Trustees, Point of Care Foundn, 2013–19.

**MONTAGUE**, Lisa Kimberley; Group Chief Executive Officer, Walker Greenbank plc, since 2019; b Stockport, 8 Aug. 1963; d of Derrick Bingham and Jillian Bingham; m 2001, Simon Charles Francis Montague; one s two d. Educ: Macclesfield High Sch. for Girls; Middlesex Poly. Sales Vice Pres., Cerruti 1881 USA, 1989–92; Internat. Sales Dir, Cerruti 1881 GmbH, 1992–95; Man. Dir, Cerruti 1881 UK, 1995–2000; Chief Operating Officer, Mulberry Gp plc, 2000–09; Pres. and CEO, Loewe S.A., 2009–16; CEO, Aspinal of London, 2017–18. MInstD. Recreations: equitation, yoga, travel. E: montaguelisa@hotmail.com. Club: Soho House.

**MONTAGUE**, Robert Joel, CBE 1990; Founder, Chairman and Chief Executive, Axis Intermodal Ltd, since 1999; Founder, The North American Guitar, 2010; b 22 June 1948; s of late Robert and of Freda Montague; m 1972 (marr. diss.); two s one d; m 1990, Silke Kruse; two s one d. Educ: Bedstone Sch., Shropshire; Caius Sch., Brighton. Esso Petroleum Co. Ltd, 1964–69; Cables Montague Ltd, 1969–80; Founder, Chm. and Chief Exec., Tiphook plc, 1978–94. Recreations: children, fishing, opera, ballet, guitar.

**MONTAGUE**, Air Cdre Ruth Mary Bryceson; Director, Women's Royal Air Force, 1989–94; b 1 June 1939; d of late Griffith John Griffiths and Nancy Bryceson Griffiths (née Wrigley); m 1966, Roland Arthur Montague (d 2015). Educ: Cavendish Grammar Sch. for Girls, Buxton; Bedford Coll., Univ. of London (BSc). Commissioned RAF, 1962; UK and Far East, 1962–66; UK, 1966–80; HQ Strike Command, 1980–83; RAF Staff Coll., 1983–86; Dep. Dir, WRAF, 1986–89. ADC to the Queen, 1989–94. Mem., Council and F and GP Cttee, RAF Benevolent Fund, 1994–2003; Chm., Adv. Bd, Princess Marina House Care Home, 2003–07. Mem. Council, Royal Holloway, London Univ., 1994–2003 (Hon. Fellow, 2006). FRSA 1993. Badge, Order of Mercy, 2008. Recreations: cookery, tapestry, gardening. Address: c/o National Westminster Bank, PO Box 873, 7 High Street, Marlow, Bucks SL7 1BZ. Club: Royal Air Force.

**MONTAGUE**, Sarah Anne Louise, (Lady Brooke); Presenter, World At One, BBC Radio 4, since 2018; b 8 Feb. 1966; d of late Col John and Mary Montague; m 2002, Sir (Richard) Christopher Brooke, Bt, qv; three d, and one step d. Educ: Blanchelande Coll., Guernsey; Univ. of Bristol (BSc Hons Biol.). County Natwest, 1987–89; Charles Tyrwhitt Shirts, 1990–91; Channel TV, 1991–94; Reuters, 1994–95; Sky News, 1995–97; BBC, 1997–: BBC News 24, 1997–2001; Hardtalk, 1999–; BBC Newsnight, 2000; BBC Breakfast, 2001–02; Today Programme, BBC Radio 4, 2002–18. Recreations: musicals, diving, ski-ing, jigsaws, gardens. E: Sarah.Montague@bbc.co.uk.

**MONTEAGLE OF BRANDON**, 7th Baron cr 1839; **Charles James Spring Rice**; b 24 Feb. 1953; o s of 6th Baron Monteagle of Brandon and of Anne Spring Rice (née Brownlow); S father, 2013; m 1987, Mary Teresa Glover; four d. Educ: Harrow. Heir: uncle Hon. Michael Spring Rice [b 18 Feb. 1935; m 1959, Fiona Sprot; one s one d].

**MONTEFIORE**; see Sebag-Montefiore.

**MONTEITH, Brian;** Editor, ThinkScotland.org; Communications Director, Global Britain; Member (Brexit) North East Region, European Parliament, since 2019; *b* 8 Jan. 1958; *s* of Donald MacDonald Monteith and Doreen Campbell Monteith (*née* Purves); *m* 1984, Shirley Joyce Marshall (marr. diss.); twin *s*; *m* Jacqueline Anderson. *Educ:* Portobello High Sch.; Heriot-Watt Univ. Chm., Fedn of Conservative Students, 1982–83; Public Relations Consultant: Michael Forsyth Associates, London, 1983–84 and 1985–86; Dunseath Stephen Associates, Edinburgh, 1984–85; Man. Dir, Leith Communications Ltd, 1986–91; PR Dir, Forth Mktg Ltd, 1991–94; Scottish Dir, Communication Gp, 1994–96; sole proprietor and Consultant, Dunedin PR, 1996–99. Scottish Parliament: Mem., Scotland Mid and Fife, 1999–2007 (C 1999–2005, Ind 2005–07); Convener, Audit Cttee, 2003–07; Cons. spokesman on educn, culture and sport, 1999–2003, on finance and local govt, 2003–05. Mem., Tuesday Club. Chm. Trustees, ESU Scotland, 2009–14. *Publications:* Paying the Piper: from a taxing lament to a rewarding jig, 2007; The Bully State: the end of tolerance, 2009; The Full Monty, 2009. *Recreation:* football. *Club:* Duddingston Golf (Edinburgh).

**MONTEITH, Very Rev. David Robert Malvern;** Dean of Leicester, since 2013; *b* Enniskillen, NI, 5 June 1968; *s* of Thomas Malvern Monteith and Mary, (Molly), Louise Monteith (*née* Johnston); civil partnership 2008, David Hamilton. *Educ:* Portora Royal Sch., Enniskillen; St John's Coll., Durham (BSc Zool. 1989); St John's Coll., Univ. of Nottingham (BTh 1992; MA Mission and Ministry 1993). Ordained deacon, 1993, priest, 1994; Asst Curate, All Saints', Kings Heath, Birmingham, 1993–97; Asst Curate, 1997–2000, Associate Vicar, 2000–02, St Martin-in-the-Fields; Priest-in-charge, Holy Trinity, Wimbledon, 2002–09; Area Dean of Merton, Dio. of Southwark, 2004–09; Team Rector, Merton Priory Team, 2009; Canon Chancellor, Leicester Cath., 2009–13. Chair of Trustees, St Philip's Centre for Interfaith Dialogue, Leicester, 2012–17. Hon. LLD Leicester, 2016. Gov., Leicester GS Trust, 2017–. *Recreations:* visual arts, contemporary poetry, theatre, gardening. *Address:* St Martins House, 7 Peacock Lane, Leicester LE1 5PZ. *T:* (0116) 261 5356. *E:* david.monteith@leccofe.org.

**MONTGOMERIE,** family name of **Earl of Eglinton and Winton**.

**MONTGOMERIE, Lord; Rhuridh Seton Archibald Montgomerie;** *b* 4 March 2007; *s* and *heir* of 19th Earl of Eglinton and Winton, *qv.*

**MONTGOMERIE, Colin Stuart,** OBE 2005 (MBE 1998); professional golfer, since 1987; *b* Glasgow, 23 June 1963; *s* of James Montgomerie; *m* 1st, 1990, Eimear Wilson (marr. diss. 2004); one *s* two *d;* 2nd, 2008, Gaynor Knowles (marr. diss. 2017). *Educ:* Strathallan Sch., Perth; Leeds Grammar Sch.; Houston Baptist Univ., Texas. Wins include: Scottish Amateur Stroke-Play Championship, 1985; Scottish Amateur Championship, 1987; Portuguese Open, 1989; Scandinavian Masters, 1991, 1999, 2001; Dutch Open, 1993; Volvo Masters, 1993, (jtly) 2002; Spanish Open, 1994; English Open, 1994; German Open, 1994, 1995; Lancôme Trophy, 1995; Alfred Dunhill Cup, 1995; Million Dollar Challenge, 1996; European Masters, 1996; Dubai Desert Classic, 1996; Irish Open, 1996, 1997, 2001; King Hassan II Trophy, 1997; European Grand Prix, 1997; World Cup (Individual), 1997; World Championship of Golf, 1997; PGA Championship, 1998, 1999, 2000; German Masters, 1998; British Masters, 1998; Benson & Hedges Internat. Open, 1999; Loch Lomond Invitational, 1999; BMW Internat. Open, 1999; Cisco World Matchplay, 1999; French Open, 2000; Skins Game, USA, 2000; Australian Masters, 2001; TCL Classic, 2002; Macau Open, 2003; Caltex Masters, Singapore, 2004; Dunhill Links Championship, 2005; Hong Kong Open, 2006; European Open, 2007; World Cup (Team), 2007; Senior USPGA Championship, 2014, 2015; 1st in European Order of Merit, annually, 1993–99, 2005. Member: Alfred Dunhill Cup team, 1988, 1991–2000; World Cup Team, 1988, 1991–93, 1997–99, 2006–07, 2008; Ryder Cup team, 1991, 1993, 1995, 1997, 1999, 2002, 2004, 2006, Captain, 2010; UBS Cup Team, 2003, 2004; Seve Trophy team, 2000, 2002, 2003, 2005, 2007. Coach of the Year, BBC Sports Personality of the Year, 2010. *Publications:* (with Lewine Mair) The Real Monty (autobiog.), 2002; The Thinking Man's Guide to Golf, 2003; Monty: the autobiography, 2012. *Address:* c/o IMG, Building 6, Chiswick Park, 566 Chiswick High Road, W4 5HR.

**MONTGOMERIE, Timothy Hugh;** Founder and Editor, UnHerd, 2017–18; *b* Barnstaple, N Devon, 24 July 1970. *Educ:* King's Sch., Gütersloh, Germany; Univ. of Exeter (BA Econs and Geog. 1992). COS to Rt Hon. Iain Duncan Smith, 2003; Founder, Centre for Social Justice, 2004; Founder and Ed., conservativehome.com, 2005–13; Comment Ed., The Times, 2013–14. Sen. Fellow, Legatum Inst., 2015. *Recreation:* season ticket holder at Manchester United.

**MONTGOMERY,** family name of **Viscount Montgomery of Alamein**.

**MONTGOMERY OF ALAMEIN,** 2nd Viscount *cr* 1946, of Hindhead; **David Bernard Montgomery,** CMG 2000; CBE 1975; Chairman, Baring Puma Fund, 1991–2002; *b* 18 Aug. 1928; *s* of 1st Viscount Montgomery of Alamein, KG, GCB, DSO, and Elizabeth (*d* 1937), *d* of late Robert Thompson Hobart, ICS; *S father,* 1976; *m* 1st, 1953, Mary Connell (marr. diss. 1967); one *s* one *d;* 2nd, 1970, Tessa, *d* of late Gen. Sir Frederick Browning, GCVO, KBE, CB, DSO, and Lady Browning, DBE (Dame Daphne du Maurier). *Educ:* Winchester; Trinity Coll., Cambridge (MA). Shell International, 1951–62; Dir, Yardley International, 1963–74; Man. Dir, Terimar Services (Overseas Trade Consultancy), 1974–99; Dir, Korn/Ferry International, 1977–93; Chm., Antofagasta (Chile) and Bolivia Railway Co., 1980–82; Dir, NEI, 1981–87. Mem., Exec. Cttee, British Gp, IPU, 1987–99, 2008–13; Deleg., OSCE Parly Assembly, 1991–2000. Elected crossbench Mem., H of L, 2005–15; Chm., London Gp, H of L, 2007–12. Editorial Adviser, Vision Interamericana, 1974–94. Chm., Economic Affairs Cttee, Canning House, 1973–75; Pres., British Industrial Exhibition, São Paulo, 1974. Councillor, Royal Borough of Kensington and Chelsea, 1974–78. Hon. Consul, Republic of El Salvador, 1973–77. President: Anglo-Argentine Soc., 1977–87; Anglo-Belgian Soc., 1994–2006; Chairman: Hispanic and Luso Brazilian Council, 1978–80 (Pres., 1987–94); Brazilian Chamber of Commerce in GB, 1980–82; European Atlantic Gp, 1992–94 (Pres., 1994–97). Pres., Cambridge Univ. Engrs Assoc., 2001–06. Patron: D-Day and Normandy Fellowship, 1980–95; 8th Army Veterans Assoc., 1985–2002. President: Redgrave Theatre, Farnham, 1977–89; Restaurateurs Assoc. of GB, 1982–90 (Patron, 1991–99); Acad. of Food and Wine Service, 1995–98; Centre for International Briefing, Farnham Castle, 1985–2003. Pres., Amesbury Sch., 1992– (Gov., 1976–92). Gran Oficial: Orden Bernardo O'Higgins (Chile), 1989; Orden Libertador San Martin (Argentina), 1992; Orden Nacional Cruzeiro do Sul (Brazil), 1993; Orden de Isabel la Católica (Spain), 1993; Commander's Cross, Order of Merit (Germany), 1993; Order of Aztec Eagle (Mexico), 1994; Order of Leopold II (Belgium), 1997; Orden de San Carlos (Colombia), 1998; Orden del Libertador (Venezuela), 1999. *Publications:* (with Alistair Horne) The Lonely Leader: Monty 1944–45, 1994. *Heir: s* Hon. Henry David Montgomery [*b* 2 April 1954; *m* 1980, Caroline (*d* 2014), *e d* of Richard Odey, Hotham Hall, York; three *d*]. *Clubs:* Garrick, Canning.

**MONTGOMERY, Alan Everard,** CMG 1993; PhD; HM Diplomatic Service, retired; Associate Member, General Medical Council, 2009–12; *b* 11 March 1938; *s* of Philip Napier Montgomery and Honor Violet Coleman (*née* Price); *m* 1st, 1960, Janet Barton (*d* 1994); one *s* one *d;* 2nd, 1999, Florence Belle Liebst. *Educ:* Royal Grammar Sch., Guildford; County of Stafford Training Coll. (Cert. of Educn); Birkbeck Coll., London (BA Hons, PhD). Served Middx Regt, 1957–59. Teacher, Staffs and ILEA, 1961–65; Lectr, Univ. of Birmingham, 1969–72; entered FCO, 1972; 1st Secretary: FCO, 1972–75; Dhaka, 1975–77; Ottawa, 1977–80; FCO, 1980–83; Counsellor GATT/UNCTAD, UKMIS Geneva, 1983–87; Counsellor, Consul-Gen. and Hd of Chancery, Jakarta, 1987–89; Head of Migration and Visa Dept, FCO, 1989–92; Ambassador to the Philippines, 1992–95; High Comr to Tanzania, 1995–98. Trade Policy Advr, Commonwealth Business Council, 1998–99. Mem., Fitness to Practise Cttee (formerly Professional Conduct Cttee), GMC, 2000–08, 2009–12; Lay Member: Immigration Services Tribunal, 2001–08; Complaints Commn, 2001–04, Professional Standards Cttee, 2004–05, Rules Cttee, 2006, Gen. Council of the Bar; Professional Conduct Panel, RICS, 2003–07; Professional Conduct Panel, British Assoc. for Counselling and Psychotherapy, 2003–08; Ind. Mem., Surrey Police Authy Misconduct Tribunals, 2004–10. Mem. Bd, FARM Africa, 1998–2001. Gp Leader, RCDS Africa tour, 2001–03. *Publications:* (contrib.) Lloyd George: 12 essays, ed A. J. P. Taylor, 1971; (contrib.) Commonwealth Banking Almanac, 1999; contrib. Cambridge Hist. Jl, 1972. *Recreations:* historic buildings, jazz, theatre, opera, gardening.

**MONTGOMERY, Sir (Basil Henry) David,** 9th Bt *cr* 1801, of Stanhope; CVO 2007; Lord-Lieutenant of Perth and Kinross, 1996–2006; Chairman, Forestry Commission, 1979–89; *b* 20 March 1931; *s* of late Lt-Col H. K. Purvis-Montgomery, OBE, and of Mrs C. L. W. Purvis-Russell-Montgomery (*née* Maconochie Welwood); *S uncle,* 1964; *m* 1956, Delia (*d* 2019), *o d* of Adm. Sir (John) Peter (Lorne) Reid, GCB, CVO; one *s* four *d* (and one *s* decd). *Educ:* Eton. National Service, Black Watch, 1949–51. Member: Nature Conservancy Council, 1973–79; Tayside Regional Authority, 1974–79. Comr, Mental Welfare Commn for Scotland, 1990–91. Trustee, Municipal Mutual Insurance Ltd, 1980–96. Hon. LLD Dundee, 2017. DL Kinross-shire, 1960, Vice-Lieutenant 1966–74; JP 1966; DL Perth and Kinross, 1975. *Heir: s* James David Keith Montgomery [*b* 13 June 1957; *m* 1983, Elizabeth, *e d* of late E. Lyndon Evans, Pentyrch, Mid-Glamorgan; one *s* one *d.* Served The Black Watch, RHR, 1976–86]. *Address:* Burleigh House, Milnathort, Kinross KY13 9SR. *T:* (01577) 863467.

**MONTGOMERY, Vice Adm. Sir Charles (Percival Ross),** KBE 2012 (CBE 2006); Director General, UK Border Force, Home Office, 2013–17; *b* 12 April 1955; *s* of Phillip Stuart Montgomery and Eileen Beryl Montgomery; *m* 1982, Adrienne Julie; three *s* one *d*. *Educ:* Univ. of Sheffield (BEng Hons 1976). CO HMS Beaver, 1991–93; Directorate of Defence Policy, 1993–95; Private Sec. to Sec. of State, 1995–97; Trng Dir, Naval Recruiting and Trng Agency, 1997–2000; Hd, NRTA Estate Rev. Team, 2000; Asst Dir of Naval Staff (Strategy), 2000–02; rcds, 2003; Dir Naval Personnel Strategy, 2003–06; Cdre Maritime Warfare Sch. and CO HMS Collingwood, 2006–07; Naval Sec. and COS (Personnel) to C-in-C Fleet, 2007–10; Second Sea Lord and C-in-C Naval Home Comd, 2010–12; Flag ADC to the Queen, 2010–12. Chm. Bd, Greenwich Hosp., 2010–12. Chm., King Alfred Multi-Acad. Trust, 2016–. Younger Brother, Trinity House, 2007–. President: RN Hockey Assoc., 2009–12; RN Lawn Tennis Assoc., 2010–12; Combined Services Lawn Tennis Assoc., 2010–12; Combined Services Hockey Assoc., 2011–12; RN Benevolent Trust, 2013–; Vice-Pres., RN Rugby Union; Smile Support, 2013–. Patron, Battleback, 2010–. CCMI 2012; FCIPD 2012. Hon. Freeman, Wheelwrights' Co., 2014. Hon. DEng Sheffield, 2012. *Recreations:* cricket, golf, Rugby, hockey, gardening, outdoor pursuits. *Clubs:* Royal Navy of 1765 and 1785, Army and Navy.

**MONTGOMERY, Clare Patricia;** QC 1996; a Recorder, since 2000; a Deputy High Court Judge, since 2003; a Judge of the Courts of Appeal of Jersey and Guernsey, since 2007; *b* 29 April 1958; *d* of Stephen Ross Montgomery and Ann Margaret Barlow; *m* 1991; two *d*. *Educ:* Millfield Sch.; UCL (LLB). Called to the Bar, Gray's Inn, 1980, Bencher, 2002. An Asst Recorder, 1999–2000. Mem., Supplementary Panel (Common Law), 1992–96. *Publications:* (ed) Archbold Criminal Pleading Evidence and Practice, annually, 1993–2014; (ed) Fraud: criminal law and procedure, 2008; (ed) The Law of Extradition and Mutual Assistance, 2013. *Address:* Matrix Chambers, Gray's Inn, WC1R 5LN. *T:* (020) 7404 3447.

**MONTGOMERY, Sir David;** see Montgomery, Sir B. H. D.

**MONTGOMERY, David,** CMG 1984; OBE 1972; Foreign and Commonwealth Office, 1987–91; *b* 29 July 1927; *s* of late David Montgomery and Mary (*née* Walker Cunningham); *m* 1955, Margaret Newman; one *s* one *d*. RNVR, 1945–46; Royal Navy, 1946–48. Foreign Office, 1949–52; Bucharest, 1952–53; FO, 1953–55; Bonn, 1955–58; Düsseldorf, 1958–61; Rangoon, 1961–63; Ottawa, 1963–64; Regina, Saskatchewan, 1964–65; FCO, 1966–68; Bangkok, 1968–72; Zagreb, 1973–76; FCO, 1976–79; Dep. High Comr to Barbados, 1980–84, also (non-resident) to Antigua and Barbuda, Dominica, Grenada, St Kitts and Nevis, St Lucia, St Vincent and the Grenadines, 1980–84; FCO, 1984–85. *Address:* London, SW15.

**MONTGOMERY, David John;** Chairman, Local TV Ltd, since 2017; Director, National World Ltd, since 2016; *b* 6 Nov. 1948; *s* of William John and Margaret Jean Montgomery; *m* 1st, 1971, Susan Frances Buchanan Russell (marr. diss. 1987); 2nd, 1989, Heidi Kingstone (marr. diss. 1997); 3rd, 1997, Sophie Countess of Woolton, *d* of Baron Birdwood; one *s* one *d*. *Educ:* Queen's University, Belfast (BA Politics/History). Sub-Editor, Daily Mirror, London/Manchester, 1973–78; Assistant Chief Sub-Editor, Daily Mirror, 1978–80; Chief Sub-Editor, The Sun, 1980; Asst Editor, Sunday People, 1982; Asst Editor, 1984, Editor, 1985–87, News of the World; Editor, Today, 1987–91 (Newspaper of the Year, 1988); Man. Dir, News UK, 1987–91; Chief Exec., 1991, Dir, 1991–, London Live Television; Chief Exec., Mirror Gp Newspapers, 1992–99; Exec. Chm., 2000–09, Chief Exec., 2009–11, Mecom UK Mgt Ltd, later Mecom Gp plc; CEO, Local World Ltd, 2013–16 (Exec. Chm., 2012–13). Director: Satellite Television PLC, 1986–91; News Group Newspapers, 1986–91; Caledonian Publishing Co. (Glasgow Herald & Times), 1991–92; Donohue Inc., 1992–95; Newspaper Publishing (The Independent, Independent on Sunday), 1994–98; Scottish Media Gp (formerly Scottish Television), 1995–99; Press Assoc., 1996–99; Chairman: Tri-mex Gp, 1999–2002; Yava, 2000–03; Africa Lakes plc, 2000–07; West 175 Media plc, 2002–06; Moyle Hldgs Ltd, 2003–08; NI Energy Hldgs, 2005–08; Berliner Verlag (Germany), 2005–09; Media Gp Limburg (Netherlands), 2006–08; RSDB (Netherlands), 2006–09; Royal Wegener (Netherlands), 2009–11. Pres., Integrated Educn Fund Develt Bd (NI), 2000–. Member: QUB Foundn Bd, 2002–05; Campaign for Peace and Democratic Reconstruction for NI, 2002–; Chm., Team NI, 2003–08. *Address:* 15 Collingham Gardens, SW5 0HS.

**MONTGOMERY, Prof. Hugh Edward,** MD; FRCP; Director, Centre (formerly Institute) for Human Health and Performance, since 2005, and Professor of Intensive Care Medicine, since 2008, University College London; *b* Plymouth, 20 Oct. 1962; *s* of Nelson and Bridget Montgomery; *m* 2001, Mary Limebury (*d* 2019); two *s*. *Educ:* Plymouth Coll.; Middlesex Hosp., Univ. of London (BSc Physiol./Neuropharmacol. 1984; MB BS 1987; MD 1997). FRCP 2007; FFICM 2011. House Physician, Whittington Hosp., 1987; House Surgeon, Battle Hosp., Reading, 1988; Senior House Officer: Hammersmith Hosp., 1988–89; St Bartholomew's Hosp., 1989–90; Intensive Care Unit and Chronic Respiratory Unit, St Thomas' Hosp., 1990; MO, CJM Hosp., Kwazulu, Africa, 1990–91; Registrar: Medical and Cardiol., St Peters Hosp., Chertsey, 1991–92; Cardiol., St George's Hosp.,

1992–93; BHF Res. Fellow and Clin. Lectr, Hatter Inst., 1993–95; Sen. Registrar, Intensive Care Unit, UCLH 1995–97, 1997–98; University College London: Res. Fellow, Cardiovascular Genetics, 1995–96; Lectr, Intensive Care, 1996–97; Res. Fellow, Cardiol., 1997–98; SHO, Dept of Anaesthetics, St Helier's Hosp., Surrey, 1997; Specialist Registrar, Cardiol. and Gen. Medicine, 1998–2000; Consultant Intensivist: UCLH, 2002–06; Whittington Hosp., 2006–. Consultant, Deepmind Health, 2015–. Leader, Project Genie, 2004–; London Leader, GLA, 2008–. Chair: Lancet Commn Climate Change and Health, 2013–15; Lancet Countdown Climate Change and Health, 2016–. Member: Bd, UK Climate and Health Council, 2008–; Steering Gp, Natural Capital Initiative, 2009–17. TV writer and presenter: Royal Instn Christmas Lectures, 2007; Who Sank the Mary Rose?, 2008. Patents: Patient Controlled Hydration, 2016; A novel particulate removal system, 2016. *Publications:* (ed) 100 Questions in Cardiology, 2000; My First MRCP Book, 2003; (ed) Puzzling Out Medicine series (10 books), 2005; (ed) Surviving Prescribing, 2006; Control (fiction), 2019; *for children:* The Voyage of the Arctic Tern, 2002; Cloudsailors, 2005; The Genie in the Bottle, 2006; contrib. book chapters and scientific jls incl. Nature. *Recreations:* mountaineering, hill-walking, diving, writing. *Address:* UCL Centre for Human Health and Performance, 1st Floor, Institute for Sport, Exercise and Health, 170 Tottenham Court Road, W1T 7HA. *E:* h.montgomery@ucl.ac.uk.

**MONTGOMERY, John;** Sheriff of South Strathclyde, Dumfries and Galloway, since 2003, at Ayr since 2005; *b* 17 Sept. 1951; *s* of Robert and Jessie Montgomery; *m* 1978, Susan Wilson Templeton; one *s* three *d. Educ:* Stevenston High Sch.; Ardrossan Acad.; Glasgow Univ. (LLB Hons). NP. Solicitor, 1976–2003. Temp. Sheriff, 1995–99; Sheriff (pt-time), 2000–03. *Recreations:* family, walking, gardening, travel. *Address:* Sheriff Court, Wellington Square, Ayr KA7 1DR.

**MONTGOMERY, John Duncan;** Member, Monopolies and Mergers Commission, 1989–95; *b* 12 Nov. 1928; *s* of Lionel Eric Montgomery and Katherine Mary Montgomery (*née* Ambler); *m* 1956, Pauline Mary Sutherland; two *d. Educ:* King's College Sch., Wimbledon; LSE (LLB, LLM). Admitted Solicitor 1951; Treasury Solicitor's Dept, 1960–68; Legal Adviser, Beecham Products, 1974–75; Head, Legal Div., Shell UK, 1975–88 and Company Sec., Shell UK, 1979–88. Former Chm., Youth Orgns, Merton. Freeman, City of London, 1987; Mem., Loriners' Co., 1988. JP SW London, 1985–98. *Recreations:* dinghy sailing, photography. *Address:* 6 White Lodge Close, Sutton, Surrey SM2 5TQ. *Clubs:* MCC; Surrey CC.

**MONTGOMERY, John Matthew;** Clerk of the Salters' Company, 1975–90; *b* 22 May 1930; *s* of Prof. George Allison Montgomery, QC, and Isobel A. (*née* Morison); *m* 1956, Gertrude Gillian Richards (*d* 2008); two *s* one *d. Educ:* Rugby Sch.; Trinity Hall, Cambridge (MA). Various commercial appointments with Mobil Oil Corporation and First National City Bank, 1953–74. Member Council: Surrey Trust for Nature Conservation Ltd, 1965–89 (Chm., 1973–83; Vice-Pres., 1983–); Royal Soc. for Nature Conservation 1980–89; Botanical Soc. of British Isles, 1991–95; Founder Mem., London Wildlife Trust, 1981–. Member, Executive Committee: Nat. Assoc. of Almshouses, 1980–91; Age Concern Gtr London, 1985–96 (Chm., 1988–91; Vice-Pres., 1996–2001). *Recreation:* various natural history interests. *Address:* 36 Gibson Court, 33 Manor Road North, Hinchley Wood, Esher, Surrey KT10 0AW. *T:* (020) 8398 5038.

**MONTGOMERY, Sir Jonathan (Robert),** Kt 2019; Professor of Health Care Law, University College London, since 2013; Chairman, Oxford University Hospitals NHS Foundation Trust, since 2019; *b* 29 July 1962; *s* of Robert William Montgomery and Margaret Elizabeth Montgomery (*née* Exell); *m* 1986, Elsa Mary Wells Harnett; two *d. Educ:* King's College Sch., Wimbledon; Gonville and Caius Coll., Cambridge (BA 1983; LLM 1984). Lectr, 1984–98, Reader, 1998–2001, Prof. of Health Care Law, 2001–13, Univ. of Southampton. Non-exec. Dir, 1992–98, Chm., 1998–2001, Southampton Community Health Services NHS Trust; Chairman: W Hants NHS Trust, subseq. Hants Partnership NHS Trust, 2001–04; Hants and IoW Strategic HA, 2004–06; Hampshire PCT, 2006–13; Health Res. Authy, 2012–19. Member: Med. Ethics Cttee, BMA, 2003–08; Ethics Adv. Gp to Care Records Develt Bd, NHS Prog. for IT, 2004–06; Working Party on Ethics of Public Health, Nuffield Council on Bioethics, 2006–07; Cttee on the Ethical Aspects of Pandemic Influenza, 2006–; Organ Donation Taskforce, 2008–09; Morecambe Bay Investigation, 2014–15; Expert Adv. Gp, Healthcare Safety Investigation Branch, 2015–16; Eur. Gp on Ethics in Sci. and Emerging Technologies, 2017–. Chairman: Adv. Cttee on Clinical Excellence Awards, 2005–14; Working Party on a Strategy for Brain Tissue Banking, UK Clinical Res. Collaboration, 2007–08; Scientific Steering Cttee, Brain Banks UK, 2009–12; Human Genetics Commn, 2009–12; Nuffield Council of Bioethics, 2012–17; Task and Finish Gp, Rev. of Confidentiality Guidance, GMC, 2015–16. Comr, Commn of Inquiry into the Future of Adult Social Care, Hants CC, 2008. Non-exec. Dir, Health Data Res. UK, 2018–. Chm., Winchester Diocesan Council for Social Responsibility, 1997–98; Lay Examining Chaplain for Bishop of Portsmouth, 2003–. Patron, CISters (Childhood Incest Survivors), 2004–. Trustee, TADIC (Teenage Drop-in Centre, Hedge End), 2008–10. Annual Health Ethics and Law Lect., Univ. of Southampton, 2015; George Griffin Lect., 2017, J. Kenyon Mason Lect., 2017, Assoc. Physicians GB and Ireland; Liverpool Univ. Health Partnership Annual Lect., 2017; Annual Lect., Res. Inst. Ethics and Law, Swansea Univ., 2018. General Editor: (with G. Howells) Butterworths Family Law Service, 1996–; Butterworths Family and Child Law Bulletin, 1997–2006; Consultant Ed., Halsbury's Laws of England: Medical Professions vol., 5th edn 2011. Hon. FRCPCH 2005. *Publications:* Health Care Law, 1997, 2nd edn 2003; (with P. Alderson) Health Care Choices: making decisions with children, 1996; numerous book chapters and contribs to learned jls. *Recreations:* family and friends, active member of the Church of England, church youth work, lacrosse (Cambridge Univ. Lacrosse Club, 1982–84; Southampton Univ. Men's Lacrosse Club, 1984–88, 2007–08; Southampton City Lacrosse Club, 2008–15). *Address:* Faculty of Laws, University College London, 104 Bentham House, Endsleigh Gardens, WC1H 0EG. *E:* Jonathan.Montgomery@ucl.ac.uk.

**MONTGOMERY, Joseph,** CB 2006; Chairman, Re Ltd, since 2015; Member, Civil Service Commission, since 2017; *b* 1 Feb. 1961. *Educ:* Becket Sch., Nottingham; Aston Univ. (BSc 1983). Asst Sec., Cadbury Trust, 1986–89; Leader, Deptford Task Force, DTI, 1989–92; Chief Exec., Deptford City Challenge, 1992–94; Dir, Leisure, Economy and Envmt, 1994–99, Exec. Dir for Regeneration, 1999–2001, Lewisham BC; Director General: Neighbourhood Renewal Unit, DTLR, then at ODPM, subseq. Tackling Disadvantage Gp, ODPM, then at DCLG, 2001–06; Regions (formerly Places) and Communities, DCLG, 2006–11; Chief Exec. for Europe, Urban Land Inst., 2011–14. Chm., Youth Futures Foundn, 2019–. *Address:* Re Ltd, 9th Floor, Barnet House, 1255 High Road, Barnet, N20 0EJ.

**MONTGOMERY, Kristina Aileen;** QC 2013; **Her Honour Judge Montgomery;** a Circuit Judge, since 2014; *b* 17 Jan. 1971; *d* of Stuart Montgomery and Eva Montgomery; *m* 2006, Matthew Barnes; one *s.* Called to the Bar, Middle Temple, 1993; a Recorder, 2010–14. *Address:* Oxford Combined Court and Family Hearing Centre, St Aldates, Oxford OX1 1TL.

**MONTGOMERY, Susannah;** HM Diplomatic Service; Head, Foreign and Security Policy Unit, Foreign and Commonwealth Office, since 2017. *Educ:* Univ. of Cambridge. Joined FCO, 1995; Vice Consul, Almaty, 1996; Second Sec. (Pol), Moscow, 1997; Actg Hd of Mission, Minsk, 1998; Second Sec. (Pol), UK Mission to the UN, NY, 1999–2000; on secondment to DFID, 2001; Ops Manager, Finance Directorate, FCO, 2002–04; Hd, Nuclear Safety, Sci. and Envmt Team, Moscow, 2004–05; Strategic Policy Advr, Policy Planners, FCO, 2005–07; Hd, Eur. Prog. Team, FCO, 2007–08; High Comr, Gambia, 2008–09; Advr, Parly Relations Team, 2010; Communications Manager, Paris, 2011; Ambassador to Slovakia, 2011–14; Lead, Good Governance Fund, 2015–17. *Recreation:* archery. *Address:* c/o Foreign and Commonwealth Office, King Charles Street, SW1A 2AH.

**MONTGOMERY CAMPBELL, Sir Philip Henry;** *see* Campbell.

**MONTGOMERY CUNINGHAME, Sir John Christopher Foggo,** 12th Bt *cr* 1672, of Corsehill, Ayrshire and Kirktonholm, Lanarkshire; Director, Primentia Inc., and other companies; *b* 24 July 1935; 2nd *s* of Col Sir Thomas Montgomery-Cuninghame, 10th Bt, DSO (*d* 1945), and of Nancy Macaulay (his 2nd wife), *d* of late W. Stewart Foggo, Aberdeen (she *m* 2nd, 1946, Johan Frederik Christian Killander); *b* of Sir Andrew Montgomery-Cuninghame, 11th Bt; *S* brother, 1959; *m* 1964, Laura Violet, *d* of Sir Godfrey Nicholson, 1st Bt; three *d. Educ:* Fettes; Worcester Coll., Oxford (MA). 2nd Lieut, Rifle Brigade (NS), 1955–56; Lieut, London Rifle Brigade, TA, 1956–59. *Recreation:* fishing. *Heir:* none. *Address:* The Old Rectory, Brightwalton, Newbury, Berks RG20 7BL.

**MONTI, Dr Mario;** Senator-for-Life, Italy, since 2011; Prime Minister of Italy, 2011–13; *b* 19 March 1943; *m* 1970, Elsa Antonioli; one *s* one *d. Educ:* Bocconi Univ. (Dr); Yale Univ. Bocconi University, Italy: Asst, 1965–69; Prof. of Monetary Theory and Policy, 1971–85; Prof. of Economics and Dir, Economics Inst., 1985–94; Founder, Paolo Baffi Centre for Monetary and Financial Economics, 1985; Rector, Innocenzo Gasparini Inst. of Economic Res., 1989–94; Pres., 1994–. Mem., European Commn, 1995–2004. Chm., 2005–08, Hon. Pres., 2008–, Brussels European and Global Econ. Lab. (Bruegel). *Address:* Italian Senate, Piazza Madama, 00186 Rome, Italy.

**MONTREAL, Bishop of,** since 2015; **Rt Rev. Mary Irwin-Gibson;** *b* Sarnia, Ont, 23 Oct. 1955; *d* of George A. Irwin and Joan Irwin (*née* McKenzie); *m* 1978, Mark Gibson; two *d. Educ:* McGill Univ. (BTh 1979); Montreal Diocesan Theol Coll. (DipMin 1981); Univ. de Québec à Montréal (MBA 2005). Ordained deacon, 1981, priest, 1982; Diocese of Montreal: Asst Curate, Parish of Vaudreuil, 1981–84; Rector, Parish of Dunham-Frelighsburg, 1984–91; Regl Dean, Bedford, 1988–91; Rector, Parish of Ste-Agathe, 1991–2009; Regl Dean, Laurentians, 1993–97; Archdeacon, St Andrews, Ont, 2000–06; Dean of Ontario and Rector, St George's Cathedral, Dio. Ontario, 2009–15. *Address:* Anglican Diocese of Montreal, 1444 Union Avenue, Montreal, QC H3A 2B8, Canada. *T:* (514) 8436577, ext. 234, *Fax:* (514) 8433221. *E:* bishops.office@montreal.anglican.ca.

**MONTROSE, 8th Duke of,** *cr* 1707; **James Graham;** Lord Graham 1445; Earl of Montrose 1505; Bt (NS) 1625; Marquis of Montrose 1644; Duke of Montrose, Marquis of Graham and Buchanan, Earl of Kincardine, Viscount Dundaff, Lord Aberuthven, Mugdock, and Fintrie 1707; Earl and Baron Graham (Eng.) 1722; *b* 6 April 1935; *e s* of 7th Duke of Montrose, and Isobel Veronica (*d* 1990), *yr d* of Lt-Col T. B. Sellar, CMG, DSO; *S* father, 1992; *m* 1970, Catherine Elizabeth MacDonell (*d* 2014), *d* of late Captain N. A. T. Young, and of Mrs Young, Ottawa; two *s* one *d. Educ:* Loretto. Elected Mem., H of L, 1999; Opposition Whip, H of L, 2001–11; Opposition spokesman on Scottish affairs, 2001–11. Captain, Royal Company of Archers (Queen's Body Guard for Scotland), 2005–14 (Mem., 1965–). Area Pres., Scottish NFU, 1986 (Mem. Council, 1981–86 and 1987–90); President: RHASS, 1997–98; Nat. Sheep Assoc., 2011–17. ARAgS 2009, FRAgS 2013. OStJ 1978. *Heir: s* Marquis of Graham, *qv. Address:* Garden Cottage, Auchmar, Drymen, Glasgow G63 0AG. *T:* (01360) 660307.

**MONTY, Simon Trevor;** QC 2003; **His Honour Judge Monty;** a Circuit Judge, since 2018; a Deputy High Court Judge, since 2013; *b* 9 Dec. 1959; *s* of Cyril Monty and Gina (*née* Dixon); *m* 1985, Susan Andrea Goldwater; two *s* one *d. Educ:* Alleyn's Sch., Dulwich; Manchester Univ. (LLB Hons 1981). Called to the Bar, Middle Temple, 1982, Bencher, 2004; in practice as barrister, 1983–2018, specialising in professional negligence litigation; a Recorder, 2010–18. *Publications:* (contrib.) Jackson & Powell's Professional Liability Precedents, 2000. *Recreations:* ski-ing, music, walking. *Address:* Central London County Court, Thomas More Building, Royal Courts of Justice, Strand, WC2A 2LL.

**MOODY, Prof. Christopher John,** PhD, DSc; CChem, FRSC; Sir Jesse Boot Professor of Chemistry, University of Nottingham, since 2005; *b* Manchester, 30 Dec. 1951; *s* of Geoffrey Moody and Sheila Moody; *m* 1976, Barbara Moore; three *d. Educ:* Manchester Grammar Sch.; King's Coll. London (BSc 1973); Univ. of Liverpool (PhD 1976); Univ. of London (DSc 1989). Royal Soc. Postdoctoral Fellow, ETH, Zürich, 1976–77; Sen. Chemist, Roche, 1977–79; Lectr, then Reader, Imperial Coll. London, 1979–89; Professor of Organic Chemistry: Loughborough Univ., 1990–96; Univ. of Exeter, 1996–2005. *Publications:* (with L. M. Harwood) Experimental Organic Chemistry, 1989, 3rd edn 2017; (with G. H. Whitham) Reactive Intermediates, 1992; over 435 papers in learned jls. *Recreations:* sport, walking. *Address:* School of Chemistry, University of Nottingham, University Park, Nottingham NG7 2RD. *T:* (0115) 846 8500.

**MOODY, Clare Miranda;** Member (Lab) South West Region and Gibraltar, European Parliament, 2014–19; *b* Chipping Norton, 30 Oct. 1965; *d* of Raymond and Joan Moody. *Educ:* Univ. of Kent (BA Industrial Relns). Trade union officer, UNIFI, Amicus then Unite, 1994–2014. Advr, Prime Minister's Policy Unit, 10 Downing St, 2008–10. Vice Chm., Security and Defence Sub-Cttee; Member: Cttee on Foreign Affairs; Cttee on Industry, Res. and Energy; Cttee on Women's Rights and Gender Equality. Contested (Lab): SW Reg., EP, 2004; Salisbury, 2005; SW Reg., EP, 2019.

**MOODY, David Barker,** CVO 2014; Lord-Lieutenant of South Yorkshire, 2004–15; *b* 7 April 1940; *s* of Norman William Barker Moody and Dorothy Moody (*née* Beetham); *m* 1966, Carolyn Susan Lindop Green; one *s* two *d* (and one *d* decd). *Educ:* Worksop Coll.; Pembroke Coll., Oxford (MA Mod. Hist.); London Business Sch. (Sloan Fellow 1971). Asst Master, Sussex House Prep. Sch., 1959–60; graduate apprentice, United Steel Cos Ltd, 1963–64; Samuel Fox & Company Limited: Mgt Develt Officer, 1964–70; Manager Billet Finishing, 1970–72; Sales Manager, 1972–75; Commercial Dir, Spartan Redheugh Ltd, 1975–81; Chm. and Man. Dir, Spartan Sheffield Ltd, 1981–99; Chm., J. Shipman Properties Ltd, 1998–. Chm., S Yorks Investment Fund, 2001–10; President: Sheffield Chamber of Commerce and Industry, 1998–99; S Yorks Community Foundn, 2004–15; Army Benevolent Fund S Yorks, 2004–15; Wentworth Castle and Stainborough Park Heritage Trust, 2004–; Friends of Sheffield Cathedral, 2006–15 (Vice-Pres., 2004–06); Vice-Pres., S and W Yorks, RBL, 2004–15. Governor: Worksop Coll., 1975–2010 (Chm. of Govs, 1992–2001); Ranby House Sch., 1975–2010 (Chm. of Govs, 1992–2001); Fellow and Dir, Woodard Schs Ltd, 1981–2005. High Sheriff, S Yorks, 2003–04. Hon. Freeman, Metropolitan Bor. of Barnsley, 2016. *Recreations:* Burgundy, grandchildren, landscape, Romanesque, Schubert. *Address:* Ivas Wood, Round Green Lane, Stainborough, Barnsley, Yorks S75 3EL. *T:* (01226) 205325, *Fax:* (01226) 785420. *Club:* Royal Over-Seas League.

**MOODY, Ian Charles Hugh,** OBE 1996; DL; Commissioner-in-Chief, St John Ambulance, 1991–95; *b* 25 April 1928; *s* of William Thomas Charles Moody and Roberta (*née* Baxter); *m* 1952, Angela de Lisle Carey (*d* 2007); one *s* two *d. Educ:* Cheltenham Coll.; RMA, Sandhurst. Served RWF, 1947–50. Industrial relations and personnel appointments with: Compania Shell de Venezuela, 1951–54; Shell Trinidad Ltd, 1954–59; Shell BP Nigeria Ltd, 1959–60; PT Shell Indonesia, 1960–64; Pakistan Shell Oil Ltd, 1964–68; Personnel Manager, Shell Nigeria Ltd, 1968–72; Employee Relations, Shell Internat. Petroleum Co. Ltd, 1974–76; Personnel Manager, Shell Internat. Trading Co., 1976–83; retd 1983. St John Ambulance, Devon: Comr, 1983–88; Comdr, 1988–91; Chm., 1995–98. Chm., E Devon Cons. Assoc., 1997–2000. FCIPD. DL Devon, 1991. KStJ 1991. *Recreations:* cricket, sailing, gardening. *Address:* The Queen Anne House, The Strand, Lympstone, Devon EX8 5JW. *T:* (01395) 263189. *Club:* MCC.

**MOODY, Neil Robert;** QC 2010; *b* Winchester, 1 Aug. 1965; *s* of Geoffrey and Janet Moody; *m* 1995, Nicola Ball; one *s* two *d. Educ:* Maidstone Grammar Sch.; University Coll., Oxford (BA 1987; MA 1992); Poly. of Central London (Dip. Law 1988). Called to the Bar, Gray's Inn, 1989; in practice as barrister, 1990–, specialising in commercial and common law; Hd of Chambers, 2015–19. *Recreations:* ski-ing, sailing. *Address:* 2 Temple Gardens, EC4Y 9AY. *T:* (020) 7822 1200. *E:* nmoody@2tg.co.uk. *Clubs:* MCC; Salterns Sailing (Lymington).

**MOODY, Patrick Thomas Robert;** HM Diplomatic Service; Ambassador to the United Arab Emirates, since 2018; *b* Berlin, 17 March 1966; *s* of Col A. M. T. Moody and Tanya Moody (*née* Pulley); *m* 1996, Atalanta Sturdy; one *s* one *d. Educ:* Sherborne Sch.; New Coll., Oxford (BA Juris. 1988). Entered FCO, 1988; Asst Desk Officer, Gibraltar and Cyprus, FCO, 1988–90; Second Sec. (Press and Political), Mexico City, 1990–93; Head: Bosnia Team, FCO, 1994–96; Money Laundering and Financial Crime Team, FCO, 1996–97; Policy Team, Jt Export Promotion Dept, FCO, 1997–98; First Sec. and Hd, Ext. Relns Team, UK Delegn, NATO, Brussels, 1998–2002; Dep. Hd, Africa Dept (Equatorial), FCO, 2003–06; Dep. High Comr, Kuala Lumpur, 2006–09; HCSC, 2010; Dir, Internat. Policy, UK Border Agency, 2010–11, Hd, Border Security Unit, 2011–12, Home Office; Hd, Pakistan and Afghanistan Dept, and Actg Dir, S Asia and Afghanistan Directorate, FCO, 2012–14; Dep. High Comr, Islamabad, 2014–17; Addnl Dir, Asia-Pacific Directorate, FCO, 2017–18. *Recreations:* fishing, tennis. *Address:* c/o Foreign and Commonwealth Office, King Charles Street, SW1A 2AH. *E:* patrick.moody@fco.gov.uk.

**MOODY-STUART, Sir Mark,** KCMG 2000; PhD; FGS; FRGS; Director, Shell Transport and Trading Company plc, 1991–2005 (Chairman, 1997–2001); Chairman: Anglo American plc, 2002–09; Hermes Equity Ownership Services, 2009–16; *b* 15 Sept. 1940; *s* of Sir Alexander Moody-Stuart, OBE, MC and Judith (*née* Henzell); *m* 1964, Judith McLeavy; three *s* one *d. Educ:* Shrewsbury Sch.; St John's Coll., Cambridge (MA, PhD; Hon. Fellow, 2001). Joined Shell, 1966; worked for various Shell companies in: Holland, 1966; Spain, 1967; Oman, 1968; Brunei, 1968–72; Australia, 1972–76; UK, 1977–78; Brunei, 1978–79; Nigeria, 1979–82; Turkey, 1982–86; Malaysia, 1986–89; Holland, 1990–94; Gp Man. Dir, 1991–2001, Chm., Cttee of Man. Dirs, 1998–2001, Royal Dutch/ Shell Group. Director: HSBC Hldgs plc, 2001–10; Accenture, 2001–15; Saudi Aramco, 2007–; Zamyn, 2010–. Co-Chm., G-8 Task Force on Renewable Energy, 2000–01. Member: UN Sec.-Gen's Adv. Council on Global Compact, 2001–04; Bd, Global Reporting Initiative, 2001–07; UN Global Compact Bd, 2006– (Vice Chm., 2007–18); Adv. Bd, Envision Energy, 2012–; Chairman: Global Business Coalition for HIV/AIDS, TB and Malaria, 2002–11; Global Compact Foundn, 2006–; Innovative Vector Control Consortium, 2008–18; FTSE Envmtl, Social and Governance Adv. Cttee, 2015–; Hon. Co-Chm., Internat. Tax and Investment Center, 2011–. Vice-Pres., 1997–2001, Pres., 2001–08, Liverpool Sch. of Tropical Medicine; Mem. Bd, Internat. Inst. for Sustainable Develt, 2002–11. Gov., Nuffield Hosps, 2001–08. Trustee, St George's House, Windsor, 2011–17. Mem., Soc. of Petroleum Engrs, 1990–; FGS 1966 (Pres., 2002–04); FInstPet 1997 (Cadman Medal, 2001); FRGS 1999. Hon. FIChemE 1997. Hon. DBA Robert Gordon, 2000; Hon. LLD Aberdeen, 2004; Hon. DSc London, 2007. *Publications:* Responsible Leadership: lessons from the front line of sustainability and ethics, 2014; papers in Geol Mag., Jl of Sedimentary Petrology, Bull. Amer. Assoc. Petrology and Geol., Norsk Polarinstitut, Proceedings of Geologists' Assoc., Corporate Environmental Strategy, Jl Corporate Citizenship. *Recreations:* sailing, travel, reading. *Address:* 9 Gun House, 122 Wapping High Street, E1W 2NL. *Clubs:* Travellers, Cruising Association.
*See also* T. Moody-Stuart.

**MOODY-STUART, Thomas;** QC 2016; *b* Seria, Brunei, 17 Nov. 1970; *s* of Sir Mark Moody-Stuart, *qv*; *m* 2005, Selina Taylor; four *s. Educ:* Windlesham House; Shrewsbury Sch.; Gonville and Caius Coll., Cambridge (BA 1st Cl. Natural Scis 1993). Called to the Bar, Middle Temple, 1995; in practice as barrister specialising in intellectual property, 1995–. Trustee, Reading Agency, 2011–. *Publications:* (jtly) Encyclopedia of Patent Law; (jtly) Kerly's Law of Trade Marks and Trade Names, 15th edn 2011. *Recreations:* weak puns, science fiction, resisting entropy. *Address:* 8 New Square, Lincoln's Inn, WC2A 3QP. *T:* (020) 7405 4321. *E:* tom.moodystuart@8newsquare.co.uk.

**MOOLLAN, Sir (Abdool) Hamid (Adam),** Kt 1986; GOSK 2010; QC (Mauritius) 1976; Chairman, Law Reform Commission, Mauritius, 1996–2003; *b* 10 April 1933; *s* of Adam Sulliman Moollan and Khatija Moollan; *m* 1966, Sara Sidiot; three *s. Educ:* Soonee Surtee Musalman Society Aided School; Royal College School; King's College London (LLB); Faculté de Droit, Univ. de Paris. Called to the Bar, Middle Temple, 1956; joined Mauritian Bar, 1960. Chm., Bar Council, Mauritius, 1970, 1993, 2010–11. Mem., Presidential Commn for reform of judicial and legal system, Mauritius, 1997. *Recreations:* tennis, horse racing, hunting, fishing. *Address:* (home) 61 Floreal Road, Vacoas, Mauritius. *T:* 6864983; (chambers) 43 Sir William Newton Street, Port-Louis, Mauritius. *T:* 2126913. *E:* sirhamid@chambers.sirhamid.intnet.mu. *Clubs:* Royal Over-Seas League; Mauritius Gymkhana, Mauritius Turf.
*See also* S. A. H. Moollan.

**MOOLLAN, Salim Abdool Hamid;** QC 2016; *b* Réduit, Mauritius, 26 July 1971; *s* of Sir (Abdool) Hamid (Adam) Moollan, *qv*; *m* 2005, Manuela, *d* of Count Dominique Frémy, France; three *s. Educ:* Ecole Polytechnique, Paris (Masters in Maths); Inst. d'Etudes Politiques, Paris (Masters in Political Sci.); Downing Coll., Cambridge (BA Law 1997). Called to the Bar, Middle Temple, 1998; in practice as barrister specialising in commercial and arbitration law, 1998–. Chm., 2011–12, Vice Chm., 2013–14, UN Commn on Internat. Trade Law. Vice-Pres., Internat. Chamber of Commerce Court of Arbitration, 2009–15. *Publications:* contribs to Arbitration Internat., Revue de l'Arbitrage. *Recreations:* classical music and opera, horse riding. *Address:* Essex Court Chambers, 24 Lincoln's Inn Fields, WC2A 3EG. *T:* (020) 7813 8000. *Clubs:* Oxford and Cambridge, Royal Over-Seas League.

**MOON, Angus;** *see* Moon, P. C. A.

**MOON, Sir Humphrey,** 7th Bt *cr* 1887, of Copsewood, Stoke, Co. Warwick; *b* Puddington, Cheshire, 9 Oct. 1919; *s* of Jasper Moon (*d* 1975) (*ggs* of 1st Bt) and Isabel (*née* Logan); *S* brother, 2017; *m* 1st, 1955, Diana Hobson (marr. diss. 1964); two *d*; 2nd, 1964, Elizabeth Anne (*d* 1994), *d* of late George Archibald Drummond Angus and widow of Henry James Butler; one *d. Educ:* Sedburgh Sch. Various. *Recreation:* bridge. *Heir:* none. *Club:* Probus.

**MOON, Madeleine;** MP (Lab) Bridgend, since 2005; *b* 27 March 1950; *d* of Albert Edward and Hilda Ironside; *m* Stephen John Moon (*d* 2015); one *s. Educ:* Madeley Coll. (Cert Ed 1971); Keele Univ. (BEd 1972); University Coll., Cardiff (CQSW, DipSW 1980). Social Services Directorate: Mid Glamorgan CC, 1980–96; City and Co. of Swansea, 1996–2002; Care Standards Inspectorate for Wales, 2002–05. Member (Lab): Porthcawl Town Council, 1990–2000 (Mayor, 1992–93, 1995–96); Ogwr BC, 1991–96; Bridgend CBC, 1995–2005. PPS to Minister of State, DCSF, 2007–08, to Minister of State, DECC, 2008–10. Member: Envmt, Food and Rural Affairs Select Cttee, 2005–07; Defence Select Cttee, 2009–; Panel of Chairs, 2015–. Pres., NATO Parly Assembly, 2017–. *Recreations:* travel, theatre, films, reading, walking, looking for things I have put in a safe place! *Address:* House of Commons, SW1A 0AA. *E:* moonm@parliament.uk.

**MOON, Mary Marjorie;** Head Mistress, Manchester High School for Girls, 1983–94; *b* 28 Sept. 1932; *d* of Clement Alfred Moon and Mabel Moon (*née* Berks). *Educ:* King Edward's Grammar Sch. for Girls, Camp Hill, Birmingham; Univ. of Manchester (BA Hons, MEd); Univ. of London Inst. of Education (PGCE); Buckinghamshire New Univ. (BA Creative Arts 2013). Asst English Teacher, 1955–59, Head of English Dept, 1959–63, Orme Girls' Sch., Newcastle-under-Lyme; Head of English, Bolton Sch. (Girls' Div.), 1963–71; Head Mistress, Pate's Grammar Sch. for Girls, Cheltenham, 1971–83. Mem. Court, Univ. of Manchester, 1985–2000. *Recreations:* photography, sketching, travel.

**MOON, Michael,** RA 1994; artist; *b* 9 Nov. 1937; *s* of Donald and Marjorie Moon; *m* 1977, Anjum Khan; two *s. Educ:* Chelsea Sch. of Art; RCA. One-man shows include: Tate Gall., 1976; Waddington Galls, London, 1969, 1970, 1972, 1978, 1984, 1986, 1992; Macquarie Galls, Sydney, 1982; Christine Abrahams Gall., Melbourne, 1983; Pace Prints, NY, 1987; Kass/Meridien Gall., Chicago, 1988; Linda Goodman Gall., Johannesburg, 1994; Alan Cristea Gall., 1996; Serge Sirocco Gall., San Francisco, 1997; work in public collections include: Tate Gall.; Australian Nat. Gall., Canberra; Mus. of WA, Perth; Art Gall. of NSW, Sydney; Power Inst., Sydney; Walker Art Gall., Liverpool; Birmingham City Art Gall.; V&A Mus. *Address:* 61 Kirkwood Road, SE15 3XU. *T:* (020) 7639 6651.

**MOON, Sir Peter Wilfred Giles Graham-,** 5th Bt *cr* 1855; *b* 24 Oct. 1942; *s* of Sir (Arthur) Wilfred Graham-Moon, 4th Bt, and 2nd wife, Doris Patricia, *yr d* of Thomas Baron Jobson, Dublin; *S* father, 1954; *m* 1st, 1967, Sarah Gillian Chater (marr. diss.) (formerly *m* Major Antony Chater; marr. diss. 1966), *e d* of late Lt-Col Michael Lyndon Smith, MC, MB, BS, and Mrs Michael Smith; two *s*; 2nd, 1993, Mrs Terry de Vries, Cape Town, S Africa; 3rd, 1997, Noodaeng Samigran, Thailand; one *d. Recreations:* shooting, golf. *Heir:* *s* Rupert Francis Wilfred Graham-Moon, *b* 29 April 1968. *Clubs:* Royal Cork Yacht; Ecurie Cod Fillet.

**MOON, (Philip Charles) Angus;** QC 2006; barrister; *b* 17 Sept. 1962; *s* of Charles Moon and Liggy Quyke; *m* 1996, Florence; one *s* three *d. Educ:* King's Coll., Taunton; Christ's Coll., Cambridge (BA 1984). Called to the Bar, Middle Temple, 1986; in practice as a barrister, 1986–, specialising in medical and employment law. Editor, Medical Law Reports (Life Sciences Law Medical), 1998–. *Publications:* medical law reports. *Recreation:* novels of Elmore Leonard. *Address:* Serjeants' Inn Chambers, 85 Fleet Street, EC4Y 1AE. *T:* (020) 7427 5000.

**MOON, Richard John,** PhD; HM Diplomatic Service; Deputy Ambassador, Jordan, since 2019; *b* 3 Jan. 1959; *s* of late John Frederick Moon and Caroline Bowden Moon; *m* 1987, Sandra Sheila Francis Eddis (*d* 2009); one *s* one *d*; *m* 2018, Claire Eleanor Wylie. *Educ:* Chace Sch., Enfield; Wadham Coll., Oxford (MA); London Sch. of Econs (PhD 1994). Joined FCO, 1983; Second Sec., Jakarta, 1984–88; First Sec., FCO, 1988–93, Rome, 1993–97; FCO, 1997–99; UK Mission to UN, NY, 1999–2005; UK Delegn to OECD, Paris, 2005–07; Ambassador to Latvia, 2007–09; Project Dir, Strategy and Resource Gp, FCO, 2009–10; UK Mem., Adv. Cttee on Admin. and Budgetary Questions, UN, NY, 2011–16; Dep. Ambassador, Afghanistan, 2016–18. *Recreations:* history of art, marathon running. *Address:* c/o Foreign and Commonwealth Office, King Charles Street, SW1A 2AH.

**MOONCEY, Ebraham Mohamed; His Honour Judge Mooncey;** a Circuit Judge, since 2009; *b* Jogwad, Gujarat, India; *s* of late Mohamed and Amina Gantawala-Patel; *m*; four *c. Educ:* Charnwood Primary Sch. and Jun. Sch., Leicester; Stoneygate Coll., Leicester; Linwood Secondary Modern Sch., Leicester; Gateway Sixth Form Coll., Leicester; Kingston Poly. (LLB Hons); Inns of Court Sch. of Law. Called to the Bar, Gray's Inn, 1983; a Recorder, 2004–09. Mem., Criminal Sub-cttee, Council of Circuit Judges, 2014–. Tutor Judge, Judicial Coll., 2016–. *Recreations:* tennis, gardening.

**MOONEY, Bel;** writer and broadcaster; *b* 8 Oct. 1946; *d* of Edward and Gladys Mooney; *m* 1st, 1968, Jonathan Dimbleby, *qv* (marr. diss. 2006); one *s* one *d*; 2nd, 2007, Robin Allison-Smith. *Educ:* Trowbridge Girls' High School; University College London (1st cl. Hons, Eng. Lang. and Lit., 1969; Fellow 1994). Freelance journalist, 1970–79; columnist: Daily Mirror, 1979–80; Sunday Times, 1982–83; The Listener, 1984–86; The Times, 2005–07; Daily Mail, 2007–; Ed., Proof mag. (SW Arts), 2000–01; *television:* interview series: Mothers By Daughters, 1983; The Light of Experience Revisited, 1984; Fathers By Sons, 1985; Grief, 1995; various series for BBC Radio 4 (Sandford St Martin Trust award for Devout Sceptics, 1994) and films for BBC TV and Channel 4. Member, Board: Friends of Gt Ormond St, 1994–98; Theatre Royal, Bath, 2009–14. Governor, Bristol Polytechnic, 1989–91. Hon. Fellow, Liverpool John Moores Univ., 2002. Hon. DLitt Bath, 1998. *Publications: novels:* The Windsurf Boy, 1983; The Anderson Question, 1985; The Fourth of July, 1988; Lost Footsteps, 1993; Intimate Letters, 1997; The Invasion of Sand, 2005; *for children:* Liza's Yellow Boat, 1980; I Don't Want To!, 1985; The Stove Haunting, 1986; I Can't Find It!, 1988; It's Not Fair!, 1989; A Flower of Jet, 1990; But You Promised!, 1990; Why Not?, 1990; I Know!, 1991; The Voices of Silence, 1994; I'm Scared!, 1994; I Wish!, 1995; The Mouse with Many Rooms, 1995; Why Me?, 1996; The Green Man, 1997; Joining the Rainbow, 1997; I'm Bored, 1997; I Don't Want to Say Yes!, 1998; You Promised You Wouldn't be Cross, 1999; It's Not My Fault, 1999; So What?, 2002; Kitty's Big Ideas, 2002; Kitty's Friends, 2003; Mr Tubs is Lost, 2004; Who Loves Mr Tubs?, 2006; Big Dog Bonnie, 2007; Best Dog Bonnie, 2007; Bad Dog Bonnie, 2008; Brave Dog Bonnie, 2008; Busy Dog Bonnie, 2009; Bright Dog Bonnie, 2010; *miscellaneous:* The Year of the Child, 1979; Differences of Opinion (collected journalism), 1984; (with Gerald Scarfe) Father Kismass and Mother Claws, 1985; Bel Mooney's Somerset, 1989; From This Day Forward (Penguin Book of Marriage), 1989; Perspectives for Living, 1992; Devout

Sceptics, 2003; (ed) Mothers and Daughters, 2006; Small Dogs Can Save Your Life (memoir), 2010; Lifelines (collection), 2015; Goodbye Pet & See You in Heaven (memoir), 2016. *Recreations:* family, books, art, churches, the countryside, riding pillion on a Harley-Davidson. *Address:* c/o Daily Mail, 2 Derry Street, W8 5TS. *T:* (020) 7938 6000.

**MOONEY, Giles Joseph;** QC 2019; *b* Nottingham, 28 Feb. 1974; *s* of Leonard and Rosemary Mooney; *m* 2007, Emma Templar; one *s* two *d*. *Educ:* Charterhouse; King's Coll. London (BA Hons Hist.). Called to the Bar, Gray's Inn, 1998; in practice as barrister, St Ives Chambers, 1999–2004, 9 Gough Sq. Chambers, 2004–. *Recreations:* history, show jumping, cricket. *Address:* 9 Gough Square, EC4A 3DG. *T:* (020) 7832 0500. *E:* gmooney@9goughsquare.co.uk.

**MOONEY, Kevin Michael;** Partner, Simmons & Simmons, since 1972; *b* Hammersmith, 14 Nov. 1945; *s* of John Mooney and Bridget Mooney; *m* 1972, Maureen O'Hara; two *s* one *d*. *Educ:* Cardinal Vaughan Grammar Sch., Kensington; Univ. of Bristol (LLB). Admitted solicitor, 1971. Chairman: Ind. Panel on Classification of Borderline Products, 2008–13; Ind. Panel on the Advertising of Medicines, 2009–13; Rules Cttee, Unitary Patent Court, 2012–. Member: EC Expert Cttee on the Unitary Patent System, 2009–12; Expert Gp advising Preparatory Cttee on implementation of Unitary Patent Court, 2014–. *Recreations:* golf, farming in Majorca, supporting Queens Park Rangers. *Address:* 11 Trafalgar Road, Twickenham, Middx TW2 5EJ. *T:* (020) 8894 3398, (020) 7825 4480, *Fax:* (020) 7628 2070. *E:* kevin.mooney@simmons-simmons.com.

**MOONEY, Patricia L.;** *see* Lewsley-Mooney.

**MOONEY, Stephen John; His Honour Judge Mooney;** a Circuit Judge, since 2019; *b* Manchester, 9 April 1965; *s* of Anthony Mooney and Linda Mooney; *m* 1995, Penelope Wolfenden; one *s* one *d*. *Educ:* Wilmslow Grammar Sch., then Harefield High Sch.; Univ. of Hull (LLB Hons). Called to the Bar, Inner Temple, 1987; barrister, Albion Chambers, Bristol, 1987–2019. Legally Qualified Chair: Police Misconduct Proceedings, 2016–19; Med. Practitioners Tribunal Service, 2017–19. *Recreations:* musician (plays clarinet and saxophone), men's lacrosse player, walker of Labradors, cold water swimmer. *Address:* Lewes Combined Court Centre, The Law Courts, High Street, Lewes BN7 1YB.

**MOONIE,** family name of **Baron Moonie**.

**MOONIE,** Baron *cr* 2005 (Life Peer), of Bennochy in Fife; **Lewis George Moonie;** *b* 25 Feb. 1947; *m* 1971, Sheila Ann Burt; two *s*. *Educ:* Grove Acad., Dundee; St Andrews Univ. (MB ChB 1970); Edinburgh Univ. (MSc 1981). MRCPsych 1979; MFCM 1984. Psychiatrist, Ciba-Geigy, Switzerland, and Organon Internat., Netherlands; Sen. Registrar (Community Medicine), subseq. Community Medicine Specialist, Fife Health Bd. Mem., Fife Regl Council, 1982–86. MP (Lab and Co-op) Kirkcaldy, 1987–2005. Opposition front bench spokesman on technology, 1990–92, on science and technol., 1992–97, and on industry, 1994–97; Parly Under-Sec. of State, 2000–03, and Minister for Veterans Affairs, 2001–03, MoD. Member: Social Services Select Cttee, 1987–89; Treasury Select Cttee, 1998–2000; H of C Commn, 1997; H of L Select Cttee on Econ. Affairs, 2007–12; Chm., Finance and Services Cttee, 1997–2000. Non-exec. Dir, Bwin.Party plc (formerly PartyGaming), 2007–. *Address:* House of Lords, SW1A 0PW.

**MOOR, Jonathan Edward,** CBE 2011; FCA, CPFA; Vice-President, Finance and Corporate Management Branch, and Chief Financial Officer, Canada Border Services Agency (on secondment), since 2018; *b* 23 June 1964; *s* of late Rev. David Drury Moor and Evangeline Moor (*née* White); *m* 1st, 1990, Sara Louise Stratton (marr. diss. 2015); three *d*; 2nd, 2016, Catherine Hawara. *Educ:* Canford Sch.; Univ. of Kent at Canterbury (BA Hons (Geog.) 1985). ACA 1989, FCA 2000; CPFA 2016. Trainee, subseq. Audit Manager, Touche Ross & Co., 1985–91; Audit Manager, Dist Audit, 1991–94; Audit Commission: Resources Sen. Manager, 1994–97; Associate Dir of Finance and Corporate Planning, 1997–2000; Finance Dir, 2000–03; Department for Transport: Finance Dir, 2003–04, Dir of Strategy and Resources, 2004–05, Driver, Vehicle and Operator Gp; Dir of Airports Strategy, 2006–08; Dir Gen., Civil Aviation, 2009–13; Dir Gen., Resources and Strategy, DfT, 2013–17; Acting Perm. Sec., 2017. *Recreations:* travel, DIY, family. *Address:* Canada Border Services Agency, 191 Laurier Avenue West, Ottawa, ON K1A 0L8, Canada. *T:* (613) 9488604. *E:* Jonathan.Moor@cbsa-asfc.gc.ca.
See also Hon. Sir P. D. Moor.

**MOOR, Hon. Sir Philip Drury,** Kt 2011; **Hon. Mr Justice Moor;** a Judge of the High Court of Justice, Family Division, since 2011; Family Division Liaison Judge for Kent, Surrey and Sussex, since 2017, and for Thames Valley, since 2019; *b* 15 July 1959; *s* of late Rev. David Drury Moor and Evangeline Moor (*née* White); *m* 1987, Gillian Stark; two *d*. *Educ:* Canford Sch.; Pembroke Coll., Oxford (MA; Hon. Fellow 2014). Called to the Bar, Inner Temple, 1982, Bencher, 2004; QC 2001; a Recorder, 2002–11; a Dep. High Ct Judge, 2009–11; Family Div. Liaison Judge for Wales, 2012–17. Hd of Chambers, 2007–11. Chair, High Ct Judges' Assoc., 2016–18; Member: Cttee, Family Law Bar Assoc., 1987–2009 (Actg Treas., 2000–01; Vice-Chm., 2002–03, Chm., 2004–05); Gen. Council of the Bar, 1987–89, 2004–05 (Mem., 2002–03, Vice-Chm., 2003, Professional Standards Cttee); Council of Legal Educn, 1988–91 (Mem. Bd of Examrs, 1989–92). Chm., Inner Temple Scholarship Cttee, 2010–12. Gov., Royal Russell Sch., Croydon, 2009–. Trustee, Gingerbread, 2010–11. *Recreations:* cricket, Association football, Rugby football. *Address:* Royal Courts of Justice, Strand, WC2A 2LL. *Club:* MCC.
See also J. E. Moor.

**MOOR, Dr Robert Michael,** FRS 1994; Head of Protein Function Laboratory, Babraham Institute, 1996–99; *b* 28 Sept. 1937; *s* of Donald C. Moor and Gwendolen (*née* Whitby); *m* 1962, Felicia Alison Elizabeth Stephens; four *d*. *Educ:* Estcourt, Natal, S Africa; Gonville and Caius Coll., Cambridge Univ. (PhD 1965; ScD). Senior Scientist, ARC Unit of Reproductive Physiology and Biochemistry, 1965–86; Head, Dept of Molecular Embryology, AFRC Inst. of Animal Physiology and Genetics Res., 1986–93; Dep. Dir, Babraham Inst., 1993–97. Hon. Fellow, Italian Vet. Assoc., 1990. Hon. Dr Univ. of Milan, 1990. *Publications:* numerous contribs to learned jls. *Recreations:* mountaineering, music. *Address:* 19 Thornton Close, Cambridge CB3 0NF. *T:* (01223) 276669. *Club:* Alpino Italiano (Milan).

**MOORCOCK, Michael John;** author, since 1956; *b* 18 Dec. 1939; *s* of Arthur Moorcock and June Moorcock (*née* Taylor); *m* 1st, 1962, Hilary Bailey (marr. diss. 1978); one *s* two *d*; 2nd, 1978, Jill Riches (marr. diss. 1983); 3rd, 1983, Linda Mullens Steele. *Educ:* Michael Hall, Sussex; Pitman's Coll., Surrey. Ed., Tarzan Adventures, 1956–58; Asst Ed., Sexton Blake Lby, 1959–61; travelled as singer/guitarist in Scandinavia and W Europe, 1961–62; ed. and pamphlet writer for Liberal Party pubns dept, 1962–63; Ed., New Worlds, 1963–80 (Publisher, 1980–); writer and vocalist for Hawkwind, 1971–; writer, vocalist and fretted instruments for Deep Fix; vocalist and instrumentalist for Robert Calvert; writer for Blue Oyster Cult, and associated with various other bands. Has made recordings, incl. An Alien Heat, with Albert Bouchier, 2018, Live from the Terminal Café, 2019. *Publications:* books include: Byzantium Endures, 1981; The Laughter of Carthage, 1984; Mother London, 1988; Jerusalem Commands, 1992; Blood, 1994; Fabulous Harbours, 1995; The War Amongst the Angels, 1996; Tales from the Texas Woods, 1997; King of the City, 2000; (with Storm Constantine) Silverheart, 2000; London Bone, 2001; The Dreamthief's Daughter, 2001; Firing the Cathedral, 2002; The Skrayling Tree, 2003; The Life and Times of Jerry Cornelius, 2003; The Vengeance of Rome, 2006; The Metatemporal Detective, 2007; Elric: the stealer of souls, 2008; The Best of Michael Moorcock, 2009; Hawkmoon: the mad god's amulet, 2010; Into the Media Web: selected short non-fiction, 1956–2006, 2010; London Peculiar, 2011; The Whispering Swarm, 2015; Pegging the President, 2018; The Woods of Arcady, 2019; Kaboul et Autres Souvenirs de la Troisième Guerre Mondiale, 2018; various omnibus edns of novels; ed numerous anthologies, collections and short stories. *Recreations:* walking, mountaineering, travel. *Address:* 185 rue St Maur, 75010 Paris, France; c/o Nomads Association, 21 Honor Oak Road, Honor Oak, SE23 3SH; c/o Hoffman, 77 Boulevard St Michel, 75005 Paris, France. *Club:* Royal Over-Seas League.

**MOORCRAFT, Dennis Harry;** Under-Secretary, Inland Revenue, 1975–81; *b* 14 Aug. 1921; *s* of late Harry Moorcraft and Dorothy Moorcraft (*née* Simmons); *m* 1945, Ingeborg Utne (*d* 2000), Bergen, Norway; one *s* one *d*. *Educ:* Gillingham County Grammar Sch. Tax Officer, Inland Revenue, 1938. RNVR, 1940–46. Inspector of Taxes, 1948; Sen. Inspector of Taxes, 1956; Principal Inspector of Taxes, 1963. *Recreations:* gardening, garden construction, croquet, music.

**MOORCROFT, David Robert,** OBE 1999 (MBE 1983); Co-Founder, pointfourone sports consultancy, 2007; Chief Executive, UK Athletics, 1997–2007; *b* 10 April 1953; *s* of Robert Moorcroft and Mildred Moorcroft (*née* Hardy); *m* 1975, Linda Ann, *d* of John Ward; one *s* one *d*. *Educ:* Woodlands Comp. Sch.; Tile Hill Coll. of Further Educn; Loughborough Univ. (BEd 1976). School teacher, 1976–81. Athlete: Olympic Games: finalist, 1,500m, Montreal, 1976; semi-finalist, 5,000m, Moscow, 1980; finalist, 5,000m, Los Angeles, 1984; Commonwealth Games: Gold Medal, 1,500m, Edinburgh, 1974, Edmonton, 1978; Gold Medal, 5,000m, Brisbane, 1982; European Championships: Bronze Medal, 1,500m, Prague, 1978; Bronze Medal, 5,000m, Athens, 1982; Europa Cup: Gold Medal, 5,000m, Zagreb, 1981; set world record for 5,000m, Oslo, 1982, European record for 3,000m, Crystal Palace, 1982. Commentator, BBC TV and radio, 1983–97. Chief Executive: Coventry Sports Foundn, 1981–95 (Trustee, 1995–); British Athletic Federation Ltd, 1997; UK Athletics 98, 1998.

**MOORCROFT, Sir William,** KBE 2008; Principal, Trafford College (formerly South Trafford College), 2003–16; *b* Liverpool, 17 Feb. 1958; *s* of Robert and Diane Jane Moorcroft; *m* 1990, Wendy Anne Clarehugh; one *s*. *Educ:* Manchester Metropolitan Univ. (MA Mgt); Bolton Inst. (Cert Ed). MHCIMA 1992. Exec. Chef, Littlewoods Orgn, 1979–83; Lectr, Southport Coll., 1983–91; Nat. Chief Verifier, City & Guilds, 1991–94; Hd of Dept, 1994–97, Vice Prin., 1997–2002, South Trafford Coll., subseq. Trafford Coll. Member, Board: Learning and Skills Improvement Service, 2008–; Lancs County Cricket Foundn. *Recreation:* golf. *Club:* Southport and Ainsdale Golf.

**MOORE,** family name of **Earl of Drogheda**.

**MOORE, Viscount; Benjamin Garrett Henderson Moore;** *b* 21 March 1983; *s* and heir of Earl of Drogheda, *qv*. *Educ:* Pro Corda; Eton; Peterhouse, Cambridge; Universität der Künste Berlin. *Address:* 40c Ledbury Road, W11 2AB.

**MOORE, Prof. Adrian William,** DPhil; Professor of Philosophy, University of Oxford, since 2004; Fellow, since 1988, and Vice-Principal, since 2017, St Hugh's College, Oxford; *b* Kettering, 29 Dec. 1956; *s* of Victor George Moore and Audrey Elizabeth Moore. *Educ:* Manchester Grammar Sch.; King's Coll., Cambridge (BA 1978); Balliol Coll., Oxford (BPhil 1980; DPhil 1982). Lectr in Philosophy, University Coll., Oxford, 1982–85; Jun. Res. Fellow in Philosophy, King's Coll., Cambridge, 1985–88; Leverhulme Maj. Res. Fellow, 2006–09. Pres., Aristotelian Soc., 2014–15. Delegate of OUP, 2014–. Jt Ed., Mind jl, 2014–. *Publications:* The Infinite, 1990, 3rd edn 2019; Points of View, 1997; Noble in Reason, Infinite in Faculty: themes and variations in Kant's moral and religious philosophy, 2003; The Evolution of Modern Metaphysics: making sense of things, 2012; Language, World, and Limits: essays in philosophy of language and metaphysics, 2019. *Recreation:* Manchester City supporter. *Address:* St Hugh's College, Oxford OX2 6LE. *T:* (01865) 274953. *E:* adrian.moore@philosophy.ox.ac.uk.

**MOORE, Alan Edward,** CBE 1980; Deputy Chairman: Lloyds TSB Group plc, 1998–2003 (Director, 1995–2003); Lloyds Bank Plc, 1999–2003 (Director, 1989–2003); TSB Bank plc, 1998–2003; *b* 5 June 1936; *s* of late Charles Edward and Ethel Florence Moore; *m* 1961, Margaret Patricia Beckley; one *s* one *d*. *Educ:* Berkhamsted Sch. FCIB, FCIS, FCT. Glyn Mills & Co., then Williams & Glyn's Bank, London, 1953–74; Dir Gen., Bahrain Monetary Agency, 1974–79; Dir and Treas., Lloyds Bank Internat., 1980–84; Dir of Treasury, Lloyds Bank, 1985–88; Dir of Corporate Banking and Treasury, Lloyds Bank, 1988–94; Dep. Chief Exec. and Treas., Lloyds Bank, 1994–98; Dep. Gp Chief Exec. and Treas., Lloyds TSB Gp plc, 1995–98. *Recreations:* photography, railway history, travel.

**MOORE, Anthony Michael Frederick, (Anthony Michaels-Moore);** baritone; *b* 8 April 1957; *s* of John Moore and Isabel (*née* Shephard); *m* 1st, 1980, Ewa Migocki (marr. diss. 2004); one *d*; 2nd, 2010, Emily Doyle Schluter; one *s* one *d*. *Educ:* Newcastle Univ. (BA Hons 1978); Royal Scottish Acad. of Music and Drama. First British winner, Pavarotti Comp., 1985. Débuts: Opera North, 1986; Royal Opera House, Covent Garden, 1987; Vienna State Opera, 1993; La Scala, Milan, 1993; Paris Opera, 1994; Buenos Aires, 1996; Metropolitan, NY, 1996; San Francisco, 1997; Chicago, 2000; Glyndebourne, 2001. *Rôles* include: Marcello, Belcore, Escamillo, Posa, Hamlet, Falke, Lescaut, Simon Boccanegra, Scarpia, Figaro, Orestes, Onegin, Rigoletto, Macbeth, Montforte, Ford, Ezio, Iago, Carlo. Recordings incl. Carmina Burana, Lucia di Lammermoor, Falstaff, Aroldo, and La Favorite. Royal Philharmonic Soc. Award, 1997. *Recreations:* road bikes, cricket, swimming, spicy food. *Address:* c/o Fletcher Artists Management, 14 Murray Street, Apartment 124, New York, NY 10007, USA.

**MOORE, Prof. Brian Cecil Joseph,** PhD; FRS 2002; FMedSci; Professor of Auditory Perception, University of Cambridge, 1995–2014, now Emeritus; Fellow of Wolfson College, Cambridge, 1983–2013, now Emeritus; *b* 10 Feb. 1946; *s* of Cecil George Moore and Maria Anna Moore. *Educ:* St Catharine's Coll., Cambridge (BA Nat. Sci. 1968; PhD Exptl Psychol. 1971). Lectr in Psychology, Reading Univ., 1971–77; Vis. Prof., Brooklyn Coll., NY, 1973–74; University of Cambridge: Lectr in Experimental Psychology, 1977–89; Reader in Auditory Perception, 1989–95. Erskine Fellow, Univ. of Canterbury, NZ, 2017. Hon. Life Mem., British Soc. of Audiology, 2019. FMedSci 2001. Fellow: Acoustical Soc. of America, 1985; Audio Engrg Soc., 2016; Hon. Fellow, Belgian Soc. of Audiology, 1997; Hon. Fellow, British Soc. of Hearing Aid Audiologists, 1999. Hon. Dr Adam Mickiewicz Univ., Poland, 2015. *Publications:* An Introduction to the Psychology of Hearing, 1977, 6th edn 2012; Frequency Selectivity in Hearing, 1986; Perceptual Consequences of Cochlear Damage, 1995; Hearing, 1995; Cochlear Hearing Loss, 1998, 2nd edn 2007; The Perception of Speech: from sound to meaning, 2007; Multistability in Perception: binding sensory modalities, 2012; Auditory Processing of Temporal Fine Structure: effects of age and hearing loss, 2014; Hearing Aids, 2016. *Recreations:* music, playing the guitar, bridge, fixing things. *Address:* Department of Experimental Psychology, University of Cambridge, Downing Street, Cambridge CB2 3EB. *T:* (01223) 333574.

**MOORE, Charles Hilary;** journalist and author; Consulting Editor, The Telegraph Group, since 2004; *b* 31 Oct. 1956; *s* of late Richard and of Ann Moore; *m* 1981, Caroline Mary Baxter; twin *s* and *d*. *Educ:* Eton Coll.; Trinity Coll., Cambridge (MA Hons History). Joined editorial staff of Daily Telegraph, 1979, leader writer, 1981–83; Assistant Editor and political columnist, 1983–84, Editor, 1984–90, The Spectator; weekly columnist, Daily Express, 1987–90; Dep. Editor, Daily Telegraph, 1990–92; Editor: The Sunday Telegraph, 1992–95; The Daily Telegraph, 1995–2003. Chm., Policy Exchange, 2005–11. Chm., Rectory Soc., 2005–. Pres., S of England Agricl Soc., 2016–17. Ind. Mem., H of L Appts Commn, 2019–. Mem. Council, Benenden Sch., 2000–09. Hon. PhD Buckingham, 2006. Luca de Tena Prize, 2011. *Publications:* (ed with C. Hawtree) 1936, 1986; (with A. N. Wilson and G. Stamp) The Church in Crisis, 1986; (ed with Simon Heffer) A Tory Seer: the selected journalism of T. E. Utley, 1989; Margaret Thatcher: the authorized biography, vol. 1: Not For Turning, 2013 (Elizabeth Longford Prize for Histl Biog., Paddy Power Political Book of Year, 2014), vol. 2: Everything She Wants, 2015, vol. 3: Herself Alone, 2019. *Recreation:* hunting. *Address:* c/o The Daily Telegraph, 111 Buckingham Palace Road, SW1W 0DT. *T:* (020) 7931 2000. *Clubs:* Beefsteak, White's.

**MOORE, Charlotte;** Director of Content, BBC, since 2016; *b* Guildford, 19 June 1968; *d* of Graham and Joanna Moore; *m* 2002, Johann Perry; one *s* one *d*. *Educ:* Wycombe Abbey Sch.; Bristol Univ. (BA Hist.). Freelance producer and director, 1992–2003, including: Series Prod., Seekers of Lost Treasure, Discovery Channel US, 1995; Series Prod., Prohibition, BBC 2/A&E, 1997; Prod. and Dir, Children's Hospital, BBC 1, 1998; Series Prod. and Dir, Lagos Airport, Channel 4, 1999; Series Prod. and Dir, Living with Cancer, BBC1, 2001; Prod. and Dir, Great Britons: Winston Churchill, BBC 2, 2002; Dir, Contemp. Factual, IWC Media, 2003–06; Commng Ed., Documentaries, 2006–09, Hd of Commng, Documentaries, 2009–13, BBC; Controller, BBC One, 2013–16. *Address:* BBC Broadcasting House, Portland Place, W1A 1AA. *E:* charlotte.moore@bbc.co.uk.

**MOORE, Air Vice-Marshal Christopher John;** Director Service Operations, Information Systems and Services, Joint Forces Command, since 2018; *b* Isleworth, Middx, 7 Nov. 1968; *s* of Colin and Mary Moore. *Educ:* Dartmouth Comprehensive Sch.; Torbay Tech. Coll.; Salford Univ. (BEng Hons 1990); King's Coll. London (MA). Joined RAF, 1987; OC, Engrg Support Sqdn for Chinook helicopters, 2001–03; MoD, 2003–05; acsc 2006; Capability Mgt, MoD, 2006–07; Chief Operational Communications and Inf. Systems Planner, Afghanistan, MoD, 2007–08; Strategic Resources Planning, MoD, 2008–09; OC, Tactical Communications Wing, 2009–11; Gp Captain, IT Cyber and Communications, 2011–13; HCSC 2013; CO, 90 Signals Unit, 2013–14; AO A6, then A6 Force Comdr, 2014–16; Hd, Operate and Defend, Information Services and Systems, MoD, 2016–18. *Recreations:* former professional Rugby Union player with Bristol; representative honours for RAF, Combined Services, England Universities and England students. *T:* (030) 6770 1950. *E:* moore.c@sky.com.

**MOORE, Damien;** MP (C) Southport, since 2017; *b* Workington, 26 April 1980; *s* of Thomas William Moore and Joan Burland. *Educ:* Stainburn Sch.; Univ. of Central Lancashire (BA Hist. 2005). Retail manager, Asda, 2007–17. Mem. (C), Preston CC, 2012–18. Contested (C) Southport, 2015. *Recreations:* visiting historic sites, cooking. *Address:* House of Commons, SW1A 0AA. *T:* (020) 7219 1162. *E:* damien.moore.mp@parliament.uk.

**MOORE, David James Ladd;** Partnership Secretary, Freshfields, 1993–98; *b* 6 June 1937; *s* of James and Eilonwy Moore; *m* 1968, Kay Harrison; two *s*. *Educ:* King Edward VI Sch., Nuneaton; Brasenose Coll., Oxford (BA); Birkbeck Coll., Univ. of London (BA (History of Art) 2003; MA History 2005). PO, 1961–67 (Asst Principal 1961, Principal 1966); Cabinet Office, 1967–69; HM Treasury, 1969–80 (Asst Sec. 1973); Under Secretary: Cabinet Office, 1980–82; HM Treasury, 1982–83; Inland Revenue (Principal Finance Officer), 1983–85; HM Treasury, 1985–93. *Recreations:* cinema, history of art, theatre. *Address:* 183 Hampstead Way, NW11 7YB.

**MOORE, Prof. David Robert,** PhD; Professor of Otolaryngology and Neuroscience, University of Cincinnati, since 2013; Director, Communication Sciences Research Center, Cincinnati Children's Hospital, since 2013; *b* 19 July 1953; *s* of William Leonard Moore and Joan Moore (*née* Kerr); *m* 1976, Victoria Doloughan (marr. diss. 2014); one *d*. *Educ:* Monash Univ., Victoria (BSc; PhD). NIH Internat. Fellow, Univ. of Calif, Irvine, 1983–84; University of Oxford: MRC Sen. Fellow, 1986–89; Res. Lectr, 1989–96; Reader, 1996–99; Prof. of Auditory Neurosci., 1999–2002; Dir, MRC Inst. of Hearing Res., 2002–13. Co-Founder, NIHR Nottingham Hearing Biomed. Res. Unit, 2008. Vis. Prof., Univ. of Washington, Seattle, 1992; Vis. Schol., Center for Neural Sci., NY Univ., 1997. *Publications:* numerous peer-reviewed scientific contribs to internat. jls. *Recreations:* food and wine, cycling, art and architecture. *Address:* Communication Sciences Research Center, Cincinnati Children's Hospital Medical Center, 3333 Burnet Avenue, Cincinnati, OH 45229–3026, USA. *Club:* Yarragon Axe (Victoria, Australia).

**MOORE, Derry;** *see* Drogheda, Earl of.

**MOORE, Most Rev. Desmond Charles,** KBE 1996; former Bishop of Alotau, Papua New Guinea (RC); *b* Adelaide, 12 May 1926; *s* of Edwin John Moore and Margaret Mary Leahy. *Educ:* Christian Brothers Sch., Adelaide; Adelaide Univ.; Sacred Heart Monastery, Croydon, Vic. Entered novitiate, 1950, professed mem., 1951–, Congregation of Missionaries of the Sacred Heart of Jesus; ordained priest, 1957; Bursar and Assistant to Novice Master, St Mary's Towers Monastery, Douglas Park, 1958–61; Assistant to Parish Priest, Port Moresby, PNG, 1961–62; first Parish Priest, Boregaina Village, Rigo, 1962–67; Parish Priest, St Joseph's, Boroko, and Religious Superior, Missionaries of the Sacred Heart of Jesus, dio. of Port Moresby, 1967–70; cons. Bishop of Sideia, 1970, name of dio. changed to Alotau, 1977; retired, 2001. *Address:* Sacred Heart Monastery, 1 Roma Avenue, Kensington, NSW 2033, Australia. *T:* (2) 96627188, *T:* and *Fax:* (2) 93865206. *E:* desmondmoore@gmail.com.

**MOORE, His Honour (Douglas) Marks;** a Circuit Judge, 2007–18; *b* 31 Jan. 1950; *s* of Douglas Moore and Josephine Moore (*née* Ritchie); *m* 1st, 1983, Susan Clayton (marr. diss. 2010); one *s* three *d*; 2nd, 2013, Maria Paris-Ketting. *Educ:* Regent House Sch., NI; Queen's Univ., Belfast (BA 1972; Dip. Soc. Anthropol. 1973); RMA Sandhurst; Inns of Court Sch. of Law. Subaltern, Irish Guards, 1974–76. Called to the Bar, 1979; Tenant in Chambers of Roy Amlot, QC, 6 King's Bench Walk; Recorder, 1998–2007; Senior Trial Attorney, Office of the Prosecutor: Internat. Criminal Tribunal for Rwanda, 2001–03, with responsibility for prosecution of former members of Hutu Govt and for the Special Investigation concerning alleged atrocities committed by the Rwandan Patriotic Front; Internat. Criminal Tribunal for Yugoslavia, The Hague, 2005–07, with responsibility for prosecution of former sen. Yugoslav officers involved in atrocities in Vukovar, Croatia. *Recreations:* salmon fishing, golf, reading, travel. *Clubs:* Cavalry and Guards; Muthaiga Country (Kenya).

**MOORE, Emma Sophie;** Chief Operating Officer, Border Force, Home Office, since 2017; *b* Reading, 22 Feb. 1981; *d* of Martin Alan Taylor-Smith and Rosanna Theresa Daphne Taylor-Smith; *m* 2005, Nicholas Christopher Moore; one *s* one *d*. *Educ:* Lake Forest High Sch., Lake Forest, Ill; Dover-Sherborn Regl High Sch., Sherborn, Mass; Sevenoaks Sch., Kent; Durham Univ. (BA Hons Econs). Regl Sales Manager, RDM Factors Ltd, 2002–05; Manager, Invoice Finance Brokerage, Xbridge Ltd, 2005–06; Business Develt Manager, Royal Bank of Scotland plc, 2006–07; Partner, Invoice Finance, Clydesdale Bank plc, 2007–12; G4S plc: Sen. Consultant, G4S Secure Solutions, 2012–14; Bid Dir, Corporate Develt, 2014; Dir, Local Govt, 2014–15; Chief Operating Officer, G4S Health, and Sen. Information Risk Officer, G4S Public Services, 2015–17. *Recreations:* family time, current affairs, box sets, learning to paint. *Address:* Home Office, 12th Floor, Apollo House, 36 Wellesley Road, Croydon CR9 2BY. *E:* emma.moore2@homeoffice.gov.uk.

**MOORE, Sir Francis Thomas, (Sir Frank),** Kt 1983; AO 1991; Chairman, Asia-Pacific Economic Cooperation International Centre for Sustainable Tourism, 2000; *b* 28 Nov. 1930; *m* 1972, Norma Shearer (*d* 2018); two *s*. *Educ:* Nudgee Coll. Licensed Valuer, 1952–2008; Man. Dir, Radio Broadcasting Network of Queensland, 1957–78; Director: Universal Telecasters Qld Ltd, 1961–80; Trust Co. Australia Ltd, 1983–96; Chm., Nature Resorts Ltd, 1997–2002. Chairman: Queensland Tourist and Travel Corp., 1979–90; Tourism Council of Australia (formerly Australian Tourism Industry Assoc.), 1983–95; Nat. Centre for Studies in Travel and Tourism, 1987–94; Taylor Byrne Tourism Gp, 1990–2002; Tourism Forecasting Council, 1996–2003; Co-op. Res. Centre for Sustainable Tourism, 1997–2008; Dir, Gold Coast Airport Ltd, 2001–04; Mem., World Travel and Tourism Council, 1992. Queen Elizabeth II Silver Jubilee Medal, 1977; Centenary Medal (Australia), 2001. *E:* ftmoore@powerup.com.au.

**MOORE, Gaynor Elizabeth;** *see* Lloyd, G. E.

**MOORE, Gillian,** CBE 2018 (MBE 1994); Director of Music, Southbank Centre, since 2015; broadcaster and writer; *b* 20 Feb. 1959; *m* 2001, Bruce Nockles; one *s* one *d*. *Educ:* Univ. of Glasgow (BMus Hons 1980); Univ. of York (MA 1981). Educn Officer, London Sinfonietta, 1983–93; Hd of Educn, Southbank Centre, 1993–98; Artistic Dir, ISCM World Music Days, 1998; Dir, London Sinfonietta, 1998–2006; Hd of Contemporary Culture, 2006–11, Hd of Classical Music, 2011–15, Southbank Centre. Member, Council: RCM; Royal Philharmonic Soc. Mem., Cttee, Queen's Medal for Music, 2014–. Hon. ARAM, 2003. FRCM. Hon. FGS. Hon. DMus Brunel, 2006; Hon. Dr Goldsmiths, Univ. of London, 2017. *Publications:* The Rite of Spring: music of modernity, 2019. *Address:* Southbank Centre, Belvedere Road, SE1 8XX. *T:* (020) 7921 0897. *E:* gillian.moore@southbankcentre.co.uk.

**MOORE, Graham,** QPM 1997; Chief Constable, West Yorkshire Police, 1998–2002; *b* 15 Jan. 1947; *s* of Graham and Kate Moore; *m* 1965, Susan Fletcher; one *s* one *d*. *Educ:* Brunts GS, Mansfield; Warwick Univ. (BA Hons Philosophy and Lit. 1975). Professional musician; Police Constable, Birmingham City Police, 1969–72; Inspector of Taxes, Inland Revenue, 1975–77; joined W Midlands Police, 1977; Asst Chief Constable, S Yorks Police, 1991–94; Dep. Chief Constable, Cambs Constabulary, 1994–98. *Recreations:* music, literature, fine arts.

**MOORE, Prof. Dame Henrietta (Louise),** DBE 2016; PhD; FBA 2007; Professor of Culture, Philosophy and Design, and Director, UCL Institute for Global Prosperity, University College London, since 2014; *b* Saunderton, 18 May 1957; *d* of Stephen Andrew Moore and Josephine Anne Jane Mary Moore. *Educ:* Univ. of Durham (BA Archaeol. and Anthropol. 1979); Newnham Coll., Cambridge (PhD 1983). Field Dir, UNA, Burkina Faso, 1983–84; Curatorial Asst for Anthropol., Univ. Mus. of Archaeol. and Anthropol., Cambridge, 1984–85; Lectr in Soc. Anthropol., Univ. of Kent, Canterbury, 1985–86; Lectr in Soc. Anthropol., 1986–88, Manager, African Studies Centre, 1987–90, Univ. of Cambridge; Lectr and Dir of Studies in Soc. Anthropol., Girton Coll., 1986–88; Fellow and Lectr in Anthropol. and Soc. and Pol Scis, Pembroke Coll., 1989–90; London School of Economics and Political Science: Lectr, 1990–93, Reader, 1993–97, in Soc. Anthropol.; Prof. of Soc. Anthropol., 1997–2008; Dir, Gender Inst., 1994–99; Dir, Culture and Communication Prog., Centre for Global Governance, 2005–11; Gov., 1999–2005; Dep. Dir, 2002–05; William Wyse Prof. of Social Anthropology, Univ. of Cambridge, 2008–14; Fellow, Jesus Coll., Cambridge, 2009–14. Fellow: Centre for Globalization and Policy Res., Sch. of Public Affairs, UCLA, 2005–11; Goodenough Coll., Univ. of London, 2005–; Maj. Res. Fellow, Leverhulme Trust, London, 2007–10. Visiting Professor: Univ. of Bergen, 1988; Univ. of Bremen, 1990; Univ. of Calif, Berkeley, 1994, 1997; Univ. of Porto, 2004; Vis. Lectr, Univ. of Witwatersrand, 1992. Co-Founder and Chm. Bd, SHM Productions Ltd, 1996–; Founder Trustee, SHM Foundn, 2007–. Member: Adv. Bd for Global Coalition on Africa, Min. of For. Affairs, Netherlands, 1994–95; Educn Cttee, Catholic Inst. for Internat. Relns, 1995–98; Bd of Res. Counsellors, Foundn for Advanced Studies on Internat. Devel, Tokyo, 1996–99; Bd of Social Enterprise, London, 2002–04; Scientific Council, Eur. Res. Council, 2009–13; Scientific Adv. Council, DEFRA, 2016–; Chm. Wkg Gp, Best Practice for Social Enterprise, DTI, 2001–02. FRAI 1981 (Mem. Council, 1989–92); Member: African Studies Assoc., 1986– (Mem. Council, 1986–89); Assoc. of Social Anthropologists of UK and Commonwealth, 1986– (Hon. Sec., 1991–94); Amer. Assoc. of Anthropologists, 2004–; Council, British Acad., 2012–15. Pres., British Inst. in Eastern Africa, 2016–. Trustee, Barbican Centre, 2011–. FRSA 2000; FAcSS (AcSS 2001); MInstD 2002. *Publications:* Space, Text and Gender: an anthropological study of the Marakwet of Kenya, 1986, 2nd edn 1996; Feminism and Anthropology, 1988; (with M. A. Vaughan) Cutting Down Trees: gender, nutrition and change in the Northern Provinces of Zambia, 1890–1990, 1994 (Herskovits Prize, African Studies Assoc., USA, 1995); A Passion for Difference: essays in anthropology and gender, 1994; (ed) The Future of Anthropological Knowledge, 1996; (ed) Promoting the Health of Children and Young People: setting a research agenda, 1998; (ed jtly) Those Who Play with Fire: gender and fertility in Africa, 1999; (ed) Anthropological Theory Today, 1999; (ed with D. T. Sanders) Magical Interpretations, Material Realities: modernity, witchcraft and the occult in post colonial Africa, 2001; (with Ed Mayo) The Mutual State and How to Build It, 2001; (ed with D. T. Sanders) Anthropology in Theory: issues in epistemology, 2005; The Subject of Anthropology: gender, symbolism and psychoanalysis, 2007; (ed with David Held) Cultural Politics in a Global Age: uncertainty, solidarity and innovation, 2008; Still Life: hopes, desires and satisfactions, 2011; (ed with N. Long) Sociality: new comparative approaches, 2012; (ed with P. Aggleton, P. Boyce and R. Parker) Understanding Global Sexualities, 2012; (ed with M. Kaldor and S. Selchow) Global Civil Society 2012: ten years of critical reflection, 2012; (ed with N. Long) The Social Life of Achievement, 2013; (ed with J. Cook and N. Long) The State We're In: reflecting on democracy's troubles, 2016. *Recreations:* relaxing, thinking, theatre, opera, walking. *Address:* UCL Institute for Global Prosperity, University College London, Gower Street, WC1E 6BT. *Clubs:* Groucho, Academicians' Room.

**MOORE, Rt Rev. Henry Wylie;** General Secretary, Church Missionary Society, 1986–89; Assistant Bishop, Durham, 1990–94; *b* 2 Nov. 1923; *m* 1951, Betty Rose Basnett; two *s* three *d*. *Educ:* Univ. of Liverpool (BCom 1950); Wycliffe Hall, Oxford; MA (Organization Studies) Leeds, 1972. LMS Railway Clerk, 1940–42. Served War with King's Regt (Liverpool), 1942–43; Rajputana Rifles, 1943–46. Curate: Farnworth, Widnes, 1952–54; Middleton, 1954–56; CMS, Khuzistan, 1956–59; Rector: St Margaret, Burnage, 1960–63; Middleton, 1963–74; Home Sec. and later Executive Sec., CMS, 1974–83; Bishop in Cyprus and the Gulf, 1983–86. *Recreation:* family life. *Address:* Flat 20, Fosbrooke House, 8 Clifton Drive, Lytham FY8 5RQ.

**MOORE, James Antony Axel Herring,** OBE 1998; Executive Director, US-UK Educational Commission (Fulbright Commission), 1993–2002; *b* 1940; *s* of late Lieut A. D. W. Moore, RN (killed HMS Audacity, 1941) and Agneta Moore (*née* Wachtmeister); *m* 1964, Marianne Jerlström; two *s* one *d*. *Educ:* Wellington Coll.; Trinity Coll., Cambridge (MA); London Univ. Inst. of Educn (PGCE). Teacher: Norway, 1962–63; Thailand, 1964–67; British Council: Warsaw, 1967–70; Beirut, 1971–73; Ottawa, 1973–75; London, 1975–80; Chinese lang. trng, 1980–81; Director: Manila, 1981–85; Copenhagen, 1985–89; General Manager, Fellowships and Scholarships, 1990–93. *Recreations:* music, ski-ing, walking, languages. *Address:* 7 Brook Lane, Lindfield, Haywards Heath RH16 1SF.
See also Vice-Adm. Sir M. A. C. Moore.

**MOORE, Jeremy Patrick,** CB 2016; Director General, Strategy, Policy and Analysis, Department for Work and Pensions, 2013–17; *b* London, 24 July 1956; *s* of James Patrick Moore and Jocelyn Ann Inrig; *m* 1989, Barbara Joan Richards. *Educ:* St George's Coll., Weybridge; London Sch. of Econs and Pol Sci. (BSc Econ; Bassett Meml Prize, 1978; MSc 1979); Alliance Française, Paris; London Univ. ext. (BA Italian 2009; Dr Guenther Prize, 2009). Res. admin posts, 1980–87, Principal Finance Officer, 1987–89, ESRC; policy posts, 1989–93, Dep. Dir, and Hd, Student Support Policy, 1993–98, DES, then DfE, later DfEE; Hd, Envmt, Transport and Regions Spending Team, HM Treasury, 1998–2000; Hd, Structural Unemployment Policy Div., DfEE, 2000–01; Department for Work and Pensions: Dep. Dir, Strategy and Planning, 2001–04; Director: Planning and Performance Mgt, 2005–09; Labour Market Policy, 2009–11; Disability Policy, and Office for Disability Issues, 2011–13. Chair, BPDTS Ltd, 2019–. Non-exec. Dir, Student Loans Co., 1994–98. Trustee and Member, Board: Learning and Work Initiative, 2018–; Shaw Trust, 2018–. *Recreations:* French and Italian culture and literature, visiting Canada, Turkish language. *E:* jeremypmoore@btinternet.com.

**MOORE, John, (Jonathan Moore);** actor; writer; director; *b* 25 Nov.; *s* of Richard and Nora Moore. *Educ:* St Elphege's, Wallington; Roundshaw Sch., Wallington; Croydon Art Coll. *Writer: plays:* 1st play aged 11, Hornus' Poem; Sea Change, 1977; Obstruct the doors, cause delay and be Dangerous..., 1980; Street Captives, Edinburgh Fest., transf. Royal Exchange, 1981; Treatment, Donmar, 1982 (Edinburgh Fest. Fringe First award; also BBC TV Film); The Hooligan Nights (NT commn), 1985; Behind Heaven, Royal Exchange (commd), transf. Donmar, 1986; Regeneration, 1989; This Other Eden, Soho Th., 1990; Fall From Light, 2002; Mad God (adaptation of The Bacchae, commd by Royal Exchange), 2003–05, 2014; Inigo (also dir), White Bear Th., transf. Pleasance Main House, 2015; *television:* Crown Court (Granada TV), 1982; *libretto:* Stewart Copeland's Horse Opera (televised, also actor), 1992; The Invention of Morel, Chicago Opera Theater, 2017, Long Beach Opera, 2018; Savage Winter, Pittsburgh Opera, transf. Brooklyn Acad. of Music, 2018; *directed:* Turnage's Greek (world premiere; co-writer of adaptation from play), Munich Biennale (Best Libretto award), Edinburgh Internat. Fest., 1988, ENO, 1990 (co-dir. BBC TV film, Royal Phil. Soc. Best Film award), revival, Grimeborn Opera Fest., Arcola Th., 2018; Elegy for Young Lovers, La Fenice, Venice, 1989; 63 Dream Palace, Munich Biennale (Best Dir award) and German TV, 1990; Baa Baa Black Sheep, Opera North, Cheltenham Fest., BBC TV, 1993; Cask of Amontillado, Holders, Barbados, 1993; East and West (also writer of text), Almeida, 1994; Life with An Idiot, ENO, Scottish Opera, 1995; James MacMillan's Ines de Castro, Scottish Opera, Edinburgh Internat. Fest., BBC TV, 1996; Dance Marathon, Basel Ballet, 1996; Inkle and Yarico, Holders Easter Season, Barbados, 1997; Mottke the Thief (also writer of adaptation from novel by Schalom Asch), Bonn Opera, 1998; Nyman's Facing Goya, Santiago del Compostela, Perrelada Fest., 2001; Die Versicherung, State Th., Darmstadt, 2002; Magic Flute (also trans. of spoken text), Scottish Opera, 2003; Sex, Chips and Rock 'n' Roll, Royal Exchange, 2005; The Soldier's Tale (also actor), Savannah Fest., Georgia, 2006; The Ballad of Elizabeth Sulky Mouth, Greenwich, 2006; The Revenger's Tragedy, Royal Exchange, 2008; House of Bernarda Alba, Battersea Arts Centre Main House, 2009; Crimes in Hot Countries, RADA, 2009; Our Lady of Sligo, RADA, 2010; Shadowball, Mermaid Th., 2010; Faith and Cold Reading, Live Th., Newcastle, 2011; Tell Tale Heart, ROH, 2011; Ashes and Sand, RADA, 2011; The Acid Test, RADA, 2012; Betrayal, RADA, 2013; Glengarry Glenross, Jacksons Lane Th., 2012; What You Will, Shakespeare's Globe, Cultural Olympiad, 2012; Sonnet Walks, Shakespeare's Globe, 2013–14; Unprotected, Courtyard Th., Hoxton, 2014; A Midsummer Night's Dream, Oval House, 2015; *actor: theatre* includes leading roles in: Class Enemy, Oxford Playhouse, transf. Young Vic, 1979; The Gorky Brigade, Royal Court, 1980; I Die for None of Them (one-man play), Edinburgh Fringe Fest., 1980, 1981 (Fringe First Award); Treatment, Gate, 1981, Donmar, 1982, Edinburgh Fest., 1986; Venice Preserv'd, Almeida, 1982; Arrivederci Millwall, Albany Empire, 1985; Behind Heaven, Royal Exchange, Donmar, 1986; The Art of Success, RSC, 1987; The Idiot, Barbican, 1990; Narrator, The Raven, Teatro Manzoni, Milan, 1990, Teatro Dell'Elfo, Milan, 2012; Dead Funny, Salisbury Playhouse, Th. Clwyd, 1998; Misalliance, 1998, The School of Night, 1999, Chichester Fest. Th.; A Midsummer Night's Dream, 2001, Macbeth, 2002, Arcola; Round the Horne, West End and No 1 UK tour, 2004; 2Graves (one-man play), Edinburgh Fest., transf. Arts Th., 2006; Holding Fire!, Shakespeare's Globe, 2007; Don Juan Comes Back From The War, New Diorama Th., 2014; *television* includes leading roles in: Treatment, 1984; Inside Story, 1986; Bleak House, 1986; Jack the Ripper (series), 1988; Roger Roger (two series), 1999, 2003; The People's Harry Enfield, 2001; Foyle's War, 2003; Cruel Train, 2004; City of Vice (series), 2007, Criminal Justice (series), 2008; Midsomer Murders (series), 2008; Sharpe's Peril (series), 2009; Holby City, 2013; *films* include: My Beautiful Laundrette, 1985; Golden Brown, 2011; 2 Graves, 2013. Collaborated on theatre pieces with Ludovico Einaudi, Stewart Copeland, Daniel Hope, band Test Dept, master percussionist Stomu Yamashta, jazz pianist Uri Caine, Eddy Grant, and mems of rock band Killing Joke and Jah Wobble; contrib. to BBC TV and radio arts discussion progs. Founder Mem. And Dir, New London Actors, 1980–84. Writer-in-Residence, Albany Empire, Deptford, 1985. Vis. Sen. Lectr, RCM, 2006; Guest Lectr, 2006, Vis. Lectr, 2010, Drama Centre, London; Vis. Lectr, RADA, 2009–13. Mem., Artistic Adv. Cttee, RADA, 2013–. Directed Shakespeare and screen acting workshops, Actor's Centre. KHS 2016. *Publications:* Jonathan Moore: three plays, 2002; Inigo, 2015 (trans. Spanish, 2016). *Recreations:* meditation, interior landscape gardening, football. *Address:* (writing and directing) c/o Julia Kreitman, The Agency, 24 Pottery Lane, Holland Park, W11 4LZ. *T:* (020) 7727 1346. *E:* info@theagency.co.uk; (acting) c/o Rebecca Singer Management, 79 Sutton Court Road, W4 3EQ. *T:* 07801 259963, (020) 8742 7747. *E:* office@rebeccasingermanagement.com; (opera directing) Robert Gilder and Co, N102, Vox Studios, 1–45 Durham Street, SE11 5JH. *T:* (020) 7580 7758, *Fax:* (020) 7580 7739. *W:* www.jonathanmooreuk.com.

**MOORE, Hon. John Colinton,** AO 2004; *b* Rockhampton, Qld, 16 Nov. 1936; *s* of Thomas R. Moore and Doris (*née* Symes); *m* 1st, 1965 (marr. diss.); two *s* one *d*; 2nd, 1980, Jacqueline Sarah, *d* of Hon. Sir William John Farquhar McDonald and Evelyn S. McDonald. *Educ:* Southport Jun. Sch., Qld; Armidale Sch., NSW; Univ. of Queensland (BCom; AAUQ). AASA. Stockbroker, 1960; Mem., Brisbane Stock Exchange, 1962–74. Former Director: Wm Brandt & Sons (Aust.); Phillips; First City; Brandt Ltd (PFCB Ltd); Merrill Lynch, Pierce, Fennell & Smith (Aust.) Ltd; Citi-national Ltd; Agricl Investments Aust. Ltd. MP (L) Ryan, Qld, 1975–2001; Fed. Minister for Business and Consumer Affairs, 1980–82; Opposition spokesman: for Finance, 1983–84; for Communications, 1984–85; for Northern Develt and Local Govt, 1985–87; for Tspt and Aviation, 1987; for Business and Consumer Affairs, 1987–89; for Business Privatisation and Consumer Affairs, 1989–90; Shadow Minister for Industry and Commerce, and Public Admin, 1995–96; Minister for Industry, Sci. and Tourism, 1996–98; Vice-Pres., Exec. Council, 1996–98; Minister for Defence, 1998–2001. Member: various Govt cttees, 1984–96; various internat. delegns. Queensland Liberal Party: Vice-Pres. and Treas., 1967–73; Pres., 1973–76 and 1984–90; Mem., Qld State Exec., Liberal Party of Aust., 1966–91 and 1996–98. Mem. Council, Order of Australia, 1996–98. Mem., Anti-Cancer Council of Qld, 1972. *Recreations:* tennis, cricket, reading, golf. *Address:* PO Box 1573, Toowong, Qld 4066, Australia. *Clubs:* Queensland, Brisbane, Tattersall's (Brisbane); Queensland Turf.

**MOORE, John David;** Headmaster, St Dunstan's College, Catford, 1993–97; *b* 16 Feb. 1943; *s* of John and Hilda Moore; *m* 1966, Ann Medora; one *s* one *d*. *Educ:* St John's Coll., Cambridge (BA Classics 1965; MA 1969); CertEd Cambridge Univ., 1966. Classics Master, Judd Sch., Tonbridge, 1966–69; trainee commodity trader, Gill and Duffus Ltd, 1969–70; English Master, Skinners' Sch., Tunbridge Wells, 1970–74; Head of General Studies and English Master, King's Sch., Macclesfield, Ches., 1974–80; Dep. Headmaster, Carre's Grammar Sch., Sleaford, Lincs, 1981–86; Headmaster, Ilford County High Sch. for Boys, London Borough of Redbridge, 1986–93. Member Committee: S Lakeland Carers, 1998–2001 (Chm., 1999–2001); Old Bradfordian Assoc., 1999– (Pres., 2003–06). Governor: Heron Hill Primary Sch., Kendal, 1998–2007; King's Sch., Macclesfield, 2000–12 (Mem., Govs' Educn Sub-Gp, 1998–2012; Chm., Educn Cttee, 2006–12). Freeman, City of London, 1996. *Publications:* Haec Egimus - All This We Did: a history of Bradford Grammar School, 1949–63, 2011. *Recreations:* cricket, walking, theatre, music. *Address:* 24 Castle Nurseries, Chipping Campden, Glos GL55 6JT.

**MOORE, Prof. John Halstead Hardman,** CBE 2017; PhD; FBA 1999; George Watson's and Daniel Stewart's Professor of Political Economy, University of Edinburgh, since 2000; Professor of Economic Theory, London School of Economics, since 1990 (quarter-time since 2000); *b* 7 May 1954; *s* of Frank Moore, OBE and Audrey Jeanne Moore (*née* Halstead); *m* 1986, Dr Susan Mary Hardman; one *s* one *d*. *Educ:* Dorking County Grammar Sch.; Fitzwilliam Coll., Cambridge (BA 1st cl. Hons Maths 1976; MA 1983); LSE (MSc 1980; PhD 1984). Exec. Engr, Dundee Telephone Area, 1976–78; Temp. Lectr in Econs, LSE, 1980–81; Lectr, Birkbeck Coll., London Univ., 1981–83; Lectr, 1983–87, Reader, 1987–90, LSE. Vis. Asst Prof., MIT, 1986–87; Vis. Prof., Princeton Univ., 1991–92; Prof., St Andrews Univ., 1997–2000 (quarter-time); Leverhulme Personal Res. Prof., 1998–2003; ESRC Professorial Fellow, 2004–07. Ed., Rev. of Economic Studies, 1987–91. Lectures: Walras-Bowley, 1996, Marschak, 2002, Econometric Soc.; Clarendon, Oxford Univ., 2001; Schumpeter, European Econ. Assoc., 2006; Max Weber, European Univ. Inst., 2006; Bernoulli, Univ. of Basel, 2007; Keynes Lectr, British Acad., 2007. Pres., REconS, 2015–16; Fellow: Econometric Soc., 1989 (Pres., 2010); Royal Soc. of Edinburgh, 2003. Foreign Hon. Member: Amer. Econ. Assoc., 2001; Amer. Acad. of Arts and Scis, 2002. Yrjö Jahnsson Award, European Econ. Assoc., 1999. *Publications:* articles on econs. *Recreations:* music, mountains. *Address:* School of Economics, University of Edinburgh, 31 Buccleuch Place, Edinburgh EH8 9JT; London School of Economics, Houghton Street, WC2A 2AE.

**MOORE, Jonathan;** *see* Moore, John.

**MOORE, Dame Julie,** DBE 2012; Professor of Healthcare Systems, Warwick Manufacturing Group, University of Warwick, since 2018; *b* Liverpool, 18 Aug. 1958; *d* of Edward James and Kathleen Mary Moore; civil partnership 2006, Lesley Ann Pattenson. *Educ:* BSc; Univ. of Leeds (MA Health Services Studies). Registered Nurse, then nurse manager, later nursing dir, Leeds; gen. mgt posts, 1977–98; Dir, Leeds Teaching Hosps NHS Trust, 1998–2002; Exec. Dir of Ops, 2002–06, CEO, 2006–18, University Hosps Birmingham NHS Foundn Trust. Hon. Prof., Univ. of Warwick, 2013–18. Hd, Educn and Trng Gp, NHS Future Forum, 2011–. Mem., Commn on Living Standards; former Mem., MoD/DoH Partnership Bd; Ind. Mem., OSCHR, 2010–16. Member: Nat. Organ Donation Taskforce, 2007–08; Nuffield Steering Gp on New Frontiers in Efficiency, 2009; Public Service Leadership Taskforce, 2018–. Former Mem., Internat. Adv. Bd, Univ. of Birmingham Business Sch.; Mem. Bd, Mktg Birmingham. Gov., Birmingham City Univ. *Recreations:* travel, music, history. *Address:* Warwick Manufacturing Group, International Manufacturing Centre, University of Warwick, Coventry CV4 7AL.

**MOORE, Katharine Elizabeth;** Her Honour Judge Katharine Moore; a Circuit Judge, since 2014. *Educ:* Downing Coll., Cambridge (BA 1994). Called to the Bar, Middle Temple, 1995; a Recorder, 2009–14. *Address:* Norwich Crown Court, The Law Courts, Bishopsgate, Norwich NR3 1UR.

**MOORE, Mark Jonathan,** MA; Headmaster, Akademeia High School, Warsaw; *b* 25 April 1961; *s* of Dennis and Sheila Moore; *m* 1989, Joanna Hawley; two *s* two *d*. *Educ:* Wolverhampton Grammar Sch.; Downing Coll., Cambridge (BA Hons English 1983; PGCE 1984; MA 1987). Assistant Master: Marlborough Coll., 1984–87; Eton Coll., 1987–94; Hd of English, Radley Coll., 1994–2005; Head of Coll., Clifton Coll., 2005–15. *Recreations:* ball games, reading, talking. *Clubs:* Jesters; Hawks (Cambridge).

**MOORE, Marks;** *see* Moore, D. M.

**MOORE, Martin Luke;** QC 2002; *b* 25 April 1960; *s* of late Brig. Peter Neil Martin Moore, DSO (and two Bars), MC, and Enid Rosemary Moore; *m* 1985, Caroline Mary Mason; three *d*. *Educ:* Winchester Coll.; Lincoln. Coll., Oxford (BA Hons). Called to the Bar, Lincoln's Inn, 1982, Bencher, 2010; in practice, specialising in company law litigation and advice. *Address:* Hurst Farm, Hurst Lane, Privett, Hants GU34 3PL. *T:* (01420) 588660; Erskine Chambers, 33 Chancery Lane, WC2A 1EN. *T:* (020) 7242 5532. *E:* mmoore@erskinechambers.com.

**MOORE, Vice Adm. Sir Michael (Antony Claës),** KBE 1997; LVO 1981; Chief Executive (formerly Director General), Institution of Mechanical Engineers, 1998–2007; *b* 6 Jan. 1942; *s* of Lieut A. D. W. Moore, RN (killed HMS Audacity, 1941) and Agneta Moore (*née* Wachtmeister); *m* 1969, Penelope Jane, JP, *d* of Rear-Adm. Frederick Charles William Lawson, CB, DSC and Bar; one *s* three *d*. *Educ:* Wellington Coll.; RNC Dartmouth. Swedish Naval Interpreter. Joined RN, 1960; served HM Ships Gurkha, Britannia and Ashton, 1963–67; Flag Lieut to Comdr FEF, Singapore, 1967–68; i/c HMS Beachampton, 1969; qualified as Navigator, 1970; HM Ships Tenby, Brighton, Plymouth and Tartar (i/c), 1970–77; Naval Ops, MoD, 1977–79; HMY Britannia, 1979–81; Captain,

1981; Naval Asst to Chief of Fleet Support, MoD, 1981–82; i/c HMS Andromeda, and Capt. 8th Frigate Sqn, 1983–84; i/c Ops, Northwood MHQ, 1985–87; Dir, Naval Warfare, MoD, 1988–90; Rear Adm., 1990; Maritime Advr to SACEUR, 1990–93; Vice Adm. 1994; C of S to Comdr Allied Naval Forces Southern Europe, 1994–97. Chm., Forces Pension Soc. (formerly Officers' Pension Soc.), 2006–11. Dir, Tall Ships Youth Trust, 2010–16; Pres., Friends of RN Mus. and HMS Victory, 2012–18. Hon. Fellow: Swedish Royal Soc. of Naval Scis, 1992; IMechE 2006. Younger Brother, Trinity House, 1988. *Address:* Churchill Cottage, Castle Street, Portchester, Hants PO16 9QW.

*See also J. A. A. H. Moore.*

**MOORE, Prof. Michael Arthur,** DPhil; FRS 1989; Professor of Theoretical Physics, University of Manchester, 1976–2011, now Emeritus; *b* 8 Oct. 1943; *s* of John Moore and Barbara Atkinson; *m* 1967, Susan Eadington; three *s* one *d. Educ:* Huddersfield New Coll.; Oriel Coll., Oxford (BA 1964; DPhil 1967). Prize Fellow, Magdalen Coll., Oxford, 1967–71; Res. Associate, Univ. of Illinois, USA, 1967–69; Lectr in Physics, Univ. of Sussex, 1971–76. *Publications:* papers in scientific jls. *Recreation:* tennis. *Address:* The Schuster Laboratory, The University, Manchester M13 9PL.

**MOORE, Rt Hon. Michael (Kenneth),** ONZ 2000; PC 1990; Director-General, World Trade Organisation, 1999–2002; Ambassador of New Zealand to the United States of America, 2010–15; *b* 28 Jan. 1949; *m* 1975, Yvonne (*née* Dereany). *Educ:* Dilworth Sch.; Bay of Islands College (only Minister in Labour Govt without a degree). Worked as social worker, builder's labourer, meat freezing worker and printer; MP (Lab) Eden 1972–75 (youngest NZ MP ever elected); MP (Lab) Papanui, later named Christchurch North, then Waimakariri, 1978–99; spokesperson on housing, regional, small town and community development, the environment, tourism, recreation and sport, overseas trade and marketing, external relations and trade, finance; Minister of Foreign Affairs and Trade, 1990; trade missions led incl. Japan, Europe, Soviet Union, Pakistan, Turkey; Prime Minister of NZ, Sept.–Oct. 1990; Leader of the Opposition, 1990–93. Adjunct Prof., Faculty of Law and Mgt, La Trobe Univ., 2003–. Hon. DCom: Lincoln, NZ; Auckland Univ. of Technol.; Hon. DEc People's Univ. of China; Hon. Dr Canterbury, Christchurch; Hon. DIur La Trobe. *Publications:* On Balance, 1980; Beyond Today, 1981; A Pacific Parliament, 1982; The Added Value Economy, 1984; Hard Labour, 1987; Fighting for New Zealand, 1993; Children of the Poor, 1996; A Brief History of the Future, 1998; A World Without Walls, 2003; Saving Globalization, 2009.

**MOORE, Rt Hon. Michael (Kevin);** PC 2010; Director General, British Private Equity and Venture Capital Association, since 2019; *b* 3 June 1965; *s* of Rev. (William) Haisley Moore and Geraldine Anne, (Jill), Moore; *m* 2004, Alison Louise Hughes; one *s* one *d. Educ:* Strathallan Sch.; Jedburgh Grammar Sch.; Univ. of Edinburgh (MA Jt Hons Politics and Modern Hist.). CA 1991. Research Asst to Archy Kirkwood, MP, 1987–88; with Coopers & Lybrand, Edinburgh, 1988–97 (a Manager, corporate finance). MP (Lib Dem) Tweeddale, Ettrick and Lauderdale, 1997–2005, Berwickshire, Roxburgh and Selkirk, 2005–15; contested (Lib Dem) same seat, 2015. Lib Dem spokesman on defence, 2005–06; on foreign affairs, 2006–07, on internat. develt, 2007–10; Sec. of State for Scotland, 2010–13. Mem., Select Cttee on Scottish affairs, 1997–99. Sen. Advr, PwC, 2016–19. Parly Vis. Fellow, St Antony's Coll., Oxford, 2003–04; Vis. Prof., Internat. Public Policy Inst., Univ. of Strathclyde, 2016–. Non-exec. Dir, Edinburgh Business Sch., Heriot-Watt Univ., 2017–. Gov. and Vice-Chm., Westminster Foundn for Democracy, 2002–05; Mem. Council, Chatham House, 2004–10; Gov., Ditchley Foundn, 2010–. Chm., Borders Book Fest., 2015–; Trustee, Tweed Foundn, 2015–18. *Recreations:* jazz, music, films, Rugby, hill-walking.

**MOORE, Michael Rodney Newton,** CBE 1996; Chairman, Which? Ltd, 1997–2008; Director, HBOS Financial Services, 2001–09; *b* 15 March 1936; *s* of Gen. Sir Rodney Moore, GCVO, KCB, CBE, DSO, PMN and Olive Marion (*née* Robinson); *m* 1986, Jan, *d* of Paul and Lilian Adorian; one *s. Educ:* Eton; Magdalen College, Oxford (MA); Harvard Business Sch. (MBA). Nat. Service Commission, Grenadier Guards, 1957–59, serving in Cyprus, Lebanon, UK. Called to the Bar, Gray's Inn, 1961; practised until 1964; joined Hill Samuel & Co., 1966 (Dir, 1970–71); subseq. Chm./Dir, various UK, USA & Swedish cos; Chairman: Royston Lead, 1975–81; Tomkins, 1984–95; Quicks Gp, 1992–2002; Linx Printing Technologies, 1993–2005; London Internat. Gp, 1994–99; Warm Zones, 2001–04; Dir, Sir John Soane's Mus. Soc., 2004–05. Mem. Council of Mgt, Consumers' Assoc., 1997–2003. Trustee, Public Concern at Work, 1996–2003. Chm., NSPCC, 1988–95. *Recreations:* visiting ruins, opera, photography, reading. *Clubs:* Garrick, Pratt's, Boodle's.

**MOORE, Michael S.;** *see* Stuart-Moore.

**MOORE, Miranda Jayne, (Mrs J. M. Haslam);** QC 2003; *b* 4 Jan. 1961; *d* of Bryan John Moore and Anne Rosemary Janet Spokes Moore; *m* 1987, Jonathan Mark Haslam; one *s* one *d. Educ:* Univ. of Aston (BSc 1st Cl. Hons Business Studies). Called to the Bar, Lincoln's Inn, 1983, Bencher, 2012; in practice as barrister, specialising in criminal law, 1984–. *Recreations:* dancing, theatre, shopping. *Address:* 5 Paper Buildings, Temple, EC4Y 7HB. *T:* (020) 7583 6117. *E:* clerks@5pb.co.uk.

**MOORE, Dr (Sir) Peter Alan Cutlack,** (4th Bt *cr* 1919, has established his claim but does not use the title); Director, Peter Moore Consulting Ltd, since 2004; *b* Bristol, 21 Sept. 1951; *o s* of Dr (Sir) Norman Winfrid Moore (3rd Bt) and Dr Janet Moore (née Singer); *S* father, 2015; *m* 1989, Pamela Michele Edwardes; one *s* one *d. Educ:* Eton Coll.; Trinity Coll., Cambridge (BA 1973, MA 1977); Univ. of Oxford (DPhil 1980). MInstP; CPhys 1985. With BP, 1978–2003: roles in res., planning, oil trading, business develt in E Asia and HR; EU exec. trng prog., Japan, 1982–83; consultant on strategy and governance in internat. develt, 2004–. Vice Chm., ActionAid UK, 2003–08. *Recreation:* community groups for international development. *Heir:* *s* Paul Edwardes Moore, *b* 11 Nov. 1990. *Address:* 23 Mount Pleasant Road, NW10 3EG.

**MOORE, Peter Robert;** Chief Executive Officer, Liverpool Football Club, since 2017; *b* Liverpool, 16 March 1955; *s* of Terence and Marilyn Moore; *m* 2018, Deborah Dubois; one *s* three *d. Educ:* Keele Univ. (BEd); California State Univ. (MEd). Phys. Education Teacher, Ysgol Dinas Bran, Llangollen, 1977–81; Sales Rep., 1981–84, Sales Manager, 1984–88, Pres., 1988–92, Patrick USA; Sen. Vice Pres., Reebok Internat., 1992–98; Pres. and Chief Operating Officer, Sega of America, 1998–2003; Corporate Vice Pres., Microsoft, 2003–07; Pres., 2007–11, Chief Operating Officer, 2011–17, EA Sports. *Address:* Axholme, Noctorum Road, Prenton, Wirral, Merseyside CH43 9UQ. *T:* 07511 100388. *E:* prmoore55@liverpoolfc.com.

**MOORE, Philip John,** BMus; FRCO; Organist and Master of the Music, York Minster, 1983–2008, now Organist Emeritus; President, Royal College of Organists, 2015–17; *b* 30 Sept. 1943; *s* of late Cecil and Marjorie Moore; one *s* two *d*; *m* 2018, Alison, *d* of Dr Alexander Hunter. *Educ:* Maidstone Grammar Sch.; Royal Coll. of Music (ARCM; GRSM 1965); BMus Dunelm 1975. FRCO 1965. Asst Music Master, Eton Coll., 1965–68; Asst Organist, Canterbury Cathedral, 1968–74; Organist and Master of the Choristers, Guildford Cathedral, 1974–83. Hon. FRSCM 2005; Hon. FGCM 2006; Hon. Fellow, Acad. of St Cecilia, 2007. Hon. Dr York, 2014. Order of St William of York, 2008. Cranmer Award for Worship, Lambeth Palace, 2016. *Publications:* anthems, services, cantatas, organ music, song cycles, chamber music, orchestral music. *Recreations:* collecting fountain pens, collecting Imari, cooking, log fires, architecture, cars, art, reading. *Address:* Rectory Cottage, Barton-le-Street, Malton YO17 6PN.

**MOORE, Philip Wynford,** TD 1994; Group Finance Director, Liverpool Victoria Friendly Society, 2010–17; *b* 5 Jan. 1960; *s* of Cecil Philip John Moore and late Christine Margaret Moore; *m* 1995, Amanda Lawson; two *d. Educ:* St Albans Sch.; Clare Coll., Cambridge (BA Maths 1982; MA 1986). AIA 1986, FIA 1988. Life Dept, Commercial Union Insce Co., 1982–87; Managing Consultant, William M. Mercer, 1987–89; Coopers & Lybrand: leader of life actuarial practice, London, 1989–95; Partner, Financial Instns Gp, Coopers & Lybrand Consulting (East Asia), leader, E Asia Insce Consultancy practice, Hong Kong, 1995–98; Finance Dir and Actuary, National Provident Instn, 1998–2000; Corp. Dir of Finance and Hd of Mergers and Acquisitions, AMP (UK) plc, 2000–03; Gp Finance Dir, 2003–06, Gp Chief Exec., 2007, Friends Provident plc; Interim Chief Finance Officer, HMRC, 2008; Gp Finance Partner, 2008–10, and Chief Risk Officer, 2009–10, Pensions Corp. LLP. Non-executive Director: RAB Capital plc, 2009–11 (Chm., Audit Cttee, 2009–11); Towergate Insurance Ltd (formerly Towergate Partnership Co. Ltd), 2011–17 (Chm., Audit Cttee, 2011–17; Sen. Ind. Dir, 2013–15); Bank of Ireland (UK) plc, 2018–; Codan A/S and Codan Forsikring A/S, 2018– (Chm., Audit and Risk Cttee, 2018–). Mem., Educn Leadership Team, BITC, 2006–10. Trustee: Childhood Eye Cancer Trust, 2007–13 (Chm., 2008–13); RBL, 2014– (Chm., Finance Cttee, 2014–). Gov., Aylward Acad., 2011– (Chm., Achievement and Standards Cttee, 2014–17; Vice Chm., 2016–17; Chm. of Govs, 2017). *Recreations:* family, flying (private pilot's licence), ski-ing, running. *Club:* Honourable Artillery Company.

**MOORE, Air Vice-Marshal Richard Charles,** MBE 1989; Director, D&MM Associates Ltd, since 2014; Air Officer Administration, and Air Officer Commanding Directly Administered Units, 2003–05; *b* 5 Aug. 1950; *s* of Ernest William Moore and Hilda Margaret Moore (*née* Edwards); *m* 1977, Judith Ellen Owen; two *s. Educ:* Open Univ. (BSc Systems); RAF Staff Coll. Joined RAF, 1970; OC 16 Sqdn, 1983–85, 6 Wing, 1988–91, RAF Regt; MoD Staff appts, Regt 26 (RAF), 1985–88, Air Plans (LTC), 1991–95; Officer Commanding: Defence Nuclear Biol and Chem. Centre, 1995–97; RAF Honington, 1997–99; Comdt Gen., RAF Regt, 1999–2001; Team Leader, Ground Based Air Defence Integrated Project, Defence Procurement Agency, 2001–03. Dir, Network Enabled Solutions, QinetiQ Ltd, 2008–14. Chm., RAF Bobsleigh, Luge and Skeleton Bobsleigh Assoc., 1997–2006. *Recreation:* offshore sailing. *Address:* c/o RAF High Wycombe, Bucks HP14 4UE.

**MOORE, Richard Hobart John de Courcy,** FCA; Managing Partner, 1987–2004, and Senior Partner, 1989–2017, Moore Stephens; Chairman, Moore Stephens International Ltd, since 2005; *b* 31 Aug. 1949; *s* of late Hobart Harold de Courcy Moore and Elizabeth Helen Moore; *m* 1977, Lucy Annabelle Sefton-Smith; one *s* one *d. Educ:* Stowe Sch. ACA 1972, FCA 1979. Moore Stephens LLP, 1968–2019, Partner, 1975–2019. Dir, Moore Family Office Ltd, 2019–. Comr, Royal Hospital Chelsea, 2006–12. Treas., Shipwrights' Co., 1989–. *Recreations:* Real tennis, cricket. *Address:* 11 Chelsea Park Gardens, SW3 6AF. *T:* (020) 7352 7594. *Clubs:* Boodle's, MCC, Hurlingham, Queen's.

**MOORE, Richard Peter,** CMG 2017; HM Diplomatic Service; Director-General, Political, Foreign and Commonwealth Office, since 2018; *b* Tripoli, Libya, 9 May 1963; *s* of John Robert Moore and (Norah) Patricia Moore (*née* Buckley); *m* 1985, Margaret Patricia Isabel, (Maggie), Martin; one *s* one *d. Educ:* St George's Coll., Weybridge; Worcester Coll., Oxford (BA (Hons) PPE); Kennedy Sch. of Govt, Harvard Univ. (Kennedy Schol.); Stanford Graduate Sch. of Business (Stanford Exec. Prog. 2007). Joined FCO, 1987; Third Sec., Hanoi, 1988; Second Sec. (Pol), Ankara, 1990; Consul (Pol and Press), Istanbul, 1991–92; Desk Officer, Iran, FCO, 1992–95; First Sec., Islamabad, 1995–98; Section Hd, Security Policy Gp, FCO, 1998–2001; Counsellor, Kuala Lumpur, 2001–05; Dep. Dir, Middle East, 2005–08, Dir, Progs and Change, 2008–10, Dir, Europe, Latin America and Globalisation, 2010–12, FCO; Ambassador to Turkey, 2014–17; Dep. Nat. Security Advr (Intelligence, Security and Resilience), 2018. *Recreations:* golf, watching cricket and Rugby, reading, TV, travel. *Address:* c/o Foreign and Commonwealth Office, King Charles Street, SW1A 2AH. *E:* richard.moore@fco.gov.uk. *Clubs:* Garrick, Vincent's, MCC.

**MOORE, Sir Richard William,** 4th Bt *cr* 1932; *b* 8 May 1955; *s* of Sir William Roger Clotworthy Moore, 3rd Bt, TD and Gillian Moore (*née* Brown); *S* father, 2019; *m* 1985, Karyn Furness; three *d.* Lieut Royal Scots, 1974.

**MOORE, His Honour Robert Jeffery,** a Circuit Judge, 1995–2017; a Deputy Circuit Judge, since 2017; *b* 1947; *s* of Jeffery Moore and Doreen Moore; *m* 1979, Susan Elaine Hatcliffe; two *s. Educ:* Loughborough Grammar Sch.; Univ. of Manchester (LLB Hons 1968); Council of Legal Educn (Bar Finals 1969). Called to the Bar, Gray's Inn, 1970; practised on North Eastern Circuit, from Sheffield, 1971–80 and from 11 Kings Bench Walk, Temple, 1980–95; Ethnic Minorities Liaison Judge for S Yorks and Humberside (formerly Sheffield), 1998–2004. Mem., Written Examinations and Interview Panel, Judicial Appts Commn, 2008–11. *Recreations:* travel, especially with family, golf, Leicester Tigers, Sheffield Hospitals' radio. *Address:* The Law Courts, 50 West Bar, Sheffield S3 8PH. *Clubs:* Sloane; Sickleholme Golf (Bamford).

**MOORE, Prof. Roger Kenneth,** PhD; Professor of Spoken Language Processing, University of Sheffield, since 2004; *b* Swanage, 26 Feb. 1952; *s* of Kenneth Moore and Rosemary Moore; *m* 1987, Jenifer Younger; one *s. Educ:* Swanage Grammar Sch.; Univ. of Essex (BA Hons Computers and Communications Engrg 1973; MSc 1974; PhD 1976). FIOA 1987. Postdoctoral Researcher, UCL, 1976–80; Section Leader, RSRE, 1980–85; Hd, Speech Res. Unit, DERA, 1985–99; Chief Scientific Officer, 20/20 Speech Ltd, 1999–2004. Visiting Professor: Psychol. and Lang. Scis, UCL, 1990–; Bristol Robotics Lab., UWE, 2011–. Fellow, Internat. Speech Communication Assoc., 2008. Editor-in-Chief, Jl of Computer Speech and Lang., 1985–. *Publications:* (jtly) The Eagles Handbook of Standards and Resources for Spoken Language Systems, 1997; (jtly) Handbook of Multimodal and Spoken Dialogue Systems: resources, terminology and product evaluation, 2000; over 25 articles in acad. jls incl. Nature Scientific Reports, Speech Communication, Computer Speech and Lang., Phonetics, Connection Sci., IEEE Trans. on Computers, Artificial Intelligence Res. *Recreations:* photography, running. *Address:* Department of Computer Science, University of Sheffield, Regent Court, 211 Portobello, Sheffield S1 4DP. *T:* (0114) 222 1807. *E:* r.k.moore@sheffield.ac.uk.

**MOORE, Rosalyn Elaine, (Mrs Stephen Littler);** Chief Executive Officer, Parish Nursing Ministries UK, since 2015; *b* Castleford, 1 March 1957; *d* of Harold Moore and Sheila Moore (*née* Turner); *m* 1998, Stephen Littler; one *s* two *d. Educ:* Normanton Grammar Sch.; Leeds Metropolitan Univ. (BSc Hons Nursing); Open Univ. (MA Educn and Leadership). SRN 1981; RNT 1989. Staff Nurse, Castleford and Normanton District Hosp., 1981–84; Paediatric Staff Nurse, Pontefract and Pinderfields Hosps, 1984–87; Nurse Tutor, Pinderfields Hosp., Wakefield, 1987–89; Hd, Adult Nursing, later Postgrad. Educn,

Leeds Coll. of Health, subseq. Univ. of Leeds, 1989–96; Asst Dir of Nursing and Professional Develt Lead, Pinderfields and Pontefract NHS Trust, 1996–99; Chief Nurse and Ops Manager, NHS Direct, W Yorks, and Dep. Dir, W Yorks Metropolitan Ambulance Service, 1999–2002; Nat. Dir for Quality and Learning, and Dep. Clin. Dir, NHS Direct, 2002–04; Professional Nursing Officer, DoH, 2004–09; Dir of Nursing, NHS Connecting for Health, 2009–10; Chief Nursing Officer, Scotland, and Dir for Patients, Public and Health Professions, Scottish Govt, 2010–14.

**MOORE, Rear-Adm. Simon,** CB 2000; Chief Executive, Action Medical Research (formerly Action Research), 2001–09; *b* 25 Sept. 1946; *s* of Ronald and Christine Moore; *m* 1978, Catherine Sarcelet; three *d*. *Educ:* Brentwood Sch. Joined RN 1964; in command, HM Ships: Walkerton, 1974–75; Rhyl, 1983; Berwick, 1984–85; Asst Dir, Defence Policy, MoD, 1988–91; in command, HMS Fearless, 1991–93; Captain, BRNC, Dartmouth, 1993–95; Dir, Intelligence Regl Assessments, 1995–97; ACDS (Ops), MoD, 1997–2000. Pres., London Flotilla, 1999–2005. Gov., Hurstpierpoint Coll., 2001–13 (Chm. of Govs, 2003–13). Trustee: Assoc. of Med. Res. Charities, 2008–13; British Youth Opera, 2008–16; SGS Foundn Trust, 2014–. Chm., Chanctonbury Chorus, 2010–18. Liveryman, Curriers' Co., 2006–. *Recreations:* music, choral singing, theatre.

**MOORE, Terence,** CBE 1993; business consultant, 1995–2010; Group Managing Director and Chief Executive Officer, Conoco Ltd, 1987–95; *b* 24 Dec. 1931; *s* of Arthur Doncaster Moore and Dorothy Irene Gladys (*née* Godwin); *m* 1955, Tessa Catherine (*née* Wynne) (separated 1990); two *s* one *d*. *Educ:* Strand Sch., London; BScEcon, Univ. of London; Harvard (AMP). ACII 1958; AICS 1959. Shell Internat. Petroleum Co., 1948–64; Locana Corp. Ltd (investment bank), 1964–65; Conoco Ltd, 1965–95: Dep. Man. Dir, Marketing and Operations, 1975; Man. Dir, Supply and Trading, Europe, 1979. Director: Conoco Pension Trustees Ltd, 1996–2003; James Fisher & Son plc, 1998–2004. Pres., Oil Industries Club, 2003–09; Hon. Sec., Inst. of Petroleum, 1995–2001. Gov., Greenwich Theatre, 1991–97 (Vice Chm. Govs, 1992–93). Chm., St Katherine and Shadwell Trust, 1999. *Publications:* articles in industry jls. *Recreations:* music, theatre, walking, family and friends. *Address:* 67 Merchant Court, Thorpes Yard, 61 Wapping Wall, E1W 3SJ. *T:* and *Fax:* (020) 7481 0853. *E:* t.moore@talktalk.net.

**MOORE, Prof. Terry,** PhD; FRAS, FRIN, FCInstCES, CEng; Professor of Satellite Navigation, since 2001, Director, Nottingham Geospatial Institute (formerly Institute of Engineering Surveying and Space Geodesy), since 2003, and Lead for Transport Technologies Research Priority Area, since 2016, University of Nottingham; *b* 3 May 1961; *s* of Colin Leonard and Edna Moore; *m* 1985, Ingrid Tamara Rejent; one *s* one *d*. *Educ:* Univ. of Nottingham (BSc 1st Cl. Civil Engrg 1982; PhD Space Geodesy 1986). FRAS 1983; FRIN 1995; FCInstCES 2009; CEng 2019. University of Nottingham: Res. Fellow, 1985–88; Lectr, 1989–97; Reader in Satellite Navigation, 1997–2000; Dep. Hd, Sch. of Civil Engrg, 2008–10; Associate Dean, Faculty of Engrg, 2011–15. Special Prof., Chinese Acad. of Surveying and Mapping, 2004–. Mem., US Nat. Space-Based Positioning, Navigation and Trng Adv. Bd, 2019–. Vice Pres., 2008–10 and 2014–18, Pres., 2018–, Royal Inst. of Navigation. Associate Fellow, Remote Sensing and Photogrammetry Soc., 2001. Fellow, US Inst. of Navigation, 2013. Harold Spencer-Jones Gold Medal, 2013, J. E. D. Williams Medal, 2016, Royal Inst. of Navigation; Johannes Kepler Award, Inst. of Navigation, USA, 2017. *Publications:* chapters in: Sovereign Limits Beneath the Oceans: delimiting the new continental shelf, 1999; Guidelines for the use of GPS in Surveying and Mapping, 2003; Springer Handbook of Global Navigation Satellite Systems, 2017; Multi-Technology Positioning, 2017; contrib. papers to learned jls incl. Jl Navigation, Survey Rev., IEE Digest, GPS Solutions, Internat. Hydrographic Rev., Advances in Astronautical Scis, Hydro Internat., IALA Bulletin, Jl Surveying Engrg, Jl Satellite Positioning, Navigation and Communication, Jl British Interplanetary Soc., Navigation, Prequisas, Revista Brasileira de Cartografia, Space Communications Jl, Jl of Engrg and Technol Scis, Jl of Computer Sci., Internat. Jl of Advancements in Tech., Gyroscopy and Navigation, Lecture Notes in Geoinformation and Cartography, Jl of Mobile Multimedia, Jl of Location Based Services, Jl of Applied Geodesy, Geo-spatial Information Sci., Proceedings of IEEE, Pervasive and Mobile Computing, Measurement, Jl of the International Measurement Confederation, GPS World, Sensors, Cognition Technology and Work, Progress in Aerospace Scis, Jl Ambient Intelligence and Humanized Computing, Computer Sci. Rev. *Recreations:* mountaineering, hill walking and other outdoor activities, travelling and caravanning, music (singing and playing guitar), reading, sport, Season Ticket holder for Sheffield United FC. *Address:* Nottingham Geospatial Institute, Nottingham Geospatial Building, University of Nottingham Innovation Park, Nottingham NG7 2TU. *T:* (0115) 951 3886, *Fax:* (0115) 951 3881. *E:* terry.moore@nottingham.ac.uk. *Club:* Austrian Alpine (Section Britannia).

**MOORE, Trevor Charles;** HM Diplomatic Service, retired; *b* Freetown, Sierra Leone, 19 Jan. 1958; *s* of Samuel Robert William Moore and Janet Joan Moore; *m* 1991, Diane Elizabeth Burns; three *s*. *Educ:* Manchester Univ. (BA Jt Hons American and Russian Studies). Joined HM Diplomatic Service, 1980; Third Sec., Belgrade, Yugoslavia, 1983–86; Vice-Consul, NY, 1986–87; Second Sec., (Pol.-Mil.), Washington, 1987–89; FCO, London, 1989–97; First Sec. (Comprehensive Nuclear Test Ban Treaty), Vienna, 1997–2001; Deputy Head: Latin America and Caribbean Dept, FCO, 2001–04; Counter-Proliferation Dept, FCO, 2004–07; Human Rights, Democracy and Governance Gp, FCO, 2007–08; Ambassador to Tajikistan, 2009–12; Finance Directorate, FCO, 2012; Special Projects Officer, Syria Team, FCO, 2012–13. Strategic Develt Consultant, Dio. of London, 2014–15. *Recreations:* walking (Gold Duke of Edinburgh Award), reading (American and Russian literature), opera.

**MOORE, Maj. Gen. William Hewitt,** CBE 2004; Chief Executive Officer, The Portman Estate, 2011–18; executive coach and leadership development, since 2018; *b* 24 Feb. 1958; *s* of Brian and Eileen Moore; *m* 1986, Jane Moore; two *s*. *Educ:* Univ. of Salford (BA Hons Pols and Hist. of Industrial Soc. 1979). Battery Comdr 1 Parachute Battery (Bull's Troop), RHA, 1992–94; Directing Staff, Army Staff Coll., 1994–96; CO 7th Parachute Regt, RHA, 1996–98; Col Force Develt, 1998–2001; Commander: Sierra Leone Armed Forces, 2001; 19 Mechanised Bde, 2001–03 (Sierra Leone and Iraq); Dir Equipment Capability (Ground Manoeuvre), MoD, 2004–07; Dir Gen. Logistics, Support and Equipment, HQ Land Forces, 2007–08; Dep. Comdg Gen. Multi Nat. Corps, Iraq, 2009; Dir (Battlespace Manoeuvre) and Master Gen. of the Ordnance, 2010–11. Founder and Chm., West End Security Gp, 2016–. Co-Chm., nat. counter terrorism prog. bd, Step Change, 2018–. Mem. Council, Forces Pension Soc., 2017–. Dir, Inter Services T20, Lord's, 2010–12. Trustee, Malvern Coll., 2005–14. CMgr 2011; CCMI 2016. QCVS 2001. Cross of Merit (Czech Republic), 2003; Officer, Legion of Merit (USA), 2011. *Publications:* articles in RUSI, British Army Rev. *Recreations:* trekking, cycling, cricket, rock music, outwitting the dog.

**MOORE-BICK, Maj. Gen. John David,** CBE 1997 (OBE 1991); DL; FICE; FCIL; General Secretary, Forces Pension Society, 2007–15; *b* 10 Oct. 1949; *s* of late John Ninian Moore-Bick and Kathleen Margaret Moore-Bick (*née* Beall); *m* 1973, Anne Horton; one *d*. *Educ:* Stonegate Sch.; Skinners'; St Catherine's Coll., Oxford (BA (Forestry), MA). Commissioned RA (V) 1969, regular commission, 1971; transf. to RE, 1972; served 45 Commando Gp, Junior Leaders' Regt RE and 23 Amphibious Engr Sqdn, 1972–79; Führungsakademie der Bundeswehr, 1979–82; HQ UKLF, 1982–84; Falkland Is, 1984–85; 26 Armd Engr Sqdn, 1985–86; Asst to Chm., NATO Mil. Cttee, 1986–88; 21 Engr Regt, Germany, and Gulf War, 1988–91; Chief Engr, Multi National Airmobile Div., 1991; Col Army Plans, MoD, 1991–94; Chief Engr, ARRC, 1994–95 and Implementation Force, Sarajevo, 1995–96; Dir, Army Staff Duties, MoD, 1996–99; Leader, MoD Study into Future of Shrivenham/Watchfield, 1999; MA to High Rep., Sarajevo, 2000; GOC UK Support Comd (Germany), 2001–03; Special Defence Advr, Serbia and Montenegro, 2003–04. Hon. Colonel: 39 (Skinners') Signal Regt, 2001–06; Sussex ACF, 2007–; Col Comdt, RE, 2002–12; Sqdn Col, 56 Signal Sqdn (V), 2011–14. Chm., RE Assoc., 2007–12. Patron, Eastbourne Scottish Pipe Band, 2006–; Chm., Blythe Sappers, 2010. Chm. Govs, Skinners' Sch., 2005–15; Gov., Plumpton Coll., 2016–. FICE 1997; FCIL (FIL 2003). Liveryman, Skinners' Co., 1988– (First Warden, 2007–08; Master, 2008–09; Chm., Lawrence Atwell's Charity, 2016–). DL 2006, High Sheriff, 2018, E Sussex. 1st Cl. Service Order (Hungary), 1996. *Recreations:* Eastern Europe and Germany, Kent and Sussex Weald. *Address:* Castle Well, Ewhurst Green, E Sussex TN32 5TD. *Club:* Army and Navy.

*See also Rt Hon. Sir M. J. Moore-Bick.*

**MOORE-BICK, Rt Hon. Sir Martin (James),** Kt 1995; PC 2005; a Lord Justice of Appeal, 2005–16; *b* 6 Dec. 1946; *s* of late John Ninian Moore-Bick and Kathleen Margaret Moore-Bick (*née* Beall); *m* 1974, Tessa Penelope Gee; two *s* two *d*. *Educ:* The Skinners' Sch., Tunbridge Wells; Christ's Coll., Cambridge (MA; Hon. Fellow, 2009). Called to the Bar, Inner Temple, 1969, Bencher, 1992 (Treas., 2015); QC 1986; a Recorder, 1990–95; a Judge of the High Ct of Justice, QBD, 1995–2005; Dep. Hd of Civil Justice, 2007–12; Vice-Pres., Court of Appeal, Civil Div., 2014–16. Chm., Legal Services Consultancy Panel, 2005–09; Chair, Public Inquiry into Grenfell Tower Fire, 2017–. *Recreations:* early music, gardening, reading. *Address:* 20 Essex Street, WC2R 3AL. *E:* MMoore-Bick@20essexst.com.

*See also Maj. Gen. J. D. Moore-Bick.*

**MOORE-BRABAZON,** family name of **Baron Brabazon of Tara**.

**MOORE-BRIDGER, Timothy Peter,** MA; Headmaster, King Edward VI Grammar School, Stratford-upon-Avon, 1997–2010; *b* 11 May 1945; *s* of Harry Charles and Winifred Jane Moore-Bridger; *m* 1980, Iwona Elzbieta Joanna (*née* Barycz); one *s* two *d*. *Educ:* Oswestry Sch., Shropshire; Queens' Coll., Cambridge (MA Mod. and Medieval Langs). Asst Master teaching French, Latin, Italian, Ancient History, St Paul's Sch., Barnes, 1967–88; Dep. Headmaster, Nottingham High Sch., 1988–97. Trustee: Shakespeare Birthplace Trust, 1997–2010; Hampton Lucy Grammar Sch. Trust, 2001–10. Gov., Oswestry Sch., 2011– (Vice Chm., 2013–). *Recreations:* attending and supporting RSC productions, singing in Stratford-upon-Avon Choral Society, gardening, studying with Oxford University Centre for Continuing Education.

**MOORE-GILLON, Dr John Christopher,** FRCP; Consultant Physician, King Edward VII's Hospital Sister Agnes, since 2007; *b* London, 2 Jan. 1953; *s* of John Alec Moore-Gillon and Daphne Moore-Gillon; *m* 1980, Victoria Kirby, FRCS; one *s* two *d*. *Educ:* Tiffin Sch.; St Catharine's Coll., Cambridge (BA 1973); St Thomas's Hosp. Med. Sch. (MB (Dist.) BChir 1976; MD 1987); Univ. of London ext. (LLB 2003). MRCP 1978, FRCP 1992. Hse Officer, St Thomas's and Kingston Hosps, 1976–77; Sen. Hse Officer, St Thomas's and Royal Brompton Hosps, 1977–78; Med. Registrar, Kingston and St Thomas's Hosps, 1978–80; Res. Fellow, 1980–83, Lectr, 1983–88, Dept of Medicine, St Thomas's Hosp. Med. Sch.; Sen. Registrar, London Chest Hosp., 1985–88; Sen. Lectr and Hon. Consultant Physician, Med. Coll. of St Bartholomew's Hosp., 1988–92; Consultant Physician: St Bartholomew's Hosp., 1992–2010; Royal London Hosp., 1998–2010, now Emeritus Consultant. Hon. Sec., British Thoracic Soc., 1992–94; British Lung Foundation: Chm., 1994–99; Pres., 2001–07; Vice-Pres., 2007–; Hon. Med. Advr, 2010–. Liveryman, Soc. of Apothecaries, 1989 (Sen. Warden, 2013–14; Master, 2014–15). *Publications:* contrib. book chapters, rev. articles and scientific papers on respiratory medicine. *Recreations:* music, theatre, time with family and friends. *Address:* 37 Devonshire Street, W1G 6QA. *T:* (020) 7339 3089, *Fax:* (020) 7339 3088. *E:* john@moore-gillon.com. *Clubs:* Athenæum, Garrick.

**MOORE-GWYN, Alison Frances,** LVO 2013; Chief Executive Officer, Fields in Trust (National Playing Fields Association), 2004–12; *b* 25 March 1950; *d* of late Clifford George White and Joyce Beatrice White (*née* Lawley); *m* 1974, David Moore-Gwyn; two *s* one *d*. *Educ:* Berkhamsted Sch. for Girls; Girton Coll., Cambridge (BA 1971). Admitted solicitor, 1976; served articles, Clifford Turner. Trustee, NPFA, 1990–2004 (Chm., 2000–04). Trustee: Orders of St John Care Trust, 2000–10; St Endellion Easter Fest., 2004–17. Gov., Berkhamsted Collegiate Sch., 1979–2013 (Vice Chm., 1997–2013). Trustee: Countryside Educn Trust, 2014–; Fortune Centre for Riding Therapy, 2014–; Vintage Music, 2014–; Endelienta, 2017–. Mem., New Forest Beekeepers' Assoc. *Recreations:* singing and enjoyment of music, fine art, reading, travel, gardening, beekeeping, sailing in fine weather only. *E:* alisonmooregwyn@gmail.com. *Club:* Beaulieu River Sailing.

*See also D. C. S. White.*

**MOORE-WILTON, Maxwell William,** AC 2001; Chairman and Director, Sydney Airports Ltd (formerly Macquarie Airports Management Ltd, then MAp Airports Ltd), 2006–15; Chairman, Southern Cross Media Group (formerly Executive Chairman, Macquarie Media Group), 2007–15; *b* 27 Jan. 1943; *s* of William Moore-Wilton and Cavell Little; *m* 1966, Janette Costin; one *s* one *d*. *Educ:* St Joseph's Coll., Qld; Univ. of Queensland (BEc). Commonwealth Department of Trade, Australia, 1964–78: Minister, Delegn for Trade Negotiations, Geneva, 1974–76; First Asst Sec., Policy Develt/Commodity Policy, 1976–78; Dep. Sec., Commonwealth Dept of Primary Industry, 1980–81; Gen. Manager, Australian Wheat Bd, Melbourne, 1981–84; Man. Dir, Australian Nat. Line, Melbourne, 1984–88; Chm., NSW Egg Corp., 1987–89; Chief Exec., Maritime Services Bd of NSW, 1989–91; Dir-Gen., NSW Dept of Transport, 1991–94; Chief Exec., Roads and Traffic Authy of NSW, 1994–95; Chm., Public Transport Corp., Vic, 1995–96; Nat. Dir, Policy Co-ordination and Priorities Rev., Australian Stock Exchange Ltd, 1995–96; Sec., Dept of Prime Minister and Cabinet, Australia, 1996–2002; Exec. Chm. and CEO, 2003–06, Chm., 2006–15, Southern Cross Airports Corp. Hldgs (formerly Sydney Airport Corp.) Ltd; Exec. Dir, Macquarie Bank, 2006–08. Mem. Bd, Infrastructure NSW, 2011–. Mem. Bd, Chris O'Brien Lifehouse, 2007–. Centenary Medal, Aust., 2003. *Recreations:* reading, swimming. *Address:* 8 Beatrice Street, Clontarf, NSW 2093, Australia. *Club:* Australian (Sydney).

**MOOREHEAD, Caroline Mary,** OBE 2005; FRSL; writer; *b* 28 Oct. 1944; *d* of Alan Moorehead and Lucy (*née* Milner); *m* 1967, Jeremy Swift (marr. diss. 2001); one *s* one *d*. *Educ:* Sorbonne, Paris; University Coll. London (BA Hons 1965). Reporter, Time magazine, 1968–70; Feature Writer, Telegraph magazine, 1970–71; Feature Ed., TES, 1971–74; Feature Writer, The Times, 1973–85; Human Rights Columnist and Feature Writer, Independent, 1985–91; Associate Producer, BBC human rights TV series, 1988–99. Royal Literary Fund Fellow, 2003–05. Trustee: Council, PEN, 1992–97; London Liby, 1994–97; Index on Censorship, 1994–2005; British Inst. for Human Rights, 1995–2004; Soc. of Authors, 1996–99; RSL, 1996–2001; Helen Bamber Foundn, 2005–; Interights, 2005; Mem., Eminent Persons Mission to USSR, 1994; Co-Founder, Africa and Middle East Refugee Assistance, 2003–. FRSL 1998. *Publications:* Fortune's Hostages, 1980; Sidney

Bernstein: a biography, 1984; Freya Stark: a biography, 1987; (ed) Beyond the Rim of the World: the letters of Freya Stark, 1989; Troublesome People, 1991; (ed) Betrayed: children in today's world, 1994; Schliemann and the Lost Treasures of Troy, 1994; Dunant's Dream: war, Switzerland and the Red Cross, 1998; Iris Origo: Marchesa of the Val d'Orcia, 2000; Martha Gellhorn: a life, 2003; Human Cargo: a journey among refugees, 2005; (ed) Letters of Martha Gellhorn, 2006; Dancing to the Precipice: Lucie de la Tour du Pin and the French Revolution, 2009; Humanity in War, 2009; A Train in Winter, 2011; Village of Secrets: defying the Nazis in Vichy France, 2014; A Bold and Dangerous Family, 2017. *Recreations:* travel, music. *Address:* c/o Clare Alexander, Aitken Alexander Associates, 291 Gray's Inn Road, WC1X 8EB.

**MOOREHEAD, Susanna Mary Davies,** PhD; HM Diplomatic Service; Chair, Development Assistance Committee, Organisation for Economic Cooperation and Development, Paris, since 2019; *b* London, 22 April 1957; *d* of George Eveleigh Davies and Mary Elizabeth Davies (*née* Jenkins); *m* 1988, Richard McCrae Moorehead (*d* 1998); two *d. Educ:* Univ. of York (BA 1st Cl. Hist. and Politics 1979); London Sch. of Econs and Pol Sci. (MSc (Econ) Internat. Relns 1980; PhD Internat. Relns 1983). Project Dir, Save the Children Fund (UK) in Mali, W Africa, 1986–89; Dep. Dir and Fellow, Inst. of Develt Studies, Sussex, 1989–97; Res. Prog. Dir, Inst. of Develt Studies, Jaipur, India, 1997–98; Department for International Development: Head: Econ. and Social Res., 1999–2001; Asia Regl Policy, 2001–03; Governance and Sustainable Develt, 2003–04; Minister (Develt) and Hd, DFID India, Delhi, 2005–08; Exec. Dir for UK, World Bank Gp, Washington, 2008–12; Dir, W and Southern Africa, DFID, 2012–15; Ambassador to Ethiopia and to Djibouti (non-res.), and Perm. Rep. of UK to African Union, 2016–19. FRSA. DUniv York, 2014. *Publications:* as Susanna Davies: (with M. Buchanan-Smith) Famine Early Warning and Responses: the missing link, 1995; Adaptable Livelihoods: coping with food insecurity in the Malian Sahel, 1996. *Recreations:* pretending to be an interior designer, creating risotto from what's left in the fridge, getting lost when driving outside Zone 2, watching bad period dramas, making lists. *Address:* Organisation for Economic Cooperation and Development, 2 rue André-Pascal, 75775 Paris CEDEX 16, France. *T:* (1) 45249070. *E:* Susanna.Moorehead@oecd.org. *W:* www.twitter.com/DACchairOECD.

**MOORES, Dame Yvonne,** DBE 1999; Chief Nursing Officer and Director of Nursing, Department of Health, 1992–99; *b* 14 June 1941; *d* of late Tom Abraham Quick and Phyllis Quick (*née* Jeremiah); *m* 1st, 1969, Bruce Holmes Ramsden; 2nd, 1975, Brian Moores. *Educ:* Itchen Grammar Sch., Southampton; Royal South Hampshire Hosp. (RGN); Southampton Gen. Hosp. (RM). Ward Sister, Whittington Hosp. and Royal Hampshire County Hosp., 1964–70; Principal Nursing Officer: N London HMC, 1971–72; W Manchester, 1973–74; Dist Nursing Officer, N Manchester, 1974–76; Area Nursing Officer, Manchester AHA, 1976–81; Chief Nursing Officer: Welsh Office, 1982–88; Scottish Office, Home and Health Dept, 1988–92. Vice-Chm., NHS Supply Council, 1979–82; Pres., Infection Control Nurses Assoc., 1987–90; Mem., WHO Global Adv. Gp for Nursing and Midwifery, 1992–97 (Chair, 1994–97); Vis. Prof., Sheffield Univ., 1996–99. Chm., Macmillan Cancer Unit Appeal, Calderdale, 2000–01. Dep. Chair, Cttee of Univ. Chairs, 2003–04. Bd Mem., Leadership Foundn for Higher Educn, 2005–07. Non-executive Director: NHBC, 2004–11 (Chm., Pensions Bd, 2007–18); Poole Hosp. NHS Trust, 2006–14 (Vice-Chm., 2010–14). Mem. Council, Southampton Univ. 1994–2006 (Chm., 2000–06); Pro-Chancellor, Bournemouth Univ., 2006–13. Mem., Internat. Award Cttee, Princess Srinagarindra Award, 2000–. Chair, Florence Nightingale Foundn, 2019–. Patron: Assoc. for Continence Advice, 2005–11; Poole Hosp. Africa Link, 2010–; Forest Holme Hospice Charity, 2015–18. Mem., Policy Steering Cttee, Ferndown Golf Club, 2007–10. Hon. Fellow, Coll. of Med., Univ. of Wales, 1995. Hon. FRSPH (Hon. FRSH); Hon. FFPHM 1996; Hon. FRCP. Hon. DSc: Portsmouth, 1993; Huddersfield, 1997; Bradford, 1998; DUniv: Central England, 2001; Southampton, 2006; Hon. DCL Northumbria, 1995; Hon. MA De Montfort, 1995; Hon. DEd Bournemouth, 2014. Dist. Lifetime Achievement Award, Sigma Theta Tau Internat. Honor Soc. of Nursing, 2017. *Recreations:* bridge, golf, knitting, cooking. *Address:* 3 Yeatton House, Hordle Lane, Hordle, Lymington, Hants SO41 0HW.

**MOOREY, Adrian Edward;** independent consultant, since 2003; *b* 4 May 1946; *s* of Edward Alfred Moorey and Lily Elizabeth Moorey; *m* 1st, 1969, Sandra Ann Jeffrey (marr. diss.); one *s*; 2nd, 1987, Lesley Nicola Hancock; one *s* one *d. Educ:* Sir Joseph Williamson's Mathematical Sch., Rochester. Advertising and Marketing Asst, Lonsdale-Hands Orgn, 1964–67; Asst Information Officer, 1967–69, Inf. Officer, 1969–72, Home Office; Press Officer, PM's Office, 1973; Department of Employment: Sen. Press Officer, 1974–75; Chief Press Officer, 1976–81; Head of Inf., 1982–86; Director of Information: DTI, 1987–90; Home Office, 1990–94; Dir, Corporate and Govt Affairs, Cable and Wireless plc, 1995–99; Corporate Communications Dir, CAA, 1999–2001; Dir of Communications, NATS, 2001–03. *Recreations:* cricket, golf. *Address:* Ellesmere House, 56 Bloomfield Avenue, Bath BA2 3AE.

**MOOREHEAD, Prof. Richard Lewis,** FAcSS; Professor of Law and Head, Law School, University of Exeter, since 2019; *b* Ashington, Northumberland, 12 Feb. 1969; *s* of Lewis Moorhead and Elizabeth Moorhead (*née* Dalton); *m* 2011, Dr Leanne Smith; one *s* two *d. Educ:* Hanley Castle High Sch.; Univ. of Warwick (LLB Hons Law). Admitted solicitor, 1995. Res. Associate, Univ. of Liverpool, 1990–91, 1992–93; trainee solicitor, 1993–95, solicitor, Irwin Mitchell, 1995–96; Res. Fellow, Inst. of Advanced Legal Studies, 1996–97; Lectr, Univ. of Birmingham, 1997–98; Res. Fellow, 1998–2000, Sen. Res. Fellow, 2000–02, Inst. of Advanced Legal Studies; Sen. Lectr, 2002–04, Prof. of Law, 2004–12, Cardiff Univ.; Prof. of Law and Professional Ethics, 2012–19, Vice Dean (Res.), 2016–19, UCL. Member: Legal Services Consultative Panel, 2001–06; Civil Justice Council, 2006–11; Data Evidence and Sci. Bd, MoJ, 2018–. FAcSS 2019. *Publications:* After Universalism: reengineering access to justice, 2003; Litigants in Person in First Instance Proceedings, 2005; Judgecraft, 2007; Damage-based Contingency Fees in Employment Cases, 2008; Something for Nothing, 2009; Designing Ethics Indicators for Legal Services, 2012; Mapping the Moral Compass, 2016; In-House Lawyers' Ethics: institutional logics, legal risk and the tournament of influence, 2018. *Recreations:* running, blogging, film, poetry. *Address:* Law School, University of Exeter, Amory Building, Rennes Drive, Exeter EX4 4RJ.

**MOORHOUSE, Barbara Jane;** Chief Operating Officer, Westminster City Council, 2011–13 (Strategic Director, Finance and Performance, 2010–11); *b* 21 Nov. 1958; *d* of Andre and Rosalind Moorhouse; *m* 2001, Mike Brittain. *Educ:* St Catherine's Coll., Oxford (BA Hons PPE 1981). FCMA 1990; ACT 1999. European Finance Dir, Courtaulds plc, 1986–90; Regulatory Dir, South West Water plc, 1991–95; Finance Dir, Johnson Controls Inc., 1995–96; Gp Finance Dir, Morgan Sindall plc, 1997–98; Interim Exec., Mondex Internat., Jigsaw plc and Energis plc, 1998–2000; Gp Finance Dir, Kewill Systems plc, 2000–02; Chief Financial Officer, Scala Business Solutions NV, 2003–04; Dir Gen., Finance, DCA, subseq. Finance and Commercial, MoJ, 2005–07; Dir Gen., Corporate Resources, DfT, 2007–09. Chair, Rail Standards and Safety Bd, 2019–. Chair, OPM Gp, 2009–12; non-executive Director: CSA, 2003–06; Agility Trains, 2015–; IDOX plc, 2016–19; Microgen plc, 2017–; Balfour Beatty plc, 2017–. Mem., Financial Reporting Rev. Panel, 2004–13; Ind. Dir, Lending Standards Bd, 2014–19. Lay Mem., Strategy and Finance, W Hants CCG, 2013–17. Trustee, Guy's and St Thomas' Charity, 2015–. *Recreations:* horse-riding, ballroom dancing, walking, ski-ing.

**MOORHOUSE, George;** *see* Moorhouse, M. G. C.

**MOORHOUSE, Judith Helen,** OBE 2008; Chair, General Teaching Council England, 2004–09; *b* Eastleigh, Hants, 31 Oct. 1949; *d* of Edward and Joan Moorhouse. *Educ:* Coll. of Sarum St Michael, Salisbury (Cert Ed). Teacher of English: Fairoak Sch., Hants, 1971–72; Shackleton Sch., Fallingbostel, W Germany, 1972–73; Toynbee Sch., Eastleigh, 1973–74; Teacher of English, 1974–2010, Hd of Year, 1995–2010, Richmond Sch., N Yorks. National Union of Teachers: Exec. Mem., 1998–2004, 2008–10; Chm., Educn and Equal Opportunities Cttee, 2000–04; Pres., 2006–07. Mem., Governing Council, Nat. Coll. for Sch. Leadership, 2005–09; Specialist Schools and Academies Trust: Mem. Council, 2004–07; Trustee, 2007–12; Chm., Finance and Gen. Purposes Cttee, 2010–12. Non-exec. Dir, Teachers Assurance, 2008–11; Trustee/Director: Teachers Gp Educnl Trust, 2013–; Richmond N Yorks YMCA, 2014–18. Nat. Examr of Accounts, NUT, 2012–18. Chair, Richmondshire Choral Soc., 2016–19. *Recreations:* basking on Greek beaches, far-flung travel, trade unionism and equal rights, singing - from blues to requiem masses, indiscriminate reading. *Address:* 67 Frenchgate, Richmond, N Yorks DL10 7AE. *T:* (01748) 825106, 07909 542283. *E:* judy@hmoorhouse.plus.com.

**MOORHOUSE, (Kathleen) Tessa;** a District Judge (formerly Registrar), Family Division of the High Court of Justice, 1982–2004; a Deputy District Judge, since 2004; *b* 14 Sept. 1938; *d* of late Charles Elijah Hall, MRCVS and Helen Barbara Hall; *m* 1959, Rodney Moorhouse. *Educ:* Presentation Convent, Derbyshire; Leeds Univ.; King's Coll., London. Called to the Bar, Inner Temple, 1971. Asst, Jardine's Bookshop, Manchester, 1953–56; student, Leeds Univ., 1956–59; teacher of educationally subnormal, 1959–61; student, King's Coll., London, 1961–62; Classifier, Remand Home, 1962–64; Lectr in Law, 1964–71; barrister in practice, 1971–82. *Address:* 1st Avenue House, 42–49 High Holborn, WC1V 6NP. *T:* (020) 7947 6000; Coram Chambers, Fulwood Place, WC1V 6HG.

**MOORHOUSE, His Honour (Michael) George (Currer);** a Circuit Judge, 2001–15; *b* 29 June 1946; *s* of Reginald Currer Moorhouse and Betty Moorhouse; *m* 1970, Jane Mary Ross; one *s* three *d. Educ:* Ampleforth Coll. Admitted solicitor, 1970; in private practice, 1970–2001; Partner, R. C. Moorhouse Co., subseq. Keeble Hawson Moorhouse, 1975–2001. *Recreations:* gardening, sport, walking.

**MOORHOUSE, Tessa;** *see* Moorhouse, K. T.

**MOOSA, Nazo;** Founder and Managing Partner, v|t partners, since 2017; *b* Kabul, Afghanistan, 1 Feb. 1970; *d* of Mahbuba Moosa and M. Daoud Moosa. *Educ:* Univ. of Calif, Los Angeles (BA 1992); Columbia Business Sch. (MBA 1999). Associate, JH Partners, 1999–2000; Dir, Carlyle Gp, 2000–12; Man. Partner, C5 Capital, 2013–16. Member, Board: Transics, 2004–06; LBi (formerly Big Mouth Media), 2006–12; Metrasens, 2013–16; Arts Council England, 2013–17; Charity Commn, 2013–14. *Address:* v|t partners, 20 North Audley Street, W1K 6WE. *T:* 07799 472292.

**MORADIFAR, Kambiz; His Honour Judge Moradifar;** a Circuit Judge, since 2016. Called to the Bar, Gray's Inn, 1998; in practice as barrister, specialising in family and matrimonial law, 1998–2016; a Recorder, 2012–16. *Recreations:* ski-ing, mountaineering, climbing, fencing, scuba diving. *Address:* Reading County Court, 160–163 Friar Street, Reading, Berks RG1 1HE.

**MORAES, Claude Ajit;** Member (Lab) London Region, European Parliament, since 1999; *b* 22 Oct. 1965; *s* of H. I. Moraes and Theresa (*née* Aranha); *m* Bharti Patel; one *s. Educ:* St Modan's High Sch., Stirling; Univ. of Dundee (LLB 1988); Birkbeck Coll., Univ. of London (MSc 1989). Res. Asst to John Reid, MP and Paul Boateng, MP, 1987–89; postgrad. study in internat. law, LSE, 1990–91; Nat. Policy Officer, TUC, 1989–92; Dir, Jt Council for Welfare of Immigrants, 1992–98; Chief Exec., Immigrants' Aid Trust, 1992–98. European Parliament: Socialist and Democrat Gp spokesperson on Civil Liberties, Justice and Home Affairs, 2009–14; Chm., Civil Liberties, Justice and Home Affairs Cttee, 2014–19. Dep. Leader, European PLP, 2009–14. Comr, CRE, 1998–99. Mem., Council, Liberty, 1997–2005. Columnist, Tribune, 1998–2005. Mem. Council, Toynbee Hall, 1995–98. Patron, Refugee Therapy Centre, 2000–. Contested (Lab) Harrow W, 1992. FRSA 1998. MEP of Year, Justice and Civil Liberties, Dods and Parliament Mag., 2011. *Publications:* (jtly) Social Work and Minorities: European perspectives, 1998; (jtly) The Politics of Migration, 2003; (jtly) The European Union after the Treaty of Lisbon, 2012; contributed: Full Employment and the Global Economy, 2004; Perspectives on Migration, 2005; Immigration under Labour, 2010; Roma: a European minority, 2011; contrib. jls and nat. newspapers. *Recreations:* Scottish literature, chess, films, listening to BBC Radio 4 and 6, World Service, BBC London Radio and my MP3 player. *Address:* European Parliament, Rue Wiertz, 1047 Brussels, Belgium. *T:* (Brussels) (2) 2845553. *E:* claudemoraes@aol.com.

**MORAN,** 3rd Baron *cr* 1943; **James McMoran Wilson;** Founder and Chairman, Source Squared, since 2006; *b* York, England, 6 Aug. 1952; *s* of 2nd Baron Moran, KCMG and Shirley Rowntree Wilson (*née* Harris); *S* father, 2014; *m* 1980, Hon. Jane Hepburne-Scott, *d* of 1st Lord Polwarth, TD; two *s. Educ:* Eton Coll.; Trinity Coll., Cambridge (BA 1974; MA 1979). With Econ. Intelligence Dept, Bank of England, 1974–75; First Nat. Bank of Boston, 1977–83; Partner, Boston Ventures, 1983–2005. *Recreations:* fishing, sailing, running. *Heir: er s* Hon. David Andrew McMoran Wilson, *b* 6 Nov. 1990. *Address:* 65 Upland Road, Brookline, MA 02445, USA. *Clubs:* Flyfishers'; Somerset (Boston).

**MORAN, Andrew Gerard;** QC 1994; international maritime and commercial arbitrator, since 2016; a Recorder, since 1997; Deemster, High Court of Isle of Man, since 2002; a Deputy High Court Judge, since 2005; *b* 19 Oct. 1953; *s* of Francis Michael Moran and Winifrede Moran; *m* 1977, Carole Jane Sullivan; six *s* one *d. Educ:* West Park Grammar Sch., St Helens, Lancs; Britannia Royal Naval Coll., Dartmouth; Balliol Coll., Oxford (BA Law). Called to Bar, Gray's Inn, 1976, Bencher, 2005. FCIArb; Fellow: Singapore Inst. Arbitrators; Hong Kong Inst. Arbitrators. *Recreations:* family, sport, travel, sailing. *Address:* Arbitration Chambers, 32 Maxwell Road, #02–#03, Singapore 069115; 6 Pump Court, Temple, EC4Y 7AR. *T:* (020) 7797 8400, *Fax:* (020) 7797 8401.

**MORAN, Andrew John;** QC 2016; *b* London, 9 May 1962; *s* of Joseph Michael Moran, CB, QC and Margaret Mary Moran; *m* 2002, Michele Caroline Giddens; one *s* one *d. Educ:* Wimbledon Coll.; University Coll. London (LLB); New Coll., Oxford (BCL). Called to the Bar, Middle Temple, 1989, Bencher, 2018. *Publications:* Commercial Litigation in Anglophone Africa, 2018. *Recreations:* reading, cycling, riding. *Address:* Serle Court, 6 New Square, Lincoln's Inn, WC2A 3QS. *T:* (020) 7242 6105. *E:* amoran@serlecourt.co.uk. *Club:* Soho House.

**MORAN, Catherine Elizabeth, (Caitlin);** author; columnist, The Times, since 1992; *b* Brighton, 5 April 1975; *d* of John Moran and Margaret Moran; *m* 1999, Peter Paphides; two *d. Educ:* none. Melody Maker, 1992–95; presenter, Naked City, Channel 4, 1992–93; co-writer, Raised by Wolves, Channel 4, 2015. Columnist of the Year, 2010, Critic of the

Year, 2011, Interviewer of the Year, 2011, British Press Awards; Columnist of the Year, British Soc. of Mag. Editors' Awards, 2013, 2014. *Publications:* The Chronicles of Narmo, 1990; How To Be a Woman, 2011 (Book of the Year, Galaxy Book Awards); Moranthology, 2012; How to Build a Girl, 2014; How to Be Famous, 2018. *Recreations:* hair biggening, cava, eyeliner, The Struggle. *E:* (literary agent, Georgia Garrett) Georgia@rcwlitagency.com, (screenwriting agent, Nick Marston), nick@curtisbrown.co.uk.

**MORAN, Christopher John;** Chairman, Christopher Moran Group of Companies, since 1970; *b* 16 Jan. 1948; *s* of late Thomas Moran and Iva Mary Moran (*née* Alcock); *m* 1981, Helen Elisabeth Taylor (marr. diss. 1999); two *s* (twins). *Educ:* Owen's Grammar Sch. Chm., C&UCO Properties Ltd, 2009–. Chairman: Finance Bd, LSO, 2004–; Co-operation Ireland (GB), 2004–; Co-operation Ireland, 2006–; Member: Consultative Cttee, Dulwich Picture Gall., 1993–96; Thames Adv. Bd, 1994–97; Adv. Council, LSO, 2008–. Trustee: UCL Hosps Charitable Foundn, 1999– (Chm., 2003–); Exec. Cttee, CCJ, 2003– (Vice Chm., 2008–16; Vice-Pres., 2016–); Mary Rose Trust, 2004–; LSO Endowment Trust, 2007–; Prince's Charities Council, 2009–. Freedom, City of London, 2017. Hon. LLD Ulster, 2014. FRSA 2005. *Recreations:* architecture, opera, art, politics, country pursuits. *Address:* c/o Crosby Hall, Cheyne Walk, SW3 5AZ.

**MORAN, David John;** HM Diplomatic Service; Head, Global Economic Issues Department, Foreign and Commonwealth Office, since 2018; *b* 22 Aug. 1959; *s* of late Thomas Henry Moran and of Donna Lois Moran (*née* Zastrow); *m* 1993, Carol Ann Marquis. *Educ:* Stoke Brunswick Sch.; Tonbridge Sch.; Willamette Univ., Salem, Oregon (BA); Univ. of Sussex (MA). Oregon State Employment Div., 1979–80, 1982–83; DTI, 1985; ODA, 1985–88; Second Sec., E Africa Office, ODA, Nairobi, 1988–91; Hd of Section, Econ. Relns Dept, FCO, 1991–93; First Sec., Moscow, 1993–96; Head: France and Switzerland Section, FCO, 1996–98; EU Charter of Rights Section, EU Dept (Internal), 1998–2000; Dep. UK Perm. Rep. to OECD, Paris, 2001–05; Ambassador to Uzbekistan, 2005–07; Counsellor, FCO, 2007–08; on loan to Cabinet Office, 2008–09; Ambassador to Kazakhstan and (non-resident) to Kyrgyz Republic, 2009–12; Chargé d'Affaires to Georgia (with personal rank of Ambassador), 2013; Ambassador to Switzerland and (non-resident) to Liechtenstein, 2014–17; Whitehall Preparedness and No Deal Planning, EU Exit Strategy Dept, Europe Directorate, FCO, 2017–18. *Recreations:* writing and listening to music, reading, theatre, swimming, football. *Address:* c/o Foreign and Commonwealth Office, King Charles Street, SW1A 2AH.

**MORAN, Rt Rev. Mgr John,** CBE 1985; Principal RC Chaplain and Vicar General (Army), 1981–85; *b* 3 Dec. 1929; *s* of Thomas Moran and Gertrude May (*née* Sheer). *Educ:* De La Salle Coll., Sheffield; Ushaw Coll., Durham. Ordained priest, Leeds Diocese, 1956; Curate, Dewsbury, 1956–60; Prison Chaplain, Armley, 1960–61; commissioned Army Chaplain, 1961; service in BAOR, Singapore, Malaya, Hong Kong, UK; Chaplain, RMA Sandhurst, 1968–70, Staff Chaplain, 1970–71; Senior Chaplain, HQ BAOR, 1977–79, and HQ UKLF, 1979–80. *Recreations:* music, rivers, clocks.

**MORAN, Layla;** MP (Lib Dem) Oxford West and Abingdon, since 2017; *d* of James and Randa Moran. *Educ:* Imperial Coll. London (BSc Physics 2003); Brunel Univ. (PGCE 2006); Inst. of Educn, Univ. of London (MA Comparative Educn 2008). Teacher of Maths and Physics, Middle Sch., Internat. Sch. of Brussels, 2003–07; Teacher of Physics, Southbank Internat. Sch., 2007–13; Acad. Develt Manager, Oxford Study Courses Ltd, 2012–17. Lib Dem Shadow Sec. of State for Educn, Sci. and Young People, 2017–. Mem., Public Accounts Cttee, H of C, 2017–. Contested (Lib Dem): Battersea, 2010; Oxford West and Abingdon, 2015. *Address:* House of Commons, SW1A 0AA.

**MORAN, Air Vice-Marshal Manus Francis;** Royal Air Force, retired; *b* 18 April 1927; *s* of John Thomas Moran and Katherine Mary (*née* Coyle); *m* 1955, Maureen Elizabeth Martin, *o d* of Martin Dilks; one *s* three *d* (and one *s* decd). *Educ:* Mount St Joseph Abbey, Roscrea; University College Dublin (MB ChB, BAO 1952; MCh 1964); DLO, RCP and RCS, 1963. St Vincent's Hosp., Dublin, 1952; GP, Lutterworth, 1953–54; joined RAF 1954; Department of Otorhinolaryngology: served London, 1955–56; Wroughton, 1956–58; Weeton, 1958–59; Akrotiri, 1959–61; Halton, 1963–65; Consultant in ORL, RAF, 1965; served Changi, Singapore, 1965–68; Vis. Consultant, Johore Bahru Gen. Hosp., 1966–68; Nocton Hall, 1968–75; Wegberg, 1975–78; Wroughton, 1978–83; Consultant Adviser in ORL (RAF), 1983–88; Dean of Air Force Medicine, 1988–90; Sen. Consultant, RAF, 1990–91; Civilian Consultant in ORL, RAF Hosp., Wroughton, 1991–95. QHP, 1988–91. Lectr in ORL, IAM Farnborough, for Dip. in Aviation medicine, RCP, 1983–88. Consultant: Nuffield Hosp., Leicester, 1992–2000; Met. Police, 1994–2003. Chm., Gen. Cttee, 8th British Acad. Conf. in ORL, 1987–91. Member: Irish Otological Soc.; Midland Inst. of Otology (Vice-Pres., 1971, 1975); Otology Section, RSM (Vice-Pres., Section of Laryngology, 1988–91, Pres., 1991–92); Council, British Assoc. of Otolaryngologists, 1983–88; Joseph Soc., BMA; BS Cttee on Auditory Alarms in med. monitoring equipment, 1983–88; Bd, Co-operation North, 1992–97. Special Trustee, Royal Nat. Throat, Nose and Ear Hosp., 1993–99. Mem. Editl Bd, Amer. ENT Jl, 1982–92. FRAeS 1996. Hon. FRCSI 1991. Liveryman, Apothecaries' Soc. (Chm., Livery Cttee, 1994–96); Freeman, City of London. CStJ 1990. Med. Soc. (UCD) Gold Medal, 1951; Lady Cade Medal, RCS, 1980. *Publications:* Upper Respiratory Problems in Yellow Nail Syndrome (jtly), 1976; contribs to learned jls on ORL applied to aviation medicine, uraemic rhinitis, vestibular dysfunction, acoustic trauma and hearing conservation. *Recreations:* preservation of rural amenities, walking, poetry, theology, power boating. *Address:* The Old Forge House, Marston Meysey, Cricklade, Wilts SN6 6LQ. *T:* (01285) 810511. *Club:* Royal Air Force.

**MORAN, Margaret;** *b* 24 April 1955; *d* of Patrick John, (Jack), Moran and Mary (*née* Murphy). *Educ:* Birmingham Univ. (BSocSc). Dir, Housing for Women, 1987–97. Mem., Lewisham BC, 1984–96 (Chairman: Housing Cttee, 1985–91; Direct Lab. Cttee, 1991; Leader, 1995–96). Dep. Chm., AMA, 1994 (Chm., Housing Cttee, 1992). Contested (Lab) Carshalton and Wallington, 1992. MP (Lab) Luton S, 1997–2010. PPS to Minister for Cabinet Office, 1999–2003; an Asst Govt Whip, 2003–05. Member: NI Select Cttee, 1997–98; Public Admin Select Cttee, 1999.

**MORAN, Rt Rev. Peter Antony;** Bishop of Aberdeen, (RC), 2003–11; *b* 13 April 1935; *s* of Joseph Moran and Gertrude Moran (*née* O'Callaghan). *Educ:* St Aloysius' Coll., Glasgow; Pontifical Gregorian Univ., Rome (PhL 1955; STL 1959); Univ. of Glasgow (MA Hons (Classics) 1963); Univ. of Aberdeen (MEd 1968). Ordained priest, 1959; schoolmaster, Blairs Coll., Aberdeen, 1964–86; Parish Priest: Blairs, 1979–93; Inverurie, 1993–2003; Diocesan Administrator, Aberdeen, 2002–03. *Recreations:* modern languages, dinghy sailing, walking, music, sketching.

**MORAN, Robert Andrew Victor, (Bob);** Lead Political Cartoonist and Animator, Daily Telegraph, since 2018; *b* Taunton, Som, 20 March 1986; *s* of Tom and Jane Moran; *m* 2012, Sally Pawson; one *s* one *d*. *Educ:* Wellington Sch., Som; University Coll., Falmouth (BA Hons Illustration 2008). Cartoonist, as 'Bob', Second Political Cartoonist, Daily Telegraph, 2011–17. *Recreations:* music, cinema, coffee, kitchen discos, cryptic crosswords, Ambassador for Baby Lifeline charity. *Address:* c/o Daily Telegraph, 111 Buckingham Palace Road, SW1W 0DT. *E:* bob.moran@telegraph.co.uk.

**MORAN, Terence Anthony,** CB 2007; Chairman, Hull University Teaching Hospitals (formerly Hull and East Yorkshire Hospitals) NHS Trust, since 2017; *b* Rotherham, 23 April 1960; civil partnership 2010, Stuart Hayes. *Educ:* St Joseph's Prim. Sch., Rawmarsh; Rawmarsh Comp. Sch.; Harvard Business Sch. (AMP 2006). Joined Civil Service, 1977; clerical asst, DHSS, 1977; Private Secretary: to Dir, Social Security Ops, 1990–91; to Chief Exec., Benefits Agency, 1992–96; Area Dir, Yorks, Benefits Agency, 2001–02; Dir, NW Reg., Jobcentre Plus, 2002–04; Chief Exec., Disability and Carers Service, 2004–07; Interim Chief Exec., Pension Service, 2007–08; Chief Exec. and Dir Gen., Pension, Disability and Carers Service, 2008–10, Dir Gen., Universal Credit, 2010–11, Chief Operating Officer, 2011–13, Second Perm. Sec., 2012–13, DWP. Non-exec. Dir, Mid Yorks Hosps NHS Trust, 2015–17. Chm., Together for Short Lives, 2014–17; Trustee: Nat. Bd, Victim Support, 2006–08; Nat. Bd, Social Care Inst. for Excellence, 2013–17; CatZero, 2019. *Recreations:* sports, music, gardening, walking, baking.

**MORAN, Vincent John;** QC 2011; a Recorder, since 2010; *b* Dartford, 6 Feb. 1966; *s* of John and Anne Moran; *m* 1997, Alison Thraves; two *s* two *d*. *Educ:* Dartford Grammar Sch.; Clare Coll., Cambridge (BA 1987); City Univ. (DipLaw 1990). Called to the Bar, Gray's Inn, 1991, Bencher, 2017; in practice as a barrister, specialising in construction law and professional negligence. *Publications:* (ed) Chitty on Contracts, 29th edn 2004 to 31st edn 2012; (contrib.) Keating on Construction Contracts, 8th edn 2006 to 10th edn 2016. *Recreations:* cricket, history, The Edgar Wallace. *Address:* Keating Chambers, 15 Essex Street, WC2R 3AA. *T:* (020) 7544 2600. *E:* vmoran@keatingchambers.com.

**MORATINOS CUYAUBÉ, Miguel Angel,** Knight, Order of Civil Merit (Spain); Minister of Foreign Affairs, Spain, 2004–10; High Representative for Alliance of Civilizations, United Nations, since 2019; *b* 8 June 1951; *m* Dominique Maunac; three *c*. *Educ:* Madrid (Law and Political Sci. degree); Diplomatic Sch. (Dip. Internat. Studies). Spanish Diplomatic Service: Dir-Hd, E Europe Co-ordination Desk, 1974–79; First Sec., 1979–80, Chargé d'affaires, 1980–84, Yugoslavia; Political Advr, Rabat, 1984–87; Dep. Dir Gen. for N Africa, 1987–91; Director General: Inst. for Co-operation with the Arab World, 1991–93; of Foreign Policy for Africa and ME, 1993–96; Ambassador, Israel, 1996; EU Special Rep. for the ME Peace Process, 1996–2003. Comdr, Order of Ouissam Alaouite (Morocco). *Publications:* The European Security and the Mediterranean, 1990; Mediterranean: a forgotten sea, 1990; Mediterranean and Middle East, 1995. *Recreations:* tennis, football.

**MORAUTA, Rt Hon. Sir Mekere,** KCMG 2009; Kt 1991; MP (Ind) Moresby North-West, Papua New Guinea, since 2017; Chairman, Papua New Guinea Sustainable Development Program Ltd, since 2012; *b* 12 June 1946; *s* of Morauta Hasu and Morikoai Elavo; *m* Roslyn; two *s*. *Educ:* Univ. of Papua New Guinea (BEcon); Flinders Univ., SA. Res. Officer (Manpower Planning), Dept of Labour, 1971; Economist, Office of the Economic Advr, 1972; Sec. for Finance, Govt of PNG, 1973–82; Man. Dir, PNG Banking Corp., 1983–92; Gov., Bank of Papua New Guinea, 1993–94; Executive Chairman: Delta Seafoods, 1994–97; Morauta and Associates (Publishing), 1994–97. MP Moresby NW, 1997–2012 (People's Democratic Movement, 1997–2002, PNG Party, 2002–12); Minister: for Planning and Implementation, PNG, 1997–98; for Fisheries and Marine Resources, 1998–99; Prime Minister and Minister for Treasury, 1999–2002; Leader of the Opposition, 2007–10; Minister for Public Enterprises, 2011. Chm., Nat. Airline Commn, 1992–94. Mem. Bd, Angco; formerly Director: Highlands Gold (PNG); PNG Associated Industries; Thomas Nationwide Transport (PNG); James Barnes PNG; numerous public and commercial bodies. Former Mem. Fund Raising Cttees, Salvation Army and Red Cross. Hon. DTech Univ. of Technology, PNG, 1987; Hon. DEc PNG, 2001. *Publications:* numerous papers on economic and allied subjects. *Address:* National Parliament, Parliament House, Waigani, NCD 131, Papua New Guinea.

**MORAVIEC, Paul;** Chief Executive Officer, ConvaTec Group plc, 2014–18; *b* Reading, 5 April 1958; *s* of Victor Moraviec and Joan Moraviec; *m* 1984, Nicola; two *d*. *Educ:* Kingston Univ. (MA Mktg 1994). Vice President International: Johnson & Johnson, 1994–2001; Abbott Laboratories, 2001–07; CEO, ProSurgics Ltd, 2007–09; Pres., EMEA, ConvaTec, 2009–14. *Recreation:* motor sport.

**MORAY, 21st Earl of,** *cr* 1562; **John Douglas Stuart;** Lord Abernethy and Strathearn, 1562; Lord Doune, 1581; Lord St Colme, 1611; Baron Stuart (GB), 1796; *b* 29 Aug. 1966; *o s* of 20th Earl of Moray and of Lady Malvina Murray, *er d* of 7th Earl of Mansfield and Mansfield; *S* father, 2011; *m* 2000, Catherine Jane, *d* of Prof. Wilfred Alan Lawson; two *s*. *Educ:* Loretto School, Musselburgh; University Coll. London (BA Hist. of Art). *Heir: s* Lord Doune, *qv*. *Address:* Doune Park, Doune, Perthshire FK16 6HA; Darnaway Castle, Forres, Moray.

**MORAY, ROSS AND CAITHNESS, Bishop of,** since 2007; **Most Rev. Mark Jeremy Strange;** Primus of the Scottish Episcopal Church, since 2017; *b* 2 Nov. 1961; *s* of Edward Strange and Dorothy Strange (*née* Tinker); *m* 1983, Jane Elizabeth; one *s* two *d*. *Educ:* Aberdeen Univ. (LTh); Lincoln Theol Coll. (Cert. in Ministry and Mission). Cathedral Verger, Worcester Cathedral, 1984–87; ordained deacon, 1989, priest, 1990; Curate, St Barnabas and Christchurch, Worcs, 1989–92; Vicar, St Wulstan, Warndon, Worcs, 1992–98; Rector, Holy Trinity, Elgin, 1998–2007; Priest-in-charge: St Margaret's, Lossiemouth, 1998–2007; St Michael's, Dufftown, 2004–07; St Margaret's, Aberlour, 2004–07. Canon, 2000–07; Provost, 2014–17, St Andrew's Cathedral, Inverness. Convenor, Scottish Episcopal Youth Network, 2002–; Synod Clerk, Moray, Ross and Caithness, 2003–07. Moray Scout Association: Area Comr, 1998–2001; Area Chaplain, 2001–09; Chaplain, Elgin ATC, 2004–07. Chair, Elgin Community Planning Workers Gp, 2002–09. Hon. DD Univ. of South, Sewanee. Companion, Meml of Merit of King Charles the Martyr, 2017. *Recreations:* hill-walking, beach-combing, whisky-tasting. *Address:* Bishop's House, Arpafeelie, North Kessock, Inverness IV1 3XD. *E:* bishop@moray.anglican.org.

**MORAY, ROSS AND CAITHNESS, Dean of;** *see* Simpson, Very Rev. A. J.

**MORBEY, Gillian Ann,** OBE 1995; Chief Executive, 2010–18, Consultant, since 2018, Sense and Sense International; *b* Glasgow, 11 June 1953; *d* of Henry and Valerie Kay; *m* 1973, Jerry Morbey; one *s* one *d*. *Educ:* BA Hons Psychol. 1984. RGN 1974. Student Nurse, 1971–74, Staff Nurse, 1974–81, NHS; CEO and Founder, Sense Scotland, 1985–2010. Mem., All Party Disability Gp, 1994. Vice Chair, then Chair, Glasgow Council for Voluntary Sector, 1989–95. Mem., Nat. Disability Council, 2000. Pres., Deafblind Internat., 2011–19. Trustee, Family Fund Trust, 1995–97 (Vice Chair, 1997–2001). FRSA. Scottish Social Entrepreneur of Year, 2005. *Recreations:* walking, gardening, reading. *Address:* Sense, 101 Pentonville Road, N1 9LG. *T:* 0845 127 0060, *Fax:* 0845 127 0061. *E:* Gillian.Morbey@sense.org.uk.

**MORCOM, Christopher;** QC 1991; *b* 4 Feb. 1939; *s* of late Dr Rupert Morcom and Mary Morcom (*née* Carslake); *m* 1966, Diane, *d* of late Jose Antonio Toledo and Winifred Anne (*née* Wardlaw); one *s* two *d*. *Educ:* Sherborne Sch.; Trinity Coll., Cambridge (BA Hons 1961; MA 1964). Called to the Bar, Middle Temple, 1963 (Cert. Honour, Astbury Scholar; Bencher, 1996); Barrister, Mauritius, 1979–. Member: Senate, Law Soc. Jt Wkg Party on

Intellectual Property Law, 1976–; Standing Adv. Cttee on Industrial Property, 1990–2001; Council, Intellectual Property Inst., 1991–. Chm., Competition Law Assoc., 1985–99. Pres., Ligue Internationale du Droit de la Concurrence, 1996–98 (Vice Pres., 1994–96; Hon. Pres., 2000). Chm., Bar Musical Soc., 1991–2008. *Publications:* Service Marks: a guide to the new law, 1987; A Guide to the Trade Marks Act 1994, 1994; (jtly) The Modern Law of Trade Marks, 2000, 5th edn 2016; legal articles in Law Soc. Gazette, Counsel, European Intellectual Property Rev. *Recreations:* music, walking. *Address:* Hogarth Chambers, 5 New Square, Lincoln's Inn, WC2A 3RJ. *T:* (020) 7404 0404. *Clubs:* Athenæum, Noblemen and Gentlemen's Catch.

**MORDAUNT, Rt Hon. Penelope Mary;** PC 2017; MP (C) Portsmouth North, since 2010; *b* Torquay, 4 March 1973; *d* of John Edward Patrick Mordaunt and late Jennifer Mordaunt and step *d* of Sylvia Mordaunt. *Educ:* Oaklands RC Comprehensive Sch., Waterlooville; Reading Univ. (BA Hons Philosophy 1995). Aid worker, 1991–92; spokesman, Freight Transport Assoc., 1997–99; Hd, Foreign Press, George Bush's presidential campaign, 2000; Hd of Broadcasting, Cons. Party, 1999–2001; Director: RBKC, 2001–03; Media Intelligence Partners, 2004–06; Diabetes UK, 2006–09. Dep. Dir, Big Lottery Fund, 2003–05. Parly Under-Sec. of State, DCLG, 2014–15; Minister of State, MoD, 2015–16; Minister of State (Minister for Disabled People, Work and Health), DWP, 2016–17; Sec. of State for Internat. Develt, 2017–19, for Defence, 2019; Minister for Women and Equalities, 2018–19. *Recreations:* astronomy, painting, hospital volunteer, RNR, dance and music. *Address:* House of Commons, SW1A 0AA. *E:* penny.mordaunt.mp@parliament.uk.

**MORDAUNT, Sir Richard (Nigel Charles),** 14th Bt *cr* 1611; documentary film producer; founder: Lusia Films UK, 1965; Coolamon Films Australia, 1994; *b* 12 May 1940; *s* of Lt-Col Sir Nigel John Mordaunt, 13th Bt, MBE, and Anne (*d* 1980), *d* of late Arthur F. Tritton; *S* father, 1979; *m* 1st, 1964, Myriam Atchia (decd); one *s* one *d*; 2nd, 1995, Diana Barbara (*née* Davis); one step *d*. *Educ:* Wellington. Producer, award-winning documentaries, England and Australia, 1965–. *Heir: s* Kim John Mordaunt [*b* 11 June 1966; *m* 2006, Sylvia Wilczynski; one *s*]. *Address:* 12 Wareham Street, Suffolk Park, NSW 2481, Australia.

**MORDEN, Jessica;** MP (Lab) Newport East, since 2005; *b* 29 May 1968; *d* of Mick and Margaret Morden. *Educ:* Croesyceiliog Comp. Sch., Cwmbran; Univ. of Birmingham (BA Hons Hist. 1989). Researcher: to Huw Edwards, MP, 1991–92; to Llew Smith, MP, 1992–93; Organiser, SE Wales, Welsh Lab. Party, 1993–98; Elections Officer, Labour Party, 1998–99; Gen. Sec., Welsh Labour Party, 1999–2005. An Opposition Whip, 2015–. Member: Welsh Affairs Cttee, 2005–07, 2010–15; Justice Cttee, 2007–10; Speaker's Cttee on Electoral Commn, 2010–; Cttee of Selection, 2016–17; Admin Cttee, 2017–. *Recreations:* gym, film. *Address:* House of Commons, SW1A 0AA. *T:* (020) 7219 6213, (constituency) (01633) 841725. *E:* jessica.morden.mp@parliament.uk. *Club:* Ringland Labour (Newport).

**MORDUE, Jane Margaret;** strategic management consultant and coach, 2001–15; Chief Executive, Comparative Clinical Science Foundation, 2005–15; *b* 8 June 1953; *d* of late James Gibson Jones and Margaret Jones (*née* Finlayson); *m* 1st, 1990, Prof. Alan Osborn Betts (*d* 2005); 2nd, 2007, Howard James Mordue. *Educ:* Univ. of Leeds (BA); Cornell Univ. (EDP); INSEAD (AMP). MHSM. PA to Man. Dir, Fairclough Ltd, Leeds, 1976–79; University of London: PA to Principal and Information Officer, RVC, 1979–85; Admin. Assistant to Vice-Chancellor and Dep. Public Relations Officer, 1985–88; Sec., BPMF, 1988–96; Sec.-Gen., Law Soc., 1996–2000; Chm., Thames Valley Strategic HA, 2002–04. Vice-Chm., Gangmasters Licensing Authy, 2005–15. Member: Cttee, Healthwatch England, 2012–18 (Chair, 2016–18); Bd, Care Quality Commn, 2016–18. Mem., Bd of Trustees, 2008–13, Vice Chm., 2010–13, Citizens Advice (Chm., SE Area (formerly Region) Cttee, 2004–09; Chm., Rural Issues Gp, 2015–); Chm., Rotary District 1260 Vocational Cttee, 2014–18 (Asst Gov., 2018–19; Dist Gov. Nominee, 2019–). CDir 2004; FInstD 2015. FRSA 1996; FIHM 2003. Liveryman, City of London, 2004; Mem., Mgt Consultants' Co., 2006. *Recreations:* travel, music, photography. *Address:* 5 Carisbrooke Court, Buckingham MK18 1TU. *Club:* Athenæum.

**MORE, Michael John,** CBE 2008; PhD; Chief Executive, Westminster City Council, 2008–13; *b* 21 May 1955; *s* of late Norman More and of Kathleen Mary More; *m* 1982, Sue Jordan; two *s*. *Educ:* Univ. of Hull (BA 1st Cl. Hons; PhD 1982). CPFA 1985. Audit trainee, Nat. Audit Office, 1981–86; Cambridgeshire County Council: Audit Manager, 1986–90; Asst Dir, 1990–96; Hd of Finance, 1996–99; Dir of Resource Mgt, 1999–2002, Chief Exec., 2002–08; Suffolk CC; Clerk to Lord Lieut of Suffolk, 2002–08. Non-exec. Dir, Univ. Campus, Suffolk, 2005–08. Chm., Prince's Trust, Suffolk, 2006–08. Mem., Olympic Games Transport Bd, 2010–12; Mem. Bd, Cambridge Univ. Hosps NHS Foundn Trust, 2013– (Vice Chair, 2015–17; Sen. Ind. Dir, 2016–17; Chair, 2017–); Mem. Gp Bd and Chm., Audit Cttee, L&Q Housing Assoc., 2015–. Dir, Cambridge Univ. Health Partners, 2017–. Trustee: Ipswich Town FC Sports and Educn Trust, 2004–08; Addenbrooke's Charitable Trust, 2015–17. FRSA. DUniv: E Anglia, 2009; Essex, 2009. *Publications:* press articles and papers in various analytical philosophy jls. *Recreations:* family, gardens, music, reading, analytical philosophy and logic, horse racing, football.

**MORELAND, Claire Josephine,** MA; DL; Principal, Chetham's School of Music, 1999–2016; *b* 2 Aug. 1958; *d* of late Peter Alfred White and Eileen Beatrice White (*née* Kidston); *m* 1st, 1982, John Moreland (marr. diss. 1999); (one *s* decd); 2nd, 2004, Richard Hickman (marr. diss. 2011). *Educ:* Devonport High Sch. for Girls; St Hugh's Coll., Oxford (MA Modern Langs, PGCE). Asst teacher, Sevenoaks Sch., 1981–84; Hd of German, Croydon High Sch. for Girls, 1984–88; Rugby School: asst teacher, 1988–92; Housemistress, 1992–97; Dep. Head, 1997–99. Chm., Bd of Dirs, Bolton Octagon Th., 2016–. Hon. DArts Bolton, 2017. DL Gtr Manchester, 2012. *Publications:* Schreib mir Bitte, 1982. *Recreations:* literature, music, outdoor pursuits, finding silver linings.

**MORELAND, Robert John;** management consultant; Member, Economic and Social Committee, European Community, 1986–98 (Chairman, Regional Policy and Town and Country Planning Section, 1990–98); *b* 21 Aug. 1941; *s* of late Samuel John Moreland and Norah Mary, (Molly) (*née* Haines). *Educ:* Glasgow Acad.; Dean Close Sch., Cheltenham; Univ. of Nottingham (BA Econs); Inst. of World Affairs, Conn, and Warwick Univ. (postgrad. work). Civil Servant, Govt of NS, Canada, 1966–67, Govt of NB, 1967–72; Sen. Economist, W Central Scotland Planning Study, 1972–74; Management Consultant, Touche Ross and Co., London, 1974–. Member (C): for Knightsbridge, Westminster CC, 1990–98 (Chief Whip, 1993–94; Chm. of Envmt, 1994–95; Chm., Planning and Envmt, 1995–97); Gloucester CC, 2001–02. Contested (C): Pontypool, Oct. 1974; GLA, 2000. Mem. (C) Staffs, European Parlt, 1979–84, contested same seat, 1984; Chm., Eur. Cttee, Bow Gp, 1977–78; Dep. Chm., Conservative Gp for Europe, 2006–09 (Vice-Chm., 1985–88, 2003–06; Treas., 2000–03). Dep. Chm., 1998–2000, Chm., 2000–, London Europe Soc. Treas., European Movement, 2003–08. Dir, Albert Meml Trust, 1997–2000. Gov., Archbishop Tenison's Sch., Kennington Oval, 1992– (Chm., 2003–11). Mem. Bd, S Wales and Severn Partnership, Canal and River Trust, 2012–. *Publications:* Climate Change, 2000; contrib. to Crossbow. *Recreations:* tennis, ski-ing, watching cricket and Rugby, golf. *Address:* 3 The Firs, Heathville Road, Gloucester GL1 3EW. *T:* 07803 012683. *E:* horseferry@yahoo.com. *Clubs:* MCC; Gloucestershire CC.

**MORELL, Purni;** theatre maker; Artistic Director, Unicorn Theatre, 2011–18; *b* London, 4 Aug. 1972; *d* of Pravat Mukherjee and Lydia Allegoet. *Educ:* James Allen's Girls' Sch.; Univ. of Glasgow (MA Hons Hist.). Literary Manager, Berkeley Repertory Th., 1999–2001; producer, gryllus, 2004–07; Hd of Studio, National Th., 2007–11. Numerous freelance projects as dir, translator and producer. *Recreation:* marine ecology and conservation.

**MORENO, Glen Richard;** Chairman, Virgin Money, 2015–18; *b* 24 July 1943; *s* of John Moreno and Ellen (*née* Oberg); *m* 1966, Cheryl Eschbach. *Educ:* Stanford Univ. (BA with Dist. 1965); Univ. of Delhi (Rotary Foundn Fellow 1966); Harvard Law Sch. (JD 1969). Gp Exec., Citigroup, 1969–87; Pres., 1987–92, Dir, 1987–, Fidelity Internat.; Chm., Pearson plc, 2005–15; Senior Independent non-executive Director: Man Gp plc, 1994–2009; Lloyds Banking Gp, 2010–12; Acting Chm., UK Financial Investments Ltd, 2009. Dep. Chm., Financial Reporting Council, 2010–14. Sen. Advr, HSBC, 2014–. Gov., Ditchley Foundn, 1983–. Dir, RADA, 2007–18. *Recreations:* reading, shooting, Angus cattle breeder, vintner. *Clubs:* Farmers, National Liberal, Naval and Military.

**MORETON,** family name of **Earl of Ducie**.

**MORETON, Lord; James Berkeley Moreton;** *b* 6 May 1981; *s* and *heir* of 7th Earl of Ducie, *qv*.

**MORETON, Catherine Jane;** *see* Bell, C. J.

**MOREY, Anthony Bernard Nicholas,** CBE 1993; HM Diplomatic Service, retired; *b* 6 Dec. 1936; *s* of late Bernard Rowland Morey and Madeleine Morey; *m* 1961, Agni Campbell Kerr; two *s* one *d*. *Educ:* Wimbledon Coll. Nat. service, 1955–57. FO, 1957–60; Kuwait, 1960–62; FO, 1962–65; Madras, 1965–66; FO, 1966; Tehran, 1967; Kabul, 1968–71; FCO, 1971–72; Washington, 1972–76; Zagreb, 1976–80; Lagos, 1980–83; seconded to Guinness Mahon, 1983–85; Counsellor and Consul General, Moscow, 1985–88; Dep. High Comr, Madras, 1989–91; Ambassador to Mongolia, 1991–93; Dep. High Comr, Calcutta, 1993–96. *Recreations:* gardening, music, cats. *Address:* Lattice House, Castleton, Sherborne, Dorset DT9 3SA. *Club:* Royal Calcutta Turf.

**MOREY, Caroline;** *see* Douglas, C.

**MORFEY, Dr Kathryn Margaret Victoria;** Consultant, Warner Goodman & Streat, 2000–02 (Associate Solicitor, 1991–2000); *b* 26 May 1942; *d* of Sidney Charles Waterton and Catherine Margaret Waterton (*née* Lilley); *m* 1963, Christopher Leonard Morfey; one *d* (one *s* decd). *Educ:* Newnham Coll., Cambridge (BA 1963; MA 1968); Univ. of Southampton (PhD 1968; LLB 1977). Admitted Solicitor, 1980. Lecturer: Univ. of Bristol, 1963; Univ. of Southampton, 1967–69; Nat. Childbirth Trust Orgnr, 1970–75; solicitor in private practice, 1980–2002. Mem., Sch. Admission Appeal Panel, 2003–. Member: Gen. Synod, C of E, 1990–2000; Legal Adv. Commn, C of E, 1991–93; Cathedrals Fabric Commn for England, 1991–96; Cathedrals Statutes Commn, 1996–2000; Vice-Pres., Winchester Diocesan Synod, 1997–2003. Gov., King Alfred's Coll. of Higher Educn, 1992–99. *Recreations:* visiting other people's gardens, choral music.

**MORGAN;** *see* Elystan-Morgan.

**MORGAN,** family name of **Baron Morgan**.

**MORGAN, Baron** *cr* 2000 (Life Peer), of Aberdyfi in the co. of Gwynedd; **Kenneth Owen Morgan,** FBA 1983; FRHistS; Principal, then Vice-Chancellor, University College of Wales, Aberystwyth and Professor in the University of Wales, 1989–95, Emeritus Professor, 1999 (Research Professor, 1995–99); Vice-Chancellor, then Senior Vice-Chancellor, University of Wales, 1993–95; *b* 16 May 1934; *s* of David James Morgan and Margaret Morgan (*née* Owen); *m* 1st, 1973, Jane Keeler (*d* 1992); one *s* one *d*; 2nd, 2009, Elizabeth Gibson, Bordeaux. *Educ:* University College School, London; Oriel College, Oxford (MA, DPhil 1958, DLitt 1985; Hon. Fellow, 2003). University College (later University of Wales), Swansea: Lectr in History Dept, 1958–66 (Sen. Lectr, 1965–66); Hon. Fellow, 1985; Hon. Prof., 1995–; Fellow and Praelector, Modern Hist. and Politics, Queen's Coll., Oxford, 1966–89 (Hon. Fellow, 1992); Faculty Lectr, 1995–2009. Supernumerary Fellow, Jesus Coll., Oxford, 1991–92. Amer. Council of Learned Socs Fellow, Columbia Univ., 1962–63; Visiting Professor: Columbia Univ., 1965; Univ. of S Carolina, 1972; Univ. of Witwatersrand, 1997, 1998 and 2000; Vis. Benjamin Meaker Prof., Univ. of Bristol, 2000; Vis. Prof., Inst. of Contemporary British History, KCL, 2011–; Vis. Lectr, Univ. of Texas, 1994, 1999, 2007, 2010, 2014. Lectures: O'Donnell, Univ. of Wales, 1981; Neale, UCL, 1986; Dodd, UCNW (Bangor), 1992, Univ. of Wales, Bangor, 2005; BBC (Wales), 1995; Prothero, RHistS, 1996; Merlyn-Rees, Univ. of Glamorgan, 2002; Presidential, Univ. of Rouen, 2003; Ford Special, Univ. of Oxford, 2005; London Guildhall, 2006; Gresham Coll., 2007; 10 Downing St, 2014, 2017; Speaker's House, 2011, 2015; Soc. des Anglicistes de l'Enseignement Supérieur, Limoges, 2012; KCL Constitutional Law, 2017; Keir Hardie Meml, 2014; Hist. of Parlt Trust, 2016; Branthurst, Johannesburg, 2019. Member: Bd of Celtic Studies, 1972–2003; Council, Nat. Library of Wales, 1991–95. Member: H of L Select Cttee on the Constitution, 2001–04, 2015–19; Jt Select Cttee on Draft Constitutional Renewal Bill, 2008. Chairman: Fabian Soc. Commn on the Monarchy, 2002–03; University Cttee on Student Radicalisation, 2015. Trustee: History of Parlt Trust, 2002–19; Cttee for Defence of British Univs, 2013–. Mem., Yr Academi Gymreig. FRHistS 1964 (Mem. Council, 1983–86). Editor, Welsh History Review, 1961–2003; Jt Editor, 20th Century British History, 1994–99. Hon. Mem., Gorsedd of Bards, Nat. Eisteddfod, 2008. Founding FLSW 2010. Hon. Fellow: Univ. of Wales, Cardiff, 1997; Trinity Coll., Carmarthen, 1998. Hon. DLitt: Wales, 1997; Glamorgan, 1997; Greenwich, 2004; Dr *hc* Tours, 2017. Gold Medal, Hon. Soc. of Cymmrodorion, 2009; Lifetime Achievement Award, All-Party Parly Gp on Hist. and Archives, 2014; Welsh Parliamentarian of Year Award, 2014. *Publications:* Wales in British Politics, 1963, 3rd edn 1980; David Lloyd George: Welsh radical as world statesman, 1963, 2nd edn 1982; Freedom or Sacrilege?, 1966; Keir Hardie, 1967; The Age of Lloyd George, 1971, 3rd edn 1978; (ed) Lloyd George: Family Letters, 1973; Lloyd George, 1974; Keir Hardie: radical and socialist, 1975 (Arts Council prize, 1976), 3rd edn 1997; Consensus and Disunity, 1979, 2nd edn 1986; (with Jane Morgan) Portrait of a Progressive, 1980; Rebirth of a Nation: Wales 1880–1980, 1981, new edn 1998 (Arts Council prize, 1982); David Lloyd George, 1981; Labour in Power 1945–1951, 1984, 2nd edn 1985; (ed jtly) Welsh Society and Nationhood, 1984; (ed) The Oxford Illustrated History of Britain, 1984, new rev. edn 2009; (ed) The Sphere Illustrated History of Britain, 1985; Labour People, 1987, new edn 1992; (ed) The Oxford History of Britain, 1989, new updated edn 2020; The Red Dragon and the Red Flag, 1989; The People's Peace: British History 1945–1990, 1991, new edn as The People's Peace: British History since 1945, 2001, new updated edn 2020; Academic Leadership, 1991; Modern Wales: politics, places and people, 1995; Britain and Europe, 1995; Steady As She Goes, 1996; (ed) The Young Oxford History of Britain & Ireland, 1996, rev. edn 2005; Callaghan: a life, 1997; (ed jtly) Crime, Protest and Police in Modern British Society, 1999; The Twentieth Century, 2000; The Great Reform Act, 2001; Universities and the State, 2002; Michael Foot: the life, 2007; Ages of Reform, 2011; (contrib.) The Global Lincoln, 2011; Eminent Parliamentarians, 2012; (ed) David Lloyd George, 2013; Revolution to Devolution, 2014; Labour Leaders, 2015; Kenneth O. Morgan: my histories,

2015; (contrib.) Harold Wilson, 2016; (contrib.) The Rights and Aspirations of Magna Carta, 2009; (contrib.) Making Social Democrats, 2018; (contrib.) Britain and Brexit, 2018; many articles, reviews etc; many contribs to Oxford DNB. *Recreations:* music, architecture, sport, travel. *Address:* The Croft, 63 Millwood End, Long Hanborough, Witney, Oxon OX29 8BP. *T:* (01993) 881341. *Club:* Reform.

**MORGAN OF DREFELIN,** Baroness *cr* 2004 (Life Peer), of Drefelin in the County of Dyfed; **Delyth Jane Morgan;** Chief Executive, Breast Cancer Now and Breast Cancer Care (formerly Breast Cancer Now), since 2015; *b* 30 Aug. 1961; *d* of late Julian Morgan and Ann Morgan; *m* 1991, Jim Shepherd; one *d*. *Educ:* Bedford Coll., London, then UCL (BSc Physiol.; Fellow, 2005). Campaigns Co-ordinator, Shelter, 1986–88; Director: Workplace Nurseries Campaign, 1988–92; Commns, Nat. Asthma Campaign, 1992–96; Chief Executive: Breakthrough Breast Cancer, 1996–2005; Breast Cancer Campaign, 2011–15. Founding Mem., Long Term Conditions Alliance (Vice-Chm., 1996; Chm., 1996–98; Trustee, 1994–2000); Chm., DoH Primary Task Gp, Patient Choice, 2003; Member: NHS Nat. Cancer Taskforce, 2000–05; NHS Modernisation Bd, 2002–05. A Baroness in Waiting (Govt Whip), 2007–10; Parly Under-Sec. of State, DIUS, 2008, DCSF, 2008–10. House of Lords: Member: Select Cttee on Merit of Statutory Instruments, 2005–07; Jt Cttee on Draft Children (contact) and Adoption Bill, 2005–; Vice Chair, All Party Gp on Breast Cancer, 2005–07. Mem. Exec. Council, Assoc. Med. Res. Charities, 1999–2004. Fellow, Cardiff Univ., 2005. *Address:* House of Lords, SW1A 0PW.

**MORGAN OF ELY,** Baroness *cr* 2011 (Life Peer), of Ely in the City of Cardiff; **(Mair) Eluned Morgan;** Member (Lab) Mid and West Wales, National Assembly for Wales, since 2016; Minister for International Relations and the Welsh Language, since 2018; *b* 16 Feb. 1967; *d* of late Rev. Bob Morgan and of Elaine Morgan; *m* 1996, Rev. Dr Rhys Jenkins, one *s* one *d*. *Educ:* Atlantic Coll.; Univ. of Hull (BA). Stagiaire with Socialist Gp, Europe. Parlt, 1990; with S4C, 1991; researcher and reporter, Agenda TV, 1992; documentary researcher, BBC TV, 1993. MEP (Lab) Mid and W Wales, 1994–99, Wales, 1999–2009; Mem., Industry, Res. and Energy Cttee, EP, 2004–09. Shadow spokesperson for Wales and Foreign Affairs, H of L, 2013–16. Minister for Welsh Lang. and Lifelong Learning, Welsh Govt, 2017–18. Dir of Develt (formerly Head of Low Carbon Business Develt) for Wales, SSE plc (formerly Scottish and Southern Energy plc), 2009–13. Chm., Cardiff Business Partnership, 2013–14; Welsh Chm. and Trustee, Live Music Now, 2012–16. Hon. Distinguished Prof., 2010, and Fellow, 2012–, Cardiff Univ. *Recreations:* walking, reading. *Address:* National Assembly for Wales, Cardiff Bay, Cardiff CF99 1NA. *E:* Eluned.Morgan@assembly.wales.

**MORGAN OF HUYTON,** Baroness *cr* 2001 (Life Peer), of Huyton in the County of Merseyside; **Sally Morgan;** Master, Fitzwilliam College, Cambridge, since 2019; *b* 28 June 1959; *d* of Albert Edward Morgan and Margaret Morgan; *m* 1984, John Lyons; two *s*. *Educ:* Belvedere Girls' Sch., Liverpool; Durham Univ. (BA Geog. Hons); Univ. of London (PGCE, MA Educ.). Secondary Sch. Teacher, 1981–85; Labour Party: Student Organiser, 1985–87; Sen. Targetting Officer, 1987–93; Dir, Campaigns and Elecns, 1993–95; Head of Party Liaison for Leader of the Opposition, 1995–97; Pol Sec. to the Prime Minister, 1997–2001; Minister of State, Cabinet Office, 2001; Dir of Pol and Govt Relations, Prime Minister's Office, 2001–05. Mem. Bd, Olympic Delivery Authy, 2005–14. Chm., Royal Brompton and Harefield NHS Foundn Trust, 2017–. Non-executive Director: Dixons Carphone (formerly Carphone Warehouse) plc, 2005–17; Southern Cross Healthcare Plc, 2006–11; Infinis Energy plc, 2014–16; Countryside Properties, 2015–. Chm., Ofsted, 2011–14. Advr to Bd, Absolute Return for Kids, 2005–; Member, Advisory Panel: Lloyds Pharmacy, 2006–10; Virgin Hldg Co., 2011–15. Mem. Council, KCL, 2014–. *Recreations:* relaxing with family and friends, cooking, gardening.

**MORGAN, Alasdair Neil;** Member (SNP) Scotland South, Scottish Parliament, 2003–11 (Galloway & Upper Nithsdale, 1999–2003); *b* 21 April 1945; *s* of Alexander Morgan and Emily Morgan (*née* Wood); *m* 1969, Anne Gilfillan; two *s*. *Educ:* Breadalbane Acad., Aberfeldy; Univ. of Glasgow (MA Hons 1968); Open Univ. (BA Hons 1990). IT Project Manager, Lothian Reg., 1986–96; IT Consultant, W Lothian Council, 1996–97. Contested (SNP) Dumfries, 1992. MP (SNP) Galloway and Upper Nithsdale, 1997–2001. Mem., Select Cttee on Trade and Industry affairs, 1997–2001. Scottish Parliament: Mem., Rural Affairs Cttee, 1999–2000; Convenor, Justice I Cttee, 2000–01; Mem., Finance Cttee, 2001–03; Convenor, Enterprise and Culture Cttee, 2003–04; Vice Convenor, Finance Cttee, 2004–05; Mem., European and External Relations Cttee, 2007–08; Dep. Presiding Officer, 2007–11; Mem., Rural Affairs and Envmt Cttee, 2008–11. Scottish National Party: Nat. Treas., 1983–90; Sen. Vice Convenor, 1990–91; Nat. Sec., 1992–97; Vice Pres., 1997–2004; Leader, Parly Gp, 1999–2001; Chief Whip, Scottish Parly Gp, 2005–07. Trustee, Scottish Parly Pension Fund, 2009–18. Mem., Electoral Commn, 2014–. *Recreation:* hill walking. *Address:* 2 Park Place, Dunfermline KY12 7QJ.

**MORGAN, Alastair William James,** CMG 2019; Coordinator, United Nations 1718 (DPRK Sanctions) Panel of Experts, New York, since 2019; *b* Camberley, 28 May 1958; *s* of late Col Geoffrey Charles Purday Morgan, OBE, DL and of Dr Barbara Hilary Morgan; *m* 1988, Ayako Nakamura; one *s* two *d*. *Educ:* St Andrew's Sch., Pangbourne; Sherborne Sch.; Trinity Coll., Cambridge (BA 1979; MA 1983). Lectr, Gakushuin Univ., Tokyo, 1983–85; with Department of Trade and Industry, later Department for Business, Innovation and Skills, subseq. Department for International Trade, 1985–2019: Insce Div., 1985–86; Aerospace Div., 1986–88; Private Sec. to Minister for Trade and Industry, 1988–89; Principal, Financial Services Div., 1991; Japanese lang. trng, 1991–92; First Sec. Tokyo, 1992–96; Hd, UK Mergers Section, DTI, 1996–99; Actg Chief Exec. and Dir of Ops, Invest in Britain Bureau, 1999–2001; Sen. Advr to Japanese Min. of Econ., Trade and Industry, Tokyo, 2001–02; Counsellor, Tokyo, 2002–06; Mandarin lang. trng, 2006; Counsellor, Beijing, 2007–10; Consul-Gen., Guangzhou, 2010–14; Ambassador to Democratic People's Republic of Korea, 2015–18; Sen. Advr, FCO, 2019. Sen. Vis. Res. Fellow, KCL, 2019–. *Recreations:* walking, reading, oriental languages. *E:* alastair.morgan@un.org.

**MORGAN, Anthony Hugh,** CMG 1990; HM Diplomatic Service, retired; Consul-General, Zürich, Director of British Export Promotion in Switzerland and Consul-General, Liechtenstein, 1988–91; *b* 27 March 1931; *s* of late Cyril Egbert Morgan and late Muriel Dorothea (*née* Nash); *m* 1957, Cicely Alice Voysey (*d* 2011); two *s* one *d*. *Educ:* King's Norton Grammar Sch.; Birmingham Univ. (BA 1952). Served HM Forces (RAF Educn Br.), 1952–55. Joined HM Foreign (later Diplomatic) Service, 1956; Cairo, then Cyprus, 1956; Khartoum, 1957; FO, 1959; Saigon, 1962; Second Sec., 1963; UK Delegn to NATO, 1965; First Sec., 1968; FCO, 1969; First Sec. and Head of Chancery, Calcutta, 1973; FCO, 1976; Dep. Head of Inf. Policy Dept, 1977; Counsellor: (Information), Brussels, 1977–79; (Commercial), Copenhagen, 1979–82; Vienna, 1982–88. Comdr, Order of Dannebrog, Denmark, 1979. *Recreations:* listening to music, looking at pictures. *Club:* Royal Air Force.

**MORGAN, Arthur William Crawford;** *see* Morgan, T.

**MORGAN, Most Rev. Dr Barry Cennydd;** Bishop of Llandaff, 1999–2017; Archbishop of Wales, 2003–17; *b* 31 Jan. 1947; *s* of Rees Haydn Morgan and Mary Gwyneth Morgan; *m* 1969, Hilary Patricia Lewis (*d* 2016); one *s* one *d*. *Educ:* Ystalyfera Grammar Sch.; University Coll. London (BA Hons History 1969); Selwyn Coll., Cambridge (BA Hons Theol. 1971); Westcott House, Cambridge. MA Cantab 1974; PhD Wales 1986. Priest, Llandaff, 1973; Curate, St Andrew's Major, Dinas Powis, 1972–75; Chaplain, Bryn-y-Don Community Sch., 1972–75; Chaplain and Lectr, St Michael's Coll., Llandaff, 1975–77; Lectr, University Coll., Cardiff, 1975–77; Warden of Church Hostel, Bangor, Anglican Chap., UCNW and Lectr in Theology, UCNW, 1977–84; Rector of Wrexham, 1984–86; Archdeacon of Merioneth and Rector of Criccieth, 1986–92; Bishop of Bangor, 1993–99. Editor, Welsh Churchman, 1975–82. Exam. Chaplain to Abp of Wales, 1978–82, to Bp of Bangor, 1983; Diocese of Bangor: In-Service Trng Officer, 1979–84; Warden of Ordinands, 1982–84; Canon of Bangor Cathedral, 1983–84. Member: Archbishop's Doctrinal Commn, 1982–93 (Chm. 1989–93); Crown Nominations Commn, 2012; Chm., Div. of Stewardship, Provincial Bd of Mission, 1988–95. Pres., Welsh Centre for Internat. Affairs, 2004–10. Vice-Chairman: Nat. Soc., 1999; Bible Soc., 1999. Fellow, Woodard Corp., 2001–. Pro-Chancellor, Univ. of Wales, 2006–. FLSW 2013. Hon. Fellow: Bangor Univ., 1994; UWIC, 2003; Lampeter Univ., 2004; Cardiff Univ., 2004; Swansea Univ., 2009; Trinity Univ. Coll., Carmarthen 2009. Hon. DLitt Cardiff Metropolitan, 2015; Hon. DD Wales, 2017. *Publications:* O Ddydd i Ddydd, Pwyllgor Darlleniadau Beiblaidd Cyngor Eglwysi Cymru, 1980; History of the Church Hostel and Anglican Chaplaincy at University College of North Wales, Bangor, 1986; Concepts of Mission and Ministry in Anglican University Chaplaincy Work, 1988; Strangely Orthodox: R. S. Thomas and his poetry of faith, 2006. *Recreation:* golf. *Address:* Crud yr Allt, Westbourne Crescent, Cardiff CF14 2BL.

**MORGAN, Brian David Gwynne,** FRCS; Consultant Plastic Surgeon, University College Hospital, London and Mount Vernon Hospital, 1972–98; *b* 2 March 1935; *s* of Brig. John Gwynne Morgan and Ethel Lilian Morgan; *m* 1962, Sally Ann Lewis; one *s* two *d*. *Educ:* Wycliffe Coll., Glos; University College Hosp., London (MB BS). FRCS 1963. University College Hospital: pre-registration house appts, 1959–61; Casualty Officer, 1961; Registrar in Surgery, St Richard's Hosp., Chichester, 1962–64; Registrar in Surgery, 1964–66, Sen. Registrar, 1967, UCH; Plastic Surgery Registrar and Sen. Registrar, Mt Vernon Hosp., 1967–70; Consultant Plastic Surgeon, Shotley Bridge, Durham, 1970–72. Hon. Archivist, British Assoc. of Plastic, Reconstructive and Aesthetic Surgeons, 1999–2015. Mem. Council, RCS, 1991–99 (Trustee, Hunterian Collection, 2000–14). Fellow, UCL, 1992. *Publications:* Essentials of Plastic and Reconstructive Surgery, 1986. *Recreations:* water-colour painting, sailing, jazz trombone. *Address:* Stockers House, Stockers Farm Road, Rickmansworth, Herts WD3 1NZ. *T:* (01923) 773922. *E:* brianandsallymorgan@btinternet.com.

**MORGAN, Bruce;** District Judge (Magistrates' Courts), West Mercia, 2003–11; *b* 30 March 1945; *s* of Francis William Morgan, DFC, and Phyllis Marie Morgan; *m* 1988, Sandra Joy Beresford; twin *d*. *Educ:* Oswestry School; Open Univ. (BA 1994). Solicitor of Supreme Court. Articled Clerk, Stourbridge, Worcs, 1964–69; Asst Solicitor, London, SE10, 1969–72; Partner with Lickfolds Wiley & Powles, 1973–86. Member: London Criminal Courts Solicitors Assoc. Cttee, 1971–73; Criminal Law Cttee, Westminster Law Soc., 1981–86; No 14 Area Regl Duty Solicitors Cttee, 1986–87; Metropolitan Stipendiary Magistrate, 1987–89; Stipendiary Magistrate, subseq. Dist Judge (Magistrates' Courts), W Midlands, 1989–2003. Ind. Prison Adjudicator, 2001–13. Member: Birmingham Magistrates' Court Cttee, 1990–93; Birmingham Magistrates' Bench Cttee, 1990–2003; Midland Mem., Nat., subseq. HM, Council of Dist Judges (Magistrates' Courts) (formerly Jt Council of Stipendiary Magistrates), 1995–2003; Member: W Mercia Area Judicial Forum, 2005–11; W Mercia Judicial Issues Gp, 2005–11. Member: British Acad. of Forensic Sci., 1970; Legal Medico Soc., 1970–2012; Our Soc., 1994–. Vice Chm., Cleobury North PCC, 1996–2010. Member: Ludlow Rotary Club, 1969–98; Shropshire Soc. in London, 2008–; Knighton Rotary Club, 2015–; Chm., Greenwich Round Table, 1983–84. Governor, Oswestry Sch., 1996–2013 (Vice Chm., 1996–2000, 2007–13). *Publications:* various articles in legal journals. *Recreations:* tennis, cricket, gardening, attending auctions, cooking. *Clubs:* Reform; Worcestershire Cricket.

**MORGAN, Vice-Adm. Sir (Charles) Christopher,** KBE 1996; Director General, Chamber of Shipping, 1997–2003; Director, CM Shipping Consultants Ltd, 2003–09; *b* 11 March 1939; *s* of late Captain Horace Leslie Morgan, CMG, DSO, RN and Kathleen Hilda Morgan; *m* 1970, Susan Caroline Goodbody; three *d*. *Educ:* Clifton College; BRNC Dartmouth. Joined RN, 1957; served Brunei, 1962–66; HMS Greatford in Comd, 1966; Specialist Navigation Course, 1967; HMS Eskimo in Comd, 1976; NDC 1978; Comdr Sea Training, 1979; MoD, 1981–83; RCDS, 1984; Captain 5th Destroyer Sqdn (HMS Southampton), 1985–87; Staff, Jt Service Defence Coll., 1987–89; Naval Sec., 1990–92; Flag Officer, Scotland, Northern England and NI, 1992–96. Younger Brother of Trinity House, 1977. Governor: Clifton Coll., 1994–2018; Sherborne Sch. for Girls, 2004–10. Chm. Trustees, Royal Naval Benevolent Soc., 1996–2005; Gov., Tancred Soc., 1996–2019. Member, Council: King George's Fund for Sailors, 1997–2003; RNLI, 2002–10 (Vice-Pres., 2009–); Chm., Bubbly charity, 2005–14. Freeman, Co. of Master Mariners, 1999; Liveryman, Shipwrights' Co., 2000. FCMI; FRIN 1996; MInstD 1996. *Recreations:* family, golf, tennis, Rugby, wine, gardening. *Address:* c/o Lloyds, 75 Cheap Street, Sherborne, Dorset. *Clubs:* Army and Navy; Royal North Devon Golf.

**MORGAN, Rt Hon. Sir (Charles) Declan,** Kt 2004; PC 2009; Lord Chief Justice of Northern Ireland, since 2009; *b* 14 Jan. 1952; *m*; three *c*. *Educ:* St Columb's Coll., Londonderry; Peterhouse, Cambridge (BA 1974; Hon. Fellow, 2010); Queen's Univ., Belfast. Called to the Bar, NI, 1976; QC (NI) 1993; Sen. Crown Counsel, 2002–04; a Judge of the High Ct of Justice, NI, 2004–09. Chairman: Law Reform Adv. Cttee, 2004–07; NI Law Commn, 2007–09; NI Judicial Appts Commn, 2009–. Hon. Bencher, Middle Temple, 2012. *Address:* Royal Courts of Justice, Chichester Street, Belfast BT1 3JF.

**MORGAN, Charles Peter Henry;** DL; Chairman and Chief Executive Officer, Morgan Motor Co. Ltd, 2009–13; *b* 29 July 1951; *s* of Peter and Jane Morgan; *m* 2003, Kira Kopylova; one *s* one *d*, and one *s* two *d* from previous marriage. *Educ:* Sussex Univ. (BA Hons Hist. of Art 1971); Coventry Univ. (MBA Engng Mgt 1994). News film cameraman, ITN, 1974–82; Co-founder and Dir, Television News Team Ltd, 1982–85; Morgan Motor Co. Ltd: Marketing Dir, 1985–99; Man. Dir, 1999–2004; Dir, Corporate Strategy, 2004–09. Hon. DBA Coventry, 2003. Silver Nymph award for news TV film, Montreux Internat. TV Fest., 1978. DL Worcs 2010. Hon. MA Worcester, 2008; Hon. DTech Loughborough, 2009; Hon. DBus Southampton Solent, 2010; DUniv Birmingham City, 2011. *Publications:* (with Gregory Houston Bowden) Morgan 100 Years, 2008 (German Motor Press Club Book Prize, 2010). *Recreations:* ski-ing, architecture and design, painting. *Address:* c/o Morgan Motor Co. Ltd, Pickersleigh Road, Malvern Link, Worcs WR14 2LL. *T:* (01684) 573104. *Clubs:* Academy; British Racing Drivers'; St Moritz Tobogganing.

**MORGAN, Christine Lesley**; Head of Radio, BBC Religion and Ethics, since 2009; *b* 4 May 1958; *d* of Gerald Potts and Brenda Austin Potts (*née* Bell); *m* 1st, 1979, Christopher Harry Morgan (marr. diss. 1987); 2nd, 2000, Paul Vallely, *qv*; one *s*. *Educ*: Ormskirk Grammar Sch.; Southport Coll.; FE Teaching Dip. AEWVH 1987. Joined WRAF, 1976: HQ Strike Comd, 1976–78; Personal Staff of Chief of Air Staff, MoD, 1978–79; Design Team, Airmen's Comd Sch., Hereford, 1979–80; Personnel Asst to Purchasing Dir, H. P. Bulmer Ltd, 1980–83; Lectr in Business Studies, Royal Nat. Coll. for the Blind, 1983–87 (devised RNCB Nat. Work Experience Scheme, 1987); joined BBC Religious Broadcasting, 1987; Producer, Radio 4 Sunday, 1991–93; Producer, 1992–2004, Ed., 2004–, Thought for the Day; Series Producer: Sunday Radio 4, 1993–95; Heart and Soul, BBC TV, 1995; Producer: The Choice, 1995; File on 4, 1995–96; Heart of the Matter, BBC TV, 1998 (Series Producer, 1999–2001); Everyman, Letters to the Yorkshire Ripper, BBC TV, 2001; The Celibacy Debate, BBC TV; Exec. Producer, Music and Worship Progs, Religion and Ethics, 2002–04; Exec. Producer, Religion and Ethics, BBC Radio, 2004–09; Editor: Faith in Africa, 2005; Humphrys in Search of God, 2006; The King James Bible, 2011; The People's Passion, 2012. MA Lambeth, 2008. Sanford St Martin Award, 1992, 2007, 2011; Sony Bronze Award, 1995; Silver Award, Med. Radio of the Year, 1998; VLV New Prog. Award, 2007; Jerusalem Trust Award, 2007. *Recreation*: Thomas. *Address*: BBC Religion and Ethics, Dock House, MediaCityUK, Salford M50 2LH.

**MORGAN, Rt Rev. Christopher Heudebourck**; Area Bishop of Colchester, 2001–13; an Honorary Assistant Bishop, Diocese of Chichester, since 2014; *b* 23 March 1947; *m* 1975, Anne Musgrave; one *s* one *d*. *Educ*: City of Bath Boys' Sch.; Kelham Theol Coll.; Lancaster Univ. (BA 1973); Heythrop Coll., London (MTh 1991). Ordained deacon, 1973, priest, 1974; Curate, St James the Great, Birstall, 1973–76; Chaplain to EC staff, and Asst Chaplain, Holy Trinity Ch, Brussels, 1976–80; Team Vicar, St George, Redditch, and part-time Industrial Chaplain, 1980–85; Vicar, Sonning, 1985–96; Gloucester Diocesan Officer for Ministry, and a Residentiary Canon, Gloucester Cathedral, 1996–2001. Principal, Berks Christian Trng Scheme, 1985–89; Dir, Pastoral Studies, St Albans and Oxford Diocesan Ministry Course, 1992–96. *Recreations*: hill walking, improving at golf, music, grandchildren. *Address*: 6 Wellington Court, Grand Avenue, Worthing, W Sussex BN11 5AB.

**MORGAN, Christopher John; His Honour Judge Christopher Morgan**; a Circuit Judge, since 2015; *b* St Neots, Cambs, 18 Dec. 1963; *s* of John Willingdon Morgan and Anne Morgan; partner 1987, Julia Mary Gooch; one *d* (one *s* decd); *m* 2017, Tracy Jane Watts (*née* Law); one *s* one *d*. *Educ*: Poly. of Central London (LLB Hons 1986); Council of Legal Educn. Called to the Bar, Middle Temple, 1987; in practice as barrister specialising in criminal law, 1987–2015; a Recorder, 2009–15. *Recreations*: road cycling, gardening, family, literature, music, walking, wine. *Address*: Chelmsford Crown Court, PO Box 9, New Street, Chelmsford, Essex CM1 1EL.

**MORGAN, Claire**; *see* Durkin, C.

**MORGAN, David**; *see* Morgan, F. D.

**MORGAN, Prof. David Owen**, PhD; FRS 2012; Professor, since 1997, and Vice Chair, since 1998, Department of Physiology, and Professor, Department of Biochemistry and Biophysics, since 1997, University of California, San Francisco. *Educ*: Univ. of Calgary (BSc Animal Biol. 1980); Univ. of California, San Francisco (PhD 1986). Postdoctoral Fellow, 1986–89, Asst Prof., 1989–95, Associate Prof., 1995–97, University of California, San Francisco. *Publications*: The Cell Cycle: principles of control, 2006; articles in jls. *Address*: Department of Physiology, Box 2200, University of California at San Francisco, 600 16th Street, San Francisco, CA 94158–2517, USA.

**MORGAN, David Thomas**; land and development consultant; *b* 22 Jan. 1946; *s* of Janet Catherine and Noel David Morgan; *m* 1968, Quita Valentine; two *d*. *Educ*: Alleyne's Grammar School, Stevenage; Univ. of Newcastle upon Tyne (BA Hons Land Use Studies 1968). MRTPI 1971–2008. Somerset CC, 1968–70; Worcs CC, 1970–71; Peterborough Develt Corp., 1971–81; Housing Develt Manager, 1981–85, Dir, Planning Services, 1985–87, LDDC; Chief Exec., Black Country Develt Corp., 1987–98. Mem., Inland Waterways Amenity Adv. Council, 1997–2006. *Recreation*: painting and drawing. *Address*: 3 Riverside Court, Caunsall, near Kidderminster, Worcs DY11 5YW. *T*: (01562) 851688.

**MORGAN, David Wynn; His Honour Judge David Wynn Morgan**; a Circuit Judge, since 2000; *b* 18 April 1954; *s* of late Arthur Islwyn Lewis Morgan and of Mary Morgan (*née* Wynn); *m* 1982, Marian Eléna Lewis; one *s* one *d*. *Educ*: Kingswood Sch., Bath; Balliol Coll., Oxford (BA Jurisprudence). Called to the Bar, Gray's Inn, 1976; practised on Wales and Chester Circuit, 1977–2000; Asst Recorder, 1991–95, Recorder, 1995–2000. Mem., Parole Bd, 2002–09. *Recreations*: music, reading, being in Pembrokeshire. *Address*: The Crown Court, Cathays Park, Cardiff CF10 3PG.

**MORGAN, Rt Hon. Sir Declan**; *see* Morgan, Rt Hon. Sir C. D.

**MORGAN, Prof. Derec Llwyd**, DPhil, DLitt; FLSW; Vice-Chancellor and Principal, University of Wales, Aberystwyth, 1995–2004; Senior Vice-Chancellor, 2001–04, Professor Emeritus, since 2004, University of Wales; *b* 15 Nov. 1943; *s* of Ewart Lloyd Morgan and Margaret Morgan; *m* 1965, Jane Edwards; one *d*. *Educ*: Amman Valley GS; UCNW, Bangor (BA; Hon. Fellow, 1996); Jesus Coll., Oxford (DPhil; Hon. Fellow, 1999); DLitt Wales, 1999. Res. Fellow, Univ. of Wales, 1967–69; Lectr, UCW, Aberystwyth, 1969–74; University College of North Wales, Bangor: Lectr, 1975–80, Sen. Lectr, 1980–83, Reader, 1983–89, Dept of Welsh; Dir, Research Centre Wales, 1985–89; Prof. of Welsh, 1989–95, and Vice-Principal, 1994–95, UCW, Aberystwyth. Supernumerary Fellow, 1997–98, Welsh Supernumerary Fellow, 2003–04, Jesus Coll., Oxford. Member: Bd of Celtic Studies, Univ. of Wales, 1990–96; Court and Council, Nat. Library of Wales, 1995–2007; Governing Body, Inst. of Grassland and Environmental Res., 1995–2004. Member: Gen. Adv. Council, BBC, 1984–90; Broadcasting Council for Wales, 1990–95; ITC, 1999–2003. Chm., Rowntree Commn on Rural Housing in Wales, 2007–08. Royal National Eisteddfod of Wales: Chm. Council, 1979–82, 1985–86; Chm. Exec. Cttee, Ynys Môn, 1983; Pres. Court, 1989–93. Chairman: All-Wales Cultural Forum, 1999; Celtic Film and Television Festival, 2000; Exec. Cttee, James Pantyfedwen Foundn, 2011–; Anglesey Language Forum, 2013–18; Exec. Cttee, Anglesey Nat. Eisteddfod, 2017. Non-executive Director: PO Bd, Wales and the Marches, 1996–2000; Menter a Busnes, 1997–2000. Trustee: James Pantyfedwen Foundn, 2004–; Sir Kyffin Williams Trust, 2017– (Chm., 2006–16); Oriel Môn Trust, 2018–. Founding FLSW 2010 (Mem. Council, 2009–12). Hon. Fellow, Trinity UC, 2009. DUniv Wales, 2006. *Publications*: Y Tân Melys, 1966; Pryderi, 1970; Barddoniaeth Thomas Gwynn Jones: astudiaeth, 1972; Kate Roberts, 1974, 2nd edn 1991; (ed) Cerddi '75, 1975; Iliad Homer, 1976; (ed) Adnabod Deg, 1977; Gwna yn Llawen, Wr Ieuanc, 1978; Y Diwygiad Mawr, 1981 (trans., The Great Awakening in Wales, 1988); Williams Pantycelyn, 1983; Pobl Pantycelyn, 1986; (ed) Glas y Nef: cerddi ac emynau John Roberts Llanfwrog, 1987; Cefn y Byd, 1987; (ed) Emynau Williams Pantycelyn, 1991; (ed) Meddwl a Dychymyg Williams Pantycelyn, 1991; Ni cheir byth wir lle bo llawer o feirdd, 1992; Charles Edwards, 1994; Y Beibl a Llenyddiaeth Gymraeg, 1998; John Roberts Llanfwrog: pregethwr, bardd, emynydd, 1999; (contrib.) Gogoneddus Arglwydd, Henffych Well, 2000; Nid hwn mo'r llyfr terfynol: Hanes Llenyddiaeth Thomas Parry, 2004; (ed) Kyffin: a celebration, 2007; Tyred i'n Gwaredu, 2010; (ed) Daniel Owen's Fireside Tales, 2011; Y Brenhinbren: bywyd a gwaith Thomas Parry 1904–1985, 2013; (ed) Emlyn Hooson: essays and reminiscences, 2014; Bachgendod Isaac, 2017. *Recreations*: cricket, gardening, fortunes and misfortunes of Swansea City AFC, reading. *Address*: Carrog Uchaf, Tregaian, Llangefni, Anglesey LL77 7UE. *Clubs*: Premier (Glamorgan County Cricket); Rygbi Llangefni.

**MORGAN, Dianne**; *see* Edwards, Dianne.

**MORGAN, Douglas**, IPFA; County Treasurer, Lancashire County Council, 1985–92; *b* 5 June 1936; *s* of late Douglas Morgan and Margaret Gardner Morgan; *m* 1960, Julia (*née* Bywater); two *s*. *Educ*: High Pavement Grammar Sch., Nottingham. IPFA 1963 (4th place in final exam. and G. A. Johnston (Dundee) Prize). Nat. Service, RAF, 1954–56. Nottingham CBC, 1952–61; Herefordshire CC, 1961–64; Berkshire CC, 1964–67; Asst Co. Treas., W Suffolk CC, 1967–70; Asst, later Dep., Co. Treas., Lindsey CC, 1970–73; Dep. Co. Treas., Lancashire CC, 1973–85. Chm., NW & N Wales Region, CIPFA, 1985–86; Pres., NW & N Wales Region, Students' Soc., CIPFA, 1989–90. Treas., Lancs Cttee, Royal Jubilee & Prince's Trust, 1985–92; Hon. Treasurer: Lancs Playing Fields Assoc., 1985–92; NW Region Library System and NW Sound Archive, 1986–92; Mem., Exec. Cttee, Lancs Union of Golf Clubs, 1998–2002. FRSA. *Publications*: articles for Public Finance & Accountancy and other local govt jls. *Recreations*: golf and "collecting" golf courses, jazz. *Address*: 8 Croyde Road, St Annes-on-Sea, Lancs FY8 1EX. *T*: (01253) 725808. *Club*: Fairhaven Golf (Centenary Captain, 1995–96).

**MORGAN, Emma Victoria, (Mrs Paul Monaghan)**; Creative Director, Factual, Firecracker Films, since 2017; *b* Chiswick, London, 13 March 1967; *d* of Geoffrey Thomas Morgan, *qv*; *m* 2001, Paul Monaghan; two *d*. *Educ*: Waldegrave Sch. for Girls; Richmond Upon Thames Coll.; Univ. of Hull (BA Jt Hons English and Drama 1989); Welsh Coll. of Music and Drama (Dip. Acting 1990). Professional actress, 1990–96; freelance producer, 1996–2002; Twofour: Devlt Producer, 2002–04; Exec. Producer, 2004–11; Hd, Documentaries, 2005–09; Hd, Develt, 2009–11; Exec. Producer, Dir, Develt, Mentorn Media, 2011–14; Creative Dir, Watershed TV, Warner Bros Television UK, 2014; Exec. Producer and Hd of Popular Factual, Oxford Scientific Films, 2015–17. Diversity Mentor, Channel 4, 2006–14. BAFTA: Mem., TV Cttee, 2014– (Dep. Chair, 2015–17); Co-Chair, Break Through Brits TV and Film Cttee, 2015; Trustee, 2015–17. Mem., Adv. Panel, Factual Develt and Prodn Dip., Nat. Film and TV Sch., 2015. Productions include: for Channel 4: The F***ing Fulfords, 2004; Why Men Wear Frocks, 2005; Crip on a Trip, 2006; The Fried Chicken Shop, 2013; Angry White and Proud, 2015; Messages Home: Lost Films of the British Army, 2016; A Very British Hotel, 2017; How the Other Kids Live, 2019; Mums Make Porn, 2019; for ITV: Saving Ed Mitchell, 2008; for BBC: Edwardian Insects on Film, 2013; Free Speech, 2014; for UKTV: Emma Willis: Delivering Babies, 2018; Stacey Dooley Sleep Over, 2019. *Recreations*: yoga, theatre and cinema, visiting art galleries, gardening, family life and walking the toy poodle. *Address*: Firecracker Films, 5th Floor, No 1 Smiths Square, 77–85 Fulham Palace Road, W6 8JA. *T*: (020) 3837 7780. *E*: emma.morgan@firecrackerfilms.com.

**MORGAN, (Evan) Roger**; Senior Clerk, Science & Technology Committee, House of Lords, 1999–2003; *b* 18 April 1945; *s* of late Evan and Stella Morgan; *m* 1st, 1967 (marr. diss.); one *s* one *d*; 2nd, 1997, Lesley Greene (*née* Smith). *Educ*: Whitgift Sch., South Croydon; Battersea Coll. of Advanced Technol. Main career spent within DES, then Dept for Educn, later Dept for Educn and Employment: Under Sec., Further Educn, 1991–94, Internat. Relns and Youth, 1994–95; Asst Dir, Internat. Dept for Educn and Employment, 1995–97. Various voluntary post-retirement positions, 2003–. *Recreations*: making music, cycling, local history. *E*: morgan.roger@btopenworld.com.

**MORGAN, Francis Vincent**; General Secretary, Association of Governing Bodies of Independent Schools (formerly Governing Bodies Association and Governing Bodies of Girls' Schools Association), 1998–2003; *b* 22 June 1936; *s* of Joseph Michael Morgan and Monica Morgan; *m* 1965, Annette Mary Tolhurst; one *s*. *Educ*: St Edward's Coll., Liverpool; Univ. of Liverpool (Oliver Lodge Prize; BSc 1958); St John's Coll., Cambridge (PGCE 1959); Chelsea Coll., Univ. of London (MEd 1974). Asst master, Stonyhurst Coll., 1959–62; various posts, Redrice Sch., Andover, 1962–68; Lectr in Physical Scis, Homerton Coll., Cambridge, 1968–70; Schs Advr, Borough of Southend-on-Sea, 1970–73; Head: Sacred Heart Sch., Tunbridge Wells, 1973–78; St Mary's Catholic Sch., Bishop's Stortford, 1978–84; Schs Officer, Archdio. Westminster, 1984–86; Dir of Educn, RC Dio. Brentwood, 1986–90; Dir, United Westminster Schs and Royal Foundn of Grey Coat Hosp., 1990–98. Mem., Ind. Schs Pension Scheme Cttee, 1996–2001. Governor: Stonyhurst Coll., 1986–91; New Hall Sch., Chelmsford, 1992–2001 (Chm., 1995–2001); Westminster Cathedral Choir Sch., 1998–2010; Sutton Valence Sch., 1998–2004; St Mary's Sch., Ascot, 2002–11; St Mary's Sch., Cambridge, 2010–14 (Chm., 2012–14); Trustee: St Mary's Sch., Hampstead, 1992–2001; United Westminster Schs, 2000–06; Eastern Counties Educnl Trust (formerly Royal Eastern Counties Schs), 2002–12. *Recreations*: contemporary novels, biographies, chess, bridge, Haydn symphonies. *Address*: 34 Ashley Road, Newmarket, Suffolk CB8 8DA. *T*: (01638) 602313. *Club*: Athenæum.
*See also* J. A. Morgan.

**MORGAN, Prof. Frank**, OBE 2012; Vice-Chancellor, Bath Spa University (formerly Bath College of Higher Education, then Bath Spa University College), 1996–2011; *b* Stockport, 23 Nov. 1952; *s* of George Morgan and Hilda Morgan; *m* 1989, Gurcharan Kaur Dhillon; two *s*. *Educ*: Bridge Hall Sch., Stockport; University Coll. London (BA 1974); City Univ. Business Sch. (MSc 1976); Preston Poly. (CPFA 1981). Greater Manchester Transport, 1976–80; Accountant, London Bor. of Southwark, 1980–83; Hd, Finance, North East London Poly., 1983–86; Dep. Dir, Bath Coll. of Higher Educn, 1986–96. Gov., Bridgwater Coll., Som. *Recreations*: studying seventeenth century French plays, watching Rugby League, exploring England's industrial heritage.

**MORGAN, (Frederick) David**, OBE 2008; DL; President, International Cricket Council, 2008–10 (Director, since 2003); *b* 6 Oct. 1937; *s* of Frederick Barlow Morgan and Caroline Morgan (*née* Constable); *m* 1960, Ann Cruickshank; one *s*. *Educ*: Thomas Richards Technical Sch., Tredegar; Henley Management Coll. (Gen. Mgt Prog. 1975). British Steel: Works Manager, Hot Sheet Finishing and Cold Rolling, Llanwern, 1977–84; Regl Sales Manager, SW and Wales, Strip Products, 1984–85; Commercial Manager, Electricals, 1985–90; Commercial Dir, European Electrical Steels, 1991–2001. Dir, Newport Develt Bd, 1997–2002. Chm., Wkg Party on setting up ECB (reported 1996); Dep. Chm., 1997–2002, Chm., 2003–07, ECB; conducted review of business of domestic cricket in England and Wales (reported 2012). Vice Pres., Friends of Newport Cathedral Choir, 2010–. DL Gwent, 2009. Hon. Fellow, Univ. of Wales, 2011. Chancellor's Medal, Univ. of Glamorgan, 2004. *Recreations*: grandchildren, music, Church liturgy, Rugby, wine, newspapers. *Address*: 49 Old Hill Crescent, Christchurch, Newport NP18 1JL. *T*: (01633) 420485. *E*: fdm53a@gmail.com. *Clubs*: MCC (Pres., 2014–15); Glamorgan CC (Chm., 1994–98; Pres., 2013–17; Mem., Nominations Gp, 2017–), Worcestershire CC, Surrey CC (Hon. Life Vice-Pres., 2010; Chm., Master's Club, 2018–).

**MORGAN, Gareth;** Chief Constable, Staffordshire Police, since 2017; *b* Stirling, 29 July 1966. *Educ:* Univ. of Birmingham (BA Social Scis 1987); FBI Nat. Acad. Prog. West Midlands Police, 1987–2011; Accelerated Promotion Scheme, 1996; Inspector, 1996; Detective Chief Inspector, 2000; Superintendent, 2002; on secondment to Home Office, 2002–03; Strategic Comd Course, 2011; COS to Pres., ACPO, 2011–12; Asst Chief Constable, Warwickshire Police and W Mercia Police, 2012–14; Dep. Chief Constable, Avon and Som Police, 2014–17. *Recreations:* gardening, cooking, Star Wars, walking, classical music. *Address:* Staffordshire Police Headquarters, PO Box 3167, Stafford ST16 9JZ. *T:* (01785) 232120. *E:* gareth.morgan@staffordshire.pnn.police.uk.

**MORGAN, Geoffrey Thomas,** CB 1991; Under Secretary, Cabinet Office, 1985–91; *b* 12 April 1931; *s* of late Thomas Evan Morgan and Nora (*née* Flynn); *m* 1960, Heather, *d* of late William Henry Trick and of Margery Murrell Wells; two *d. Educ:* Roundhay Sch. National Service, Royal Signals, 1950–52; joined Civil Service, 1952; served in Mins of Supply and Aviation, 1952–65; HM Treasury, 1965–68 and 1981–83; CSD, 1968–81; seconded to Arthur Guinness Son & Co., 1970–72; Cabinet Office, 1983–91; Adviser to: World Bank in Washington, 1977–78; UN in NY, 1987–88; official missions to: People's Republic of China in Beijing, 1988, 1991; Govt of Hungary in Budapest, 1990–2000; Govt of Jamaica in Kingston, 1991; South Africa, 1991–95; Czech Republic, 1996–2000; Chile, 1998. Chm., Public Admin Cttee, WEU, 1990–91. Advr, Coopers & Lybrand, subseq. PricewaterhouseCoopers, 1991–2000. Panel Chm., CSSB, 1991–95; Chm., Internat. Adv. Panel, Civil Service Coll., 1998–2001. Trustee, Whitehall and Industry Gp, 1991–94. Trustee, Twickenham Mus., 2002–14. FRSA 1996. *Recreation:* enjoying life with grandchildren. *E:* morganongreen@gmail.com. *Clubs:* Athenæum; Lensbury (Teddington).
*See also E. V. Morgan.*

**MORGAN, Dame Gillian (Margaret),** DBE 2004; FRCP, FFPH; Permanent Secretary, Welsh Government (formerly Welsh Assembly Government), 2008–12; Chair, NHS Providers, since 2014; *b* 23 July 1953. *Educ:* University Coll. Hosp. Medical Sch. (MB BS 1976). DRCOG 1981; FFPH (FFPHM 1996); FRCP 1998; MRCGP 2008; CCMI 2008. Leicestershire Health Authority: Dir of Quality and Contracts, 1989–91; Dir of Public Health, 1991–94; Chief Exec., North and East Devon HA, 1995–2002; Chief Exec., NHS Confederation, 2002–08. Chairman: Compli With Us Ltd, 2012–13; Clinical Bd, London Cancer Alliance, 2012–13; Alzheimer's Soc., 2013–15; Foundn Trust Network, 2014–18. Advr, de Poel, 2013–. Trustee, Lloyds Bank Foundn, 2017–. Hon. Fellow, Trinity Univ. Coll., 2009. Hon. DSc City, 2006. *Recreation:* sailing.

**MORGAN, Sir Graham,** Kt 2000; independent health care advisor, 2007–17; *b* 20 Aug. 1947; *s* of Islwyn and Phyllis Morgan; civil partnership 2006, Raymond Willetts. *Educ:* Treorchy Secondary Modern Sch.; Llandough Hosp. (RGN 1969). Staff Nurse: Llandough Hosp., Cardiff, 1969; Royal Marsden Hosp., 1970–72; Charge Nurse, St Mary's Hosp., Paddington, 1972–74; Nursing Officer, KCH, 1974–83; Asst Dir of Nursing, St Charles' Hosp., 1983–91; Special Nurse Advr, 1991–94, Dir of Nursing and Quality, 1994–99, Central Middlesex Hosp.; Exec. Dir of Nursing, 1999–2005, Dir of Clinical Strategy, 2005–07, NW London Hosps NHS Trust. Ordained priest, 1984; NSM, St Michael and All Angels, Bedford Park, 2003–. Dir and Trustee, St Margaret's Convent and St Mary's Nursing Home (formerly St Mary's Convent and Nursing Home), Chiswick, 2006–. *Publications:* (with Amanda Layton) Nuts and Bolts of Protocols, 1998; articles in various health care jls. *Recreations:* opera, dining out. *Address:* 24 Charleville Court, Charleville Road, W14 9JG. *Club:* National Liberal.

**MORGAN, His Honour Hugh Marsden;** a Circuit Judge, 1995–2010; *b* 17 March 1940; *s* of late Hugh Thomas Morgan, Cyncoed, Cardiff and Irene Morgan (*née* Rees); *m* 1967, Amanda Jane Tapley; two *s* one *d. Educ:* Cardiff High Sch.; Magdalen Coll., Oxford (Demy; BCL; MA Jurisp.). Tutor in Jurisprudence, St Edmund Hall and Pembroke Coll., Oxford, 1963–64. Called to the Bar, Gray's Inn, 1964; in practice: Midland Circuit, 1965–71; SE Circuit, 1971–95; Asst Recorder, 1983–87; Recorder, 1987–95. Member: Matrimonial Causes Rule Cttee, 1989–91; Family Proceedings Rule Cttee, 1991–93; Fees and Legal Aid Cttee, Senate and Bar Council, 1976–82; London Family Justice Council, 2005–10. Mem., Wine Cttee, SE Circuit, 1986–88. Mem. Cttee, Family Law Bar Assoc., 1976–89. *Recreations:* dabbling in artistic pursuits with friends, enjoying opera, ballet, cinema, lunching, wining and dining, family, travel. *Address:* c/o HM Courts and Tribunals Service, 102 Petty France, SW1H 9AJ.

**MORGAN, Ven. Ian David John;** Archdeacon of Suffolk, since 2012; *b* Hereford, 6 Jan. 1957; *s* of David and Margaret Morgan; *m* 1991, Tracey; two *s* one *d. Educ:* Wallingford Sch.; LTCL 1975; Univ. of Hull (BA Hons Music 1978); Ripon Coll., Cuddesdon. Ordained deacon, 1983, priest, 1984; Curate: Holy Trinity, Hereford, 1983–86; St Nicholas and St Mary de Haura, Shoreham by Sea, 1986–88; Producer, Presenter and Sen. Producer, BBC Local and Network Radio, 1988–92; Vicar, All Hallows, Ipswich, 1992–95; Rector, St Mary at Stoke and St Peter, Stoke Park with St Francis and St Clare (SW Ipswich Team Ministry), 1995–2012; Rural Dean of Ipswich, 2008–12. Hon. Canon, St Edmundsbury Cath., 2009–. Chair of Governors: Stoke High Sch., 1996–2012; Suffolk One Sixth Form Coll., 2011–. Chair, Suffolk Academies Trust, 2016–. Musical Dir, Abbot Consort of Voices, 2005–13. *Recreations:* supporter of Welsh Rugby, England cricket and Brighton and Hove Albion, cooking, Rotary (Pres., Ipswich Club, 2007–08), falling asleep whilst reading at the beach hut. *Address:* The Archdeaconry, Church Road, Marlesford, Suffolk IP13 0AT. *T:* (01728) 746863. *E:* archdeacon.ian@cofesuffolk.org.

**MORGAN, Sir Ian Parry David H.;** *see* Hughes-Morgan.

**MORGAN, Ioan,** CBE 2007; Principal, Warwickshire College, 1997–2010; *b* 4 April 1953; *s* of John and Marjorie Morgan; *m* 1976, Sandra Evans; two *s* one *d. Educ:* Univ. of Wales, Aberystwyth (BSc Hons 1975); London Univ. (CertEd 1978). CBiol 1980. Principal: Cambridgeshire Coll. of Agric. and Hort., 1985–89; Pembrokeshire Coll., 1989–97. Chm., 157 Gp of Colls, 2006. Mem., Commn for Skills and Employment, 2007–09; Further Educn Strategic Advr, Pearson/Educn Develt Internat., 2010–; Interim Principal: Dearne Valley Coll., Rotherham, 2012; Lewisham Southwark Coll., 2014–15; Peterborough Coll., 2015; Farnborough Coll. and Tresham Coll., 2016–17; Dep. Further Educn Comr for England, 2018. Freelance consultant in further educn, 2020–. FCGI. *Recreations:* dogs, countryside, Rugby, cricket, travel. *T:* (01926) 717306, 07740 419335. *E:* Ioan.Morgan@live.co.uk.

**MORGAN, Jane Sara;** *see* Gandee, J. S.

**MORGAN, Janet;** *see* Balfour of Burleigh, Lady.

**MORGAN, Jeremy;** *see* Morgan, T. J.

**MORGAN, John;** *see* Morgan, W. J.

**MORGAN, John Alfred;** Director, Eleco Holdings plc, 1997–2001; *b* 16 Sept. 1931; *s* of late Alfred Morgan and Lydia Amelia Morgan; *m* 1959, Janet Mary Sclater-Jones; one *d. Educ:* Rugeley Grammar Sch.; Peterhouse, Cambridge (BA). Investment Research, Cambridge, 1953–59; Investment Manager, S. G. Warburg & Co. Ltd, 1959–67; Director: Glyn, Mills & Co., 1967–70; Williams & Glyn's Bank Ltd, 1970–76; Rothschild Asset Management, 1976–78; Central Trustee Savings Bank Ltd, 1982–86; Zurich Life Assce Co. Ltd, 1970–87; Sealink UK Ltd, 1983–85; Caviapen Investments Ltd, 1993–97; Yamaichi Bank (UK) plc, 1994–98. Gen. Manager, British Railways Pension Funds, 1978–86; Chief Exec., IMRO, 1986–93. Chm., Post Office Users' Nat. Council, 1978–82. *Recreations:* music, contemporary art. *Club:* Reform.

**MORGAN, His Honour John Ambrose;** a Circuit Judge, 1990–2003; a Deputy Circuit Judge, 2003–09; *b* 22 Sept. 1934; *s* of Joseph Michael Morgan and Monica Morgan; *m* 1970, Rosalie Mary Tyson; two *s. Educ:* St Edward's Coll., Liverpool; Univ. of Liverpool (Emmott Meml Scholar 1953; Alsopp Prizewinner 1953; LLB 1955). Law Soc. Finals 1957 (Local Govt Prize). Nat. Service, RAF, 1958–60. Admitted Solicitor, 1958; practised in local govt and private practice, 1960–70; called to the Bar, Gray's Inn, 1970; N Circuit, 1970–90; Dep. Stipendiary Magistrate, 1982; Asst Recorder, 1983; Recorder, 1988. Chm. of Govs, St Edward's Coll., Liverpool, 1987–95. *Recreations:* Rugby Union football (Pres., Liverpool RFU, 1980–82), golf, cricket, music, amateur operatics. *Address:* Tarnbrick, 80 Beech Lane, Liverpool L18 3ER. *Clubs:* Athenæum (Liverpool) (Pres., 2010); Liverpool St Helen's Rugby Football, Woolton Golf, Sefton Cricket (Pres., 2003–06).
*See also F. V. Morgan.*

**MORGAN, John Christopher;** Chief Executive, Morgan Sindall Group plc, 1994–99 and since 2012 (Executive Chairman, 2000–12); *b* 31 Dec. 1955; *m* 1984, Rosalind Kendrew; two *s* one *d. Educ:* Peter Symonds Grammar Sch., Winchester; Univ. of Reading (BSc Estate Mgt 1977); Open Univ. (MBA 1994). Chairman: Morgan Lovell, 1977–94; Johnsons Freshly Squeezed Juice Ltd, 1985–96; Genetix plc, 2000–08. *Address:* Morgan Sindall Group plc, Kent House, 14–17 Market Place, W1W 8AJ. *T:* (020) 7307 9200.

**MORGAN, Jonathan;** Managing Consultant, Insight Wales Consulting Ltd, since 2011; Consultant, Practice Solutions Ltd, since 2011; *b* 12 Nov. 1974; *s* of Barrie and Linda Morgan. *Educ:* Bishop of Llandaff Church in Wales Sch., Cardiff; Cardiff Univ. (LLB Hons Law & Politics; MSc Econ European Policy). European Funding Officer, Cardiff Further Educn Coll., 1998–99. National Assembly for Wales: Mem. (C) S Wales Central, 1999–2007, Cardiff N, 2007–11; contested (C) Cardiff N, 2011. *Recreations:* theatre, golf, music. *Club:* Merthyr Conservative (Merthyr Tydfil).

**MORGAN, Julie;** Member (Lab) Cardiff North, National Assembly for Wales, since 2011; Deputy Minister for Health and Social Services, since 2018; *b* 2 Nov. 1944; *d* of late Jack Edwards and of Grace Edwards; *m* 1967, Rt Hon. (Hywel) Rhodri Morgan (*d* 2017); one *s* two *d. Educ:* Howell's Sch., Llandaff; KCL (BA Hons); Manchester Univ.; Cardiff Univ. (DipSocAdmin, CQSW). Sen. Social Worker, Barry, S Glam. Social Services, 1980–83; Principal Officer and Develt Officer, W Glam. CC, 1983–87; Asst Dir, Child Care, Barnardo's, 1987–97. Member (Lab): S Glam. Council, 1985–96; Cardiff UA, 1996–97. Contested (Lab) Cardiff N, 1992. MP (Lab) Cardiff North, 1997–2010; contested (Lab) same seat, 2010. *Address:* Lower House, Michaelston-le-Pit, Dinas Powys CF64 4HE; National Assembly for Wales, Cardiff Bay, Cardiff CF99 1NA. *W:* www.juliemorgan.org.

**MORGAN, Karen Jane,** OBE 1999; DL; Chairman of Trustees, The Converging World, since 2007; *b* 28 June 1945; *d* of Walter Anderson Caldwell and Jean Drummond Caldwell (*née* Hislop); *m* 1st, 1977, (Malcolm) John Methven (later Sir John Methven; he *d* 1980); three step *d*; 2nd, 1988, Andrew John Mandle Morgan; two step *s* two step *d. Educ:* St Leonard's Sch., St Andrews; Univ. of Edinburgh (BSc 1st Cl. Hons Chemistry). ICI Ltd, 1968–81. Director: Latchways Ltd, 1982–85; Southdown Bldg Soc., 1990–92 (Vice-Chm., 1991–92); Associate, Solomon Hare LLP, 1993–2005. Dir, Wessex Water Services Ltd, 1998–2005. Member: Bd, NRA, 1989–95; Bd, EA, 1995–98; Envmt Cttee, RSA, 1999–2005; Council, NERC, 2002–08. Trustee, 1992–2007, Vice-Chm., 2001–07, Water Aid; Chm., EcoAlert Ltd, 2007–10; Chm. and Dir, Sustainable Engine Systems Ltd, 2010–13; Chm., Aspire Glos Ltd, 2015–18. Mem. Council, CNAA, 1982–88; Comr, Fulbright Commn, 1983–87; Mem., Bd of Govs, Bristol Poly., 1989–92; University of West of England: Mem., 1992–2003, Dep. Chm., 1994–97, Chm., 1998–2003, Bd of Govs; Pro Chancellor, 2004–10; Mem., 1998–2003, Dep. Chm., 2000–02, Cttee of Univ. Chairmen; Member: Commn on Univ. Career Opportunity, 1999–2000; Jt Equality Steering Gp, 2001–03; Equality Challenge Unit Mgt Bd, 2003–06. Dir, At-Bristol, 2000–11; Trustee, Plymouth Marine Lab., 2005–12. Chm., Appeal Cttee, 2004–07, Vice Pres., 2007–, Penny Brohn Cancer Care (formerly Bristol Cancer Help Centre). Member: Governing Body, Colston's Collegiate Sch., 2004–13 (Chm., 2010–13); Governing Council, RAU (formerly RAC), Cirencester, 2004–13 (Vice Chm., 2005–10); Council, RSA, 2005–09; Adv. Bd, Cabot Inst., Univ. of Bristol, 2010–15; Council, Univ. of Gloucestershire, 2012– (Vice-Chair, 2015–). Trustee: Bath Festivals Trust, 1993–98; Colston's Foundn, 2010–; Friends of Cotswolds, 2014–; The Door, 2017–; Caring for Communities and People, 2019–; Patron, Ruskin Mill Trust, 2015–. FRSA 1998. Hon. DEd UWE, 2004. DL Glos, 2007. Freeman, 2001–03, Liveryman, 2003–12, Co. of Water Conservators; Mem., Soc. of Merchant Venturers, 2003–; Mem., Hon. Co. of Glos, 2008–. *Publications:* (contrib.) Time of Flight Mass Spectrometry, 1969. *Recreations:* music, sailing, ski-ing, travelling, water. *Address:* Little Skiveralls, Chalford Hill, Stroud, Glos GL6 8QJ. *Clubs:* Reform; Kandahar Ski; Downhill Only Ski; Royal Western Yacht, Clyde Cruising.

**MORGAN, Lisa Jayne;** Founder Director, Morgan-Knox Ltd, since 2010; *b* 28 May 1970; *m*; two step *d*. Buyer, Tandy, 1989–93; Gp Software Buyer, Dixons, 1993–97; GAME Group, 1997–2010: Hd, Buying, Electronics Boutique, 1997–98; Buying and Mktg Dir, 1998–2000; Commercial Dir, 2000–03; Dep. Chief Exec., 2003–06; Chief Exec., 2006–10. *Recreations:* horses, cooking, spending time with family.

**MORGAN, Dr Llewelyn William Goronwy;** Professor of Classical Languages and Literature, University of Oxford, since 2014; Tutorial Fellow in Classics, since 1997, and Vice-Principal, since 2018, Brasenose College, Oxford; *b* St Helens, 25 June 1968; *s* of William Geraint Morgan and Jill Morgan; *m* 1995, Andrea Mae Swinton; two *s. Educ:* Liverpool Coll.; Corpus Christi Coll., Oxford (BA 1990; MA); Trinity Coll., Cambridge (PhD 1995). Lectr, Dept of Classics, UCD, 1994–97; Lectr in Classical Langs and Lit., Univ. of Oxford, 2002–14. Philip Leverhulme Prize, 2004. *Publications:* Patterns of Redemption in Virgil's Georgics, 1999; Musa Pedestris: metre and meaning in Roman poetry, 2010; The Buddhas of Bamiyan, 2012. *Recreations:* walking the dog, broadcasting my love for the Greco-Latin classics across social media, anything but marking. *Address:* Brasenose College, Oxford OX1 4AJ. *T:* (01865) 277890. *E:* llewelyn.morgan@bnc.ox.ac.uk.

**MORGAN, Loraine;** District Judge (Magistrates' Courts) (formerly Metropolitan Stipendiary Magistrate), 1995–2019; *b* 2 Dec. 1953; *d* of late Enrico Bellisario and Elizabeth Bellisario (*née* Coyle); *m* 1976, Captain Dai Morgan, RN. *Educ:* St Augustine's Priory, Ealing; Univ. of Exeter; Coll. of Law, Guildford. Admitted Solicitor, 1981; Partner, Reynolds & Hetherington, Fareham 1982–86, Allsworth & Spears, Fareham, 1986–88; Solicitor Advocate, 1988–95; Co-founder and Dir, Just Advocates Ltd, 1991–95; Plate Judge Advocate, 1996–2001; Asst Recorder, 1999–2000; a Recorder, 2000. Mem., Crown Court Rules Cttee, 1994. Vice-Pres., Bracton Law Soc., 1974–75; Cttee Mem., Hampshire Inc. Law Soc., 1990–94; Sec. and Chm., Southampton Criminal Courts Solicitors' Assoc., 1990–94; Vice-Chm., Criminal Law Solicitors' Assoc., 1991–94. *Recreations:* good wine, good food, the company of good friends. *Club:* Army and Navy.

**MORGAN, Marilynne Ann,** CB 1996; Solicitor to the Departments for Work and Pensions (formerly of Social Security) and of Health, and Head of Law and Special Policy Group, Department for Work and Pensions (formerly Department of Social Security), 1997–2004; *b* 22 June 1946; *d* of late J. Emlyn Williams and Roma Elizabeth Williams (*née* Ellis); *m* 1970, Nicholas Alan, *e s* of Rear-Adm. Sir Patrick Morgan, KCVO, CB, DSC. *Educ:* Gads Hill Place, Higham-by-Rochester; Bedford Coll., Univ. of London (BA Hons History). Called to the Bar, Middle Temple, 1972, Bencher, 2002 (Lent Reader, 2012). Res. Asst, Special Historical Sect., FCO, 1967–71; Department of Health and Social Security: Legal Asst, 1973; Sen. Legal Asst, 1978; Asst Solicitor, 1982; Under Sec. and Principal Asst Solicitor, 1985–91, DSS, 1988–91, DoE, 1991–92; Department of the Environment: Solicitor and Legal Advr, 1992–97; Chm., Departmental Task Force, 1994–95; Sen. Dir, Legal and Corporate Services Gp, 1996–97. Non-exec. Dir, Treasury Solicitor's Dept, 2004–10. Vice-Chm. 1983–84, Chm. 1984–86, Legal Sect. of Assoc. of First Div. Civil Servants. Mem., General Council of the Bar, 1987–92. Hon. Legal Advr, CS Sports Council, 2006–. Trustee/Director: Alzheimer's Soc., 2003–09 (Chm., Nominations Cttee, 2005–11); Ambache Orchestra, 2003–06; Alzheimer's Brain Bank UK, 2006–11; Bucks Historic Churches Trust, 2013–; Trustee, Middle Temple Charity Funds, 2014–; Chm., Friends of Bucks Historic Churches, 2008–. *Publications:* contributor, Halsbury's Laws of England, 1982, 1986; articles in learned jls. *Recreation:* homely pursuits. *Club:* University Women's (Trustee, 2009–19; Chm. Trustees, 2011–19).

**MORGAN, Martin Gerard;** Principal Social Worker, Child Care Social Services, Belfast Trust, since 2008; *b* 25 Oct. 1966; *s* of Robert Morgan and Kathleen Morgan; *m* 2001, Dympna O'Hara. *Educ:* Queen's Univ., Belfast (BA Hons Inf. Mgt; MSW; DipSW). Child Protection Investigation Team, 2002–03, Sen. Social Worker, 2005–08, Child Care Social Services. Mem. (SDLP), Belfast City Council, 1993–2005; Lord Mayor of Belfast, 2003–04. Pt-time columnist on NI politics. *Recreations:* golf, athletics, reading political biographies.

**MORGAN, Prof. Mary Susanna,** PhD; FBA 2002; Professor of the History and Philosophy of Economics, London School of Economics and Political Science, University of London, since 1999. *Educ:* LSE (BSc 1978; PhD 1984). Res. Asst to Economist, Citibank, London, 1973–75; Exchange Control Dept, Bank of England, 1978–79; Res. Officer, Dept of Econs, LSE, 1979–82, 1983–84; Lectr, Dept of Econs and Related Studies, Univ. of York, 1984–87; Vis. Asst Prof., Dept of Econs, Duke Univ., 1987; Lectr, Dept of Econ. History, 1988–94, Reader in History of Econs, 1994–99, Chm., Dept of Econ. Hist., 2002–05, LSE. Prof. of History of Econ. Thought and Philosophy of Econ. Sci., Univ. of Amsterdam (part-time), 1992–99. *Publications:* (ed jtly) The Probabilistic Revolution, vol. II: ideas in the sciences, 1987; The History of Econometric Ideas, 1990; (ed jtly) Higgling: transactors and their markets in the history of economics, 1994; (jtly) The Foundations of Econometric Analysis, 1995; (ed jtly) From Interwar Pluralism to Post-War Neoclassicism, 1998; (jtly) Methodology and Tacit Knowledge, 1999; (ed jtly) Models as Mediators, 1999; (ed jtly) Empirical Models and Policy Making, 2000; (ed jtly) The Age of Economic Measurement, 2001; (ed jtly) How Well Do Facts Travel?, 2011; The World in a Model: how economists work and think, 2012; articles in jls. *Address:* Department of Economic History, London School of Economics and Political Science, Houghton Street, WC2A 2AE.

**MORGAN, Matthew Spencer Richard;** Headmaster, Sir Thomas Rich's School, Gloucester, since 2013; *b* Oxford, 28 Sept. 1975; *s* of Richard Arthur George Morgan and Diana Elizabeth Morgan. *Educ:* Bedford Sch.; Royal Holloway, Univ. of London (BSc Hons 1997); Hughes Hall, Cambridge (PGCE 1998); Oxford Brookes Univ. (MA Educn (Distinction) 2002). NPQH 2006; CGeog 2009. Teacher of Geog., 1998–2003, Sen. Teacher, 2003–07, Royal Latin Sch., Buckingham; Dep. Headmaster, Sir Thomas Rich's Sch., 2007–13. FRGS 2006. *Publications:* (contrib.) Assessment in RE: a practical guide, 2019; articles in Teaching Geography, 2000–07. *Recreations:* walking, cooking, conducting. *Address:* Sir Thomas Rich's School, Oakleaze, Longlevens, Gloucester GL2 0LF. *T:* (01452) 338431. *E:* mm@strs.org.uk.

**MORGAN, Michael David;** Development Director, Anglia Housing Association Group, 1993–98; *b* 19 Jan. 1942; *s* of Edward Arthur and Winifred Maud Morgan; *m* 1980, Ljiljana Radojcic; three *d*. *Educ:* Royal Liberty Sch., Romford; Prince Rupert Sch., Wilhemshaven, FRG; Coll. of Estate Management, London Univ. (BSc Est. Man.). FRICS. Sheffield City Council, 1964–67; Derby Borough Council, 1967–70; Telford Develt Corp., 1970–92 (Chief Exec. and Gen. Manager, 1986–92, retd). *Recreations:* cricket, jogging, gardening.

**MORGAN, Prof. Michael John,** PhD, ScD; FRS 2005; Professor of Visual Psychophysics, City, University of London (formerly City University), since 2000; *b* 25 Aug. 1942; *m* 1996, Prof. Linda Partridge (*see* Dame L. Partridge). *Educ:* Queens' Coll., Cambridge (BA 1964; PhD 1969; ScD 1994). Asst in Res., 1965–71, Lectr, 1971–78, Univ. of Cambridge; Fellow, Queens' Coll., Cambridge, 1967–74; Professor of Psychology: Univ. of Durham, 1978–81; UCL, 1981–89; Professorial Fellow, Univ. of Edinburgh, 1989–93; Prof. of Visual Psychophysics, UCL, 1993–2000. *Publications:* Molyneux's Question: vision, touch and the philosophy of perception, 1977; The Space Between Our Ears, 2003; contrib. learned jls. *Address:* Division of Optometry and Visual Science, City, University of London, Northampton Square, EC1V 0HB.

**MORGAN, Rt Hon. Nicola (Ann), (Rt Hon. Nicky);** PC 2014; MP (C) Loughborough, since 2010; Secretary of State for Digital, Culture, Media and Sport, since 2019; *b* Kingston upon Thames, 10 Oct. 1972; *d* of Peter M. Griffith and Jennifer C. Griffith; *m* 2000, Jonathan Morgan; one *s*. *Educ:* Surbiton High Sch.; St Hugh's Coll., Oxford (MA Law); Guildford Law Sch. Admitted as solicitor, 1996; in practice as solicitor, specialising in corporate law: Theodore Goddard, 1994–97; Allen & Overy, 1998–2002; Travers Smith, 2002–10. An Asst Govt Whip, 2012–13; Economic Sec., 2013–14, Financial Sec., 2014, HM Treasury; Sec. of State for Educn, and Minister for Women and Equality, 2014–16. Chm., Treasury Select Cttee, 2017–19. *Publications:* Taught not Caught: educating for 21st century character, 2017. *Recreations:* running, ski-ing, spending time with family. *Address:* House of Commons, SW1A 0AA. *T:* (020) 7219 7224, (constituency) (01509) 262723. *E:* nicky.morgan.mp@parliament.uk.

**MORGAN, Patrick;** HM Diplomatic Service, retired; Ambassador to El Salvador, 1999–2003; *b* 31 Jan. 1944; *s* of Matthew Morgan and Margaret (*née* Docherty); *m* 1966, Marlene Collins Beaton (*d* 2011); two *s* three *d*. *Educ:* St Columba's High Sch., Greenock. BoT, 1963–64; CRO, 1964–65; FCO, 1965–67; British Embassy: Bonn, 1967–69; Kuwait, 1969–71; La Paz, 1972–75; FCO, 1975–79; British Embassy: Washington DC, 1979–83; Jakarta, 1983–86; FCO, 1987–92; Ambassador to Honduras, 1992–95; Counsellor and Dep. Hd of Mission, Abu Dhabi, 1995–98; Counsellor, FCO, 1998–99. Governor, Al Khubairat Community Sch., Abu Dhabi, 1995–98. *Recreations:* swimming, reading, music, travel. *Address:* 4 Den Close, Beckenham, Kent BR3 6RP.

**MORGAN, Hon. Sir Paul (Hyacinth),** Kt 2007; **Hon. Mr Justice Morgan;** a Judge of the High Court, Chancery Division, since 2007; *b* 17 Aug. 1952; *s* of Daniel Morgan and Veronica Mary (*née* Elder); *m* 1980, Sheila Ruth Harvey; three *s*. *Educ:* St Columb's Coll., Londonderry; Peterhouse, Cambridge (BA 1974; MA 1979). Called to the Bar, Lincoln's Inn, 1975, Bencher, 2001. QC 1992; a Dep. High Court Judge, 2001–07. Dep. Chm., Agricl Land Tribunal, 1999–2007. *Publications:* (ed jtly) Megarry on Rent Acts, 11th edn, 1988; (ed jtly) Woodfall on Landlord and Tenant, 28th edn, 1990 (looseleaf); (ed jtly) Gale on Easements, 18th edn 2008 to 20th edn (ed) 2017; (ed jtly) Fisher & Lightwood's Law of Mortgage, 13th edn 2010 and 14th edn 2014. *Address:* Rolls Building, 7 Rolls Building, Fetter Lane, EC4A 1NL.

**MORGAN, Prof. Peter John,** PhD; FRSE; Director, Rowett Institute of Nutrition and Health (formerly Rowett Research Institute), since 1999, and Professor, since 2008, University of Aberdeen (Vice-Principal, 2008–14); *b* 23 Feb. 1956; *s* of Dr John W. W. Morgan and Patricia M. Morgan; *m* 1991, Prof. Denise Kelly; one *s* one *d*. *Educ:* Queen Mary Coll., London (BSc); Univ. of Aberdeen (PhD 1981). FRSE 2002. AFRC post-doctoral res. asst, Dept of Zool., Univ. of Aberdeen, 1981–85; Rowett Research Institute, Aberdeen: SSO, 1985–89; PSO, 1989–96; Leader, Molecular Neuroendocrinology Res. Gp, 1991–97; Head, Molecular Neuroendocrinology Unit and Mem., Sen. Mgt Gp, 1997–99. Hon. Prof., Dept of Zoology, Univ. of Aberdeen, 1999–2008. Trustee, Rowett Res. Inst. Charity, 2008–. *Recreations:* music (pianist), squash, swimming, travel. *Address:* Rowett Institute of Nutrition and Health, University of Aberdeen, Foresterhill, Aberdeen AB25 2ZD. *T:* (01224) 438663.

**MORGAN, Peter William Lloyd,** MBE 2003; Director-General, Institute of Directors, 1989–94; *b* 9 May 1936; *s* of late Matthew Morgan and of Margaret Gwynneth (*née* Lloyd); *m* 1964, Elisabeth Susanne Davis; three *d*. *Educ:* Llandovery Coll.; Trinity Hall, Cambridge. Joined IBM UK Ltd, 1959; Data Processing Sales Dir, 1971–74; Gp Dir of Marketing, IBM Europe, Paris, 1975–80; Executive Director: IBM UK Ltd, 1983–87; IBM UK Holdings Ltd, 1987–89; National Provident Institution: Dir, 1990–99; Chm., 1996–99; Underwriting Mem., 1987–, Ext. Mem. Council, 2000–09, Lloyd's. Chairman: South Wales Electricity PLC, 1996 (Dir, 1989–96); Pace Micro Technology plc, 1996–2000; Director: Hyder Consulting (formerly Firth Holdings) plc, 1994–2009; Baltimore Technologies plc (formerly Zergo Holdings), 1994–2003 (Dep. Chm., 1998–2000; Chm., 2000–03); Assoc. of Lloyd's Mems, 1997–2015 (Chm., 2010–12); Oxford Instruments plc, 2000–09; Strategic Thought Gp plc, 2004–12 (Chm., 2004–09). Public Mem., Network Rail, 2012–15. Mem., European Econ. and Social Cttee, Brussels, 1994–2002, 2006–15. Liveryman, Co. of Inf. Technologists, 1992– (Master, 2002–03). Radical of the Year, Radical Soc., 1990. *Publications:* Alarming Drum, 2005. *Recreations:* history, travelling, gardening, country house opera, drinking wine, watching Rugby, walking dogs. *Address:* Fairwood, Grayswood Road, Haslemere, Surrey GU27 2BU. *Club:* Oxford and Cambridge.

**MORGAN, Piers Stefan;** broadcaster and journalist; *b* 30 March 1965; *s* of Glynne and Gabrielle Pughe-Morgan; *m* 1st, 1991, Marion Elizabeth Shalloe (marr. diss. 2008); three *s*; 2nd, 2010, Celia, *d* of George Gordon Harvey Walden, *qv*; one *d*. *Educ:* Chailey Comprehensive Sch.; Lewes Priory Sixth Form Coll.; Harlow Journalism Coll. With Lloyd's of London, 1985–87; Reporter, Surrey and S London Newspapers, 1987–89; Showbusiness Editor, The Sun, 1989–94; Editor: News of the World, 1994–95; Daily Mirror, 1995–2004. Judge, TV series: America's Got Talent, 2006–10; Britain's Got Talent, 2007–10; Presenter, TV Series: Piers on…, 2009; Piers Morgan's Life Stories, 2009–; When Piers Met…, 2009; Piers Morgan Live, CNN, 2011–14; Killer Women with Piers Morgan, 2016, 2017; Serial Killers with Piers Morgan, 2017–; Co-Presenter, Good Morning Britain, 2015–. Editor of the Year, Newspaper Focus Awards, 1994. *Publications:* Private Lives of the Stars, 1990; Secret Lives of the Stars, 1991; Phillip Schofield: to dream a dream, 1992; Take That: our story, 1993; Take That: on the road, 1994; Va Va Voom: a fan's diary of Arsenal's invincible season, 2004; The Insider: the private diaries of a scandalous decade, 2005; Don't You Know Who I Am?, 2007; God Bless America: misadventures of a big mouth Brit, 2009; Shooting Straight, 2013. *Recreations:* cricket, Arsenal FC.

**MORGAN, Richard Hugo Lyndon;** QC 2011; *b* London, 30 April 1963; *s* of John and Anne Lyndon Morgan; *m* 1996, Monica Marie Coombs; one *s* one *d*. *Educ:* St Edward's Sch., Oxford; St Edmund Hall, Oxford (sent down); Univ. of Buckingham (LLB 1985); Fitzwilliam Coll., Cambridge (LLM 1987). Called to the Bar, Gray's Inn, 1988; in practice as barrister, 1989–. Trustee/Dir, Action for Stammering Children (formerly Assoc. for Res. into Stammering in Childhood), 2006–13. *Recreations:* travel, casual sport, family and friends. *Address:* Maitland Chambers, 7 Stone Buildings, Lincoln's Inn, WC2A 3SZ. *T:* (020) 7406 1200, *Fax:* (020) 7406 1300. *E:* rmorgan@maitlandchambers.com.

**MORGAN, Richard Martin,** MA; Warden, Radley College, 1991–2000; *b* 25 June 1940; *s* of His Honour Trevor Morgan, MC, QC, and late Leslie Morgan; *m* 1968, Margaret Kathryn, *d* of late Anthony Agutter and of Mrs Launcelot Fleming; three *d*. *Educ:* Sherborne Sch.; Caius Coll., Cambridge (MA, DipEd); York Univ. Assistant Master, Radley Coll., 1963; Housemaster, 1969; Headmaster, Cheltenham College, 1978–90. Member, Adv. Council, Understanding British Industry, 1977–79. Pres., Mencap, S Wilts, 2004–12; Chm., Prince's Trust, Salisbury, 2004–08. Governor: Clifton Coll., 2001– (Chm., 2014–16); Sherborne Sch., 2002–10. JP Glos, 1978–90. *Recreations:* reading, music, Anthony Powell Soc. *Address:* Warmans, Bodenham, Salisbury, Wilts SP5 4EU. *T:* (01722) 338868. *Clubs:* Free Foresters, Jesters'.

**MORGAN, Robin Milne;** Principal: Daniel Stewart's and Melville College, Edinburgh, 1977–89; The Mary Erskine School, 1979–89; *b* 2 Oct. 1930; *o s* of Robert Milne Morgan and Aida Forsyth Morgan; *m* 1955, Fiona Bruce MacLeod Douglas (*d* 2008); three *s* one *d*. *Educ:* Mackie Academy, Stonehaven; Aberdeen Univ. (MA); London Univ. (BA, External). Nat. Service, 2nd Lieut The Gordon Highlanders, 1952–54; Asst Master: Arden House Prep. Sch., 1955–60; George Watson's Coll., 1960–71; Headmaster, Campbell Coll., Belfast, 1971–76. *Recreations:* music, archaeology, fishing, entertaining my ten grandchildren. *Address:* 1c Old Mansion House, Newbyth, East Linton, E Lothian EH40 3DU.

**MORGAN, Robin Richard;** author and journalist; Editor, The Sunday Times Magazine, 1992–93 and 1995–2009; Chief Executive Officer, Iconic Images Inc., since 2013; Managing Director, Morgan Media Partners, since 2013; *b* 16 Sept. 1953; *s* of Raymond Morgan and Jean Edith Bennett; *m*; two *s* one *d*. *Educ:* King Edward VI Grammar Sch., Stourbridge, W Midlands. County Express, Stourbridge, 1971–73; Evening Echo, Hemel Hempstead, 1973–79; Sunday Times, London, 1979–89: Reporter, 1979–83; Dep. News Editor, 1983–85; Insight Editor, 1985–87; Features Editor, Sunday Times, 1987–89; Editor, Sunday Express, 1989–91; Associate Editor, Sunday Times, 1991–92; Editorial Dir designate, Reader's Digest, 1993–94. Contributing Editor: GQ Magazine, 1999–2003; Departures Magazine, 2009–. Campaigning Journalist of the Year: (commended) 1982; (winner) 1983. *Publications:* (jtly) The Falklands War, 1982; (jtly) Rainbow Warrior, 1986; (jtly) Bullion, 1988; (ed) Manpower, 1988; (jtly) Ambush, 1989; (jtly) The Book of Movie Biographies, 1997; (ed) Sinatra: Frank and friendly, 2007; The Eltonography, 2008; All About Bond, 2012; (jtly) 1963: The Year of the Revolution: how youth changed the world, 2013; (jtly) Sinatra, 2015; (jtly) Two Days That Rocked the World, 2015; (jtly) Breaking Stones: a band on the brink of stardom, 2016; (jtly) Bowie By O'Neill, 2016; (jtly) Groupies and Other Electric Ladies, 2016; (jtly) Essential Marilyn Monroe: Milton H. Greene - 50 sessions, 2017; (jtly) Burning Desire: the Jimi Hendrix experience through the lens of Ed Caraeff, 2017; (jtly) Iggy and the Stooges: one night at The Whisky 1970, 2017; (jtly)

Picturing Prince: an intimate portrait, 2017; (jtly) When Ziggy Played The Marquee, 2017; (jtly) Through Her Lens: the photographs of Eva Sereny, 2018; (jtly) Led Zeppelin Live: 1975–77, 2018. *Recreations:* cinema, US politics, modern American fiction, travel. *Address:* Iconic Images Inc., 63 Lisson Street, NW1 5DA.

**MORGAN, Prof. Rodney Emrys;** Professor of Criminal Justice, University of Bristol, 1990–2001, now Emeritus; Visiting Professor: Cardiff University, 2008–13; University of Sussex, since 2012; *b* 16 Feb. 1942; *s* of William Emrys Morgan and Jessmine Lilian (*née* Reed); *m* 1966, Karin Birgitta Lang; three *s*. *Educ:* Haberdashers' Aske's Sch., Mill Hill; Paston Sch., N Walsham; Univ. of Southampton (BSc; Dip. Applied Social Studies). Lectr, Univ. of Southampton, 1971–72; Lectr, then Sen. Lectr, Univ. of Bath, 1972–89; University of Bristol: Reader, 1989–90; Dean of Law, 1992–95. HM Chief Inspector of Probation for England and Wales, 2001–04; Chm., Youth Justice Bd for England and Wales, 2004–07; Advr on criminal justice inspection, MoJ, 2007–11. Visiting Fellow: Univ. of Oxford, 1985–87; Human Rights Implementation Centre, Univ. of Bristol, 2013–; Centre for Internat. Prison Studies, Univ. of Essex, 2013–; Visiting Professor: Univ. of WA, 1991; Univ. of Freiburg, 1995; Univ. of Onati, 1996; Harvard Univ., 1996; LSE, 2007–11. Mem., Daniel Morgan Ind. Panel, 2014–19. Mem., Academic Adv. Cttee, Cumberland Lodge, 2010–16. Trustee: King's Coll. Centre for Criminol Res., 2003–11; Inst. for Criminal Policy Res., Birkbeck, Univ. of London, 2003–12; Police Foundn, 2006–; Dance Utd, 2006–14; Bath Philharmonia, 2007–15; Bath Alcohol and Drugs Adv. Service, 2007–12; Bath Festivals Trust, 2008–13; Criminal Justice Alliance, 2019–; Pres., Mentoring Plus, 2007–. *Publications:* (ed jtly) Oxford Handbook of Criminology, 1994, 5th edn 2012; The Politics of Sentencing Reform, 1995; The Future of Policing, 1997; Preventing Torture, 1998; Protecting Prisoners, 1999; Crime Unlimited, 1999; Combating Torture in Europe, 2001; Handbook of Probation, 2007; Preventing Torture in Europe, 2018; contrib. numerous articles to law, social policy and criminology jls. *Recreations:* sailing, theatre, music, walking, gardening, taking risks. *Address:* Beech House, Lansdown Road, Bath BA1 5EG. *T:* (01225) 316676. *E:* karin.rod@freeuk.com.

**MORGAN, Roger;** *see* Morgan, E. R.

**MORGAN, Sadie;** Founding Director, dRMM, since 1995; *b* Kent, 28 Feb. 1969; *d* of Jack Morgan and Caroline Morgan (*née* Darke); two *d*. *Educ:* Kingston Poly. (BA Hons Interior Design); Royal Coll. of Art (MA Interior Design). Vis. Prof., Univ. of Westminster, 2017–. Mayor's Design Advr, GLA, 2017–. Member: Nat. Infrastructure Commn, 2015–; Thames Estuary 2050 Growth Commn, 2016–18. Ind. Design Chair, HS2, 2015–. Mem., Adv. Bd, Central London Partnership 2012 Legacy Strategic Taskforce, 2010. Chair of Examiners: Cardiff Univ., 2009–11; Sch. of Architecture, Kent Univ., 2011–; Ext. Examr, Univ. of Westminster, 2011–15. Member: Advisory Board: RIBA Nat. Awards Adv. Panel, 2013–; Degree Awarding Powers, AA, 2014; Validation Bd, MA Interior Design, RCA, 2010; Bd, Homes England, 2019–. Non-exec. Dir, Major Projects Assoc., 2017–. Architecture Association: Pres., 2013–15; Chair, Past Presidents' Adv. Council, 2013–; Hon. Treas., Council, 2009–12; Dir, AA Pubns, 2013–. Mem., Adv. Bd, London Fest. Arch., 2008. Trustee, Creative Educn Trust, 2013–15 (Chm., Estates and Bldg Cttee, 2013–15). FRSA 2012. Hon. Dr Southbank, 2016. *Recreations:* cycling, sailing. *Address:* dRMM Ltd, 136–148 Magdalen House, Tooley Street, SE1 2TU. *T:* (020) 7803 0777. *E:* mail@drmm.co.uk.

**MORGAN, Sarah Mary;** QC 2011; a Recorder, since 2009; *b* Pembroke, 17 Sept. 1964; *d* of Malcolm Morgan and Georgina Morgan (*née* Duhig). *Educ:* Brunel Univ. (LLB Hons). Called to the Bar, Gray's Inn, 1988. *Recreations:* being, as often as possible, in the Caribbean Sea. *Address:* 1GC | Family Law, 10 Lincoln's Inn Fields, WC2A 3BP. *T:* (020) 7797 7900, *Fax:* (020) 7797 7929. *E:* morgan@1gc.com.

**MORGAN, Dame Shan (Elizabeth),** DCMG 2017 (CMG 2012); Permanent Secretary, Welsh Government, since 2017; *b* 12 March 1955; *d* of Air Cdre Alun Morgan, CBE and Yvonne Morgan (*née* Davies). *Educ:* South Park High Sch., Lincoln; High Wycombe Grammar Sch.; Royal Latin Sch.; Univ. of Kent (BA Hons 1977). Manpower Services Commn, subseq. Employment Dept, then DfES, 1977–97; Eur. Commn DG V, 1984–87; Pvte Sec. to Perm. Sec., Dept of Employment, 1990–92; Govt Office for London, 1992–94; UK Govt Deleg. to ILO Governing Body, 1994–97; seconded to FCO, 1997; First Sec., Labour and Social Affairs, Paris, 1997–2001; Counsellor, Social, Envmtl and Regl Affairs, UK Perm. Repn, Brussels, 2001–06; transferred FCO, 2006; Dir, EU, FCO, 2006–08; Ambassador to Argentina and (non-resident) to Paraguay, 2008–12; Dep. Perm. Rep., UK Repn to the EU, 2012–17. FRSA. Hon. DCL Kent, 2014. *Recreations:* walking, learning Welsh, cycling. *Address:* Welsh Government, Cathays Park, Cardiff CF10 3NQ.

**MORGAN, Stephen;** MP (Lab) Portsmouth South, since 2017; *b* Portsmouth, 1981; *s* of Trevor Morgan. *Educ:* Priory Sch., Southsea; Portsmouth Coll.; Univ. of Bristol (BA Politics and Sociol.); Goldsmith's Coll., London (MA Politics). Strategy Advr, Chief Exec.'s Office, 2003–06, Projects Manager, 2006–08, Portsmouth CC; Hd, Community Engagement, RBK&C, 2008–15; Chief Exec., Basingstoke Voluntary Action, 2015–17. Mem. (Lab), Portsmouth CC, 2016–. *Address:* House of Commons, SW1A 0AA.

**MORGAN, Stephen Peter,** CBE 2016 (OBE 1992); Chairman: Redrow plc, 2009–19 (Founder and Chairman, Redrow Group plc, 1974–2000); Bridgemere Group of Companies, since 1996; *b* 25 Nov. 1952; *s* of Peter and Mary Morgan; *m* 1st, 1973, Pamela Borrett; one *s* one *d*; 2nd, 2002, Fiona Elspeth, (Didy) Boustead; one *s* one *d*; 3rd, 2016, Sally Julia Ffoulkes-Davies (*née* Findlay). *Educ:* Colwyn High Sch.; Liverpool Poly. Founded Redrow Gp plc, 1974. Owner, Carden Park Hotel, nr Chester, 2006–; owner, Wolverhampton Wanderers FC, 2007–16 (Chm., 2007–15). Founder, 2001, Chm. of Trustees, 2002–, Steve Morgan Foundn (over £300 million donated to good causes). FCIOB 2000. Hon. Fellow: John Moores Univ., 1993; NE Wales Inst. of Higher Educn, 1993; Cardiff Univ., 2005; Wolverhampton Univ., 2010. Hon. DBA Chester, 2016. *Publications:* The Redrow Way, 1999. *Recreations:* football, Rugby, ski-ing, walking, golf.

**MORGAN, Sir Terence Keith, (Sir Terry),** Kt 2016; CBE 2009; FREng, FIET; Chairman, Ricardo plc, since 2014; *b* 28 Dec. 1948; *s* of Keith and Ivy Morgan; *m* 1970, Ann Jones; one *s* one *d*. *Educ:* Univ. of Birmingham (MSc 1977). FIET (FIEE 1990); FREng (FEng 1995). Leyland Bus Co., 1980–85; Production Dir, Land Rover, 1985–91; Man. Dir, Land Rover Vehicles, Rover Gp, 1991–95; BAE Systems: Man. Dir, Royal Ordnance, 1995–97; Gp HR Dir, 1997–2000; Gp Man. Dir Ops, 2000–02; CEO, Tube Lines Ltd, 2002–09. Chairman: Crossrail, 2009–18; London City Airport, 2017–18; HS2 Ltd, 2018, Chm., Nat. Coll. for High Speed Rail. *Recreations:* Rugby, golf.

**MORGAN, (Thomas) Jeremy;** QC 2003; *b* 18 Aug. 1948; *s* of Thomas Morgan and Jean Morgan (*née* Campbell); *m* 1998, Delia Dumaresq; one *d*, and one step *s*. *Educ:* Loretto Sch.; Exeter Coll., Oxford (BA Greats); Univ. of Kent (BA Law). FCIArb 1998. Admitted solicitor, 1976; Solicitor: Garratt Lane Law Centre, Wandsworth, 1976–80; Southwark Law Project, 1980–82; sole practitioner, 1982–89; called to the Bar, Middle Temple, 1989; in practice as barrister, 1990–2013. Mem., Treasury Panel of Counsel, 1997–2003. *Recreations:* Italy, cinema, windsurfing, ballet.

**MORGAN, Most Rev. Thomas Oliver;** Archbishop of Saskatoon and Metropolitan of the Ecclesiastical Province of Rupert's Land, 2000–03; Interim Rector and Dean, St John's Cathedral, Saskatoon, 2006–07 and 2011–12; *b* 20 Jan. 1941; *s* of Charles Edwin Morgan and Amy Amelia (*née* Hoyes); *m* 1963, Lillian Marie (*née* Textor); two *s* one *d*. *Educ:* Univ. of Saskatchewan (BA 1962); King's College, London (BD 1965); Tyndale Hall, Bristol (GOE 1966). Curate, Church of the Saviour, Blackburn, Lancs, 1966–69; Rector: Porcupine Plain, Sask, Canada, 1969–73; Kinistino, 1973–77; Shellbrook, 1977–83; Archdeacon of Indian Missions, Saskatchewan, 1983–85; Bishop of Saskatchewan, 1985–93; Bishop of Saskatoon, 1993–2003. Hon. DD Coll. of Emmanuel and St Chad, Saskatoon, 1986.

**MORGAN, Tony;** Chief Executive, Industrial Society, 1994–2000; *b* 24 Aug. 1931; *s* of Arthur James and Violet Morgan; *m* 1955, Valerie Anne Williams; three *s*. *Educ:* Hereford High Sch.; Westcliff High Sch. Chm. and Chief Exec. Officer, Purle Bros Holdings, 1964–71; Dep. Chm., Wimpey Waste Management, 1974–81; Dir, Redland plc, 1971–73; Founder and Dir, Morgan Hemingway Investment Bank, 1973–78; working in California for non-profit organisations, incl. Hunger Project and Breakthrough Foundn, 1981–84; Chm., Wistech, 1984–90; Dir, Wraytech UK, 1996–99. Governor, BBC, 1972–77. Non-exec. Chm., Octopus Apollo VCT3 (formerly Octopus Protected VCT) plc, 2006–17 (non-exec. Dir, 2012–17); non-executive Director: Alexander Corp., 1990–99; Quickheart Ltd, 2001–; Phoenix Venture Capital Trust, 2003–10; Re-Energy plc, 2006–09; Partner, Latitude Strategy Consulting, 2000–05. Sailed Olympic Games, Tokyo; Silver Medal, Flying Dutchman, 1964; Jt Yachtsman of the Year, 1965; Member: British Olympic Yachting Appeal, 1970; Royal Yachting Assoc. Council, 1968–72. Chairman: Hunger Project Trust, 1984–89; Grit (formerly Youth at Risk), 1996–. FRSA. *Publications:* various technical papers. *Recreations:* squash, ski-ing, sailing, gardening, rowing. *Address:* The Old Dairy, Model Farm, Sutton Road, Cookham SL6 9QX. *T:* (01628) 529635. *Club:* Royal Thames Yacht.

**MORGAN, Rt Rev. Mgr Vaughan Frederick John,** CBE 1982; Parish Priest, St Teresa's Charlbury, 1997–2007; *b* Upper Hutt, New Zealand, 21 March 1931; *o s* of late Godfrey Frederick Vaughan Morgan and Violet (Doreen) Vaughan Morgan. *Educ:* The Oratory Sch., S Oxon; Innsbruck Univ. Ordained, 1957; Archdiocese of St Andrews and Edinburgh, 1959–62; entered Royal Navy as Chaplain, 1962; Prin. RC Chaplain (Naval), and Vicar Gen. for RN, 1979–84; Chaplain, The Oratory Sch., 1984–97. Chaplain to High Sheriff of Oxfordshire, 2000–01. Prelate of Honour to HH Pope John Paul II, 1979. *Publications:* contribs to journals. *Recreations:* music, swimming, painting, heraldry. *Address:* Flat 28, Diamond Court, 153 Banbury Road, Oxford OX2 7AA. *T:* (01865) 516672. *Club:* Army and Navy.

**MORGAN, Prof. William Basil;** Professor of Geography, 1971–92, Professor Emeritus, since 1988, and Head of Geography Department, 1982–87, King's College London; *b* 22 Jan. 1927; *s* of William George Morgan and Eunice Mary (*née* Heys); *m* 1954, Joy Gardner (*d* 2004); one *s* one *d*. *Educ:* King Edward's Sch., Birmingham; Jesus Coll., Oxford (MA); PhD Glasgow. Assistant, Glasgow Univ., 1948; Lecturer: University Coll., Ibadan, Nigeria, 1953; Univ. of Birmingham, 1959; Reader in Geography, KCL, 1967. Participant in various UN university res. projects and conferences. *Publications:* (with J. C. Pugh) West Africa, 1969; (with R. J. C. Munton) Agricultural Geography, 1971; Agriculture in the Third World: a spatial analysis, 1978; (with R. P. Moss) Fuelwood and rural energy production and supply in the humid tropics, 1981; contribs to geographical and other learned jls and to various conf. collections. *Recreation:* development geography. *Address:* 57 St Augustine's Avenue, South Croydon, Surrey CR2 6JQ. *T:* (020) 8688 5687. *E:* williammorgan@sky.com.

**MORGAN, Prof. (William) John,** PhD; Professor of Comparative Education, 1995–2015, and UNESCO Professor of Political Economy of Education, 2005–15, University of Nottingham, now Emeritus Professor; Hon. Professor, Cardiff University, since 2015; *b* Rhymney, Wales, 4 Nov. 1946; *s* of late Glyndwr Morgan and Kathleen Morgan (*née* Evans); *m* 1975, Joyce Roberts; one *s* one *d*. *Educ:* Lewis Sch., Pengam (Hugh Griffiths Hist. Prize; R. W. Jones Meml Prize); University Coll. of Swansea (Open Scholar; BA Jt Hons 1968; PGCE 1969); Jesus Coll., Oxford (Postgrad. Res.); University Coll., Cardiff (MEd 1979; Naughton Faculty Prize); Univ. of Nottingham (PhD 1994). Tutor Organiser, WEA, 1971–73; Lectr, then Sen. Lectr, Coll. of Technol., Cardiff, 1973–79; University of Nottingham: Lectr, then Sen. Lectr, 1979–95; Actg Dir, Inst. of Asian Pacific Studies, 1996–99; Dir, Centre for Comparative Educn Res., 1999–2009. Hon. Res. Fellow, University Coll. of Swansea, 1987; Visiting Professor: Univ. of Kerala, 1994; Centre for Adv. Studies in Soc. Scis, Univ. of Cordoba, Argentina, 1996; Comparative Educn Soc. of Asia and Waseda Foundn, 1998; Univ. of Debrecen, 2005; Univ. of Helsinki, 2009; Inst. of Higher Educn, Beihang Univ., China, 2014; Vis. Professorial Fellow, Commonwealth Studies Inst., Sch. of Advanced Study, Univ. of London, 2002–05; Dist. Prof., Internat. Inst. of Adult and Lifelong Educn, 2008; Sen. Fellow, China Policy Inst., 2008; Leverhulme Emeritus Fellow, 2017. Mem., Commonwealth Scholarship Commn, 2002–08 (Chair: Academic Staff Fellowships Cttee; Professional Fellowships Cttee); Steering Cttee, UNESCO Peace Prog. for Palestinian Higher Educn, 2007; Chm., UK Nat. Commn, UNESCO, 2010–13 (Dir, 2007–10); Convener, UNESCO Dir Gen.'s Consultation for Europe and N America, 2010; Co-Chair, UNESCO Dir Gen.'s Sen. Experts' Panel on Rethinking Educn in the 21st Century, 2013. Member, Executive Committee: Council for Educn in the Commonwealth, 1999–2002; British Assoc. of Internat. and Comparative Educn, 2002–05; Internat. Adv. Bd, Centre for Res. in Contg Educn and Lifelong Learning, Univ. of Hong Kong, 2007; Mem. Council and Trustee, Royal Anthropological Inst., 2017–; Mem. Council and Trustee, Learned Soc. of Wales, 2017–. Mem., Hocart Prize Judges' Panel, 2017–. Hon. Sec., Internat. Soc. for Comparative Adult Educn, 1990–93. Gov., Portland Coll. for the Disabled, 1991–93 (Chm., Educn and Trng Cttee, 1991–93). Patron, Landmine Disability Support Trust, 2007–. James A. Draper Meml Lectr, New Delhi, 2009. FRSA 1979; FRAI 1989; FLSW 2012; FRHistS 2016. Hon. DSc Inst. of Sociol., Russian Acad. of Scis, 2010. Vice Chancellor's Achievement Medal, Univ. of Nottingham, 2014. Mem., editl bds of various internat. jls. *Publications:* (ed) The Welsh Dilemma: some essays on nationalism in Wales, 1973; (with N. T. Scott) Unemployed Graduates: a wasted national resource, 1987; (ed) Politics and Consensus in Modern Britain, 1988; (ed with B. Hake) Adult Education, Public Information and Ideology, 1989; Social Welfare in the British and West German Coal Industries, 1989; (ed jtly) Access and Delivery in Continuing Education: a guide to contemporary literature, 1992; (ed with P. Preston) Raymond Williams: politics, education, letters, 1993; (ed jtly) Access and Delivery in Continuing Education: first supplement, 1995; (ed with J. Muckle) Post-school Education and the Transition from State Socialism, 2001; (ed with S. W. Livingstone) Law and Opinion in 20th Century Britain and Ireland, 2003; Communists on Education and Culture, 2003; (jtly) Teacher Mobility, Brain Drain and Educational Resources in the Commonwealth, 2006; Place, Inequality and Recognition: key concepts in contemporary citizenship, 2008; (ed with B. Wu) Higher Education Reform in China, 2011; (with A. Guilherme) Buber and Education, 2013; (ed with B. Wu) Chinese Higher Education Reform and Social Justice, 2015; (ed with Q. Gu and F. Li) Handbook of Education in China, 2017; (with A. Guilherme) Philosophy, Dialogue, and

Education: nine modern European philosophers, 2018; (jtly) Civil Society, Social Change, and a New Popular Education in Russia, 2019; articles in jls and book chapters. *Recreations:* reading, music, Rugby, grandchildren. *Address:* Wales Institute of Social and Economic Research, Data and Methods, School of Social Sciences, Cardiff University, 38 Park Place, Cardiff CF10 3BB. *T:* (029) 2087 9338. *E:* MorganJ74@cardiff.ac.uk. *Club:* Royal Over-Seas League.

**MORGAN-WEBB, Dame Patricia,** DBE 2000; Co-founder and Chief Executive, Morgan Webb Education Ltd, 2003–11; *m* 1992, Christopher J. Webb. Principal and Chief Exec., Clarendon Coll., 1991–98; Chief Exec., New Coll. Nottingham, 1998–2003. Member: Bd, QCA, 1997–2002; E Midlands Regl Cttee, FEFC; Derbys Learning and Skills Council, 2000. Mem. Bd, E Midlands Develt Agency, 1998–2004; Dir, Gtr Nottingham TEC. Gov., Walsall Coll., 2012–; Dir, Bd, St George's Free Sch., Newtown, Birmingham, 2013–. Trustee, S Staffs CAB, 2013–; Pres., Roots and Renewal Foundn, 2013–. *Address:* Church Hill Cottage, Church Hill, Longdon Green WS15 4PU.

**MORIARTY, Clare Mary,** CB 2016; Permanent Secretary, Department for Exiting the European Union, since 2019; *b* 6 April 1963; *d* of Michael John Moriarty, *qv*; *m* 2001, James MacDonald; one *s* one *d*, and one step *s* two step *d*. *Educ:* North London Collegiate Sch.; Balliol Coll., Oxford (BA Hons Maths 1985). FCCA 1995. Joined DHSS, 1985; Cycle Internat., Ecole Nat. d'Admin, Paris, 1990–91; Prin. Private Sec. to Sec. of State for Health, 1994–97; Hon. Sen. Res. Fellow, Sch. of Public Policy, UCL, 1997–98; Hd, NHS Foundn Trust Unit, DoH, 2002–04; Whole Systems Dir, Portsmouth and SE Hampshire Health and Social Care Community, 2004–05; Constitution Dir, DCA, later MoJ, 2005–08; Dir (Projects), DoH, 2008–09; Dir Gen., Corporate Support Functions, later Corporate Gp, DfT, 2009–12; Dir Gen., Rail Gp, then Rail Exec., DfT, 2013–15; Perm. Sec., DEFRA, 2015–19. *Recreations:* family, singing, cycling, mountain walking, restoring and maintaining hill farm in Connemara, Ireland. *Address:* Department for Exiting the European Union, 70 Whitehall, SW1A 2AA. *E:* clare.moriarty@dexeu.gov.uk.

**MORIARTY, Gerald Evelyn;** QC 1974; a Recorder of the Crown Court, 1976–98; *b* 23 Aug. 1928; *er s* of late Lt-Col G. R. O'N. Moriarty and Eileen Moriarty (*née* Moloney); *m* 1961, Judith Mary, *er d* of Hon. William Robert Atkin; four *s*. *Educ:* Downside Sch.; St John's Coll., Oxford (MA). Called to the Bar, Lincoln's Inn, 1951, Bencher, 1983. *T:* (01284) 789232. *Club:* Reform.

**MORIARTY, Brig. Joan Olivia Elsie,** CB 1979; RRC 1977; Matron-in-Chief and Director of Army Nursing Services, 1976–80; *b* 11 May 1923; *d* of late Lt-Col Oliver Nash Moriarty, DSO, RA, and Mrs Georgina Elsie Moriarty (*née* Moore). *Educ:* Royal Sch., Bath; St Thomas' Hosp. (nursing); Queen Charlotte's Hosp. (midwifery). SRN. VAD, Somerset, 1941–42; joined QAIMNS (R), 1947; Reg. QAIMNS (later QARANC), 1948, retired Jan. 1981; appts incl.: Staff Captain, WO; Instr, Corps Trng Centre; Liaison Officer, MoD; served in UK, Gibraltar, BAOR, Singapore, Malaya, Cyprus; Matron, Mil. Hosp., Catterick, 1973–76; Comdt, QARANC Trng Centre, Aldershot, 1976. Major 1960; Lt-Col 1971; Col 1973; Brig. 1977. QHNS, 1977–80. OStJ 1977.

**MORIARTY, Prof. Michael,** PhD; FBA 2006; Drapers Professor of French, University of Cambridge, since 2011 (Head, Department of French, 2012); Fellow, Peterhouse, Cambridge, since 2011; *b* 27 May 1956; *s* of Martin Moriarty and Ellen Moriarty (*née* O'Connor); *m* 1992, Morag Elizabeth Shiach; two *s*. *Educ:* Warwick Sch.; St John's Coll., Cambridge (BA 1978, MA 1982; PhD 1984). Asst Lectr, 1986–90, Lectr, 1990–95, Dept of French, Univ. of Cambridge; Res. Fellow, 1982–85, Lectr in French and Dir of Studies in Mod. Langs, 1985–95, Gonville and Caius Coll., Cambridge; Prof. of French Lit. and Thought, 1995–2005, Centenary Prof., 2005–11, QMUL. Member: Panel 51 (French), RAE 2001; Sub-panel 52 (French), RAE 2008. Chm., Soc. for Seventeenth-Century French Studies, 2012–16. Chevalier, Ordre des Palmes Académiques (France), 2010. *Publications:* Taste and Ideology in Seventeenth Century France, 1988; Roland Barthes, 1991; Early Modern French Thought: the Age of Suspicion, 2003; Fallen Nature, Fallen Selves: Early Modern French Thought II, 2006 (Jl Hist. of Philosophy Prize for best book on hist. of western philosophy); Disguised Vices: theories of virtue in early modern French thought, 2011 (R. H. Gapper Book Prize, Soc. of French Studies, 2012); (ed with N. Hammond) Evocations of Eloquence: rhetoric, literature and religion in early modern France, essays in honour of Peter Bayley, 2012; contrib. articles to French Studies, Romance Studies, etc. *Recreations:* walking, listening to music, crosswords. *Address:* Peterhouse, Trumpington Street, Cambridge CB2 1RD. *T:* (01223) 338254. *E:* mm10005@cam.ac.uk.

**MORIARTY, Michael John,** CB 1988; Deputy Chairman, Radio Authority, 1994–2000 (Member, 1991–2000); Deputy Under-Secretary of State and Principal Establishment Officer, Home Office, 1984–90; *b* 3 July 1930; *er s* of late Edward William Patrick Moriarty, OBE, and May Lilian Moriarty; *m* 1960, Rachel Milward, *d* of late J. S. Thompson and Isobel F. Thompson; one *s* two *d*. *Educ:* Reading Sch., Reading; St John's Coll., Oxford (Sir Thomas White schol.; MA Lit. Hum.). Entered Home Office as Asst Principal, 1954; Private Sec. to Parliamentary Under-Secretaries of State, 1957–59; Principal, 1959; Civil Service Selection Bd, 1962–63; Cabinet Office, 1965–67; Asst Sec., 1967; Private Sec. to Home Sec., 1968; Head of Crime Policy Planning Unit, 1974–75; Asst Under-Sec. of State, 1975–84; seconded to NI Office, 1979–81; Broadcasting Dept, 1981–84. UK Representative, 1976–79, and Chm., 1978–79, Council of Europe Cttee on Crime Problems. Sub-Treas., Chichester Cathedral, 1991–; a Church Comr, 1996–98. *Recreations:* music, walking, local interests. *Address:* 22 Westgate, Chichester, West Sussex PO19 3EU. *T:* (01243) 789985.
*See also C. M. Moriarty.*

**MORIARTY, Stephen;** QC 1999; *b* 14 April 1955; *s* of George William Moriarty and Dorothy Violet Moriarty (*née* Edwards); *m* 1988, Dr Susan Clare Stanford. *Educ:* Chichester High Sch. for Boys; Brasenose Coll., Oxford (BCL, MA; Vinerian Schol. 1978). Univ. Lectr in law, and Fellow and Tutor in Law, Exeter Coll., Oxford, 1979–86; called to the Bar, Middle Temple, 1986, Bencher, 2009; in practice at the Bar, 1986–; Hd, Fountain Court Chambers, 2013–18. Chm., Commercial Bar Assoc., 2011–13. Mem., Bar Council, 2011–13. *Recreations:* theatre, opera, cycling. *Address:* Fountain Court Chambers, Fountain Court, Temple, EC4Y 9DH. *T:* (020) 7583 3335. *Club:* Reform.

**MORICE, Prof. Peter Beaumont,** DSc, PhD; FREng, FICE, FIStructE; Professor of Civil Engineering, University of Southampton, 1958–91, now Emeritus; *b* 15 May 1926; *o s* of Charles and Stephanie Morice; *m* 1st, 1952, Margaret Ransom (marr. diss. 1986); one *s* two *d*; 2nd, 1986, Rita Corless (*née* Dunk) (*d* 2006). *Educ:* Barfield Sch.; Farnham Grammar Sch.; University of Bristol; University of London. Surrey County Council, 1947–48; Research Div., Cement and Concrete Assoc., 1948–57. Vis. Prof., Ecole Nat. des Ponts et Chaussées, Paris; Mem. Foundn Cttee, Sultan Qaboos Univ., Oman, 1980–86. FREng (FEng 1989). Compagnon du Beaujolais, 1987. Order of Sultan Qaboos (Oman), 1986. *Publications:* Linear Structural Analysis, 1958; Prestressed Concrete, 1958; papers on structural theory in various learned journals. *Recreations:* sailing, DIY, reading, listening to music, painting. *Address:* 12 Abbotts Way, Highfield, Southampton SO17 1QT. *T:* (023) 8055 7641, 07429 492356.

**MORISON, Hugh,** CBE 2002; Chief Executive (formerly Director General), Scotch Whisky Association, 1994–2003; *b* 22 Nov. 1943; *s* of Archibald Ian Morison and Enid Rose Morison (*née* Mawer); *m* 1st, 1971, Marion Smithers (marr. diss. 1993); two *d*; 2nd, 1993, Ilona Bellos (*née* Roth). *Educ:* Chichester High School for Boys; St Catherine's Coll., Oxford (MA English Language and Literature; DipEd). Asst Principal, SHHD, 1966–69; Private Sec. to Minister of State, Scottish Office, 1969–70; Principal: Scottish Educn Dept, 1971–73; Scottish Economic Planning Dept, 1973–74; Offshore Supplies Office, Dept of Energy, 1974–75; Scottish Economic Planning Dept, 1975–82, Asst Sec., 1979; Gwilym Gibbon Res. Fellow, Nuffield Coll., Oxford, 1982–83; Scottish Development Dept, 1983–84; Under Secretary: SHHD, 1984–88; Industry Dept for Scotland, subseq. Scottish Office Industry Dept, 1988–93. Director: The Weir Gp, 1989–93; Praban na Linne Ltd, 2005–06. Member: Health Appts Adv. Cttee (Scotland), 1995–2000; Exec. Cttee, Barony Housing Assoc., 1996–2010 (Chm., 2005–09). Chm., Scottish Business and Biodiversity Gp, 1998–2003. Prés., 2001–03, Prés. d'honneur, 2003–, Confédn Eur. des Producteurs de Spiritueux. Gov., UHI (formerly UHI Millennium Inst.), 2004–13. Chm., Letterfearn Moorings Assoc., 2001–. *Publications:* The Regeneration of Local Economies, 1987; (with Ilona Bellos) Dauphiné, 1991; The Feelgood Fallacy, 2008. *Recreations:* hill walking, cycling, sailing, playing the euphonium, looking at ruins. *Address:* 12 Sunbury Place, Edinburgh EH4 3BY. *T:* (0131) 225 6568. *Club:* New (Edinburgh).

**MORISON, Prof. John William Edgar,** PhD; Professor of Jurisprudence, Queen's University, Belfast, since 1996; *b* 8 March 1958; *s* of John Edgar Morison and Ellen McCracken Morison; *m* 1984, Susan Royal; two *d*. *Educ:* Brackenber House; Campbell Coll.; University of Wales, Cardiff (LLB 1979; PhD 1985). Queen's University, Belfast: Lectr in Law, 1984–94; Reader in Law, 1994–96; Hd, Sch. of Law, 2003–07. Mem., NI Judicial Appointments Commn, 2003–12; Ind. Bd Mem., NI Legal Services Commn, subseq. Legal Services Agency NI, 2014–18. Dir, European Public Law Centre, Athens, 1996–. MRIA 2009. *Publications:* (with P. Leith) The Barrister's World and the Nature of Law, 1992; (with S. Livingstone) Reshaping Public Power: Northern Ireland and the British constitutional crisis, 1995; (ed jtly) Judges, Transition and Human Rights, 2007; (ed jtly) Values in Global Administrative Law, 2011. *Recreations:* collecting art, dog walking. *Address:* School of Law, Queen's University, Belfast BT7 1NN. *E:* j.morison@qub.ac.uk.

**MORISON, Hon. Sir Thomas (Richard Atkin),** Kt 1993; a Judge of the High Court of Justice, Queen's Bench Division, 1993–2007; *b* 15 Jan. 1939; *s* of Harold Thomas Brash Morison and Hon. Nancy Morison; *m* 1963, Judith Rachel Walton Morris (marr. diss. 1992); one *s* one *d*; *m* 1993, Caroline Yates. *Educ:* Winchester Coll.; Worcester Coll., Oxford, 1959–62 (MA). Passed final Bar examinations, 1959; called to the Bar, Gray's Inn, 1960, Bencher, 1987; pupil in Chambers, 1962–63; started practice, 1963; QC 1979; a Recorder, 1987–93. *Recreations:* reading, gardening, cooking.

**MORITZ, Sir Michael J.,** KBE 2013; venture capitalist; President and Chairman, Sequoia Capital, since 2012 (Managing Partner, 1986–2012); *b* Cardiff, 12 Sept. 1954; *s* of Prof. Alfred. Moritz and Doris Moritz; *m* Harriet Heymen; two *c*. *Educ:* Howardian High Sch., Cardiff; Christ Church, Oxford (BA 1976); Wharton Sch., Univ. of Pennsylvania (MBA). Journalist, Time Inc.; Co-founder, Technologic Partners; Partner and venture capitalist, Sequoia Capital Israel, 1986. Chm., LUXIM Corp.; directorships include: Flextronics Internat. Ltd, 1993–2005; Yahoo!, 1995–2003; Saba Software, 1998–2006; eToys Inc., 1998–; PayPal, 1999–2002; Google Inc., 1999–2007; RedEnvelope Inc., 1999–2005 (Chm., 2003–05); GameFly Inc., 2002–; 24/7 Customer, 2003–; Green Dot Corp., 2003–; Kayak Software Corp. (formerly Kayak.com), 2005–; Sugar Inc., 2007–; Kiarna AB, 2010–; LinkedIn Corp., 2011–; Zappos.com Inc.; Nightfire Software Inc.; Maplebear Inc., 2013–. Hon. Fellow, Cardiff Univ., 2010. *Publications:* (with B. Seaman) Going for Broke: the Chrysler Story, 1981; The Little Kingdom: the private story of Apple Computer, 1984; Return to the Little Kingdom: Steve Jobs, the creation of Apple and how it changed the world, 2009; (with Sir Alex Ferguson) Leading, 2015. *Address:* Sequoia Capital, 2800 Sand Hill Road, Suite 101, Menlo Park, CA 94025, USA.

**MORLAND, Edward;** Chief Executive, Health & Safety Laboratory, 2005–15; *b* 23 June 1957; *s* of Albert Edward Morland and Eva Doris Morland; *m* 1977, Lynda Hockenhull; one *s* one *d*. *Educ:* Wade Deacon Grammar Sch.; Manchester Poly. (BSc 1st Cl. Hons Physics 1982); UMIST (MSc Mgt Sci. 1994). FInstP 2006. Res. Scientist, UKAEA, 1975–92; Mktg Manager, AEA Technology, 1992–97; Commercial Dir, then Ops Dir, 1997–2003, Chief Exec., 2003–05, AEA Rail. FRSA 2005; FRSocMed 2007. *Publications:* (jtly) Mechanical Testing, 1988. *Recreations:* reading history, supporting Manchester United, playing strategy games, hill walking with my wife.

**MORLAND, Martin Robert,** CMG 1985; HM Diplomatic Service, retired; consultant with Hardcastle and Co. Ltd, 1996–2002; *b* 23 Sept. 1933; *e s* of Sir Oscar Morland, GBE, KCMG and late Alice, *d* of Rt Hon. Sir Francis Oswald Lindley, PC, GCMG; *m* 1964, Jennifer Avril Mary Hanbury-Tracy (*d* 2018); two *s* one *d*. *Educ:* Ampleforth; King's Coll., Cambridge (BA). Nat. Service, Grenadier Guards, 1954–56; British Embassy, Rangoon, 1957–60; News Dept, FO, 1961; UK Delegn to Common Market negotiations, Brussels, 1962–63; FO, 1963–65; UK Disarmament Delegn, Geneva, 1965–67; Private Sec. to Lord Chalfont, 1967–68; European Integration Dept, FCO, 1968–73; Counsellor, 1973–77, Rome (seconded temporarily to Cabinet Office to head EEC Referendum Information Unit, 1975); Hd of Maritime Aviation and Environment Dept, FCO, 1977–79; Counsellor and Head of Chancery, Washington, 1979–82; seconded to Hardcastle & Co. Ltd, 1982–84; Under-Sec., Cabinet Office, 1984–86; Ambassador to Burma, 1986–90; Ambassador and UK Perm. Rep. to Office of UN and other internat. orgns, Geneva, 1990–93; Dir, Public Affairs, BNFL, 1994–96. Mem. Cttee, Supporters of Nuclear Energy, 2005–11. Chm. Govs, Westminster Cathedral Choir Sch., 2001–08. Chm., Prospect Burma, 1994–2012. *Address:* Prospect House, Shaftesbury Road, East Knoyle, Salisbury SP3 6AR. *E:* m.morland731@btinternet.com.

**MORLAND, Sir Michael,** Kt 1989; a Judge of the High Court of Justice, Queen's Bench Division, 1989–2004; *b* 16 July 1929; *e s* of Edward Morland, Liverpool, and Jane Morland (*née* Beckett); *m* 1961, Lillian Jensen, Copenhagen; one *s* one *d*. *Educ:* Stowe; Christ Church, Oxford (MA). 2nd Lieut, Grenadier Guards, 1948–49; served in Malaya. Called to Bar, Inner Temple, 1953, Bencher 1979; Northern Circuit; QC 1972; a Recorder, 1972–89; Presiding Judge, Northern Circuit, 1991–95. Mem., Criminal Injuries Compensation Bd, 1980–89. Mem., Gardiner Cttee on measures to deal with terrorism in NI, 1974; Chairman: Cttee of Inquiry for DHSS in case of Paul Brown, 1980; Public Inquiry for NI Office into death of Rosemary Nelson, 2004–11.

**MORLAND, Sir Robert (Kenelm),** Kt 1990; General Manager, Exports: Tate & Lyle Sugars, 1987–93; Tate & Lyle International, 1987–93; Director, Tate & Lyle Norway A/S, 1987–93; *b* 7 April 1935; *s* of late Kenelm and Sybil Morland; *m* 1st, 1960, Eve Charters (marr. diss. 1965); one *s*; 2nd, 1972, Angela Fraser; one *s*. *Educ:* Birkenhead Sch.; Rydal Sch., Colwyn Bay. Joined Tate & Lyle, 1953; held various managerial positions. Member: Cheshire Riverboard Authy, 1962–65; Birkenhead Nat. Assistance Bd, Adv. Cttee, 1962–65. Dir, 1996–98, Associate non-exec. Dir, 1999–2001, Kingston and Richmond HA; Bd Mem., Thames Health Primary Care Gp, 1999–2001; non-executive Director: Teddington, Twickenham and Hamptons PCT, 2001–02; Richmond and Twickenham

PCT, 2002–04; Age Concern, Richmond upon Thames, 2004–05, Glos, 2005–11. Member: Birkenhead CBC, 1959–65; Richmond upon Thames BC, 1968–71. Contested (C) Birkenhead, 1964. Chairman: Birkenhead Young Conservatives, 1955–58; Kew Conservatives, 1971–74; Richmond and Barnes (now Richmond Park) Cons. Assoc., 1975–79 (Dep. Pres., 1985–98); Cons. Docklands Action Cttee, 1990–92; Greenwich and Lewisham Cons. Action Gp, 1993–94; Dep. Chm., Nat. Trade and Industry Forum, Cons. Party, 1991–96; Vice-President: Gtr London Conservatives, 1990– (Dep. Chm., 1978–81; Jt Hon. Treas., 1981–87; Chm., 1987–90); Newham S Cons. Assoc., 1989–96; Member: Cons. Nat. Union Exec. Cttee, 1978–93; Cons. Bd of Finance, 1981–87. Ind. Mem., Standards Cttee, Cotswolds Conservation Bd, 2005–12. Dir, Friends of the Cotswolds, 2007–12. Chairman: St Mary's Drama Gp, Hampton, 1999–2001 (Vice Chm., 1996–99); Friends of St Edward's Parish Ch, Stow-on-the-Wold, 2008–14; N Cotswold Probus, 2013–14. Vice Pres., Gloucestershire CCC, 2007–. *Recreations*: theatre, travel, cricket, horseriding. *Club*: Carlton.

**MORLEY**; *see* Hope-Morley, family name of Baron Hollenden.

**MORLEY, 7th Earl of,** *cr* 1815; **Mark Lionel Parker**; *b* 22 Aug. 1956; *o s* of 6th Earl of Morley, KCVO and of Johanna Katherine, *d* of Sir John Molesworth-St Aubyn, 14th Bt, CBE; *S* father, 2015; *m* 1983, Carolyn Jill, *d* of Donald McVicar, Meols, Wirral, Cheshire; three *d*. *Educ*: Eton. Commissioned, Royal Green Jackets, 1976. *Heir*: cousin Edward Geoffrey Parker [*b* 15 Oct. 1967; *m* 1992, Alice Victoria, *d* of Thomas Elliott; one *s* one *d*]. *Address*: Pound House, Yelverton, Devon PL20 7LJ.

**MORLEY, Dame Carol Mary**; *see* Black, Dame C. M.

**MORLEY, Catherine**; *see* Pepinster, C.

**MORLEY, David Howard**; Global Senior Partner, Allen & Overy LLP, Solicitors, 2008–16; Chairman: Elaghmore LLP, since 2017; Vannin Capital, since 2018; *b* 21 Sept. 1956; *s* of Glyn and Yvonne Morley; *m* 1982, Sue (*née* Radcliffe); two *s* two *d*. *Educ*: St John's Coll., Cambridge (BA 1979). Admitted solicitor, 1982. Joined Allen & Overy, 1980: Partner, 1988; Hd, Banking Practice, 1998–2003; Worldwide Man. Partner, 2003–08. *Recreations*: cycling, ski-ing, sailing.

**MORLEY, David John**; HM Diplomatic Service, retired; High Commissioner to The Gambia, 2011–14; *b* Reading, 23 Oct. 1954; *s* of John Morley and Jean Morley; *m* 1978, Jacqueline Ann Wells. *Educ*: St Peter's Primary Sch., Reading; Bulmarshe Grammar Sch., Reading. Joined FCO, 1973; Third Sec., Kaduna, 1980–83; Second Sec., Moscow, 1990–93; Dep. High Comr, Mbabane, 1997–99; First Sec., UK Delegn to NATO, Brussels, 1999–2001; Adminr, Tristan da Cunha, 2007–10. *Recreations*: fishing, walking, travelling, dining.

**MORLEY, Elliot Anthony**; *b* 6 July 1952; *m* 1975; one *s* one *d*. *Educ*: St Margaret's C of E High Sch., Liverpool. Special needs teacher, comprehensive sch., Hull; head of individual learning centre, until 1987. Mem., Kingston upon Hull City Council, 1979–85; Chair, Hull City Transport Cttee, 1981–85. Contested (Lab) Beverley, 1983. MP (Lab) Glanford and Scunthorpe, 1987–97, Scunthorpe, 1997–2010. Opposition front bench spokesman on food, agriculture and rural affairs, 1989–97; Labour spokesperson on animal welfare, 1992–97; Parly Sec., MAFF, then DEFRA, 1997–2003; Minister of State (Minister for the Envmt), DEFRA, 2003–06. Mem., Select Cttee for Agriculture, 1987–90; Dep. Chair, PLP Educn Cttee, 1987–90. Vice-Pres., Wildlife and Countryside Link, 1990–97; Member of Council: RSPB, 1989–93; British Trust for Ornithology, 1992–95 (Vice-Pres., until 2009). Hon. Pres., N Lincs RSPCA, until 2010. Hon. Vice-Pres., Assoc. of Drainage Authorities, until 2010. Hon. Fellow, Univ. of Lincoln (formerly Lincs and Humberside Univ.). Hon. FICE. *Recreations*: ornithology, the environment, the countryside.

**MORLEY, Iain Charles**; QC 2009; a Judge of the High Court of the Eastern Caribbean assigned to Antigua and Montserrat, since 2016; Judge, Eastern Caribbean Sexual Offences Model Court; *b* Dublin, 21 Oct. 1965; *s* of Charles Trevor Morley and Teresa Ann Morley (*née* Forken); *m* 1989, Jillian Helen Prickett (separated); two *s* one *d*. *Educ*: Lady Margaret Hall, Oxford (MA 1987). Called to the Bar: Inner Temple, 1988, Bencher, 2010; Eire, 1993; Pegasus Schol. 1993; in practice specialising in criminal law, London, 1989–2004; Prosecutor, UN Internat. Criminal Tribunal for Rwanda, Arusha, Tanzania, 2005–09; Sen. Trial Counsel, Special Tribunal for Lebanon, The Hague, 2009–12. Exec. Mem., SE Circuit, 2013–16. Co-Chm., E Caribbean Supreme Court Sentencing Guidelines Cttee. Member: Inner Temple Advocacy Cttee, 1993–; Internat. Cttee, Advocacy Training Council, 2012–; Chair, Inner Temple Student Socs, 2013–16. *Publications*: The Devil's Advocate, 2005, 3rd edn 2015. *Recreations*: cinema, opera, travels, fell-walking, sailing.

**MORLEY, Michael John**; Chief Executive, Coutts & Co., London, 2009–16; *b* Bushey, Middx, 18 May 1957; *s* of John Lewis Morley and Jean Elizabeth Bentley Morley (*née* Morris); *m* 1991, Conchita Amell de la Morena; two *s*. *Educ*: Merchant Taylors' Sch., Northwood; Christ's Coll., Cambridge (BA Mod. and Medieval Langs 1979). Lloyds Bank Internat., 1980–86; Hd, Fixed Income, Enskilda Securities, 1986–94; Man. Dir and Hd, UK Private Banking, Merrill Lynch, 1994–2002; CEO, Barclays Wealth Internat., 2002–07; Man. Dir, Singer and Friedlander Investment Mgt, 2007–08. *Recreations*: playing the piano, ski-ing, walking around London, my family.

**MORLEY, Oliver Charles Fenton,** CBE 2017; Chief Executive, Pension Protection Fund, since 2018; *b* London, 22 June 1971; *s* of Michael and Delia Morley; *m* 1997, Susan Dandridge; two *s* two *d*. *Educ*: Jesus Coll., Cambridge (BA Econs 1993); London Business Sch. (MBA 1998). Shipping Exec., Maersk Line, 1993–96; Consultant, CSC Index/Kalchas, 1998–99; Reuters: Hd, Treasury Strategy, 2000–02; Hd, Sales Ops, 2002–04; Hd, Nordic Sales, 2005–06; Hd, Customer Experience, 2007–08; Dir, Commercial Services, 2008–10, Chief Exec., Keeper of the Public Records and Historical Manuscripts Comr, 2010–13, Nat. Archives; Chief Exec., DVLA, Dft, 2013–18. *Recreations*: food, wine, history, ski-ing, running. *Address*: Pension Protection Fund, 12 Dingwall Road, Croydon, Surrey CR0 2NA.

**MORNINGTON, Earl of; Arthur Gerald Wellesley**; *b* 31 Jan. 1978; *er s* and *heir* of Duke of Wellington, *qv*; *m* 2005, Jemma Madeleine, *d* of John Edward Aitken Kidd; two *s* one *d* (of whom one *s* one *d* are twins). *Educ*: Eton Coll.; Christ Church, Oxford. A Page of Honour to HM Queen Elizabeth the Queen Mother, 1993–95. *Heir*: *s* Viscount Wellesley, *qv*. *Address*: The Old Rectory, Stratfield Saye, Hants RG7 2DA.

**MORPHET, David Ian**; author; *b* 24 Jan. 1940; *s* of late Albert and Sarah Elizabeth Morphet; *m* 1968, Sarah Gillian Sedgwick; two *s* one *d*. *Educ*: King James's Grammar Sch., Almondbury, Yorks; St John's Coll., Cambridge (History Schol.; English Tripos, class I, Pts I and II). Foreign Office, 1961; Vice Consul, Taiz, 1963; Doha, 1963–64; FO, 1964–66; Asst Private Sec. to Foreign Secretary, 1966–68; First Sec., Madrid, 1969–72; Diplomatic Service Observer, CS Selection Board, 1972–74; transf. to Dept of Energy, 1974; Asst Sec., 1975; Dep. Chm., Midlands Electricity Board (on secondment), 1978–79; Under-Secretary: Electricity Div., 1979–83; Energy Policy Div., 1983–85; Atomic Energy Div., 1985–89; UK Governor: Internat. Energy Agency, Paris, 1983–85; IAEA, Vienna, 1985–89. Director: BICC Cables Ltd, 1981–89; Planning and Develt, Balfour Beatty Ltd, 1989–91; Govt Affairs, BICC plc, 1992–95; Barking Power Ltd, 1993–2001; Dir Gen., Railway Forum, 1997–2000. Chm., Export Finance Cttee, CBI, 1992–96; Mem. Council, CBI, 1995–96 and 1997–2001. Founder Mem. and Chm., Nat. Schizophrenia Fellowship, 1977–83. *Publications*: Louis Jennings, MP: editor of The New York Times and Tory democrat, 2001; (ed) St John's College, Cambridge: excellence and diversity, 2007; *poetry*: Seventy-Seven Poems, 2002; The Angel and the Fox, 2003; Approaching Animals from A to Z, 2004; 39 Ways of Looking, 2005; The Silence of Green, 2007; The Maze: a daydream in five cantos, 2009; The Intruders and Other Poems, 2010; Lyrics from the Periodic Table, 2011; A Sequence from the Cyclades, 2012; Night Train to Utopia, 2013; Satires and Legacies, 2014; Homecoming by Microlight: landscapes and satires, 2015; Brief Encounters, 2016; The Wranglers and other poems, 2017; Another Planet Earth: new and selected poems, 2018; (ed) Poetry at the Athenaeum: an anthology, 2019. *Address*: 11 Daisy Lane, SW6 3DD. *Club*: Athenæum.

**MORPHET, Richard Edward,** CBE 1998; Keeper, Modern Collection, Tate Gallery, 1986–98; *b* 2 Oct. 1938; *s* of Horace Taylor Morphet and Eleanor Morphet (*née* Shaw); *m* 1965, Sarah Francis Richmond, (Sally Morphet, CMG) (*d* 2014); two *d*. *Educ*: Bootham Sch., York; London Sch. of Economics (BA Hons History). Fine Arts Dept, British Council, 1963–66; Tate Gallery: Asst Keeper, 1966–73; Dep. Keeper, Modern Collection, 1973–86. Exhibitions (curator and author/editor of catalogue) include: Richard Hamilton, Tate, 1970; Bernard Cohen, Hayward, 1972; William Turnbull, Tate, 1973; Art in One Year: 1935, Tate, 1977; Meredith Frampton, Tate, 1982; Cedric Morris, Tate, 1984; The Hard-Won Image, Tate, 1984; Richard Hamilton, Tate, 1992; R. B. Kitaj, Tate, 1994; Encounters: New Art from Old, National Gallery, 2000; other exhibition catalogues include: Roy Lichtenstein, Tate, 1968; Andy Warhol, Tate, 1971; Howard Hodgkin, Arts Council, 1976; Leonard McComb, Serpentine, 1983; contribs to exhibn catalogues on Late Sickert, Hayward, 1981 and The Art of Bloomsbury, Tate, 1999. *Publications*: Jonathan Leaman, 2002; contrib. books on Eric Ravilious, 1983, Anthony Gross, 1992, and Ann Stokes, 2009; contrib. Apollo, Burlington Mag., Studio International, TLS, etc. *E*: morphet234@gmail.com.

**MORPHY, Leslie Ann,** OBE 2010; Chief Executive, Crisis UK, 2006–14; *b* 23 Jan. 1949; *d* of Hugh Webster Morphy and Grace Clara Morphy; *m* 1981, Bob Deffee; one *s* one *d* (and one *d* decd). *Educ*: London Sch. of Econs (BSc Econ); Birkbeck Coll., London (MSc). Researcher, Penguin, 1971–72; Mgr, NUS, 1972–78; freelance consultancy, 1983–89; Dir, Broadcasting Support Services, 1978–83; Hd, R&D, Basic Skills Agency, 1989–96; Dir, Prince's Trust, 1996–2006. Non-executive Director: Home Gp, 2013–; Surrey and Borders Partnership NHS Foundn Trust, 2015–. Chair, Pathway, 2015–. Gov., Oxford Brookes Univ., 2011– (Vice Chair, 2013–16; Chair, 2016–). *Recreations*: being with my family, theatre, reading novels, growing things. *Address*: 4 West Park Road, Kew Gardens, Richmond, Surrey TW9 4DA. *T*: 07867 515541. *E*: leslieamorphy@gmail.com.

**MORPURGO, Sir Michael (Andrew Bridge),** Kt 2018; OBE 2006 (MBE 1999); DL; writer; Joint Founder Director, Farms for City Children, since 1976; Children's Laureate, 2003–05; *b* 5 Oct. 1943; *s* of Tony Valentine Bridge and late Catherine Noel Kippe (*née* Cammaerts), and step *s* of late Jack Eric Morpurgo; *m* 1963, Clare (MBE 1999), *d* of Sir Allen Lane, founder, Penguin Books; two *s* one *d*. *Educ*: King's Sch., Canterbury; RMA Sandhurst; King's Coll., London (AKC, BA 1967; FKC 2001). Primary school teacher, 1967–75; with Clare Morpurgo founded Farms for City Children and opened Nethercott House farm, 1976; opened Treginnis Isaf, 1989, Wick Court, Glos, 1998. Co-writer/presenter, The Invention of Childhood (series), BBC Radio 4, 2006. DL Devon, 2015. Hon. DEd: Plymouth, 2002; UCE, 2007; Hon. DLitt: Exeter, 2004; Herts, 2006; Hon. MA Worcester, 2007 (with Clare Morpurgo). Bookseller Assoc. Writer of the Year, 2005. Chevalier des Arts et des Lettres, 2004. *Publications*: over 100 books for children, including: Friend or Foe, 1978; (with Ted Hughes) All Around the Year, 1979; The Nine Lives of Montezuma, 1980; The White Horse of Zennor, 1982; War Horse, 1984 (performed NT, 2007–08; filmed, 2012); Twist of Gold, 1986; Mr Nobody's Eyes, 1989; Why the Whales Came (Silver Pencil award, Holland), 1989 (screenplay, When the Whales Came, 1991; performed Alibi Th., 1995); My Friend Walter, 1990 (screenplay, 1994); Little Foxes, 1992; The Marble Crusher, 1992; King of the Cloud Forests, 1992 (Cercle d'Or, Montreuil, 1994; Prix Sorcière, 1995); The War of Jenkins Ear, 1992 (Best Book award, Amer. Liby Assoc., 1996); Blodin the Beast, 1993; Waiting for Anya, 1993; The Sandman and the Turtles, 1994; The Dancing Bear, 1995; The Wreck of the Zanzibar, 1995 (Whitbread Children's Award, and Children's Book Award, Fedn of Children's Books, 1996; IBBY Honour Book, 1998); Arthur High King of Britain, 1995; Sam's Duck, 1996; Muck and Magic, 1996; The Butterfly Lion, 1996 (Writers' Guild Award, 1996; Smarties Prize, 1997; performed Barn Th., 2019); The Ghost of Grania O'Malley, 1996; Robin of Sherwood, 1997; Farm Boy, 1997; Red Eyes at Night, 1997; Beyond the Rainbow Warrior, 1997; Escape from Shangri-la, 1998; Joan of Arc of Domrémy, 1998; Wartman, 1998; The Rainbow Bear, 1999 (Children's Book Award, Nat. Assoc. of Teachers of English); Kensuke's Kingdom, 1999 (Children's Book Award, Prix Sorcière, Prix Lire au Collège; performed Polka Th., 2002); Wombat Goes Walkabout, 1999 (Prix Sorcière); Animal Stories, 1999; Dear Olly, 2000; The Silver Swan, 2000; Black Queen, 2000; Tom's Sausage Lion, 2000; From Hereabout Hill, 2000; Billy the Kid, 2000 (performed Unicorn Th., 2006); Classic Boys' Stories, 2000; Toro! Toro!, 2001; More Muck and Magic, 2001; Because a Fire was in my Head, 2001; Out of the Ashes, 2001 (Children's Book Award); The Last Wolf, 2002; The Sleeping Sword, 2002; Cool, 2002; Mr Skip, 2002; Gentle Giant, 2003; Private Peaceful, 2003 (Children's Book Award, Blue Peter Award, Prix Sorcière; performed Bristol Old Vic, 2004); Little Albatross, 2003; Dolphin Boy, 2004; It's a Dog's Life, 2004, (with Patrick Benson), 2010; Sir Gawain and the Green Knight, 2004; Aesop's Fables, 2004; Cockadoodle-doo Mr Sultana!, 2004; (with Jane Feaver) Cock Crow, 2004; The Best Christmas Present in the World, 2004; The Amazing Story of Adolphus Tips (Sheffield Book Award), 2005 (theatre adaptation, 2015); I Believe in Unicorns, 2005; (with Michael Foreman) Beowulf, 2006; Singing for Mrs Pettigrew, 2006; Alone on a Wide Wide Sea, 2006 (Ind. Booksellers' Children's Book of Yr, 2007); (with Quentin Blake) On Angel Wings, 2006; (with Michael Foreman) The Mozart Question, 2007; Born to Run, 2007; (with Emma Chichester Clark) Hansel and Gretel, 2008; (with Michael Foreman) Kaspar, Prince of Cats, 2008; (with Christian Birmingham) This Morning I Met a Whale, 2008; Running Wild, 2009 (performed Chichester Festival Th., 2016, transf. Regent's Park Open Air Th.); (with Emma Chichester Clark) Best of Times, 2009; (with Michael Foreman) Not Bad for a Bad Lad, 2010; (with Michael Foreman) An Elephant in the Garden, 2010; Shadow, 2010; (with Emma Chichester Clark) The Pied Piper of Hamelin, 2011 (musical adaptation, 2015); A Medal For Leroy, 2012; Jo-Jo the Melon Donkey, 2013; (with François Place) Meeting Cézanne, 2013; Listen to the Moon, 2014; (with Michael Foreman) An Eagle in the Snow, 2015; Such Stuff (non-fiction), 2016; The Giant's Necklace, 2016; Toto: the dog-gone amazing story of the Wizard of Oz, 2017; Lucky Button, 2017; Flamingo Boy, 2018; In the Mouth of the Wolf, 2018; Poppy Field, 2018; The Snowman, 2018; Our Jacko, 2018; libretti: Solar, 1981; Scarecrow (music by Phyllis Tate), 1982; *relevant publication*: Michael Morpurgo: war child to war horse, by Maggie Fergusson, 2012. *Recreations*: dreaming, travelling. *Address*: c/o David Higham Associates, 7th Floor, Waverley House, 7–12 Noel Street, W1F 8GQ. *Club*: Chelsea Arts.

**MORPUSS, Guy;** QC 2008; b Worcester, 13 March 1969; s of Richard and Rosemarie Morpuss; m 1999, Julie Davies; two s. Educ: Hillcrest High Sch., South Africa; Univ. of Birmingham (LLB 1st Cl. Hons). Called to the Bar, Lincoln's Inn, 1991; in practice as barrister specialising in commercial litigation, 1991–. Recreations: running, travelling, skiing, music. Address: Macfarlanes LLP, 20 Cursitor Street, EC4A 1LT.

**MORRELL, David William James;** Scottish Legal Services Ombudsman, 1991–94; b 26 July 1933; s of Rev. W. W. Morrell, MBE, TD and Grace Morrell; m 1960, Margaret Rosemary Lewis; two s one d. Educ: George Watson's Coll., Edinburgh; Univ. of Edinburgh (MA Hons, LLB). Law Apprentice, Edinburgh, 1954–57; Admin. Asst, Univ. of Durham, 1957–60; Asst Registrar and Graduate Appts Officer, Univ. of Exeter, 1960–64; Sen. Asst Registrar, Univ. of Essex, 1964–66; Academic Registrar, 1966–73, Registrar, 1973–89, Univ. of Strathclyde; Lay Observer for Scotland, 1989–91. OECD Consultant on management in higher educn, 1990. Vice-Chm., Lomond Healthcare NHS Trust, 1995–99 (Chm., 1995–96); Mem., Argyll and Clyde Health Bd, 1999–2001. Governor: Univ. of Paisley (formerly Paisley Coll.), 1990–2002 (Vice-Chm., 1992–97, Chm., 1997–2002); Scottish Centre for Children with Motor Impairments, 1994–97; Chm., Conf. of Scottish Centrally-Funded Colls, 1997–2000. DUniv Paisley, 2005. Publications: papers on higher education and on provision of legal services. Recreations: hill-walking, fishing. Address: 29 Barclay Drive, Helensburgh, Dunbartonshire G84 9RA. T: (01436) 674875.

**MORRELL, Leslie James,** OBE 1986; JP; Chairman, Northern Ireland Water Council, 1982–93; b 26 Dec. 1931; s of James Morrell; m 1958, Anne Wallace, BSc; two s one d. Educ: Portora Royal Sch., Enniskillen; Queen's Univ., Belfast. BAgric 1955. Member: Londonderry CC, 1969–73; Coleraine Bor. Council, 1973–77; Mem. (U) for Londonderry, NI Assembly, 1973–75; Minister of Agriculture, NI Exec., 1973–74; Dep. Leader, Unionist Party of NI, 1974–80. Mem., BBC Gen. Adv. Cttee, 1980–86; Chm., BBC NI Agricl Adv. Cttee, 1986–91. Chm., NI Fedn of Housing Assocs, 1978–80; Member, Board: Oaklee Homes, 2003–09; Oaklee Housing Trust, 2006–18; Company Sec., Choice Housing Ireland (formerly Oaklee Trinity) Ltd, 2014–16 (Hon. Pres., 2016–). Hon. Secretary: Oaklee Gp (formerly Housing Assoc., then Homes Gp), 1992–2014 (James Butcher Housing Assoc. (NI), 1981–92 (Chm., 1976–81)); James Butcher Retirement Homes Ltd, 1985–95; Oaklee Care and Support Services Ltd, Oaklee Enterprises and Oaklee Employment Services, 2009. Mem. Exec., Assoc. of Governing Bodies of Voluntary Grammar Schs, 1978–84; Chm., Virus Tested Stem Cutting Potato Growers Assoc., 1977–88. JP Londonderry, 1966. Lifetime Achievement Award, Chartered Inst. of Housing, 2017. Address: Dunboe House, 133 Quilly Road, Castlerock, Coleraine BT51 4UB. T: (028) 7084 8352.

**MORRELL, Paul Dring,** OBE 2009; Principal, Paul Morrell Consulting, since 2007; b Doncaster, Yorks, 28 Feb. 1948; s of David Dring Morrell and Joan Hannah Morrell (née Rankin); m 1978, Shirley Irene Betney. Educ: Oundle Sch.; Coll. of Estate Mgt, Univ. of Reading (BSc 1970). ARICS 1975, FRICS 1986; FICE 2011. Davis Langdon, chartered quantity surveyors, 1971–2007, Sen. Partner, 1999–2004. Chief Construction Advr, BIS, 2009–12. Mem., CABE, 2000–08 (Dep. Chm., 2007–08). Mem., Mgt Bd, British Council for Offices, 1999–2008 (Pres., 2004–05). Mem. Bd, Siobhan Davies Dance Co., 2002–17 (Chm., 2007–17); Gov., RSC, 2006– (Mem. Bd, 2006–13); Trustee and Mem. Bd, Bristol Old Vic Th., 2013–; Trustee and Dep. Chm., Garden Bridge Trust, 2013–19; Trustee and Member, Board: BAFTA, 2015–; Royal Opera House, 2016–. Vis. Prof., Nottingham Trent Univ., 2012–18. Hon. FRIBA 2000; Hon. Fellow, College of Estate Mgt, 2011; Hon. FAPM 2012; Hon. FABE 2012. Publications: regular columnist on matters relating to construction incl. Mgt Today and Building Mag. Recreations: sailing, opera, theatre, contemporary dance. Address: 4 Caithness Road, W14 0JB. T: (020) 7602 6082. E: paul.morrell@btinternet.com.

**MORRELL, Rev. His Honour Peter Richard;** a Circuit Judge, 1992–2009; a Judge, Mental Health Tribunal, 2001–14; b 25 May 1944; s of Frank Richard Morrell and Florence Ethel Morrell; m 1970, Helen Mary Vint Collins; two d. Educ: Westminster Sch.; University Coll., Oxford (MA). Admitted Solicitor, 1970; called to the Bar, Gray's Inn, 1974; a Recorder, 1990–92. C of E Reader, 2005–07, ordained deacon, 2008, priest, 2009, Peterborough Dio.; permission to officiate: Dio. of Peterborough, 2012–; Dio. of Europe, 2009–. Publications: The Rector of Pepynbridge, 2015; The Islamist of Pepynbridge, 2015; The Russells of Thornhaugh, 2015; The Honourable Member for Pepynbridge, 2016; From the Pulpit, Home and Abroad, 2018. Recreations: shooting, fishing, Spain. Address: Swallow Cottage, Apethorpe Road, Nassington, Peterborough PE8 6QT. T: 07860 573597.

**MORREY, Rev. William Reginald;** Faith Communities Adviser, Action for Children, 2008–14; b 24 March 1953; s of Claude William Morrey and Joan Morrey; m 1976, Vicki Mountford; two s. Educ: Birmingham Univ. (BA Theol. 1974); Queen's Coll., Birmingham; Westhill Coll., Birmingham (Cert. in Community and Youth Work 1976). Minister: Bideford, 1976–79; Ecclesall, Sheffield, and Chaplain to Children's Hosp., 1979–84; Halifax, 1984–87; Supt Minister, Bangor and Chaplain to UCNW, Bangor, and to RAF Valley, 1987–94; Co-ordinator, Council for Methodism in Wales, 1994–97; Chm., S Wales Dist, Methodist Ch, 1997–2007; Chair, Wales Synod, Methodist Ch in Wales, 2007–08. Pres., Methodist Conference, 2004–05; Chair, Methodist Council, 2006–09. Foundn Trustee, N Wales Deaf Assoc., 1994–97; Chm., NCH Cymru, 2005–07; Faith Communities Advr, Action for Children, 2008–14. Chm., Amelia Trust Farm, 2011–18. Publications: Seeing is Hearing: reflections on being deafened, 1995. Recreations: badminton, squash, walking, watching Rugby. Address: c/o Methodist Church Conference Office, 25 Marylebone Road, NW1 5JR.

**MORRICE, Graeme;** b Edinburgh, 23 Feb. 1959. Educ: Mauldeth Road Primary Sch.; Parrs Wood High Sch.; Broxburn Acad.; Napier Univ. (SHND Business Studies). Mem. (Lab) W Lothian Council, 1987–2012 (Leader, 1995–2007). MP (Lab) Livingston, 2010–15; contested (Lab) same seat, 2015.

**MORRICE, Jane;** Northern Ireland Member, European Economic and Social Committee, since 2006 (Vice President, 2013–15); Deputy Chief Equality Commissioner for Northern Ireland, 2008–15; b 11 May 1954; d of George Eric Morrice and Irene (née Cleland); m 1988, Paul Robinson (d 2009); one s. Educ: Univ. of Ulster (BA Hons W Eur. Studies 1977). Journalist, Brussels, specialising in internat. economy and Third World; business and labour relns corresp., 1980–87; BBC TV and Radio in NI, 1987–92; Head, Eur. Commn Office in NI, 1992–97; Mem., Eur. Commn Task Force preparing special support prog. for peace and reconciliation in NI and border counties of Ireland, 1992–97; Mem. (NI Women's Coalition) N Down, 1998–2003, and Dep. Speaker, 1999–2002, NI Assembly. Mem., NI Adv. Cttee, Ofcom, 2004–07. Bd Mem., Laganside Corp., 1998–2007. Publications: North/South Dialogue, 1984; The Lomé Convention From Politics to Practice, 1985. Recreations: writing, swimming, tennis, photography. Address: 18 Ballyholme Esplanade, Bangor, Co. Down BT20 5LZ.

**MORRICE, Philip;** HM Diplomatic Service, retired; director and consultant, various companies in Australia and UK; Director: Philip Morrice Consulting Pty Ltd, since 1999; TFG International Pty Ltd, since 2001; MyWhiskyJourneys Pty Ltd, since 2017; b 31 Dec. 1943; s of late William Hunter Morrice and Catherine Jane Cowie; m 1988, Margaret Clare Bower (marr. diss. 2014); one s one d. Educ: Robert Gordon's College, Aberdeen; Univ. of Besançon; École Nat. d'Administration, Paris; London Business Sch. Entered HM Diplomatic Service, 1963; served Kuala Lumpur, 1964–67; CO, later FCO, 1967–69; Caracas, 1969–72; First Sec., UK Delegn to OECD, Paris, 1973–75; First Sec. (Energy), UK Perm. Rep. to EC, Brussels, 1975–78; FCO, 1978–81; First Sec. (Commercial), later Counsellor (Comm.), Rome, 1981–85; Counsellor (Econ. and Comm.), Lagos, 1986–88; Minister-Counsellor, Consul-Gen. and Dir of Trade Promotion, Brasilia, 1988–92; Director, Anglo-Taiwan Trade Cttee, subseq. British Trade and Cultural Office, Taipei (on secondment), 1992–95; Consul-Gen., Sydney, and Dir Gen. of Trade and Investment Promotion in Australia, 1995–99. Dir, KPMG Consulting, 1999–2001. Publications: The Schweppes Guide to Scotch, 1983; The Whisky Distilleries of Scotland and Ireland, 1987; The Teacher's Book of Whisky, 1993; numerous articles. Recreations: travel, tennis, golf, sailing. Address: PO Box 44, Edgecliff, NSW 2027, Australia. T: 0408664021. E: philip.morrice@tfginternational.com. Clubs: Royal Automobile; Union (Sydney); Royal Sydney Golf.

**MORRILL, Rev. Prof. John Stephen,** DPhil; FRHistS; FBA 1995; Professor of British and Irish History, University of Cambridge, 1998–2015, now Emeritus; Fellow, Selwyn College, Cambridge, since 1975; b 12 June 1946; s of William Henry Morrill and Marjorie (née Ashton); m 1968, Frances Mead (d 2007); four d. Educ: Altrincham County Grammar Sch.; Trinity Coll., Oxford (BA 1967; MA, DPhil 1971; Hon. Fellow, 2006). FRHistS 1977. Keasbey Lectr in Hist., 1970–71, Jun. Res. Fellow, 1971–74, Trinity Coll., Oxford; Coll. Lectr in Hist., St Catherine's Coll., Oxford, 1973–74; Lectr in Mod. Hist., Univ. of Stirling, 1974–75; Cambridge University: Asst Lectr and Lectr, Faculty of History, 1975–92; Reader in Early Modern Hist., 1992–98; Dep. Dir, Centre for Arts, Humanities and Social Scis, 2001–04; Selwyn College, Cambridge: Dir of Studies in Hist., 1975–91; Tutor, 1979–91; Admissions Tutor, 1983–87; Sen. Tutor, 1987–91; Vice Master, 1994–2004. Vice-President: RHistS, 1993–97; British Acad., 2001–09; Mem., AHRB, 1999–2004 (Convenor, History Panel, 1999–2002; Chair, Res. Cttee, 2002–04). Ordained permanent deacon, RC Ch, 1996. Foreign Mem., Finnish Acad. of Arts and Scis, 2002. Centenary Fellow, Historical Assoc., 2006. FRSA 2008. Hon. MRIA 2010. Hon. DLitt UEA, 2002; DUniv Surrey, 2002. Publications: Cheshire 1630–1660, 1974; The Revolt of the Provinces 1630–1650, 1976, rev. edn 1980; The Cheshire Grand Jury 1625–1659, 1976; (with G. E. Aylmer) The Civil Wars and Interregnum: sources for local historians, 1979; Seventeenth-Century Britain, 1980; (ed) Reactions to the English Civil War, 1982; (ed) Land Men and Beliefs, 1985; Charles I, 1989; Oliver Cromwell and the English Revolution, 1990; (ed) The National Covenant in its British Context, 1990; (ed) The Impact of the English Civil War, 1991; (ed) Revolution and Restoration, 1992; The Nature of the English Revolution, 1993; (with P. Slack and D. Woolf) Public Men and Private Conscience in Seventeenth-Century England, 1993; (ed) The Oxford Illustrated History of Tudor and Stuart Britain, 1996; (with B. Bradshaw) The British Problem 1534–1707: state formation in the Atlantic Archipelago, 1996; Revolt in the Provinces: the English people and the tragedies of war, 1998; (jtly) Soldiers and Statesmen of the English Revolution, 1998; Oliver Cromwell, 2007; contribs to learned jls. Recreations: classical music, whisky and whiskey, cricket. Address: Selwyn College, Cambridge CB3 9DQ; 1 Bradford's Close, Bottisham, Cambs CB25 9DW. T: (01223) 811822.

**MORRIS,** family name of **Barons Killanin, Morris, Morris of Aberavon, Morris of Handsworth, Morris of Kenwood** and **Naseby.**

**MORRIS,** 4th Baron cr 1918, of St John's in the Dominion of Newfoundland and of the City of Waterford; **Thomas Anthony Salmon Morris;** b 2 July 1982; s of 3rd Baron Morris and of his 3rd wife, Juliet Morris (née Buckingham); S father, 2011. Heir: b Hon. John Michael Morris, b 1 Aug. 1983.

**MORRIS OF ABERAVON,** Baron cr 2001 (Life Peer), of Aberavon in the County of West Glamorgan and of Ceredigion in the County of Dyfed; **John Morris,** KG 2003; Kt 1999; PC 1970; QC 1973; Chancellor, University of South Wales (formerly University of Glamorgan), 2001–13; Lord-Lieutenant of Dyfed, 2002–06; b Nov. 1931; s of late D. W. Morris, Penywern, Talybont, Cardiganshire and Mary Olwen Ann Morris (later Lewis); m 1959, Margaret M., d of late Edward Lewis, OBE, JP, of Llandysul; three d. Educ: Ardwyn, Aberystwyth; University Coll. of Wales, Aberystwyth; Gonville and Caius Coll., Cambridge (LLM; Hon. Fellow); Academy of International Law, The Hague; Holker Senior Exhibitioner, Gray's Inn. Commissioned Royal Welch Fusiliers and Welch Regt. Called to the Bar, Gray's Inn, 1954, Bencher, 1985; a Recorder, 1982–97. MP (Lab) Aberavon, Oct. 1959–2001. Parly Sec., Min. of Power, 1964–66; Jt Parly Sec., Min. of Transport, 1966–68; Minister of Defence (Equipment), 1968–70; Sec. of State for Wales, 1974–79; opposition spokesman on legal affairs and Shadow Attorney Gen., 1979–81 and 1983–97; Attorney General, 1997–99. Member: Cttee of Privileges, 1994–97; Select Cttee on Implementation of Nolan Report, 1995–97; Adv. Cttee on Business Appointments, 2002–09. Dep. Gen. Sec. and Legal Adviser, Farmers' Union of Wales, 1956–58. Member: UK Delegn Consultative Assembly Council of Europe and Western European Union, 1963–64, 1982–83; N Atlantic Assembly, 1970–74. Chairman: Nat. Pneumoconiosis Jt Cttee, 1964–66; Jt Review of Finances and Management, British Railways, 1966–67; Nat. Road Safety Advisory Council, 1967. Mem. Council, Prince's Trust (Cymru), 2002–08. Pres., London Welsh Trust, 2001–09; Mem., London Welsh Assoc. Patron, London Welsh Lawyers, 2010–; Trustee, Foundn of St George's, Windsor, 2013–. David Lloyd George Meml Lect., Criccieth Fest., N Wales, 2007; Youard Lect., Swansea Univ., 2011; Annual Lect. for Political Archives, Nat. Liby of Wales, 2013. Hon. Fellow: UCW, Aberystwyth; Trinity Coll., Carmarthen; UC, Swansea; Univ. of Wales, Lampeter, 2009. Hon. LLD: Wales, 1985; S Wales, 2014. Lifetime Achievement Award, Wales Yearbook Awards, 2011. Publications: Fifty Years in Politics and the Law, 2011. Address: House of Lords, SW1A 0PW. Club: Garrick.

See also D. W. Morris.

**MORRIS OF BOLTON,** Baroness cr 2004 (Life Peer), of Bolton in the County of Greater Manchester; **Patricia Morris,** OBE; DL; b 16 Jan. 1953; d of late James Sydney Whittaker, Bolton; m 1978, His Honour William Patrick Morris, qv; one s one d. Educ: Bolton Sch. Girls' Div.; Clifton and Didsbury Colls of Educn. Personal Assistant: to N Regl Dir, Slater Walker Ltd, 1974–75; to Chevalier Dr Harry D. Schultz, 1975; Fund Manager, PPS, 1975–77; Technical Analyst: Foster & Braithwaite, 1977–78; Charlton, Seal, Dimmock & Co., 1979–83; Policy and Political Advr to a Cons. MEP, 1999–2001. Mem., Cons. Women's Nat. Cttee, 1989; Vice-Chm., Cons. Party, 2001–05. Contested (C) Oldham Central and Royton, 1992. Opposition Whip, H of L, 2004–10; opposition spokesman on women, 2005–10, on children and families, 2005–08, on educn, 2005–08, H of L. Dep. Chm., Salford Royal Hosps NHS Trust, 1993–97; Advr to Abbot of Ampleforth, 1998–2004. President: Nat. Benevolent Instn, 2006–; World Travel Market, 2009–; Co-Chm., Women in Public Policy, 2007–; Patron, OXPIP, 2006; Trustee: Disability Partnership, 2007–; UNICEF, 2007; Transformation Trust, 2009. Mem. Cttee, Patrons and

Associates, Manchester City Art Galls, 1982–94; Mem., Manchester N Valuation and Community Charge Tribunal, 1988–92; Chm., Bolton Cancer Res. Campaign, 1992–95; Mem. Bd Mgt, 1994–97, Dir, 1997–2002, Bolton Lads' and Girls' Club. Gov. and Trustee, Bolton Sch., 1992. Chancellor, Univ. of Bolton, 2010–13. DL Greater Manchester, 2008. *Address:* House of Lords, SW1A 0PW.

**MORRIS OF HANDSWORTH**, Baron *cr* 2006 (Life Peer), of Handsworth in the County of West Midlands; **William Manuel Morris**, Kt 2003; OJ 2002; General Secretary, Transport and General Workers Union, 1992–2003 (Deputy General Secretary, 1986–92); *b* 19 Oct. 1938; *s* of William and Una Morris; *m* 1957, Minetta (*d* 1990); two *s*. *Educ:* Mizpah Sch., Manchester, Jamaica; Handsworth Tech. Coll. Hardy Spicer Engineering, 1954. Joined TGWU, 1958: Shop Steward, 1962; Mem. Gen. Exec. Council, 1971–72; Dist Officer, Nottingham, 1973; Dist Sec., Northampton, 1976; Nat. Sec., Passenger Services, 1979–85. Mem., TUC Gen. Council, 1988–2003. Non-exec. Dir, Bank of England, 1998–2006. Chm., Morris Inquiry, Metropolitan Police Authy, 2004. Member: Commn for Racial Equality, 1977–87; IBA Gen. Adv. Council, 1981–86; Bd, ITF, 1986–2003; Road Transport ITB, 1986–92; Prince's Youth Business Trust, 1987–90; BBC General Adv. Council, 1987–88; Employment Appeals Tribunal, 1988–2009; Economic and Social Cttee, EC, 1990–92; NEDC, 1992; ACAS, 1997–2003; Royal Commn on H of L reform, 1999; Commn for Integrated Transport, 1999–2005; Architects' Registration Bd, 2001–05; Panel on Takeovers and Mergers, 2005–18. Chair, Midland Heart Housing Assoc., 2007–14. Vice Chm., Jamaica Nat. Money Services, 2007–11. Vis. Prof., Thames Valley Univ., 1997–2005. Chancellor: Univ. of Technology, Jamaica, 2000–10; Staffordshire Univ., 2004–11. Member: Governing Body, Atlantic Coll., 1994–2004; Court: Luton Univ., 1994–2006; Univ. of Northampton (formerly Nene Coll., later UC Northampton), 1996–2005. Member: Bd of Govs, London South Bank (formerly S Bank) Univ., 1997–2005; Univ. Assembly, Greenwich Univ., 1997–2001; Trustee Bd, Open Univ. Foundn, 1997–2006. Mem., Cricket Bd for England and Wales, 2004–15. Trustee, Performances Birmingham Ltd, 2008–15. DL Stafford, 2008. Hon. FRSA, 1992; Hon. FCGI, 1992. Hon. LLD: South Bank, 1994; Teesside, 1997; Univ. of Technol., Jamaica, 2000; Luton, 2000; Birmingham, Warwick, 2002; Nottingham, 2005; DUniv: Leeds Metropolitan, 1996; Middlesex, Stafford, 2002; Hon. DLitt: Westminster 1997; Hull, 2007; Hon. DBA Greenwich, 1997; Hon. Dr Thames Valley, 1997; Hon. DLit London South Bank, 2007; MUniv Open, 1995; Hon. MA UC Northampton, 2001. *Recreations:* walking, gardening, watching sports. *Address:* House of Lords, SW1A 0PW. *E:* morrisw@parliament.uk.

**MORRIS OF KENWOOD**, 3rd Baron *cr* 1950, of Kenwood; **Jonathan David Morris**; company director; *b* 5 Aug. 1968; *s* of 2nd Baron Morris of Kenwood and of Hon. Ruth (CBE 2014), *d* of Baron Janner; *S* father, 2004; *m* 1996, Melanie, *d* of Robin Klein; two *s*. *Educ:* St Paul's Sch.; Leicester Univ. *Heir: s* Hon. Benjamin Julian Morris, *b* 5 Nov. 1998.

**MORRIS OF YARDLEY**, Baroness *cr* 2005 (Life Peer), of Yardley in the county of West Midlands; **Estelle Morris**; PC 1999; *b* 17 June 1952; *d* of Rt Hon. Charles Richard Morris, PC and of Pauline Morris. *Educ:* Whalley Range High Sch., Manchester; Coventry Coll. of Educn (TCert); BEd Warwick Univ. Teacher, 1974–92. Councillor, Warwick DC, 1979–91 (Labour Gp Leader, 1981–89). MP (Lab) Birmingham, Yardley, 1992–2005. An Opposition Whip, 1994–95; opposition front-bench spokesman on educn, 1995–97; Parly Under-Sec. of State, 1997–98, Minister of State, 1998–2001, DFEE; Sec. of State for Educn and Skills, 2001–02; Minister of State (Minister for the Arts), DCMS, 2003–05. Hon. Fellow: St Martin's Coll., Lancaster, 2006; Goldsmiths, Univ. of London, 2018. Hon. DLitt: Warwick, 2002; Bradford, 2005; Chester, 2011; Hon. DEd: Wolverhampton, 2004; Manchester Metropolitan, 2007; Sunderland, 2008; Hon. DArts Leeds Metropolitan, 2004; DUniv: Birmingham, 2006; Open, 2011. *Address:* House of Lords, SW1A 0PW.

**MORRIS, Alan Douglas;** independent consultant on anti-corruption and regulatory compliance; Director, Anti-Corruption Advisory, PricewaterhouseCoopers, 2007–11; *b* 15 Sept. 1956; *s* of Leslie John Morris and Gladys Josephine Morris; *m* 1st, 1984, Barbara Caroline Alexandra Welsh (marr. diss. 1998); two *d*; 2nd, 1999, Anne Marie Stebbings (marr. diss. 2008). *Educ:* John Ruskin Grammar Sch., Croydon; Magdalene Coll., Cambridge (MA, LLM). FCMA. Joined Tate & Lyle, 1978; Esso Petroleum, 1981–84; Financial Controller: RBC Systems, 1984–87; MI Group, 1987–88; Simmons & Simmons: Finance Dir, 1988–96; Man. Dir, 1997–99; PricewaterhouseCoopers: Hd of Operations—Legal, 2000–04; Hd of Performance Improvement Consulting, Gatwick Region, 2004–07. Liveryman, Drapers' Co., 2005– (Mem., Ct of Assts, 2011–; Second Master Warden, 2016–17; Chm., Multi-Academy Trust, 2014). *Recreations:* acting, shooting, bridge, reading. *Address:* Waterloo Farm, Waterloo Lane, Stourton Caundle, Dorset DT10 2JF. *Club:* MCC.

**MORRIS, Albert**, FCIB; Director, 1989–94, and Deputy Group Chief Executive, 1992–94, National Westminster Bank; *b* 21 Oct. 1934; *m* 1987, Patricia Lane (*d* 2005). *Educ:* Skerry's Coll., Liverpool; City of Liverpool Coll. of Commerce; Admin. Staff Coll., Henley; MIT. National Westminster Bank: Head of Money Transmission, 1979–83; Dep. Gen. Manager, 1983–85, Gen. Manager, 1985–88, Management Services Div.; Chief Exec., Support Services, 1989–92. Director: NatWest Estate Management & Development Ltd, 1989–94; National Westminster Life Assce Ltd, 1992–94; Regent Associates, 1995–; Metroline plc, 1997– (Chm., 1997–2000); Chairman: BACS Ltd, 1985–94; Centre-file Ltd, 1988–94; Lorien plc, 1998–2007; Macro 4 plc, 2000–07; Inbucon Ltd, 2007–08. Founding Mem., 1985–87 and Mem. Council, 1990–94, UK Banking Ombudsman Scheme; Chm., APACS, 1993–94 (Dep. Chm., 1991–93; Dir, APACS Admin Ltd, 1987–94). Mem. Adv. Council, Sema Group, 1995–96; Special Advr, Ibos Ltd, 1995–96; non-exec. Mem., DSS Departmental Bd, 1993–97; Mem., Adv. Bd, Integral Specialist Services Ltd. Hon. Treas., Kingwood Trust, 1996–2000. CCMI; FCIB 1984 (Mem. Council, 1989–); FRSA 1989. Freeman, City of London, 1992; Liveryman, 1992–, Trustee, 2002–, Charity Dir and Chm. of Audit Cttee, Co. of Information Technologists. *Recreations:* golf, work, politics. *Address:* Stonebridge, 74 West Common, Harpenden, Herts AL5 2LD.

**MORRIS, Alfred Cosier**, CBE 2003; DL; Chairman, Higher Education Associates Ltd, since 2011; *b* 12 Nov. 1941; *s* of late Stanley Bernard Morris, Anlaby, E Yorks, and Jennie Fletcher; *m* 1970, Annette, *er d* of Eamonn and May Donovan, Cork, Eire; one *d*. *Educ:* Hymers Coll., Hull (E Riding Scholar); Univ. of Lancaster (MA Financial Control 1970). FCA; FSS. Articled clerk to Oliver Mackrill & Co., 1958–63; Company Sec., Financial Controller and Dir, several cos, 1963–71; Sen. Leverhulme Res. Fellow in Univ. Planning and Orgn, Univ. of Sussex, 1971–74; Vis. Lectr in Financial Management, Univ. of Warwick, 1973; Group Management Accountant, Arthur Guinness Ltd, 1974–76; Management Consultant, Deloitte Haskins & Sells, 1976–77; Financial Adviser, subsids of Arthur Guinness, 1977–80; Dep. Dir, Polytechnic of the South Bank, 1980–85, Acting Dir, 1985–86; Dir, Bristol Poly., 1986–92; Vice Chancellor: UWE, Bristol, 1992–2005; Univ. of Wales, Lampeter, 2008–09; (interim) London Metropolitan Univ., 2009–10. Strategic Advr, Kaplan UK, 2010–11. Adviser to H of C Select Cttee on Educn, Sci. and Arts, 1979–83. Chm., PCFC Cttee on Performance Indicators in Higher Educn, 1989–90; Member: CNAA, 1988–93; HEFCW, 1992–2000 (Chm., Audit Cttee, 1997–2000); Higher Educn Quality Council, 1992–94; South West Arts, 1994–2000; Bd, Westec,

1995–98; FEFCE, 1997–99 (Chm., Audit Cttee, 1997–99). Dir, Bristol and West, 1992–2002. Dir, SW Urban Regeneration Fund, 2003–08. Chairman: Bristol Old Vic Trust, 1992–94; Patrons of Bristol Old Vic, 1993–2008; Mem. Council, Bristol Old Vic Theatre Sch., 2006–10; Chm., N Bristol NHS Trust, 2006–08; Mem., SW of England RDA, 1998–2002; Trustee: Bristol Cathedral Trust, 1988–2007; John Cabot's Matthew Trust, 1996–2002; Bristol Charities, 2006–14; Mem. Exec. Cttee, Bristol Soc., 1992–2011. President: City Acad. Bristol, 2003–06; Hartpury Coll., Glos, 2008–; Director: eUnivs Holding Co., 2002–04; Hult Internat. Business Sch., 2015–. Member: Council, Clifton High Sch., 1995–2004; Representative Body, Ashridge Trust, 2015–. Vice-Chairman: Univ. of Law, 2015–; Arden Univ., 2016–. Patron: DAVAR, 1999–2010; Fast Track Trust, 2000–10; Bristol Drugs Project, 2002–10; Trustee: Quartet Community (formerly Gtr Bristol) Foundn, 1999–2004 (Chm., 1999–2000); Patrons of the RWA, 2000–06; Mem. Council, RWA, 2009–10. Ringer, Antient Soc. of St Stephen's Ringers, 2007–; Mem., Soc. of Merchant Venturers of Bristol, 2004–; Pres., Dolphin Soc., 2008–09; Chair, Trinity St David Trust, 2009–10. DL, 2002, High Sheriff, 2006–07, Glos. Hon. Fellow: Humberside Univ., 1990; RWA, 2001. Hon. LLD: Bristol, 1993; UWE, 2006; Gloucestershire, 2007. *Publications:* (ed jtly and contrib.) Resources and Higher Education, 1982; articles and contribs to jls on higher educn. *Recreations:* sailing, wind-surfing. *Address:* Park Court, Sodbury Common, Old Sodbury BS37 6PX. *T:* 07837 949996. *Club:* Salcombe Yacht.

**MORRIS, Andrew Bernard;** non-executive Chairman, Event Academy Ltd, since 2017; *b* 16 Oct. 1952; *s* of Sam and Golda Morris; *m* 1976, Jennifer Maizner; one *s* two *d*. *Educ:* Christ's Coll., London; Coll. for Distributive Trades; Harvard Business Sch. Sales and Marketing Dir, City Industrial Ltd, 1980–84; Jt Man. Dir, 1984–86, Man. Dir, 1986–89, Sales and Mktg Dir, 1989–99, Business Design Centre; CEO, 1999–2004, non-exec. Chm., 2004, Earls Court & Olympia Gp Ltd; Chief Exec., NEC Gp, 2004–06; Chm., 2009–11, Chief Exec., 2011–16, Acad. for Chief Executives Ltd. Non-executive Director: Business Design Centre, 1999–; Ingenious Media Live VCT, 2005–. Non-executive Chairman: Brand Events, 2007–11; World Photography Awards, 2007–11. *Publications:* Business to Go, 2012. *Recreations:* tennis, cycling, reading, contemporary art.

**MORRIS, Prof. Andrew David**, CBE 2018; MD; FRCPE, FRCPGlas; FRSE; FMedSci; Professor of Medicine and Vice Principal, Data Science, University of Edinburgh, since 2014; Director, Health Data Research UK, since 2017; *b* York, 7 Oct. 1964; *s* of David Morris and Beryl Morris; *m* 1994, Elspeth Riddell; one *s* two *d*. *Educ:* Royal Grammar Sch., Newcastle Upon Tyne; Robert Gordon's Coll., Aberdeen; N Berwick High Sch.; Univ. of Glasgow (MB ChB 1987; MSc Clin. Pharmacol. 1992; MD 1994). FRCPE 1994; FRCPGlas 1994. Lectr in Medicine, Univ. of Glasgow, 1990–94; University of Dundee: Sen. Lectr, 1994–96; Reader, 1996–2000; Prof. of Diabetic Medicine, 2000–10; Prof. of Medicine, 2010–14; Dean of Medicine, 2012–14; Hon. Prof., 2014–; Lead Clinician for Diabetes, Scotland, 2002–06; Chief Scientist, Health Dept, Scottish Govt, 2012–17; Dir, Usher Inst. of Population Health Sci. and Informatics, 2014–17, Vice-Principal of Data Sci., 2014–17, Univ. of Edinburgh. Mem., Assoc. of Physicians of GB and Ire., 2004. FRSE 2006; FMedSci 2009. *Publications:* 300 articles in jls on diabetes, epidemiology informatics and genetics. *Recreation:* golf. *Address:* University of Edinburgh, No 9 Edinburgh Bioquarter, 9 Little France Road, Edinburgh EH16 4UX. *T:* (0131) 651 7849. *E:* Andrew.Morris@ed.ac.uk; Health Data Research UK, Gibbs Building, 215 Euston Road, NW1 2BE. *E:* andrew.morris@hdruk.ac.uk. *Club:* Royal and Ancient Golf.

**MORRIS, Andrew James;** HM Diplomatic Service, retired; High Commissioner, Kingdom of Tonga, and Consul for Pacific Islands under American sovereignty South of the Equator, 1994–98; *b* 22 March 1939; *s* of late Albert Morris and of Clara Morris; *m* 1961, Ann Christine Healy; two *s*. Served Army, 1960–64. Entered FO, 1964; served Kuwait, Salisbury, Sofia, Muscat, and San Francisco, 1965–78; Consul, Los Angeles, 1978–82; FCO, 1982–86; First Sec., Kaduna, 1986–89; Dep. High Comr, Port Moresby, 1989–93; First Sec., FCO, 1993–94. *Recreations:* golf, travel.

**MORRIS, Anne;** see Molyneux, A.

**MORRIS, Anne Marie;** MP for Newton Abbot, since 2010 (C, 2010–17, Ind, 2017, C, since 2017); *b* London, 1957; *d* of late John Backes and of Margaret Agg. *Educ:* Hertford Coll., Oxford (BA PPP/Juris.); Open Univ. (MBA 1997); Harvard Univ. (Leadership Prog. 2004). Admitted solicitor, 1982; trainee solicitor, Withers, London, 1981–83; Corporate Finance Lawyer, Norton Rose, London, 1983–85; Corporate, Commercial, Banking Lawyer, Crossman Block, London, 1985; Asset Finance Lawyer, Sinclair Roche & Temperley, Singapore, 1986–88; Corporate Finance Lawyer, 1988–90, Hd, Educn and Trng, 1990–93, Allen & Overy; Dir, Professional and Business Develt, Baker & McKenzie, 1993–95; Dir, Mktg and Business Develt, Simmons & Simmons, 1995–97; Mktg Dir, Tax and Legal Services, EMEA, PricewaterhouseCoopers, 1997–99; Global Marketing Director: Ernst & Young, 1999–2002; Linklaters, 2002–05; Man. Dir, Manteion Ltd, 2005–. Mem., W Sussex CC, 2005–07 (Chm., Health Overview and Scrutiny Cttee). PPS, BIS, 2015–16. Member: Work and Pensions Select Cttee, 2012–15; Public Accounts Select Cttee, 2016–17, 2018–. Founder and Chair, All Party Parly Gp for Micro Businesses, 2011–15, on Rural Health and Social Care, 2016–, on Business Brexit, 2016–; Access to Medicines and Medical Devices, 2018–; Chair, All Party Parly Gp for Small Businesses, 2015. Sec., Bolney Br., Arundel and S Downs Cons. Assoc., 2003. Member: Cttee, Nat. Legal Educn and Trng Gp, 1990–94 (Chm., 1990–94); Lord Chancellor's Adv. Gp on Legal Educn, 1992–93; Cttee, Nat. Professional Services Mktg Gp, 1994–97; wkg party to develop personal mgt standards, Law Soc., 1994–95; Bd, Eur. Mentoring and Coaching Council, 2008–09; Specialist Assessor, Law, HEFC, 1992–93. Mem. Bd of Studies, Oxford Inst. of Legal Practice, 1990–2004; non-exec. Mem. Bd, Southampton Univ., 2005–06. Associate Gov., Rydon Sch., 2010–; former Gov., Newton Abbot Coll. FRSA 2000; FCIM 2002; MInstD 2001. *Address:* Templer House, Sandford Orleigh, Newton Abbot, Devon TQ12 2SQ. *T:* (01626) 368277. *E:* annemarie@annemariemorris.co.uk.

**MORRIS, His Honour Anthony Paul;** QC 1991; a Senior Circuit Judge, 2003–17; *b* 6 March 1948; *s* of late Isaac Morris Morris and Margaret Miriam Morris; *m* 1975, Jennie Foley; two *s*. *Educ:* Manchester Grammar Sch.; Keble Coll., Oxford (MA). Called to the Bar, Gray's Inn, 1970, Bencher, 2001; practising on Northern Circuit, 1970–2003. A Recorder of the Crown Court, 1988–2003. *Recreations:* travel, the arts, tennis, golf, bridge, Manchester United FC, Aldeburgh. *Clubs:* Garrick; Old Bailey Judges' Golfing Society.

**MORRIS, Carolyn;** see Quinn, C.

**MORRIS, Air Vice Marshal Christopher Brian**, CB 2012; QHS 2006; Chief of Staff Health (HQ Air Command), and Director General Medical Services, Royal Air Force, 2009–12; *b* Wrexham, 5 March 1952; *s* of Richard L. Morris and Patricia Morris; *m* 1975, Linda Goodman; two *s*. *Educ:* Hurstpierpoint Coll.; King's Coll. London; Westminster Med. Sch. (MB BS 1975); Birmingham Univ. (MMedSci 1995). DAvMed 1986; FFOM 2003. Joined RAF, 1972; med. cadet, 1972–75; SMO, RAF Laarbruch, 1988–91; Comd Flight Med. Officer (HQ Strike Comd), 1991–94; OC, Aviation Medicine Trng Centre, 1995–99; Asst Dir, Med. Policy (Surgeon Gen.'s Dept), 2000–03; ACOS Health, HQ

Personnel and Trng Comd, then HQ Air Comd, 2006–09. OStJ 2007. Cdre, Fisher Owners Assoc. Pres., RAF Medical Bd, 2003–06. Med. Advr, RAF Benevolent Fund, 2012–. Richard Fox Linton Meml Prize, RAF Medical Services, 1993. *Recreation:* offshore sailing. *Address:* Cornwall. *Club:* Royal Air Force.

**MORRIS, Rev. Prof. Colin,** FBA 2007; Professor of Medieval History, University of Southampton, 1969–92, now Emeritus; *b* 16 Sept. 1928; *s* of Henry Morris and Catherine Victoria Morris; *m* 1956, Brenda Gale; two *s* one *d*. *Educ:* Queen's College, Oxford (BA Modern Hist. 1st cl. 1948; BA Theol. 1st cl. 1951; Hon. Fellow, 2009); Lincoln Theol Coll. Ordained deacon, 1953; priest, 1954. Fellow and Chaplain, Pembroke Coll., Oxford, 1953–69. Pres., Ecclesiastical Hist. Soc., 1998–2000. FRHistS 1970. *Publications:* The Discovery of the Individual, 1972; The Papal Monarchy: the Western Church from 1050 to 1250, 1989; (ed with P. Roberts) Pilgrimage: the English experience from Becket to Bunyan, 2002; The Sepulchre of Christ and the Medieval West, 2005. *Recreations:* travel, liturgy, family and friends. *Address:* 14 Guildhall Apartments, 10 Park Walk, Southampton SO14 7BL. *T:* (023) 8033 3944. *E:* pr.colin.morris@gmail.com.

**MORRIS, David;** *see* Morris, William D.

**MORRIS, David;** MP (C) Morecambe and Lunesdale, since 2010; *b* Leigh, Lancs, 3 Jan. 1966; *s* of Captain Alan Lewis Morris and Vera White; *m* (marr. diss.); two *s*. *Educ:* St Andrew's Sch., Nassau. Company director, 1990–2010. Contested (C): Blackpool S, 2001; Carmarthen W and S Pembrokeshire, 2005. Mem., Select Cttee on Sci. and Technol., 2010–14, on Political and Constitutional Reform, 2014–15, on Public Admin and Constitutional Affairs, 2017–. PPS to Sec. of State for Wales, 2014–16, to Sec. of State for Scotland, 2016–17, to Sec. of State for NI, 2017–18, to Sec. of State for Educn, 2018–. Chairman, All-Party Groups: Bahamas, 2014–; Bovine TB, 2014–15; Coastal and Marine, 2014–15; Parly Space Cttee, 2015–; Classic Rock and Blues, 2015–. UK Govt Self Employment Ambassador, 2014–. Chm., Cons. Friends of Nuclear Energy, 2010–. Lt Comdr, RN, Parly Armed Forces Scheme, 2010. Master Mariner, 2014. *Recreations:* music, classic cars. *Address:* House of Commons, SW1A 0AA. *T:* (020) 7219 7234.

**MORRIS, His Honour David Griffiths;** a Circuit Judge, 1994–2012; *b* 10 March 1940; *s* of Thomas Griffiths Morris and Margaret Eileen Morris; *m* 1971, Carolyn Mary (*née* Miller); one *s* one *d*. *Educ:* Abingdon Sch.; King's Coll., Univ. of London (LLB Hons). Called to the Bar, Lincoln's Inn, 1965, Bencher, 1999. Pupillage in London (Temple and Lincoln's Inn), 1965–67; Tenant in London Chambers (Temple), 1967–72; Tenant in Cardiff Chambers, 1972–94; Asst Recorder, 1979–84; Local Junior for Cardiff Bar, 1981–87; Head of Chambers, 1984–94; a Recorder, 1984–94. Judicial Member: Gwent Probation Bd, 1998–; Gwent Courts Bd, 2004–07; SE Wales Courts Bd, 2007–. Founder Member: Llantwit Major Round Table and 41 Clubs; Llantwit Major Rotary Club (Pres., 1984–85); Llanmaes Community Council, 1982–84; Mem., Bd of Trustees, Torfaen Mus. Trust, 2011–. *Recreations:* Rugby Union football, cricket, swimming, theatre, reading, gardening, family. *Address:* Bryn Hafren, Newport Road, Castleton, Cardiff CF3 2UN. *T:* (01633) 681244. *Clubs:* Cardiff and County, United Services Mess (Cardiff); Pontypool Rugby Football (Past Pres.).

**MORRIS, David Richard,** CEng, FIMechE; Chairman, Northern Electric plc, 1989–97; *b* 25 July 1934; *s* of Frederick George Morris and Marjorie Amy (*née* Brown); *m* 1961, (Ann) Carole Birch; two *s* one *d*. *Educ:* Imperial College (BScEng). ACGI. Graduate Engrg apprenticeship, D. Napier & Son, Divl Chief Develt Engr and Gen. Manager, 1956–69, English Electric; Divl Gen. Manager and Divl Dir, General Electric Co., 1969–75; Subsid. Co. Man. Dir, Sears Holdings plc, 1975–80; Delta Group plc: Divl Man. Dir, 1980–84; Gp Exec. Dir, 1984–88. FRSA. *Recreations:* sailing, golf, tennis, gardening.

**MORRIS, Capt. David Simon,** RN; Partner, Kalbarri Thames Charters, since 2019; *b* 4 Feb. 1951; *s* of late Basil Charles Owen Morris and Alice Joan Morris (*née* Crump); *m* 1987, Susie Turner; two *d*. *Educ:* Sedbergh Sch.; BRNC, Dartmouth. Joined RN, 1971; specialised in submarines and navigation; served in HM Ships Gavinton, Albion, Norfolk, Olympus, Repulse, Resolution, Osiris, Ocelot, 1971–82; Flag Lieut to Flag Officer Submarines, 1978–80; qualified Submarine Commnd, 1983; Exec. Officer, HMS Churchill, 1983–85; Defence Intelligence, MoD, 1985–87; commanded: HMS Onyx, 1987–89; HMS Revenge, 1991; HMS Renown (P), 1992–94; Dir, UK Strategic Targeting Centre, 1994–96; Cabinet Office, 1996–99; Dep. ACOS (Progs and Policy) to C-in-C Fleet, 1999–2001; Asst Dir, Directorate of Naval Ops and Strategic Plans, MoD, 2001–04; Navy Job Evaluation Judge, 2004–05. MNI 2004–09. Clerk to Salters' Co., 2006–18; Co. Sec., Salters' Mgt Co Ltd, 2006–18; Dir, Salters' Educn Resources Ltd, 2015–18; Trustee, Salters' Co. Pension Scheme, 2006–18. Technical Deleg. (Alpine, Constituent), 1995–2001; Chairman: Combined Services Winter Sports Assoc. (Alpine), 1999–2004; British Alpine Racing Ski Club, 2008–10; Dir, Kandahar Ski Club, 2001–06. Freeman, Master Mariners' Co., 2004–11. Friend of RN Submarine Mus., 1999–. *Recreations:* ski-ing, vintage cars and boats, sailing, tennis, countryside. *Address:* 90 Fernside Road, SW12 8LJ. *T:* (020) 8673 9798. *E:* dsmorris58@gmail.com, kalbarricharters@gmail.com. *Clubs:* Hurlingham, Royal Navy of 1765 and 1785; Thames Vintage Boat; Royal Naval Sailing Assoc.; Rampart Owners; Kandahar Ski.

**MORRIS, Prof. David William,** PhD; FRAgS; sheep farmer, since 1983; agricultural consultant, since 1986; *b* 7 Dec. 1937; *s* of late David William Morris and Mary Olwen Ann Lewis; *m* 1966, Cynthia Cooper; one *s* one *d*. *Educ:* Ardwyn Grammar Sch.; UC of Wales (BSc Agric.); Univ. of Newcastle upon Tyne (PhD). FRAgS 1974. Develt Officer, Agric. Div., ICI, 1963–64; Asst Dir, Cockle Park Exptl Farm, Newcastle upon Tyne Univ., 1964–68; Farms Manager for Marquis of Lansdowne, Bowood, Wilts, 1968–70; Principal, Welsh Agricl Coll., Aberystwyth, 1970–83; Prof. of Agric., UC Wales, Aberystwyth, 1979–83. Churchill Fellowship, 1973. Chm., Lleyn Sheep Soc., 2005–07 (Treas., 2010–14); Hon. Life Mem., British Charollais Sheep Soc., 2001. John Gittins Meml Award, Royal Welsh Agricultural Soc., 2014. *Publications:* Practical Milk Production, 1976, 3rd edn 1977; (with M. M. Cooper) Grass Farming, 5th edn 1984. *Recreation:* farming. *Address:* Yr Ostrey, St Clears, Carmarthen, Carmarthenshire SA33 4AJ. *T:* (01994) 230240.
*See also Baron Morris of Aberavon.*

**MORRIS, Sir Derek (James),** Kt 2003; DPhil; Provost of Oriel College, Oxford, 2004–13 (Fellow and Tutor in Economics, 1970–98, now Hon. Fellow); *b* 23 Dec. 1945; *s* of Denis William and Olive Margaret Morris; *m* 1975, Susan Mary Whittles; two *s*. *Educ:* Harrow County Grammar Sch.; St Edmund Hall, Oxford (MA; Hon. Fellow); Nuffield Coll., Oxford; DPhil. Research Fellow, Centre for Business and Industrial Studies, Warwick Univ., 1969–70; Tutor and Sen. Tutor, Oxford University Business Summer Sch., 1970–78; Visiting Fellow, Oxford Centre for Management Studies, 1977–81; Economic Dir, Nat. Economic Develt Office, 1981–84; Oxford University: Sir John Hicks Res. Fellow, 1991–92; Chm., Social Studies Bd, 1993–94; Reader in Econs, 1996–98; Chm., Competition (formerly Monopolies and Mergers) Commn, 1998–2004 (Mem., 1991–2004; Dep. Chm., 1995–98). Vis. Lectr, Univ. of Calif, Irvine, 1986–87. Mem., Cttee of Inquiry into the Future of Cowley, 1990; Chm., Morris Review of Actuarial Profession, 2004–05; Mem., Cttee on Standards in Public Life, 2008–14. Gov., NIESR, 1997–. Chm., Oxford Economic Forecasting, 1984–98; Dir, Oxford China Economics Ltd, 1993–97; non-exec. Dir, Lucida plc, 2009–14 (Chm., 2013–14); Sen. Consultant, Frontier Economics, 2009–; Sen. Econ. Consultant on Chinese Econ. Reform, Cairncross Foundn, 2013–. Chairman, Trustees: OUP Pension Fund, 2006–16; Cheviot Pensions Master Trust, 2017–. Member Editorial Board: Oxford Economic Papers, 1984–97; Annual Register of World Events, 1985–97; Asst Editor, Jl of Industrial Economics, 1984–87; Associate Editor, Oxford Review of Economic Policy, 1985–98. Hon. Fellow, TCD, 2004. Hon. DCL: UC Dublin, 2004; UEA, 2005; Hon. DSc Cranfield, 2006. *Publications:* (ed) The Economic System in the UK, 1977, 3rd edn 1985; (with D. Hay) Industrial Economics, Theory and Evidence, 1979, 2nd edn 1991; (with D. Hay) Unquoted Companies, 1984; (ed jtly) Strategic Behaviour and Industrial Competition, 1987; (with D. Hay) State-Owned Enterprises and Economic Reform in China 1979–87, 1993; (as Harry Armstrong) Pawn's Gambit, 2012; articles on unemployment, trade policy and performance, productivity growth, industrial policy, macroeconomic policy, the Chinese economy, exchange rates, profitability, the stock market and corporate control. *Recreations:* ski-ing, Rugby, reading history. *Clubs:* Reform, Oxford and Cambridge.

**MORRIS, Desmond John,** DPhil; writer on animal and human behaviour; artist; *b* 24 Jan. 1928; *s* of late Capt. Harry Howe Morris and Dorothy Marjorie Fuller Morris (*née* Hunt); *m* 1952, Ramona Baulch (*d* 2018); one *s*. *Educ:* Dauntsey's Sch.; Birmingham Univ. (BSc); Magdalen Coll., Oxford (DPhil). Postdoctoral research in Animal Behaviour, Dept of Zoology, Oxford Univ., 1954–56; Head of Granada TV and Film Unit at Zool Soc. of London, 1956–59; Curator of Mammals, Zool Soc. of London, 1959–67; Dir, Inst. of Contemp. Arts, London, 1967–68; Research Fellow, Wolfson Coll., Oxford, 1973–81. Chm. of TV programmes: Zootime (weekly), 1956–67; Life (fortnightly), 1965–68; TV series: The Human Race, 1982; The Animals Roadshow, 1987–89; The Animal Contract, 1990; Animal Country, 1991–95; The Human Animal, 1994; The Human Sexes, 1997. 54 solo exhibitions of paintings in England, France, Belgium, Holland, Spain, Portugal and USA, 1948–; works in public collections in England, Scotland, Italy, Israel and USA. Hon. FLS 2006; Hon. FZS 2012. Hon. DSc Reading, 1998; Dr *hc* Malta, 2015. *Publications:* (Jt Ed.) International Zoo Yearbook, 1959–62; The Biology of Art, 1962; The Mammals: A Guide to the Living Species, 1965; (with Ramona Morris) Men and Snakes, 1965; (with Ramona Morris) Men and Apes, 1966; (with Ramona Morris) Men and Pandas, 1966; The Naked Ape, 1967; (ed) Primate Ethology, 1967; The Human Zoo, 1969; Patterns of Reproductive Behaviour, 1970; Intimate Behaviour, 1971; Manwatching: a field guide to human behaviour, 1977; (jtly) Gestures: their origins and distribution, 1979; Animal Days (autobiog.), 1979; The Giant Panda, 1981; The Soccer Tribe, 1981, 2nd edn 2016; Inrock (novel), 1983; The Book of Ages, 1983; The Art of Ancient Cyprus, 1985; Bodywatching: a field guide to the human species, 1985; The Illustrated Naked Ape, 1986; Catwatching, 1986; Dogwatching, 1986; The Secret Surrealist, 1987; Catlore, 1987; The Human Nestbuilders, 1988; The Animals Roadshow, 1988; Horsewatching, 1988; The Animal Contract, 1990; Animal-Watching, 1990; Babywatching, 1991; Christmas Watching, 1992; The World of Animals, 1993; The Human Animal, 1994; The Naked Ape Trilogy, 1994; Bodytalk: a world guide to gestures, 1994; The Illustrated Catwatching, 1994; Illustrated Babywatching, 1995; Catworld: a feline encyclopedia, 1996; Illustrated Dogwatching, 1996; The Human Sexes, 1997; Illustrated Horsewatching, 1998; Cool Cats: the 100 cat breeds of the world, 1999; Body Guards: protective amulets and charms, 1999; The Naked Eye: travels in search of the human species, 2000; Dogs: the ultimate dictionary of over 1,000 dog breeds, 2001; Peoplewatching, 2002; The Nature of Happiness, 2004; The Naked Woman: a study of the female body, 2004; Watching: encounters with humans and other animals, 2006; The Naked Man: a study of the male body, 2008; Baby: the amazing story of the first two years of life, 2008; (with S. Parker) Planet Ape, 2009; Owl, 2009; Child: how children think, learn and grow in the early years, 2010; Monkey, 2013; The Artistic Ape: three million years of art, 2013; Leopard, 2014; Headworks, 2014; Bison, 2015; The Boats of Malta: the art of fishermen, 2016; Cats in Art, 2017; Sixty-Nine Surrealists, 2017; The Lives of the Surrealists, 2018; Bodyworks, 2019; Postures: body language in art, 2019; numerous papers in zoological jls. *Recreations:* book-collecting, archæology. *Address:* c/o Silke Bruenink Agency, Margit-Schramm-Strasse 12, 80639 Munich, Germany. *W:* desmond-morris.com.

**MORRIS, Desmond Victor;** HM Diplomatic Service, retired; *b* 26 June 1926; *s* of late John Walter Morris and Bessie (*née* Mason); *m* 1st, 1951, Peggy Iris Mumford (*d* 2014); two *d*; 2nd, 1961, Patricia Irene Ward, *d* of Charles Daniel and Emma Camwell; one *d*. *Educ:* Portsmouth Southern Secondary Sch. for Boys; Durham Univ. (RAF Aircrew Cadets Short Course). Served RAF, 1945–48. Joined HM Diplomatic Service, 1948; served at Seattle, Budapest, Saigon; Inf. Officer and Second Sec., Addis Ababa; Second Sec., Berne; Consul and First Secretary: Ankara; Pretoria; Dep. and Actg High Comr, Georgetown, 1973–78; Dep. and Actg Head of Accommodation and Services Dept, FCO, 1979–82; Consul-Gen. and Counsellor (Administration), Washington, 1982–86.

**MORRIS, Dr Elizabeth Mary,** OBE 2000; PhD; Emeritus Associate, Scott Polar Research Institute, since 2016 (Senior Associate, 2006–16); *b* London, 7 Sept. 1946; *d* of James Creed Morris and Jessie Margaret Morris. *Educ:* Univ. of Bristol (BSc Physics; PhD Physics 1972). Institute of Hydrology: Higher SO, 1975–76; Sen. SO, 1976–80; Principal SO, 1980–86; British Antarctic Survey: Hd, Ice and Climate Div., 1986–99; Res. Activities Co-ordinator, 1999–2000; Arctic Sci. Advr, NERC, 2000–06 (on secondment). Vis. Prof., Earth Systems Sci. Centre, 1996–2010, Prof. of Ice Physics, 2015, Univ. of Reading. President: Internat. Commn on Snow and Ice, 1995–2001; Internat. Glaciological Soc., 2002–05. Hon. DSc Bristol, 2015. Polar Medal, 2003; Richardson Medal, Internat. Glaciological Soc., 2016. *Publications:* contrib. papers to learned jls on glacier flow, snow physics, boundary layer meteorology and hydrology. *Recreations:* climbing, communal living. *Address:* Scott Polar Research Institute, University of Cambridge, Lensfield Road, Cambridge CB2 1ER. *T:* (01223) 336568. *E:* emm36@cam.ac.uk. *Clubs:* Cambridge Climbing and Caving; Austrian Alpine.

**MORRIS, Frances Mary;** Director, Tate Modern, since 2016; *b* London, 13 Jan. 1959; *d* of late Alan Croft Faulkner Morris and of Elizabeth Villar; *m* 1989, Martin Caiger-Smith; two *s* one *d*. *Educ:* King's Coll., Cambridge (BA 1st cl. 1982; Hon. Fellow); Courtauld Inst. of Art (MA Hist. of Art 1983). Curator, Tate Gall., 1987–97; Art Prog. Curator, Tate Gall. of Modern Art, 1997–2000; Hd of Displays, and Curator, Modern and Contemp. Art, Tate Modern, 2000–07; Hd of Collections, then Dir of Collection, Internat. Art, Tate, 2007–16. Member: Bd, Internat. Cttee for Mus and Collections of Modern Art, ICOM, 2000–; Adv. Cttee, Serralves Mus. of Contemp. Art, Porto; Bd, Fruitmarket Gall., Edinburgh. Hon. Dr: UAL; RCA; York; Essex; Edinburgh. *Publications:* Paris Post War: art and existentialism, 1993; (with S. Morgan) Rites of Passage, 1995; (with R. Flood) Zero to Infinity: Arte Povera 1962–72, 2001; (with Christopher Green) Jungles in Paris, 2005; Tate Modern: the handbook, 2006; Louise Bourgeois, 2007; Yayoi Kusama, 2012; Agnes Martin, 2016; Giacometti, 2017. *Recreations:* sailing, walking. *Address:* Tate Modern, Bankside, SE1 9TG. *T:* (020) 7401 5220. *E:* frances.morris@tate.org.uk.

**MORRIS, Hon. Frederick Reginald;** President of the High Court, Republic of Ireland, 1998–2001; *b* 1 Dec. 1929; *s* of Michael Archdale Morris and Mary Archdale Morris (*née* Guiry); *m* 1965, Valerie Rose Farrell; two *d*. *Educ:* Glenstall Abbey Sch.; University Coll., Dublin; King's Inns, Dublin. Called to the Irish Bar, 1959 (Bencher, 1990), Inner Bar, 1973,

Hon. Bencher, King's Inns, 2001; called to the Bar, Middle Temple, 1969, Hon. Bencher, 1999; Judge, High Court in Ireland, 1990–98; Mem., Council of State, 1998–2001. Chm., Tribunal of Inquiry into allegations of misconduct by mems of An Garda Síochána. Trustee, Acad. of Eur. Law, Trier. Freeman, City of Waterford, 1963. *Recreations*: sailing, golf, Rugby. *Address*: 17 Leeson Village, Upper Leeson Street, Dublin 4, Republic of Ireland; Four Courts, Dublin 7, Republic of Ireland. *Clubs*: Royal Irish Yacht (Dun Laoghaire); Milltown Golf (Dublin), Blainroe Golf (Co. Wicklow); University College Dublin Rugby.

**MORRIS, Gareth;** see Morris, John G.

**MORRIS, Prof. Gareth Alun,** DPhil; FRS 2014; FRSC; Professor of Physical Chemistry, University of Manchester, since 1998; *b* Harrogate, 6 July 1954; *s of* Mervyn Morris and Margaret Alice Morris (*née* Burley); *m* 1983, Mary Isabella Ayre Care; two *d*. *Educ*: Royal Grammar Sch., Newcastle upon Tyne; Magdalen Coll., Oxford (MA Nat. Sci.; DPhil 1978). CChem 1986; MRSC 1986, FRSC 2016. Fellow, Magdalen Coll., Oxford, 1978–81; Izaak Walton Killam Postdoctoral Res. Fellow, Univ. of British Columbia (on leave of absence), 1978–79; Lectr, 1982–89, Reader, 1989–97, in Physical Chem., Univ. of Manchester. Leverhulme Res. Fellow, 1996–97; Vis. Prof., Univ. Pierre et Marie Curie, 2010. *Publications*: approx. 250 articles in learned jls, book chapters. *Recreations*: literature, music (especially guitar and lute), allotments, birdwatching. *Address*: School of Chemistry, University of Manchester, Oxford Road, Manchester M13 9PL. *T*: (0161) 275 4665. *E*: g.a.morris@manchester.ac.uk.

**MORRIS, Gillian Susan,** PhD; barrister in private practice; *b* 30 March 1953; *d of* late Edgar and Eve Morris; *partner*, David Millett. *Educ*: Univ. of Bristol (LLB Hons 1974); Churchill Coll., Cambridge (PhD 1978). Lectr in Law, Nottingham Univ., 1977–79; Sen. Lectr in Law, Poly. of N London, 1980–88; Lectr, 1988–91, Reader, 1991–93, Prof. of Law, 1993–2003, Prof. Associate, 2003–08, Brunel Univ. Honorary Professor: Univ. of Warwick, 2007–12; UCL, 2013–. Called to the Bar, Inner Temple, 1997. Labour Law Expert for ILO, 1990–; Legal Expert Advr to EC, later EU, 1991–. Chair, Rev. Body for Nursing and Other Health Professions, later NHS Pay Rev. Body, 2005–11; Deputy Chair: Central Arbitration Cttee, 2000–; Police Negotiating Bd and Police Adv. Bd for England and Wales, 2005–14; Mem., Panel of Arbitrators, ACAS, 2007–. *Publications*: Strikes in Essential Services, 1986; (with S. Fredman) The State as Employer: labour law in the public services, 1989; (with T. J. Archer) Trade Unions, Employers and the Law, 1992, 2nd edn 1993; (with S. Deakin) Labour Law, 1995, 6th edn 2012; (with T. J. Archer) Collective Labour Law, 2000; contrib. articles to legal jls. *Recreations*: walking, swimming, travel, the arts. *Address*: Matrix Chambers, Griffin Building, Gray's Inn, WC1R 5LN. *Club*: Lansdowne.

**MORRIS, Grahame;** MP (Lab) Easington, since 2010; *b* 13 March 1961; *s of* late Richard and Constance Morris; *m* 1986, Michelle Hughes; two *s*. *Educ*: Peterlee Howletch Secondary Sch.; Newcastle Coll. (BTEC ONC); Newcastle Poly. (BTEC HNC Med. Lab. Scis). Med. lab. SO, Sunderland Royal Infirmary, 1980–87; researcher and constituency caseworker to John Cummings, MP, 1987–2010. Non-exec. Dir, City Hosps Sunderland NHS Trust, 1997–2005. Mem. (Lab) Easington DC, 1987–2003. Opposition Whip, 2015–16; Shadow Sec. of State for Communities and Local Govt and Shadow Minister for Constitnl Convention, 2016. Member: Health Select Cttee, 2010–15; Transport Select Cttee, 2018–. *Address*: House of Commons, SW1A 0AA.

**MORRIS, Grant,** OBE 1994; RCNC; Commercial Director, NATO Eurofighter and Tornado Management Agency, 2008–11; Director, Foxborough Consultancy, 2011–14; *b* 28 May 1951; *s of* Leslie and Gena Morris; *m* 1975, Amanda Morgan; two *s* one *d*. *Educ*: Univ. of Bath (BSc Hons Engrg 1974). RCNC 1976; CEng, MIMechE 1979; MCIPS 2003. Proj. Manager, HMS Ocean, 1994–96; MoD, 1996; HQ QMG, 1997; Internat. Relns, MoD, 1997–2000; rcds, 2001; Dir Commercial, 2002–06, Dir Gen. Commercial, 2006–07, Defence Logistics Orgn; Dir Gen. Commercial, Defence Equipment and Support, MoD, 2007–08. Member: RYA (instructor, 1997–); RNSA. *Recreations*: sailing, diving, cookery, travel, ski-ing, mountain biking. *Address*: Foxborough Cottage, North Road, Bath BA2 6HW. *E*: foxys.morris@gmail.com.

**MORRIS, Prof. Howard Redfern,** FRS 1988; Professor of Biological Chemistry, Imperial College London, 1980–2001, now Professor Emeritus and Senior Research Investigator; Founder Chairman and Chief Scientific Officer, BIOPHARMASPEC Group, since 2014; *b* 4 Aug. 1946; *s of* Marion Elizabeth and Herbert Morris, Bolton, Lancs; *m* 1st, 1969, Lene Verny Jensen (marr. diss.); two *d*; 2nd, 1988, Maria Panico; one *s* one *d*. *Educ*: Univ. of Leeds (BSc 1967; PhD 1970). SRC Fellow, Cambridge, 1970–72; Scientific Staff, MRC Lab. of Molecular Biol., Cambridge, 1972–75; Imperial College: Lectr, Dept of Biochem., 1975–78; Reader in Protein Chem., 1978–80; Hd, Dept of Biochem., 1985–88; Chm., Div. of Life Sciences, 1985–88. Founder Chm. and Chief Scientific Officer, M-Scan Gp, analytical chem. and biochem. consultants, 1979–2010. Visiting Professor: Univ. of Virginia, 1978; Soviet Acad. of Scis, 1982; Univ. of Naples, 1983; Life Scis Div., E. I. Dupont, USA, 1984–85; Dow Lectr in Analytical Chem., Univ. of British Columbia, 1989–90. Royal Soc. Rep. to Council, Inst. of Cancer Res., 1994–98 (Council Mem. and Trustee, 1994–2004); Mem., Audit Cttee, Inst. of Cancer Res., 2013–17; Mem., Sectional Cttee on Gen. and Hon. Candidates for Fellowship, Royal Soc. Mem., EMBO, 1979–. Dr *hc* Univ. of Naples, Federico II, 2005; Hon. DSc Leeds, 2015. BDH Gold Dist. Medal and Prize for Analytical Biochem., Biochem. Soc., 1978; Medal and Prize for macromolecules and polymers, RSC, 1982; Gold Medal for dist. contribs to biopolymer sequencing and mass spectroscopy, Univ. of Naples/CNR Italy, 1989; Rector's Award for Excellence in Teaching, 1996, 2001; Blaise Pascale Medal and Prize for Life Scis and Medicine, Eur. Acad. of Scis, 2010; Franklin Medal and Prize for contribs to mass spectrometer design, Inst. of Physics, 2012; Royal Medal, Royal Soc., 2014. *Publications*: (ed) Soft Ionisation Biological Mass Spectrometry, 1981; some 450 contribs to learned jls, on mass spectrometry, incl. develt of Q-TOF instrumentation, protein, glycoprotein and natural product structure elucidation, including Enkephalin (the first endorphin), SRS-A leukotrienes, interleukin 2 and calcitonin gene related peptide. *Recreations*: travel, guitar. *Address*: Department of Life Sciences, Faculty of Natural Sciences, Sir Ernst Chain Building, Imperial College London, SW7 2AZ. *T*: (020) 7594 5221, *Fax*: (020) 7225 0458. *E*: h.morris@imperial.ac.uk.

**MORRIS, Hugh Colin,** FRCO; Director, Royal School of Church Music, since 2018; *b* Oxford, 18 Feb. 1977; *s of* Geoffrey and Jennifer Morris; *m* 2001, Sarah Reynolds; two *d*. *Educ*: Abingdon Sch.; Magdalene Coll., Cambridge (Organ Scholar; BA Music 1998). FRCO 2002; DipCHD. Teacher of Music, King's Sch., Tynemouth, 2001–09; Asst Organist, Hexham Abbey, 2001–09; Lectr and Tutor in Harmony, Newcastle Univ., 2002–09; Teacher of Music, Bournemouth Sch. for Girls, 2009–15; Director of Music: Christchurch Priory, 2009–15; Derby Cathedral, 2015–18. *Recreations*: music, walking, taming the garden, eating Sarah's cooking. *Address*: Royal School of Church Music, 19 The Close, Salisbury SP1 2EB. *T*: (01722) 424848. *E*: hmorris@rscm.com.

**MORRIS, Ian;** see Morris, His Honour James I.

**MORRIS, Prof. Ian Matthew,** PhD; Jean and Rebecca Willard Professor of Classics, Stanford University, since 1995; Fellow, Stanford Archaeology Center, since 2000; Senior Fellow, LSE IDEAS, since 2015; *b* Stoke-on-Trent, Staffs, 27 Jan. 1960; *s of* Noel and Barbara Morris; *m* 1989, Kathy St John. *Educ*: Alleynes Comprehensive Sch., Stone; Birmingham Univ. (BA 1st Cl. Hons 1981); Cambridge Univ. (PhD 1985). Res. Fellow, Jesus Coll., Cambridge, 1985–87; Asst Prof., 1987–90, Associate Prof., 1990–95, Hist. and Classics, Univ. of Chicago. Dir, Stanford excavations at Monte Polizzo, Sicily, 2000–07. Guggenheim Fellow, 2002–03; Nat. Fellow, Hoover Instn, 2013–14. Corresp. FBA 2013. Hon. Dr: De Pauw, 2012; Birmingham, 2014. *Publications*: Burial and Ancient Society, 1987; Death-Ritual and Social Structure in Classical Antiquity, 1992 (trans. Greek, 1997); (ed) Classical Greece: ancient histories and modern archaeologies, 1994; (with B. Powell) A New Companion to Homer, 1997; Archaeology as Cultural History, 2000; (with B. Powell) The Greeks: history, culture and society, 2005, 2nd edn 2009; (with J. Manning) The Ancient Economy: evidence and models, 2005; (jtly) The Cambridge Economic History of the Greco-Roman World, 2007; (with W. Scheidel) The Dynamics of Ancient Empires, 2009; Why the West Rules - for Now, 2010; The Measure of Civilization, 2013; War! What is it Good For?, 2014; Foragers, Farmers, and Fossil Fuels, 2015. *Recreations*: dogs, cats. *Address*: Department of Classics, Building 110, Stanford University, Stanford, CA 94305, USA. *T*: 8313380653. *E*: imorris@stanford.edu.

**MORRIS, Jack Anthony,** CBE 2016 (OBE 2005); Chairman, Business Design Centre Group Ltd, since 1992; *b* London, 23 June 1956; *s of* Sam and Golda Morris; *m* 1983, Susan Lee; two *s* (one *d* decd). *Educ*: Christ's Coll. Sch., Finchley. Trainee accountant, Pridie Brewster Chartered Accountants, 1975–78; Business Design Centre Group Ltd: Gp Financial Controller, 1979–83; Gp Finance Dir, 1983–86; Dep. Chm., 1986–91. Dir, Earls Court and Olympia Gp Ltd, 1999–2004. Mem., London Skills and Employment Bd, 2006–11, London Enterprise Panel, 2012–16, Mayor of London; Co Vice Chair, London Councils Young People's Educn and Skills, 2010–17; Chm., Islington Business Bd, 2009–19. Mem. Council, CBI London Reg., 1992–99. Chm., City and Islington Coll., 1996–2014. Chairman: Morris Charitable Trust, 1989–; Anne Frank Trust UK, 1999–2003; Ben Kinsella Trust, 2010–13; Islington Giving Appeal, 2010–; Brain Tumour Charity, 2018–. FInstD 1998; FRSA 2007. Hon. DSc City Univ., London, 2008. *Recreations*: family, cycling, classic cinema, film music, art and design, charity and voluntary work. *Address*: Business Design Centre, 52 Upper Street, Islington, N1 0QH. *T*: (020) 7359 3535.
*See also A. B. Morris.*

**MORRIS, James;** see Morris, Jan.

**MORRIS, Air Vice-Marshal James,** CBE 1984 (OBE 1977); Chief Executive, Scottish Society for the Prevention of Cruelty to Animals, 1991–2001; *b* 8 July 1936; *s of* late James and Davina Swann Morris; *m* 1959, Anna Wann Provan; three *s*. *Educ*: Kirkcaldy High Sch.; Edinburgh Univ. (BSc). Commnd RAF, 1957; Flying/Staff Duties, RAF, USN, RN, 1960–72; Sqn Comdr 201 Sqdn, 1975–77; psc 1978; Station Comdr RAF Kinloss, 1981–84; Dir Operational Requirements (Air), MoD, 1986–89; AO Scotland and NI, 1989–91. President: Scottish Area, RAFA, 1991–2006; Scottish Union Jack Assoc., 1995–2006. Regl Chm., Scottish and NI Air Cadets, 1995–97. HM Comr, Queen Victoria Sch., Dunblane, 1995–2005. Mem., Governing Bd, Scottish Food Quality Certification Ltd, 1998–2001; Chm., Mgt Bd, RAF Benevolent Fund Home, Alastrean House, 2001–05. *Recreation*: golf. *Address*: 22 The Inches, Dalgety Bay, Fife KY11 9YG. *Club*: Royal Air Force.

**MORRIS, James;** MP (C) Halesowen and Rowley Regis, since 2010; an Assistant Government Whip, since 2019; *b* Nottingham, 4 Feb. 1967; *m* 1995, Anna Mellitt; one *s* one *d*. *Educ*: Nottingham High Sch.; Univ. of Birmingham (BA 1st cl. Eng. Lit.); Univ. of Oxford (postgrad.); Cranfield Sch. of Mgt (MBA). IT/software entrepreneur, 1996–2006; Managing Director: Torington Interactive, 1996–2001; Vice-Versa Ltd, 2001–06; Chief Exec., Localis, 2008–10. PPS to Minister for Employment, 2014–15, to Minister for Europe, 2015–16, to Sec. of State for Health, 2016–17, to First Sec. of State and Minister for Cabinet Office, 2017–19. Mem., Communities and Local Govt Select Cttee, 2010–14; Chm., All Party Parly Gp for Mental Health, 2012–15. *Publications*: (ed jtly) Big Ideas: building on Conservative fundamentals, 2008; (ed jtly) Million Vote Mandate, 2008; (ed jtly) Can Localism Deliver?, 2009. *Recreations*: spending time with family, cricket, theatre, music. *Address*: House of Commons, SW1A 0AA. *T*: (020) 7219 7080. *E*: james.morris.mp@parliament.uk.

**MORRIS, His Honour (James) Ian;** a Circuit Judge, 1994–2007; *b* 6 Feb. 1944; *s of* late Thomas Orlando Morris and Pearl Morris; *m* 1st, 1966, Maureen Burton (marr. diss. 1978); one *s* one *d*; 2nd, 1979, Christine Dyson (*d* 1980); 3rd, 1982, Alison Turner (marr. diss. 1988); 4th, 1998, Jane Boddington. *Educ*: King Henry VIII Grammar Sch., Coventry; Corpus Christi Coll., Oxford (BA Jurisp. 1967; MA 1970). Called to the Bar, Inner Temple, 1968; Asst Recorder, 1984, Recorder, 1988–94, Midland and Oxford Circuit; Liaison Judge, Hereford and Worcs Magistracy, 1997–2004; Jt Liaison Judge, W Mercia Magistracy, 2004–06; a Dep. High Court Judge, 1998–2005; Designated Family and Adoption Judge for Hereford and Worcs, 1998–2005. Mem., Judicial Appts Commn, 2007–09. Chm., W Mercia Area Judicial Forum, 2005–06. Chairman: Sandwell AHA Enquiry, 1979; Rubery Hosp. Enquiry for RHA, 1981; Bromsgrove Hosp. Enquiry, 1982; Solihull Hosp. Enquiry for RHA, 1984; RHA Counsel, Cttee of Enquiry, Legionnaires' Disease, Stafford, 1985. Mem., Wkg Party on Arrangements for Admission of Accused and Convicted Persons to Mental Hosp., 1985–89. Founder and first Chm., Birmingham Cancer Support Gp, 1984. Executive Chairman: link-global ltd, 2007–16; Warmamask Ltd, 2007–15. Chm., Bromsgrove Internat. Musicians' Competition, 2017– (Exec. Chm., 2013–17). Hon. Pres., Council of Valuation Tribunal Members in England, 2006–10. Sen. Hon. Coach (Loughborough), AAA, 1965. *Publications*: Just a Grain of Sand (poetry), 2004; Palmers Hill (historical fiction), 2009; contrib. Internat. Jl of Child Abuse and Neglect. *Recreations*: writing, music, walking. *Address*: c/o Worcester Crown Court, Foregate Street, Worcester.

**MORRIS, Jan,** CBE 1999; MA Oxon; FRSL; writer; *b* 2 Oct. 1926. Commonwealth Fellow, USA, 1953; Editorial Staff, The Times, 1951–56; Editorial Staff, The Guardian, 1957–62. Fellow, Yr Academi Gymreig; Mem., Gorsedd of Bards, Nat. Eisteddfod of Wales. Hon. FRIBA 1998; Hon. FLSW 2016. Hon. Fellow: UCW, 1992; UCNW, 2003; Hon. Student, Christ Church, Oxford, 2002. Hon. DLitt: Wales, 1993; Glamorgan, 1996. PEN Lifetime Award, 2005; Wales World-Wide Award, Ninnau and Cambria magazines, 2007; Honourable Soc. of Cymmrodorion Medal, 2016. *Publications*: (as James Morris or Jan Morris): Coast to Coast, 1956; Sultan in Oman, 1957; The Market of Seleukia, 1957; Coronation Everest, 1958; South African Winter, 1958; The Hashemite Kings, 1959; Venice, 1960, 3rd edn 1993; The Upstairs Donkey, 1962 (for children); The World Bank, 1963; Cities, 1963; The Presence of Spain, 1964, rev. edn (as Spain), 1988; Oxford, 1965, 2nd edn 1986; Pax Britannica, 1968; The Great Port, 1970; Places, 1972; Heaven's Command, 1973; Conundrum, 1974; Travels, 1976; Farewell the Trumpets, 1978; The Oxford Book of Oxford, 1978; Destinations, 1980; My Favourite Stories of Wales, 1980; The Venetian Empire, 1980, 2nd edn 1988; The Small Oxford Book of Wales, 1982; A Venetian Bestiary, 1982; The Spectacle of Empire, 1982; (with Paul Wakefield) Wales, The

First Place, 1982; (with Simon Winchester) Stones of Empire, 1983; The Matter of Wales, 1984, revd edn as Wales, 1998; Journeys, 1984; Among the Cities, 1985; Last Letters from Hav, 1985; (with Paul Wakefield) Scotland, The Place of Visions, 1986; Manhattan '45, 1987; Hong Kong, 1988, 3rd edn 1996; Pleasures of a Tangled Life, 1989; (with Paul Wakefield) Ireland, Your Only Place, 1990; Sydney, 1992; O Canada!, 1992; Locations, 1992; (ed) Travels with Virginia Woolf, 1993; (with Twm Morys) A Machynlleth Triad, 1994; Fisher's Face, 1995; Fifty Years of Europe: an album, 1997; Lincoln: a foreigner's quest, 1999; (with Twm Morys) Our First Leader, 2000; Trieste and the Meaning of Nowhere, 2001; A Writer's House in Wales, 2002; A Writer's World, 2003; Hav, 2006; Europe, 2006; Contact!, 2009; Ciao, Carpaccio!, 2014; Battleship Yamato, 2018; In My Mind's Eye, 2018. *Address*: Trefan Morys, Llanystumdwy, Gwynedd, Cymru/Wales LL52 0LP. *T*: (01766) 522222. *E*: jan.morris1@yahoo.com.

**MORRIS, Rev. Dr Jeremy Nigel;** Master, Trinity Hall, Cambridge, since 2014; *b* London, 22 Jan. 1960; *s* of David and Diana Morris; *m* 1992, Alexandra Davidson; one *s* two *d*. *Educ*: Balliol Coll., Oxford (BA 1981; DPhil 1985); Clare Coll., Cambridge (BA 1992); Westcott House, Cambridge (Cert. of Theol. for Ministry 1993). Scholarship Officer, Assoc. of Commonwealth Univs, 1985–87; Sen. Admin. Officer, LSE, 1987–90; Curate, St Mary's, Battersea, 1993–96; Vice-Principal, Westcott House, Cambridge, 1996–2001; Dean: Trinity Hall, Cambridge, 2001–10; of Chapel, King's Coll., Cambridge, 2010–14. Hon. Canon, Ely Cathedral, 2019–. *Publications*: Religion and Urban Change: Croydon 1840–1914, 1993; (ed with N. Sagovsky) The Unity We Have and the Unity We Seek, 2003; F. D. Maurice and the Crisis of Christian Authority, 2005; The Church in the Modern Age, 2007; (ed with D. Dormor) An Acceptable Sacrifice?: homosexuality and the Church, 2007; To Build Christ's Kingdom: an F. D. Maurice reader, 2007; The High Church Revival in the Church of England: arguments and identities, 2016; (ed) The Oxford History of Anglicanism, vol. 4: Global Western Anglicanism c1910 to present, 2017; contrib. articles to jls incl. Anglican Histl Rev., Histl Jl, Jl Ecclesiastical Hist., Theol. *Recreations*: piano, walking, historic buildings, riding. *Address*: Trinity Hall, Trinity Lane, Cambridge CB2 1TJ. *T*: (01223) 332540, *Fax*: (01223) 765157. *E*: master@trinhall.cam.ac.uk.

**MORRIS, Jill,** CMG 2015; HM Diplomatic Service; Ambassador to Italy and (non-resident) to San Marino, since 2016; *b* 14 Aug. 1967; *d* of Gerald Morris and Marjorie Morris. Entered FCO, 1990; Desk Officer, UN Dept, FCO, 1999–2000; Second Sec., Nicosia, 2001–05; Ext. Relns Desk Officer, 2005–06, Counsellor, 2006–08, UK Repn to EU, Brussels; Foreign and Commonwealth Office: Head: Consular Strategy Dept, 2008–10; Counter-Proliferation Dept, 2011; Dir, Europe, 2012–15. *Address*: c/o Foreign and Commonwealth Office, King Charles Street, SW1A 2AH.

**MORRIS, John Cameron;** QC (Scot.) 1996; All Scotland Floating Sheriff at Edinburgh, since 2014 (Sheriff of South Strathclyde, Dumfries and Galloway at Airdrie, 1998–2014); Appeal Sheriff, Sheriff Appeal Court, since 2015; *b* 11 April 1952; *s* of Thomas and Louise Morris. *Educ*: Allan Glen's Sch., Glasgow; Strathclyde Univ. Solicitor, Scotland, 1976–84; admitted Advocate, Scottish Bar, 1985; called to the Bar, Inner Temple, 1990. Crown Counsel, Scotland, 1989–92. Temp. Sheriff, 1992–98; Temp. High Ct Judge, 2008–. *Recreations*: golf, music, reading. *Address*: Sheriff Court House, 27 Chambers Street, Edinburgh EH1 1LB.

**MORRIS, Prof. (John) Gareth,** CBE 1994; FRS 1988; FRSB; FLSW; Professor of Microbiology, University of Wales, Aberystwyth, 1971–2000, now Emeritus; *b* 25 Nov. 1932; *s* of Edwin Morris and Evelyn Amanda Morris (*née* Griffiths); *m* 1962, Áine Mary Kehoe (*d* 2013); one *s* one *d*. *Educ*: Bridgend Grammar Sch.; Univ. of Leeds; Trinity Coll. Oxford. DPhil. FRSB (FIBiol 1971). Guinness Res. Fellow, Univ. of Oxford, 1957–61; Rockefeller Fellow, Univ. of Calif at Berkeley, 1959–60; Tutor in Biochem., Balliol Coll. Oxford, 1960–61; Lectr, subseq. Sen. Lectr, Univ. of Leicester, 1961–71. Vis. Associate Prof., Purdue Univ., USA, 1965. Member: UGC, 1981–86; Royal Commn on Environmental Pollution, 1991–99. FLSW 2011. *Publications*: A Biologist's Physical Chemistry, 1968, 2nd edn 1974; contribs on microbial biochemistry and physiology. *Recreations*: gardening, walking. *Address*: 48 Homeforge House, Goldwire Lane, Monmouth NP25 5HA. *T*: (01600) 713951.

**MORRIS, John Michael Douglas;** General Secretary, 1986–99, and Company Secretary, 1990–99, Hon. Consultant, since 2000, British Boxing Board of Control; *b* 10 Aug. 1935; *s* of Charles Edward Douglas Morris and Mary Kathleen (*née* Murphy); *m* 1958, Jill Margaret Walker; two *s* two *d*. *Educ*: Towcester GS; John Fisher Sch.; Dulwich Coll. Reporter, Northampton Chronicle & Echo, 1953–60; Sports sub-editor, Evening Standard, 1960–67; Gp Sports Editor, United Newspapers, 1967–77; freelance writer and publican, 1977–79; John Morris Sports Agency, Northampton, 1979–86. Co. Sec., European Boxing Union, 1991–99; Mem., Bd of Govs, World Boxing Council, 1986–99 (Consultant, 2000–). Commissioner of the Year: World Boxing Council, 1987, 1989, 1994, and 1997; World Boxing Assoc., 1988. Pres., Nat. Schs Amateur Boxing Assoc., 2002–. Chair: Towcester and Dist Local History Soc., 2007–17; Towcester Area World War One Commemoration Cttee, 2013–19; Chair of Trustees, Northampton Town FC Charitable Foundn, 2009–. Pres., Northampton Amateur Boxing Club, 2003– (Founder Sec., 1953). *Publications*: Play Better Tennis (instructional booklet), 1969; Come in No 3: biography of cricketer David Steele, 1977; Box On: biography of boxing referee Harry Gibbs, 1981. *Recreations*: amateur drama, reading, all sport. *Address*: 24 Richmond Court, Towcester, Northants NN12 6DT. *T*: (01327) 350297. *E*: johnmorris2736@gmail.com.

**MORRIS, Sir Keith (Elliot Hedley),** KBE 1994; CMG 1988; HM Diplomatic Service, retired; *b* 24 Oct. 1934; *m* 1st, Maria del Carmen Carratala (*d* 2008); two *s* two *d*; 2nd, 2013, Maria Samuel; one step *d*. Entered Foreign Office, 1959; served Dakar, Algiers, Paris, Bogota; First Sec., FCO, 1971–76; Counsellor (Commercial), Warsaw, 1976–79; Minister-Counsellor, Mexico City, 1979–84; Head of Personnel Policy Dept, FCO, 1984–85; rcds, 1986; Minister (Commercial) and Consul-Gen., Milan, 1987–90; Ambassador to Colombia, 1990–94. Mem., Internat. Adv. Bd, Parra Rodriguez (formerly Parra, Rodriguez & Cavelier, then Rodriguez y Cavelier, later Parra Rodriguez Sanin), Bogota, 2003–. Dir, British and Colombian Chamber of Commerce, 1999– (Chm., 1996–99). Mem., Adv. Panel, Transform Drug Policy Foundn, 2016–. *Recreations*: history, hill walking. *Club*: Polish Hearth.

**MORRIS, Kenneth;** Managing Director, Nirvana Europe Ltd, since 1999; *b* 17 April 1947; *s* of Thomas and Phyllis Morris; *m* 1988, Veronica Ann Young; two *s*. *Educ*: George Stephenson Grammar Sch., West Moor, Newcastle upon Tyne. Group Accountant, Newcastle upon Tyne CBC, 1972; Management Accountant, Tyne and Wear CC, 1974; Chief Accountant, 1976, Dep. Dir of Finance, 1982, Gateshead MBC; County Treasurer, 1988, Man. Dir, 1992–99, Northumberland CC. *Recreations*: sport, reading, music. *Address*: 3 Bank Top, Earsdon, Whitley Bay, Tyne and Wear NE25 9JS. *T*: (0191) 253 4907; (office) Osprey House, Kingfisher Way, Silverlink Business Park, Wallsend NE28 9NX. *T*: (0191) 257 1750.

**MORRIS, Mali,** RA 2010; artist; *b* Caernarfon, N Wales, 5 Feb. 1945; partner, Stephen Lewis. *Educ*: Univ. of Newcastle upon Tyne (BA Hons Fine Art 1968); Univ. of Reading (MFA 1970). Lectr in Painting, Sunderland Poly., 1970–72; Sessional Lectr, Dept of Fine Art, Univ. of Reading, 1975–90; Sen. Lectr (pt-time) in Painting, Chelsea Coll. of Art, London Inst., then Univ. of the Arts London, 1991–2005. Vis. Lectr at many UK college depts of fine art, 1972–90. External Examiner: Manchester Poly.; Slade Sch. of Art, 1996–99; Wimbledon Sch. of Art, 1999–2003; RCA, 2003–06; Univ. of Newcastle upon Tyne, 2012–14; Slade Sch. of Art, UCL, 2014–. Chm., Selection Panel, Jerwood Contemporary Painters, 2009; Selector and Mentor, Jerwood Painting Fellowships, 2012–13; Mem. Selection Panel, John Moores Painting Prize China, 2014. First solo exhibns, Serpentine Gall., 1977 and Ikon Gall., Birmingham, 1979; *solo exhibitions* include: Gall. Saoh, Tokyo, 2000; Spica Mus., Tokyo, 2004; Omotesando Gall., Tokyo, 2005; Robert Steele Gall., NY, 2005, 2007; Poussin Gall., London, 2005, 2008; Friends Room, Royal Acad., 2010; The Cut, Halesworth, 2011; Mostyn Gall., Llandudno, 2012; Eagle Gall., London, 2012; Fold Gall., London, 2017; Royal Acad., 2019; *group exhibitions* include: Walker Art Gall., Liverpool, 1980, 1989, 2003; Whitechapel Gall., 1977, 1983, 1985, 1986, 1988, 1992, 1994; Hayward Gall., 1980; Serpentine Gall., 1987; Barbican, 1988; Antwerp, 1997; RA Summer Show, 2008–17; Hidde van Seggelen Gall., London, 2012; Laing Art Gall., Newcastle Upon Tyne, 2013; Nat. Museum Wales, Cardiff, 2013; Eagle Gall., London, 2013, 2017; Ikon Gall., Birmingham, 2014; Pulchri, The Hague, 2014; Pallant House, Chichester, 2014; Flowers NY, USA, 2014; Kapil Jarawala Gall., London, 2014, 2015; Linden Hall Gall., Deal, 2015, 2016, 2017; University Greenwich Gall., 2015; Seventeen Gall., London, 2016; Fold Gall., London, 2016; Hepworth, Wakefield, 2016; Syson Gall., Nottingham, 2017; *work in public collections* incl. Arts Council England, British Council, Contemp. Arts Soc., Govt Art Collection, Whitworth Art Gall., Manchester, Nat. Mus. Wales, Cardiff, RA, Pallant House, Chichester, Fitzwilliam Mus., Cambridge. Trustee, Poetry London, 2013–. *Publications*: Mali Morris New Paintings, 1992; Mali Morris Paintings, 1994; The Singular and the Painterly, Mali Morris's Recent Work, 2002; Mali Morris New Paintings, 2008; (contrib.) A Sore Head, 2015; Mali Morris: painting, 2019; exhibn catalogues; contribs to Turps Banana, RA Mag. *W*: www.malimorris.co.uk.

**MORRIS, Mark William;** American choreographer, director and dancer; Founder and Artistic Director, Mark Morris Dance Group, since 1980; *b* Seattle, 29 Aug. 1956; *s* of William Morris and Maxine Crittenden Morris. Dir of Dance, Théâtre Royal de la Monnaie, 1988–91; Jt Founder, White Oak Dance Project, 1990; has choreographed more than 120 modern dance works for Mark Morris Dance Gp, including: L'Allegro, il Penseroso ed il Moderato, 1988; Dido and Aeneas (opera), 1988; The Hard Nut, 1991; Four Saints in Three Acts, 2000; V, 2001; All Fours, 2003; Mozart Dances, 2007; Socrates, 2010; Pepperland, 2017; (with Silkroad Ensemble) Layla and Manjun, 2018; Sport, 2019; choreography for other companies includes: ballets: Drink to Me Only With Thine Eyes, Amer. Ballet Theatre, 1988; Ein Herz, Paris Opera Ballet, 1990; Gong, Amer. Ballet Th., 2001; Sylvia, San Francisco Ballet, 2004; operas: Nixon in China, Houston Grand Opera, 1987; Orfée et Euridice, Seattle Opera, 1988; The Death of Klinghoffer, Théâtre de la Monnaie, 1991; The Indian Queen, ENO, 2015; dir, Die Fledermaus, Seattle Opera, 1990; dir and choreographed, Platée, Royal Opera, 1997; King Arthur, ENO, 2006. Fellow, MacArthur Foundn. Awards include: Laurence Olivier Award for Best New Dance Prodn, 1998, for Outstanding Achievement in Dance, 2002; Critics Circle UK Dance Awards for Best Foreign Dance Co. and Best Modern Choreography, 2003; NY Dance and Perf. Award, 2007; Dist. Artist Award, Internat. Soc. for Performing Arts, 2012; Outstanding Achievement in Arts Award, ArtsFund, 2016. *Address*: Mark Morris Dance Group, 3 Lafayette Avenue, Brooklyn, NY 11217–1415, USA.

**MORRIS, Michael Clough;** a District Judge (Magistrates' Courts), 2002–15; *b* 28 Dec. 1946; *s* of Alfred Morris and Mary Morris, MBE, JP; *m* 1973, Hilary; three *s* one *d*. *Educ*: Calday Grange Grammar Sch., W Kirby; Univ. of Leeds (LLB Hons). Admitted solicitor, 1972; Partner, Wilkes Partnership, Birmingham, 1977–2002; Dep. Stipendiary Magistrate, 1995–2002. Birmingham Law Society: Chm., Criminal Law Cttee, 1994–2001; Dep. Vice Pres., 2001–02. Exec. Gov., Solihull Sch., 2006– (Vice-Chm., Govs, 2010–). *Recreations*: fell-walking, golf, Freemasonry.

**MORRIS, Michael Jeremy,** MBE 2012; Director, Cultural Industry Ltd, since 1988; Co-Director, Artangel, since 1991; *b* 30 March 1958; *s* of Lawrence and Monica Morris; *m* 1991, Sarah Culshaw; one *s* one *d*. *Educ*: Oundle Sch.; Keble Coll., Oxford (BA Hons); Tavistock Centre for Couple Relationships (Postgrad. Dip. Psychodynamic Marital and Couple Therapy 2008). Dir, Performing Arts, ICA, 1984–88. Director: Artangel Media Ltd, 2000–; Shockheaded Peter Ltd, 2000–02. Mem., Arts Adv. Panel, British Council, 1983–86. Artistic Associate: Lyric Th., 1999–2004; RNT, 2003–; Manchester Internat. Fest., 2006–; Artistic Advr, 14–18 NOW, 2013–18. Associate Producer, Ex Machina/Robert Lepage, 1999–. Mem. Council, Tate Modern, 2005–. Trustee, Longplayer Trust, 2001–. Ambassador, School of Life, London, 2008–. Couples Therapist, Tavistock Centre for Couple Relationships, 2007–. Mem., British Assoc. for Counselling and Psychotherapy, 2009–. Hon. Fellow, Goldsmiths, Univ. of London, 2012. Chevalier, Ordre National du Québec, 2002. *Publications*: (with J. Lingwood) Off Limits: 40 Artangel projects, 2002; (with J. Lingwood) Inside: artists and writers in Reading Prison, 2017. *Recreations*: collecting unusual stringed instruments, accordions and cookery books, table tennis. *Address*: Artangel, 31 Eyre Street Hill, EC1R 5EW. *T*: (020) 7713 1400. *E*: info@artangel.org.uk. *Clubs*: Two Brydges, Arts.

**MORRIS, Michael Sachs;** Director-General, British Insurance Brokers' Association, 1980–85; *b* 12 June 1924; *s* of late Prof. Noah Morris, MD, DSc, and Hattie Michaelis; *m* 1952, Vera Leonie, *m d* of late Paul and Lona Heller; one *s* one *d*. *Educ*: Glasgow Acad.; St Catharine's Coll., Cambridge. Wrangler, 1948. Scientific Officer, Admty Signals Estabt, 1943–46; Asst Principal, BoT, 1948; idc 1970; Under Secretary: Insurance Div., DoT, 1973; Shipping Policy Div., DoT, 1978–80. Chairman: NATO Planning Bd for Ocean Shipping, 1978–80; Consultative Shipping Gp, 1979–80. Mem., Barnet Health Authy, 1985–90. *Recreation*: sitting in the sun. *Address*: 5 Sunrise View, The Rise, Mill Hill, NW7 2LL. *T*: (020) 8959 0837. *Club*: Oxford and Cambridge.

**MORRIS, Norma Frances,** PhD; Research Fellow, University College London, 1995–2018, now Hon. Research Associate; *b* 17 April 1935; *d* of Henry Albert Bevis and Lilian Eliza Bevis (*née* Flexon); *m* 1960, Samuel Francis Morris; one *s* two *d*. *Educ*: Ilford County High Sch. for Girls; University College London (BA, MA), Univ. of Twente, Netherlands (PhD). Assistante Anglaise, Paris, 1956–57; Asst Lectr, Univ. of Hull, 1959–60; MRC, 1960–95, Admin. Sec., 1989–95. Member: Nat. Biol Standards Bd, 1990–98; Gen. Chiropractic Council, 2002–04 (Chm., 1998–2002); British Acupuncture Accreditation Bd, 2004–14; Bd, Campaign for Sci. and Engrg, 2004–14; Compass Collaborative Adv. Gp, 2007–11. Trustee, Patients' Assoc., 2004–06. *Publications*: contribs to sci. policy and med. sociol. books and jls. *Recreations*: canoeing, opera, edible fungi. *Address*: 15 Osten Mews, SW7 4HW. *T*: (020) 7370 4565.

**MORRIS, Peter Christopher West**; solicitor; consultant with Sussex Defence Solicitors, 2008–16; *b* 24 Dec. 1937; *s of* C. T. R. and L. B. Morris; *m* 1st, 1959, Joy (marr. diss.); two *s* one *d*; 2nd, 1987, Terese; one step *s* two step *d*. *Educ*: Seaford Coll.; Christ's Coll., Cambridge, 1958–61 (MA, LLB). Hockey Blue, 1959, 1960, 1961; Hockey for Wales, 1962–65. National Service, 1956–58. Admitted Solicitor, 1965; Partner with Wild Hewitson & Shaw, 1967; a Recorder of the Crown Court, 1980–84; voluntary removal from Roll of Solicitors, 1982; Barrister, Middle Temple, 1982–84; company dir, 1985–93; name restored to Roll of Solicitors, 1993; Partner with Morris and Rogers, 1998–2003, with Morris and Warren, 2003–05 (Consultant, 2005–07). *Recreations*: golf, Arsenal Football Club. *Club*: Hawks (Cambridge).

**MORRIS, Sir Peter (John)**, AC 2004; Kt 1996; FRS 1994; President, Royal College of Surgeons of England, 2001–04; Nuffield Professor of Surgery, Chairman, Department of Surgery and Director, Oxford Transplant Centre, Oxford University, 1974–2001, now Emeritus Professor; Fellow of Balliol College, 1974–2001, now Emeritus Fellow; Director, Centre for Evidence in Transplantation, Royal College of Surgeons of England and London School of Hygiene and Tropical Medicine, 2005–16, and Hon. Professor, London School of Hygiene and Tropical Medicine, since 2005; *b* 17 April 1934; *s of* Stanley Henry and Mary Lois Morris; *m* 1960, Mary Jocelyn Gorman; three *s* two *d*. *Educ*: Xavier Coll., Melbourne; Univ. of Melbourne (MB, BS, PhD). FRCS, FRACS, FACS, FRCP, FRCSGlas. Jun. surg. appts at St Vincent's Hosp., Melbourne, Postgrad. Med. Sch., London, Southampton Gen. Hosp. and MGH Boston, 1958–64; Research Fellow, Harvard Med. Sch., 1965–66; Asst Prof. in Surgery, Med. Coll. of Virginia, 1967; 2nd Asst in Surgery, Univ. of Melbourne, 1968–69, 1st Asst 1970–71; Reader in Surgery, Univ. of Melbourne, 1972–74. WHO Consultant, 1970–84; Cons. to Walter and Eliza Hall Inst. of Med. Res., 1969–74. Chairman: Nat. Kidney Res. Fund, 1986–90; Council, British Heart Foundn, 2003–09; Inst. of Health Scis, Oxford Univ., 2000–04; Member: MRC, 1983–87; Oxford RHA, 1988–90; Council, RCS, 1991–2004 (Vice Pres., 2000–01); Council, ICRF, 1995–2001. President: Transplantation Soc., 1984–86; British Soc. for Histocompatibility and Immunogenetics, 1993–95; Eur. Surgical Assoc., 1996–98; Internat. Surgical Soc., 2001–03; Medical Protection Soc., 2007–10. Hunterian Prof., RCS, 1972. Lectr, Coll. de France, 1982; Rudin Prof., Columbia Univ., NY, 1983; USA Nat. Kidney Foundn Prof., 1986; Nimmo Vis. Prof., Univ. of Adelaide, 1993; Ho Tam Kit Hing Vis. Prof., Univ. of Hong Kong, 1994; Waltman Walters Vis. Prof., Mayo Clinic, 1994; G. T. Diethelm Prof., Univ. of Alabama, 2002; Honorary Professor: LSHTM, 2005; Warwick Univ., 2007. Lectures: Gibson, Columbia Univ., 1969; Deryl Hart, Duke Univ., 1979; Finlayson, RCPSG, 1984; Kinmonth, RCS, 1986; Loewenthal, Univ. of Sydney, 1987; Marjorie Budd, Univ. of Bristol, 1989; Champ Lyons, Univ. of Alabama, 1989; Fraser Meml, Univ. of Edinburgh, 1990; Bennett, TCD, 1991; Graham, Washington Univ., 1991; Murdoch Meml, Aberdeen Univ., 1991; Shaw, RCPE, 1991; Pybus Meml, N of Eng. Surg. Soc., 1992; Gallie, Royal Coll. of Physicians and Surgeons, Canada, 1992; Agnew, Univ. of Penn, 1993; Grey Turner, Internat. Surg. Soc., 1993; Gordon Taylor, RCSEd, 1995; Fred Belzer, Univ. of Wisconsin, 1998; Martin, Emory Univ., 1999; Ceppellini, Eur. Foundn for Immuno-Genetics, 1999; Paul Russell, Harvard Med. Sch., 2000; Dist. Lectr, Stanford Univ., 2001; Syme Oration, RACS, 2002; Rienhoff, Johns Hopkins Med. Sch., 2003; Hunterian Oration and Medal, RCS, 2005; Pehr Edman, St Vincent's Med. Res. Inst., Melbourne Univ., 2005; Bryant Stokes, Royal Perth Hosp., 2006; Dunphy, UCSF, 2008; Raj Yadav Oration, Delhi, 2008; Alexander, Univ. of Cincinnati, 2010; Halford Oration, Melbourne Univ., 2012. Pres., Med. Protection Soc., 2007–15; Governor: PPP Foundation (formerly PPP Healthcare Med. Trust), 1998–2003; Garfield Weston Foundn, 1998–; Trustee, Roche Organ Transplantation Res. Foundn, 1998–2004. Chm., Order of Australia Assoc., UK/Europe, 2008–13. Founder FMedSci 1998. Hon. Fellow: Amer. Surgical Assoc., 1982; Asian Surg. Soc., 1989; German Surgical Soc., 2003; Acad. of Med., Singapore, 2004; RCSI, 2006; Hon. FACS 1986; Hon. FRACS, 1995; Hon. FRCSE 1995; Hon. FDSRCS 2003; Hon. Mem., Amer. Soc. of Transplant Surgeons, 1993; Foreign Member: Nat. Acad. of Medicine (formerly Inst. of Medicine, Nat. Acad. of Sci.), 1997; Amer. Phil Soc., 2002. Hon. DSc: Hong Kong, 1999; Imperial Coll. London, 2003; Hon. DLaws Melbourne, 2012. Selwyn Smith Prize, Univ. of Melbourne, 1971; Cecil Joll Prize, RCS, 1988; Lister Medal, RCS, RCSE, Irish Coll. of Surgeons and Royal Soc., 1997; Maharshi Sushruta Award, Inst. of Kidney Disease, Ahmedabad, 2004; Neil Hamilton Fairley Medal, RCP, 2005; Medawar Prize, Transplantation Soc., 2006; Pioneer Award, Amer. Soc. of Transplant Surgeons, 2006; Internat. Surgical Soc. Prize, 2007. Editor, Transplantation, 1979–2014. *Publications*: Kidney Transplantation: principles and practice, 1979, 7th edn 2014; Tissue Transplantation, 1982; Transient Ischaemic Attacks, 1982; (ed jtly) Progress in Transplantation, vol. 1 1984, vol. 2 1985, vol. 3 1986; (ed jtly) Oxford Textbook of Surgery, 1994, 2nd edn 2000; (ed) Transplantation Reviews, 1987–2002; numerous sci. articles and chapters in books concerned mainly with transplantation and surgery. *Recreations*: golf, tennis, cricket. *Address*: 19 Lucerne Road, Oxford OX2 7QB. *Clubs*: Oxford and Cambridge, MCC; Frilford Heath Golf (Oxford); Oxfordshire County Cricket; Melbourne Cricket (Melbourne); Barwon Heads Golf (Barwon Heads, Vic.).

**MORRIS, Reyahn**; *see* King, R.

**MORRIS, Richard Charles**; HM Diplomatic Service; Ambassador to Nepal, 2015–19; *b* Worcester, 1 Nov. 1967; *s of* John and Kathleen Morris; *m* 1992, Alison Waring; two *s* one *d*. *Educ*: University Coll. of Wales, Aberystwyth (BA Hons English Lit.); Univ. of Illinois (Schol.); Aston Univ. (MBA). Entered FCO, 1990; Assistant Desk Officer: Non-Proliferation and Defence Dept, 1990–91; Cultural Relns Dept, 1991–92; temp. duty to UKMIS to UN, NY, 1993; Third Sec. (Pol), Ottawa, 1993–96; Second Sec. (Pol), Bridgetown, 1996–2000; Head: Resource Accounting and Budgeting Team, FCO, 2000–01; Assistance Gp, Consular Directorate, FCO, 2001–04; Dep. Hd of Mission and Consul Gen., Mexico City, 2005–08; Consul-Gen., Sydney and Dir-Gen., Trade and Investment, Australasia, 2008–12; Hd, Pacific Dept, FCO, 2013–15. FCIM; FRSA. *Recreations*: long distance running, reading. *Address*: Foreign and Commonwealth Office, King Charles Street, SW1A 2AH. *E*: Richard.morris@fco.gov.uk.

**MORRIS, Richard Francis Maxwell**; Chief Executive, Associated Board of the Royal Schools of Music, 1993–2009; *b* 11 Sept. 1944; *s of* late Maxwell Morris and Frederica (*née* Abelson); *m* 1st, 1974, Sarah Quill (marr. diss. 1978); 2nd, 1983, Marian Sperling; two *d*. *Educ*: Eton Coll.; New Coll., Oxford (MA); Coll. of Law, London; Acad. of Exec. Coaching (Dip. 2010). Solicitor, Farrer & Co., 1967–71; Legal Advr and Banker, Grindlay Brandts, 1971–75; Corporate Finance Manager, S. G. Warburg & Co., 1975–79; Hodder and Stoughton: Group Finance Dir, 1979; Man. Dir, Educnl and Acad. Publishing, 1987; Jt Man. Dir, 1989–91; Dir, The Lancet, 1986–91; Man. Dir, Edward Arnold, 1987–91. Director: Invicta Sound, 1984–91; Southern Radio, 1991–92; Magma Poetry, 2010–15; Mem., Develt Bd, Arvon Foundn, 2008–. Mem., Nat. Exec., Eur. Movement, 2018–. Mem. Council, Kent Opera, 1985–90; Founder, Almavíva Opera, 1989–2002. Chairman: Music Educn Council, 1998–2001 (Mem. Exec. Cttee, 1995–); Henri Oguike Dance Co., 2009–12; Dep. Chm., Steering Bd, GLA Music Educn Prog., 2010–17; Co-Founder and Vice-Chm., Mayor of London's Fund for Young Musicians, 2011–. Trustee: Council for Dance Educn and Trng, 1999–2005; Kent Music (formerly Kent Music Sch.), 2001–14; Yehudi Menuhin Sch., 2004– (Dep. Chm., 2010–11; Chm., 2011–); Music Preserved, 2010–14; Music Mark, 2014–17. Hon. RCM 1994; Hon. RNCM 2001; Hon. FRAM 2007. Lifetime Achievement Award, Music Teacher Awards, 2015. *Recreations*: music, wine, visual arts. *Address*: Holdfast House, Edenbridge, Kent TN8 6SJ. *T*: (01732) 862439. *Club*: Athenæum.

**MORRIS, Prof. Richard Graham Michael**, CBE 2007; FRS 1997; Professor, since 1993, Royal Society Wolfson Professor, since 2006, of Neuroscience, and Director, Centre for Cognitive and Neural Systems, since 2005, Edinburgh University (Chairman, Department of Neuroscience, 1998–2002); Head, Neuroscience and Mental Health, Wellcome Trust, 2007–10 (Senior Neuroscience Adviser, 2010); *b* 27 June 1948; *s of* Robert Walter and Edith Mary Morris; *m* 1st, 1985, Hilary Ann Lewis (marr. diss. 2010); two *d*; 2nd, 2015, Mónica Muñoz-Lopez; one *s*. *Educ*: Trinity Hall, Cambridge (BA 1969; MA 1971); Univ. of Sussex (DPhil 1974). Addison Wheeler Fellow, Univ. of Durham, 1973–75; BM (Nat. History), 1975–76; BBC Science and Features Dept, 1977; Lectr, Univ. of St Andrews, 1977–86; Reader, Dept of Pharmacology, Univ. of Edinburgh, 1986–93. Visiting Professor: MIT, 1991; Nat. Centre for Biol Scis, Bangalore, 2014–. Royal Society Leverhulme Fellow, 1996; Gatsby Res. Fellow, 1997. Hon. Prof., Norwegian Univ. of Sci and Technol., 2000–13; Caro Almela Hon. Prof. of Neurobiol., CSIC-UMH, Alicante 2014–. Lectures: Lansdown, Univ. of Victoria, BC, 1994; Segerfalk, Univ. of Lund, 1995; Swammerdam, 1996, Frijda, 2004, Netherlands Royal Acad.; Decade of the Brain, BNA, 1998; Feigen, Stanford Univ., 1998; Henry Dryerre Prize, RSE, 1998; Jerzy Konorski, Gdansk, 1999; Zotterman (and medal), Swedish Physiol. Soc., 1999; American Med. Alumnus, St Andrews Univ., 2003; Craik, Univ. of Cambridge, 2004; Presidential, Soc. for Neurosci., 2009; Indian Inst. of Science, Bangalore, 2012; Kavli Prize Ceremony, Oslo, 2014; Plenary, British Neurosci. Assoc., 2015; Spanish Neurosci. Soc., 2015. Invited Lectr, Peking Univ. and Chinese Nat. Acad. of Sci., Beijing, 2001, 2002. Member: Neuroscis Grants Cttee, MRC, 1981–85; Neuroscis and Mental Health Bd, MRC, 1993–97; Innovation Bd, MRC, 1997–2000; Strategy Develt Gp, MRC, 2000–04; Scottish Sci. Adv. Council, 2004–06; President's Adv. Gp, Weizmann Inst., Israel, 2006–08; Bd of Rev. Eds, SCIENCE Mag., 2007–18. Member, Scientific Advisory Board: Alzheimer's Res. Trust, 2004–08; RIKEN Brain Scis Inst., Japan, 2002–08, 2018–; MPI Martinsried, Germany, 2000–05; Picower Inst., MIT, 1998–2011; Branco Weiss Sci. in Soc. Fellowship, Switzerland; Shanghai Inst. for Neurosci.; MPI Biol Cybernetics, Tübingen, Germany. Chm., Brain Res. Assoc., 1990–94; Guarantor of Brain; Hon. Sec., Exptl Psychol. Soc., 1985–89; Pres., Fedn of European Neurosci. Socs, 2006–08 (Pres. of Trust Fund, 2012–). Chairman: Univ. Res. Fellowships Cttee B, 2011–14, Hooke Cttee, 2013–, Royal Soc.; Brain Prize Selection Cttee, Lundbeck Foundn, 2019–. Trustee, MQ: Transforming Mental Health, 2010–17. Mem., RYA. FRSE 1994; Founder FMedSci 1998; Foreign Fellow: Amer. Acad. of Arts and Scis, 2004; AAAS 2007; Norwegian Acad. of Sci. and Letters, 2007. Outstanding Achievement in Neurosci., British Neurosci. Assoc., 2002; EJN Prize, Fedn of Eur. Neuroscis, 2004; Feldberg Prize, Feldberg Foundn, 2006; Santiago-Grisolia Award, Valencia, 2007; Fondation IPSEN, Neuronal Plasticity Prize, 2013; Royal Medal, RSE, 2014; Brain Prize, 2016; Chancellor's Award, Univ. of Edinburgh, 2019. *Publications*: (ed) Parallel Distributed Processing, 1988; The Hippocampus Book, 2007; contrib. to academic jls and books (230 publications). *Recreation*: sailing. *Address*: Centre for Cognitive and Neural Systems, University of Edinburgh College of Medicine, 1 George Square, Edinburgh EH8 9JZ. *T*: (0131) 650 3520. *E*: r.g.m.morris@ed.ac.uk.

**MORRIS, Richard Keith**, OBE 2003; FSA; archaeologist, writer, composer; Research Professor, University of Huddersfield, 2010–15, now Emeritus; *b* 8 Oct. 1947; *s of* John Richard Morris and Elsie Myra (*née* Wearne); *m* 1972, Jane Whiteley; two *s* one *d*. *Educ*: Denstone Coll., Staffs; Pembroke Coll., Oxford (MA); Univ. of York (BPhil). FSA 1982; MIFA 1986, Hon. MIFA 2001. Musician, 1971–72; Res. Assistant, York Minster Archaeol. Office, 1972–75; Churches Officer, 1975–77, Res. Officer, 1978–88, Council for British Archaeol.; Hon. Lectr, Sch. of History, Univ. of Leeds, 1986–88; Lectr, Dept of Archaeol., Univ. of York, 1988–91; Dir, Council for British Archaeology, 1991–99 (Hon. Vice-Pres., 2001); Dir, Inst. for Medieval Studies, 2003–10, Prof. for Research in the Historic Envmt, 2007–10, Univ. of Leeds. Comr, English Heritage, 1996–2005; Chairman: Ancient Monuments Adv. Cttee for England, 1996–2000; Historic Settlements and Landscapes Adv. Cttee, 2001–03; Bede's World, 2001–08; English Heritage Adv. Cttee, 2003–05; Heritage Lottery Fund Expert Panel, 2005–11; Blackden Trust, 2005–16. Trustee: Nat. Heritage Meml Fund, 2011–18; York Archaeological Trust, 2011–19. Pres., Soc. for Church Archaeol., 2001–05. Hon. Vis. Prof., Univ. of York, 1995. Frend Medal, Soc. of Antiquaries of London, 1992. *Publications*: Cathedrals and Abbeys of England and Wales, 1979; The Church in British Archaeology, 1983; Churches in the Landscape, 1989; (jtly) Guy Gibson, 1994; Cheshire, VC, OM, 2000; (jtly) Breaching the German Dams, 2008; (jtly) The Archaeology of English Battlefields, 2012; Time's Anvil: England, archaeology and the imagination, 2013; Yorkshire, 2018. *Recreations*: aviation history, natural history, dog walking, gliding. *Address*: Appletrees, 6 Park Farm, Leathley, N Yorks LS21 2JU. *T*: (01423) 504219.

**MORRIS, Air Vice-Marshal Richard Vaughan**, CBE 2000; AFC 1991; Chief of Staff and Deputy Commander-in-Chief, HQ Personnel and Training Command, Innsworth, 2000–01; *b* 24 Sept. 1949; *s of* Edgar Morris and Iona Morris (*née* Clement); *m* 1969, Sheena Blundell; two *s*. *Educ*: John Bright Grammar Sch., Llandudno. XV Sqn, Laarbruch, 237 OCU, Honington, 16 Sqn, Laarbruch, 1971–80; Tri-Nat. Tornado Trng Estabt, Cottesmore, 1980–82; PSO to ACAS, MoD, 1984–87; OC 14 Sqn, Bruggen, 1988–91; Comdr, British Forces Op. Jural, 1992; Station Comdr, Honington, 1993–94; Policy HQ Allied Forces Northwestern Europe, 1994; rcds, 1995; Comdt, Air Warfare Centre, Waddington, 1996–98; SASO, HQ 1 Gp, High Wycombe, 1998–2000; Comdr, British Forces Op. Desert Fox, 1998, Op. Allied Force, 1999; retired 2002. *Recreations*: golf, hill walking. *Address*: c/o Lloyds Bank, 65 High Street, Stamford PE9 2AT.

**MORRIS, Robert Matthew**, CVO 1996; Assistant Under Secretary of State, Home Office, 1983–97; *b* 11 Oct. 1937; *s of* late William Alexander Morris and of Mary Morris (*née* Bryant); *m* 1965, Janet Elizabeth Gillingham; two *s* one *d*. *Educ*: Handsworth Grammar Sch.; Christ's Coll., Cambridge (Exhibnr (Hist.)); Open Univ. (PhD 2004). S Staffords Regt, 1956–58. Joined Home Office, 1961; Asst Private Sec. to Home Sec., 1964–66; CSD, 1969–71; Sec. to NI (Compton) Inquiry, 1971; Principal Private Sec. to Home Sec., 1976–78; Sec. to UK Prison Services Inquiry (May Cttee), 1978–79; Head of Crime Policy Planning Unit, 1979–81; Asst Under Sec. of State, Fire and Emergency Planning, 1983, Immigration Policy, Nationality and Passports, 1986, Criminal Justice and Constitutional, 1991; Registrar, Baronetage, 1991–96. Mem. Council, Internat. Social Service UK, 1998–2005. Sec. to (Hurd) Review of See of Canterbury, 2000–01. Governor: Mayfield Sch., 1978–83; Spencer Park Sch., 1980–86. Hon. Sen. Res. Fellow, Constitution Unit, Sch. of Public Policy, subseq. Dept of Political Sci., UCL, 1999–. *Publications*: Church and State in 21st Century Britain: the future of Church establishment, 2009; Reforming the Police in the Nineteenth Century, 2014; articles on criminal justice (especially police) history, and constitutional politics of religion. *Address*: 4 Desenfans Road, SE21 7DN.

**MORRIS, Rt Rev. Roger Anthony Brett**; *see* Colchester, Area Bishop of.

**MORRIS, Rear-Adm. Roger Oliver,** CB 1990; Hydrographer of the Navy, 1985–90; *b* 1 Sept. 1932; *s* of Dr Oliver N. Morris and H. S. (Mollie) Morris (*née* Hudson). *Educ:* Mount House School, Tavistock; Royal Naval College, Dartmouth. Entered Royal Navy, 1946, commissioned 1952; specialised in Hydrographic Surveying, 1956; commanded HM Ships Medusa, Beagle, Hydra, Fawn, Hecla, Hydra, 1964–80; RCDS 1978; Director of Hydrographic Plans and Surveys, 1980–81; Asst Hydrographer, 1982–84. Chm. of Council, Soc. for Nautical Res., 1989–94; Vice-Pres., Royal Inst. of Navigation, 1991–92; Pres., World Ship Soc., 1997–2000. *Publications:* Charts and Surveys in Peace and War, 1995. *Recreations:* heraldry, opera, bird watching. *Address:* Orchard House, Quantock View, Bishops Lydeard, Somerset TA4 3AW.

**MORRIS, Prof. Russell Edward,** DPhil; FRS 2016; Bishop Wardlaw Professor of Chemistry, University of St Andrews, since 2016 (Professor of Structural and Materials Chemistry, 2000–16); *b* St Asaph, Wales, 8 June 1967; *s* of Merfyn Morris and Ursula Patricia Morris; *m* 2002, Silke Frauke Karen Wewetzer; one *s* one *d. Educ:* Ysgol Glan Conwy; Ysgol Dyffryn Conwy, Llanrwst; Oriel Coll., Oxford (BA Chem. 1989; MA; DPhil 1992). Postdoctoral Researcher, UCSB, 1992–95; RSE Research Fellow, 1995–98, Reader in Chemistry, 1998–2000, Univ. of St Andrews. FRSE 2008; FLSW 2012. *Publications:* over 200 articles in learned jls. *Recreations:* first class cricketer (1987–91), Blues in football and cricket at University of Oxford, guitar. *Address:* School of Chemistry, University of St Andrews, Purdie Building, North Haugh, St Andrews, Fife KY16 9ST. *T:* (01334) 463818, *Fax:* (01334) 463808. *E:* rem1@st-and.ac.uk.

**MORRIS, Sean Robert; His Honour Judge Sean Morris;** a Circuit Judge, since 2008; *b* Bingley, W Yorks, 17 Oct. 1958; *s* of John Morris and Margaret Morris. *Educ:* Fulneck Sch., Leeds; Benton Park Grammar Sch., Leeds; Leeds Poly. (BA Hons Law). Pres., Students Union, 1981–82. Called to the Bar, Lincoln's Inn, 1983; in practice as barrister specialising in crime, 6 Park Square Chambers, Leeds, 1983–2008; a Recorder of the Crown Court, 2003–08; Resident Judge, Lincoln Crown Court, 2010–14. Hon. Recorder of Lincoln, 2011–14. *Recreations:* cooking, eating real curry, walking to country pubs. *Address:* Teesside Combined Court Centre, Russell Street, Middlesbrough TS1 2AE.

**MORRIS, Sir Sennen John,** 12th Bt *cr* 1806, of Clasemont, Glamorganshire; *b* 5 June 1995; *s* of Sir Allan Lindsay Morris, 11th Bt and of Cheronne Denise Morris (*née* Whitford); *S* father, 2016, but his name does not appear on the Official Roll of the Baronetage. *Heir:* brother Chace James Morris, *b* 1997.

**MORRIS, Simon C.;** see Conway Morris.

**MORRIS, Prof. Stephen,** PhD; RAND Professor of Health Services Research, University of Cambridge, since 2019; *b* Jarrow, 2 May 1971; *s* of Christopher William Morris and Christine Morris; *m* 1998, Deborah Mary Georgina Rowntree; two *d. Educ:* Bishop's Stortford High Sch.; Univ. of Nottingham (BA 1993); Univ. of York (MSc 1994); City Univ., London (PhD 2002). Lectr, City Univ., London, 1994–2002; Sen. Lectr, Imperial Coll. London, 2002–06; Reader, Brunel Univ., 2006–09; Prof. of Health Econs, UCL, 2009–19. *Publications:* (jtly) Economic Analysis in Health Care, 2007, 2nd edn 2012; contribs to learned jls on health econs. *Recreations:* running ultra marathons, drinking coffee, reading science fiction and fantasy novels. *Address:* Primary Care Unit, Department of Public Health and Primary Care, University of Cambridge, Institute of Public Health, Forvie Site, Robinson Way, Cambridge CB2 0SR. *T:* (01223) 748605. *E:* sm2428@medschl.cam.ac.uk.

**MORRIS, Sir Stephen Nathan,** Kt 2016; **Hon. Mr Justice Morris;** a Judge of the High Court of Justice, Queen's Bench Division, since 2016; *b* 18 May 1957; *s* of late Jack Ellis Morris and June Audrey Morris (*née* Livingstone). *Educ:* Bradford Grammar Sch.; Christ's Coll., Cambridge (BA 1979, MA 1982). Called to the Bar, Lincoln's Inn, 1981; in private practice at the bar, 1983–2016; Jun. Counsel to the Crown (A Panel), 1999–2002; QC 2002; Asst Recorder, 1998–2000; Recorder, 2000–16; Dep. High Court Judge, 2004–16. *Publications:* (contrib.) Plender: European Court Practice and Precedent, 1998; (contrib.) Bar Council Practitioners' Handbook of EC Law, 1998; (contrib.) Bellamy & Child: European Community Law of Competition, 5th edn 2001. *Recreations:* ski-ing, theatre, gardening, cooking. *Address:* Royal Courts of Justice, Strand, WC2A 2LL. *Club:* Royal Automobile.

**MORRIS, Thomas Alun, (Tom),** OBE 2016; Artistic Director, Bristol Old Vic, since 2009; *b* Stamford, Lincs, 1964; *s* of Michael and Rosemary Morris; *m* 2011, Kate McGrath; one *s* one *d. Educ:* Stonyhurst Coll.; Pembroke Coll., Cambridge (BA Hons English Lit. 1982; MA 1986). Formerly broadcaster and arts journalist for Independent, Sunday Times, Guardian, BBC Radio 4 and Time Out; Artistic Dir, Battersea Arts Centre, 1995–2004; Associate Dir, NT, 2004–09. Productions include: as *writer/adaptor:* with Carl Heap: Tom Tom, 1987; Battersea Arts Centre: Ben Hur, 2002; Jason and the Argonauts, 2003; The World Cup Final 1966, and tour, 2004; The Wooden Frock, Kneehigh Th., 2004; with Emma Rice: (also dir) Disembodied, nat. tour, 2005; Nights at the Circus, Lyric, Hammersmith, 2006; (with David Glass) A Matter of Life and Death by Samuel Beckett, NT, 2007; A Christmas Carol by Charles Dickens, Bristol Old Vic, 2018; as *director:* Battersea Arts Centre: All that Fall, 1996; Trio, 1996; Othello Music, 1997; Oedipus the King, 1998; Macbeth, 1999; To the Island with the Goose, 1999; Unsung, 2000; Oogly Boogly, tour, 2004; (with Marianne Elliott) (also prod.) War Horse, NT, 2007, transf. NY, 2011 ((jtly) Tony Award for Best Direction, 2011); Bristol Old Vic: Juliet and Her Romeo, 2011; Swallows and Amazons, transf. Vaudeville and tour, 2011; The Little Mermaid, 2013; A Midsummer Night's Dream, 2014; World Cup Final 1966, 2014; The Crucible, 2015; King Lear, 2016; The Grinning Man, 2016; Messiah, 2017; Touching the Void, 2018; opera: Battersea Arts Centre: Passions, 2001; Kombat Opera Klubneit, 2002; Newsnight: the opera, 2003; The Death of Klinghoffer, ENO, 2012; as *producer:* Matters of Life and Death Season, Battersea Arts Centre, 2000; Jerry Springer: the opera, 2001; Coram Boy, NT, 2005. *Recreations:* cricket, journalism, unusual music. *Address:* Bristol Old Vic, King Street, Bristol BS1 4ED.

**MORRIS, Timothy Colin;** HM Diplomatic Service, retired; strategy consultant, since 2018; *b* 17 Sept. 1958; *s* of late Maj. Charles Anthony Morris and Sheila Ann Margaret Morris (*née* Watson); *m* 1996, Patricia Tena; three *s. Educ:* Winchester Coll.; Queen's Coll., Oxford (BA 1st Cl. Hons Modern Langs (French and Spanish) 1981). Joined HM Diplomatic Service, 1981; Japanese lang. trng, 1982–84; Second Sec., Commercial, Tokyo, 1984–87; FCO, 1987–89; Hd, Exports to Japan Unit, DTI, 1989–91; First Sec. and Hd, Political Section, Madrid, 1991–95; Dep. Hd, UN Dept, FCO, 1996–98; Counsellor, Trade and Investment, Tokyo, 1998–2002; Dep. Hd of Mission, Lisbon, 2003–04; Hd, Internat. Orgns Dept, FCO, 2005–08; Ambassador to Morocco and (non-resident) to Mauritania, 2008–12; Hd of Sahel Task Force, FCO, 2012–13; UK Special Envoy for S Sudan, 2014; temp. Hd of Mission, Kinshasa, 2014–15; Ambassador to Republic of S Sudan, 2015–17; Sen. Trade Advr on Africa, FCO, 2017–18. *Recreations:* music, literature. *Club:* Oxford and Cambridge.

**MORRIS, Rev. Canon Timothy David;** Priest Ministry Developer, Pembina Hills Parish, Diocese of Rupert's Land, Canada, 2008–10; *b* 17 Aug. 1948; *s* of Joseph Ernest and Mabel Elizabeth Morris; *m* 1st, 1972, Dorothy Helen Ralph (marr. diss. 1987); one *d*; 2nd, 1988, Irene Elizabeth Lyness. *Educ:* King Edward's Grammar Sch., Bath; Coll. of Estate Management, London Univ. (BSc Econs); Trinity Coll., Bristol and Bristol Univ. (DipTh). Asst Estate Surveyor, Min. of Public Building and Works, Edinburgh, 1969–72; Curate, St Thomas's Church, Edinburgh, 1975–77; Rector: St James's Episcopal Church, Leith, Edinburgh, 1977–83; St Ninian's, Troon, Ayrshire, 1983–85; St Peter's, Galashiels, 1985–2002; Church of the Good Shepherd, Murrayfield, 2002–08; Priest, St Salvador's Church, Stenhouse, 2003–08; Dean, Dio. Edinburgh, Episcopal Ch in Scotland, 1992–2001. Hon. Canon, St Mary's Cathedral, Edinburgh, 2002–. HM Lay Inspector of Educn, 2003–08. Chm., Bd of Mgt, Positive Help, Edinburgh, 2003–08. Chm., Foulden Village Hall Cttee, Berwickshire, 2015–. Trustee, Gunsgreen House, Eyemouth, 2013–. *Recreations:* music, Rugby Union, cricket, gardening, curling, cross-country ski-ing. *Address:* 2 The Firs, Foulden Newton, Berwick-upon-Tweed TD15 1UL. *T:* (01289) 386615.

**MORRIS, Prof. Timothy John,** PhD; Professor of Management Studies, Oxford University, and Fellow, Green Templeton College (formerly Templeton College), Oxford, since 2002; *b* 21 Jan. 1953; *s* of Ernest Joseph Morris and Dorothy Beatrice Morris; *m* 1999, Dr Helen Margaret Lydka; one *s* one *d* (and one *d* decd). *Educ:* Eltham Coll., London; Jesus Coll., Cambridge (BA Hons 1975); London Sch. of Econs (MSc 1980; PhD 1984); Nuffield Coll., Oxford; MA Oxon 2002. Faculty, London Business Sch., 1988–2000; Prof. of Organisational Behaviour, Imperial Coll. London, 2000–02; Dir, Clifford Chance Centre for Mgt of Professional Service Firms, Oxford Univ., 2003–05 and 2007–08; various admin. posts, Saïd Business Sch., Univ. of Oxford, 2007–17. *Publications:* (jtly) The Car Industry: labour relations and industrial adjustment, 1985; Innovations in Banking: business strategies and employee relations, 1986; (jtly) Union Business, 1993; (jtly) Career Frontiers: new conceptions of working lives, 2000; numerous articles in scholarly jls and chapters in edited collections on innovation and change in professional orgns and the role of the CEO. *Recreations:* cinema, running, swimming, contemporary fiction. *Address:* Saïd Business School, Oxford OX1 1HP. *T:* (01865) 288954, *Fax:* (01865) 288805. *E:* tim.morris@sbs.ox.ac.uk.

**MORRIS, Sir Trefor (Alfred),** Kt 1996; CBE 1992; QPM 1985; HM Chief Inspector of Constabulary, 1993–96; Chairman, Police Information Technology Organisation, 1996–2000; Adviser, British Transport Police Committee, 1996–2001; *b* 22 Dec. 1934; *s* of late Kenneth Alfred Morris and Amy Ursula (*née* Burgess); *m* 1958, Martha Margaret (*née* Wroe); two *d. Educ:* Ducie Technical High School, Manchester; Manchester University (Dip. Criminology); Nat. Exec. Inst., USA. Constable to Chief Superintendent, Manchester City Police, Manchester and Salford Police, Greater Manchester Police, 1955–76; Asst Chief Constable, Greater Manchester Police, 1976–79; Dep. Chief Constable, 1979–84, Chief Constable, 1984–90, Herts; HM Inspector of Constabulary, 1990–93. Trustee, Police Foundn, 1993–96. Pres., Police Mutual Assurance Soc., 1994–97. Member: St Albans Diocesan Synod, 1989–96; PCC, St Mary's Church, Abergavenny, 1997–; Governing Body, Church in Wales, 2003–09. Chairman: St Mary's Priory Develt Trust, 1999–; St Mary's Priory House Co. Ltd, 2009–. Churchwarden, St Mary's Priory Church, 2010–13. Vice President: Herts Scouts, 1989–; Police Athletics Assoc.; Pres., Luton, N Herts Inst. of Mgt; Pres., Beaufort Male Choir, 2010–13. Chm., Bryn-y-Cwm Community Forum, 2004–08. Dir, Abergavenny Food Fest. Co. Ltd, 1999–2016. Trustee, Hospice of the Valleys, 1997–2005. CCMI (CBIM 1986). FRSA 1993. OStJ 1984. *Recreations:* music, golf, wine, walking, gardening, medieval history. *Clubs:* Royal Over-Seas League; Monmouthshire Golf (Captain, 2005–06).

**MORRIS, Ulrike Luise;** see Tillmann, U. L.

**MORRIS, Warwick;** HM Diplomatic Service, retired; consultant on Asian Affairs; *b* 10 Aug. 1948; *e s* of late Clifford Morris and Patricia Morris (*née* O'Grady), JP; *m* 1972, Pamela Jean Mitchell, MBE; one *s* two *d. Educ:* Bishop's Stortford Coll. VSO, Cameroon, 1967–68; entered Diplomatic Service, 1969; Third Sec., Paris, 1972–74; Korean lang. trng, Yonsei Univ., Seoul, 1975–76; Second Sec., Seoul, 1977–79; FCO, 1979–83; First Sec., 1982; First Sec. (Commercial), Mexico City, 1984–87; Head of Chancery, Seoul, 1988–91; Dep. Head, Far Eastern Dept, FCO, 1991–93; Counsellor, 1993, Head, 1994, Permanent Under Sec.'s Dept, FCO; Econ. and Commercial Counsellor, New Delhi, 1995–98; RCDS, 1999; Ambassador: to Vietnam, 2000–03; to South Korea, 2003–08. Korea and Vietnam Advr to Lloyd's, 2008–12; non-executive Director: PCA Life Korea, 2008–13; Prudential Vietnam, 2013–; Advr, KOTRA UK, 2010–15. Member, Board: Locate in Kent, 2009–15 (Chm., 2012–15); Kent Ambassador, 2010–. Hon. Pres., British Korean Law Assoc., 2008–; Chm., British Korean Soc. (formerly Anglo-Korean Soc.), 2011–18; Chm., Vietnam-UK Network, 2018– (Founder, 2013; Vice Chm., 2013–18). Hon. Fellow, Robinson Coll., Cambridge, 2011. *Recreations:* sport, travel, philately. *Address:* Rosewood, Stonewall Park Road, Langton Green, Kent TN3 0HD.

**MORRIS, Prof. (William) David,** PhD, DSc(Eng); Professor of Mechanical Engineering, University of Wales, Swansea (formerly University College of Swansea), 1985 (Head of Department, 1985–91 and 1995); *b* 14 March 1936; *s* of late William Daniel and Elizabeth Jane Morris; *m* 1959, Pamela Eira Evans (*d* 2008); two *s* one *d. Educ:* Queen Mary College, London (1st Cl. Hons BSc Eng); UC of Swansea, Wales (PhD); Univ. of London (DSc(Eng)). CEng, FIMechE, FIET. Bristol Siddeley Engine Co., 1958–60; James Clayton Res. Fellow, Univ. of Wales, Swansea, 1960–63; Lectr, Dept of Mech. Engrg, Univ. of Liverpool, 1963–67; Lectr, 1967–72, Reader, 1972–79, Sch. of Engrg, Univ. of Sussex; J. H. Fenner Prof. of Mech. Engrg and Head, Dept of Engrg Design, Univ. of Hull, 1979–85; Vice Principal, UC Swansea, 1991–93. *Publications:* Differential Equations for Engineers and Applied Scientists, 1979; Heat Transfer and Fluid Flow in Rotating Coolant Channels, 1981. *Recreations:* oil painting, DIY, walking.

**MORRIS, His Honour William Patrick;** a Circuit Judge, 1995–2012; Resident Judge, Bolton Crown Court, 2002–12; Honorary Recorder of Bolton, 2008–12; *b* 17 March 1947; *s* of His Honour Sir William Gerard Morris and Mollie Morris; *m* 1978, Patricia Whittaker (*see* Baroness Morris of Bolton); one *s* one *d. Educ:* Ampleforth Coll.; Gonville and Caius Coll., Cambridge (BA 1968, MA). Called to the Bar, Lincoln's Inn, 1970; a Recorder, 1988–95. *Recreations:* fishing, gardening, walking, watching Bolton Wanderers.

**MORRISON,** family name of **Viscount Dunrossil** and of **Baron Margadale**.

**MORRISON, Alasdair;** Chairman, MG Alba, 2008–11; Director, UBC Group, 2007; *b* 18 Nov. 1968; *m*; one *s* one *d*. Former Western Isles correspondent, BBC; former Editor, New Gael newspaper. Mem. (Lab) Western Isles, Scottish Parlt, 1999–2007. Dep. Minister for Enterprise in the Highlands and Islands and Gaelic, 1999–2001, for Enterprise and Lifelong Learning and Gaelic, 2001, Scottish Exec. Dir, Harris Tweed Hebrides LLP, 2011–12. Contested (Lab) Western Isles, 2015.

**MORRISON, Sir (Alexander) Fraser,** Kt 1998; CBE 1993; Deputy Chairman, Clydesdale Bank plc, 1999–2004 (Director, 1994–2004); Chairman: Teasses Capital Ltd, since 2003; Duthus Investments Ltd, 2013–18; *b* 20 March 1948; *s* of late Alexander Ferrier Sharp Morrison and of Catherine Colina (*née* Fraser); *m* 1972, Patricia Janice Murphy; one *s* two *d. Educ:* Tain Royal Acad.; Univ. of Edinburgh (BSc Hons Civil Engrg). CEng, FICE 1993; Eur Ing 1993; MCIHT (MIHT 1982); FCIOB 1995. Morrison Construction Gp, subseq. Morrison: Dir, 1970; Man. Dir, 1976–96; Chm., 1984–96; Exec. Chm., 1996–2000. Director: Shand Ltd, 1978–89; Alexander Shand Holdings Ltd, 1982–86; RMJM Ltd, 2007–13 (Chm., 2007–13); Chairman: Ramco Hldgs, 2005–13; Vermilion Hldgs, 2007–16. Chm., Highlands & Islands Enterprise, 1992–98. Federation of Civil Engineering Contractors: Chm., Scottish Sect., 1991–92; Chm., Nat. Fedn, 1993–94; Vice Pres., 1994–96. Chm., American Patrons, Nat. Liby and Galls of Scotland, 2011–17. Chairman: Bd of Governors, Univ. of Highlands and Is Project, 1998–2001; Council St Leonard's Sch., St Andrews, 1999–2007. Internat. Pres., Chief Execs Orgn, 2009–10 (Dir, 2003–13). FRSA 1990; FScotvec 1994. Hon. DTech: Napier, 1995; Glasgow Caledonian, 1997; DUniv Open, 2000. *Recreations:* shooting, golf, music, art. *Address:* Teasses House, near Ceres, Leven, Fife KY8 5PG. *T:* (01334) 828048; 14 East 75th Street, New York, NY 10021, USA. *T:* (212) 744 2697. *Clubs:* New (Edinburgh); Royal & Ancient Golf (St Andrews).

**MORRISON, Alistair Neil;** photographer; *b* Lima, Peru, 4 Nov. 1956; *s* of James and Eileen Morrison; *m* 1st, 1980, Janis Anne Edwards (marr. diss. 1990); one *s* one *d*; 2nd, 2005, Louise Mary Bader (marr. diss. 2013); one *s* one *d*; 3rd, 2019, Lara Antonella Henderson. *Educ:* Ardingly Coll., Sussex; Harrow Coll. (BA Hons Photography, Film and TV). Photographs exhibited in NPG, London; exhibitions: Twenty for Today, 1985, Olympians, 1992, NPG; Time to Reflect, 2000; Retrospective, New Lodge, Windsor, 2006; Nudes: a country collection, Linley, Belgravia, 2008; Actors Last Supper, NPG, 2013; The Adoration Trilogy: searching for Apollo, V&A Mus., 2017. *Publications:* Time to Reflect I, 2000; Time to Reflect II, 2008; Hidden Gems, 2009. *Recreations:* art and photography galleries, all music, sun, sea, sand.

**MORRISON, Amanda Mary;** *see* Doyle, A. M.

**MORRISON, (Andrew) Neil,** CBE 1997; QFSM 1989; HM Chief Inspector of Fire Services for Scotland, 1994–99; *b* 8 Sept. 1937; *e s* of late Andrew Steel Morrison and Margueritta Wilkin Caird; *m* 1963, Kathleen Rutherford; one *s. Educ:* Arbroath High Sch.; Dundee Coll. of Technol. FIFireE 1991. Angus Fire Brigade: Fireman, 1962–70; Leading Fireman, 1970–71; Sub-officer, 1971–74; Station Officer, 1974–75; Tayside Fire Brigade: Station Officer, 1975–76; Asst Divl Officer, 1976; Divl Officer, Grade III, 1976–79; Divl Officer, Grade I, 1979–80; Grampian Fire Brigade: Dep. Firemaster, 1980–85; Firemaster, 1985–93. Hon. DTech Robert Gordon Univ., 1994. *Recreations:* curling, golf, hill-walking, swimming. *Address:* 18 Slateford Gardens, Edzell, Angus DD9 7SX. *T:* (01356) 648768.

**MORRISON, Very Rev. Angus,** PhD; Moderator of the General Assembly of the Church of Scotland, 2015–16; Chaplain to the Queen in Scotland, since 2006; *b* 30 Aug. 1953; *s* of Norman Morrison, MBE and Mary Ann Morrison; *m* 1983, Marion Jane Matheson; three *s* one *d. Educ:* Glasgow Univ. (MA Hons 1976); London Univ. (BD Hons 1993 ext.); Edinburgh Univ. (PhD 2001). Minister, Free Presbyterian Church of Scotland: Oban, 1979–86; Edinburgh, 1986–89; Minister: Associated Presbyterian Chs, Edinburgh, 1989–2000; St Columba's Old Parish Ch, Stornoway, 2000–11; Orwell and Portmoak Parish Ch, Kinross-shire, 2011–. Moderator: Gen. Assembly, Associated Presbyterian Chs, 1998–99; C of S Presbytery of Lewis, 2003–04; Chaplain, Nicolson Inst., Stornoway, 2003–; Chaplain to Lord High Comr to Gen. Assembly of C of S, 2005, 2006; Nat. Chaplain, Girls' Brigade, Scotland, 2016–. C of S Ecumenical Delegate to Gen. Synod of C of E, 2016–; Co-Chm., Columba Declaration Contact Gp, 2016–. Convener: C of S Mission and Discipleship Council, 2005–09; Gaelic Gp, C of S, 2016–. Mem., C of S Special Commn on Same-Sex Relationships and the Ministry, 2009–11. Chm., Novum Trust, 2014–; Pres., Scottish Churches Disability Gp, 2016–. Vis. Scholar, Princeton Theol Seminary, 2009; Vis. Lectr, United Theol Coll., Bangalore, 2012. DD Glasgow, 2018. *Publications:* (contrib.) Dictionary of Scottish Church History and Theology, 1993; (contrib.) Oxford DNB; (ed) Tolerance and Truth: the spirit of the age or the spirit of God?, 2007; (contrib.) Dizionario di Teologia Evangelica, 2007. *Recreations:* walking, reading, listening to music, cycling. *Address:* 41 Auld Mart Road, Milnathort, Kinross-shire KY13 9FR. *E:* angusmorrison3@gmail.com.

**MORRISON, Anne Catherine;** Chair, Governing Body, Pearson College London, since 2017; *b* 18 Aug. 1959; *d* of late George Charles Morrison and of Persis Mae Morrison (*née* Ross); *m* 1989, Robert John Jarvis Johnstone; one *d. Educ:* Richmond Lodge Sch., Belfast; Churchill Coll., Cambridge (MA Eng. Lit). Gen. Trainee, BBC, 1981–83; Researcher and Dir, Documentary Features, BBC TV, 1983–87; Prod., Holiday, 1987–88; Series Prod., Crimewatch UK, 1988–90; Chief Assistant, Documentary Features, 1990–92; Exec. Prod., Taking Liberties, and Rough Justice, 1992; Dep. Head, 1992–94, Hd, 1994–96, Features, BBC TV; BBC Production: Head of Consumer and Leisure, 1996–98; Head of Features and Events, 1998–2000; Controller, Leisure and Factual Entertainment, 2000–01, General Factual Gp, 2001–02, Documentaries and Contemp. Factual, 2002–06, Network Production, 2006–09, BBC TV; Dir, BBC Acad., 2009–14; Exec. Prod., Manolo: the boy who made shoes for lizards, 2016–17; Sen. Hearing Mgr, BBC, 2018–. Mem., Editl Review Bd, Top Gear Mag., 2018–. Mem., Communication and Engagement Cttee, British Acad., 2017–. Mem. Bd, Women in Film and TV, 2017–. Trustee: BAFTA, 2010–17 (Mem., TV Cttee, 2008–13; Chairman: Learning and Events Cttee, 2010–14; Internat. Cttee, 2017–; Dep. Chm., 2013–14, 2016–17; Chm., 2014–16); Charleston Trust, 2015–; Watersprite Internat. Student Film Fest., 2015–. Patron, Medical Aid Films, 2016–. Mem. Bd, London & Partners, 2015–17. Gov., UAL, 2015–17. Hon. DArts Nottingham Trent, 2018. *Recreations:* reading, dancing, films, improving my Italian. *Address:* Pearson College London, 190 High Holborn, WC1V 7BH.

**MORRISON, Blake;** *see* Morrison, P. B.

**MORRISON, Dennis John;** Regional Director, Government Office for the East Midlands, 1998–2002; Special Professor, Faculty of the Built Environment, University of Nottingham, 2000–10; *b* 20 May 1942; *s* of Leonard Tait Morrison and Alice Morrison; *m* 1967, Frances Joan Pollard; one *s* one *d. Educ:* Ashton-upon-Mersey Boys' School; Lymm Grammar School; Manchester Univ. (BA, DipT&CP). MRTPI. Planning appointments: Lancs CC, 1966–70; Welsh Office, Cardiff, 1970–75; NW Region, DoE, Manchester, 1975–81; Regional Controller, NW Enterprise Unit, DoE, 1981–84; Regional Controller (Urban and Economic Affairs), Merseyside Task Force, Liverpool, 1984–89; Regl Dir, Depts of Envmt and Transport, E Midlands Region, 1989–94; Dir, Envmt and Transport, Govt Office for E Midlands, 1994–97; Regl Dir, Govt Office for Merseyside, 1997–98. Mem., Adv. Bd, Highways Agency, 1999–2003; Bd Mem., Industrial Trust E Midlands, 2000–10. Non-exec. Dir, Independent Decision Makers Ltd, 2002–09. Mem., Exec. Cttee, Liverpool Cathedral, 1986–. Trustee, 2005–14, Arkwright Soc. (Vice. Pres., 2008–12). FRGS. Hon. Mem., Bromley House Library, Nottingham. *Recreations:* antiquarian book collecting, horology, antique barometer restoration, hill walking, gardening, cooking, people watching. *Address:* Bowdon, Cheshire.

**MORRISON, Fiona Jane;** Owner, Fiona Morrison Professional Services Ltd, since 2018; President, Institute and Faculty of Actuaries, 2015–16; *b* Stevenage, 2 May 1957; *d* of John Black, (Ian), Morrison and Marion Lilian Morrison (*née* Morgan, later Bicknell); *m* 1984, Dr Eivind James Dullforce (*d* 2006). *Educ:* Dauntsey's Sch., Devizes; Selwyn Coll., Cambridge (BA 1979). FIA 1984. Joined Lane Clark & Peacock LLP, 1979, Partner, 1984–2018. Institute of Actuaries, later Institute and Faculty of Actuaries: Member: Council, 2001–07 and 2008–17; Regulation Bd, 2008–17; Pres.'s Award, 2012. Chm., Staple Inn Actuarial Soc., 2008–10. Pres., Selwyn Coll. Alumni Assoc., 2012–13. Trustee, Oxford and Cambridge Rowing Foundn, 2015–. Liveryman, Actuaries' Co., 1996 (Court Asst, 2012–17; Master, 2019–); Trustee, Co. of Actuaries Charitable Trust, 2004–12; Chm., Oxford and Cambridge Rowing Foundn, 2017–. *Recreations:* ski touring, rowing. *E:* fiona@fionamorrison.org. *Clubs:* Oriental; Leander.

**MORRISON, Sir Fraser;** *see* Morrison, Sir A. F.

**MORRISON, Fraser;** *see* Morrison, R. F.

**MORRISON, Sir George Ivan, (Sir Van),** Kt 2015; OBE 1996; singer and songwriter; *b* Belfast, 31 Aug. 1945; *s* of George Morrison and Violet Morrison; *m* 1967, Janet Planet (marr. diss. 1973); one *d*; *m* Michelle Rocca; one *s* one *d.* Singer with Them, 1964–67; solo singer, 1967–. *Albums include:* with Them: Them, 1965; Them Again, 1966; solo: Blowin' Your Mind, 1967; Astral Weeks, 1968; Moondance, 1970; His Band and Street Choir, 1970; Tupelo Honey, 1971; St Dominic's Preview, 1972; Hard Nose the Highway, 1973; Veedon Fleece, 1974; A Period of Transition, 1977; Wavelength, 1978; Into the Music, 1979; Common One, 1980; Beautiful Vision, 1982; Inarticulate Speech of the Heart, 1983; A Sense of Wonder, 1985; No Guru, No Method, No Teacher, 1986; Poetic Champion Compose, 1987; Irish Heartbeat, 1988; Avalon Sunset, 1989; Enlightenment, 1990; Hymns to the Silence, 1991; Bang Master, 1991; Too Long in Exile, 1993; A Night in San Francisco, 1994; Days Like This, 1995; How Long Has This Been Going On, 1995; The Healing Game, 1996; Tell Me Something, 1996; The Philosopher's Stone, 1998; The Masters, 1999; Back on Top, 1999; Down the Road, 2002; What's Wrong with this Picture, 2003; Magic Time, 2005; Keep it Simple, 2008; Born to Sing: No Plan B, 2012; Duets: reworking the catalogue, 2015; Keep Me Singing, 2016; Versatile, 2017; Roll with the Punches, 2017. Hon. Freeman, Belfast, 2013. *Address:* Exile Productions Ltd, 2nd Floor, 88–90 Baker Street, W1U 6TQ.

**MORRISON, Graham,** OBE 2016; RIBA; Founder and Partner, Allies and Morrison, Architects, since 1983; *b* Kilmarnock, Scotland, 2 Feb. 1951; *s* of Robert Morrison and Robina Sandison Morrison; one *s* one *d. Educ:* Brighton Coll.; Jesus Coll., Cambridge (MA; Brancusi Prize 1972; DipArch 1975). RIBA 1976. *Projects completed* include: Clove Bldg, London, 1990 (RIBA Award 1991); Sarum Hall Sch., London, 1995 (RIBA Award, Civic Trust Award, 1996); Nunnery Square, Sheffield, 1995 (RIBA Award 1996); British Embassy, Dublin, 1995 (RIBA Award 1997); Rosalind Franklin Bldg, Newnham Coll., Cambridge, 1995 (RIBA Award 1996); Abbey Mills Pumping Station, Stratford (RIBA Award), 1997; Rutherford Information Services Bldg, Goldsmiths Coll., London, 1997 (RIBA Award 1998); Blackburn Hse, London, 1999 (RIBA Award 2000); Blackwell, Cumbria, 2003 (RIBA Award, Civic Trust Award, 2003); extension to Horniman Mus., 2004 (RIBA Award, Civic Trust Award, 2004); 85 Southwark Street, London, 2004 (London Civic Trust Award, Bldg of Year Award, RIBA London, Nat. Winner for Corporate Workplace Bldg, British Council for Offices Awards, 2004); BBC Media Village, White City, 2003 (RIBA Award 2005; Civic Trust Award 2006); Fitzwilliam Coll. Gatehouse and Auditorium, 2004 (RIBA Award 2005; Civic Trust Award 2007); City Lit, 2004 (Civic Trust Award 2006); The Finlay Bldg, Merton Coll., 2004 (Civic Trust Award 2007); Girton Coll. Liby, Cambridge, 2005 (RIBA Award 2006; Civic Trust Award 2007); Farnborough Business Park, Hants, 2006 (RIBA Award 2007); WWT Vis. Centre and Footbridge, Welney, 2006 (Civic Trust Award 2007); Royal Festival Hall restoration, 2007; Planetarium, Royal Observatory, Greenwich, 2007 (RIBA Award 2008; Civic Trust Award 2008); Bankside 123, 2007 (RIBA Award 2010); Paradise Street, Liverpool One, 2009 (RIBA Award 2009); Charles Street Car Park, Sheffield, 2009 (RIBA Award 2009); One Vine Street, The Quadrant, Regent Street, 2009 (RIBA Award 2009); Highbury Square, 2009 (RIBA Award 2010); Mint Hotel, Leeds (RIBA Award 2011); Royal Albert Meml Mus., 2013 (RIBA Award 2013); Simon Smith Bldg, 2013 (RIBA Award 2013); Rambert London, 2014 (RIBA Award 2014); Ash Court, Girton Coll., Cambridge, 2014 (RIBA Award 2014); 100 Bishopsgate, 2019; St Peter's Coll., Oxford; Darwin Coll., Cambridge; *Masterplans* include: London 2012 Stratford and Legacy London, 2012 (RIBA Nat. Award 2013); Beirut districts; Wood Wharf, Canary Wharf; Irfan, Oman, 2017. *Exhibitions* include: New British Architecture, Japan, 1994; Allies and Morrison Retrospective, USA Schs of Architecture, 1996–98; exhibns in Helsinki, Delft, Strasbourg, 1999. Special Prof. of Architecture, Univ. of Nottingham, 2004–05. Member: RIBA Council, 1992–95; Architecture Adv. Cttee, Arts Council, 1996–97; Royal Fine Art Commn, 1998–99; Design Review Cttee, CABE, 2000–04; Historic England (formerly English Heritage): Member: London Adv. Cttee, 2001–13; Urban Panel, 2009–16; Comr, 2011–15; Adv. Cttee, 2013–16. Chm., S Downs Nat. Park Design Review Panel, 2015–; Mem., S Downs Nat. Park Authy, 2018–. External Examiner: Univ. of Cambridge, 1994–97; Univ. of Portsmouth, 2003–05; Bartlett Sch. of Architecture, 2010–11. Dir, RIBA Jl, 1993–97. Masterplanning Architect of the Year and Public Bldg Architect of the Year, 2007, Masterplanning and Public Realm Architect of the Year, 2015, Education Architect of the Year, 2015, Bldg Design Awards. *Publications:* Contributor: Allies and Morrison, 1996; Allies and Morrison vol. 1, 2011, vol. 2, 2019; The Fabric of Place, 2013. *Address:* Allies and Morrison, 85 Southwark Street, SE1 0HX. *T:* (020) 7921 0100, *Fax:* (020) 7921 0101. *E:* gmorrison@alliesandmorrison.com.

**MORRISON, His Honour Sir Howard (Andrew Clive),** KCMG 2015; CBE 2007 (OBE 1988); QC 2001; a Circuit Judge, 2004–19; a Judge of the International Criminal Court, The Hague, since 2011 (a Judge of Appeals Division, since 2016); *b* 20 July 1949; *s* of Howard Edward Morrison and Roma Morrison; *m* 1980, Kathryn Margaret Moore; one *s* one *d. Educ:* London Univ. (LLB); Inns of Court Sch. of Law. Volunteer, Ghana, 1968–69, Desk Officer, Zambia and Malawi, 1975–76, VSO. Subaltern, Queen's Regt, 1970–74. Called to the Bar: Gray's Inn, 1977, Bencher, 2006; Fiji, 1988; Eastern Caribbean, 1990; in practice on Midland and Oxford Circuit, 1977–85; Resident Magistrate, then Chief Magistrate, Fiji, 1985–87; concurrently Sen. Magistrate for Tuvalu and locum Attorney Gen. of Anguilla, 1988–89; in practice on Midland and Oxford Circuit, 1989–2004; a Recorder, 1994–2004; engaged in defending in UN War Crime Tribunals, The Hague and Arusha, 1998–2004; Sen. Judge, Sovereign Base Areas, Cyprus, 2007–; Judge, Special Tribunal for Lebanon, 2010; Permanent Judge, UN Internat. Criminal Tribunal for former Yugoslavia, The Hague, 2010–. Advocacy Teacher/Trainer, Gray's Inn, 1994–. Holding Redlich Dist. Vis. Fellow, Monash Univ., 2007; Hon. Prof. of Law, Leicester Univ., 2012–; Sen. Fellow, Lauterpacht Centre for Internat. Law, Cambridge Univ., 2013–; Vis. Prof., Northumbria Univ., 2018. Lectures on internat. humanitarian law, Europe, Africa, Middle East, USA and Australia. Member: Race Relations Cttee, 1996–2002, Equal Opportunities Cttee, 2002–03, Bar Council; IBA; Commonwealth Judges and Magistrates Assoc.; Justice; British Inst. for Internat. and Comparative Law; Adv. Bd, Jl of Internat. Criminal Law, 2008–; Adv. Bd, Internat. Criminal Law Network, 2012–. Member, Bar: Fiji; E Caribbean.

Mem., RUSI. FRGS 1991; FRSA 2018. Hon. LLD Leicester, 2014. *Publications:* numerous legal articles, mainly on internat. criminal law. *Recreations:* travel, flying, sailing, ski-ing, hill walking. *Address:* The 36 Group, 4 Field Court, Gray's Inn, WC1R 5EF. *Clubs:* Royal Over-Seas League; Portsmouth Offshore Group.

**MORRISON, Air Vice Marshal Ian Craig,** CBE 2011; FRAeS; FCMI; Director General, Saudi Arabian Programme, 2012–18; *b* Lancs, 15 Oct. 1959; *s* of Thomas David Morrison and Patricia Morrison; *m* 1996, Samantha Jayne McKie Edwards; one *s* one *d*. *Educ:* Winton High Sch.; Eccles Sixth Form Coll.; Open Univ.; Royal Coll. of Defence Studies. Commnd officer RAF, 1979; RAF aircrew and mil. duties incl. qwi, 1979–2000, RAF Staff Coll., 1995–96; Comdr XXV (Fighter) Sqn, 2000–03; Dep. Principal SO to UK CDS, MoD, 2003–04; Station Comdr, RAF Leeming, 2004–06; Dep. Comdr British Forces, Afghanistan, 2006; Dir RAF Operation Trng, 2007–09; Comdr UK Air Command Coordination Exec., ISAF HQ Kabul, Afghanistan, 2008; Asst COS, Air Capability, 2009–11; COS Capability HQ Air Comd, 2011–12; Actg Air Marshal, 2014–18. Trustee: Queen's Cottages Almshouse charity, 2011–18; Harrison Homes Charity, 2012–. Upper Liveryman, Hon. Co. of Air Pilots (formerly GAPAN), 2011. FRAeS 2011; FCMI 2012; FInstD 2012. *Recreations:* dinghy sailing, running, fly fishing, family. *Club:* Royal Air Force.

**MORRISON, Dr James,** RSA 1992 (ARSA 1973); RSW 1968; painter in oil and water colours; *b* 11 April 1932; *s* of John Morrison and Margaret Thomson; *m* 1955, Dorothy McCormack (*d* 2005); one *s* one *d*; partner, Ann Keddie. *Educ:* Hillhead High Sch., Glasgow; Glasgow Sch. of Art (DA). Vis. Artist, Hospitalfield House, 1962, 1963; Duncan of Jordanstone College of Art, Dundee: Member of Staff, 1965–87; Head of Dept, 1978–87; Mem. Board, 1988–. Council Mem., Soc. of Scottish Artists, 1964–67; Keeper of the Collection, Royal Scottish Acad., 1992–. Mem., Inst. of Contemporary Scotland, 2000. Painting in Europe, USA and Canada, 1968–; painting in the High Arctic, 1990–96; painting in Africa, 1998; one-man exhibitions: Scotland, London, Italy, Germany, Canada, 1956–; Scottish Gall., Edinburgh, 2012; Fleming Gall., London, 2013; numerous works in public and private collections, UK and overseas. Torrance Award, RGI, 1958; Arts Council Travelling Award, 1968. DUniv Stirling, 1986. *Publications:* Aff the Squerr, 1976, 2nd edn 1990; Winter in Paris, 1991. *Recreation:* playing recorder in a chamber music group. *Address:* Craigview House, Usan, Montrose, Angus DD10 9SD. *T:* (01674) 672639.

**MORRISON, James;** *see* Morrison, J. J. H.

**MORRISON, Janet Rachel;** Chief Executive, Black Stork Charity, since 2019; *b* 13 April 1964; *d* of Alastair and Jennifer Morrison; one *s* one *d*. *Educ:* Univ. of Nottingham (BA Hons Pols 1985); Virginia State Univ. (MA Pol Sci. 1986). Dir, Policy and Res., NCVO, 1995–97; Sen. Policy Advr, BBC, 1997–99; Dep. Chief Exec., NESTA, 1999–2007; Chief Exec., IndependentAge, 2007–19. Member: Deregulation Task Force for Charities, 1994; Deakin Commn Charity Law Cttee, 1995. Chm., Baring Foundn, 2014– (Trustee, 2008–; Vice Chm., 2010–14); Mem., Campaign to End Loneliness, 2011–19 (Chm., 2017); Dir, ReConnections Ltd, 2015–18; Chm., Assoc. of Charitable Foundations, 2018–. *Recreations:* family, arts, comedy, walking, travel. *Address:* 27 Muswell Road, N10 2BS; Black Stork Charity, 70 Grosvenor Street, W1K 3JP. *T:* (020) 7408 0988. *E:* janet.morrison@grosvenor.com.

**MORRISON, Jasper,** RDI 2001; designer; *b* 11 Nov. 1959; *s* of Alec and Dinah Morrison; *m* 2011, Junko Tamura. *Educ:* Kingston Polytechnic; RCA (MA Design). Established Office for Design, 1986. *Publications:* Jasper Morrison: designs, projects and drawings 1981–1989, 1990; A World Without Words, 1992, 2nd edn 1998; A New Tram for Hanover, 1997; Everything But the Walls, 2002, 2nd edn 2006; (with Naoto Fukasawa) Super Normal, 2007; The Good Life, 2014; A Book of Things, 2015; The Hard Life, 2017. *Address:* 24B Kingsland Road, E2 8DA. *T:* (020) 7739 2522.

**MORRISON, Ven. John Anthony;** Archdeacon of Oxford, 1998–2005, now Archdeacon Emeritus; a Residentiary Canon of Christ Church, Oxford, 1998–2005, now Canon Emeritus; *b* 11 March 1938; *s* of late Major Leslie Claude Morrison and Mary Sharland Morrison (*née* Newson-Smith); *m* 1968, Angela, *d* of late Major Jonathan Eric Bush; two *s* one *d*. *Educ:* Haileybury; Jesus Coll., Cambridge (BA 1960; MA 1964); Lincoln Coll., Oxford (MA 1968); Chichester Theol. Coll. Ordained deacon 1964, priest 1965; Curate: St Peter, Birmingham, 1964–68; St Michael-at-the-Northgate, Oxford, 1968–74; Chaplain, Lincoln Coll., Oxford, 1968–74; Vicar, Basildon, Berks, 1974–82; RD Bradfield, 1978–82; Vicar, Aylesbury, Bucks, 1982–89. Team Rector, 1989–90; RD Aylesbury, 1985–89; Archdeacon of Buckingham, 1990–98. Examining Chaplain to Bishop of Oxford, 1972–78. Mem., Gen. Synod, 1980–90, 1998–2000. Sen. Treas.; Corp. of Sons of the Clergy, 2005–08 (Treas., 2002–08). County Chaplain: Bucks, 1990–98, Oxon, 1998–2007, RBL; Bucks, 1990–98, Oxon, 1998–2007, St John Ambulance. Master, Spectacle Makers' Co., 2006–07. Hon. Chaplain, 007 Past Masters Assoc., 2007–. *Address:* 39 Crown Road, Wheatley, Oxford OX33 1UJ. *T:* (01865) 876625. *E:* morrison039@btinternet.com. *Clubs:* Leander (Henley-on-Thames); Vincent's (Oxford).

**MORRISON, (Jonathan) James (Howard),** CMG 2015; Chef de Cabinet, European Commissioner for Security Union, European Commission, since 2016; *b* Sale, Cheshire, 31 Dec. 1967; *s* of Kenneth and Norma Morrison; *m* 1994, Helen Pope; three *d*. *Educ:* Stockport Grammar Sch.; Birmingham Univ. (BA Hons); Ashridge Business Sch. (MBA). Home Office, 1989–91; HM Diplomatic Service, 1991–2008: UN Dept, 1991–94; Third, later Second, then First Sec., UK Perm. Repn, Brussels (Ext. Relns), 1994–99; press spokesman on EU issues, FCO, 1999–2000; Private Sec. to Minister for Europe, 2000–03; Eur. corresp. and Hd, Common Foreign and Security Policy Dept, 2003–04; Counsellor, UK Perm. Repn, Brussels, 2004–05; on loan to Ashridge Business Sch. as Strategy Tutor and Prog. Manager, 2006–07; Sen. Advr to Minister for Europe, 2007–08; Chef de Cabinet, Eur. Comr for Trade, EC, 2009; COS to EU High Rep. for Foreign and Security Policy and Vice Pres. of EC, 2009–14; Dir, Policy Coordination, Secretariat General, EC, 2014–16. *Recreations:* walking, classic cars, family. *Address:* European Commission, Rue de la Loi 200, 1040 Brussels, Belgium. *E:* james.morrison@ec.europa.eu. *Club:* Goodwood Road Racing.

**MORRISON, Leslie;** Chief Executive Officer, Invest Northern Ireland, 2001–09; *b* 29 Jan. 1948. *Educ:* Queen's Univ., Belfast (BA Hons Mod. Languages 1971). Man. Dir, J. P. Morgan & Co., 1983–2001. Chairman, Advisory Committee: Invest Growth Fund, 2011–17; Techstart NI, 2014–; Mem., Investment Cttee, Crescent Capital III LLP, 2014–.

**MORRISON, Hon. Mary Anne,** GCVO 2013 (DCVO 1982; CVO 1970); Woman of the Bedchamber to the Queen, since 1960; *b* 17 May 1937; *o d* of 1st Baron Margadale, TD. *Educ:* Heathfield School.

**MORRISON, Murdo,** FRAeS; Head of Strategic Content, Flightglobal, since 2015; *b* 22 June 1964; *s* of late John and of Mairi Morrison; *m* 1994, Juliet Parish; one *s* one *d*. *Educ:* Nicolson Inst., Stornoway; Glasgow Univ. (MA Hons Politics 1986); University Coll., Cardiff (Dip. Journalism 1987). Journalist, Commercial Motor, 1987–92; Editor, Car & Accessory Trader, 1992–94; Dep. Editor, Printweek, 1994–95; Editor: Planning Week, 1995; Motor Trader, 1995–2001; Man. Ed., 2001, Ed., 2001–15, Flight Internat. Governor, Middle Street Primary Sch., Brighton, 1998–2006 (Chm. of Govs, 2001–06). FRAeS 2010. *Recreation:* football (Brighton & Hove Albion). *Address:* Reed Business Information, Quadrant House, The Quadrant, Sutton, Surrey SM2 5AS. *T:* (020) 8652 4395, *Fax:* (020) 8652 3850. *E:* murdo.morrison@flightglobal.com.

**MORRISON, Neil;** *see* Morrison, A. N.

**MORRISON, Nigel Murray Paton;** QC (Scot.) 1988; Sheriff of Lothian and Borders at Edinburgh, 1996–2017; Temporary Judge, Court of Session and High Court of Justiciary, since 2013; Appeal Sheriff, Sheriff Appeal Court, 2015–17; Sheriff and Appeal Sheriff (part-time), since 2017; *b* 18 March 1948; *o s* of late David Paton Morrison, FRICS, FLAS and Dilys Morrison. *Educ:* Rannoch School. Called to the Bar, Inner Temple, 1972; admitted Scottish Bar, 1975; Asst Editor, Session Cases, 1976–82; Asst Clerk, Rules Council, 1978–84; Clerk of Faculty, Faculty of Advocates, 1979–87; Standing Junior Counsel to Scottish Develt Dept (Planning), 1982–86; Temporary Sheriff, 1982–96; Second (formerly Junior) Counsel to Lord President of Court of Session, 1984–89; First Counsel to Lord President, 1989–96; Counsel to Sec. of State under Private Legislation Procedure (Scotland) Act 1936, 1986–96. Chairman: Social Security Appeal Tribunals, 1982–91; Medical Appeal Tribunals, 1991–96. Dir of Judicial Studies, Judicial Studies Cttee, 2000–04. Pres., Sheriffs' Assoc., 2011–13 (Vice Pres., 2009–11). Trustee, Nat. Library of Scotland, 1989–98. Editor: Greens Civil Practice Bulletin, 1995–2003; Greens Litigation Styles, 1998–2003. *Publications:* (jtly) Greens Annotated Rules of the Court of Session, 1994; (ed jtly) Sentencing Practice, 2000; contribs to Stair Memorial Encyclopaedia of the Laws of Scotland, Macphail on Sheriff Court Practice, 2nd edn. *Recreations:* music, riding, being taken for walks by my dogs. *Address:* Sheriff Court House, 27 Chambers Street, Edinburgh EH1 1LB. *T:* (0131) 225 2525. *Club:* New (Edinburgh).

**MORRISON, (Philip) Blake,** FRSL; poet, novelist and critic; *b* 8 Oct. 1950; *s* of Arthur Blakemore Morrison and Agnes O'Shea; *m* 1976, Katherine Ann Drake; two *s* one *d*. *Educ:* Ermysted's Grammar Sch., Skipton; Nottingham Univ. (BA); McMaster Univ. (MA); University College London (PhD; Fellow, 2006). FRSL 1988. Poetry and fiction editor, TLS, 1978–81; Dep. Literary Editor, 1981–86, Literary Editor, 1987–89, Observer; Literary Editor, 1990–94, Staff writer, 1994–95, Independent on Sunday. Prof. of Creative and Life Writing, Goldsmiths Coll., London Univ., 2003–. Writer: of plays, The Man with Two Gaffers, 2006, Lisa's Sex Strike, 2007; We Are Three Sisters, 2011; For Love or Money (adaptation), 2017; of opera libretto, Elephant and Castle, 2007. Eric Gregory Award, 1980; Somerset Maugham Award, 1984; Dylan Thomas Meml Prize, 1985; E. M. Forster Award, 1988. *Publications:* The Movement: English poetry and fiction of the 1950s, 1980; (ed jtly) The Penguin Book of Contemporary British Poetry, 1982; Seamus Heaney, 1982; Dark Glasses, 1984; The Ballad of the Yorkshire Ripper, 1987; The Yellow House, 1987; And When Did You Last See Your Father, 1993 (Waterstone's/Volvo/Esquire Non-Fiction Award, 1993; J. R. Ackerley Award, 1994); The Cracked Pot, 1995; (ed jtly) Mind Readings, 1996; As If, 1997; Too True, 1998; Dr Ox's Experiment (opera libretto), 1998; Selected Poems, 1999; The Justification of Johann Gutenberg, 2000; Things My Mother Never Told Me, 2002; Oedipus and Antigone (translations), 2003; South of the River, 2007; The Last Weekend, 2010 (televised 2012); We are Three Sisters, 2011; A Discoverie of Witches (poetry), 2012; This Poem…, 2013; Shingle Street (poetry), 2015; (contrib.) Dear Stranger: letters on the subject of happiness, 2015; The Executor, 2018. *Recreations:* football, tennis, running. *Address:* c/o United Agents, 12–26 Lexington Street, W1F 0LE. *T:* (020) 3214 0800.

**MORRISON, Richard Duncan;** Columnist, since 1999, Chief Music Critic, since 2001, The Times; *b* 24 July 1954; *s* of Donald and Mary Morrison; *m* 1st, 1977, Marian Plant (marr. diss. 2011); two *s* one *d*; 2nd, 2013, Anna Louise Elisabeth Tilbrook (marr. diss. 2018); 3rd, 2018, Anna Wanda Baziuk; one *d*. *Educ:* University Coll. Sch.; Magdalene Coll., Cambridge (MA). Asst Editor, Classical Music magazine, 1977–83; Dep. Editor, Early Music magazine, 1984–88; The Times: Music Critic, 1984–89; Dep. Arts Editor, 1989–90; Arts Editor, 1990–99. Dir of Music, St Mary, Hendon, 1976–. FRSA 1995. *Publications:* Orchestra: the LSO: a century of triumphs and turbulence, 2003. *Recreations:* walking, organ-playing. *Address:* 88a Willesden Lane, NW6 7TA. *T:* 07770 381928.

**MORRISON, His Honour (Robert) Fraser;** a Circuit Judge, 2009–17; a Deputy Circuit Judge, since 2017; *b* Hitchin, 10 Feb. 1952; *s* of Robert Morrison and Mary Morrison; *m* 1975, Sheila Joanna Brand; two *s*. Admitted solicitor, 1975; solicitor in private practice, 1975–2008; Asst Recorder, 1995–99; Dep. Dist Judge, 1997–2009; Recorder, 1999–2009; Tribunal Judge, Mental Health Rev. Tribunals, 2018–. *Recreations:* sport, good company. *Club:* Hertford.

**MORRISON, Hon. Sara Antoinette Sibell Frances, (Hon. Mrs Sara Morrison);** *b* 9 Aug. 1934; *d* of 2nd Viscount Long and of Laura, Duchess of Marlborough; *m* 1954, Hon. Charles Andrew Morrison (marr. diss. 1984; he *d* 2005); one *s* one *d*. *Educ:* in England and France. Gen. Electric Co., 1975–98 (Dir, 1980–98); Non-executive Director: Abbey National plc (formerly Abbey Nat. Building Soc.), 1979–95; Carlton TV, 1992–98; Kleinwort Charter Trust, 1993–2002. Chairman: Nat. Council for Voluntary Orgns (formerly Nat. Council of Social Service), 1977–81; Nat. Adv. Council on Employment of Disabled People, 1981–84. County Councillor, then Alderman, Wilts, 1961–71; Chairman: Wilts Assoc. of Youth Clubs, 1958–63; Wilts Community Council, 1965–70; Vice-Chairman: Nat. Assoc. Youth Clubs, 1969–71; Conservative Party Organisation, 1971–75; Member: Governing Bd, Volunteer Centre, 1972–77; Annan Cttee of Enquiry into Broadcasting, 1974–77; Nat. Consumer Council, 1975–77; Bd, Fourth Channel TV Co., 1980–85; Video Appeals Cttee (Video Recordings Act, 1984), 1985–; Governing Council, Family Policy Studies Centre, 1983–99; Nat. Radiological Protection Bd, 1989–97; Council, PSI, 1980–93; Governing Body, Imperial Coll., London, 1986–2002 (Hon. Fellow 1993); UK Round Table on Sustainable Develt, 1995–98; Chm., WWF UK, 1998–2002; Dep. Chm., 2000–05, Vice Pres. Emeritus, 2005–, WWF Internat.; Chm., Council, Univ. of Bath, 2004–06. Life FRSA 1986; FCGI 2005. Hon. DBA Coventry, 1994; Hon. LLD De Montfort, 1998; Hon. DSc Buckingham, 2000. *Address:* Wyndham's Farm, Wedhampton, Devizes, Wilts SN10 3RR. *T:* (01380) 840221; 16 Groom Place, SW1X 7BA. *T:* (020) 7245 6553.

**MORRISON, Sophia Kizito, (Sophie);** *see* Linden, S. K.

**MORRISON, Stephen Roger;** non-executive Chairman, All3Media, 2013–14 (Chief Executive, 2003–12); *b* 3 March 1947; *s* of Hyman Michael Morrison and Rebecca (*née* Zolkwer); *m* 1979, Gayle Valerie Broughall; three *d*. *Educ:* High Sch., Glasgow; Edinburgh Univ. (MA Hons); Nat. Film Sch., Beaconsfield (ANFS). BBC Scotland (Radio and TV), 1970; Granada Television: Producer/Dir, Northern Documentary Unit, 1974; Ed., Granada Regl Progs, 1977; Hd of Arts and Features, 1981; Dir of Programmes, 1987–92; Man. Dir, Broadcasting, 1992–94; Man. Dir, 1993–94; Man. Dir, LWT, 1994–96; Chief Exec., Granada Media Gp, 1996–2002. Feature Films Producer: The Magic Toyshop, 1986; The Fruit Machine, 1988; (Exec. Producer) My Left Foot, 1989 (2 Acad. Awards); (Exec. Producer) The Field, 1990; Jack and Sarah, 1995; August, 1996. Mem. for Scotland, BBC Bd, 2017–. Rector, Univ. of Edinburgh, 2015–18. *Recreations:* walking, reading, films and theatre, talking and dining, touring delicatessens. *Club:* Garrick.

**MORRISON, Van;** see Morrison, G. I.

**MORRISON-BELL, Sir William (Hollin Dayrell),** 4th Bt cr 1905; solicitor and farmer; b 21 June 1956; s of Sir Charles Reginald Francis Morrison-Bell, 3rd Bt and of Prudence Caroline, d of late Lt-Col W. D. Davies, 60th Rifles (she m 2nd, Peter Gillbanks); S father, 1967; m 1984, Cynthia Hélène Marie White; one s one d. Educ: Eton; St Edmund Hall, Oxford. Heir: s Thomas Charles Edward Morrison-Bell, b 13 Feb. 1985. Address: Highgreen, Tarset, Hexham, Northumberland NE48 1RP. T: (01434) 240223; 28 Batoum Gardens, W6 7QD. T: (020) 7602 1363.

**MORRISON-LOW, Sir Richard Walter;** see Low, Sir R. W. M.

**MORRISSEY, David;** actor, director and producer; Director, Dolally Pictures, since 2017; b Liverpool, 21 June 1964; s of Joseph and Joan Morrissey; m 2006, Esther (separated 2016), d of Lucian Freud, OM, CH; two s one d. Educ: St Margaret Mary's Sch., Liverpool; De La Salle Grammar Sch., Liverpool; Royal Acad. of Dramatic Art. Actor: stage includes: Le Cid, Twelfth Night, UK tour and Donmar Warehouse, 1986; King John, Richard III, Edward IV, 1988, RSC; Peer Gynt, Nat. Th., 1990; Much Ado About Nothing, Queen's, 1993; Three Days of Rain, Donmar Warehouse, 1999; In a Dark Dark House, Almeida, 2008; Macbeth, Everyman, Liverpool, 2011; Hangmen, Royal Court, 2015; Julius Caesar, Bridge Th., 2018; the end of history…, Royal Court, 2019; films include: Waterland, 1992; Being Human, 1993; Hilary and Jackie, 1998; Fanny and Elvis, 1999; The Suicide Club, Some Voices, 2000; Captain Corelli's Mandolin, 2001; Stoned, 2005; Derailed, Basic Instinct 2, 2006; The Reaping, The Water Horse, 2007; The Other Boleyn Girl, Is Anybody There?, 2008; Blitz, 2011; television includes: One Summer, 1983; Framed, 1992; Between the Lines, 1993; The Knock, Finney, 1994; Out of the Blue, 1996; Holding On, 1997; Our Mutual Friend, 1998; State of Play, The Deal, 2003 (Best Actor, RTS Awards); Blackpool, 2004; Cape Wrath, 2007; Sense and Sensibility, 2008; Red Riding, 2009; Mrs Mandela, 5 Days, U Be Dead, 2010; South Riding, 2011; The Field of Blood, 2011, 2013; The Walking Dead (series), 2012–14; The 7:39, The Driver (also prod.), 2014; The Extant (series), 2015; The Missing, 2016; Britannia, The City & the City, 2018; director: films: Bring Me Your Love (also prod.), 2000; Don't Worry About Me (also writer and prod.), 2009; The Ones Below, 2016; television: Sweet Revenge, 2001; Passer By, 2004; Thorne: Sleepyhead (also prod.), 2010; Thorne: Scaredy Cat (also prod.), 2010; Richard II, 2012. Recreations: horse riding, tennis, golf, football. Address: c/o Troika, 180 Great Portland Street, W1W 5QZ. T: (020) 7336 7868. E: info@troikatalent.co.uk. Clubs: One Alfred Place, Garrick, Soho House.

**MORRISSEY, Gerry Anthony;** Head, BECTU sector, Prospect (formerly General Secretary, Broadcasting, Entertainment, Cinematograph and Theatre Union), 2007–18; b 12 April 1960; s of Jimmy and Peggy Morrissey; m 1996, Susan Caird; one s one d. Educ: Christian Brothers Secondary Sch., Tipperary Town. Storeman, BBC, 1976–88; Broadcasting and Entertainments Trade Alliance, subseq. Broadcasting, Entertainment, Cinematograph and Theatre Union: full-time Union Official, 1988–91; Supervisory Official, 1991–99; Asst Gen. Sec., 1999–2007. Exec. Mem., Union Network Internat., 2002; Pres., UNI MEI, 2011. Recreations: tennis, badminton, running, Arsenal Football Club, National Hunt racing.

**MORRISSEY, Dame Helena (Louise),** DBE 2017 (CBE 2012); Head of Personal Investing, Legal & General Investment Management, since 2017; b Altrincham, Cheshire; d of Anthony Atkins and Jacqueline Atkins; m 1990, Richard Morrissey; three s six d. Educ: Fitzwilliam Coll., Cambridge (BA Hons 1987). Schroders, NY, 1987–90; Schroders Investment Mgt, 1991–93; Newton Investment Management: Global Bond Fund Manager, 1994–2004; Head of Fixed Income, 1999–2001; CEO, 2001–16. Mem., Practitioner Panel, FSA, 2007–13. Dir, Investment Mgt Assoc., 2005–12. Chair: Corporate Bd, RA, 2012–15; Investment Assoc., 2014–; Mem., Endowment Fund Investment Bd, Univ. of Cambridge, 2012–15; Ext. Mem., Financial Services Trade and Investment Bd, 2015–. Founder and Chm., 30% Club, 2010–15. Fellow, Eton Coll., 2018–. Publications: A Good Time to be a Girl, 2018. Address: Legal & General, 1 Coleman Street, EC2R 5AA.

**MORRITT, Rt Hon. Sir (Robert) Andrew,** Kt 1988; CVO 1989; PC 1994; Chancellor of the High Court, 2005–13 (Vice-Chancellor of the Supreme Court, 2000–05); Vice-President of the Court of Protection, 2005–13; b 5 Feb. 1938; s of Robert Augustus Morritt, MBE and Margaret Mary Morritt (née Tyldesley Jones); m 1962, Sarah Simonetta, d of late John Ralph Merton, MBE; two s. Educ: Eton Coll.; Magdalene Coll., Cambridge (BA 1961; Hon. Fellow, 2009). 2nd Lieut Scots Guards, 1956–58. Called to the Bar, Lincoln's Inn, 1962 (Bencher, 1984; Treas., 2005); QC 1977. Junior Counsel: to Sec. of State for Trade in Chancery Matters, 1970–77; to Attorney-Gen. in Charity Matters, 1972–77; Attorney General to HRH The Prince of Wales, 1978–88; a Judge of High Court of Justice, Chancery Div., 1988–94; a Lord Justice of Appeal, 1994–2000. Vice-Chancellor of Co. Palatine of Lancaster, 1991–94. Member: Gen. Council of the Bar, 1969–73; Adv. Cttee on Legal Educn, 1972–76; Top Salaries Review Body, 1982–87. Pres., Council of the Inns of Court, 1997–2000. Recreations: fishing, shooting. E: ramorritt@outlook.com. Club: Garrick.

**MORROW, Baron** cr 2006 (Life Peer), of Clogher Valley in the county of Tyrone; **Maurice George Morrow;** Chairman, Democratic Unionist Party; s of Ernest and Eliza Jane Morrow; m 1976, Jennifer Reid; two d. Educ: Drumglass High Sch.; East Tyrone Coll. of Further and Higher Educn. Mem. (DemU) Fermanagh and S Tyrone, NI Assembly, 1998–2017; contested (DemU) same seat, 2017. Minister for Social Develt, NI, 2000–01 and 2016. Mem. (DemU) Dungannon and S Tyrone BC. Address: House of Lords, SW1A 0PW.

**MORROW, Cdre Anthony John Clare,** CVO 1997; RN; Clerk to the Butchers' Company, 2003–14; Extra Equerry to the Queen, since 1998; b 30 March 1944; s of late Capt. John Geoffrey Basil Morrow, CVO, DSC, RN and Dorothy April Bettine (née Mather); m 1st, 1969 (marr. diss. 1987); two d; 2nd, 1982 (marr. diss 2010); one s one d. Educ: Summer Fields, Oxford; Nautical Coll., Pangbourne; BRNC, Dartmouth. Entered RN, 1962: qualified Signals Officer, HMS Mercury, 1971; Lt-Comdr 1972; on staff of C-in-C Fleet, Signals Officer, HM Yacht Britannia, 1976–78; commanded HMS Lindisfarne, 1978–79; Comdr 1979; on staff, UK Mil. Rep. to NATO, 1980–83; commanded HMS Active, 1983–85; RN Exchange to CNO, US Navy, Washington, 1985–87; MoD, 1987–88; Capt. 1988; Captain, HMS Mercury, 1988–91; commanded Fourth Frigate Sqdn, HMS Active, 1991–93; ACOS, Plans and Policy, CINCHAN, Eastern Atlantic, 1993–94; Commodore Royal Yachts, 1995–98; retired 1998. Gen. Manager, W. & F. C. Bonham & Sons Ltd, 1999. Chm., Assoc. of Royal Yachtsmen, 1998–. Mem., RNSA. Younger Brother, Trinity House, 1996. Recreations: outdoor activities, sports. Clubs: Royal Yacht Squadron, Royal London Yacht; Bosham Sailing; Imperial Poona Yacht.

**MORROW, Clare;** Chair of Trustees, Yorkshire Film Archive, since 2016; b Hanover, 16 Sept. 1960; d of Gordon and Penelope Anne Brocklehurst; m 1st, 1981, John Morrow (marr. diss. 1992); one s one d; 2nd, 1992, Russell Peasgood; one d. Educ: Christ's Coll., Cambridge (BA Law and English 1983). NCTJ qualif. in Law, Public Admin, Newspaper Practice and Shorthand; Nat. Exam Bd in Occupational Safety and Health Cert. Reporter and producer: BBC Radio Humberside, 1986–92; BBC TV Leeds, 1990–92; news producer, 1992–95, Ed., Calendar, 1995–2001, Controller, News and Regl Progs, Yorks TV, later ITV Yorks, 2002–07; Chair, Welcome to Yorks, 2008–15. Non-executive Director: Rugby Football League, 2008–18; Leeds Teaching Hosps NHS Trust, 2010–14; Bettys and Taylors Gp, 2014–. Chm., Hollybank Trust, 2017–; Trustee: W Yorks Playhouse, 2001–10; Sheffield Theatres, 2012–15. T: 07702 565752. E: clare2morrowmedia@btinternet.com.

**MORROW, His Honour Graham Eric;** QC 1996; a Circuit Judge, 2006–16; b 14 June 1951; s of George Eric Morrow and Freda Morrow; m 1987, Rosalind Nola Ellis; one s, and two step d. Educ: Liverpool Coll. (Foundation Mem., 2006); Univ. of Newcastle upon Tyne (LLB). Called to the Bar, Lincoln's Inn, 1974; Asst Recorder, 1990; a Recorder, 1997–2006. Trustee, Royal Sch. for the Blind, Liverpool, 2003–. Dir, Morrow's (Outfitters) Ltd, 2016–. Recreations: cycling, swimming, ski-ing.

**MORROW, Dr Joseph John,** CBE 2018; QC (Scot.) 2015; Lord Lyon King of Arms, since 2014; Vice Lord-Lieutenant, City of Dundee, since 2009; Chancellor, Diocese of Moray, Ross and Caithness, since 2018; b 12 Dec. 1954. Team Rector, St Martin's/St John's Ch, Dundee; Chaplain, St Paul's Cathedral, Dundee (now Hon. Canon). Solicitor in private practice and voluntary sector; joined Faculty of Advocates, 2000, non-practising Mem., 2007. First-tier Tribunal Judge (Asylum and Immigration). President: Mental Health Tribunal for Scotland, 2008– (Convener, 2005–08); Additional Support Needs Tribunals for Scotland, 2011–14; Mem. Bd, Scottish Courts and Tribunals Service, 2014–19. Mem. Bd, Scottish Children's Reporter Admin, 2002–10. Mem. (Lab), Dundee CC, 2003–09. Grand Master, Grand Lodge of Scotland, 2004–05; First Grand Principal, Supreme Grand Royal Arch Chapter of Scotland, 2018–. Chancellor, St John Priory of Scotland, 2018–. Hon. LLD Edinburgh Napier, 2016. KStJ 2015 (OStJ 1996). Address: Court of the Lord Lyon, HM New Register House, Edinburgh EH1 3YT.

**MORSE, Sir Amyas (Charles Edward),** KCB 2014; Comptroller and Auditor General, National Audit Office, 2009–19; b Edinburgh. CA. Coopers & Lybrand: leader, practice in Scotland; Manager, London City Office; Exec. Partner, UK; Global Leader, Assce Practice, then Global Mktg Partner (Ops), PricewaterhouseCoopers; Defence Commercial Dir, MoD, 2006–09.

**MORSE, Richard South;** Chairman, Woodard Corporation, since 2016; b London, 24 Jan. 1959; s of Sir (Christopher) Jeremy Morse, KCMG and Belinda Morse; m 1985, Christine James; two s one d. Educ: Winchester Coll.; New Coll., Oxford (BA Lit.Hum.). Man. Dir, Kleinwort Benson, 1981–2000; Dep. Dir Gen., Ofgem, 2000–01; Partner, Greenhill & Co., 2001–10; Partner, Opus Corporate Finance, 2011–. Chm., John Laing Envmtl Assets Gp Ltd, 2014–; Dep. Chm., Bazalgette Tunnel Ltd, 2015–. Hon. Fellow, Ripon Coll. Cuddesdon, 2010. Recreations: music and opera, crosswords, golf, tennis. Address: The Deane House, Sparsholt, Winchester SO21 2LR. T: (office) (020) 7025 3600. E: morse.bms@gmail.com. Club: Portland.

**MORSHEAD, Timothy Francis;** QC 2011; b London, 16 Dec. 1969; s of late Rev. Ivo Morshead and Anne Morshead; m 2003, Penrose Foss; one s one d. Educ: Marlborough Coll.; Pembroke Coll., Oxford (BA 1991); City Univ. (DipLaw 1993). Called to the Bar, Lincoln's Inn, 1995; in practice as a barrister, specialising in commercial property and public law; Mem., Attorney Gen.'s Panel of Counsel, 2001–11. Recreations: bicycling, photography. Address: Landmark Chambers, 180 Fleet Street, EC4A 2HG. T: (020) 7430 1221.

**MORT, His Honour Timothy James;** a Circuit Judge, 1996–2017; b 4 March 1950; s of Dr Philip Mort and Sybil Mort; m 1979, Philippa Mary Brown; one s three d. Educ: Clifton Coll., Bristol; Emmanuel Coll., Cambridge (Schol.; MA Law Tripos 1971). Called to the Bar, Middle Temple, 1972; in practice, Northern Circuit, 1972–96. Recreations: tennis, Real tennis, music. Club: Manchester Tennis and Racquet.

**MORTADA, Rami;** Ambassador of Lebanon to the Court of St James's, since 2017; b Beirut, 1970; m 1997, Jamal Yehia; one s one d. Educ: American Univ. of Beirut (BA Pol Sci.); Lebanese Univ., Beirut (Law degree); Univ. René Descartes, Paris (DEA Internat. Law). Entered Foreign Service of Lebanon, 1994; Min. of Foreign Affairs, Beirut, 1994–96; Muscat, Sultanate of Oman, 1996–98; Paris, 1998–2000; Consul Gen., NY, 2000–04; Hd, Cabinet of Minister of Foreign Affairs and Emigrants, Beirut, 2004–09; Chargé d'Affaires, Syria, 2009–13; Ambassador to Belgium and EU, 2013–17. Officier, Ordre Nat. du Mérite (France), 2009; Grand Croix, Ordre de la Couronne (Belgium), 2018. Recreations: dogs, pets. Address: Embassy of Lebanon, 21 Kensington Palace Gardens, W8 4QN. T: (020) 7727 6696, Fax: (020) 7243 1699. E: emb.leb@btinternet.com.

**MORTENSEN, Prof. Neil James McCready,** MD; FRCS; Professor of Colorectal Surgery, University of Oxford, since 1999; Fellow, Green Templeton College (formerly Green College), Oxford, since 2005; Consultant Colorectal Surgeon, John Radcliffe Hospital, Oxford, since 1986; Honorary Consultant Colorectal Surgeon, Oxford University Hospitals, since 2016; b 16 Oct. 1949; s of late Peter Mortensen and of Rhoda Mortensen; m 1973, Jane Baker; one s two d. Educ: Hampton Sch.; Univ. of Birmingham Medical Sch. (MB ChB 1973); Univ. of Bristol (MD 1977). FRCS 1977; FRCSI 2016. Consultant Sen. Lectr, Univ. of Bristol and Bristol Royal Infirmary, 1981–86; Reader in Colorectal Surgery, Univ. of Oxford, 1994–99. Treas. and Dir, 1996–2004, Chm., 2004–13, British Jl of Surgery Soc.; President: Assoc. of Coloproctology, GB and Ire., 2002–03; Coloproctology Sect., RSocMed, 2003–04; Ileostomy Assoc., 2009–. Chm., Occtopus, 2017–. Trustee and Mem. Council, RCS, 2013– (Vice Pres., 2017–). FRCPSGlas 2007; Hon. FRCSE 2009; Hon FRCSI 2016. Editor in Chief: Bull. RCS, 2015–; Colorectal Disease, 2015–. Publications: An Atlas of Rectal Endosonography, 1991; Restorative Proctocolectomy, 1993; Ulcerative Colitis and Crohn's Disease, 1993; Controversies in Inflammatory Bowel Disease, 2001; Anorectal and Colonic Disease, 2010; original articles on all aspects of colorectal surgery and colorectal disease. Recreations: Real tennis, opera, farming. Address: Department of Colorectal Surgery, Churchill Hospital, Oxford OX3 7LE. T: (01865) 235613.

**MORTIMER, Hon. Barry;** see Mortimer, Hon. J. B.

**MORTIMER, Edward,** CMG 2010; freelance writer and consultant; Distinguished Fellow, All Souls College, Oxford, since 2013; b Burford, 22 Dec. 1943; s of Robert Cecil Mortimer and Mary Hope Mortimer (née Walker); m 1968, Elizabeth Anne Zanetti; two s two d. Educ: Eton Coll.; Balliol Coll., Oxford (BA 1965; Hon. Fellow 2004). Asst d'Anglais, Lycée Faidherbe, St Louis-du-Sénégal, 1962; Fellow, All Souls Coll., Oxford, 1965–72, 1984–86, 2006–08; Asst Paris Corresp., 1967–70, Foreign Specialist and Leader Writer, 1973–85, The Times; For. Affairs Ed., FT, 1987–98; Chief Speechwriter and Dir of Communications, Exec. Office of the Sec.-Gen., UN, 1998–2006; Sen. Vice Pres. and Chief Prog. Officer, 2007–11, Sen. Prog. Advr, 2012–, Salzburg Global Seminar. Sen. Associate, Carnegie Endowment, NY, 1980–81. Res. Associate, IISS, 1990–91. Rapporteur, Gp of Eminent Persons, Council of Europe, 2011. Hd, Ind. Review, BBC coverage of Arab Spring, 2012. Pres., British Assoc. of Former UN Civil Servants, 2011–17; Chair: Sri Lanka Campaign for Peace and Justice, 2009–15; 21st Century Trust, 2011–; Ind.

Diplomat UK, 2012–; Children's Radio Foundn UK, 2015–19 (Trustee). Leonard Stein Lectr, Balliol Coll., Oxford, 2012. Hon. Prof., Univ. of Warwick, 1993–98. Hon. DLitt Exeter, 1999. *Publications:* France and the Africans, 1969; Faith and Power: the politics of Islam, 1982; The Rise of the French Communist Party, 1984; Roosevelt's Children 1987 (US edn as The World that F.D.R. Built, 1989); European Security after the Cold War, 1992; (ed with Robert Fine) People, Nation and State, 1999; (with T. Garton Ash and K. Öktem) Freedom in Diversity, 2013. *Recreations:* talking, walking, reading aloud, going to the theatre. *Address:* 79 Witney Street, Burford, Oxon OX18 4RX. *E:* edward.mortimer@all-souls.ox.ac.uk. *Clubs:* Groucho, Frontline.

**MORTIMER, James Edward;** Deputy Director and Treasury Officer of Accounts, 1995–2000; *b* 9 Nov. 1947; *s* of late James Edward Mortimer and Renee Mabel Mortimer (*née* Horton); *m* 1969, Lesley Patricia Young. *Educ:* Latymer Upper Sch.; Wadham Coll., Oxford (MA, BPhil). HM Treasury, 1971–2000: Economic Advr, 1974–81; Principal, 1981–83; Grade 5, 1983–91; Under Sec., 1991–2000; Head of Aid and Export Finance Gp, 1991–95. *Recreations:* football, golf, cricket, birdwatching, cinema. *Address:* 21 Hogarth Way, Hampton, Middlesex TW12 2EL. *Clubs:* Royal Automobile; Old Latymerians Association.

**MORTIMER, Hon. (John) Barry,** OBE 2019; GBS 1999; QC 1971; mediator and arbitrator; a Non-Permanent Judge, Court of Final Appeal, Hong Kong, 1997–2015; a Judge, Court of Appeal, Brunei Darussalam, since 2005 (President, 2010–18); *b* 7 Aug. 1931; *s* of late John William Mortimer and Maud (*née* Snarr) Mortimer; *m* 1958, Judith Mary (*née* Page) (*d* 2013); two *s* two *d. Educ:* St Peter's School, York (Headmasters' Exhibitioner 1945); Emmanuel College, Cambridge; BA 1955, MA 1959. Commissioned into 4 RTR, 1951; served in Egypt, 1951–52; 45/51 RTR (TA), 1952–57. Called to the Bar, Middle Temple, 1956 (Bencher, 1980; Master Reader, 2003); Harmsworth Law Scholar 1957; Prosecuting Counsel on NE Circuit: to Post Office, 1965–69; to Inland Revenue, 1969–71; a Recorder, 1972–87; Judge, Supreme Court of Hong Kong, 1985–93; a Justice of Appeal, Court of Appeal, Supreme (later High) Court of Hong Kong, 1993–99 (a Vice-President, 1997–99). Chancellor, Dio. of Ripon, 1971–85. Chairman: Mental Health Review Tribunal, 1983–85; Overseas Trust Bank (Compensation) Tribunal, 1986–87; Member: Bar Council, 1970–75; Senate, 1979–85; Law Reform Commn, Hong Kong, 1990–99 (Chm., Sub-cttee on Privacy and Data Protection); Judicial Studies Bd, 1996–99; Vice Chm., Advocacy Inst. of Hong Kong, 1997–99; Chm., Criminal Court Users Cttee, 1998–99; Dir of Advocacy, Middle Temple, 2004–06. Chm., Envmtl Impact Assessment Appeal Bd, Kowloon Canton Railway Corp. Spur Line Appeal, 2001. Dir, City Disputes Panel Ltd, 2000–05. Hon. Diplomate, Amer. Bd of Trial Advocates, 1994. Order of the Crown, First Class, SPMB, (Brunei), 2019. *Recreations:* reading, shooting, tennis. *Address:* The Grange, Staveley, Knaresborough, N Yorks HG5 9LD; 21 Fl., HK Diamond Exchange Building, 8–10 Duddell Street, Central, Hong Kong. *Clubs:* Travellers; Hong Kong.

**MORTIMER, Robin John David;** Chief Executive, Port of London Authority, since 2014; *b* Norwich, 8 June 1972; *s* of David and Valerie Mortimer; *m* 1999, Katie Luther; one *s* one *d. Educ:* Norwich Sch.; Queen's Coll., Oxford (BA Modern Hist.); Sch. of Oriental and African Studies, Univ. of London (MSc Develt Studies 1999). Department of the Environment, later Department of the Environment, Transport and the Regions: fast stream postings in local govt finance and internat. trade and envmt, 1994–96; Private Sec. to Sec. of State, 1996–98; Policy Advr on Gt Lakes region, DFID, 1999–2000; Department of the Environment, Transport and the Regions, later Department for Environment, Food and Rural Affairs: Hd, Water Industry Team, 2000–01; Private Sec. to Sec. of State, 2001–03; Hd, Rural Strategy Div., 2004–06; Dep. Dir, Office of Climate Change, 2006–07; Dir, Envmt and Rural Gp, 2007–14. *Recreations:* running, music, reading, cooking, history. *Address:* Port of London Authority, Pinnacle House, 23–26 St Dunstan's Hill, EC3R 8HN.

**MORTIMORE, Prof. Peter John,** OBE 1994; PhD; FBPsS; independent educational consultant; Director, Institute of Education, London University, 1994–2000 (Professor of Education, 1990–2000, now Emeritus); *b* 17 Jan. 1942; *s* of late Claude Mortimore and Rose Mortimore; *m* 1965, Jo Hargaden; three *d. Educ:* Chiswick County Grammar Sch.; St Mary's Coll., Strawberry Hill; Birkbeck Coll., London Univ. (BSc, Hon. Fellow 2001); Inst. of Education (MSc; Hon. Fellow 2008); Inst. of Psychiatry (PhD). CPsychol 1989; FBPsS 1989. Teacher, Sacred Heart Sch., SE5, 1964–66; Teacher and Head of Dept, Stockwell Manor Sch., SW9, 1966–73; Res. Officer, Inst. of Psychiatry, 1975–78; Mem., HM Inspectorate, 1978; Inner London Education Authority: Dir, Res. and Stats Br., 1979–85; Asst Educn Officer (Secondary Schs), 1985–87; Prof. of Educn, Lancaster Univ., 1988–90; Dep. Dir, London Univ. Inst. of Educn, 1990–94; Pro-Vice-Chancellor, London Univ., 1999–2000; Prof. of Educn, Univ. of Southern Denmark, 2008–09. Member: Educn Res. Bd, SSRC, 1981–82; Educn and Human Develt Cttee, ESRC, 1982–85; Univ. of London Exams and Assessment Council, 1991; Trustee, VSO, 1992–2002. Consultant, OECD, 2003–07. Governor: SOAS, 1993–98; Birkbeck Coll., 1998–2000. Monthly columnist, Guardian Education, 2006–. Hon. FCP 1994; AcSS 2000. FRSA 1990. Hon. DLitt Heriot-Watt, 1998; Hon. PhD Southern Denmark, 2008. *Publications:* (jtly) Fifteen Thousand Hours: secondary schools and their effects on children, 1979; (jtly) Behaviour Problems in Schools, 1984; (jtly) Secondary School Examinations, 1986; (jtly) School Matters: the junior years, 1988; (jtly) The Primary Head: roles, responsibilities and reflections, 1991; The Secondary Head: roles, responsibilities and reflections, 1991; (jtly) Managing Associate Staff, 1994; (jtly) Planning Matters, 1995; (jtly) Living Education, 1997; (jtly) Forging Links, 1997; Road to Improvement, 1998; (jtly) Understanding Pedagogy, 1999; (jtly) Culture of Change, 2000; (jtly) Improving School Effectiveness, 2001; Education under Siege, 2013. *Recreations:* theatre, art, music, walking.

**MORTIMORE, Simon Anthony;** QC 1991; *b* 12 April 1950; *s* of late Robert Anthony Mortimore and Katherine Elizabeth Mackenzie Mortimore (*née* Caine); *m* 1983, Fiona Elizabeth Jacobson; one *s* one *d. Educ:* Westminster School; Exeter Univ. (LLB). Called to the Bar, Inner Temple, 1972; in practice at the Bar, 1972–2017; Associate Mem., 3–4 South Square, 2017–. Mem., ACCA Disciplinary Panel, 2003–07. Chm., Peasmarsh Chamber Music Fest., 2012–; Dir, Opera Rara, 2015–. *Publications:* contribs to Bullen and Leake and Jacobs Precedents of Pleading, 13th edn 1990; Insolvency of Banks, 1996; (ed) Company Directors: duties, liabilities and remedies, 2009, 3rd edn 2017. *Recreations:* opera, general cultural interests, travel, golf. *Address:* 3–4 South Square, Gray's Inn, WC1R 5HP. *T:* (020) 7696 9900. *Clubs:* Hurlingham, Brooks's; Royal St George's Golf (Captain, 2019–20), Rye Golf.

**MORTON,** 23rd Earl of, *cr* 1458 (*de facto* 22nd Earl, 23rd but for the Attainder); **John Stewart Sholto Douglas;** Lord Aberdour 1458; *b* 17 Jan. 1952; *s* of 22nd Earl of Morton and Sheila Mary Douglas (*née* Gibbs); *S* father, 2016; *m* 1985, Amanda, *yr d* of David Mitchell, Kirkcudbright; one *s* two *d. Educ:* Dunrobin Castle School. Studied Agriculture, Aberdeen Univ. Partner, Dalmahoy Farms, Kirknewton. Pres., Convention of Baronage of Scotland. *Heir: s* Lord Aberdour, *qv. Address:* Haggs Farm, Kirknewton, Midlothian EH27 8EE.

**MORTON, Alison Margaret;** *see* Kinnaird, A. M.

**MORTON, His Honour (David) Christopher;** a Circuit Judge, 1992–2008; *b* 1 Dec. 1943; *s* of Rev. Alexander Francis Morton and Esther Ann Morton; *m* 1970, Sandra Jo Kobes; three *s* one *d. Educ:* Worksop Coll., Notts; Fitzwilliam Coll., Cambridge (BA, LLB). Called to the Bar, Inner Temple, 1968; Wales and Chester Circuit; practised in Swansea, 1969–92. *Recreations:* Welsh affairs, railways, family. *Club:* Royal Over-Seas League.

**MORTON, George Martin;** Principal (formerly Senior) Planner, Trafford Borough Council, 1986–99; *b* 11 Feb. 1940; *s* of Rev. Thomas Ralph Morton, DD, and Janet Maclay MacGregor Morton (*née* Baird). *Educ:* Fettes Coll. Edinburgh; Edinburgh Coll. of Art; Glasgow Univ. Member: Manchester City Council, 1971–74; Greater Manchester Council, 1973–77. Sec., Tameside and Glossop CHC, 1984–86. MP (Lab) Manchester, Moss Side, July 1978–1983; an Opposition Whip, 1979–83. *Address:* 4 St Annes Road, Manchester M21 8TD. *T:* (0161) 881 8195.

**MORTON, Prof. John,** OBE 1998; PhD; FRS 2011; FBPsS; Director, Cognitive Development Unit, Medical Research Council, 1982–98; Hon. Professor, University College London, since 1998 (Hon. Fellow, 2012); *b* 1 Aug. 1933; *s* of late Winston James Morton and Mary Winifred Morton (*née* Nutter); *m;* one *d; m* 3rd, 1985, Guinevere Tufnell. *Educ:* Nelson Grammar Sch.; Christ's Coll., Cambridge (BA, MA); Reading Univ. (PhD 1961). FBPsS 1974 (Hon. FBPsS 1997). Scientist, MRC Applied Psychology Unit, Cambridge, 1960–82. Res. Fellow, Univ. of Michigan, 1967; Res. Associate and Lectr, Yale Univ., 1967–68; Vis. Scientist, MSH Paris, 1974–75; Max Planck Ges., Nijmegen, 1977–80; Visiting Professor: Cornell Univ., 1980; UCL, 1982–98; Vis. Fellow, Tokyo Metropolitan Inst. of Gerontology, 1981. Pres., EPsS, 1998–2000 (Hon. Mem., 2001). MAE 1990. President's Award, BPsS, 1988; Ipsen Prize in neural plasticity, Ipsen Foundn, 2001. *Publications:* (ed) Biological and Social Factors in Psycholinguistics, 1971; (ed jtly) Psycholinguistics: Developmental and Pathological, Series I, 1977, Series II, 1979; (with M. Johnson) Biology and Cognitive Development, 1991; (ed jtly) Development Neurocognition, 1993; (ed jtly) The Acquisition and Dissolution of Language, 1994; (ed jtly) Cognitive Science: an introduction, 1996; Understanding Developmental Disorders: a causal modelling approach, 2004; articles in sci. jls. *Recreations:* theatre, cooking, Tower Theatre Company, chocolate, Burnley FC. *Address:* (office) Institute of Cognitive Neuroscience, University College London, Alexandra House, 17–19 Queen Square, WC1N 3AR. *T:* (020) 7679 1156.

**MORTON, John,** DPhil; FCGI; FRAeS; FIMMM; CEng; Stipendiary Lecturer, University College, Oxford, since 2017 (Lecturer, 2009–12; Senior Lecturer, 2012–17); Senior Lecturer, Worcester College, Oxford, since 2015; *b* Gateshead, 11 Dec. 1949; *s* of John Morton and Emmeline Morton (*née* Watson); *m* 1977, Maria Rosario Larrarte; two *s. Educ:* Grammar Sch. for Boys, Gateshead; St Catharine's Coll., Cambridge (BA 1971); Exeter Coll., Oxford (DPhil 1975); Stanford Graduate Sch. of Business. CEng 1978. Vis. Researcher, Escuela Técnica Superior de Ingenieros de Caminos, Canales y Puertos, Madrid (Royal Soc. Study Visit Award), 1979; Lectr, Dept of Aeronautics, Imperial Coll. London, 1979–85; Sen. Res. Associate, NASA Langley Res. Center, USA, 1986; Prof., Dept of Engrg Sci. and Mechanics, 1986–93, Dir, Center for Composite Materials and Structures, 1991–93, Virginia Tech.; Defence Research Agency, subseq. Defence Evaluation and Research Agency: Dir, Structural Materials Centre, 1993–97; Dir, Mechanical Scis Sector, 1998–2001; Chief Operating Officer, Future Systems and Technol., QinetiQ, 2001–05; Chief Exec., Engrg and Technol. Bd, 2005–08. Sen. Res. Fellow, Dept of Engrg Sci., Univ. of Oxford, 2009–12; Sen. Res. Investigator, Imperial Coll. London, 2012–16. Man. Dir, Oxcomp Ltd, 2011–13; Corporate Develt Dir, A. L. Technol. Investment Co. Ltd, 2017–19. Vis. Scientist, Univ. Libre de Bruxelles, 1992; Prof. invité, Ecole polytechnique fédérale de Lausanne, 1992; Visiting Professor: Dept of Aeronautics, Imperial Coll. London, 1995–; Univ. of Oxford, 2016–. Mem., Foresight Panel for Materials, OST, 1994–97. Chm., Women into Sci., Engrg and Construction, 2007–08. Mem. Council, IMMM, 2004–08. FIMMM 1992; FRAeS 1998; FCGI 2008; FRSA 2019. Liveryman, Co. of Engineers, 2006. (Jtly) Donald Julius Groen Prize, 1991 and 1995, (jtly) William Sweet Smith Prize, 1991, IMechE. *Publications:* articles on fracture mechanics, structural mechanics and the mechanics of composite materials. *Recreations:* tennis, gardening. *Address:* 129 High Street, Odiham RG29 1NW. *E:* john.morton@univ.ox.ac.uk. *Club:* Oxford and Cambridge.

**MORTON, John David Peter;** writer and director for television and radio, since 1992; *b* Sutton Bonnington, Notts, 22 Jan. 1957; *s* of Harold and Josephine Morton; *m* 1997, Helen Atkinson Wood. *Educ:* Kingsbridge Sch., S Devon; Univ. of Leicester (BA Hons English Lit. 1979); Hughes Hall, Cambridge (PGCE 1980); Univ. of Kent (MA Modern English Lit. 1981). English teacher, Peter Symonds' Coll., Winchester, 1981–92. Writer for BBC Radio: People Like Us, 1995; Mightier than the Sword, 1995; The Sunday Format, 1996; writer for BBC TV: (with C. Langham) Kiss Me Kate, 1998; writer and director for BBC Television: People Like Us, 1999; The Gist, 2001; (with T. Roche) Broken News, 2005; Twenty Twelve, 2010; W1A, 2014, 2015, 2017. *Recreations:* walking, tennis, squash, thinking. *Address:* c/o Curtis Brown, Haymarket House, 28–29 Haymarket, SW1Y 4SP.

**MORTON, Kathryn Mary Stuart,** CB 2002; Solicitor and Director General, Legal Services, Department for Environment, Food and Rural Affairs, 2001–02; *b* 2 June 1946; *d* of late Samuel Stuart Morton and Joan Alice Bessie Morton (*née* Tapscott). *Educ:* Ealing Grammar Sch. for Girls; Univ. of Sussex (BA). Admitted Solicitor, 1980. Leverhulme Res. Scholarship, India, 1967–68; Res. Asst, Lancaster Univ., 1969–71; Res. Officer, ODI, 1971–74; Res. Associate, ODI, and free-lance economist, 1974–80; with Bird & Bird, 1978–82; OFT, 1982–85; DTI, 1985–97, Under Sec. (Legal), subseq. Dir, 1992–97; Legal Advr and Solicitor, MAFF, 1997–2002. *Publications:* Aid and Dependence, 1975; (with Peter Tulloch) Trade and Developing Countries, 1977. *T:* (020) 7226 2332. *E:* kmsmorton@waitrose.com.

**MORTON, Keith Farrance;** QC 2011; *b* London, 8 Feb. 1966; *s* of Ian Francis Morton and Edna Hilda Morton (*née* Farrance). *Educ:* Earlham High Sch., Norwich; Univ. of Hull (BSc Econs 1987); City Univ. (DipLaw 1989); Inns of Court Sch. of Law. Called to the Bar, Lincoln's Inn, 1990; Mem., Temple Garden Chambers, 1990–, Hd of Chambers, 2016–; Treasury Counsel (Civil), 1997–2011. *Recreations:* architecture, music, cycling. *Address:* Temple Garden Chambers, 1 Harcourt Buildings, Temple, EC4Y 9DA. *T:* (020) 7583 1315. *E:* kmorton@tgchambers.com. *Clubs:* Two Brydges, Garrick.

**MORTON, Prof. Keith William;** Professor of Numerical Analysis, and Professorial Fellow of Balliol College, Oxford University, 1983–97, now Emeritus Professor, Oxford University and Emeritus Fellow, Balliol College; Professor of Mathematics (part-time), University of Bath, 1998–2005; *b* 28 May 1930; *s* of Keith Harvey Morton and Muriel Violet (*née* Hubbard); *m* 1952, Patricia Mary Pearson; two *s* two *d. Educ:* Sudbury Grammar Sch.; Corpus Christi Coll., Oxford (BA 1952; MA 1954); New York Univ. (PhD 1964). Theoretical Physics Div., AERE, Harwell, 1952–59; Res. Scientist, Courant Inst. of Mathematical Sci., NY Univ., 1959–64; Head of Computing and Applied Maths, Culham Lab., UKAEA, 1964–72; Prof. of Applied Maths, Reading Univ., 1972–83. Fellow, SIAM, 2011. IMA Gold Medal, 2002; De Morgan Medal, LMS, 2010. *Publications:* (with R. D. Richtmyer) Difference Methods for Initial-value Problems, 1967; (ed with M. J. Baines) Numerical Methods for Fluid Dynamics, Vol. I 1982, Vol. II 1986, Vol. III 1988, Vol. IV

1993, Vol. V 1995; (with D. F. Mayers) Numerical Solution of Partial Differential Equations: an introduction, 1994, 2nd edn 2005; Numerical Solution of Convection-Diffusion Problems, 1996; numerous articles on numerical analysis and applied maths in learned jls. *Recreations:* reading, walking, gardening, listening to music. *Address:* Roscarrock, 48 Jack Straw's Lane, Headington, Oxford OX3 0DW. *T:* (01865) 768823. *E:* morton@maths.ox.ac.uk.

**MORTON, Patricia Ann**; *see* Jacobs, P. A.

**MORTON, Paul Victor**; Tax Director, Office of Tax Simplification, HM Treasury, 2017–19; *b* Chelmsford, Essex; *s* of Alan and Margaret Morton; *m* 1990, Karen Sherer; two *d. Educ:* University Coll. London (BSc Microbiol.). HM Inspector of Taxes, 1982–85; Tax Manager: Peat Marwick Mitchell & Co., 1985–89; Shell, 1989–2005; Hd, Gp Tax, Reed Elsevier, 2005–17. Fellow, Chartered Inst. of Taxation, 2005. *Recreations:* music, opera, maths, physics.

**MORTON, Wendy**; MP (C) Aldridge-Brownhills, since 2015; Parliamentary Under-Secretary of State, Ministry of Justice, since 2019; *b* Northallerton, 1967; *d* of Thomas and Edna Hunter; *m* 1990, David Morton. *Educ:* Wensleydale Sch., N Yorks; Open Univ. (MBA). Exec. Officer, FCO, 1987–89; sales and marketing: HMCO Europe; Centrostyle; Dir, DM Electronics Ltd, 1991–2018. An Asst Govt Whip, 2018–19. *Recreations:* walking, running, cooking, Rotary. *Address:* House of Commons, SW1A 0AA. *T:* (020) 7219 8784. *E:* wendy.morton.mp@parliament.uk.

**MORTON, Very Rev. Dr William Wright**; DL; Dean, St Patrick's Cathedral, Dublin, since 2016; *b* Banbridge, Co. Down, 23 July 1956; *m* 1988, Rosemary Emily Alexandra Todd; three *s. Educ:* Newry High Sch.; Trinity Coll., Dublin (BTh 1988; MA 1995); Queen's Univ. Belfast (PhD 1996); Ulster Univ. (MMus). ALAM. Ordained deacon, 1988, priest, 1989; Curate, Christ Church, Drumachose, 1988–91; Conwal, Donegal, 1991–97; Bishop's Domestic Chaplain, 1992–97; Dean of Derry, 1997–2016. Canon: Raphoe Cathedral, 1994–97; St Patrick's Cathedral, 2013–16. DL City of Londonderry, 2014. FRSA. Hon. DLitt Ulster, 2018. *Recreations:* listening to classical music, playing classical organ. *Address:* St Patrick's Cathedral, St Patrick's Close, Dublin 8, Ireland. *T:* (home) 4755449, (office) 4539472. *E:* dean@stpatrickscathedral.ie. *Club:* Kildare Street and University (Dublin).

**MORTON JACK, His Honour David**; a Circuit Judge, 1986–2008; *b* 5 Nov. 1935; *o s* of late Col W. A. Morton Jack, OBE, and late Mrs Morton Jack (*née* Happell); *m* 1972, Rosemary, *o d* of F. G. Rentoul; four *s. Educ:* Stowe (scholar); Trinity Coll., Oxford (Cholmeley Schol., MA). 2nd Lieut, RIrF, 1955–57. Called to the Bar, Lincoln's Inn, 1962; a Recorder of the Crown Court, 1979–86. *Recreations:* country pursuits, sheep-keeping, reading, music, gardens. *Club:* Travellers.

**MOSCO, Les**; Chief Executive Officer (formerly Managing Director), Commercial Strategies (formerly Purchasing Strategies) Ltd, 2003–18; Founder, Les Mosco Consultancy; *b* Manchester, 15 July 1954; *s* of late Bernard Mosco and Stella Mosco; *m* 1979, Barbara Baum; one *s* one *d. Educ:* Queen Elizabeth's Grammar Sch., Middleton, Manchester; Sheffield Univ. (BSc 1st Cl. Hons Physics). FCIPS 1992. Various posts, British Coal, 1975–89; Asst Sec., Scottish Office, 1989–92; Gp Purchasing Dir, Natwest Bank, 1992–98; Supply Chain Exec., Amerada Hess, 1998–2000; Supply Chain Dir, Railtrack, then Network Rail, 2000–03; Dir, Commercial, Defence Equipment and Support, 2007–11, Dir, Commercial, 2011–14, MoD. Non-executive Director: Transport for Greater Manchester, 2015–; Hellios Information Mgt Ltd, 2016–. Trustee: Victim Support, 2014–; Chiltern Soc., 2015–; We Love Manchester Emergency Fund, 2017–18. MInstD. *Recreations:* walking and cycling in the Chilterns and London, watching film (especially in Rex Cinema, Berkhamsted), travel, current affairs. *Address:* 3 Rothschild Court, Hamberlins Lane, Northchurch, Berkhamsted, Herts HP4 3TD. *T:* 07799 718283. *E:* lesmosco@hotmail.com.

**MOSCOVICI, Pierre**; Member, European Commission, 2014–19; *b* Paris, 16 Sept. 1957; *s* of Serge Moscovici and Marie Moscovici (*née* Bromberg). *Educ:* Lycée Condorcet; Univ. Paris I–Panthéon Sorbonne (Master in econs and pol sci.; DEA); École nationale d'admin. Auditor, 1984–88, Advr, 1988–89, French Court of Audit; Hd of Mission, Office of Minister of Educn, 1989–90; Hd of Finance, Commissariat général du Plan, 1990–93; MEP, 1994–97; Mem. for Doubs, French Nat. Assembly, 1997, 2007–12, 2014; Minister for Eur. Affairs, 1997–2002; Chief Advr, Court of Audit, 2003; MEP, 2004–07; Minister for Economy and Finance, 2012–14. Member: Doubs Council, 1994–2001; Montbéliard Council, 1995–2008; Franche-Comté Regl Council, 1998–2004; Valentigney Council, 2008–14; Pres., Gtr Montbéliard Authy, 2008–12. *Publications:* (jtly) L'Heure des choix, 1991; A la recherche de la gauche perdue, 1994; (jtly) Quelle économie pour l'emploi, 1995; L'Urgence, plaidoyer pour une autre politique, 1997; Au coeur de l'Europe, 1999; L'Europe, une puissance dans la mondialisation, 2001; Un an après, 2003; Les 10 Questions qui fâchent les Européens, 2004; L'Europe est morte, vive l'Europe!, 2006; La France dans un monde dangereux, 2007; Le Liquidateur, 2008; Mission impossible?, 2009; Défaite interdite, 2011; Combats: pour que la France s'en sorte, 2013; Dans ce clair-obscur surgissent les monstres, 2018.

**MOSELEY, Elwyn Rhys**, CBE 2003; Commissioner for Local Administration in Wales (Ombudsman), 1991–2003; *b* 6 Aug. 1943; *s* of late Rev. Luther Moseley and Megan Eiluned Moseley (*née* Howells); *m* 1968, Annick Andrée Guyomard; two *s* one *d. Educ:* Caterham Sch.; Queens' Coll., Cambridge (MA). Solicitor. Asst Solicitor, Newport CBC, 1969–72; Sen. Asst Solicitor, Cardiff CBC, 1972–74; Cardiff City Council: City Solicitor, 1974–91; Dep. Chief Exec., 1979–91; Dir of Admin. and Legal Services, 1987–91.
*See also* T. H. Moseley.

**MOSELEY, His Honour Hywel**; *see* Moseley, His Honour T. H.

**MOSELEY, Joyce**, OBE 2007; Chief Executive, Catch22 (formerly Rainer), 1999–2011; *b* 12 Jan. 1947; *d* of late Harry Moseley and Kathleen Moseley (*née* Dalton); *m* 1995, Anthony Allen. *Educ:* Manchester High Sch. for Girls; Bedford Coll., Univ. of London (BScSoc Hons 1968 and Applied Social Studies 1970); Univ. of Surrey (MSc Social Res. 1984). Social worker and Sen. Social Worker, London Borough of Ealing, Sen. Social Worker and Area Manager, London Borough of Islington, 1974–86; Asst Dir, Herts CC, 1986–91; Dir of Social Services, London Borough of Hackney, 1991–97; consultancy, 1997–99. Chm., HCT Gp, 2010–16. Mem., Youth Justice Bd for England and Wales, 1998–2004; Chm., Transition to Adulthood Alliance, 2012–. Non-exec. Dir, Tavistock and Portman NHS Foundn Trust, 2009–14. Trustee: Warren House Gp, Dartington Service Design Lab (formerly Social Res. Unit), 2012–19 (Chair, 2014–19); Halesworth Campus Trust, 2016–. *Publications:* Other People's Children, 1976; contrib. articles and chapters to social care pubns. *Recreations:* theatre, walking, food and wine. *Club:* Two Brydges.

**MOSELEY, His Honour (Thomas) Hywel**; QC 1985; a Circuit Judge, 1989–2004; *b* 27 Sept. 1936; *s* of late Rev. Luther Moseley and Megan Eiluned Moseley; *m* 1960, Monique Germaine Thérèse Drufin (separated 2009); three *d. Educ:* Caterham Sch.; Queens' Coll., Cambridge (MA, LLM). Called to the Bar, Gray's Inn, 1964; in private practice, Cardiff, 1965–89, and London, 1977–89; a Recorder, 1981–89. Lectr in Law, 1960–65, Prof. of Law, 1970–82, UCW, Aberystwyth. Mem., Insolvency Rules Cttee, 1993–97. *Publications:* (with B. Rudden) Outline of the Law of Mortgages, 4th edn 1967. *Recreation:* reading. *Address:* Nantceiro, Llanbadarn Fawr, Aberystwyth, Ceredigion SY23 3HW. *T:* (01970) 623532.
*See also* E. R. Moseley.

**MOSER, Dr Michael Edward**; conservationist and specialist international advisor on environment, UN Development Programme, Iran, Mongolia, The Maldives and China, and other international organisations; *b* 16 July 1956; *s* of late Roger Michael Moser and Noreen Moser (*née* Wane); *m* 1983, Joanna Jocelyn Stewart-Smith; three *d. Educ:* Shrewsbury Sch.; Durham Univ. (1st cl. Hons Ecol.; PhD). David Lack Studentship, BOU, 1980–82; British Trust for Ornithology: Estuaries Officer, 1983–86; Dir of Develt, 1986–88; Dir, Internat. Waterfowl and Wetlands Res. Bureau, then Wetlands Internat., 1988–99; English Nature: Mem., Council, 1999–2006; Dep. Chm., 2004–05; Acting Chm., 2005–06; Mem., UK Jt Nature Conservation Cttee, 2001–06. Member, Council: Tour du Valat, Centre for Mediterranean Wetlands, Camargue, France, 1990–2014; RSPB, 2001–06; Chairman: N Devon UNESCO Biosphere Reserve Partnership, 2007–12; SW Forestry and Woodlands (formerly SW Region) Adv. Cttee, Forestry Commn, 2007–17; N Devon Biosphere Nature Improvement Gp, 2013–; Member, Board: Devon Wildlife Trust, 2014–; MAVA Foundn for Nature, Switzerland, 2015–. *Publications:* (with C. M. Finlayson) Wetlands, 1991. *Recreations:* natural history, travel, fly fishing, woodland management. *Address:* West Week Farm, Week, Chulmleigh, Devon EX18 7EE.

**MOSER, Philip Curt Harold**; QC 2012; *b* Vienna, 20 July 1968; *s* of Peter Moser and Maud Moser (now Fuerst); *m* 2003, Anne, *d* of Prof. Olle Isaksson and Eva Isaksson; one *s* one *d. Educ:* Vienna Internat. Sch.; Robinson Coll., Cambridge (BA 1990; MA); Inns of Court Sch. of Law. Called to the Bar: Inner Temple, 1992, Bencher, 2012; NI, 2016; Mediator, 2003; Jun. Counsel to the Crown, 2008–12; Jt Head, Monckton Chambers, 2016–. Arbitrator: Centre for Arbitration and Dispute Resolution, Switzerland, 2015; London Court of Internat. Arbitration, 2015–. University of Cambridge: Supervisor in EC Law, Robinson Coll., 1995–97; Res. Associate, Centre for Eur. Legal Studies, 1996–98. Fellow, Eur. Law Inst., 2012–. Bar Council Rep. to Fedn of Eur. Bars, 2001–07; UK Mem., Council, Internat. Criminal Bar, 2003–07 (Chm., Election and Constitution Cttees, 2003–07); Member: Cttee, Bar Eur. Gp, 1998– (Vice-Chm., 2018–); Bar Liaison Cttee, Inner Temple, 2003–12; Cttee, UK Assoc. of Eur. Law, 2005–; Internat. Relns Cttee, 2000–08, Training for the Bar Cttee, 2012–13, Brexit Working Gp, 2016– (Vice-Chm., 2018–), Bar Council. Gov., St Joseph's Sch., Camden, 1995–2003. Mem., Editl Bd, European Law Reports, 1999–2012; Ed., The European Advocate, 2000–. *Publications:* (ed) Making Community Law, 2008; contrib. chapters to books on EU Law and articles in legal jls. *Address:* Monckton Chambers, 1 & 2 Raymond Buildings, Gray's Inn, WC1R 5NR. *T:* (020) 7405 7211, *Fax:* (020) 7405 2084. *E:* pmoser@monckton.com.

**MOSES, Rev. Alan**; *see* Moses, Rev. L. A.

**MOSES, Rt Hon. Sir Alan (George)**, Kt 1996; PC 2005; a Lord Justice of Appeal, 2005–14; Chairman, Independent Press Standards Organisation, 2014–19; *b* 29 Nov. 1945; *s* of late Eric George Rufus Moses, CB and of Pearl Moses (*née* Lipton); *m* 1992, Dinah Victoria Casson, *qv*; two *s* one *d* by a previous marriage. *Educ:* Bryanston Sch.; University Coll., Oxford (Quondam Exhibnr; BA). Called to the Bar, Middle Temple, 1968, Bencher, 1994; Mem., Panel of Junior Counsel to the Crown, Common Law, 1981–90; Junior Counsel to Inland Revenue, Common Law, 1985–90; a Recorder, 1986–96; QC 1990; a Judge of the High Ct, QBD, 1996–2005; Presiding Judge, SE Circuit, 1999–2002. Mem., Ct of Appeal, Cayman Islands, 2015–. Chm., Spoliation Adv. Panel, 2015–. Prof. of Law, 2006–, Mem. Council, 2007–13, RA; Mem. Bd, Royal Acad. Schs, 2015–19. Mem. Cttee, London Library, 2003–06. Chm., Spitalfields Music, 2009–15. Trustee: Koestler Award Trust, 2004–06 (Advr, 2006–); Pilgrim Trust, 2006–16; Solomon's Knot, 2018–. *Club:* Union Socialista La Serra (Italy).

**MOSES, Dinah Victoria, (Lady Moses)**; *see* Casson, D. V.

**MOSES, Very Rev. Dr John Henry**, KCVO 2006; Dean of St Paul's, 1996–2006, now Emeritus; Dean, Order of St Michael and St George, and Dean, Order of the British Empire, 1996–2006; *b* 12 Jan. 1938; *s* of late Henry William Moses and Ada Elizabeth Moses; *m* 1964, Susan Elizabeth; one *s* two *d. Educ:* Ealing Grammar School; Nottingham Univ. (Gladstone Meml Prize 1958; BA History 1959; PhD 1965); Trinity Hall, Cambridge (Cert. in Education 1960); Lincoln Theological Coll. Ordained deacon 1964, priest 1965; Asst Curate, St Andrew, Bedford, 1964–70; Rector of Coventry East Team Ministry, 1970–77; Examining Chaplain to Bishop of Coventry, 1972–77; Rural Dean of Coventry East, 1973–77; Archdeacon of Southend, 1977–82; Provost of Chelmsford, 1982–96. Vis. Fellow, Wolfson Coll., Cambridge, 1987. Mem., Gen. Synod, 1985–2005; Church Comr, 1988–2006; Mem., ACC, 1997–2005. Chm. Council, Centre for Study of Theology, Essex Univ., 1987–96; Rector, Anglia Poly. Univ., 1992–96. Select Preacher, Oxford Univ., 2004–05. Vice-Pres., City of London Fest., 1997–2006. Freeman, City of London, 1997; Liveryman: Feltmakers' Co., 1998–; Plaisterers' Co., 1999–; Masons' Co., 2005–; Hon. Freeman: Water Conservators' Co., 2000–; Weavers' Co., 2011–. Hon. Dr Anglia Poly. Univ., 1997; Hon. DD: Nottingham, 2007; Grad. Theol Foundn, Indiana, 2010. OStJ 2003. Order of Al Istiqlal of Hashemite (Jordan), 2002. *Publications:* The Sacrifice of God, 1992; A Broad and Living Way, 1995; The Desert, 1997; One Equall Light: an anthology of the writings of John Donne, 2003; The Language of Love, 2007; Divine Discontent: the prophetic voice of Thomas Merton, 2014; The Art of Thomas Merton, 2018. *Address:* Chestnut House, Burgage, Southwell, Notts NG25 0EP. *T:* (01636) 814880. *E:* johnmoses.southwell@gmail.com. *Club:* Athenæum.

**MOSES, Rev. (Leslie) Alan**; Vicar of All Saints', Margaret Street, London, since 1995; *b* 3 Nov. 1949; *s* of Leslie Moses and Edna (*née* Watson); *m* 1971, Theresa Frances O'Connor; one *s* one *d. Educ:* Univ. of Hull (BA Hons History); Univ. of Edinburgh (BD Hons); Edinburgh Theol Coll.; King's Coll., London (MA Systematic Theol. 2001). Ordained deacon 1976, priest 1977; Asst Curate, Old St Paul's, Edinburgh, 1976–79; Rector, St Margaret of Scotland, Leven, 1979–85; Priest-in-Charge, St Margaret of Scotland, Edinburgh, 1986–92; Rector, Old St Paul's, Edinburgh, 1985–95; Priest-in-Charge, The Annunciation, Bryanston St, 2006–10. Area Dean of Westminster-St Marylebone, 2001–; Preb., St Paul's Cathedral, 2010–. Mem., Gen. Synod of C of E, 2005–15, 2009–10, 2010–; Chair, Hse of Clergy, Dio. of London, 2013–. Chm., USPG: Anglicans in World Mission (formerly USPG), 2006–09 (Trustee (formerly Gov.), 1997–2009; Hon. Vice-Pres., 2009). *Recreations:* reading, visiting museums, galleries, churches and other buildings, exploring places. *Address:* The Vicarage, 7 Margaret Street, W1W 8JQ. *T:* (020) 7636 1788. *E:* alanmoses111@gmail.com.

**MOSES, Stephen Colin**; QC 2016; *b* Bletchley, 3 Sept. 1971; *s* of Colin Moses and Greta Moses. *Educ:* Appleton Sch.; South East Essex Sixth Form Coll.; West London Coll. (LLB Hons Univ. of London 1996). Called to the Bar, Gray's Inn, 1997; in practice as a barrister, specialising in crime, 1997–; Dir, Furnival Chambers, 2013–. *Recreations:* theatre, ski-ing, charity fundraising, creator of 'Strictly Furnival'. *Address:* Furnival Chambers, 32 Furnival Street, EC4A 1JQ. *T:* (020) 7405 3232, *Fax:* (020) 7405 3322. *E:* smoses@furnivallaw.co.uk.

**MOSEY, Prof. David**, PhD; Professor of Law and Director, Centre of Construction Law, King's College London, since 2013; *b* London, 28 Oct. 1954; *s* of Victor and Vera Mosey; *m* 1980, Cécile Baland; two *s*. *Educ:* University Coll., Cardiff (LLB Hons 1976); King's Coll. London (PhD 2007). Admitted Solicitor, 1980; Legal Advr, Govt of Kingdom of Bahrain, 1980–84; Partner, Trowers & Hamlins, Solicitors, 1984–2013 (Resident Partner, Sultanate of Oman, 1988–91; Hd of Projects and Construction, 1992–2013). Sen. Fellow, Melbourne Law Sch., 2015–18; CEM Fellow, Dept of Engrg, Univ. of Cambridge, 2017–. Hon. Legal Advr to British Ambassador, Oman, 1988–91. Jt Hd, Nat. Change Agent Prog., UK Govt, 2005–11; Lead Mentor, Two Stage Open Book procurement, Cabinet Office, 2013–18. Mem., Comitato Scientifico, Milan Centre of Construction Law and Mgt, 2018–. Chair, British Scholarships for Oman, 1988–91. Mem., Poetry Soc., 2015–18. Achiever of the Year, Constructing Excellence, 2009; Assoc. of Consultant Architects Medal, 2015. *Publications:* PPC 2000: suite of standard form contracts for project partnering and alliancing, 2000, rev. edn 2013; Early Contractor Involvement in Building Procurement, 2009; FAC-1: Framework Alliance Contract, 2016; TAC-1: Term Alliance Contract, 2016; Enabling BIM Through Procurement and Contracts, 2016; Collaborative Construction Procurement and Improved Value, 2019. *Recreation:* having a laugh with the legions of other performing drummers, guitarists and poets. *Address:* King's College London, The Old Watch House, Strand, WC2R 2LS. *T:* (020) 7848 1661. *E:* david.mosey@kcl.ac.uk. *Club:* Henley Sailing.

**MOSEY, Roger**; Master, Selwyn College, Cambridge, since 2013; *b* 4 Jan. 1958; *s* of late Geoffrey Mosey and Marie Mosey (*née* Pilkington). *Educ:* Bradford Grammar Sch.; Wadham Coll., Oxford (MA Mod. Hist. & Mod. Langs); INSEAD (AMP 1999). Producer, Pennine Radio, 1979; Reporter, BBC Radio Lincolnshire, 1980; Producer: BBC Radio Northampton, 1982; Today programme, BBC Radio Four, 1984; BBC New York office, 1986; Editor: PM prog., 1987; World At One, 1989; Today prog., BBC Radio Four, 1993 (Sony Radio Gold Awards, 1994, 1995); Controller, BBC Radio Five Live, 1996–2000 (Sony Radio Gold Award, 1998); Acting Dir, BBC Continuous News, 1999; Hd of TV News, BBC, 2000–05; Dir of Sport, BBC, 2005–09; Dir of London 2012, BBC, 2009–12; Acting Dir of TV, BBC, 2012–13; Editorial Dir, BBC, 2013. Dir, Parly Broadcasting Unit Ltd, 1999–2003; Mem. Exec. Bd, European Broadcasting Union, 2011–13. Board Member: Union Dance, 2001–05; Invictus Games, 2013–15. Trustee: Nat. Media Mus., 2008–13; RIBA, 2010–14; Syndic, Fitzwilliam Mus., 2015–. Chair, Council, Bishop Grosseteste Univ., 2013–16. Fellow, Radio Acad., 1999; FRTS 2013. Hon. DLitt Lincoln, 2011; DUniv Bradford, 2013. *Publications:* Getting Out Alive, 2015; contrib. New Statesman, Financial Times, Guardian, Daily Mail, Sunday Times. *Recreations:* football (Arsenal and Bradford City), political history, music, walking with basset hounds. *Address:* Master's Lodge, Selwyn College, Cambridge CB3 9DQ. *T:* (01223) 335890. *E:* master@sel.cam.ac.uk.

**MOSHINSKY, Elijah**; opera and theatre producer and director; *b* 8 Jan. 1946; *s* of Abraham and Eva Moshinsky. *Educ:* Melbourne Univ. (BA); St Antony's Coll., Oxford. Apptd to Royal Opera House, 1973: work includes original productions of: Peter Grimes, 1975; Lohengrin, 1978, 1997; The Rake's Progress, 1979; Macbeth, 1981; Samson and Dalila, 1981; Tannhäuser, 1984; Otello, 1987; Die Entführung aus dem Serail, 1987; Attila, 1990; Simon Boccanegra, 1991; Stiffelio, 1993; Aida, 1994; I Masnadieri, 1997; Il Trovatore, 2002; for ENO: Le Grand Macabre, 1982; The Mastersingers of Nuremberg, 1984; The Bartered Bride, 1985, 1986; for Australian Opera: A Midsummer Night's Dream, 1978; Boris Godunov, 1980; Il Trovatore, 1983; Werther, Rigoletto, 1990; Les Dialogues des Carmélites; for Metropolitan Opera, NY: Un Ballo in Maschera, 1980; Samson, 1987; Ariadne auf Naxos, 1993; Otello, 1994; The Makropulos Case, 1996; The Queen of Spades; Samson et Dalila, 1998; other opera productions include: Wozzeck, 1976; Antony and Cleopatra, Chicago, 1990; I Vespri Siciliani, Grand Théâtre, Geneva; La Bohème, 1989, La Forza del Destino, 1990, Scottish Opera; Beatrice and Benedict, 1994, Cavalleria Rusticana and Pagliacci, 1996, WNO; Die Meistersinger von Nürnberg, 1994, Holland Fest.; Benvenuto Cellini, 50th Maggio Musicale, Florence, 1987; The Turn of the Screw, Broomhill Opera, 2000; Giovanna d'Arco, Buxton, 2015. Producer: Three Sisters, Albery, 1987; Light up the Sky, Globe, 1987; Ivanov, Strand, 1989; Much Ado About Nothing, Strand, 1989; Another Time, Wyndham's, 1989; Shadowlands, Queen's, 1989; Cyrano de Bergerac, Theatre Royal, Haymarket, 1992; Lord of the Flies, 1995, Richard III, 1998, RSC; productions at National Theatre: Troilus and Cressida, 1976; The Force of Habit, 1976; productions for the BBC: All's Well That Ends Well, 1980; A Midsummer Night's Dream, 1981; Cymbeline, 1982; Coriolanus, 1984; Love's Labour's Lost, 1985; Ghosts, 1986; The Rivals, 1987; The Green Man, 1990; Genghis Cohn, 1993; Danton, 1994. Director: Matador, Queen's, 1991; Beckett, Haymarket, 1991; Reflected Glory, Vaudeville, 1992; Old Wicked Songs, Gielgud, 1996; The Female Odd Couple, Apollo, 2001; Sleuth, Apollo, 2002. *Recreations:* telephone conversation, writing film scripts. *Club:* Garrick.

**MOSIEWICZ, Muriel Anita**; *see* Robinson, Muriel A.

**MOSIMANN, Anton**, OBE 2004; DL; Owner, Mosimann's (formerly Belfry Club), since 1988; Principal, Mosimann Academy, London, since 1996; *b* 23 Feb. 1947; *s* of Otto and Olga Mosimann; *m* 1973, Kathrin Roth; two *s*. *Educ:* private school in Switzerland; youngest Chef to be awarded Chef de Cuisine Diplôme; 3 degrees. Served apprenticeship in Hotel Baeren, Twann; worked in Canada, France, Italy, Japan, Sweden, Belgium, Switzerland, 1962–; cuisinier at: Villa Lorraine, Brussels; Les Près d'Eugénie, Eugénie-les-Bains; Les Frères Troisgros, Roanne; Paul Bocuse, Collonges au Mont d'Or; Moulin de Mougins; joined Dorchester Hotel, 1975, Maître Chef des Cuisines, 1976–88; Chef to VIPs at Olympics in Beijing, Vancouver, London, Sochi and Rio de Janeiro. Channel Four TV series: Cooking with Mosimann, 1989; Anton Mosimann Naturally, 1991; Swiss TV series: Healthy Food, 1997; Swiss Regional Cooking, 1998. Mem., Internat. Adv. Bd, Ecole Hôtelière, Lausanne, 2011–. World Pres., Les Toques Blanches Internationales, 1989–93; Hon. Member: Chefs' Assoc., Canada, Chicago, Japan, Switzerland, S Africa; World Assoc. of Chefs' Socs, 2008; Cercle des Chefs de Cuisine, Berne, 2008; Club Chefs des Chefs, 2008; Goldenen Fisch Assoc., 2019; Hon. Judge, Swiss Golden Kock, Berne, 2011–17. Freeman, City of London, 1999. DL Greater London, 2011. Royal Warrant Holder as Caterer to the Prince of Wales, 2000; Pres., Royal Warrant Holders' Assoc., 2006–07. Hon. Prof., Thames Valley Univ., 2004. Disciple d'Escoffier of Great Britain, 2008. Johnson & Wales University, RI: Dr of Culinary Arts *hc*, 1990; Hon. DSc Bournemouth Univ., 1998. Restaurateur of the Year, 2000. Numerous Gold Medals in Internat. Cookery Competitions; Catey Chef Award, Caterer and Hotelkeeper, 1985; Personnalité de l'année award, 1986; Glenfiddich Awards Trophy, 1986; Chevalier, Ordre des Coteaux de Champagne, 1990; Grand Cordon Culinaire, Conseil Culinaire Français de Grande Bretagne, 1994; Swiss Culinary Ambassador of the Year, Hotel & Restaurant Assoc. of Switzerland, 1995; Catey Lifetime Achievement Award for Catering, Caterer and Hotelkeeper, 2004; Davos Tourism Award for World Econ. Forum, 2010; Internat. Chef Days Lifetime Achievement Award, 2010; Asia Pacific Brands Foundn, Brand Personality Award, 2010; Hon. Cross, Fedn Cuisinier Exclusive d'Europe, 2012; Médaille du Mérite, Société Suisse des Cuisiniers, 2012; Gastronomische Akademie Deutschlands Rumohr Ring, 2013; Lifetime Achievement Award, Hotelympia, 2016; Lifetime Chef Award and Gold Medal, Verband der Köche Deutschlands, 2016; Flamme de l'Accueil, Assoc. Gastrosuisse, 2019. Officier, Ordre Nat. du Mérite Agricole (France), 2006 (Chevalier, 1988). *Publications:* Cuisine à la Carte, 1981; A New Style of Cooking, 1983; Cuisine Naturelle, 1985; Anton Mosimann's Fish Cuisine, 1988; The Art of Anton Mosimann, 1989; Cooking with Mosimann, 1989; Anton Mosimann Naturally, 1991; The Essential Mosimann, 1993; Mosimann's World, 1996; Mosimann's Fresh, 2006; Five Centuries of Culinary History, 2012; 25 Years of Mosimann's, 2013; Life is a Circus (autobiog.), 2017. *Recreations:* classic cars and participating in rallies around the world, collecting antiquarian cookery books, enjoying fine wine, passionate about food and travelling, especially to the food markets of the Far East. *Address:* c/o Mosimann's, 11B West Halkin Street, SW1X 8JL. *T:* (020) 7235 9625. *Clubs:* Garrick, Reform.

**MOSLEY,** family name of **Baron Ravensdale**.

**MOSLEY, Max Rufus**; President, 1993–2009, Honorary President, Fédération Internationale de l'Automobile, since 2009 (Member of Senate, 1993–2013); Chairman, Global New Car Assessment Programme, 2011–17; *b* 13 April 1940; *s* of Sir Oswald Mosley, 6th Bt and Hon. Diana (*d* 2003), *d* of 2nd Baron Redesdale; *m* 1960, Jean Taylor; one *s* (and one *s* decd). *Educ:* abroad; Christ Church, Oxford (MA Natural Sciences). Sec., Oxford Union Society, 1961. Called to the Bar, Gray's Inn, 1964; Dir, March Cars, 1969–79; Legal Adviser, Formula One Constructors' Assoc., 1971–82; Pres., Fédn Internat. du Sport Automobile, 1991–93 (Pres., Manufacturers' Commn, FISA, 1986–91). Chm., Eur. New Car Assessment Prog., 1997–2004; EU Commission: Co-founder, e-Safety Forum, 2003; Mem., High Level Gp, CARS 21 (Competitive Automotive Regulatory System for the 21st century), 2005–09. Hon. Mem., ERTICO Intelligent Transport Systems Europe, 2007 (Vice-Chm., 1999–2001, Chm., 2001–04, Supervisory Bd; Pres. and spokesperson, 2004–07). Mem. Bd of Trustees, 2001–14, Chm., Programmes Cttee, 2001–12, FIA Foundn for the Automobile and Society; Chm., Towards Zero Foundn, 2016–18 (Pres. Emeritus, 2019); Patron, eSafety Aware, 2006–09. Hon. President: Automobile Users' Intergroup, EP, 1994–99; Nat. Road Safety Council NGO, Armenia, 2005. Founder Mem., Inst du Cerveau et de la Moelle Epinière, 2005. Hon. DCL Northumbria, 2005. Gold Medal, Castrol/Inst. of Motor Industry, 2000; Quattroruote Premio Speciale per la Sicurezza Stradale (Italy), 2001; Goldene VdM-Dieselring (Germany), 2001. Grande Ufficiale dell' Ordine al Merito (Italy), 1994; Order of Madarski Konnik, 1st degree (Bulgaria), 2000; Order of Merit (Romania), 2004; Huésped Ilustre de Quito (Ecuador), 2005; Chevalier de la Légion d'Honneur (France), 2005; Commandeur de l'Ordre de Saint Charles (Monaco), 2006. *Publications:* Formula One and Beyond (autobiog.), 2015 (Sports Autobiog. of the Year, Cross Sports Book Awards, 2016). *Recreations:* snow-boarding, walking. *Address:* Palais Solemar, 8 avenue des Citronniers, MC 98000, Monaco.

**MOSLEY, Stephen James**; *b* Solihull, 22 June 1972; *m* 1997, Caroline Smith; one *s* one *d*. *Educ:* King Edward's Sch., Birmingham; Univ. of Nottingham (BSc Chem. 1993). With IBM (UK) Ltd, 1993–97; Director: Weblong Ltd, 1997–2010, 2015–; Streamfolder Ltd, 2004–10, 2015–; Severn Industrial Estates Ltd, 2004–10, 2015–; Startup Technology Ltd, 2015–. Member (C): Chester CC, 2000–09; Cheshire CC, 2005–09. MP (C) City of Chester, 2010–15; contested (C) same seat, 2015.

**MOSS, Andrew Jonothan**; Headmaster, Gordon's School, Woking, since 2010; *b* Southport, 10 Aug. 1968; *s* of Eric Moss and Christine Moss; *m* 1998, Tracey Louise Smith (marr. diss. 2010); two *d*. *Educ:* Ormskirk Sch.; Liverpool Poly. (BScSci 1989); Univ. of Manchester (MEd 1999). Teacher of Economics, Business and IT: St Nicholas Sch., Cheshire, 1992–95; Rochester Grammar Sch., 1995–96; Trent Coll., 1996–2001; Wymondham Coll., 2001–04; Sea View Sch., Fife, 2004–05; Hayling Coll., 2005–07; Cognita Schs Gp, 2007–10. *Recreations:* ski-ing, caving, badminton, trying to make bread, work. *Address:* 23 Guildford Road, West End, Woking GU24 9QH.

**MOSS, His Honour Christopher John**; QC 1994; a Senior Circuit Judge, 2002–18; *b* 4 Aug. 1948; *s* of John (Jack) Gordon Moss and Joyce (Joy) Mirren Moss (*née* Stephany); *m* 1st, 1971, Gail Susan Pearson (marr. diss. 1987); one *s* two *d*; 2nd, 1988, Tracy Louise Levy (marr. diss. 1997); one *s* one *d*; 3rd, 1999, Lisa Annette O'Dwyer; two *d*. *Educ:* Bryanston Sch.; University Coll. London (LLB). Called to the Bar, Gray's Inn, 1972, Bencher, 2002; a Recorder, 1993–2002. *Recreation:* playing the piano and accordion.

**MOSS, David Christopher**, FCILT; Chairman, Iford Arts Ltd, since 2018; *b* 17 April 1946; *s* of Charles Clifford Moss and Marjorie Sylvia Moss (*née* Hutchings); *m* 1971, Angela Mary Wood; one *s*. *Educ:* King's Sch., Chester; Magdalene Coll., Cambridge (BA 1968; MA). Asst Principal, MPBW, 1968; Principal, 1972, DoE, and subseq. Dept of Transport and HM Treasury; Asst Sec., 1980, Dept of Transport and DoE; Under Sec., Internat. Aviation, Dept of Transport, 1988–93; Railtrack: Commercial Dir, 1993–95; European Affairs Dir, 1995–98; Dir Gen. (Europe), 1998–2001. Pres., European Civil Aviation Conf., 1990–93; Bd Chm., Jt Aviation Authorities, 1990–93. Chairman: Bradford on Avon Preservation Trust Ltd, 2004–17; Bradford on Avon Stn Footbridge Canopy Project, 2018–; Wilts Victoria County History Trust, 2018–. FCILT (FCIT 1998). *Recreations:* opera, ecclesiastical architecture, wine. *Club:* Oxford and Cambridge.

**MOSS, David John**; Chairman: Royal Bournemouth and Christchurch NHS Foundation Trust, since 2017; Poole Hospital NHS Foundation Trust, since 2019; *b* 23 May 1947; *s* of late John Henry Moss and Doris (*née* Fenna); *m* 1975, Susan Elizabeth Runnalls; three *s*. *Educ:* Sevenoaks Sch.; St John's Coll., Cambridge (MA); Poly. of Central London (Dip. Management Studies). IPFA; MHSM; FCMA. Management Trainee and Management Accounting, Philips Lamps, 1968–73; Asst Finance Officer, St Thomas' Hosp., 1973–74; Dist Finance Officer, Enfield Health Dist, 1974–79; Dist Treasurer, E Dorset HA, 1979–86; General Manager: Poole Gen. Hosp., 1986–88; Southampton Gen. Hosp., 1988–91; Southampton Univ. Hosps, 1991–93; Chief Exec., Southampton Univ. Hosps Trust, 1993–2004; Programme Dir, NHS Pay Reform, then Dep. Dir, Workforce, DoH, 2003–07. Chm., UK Univ. Hosp. Forum, 2001–03. Mem., Audit Commn, 2001–07. Chm., Bd of Govs, Ferndown Upper Sch., 2009–16. FRSA 1994; FCMI. *Publications:* (jtly) Managing Nursing, 1984; articles in professional jls. *Recreations:* cricket, golf, tennis, Rugby, history, opera, walking.

**MOSS, (Sir) David John E.**; *see* Edwards-Moss.

**MOSS, Sir David Joseph**, KCVO 1998; CMG 1989; HM Diplomatic Service, retired; High Commissioner in Kuala Lumpur, 1994–98; *b* 6 Nov. 1938; *s* of Herbert Joseph and Irene Gertrude Moss; *m* 1961, Joan Lillian Moss; one *d* (one *s* decd). *Educ:* Hampton Grammar Sch.; Open Univ. (BA Hons 2007). CS Commn, 1956; FO, 1957; RAF, 1957–59; FO, 1959–62; Third Sec., Bangkok, 1962–65; FO, 1966–69; First Sec., La Paz,

1969–70; FCO, 1970–73; First Sec. and Head of Chancery, The Hague, 1974–77; First Sec., FCO, 1978–79, Counsellor, 1979–83; Counsellor, Hd of Chancery and Dep. Perm. Rep., UK Mission, Geneva, 1983–87; Asst Under-Sec. of State, FCO, 1987–90; High Comr, New Zealand, 1990–94. *Recreations:* reading, listening to music. *Club:* Royal Over-Seas League.

**MOSS, Elaine Dora;** Children's Books Adviser to The Good Book Guide, 1980–86; *b* 8 March 1924; *d* of Percy Philip Levy and Maude Agnes Levy (*née* Simmons); *m* 1950, John Edward Moss, FRICS, FAI; two *d*. *Educ:* St Paul's Girls' Sch.; Bedford Coll. for Women (BA Hons); Univ. of London Inst. of Educn (DipEd); University College London Sch. of Librarianship (ALA). Teacher, Stoatley Rough Sch., Haslemere, 1945–47; Asst Librarian, Bedford Coll., 1947–50; freelance journalist and broadcaster (Woman's Hour, The Times, TES, TLS, The Spectator, Signal, etc.), 1956–; Editor and Selector, NBL's Children's Books of the Year, 1970–79; Librarian, Fleet Primary Sch., ILEA, 1976–82. Eleanor Farjeon Award, 1976. *Publications:* texts for several picture books, incl. Polar, 1976; catalogues for Children's Books of the Year, 1970–79; Picture Books for Young People 9–13, 1981, 3rd edn 1992; Part of the Pattern: a personal journey through the world of children's books 1960–1985, 1986; (with Nancy Chambers) The Signal Companion, 1996. *Recreations:* walking, art galleries, reading, ballet. *Address:* 14 Kekewich House, 1 View Road, N6 4DJ.

**MOSS, Kate;** fashion model, business owner and entrepreneur; *b* 16 Jan. 1974; *d* of Peter Edward Moss and Linda Rosina Moss (*née* Shephard); one *d* by Jefferson Hack; *m* 2011, Jamie Hince (marr. diss. 2016). *Educ:* Riddlesdown High Sch., Purley. Modelling contracts with Calvin Klein, 1992–2000, 2006–; campaigns incl. Burberry, Chanel, Dior, Dolce & Gabbana, Gucci, Katherine Hamnett, Rimmel, H. Stern, Versace, Louis Vuitton, Yves Saint Laurent, Alexander McQueen; fashion design collaborations: with Topshop, 2007–10 and 2014; with Equipment, 2016; founder, The Kate Moss Agency, 2016. Fashion Personality of the Year, 1995, Model of the Year, 2001, 2006, Special Recognition Award, 2013, British Fashion Awards. *Publications:* Kate, 1995; (jtly) Kate, 2012. *Address:* Kate Moss Agency, 25A Old Compton Street, Soho, W1D 5JN.

**MOSS, Ven. Leonard Godfrey;** Archdeacon of Hereford and Canon Residentiary of Hereford Cathedral, 1991–97, now Archdeacon Emeritus; *b* 11 July 1932; *s* of Clarence Walter Moss and Frances Lilian Vera Moss; *m* 1954, Everell Annette (*née* Reed) (*d* 2012); one *s* one *d* (and one *s* decd). *Educ:* Regent St Poly., London; King's Coll., London and Warminster (BD, AKC 1959). Quantity Surveyor's Asst, L. A. Francis and Sons, 1948–54; RE (National Service), 1954–56. Ordained: deacon, 1960; priest, 1961; Assistant curate: St Margaret, Putney, 1960–63; St Dunstan, Cheam, 1963–67; Vicar: Much Dewchurch with Llanwarne and Llandinabo, 1967–72; Marden with Amberley and Wisteston, 1972–84; Hereford Diocesan Ecumenical Officer, 1969–83; Prebendary of Hereford Cathedral, 1979–97; Bishop of Hereford's Officer for Social Responsibility and Non-Residentiary Canon of Hereford Cathedral, 1984–91; Priest-in-charge, Marden with Amberley and Wisteston, 1992–94. Proctor in Convocation, 1970–97. Order of St Ethelbert, Dio. Hereford, 2016. *Publications:* (contrib.) The People, the Land and the Church, 1987; articles and reviews in theol jls. *Recreations:* adult education, reading, listening to music, theatre. *Address:* 10 Saxon Way, Ledbury, Hereford HR8 2QY. *E:* lgmoss@btinternet.com.

**MOSS, Malcolm Douglas;** *b* 6 March 1943; *s* of late Norman Moss and Annie Moss (*née* Gay); *m* 1965, Vivien Lorraine (*née* Peake) (*d* 1997); two *d*; *m* 2000, Sonya Alexandra McFarlin (*née* Evans); one step *s* one step *d*. *Educ:* Audenshaw Grammar Sch.; St John's Coll., Cambridge (BA 1965, MA 1968). Teaching Cert 1966. Asst Master, 1966–68, Head of Dept, 1968–70, Blundell's Sch.; Insurance Consultant, 1970–72, Gen. Manager, 1972–74, Barwick Associates; Chairman: Mandrake Gp plc, 1986–88; Mandrake Associates Ltd (formerly Mandrake (Insurance and Finance Brokers)), 1986–93 (Dir, 1974–94); Fens Business Enterprise Trust, 1983–87 (Dir, 1983–94). Mem., Cambs CC, 1985–88. MP (C) NE Cambs, 1987–2010. PPS to Minister of State, FO, 1991–93, to Sec. of State for NI, 1993–94; Parly Under-Sec. of State, NI Office and Minister for Health and Envmt, 1994–97; opposition front bench spokesman on NI, 1997–99; on MAFF, 1999–2001; opposition spokesman, for local govt and regions, 2001–02, for aviation and rural transport, 2002, for arts and tourism, 2002–03, for home and constitutional affairs, 2003–05, for tourism, licensing and gambling, 2005–06. Mem., Foreign Affairs Select Cttee, 2006–10; Treas., Swiss All Party Parly Gp, 1987–89; Sec., Anglo-Bermuda All Party Parly Gp, 1989–91; Sec., 1988–91, Vice Chm., 1991–93, Cons. Backbench Energy Cttee. Chairman: SLL White Horses Charity, 2010–17; Nat. Casino Forum, 2011–15. Chm., Glapthorn Parish Council, 2016–. *Recreations:* tennis, ski-ing, amateur dramatics, gardening.

**MOSS, Peter Jonathan; His Honour Judge Peter Moss;** a Circuit Judge, since 2004; *b* 29 March 1951; *s* of John Cottam Moss and Joyce Alison Moss (*née* Blunn); *m* (marr. diss.); three *s*; *m* 2010, Tertia Elizabeth, *d* of Alan Norman Mackesy and Janice Emily Mackesy, Glos. *Educ:* Charterhouse. Called to the Bar, Lincoln's Inn, 1976. Legal Mem., Mental Health Review Tribunal, 1994–2009; Asst Recorder, 1999–2000, Recorder, 2000–04. *Recreations:* golf, cricket, ski-ing, fishing. *Address:* Guildford Crown Court, Bedford Road, Guildford GU1 4ST. *Clubs:* MCC; New Zealand Golf.

**MOSS, His Honour Ronald Trevor;** a Circuit Judge, 1993–2009; *b* 1 Oct. 1942; *s* of Maurice and Sarah Moss; *m* 1971, Cindy (*née* Fiddleman); one *s* one *d*. *Educ:* Hendon County Grammar School; Nottingham University (Upper Second BA; Hons Law). Admitted Solicitor, 1968; Partner, Moss Beachley, solicitors, 1973–84; Metropolitan Stipendiary Magistrate, 1984–93; Asst Recorder, 1986–90; Recorder, 1990–93; Luton Crown Court, 1993–2005, Resident Judge, 2001–05; Harrow Crown Court, 2005–09. Chm., Inner London Juvenile Courts, subseq. Inner London Youth and Family Panel, 1986–93. Mem. Cttee, London Criminal Courts Solicitors' Assoc., 1982–84. *Recreations:* golf, bridge, Watford Football Club. *Club:* Moor Park Golf.

**MOSS, Sir Stephen (Alan),** Kt 2006; Chief Executive, Queen's Medical Centre, Nottingham, 2003–05; *b* 15 May 1947; *s* of George Ernest Moss and Dorothy May Moss. *Educ:* Kingsmead Sch., Hednesford; Wolverhampton Sch. of Nursing (RN; OND); Univ. of London (DN). Nursing Officer: Royal Hosp., Wolverhampton, 1973–75; Dudley Rd Hosp., Birmingham, 1975–77; Sen. Nursing Officer, subseq. Dir of Nursing, Derbys Royal Infirmary, 1977–84; Dir of Nursing, Queen's Med. Centre, Nottingham, 1984–2003. Member: Sheffield HA, 1987–91; Commn for Health Improvement, 1999–2004; Chm., Mid Staffs NHS Foundn Trust, 2009–12; non-executive Director: Derby Teaching Hosps (formerly Derby Hosps) NHS Foundn Trust, 2013–; Health Educn England, 2014–. Chm., Trust Nurses Assoc., subseq. Nurse Dirs Assoc., 1997–2003. Hon. LLD Nottingham, 2011; DUniv Derby, 2016. *Recreations:* walking, pottering, antiques, theatre, travel. *Address:* 7 Hall Lane, Nether Heage, Belper, Derbys DE56 2JW. *T:* (01773) 270967. *E:* stephenm0109@yahoo.com.

**MOSS, Stephen Hodgson;** freelance naturalist, author, broadcaster and wildlife television producer; Senior Lecturer in Creative Writing, Bath Spa University, since 2015; *b* London, 26 April 1960; *s* of late Franco Clerici and Kathleen Mary Hodgson Moss; *m* 1st, 1985, Jane Freeth (marr. diss. 2001); two *s*; 2nd, 2001, Suzanne Dolan; two *s* one *d*. *Educ:* Hampton Grammar Sch., Middx; Gonville and Caius Coll., Cambridge (BA English 1982). Television producer, BBC Educn Dept, 1982–97; Series Producer, BBC Natural History Unit, 1997–2011. Programmes include: Birding with Bill Oddie, 1997, 1998, 2000; Big Cat Diary, 1998; Bill Oddie Goes Wild, 2001, 2002, 2003; Springwatch, 2005–11 (RTS Award, 2005); (co-presenter) A Guide to Garden, Woodland, Coastal, Farmland, Wetland, Mountain and Moorland Birds, BBC Radio 4, 2007–13; The Nature of Britain, 2007; Autumnwatch, 2008; Birds Britannia, 2010; Big British Wildlife Revival, 2013; Hive Alive, 2014. President: Somerset Wildlife Trust, 2014– (Vice-Pres., 2011–14); Somerset Ornithological Soc., 2016–; Mem. Council, RSPB, 2015–. Author of Report for NT, Natural Childhood, 2012. Hon. Prof., Business Sch. and Sch. of History, Univ. of Nottingham, 2011–. Dilys Breese Medal, British Trust for Ornithology, 2009. *Publications:* Birds and Weather, 1995; Attracting Birds to your Garden, 1997; The Garden Bird Handbook, 2003; How to Birdwatch, 2003; Understanding Bird Behaviour, 2003; A Bird in the Bush, 2004; How to Watch Wildlife, 2005; Everything You Always Wanted to Know about Birds, 2005; This Birding Life, 2005; Remarkable Birds, 2007; A Sky Full of Starlings, 2008; The Bumper Book of Nature, 2009; (contrib.) Handbook of the Birds of the World, vol. 14, 2009; Birds Britannia, 2011; Wild Hares and Hummingbirds: the natural history of an English Village, 2011; Springwatch Guide to British Wildlife, 2012; (ed) Hedgerows Heaped With May: the Daily Telegraph book of the countryside, 2013; The Great British Year, 2013; (with Brett Westwood) Tweet of the Day, 2014 (Thomson Reuters Award for Communicating Zoology, 2014); Wild Kingdom: bringing back Britain's wildlife, 2016; Highlands: Scotland's wild heart, 2016; (with Brett Westwood) Natural Histories, 2016; Planet Earth II, 2016; (with Brett Westwood) Wonderland: a year of Britain's wildlife, day by day, 2017; The Robin: a biography, 2017; Mrs Moreau's Warbler: how birds got their names, 2018; Dynasties: the rise and fall of animal families, 2018; The Wren: a biography, 2018. *Recreations:* birding, natural history, collecting wildlife books, family life. *Address:* Mill Batch, Blackford Road, Mark, Highbridge, Som TA9 4NR. *T:* (01278) 641283, 07712 528179. *E:* stephenmoss@live.com.

**MOSS, Stephen Raymond;** writer with The Guardian; *b* 30 July 1957; *s* of Raymond Moss and Catherine Moss (*née* Croome); *m* 1984, Helen Bonnick; one *s*. *Educ:* Balliol Coll., Oxford (BA Modern Hist. 1978); Birkbeck Coll., London (MA Victorian Studies 1986). Editor with Kogan Page Publishers Ltd, 1979–81; Editor: Managing Your Business, 1981–83; Marketing and Direction, 1983–89; joined The Guardian, 1989: Dep. Arts Ed., 1991–93; Dep. Features Ed., 1994–95; Literary Ed., 1995–98. *Publications:* (ed) Pass Notes, 1994; (ed) Wisden Anthology 1978–2006: cricket's age of revolution, 2006; The Rookie: an odyssey through chess (and life), 2016. *Recreations:* chess, cricket, music. *Address:* c/o The Guardian, Kings Place, 90 York Way, N1 9GU. *E:* stephen.moss@theguardian.com.

**MOSS, Sir Stirling,** Kt 2000; OBE 1959; FIE; racing motorist, 1947–62, retired; Managing Director, Stirling Moss Ltd; Director, Stirling Products Ltd; *b* 17 Sept. 1929; *m* 1st, 1957, Kathleen Stuart (marr. diss. 1960), *y d* of F. Stuart Molson, Montreal, Canada; 2nd, 1964, Elaine (marr. diss. 1968), 2nd *d* of A. Barbarino, New York; one *d*; 3rd, 1980, Susan, *y d* of Stuart Paine, London; one *s*. *Educ:* Haileybury and Imperial Service Coll. Brit. Nat. Champion, 1950, 1951, 1952, 1954, 1955, 1956, 1957, 1958, 1959, 1961; Tourist Trophy, 1950, 1951, 1955, 1958, 1959, 1960, 1961; Coupe des Alpes, 1952, 1953, 1954; Alpine Gold Cup (three consecutive wins), 1954. Only Englishman to win Italian Mille Miglia, 1955. Competed in 529 races, rallies, sprints, land speed records and endurance runs, finished in 387 and won 211; drove 108 different cars. Successes include Targa Florio, 1955; Brit. Grand Prix, 1955, 1957; Ital. GP, 1956, 1957, 1959; NZ GP, 1956, 1959; Monaco GP, 1956, 1960, 1961; Leguna Seca GP, 1960, 1961; US GP, 1959, 1960; Aust. GP, 1956; Bari GP, 1956; Pescara GP, 1957; Swedish GP, 1957; Dutch GP, 1958; Argentine GP, 1958; Morocco GP, 1958; Buenos Aires GP, 1958; Melbourne GP, 1958; Villarreal GP, 1958; Caen GP, 1958; Portuguese GP, 1959; S African GP, 1960; Cuban GP, 1960; Austrian GP, 1960; Cape GP, 1960; Watkins Glen GP, 1960; German GP, 1961; Modena GP, 1961. Twice voted Driver of the Year, 1954 and 1961. *Publications:* Stirling Moss's Book of Motor Sport, 1955; In the Track of Speed, 1957; Stirling Moss's Second Book of Motor Sport, 1958; Le Mans, 1959; My Favourite Car Stories, 1960; A Turn at the Wheel, 1961; All But My Life, 1963; Design and Behaviour of the Racing Car, 1964; How to Watch Motor Racing, 1975; Motor Racing and All That, 1980; My Cars, My Career, 1987; (with D. Nye) Fangio: a Pirelli album, 1991; Great Drives in the Lakes and Dales, 1993; (with C. Hilton) Stirling Moss's Motor Racing Masterpieces, 1994; All My Races, 2009; (with S. Taylor) My Racing Life, 2015; *relevant publications:* Stirling Moss, by Robert Raymond, 1953; Racing with the Maestro, by Karl Ludvigsen, 1997; Stirling Moss: the authorised biography, by Robert Edwards, 2001. *Recreations:* historic racing, designing, model making. *Address:* (business) Stirling Moss Ltd, 46 Shepherd Street, W1J 7JN; (residence) 44 Shepherd Street, W1J 7JN. *Clubs:* Royal Automobile; British Racing Drivers' (Silverstone); British Automobile Racing (Thruxton); British Racing and Sports Car (W Malling, Kent); Road Racing Drivers of America, 200 mph (Bonneville, USA); Internationale des Anciens Pilotes des Grand Prix (Bergamo); Chm. or Pres. of 36 motoring clubs.

**MOSS, Timothy James,** CBE 2016; Chief Executive and Comptroller General, UK Intellectual Property Office, since 2017; *b* London; *s* of Prof. James Moss and Mary Moss; *m* 1996, Rachel; one *s* one *d*. *Educ:* Gonville and Caius Coll., Cambridge (BA 1988); Swansea Univ. (MBA 2002). Location Manager, Delta Crompton Cables, 1990–99; Manufacturing Manager: Norsk Hydro, Alupres, 1999; Pirelli Cables, 1999–2001; Dep. Dir of Ops, 2002–04, Dir, Corporate Strategy, 2004–12, Registrar of Companies for England and Wales and Chief Exec., 2012–17, Companies House. *Address:* Intellectual Property Office, Concept House, Cardiff Road, Newport NP10 8QQ.

**MOSSE, Prof. David,** DPhil; FBA 2013; Professor of Social Anthropology, since 2007, and Head, Department of Anthropology and Sociology, since 2012, School of Oriental and African Studies, University of London; *s* of Charles Riou Mosse and Veronica Mosse (*née* Bain); *m* 1981, Julia Caroline Cleves (marr. diss.; she *d* 2007); two *s*; *m* 2003, Siobhan Nicole Stamp. *Educ:* New Coll., Oxford (BA; DPhil Social Anthropol.). Rural develt consultant; Regl Rep. for S India, Oxfam, 1987–91; social develt advr for internat. develt agencies incl. DFID; Lectr in Social Anthropol., 1997–2007, Mem., Governing Body, 2013–, SOAS, Univ. of London. Member, Editorial Board: World Develt; Amer. Ethnologist; Jl Develt Studies. *Publications:* The Rule of Water: statecraft, ecology and collective action in South India, 2003; Cultivating Development, 2005; (ed with D. Lewis) The Aid Effect, 2005; (ed with D. Lewis) Development Brokers and Translators, 2006; (ed) Adventures in Aidland, 2011; The Saint in the Banyan Tree, 2012; contribs to learned jls. *Address:* Department of Anthropology and Sociology, School of Oriental and African Studies, University of London, Thornhaugh Street, Russell Square, WC1H 0XG.

**MOSSE, Katharine Louise, (Kate),** OBE 2013; novelist, non-fiction writer and playwright; *b* 20 Oct. 1961; *d* of late Richard Hugh Mosse and Barbara Mary Mosse; *m* 2001, Gregory Charles Mosse (*né* Dunk); one *s* one *d*. *Educ:* New Coll., Oxford (BA Hons 1984, MA 1994). Publisher, 1984–92; Exec. Dir, Chichester Fest. Th., 1998–2001; presenter, BBC 4 and BBC2 TV and BBC Radio 4, 2000–. Dir, Mosse Associates Ltd, 2003–. Founder Dir (formerly Co-founder and Hon. Dir), Orange, later Women's, then Baileys Women's Prize for Fiction, subseq. Women's Prize for Fiction, 1996–; Co-dir, Chichester Writing Festival, 2006–12; Mem. Bd, RNT, 2011–19 (Dep. Chair, 2014–19).

Mem., Exec. Bd, Women of the World, 2011–. Vis. Prof., Univ. of Chichester, 2019–; Fellow, Writer's House, Amsterdam, 2019. Trustee, Weald and Downland Open Air Mus., Sussex, 2009–11; Patron, Fishbourne Centre, 2010–. Pres., Consort of Twelve, 2013–. Hon. MA UC Chichester, 2006. *Publications:* Becoming a Mother, 1993, rev. 10th edn 2016; The House: behind the scenes at the Royal Opera House, Covent Garden, 1995; Eskimo Kissing, 1996; Crucifix Lane, 1998; Labyrinth, 2005; Sepulchre, 2007; Syrinx (play), 2009; The Winter Ghosts, 2009; Endpapers (play), 2011; Chichester Festival Theatre at Fifty, 2012; Citadel, 2012; The Mistletoe Bride & Other Haunting Tales, 2013; The Taxidermist's Daughter, 2014 (play adaptation, 2020); The Old Timers (play), 2015; The Burning Chambers, 2018; (ed) I am Heathcliff (anthology), 2018; The City of Tears, 2020. *Recreations:* family and friends, reading, theatre, walking, running, swimming, cycling. *Address:* c/o The Soho Agency, 16–17 Wardour Mews, Soho, W1F 8AT. *E:* Mark@thesohoagency.co.uk.

**MOSSON, Alexander Francis;** Member (Lab), Glasgow City Council, 1984–2007; Lord Provost and Lord-Lieutenant of Glasgow, 1999–2003; *b* 27 Aug. 1940; *m* 1971, Maureen Sweeney; four *s* three *d. Educ:* St Patrick's Primary Sch.; St Mungo's Acad. Glasgow Corporation, 1955; apprentice boilermaker, Barclay Curle, 1956; plater, Alexander Stephens, 1959; insulating engineer, 1963. Active Trade Unionist from age of 17; Glasgow City Council: Convener, Environmental Services, 1995–99; Bailie, 1992–99; Dep. Lord Provost, 1996–99. Chm., Glasgow City Mktg Bureau, 2003–07. Hon. FRCPSGlas 2003; Hon. FCLIP Scotland, 2003. Hon. LLD: Glasgow, 2001; Caledonian, 2002; Strathclyde, 2003. OStJ 2000. Golden Jubilee Medal, 2002. *Recreations:* painting with water colours and oils, watching football, researching Scottish and Middle East politics and history. *Address:* 1 Danes Drive, Glasgow G14 9HZ.

**MÖST, Franz W.;** *see* Welser-Möst.

**MOSTESHAR, Prof. Sa'id;** barrister and attorney-at-law; Director, since 2008, and Professor of International Space Policy and Law (formerly Professor of International Space Law), since 2009, London Institute of Space Policy and Law; *b* Tehran, Iran; *s* of Mohammad Ali Mosteshar and Mahmonir Mosteshar. *Educ:* Univs of Southampton, London and Oxford; degrees and qualifications in physics, econometrics, law and accountancy. FCA 1972; MCIArb 2008; FRAeS 2013. Called to the Bar, Lincoln's Inn, 1975; admitted to State Bar of Calif and US Federal Bar, 1981; in practice as barrister: Chambers of Gerald Owen, QC, 1975–78; Chambers of Peter Whiteman, QC, 1978–82; Chambers of Sa'id Mosteshar, 1982–; on secondment: as Hd, Space Unit, Clifford Chance, 1986–88; as Chief Legal Officer and Actg CEO, Tachyon Inc., 2000–01. Prof. of Global Communications Policy, UCSD, 1995–2002; Sen. Associate Res. Fellow, Inst. of Advanced Legal Studies, London Univ., 2008–. Vis. Fellow, LLM Tutor, UCL, 1992–94. Advr to govts incl. UK and its Delegn, Legal Sub-cttee, Cttee on Peaceful Uses of Outer Space, UN, 2010–. Mem., UK Space Leadership Council, 2010–16. Mem., Editl Bd, Space Regulation Liby, 2010–. Distinguished Service Award, Internat. Inst. of Space Law, 2016. *Publications:* Company Taxation, 1983; Satellite and Cable Television: international protection, 1984, 2nd edn 1986; Satellite Communications, 1986; (contrib.) Encyclopaedia of Information Technology, 1990; European Community Telecommunications Regulation, 1993; Research and Invention in Outer Space: liability and intellectual property rights, 1995; (contrib.) Outlook on Space Law in the Next Thirty Years, 1997; (contrib.) Air and Space Law in the Twenty-first Century, 2001; (contrib.) National Regulation of Space Activities, 2010; (contrib.) Earth Observation Evidence and the Law, 2012; (contrib.) Commercialisation of Space, 2015; (contrib.) Small Satellites: chances and challenges, 2016; (contrib.) Handbook of Space Law, 2016; (contrib.) Oxford Research Encyclopaedia of Planetary Science, 2018; contribs to econometrics, accountancy and legal jls. *Address:* Charles Clore House, Russell Square, WC1A 5DR. *T:* (020) 7175 0550. *E:* SM@SpaceLaw.co.

**MOSTYN,** 7th Baron *cr* 1831, of Mostyn, co. Flint; **Gregory Philip Roger Lloyd Mostyn;** Bt 1778; *b* London, 31 Dec. 1984; *o s* of 6th Baron Mostyn and of Denise Suzanne (*née* Duvanel); *S* father, 2011. *Educ:* Durham Univ. (BA Hons Modern Hist. 2006); City Univ. (MSc Real Estate 2015). With Interac, 2007, Ladbrokes, 2008–09, Sportradar, 2009–10. *Recreations:* pool, chess, snooker, football. *Heir: cousin* Roger Hugh Lloyd Mostyn [*b* 1 Dec. 1941; *m* 1967, Mary Frances Elderton (marr. diss.); three *s*]. *Address:* Mostyn Hall, Holywell CH8 9HN. *T:* 07745 862941. *E:* lordmostyn@mostynestates.co.uk.

**MOSTYN, Hon. Sir Nicholas Anthony Joseph Ghislain,** Kt 2010; **Hon. Mr Justice Mostyn;** a Judge of the High Court of Justice, Family Division, since 2010; *b* 13 July 1957; *s* of Jerome John Joseph Mostyn and Mary Anna Bridget Mostyn (now Learoyd); *m* 1981, Lucy Joanna Willis (marr. diss. 2012); three *s* one *d*; *m* 2019, Elizabeth Anne Clarke. *Educ:* Ampleforth; Bristol Univ. (LLB). Called to the Bar, Middle Temple, 1980, Bencher, 2005; QC 1995; Asst Recorder, 1997–2000; Recorder, 2000–10; Dep. High Court Judge, 2000–10. *Publications:* Child's Pay, 1993, 3rd edn 2002; At a Glance, annually, 1992–; Financial Remedies Practice, annually, 2011–. *Recreations:* Wagner, Southampton FC, skiing. *Address:* Royal Courts of Justice, Strand, WC2A 2LL. *Club:* MCC.

**MOSTYN, Sir William Basil John,** 15th Bt *cr* 1670, of Talacre, Flintshire; *b* 15 Oct. 1975; *s* of Sir Jeremy John Anthony Mostyn, 14th Bt and of Cristina, *o d* of Marchese Orengo, Turin; *S* father, 1988; *m* 2009, Sejal Asar; two *s*. *Heir: s* Rohan Jeremy Mostyn, *b* 27 July 2010. *Address:* 76 Chelmsford Road, South Woodford, E18 2PP.

**MOTE, Ashley;** author; Member (UK Ind, then Ind) South East Region, European Parliament, 2004–09; *b* 25 Jan. 1936; *m* 1972, Anna-Nicola Goddard; one *s* one *d. Educ:* City of London Freemen's Sch. Army, 1954–56. Journalist, Picture Post, then Farmers' Weekly, 1956–61; communications specialist, 1961–68; Unilever, 1968–72; founder, internat. marketing co., 1972–90. Writer and broadcaster; columnist, Compass, 2004–07. Mem., Hambledon Club (Pres., 1998–2007). *Publications:* The Glory Days of Cricket: biography of Broadhalfpenny Down, 1998, 2nd edn 2014; (ed) John Nyren's The Cricketers of my Time - the original version, 1998; (jtly) The Winning Edge: the secrets and techniques of the world's best cricketers, 2001; Vigilance: a defence of British liberty, 2001; OverCrowded Britain: our immigration crisis exposed, 2003; J'Accuse…!, 2008; We Want Our Country Back, 2009; Light in Dark Places, 2010; A Mote in Brussels' Eye, 2013.

**MOTH, Rt Rev. (Charles Phillip) Richard;** *see* Arundel and Brighton, Bishop of, (RC).

**MOTHERWELL, Bishop of, (RC),** since 2014; **Rt Rev. Mgr Joseph Toal;** *b* Inverness, 13 Oct. 1956; *s* of Patrick Toal and Mary Toal (*née* MacInnes). *Educ:* Royal Scots Coll., Valladolid, Spain (STB 1980). Ordained priest, 1980; Asst Priest, St Peter's, Daliburgh, S Uist, 1980–83; Prof., St Mary's Coll., Blairs, Aberdeen, 1983–86; Parish Priest: St Michael's, S Uist, 1986–91; St Kieran's, Campbeltown, 1991–93; St Mary's, Benbecula, 1993–99; Spiritual Dir, Royal Scots Coll., Salamanca, 1999–2004; Rector, Salamanca, 2004–08; Bishop of Argyll and the Isles, (RC), 2008–14. *Address:* c/o Diocese of Motherwell, Coursington Road, Motherwell ML1 1PP.

**MOTHERWELL, Prof. William Branks,** PhD, DSc; FRS 2004; FRSE 2007; Alexander Williamson Professor of Chemistry (first incumbent), University College London, 1993–2012, now Emeritus; Visiting Researcher, Imperial College London, since 2012; *b* 10 May 1947; *s* of James Motherwell, BEM and Mary Motherwell (*née* Jarvie); *m* 1977, Dr Robyn Suzanne Hay; one *d. Educ:* Univ. of Glasgow (BSc 1st cl. 1969; PhD 1972; Carnegie Schol.); Univ. of London (DSc 1999). CChem; FRSC 1999. ICI Fellow, Univ. of Stirling, 1972–75; Schering-Plough Fellow, Imperial Coll., London, 1975–77; chargé de recherche, Inst. de Chimie des Substances Naturelles, CNRS, Gif-sur-Yvette, 1977–83; Lectr, 1983–90, Reader, 1990–93, Imperial Coll., London. Visiting Professor: Univ. of Paris, 1993; Univ. of Auckland, 1996; Université Bordeaux, 1998; Univ. of Rouen, 2002. Mem., Exec. Editl Bd, Tetrahedron, 1993–2013. Corday-Morgan Medal, 1983, Bader Award, 1991, Tilden Medal, 1999, Royal Soc. of Chemistry; Prix Franco-Britannique, French Chemical Soc., 2015. *Publications:* over 200 scientific papers in learned jls. *Recreations:* music, walking, golf. *Address:* Department of Chemistry, Christopher Ingold Laboratories, University College London, 20 Gordon Street, WC1H 0AJ. *T:* (020) 7679 7533. *E:* w.b.motherwell@ucl.ac.uk.

**MOTION, Sir Andrew,** Kt 2009; writer; Homewood Professor of the Arts, Johns Hopkins University, Baltimore, since 2015; Poet Laureate, 1999–2009; *b* 26 Oct. 1952; *s* of late Andrew Richard Motion and Catherine Gillian Motion; *m* 1st, 1973, Joanna Jane Powell (marr. diss. 1983); 2nd, 1985, Janet Elisabeth Dalley (marr. diss. 2009); two *s* one *d*; 3rd, 2010, Kyeong-Soo Kim. *Educ:* Radley Coll.; University Coll., Oxford (BA 1st Cl. Hons, MLitt; Hon. Fellow, 1999). Lectr in English, Univ. of Hull, 1977–81; Editor of Poetry Review, 1981–83; Poetry Editor, 1983–89, Editl Dir, 1985–87, Chatto & Windus; Prof. of Poetry, UEA, 1995–2003; Prof. of Creative Writing, RHUL, 2003–15. Mem., Arts Council of England, subseq. Arts Council England, 1996–99 (Chm., Literature Adv. Panel, 1996–2003); Chm., MLA, 2008–12. Co-founder and co-dir, Poetry Archive, 2005–. Pres., CPRE, 2012–15. FRSL 1982; FRSA 2000. Hon. Fellow, Homerton Coll., Cambridge, 2014. Hon. DLitt: Hull, 1996; Exeter, 1999; Brunel, 2000; Anglia, 2001; Sheffield Hallam, 2003; Sheffield, 2005; Aberdeen, 2006; Chester 2008; Robert Gordon, Aberdeen, 2009; Durham, 2018; DUniv Open, 2002. *Publications: poetry:* The Pleasure Steamers, 1978, 4th edn 1999; Independence, 1981; The Penguin Book of Contemporary British Poetry (anthology), 1982; Secret Narratives, 1983; Dangerous Play, 1984 (Rhys Meml Prize); Natural Causes, 1987 (Dylan Thomas Award); Love in a Life, 1991; The Price of Everything, 1994; Salt Water, 1997; Selected Poems, 1998; Public Property, 2002; The Cinder Path, 2009; The Customs House, 2012 (Wilfred Owen Prize, 2014); Peace Talks, 2015 (Ted Hughes Award); Essex Clay, 2018; *criticism:* The Poetry of Edward Thomas, 1981; Philip Larkin, 1982; (ed) William Barnes: selected poems, 1994; Thomas Hardy: selected poems, 1994; Ways of Life: on places, painters and poets, 2008; *biography:* The Lamberts, 1986 (Somerset Maugham Award, 1987); Philip Larkin: a writer's life, 1993 (Whitbread Award, 1993); Keats, 1997; Wainewright the Poisoner, 2000; In the Blood (autobiog.), 2006; *novels:* The Pale Companion, 1989; Famous for the Creatures, 1991; The Invention of Dr Cake, 2003; Silver: return to Treasure Island, 2012; The New World, 2014. *Address:* c/o Faber & Faber, Bloomsbury House, 74–77 Great Russell Street, WC1B 3DA.

**MOTO, Dr Francis;** Ambassador of Malaŵi to Brazil, 2010–15; *b* 28 Feb. 1952; *s* of Bwanali and Rufina Moto; *m* 1982, Elizabeth Inglis; two *s* one *d* (and one *s* decd). *Educ:* Univ. of Malaŵi (DipEd; BEd); SOAS, Univ. of London (MA); PhD University Coll. London 1989. Chancellor College, University of Malaŵi: Staff associate, 1977–80; Lectr, 1980–90; Sen. Lectr, 1990–99; Associate Prof., 1999–2006; Hd of Dept and Dean of Faculty, 1985–2006; Vice Principal, 1994–98, Principal, 1998–2005, Univ. of Malaŵi; High Comr to UK and Republic of Ireland, 2006–10. Mem. Bd, Malawi Privatisation Commn, 2003–05. Chm., Women and Law in Southern Africa (Trustee, Regl Bd), 1998–2005. Mem. Bd, Malawi Inst. of Educn, 1998–2005. Chm., Malawi Nat. Day of Educn, 2000–04. Malaŵi Govt Scholarship Award, 1972, 1978; Commonwealth Scholarship Award, 1986. *Publications:* Nzeru Umati Zako Nzokuuza, 1987; Gazing at the Setting Sun, 1994; Trends in Malawian Literature, 2001; Topics in Language, Power and Society, 2007; contribs to Studies in African Linguistics, Jl Contemporary African Studies, Jl Humanities, Jl Social Sci., Nordic Jl African Studies. *Recreations:* football, golf, lawn tennis, squash, dancing, table tennis. *Clubs:* Gymkhana (Zomba); Blantyre Sports; Lilongwe Golf, Limbe Country.

**MOTSON, John Walker,** OBE 2001; BBC TV Sports Commentator, 1971–2018; *b* 10 July 1945; *s* of late William and Gwendoline Motson; *m* 1976, Anne Jobling; one *s. Educ:* Culford Sch., Bury St Edmunds. Barnet Press, 1963–67; Morning Telegraph, Sheffield, 1967–68; BBC Radio Sport, 1968–71 and 2001–18; BBC TV Sport, 1971–2018; talkSPORT, 2018–. Commentator: 29 FA Cup Finals, 1977–2008; 8 World Cup Final Series, including 6 Finals, 1974–2006; 8 European Championships, 1976–2008. Commentator of the Year, RTS, 2004; Special Award, BAFTA, 2018. *Publications:* Second to None: great teams of post-war soccer, 1972; (with J. Rowlinson) History of the European Cup, 1980; Motty's Diary: a year in the life of a commentator, 1986; Match of the Day: the complete record, 1992, 1994; Motty's Year, 2004; Motson's National Obsession, 2004; Motson's FA Cup Odyssey, 2005; Motson's World Cup Extravaganza, 2006; Motty: 40 years in the commentary box (autobiog.), 2009; World Cup Motty, 2018. *Recreation:* running half-marathons. *Address:* c/o Jane Morgan Management, Argentum, 2 Queen Caroline Street, W6 9DX. *T:* (020) 3178 8071. *Club:* Cricketers'.

**MOTT, Sir David Hugh,** 4th Bt *cr* 1930, of Ditchling, co. Sussex; *b* 1 May 1952; *o s* of Sir John Harmar Mott, 3rd Bt and Elizabeth Mott (*née* Carson); *S* father, 2015; *m* 1st, 1980, Amanda Jane (marr. diss. 2007), *d* of Lt-Comdr D. W. P. Fryer, RN; two *s*; 2nd, 2013, Vivian Nanzhou Yuan, *d* of Chen Shangren. *Educ:* Univ. of London (PhD Artificial Intelligence). *Heir: s* Matthew David Mott, *b* 13 March 1982.

**MOTT, John Charles Spencer,** FREng; Chairman, William Sindall plc, 1990–94 (Director, 1989–94); *b* Beckenham, Kent, 18 Dec. 1926; *m* 1953, Patricia Mary (*née* Fowler); two *s. Educ:* Balgowan Central Sch., Beckenham, Kent; Brixton Sch. of Building; Battersea Polytechnic; Rutherford Coll. of Technology, Newcastle upon Tyne; Wolfson Coll., Cambridge (BA English 1999; MA English 2004). FICE, FIStructE. Served war, Lieut, Royal Marines, 1943–46. Indentured as Engr with L. G. Mouchel & Partners, 1949–52; joined Kier Ltd, 1952; Agent on heavy civil engrg contracts, 1952–63; Chairman: French Kier Holdings plc, 1974–86 (Dir, on merger, 1973, Chief Exec., 1974–84); May Gurney Hldgs Ltd, 1986–89. Director: Kier Ltd, 1963; J. L. Kier & Co. Ltd (Holding Co.), 1968; RMC plc, 1986–94. Mem. Council, Fellowship of Engrg, 1983–86; Mem. Council, 1973–75, 1986–87, and Vice Pres., 1986–87, ICE; Mem., Bragg Cttee on Falsework, 1972–74. *Club:* Danish.

**MOTT, Prof. Martin Gerard,** FRCP, FRCPCH; Cancer and Leukemia in Children Professor of Paediatric Oncology, 1990–2000, now Emeritus, and Dean of Clinical Medicine and Dentistry, 1997–2000, University of Bristol; *b* 30 Nov. 1941; *s* of Mervyn Gerard Mott and Frances Emily Davis; *m* 1964, Patricia Anne Green; one *s* two *d. Educ:* Wimbledon Coll.; Univ. of Bristol (BSc 1963; MB ChB 1966; DSc 1991). FRCP 1983; FRCPCH 1996. Research Fellow, Univ. of Texas (M. D. Anderson Hosp.), 1972; Vis. Asst

Prof., Stanford Univ., 1974–76; Sen. Lectr, then Reader, Univ. of Bristol, 1976–90. Founder Mem., UK Children's Cancer Study Gp, 1977–. International Society of Paediatric Oncology: Hon. Sec., 1979–82; Pres., Eur. Continental Branch, 1999–2000; Mem., GMC, 1999–2000. *Publications:* numerous contribs to learned jls on topics relating to childhood cancer. *Recreations:* music, ornithology. *Address:* 6 Wyecliffe Road, Henleaze, Bristol BS9 4NH. *T:* (0117) 962 1476.

**MOTT, His Honour Michael Duncan;** a Circuit Judge, 1985–2006; a Deputy Circuit Judge, 2006–12; *b* 8 Dec. 1940; *s* of late Francis J. Mott and Gwendolen Mott; *m* 1970, Phyllis Ann Gavin; two *s. Educ:* Rugby Sch.; Caius Coll., Cambridge (Exhibnr, MA). Called to Bar, Inner Temple, 1963; practised Midland and Oxford Circuit, 1964–69; Resident Magistrate, Kenya, 1969–71; resumed practice, Midland and Oxford Circuit, 1972; a Deputy Circuit Judge, 1976–80; a Recorder, 1980–85. *Recreations:* golf, travel, music, helping in the village shop. *Club:* Cambridge Union Society.

**MOTT, Philip Charles;** QC 1991; a Recorder of the Crown Court, since 1987; a Deputy High Court Judge, since 1998; *b* 20 April 1948; *s* of Charles Kynaston Mott and Elsie (*née* Smith); *m* 1977, Penelope Ann Caffery (marr. diss. 2011); two *d. Educ:* King's Coll., Taunton; Worcester Coll., Oxford (MA). Called to the Bar, Inner Temple, 1970, Bencher, 2006; in practice on Western Circuit, 1970–, Leader, 2004–07. Chm., Mental Health Review Tribunal (Restricted Patients Panel), 2000–16. Bar Council: Member: Legal Services Cttee, 2004–05; Advocacy Trng Council, 2004–12; Carter Response Gp, 2005–07; Bar Policy and Research Group: Vice-Chm., 2006; Mem., Gen. Mgt Cttee, 2007–08. *Recreations:* the countryside, growing trees, sailing. *Address:* Outer Temple Chambers, 222 Strand, WC2R 1BA. *T:* (020) 7353 6381. *Clubs:* Bar Yacht, Perculi Sailing.

**MOTTELSON, Prof. Ben R.,** PhD; Danish physicist; Professor, Nordic Institute for Theoretical Atomic Physics, Copenhagen, 1957, now Emeritus; *b* Chicago, Ill, USA, 9 July 1926; *s* of Goodman Mottelson and Georgia Mottelson (*née* Blum); became a Danish citizen, 1971; *m* 1948, Nancy Jane Reno (*d* 1975); two *s* one *d*; *m* 1983, Britta Marger Siegumfeldt. *Educ:* High Sch., La Grange, Ill; Purdue Univ. (officers' trng, USN, V12 program; BSc 1947); Harvard Univ. (grad. studies, PhD 1950). Sheldon Trav. Fellowship from Harvard at Inst. of Theoretical Physics, Copenhagen (later, the Niels Bohr Inst.), 1950–51. His Fellowship from US Atomic Energy Commn permitted continuation of work in Copenhagen for two more years, after which he held research position in CERN (European Organization for Nuclear Research) theoretical study group, formed in Copenhagen. Visiting Prof., Univ. of Calif at Berkeley, Spring term, 1959. Mem., Royal Danish Acad. of Scis and Letters, 1958. Nobel Prize for Physics (jtly), 1975; awarded for work on theory of Atomic Nucleus, with Dr Aage Bohr (3 papers publ. 1952–53). *Publications:* Nuclear Structure, vol. I, 1969; vol. II, 1975 (with A. Bohr); (jtly) The Principle Behind Quantum Mechanics, 2004; contrib. Rev. Mod. Phys (jt), etc. *Address:* Nordisk Institut for Teoretisk Fysik, Blegdamsvej 17, 2100 Copenhagen, Denmark.

**MOTTISTONE,** 6th Baron *cr* 1933, of Mottistone, Southampton; **Christopher David Peter Seely;** *b* 1 Oct. 1974; *s* of 5th Baron Mottistone and Joyce Seely (*née* Cairns); *S* father, 2013. *Heir:* half-*b* Hon. Richard William Anthony Seely, *b* 1988.

**MOTTRAM, Lesley Anne;** a District Judge (Magistrates' Courts), since 2005; *b* 3 May 1952; *d* of Fred and Peggy Pugh; *m* 1981, Michael Martin; one *s. Educ:* Priory Sch. for Girls, Shrewsbury; LLB Hons. Admitted solicitor, 1976; solicitor, specialising in criminal advocacy, West Midlands, 1977–2005. *Address:* Coventry Magistrates' Court, Little Park Street, Coventry CV1 2SQ. *T:* (024) 7650 0666.

**MOTTRAM, Sir Richard (Clive),** GCB 2006 (KCB 1998); Chairman, Amey plc, 2008–17; *b* 23 April 1946; *s* of John Mottram and Florence Yates; *m* 1971, Fiona Margaret Erskine; three *s* one *d. Educ:* King Edward VI Camp Hill Sch., Birmingham; Univ. of Keele (1st Cl. Hons Internat. Relns). Entered Home Civil Service, 1968, assigned to Ministry of Defence: Asst Private Sec. to Sec. of State for Defence, 1971–72; Cabinet Office, 1975–77; Ministry of Defence: Private Sec. to Perm. Under Sec., 1979–81; Private Sec. to Sec. of State for Defence, 1982–86; Asst Under Sec. of State, 1986–89; Dep. Under Sec. of State (Policy), 1989–92; Permanent Secretary: Office of Public Service and Sci., 1992–95; MoD, 1995–98; DETR, then DTLR, 1998–2002; DWP, 2002–05; Perm. Sec., Intelligence, Security and Resilience, and Chm., Jt Intelligence Cttee, Cabinet Office, 2005–07; Chm., DSTL, 2008–14. Pres., Commonwealth Assoc. for Public Admin and Mgt, 2000–02. Mem. Internat. Adv. Bd, Garda World, 2008–15. Vis. Prof., LSE, 2008–. Governor: Ditchley Foundn, 1996–2019 (Vice Chm., Council of Mgt, 2010–13; Hon. Gov., 2019); Ashridge Business Sch. (formerly Ashridge Mgt Coll.), 1998–2015. Trustee, Royal Anniversary Trust, 2010–. AcSS 2000. Hon. DLitt Keele, 1996. *Recreations:* cinema, theatre. *E:* rcmottram@googlemail.com.

**MOTTRAM, Toby Trevor Fury,** PhD; CEng, FREng; engineer and inventor of robotic milking, rumen telemetry and automated cow fertility management; Founder and Managing Director, eCow Ltd, since 2007; Founder and Chief Technology Officer, Milkalyser Ltd, since 2016; *b* Honiton, Devon, 12 Feb. 1952; *s* of Kenneth Mottram and Mary Fury Mottram; *m* 1st, 1971, Penny Jenkins (marr. diss. 2010); one *s* two *d*; 2nd, 2016, Catherine Hendrick (marr. diss. 2018). *Educ:* Barony Coll., Dumfries (Agricl Apprenticeship 1975); Open Univ. (BA Hons 1st Cl. Agric. and Engrg 1986; BSc Software Develt and eCommerce 2014); Silsoe Coll., Cranfield Inst. of Technol. (MSc Agricl Machinery Engrg 1987; PhD Automation of Milking 1992). CEng 1993; FIAgrE 2015. Proj. Leader (Sen. Scientist), 1989–98, Proj. Leader (Principal Scientist), Bio-Engrg Div., 1998–2005, Silsoe Res. Inst.; Prog. Manager for Condition Based Monitoring, 2005–07, Tech. Authority, Scottish Enterprise, 2007–09, ITITechmedia Ltd; Coordinator, Agricl Greenhouse Gas R&D projects, DEFRA, 2010–13; Douglas Bomford Trust Prof. in Farm Mechanisation, RAU, Cirencester, 2012–17. BBSRC/RSE Enterprise Fellow, 2015–16. Member: British Soc. of Animal Sci.; Royal Assoc. of British Dairy Farmers. FREng 2016. *Publications:* (contrib.) Quantitative Aspects of Ruminant Digestion and Metabolism, 2nd edn 2005; over 50 articles in jls. *Recreations:* walking the pilgrim routes of Europe, sailing, following Exeter Chiefs. *Address:* c/o Milkalyser Ltd, Science Park Centre, Babbage Way, Clyst Honiton, Exeter EX5 2FN. *E:* toby@milkalyser.com. *Club:* Lympstone Sailing (Exmouth).

**MOULD, Christopher Peter;** Chief Executive Officer, FSCI (UK), since 2017; Partner, Shaftesbury Partnership Ltd, since 2010; *b* Fareham, Hants, 30 Nov. 1958; *s* of Peter Sidney Mould and Phyllida Mould (*née* Ormond); *m* 1979, Angela Geraldine Druce; four *d. Educ:* Royal Grammar Sch., High Wycombe; Magdalen Coll., Oxford (BA Modern Hist.); London Sch. of Econs and Pol Sci. (MSc Social Policy and Planning in Developing Countries (Dist.)). DipHSM. Fund raiser, City of London, LEPRA, 1981–82; Planning Asst, NE Thames RHA, 1982–83; Hd, Planning and Information, 1983–85, Asst Dist Gen. Manager, 1985–86, Southend HA; Hosp. Manager, Southend Hosp., Essex, 1986–88; Unit Gen. Manager, then Chief Exec., S Beds Community Health Services NHS Trust, 1988–92; Dist Gen. Manager, Salisbury HA, and Chief Exec., Salisbury Health Care NHS Trust, 1992–2001; on secondment as Prog. Dir for Strategic Change in Wilts and Swindon, then Interim Dir of Educn and Trng, NHS Exec. SW, 1998–99; Chief Exec., Centrex, Central Police Trng and Develt Authy, 2001–03; ind. consultant in transformation and strategic change, 2004–10; Exec. Dir, 2007–11, Exec. Chm., 2011–14, Trussell Trust (Trustee, 2004–17; Chm., 2004–16). Chm., Healthwork UK, Health Care Nat. Trng Orgn, 1998–2001. Founder and Chm., Foundn for Social Change and Inclusion, 2008–; non-exec. Chm., Franchising Works, 2010–; Chm., Evidence to Impact, 2018–. *Recreations:* long-distance running, mountaineering, conference speaking, Christian preaching. *Address:* 96 Harnham Road, Salisbury, Wilts SP2 8JW. *T:* (01722) 333937, 07881 624887. *E:* chris@chrismould.co.uk.

**MOULD, Philip Jonathan Clifford,** OBE 2005; art dealer, writer, broadcaster and conservationist; Director, Philip Mould & Co. (formerly Historical Portraits Ltd), since 1987; *b* Clatterbridge, Cheshire; *s* of Anthony Mould and Catherine Mould; *m* 2004, Catherine Mary Morgan; one *s. Educ:* Kingsmead Sch., Hoylake; Worth Abbey Sch., Crawley; Univ. of East Anglia (BA Hons). Works of Art Advr, H of C and H of L, 1988–2011. Television work includes: writer and presenter, Changing Faces, 1988; an expert, Antiques Roadshow, 2008–; co-presenter, Fake or Fortune, 2011–. Pres., Kids in Museums, 2016– (Chm., 2011–14); Mem., English Heritage Blue Plaques Panel, 2014–; Trustee, English Heritage Trust, 2011–. Pres., Plantlife, 2010– (Chm., Trustees, 2002–07). Patron, Fight for Sight, 2010–. FLS 2011. Hon. DLitt UEA, 2013. *Publications:* Sleepers: in search of lost old masters, 1995; Sleuth: the amazing quest for lost art treasures, 2009. *Recreations:* tennis, un-cleaned pictures, fishing, shooting, ancient meadows. *Address:* Philip Mould & Co., 18–19 Pall Mall, SW1Y 5LU. *T:* (020) 7499 6818. *E:* art@philipmould.com. *Clubs:* Garrick, Buck's.

**MOULD, Timothy James;** QC 2006; barrister; a Deputy High Court Judge, since 2018; *b* 22 May 1960; *s* of John and Dorothy Mould; partner, Debbie Field; one *s* one *d. Educ:* Blueboys Sch., Minchinhampton; Wycliffe Coll. Jun. Sch.; Rugby Sch.; Queen's Coll., Oxford (BA Hons Lit. Hum. 1982); Poly. of Central London (Dip. Law 1986). Called to the Bar, Gray's Inn, 1987, Bencher; in practice as a barrister, 1987–, specialising in planning and administrative law. *Publications:* (ed) Encyclopedia of Rating and Local Taxation, 2007. *Recreations:* music, cricket, keeping calm, travel, food and wine in Italy. *Address:* Landmark Chambers, 180 Fleet Street, EC4A 2HG. *T:* (020) 7430 1221. *E:* tmould@landmarkchambers.co.uk.

**MOULDEN, Peter Ronald;** a Judge of the Upper Tribunal (Immigration and Asylum Chamber) (formerly a Vice President, Immigration Appeal Tribunal, later a Senior Immigration Judge, Asylum and Immigration Tribunal), 2000–15; Resident Senior Immigration Judge, Field House, London, 2006–10; *b* 31 Jan. 1945; *s* of Ronald Charles and Kathleen Norah Bell Moulden; *m* 1970, Elaine Williams; one *s* one *d. Educ:* Cranleigh Sch. In practice as solicitor, 1969–99; Adjudicator, Immigration Appeal Tribunal, 1999–2000. Craft-owning Freeman, Co. of Watermen and Lightermen, 2006. *Recreation:* history and biography. *Club:* Savile.

**MOULE, John Stuart;** Warden, Radley College, since 2014; *b* Shrewsbury, 29 May 1971; *s* of Barry and Sheila Moule; *m* 1993, Diana; one *s* two *d. Educ:* Orleton Park Comprehensive Sch.; Telford New Coll.; Lady Margaret Hall, Oxford (BA 1st Cl. Hons Hist.). Teacher, Dean Close Sch., Cheltenham, 1993–98; Hd of Hist., 1998–2000, House Master, Walpole, 2000–05, Stowe Sch.; Vice Master, 2006–08, Head Master, 2008–14, Bedford Sch. *Recreations:* theology, political biography, P. G. Wodehouse, armchair sports viewing, theatre. *Address:* Radley College, Abingdon, Oxon OX14 2HR. *Club:* East India.

**MOULTON, Jonathan Paul;** Chairman, Better Capital GP and 12 GP Ltd, since 2009; *b* 15 Oct. 1950; *s* of Cecil Moulton and Elsie Moulton (*née* Pointon); *m* 1974, Pauline Dunn; one *s* one *d. Educ:* Univ. of Lancaster (BA Chem.). FCA 1977. Coopers & Lybrand: Manager, Liverpool, 1972–78; Manager in M&A gp, NY, 1978–80; Citicorp Venture Capital: NY, 1980–81; Man. Dir, London, 1981–85 (Mem., French and German Investment Cttees); Founder and Managing Partner, Schroder Ventures, London, 1985–94 (Mem., French and German Investment Cttees); Dir in Charge of Leveraged Buy-outs, Apax Partners, London, 1994–97 (Mem., Internat. Operating Cttee); Founder and Man. Partner, Alchemy Partners LLP, 1997–2009. Chm., Internat. Stock Exchange (formerly CI Securities Exchange), 2013–; non-executive Chairman: finnCap, 2009–; AMR Centre. Mem., Regl Growth Fund, 2011–. Founder, J P Moulton Charitable Foundn, 2004. Trustee, UK Stem Cell Foundn, 2005–. Fellow, Soc. of Turnaround Professionals, 2000. *Recreations:* tennis, bridge, chess.

**MOUND, Laurence Alfred,** DSc; FRES; Hon. Research Fellow, CSIRO Australian National Insect Collection (formerly Division of Entomology, Commonwealth Scientific and Industrial Research Organisation, then CSIRO Entomology, later CSIRO Ecosystem Sciences), since 1996; Research Associate, Natural History Museum (formerly British Museum (Natural History)), since 1992 (Keeper of Entomology, 1981–92); *b* 22 April 1934; *s* of John Henry Mound and Laura May Cape; *m* 1st, 1958, Agnes Jean Solari (marr. diss. 1985); one *s* two *d*; 2nd, 1987, Sheila Helen Halsey (marr. diss. 1994); 3rd, 2004, Alice Wells. *Educ:* Warwick Sch.; Sir John Cass Coll., London; Imperial Coll., London (DIC); DSc London; Imperial Coll. of Tropical Agriculture, Trinidad (DipTA). Nigerian Federal Dept of Agricl Research, 1959–61; Rockefeller Studentship, Washington and Calif, 1961; Empire Cotton Growing Corp., Republic of Sudan, 1961–64; Sen. Scientific Officer, BM (NH), 1964–69; Australian CSIRO Research Award, 1967–68; PSO, 1969–75, Dep. Keeper, Dept of Entomology, BM (NH), 1975–81. Sec., 1976–88, Vice-Chm., 1988–92, Council for Internat. Congresses of Entomology; Consultant Dir, Commonwealth Inst. of Entomology, 1981–92. Hon. Prof., Sch. of Pure and Applied Biology, Univ. of Wales at Cardiff, 1990–96; McMaster Res. Fellow, CSIRO, 1995–96. Editor, Jl of Royal Entomological Soc. of London, 1973–81 (Vice-Pres., RES, 1975–76). Numerous expedns studying thrips in tropical countries. *Publications:* over 420 technical books and papers on biology of thrips and whitefly, incl. Whitefly of the World (with S. H. Halsey), Thrips of Central and South America (with R. Marullo), and Evolution of Ecological and Behavioural Diversity (with B. Crespi and D. Morris). *Recreation:* thrips with everything. *Address:* c/o CSIRO Australian National Insect Collection, GPO Box 1700, Canberra, ACT 2601, Australia. *T:* (2) 62464280, *Fax:* (2) 62464264. *E:* laurence.mound@csiro.au.

**MOUNSTEPHEN, Rt Rev. Philip Ian;** see Truro, Bishop of.

**MOUNT, Ferdinand;** see Mount, W. R. F.

**MOUNT, Harry Francis Gregory;** Editor, The Oldie magazine, since 2017; *b* London, 2 Sept. 1971; *s* of (William Robert) Ferdinand Mount, *qv. Educ:* Westminster Sch.; Magdalen Coll., Oxford (MA); Courtauld Inst. (MA). Called to the Bar, Middle Temple, 1998. Leader Writer and NY corresp., Daily Telegraph, 2000–06; contributor, Daily Mail, Spectator, Sunday Times and TLS, 2006–. *Publications:* (ed) Auberon Waugh: closing the circle, 2001; My Brief Career, 2004; Amo, Amas, Amat and All That, 2006; Carpe Diem: put a little Latin in your life, 2007; A Lust for Window Sills, 2008; How England Made the English, 2012; (ed) The Wit and Wisdom of Boris Johnson, 2013; The King and I: how Elvis shaped my life, 2013; Harry Mount's Odyssey: Ancient Greece in the footsteps of

Odysseus, 2015; Summer Madness: how Brexit split the Tories, destroyed Labour and divided the country, 2017. *Recreations:* bicycling, newspapers and magazines, church-crawling. *Address:* 62 Caversham Road, NW5 2DS. E: harry.mount@hotmail.co.uk. *Clubs:* Academy, Beefsteak.

**MOUNT, Peter William,** CBE 2007; CEng; Chairman, Central Manchester and Manchester Children's University Hospitals NHS Trust, 2001–14; *b* 14 Jan. 1940; *s* of William J. and Bridie Mount; *m* Margery; three *c*. *Educ:* De La Salle Sch., Manchester; UMIST (BSc Tech); Univ. of Vienna (short prog.). MIMechE. Prodn Engr, Rolls Royce Ltd, 1961–66; Mgt Consultant, PricewaterhouseCoopers, 1966–72; Project Dir, Chloride Industrial Batteries, 1972–78; Man. Dir, Chloride Ireland, 1978–81; various Bd appts then CEO, Thorn EMI Fire Protection Ltd and Dir, Thorn Security Ltd, 1984–93. Chairman: Salford Royal Hosps NHS Trust, 1983–2001; Greater Manchester NHS Workforce, 1993–2004; NHS Confederation, 2003–07. Member: Audit Cttee, DoH, 2002–08; Bd, Sector Skills Develt Agency, 2002–06 (Chm., Audit Cttee, 2002–06). Dep. Chm., Oldham TEC, 1987–93. Mem. Court, subseq. Gen. Assembly, Univ. of Manchester, 1995–. Founder and Chm. Trustees, charity working with Uganda schs. Co-holder of patent relating to gold processing. RHS Award, 1990. *Publications:* (jtly) Absenteeism in Industry, 1980. *Recreations:* walking, ski-ing, cars, computers, making and fixing things, music, good food, taking grandchildren for walks in the park. *Address:* 6 The Ceal, Compstall, Stockport, Cheshire SK6 5LQ. T: (0161) 427 4260. E: pwmount@me.com.

**MOUNT, (William Robert) Ferdinand,** (3rd Bt *cr* 1921, of Wasing Place, Reading, Berks, but does not use the title); author and journalist; Editor, Times Literary Supplement, 1991–2002; *b* 2 July 1939; *s* of Robert Francis Mount (*d* 1969), 2nd *s* of Sir William Arthur Mount, 1st Bt, CBE and his 1st wife, Lady Julia Pakenham (*d* 1956), *d* of 5th Earl of Longford; *S* uncle, 1993; *m* 1968, Julia Margaret, *d* of late Archibald Julian and Hon. Mrs Lucas; two *s* one *d* (and one *s* decd). *Educ:* Eton; Christ Church, Oxford. Has worked for Sunday Telegraph, Conservative Research Dept, Daily Sketch, National Review, Daily Mail, The Times; Political Columnist: The Spectator, 1977–82 and 1985–87; The Standard, 1980–82; Daily Telegraph, 1984–90; Sunday Times, 1997–2004; Head of Prime Minister's Policy Unit, 1982–83. Vice-Chm., Power Commn, 2005–06. Chm., Friends of British Liby, 2013–. FRSL 1991 (Mem. Council, 2002–05); FSA 2009. *Publications:* Very Like a Whale, 1967; The Theatre of Politics, 1972; The Man Who Rode Ampersand, 1975; The Clique, 1978; The Subversive Family, 1982; The Selkirk Strip, 1987; Of Love and Asthma, 1991 (Hawthornden Prize, 1992); The British Constitution Now, 1992; Umbrella, 1994; The Liquidator, 1995; Jem (and Sam): a revenger's tale, 1998; Fairness, 2001; Mind the Gap, 2004; Heads You Win, 2004; The Condor's Head, 2007; Cold Cream: my early life and other mistakes, 2008; Full Circle: how the classical world came back to us, 2010; The New Few: or a very British oligarchy, 2012; The Tears of the Rajas: mutiny, money and marriage in India 1805–1905, 2015; English Voices: lives, landscapes, laments, 2016; Prime Movers: from Pericles to Gandhi, 2018. *Heir: s* William Robert Horatio Mount [*b* 12 May 1969; *m* 1997, Deborah Grey; two *s*]. *Address:* 17 Ripplevale Grove, N1 1HS. T: (020) 7607 5398.
*See also* H. F. G. Mount.

**MOUNT CHARLES, Earl of;** Alexander Burton Conyngham; Director, Slane Castle Irish Whiskey Ltd, since 2009; *b* 30 Jan. 1975; *s* and *heir* of Marquess Conyngham, *qv*; *m* 2007, Carina Suzanne, *d* of late Nicholas George Bolton; two *s* one *d*. *Educ:* Trinity Coll., Dublin (BA History of Art 1997); Univ. of Cape Town (MBA 2005). Pernod Ricard; Christie's. *Heir: s* Viscount Slane, *qv*. *Address:* Slane Castle, Co. Meath, Eire.

**MOUNT EDGCUMBE, 8th Earl of,** *cr* 1789; **Robert Charles Edgcumbe;** Baron Edgcumbe, 1742; Viscount Mount Edgcumbe and Valletort, 1781; Farm Manager, for Lands and Survey, New Zealand, 1975–84; *b* 1 June 1939; *s* of George Aubrey Valletort Edgcumbe (*d* 1977) and of Meta Blucher, *d* of late Robert Charles Lhoyer; *S* uncle, 1982; *m* 1st, 1960, Joan Ivy Wall (marr. diss. 1988); five *d*; 2nd, 2017, Beryl Joyce Cottrell. *Educ:* Nelson College. Career from farm worker to farm manager, managing first farm, 1960; taking up family seat in Cornwall, 1984. *Recreations:* hunting game, restoring classic cars. *Heir:* half-*b* Piers Valletort Edgcumbe [*b* 23 Oct. 1946; *m* 1971, Hilda Warn (marr. diss.); two *d*]. *Address:* Empacombe House, Cremyll, Cornwall PL10 1HZ.

**MOUNTAIN, Sir Edward (Brian Stanford),** 4th Bt *cr* 1922, of Oare Manor, Co. Somerset, and Brendon, Co. Devon; Member (C) Highlands and Islands, Scottish Parliament, since 2016; *b* 19 March 1961; *er s* of Sir Denis Mortimer Mountain, 3rd Bt and Hélène Fleur Mary Mountain (*née* Kirwan-Taylor); *S* father, 2005; *m* 1987, Charlotte Sarah Jesson, *d* of His Honour Henry Pownall, QC; two *s* one *d*. *Educ:* King's School, Bruton; RMA Sandhurst; Sparshott Coll. (Dip. Farm Mgt); RAC, Cirencester (BSc Rural Land Mgt 1995). Commnd Army, 1981, Blues and Royals; Captain, 1983; Major, 1991. Joined Bidwells, 1995. Contested (C): Caithness, Sutherland and Ross, Scottish Parlt, 2011; Inverness, Nairn, Badenoch and Strathspey, 2015. *Recreations:* shooting, fishing. *Heir: s* Thomas Denis Edward Mountain, *b* 14 Aug. 1989. *Address:* Delfur Lodge, Orton, Morayshire IV32 7QQ. T: (01542) 860374.

**MOUNTBATTEN,** family name of **Marquess of Milford Haven.**

**MOUNTBATTEN OF BURMA, 3rd Earl** *cr* 1947; **Norton Louis Philip Knatchbull;** Bt 1641; Baron Brabourne *cr* 1880; Viscount Mountbatten of Burma, 1946; Baron Romsey, 1947; *b* 8 Oct. 1947; *s* of 7th Baron Brabourne, CBE and Countess (2nd in line) Mountbatten of Burma, CBE, CD; *S* father, 2005, and mother, 2017; *m* 1979, Penelope M. M. Eastwood; one *s* one *d* (and one *d* decd). *Educ:* Dragon School, Oxford; Gordonstoun; University of Kent (BA Politics). *Heir: s* Lord Brabourne, *qv*. *Address:* Broadlands, Romsey, Hants SO51 9ZD.

**MOUNTEVANS, 4th Baron** *cr* 1945, of Chelsea; **Jeffrey Richard de Corban Evans;** Lord Mayor of London, 2015–16; *b* Gothenburg, Sweden, 13 May 1948; *yr s* of 2nd Baron Mountevans and Deirdre Grace (*d* 1997), *d* of John O'Connell, Cork; *S* brother, 2014; *m* 1972, Hon. Juliet, *d* of 2nd Baron Moran, KCMG; two *s*. *Educ:* Nautical Coll., Pangbourne; Pembroke Coll., Cambridge (BA Econs 1971). H. Clarkson & Co., later Clarkson Platou: shipbroker, 1972–2017; tanker broker, 1972–79; Gas Div., 1979–2000; Dir, 1989; Hd, Gas and Specialized Tankers, 2000–01; Man. Dir, Gas, 2001–14. Director: Maritime London, 2011– (Chm., 2013–); Maritime UK, 2017– (Chm., 2014–15). Chm., Maritime Growth Study, 2015. Pres., Inst. of Chartered Shipbrokers, 2018–. Elected Mem., H of L, 2015. Mem. Council, White Ensign Assoc., 2003–; Trustee: Seafarers UK (King George's Fund for Sailors), 2011–; Mansion House Scholarship Scheme, 2011–; St Paul's Cathedral Chorister Trust, 2013–18; President: City of London Sea Cadet Corps, 2007–; Captain Scott Soc., Cardiff, 2017–; Hon. Pres., Canning House, 2018–. Magistrate, Central London Bench, 2007–14. Gov., City of London Acad., Islington, 2008–16; Almoner, Christ's Hospital Sch., 2010–18. Church Warden, St Lawrence Jewry next Guildhall, 2009–18. Alderman, Ward of Cheap, City of London, 2007–18; Sheriff, City of London, 2012–13. Liveryman: Shipwrights' Co., 1979– (Prime Warden, 2006–07); World Traders' Co., 2010–; Goldsmiths' Co., 2012–; Wheelwrights' Co., 2013–; Security Professionals' Co., 2014–. KStJ 2015. Hon. Capt., RNR, 2017–. Younger Brother, Trinity House, 2014–. Hon. Dr Maritime Sci., City, 2015; Hon. Dr Maritime Business, Korea Maritime and Ocean Univ., 2016. *Recreations:* matters maritime, cross-country ski-ing, Antarctic exploration, Scandinavia, France. *Heir: s* Hon. Alexander Richard Andvord Evans [*b* 23 July 1975; *m* 2007, Emma Williams]. *Address:* House of Lords, SW1A 0PW. *Club:* Ward of Cheap (Patron, 2007–).

**MOUNTFIELD, Helen;** QC 2010; a Recorder, since 2010; a Deputy High Court Judge, since 2013; Principal, Mansfield College, Oxford, since 2018; *b* London, 14 March 1967; *d* of Sir Robin Mountfield, KCB and of Anne Mountfield; *m* 2005, Dr Damian Tambini; three *d*. *Educ:* Crown Woods Comp. Sch.; Magdalen Coll., Oxford (BA 1st Cl. Hons Mod. Hist.); City Univ. (DipLaw); King's Coll., London (Dip Eur. Law). Called to the Bar, Gray's Inn, 1991 (Reid and Holker Schol.), Bencher, 2014; Founder Mem., Matrix Chambers, 2000–. Mem., Justice Council, 2014–. Mem., RSA Commn on Drugs Policy, 2010; Co-Chm., Ind. Commn on Future of Work, 2016–17. Trustee: Birthrights, 2013–16; Equal Rights Trust, 2014–; Nat. Campaign for Arts, 2016–; Inst. for the Future of Work, 2018–. *Publications:* (jtly) Blackstone's Guide to the Human Rights Act 1998, 1998, 7th edn 2015; (contrib.) The White Book, 2006; (contrib.) Oxford Guide to the Law, 2009; (contrib.) Complexity's Embrace: the international law implications of Brexit, 2018. *Address:* Matrix, Griffin Building, Gray's Inn, WC1R 5LN. T: (020) 7404 3447, *Fax:* (020) 7404 3448. E: helenmountfield@matrixlaw.co.uk; Mansfield College, Mansfield Road, Oxford OX1 3TF. T: (01865) 270999. E: helen.mountfield@mansfield.ox.ac.uk.

**MOUNTFIELD, Peter;** Executive Secretary, Development Committee, World Bank, 1991–95; *b* 2 April 1935; *s* of late Alexander Stuart Mountfield and Agnes Elizabeth (*née* Gurney); *m* 1958, Evelyn Margaret Smithies (*d* 2010); three *s*. *Educ:* Merchant Taylors' Sch., Crosby; Trinity Coll., Cambridge (BA); Graduate Sch. of Public Admin, Harvard. RN, 1953–55. Asst Principal, HM Treasury, 1958; Principal, 1963; Asst Sec., 1970; Under Secretary: Cabinet Office, 1977; HM Treasury, 1980–91. *Recreations:* reading, walking, looking at buildings. *Address:* 1 Summerbank, Rockdale Road, Sevenoaks, Kent TN13 1BU. T: (01732) 462958. E: petermountfield@hotmail.com.

**MOUNTFORD, Carol Jean, (Kali);** *b* 12 Jan. 1954; *m*; one *s* one *d*; *m* 1995, Ian Leedham. *Educ:* Crewe and Alsager Coll. (BA SocSc ext.). Civil Service posts, Dept of Employment, 1975–96. Mem., Dept of Employment Exec. Cttee, CPSA, 1986. Mem. (Lab) Sheffield CC, 1992–96. MP (Lab) Colne Valley, 1997–2010. Parliamentary Private Secretary: to Minister for Work, 2003–04; to Immigration Minister, 2004–05; to Chief Sec. to Treasury, 2005–06; to Sec. of State for Defence, 2006–08. Mem., Treasury Select Cttee, 2001–03.

**MOUNTFORD, Roger Philip;** Chairman: HgCapital Trust plc, since 2005 (non-executive Director, since 2004); Lafarge UK Pension Plan, since 2017; *b* Wimbledon, 5 June 1948; *s* of Stanley W. A. Mountford and Evelyn Mountford (*née* Richardson); *m* 1981, Jane Stanton; three *d*. *Educ:* Kingston Grammar Sch.; London Sch. of Econs and Pol Sci. (BSc Econ 1971); Stanford Business Sch. (MS Mgt 1980). ACIB 1976. Merchant banker, Hambros Bank, subseq. SG Hambros, 1971–2000: Dir, 1984–98; Man. Dir, 1998–2000; Man. Dir, Hambro Pacific Ltd, Hong Kong, 1983–89. Chairman: CAA Pension Scheme, 2003–13; Housing Finance Corp., 2007–13; Allied Domecq Pension Fund, 2013–17; non-executive Director: Dover Harbour Bd, 2001–12 (Chm., 2011–12); CAA, 2003–13; High Speed Two (HS2) Ltd, 2015–. Member: C of E Pensions Bd, 2012–; Finance Adv. Cttee, Westminster Abbey, 2013–. Chm., LSE Enterprise Ltd, 2004–14; Mem. Council, LSE, 2014–. Chm., Fedn of Cons. Students, 1970–71. FRSA. *Recreations:* opera, music, theatre. *Clubs:* Carlton; Hong Kong, Hong Kong Jockey (Hong Kong).

**MOUNTGARRET, 18th Viscount** *cr* 1550 (Ire.); **Piers James Richard Butler;** Baron (UK) 1911; *b* 15 April 1961; *s* of 17th Viscount Mountgarret and Gillian Margaret (*née* Buckley); *S* father, 2004; *m* 1st, 1995, Laura Brown Gary (marr. diss. 2000); two *d*; 2nd, 2006, Fenella Mary, *d* of David and Mary Fawcus; one *s* one *d*. *Educ:* Eton; St Andrews Univ. *Heir: s* Hon. Theo Oliver Stafford Butler, *b* 11 Oct. 2015.

**MOUSLEY, Timothy John;** QC 2003; His Honour Judge Mousley; a Circuit Judge, since 2013; *b* 29 April 1956; *s* of late James Silvester and Patricia Mary Mousley; *m* 1st, 1981 (marr. diss. 2008); two *d*; 2nd, 2016, Elisabeth. *Educ:* Peter Symonds Sch., Winchester; Univ. of Keele (BA Hons Law and Econs). Called to the Bar, Middle Temple, 1979; barrister on Western Circuit, 1980–2013; a Recorder, 1998–2013. *Recreations:* sport (watching), gardening. *Address:* Portsmouth Combined Court Centre, Winston Churchill Avenue, Portsmouth PO1 2EB. *Clubs:* Southampton Football; Hampshire County Cricket; West Tytherley Wine.
*See also* W. H. Mousley.

**MOUSLEY, William Howard;** QC 2011; a Recorder, since 2009; *b* London, 9 Jan. 1963; *s* of James Silvester Mousley and Patricia Mary Mousley; *m* 1988, Elaine Claire Delves; one *s* one *d*. *Educ:* Montgomery of Alamein Sch., Winchester; Peter Symonds Coll., Winchester; Univ. of Warwick (LLB Hons Law 1985). Called to the Bar, Middle Temple, 1986; in practice as a barrister, specialising in criminal law, 1987–. Vice-Pres., Winchester RFC, 2009–. *Recreations:* singing and playing harmonica in "Foolish Behaviour", coaching and watching Rugby, cricket, embracing baldness. *Address:* 2 King's Bench Walk, Temple, EC4Y 7DE. T: (020) 7353 1746, *Fax:* (020) 7583 2051. E: wmousley@2kbw.com. *Clubs:* Winchester Rugby Football, Scrummagers Cricket.
*See also* T. J. Mousley.

**MOUTRAY, Stephen;** Member (DemU) Upper Bann, Northern Ireland Assembly, 2003–16; *b* 25 Feb. 1959; *s* of William and Lena Moutray; *m* 1985, Myrtle Taylor; two *s* one *d*. *Educ:* Kingspark Primary Sch.; Lurgan Jun. High Sch.; Lurgan Coll. Company dir (retail); sub postmaster. Mem. (DemU), Craigavon BC, 2001–13, 2018–. *Recreations:* walking, swimming, collecting autographed biographies, travelling. E: stephenmoutray@btinternet.com.

**MOVERLEY, Prof. John,** OBE 2004; FRAgS, FIAgrE; Chairman: Amenity Forum, since 2009; West Midlands Advisory Committee, Forestry Commission, since 2010; self-employed consultant, writer and speaker on food issues; *b* Thornton, Yorks, 15 Feb. 1950; *s* of Robert John and Elsie Maria Moverley; *m* 1973, Elizabeth Ann; two *s*. *Educ:* Pocklington Sch.; St Catharine's Coll., Cambridge (Scholar; BA 1971; Wood Prize for Agric. 1971). FRAgS 2006; FIAgrE 2006. Mgt consultant, 1971–74; Lectr and Res. Fellow, Univ. of Nottingham, 1974–77; Sen. Lectr in Mgt, Bishop Burton and Shuttleworth Colls, 1977–86; Dep. Principal, Bicton Coll., 1986–88; Principal, Lincolnshire Coll. of Agric. and Hort., 1988–97; Principal and Chief Exec., Myerscough Coll., 1997–2005; Chief Exec., RASE, 2005–08. Pro Vice Chancellor and Prof., De Montfort Univ., 1994–97. Director: Azurance Ltd, 2010–; Greenwatt Rural Services, 2011–. Member: Editl Bd, Internat. Supermarket News; Severn and Wye Flood and Coastal Cttee, 2012–; Mem. Adv. Gp, Winterbourne House and Gardens, 2015–; Trustee: and Mem. Bd, BASIS Registration Ltd, 2009–; Community Forest Trust, 2013–. Gov., Moreton Morrell C of E Sch., 2013–. Hon. Fellow: Univ. of Central Lancashire, 2005; Myerscough Coll., 2005. *Publications:* Microcomputers and Agriculture, 1984; From Village Pump to Royal Appointment, 2012; numerous papers and articles. *Recreations:* sport, garden. *Club:* Farmers.

**MOVERLEY SMITH, Stephen Philip**; QC 2002; *b* 10 Jan. 1960; *s* of Philip Smith and Carol Smith (*née* Moverley); *m* 1990, Caroline Topping; three *s*. *Educ:* Reading Sch.; Pembroke Coll., Oxford (MA). Called to the Bar, Middle Temple, 1985; in practice, specialising in international trust, company and commercial litigation and arbitration. *Recreations:* sailing, tennis, mountain walking, cycling. *Address:* 24 Old Buildings, Lincoln's Inn, WC2A 3UP. *T:* (020) 7691 2424, *Fax:* 0870 460 2178. *E:* sms@xxiv.co.uk.

**MOWAT, Ashley;** *see* Mowat, N. A. G.

**MOWAT, David John;** *b* Rugby, 1957; *s* of John and Pat Mowat; *m* 1983, Veronica Mann; one *s* three *d*. *Educ:* Lawrence Sheriff Grammar Sch., Rugby; Imperial Coll., London (BSc Civil Engrg). ACA 1981. Chartered Accountant, 1981–2002, Partner, 1989–2002, Arthur Andersen, London; Global Man. Partner for Energy, Accenture, 2002–05. Mem. (C) Macclesfield BC, 2007–08. MP (C) Warrington S, 2010–17; contested (C) same seat, 2017. PPS to Financial Sec. to HM Treasury, 2012–16; Parly Under-Sec. of State, DoH, 2016–17. *Recreations:* chess, golf, Rugby Union and League, theatre. *Clubs:* Carlton; Warrington.

**MOWAT, David McIvor;** JP; consultant, business columnist and commentator; Managing Director, Iatros Ltd, 1994–2015; *b* 12 March 1939; *s* of Ian M. Mowat and Mary I. S. Steel; *m* 1964, Elinor Anne Birtwistle (*d* 2008); three *d*. *Educ:* Edinburgh Academy; University of Edinburgh (MA); BA Open Univ., 1984. Chief Executive: Edinburgh Chamber of Commerce and Manufactures, 1967–90; Chamber Developments Ltd, 1971; Edinburgh's Capital Ltd, 1986; Who's Who in Business in Scotland Ltd, 1989–90. Dir, St Andrews Golf Club Manufacturing Ltd, 1994–2011. Dep. Chm., Edinburgh Tourist Gp, 1985–90. Pres., British Chambers of Commerce Execs, 1987–89. JP Edinburgh, 1969. FRSA. *Address:* 37 Orchard Road South, Edinburgh EH4 3JA. *T:* (0131) 332 6865.

**MOWAT, Her Honour Mary Jane Stormont;** a Circuit Judge, 1996–2014; *b* 7 July 1948; *d* of late Duncan McKay Stormont Mowat and Jane Archibald Mowat (*née* Milne); *m* 1973, Prof. the Hon. Nicholas Michael John Woodhouse, *qv*, 2nd *s* of 5th Baron Terrington, DSO, OBE; one *s*. *Educ:* Sherborne Sch. For Girls; Lady Margaret Hall, Oxford (MA). Called to the Bar, Inner Temple, 1973. *Recreations:* music, walking, reading, riding.

**MOWAT, Prof. (Norman) Ashley (George),** LVO 2009; FRCP, FRCPE, FRCPGlas; Consultant Physician and Gastroenterologist, Aberdeen Royal Infirmary, 1975–2008; Professor in Medicine, Aberdeen University Medical School, 2002–08; Physician to the Queen in Scotland, 2001–08; *b* 11 April 1943; *s* of William Mowat and Isabella Parker Mowat (*née* Mair); *m* 1966, Kathleen Mary Cowie; one *s* two *d*. *Educ:* Fordyce Acad.; Aberdeen Univ. (MB ChB). MRCP 1971, FRCP 1984; FRCPE 1991; FRCPGlas 2002. Hse Officer, SHO, then Registrar, Trng, Aberdeen Teaching Hosps, 1966–72; Lecturer: in Medicine, Aberdeen Univ., 1972–73; in Gastroenterol., and Res. Fellow, St Bartholomew's Hosp., London, 1973–74; Clinical Sen. Lectr in Medicine, Aberdeen Univ. Med. Sch., 1975–2002. Vis. Physician to Shetland Is, 1975–94. President: Scottish Soc. of Gastroenterology, 2002–04; Scottish Soc. of Physicians, 2004–05. Chm., Three Harbours Assoc./Cullen Sea Sch., 2014–. DL Banffshire, 2013. *Publications:* (ed jtly) Integrated Clinical Sciences: gastroenterology, 1985; numerous contribs to med. and gastroenterol. jls. *Recreations:* sailing, photography, golf, reading. *Address:* York House, York Place, Cullen, Buckie AB56 4UW.

**MOWBRAY, 27th Baron** *cr* 1283, **SEGRAVE, 28th Baron** *cr* 1283, **AND STOURTON,** 24th Baron *cr* 1448, of Stourton, co. Wilts; **Edward William Stephen Stourton;** *b* 17 April 1953; *s* of Charles Edward Stourton, CBE, 26th Baron Mowbray, 27th Baron Segrave and 23rd Baron Stourton, and Hon. Jane de Yarburgh Bateson, *oc* of 5th Baron Deramore; *S* father, 2006; *m* 1980, Penelope Lucy, *e d* of Dr Peter Brunet; one *s* four *d*. *Educ:* Ampleforth. *Heir: s* Hon. James Charles Peter Stourton, *b* 12 Dec. 1991.

**MOWBRAY, John;** *see* Mowbray, W. J.

**MOWBRAY, Sir John Robert,** 6th Bt *cr* 1880; DL; *b* 1 March 1932; *s* of Sir George Robert Mowbray, 5th Bt, KBE, and Diana Margaret, *d* of Sir Robert Heywood Hughes, 12th Bt; *S* father, 1969; *m* 1957, Lavinia Mary, *d* of late Lt-Col Francis Edgar Hugonin, OBE, Stainton House, Stainton in Cleveland, Yorks; three *d*. *Educ:* Eton; New College, Oxford. DL Suffolk, 1993. *Address:* The Hill House, Duffs Hill, Glemsford, Suffolk CO10 7PP. *T:* (01787) 281930.

**MOWBRAY, (William) John;** QC 1974; *b* 3 Sept. 1928; *s* of James Mowbray, sugar manufr and Ethel Mowbray; *m* 1960, Shirley Mary Neilan; one *s* three *d*. *Educ:* Upper Canada Coll.; Mill Hill Sch.; New Coll., Oxford (BA Jurisprudence 1952); Heythrop Coll. (BA Theol. 2008; MA Dist. 2009; PhD 2016). Called to Bar, Lincoln's Inn, 1953 (Bencher, 1983); called to Bahamian Bar, 1971, to Eastern Caribbean Bar, 1992. Chairman: Chancery Bar Assoc., 1985–94; Westminster Assoc. for Mental Health, 1981–88 (Trustee, 1999–2011); Westminster Christian Council, 1986–87 (Vice-Chm., 1984–85). Trustee, IMPACT, 2002–19. *Publications:* Lewin on Trusts, 16th edn 1964, 18th edn 2008; Estate Duty on Settled Property, 1969; articles in jls. *Recreations:* music, observing nature in Sussex garden. *Club:* Travellers.

**MOWL, Colin John,** CB 2004; Executive Director, Macroeconomics and Labour Market Office for National Statistics, 2002–08; *b* 19 Oct. 1947; *s* of late Arthur Sidney and Ada Mowl; *m* 1980, Kathleen Patricia Gallagher; one *s* one *d*. *Educ:* Lawrence Sheriff Sch., Rugby; LSE (BSc Econs, MSc). Econ. Asst, MoT, 1970–72; Sen. Econ. Asst, Econ. Advr, HM Treasury, 1972–83; Res. Manager, Forex Research Ltd, 1983; HM Treasury: Sen. Econ. Advr, 1983–90; Grade 3, and Hd, Econ. Analysis and Forecasting Gp, later Dep. Dir, Macroecon. Policy and Prospects, 1990–95; Dep. Dir, subseq. Dir, Budget and Public Finances, 1995–2002. *Publications:* various Treasury working papers. *Recreations:* spending time with four grandchildren, holiday home in lower Normandy, medieval and Second World War history of Normandy, commemoration of British and Commonwealth airmen buried in French community cemeteries, attending and setting quizzes. *E:* colin.mowl@gmail.com.

**MOWLL, Rev. (John) William (Rutley);** Chaplain to the Queen, 2000–12; *b* 24 March 1942; *s* of late Wilfred Rutley Mowll and Mary Giffard (*née* Holden); *m* 1966, Susan Frances Lisle Bullen; two *s*. *Educ:* Canterbury Cathedral Choir Sch.; King's Sch., Canterbury; Sarum Theol Coll. Ordained deacon, 1966, priest, 1967; Curate: Church of the Ascension, Oughtibridge, dio. Sheffield, 1966–69; St James, Hill, dio. Birmingham, 1969–72; Industrial Chaplain and Vicar, Upper Arley, 1973–78; Priest-in-Charge, 1978–81, Rector, 1981–83, Upton Snodsbury; Vicar, Boughton-under-Blean with Dunkirk, 1983–2007, also Hernhill, 1989–2007; Rural Dean, Ospringe, Faversham, 1995–2001; Hon. Minor Canon, Canterbury Cathedral, 1995–2002; Chaplain to High Sheriff of Kent, 2001–02. Occasional Lectr, Nat. Maritime Mus. Mem., Soc. for Nautical Res., 1986–; Life Mem., HMS Warrior 1860; Hon. Mem., Guild of Master Craftsmen, 1984–. Model ships on display: SS Great Britain, Brunel Inst. Library, Bristol; HMS Warrior 1860, Victory Gate, Portsmouth, then Portsmouth Civic Centre; PS Sirius 1838, Amer. Philatelic Soc. Bldg, Pennsylvania. *Publications:* SS Great Britain: the model ship, 1982; HMS Warrior 1860: building a working model warship, 1997; (contrib.) Building Model Warships of the iron and steel era (ed P. Beisheim), 2002; Thunderer: building a model Dreadnought, 2010; HMS Gannet 1878: ship and model, 2018; contrib. Ships in Scale mag., 2012–13, 2015–. *Recreations:* practising musician, amateur playwright, engineer in miniature craftwork, specialising in model ships. *Address:* Holly Cottage, Water Lane, Ospringe, Faversham, Kent ME13 8TS. *T:* (01795) 597597.

**MOWSCHENSON, Terence Rennie;** QC 1995; a Recorder, since 2000; a Deputy High Court Judge, since 2003; *b* 7 June 1953; *s* of Henry and Hanny Mowschenson; *m* 1992, Judith Angela Strang. *Educ:* Eagle Sch., Umtali, Rhodesia; Peterhouse, Marandellas, Rhodesia; Queen Mary Coll., London (LLB Hons 1975); Exeter Coll., Oxford (BCL Hons 1976). FCIArb. Called to the Bar, Middle Temple, 1977, Bencher, 2003; Asst Recorder, 1997–2000. Part-time Judge (formerly Chairman): Claims Mgt Tribunal, 1996–; Financial Services and Markets Act Tribunal, 2002–; Pension Regulator Tribunal, 2005–. Chm., Barristers' Benevolent Assoc., 1999– (Hon. Sec., 1995–97, Hon. Treas., 1997–99). Fellow, Internat. Acad. of Trial Lawyers, 2019. *Recreations:* opera, reading, travel. *Address:* Wilberforce Chambers, 8 New Square, Lincoln's Inn, WC2A 3QP. *T:* (020) 7306 0102. *Clubs:* Royal Automobile, Garrick.

**MOXHAM, Prof. John,** MD; FRCP; Professor of Respiratory Medicine, King's College London School of Medicine; Consultant Physician, King's College Hospital, 1982–2015, now Hon. Consultant; Director of Clinical Strategy, King's Health Partners Academic Health Sciences Centre, since 2009; Director, Value Based Health Care, since 2018; *b* 9 Dec. 1944; *s* of late Wilson Moxham and Marie Moxham (*née* Bland), Evesham, Worcs; *m* 1978, Nicola Seaman; three *d*. *Educ:* Prince Henry's Grammar Sch., Evesham; LSE (BSc (Econ) 1967); UCH Med. Sch. (MB BS 1973; MD 1982). MRCP 1975, FRCP 1987. Lectr in Medicine, UCH, 1978–80; Sen. Registrar, Brompton and St James' Hosp., London, 1980–82. King's College School of Medicine and Dentistry, then Guy's, King's and St Thomas' School of Medicine, King's College London, subseq. King's College London School of Medicine: Prof. of Respiratory Medicine, 1990–; Dean: for Med. Student Admissions, 1991–96, Faculty of Clin. Medicine, 1997–98; KCH Campus, 1998–2000; Vice-Dean, 2000–03; Medical Dir, 2003–09. Chm., Consultants' Cttee, KCH, 1995–97; non-exec. Dir, KCH NHS Trust, 2000–03. Chm., Doctors for Tobacco Law, 1991–97; Chm., 1996–98, 2009–19, Mem. Bd, 2006–, ASH; Mem., Ind. Inquiry into Access to Healthcare for People with Learning Disabilities, 2007–08. Thoracic Society: Scientific Meetings Sec., 1988–90; Mem. Exec., 1988–93; Chm., Tobacco Cttee, 1990–93. Bertram Louis Abrahams Lect., RCP, 2007; Moran Campbell Lect., British Thoracic Soc., 2013; Halliburton Lect. in Physiology, KCL, 2016. Gov., James Allen's Girls' Sch., 2004–14. Eur. Respiratory Soc. Congress Award, 2012. Hon. MFPH 2015. *Publications:* (ed jtly) Textbook of Medicine, 1990, 4th edn 2002; res. papers on clinical physiol., particularly ventilatory failure, respiratory muscle function and breathlessness. *Recreations:* family, art, good beer, mooching around London. *Address:* 17 Maude Road, Camberwell, SE5 8NY. *T:* (020) 7703 4396. *E:* john.moxham@kcl.ac.uk.

**MOXON, Most Rev. Sir David John,** KNZM 2014; Archbishop of Canterbury's Representative to the Holy See, and Director, Anglican Centre in Rome, 2013–17; *b* 6 Sept. 1951; *s* of John Rosher Moxon and Joan Moxon; *m* Tureiti; two *s* two *d*. *Educ:* Freyberg High Sch., Palmerston North; Massey Univ. (MA Hons); Oxford Univ. (MA); Univ. of Waikato (Cert. Maori Studies 1991). Volunteer service abroad (school leaver scheme), 1970; Univ. Tutor, Educn Dept, Massey Univ., 1974–75; Curate, St Luke's, Havelock North, 1978–81; Vicar, St George's, Gate Pa, Tauranga, 1981–87; Dir, Theol Educn by Extension Unit, Anglican Church of Aotearoa, NZ and Polynesia, 1987–93; Bishop of Waikato, 1993–2013; Archbishop and Co-Primate, Anglican Church in Aotearoa, NZ and Polynesia, 2006–13. Hon. Ambassador, City of Hamilton, 2013. Fellow, St Margaret's Coll., Univ. of Otago, 2006. Hon. Fellow, St Peter's Coll., Oxford, 2006. Hon. LTh Aotearoa; Hon. DLitt Massey, 2015; DUniv Waikato, 2016. Gold Duke of Edinburgh Award, 1969. *Recreations:* playing flute, reading, tramping, swimming.

**MOXON, Prof. (Edward) Richard,** FMedSci; FRS 2007; Action Research Professor of Paediatrics, University of Oxford, 1984–2008, now Emeritus Professor; Fellow, Jesus College, Oxford, 1984–2008, now Emeritus; Head, Molecular Infectious Diseases Group, Institute of Molecular Medicine, John Radcliffe Hospital, Oxford, 1988–2008; Founder and Chairman, Oxford Vaccine Group, 1994–2008; *b* 16 July 1941; *s* of late Gerald Richard Moxon and of Margaret Forster Mohun; *m* 1973, Marianne Graham; two *s* one *d*. *Educ:* Shrewsbury Sch.; St John's Coll., Cambridge (Keasby Award, 1961; BA 1963); St Thomas' Hosp. (MB, BChir 1966); MA Oxon 1984. MRCP 1968, FRCP 1984; FRCPCH 1997. Surgical House Officer, Kent and Canterbury Hosp., 1966; Medical House Officer, Peace Meml Hosp., Watford, 1966; Pathologist, St Thomas' Hosp., 1967; Sen. House Officer in Paediatrics: Whittington Hosp., 1968; Hosp. for Sick Children, Gt Ormond St, 1969; Children's Hosp. Medical Center, Boston, Mass, USA; Asst Resident in Pediatrics, 1970; Res. Fellow in Infectious Diseases Div., 1971–74; Johns Hopkins Hosp., Baltimore, Md, USA: Asst Prof. in Pediatrics, 1974–80; Associate Prof. in Pediatrics, 1980–84; Chief, Eudowood Div. of Pediatric Infectious Diseases, 1982–84. Vis. Scientist, Washington Univ., St Louis, 1990–91; Burroughs-Wellcome Vis. Prof., Allegheny Univ. of Health Scis, Philadelphia, 1999. Lectures: Mitchell, RCP, 1992; Blackfan, Children's Hosp. Med. Center, Boston, Mass, 1994; Teale, RCP, 1998; Dolman, Univ. of BC, 1999; Hattie Alexander Meml, Columbia, 2005; Award, Eur. Soc. of Clin. Microbiol. and Infectious Diseases, 2007; Fred Griffith Review, Soc. for Gen. Microbiol., 2007. Convenor, BPA Immunology and Infectious Diseases Gp, 1984–89; Chm., MRC Sub-Cttee, Polysaccharide Vaccines, 1986–90; Member: Steering Gp, Encapsulated Bacteria, WHO, 1987–93; Amer. Soc. Clinical Investigation. Founder FMedSci 1998; Fellow: Amer. Soc. of Microbiol., 2001; Infectious Diseases Soc. of America, 2002. Bill Marshall Award, ESPID, 2005. *Publications:* (with D. Isaacs): Neonatal Infections, 1991; A Practical Approach to Pediatric Infectious Diseases, 1996; Longman Handbook of Neonatal Infections, 1999; contribs to: Mandell's Principles and Practice of Infectious Diseases, 2nd edn 1985, 4th edn 1995; Forfar and Arneil's Textbook of Paediatrics, 4th edn 1992, 5th edn 1998; Oxford Textbook of Medicine, 3rd edn 1996, 4th edn 2000; editorial adviser: Lancet's Modern Vaccines, 1991; Lancet's Vaccine Octet, 1997; Yu, Merigan, Barrière, Antimicrobial Therapy and Vaccines, 1998; Stearns' Evolution in Health and Disease, 1998; many articles in learned jls on molecular microbiol., paediatric vaccines and infectious diseases, esp. relating to *Haemophilus influenzae* and *Neisseria meningitidis*. *Recreations:* music, tennis, golf, wines. *Address:* 9A North Parade Avenue, Oxford OX2 6LX.

**MOXON BROWNE, Robert William;** QC 1990; a Recorder, since 1991; a Deputy Judge of the Technology and Construction Court (formerly Deputy Official Referee), since 1992; a Deputy Judge of the High Court, since 1999; *b* 26 June 1946; *s* of late Kendall Edward Moxon Browne and Sheila Heron Moxon Browne; *m* 1968, Kerstin Elizabet Warne; one *s* one *d*. *Educ:* Gordonstoun School; University College, Oxford (BA). Called to the Bar, Gray's Inn, 1969; specialises in commercial and insurance law in London and on Western Circuit. Dir, Sirius Projects Ltd, 2005–. *Recreations:* walking, gardening, wine. *Address:* 2 Temple Gardens, EC4Y 9AY. *T:* (020) 7822 1200.

**MO YAN;** *see* Guan Moye.

**MOYERS, Bill D.**; journalist; President, Schumann Media Center (formerly Florence and John Schumann Foundation), since 1990; *b* 5 June 1934; *s* of John Henry Moyers and Ruby Moyers (*née* Johnson); *m* 1954, Judith Suzanne Davidson; two *s* one *d*. *Educ*: High Sch., Marshall, Texas; N Texas State Univ.; Univ. of Edinburgh; Southwestern Theological Seminary. BJ 1956; MDiv 1959. Personal Asst to Senator Lyndon B. Johnson, 1959–60; Executive Asst for US Vice Presidential Campaign, 1960–61; US Peace Corps: Founding Organizer, 1961; Dep. Dir, 1962–63. Special Asst to President Johnson, 1963–66; Press Sec., 1965–67; Publisher of Newsday, Long Island, 1967–70; Exec. Ed., Bill Moyers' Jl, Public Broadcasting Service, 1971–76, 1978–81; Sen. Correspondent, CBS Reports, 1976–78; Sen. News Analyst, CBS Evening News, 1981–86; Founder and Man. Ed., Public Affairs Television Inc., 1987–2015. Contributing Editor, Newsweek Magazine. Over thirty-five Emmy Awards, incl. most outstanding broadcaster, 1978; Lowell Medal, 1974; ABA Gavel Award for distinguished service to American system of law, 1974; ABA Cert. of Merit, 1975; Awards for The Fire Next Door: Monte Carlo TV Festival Grand Prize, Jurors Prize and Golden Nymph Award, 1978; Robert F. Kennedy Journalism Grand Prize, 1978; Christopher Medal, 1978; Sidney Hillman Prize for Distinguished Service, 1978, 1981, 1987; Distinguished Urban Journalism Award, Nat. Urban Coalition, 1978; George Polk Award, 1980, 1986, 2008; Alfred I. du Pont—Columbia Univ. Award, 1980, 1988, 1992, 1999; Peabody Award, 1978, 1980, 1984, 1985, 1988, 1989, 1998, 1999; Edward R. Murrow Award, 1980; State Univ. of NY Regents Medal of Excellence, 1984; Career Achievement Award, Internat. Documentary Assoc., 1991; Walter Cronkite Award for Excellence in Journalism, 1995; Nelson Mandela Award for Health and Human Rights, 1996; Charles Frankel Prize in the Humanities, NEH, 1996; Peabody Award for Lifetime Achievement, 2003; PEN USA Courageous Advocacy Award, 2005; Emmy Lifetime Achievement Award, 2006. *Publications*: Listening to America, 1971; Report from Philadelphia, 1987; The Secret Government, 1988; Joseph Campbell and the Power of Myth, 1988; A World of Ideas, vol. 1, 1989, vol. 2, 1990; Healing and the Mind, 1993; Language of Life, 1995; Genesis, 1996; Fooling With Words, 1999; Moyers on America, 2004; Moyers on Democracy, 2008; Bill Moyers' Journal: the conversation continues, 2012. *Address*: (office) 250 West 57th Street, Suite 715, New York, NY 10107–0003, USA.

**MOYES, David William**; Manager, West Ham United Football Club, 2017–18; *b* 25 April 1963; *m* Pamela; one *s* one *d*. Football player: Celtic, 1980–83; Cambridge United, 1983–85; Bristol City, 1985–87; Shrewsbury Town, 1987–90; Dunfermline Athletic, 1990–93; Hamilton Academical, 1993; Preston North End, 1993–98; Manager: Preston North End, 1998–2002 (Div. 2 Champions, 2000); Everton FC, 2002–13; Manchester United FC, 2013–14; Real Sociedad FC, 2014–15; Sunderland AFC, 2016–17. Manager of Year, League Managers Assoc., 2003, 2005.

**MOYES, James Christopher**; Founder and Director, Momart Ltd, Fine Arts Services and Shipping Co., 1971–99; working artist in all media, since 1999; *b* 29 April 1943; *s* of Albert Jack Moyes and Catherine Louise Moyes; *m* 1st, 1969, Elizabeth McKee (marr. diss. 1981); one *d*; 2nd, 1987, Joanna Margaret Price (marr. diss. 2000); two *d*; 3rd, 2006, Alison Jane Winfield-Chislett (marr. diss. 2010). *Educ*: Univ. of Kent (BA); Slade Sch. of Art (MA 1999). Visiting Lecturer: Essex Univ., 1988–98; UEA, 1988–98; Associate Vis. Lectr in Mus. Studies, Leicester Univ., 1990–2000. Vice Chm., Contemporary Arts Soc., 1996–99. Royal Warrant Holder, 1993 (re-assigned to Momart 1999). Patron, Foundling Mus., 2014–. Liveryman, Arts Scholars' Co., 2017–. *Recreation*: rowing. *Address*: Studio #4, Ropewalk Mews, 118 Middleton Road, E8 4LR. *Club*: Quintin Boat.

**MOYES, Dr William**; Chairman: General Dental Council, since 2013; Gambling Commission, since 2016; *b* 18 Sept. 1949; *s* of William Moyes and Catherine (*née* Brannan); *m* 1971, Dr Barbara Ann Rice; one *s*. *Educ*: Lawside Acad., Dundee; Univ. of Edinburgh (BSc Chem. 1971; PhD Theoretical Chem. 1977); London Business Sch. (Public Sector Mgt Prog. 1988). DoE, 1974–76; Dept of Transport, 1976–80; Cabinet Office Econ. Secretariat, 1980–83; Finance Div., Scottish Office, 1983–85; Scottish Educn Dept, 1985–87; Dept of Agric. and Fisheries for Scotland, 1987–90; Dir, Strategic Planning and Performance Mgt, Mgt Exec., NHS in Scotland, 1990–94; Hd, Infrastructure Finance, Bank of Scotland, 1994–2000; Dir-Gen., British Retail Consortium, 2000–04. Director: British Linen Investments Ltd, 1996–2000; Catalyst Healthcare Gp, 1996–2000; Summit Healthcare Gp, 1997–2000; Community Health Facilities (Oxford) Ltd, 1998–2000; Eurocommerce, 2001–04 (also Mem., Steering Cttee); BRC Trading Ltd, 2002–04; Skills Mart Ltd, 2002–04; Mem. Bd, Priory Hosp. Gp, 2011–16. Exec. Chm., Monitor, Independent Regulator of NHS Foundn Trusts, 2004–10; Mem. Bd, OFT, 2010–14; Associate, Inst. for Govt, 2010–13; Mem. Bd, Albertus Inst., 2015–18. Lay Mem., Legal Services Bd, 2008–15. Mem. Council, Univ. of Surrey, 2004–. Dir, BLISS (Nat. Charity for Newborn), 2002–04. Trustee: Nuffield Trust, 2008–12; Catholic Trust for England and Wales, 2010–16. Gov., Heythrop Coll., 2011–14 (Chm., Governing Body, 2012–14). Chm., St Mary's Music Sch., Edinburgh, 2015–18. *Publications*: contrib. papers to scientific jls. *Recreations*: good food, gardening, theatre, hill walking.

**MOYLAN-JONES, Rear-Adm. Roger Charles**, CEng, FIMechE; Director General Aircraft (Navy), 1992–95; *b* 18 April 1940; *s* of Brian Percy Jameson Moylan-Jones and Louie-Mae (*née* Brown); *m* 1961, Mary Howells; two *s* one *d*. *Educ*: King Edward VI Grammar Sch., Totnes; BRNC, Dartmouth; RNEC, Manadon (BSc Eng 1964). CEng, FIMechE 1990. Joined BRNC Dartmouth, 1958; service in 766, 890, 360 Sqdns and HMS Ark Royal, 1965–69; HMS Ganges, 1969–71; Air Engineering Officer, 706 Sqdn and 819 Sqdn; Staff of Flag Officer Carriers and Amphibious Ships, 1971–77; ndc 1978; Staff of: Flag Officer, Naval Air Comd, 1978–80; Dep. Chief of Defence Staff (OR), 1981–82; CSO to FONAC, 1983–84; Capt., HMS Daedalus, 1984–86; RCDS 1987; Director: Aircraft Support Policy (Navy), 1988–89; Naval Manning and Trng (Engrg), 1989–91. Capt., RN and Combined Services CC, 1969–73, 1982, 1983; Pres., RNCC, 1993–95 (Chm., 1985–89; Life Vice Pres., 1995). President: Devon Assoc. of Cricket Officials, 2009–15; Devon CCC, 2010– (Chm., 1997–2010; Hon. Life Mem., 2014); Minor Counties Cricket Assoc., 2015–17; Chm., Devon Cricket Bd, 1997–2003; Mem., ECB Mgt Bd, 2000–05; Dir, ECB Ltd, 2000–05. Trustee and Dir, England and Wales Cricket Trust, 2006–. *Recreations*: cricket, travel. *Clubs*: Army and Navy, MCC; I Zingari, Free Foresters, Forty.

**MOYLE, Lloyd Cameron R.**; *see* Russell-Moyle.

**MOYNE**, 3rd Baron *cr* 1932, of Bury St Edmunds; **Jonathan Bryan Guinness**; *b* 16 March 1930; *s* of 2nd Baron Moyne and Hon. Diana (*née* Mitford, later Hon. Lady Mosley) (*d* 2003); *S* father, 1992; *m* 1st, 1951, Ingrid Wyndham (marr. diss. 1962); one *s* one *d* (and one *s* decd); 2nd, 1964, Suzanne Phillips (*née* Lisney); one *s* one *d*; one *s* two *d* by Susan Mary Taylor. *Educ*: Eton; Oxford (MA, Mod. Langs). Journalist at Reuters, 1953–56. Merchant Banker: trainee at Erlangers Ltd, 1956–59, and at Philip Hill, 1959–62; Exec. Dir, 1962–64, non-exec. Dir, 1964–91, Leopold Joseph; Dir, Arthur Guinness Son & Co. Ltd, 1961–88. CC Leicestershire, 1970–74; Chairman, Monday Club, 1972–74. *Publications*: (with Catherine Guinness) The House of Mitford, 1984; Shoe: the Odyssey of a Sixties Survivor, 1989; Requiem for a Family Business, 1997. *Heir*: *s* Hon. Valentine Guy Bryan Guinness [*b* 9 March 1959; *m* 1986, Lucinda Jane, OBE (marr. diss. 2013), *o d* of Sir Miles Rivett-Carnac, 9th Bt; two *d*]. *Address*: Linley Lodge, Linley, Bishop's Castle, Shropshire SY9 5HL.
*See also* Hon. D. W. Guinness, Earl of Wemyss and March.

**MOYNIHAN**, family name of **Baron Moynihan**.

**MOYNIHAN**, 4th Baron *cr* 1929, of Leeds, co. York; **Colin Berkeley Moynihan**; Bt 1922; Founding Partner, CMA Consultants, since 1994; Director, Rowan Companies Inc., 1996–2015; Chairman, British Olympic Association, 2005–12; *b* 13 Sept. 1955; *s* of 2nd Baron Moynihan, OBE, TD, and of June Elizabeth (who *m* 1965, N. B. Hayman), *d* of Arthur Stanley Hopkins; *S* half-brother, 1997; *m* 1992, Gaynor-Louise Metcalf (marr. diss. 2016); two *s* one *d*. *Educ*: Monmouth Sch. (Music Scholar); University Coll., Oxford (BA PPE 1977, MA 1982). Pres., Oxford Union Soc., 1976. Personal Asst to Chm., Tate & Lyle Ltd, 1978–80; Manager, Tate & Lyle Agribusiness, resp. for marketing strategy and develt finance, 1980–82; Chief Exec., 1982–83, Chm., 1983–87, Ridgways Tea and Coffee Merchants; external consultant, Tate & Lyle PLC, 1983–87. Chm. and CEO, Consort Resources Ltd, 2000–03; Exec. Chm., Clipper Windpower Marine Ltd, 2005–07; Chairman: Pelamis Wave Power (formerly Ocean Power Delivery), 2005–11; Hydrodec Gp plc, 2012–; Buckthorn Partners LLP, 2014–. Dir, Inst. of Petroleum, 2001–03. MP (C) Lewisham East, 1983–92; contested (C) Lewisham East, 1992. Political Asst to the Foreign Sec., 1983; PPS to Minister of Health, 1985, to Paymaster General, 1985–87; Parly Under-Sec. of State (Minister for Sport), DoE, 1987–90; Parly Under-Sec. of State, Dept of Energy, 1990–92. Chm., All-Party Parly Gp on Afghanistan, 1986; Vice Chm., Cons. Food and Drinks Sub-Cttee, 1983–85; Sec., Cons. Foreign and Commonwealth Affairs Cttee, 1983–85. Member: Paddington Conservative Management Cttee, 1980–81; Bow Group, 1978–92 (Mem., Industry Cttee, 1978–79, 1985–87); Chm., Trade & Industry Standing Cttee, 1983–87. Elected Mem., H of L, 1999. Sen. Opposition spokesman on foreign affairs, H of L, 1999–2002; Chm., Cons. Campaigning Bd, 2004–05; special advr to Leader of the Opposition, 2003–05 (Treas., Leadership Campaign Fund, 2003). Chm., Sydney Olympic UK Business Task Force, 1995–97; Member: Sports Council, 1982–85; Major Spectator Sports Cttee, CCPR, 1979–82; CCPR Enquiry into Sponsorship of Sport, 1982–83; Exec. Cttee, Assoc. Nat. Olympic Cttees, 2006–10; IOC Internat. Relations Cttee, 2008–14; Dir, LOCOG, 2005–13; Steward, British Boxing Bd of Control, 1979–87. Trustee: Oxford Univ. Boat Club, 1980–84; Sports Aid Trust, 1983–87; Governor, Sports Aid Foundn (London and SE), 1980–82. Pres., British Water Ski, 2006–. Mem. Council, Royal Commonwealth Soc., 1980–82. Hon. Sec., Friends of British Council. Freeman, City of London, 1978; Liveryman, Worshipful Co. of Haberdashers, 1981 (Second Warden, 2015–16). Patron, Land & City Families Trust. Oxford Double Blue, Rowing and Boxing, 1976 and 1977; World Gold Medal for Lightweight Rowing, Internat. Rowing Fedn, 1978; Olympic Silver Medal for Rowing, 1980; World Silver Medal for Rowing, 1981. *Recreations*: collecting Nonesuch Books, music, sport. *Heir*: *s* Hon. Nicholas Ewan Berkeley Moynihan, *b* 31 March 1994. *Address*: Room 3–19, Millbank House, House of Lords, SW1A 0PW. *T*: (020) 7219 5879. *E*: moynihanc@parliament.uk. *Clubs*: Ivy; Kandahar Ski; Leander (Henley-on-Thames); Vincent's (Oxford).

**MOYNIHAN, Sir Daniel**, Kt 2012; EdD; Chief Executive, Harris Federation of London Schools, since 2006; *b* London, 29 Jan. 1960; *s* of Edmund and Bridget Moynihan; *m* 1987, Jane Margaret Iles; one *s* one *d*★. *Educ*: St George's RC Sch., Maida Vale; University Coll. London (BSc Econ. 1982); Inst. of Educn, London Univ. (PGCE Dist. 1984; MA Educnl Admin 1996; EdD 2002). Head of Econs, Bishop Challoner Sch., 1984–88; Head of Business Studies, Kingsbury High Sch., Brent, 1988–90; Asst Principal, 1990–96, Vice Principal, 1996–99, Leigh City Technol. Coll., Dartford; Headteacher, Valentines High Sch., Ilford, 1999–2004; Principal, Harris City Technol. Coll., 2005–08. Chm., Educn Hons Cttee, Cabinet Office, 2013–. Hon. Fellow, Harris Manchester Coll., Oxford, 2018. *Publications*: (with B. Titley) Economics: a complete course, 1987, 3rd edn 2000; Advanced Business, 1995, 2nd edn 2001; Intermediate Business, 1996; (with B. Titley) Economics: a complete course for Cambridge IGCSE and O Level, 2007; (with B. Titley) Complete Economics for IGCSE and O Level, 2012, 3rd edn 2018. *Recreations*: art, history, politics, travel. *Address*: Harris Federation, 4th Floor, Norfolk House, Wellesley Road, Croydon CR0 1LH. *E*: Dan.moynihan@harrisfederation.org.uk, D.Moynihan1@btinternet.com.

**MOYNIHAN, Jonathan Patrick**, OBE 1994; Chairman and Joint Principal, Ipex Capital, since 2008; *b* Cambridge, 21 June 1948; *s* of Sir Noël Henry Moynihan and Margaret Mary Moynihan (*née* Lovelace); *m* 1980, Patricia Underwood; one step *d*. *Educ*: Balliol Coll., Oxford (Lazarus Fletcher and Agnes Ward Schol. in Maths; MA 1975; Foundn Fellow 1999); Poly. of N London (MSc 1974); Massachusetts Inst. of Technol. (SM 1977). Track Records, 1970–71; Relief and Rehabilitation Organiser: War on Want, Calcutta, 1971; SCF, Orissa and Bangladesh, 1971–72; Product Manager, Roche Products Ltd, London, 1972–76; Associate, McKinsey & Co., Amsterdam, 1977–79; Vice Pres., Strategic Planning Associates, Washington DC, 1979–81; Pres., Moynihan Strategy Consultants, NY, 1981–82; Man. Vice Pres., First Manhattan Consulting Gp, NY, 1982–92; Chief Exec., 1992–99, Exec. Chm., 1994–2013, PA Consulting Gp. Chairman: UbiNetics, 1995–2005; Cubiks, 1998–2005; Meridica, 2000–05; ImPAct Executives, 2000–03; Aegate, 2003–10 (non-exec. Dir, 2011–17); ProcServe Ltd, 2005–16; PlaqueTec Ltd, 2007–18; Semblant Ltd, 2008–18. Mem., Overseas and Welfare Cttee, SCF, 1972–76. Member: Dean's Council, Sloan Sch., MIT, 1997–2011; Dean's Adv. Gp, Saïd Business Sch., 1999–2006; Vice Chancellor's Circle, Oxford Univ., 2010–; Adv. Council, Inst. of Econ. Affairs, 2017–19. Chm., Balliol Campaign Bd, 1995–2007. Founder Chm., Helen Bamber Foundn, 2005–07. Mem. Council, Royal Albert Hall, 2012–19 (Pres., 2015–19). Hon. Fellow, Gray's Inn, 2012–16. Dist. Friend of Oxford, 2010–. *Recreation*: economics. *Address*: 41 Chelsea Square, SW3 6LH. *T*: (020) 7376 6767, *Fax*: (020) 7376 6777. *E*: jon@moyni.biz. *Clubs*: Travellers, Carlton, MCC, Academy, 5 Hertford Street, Coya.

**MOZAYEN, (Ann) Rosemary**; *see* Arnott, A. R.

**MOZUMDER, Air Vice-Marshal Aroop Kumar**, CB 2015; Commander Defence Primary Healthcare, Joint Forces Command, 2013–15; Director General Royal Air Force Medical Services, 2011–15; Farmington Fellow, Harris Manchester College, Oxford, since 2015; *b* London, 24 April 1956; *s* of Sailendra Mohon Mozumder and Gouri Mozumder; *m* 1984, Jane Edgcumbe; one *s* two *d*. *Educ*: Latymer Upper Sch.; Charing Cross Hosp. Med. Sch., London (MB BS 1979; MSc 1998). DRCOG 1983; DTM&H 1985; DAvMed 1993; DMCC 2004; FRCGP 2013; FFPH 2016. MO, Save the Children, 1984–86; Royal Air Force: MO, 1987–2015; Inspector Gen., Defence Med. Services, 2009–11. QHP 2008–15. GP Advr, Care Quality Commn, 2015–. Trustee: Headley Court Charity, 2013–16; Help for Heroes, 2014–17. Pres., Faculty of Conflict and Catastrophe Medicine, Apothecaries' Soc., 2012– (Mem., Ct of Assts, 2012–; Dean, 2017–). President: RAF Real Tennis, 2011–15; RAF Lawn Tennis, 2013–15. CDir 2014. Hon. Air Cdre, 605 Squadron, RAuxAF, 2015–. OStJ 2001. *Publications*: (contrib.) Conflict and Catastrophe Medicine, 2nd edn 2008, 3rd edn (contrib. ed.) 2013. *Clubs*: Royal Air Force; Royal Society of Medicine.

**MPUCHANE, Samuel Akuna;** in business in Botswana, since 1991; *b* 15 Dec. 1943; *s* of Chiminya Thompson Mpuchane and Motshidiemang Phologolo; *m* Sisai Felicity Mokgokong; two *s* one *d*. *Educ*: Univ. of Botswana, Lesotho and Swaziland (BA Govt and Hist.); Southampton Univ. (MSc Internat. Affairs). External Affairs Officer, 1969–70; First Secretary: Botswana Mission to UN, 1970–71; Botswana Embassy, Washington, 1971–74; Under Sec., External Affairs, 1974–76; on study leave, 1976–77; Dep. Perm. Sec., Min. of Mineral Resources and Water Affairs, 1977–79; Admin. Sec., Office of Pres., 1979–80; Perm. Sec., Min. of Local Govt and Lands, 1980–81; High Comr for Botswana in UK, 1982–85; Perm. Sec. for External Affairs, 1986–90. Director, 1991–: Builders World; Building Materials Supplies; Royal Wholesalers; Parts World; Trade World; Blue Chip Investments; Continental Star Caterers; Minaras Investments (Pty) Ltd; Keystone Investments (Pty) Ltd; 21st Century Hldgs (Pty) Ltd; Kan Bw (Pty) Ltd. Mem. Bd Trustees, Univ. of Botswana Foundn, 2000–. Order of White Rose and of the Lion (Finland), 2018. *Recreations*: playing and watching tennis, watching soccer.

**MROZ, Ann Dorota;** Digital Publishing Director, TES Global (formerly TSL Education), since 2012, and Editor, TES (formerly Times Educational Supplement), since 2013; *b* London, 31 Jan. 1959; *d* of Bolesław Mroz and Maria Mroz; one *d* one *s*. *Educ*: Orange Hill Grammar Sch., Edgware; London Coll. of Printing (NCTJ Proficiency Cert.); Henley Coll. (Cert. Mgt). Times Higher Education Supplement, later Times Higher Education, 1994–2012: Sub-Editor, later Chief Sub-Editor; Dep. Editor, 2007–08; Editor, 2008–12. FRSA. *Recreations*: riding hobby horses, swimming against the tide, sailing too close to the wind. *Address*: TES Global, 26 Red Lion Square, WC1R 4HQ. *T*: (020) 3194 3326. *E*: ann.mroz@tes.com.

**MSAKA, Bright,** SC; Minister of Education, Science and Technology, Malaŵi; Vice President, Eastern Region, since 2014; *m* Primrose; three *c*. NP; Practised law, specialising in commercial litigation and tort; Lectr in Law, Univ. of Malaŵi; Examr of Co. Law, ACCA; High Comr of Malaŵi in UK, and concurrently Ambassador to Finland, Iceland, Norway, Portugal, Spain, Sweden, 1998–2003; Chief Sec. for Pres. and Cabinet, 2004; Minister of Natural Resources, Energy and Mining. *Address*: Ministry of Education, Science and Technology, Capital Hill Circle, Private Bag 328, Capital City, Lilongwe 3, Malaŵi.

**MTETEMELA, Most Rev. Donald Leo;** Member, Constituent Assembly of Tanzania, 2014; Archbishop of Tanzania, 1998–2008; *b* Nov. 1947; *s* of Weston Mtetemela and Anjendile Mtetemela; *m* 1970, Gladys Matonya; three *s* four *d*. *Educ*: Dodoma Secondary Sch.; St Philip's Theol Coll., Kongwa (LTh); Wycliffe Hall, Oxford; DipTh London Univ. Ordained, 1971; Pastor, 1971–82; Asst Bishop, Central Tanganyika, 1982–90; Bishop of Ruaha, 1990–2010. Chancellor, St John's Univ. of Tanzania. Member: Windsor Continuation Gp, 2008; Bd, CMS-Africa, 2012– (Chm., 2016–); Advr, Primates Council, Global Anglican Future Conf., 2015–. Founder and Chm., Mama Bahati Foundn, 2006–. *Publications*: Nioneshe Kiongozi Mwadilifu (Show Me a Leader with Moral Integrity), 2014.

**MUBARAK, (Mohammed) Hosny,** Hon. GCMG 1985; President of Egypt, 1981–2011 (Vice President, 1975–81; Prime Minister, 1981–82); *b* 4 May 1928; *m* Suzanne Thabet; two *s*. *Educ*: Military Acad.; Air Force Acad. Joined Egyptian Air Force, 1950; Flight Instr, 1952–59, Dir Gen., 1967–69, Air Force Acad.; COS, 1969–72, C-in-C, 1972–75, Air Force; Lt Gen. 1973. Chm., OAU, 1989–90. National Democratic Party: Vice Chm., 1976–81; Sec. Gen., 1981–82; Chm., 1982–2011.

**MUCH, Ian Fraser Robert;** Chief Executive, De La Rue plc, 1998–2004; *b* 8 Sept. 1944; *s* of Alan Fraser Much and Helen Isabella Much (*née* Barker); *m* 1978, Perena Amanda Richards; two *d*. *Educ*: Haileybury and ISC; Lincoln Coll., Oxford (MA Jurisp.). The Metal Box Co., 1966–73; Selkirk Metalbestos, 1974–78; Household International Inc., 1978–84; Factory Manager, Nampa, Idaho, 1978–80; Vice-Pres., Gen. Manager, Greensboro, N Carolina, 1980–84; BTR: Man. Dir, Dunlop Aviation Div., 1985–87; Gp Chief Exec., 1987–88; Dir, BTR Industries; T & N: Exec. Dir, 1988–98; Man. Dir, Engineering & Industrial, 1990–91, Bearings and Industrial, 1991–95; Chief Exec., Ops, 1995–96; Chief Exec., 1996–98. Non-executive Director: Manchester United plc, 2000–05; Chemring, 2004–16; Simplyhealth (formerly HSA) Gp, 2005–09; Senior plc, 2005–14; BTG plc, 2010–. Gov., Haileybury and ISC, 2005–14; Chm. Govs, Royal School, Surrey, 2013–. Chm., Campaign Cttee, Lincoln Coll., Oxford, 2005–10. *Recreations*: ski-ing, tennis, squash, golf, swimming, bridge, theatre.

**MUCHLINSKI, Prof. Peter Thomas;** Professor of International Commercial Law, School of Oriental and African Studies, University of London, 2005–16, now Emeritus; *b* 18 Oct. 1957; *s* of late Franciszek Ksawery Muchlinski and Maria Irena Muchlinska. *Educ*: London Sch. of Econs (LLB); Christ's Coll., Cambridge (LLM). Called to the Bar, Lincoln's Inn, 1981; Res. Officer, British Inst. of Human Rights, 1979–80; Lectr in Law, Univ. of Kent at Canterbury, 1981–83; Lectr in Law, 1983–96, Sen. Lectr, 1996–98, LSE; Drapers Prof. of Law, QMW, Univ. of London, 1998–2001; Prof. of Law and Internat. Business, Kent Law Sch., Univ. of Kent, 2001–05. Principal Advr on investment law, Div. of Investment and Enterprise, UNCTAD, 1997–2012. *Publications*: Multinational Enterprises and the Law, 1995, 2nd edn 2007; (ed jtly) Oxford Handbook of International Investment Law, 2008; contrib. articles to jls incl. Yearbook of Internat. Investment Law and Policy, Cambridge Jl of Economics, Modern Law Rev., Internat. and Comparative Law Qly, Internat. Affairs, Business Ethics Qly, Indiana Jl of Global Legal Studies, Yearbook of Japanese Assoc. of Internat. Econ. Law, Politeia, German Law Jl; Eur. Yearbook of Internat. Econ. Law. *Recreations*: allotment gardening, history. *Address*: School of Law, School of Oriental and African Studies, Thornhaugh Street, Russell Square, WC1H 0XG.

**MUDD, (William) David;** consultant on tourism, transport and communications; cruise lecturer; *b* 2 June 1933; *o s* of Capt. W. N. Mudd and Mrs T. E. Mudd; *m*; one *s* one *d* (and one step *d*). *Educ*: Truro Cathedral Sch. Journalist, Broadcaster, TV Commentator; work on BBC and ITV (Westward Television). Editor of The Cornish Echo, 1952; Staff Reporter: Western Morning News, 1952–53 and 1959–62; Tavistock Gazette, 1963. Mem., Tavistock UDC, 1963–65. MP (C) Falmouth and Camborne, 1970–92. PPS, Dept of Energy, 1979–81; Mem., Transport Select Cttee, 1982–92. Secretary: Conservative West Country Cttee, 1973–76; Conservative Party Fisheries Sub-Cttee, 1974–75, 1981–82. Contested (Ind.) Falmouth and Camborne, 2005. Patron, Court Interpreters' Assoc., Supreme Court of Hong Kong, 1979–97. *Publications*: Cornishmen and True, 1971; Murder in the West Country, 1975; Facets of Crime, 1975; The Innovators, 1976; Down Along Camborne and Redruth, 1978; The Falmouth Packets, 1978; Cornish Sea Lights, 1978; Cornwall and Scilly Peculiar, 1979; About the City, 1979; Home Along Falmouth and Penryn, 1980; Around and About the Roseland, 1980; The Cruel Cornish Sea, 1981; The Cornish Edwardians, 1982; Cornwall in Uproar, 1983; Around and About the Fal, 1989; Around and About the Smugglers' Ways, 1991; Strange Stories of Cornwall, 1992; Dartmoor Reflections, 1993; The Magic of Dartmoor, 1994; Let the Doors be Lock'd, 2000; Better with a Pinch of Salt, 2003; Sugar 'n' Spice, 2005; The Sign of the Balloon, 2006; Clarence the Cornish Chough, 2008; How Zacci Met the Queen, 2011. *Recreations*: jig-saw puzzles, photography. *Address*: The Retreat, Down Park Drive, Tavistock, Devon PL19 9AH. *Club*: West Devon.

**MUDDIMAN, Noel,** CBE 1992 (OBE 1985); Director: CF Solutions Ltd, since 2003; Motability, 1995–2004 (Member of Council, since 2004); *b* 17 Dec. 1943; *s* of late Flora Muddiman (*née* Holdsworth), and step *s* of late Arthur George Muddiman; *m* 1969, Patricia Anne Sevage; two *s*. *Educ*: Borden Grammar Sch.; RMA, Sandhurst. Commnd RCT, 1965; regtl posts in Germany, UK, Singapore; Staff Coll., Camberley, 1975; ndc, 1981; CO, 25 Transport and Movements Regt, RCT, 1983–85; Head of Personnel and Logistics, Falkland Islands, 1985–86; Principal Logistic Planner, British Forces Germany, 1987–90; Commander: Transport and Movements, BAOR, 1990–92; Logistic Support Gp (ME), 1991; rcds, 1992; Comdt, Army Sch. of Transport, 1993–95, retd. Non-exec. Dir, Metropole Search Partners Ltd, 2012–. Norwegian Gulf War Medal, 1995. *Publications*: (jtly) Blackadder's War, 1995. *Recreations*: gardening, walking, photography.

**MUDDIMER, Robert Michael;** Deputy Chairman, Tomkins plc, 1996–97 (Director, 1986–97); Chairman, Gates Rubber Co., 1996–97; *b* 30 Jan. 1933; *m* 1959, Marguerite Conroy; two *s* one *d*. *Educ*: Kibworth Grammar Sch.; Univ. of Nottingham (BSc Mech. Eng 1956). FIET (FIMfgE 1966). Materials Mgt, Lansing Bagnall, 1965–68; Director: BTR Ind. Ltd, 1969–80; Molins Tobacco Ind. Ltd, 1981–86; Chm., Rank Hovis McDougall, 1992–96. *Recreations*: golf, sailing, wooden clockmaking.

**MUDIE, Colin Crichton,** RDI 1995; CEng; FRINA, FRIN; Principal Partner, Colin Mudie, Naval Architects and Yacht Designers, 1958–2014; *b* 11 April 1926; *s* of John Mudie and Janet Somerville Mudie (*née* Jack); *m* 1954, Rosemary Horder; one *s*. *Educ*: George Watson's, Edinburgh; Whitgift Sch.; University Coll., Southampton. CEng 1971; FRINA 1971; FRIN 1972 (Hon. FRIN 2004). Design apprentice: British Power Boat Co., Southampton, 1942–46; Laurent Giles & Partners Ltd, 1946–49; various marine projects incl. Sopranino voyage, 1951–52 and Small World transatlantic balloon flight, 1958–59. Winston Churchill Fellowship, 1968. Design work includes sail trng vessels, reproduction, expedition and exploration boats, power boats, sailing yachts, motor cruisers, etc; designer of sail trng ship, Young Endeavour, GB's gift to Australia for 1988 Bicentennial. Member: Cttee of Mgt, RNLI, 1987–2001 (Vice-Pres., 1997–2001, now Life Vice-Pres.); Council, RINA, 1988–97. Associate Mem., Acad. de Marinha, Portugal, 1995. FRSA 1996. Award for sail trng brig Royalist, Lloyd's Register of Shipping, 1971; Small Craft Medal, RINA, 1984; Award for sail trng barque Lord Nelson, British Design Council, 1993. *Publications*: Sopranino (with P. Ellam), 1953; Motor Boats and Boating, 1972; Power Boats, 1975; with Rosemary Mudie: The Story of the Sailing Ship, 1975; Power Yachts, 1977; The Sailing Ship, 1984; Sailing Ships, 2000; contrib. papers at various symposia, and articles and illustrations to professional, yachting and other jls. *Recreations*: reading, watching model yachts at Setley Pond, Lymington. *Address*: Bywater Lodge, Undershore Road, Lymington, Hants SO41 5SB. *T*: (01590) 672047. *Clubs*: Royal Lymington Yacht, Lymington Town Sailing; Ocean Cruising.

**MUDIE, George Edward;** *b* 6 Feb. 1945. *Educ*: state schs. Former Mem. (Lab) Leeds CC, and Leader of Council. MP (Lab) Leeds E, 1992–2015. Treasurer of HM Household (Dep. Chief Govt Whip), 1997–98; Parly Under-Sec. of State, DfEE, 1998–99; an Asst Govt Whip, 2009–10; Opposition Whip, 2010–13. Mem., Treasury Select Cttee, 2001–14.

**MUELLBAUER, Prof. John Norbert Joseph,** PhD; FBA 1997; Professor of Economics, University of Oxford, 1997–2011, now Emeritus; Senior Research Fellow: Nuffield College, Oxford, since 2011 (Fellow in Economics, 1981–2011); Institute for New Economic Thinking at Oxford Martin School, since 2011; Research Fellow, Centre for Economic Policy Research; *b* 17 July 1944; *s* of late Prof. Norbert J. Muellbauer and Edith Heinz; *m* 1999, Dr Janine Aron; one *d*; one *s* from previous marriage. *Educ*: King's Coll., Cambridge (MA 1965); Univ. of Calif at Berkeley (PhD 1975). Lectr in Economics, Univ. of Warwick, 1969–72; Lectr, 1972–75, Reader, 1975–77, Prof., 1977–81, in Economics, Birkbeck Coll., London Univ. Member: Gp of Outside Ind. Economists advising the Chancellor of the Exchequer, 1989; Retail Price Index Adv. Cttee, 1993–95. Wim Duisenberg Vis. Fellow, Eur. Central Bank, 2012–13; Fellow, S African Reserve Bank, 2018–19. Fellow, Econometric Soc., 1976. Medal, Helsinki Univ., 1980. *Publications*: (with Angus Deaton) Economics and Consumer Behaviour, 1980; articles in Financial Times, Amer. Econ. Review, Econometrica, Econ. Jl, etc. *Recreations*: music, tennis. *Address*: Nuffield College, Oxford OX1 1NF. *T*: (01865) 278583.

**MUELLER, Rudolf Gottfried,** Hon. CBE 1997; Chairman, Chiltern Participations UK Ltd, 2004–06; *b* 28 May 1934; Swiss national; *m* Christiane Béroud; two *s*. *Educ*: primary and secondary schools, St Gallen, Switzerland; Internat. Management Inst., Geneva. Swiss Fed. Commercial Dip. 1953; grad. 1969 from Univ. of Geneva with dip. equivalent to MBA. James Capel & Co., 1969–77; joined Union Bank of Switzerland, 1977: Chm. and Chief Exec., UBS UK, 1989–96; Mem., Exec. Bd, UBS Gp, 1991–96; non-exec. Chm., UBS UK, 1996–98; Chairman: WJB Chiltern Gp plc (formerly Chiltern Gp plc), 1998–2003; WJB Chiltern Wealth Mgt Services Ltd, 2004–06. Non-executive Director: Lend Lease Corp. Ltd, 1996–2002; TI Gp, 1996–2000. Chm., Swiss Options Financial Futures Exchange, Zürich, 1986–88; Dir, London Stock Exchange, 1991–95. Chm. of Bd of Trustees, Rix Centre, 2004–10. Member of Board: Internat. Mgt Inst., Kiev, 1993–2005; Royal Opera House Trust, 1992–97; Dir, Royal Opera House, 1996–98. Hon. DBA East London, 2005. *Recreations*: golf, ski-ing, hiking, oenology.

**MUFF,** family name of **Baron Calverley**.

**MUGGERIDGE, Rev. Sara Ann, (Sally), (Mrs R. D. Williams);** Chief Executive, Industry and Parliament Trust, 2003–10; Curate, St Stephen Walbrook, City of London, 2015–17; Licensed Priest, Canterbury, since 2018; *b* 10 Sept. 1949; *d* of John Raymond Muggeridge, MBE and Sylvia Barbara Ann (*née* Jenkins); *m* 1969, Richard David Williams; one *s* two *d*. *Educ*: Aida Foster Stage Sch.; S Hampstead High Sch.; Guildhall Sch. of Music and Drama (Cert. Acting); Westfield Coll., London (BA Hons); Henley Mgt Coll. (Co. of Marketors Award 1992; MBA); Univ. of Kent (Cert. Applied Christian Theol., 2010); Canterbury Christ Church Univ. (FdA Theol., 2013). Mktg Manager, British Telecom plc, 1985–91; Cable & Wireless plc: Mktg Dir, Mercury Communications, 1991–93; Mgt Develt Dir, 1993–96; HR Dir, Asia, 1996–99; Mgt Develt Dir, Pearson plc, 1999–2003. Non-exec. Dir, Total Upstream UK Ltd, 2010–15. Chartered Institute of Marketing: Mem. Council, 1985–95; Pres., CIM Singapore, 1996–98; Exec. Vice-Pres., 1999–2004; Mem., Academic Senate, 2007–13. Member: Bd, Southern Arts, 1992–96; Council for Excellence in Mgt and Leadership, 2000–02; Consultative Cttee, Three Faiths Forum, 2008–. Church Comr and Gov., C of E, 2014–; ordained deacon, 2015, priest, 2016; Chaplain, Lady Masters Assoc., 2016–. Mem., House of Laity, Gen. Synod, 2010–15. Trustee: Pearson Gp Pensions Ltd, 1999–2003; Tutu Foundn UK, 2003–13 (Vice Patron, 2013–); Foundn for Church Leadership, 2003–11 (Vice Pres., 2011–13). Internat. Pres., Malcolm Muggeridge Soc., 2003–. Mem. Council, Univ. of Kent, 2006–12. Fellow, Industry and Parlt Trust, 1995; FCIM 1988; FCIPD 1996; FRSA 1995; FInstD 2011. Hon. Life Mem., Acad. of Mktg, 2013. President's Award, CIM, 1999; Voluntary Sector Achiever of the Yr, Woman of the Yr Awards, 2007; World of Difference Award, Internat. Alliance of Women, 2015. *Films*: acted in The Hallelujah Handshake, 1970, and The Yes Girls, 1971; contrib. Timeshift: Malcolm Muggeridge (TV), 2003. Mem., House of Laity, Gen. Synod, 2010–. Freeman, City of London, 1995. Master, Marketors' Co., 2013. *Publications*: contributor: The Laterite Road, 2005; Conversion: the spiritual journey of a twentieth century pilgrim,

2005; Seeing Through the Eye, 2005; Something Beautiful for God, 2009; Jesus: the Gospel according to Saint Mugg, 2016. *Recreations:* choral singing, preaching, theatre and the arts, entertaining grandchildren and English Setter. *E:* revdsallymuggeridge@gmail.com. *Club:* Farmers.

**MUGGLETON, Prof. Stephen Howard,** PhD; FREng; Professor of Machine Learning, since 2001 and Royal Academy of Engineering/Syngenta Research Professor of Machine Learning, since 2013, Imperial College London; *b* Salisbury, Southern Rhodesia, 6 Dec. 1959; *s* of late Prof. Louis Miles Muggleton and (Alice) Sylvia Muggleton; *m* 1988, Thirza Ana Castello-Cortes; one *d. Educ:* George Watson's Coll., Edinburgh; Univ. of Edinburgh (BSc Hons 1983; PhD 1986). Res. Fellow, Turing Inst., Glasgow, 1987–92; Res. Fellow, Wolfson Coll., Oxford, 1992–97; EPSRC Advanced Res. Fellow, Computing Lab., 1992–97; Reader, 1997, Univ. of Oxford; Prof. of Machine Learning, Dept of Computing, Univ. of York, 1997–2001; Imperial College London: EPSRC Prof. of Computational Bioinformatics, 2001–06; Dir, Modelling, BBSRC Centre for Integrative Systems Biol., 2005–10; RAEng/Microsoft Res. Prof. of Machine Learning, 2007–12; Dir, Syngenta University Innovation Centre, 2008–. Hon. Lectr, Univ. of Strathclyde, 1991–92; Fujitsu Vis. Associate Prof., Univ. of Tokyo, 1993. FAAAI 2002; FBCS 2008; FIET 2008; FREng 2010; FRSB (FSB 2011); Fellow, Eur. Coordinating Cttee for Artificial Intelligence, 2014. Ed.-in-Chief, Machine Intelligence series, 2000–. *Publications:* Inductive Acquisition of Expert Knowledge, 1990; (ed) Inductive Logic Programming, 1992; (ed jtly) Machine Intelligence, vol. 13, 1994, vol. 14, 1995, vol. 15, 1999; (ed jtly) Elements of Computational Systems Biology, 2010; (ed jtly) Latest Advances in Inductive Logic Programming, 2015; articles in jls incl. New Generation Computing, Jl of Logic Programming, Machine Learning, Artificial Intelligence, AI Communications, Procs of Royal Soc., Nature, Jl Molecular Biol. *Recreations:* reading, walking, listening to music, watching films. *Address:* Department of Computing, Imperial College London, 180 Queen's Gate, SW7 2RH.

**MUGHAL, Sajda,** OBE 2015; Chief Executive Officer, JAN Trust, since 2008; *b* Nairobi, Kenya; two *d. Educ:* sch. in N London; BA Business Mgt. Author of reports: Consent Matters: towards effective prevention of forced marriages within the Pakistani community in the UK, 2012; Internet Extremism: working towards a community solution, 2013. *Recreations:* reading, keeping fit, travelling, current affairs. *Address:* c/o JAN Trust, 8–10 Bedford Road, Wood Green, N22 7AU. *E:* info@jantrust.org.

**MUHEIM, Franz Emmanuel;** President, Swiss Red Cross, 1996–2001; Vice-President, International Federation of Red Cross and Red Crescent Societies, 1996–2001; Swiss Ambassador to the Court of St James's, 1989–94; *b* 27 Sept. 1931; *s* of Hans Muheim and Hélène (*née* Ody); *m* 1962, Radmila Jovanovic. *Educ:* Univs of Fribourg (LèsL), Geneva and Paris (arts degree). Joined Swiss Federal Dept of Foreign Affairs, 1960; served successively in Belgrade, Rabat and London, 1961–70; Council of Europe, UN and Internat. Orgns Sect., Dept of Foreign Affairs, Berne, 1971–77; Dep. Head of Mission, Minister Plenipotentiary, Washington, 1978–81; Dep. Dir of Political Affairs and Head of Political Div. Europe and N America, with rank of Ambassador, Berne, 1982–83; Dir, Internat. Orgns, Dept of Foreign Affairs, 1984–89. Head of Swiss delegns to internat. confs, *inter alia* UNESCO, ESA, Red Cross, Non-Aligned Movement. Fellow, Center for Internat. Affairs, Harvard Univ., 1981–82; Prof., Bologna Center, Johns Hopkins Univ., 1995–96. *Publications:* (ed jtly) Einblick in die Schweizerische Aussenpolitik: festschrift für Staatssekretär Raymond Probst, 1984; Multilateralism Today: festschrift zum 70. Geburtstag von a. Ständerat Franz Muheim, 1993; Traces d'un passant, 2019. *Recreations:* walking, mountaineering, ski-ing, photography, music. *Address:* Route des Chesaux 40, 1646 Echarlens, Switzerland. *T:* (026) 9152474, 07946 75056, *Fax:* (026) 9152450.

**MUIR, Prof. Alexander Laird,** MD; FRCPE, FRCR, FRCSE; Professor of Postgraduate Medicine, University of Edinburgh, 1990–99; Honorary Consultant Physician, Edinburgh Royal Infirmary, 1974–99; Honorary Physician to the Army in Scotland, 1986–99; *b* 12 April 1937; *s* of Andrew Muir and Helena Bauld; *m* 1968, Berenice Barker Snelgrove, FRCR; one *s* one *d. Educ:* Morrison's Acad.; Fettes Coll.; Univ. of Edinburgh. MB ChB, MD 1970; FRCPE 1975 (MRCPE 1967); FRCR 1986; FRCSE 1994. MO, British Antarctic Survey, 1963–65; MRC Fellow, McGill Univ., 1970–71; Consultant Physician, Manchester Royal Infirmary, 1973–74; Edinburgh University: Sen. Lectr in Medicine, 1974; Reader in Medicine, 1981–89; Postgrad. Dean of Medicine, 1990–99. Physician to the Queen in Scotland, 1985–96. Canadian MRC Vis. Scientist, Univ. of British Columbia, 1982. Chm. and Med. Dir, Jt Cttee for Higher Med. Trng, 1998–2001; Mem., Admin of Radioactive Substances Adv. Cttee, 1986–91. Vice-Pres., RCPE, 1994–97. Founder FMedSci 1998. Member Editorial Board: Thorax, 1981–86; British Heart Jl, 1986–90. *Publications:* contribs on physiology and diseases of heart and lungs to medical books, symposia and jls. *Recreations:* gardening, reading, golf. *Address:* Easter Rubislaw, 31/9 Hermitage Drive, Edinburgh EH10 6BY.

**MUIR, Gregor;** Director of Collection, International Art, Tate, since 2017; *b* London, 29 Nov. 1964; *s* of John and Maura Muir. *Educ:* Camberwell Sch. of Arts and Crafts (BA Hons Fine Art, Painting 1987). Ind. writer, critic and curator, 1987–93; ind. writer and curator, 1993–97; Dir, Lux Gall., Hoxton Sq., 1997–2001; Kramlich Curator of Contemp. Art, Tate, 2001–03; Dir, Hauser & Wirth, London, 2004–10; Exec. Dir, ICA, 2011–16. *Publications:* Lucky Kunst: the rise and fall of young British art, 2009, 2nd edn 2010. *Recreations:* art, architecture, design, food, music. *Address:* Tate Modern, Bankside, SE1 9TG.

**MUIR, (Sir) Richard James Kay,** (4th Bt cr 1892, of Deanston, Perthshire); *S* father, 1994, but does not use the title and his name is not on the Official Roll of the Baronetage; *b* 25 May 1939; *s* of Sir John Harling Muir, 3rd Bt, TD and Elizabeth Mary, *e d* of Frederick James Dundas; *m* 1st, 1965, Susan Elizabeth (marr. diss. 1974), *d* of George A. Gardener; two *d*; 2nd, 1975, Lady Linda Mary Cole, *d* of 6th Earl of Enniskillen, MBE; two *d. Heir: b* Ian Charles Muir [*b* 16 Sept. 1940; *m* 1967, Fiona Barbara Elspeth, *d* of Major Stuart Mackenzie; three *d*].

**MUIR, Richard John Sutherland,** CMG 1994; HM Diplomatic Service, retired; *b* 25 Aug. 1942; *s* of John Muir and Edna (*née* Hodges); *m* 1966, Caroline Simpson; one *s* one *d. Educ:* The Stationers' Co.'s Sch.; Univ. of Reading (BA Hons). Entered HM Diplomatic Service, 1964; FO, 1964–65; MECAS, Lebanon, 1965–67; Third, then Second Sec. (Commercial), Jedda, 1967–70; Second Sec., Tunis, 1970–72; FCO, 1972–75; First Sec., Washington, 1975–79; seconded to Dept of Energy, 1979–81; Dir-Gen., British Liaison Office, Riyadh, 1981–85; FCO 1985–94: Hd of Information Dept, 1987–90; Principal Finance Officer and Chief Inspector, 1991–94; Ambassador: to Oman, 1994–99; to Kuwait, 1999–2002. Vice Pres., Anglo-Omani Soc., 2012– (Chm., 2004–12); Chm., Sir William Luce Meml Fund, 2007–; Dir, Altajir Trust, 2007–. Order of Na'aman (1st Class) (Oman), 2013.

**MUIR, Tom;** Under Secretary, Textiles and Retailing Division, Department of Trade and Industry, 1992–94; *b* 15 Feb. 1936; *s* of late William and Maria Muir; *m* 1968, Brenda Dew; one *s* one *d. Educ:* King Edward VI Sch., Stafford; Leeds Univ. (BA Econs 1962). FCIS 1994. English Electric Co. Ltd, 1954–59; BoT, 1962–68; UK Perm. Delegn to OECD (on secondment to HM Diplomatic Service), 1968–71; DTI, 1972–75; UK Perm. Repn to EC,

1975–79 (on secondment); DoI, 1979–81; Dept of Trade, 1981–83; DTI, 1983–94: Under Sec., Insce Div., 1982–87, Overseas Trade Div. 4, 1987–89, Internat. Trade Policy Div., 1989–92. Dir, British Retail Consortium, 1995–97. Inquiry Sec., then Inquiry Manager, Competition Commn, 1999–2008. Chm., Fedn of British Artists (Mall Galls), 1998–2001. *Recreations:* walking, reading, looking at buildings and pictures, opera.

**MUIR MACKENZIE, Sir Alexander (Alwyne Henry Charles Brinton),** 7th Bt cr 1805; *b* 8 Dec. 1955; *s* of Sir Robert Henry Muir Mackenzie, 6th Bt and Charmian Cecil de Vere (*d* 1962), *o d* of Col Cecil Charles Brinton; *S* father, 1970; *m* 1984, Susan Carolyn (marr. diss. 2015), *d* of late John David Henzel Hayter; one *s* one *d. Educ:* Eton; Trinity Coll., Cambridge. *Heir: s* Archie Robert David Muir Mackenzie, *b* 17 Feb. 1989.

**MUIR WOOD, Prof. David,** PhD; FREng, FICE, FRSE; Professor of Civil Engineering, University of Bristol, 1995–2009, now Emeritus; Professor of Geotechnical Engineering, University of Dundee, 2009–14, now Emeritus; Professor affilierad, Geotechnical Engineering, Chalmers University of Technology, Gothenburg, Sweden, since 2014; *b* 17 March 1949; *s* of Sir Alan Muir Wood, FRS, FREng and Winifred L. Wood; *m* 1978, Helen Rosamond Piddington; two *s. Educ:* Royal Grammar Sch., High Wycombe; Peterhouse, Cambridge (BA 1970, MA 1974; PhD 1974). FICE 1992; FREng (FEng 1998); FRSE 2012. University of Cambridge: res. student, Engrg Dept, 1970–73; William Stone Res. Fellow, Peterhouse, 1973–75; Fellow, Emmanuel Coll., 1975–87; Demonstrator/Lectr in Soil Mechanics, Engrg Dept, 1975–87; University of Glasgow: Cormack Prof. of Civil Engrg, 1987–95; Hd, Dept of Civil Engrg, 1991–93; Dean, Faculty of Engrg, 1993–94; University of Bristol: Hd, Dept of Civil Engrg, 1997–2002; Dean, Faculty of Engrg, 2003–07. Royal Soc. Res. Fellow, Norwegian Geotechnical Inst., Oslo, 1975; Royal Soc. Industry Fellow, Babtie Gp, 1995–96. Visiting Professor: Politecnico di Milano, 2014; Dresden Tech. Univ., 2015; Univ. of Innsbruck, 2016; Yokohama Nat. Univ., 2017; Northwestern Univ., Illinois, 2018. Hon. Editor, Géotechnique, 1991–93. Associate, Geotechnical Consulting Gp, 1983–. Chm., Scottish Geotechnical Gp, 1991–93. Elder: Cairns Ch of Scotland, Milngavie, 1993–98; Monikie and Newbigging, Murroes and Tealing, Ch of Scotland, 2011–. (Jtly) British Geotechnical Soc. Prize, 1978. *Publications:* (with R. J. Mair) Pressuremeter Testing: methods and interpretation, 1987; Soil Behaviour and Critical State Soil Mechanics, 1990; (jtly) Piled Foundations in Weak Rock, 1999; Geotechnical Modelling, 2004; Soil Mechanics: a one-dimensional introduction, 2009; A very short introduction to civil engineering, 2012; contrib. numerous papers to professional jls and confs. *Recreations:* music, opera, travel, photography. *Address:* University of Dundee, Division of Civil Engineering, Fulton Building, Dundee DD1 4HN. *E:* dmuirwood@dundee.ac.uk; Kirklands, Kirkton of Monikie, Broughty Ferry, Angus DD5 3QN. *T:* (01382) 370685.

**MUIRDEN, Catherine Mary;** People Director (formerly Director of Human Resources, Retail), Co-operative Foods, since 2014; *b* Inverness, 19 Sept. 1962; *d* of Rev. John R. Muirden and J. Christine Muirden; *m* 1998, Werner Keschner; one *s. Educ:* Inverness Royal Acad.; Edinburgh Univ. (MA Gen. Arts 1984). Marks & Spencer: personnel mgt appts, 1984–93; Econ. and Strategic Develt Unit, London Bor. of Croydon (on secondment), 1993–94; store manager, 1994–98; Divl Personnel Manager, 1998–2000; Regl Hd of HR, 2000–02; Gp Hd of Recruitment, 2002–05; Divl Hd of HR, 2005–07; HR Dir, UK Retail and Business Bank, Barclays plc, 2007–14. Non-exec. Dir, Crieff Hydro Gp of Hotels, 2014–18. Chair, Fruitmarket Gall., Edinburgh, 2014–17 (Mem. Bd, 2005–17); Mem. Bd, Scottish Ballet, 2019–. Trustee: Nat. Galleries of Scotland, 2012–; Elevation Networks, 2012–15. FRSA 2006. *Recreations:* early morning swimming, gardening, contemporary art, good food and drink. *E:* kittykeschner@icloud.com. *Club:* New (Edinburgh).

**MUIRHEAD, Alastair William;** Senior Adviser, Phoenix Equity Partners, since 2018 (Partner, 2001–18); *b* Sheffield, 12 Sept. 1953; *s* of William Calliope Muirhead and Joan Andrade Muirhead; *m* 1980, Linda Anne; three *d. Educ:* Tonbridge Sch.; St John's Coll., Oxford (Schol.; MA Hons Natural Scis (Chem.)). Man. Dir, Charterhouse Bank, 1989–96; Partner, Phoenix Gp, 1996–97; Managing Director: Donaldson Lufkin & Jenrette, 1997–2000; Credit Suisse, 2000–01. Trustee, 2008–19, Treas., 2013–19, RHS. *Recreations:* gardening, hill walking, fly fishing, golf. *Address:* Phoenix Equity Partners, 123 Victoria Street, SW1E 6DE. *T:* (020) 7434 6999. *Clubs:* Hankley Common Golf; Houghton.

**MUIRHEAD, Geoffrey,** CBE 2004; FCILT, FICE; Group Chief Executive, Manchester Airports Group, 2001–10; *b* 14 July 1949; *s* of John Thomas Muirhead and Irene Clarke; *m* 1972, Clare Elizabeth Parker; one *d. Educ:* Teesside Polytechnic. FCIT 1994; FICE 1998. Started career with British Steel; subseq. senior positions with William Press, Simon Carves, Fluor and Shand, incl. posts in Saudi Arabia, Belgium, Eire; Manchester Airport: Dir, Develt, 1988; Dir, Business Develt, 1992; Chief Exec., 1993–2001. Past Pres., Airports Council Internat. Europe. Mem., NW Business Leadership Team, 1993–2010 (Dep. Chm., 2006–10); Exec. Mem., NW Regl Assembly, 2006–08; Mem. Leaders Bd, 4NW. Associate Mem., Greater Manchester Chamber of Commerce and Industry, 2001 (Past Pres.). Chm., Ask Developments, 2010. Mem. Bd, Manchester Metropolitan Univ. FRSA 1996. Hon. DBA: Manchester Metropolitan, 2003; Teesside, 2005; Hon. DSc Salford, 2004. *Recreations:* golf, travel.

**MUIRHEAD, Dame Lorna (Elizabeth Fox),** DCVO 2017; DBE 2000; Lord-Lieutenant of Merseyside, 2006–17; Midwifery Sister, Liverpool Women's Hospital (formerly Liverpool Maternity Hospital), 1966–69 and 1974–2005; President, Royal College of Midwives, 1997–2004; *b* 13 Sept. 1942; *d* of Donald Fox and Joan Mary (*née* Harper); *m* 1966, Ronald A. Muirhead; one *s* one *d. Educ:* in Shropshire and Warwickshire. SRN 1963; SCM 1965; MTD 1970; FRCOG 2001. Nurse trng, Hallam Hosp., W Bromwich, 1960–63; midwifery trng, Hallam Hosp. and Marston Green Maternity Hosp., 1964–65; Staff Midwife, Liverpool Maternity Hosp., 1965–66; Midwifery Sister Tutor, 1969–71; part-time Lectr, Liverpool Poly., 1975–80; Sen. Lectr, British Shipping Fedn med. course, 1975–85; frequent Lectr at Univ. and Royal Coll. Midwives seminars and study days, 1980–. DL Merseyside, 2003. Fellow, Royal Coll. Midwives, 2005. Hon. Fellow, Liverpool John Moores Univ., 2001. Hon. LLD Liverpool, 2010; Hon. DHumLit Liverpool Hope, 2016. CStJ 2008. *Publications:* chapter on A Midwife's Role in Epidural Analgesia, in Epidural Analgesia in Obstetrics, ed A. Doughty, 1980. *Recreations:* choral singing, music, poetry, restoration of old furniture. *T:* (0151) 224 4000.

**MUIRHEAD, Oona Grant,** CBE 2000 (OBE 1992); business consultant, since 2012; Business Adviser, Policy Connect, since 2017; *b* 29 Jan. 1956; *d* of Michael and Marion Muirhead. *Educ:* Univ. of Birmingham (BA Hons Russian; Dip. Vocational Techniques for Prof. Linguist). Ministry of Defence, 1979–2003: Defence Intelligence Service, 1979; various policy and operational posts, 1985–95; (first) Pol Advr to Chief of Jt Ops, 1995–97; Dir, Inf. Strategy and News, 1997–2000; rcds, 2000; DG, Mgt and Orgn, 2001–03; Prog. Dir for Modernising Rural Delivery, DEFRA, 2003–05; Dir of Strategy and Communications, LGA, 2005–07; Dir, Land Use Proj., DEFRA, 2007; South East England Development Agency: Exec. Dir, Skills and Sustainable Prosperity Directorate, 2007–09; Gp Exec. Dir, Strategy and Resources, 2009–11; Chief Exec., 2011–12; Dir, 2012, Mem., Exec. Bd, 2013–16, Security in Complex Envmts Gp, ADS Gp Ltd; Man. Dir, Muirhead

Ltd, 2012–16; Advr, Aegis Defence Services, 2012–15. Member, Board: Office for Nuclear Regulation, 2014– (Chair, Security Cttee, 2014–); MSS Global, 2016–. Trustee, RN and RM Charity, 2013–18. *Recreations:* gardening, golf, walking, decorating/DIY, opera, the Archers omnibus, reading mental chewing-gum, sailing. *Address:* Battersea, SW11 3GL.

**MUIRHEAD, William Donald;** Sheriff of Lothian and Borders at Livingston, 2009–13 (at Linlithgow, 2000–09); *b* 21 March 1948; *s* of William Ingram Muirhead and Phyllis Jessie Muirhead; *m* 1976, Maria de los Angeles Cabieces; one *s* two *d*. *Educ:* Melville Coll.; Edinburgh Univ. (LLB Hons). Solicitor, Aitken Nairn WS, 1972–2000. Pt-time Sheriff, 1993–99. *Recreations:* golf, music, hill walking, fishing. *Club:* Bruntsfield Links Golf.

**MUIRHEAD, William Mortimer,** AM 2013; Agent General for South Australia in London, since 2007; Founding Partner and Executive Director, M&C Saatchi, since 1995; *b* Adelaide, SA, 11 July 1946; *s* of Denis and Lorna Muirhead; *m* 1971, Jeanne Elizabeth Meins; three *s*. *Educ:* Armidale Sch., Armidale, NSW; St Dunstan's Coll., London. Jackson Wain/Leo Burnett, 1966–70; Account Exec., Ogilvy & Mather, 1970–72; Account Dir, subseq. Gp Account Dir, Saatchi & Saatchi, 1972–89; Chm. and Chief Exec., Saatchi & Saatchi Advertising UK, 1989–92; Chm., Saatchi & Saatchi Europe, 1992–94; Chief Exec. and Pres., Saatchi & Saatchi Advertising Worldwide, NY, 1994–95. *Recreations:* tennis, skiing, golf, music, travel. *Address:* Australia Centre, Strand, WC2B 4LG. *T:* (020) 7520 9100. *E:* bill.muirhead@south-aus.eu. *Clubs:* Royal Automobile, Thirty, South Australia.

**MUIRHEAD-ALLWOOD, Sarah Kathryn,** FRCS; Consultant Orthopaedic Surgeon: Royal National Orthopaedic Hospital, 1991–2012, now Hon. Consultant; King Edward VII's Hospital for Officers, since 1993; *b* 4 Jan. 1947; *c* of late Maj. W. R. Muirhead and of Joyce Muirhead (*née* Forster); *m* 1983; two *s*. *Educ:* Wellington; St Thomas' Hosp. Med. Sch. (BSc, MB BS). MRCS, FRCS, LRCP. St Thomas' Hospital: House Surg., 1971–72; Sen. House Officer, 1972–73; Anatomy Demonstrator, 1973; Sen. House Officer, Stoke Mandeville Hosp., 1973–74; Registrar: UCH, 1974–77; Charing Cross Hosp., 1977–78; Sen. Registrar, Queen Mary's Hosp., Roehampton, Westminster Hosp., Royal Nat. Orthopaedic Hosp., UCH, 1978–84; Consultant Orthopaedic Surgeon, Whittington Hosp., 1984–2004; estabd London Hip Unit, 2002. Hon. Sen. Clin. Lectr, UCL, 1984; Hon. Consultant: St Luke's Hosp. for the Clergy, 1984; Hosp. of St John and St Elizabeth. Member: British Orthopaedic Assoc., 1980; BMA, 1983; British Hip Soc., 1989; European Hip Soc., 1993; Internat. Hip Soc., 2009. Freeman, City of London, 2009; Liveryman, Gold and Silver Wyre Drawers' Co., 2009. *Publications:* contributions to: Joint Replacement—State of the Art, 1990; Recent Advances in Orthopaedic Surgery, 1991; Gray's Anatomy, 1995. *Recreations:* golf, sailing. *Address:* The London Hip Unit, 4th Floor, 30 Devonshire Street, W1G 6PU. *T:* (020) 7908 3709. *E:* londonhip@aol.com.

**MUIRHEAD-ALLWOOD, William Forster Gillespie;** *see* Muirhead-Allwood, S. K.

**MUKARJI, Dr (Satyanand) Daleep,** Hon. OBE 2008; Chairman, Y Care International, 2010–15; *b* 22 Feb. 1946; *m* Azra Latifi; one *s* two *d*. *Educ:* Christian Med. Coll., Vellore, India (MB BS); London Sch. of Hygiene and Tropical Med. (DTPH); LSE (MSc). Med. Superintendent, Mission Hosp., Andhra Pradesh, India, 1972; MO and Project Dir, Leprosy Hosp., Dichpalli, 1973; Programme Dir, Rural Unit for Health and Social Affairs, Christian Med. Coll., Vellore, 1977–85; Gen. Sec., Christian Med. Assoc. of India, 1985–94; Exec. Sec., Urban Rural Mission, 1994–96, Health, Community and Justice, 1997–98, WCC, Geneva; Dir, Christian Aid, 1998–2010; Chm., Overseas Develt Inst., 2010–12. *Recreations:* music, theatre, cinema. *Address:* 7 Torrington Grove, N12 9NA.

**MUKHAMEDOV, Irek Javdatovich,** OBE 2000; ballet dancer; Principal Ballet Master and Character Artist, English National Ballet, since 2015; *b* 1960; *s* of Djavdat Rasulievich Mukhamedov and Rashida Nizamovna; *m* 1990, Maria Zubkhova; one *s* one *d*. *Educ:* Moscow Choreographic Inst. Soloist, Moscow Classical Co., 1978–81; Bolshoi Ballet, 1981–90; Principal, 1990–99, Guest Artist, 1999–2001, Royal Ballet Co.; founded Mukhamedov & Co., 1991; Artistic Co-ordinator, 2006–07, Artistic Dir, 2007–10, Greek Nat. Opera Ballet; Artistic Dir, Slovenian Nat. Theatre Ballet, 2010–14. Vice Pres., Arts Educnl Sch., Tring, 2002–. *Leading rôles* in ballets including: Spartacus, Ivan the Terrible, Raymonda, La Bayadère, La Fille mal gardée, Manon, Giselle, Mr Worldly Wise, Mayerling, Different Drummer, Fearful Symmetries, Nutcracker, Les Biches, Prodigal Son, Othello, Cheating, Lying, Stealing, L'Après-midi d'un faune, The Crucible; musical: On Your Toes; *rôles created* include: Boris in The Golden Age; Vershinin in Winter Dreams; the foreman in the Judas Tree. *Address:* c/o English National Ballet, Markova House, 39 Jay Mews, SW7 2ES.

**MUKHERJEE, Avik; His Honour Judge Mukherjee;** a Circuit Judge, since 2015; *b* Bolton, Lancs, 27 Feb. 1967; *s* of Soreen Mukherjee and Rina Mukherjee; *m* 2002, Rosaline Louise, (Roz), Kings; one *s*. *Educ:* Fartown High Sch., Huddersfield; Huddersfield New Coll.; Trent Poly., Nottingham (LLB Hons). Called to the Bar, Gray's Inn, 1990; a Recorder, 2009–15; Diversity and Community Relns Judge, 2016–; Mental Health Rev. Tribunal Judge, 2017–. Hon. Prof., Nottingham Trent Univ., 2016–. Hon. LLD Nottingham Trent, 2018. *Recreations:* classic rock music, gigs, football, running. *Address:* Birmingham Crown Court, 1 Newton Street, Birmingham B4 7NA. *T:* (0121) 681 3300, 0870 324 0273.

**MUKHERJEE, Pranab Kumar,** Bharat Ratna, 2019; President of India, 2012–17; *b* 11 Dec. 1935; *s* of Kamda Kinkar Mukherjee, of an illustrious family which was involved actively in the Freedom Movement of India; *m* 1957, Suvra Mukherjee; two *s* one *d*. *Educ:* Vidyasagar Coll., Suri; Calcutta Univ. (MA (Hist. and Pol Sci.); LLB). Elected Mem., W Bengal, Rajya Sabha, 1969, re-elected 1975, 1981, 1993, 1999; Leader, Rajya Sabha, 1980–85; Mem., and Leader of the House, Lok Sabha, 2004–12. Dep. Minister, Mins of Industrial Develt and of Shipping and Transport, 1973–74; Minister of State, Finance Min., 1974–77; Cabinet Minister i/c of Mins of Commerce, Steel and Mines, 1980–82; became youngest Minister to hold Finance Portfolio in Independent India, 1982–85; Dep. Chm., Planning Commn, 1991–93; Commerce Minister, 1993–95; Minister of External Affairs, 1995–96 and 2006–09; Minister of Defence, 2004–06; Minister of Finance, 2009–12. Spokesman, All India Congress Cttee, 1991; Chm., Central Election Campaign Cttee of Congress Party, 1984, 1991, 1996, 1998. *Publications:* Crisis in Democracy; An Aspect of Constitutional Problems in Bengal, 1967; Mid-Term Poll, 1969; Beyond Survival: an emerging dimension of Indian economy, 1984; Off the Track: an analysis of Indian economy, 1987; Saga of Struggle and Sacrifice, 1992; Challenges before the Nation, 1992. *Recreations:* music, gardening, reading.

**MUKHERJEE, Shiv Shankar;** High Commissioner for India in the United Kingdom, 2008–09; *b* Bihar, India, 1 Aug. 1949; *s* of Ananga Mukherjee and Sumita Devi Mukherjee (*née* Chakravarti); *m* 1972, Nalini Kapoor; one *s* one *d*. *Educ:* St Stephen's Coll., Univ. of Delhi (BSc Chemistry 1970; MSc). Attaché, then Under Sec., Bangladesh, Min. of External Affairs, India, 1973–75; Second Sec., then First Sec., Damascus, 1975–79; First Sec., Brussels, 1979–82; Dep. High Comr, Lusaka, 1982–85; Counsellor (Press), Washington, 1985–88; Dir (Ext. Publicity), Min. of External Affairs, 1988–89; Hd, India Observer Mission, 1989–90, High Comr, 1990–92, Windhoek; Jt Sec. (Ext. Publicity), Min. of External Affairs, 1992–94; Dir Gen., Indian Council for Cultural Relns, 1994–95; Minister (Press Inf. and Culture), Washington, 1995–98; Ambassador, Cairo, 1998–2000; High Comr, Pretoria, 2000–04; Ambassador, Kathmandu, 2004–08. Member: India Habitat Centre, 1993–; India Internat. Centre, 1993–; IUCN Project Adv. Cttee. Vice-Chm., Bd of Trustees, Asian Univ. for Women, Bangladesh, 2017–. Hon. Fellow, SOAS, 2010. *Recreations:* reading, golf, chess. *Clubs:* Delhi Press, Delhi Gymkhana.

**MUKWASHI, Amanda Khozi;** Chief Executive, Christian Aid, since 2018; *b* Twickenham, 30 May 1969; *d* of Andrew Weston Khozi and Juliet Moyo; *m* 1994, Daniel Mukwashi; one *s* one *d*. *Educ:* Univ. of Zambia (LLB Internat. Trade and Investment); Univ. of Warwick (Chevening Scholar; LLM Internat. Econ. Law). Coordinator, Common Mkt for E and S Africa, 1992–97; Hd, Progs. and External Relns, Skillshare Internat., 2002–11; Dir, Policy, VSO, 2011–12; Chief, Knowledge and Innovation, UN, 2012–18. Pres., Akina Mama wa Afrika, 2008–11. *Recreations:* visiting old churches, cathedrals, museums, listening to gospel music, laughing and joking, love comedy. *Address:* Christian Aid, 35–41 Lower Marsh, Lambeth, SE1 7RL. *T:* (020) 7523 2259, *Fax:* (020) 7523 2354. *E:* amukwashi@christian-aid.org.

**MUKWENA, Prof. Royson Mabuku,** PhD; Executive Director, National Institute of Public Administration, Zambia, since 2015; *b* Kalomo Dist, Zambia, 29 Feb. 1960; *s* of Alexander Mukwena and Vailet Mukwena; *m* 1986, Ruth Kanjanga Phiri; two *s* one *d*. *Educ:* St Marks Secondary Sch.; Univ. of Zambia (BA Public Admin 1983, MA Public Admin 1988); Univ. of Manchester (PhD Public Admin 1998). Lectr, Nat. Inst. of Public Admin, Zambia, 1985–86; Personnel Officer, Zambia Electricity Supply Corp. Ltd, 1987–88; Lectr in Public Admin, Univ. of Zambia, 1988–93; University of Namibia: Lectr, 1998–2002; Prof. of Public Admin, 2002–05; Hd, Dept of Political and Admin. Studies, 2005; Dep. Dean, 2001–03, Actg Dean, 2004, Faculty of Econs and Mgt Sci.; High Comr to Tanzania, and Ambassador (non-resident) to Burundi, Rwanda, Uganda, Union of the Comoros and Internat. Conf. on Great Lakes Reg., 2005–09; High Comr in UK and (non-resident) Ambassador to the Holy See and Ireland, 2009–12; Exec. Dir, Orgn for Social Sci. Res. in Eastern and Southern Africa, 2012; Dir, Res. and Postgrad. Studies, 2013–15, Dean, Sch. of Social Scis, 2014–15, Mulungushi Univ., Zambia. *Publications:* (ed with D. Olowu) Governance in Southern Africa and Beyond: experiences of institutional and public policy reform in developing countries, 2004; (ed with T. O. Chirawu) Decentralisation and Regional and Local Government in Namibia, 2008; (ed with F. Sumaili) Zambia at Fifty Years, 2016; chapters in books; articles in learned jls. *Recreation:* soccer fan (Manchester United). *E:* roymukwena@yahoo.com.

**MULCAHY, Sir Geoffrey (John),** Kt 1993; Chairman: Javelin Group Ltd, 2003–14; British Retail Consortium, 2006–09; *b* 7 Feb. 1942; *s* of Maurice Frederick Mulcahy and Kathleen Love Mulcahy; *m* 1965, Valerie Elizabeth; one *s* one *d*. *Educ:* King's Sch., Worcester; Manchester Univ. (BSc). Harvard Univ. (MBA). Esso Petroleum, 1964–74; Norton Co., 1974–77; British Sugar, 1977–83; Woolworth Holdings, subseq. Kingfisher, 1983–2002: Gp Man. Dir, 1984–86; Chief Exec., 1986–93; Chm., 1990–95; Chief Exec., 1995–2002. Non-executive Director: Instore plc, 2004–06; Homsway Gp (China), 2004–07; Chelsea and Westminster Hosp. Foundn Trust, 2011–15. Operating Partner, Global Leisure Partners, 2009–14. Trustee: Foundn for Credit Counselling, 2008–18; StepChange Debt Charity, 2009–18. *Recreations:* sailing, squash, Real Tennis, tennis. *Clubs:* Lansdowne, Royal Automobile, Royal Thames Yacht, Queen's; Royal Southern Yacht, Royal Yacht Squadron.

**MULCAHY, Leigh-Ann Maria;** QC 2009; a Deputy High Court Judge, since 2016; *b* London, 15 Oct. 1969; *d* of William and Margaret Mulcahy; *m* 2010, Dr Mark Ford; one *d*. *Educ:* Becket Sch., Nottingham; Jesus Coll., Cambridge (BA 1991); York Univ., Canada (LLM); Inns of Court Sch. of Law; King's Coll. London (Postgrad. Dip. EU Law). Called to the Bar, Inner Temple, 1993; in practice as barrister, specialising in commercial, inscc and public law; Jun. Counsel to Crown, 1998–2009; First Counsel to Welsh Govt, 2013–16; Sen. Decision Maker, Guernsey Financial Services Commn, 2014–. *Publications:* (Gen. Ed.) Human Rights and Civil Practice, 2001; (ed) The Law and Regulation of Medicine, 2008; (ed) Jackson and Powell on Professional Liability, 5th edn, 2002 to 8th edn, 2016. *Recreations:* travel, fitness, theatre. *Address:* Fountain Court Chambers, Temple, EC4Y 9DH. *T:* (020) 7583 3335. *E:* lm@fountaincourt.co.uk.

**MULCAHY, Prof. Linda Mary,** PhD; Professor of Socio-Legal Studies, University of Oxford, since 2019; Fellow, Wolfson College, Oxford, since 2019; *b* High Wycombe, 1 Jan. 1962; *d* of Seàn Mulcahy and Euphemia Shirley Mulcahy; *m* 1990, Richard Emmott; two *s*. *Educ:* Lady Verney High Sch.; Wycombe High Sch.; Univ. of Southampton (LLB Hons); London Sch. of Econs and Pol Sci. (LLM Legal Theory); Univ. of London (PhD 1993). Postgrad. Cert. Art Hist.). Research Assistant: Univ. of Bristol, 1986–88; Law Commn, 1987–88; Res. Fellow, Univ. of Oxford, 1988–92; Sen. Res. Fellow, South Bank Univ., 1992–96; Reader, Univ. of North London, 1996–2000; Anniversary Reader, Anniversary Chair and Dean of Arts, Birkbeck, Univ. of London, 2000–10; Prof. of Law, LSE, 2010–18. Pres., Socio-Legal Studies Assoc., 1998–2001. *Publications:* Disputing Doctors: the socio-legal dynamics of complaints about doctors, 2003; (ed with S. Wheeler) Feminist Perspectives on Contract, 2005; Contract Law in Perspective, 5th edn 2008; (with Carl Stychin) Legal Methods and Systems, 4th edn 2010; Legal Architecture: justice, due process and the place of law, 2010. *Recreation:* art history and design. *Address:* Wolfson College, Linton Road, Oxford OX2 6UD.

**MULCAIR, Hon. Thomas J.;** PC (Can.) 2012; Professor of Political Science, University of Montreal, since 2018; *b* Ottawa, 24 Oct. 1954; *s* of Harry Donnelly Mulcair and Jeanne Marie Mulcair (*née* Hurtubise); *m* 1976, Catherine P. Pinhas; two *s*. *Educ:* McGill Univ. (BCL 1976; LLB 1977). Legislative counsel, Québec Justice, 1978–80; Dir, Affaires juridiques, Conseil de la langue Française, 1980–83; Dir, Legal Affairs, Alliance Québec, 1983–85; Partner, Donald and Duggan, 1985–87; Legal Revisor, Attorney Gen. of Manitoba, 1985–87; Pres., Office des Professions du Québec, 1987–93. Mem., Nat. Assembly of Québec, 1994–2007; Minister of Sustainable Develt, Envmt and Parks, Québec, 2003–06; MP (NDP) Outremont, 2007–18; Leader of the Opposition, 2012–15. Leader, NDP, Canada, 2012–17. Pres., English-speaking Catholic Council, 1987 (Mem., Bd of Dirs, 1984–87). Chm. Bd, Jour de la Terre (Earth Day), 2018–; Member, Board of Directors: Council on Licensure, Enforcement and Regulation, 1991–95; Opération Enfant Soleil Children's Hosp. Telethon, 1991–2003; St Patrick's Soc. of Montreal, 1991–2003, 2007–; Montreal Oral Sch. for the Deaf, 1993–2003; La Marois Country Club, 1993–97. Fellow, Centre for Internat. Studies; Sen. Fellow, Raoul Wallenberg Centre for Internat. Studies for Human Rights. *Publications:* Bibliographie sur la rédaction et l'interprétation des textes législatifs, 1980. *Recreations:* swimming, ice hockey, snowshoeing, golf. *Address:* Political Science Department, University of Montreal, PO Box 6128 Downtown Branch, Montreal, QC H3C 3J7, Canada.

**MULDER, (Robert) Frederick,** CBE 2012; PhD; Director, Frederick Mulder Ltd, dealers in European original prints, since 1972; *b* 24 June 1943; *s* of William Eldred Bowman and Kathleen Elsie Delarue; *m* 1971, Valerie Ann Townsend (marr. diss. 2000); one *s* one *d* (and one *s* decd); one *s*. *Educ:* Eston High Sch., Sask.; Univ. of Saskatchewan (BA Hons Eng. 1965); Brown Univ., Providence, RI (MA Philos. 1967; PhD Philos. 1971); Linacre Coll.,

Oxford. Dir, P. and D. Colnaghi, 1972–75. Chm. of Trustees, Frederick Mulder Foundn (formerly Frederick Mulder Trust, then Prairie Trust), 1986–; Founding Chm., The Funding Network, 2002–12; Trustee: Gaia Foundn, 1988–91; Network for Social Change, 1995–98; Oxford Res. Gp, 2000–06. *E*: fm@frederickmulder.com.

MULDOON, Bristow Cook; Head of Policy Advice, Press and Parliamentary Affairs, Royal Society of Edinburgh and Royal Society of Chemistry, 2007–18; *b* 19 March 1964; *s* of late Bristow Cook Muldoon and of Annie McKenzie Muldoon (*née* McCallum); *m* 1988, Catherine Sloan McMillan; three *s*. *Educ*: Cumbernauld High Sch.; Univ. of Strathclyde (BSc Hons Chem.); Open Univ. (BA Hons). Manager in rail industry, 1986–99; business analyst, Great North Eastern Rly, 1997–99. Member (Lab): Lothian Regl Council, 1994–96 (Vice-Chm., Econ. Develt); West Lothian Council, 1995–99 (Convener, Community Services). Mem. (Lab) Livingston, Scottish Parlt, 1999–2007. Non-exec. Dir, West Lothian NHS Trust, 1997–99. Member: Labour Party; Co-Op Party; TSSA. *Recreations*: golf, music, football, reading. *Club*: Uphall Golf.

MULDOON, Prof. Paul; Howard G. B. Clark Professor in the Humanities, Princeton University, since 1998; *b* Portadown, NI, 20 June 1951; *s* of late Patrick Muldoon and Brigid (*née* Regan); *m* 1987, Jean Hanff Korelitz; one *s* one *d*. *Educ*: St Patrick's Coll., Armagh; Queen's Univ., Belfast (BA Eng. Lang. and Lit. 1973). BBC Northern Ireland: Producer, Arts Progs (Radio), 1973–78, Sen. Producer, 1978–85; TV Producer, 1985–86; Judith E. Wilson Vis. Fellow, Cambridge Univ., 1986–87; Creative Writing Fellow, UEA, 1987; Lecturer: Sch. of the Arts, Columbia Univ., 1987–88; Creative Writing Program, Princeton Univ., 1987–88; Writer-in-residence, 92nd Street Y, NY, 1988; Roberta Holloway Lectr, Univ. of Calif, Berkeley, 1989; Vis. Prof., Univ. of Mass, Amherst, 1989–90; Princeton University: Lectr, 1990–95; Prof., 1995–98; Dir, Creative Writing Program, 1993–2002; Vis. Prof., Bread Loaf Sch. of English, Middlebury, Vt, 1997–; Prof. of Poetry, Univ. of Oxford, 1999–2004; Fellow, Hertford Coll., Oxford, 1999–2004, now Hon. Fellow. Poetry Ed., New Yorker, 2007–17. Pres., Poetry Soc. of GB, 1996–2005. Mem., Aosdána, 1980–. FRSL 1981; John Simon Guggenheim Meml Fellow, 1990; Fellow: American Acad. of Arts and Scis, 2000; American Acad. of Arts and Letters, 2008. Readings of work throughout Europe, USA and Canada, Japan and Australia. Eric Gregory Award, 1972; Sir Geoffrey Faber Meml Award, 1980 and 1991; T. S. Eliot Prize for Poetry, 1994; Award in Literature, AAAL, 1996; Poetry Prize, Irish Times, 1997; Shakespeare Prize, 2004; Queen's Gold Medal for Poetry, 2017. *Publications*: *poetry*: Knowing My Place, 1971; New Weather, 1973; Spirit of Dawn, 1975; Mules, 1977; Names and Addresses, 1978; Immram, 1980; Why Brownlee Left, 1980; Out of Siberia, 1982; Quoof, 1983; The Wishbone, 1984; Selected Poems 1968–83, 1986; Meeting the British, 1987; Selected Poems 1968–86, 1987; Madoc: a mystery, 1990; Incantata, 1994; The Prince of the Quotidian, 1994; The Annals of Chile, 1994; Kerry Slides, 1996; New Selected Poems 1968–94, 1996; Hopewell Haiku, 1997; The Bangle (Slight Return), 1998; Hay, 1998; Poems 1968–1998, 2001; Moy Sand and Gravel, 2002 (Pulitzer Prize, 2003); Horse Latitudes, 2006; Maggot, 2010; One Thousand Things Worth Knowing, 2015; Selected Poems 1968–2014, 2016; Frolic and Detour, 2019; *drama*: Monkeys (TV play), 1989; Shining Brow (opera), 1993; Six Honest Serving Men (play), 1995; Bandanna (opera), 1999; *essays*: Getting Round: notes towards an Ars Poetica, 1998; To Ireland, I, 2000; The End of the Poem, 2006; *for children*: The O-O's Party, 1981; The Last Thesaurus, 1995; The Noctuary of Narcissus Batt, 1997; *translations*: The Astrakan Cloak, by Nuala Ní Dhomhnaill, 1993; (with R. Martin) The Birds, by Aristophanes, 1999; *edited*: The Scrake of Dawn, 1979; The Faber Book of Contemporary Irish Poetry, 1986; The Essential Byron, 1989; The Faber Book of Beasts, 1997; contribs to poetry anthologies; works trans. into numerous langs. *Recreations*: tennis, electric guitar. *Address*: c/o Faber & Faber, Bloomsbury House, 74–77 Great Russell Street, WC1B 3DA. *Clubs*: Athenæum, Groucho.

MULDOWNEY, Diane Ellen, (Mrs Dominic Muldowney); *see* Trevis, D. E.

MULDOWNEY, Dominic John; composer; Music Director, Royal National (formerly National) Theatre, 1976–97; *b* 19 July 1952; *s* of William and Barbara Muldowney; *m* 1986, Diane Ellen Trevis, *qv*; one *d*. *Educ*: Taunton's Grammar School, Southampton; York Univ. (BA, BPhil). Composer in residence, Southern Arts Association, 1974–76; composer of chamber, choral, orchestral works, including work for theatre, ballet and TV. *Compositions include*: Piano Concerto, 1983; The Duration of Exile, 1984; Saxophone Concerto, 1985; Sinfonietta, 1986; Ars Subtilior, 1987; Lonely Hearts, 1988; Violin Concerto, 1989; Three Pieces for Orchestra, 1990; Percussion Concerto, 1991; Oboe Concerto, 1992; Trumpet Concerto, 1993; Concerto for 4 Violins, 1994; The Brontës (ballet), 1995; Trombone Concerto, 1996; Clarinet Concerto, 1997; Irish Love Songs, 1998; The Fall of Jerusalem (oratorio), 1999; Piano Concerto No. 2, 2002; Red Razzmatazz (opera), 2005; War Oratorio (film), 2007; Tsunami (song cycle), 2008; Checkpoint Charlie, 2009; Ostalgie, 2011; English Song Book, 2015; Krieg der Welten, 2015; Hey Presto!, 2016. *Recreation*: driving through France and across America.

MULFORD, Dr David Campbell; Distinguished Visiting Fellow, Hoover Institution, Stanford University, since 2017; *b* Rockford, Ill, 27 June 1937; *s* of Robert Lewis Mulford and Theodora Henie Moellenhauer Mulford; *m* 1985, Jeannie Louise Simmons; two *s*. *Educ*: Lawrence Univ., Wisconsin (BA Econs *cum laude* 1959); Univ. of Cape Town; Boston Univ. (MA Pol Sci. 1962; Dist. Alumni Award, 1992); St Antony's Coll., Oxford (DPhil 1966). Special Asst to Sec. and Under Sec., US Treasury, 1965–66; Man. Dir and Head, Internat. Finance, White, Weld & Co., Inc., 1966–74; Sen. Investment Advr, Saudi Arabian Monetary Agency, 1974–84, on secondment; Under Sec. and Asst Sec. for Internat. Affairs, US Treasury, 1984–92 (sen. advr on financial assistance to former Soviet Union states; head of internat. debt strategy; led US delegn to negotiate estabt of EBRD); Mem. Exec. Bd, 1992–2003, Chm. Europe, 1993–99, Chm. Internat., 1999–2003, Credit Suisse First Boston; US Ambassador to India, 2004–09; Vice-Chm. Internat., Credit Suisse, 2009–16. Mem., Council on Foreign Relations, 1972–; Affiliate, Center for Strategic and Internat. Studies, Washington, 1992–. Hon. LLD Lawrence, Wisconsin, 1984. Alexander Hamilton Award, USA, 1992. Légion d'Honneur (France), 1990; Order of May (Argentina), 1993; Officer's Cross, Medal of Merit (Poland), 1995. *Publications*: Northern Rhodesia General Election, 1962; Zambia: the politics of independence, 1967; Packing for India: a life of action in global finance and diplomacy, 2014. *Recreations*: golf, running, canoeing. *Club*: Metropolitan (Washington).

MULGAN, Geoffrey John, CBE 2004; PhD; Chief Executive, National Endowment for Science, Technology and the Arts, 2011–19; *b* 28 Aug. 1961; *s* of Anthony Philip Mulgan and Catherine Mulgan (*née* Gough); *m* 1998, Rowena Young (marr. diss. 2017); one *s* one *d*. *Educ*: Balliol Coll., Oxford (MA 1982); Central London Poly. (PhD 1990). Investment Exec., Greater London Enterprise, 1984–86; Harkness Fellow, MIT, 1986–87; Consultant, and Lectr in Telecommunications, Central London Poly., 1987–90; Special Advr to Gordon Brown, MP, 1990–92; Fellow, BFI, 1992–93; Co-Founder and Dir, Demos, 1993–97 (Chm., Adv. Council, 1998–); Mem., Prime Minister's Policy Unit, 1997–2000; Director: Perf. and Innovation Unit, Cabinet Office, 2000–02; Prime Minister's Forward Strategy Unit, 2001–02; Strategy Unit, Cabinet Office, 2002–04; Head of Policy, Prime Minister's Office, 2003–04; Dir, Inst. of Community Studies, later The Young Foundn, 2004–11; Dir, Big Society Capital, 2011–15. Co-Chair, London Enterprise Panel, Digital Creative, Sci. and Technol. Wkg Gp, 2013–16. Member: Health Innovation Council, 2008–10; Prime Minister's Council on Social Action, 2008–10. Chm., internat. adv. cttee for Mayor of Seoul, 2016–; Member: Adv. Cttee on Innovation, UAE Govt, 2016–; Adv. Cttee on Innovation, Scottish Govt, 2017–; Internat. Adv. Cttee, SITRA (Finland), 2017–; Bd, Reimagine Europa, 2018–. Visiting Professor: UCL, 1996–; LSE, 2004–; Melbourne, 2006–; Lectr, 2009–17, Vis. Prof., 2017–, China Exec. Leadership Acad.; Sen. Vis. Scholar, Harvard Univ., 2015–18. Mem., Design Council, 2006–10. Chairman: Involve, 2005–10; Social Innovation Exchange, 2010–; Studio Schs Trust, 2012–17; WEF Global Futures Council on innovation and entrepreneurship, 2016–18; Mem. Bd, Luton Culture, 2017–. Pres., Nesta Italia, 2018–. Trustee: Political Qly, 1995–2005; Work Foundn, 2005–10. *Publications*: Saturday Night or Sunday Morning, 1987; Communication and Control, 1990; Politics in an Antipolitical Age, 1994; (ed) Life After Politics, 1997; Connexity, 1997; Good and Bad Power: the ideals and betrayals of government, 2006; The Art of Public Strategy, 2009; The Locust and the Bee: predators and creators in capitalism's future, 2013; Big Mind: how collective intelligence can change our world, 2017. *Recreation*: making music.

MULHALL, Daniel; Ambassador of Ireland to the United States of America, since 2017; *b* Waterford, 8 April 1955; *s* of Thomas and Alice Mulhall; *m* 1982, Greta Lothian; one *s* one *d*. *Educ*: University Coll., Cork (BA 1975; HDE 1978; MA 1979). Entered Dept of Foreign Affairs, Ireland, 1978; Third Secretary: Dept of Foreign Affairs, 1978–80; New Delhi, 1980–83; Dept of Foreign Affairs, 1983–87; First Secretary: Vienna, 1987–89; Dept of Foreign Affairs, 1989–90; Perm. Repn of Ireland to EU, Brussels, 1990–94; on secondment to Forum for Peace and Reconciliation, 1994–95; Press Section, Dept of Foreign Affairs, 1995–98; Consul Gen., Edinburgh, 1998–2001; Ambassador to Malaysia, and concurrently to Laos, Thailand and Vietnam, 2001–05; Dir Gen., EU Div., Dept of Foreign Affairs, 2005–09; Ambassador: to Germany, 2009–13; to Court of St James's, 2013–17. *Publications*: A New Day Dawning: a portrait of Ireland in 1900, 1999; (ed jtly) The Shaping of Modern Ireland, 2016; contrib. articles to jls on hist. and lit. *Recreations*: Irish history, literature, sport. *Address*: Embassy of Ireland, 2234 Massachusetts Avenue NW, Washington, DC 20008, USA. *Clubs*: Athenæum, Royal Automobile, Travellers, Caledonian.

MULHOLLAND, family name of Baron Dunleath.

MULHOLLAND, Rt Hon. Lord; Francis Mulholland, (Frank), CBE 2017; PC 2011; a Senator of the College of Justice in Scotland, since 2016; a Judge of the Upper Tribunal (Asylum and Immigration Chamber), since 2019; *b* 18 April 1959; *s* of Charles and Jean Mulholland; *m* 1988, Marie Quinn; one *s*. *Educ*: Columba High Sch., Coatbridge; Univ. of Aberdeen (LLB Hons; DipLP); Univ. of Edinburgh (MBA 1997). Trainee solicitor, Bird Semple & Crawford Heron, 1982–84; Procurator Fiscal Depute: Greenock, 1984–87; Glasgow, 1987–91; NP 1992; SSC 1993; Crown Office: Solicitor: High Court Unit, 1991–94; Appeals Unit, 1994–97; Advocate Depute, 1997–2000; Asst Procurator Fiscal, 2000–01, Procurator Fiscal, 2001–03, Edinburgh; Sen. Advocate Depute, 2003–06; QC (Scot.) 2005; Area Procurator Fiscal, Lothian and Borders, 2006–07; Solicitor Gen. for Scotland, 2007–11; Lord Advocate for Scotland, 2011–16. Admitted Mem., Faculty of Advocates, 2008. Accredited advocacy trainer, Nat. Inst. for Trial Advocacy, 2006–. Mem., Parole Bd for Scotland, 2019–. *Recreations*: football, golf, squash, military history. *Address*: Court of Session, Parliament House, Edinburgh EH1 1RQ.

MULHOLLAND, Clare, OBE 1998; Vice Chairman of Council, Communications Regulatory Agency (formerly Independent Media Commission), Bosnia and Herzegovina, 1998–2005; *b* 17 June 1939; *d* of James Mulholland and Elizabeth (*née* Lochrin). *Educ*: Notre Dame High Sch., Glasgow; Univ. of Glasgow (MA Hons). Gen. trainee, then Press Officer, ICI, 1961–64; Press Officer: Granada Television, 1964–65; TWW, 1965–68; Press Officer, then Educn Officer, HTV, 1968–71; Independent Broadcasting Authority, later Independent Television Commission, 1971–97: Reg. Exec., Bristol, 1971–77; Reg. Officer, Midlands, 1977–82; Chief Asst, Television, 1982–83; Dep. Dir of Television, 1983–91; Dir of Programmes, 1991–96; Dep. Chief Exec., 1996–97; internat. broadcasting consultant, 1998–2008. Member: Arts Council of GB, 1986–94; Scottish Film Prodn Fund, 1984–90; Lottery Film Panel, Arts Council of England, 1997–2000. FRTS 1988. *Recreations*: travel, theatre, cinema.

MULHOLLAND, Prof. Clive William, PhD; CSci; Principal and Vice Chancellor, University of the Highlands and Islands, 2014–19. *Educ*: Univ. of Ulster (BSc 1st Cl. Hons 1988; PhD Biochem. 1993). CSci 2004. Academic, 1997–2001, Dir, Lifelong Learning, 2001–07, and Prof. of Technol. Enhanced Learning, Univ. of Ulster; Dep. Vice Chancellor, Univ. of S Wales (formerly Glamorgan), 2007–14. Pres., Network of Excellence in Island Univs, 2016. FIBMS 1992; FRSA 2012; SFHEA 2013.

MULHOLLAND, Francis; *see* Mulholland, Rt Hon. Lord.

MULHOLLAND, Gregory Thomas; Director, Greg Mulholland Communications; *b* 31 Aug. 1970; *m* 2004, Raegan Melita Hatton; three *d*. *Educ*: St Ambrose Coll., Altrincham; Univ. of York (BA 1991; MA 1995). Account handler, several marketing and sales promotion agencies, 1997–2002. Mem. (Lib Dem), Leeds CC, 2003–05 (Lead Mem., Corp. Services and Metro (W Yorks PTA)). MP (Lib Dem) Leeds NW, 2005–17; contested (Lib Dem) same seat, 2017.

MULHOLLAND, James Malachi; QC 2011; a Recorder, since 2007; *b* Manchester, 24 July 1964; *s* of James Gerard Mulholland and Martina Veronica Mulholland (*née* Barron); *m* 2005, Kate Fowler; one *s* one *d*. *Educ*: Cardinal Langley Grammar Sch., Rochdale; Univ. of Leeds (LLB Hons 1985). Called to the Bar, Inner Temple, 1986; in practice as a barrister in criminal and regulatory law, specialising in serious fraud work. *Recreations*: political biographies, history, classical music, conversation, walking, Manchester United. *Address*: 23 Essex Street, WC2R 3AA. *T*: (020) 7413 0353. *E*: jamesmulhollandqc@23es.com.

MULKERN, John, CBE 1987; JP; international airport and aviation consultant, since 1987; *b* 15 Jan. 1931; *s* of late Thomas Mulkern and Annie Tennant; *m* 1954, May Egerton (*née* Peters); one *s* three *d*. *Educ*: Stretford Grammar Sch.; Dip. Govt Admin of Local Govt Exam. Bd, London; Harvard Business Sch. (AMP 1977). Ministries of Supply and Aviation, Civil Service, 1949–65: Exec. Officer, finally Principal, Audit, Purchasing, Finance, Personnel and Legislation branches; British Airports Authority, 1965–87: Dep. Gen. Man., Heathrow Airport, 1970–73; Dir, Gatwick Airport, 1973–77; Man. Dir and Mem. of Bd, 1977–87. Chairman: British Airports International Ltd, 1978–82; Manchester Handling Ltd, 1988–94; Granik Ltd, 1990–91 (Pres., 1992–94); Director: London Luton Airport Ltd, 1991–2000; Reliance Aviation Security Ltd, 1992–94. President: Western European Airports' Assoc., 1981–83; Internat. Civil Airports Assoc. (Europe), 1986; Chm., Co-ordinating Council, Airports Assocs, 1982; Mem. Bd, Airport Operators Council Internat., 1978–81. Mem., Surrey Probation Cttee, 1996–2001. Trustee: Surrey Springboard, 1997–2001; BAA Pension Trust Co. Ltd, 1997–2000. Mem., Middlesex and Surrey Soc., 1995–2009. FCILT 1973 (Mem. Council, 1979–82); CCMI (CBIM 1981); FInstD 1982. JP Surrey, 1988. *Recreations*: family pursuits, opera, classical recorded music.

MULL, Very Rev. Gerald S.; *see* Stranraer-Mull.

MULLALLY, Rt Rev. and Rt Hon. Dame Sarah Elisabeth; *see* London, Bishop of.

**MULLALY, Terence Frederick Stanley**; art historian and critic; b 14 Nov. 1927; s of late Col B. R. Mullaly (4th s of Maj.-Gen. Sir Herbert Mullaly, KCMG, CB, CSI) and Eileen Dorothy (née Stanley); m 1949, Elizabeth Helen (née Burkitt). Educ: in India, England, Japan and Canada; Downing Coll., Cambridge (MA). FSA 1977; FRNS 1981 (Mem. Council, 1993–95); FSAScot 1995. Archæological studies in Tripolitania, 1948, and Sicily, 1949; has specialised in study of Italian art, particularly Venetian and Veronese painting of 16th and 17th centuries; lecturer and broadcaster; Art Critic, Daily Telegraph, 1958–86. Vis. Prof., Finch Coll., NY, 1967–72. President: Brit. Section, Internat. Assoc. of Art Critics, 1967–73; British Art Medal Soc., 1986–98 (Vice Chm., 1982–86; Vice-Pres., 1998–); Member: Adv. Cttee, Cracow Art Festival, 1974, Palermo Art Festival, 1976; UK Delegn, Budapest Cultural Forum, 1985; Cttee, FIDEM Congress, 1992; Comitato Scientifico, Arte Documento; Council: Attingham Summer Sch. Trust, 1984–90; Derby Porcelain Internat. Soc., 1985–; Friends, Univ. of Cyprus, 1995– (Vice Chm., 1998–); Artistic Adviser, Grand Tours, 1974–90; Director: Grand Tours, 1980–90; Specialtours, 1986. Editor, Jl of British-Italian Soc., 1995–. FRSA 1969. Commendatore, Ordine Al Merito, Italy, 1974 (Cavaliere Ufficiale, 1964); l'Ordre du Mérite Culturel, Poland, 1974; Order of Merit of Poland (Silver Medal), 1978; Bulgarian 1300th Anniversary Medal, 1981; Sacro Militare Ordine Costantiniano di S Giorgio (Silver Medal), 1982; Premio Pietro Torta per il restauro di Venezia, 1983; Socio Straniero, Ateneo Veneto, 1986. Publications: Ruskin a Verona, 1966; catalogue of exhibition, Disegni veronesi del Cinquecento, 1971; contrib. to catalogue of exhibition Cinquant'anni di pittura veronese: 1580–1630, 1974; ed and contrib. to catalogue of exhibition, Modern Hungarian Medal, 1984; contrib. to Affreschi del Rinascimento a Verona: interventi di restauro, 1987; Caterina Cornaro, Queen of Cyprus, 1989; catalogue of exhibn, Zofia Demkowska, 1997; (jtly) Cyprus: the legacy, 1999; contribs to DNB and on history of art, to Burlington Magazine, Master Drawings, Arte Illustrata, Arte Documento, Antologia di Belle Arti, The Minneapolis Inst. of Arts Bulletin, Bull. Univ. of New Mexico Art Mus., British Numismatic Jl, Numismatic Chronicle, Jl of British Art Medal Soc., Apollo, etc. Recreations: numismatics, Eastern Europe. Address: Waterside House, Pulborough, Sussex RH20 2BH. T: (01798) 872104.

**MULLAN, Diya**; see Sen Gupta, D.

**MULLAN, Prof. John Dermot**, PhD; Professor of English, since 2005, and Lord Northcliffe Professor of Modern English Literature, since 2016, University College London; b London, 6 Aug. 1958; s of Dermot Mullan and Antonia Mullan; m 2000, Harriet Stewart; one s two d. Educ: Downside Sch.; King's Coll., Cambridge (BA 1980; PhD 1984). Res. Fellow, Jesus Coll., 1984–87, Lectr, Fitzwilliam Coll., 1987–94, Cambridge; Lectr, 1994–98, Sen. Lectr, 1998–2005, in English, UCL. Vis. Prof., Univ. of Munich, 1993. Publications: Sentiment and Sociability, 1988; (ed) Eighteenth-Century Popular Culture, 2000; How Novels Work, 2006; Anonymity: a secret history of English literature, 2007; What Matters in Jane Austen?, 2012. Recreations: eating, walking, swimming in the sea, going to the theatre. Address: Department of English Language and Literature, University College London, Gower Street, WC1E 6BT. E: j.mullan@ucl.ac.uk.

**MULLARD, Prof. Christopher Paul**, CBE 2005; PhD; DL; Chairman and Chief Executive Officer, Focus Consultancy, since 1994; b 23 Nov. 1944; m Mike-Madelaine Elmont; one s two d. Educ: Park House Secondary Modern Sch., Newbury; Westminster City Coll., London; Univ. of Durham (MA 1975; PhD 1980). Northern Sec., CARD, 1964–68; Principal Community Relns Officer, Tyne and Wear, 1968–73; researcher and pt-time Lectr in Sociol., Univ. of Durham, 1973–76; Sen. Lectr in Sociol., King Alfred's Coll., Winchester, 1976–77; Lectr, Dept of Sociol. of Educn, Univ. of London Inst. of Educn, 1977–80; Dir, Race Relns Policy and Practice Res. Units, Univ. of London Inst. of Educn and LSE, 1980–86; University of Amsterdam: Royal Prof. in Ethnic Studies and Educn, and Dir, Centre for Race and Ethnic Studies, 1984–91; Advr to Senate, 1991–94. Mem., Widening Participation and Student Opportunity Strategy Adv. Cttee (formerly Widening Access and Participation Strategy Adv. Cttee), HEFCE, 2010–14; Ext. Affiliate, PURAI—Global Indigenous Res. and Diaspora, Univ. of Newcastle, Australia, 2014–. Foundn Dir, Focus Inst. on Rights and Social Transformation, 2004–. Chm., Zebra Investment Trading Ltd, 2018–; Dir, Aion Ltd, 2019–. Chairman: Bernie Grant Trust, 2000–11 (Trustee, 2012–); London Notting Hill Carnival Ltd, 2002–08; Commn on African and Caribbean Families in Britain, 2010–15; Ladybird Economic Advancement Partnership, 2014–; Mem., Dep. Prime Minister's Bicentenary Adv. Gp on Commemorating the Abolition of the Slave Trade, 2006–08; Patron: Caribbean Women's Standing Conf., 2001–17; Caribbean Develt Trust (UK), 2005–14; Internat. Judge, Shanghai Tourism Festival Parade, 2005–15; African Fellowship Trust, 2015–. Chm., Liliesleaf Trust UK, 2019–. Vis. Prof., 2007–, Gov., 2008–16, Royal Agricl Univ. (formerly Coll.). Hon. Consul for South Africa, 2006–. FRSA 2005; MInstD 1998. DL Wilts, 2007. Hon. LLD Exeter, 2009. Publications: Black Britain, 1973; Aborigines in Australia Today, 1974; On Being Black in Britain, 1975; Anti-Racist Education: the three O's, 1984; Race, Power and Resistance, 1985; De Plurale Kubus, 1990; Antirassistische Erziehung, 1991. Recreations: gardening, theatre, golf, travel. Club: Reform.

**MULLARKEY, Thomas**, MBE 1996; Chief Executive, British Chiropractic Association, since 2019; b 1 April 1957; s of Patrick and Teresa Mullarkey; m 1982, Sue Hamilton; two s. Educ: Maidstone Grammar Sch.; Univ. of Lancaster (BA Orgn Studies 1978); RMA, Sandhurst; Indian Defence Services Staff Coll. (MSc Defence Studies 1992). Army officer, RA, 1975–95; service in UK, Germany, NI, Canada, India and Rwanda (co-ordinated UN restoration plan). Gen. Manager Projs, SBC Warburg, 1995–96; Gen. Manager, then Dir, Special Projs, XVII Commonwealth Games, Manchester, 1996–2001; Chief Executive: Nat. Security Inspectorate, 2002–06; RoSPA, 2006–17. Publications: A Thousand Hills: a story of crisis in Rwanda, 2001. Recreations: sailing, cycling, the hills, writing, military and naval history.

**MULLEE, Patrick**; HM Diplomatic Service, retired; Ambassador to Ecuador, 2012–16; b 8 Oct. 1954; s of Patrick and Teresa Mullee; m 1987, Joanna Louise, d of Philip Hughes Johnson and Diana Ruth Chase; two d. Joined FCO, 1974; Prague, 1976–77; Caracas, 1977–80; Latin America and Africa floater, 1980–84; Policy Planning Staff, FCO, 1985–88; Vice-Consul, San José, 1988–91; Second Sec. (Chancery/Inf.), Bridgetown, 1991–95; Second, later First Sec., Eastern Caribbean Desk, FCO, 1995–97; Dep. Hd, Personnel Mgt Unit, FCO, 1997–2000; Dep. Hd of Mission and HM Consul, Quito, 2000–03; HR Manager, Directorate Gen. for Defence and Intelligence, FCO, 2003–07; Ambassador to Uruguay, 2008–12. Recreations: football, golf, mountains. Clubs: Wanderers Masters Football (Barbados); Worcestershire Golf.

**MÜLLER, Alex**; see Müller, K. A.

**MULLER, Franz Joseph**, QC 1978; a Recorder of the Crown Court, 1977–2008; b England, 19 Nov. 1938; yr s of late Wilhelm Muller and Anne Maria (née Ravens); m 1985, Helena (High Sheriff, S Yorks, 2009–10), y d of Mieczyslaw Bartosz; two s. Educ: Mount St Mary's Coll.; Univ. of Sheffield (LLB). Called to the Bar, Gray's Inn, 1961, Bencher, 1994; called to NI Bar, 1982. Graduate Apprentice, United Steel Cos, 1960–61; Commercial Asst, Workington Iron and Steel Co. Ltd, 1961–63. Commenced practice at the Bar, 1964; Head of Chambers, 11 King's Bench Walk, Temple, 1984–2005. Non-executive Director: Richards of Sheffield (Holdings) PLC, 1969–77; Satinsteel Ltd, 1970–77; Joseph Rodgers and Son Ltd and Rodgers Wostenholm Ltd, 1975–77. Recreations: the Georgians, fell walking, being in Greece, listening to music. Address: Slade Hooton Hall, Laughton en le Morthen, S Yorks S25 1YQ; KBW, The Engine House, 1 Foundry Square, Leeds LS11 5DL. T: (0113) 297 1200.

**MÜLLER, Herta**; writer; b Nitzkydorf, Romania, 17 Aug. 1953; m Richard Wagner (marr. diss. 1988); m 1990, Dr Harry Merkle. Educ: Univ. of Timisoara (German and Romanian Lit.). Translator, machine construction factory, Timisoara, 1976–79. Emigrated to Germany, 1987. Awards include: Deutscher Kritikerpreis, 1992; Kleist Preis, 1994; Literaturpreis Aristeion, EU, 1995; Dublin Literary Award, Internat. IMPAC, 1998; Franz Kafka Literaturpreis, 1999; Nobel Prize for Literature, 2009; Franz Werfel Preis, 2009; Heinrich-Böll-Preis, 2015. Publications: Drückender Tango, 1984; Der Mensch ist ein großer Fasan auf der Welt, 1986; Barfüßiger Februar, 1987; Reisende auf einem Bein, 1989; Der Teufel sitzt im Spiegel, 1991; Eine warme Kartoffel ist ein warmes Bett, 1992; Der Wächter nimmt seinen Kamm, 1993; Hunger und Seide (essays), 1995; In der Falle. Bonner Poetikvorlesungen, 1996; Der fremde Blick oder Das Leben ist ein Furz in der Laterne, 1999; Im Haarknoten wohnt eine Dame, 2000; Heimat ist das, was gesprochen wird, 2001; Der König verneigt sich und tötet, 2003; Die blassen Herren mit den Mokkatassen, 2005; Cristina und ihre Attrappe, oder Was (nicht) in den Akten der Securitate steht, 2009; Lebensangst und Worthunger, 2010; Immer derselbe Schnee und immer derselbe Onkel (essays), 2011; Vater telefoniert mit den Fliegen, 2012; Mein Vaterland war ein Apfelkern, 2014; Im Heimweh ist ein blauer Saal, 2019; novels: Niederungen, 1982; Der Fuchs war damals schon der Jäger, 1992; Herztier, 1994; Heute wär ich mir lieber nicht begegnet, 1997; Atemschaukel, 2009; in Romanian: Este sau nu este Ion, 2005; works trans. into numerous languages. Address: Carl-Hanser-Verlag, Postfach 860420, 81631 München, Germany.

**MÜLLER, Prof. (Karl) Alex**, PhD; physicist at IBM Zurich Research Laboratory, 1963; b 20 April 1927. Educ: Swiss Federal Institute of Technology, Zürich (PhD 1958). FInstP 1998. Battelle Inst., Geneva, 1958–63; Lectr, 1962, Titular Prof., 1970, Prof., 1987–2009, now Prof. Emeritus, Univ. of Zürich; joined IBM Res. Lab., Zurich, 1963: Manager, Physics Dept, 1972–85; IBM Fellow, 1982–85, IBM Fellow Emeritus, 1992–98; researcher, 1985–. Hon. degrees from twenty European and American univs. Prizes and awards include Nobel Prize for Physics (jtly), 1987. Publications: over 600 papers on ferroelectric and superconducting materials. Address: Physik-Institut, Universität Zürich-Irchel, Winterthurerstrasse 190, 8057 Zürich, Switzerland.

**MULLIGAN, (Margaret) Mary**; Churches Development Officer, Christian Aid; b Liverpool, 12 Feb. 1960; m 1982, John Mulligan; two s one d. Educ: Notre Dame High Sch., Liverpool; Manchester Univ. (BA Hons Econs and Social Studies 1981). Retail and personnel mgt, 1981–86. Member (Lab): Edinburgh DC, 1988–95 (Chm., Housing Cttee, 1992–97; City of Edinburgh Council, 1995–99. MSP (Lab) Linlithgow, 1999–2011; contested (Lab) same seat, 2011. Scottish Executive: PPS to First Minister, 2000–01; Dep. Minister for Health and Community Care, 2001–03, for Communities, 2003–04. Scottish Parliament: Chm., Educn, Sports and Culture Cttee, 1999–2000; Mem., Local Govt and Communities Cttee, 2008–11. Recreations: music, theatre, watching sports.

**MULLIKEN, Anthony Morris St John**; Co-founder, 1989, and Chairman, since 2006, Midas Public Relations (Partner and Joint Managing Director, 1989–2006); b Windsor, 17 Jan. 1950; s of Robert Edward Mulliken and Joan Kathleen Mulliken (née Laley); m 1978, Pamela. Educ: Homelands, Torquay; St Luke's Coll., Exeter. Partner, Pengelly Mulliken Publicity, 1975–89. Freeman, City of London, 2002. Recreations: tennis, squash, alpacas. Address: Sharcott Barracks, Drove Road, Sharcott Pewsey, Wilts SN9 5NJ. T: (01672) 564112. E: tony.mulliken@midaspr.co.uk. Club: Ivy.

**MULLIN, Christopher John, (Chris)**; author, journalist, politician; b 12 Dec. 1947; s of Leslie and Teresa Mullin; m 1987, Nguyen Thi Ngoc, d of Nguyen Tang Minh, Kontum, Vietnam; two d. Educ: Univ. of Hull (LLB). Freelance journalist, travelled extensively in Indo-China and China; sub editor, BBC World Service, 1974–78; Editor, Tribune, 1982–84. Executive Member: Campaign for Labour Party Democracy, 1975–83; Labour Co-ordinating Cttee, 1978–82. Contested (Lab): Devon N, 1970; Kingston upon Thames, Feb. 1974. MP (Lab) Sunderland S, 1987–2010. Parliamentary Under-Secretary of State: DETR, 1999–2001; DFID, 2001; FCO, 2003–05. Chm., Home Affairs Select Cttee, 1997–99, 2001–03; Mem., Standards and Privileges Cttee, 2007–10. Chm., All Party Vietnam Gp, 1988–99; Sec., British Cambodia All Party Gp, 1992–99; Hon. Sec., British Tibet All Party Gp; Chm., PLP Civil Liberties Gp, 1992–97. Mem., Northumberland Nat. Park Authy, 2017–. Chm., Internat. Alert, 2016–18. Trustee: Prison Reform Trust, 2006–10; N of England Civic Trust, 2011–; Chillingham Wild Cattle Trust, 2014–; Patron: Joe Homan Charity, 2011–. Chm., Heritage Lottery Fund NE, 2011–17; Pres., Northumbria Wildlife Trust, 2012–. Judge, Man Booker Prize, 2011. Mem. Council, Winston Churchill Meml Trust, 2012–. Vis. Lectr, Sch. of Geog., Politics and Sociol., Univ. of Newcastle, 2010–; Associate, Sch. of Business, Edinburgh Univ., 2016–. Hon. Fellow, Sch. of Govt and Internat. Affairs, Univ. of Durham, 2010. Hon. LLD City, 1992; Hon. DLitt Sunderland, 2010; Hon. DLaws Hull, 2011; Hon. DCL Newcastle, 2011; Hon. Dr Essex, 2011. Editor: Arguments for Socialism, by Tony Benn, 1979; Arguments for Democracy, by Tony Benn, 1981. Publications: novels: A Very British Coup, 1982 (televised 1988); The Last Man Out of Saigon, 1986; The Year of the Fire Monkey, 1991; The Friends of Harry Perkins, 2019; non-fiction: Error of Judgement—the truth about the Birmingham bombings, 1986, rev. edn 1997; A View from the Foothills: diaries 1999–2005, 2009; Decline and Fall: diaries 2005–2010, 2010; A Walk-On Part: diaries 1994–1999, 2011; Hinterland: a memoir, 2016; pamphlets: How to Select or Reselect your MP, 1981; The Tibetans, 1981. E: chris@chrismullinexmp.com. W: www.chrismullinexmp.com, www.twitter.com/chrismullinexmp.

**MULLIN, John**; Deputy Head of Sport, Telegraph Media Group, since 2016 (Head of Sport News, 2015–16); b Bellshill, 22 March 1963; s of John and Helen Mullin; m 1995, Maggie O'Kane; one s two d. Educ: Seafar Primary Sch., Cumbernauld; Hutchesons' Grammar Sch.; Glasgow Univ. (MA Politics and Econs 1984); City Univ., London (Dip. Newspaper Journalism 1985). The Guardian: reporter, 1990–96; Night Ed., 1996–97; Ireland corresp., 1997–2000; Dep. Ed., The Scotsman, 2000–03; Exec. Ed., The Independent, 2003–07; Dep. Ed., 2007–08, Ed., 2008–13, Independent on Sunday; Referendum Ed., BBC Scotland, 2013–14.

**MULLIN, (William Arthur) Roger**. Educ: Univ. of Edinburgh (MA Hons Sociol. 1977); Stow Coll., Glasgow (HNC Electrical and Electronic Engrg). Tutor in Social Scis, Univ. of Edinburgh, 1977–79; Lectr in Industrial Sociol., W Lothian Coll., 1979–80; Sen. Lectr and Depute Hd, Centre for Industrial Studies, Glenrothes Coll., 1980–85; Hd of Dept, Stevenson Coll. of FE, 1985–86; Sen. Partner, Roger Mullin Associates, 1986–99; Man. Dir, Inter-ed Ltd, 1993–2012; freelance writer, researcher, 2014–15. Consultant to orgns incl. UNESCO, UNFAO, UNIDO, UNDP, ILO, IBRD and Asian Develt Bank. Associate Lectr and Ext. PhD Supervisor, Open Univ., 1978–2002; MBA Ext. Lectr and thesis supervisor, Stirling Univ., 2001–15. Director: Red Lead Arts Ltd, Belfast, 2004–05; Momentous Change Ltd, 2012–14. Hon. Prof., Stirling Univ. Mgt Sch., 2010–15. MP (SNP) Kirkcaldy and Cowdenbeath, 2015–17; contested (SNP) same seat, 2017. Internat.

Progs Advr, Australian Acad., 1996–97; Columnist, TES Scotland. Advr to Lifelong Learning Inquiry, Enterprise and Lifelong Learning Cttee, Scottish Parlt, 2001–02. Member: Industrial Adv. Panel, Inst. of Biomed. and Life Scis, Univ. of Glasgow, 1997–2003; Internat. Adv. Gp, ICOD Canada. Chm., Bd of Trustees, Stirling Univ. Student Union, 2010–11. Hon. Pres., Univ. of Paisley, 1995–98. MIPD 1988. *Publications:* (contrib.) Multi-Party Britain, 1979; (contrib.) The Referendum Experience, Scotland 1979, 1981; Career Goals and Educational Attainment: what is the link?, 2004; (contrib.) Public and Third Sector Leadership, 2014; contrib. Bull. Scottish Politics.

**MULLINS, Andrew Oliver**; Chief Executive, Informa Connect (formerly Knowledge and Networking) Division, Informa plc, since 2014; *b* Woolwich, 21 March 1964; *s* of Gerald Oliver Mullins and Caroline Sylvia Mary Mullins; *m* 1992, Lucinda Harriet Nelson; two *s. Educ:* Yardley Court Prep. Sch.; Cranbrook Sch.; Bristol Univ. (BSc Hons Econs). Brand manager, Unilever, 1986–95; Global Brand Dir and Man. Dir, UDV Amsterdam, Diageo, 1995–2001; Mktg Dir and Gen. Manager, News Internat., 2001–07; Managing Director: Associated Newspapers, 2007–09; Evening Standard Ltd, 2007–14; Independent Print Ltd, 2010–14; CEO, London Live ESTV, 2013–14 (non-exec. Dir, 2014–). Non-executive Director: Which?, 2011–16; Evening Standard, 2014–; Independent Print Ltd, 2014–; ITN, 2018–. *Recreations:* golf, cycling, ski-ing. *E:* andrew.mullins@informa.com. *Clubs:* Dulwich and Sydenham Golf, Band of Brothers Cricket.

**MULLINS, Charlie**, OBE 2015; Founder and Chief Executive Officer, Pimlico Plumbers Ltd, since 1979; *b* St Pancras, 28 Oct. 1952; *m* Julie Shirley; two *s* two *d. Educ:* Tower Bridge Comprehensive Sch. C&G Plumbing and Advanced Plumbing. Featured on television programmes: Posh Plumbers, BBC, 2004; Secret Millionaire, Channel 4, 2009; Show Me Your Money, Channel 4, 2012; How Did You Get So Rich?, Channel 4, 2017; Judge, BBC Young Plumber of the Year, 2010. Patron, Women on the Tools, 2015–. SE England Apprenticeship Ambassador, 2013. *Publications:* Bog-Standard Business, 2015. *Recreation:* boxing. *Address:* Pimlico Plumbers Ltd, Pimlico House, 1 Sail Street, SE11 6NQ. *T:* (020) 7928 8888. *E:* charlie@pimlicoplumbers.com.

**MULLINS, Rt Rev. Daniel Joseph**; Bishop of Menevia, (RC), 1987–2001, now Emeritus; *b* 10 July 1929; *s* of Timothy Mullins. *Educ:* Mount Melleray; St Mary's, Aberystwyth; Oscott Coll.; UC of S Wales and Mon, Cardiff (Fellow, University Coll., Cardiff). Priest, 1953; Curate at: Barry, 1953–56; Newbridge, 1956; Bargoed, 1956–57; Maesteg, 1957–60; Asst Chaplain to UC Cardiff, 1960–64; Sec. to Archbp of Cardiff, 1964–68; Vicar General of Archdiocese of Cardiff, 1968; Titular Bishop of Stowe and Auxiliary Bishop in Swansea, 1970–87. Pres., Catholic Record Soc. Hon. Fellow, St David's University Coll., Lampeter, 1987. *Recreations:* golf, walking.

**MULLINS, Edwin Brandt**; author, journalist and film-maker; *b* 14 Sept. 1933; *s* of late Claud Mullins and Gwendolen Mullins, OBE; *m* 1st, 1960, Gillian Brydone (*d* 1982); one *s* two *d*; 2nd, 1984, Anne Kelleher. *Educ:* Midhurst Grammar Sch.; Merton Coll., Oxford (BA Hons, MA). London Editor, Two Cities, 1957–58; Sub-editor and Art Correspondent, Illustrated London News, 1958–62; Art Critic: Sunday Telegraph, 1962–69; Telegraph Sunday Magazine, 1964–86; contributor, 1962–, to The Guardian, Financial Times, Sunday Times, Director, Apollo, Art and Artists, Studio, Radio Times, TV Times, Country Living. Scriptwriter and presenter of numerous TV documentaries for BBC, Channel 4 and RM Arts, Munich, incl. 100 Great Paintings, The Pilgrimage of Everyman, Gustave Courbet, Fake?, Prison, The Great Art Collection, A Love Affair with Nature, Masterworks, Paradise on Earth, Montparnasse Revisited, Dürer, Out of the Dark Ages—a tale of four Emperors, Georges de la Tour—Genius Lost and Found, Van Gogh in England, The Changing of the Avant-Garde. *Publications:* Souza, 1962; Wallis, 1967; Josef Herman, 1967; Braque, 1968; The Art of Elisabeth Frink, 1972; The Pilgrimage to Santiago, 1974, repr. 2001; (ed) Great Paintings, 1981; (ed) The Arts of Britain, 1983; The Painted Witch, 1985; A Love Affair with Nature, 1985; The Royal Collection, 1992; Alfred Wallis: Cornish Primitive, 1994; In Search of Cluny—God's Lost Empire, 2006; Avignon of the Popes: city of exiles, 2007; The Carmargue: portrait of a wilderness, 2009; Roman Provence, a History and Guide, 2011; Van Gogh: the asylum year, 2015; Swimming with Dali, and Other Encounters with Artists, 2016; The Four Roads to Heaven: France and the Santiago Pilgrimage, 2017; In Search of Art: adventures and discoveries, 2018; *novels:* Angels on the Point of a Pin, 1979; Sirens, 1983; The Golden Bird, 1987; The Lands of the Sea, 1988; Dear Venus, 1992; With Much Love, 1993; All My Worldly Goods, 1994; The Outfit, 1995; The Devil's Work, 1996. *Recreation:* friendship. *Address:* 27 Bracken Gardens, Barnes, SW13 9HW.

**MULLIS, Marjorie**; *see* Allthorpe-Guyton, M.

**MULLOVA, Viktoria**; violinist; *b* 27 Nov. 1959; *d* of Juri Mullov and Raisa Mullova; one *s* two *d. Educ:* Central Music Sch., Moscow; Moscow Conservatory. First prize, Sibelius Competition, Helsinki, 1980; Gold Medal, Tchaikovsky Competition, Moscow, 1982; left USSR, 1983. Has performed with most major orchestras; many festival appearances. Recordings include: violin concertos: Bach, Brahms, Tchaikovsky, Sibelius, Mendelssohn, Stravinsky, Bartok No 2, Shostakovich No 1, Prokoviev No 2, Paganini No 1; Bach partitas; sonatas for violin and piano: Bach, Janácek, Prokofiev, Debussy, Brahms; Vivaldi, Four Seasons; Through the Looking Glass (arrangements of works by Miles Davis, Weather Report and Youssou N'Dour). *Address:* c/o Askonas Holt, 15 Fetter Lane, EC4A 1BW.

**MULQUEENY, Emma Elizabeth**, OBE 2016; Chief Executive Officer, Elbi Digital, since 2016; *b* Sidcup, Kent, 12 July 1971; *d* of Ken Knight and Sara Nicholls; *m* (marr. diss.); two *d. Educ:* St James Independent Sch. for Girls; Univ. of Surrey. Jillaroo and gold mine work, Australia, 1992–97; freelance consultancy, 1997–2004; Manager: Online Content, Bd of Inland Revenue, 2004–06; Strategic Communication, Cabinet Office, 2005–07; Hub Mum, FCO, 2007–08; Hd, Digital, Home Office, 2008–10; Curator, Open Platform, The Guardian, 2010–11. Founder and CEO, 2009–14, Chm., 2014–17, Rewired State Gp. Mem., Exec. Cttee, British Interactive Media Assoc., 2011–. Member: Lord Mayor of London's Digital Adv. Bd, 2011–; Adv. Bd, Design Council, 2011–; Mozilla Learning Adv. Gp, 2012–; Comr, Speaker's Commn on Digital Democracy, 2014–. FRSA 2014. Fellow, Openforum Acad., 2011–; Google Fellow, 2014. *Recreations:* cooking, reading, travelling. *Address:* Mulqueenys, 3 Waterside Mews, Guildford GU1 1LA. *T:* 07730 570647. *Club:* Blacks.

**MULREADY, Rt Rev. David Gray**; Bishop of North West Australia, 2004–11; Minister, Diocese of Sydney, since 2011; *b* 13 Sept. 1947; *s* of Norman Benson Mulready and Edna Faith Mulready (*née* Osborne); *m* 1971, Maureen Jane Mulready (*née* Lawrie); two *s* one *d. Educ:* Newington Coll., Sydney; Moore Theol Coll., Sydney (ThL 1971); Melbourne Coll. of Divinity (DipRE 1973). Ordained deacon and priest, 1971; Assistant Minister: Camden, 1971–73; Eastwood, 1973–74; Rector: Tambar Springs, 1974–77; Walgett, 1977–81; Manilla, 1981–85; Gunnedah, 1985–89; State Dir, Bush Ch Aid Soc., 1989–93; Rector, Penrith, 1993–2000; Rector and Sen. Canon, St John's Cathedral, Parramatta, 2000–04. *Recreations:* family, gardening, photography, travel, reading. *Address:* 28 Croft Place, Gerringong, NSW 2534, Australia. *T:* (2) 42342346.

**MULRONEY, Rt Hon. (Martin) Brian**; PC (Can.) 1984; CC 1998; Senior Partner, Norton Rose Fulbright Canada LLP (formerly Ogilvy Renault, then Norton Rose OR), since 1993; *b* 20 March 1939; *s* of Benedict Mulroney and Irene O'Shea; *m* 1973, Mila Pivnicki; three *s* one *d. Educ:* St Francis Xavier Univ. (BA); Université Laval (LLL). Partner, Ogilvy, Renault (Montreal law firm), 1965–76; Pres., Iron Ore Co. of Canada, 1976–83. MP (Progressive Conservative): Central Nova, 1983–84; Manicouagan, 1984–88; Charlevoix, 1988–93. Leader of the Opposition, 1983–84; Prime Minister of Canada, 1984–93. Royal Comr, Cliche Commn investigating violence in Quebec construction industry, 1974. Director: Barrick Gold Corp.; Trizec Properties Inc. (formerly TrizecHahn Corp.); Archer Daniels Midland Co.; Cendant Corp.; Quebecor Inc. (Chm., 2014–); Quebecor World Inc.; Acreage Hldgs, 2018–. Member, International Advisory Council: China Internat. Trust and Investment Corp.; J P Morgan Chase & Co.; Independent News and Media plc. Trustee, Montreal Heart Inst. Hon. LLD: St Francis Xavier Univ., 1979; Meml Univ., 1980. *Publications:* Where I Stand, 1983. *Recreations:* tennis, swimming.

**MULVANY, Patrick Mowbray**; Director, Kamayoq, since 2012; *b* Eastbourne, 12 July 1946; *s* of Brian Mulvany and Barbara Mulvany; *m* 1972, Annabel Royes; two *s* one *d* (and one *s* decd). *Educ:* Eastbourne Coll.; St John's Coll., Oxford (MA Agriculture 1969). CBiol 1977. Develt worker, Catholic Inst. for Internat. Relns, Honduras, 1969–72; Higher Scientific Officer, Nat. Inst. for Res. in Dairying, Reading, 1973–79; Sen. Policy Advr, Practical Action (formerly Intermediate Technol. Develt Gp), 1979–2012. Chm., UK Food Gp, 2002–14. Evaluations of: GRAIN, 2007; Friends of the Earth Internat., 2008; Via Campesina, 2010; S Africa Develt Community Seed Security Network, 2013; Civil Soc. Mechanism/Cttee on World Food Security, 2017; UN Envmt Agricl Biodiversity Prog. in Central Asia, 2017; African Centre for Biodiversity, 2019. Member: Biosci. for Society Strategy Panel, BBSRC, 2013–; Food Ethics Council, 2014–; ECOROPA, 2014–; Etc Group, 2015–. Trustee: Oxfam, 1986–92; Action Aid, 1994–2001; Catholic Inst. for Internat. Relns, 1980–85 and 1993–2001; Sustain: the alliance for better food and farming, 2005–17. Co-Chm., Consultative Gp on Internat. Agricl Res.–NGO Cttee, 2002–03. Hon. Res. Fellow, Centre for Agroecology, Water and Resilience, Coventry Univ., 2017–. *Publications:* contrib. books, jls, confs and papers on issues concerning governance of technol., agricl biodiversity and food sovereignty. *Recreations:* music, growing food, travel, family. *T:* (020) 7193 7283. *E:* patrick.mulvany@coventry.ac.uk.

**MULVEY, Prof. Laura Mary Alice**, FBA 2000; Professor of Film and Media Studies, Birkbeck, University of London, since 1999; *b* 15 Aug. 1941. *Educ:* St Paul's Girls' Sch.; St Hilda's Coll., Oxford (BA). Teacher of film studies and film practice; responsible for Birkbeck Coll. MA in Film and TV History and Theory. Co-director: six films with Peter Wollen; (with Mark Lewis) Disgraced Monuments, 1994. *Publications:* Visual and Other Pleasures, 1989, 2nd edn 2009; Citizen Kane, 1993, 2nd edn 2013; Fetishism and Curiosity, 1996, 2nd edn 2013; Death Twenty-four Times a Second: stillness and the moving image, 2006; articles and chapters in books. *Address:* School of History of Art, Film and Visual Media, Birkbeck, University of London, 43 Gordon Square, WC1H 0PD.

**MULVILLE, James Thomas**; Managing Director, Hat Trick Productions, since 1985; *b* 5 Jan. 1955; *s* of late James Lawrence Mulville and of June Mulville; *m* 1st, 1974, Julia Kelly; 2nd, 1987, Denise O'Donoghue, *qv* (marr. diss. 1998); 3rd, 1999, Karen Page; three *s* one *d. Educ:* Alsop Comprehensive Sch., Liverpool; Jesus Coll., Cambridge (BA Hons; Pres., Cambridge Footlights, 1976–77). With BBC Light Entertainment as writer and producer, 1978–82; Jt Founder, Hat Trick Prodns, 1985; co-writer and performer: Who Dares Wins (series), Channel 4, 1983–88; Chelmsford 123, Channel 4, 1987–90; actor: That's Love, 1987–91; GBH, 1991. FRTS 2001. Hon. DLit Liverpool. *Publications:* (jtly) Who Dares Wins, 1986. *Recreations:* my children, family, friends, films, Everton Football Club, shooting. *Address:* c/o Hat Trick Productions, 33 Oval Road, NW1 7EA. *T:* (020) 7434 2451.

**MUMBENGEGWI, Hon. Simbarashe Simbanenduku**; MP, Republic of Zimbabwe, since 2005; Minister of State for Presidential Affairs and Monitoring of Government Programmes, since 2017; *b* Chivi, Zimbabwe, 20 July 1945; *s* of late Chivandire Davis Mumbengegwi and Dzivaidzo Shuvai Mumbengegwi; *m* 1983, Emily; one *s* four *d. Educ:* Fletcher High Sch., Gweru, Zimbabwe; Monash Univ., Melbourne (BA Gen., BA Combined Hons, DipEd, MEd). Teacher, Dadaya Secondary Sch., Zvishavane, and schools in Melbourne, then Tutor in Politics at colls in Melbourne, 1966–78; MP: Midlands Province, 1980–85; Shurugwi Constituency, Midlands Province, 1985–90; Dep. Speaker and Chm. of Cttees, House of Assembly, Parlt of Zimbabwe, 1980–81; Dep. Minister of Foreign Affairs, 1981–82; Minister: of Water Resources and Develt, 1982; of Nat. Housing, 1982–84; of Public Construction and Nat. Housing, 1984–88; of Transport, 1988–90; Ambassador and Perm. Rep. of Zimbabwe to UN, NY, 1990–95; Vice-Pres., UN Gen. Assembly, 1990–91; Mem., UN Security Council, 1991–92 (Pres. at height of Gulf War, 1991, and 1992); Ambassador to Belgium, Netherlands, Luxembourg and Perm. Rep. to EU, Brussels, 1995–99; Perm. Rep. to Orgn for Prohibition of Chem. Weapons, The Hague, 1997–99 (Mem. Council, 1997–99); High Comr, later Ambassador, to UK, and Ambassador to Ireland, 1999–2005; Minister of Foreign Affairs, 2005–17. Participated in numerous ministerial confs and Heads of State summits of OAU, 1981–94; Hd of delegns to all annual confs of UN Commn for Human Settlements, 1983–88; served on numerous UN and ACP cttees. Mem., Youth Leagues of Nat. Democratic Party, ZAPU and ZANU, 1960–64; ZANU activist in exile, 1966–72; Zimbabwe African National Union: Dep. Chief Rep., 1973–76, Chief Rep., 1976–78, Australia and Far East; Chief Rep. to Zambia, 1978–80; ZANU-Patriotic Front: Provincial Treas., Midlands Province, 1981–84; Mem., Central Cttee, 1984–94, 2006– (Dep. Sec. for Publicity and Inf., 1984–89). *Recreations:* reading, photography, jogging, tennis, golf, swimming. *Address:* Ministry of State for Presidential Affairs, Munhumutapa Building, Harare, Zimbabwe.

**MUMFORD, Rev. David Christopher**; Rector, St Andrew's, Brechin, and St Drostan's, Tarfside, 2007–15; Dean of Brechin, 2008–12; *b* 14 Jan. 1947. *Educ:* Merton Coll., Oxford (MA 1974); York Univ. (MSW 1981; CQSW 1981); Lincoln Theol Coll. Ordained deacon, 1986, priest, 1987; Assistant Curate: St Mark's, Shiremoor, Newcastle, 1986–89; St Augustine's, North Shields, 1989–91; Vicar, St Anthony, Byker, 1991–97; Rural Dean, Newcastle E, 1996–97; Vicar, St Peters, Cowgate, 1997–2002; Internat. Co-ordinator, Internat. Fellowship of Reconciliation, 2002–07. *Address:* 10 Temple Mains Steading, Innerwick, Dunbar, E Lothian EH42 1EF. *T:* (01368) 840361. *E:* dmumford@phonecoop.coop.

**MUMFORD, David Stewart**; QC 2016; *b* Edinburgh, 6 March 1975; *s* of John and Fiona Mumford; *m* 2006, Jane Christina Rankin; three *d. Educ:* King's Coll. Sch., Wimbledon; Magdalen Coll., Oxford (BA Lit. Hum.; MA); City Univ. (DipLaw); Inns of Court Sch. of Law. Called to the Bar, Lincoln's Inn, 2000; in practice as barrister, specialising in commercial and chancery litigation, 2001–. *Recreations:* writing and producing electronic music, science literature. *Address:* Maitland Chambers, 7 Stone Buildings, Lincoln's Inn, WC2A 3SZ. *T:* (020) 7406 1200. *E:* dmumford@maitlandchambers.com.

**MUMFORD, Prof. Karen Ann**, CBE 2016; PhD; Professor of Economics, University of York, since 2009; *b* Australia, 1962; *m* 1991, Prof. Peter Nigel Smith; one *s* one *d*. *Educ*: Macroberston Girls High Sch.; Macquarie Univ. (BEc Hons 1984); Australian Nat. Univ. (PhD 1991). Harkness Fellow, Princeton, Dartmouth and Harvard Univs, 1990, 1991; Lecturer: ANU, 1991–92; Univ. of Warwick, 1992–95; University of York: Lectr, 1995–99; Sen. Lectr, 1999–2004; Reader in Econs, 2004–08. Chm., Women's Cttee, 2009–16, Mem., Exec. Cttee, 2010–16, REconS. *Recreations*: walking, reading. *Address*: Department of Economics, University of York, York YO10 5DD. *T*: (01904) 323756. *E*: karen.mumford@york.ac.uk.

**MUMFORD, Peter Taylor;** theatre lighting and stage designer; television and stage director; Chairman, Association of Lighting Designers (UK), 2011–17; *b* 12 Dec. 1946; *s* of late John and Doreen Mumford; *m* 1st, 1969, Mary Davida Becket (*d* 1992); three *s*; 2nd, 1995, Tana Marie Lester (marr. diss. 2009); one *d*; 3rd, 2009, Alexandra Thompson. *Educ*: Central Sch. of Art (DipAD Theatre Design). Founding Mem., exptl theatre gp, Moving Being, late 1960s; freelance theatre artist, lighting and designing operas, plays and ballets, worldwide, 1978–; lighting designs for numerous productions, including: Fearful Symmetries, Royal Ballet, 1994; The Glass Blew In, Siobhan Davies Dance Co., 1995 (Olivier Award for Outstanding Achievement in Dance (for lighting design)); The Merchant of Venice, NT, 1999; Vincent in Brixton, NT, transf. Playhouse Th., 2002, transf. NY, 2003; Bacchai, NT, 2003 (Olivier Award for Best Lighting Designer); Peter Pan, Northern Ballet Th., 2005; Midsummer Marriage, Lyric Opera, Chicago, 2005; Cinderella, for Scottish Ballet, 2005; Madame Butterfly, for ENO, 2005–06, and Metropolitan Opera, NY, 2006; Eugene Onegin, Royal Opera House, 2006; The Rose Tattoo, NT, 2007; The Hothouse, NT, 2007; Fiddler on the Roof, Savoy Th., 2007; The Seagull, Royal Ct, 2007, transf. NY, 2008; Carousel, Savoy Th., 2008; Peter Grimes, Metropolitan Opera, NY, 2008; A View from the Bridge, Duke of York's, 2009; E=mc$^2$, Sadler's Wells, 2009; All's Well That Ends Well, NT, 2009; Metropolitan Opera 125th Anniversary Gala, NY, 2009; Carmen, Metropolitan Opera, NY, 2010; A Midsummer Night's Dream, Rose Th., Kingston upon Thames, 2010; An Ideal Husband, Vaudeville, 2010; A Streetcar Named Desire, Guthrie Th., Minneapolis, 2010; Bedroom Farce, Duke of York's and tour, 2010; Capriccio, Grange Park Opera, 2010; Elegy for Young Lovers, ENO at Young Vic, 2010; Enlightenment, Hampstead Th., 2010; Faust, ENO, 2010; La Spinalba, Guildhall Sch. of Music and Drama, 2010; Pictures from an Exhibition, Sadler's Wells, 2010; Pieces of Vincent, Arcola Th., 2010; Sucker Punch, Royal Court, 2010 (Knight of Illumination Award, Best Lighting for Drama); Tosca, Grange Park Opera, 2010; Twelfth Night, NT, 2011; Lucrezia Borgia and The Damnation of Faust, ENO, 2011; Punch and Judy, Opera Genève, 2011; Much Ado About Nothing, Wyndham's, 2011; Top Hat, UK tour, 2011; Faust, Metropolitan Opera, 2011, Eugene Onegin, LA Opera, 2011; King Kong, Regent Th., Melbourne, 2013 (Green Room Award for Lighting Design, Helpmann Award for Lighting Design), Broadway Th., NY, 2018; Ghosts, Almeida, 2013; Women on the Verge of a Nervous Breakdown, Playhouse, 2015; The Flying Dutchman, Opera North, 2015; Andre Chénier, Opera North, 2016; Escaped Alone, Royal Court Th., 2017, transf. Harvey Th. Brooklyn, NY, 2017; Faust, Vilnius City Opera, 2017; The Children, Royal Court Th., NY, 2017; Forty Second Street, Drury Lane Th., 2017; The Ferryman, Royal Court Th., 2017, transf. Gielgud Th., 2017, transf. Bernard B Jacobs Th., NY, 2018; Carmen, Grange Opera, 2017; The Damnation of Faust, Schiller Th., Berlin, 2017; Corybantic Games, ROH, 2018; John, NT, 2018; Long Day's Journey into Night, Wyndham's, 2018, transf. Brooklyn Acad. of Music, NY, 2018; My Name is Lucy Barton, Bridge Th., 2018; The Way of the World, Donmar Warehouse, 2018; Katya Kabanova, Opera North, 2019; The Queen of Spades, Vilnius City Opera, 2019; Beauty and Sadness, Chamber Opera, Hong Kong, 2019; Jude, Hampstead Th., 2019; dir/designer of concert version of Ring Cycle, Opera North, 2011– (dir of film for BBC, 2016); also set and lighting designs for Northern Ballet; dir, dance and music films for TV, incl. adaptations of Matthew Bourne's Swan Lake, and series of short films, 48 Preludes and Fugues (J. S. Bach). *Recreation*: fly fishing when the opportunity arises. *Address*: South Dock Marina, Rope Street, SE16 7SZ. *E*: mumf1@mac.com. *W*: www.petermumford.info.

**MUMMERY, Christopher John L.;** *see* Lockhart-Mummery.

**MUMMERY, Rt Hon. Sir John Frank,** Kt 1989; PC 1996; DL; a Lord Justice of Appeal, 1996–2013; Deputy Chairman, Takeover Appeal Board, since 2014; *b* 5 Sept. 1938; *s* of late Frank Stanley Mummery and Ruth Mummery (*née* Coleman), Coldred, Kent; *m* 1967, Elizabeth Anne Lamond Lackie (*d* 2016), *d* of late Dr D. G. L. Lackie and Ellen Lackie (*née* Easterbrook), Edinburgh; one *s* one *d*. *Educ*: Oakleigh House, Dover; Dover County Grammar Sch.; Pembroke Coll., Oxford, 1959–63 (MA, BCL; Winter Williams Prize in Law; Hon. Fellow, 1989). National Service, The Border Regt and RAEC, 1957–59. Called to Bar, Gray's Inn (Atkin Schol.), 1964 (Bencher, 1985; Treas., 2005). Treasury Junior Counsel: in Charity Matters, 1977–81; Chancery, 1981–89; a Recorder, 1989; a Judge of the High Court, Chancery Div., 1989–96. President: Employment Appeal Tribunal, 1993–96; Investigatory Powers Tribunal, 2000–13; Clergy Discipline Tribunals, 2003–13; Chm., Clergy Discipline Commn, 2003–13; Member: Court of Ecclesiastical Causes Reserved, 2006–13; Faculty Rule Cttee, 2015–. Member, Senate of Inns of Court and Bar, 1978–81; Pres., Council of Inns of Court, 2000–03. Member: Justice Cttee on Privacy and the Law, 1967–70; Legal Adv. Commn, Gen. Synod of C of E, 1988–2013; Council of Legal Educn, 1989–92; leader, Rev. of Competition Appeal Tribunal Procedure, 2014. Chm. Trustees, CAB, Royal Courts of Justice, 2003–13. Gov., Inns of Court Sch. of Law, 1996–2001; Mem. Council, Pegasus Scholarship Trust, 1997–2013; Mem. Adv. Bd, British Inst. of Internat. and Comparative Law, 2001–13. Trustee, Wye Rural Museum Trust, 2008–. DL Kent, 2008–13. Hon. Fellow, Soc. for Advanced Legal Studies, 1997; Hon. Mem., Soc. of Legal Scholars, 1998; Hon. President: Employment Law Bar Assoc., 2003–13; Charity Law Assoc., 2004–15. Hon. Fellow, Oxford Inst. of Intellectual Property, 2013. Hon. LLD: De Montfort, 1998; City, 2002; DUniv: Canterbury Christ Church, 2014; Derby, 2016. *Publications*: (co-ed) Copinger and Skone James on Copyright, 12th edn 1980, 13th edn 1991. *Recreation*: walks with family, friends and alone.

**MUNBY, Rt Hon. Sir James (Lawrence),** Kt 2000; PC 2009; President of the Family Division, 2013–18; *b* 27 July 1948; *s* of Denys Lawrence Munby and Mary Munby (*née* Dicks); *m* 1977, Jennifer Anne Lindsay Beckhough; one *s* one *d*. *Educ*: Magdalen College Sch., Oxford; Wadham Coll., Oxford (BA). Called to the Bar, Middle Temple, 1971 (Bencher, 2000); QC 1988; a Judge of the High Court of Justice, Family Div., 2000–09; a Lord Justice of Appeal, 2009–13. Chm., Law Commn, 2009–12. Chm., Nuffield Family Justice Observatory, 2019–. *Address*: c/o Royal Courts of Justice, Strand, WC2A 2LL.

**MUNBY, Stephen Thurston,** CBE 2010; education consultant, since 2017; *b* North Shields, 25 Aug. 1956; *s* of Robert Munby and Hilda Munby; *m* 2005, Jacqueline Rothery. *Educ*: Royal Grammar Sch., Newcastle upon Tyne; Univ. of Reading (BA Hons Philos.); Univ. of Birmingham (PGCE); Manchester Metropolitan Univ. (MEd). Teacher of History and English, Fairfax Sch., Sutton Coldfield, then Teacher of History, Lord Lawson High Sch., Gateshead, 1978–85; TVEI support teacher, 1985–86; Sen. Lectr, Sunderland Poly., 1986–87; consultant, assessment and recording of achievement, 1987–89; Inspector, then Manager, Sch. Adv. Service, Oldham BC, 1989–97; Asst Dir, Blackburn with Darwen BC, 1997–2000; Dir, Educn and Lifelong Learning, Knowsley BC, 2000–05; Chief Exec., Nat. Coll. for Sch. Leadership, 2005–12; Chief Exec., CfBT Educn Trust, then Educn Develt Trust, 2012–17. Vis. Prof., UCL, 2017–. Chm., Nat. Teaching Awards Trust, 2017–. Hon. DArts Bedfordshire, 2010; DUniv Bishop Grosseteste University Coll., Lincoln, 2011. *Publications*: Assessing and Recording Achievement, 1989; Imperfect Leadership: a book for leaders who know they don't know it all, 2019. *Recreations*: supporting Newcastle United Football Club, walking, listening to Leonard Cohen and Bob Dylan music. *E*: steve@munbyeducation.co.uk.

**MUNDAY, Christopher Charles;** Strategic Director, Children and Young People, Barnet Borough Council, since 2015; *b* Eastwood, Essex, 12 Aug. 1967; *s* of Robert Charles Munday and Brenda Munday; *m* 2003, Danel Malherbe; two *s* one *d*. *Educ*: North East London Poly. (BSc); London Sch. of Hygiene and Tropical Medicine (MSc); Univ. of Warwick (MBA); Inst. of Educn (MA). Mission Partner, Church Missionary Soc., 1988–93; Youth Worker (Health), Southend Locality Youth Service, 1993–95; Health Promotion Manager, South Essex HA, 1995–98; Children's Quality Manager, Southend BC, 1998–2004; Children's Trust Manager, Tower Hamlets Council, 2004–06; service and divl dir roles, Bucks CC, 2006–15. FRSA. *Recreations*: supporting West Ham United, family time. *Address*: 30 Nathaniel Walk, Tring, Herts HP23 5DG. *T*: (01442) 824388. *E*: d.munday@me.com.

**MUNDAY, Janice Margaret,** CBE 2013; Director, Advanced Manufacturing and Services, Department for Business, Innovation and Skills, 2010–16; *d* of late Richard Munday and of Margaret Elliott (*née* Rogers); partner, Martin Edward Stanley, *qv*; one *s* (and one *s* decd). Public Service Delivery, Cabinet Office, 1989–92; Accountancy Policy, DTI, 1992–95; Dir of Policy, Charity Commn, 1995–96; Department of Trade and Industry: Dir of Policy, Consumer Affairs, 1999–2000; Dir, Participation and Skills, then Head, Employment Relns, 2000–07 (Dir, Employment Relns, 2003–07); Dir, Business Support Simplification Project, then Solutions for Business/BSSP, later Solutions for Business, Low Carbon and Services, BERR, subseq. BIS, 2007–10. Non-executive Director: Inogesis (formerly VTC Gp), 2016–; Sheffield Forgemasters, 2016–. Principal Fellow, Warwick Manufg Gp, 2017–. Ambassador for Industrial Cadets, 2018–. *Recreations*: enjoying London, gardening, dog walking. *E*: Janice.M.Munday@gmail.com.

**MUNDAY, Stephen Charles Richard,** CBE 2013; Executive Principal, Comberton Village College, and Chief Executive, Cam Academy Trust (formerly Comberton Academy Trust), since 2011; *b* Barking, Essex, 4 Aug. 1964; *s* of Brian and Jill Munday; *m* 1989, Elizabeth Marion Darling; one *s* two *d*. *Educ*: Simon Langton Grammar Sch. for Boys, Canterbury; St John's Coll., Cambridge (BA Econs 1986); Inst. of Educn, Univ. of London (PGCE; MA). Teacher of Econs, 1987–94, Hd of Sixth Form, 1989–94, Bishop's Stortford High Sch.; Dep. Hd, Saffron Walden Co. High Sch., 1994–2000. Member: Teaching Schs' Council, 2014–; E of England and N-E London Headteacher Bd, 2014–; Chm., Initial Teacher Trng Expert Gp to produce prog. of core content for ITT in England, 2015–16; Pres., Chartered Coll. of Teaching, 2018–. Hon. DEd Anglia Ruskin, 2009. *Publications*: Current Developments in Economics, 1996; Markets and Market Failure, 2000; (with C. Bamford) Markets, 2001. *Recreations*: sport, especially golf and cricket, local church. *Address*: Comberton Village College, West Street, Comberton, Cambridge CB23 7DU. *T*: (01223) 262503. *E*: thecollege@comberton.cambs.sch.uk. *Club*: Gog Magog Golf (Cambridge).

**MUNDELL, Prof. Carole Gibson,** PhD; FInstP; Professor of Extragalactic Astronomy, since 2007 and Head of Astrophysics, since 2015, University of Bath (Head, Department of Physics, 2016–18); Chief Scientific Adviser, Foreign and Commonwealth Office, since 2018; *b* Sheffield, 17 Aug. 1969; *d* of Robert Mundell and Hilda Mundell (*née* Gibson); *m* 1998, Dr David Leslie Shone; two *s*. *Educ*: Penketh High Sch., Warrington; Priestley Sixth-Form Coll., Warrington; Univ. of Glasgow (BSc Hons 1992); Univ. of Manchester (PhD 1995). FInstP 2017. PPARC Postdoctoral Res. Fellow, Jodrell Bank, Univ. of Manchester, 1995–97; Postdoctoral Res. Associate, Dept of Astronomy, Univ. of Maryland, 1997–99; Astrophysics Research Institute, Liverpool John Moores University: Royal Soc. Univ. Res. Fellow, 1999–2009; Res. Councils UK Fellow, 2005–11; Prof. of Extragalactic Astronomy, 2007–15. Royal Soc. Wolfson Res. Merit Award, 2011–16. Mem. Council, STFC, 2015–18; Chair, Skills and Engagement Adv. Bd, 2015–. Woman of the Year, FDM Everywoman in Technol. Awards, 2016. *Publications*: contrib. papers in fields of active galaxies and gamma ray bursts to peer-reviewed jls incl. Nature, Sci., Astrophysical Jl and Monthly Notices of RAS. *Recreations*: music, reading, tae kwon do, knitting, family. *Address*: Department of Physics, University of Bath, Claverton Down, Bath BA2 7AY. *E*: c.g.mundell@bath.ac.uk.

**MUNDELL, Rt Hon. David (Gordon);** PC 2010; MP (C) Dumfriesshire, Clydesdale and Tweeddale, since 2005; *b* 27 May 1962; *s* of Dorah Mundell; *m* 1987, Lynda Jane Carmichael (marr. diss. 2012); two *s* one *d*. *Educ*: Lockerbie Acad.; Edinburgh Univ. (LLB Hons 1984); Univ. of Strathclyde Business Sch. (MBA 1991). Trainee Solicitor, Tindal Oatts, Glasgow, 1985–87; Solicitor, Maxwell Waddell, Glasgow, 1987–89; Sen. Corporate Lawyer, Biggart Baillie & Gifford, Glasgow, 1989–91; Group Legal Advr Scotland, BT, 1991–98; Head of Nat. Affairs, BT Scotland, 1998–99. MSP (C) S of Scotland, 1999–2005. Shadow Sec. of State for Scotland, 2005–10; Parly Under-Sec. of State, 2010–15, Sec. of State, 2015–19, Scotland Office. Member: Law Soc. of Scotland, 1986–; Law Soc., 1992–. *Recreations*: family and friends, travel. *Address*: House of Commons, SW1A 0AA.
*See also* O. G. W. Mundell.

**MUNDELL, Oliver Gordon Watson;** Member (C) Dumfriesshire, Scottish Parliament, since 2016; *b* Irvine, 1 Dec. 1989; *s* of Rt Hon. David (Gordon) Mundell, *qv*; *m* 2015, Catherine Easton. *Educ*: Moffat Acad.; Univ. of Edinburgh (LLB Hons). Worked for Royal Dutch Shell. *Address*: Scottish Parliament, Edinburgh EH99 1SP.

**MUNDELL, Prof. Robert Alexander,** CC 2003; PhD; Professor of Economics, Columbia University, 1974, now Emeritus; *b* 24 Oct. 1932; *s* of William Campbell Mundell and Lila Teresa Mundell; *m* 1st, 1957, Barba Sheff (*d* 1972); 2nd, 1998, Valerie S. Natsios; one *s*. *Educ*: Univ. of BC; MIT (PhD); London Sch. of Econs; Univ. of Chicago. Instructor, Univ. of BC, 1957–58; economist, Royal Commn on Price Spreads of Food Products, Ottawa, 1958; Asst Prof. of Econs, Stanford Univ., 1958–59; Prof. of Econs, Johns Hopkins Univ., Sch. of Advanced Internat. Studies, Bologna, 1959–61; Sen. Economist, IMF, 1961–63; Prof. of Internat. Econs, Grad. Inst. Internat. Studies, Geneva, 1965–75; Professor of Economics: Univ. of Chicago, 1966–71; Univ. of Waterloo, Ont., 1972–74. Vis. Prof. of Econs, McGill Univ., 1963–64, 1989–90; First Rockefeller Vis. Res. Prof. of Internat. Econs, Brookings Inst., 1964–65; Guggenheim Fellow, 1971; Annenburg Dist. Schol. in Residence, Univ. of Southern Calif, 1980; Richard Fox Vis. Prof. of Econs, Univ. of Penn, 1990–91. Ed., Jl Pol Econ., 1966–71. Pres., N American Econ. and Financial Assoc., 1974–78. Hon. Dr: Paris, 1992; People's Univ. of China, 1995. Nobel Prize for Econs, 1999. *Publications*: The International Monetary System: conflict and reform, 1965; Man and Economics, 1968; International Economics, 1968; Monetary Theory: interest, inflation and growth in the world economy, 1971; contrib. learned jls. *Recreations*: painting, tennis, hockey, ski-ing, history. *Address*: 35 Claremont Avenue #5N, New York, NY 10027–6815, USA. *T*: (212) 7490630; Palazzo Mundell, Strada di Santa Columba 2–4, Santa Columba, Siena 53100, Italy. *Club*: Reform.

**MUNDIE, Douglas Stewart;** Managing Director, Saltire Business Solutions Ltd, since 2004; *b* Glasgow, 26 July 1952; *s* of Robert Hunter Mundie and Norah Mundie (*née* Carswell); *m* 1981, Elizabeth Lesley Rae; two *s* one *d*. *Educ*: Glasgow Acad.; Univ. of St Andrews (MA Hons 1974); Manchester Business Sch. (EDP 1987). Sales Mgt, Metal Box plc, 1974–82; Commercial Manager, Metal Box plc, 1982–85; Gp Mkt Develt Manager, Lin Pac Plastics Internat. Ltd, 1985–88; Man. Dir, Bonar Flexibles Ltd, 1988–92; Gen. Manager, Borden Rigid Plastics Edinburgh, 1992–97; Divl Sales Mktg Dir, M. Y. Plastics Ltd, 1997–2000; Chief Exec., Technol. Ventures Scotland, 2000–04; Chm., Fusion (Scotland) Ltd, 2003–08; Man. Dir, Sea Mammal Res. Unit Ltd, 2006–11; Gp Commercial Dir, SOI Gp Ltd, 2011–13. Mem. Bd, SFC, 2014– (Dep. Chair, 2018–; Chairman: Remuneration Cttee, 2015–; Capital Decision Point Cttee, 2016–). Gov., and Convener, Audit Cttee, Court of Univ. of St Andrews, 1994–2004. Chm., Fife Br., Inst. of Dirs, 2002–06 (Mem. Council, 2002–). Trustee, St Andrews Harbour Trust, 2018–. *Recreations*: sailing, Rugby, golf, family, coastal rowing. *Address*: c/o Scottish Further and Higher Education Funding Council, Apex 2, 97 Haymarket Terrace, Edinburgh EH12 5HD. *T*: (0131) 313 6500. *E*: douglas.mundie@gmail.com. *Club*: New (St Andrews).

**MUNDY, Prof. Anthony Richard,** FRCP, FRCS; Professor of Urology, University of London, since 1991; Director, Institute of Urology (formerly Institute of Urology and Nephrology), University College London, since 1996; Medical Director, UCL Hospitals NHS Foundation Trust, since 2000; *b* 25 April 1948; *s* of Peter Gordon Mundy and Betty (*née* Hall); *m* 1st, 1970, Sheila Peskett; 2nd, 1975, Marilyn Ashton; one *s* one *d*; partner, Debra Hendley; one *d*. *Educ*: Mill Hill Sch.; St Mary's Hosp. Medical Sch., London (MB BS Hons 1971); MS London 1982. MRCP 1974, FRCP 1996; FRCS 1975. House Surgeon, St Mary's Hosp., London, 1971; House Physician, Barnet General Hosp., 1972; Casualty Officer, St Mary's Hosp., London, 1973; Surgical Registrar, Orsett Hosp., 1973–75; Guy's Hospital: Sen. Registrar, Surgery, 1975–78, Urology, 1978–81; Consultant Urologist, 1981–99; Consultant Urologist, St Peter's Hosps and UCL Hosps, 1986–. Vis. Consultant Urologist, St Luke's Hosp., subseq. Mater Dei Hosp., Malta, 1984–. Jack McAninch Vis. Prof., Univ. of San Francisco, 2015; Vis. Prof., Univ. of Oman, 2018. Lectures: Pradke, Pune, India, 1992; Sir Ernest Finch, Sheffield, 1994; Bodo von Garrelts, Stockholm, 1995; Ballenger, Puerto Rica, 1996; Ian Aird, Imperial Coll., 1999; Grey Turner, Newcastle, 1999; C. E. Alken, Dusseldorf, 1999; Rovsing, Copenhagen, 2000; British Assoc. of Urol Surgeons, 2001, 2009; Hunterian Oration, RCS, 2007; Moynihan, RCS/Assoc. of Surgeons of GB and Ireland, 2009; Vicary, RCS, 2016. Hon. Prof. of Medicine, Univ. of Crete, 2009–. Pres., British Assoc. of Urol Surgeons, 2006–08 (Mem. Council, 1990–93, 1995–2001; Vice-Pres., 2003–06); Member: Exec. Cttee, Eur. Assoc. of Urol., 1994–2000 (Mem., Acad., 2000–); Council, RCS, 2000–10; Founder Mem., Genito-Urinary Reconstructive Surgeons, 1984–; Convenor, Urol Res. Soc., 1984–; Fellow, Urological Soc. of Australia and NZ, 2011; Hon. FRACS 2013; Hon. FACS. Hon. Member, Urological Society (of Australasia, 1986; of HK, 1989; of Singapore, 1990; of Malaysia, 1994; of S Africa, 1998; of Holland, 1990; of Germany, 2011; Internat. Mem., Amer. Assoc. of Genito-Urinary Surgeons, 2004–. Hon. PhD Crete, 2009. St Peter's Medal, British Assoc. of Urol Surgeons, 2002; Distinguished Career Award, Société Internationale d'Urologie, 2018. *Publications*: Urodynamics: principles, practice and application, 1984, 2nd edn 1994; Current Operative Surgery: Urology, 1987; Neuropathic Bladder in Childhood, 1991; Urodynamic and Reconstructive Surgery of the Lower Urinary Tract, 1994; Scientific Basis of Urology, 1999, 3rd edn 2010; Succeeding as a Hospital Doctor, 2000, 3rd edn 2007; articles on reconstructive urology in various urological jls. *Recreations*: home, wine, history. *Address*: Sunnylands, 57 Harrington Lane, Pinhoe, Exeter EX4 8NY. *E*: tony.mundy1@btinternet.com.

**MUNDY, (Barbara) Helen;** *see* Dean, B. H.

**MUNDY, (James) Toby;** Founding Director, Toby Mundy Associates Ltd, since 2014; Executive Director, Baillie Gifford Prize (formerly Samuel Johnson Prize) for Non-Fiction, since 2015; Partner, Jericho Chambers LLP, since 2016; *b* London, 11 Nov. 1968; *s* of Stuart Mundy and Olga Mundy; *m* 1995, Charis Evans; one *s* one *d*. *Educ*: Royal Holloway Coll., Univ. of London (BA 1st Cl. Hons Eng. Lit.); Queen Mary and Westfield Coll., Univ. of London (MA Dist. Lit. and Lang.). Editor, HarperCollins Publishers, 1991–97; Publishing Dir, Weidenfeld & Nicolson, 1997–2000; Founder, Chm. and Chief Exec., Atlantic Books Ltd, 2000–14. Non-exec. Dir, Prospect Publishing Ltd, 2005–11. Chm., Bd of Trustees, Wimbledon Bookfest, 2016– (Trustee, 2014–); Mem., Adv. Bd, DEMOS, 2014–15. Hon. DArt Bournemouth, 2004. *Recreations*: walking, food and wine, cinema, music. *Address*: Toby Mundy Associates Ltd, 38 Berkeley Square, W1J 5AE. *T*: (020) 3713 0067. *E*: tobymundy@tma-agency.com. *Club*: Union.

**MUNDY, Jo A.;** *see* Shapcott, J. A.

**MUNDY, John Kennedy;** Sheriff of Tayside, Central and Fife, since 2011; *b* Glasgow, 20 Sept. 1958; *s* of Thomas Mundy and Margaret Mundy; *m* 1987, Fiona Margaret Brown; two *s*. *Educ*: Montgomery of Alamein Sch., Winchester; Balfron High Sch., Stirlingshire; Univ. of Dundee (LLB, DipLP 1981). Admitted as solicitor, 1983; admitted to Faculty of Advocates, 1987. Legal Assessor: GMC, 2007–11; NMC, 2007–11; Chm., Investigating Cttee, Gen. Osteopathic Council, 2009–11. *Recreations*: euphonium, guitar, golf, curling. *Address*: Falkirk Sheriff Court, Main Street, Camelon, Falkirk FK1 4AR.

**MUNDY, Toby;** *see* Mundy, J. T.

**MUNGLANI, Rajesh,** FRCA; Consultant in Pain Medicine, St Thomas' Hospital, since 2016; *b* 31 Aug. 1962; *s* of Balwani Rai Munglani and Krishna Gulati; *m* 1989, Dr Jane Bolland; four *d*. *Educ*: St George's Hosp., Univ. of London (MB BS 1985); DCH 1989. FRCA 1990. Clin. Lectr, 1993–96, Lectr in Anaesthesia and Pain Mgt, 1997–2000, Univ. of Cambridge; Consultant in Anaesthesia and Pain Mgt, Addenbrooke's Hosp., Cambridge, 1997–2000; Consultant in Pain Medicine, West Suffolk Hosp., Bury St Edmunds, 2000–16. John Farman Prof., RCAnaes, 1997. Founder and Dir, Healing the Person Ltd, 2009. British Pain Society: Exec. Officer, Interventional Pain Medicine Special Interest Gp, 2010–; co-founder and Sec., Medicolegal Special Interest Gp, 2011–13; Mem. Council, 2011–14; Ed., Pain News, 2018–. Founder, Cambridge Annual Medico-Legal Conference, 2011–; co-founder, Cambridge Medico-Legal Forum, 2012–. Fellow, Faculty of Pain Medicine, RCAnaes, 2008; Mem. Council, Pain Section, RSocMed, 2014–. Founder and Chief Ed., Jl of Observational Pain Medicine, 2012–. *Publications*: Pain: current understanding, emerging therapies and novel approaches to drug discovery, 2001; contrib. numerous papers and chapters on scientific basis of chronic pain, spinal pain incl. whiplash and complex regional pain syndromes. *Recreations*: walking in the Lake District, reading. *Address*: Spire Cambridge Lea Hospital, 30 New Road, Impington, Cambridge CB24 9EL. *T*: (01223) 479024. *E*: sue.sanalitro@gmail.com. *Club*: Carlton.

**MUNIR, (Ashley) Edward,** PhD; Barrister; Under Secretary, Ministry of Agriculture, Fisheries and Food, 1982–92; *b* 14 Feb. 1934; *s* of late Hon. Sir Mehmed Munir Bey, Kt, CBE, and late Lady (Vessime) Munir; *m* 1960, Sureyya S. V. Dormen; one *s*. *Educ*: Brentwood Sch.; St John's Coll., Cambridge (MA 1957); King's Coll., London (PhD 1992). Called to the Bar, Gray's Inn, 1956. Practised as barrister, 1956–60, 1992–; Crown Counsel, 1960–64; entered Govt Legal Service, 1964; Asst Solicitor, MAFF, 1975–82. *Publications*: Perinatal Rights, 1983; Fisheries after Factortame, 1991; Mentally Disordered Offenders, 1993. *Recreations*: walking, music. *Address*: (chambers) 5 St Andrew's Hill, EC4V 5BY. *T*: (020) 7332 5400. *Club*: Oxford and Cambridge.

**MUNN, Geoffrey Charles,** OBE 2013; MVO 2018; FSA, FLS; jewellery historian, television presenter and writer; Managing Director, Wartski Ltd, 1990–2018; *b* Hastings, 11 April 1953; *s* of Stewart Hayden Munn and Heather Rosemary Munn (*née* Hollingsworth); *m* 1983, Caroline Watney, MA; two *s*. *Educ*: Steyning Grammar Sch., Sussex. Joined Wartski, 1972, Dir, 1981. Contributor, Antiques Roadshow, 1989–. Chm., Friends of British Antique Dealers' Assoc. Trust, 2016–. Ambassador: Samaritans, 1990–; Pancreatic Cancer UK, 2011–; Patron: Lowestoft Samaritans, 1994–; Sotterley Chapel Preservation Trust, 2005–; Nat. Osteoporosis Soc., 2016–. Curator, loan exhibns at Wartski, and Tiaras exhibn at V&A Mus., 2002. Actor in film, Joe's Palace, 2007. Freeman, Goldsmiths' Co., 1986 (Liveryman, 2005; Mem., Ct of Assts, 2014; Fourth Warden, 2016). FSA 1991; FLS 2014. FRSA 2012. *Publications*: Castellani and Giuliano: revivalist jewellers of the nineteenth century, 1984; (with C. Gere) Artists' Jewellery: Pre-Raphaelite to Arts and Crafts, 1989, 2nd edn 1996; The Triumph of Love: jewellery 1530–1930, 1993; Tiaras: a history of splendour, 2001, 6th edn 2018; Tiaras Past and Present, 2002; Southwold: an earthly paradise, 2006, 2nd edn 2017; Wartski: the first one hundred and fifty years, 2015; contribs to specialist press on hist. of jewellery and drawings of J. W. M. Turner, Edward Lear and D. G. Rossetti. *Recreations*: mudlarking and metal detecting, Bonsai, running, cycling, cooking, museums and art galleries. *W*: geoffreymunn.art. *Clubs*: Garrick, Arts, Two Brydges; Southwold Sailors' Reading Room.

**MUNN, Dr Helen Louise;** Executive Director, Academy of Medical Sciences, since 2009; *b* Cardiff, 11 Jan. 1978; *d* of late William Munn and of Janet Munn; *m* 2008, Alex Grant; one *s* two *d*. *Educ*: Howell's Sch., Llandaff; Cheltenham Ladies' Coll.; Queen's Coll., Oxford (BSc Biol Scis); Univ. of Edinburgh (PhD Molecular Scis 2003). Joined Acad. of Med. Scis, 2004; Policy Officer, 2004–06; Policy Manager, 2006–07; Policy Dir, 2007–09. *Recreations*: theatre, travel, novels, friends. *Address*: Academy of Medical Sciences, 41 Portland Place, W1B 1QH. *T*: (020) 3141 3201. *E*: helen.munn@acmedsci.ac.uk.

**MUNN, Meg;** consultant; Independent Chair, National Safeguarding Panel, Church of England, since 2018; *b* 24 Aug. 1959; *d* of late Reginald Edward Munn and Lillian Seward; *m* 1989, Dennis Clifford Bates. *Educ*: Univ. of York (BA Hons Language); Univ. of Nottingham (MA Social Work; CQSW); Open Univ. (Dip. Mgt Studies). Social Work Assistant, Berkshire, 1981–84; Social Worker, 1986–90, Sen. Social Worker, 1990–92, Nottinghamshire; Dist Manager, Barnsley, 1992–96; Children's Service Manager, Wakefield, 1996–99; Asst Dir of Children's Services, Social Services, York, 1999–2000. MP (Lab and Co-op) Sheffield, Heeley, 2001–15. PPS, DFES, 2003–05; Parliamentary Under-Secretary of State: DTI, 2005–06; DCLG, 2006–07; FCO, 2007–08. All Party Parliamentary Groups: Chair: Kurdistan Region in Iraq, 2008–15; Methodist, 2010–15; Child Protection, 2010–15; Vice-Chair: Women in Enterprise, 2010–15; Engrg and IT, 2010–15; Yorks and N Lincs, 2011–15. Chair, 2008–10, Vice-Chair, 2010–12, Westminster Foundn for Democracy; Pres., Co-operative Congress, 2006. Mem., Mgt Cttee, Wortley Hall Ltd, 1994–2000; Chair Cttee, Barnsley Br., CRS Ltd, 1997–2001. Non-exec. Dir, Phone-paid Services Authy, 2017–. Gov., Sheffield Hallam Univ., 2015– (Dep. Chair, 2017–). CMgr 2012; FCMI. *Publications*: (ed jtly) Family Fortunes: the new politics of childhood, 2004; (ed) Unlocking Potential: perspectives on women in science, engineering and technology, 2011. *Recreations*: tennis, swimming, gardening.

**MUNNS, Victor George;** Counsellor (Labour), Washington, 1983–86; *b* 17 June 1926; *s* of Frederick William Munns and Lilian Munns; *m* 1952, Pamela Ruth Wyatt; two *s*. *Educ*: Haberdashers' Aske's, Hatcham; University Coll., London (BA). Served HM Forces (Army Intell.), 1945–48. Min. of Labour Employment Service, 1951–61; ILO, Trinidad and Belize, 1962–63; Sec., Shipbldg Industry Trng Bd, 1964–66; Res. Staff, Royal Commn on Trade Unions, 1966; Principal, Dept of Employment (Indust. Trng and Indust. Relations), 1967–72; Dep. Chief Officer, Race Relations Bd, 1973–74; Sec., Health and Safety Commn, 1974–77; Asst Sec., Health and Safety Exec., 1977–82. Dir, Nailsworth Festival, 1992–96. *Club*: Royal Over-Seas League.

**MUÑOZ-DEACON, Julio;** Ambassador of Peru to the Court of St James's, 2012–15, and to Ireland, 2014–15; *b* 17 July 1950; *s* of Julio Ernesto Muñoz and Hortensia Deacon; *m* 1982, Marcela Chávez; one *s* one *d*. *Educ*: Pontifical Catholic Univ. of Peru (Arts and Humanities); Diplomatic Acad. of Peru (BA Internat. Relns 1978). Diplomatic Service, Peru: joined as Third Sec. of Chancery, Gen. Directorate of Protocol, 1974; Third Sec., 1976–78, Second Sec., 1978, Venezuela; Second Sec., 1979–82, First Sec., 1982, Perm. Mission to OAS, Washington, DC; Hd, Gen. Secretariat's Cabinet, 1982; First Sec., 1985, Counsellor, 1986, Minister Counsellor, 1988, Perm. Mission to Internat. Agencies, Geneva; Integration Dir, Under-Secretariat for Econ. Affairs, Cooperation and Integration, 1991; Sub-regl Orgns Dir, Gen. Directorate of Multilateral Affairs, 1992; Gen. Dir, Tech. Office of Integration, 1993; Minister, Belgium, Luxembourg and EU, 1994–96; Ambassador to Czech Republic, 1996–99; Econ. Orgns Dir, Under-Secretariat of Multilateral and Special Affairs, 1999–2000; Asia and Oceania Dir, Under-Secretariat of Europe, Africa, Asia and Oceania Affairs, 2000; Admin Gen. Dir, 2002; Advr on Admin to Minister of Foreign Affairs, 2002; Ambassador, Perm. Rep. to Council, ICAO, Montreal, 2002–07; Information Physical Security Advr to Minister of Foreign Affairs, 2007–08; Admin Under-Sec., 2008–09; Gen. Sec., Min. of Foreign Affairs, 2009–10; Ambassador to Germany, 2011–12. *Clubs*: Travellers, Athenæum.

**MUNRO, Sir Alan (Gordon),** KCMG 1990 (CMG 1984); HM Diplomatic Service, retired; *b* 17 Aug. 1935; *s* of late Sir Gordon Munro, KCMG, MC and Lilian Muriel Beit; *m* 1962, Rosemary Grania Bacon; twin *s* two *d*. *Educ*: Wellington Coll.; Clare Coll., Cambridge (MA). MIPM. Mil. Service, 4/7 Dragoon Guards, 1953–55; Middle East Centre for Arab Studies, 1958–60; British Embassy, Beirut, 1960–62; Kuwait, 1961; FO, 1963–65; Head of Chancery, Benghazi, 1965–66 and Tripoli, 1966–68; FO, 1968–73; Consul (Commercial), 1973–74, Consul-Gen., 1974–77, Rio de Janeiro; Head of E African Dept, FCO, 1977–78; Head of Middle East Dept, FCO, 1979; Head of Personnel Ops Dept, FCO, 1979–81; Regl Marketing Dir (ME), MoD, 1981–83; Ambassador to Algeria, 1984–87; Dep. Under-Sec. of State, ME/Africa, FCO, 1987–89; Ambassador to Saudi Arabia, 1989–93. Director: Schroder Asseily & Co. Ltd, 1993–2000; Middle East Internat., 1997–2006; Dabbagh Gp (Jedda), 1998–2001; Internat. Trade & Investment Missions Ltd, 1998–2002; Advr, Tate and Lyle; Dir, Arab-British Chamber of Commerce, 2007– (Vice-Chm., 1993–2007). Gov., Imperial Coll., 1994–2001; Chm., Imperial Coll. Trust, 2009–10. Chairman: Soc. for Algerian Studies, 1994–2010; Saudi-British Soc., 2003–07; Beit Trust for Central Africa; Vice Chm., BRCS, 1994–2001; Chm., Jt Cttee, Red Cross and St John, 2001–11. Order of King Abdul Aziz (Saudi Arabia), 1993; OStJ 2006. *Publications*: An Arabian Affair (Arab Storm): politics and diplomacy behind the Gulf War, 1996, 2nd edn 2006; (contrib.) Envoys to the Arab World, 2009; Keep the Flag Flying: a diplomatic memoir, 2012; reviews and articles on Middle East. *Recreations*: historic buildings, gardening, music, history. *Club*: Travellers.

**MUNRO, Dr Alan James**; Fellow, since 1962, and Master, 1995–2002, Christ's College, Cambridge; b 19 Feb. 1937; s of John Bennet Lorimer Munro, CB, CMG and Gladys, (Pat), Maie Forbes Munro (née Simmons); m 1960, Mary, d of John Gibson Robertson, Dumfries; two s. Educ: Edinburgh Acad.; Christ's Coll., Cambridge (BA 1960; MA; PhD 1964). Nat. Service, 2nd Lt Queen's Own Cameron Highlanders, 1955–57; Demonstrator, 1963–67, Lectr, 1967–68, Dept of Biochemistry, Cambridge Univ.; Scientific Officer, MRC Lab. of Molecular Biology, Cambridge, 1968–71; Lectr, 1971–80, Reader, 1980–89, in Immunology, Dept of Pathology, Cambridge Univ.; Jt Founder and Scientific Dir, Cantab Pharmaceuticals plc, 1989–95. Director: Babraham Inst. Ltd, 1996–2002; Blackwell Science Ltd, 1997–2001; Genome Research Ltd, 1997–2001; Blackwell Publishing Ltd, 2001–07; Paradigm Therapeutics Ltd, 2002–07; Chm., Lorantis Holdings Ltd, 2000–03. Fulbright Travel Schol. and Vis. Scientist, Salk Inst., La Jolla, Calif, 1965–66; Boerhaave Prof., Univ. of Leiden, 1976–77. Chm., Link Cttee on Cell Engrg, DTI, 1994–2002. Gov., Lister Inst. of Preventive Medicine, 1996–2002. *Publications*: (jtly) The Immune System, 1981; papers in scientific jls on immunology and molecular biology. *Address*: Christ's College, Cambridge CB2 3BU.
*See also B. S. Munro.*

**MUNRO, Alice Ann**; writer; b Wingham, Canada, 10 July 1931; d of Robert Eric Laidlaw and Anne Clarke (née Chamney); m 1st, 1951, James Munro (marr. diss. 1972); three d (and one d decd); 2nd, 1976, Gerald Fremlin (d 2013). *Educ*: Lower Town Sch., Wingham; Univ. of Western Ontario (Schol.). Founded Munro's Books, 1963. Writer-in-Residence, Univ. of Western Ontario, 1974–75. Contrib. stories to mags incl. Mayfair, Queen's Qly, Canadian Forum, Chatelaine, New Yorker, Harper's, London Rev. of Books, New Statesman. Hon. Dr Western Ontario, 1976. Gov. Gen.'s Award for Fiction, Canada, 1968, 1978, 1982; Man Booker Internat. Prize, 2009; Trillium Book Award, Govt of Ontario, 2012; Nobel Prize for Literature, 2013. *Publications*: Dance of the Happy Shades, 1968; Lives of Girls and Women: a novel, 1971; Something I've Been Meaning to Tell You, 1974; Who Do You Think You Are?: stories, 1978; The Moons of Jupiter: stories, 1982; The Progress of Love, 1986; Friend of My Youth: stories, 1990; Open Secrets, 1994; Selected Stories, 1996; The Love of a Good Woman: stories, 1998; Queenie: a story, 1999; Hateship, Friendship, Courtship, Loveship, Marriage: stories, 2001; Vintage Munro, 2004; Runaway: stories, 2004; Carried Away: a selection of stories, 2006; The View from the Castle Rock: stories, 2006; Away From her, 2007; Too Much Happiness: stories, 2009; New Selected Stories, 2011; Dear Life: stories, 2012; Lying Under the Apple Tree, 2014. *Address*: c/o William Morris Endeavor, 11 Madison Avenue, New York, NY 10010, USA.

**MUNRO, Dr (Bruce) Sean**, FRS 2011; Head, Division of Cell Biology, Medical Research Council Laboratory of Molecular Biology, Cambridge, since 2012; b Cambridge, 19 Aug. 1961; s of Dr Alan James Munro, qv; m 2004, Dr Katja Roeper; two s. *Educ*: Netherhall Sch.; University Coll., Oxford (BA 1983); Trinity Coll., Cambridge (PhD 1987). Postdoctoral Fellow, Harvard Univ., 1987–89; Mem., Scientific Staff, MRC Lab. of Molecular Biol., Cambridge, 1989–. Jun. Res. Fellow, Trinity Coll., Cambridge 1986–92. Mem. EMBO 1997 (Mem. Council, 2000–06); FAAAS 2012. Dir, Co. of Biologists Ltd, 2012–. *Publications*: papers in scientific jls on molecular and cell biology. *Recreations*: entertaining my children, cooking, politics. *Address*: MRC Laboratory of Molecular Biology, Francis Crick Avenue, Cambridge CB2 0QH. T: (01223) 267028.

**MUNRO, Colin Andrew**, CMG 2002; HM Diplomatic Service, retired; international affairs consultant, since 2007; Associate, Ambassador Partnership LLP, since 2010; Chairman, UK Citizens in Austria, since 2017; b 24 Oct. 1946; s of Capt. Frederick Bertram Munro and Jane Eliza (née Taylor); m 1967, Ehrengard Maria Heinrich; two s. *Educ*: George Watson's Coll., Edinburgh; Edinburgh Univ. (MA Hons Mod. Langs 1968); King's Coll., London (MA Internat Studies 2002). Asst Principal, Bd of Inland Revenue, 1968–69; FCO, 1969–71; Third, later Second, Sec., Bonn, 1971–73; Second, later First, Sec., Kuala Lumpur, 1973–77; FCO, 1977; Private Sec. to Minister of State, 1979–80; Hd of Chancery, Bucharest, 1981–82; FCO, 1983; Asst Head of W European Dept, 1985–87; Dep. Hd of Mission, E Berlin, 1987–90; Consul Gen., Frankfurt, 1990–93; Hd of OSCE and Council of Europe Dept, FCO, 1993–97; Ambassador to Republic of Croatia, 1997–2000; Dep. High Rep., Mostar, 2001; rcds, 2002; UK Perm. Rep. to OSCE, Vienna, 2003–07. *Publications*: (contrib.) Korea and East Asia, 2013; contrib. Jl of Prince Albert Soc., Jl of Inst. of Contemp. British Hist., Jl of Vienna Univ. Inst. for Peace Research, Bulletin of German Historical Inst. London. *Recreations*: sports especially hockey, cricket, ski-ing, golf, history, music. *Clubs*: Reform; Royal Selangor (Kuala Lumpur); Rotary (Vienna North East).

**MUNRO, Dominic James**; Director for Fair Work, Employability and Skills, Scottish Government, since 2016; b Reading, 22 July 1974; s of Alasdair and Mary Munro; m 2003, Gillian Atkins; two s one d. *Educ*: Cowes High Sch., IoW; Univ. of Dundee (MA Econs 1996); Univ. of York (MSc Econ. and Social Policy Analysis 1997). Asst Economist, DTI, 1997–99; Economic Adviser: ECGD, 1999–2003; HM Treasury, 2003–05; Scottish Government: Sen. Economist, 2005–09; Dep. Dir, Communities and Justice Analytical Services, 2009–13; Dep. Dir, Better Homes, 2013–16. *Recreations*: creative writing, hill-walking, football. *Address*: Scottish Government, St Andrew's House, Regent Road, Edinburgh EH1 3DG. T: (0131) 244 5510. E: dominic.munro@gov.scot.

**MUNRO, Prof. Eileen Margaret**, CBE 2012; PhD; Professor of Social Policy, London School of Economics and Political Science, 2008–18, now Emeritus; b Cirencester, 21 Oct. 1950; d of late Patrick Higgins and Margaret Higgins; m 1974, Alexander James Munro (marr. diss. 2000); three d. *Educ*: Cirencester Grammar Sch.; Univ. of Exeter (BA Hons Philos. 1971); Univ. of Edinburgh (Dip. Social Admin 1972); Univ. of Southampton (CQSW 1973); London Sch. of Econs and Pol Sci. (MSc Logic and Scientific Methods 1981; PhD 1990). Med. Social Worker, St Mary's Hosp., London, 1973–74; Social Worker, Leics Social Services Dept, 1974–75; Psychiatric Social Worker, Maudsley Hosp., London, 1975–79; London School of Economics and Political Science: Res. Fellow, 1993–95; Lectr, 1995–2003; Reader, 2003–08; Gov., 2007–. Zellerbach Prof., Univ. of Calif, Berkeley, 2005. Led ind. govt review of child protection in England, 2010–11 (report, Munro Review of Child Protection: a child-centred system, 2011). Hon. DLitt Tavistock Inst., UEL, 2012. *Publications*: Understanding Social Work: an empirical approach, 1998; Effective Child Protection, 2002, 2nd edn 2008; Child Protection, 2007; (jtly) Learning Together to Safeguard Children, 2008; articles in Children and Youth Services Rev., British Jl of Social Work, Child Abuse and Neglect, Health, Risk and Society, Risk Analysis, British Jl of Psychiatry, Jl of Forensic Psychiatry. *Address*: London School of Economics and Political Science, Houghton Street, WC2A 2AE. E: E.Munro@lse.ac.uk.

**MUNRO, Graeme Neil**, CVO 2005; Director and Chief Executive, Historic Scotland, 1991–2004; b 28 Aug. 1944; s of Daniel Munro and Nancy Kirkwood (née Smith); m 1972, Nicola Susan Wells (see N. S. Munro); one s one d. *Educ*: Daniel Stewart's Coll., Edinburgh; Univ. of St Andrews (MA Hons 1967). Joined Scottish Office as Asst Principal, 1968; Scottish Development Department: Housing, 1968; Planning, 1968–70; Private Sec. to Head of Dept, 1971; Principal, Roads, 1972–74; Scottish Home and Health Department: Hosp. Services, 1974–76; Criminal Justice, 1976–79; Assistant Secretary: Dept of Agriculture and Fisheries for Scotland (Fisheries), 1979–83; NHS Funding, Scottish Home and Health Dept, 1983–87; Management and Orgn, Scottish Office Central Services, 1987–90; Dir, Historic Buildings and Monuments, Scotland, 1990–91. Member: Council, Cockburn Assoc. (Edinburgh Civic Trust), 2005–11 (former Mem., Mgt and Finance Cttee); Mgt Cttee, Rosslyn Chapel Trust, 2005–16 (Dep. Chm., 2007–16); Trustee, Historic Scotland Foundn, 2007–17 (Chm., 2011–16). Comr, Queen Street Gardens, 2011–. *Recreations*: gardening, walking, travel, reading. *Address*: 15 Heriot Row, Edinburgh EH3 6HP. T: (0131) 556 3201. E: gandnmunro@hotmail.com.

**MUNRO, Sir Ian Kenneth**, 17th Bt cr 1634, of Foulis-Obsdale, Ross-shire; b 5 April 1940; s of Sir Kenneth Munro, 16th Bt and Olive Freda (née Broome); S father, 2004, but his name does not appear on the Official Roll of the Baronetage. *Heir*: cousin Godfrey Roland Munro [b 1 July 1938; m 1985, Julie Pamela Gosling; two s one d].

**MUNRO, Jamie Ross**; Joint Founder and Managing Director, Greenbird Media Ltd, since 2012; b Reading, 14 June 1971; s of Ian and Pauline Munro; m Pippa Dalley; two d. *Educ*: Chiltern Edge Sch.; Henley Coll.; Wolverhampton Univ. (BA Hons). Sales Support Exec., BBC Worldwide (Americas), 1994–95; Sales Exec., BBC Library Sales, 1995–96; Publishing Licensing Manager, BBC Worldwide, 1996–98; Commercial Dir, Drama, Entertainment and Children's, BBC Commercial Agency, 1998–2005; involved in sale of Strictly Come Dancing and What Not To Wear to USA; Commercial Dir and Sen. Vice Pres., Internat. Prodn, Tiger Aspect Prodns, 2005–08 (progs incl. two series of Make Me a Supermodel); Jt Man. Dir, Shine TV, 2008–12. *Recreations*: karaoke, watching England and Harlequins play Rugby, TV. *Clubs*: Groucho, Soho House, Ivy.

**MUNRO, Julia Henrietta**; University Librarian, University of Reading, 2001–18; b 21 Dec. 1952; d of Leslie H. and Joan B. Tebbitt; m 1975, Dr Peter M. G. Munro; one s one d. *Educ*: Imperial Coll., London (BSc 1975); City Univ. (MSc 1977); Univ. of Reading (MBA 2000). ARCS 1975; MCLIP 2002. Grad. trainee liby asst, Poly. of Central London, 1975–76; Assistant Librarian: Paediatric Res. Unit, Guy's Hosp. Med. Sch., 1977–79; Centre for Envmtl Technol., Imperial Coll., London, 1979–84; UCL, 1984–93; Dep. Librarian, Univ. of Reading, 1993–2001. Mem., Lifelong Learning UK Sector Skills Council, 2005–11. *Recreation*: family life with a neurotic Weimaraner and a punk cat.

**MUNRO of Lindertis, Sir Keith Gordon**, 7th Bt cr 1825; Resort Manager, Sugarbush Resort, Vermont; b Norwalk, Conn, USA, 3 May 1959; o s of Sir Alasdair Thomas Ian Munro of Landertis, 6th Bt and of Marguerite Lilian Munro (née Loy); S father, 2014; m 1989; one s one d. *Educ*: Univ. of New Hampshire (Restaurant Mgt). Chef for 36 years. *Recreations*: ski-ing, shooting, fishing, moto riding. *Heir*: s Zachary Adrian, (Zak) Munro, b 2 Oct. 1992. *Address*: PO Box 724, Waitsfield, VT 05673, USA. T: (802) 7932339. E: delilama59@yahoo.com.

**MUNRO, Neil Christopher**, CBE 2003; Head, Customer Contact Transformation Programme, HM Revenue and Customs, 2006–07; b 25 July 1947; s of late Alan and Jean Munro; m 1987, Caroline Anne Virginia Smith; two d. *Educ*: Wallasey Grammar Sch.; St John's Coll., Oxford (BA Hons Mod. Hist., MA). MCIPD (MIPD 1993). Board of Inland Revenue, subsequently HM Revenue and Customs, 1970–2007: various posts in tax policy and mgt work; seconded to CBI as Head, Taxation Dept, 1978–80; Dep. Dir of Personnel, 1991–94; Director: Mgt Services, 1994–96; Tax Law Rewrite Project, 1996–2001; Revenue Policy: Corporate Services, 2001–05; Better Guidance Prog., 2005–06. *Recreations*: modern literature, music, football, cooking, family history. *Address*: 66 Lavington Road, Ealing, W13 9LS. E: neilmunro47@gmail.com.

**MUNRO, Nicola Susan**, CB 2006; Head of Scottish Executive Development Department, 2001–07; b 11 Jan. 1948; d of Ernest Derek Wells and Barbara Gurney Wells; m 1972, Graeme Neil Munro, qv; one s one d. *Educ*: Harrogate Grammar Sch.; Univ. of Warwick (BA Hons History). Scottish Office, later Scottish Executive, 1970–2007: Head of Div. (hosp. services, food, med. educn), Scottish Home and Health Dept, 1986–89; Head of Div. (urban and local economic policy), Scottish Office Industry Dept, 1989–92; Head of Div. (curriculum, assessment, careers service, educn industry links), Scottish Office Educn Dept, 1992–95; Under-Sec., Public Health Policy, Scottish Office, then Scottish Exec., Dept of Health, 1995–2000; Hd of Envmt Gp, Scottish Exec. Rural Affairs Dept, 2000–01. Member: Scottish Consumer Council, subseq. Consumer Focus Scotland, 2008–14; Scottish Refugee Council, 2008–15; Consumer Adv. Panel, Office of Rail and Road (formerly Rail Regulation), 2010–16; Scottish Wildlife Trust, 2015–. *Recreations*: reading, travel, gardening, family, friends. *Address*: 15 Heriot Row, Edinburgh EH3 6HP.

**MUNRO, Sarah Belinda McLeod**; QC 2002; Her Honour Judge Munro; a Circuit Judge, since 2011; Senior Circuit Judge, Central Criminal Court, since 2017; b Southampton, 29 Sept. 1960; d of John and Margaret Munro; m 2013, Chris Doe; one s. *Educ*: St Swithun's, Winchester; Univ. of Exeter (BA Hons Classics); Poly. of Central London (DipLaw); Council of Legal Educn. Called to the Bar, Inner Temple, 1984, Bencher, 2016; Recorder, 2000–11; authorised to try murder cases, 2013; authorised to sit in Ct of Appeal, Criminal Div., 2013. Judicial Mem., Sentencing Council, 2013–. *Recreations*: golf, dog walking, cooking, watching sport, ski-ing. *Address*: Central Criminal Court, Old Bailey, EC4M 7EH.

**MUNRO, Sean**; see Munro, B. S.

**MUNROE-BLUM, Prof. Heather Anne Elise Lilian**, OC 2003; OQ 2009; PhD; FRSC; Principal and Vice-Chancellor, and Professor of Epidemiology and Biostatistics, McGill University, 2003–13, now Emeritus; Chairman, Canada Pension Plan Investment Board, since 2014 (Director, since 2011); Chairman, Corporate Governance Committee, since 2014); Director, Royal Bank of Canada, since 2011; b 25 Aug. 1950; d of Donald Munroe and late Dorothy Munroe; m 1970, Leonard Blum, screenwriter; one d. *Educ*: McMaster Univ. (BA, BSW 1974); Wilfrid Laurier Univ. (MSW 1975); Univ. of NC, Chapel Hill (PhD with Dist. 1983). Psychiatric Social Worker and Social Work Supervisor, McMaster Univ. Med. Centre and St Joseph's Hosp., 1975–79; McMaster University: Clinical Lectr, 1976–79, Asst Clinical Prof., 1979–84, Dept of Psychiatry; Asst Prof., Depts of Psychiatry and Clinical Epidemiol. and Biostatistics, 1984–89; University of Toronto: Prof., and Dean, Faculty of Social Work, 1989–93; Prof., and Vice-Pres., Res. and Internat. Relns, 1994–2002. Asst Prof., Dept of Social Work, Atkinson Coll., York Univ., 1982–84; Continuing Sen. Fellow, Massey Coll. 2010– (Associate Fellow, 1990–93; Associate Sen. Fellow, 1998–2000; Sen. Fellow, 2000–10). Director: Neurosci. Canada Partnership, 2001–05 (Hon. Mem., 2005–); Neurosci. Canada Foundn, 2001–; McGill Univ. Health Centre, 2003–13; Gairdner Foundn, 2014–. Member: Assoc. of Univs and Colls of Canada, 2003–13 (Chair, Standing Adv. Cttee on Univ. Res.; Mem., Exec. Cttee, 2007–13); Assoc. of Amer. Univs, 2003–13; Conf. des recteurs et des principaux des Univs de Québec, 2003–13 (Vice Pres., 2005; Pres., 2007–13); Adv. Bd, 2014–, Bd, 2015–, Center for Advanced Study in Behavioral Scis, Stanford Univ. Fellow, Assoc. for Clinical Psychosocial Res., 1991; FRSC, 2002. Dr hc: Montréal, 2004; Edinburgh, 2005; École Normale Supérieure de Lyon, 2005; Hon. LLD: Toronto, 2005; Wilfrid Laurier, 2005; McMaster, 2007; Hon. DSc: N Carolina at Chapel Hill, 2008; Ottawa, 2008; McGill, 2017; Hon. DLit: Glasgow, 2013; Western, 2014. Outstanding Alumni Award, Sch. of Public Health, Univ. of NC, Chapel Hill, 1992; Dist. Alumni Award, McMaster Univ., 1995. *Publications*: (jtly) Schizophrenia in Focus: a psychosocial approach to treatment and rehabilitation, 1983; (jtly)

PDQ Epidemiology, 1989; (ed jtly) Borderline Personality Disorder: an empirical perspective, 1992; (with E. Marziali) Interpersonal Group Psychotherapy for Borderline Personality Disorder, 1994; Growing Ontario's Innovation System: the strategic role of university research, 1999; contribs to books and numerous articles in learned jls. *Club:* Mount Royal.

**MUNROW, Roger Davis,** CB 1993; Chief Master of the Supreme Court of Judicature (Chancery Division), 1986–92, retired (Master, 1985–86); *b* 20 March 1929; *s* of late William Davis Munrow, CBE and Constance Caroline Munrow (*née* Moorcroft); *m* 1st, 1957, Marie Jane Beresford (*d* 2001); three *d*; 2nd, 2001, Norma Eileen Boucher (*d* 2014). *Educ:* Bryanston School; Oriel College, Oxford (MA). Solicitor. Entered Treasury Solicitor's Dept as Legal Assistant, 1959; Senior Legal Assistant, 1965; Assistant Treasury Solicitor, 1973; Principal Asst Treasury Solicitor, 1981. *Address:* 5 Mallard Close, Harnham, Salisbury, Wilts SP2 8JB.

**MUNT, Tessa;** *b* Surrey, 16 Oct. 1959; *m* 1992, Martin Munt; one *s* one *d* and one step *d*. *Educ:* Reigate Co. Sch. for Girls; Sutton High Sch. Lectr, SE Essex Coll. of Arts and Technol., 1992–94; Adminr, Holiday Explorers, 1994; supply teacher, Samuel Ward Upper Sch., Haverhill, 1994–95; Manager, Community Resource Unit, Suffolk Social Services, 1994–96; PA to Phil Edmonds, 1996–98; fee-earner: Franks Charlesly and Co., 1996–98; Jay Benning and Pelts, 1998–99; Forsters, 1999–. Contested (C): S Suffolk, 2001; Ipswich, Nov. 2001; Wells, 2005. MP (Lib Dem) Wells, 2010–15; contested (Lib Dem) same seat, 2015, 2017. PPS to Sec. of State for Business, Innovation and Skills, 2012–15. Member, Select Committee: on Educn, 2010–12; on Admin, 2010–15. Mem. (Lib Dem), Somerset CC, 2017–. Hon. Pres., Liberal Youth, 2016–.

**MURAD, Prof. Ferid,** MD, PhD; University Professor, Department of Biochemistry and Molecular Biology, and Director, Institute of Molecular and Cellular Signalling, George Washington University, since 2011; Adjunct Professor, Department of Medicine, Stanford University and Senior Research Adviser, Palo Alto VA Hospital, since 2017; *b* 14 Sept. 1936; *s* of John Murad and Josephine Bowman; *m* 1958, Carol A. Leopold; one *s* four *d*. *Educ:* DePauw Univ. (BA 1958); Sch. of Medicine, Western Reserve Univ. (MD 1965; PhD 1965). University of Virginia: Dir, Clin. Res. Center, Sch. of Medicine, 1971–81; Prof., Depts of Internal Medicine and Pharmacology, 1975–81; Stanford University: Prof., Depts of Internal Medicine and Pharmacology, 1981–88; acting Chm., Dept of Medicine, 1986–88; Adjunct Prof., Dept of Pharmacology, Northwestern Univ., 1988–96; Prof. and Chm., Dept of Integrative Biol., Pharmacol. and Physiol., Houston Medical Sch., 1997–2011, and Dir, Inst. of Molecular Med., Houston, 1999–2011, Univ. of Texas. MNAS. Ciba Award, 1988; Albert and Mary Lasker Foundn Award for Basic Res., 1996; Nobel Prize in Medicine or Physiology, 1998; American Clinical Soc. Award; American Assoc. Medical Sch. Res. Award. *Publications:* ed. and jt ed. of 27 books; contrib. 470 research pubns. *Recreations:* golf, carpentry. *Address:* Palo Alto Veterans Institute for Research, 3801 Miranda Avenue, Building 101, Room A2–210, Palo Alto, CA 94304–0038, USA.

**MURAKAMI, Takashi;** artist; *b* Tokyo, 1 Feb. 1962. *Educ:* Tokyo National Univ. of Fine Arts and Music (BFA 1986; MFA 1988; PhD 1993). Works include fine art pieces, design collaborations and curatorial projects. *Solo exhibitions* include: Bard Coll. Center for Curatorial Studies, NY, 1999; Mus. of Contemp. Art, Tokyo, and Mus. of Fine Arts, Boston, 2001; Fondation Cartier pour l'art contemporain, Paris, 2002; Rockefeller Center, NY, 2003; Fondazione Sandretto Re Rebaudengo, Turin, 2005; (retrospective) Mus. of Contemp. Art, LA, 2007; Gagosian Gall., London, 2009; (retrospective) Mus. of Contemp. Art, Chicago, 2017. Dir of film, Jellyfish Eyes, 2013. *Publications:* Superflat, 2000; (jtly) My Reality: contemporary art and the culture of Japanese animation, 2001; (ed) Little Boy: the arts of Japan's exploding subculture, 2004. *Recreation:* cactus growing. *Address:* Kaikai Kiki Co. Ltd, Motoazabu Crest Building, B1F 2–3–30 Motoazabu, Minato-ku, Tokyo 106–0046, Japan.

**MURDIN, Paul Geoffrey,** OBE 1988; PhD; FInstP; Senior Fellow, Institute of Astronomy, Cambridge University, since 2002; *b* 5 Jan. 1942; *s* of Robert Murdin and Ethel Murdin (*née* Chubb); *m* 1964, Lesley Carol Milburn; two *s* one *d*. *Educ:* Trinity School of John Whitgift; Wadham Coll., Oxford (BA Physics); Univ. of Rochester, NY (PhD Physics and Astronomy). FRAS 1970; FInstP 1992. Res. Associate, Univ. of Rochester, 1970–71; Sen. Res. Associate, Royal Greenwich Observatory, 1971–74; Sen. Res. Scientist, Anglo-Australian Observatory, NSW, 1975–78; Royal Greenwich Observatory: Prin. Sci. Officer, 1979–81; Hd of La Palma Operations, 1981–87; Hd of Astronomy Div., 1987–90; Dir, Royal Observatory, Edinburgh, 1991–93; Head of Astronomy, PPARC, and Dir of Sci., BNSC, 1994–2001. Sen. Mem., Wolfson Coll., Cambridge, 1990–; Vis. Prof., Liverpool John Moores Univ., 2002–. Mem. Bd of Trustees, Nat. Maritime Museum, 1990–2001. Pres., Faulkes Telescope Corp., 1999–2005. Member: Royal Astronomical Soc., 1963– (Councillor, 1997–99, 2012–16; Vice-Pres., 2000–01; Treas., 2001–11); European Astronomical Soc., 1991– (Vice-Pres., 1991–93; Pres., 1993–97). RAS Service Award, 2012; Donald E. Osterbrock Prize, Amer. Astronomical Soc., 2017. *Publications:* The Astronomer's Telescope (with Patrick Moore), 1963; Radio Waves from Space, 1969; (with L. Murdin) The New Astronomy, 1974; (with D. Allen and D. Malin) Catalogue of the Universe, 1980; (with D. Malin) Colours of the Stars, 1985; End in Fire, 1989; Encyclopedia of Astronomy & Astrophysics, 2001; Firefly Encyclopedia of Astronomy, 2004; Full Meridian of Glory, 2009; Secrets of the Universe, 2009; Pursuit of Gazelles, 2011; Mapping the Universe: the interactive history of astronomy, 2012; Are we being watched?: the search for life in the Cosmos, 2013; Planetary Vistas: the landscapes of other worlds, 2015; Rock Legends: asteroids and their discoverers, 2016; Handbook of Supernovae, 2017; Universe: exploring the astronomical world, 2017; The Secret Lives of Planets, 2019; over 150 pubns in astronom. and other sci. jls, principally Monthly Notices of RAS. *Recreations:* writing, music, natural history, history of art. *Address:* Institute of Astronomy, Madingley Road, Cambridge CB3 0HA. *E:* paul@murdin.com.

**MURDOCH, Prof. Alison Pamela,** MD; FRCOG; FRSB; Professor of Reproductive Medicine, University of Newcastle upon Tyne, since 2003 (part-time, since 2016); Consultant Gynaecologist, Newcastle Hospitals NHS Trust, since 1991; *b* 12 Feb. 1951; *d* of John Peter Smith and Ruby Smith (*née* Easton); *m* 1972, Ian James Murdoch; two *s* two *d*. *Educ:* Univ. of Edinburgh (BSc 1972; MB ChB 1975; MD 1987). MRCOG 1982, FRCOG 2001; FRSB (FSB 2012). Early career researching in field of reproductive endocrinology; estabd clinic for infertility treatment, NE England, leading to regl clin. service, Newcastle Fertility Centre at Life. Res. interests now relate to human pre-implantation embryology, mitochondrial transfer techniques and regulatory issues of egg and embryo donation to res. Founder Mem., Newcastle Embryonic Stem Cell Gp, 2001–; Chm., British Fertility Soc., 2002–06; Member: Nuffield Council on Bioethics, 2007–13; Adv. Cttee on Safety of Blood, Tissues and Organs, 2013–. *Address:* Newcastle Fertility Centre at Life, International Centre for Life, Times Square, Newcastle upon Tyne NE1 4EP. *T:* (0191) 213 8211.

**MURDOCH, Elisabeth, (Mrs K. T. Tyson);** Founder and Chair: Vertical Networks; Locksmith Animation Ltd; Freelands Foundation; Freelands Ventures; *b* 22 Aug. 1968; *d* of Keith Rupert Murdoch, *qv* and Anna Murdoch Mann (*née* Torv); *m* 1st, 1994, Elkin Kwesi Pianim; two *d*; 2nd, 2001, Matthew Rupert Freud, *qv* (marr. diss. 2015); one *s* one *d*; 3rd, 2017, Keith Thomas Tyson. *Educ:* Vassar Coll., NY (BA). Dir of Programming, KSTU-TV, 1994–95; Pres. and CEO, EP Communications, 1995–96; Man. Dir, BSkyB Plc, 1996–2001; Chief Exec., 2001–12, Chm., 2001–14, Shine Ltd, later Shine Gp. Non-exec. Dir, Jimmy Choo, 2015–. Trustee, Tate, 2008–16; Mem., Nat. Council, Arts Council England, 2017–. McTaggart Lectr, Edinburgh Internat. TV Fest., 2012.

**MURDOCH, His Honour Gordon Stuart;** QC 1995; a Circuit Judge, 2002–15; *b* 7 June 1947; *s* of late Ian William Murdoch and Margaret Henderson McLaren Murdoch; *m* 1976, Sally Kay Cummings; two *s*. *Educ:* Falkirk High Sch.; Sidney Sussex Coll., Cambridge (MA, LLB). Called to the Bar, Inner Temple, 1970; a Recorder, 1995–2002. *Recreations:* music, walking.

**MURDOCH, John Derek Walter;** Director of Art Collections, The Huntington Library, Art Collections and Botanical Gardens, California, 2002–12; Visiting Scholar, Ecole du Louvre, 2013; *b* 1 April 1945; *s* of James Duncan and Elsie Elizabeth Murdoch; *m* 1st, 1967, Prue Smijth-Windham (marr. diss. 1986); one *s* two *d*; 2nd, 1990, Susan Barbara Lambert, *qv* (marr. diss. 2007); 3rd, 2007, Allison Browne Freeman; one *s* two *d*. *Educ:* Shrewsbury Sch.; Magdalen Coll., Oxford (BA); King's Coll., London (MPhil). Asst Keeper, Birmingham City Art Gall., 1969–73; Victoria & Albert Museum: Asst, then Dep. Keeper, Dept of Paintings, 1973–86; Keeper of Prints, Drawings, Photographs and Paintings, 1986–89; Asst Dir in charge of Collections, 1989–93; Dir, Courtauld Inst. Gall., 1993–2002. Vis. Fellow, British Art Center, Yale Univ., 1979. Trustee: William Morris Gall., Walthamstow, 1975–2002 (Dep. Chm., 1997–2002); Dove Cottage, Grasmere, 1982–2002. *Publications:* David Cox, 1970; Byron, 1974; English Watercolours, 1977; The English Miniature, 1981; Discovery of the Lake District, 1984; A Sort of National Property, 1985; Painters and the Derby China Works, 1986; Seventeenth Century Portrait Miniatures in the Collection of the Victoria and Albert Museum, 1997; contrib. to Rev. of English Studies, Jl of Warburg and Courtauld Insts, Burlington Magazine, Apollo. *Address:* 34 Effingham Street, Ramsgate, Kent CT11 9AT.

**MURDOCH, (Keith) Rupert,** AC 1984; publisher; Executive Chairman, News Corporation, United States, since 2013 (Chief Executive Officer, 1979–2013; Chairman, 1991–2013); Executive Chairman, 21st Century Fox, since 2013 (Chief Executive, 2013–15); *b* 11 March 1931; *s* of late Sir Keith Murdoch and Dame Elisabeth Joy Murdoch, AC, DBE; *m* Patricia Booker (marr. diss.); one *d*; *m* 1967, Anna Torv (marr. diss. 1999); two *s* one *d*; *m* 1999, Wendi Deng (marr. diss. 2013); two *d*; *m* 2016, Jerry Hall. Dir, News International plc, UK, 1969–2012 (Chm., 1969–87 and 1994–95; Chief Exec., 1969–81; Man. Dir, 1982–83); Chm., News America Publishing Inc.; Dir, Times Newspapers Hldgs Ltd, 1981–2012 (Chm., 1982–90 and 1994–2012); Chm. and Chief Exec. Officer, Fox Entertainment Gp Inc., 1998–; Chm., British Sky Broadcasting, 1999–2007. KSG 1998. *Address:* News Corporation, 1211 Avenue of the Americas, New York, NY 10036, USA. *See also* E. *Murdoch.*

**MURE, James Douglas McFarlane Haye;** QC (Scot.) 2009; *b* Edinburgh, 4 Dec. 1962; *s* of Douglas Mure and Betteane Mure; *m* 1992, Lesley Miller; one *s* two *d*. *Educ:* Edinburgh Acad.; Clare Coll., Cambridge (BA Hons Hist. 1984; MA 1987); Edinburgh Univ. (LLB 1991; DipLP 1992). HM Diplomatic Service, 1984–88; admitted Faculty of Advocates, 1995; Standing Jun. Counsel, 2001–07, First Standing Jun. Counsel, 2007–09, Scottish Exec., later Scottish Govt. *Recreations:* music, singing. *Address:* Faculty of Advocates, Parliament House, Edinburgh EH1 1RF.

**MURERWA, Dr Herbert Muchemwa;** Chairman, Zesa Holdings, since 2014; *b* 31 May 1941; *m* 1969, Ruth Chipo; one *s* four *d*. *Educ:* Harvard Univ.; EdD (Educational Planning). Economic Affairs Officer, UN Economic Commission for Africa, Addis Ababa, 1978–80; Permanent Sec., Min. of Manpower Planning, 1980–81; Permanent Sec., Min. of Labour and Social Services, 1982–84; High Comr for Zimbabwe in UK, 1984–90; MP (Zanu PF) Goromonzi, 1990–2008; Minister: for the Envmt and Tourism, 1990–95; of Industry and Commerce, 1995–96; of Finance, 1996–2000 and 2002–07; of Higher Educn and Technol., 2000–01; of Internat. Trade and Technol., 2001–02; of Higher and Tertiary Educn, 2004; Mem. of Senate (Zanu PF) Goromonzi, 2008–13; Minister of Lands and Rural (formerly Land) Resettlement, 2009.

**MURFIN, Dr David Edward;** Principal in general medical practice, Ammanford, 1974–2006; *b* 15 June 1946; *s* of late Walter Murfin and Elizabeth Ann Murfin; *m* 1972, Ann Margaret Lewis (*d* 2017); one *s* one *d*. *Educ:* Gowerton Boys' Grammar Sch.; King's Coll. London; St George's Hosp., London. Adviser to ABPI, 1991–2006. Mem. Council, RCGP, 1984–90 and 1993–96 (Vice Pres., 1994–96); Mem., Standing Cttee on Medicines, RCPCH, 1996–2001. Mem. Cttee, Retired Fellows Soc., RSocMed, 2015– (Sec., 2016–). *Recreations:* reading, walking, cycling. *Address:* Longmeadow, 30 Llandeilo Road, Llandybie, Ammanford, Carmarthen SA18 3JB. *T:* (01269) 850914.

**MURFITT, Catriona Anne Campbell; Her Honour Judge Murfitt;** a Circuit Judge, since 2007; *b* London, 16 Jan. 1958; *d* of Dr A. Ian Campbell Murfitt and Anne Murfitt (*née* Ritchie); partner, Iain Hutton-Jamieson. *Educ:* St Mary's Sch. Ascot; Leicester Poly. Sch. of Law (BA Hons Law). Called to the Bar, Gray's Inn, 1981; practised at Family Bar, 1 Mitre Court, then 1 Hare Court, 1981–2007; Asst Recorder, 1998–2000; Recorder, 2000–07. Mem. Cttee, Family Law Bar Assoc., 1997–2003; Mem., Professional Complaints and Conduct Cttee, Bar Council, 2001–04. *Recreations:* creating a garden, art, landscapes, architecture, sacred choral music, textiles, ski-ing. *Address:* c/o Chelmsford County Court, Priory Place, New London Road, Chelmsford, Essex CM2 0PP. *T:* (01245) 295380. *E:* catriona.murfitt@googlemail.com.

**MURGATROYD, Prof. Walter,** PhD; Professor of Thermal Power, Imperial College of Science and Technology, 1968–86, now Professor Emeritus; Rockefeller International Fellow, Princeton University, 1979; *b* 15 Aug. 1921; *m* 1952, Denise (*née* Schlumberger) (*d* 2014); one *s* one *d* (and one *s* decd). *Educ:* St Catharine's Coll., Cambridge. BA 1946, PhD 1952. Hawker Aircraft Ltd, 1942–44; Rolls Royce Ltd, 1944–46; Univ. of Cambridge, 1947–54; UK Atomic Energy Authority, Harwell, 1954–56; Head of Dept of Nuclear Engineering, Queen Mary Coll., Univ. of London, 1956–67, and Dean of Engineering, 1966–67. Member: British-Greek Mixed Commn, 1963–78; British-Belgian Mixed Commn, 1964–78; British-Austrian Mixed Commn, 1965–78. Specialist Adviser to H of C Select Cttee on Energy, 1980–90. *Publications:* contrib. to various scientific and technical journals. *Recreation:* music.

**MURIA, Sir (Gilbert) John Baptist,** Kt 1995; Chief Justice, Kiribati, since 2011; *b* 2 Feb. 1953; *s* of late John Baptist Manumate and of Adriana Gala; *m* 1982, Rosemary Kekealu; one *s* three *d*. *Educ:* Univ. of Papua New Guinea (LLB). Called to the Bar: PNG, 1980; Solomon Is, 1981. Sen. Crown Counsel, Solomon Is, 1980; Sen. Legal Officer, 1981–83; Chief Legal Officer, 1984–87; Dep. Public Solicitor, 1987–89; Public Solicitor, 1989–91;

Actg Attorney Gen., 1989; Puisne Judge, High Court of Solomon Is, 1991–93; Chief Justice, Solomon Is, 1993–2003; a Judge of Supreme Court, Belize, 2007–10. Chancellor, Solomon Islands Nat. Univ., 2013–. *Address:* High Court of Kiribati, Betio, Tarawa, Republic of Kiribati.

**MURIE, John Andrew,** MD; FRCSGlas, FRCSE; Consultant Vascular Surgeon: Spire Murrayfield Hospital, since 1989; Royal Infirmary of Edinburgh, 1989–2014; Professor of Surgery, National University of Malaysia, 2011–14; *b* 7 Aug. 1949; *s* of John Andrew Murie and Jessie Murie (*née* Sutherland); *m* 1977, Edythe Munn; one *d*. *Educ:* Univ. of Glasgow (BSc 1st Cl. Hons Biochem. 1971; MB ChB Hons 1975; MD 1984); MA Oxon 1984. FRCSGlas 1979; FRCSE 1993. Clin. Reader in Surgery, Nuffield Dept of Surgery, Univ. of Oxford and Fellow, Green Coll., Oxford, 1984–89; Hon. Consultant Surgeon, John Radcliffe Hosp., Oxford, 1984–89; Clin. Dir, Gen. and Vascular Surgery, Royal Infirmary of Edinburgh, 1995–2000; Hon. Sen. Lectr, Univ. of Edinburgh, 1989–2011. British Journal of Surgery: Mem. Editl Team, 1989–96; Jt Sen. Ed., 1996–2002; Editor in Chief, 2002–10. Mem., Nat. Panel of Specialists, NHS Scotland, 2000–05. Member of Council: Assoc. of Surgeons of GB and Ireland, 1994–99 (Hon. Editl Sec., 1996–99); Vascular Surgical Soc. of GB and Ireland, 1998–2001; RCPSG, 1998–2006. *Publications:* (ed with J. J. Earnshaw) The Evidence for Vascular Surgery, 1999, 2nd edn 2006; contrib. numerous chapters in textbooks and papers in learned jls on general theme of surgery (particularly vascular surgery). *Recreations:* golf, reading, food and wine. *Address:* Spire Murrayfield Hospital, 122 Corstorphine Road, Edinburgh EH12 6UD. *T:* (0131) 334 0363; 28 Mortonhall Road, Edinburgh EH9 2HN.

**MURLEY, Richard Andrew;** Managing Director, since 2006 and Executive Vice Chairman, since 2010, N. M. Rothschild & Sons Ltd; *b* 7 Jan. 1957; *s* of Alan and Anne Murley; *m* 1986, Penelope Wiseman; two *s* one *d*. *Educ:* Christ Church, Oxford (MA). Admitted solicitor, 1981; with Linklaters & Paines, 1979–81; Dir, Kleinwort Benson Ltd, subseq. Dresdner Kleinwort Benson, 1981–98; Man. Dir, Goldman Sachs Internat., 1998–2006; Dir Gen., Panel on Takeovers and Mergers, 2003–05; Co-Hd, UK Investment Banking, N. M. Rothschild & Sons Ltd, 2006–10. Chm., United Trust Bank Ltd, 2016–. Member: Financial Reporting Review Panel, 2003–14; Code Cttee, Panel on Takeovers and Mergers, 2012– (Chm., 2017–). Dir, University Coll. London Hosps NHS Foundn Trust, 2008–17 (Chm., 2010–17). Mem., UKRI-MRC (formerly MRC), 2017–. Trustee: Crisis, 2012–19; RSM, 2016–; Macmillan Cancer Support, 2017– (Chair, 2019–). *Recreations:* golf, sailing, gardening. *Address:* N. M. Rothschild & Sons Ltd, New Court, St Swithin's Lane, EC4N 8AL. *T:* (020) 7280 5000.

**MURNAGHAN, Dermot John;** Presenter, Sky News Today, since 2008; *b* 26 Dec. 1957; *s* of late Vincent Murnaghan and of Wendy Murnaghan (*née* Bush); *m* 1989, Maria Keegan; one *s* three *d*. *Educ:* Sussex Univ. (BA 1979, MA History 1980); City Univ. (Postgrad. Dip. Journalism, 1983). Presenter, Business Prog., Channel 4, 1984–88; correspondent, EBC Switzerland, 1988–89; presenter: Channel 4 Daily, 1989–92; Lunchtime News, ITN, 1992–99; ITV Nightly News, 1999–2001; ITV Evening News, 2001–02; BBC Breakfast, 2002–07; presenter: The Big Story, ITV, 1993–97; Britain's Most Wanted, ITV, 1997–2002; Eggheads, BBC2, 2003–14. Interview of the Year Award, RTS, 1998; Newscaster of the Year Award, TRIC, 2000. *Recreations:* running, film, football, sailing, chess. *Address:* Sky News, British Sky Broadcasting, Grant Way, Isleworth, Middx TW7 5QD.

**MURPHY,** Baroness *cr* 2004 (Life Peer), of Aldgate in the City of London; **Elaine Murphy,** MD, PhD; FRCPsych; Chairman, Council, St George's, University of London, 2006–10; academic psychiatrist, 1983–2006; social historian, since 2000; *b* Nottingham, 16 Jan. 1947; *d* of Roger Lawson and Nell Lawson (*née* Allitt); *m* 1st, 1969, John Matthew Murphy (marr. diss. 2001); 2nd, 2001, Michael Alfred Robb, *qv*. *Educ:* Univ. of Manchester Med. Sch. (MB, ChB 1971; MD 1979); PhD UCL 2000. FRCPsych 1986. Prof. of Psychiatry of Old Age, UMDS of Guy's and St Thomas' Hosps, 1983–96; Res. Fellow, Wellcome Inst. for History of Medicine, 1996–2005; Dist Gen. Manager, Lewisham and N Southwark HA, 1988–90; Chairman: City and Hackney NHS Trust, 1996–99; E London and the City HA, 1999–2002; NE London Strategic HA, 2002–06. Vice-Chm., Mental Health Act Commn, 1988–94. Hon. Prof. of Old Age Psychiatry, QMW, 1995–2006. *Publications:* Dementia and Mental Illness in Older People, 1986, 2nd edn 1993; Affective Disorders in the Elderly, 1986; After the Asylums, 1991; The Moated Grange, 2015; Monks Hall: the history of a Waveney Valley manor, 2018; papers on mental disorder, social policy and social history. *Recreations:* Italy, social history research. *Address:* House of Lords, SW1A 0PW.

**MURPHY OF TORFAEN,** Baron *cr* 2015 (Life Peer), of Abersychan in the County of Gwent; **Paul Peter Murphy;** PC 1999; *b* 25 Nov. 1948; *s* of late Ronald and Marjorie Murphy. *Educ:* St Francis RC Primary Sch., Abersychan; West Monmouth Sch., Pontypool; Oriel Coll., Oxford (MA; Hon. Fellow, 2000). Management Trainee, CWS, 1970–71; Lectr in History and Govt, Ebbw Vale Coll. of Further Education, 1971–87. Mem., Torfaen Borough Council, 1973–87 (Chm., Finance Cttee, 1976–86); Sec., Torfaen Constituency Labour Party, 1974–87. MP (Lab) Torfaen, 1987–2015. Opposition front bench spokesman for Wales, 1988–94; on NI, 1994; on for. affairs, 1994–95; on defence, 1995–97; Minister of State, NI Office, 1997–99; Secretary of State: for Wales, 1999–2002 and 2008–09; for NI, 2002–05. Chm., Intelligence and Security Cttee, 2005–08. Vis. Parly Fellow, St Antony's Coll., Oxford, 2006–07. Hon. Fellow, Glyndŵr Univ., Wrexham, 2009. DUniv S Wales, 2014; Hon. DLitt Wales Trinity Saint David, 2018. *Recreation:* music. *Address:* House of Lords, SW1A 0PW. *E:* murphyrighthon@aol.com. *Clubs:* Oxford and Cambridge; St Joseph's (St Dials).

**MURPHY, Andrew John;** Sheriff of Tayside Central and Fife at Falkirk, 1991–2005; *b* 16 Jan. 1946; *s* of Robert James Murphy and Robina Murphy (*née* Scott); *m* 1980, Susan Margaret Thomson; two *s* two *d*. *Educ:* Allan Glen's School, Glasgow; Edinburgh Univ. (MA, LLB). 2nd Lieut RA (V), 1971–73; Flt Lieut RAF, 1973–75. Admitted to Faculty of Advocates, Scottish Bar, 1970; called to Bar, Middle Temple, 1990; Crown Counsel, Hong Kong, 1976–79; Standing Junior Counsel to Registrar General for Scotland, 1982–85; Temporary Sheriff, 1983–85; Sheriff of Grampian, Highland and Islands at Banff and Peterhead, 1985–91. *Address:* c/o Advocates Library, Parliament House, Edinburgh EH1 1RF.

**MURPHY, Brian Gordon;** Building Societies' Ombudsman, 1992–99; *b* 18 Oct. 1940; *s* of Albert and Doris Murphy; *m* 1973, Judith Ann Parkinson. *Educ:* Mill Hill Sch. Articled Smiles & Co.; admitted Solicitor, 1966; with Roythorne & Co. and Russell & DuMoulin, Canada; Partner: Knapp Fishers, 1968–87; Farrer & Co., 1987–92. Pt-time Chm., Employment (formerly Industrial) Tribunals, 1991–92 and 2000–03. Vice-Chm., Incorp. Council of Law Reporting for Eng. and Wales, 1992–96; Mem. Council, Law Soc., 1982–93 (Chm., Employment Law Cttee, 1987–90); Pres., Westminster Law Soc., 1983–84. *Recreations:* golf, theatre, photography, travel. *Club:* Phyllis Court (Henley).

**MURPHY, Christopher Philip Yorke;** political lecturer; *b* 20 April 1947; *s* of Philip John and Dorothy Betty Murphy; *m* 1969, Sandra Gillian Ashton. *Educ:* Devonport High Sch.; The Queen's Coll., Oxford (MA). Formerly Associate Dir, D'Arcy MacManus & Masius. President, Oxford Univ. Conservative Assoc., 1967; held number of Conservative Party offices, 1968–72. Parish Councillor, Windlesham, Surrey, 1972–76. Contested (C): Bethnal Green and Bow, Feb. 1974, Oct. 1974. MP (C) Welwyn Hatfield, 1979–87. Vice-Chairman: Parly Urban and New Town Affairs Cttee, 1980–87; Parly Arts and Heritage Cttee, 1981–86; Mem., Select Cttee on Statutory Instruments, 1980–87 (rep of cttee on Commonwealth Delegated Legislation Cttee, 1980–87); UK Delegate to Council of Europe/WEU, 1983–87 (Hon. Associate, 1988). Vice-President: C of E Artistic Heritage Commn, 1984–87; C of E Youth & Drugs Commn, 1986–87. Member: Nat. Cttee for 900th Anniversary of Domesday Book, 1986; Chief Pleas of Sark (Parlt), 1989–90 (Vice-Pres., Internat. Cttee of Chief Pleas, 1989–90); Arts Council of Bailiwick of Guernsey, 1988–90; Council, Société Guernesiaise, 1988–90. Life Mem., CPA, 1987. Hon. Sec., Société Sercquiaise, 1988–90. Sec., Sodor & Man Diocesan Synod, and Bishop's Advr, 1991–2000; Chapter Clerk, St German's Cathedral, 1992–2000; Diocesan Sec., Dio. of Sodor and Man, 1993–2000; Secretary: Diocesan Bd of Finance, 1993–2000; Church Comrs for IOM, 1993–2000; Legislative Cttee, 1997–2000; DAC for Care of Churches, 1997–2000. FRSA. Freeman, City of London, 1984. Hon. Citizen, Cork, 1985. *Recreations:* arts, heritage, travel, conservation, walking. *Club:* Oxford Union Society.

**MURPHY, Conor Terence;** Member (SF) Newry and Armagh, Northern Ireland Assembly, 1998–July 2012 and since June 2015; *b* 10 July 1963; *m* Catherine; one *s* one *d*. *Educ:* St Colman's Coll., Newry; Univ. of Ulster; Queen's Univ., Belfast (MA). Mem. (SF), Newry and Mourne DC, 1989–97. Minister for Regl Develt, NI, 2007–11. Contested (SF) Newry and Armagh, 2001. MP (SF) Newry and Armagh, 2005–15. *Address:* Northern Ireland Assembly, Parliament Buildings, Ballymiscaw, Stormont, Belfast BT4 3XX.

**MURPHY, Denis;** *b* 2 Nov. 1948; *s* of late John Murphy and of Josephine Murphy; *m* (separated); one *s* one *d*. *Educ:* St Cuthbert's Grammar Sch., Newcastle upon Tyne; Northumberland Coll. Apprentice electrician, 1965–69; underground electrician, Ellington Colliery, 1969–94. Mem. (Lab) Wansbeck DC, 1990–97 (Leader, 1994–97). MP (Lab) Wansbeck, 1997–2010.

**MURPHY, Dervla;** writer; *b* 28 Nov. 1931; *d* of Fergus Murphy and Kathleen Rochfort-Dowling; one *d*. *Educ:* Ursuline Convent, Waterford. American Irish Foundn Literary Award, 1975; Christopher Ewart-Biggs Meml Prize, 1978; Irish Amer. Cultural Inst. Literary Award, 1985. *Publications:* Full Tilt, 1965, 11th edn 1995; Tibetan Foothold, 1966, 5th edn 2000; The Waiting Land, 1967, 7th edn 1998; In Ethiopia with a Mule, 1968, 7th edn 1994; On a Shoe String to Coorg, 1976, 7th edn 1995; Where the Indus is Young, 1977, 7th edn 1995; A Place Apart, 1978, 4th edn 1987; Wheels Within Wheels, 1979, 6th edn 2001; Race to the Finish?, 1981, 2nd edn 1982; Eight Feet in the Andes, 1983, 7th edn 1994; Muddling Through in Madagascar, 1985, 6th edn 1998; Ireland, 1985; Tales from Two Cities, 1987, 5th edn 1999; (ed) Embassy to Constantinople, the Travels of Lady Mary Wortley Montague, 1988; In Cameroon with Egbert, 1989; Transylvania and Beyond, 1992, 4th edn 1993; The Ukimwi Road, 1993, 3rd edn 1994; South from the Limpopo, 1997, 3rd edn 1998; Visiting Rwanda, 1998; One Foot in Laos, 1999, 2nd edn 2000; Through the Embers of Chaos: Balkan journeys, 2002, 2nd edn 2003; Through Siberia by Accident, 2005, 2nd edn 2006; Silverland: beyond the Urals, 2006, 2nd edn 2007; The Island that Dared: Cuban journeys, 2008, 2nd edn 2010; Encounters in Gaza, 2012; Between River and Sea: encounters in Israel and Palestine, 2015. *Recreations:* reading, music, cycling, swimming, walking. *Address:* The Old Market, Lismore, Co. Waterford, Ireland.

**MURPHY, Fiona Clare;** barrister, Doughty Street Chambers, since 2013; *b* Belfast, 17 June 1966; *d* of Eugene Murphy and Rosaleen Murphy; partner, 2001, Sam Craig. *Educ:* Dominican Coll., Fort William; London Sch. of Econs and Pol Sci. (LLB); Coll. of Law. Admitted Solicitor, 1993; Solicitor, B. M. Birnberg & Co., 1992–98; Founder Partner, Bhatt Murphy, 1998–2013; called to the Bar, Gray's Inn, 2013. Member: Police Action Lawyers Gp, 1990–; Inquest Lawyers Gp, 1992–. *Recreations:* art and architecture, open spaces. *Address:* Doughty Street Chambers, 53–54 Doughty Street, WC1N 2LS. *T:* (020) 7404 1313, *Fax:* (020) 7404 2283. *E:* f.murphy@doughtystreet.co.uk.

**MURPHY, Foster;** *see* Murphy, R. S. F.

**MURPHY, Gerard Martin,** PhD; Chairman: Blackstone Group International Partners LLP (formerly Blackstone Group International Ltd), since 2009 (Senior Managing Director, 2008–17); Tate & Lyle plc, since 2017; Burberry plc, since 2018; *b* 6 Nov. 1955; *m*; two *s*. *Educ:* University Coll., Cork (BSc, PhD 1980); University Coll., Dublin (MBS 1983). Various exec. posts in Ireland, UK and USA, Grand Metropolitan plc, 1978–91; Chief Executive Officer: Greencore Group plc, 1991–95; NFC plc, subseq. Exel plc, 1995–2000; Carlton Communications plc, 2000–03; Kingfisher plc, 2003–08. Non-executive Director: Novar plc (formerly Caradon plc), 1997–2003; Abbey National plc, 2004–05; Reckitt Benckiser plc, 2005–08; British American Tobacco plc, 2009–17. *Address:* Blackstone Group International Partners LLP, 40 Berkeley Square, W1J 5AL.

**MURPHY, Prof. Gillian,** PhD; FMedSci; Professor of Cancer Cell Biology, 2002–14, now Emeritus, and Deputy Head, Department of Oncology, 2002–14, University of Cambridge (Hon. Visitor, Department of Oncology, since 2014); Fellow of Wolfson College, Cambridge, 2003–13, now Emeritus; *b* 25 May 1946; *d* of Donald Ralph Emery and Joan Edwina Emery. *Educ:* Univ. of Birmingham (BSc Biochem.; PhD Biochem. 1971). Nato Sci. Fellow, 1972–74; Res. Fellow, 1974–87, Arthritis Res. Campaign Sen. Fellow, 1987–97, Strangeways Res. Lab., Cambridge; Prof. of Cell Biol., Dept of Biol Sci., UEA, 1995–2002 (Hon. Prof., Biol Scis, 2002). Hon. Vis. Prof. of Biochem., Univ. of Hong Kong, 2000. Member: Biochem. Soc., 1975; Amer. Soc. for Biochem. and Molecular Biol. FMedSci 2005. *Recreations:* gardening, walking, handicrafts, music. *Address:* Cancer Research UK Cambridge Institute, Li Ka Shing Centre, Robinson Way, Cambridge CB2 0RE. *E:* gm290@cam.ac.uk.

**MURPHY, Ian Patrick;** QC 1992; a Recorder, 1990–2016; *b* 1 July 1949; *s* of Patrick Murphy and Irene Grace (*née* Hooper); *m* 1974, Penelope Gay; two *d*. *Educ:* St Illtyd's Coll., Cardiff; LSE (LLB). Chartering Clerk, Baltic Exchange, 1970–71; called to the Bar, Middle Temple, 1972, Bencher, 2001; in practice as a barrister, 1972–2016; Asst Recorder, 1986–90. *Recreations:* golf, ski-ing, cricket, family time with daughters, Anna Sumner and Charlotte Murphy and grandchildren Isabel, Arthur and Beatrix Sumner. *Address:* 3 Llandaff Chase, Llandaff, Cardiff CF5 2NA. *Clubs:* Cardiff County; Royal Porthcawl Golf.

**MURPHY, Rt Hon. James;** PC 2008; *b* 23 Aug. 1967; *s* of Jim Murphy and Anne Murphy. *Educ:* Bellarmine Secondary Sch., Glasgow; Milnerton High Sch., Cape Town. Dir, Endsleigh Insurance, 1994–96; Project Manager, Scottish Lab. Party, 1996–97. MP (Lab) Eastwood, 1997–2005, E Renfrewshire, 2005–15; contested (Lab) same seat, 2015. PPS to Sec. of State for Scotland, 2001–02; an Asst Govt Whip, 2002–03; a Lord Comr of HM Treasury (Govt Whip), 2003–05; Parly Sec., Cabinet Office, 2005–06; Minister of State: DWP, 2006–07; (Minister for Europe), FCO, 2007–08; Sec. of State for Scotland, 2008–10; Shadow Sec. of State for Scotland, 2010, for Defence, 2010–13, for Internat. Affairs, 2013–14; Leader, Scottish Labour Party, 2014–15. Parly Spokesman, Scottish PFA. Chm., Labour Friends of Israel, 2001–02. Pres., NUS, 1994–96. *Publications:* (as Jim Murphy) The Ten Football Matches that Changed the World, 2014.

**MURPHY, Joe**; Political Editor, London Evening Standard, since 2004; *b* Lincs, 20 Sept. 1964; *s* of J. F., (Frank), Murphy and Iris Dove; *m* 1997, Joy Copley; one *d*. Leicester Mercury, 1985–89; Coventry Evening Telegraph, 1989; Central Press, 1989–92; Political Reporter, The Sun, 1992–94; Political Corresp./Political Editor, Mail on Sunday, 1994–99; Political Editor, Sunday Telegraph, 1999–2002; Whitehall Editor, London Evening Standard, 2002–04. *Recreation:* sailing. *Club:* Dinghy Cruising Association.

**MURPHY, (John) Philip**; writer and lecturer, since 2018; *b* 3 June 1958; *s* of Robert Anthony Murphy and Cecily Vaughan Murphy (*née* Nicholson); *m* 1st, 1983, Elizabeth McManus (marr. diss. 1988); 2nd, 1991, Sophie Annabel Davies; one *s* one *d*. *Educ:* St Cuthbert's Grammar Sch., Newcastle upon Tyne; Hertford Coll., Oxford (BA 2nd Cl. Hons French and Latin); City Univ. (Postgrad. Dip. in Practical Journalism); LSE (Dip. Macro- and Micro-Econs). Reporter: Southern Evening Echo, Southampton, 1981–83; and local govt corresp., The Journal, Newcastle upon Tyne, 1983–86; Lobby Corresp., Thomson Newspapers, 1986–87; Political Editor, Yorkshire Post, 1987–96; Press Assoc., 1996–98; Exec. Dir (Communications), Arts Council of England, 1998–99; Asst Gen. Sec. and Dir of Media Communications, Labour Party, 1999–2000; Special Advr to Prime Minister, 2000–01; BG Group: Govt Affairs Manager, 2001–02; Hd of Govt and Public Affairs, and Dep. Hd of Policy and Corporate Affairs Dept, 2003–06; Hd of Policy and Corporate Affairs—Europe and Central Asia, 2006–11; Hd of Partner Relations (Europe), 2010–12; Vice-Pres., Corporate Policy, 2012–13; Vice-Pres. and Global Hd of Govt and Public Affairs, 2013–16; Exec. Vice-Pres. and Hd of Govt and Partner Relns, Vanwall Energy, 2016–17; Man. Dir, Vidhya Gp, 2017–18. *Publications:* (with R. Caborn) Regional Government for England: an economic imperative, 1995. *Recreations:* art from the late 19th century, music, allotment. *Clubs:* Wisley Golf; Old Thorns Golf.

**MURPHY, Sir Jonathan (Michael)**, Kt 2014; QPM 2007; DL; Professor of Advanced Policing Studies, Liverpool John Moores University, since 2016; *b* Liverpool, 17 June 1958; *s* of William Michael Murphy and Martha Iris Murphy; *m* 1981, Janet Astbury; one *s* one *d*. *Educ:* Liverpool Univ. (LLB Hons 1990); Cambridge Univ. (Dip. Applied Criminol. 2001). Merseyside Police: Police Cadet, 1975–76; Constable, Liverpool City and Operational Support Gp, 1976–82; Detective Constable, 1982–84; Uniform Patrol Sergeant, 1984–85; Detective Sergeant, 1985–92; Detective Inspector Force Intelligence, 1992–95; Head, Criminal Investigation Dept, Wallasey, 1995–96, Liverpool City Centre area, 1996–97; Detective Superintendent, 1997–98; Detective Chief Superintendent, 1998–99; Force Ops Manager, 1999–2001; Asst Chief Constable (Hd of Ops), Nat. Crime Squad, 2002–04; Dep. Chief Constable, 2004–07, Chief Constable, 2010–16, Merseyside Police; Nat. Hd, Crime Business Area, ACPO, 2010–16 (Co-ordinator, Serious and Organised Crime, 2007–10). DL Merseyside, 2017. Fulbright Police Fellowship, Univ. of Calif, 1995. Advanced Fellow, RUSI, 2016. Hon. Fellow, Liverpool John Moores Univ., 2014. Hon DLaws Liverpool, 2016. *Recreations:* ski-ing, reading. *Address:* Liverpool Centre for Advanced Policing Studies, Liverpool John Moores University, 80–98 Mount Pleasant, Liverpool L3 5UZ. *E:* j.m.murphy@ljmu.ac.kuk.

**MURPHY, Laurence**; QC (Scot.) 2000; *b* 12 April 1958; *s* of William John Murphy and Alison Boyd Spindlow or Murphy; *m* 1989, Christine Marie Cecile Germaine Boch; one *s* one *d*. *Educ:* Univ. of Glasgow (MA (Hons) 1980; LLB 1982). Solicitor, 1983–89; Advocate, 1990–. *Recreations:* golf, tennis, walking, music, travel. *Address:* Advocates' Library, Parliament House, Edinburgh EH1 1RF. *T:* (0131) 226 2881.

**MURPHY, Prof. Michael Furber**, MD; FRCP, FRCPath, FFPath; Professor of Blood Transfusion Medicine, University of Oxford, since 2004; Consultant Haematologist: Oxford University Hospitals NHS Foundation Trust (formerly Oxford Radcliffe Hospital NHS Trust), since 1996; NHS Blood and Transplant (formerly National Blood Service), since 1996; *b* Liverpool, 2 May 1951; *s* of Arthur Furber Murphy and Jean Marjorie Murphy (*née* Frazer); *m* 1984, Elizabeth Sarah Green; one *s* one *d*. *Educ:* Malvern Coll.; St Bartholomew's Hosp. Med. Coll., London (MB BS 1973); Univ. of London (MD 1988). MRCP 1976, FRCP 1993; MRCPath 1982, FRCPath 1994; FFPath 2015. St Bartholomew's Hospital, London: Registrar, then Sen. Registrar in Haematol., 1978–84; Sen. Lectr in Haematol. and Consultant Haematologist, 1985–96. Chairman: NICE Guideline and Develt Gp for Blood Transfusion, 2013–15; Biomedical Excellence for Safer Transfusion Collaborative, 2014–18. Mem., Bd of Dirs, Amer. Assoc. of Blood Banks, 2011– (Vice-Pres., 2016–17; Pres., 2018–19). *Publications:* (ed jtly) Practical Transfusion Medicine, 2005, 5th edn 2017; over 200 articles in scientific jls. *Recreations:* golf, running, theatre. *Address:* NHS Blood and Transplant, John Radcliffe Hospital, Oxford OX3 9BQ. *T:* (01865) 387902, *Fax:* (01865) 387975. *E:* mike.murphy@nhsbt.nhs.uk. *Clubs:* Frilford Heath Golf, St Enodoc Golf.

**MURPHY, Michael James, (Mick)**; Member (SF) South Down, Northern Ireland Assembly, 1998–2003; *b* Banbridge, 6 Feb. 1942; *s* of Michael and Mary Theresa Murphy; *m* 1965, Carole Trainor; six *d*. *Educ:* Legannay Sch., Leitrim, Co. Down. Publican in Rostrevor, 1978–91. Elected Mem. (SF) Newry and Mourne DC, 1996–2014; Mem. (SF) NI Forum, 1996–98. Contested (SF) S Down, 2001. *Recreations:* Gaelic games, Irish culture.

**MURPHY, Prof. Michael Joseph**, FBA 2002; Professor of Demography, London School of Economics and Political Science, since 1997; *b* 19 March 1947. *Educ:* Trinity Coll., Cambridge (BA 1969); Univ. of York (BPhil). Statistician, CSO, 1971–78; Res. Fellow, LSHTM, 1978–80; Lectr, LSE, 1980–97. *Publications:* contrib. learned jls. *Address:* Department of Social Policy, London School of Economics and Political Science, Houghton Street, WC2A 2AE.

**MURPHY, His Honour Michael Joseph Adrian**; QC 1993; a Circuit Judge, 1999–2016; *b* 1 Oct. 1949; *s* of late Patrick Joseph Murphy, Hirwaun, Mid-Glam., and Frances Murphy; *m* 1973, Rosemary Dorothy Aitken; three *s* one *d*. *Educ:* Aberdare Grammar Sch., Mid-Glam.; Sheffield Univ. (LLB, MA). Called to the Bar, Inner Temple, 1973. A Recorder, 1989–99.

**MURPHY, Dame Olwen**; *see* Hufton, Dame O.

**MURPHY, Patrick James**, CMG 1985; HM Diplomatic Service, retired; Adviser on Central Europe, British Consultancy Charitable Trust, 2005–12; *b* 11 March 1931; *e s* of late Dr James Murphy and Cicely Mary (*née* Crowley); *m* 1st, 1959, Barbara May Healey-Purse (marr. diss. 1969); two *s*; 2nd, 1974, Jutta Ulrike Oehlmann; one *s*. *Educ:* Cranbrook School; Gonville and Caius College, Cambridge (BA; Geography Tripos). Served RAF, 1950–52. Oxford and Cambridge Far Eastern Expedition, 1955–56; BBC Gen. Overseas Service, 1956; Joined FO, 1957; Frankfurt, 1958; Berlin, 1959; FO, 1962; Second Sec. (Commercial), Warsaw, 1962; First Sec., FO, 1965; First Sec. (Commercial) and Consul, Phnom Penh, 1966; Consul, Düsseldorf, 1969; Consul, Hamburg, 1971; FCO, 1974; First Sec., Vienna, 1977; Counsellor, FCO, 1981–87. Advr, Sultanate of Oman, 1987–90; Consultant, HM Diplomatic Service, 1990–95; Regl Dir for Poland and the Baltic States, 1995–2005, Czech and Slovak Republics, 1997–2005, and Belarus, 2000–05, BESO. Mem. Council, Polish Corps of Volunteer Experts, 2006–. Officer's Cross, Order of Merit (Poland), 2000. *Recreations:* history, travel, wine, Irish life. *Address:* Flat 8, Glebe Court, The Glebe, Blackheath, SE3 9TH. *T:* (020) 8852 2483. *Club:* Royal Air Force.

**MURPHY, Patrick Wallace**; agricultural consultant, 1996–2006; Under Secretary, Land Use, Conservation and Countryside Group, Ministry of Agriculture, Fisheries and Food, 1994–96; *b* 16 Aug. 1944; *s* of Lawrence Vincent Murphy and Agnes Dunn; *m* 1972, Denise Lillieth Fullarton-Fullarton; two *s*. *Educ:* St Chad's College, Wolverhampton; Trinity Hall, Cambridge (BA Hons). Joined MAFF, 1966; Asst Private Sec. to Minister of Agriculture, Fisheries and Food, 1970; First Sec. (Agriculture and Commercial), British Embassy, Washington, 1974–78; Controller of Plant Variety Rights, 1978–82; Head, Land Use and Tenure Div., 1982–86; Under Sec., 1986; Head, Milk and Potatoes Gp, 1986–89; Hd of Pesticides, Vet. Medicines, Emergencies and Biotechnol. Gp, 1989–93; Hd of EC Gp, 1993–94. Non-exec. Dir, IDV (UK), 1985–88. Chm., I'Anson Cricket Competitions, 2006–12. Chm., Elstead Parish Council, 2011–. *Recreations:* cricket, walking, gardening.

**MURPHY, Peter John**; QC 2002; a Recorder, since 2000; *b* 20 May 1958; *s* of John James Murphy and Joan Murphy; *m* 1997, Ceri Louise Phillips; two *s* three *d*. *Educ:* Leicester Univ. (LLB Hons). Joined chambers, Cardiff, 1980; called to the Bar, Gray's Inn, 1980; an Asst Recorder, 1997–2000. *Recreations:* amateur dramatics and singing, numerous sporting activities incl. swimming, football and squash, avid reader.

**MURPHY, His Honour Peter William**; writer; a Circuit Judge, 2007–15; Resident Judge, Peterborough Crown Court and Honorary Recorder of Peterborough, 2014–15; *b* Boston, Lincs, 10 Feb. 1946; *s* of William Joseph Murphy and Rhiannon Murphy (*née* Rees); *m* 1992, Christine Service; one *s*, and one step *s*. *Educ:* Queen Elizabeth's Grammar Sch., Blackburn; Downing Coll., Cambridge (BA 1966; LLB 1967; MA 1970). Called to the Bar: Middle Temple, 1968, Bencher, 2013 (Autumn Reader, 2018); Calif, 1981; Texas, 1985; private practice, London, 1970–78; Principal Lectr, Inns of Court Sch. of Law, 1978–80; private practice, San Francisco, 1980–84; Prof. of Law, South Texas Coll. of Law, 1984–2007; Trial and Appellate Counsel, Internat. Criminal Tribunal for Former Yugoslavia, 1998–2007. Trustee, Amer. Inns of Court Foundn, 1985–99, now Emeritus. Vis. Prof., L'Ecole nat. de la magistrature, 2009–. Founding Editor-in-Chief, Blackstone's Criminal Practice, 1991–2007. *Publications:* A Practical Approach to Evidence, 1980, 12th edn as Murphy on Evidence, 2011; Evidence Proof and Facts: a book of sources, 2003; *novels:* Removal, 2012; A Higher Duty, 2013; Test of Resolve, 2014; A Matter for the Jury, 2014; And is there Honey still for Tea?, 2015; The Heirs of Owain Glyndwr, 2016; Calling Down the Storm, 2017; One Law for the Rest of Us, 2018; *short stories:* Walden of Bermondsey, 2017; Judge Walden: Back in Session, 2018; numerous law review articles. *Recreations:* theatre, music, watching sports (Blackburn Rovers, Harlequins and Wales), chess, snooker. *Club:* Reform.

**MURPHY, Philip**; *see* Murphy, J. P.

**MURPHY, Prof. Richard James**, FCA; Professor of Practice in International Political Economy, City, University of London, since 2015; Director, Tax Research LLP, since 2005; *b* Romford, Essex, 21 March 1958; *s* of William Patrick Murphy and late Barbara Jean Murphy; *m* 1999, Jacqueline Anne Walsh; two *s*. *Educ:* Southampton Univ. (BScSoc Business Econs and Accountancy 1979). ACA 1982, FCA 1993. With Chartered Accountants, Peat Marwick Mitchell & Co., London, 1979–83, Shelley Pinnick & Co., London, 1983–84; Principal, R J Murphy & Co., London, 1985–89; Sen. Partner, Murphy Deeks Nolan, London, 1989–2000; Principal, Fulcrum, Chartered Accountants, 2000–. Adviser: Tax Justice Network, London, 2003–10; TUC, 2008–12; PCS, 2009–14. Academic, visiting or research Fellowships at: Univ. of Portsmouth Business Sch., 1997–2000; Centre for Global Political Econ., Univ. of Sussex, 2005–08; Tax Res. Inst., Univ. of Nottingham, 2006–09. Director: Fair Tax Mark, 2013–; Cambridge Econometrics Ltd, 2017–; Green New Deal Gp Ltd, 2019–; Corporate Accountability Network, 2019–. FRSA. Blogger at www.taxresearch.org.uk/Blog. *Publications:* (jtly) Tax Havens: at the heart of globalization, 2009; The Courageous State, 2011; Over Here and Undertaxed, 2013; The Joy of Tax, 2015; Dirty Secrets: how tax havens destroy the economy, 2017; contrib. articles to jls incl. Accountancy, Accountancy Age, AccountingWEB (contrib. ed.), Tax Notes Internat. *Recreations:* my family, transport history, railway modelling, walking Hector, a cocker spaniel, holidaying in England, birdwatching. *Address:* Tax Research LLP, 33 Kingsley Walk, Ely, Cambs CB6 3BZ. *T:* (01353) 665405. *E:* richard.murphy@taxresearch.org.uk. *W:* www.taxresearch.org.uk/Blog.

**MURPHY, (Robert Somerville) Foster**; Principal, Charitable Futures, 2002–14; Chief Executive, Abbeyfield Society, 1992–2002; *b* 1 June 1940; *s* of Robert Somerville Foster Murphy and Eva Constance (*née* Harvey); *m* 1964, Patricia Mary Hamilton; one *s* one *d*. *Educ:* Dublin Univ. (MA); Downing Coll., Cambridge (MA); London Univ. (Dip. SocScis (ext.)). Irish Sec., SCM, 1965–67; Youth Sec., BCC, 1967–72; Youth Sec., subseq. Head of Div., then Dep. Dir, NCVO, 1972–81; Dir, Volunteer Centre, UK, 1981–92. Board Member: Innisfree HA, 1993–99; Internat. Assoc. for Homes & Services for the Aging, 1994–2003; Centre for Policy on Ageing, 1997–2002 (Chm., 2000–02); Citizen's Advice Notes Trust, 2002–05; Abbeyfield Internat., 2002–11 (Vice Chm., 2005–09); Vegetarian Housing Assoc., 2004–07. Voluntary Advr, Officers' Assoc., 2003–16. *Publications:* (jtly) Integrating Care, Housing and Community, 1998; Collected Poems, 2018; Collection 2, 2019. *Recreations:* opera, gardening, keeping fit. *Address:* 64 Callander Road, SE6 2QE. *E:* foster.murphy.uk@gmail.com.

**MURPHY, Rory**; Director, Carom Ltd, since 2005; *b* 23 April 1955; *s* of Philip Murphy and Noreen Murphy (*née* Sheahan); *m* 1976, Catherine Deane; two *s*. *Educ:* Bishop Bright RC Grammar Sch., Leamington Spa. Photographer, Pitt Rivers Mus., Oxford, 1972–84 (on secondment as Union Official, 1979–84); Nat. Sec., ASTMS, Ireland, 1984–87; Asst Gen. Sec., ASTMS, later MSF, 1987–89; Chief Exec., Finers, Solicitors, 1989–90; Dir of Industrial Relations, Royal Coll. of Midwives, 1990–95; Gen. Sec., NatWest Staff Assoc., 1995–99; Jt Gen. Sec., UNIFI, 1999–2004; Asst Gen. Sec., Amicus, 2004–05; Hd of Commercial Health and Wellbeing, First Assist, 2006–07; Dir of People Management, PBLSat, 2007–08; Trade Union and Govt Advr, Swiss Re, 2008–09. Chm., Merchant Navy Officers Pension Fund. *Recreations:* football (Arsenal), theatre, art, archaeology.

**MURPHY, Dr Simon Francis**; non-executive Chairman, Sandwell Local Improvement Finance Trust Company Ltd, since 2005; *b* 24 Feb. 1962; *s* of Patrick Joseph Murphy and Mary Frances Murphy; *m* 1992, Bridget Lee Brickley; one *s* one *d* (and one *s* decd). *Educ:* Sacred Heart Coll., Droitwich; N Worcs Coll., Bromsgrove; UCW, Aberystwyth (BSc Econ 1983; PhD 1986). Tutor, Dept of Political Sci., UCW, Aberystwyth, 1984–86; Asst to Leader of Labour Gp, Wolverhampton MBC, 1986–89; Head of Research, Office of John Bird, MEP, 1989–94. MEP (Lab) Midlands W, 1994–99, W Midlands Reg., 1999–2004. Whip, 1996–98, Leader, 2000–02, European PLP; Vice-President: Socialist Gp, EP, 2000–02; Eurogroup for Animal Welfare & Conservation, 1997–99. Contested (Lab) Wolverhampton SW, 1992. Chief Exec., Birmingham Forward, 2004–06; City Region Dir, Urban West Midlands, 2006–11. Dir, W Midlands Develt Agency, 1997. Dir, Capital Ventures Mgt Ltd, 2004–06; non-exec. Dir, Eur. Bd, iSoft Gp plc, 2003–06; Dir and Trustee, Groundwork W Midlands, 2013– (Chm., Finance and Audit Cttee, 2014–); Exec. Consultant, Shakespeares LLP, 2011–14; Business Develt Consultant, Waterhouse Search, 2011–14; Associate, Deloitte, 2011–13; Interim Chief Executive Officer: Worcester Community Trust, 2013–15; Groundwork N Ireland, 2015; Interim Dir, Develt and Sales, ExtraCare Charitable Trust, 2016–18. Co-Founder and Chair, Worcs Social and Econ.

Inclusion Consortium (Fusion), 2014–15. Member: Better Regulation Commn (formerly Task Force), 2005–06; MG Rover Task Force, 2005–06; Technol. Transfer Fund Investment Gp, Advantage W Midlands, 2005–06. Non-executive Director: Worcs LEP, 2014–17; Dudley and Walsall NHS Mental Health Trust, 2015– (Chm., Quality and Safety Cttee, 2015–18; Sen. Ind. Dir, 2016–; Chm., Finance and Perf. Cttee, 2018–); Birmingham Community Health Care NHS Foundn Trust, 2017–18. Interim Chair, Worcs Food and Drink, 2017–. Gov., Univ. of Wolverhampton, 1996–99. W Mercia Police and Crime Comr candidate (Lab), 2012. Dir of Junior Cricket, Old Elizabethans' Cricket Club, Worcester, 2018–. *Publications:* (contrib.) Contemporary Minority Nationalisms, ed M. Watson, 1990; (contrib.) European Governance, 2002; Views from the UK on democracy, participation and policy-making in the EU; articles in Waterlog Mag. *Recreations:* running, reading, cooking, fishing, watching sport, triathlons.

**MURPHY, Stephen David;** General Secretary, Union of Construction, Allied Trades and Technicians, 2012–15; *b* Chesterfield, Derbys, 8 April 1961; *s* of Thomas and Avis Murphy; *m* 1987, Angela Phillips; two *d*. *Educ:* Newbold Green Sch., Chesterfield. C&G Bricklaying. Bricklayer, 1978–97; shop steward, 1989–97; Union of Construction, Allied Trades and Technicians: Develt Officer, 1997–2001; Regl Organiser, 2001–05; Regl Sec., Midlands, 2005–11, Yorks, 2011–12. Mem., Lab. Party, 1997–. *Recreations:* Sheffield Wednesday, hill walking.

**MURPHY, Steven;** Founder and Managing Partner, Murphy and Partners, since 2015; *b* New York, 17 March 1954; *s* of Edward Murphy and Gloria Murphy (*née* Suglia); *m* 1978, Annie Pleshette; one *s* one *d*. *Educ:* Georgetown Univ., Washington, DC (BA Eng. Lit.). Div. Pres., Simon & Schuster, 1985–91; Pres., EMI Music/Angel Records, 1991–98; Exec. Vice Pres. and Man. Dir, Disney Publishing, 1998–2000; Chief Operating Officer, 2000–02, Chief Exec. and Pres., 2002–09, Rodale Inc.; CEO, Christie's Internat. plc, 2010–14. Trustee, V&A Mus., 2017–. *Recreations:* horse riding, yoga, art, reading, music, theatre. *Clubs:* Arts, Harry's Bar, Annabel's, 5 Hertford Street.

**MURPHY, Stuart Neil Luke;** Chief Executive, English National Opera, since 2018; *b* 6 Nov. 1971; *s* of David Francis Murphy and Patricia Mary Murphy (*née* Downing); *m* 2002 (marr. diss. 2005); two *s*; partner, 2014, David Clews. *Educ:* St Mary's RC Sch., Ilkley; Clare Coll., Cambridge (MA Pol Geog.). Joined BBC, 1993; worked on comedy, documentaries, entertainment shows, 1993–96; Producer: MTV Europe, 1997; Big Breakfast, Channel 4, 1997; BBC: Strategic Develt Exec., TV, 1998; Broadcast Develt Exec., 1999–2002; launched UK Play, music and comedy channel, 1999; Hd of Programming, 1999–2001, Channel Controller, 2001–03, BBC Choice; Launch Controller, BBC 3, 2003–05; commissioned Little Britain, Gavin and Stacey, Nighty Night, Bodies, The Mighty Boosh, Torchwood; Creative Director: RDF Media, 2006; Twofour Broadcast, 2006–09; Sky: Dir of Programming, Sky1, 2009–12; Launch Dir, Sky Atlantic, 2011; Dir, Entertainment Channels, 2012–15; commissioned A League of Their Own, An Idiot Abroad, Stella, Hunderby, Penny Dreadful, Fortitude, The Last Panthers, Moone Boy, Patrick Melrose; acquired Modern Family, Game of Thrones, Mad Men, The Affair. Board Director: Nickelodeon, 2013; Jaunt, 2014–15; A&E Networks UK, 2015; Nat. Opera Studio, 2019. *Recreations:* travelling to unusual places with my teenage sons, Russian, classical music, Rugby, horror films, silly comedies. *Club:* Ivy.

**MURPHY, Thomas,** CBE 1991; Managing Director, Civil Aviation Authority, 1987–95; *b* 13 Nov. 1928; *s* of Thomas Murphy and Elizabeth Gray Murphy (*née* Leckie); *m* 1962, Sheila Jean Dorothy Young; one *s* three *d*. *Educ:* St Mirin's Acad., Paisley; Glasgow Univ. (MA Hons). Served Royal Artillery, 1951–53. Marks and Spencer, 1953–55; British Petroleum, 1955–86: appts in Territory of Papua New Guinea, Trinidad, Scotland, Algeria, USA, 1955–68; Asst Gen. Man., BP Tanker Co., 1968–76; Gen. Man., Gp Personnel, 1976–81; Advr, Organisation Planning, 1981–86. Non-executive Director: CAA, 1986–87; Parity plc, 1997–2001; Oriel Gp plc, 1998. Internat. Sen. Managers Programme, Harvard Business Sch., 1973. *Recreations:* walking, coarse golf, destructive gardening. *Address:* Woodruffe, Onslow Road, Sunningdale, Berks SL5 0HW. *T:* (01344) 623261.

**MURPHY, Thomas James;** journalist, singer and actor; *b* 26 June 1956; *s* of James Murphy and Beatrice Murphy (*née* Strand); *m* 1976, Janet Sallis; four *s*. *Educ:* Salesian Sch., Chertsey; Sussex Univ. (BA History); Warwick Univ. (MBA); Royal Acad. of Music (Cert.). Kitchen porter and factory labourer, 1977; trainee journalist, Slough Observer, 1978; Sports editor, Buckinghamshire Advertiser, 1981; Editor: Staines Informer, 1983; East Grinstead Courier, 1984; Sub-editor, The Independent, 1986; Dep. Chief sub-editor, London Evening News, 1987; Editor, The Universe, 1988–90; journalist, The Times, 1990. Various theatrical roles incl. Swing in Gypsy, Savoy Th., 2015. *Recreation:* swimming.

**MURRAY;** see Erskine-Murray.

**MURRAY,** family name of **Duke of Atholl, Earl of Dunmore** and **Earl of Mansfield and Mansfield.**

**MURRAY, Alan James;** Chief Executive Officer, Hanson plc, 2002–07; *b* 12 May 1953; *s* of James and Elsie Murray; *m* 2002, Pamela Clark. *Educ:* Lancaster Univ. (BA Hons Econ.). FCMA 1988. Finance Dir, Burton Gp, 1985–88; Hanson plc, 1988–2007: Finance Director: ARC General Products and S Region, 1993–94; Hanson Brick UK, 1994–95; Asst Finance Dir, 1995–97; Finance Dir, 1997–98; Chief Exec., Hanson Building Materials America, 1998–2002. Non-executive Director: Internat. Power plc, 2007–11; HeidelbergCement AG, 2010–17; Ferguson (formerly Wolseley) plc, 2013–; Owens-Illinois Inc., 2015–. *Recreations:* cinema, music, travel.

**MURRAY, Alexander,** FRHistS; FBA 1995; Fellow and Praelector in Modern History, University College, Oxford, 1980–2001, now Emeritus Fellow; *b* 14 May 1934; second *s* of late Stephen Hubert Murray and Margaret (*née* Gillett). *Educ:* Bedales Sch., Petersfield; New Coll., Oxford (BA Mod. Hist.; BPhil European Hist.). FRHistS 1971. Served RA, 1953–55. Asst Lectr in Medieval Hist., Univ. of Leeds, 1961–63; University of Newcastle upon Tyne: Lectr, 1963–77; Sen. Lectr, 1977–80; Public Orator, 1973–76; Chm., Faculty of Modern Hist., Univ. of Oxford, 1992–93. Directeur des Études Associé, École des Hautes Études en Sciences Sociales, Paris, 1986; Vis. Prof. of Medieval Hist., Harvard Univ., 1989–90. Mem., NYO, 1951–53. Dir and Trustee, Magdalena Consort, 2010–17. Gov., Bedales Sch., 1986–94. *Publications:* Reason and Society in the Middle Ages, 1978; The Violent Against Themselves, 1998; (ed) Sir William Jones, 1998; The Curse on Self-Murder, 2000; Doubting Thomas in Medieval Exegesis and Art, 2006; Conscience and Authority in the Medieval Church (essays), 2015; contrib. learned jls and collections. *Recreations:* music, walking. *Address:* University College, Oxford OX1 4BH.

**MURRAY, Sir Andrew (Barron),** Kt 2017; OBE 2013; professional tennis player, since 2005; *b* Dunblane, Scotland, 15 May 1987; *s* of William Murray and Judy Murray; *m* 2015, Kim Sears; two *d*. Winner: singles titles: San Jose, 2006, 2007; St Petersburg, 2007, 2008; ATP Masters Series Madrid, 2008, 2015; ATP Masters Series Cincinnati, 2008, 2011; Marseille, 2008; Doha, 2008, 2009; Valencia, 2009, 2014; ATP World Tour Masters 1000 Canada, 2009, 2010; Queen's, London, 2009, 2011, 2013, 2015, 2016; ATP World Tour Masters 1000 Miami, 2009, 2013; Rotterdam, 2009; ATP World Tour Masters 1000 Shanghai, 2010, 2011, 2016; Tokyo, 2011; Bangkok, 2011; Brisbane, 2012, 2013; US Open, 2012; Wimbledon, 2013, 2016; Shenzhen Open, 2014; Vienna, 2014, 2016; Munich, 2015; Italian Open, 2016; China Open, 2016; ATP World Tour Masters 1000 Paris, 2016; Barclays ATP World Tour Finals, London, 2016; doubles titles: Valencia, 2010; Tokyo, 2011; Queen's, London, 2019. Gold Medal, Men's Singles, Silver Medal, Mixed Doubles, London Olympics, 2012; Gold Medal, Men's Singles, Rio de Janeiro Olympics, 2016. Mem., winning GB Davis Cup team, 2015. Ranked No 1, ATP World Tour rankings, 2016. BBC Sports Personality of the Year, 2013, 2015, 2016. *Publications:* Andy Murray: seventy-seven: my road to Wimbledon glory, 2013. *Address:* c/o Matt Gentry, 77 Sports Management, Chester House, Fulham Green, 81–83 Fulham High Street, SW6 3JA. *T:* 07736 300694.

**MURRAY, Andrew Robin;** HM Diplomatic Service, retired; Ambassador to Uruguay, 1998–2001; *b* 21 Sept. 1941; *s* of Robert Alexander Murray and Jean Agnes Murray (*née* Burnett); *m* 1965, Irene Dorothy Foy; one *s* one *d*. *Educ:* Glenalmond; Edinburgh Univ. (MA Hons 1965). Economist with Govt of Ontario, Canada, 1966; investment analyst, ICFC, 1969; joined HM Diplomatic Service, 1973; First Sec., Islamabad, 1975–78; Head of Chancery, Buenos Aires, 1979–81; FCO, 1982–84; Counsellor, UKMIS to UN, 1984–88; Counsellor and Dep. Head of Mission, Caracas, 1988–91; FCO, 1991–93; Counsellor (Econ. and Commercial), Stockholm, 1993–97. *Recreation:* sporadic sport.

**MURRAY, Anil Peter;** His Honour Judge Murray; a Circuit Judge, since 2015; *b* Sunderland, 25 Nov. 1966; *s* of Thomas Edward Murray and Margaret Rose Murray; *m* 1991, Elizabeth Tansey; two *d*. *Educ:* Hull Univ. (LLB Hons). Called to the Bar, Middle Temple, 1989; in practice as barrister specialising in criminal law, 1989–2015; a Recorder, 2012–15. *Recreations:* sailing, walking. *Address:* Liverpool Crown Court, Queen Elizabeth II Law Courts, Derby Square, Liverpool L2 1XA.

**MURRAY, Ann,** Hon. DBE 2002; mezzo-soprano; *b* Dublin, 27 Aug. 1949; *m* 1981, Philip Gordon Langridge, CBE (*d* 2010); one *s*. *Educ:* Royal Manchester Coll. of Music. Roles include: *for English National Opera:* Ariodante; Beatrice; Charlotte; Rosina; Xerxes; *for Royal Opera:* Cherubino; Composer; Donna Elvira; Dorabella; Idamante; Marcellina; Mrs Grose in The Turn of the Screw; Oktavian; The Witch in Hansel und Gretel; *other roles:* Cecilio; Cenerentola; Countess in The Queen of Spades; Iphigénie; Nicklausse; Sextus. Many recitals and concerts (European recital tours, 1990, 1993, 1994); festival appearances incl. Aldeburgh, Edinburgh, Munich, Salzburg, Glyndebourne. Prof. of Singing, RAM, 2010–. Hon. FRAM 1999. Hon. DMus NUI, 1997. *Address:* c/o Askonas Holt Ltd, 15 Fetter Lane, EC4A 1BW.

**MURRAY, Christine;** Editor-in-chief, The Developer, since 2018; *b* Oakville, Ont, 16 Nov. 1977; *d* of Norman Murray and Nerina Murray; *m* 2007, Richard Marks; one *s* one *d*. *Educ:* Univ. of Toronto (BA Eng. Lit. 2000); Concordia Univ., Montreal (MA Eng. Lit. and Creative Writing 2005). Res. Asst, Flare mag., 2000–01; Actg Editl Asst, i-D mag., 2001–03; Montreal Correspondent, Fashion Qly, 2003–05; Ukula Magazine: Fashion and Design Editor, 2005–07; Editl Dir, 2007; Architects' Journal: Sen. Editor, The Critics, 2007–08; Dep. Editor, 2008–10; Editor, 2010–15; Editor, The Architectural Review, 2015–16; Content Dir, Drapers and Retail Jeweller, 2016; Editor-in-Chief, The Architectural Review and The Architects' Jl, 2016–18. FRSA. Hon. FRIBA 2017. *Recreations:* writing, fact collecting, reading and chasing the horizon. *E:* tcmurray@gmail.com.

**MURRAY, Clare Mary;** Founder and Managing Partner, CM Murray LLP, since 2006; *b* Hartlepool, 22 Jan. 1969; *d* of Aidan and Margaret Murray; *m* 2007, Klayton Palmer; one *s* one *d*. *Educ:* St Joseph's RC Sch., Hebburn, Tyne and Wear; St Anthony's RC Girls' Sch., Sunderland; Queen Mary and Westfield Coll., Univ. of London (LLB Hons 1990); Graduate, Goldman Sachs 10,000 Small Businesses Prog., 2017. Trainee, then Asst Solicitor, Eversheds (James & Lewis), 1991–96; Asst Solicitor, then Partner, Fox Williams, 1996–2005; Specialist Advr, Women and Equalities Select Cttee, Sexual Harassment in the Workplace Inquiry, H of C, 2018–19. *Publications:* (contrib.) The Law of Limited Liability Partnerships. *Recreations:* theatre, music, cinema, Scrabble. *Address:* CM Murray LLP, 36–38 Cornhill, EC3V 3NG. *T:* (020) 7933 9133, 07957 383079. *E:* clare.murray@cm-murray.com.

**MURRAY, Craig John;** writer and broadcaster; *b* 17 Oct. 1958; *s* of Robert Cameron Brunton Murray and Poppy Katherine Murray (*née* Grice); *m* 1st, 1984, Fiona Ann Kennedy (marr. diss. 2008); one *s* one *d*; 2nd, 2009, Nadira Alieva; one *s*. *Educ:* Paston Grammar Sch.; Univ. of Dundee (MA Hons). HM Diplomatic Service, 1984–2004: Second Sec., Lagos, 1986–89; FCO, 1990–94; First Sec., Warsaw, 1994–98; FCO, 1998–99; Dep. High Comr, Ghana, 1999–2002; Ambassador to Republic of Uzbekistan, 2002–04. Rector, Dundee Univ., 2007–10. Hon. Res. Fellow, Sch. of Law, Univ. of Lancaster, 2006–10. Contested: (Ind.) Blackburn, 2005; (Put an Honest Man into Parliament) Norwich North, July 2009. *Publications:* Murder in Samarkand, 2006; Dirty Diplomacy, 2007; Influence Not Power, 2007; The Catholic Orangemen of Togo, 2008; Sikunder Burnes: master of the great game, 2015. *Recreations:* drinking, gossiping, reading, Celtic music, football, cricket. *Address:* 63 Oxgangs Road, Edinburgh EH10 7BD. *W:* www.craigmurray.org.uk. *Clubs:* Gin Dobry (Poznan); Imperial (Ekaterinburg).

**MURRAY, Dale Jane,** CBE 2013; strategy adviser and non-executive director; *b* Palmerston North, NZ, 15 Jan. 1970; *d* of William Anderson and Beverley Ramsay; *m* 1997, Simon Murray; three *s*. *Educ:* Auckland Inst. of Technol. (Nat. Dip. Accountancy 1992); London Business Sch., Univ. of London (MBA 2001). CA 1993; FCA 2013. Accountant, Price Waterhouse, 1987–92; Manager, Accounting and Admin, BellSouth NZ Ltd, 1992–95; Finance Manager, Pearson Television Ltd, 1995–99; Jt Man. Dir, Omega Logic Ltd, 1999–2003; CEO, Eposs Ltd, 2003–05; business angel investor, 2006–12. Non-executive Director: Sussex Place Ventures, 2012–19; UKTI, 2012–15; BIS, 2013–16; Xero, 2018–; Cranemere Gp, 2019–. Fellow, Coll. of Chartered Accountants Australia and NZ, 2013. *Recreations:* family, ski-ing, cycling, gardening. *E:* info@dalemurray.net.

**MURRAY, Sir David (Edward),** Kt 2007; Chairman, Murray Capital Ltd, since 2012; director of companies; *b* 14 Oct. 1951; *s* of late David Ian Murray and of Roma Murray; *m* 1st, 1972, Louise V. Densley (*d* 1992); two *s*; 2nd, 2011, Kae A. Tinto. *Educ:* Fettes Coll.; Broughton High Sch. Formed: Murray International Metals Ltd, 1976; Murray International Holdings Ltd, 1981, Chm., 1981–2015; Murray Foundn, 1996. Young Scottish Businessman of the Year, 1984. Chairman: UK2000 (Scotland), 1987; Rangers FC, 1988–2002, 2004–09. Gov., Clifton Hall Sch., 1987. DUniv Heriot-Watt, 1986; Dr *hc* Edinburgh, 2008. *Recreations:* watching sport, collecting and producing wine (Chevalier du Tastevin, 2006). *Address:* Murray Capital Ltd, 26 Charlotte Square, Edinburgh EH2 4ET. *T:* (0131) 243 2100.

**MURRAY, David Edward,** FRICS; management consultant, since 1997; Deputy Chief Executive (Property), Crown Estate, 1993–97; *b* 22 Jan. 1944; *s* of late Thomas and Emily Murray; *m* 1968, Barbara Collins, *d* of late Sir Geoffrey and Lady Collins, Dorset; two *s*. *Educ:* Abbotsholme Sch., Derbys; Manor Park Sch., Hants; Hammersmith Sch. of Art & Building. AIQS 1970; Dip. Constr. Econs 1975; FRICS 1983. Sir Robert McAlpine & Sons, 1962–67; Planning & Transportation Dept, GLC, 1968–72; Royal County of

Berkshire: Gp Quantity Surveyor, 1972–77; Co. Quantity Surveyor, 1977–88; Dir of Property, 1988–93. External Examiner: Coll. of Estate Mgt, 1978–92; Univ. of Portsmouth, 1994–98. Pres., Soc. of Chief Quantity Surveyors in Local Govt, 1979; Royal Institution of Chartered Surveyors: Chm., Quantity Surveyor's R&D Cttee, 1983–84; Mem., Divl Council, 1975–; Trng Advr, 1998–; Mem., several panels and wkg parties. *Publications:* Cost Effectiveness in Property Management, 1984; Artificial Intelligence in Property Portfolio Management, 1988; papers on property mgt and procurement to various UK confs. *Recreations:* sport (especially sailing), reading, music. *Address:* Highcroft, 18 Highclere Drive, Camberley, Surrey GU15 1JY. *T:* (01276) 24345. *Club:* Parkstone Yacht (Dorset).

**MURRAY, Rt Rev. David Owen;** Assistant Bishop of Perth, Southern Region, Western Australia, 1991–2006; Director, Centre for Spirituality, St George's Cathedral, Perth, since 2007; *b* 23 Dec. 1940; *s* of George Lawrence Murray and Winifred Eva (*née* Morgan); *m* 1971, Janet Mary Chittleborough; two *s*. *Educ:* Swanbourne State Sch.; Claremont High Sch.; St Michael's House, Crafers, SA (Kelham, Aust.) (ThL 1968). Jun. Postal Officer, 1955; Postal Clerk, 1957–65. Ordained deacon, 1968, priest, 1969; Asst Curate, Bunbury, 1968–70; Rector: Lake Grace, 1970–74; Jerramungup, 1974–79; Mt Barker, 1979–83; Chaplain to the Bishop of Bunbury, 1978–83; Rector: S Perth, 1983–88; Fremantle, 1988–94; Archdeacon of Fremantle, 1988–91; Administrator during Abp's absences, Dio. of Perth, 1995–2006; Protector of The Little Brothers of Francis, Tabulam, NSW, 1996–2006; Coordinator of Archbishop's Spiritual Dirs, Dio. of Perth, 2006–19; permission to officiate, Dio. of Bunbury, WA, 2010–. Perth Diocesan Trustee, 1992–2006. Episcopal Rep. for Australia and NZ Adv. Council to Anglican Religious Communities, 1993–2006; Mem., ANZ Regl Cttee, St George's Coll., Jerusalem, 2000–06. Mem., Governance Cttee and Mgt Council, St Hilda's Anglican Sch. for Girls, Mosman Park, WA, 2002–04; Mem., Council of Mgt, Peter Carnley Anglican Community Sch., 2007–15 (Dep. Chm., 2007–15); Chair: Bldgs and Grounds Cttee, 2008–15; Future Cttee, 2010–15). Mem., Morsecodians Fraternity of WA. *Recreations:* bagpipe playing, bush walking, swimming, cycling, theatre, opera, concerts, reading, entertaining. *Address:* Villa 15, St Mary's Close, 9 Ridge Street, South Perth, WA 6151, Australia.

**MURRAY, Air Vice-Marshal Hon. David Paul,** CVO 2012; OBE 1999 (MBE 1996); Controller, Royal Air Force Benevolent Fund, since 2016; *b* London, 8 April 1960; *s* of Baron Murray of Epping Forest, OBE, PC and of Heather Murray; *m* 1984, Moira Roche; one *s* one *d*. *Educ:* RAF Coll., Cranwell. Commnd RAF, 1980; Stn Comdr, RAF Halton, 2000–02; Comdr, Winchester Garrison and Comdt, Defence Coll. of Police, 2002–05; ACOS Trng, 2006–09; rcds 2009; Hd, Defence Personnel Strategy and Progs, MoD, 2009–10; ACDS (Personnel and Trng) and Defence Services Sec., 2010–12. Controller, SSAFA, 2012–16. *Recreations:* reading, walking, British history and politics. *Address:* Royal Air Force Benevolent Fund, 67 Portland Place, W1B 1AR. *T:* (020) 7307 3301. *E:* david.murray@rafbf.org.uk. *Club:* Royal Air Force.

**MURRAY, Denis James,** OBE 1997; Ireland Correspondent, BBC, 1988–2008; *b* 7 May 1951; *s* of late James and Helen Murray; *m* 1978, Joyce Linehan; two *s* two *d*. *Educ:* St Malachy's Coll., Belfast; Trinity Coll., Dublin (BA Respondency 1993); Queen's Univ., Belfast (HDipEd). Grad. Trainee, then Reporter, Belfast Telegraph, 1975–77; Belfast Reporter, RTE, 1977–82; BBC: Dublin Correspondent, 1982–84; NI Political Correspondent, 1984–88. *Publications:* (contrib.) BBC Guide to 1997 General Election, 1997. *Recreations:* music, reading, sport, family!

**MURRAY, Diana Mary,** CBE 2019; FSA; FSAScot; FRSE, FRSGS; Senior Executive, Historic Environment Scotland, 2015–16; *b* 14 Sept. 1952; *d* of Keith and Mary Collyer; *m* 1987, Robin Murray; two *d*. *Educ:* King Edward VI Camp Hill Sch. for Girls, Birmingham; Univ. of Cambridge (MA 1974). MCIfA (MIFA 1984); FSAScot 1977; FSA 1986. Royal Commission on the Ancient and Historical Monuments of Scotland: Res. Asst, 1976–83; Hd, NMRS recording section, 1983–90; Curator of Archaeology Record, 1990–95; Curator Depute, NMRS, 1995–2004; Sec., Royal Commn on Ancient and Histl Monuments of Scotland, 2004–15. Chm., Inst. of Field Archaeologists, 1995–96. Trustee: Nat. Trust for Scotland, 2011–14; Royal Botanic Garden Edinburgh, 2014–; Scottish Waterways Trust, 2014–18; Scottish Seabird Centre, 2014–; Scottish Internat. Educn Trust, 2015–; Arts and Business Scotland, 2016– (Chair, 2016–); Chair, Scottish Assoc. of Marine Sci., 2019–. JP E Lothian, 2000–07. FRSGS 2016; FRSE 2016. *Recreations:* choral singing, gardening. *Address:* The Rowans, 15 Manse Road, Dirleton, East Lothian EH39 5EL. *E:* diana.murray@rowanberry.co.uk.

**MURRAY, Duncan Law;** Sheriff Principal of North Strathclyde, since 2014; *b* 5 May 1959; *s* of James Duncan Murray and Catherine Margaret Law or Murray; *m* 1988, Ianthe Elizabeth Lee Craig; two *s* one *d*. *Educ:* Aberdeen Grammar Sch.; Aberdeen Univ. (LLB Hons 1980). Robson McLean Paterson: apprentice, 1980–82; Asst, 1982–85; Partner, Robson McLean, 1985–2002; Partner, 2002–14, Chief Exec., 2011–13, Morton Fraser, Solicitors. Part-time Sheriff, 2006–14. Pres., Law Soc. of Scotland, 2004–05. *Recreations:* golf, ski-ing, hill-walking, family. *Address:* Sheriff Court House, St James Street, Paisley PA3 2HW. *T:* (0141) 847 6746, *Fax:* (0141) 889 1748. *Club:* Luffness New Golf.

**MURRAY, Hon. Sir Edward (Henry),** Kt 2018; **Hon. Mr Justice Murray;** a Judge of the High Court, Queen's Bench Division, since 2018; *b* Washington, DC, 4 May 1958; *s* of Joseph Murray and Margaret Murray (*née* Gibson); *m* 1984, Andrea Stang (marr. diss. 2018); one *d*. *Educ:* St Anselm's Abbey Sch.; Trinity Coll., Dublin (MA 1980). Harvard Law Sch. (JD *cum laude* 1985). Admitted to the Bar, State of NY, 1986; Associate, Sidley & Austin, 1986–90; admitted as solicitor, 1992; Allen & Overy: Associate, 1990–93; Partner, 1993–2013; Consultant, 2013–18; Recorder, 2009–18; Dep. High Court Judge, 2013–18. Bencher, Middle Temple, 2018. Vis. Lectr, then Vis. Professorial Fellow, 2004–16, Vis. Prof., 2016–18, Centre for Commercial Law Studies, QMUL; Vis. Lectr, Univ. Panthéon-Assas (Paris II), 2002–18. Member: Treasury Banking Liaison Panel, 2009–13; Panel of Recognised Internat. Mkt Experts in Finance, 2012–18. Mem., Forum Gp on Collateral, EC, 1999–2000. Counsel, City of London Jt Wkg Gp on Eur. Monetary Union Legislation, 1997–98. Mem., Adv. Cttee, Commercial Law Centre, Harris Manchester Coll., Oxford, 2014–. Member, Editorial Board: Capital Mkts Law Jl, 2006–; Law and Financial Mkts Rev., 2007–18. *Publications:* (ed jtly) A History of the Dublin University Cricket Club, 1982; contrib. articles and book chapters on financial law topics. *Recreations:* music, language learning, film, reading, travel, tennis. *Address:* Royal Courts of Justice, Strand, WC2A 2LL. *Clubs:* City University, Roehampton; Harvard (New York City).

**MURRAY, Elaine Kildare,** PhD; Member (Lab) and Leader, Dumfries and Galloway Council, since 2017; *b* 22 Dec. 1954; *d* of Kenneth and Patricia Murray; *m* 1986, Jeffrey Leaver; two *s* one *d*. *Educ:* Edinburgh Univ. (BSc 1st Cl. Hons Chemistry); Cambridge Univ. (PhD Physical Chemistry 1980). Res. Fellow, Cavendish Lab., Cambridge, 1979–82; Researcher, Royal Free Hosp., London, 1982–84; SSO, Inst. of Food Res., Reading, 1984–87; Asst to Alex Smith, MEP, 1990–93; Associate Lectr, Open Univ., 1992–99. MSP (Lab): Dumfries, 1999–2011; Dumfriesshire, 2011–16. Scottish Executive: Dep. Minister for Tourism, Culture and Sport, 2001–03; Shadow Minister for Enterprise, 2007–08, for Envmt, 2008–11, for Rural Affairs and Envmt, 2011–12, for Housing and Transport, 2012–14, for Community Safety, 2014–16. Scottish Parliament: Vice Convener, Finance Cttee, 2007–08; Mem., Rural Affairs, Climate Change and Envmt Cttee (formerly Rural Affairs and Envmt Cttee), 2008–11; Mem. Finance Cttee, 2012–13; Mem., Infrastructure and Capital Investment Cttee, 2013–14; Vice Convenor, Justice Cttee, 2014–16. Contested (Lab) Dumfriesshire, Scottish Parlt, 2016. *Recreations:* cooking, spending time with my family and pets, exercise, music, reading, gardening.

**MURRAY, Gordon;** *see* Murray, I. G.

**MURRAY, Prof. Gordon Cameron,** RIBA; PPRIAS; Partner, Ryder Architecture (formerly Director, GMA Ryder), since 2012; Professor of Architecture and Urban Design, University of Strathclyde, 2007–15 (Visiting Professor, 2002–07 and since 2016; Head, School of Architecture and Building Science, 2007–12); *b* 26 July 1952; *s* of James and Jessie Murray; *m* 1975, Sharon Boyle; two *d*. *Educ:* Univ. of Strathclyde (BSc, BArch). MCIArb; RIBA 1988; MRTPI 2010; FRIAS. Assistant Architect: Richard Moira, Betty Moira & James Wann, 1974; Dept of Architecture and Related Services, 1975–77; Project Architect, Sinclair and Watt Architects, 1978–79; Sen. Architect, Cunningham Glass Partnership, 1979–87; Partner: Cunningham Glass Murray Architects, 1987–92; Glass Murray Architects, 1992–99; Partner, Gordon Murray + Alan Dunlop Architects, 2000–10; Principal, Gordon Murray Architects, 2010–12. External Examiner: Univ. of Ulster, 2004–08, Univ. of Bath, 2011–15; Univ. of Manchester, 2015–; Univ. of Dundee, 2016–. Panel Mem., Architecture and Design Scotland, 2007–. Chairman: Technologies' Excellence Gp, Curriculum for Excellence, 2009–10; Standing Council of Hds of UK Schs of Architecture, 2010–12. President: Glasgow Inst. of Architects, 1998–2000; RIAS, 2003–05. Mem. Bd, Lighthouse Trust, 2003–09. *Publications:* An Integrated Transport System for Greater Glasgow, 1977; (with A. Sloan) James Miller, Architect: a monograph, 1990; (contrib.) Challenging Contextualism: the work of gm+ad architects, 2002; Curious Rationalism, 2006; (contrib.) Adaptive Architecture: changing parameters and practice, 2017; (contrib.) Defining Contemporary Professionalism: for architects in practice and education, 2019. *Recreations:* cinema, art, saxophone, jazz, travel, books. *Address:* Ryder Architecture, 221 West George Street, Glasgow G2 2ND. *T:* (0141) 285 0230. *E:* gmurray@ryderarchitecture.com.

**MURRAY, Ian;** MP (Lab) Edinburgh South, since 2010; *b* Edinburgh, 10 Aug. 1976; *s* of James Brownlie Murray and Lena Murray. *Educ:* Wester Hailes Educn Centre; Univ. of Edinburgh (MA Hons Social Policy and Law). Investment Administrator: WM Co., 1998; AEGON UK, 1998–99; Dir, Ops, Worldart.com, 2000–02; Dir, 100mph Events Ltd, 2002–; Partner, Alibi Bars LLP, 2005–11. Mem. (Lab) Edinburgh CC, 2003–10. PPS to Shadow Sec. of State for Culture, Media and Sport, 2010–11; Shadow Minister for Employee Relns, Postal and Consumer Affairs, 2011–13, for Trade and Investment (incl. Employment Relns and Postal Affairs), 2013–15; Shadow Sec. of State for Scotland, 2015–16. Member: Business, Innovation and Skills Select Cttee, 2010–11; Envmtl Audit Select Cttee, 2010–12; Foreign Affairs Select Cttee, 2016–; Scottish Affairs Select Cttee, 2016–17. *Address:* (office) 31 Minto Street, Edinburgh EH9 2BT. *T:* (0131) 662 4520, *Fax:* (0131) 662 1990. *E:* ian.murray.mp@parliament.uk.

**MURRAY, (Ian) Gordon,** CBE 2019; Chief Executive Officer and Technical Director, Gordon Murray Design Ltd, since 2007; *b* 18 June 1946; *s* of William and Roma Murray; *m* 1970, Stella Gane; one *s*. *Educ:* Natal Tech. Coll., SA. Moved to England, 1969, to work in motor racing; joined Brabham, 1970: design draughtsman, 1970–73; Chief Designer, 1973–74; Technical Dir, 1974–86 (design innovations incl. fan car, 1978, and hydro-pneumatic suspension, 1981; 22 Grand Prix wins; 2 World Drivers' Formula 1 Championships, first turbo-powered World Championship, 1983); Technical Dir, McLaren Internat., 1986–90 (29 Grand Prix wins; 2 World Drivers' Formula 1 Championships; 2 World Formula 1 Constructors' Championships); Technical Dir, McLaren Cars Ltd, 1990–2004: designed and prod McLaren F1 road car (Fastest Road Car, 1992; GTR version won 2 championships, and Le Mans 1995). Hon. Prof., Durban Inst. of Technology, 2003–. John Bolster Award, Autosport Awards for Technical Achievement, 2014. *Recreations:* motor-cycles, music, food and fine wine, architecture. *Address:* Gordon Murray Design Ltd, Wharfside, Broadford Park, Shalford, Surrey GU4 8EP.

**MURRAY, Irena, (Mrs Eric Ormsby),** PhD; Sir Banister Fletcher Director (formerly Librarian), British Architectural Library, Royal Institute of British Architects, 2004–13, now Senior Research Fellow; *b* 3 July 1946; *d* of Jiri and Hana Žantovský; *m* 1995, Dr Eric Ormsby; two step *s*. *Educ:* Charles Univ., Prague (BA 1968); Univ. of Western Ontario, London (MLS 1970); Ecole des Chartes, Paris; McGill Univ., Montreal (MArch 1991; PhD 2003). Bibliographer, Nat. Liby of Canada, 1972; Curator, Nat. Archives of Canada, 1973; McGill University: Librarian, 1973–80; Dir, Art and Arch. Liby, 1981–96; Chief Curator, Rare Books and Special Collections, 1996–2004. FRSA. Hon. FRIBA 2014. *Publications:* (ed) Moshe Safdie: buildings and projects 1967–1992, 1996; (trans.) Karel Teige, Modern Architecture in Czechoslovakia, 2000; (ed) Looking at European Architecture, 2007; (ed) Le Corbusier and Britain, 2008; (ed) Palladio and His Legacy: a transatlantic journey, 2010. *Recreations:* reading, writing, walking. *Address:* c/o Royal Institute of British Architects, 66 Portland Place, W1B 1AD. *T:* (020) 7307 3644, *Fax:* (020) 7307 3719.

**MURRAY, Prof. James Dickson,** FRS 1985; FRSE 1979; Professor of Mathematical Biology, 1986–92, now Emeritus Professor, and Director, Centre for Mathematical Biology, 1983–92, University of Oxford; Professorial Fellow, 1986–92, Hon. Fellow, 2000, Corpus Christi College, Oxford; Senior Scholar, Princeton University, 2010–19; *b* 2 Jan. 1931; *s* of Peter and Sarah Murray; *m* 1959, Sheila (*née* Campbell); one *s* one *d*. *Educ:* Dumfries Acad.; Univ. of St Andrews (BSc 1953; Carstairs Medal; Miller Prize; PhD 1956); Univ. of Oxford (MA 1961; DSc 1968). FRSB (FIBiol 1988); FIMA 2009. Lectr, Applied Maths, King's Coll., Durham Univ., 1955–56; Gordon MacKay Lectr and Res. Fellow, Tutor in Applied Maths, Leverett House, Harvard, 1956–59; Lectr, Applied Maths, UCL, 1959–61; Fellow and Tutor in Maths, Hertford College, Oxford, 1961–63; Res. Associate, Harvard, 1963–64; Prof. of Engineering Mechanics, Univ. of Michigan, 1964–67; Prof. of Maths, New York Univ., 1967–70; Fellow and Tutor in Maths, 1969–85, Sen. Res. Fellow, 1985–86, Corpus Christi Coll., Oxford; Reader in Maths, Univ. of Oxford, 1972–86. Vis. Fellow, St Catherine's Coll., Oxford, 1967; Guggenheim Fellow, Pasteur Inst., Paris, 1968; Visiting Professor: Nat. Tsing Hua Univ., 1975; Univ. of Florence, 1976; MIT, 1979; Winegard Prof., Univ. of Guelph, 1979; Univ. of Utah, 1979, 1985; Ida Beam Prof., Univ. of Iowa, 1980; Univ. of Heidelberg, 1980; CIT, 1983; Univ. of Angers, 1993; La Chaire Européenne, Univ. of Paris, 1994, 1995, 1996; Stan Ulam Vis. Schol., Univ. of Calif. Berkeley's Los Alamos Nat. Lab., 1985; Philip Prof., 1988–94, Boeing Prof., 1997–2000, Prof. Emeritus, 2000, Univ. of Washington (endowed Chair, James D. Murray Prof. of Applied Maths and Neuropathol., est. in perpetuity in his honour, 2007); Hon. Prof., City Univ. of Hong Kong, 2013–. Lectures: Scott Hawkins, Southern Methodist Univ., Dallas, 1984; Lansdowne, Univ. of Victoria, 1990; Pinkham, Swedish Hosp., Seattle, 1992 and 1998; Dist. Lecture Series, Emory Univ., 1992; Curle, Univ. of St Andrews, 1994; Smith, St Catherine's Coll., Oxford, 1994; Class of '62, Williams Coll., 1995; Faculty, 1998, Boeing Distinguished, 2011, Univ. of Washington, 1998; Bakerian, Royal Soc., 2009; Rees, Univ. of Delaware, 2009; Sears, Woods Hole Oceanographic Inst., 2010; Leonardo da Vinci Prize Lectr and Medal, Eur. Acad. of Scis, Milan, 2011; Turing Centenary Conf., Microsoft Res. Lectr, Univ. of Cambridge, and Plenary Lectr, Univ. of Princeton, 2012;

Inaugural Hooke, Univ. of Oxford, 2014; 21st Anniversary Pekeris, Weizmann Inst., 2014. Math. Comr, SERC, 1985–88; Founding Pres., European Soc. for Mathematical and Theoretical Biol., 1991–94; Member: Bd of Dirs, Soc. for Mathematical Biol., USA, 1986–89; ESF Network Cttee, 1991–94. For. Mem., Acad. des Scis, France, 2000; Hon. Mem., Edinburgh Mathematical Soc., 2008. Hon. DSc: St Andrews, 1994; Strathclyde, 1999; Hon. Dr Math: Milan, 2004; Waterloo, 2006; Hon. LLD Dundee, 2011. Naylor Lect. and Prize in Applied Math., London Math. Soc., 1989; Akira Okubo Prize, Soc. for Mathematical Biol., USA, 2005; Gold Medal, IMA, 2009; William Benter Prize in Applied Maths, City Univ. of Hong Kong, 2012. *Publications:* Asymptotic Analysis, 1974, 3rd edn 1996; Nonlinear Differential Equation Models in Biology, 1977 (trans. Russian 1983); (ed with S. Brenner and L. Wolpert) Theories of Biological Pattern Formation, 1981; (ed with W. Jäger) Modelling of Patterns in Space and Time, 1984; Mathematical Biology, 1989, 3rd edn in 2 vols, vol. I 2002 (trans. Polish 2006, Russian 2009, Chinese 2016, Japanese 2017), vol. II 2003 (trans. Russian 2010, Chinese 2016); (ed with H. G. Othmer and P. K. Maini) Experimental and Theoretical Advances in Biological Pattern Formation, 1993; (jtly) The Mathematics of Marriage, 2002; My Gift of Polio: an unexpected life from the rural hills of Scotland to the hallowed halls of Oxford and beyond (memoir), 2018; several hundred articles in learned jls on the application of maths in biomed. scis.

**MURRAY, Janice;** Director General (formerly Director), National Army Museum, 2010–17; *b* Newcastle-upon-Tyne, 15 Aug. 1957; *d* of Harold and Irene Blair; *m* 1st, 1982, Terence Christopher Murray (*d* 2000); two *s*; 2nd, 2004, David John Stockdale. *Educ:* Dame Allan's Girls' Sch.; Univ. of Warwick (BA Hons Hist.); Univ. of Leicester (Postgrad. Cert. Mus. Studies). Curator, Mus. and Art Gall., St Helen's, 1982–86; Keeper of Human Hist., Dundee Art Galls and Museums, 1986–96; Arts and Heritage Manager, Dundee CC, 1996–2002; Dep. Hd, Nat. Rlwy Mus., York, 2002–08; Chief Exec., Royal Armouries, 2009–10. Mem. Bd, Internat. Cttee of Museums and Collections of Arms and Military History, 2013–. Trustee, Bowes Mus., 2019–. Mem., Co. of Merchant Adventurers of City of York, 2019–. FRSA. *Recreations:* gardening, hardy plants, contemporary glass, bagging bargains. *E:* murray.stockdale@icloud.com.

**MURRAY, Dame Jennifer Susan, (Dame Jenni),** DBE 2011 (OBE 1999); Presenter, Woman's Hour, BBC Radio 4, since 1987; *b* 12 May 1950; *d* of Alvin Bailey and Win Bailey (*née* Jones); *m* 1971, Brian Murray (marr. diss. 1978); partner, David Forgham-Bailey; two *s*. *Educ:* Barnsley Girls' High Sch.; Hull Univ. (BA Hons French/Drama). BBC Radio Bristol, 1973–78; BBC TV South, 1978–82; BBC Newsnight, 1982–85; BBC Radio 4 Today, 1985–87. Vis. Prof., London Inst., 2000–. TV documentaries include: Everyman: Stand By Your Man, 1987, Breaking the Chain, 1988, As We Forgive Them, 1989; The Duchy of Cornwall, 1985, Women in Politics, 1989; Here's Looking At You, 1991; Presenter: Points of View, 1993; This Sunday, 1993–95; Dilemmas, 1994; The Turning World, 1998–2001; The Message, BBC Radio 4, 2001. Weekly columnist, The Express, 1998–2000. Pres., Fawcett Soc., 2001–; Patron: FPA, 2002–; Breast Cancer Campaign; non-exec. Dir, The Christie, 2011–14. Hon. DLitt Bradford, 1994; DUniv Open, 1999; Hon. Dr: Sheffield; Bristol; St Andrews; Huddersfield; Salford. *Publications:* The Woman's Hour Book of Humour, 1993; The Woman's Hour: a history of British women 1946–1996, 1996; Is It Me Or Is It Hot In Here, 2001; That's My Boy!, 2003; Memoirs of a Not So Dutiful Daughter, 2008; My Boy Butch, 2011; A History of Britain in 21 Women, 2016; Fat Cow, Fat Chance, 2020; Votes for Women!: the pioneers and heroines of female suffrage, 2018; contrib. to newspapers and periodicals. *Recreations:* reading, theatre, riding. *Address:* c/o Woman's Hour, BBC, Broadcasting House, Portland Place, W1A 1AA. *T:* (020) 7765 4314.

**MURRAY, Prof. John Joseph,** CBE 1997; PhD; FDSRCS; FMedSci; Dean of Dentistry, University of Newcastle upon Tyne, 1992–2002, now Professor Emeritus; Clinical Director, Dental Hospital, Royal Victoria Infirmary NHS Trust, Newcastle upon Tyne, 1995–2002; *b* 28 Dec. 1941; *s* of late John Gerald Murray, Bradford, and Margaret Sheila (*née* Parle); *m* 1967, Valerie (*d* 2002), *d* of late Harry and Lillie Aiden; two *s*. *Educ:* St Bede's Grammar Sch., Bradford; Univ. of Leeds (BChD 1966; MChD 1968; PhD 1970); FDSRCS 1973; MCCDRCS 1989. Res. Fellow in Children's and Preventive Dentistry, Leeds Univ., 1966–70; Sen. Lectr in Children's Dentistry, 1970–75, Reader, 1975–77, Inst. of Dental Surgery, London; University of Newcastle upon Tyne: Prof. of Child Dental Health, 1977–92; Dental Postgrad. Sub-Dean, 1982–92. Chm., Cleft Lip and Palate Cttee, Clinical Standards Adv. Gp, 1998. Chm., Educn Cttee, GDC, 1999–2003. Mem., Children's Task Force, DoH, 2002–05. Chm., Multi-professional Postgrad. Dental Educn Cttee, Northern Deanery, NHS North East, 2007–14. Founder FMedSci 1998. Hon. MFPHM 1998. John Tomes Medal, BDA, 1993; H. Trendley Dean Award, Internat. Assoc. Dental Res., 1997; Colyer Gold Medal, RCS, 1999. *Publications:* (jtly) The Acid Etch Technique in Paedodontics and Orthodontics, 1985; Fluorides in Caries Prevention, 1976, 3rd edn (jtly) 1991; Appropriate Use of Fluorides for Human Health, 1985; The Prevention of Dental Disease, 1983, 4th edn 2003 as The Prevention of Oral Disease. *Recreations:* bridge, Newcastle United Football Club, golf, photography. *Address:* 6 Regency Way, Darras Hall, Ponteland, Newcastle upon Tyne NE20 9AU. *T:* (01661) 871035. *Club:* Ponteland Golf (Capt. 2006; Chm., 2007–10; Pres., 2018–).

**MURRAY, John Loyola; Hon. Mr Justice John Murray;** Chief Justice of Ireland, 2004–11; Senior Ordinary Judge, Supreme Court of Ireland, 2011–15; Chancellor, University of Limerick, 2013–17; *b* 27 June 1943; *s* of Cecil Murray and Catherine (*née* Casey); *m* 1969, Gabrielle Walsh; one *s* one *d*. *Educ:* Crescent Coll.; Rockwell Coll.; University Coll. Dublin and King's Inns (Barrister-at-Law). Called to the Bar, Supreme Court, Ireland, 1967, Bencher, 1985; called to the Inner Bar, 1981; Attorney Gen. of Ireland, Aug.–Dec. 1982; in private practice at the Bar of Ireland, 1982–87; Attorney Gen., 1987–91; Judge of Court of Justice of European Union, 1991–99; Judge, Supreme Court of Ireland, 1999–2015. Mem., Council of State, 1982, 1987–91, 2004–. Vis. Lectr, Georgetown Univ. Summer Sch., Heidelberg and Florence, 1994–2002; Vis. Prof. of Law, Univ. of Louvain, 1997–2000; Adjunct Prof. of Law, Univ. of Limerick, 2012–13. Hon. Co-chair, Internat. Law Inst., Washington, 1996–. Chairman: Bd, Courts Service, 2004–11; Judicial Appts Adv. Bd, 2004–11. Chairperson: Anti-Fraud Cttee, Eur. Central Bank, 2000–03; Ethical Cttee, EC, 2004–07. Governor: Marsh's Liby, Dublin, 2004–11; St Patrick's Hosp., Dublin, 2004–11. Hon. LLD: Limerick, 1993; New England Sch. of Law, 2006; Hon. Dr Wake Forest, NC, 2014. Grand Cross, OM (Luxembourg), 1991. *Publications:* legal articles in law jls and other pubns. *Clubs:* Athenæum; Fitzwilliam Lawn Tennis (Dublin); Royal Irish Yacht.

**MURRAY, Kevin;** executive leadership coach, communications adviser, author and speaker; Special Adviser, Chime Communications, since 2018; *b* Bulawayo, Rhodesia, 9 June 1954; *s* of Ian and Shirley Murray; *m* 1978, Elisabeth Anne Mary Whalley; one *s* one *d*. *Educ:* Hyde Park High Sch., Johannesburg. The Star, Johannesburg: court reporter and crime reporter, 1973–76; Foreign corresp., Argus Co., London, 1977–78; Air corresp. and Transport Ed., 1978–80; News Ed., 1980–81; Gp Pubns Ed. and PR Exec., Barlow Rd Ltd, Johannesburg, 1981–82; Man. Ed., Leadership SA Mag., 1982–83; Dir, Mktg and Advertising, Churchill Murray Pubns, Johannesburg, 1984–85; Managing Director: Kestrel Pubns, 1985–87; Shearwater Communications, 1987–88; Gp Public Relns Manager, Bayer plc, UK, 1988–92; Director: Corporate Communications, UKAEA, 1992–94; Corporate Affairs, AEA Technol., 1994–96; of Communications, British Airways, 1996–98; Sen. Consultant, 1998–99, Man. Dir, 1999–2002, Bell Pottinger Consultants; Chief Exec., 2002–05, Chm., 2005–12, Bell Pottinger Gp; Chm., Good Relations Gp, 2012–17. FCIPR 2005. *Publications:* The Language of Leaders, 2011; Communicate to Inspire: a guide for leaders, 2015; Blood of the Rose (novel), 2014; People with Purpose, 2017; The Charismatic Leader, 2020. *Recreations:* golf, cinema, walking, cycling. *Address:* Kevin Murray & Co, Beechwood House, Slade End, Brightwell-cum-Sotwell OX10 0RD. *T:* (01491) 825816. *E:* kevin@kevinmurrayandco.com. *Club:* Frilford Heath Golf (Dir, 2016–).

**MURRAY, Prof. Leo Gerard;** Director, Cranfield School of Management, 1986–2003; *b* 21 May 1943; *s* of Patrick and Teresa Murray; *m* 1970, Pauline Ball; one *s* one *d*. *Educ:* St Aloysius' Coll., Glasgow; Univ. of Rennes; Glasgow Univ. (MA Hons 1965). British Petroleum Co., 1965–67; Courtaulds Gp, 1968–75; A. T. Kearney Ltd, 1975–79; Rothmans International Ltd, 1979–86: Man. Dir, Murray Sons & Co. Ltd, 1979–82; Dir, Overseas Mfg and Licensing, 1982–85; Dir, ME Region, 1985–86. Pro Vice-Chancellor, Cranfield Inst. of Technology, then Univ., 1992–95. Mem., Textile Sector Gp, NEDO, 1987–88. Chairman: ICL Cranfield Business Games Ltd, 1987–92; Cranfield Conference Centre, 1993–2003; Man. Dir, Cranfield Management Develt Ltd, 1993–2003; Chm., Fairways Solicitors, 2001–03. Board Member: E of England Develt Agency, 2000–06; E of England Internat., 2004–06. Non-exec. Dir, Spectris plc, 2003–06. Director and Treasurer: Council of Univ. Management Schs, 1987–92; Assoc. of Business Schs, 1992–93 and 1999–2003; Bd Mem., Eur. Foundn for Mgt Develt, 2000–03; Membre: Conseil d'Orientation, Ecole Internat. d'Affaires, Marseilles, 1988–91; Conseil d'Admin, Univ. Technique de Compiègne, 1996–99; Conseil d'Admin, Reims Mgt Sch., France, 2009–12; Internat. Adv. Bd, Lingnan University Coll., China, 2010–. Vice-Pres., Strategic Planning Soc., 1992–99. Chairman: Bd, Euro-Arab Management Sch., Granada, Spain, 2003–06; Govs, Nat. Centre for Languages, 2004–05. Trustee: Blind in Business, 1992–2005; Macintyre Charitable Trust, 2003–08. FCIM 1988; FRSA 1989; CCMI 2000. *Recreations:* family, golf. *Address:* The Beeches, 2 Church Lane, Lathbury, Bucks MK16 8JY. *T:* (01908) 615574. *Club:* Woburn Golf and Country.

**MURRAY, Michael Thomas;** HM Diplomatic Service, retired; *b* 13 Oct. 1945; *s* of late Robert Murray and Anne Clark Murray (*née* Leech); *m* 1968, Else Birgitta Margareta Paues; one *s* one *d*. *Educ:* Bedlington Grammar Sch. Joined FO, 1964; DSAO, 1964; Prague, 1967; Vienna, 1971; Vice-Consul (Commercial), Frankfurt, 1973; Second Sec. (Develt), Khartoum, 1977; FCO, 1980; First Sec. and Hd of Chancery, Banjul, 1983; FCO, 1988; First Sec. (Develt/Econ.), Lusaka, 1995; on loan to DFID, Lusaka, 1998; Dep. Consul Gen., Chicago, 1999; Ambassador to Eritrea, 2002–06. Member: Cttee, Friends of Bellingham Surgery, 2007–; New Leader Project, Northumberland Uplands Local Action Gp, 2008–. *Recreations:* living lightly; coarse, chemical-free horticulture; my logpile, golf, arts and crafts. *Address:* The Old Rectory, Falstone, Hexham, Northumberland NE48 1AE. *Clubs:* Laholms Golf (Sweden); Hexham Golf.

**MURRAY of Blackbarony, Sir Nigel Andrew Digby,** 15th Bt *cr* 1628; farmer; *b* 15 Aug. 1944; *s* of Sir Alan John Digby Murray of Blackbarony, 14th Bt, and of Mabel Elisabeth, *d* of late Arthur Bernard Schiele, Arias, Argentina; *S* father, 1978; *m* 1980, Diana Margaret, *yr d* of late Robert C. Bray, Arias, Argentina; one *s* two *d*. *Educ:* St Paul's School, Argentina; Salesian Agricl Sch., Argentina; Royal Agricultural Coll., Cirencester. Farms dairy cattle, crops and bees. Lay Minister. *Heir:* *s* Alexander Nigel Robert Murray [*b* 1 July 1981; *m* 2016, Veronica Ines Santana Mackinley. *Educ:* Univs of Buenos Aires and Favaloro]. *Address:* Establecimiento Tinamú, cc 57, 2624 Arias, Provincia de Córdoba, Argentina. *T:* (03468) 441231, 449801.

**MURRAY, Norman Loch,** CA; FRSE; Chairman: Edrington Group Ltd, 2013–17 (Director, 2012–13); Scottish Ballet, since 2013; President, Institute of Chartered Accountants of Scotland, 2006–07; *b* 17 March 1948; *er s* of Thomas Loch Murray and May Fox Murray (*née* Davidson); *m* 1973, Pamela Anne Low; two *s*. *Educ:* George Watson's Coll., Edinburgh; Heriot-Watt Univ. (BA 1971); Harvard Business Sch. (PMD 1987). CA 1976. Grad. trainee, Scottish & Newcastle Breweries, 1971–73; CA apprentice, Arthur Young McLelland Moores & Co., Edinburgh, 1973–76; Dep. Manager, Peat, Marwick, Mitchell & Co., Hong Kong, 1976–80; Asst Lectr, Accountancy and Finance, Heriot-Watt Univ., 1980; Manager, Royal Bank Develt Capital Ltd, 1980–84; Dir, Charterhouse Develt Capital Ltd, 1984–89; Dep. Chief Exec., 1989–96, Chief Exec., 1996–97, Chm., 1998, Morgan Grenfell Private Equity Ltd; Director: Morgan Grenfell & Co. Ltd, 1989–98; Morgan Grenfell Asset Mgt Ltd, 1997–98. Non-executive Director: Taunton Cider Co. Ltd, 1991–93; Bristow Helicopter Gp Ltd, 1991–96; Penta Capital Partners Hldgs Ltd, 1999–2007; Robert Wiseman Dairies plc, 2003–11; Greene King plc, 2004–12; Chm., Cairn Energy plc, 2002–11 (Dir, 1999–2011); Dep. Chm., Cairn India Ltd, 2006–08; Chm., Petrofac Ltd, 2011–14. Mem. Council, 1992–97, Chm., 1997–98, British Venture Capital Assoc. Mem. Council, 1992–98, Sen. Vice-Pres., 2005–06, ICAS (Chm., Ethics Bd, 2015–). Chm., Audit Firm Governance Wkg Gp, Financial Reporting Council, 2008–10 (reported, 2010). Chm., Governing Council, George Watson's Coll., 2004–09 (Gov., 1994–2004). Gov., St Columba's Hospice, 1998–2003 (Chm., Investment Cttee, 1998–2003). Hon. Prof., Heriot-Watt Univ., Edinburgh, 2008–. FRSE 2015; FRSA 2018. *Publications:* (jtly) Making Corporate Reports Valuable, 1988. *Recreations:* climbing and hill walking, classic cars, golf, squash, travel, silviculture, addressing the haggis. *Address:* Ettrick, 8 Pentland Avenue, Colinton, Edinburgh EH13 0HZ. *Clubs:* Harvard Business School of London; New (Edinburgh); Luffness New Golf; Royal Hong Kong Yacht.

**MURRAY, Sir Patrick (Ian Keith),** 12th Bt *cr* 1673; *b* 22 March 1965; *s* of Sir William Patrick Keith Murray, 11th Bt, and of Susan Elizabeth (who *m* 1976, J. C. Hudson, PhD), *d* of Stacey Jones; *S* father, 1977. *Educ:* Christ College, Brecon, Powys; LAMDA. *Heir:* kinsman Major Peter Keith-Murray, Canadian Forces [*b* 12 July 1935; *m* 1960, Judith Anne, *d* of late Andrew Tinsley; one *s* one *d*].

**MURRAY, Rev. Paul B.;** *see* Beasley-Murray.

**MURRAY, Peter,** OBE 2010; FRICS; Founder and Chair: Ormiston Trust, since 1969; Ormiston Academies Trust, since 2009; *b* London, 10 May 1937; *s* of George and Ethel Murray; *m* 1st, Judith (*d* 2007); two *s*; 2nd, 2010, Diana. *Educ:* Ibstock Place Sch.; Canford Sch.; Stanford Univ.; Coll. of Estate Mgt. FRICS. Founder: Ormiston Families, 1980; Gateway Acad., 2009; Birmingham Ormiston Acad., 2010. Co-Founder, Assoc. of Charitable Foundns. *Recreations:* chess, tennis. *Address:* Ormiston Trust, 1 Bell Yard, WC2A 2JR. *T:* (020) 7266 7940.

**MURRAY, Peter Gerald Stewart;** Chairman, Wordsearch, 2004–14 (Managing Director, 1983–2004); Founder Director, London Architecture Biennale, 2004, 2006; Chairman, New London Architecture, since 2012 (Exhibition Director, 2005–12); Director, London Festival of Architecture, 2008, 2010, 2012; *b* 6 April 1944; *s* of Stewart and Freda Murray; *m* 1967, Jane Wood; two *s* two *d*. *Educ:* King's Coll., Taunton; Sch. of Architecture, Royal West of England Acad., Bristol; Dept of Architecture, Univ. of Bristol; Architectural Assoc. Sch. of Architecture. Editor, Building Design, 1974–79; Editor, RIBA Jl, and Man. Dir, RIBA Magazines Ltd, 1979–84; founded Wordsearch Ltd and launched Blueprint mag.,

1983. Editor, Pidgeon Digital, 2007–; Editor-in-Chief, New London Qly, 2010–. Mem., Mayor of London's Design Adv. Gp, 2012–16; Mayor's Design Advocate, 2017–. Mem. Council, 1987–90, Hon. Sec., 1989–90, AA; Mem. Architecture Cttee, RA, 2000–06. Exhibition Co-organiser: New Architecture: the work of Foster, Rogers and Stirling, RA, 1986; Living Bridges: the inhabited bridge, past, present and future, RA, 1996; New City Architecture, Broadgate, 2004. Vis. Prof., IE Univ., Madrid, 2011–17. Dir, Assoc. of Architecture Organisations, 2017–. Non-exec. Dir, Be First Ltd, 2018–. Trustee, Bannister Fletcher, 1984–86. Dep. Chm., Bedford Park Soc., 1998– (Hon. Sec., 1998–2013); Chm., London Soc., 2014–. Trustee, Cycle to Cannes, charity cycle ride, 2009–14 (Dir, 2006–09). Academician, Acad. of Urbanism, 2012. FRSA 1990. Hon. FRIBA 2000. Liveryman, Chartered Architects' Co., 2008 (Mem. Ct of Assts, 2010–; Master, 2015–16). *Publications*: Modern Architecture in Britain, 1984; Contemporary British Architects, 1995; Living Bridges (exhibn catalogue), 1996; New Urban Environments, 1997; The Saga of Sydney Opera House, 2004; Architecture and Commerce, 2005; 50 Years of London Architecture, 2010; A Passion to Build, 2012; The Leadenhall Building, 2016. *Recreations*: cycling, wood turning, looking at buildings, sketching, London. *Address*: 31 Priory Avenue, Bedford Park, W4 1TZ. *E*: pgsmurray@mac.com. *Clubs*: Athenæum, Architecture (Hon. Sec., 1978–2013), City Livery.

**MURRAY, Richard Dixon,** CB 2012; Chief Executive, The King's Fund, since 2019 (Director of Policy, 2014–19); *b* Bristol, 23 March 1965; *s* of Gerald Roy Murray and Jean Margaret Murray; civil partnership 2012, Tom Johnston Penman. *Educ*: Wellsway Comp. Sch.; Brasenose Coll., Oxford (BA Mod. Hist. and Econs 1986). Sen. Lectr, London Guildhall Univ., 1990–93; Econ. Advr, DoH, 1993–98; McKinsey & Co., 1998–2002; Department of Health: Sen. Econ. Advr, 2002–06; Dir, Finance and Strategy, 2006–13, and Chief Economist and Dir of Strategy, 2011–13; Chief Economist, NHS Commissioning Bd, 2013–14. *Recreations*: RSPB, Victorian literature, travel, ballet. *Address*: The King's Fund, 11–13 Cavendish Square, W1G 0AN. *T*: (020) 7307 2598. *E*: r.murray@kingsfund.org.uk.

**MURRAY, Sir Robert Sydney, (Sir Bob),** Kt 2010; CBE 2002; FCCA; Chairman and Founder: Sterling Capitol, since 1991; Omega International Group, since 1992; *b* Newcastle upon Tyne, 3 Aug. 1946; *s* of Sydney and Elsie Murray; *m* Susan Diane Gorman; one *s* two *d*. *Educ*: Consett Jun. Sch.; Annfield Plain Secondary Mod. Sch.; Consett Tech. Coll.; Newcastle Poly.; Leeds Poly. FCCA 1972. Dir and Founder, Spring Ram, 1978–89; Director: FKI plc, 1991–99; Wembley Nat. Stadium, 2002. Dir, 1984–2006, Chm., 1986–2006, Life Pres., 2006, Sunderland AFC. Dir, Stadia Bd, Football Foundn, 2004. Project Dir, 2008–15, Advr, 2015–, Nat. Football Centre; Advr, Wembley Nat. Stadium, 2015–. Chm. Trustees, Sunderland AFC Foundn of Light, 2001–; Trustee, Academy 360, 2005–16. Chancellor, Leeds Beckett (formerly Leeds Metropolitan) Univ., 2013–. Hon. Fellow, Sunderland Univ., 1991. Hon. DBA: Sunderland Univ., 1997; Leeds Metropolitan, 2008. Internat. Ambassador for Derwentside, Derwentside Council, 1999; Worldwide Ambassador for Sunderland, 2005. Freedom, City of Sunderland, 2011. *Recreations*: family, friends, travel, charity work, keeping fit and sport; enjoy spending time with my many entertaining and loyal friends; passionate about helping people to fulfil their potential in the communities where I have lived, specifically in NE of England; great believer in lifelong education and learning; last, but not least, football, especially Sunderland AFC. *E*: nicki@themurrayfamilyoffice.com.

**MURRAY, Sir Robin (MacGregor),** Kt 2011; MD; FRS 2010; Professor of Psychiatric Research, Institute of Psychiatry, Psychology and Neuroscience (formerly Institute of Psychiatry), King's College London, since 2009 (Professor of Psychiatry, 1999–2009); *b* 31 Jan. 1944; *s* of James Alistair Campbell Murray and Helen Murray; *m* 1st, 1971, Shelagh Harris (marr. diss. 2013); one *s* one *d*; 2nd, 2014, Marta Di Forti. *Educ*: Royal High Sch., Edinburgh; Glasgow Univ. (MB, ChB 1968; MD 1974). MRCP 1971; MRCPsych 1976; MPhil London, 1976; DSc London, 1989. Registrar, Dept of Medicine, Univ. of Glasgow/Western Infirmary, 1971; Sen. House Officer, successively Registrar and Sen. Registrar, Maudsley Hosp., 1972–76; Vis. Fellow, National Inst. of Health, Washington, DC, 1977; Institute of Psychiatry, 1978–: Sen. Lectr, 1978–82; Dean, 1982–89; Prof. of Psychol Medicine, KCL, 1989–99. Pres., Assoc. of European Psychiatrists, 1995–96. For. Mem., Inst. of Medicine, USA, 2004. Founder FMedSci 1998. *Publications*: (jtly) Essentials of Postgraduate Psychiatry, 1979; (jtly) Misuse of Psychotropic Drugs, 1981; Lectures on the History of Psychiatry, 1990; Schizophrenia, 1996; Neurodevelopment and Adult Psychopathology, 1997; Psychosis in the Inner City, 1998; (jtly) First Episode Psychosis, 1999; (ed jtly) Comprehensive Care of Schizophrenia, 2000; (jtly) An Atlas of Schizophrenia, 2002; Marijuana and Madness, 2004; articles on schizophrenia, depression, brain imaging and psychiatric genetics. *Recreations*: Scottish and Jamaican music, swimming, walking labrador.

**MURRAY, Roger;** Chairman, Fuerst Day Lawson Holdings, 1998–2008; *b* 8 June 1936; *s* of Donald Murray and Nancy (*née* Irons); *m* 1960, Anthea Mary (*née* Turnbull); one *s* three *d*. *Educ*: Uppingham Sch.; Brasenose Coll., Oxford (MA). RNVR (Sub-Lieut), 1954–56. Joined Cargill Inc., Minneapolis, 1959; President: Cargill Canada, 1973; Cargill Europe Ltd, 1982–97; Chm., Cargill plc, 1982–97; Mem., Management Cttee, Cargill Inc., 1986–97. Dir, various Canadian cos, 1975–82. Chairman: JP Morgan Fleming Emerging Markets IT, 1994–2003; Pacific Rim Palm Oil Ltd (Mauritius), 2001–05. Mem. Bd, Commonwealth Develt Corp., 1997–2000. Canadian and British citizen. Ind. Mem., Chatham House, 1999–. FRGS 1990. *Recreations*: sailing, ski-ing, mountaineering, golf. *Address*: 25 Addison Avenue, Holland Park, W11 4QS. *T*: (020) 7603 3904. *Clubs*: Denham Golf; Alpine; Royal Lake of the Woods Yacht (Kenora, Ont) (Cdre, 2008–11).

**MURRAY, Sir Rowland William,** 15th Bt *cr* 1630, of Dunerne, Fifeshire; *b* 22 Sept. 1947; *s* of Sir Rowland William Patrick Murray, 14th Bt and Josephine Margaret Murray (*née* Murphy) (*d* 1989); *S* father, 1994, but his name does not appear on the Official Roll of the Baronetage; *m* 1970, Nancy Diane, *d* of George C. Newberry; one *s* one *d*. *Educ*: Georgia State Univ. (SB 1974). Sen. Vice Pres. and Managing Broker, Berkshire Hathaway Home Services Georgia Properties. Mem., Atlanta Bd of Realtors. *Recreations*: golf, gardening, travel. *Heir*: *s* Rowland William Murray IV, *b* 31 July 1979. *Address*: 2565 Habersham Road NW, Atlanta, GA 30305–3577, USA. *T*: (404) 2662408. *Clubs*: Midtown Atlanta Rotary, Atlanta High Museum of Art, Atlanta Botanical Gardens.

**MURRAY, Ruth Hilary;** *see* Finnegan, R. H.

**MURRAY, Sara Elizabeth,** OBE 2012; Founder and Chief Executive, Buddi, since 2004; *b* Lancs, 2 Nov. 1968; *d* of Anthony Murray and Patricia Murray; one *d*. *Educ*: Malvern Girls' Coll.; St Hilda's Coll., Oxford (BA Hons PPP 1990); Univ. of Lausanne (Adv. Dip. French 1992). Founder and Chief Executive Officer: Ninah Consulting, 1992–2003; Inspop.com Ltd, 1998–2002; Dir, Business Develt, Zenith Optimedia, 2002–03. Non-executive Director: Schering Health Care, 2002–07; Boohoo.com plc, 2016–. Member: Governing Bd, Technol. Strategy Bd, later Innovate UK, 2009–16; Business Sec.'s Entrepreneurs' Forum, 2010–. Mem., Founding Bd, Seedcamp, 2007–. Mem., Develt Council, NPG, 2011–16. Mem. Council, Imperial Coll. London, 2015–. Hon. DBus Plymouth, 2011. Entrepreneur of the Year, Orange Nat. Business Awards, 2009. *Recreations*: Private Pilot Licence (Helicopters) - helicopter flying in perfect weather, sailing, fishing, shooting, ski-ing. *E*: ceo@buddi.co.uk. *Clubs*: Queen's, Groucho.

**MURRAY, Very Rev. Sarah Elisabeth;** Provost of St Andrew's Cathedral, Inverness, since 2017; *b* Newport, Isle of Wight, 3 Dec. 1970; *d* of Francis William Martin and Elizabeth Anne Bright; *m* 2004, John Morgan Murray; one *s*. *Educ*: St Mary's Hall, Brighton; Univ. of Sussex; Univ. of Aberdeen (BTh 2012). Ordained deacon, 2013, priest, 2014; Asst Curate, Isla Deveron Gp, 2013–16; Vice-Provost, St Andrew's Cathedral, Inverness, 2016–17. *Address*: Inverness Cathedral, 9–11 Kenneth Street, Inverness IV3 5NR. *T*: (01463) 225553. *E*: provost@invernesscathedral.org.

**MURRAY, Sheryll;** MP (C) South East Cornwall, since 2010; *b* Millbrook, Cornwall, 4 Feb. 1956; *d* of Edgar and Elaine Hickman; *m* 1986, Neil Murray (*d* 2011); one *s* one *d*; *m* 2019, Bob Davidson. *Educ*: Torpoint Sch. Insce underwriter, 1972–88; GP receptionist, 1990–2010. Mem. (C) Cornwall CC, 2001–05. PPS to Sec. of State for Envmt, Food and Rural Affairs, 2016–17. Member: Envmtl Audit Cttee, 2010–12; Envmt, Food and Rural Affairs Cttee, 2012–15, 2017–. *Address*: (office) The Parade, Liskeard, Cornwall PL14 6AF. *T*: (01579) 344428. *E*: sheryll@sheryllmurray.com.

**MURRAY, Simon Anthony,** CEng; consultant; non-executive Director, East West Rail Company Ltd, since 2019; *b* 31 Aug. 1951; *s* of Frank Murray and Barbara (*née* Williams); *m* 1st, 1974, Anne Humphrey (marr. diss. 1982); 2nd, 1983, Lindsay Maxwell (marr. diss. 2004); two *s* one *d*. *Educ*: Welbeck Coll.; Imperial Coll., London (BSc). CEng 1978; MICE 1978; FCGI 1999. Ove Arup & Partners: S Africa, 1975–77; Kenya, Zimbabwe, Hong Kong and London, 1977–89; Dir, 1990–94; Man. Dir, Gp Technical Services, BAA plc, 1995–98; Dir, Major Projects and Investment, Railtrack plc, 1999–2001. Non-executive Director: Ascot Authority (Hldgs) Ltd, 2000–06; Manchester Airport Develts Ltd, 2002–04; Highways England (formerly Highways Agency), 2012–19; Chm., Geoffrey Osborne Ltd, 2003–12. Mem., EPSRC, 1998–2001. *Recreations*: walking, gym, reading, wine. *Address*: 150 Langton Way, Blackheath, SE3 7JS.

**MURRAY, Susan Elizabeth, (Mrs M. Weston);** Senior Independent Director, Mitchells & Butlers plc, since 2019; *m* 1989, Michael Weston; one step *d*. *Educ*: Communications, Advertising and Mktg Dip. 1978. Colgate-Palmolive, 1979–82; General Foods, then Kraft General Foods, 1982–89; Duracell, 1989–92; Worldwide Pres. and CEO, Pierre Smirnoff Co., 1992–98; Chief Exec., Littlewoods Stores, Littlewoods, 1998–2004. Non-exec. Chm., Farrow and Ball, 2007–14; non-executive Director: Enterprise Inns plc, 2004–14; Imperial Tobacco Gp plc, 2004–14; Wm Morrison Supermarkets plc, 2005–10; SSL International plc, 2005–08; Compass Group plc, 2007–17; Pernod Ricard SA, 2010–14; 2 Sisters Food Gp, 2015–19. Council Mem. and Dir, ASA, 2003–09. *Recreations*: cycling, walking, theatre. *E*: info@susan-murray.com. *Clubs*: Forum UK, Women's Advertising Club of London.

**MURRAY HILL, Hilary;** Chief Executive Officer, Hachette Children's Group, since 2015; *b* Gloucester; *d* of Kenneth Cohen and Sylvia Cohen (*née* Luton); *m* 2001, Piers Murray Hill. *Educ*: Mark Rutherford Upper Sch.; Poly. of the South Bank, London (BSc Soc. Sci. 1986). Publishing Admin Manager, Reed Elsevier, 1988–92; Mktg Manager, Carlton Publishing Gp, 1992–2000; UK Sales and Mktg Dir, Usborne Publishing Ltd, 2000–05; Scholastic Children's Books: UK Sales and Mktg Dir, 2005–09; Man. Dir, 2009–14; Man. Dir, Egmont Books, 2014. Chair, Children's Publishers Gp, Publishers Assoc., 2018–. *Recreations*: reading, cooking, music. *Address*: Hachette Children's Group, Carmelite House, 50 Victoria Embankment, EC4Y 0DZ. *T*: (020) 3122 6600. *E*: hilary.murrayhill@hachettechildrens.co.uk.

**MURRAY WELLS, James Nicholas,** OBE 2015; Industry Head, Retail, Google, since 2013; *b* Westminster, London, 21 March 1983; *s* of late Simon Henry Murray Wells and of Alison Benedict Murray Wells. *Educ*: Harrow Sch.; Univ. of the West of England (BA Hons Eng.). Founder and Executive Chairman, Glasses Direct, 2004–13. Co-Founder, StartUp Britain, 2011–13. Queen's Award for Enterprise Promotion, 2009. *Address*: Google, 1–13 St Giles High Street, WC2H 8AG.

**MURRELL, Geoffrey David George,** CMG 1993; OBE 1987; HM Diplomatic Service, retired; *b* 19 Dec. 1934; *s* of Stanley Hector Murrell and Kathleen Murrell (Martin); *m* 1962, Kathleen Ruth Berton; one *s* three *d*. *Educ*: Minchenden Grammar School, Southgate; Lincoln Coll., Oxford (BA French and Russian, MA). FCO Research Dept, 1959–61; Moscow, 1961–64; FCO, 1964–68; Moscow, 1968–70; Head, Soviet Section, FCO Research Dept, 1970–75; First Sec., Belgrade, 1975–78; Regional Dir, Soviet and East European Region, Research Dept, 1978–83; Counsellor, Moscow, 1983–87; Counsellor, Res. Dept, FCO, 1987–91; Minister-Counsellor, Moscow, 1991–94. *Publications*: Russia's Transition to Democracy, 1996. *Recreations*: guitar, Russian and Italian literature.

**MURRIN, Orlando Richard Charles;** writer and journalist, food writer and hôtelier; Director and owner, Project Unleash Ltd; *b* 1 April 1958; *s* of late Patrick John Murrin and Patricia Mary, *d* of W. J. Skardon, OBE, MI5. *Educ*: Blundell's Sch., Devon; Magdalene Coll., Cambridge (Exhibnr; BA Hons English; MA). Radio 3 Sub-Editor, Radio Times, 1980–83; Chief Sub Ed., Living mag., 1983–85; Asst Ed., Country Homes and Interiors, 1985–87; advertising copywriter, 1987–90; Dep. Ed., Living mag., 1990–93; Ed., Woman and Home, 1993–96; Ed., BBC Good Food mag., 1997–2004; founding Ed., Olive mag., 2004; Editl Dir, Food Gp, BBC Magazines, 2004–. Proprietor (with Peter Steggall): Le Manoir de Raynaudes, a gastronomic maison d'hôtes, 2004–09; Langford Fivehead, boutique hotel, 2010–12. Clever Cook column, Daily Express, 1997–2002. Pres., Guild of Food Writers, 2019–. Pianist, Kettners Restaurant, 1983–2002. *Publications*: The Clever Cookbook, 1999; The Can't Go Wrong Cookbook, 2002; The No-cook Cookbook, 2003; A Table in the Tarn, 2008. *Recreation*: the life and legacy of Romanian pianist Dinu Lipatti (1917–1950). *Address*: 5a North Street, Heavitree, Exeter EX1 2RH.

**MURRISON, Rt Hon. Dr Andrew (William);** PC 2019; MP (C) South West Wiltshire, since 2010 (Westbury, 2001–10); Minister of State, Foreign and Commonwealth Office and Department for International Development, since 2019; *b* 24 April 1961; *s* of William Gordon Murrison, RD and Marion Murrison (*née* Horn); *m* 1994, Jennifer Jane Munden; five *d*. *Educ*: Harwich High Sch.; The Harwich Sch.; BRNC Dartmouth; Bristol Univ. (MB ChB 1984; MD 1996); Hughes Hall, Cambridge (DPH 1996). MFOM 1994. Med. Officer, RN, 1981–2000, 2003 (Surg. Comdr); Med. Officer, RNR; Consultant Occupational Physician, 1996–2001. Opposition front bench spokesman on health, 2003–05, on defence, 2005–10; PPS to Sec. of State for Health, 2010–12; Parly Under-Sec. of State, MoD, 2012–14, NI Office, 2014–15. Mem., Jt Select Cttee on Nat. Security Strategy, 2015–17; Chm., Select Cttee on NI Affairs, 2017–19; Chm., All Party Parly Gp on Morocco, 2010–12, on Clinical Mgt, 2017–. Prime Minister's Special Rep., Centenary Commemoration of First World War, 2011–19; Trade Envoy to Morocco and Tunisia, 2016–19. Chm., Internat. Develt Gp, Hughes Hall, Cambridge, 2016–19. *Publications*: Tommy This an' Tommy That, 2011; Redemption, 2017; contribs to various biomed. pubns. *Recreations*: sailing, ski-ing. *Address*: House of Commons, SW1A 0AA.

**MURSELL, Rt Rev. (Alfred) Gordon;** Bishop Suffragan of Stafford, 2005–10; b 4 May 1949; s of late Philip Riley Mursell and Sheena Nicholson Mursell; m 1989, Anne Muir. *Educ:* Ardingly Coll.; Brasenose Coll., Oxford (MA 1974; BD 1987). ARCM 1975. Ordained deacon, 1973, priest, 1974; Curate, St Mary Walton, Liverpool, 1973–77; Vicar, St John, E Dulwich, 1977–87; Tutor, Salisbury and Wells Theol Coll., 1987–91; Team Rector, Stafford, 1991–99; Provost, subseq. Dean, of Birmingham, 1999–2005. Hon. DD Birmingham, 2005. *Publications:* Theology of the Carthusian Life, 1988; Out of the Deep: prayer as protest, 1989; The Meditations of Guigo I, Prior of the Charterhouse, 1995; The Wisdom of the Anglo-Saxons, 1997; English Spirituality, 2001; (Gen. Ed.) The Story of Christian Spirituality: two thousand years, from East to West, 2001; Praying in Exile, 2005; (with Jonathan Lawson) Hearing the Call, 2014. *Recreations:* music, hill-walking. *Address:* The Old Manse, Borgue, Kirkcudbright DG6 4SH. *T:* (01557) 870307. *E:* gordon.mursell@btinternet.com. *Club:* Athenæum.

**MURTHY, Krishnan G.;** see Guru-Murthy.

**MURTON, Dr John Evan;** HM Diplomatic Service; Ambassador to the Democratic Republic of Congo, and (non-resident) to the Republic of Congo and to the Central African Republic, since 2017; b 18 March 1972; s of Stewart Anthony Murton and Marion Elizabeth Murton; m 1st, 1998, Sarah Elizabeth Harvey (marr. diss. 2015); two s one d; 2nd, 2017, Zoe Ellen Burden; one s. *Educ:* Sidney Sussex Coll., Cambridge (BA Geog. 1994); Darwin Coll., Cambridge (PhD 1997). Entered FCO, 1997; UN Dept, FCO, 1997; Japanese lang. trng, 1998; Second Sec., Global Issues, 2000–03, First Sec., Energy and Envmt, 2003–04, Tokyo; Dep. Dir, NATO Sec. Gen.'s Private Office, 2004–07; High Comr, Mauritius, and Ambassador to Madagascar and The Comoros, 2007–10; Hd, Indian Ocean Network, FCO, 2009–10; Hd, E Asia and Pacific Dept, FCO, 2010–13; Dep. High Comr, Nairobi, and Perm. Rep. to UN in Nairobi, 2013–17. *Recreations:* hiking, ski-ing, playing guitar badly. *Address:* c/o Foreign and Commonwealth Office, King Charles Street, SW1A 2AH. *E:* john.murton@fco.gov.uk.

**MUSCAT, Hon. Dr Joseph,** Hon. KCMG 2015; CH National Order of Merit (Malta), 2013; Prime Minister of Malta, since 2013; Leader, Labour Party, since 2008; b Pieta, Malta, 22 Jan. 1974; s of Saviour and Grace Muscat; m 2001, Michelle; twin d. *Educ:* St Francis Sch., State Primary Sch., St Paul's Bay; Stella Maris Sch., Balzan; St Aloysius Coll., B'Kara; Univ. of Malta (BCom Mgt and Public Policy; BA Hons Public Policy; MA Eur. Studies); Univ. of Bristol (PhD Mgt Res. 2007). Journalist, then Asst Hd of News, One Radio and One TV, 1992–97; Mkt Intelligence Manager, Inst. for Promotion of Small Enterprise, 1997–99; Investment Advr, Crystal Finance Investments, reps in Malta of UBS Bank, Switzerland, 2000–04; first Ed., maltastar.com, Lab. Party's online newspaper, 2001–04. Mem., Central Admin of Labour Party as Educn Sec., 2001–03; MEP (Lab), Malta, 2004–08; Leader of Opposition, Parlt of Malta, 2008–13. Mem., Nat. Exec., Labour Party, 1994–2001; Dep., then Actg Chairperson, Labour Youth Forum, 1997. Grand Cross, Order of Honour (Greece), 2013. *Address:* Auberge de Castille, Valletta, Malta. *T:* 22002400. *E:* joseph.muscat@gov.mt.

**MUSCATELLI, Prof. Sir (Vito) Antonio,** Kt 2017; PhD; FRSE; Principal and Vice-Chancellor, University of Glasgow, since 2009; b 1 Jan. 1962; s of Ambrogio and Rosellina Muscatelli; m 1986, Elaine Flood; one s one d. *Educ:* High Sch., Glasgow; Univ. of Glasgow (MA Hons; Logan Prize; PhD). University of Glasgow: Lectr, then Sen. Lectr, 1984–94; Daniel Jack Prof. of Pol Economy, 1994–2007; Dean, Fac. of Soc. Scis, 2000–04; Vice-Principal (Strategy and Budgeting, then Strategy and Advancement), 2004–07; Principal and Vice-Chancellor, Heriot-Watt Univ., 2007–09. Visiting Professor: Univ. of Parma, 1989; Catholic Univ. of Milan, 1991–97; Univ. of Bari, 1995–2004; Res. Fellow, CESifo Res. Inst. Munich, 1999–. Adv. Panel of Econ. Consultants, Sec. of State for Scotland, 1998–2000; Special Advr, H of C Treasury Select Cttee, 2007–10; Mem., Council of Econ. Advrs, Scottish Govt, 2015–; Chm., Commn on Econ. Growth for Glasgow City Reg. (formerly Glasgow and Clyde Valley Commn on Urban Econ. Growth), 2015–; Chair, Scottish Govt's Standing Council on Europe, 2016–. Member: Res. and Knowledge Transfer Cttee, SFC, 2005–08; HEFCE RAE Panel, 2001, 2008; Res. Grants Bd, ESRC, 2002–07; Bd, Glasgow City Mktg Bureau, 2009–16; Bd, SFC, 2012–; Chair, Res. and Commercialisation Cttee, 2007–08, 2012–14, Convener, 2008–10, Universities Scotland; Vice-Pres., Universities UK, 2008–10 (Mem. Bd, 2013–19); Director: Russell Gp of Univs, 2009– (Chm., 2017–); Universitas 21 Gp of Univs, 2009–16; Nat. Centre for Univs and Business, 2013–17; Bd, Univs Superannuation Scheme, 2015–; Glasgow Life, 2016–. Council, Royal Econ. Soc., 2002–06. Trustee, CASE (Europe), 2013–19 (Chm., 2017–19); Dir, Beatson Inst., 2014–. Dir, High Sch. of Glasgow, 2000–. Hon. Pres., David Hume Inst., 2014–. FRSE 2003; FAcSS (AcSS 2004); FRSA 1995. Editor, Scottish Jl of Political Economy, 1989–2003. Hon. LLD McGill, 2012. Commendatore (Italy), 2009. *Publications:* (jtly) Macroeconomic Theory and Stabilisation Policy, 1988; (ed) Economic and Political Institutions in Economic Policy, 1996; Monetary Policy; Fiscal Policies and Labour Markets; Macroeconomic Policy Making in the EMU, 2004. *Recreations:* music, literature, football, strategic games. *Address:* University of Glasgow, Glasgow G12 8QQ.

**MUSEVENI, Lt-Gen. Yoweri Kaguta;** President of the Republic of Uganda, since 1986; b 1944; s of Amos and Esteri Kaguta; m 1973, Janet Kataaha; one s three d. *Educ:* primary and secondary schs in Uganda; Univ. of Dar-es-Salaam, Tanzania (BA). Asst Sec. for Research in President's Office, 1970–71; Hd of Front for National Salvation and anti-Idi Amin armed gp, 1971–79; Minister of Defence, 1979–80, and Vice Chm. of ruling Military Commn; Chm., Uganda Patriotic Movement; Chm., High Comd of Nat. Resistance Army, 1981–86. *Publications:* What is Africa's Problem? (essays), 1992; Sowing the Mustard Seed: the struggle for freedom and democracy in Uganda (autobiog.), 1997. *Recreations:* karate, football. *Address:* Office of the President, Parliamentary Buildings, PO Box 7168, Kampala, Uganda. *T:* (41) 234522/234503.

**MUSGRAVE, Sir Christopher John Shane,** 8th Bt cr 1782, of Tourin, Waterford; b 23 Oct. 1959; er s of Sir Richard Musgrave, 7th Bt and of Maria (née Cambanis); S father, 2000. *Educ:* Cheltenham. *Heir:* b Michael Shane Musgrave [b 30 Jan. 1968; m 2005, Juana, d of Juan Larreta; one s].

**MUSGRAVE, Sir Christopher (Patrick Charles),** 15th Bt cr 1611; gentleman farmer; b 14 April 1949; s of Sir Charles Musgrave, 14th Bt and of Olive Louise Avril, o d of Patrick Cringle, Norfolk; S father, 1970; m 1st, 1978 (marr. diss. 1992); two d; 2nd, 1995, Carol, d of Geoffrey Lawson. *Recreations:* painting, model-making, sustainability. *Heir:* b Julian Nigel Chardin Musgrave [b 8 Dec. 1951; m 1975 (marr. diss. 1999); two d]. *Address:* Wern Uchaf Farm, Capel Seion Road, Pontyberem, Llanelli SA15 5AT.

**MUSGRAVE, Lucy Ellen,** OBE 2019; Director, Publica, since 2010; b Leamington Spa, 4 Oct. 1966; m 1997, Zadoc Rogers; four d. *Educ:* Univ. of Manchester (BA Hons Hist. of Art); Goldsmiths' Coll., Univ. of London (MA (Hons) Culture, Community and Society 1991). Journalist and Architl Corresp., Scotland on Sunday, 1991–94; Researcher, BBC, 1994; Associate Dir, 1994–97, Dir, 1997–2002, Architecture Foundn; Co-Founder and Dir, General Public Agency, 2003–10. Member: Urban Sounding Bd, ODPM, 2001–03; Public Realm Adv. Gp, GLA, 2002–03; Design Panel, HS2, 2015–18; Expert Adv. Gp, 2016–, Design Task Force, 2018–, Nat. Infrastructure Commn; Barbican Centre Bd, 2017–. Mayor's Design Advocate, 2017–. Mem. Bd, City Property Assoc., 2015–16. Trustee: Photographers' Gall., 2000–05; Sheila McKechnie Foundn, 2004–14; Tree Council, 2014–16. Freeman, Chartered Architects' Co., 2016. Hon. FRIBA 2001. *Publications:* (with Clare Cumberlidge) Design and Landscape for People: new approaches to urban renewal, 2007. *Recreations:* trees, table tennis, sailing, ski-ing. *Address:* Publica, 7th Floor, 3 Finsbury Avenue, EC2M 2PA. *T:* (020) 7490 3986. *E:* lucy@publica.co.uk.

**MUSGRAVE, Rosanne Kimble,** MA; educational consultant, since 2000; Headmistress, Blackheath High School (GDST), 1989–2000; b 31 Jan. 1952; d of late Gp Captain John Musgrave, DSO, and Joanne Musgrave. *Educ:* Cheltenham Ladies' Coll.; St Anne's Coll., Oxford (MA); MA Reading Univ.; PGCE London Univ. Assistant teacher of English: Latymer Grammar Sch., 1976–79; Camden School for Girls (ILEA), 1979–82; Head of English: Channing Sch., Highgate, 1982–84; Haberdashers' Aske's School for Girls, Elstree, 1984–89. Pres., GSA, 1999; Dir of Member Support, 2008–11, Dep. Gen. Sec., 2011–13, Ind. Schs Specialist, 2013–14, ASCL. Corporate Mem., Cheltenham Ladies' Coll., 1989; Gov., St Albans High Sch., 1996–2018. FRSA 1994. Freeman, City of London, 1993. *Recreations:* letterpress printing, cooking. *Address:* 14 Fortis Green, N2 9EL.

**MUSGRAVE, Thea,** CBE 2002; composer; b 27 May 1928; d of James P. Musgrave and Joan Musgrave (née Hacking); m 1971, Peter Mark, conductor, s of Irving Mark, NY. *Educ:* Moreton Hall, Oswestry; Edinburgh Univ.; Paris Conservatoire; privately with Nadia Boulanger. Dist. Prof., Queens Coll., CUNY, 1987–2002. *Works include:* Cantata for a summer's day, 1954; The Abbot of Drimock (Chamber opera), 1955; Triptych for Tenor and orch., 1959; Colloquy for violin and piano, 1960; The Phoenix and the Turtle for chorus and orch., 1962; The Five Ages of Man for chorus and orch., 1963; The Decision (opera), 1964–65; Nocturnes and arias for orch., 1966; Chamber Concerto No. 2, in homage to Charles Ives, 1966; Chamber Concerto No 3 (Octet), 1966; Concerto for orchestra, 1967; Music for Horn and Piano, 1967; Clarinet Concerto, 1968; Beauty and the Beast (ballet), 1968; Night Music, 1969; Memento Vitae, a concerto in homage to Beethoven, 1970; Horn concerto, 1971; From One to Another, 1972; Viola Concerto, 1973; The Voice of Ariadne (opera), 1972–73; Rorate Coeli, for chorus, 1974; Space Play, 1974; Orfeo I and Orfeo II, 1975; Mary, Queen of Scots (opera), 1976–77 (chamber music version, 2015); Christmas Carol (opera), 1979; An Occurrence at Owl Creek Bridge (radio opera), 1981; Peripeteia (orchestral), 1981; Harriet, the Woman called Moses (opera), 1984; Black Tambourine for women's chorus and piano, 1985; Pierrot, 1985; For the Time Being for chorus, 1986; The Golden Echo, 1987; Narcissus, 1988; The Seasons (orchestral), 1988; Rainbow (orchestral), 1990; Simón Bolivar (opera), 1993; Autumn Sonata, 1993; Journey through a Japanese Landscape (marimba concerto), 1993; Wild Winter, 1993; On the Underground (vocal), 1994; Helios (oboe concerto), 1995; Phoenix Rising (orchestral), 1997; Lamenting with Ariadne, 2000; Pontalba (opera), 2003; Turbulent Landscapes (orchestral), 2004; Wood, Metal and Skin (percussion concerto), 2004; Journey Into Light (soprano and orch.), 2005; Voices of Power and Protest, 2006; Two's Company (concerto for percussion and oboe), 2007; Green (for 12 strings), 2007; Cantilena (for oboe and string trio), 2008; Poets in Love (for tenor, baritone and piano), 2009; Sunrise (for flute, viola and harp), 2009; Ithaca (for unaccompanied chorus); 2009; Towards the Blue (clarinet solo with wind quartet and string quartet), 2010; Dawn (oboe solo), 2012; Loch Ness—a postcard from Scotland (orchestral), 2012; Largo in Homage to B.A.C.H. (for string orch.), 2013; The Voices of Our Ancestors (for chorus, organ and brass quintet), 2014; Night Windows (for solo oboe and 15 strings), 2016; D.E.S.—In Celebration (cello solo), 2016; La Vida es Sueño (dramatic monologue for baritone and piano), 2016; Missa Brevis (for choir and organ), 2017; From Darkness into the Light (for solo cello and chamber orch.), 2017; Trumpet Concerto, 2019. Performances and broadcasts: UK, France, Germany, Switzerland, Scandinavia, USA, USSR, etc, Edinburgh, Cheltenham, Aldeburgh, Zagreb, Venice and Warsaw Festivals. Hon. MusDoc, CNAA. Queen's Medal for Music, 2018. *Address:* c/o Novello & Co. Ltd, 14–15 Berners Street, W1T 3LJ.

**MUSGROVE, Harold John;** Chairman, Worcester Acute Hospitals NHS Trust, 1999–2003; b 19 Nov. 1930; s of Harold Musgrove; m 1958, Jacquelin Mary Hobbs; two s two d. *Educ:* King Edward Grammar Sch., Birmingham; Birmingham Tech. Coll. Nat. Cert. of Mech. Engrg; Harvard Univ. (Sen. Mgt Course). Apprentice, Austin Motor Co., 1945; held various positions, incl. Chief Material Controller (Commission as Navigator, RAF, during this period); Senior Management, Truck and Bus Group, Leyland Motor Corp., 1963–78; Austin Morris: Dir of Manufacturing, 1978–79; Man. Dir, 1979–80; Chm. and Man. Dir, 1980–81; Chm., Light Medium Cars Group, 1981–82; Chm. and Chief Exec., Austin Rover Gp, 1982–86; Chloride plc: Dir, 1989–92; Chm., Industrial Battery Sector, 1989–91; Chm., Power Supplies and Lighting Gp, 1991–92. Non-exec. Dir, Metalrax plc, 1986–2003. Chairman: W Midlands Ambulance Service, 1992–94; Birmingham Heartlands Hosp. NHS Trust, 1994–96; Birmingham Heartlands and Solihull (Teaching) NHS Trust, 1996–99. Pres., Birmingham Chamber of Industry and Commerce, 1987–88. Pres., Aston Villa FC, 1986–98. FIMI 1985. DUniv Birmingham, 2000. Midlander of the Year Award, 1980; IProdE Internat. Award, 1981; Soc. of Engineers Churchill Medal, 1982. *Recreations:* golf, soccer. *Address:* Orchard Cottage, Laverton, Broadway, Worcs WR12 7NA.

**MUSHARRAF, Gen. Pervez;** President of Pakistan, 2001–08; Chief of Army Staff, 1998–2007; b 11 Aug. 1943; s of late Syed Musharraf Uddin; m 1968, Sehba Farid; one s one d. *Educ:* St Patrick's High Sch., Karachi; Forman Christian Coll., Lahore. Pakistan Mil. Acad., 1961; commnd Artillery Regt, 1964; Dir Gen., Mil. Ops, 1993–95; Chm., Jt Chiefs of Staff Cttee, 1999–2001; Chief Exec. of Pakistan, 1999–2002. *Publications:* In the Line of Fire (autobiog.), 2006.

**MUSKERRY,** 9th Baron cr 1781 (Ire.); **Robert Fitzmaurice Deane;** Bt 1710 (Ire.); b 26 March 1948; s of 8th Baron Muskerry and Betty Fairbridge, e d of George Wilfred Reckless Palmer; S father, 1988; m 1975, Rita Brink, Pietermaritzburg; one s two d. *Educ:* Sandford Park School, Dublin; Trinity Coll., Dublin (BA, BAI). *Heir:* s Hon. Jonathan Fitzmaurice Deane, b 7 June 1986. *Address:* 725 Ridge Road, Berea, Durban 4001, South Africa.

**MUSSON, Rear Adm. (John Geoffrey) Robin,** CB 1993; Senior Naval Directing Staff, Royal College of Defence Studies, 1990–93; Chief Naval Supply and Secretariat Officer, 1991–93; b 30 May 1939; s of late Geoffrey William Musson and Winifred Elizabeth Musson (née Whyman); m 1965, Joanna Marjorie Ward; two s one d. *Educ:* Luton Grammar Sch.; BRNC, Dartmouth. Entered RN, 1957; served HM Ships: Bulwark, 1960–61; Decoy, 1961–62; 2nd Frigate Sqdn, 1964–65; HM Ships: Cavalier, 1966–67; Forth, 1967–69; Kent, 1975–76; NDC, 1979; MA, VCDS (Personnel and Logistics), 1980–81; Sec. to Chief of Fleet Support, 1982–83; CSO (Personnel and Admin), FONAC, 1984–86; Dir, Naval Officer Appts (Supply and WRNS), 1986–88; Captain, HMS Cochrane, 1988–90; retd, 1993. Admiralty Bd Gov., Royal Naval Benevolent Trust, 1995–2002. Gov. (formerly Mem. Cttee of Mgt), Royal Hosp. Sch., Holbrook, 1995–2002. Sec., Salisbury Dio. Sudan Link, 1995–2001. Freeman, City of London, 1993. *Recreations:* Scottish country dancing, mending things, history.

**MUSSON, John Nicholas Whitaker**; Warden of Glenalmond College (formerly Trinity College, Glenalmond), 1972–87; *b* 2 Oct. 1927; *s* of late Dr J. P. T. Musson, OBE and Gwendoline Musson (*née* Whitaker); *m* 1953, Ann Preist (*d* 2004); one *s* three *d*. *Educ*: Clifton Coll.; Brasenose Coll., Oxford (BA Hons Mod. Hist., 1951; MA). Served with Welsh Guards and Lancs Fusiliers, 1945–48 (commnd). HM Colonial Service, later HM Overseas Civil Service, 1951–59: District Officer, N Nigeria; Instructor, Inst. of Administration, N Nigeria; Staff Dept, British Petroleum, London, 1959–61; Asst Master and Housemaster, Canford Sch., 1961–72. Chm., Scottish Div. HMC, 1981–83; Scottish Dir, ISCO, 1987–93. Governor: Clifton Coll., 1989– (Mem. Council, 1989–95); George Watson's Coll., Edinburgh, 1989–98. Mercy Corps Europe/Scottish European Aid: Dir and Trustee, 1996–2000; served in Bosnia and Herzegovina, resident in Sarajevo; Vice-Chm., Mercy Corps Europe (Aid Internat.), 2000–07. *Recreations:* travel, art, Egyptology, watching Rugby. *Address:* Edinburgh. *Club:* New (Edinburgh).

**MUSSON, Rear Adm. Robin;** *see* Musson, Rear Adm. J. G. R.

**MUSTARD, Simon;** HM Diplomatic Service; High Commissioner to Sierra Leone, since 2019; *b* Wakefield, 3 Aug. 1971; *s* of Colin Mustard and Lynne Carter (*née* Cooke); *m* 2003, Mary Roberton; two *s*. *Educ*: Univ. of Aberdeen (MA Hons). Police officer, Lothian and Borders Police, 1994–2001; joined FCO, 2001; Envmt Policy Dept, FCO, 2001–02; Political Officer, High Commn, Belize, 2002–05; Second Sec., Washington, 2005–08; Pte Sec. to Minister of State and Foreign Sec., 2008–09; Hd of Team, Counter Proliferation Dept, FCO, 2009–11; Dep. Hd, Consular Directorate, 2011–13; Dep. Hd of Mission, Jordan, 2013–16; High Comr to Malawi, 2016–17; Hd, Africa Central/Southern Dept, and Great Lakes Special Envoy, FCO, 2017–19. Mem., Linacre Inst., 2015–. *Recreations:* Rugby, running, music, Newcastle United, school governor. *Address:* c/o Foreign and Commonwealth Office, King Charles Street, SW1A 2AH. *E:* simon.mustard@fco.gov.uk. *Clubs:* Royal Over-Seas League; Mowden Park Rugby.

**MUSTHAPHA, (Mohamed) Faisz;** High Commissioner for Sri Lanka in the United Kingdom, 2002–05; *b* 5 Dec. 1940; *s* of Seyed Mohamed Musthapha and Masooda Musthapha; *m* 1967, Fathima Fatheena; one *s* one *d*. *Educ*: Trinity Coll., Kandy; Univ. of Ceylon (LLB); Sri Lanka Law Coll. Advocate of the Supreme Court of Sri Lanka, 1965–; President's Counsel, 1988; Dep. DPP, 1976–78. Chairman: and Mem., Finance Commn of Sri Lanka, 1987–90; Human Rights Commn, Sri Lanka, 1998–2000; Mem., Law Commn of Sri Lanka, 1997–2000. Dir, Amana Investments Ltd, 1996; Chm., Amana Thakaful Ltd (Risk Mgt Co.), 1998–. Mem., Council of Legal Educn, 1997–2000. Legal Advr, All Party Conf., 1987. Member: Sri Lanka Delegn to Thimpu Talks, Bhutan, 1987; Sri Lankan Gp, Internat. Court of Arbitration, The Hague, 1996. Mem., Bar Assoc. of Sri Lanka (Dep. Pres., 1986–98). Chm., Amal Internat. Sch., 1990–2000. *Publications:* contribs on Islam and law. *Recreations:* reading, bird watching, badminton. *Address:* 35 Kaviratne Place, Colombo 6, Sri Lanka. *T:* (11) 2586963, *Fax:* (11) 5555048. *E:* faiszmusthapha@sltnet.lk.

**MUTHALAGAPPAN, Kumar Periakaruppan,** OBE 2009; FCA; Director, Paramount Hotel Collection, 1997; Chief Executive Officer, MeDiNova Clinical Research and Medical Services, since 2011; *b* India, 2 June 1960; *s* of Muthu and Meena Muthalagappan; *m* 1988, Kannahi Sivanantham; two *s* one *d*. *Educ*: Univ. of Warwick (BSc Hons Accounting and Financial Analysis). FCA 1996. Senior Manager, KPMG, 1983–97. Member Board: Heart of England Tourist Bd, 2000–04; Visit Britain, 2002–10. Member, Board: Olympic Delivery Authy, 2006–14; Advantage W Midlands, 2009–12; Alexandra Palace, 2010–12; Age UK (Mem. Fundraising Bd, 2012). Mem. Council, Univ. of Warwick, 2007–10. Chm., City of Birmingham Symphony Orch., 2007–12; Mem. Bd, Belgrade Th., 2000–04. *Recreations:* music, history, sport, gardening. *Address:* 149 Warwick Road, Kenilworth, Warwicks CV8 1HY. *T:* (01926) 851156, *Fax:* (01926) 854420. *E:* kumar@muthalagappan.com.

**MUTI, Riccardo,** Hon. KBE 2000; Music Director, Chicago Symphony Orchestra, since 2010 (Music Director designate, 2009–10); *b* 28 July 1941; *m* 1969, Cristina Mazzavillani; two *s* one *d*. *Educ*: Diploma in pianoforte, Conservatorio di Napoli; Diploma in conducting and composition, Milan. Principal Conductor, Orchestra Maggio Musicale Fiorentino, 1969–80; Principal Conductor, 1972–82, Music Dir, 1979–82, New Philharmonia, later Philharmonia Orchestra, London; Philadelphia Orchestra: Principal Guest Conductor, 1977–80; Principal Conductor and Music Dir, 1980–92; Conductor Laureate, 1992–2003; Music Dir, La Scala, Milan, 1986–2005. Concert tours in USA with Philadelphia Orch.; concerts at Salzburg, Edinburgh, Lucerne, Flanders, Vienna and Ravenna Festivals; concerts with Berlin Philharmonic, Vienna Philharmonic, Concertgebouw Amsterdam, NY Philharmonic, Bayerisches Rundfunk SO, Filarmonica della Scala, Israel Philharmonic, Boston SO, Chicago SO; opera in Florence, Salzburg, Vienna, Munich, Covent Garden, Milan, Ravenna, Venice. Founder, Luigi Cherubini Youth Orch., 2004. Hon. degrees from Univs of Bologna, Urbino, Milan, Lecce and Tel Aviv, and univs in England and USA. Recording prizes from France, Germany, Italy, Japan and USA. Accademico: dell'Accademia di Santa Cecilia, Rome; dell'Accademia Luigi Cherubini, Florence. Hon. Citizen: Milan; Florence; Sydney; Ravenna. Grande Ufficiale, Repubblica Italiana; Cavaliere, Gran Croce (Italy), 1991; Verdienstkreuz, 1st class (Germany), 1976; KM; Ehrenkreuz (Austria).

**MUTTER, Anne-Sophie;** violinist. *Educ*: studied with Prof. Aida Stucki in Switzerland. Début with Herbert von Karajan, Salzburg, 1977; soloist with major orchestras of the world; also plays with string trio and quartet; has given first performances and recorded many works for violin by contemporary composers incl. Lutosławski, Moret, Penderecki, Gubaidulina, Rihm, Dutilleux, Currier, Chin, Williams and Previn. Guest teacher, RAM, 1985. Founder: Rudolf Eberle Foundn, 1987; Anne-Sophie Mutter Foundn, 1997. Hon. Pres., Univ. of Oxford Mozart Soc., 1983. Hon. Mem., Beethoven Soc., 1996. FHMAAS 2013. Hon. Fellow, Keble Coll., Oxford, 2015. Hon Dr Norwegian Univ. of Sci. and Technol., 2010. Prizes and awards include: Jugend Musiziert Prize (FRG) for: violin, 1970 and 1974; piano, 1970; Künstler des Jahres Deutscher Schallplattenpreis, 1979; Grand Prix Internat. du Disque, Record Acad. Prize, Tokyo, 1982; Internat. Schallplattenpreis, 1993; Grammy, 1994, 1999, 2000, 2004; Siemens Music Prize, 2008; Polar Music Prize, 2019. Bundesverdienstkreuz (1st Cl.), 1987; Cross of Honour for Sci. and Art (Austria), 2001; Gold Medal for Merits in the Fine Arts (Spain), 2016; Commander, Order of the Arts and Lit. (France), 2017; Grand Officer, Order of Cultural Merit (Romania), 2017; Gloria Artis Medal (Poland), 2018. *Recreations:* graphic arts, sport.

**MUTTRAM, Roderick Ian,** FREng; Founder and Managing Director, Fourth Insight Ltd, since 2012; *b* 15 Jan. 1952; *s* of late Wilfred Reginald Muttram, DSC, RN and Dorothy May Muttram (*née* Best); *m* 1974, Jane Elisabeth Sinkinson; four *d*. *Educ*: St Bartholomew's Grammar Sch., Newbury; Victoria Univ. of Manchester (BSc Hons); Manchester Metropolitan Univ. (DMS). FIET (FIEE 1994). Gp Engrg and Quality Dir, Ferranti Instrumentation Gp, 1986–90; Dir and Gen. Manager, Defence Systems Div., Thorn EMI Electronics, 1990–93; Railtrack plc: Director: Electrical Engrg and Control Systems, 1994–97; Safety and Standards, 1997–2000; Dir, Railtrack Gp plc, 1997–2000; CEO, Railway Safety, 2000–03; ind. engrg and safety consultant, 2003; Vice-Pres., Bombardier Transportation (UK) Ltd, 2003–12. Adv. Prof., Beijing Jiaotong Univ., 2016. Chm., Rail Industry Trng Council, 2001–03. Chm., Supervisory Bd, Eur. Rail Res. Inst., Netherlands, 1994–2003; Vice-Chm., Eur. Rail Res. Adv. Council, 2004–05; Dir, Assoc. Européenne pour l'Interopérabilité Ferroviaire, 2004–06. Mem., Smeatonian Soc. of Civil Engrs, 2017– (Asst Hon. Treas., 2019–). Freedom, City of London, 2004; Liveryman, Co. of Engineers, 2005. FREng 2012; FInstD 2008; FRSA 2014. *Publications:* (contrib.) The Yellow Book on Engineering Safety Management, 1996; numerous conf. papers in UK, Japan, Australia, USA; contrib. numerous papers to Jl Rail and Rapid Transit (IMechE), Japan Railway Tech. Rev., IEE Summer Schs. *Recreations:* small bore rifle shooting, motor vehicle restoration. *Address:* Fourth Insight Ltd, The Cottage, The Street, Ewhurst, Cranleigh, Surrey GU6 7QA. *T:* (01483) 277218. *E:* ext.rod.muttram@rail.bombardier.com, fourthinsight@aol.com.

**MUTTUKUMARU, Christopher Peter Jayantha,** CB 2006; DL; barrister; General Counsel, Department for Transport, 2011–13; *b* 11 Dec. 1951; *y s* of late Maj. Gen. Anton Muttukumaru, OBE and of Margaret Muttukumaru; *m* 1976, Ann Elisabeth Tutton; two *s*. *Educ*: Xavier Coll., Melbourne; Jesus Coll., Oxford (BA, MA). Called to the Bar, Gray's Inn, 1974, Bencher, 2010; in practice at the Bar, 1976–83 and 2014–18; Treasury Solicitor's Dept, 1983–88; Law Officers' Dept, 1988–91; Head of Employment Litigation Sect., Treasury Solicitor's Dept, 1991–92; Sec., Scott Inquiry into Export of Defence and Defence-related Equipment to Iraq, 1992–96; Treasury Solicitor's Department: Dep. Legal Advr, MoD, 1996–98; Legal Advr to DCMS, 1998–99; Dir, Legal (Commercial, Envmt, Housing and Local Govt), DETR, 1999–2001; Legal Dir (Transport), DTLR, 2001–02; Legal Services Dir, 2002–11, Legal Advr, 2003–11, DfT. Consultant, Eversheds Sutherland (Internat.) LLP. Mem. Adv. Bd, Law Sch., City Univ., 2008– (Vice Chm., 2012–15). Mem., Academic Council, Fundación para la Investigación sobre el Derecho y la Empresa, 2017–. Gov., Eltham Coll., London, 1999–2012 (Vice-Chm., Govs, 2006–12). DL Gtr London, 2017. Hon. DLaws City, 2012. Mem., Editl Adv. Bd, Nottingham Law Jl; Chm., Strategic Editl Bd, Navigating Brexit, 2018–. *Recreations:* reading, cricket (watching), photography, sunflowers. *E:* cpjmk99@outlook.com.

**MWINYI, Ndugu Ali Hassan;** President, United Republic of Tanzania, 1985–95; *b* 8 May 1925; *s* of late Hassan Mwinyi Chande and Asha Mwinyishehe; *m* 1960, Siti A. Mwinyi (*née* Abdulla); five *s* four *d*. *Educ*: Mangapwani Sch. and Dole Sch., Zanzibar; Teachers' Training Coll., Zanzibar; Durham Univ. Inst. of Education. Primary sch. teacher, head teacher, Tutor, Principal, Zanzibar, 1945–64; Acting Principal Sec., Min. of Educn, 1964–65; Dep. Gen. Manager, State Trading Corp., 1965–70; Minister of State, President's Office, Dar es Salaam, 1970–72; Minister for Health, 1972–75; Minister for Home Affairs, 1975–77; Ambassador to Egypt, 1977–81; Minister for Natural Resources and Tourism, 1982–83; Minister of State, Vice-President's Office, 1983; Vice-Pres., Union Govt, 1984. Chama Cha Mapinduzi (Revolutionary Party): Member, 1977; Nat. Exec. Cttee, 1982; Central Cttee, 1984; Vice-Chm., 1984–90; Chm., 1990–96; Mem., Afro-Shirazi Party, 1964. Chairman: Zanzibar Film Censorship Bd, 1964–65; E African Currency Bd, Zanzibar, 1964–67; Nat. Kiswahili Council, 1964–77; Tanzania Food and Nutrition Council, 1974–76. Mem., Univ. Council of Dar es Salaam, 1964–65. *Address:* c/o State House, Dar es Salaam, United Republic of Tanzania.

**MYER, Sidney Baillieu,** AC 1990; MA Cantab; Chairman, Myer Emporium Ltd, 1978–86 (Director, 1955–86); Deputy Chairman, Coles Myer Ltd, 1986–94; Director: Myer Foundation, 1959, now Emeritus (Chairman, 1992–95; Vice-President, 1959–92); N. M. Rothschild Australia Holdings (formerly N. M. Rothschild & Son (Australia) Pty Ltd), 1993–2003; *b* 11 Jan. 1926; *s* of late Sidney Myer and late Dame (Margery) Merlyn Baillieu Myer, DBE; *m* 1955, Sarah J., *d* of late S. Hordern; two *s* one *d*. *Educ*: Geelong Grammar Sch.; Pembroke Coll., Cambridge (MA). Sub-Lieut, RANVR, 1944–46. Joined Myer Emporium, 1953. Director: Myer Family Office Ltd (formerly Myer Family Co. Pty Ltd), 1953; Elders IXL Ltd, 1972–90; Cadbury Schweppes Aust. Ltd, 1976–82; Commonwealth Banking Corp., 1979–83; Network Ten Holdings Ltd and associated Cos, 1985–87; Chm., Nat. Mutual Life Assoc. of Australasia, 1988–92 (Dir, 1978–85 and 1986–92). Dir, Howard Florey Inst. of Experimental Physiology and Medicine, 1971–2002 (Pres., 1988–92); Part-time Mem. Executive, CSIRO, 1981–85. Pres., French Chamber of Commerce (Vic), 1962–64; Rep. Chm., Aust.-Japan Foundn, 1976–81; Member: Consultative Cttee on Relations with Japan, 1978–81; Aust.-China Council, 1979–81; Nat. Bicentennial Sci. Centre Adv. Cttee, 1986–89; Nat. Adv. Cttee on Ageing, 2002–04; Future Melbourne Reference Gp, 2007–08; Chm., Asia Soc. AustralAsia Centre, 2009–; participant, Rural Industries and Communities Aust. 2020 summit, 2008. Councillor: Aust. Conservation Foundn, 1964–73; Vic. Coll. of Arts, 1973–78; Chm., Art Foundn of Vic., 1986–88; Vice-Pres., Nat. Gall. Soc. of Vic., 1964–68; Dir, Tasman Inst., 1990–98; Trustee: Sidney Myer Fund, 1958–2001 (Chm. Trustees, 1992–2001); Nat. Gall. of Vic., 1973–83, now Trustee Emeritus (Vice-Pres., 1977–83); Victorian Tapestry Foundn, 1995–; Chm., Commonwealth Research Centres of Excellence Cttee, 1981–82. Hon. LLD Melbourne, 1993. Centenary Medal (Australia), 2003. Officier de la Légion d'Honneur (France), 2007 (Chevalier, 1976). *Recreations:* tennis, ski-ing, viticulture. *Clubs:* Leander (Henley-on-Thames); Australian (Melbourne).

**MYERS, Anthea Elizabeth Joy;** *see* McIntyre, A. E. J.

**MYERS, David;** Director, Shared Services Programme, Cabinet Office, 2005–07; *b* 28 March 1965; *s* of Frederick Myers and Beryl Adelaide Myers; *m* 1991, Janice Adele Harrison; three *d*. *Educ*: Highfield Sch., Liverpool; Univ. of Lancaster (BA Hons Econ 1st Cl 1987). British Gas plc, 1988–90; Rolls-Royce plc, 1990–92; KPMG, 1992; ICI Pharmaceuticals, 1993–96; Change Prog. Manager, Mil. Aircraft, BAe, 1996–98; Dir of IT, BAe Regl Aircraft, 1998–2000; Dir of IT and Business Change, BAE SYSTEMS Avionics, 2000–02; e-Business Dir, DEFRA, 2003–05. *Recreations:* landscape gardening, following St Helens Rugby League, exploring West Indies.

**MYERS, (Denis) Kevin,** CBE 2015; Director-General, Regulation, Health and Safety Executive, 2015–16; President, International Association of Labour Inspection, since 2014 (Secretary General, 2011–14); *b* 30 Sept. 1954; *s* of Stephen Myers and Bridget Myers (*née* McSweeney); *m* 1976, Jan Hannan; four *s* one *d*. *Educ*: St Bonaventure's Sch., Forest Gate; Luton Coll. of Technol. (BSc Hons Biochem. and Envmtl Biol.). Joined Health and Safety Exec., 1976, various posts in London, E Anglia and SW, 1976–93; Policy Officer, DG XI, Eur. Commn, 1993–95; Health and Safety Executive: Regl Dir, Home Counties Reg., 1997–2002, Chief Inspector of Construction, 2000–05; Dir, Hazardous Installations, 2005–08; Dep. Chief Exec., 2008–13 and 2014–15, Actg Chief Exec., 2013–14. Non-exec. Dir, Office for Nuclear Regulation, 2011–14; Mem., Singapore Govt Internat. Adv. Panel for Workplace Safety and Health, 2013–. Trustee: British Safety Council, 2009–17; Mates in Mind, 2016–. *Recreations:* family, Italy, football (West Ham United FC), cricket, opera.

**MYERS, Sir Derek (John),** Kt 2014; Chief Executive: Royal Borough of Kensington and Chelsea, 2000–13; London Borough of Hammersmith and Fulham, 2011–13; Lead Commissioner, Rotherham Metropolitan Borough Council, 2015–17; *b* 15 Aug. 1954; *s* of Alfred and Elsie Myers; *m* 1992, Anne Mercer; one *s* one *d*. *Educ*: Univ. of Manchester (BA Econs 1976; Dip. Social Work 1977); Univ. of London (LLB 1988). Social Services: Essex CC, 1977–86; Hillingdon LBC, 1986–92; Dir of Social Services, 1992–97, Chief Exec.,

1997–2000, London Borough of Hounslow; Town Clerk, RBK&C, 2000–11. Chm., Soc. of Local Authority Chief Execs, 2008–12. Mem., Adv. Bd, Public Health England, 2013–. Chm. Trustees, Shelter, 2013–17; Trustee, Royal Botanic Gdns, Kew, 2013–. *Recreations:* tennis, cooking, hill-walking.

**MYERS, Dominic Peter;** European Publishing Director, Amazon Media EU, since 2014; *b* Street, 13 Aug. 1962; *s* of Neville and Pat Myers; *m* 2001, Heike Diederichs; three *d*. *Educ:* Wadham Coll., Oxford (BA Eng. Lang. and Lit. 1984). Marks & Spencer, 1986–91; Somerfield, 1992–98; Managing Director: Hasbro Interactive, 1999–2000; Blackwell UK, 2002–05; HMV Group: Strategy Dir, Waterstone's, 2006–07; Gp Develt Dir, 2007–10; Man. Dir, Waterstone's, 2010–11. Non-executive Chairman: txt2buy Ltd, 2011–12; Bounts.it, 2013–14; Dir, Bear and Horn Ltd, 2011–; non-exec. Dir, Sainsbury's eBooks, 2012–14. *Recreation:* three daughters - keeps me busy.

**MYERS, Geoffrey,** CBE 1984; CEng; FCILT; Chairman, TRANSAID, 1988–95; Vice-Chairman, British Railways Board, 1985–87 (Member, 1980–87); *b* 12 July 1930; *s* of Ernest and Annie Myers; *m* 1959, Patricia Mary (*née* Hall); two *s*. *Educ:* Belle Vue High Sch.; Bradford Technical Coll. (BScEng London). CEng, MICE 1963; FCILT (FCIT 1973). RE, 1955–57. British Rail: civil engrg positions, 1957–64; Planning Officer, N Eastern Reg., 1964–66; Divl Movements Manager, Leeds Div., 1966–68; Dir of Studies, British Transport Staff Coll., 1968–70; Divl Man., Sheffield, 1970–76; Dep. Gen. Man., Eastern Reg., 1976–77, Gen. Man., 1977–78; Dir of Strategic Develt, 1978–80; Dep. Chief Exec. (Railways), 1983; Jt Managing Dir (Railways), 1984–85. Pres. Council, CIT, 1986–87. Bd Mem., TRANSAID Worldwide, 1998–2000. Mem. Council, Save the Children (UK), 1993–2000; Pres., White Rose Children's Charity, 1995–2017. Hon. DEng Bradford, 1988. OStJ 1979. *Recreations:* golf, walking. *Address:* 30 Emmandjay Court, Valley Drive, Ben Rhydding, Ilkley, W Yorks LS29 8PF. *T:* (01943) 605241.

**MYERS, John David;** Chairman of Industrial Tribunals, 1982–97 (Regional Chairman for Newcastle, 1994–97); part-time Chairman of Employment Tribunals, 1998–2005; *b* 30 Oct. 1937; *s* of Frank and Monica Myers; *m* 1974, Anne McGeough (*née* Purcell), *widow of* J. T. McGeough; one *s*. *Educ:* Marist College, Hull; Hull University. LLB Hons. Called to the Bar, Gray's Inn, 1968. Schoolmaster, 1958–64; University, 1964–67; pupillage with J. D. Walker (later Judge Walker); practice at Hull, 1969–82 (Junior, NE Circuit, 1975–76). Northumberland worker, Age UK, 2004–13. *Recreations:* cooking, oenology, bridge. *Club:* Alnmouth Golf.

**MYERS, Kevin;** *see* Myers, D. K.

**MYERS, Martin Trevor,** FRICS; Chairman, Mountgrange Capital plc, 2002–09; Senior Partner, Mountgrange Real Estate Opportunity Fund, 2007; *b* 24 Sept. 1941; *s* of Bernard Myers and Sylvia Marjorie Myers (*née* Pearman); *m* 1981, Nicole Josephine Yerna; one *s* one *d*. *Educ:* Arnold House, St John's Wood; Latymer Upper Sch.; Coll. of Estate Management, London Univ. (BSc). FRICS 1975. Jones Lang Wootton, 1965–83: Partner, 1969; Proprietary Partner, 1972; Chm. and Chief Exec., Arbuthnot Properties, 1983; merged with Imry Property Holdings, 1987, and with City Merchant Developers, 1988; Chief Exec. and Man. Dir, Imry Holdings Ltd, 1989–97; Exec. Dep. Chm., Trillium Gp, 1998–2001. Trustee, Royal Marsden Cancer Campaign, 2003–09. *Recreations:* golf, shooting, exercise. *Club:* Turf.

**MYERS, Dr Norman,** CMG 1998; Managing Director, Norman Myers' Scientific Consultancy, 1982; *b* 24 Aug. 1934; *s* of John Myers and Gladys Myers (*née* Haworth); *m* 1965, Dorothy Mary Halliman (separated 1992); two *d*. *Educ:* Keble Coll., Oxford (BA 1957; MA 1963); Univ. of Calif, Berkeley (PhD 1973). Dist Officer, Kenya Colonial Admin, 1958–61; high sch. teacher, Nairobi, 1961–65; freelance writer, professional photographer and lectr on African wildlife, Kenya, 1966–69; consultant in envmt and develt, from 1972: projects for develt orgns and res. bodies, incl. World Bank, UN agencies, OECD, EC, US Depts of State and Energy, NASA, US Nat. Acad. of Scis. Hon. Vis. Fellow, Green Templeton (formerly Green) Coll., Oxford, 1992; Adjunct Prof., Duke Univ., 1997; Prof. at Large, Univ. of Vermont, 2007; Ext. Fellow, 21st Century Sch., Oxford, 2008; Vis. Prof., Univs of Kent, Utrecht, Cape Town, Calif, Texas, Michigan, Cornell, Harvard and Stanford. For. Associate, US NAS, 1994; FWAAS 1989; FAAAS 1990; FRSA 1993; FLS 1993; Fellow, Royal Instn, 1997; Ext. Fellow, Saïd Business Sch., Oxford Univ., 2005. Hon. DSc Kent, 2003. Numerous awards for work in environment and development, including Volvo Envmt Prize, 1992; Pew Fellowship in Envmt, 1994; UNEP Sasakawa Envmt Prize, 1995; Blue Planet Prize, Asahi Glass Foundn, Japan, 2001. *Publications:* The Long African Day, 1972; The Sinking Ark, 1979 (trans. Japanese and Hungarian); Conversion of Tropical Moist Forests, 1980; A Wealth of Wild Species, 1983; The Primary Source: tropical forests and our future, 1984, rev. edn 1992; The Gaia Atlas of Planet Management, 1984 (trans. 11 langs), 2nd edn 2005; (ed jtly) Economics of Ecosystem Management, 1985; Future Worlds: challenge and opportunity in an age of change, 1990; Population, Resources and the Environment: the critical challenges, 1991; (ed) Tropical Forests and Climate, 1992; Ultimate Security: the environmental basis of political stability, 1993, 2nd edn 1996; Scarcity or Abundance: a debate on the environment, 1994 (trans. Italian); Environmental Exodus: an emergent crisis in the global arena, 1995; (jtly) Biodiversity Hotspots, 1999; Towards a New Greenprint for Business and Society, 1999; Food and Hunger in Sub-Saharan Africa, 2001; (jtly) Perverse Subsidies: how tax dollars can undercut the environment and the economy, 2001; New Consumers: the influence of affluence on the environment, 2004; The Citizen is Willing but Society Won't Deliver: the problem of institutional roadblocks, 2008; contrib. numerous professional papers in scientific jls incl. Science, Nature, Population and Develt Rev., Jl Envmtl Econs & Mgt, Internat. Jl Social Econs. *Recreations:* professional photography, marathon running, mountaineering. *Club:* Achilles.

**MYERS, Robert William;** Chairman, Robert Myers Associates, Landscape Architects, since 2006; *b* London, 19 May 1969; *s* of His Honour Mark Myers and Katherine Myers; *m* 1997, Clare Burlton; three *s*. *Educ:* Highgate Sch., London; Girton Coll., Cambridge (BA Hons Geog. 1990); Univ. of Central England (Dip. Landscape Architecture). Dir, Elizabeth Banks Associates, 1998–2005. Major projects include: design of Wellcome Trust Genome Campus, Hinxton Hall, 1998; new courtyard and gdns, Southwark Cath., 2001; design of Duke of York Sq., King's Rd, Chelsea, 2003; design of gdns at Tregothnan, Cornwall, 2004; landscape strategy and plan for The Backs, Cambridge, 2007; gdns, Clare Coll., Cambridge, 2009; Hereford Cathedral Close, 2011; Exeter Cathedral Green, 2011; RHS Wisley Bowes-Lyon Rose Garden, 2012; Magic Garden, Hampton Court Palace, 2016; Clandon Park, 2018. RHS Chelsea Flower Show Gold Medals for: Sir Hans Sloane Gdn, 2003; Costiera dei Fiori Gdn, 2006; Fortnum and Mason Gdn, 2007; Cadogan Estates Gdn, 2008; CRUK Gdn, 2010; Brewin Dolphin Garden, 2013. CMLI 1994. *Recreations:* sailing, ski-ing, cricket, playing trumpet and jazz piano. *Address:* Robert Myers Associates, Pensons Yard, Stoke Bliss, Tenbury Wells, Worcs WR15 8RT. *T:* (01885) 227377. *E:* robert@robertmyers-associates.co.uk.

**MYERSON, His Honour Arthur Levey;** QC 1974; a Circuit Judge, 1978–99; *b* 25 July 1928; *o s* of Bernard and Eda Myerson; *m* 1960, (Elaine) Shirley Harris; two *s*. *Educ:* Blackpool Grammar Sch.; Queens' Coll., Cambridge (BA 1950; LLB 1951); BA (Open Univ.) 1985. RAF, 1946–48. Called to the Bar, 1952; a Recorder of the Crown Court, 1972–78; Resident Judge, York Crown Court, 1996–99. Pres., HM Council of Circuit Judges, 1991. *Recreations:* walking, reading, fishing. *Address:* 20 Sandmoor Lane, Leeds LS17 7EA.
*See also* D. S. Myerson.

**MYERSON, (David) Simon;** QC 2003; a Recorder, since 2001; *b* 22 Oct. 1962; *s* of His Honour Arthur Levey Myerson, *qv*; *m* 1987, Nicole Maurice; four *d*. *Educ:* Carmel Coll.; Downing Coll., Cambridge (MA). Called to the Bar, Middle Temple, 1986, Bencher, 2013. *Recreations:* walking, reading, sailing. *Address:* 12 Byrom Street, Manchester M3 4PP. *T:* (0161) 829 2100, *Fax:* (0161) 829 2101; St Paul's Chambers, Park Row House, 19–20 Park Row, Leeds LS1 5JF. *T:* (0113) 245 5866, *Fax:* (0113) 245 5807. *E:* simon.myerson@me.com.

**MYERSON, Prof. Jeremy;** Helen Hamlyn Professor of Design, Royal College of Art, since 2008 (Professor of Design Studies, 2003–08); Director: Helen Hamlyn Centre for Design, 1999–2015; InnovationRCA, 2004–09); Director, Worktech Academy, since 2015; *b* 6 Aug. 1956; *s* of Alexander and Maxine Myerson; *m* 1986, Wendy Smith; two *s*. *Educ:* Hull Univ. (BA Hons). Royal Coll. of Art (MA). Editor: Creative Rev., 1984–86; Design Week, 1986–89; freelance writing and consultancy, 1989–95; Prof. of Contemporary Design, De Montfort Univ., 1995–98. Mem. Bd, Design Council, 2009–11. Trustee: Gordon Russell Trust, 1994–2011; Audi Design Foundn, 2004–10. *Publications:* (jtly) Conran Design Guides to Tableware, Lighting, Home Office and Kitchenware, 1990; Gordon Russell: designer of furniture, 1992; Beware Wet Paint: designs by Alan Fletcher, 1996; New Public Architecture, 1996; (jtly) New Workspace New Culture: office design as a catalyst for change, 1998; (jtly) The Creative Office, 1999; Making The Lowry, 2000; IDEO: masters of innovation, 2001; (jtly) Rewind: 40 years of design and advertising, 2002; (jtly) The 21st Century Office, 2003; Space to Work: new office design, 2006; New Demographics New Workspace, 2010; Life of Work: what office design can learn from the world around us, 2014; New Old: designing for our future selves, 2017. *Recreations:* architecture, jazz, football. *Address:* Royal College of Art, Helen Hamlyn Centre for Design, 4 Hester Road, SW11 4AN. *T:* (020) 7233 7705. *E:* jeremy.myerson@rca.ac.uk.

**MYERSON, Julie Susan Emilia;** novelist and critic; *b* Nottingham, 2 June 1960; *d* of late Geoffrey Pike and Maritza Simpson (*née* Jackson); *m* 2005, Jonathan Scott Myerson; two *s* one *d*. *Educ:* Nottingham Girls' High Sch.; Univ. of Bristol (BA Hons English). Publicist, Press Office, National Th., 1983–87; publicist, Walker Books, 1988–93. *Publications:* Sleepwalking, 1994; The Touch, 1996; Me and the Fat Man, 1998; Laura Blundy, 2000; Something Might Happen, 2002; Home: the story of everyone who ever lived in our house, 2004; Not a Games Person, 2005; The Story of You, 2006; Out of Breath, 2008; The Lost Child, 2009; Then, 2011; The Quickening, 2013; The Stopped Heart, 2016. *Recreation:* gardening. *Address:* c/o Karolina Sutton, Curtis Brown Group, Haymarket House, 28–29 Haymarket, SW1Y 4SP.

**MYERSON, Prof. Roger Bruce,** PhD; Professor of Economics, since 2001, and David L. Pearson Distinguished Service Professor of Global Conflict Studies, since 2018, University of Chicago (Glen A. Lloyd Distinguished Service Professor, 2007); *b* Boston, Mass, 29 March 1951; *m* 1982, Regina Weber; one *s* one *d*. *Educ:* Harvard Univ. (AB *summa cum laude*, SM Applied Maths 1973; PhD Applied Maths 1976). Northwestern University: Asst Prof. of Managerial Econs and Decision Scis, 1976–79; Associate Prof., 1979–82; Prof., 1982–2001. Vis. Prof. of Econs, Univ. of Chicago, 1985–86, 2000–01; Vis. Researcher, Univ. Bielefeld, 1978–79. Fellow: Econometric Soc., 1983 (Mem. Council, 1996–2002, 2005–07; Vice Pres., 2007–08; Pres., 2009); American Acad. of Arts and Scis, 1993. (Jtly) Nobel Prize in Econ. Scis, 2007. *Publications:* Game Theory: analysis of conflict, 1991 (trans. Chinese, 2001); Probability Models for Economic Decisions, 2005; *contributor:* Auctions, Bidding and Contracts, 1983; Social Goals and Social Organization, 1985; Game Theoretic Models of Bargaining, 1985; The Shapley Value, 1988; The New Palgrave: allocation, information and markets, 1989; Negotiation Analysis, 1991; Rational Interaction, 1992; Political Economy: institutions, competition and representation, 1993; Handbook of Game Theory, vol. 2, 1994; Advances in Economic Theory and Econometrics, vol. 1, 1997; Economics of Transnational Commons, 1997; Passion and Craft: how economists work, 1998; contrib. articles to newspapers and papers to learned jls, incl. Internat. Jl Game Theory, Econometrica, Games and Econ. Behavior, Social Choice and Welfare, Jl Econ. Theory, Amer. Econ. Rev. *Address:* Harris School of Public Policy, University of Chicago, 1307 East 60th Street, Chicago, IL 60637, USA.

**MYERSON, Simon;** *see* Myerson, D. S.

**MYKURA, Dr Hamish Finlayson;** Executive Vice President, Programming and Development, National Geographic Global Networks, since 2012; *b* Edinburgh, 28 March 1962; *s* of Dr Walter Mykura and Alison Mykura; *m* 1997, Janey Patricia Winifred Walker, *qv*; twin *d*. *Educ:* George Heriot's Sch., Edinburgh; Univ. of Aberdeen (MA 1984); Univ. of Manchester (PhD 1989). Prodn trainee, BBC, 1989–91; documentaries producer, BBC Radio, 1991–92; prod. and dir, BBC TV, 1992–2000; Dir, Blakeway Prodns, 2000–01; Channel 4 Television: Commng Ed. for Hist., 2001–03; Hd of Hist., Sci. and Religion, 2003–07; Hd of Documentaries and More4, 2008–12. FRGS 2017; FRSA. *Recreations:* hill walking, travel writing, classic cars of the 1970s and 80s. *Address:* National Geographic Channel, 10 Hammersmith Grove, W6 7AP. *E:* hamish.mykura@natgeo.com.

**MYKURA, Janey Patricia Winifred;** *see* Walker, J. P. W.

**MYLAND, Howard David,** CB 1988; Deputy Comptroller and Auditor General, National Audit Office, 1984–89; *b* 23 June 1929; *s* of John Tarrant and Frances Grace Myland; *m* 1951, Barbara Pearl Mills (*d* 2013); two *s* one *d*. *Educ:* Fairfields Schs; Queen Mary's Sch., Basingstoke. Served Intelligence Corps, 1948–50. Entered Exchequer and Audit Dept, 1948; Dep. Dir of Audit, 1972; Dir of Audit, 1977; Dep. Sec. of Dept, 1979; an Asst Auditor Gen., National Audit Office, 1984. Chairman: Valentine Court Ltd, 1998–2004; Brompton Court Ltd, 2005–09. Concert Patron, Bournemouth SO, 2016–. Fellow, CIPFA, 2018 (Mem., 1979). Mem., Basingstoke Round Table, 1962–70. *Publications:* Public Audit Law—Key Development Considerations, 1992. *Recreations:* travel, classical music, contract bridge.

**MYLES, Lynda Robbie;** independent film producer, Pandora Productions, since 1991; Head, Fiction Direction, National Film and Television School, 2004–17; *b* 2 May 1947; *d* of late Alexander Watt Myles and Kathleen Kilgour Myles (*née* Polson); *m* 1972, Dr David John Will (marr. diss. 1978). *Educ:* Univ. of Edinburgh (MA Hons Mental Philosophy). Dir, Edinburgh Internat. Film Fest., 1973–80; Curator of Film, Pacific Film Archive, Univ. of Calif, Berkeley, 1980–82; Film Consultant, Channel Four TV, 1982–83; Producer, Enigma Films, 1983–86; Sen. Vice-Pres., Creative Affairs (Europe), Columbia Pictures, 1986–88; Commng Ed. for Drama, BBC TV, 1989–91. Co-Exec. Dir, East-West Producers' Seminar, 1990–94. Producer: Defence of the Realm, 1986; The Commitments, 1991; The

Snapper, 1993; The Van, 1995; The Life of Stuff, 1997; When Brendan Met Trudy, 2000; (jtly) Killing Me Softly, 2001. Chair (first), Women in Film and TV, 1990–91; Member: Bd, Ateliers du Cinéma Européen, 1998–2016; Bd, European Film Acad., 2016–18; Film Cttee, BAFTA, 2016–18. Gov., BFI, 1993–96. BFI Award, 1981. *Publications:* (with M. Pye) The Movie Brats, 1978. *Address:* Pandora Productions, 35A Princedale Road, W11 4NP. *T:* (020) 7243 3013. *Clubs:* Groucho, Union, Academician's Room.

**MYLNE, Dawn;** see Chatty, D.

**MYLNE, Nigel James;** QC 1984; a Recorder, 1985–2004; *b* 11 June 1939; *s* of late Harold James Mylne and Dorothy Evelyn Mylne (later D. E. Hogg); *m* 1st, 1967, Julie Phillpotts (marr. diss. 1977); two *s* one *d*; 2nd, 1979, Judith Hamilton (marr. diss. 1997); one *s*; 3rd, 2009, Susan Walker, *d* of Maj. Derek Stuart Holmes. *Educ:* Eton College. National Service, 10th Royal Hussars, 1957–59. Called to the Bar, Middle Temple, 1963, Bencher, 1995. Immigration Judge, 1997–2009; Pres., Mental Health Review Tribunals, 1999–2009. *Recreation:* beekeeping. *Address:* Langleys, Brixton Deverill, Wiltshire BA12 7EJ. *T:* (01985) 840351. *E:* nigelmylne@btinternet.com. *Club:* Pratt's.

**MYLONAS, Michael John;** QC 2012; *b* 11 June. *Educ:* Haileybury Jun. Sch.; Eton Coll.; Univ. of Buckingham (LLB Hons 1987); Inns of Court Sch. of Law. Called to the Bar, Gray's Inn, 1988; in practice as a barrister, 1988–. *Publications:* (contrib.) Medical Law Reports, 2000–10; (contrib.) APIL, Clinical Negligence, 2007; (contrib.) Medical Treatment Decisions and the Law, 2010 (2nd edn 2016).

**MYLREA, (Anthony) Paul;** Director of Communications, University of Cambridge, since 2013; Fellow, Wolfson College, Cambridge, since 2013; *b* 21 March 1956; *s* of late Thomas Aloysius Mylrea and Joan Mylrea (*née* Wilcox, latterly Taylor, stage name Joan Campion); *m* 1986, Frances Lowndes; one *s* two *d*. *Educ:* St Bede's Coll., Manchester; Univ. of Birmingham (BA Hons French 1978); Open Univ. (MBA 2003). Reuters: Corresp., London, Germany, Luxembourg, Belgium and Brazil, 1982–90; Chief Corresp., Chile, Bolivia and Peru, 1990–94; UK Political Corresp., 1994–97; Dep. Editor, 1997–99, Editor, 1999–2002, www.alertnet.org; Hd, Media, Oxfam GB, 2002–04; Dir, Gp Media, Transport for London, 2004–07; Dir, Communications, DFID, 2007–10; Hd, Press and Media Relns, 2010–11, Dir of Communications, 2011–12, Dir of Public Affairs, 2012–13, BBC. Associate Lectr, OU Business Sch., 2005–13. *Recreations:* swimming in cold water, scuba diving. *Address:* University of Cambridge, The Old Schools, Trinity Lane, Cambridge CB2 1TN. *T:* (01223) 765539. *E:* paul.mylrea@admin.cam.ac.uk.

**MYNERS,** family name of **Baron Myners.**

**MYNERS,** Baron *cr* 2008 (Life Peer), of Truro in the County of Cornwall; **Paul Myners,** CBE 2003; Partner and UK Chairman, Cevian Capital, since 2011; *b* 1 April 1948; adopted *s* of late Thomas Russell Myners and of Caroline Molly Myners; *m* 1995, Alison Agnes Isabel Macleod (*see* Lady Myners); one *s* one *d*, and three *d* by a previous marriage. *Educ:* Truro Sch., Cornwall; Univ. of London Inst. of Educn (BEd); Stanford Sch. of Business (SEP 1995). Daily Telegraph, 1970–74; N. M. Rothschild & Sons Ltd, 1974–85 (Dir, 1979); Gartmore plc: Chief Exec., 1985–93, 1999–2000; Chm., 1987–2001; Chairman: Guardian Media Gp plc, 2000–08; Land Securities PLC, 2006–08; Edelman UK, 2015–; Chm. and Dir, Nomad Hldgs Ltd, 2014–; Vice Chm., Global Counsel LLP, 2016–; non-exec. Chm., Autonomous Res. LLP, 2011–. Financial Services Sec., HM Treasury, 2008–10. Dep. Chm., PowerGen plc, 1999–2001; Exec. Dir, Nat. Westminster Bank, 1997–2000; non-executive Director: Orange plc, 1996–99; Coutts Group, 1997–2000; Guardian Newspapers Ltd, 2001–08; mmO₂ plc (formerly BT Wireless), 2001–04; Marks and Spencer, 2002–06 (Chm., 2004–06); Bank of New York, 2002–06; RIT Capital, 2010–; Ecofin Water and Power Opportunities plc, 2012–16; Co-operative Gp, 2013–14; MegaFon, 2013–; Mem., Ct of Dirs, Bank of England, 2005–08; Advr, Govt of Singapore Investment Corp., 2006–08; Chm., Personal Accounts Delivery Authy, DWP, 2007–08. Member: Financial Reporting Council, 1995–2004; Company Law Review Consultative Cttee, 1998–2000; Commn on English Prisons, 2007–08; Commn on Vulnerable Employment, 2007–08; Chm., Low Pay Commn, 2006–08. Vis. Fellow, Nuffield Coll., Oxford, 2007–; Exec. Fellow, London Business Sch., 2013–. Chancellor, Univ. of Exeter, 2016–. Chm. of Court and Council, LSE, 2015–16. Mem., Adv. Council, LSO, 1993–2003. Trustee: Nat. and Cornwall Maritime Mus. Trust, 1998–2004; Royal Acad. Trust, 2000–03; Tate Gall., 2003–08 (Chm., 2004–08; Chm. Council, Tate St Ives, 2001–08); Glyndebourne, 2003–08; Smith Inst., 2003–08; Charities Aid Foundn, 2003–04; Nat. Gallery, 2007–08. FRSA 1994. Hon. LLD Exeter, 2003. Freeman, City of London, 1996. *Publications:* Developing a Winning Partnership, 1995; Creating Quality Dialogue, 1999; Institutional Investment in the UK: a review for HM Treasury, 2001. *Recreations:* family, contemporary art, opera, Rugby football. *Address:* House of Lords, SW1A 0PW. *Clubs:* City of London, Oriental; Hong Kong; Royal Cornwall Yacht.

**MYNERS, Lady; Alison Agnes Isabel Myners;** psychotherapeutic counsellor, since 2013; Chair, Royal Academy Development Trust, Royal Academy of Arts, since 2018; *b* Surrey, 20 Nov. 1959; *d* of Angus James Macleod and Mary McKay Macleod; *m* 1995, Paul Myners (*see* Baron Myners); one *s* one *d*, and three step *d*. *Educ:* Lady Eleanor Holles Sch., Hampton; City of London Poly. (Bi-lingual Sen. Sec. Dip.); Regent's Univ. London (Dip. Psychotherapy and Psychol. of Counselling). Chair, Corporate Develt Bd, Women's Aid, 2005–07. Chair: Royal Acad. Schs' Patrons, 2003–06; Contemp. Art Soc., 2006–10; Inst. of Contemp. Arts, 2010–16. Trustee, Royal Acad. of Arts, 2003–08, Emeritus Trustee, 2009. Mem. Cttee, Action on Addiction, 1997–2000. Mem. Bd, Mustique Co. Ltd, 2017– (Chm., Audit Cttee, 2017–); Mem., Develt Bd, Space Studios, 2018–. Mem., Adv. Bd, Prix Pictet, 2009–. Mem., British Assoc. for Counselling and Psychotherapy, 2015. Mem., RIIA. Cultural Champion Award, Arts & Business, 2012. Mem., St James's Roundtable, Chatham House. *Recreations:* family, art, tennis, cycling, walking. *Clubs:* Soho House; St Mawes Sailing; Trebah Tennis.

**MYNORS, Charles Baskerville,** PhD; author, since 1983; lawyer, Law Commission, since 2016, on secondment to Welsh Government, since 2018; Chancellor, Diocese of Worcester, since 1998; *b* Normandy, Surrey, 27 Aug. 1953; *s* of David Rickards Baskerville Mynors, OBE and Mary Laurence Mynors (*née* Garton); *m* 1978, Janet Lennox Mynors (*née* Wardrop); one *s* one *d* (and one *d* decd). *Educ:* Eton Coll.; Corpus Christi Coll., Cambridge (MA Architecture); Univ. of Sheffield (MA Town and Regl Planning); Poly. of Central London (DipLaw); Univ. of Cambridge (PhD Law 2010). MRTPI 1979, FRTPI 1989; MRICS 1986, FRICS 2008; IHBC 1997. Planning Officer, Royal Borough of Kensington and Chelsea, 1977–86; called to the Bar: Middle Temple, 1988, Bencher, 2017; NI, 2002; in practice as a barrister, Francis Taylor Bldg, 1989–2016. Member: Estates Cttee, Middle Temple, 1998–; Bar Council Disability Gp, 2004–16; Legal Adv. Commn, Gen. Synod, 2011–. Sen. Res. Fellow, De Montfort Univ., Leicester, 1995–98; Vis. Prof., Oxford Brookes Univ., 2005–; Vis. Lectr, Univ. of Bath, 2012–. Mem., Advisory Panel, Prince's Regeneration Trust, 2009–18. Trustee: Overseas Bishoprics Fund, 1997– (Chair, 2013–); Tree Advice Trust, 2012–14; Chm., Complaints Appeal Bd, Inst. of Chartered Foresters, 2008–16. Hon. FICFor, 2017. Member, Editorial Board: Jl of Architectural Conservation, 1995–; Jl of Planning and Envmt Law, 1998–; Ed., Planning and Envmtl Law Bulletin, 1992–96 (Gen. Ed., 1996–98, Consultant Ed., 1998–2002). *Publications:* Urban Conservation and Historic Buildings: a guide to the legislation, 1983; Planning Applications and Appeals: a guide for architects and surveyors, 1987; Listed Buildings and Conservation Areas, 1989, 5th edn (with Nigel Hewitson) as Listed Buildings and Other Heritage Assets, 2017; Planning Control and the Display of Advertisements, 1992; (contrib.) Law, Policy and Development in the Rural Environment, 1999; The Law of Trees, Forests and Hedges, 2002, 2nd edn 2011; The Control of Outdoor Advertising and Graffiti, 2009; (contrib.) Gardens and Landscapes in Historic Building Conservation, 2014; (contrib.) Modern Studies in Property Law, vol. 8, 2015; Changing Churches: a practical guide to the faculty system, 2016; numerous jl articles. *Recreations:* church activities, learning a little Welsh, trying to find the time to learn the harp. *Address:* 16 Elm Crescent, W5 3JW. *T:* (020) 8579 3579. *E:* cmynors@gmail.com.

**MYNORS, Sir Richard (Baskerville),** 2nd Bt *cr* 1964, of Treago, Co. Hereford; landowner; *b* 5 May 1947; *s* of Sir Humphrey Charles Baskerville Mynors, 1st Bt and Lydia Marian (*d* 1992), *d* of Sir Ellis Minns, LittD, FSA, FBA; *S* father, 1989; *m* 1970, Fiona Bridget, *d* of late Rt Rev. G. E. Reindorp; three *d*. *Educ:* Marlborough; Royal College of Music (ARCM, ARCO); Corpus Christi Coll., Cambridge (MA). Asst Director of Music, King's School, Macclesfield, 1970–73; Director of Music: Wolverhampton Grammar School, 1973–81; Merchant Taylors' School, Crosby, 1981–88; Belmont Abbey Sch., Hereford, 1988–89. *Heir:* none. *Address:* The Dower House, Treago, St Weonards, Hereford HR2 8QB. *T:* (01981) 580208.

**MYNOTT, Adam Robert John;** Vice-President, Media Affairs Europe, Huawei Technologies, since 2015 (Director of Media Affairs, 2014–15); *b* 21 Oct. 1957; *s* of Michael J. Mynott and Rosalind S. Mynott; *m* 1987, Carol Elizabeth Schug; two *s* one *d*. *Educ:* Eastbourne Coll.; Univ. of Exeter (BA Hons Philos. 1980); London Coll. of Printing (Postgrad. Dip. Radio Journalism 1982). BBC: Producer, Today Prog., 1986–90; gen. news reporter, 1990–94; Sports Corresp., 1994–2001; S Asia Corresp., Delhi, 2001–04; E Africa Corresp., Nairobi, 2004–08; World Affairs Corresp., 2008–11; Dir of Media Relns, G4S plc, 2011–14. *Publications:* The Battle for Iraq, 2003. *Recreations:* news and current affairs, starting DIY projects. *Address:* Huawei Technologies, 16 Old Queen Street, Westminster, SW1H 9HP. *E:* adam.mynott@gmail.com. *Clubs:* Free Foresters, Sou'westers.

**MYNOTT, Dr (Roger) Jeremy;** Chief Executive of the Press, Secretary of the Press Syndicate and University Printer, Cambridge University Press, 1999–2002; Fellow, Wolfson College, Cambridge, 1999–2009, now Emeritus; *b* 15 Feb. 1942; *s* of Clifford Harry Mynott and Margaret Mynott (*née* Ketley); *m* 2000, Diane Speakman. *Educ:* Colchester Royal Grammar Sch.; Corpus Christi Coll., Cambridge (BA 1964; MA 1968; PhD 1968). Schoolmaster, Magdalen Coll. Sch., Oxford, 1964–65; Cambridge University Press, 1968–2002: sub-editor, 1968–69; editor, 1969–73; sen. editor, 1973–75; Associate Dir, 1975–79; Editl Dir, Humanities and Social Scis, 1979–81; Dir, Publishing Develt, 1981–85; Press Editl Dir Worldwide, 1985–92; Man. Dir, Publishing Div. and Dep. Chief Exec., 1992–99. FRSA 1990. Founder Mem., New Networks for Nature, 2009–. *Publications:* Little Thurlow 2000, 1999; Walks Round the Thurlows, 2005; Birdscapes, 2009; Thurlow 2010, 2010; (ed and trans.) Thucydides: the War of the Peloponnesians and the Athenians, 2013; Knowing your Place, 2016; Birds in the Ancient World: winged words, 2018. *Recreations:* natural history (especially ornithology), walking, philosophy. *W:* www.jeremymynott.org.

**MYRES, Rear-Adm. John Antony Lovell,** CB 1993; Hydrographer of the Navy, 1990–94; *b* 11 April 1936; *yr s* of late Dr John Nowell Linton Myres, CBE and Joan Mary Lovell Myres (*née* Stevens); *m* 1965, Alison Anne, *d* of late Lieut David Lawrence Carr, RN (killed in action 1941) and Mrs James Pertwee; two *s* (and one *s* decd). *Educ:* Winchester College. FRICS 1975–95; FRGS 1993–97; FRIN 1994–97. Entered RN 1954; specialised Hydrographic Surveying, 1959; CO HM Ships Woodlark, 1969–71, Fox, 1972–73, Hecla, 1974, 1978–79, 1981–82; Hydrographer, RAustN, 1982–85. Sec., UK Polar Medal Assessment Cttee, 1994–2011. Pres., Orders and Medals Res. Soc., 1997–2001. Vice Pres., RNLI, 2006–. Younger Brother of Trinity House, 1990. Freeman, City of London, 1990; Liveryman, Chartered Surveyors' Co., 1990–97. Guild Burgess of Preston, 1952. *Publications:* (jtly) British Polar Exploration and Research: a historic and medallic record with biographies, 2000; The First and Second Arctic Medals (1818–1876): with biographies of their recipients, 2019; articles in professional jls. *Recreations:* naval and medallic history, gardening. *Address:* The Gables, 43 Abingdon Road, Dorchester-on-Thames, Oxfordshire OX10 7JZ. *Club:* Antarctic.

**MYRTLE, Brig. Andrew Dewe,** CB 1988; CBE 1979 (MBE 1967); Chief Executive and Secretary, Tennis and Rackets Association, 1989–2001; *b* 17 Dec. 1932; *s* of Lt-Col John Young Elphinstone Myrtle, DSO, KOSB (killed in action in World War II) and late Doreen May Lake; *m* 1973, Mary Rose Ford; two *d*. *Educ:* Horris Hill Prep. Sch.; Winchester Coll.; RMA, Sandhurst (Sword of Honour and Infantry Prize); Army Staff Coll. Co. Comdr, 1 KOSB, 1964–66; Bde Major, 24 Infantry Bde, 1966–68; Co. Comdr, 1 KOSB, 1968–69, CO, 1 KOSB, 1969–71; MA to Adjt Gen., 1971–74; Comdt, Jun. Div., Staff Coll., 1974–77; Comd 8 Infantry Bde, 1977–79; student, RCDS, 1979; DDMO, MoD, 1980–83; Asst Comdt, RMA, Sandhurst, 1983–85; Comdr Land Forces, Cyprus, 1986–88. Col, KOSB, 1980–85. ADC to the Queen, 1985–88. *Recreations:* golf, fly-fishing. *Address:* Pen Guen, Stonor, Henley-on-Thames, Oxon RG9 6HB. *Clubs:* MCC; Huntercombe Golf; Queen's.

# N

**NAAS, Lord**; Richard Thomas Bourke; *b* 7 Dec. 1985; *s* and *heir* of Earl of Mayo, *qv*.

**NADER, Ralph**; author, lecturer, lawyer, consumer advocate; *b* Winsted, Conn, USA, 27 Feb. 1934; *s* of Nadra Nader and Rose (*née* Bouziane). *Educ*: Gilbert Sch., Winsted; Woodrow Wilson Sch. of Public and Internat. Affairs, Princeton Univ. (AB *magna cum laude*); Harvard Univ. Law Sch. (LLB). Admitted to: Bar of Conn, 1958; Bar of Mass, 1959; US Supreme Court Bar, 1963. Served US Army, 1959. Law practice in Hartford, Conn, 1959–; Lectr in History and Govt, Univ. of Hartford, 1961–63; Lectr, Princeton Univ., 1967–68. Member: Amer. Bar Assoc., 1959–; AAAS, 1964–; Phi Beta Kappa. Has pursued actively better consumer protection and improvement in the lot of the American Indian; lobbied in Washington for safer food, drugs, air, water and against nuclear reactors; played very important role in work for passing of: National Traffic and Motor Vehicle Safety Act, 1966; Wholesome Meat Act, 1967; Occupational Safety and Health Act, 1970; Safe Drinking Water Act, 1974; Freedom of Information Act, 1974; National Cooperative Bank Act, 1978. Candidate for Presidency of the USA (Green) 1996 and 2000, (Ind) 2004 and 2008. Nieman Fellows Award, 1965–66; named one of the Ten Outstanding Young Men of the Year by US Jun. Chamber of Commerce, 1967. *Publications*: Unsafe at Any Speed: the designed-in dangers of the American automobile, 1965, rev. edn 1991; (jtly) What to do with Your Bad Car, 1971; Working on the System: a manual for citizen's access to federal agencies, 1972; (jtly) Action for a Change, 1972; (jtly) Whistleblowing, 1972; (jtly) You and Your Pension, 1973; (ed) The Consumer and Corporate Accountability, 1973; (co-ed) Corporate Power in America, 1973; (jtly) Taming the Giant Corporation, 1976; (co-ed) Verdicts on Lawyers, 1976; (jtly) Menace of Atomic Energy, 1977; (co-ed) Who's Poisoning America?, 1981; (jtly) The Big Boys: power and position in American business, 1986; (jtly) Winning the Insurance Game, 1990; (jtly) No Contest, 1996; Only the Super-Rich Can Save Us! (novel), 2009; Getting Steamed to Overcome Corporatism, 2011; The Seventeen Solutions: bold ideas for our American future, 2012; Told You So, 2013; Unstoppable: the emerging left-right alliance to dismantle the corporate state, 2014; Return to Sender, 2015; Breaking Through Power, 2016; Animal Envy, 2016; To The Ramparts, 2018; How the Rats Re-Formed the Congress, 2018; contrib. articles to many magazines; has weekly syndicated newspaper column. *Address*: PO Box 19312, Washington, DC 20036, USA.

**NAGAI, Kiyoshi**, PhD; FRS 2000; Member, since 1981, and Senior Scientist, MRC Laboratory of Molecular Biology; Fellow, Darwin College, Cambridge, since 1993; *b* 25 June 1949; *s* of Prof. Otoji Nagai and Naoko Nagai; *m* 1974, Yoshiko Majima; one *s* one *d*. *Educ*: Toin High Sch.; Osaka Univ. (BSc 1972; MSc 1974; PhD 1978). Thomas Usher Res. Fellow, Darwin Coll., Cambridge, 1981–83. Mem., EMBO, 2000. Novartis Medal and Prize, Biochem. Soc., 2000. *Publications*: (jtly) RNA: protein interactions, 1994; res. pubns and reviews in scientific jls. *Recreations*: playing cello in chamber groups, reading. *Address*: MRC Laboratory of Molecular Biology, Francis Crick Avenue, Cambridge CB2 0QH. *T*: (01223) 267077. *E*: kn@mrc-lmb.cam.ac.uk.

**NAGANO, Kent George**; conductor; Music Director, Montréal Symphony Orchestra, 2006–Aug. 2020; Principal Guest Conductor, Gothenburg Symphony Orchestra, since 2012; General Music Director, Hamburg State Opera and Chief Conductor, Hamburg Philharmonic State Orchestra, since 2015; *b* 22 Nov. 1951; *s* of George Kimiyoshi Nagano and Ruth Okamoto; *m* Mari Kodama; one *d*. *Educ*: Univ. of Calif. Music Director: Opéra de Lyon, 1988–98; Hallé Orch., 1991–2000; Artistic Dir, Deutsches Symphonie-Orchester Berlin, 2000–06; Music Director: LA Opera, 2001–06; Bayerische Staatsoper, 2006–13. Has performed with: Boston Symphony Orch., 1984; Paris Opera (World Première, St François d'Assise, by Messiaen); Metropolitan Opera; Salzburg Fest.; Vienna Philharmonic; Berlin Philharmonic; NY Philharmonic; also World Premières: Death of Klinghoffer by John Adams, Brussels, Lyon and Vienna; L'Amour de loin by Saariaho; A White House Cantata by Bernstein; Das Gehege by Wolfgang Rihm; Alice in Wonderland by Unsuk Chin; Babylon by Jörg Widmann; Stilles Meer by Toshio Hosokawa, Turangalîla (ballet) by John Neumeier, Hamburg, 2016. Gramophone Record of Year, 1990; Gramophone Opera Award, 1993; Grammy Award, 1995, 2001, 2011. *Address*: c/o HarrisonParrott, The Ark, 201 Talgarth Road, W6 8BJ.

**NAGDA, Kanti**; Manager, Sangat Advice Centre, Harrow, since 1998; *b* 1 May 1946; *s* of Vershi Bhoja Nagda and Zaviben Nagda; *m* 1972, Bhagwati Desai; two *s*. *Educ*: City High Sch., Kampala, Uganda; Coll. of Further Educn, Chippenham, Wilts; E African Univ., Uganda; Cassio Coll., Watford. Sec.-Gen., Confedn of Indian Organisations (UK), 1975–98; Manager, Sancroft Community Centre, 1982–98. Pres., Nat. Congress of Gujarati Orgns, 1992–95; Chair, NW London Community Foundn, 2011–12. Exec. Cttee Member: Harrow Community Relations Council, 1974–76; Gujarati Literary Acad. (GB), 1976–82. President: Uganda Art Circle, 1968–71; Anglo Indian Circle, 1973–82 and 1985–88; Indian Cricket Club, Harrow, 1976–80; Greenford (Willow Tree) Lions Club, 1988–89. Trustee, Karma Yoga Foundn, 2009–. Hon. Editorial Consultant, International Asian Guide & Who's Who, 1975–95; Asst Editor, Oshwal News, 1977–84. Mem., Rose of England Lodge, 2010–. *Publications*: Muratiyo Ke Nokar (Gujarati novel), Kenya 1967; stories and articles in newspapers and jls. *Recreations*: cricket, photography. *Address*: 170 Tolcarne Drive, Pinner, Middx HA5 2DR. *T*: (020) 8429 2636. *Club*: Greenford Lions (Sec., 2012).

**NAGEL, William**, CMG 2002; Chairman, W. Nagel (International Diamond Brokers), since 1955; *b* 17 Jan. 1925; *m* 1960, Ruth Marion Josephine Yvonne Tand; one *s* three *d*. *Educ*: University Coll. London (LLB Hons 1949). Called to the Bar, Lincoln's Inn, 1949; post-grad. res. in Public Internat. Law, Fitzwilliam House, Cambridge Univ., 1950–53; Public Internat. Law Course, Internat. Court of Justice, The Hague, 1954; apptd Official Broker, De Beers, 1959. Special Advr to Minister of Foreign Affairs, Romania, 1992. Member: ESU; Foreign Press. Assoc.; RIIA. Freeman, City of London, 1988. Comdr, Order of the Crown (Belgium), 1996; Officer's Cross, Order of Merit (Germany), 2000; Comdr, Nat. Order Serviciul Credincios (Romania), 2002. *Address*: 10 Ely Place, EC1N 6RY. *T*: (020) 7242 9636, *Fax*: (020) 7430 0990. *E*: wn@wnagel.com.

**NAGHDI, Yasmine**; Principal Ballerina, Royal Ballet, since 2017; *b* Royal Borough of Kensington and Chelsea, London, 25 March 1992; *d* of Kamran and Sabine Naghdi. *Educ*: Hill House Internat. Sch.; Royal Ballet Sch. Royal Ballet: Artist, 2010–12; First Artist, 2012–14; Soloist, 2014–16; First Soloist, 2016–17. *Recreations*: travelling, art and contemporary architecture, independent cinema. *Address*: c/o Royal Ballet, Royal Opera House, Bow Street, Covent Garden, WC2E 9DD. *E*: yasminenaghdi@gmail.com. *Club*: Soho House.

**NAGLE, Terence John**, FRICS; Director, Wynnstay Properties plc, 1998–2017; *b* 10 Nov. 1942; *s* of Richard and Bridget Nagle; *m* 1974, Elizabeth Mary Millett; two *s* two *d*. *Educ*: Ottershaw Sch.; St John's Seminary, Wonersh (BTh). FRICS 1964. Property Dir, 1984–93, Man. Dir, 1993–97, Brixton Estate plc. *Recreations*: gardening, sitting on committees. *Address*: Pitch Place House, Worplesdon, Guildford, Surrey GU3 3LQ. *T*: (01483) 232036.

**NAGLER, Neville Anthony**, OBE 2011; Executive Director, Taxation Disciplinary Board, 2007–15; *b* 2 Jan. 1945; *s* of late Gerald and Sylvia Nagler; *m* 1971, Judy Mordant; one *s* one *d*. *Educ*: Christ's Coll., Finchley; Jesus Coll., Cambridge (MA); Cert. in Public Services Mgt, 2000. Asst Principal, HM Treasury, 1967–70; Private Sec. to Chancellor of Exchequer, 1970–71; Principal, 1972; transferred to Home Office, 1975; Asst Sec., Race Relations and Equal Opportunities, 1980–83; Head, Drugs and Extradition Div., 1983–88; Asst Sec., Home Office Finance Div., 1988–91; Chief Exec., subseq. Dir Gen., 1991–2004, Interfaith Consultant, 2005–07, Bd of Deputies of British Jews; Dir, Sternberg Foundn, 2005–06. Vice Chm., Inter Faith Network for UK, 2005–07. Lay Member: Disciplinary Tribunals, Council of Inns of Ct, 2005–12; Investigation Cttee, CIMA, 2007–13; Mem., Lord Chancellor's Adv. Cttee for JPs in NW London, 2006–14. UK Rep. to UN Commn on Narcotic Drugs, 1983–88; Chm., Council of Europe Pompidou Gp, 1984–88. Haldane Essay Prize, Haldane Soc., 1979; Cert. of Appreciation, US Drug Enforcement Admin, 1988. *Publications*: articles in Public Administration and UN Jl of Narcotic Drugs. *Recreations*: listening to music, theatre, walking. *Address*: 21 Regency House, 269 Regent's Park Road, N3 3JZ. *T*: (020) 8346 8083.

**NAGPAUL, Dr Chaand**, CBE 2015; FRCGP; General Practitioner, since 1989 and Senior Partner, since 1995, Honeypot Medical Centre, Stanmore; Chair of Council, British Medical Association, since 2017; *b* Nairobi, Kenya, 18 Feb. 1961; *m* 1992, Dr Meena Thakur; one *s* one *d*. *Educ*: St Bartholomew's Hosp. Med. Coll. (BSc Hons 1993; MB BS 1985). MRCGP 1990, FRCGP 2002. Negotiator, 2007–13, Chair, 2013–17, GP Cttee, BMA. *Recreations*: jazz music, photography. *Address*: British Medical Association, BMA House, Tavistock Square, WC1H 9JP. *T*: (020) 7383 6100. *E*: cnagpaul@bma.org.uk.

**NAHM, Prof. Werner**, PhD; FRS 2011; Senior Professor of Theoretical Physics, and Director, School of Theoretical Physics, Dublin Institute for Advanced Studies, since 2002; *b* 1949. *Educ*: Ludwigs Maximilian Univ., Munich (Dip. Physics 1970); Bonn Univ. (PhD 1972). Postdoctoral res., Bonn Univ., 1972–75; Fellow and staff mem., CERN, 1976–82; Heisenberg Fellow, Bonn Univ., 1982–86; Associate Prof., Univ. of Calif, Davis, 1986–89; Prof., Bonn Univ., 1989–2002. Ext. Scientific Mem., Max-Planck-Inst. für Mathematik. Gothenburg Lise Meitner Prize, Univ. of Gothenburg, 2012; Max Planck Medal for Theoretical Physics, German Phys. Soc., 2013; Gold Medal for Phys. and Math. Scis, RIA, 2014. *Address*: School of Theoretical Physics, Dublin Institute for Advanced Studies, 10 Burlington Road, Dublin 4, Ireland.

**NAHORSKI, Prof. Stefan Ryszard**, PhD; FMedSci; Professor of Pharmacology, 1984–2006, now Emeritus, and Head of Department of Cell Physiology and Pharmacology, 1993–2006, University of Leicester; *b* 10 Dec. 1945; *s* of Stanislaw Nahorski and Linda Nahorska; *m* 1969, Catherine Mary Gower; one *s* two *d*. *Educ*: St Boniface's Coll., Plymouth; Univ. of Southampton (BSc Hons); Portsmouth Sch. of Pharmacy (PhD 1971). Research Asst, Portsmouth, 1968–71; MRC Fellow, Sheffield, 1971–75; University of Leicester: Lectr in Pharmacology, 1976–81; Reader, 1981–84. Gov., Cornwall Coll., 2008–12. Founder FMedSci 1998. John Vane Medal, British Pharmacological Soc., 2004. *Publications*: Pharmacology of Adrenoceptors, 1985; Transmembrane Signalling, 1990; numerous research papers to learned jls. *Recreations*: tennis, walking, watching (supporting) soccer, sea angling.

**NAHUM, Peter John**; art advisor and dealer, Peter & Renate Nahum Agency, London, since 2009; *b* 19 Jan. 1947; *s* of Denis E. Nahum and Allison Faith Nahum (*née* Cooke); *m* 1987, Renate Angelika Meiser. *Educ*: Sherborne. Peter Wilson's Sotheby's, 1966–84; British Paintings Dept, Sotheby's, Belgravia, 1971–84, Sen. Dir, 1977–84; regular contributor to Antiques Road Show, BBC TV, 1980–2001; Peter Nahum at Leicester Galleries, London, 1984–2009. *Publications*: Prices of Victorian Paintings, Drawings and Watercolours, 1976; Monograms of Victorian and Edwardian Artists, 1976; Cross Section, British Art in the 20th Century, 1988; British Art in the Twentieth Century, 1989; Burne-Jones, The Pre-Raphaelites & Their Century, 1989; Burne-Jones: a quest for love, 1993; Fairy Folk in Fairy Land, 1997; Pre-Raphaelite . Symbolist . Visionary, 2001; Medieval to Modern, 2003; The Ruralists: a celebration, 2007; Ancient Landscapes, Pastoral Visions, 2008; Past and Present: Edward Burne-Jones, his medieval sources and their relevance to his personal journey, 2009. *Recreations*: reading, art, sailing, photography and street photography, gardening, theatre, travel, walking. *Address*: 5 Bloomsbury Square, WC1A 2TA. *T*: (020) 7242 1126. *E*: peternahum@leicestergalleries.com.

**NAILATIKAU, Brig.-Gen. Hon. Ratu Epeli**, LVO 1977; OBE 1979; CSM 1995; MSD 1988; President of Fiji, 2009–15; UNAIDS Regional Goodwill Ambassador for the Pacific, since 2015; Speaker, Parliament of Fiji, since 2019; *b* 5 July 1941; *s* of Ratu Sir Edward Cakobau, KBE, MC, ED and Adi Lady Vasamaca Tuiburelevu; *m* 1981, Adi Koila Nailatikau (*née* Mara), *d* of Ratu Sir Kamisese Mara, GCMG, KBE, CF, MSD, PC; one *s* one *d*. *Educ*: Levuka Public Sch.; Queen Victoria Sch., Fiji; Wadham Coll., Oxford. Enlisted in Royal Fiji Military Forces, 1962; commnd Fiji Infantry Regt, 1963; seconded to First Bn, Royal NZ Infantry Regt, Malaysia and Borneo, 1966; ADC to Governor of Fiji, 1968–69; Foreign Service Course, Oxford Univ., 1969–70; Second Secretary: Fiji High Commn, Canberra, 1970–72; Fiji Mission to UN, 1973–74; Australian Army Staff

**NAIRN, Sir Michael,** 4th Bt cr 1904; b 1 July 1938; s of Sir Michael George Nairn, 3rd Bt, TD, and Helen Louise, yr d of Major E. J. W. Bruce, Melbourne, Aust.; S father, 1984; m 1st, 1972, Diana (d 1982), er d of Leonard Francis Bligh, NSW; two s one d; 2nd, 1986, Sally Jane, d of Major W. P. S. Hastings. Educ: Eton; INSEAD. Heir: s Michael Andrew Nairn [b 2 Nov. 1973; m 2009, Maya, er d of Peter Gill, San Antonio, Texas]. Club: Caledonian.

**NAIRN,** Queenscliffe, 1976 (psc); CO Fiji Bn, Fiji Infantry Regt serving with UNIFIL, 1978–79; Jt Services Staff Coll., Canberra, Australia, 1980 (jssc); Sen. Plans Officer, UNIFIL HQ, 1981; CS, 1981–82, Comdr, 1982–87, Royal Fiji Mil. Forces; Ambassador of Fiji to UK, and concurrently Ambassador to Denmark, Germany, Israel, the Holy See and Egypt, 1988–96; Roving Ambassador to Pacific Island countries, 1998; Perm. Sec. for Foreign Affairs and External Trade, Fiji, 1999; Mem., Military Council, May–July 2000; Deputy Prime Minister and Minister for Fijian Affairs: Interim Govt, July 2000–March 2001; Caretaker Govt, March–Sept. 2001; Speaker, House of Reps, Fiji, 2001–06; Minister, Interim Government: for Foreign Affairs and External Trade, 2007–08; for Foreign Affairs, Internat. Co-operation and Civil Aviation, 2008; for Indigenous Affairs, Provincial Develt and Multi-Ethnic Affairs, 2008–09. Fiji Equerry: to the Prince of Wales during Fiji Independence visit, 1970; to the Queen during Jubilee visit, 1977. Hon. Col 1st Bn Fiji Infantry Regt, 1996. OStJ 1985. Civil Service Medal (Fiji), 1995. Recreations: golf, tennis. Address: c/o Government House, Berkley Crescent, PO Box 2513, Government Buildings, Suva, Fiji.

**NAIRN, Martin John L.;** see Lambie-Nairn.

**NAIRN, Nicholas Cameron Abel;** chef; Chief Executive Officer and owner: Nairn Enterprises, since 1990; Nick Nairn Consulting, since 2008; Chief Executive Officer, owner and Senior Tutor, Nick Nairn Cook School, Port of Menteith, since 2000, and Aberdeen, 2012–18; b Stirling, 12 Jan. 1959; s of James Nairn and Irene Nairn; m 2001, Holly Anderson; one s one d. Educ: McLaren High Sch.; Glasgow Coll. of Nautical Studies (Deck Officer Cl. 1 1984). Naval officer, Merchant Navy, 1976–83; owner and Head Chef: Braeval Restaurant, 1986– (Michelin Star, 1991); Nairns Restaurant with Rooms, 1997–. Television presenter: Wild Harvest, 1996; Ready Steady Cook, 1996–2010; Landward, 2007–; Paul and Nick's Big Food Trip, 2012–. Founder Mem., Scottish Chefs Assoc., 1991; Fellow, Master Chefs of GB, 2003. DUniv Stirling, 2007. Scottish Chef of the Year, 1996. Publications: Wild Harvest, 1996; Wild Harvest 2, 1997; Island Harvest, 1998; Nick Nairn's Top 100 Salmon Recipes, 2002; New Scottish Cookery, 2002; (jtly) The Ready Steady Cook Book, 2003; Nick Nairn's Top 100 Chicken Recipes, 2004; (jtly) Great British Menu, 2006; Fish 'n' Tips, 2006; Nick Nairn Cook School, 2008. Recreations: hillwalking, cycling, mountain biking, spending time with my family. Address: Nick Nairn Cook School, Port of Menteith, Stirling FK8 3JZ. T: (01877) 389900. E: info@nicknairncookschool.com.

**NAIRN, Sir Robert Arnold S.;** see Spencer-Nairn.

**NAIRN, Prof. Tom C.;** Professor of Nationalism and Global Diversity, Royal Melbourne Institute of Technology, 2002–10; b 2 June 1932; s of David Robertson Nairn and Katherine Herd Cunningham; partner, Millicent Petrie. Educ: Dunfermline High Sch.; Univ. of Edinburgh (MA Philosophy 1956); Scuola Normale Superiore, Pisa; Univ. de Dijon. Lectr in Social Philosophy, Univ. of Birmingham, 1962–64; Lectr in Gen. Studies, Hornsey Coll. of Art, 1966–69; Fellow, Transnational Inst., Amsterdam, 1972–75; Dir, Scottish Internat. Inst., Edinburgh, 1976–80; work in commercial TV, Glasgow, 1992–94; Researcher with Ernest Gellner, Centre for Nationalism Studies, Prague Coll. of the Central European Univ., 1994–95; Lectr in Nationalism Studies, Grad. Sch., Univ. of Edinburgh, 1994–99. Inst. of Advanced Studies Fellow, University Coll., Durham Univ., 2009. Hon. DSc Edinburgh, 2016. Publications: The Beginning of the End (with Angelo Quattrocchi), 1968; The Left Against Europe, 1975; The Break-up of Britain, 1977, new edn 2003; The Enchanted Glass: Britain and Monarchy, 1988; Faces of Nationalism, 1998; Pariah: misfortunes of the British kingdom, 2001; (with Paul James) Global Matrix, 2005; Old Nations, Auld Enemies, New Times (essays), 2014, 2nd edn 2020.

**NAIRN-BRIGGS, Very Rev. George Peter;** DL; Dean (formerly Provost) of Wakefield, 1997–2007, now Dean Emeritus; b 5 July 1945; s of Frederick and Gladys Nairn-Briggs; m 1968, Candida Vickery; one s one d. Educ: Slough Tech. High Sch.; King's Coll., London (AKC 1969); St Augustine's Coll., Canterbury. Local authority housing, 1963–64; Press Officer, MAFF, 1964–66; ordained deacon, 1970, priest, 1971; Curate: St Laurence, Catford, 1970–73; St Saviour, Raynes Park, 1973–75; Vicar: Christ the King, Salfords, 1975–81; St Peter, St Helier, dio. Southwark, 1981–87; Bishop's Advr for Social Responsibility, Wakefield, 1987–97; Canon Residentiary, Wakefield Cathedral, 1992–97. A Church Comr, 2004–07. Chm., Standards Cttee, Wakefield MDC, 2002–. Mem., Gen. Synod of C of E, 1980–2007. DL W Yorks, 2006. Publications: Love in Action, 1986; Serving Two Masters, 1988; It Happens in the Family, 1992; contrib. to magazines and jls. Recreations: reading, buying antiques, travel. Address: Abbey House, 2 St James Court, Park Avenue, Wakefield WF2 8DN. T: (01924) 291029.

**NAIRNE, Alexander Robert, (Sandy),** CBE 2011; curator and writer; Director, National Portrait Gallery, 2002–15; b 8 June 1953; s of Rt Hon. Sir Patrick Dalmahoy Nairne, GCB, MC, PC; partner 1981, m 2006, Sylvia Elizabeth, (Lisa), Tickner, qv; one s one d. Educ: Radley Coll.; University Coll., Oxford (BA Modern History and Economics 1974; MA; Hon. Fellow 2006). Asst Dir, Museum of Modern Art, Oxford, 1974–76; Research Asst and Asst Keeper, Tate Gallery, 1976–79; Dir of Exhibitions, Inst. of Contemporary Arts, 1980–83; writer and associate producer, State of the Art, TV series, Channel 4, 1985–87; Dir of Visual Arts, Arts Council, 1987–92; Sen. Res. Fellow, Getty Grant Prog., 1992–93; Dir, Public and Regl Services, 1994–98, Dir, Nat. Progs, 1998–2002, Tate Gall. Member: Fabric Adv. Cttee, St Paul's Cathedral, 1996– (Chm., 2011–); Adv. Gp, Govt Art Collection, 2002–15; London Cultural Strategy Gp, 2009–10; Banknote Character Adv. Cttee, Bank of England, 2015–. Trustee, Artangel, 1993–2006. Vis. Fellow, Clark Art Inst., Mass, 2007. Gov., Middx Univ., 1994–2003 (Dep. Chm., 1999–2000); Member Council: RCA, 2001–10; British Sch. in Rome, 2001–10; Museums Assoc., 2005–08 (Vice Pres., 2006–08); Paul Mellon Centre, 2007–12; Mem. Art Gp, Maggie's Cancer Care Centres, 2010– (Chm., 2011–). Trustee: Seafarers' Hosp. Soc., 1984– (Dep. Chm., 2018–); Clore Leadership Prog., 2014–19 (Chm., 2014–19); Samuel Courtauld Trust, Courtauld Inst., 2014–; Nat. Trust, 2015–. Sen. FRCA 2010; FSA 2012. Hon. DArts: Middx, 2005; De Montfort, 2008; London, 2012; Hon. Dr Norwich Univ. of the Arts, 2015. Publications: State of the Art, 1987; Thinking about Exhibitions, 1996; The Portrait Now, 2006; Art Theft and the Case of the Stolen Turners, 2011; 21st Century Portraits, 2013. Recreation: racing punting. Address: 43 Lady Somerset Road, NW5 1TY. Clubs: Chelsea Arts; Hampstead Heath Croquet; Leander (Henley).

See also A. Nairne.

**NAIRNE, Andrew,** OBE 2019; Director, Kettle's Yard, University of Cambridge, since 2011; b 10 Feb. 1960; s of Rt Hon. Sir Patrick Dalmahoy Nairne, GCB, MC, PC; m 1995, Nicola Dandridge, qv; two s. Educ: Radley Coll.; Univ. of St Andrews (MA Art Hist. 1983). Asst Curator, Kettle's Yard, Cambridge, 1984–85; Dep. Dir, Ikon Gall., Birmingham, 1985–86; Exhibns Dir, Centre for Contemp. Arts, Glasgow, 1986–92; Visual Arts Dir, Scottish Arts Council, Edinburgh, 1992–97; Dir, Dundee Contemp. Arts, 1997–2001; Dir, Modern Art Oxford, 2001–08; Exec. Dir, Arts (formerly Arts Strategy), Arts Council England, 2008–11. Vis. Fellow, Nuffield Coll., Oxford, 2002–10. Chm., Visual Arts and Galls Assoc., 2005–07. FRSA 1997. Recreation: running. Address: 15 Grazebrook Road, N16 0HU. T: 07795 580108.

See also A. R. Nairne.

**NAIRNE, Nicola;** see Dandridge, N.

**NAIRNE, Sandy;** see Nairne, A. R.

**NAIRNE, Sylvia Elizabeth, (Lisa);** see Tickner, S. E.

**NAISMITH, Prof. James Henderson,** PhD, DSc; FRS 2014; FRSE; FMedSci, FRSC, FRSB; Professor of Structural Biology, University of Oxford, since 2017; Director, Research Complex at Harwell, since 2017; Senior Research Fellow, Jesus College, Oxford, since 2017; Director, Rosalind Franklin Institute, since 2017; b Bellshill, 26 July 1968; s of Duncan Naismith and Frances Naismith; m 1993, Rachel Middleton; one s one d. Educ: Hamilton Grammar Sch.; Univ. of Edinburgh (BSc 1st Cl. Chem. 1989); Univ. of Manchester (PhD Structural Chem. 1992); Univ. of St Andrews (DSc Structural and Chemical Biol. 2016). FRSC 2002; FRSB (FSB 2009). NATO Fellow, Lab. of Stephen Sprang, Univ. of Texas Southwestern, 1993–94; University of St Andrews: Lectr, 1995–98; Reader, 1998–2001; Prof. of Chemical Biol., 2001–17; Dir, Biomed. Scis Res. Complex, 2011–16. Mem., EMBO, 2009–. FRSE 2005; FMedSci 2012; FAAAS 2016. Publications: papers in learned jls. Recreations: family, American Civil War, Chinese art, work. Address: Division of Structural Biology, University of Oxford, Henry Wellcome Building for Genomic Medicine, Roosevelt Drive, Oxford OX3 7BN. T: (01865) 287546. E: naismith@strubi.ox.ac.uk.

**NAJIM, Omar;** Senior Advisor, Health Authority-Abu Dhabi, since 2014; b Baghdad, 10 Nov. 1973; m 2009, Hadeel Alwash; two c. Educ: Al-Mansour High Sch. for Boys, Baghdad; Univ. of Baghdad (MB ChB); Imperial Coll. London (MSc Surgical Technol.). Surgeon in training, NHS, 2001–07; Dep. Dir, Med. Workforce Develt, NHS NW, 2007–09; Leadership Fellow, NHS Inst. for Innovation and Improvement, 2009–10; Sen. Operation Manager, St George's Hosp. NHS Trust, London, 2010–11; Hd, Delivery Improvement, McKinsey Hospital Inst., 2011–14. Mem., BMA (Chm., Civil and Public Services Cttee). Publications: contribs to BMJ, British Jl Hosp. Medicine, Head and Neck Jl, Clin. Voice, Philosophy Now, Jl Neurosurgery. Recreations: horse-riding, fencing, reading, squash, creating stories about strangers.

**NAJSAREK, Paul;** Chief Executive, Ealing Borough Council, since 2016; b 13 March 1967; s of Otto Marian Najsarek and Barbara Najsarek; m 1999, Concetta Maida; two s. Educ: St Thomas Aquinas High Sch., Manchester; Xaverian Sixth Form Coll., Manchester; Univ. of Liverpool (BA Politics and Philos.); Univ. of York (MA Political Hist.); Open Univ. (MBA). Hd, Policy, Audit Commn, 2004; Corporate Dir, 2008–13, Actg Chief Exec., 2013–15, Harrow LBC; Chief Exec., Bolton MBC, 2015. Mem. Bd, What Works Centre for Wellbeing CIC, 2017–; Spokesperson for Community Wellbeing, Soc. of Local Govt Chief Execs. Recreations: cinema, reading, travel, football, cricket.

**NAKASONE, Yasuhiro;** Prime Minister of Japan, 1982–87; Chairman, Institute for International Policy Studies (formerly International Institute for Global Peace), since 1988; Founder and President, Asia Pacific Parliamentary Forum, 1993–2003 (Hon. President, since 2004); b 27 May 1918; 2nd s of Matsugoroh Nakasone; m 1945, Tsutako Kobayashi (d 2012); one s two d. Educ: Faculty of Law, Imperial Univ. (graduate). Joined Min. of Home Affairs, 1941; commd as Lt-Comdr, 1945. Mem., House of Representatives (elected 20 consecutive times), 1947–2003; Minister of State, Dir-Gen. of Science and Technology Agency, 1959–60; Minister of Transport, 1967–68; Minister of State, Dir-Gen. of Defence Agency, 1970–71; Minister of Internat. Trade and Industry, 1972–74; Minister of State for Admin. Management Agency, 1980–82. Chm. Exec. Council, 1971–72, Sec. Gen., 1974–76, Liberal Democratic Party. Hon. DHL, Johns Hopkins, 1984; Hon. Dr Louis Pasteur, Strasbourg, 1999. Médaille de la Chancellerie, Univs of Paris. Publications: The Ideals of Youth, 1947; Japan Speaks, 1954; The New Conservatism, 1978; Human Cities—a proposal for the 21st century, 1980; Anthology of Haiku by Nakasone Yasuhiro, 1985; Politics and My Life (autobiog.), 1992; Tenchiyujou (autobiography), 1996; The Making of the New Japan, 1999; Japan: a state strategy for the twenty-first century, 2002; Japanese Prime Ministership as a Science, 2004; Meditations, 2004; Anthology of Haiku 2009 by Nakasone Yasuhiro, 2009; My Last Word on Conservatism, 2010; Japanese Foreign Policy since 1945, 2012. Address: Toranomon 3–2–2, 30 Mori Building, Minato-ku, Tokyo 105–0001, Japan.

**NALL, Sir Edward William Joseph,** 3rd Bt cr 1954, of Hoveringham, co. Nottingham; b 24 Oct. 1952; er s of Sir Michael Joseph Nall, 2nd Bt and of Angela Loveday Hanbury (née Coryton); S father, 2001; m 2004, Helen Fiona Batterbury (née Fergusson); one d. Educ: Eton. Commnd 13th/18th Royal Hussars (QMO), subseq. Light Dragoons, 1973; Major, 1985; retd, 1993. Heir: b Alexander Michael Nall [b 3 July 1956; m 1982, Caroline Jane Robinson; one s one d]. Address: Hoveringham Hall, Hoveringham, Nottingham NG14 7JR.

**NALL-CAIN,** family name of **Baron Brocket.**

**NALLY, Edward;** Consultant, Fieldings Porter, Bolton, since 2014 (Partner, 1982–2014); b 18 Jan. 1956; s of Edward and Sarah Nally; m 1977, Julie Fagan; one s one d. Educ: De La Salle Grammar Sch., Salford; Nottingham Univ. (LLB Hons). Solicitor. Diocesan Solicitor, Salford RC Dio., 1983–. Dep. Vice-Pres., 2002–03, Vice-Pres., 2003–04, Pres., 2004–05, Law Soc. Member: Judicial Appts Commn, 2006–11; Legal Services Bd, 2011–15; Solicitors Disciplinary Tribunal, 2009– (Pres., 2016–); QC Appts Panel, 2016–. Governor: Coll. of Law, 2004–12; Legal Educn Foundn, 2012–. Chm. of Governors, Pendleton Sixth Form Coll., Salford, 2000–07. Recreations: golf, walking, avid Bolton Wanderers football supporter. Address: Fieldings Porter, Silverwell House, Silverwell Street, Bolton BL1 1PT. T: (01204) 540900, Fax: (01204) 397254. E: edward.nally@fieldingsporter.co.uk. Club: Royal Automobile.

**NAMALIU, Rt Hon. Sir Rabbie (Langanai),** KCMG 1996 (CMG 1979); GCL 2008; CSM 2006; PC 1989; MP for Kokopo (Pangu Pati), Papua New Guinea, 1982–2007; Chancellor, University of Natural Resources and Environment, Vudal, 2007–11; b 3 April 1947; s of Darius Namaliu and Utul Ioan; m 1978, Margaret Nakikus (d 1993); two s, and one step d; m 1999, Kelin Tavul (marr. diss. 2004); one s two d; m 2005, Darusila Watangia. Educ: Univ. of Papua New Guinea (BA); Univ. of Victoria, BC (MA). Senior Tutor, later Lectr in History, Univ. of Papua New Guinea, 1973; Principal Private Sec. to Chief Minister (Hon. Michael Somare), 1974–75; Vis. Pacific Fellow, Centre for Pacific Studies, Univ. of California, Santa Cruz, 1975; Provincial Comr, East New Britain Province, 1976; Chm., Public Services Commn, 1976–79; Exec. Officer to Leader of the Opposition (Rt Hon. Michael Somare), 1980–81; Minister for Foreign Affairs and Trade, 1982–84, for Primary Industry, 1985; Dep. Leader, 1985–88, Parliamentary Leader, 1988–93, Pangu Pati; Leader of the Opposition, May–July 1988; Prime Minister, PNG, 1988–92; Leader of the

Opposition, 1992–93; Speaker of Nat. Parlt, 1994–97; Senior Minister of State, 1997–98; Minister: for Petroleum and Energy, 1998–99; for Foreign Affairs and Immigration, 2002–06; for the Treasury, 2006–07. Non-executive Director: Era Resources Inc. (formerly Marengo Mining Ltd), 2008–17; Kina Securities Ltd, 2008–17; Bougainville Copper Ltd, 2011–; Interoil Corp. PNG, 2012–17; Post Courier, PNG, 2013–; Yandera Mining Ltd, 2017–; Chm., Kina Asset Management Ltd, 2009–17; Chm., Kramer Ausenco, 2010–. Patron, Youth with a Mission Medical Ships Prog., 2012–. Hon. LLD Univ. of Victoria, BC, 1983. *Recreations:* swimming, walking, reading. *Address:* PO Box 144, Kokopo 613, East New Britain Province, Papua New Guinea. *E:* rnamaliu@datec.net.pg.

**NANCOLLAS, Sarah Catherine;** Chief Executive, World Association of Girl Guides and Girl Scouts, since 2018; *b* London, 8 Aug. 1961; *d* of Henry John Nancollas, MBE and late Freda Nancollas. *Educ:* Simon Langton Grammar Sch. for Girls; Univ. of Nottingham (BSc Hons Civil Engrg 1983). Shift Controller, Northfleet, 1983–85, Distribution Manager, Plymstock, 1985–87, Blue Circle Cement; Sen. Mgt Consultant, Price Waterhouse, 1987–89; Implementation Manager, 1989–91, Distribution Manager Gen. Chemicals, 1991–92, BP Chemicals; Transport Advr, Save the Children UK, 1993–98; Chief Exec., Transaid, 1998–2003; Exec. Dir, Project Hope, 2003–04; Chief Executive: Canon Collins Trust, 2004–10; LEPRA Health in Action, later Lepra, 2010–17; Variety, the Children's Charity, 2017–18. Trustee: DHL UK Foundn, 2004–11; Skillshare Internat., 2004–11; ILEP, 2010–16. *Recreations:* landscape photography, watching athletics, Formula 1 and cricket. *Address:* World Association of Girl Guides and Girl Scouts, Olave Centre, 12C Lyndhurst Road, NW3 5PQ. *T:* (020) 7433 6432. *E:* sarah.nancollas@variety.org.uk.

**NANDY, Dipak;** Head of Equal Opportunities, Social Services Department, Nottinghamshire County Council, 1992–2001; *b* 21 May 1936; *s* of B. C. Nandy and Leela Nandy; *m* 1st, 1964, Margaret Gracie (decd); 2nd, 1972, Hon. Luise Byers (marr. diss. 1991); two *d*. *Educ:* St Xavier's Coll., Calcutta; Univ. of Leeds (BA 1st Cl. Hons English Literature, 1960; C. E. Vaughan Research Fellowship, 1960–62). Lectr, English Literature, Univ. of Leicester, 1962–66; Lectr and Fellow of Rutherford College, Univ. of Kent at Canterbury, 1966–68; founder-Director, The Runnymede Trust, 1968–73; Vis. Fellow, Adlai Stevenson Inst. of International Affairs, Chicago, 1970–73; Research Fellow, Social and Community Planning Research, 1973–74; special consultant on discrimination, Home Office, 1975; Dep. Chief Exec., Equal Opportunities Commn, 1976–86; Chief Exec., Intermediate Technology Develt Gp, 1986–88; Hon. Lectr in Social Policy, Univ. of Birmingham, 1989–95; Financial and Admin. Dir, RSP, Queen Elizabeth House, Oxford, 1991. Member: Cttee of Inquiry into Future of Broadcasting, 1974–77; Council, Nat. Assoc. Citizens' Advice Bureaux, 1983–86; BBC: Chm., Asian Programmes Adv. Cttee, 1983–88; Mem., General Adv. Council. Member: Council, Northern Chamber Orch., 1980–84; Royal Nat. Theatre Bd, 1991–97; Governor, BFI, 1984–87. Mem. Ct, Leicester Univ., 2002–08. Trustee, CSV, 1981–91. Hon. Liaison, Employment and Labour Law Sect., Amer. Bar Assoc., 1980–. *Publications:* numerous essays in books, periodicals and newspapers on literature, political thought, race relations, urban problems, equality for women, broadcasting policy and development issues. *Recreations:* collecting records, opera, computing.
See also L. E. Nandy.

**NANDY, Lisa Eva;** MP (Lab) Wigan, since 2010; *b* Manchester, 9 Aug. 1979; *d* of Dipak Nandy, *qv*. *Educ:* Parrs Wood Comp. Sch., Manchester; Univ. of Newcastle upon Tyne (BA Hons Pols 2001); Birkbeck, Univ. of London (MSc Pols and Govt 2005). Researcher to Neil Gerrard, MP, 2001–03; Policy Researcher, Centrepoint, 2003–05; Policy Advr, Children's Soc., 2005–10. Mem. (Lab) Hammersmith and Fulham LBC, 2006–10. Shadow Minister for Children and Families, 2012–15; Shadow Sec. of State for Energy and Climate Change, 2015–16. *Recreations:* theatre, Rugby League. *Address:* House of Commons, SW1A 0AA. *T:* (020) 7219 7188. *E:* lisa.nandy.mp@parliament.uk.

**NANSON, Maj. Gen. Paul Anthony Edward,** CBE 2015 (MBE 2002); QCVS 1996; Commandant, Royal Military Academy, Sandhurst, since 2015; General Officer Commanding Army Recruiting and Initial Training Command, 2018–April 2020; *b* Ormskirk, Lancs, 10 May 1965; *s* of Roy and Pam Nanson; *m* 1998, Louise Hatfield; one *s* one *d*. *Educ:* Merchant Taylors' Sch., Crosby; Royal Mil. Acad. Sandhurst. Commnd 1986; Platoon Comdr, 3rd Bn RRF, then Trng Regt, Queen's Div., 1986–89; Adjt, 2nd Bn RRF, 1993–95; Co. Comdr, 2nd Bn, Royal Anglian Regt, 1996–98; acsc, 1998–2000; COS, 102 Logistics Bde, 2000–02; Co. Comdr, 1st Bn RRF, 2002–04; Mem., Directing Staff, JSCSC, 2004–06; CO, 1st Bn RRF, 2006–08; COS, 1st (UK) Armd Div., 2009–11; Comdr, 7th Armd Bde, 2011–13; Dep. Comdr Regl Comd (SW), 2013–14; Dir, Army Div., JSCSC, 2014–15. Col, RRF, 2015–. *Recreations:* hill walking, cooking, running, family. *Club:* Ormskirk Golf.

**NAPIER,** family name of **Lord Napier and Ettrick** and **Baron Napier of Magdala**.

**NAPIER,** 15th Lord *cr* 1627 (Scot.), **AND ETTRICK,** 6th Baron *cr* 1872 (UK); **Francis David Charles Napier;** (12th) Bt (Napier, formerly Scott) of Thirlestane (NS) 1666; Chief of the Name and Arms of Napier; established Napier Garden Planning, 1999; *b* 3 Nov. 1962; *er s* of 14th Lord Napier (and 5th Baron Ettrick), KCVO, and of Delia Mary (*née* Pearson); *S* father, 2012; *m* 1993, Zara Jane, *o d* of Hugh McCalmont, Newmarket, Suffolk; one *s* one *d*. *Educ:* Stanbridge Earls School; South Thames Coll., Wandsworth, 1986–87 (City and Guilds Computer Diploma); Otley Coll., Ipswich (Nat. Cert Hort. Garden Design and Construction 1999). With a Lloyd's agency, 1984–92; with Heath Bloodstock Ltd, 1992–97. Member: Standing Council of Scottish Chiefs, 2011–; Standing Council of the Baronetage, 2014–; Assoc. of Conservative Peers, 2017–. Mem., Montrose Soc., 2010–. *Recreations:* travelling, horse-racing, cycling, gardening. *Heir: s* Master of Napier, *qv*. *Address:* Gowan Cottage, Westley Waterless, Newmarket, Suffolk CB8 0RQ. *Clubs:* Pratt's; Forest.

**NAPIER, Master of; Hon. William Alexander Hugh Napier;** *b* 10 June 1996; *s* and heir of Lord Napier and Ettrick, *qv*. *Educ:* King's Ely; MPW Cambridge.

**NAPIER OF MAGDALA,** 6th Baron *cr* 1868; **Robert Alan Napier;** *b* 6 Sept. 1940; *s* of 5th Baron Napier of Magdala, OBE, and Elizabeth Marian, *y d* of E. H. Hunt, FRCS; *S* father, 1987; *m* 1964, Frances Clare, *d* of late Alan Frank Skinner; one *s* one *d*. *Educ:* Winchester College; St John's Coll., Cambridge (BA 1st cl. Hons 1962; MA 1966). *Heir: s* Hon. James Robert Napier, *b* 29 Jan. 1966. *Address:* The Coach House, Kingsbury Street, Marlborough, Wilts SN8 1HU. *T:* (01672) 512333. *Club:* Leander (Henley-on-Thames).

**NAPIER, Brian William;** QC (Scot.) 2002; PhD; *b* 9 Jan. 1949; *s* of George Napier and Isobella Ramsey Ross Napier; *m* 1st, 1971, Helen Marjorie Mercer (marr. diss. 2001); one *s* one *d*; 2nd, 2007, Elizabeth Clarke; one *s*. *Educ:* George Watson's Coll., Edinburgh; Univ. of Edinburgh (LLB 1971); Queens' Coll., Cambridge (MA 1974; PhD 1976). Res. Fellow, 1974, Fellow, 1974–89, Queens' Coll., Cambridge; Asst Lectr, 1975–79, Lectr, 1979–89, Univ. of Cambridge; Prof. of Law, Queen Mary and Westfield Coll., Univ. of London, 1989–96, Vis. Prof., 1996–; called to the Bar, Middle Temple, 1990 and Gray's Inn. Prof. Associé, Univs of Paris 1 and 2, 1980–81. Joint Editor: Harvey on Industrial Relations and Employment Law, 1988–; Transfer of Undertakings, 1999–. *Recreations:* walking, music. *Address:* c/o Faculty of Advocates, Parliament House, Edinburgh EH1 1RF. *T:* (0131) 260 5654.

**NAPIER, Sir Charles Joseph,** 6th Bt *cr* 1867, of Merrion Square, Dublin; Founder and Director, Kilmeston Communications, since 2012; Co-founder and Director, Atlas Communications Partners, since 2015; *b* 15 April 1973; *o s* of Sir Robin Surtees Napier, 5th Bt and of Jennifer Beryl (who *m* 2001, Major Donald Black, MC (who *d* 2009)), *d* of H. Warwick Daw; *S* father, 1994; *m* 2003, Imelda Blanche Elisabeth, *d* of late John Trafford and of Amanda Trafford; two *s* one *d*. *Educ:* Eton; Univ. of Edinburgh (MA Hons; Fencing Blue). Scottish European Aid, 1995–96; Corporate Fundraiser, MIND, 1997–98; Appeal Dir, 1998–99, and Mem. Mgt Cttee, 2001–09, Downside Settlement, Bermondsey; public affairs, The Policy Partnership, 1999–2006; Account Dir, PPS Gp, 2006; Associate Director: Quintus Public Affairs, 2006–09; Luther Pendragon, 2009–12. Mem. (Lab), Hammersmith and Fulham LBC, 2002–06. Governor: Peterborough Primary Sch., Fulham, 2000–08; Brackenbury Primary Sch., Hammersmith, 2014–16. *Recreation:* fishing. *Heir: s* Finnian John Lennox Napier, *b* 14 Feb. 2006. *Address:* 23 West Lodge Avenue, W3 9SE.

**NAPIER, Iain John Grant;** Chairman, McBride plc, 2007–16; *b* 10 April 1949. *Educ:* Eastwood High Sch., Newton Mearns. FCMA. Whitbread plc; Ford Motor Co.; joined Bass plc, 1989; Mktg and Commercial Dir, Bass Leisure Retail, 1989–93; Gp HR Dir, 1993–94; Chief Exec., Bass Leisure Div., 1994–96; Chm., Chateaux Lascombes wine estate, Bordeaux; Chief Exec., Bass Brewers and Bass International Brewers, 1996–2000; Chm., Bass Ireland; Dir, Bass plc, until 2000; Mem. Exec. Mgt Cttee, Interbrew SA, until 2001; Chief Exec., Taylor Woodrow plc, 2002–07; Chm., Imperial Tobacco Gp plc, 2007–14 (non-exec. Dir, 2000–14; Jt Vice Chm., 2004–07). Former non-executive Director: BOC Gp plc; Perry Gp; Henderson Investors plc; St Modwens Properties plc; Tomkins plc; non-executive Director: Collins-Stewart plc, 2007–09; John Menzies plc, 2008–16 (Chm., 2010–16); Molson Coors Brewing Co., 2008–; William Grant and Sons Hldgs Ltd, 2009–.

**NAPIER, John,** RDI 1996; stage designer; *b* 1 March 1944; *s* of James Edward Thomas Napier and Lorrie Napier (*née* Godbold); *m* 1st, Andreane Neofitou; one *s* one *d*; 2nd, Donna King; one *s* one *d*; 3rd, Caroline McGee. *Educ:* Hornsey Coll. of Art; Central Sch. of Arts and Crafts. Designed 1st production, A Penny for a Song, Phoenix, Leicester, 1967; *London productions:* Fortune and Men's Eyes, 1968; The Ruling Class, The Fun War, Muzeeka, George Frederick (ballet), La Turista, 1969; Cancer, Isabel's a Jezebel, 1970; Mister, The Foursome, The Lovers of Viorne, Lear, 1971; Jump, Sam Sam, Big Wolf, 1972; The Devils (ENO), Equus, The Party, 1973; Knuckle, 1974; Kings and Clowns, The Travelling Music Show, 1978; The Devils of Loudon, Lohengrin (Covent Garden); King John, Richard II, Cymbeline, Macbeth, Richard III, 1974; Hedda Gabler, 1975; Much Ado About Nothing, The Comedy of Errors, King Lear, Macbeth, 1976; A Midsummer Night's Dream, As You Like It, 1977; The Merry Wives of Windsor, Twelfth Night, Three Sisters, Once in a Lifetime, 1979; The Greeks, Nicholas Nickleby (SWET award, Tony Award), 1980; Cats (Tony award), 1981, revival 2014; Henry IV Parts I and II, Peter Pan, 1982; Macbeth (Covent Garden), 1983; Starlight Express, 1984 (Tony Award, 1987); Les Misérables, 1985 (Tony Award, 1987); Time, 1986; Miss Saigon, 1989; Children of Eden, 1990; Trelawny of the 'Wells', 1993; Sunset Boulevard, 1993 (Tony Award, 1995); Burning Blue, 1995 (Olivier award, 1996); The Tower, 1995; Jesus Christ Superstar, 1996; Who's Afraid of Virginia Woolf?, 1996; An Enemy of the People, 1997; Peter Pan, 1997; Martin Guerre, 1998; Candide, 1999; South Pacific, 2001; Skellig, 2003; Aladdin, 2004, 2005; Equus, 2007, transf. NY, 2008; Disconnect, 2010; Birdsong, 2010; *Glyndebourne:* Idomeneo, 1983; *WNO:* Don Giovanni, 2011; *USA:* Siegfried & Roy Show (Las Vegas; also co-dir), 1990; Jane Eyre (NY), 2000; Nabucco (Met. Opera), 2001; film designs incl. Hook, 1991; numerous designs for stage productions in Europe, Japan, Australia, USA and for TV; exhibition: Stages, Beyond the Fourth Wall, Towner Art Gall., Eastbourne, 2015–16. Cameron Mackintosh Vis. Prof. of Contemporary Theatre, Univ. of Oxford, 2001. Hon. Fellow, London Inst., 2001. American Acad. of Achievement, 1994. *Recreations:* photography, sculpture. *Address:* c/o Macnaughton Lord Representation, 16 Crucifix Lane, SE1 3JW.

**NAPIER, John Alan;** Chairman: RSA Insurance Group (formerly Royal & Sun Alliance Insurance Group) plc, 2003–12; Aegis Group plc, 2008–13; *b* 22 Aug. 1942; *s* of late William Napier and Barbara Napier (*née* Chatten); *m* 1st, 1961, Gillian Reed (marr. diss. 1977); two *s* one *d*; 2nd, 1992, Caroline Denning; one *d*, and two step *s* one step *d*. *Educ:* Colchester Royal Grammar Sch.; Emmanuel Coll., Cambridge (MA Econs). Jun. and middle mgt, Internat. Publishing Corp. and Reed Internat., 1960–69; Managing Director: Index Printers, 1969–72; QB Newspapers, 1972–76; Exec. Dir (Australia), James Hardie Industries, 1976–86; Group Managing Director: AGB plc, 1986–90; Hays plc, 1991–98; Chairman: Booker plc, 1998–2000; Kelda Gp plc, 2000–08. *Recreations:* rural matters, outdoor activities, people, philosophy. *Club:* Reform.

**NAPIER, Sir John Archibald Lennox,** 14th Bt *cr* 1627 (NS), of Merchistoun; *b* 6 Dec. 1946; *s* of Sir William Archibald Napier, 13th Bt and Kathleen Mabel, *d* of late Reginald Greaves; *S* father, 1990; *m* 1969, Erica, *d* of late Kurt Kingsfield; one *s* one *d*. *Educ:* St Stithians; Witwatersrand Univ., Johannesburg. MSc(Eng); PhD. *Heir: s* Hugh Robert Lennox Napier, *b* 1 Aug. 1977. *Address:* Merchistoun, PO Box 65177, Benmore 2010, Republic of South Africa.

**NAPIER, Maj.-Gen. Lennox Alexander Hawkins,** CB 1983; OBE 1970; MC 1957; Vice Lord-Lieutenant of Gwent, 1995–2004; Inspector of Public Inquiries, 1983–98; *b* 28 June 1928; *s* of Major Charles McNaughton Napier and D. C. Napier; *m* 1959, Jennifer Dawn Wilson; one *s* two *d*. *Educ:* Radley; RMA Sandhurst. Joined Army, 1946; commnd into South Wales Borderers, 1948; commanded 1st Bn S Wales Borderers and 1st Bn Royal Regt of Wales, 1967–70; Instructor, JSSC, 1970–72; served Min. of Defence, 1972–74; Brigade Commander, Berlin Infantry Bde, 1974–76; Prince of Wales's Division: Divisional Brigadier, 1976–80; Col Commandant, 1980–83; GOC Wales, 1980–83. Col, The Royal Regt of Wales, 1983–89; Hon. Col, Cardiff Univ. OTC, 1985–92. Chm., Central Rail Users Cttee, 1985–95. Gwent: DL 1983; High Sheriff 1988. OStJ 1969. *Recreations:* shooting, gardening. *Address:* Parade House, The Parade, Monmouth NP25 3PA.

**NAPIER, Michael;** see Napier, T. M.

**NAPIER, Paul James;** Publishing Director, JPIMedia Ltd, since 2018; *b* 3 Oct. 1966; *s* of Dennis Napier and Brenda Napier (*née* Duthie); *m* 1996, Lara Katya Balmforth; one *s* one *d*. *Educ:* Kettering Boys' Sch.; Univ. of York (BA Hons English and Related Lit. 1989); Heriot-Watt Univ. (MBA 2000). Ed., Banbury Guardian, 1997–2001; Ed.-in-Chief, Bucks Herald, 2001; Editor: Scarborough Evening News, 2001–03; Hartlepool Mail, 2003–06; Yorkshire Evening Post, 2006–12; Gp Editl Develt Dir, 2012–15, Dir, Digital Newsbrand Products, 2015–17, Publishing Dir, 2017–18, Johnston Press plc. *Recreations:* family, reading, running.

**NAPIER, Robert Stewart,** CBE 2011; DL; Chairman, Homes and Communities Agency, 2008–15; *b* 21 July 1947; *s* of Andrew Napier and Lilian V. Napier (*née* Ritchie); *m* 1977, Patricia Stewart; one *d*. *Educ:* Sedbergh School; Sidney Sussex College, Cambridge (BA

1969; MA 1971); Harvard Business School (AMP 1987). RTZ Corp., 1969–73; Brandts, 1973–75; Fisons, 1975–81; Redland: Finance Dir, 1981–87; Man. Dir, 1987–97; Chief Exec., 1991–97; Chief Exec., WWF-UK, 1999–2007. Director: United Biscuits (Hldgs), 1992–2000; Rentokil Initial plc, 1996–99; Anglian Water Services Ltd, 2002–15; Anglian Water Gp, 2015– (Chm., 2015); English Partnerships, 2004–08 (Chm., 2008); Lafarge UK Pension Trustees Ltd, 2014–17; Manchester Airport Gp, 2015–; Chm., Met Office, 2006–12. Pres., Nat. Council of Building Material Producers, 1996–97; Chairman: CBI Transport Policy Cttee, 1995–97; Alliance of Construction Product Suppliers, 1996–97. Chm., Green Fiscal Commn, 2007–09. Chm. of Trustees, St Mungo's, 2016–; Trustee: World in Need, 1988–91; ACET, 1991–94; CRASH, 1994–99 (Chm., 1998–99); Baynards Zambia Trust, 1996–; Carbon Disclosure Project, 2005–11 (Chm., 2008–11); Watts Gall., 2006–; UNEP-World Conservation Monitoring Centre, 2007–17 (Chm., 2008–17); S Georgia Heritage Trust, 2007–08. Mem., Oversight Cttee, 2012–14, Trustee, Bd, 2014–17, RCS. Governor: Reigate Grammar Sch., 1995–2002; Sedbergh Sch., 1998–2011 (Chm., 2000–11). High Sheriff, 2017–18, DL, 2017, Surrey. Hon. FRCS 2014. Hon. Organist, Grytviken Church, S Georgia. *Recreations:* hill walking, escaping to Scotland, the works of John Buchan.

**NAPIER, (Thomas) Michael**, CBE 2005; solicitor (non-practising); President, Law Society, 2000–01; Attorney-General's pro bono envoy, 2002–15; Consultant, Michael Napier Consulting Ltd, since 2012; non-executive Director, Harbour Litigation Funding Ltd, 2013–19, now Chairman Emeritus; *b* 11 June 1946; *s* of late Montague Keith Napier and Mary Napier; *m* 1969, Denise Christine Willey (*d* 2016); one *s* two *d*. *Educ:* Loughborough GS; Manchester Univ. (LLB 1967). Articled clerk, Moss Toone & Deane, Loughborough, 1968–70; admitted Solicitor, 1970; Asst Solicitor, W. H. Thompson, Manchester, 1970–72; Partner 1973, Chm. and Sen. Partner, 1983–2012, Irwin Mitchell; Jt Sen. Partner, Pannone Napier, 1985–94. Mem., Mental Health Act Commn, 1983–92 (Jt Vice-Chm., 1985–88; Chm., NE Reg., 1985–90). Vis. Prof., Nottingham Law Sch., 1992–. Jt Founder, 1990, Pres., 1994–96, Assoc. of Personal Injury Lawyers; Member: Council, Law Soc., 1993–2005; Council, Justice, 1995–2009; Civil Justice Council, 1998–2008. Bd Mem., Galleries of Justice, 2001–04. Chm., Adv. Cttee, Rampton Hosp., 1992–96. Trustee, Thalidomide Trust, 2001–14 (Vice Chm., 2007–14). Editorial Consultant: Personal Injury Compensation (formerly Personal Medical Injuries Law Letter), 1985–2012; Med. Law Rev., 1994–2012; Ind. Lawyer, 2002–08. Hon. Bencher, Gray's Inn, 2005; Hon. QC 2006. Freeman, Co. of Cutlers in Hallamshire, 1992. FICPD 2004; FRSA 2005. Hon. LLD: Nottingham Trent, 2001; Sheffield, 2002; Coll. of Law, 2012. *Publications:* (jtly) Conditional Fees: a survival guide, 1995, 2nd edn 2001; (jtly) Recovering Damages for Psychiatric Injury, 1995; (Consulting Ed.) Litigation Funding, 1999; (contrib.) Blackstone's Civil Practice, 2004; contrib. legal books and jls. *Recreation:* mountain biking in Norfolk. *Address:* Windmill Hill, 18 Hindringham Road, Great Walsingham, Norfolk NR22 6DR. *T:* (01328) 820213. *Club:* Athenæum.

**NAPTHINE, Hon. Denis Vincent**; company director and broadcaster; MLA (L) South West Coast, Victoria, Australia, 2002–15 (Portland, 1988–2002); Premier of Victoria, 2013–14; Leader, Liberal Party of Victoria, 2013–14; *b* Winchelsea, Victoria, 6 March 1952; *s* of Len and Theresa Napthine; *m* 1977, Peggy Rayner; three *s*. *Educ:* Chanel Coll., Geelong; Univ. of Melbourne (BVSc; MVSc); Deakin Univ. (MBA). Vet, 1975–88, incl. Dist Veterinary Officer, Hamilton, Regl Veterinary Officer, SW Victoria, then Manager, Hamilton complex of Dept of Agric. and Rural Affairs, Victoria. Shadow Minister for Sport, Recreation and Racing, 1991–92; Parly Sec. for Health, 1992–96; Minister for Youth and Community Services, 1996–99; Leader of Opposition, 1999–2002; Shadow Minister: for Regl and Rural Develt, 2002, and for State and Regl Develt, 2002–04; for Rural and Regl Develt, 2004–05; for Water, and for Agric., 2005–06; for Regl and Rural Develt, 2006–08; for Ports and for Racing, 2006–10; for Regl Cities, 2008–10; Minister for Major Projects, and for Ports, 2010–13; Minister for Racing, and Minister for Regl Cities, 2010–14. Treas., 1999, Leader, 1999–2002, Liberal Party of Vic. *Recreations:* walking, reading, horseracing, travel. *Address:* Port Fairy, Vic 3284, Australia.

**NARAIN, Sase**, OR 1976; CMG 1969; SC (Guyana) 1985; JP (Guyana); solicitor/ attorney-at-law; Speaker of the National Assembly, Guyana, 1971–92; Chairman, National Bank of Industry and Commerce (Guyana), 1986–93; *b* 27 Jan. 1925; *s* of Oudit and Sookdai Naraine; *m* 1952, Shamshun Narain (*née* Rayman); four *s*. *Educ:* Modern Educational Inst.; Gibson and Weldon Law Tutors. Solicitor, admitted in England and Guyana, 1957. Town Councillor, City of Georgetown, 1962–70; Member: History and Arts Council, 1969; Republic Cttee of Guyana, 1969; Pres., Guyana Sanatan Dharma Maha Sabha, 1963–94. Comr for Oaths to Affidavits, 1961; Notary Public, 1968. Dep. Chm., Public Service Commn, Guyana, 1966–71; Mem., Police Service Commn, 1966–71. Chm., Berger Paints (Guyana), 1966–78; Dir, Pegasus Hotels of Guyana, 1987–90. Member: Nat. Awards Cttee of Guyana, 1970–92; Bd of Governors, President's Coll., Guyana, 1985–88. JP 1962. *Recreations:* golf, cricket, swimming. *Address:* 14b New Garden Street, Queenstown, Georgetown, Demerara, Guyana. *T:* (2) 261409. *Clubs:* Georgetown Cricket, Everest Cricket (Guyana).

**NARASIMHA, Prof. Roddam**, FRS 1992; Academy Professor, CSIR Academy of Scientific and Industrial Research, Jawaharlal Nehru Centre for Advanced Scientific Research, since 2013 (Chairman, 1990–2009); INSA Golden Jubilee Research Professor, 1991–94; ISRO K. R. Ramanathan Distinguished Professor, 1995–2000; Honorary Professor, 2009–13; DST Year-of-Science Professor, 2013–18); Honorary Distinguished Professor, Indian Space Research Organization, since 2013; *b* 20 July 1933; *s* of Prof. R. L. Narasimhaiya and Smt R. N. Leela Devi; *m* 1965, Dr Neelima S. Rao; two *d*. *Educ:* University Coll. of Engineering, Bangalore (BE 1953); Indian Inst. of Science (DIISc 1955; AIISc 1957); California Inst. of Technology (PhD 1961). Res. Fellow, CIT, 1961–62; Indian Institute of Science: Asst and Associate Prof., 1962–70; Prof., 1970–98, and Chm., 1982–84, Dept of Aerospace Engrg; Dean of Engrg Faculty, 1980–82; Chm., 1982–89, Prof., 1982–98, Centre for Atmospheric and Oceanic Scis (formerly Centre for Atmospheric Scis); Dir, Nat. Aeronautical Lab., subseq. Nat. Aerospace Labs, Bangalore, 1984–93; Dir, Nat. Inst. of Advanced Studies, Bangalore, 1997–2004. Chief Project Co-ordinator, Hindustan Aeronautics Ltd, 1977–79. Visiting appointments: Univ. Libre, Brussels, 1970; Strathclyde Univ., 1971–72; NASA Langley, 1990–93; Leverhulme Fellow, Univ. of Adelaide, 1975; Sherman Fairchild Distinguished Scholar, CIT, 1982–83, 1986; Clark B. Millikan Vis. Prof., CIT, 1985–; Jawaharlal Nehru Vis. Prof., Cambridge, 1989–90. Member: Sci. Adv. Council to the Prime Minister, 1985–89 and 2004–14, to the Cabinet, 1997–99, to Govt of India, 2000–03; Space Commn, Govt of India, 1989–2012. Pres., Indian Acad. of Scis, 1992–94. Fellow: Indian Nat. Sci. Acad., 1979; Third World Acad. of Scis, Italy, 1989; Foreign Associate: US Nat. Acad. of Engrg, 1989; US Nat. Acad. of Sci., 2000; Hon. Fellow: Aer. Soc. of India, 1985; Indian Inst. of Sci., 2008; Energy Hon. Mem., Amer. Acad. Arts and Scis, 1999; Distinguished Alumnus: CIT, 1986; Indian Inst. of Sci., 1988. Bhatnagar Prize in Engrg, CSIR, India, 1976; Gujar Mal Modi Award for Sci., 1990; Srinivasa Ramanujan Medal, Indian Sci. Congress, 1998; Fluid Dynamics Award, Amer. Inst. Aeronautics and Astronautics, 2000; Lifetime Contribution in Engrg Award, Indian Nat. Acad. of Engrg, 2003; Trieste Sci. Prize, World Acad. of Scis, 2008; Lifetime Excellence Award in Earth System Scis, Min. of Earth Scis, 2013. Kannada Rajyotsava Award, Karnataka, 1986; Padmabhushan, 1987, Padma Vibhushan, 2013, India. *Publications:* (ed) Computer Simulation, 1979; (ed) Turbulence Management and Relaminarisation, 1987; (ed) Developments in Fluid Mechanics and Space Technology, 1988; Surveys in Fluid Mechanics, vol. III, 1993; The Monsoon Trough Boundary Layer, 1997; Verses for the Brave, 2000; (ed) The Dynamics of Technology, 2003; (ed jtly) Encyclopaedia of Classical Indian Sciences, 2007; (ed) Nature and Culture, 2011; numerous sci. papers in learned jls. *Recreations:* history, walking, music. *Address:* Jawaharlal Nehru Centre for Advanced Scientific Research, Jakkur, Bangalore 560064, India. *T:* (80) 22082999, *Fax:* (80) 22082951.

**NARASIMHAN, Prof. Mudumbai Seshachalu**, PhD; FRS 1996; *b* 7 June 1932; *s* of Seshachalu Iyengar and Padmasani; *m* 1962, Sakuntala Raman; one *s* one *d*. *Educ:* Madras Univ. (BA Hons); Bombay Univ. (PhD 1960). Tata Institute, Bombay: Associate Prof., 1963–65; Prof., 1965–75; Sen. Prof., 1975–90; Prof. of Eminence, 1990–93; Hon. Fellow, 1994; Dir of Maths, Internat. Centre, subseq. Abdus Salam Internat. Centre, for Theoretical Physics, Trieste, 1992–98; Prof. of Geometry, Scuola Internazionale Superiore di Studi Avanzati, Trieste, 2000. S. S. Bhatnagar Prize in Mathematical Scis, CSIR, 1975; Meghnad Saha Award, Univ. Grants Commn, 1978; Award for Maths, Third World Acad. of Scis, 1987; Srinivasa Ramanujan Medal, INSA, 1988; C. V. Raman Birth Centenary Award, Indian Sci. Congress, 1994; King Faisal Internat. Prize for Sci., 2006. Chevalier, Ordre National du Mérite (France), 1989; Padma Bhushan (India), 1990. *Address:* TIFR Centre, PO Box 1234, IISc Campus, Bangalore 560012, India.

**NARAYAN, Prof. Ramesh**, FRS 2006; FAAAS; Thomas Dudley Cabot Professor of the Natural Sciences, Center for Astrophysics | Harvard & Smithsonian (formerly Harvard-Smithsonian Center for Astrophysics), Harvard University; *s* of Prof. Gopalasamudram Narayana Ramachandran, FRS. *Educ:* St Patrick's Sch., Adyar; Madras Christian Coll.; National Aeronautical Labs, Bangalore; Calif Inst. of Technol. FAAAS 2010; MNAS, 2013. Arizona Univ., 1986–91; joined Harvard Univ., 1991. Fellow, World Acad. of Scis, 2015. *Publications:* articles in jls. *Address:* Center for Astrophysics | Harvard & Smithsonian, 60 Garden Street, Cambridge, MA 02138, USA.

**NARAYANAN, Ravi**, Hon. CBE 2009; Chairman: Asia-Pacific Water Forum, since 2013 (Vice-Chairman, 2006–13); Water Integrity Network Association, since 2013; *b* 20 June 1943; *s* of Vaidyanatha and Kanti Narayanan; *m* 1973, Geetha Subramanan; one *s* one *d*. *Educ:* Delhi Univ. (BSc Hons); Peterhouse, Cambridge (BA 1966, MA 1968). Dir, ActionAid India, 1985–92; Hd, Internat. Ops, 1992–94, Dir, Asia Progs, 1994–99, ActionAid; Dir and Chief Exec., WaterAid, 1999–2005. Sen. Associate, Nat. Inst. of Advanced Studies, Bangalore, India. Mem., UK Delegn to Second World Water Forum, The Hague, 2000; NGO Advr to EC Delegn to World Summit of Sustainable Develt, Johannesburg, 2002. Member: World Panel on Financing Water Infrastructure, 2002–03; Millennium Project UN Taskforce on Water and Sanitation, 2004–05; Water Supply and Sanitation Collaborative Council, Geneva; Chm., Internat. Steering Cttee, Water Integrity Network, 2010–13. Life Mem., Internat. Water Acad., Norway, 2005. *Address:* 6 Palace Cross Road, Bangalore, 560020 Karnataka, India.

**NAREY, Sir Martin (James)**, Kt 2013; DL; Chair, Portman Group, since 2013; *b* 5 Aug. 1955; *s* of John and Ellenor Narey; *m* 1978, Jan Goudy; one *s* one *d*. *Educ:* Sheffield Poly. (BA Public Admin). Assistant Governor: HM Young Offender Inst. Deerbolt, 1982–86; Frankland, 1986–90; Gov. IV, Prison Service HQ, 1990–91; Home Office: Private Sec. to Minister of State, 1991–92; Criminal Policy, 1992–94; Head, Co-ordination of Computerisation in the Criminal Justice System Unit, 1994–96; Head of Crime Prevention Agency, 1996; Reviewer of Delay in the Criminal Justice System, 1996–97; HM Prison Service: Head of Security Policy, 1997–98; Dir of Regimes, 1998; Dir-Gen., 1999–2003; Perm. Under-Sec. of State, Home Office, 2003–05 (Comr for Correctional Services, 2003–04, Chief Exec., Nat. Offender Mgt Service, 2004–05); Chief Exec., Barnardo's, 2005–11. Non-executive Board Member: Scarborough and NE Yorks NHS Trust, 2009–12; Fabrick Housing Assoc., Middlesbrough, 2012–15; MoJ, 2015–17. Mem. Bd, Unilink plc, 2015–. Mem. Council, ASA, 2011–17. Chairman: End Child Poverty Coalition, 2006–09; Ind. Commn on Social Mobility, 2009; Portman Gp Complaints Panel, 2013; Adoption Leadership Bd, 2014–; Brain Tumour Charity, 2015–. Govt Advr on Children, 2011–18. Mem. Bd, The Sage Gateshead, 2016– (Dep. Chm., 2017–); Chair, Yorkshire Coast Opportunity Area; Pres., Whitby Art Soc. Chm., Corp., Redbridge Coll., 2008–10. Visiting Professor: Sheffield Hallam Univ., 2006–; Durham Univ., 2011–; Manchester Metropolitan Univ., 2017–; Vis. Scholar, Inst. of Criminol., Univ. of Cambridge, 2011–. DL N Yorks, 2015. DUniv Sheffield Hallam, 2003; Hon. LLD Teesside, 2007; Hon. DLitt, Manchester Metropolitan, 2012. Chartered Mgt Inst. Gold Medal for Leadership, 2003. *Publications:* review of delay in criminal justice system, report into security at the Maze Prison, report of Ind. Commn on Social Mobility, 2009; Adoption: a blueprint for the nation's lost children (Times report), 2011; Making the Education of Children's Social Workers Consistently Effective (DfE), 2014; Residential Care in England (DfE), 2016; Fostering in England (review for DfE), 2018. *Recreations:* planning holidays, watching Middlesbrough FC, being with Ezra, Abby and Sid. *Address:* 34A Bagdale, Whitby, N Yorks YO21 1QL. *E:* nareymartin@gmail.com.

**NARUEPUT, Owart S.;** *see* Suthiwart-Narueput.

**NASEBY, Baron** *cr* 1997 (Life Peer), of Sandy in the co. of Bedfordshire; **Michael Wolfgang Laurence Morris**; PC 1994; *b* 25 Nov. 1936; *m* 1960, Dr Ann Appleby (Dr Ann Morris, MB, BS, MRCS, MRCP); two *s* one *d*. *Educ:* Bedford Sch.; St Catharine's Coll., Cambridge (BA Hons Econs; MA). Trainee to Marketing Manager, UK, India and Ceylon, Reckitt & Colman Gp, 1960–63; Service Advertising Ltd, 1964–68; Marketing Exec. to Account Supervisor, Horniblow Cox-Freeman Ltd, 1968–71, Dir 1969–71; Dir, Benton & Bowles Ltd, 1971–81; Proprietor: A. M. International, 1980–92; Julius International Consultants, 1997–2008. Non-executive Director: Tunbridge Wells Equitable Friendly Soc., 1992–2005 (Chm., 1998–2005); Mansell plc, 1998–2003; Invesco Recovery Trust 2005 plc, 1998–2005 (Chm., 2003–05); Chm., Invesco Recovery Trust 2011 plc, 2005–11. Contested (C) Islington North, 1966. Islington Council: Councillor, 1968–70; Alderman, 1970–74; Chm. of Housing, 1968; Leader, 1969–71. MP (C) Northampton South, Feb. 1974–1997; contested (C) same seat, 1997. PPS to Minister of State, NI Office, 1979–81; Chm. of Ways and Means and Dep. Speaker, H of C, 1992–97. Member: Public Accounts Cttee, 1979–92; Select Cttee on Energy, 1982–85; Chairman's Panel, 1984–92; Mem. Council, Europe and Western European Union, 1983–91; Chairman: British Sri Lanka Cttee, 1975–92 and 1997–2015 (Pres., 2015–); British Singapore Cttee, 1985–92 (Vice-Chm., 1997–); British Malaysia Cttee, 1987–92; British Burma Cttee, 1989–92; British Maldives Cttee, 2004–09; formerly: Vice-Chm., British Indonesia Cttee; Treas., British ASEAN and Thai Cttees; Secretary: British Venezuela Cttee; Cons. Housing and Local Govt Cttee, 1974–76; Cons Trade Cttee, 1974–76; Cons. Environment Cttee, 1977–79; Vice-Chm., Cons. Energy Cttee, 1981–92; Founder, Parly Food and Health Forum. Captain, Parly Golf Soc., 1988–91 (Pres., 2009–). Chm. Trustees, Victoria County History for Northamptonshire, 1994–2008; Joint Patron: Naseby Battlefield Trust, 2005–13; Cromwell Mus., 2014–. Founder and Pres., UK Br., Cofradia del Vino Chileno, 2005–. Chm., Govs, Bedford Sch., 1989–2002 (Governor, 1982–2002).

Hon. Fellow, Univ. of Northampton, 2007. Ratna (Sri Lanka), 2005; Bernardo O'Higgins Medal (Chile), 2013. *Publications:* (jtly) Helping the Exporter, 1967; (contrib.) Marketing below the Line: studies in management, 1972; The Disaster of Direct Labour, 1978. *Recreations:* restoration work, cricket, tennis, golf, budgerigars, forestry. *Address:* Caesar's Camp, Sand Lane, Sandy, Beds SG19 2AD. *T:* (01767) 680388. *Clubs:* Carlton, MCC, Lord's Taverners; All England Lawn Tennis and Croquet; John O'Gaunt Golf; Northamptonshire CC (Patron, 2006–09, Pres., 2009–).

**NASH,** family name of **Baron Nash.**

**NASH,** Baron *cr* 2013 (Life Peer), of Ewelme in the County of Oxfordshire; **John Alfred Stoddard Nash;** *b* Bahrain, 22 March 1949; *s* of Lewis John and Josephine Nash; *m* 1983, Caroline Jennifer Paul; one *s* one *d. Educ:* Milton Abbey Sch.; Corpus Christi Coll., Oxford (MA Law). Called to the Bar, Inner Temple, 1972. Chm., 1988–2002, non-exec. Partner, 2002–12, Sovereign Capital. Non-exec. Dir, 2010–13, Parly Under-Sec. of State, 2013–17, DfE. Chm., British Venture Capital Assoc., 1988–89. Chairman: Future (charity), 2005–; Pimlico Acad., 2008–. *Recreation:* golf. *Clubs:* Athenæum, Turf.

**NASH, Prof. Anthony Aubrey,** PhD; Professor of Veterinary Pathology, 1994, and Head, Centre for Infectious Diseases, University of Edinburgh, now Emeritus Professor of Infectious Diseases; *b* 6 March 1949; *s* of Alfred Nash and Mabel Evelyn Nash (*née* Garrett); *m* 1979, Marion Eileen Bazeley; four *d. Educ:* Queen Elizabeth Coll., London (BSc Hons 1970); Univ. of Birmingham (MSc 1971; PhD 1976). Lecturer: in Immunology, Dept of Pathology, Univ. of Cambridge, 1984–94; in Pathology, Newnham Coll., Cambridge, 1987–94. Eleanor Roosevelt Fellow, Dept of Immunology, Scripps Clinic and Res. Foundn, Calif, 1989–90. Member Council: Soc. for Gen. Microbiology, 2000–04; BBSRC, 2002–05. FMedSci 1999; FRSE 2005. *Publications:* (jtly) Mims' Pathogenesis of Infectious Disease, 5th edn, 1999, 6th edn, 2015; over 100 articles in learned jls. *Recreations:* family, Leicester City Football Club. *Address:* Roslin Institute, University of Edinburgh, Easter Bush, Edinburgh EH25 9RG. *T:* (0131) 651 9177.

**NASH, David John,** OBE 2004; RA 1999; sculptor, primarily in wood; Research Fellow, University of Northumbria, 1999–2003; *b* 14 Nov. 1945; *s* of Lt-Col William Charles Nash and Dora Lillian Nash; *m* 1972, Claire Langdown; two *s. Educ:* Brighton Coll.; Kingston Sch. of Art (Higher DipAD); Chelsea Sch. of Art. Has worked in Blaenau Ffestiniog, 1967–; over 100 solo shows world wide; 100 works in internat. public collections incl. Tate Gall., Guggenheim, NY, Nat. Mus. of Wales and Metropolitan Mus., Japan. Hon. Dr: Art and Design, Kingston, 1998; Humanities and Letters, W Glamorgan, 2002. Wollaston Prize, RA, 2016; Marsh Award for Excellence in Public Sculpture, Marsh Christian Trust, 2016. *Publications:* Wood Primer, 1987; Forms into Time, 1996; Black and Light, 2001; The Return of Art to Nature, 2003; (ed jtly) David Nash at the Yorkshire Sculpture Park, 2010; *relevant publication:* David Nash, by Norbert Lynton, 2007; David Nash: a natural gallery, by Michelle Payne, 2013. *Address:* Capel Rhiw, Blaenau Ffestiniog, Gwynedd, N Wales LL41 3NT.

**NASH, David Percy,** FCA; *b* 24 May 1940; *s* of Percy and Kathleen Nash; *m* 2011, Lindsey Jane Thomas; two *s* by a previous marriage. *Educ:* Enfield Grammar Sch. FCA 1962. ICI plc, 1965–87; Gp Finance Dir, Cadbury Schweppes plc, 1987–89; Gp Finance Dir, 1989–93, Chm. and CEO, Food and Retailing Sector, 1993–95, Grand Metropolitan plc. Chairman: Kenwood Appliances plc, 1996–2001; Amicus Healthcare Gp Ltd, 1996–97; Niceopen Ltd, 1997; General Healthcare Gp Ltd, 1998–2000; Cable & Wireless Communications plc, 1998–2000; non-executive Director: IMRO, 1993–98; Cable and Wireless plc, 1995–2002 (Dep. Chm., 2002); Energy Gp plc, 1996–98; AXA UK plc, 1996–2001. Hon. Treas., Prince of Wales's Internat. Business Leaders' Forum, 1990–2007. *Recreations:* horseracing, cycling. *Club:* Royal Motor Yacht.

**NASH, Ellison;** *see* Nash, His Honour T. M. E.

**NASH, Frances Clare, (Mrs A. N. Simpson),** CB 2019; Director, Legal Services, Department for Work and Pensions, since 2016; *b* 29 Dec. 1960; *d* of late Prof. Walter Nash and Doreen Mary Nash (*née* Richardson); *m* 2012, Anthony Nicholas Simpson. *Educ:* Forest Fields Coll., Nottingham; Jesus Coll., Oxford (BA 1982, MA); University Coll. London (LLM 1994). Admitted solicitor, 1986; private practice, 1986–87; Legal Dept, MAFF, 1987–93; Legal Secretariat to Law Officers, 1993–95; Legal Dept, MAFF, 1995–99; Dep. Legal Advr, MoD, 1999–2002; Dir, Legal Services, DEFRA, 2002–04; Hd, European Div., Treasury Solicitor's Dept, 2004–08; Dir, Personal Tax and Ops, HMRC, 2008; Dir, Legal Services, MoD, 2009–16. *Recreations:* gardening, tropical fishkeeping, international travel. *Address:* Department for Work and Pensions, Caxton House, Tothill Street, SW1H 9NA. *E:* Frances.Nash@dwp.gov.uk.

**NASH, John Edward;** Member, Supervisory Board, Bank Winter AG, Vienna, 1996; Chairman, S. G. Warburg Bank AG, 1980–87 (Director, 1977–87; Deputy Chairman, 1977–80); *b* 25 June 1925; *s* of Joseph and Madeleine Nash; *m* 1st, 1947, Ralda Everard Herring (*d* 2006); two *s* two *d*; 2nd, 2009, Fiona Hood-Stewart. *Educ:* Univ. of Sydney (BEc); Balliol Coll., Oxford (BPhil). Teaching Fellow in Economics, Sydney Univ., 1947. Exec. Dir, Samuel Montagu & Co. Ltd, 1956; also Director, 1960–73: British Australian Investment Trust; Montagu Trust Ltd; Midland Montagu Industrial Finance Ltd; Capel Court Corp. (in Melb.); resigned all directorships on appt to Brussels, 1973; Dir of Monetary Affairs, EEC, 1973–77; Director: Reckitt & Colman plc, 1966–73 and 1977–86; S. G. Warburg & Co. Ltd, 1977–86; Mem. Adv. Bd, Bank S. G. Warburg Soditic AG, 1987–94. Dir, Oxford Univ. Business Summer Sch., 1965; Research Fellow, Nuffield Coll., Oxford (part-time), 1966–69. Hon. Treasurer, PEP, 1964–73. Mem. Bd of Trustees, WWF Internat., 1979–92, 1993–94 (Hon. Treas., 1985–92). *Recreations:* golf, horse-racing, music. *Address:* Chalet Gstelli, 3785 Gsteig bei Gstaad, Switzerland. *T:* (33) 7551162, *Fax:* (33) 7551132. *Clubs:* Turf, MCC; University (Sydney).

**NASH, Jonathan Scott;** QC 2006; *b* 16 Oct. 1962; *s* of late Bryan Whatmore Nash and of Jean Nash (*née* Cowie); *m* 1st, 1995, Constance Chanteux (marr. diss. 2003); two *s*; 2nd, 2012, Magdalena Popowicz. *Educ:* Reigate Grammar Sch.; St John's Coll., Oxford (BA Modern Hist. 1984). Called to the Bar, Gray's Inn, 1986; in practice at the Bar, 1987–, specialising in commercial law. *Recreations:* music, boxing, books. *Address:* 3 Verulam Buildings, Gray's Inn, WC1R 5NT. *T:* (020) 7269 1106. *E:* jnash@3vb.com. *Clubs:* Travellers, Home House, Arts.

**NASH, Prof. Jordan,** PhD; Dean, Faculty of Science, Monash University, Australia, since 2017; *b* New York, 14 June 1962; *s* of Kenneth and Carole Nash; *m* 2014, Carmen Curreli; one *s*, and one *s* one *d* by a previous marriage. *Educ:* Carnegie Mellon Univ. (BSc Physics 1983); Stanford Univ. (PhD Physics 1990). Imperial College London: Lectr in Physics, 1993–2000; Reader in Physics, 2000–07; Prof. of Physics, 2007–17; Hd, High Energy Physics Gp, 2007–14; Hd, Dept of Physics, 2014–17. Sen. Staff Scientist, CERN, 2003–18. Mem., STFC, 2015–18. Mem. Bd, Old Oak Park Royal Develt Corp., 2015–17. *Publications:* contribs to jls as mem. of Mark II, ALEPH, BaBar and CMS experiments. *Recreations:* cycling, swimming, binge reading, programming. *Address:* Faculty of Science, 14 Rainforest Walk, Clayton Campus, Monash University, Vic 3800, Australia.

**NASH, Pamela;** Chief Executive Officer, Scotland in Union, since 2017; *b* Bellshill, 1984; *d* of David Nash and late Kathleen Nash. *Educ:* St Margaret's Sch., Airdrie; Glasgow Univ. (MA Politics). Mem. for Airdrie and Shotts, Scottish Youth Parlt, 2007–09; Parly researcher to John Reid, MP, 2007–10. MP (Lab) Airdrie and Shotts, 2010–15; contested (Lab) same seat, 2015. PPS to Shadow Sec. of State for NI, 2010–13, to Shadow Sec. of State for Scotland, 2011–12, to Shadow Sec. of Internat. Develt, 2013–15. Member: Select Cttee on Sci. and Technol., 2010–15, Scottish Affairs, 2012–15; All Party Parly Gp for MS, 2010–15, Africa, 2010–15, Great Lakes, 2010–15, British-American, 2010–15, UAE, 2010–15, UN, 2010–15; Chair, All Party Parly Gp on HIV and AIDS, 2011–15, Belarus, 2012–15, Youth Unemployment, 2013–15. Hd of Policy and Campaigning, HIV Scotland, 2016–17.

**NASH, Peter Philip,** DPhil; Director, Transmissible Spongiform Encephalopathies and Zoonoses, Department for Environment, Food and Rural Affairs, 2002–06; *b* 18 May 1948; *s* of late Harold and Joan Nash; *m* 1977, June Mobbs; one *s* one *d. Educ:* Grove Park Grammar Sch., Wrexham; Jesus Coll., Oxford (MA, DPhil 1972). MAFF, subseq. DEFRA, 1972–; Head: Envmtl Protection Div., 1988–93; Financial Policy Div., 1993–97; Milk, Pigs, Eggs and Poultry Div., 1997–99; BSE Div., 1999–2002. *Recreations:* country walking, foreign languages, voluntary teaching of bridge, art history, family history. *T:* (020) 8349 2318.

**NASH, Philip;** Commissioner of Customs and Excise, 1986–90; *b* 14 March 1930; *s* of late John Hollett Nash and Edith Grace Nash (*née* Knee); *m* 1953, Barbara Elizabeth Bangs; one *s. Educ:* Watford Grammar School. National Service, RAF, 1949–50. HM Customs and Excise, 1950–90; on loan to Civil Service College, 1970–73; Asst Sec. and Head of Management Services, 1978–81; Asst Sec., Customs Directorate, 1981–86; Director, Customs, 1986–90. *Recreation:* family history. *Address:* Nutwood, 37 Lower Golf Links Road, Broadstone, Dorset BH18 8BQ. *T:* (01202) 601898.

**NASH, Ronald Peter,** CMG 2004; LVO 1983; HM Diplomatic Service, retired; High Commissioner, Trinidad and Tobago, 2004–06; *b* 18 Sept. 1946; *s* of John Henry Nash and Jean Carmichael Nash (*née* McIlwraith); *m* 1976, Annie Olsen; three *s. Educ:* Harefield Secondary Modern Sch.; Southall Tech. Sch.; Southall Grammar Tech. Sch.; Manchester Univ. (BA Hons). MCIL (MIL 1991). FCO, 1970; Moscow, 1974–76; UK Delegn to MBFR, Vienna, 1976–79; FCO, 1979–83; New Delhi, 1983–86; FCO, 1986–87; Dep. Hd of Mission, Vienna, 1988–92; Dep. High Comr, Colombo and (non-res.) Malé, 1992–95; Co-ordinator, Peace Implementation Conf. for Bosnia, 1995; Review of Africa Develt Prog., ODA, 1996; Hd, Human Rights Policy Dept, FCO, 1996–99; Ambassador: to Nepal, 1999–2002; to Afghanistan, 2002–03. Chm. Bd Dirs, Overseas Children's Sch., Colombo, Sri Lanka, 1994–95. *Address:* Ryecroft, 175 Hivings Hill, Chesham, Bucks HP5 2PN. *Clubs:* Royal Scots (Edinburgh); Berkhamsted Lawn Tennis and Squash.

**NASH, Stephen Thomas,** CMG 2000; HM Diplomatic Service, retired; Honorary Patron, British Georgian Society, since 2010 (Chairman, 2004–10); *b* 22 March 1942; *s* of Thomas Gerald Elwin Nash and Gwendolen Selina Nash (*née* Osmaston); *m* 2004, Rusudan Benashvili; one *d*; two *s* two *d* from former marriages. *Educ:* Cheltenham Coll.; Pembroke Coll., Cambridge (MA Econs and History); Sch. of Oriental and African Studies (Arabic Studies); Queen's Coll., Oxford (MA Ethnology). Asst Dir, British Council, Baghdad, 1965–67; FCO 1967; served Caracas, Bogotá, Bangkok (SEATO), Guatemala; Dep. High Comr, Belmopan, 1981–82; Head, Indo-China Section, FCO, 1984–86; Chargé d'Affaires, Managua, 1986–88; seconded to British Aerospace, 1989–91; EC Monitor Mission to former Yugoslavia, Zagreb, 1991; Chargé d'Affaires, Tirana, 1993–95; Ambassador: to Georgia, 1995–98; to Albania, 1998–99; to Latvia, 1999–2002. Dir-Gen., Canning House, 2002–03. OSCE Election Observation Missions: to Latvia, 2002, and 2006 (Dep. Head); to Serbia (Head of Mission), 2004; to USA (Dep. Head), 2004; to Romania (Head), 2004. Director: London Inf. Network on Conflicts and State-building, 2002–06; MEC Internat./Windsor Energy Gp, 2006–. Vice-Chm., Friends of Academic Res. in Georgia, 2003–; Board Member: Britain Estonia Latvia Lithuania Legal Assoc., 2002–07; British Latvian Assoc., 2004– (Chm., 2018–); Anglo-Albanian Assoc., 2006– (Chm., 2012–); Tbilisi Heritage Gp, 2011–. Governor: Dulwich Village C of E Infant Sch., 2008–12; St George's Sch., Tbilisi, Georgia, 2012–. Order of Honour (Republic of Georgia), 2011. *Recreations:* spending time with my children and grandchildren, choral singing, ski-ing, hill walking, gardening, viola-playing.

**NASH, His Honour Timothy Michael Ellison;** a Circuit Judge, 1994–2010; *b* 10 Dec. 1939; *s* of late Denis Frederick Ellison Nash, OBE, AE, FRCS and Joan May Andrew; *m* 1965, Gael Nash; one *s* one *d* (and two *s* decd). *Educ:* Dulwich Coll.; St Bartholomew's Hosp. Called to the Bar, Gray's Inn, 1964; Standing Counsel: DHSS, 1974–79; DTI, 1976–91; Asst Recorder, 1987–89; Recorder, 1990–94. Legal Assessor, GMC and Royal Dental Council, 1989–94; Chm., Home Office Police Appeal Tribunals, 1988–94. Metropolitan Police Special Constabulary, 1961–83. Examr, Dio. of Canterbury, 1990–94. *Recreation:* walking round in ever-increasing circles.

**NASHA, Margaret Nnananyana, (Mrs Lawrence Nasha);** MP (Democratic Party), Botswana, 1994–2014; Speaker of the National Assembly of Botswana, 2009–14; *b* 6 Aug. 1947; *d* of Sadinyana and Motlatshiping Ramontshonyana; *m* 1975, Lawrence Nasha; four *s. Educ:* Univ. of Botswana (BA 1976). Several posts as broadcaster, 1968–84; Dir of Information and Broadcasting, Botswana, 1985–89; High Comr in UK, 1989–93; Government of Botswana: Dep. Minister, 1994–97, Minister, 1997–98, of Local Govt, Lands and Housing; Minister: of Minerals, Energy and Water Affairs, 1998–99; of Local Govt, 1999–2002; of Lands and Housing, 2003; of Local Govt, until 2009; of Presidential Affairs and Public Admin, 2009. *Publications:* Madam Speaker, Sir!, 2014. *Recreations:* leisure walks, tennis.

**NASHEED, Mohamed;** President of the Maldives, 2008–12; Chairman, Maldivian Democratic Party, 2005–08; *b* Male, Maldives, 17 May 1967. *Educ:* Majeediyya Sch., Male; Overseas Sch., Colombo; Dauntsey's Sch., Wilts; Liverpool Poly. (BA Maritime Studies 1989). Helped establish Sangu, political mag., 1990 (banned within a year); arrested and jailed, 1991–93 (Amnesty Internat. prisoner of conscience); rearrested 1994, 1995; imprisoned 1996–98; elected MP for Male, 1999, subseq. stripped of seat and imprisoned 2001–03; fled Maldives, 2003; co-founded Maldivian Democratic Party (MDP) (first opposition party) in exile in Sri Lanka, 2004; granted refugee status by British Govt, 2004; returned to Maldives, 2005 to establish MDP; MDP officially recognised by Govt, June 2005; initiated campaign of non-violent civil disobedience in Maldives to pressure Govt to speed up implementation of democratic reforms, 2005–08; arrested Aug. 2006 and charged with terrorism but charges later dropped. Anna Lindh Meml Fund Prize, 2009; UNEP Champions of the Earth Laureate, 2010.

**NASMITH, Sir James Duncan D.;** *see* Dunbar-Nasmith.

**NASMYTH, Prof. Kim Ashley,** PhD; FRS 1989; Whitley Professor of Biochemistry, University of Oxford, since 2006 (Head, Department of Biochemistry, 2007); Fellow, Trinity College, Oxford, since 2006; *b* 18 Oct. 1952; *s* of James Nasmyth and Jenny Hughes; *m* 1982, Anna Dowson; two *d. Educ:* Eton Coll.; York Univ. (BA); Edinburgh Univ. (PhD). Jane Coffin Childs Postdoctoral Fellow, Dept of Genetics, Univ. of

Washington, 1978–80; Robertson Fellow, Cold Spring Harbor Lab., NY, 1980–81; Staff Mem., MRC Lab. of Molecular Biol., Cambridge, 1982–87; Unofficial Fellow, King's Coll., Cambridge, 1984–87; Sen. Scientist, 1987–96, Dir, 1997–2005, Inst. of Molecular Pathology, Vienna. Hon. Prof., Univ. of Vienna, 1995–. FMedSci 2009. MAE 1993; Member: EMBO, 1985; Austrian Acad. of Scis, 1999; Foreign Hon. Mem., Amer. Acad. of Arts and Scis, 1999. *Recreations:* climbing, ski-ing. *Address:* Department of Biochemistry, University of Oxford, South Parks Road, Oxford OX1 3QU. *T:* (01865) 275263.

**NASON, Prof. Guy Philip,** PhD; Professor of Statistics, since 2002, and Director, EPSRC Centre for Doctoral Training in Computational Statistics and Data Science, since 2019, University of Bristol; *b* Dartford, 28 Aug. 1966; *s* of Brian and Diana Nason; *m* 1999, Philippa Anne Coates; two *d. Educ:* Univ. of Bath (BSc; PhD 1992); Jesus Coll., Cambridge (Dip. Math. Stat. 1988). Postdoctoral res., Univ. of Bath, 1992–93; University of Bristol: postdoctoral res., 1993–94; Lectr in Stats, 1994–2000; Reader in Stats, 2000–02; Hd, Stats Gp, 2006–08; Hd, Sch. of Maths, 2008–12; Dir, Inst. for Statistical Sci., 2016–18. Turing Fellow, Alan Turing Inst., 2018–. Adv. Res. Fellow, 2000–05, Mem., Maths Strategic Adv. Panel, 2007–, Estabd Career Fellow, 2013–, EPSRC. Mem. Council, 2004–08, 2016–; Royal Statistical Society: Sec., Res. Section, 2002–04; Mem. Council, 2004–08, 2016–; Vice Pres., 2016–; Guy Medal in Bronze, 2001. Mem., ISI, 2015. *Publications:* Wavelet Methods in Statistics with R, 2008; contrib. papers to learned jls. *Recreations:* fine wine, building gardens. *Address:* School of Mathematics, University of Bristol, Bristol BS8 1TW. *T:* (0117) 331 8411.

**NASON, Justin Patrick Pearse,** OBE 1980; HM Diplomatic Service, retired; *b* 29 March 1937; *s* of John Lawrence Nason and Catherine Agnes (*née* McFadden); *m* 2000, Jeannine Dubois. *Educ:* Ampleforth; University Coll., Oxford. National Service, RAF, 1956–58. BICC, 1962–63; entered HM Foreign Service, 1963; FO, 1964–65; Prague, 1965–67; FCO, 1967–71; First Sec., Pretoria and Cape Town, 1971–74; Head of Chancery, Saigon, 1974–75; FCO, 1975–79; Head of Chancery, Kampala, 1979–81; Nat. Defence Coll. of Canada, 1981–82; Dep. High Comr, Colombo, 1982–85; Barclays Bank (on secondment), 1986–87; Minister Counsellor, Mexico City, 1988–90; temp. duty, Accra, 1990–91; Ambassador to Guatemala, 1991–95. *Recreation:* golf. *Club:* Oxford and Cambridge.

**NASR, Dara;** Managing Director, Twitter UK, since 2016; *b* Tehran, Iran, 16 Sept. 1975; *s* of late Homayoun Nasr and of Mina Gouran; *m* 2006, Anna Locke; two *d. Educ:* Merchant Taylors' Sch., Northwood; Queen Mary and Westfield Coll., Univ. of London (LLB Hons 1996); Coll. of Law. Sales Exec., Flextech TV, 1999–2005; Sales Mgt, Eurosport TV, 2005–07; Hd of Sales, Google UK, 2007–12; Twitter UK: Hd of Sales, 2012–14; Sales Dir, 2014–16. *Recreations:* sport (cycling, golf), family, music. *Address:* Twitter UK, 100 New Bridge Street, EC4V 6JA.

**NATALEGAWA, (Raden Mohammad) Marty (Muliana),** DPhil; Minister of Foreign Affairs, Indonesia, 2009–14; *b* 22 March 1963; *s* of Raden Sonson Natalegawa and Siti Komariyah Natalegawa; *m* 1987, Sranya Bamrungphong; two *s* one *d. Educ:* Corpus Christi Coll., Cambridge (MPhil 1986); London Sch. of Econs (BSc Hons 1989); Australian National Univ. (DPhil 1993). Agency for Policy Analysis and Develt, Dept of For. Affairs, 1986–90; Indonesian Perm. Mission to UN, NY, 1994–99, Hd of Political Sect., 1999; Department of Foreign Affairs: Dep. Dir, 1999–2000, Dir, 2001–02, for Internat. Orgns; Spokesperson of Dept, 2002–05; Chief of Staff, Office of Minister of For. Affairs, 2002–04; Dir Gen. for ASEAN Co-operation, 2003–05; Ambassador to UK and to Ireland, 2005–07; Perm. Rep. to UN, NY, 2007–09. Non-exec. Dir, Jardine Cycle & Carriage, 2015–. Foreign Service Award, 1996, 2006; Public Relns Soc. Award, 2004. *Recreations:* classic cars, football, walks. *E:* rm3n@yahoo.com.

**NATH, Sarah Joanna;** *see* Tabrizi, S. J.

**NATHAN,** family name of **Baron Nathan.**

**NATHAN,** 3rd Baron *cr* 1940, of Churt, Surrey; **Rupert Harry Bernard Nathan;** *b* 26 May 1957; *o s* of 2nd Baron Nathan and of Philippa Gertrude (*née* Solomon); *S* father, 2007; *m* 1st, 1987, Ann Hewitt (marr. diss. 1997); 2nd, 1997, Jane, *d* of D. Cooper; one *s* one *d. Educ:* Charterhouse; Durham Univ. (BA). *Heir: s* Hon. Alasdair Harry St John Nathan, *b* 27 Sept. 1999.

**NATHAN, Aparna;** QC 2019; *b* India, 1970; *d* of T. V. V. Nathan and Dr Indumathi Nathan; *m* 1999, Diarmuid Boyd; one *s* one *d. Educ:* Queen's Coll., London; United World Coll. of SE Asia, Singapore; Raffles Jun. Coll., Singapore; London Sch. of Econs and Political Sci. (LLB Hons, LLM). Inns of Court Sch. of Law. Called to the Bar, Middle Temple, 1994; in practice as a barrister specialising in tax law, Gray's Inn Tax Chambers, 1996–2014, Devereux Chambers, 2014–. Attorney Gen.'s Civil Counsel C Panel, 2010, B Panel, 2015, A Panel, 2017. Chair, Capital Gains and Investment Income Sub-Cttee, Chartered Inst. of Taxation, 2015–. Member: Addington Soc.; Revenue Bar Assoc.; Chancery Bar Assoc. Liveryman, Tax Advisers' Co. *Publications:* (jtly) McCutcheon on Inheritance Tax, 5th edn to 7th edn 2016; (contrib.) Mellows: taxation for executors and trustees. *Recreations:* theatre, Indian classical music and dance. *Address:* Devereux Chambers, Queen Elizabeth Building, Temple, EC4Y 9BS. *T:* (020) 7353 7534, *Fax:* (020) 7583 5150. *E:* nathan@devchambers.co.uk.

**NATHAN, David Brian;** QC 2002; *b* 29 Nov. 1948; *s* of Ephraim and Jenny Nathan; *m* Susan Mary Hayes; two *d;* one *s* one *d* from previous marriage. *Educ:* City of London Sch.; Manchester Univ. (LLB Hons). Called to the Bar, Middle Temple, 1971; in practice as barrister, specialising in all areas of criminal defence work, 1971–; Hd of Chambers, 9 Lincoln's Inn Fields, 2002. *Recreations:* reading, watching old movies. *Address:* 5 St Andrew's Hill, EC4V 5BZ.

**NATHAN, Peter Joseph; His Honour Judge Nathan;** a Circuit Judge, since 2005; Designated Family Judge for Surrey, since 2011; *b* 20 Dec. 1949; *s* of Laurence Nathan and Julia Nathan; *m* 1974, Denise Pomper; three *s. Educ:* Homefield Prep. Sch., Sutton; Wallington Independent Grammar Sch.; London Sch. of Economics (LLB Hons 1971, LLM 1972). Called to the Bar, Inner Temple, 1973; admitted solicitor, 1981; founder Mem., One Garden Court Family Law Chambers, 1989; Dep. Dist Judge, 1993–2005; a Recorder of the Crown Court, 2000–05. *Recreations:* walking, reading history, travel, gardening.

**NATHAN, Sara Catherine,** OBE 2008; portfolio worker, since 1998; *b* 16 Feb. 1956; *d* of late Derek Nathan and Mary Nathan (*née* Lavine); *m* 1984, Malcolm John Singer; one *s* one *d. Educ:* New Hall, Cambridge (BA Hons); Stanford Univ., Calif. (Harkness Fellow). News trainee, 1980–82; with BBC news and current affairs, incl. Results Ed., Election prog., 1992, Newsnight, Breakfast Time/News, Money Prog., 1982–93; Editor: The Magazine, BBC Radio 5, 1993–95; Channel 4 News, 1995–97; columnist, The Scotsman, 1999–2000. Ind. Editl Advr, BBC Trust, 2008–17. Chm., Animal Procedures Cttee, 2006–12. Lay Member: Professional Conduct Cttee, Bar Council, 1998–2004; Judicial Appts Commn, 2006–12; Member: HFEA, 1998–2005; Radio Authy, 1999–2003; Criminal Injuries Compensation Appeals Panel, 2000–06; Gambling Rev. Body, 2000–01; Regulatory Decisions Cttee, FSA, 2001–06; OFCOM, 2002–07 (Dep. Chm., Content Bd, 2003–06); Cttee, ICSTIS (Phonepay Plus), 2002–08; Youth Crime Commn, 2008–10; Solicitors Regulation Authy, 2010–14 (Chm., Standards Cttee, 2012–); Bd, Assoc. for TV on Demand, 2010–12; Chm., Disciplinary Tribunals, Nursing and Midwifery Council, 2012–; Public Appts Assessor, 2012–16. Sen. Hearing Manager, BBC, 2018–19. Chm., Children First Commn, Lambeth, 2000–02; Marshall Scholarship Comr, 2000–07. Trustee, Why Me?, 2010–16; Co-Founder and Trustee, Refugees At Home, 2015–. Chm., Churchfield Community Assoc., 2009–12. Mem., BAFTA. *Recreations:* finding hosts for refugees, cinema, gym. *Address:* 29 Goldsmith Avenue, W3 6HR.

**NATHAN, Stephen Andrew;** QC 1993; a Recorder, 2000–17; *b* 30 April 1947; *s* of Frederick Emil Nathan and Margot Sophie Jeanette Nathan (*née* Welch); *m* 1999, Colleen Toomey; one *s;* one *d. Educ:* Hall Sch., Hampstead; Cranleigh Sch., Surrey (Schol.); New Coll., Oxford (BA Law 1968; MA 1972). Called to the Bar, Middle Temple, 1969, Bencher, 2005; in practice at the Bar, 1969–; Asst Recorder, 1989–2000. Chm., London Common Law and Commercial Bar Assoc., 2009–11; Member: London Court of Internat. Arbitration, European Users' Council, 2011–; CEDR Exchange 2012–; Internat. Council for Commercial Arbitration, 2013–. Dep. Chm., Guild of Guide Lectrs, 1975–76; Chairman: Ponsonby Residents' Assoc., 1995–99; W Hampstead Gardens and Residents' Assoc., 2011–. *Publications:* (jtly) Employee Competition: covenants, confidentiality and garden leave, 2007, 2nd edn 2011. *Recreations:* tennis, swimming, fine cooking. *Address:* Blackstone Chambers, Blackstone House, Temple, EC4Y 9BW. *T:* (020) 7583 1770. *Club:* Royal Automobile.

**NATHANSON, Dr Vivienne Hilary;** Chair and Director, Nathanson Health Associates Ltd; *b* 9 March 1955; *d* of Norman Eric Nathanson and Margaret Nathanson (*née* Milman). *Educ:* Birkenhead High Sch., GDST; Middx Hosp. Med. Sch., Univ. of London (MB BS 1978). FRCP 2008. Med. Registrar, Glan Clwyd Hosp., 1981–84; British Medical Association: mgt trainee, 1984–86; Hd, Med. Ethics and Internat. Affairs, 1987–90; Scottish Sec., 1990–95; Hd, Professional Resources and Res. Gp, then Dir of Professional Activities, 1996–2014; Sen. Dir, BMA, 2014–15. Prof., Sch. for Health, Univ. of Durham, 2004–. Chair, Ethics Cttee, RCOG, 2015–. Hon. FFPH 2013. Hon. DSc Strathclyde, 2014. *Recreations:* bridge, opera. *Address:* 214 Princess Park Manor, Royal Drive, N11 3FS. *T:* (020) 8361 5885.

**NATKIEL, Rod;** Managing Director and Head of Production, RNA (Rod Natkiel Associates) Ltd, since 1999; Chief Executive, Fair Train, since 2016; *b* 30 Jan. 1952; *s* of late Daniel Natkiel and Marjorie Jessie (*née* Pinkham); *m* 1976, Janet Ruth Sawtell; two *s. Educ:* Kingston Grammar Sch.; Univ. of Bristol (BA Drama); Univ. of Birmingham (MBA Dist.). Theatre dir and composer, 1973–; Dir/Producer, BBC TV Entertainment, 1978–84; freelance Exec. Producer/Producer/Dir/Writer in Entertainment and Features, Drama, News and Current Affairs for all major broadcasters, 1984–; Hd of Network TV and Radio, BBC Birmingham, 1992–99; Events Creator/Prod., 2000–. Vis. Prof. in TV Studies, Univ. of Central England, 1993–99. Mem., Arts Council of England, 1997–98; Chair: W Midlands Arts Bd, 1997–2001; Screen W Midlands, 2001–03. Mem. Bd, Variety Children's Charity, 1995–; Chm., Variety Club Midlands, 1997–2000. *Recreations:* squash, cricket, theatre, cinema, DIY. *Address:* 5 Vesey Road, Sutton Coldfield, W Midlands B73 5NP. *T:* (0121) 355 2197, *Fax:* (0121) 355 8033. *E:* rod@rodnatkiel.co.uk.

**NATTRASS, Michael Henry,** FRICS; Member (UK Ind) West Midlands Region, European Parliament, 2004–14; *b* 14 Dec. 1945. Property mgt; co-founder and Sen. Partner, Nattrass Giles, chartered surveyors, 1980–2007. Former Party Chm. and former Dep. Leader, UKIP. Contested (UK Ind) S Staffordshire, 2010.

**NATWAR-SINGH, Kanwar;** Padma Bhushan, 1984; MP (Congress Party) Bharatpur: Lok Sabha, 1984–89 and 1998–99; Rajya Sabha, 2002–08; Union Minister for External Affairs, India, 2004–05; *b* 16 May 1931; *s* of Govind Singhji and Prayag Kaur; *m* 1967, Princess Heminder Kumari, *e d* of late Maharaja Yadvindra Singhji of Patiala; one *s* (one *d* decd). *Educ:* St Stephen's Coll., Delhi Univ. (BA 1st cl. hons History 1951); Corpus Christi Coll., Cambridge, 1952–54 (Hon. Fellow 2005); Peking Univ. Joined Indian Foreign Service, 1953; 3rd Sec., Peking, 1956–58; Under Sec., Ministry of External Affairs, and Private Sec. to Sec. General, 1958–61; Adviser, Indian Delegn to UN, NY, 1961–66; Rapporteur, UN Cttee on Decolonisation, 1962–66; Rapporteur, UN Trusteeship Council, 1965; Alt. Deleg. of India to UN Session for 1962; Rep. of India on Exec. Bd of UNICEF, NY, 1962–66; Dep. Sec. to Prime Minister of India, 1966–67; Dir, Prime Minister's Secretariat, New Delhi, 1967–70; Jt Sec. to Prime Minister, 1970–71; Ambassador to Poland, 1971–73; Dep. High Comr in London, 1973–77; High Comr for India in Zambia and Botswana, 1977–80; Ambassador to Pakistan, 1980–82; Sec., Min. of External Affairs, India, 1982–84; Minister of State for Steel, 1984–85, for Fertilizers, 1985–86; Union Minister of State for Foreign Affairs, 1986–89. Attended Commonwealth Heads of Govt Meetings: Jamaica, 1975; Lusaka, 1979; Member: Commonwealth Gurus Cttee, 1977; Indian Delegn to Zimbabwe Ind. Celebrations, 1980; Sec.-Gen., 7th Non-Aligned Summit, New Delhi, 1983; Chief Co-ordinator, Commonwealth Heads of State and Govt Meeting, New Delhi, 1983; Pres., UN Conf. on Disarmament and Develt, 1987; Leader, Indian Delegn to 42nd Session of UN Gen. Assembly, 1987. Dir, Air India, 1982–84. Exec. Trustee, UNITAR, 1981–86. Pres., All India Tennis Fedn, 1988–92. Hon. Res. Fellow, UCL. Hon. Dr Pol Sci. Seoul, 2005. E. M. Forster Literary Award, 1989. Comdr, Ordre Nat. du Lion (Senegal), 2005. *Publications:* E. M. Forster: A Tribute, 1964; The Legacy of Nehru, 1965; Tales from Modern India, 1966; Stories from India, 1971; Maharaja Suraj Mal, 1707–1763, 1981; Curtain Raisers, 1984; Profiles and Letters, 1997; The Magnificent Maharaja Bhupinder Singh of Patiala 1891–1938, 1997; Heart to Heart, 2003; Yours Sincerely, 2008; My China Diary, 1956–88, 2010; Walking with Lions, 2012; One Life is Not Enough (autobiog.), 2014; writes and reviews for national and international newspapers and magazines. *Recreations:* tennis, watching cricket, reading, writing, collecting books and reading them, good conversation followed by prolonged periods of reflective uninterrupted silence. *E:* knatwarsingh@yahoo.com. *Clubs:* Royal Over-Seas League (Life Mem.); India International Centre (Life Mem.), Gymkhana (Life Mem.; Pres., 1984) (Delhi).

**NATZLER, Sir David (Lionel),** KCB 2018; Clerk of the House of Commons, and Head of the House of Commons Service, 2015–19; *b* 16 Aug. 1952; *o s* of Pierre Jean Natzler and late Brenda Agnes Natzler (*née* Wrangham); *m* 1988, Hilary Joan Gauld Thompson; two *s* one *d. Educ:* Eton Coll.; Trinity Coll., Cambridge (BA 1973); Harvard Univ. (Kennedy Schol.). House of Commons: Clerk of Select Committee: on Social Services, 1981–85; on Defence, 1989–95; on Procedure, 1995–97; on Trade and Industry, 1997–2001; Principal Clerk, Select Cttees, 2001–04; Sec., H of C Commn, 2004–06; Principal Clerk, Table Office, 2006–08; Clerk of Cttees, 2008–09; Clerk of Cttee and Clerk of Legislation, 2009–11; Clerk Asst and Dir Gen., Chamber and Cttee Services, 2011–15; Actg Clerk of H of C, 2014–15. *E:* dlnatzler@gmail.com.

**NAUGHTIE, (Alexander) James,** FRSE; journalist and broadcaster; Special Correspondent, BBC Radio 4, since 2016; Books Editor, BBC News, since 2016; *b* 9 Aug. 1951; *s* of Alexander and Isabella Naughtie; *m* 1986, Eleanor Updale; one *s* two *d. Educ:* Keith Grammar Sch.; Aberdeen Univ. (MA Hons); Syracuse Univ., New York (MA). The Press and Journal, 1975–77; The Scotsman, 1977–84; The Guardian, 1984–88; Presenter: The World at One, BBC Radio 4, 1988–94; Opera News, BBC Radio 3, 1990–93; BBC

Proms, 1992–2004; Today, BBC Radio 4, 1994–2015; Bookclub, BBC Radio 4, 1998–; The New Elizabethans, BBC Radio 4, 2012. Laurence M. Stern Fellow, Washington Post, 1981. Chancellor, Stirling Univ., 2008–18. Patron: Southbank Sinfonia, 2003–; Borders Book Festival, 2005–. Ambassador, The Prince's Foundn for Children and the Arts (formerly Prince of Wales Arts and Kids Foundn), 2005–. Trustee: Booker Prize Foundn, 2010–; Great Tapestry of Scotland, 2012–. FRSE 2017. Hon. LLD: Aberdeen, 1990; St Andrews, 2001; DUniv Stirling, 2001; Hon. DLitt: Glasgow Caledonian, 2002; Napier, 2002; Edinburgh, 2006. Personality of the Year, Sony Radio Awards, 1991. *Publications*: (ed) Playing the Palace: a Westminster collection, 1984; The Rivals: the intimate story of a political marriage, 2001; The Accidental American, 2004; The Making of Music: a journey with notes, 2007; The New Elizabethans, 2012; The Madness of July (novel), 2014; Paris Spring (novel), 2016; contribs to newspapers, magazines, journals. *Recreations*: books, opera. *Address*: BBC News Centre, Broadcasting House, Portland Place, W1A 1AA. *Club*: Garrick.

**NAUGHTON, Prof. John;** academic and journalist; Senior Research Fellow, Centre for Research in the Arts, Social Sciences and Humanities, University of Cambridge, 2012–18; Fellow, Wolfson College, Cambridge, 1992, now Emeritus (Vice President, 2011–15); *b* 18 July 1946; *s* of late Peter Naughton and Pearl Naughton (*née* Moran); *m* 1st, 1968, Carol (marr. diss. 2001); two *s*; 2nd, 2002, Susan Pinniger (*d* 2002); one *s* one *d*; 3rd, 2012, Fiona Blackburn (*née* Haigh). *Educ*: University Coll., Cork (BE 1968); Emmanuel Coll., Cambridge (MA 1972). Open University: Lectr, then Sen. Lectr, 1972–2002; Prof. of Public Understanding of Technol., 2002–11, now Prof. Emeritus. Res. Fellow, Twente Univ. of Technol., Netherlands, 1997–98; Adjunct Prof., UC Cork. Television Critic: Listener, 1982–87; Observer, 1987–95; columnist, 1987–, technol. columnist, 1995–, Observer. FRSA. *Publications*: A Brief History of the Future: the origins of the internet, 1999; From Gutenberg to Zuckerberg, 2012; contrib. articles to jls, newspapers and mags. *Recreations*: photography, conversation, blogging, Provençal summers. *Address*: Wolfson College, Barton Road, Cambridge CB3 9BB. *Clubs*: Garrick, Groucho.

**NAVARRETE LÓPEZ, Jorge Eduardo;** Senior Researcher on International Affairs, National Autonomous University of Mexico, 2004–18; *b* 29 April 1940; *s* of late Gabriel Navarrete and Lucrecia López; *m* 1st, 1962, María Antonieta Linares (marr. diss. 1973); one *s*; 2nd, 1976, María de Navarrete (*d* 1985); 3rd, 1987, Angeles Salceda (marr. diss. 1994); 4th, 1996, Martha López (marr. diss. 2007). *Educ*: Nat. Sch. of Economics, Nat. Autonomous Univ. of Mexico (equivalent BA Econ.); post-graduate studies in internat. economy. Center for Latin American Monetary Studies, Mexico, 1963–65; Nat. Foreign Trade Bank, Mexico, 1966–72; joined Mexican Foreign Service, 1972; Ambassador to: Venezuela, 1972–75; Austria, 1976–77; Yugoslavia, 1977–79; Dep. Perm. Rep. to UN, NY, 1979; Under Sec. (Economics), Min. of Foreign Affairs, Mexico, 1979–85; Ambassador: to UK and Republic of Ireland, 1986–89; to China, 1989–93; to Chile, 1993–95; Under Sec. for Energy, 1995–97; Ambassador to Brazil, 1997–2000; Perm. Rep. to UN, NY, 2000–02; Ambassador to Germany, 2002–04. Former Mem., South Commn. Mem. Bd of Govt, Nat. Inst. for Bank Savings Protection. Holds decorations from Argentina, Brazil, Dominican Republic, Ecuador, Federal Republic of Germany, Italy, Panama, Poland, Sweden, Venezuela. *Publications*: The International Transfer of Technology (with G. Bueno and M. S. Wionczeck), 1969; Mexico's Economic Policy, 2 vols, 1971, 1972; Cancun 1981: the international meeting on co-operation and development, 1982; The External Debt of Latin America: issues and policies, 1987; (ed) The Deconstruction of Mexican Foreign Policy, 2005; China: the third inflection, 2007; The Global Foot-print of China: international relations of a global power, 2011; numerous essays on Mexican and Latin American economic issues, in Mexican and foreign jls. *Recreation*: chess. *Address*: Sta Margarita 214, 03100 Mexico City, Mexico.

**NAVRATILOVA, Martina;** tennis player; commentator; *b* Prague, 18 Oct. 1956; *d* of late Jana Navratilova. Left Czechoslovakia, 1975; adopted American nationality, 1981; *m* 2014, Julia Lemigova. Professional player, 1975–94. Has won 167 singles and 178 doubles titles, including 18 Grand Slam singles titles (a record 9 Wimbledon singles wins) and 41 Grand Slam doubles titles. Pres., Women's Tennis Assoc., 1979–80, 1994–95. *Publications*: Martina (autobiog.), 1985; Shape Your Self, 2006; novels (with Liz Nickles): The Total Zone, 1994; Killer Instinct, 1995; Breaking Point, 1996. *Address*: c/o International Management Group, 1360 E 9th Street, Suite #100, Cleveland, OH 44114–1782, USA.

**NAWANA, Namal Sasrika;** Chief Executive Officer, Smith & Nephew plc, since 2018; *b* Colombo, Sri Lanka, 15 Nov. 1970. *Educ*: Univ. of Adelaide (BEng Hons Mech. Engrg; MA Med. Sci.); Henley Mgt Coll. (MBA). Pres., De Puy Synthes Spine, 2011–12; Alere Inc.: Chief Operating Officer, 2012–14; CEO, 2014–17. Dir, AdvaMedDX, 2016–18; non-executive Director: Hologic Inc., 2018–; AdvaMed, 2019–. Founder: Neoenta, 2018; Innovoyce, 2019. *Recreations*: golf, yoga. *Address*: Smith & Nephew, 15 Adam Street, WC2N 6LA. *T*: (020) 7960 2201. *Club*: Pinebrook Country (Weston, MA).

**NAWAZ, Amjad; His Honour Judge Nawaz;** a Circuit Judge, since 2008; *b* Jhelum, Pakistan, 10 Feb. 1958; *s* of Choudary Mohammed Azam and Shafia Begum; *m* 1983, Shamin Akhtar; two *s* four *d* (incl. triplets). *Educ*: Univ. of Aston in Birmingham (BSc 1st Cl. Hons Managerial and Admin Scis). Called to the Bar, Lincoln's Inn, 1983; in practice as barrister, specialising in crime, chancery and commercial law, 1983–2008; Recorder, 2002–08. *Recreations*: cricket (played at University level), squash, tennis, Manchester United fan. *Address*: Wolverhampton Crown Court, Pipers Row, Wolverhampton WV1 3LQ.

**NAWAZ, Maajid;** Chairman, Quilliam Foundation, since 2008; *m* 2014, Rachel Maggart. *Educ*: Sch. of Oriental and African Studies, Univ. of London (BA Law and Arabic); London Sch. of Econs and Pol Sci. (MSc Pol Theory). Hon. Associate, Nat. Secular Soc., 2014–. Columnist, Daily Beast, 2015–. Contested (Lib Dem) Hampstead and Kilburn, 2015. FRSA 2009. *Publications*: Radical, 2012; (with S. Harris) Islam and the Future of Tolerance: a dialogue, 2015. *Address*: Quilliam Foundation, PO Box 60380, WC1A 9AZ. *T*: (020) 7182 7280. *E*: information@quilliamfoundation.org.

**NAWBATT, Akash Vedant;** QC 2017; *b* Toronto, 29 May 1976; *s* of Lal Nawbatt and Ayush Nawbatt; *m* 2009, Anoli Rayvadera; one *s*. *Educ*: Park High Sch.; Queen Elizabeth's Sch., Barnet; Jesus Coll., Cambridge (BA 1998). Called to the Bar, Gray's Inn, 1999; in practice as barrister, specialising in employment and tax. *Publications*: (Contrib. Ed.) Harvey on Industrial Relations and Employment Law, 2006–. *Recreations*: family, sport. *Address*: Devereux Chambers, Devereux Court, Temple, WC2R 3JH.

**NAYLER, Georgina Ruth;** Director, Pilgrim Trust, since 1996; *b* 16 March 1959; *d* of late Dennis Nayler and of Yvonne Nayler (*née* Loader); partner, Simon Stillwell; one *s* one *d*. *Educ*: Brentwood County High Sch. for Girls; Univ. of Warwick (BA). Joined Nat. Heritage Meml Fund, 1982: Asst Dir, 1987–88; Dep. Dir, 1988–89; Dir, 1989–95. Mem., Historic Bldgs Council for Scotland, 1990–96. Mem., Adv. Bd, Faculty of Arts, Univ. of Warwick, 2003–10. Trustee: Charlotte Bonham-Carter Charitable Trust, 2008–; Pitzhanger Manor Trust, 2013– (Dep. Chm., 2014–). *Recreation*: gardening. *Address*: c/o The Pilgrim Trust, 55a Catherine Place, SW1E 6DY.

**NAYLOR, (Andrew) Ross,** MD; FRCSE, FRCS; Consultant Vascular Surgeon, since 1995, and Professor of Vascular Surgery, since 2003, Leicester Royal Infirmary; *b* 22 March 1958; *s* of Robert Charles Naylor and Patricia Mary Naylor; *m* 1982, May Bruce MacPherson; one *s* one *d*. *Educ*: Merchiston Castle Sch., Edinburgh; Univ. of Aberdeen (MBChB (commendation) 1981; MD 1990). FRCSE 1986; FRCS 1994. House Officer, Aberdeen Hosps, 1981–82; Lectr in Pathology, Aberdeen Royal Infirmary, 1982–83; Sen. House Officer, Surgery, Aberdeen Hosps, 1983–85; Surgical Registrar, Edinburgh Hosps, 1985–88; Res. Fellow in Surgery, Edinburgh Univ., 1988–90; Lectr in Surgery, Leicester Univ., 1991–93; Consultant Vascular Surgeon, Aberdeen Royal Infirmary, 1993–95. Reader in Surgery, Leicester Royal Infirmary, 1995–2003. Hunterian Prof., RCS, 2002. Vis. Nimmo Prof., Adelaide Univ., 2018. Member Council: Vascular Soc. of GB and Ireland, 2006–12 (Pres., 2011–12); European Soc. of Vascular and Endovascular Surgery, 2010–16. Associate Ed., 2008–11, Sen. Ed., 2011–13, Ed. in Chief, 2013–16, Eur. Jl of Vascular and Endovascular Surgery. *Publications*: (ed jtly) Carotid Artery Surgery: a problem based approach, 2000; (ed jtly) Vascular Surgery: principles and practice, 2016; 74 book chapters on mgt of vascular disease; 506 pubns in peer reviewed jls, mainly relating to mgt of carotid artery disease. *Recreations*: road cycling, ski-ing, gardening. *Address*: 9 Dalby Avenue, Bushby, Leicester LE7 9RE. *T*: (0116) 258 7768, *Fax*: (0116) 258 5029. *E*: arnaylor@hotmail.com.

**NAYLOR, Bernard;** University Librarian, Southampton University, 1977–2000; President, Library Association, 2001–02; *b* 7 May 1938; *s* of William Edward Naylor and Lilian Naylor (*née* Oakes); *m* 1967, Frances Gemma Trenaman; four *s* one *d*. *Educ*: Balliol Coll., Oxford (BA 1963; MA 1965); Sch. of Librarianship and Archive Administration, University Coll. London (Dip. Lib. 1966). MCLIP (ALA 1969). Asst, Foreign Accessions Dept, Bodleian Liby, 1964–66; Librarian and Bibliographer, Univ. of London Inst. of Latin American Studies, 1966–74; Sec., Library Resources Co-ordinating Cttee, Univ. of London, 1974–77; Co-ordinator of Inf. Services, 1988–93, of Acad. Support Services, 1998–2000, Southampton Univ. Member: British Liby Adv. Cttee on Lending Services, 1978–86 (Chm., 1981–85); Council, Standing Conf. of Nat. and Univ. Libraries, 1979–82, 1984–90 (Vice-Chm., 1984–86; Chm., 1986–88); British Council Libraries Adv. Cttee, 1982–96 (Chm., 1986–95); British Liby Bd, 1995–2001. Chm., Hants Area Tech. Res. Indust. Commercial Service Exec., 1981–2000. Trustee: Nat. MSS Conservation Trust, 1995–2017; Hansard Trust, 2002–; Chartered Inst. of Liby and Inf. Professionals Benevolent Fund (formerly Liby Assoc. Benevolent Fund), 2002–17 (Chm., 2008–13; Treas., 2016–17). Chm., Laser Foundn, 2003–05. Gov., La Sainte Union Coll., Southampton, 1996–97. Mem., British Council, 1995. Hon. DLitt Southampton, 2006. *Publications*: Accounts of Nineteenth Century South America, 1969; Directory of Libraries and Special Collections on Latin America and the West Indies, 1975; articles in liby jls. *Recreations*: playing the piano (in private), learning foreign languages. *Address*: 12 Blenheim Avenue, Highfield, Southampton SO17 1DU. *T*: (023) 8055 4697.

**NAYLOR, (Charles) John,** OBE 1993; Secretary and Treasurer, then Chief Executive, Carnegie United Kingdom Trust, 1993–2003; Chair, Office of Scottish Charity Regulator, 2006–11; *b* 17 Aug. 1943; *s* of late Arthur Edgar Naylor, MBE and Elizabeth Mary Naylor; *m* 1968, Margery Thomson; two *s*. *Educ*: Royal Grammar Sch., Newcastle upon Tyne; Haberdashers' Aske's Sch., Elstree; Clare Coll., Cambridge (MA History). Jun. and sen. exec. posts in industry, 1965–75; Dir, YMCA National Centre, Lakeside, Cumbria, 1975–80; Dep. National Sec., 1980–82, Nat. Sec., 1982–93, National Council of YMCAs; mem. and chm. of YMCA European and world cttees, 1976–92. Jt Founder, Y Care Internat., 1984. Vice-Chm., Nat. Council for Voluntary Youth Services, 1985–88; Mem., Nat. Adv. Council for Youth Service, 1985–88. Chairman: Assoc. of Heads of Outdoor Educn Centres, 1979–80; MSC and DES Working Party on Residential Experience and Unemployment, 1980–81; DES Adv. Cttee for Innovation in Youth Work, 1986–92; Mem., Scottish Charity Law Review Commn, 2000–01. Member: Community Fund Scottish Cttee, 2003–04 (Chm., 2004–06); UK Bd, Big Lottery Fund, 2004–06; Audit and Risk Mgt Cttee, Nat. Trust for Scotland, 2011–. Chm., 1995–2000, Trustee, 2000–06, Brathay Exploration Gp; Trustee and Treas., The Tomorrow Project, 2000–13; Chm., Strange Town (youth theatre), 2011– (Vice Chm., 2007–11). Trustee: Med. Res. Scotland (formerly Scottish Hosps Endowment Res. Trust), 2005–13; Foundn Scotland (formerly Scottish Community Foundn), 2011–; Trustee and Director: Resilient Scotland Ltd, 2011–14; Jessica (Scotland) Trust, 2011–14. Mem. Council, UK Scout Assoc., 2005–10 (Chm., Develt Grants Bd, 2003–10; Mem., Scouts District Exec., Craigalmond, 2016–); Jt Founding Convenor, Scottish Grant Making Trust Gp, 1994–2004; Chm., RSA Scotland, 2012–14; Pres., YMCA Scotland 2012–. Mem., Clare Coll., Cambridge Alumni Council, 2010–13; Chair, Cambridge Soc. of Edinburgh, 2018–. Kirk Elder, 1998–. CCMI; FRSA. *Publications*: contribs on youth, outdoors and grant making to UK periodicals and books. *Recreations*: the outdoors (partic. mountains), travel, performing and other arts, golf. *Address*: Orchard House, 25b Cramond Glebe Road, Edinburgh EH4 6NT.

**NAYLOR, Prof. David,** OC 2006; FRSC 2004; FCAHS; Professor of Medicine, University of Toronto, since 1996 (President, 2005–13, now President Emeritus); *b* 26 Oct. 1954; *s* of Thomas Naylor and Edna (*née* Aziz); *m* 1985, Ilse Treurnicht, DPhil. *Educ*: Univ. of Toronto (MD 1978); Hertford Coll., Oxford (Rhodes Schol. 1979; DPhil 1983). FRCPC 1986. Resident in internal medicine, Univ. of Western Ontario teaching hosps, 1983–86; MRC Res. Fellow, Clinical Epidemiol., Toronto Gen. Hosp., 1987–88; University of Toronto: Asst Prof., 1988–92, Associate Prof., 1992–96, of Medicine; Dean of Medicine and Vice Provost, Relns with Health Care Instns, 1999–2005; Founding Dir, Clinical Epidemiology Prog., Sunnybrook Health Scis Centre, Toronto, 1990–96; Founding CEO, Inst. for Clinical Evaluative Scis, 1991–98. Interim Pres. and CEO, Hosp. for Sick Children, 2018–19. Chairman: Nat. Adv. Cttee on SARS and Public Health, 2003; Nat. Adv. Panel on Healthcare Innovation, 2014–15; Nat. Adv. Panel on Fundamental Sci., 2016–17; Member: Global Commn on Educating Health Professionals for the 21st Century, 2009–10; Federal Rev. of Res. and Develt (Jenkins Panel), 2010–11. Trustee, Aga Khan Univ., 2013–. FCAHS 2005. For. Associate, Inst. of Medicine, NAS, 2005. Hon. Life Mem., Canadian Public Health Assoc., 2005. Member Editorial Board: BMJ, 1996–98; Jl of American Med. Assoc., 1998–2016 (Mem., Editl Oversight Cttee, 2017–); Canadian Med. Assoc. Jl, 1998–2000. Hon. DSc: Manitoba, 2009; Alberta, 2018; Hon. LLD: Western, 2011; Calgary, 2017. F. N. G. Starr Medal, Canadian Med. Assoc., 2016; Henry G. Friesen Internat. Prize in Health Research, 2018. *Publications*: co-author of numerous books and chapters, and over 250 jl articles. *Recreations*: golf, piano. *Address*: c/o Department of Medicine, University of Toronto, Suite RFE 3–805, 200 Elizabeth Street, Toronto, ON M5G 2C4, Canada. *Club*: Scarboro Golf.

**NAYLOR, Maj.-Gen. (David) Murray,** CB 1992; MBE 1972; Director-General, Territorial Army and Organisation, Ministry of Defence, 1989–92; *b* 5 March 1938; *s* of Thomas Humphrey Naylor and Dorothy Isobel Durning Naylor (*née* Holt); *m* 1965, Rosemary Gillian Hicks Beach; three *s*. *Educ*: Eton Coll. psc, rcds. Joined Scots Guards, 1956; commnd as National Service and later as Regular Officer; commanded: 2nd Bn Scots Guards, 1976–79; 22nd Armoured Bde, 1982–83; Dep. Mil. Sec. (A), 1985–87; GOC NE Dist and Comdr 2nd Inf. Div., 1987–89. Chm., N Yorks Ambulance Service NHS Trust, 1992–97. Mem. (C), N Yorks CC, 1997–2005. DL N Yorks, 1994. Mem., Merchant

Adventurers Co. of York, 1998. Gov., St Peter's Sch., York, 1991–2005 (Chm. of Govs, 2000–05). Lay Chm., Southern Ryedale Deanery, 2008–13. Mem., Kohima Educnl Trust, 2003– (Chm., 2003–09; Pres., 2016–). Trustee, Ryedale Fest., 2012–15. Volunteer guide, York Minster, 2008–18. *Publications:* Among Friends: Scots Guards 1956–1993, 1995; England's Cathedrals by Train: discover how the Normans and Victorians helped to shape our lives, 2013; England's Historic Churches by Train: a companion volume to England's Cathedrals by Train, 2016; An Unintentional Soldier: the life of Murray Naylor (autobiog.), 2018. *Recreations:* walking, travel. *Address:* Minster Hill, Huttons Ambo, York YO60 7HJ. *T:* (01653) 695008; 07889 138381. *Club:* Cavalry and Guards.

**NAYLOR, Prof. Ernest,** OBE 1998; PhD, DSc; Lloyd Roberts Professor of Marine Zoology (formerly Lloyd Roberts Professor of Zoology), 1982–96, now Professor Emeritus, and Head of School of Ocean Sciences, 1992–96, University College of North Wales, Bangor; *b* 19 May 1931; *s* of Joseph and Evelyn Naylor; *m* 1956, Carol Gillian Bruce; two *d*. *Educ:* Swanwick Hall Grammar Sch.; Univ. of Sheffield (BSc); Univ. of Liverpool (PhD, DSc). FIBiol 1972–96. Commnd RAF, 1954–56 (Educn Br.). Successively Asst Lectr, Lectr, Sen. Lectr and Reader in Zoology, University Coll. of Swansea, Wales, 1956–71; Prof. of Marine Biology, Univ. of Liverpool, 1971–82; Dean of Sci., UCNW, Bangor, 1989–91. Visiting Professor: Duke Univ., USA, 1969, 1970; Univ. of Otago, NZ, 1982. Mem., NERC, 1976–82 (Mem., Marine Sci. and Technol. Bd, 1994–96); Specialist Adviser to H of L Select Sub-Cttee on Marine Sci. and Technology, 1985; Ind. Mem., Co-ordinating Cttee on Marine Sci. and Technology, 1988–91; Ind. Assessor, Inter-Agency Cttee on Marine Sci. and Technol., 1991–98; UK Rep., EC Adv. Cttee for Marine Science and Technol., 1989–96. President: Sect. D (Zoology), BAAS, 1982; Estuarine and Coastal Sciences Assoc., 1986–89 (Hon. Life Mem. 2001); Soc. for Exptl Biology, 1989–91 (Hon. Life Mem. 1997); Member Council: Marine Biol Assoc. of UK, 1977–80, 1982–85; Challenger Soc. for Marine Sci., 1997–98 (Hon. Life Mem. 2007). Founding Ed., Estuarine, Coastal and Shelf Science, 1972–2000. *Publications:* British Marine Isopods, 1972, 2nd edn (with Angelika Brandt) as Intertidal Marine Isopods, 2015; (co-ed with R. G. Hartnoll) Cyclic Phenomena in Marine Plants and Animals, 1979; Chronobiology of Marine Organisms, 2010; Moonstruck, 2015; over 160 papers in learned jls. *Recreations:* travel, gardening. *Address:* School of Ocean Sciences, Bangor University, Menai Bridge, Anglesey LL59 5AB. *T:* (01248) 382842. *E:* e.naylor@bangor.ac.uk.

**NAYLOR, Jennifer Mary;** *see* Higham, J. M.

**NAYLOR, John;** *see* Naylor, C. J.

**NAYLOR, Maurice;** *see* Naylor, W. M.

**NAYLOR, Maj.-Gen. Murray;** *see* Naylor, Maj.-Gen. D. M.

**NAYLOR, Sir Robert (Antony),** Kt 2008; Chief Executive, University College London Hospitals NHS Trust, 2000–16; National Adviser to UK Government on NHS Property and Estates, since 2016; *b* 13 Nov. 1949; *s* of Francis Thomas Naylor and Kathleen Mary (*née* Donellan); *m* 1974, Jane Karen Evans; one *s* one *d*. *Educ:* Presentation Coll., Reading; Thames Poly. (BSc Hons Chem. London). Grad. mgt trainee, King's Fund, 1972–74; Hosp. Sec., National Hosp., Queen Sq., 1974–77; Dist Administrator, Enfield HA, 1977–84; Chief Exec., Birmingham Heartlands and Solihull NHS Trust, 1984–2000. Chm., Shelford Gp, 2013–14; Mem., Foundn Trust Network, 2009–15. Hon. Sen. Fellow, Univ. of Warwick. *Recreations:* golf, scuba diving. *Address:* 4 Chester Terrace, Regent's Park, NW1 4ND.

**NAYLOR, Ross;** *see* Naylor, A. R.

**NAYLOR, (William) Maurice,** CBE 1973; FIHM; Director, National Association of Health Authorities, 1981–84; *b* 20 Dec. 1920; *s* of Thomas and Agnes Naylor; *m* 1948, Maureen Ann, *d* of John and Mary Walsh; one *s* two *d*. *Educ:* St Joseph's Coll., Market Drayton; Manchester Univ. (BA Admin). FIHM (FHSM 1956, Hon. FHSM 1987). War service, 1941–46, 135 Field Regt RA (FE, POW (captured at fall of Singapore), 1942–45). Parly Asst, Town Clerk's Office, Manchester, 1950–55; Asst Sec., Manchester RHB, 1955–57; Dep. Sec., 1957–63, Sec., 1963–73, Sheffield RHB; Regl Administrator, Trent RHA, 1973–81. Institute of Health Services Management: Mem., Nat. Council, 1966–86; Chm., 1974; Pres., 1975–76; Chm. Educn Cttee, 1980–86. Member: Cttee on Hosp. Supplies Orgn, 1969; Steering Cttee on Reorgn of NHS, 1973–74; Cornwall AHA, 1982–84; Chm., Patient Transport Services Working Party, 1981. Trustee, NHS Pensioners Trust, 1991–99. JP Sheffield, 1970. Hon. MBA Sheffield, 1982. *Publications:* (contrib.) Challenges for Change, 1971; Organisation of Area Health Services, 1972; (contrib. and Chm., Editl Cttee) Health Care in the United Kingdom: its organisation and management, 1982; contrib. to professional jls. *Address:* 7 Hewitt Drive, Kirby Muxloe, Leicester LE9 2EB. *T:* (0116) 239 2606.

**NAYLOR-LEYLAND, Sir Philip (Vyvian),** 4th Bt *cr* 1895, of Hyde Park House; Chairman, Milton (Peterborough) Estates Co.; *b* 9 Aug. 1953; *s* of Sir Vivyan Edward Naylor-Leyland, 3rd Bt and Hon. Elizabeth Anne Fitzalan-Howard, *yr d* of 2nd Viscount FitzAlan of Derwent, OBE (she *m* 2nd, Sir Stephen Hastings, MC, and *d* 1997); *S* father, 1987; *m* 1980, Lady Isabella Lambton, *d* of Viscount Lambton (*d* 2006); four *s* two *d*. *Educ:* Eton; RMA Sandhurst; NY Univ. Business Sch.; RAC Cirencester. 2nd Lieut, Life Guards, 1973, Lieut, 1975–76. Chm., Peterborough Royal Foxhound Show Soc., 1995– (Vice-Chm., 1988–95); Pres., Nat. Coursing Club, 1988–. Jt Master, Fitzwilliam (Milton) Hunt, 1987–. *Heir: s* Thomas Philip Naylor-Leyland [*b* 22 Jan. 1982; *m* 2011, Alice Dawson; two *s* one *d*]. *Address:* Milton, Peterborough, Cambs PE6 7AA; Nantclwyd Hall, Ruthin, Denbighshire LL15 2PR. *Clubs:* White's; Royal Air Squadron; Sunningdale Golf.

**NAYSMITH, (John) Douglas,** PhD; *b* 1 April 1941; *s* of late James Naysmith and Ina (*née* Vass); *m* 1966, Caroline (separated), *d* of late Sidney and Kate Hill; one *s* one *d*. *Educ:* Musselburgh Burgh Sch.; George Heriot's Sch., Edinburgh; Edinburgh Univ. (BSc, PhD). CBiol 1989, FRSB (FIBiol 1999). Res. Asst, Edinburgh Univ., 1966–69; Fellow, Yale Univ., 1969–70; Res. Immunologist, Beecham Res. Labs, 1970–72; University of Bristol: Res. Associate, 1972–76; Fellow, 1976–81; Lectr in Immunology, Dept of Pathology, 1981–95; Administrator, Registrar's Office, 1995–97. MP (Lab and Co-op) Bristol NW, 1997–2010. Mem. (Lab) Bristol City Council, 1981–98 and 2010–14. FRSocMed 1980.

**NAZARETH, Prof. Irwin,** PhD; FRCGP; Professor of Primary Care and Population Sciences, since 2002, and Director, Priment Clinical Trials Unit, since 2008, University College London; *b* Bombay, 12 Oct. 1958; *s* of Ignatius Nazareth and Caroline Rodrigue-Nazareth. *Educ:* Topiwala Nat. Medical Coll., Bombay (MB BS 1984); London (PhD 1997). LRCPE 1986; LRCSE 1986; LRCPSGlas 1986; DRCOG 1988; MRCGP 1989; FRCGP 2004. SHO, 1984–89; University College London: Sir Jules Thorne Res. Fellow, 1990–93; Lectr in Primary Care, 1994–95; Sen. Lectr in Primary Care Medicine, 1995–2002; Vice Dean, Primary Care, 2007–11; Dir, Gen. Practice Res. Framework, GMC, 2005–12. *Publications:* contrib. key chapters in six books on med. practice and res.; over 400 original res. papers in scientific med. jls. *Recreations:* running, travel, music. *Address:* Department of Primary Care and Population Health, University College London Medical School, Rowland Hill Street, NW3 2NF.

**NAZIR-ALI, Rt Rev. Dr Michael James;** Bishop of Rochester, 1994–2009; President, Oxford Centre for Training, Research, Advocacy and Dialogue, since 2009; *b* 19 Aug. 1949; *s* of James and Patience Nazir-Ali; *m* 1972, Valerie Cree; two *s*. *Educ:* St Paul's School and St Patrick's Coll., Karachi; Univ. of Karachi (BA 1970, Econs Sociology and Islamic History); Fitzwilliam Coll. (PGCTh 1972; MLitt 1977; Hon. Fellow, 2006) and Ridley Hall, Cambridge; St Edmund Hall, Oxford (BLitt 1974; MLitt 1981; Hon. Fellow, 1999); ThD Aust. Coll. of Theol., NSW 1985; DHLitt Westminster Coll., Penn 2004; DD Lambeth, 2005. Assistant: Christ Church, Cambridge, 1970–72; St Ebbe's, Oxford, 1972–74; Burney Lectr in Islam, Cambridge, 1973–74; Tutorial Supervisor in Theology, Univ. of Cambridge, 1974–76; Assistant Curate, Holy Sepulchre, Cambridge, 1974–76; Tutor, then Sen. Tutor, Karachi Theol Coll., 1976–81; Assoc. Priest, Holy Trinity Cathedral, Karachi, 1976–79; Priest-in-charge, St Andrew's, Akhtar Colony, Karachi, 1979–81; Provost of Lahore Cathedral, 1981–84; Bishop of Raiwind, Pakistan 1984–86; Asst to Archbp of Canterbury, Co-ordinator of Studies and Editor for Lambeth Conf., 1986–89; Director-in-Residence, Oxford Centre for Mission Studies, 1986–89; Gen. Sec., CMS, 1989–94; Asst Bishop, Southwark, 1989–94; Canon Theologian, Leicester Cathedral, 1992–94. Took seat in H of L, 1999. Mem., HFEA, 1998–2003 (Chm., Ethics and Law Cttee, 1998–2003). Sec., Archbp's Commn on Communion and Women in the Episcopate (Eames Commn), 1988–98; Chm., Wkg Party on Women in Episcopate, 2001–04; Archbishops' nominee, CCBI, 1990–94; Chairman: C of E Mission Theol Adv. Gp, 1992–2001; House of Bishops' Theol. Gp, 2004–09; Member: ARCIC II, 1991–2010; C of E Bd of Mission, 1991–94, 1996–2001; Archbps' Council, 2000–05; House of Bishops' Standing Cttee, 2000–05; Internat. Anglican-Roman Catholic Commn for Unity and Mission, 2001–; Vis. Bishop for Anglican Relations, Dio. S Carolina, 2010–. Mem. Bd, Christian Aid, 1987–97. Chm., Christian Coalition for Educn, 2015. Vis. Prof., Univ. of Greenwich, 1996–; Sen. Fellow, 2010–15, Vis. Faculty, 2015–, Wycliffe Hall, Oxford; Visiting Faculty: London Sch. of Theol.; Lahore Coll. of Theol.; Forman Christian Univ.; Alexandria Sch. of Theol.; Oxford Centre for Mission Studies, 2012–. Chm. Council, Trinity Coll., Bristol, 1996–2008. Paul Harris Rotary Fellow, 2005. Hon. DLitt: Bath, 2003; Greenwich, 2003; Hon. DD: Kent, 2004; Nashotah, 2010. Sheikh Yamani Gold Medal in Islamic Studies, Iqbal Acad. *Publications:* Islam: a Christian perspective, 1983; Frontiers in Muslim-Christian Encounter, 1987; Martyrs and Magistrates: toleration and trial in Islam, 1989; From Everywhere to Everywhere, 1990; Mission and Dialogue, 1995; The Mystery of Faith, 1995; Citizens and Exiles: Christian faith in a plural world, 1998; Shapes of the Church to Come, 2001; Understanding My Muslim Neighbour, 2002; Conviction and Conflict, 2006; The Unique and Universal Christ, 2008; Triple Jeopardy for the West, 2012; How the Anglican Communion Came to be and Where it is Going, 2013; Faith, Freedom and the Future, 2016; *edited:* Working Papers for the Lambeth Conference, 1988; The Truth shall Make you Free: report of the Lambeth Conference, 1988; Trustworthy and True: Pastoral letters from the Lambeth Conference, 1988; monographs, articles and contribs to jls. *Recreations:* cricket, hockey, table tennis, reading fiction, humour and poetry, writing poetry. *Address:* 70 Wimpole Street, W1G 8AX.

**NDOMBET-ASSAMBA, Aloun;** Chief Executive Officer, City of Kingston Sodality Co-operative Credit Union Ltd, Kingston, Jamaica, since 2016; *b* Spanish Town, Jamaica; *d* of James Wood and Gloria Wood; one *s*. *Educ:* Univ. of the West Indies (LLB Hons); Norman Manley Law Sch. (Legal Educn Cert.); Inst. of Mgt and Prodn (Dip. Human Resources Develt); Univ. of Pittsburgh (Heinz Fellow). Legal Officer and Corporate Sec., Jamaica Industrial Develt Corp., 1983–87; Personal Manager and Legal Advr, 1988–94, Gen. Manager, 1994–2002, City of Kingston Co-op Credit Union. Parliament of Jamaica: Senator, 1998–2002; Minister of State, Min. of Industry, Sci., Commerce and Technol. 2002; Minister of Industry and Tourism, 2002–05, of Tourism, Entertainment and Culture, 2005–07; MP, St Ann SE, 2002–07; High Comr of Jamaica in UK, and Ambassador (non resident) to Norway, Sweden, Denmark, Finland and Ireland, 2012–16. Man. Partner, Aloun Ndombet-Assamba & Co., Attorneys-at-Law, 2008–12. Founding Member: Lions Club, New Kingston, 1991; Women's Leadership Initiative, 2001. *Recreations:* theatre, cinema, family, travel, art, history, culture, dancing, swimming. *Address:* Grierfield Great House, Moneague, St Ann PO, Jamaica. *E:* aassamba@cokcu.com.

**NDUNGANE, Most Rev. (Winston Hugh) Njongonkulu;** President and Founder, African Monitor, since 2008; Archbishop of Cape Town and Metropolitan of Southern Africa, 1996–2008; *b* Kokstad, 2 April 1941; *s* of Foster Tunyiswa Ndungane and Tingaza (*née* Gcanca); *m* 1st, 1972, Nosipho Ngcelwane (*d* 1986); one *s* one *d*; 2nd, 1987, Nomahlubi Vokwana. *Educ:* Lovedale High Sch., Alice, E Cape; Federal Theol Seminary, Alice (Associate, 1973); King's Coll., London (AKC, BD 1978; MTh 1979; FKC 1997). Ordained deacon, 1973, priest, 1974; Assistant Priest: St Mark's, Athlone, Cape Town, 1973–75; St Mark, Mitcham, 1975–76; St Peter's, Hammersmith, 1976–77; St Mary the Virgin, Primrose Hill, 1977–79; Asst Chaplain, St George's, Paris, 1979; Rector, St Nicholas, Elsies River, Cape Town, 1980–81; Provincial Liaison Officer, CPSA, 1981–84; Principal, St Bede's Coll., Umtata, 1985–86; Provincial Canon, 1987; Chief Exec. Officer, CPSA, 1987–91; Bishop of Kimberley and Kuruman, 1991–96. Vis. Scholar, Ch Divinity Sch. of the Pacific, Berkeley, 1990–91. Chairman: SACC Church Leaders' Forum, 1997–98; Nat. Poverty Hearings, 1998; Member: Budget Gp, USPG, 1981–86; ACC, and its Standing Cttee, 1981–90; Bd, SABC, 1993– (Chm., Religious Broadcasting Panel, 1995–). Chm. Council, Univ. of Cape Town, 2008–. Hon. DD: Rhodes Univ., 1997; Protestant Episcopal Seminary, Va, 2000; Episcopal Divinity Sch., Cambridge, Mass, 2007; Hon. DHL Worcester State Coll., Mass, 2000; Hon. DSocSc Natal, 2001; Hon. PhD: Cape Town, 2003; Walter Sisulu, 2011; Hon. DLitt Witwatersrand, 2012; Hon. Dr S Africa, 2008. Grand Counsellor, Order of Baobab (S Africa), 2008. *Publications* include: The Commuter Population for Claremont, Cape, 1973; Human Rights and the Christian Doctrine of Man, 1979; A World with a Human Face: a voice from Africa, 2003; contributions to: Peace and Peacemaking, 1984; Open to the Spirit, 1987; Doing Ethics in Context, 1994; Ethics and Values: a global perspective, 1997; Change and Challenge, 1998; articles in periodicals. *Address:* African Monitor, 62 Sir Lowry Road, Woodstock 7925, Cape Town, South Africa.

**NEAD, Prof. Lynda,** PhD; FBA 2018; FRHistS; Pevsner Professor of History of Art, Birkbeck, University of London, since 2004; *b* London. *Educ:* Henrietta Barnett Sch.; Univ. of Leeds (BA 1st Cl. Hons Fine Art); University Coll. London (PhD 1986). FRHistS 2017. Res. Scholar, History of Art, Univ. of Leicester, 1982–83; Lectr, History and Theory of Art, Univ. of Kent, 1983–84; Lectr, History of Art, Birkbeck, Univ. of London, 1984–2004. Vis. Prof. of History of Art, Gresham Coll., London, 2013–14. Member: Council, Tate Britain, 2002–06; Adv. Council, Paul Mellon Centre for British Art, 2002–08, 2016–; Adv. Cttee, Leverhulme Trust Res. Awards, 2005–07; Blue Plaques Panel, English Heritage, 2016–. Trustee, V&A Mus., 2017–. MAE 2014. *Publications:* Myths of Sexuality, 1988; The Female Nude, 1992; Victorian Babylon, 2000; The Haunted Gallery, 2008; The Tiger in the Smoke, 2017. *Recreations:* cinema, sport (qualified ABAE boxing coach).

**NEAGLE, Lynne;** Member (Lab) Torfaen, National Assembly for Wales, since 1999; *b* Merthyr Tydfil, 18 Jan. 1968; *m* 1996, Huw George Lewis, *qv*; two *s*. *Educ:* Cyfarthfa High Sch., Merthyr Tydfil; Reading Univ. (BA Hons French and Italian). Vol. Housing Rights Worker, Shelter Cymru, 1991–93; Inf. Project Officer, Mid Glam Assoc. of Voluntary

Orgns, 1993–94; Res. Asst to Glenys Kinnock, MEP, 1994–97; Carers Develt Officer, Voluntary Action Cardiff, 1997–99. *Recreations:* cinema, reading, swimming. *Address:* (office) 73 Upper Trosnant Street, Pontypool, Torfaen NP4 8AU.

**NEAL, Prof. David Edgar,** CBE 2014; FRCS, FMedSci; Professor of Surgical Oncology, University of Oxford, since 2015; Professor of Surgical Oncology, University of Cambridge, 2002–14, now Emeritus, and Senior Visiting Fellow, since 2014; Honorary Consultant Urological Surgeon, Cambridge University Hospitals NHS Trust, 2002–14; Global Senior Vice President, Research (Academic), Elsevier, since 2014; *b* 9 March 1951; *s* of Norman and Beth Neal; *m* 1972, Deborah Mary Heyworth; three *d*. *Educ:* University Coll. London (BSc 1st Cl. Hons Anatomy; MB BS, MS). FRCS 1980. Tutor and Lectr in Surgery, Univ. of Leeds, 1981–83; First Asst in Urology, 1983–87, Sen. Lectr in Urological Surgery, 1988–92, Consultant Urologist, 1992–2002, Freeman Hosp., Newcastle upon Tyne; Prof. of Surgery, 1992–2002 and Dir, Med. Res., 1997–2002, Univ. of Newcastle upon Tyne. Mem., King's Fund Mgt Cttee, 1996–2002. Member: Council, RCS, 2002–12; Postgraduate Medical Educn and Trng Bd, 2003–09; Council, Acad. of Medical Scis, 2006–09. Hon. Mem., Urological Soc. Australia, 1999; Corresp. Mem., Amer. Assoc. Genito-urinary Surgeons, 1999. FMedSci 1998. St Peter's Medal, Brit. Assoc. of Urological Surgeons, 2001. *Publications:* Tumours in Urology, 1994; (jtly) Basic Science in Urology, 1999; over 100 books and chapters in books; contrib. articles to Nature, Nature Genetics, Cancer Cell, The Lancet, EMBO Jl etc; over 500 peer-reviewed articles on urology and cancer. *Recreations:* playing the classical guitar, maintenance of classic motor cycles. *Address:* Nuffield Department of Surgical Sciences, University of Oxford, Old Road Campus Research Building (off Roosevelt Drive), Headington, Oxford OX3 9DQ. *T:* (01865) 617124, *Fax:* (01865) 617125.

**NEAL, Hon. Sir Eric (James),** AC 1988; Kt 1982; CVO 1992; Governor, South Australia, 1996–2001; Chancellor, Flinders University, 2002–10; *b* 3 June 1924; *s* of James and May Neal; *m* 1950, Thelma Joan, *d* of R. E. Bowden; two *s*. *Educ:* South Australian Sch. of Mines. CEng, CPEng; FIGEM, FAIM. Boral Ltd: Dir, 1972–92; Chief Exec., 1973–87; Man. Dir, 1982–87; Chairman: Atlas Copco Australia Pty Ltd, 1989–96; Metal Manufacturers Ltd, 1990–96 (Dir, 1987–96); Director: Westpac Banking Corp., 1985–92 (Dep. Chm., 1987–88; Chm., 1989–92); John Fairfax Ltd, 1987–88; BHP Co. Ltd, 1988–94; Coca Cola Amatil Ltd, 1987–96. Mem., Australian Adv. Council, Gen. Motors, 1987–94. Mem., Cttee apptd by Fed. Govt to advise on Higher Defence Orgn, 1982. Mem., Amer. Bureau of Shipping, 1976–90; first Nat. Pres., Aust. Inst. of Co. Dirs, 1990–92. Chm. Exec. Cttee, Duke of Edinburgh's Sixth Commonwealth Study Conf. 1986; Nat. Chm., Duke of Edinburgh's Award Scheme in Australia, 1984–92; Internat. Trustee, Duke of Edinburgh's Award Internat. Assoc., 1986–97. Chief Comr, City of Sydney, 1987–88. Chm., SA Govt Veterans' Adv. Council, 2008–16. Hon. FIEAust 1985; Hon. Fellow, Aust. Inst. of Building, 1998; Emeritus Mem., Aust. Inst. of Mgt, 1998; Life FAICD 2000. Hon. DEng Sydney, 1989; DUniv: S Australia, 1996; Flinders, 2001. US Dept of Defense National Medal for Dist. Public Service, 1992; Peter Nicol Russell Meml Medal, Instn of Engrs, Australia, 2015. *Recreations:* naval history, travel, reading, shipping. *Address:* 82/52 Brougham Place, North Adelaide, SA 5006, Australia. *Clubs:* Adelaide (Adelaide); Melbourne (Melbourne).

**NEAL, Frederick Albert,** CMG 1990; FCIL; aviation consultant; UK Representative on Council of International Civil Aviation Organization, Montreal, 1983–93; *b* 22 Dec. 1932; *s* of Frederick William George Neal and Frances Elizabeth (*née* Duke); *m* 1958, Gloria Maria Moirano. *Educ:* Royal Grammar Sch., High Wycombe; Sch. of Slavonic Studies, Cambridge; Birkbeck Coll., London (BA). FCIL (FIL 1965). Min. of Supply, 1953; Asst Defence Supply Attaché, Bonn, 1958–64; Principal, Min. of Technology (subseq. DTI), 1967; Asst Sec., DTI, 1974; Counsellor (Economic and Commercial), Ottawa, 1975–80; Asst Sec., Dept of Trade, 1980–83. *Recreations:* golf, bridge, music. *Address:* 2 Hambledon Court, 19B Crescent East, Hadley Wood, Herts EN4 0EY. *Clubs:* Royal Over-Seas League; Hadley Wood Golf.

**NEAL, (Harry) Morton,** CBE 1991; FIC; Chairman, St Anselm Development Company Ltd, since 1985; *b* 21 Nov. 1931; *s* of late Godfrey French Neal and Janet Bryce Morton; *m* 1954, Cecilia Elizabeth Crawford, *d* of late Col M. Crawford, DSO; one *s* three *d*. *Educ:* Uppingham Sch.; London Univ. (BScEng); City and Guilds Coll. (ACGI). Flying Officer, RAF, 1953. Chm., Connaught Hotel Ltd, 1980–94 (Dir, 1966–97); Dir, Savoy Hotel Ltd, 1982–93. Chm., Harry Neal Ltd, 1985–2009. Member of Lloyd's. Chm., City and Guilds of London Inst., 1979–91 (Vice Pres., 1999–2004); Member: TEC, then BTEC, 1982–94; Court of City Univ., 1982–91; Delegacy, St Mary's Hosp. Med. Sch., 1993–98; Board of Governors: Imperial Coll., London, 1988–2001; Willesden Tech. Coll., 1983–86; Francis Holland Sch., 1988–2006 (Vice-Chm., 1996–2005); Mgt Cttee, Courtauld Inst. of Art, 1983–99; Court, Univ. of Herts, 2006–. Trustee: Buckminster Estate, 1969–2005; Samuel Courtauld Trust, 1989–2006; Prince of Wales Inst. of Architecture, 1991–99 (Mem., Bd of Advrs, 1993–99). President: Greater London Middx W County (formerly NW County) Scout Council, 1983–2007; City and Guilds Coll. Assoc., 1994–95; Herts Agricl Soc., 2004; City and Guilds Assoc., 2006–08. Liveryman, Carpenters' Co., 1955– (Master, 1997–98). High Sheriff, Herts, 1999–2000. FCIOB, FRSA; FCGI 1983. Hon. Fellow, Courtauld Inst. of Art, 2007; Fellow, Univ. of Herts, 2015. Chevalier de Tastevin, 1981. *Recreations:* gardening, shooting. *Address:* Great Sarratt Hall, Sarratt, Herts WD3 4PD.

**NEAL, Michael David;** Headmaster, Cranborne Chase School, 1969–83; *b* 27 Jan. 1927; *s* of David Neal, FCA; *m* 1952, Barbara Lisette (*d* 2002), *d* of late Harold Carter, MA; two *s* two *d*. *Educ:* Winchester; University Coll., Oxford (BA); BSc Open Univ. 1996. Rifle Bde, 1945–48 (Captain); Asst Master, RNC Dartmouth, 1952–54; Eton Coll., 1954–69 (Housemaster, 1963–69). Mem., Eton UDC, 1960–63. Sec., PCC, St Peter's, Titley, Hereford, 1984–2016. *Address:* Culwood House, 130 Lye Green Road, Chesham, Bucks HP5 3NH.

**NEAL, Morton;** see Neal, H. M.

**NEALE, Gordon William,** OBE 2002; consultant on disability sport, since 2010; Director of Events, Disability Sport Events (formerly Chief Executive, Disability Sport England), 1998–2010; *b* 10 April 1945; *s* of William and Lily Neale; *m* 2000, Elizabeth (*née* Irvine); one *s* one *d*. *Educ:* Beechfield Secondary Sch.; North London Univ. HM Forces, 1960–86 (GSM, Borneo, Malaya, NI; UN medal, Cyprus); Sport Develt Officer: Lee Valley Regl Park, 1986–88; English Volleyball Assoc., 1988–90; Disability Sport England, 1990–2010. Member Board: British Volleyball Fedn, 2008–; English Volleyball Assoc., 2008–; Comr, World ParaVolley, 2010– (Trustee, 2016–). Chm. of Trustees, Cedars Trust Sch. and Sports Coll., Gateshead, 2010–. Sec., Whitley Bay and N Shields Br., RBL, 2019. A torchbearer, London 2012 Olympics; commentator, London 2012 Paralympics. Silver Jubilee Medal, 1977; Peter Wardale Trophy, Volleyball England, 2014. *Recreations:* volleyball, swimming, cycling, disability sport. *Address:* 30 Holly Avenue, Whitley Bay, Tyne and Wear NE26 1ED. *T:* (0191) 252 0165, 07768 288030. *E:* mrgneale@btinternet.com. *Club:* Comrades (Whitley Bay).

**NEALE, Gregory David;** journalist, historian, broadcaster; Editor, 2000–04, and Founding Editor/Editor at large, since 2004, BBC History Magazine; Editor-in-Chief: Resurgence Trust, since 2007; Resurgence & Ecologist, since 2016 (Editor, 2014–16); *b* 1 May 1954; *s* of Lawrence Edwin Neale and Jean Alicia Neale (*née* Gilbert). *Educ:* Birkbeck Coll., London (BA Hons Hist.); Pembroke Coll., Oxford (MSt Modern Hist.). Work on newspapers, including: The Times, 1982–86; Daily Telegraph, 1987–89; Sunday Telegraph, 1989–99. Resident historian, Newsnight and The World, BBC TV, 2005–06. Editor, Oxford Today, 2007–11. Centenary Fellow, Historical Assoc., 2006. Hon. Vis. Fellow, Univ. of York, 2012–14. Editor of the Year, BSME, 2000, 2002. *Publications:* The Green Travel Guide, 1998, 2nd edn 1999; (with Tim Gopsill) Journalists: 100 years of the NUJ, 2007. *Recreations:* chess, choral singing, reading, walking, thinking about gardening. *T:* (office) (01237) 441293. *E:* greg.neale@btinternet.com. *Clubs:* Frontline; Sutton United Supporters.

**NEALE, Rt Rev. John Robert Geoffrey,** AKC; Area Bishop (formerly Suffragan Bishop) of Ramsbury, 1974–88; *b* 21 Sept. 1926; *s* of late Geoffrey Brockman Neale and Stella Beatrice (*née* Wild). *Educ:* Felsted Sch.; King's Coll., London Univ. Served War of 1939–45: Lieut RA; Army, 1944–48. Business, G. B. Neale & Co. Ltd, EC2, 1948–51. King's Coll. London, 1951–55 (Jelf Prize, 1954). Deacon, 1955, priest, 1956; Curate, St Peter, St Helier, Dio. of Southwark, 1955–58. Chaplain, Ardingly Coll., Sussex, 1958–63; Recruitment Sec., CACTM (ACCM), 1963–67; Archbishops' Rep. for ordination candidates, 1967–68; Canon Missioner, Dio. of Guildford, Hon. Canon of Guildford Cath. and Rector of Hascombe, Surrey, 1968–74; Dir, Post Ordination Trng, 1974–88; Hon. Canon of Salisbury Cathedral, 1974–88; Archdeacon of Wilts, 1974–80; Dir, Diocesan Ordinands, 1976–88; Sec., Partnership for World Mission, 1989–91; Honorary Assistant Bishop: Dio. of Bath and Wells, 1991–2008; Dio. of Bristol, 1991–2015; Dio. of Gloucester, 1996–2004. FIC 1991. *Publications:* Ember Prayer, 1965. *Address:* Shockerwick House, Bath BA1 7LL. *T:* (01225) 743636, ext. 1417.

**NEALE, Keith Douglas;** independent adviser to pension funds, 2002–15; *b* 27 March 1947; *s* of Douglas Jeffrey and Dorothy Neale; *m* 1969, Mary Williamson; one *s* one *d*. East Midlands Electricity Board, 1964; Trainee Accountant, Blackwell RDC, 1965; County Treasurer's Dept, Lindsey CC, Lincs, 1968; Asst Dir of Finance, Humberside CC, 1974; Dep. County Treasurer, 1982–87, County Treasurer, 1987–2002, Essex; Treasurer: Essex Police Authy, 1995–2002; Essex Fire Authy, 1998–2002. Treasurer: E Anglia Tourist Bd, 1987–96; E of England Tourist Bd, 1996–2006. Pres., Soc. of County Treasurers, 1998–99 (Hon. Sec., 1991–97; Vice-Pres., 1997–98); Advr, Policy Cttee, ACC, 1993–97. Member: CIPFA, 1969– (Mem., Pensions (formerly Superannuation) Panel, 1994–2003); UK Steering Cttee on Local Govt Pensions (formerly Superannuation), 1991–2002; Cttee, Nat. Assoc. of Pension Funds Investment, 1995–2000; Public Sector and Not-for-Profit Cttee, Accounting Standards Bd, 1999–2002. Freeman, City of London, 1999. *Address:* Moorfield House, 14 Hay Green, Danbury, Essex CM3 4NU. *T:* (01245) 222822.

**NEALE, Mark Frost,** CB 2010; Chief Executive, Financial Services Compensation Scheme, since 2010; *b* 7 July 1957; *s* of Sir Alan (Derrett) Neale, KCB, MBE and Joan Neale (*née* Frost); *m* 1988, Xanthe Waddington Lunghi; one *s* two *d*. *Educ:* Queen's Coll., Oxford (BA 1st Cl. Hons Modern Hist. 1979). CSD, 1980–83; DES, then DFE, 1983–95; HM Treasury, 1995–98; Head, Structural Unemployment Policy Div., DFEE, 1998–2000; Dir, Finance and Commercial and Corporate Services, Employment Service, 2000–01; Dir, Children, Poverty and Housing, then Children and Housing, DWP, 2001–03; Dir Gen., Security, Internat. and Organised Crime, Home Office, 2003–05; Man. Dir, Budget, Tax and Welfare, HM Treasury, 2005–10. Chair, Froebel Trust, 2016–. Mem. Council, Univ. of Roehampton, 2010–. *Recreation:* watching Chelsea FC. *Address:* Financial Services Compensation Scheme, Beaufort House, 15 St Botolph Street, EC3A 7QU. *Club:* Reform.

**NEALE, Michael Cooper,** CB 1987; FIMechE; *b* 2 Dec. 1929; *s* of late Frank and Edith Kathleen Neale; *m* 1956, Thelma Weare; one *s* two *d*. *Educ:* West Bridgford Grammar Sch., Nottingham; Queen Mary Coll., Univ. of London (BScEng 1st cl. Hons; MScEng). Postgraduate research on fuel injection in diesel engines, 1951–53; Engr Officer, Royal Air Force, 1953–56; joined Civil Service, 1956; Aeroplane and Armament Experimental Estabt, Boscombe Down, 1956–58; joined Nat. Gas Turbine Estabt, Pyestock, 1958; Asst Director of Engine Develt, MoD Headquarters, 1971; Dep. Director (R&D), Nat. Gas Turbine Estabt, 1973–80; Dir Gen. Engines (PE), MoD, 1980–87; Sec., Royal Commn for Exhibn of 1851, 1987–94; non-exec. dir of cos and industrial consultant, 1988–96. Hon. Treas., Castleton Church, Dorset, 2002–08. Silver medallist, RAeS, 1987. *Publications:* papers in Aeronautical Research Council reports and memoranda series and elsewhere in the technical press, mainly concerning engines. *Recreations:* old railways, cricket as it used to be played. *Address:* Quill Cottage, 32 Hound Street, Sherborne, Dorset DT9 3AA. *T:* (01935) 814332.

**NEAME, Gareth Elwin,** OBE 2016; Chief Executive Officer (formerly Managing Director), Carnival Film and Television Ltd, since 2004; *b* Beaconsfield, 8 March 1967; *s* of late Christopher Elwin Neame and Heather Marilyn Neame (*née* Wade); *m* 1995, Karen Elizabeth Hughes (marr. diss. 2001; she *d* 2010). *Educ:* Univ. of Birmingham (BA Hons Eng. and Drama 1988). Various roles in film and TV develt and prodn, 1988–93; producer, BBC drama, 1994–2000; independent producer, 1998–99; Hd, Drama Commissioning, BBC, 2000–04. Television productions include: as Producer: Truth or Dare, 1996; The Woman in White, The Missing Postman, 1997; Getting Hurt, 1998; All the King's Men, 1999; Happy Birthday Shakespeare, Take a Girl Like You; as Executive Producer: Warriors, 1999; The Wyvern Mystery, Paranoid, Lorna Doone, 2000; Station Jim, 2001; Clocking Off, 2001–02; Murder, Tipping the Velvet, The Hound of the Baskervilles, 2002; Spooks, 2002–04; Trust, Cambridge Spies, State of Play, 2003; Red Cap, 2003–04; New Tricks, 2003–05; Gunpowder, Treason and Plot, Bodies, Conviction, Outlaws, The Grid, 2004; Hustle 2004–05; The Rotters Club, Fingersmith, Rome, 20,000 Streets Under the Sky, 2005; Hotel Babylon, 2006–09; Sea of Souls, Life Line, Empathy, Whistleblowers, The Old Curiosity Shop, 2007; Midnight Man, Harley Street, 2008; The Philanthropist, 2009; Material Girl, 2010; Downton Abbey, 2010–15; Page Eight, 2011; The Hollow Crown, 2012–16; Murder on the Home Front, Dracula, 2013; The 7:39, Turks and Caicos, Salting the Battlefield, The Lost Honour of Christopher Jefferies, 2014; The Last Kingdom, 2015–; Jamestown, 2017–19; Belgravia, 2019; producer, film, Downton Abbey, 2019. Mem. Council, BAFTA, 2004–06. Ambassador, GREAT Britain Campaign, 2014–. David L. Wolper Award for Outstanding Producer, Producers Guild of America, 2012. *Recreations:* arts, literature, film and television, countryside, fine wine, travel. *Clubs:* Garrick, Savile, Beefsteak.

**NEAME, Jonathan Beale;** DL; Chief Executive, Shepherd Neame Ltd, since 2003; *b* Whitstable, 30 Jan. 1964; *s* of Robert Harry Beale Neame, *qv*; *m* 1996, Lucilla Margaret Baker; one *d*. *Educ:* Harrow (Leaving Schol.); Pembroke Coll., Cambridge (Open Exhibnr in Classics; Harris Meml Schol.; BA Hons Classics 1985; MA 1989); City Univ. (Dip. Legal Educn). Called to the Bar, Middle Temple, 1987; Associate Consultant, COBA Gp, 1987–91; Shepherd Neame Ltd: Co. Sec., 1991–94; Tenanted Trade Dir, 1994–98; Trade Dir, 1998–99; Man. Dir, 1999–2003. Non-executive Director: Invicta Radio Ltd, 1999–2004 (Chm., 2001–04); St Austell Brewery Co. Ltd, 2002–. Chm., British Beer and Pub Assoc., 2012–15. Trustee, Leeds Castle Foundn, 2011–; Chm., Visit Kent, 2015–.

Mem., Stour Fishery Assoc. Mem., Ct Assts, Brewers' Co. (Middle Warden, 2019–20). DL Kent, 2013. *Recreations:* cricket, ski-ing, Real tennis, walking, country pursuits. *Address:* Pheasant Farm, Church Road, Oare, Faversham, Kent ME13 0QB. *T:* (01795) 535366. *E:* jneame@shepherdneame.co.uk. *Clubs:* United and Cecil, MCC, Lord's Taverners; Royal St George's Golf; Kent County Cricket.

**NEAME, Robert Harry Beale,** CBE 1999; DL; President, Shepherd Neame Ltd, brewers, since 2006 (Chairman, 1971–2005); *b* 25 Feb. 1934; *s* of Jasper Beale Neame and Violet Evelyn Neame; *m* 1st, Sally Elizabeth Corben; one *s* two *d* (and one *s* decd); 2nd, 1974, Yvonne Mary Mackenzie; one *d*. *Educ:* Harrow (Head of School). Joined Shepherd Neame, 1956; Dir, 1957–2006; Dir and Chm., Faversham Laundry, 1961–70. SE Regl Dir, National Westminster Bank, 1982–92; Dir, SE Adv. Bd, Royal Insurance Co., 1988–2000; Director: Folkestone Racecourse, 1985–99 (Chm., 1988–99); Marr Taverns PLC, 1992–96; non-executive Director: Mendocino Brewing Co. (USA), 1998–2004; Merrydown plc, 1998–2004. Chairman: SE England Tourist Bd, 1979–90 (Vice-Pres., 1990–2003); Gatwick Airport Consultative Cttee, 1990–95; Member: SE RHA, 1977–78; Canterbury and Thanet RHA, 1990–94; Inland Waterways Amenities Adv. Council, 1992–98. Chairman, British Section: IULA, 1986–89; CEMR, 1986–89; Vice Chm., Consultative Council of Regl and Local Authorities, 1989. Mem. (C) for Faversham, Kent CC, 1965–89 (Leader, 1982–84). Pres., Kent CCC, 2003–04. DL 1992, High Sheriff, 2001, Kent. Hon. Alderman, Kent CC, 2010. Hon. DCL Kent, 2009. *Recreations:* cricket, squash, rackets (Army Rackets Champion, 1954), golf, shooting, ski-ing. *Address:* Dane Court Farmhouse, Kits Hill, Selling, Faversham, Kent ME13 9QP. *T:* (01227) 752284. *Clubs:* Press; MCC, Free Foresters, I Zingari, Band of Brothers, Butterflies; Kandahar Ski; Escorts, Jesters.
*See also J. B. Neame.*

**NEARS, Colin Gray,** CBE 1998; television producer; Member of Council, and Chairman of Advisory Panel on Dance, Arts Council of Great Britain, 1982–90; *b* 19 March 1933; *s* of William Charles Nears and Winifred Mildred Nears (*née* Gray). *Educ:* Ipswich Sch.; King's Coll., Cambridge (MA). Admin. Asst, RIBA, 1956; BBC, 1958–87; Producer: Schools Television, 1960; Music and Arts, 1967; Editor, Review, 1971–72. Author and director of programmes on literature, the visual arts, music and dance. Director: Royal Opera House, 1995–98 (Mem., 1990–98, Dep. Chm., 1991–98, Ballet Bd); Birmingham Royal Ballet Bd, 1993–2002 (Chm., 1993–99); Gov., Royal Ballet Sch., 1993–2000; Trustee: Royal Ballet Benevolent Fund, 1992–2016 (Chm., 2011–13); Dancers' Resettlement Fund, subseq. Dancers' Career Develt, 1991–2013; Member Board: Riverside Trust, 1991–93; Rambert Dance Co., 1993–2001. FRSA. BAFTA award for Best Specialised Programme, 1973; Prix Italia music prize, 1982. *Recreations:* reading, gardening. *Address:* 16 Ashchurch Terrace, W12 9SL. *T:* (020) 8749 3615.

**NEARY, Prof. Ian James,** DPhil; Professor in the Politics of Japan, University of Oxford, since 2008 (Director, Nissan Institute of Japanese Studies, 2006–14; Head, School of Interdisciplinary Area Studies, 2011–14); Fellow, St Antony's College, Oxford, since 2004; *b* 9 July 1951; *s* of Kenneth and Joan Neary; *m* 1979, Suzuko Anai; one *s* one *d*. *Educ:* King Edward VII Grammar Sch., Sheffield; Sheffield Univ. (BA); Kyushu Univ.; Sussex Univ. (DPhil). Lecturer: Dept of Hist. and Politics, Huddersfield Poly., 1979–84; Dept of Politics, Newcastle Univ., 1984–89; Prof. of Japanese Politics, Dept of Government, Essex Univ., 1989–2004; Lectr in Japanese Politics, Univ. of Oxford, 2004–08. Pres., British Assoc. Japanese Studies, 1991–94. *Publications:* Politics, Protest and Social Control: origins of Buraku liberation, 1989; (with J. Howells) Intervention and Technological Innovation: government and the pharmaceutical industry in the UK and Japan, 1995; Human Rights in Japan, S Korea and Taiwan, 2002; The State and Politics in Japan, 2002, 2nd edn 2019; The Buraku Issue and Modern Japan, 2010 (trans. Japanese, 2016); articles on Japan and human rights in Japan Forum, Social Res., etc. *Recreations:* running, triathlons, gardening, Witney Music Society. *Address:* Nissan Institute of Japanese Studies, 27 Winchester Road, Oxford OX2 6NA. *T:* (01865) 274570, *Fax:* (01865) 274574.

**NEARY, Prof. (James) Peter,** DPhil; FBA 2008; Professor of Economics, University of Oxford, since 2006; Fellow, Merton College, Oxford, since 2006; *b* Drogheda, Ireland, 11 Feb. 1950; *s* of late Peter Austin Neary and of Anne Rosemary Neary (*née* Loughran); *m* 1st, 1972, Frances Ruane (marr. diss. 1997); two *s*; 2nd, 1997, Mairéad Hanrahan; two *d*. *Educ:* Christian Brothers, Drogheda; Clongowes Wood Coll.; University Coll., Dublin (BA 1970; MA 1971); Univ. of Oxford (MPhil 1976; DPhil 1978). Res. Asst, Econ. and Soc. Res. Inst., Dublin, 1970–72; Trinity College, Dublin: Asst Lectr, 1972–74; Lectr, 1978–80; Fellow, 1980; Heyworth Res. Fellow, Nuffield Coll., Oxford, 1976–78; Prof. of Political Economy, University Coll., Dublin, 1980–2006. Visiting Scholar: MIT, 1978; Inst. for Internat. Econ. Studies, Stockholm, 1979; Internat. Inst. for Applied Systems Analysis, Laxenburg, 1981; Visiting Professor: Princeton Univ.; Univ. of Calif, Berkeley, 1982; Queen's Univ., Ont., 1986–88; Univ. of Ulster, Jordanstown, 1992–93; Ecole Polytechnique, Paris, 1999–2000. Chm., Economics and Econometric Sub-Panel, UK REF 2014, 2010–14. ERC Advanced Grant, 2012–17. Co-Editor, Jl of Internat. Economics, 1980–83; Associate Editor: Economic Jl, 1981–85; Econometrica, 1984–87; Rev. of Economic Studies, 1984–93; Economica, 1996–2000; Ed., European Economic Rev., 1986–90. Fellow: Centre for Econ. Policy Res., 1983; Econometric Soc., 1987 (Mem. Council, 1994–99, 2015–18); Member: Council, Royal Econ. Soc., 1984–89, 1992–97, 2016–19 (Pres., 2017–18); Eur. Econ. Assoc., 1985–92 (Pres., 2002; Fellow, 2004); President: Irish Econ. Assoc., 1990–92; Internat. Trade and Finance Soc., 1999–2000; Econs Section, BAAS, 2005. MAE 1989; Mem., RIA, 1997. Gold Medal in Soc. Scis, RIA, 2006. *Publications:* Measuring the Restrictiveness of International Trade Policy (with J. E. Anderson), 2005; (ed jtly) Natural Resources and the Macroeconomy, 1986; (ed jtly) Theory, Policy and Dynamics in International Trade, 1993; (ed) Readings in International Trade, 1995; over 100 articles, mainly on internat. economics. *Recreations:* family, travel, reading, music. *Address:* Department of Economics, Manor Road Building, Oxford OX1 3UQ.

**NEARY, Martin Gerard James,** LVO 1998; conductor and organist; Organist and Master of the Choristers, Westminster Abbey, 1988–98; Conductor, Millennium Consort Singers, since 2007; *b* 28 March 1940; *s* of late Leonard Walter Neary and of Jeanne Marguerite (*née* Thébault); *m* 1967, Penelope Jane, *d* of Sir Brian Warren and Dame Josephine Barnes, DBE; one *s* two *d*. *Educ:* HM Chapels Royal, St James's Palace; City of London Sch.; Gonville and Caius Coll., Cambridge (Organ Schol.; MA Theol. and Music). FRCO. Organist, St Mary's, Hornsey Rise, 1958; St Margaret's, Westminster: Asst Organist, 1963–65; Organist and Master of Music, 1965–71; Prof. of Organ, Trinity Coll., London, 1963–72; Organist and Master of Music, Winchester Cathedral, 1972–87. Organ Advr to dio. of Winchester, 1975–87. Conductor, Twickenham Musical Soc., 1966–72; Founder and Conductor: St Margaret's Westminster Singers, 1967–71; English Chamber Singers; Conductor, Waynflete Singers, 1972–88; Dir, Southern Cathedrals Festival, 1972, 1975, 1978, 1981, 1984, 1987; Conductor, Aspen Music Festival, 1980; Artistic Director: Paulist Choristers of California, 1999–2003; Pacific Acad. of Ecclesiastical Music, 2006–09; Dir of Music, First Congregational Ch of LA, 2001–02; Dir of Music, St Michael and All Angels, Barnes, 2013–; Guest Conductor: Australian Youth Choir, 1999–; BBC Singers; Netherlands Chamber Choir; Chief Guest Conductor: Grand Rapids Choir of Men and Boys, 2010–; Salzburg Global Seminar Faculty, 2011. Consultant, Millennium Youth Choir, RSCM, 1999–2001. President: Cathedral Organists' Assoc., 1985–88; RCO, 1988–90, 1996–98 (Mem. Council, 1982–; a Vice-Pres., 1990–); Organists Charitable Trust (formerly Organists' Benevolent League), 1988–; John Carpenter Club, 1997–98; Chm., Herbert Howells Soc., 1993–; Mem., Exec. Cttee, Help Musicians UK (formerly Musicians Benevolent Fund), 1993– (Chm., Church Services Cttee, 1993–99). Music Advr, John Lyon's Charity, 2005–. Many organ recitals and broadcasts in UK, incl. Royal Festival Hall; has conducted many premières of music by British composers incl. John Tavener's Ultimos Ritos, 1979, and Akathist, 1988, Jonathan Harvey's Hymn, 1979, and Passion and Resurrection, 1981; conducted John Tavener's Veil of the Temple, Holland Fest., 2005; with Martin Neary Singers perf. madrigals and graces at 10 Downing Street, 1970–74. Toured US and Canada, 1963, 1968, 1971, 1973, 1975, 1977, 1979, 1982, 1984, 1986, 1988, 1992, 1996, appearances incl. Carnegie Hall, Lincoln Center, Kennedy Center, Roy Thomson Hall, Walt Disney Hall; many European tours, including Russia, 1994, Ukraine, 1996; BBC Promenade Concerts, incl. organ soloist on First Night, 2004; sometime Conductor with: ECO; LSO; BBCSO; Bournemouth SO and Sinfonietta; Acad. of Ancient Music; Winchester Baroque Ensemble; Orch. of the Age of Enlightenment; Arts Council Contemporary Music Network Tour, 1993; many recordings, incl. Purcell, Music for Queen Mary, Tavener, Akathist, and The Choirboys. FRSCM 1997. Hon. FTCL 1969; Hon. RAM 1988. Hon. DMus: Southampton, 1997; Lambeth, 2012. Hon. Citizen of Texas, 1971. Prizewinner, St Alban's Internat. Organ Festival, 1963; Conducting Scholarship, Berkshire Music Center, USA, 1963; Diploma, J. S. Bach Competn, Leipzig, 1968; UK/USA Bicentennial Fellow, 1979–80; Artist-in-residence, Univ. of California at Davis, 1984, 2007. *Compositions* include: What is Man?; May the grace of Christ (Nat. Anthem arr.); O worship the Lord, 2000; All Saints Mass, 2004; Joy and Woe, 2009; Mass of the Redeemer, 2011; responses, descants, carol and hymn arrangements, incl. Make me a channel of your peace. *Publications:* edns of early organ music; contribs to organ jls. *Recreations:* watching cricket, grandparental duties. *Address:* 13 Parkwood Road, Wimbledon, SW19 7AQ. *T:* and *Fax:* (020) 3016 7439. *E:* martin@mneary.co.uk. *Club:* Garrick.

**NEARY, Most Rev. Michael;** *see* Tuam, Archbishop of, (RC).

**NEARY, Peter;** *see* Neary, J. P.

**NEATE, (Francis) Vincent (Hugh),** CA; Founder and Director, Relationship Capital Strategies Ltd, since 2016; *b* London, 22 Jan. 1968; *s* of Francis Webb Neate and Patricia Ann Neate; *m* 1990, Emma Jane Pentland; two *s*. *Educ:* Colet Court; St Paul's Sch., Barnes; Univ. of Liverpool (BA Hons Philosophy 1992). CA 1995. Accountant, James and Cowper, Newbury, 1992–95; KPMG, 1995–2016: Partner, 2007–16, Head, UK Climate Change and Sustainability, 2010–16. Mem., Global Adv. Council, Cornerstone Capital Inc., 2014–. Chair, Professional Standards Cttee, Eur. Private Equity and Venture Capital Assoc., 2009–14. Mem. Council, RIIA, 2014. Chair of Trustees, Fight for Peace UK Ltd, 2005–19; Trustee: From Babies with Love Ltd, 2012–; Keep Britain Tidy, 2019–. Gov., Richmond upon Thames Coll., 2019–. *Recreations:* reading, dog walking, gardening, drawing, ski-ing, sailing.

**NEATH, Gavin Ellis,** CBE 2007; Senior Vice President, Sustainability, Unilever plc, 2011 (Senior Vice President, Global Communications, 2008–11); *b* 5 April 1953; *s* of late Ronald William Neath and Frances Gillian Neath; *m* 2004, Ann; three *d*. *Educ:* Univ. of Manchester; Univ. of Warwick; Stanford Univ. BA American Studies; MSc Mgt Scis. Unilever: graduate trainee, 1977; Mktg Dir, Lever France, 1985–90; Category Dir Laundry, Lever Europe, 1990–94; Man. Dir, Lever Ponds (SA), 1994–98; Chm., Unilever Bestfoods UK, 1998–2004; Chm., 2004–06, Nat. Manager, 2006–08, Unilever UK. Pres., Food and Drink Fedn, 2005–07. Mem. Develt Bd, Royal Court Th., 2005–08. Dep. Chm., St Margaret's Film Club. FIGD. *Recreations:* theatre, cinema, cricket, Rugby.

**NEAVE, Sir Paul (Arundell),** 7th Bt *cr* 1795, of Dagnam Park, Essex; *b* 13 Dec. 1948; *s* of Sir Arundell Thomas Clifton Neave, 6th Bt and Richenda Alice Ione (*d* 1994), *d* of Sir Robert Joshua Paul, 5th Bt; *S* father, 1992; *m* 1976, Coralie Jane Louise, *e d* of Sir Robin Kinahan, ERD; two *s*. *Educ:* Eton. *Heir: s* Frederick Paul Kinahan Neave, *b* 25 Jan. 1981.

**NEBHRAJANI, Sharmila,** OBE 2014; Chief Executive, Wilton Park, since 2017; *d* of Vir and Jayantee Nebhrajani; one *s* one *d*. *Educ:* City of London Sch. for Girls; St Anne's Coll., Oxford (BA 1st Cl. Physiolog. Scis (Medicine); MA). Mem. ICAEW 1991. Mgt Consultant, Coopers & Lybrand, 1988–93; Strategic Planning Manager, Cable & Wireless, 1993–95; Asst Dir, Corporate Finance, Price Waterhouse, 1995–96; Hd, Corporate Planning, BBC, 1996–2000; Chief Operating Officer, BBC Future Media and Technol., 2000–08; Dir, Financial and Commercial Strategy, BBC, 2008–09; Dir of Finance and Contracting, NHS Sussex (formerly E Sussex Downs and Weald, and Hastings and Rother PCTs), 2009–11; Chief Exec., Assoc. of Medical Res. Charities, 2011–14; Chm., Human Tissue Authy, 2014–18 (Mem., 2005–07); Dir, External Affairs, MRC, 2015–17. Vice Chm., Human Fertilisation and Embryology Authy, 1998–2008. Member: Olympic Lottery Distributor, 2006–08; Audit Cttee, RSC, 2008–10; a Charity Comr, 2007–12; Audit Cttee and Ethics Cttee, Inst. of Cancer Res., 2011–14; Bd, Pension Protection Fund, 2012–18; Bd, Parly and Health Service Ombudsman, 2013–15. Non-executive Director: BMJ, 2014–; Towers Watson Master Trust Ltd, 2015–; Nat. Savings and Investments, 2017–. Trustee, Health Foundn, 2018–. Mem. Council, Univ. of Sussex, 2011–18. Yale World Fellow, 2007. *Address:* Wilton Park, Wiston House, Steyning, W Sussex BN44 3DZ.

**NEČAS, Petr;** MP (Civic Democratic), Zlin Region, 1992–2013; Prime Minister, Czech Republic, 2010–13; Leader, Civic Democratic Party, 2010–13; *b* Uherské, Hradiště, 19 Nov. 1964; *m* Radka Nečasová (marr. diss. 2013); two *s* two *d*; *m* 2013, Jana Nagyova. *Educ:* J. E. Purkyně Univ., Brno; Dr rer. nat. Mem., Foreign Affairs Cttee, Parlt of Czech Republic, 1992; Leader, Perm. Delegn to IPU and Delegn to WEU Assembly, 1992–96; First Dep. Minister of Defence, 1995–96; Shadow Minister of Defence, 1998; Dep. Prime Minister and Minister of Labour and Social Affairs, 2006–09. Civic Democratic Party: Mem., 1991–; Dep. Chm., 1999–2010. *Recreations:* politics, art.

**NEEDHAM,** family name of Earl of Kilmorey.

**NEEDHAM, John Anthony;** Second Deemster, Isle of Man, since 2018; *b* London, 12 July 1966; *s* of Eric and Evelyn Needham; *m* 1998, Helen Kneale; two *s*. *Educ:* Bishop Challoner Sch., Shortlands, Kent; Univ. of Newcastle upon Tyne (BSc Hons Geol. 1988); Coll. of Law, Chester (CPE 1991). Exec. Officer, HM Customs and Excise, 1988–89; Constable, MoD Police, 1989–90; London Borough of Redbridge: articled clerk, 1992–94; admitted as solicitor, 1994; Asst Solicitor, 1994–97; Principal Asst Solicitor, 1997–99; Clerk to Justices, 1999–2010, High Bailiff, 2010–18, Isle of Man. *Recreations:* classic car restoration, cricket spectating, dog walking, Irish traditional music. *Address:* Isle of Man Courts of Justice, Deemsters Walk, Bucks Road, Douglas, Isle of Man IM1 3AR. *T:* (01624) 685247.

**NEEDHAM, Phillip;** Chief Executive, ADAS Group (formerly ADAS Agency), 1995–2000; *b* 21 April 1940; *s* of Ephraim and Mabel Jessie Needham; *m* 1962, Patricia Ann (*née* Farr); two *s* two *d*. *Educ:* Dunstable Grammar Sch.; Univ. of Birmingham (BSc);

Imperial Coll., London Univ. (MSc, DIC). National Agricultural Advisory Service, subseq. Agricultural Development and Advisory Service, MAFF: Soil Scientist, 1961; Regional Soil Scientist, Reading, 1979; Hd of Soil Science, London, 1982; Sen. Agricl Scientist, 1985; Dep. Dir of R&D, 1987; Dir, Farm and Countryside Service and Commercial Dir, 1988–92; Dir of Ops, 1992–95. *Publications*: contribs to books and jls on various aspects of crop nutrition and soil science. *Address*: 58 Harpsden Road, Henley-on-Thames, Oxon RG9 1EG.

**NEEDLE, Clive John;** independent public policy advisor, since 1999; Director and Policy Advisor, EuroHealthNet (formerly European Network of Health Promoting Agencies), Brussels, since 2000. *Educ*: Southend High Sch.; Aston Univ. MEP (Lab) Norfolk, 1994–99; contested (Lab) Eastern Region, 1999, 2004. EU Rep., Health Action Partnerships Internat., 2010–13; Chairman: EU/EC Mental Health Platform, 2005–07; EU Public Health and Agriculture Consortium, 2011–12. Mem., Adv. Cttee on Public Health, 2012–, Adv. Gp on Tobacco, 2014–, WHO for Europe. Columnist, Eastern Daily Press, 2004–07.

**NEEL, Janet;** see Baroness Cohen of Pimlico.

**NEELY, Prof. Andrew David,** PhD; FAcSS; FIET, FREng; Director, Cambridge Service Alliance, since 2008; Professor of Manufacturing Engineering since 2015, and Pro-Vice-Chancellor, Enterprise and Business Relations, since 2017, University of Cambridge; Fellow of Sidney Sussex College, Cambridge, since 2015; *b* Guisborough, 3 June 1967; *s* of John David and Elizabeth Anne Neely; *m* 1994, Anna-Liese Stubbs; two *s* two *d*. *Educ*: St Peter's Sch., York; Univ. of Nottingham (BEng 1989; PhD 1993); MA Cantab 1999. FIET 2017. Res. Asst, Univ. of Nottingham, 1989–92; University of Cambridge: Sen. Res. Associate, 1992–95; Univ. Lectr, 1995–2000; Fellow, Churchill Coll., Cambridge, 1996–99; Prof. of Operations Mgt, Cranfield Sch. of Mgt, 2000–12; Dep. Dir, UK Advanced Inst. of Mgt Res., 2003–12; Royal Acad. of Engrg Prof. of Complex Services, 2011–15, Hd, Inst. for Manufacturing, 2015–17, Univ. of Cambridge. FAcSS 2008; FREng 2018. *Publications*: Measuring Business Performance, 1998; The Performance Prism, 2002; Managing Performance in Turbulent Times, 2011. *Address*: Institute for Manufacturing, University of Cambridge, 17 Babbage Road, Cambridge CB3 0FS. *T*: (01223) 766141. *E*: adn1000@cam.ac.uk.

**NEELY, William Robert Nicholas;** Chief Global Correspondent, NBC News, since 2013; *b* 21 May 1959; *s* of late William John Neely and of Patricia (*née* Larney); *m* 1988, Marion Kerr; two *d*. *Educ*: St Malachy's Coll., Belfast; Queen's Univ., Belfast (BA Jt Hons Eng. Lit. and Hist.). Reporter: BBC NI, 1981–86; BBC Network, 1987–88; Sky News, Jan.–June 1989; ITN, 1989–90; ITN: Washington Correspondent, 1991–97; Europe Correspondent, 1997–2002; International Editor, 2002–13. RTS News Awards, 1998 (World Cup), 2000 (European Football Championships), 2011 (Haiti earthquake); Internat. Emmy News Award, 2009 (China earthquake); BAFTA News Awards, 2009 (China earthquake), 2010 (Haiti earthquake), 2011 (Cumbria killings); Broadcasting Journalist of the Year, London Press Club, 2011. *Address*: NBC News, 200 Gray's Inn Road, WC1X 8XZ.

**NEESON, Liam;** see Neeson, W. J.

**NEESON, Séan;** Member (Alliance) Antrim East, Northern Ireland Assembly, 1998–2011; *b* 6 Feb. 1946; *s* of Patrick and Mary Neeson; *m* 1978, Carol Henderson; two *s* two *d*. *Educ*: Queen's Univ., Belfast (BA); St Joseph's Coll. of Educn, Belfast (Postgrad. Dip. in Educn 1968); Univ. of Ulster, Jordanstown (Postgrad. Dip. in Mktg 1988). Teacher, Head of History Dept, St Comgall's High Sch., Larne, 1968–85; marketing and PR consultant, 1988–98. Mem. (Alliance) Carrickfergus Council, 1977–2013; Mayor of Carrickfergus, 1993–94; Mem., NI Assembly, 1982–86. Leader, Alliance Party of NI, 1998–2001. Representative for NI: on Congress of Local and Regl Authorities in Europe, 2002; on Nat. Adv. Cttee on Historic Ships, 2007. Mem. Bd, Nat. Museums and Galleries (NI), 1998–2008. *Publications*: articles on maritime heritage in jls. *Recreation*: study of British and Irish maritime heritage. *Address*: 44 Milebush Park, Carrickfergus, Co. Antrim BT38 7QR. *T*: (028) 9336 4105.

**NEESON, William John, (Liam),** OBE 2000; actor; *b* Ballymena, NI, 7 June 1952; *s* of late Barney Neeson and of Katherine Neeson; *m* 1994, Natasha Jane Richardson, actress (*d* 2009); two *s*. Winner, NI Youth Heavyweight Boxing Championship. *Theatre* includes: The Risen, Lyric Players' Theatre, Belfast, 1976; Of Mice and Men, Abbey Theatre, Dublin; The Informer, Dublin Theatre Fest.; Translations, NT; The Plough and the Stars, Royal Exchange, Manchester; Anna Christie, Broadway, 1993; The Judas Kiss, Playhouse Theatre, 1998; The Crucible, Broadway, 2002; *films* include: Excalibur, 1981; Krull, 1983; The Bounty, 1984; Duet for One, Lamb, The Mission, 1986; A Prayer for the Dying, Suspect, 1987; The Dead Pool, The Good Mother, 1988; Darkman, Crossing the Line (retitled The Big Man, 1991), 1990; Shining Through, Under Suspicion, Leap of Faith, Husbands and Wives, 1992; Ethan Frome, 1993; Schindler's List, Nell, 1994; Rob Roy, 1995; Before and After, Michael Collins (Best Actor Award, Venice Film Fest.), 1996; Les Misérables, 1998; Star Wars Episode One: the Phantom Menace, The Haunting, 1999; Gangs of New York, K-19: The Widowmaker, 2002; Love Actually, 2003; Kinsey, Kingdom of Heaven, Batman Begins, 2005; Breakfast at Pluto, 2005; Seraphim Falls, 2007; Taken, 2008; Chloe, Clash of the Titans, The A-Team, 2010; Unknown, 2011; The Grey, Wrath of the Titans, The Dark Knight Rises, Battleship, Taken 2, 2012; Non-Stop, A Million Ways to Die in the West, A Walk Among the Tombstones, Third Person, 2014; Taken 3, Run All Night, A Christmas Star, 2015; A Monster Calls, Silence, 2017; The Commuter, Mark Felt: the man who brought down the White House, Widows, The Ballad of Buster Scruggs, 2018; Cold Pursuit, Men in Black: international, 2019; *television* includes: A Woman of Substance, 1984; Arthur the King, 1985; Miami Vice, 1986; Hold the Dream, 1986; Sweet As You Are, 1987; Next of Kin, 1989; Five Minutes of Heaven, 2009.

**NEGARA BRUNEI DARUSSALAM, HM Sultan of; Hassanal Bolkiah Mu'izzaddin Waddaulah,** DKMB, DK, PSSUB, DPKG, DPKT, PSPNB, PSNB, PSLJ, SPMB, PANB; Hon. GCMG; DMN, DK (Kelantan), DK (Johor), DK (Negeri Sembilan), DK (Pahang); Ruler of Negara Brunei Darussalam (formerly Brunei), since 1967; Prime Minister, Negara Brunei Darussalam, since its independence, Jan. 1984; Minister of Defence, since 1986 (Finance and Home Affairs Minister, 1984–86); *b* 15 July 1946; *s* of Sultan Sir Muda Omar 'Ali Saifuddien Sa'adul Khairi Waddien, DKMB, DK, GCVO, KCMG, PSSUB, PHBS, PBLI (*d* 1986); *m* 1st, 1965, Rajah Isteri Anak Saleha; two *s* four *d*; *m* 1981, Pengiran Isteri Hajjah Mariam (marr. diss. 2003); two *s* two *d*; *m* 2005, Azrinaz Mazhar Hakim (marr. diss. 2010); one *s* one *d*. *Educ*: Victoria Inst., Kuala Lumpur; RMA Sandhurst (Hon. Captain, Coldstream Guards, 1968; Hon. General 1984). Collar of the Supreme Order of the Chrysanthemum; Grand Order of Mugunghwa. *Address*: Istana Nurul Iman, Bandar Seri Begawan, Negara Brunei Darussalam.

**NEGISHI, Prof. Ei-ichi,** PhD; Herbert C. Brown Distinguished Professor of Chemistry, since 1999 and Director, Negishi-Brown Institute, since 2011, Purdue University; *b* Changchun, China, 14 July 1935; *m* Sumire Suzuki (*d* 2018); two *d*. *Educ*: Shonan High Sch.; Univ. of Tokyo (BS 1958); Univ. of Pennsylvania (Fulbright Smith-Mund Scholar, 1960; PhD 1963). Res. chemist, Iwakuni Res. Labs, Teijin Ltd, 1958–60; Postdoctoral Associate, 1966–68, Asst, 1968–72, Purdue Univ.; Asst Prof., 1972–76, Associate Prof., 1976–79, Syracuse Univ.; Purdue Univ., 1979–. Hon. DSc Purdue, 2012. (Jtly) Nobel Prize in Chemistry, 2010. Order of Culture (Japan), 2010. *Publications*: Organometallics in Organic Synthesis, vol. I, 1980; (ed) Handbook of Organopalladium Chemistry for Organic Synthesis, 2 vols, 2002; over 400 res. papers. *Address*: H. C. Brown Laboratory of Chemistry, Purdue University, 560 Oval Dreive, West Lafayette, IN 47907–2084, USA.

**NEHER, Prof. Dr Erwin;** Research Director, Max-Planck-Institut für biophysikalische Chemie, Göttingen, 1983–2011, now Emeritus; *b* 20 March 1944; *s* of Franz Xaver Neher and Elisabeth Neher; *m* 1978, Dr Eva-Maria Ruhr; three *s* two *d*. *Educ*: Technical Univ., Munich (PhD); Univ. of Wisconsin. Research Associate: Max-Planck-Inst. für Psychiatrie, Munich, 1970–72; Max-Planck-Inst. für biophysikalische Chemie, 1972–75 and 1976–83; Yale Univ., 1975–76; Fairchild Scholar, CIT, 1988–89. For. Mem., Royal Soc., 1994. Nat. and internat. sci. awards: (jtly) Nobel Prize in Physiology or Medicine, 1991. *Publications*: Elektronische Messtechnik in der Physiologie, 1974; (ed) Single Channel Recording, 1983. *Address*: Max-Planck-Institut für biophysikalische Chemie, Am Fassberg, 37077 Göttingen, Germany. *T*: (551) 2011675.

**NEIDLE, Prof. Stephen,** PhD, DSc, CChem, FRSC; independent consultant in drug discovery, since 2016; Professor of Chemical Biology and Cancer Research UK Professorial Fellow, UCL School of Pharmacy, University College London (formerly School of Pharmacy, University of London), 2002–16, now Emeritus Professor (Director of Research, 2004–12); *b* 1 July 1946; *e s* of Michael and Hetty Neidle; *m* 1971, Andrea Anne Finn; two *s* one *d*. *Educ*: Hendon County Sch.; Imperial Coll., London (BSc 1967; PhD 1970; DSc 1995). CChem, FRSC 1999. ICI Research Fellow, Univ. of London, 1970–72; Mem., Scientific Staff, Dept of Biophysics, KCL, 1972–85; Institute of Cancer Research, University of London: Reader, 1986–90; Prof. of Biophysics, 1990–2002; Dean, 1997–2002. Vis. Prof., Univ. of Rome, 2006; Dist. Visitor, Baptist Univ. of Hong Kong, 2011. Guggenheim Lect., Univ. of Reading, 2005. Cancer Research Campaign: career develt awardee, 1979–85; Life Fellow, 1985–; Dir, Biomolecular Structure Unit, 1985–2016. Bristol-Myers Squibb Lectr, SUNY, 1993; Paul Ehrlich Lectr, Société de Chimie Thérapeutique, France, 2004; Pfizer Lectr, 2010. Chairman: Chemical Biol. Forum and Mem. Council, RSC, 2002–06; Cancer Chem. Wkg Gp, Amer. Assoc. for Cancer Res., 2011–12; Member: Funding Cttee, French Nat. Cancer Inst., 2010–12; Royal Soc. Ind. Fellow Panel, 2011–15; Wellcome Trust Peer Rev. Panel, 2012–16; Royal Soc. Newton Advanced Fellowship Panel, 2015–; Medical Adv. Panel, Drinkaware UK. Chm., Bd of Tetrahedron Publications, 2011–14. Hon. Fellow, Sch. of Pharmacy, Univ. of London, 2007. Pfizer Lectr, UK, 2010; Kelland Lectr, EORTC, 2011. Award in Bio-organic and Medicinal Chem., 1999, Interdisciplinary Award, 2002, Sovnovsky Award in Cancer Therapy, 2009–10, RSC; Aventis Prize in Medicinal Chem., Aventis Pharma, France, 2004. *Publications*: DNA Structure and Recognition, 1994; (ed) Oxford Handbook of Nucleic Acid Structure, 1999; Nucleic Acid Structure and Recognition, 2002; Principles of Nucleic Acid Structure, 2007 (ed) Cancer Drug Design and Discovery, 2007, 2nd edn 2013; Therapeutic Applications of Quadruplex Nucleic Acids, 2011; approx. 500 articles on nucleic acid structure and on design of anti-cancer and anti-infective drugs, and 14 patent filings. *Recreations*: film noir, theatre, ping-pong, walking, absorbing Yiddish culture. *Address*: UCL School of Pharmacy, University College London, 29–39 Brunswick Square, WC1N 1AX. *T*: (020) 7753 5800.

**NEIGHBOUR, Roger Harvey,** OBE 2011; FRCGP; consultant in medical education, since 2003; *b* 9 June 1947; *s* of late Kenneth George Neighbour and Eileen Nora Neighbour (*née* Roberts). *Educ*: Watford Grammar Sch.; King's Coll., Cambridge (BA 1968, MA 1972); St Thomas' Hosp. (MB BChir 1971). MRCGP 1975, FRCGP 1987; DObstRCOG 1975. GP, Abbots Langley, Herts, 1974–2003. Trainer, 1977–94, and Course Organiser, 1979–86, Watford Vocational Trng Scheme. Pres., RCGP, 2003–06. Mem., 1988–2004, and Convener, 1997–2002, Panel of MRCGP Examrs. Hon. FRCP 2004; Hon. FRACGP 2006. Hon. DSc Hertfordshire, 2004. *Publications*: The Inner Consultation, 1987, 2nd edn 2004; The Inner Apprentice, 1992, 2nd edn 2004; (jtly) The Successful GP Registrar's Companion, 2003; I'm Too Hot Now, 2005; The Inner Physician, 2016; papers on med. assessment and educn, psychotherapy and Franz Schubert; contribs to British Jl of Gen. Practice, Educn for Primary Care. *Recreations*: playing the violin, music of Schubert, France, writing, armchair philosophy, trying to give up golf. *Address*: Argowan, Bell Lane, Bedmond, Herts WD5 0QS; Appt 26, La Falaise d'Hacqueville, 52 rue Saint Gaud, 50400 Granville, France.

**NEIL, Alexander;** Member (SNP) Airdrie and Shotts, Scottish Parliament, since 2011 (Central Scotland, 1999–2011); *b* 22 Aug. 1951; *s* of late Alexander Neil and Margaret Gunning Neil; *m* Isabella Kerr; one *s*. *Educ*: Dundee Univ. (MA Hons Econs 1973). Marketing Manager: Digital Equipment Corp., 1979–83; Future Technology Systems, 1983–84; Dir, Cumnock and Doon Enterprise Trust, 1983–88; Economic and Business Advr, 1988–. Dir, Prince's Scottish Youth Business Trust, 1988–90; non-exec. Dir and Chm., Network Scotland Ltd, 1989–96. Scottish Parliament: Minister for Housing and Communities, 2009–11; Cabinet Sec. for Infrastructure and Capital Investment, 2011–12, for Health and Wellbeing, 2012–14, for Social Justice, Communities and Pensioners' Rights, 2014–16. *Recreations*: reading, travel. *Address*: 26 Overmills Road, Hazelbank, Ayr KA7 3LQ. *T*: (01292) 286675.

**NEIL, Andrew Ferguson;** publisher, broadcaster and company chairman; Editor-in-Chief, since 1996, Chief Executive, since 1999, and Chairman, since 2008, Press Holdings Media Group (formerly European Press Holdings); owner of The Spectator, Spectator Australia, Spectator USA, Spectator Life and Apollo magazines), since 2004; *b* Paisley, 21 May 1949; *s* of James and Mary Neil. *Educ*: Paisley Grammar Sch.; Univ. of Glasgow (MA Hons Politics and Economics, 1971). Conservative Res. Dept, 1971–72; joined The Economist, 1973; Correspondent in Belfast, London, NY and Washington, covering politics and business, 1973–82; UK Editor, London, 1982–83; Editor, The Sunday Times, 1983–94; Exec. Editor and Chief Correspondent, Fox Network News, NY, 1994; columnist, The Sunday Times and Daily Mail, 1995–96; Contributing Editor, Vanity Fair, NY, 1995–; Ed.-in-Chief, 1996–2006, Publisher, 1999–2006, The Scotsman, Scotland on Sunday and Edinburgh Evening News. Exec. Chm., Sky TV, 1988–90; Co-Proprietor and Dir, CGA and Country Magazine, 1990–97; Chairman: World Media Rights, London, 2005–14; ITP, Dubai, 2006–17; Peters, Fraser and Dunlop, London, 2008–10. Appears regularly on various current affairs television and radio programmes in Britain and America; presenter, television: formerly of The Midnight Hour, Westminster On-Line, Is This Your Life?, Despatch Box, Thursday Night Live, Straight Talk with Andrew Neil, Sunday Politics, Daily Politics, This Week with Andrew Neil; currently of Politics Live, The Andrew Neil Show; formerly presenter, radio, Sunday Breakfast. Lord Rector, St Andrews Univ., 1999–2002. Journalist of the Year, Political Studies Assoc., 2013. *Publications*: The Cable Revolution, 1982; Britain's Free Press: Does It Have One?, 1988; Full Disclosure, 1996; British Excellence, 1998. *Recreations*: dining out in London, New York, Dubai and the Côte d'Azur, cycling. *Address*: c/o The Spectator, 22 Old Queen Street, SW1H 9HP. *Club*: Royal Automobile.

**NEIL, Dame Hilary (Anne);** see Chapman, Dame H. A.

**NEIL, Ronald John Baillie**, CBE 1999; Chief Executive, BBC Production, 1996–98; *b* 16 June 1942; *s* of John Clark Neil and Jean McMillan Taylor; *m* 1967, Isobel Anne Clark. *Educ*: High Sch. of Glasgow. Reporter, Daily Express, 1961; BBC, 1967–98: Newsreader/Reporter, Reporting Scotland, 1967; Producer, Nationwide and 24 Hours, 1969; Output Editor, Nationwide, 1973; Dep. Editor, Newsnight, 1979; Editor: That's Life, 1981; Newsnight, 1981; Breakfast Time, 1983; Six O'Clock News, 1984; TV News, 1985; Dep. Dir, 1987–88, Dir, 1988–89, News and Current Affairs; Man. Dir, Regl Broadcasting, BBC, 1989. Chm., Fundraising and Communications Cttee, 2005–13, Dep. Chm. Trustees, 2008–13, RNLI. *Recreations*: food, wine.

**NEIL-DWYER, Glenn**, FRCS, FRCSE; Consultant Neurosurgeon, Southampton University Hospitals NHS Trust, 1987–2002, now Honorary Emeritus; *b* 17 May 1938; *s* of Glen Shamrock Neil-Dwyer and Violet Agatha Hussey; *m* 1966, Jennifer Susan Edith Taylor; three *s*. *Educ*: Ruthin Sch.; St Mary's Hosp., London (MB BS; MS 1974). FRCSE 1967; FRCS 1968. Sen. House Officer, Neurosurgery, Addenbrooke's Hosp., 1968–69; Registrar, then Sen. Registrar, Wessex Neurol Centre, Southampton, 1969–74; Consultant Neurosurgeon: Cornwall Regl Hosp. and UCH (Jamaica), 1974–75; Brook Gen. Hosp., London, 1975–87; Consultant Advr in Neurosurgery to the Army, 1992–2005. Pres., Soc. of British Neurol Surgeons, 1998–2000 (Medal, 2015); Member, Council: RCS, 1998–2000; Med. Defence Union, 2000–08; Sec., Eur. Assoc. Neurosurgical Socs, 1999–2003 (Medal of Honour, 2007). Fellow, MDU, 2008. *Publications*: contrib. numerous papers to peer-reviewed jls on neurosurgical topics. *Recreations*: golf, sport, walking, travel, opera. *Address*: Annesley Glade, Bank, Lyndhurst, Hants SO43 7FD. *T*: (023) 8028 3352. *Club*: MCC.

**NEILAND, Prof. Brendan Robert**; Gallery Artist, Redfern Gallery, since 1992; Keeper of the Royal Academy, 1998–2004; *b* 23 Oct. 1941; *s* of Arthur Neiland and Joan Agnes Bessie Whiley; *m* 1970, Hilary Vivienne Salter; two *d*. *Educ*: Birmingham Sch. of Art (DipAD Hons); Royal Coll. of Art (MA). RE 1988–92 (Hon. RE 1998). Prof. of Painting, Univ. of Brighton, 1996–98. Vis. Prof. of Fine Art, Loughborough Univ., 1999. Exhibited: Angela Flowers Gall., 1970–78; Fischer Fine Art, 1978–92; Redfern Gall., 1993; retrospective exhibitions: Turlej Gall., Crakow, Poland and Sharjah Art Museum, UAE, 2006; De Montfort Univ. Gall., 2018; solo exhibitions: Redfern Gall., 2014, 2017; Galerie Belvedere, Singapore, 2015. Scholar, Crabtree Foundn, 1982. FRSA 1996. Hon. DArts de Montfort, 2013. Silver Medal, RCA, 1969; John Moores XI Prize, 1978; Daler Rowney Award, RA Summer Exhibn, 1989. *Publications*: Upon Reflection, 1997. *Recreations*: listening to the cricket commentary on Radio 4, drinking fine wines. *Address*: 2 Granard Road, SW12 8UL. *T*: and *Fax*: (020) 8673 4597. *Clubs*: Chelsea Arts, Arts.

**NEILL, Alistair Klaas**, GM 2012; Chief Executive, Herefordshire Council, since 2013; *b* 5 Nov. 1956; *s* of John and Woutertje Neill; *m* 1992, Kathryn Shapland; one *s* two *d*. *Educ*: Glasgow Univ. (MA English and Philos.; DMS in Business, distn). Marketing Manager, Unilever, 1983–88; Marketing Dir UK and CEO Asia-Pacific, BP, 1988–95; Pres. Internat. Ops, Masco Corp., 1995–2002; Chief Operating Officer, Northants CC, 2002–03; Chief Executive: Merthyr Tydfil CBC, 2003–10; Southampton CC, 2010–13. Conducted Capability Revs of DTI, later BERR, Prime Minister's Delivery Unit, 2007, and Cabinet Office, 2008. Lectr in Mgt, Warwick, Cardiff and HK Univs. MInstD 1992. Leading Wales Award, 2005, 2006; Nat. Police Public Bravery Award, 2012; Pride of Britain Award, 2012. *Publications*: Sick Pay Schemes, and Causes of Malingering, 1979. *Recreations*: my wife, children, walking in Brecon Beacons, France, playing guitar, singing woefully. *Address*: Herefordshire Council, Plough Lane, Hereford HR4 0LE. *T*: 07792 881727. *E*: alistair.neill@yahoo.co.uk. *Clubs*: Cardiff Business, Solent Business (Southampton).

**NEILL, Rev. Bruce Ferguson**; Church of Scotland Minister, Maxton and Mertoun: with St Boswells, 1996–2007; with Newtown, 2006–07; *b* 9 Jan. 1941; *s* of Thomas Ferguson Neill and Jane (*née* Bruce); *m* 1966, Ishbel Macdonald; two *s* one *d*. *Educ*: Lesmahagow Primary; Hamilton Academy; Glasgow Univ. and Trinity Coll., Glasgow (MA, BD). Probationer Asst, Drumchapel Old Parish Church, 1964–66; Minister, Dunfermline Townhill Parish Church, 1966–71; commnd as Chaplain, RN, 1971; Naval appts include: HMS Drake, 1972; RM, 1972; HMS Seahawk, 1974; HMS Cochrane, 1976; ships of 1st and 2nd Flotillas, 1979; HMS Dryad, 1981; Britannia RNC, 1983; HMS Cochrane, 1986; ships of Minor War Vessels Flotilla, 1989–91; Prin. Naval Chaplain, Church of Scotland and Free Churches, 1991–96. QHC, 1991–96. *Recreations*: gardening, hill walking, woodwork, model making.

**NEILL, John Mitchell**, CBE 1994; Chief Executive, since 1987, and Chairman, since 2012, Unipart Group of Companies; *b* 21 July 1947; *s* of Justin Bernard Neill and Johanna Elizabeth Neill; *m* 1975, Jacquelyn Anne, *d* of late Philip Brown; two *s*. *Educ*: George Heriot's Sch., Edinburgh; Univ. of Strathclyde (BA, MBA, DBA). Europe AC Delco: Planning Manager, 1969–71; Marketing Manager, 1972–73; British Leyland: Merchandising Manager, 1974–75, Sales and Marketing Dir, 1976, Parts Div.; Managing Director: Car Parts Div., 1977–78; BL Components, 1979–80; Unipart Gp, 1981–82; Gp Man. Dir, Unipart Gp Ltd, 1983–86. A Dir, Bank of England, 1996–2003. Chm., Atlantis Resources Ltd, 2013–; Dir, Charter International (formerly Charter) plc, 1994–2012; non-exec. Dir, Rolls-Royce plc, 2008–15. Dir, BITC, 1992–. Vice President: Inst. of Mktg, 2002– (Pres., 2000–01; Dep. Pres., 2001–02); Inst. of Motor Industry; BEN; Pres., SMMT, 2000–01. Trustee, Nat. Motor Mus. *Address*: Unipart Group of Companies Ltd, Unipart House, Garsington Road, Cowley, Oxford OX4 2PG.

**NEILL, Most Rev. John Robert Winder**; Archbishop of Dublin, and Primate of Ireland, 2002–11; *b* 17 Dec. 1945; *s* of Eberto Mahon Neill and Rhoda Anne Georgina Neill; *m* 1968, Betty Anne (*née* Cox); three *s*. *Educ*: Sandford Park School, Dublin; Trinity Coll., Dublin (Foundation Schol., BA 1st Cl., MA); Jesus Coll., Cambridge (MA, Gardiner Memorial Schol., Univ. of Cambridge); Ridley Hall, Cambridge (GOE). Curate Asst, St Paul's, Glenageary, Dublin, 1969–71; Lectr (Old Testament) in Divinity Hostel, 1970–71; Bishop's Vicar and Dio. Registrar, Kilkenny, 1971–74; Rector of Abbeystrewry, Skibbereen, Co. Cork, 1974–78; Rector of St Bartholomew's, and Leeson Park, Dublin, 1978–84; Lectr (Liturgy) in Theological Coll., 1982–84; Exam. Chaplain to Archbishop of Dublin, 1982–84; Dean of Christ Church Cathedral, Waterford, 1984–86; Archdeacon of Waterford, 1984–86; Bishop: of Tuam, Killala and Achonry, 1986–97; of Cashel and Ossory, 1997–2002; of Dublin and Glendalough, 2002–11. Sec., Irish House of Bishops, 1988–95; Mem., Central Cttee, WCC, 1994–2006; Pres., CTBI, 1999–2002. Hon. LLD NUI, 2003. *Publications*: contribs to Theology, New Divinity, Search, Doctrine and Life and Intercom. *Recreations*: photography, travel. *Address*: 3 Whitegate Lawn, Freshford Road, Kilkenny, R95 P92N, Ireland.

**NEILL, Nigel John Dermot, (Sam)**, DCNZM 2007; OBE 1992; actor; *b* 14 Sept. 1947; *s* of Dermot Neill and Priscilla Beatrice Neill (Ingham); *m* 1989, Noriko Watanabe; two *s* two *d*. *Educ*: Christ's Coll., Canterbury, NZ; Canterbury Univ., NZ (BA 1971). Director, NZ Nat. Film Unit, 1973–78; freelance actor, 1978–. *Films* include: My Brilliant Career, 1979; A Cry in the Dark, 1988; Dead Calm, 1989; Death in Brunswick, 1991; The Piano, Jurassic Park, 1993; In the Mouth of Madness, 1995; Restoration, 1996; The Event Horizon, 1997; Dish, 2000; Jurassic Park III, 2001; Dirty Deeds, 2003; Angel, 2007; Dean Spanley, 2008; Skin, 2009; The Vow, 2012; A Long Way Down, 2014; Backtrack, The Daughter, Hunt for the Wilderpeople, 2016; The Commuter, Sweet Country, Peter Rabbit, 2018; *television* includes: Reilly: the Ace of Spies (series), 1983; Merlin, 1998; Jessica, 2004; Mary Bryant (series), 2005; Merlin's Apprentice, 2006; The Tudors (series), 2007; Alcatraz (series), 2012; Peaky Blinders (series), 2013–14; And Then There Were None, 2015; Tutankhamun, 2016. Wine producer, Two Paddocks Wine, Queenstown, NZ, 1973–. Hon. DLitt Canterbury, NZ, 2002. *Recreations*: drinking, idling, farming, dogs, ski-ing, fly fishing, reading, ukelele, conviviality and isolation. *Address*: c/o Shanahan Management, Level 3 Berman House, 91 Campbell Street, Surry Hills, Sydney, NSW 2010, Australia.

**NEILL, Robert James Macgillivray**; MP (C) Bromley and Chislehurst, since June 2006; *b* 24 June 1952; *s* of John Macgillivray Neill and Elsie May Neill (*née* Chaston); *m* 1st, 2009, Daphne White (marr. diss. 2015); 2nd, 2018, Ann-Louise Whittaker (*née* Straker). *Educ*: London Sch. of Econs (LLB Hons 1973). Called to the Bar, Middle Temple, 1975, Bencher, 2018; barrister in private practice, 1975–2006. Member (C): Havering BC, 1974–90; Romford, GLC, 1985–86; Greater London Authority: Mem. (C) Bexley and Bromley, London Assembly, 2000–08; Leader, Cons. Gp, 2000–02, 2004–06; Chair, Planning and Spatial Develt Cttee, 2002–04. Shadow Minister for Local Govt, 2007–10; Parly Under-Sec. of State, DCLG, 2010–12. Mem., Select Cttee on Justice and Constitutional Affairs, 2006–10; Chm., Select Cttee on Justice, 2015–. Mem., UK Delegn to Parly Assembly of Council of Europe, 2012–16. Vice Chm., Cons. Party, 2012–15. Dep. Chm., Commn on London Governance, 2004–06. Leader, London Fire and Civil Defence Authy, 1985–87. Mem., Metropolitan Police Authy, 2004–08. Regl Chm., Gtr London Cons. Party, 1996–99. Contested (C) Dagenham, 1983 and 1987. Mem., UK Delegn, Cttee of Regions of EU, 2002–08. Non-exec. Dir, NE London HA, 2002–06. *Recreations*: opera, travel, sailing. *Address*: House of Commons, SW1A 0AA. *Clubs*: Carlton; Chislehurst Golf.

**NEILL, Sam;** *see* Neill, N. J. D.

**NEILSON, John Stuart**; Secretary and Registrar, Imperial College London, since 2012; *b* 31 May 1959; *s* of late Ian Neilson, ISO, and Dr Betty Neilson (*née* Harley); *m* 1985, Alison Christine Green; one *s* one *d*. *Educ*: St Paul's Sch.; Corpus Christi Coll., Cambridge (BA 1st Cl. Hons 1980; Prize for Mgt Studies, ICE, 1980). Joined Department of Energy, 1980: Second Private Sec. to Sec. of State for Energy, 1983–85; Principal, 1985; on secondment to Econ. Secretariat, Cabinet Office, 1988–89; Principal Private Sec. to Sec. of State for Energy, 1989–92; Department of Trade and Industry: Private Sec. to Minister for Energy, 1992–93; Asst Sec., 1993; Director: UK Communications Policy, 1993–97; Aerospace and Defence Industries Policy, 1997–2000; Man. Dir, Customers and Supply, Ofgem, 2000–05; Gp Dir, Sci. and Engrg Base Gp, Office of Sci. and Technol., then Res. Base, Office of Sci. and Innovation, DTI, later Res. Base, DIUS, subseq. BIS, 2005–11; Dir, Financial Mgt, MoD, 2011–12. Mem., Audit Cttee, Archbishop's Council, 2007–17; Chair Trustees, USPG, 2018–. Trustee, Royal Albert Hall, 2013–15. *Address*: Faculty Building, South Kensington Campus, Imperial College London, SW7 2AZ. *T*: (020) 7594 7272. *E*: j.neilson@imperial.ac.uk. *Club*: Athenæum.

**NEILSON, Margaret Marion**; Sheriff of Grampian, Highland and Islands at Inverness, since 2009; *b* Falkirk, 21 Feb. 1958; *d* of late Alistair Fleming Neilson and Agnes Margaret Neilson (*née* Ritchie). *Educ*: Edinburgh Univ. (MA Hons French, LLB, DipLP). Solicitor in private practice, 1984–2006; Chm., Social Security Tribunals (pt-time), 2002–09; Employment Judge (pt-time), 2005–09; Immigration Judge (pt-time), 2006–09; Sheriff (pt-time), 2006–09. *Recreations*: scuba diving, travel, pilates, hill walking. *Address*: The Sheriff Court, The Castle, Inverness IV2 3EG. *T*: (01463) 230782.

**NEISH, Andrew Graham**; QC 2009; barrister; *b* Changi, Singapore, 5 March 1964; *s* of late Andrew Stephen Neish and of Joan Neish (*née* Catterall); *m* 1st, 1991, Sara Atkinson (marr. diss. 2007); two *s*; 2nd, 2014, Dr Monica Lagazio. *Educ*: Nunthorpe Grammar Sch., York; St Andrews Univ. (MA Hons English 1986); City Univ. (Dip. Law 1987). Called to the Bar: Lincoln's Inn, 1988; BVI, 1999. MCIArb 2011. *Recreations*: reading, music (listening only, all styles), football (watching only, especially West Ham United FC), cooking, food and wine, Chinese ceramics, gin, tea, coffee, London, Italophile. *Address*: 4 Pump Court, Temple, EC4Y 7AN. *T*: (020) 7842 5555. *E*: aneish@4pumpcourt.com.

**NELIGAN, His Honour John Oliver**; a Circuit Judge, 1996–2014; *b* 21 June 1944; *yr s* of late Desmond Neligan, OBE and Penelope Anne Stabb; *m* 1971, Mary Brigid Daniel; one *s* two *d*. *Educ*: Brickwall Sch., Northiam. Admitted Solicitor, 1969; called to the Bar, Middle Temple, 1975; practised on Western Circuit; Recorder, 1994–96. Asst Comr, Boundary Commn for England, 1992–95. Mem., Mental Health Review Tribunal, 2001–11. *Recreations*: walking, painting, gardening. *Address*: Brookside Lodge, High Street, East Budleigh, Budleigh Salterton, Devon EX9 7DU.
*See also* M. H. D. Neligan.

**NELIGAN, His Honour Michael Hugh Desmond**; a Circuit Judge, 1990–2005; *b* 2 Dec. 1936; *s* of late Desmond West Edmund Neligan, OBE and Penelope Anne, *d* of Henry Mason; *m* 1965, Lynn (*née* Maidment); three *d*. *Educ*: Bradfield College; Jesus College, Cambridge. Commissioned Royal Sussex Regt, 1960–62; served East Africa with 23rd and 4th Bns, King's African Rifles. Called to the Bar, Middle Temple, 1962; Prosecuting Counsel to the Crown, 1972; Metropolitan Stipendiary Magistrate, 1987–90. *Recreations*: gardening, dog-walking.
*See also* J. O. Neligan.

**NELIS, Mary Margaret**; Member (SF) Foyle, Northern Ireland Assembly, 1998–2004; *b* 27 Aug. 1935; *d* of Denis Elliott and Catherine Coyle Elliott; *m* 1955, William Nelis; eight *s* one *d* (and one *s* decd). *Educ*: Inch Island Nat. Sch.; St Eugene's Convent Sch., Derry; Univ. of Ulster; Magee Adult Educn Faculty. Factory worker, 1949–56; Teacher, NW Coll. of Technol., Derry, then Derry Youth & Community Workshop, 1975–83. Mem., Sinn Féin, 1980–. Mem. (SF) Derry CC, 1994. Community develt, 1960–: Literacy trainee and Soc. Mem., Derry Reading Workshop, Cornhill High Sch., Derry, 1974–75; Founder Member: Foyle Hills Tenants' Assoc., 1968–73; Dove House, 1985–90; Founder Mem. and Man. Dir, Templemore Co-op., Derry, 1988–91. *Recreations*: painting, writing, music, children. *Address*: 35 Westland Avenue, Derry City, Co. Londonderry BT48 9JE. *T*: (028) 7128 6453.

**NELL**, family name of **Baroness O'Neill of Bengarve**.

**NELLIS, Helen Gwenllian**; Lord-Lieutenant of Bedfordshire, since 2012; Senior Executive Coach, since 2012; *b* 1959; *née* Jones; *m* Prof. Joseph Nellis; three *c*. *Educ*: Univ. of Keele (BA Law and Psychol. 1981; MA Criminol. and Criminal Justice 1983). Barrister; University of Buckingham: Associate Dean of Law; Prof. of Health Governance (Hon. Prof., 2007); Chair, Med. Develt Bd, 2004; Principal, Perrett Laver, 2008; Associate Dir, Harvey Nash plc, 2012. Chairman: Beds and Luton HA; Bedford Hosps NHS Trust. Chm., Luton Health Action Zone. Vice-Chm., Univ. of Luton, then Univ. of Beds. Trustee, Bedford Hosps Charity. Hon. Fellow, Univ. of Beds, 2009. DL Beds, 2007. CStJ 2018. *Address*: c/o Lieutenancy Office, Priory House, Monks Walk, Chicksands, Shefford, Beds SG17 5TQ.

**NELLIST, David;** IT manager, Citizens Advice Bureau, 2012–17 (Caseworker, Coventry Citizens Advice Bureau, 1997–2012); *b* 16 July 1952; *m* 1984, Jane Warner; one *s* three *d*. Mem., Unite (formerly Amicus). Welfare Rights Advr, Robert Zara & Co., 1992–97. Member: (Lab) W Midlands CC, 1982–86; (Socialist) Coventry CC, 1998–2012 (Leader, Socialist Gp, 1999–2010). MP (Lab, 1983–91, Ind. Lab, 1991–92) Coventry SE; contested: (Ind. Lab) Coventry SE, 1992; (Socialist) Coventry S, 1997; (Socialist) Coventry NE, 2001; (Socialist Alternative) Coventry NE, 2005, 2010; (TUSC) Coventry NW, 2015. Contested (No2EU) West Midlands, European Parlt, 2009, 2014. Mem. Nat. Cttee, Socialist Party, 1997–; Chairman: Socialist Alliance, 1998–2001; Campaign for a New Workers' Party, 2006–; Nat. Chm., Trade Unionist and Socialist Coalition, 2010–. *Address:* 33 Coundon Road, Coventry CV1 4AR. *T:* (024) 7622 9311. *E:* dave@nellist.net. *W:* www.twitter.com/davenellist.

**NELMES, Dianne Gwenllian, (Mrs I. McBride);** media and broadcasting consultant; *b* Windlesham; *d* of late James Allen Nelmes and Celandine Nelmes (*née* Kimber); *m* 1986, Ian McBride. *Educ:* Holt Co. Girls' Sch., Wokingham; Newcastle upon Tyne Univ. (BA Hons Econs/Politics 1973; Pres., Students' Union, 1973–74). Professional Cert. NCTJ 1978. Thomson grad. trainee journalist, 1974–78; journalist, on-screen reporter/presenter, BBC TV NE, 1978–83; News Ed., journalist, World in Action, Granada TV, 1983–87; Producer/Dir, Brass Tacks, BBC TV, 1987–88; Granada TV, 1988–98: Launch Ed., This Morning, 1988–89; Exec. Producer, Entertainment, 1989–92; Ed., World in Action, 1992–93; Controller: Factual Progs, 1993–96; Lifestyle Progs (launched 5 satellite-digital channels), 1996–98; Daytime, ITV Network Ltd, 1998–2000; Documentaries and Features, ITV Network, 2000–03; Dir, Daytime and Regl Programming, Granada Media, then Dir, Lifestyle Programming, Granada, later Dir, Daytime and Lifestyle Programming, ITV Prodns, 2003–08; Man. Dir, Liberty Bell Prodns, 2008–13; Creative Dir, Dinamite Prodns, 2013–. Vis. Prof., Media and Journalism, Newcastle Univ., 2008–11. Lay Mem. Council, Newcastle Univ., 2015–. Trustee, Refuge, 2006–; Lay Trustee: NUS, 2012–18; Women in Prison, 2016–18. FRTS 1996; FRSA 2002. Hon. DCL Newcastle, 2011. *Recreations:* canal boating, mountain walking, films.

**NELMES, Prof. Richard John,** OBE 2001; ScD, PhD; FRS 2003; FRSE; FInstP; Professor of Physical Crystallography, 1992–2010, now Emeritus, Honorary Professorial Fellow, since 2010, and Chairman, Centre for Science at Extreme Conditions, 2003–16, University of Edinburgh; Honorary Scientist, Science and Technology Facilities Council, ISIS Facility, Rutherford Appleton Laboratory, since 2010 (Senior Visiting Fellow, 1994–2010); *s* of late Arthur and Mabel Nelmes; *m* 1994, Tricia, *d* of late Eric and Eva Baldwin. *Educ:* Whitgift Sch., Croydon; St John's Coll., Cambridge (MA; ScD); Univ. of Edinburgh (PhD). FInstP 2001. University of Edinburgh: SRS Postdoctoral Fellow, 1969–71; Postdoctoral Res. Fellow, 1971–76; Lectr, 1976–85; Sen. Lectr, 1985–89; Reader and Professorial Fellow, 1989–92; EPSRC Sen. Fellow, 1989–94. Chm., High Pressure Gp, 1990–96, Founding Chm., Commn on High Pressure, 1996–2002, Internat. Union of Crystallography. FRSE 1995. Duddell Medal and Prize, Inst. of Physics, 2007. *Publications:* articles in scientific jls. *Recreations:* driving remote northern roads, reverie, music. *Address:* ISIS Facility, Rutherford Appleton Laboratory, Chilton, Didcot, Oxon OX11 0QX. *T:* (01235) 445285; Centre for Science at Extreme Conditions, and SUPA, School of Physics and Astronomy, University of Edinburgh, Mayfield Road, Edinburgh EH9 3JZ. *E:* r.j.nelmes@ed.ac.uk.

**NELSON,** family name of **Earl Nelson** and **Baron Nelson of Stafford**.

**NELSON, 10th Earl** *cr* 1805; **Simon John Horatio Nelson;** Baron Nelson of the Nile and of Hillborough, Norfolk, 1801; Viscount Merton, 1805; *b* 21 Sept. 1971; *s* of 9th Earl Nelson and Maureen Diana (*née* Quinn); *S* father, 2009; *m* 1999, Anna Stekerova; one *s* one *d*. *Heir: s* Viscount Merton, *qv*.

**NELSON OF STAFFORD, 4th Baron** *cr* 1960; **Alistair William Henry Nelson;** Bt 1955; family farming business, since 2007; *b* 1973; *o s* of 3rd Baron Nelson of Stafford and of Dorothy Irene Nelson; *S* father, 2006; *m* 2010, Kirsty Anne, *d* of Peter William Snowball; one *s* two *d*. *Educ:* Ampleforth Coll.; Loughborough Univ. (BEng Hons Manufacturing, Engrg and Mgt). Mech. Applications Engr, European Gas Turbines, 1995–2000; Design Engr, Farm Force Engineering Ltd, 2000–07. *Recreations:* horse trials, horse racing, shooting, ski-ing. *Heir: s* Hon. James William Henry Nelson, *b* 30 May 2015.

**NELSON, Anthony;** *see* Nelson, R. A.

**NELSON, Hon. Brendan John,** AO 2016; Director, Australian War Memorial, since 2012; *b* Coburg, Vic, 19 Aug. 1958; *s* of Desmond John and Patricia Anne Nelson; *m* 1st, 1980, Deanna (marr. diss. 1981); 2nd, 1983, Kathleen (marr. diss. 1999); one *s* one *d*; 3rd, 1999, Gillian Adamson; one step *d*. *Educ:* Modbury High Sch.; St Ignatius Coll.; Univ. of Adelaide; Flinders Univ. (BM BS 1983). FAMA 1995. Gen. med. practitioner, 1985–95, private gen. practice, Hobart, 1991–95; Dir, Hobart and Launceston After Hours Med. Service Pty Ltd, 1987–91; med. columnist, Woman's Day mag., 1995–97. Fed. Pres., AMA, 1993–95 (Fed. Vice Pres., 1991–93); Pres., Tasmanian Br., 1990–92). MP (L) Bradfield, NSW, 1996–2009; Parly Sec. to Minister of Defence, 2001; Minister: for Educn, Sci. and Trng, 2001–06; for Defence, 2006–07; Leader, Parly Liberal Party and Leader of the Opposition, 2007–08. Chm., House of Reps Standing Cttee for Employment, Educn and Trng, 1997–98, for Employment, Educn and Workplace Relns, 1998–2001. Ambassador of Australia to EU, Belgium and Luxembourg, Ambassador to NATO, and Special Rep. to WHO, 2010–12. Chm., Sydney Airport Community Forum, 1998–2001. Hon. FRACP 1995. DUniv Flinders, 2011; DLaws ANU, 2018; DUniv SA, 2019. Hon. Life Mem., RSL. Gold Medal, AMA, 1995; Centenary Medal, 2003; Bruce Shepherd Medal, Australian Doctors' Fund, 2011. Hon. Citizen, City of Ypres, 2018. *Recreations:* fishing, tennis, motorcycles, music, guitars. *Address:* Australian War Memorial, GPO Box 345, Canberra, ACT 2601, Australia.

**NELSON, Cairns Louis David;** QC 2010; a Recorder, since 2006; *b* Capel, Surrey, 1 March 1964; *s* of William and Freda Nelson; *m* 1998, Eleanor Jane Laws, *qv*; two *s* two *d*. *Educ:* King's Coll. London (LLB). Called to the Bar, Gray's Inn, 1987, Bencher, 2017. *Address:* 23 Essex Street, WC2R 3AA.

**NELSON, David Brian;** Senior Executive and Joint Head of Design, Foster + Partners, since 2007; *b* 15 April 1951; *s* of Victor Henry Nelson and Edna Mary (*née* Elliot); *m* 1977, Caroline Georgette Evans; two *d*. *Educ:* Loughborough Coll. of Art; Hornsey Coll. of Art; Royal Coll. of Art (MA). Joined Foster Associates, 1976; Dir, 1984; Partner, 1991; Dep. Chm., 2004–05. Projects, in Asia, Europe, Australia and USA, include: Century Tower, Tokyo, 1991; Amer. Air Mus., Duxford, 1997; New German Parlt, Reichstag, Berlin, 1999; Stanford Univ. Labs, Calif, 2003; Petronas Univ. of Technol., Malaysia, 2004; McLaren Technology Centre for McLaren, 2005; new Supreme Court, Singapore, 2006; Deutsche Bank Place, Sydney, Australia, 2006; transport projects: Bilbao Metro, Spain, 1995; Canary Wharf Underground Stn, 1999; N Greenwich Transport Interchange, London, 2000; Florence High-speed Rly Stn, 2010. Hon. FRIBA 2002. *Recreations:* motorsport, aviation, travel. *Address:* Foster + Partners, Riverside, 22 Hester Road, SW11 4AN. *T:* (020) 7738 0455, *Fax:* (020) 7738 1107. *E:* dnelson@fosterandpartners.com. *Club:* Architecture.

**NELSON, Deborah Louise;** *see* McAndrew, D. L.

**NELSON, Eleanor Jane;** *see* Laws, E. J.

**NELSON, Eric Victor,** LVO 1975; HM Diplomatic Service, retired; *b* 11 Jan. 1927; *s* of Victor H. H. and E. Vera B. Nelson (*née* Collingwood); *m* 1960, Maria Teresa (Marité) Paul (*d* 2008); one *d* (and one *d* decd). *Educ:* Western High School; George Washington University, Washington DC. Royal Air Force, 1945–48. Board of Trade, 1949; served FO, later FCO: Athens, Belgrade, Haiphong, Caracas; First Sec., Saigon, 1962; First Sec. and Consul, Bujumbura, 1964 (Chargé d'Affaires ai, 1966–67); FO 1968; First Sec. and Consul, Asunción, 1971; First Sec., Mexico City, 1974; FCO, 1978; seconded to Brunei Govt Service as Special Adviser to HM Sultan of Brunei, for Establishment of Brunei Diplomatic Service, 1981–84; Consul-Gen., Bordeaux, 1984–87. Order of the Aztec Eagle, Mexico, 1975. *Recreations:* photography, computer graphics, tourism, cartooning, pastel drawing, sculpture. *Address:* 8 Purberry Grove, Ewell, Surrey KT17 1LU.

**NELSON, Fraser Andrew;** Editor, The Spectator, since 2009; *b* Truro, 14 May 1973; *m* 2006, Linda; two *s* one *d*. *Educ:* Nairn Acad.; Dollar Acad.; Glasgow Univ. (MA Hist. and Politics); City Univ. (Dip. Newspaper Journalism). Journalist, Glasgow Herald, 1995; Business Corresp., The Times, 1995–2001; Political Editor: Scotsman, 2001–06; The Spectator, 2006–09. Political Commentator of the Year, Editorial Intelligence Comment Awards, 2009; Political Journalist of the Year, Press Awards, 2013; Editors' Editor of the Year, BSME Awards, 2013. *Address:* The Spectator, 22 Old Queen Street, SW1H 9HP. *T:* (020) 7961 0201, *Fax:* (020) 7961 0250. *E:* editor@spectator.co.uk.

**NELSON, Sir Jamie (Charles Vernon Hope), 4th Bt** *cr* 1912, of Acton Park, Acton, Denbigh; *b* 23 Oct. 1949; *s* of Sir William Vernon Hope Nelson, OBE and Hon. Elizabeth Ann Bevil Cary, *er d* of 14th Viscount Falkland; *S* father, 1991, but his name does not appear on the Official Roll of the Baronetage; *m* 1983, Maralyn Beverly Hedge (*née* Pyatt); one *s*. *Heir: b* Dominic William Michael Nelson [*b* 13 March 1957; *m* 1981, Sarah, *e d* of late John Neil Hylton Jolliffe; three *s* one *d*].

**NELSON, Dame Janet Laughland, (Dame Jinty Nelson),** DBE 2006; PhD; FBA 1996; FSA; Professor of Medieval History, King's College, London, 1993–2007, Emeritus Professor, 2008; *b* 28 March 1942; *d* of William Wilson Muir and Elizabeth Barnes Muir (*née* Laughland); *m* 1965, Howard George Horatio Nelson (marr. diss. 2010); one *s* one *d*. *Educ:* Keswick Sch., Cumbria; Newnham Coll., Cambridge (BA 1964; PhD 1967). King's College, London: Lectr, 1970–87; Reader, 1987–93; Dir, Centre for Late Antique and Medieval Studies, 1994–2000; FKC 2001. Chm., Adv. Bd, Inst. of Histl Res., Univ. of London, 1998–2001. Vice-Pres., British Acad., 1999–2001; FRHistS 1982 (Pres., 2000–04); FSA 2014; Corresp. Fellow, Medieval Acad. of Amer., 2000. Hon. DLitt: UEA, 2004; St Andrews, 2007; QUB, 2009; Liverpool, Nottingham, York, 2010; Glasgow, 2012. Medlicott Medal, Historical Assoc., 2019. *Publications:* Politics and Ritual in Early Medieval Europe, 1986; The Annals of St-Bertin, 1991; Charles the Bald, 1992; The Frankish World, 1996; Rulers and Ruling Families, 1999; (ed jtly) Rituals of Power, 2000; (ed jtly) The Medieval World, 2001; Courts, Elites, and Gendered Power in the Earlier Middle Ages, 2007; (ed jtly) Lay Intellectuals in the Carolingian World, 2007; (ed jtly) Reading the Bible in the Middle Ages, 2015; (ed jtly) Ravenna: its role in earlier medieval change and exchange, 2016; King and Emperor: a new life of Charlemagne, 2019. *Recreations:* music, walking, spending time with grandchildren Elias, Ruth, Martha, Miriam and John Paul. *Address:* 71 Oglander Road, SE15 4DD. *E:* jinty.nelson23@gmail.com.

**NELSON, Prof. Jenny,** PhD; FRS 2014; FInstP; Professor of Physics, Blackett Laboratory, Imperial College London, since 2006. *Educ:* Univ. of Cambridge (BA Physics 1983); Univ. of Bristol (PhD Physics 1988). FInstP 2014. Imperial College London: Postdoctoral post, Physics Dept, 1989; EPSRC Advanced Res. Fellow, 1997–2003; Lectr, 2000–03; Reader, 2003–06. RISE Leader, EPSRC, 2014. Industry Fellow, Royal Soc., 2010–13; Helmholtz Internat. Fellow, 2016. Joule Prize, 2009, Faraday Medal, 2016, Inst. of Physics; Armourers and Brasiers' Co. Prize, Royal Soc., 2012. *Publications:* The Physics of Solar Cells, 2003; contribs to learned jls. *Address:* Blackett Laboratory, Imperial College London, South Kensington Campus, SW7 2AZ.

**NELSON, Jeremy, (Jez);** Chief Executive Officer, Somethin' Else, since 2009 (Founder and Creative Director, 1991–2009); *b* London, 11 April 1964; *s* of Alan and Sheila Nelson; *m* 1997, Fran Plowright; two *s*. *Educ:* Dulwich Coll.; King's Coll., London (BSc Human Biol.); Highbury Coll., Portsmouth (Postgrad. Dip. Radio Journalism). Pirate radio DJ, 1980–84; freelance radio presenter and journalist, 1984–90; *radio:* presenter: Jazz FM, 1990–91; various BBC radio progs, 1991–, incl. Jazz on 3, 1999–; *television:* presenter, Tomorrow's World, 1996–2000; producer and exec. producer, TV documentaries, 1995–. Hon. ARAM. *Recreations:* family, jazz and all good music, Arsenal FC, swimming, cycling, Spain. *Address:* Somethin' Else, 20–26 Brunswick Place, N1 6DZ. *T:* (020) 7250 5500. *E:* jez.nelson@somethinelse.com.

**NELSON, John Frederick,** CBE 2018; DL; Chairman, Lloyd's, 2011–17; *b* 26 July 1947; *s* of George Frederick Nelson and Betty Violet Roddick; *m* 1976, Caroline Vivien Hannam; two *s* one *d*. FCA 1970. Kleinwort Benson, 1971–86, Dir, 1980; Lazard Brothers: Man. Dir, 1986–99; Vice Chm., 1990–99; Chm., Credit Suisse First Boston Europe, 1999–2002. Non-executive Director: Woolwich plc, 1998–2000; BT Gp plc, 2002–08; Kingfisher plc, 2002–11 (Dep. Chm., 2002–06 and 2009–11; Jt Dep. Chm., 2006–09); Hammerson plc, 2004–13 (Chm., 2005–13); Cazenove Gp, 2008–10; JPMorgan Cazenove Holdings, 2008–10. Senior Advr, Charterhouse Capital Partners LLP, 2006–. Chm., Chichester Harbour Trust, 2013–. Dir, ENO, 2002–10. Trustee, Nat. Gall., 2010–18; Chm., Nat. Gall. Trust, 2018–. DL W Sussex, 2017. *Recreations:* sailing, opera, ski-ing, tennis. *Clubs:* Hurlingham; Royal Yacht Squadron; Bosham Sailing.

**NELSON, John Graeme;** Chairman, Flash Forward Consulting, since 2018; *b* 19 June 1947; *s* of late Charles and Jean Nelson; *m* 1971, Pauline Dickinson; one *s* one *d* (and one *s* decd). *Educ:* Aylesbury and Slough Grammar Schs; Univ. of Manchester (BA Econ Hons). Management trainee, BR Western Reg., 1968; Asst Station Man., Liverpool Street, 1971; Area Passenger Man., Shenfield, 1973; Passenger Sales Officer, Leeds, 1977; Passenger Man., Sheffield Div., 1979; Personal Asst, Chief Exec. BRB, 1981; Parcels Man., Southern Reg., 1982; Nat. Business Man., Red Star Parcels, 1984; Gen. Man., BR Eastern Reg., 1987; Man. Dir, Network SouthEast, 1991; Gp Man. Dir, S and E, BR, 1994–97; Dir, London Develt, Railtrack, 1997; Mgt Consultant, First Class Partnerships, 1997–2015 (Chm., 1999–2012). Director: First Class Insight Ltd, 1997–2003; Renaissance Trains Ltd, 1999–2017; Hull Trains, 1999–2014; Laing Rail, 2002–06; Wrexham, Shropshire & Marylebone Railway Ltd, 2006–09; Tracsis plc, 2007–18; YourRail Ltd, 2008–09; Passenger Transport Ltd, 2011–; Member, Board: M40 Trains Ltd, 1998–2002; SE Trains (Hldgs) Ltd, 2003–06; Tracsis plc, 2007–. Chm., Tees, E and N Yorks Ambulance Service NHS Trust, 1997–2002. Member, Advisory Board: Nat. Railway Mus., 2006–12; Yorks

Rail Acad., 2007–09. *Publications:* Voters Limits: a history of London's parliamentary representation, 2015. *Recreations:* piano, football, painting, psephology. *Address:* 32 St Paul's Square, York YO24 4BD. *T:* (01904) 638659. *E:* john.nelson@post.com.

**NELSON, Marjorie J.;** *see* Jackson-Nelson.

**NELSON, Michael Edward;** Chairman, Reuter Foundation, 1982–90; General Manager, 1976–89, and Deputy Managing Director, 1981–89, Reuters Ltd; *b* 30 April 1929; *s* of late Thomas Alfred Nelson and Dorothy Pretoria Nelson; *m* 1960, Helga Johanna (*née* den Ouden); two *s* one *d*. *Educ:* Latymer Upper School; Magdalen College, Oxford (MA). Joined Reuters, London, as trainee financial journalist, 1952; assignments Asia, 1954–57; returned to London; Manager, Reuters Economic Services, 1962; Chairman, 1987–88: Reuters Asia; Reuters Europe; Reuters Overseas. Trustee: Visnews, 1990–92 (Chm., 1985–89); Internat. Inst. of Communications, 1989–95 (Chm., UK Chapter, 1989–92); Chm. Adv. Council, World Econ. Forum Jl, World Link, 1990–92. Mem., Newspaper Panel, MMC, 1989–95. External examiner, Journalism MA, Sheffield Univ., 1999–2001. Mem. Council, Internat. Assoc. for Media and Hist., 2001–09. Trustee, St Bride's Church, 1989–2009. Vice-Pres., Music Fest. of Beaulieu-sur-Mer, 2005. Hon. Res. Fellow, Univ. of Kent, 1997–. *Publications:* War of the Black Heavens: the battles of western broadcasting in the cold war, 1997; Queen Victoria and the Discovery of the Riviera, 2001; Americans and the Making of the Riviera, 2007; Castro and Stockmaster: a life in Reuters, 2011; The French Riviera: a history, 2017. *Recreations:* walking, music, history. *Address:* 40 Addison Avenue, W11 4QP. *T:* (020) 7603 1115; Domaine de la Rose, 2 Chemin des Restanques, 06650 Opio, France. *T:* 493773263. *W:* www.michaelnelsonbooks.com. *Club:* Garrick.

**NELSON, Mike,** RA 2013; sculptor; *b* Loughborough, 1967. *Educ:* Reading Univ. (BA 1st Cl. Hons Fine Art 1990); Chelsea Coll. of Art and Design (MA Sculpture 1993). Prof. of Fine Art, Kingston Univ. Sculpture Res. Fellow, Edinburgh Coll. of Art, 1998–2001; Vis. Lectr, Chelsea Coll. of Art. Represented GB at: São Paulo Biennial, 2004; Venice Biennale, 2011. *Solo exhibitions* include: Hale's Gall., London, 1995; Matt's Gall., London, 1996, 2000, 2006, 2013; Douglas Hyde Gall., Dublin, 1999, 2009; ICA, London, 2001; Mus. of Modern Art, Oxford, 2004; Turner Contemp., Margate, British Sch. at Rome, 2005; Frieze Art Fair, London, 2006; Galleria Franco Nero, Turin, 2007, 2009; Villa Arson, Nice, 2008; Statens Mus. for Kunst, Copenhagen, 2009; 303 Gall., NY, 2010, 2015; Contemp. Art Gall., Vancouver, 2013; Power Plant, Toronto, Kunsthalle Münster, Germany, 2014; *group exhibitions* include: Norwich Gall., 1997; Bonnington Gall., Nottingham, 1998; nat. touring exhibn for Hayward Gall., 2000; Tate Britain, 2001, 2019; Sydney Biennale, 2002; Kunsthalle Budapest, São Paulo, Brazil, 2004; CCA Wattis Inst. of Contemp. Arts, San Francisco, 2004, 2005; Istanbul Biennial, 2005; Galleria Franco Nero, Turin, 2006; Hayward Gall., RCA, Barbican Art Gall., 2008; Tate Triennial, Tate Britain, 2009; Singapore Biennale, 2011; Palais de Tokyo, Paris, 2014; Lyons Biennale, 2015; *work in public collections* includes: Arts Council; Hayward Gall.; British Council; Contemp. Art Soc.; Moderna Museet, Stockholm; Rennie Collection, Vancouver; Tate Collection. Charles Wollaston Award, RA, 2018. *Publications:* I, Imposter, 2011. *Address:* c/o Matt's Gallery, 42–44 Copperfield Road, E3 4RR.

**NELSON, Nicholas;** Teacher, Newlands Girls' School, Maidenhead, 2001–10; *b* 20 Jan. 1947; *s* of late Peter Nelson and Margaret Nelson; *m* 1972, Charmian Alice (*née* Bell); one *s* two *d*. *Educ:* Pudsey Grammar Sch., Yorkshire; Reading Univ. (BA (Hons) History; CertEd 1992); Birkbeck, Univ. of London (Grad. Dip. French 2013). BOAC/British Airways air cargo mgt in Japan/UK, 1969–81; DHL International (UK) Ltd: Gen. Man., 1981; Man. Dir, 1982; Regional Dir (Europe), 1987; Man. Dir, Parcels, PO, then Royal Mail Parcelforce, 1987–91; teacher, 1992–95, Head Teacher, 1995–2000, Queens' Sch., Bushey; Dir, Resources and Planning, Design Council, 2001. *Recreations:* watching cricket, trying to learn French, learning the violin.

**NELSON, Prof. Philip Arthur,** CBE 2018; PhD; CEng, FREng; FIMechE, FIET; Professor of Acoustics, University of Southampton, since 1994; Chief Executive, Engineering and Physical Sciences Research Council (on secondment), 2014–18; *b* Bishop's Stortford, 22 June 1952; *s* of David and Brenda Nelson; *m* 1979, Jennifer Mills; two *s*. *Educ:* Colchester Royal Grammar Sch.; Univ. of Southampton (BSc 1st Cl Hons Mech. Engrg; PhD Sound and Vibration Studies 1981). CEng 1992; FIMechE 1997; FREng 2002; FIET 2016. Res. develt and consulting engr, Sound Attenuators Ltd, 1978–82; University of Southampton: Lectr, Inst. of Sound and Vibration Res., 1982–88; Sen. Lectr, 1988–94; Founder Dir, Rolls-Royce Univ. Technol. Centre in Gas Turbine Noise, 1999–2001; Dir, Inst. of Sound and Vibration Res., 2001–05; Pro Vice-Chancellor, 2005–13. Vis. Prof., Penn State Univ., 1999. FIOA 1997. *Publications:* (with S. J. Elliott) Active Control of Sound, 1992; (jtly) Active Control of Vibration, 1996; contribs to refereed scientific jls. *Recreations:* golf, theatre, cinema. *Address:* Engineering, University of Southampton, Highfield, Southampton SO17 1BJ. *Club:* Hockley Golf.

**NELSON, Philip Raymond,** CMG 2005; JP; HM Diplomatic Service, retired; *b* 7 April 1950; *s* of David George Nelson and Marjorie Lilian Nelson (*née* Roberts); *m* 1st, 1971, Cynthia Lesley Elson (marr. diss. 1978); 2nd, 1992, Lyndsay Ann Halper; two *s*. *Educ:* Collyer's Sch., Horsham; Lincoln Coll., Oxford (BA Hons 1971); Fletcher Sch. of Law and Diplomacy, Tufts Univ. (AM 1972). Open Univ. (BSc Hons 2016). Joined HM Diplomatic Service, 1972; Budapest, 1974–76; Private Sec. to Sir Nicholas Henderson, Paris, 1976–79; First Secretary: Rome, 1980–83; Manila, 1990; Budapest, 1991–94; Counsellor, FCO, 1994–2005. JP Ealing, 2007, NW London Family Court, 2009, W London Family Court, 2014. *Recreations:* ski(mountaineer)ing, sailing (skippered Jolene II in Fastnet Races 2011, 2013 and 2015), cycling. *E:* ravenscourt@compuserve.com. *Club:* Royal Ocean Racing.

**NELSON, (Richard) Anthony;** *b* 11 June 1948; *o s* of late Gp Captain R. G. Nelson and of Mrs J. M. Nelson; *m* 1974, Caroline Victoria Butler; one *s* one *d*. *Educ:* Harrow Sch. (Head of School; Rothschild Scholar, 1966); Christ's Coll., Cambridge (MA (Hons) Economics and Law). N. M. Rothschild & Sons Ltd, 1969–73; Man. Dir, Salomon Smith Barney, 1997–2000; Vice-Chm., Citigroup Corporate and Investment Bank, then Citigroup Global Capital Markets, later Citigroup Global Markets, subseq. Citi, 2002–08; Chairman: Southern Water, 2002–04; Britain in Europe, 2005–07; ifs Proshare, 2007–08; Dir, Internat. Financial Services London, 2007–08. Chm., Gateway to London, 2002–08. Contested (C) E Leeds, Feb. 1974. MP (C) Chichester, Oct. 1974–1997. PPS to Minister for Housing and Construction, 1979–83, to Minister of State for the Armed Forces, 1983–85; Economic Sec., 1992–94, Minister of State, 1994–95, HM Treasury; Minister of State, DTI, 1995–97. Member: Select Cttee on Science and Technology, 1975–79; Select Cttee on Televising of Proceedings of the House, 1988–92 Dir, Chichester Fest. Th., 1983–92. Mem., Governing Body, ICC (UK), 2005–08. FRSA 1979.

**NELSON, Richard Campbell;** President, International Federation of Inspection Agencies, 1999–2018; *b* 11 Feb. 1943; *s* of Campbell Louis Nelson and Pauline (*née* Blundell); *m* 1971, Rosemary Eleanor Sterling; one *s* three *d*. *Educ:* Rugby Sch.; London Business Sch. (MSc Econs). Chartered Accountant. Dir, 1972–84, Chief Exec., 1982–84, Esperanza Ltd, subseq. Transcontinental Services Ltd; Chief Exec., Inchcape Testing Services, 1984–96; Intertek Testing Services, later Intertek Group plc: Exec. Chm., 1996–2001; Chief Exec., 1996–2005; Dep. Chm., 2005–09. Dir, Applus Services SA (formerly Applus Technologies Hldgs SLU), 2010–. *Recreations:* golf, tennis, bridge. *Address:* Flat 3, 10 Observatory Gardens, W8 7HY. *T:* (020) 7937 3457, 07775 785655. *E:* richardcnelson1@gmail.com. *Club:* Turf.

**NELSON, Dr (Richard) Stuart,** FInstP; Consultant, β Technology Ltd, 1996–2001; *b* 1 May 1937; *s* of Richard and Winifred Emily Nelson; *m* 1965, Veronica Mary Beck; one *s* two *d*. *Educ:* Univ. of Reading (BSc 1st Cl. Hons Physics, 1958; DSc 1969). FInstP 1968. Joined UKAEA, Harwell, 1958; Div. Head, Materials Develt Div., 1981; Dir, Nuclear Power Res., 1984; Dir, Northern Res. Labs, 1987–90 (including Risley, Springfield and Windscale Labs); Mem. Bd, UKAEA, 1991–96; Man. Dir, Industrial Business Gp, 1991–94, Exec. Dir, Ops, 1994–96, AEA Technology. Vis. Prof., Univ. of Sussex, 1970–. *Publications:* The Observation of Atomic Collisions in Crystalline Solids, 1968; Ion Implantation, 1973; Innovation Business, 1999; 200 papers in scientific jls. *Recreations:* hockey (played for Berkshire), golf (Club Captain, 1998), tennis. *Address:* 5 Whitehills Green, Goring, Reading, Berks RG8 0EB.

**NELSON, Hon. Sir Robert (Franklyn),** Kt 1996; a Judge of the High Court of Justice, Queen's Bench Division, 1996–2008; arbitrator and mediator, since 2009; *b* 19 Sept. 1942; *s* of late Clarence William and Lucie Margaret Nelson; *m* 1968, Anne-Marie Sabina Hall; two *s*. *Educ:* Repton; St John's Coll., Cambridge (MA). Called to the Bar, Middle Temple, 1965 (Harmsworth Entrance Exhibn, 1963), Bencher, 1993; QC 1985; a Recorder, 1986–96. Trustee, Thalidomide Trust, 2010– (Chm., 2011–). *Recreations:* cricket, opera, golf, choral singing. *Address:* 3 Verulam Buildings, Gray's Inn, WC1R 5NT. *T:* (020) 7831 8441.

**NELSON, Stephen Keith James;** Asset Management Managing Director, Infracapital, since 2013; *b* 5 Jan. 1963; *s* of late Bertram James Nelson, OBE and of Constance Nelson (*née* Dangerfield); *m* 1991, Catherine; one *s* one *d*. *Educ:* Tonbridge Sch. (Scholar); St John's Coll., Oxford (Open Scholar; MA 1st cl. Lit. Hum.). Diageo: Man. Dir, Guinness GB, 1999–2000; CEO, Guinness World Records, 2000–01; Pres., Diageo N America (SW), 2001–03; J Sainsbury plc: Trading Dir, 2003–04; Mktg Dir, 2004–05; Gp Retail Dir, BAA plc, 2005–06; CEO, BAA Ltd, 2006–08. Non-executive Director: Duchy Originals Ltd, 2009–; Office of Rail Regulation, 2011–15; Associated British Ports Hldgs, 2013–. *Recreations:* family, cycling, guitar, reading, museums, galleries.

**NELSON, Stuart;** *see* Nelson, R. S.

**NELSON, Trevor Ricardo,** MBE 2002; broadcaster, BBC, since 1996; *b* Hackney, 7 Jan. 1964; *s* of Andrew Laurent-Nelson and Willyana Nelson; *m* Anna-Marie (marr. diss.); one *s* one *d*. *Educ:* Central Foundn for Boys Grammar Sch., London; Kingsway Princeton Coll. G&M Records, 1984–87; Red Records, 1987–89; Soul II Soul Records, 1989–90; EMI/Cooltempo Records, Artists & Repertoire, 1993–98; broadcaster: Kiss FM, 1990–95; BBC Radio 1, 1996–; BBC Radio 2, 1998–; BBC 1Xtra, 2007–; MTV UK, 1998–2009. *Recreations:* massive sports fan, loves golf, big Chelsea FC fan. *Address:* c/o Money Management, 42A Berwick Street, W1F 8RZ.

**NELSON-TAYLOR, Dame Nicola (Jane),** DBE 2014; National Leader of Education, since 2010; Chief Executive Officer (formerly Executive Headteacher), Walbottle Village Primary School and Executive Teacher, Beech Hill Primary School, Newcastle upon Tyne, since 2010; *b* Newcastle upon Tyne, 9 Dec. 1971; *d* of Raymond Benjamin Nelson and Elizabeth Ann Nelson; *m* 1999, Paul Taylor (marr. diss. 2013); one *s*. *Educ:* Northumbria Univ. (BEd Hons 1994); Univ. of Newcastle upon Tyne (MEd 2002); NPQH 2002. Sen. Teacher, Shiremoor Primary Sch., 1995–2003; Dep. Head Teacher, 2003–06, Head Teacher, 2006–10, Beech Hill Primary Sch. *Recreations:* marathon running, trekking, cycling, family, friends, enjoying life, feeling the fear and doing it anyway. *Address:* Beech Hill Primary School, Linhope Road, West Denton, Newcastle upon Tyne NE5 2LW. *T:* (0191) 267 8113, *Fax:* (0191) 264 1240. *E:* Dame.nicola@beechhill.newcastle.sch.uk.

**NEMKO, Hannah;** Headteacher, Dame Alice Owen's School, since 2016; *b* London, 20 Nov. 1975; *d* of Geoffrey and Estelle Conway; *m* 2004, Barnaby Nemko; two *c*. *Educ:* Beal High Sch.; Nottingham Univ. (BA Hons 1998; PGCE 2000); Univ. de Strasbourg. Deputy Headteacher: Yavneh Coll., 2006–15; Dame Alice Owen's Sch., 2015–16. *Recreations:* family, running, reading, theatre, cooking. *Address:* Dame Alice Owen's School, Dugdale Hill Lane, Potters Bar, Herts EN6 2DU. *T:* (01707) 643441. *E:* head@damealiceowens.herts.sch.uk.

**NEOPTOLEMOS, Prof. John P.,** MD; FRCS, FMedSci; Professor of Surgery, University of Heidelberg, since 2017; *b* 30 June 1951; *m* 1974, Linda Joan Blaylock; one *s* one *d*. *Educ:* Owen's Grammar Sch., N London; Churchill Coll., Cambridge (MA); Guy's Hosp., London (MB BChir); Univ. of Leicester (MD 1985). FRCS 1981. Guy's Hosp., London, 1976–77; Leicester Royal Infirmary, 1978–84 and 1986–87; UCSD, 1984–85; Sen. Lectr, then Reader, Dept of Surgery, Univ. of Birmingham, and Consultant Surgeon, City Hosp., Birmingham, 1987–94; Prof. of Surgery, Queen Elizabeth Hosp., Birmingham, 1994–96; University of Liverpool: Prof. of Surgery, 1996–2017; Owen and Ellen Evans Chair of Surgery (formerly Cancer Studies), 2006–17; Head: Dept of Surgery, 1996–2004; Div. of Surgery and Oncology, 2004–05; Sch. of Cancer Studies, 2005–11; Hon. Consultant Surgeon, Royal Liverpool Univ. Hosp., 1996–2017; Director: Liverpool Clinical and Cancer Res. UK Trials Unit, 1997–2017; Liverpool Cancer Res. UK Centre, 2010–14; Dep. Dir, Liverpool Experimental Cancer Medicine Centre, 2007–12, 2017; Scientific Dir and Theme Leader, Liverpool Pancreas Biomedical Res. Unit, 2007–17; Sen. Investigator, 2011–17, NIHR. Hunterian Prof. of Surgery, RCS, 1987–88; Moynihan Travelling Fellow, Assoc. of Surgeons of GB and Ireland, 1988; RSM Travelling Prof., USA, 1989; British Council Lectr. Tour of Thai Med. Schs, 1990; Vis. Prof., Med. Sch., Univ. of Hong Kong, 1993; Eybers Vis. Prof., Med. Sch., Univ. of Orange Free State, S Africa, 1994; Vis. Prof., Christchurch Med. Sch., Univ. of Otago, NZ, 1995; Ext. Examr, 1996–97, Wilson Wang Vis. Prof., 1997, Chinese Univ. of Hong Kong; Visiting Professor: Univ. of Singapore, 1998; Univ. of Heidelberg, 2002; Pearce Gould Vis. Prof., UCL, 2008. Honyman Gillespie Lect., Edinburgh, 2007; Hon. Prof., 2015, Prof., Clinical Med. Sch., 2018–, Nanjing Med. Univ. Has made scientific contribs to aetiology, diagnosis and treatment of diseases of the pancreas and biliary tree. President: Pancreatic Soc. of GB and Ireland, 1994–95 (Mem. Cttee, 1987–90); Liverpool and NW Soc. of Surgeons, 2006–07. Mem. Cttee, Surgical Res. Soc., 1994–98. Chairman: Eur. Study Gp for Pancreatic Cancer, 1991–; Pancreas Cancer Sub Group, NCRI, 2004–; Treas., Eur. Digestive Surgery, 1997–2004; Member Council: Eur. Pancreatic Club, 1995–2002, 2015–17 (Sec., 1996–2002; Pres., 2015–16); United Eur. Gastroenterol. Fedn, 1997–2002 (Mem., Scientific Cttee, 2002–06); Member: World Council, Internat. Hepato-Pancreato-Biliary Assoc., 1995–98; World Council, Internat. Assoc. of Pancreatology, 1996–2004 (Pres., 2000–02); Pancreatic Cancer Progress Review Gp, Nat. Cancer Inst., 2000; Nat. Cancer Inst. Specialized Prog. of Res. Excellence for Pancreatic Cancer, 2002–03; NW Regl Res. and Develt Biomedical Res. Cttee, 2001–02; Adv. Bd, Deutsche Krebshilfe Cancer Centers, 2006–12; Panel Acad. Advrs, Commonwealth Scholarship Commn, 2007–12; Sci. Strategy Adv. Gp, CRUK, 2008–14; Scientific Res. Cttee, Nat. Cancer Inst., France, 2010–12; Scientific Cttee, Italian Assoc. for Cancer Res., 2009–16; Adv. Bd, Pancreatic Cancer UK, 2016–; Advr, Bundesministerium für Bildung und Forschung/Deutsche

Forschungsgemeinschaft, 2006–16; Clinical Lead, Develt Gp for Clinical Guidelines for Pancreatic Cancer, NICE, 2015–17. Hon. Member: S African Gastroenterology Soc., 1991; German Soc. for Surgery, 2012; Soc. for Surgery in Hungary, 2014. Freedom, City of Liverpool, 2012. FMedSci 2007. RCS USA Travelling Award, 1984; Rodney Smith Prize, RCS, 1987; Hirschberg Award for Pancreatic Cancer, American Pancreatic Assoc., 2005; Lifetime Achievement Award, Eur. Pancreatic Club, 2013; Ruth C. Brufsky Award for Excellence in Res. in Pancreatic Cancer, 2017; Henry Lynch Award for Inherited Pancreas Diseases, 2018. *Publications*: Cancer of the Pancreas, 1990, 2006; Cancer: a molecular approach, 1993; Pancreatic Cancer: molecular and clinical advances, 1996; The Pancreas, 1998, 3rd edn 2018; Acute Pancreatitis, 1999; Exocrine Pancreas Cancer, 2005; Pancreatic Cancer, 2010, 2nd edn 2018; (ed jtly) Pancreatic Cancer, Cystic Neoplasms and Endocrine Tumors: diagnosis and management, 2018; contrib. numerous scientific papers in peer-reviewed jls, incl. New England Jl of Medicine, Lancet, Jl American Med. Assoc., Jl Clin. Oncol., GUT, Annals of Surgery, Cancer Res., Gastroenterol., Proc. NAS, USA, Oncogene, Jl Nat. Cancer Inst. *Recreations*: racquet ball, Latin and ballroom dancing (Mem., Merrall's Acad. of Dance, 2003–). *Address*: Department of General Surgery, University of Heidelberg, Im Neuenheimer Feld 110, 69120 Heidelberg, Germany. *T*: (6221) 5632880, *Fax*: (6221) 565538. *E*: john.neoptolemos@med.uni-heidelberg.de. *Club*: Heswall Squash (Trustee, 2005–).

**NESBIT, Martin Alistair;** Head, Environment and Climate Governance, since 2014, and London Director, since 2016, Institute for European Environmental Policy; *b* Frimley, Surrey, 14 May 1965; *s* of James Stuart Alistair Nesbit and Pamela Scrivener Nesbit; partner, Lucy Johnson; one *s*. *Educ*: Woking Sixth Form Coll.; Clare Coll., Cambridge (BA 1987); Univ. of Bristol (MA 1989). DoE, 1988–98; UK Perm. Repn to EU, 1998–2002; DEFRA, 2002–08; DECC, 2008–09; Dir, EU and Internat. Affairs, DEFRA, 2009–14. *Recreations*: hill-walking, kayaking, long-distance paths. *Address*: Institute for European Environmental Policy, Floor 3, 11 Belgrave Road, SW1V 1RB. *W*: www.twitter.com/arrhenius.

**NESBITT, Dermot William Gibson;** Senior Lecturer, Queen's University, Belfast, 2007–12; Commissioner, Equality Commission, Northern Ireland, 2009–15; *b* 14 Aug. 1947; *s* of William Cromwell Nesbitt and Georgina Nesbitt; *m* 1970, Margaret Oriel Patterson; one *s* one *d*. *Educ*: Queen's Univ., Belfast (BSc 1st cl. Hons Econs). School Teacher, 1969–74; Lectr, Ulster Poly., 1976; Queen's Univ., Belfast, 1976–98 (Sen. Lectr and Head, Dept of Accounting and Finance). Mem., NI Forum for Political Dialogue, 1996–98. Mem. (UU) S Down, NI Assembly, 1998–2007. Jun. Minister, assisting David Trimble, 1999–2002, Minister of the Envmt, 2002, NI. Contested (UU) S Down, 1997, 2001, 2005. *Publications*: over 20 academic publications. *Recreations*: gardening, family. *Address*: 21 Downpatrick Road, Crossgar, Downpatrick, Co. Down BT30 9EQ. *T*: (028) 4483 1561.

**NESBITT, Judith;** Director (formerly Head) of National and International Partnerships, Tate, since 2010; *b* 24 March 1962; *d* of Thomas Robert Cecil Nesbitt and Joan Nesbitt (*née* Fleming); *m* 2008, Prof. Guy Lennox Claxton. *Educ*: Univ. of York (BA Hons Eng./Hist. of Art 1983); Courtauld Inst., London (MA Hist. of Art 1985). Sen. Asst Keeper, City Art Gall., Leeds, 1986–91; Exhibns Curator, Tate Gall. Liverpool, 1991–95, curated: Roy Lichtenstein, Robert Gober, 1993; Ann Hamilton, 1994; Sigmar Polke, 1995; Dir, Chisenhale Gall., 1995–98, curated shows of: Michael Landy, Pipilotti Rist, Gillian Wearing, Sam Taylor-Wood, Wolfgang Tillmans, Fernanda Gomes, Paul Noble, Thomas Hirshhorn; Hd of Programming, Whitechapel Art Gall., 1998–2000; Hd of UK Content, Eyestorm.com, 2000–01; Tate Britain: Chief Curator, 2001–10; curated: Michael Landy Semi-Detached, 2004; Peter Doig, 2008; Chris Ofili, 2010. Non-exec. Dir, Film Video Umbrella, 2011–14. Mem., Adv. Panel, Platform for Art, 2004–. Mem. Bd, Liverpool Biennial, 2017–. FRSA 2017. Hon. FRCA 1998. *Recreation*: gardening. *Address*: Tate Modern, Bankside, SE11 0TG. *T*: (020) 7401 5091. *E*: judith.nesbitt@tate.org.uk.

**NESBITT, Michael Charles,** DBA; Member (UU) Strangford, Northern Ireland Assembly, since 2011; Leader, Ulster Unionist Party, 2012–17; *b* Belfast, 11 May 1957; *s* of Alfred Charles Nesbitt and Brenda Norma Patrick; *m* 1992, Lynda Byrons; two *s*. *Educ*: Campbell Coll., Belfast; Jesus Coll., Cambridge (BA 1979); Queen's Univ., Belfast (DBA). BBC Northern Ireland: sports reporter, 1979–86; presenter, Good Morning Ulster, 1986–89; Man. Dir, Anderson Kenny PR, 1989–92; presenter and broadcast journalist, Ulster TV, 1992–2006. Comr for Victims and Survivors, NI, 2008–10. *Recreations*: literature, music, golf. *Address*: Northern Ireland Assembly, Parliament Buildings, Stormont, Belfast BT4 3XX; (office) 16 South Street, Newtownards BT23 4JT. *E*: mike.nesbitt@mla.niassembly.gov.uk.

**NESBITT, Rebecca Jane;** *see* Heaton, R. J.

**NESBITT, Simon John;** QC 2015; *b* Belfast, 27 Sept. 1966; *s* of Henry Nesbitt and Elizabeth Nesbitt; civil partnership 2007, Simon Buxton; one *d*. *Educ*: Pembroke Coll., Oxford (BA Hons 1990; MA). Admitted: Solicitor, 1994; avocat à la cour, Paris, 1997; Lovell White Durrant, subseq. Lovells LLP, then Hogan Lovells International LLP: Associate Solicitor, London and Paris, 1994–2002; Partner, 2002–13; Global Co-Hd, Internat. Arbitration, 2013–15; called to the Bar, Lincoln's Inn, 2015; arbitrator and barrister, Maitland Chambers, 2015–. FCIArb 2004. *Publications*: articles relating to arbitration in Arbitration Internat., PLC Mag., Eur. Lawyer. *Recreations*: horse riding, sailing. *Address*: Maitland Chambers, 7 Stone Buildings, Lincoln's Inn, WC2A 3SZ. *T*: (020) 7406 1200. *E*: snesbitt@maitlandchambers.com.

**NESBITT, Timothy John Robert;** QC 2018; a Recorder, since 2018; *b* London, 12 Jan. 1966; *s* of Robert Alexander George Nesbitt and Marie Louise Nesbitt (*née* Weare). *Educ*: Downside Sch.; Durham Univ. (BA 1st Cl. Hons Politics; Chancellor's Prize for highest first in year); Sch. of Oriental and African Studies, Univ. of London (LLM Law and Develt). Called to the Bar, 1991. *Recreations*: cricket, cycling, yoga, travel. *Address*: Outer Temple Chambers, 222 Strand, WC2R 1BA. *T*: (020) 7353 6381. *E*: timothy.nesbitt@outertemple.com. *Club*: MCC.

**NESS, Air Vice-Marshal Charles Wright,** CB 2009; CEng, FRAeS; Defence Adviser, Fujitsu, since 2012; *b* 6 Nov. 1957; *s* of Air Marshal Sir Charles Ernest Ness, KCB, CBE and Audrey Ness; one *d*. *Educ*: Mill Hill Sch.; Liverpool Univ. (BEng). CEng 1986; FRAeS 1998. Joined RAF, 1975; Sen. Engrg Officer, 111 Sqn, 1986–88; OC, Engrg and Supply Wing, RAF Coningsby, 1993–95; Dep. Dir, Logistics Policy (RAF), 1995–97; Hd, Aero Engines Multi-Disciplinary Gp, 1997–99; Air Cdre, Communications and Inf. Systems, 1999; COS, Equipment Support (Air), 2000–02; Harrier Integrated Project Team Leader, 2003–04; Dir, Logistics No 1 Gp, 2004–05; Hd, RAF Process and Orgn Review, 2005–06; COS, Strategy, Policy and Plans, RAF High Wycombe, 2006–07; Dir Gen., Combat Air, Defence Equipment and Support Orgn, 2007–08; Sen. Technical Advr to Charles Haddon-Cave, QC, 2008–09; Dir of Tech. Airworthiness, Military Aviation Authy, 2010–12. *Club*: Royal Air Force.

**NESS, Patrick M.;** novelist; *b* Fort Belvoir, Va, 1971; civil partnership 1999, *m* 2014, M. A. Nowell. *Educ*: Univ. of Southern Calif (BA English *summa cum laude* 1993). Writer of screenplays: A Monster Calls, 2016; Class, 2016. *Publications*: The Crash of Hennington, 2003; Topics About Which I Know Nothing, 2005; The Crane Wife, 2013; *for children*: The Knife of Never Letting Go, 2008 (Guardian Children's Fiction Prize); The Ask and the Answer, 2009 (Costa Children's Book of the Year, 2010); Monsters of Men, 2010 (Carnegie Medal, 2011); A Monster Calls, 2011 (Galaxy Nat. Book Award; Red House Children's Book Award, Carnegie Medal, 2012) (adapted for stage, 2018); More Than This, 2013; The Rest of Us Just Live Here, 2015; Release, 2017; And The Ocean Was Our Sky, 2018. *Recreations*: distance running, theatre, overpaying for imported breakfast cereal, cat harmonica. *Address*: c/o Michelle Kass Associates, 85 Charing Cross Road, WC2H 0AA. *T*: (020) 7439 1624. *E*: office@michellekass.co.uk.

**NESS, Robert;** Director, Tunisia, British Council, since 2016; *b* 30 March 1953; *s* of late Robert Mitchell Ness and of Mary Ness (*née* Connor); *m* 1st, 1985, Geraldine McKendrick (marr. diss. 2013); two *s* one *d*; 2nd, 2013, Soon Ok Shin. *Educ*: Arbroath High Sch.; Edinburgh Univ. (MA Hons; DipEd); Moray House Coll. of Educn (PGCE). Teacher, Madrid, 1978–80; joined British Council, 1981: English Tuition Co-ordinating Unit, 1981–83; Overseas Educnl Appts Dept, 1983–86; Asst Rep., Austria, 1987–89; English Lang. Div., 1989–92; Dep. Dir, SA, 1992–97; Dir, Cyprus, 1997–2000; Dir, Portugal, and Cultural Counsellor, Lisbon, 2000–03; Regl Dir, E Europe, 2003–05; Head, UK Directorate, 2005–08; Dir, Colombia, 2008–12; Dir, Hong Kong, 2012–16. *Recreations*: music (especially jazz, opera, chamber), books, running, travel. *Address*: British Council, 10 Spring Gardens, SW1A 2BN.

**NESSLING, Paul William Downs;** HM Diplomatic Service, retired; consultant, Foreign and Commonwealth Office Services, since 2013; a Special Representative of Foreign Secretary, since 2016; *b* 26 Sept. 1945; *s* of late Herbert Nessling and Mary Nessling (*née* Perry); *m* 1975, Kathryn Lynne Freeman; one *d*. *Educ*: Latymer Upper Sch., Hammersmith. Buyer, BAT, 1965–66; Department of Trade and Industry, 1967–75: on secondment as Third Sec., Chicago, 1970; Asst Private Sec. to Sec. of State, 1972–74; Private Sec. to Minister of Prices, 1974–75; on secondment as Second Sec., Bahrain, 1975–79; joined HM Diplomatic Service, 1979; Second Secretary: FCO, 1979–81; Lisbon, 1981–82; and Consul, Warsaw, 1982–84; Hd of Chancery, Aden, 1984; First Secretary: (Aid) and Dep. UK Perm. Rep. to UNEP, Nairobi, 1984–87; FCO, 1987–89; (Commercial), Harare, 1989–93; (Commercial), Muscat, 1993–96; Sarajevo, 1996–97; Dep. Dir, Jt Export Promotion Directorate, FCO, 1997–98; Dep. High Comr, Lusaka, 1998–2001; High Comr, Kingdom of Tonga, 2002–06; Team Leader, FCO Res. Analysts, 2007–12. *Recreations*: current affairs, travelling, reading, walking.

**NESTLE, Prof. Frank Oliver,** MD; FMedSci; Global Head of Immunology and Inflammation, Therapeutic Research Area and Chief Scientific Officer, North America, Sanofi, since 2016; *b* Germany, 12 March 1964; *s* of Peter and Gabriele Nestle; *m* Barbara; one *d*. *Educ*: Univ. of Wurzburg Med. Sch. (MD *summa cum laude* 1992). Bd certified physician in dermatology, allergology and clin. immunology. Consultant Physician, 1997–2000, Sen. Consultant Physician, 2000–05, Dept of Dermatol., Univ. of Zürich Hosp.; Hon. Consultant Dermatologist, St John's Inst. of Dermatol., KCL Sch. of Medicine at Guy's, King's and St Thomas' Hosp., 2005–16; Mary Dunhill Prof. of Cutaneous Medicine and Immunotherapy, KCL, 2005–17. FMedSci 2013. *Recreations*: tennis, ski-ing, cycling. *Address*: Sanofi US, 640 Memorial Drive, Cambridge, MA 02139, USA. *E*: frank.nestle@sanofi.com. *Club*: Queen's.

**NETANYAHU, Binyamin;** Prime Minister of Israel, since 2009; Member, Knesset, since 1988; *b* 21 Oct. 1949; *s* of late Cela and Benzion Netanyahu; *m* (marr. diss.); one *d*; *m* 3rd, 1991, Sara; two *s*. *Educ*: MIT (BA 1976; MBA). Mgt Consultant, Boston Consulting Gp, 1976–78; Exec. Dir, Jonathan Inst., Jerusalem, 1978–80; Sen. Manager, Rim Industries, Jerusalem, 1980–82; Dep. Chief of Mission, Washington, 1982–84; Perm. Rep. to UN, 1984–88; Deputy Minister: Ministry of Foreign Affairs, 1988–91; Prime Minister's Office, 1991–92; Prime Minister of Israel and Minister of Housing and Construction, 1996–99; Foreign Minister, 2002–03; Finance Minister, 2003–05; Leader of Opposition, 2006–09; Foreign Minister and Minister for Health, for Communications, for Regl Cooperation, 2015–. Leader, Likud, 1993–99 and 2005–. Irving Kristol Award, Amer. Enterprise Inst., 2015. *Publications*: (ed) Self-Portrait of a Hero: the letters of Jonathan Netanyahu, 1981; Terrorism: how the West can win, 1986; A Place Among the Nations: Israel and the world, 1993; Fighting Terrorism, 1996. *Address*: The Knesset, Kiryat Ben-Gurion, Jerusalem 91950, Israel.

**NETHERCOT, Prof. David Arthur,** OBE 2006; PhD, DSc; FREng, FTSE, FIStructE, FICE; Professor of Civil Engineering, 1999–2011, now Emeritus, Head of Department of Civil and Environmental Engineering, 1999–2011, and Deputy Principal, Faculty of Engineering, 2008–11, Imperial College London (formerly Imperial College of Science, Technology and Medicine, University of London); *b* 26 April 1946; *s* of late Arthur Owen Martin Nethercot and Dorothy May Nethercot; *m* 1968, Hedd Dwynwen Evans; two *d*. *Educ*: Univ. of Wales Coll. of Cardiff (BSc, PhD, DSc). FIStructE 1989; FICE 1994; FREng (FEng 1993); FCGI 2001; FTSE 2010. ICI Fellow, Univ. of Wales, 1970–71; Lectr, 1971–81, Sen. Lectr, 1981–86, Reader, 1986–89, Univ. of Sheffield; Prof. of Civil Engrg, 1989–99, Hd of Dept, 1994–99, Univ. of Nottingham. Visiting Professor: Japan Soc. for Promotion of Science, Univ. of Nagoya, 1980; Swiss Federal Inst. of Tech., Lausanne, 1990. Assessor, Grenfell Tower Public Inquiry, 2017–. President: IStructE, 2003–04 (Mem. Council, 1986–89, 1991–97; Vice-Pres., 2001–03); IABSE, 2013–16; Chm., Cttee on Bldg and Civil Engrg Structures, BSI, 2013–; Member: Cttee on Structural Use of Steel in Building, BSI, 1986–2006 (Chm., 1995–2006); Joint Bd of Moderators, 1993–2000 (Chm., 1996–98); Standing Cttee on Structural Safety, 1996–2001; Council, Royal Acad. of Engrg, 2000–03. Foreign Mem., NAE, 2015. FRSA 2002. Hon. DSc Tech. Univ., Budapest, 2019. Charles Massonnet Prize, Eur. Convention for Constructional Steelwork, 2008; Gold Medal, IStructE, 2009; Lynn Beedle Prize, Structural Stability Res. Council, 2015. *Publications*: (jtly) Design for Structural Stability, 1979, 2nd edn 1985; Limit States Design of Structural Steelwork, 1986, 3rd edn 2001; (jtly) Design of Members Subject to Combined Bending and Torsion, 1989; (jtly) Lateral Stability of Steel Beams and Columns: common causes of restraint, 1992; (jtly) The Behaviour and Design of Steel Structures to EC3, 3rd edn 2001, 4th edn 2008; (jtly) Designers Guide to EN 1993–1–1: Eurocode 3: design of steel structures, 2005, 3rd edn 2011; about 400 sci. papers on structural engrg. *Recreation*: sport. *Address*: Department of Civil and Environmental Engineering, Imperial College London, South Kensington Campus, SW7 2AZ. *T*: (020) 7594 6097, *Fax*: (020) 7594 6042.

**NETHERTHORPE,** 3rd Baron *cr* 1959, of Anston, W Riding; **James Frederick Turner;** *b* 7 Jan. 1964; *s* of 2nd Baron Netherthorpe, and Belinda, *d* of F. Hedley Nicholson; *S* father, 1982; *m* 1989, Elizabeth Curran Fahan, *d* of Edward Fahan, Connecticut; two *s* two *d*. *Educ*: Heatherdown Prep. Sch.; Harrow Sch. *Heir*: *s* Hon. Andrew James Edward Turner, *b* 24 March 1993.

**NETHSINGHA, Andrew Mark,** FRCO; conductor; Director of Music, and Fellow, St John's College, Cambridge, since 2007; University Organist, University of Cambridge, since 2016; Director and Co-Founder, St John's Sinfonia, since 2011; *b* 16 May 1968; *s* of Lucian Nethsingha and late Jane (*née* Symons); *m* 1996, Lucy Kathleen Sellwood; one *s* two *d*. *Educ*: Exeter Cathedral Sch.; Clifton Coll. (Music Schol.); Royal Coll. of Music

(ARCM); St John's Coll., Cambridge (Organ Student; BA 1990; MA 1994). FRCO 1987. Chorister, Exeter Cathedral, 1976–81; Organ Schol., St George's Chapel, Windsor Castle, 1986–87; Asst Organist, Wells Cathedral, 1990–94; Master of Choristers and Organist, Truro Cathedral, 1994–2002; Dir of Music, Gloucester Cathedral, 2002–07, Organist Emeritus, 2008. Musical Director: Three Spires Singers and Orch., 1994–2002; Gloucester Choral Soc., 2002–07; Artistic Dir, Gloucester Three Choirs Fest., 2002–07. Début: BBC Proms, 2009; Amsterdam Concertgebouw, 2009; Suntory Hall, Tokyo, 2012; Munich Herkulessaal, 2013; Verbier Fest., 2014; Esplanade, Singapore, 2015; Berlin Konzerthaus, 2017. Co-founder, St John's Cambridge imprint, Signum, 2016–. Mem., Academic Bd, RCO, 2017–. Pres., Cathedral Organists' Assoc., 2007–10. Hon. Fellow, N and Midlands Sch. of Music, 2006; Hon. FGCM, 2008; Hon. FRSCM, 2015. BBC Music Mag. Award, 2017. *Recreations:* family, reading, walking, travel. *Address:* St John's College, Cambridge CB2 1TP. *T:* (01223) 338683. *E:* an323@cam.ac.uk.

**NETTEL, Caroline Gillian;** *see* Mawhood, C. G.

**NETTEL, Julian Philip;** Director, Julian Nettel Consulting Ltd, since 2009; *b* 23 Oct. 1953; *s* of Leopold and Clare Nettel; *m* 1980, Caroline Gillian Mawhood, *qv*; two *s. Educ:* Univ. of Bristol (BA Hons Philosophy). DipHSM, MHSM 1977. Hosp. Sec., Westminster Hosp., 1983–86; General Manager, Whittington and Royal Northern Hosps, 1986–90; Ops Dir, KCH and Dulwich Hosp., 1990–92; Exec. in Residence, Faculty of Admin, Univ. of Ottawa, 1992–93; Chief Executive: Ealing Hosp. NHS Trust, 1994–99; St Mary's NHS Trust, London, 1999–2007; Barts and The London NHS Trust, 2007–09; Sen. Chief Exec. Associate, 2010–13, Chief Exec. Associate, 2015–, Harvey Nash plc; Sen. Advr, Parthenon Gp, 2010–12; Interim Man. Dir, NHS Inst. for Innovation and Improvement, 2011–12; Interim Chief Executive: Gt Ormond St Hosp. for Children NHS Foundn Trust, 2014; Moorfields Eye Hosp. NHS Foundn Trust, 2015–16. Mem., Expert Reference Gp on Renal Nat. Service Framework, DoH, 2001–03; Chm., NE London Sustainability and Transformation Prog. Bd, 2016–. Trustee, Wimbledon Coll. of Art Trust, 2009–. *Recreations:* painting, cycling, bridge, keeping fit, gardening, golf, jazz. *Address:* 35 Skeena Hill, SW18 5PW. *T:* (020) 8788 2017. *Clubs:* Royal Thames Yacht, Roehampton; Wimbledon Park Golf.

**NETTLETON, Catherine Elizabeth,** CMG 2015; OBE 1999; HM Diplomatic Service; Representative, British Office, Taipei, since 2016; *b* 13 March 1960; *d* of late Kenneth Arthur Nettleton and Olga Nettleton (*née* Musgrave). *Educ:* Exeter Univ. (BA Hons); Manchester Univ. (MA). Inland Revenue, 1982; FCO, 1983; full-time Mandarin lang. training, 1984; Vice Consul, Beijing, 1987–89; Second Sec., FCO, 1989–91; First Sec. (Political/Economic), Mexico City, 1991–95; First Sec., 1995–99, Counsellor, 1999–2000, FCO; Political/Economic Counsellor, Beijing, 2000–03; rcds, 2004; Hd, FCO Services: Presidencies, FCO, 2004–06; Ambassador to Peru, 2006–10; Ambassador to Venezuela, 2010–14; Dir of Protocol, FCO, 2015; Mandarin lang. trng, 2016. *Recreations:* walking, skiing, theatre. *Address:* c/o Foreign and Commonwealth Office, King Charles Street, SW1A 2AH.

**NEUBERGER,** family name of **Baroness Neuberger** and **Baron Neuberger of Abbotsbury.**

**NEUBERGER, Baroness** *cr* 2004 (Life Peer), of Primrose Hill in the London Borough of Camden; **Rabbi Julia Babette Sarah Neuberger,** DBE 2004; Chief Executive, The King's Fund, 1997–2004; Senior Rabbi, West London Synagogue, since 2011; Chair, University College London Hospitals NHS Foundation Trust, since 2019; *b* 27 Feb. 1950; *d* of late Walter and Alice Schwab; *m* 1973, Anthony John Neuberger; one *s* one *d. Educ:* South Hampstead High Sch.; Newnham Coll., Cambridge (BA, MA; Hon. Fellow, 2018); Leo Baeck Coll., London (Rabbinic Dip.). Lectr and Associate Fellow, Leo Baeck Coll., 1979–97; Associate, Newnham Coll., Cambridge, 1983–96; Harkness Fellow, Harvard Univ., 1991–92; Associate Fellow, King's Fund Coll., 1993–97; Bloomberg Prof. of Philanthropy and Public Policy, Divinity Sch., Harvard Univ., 2006. Rabbi, South London Liberal Synagogue, 1977–89; Chm., Rabbinic Conf., Union of Liberal and Progressive Synagogues, 1983–85. Chm., Camden and Islington Community Health Services NHS Trust, 1993–97; Member: Council, N London Hospice Gp, 1984–91; Ethics Adv. Gp, RCN, 1986–93; BMA Ethics Cttee, 1992–94; NHS Health Adv. Service, 1993–97; Council, St George's Hosp. Med. Sch., 1987–93; Chairman: Patients' Assoc., 1988–91; RCN Commn on the Health Service, 1988; Adv. Cttee, UK Clearing House on Health Outcomes, Nuffield Inst., 1992–95; Sainsbury Centre for Mental Health review of training needs of mental health workers; Vice Chair, Ind. Rev. of the Mental Health Act, 2018; Chair: Commn on the Future of Volunteering, 2006–08; Responsible Gambling Strategy Bd, 2008–12; One Housing Gp, 2009–12; Adv. Panel on Judicial Diversity, 2009–10; Prime Minister's Champion for Volunteering, 2007–09; Rev. of Liverpool Care Pathway, 2013–14. Member: Cttee on Standards in Public Life, 2001–04; Interim (formerly Voluntary) Licensing Authority for IVF, 1987–91; Human Fertilization and Embryology Authority, 1990–95; GMC, 1993–2001; MRC, 1995–2000; Exec., Anchor Housing Assoc. and Trust, 1985–87; Exec., NCVO, 1988–89; Exec., Unicef UK, 1989–91; Council, SCF, 1994–96; Bd, Citizenship Foundn, 1989–92; Council, St George's House, Windsor, 1989–94; Council, Runnymede Trust, 1989–97; Library and Information Commn, 1995–97; Bd, Inst. for Jewish Policy Res., 2006–11; a Civil Service Comr, 2001–02; Chair, Van Leer Jerusalem Inst., 2018–; DCMS Mem., Review of Funding of BBC, 1999; Governor, British Inst. of Human Rights, 1989–93; Trustee: Imperial War Mus., 1999–2006; Multifaith Secondary School Trust, 2001–; Booker Prize Foundn, 2002–11; Walter and Liesel Schwab Charitable Trust, 2003–; Urban Village, 2004–11; Jewish Care, 2004–07 and 2009–11; British Council, 2004–07; Liberal Democrats, 2005–08; New Philanthropy Capital, 2008–11; Social Market Foundn, 2012–17; Van Leer Jerusalem Inst., 2012–; Rayne Foundn, 2016–; Dep. Chm., Van Leer Gp Foundn, 2012–. Member: Nat. Cttee, SDP, 1982–88; Policy Cttee, SDP, 1983–85; Convenor, SDP/Liberal Lawyers' Working Party on Legal Services, 1985–87; Mem., Editorial Bd, *Political Qly*, 1987–93. Presenter, Choices, BBC TV, 1986 and 1987. Chancellor, Univ. of Ulster, 1993–2000. Member Council: RHBNC, 1991–93; UCL, 1993–97; Mem. Visiting Cttee, Meml Church, Harvard Univ., 1994–2000; Governor: James Allen's Girls' Sch., 1994–97; Dulwich Coll. Prep. Sch., 1995–97. Judge: Booker Prize, 1994; Orange Prize, 2010. Hon. FCGI 1997; Hon. Fellow, Mansfield Coll., Oxford, 1998. DUniv: Humberside, 1992; Stirling, 1995; Open, 1997; Hon. DSc: Ulster, 1994; Oxford Brookes, 1995; London, 2006; Hon. DLitt: City, 1994; Teesside, 1995; Hon. LLD: Nottingham, 1996; QUB, 2000; Aberdeen 2002; Hon. Dr Sheffield Hallam, 2001; Hon. DD Cambridge, 2015. *Publications:* The Story of Judaism (for children), 1986, 2nd edn 1988; (ed) Days of Decision (4 in series), 1987; Caring for Dying Patients of Different Faiths, 1987, 3rd edn 2004; (ed with John A. White) A Necessary End, 1991; Whatever's Happening to Women?, 1991; Ethics and Healthcare: the role of Research Ethics Committees in the UK, 1992; (ed) The Things That Matter (anthology of women's spiritual poetry), 1993; On Being Jewish, 1995; Dying Well: a guide to enabling a better death, 1999, 2nd edn 2004; (ed with Bill New) Hidden Assets: values and decision-making in the NHS today, 2002; The Moral State We're In, 2005; Not Dead Yet, 2008; Is That All There Is?, 2011; Antisemitism: what it is, what it isn't, why it matters, 2019; contribs to various books on cultural, religious and ethical factors in nursing, reviews for variety of jls and newspapers. *Recreations:* Irish life, opera, setting up the old girls' network, children. *Address:* House of Lords, SW1A 0PW.

**NEUBERGER OF ABBOTSBURY, Baron** *cr* 2007 (Life Peer), of Abbotsbury in the county of Dorset; **David Edmond Neuberger,** Kt 1996; PC 2004; a Justice and President of the Supreme Court of the United Kingdom, 2012–17; arbitrator; *b* 10 Jan. 1948; *s* of Prof. Albert Neuberger, CBE, FRS and Lilian Ida (*née* Dreyfus); *m* 1976, Angela, *d* of Brig. Peter Holdsworth; two *s* one *d. Educ:* Westminster; Christ Church, Oxford (MA; Hon. Student). N. M. Rothschild & Sons, 1970–73; called to the Bar, Lincoln's Inn, 1974, Bencher, 1993; QC 1987; a Recorder, 1990–96; a Judge of the High Ct of Justice, Chancery Div., 1996–2004; Supervisory Chancery Judge, Midland, Wales and Chester, and Western Circuits, 2001–04; a Lord Justice of Appeal, 2004–06; a Lord of Appeal in Ordinary, 2007–09; a non-permanent Judge, Hong Kong Court of Final Appeal, 2010–; Master of the Rolls and Hd of Civil Justice, 2009–12. Chm., Adv. Cttee on Spoliation of Art, 1999–. Chm., Schizophrenia Trust, 2003–14; Trustee: Mental Health Res. UK, 2014–; Prisoners Abroad, 2017–. Gov., Univ. of the Arts, London (formerly London Inst.), 2000–11; Chancellor, Univ. of Law, 2018–. Hon. FRS 2017. GBS 2018. *Address:* One Essex Court, Temple, EC4Y 9AR. *Club:* Garrick.

**NEVILL,** family name of **Marquess of Abergavenny.**

**NEVILL, Amanda Elizabeth,** CBE 2015; Chief Executive Officer (formerly Director), British Film Institute, 2003–20; *b* 21 March 1957; *d* of John Henry Howard King and Jill King (*née* Livett); *m* 1980, Dominic John Nevill (marr. diss. 1986); two *d. Educ:* Bar Convent, York; British Inst., Paris. Rowan Gall., London, 1978–79; Francis Kyle Gall., London, 1979–80; Bath Internat. Fest. Contemporary Art Fair, 1980–84; Adminr, 1985–90, Sec., 1990–94, Royal Photographic Soc.; Head, Nat. Mus. of Photography, Film and TV, 1994–2003. FRSA. Hon. FRPS 1994. Hon. DLit Bradford, 2000. *Address:* British Film Institute, 21 Stephen Street, W1T 1LN. *T:* (020) 7957 8903.

**NEVILLE,** family name of **Baron Braybrooke.**

**NEVILLE, Prof. (Alexander) Munro,** MD; FRCPath; Associate Director (formerly Administrator), and Research Secretary, Ludwig Institute for Cancer Research, New York and London, 1985–2005; *b* 24 March 1935; *s* of Alexander Munro and Georgina Neville; *m* 1961, Anne Margaret Stroyan Black; one *s* one *d. Educ:* Hillhead High Sch.; Univ. of Glasgow (MB ChB 1959; PhD 1965; MD 1969); Harvard Med. Sch.; DSc London, 1985. MRCPath 1969, FRCPath 1981. Med. appts, Glasgow Royal and Victoria Infirmaries, 1960–65; Res. Fellow, Harvard Med. Sch., 1965–67; Sen. Lectr in Pathology, Univ. of Glasgow, 1967–70; Hon. Consultant Pathologist, Royal Marsden Hosp., 1970–85; Prof. of Experimental Pathology, Univ. of London, 1972–85; Dean, Inst. of Cancer Research, 1982–84; Dir, Ludwig Inst. for Cancer Research, London Branch, 1975–85. Visiting Professor: of Pathol., RPMS, 1992–2006; of Med. Oncology, Imperial Coll. London, 2006–10. Hon. Treas., RCPath, 1993–98. *Publications:* The Human Adrenal Cortex, 1982; numerous papers on oncology and pathology in primary jls. *Recreations:* golf, gardening, history. *Address:* 6 Woodlands Park, Tadworth, Surrey KT20 7TL. *T:* (01737) 844113. *E:* munroneville@btinternet.com. *Club:* Banstead Downs.

**NEVILLE, Prof. Anne,** OBE 2017; PhD; FRS 2017; FREng; FRSE; RAEng Chair in Emerging Technologies, since 2009, Professor of Tribology and Surface Engineering, since 2003, and Director, Institute of Functional Surfaces, since 2013, University of Leeds; *b* Dumfries, 21 March 1970; *d* of William Neville and late Doris Neville; *m* 1999, Mark McKelvie; one *d. Educ:* Maxwelltown High Sch., Dumfries; Univ. of Glasgow (BEng 1st Cl. 1992; PhD 1995). FREng 2010. Lectr, 1995–99, Reader, 1999–2002, Prof., 2002–03, Dept of Mech. and Chem. Engrg, Heriot-Watt Univ. Ed., Tribology: Materials, Surfaces and Interfaces, 2007–. Mem., REF 2014 Panel, Gen. Engrg, 2010–13. Consultant, Oilfield Corrosion, Clariant, 2010–. Royal Soc. Wolfson Res. Merit Award Holder, 2012–17. FRSE 2005. Hon. DEng Heriot-Watt, 2017. Donald Julius Groen Prize, 2011, James Clayton Award, 2016, IMechE; Wilbur Deutsch Hunt Meml Award, Soc. of Tribologists and Lubrication Engrs, 2014; Suffrage Sci. Award, MRC, 2015; Leverhulme Medal, Royal Soc., 2016; U. R. Evans Award, Inst. of Corrosion, 2018. Hirsch Lect., Dept of Materials, Univ. of Oxford, 2019. *Recreations:* visiting islands on West coast of Scotland, hillwalking, family. *Address:* School of Mechanical Engineering, Woodhouse Lane, University of Leeds, Leeds LS2 9JT. *T:* (0113) 343 6812, 07789 712417. *E:* a.neville@leeds.ac.uk.

**NEVILLE, Dame Elizabeth (Louise),** DBE 2003; QPM 1996; DL; Chief Constable, Wiltshire Constabulary, 1997–2004; *b* 5 Feb. 1953; *d* of late Prof. Adam Matthew Neville, CBE, TD; *m* 2015, Rory Angus Cameron Carter; one *s* one *d* from former marriage. *Educ:* St Hilda's Coll., Oxford (MA; Hon. Fellow, 2006); University Coll. London (PhD). Metropolitan Police, 1973–86; Thames Valley Police, 1986–91; Asst Chief Constable, Sussex Police, 1991–94; Dep. Chief Constable, Northamptonshire, 1994–97. Non-exec. Dir, Serious Fraud Office, 2004–12. Member: Police Appeals Tribunal, 2004–08; Civil Nuclear Police Authy, 2005–12; Determinations Panel, Pensions Regulator, 2010–; Ind. Complaints Assessor, DVO Gp, subseq. Safety, Service Delivery and Logistics Gp, then Motoring and Freight Service Gp, DfT, 2004–10; Regulatory Decisions Cttee, Financial Conduct Authy, 2013–; Complaints Adjudicator, Assets Recovery Agency, 2004–08; Ind. Adjudicator, Companies House, 2007–; Appeal Officer, Regulator of Community Interest Cos, 2013–; Mem., Code Adjudication Panel (formerly Ind. Appeals Body), Phone-paid Services Authy (formerly PhonePayPlus), 2013–. Non-exec. Mem. Bd, Insolvency Service, 2013–16. Sen. Advr, Olive Gp, 2006–07. Dir, Ajay Shopfit Maintenance Ltd, 2004–08. Trustee: Cumberland Lodge (formerly King George VI and Queen Elizabeth Foundn of St Catharine's), 2001–16 (Vice Chm., 2011–16); Wiltshire Bobby Van, 2005–; Wiltshire Community Foundn, 2011–. Patron, Swindon Sanctuary, 2004–16. Mem., Bd of Govs, Stonar Sch., Wilts, 2005–11 (Vice Chm., 2011). High Sheriff, 2010–11, DL 2011, Wilts. Hon. Fellow, Univ. of Northampton, 2004. Hon. LLD Southampton Solent, 2004. *Recreations:* ski-ing, sailing. *Club:* Reform.

**NEVILLE, Helen Margaret,** PhD; FRSC; Vice President, Research and Development, Procter & Gamble, since 2010; *b* Hong Kong, 6 June 1963; *d* of Ray Coates and Yvonne Coates; *m* 1987, Mark Neville; one *s* two *d. Educ:* Durham Univ. (BSc Chem. 1984); Univ. of Southampton (PhD Organic Chem. 1987). Research and Development, Procter & Gamble: Tech. Brand Manager, Newcastle Tech. Center, 1987–89; Gp/Section Hd, 1989–97, Associate Dir, 1997–99, W Europe, Central and E Europe, Middle East and Africa; Associate Dir, Global Household Cleaning, 1999–2003, Dir, Global Hand Dish Washing, 2003–06, Brussels Innovation Center; Dir, Feminine Care, Schwalbach Tech. Center, 2006–07; Vice Pres., Hair Care, Darmstadt Innovation Center, 2007–10. Mem., EPSRC, 2013–18. Mem. Council, RSC, 2013–18. *Recreations:* travel, food and wine, fitness. *E:* neville.hm@pg.com.

**NEVILLE, (John) Oliver,** MA, PhD; Principal, Royal Academy of Dramatic Art, 1984–93; *b* 14 Aug. 1929; *s* of Frederick and Ethel Neville; *m* 1st, 1952, Shirley Hall; one *s* one *d*; 2nd, 1964, Pat Heywood. *Educ:* Price's Sch., Fareham; King's Coll., Cambridge (Le Bas Student; BA Eng. Lit., MA, PhD). After National Service, engaged in following with ultimate aim of becoming a theatre director: studied theatre design under Reginald Leefe, 1949–51; joined Old Vic Co., walking on in Tyrone Guthrie's Tamburlaine, with Donald Wolfit, 1951; studied singing with Clive Carey and Frank Titterton; seasons of rep. at York, Scarborough, Worthing, Bristol, Birmingham and Manchester, 1952–58; re-joined Old Vic Co., 1958 (roles included Warwick in Henry VI Trilogy and Claudius in Hamlet); toured America, Poland, Russia, India, Pakistan, Ceylon, with Old Vic and Bristol Old Vic, as stage dir, actor and dir; Associate Dir, Old Vic Co., 1960–62 (directed Macbeth and The Tempest); Director: Library Theatre, Manchester, 1963–66; Arts Theatre, Ipswich, 1966–69; Mature Student, Cambridge, 1969–76 (PhD on Ben Jonson's Masques and Poetry); Caroline Spurgeon Res. Fellow, Bedford Coll., London, 1977–79; Sen. Lectr in Drama, Univ. of Bristol, 1979–84. *Recreations:* mediaeval church architecture and stained-glass, gardening. *Address:* c/o Peters, Fraser & Dunlop, 55 New Oxford Street, WC1A 1BS.

NEVILLE, Munro; *see* Neville, A. M.

NEVILLE, Oliver; *see* Neville, J. O.

NEVILLE, Air Vice-Marshal Patrick, CB 1988; OBE 1976; AFC 1960; Chief of Air Staff, Royal New Zealand Air Force, 1986–89, retired; *b* 23 Sept. 1932; *s* of Patrick Joseph Neville and Helena Neville; *m* 1954, Barbara Howell; one *s* one *d*. *Educ:* Purbrook Park County High Sch. (SchCert). Commnd 1951; Navigator: RAF, 1951–55; RNZAF, 1955; CO No 14 Sqdn RNZAF, 1966–69; Base Comdr, RNZAF Base Ohakea, NZ, 1969–70; Hon. ADC to Gov. Gen., 1972; Sen. ASO, Air HQ, ANZUK Force Singapore; later, Dep. Comdr NZ Force SE Asia in Singapore, 1973–75; RNZAF Air Staff, 1975–77; Base Comdr, RNZAF Base Auckland, 1978–79; AOC RNZAF Support Gp, 1980–82; Asst CDS for Operations and Plans, Defence HQ, Wellington, 1982–83; Hd of NZ Defence Liaison Staff, London, and Defence Attaché, FRG, 1984–86. Gp Captain 1973, Air Cdre 1980, Air Vice-Marshal 1986. FNZIM; FRAeS. *Address:* 12 Mark Place, Lynmore, Rotorua 3010, New Zealand. *T:* (7) 3459650.

NEVILLE, Richard; Head of Newspapers, DC Thomson Media, since 2019 (Editor-in-Chief, Morning Newspapers, 2017–19); *b* Singapore, 2 March 1968; *s* of Brian Neville and Elspeth Neville (*née* Riddell); *m* 1997, Morag Stewart; two *s*. *Educ:* Balfron High Sch.; Napier Univ. (HND Journalism Studies). Reporter, Edinburgh Evening News, 1989–93; Asst Editor, Evening Press, York, 1993–95; reporter, Daily Record, 1995–96; News Editor, 1996–99, Dep. Editor, 1999–2000, The Scotsman; Dep. Editor, 2000–01, Editor, 2002–03, Business a.m.; Dep. Editor, Press and Journal, 2003–11; Editor, The Courier, 2011–17. *Recreations:* hillwalking, auctions, music, whisky. *Address:* D.C. Thomson & Co. Ltd, 2 Albert Square, Dundee DD1 9QJ. *T:* (01382) 575270. *E:* rneville@dctmedia.co.uk.

NEVILLE-JONES, Baroness *cr* 2007 (Life Peer), of Hutton Roof in the County of Cumbria; (Lilian) Pauline Neville-Jones, DCMG 1996 (CMG 1987); PC 2010; Prime Minister's Special Representative to Business on Cyber Security, 2011–14; *b* 2 Nov. 1939; *d* of Roland Neville-Jones and Dr Cecilia Emily Millicent Winn. *Educ:* Leeds Girls' High Sch.; Lady Margaret Hall, Oxford (BA Hons Mod. History). Harkness Fellow of Commonwealth Fund, USA, 1961–63; HM Diplomatic Service, 1963–96: Third Sec., Salisbury, Rhodesia, 1964–65; Third, later Second Sec., Singapore, 1965–68; FCO, 1968–71; First Sec., Washington, 1971–75; FCO, 1975–77; Mem. Cabinet, later Chef de Cabinet to Christopher Tugendhat, European Comr for Budget, Financial Control, Financial Instns and Taxation, 1977–82; Vis. Fellow, RIIA, and Inst. français des relations internationales, 1982–83; Head of Planning Staff, FCO, 1983–87; Minister (Econ.), 1987–88, Minister, 1988–91, Bonn; Dep. Sec., Cabinet Office (on secondment), 1991–94; Chm., Jt Intelligence Cttee, Cabinet Office, 1993–94; Political Dir and Dep. Under-Sec. of State, FCO, 1994–96; Sen. Advr to High Rep. for Bosnia (on secondment), 1996. Man. Dir, and Hd of Global Business Strategy, NatWest Markets, 1996–98; Vice Chm., Hawkpoint Partners Ltd, 1998–2000; Chm., QinetiQ Group plc, 2002–05. Shadow Security Minister and Nat. Security Advr to Leader of the Opposition, 2007–10; Minister of State (Minister for Security), Home Office, 2010–11. Chairman: Information Assurance Adv. Council, 2002–07; Adv. Panel to Bank of England on cyber security, 2015–18. Member: UKRI-EPSRC (formerly EPSRC), 2013–19; Foundn for Sci. and Technol., 2015–; Sci. and Technol. Cttee, H of L, 2015–. A Gov., BBC, 1998–2004. Member, Council: Oxford Univ., 2004–06; Lancaster Univ., 2014–; Mem. Adv. Council, City Univ., 2006–09. FRSA 1986. DUniv Open, 1998; Hon. DSc (Econ) London, 1999; Hon. DSc City, 2007. Chevalier, Légion d'Honneur, 2007. *Recreations:* antiques, cooking, gardening. *Address:* House of Lords, SW1A 0PW. *E:* nevillejonesp@parliament.uk.

NEVILLE-ROLFE, Baroness *cr* 2013 (Life Peer), of Chilmark in the County of Wiltshire; Lucy Jeanne Neville-Rolfe, DBE 2012; CMG 2005; FCIS; *b* 2 Jan. 1953; *d* of late Edmund and Margaret Neville-Rolfe; *m* Sir Richard John Packer, *qv*; four *s*. *Educ:* Somerville Coll., Oxford (BA PPE; MA; Hon. Fellow, 2003). FCIS 2010. Joined MAFF, 1973; Pvte Sec. to Minister of Agric., Fisheries and Food, 1977–79; EC Sheepmeat and Milk, 1979–86; Land Use, 1986–88; Food Safety Act, 1988–90; Head of Personnel, 1990–92; Mem., Prime Minister's Policy Unit, 1992–94; Under Sec., 1994; Dir, Deregulation Unit, DTI, then Better Regulation Unit, Cabinet Office, 1995–97; Tesco plc: Gp Dir of Corporate Affairs, 1997–2006, and Company Sec., 2003–06; Exec. Dir, Corporate and Legal Affairs, 2006–13. Non-executive Director: John Laing Construction, 1991–92; Bd of Mgt, FCO, 2000–05; Carbon Trust, 2008–13; ITV plc, 2010–14; Capita, 2017–; Health Data Res. UK, 2018–; Secure Trust Bank plc, 2018–; Thomson Reuters Founders Share Co., 2019–; Chm., Dobbies Garden Centres plc, 2007–11. Chair, Assured Food Standards, 2017–. Member: Dep. Prime Minister's Local Govt Funding Cttee, 2003–04; ESRC Panel on Cultures of Consumption, 2003–07; Corporate Leaders Gp on Climate Change, 2005–; Foresight Obesity Project, 2005–07; China Britain Business Council, 2005–13; UK India Business Council, 2008–13; Efficiency Bd, Cabinet Office, 2010–14; Strategic Adv. Gp, UKTI, 2011–13. Parly Under-Sec. of State, BIS, 2014–16, DCMS, 2015–16; Minister of State (Minister for Energy and Intellectual Property), BEIS, 2016; Commercial Sec. (Minister of State), HM Treasury, 2016–17. Member: Bd of Mgt, British Retail Consortium, 1998–2012 (Dep. Chair, 2003–12); Econs and Eur. Cttees, CBI, 1998–2012; UNICE Task Force on Enlargement, 1999–2004. Pres., EuroCommerce, 2012–15 (Vice Pres., 1998–2008). Gov., London Business Sch., 2011–. *Recreations:* cricket, racing, gardening, art, architecture, theatre. *Address:* House of Lords, SW1A 0PW.

*See also* M. T. Neville-Rolfe.

NEVILLE-ROLFE, Marianne Teresa, CB 2000; Director, P&M Hill Ltd (formerly P&M Hill Consultants Ltd), since 2004; *b* 9 Oct. 1944; *d* of late Edmund Neville-Rolfe and Margaret (*née* Evans); *m* 1st, 1972, David William John Blake (marr. diss. 1992); 2nd, 2001, Peter Andrew Hill. *Educ:* St Mary's Convent, Shaftesbury; Lady Margaret Hall, Oxford (BA). CBI, 1965–73 (Head, Brussels Office, 1971–72); Principal, DTI, 1973, Asst Sec., 1982, Under Sec., Internal European Policy Div., 1987; Chief Exec., CS Coll., and Dir, Top Management Prog., OMCS, then OPSS, Cabinet Office, 1990–94; Regl Dir, Govt Office for NW, 1994–99; Chief Exec., New East Manchester Ltd, 2000; Exec. Dir, SEEDA, 2001–04. Mem., ESRC, 2000–03. Chm., Bd of Govs, Univ. of Bolton, 2008–13; Mem., Bd of Govs, Univ. of Middx, 2014–. *Recreations:* travel, ski-ing, cycling, opera. *Address:* Angle Croft, Somerford Booths, Congleton, Cheshire CW12 2JU.

*See also* Baroness Neville-Rolfe.

NEVIN, Michael Patrick; HM Diplomatic Service; Ambassador to Iceland, since 2016; *b* 13 Jan. 1969; *m* 1997, Sawako; three *c*. Entered FCO, 1993; Asst Desk Officer, China and Taiwan, FCO, 1993–95; Riyadh, 1996; UK Mission to UN, NY, 1996; Osaka, 1996–99; Second Sec. (Chancery), Lilongwe, 1999–2003; FCO, 2003; Dep. High Comr and Counsellor (Political), Nairobi, 2008–12; High Comr to Malawi, 2012–16. *Address:* c/o Foreign and Commonwealth Office, King Charles Street, SW1A 2AH.

NEW, Maj.-Gen. Sir Laurence (Anthony Wallis), Kt 1990; CB 1986; CBE 1980; Lieutenant Governor and Captain General of the Isle of Man, and President of the Tynwald Court, 1985–90; International President, Association of Military Christian Fellowships, 1991–2002; *b* 25 Feb. 1932; *s* of Lt-Col S. W. New, MBE and Mrs C. M. New; *m* 1956, Anna Doreen Verity (CStJ, LISTD); two *s* two *d*. *Educ:* King William's College, Isle of Man. RMA Sandhurst, 1950–52; commissioned, RTR, 1952; service in Hong Kong, Germany, Malaya, Borneo; CO 4 RTR, 1971–73; Bde Major, 20th Armd Bde, 1969–70; Sec., Defence Policy Staff, 1970–71; Defence and Military Attaché, Tel Aviv, 1974–77; Col GS, MoD, 1977–79; Brig. GS (Intelligence), 1981–82; COS, Defence Intelligence Centre, Falklands Campaign, 1982; ACGS (Op. Reqs), 1983–84; ACDS (Land Systems), MoD, 1984–85; graduate Staff Coll., JSSC, RCDS. Col Comdt, RTR, 1986–93; Vice Pres., TA&VRA, 1985–90; Hon. Col I of M ACF, 1998–2002. Gen. Sec., Officers' Pensions Soc., 1990–95; Campaign Dir, War and Service Widows Parly Pensions Campaign, 1994–95. Consultant, Lagan Gp of Cos, 1998–2010; Director: Charles Brand (IOM) Ltd, 1999–2006; Lagan Construction (IOM) Ltd, 2006–10. Lectr, Sir John Cass Business Sch., City of London (formerly City Univ. Business Sch.), 1992–2002; Instructor, 2003–05, Team Dir, 2005–13, Pointman Leadership Inst.; Dir, Pointman Leadership Ltd UK, 2009–13. Licensed Reader, C of E, 1974–2013; Local Preacher, Methodist Church, IOM Dist, 2004–10; Church Warden, St Peter upon Cornhill, 1986–95; Pres., Soldiers' and Airmen's Scripture Readers Assoc., 1985–99; Vice Pres., Officers' Christian Union, 1988–93; Chm. Mgt Team, St Augustine's Ind. Anglican Church, 2016–. President: Manx Music Fest., 1985–90; Mananan Internat. Fest. of Music and the Arts, 1987–; Manx Nat. Youth Band, 1995–; Mannin Art Gp, 1996–2007; Friends of the Gaiety Theatre, 1996–2006. County Pres., St John Ambulance Brigade and Assoc., 1985–90, and 1999–2007; Patron: I of M Red Cross, 1985–90; Burma Star Assoc. (I of M), 1995–; Pres., Normandy Veterans Assoc. (I of M), 1997–; Vice-Pres., 4/7th RTR Old Comrades, 1997–2010. Pres., Fishermen's Mission, 1998–2007; Vice Patron, Royal Nat. Mission to Deep Sea Fishermen, 1999–; Patron: Choice of Living in Community Homes, 1999–2013; Friends of Chernobyl's Children, 1999–; Ramsey Lifeboat, 1999–. Chairman: Bishop Barrow's Trustees, 1985–90; Royal Jubilee and Prince's Trust (I of M), 1986–90; Pres., White House School, Wokingham, 1985–. Freeman, City of London, 1985. Church Warden, St Matthew's Church, Douglas, 2010–13. CCMI 2002 (FBIM 1979; CBIM 1986). KStJ 1986. Internat. Centurion Award, Washington, 2000. *Recreations:* family, music, water colour painting, editor of regimental website (www.4and7royaltankregiment.com). *Address:* The Granary, Ballaquark Farm, Laxey, Isle of Man IM4 7PH. *E:* generalnew@manx.net.

NEW, Terence Michael John; sculptor; President, Royal British Society of Sculptors, 2012–15; *b* Prestatyn, 6 Oct. 1945; *s* of John and Elizabeth New; *m* 1st; three *d*; 2nd, 2005, Vicki Reynolds (*d* 2008); 3rd, 2012, Diane Shiach. *Educ:* Sutton East Jun. Art Sch.; Wimbledon Sch. of Art (Foundn 1965); Hornsey Coll. of Art (DipAD 1968); Royal Coll. of Art (MA Sculpture 1971). Principal, Lectr and Dir of Sculpture, Inst. of Technol., WA, 1978–80 (Mem., Art Acquisition Panel and Mem. cttee developing MA course); sculpting and exhibiting, 1980–86; Hd of Sculpture, 1986–2001, Hd of Fine Art, 2001–10, Royal Acad. Schs, Royal Acad.; pt-time teaching posts, Birmingham, Coventry, Cardiff, Exeter, RCA, Belfast and Reading, 1986–93. External Examiner, BA (Hons): Wolverhampton Poly., 1986–89; Central St Martins Sch. of Art and Design, 1987–90; Exeter Coll. of Art, SW Poly., 1988–90; John Moores Univ., 1991–93; Ext. Advr to develop MA Course in Sculpture, Marseille Art Coll., 1989–90; Member, External Advisory Panel: on new MA in Fine Art, City and Guilds Art Sch., 2000; on ratification of BA Fine Art at Chelsea Coll. of Arts, Univ. of the Arts London, 2002; Advr, design of workshops, Coll. of Fine Arts, Univ. of Sharjah, 2002. Solo exhibitions include: Serpentine Gall., 1974; Galerie Dusseldorf, WA, 1980; Plymouth Mus. and Art Gall., 1991; Dover Street Arts Club (retrospective), 2007; Martini Arts, Turin, 2008; Fitzwilliam Mus., Cambridge, 2009; work in public collections: Sharjah Mus., UAE; Marie Curie Cancer Care, Glasgow and Solihull; Art Gall. of WA; Merck, Sharp and Dohme UK; Visual Arts Bd of Australia; Fremantle Art Gall., WA; commissions include: Allure of the Seas, Marie Curie Cancer Care; Day, Leigh and Co. Mem., Public Art Adv. Panel, Westminster Council, 1995–2010. Patron, Marie Curie. Hon. Mem., Chopin Soc. UK. Jack Goldhill Award for Sculpture, RA Summer Show, 1992, 2002. *Recreations:* reading, travelling, music, swimming, chess, horticulture. *Address:* 59 Hans Road, SW3 1RN. *T:* (020) 7823 8392. *E:* tmjnew@gmail.com. *Clubs:* Chelsea Arts, Arts, Polish Hearth.

NEW SOUTH WALES, Metropolitan of; *see* Sydney, Archbishop of.

NEWALL, family name of Baron Newall.

NEWALL, 2nd Baron *cr* 1946; Francis Storer Eaton Newall; DL; former company director and chairman of several companies; Chairman, British Greyhound Racing Board, 1985–97; *b* 23 June 1930; *o s* of 1st Baron (Marshal of the RAF Lord) Newall, GCB, OM, GCMG, CBE, AM; *S* father, 1963; *m* 1956, Pamela Elizabeth, *e d* of E. H. L. Rowcliffe, Pinkney Park, Malmesbury, Wilts; two *s* one *d*. *Educ:* Eton College; RMA Sandhurst. Commissioned into 11th Hussars (Prince Albert's Own), 1950; served in: Germany, 1950–53; Malaya, 1953–55; on staff of GHQ FarELF, Singapore, 1955–56; Adjt Royal Gloucestershire Hussars, 1956–58; retired 1961. Introduced Farriers Registration Acts and Betting Gaming and Lotteries Amendment Acts (Greyhound Racing) in House of Lords. Cons. Whip and front bench spokesman, 1976–79; Founder Mem., House of Lords all party Defence Study Group; official visits to NATO, SHAPE, Norway, Morocco, Bonn, Cyprus, BAOR, Qatar, Oman, Bahrain and Romania; Deleg. to Council of Europe and WEU, 1983–97. Mem., Select Cttee on Laboratory Animals Protection Bill. Former Pres., Soc. for Protection of Animals Abroad. Chm., British Moroccan Soc., 2000–05. Mem., Merchant Taylors' Co. (Master, 1985–86). DL Greater London, 1988. *Recreations:* sport, travel, meeting people. *Heir: s* Hon. Richard Hugh Eaton Newall [*b* 19 Feb. 1961; *m* 1st, 1996, Keira (marr. diss. 2010), *d* of Robert Glen; two *d*; 2nd, 2011, Samantha Durchslag; two *s*]. *Address:* Wotton Underwood, Aylesbury, Bucks HP18 0RZ. *Club:* Cavalry and Guards.

NEWALL, Peter; HM Diplomatic Service, retired; Ambassador to Senegal and, concurrently, to Mali, Guinea-Bissau and Cape Verde, 2004–07; *b* 20 March 1947; *s* of Bobbie and Clio Newall; *m* 1969, Marina (*née* McHugh); one *s* two *d*. *Educ:* Kent Coll., Canterbury. Joined HM Diplomatic Service, 1966; Attaché, Tehran, 1970–72; Entry Clearance Officer, New Delhi, 1972–75; Finance Dept, FCO, 1975–79; 2nd Sec. (Commercial), Belgrade, 1979–82; 1st Sec. (Commercial), Kuwait, 1982–85; Nuclear Energy Dept, FCO, 1985–89; HM Consul, Marseilles, 1989–90; Jt Mgt Officer, Geneva, 1990–95; Counter Terrorism Policy Dept, FCO, 1995–97; Non-Proliferation Dept, FCO, 1997–99; Jt Mgt Officer, Brussels, 1999–2004. Occasional election observer, EU and OSCE, 2007–11. *Recreations:* golf, ski-ing, cinema, fixing things, cycling, swimming.

**NEWARK, Archdeacon of;** see Picken, Ven. D. A.

**NEWBERRY, Patrick John,** FCA; Commissioner, Historic England, since 2018; *b* Filton, Glos, 14 Oct. 1956; *s* of Thomas Newberry and Jean Newberry (*née* Knill); *m* 1980, Jane Ware; three *s* one *d*. *Educ:* Bristol Cathedral Sch.; Univ. of Southampton (BSc Soc. Sci.). FCA 1980. Coopers and Lybrand, later PricewaterhouseCoopers, 1977–2013: Partner, 1988–2013; Global Leader, Insce Consulting, 1998–2001; Hd, UK Financial Services Consulting, and Mem., Consulting Bd, 2001–03; UK Financial Services Adv. Leader, 2003–08; Mem., Supervisory Bd, 2008–13; Hd, Private Sector Consulting, 2008–09; Chm., Financial Services Regulatory Practice, 2009–12; Commercial Man. Partner, Consulting, 2010–12. Chm., Cornish Bldgs Gp, 2019– (Vice Chm., 2016–19); non-executive Director: Unipart Expert Practices, 2013–17 (Advr, 2017–); Paragon Banking Gp plc, 2015–18; Shepherd & Wedderburn LLP, 2016–. Pres., Mgt Consultancies Assoc., 2010–11. Trustee, Georgian Gp, 2018–. Gov., Cornwall Coll. Gp, 2017–18; Mem. Adv. Bd, Duchy & Bicton Coll., 2018–. FRSA 1998. *Publications:* (contrib.) Celebrating Pevsner, 2017. *Recreations:* sailing, architectural history, Cornish history. *Address:* Pendragon House, Stoke Climsland, Cornwall PL17 8NZ. *T:* (01579) 370119. *E:* patricknewberry3@gmail.com. *Club:* Salcombe Yacht.

**NEWBERRY, Raymond Scudamore,** OBE 1989; Director, Brazil, British Council, 1990–93; *b* 8 Feb. 1935; *s* of late James Henry Newberry and Doris Ada Newberry; *m* 1967, Angelina Nance (*d* 2007); one *s* one *d*. *Educ:* Bristol Grammar Sch.; Selwyn Coll., Cambridge (BA); Univ. of Leeds (DipESL); Univ. of Bristol (DipEd). National Service, 1953–55. Lectr, Coll. of Arts, Baghdad Univ., 1959–62; British Council posts, 1962–94: Lectr, Teheran, 1963–64; Educn Officer, Calcutta, 1964–66; Head of English Dept, Advanced Teacher Trng Coll., Winneba, Ghana, 1966–70; Advr on English Lang., Min. of Educn, Singapore, 1970–74; Rep., Colombia, 1975–80; Director: North and Latin American Dept, 1980–82; America and Pacific Dept, 1982–84; Rep., Australia, 1984–89. Consultant, London Film Commn, 1996–99. Hon. Mem., Soc. of Bookbinders, 2011. *Recreation:* bookbinding. *Address:* Silverwood, Wildwood Close, Woking, Surrey GU22 8PL. *T:* (01932) 341826.

**NEWBERY, Prof. David Michael Garrood,** CBE 2012; FBA 1991; Professor of Economics, University of Cambridge, 1988–2010, now Emeritus; Fellow, Churchill College, Cambridge, since 1966; *b* 1 June 1943; *s* of late Alan James Garrood Newbery, OBE, RN and Betty Amelia Newbery; *m* 1975, Dr Terri Eve Apter; two *d*. *Educ:* Portsmouth Grammar Sch.; Trinity Coll., Cambridge (BA, MA); PhD 1976, ScD 2001, Cantab. Economist, Treasury, Tanzania, 1965–66; Cambridge University: Asst Lectr, 1966–71; Lectr, 1971–86; Reader, 1986–88; Prof. of Applied Econs, 2003–10; Dir, Dept of Applied Econs, 1988–2003; Res. Dir, Electricity Policy Res. Gp, 2005–. Associate Prof., Stanford Univ., 1976–77; Div. Chief, World Bank, Washington, 1981–83; Fellow, Centre for Economic Policy Res., 1984–; Vis. Prof., Princeton, 1985; Vis. Scholar, IMF, 1987; Ford Vis. Prof., Univ. of California, Berkeley, 1987–88; Sen. Res. Fellow, Inst. for Policy Reform, Washington, DC, 1990–96; Res. Fellow, Control and Power Res. Gp, Imperial Coll. London, 2011–15. Member: Competition (formerly Monopolies and Mergers) Commn, 1996–2003; Single Electricity Mkt Cttee, Ire., 2012–. President: European Economic Assoc., 1996 (Vice-Pres., 1994); Internat. Assoc. for Energy Economics, 2013; Mem. Council, REconS, 1984–89; Fellow, Econometric Soc., 1989 (Frisch Medal, 1990). Bd Mem., Review of Economic Studies, 1968–79; Associate Editor: Economic Jl, 1977–2000; European Economic Review, 1988–93. *Publications:* Project Appraisal in Practice, 1976; (with J. E. Stiglitz) The Theory of Commodity Price Stabilization, 1981; (with N. H. Stern) The Theory of Taxation for Developing Countries, 1987; (with I. P. Székely) Hungary: an economy in transition, 1992; Tax and Benefit Reform in Central and Eastern Europe, 1995; Privatization, Restructuring and Regulation of Network Utilities, 2000; articles in learned jls. *Recreation:* walking. *Address:* 9 Huntingdon Road, Cambridge CB3 0HH. *T:* (01223) 360216.

**NEWBERY, Freya Patricia; Her Honour Judge Newbery;** a Circuit Judge, since 2014; *b* Rustington, 1964; *d* of David Newbery and Brit Holmsen; *m* 1990, Tim Wright; one *s* one *d*. *Educ:* Felpham Comprehensive Sch.; New Hall, Cambridge (BA 1985). Called to the Bar, Middle Temple, 1986. *E:* freyanewbery@gmail.com.

**NEWBIGGING, Sir David (Kennedy),** Kt 2011; OBE 1982; Chairman: Kennedy Financial Services Ltd, since 1984; Loadpoint Ltd, since 2017; Loadpoint Bearings Ltd, since 2017; *b* 19 Jan. 1934; *s* of late David Locke Newbigging, CBE, MC and Bar, and Lucy Margaret; *m* 1968, Carolyn Susan (*née* Band); one *s* two *d*. *Educ:* in Canada; Oundle Sch., Northants. Joined Jardine, Matheson & Co. Ltd, Hong Kong, 1954; Dir, 1967; Man. Dir, 1970; Chm. and Sen. Man. Dir, 1975–83; Chairman: Hongkong & Kowloon Wharf & Godown Co. Ltd, 1970–80; Jardine Matheson & Co. Ltd, 1975–83; Jardine Fleming Holdings Ltd, 1975–83; Hongkong Land Co. Ltd, 1975–83; Hongkong Electric Holdings Ltd, 1982–83 (Dir, 1975–83); Rentokil Gp plc, 1987–94 (Dir, 1986–94); Redfearn PLC, 1988; NM UK Ltd, 1990–93; Ivory & Sime plc, 1992–95 (Dir, 1987–95); Maritime Transport Services Ltd, 1993–95; Faupel plc (formerly Faupel Trading Gp plc), 1994–2005 (Dir, 1989–2005); Equitas Holdings Ltd, 1995–98; Thistle Hotels plc, 1999–2003; Friends Provident Life Office, subseq. plc, 1998–2005 (Dir, 1993–2005; Dep. Chm., 1996–98); Talbot Hldgs Ltd, 2003–07; Synesis Life Ltd, 2006–08; Deputy Chairman: Provincial Gp plc, 1985–91 (Dir, 1984–91); Benchmark Gp plc, 1996–2004; Director: Hongkong & Shanghai Banking Corp., 1975–83; Hong Kong Telephone Co., 1975–83; Safmarine and Rennies Holdings Ltd (formerly Rennies Consolidated Holdings), 1975–85; Provincial Insurance, 1984–86; Provincial Life Insurance Co., 1984–86; CIN Management, 1985–87; PACCAR (UK) Ltd, 1986–97; Internat. Financial Markets Trading Ltd, 1986–93; United Meridian Corp., USA, 1987–98; Wah Kwong Shipping Hldgs Ltd (Hong Kong), 1992–99; Market Bd, Corp. of Lloyd's, 1993–95; Merrill Lynch & Co. Inc., USA, 1997–2007; Ocean Energy Inc., USA, 1998–2003; PACCAR Inc., USA, 1999–2006; Wah Kwong Maritime Transport Hldgs Ltd, Hong Kong, 2008–; Chm., Academic Partnerships Internat. (London) and Dir, Academic Partnerships (Dallas), 2012–15. Dir, British Coal Corp. (formerly NCB), 1984–87. Mem., Internat. Council, Morgan Guaranty Trust Co. of NY, 1977–85; Mem. Supervisory Bd, DAF Trucks NV, 1997–2000. Chairman, Council of Trustees: Mission to Seafarers (formerly Missions to Seamen), 1993–2006; Cancer Research UK, 2004–10 (Dep. Chm., 2002–04). Chm. of Trustees, Wilts Community Foundn, 1991–97; Trustee, UK Trust for Nature Conservation in Nepal (formerly King Mahendra UK Trust for Nature Conservation), 1988–. Member: Hong Kong Exec. Council, 1980–84; Hong Kong Legislative Council, 1978–82. Chairman: Hong Kong Tourist Assoc., 1977–82; Hong Kong Gen. Chamber of Commerce, 1980–82; Steward, Royal Hong Kong Jockey Club, 1975–84. JP (unofficial) Hong Kong, 1971; DL Wilts, 1993–2009; High Sheriff, Wilts, 2003–04. *Recreations:* most outdoor sports; Chinese art. *Address:* 119 Old Church Street, SW3 6EA. *T:* (020) 7352 1558. *Clubs:* Boodle's; Hong Kong (Hong Kong); Bohemian (San Francisco).

**NEWBIGIN, John Lesslie,** OBE 2015; cultural entrepreneur; consultant, since 2005; *b* Liverpool, 13 Oct. 1947; *s* of Rt Rev. James Edward Lesslie Newbigin and Helen Stewart Newbigin (*née* Henderson); *m* 1978, Juliet Grimshaw (marr. diss. 1994); two *d*. *Educ:* Queens' Coll., Cambridge (BA Hons 1970). Youth worker, ILEA, 1972–73; writer in residence, Common Stock Th., 1973–74; community worker, Avenues Unlimited, 1975–81; Manager, Brixton Young Families Housing Aid Assoc., 1981–84; Dir, London Youth Fest., 1984–85; Policy Advr, Office of the Leader of the Opposition, 1986–92; Asst to Chm., Enigma Prodns, 1992–97; Special Advr, DCMS, 1997–2000; Hd, Corporate Relns, Channel 4 TV, 2000–05. Vis. Prof., UEL, 2006–; Adjunct Prof., Univ. of Technol., Sydney, 2009–; Hon. Professor: Hong Kong Univ., 2015–; Goldsmiths, Univ. of London, 2018–. Member, Board: Keen Students Sch., 2000–12; First Light Movies Ltd, 2004–14; Cultural Industries Develt Agency, 2005–11; Mediabox, 2006–11; Becta, 2008–11; ThreeJohnsandShelagh Ltd, 2010–; London Economic Action Partnership, 2017–; Chairman: CAV Networks Ltd, 2011–18; Counterculture Partnership LLP, 2017–. Member, Advisory Board: BT Connected Earth, 2003–12; John Smith Meml Trust, 2006–10; Aluna, 2007–10; Chm., Arts and Creative Industries Adv. Gp, British Council, 2016–; Mem., London Mayor's Cultural Leadership Bd, 2017–. Chm. of Trustees, Culture 24, 2006–14; Chm., Creative England (formerly Screen England), 2010–18; Trustee: Whitechapel Art Gall., 2002–10; Theatre Royal Stratford East, 2004–09; Big Art Proj., 2007–09; Bd Dir, Battersea Arts Centre, 2013–18. *Recreations:* walking, talking, cycling, recycling. *Address:* Rock House, 14 Westfield Road, Wheatley, Oxford OX33 1NG. *T:* 07909 907739. *E:* john@newbigin.co.uk.

**NEWBOLD, Yvette Monica, (Yve);** Chair, Ethical Trading Initiative, 2000–05; *b* 6 July 1940; *d* of late Thomas Peter Radcliffe and of Anne Gertrude Radcliffe (*née* Flynn); *m* 1958, Anthony Patrick Newbold; three *s* one *d*. *Educ:* Blessed Sacrament Convent, Brighton; LLB London; Solicitor, 1970. Staff Counsel: IBM, 1968–71; Rank Xerox, 1972–79; Internat. Counsel, Xerox (USA), 1979–82; European Counsel, Walt Disney Productions, 1983–85; Co. Sec., Hanson, 1986–95; Chief Exec., Pro-Ned, 1995–97; Partner, Heidrick & Struggles, 1998–2000. Non-executive Director: BT, 1991–97; Coutts & Co., 1994–98. Chair, Inst. for Global Ethics, 2005–08 (Mem., Adv. Bd, 1997–2004); Member: Royal Commn on Criminal Justice, 1991–93; Sen. Salaries Rev. Body, 1994–97; BT Social Report Panel, 2002–05; Adv. Bd, FTSE4Good, 2003–13. Governor, London Business Sch., 1990–97.

**NEWBOROUGH,** 8th Baron *cr* 1776 (Ire.), of Bodvean; **Robert Vaughan Wynn;** Bt 1742, FRAgS; landowner and organic farmer; Chairman and Director: Rhug Ltd, since 1992; Rhug Energy Ltd, since 1992; Rhug Organic and Natural Ltd, since 2019; *b* 11 Aug. 1949; *o s* of 7th Baron Newborough, DSC and Rosamund Lavington Wynn (*née* Barbour); *S* father, 1998; *m* 1st, 1981, Sheila Christine Massey (marr. diss. 1988); one *d*; 2nd, 1988, Susan Elizabeth Hall (*née* Lloyd); one step *d*. *Educ:* Milton Abbey. Chm. and Man. Dir, Wynn Electronics, 1982–89; Dir, Country Wide Communications, 1992–. Welsh Exporter of Year, True Taste Wales, 2012; Farmer of Year, 2013, Diversification Farmer of Year, 2013, Farmers Weekly; Regl Butcher of Year, Countryside Alliance, 2013; Footprint Award, Nestlé, 2016. *Recreations:* ski-ing, sailing, golf, tennis. *Heir:* cousin Antony Charles Vaughan Wynn [*b* 2 May 1949; *m* 1st, 1973, Jane Slane Sloan (*née* Thompson) (marr. diss. 1986); 2nd, 1996, Mrs Victoria Jane Domenge, *e d* of Lt-Gen. Sir Derek Boorman, *qv*]. *Address:* Rhug Hall, Corwen, Denbighshire LL22 0EH.

**NEWBURGH,** 12th Earl of, *cr* 1660 (Scot.); **Principe Don Filippo Giambattista Francesco Aldo Maria Rospigliosi;** Viscount Kynnaird, Baron Levingston of Flacraig, 1660; 11th Prince Rospigliosi (Holy Roman Empire), 11th Duke of Zagarolo, 14th Prince of Castiglione, Marquis of Giuliana, Count of Chiusa, Baron of La Miraglia and Valcorrente, Lord of Aidone, Burgio, Contessa and Trappeto, and Conscript Roman Noble, Patrician of Venice, Genoa, Pistoia, Ravenna and Ferrara; *b* 4 July 1942; *s* of 11th Earl of Newburgh and of Donna Giulia, *d* of Don Guido Carlo dei Duchi Visconti di Mondrone, Count of Lonate Pozzolo; *S* father, 1986; *m* 1972, Baronessa Donna Luisa, *d* of Count Annibale Caccia Dominioni; one *d*. *Heir: d* Princess Donna Benedetta Francesca Maria Rospigliosi, Mistress of Newburgh [*b* 4 June 1974; *m* 1999, Piero Riccardo Maria Albertario (marr. diss. 2018); two *s*]. *Address:* Piazza Sant'Ambrogio 16, 20123 Milan, Italy.

**NEWBY,** family name of **Baron Newby**.

**NEWBY,** Baron *cr* 1997 (Life Peer), of Rothwell in the co. of West Yorkshire; **Richard Mark Newby,** OBE 1990; PC 2014; *b* 14 Feb. 1953; *s* of Frank and Kathleen Newby; *m* 1978, Rev. Canon the Hon. Ailsa Ballantyne, *yr d* of Baron Thomson of Monifieth, KT PC; two *s*. *Educ:* Rothwell Grammar Sch.; St Catherine's Coll., Oxford (MA). HM Customs and Excise: Administration trainee, 1974; Private Sec. to Permanent Sec., 1977–79; Principal, Planning Unit, 1979–81; Sec. to SDP Parly Cttee, 1981; joined SDP HQ Staff, 1981; Nat. Sec., SDP, 1983–88; Exec., 1988–90; Dir of Corporate Affairs, 1991, Rosehaugh plc; Director: Matrix Public Affairs Consultants, subseq. Matrix Communications Consultancy Ltd, 1992–99; Flagship Gp, 1999–2001; non-exec. Dir, Elmwood Design Ltd, 2004–09; Chm., Live Consulting Ltd, 2011–12. Chair, Internat. Develt through Sport, UK, 2007–12; Chm., Sport for Life, 2009–12. Dep. Chm., Lib Dem Gen. Election Team, 1995–97; Chief of Staff to Rt Hon. Charles Kennedy, 1999–2006. Lib Dem spokesman on Treasury affairs, 1998–2010, Lib Dem Chief Whip, 2012–16, Lib Dem Leader, 2016–, H of L; Govt spokesman on HM Treasury, H of L, 2012–15; Captain of the Yeoman of the Guard (Dep. Chief Whip, H of L), 2012–15. Member: Select Cttee on Monetary Policy Cttee of Bank of England, 1998–2000; Select Cttee on Economic Affairs, 2001–03; Ecclesiastical Cttee, 2002–12; Chm., All Party Social Enterprise Gp, 2010–12 (Dep. Chm., 2003); Co-Chair, Lib Dem Parly Treasury Policy Cttee, 2010–12; Treas., Associate Parly Gp on Corporate Responsibility, 2009–12. *Recreations:* family, football, cricket, walking. *Address:* St Peter's House, Minster Close, Ripon HG4 1QP. *Club:* MCC.
See also C. Thomson.

**NEWBY, Sir Howard (Joseph),** Kt 2000; CBE 1995; DL; Vice Chancellor, University of Liverpool, 2008–15; *b* 10 Dec. 1947; *s* of Alfred Joseph Newby and Constance Annie (*née* Potts); *m* 1st, 1970, Janet Elizabeth (*née* Craddock) (marr. diss. 2003); two *s*; 2nd, 2005, Sheila Mary Watt (*née* Mann); one step *s* one step *d*. *Educ:* John Port Grammar Sch., Etwall, Derbyshire; Atlantic Coll., St Donat's, Glamorgan; Univ. of Essex (BA, PhD). University of Essex: Lectr in Sociology, 1972–75; Sen. Lectr, 1975–79; Reader, 1979–83; Prof. of Sociology, 1983–88; Dir, Data Archive, 1983–88, Chm. and Chief Exec., 1988–94, ESRC; Vice-Chancellor, Southampton Univ., 1994–2001; Chief Exec., HEFCE, 2001–06; Vice Chancellor, UWE, 2006–08. Prof. of Sociology and Rural Sociology, Univ. of Wisconsin-Madison, 1980–83; visiting appointments: Univ. of NSW, 1976; Sydney, 1976; Newcastle upon Tyne, 1983–84. Chm., CEST, 1995–99; Pres., CVCP, 1999–2001. Member: UFC, 1991–93; Rural Develt Commn, 1991–99; South and West RHA, 1994–96; ESTA, 1997–98; Railway Heritage Cttee, 1999–2013; Council, Hong Kong UGC, 2015–. Chm. Bd, Nat. Railway Mus., 2008–15; Trustee: Sci. Mus. Gp (formerly Nat. Mus. of Sci. and Industry), 2007–15; Nat. Football Mus., 2008–12. Gov., BFI, 2008–12. Hon. Fellow: Univ. of Wales, Cardiff, 1996; Liverpool John Moores Univ., 2015. Hon. DLitt: City of London Poly., 1991; South Bank Univ., 1992; Surrey, 1992; Portsmouth, 1992 (Hon. Fellow, Portsmouth Poly., 1991); Ulster, 1994; Stirling, 2002; DU: Essex, 2000; Leicester, 2002; Hon. DSocSci Southampton, 2002; DUniv Derby, 2006. DL Merseyside, 2014. *Publications:* (jtly) Community Studies, 1971; The Deferential Worker, 1977; (jtly) Property, Paternalism and Power, 1978; Green and Pleasant Land?, 1979, 2nd edn 1985;

(jtly) The Problem of Sociology, 1983; (jtly) Aproximación Teorética a la Sociologia Rural, 1983; Country Life, 1987; The Countryside in Question, 1988; (jtly) Social Class in Modern Britain, 1988; *edited jointly:* The Sociology of Community, 1974; Doing Sociological Research, 1977; International Perspectives in Rural Sociology, 1978; The Rural Sociology of the Advanced Societies, 1980; Political Action and Social Identity, 1985; Restructuring Capital, 1985; The National Trust: the next hundred years, 1995; over 50 papers in learned jls. *Recreations:* sharing everything in married life, especially time with our family, walks and cycle rides, Derby County and railway interests.

**NEWCASTLE, Bishop of,** since 2015; **Rt Rev. Christine Elizabeth Hardman;** *b* 27 Aug. 1951; *d* of Wynford Atkins and Margaret Elizabeth Atkins; *m* 1971, Roger John Hardman; two *d. Educ:* Queen Elizabeth's Girls' Grammar Sch., Barnet; Univ. of London (BScEcon (ext.) 1973); Westminster Coll., Oxford (MTh 1994). Ordained deaconess 1984, deacon 1987, priest 1994; Deaconess, Markyate Street, 1984–88; Course Dir, St Albans MTS, later St Albans and Oxford Ministry Course, 1988–96; Vicar, Holy Trinity, Stevenage, 1996–2001; RD Stevenage, 1999–2001; Archdeacon of Lewisham, later Archdeacon of Lewisham and Greenwich, 2001–12; Hon. Asst Priest, Southwark Cathedral, 2012–15. Took seat in H of L, 2016. Mem., Gen. Synod, C of E, 2005–. Prolocutor, Lower House of the Convocation of Canterbury, 2010–15. *Recreations:* cycling, running, cinema, theatre. *Address:* Bishop's House, 29 Moor Road South, Newcastle upon Tyne NE3 1PA. *T:* (0191) 285 2220. *E:* bishop@newcastle.anglican.org.

**NEWCASTLE, Dean of;** *see* Miller, Ven. G. V.

**NEWCASTLE, (NSW), Bishop of,** since 2018; **Rt Rev. Dr Peter Derrick James Stuart;** *b* Alnwick, Northumberland, 23 Jan. 1963; *s* of William Derrick Stuart and Doris Mabel Stuart (née Jones); *m* 1991, Nicola Mary Wright; one *s* one *d. Educ:* Univ. of Tasmania (BCom 1985); Melbourne Coll. of Divinity (BD 1990); Univ. of Technol., Sydney (MM 2001); Flinders Univ. (EdD 2011); Inst. of Company Dirs Australia. Audit Asst, Price Waterhouse & Co., 1981–83; Audit Officer, Commonwealth Audit Office, 1985; Asst to Diocesan Registrar, Melbourne, 1985–87; ordained deacon, 1989, priest, 1990; Archdeacon of Clarence, 1997–2001; Archdeacon of Ministry Develt, Dio. of Adelaide, 2001–07; Archdeacon of Adelaide, 2007–09; Asst Bishop of Newcastle, 2009–18. Principal, St Barnabas Theol Coll., Adelaide, 2002–09. *Recreations:* watching soccer and musical theatre. *Address:* Level 3, 134 King Street, Newcastle, NSW 2300, Australia. *T:* (2) 49263733. *E:* bishoppeter@newcastleanglican.org.au. *Club:* Newcastle.

**NEWCOMBE, Andrew Bennett;** QC 2010; *b* Merton, London, 6 Feb. 1953; *s* of Guy Bennett Newcombe and Sheila Kathleen Newcombe (née Saunders); *m* 1992, Freda Bush. *Educ:* Kingston Grammar Sch.; Durham Univ. (BA 1974). Officer, Royal Marines, 1974–85: 42 Cdo RM, 1975–77; ADC to C-in-C AFNORTH, 1977–78; flying duties with Fleet Air Arm and 3 Cdo Bde Air Sqdn, 1979–84, served Falklands (despatches, 1982); Bde Intelligence Officer, 3 Cdo Bde, 1984–85. Called to the Bar, Middle Temple, 1987, King's Inns, Dublin, 1995; in practice as a barrister, 1987–2018. Liveryman, Gunmakers' Co., 2011–. *Recreations:* exercising the whippet, shooting, occasional polo, novice's interest in 17th and 18th century ceramics. *Club:* Naval and Military.

**NEWCOME, Rt Rev. James William Scobie;** *see* Carlisle, Bishop of.

**NEWCOMEN, Nigel Thomas,** CBE 2011; Prisons and Probation Ombudsman, 2011–18; *b* London, 14 June 1955; *s* of Rosalind Newcomen; *m* 1978, Susie Gammon; three *s. Educ:* St Christopher, Letchworth; Kent Univ. (BA Hons); London Sch. of Econs and Pol Sci. (LLM); Surrey Univ. (MSc). Sessional Community Service Supervisor, 1976–78, Community Service Officer, 1978–79, Inner London Probation Service; Res. Officer, Univ. of Sussex, 1980–81; Sen. Community Service Officer (pt-time), 1981–85, Hd of Res. and Information, 1985–91, SW London Probation Service; Lectr (pt-time), Chelsea Coll., Univ. of London, 1982–85; Hd of Section, Directorate of Inmate Activities, 1991–93, Lead, Criminal Justice Bill Team, Directorate of Services, 1993–94, Prison Service; Hd of Protective Security, 1994, Private Sec. to Home Sec., 1994–96, Home Office; Business Manager, Directorate of Prison Health Care, 1996; Hd of Secretariat, 1996–99, Asst Dir and Hd of Gp, Sentence Mgt Gp, 1999–2003, Prison Service; Dep. Chief Inspector of Prisons, 2003–11. *Recreations:* travel, sport, arts, allotment gardening. *E:* nigelnewcomen1@gmail.com.

**NEWDEGATE;** *see* FitzRoy Newdegate, family name of Viscount Daventry.

**NEWELL, Christopher William Paul;** Principal Legal Advisor to Director of Public Prosecutions, 2005–09; *b* 30 Nov. 1950; *s* of Nicolas Gambier Newell and Edith Alice Newell (née Edgill); *m* 1998, Teresa Mary Martin; one *d. Educ:* Wellington College; Southampton Univ. (LLB Hons). Called to the Bar, Middle Temple, 1973; Department of Director of Public Prosecutions: Legal Asst, 1975–78; Sen. Legal Asst, 1978–79; Law Officers' Dept, 1979–83; Sen. Legal Asst, DPP, 1983–86; Asst DPP, 1986; Branch Crown Prosecutor, Crown Prosecution Service, 1986–87; Asst Legal Sec., Law Officers' Dept, 1987–89; Crown Prosecution Service: Dir of HQ Casework, 1989–93; Dir (Casework), 1993–95; Dir, Casework Evaluation, 1995–98; Dir, Casework, 1998–2005. Sen. Vice-Chm., Criminal Law Cttee, IBA, 2002–06 (Vice-Chm., 2000–02). Trustee: Nat. Deaf Children's Soc., 2001–08; Centre for Accessible Envmts, 2001–08 (Vice-Chm., 2004–08); Crime Reduction Initiatives, 2001–11; Friends of W Byfleet Health Centre, 2009– (Chm., 2012–18). Mem., Wisley with Pyrford PCC, 2010–16, 2017– (Vice Chm., 2013–16). Gov., Pyrford C of E Primary Sch., 2008–; Trustee: Friends of Pyrford Primary Sch., 2009–13 (Chm., 2012–13); Newark Multi-Acad. Trust, 2018–. Vice Chm., Pyrford & Wisley Flower Show, 2015 (Hon. Vice-Pres., 2019–). *Recreations:* sport, travel.

**NEWELL, David Richard,** OBE 2017; Chief Executive, Newsmedia Association, since 2014 (Director: Newspaper Society, 1997–2014); Newspaper Publishers Association, 2007–14); *b* 21 Sept. 1951; *s* of late Dick Newell and Davida Newell (née Juleff); *m* 1978, Cora Sue Feingold; one *d. Educ:* Shrewsbury Sch.; Birmingham Univ. (LLB Hons 1973); Southampton Univ. (MPhil 1976). US, UK and British Council res. grants, 1974–81. Admitted Solicitor, 1978; Lawford & Co., 1976–78; Lectr in Law, Leicester Univ., 1978–86 (Postgrad. Tutor, 1979–84; Dir, Employment Law Postgrad. prog., 1983–86); Hon. Legal Advr, Leicester Legal Advice Centre, 1979–84; Hd of Govt and Legal Affairs, 1984–96, Dep. Dir, 1992–97, Newspaper Soc. Sec., Parly and Legal Cttee, Guild of Editors, 1984–97; Member: Advertising Assoc. Cttees, 1984–; Council, Campaign for Freedom of Information, 1990–2010 (Award for campaigning against official secrecy, 1989); Employment and Media Cttees, Law Soc., 1990–97; Council, World Assoc. of Newspapers, 1997–; Chm., Legal Framework Cttee, 1995–98, Bd Mem., 1996–2015, European Newspaper Publishers' Assoc. Director: ABC, 1997–; Press Standards Bd of Finance, 1997–2015; Advertising Standards Bd of Finance, 1998–; Nat. Readership Survey, 2014–15; Mem. Bd, News Media Europe, 2016–. Sec., Regulatory Funding Co., 2014–. Special Award, UK Press Gazette, 1988; Newspaper Industry Award, 2009. *Publications:* The New Employment Legislation: a guide to the Employment Acts 1980 and 1982, 1983; Understanding Recruitment Law, 1984; (jtly) How to Study Law, 1986, 8th edn 2017; (jtly) Financial Advertising Law, 1989; (jtly) Aspects of Employment Law, 1990; (jtly) Law for Journalists, 1991; (jtly) Tolley's Employment Law, 1994, 3rd edn 2010; (jtly) The Law of Journalism, 1995; research papers and articles on employment law, media and legal policy issues. *Recreations:* country and seaside walks, sailing, tennis. *Address:* Newsmedia Association, 292 Vauxhall Bridge Road, SW1V 1AE. *T:* (020) 7963 7480.

**NEWELL, Donald,** FRICS; Co-Chairman, Europe Middle East Africa Division, CB Richard Ellis Services Inc., USA, 1998–2000; *b* 31 Aug. 1942; *s* of Stephen Newell and Ida Laura Newell (née Hatch); *m* 1968, Rosemary Litler-Jones; one *s* two *d. Educ:* Cheshunt Grammar Sch. FRICS 1968. Lander Bedells & Crompton, 1961–68; Hillier Parker May & Rowden, Chartered Surveyors, 1968–98: Partner, 1973–98; Man. Partner, 1986–90; Sen. Partner, 1990–98. Director: Oncor Internat., USA, 1995–98; CB Hillier Parker, 1998–2000; non-executive Director: London Merchant Securities PLC, 1998–2007; Derwent London plc, 2007–11. Dir, Paddington Business Improvement Dist Ltd, 2005–10. Pres., Brit. Council for Offices, 1991–92. Liveryman, Co. of Pattenmakers, 1979– (Master, 2004–05); Chartered Surveyors, 1993–. *Recreation:* sport. *Clubs:* Buck's, MCC.

**NEWELL, Rev. Canon Edmund John,** DPhil; Principal, King George VI and Queen Elizabeth Foundation of St Catharine's, Cumberland Lodge, since 2013; *b* 9 Sept. 1961; *s* of Kenneth Ernest Newell and late Mary Newell (née James); *m* 1989, Susan Georgina Greer; one *s* one *d. Educ:* Ilfracombe Sch.; University Coll. London (BScEcon 1983); Nuffield Coll., Oxford (DPhil 1988; MA 1989); Oxford Ministry Course; Ripon Coll., Cuddesdon. Prize Res. Fellow, 1987, British Acad. Postdoctoral Fellow, 1989–92, Nuffield Coll., Oxford. Ordained deacon, 1994, priest, 1995; Curate, Deddington with Barford, Clifton and Hempton, 1994–98; Domestic Chaplain and Res. Asst to Bp of Oxford, 1998–2001; Chaplain, Headington Sch., Oxford, 1998–2001; Canon Residentiary, 2001–08, Chancellor, 2003–08, St Paul's Cathedral; Residentiary Canon and Sub Dean, Christ Church, Oxford, 2008–13, now Hon. non-Residentiary Canon. Dir, St Paul's Inst., 2003–08. Associate Mem., Nuffield Coll., Oxford, 2013–. FR.HistS 1998; FRSA 2008. *Publications:* (ed) Seven Words for the 21st Century, 2002; (ed with Claire Foster) The Worlds We Live In, 2005; (with Sabina Alkire) What Can One Person Do?, 2005; (ed) Seven Words for Three Hours: a Good Friday meditation in words and music, 2005; (with John N. Reynolds) Ethics in Investment Banking, 2011; Choice, 2012; The Sacramental Sea, 2019; contribs to books, articles in learned jls and newspapers. *Recreations:* cartooning, sport, music, exploring coastlines and islands. *Address:* Cumberland Lodge, The Great Park, Windsor, Berks SL4 2HP.

**NEWELL, Dame Jane;** *see* Newell, Dame P. J.

**NEWELL, Michael Cormac;** film director; *b* 28 March 1942; *s* of Terence William Newell and Mollie Louise Newell; *m* 1979, Bernice Stegers; one *s* one *d. Educ:* St Albans Sch.; Magdalene Coll., Cambridge (MA). Television dir, Granada TV, 1964–70: Ready When You Are Mr Magill; Baa Baa Black Sheep; Charm; freelance television dir, 1970–80: Melancholy Hussar; Just Your Luck; Destiny; Mr and Mrs Bureaucrat; Gift of Friendship; *films* include: Man in the Iron Mask, 1976; The Awakening, 1979; Dance with a Stranger, 1984 (Prix de la Jeunesse, Cannes); Good Father, 1986 (Prix Italia); Sweet and Sour, 1988; Into the West, 1992; Four Weddings and a Funeral, 1994 (Best Dir, BAFTA Awards, 1995); An Awfully Big Adventure, 1995; Donnie Brasco, 1997; Pushing Tin, 1999; Mona Lisa Smile, 2004; Harry Potter and the Goblet of Fire, 2005; Love in the Time of Cholera, 2008; Prince of Persia: The Sands of Time, 2010; Great Expectations, 2012; The Guernsey Literary and Potato Peel Pie Society, 2018; executive producer, Photographic Fairies, 1997; Best Laid Plans, 200 Cigarettes, 1999; High Fidelity, Traffic, 2000. Hon. DA Herts, 2005. *Recreations:* walking, reading (anything but fiction). *Address:* c/o Independent Talent Group Ltd, 40 Whitfield Street, W1T 2RH.

**NEWELL, Rt Rev. Phillip Keith,** AO 1993; Bishop of Tasmania, 1982–2000; *b* 30 Jan. 1930; *s* of Frank James and Ada Miriam Newell; *m* 1959, Merle Edith Callaghan; three *s. Educ:* Univ. of Melbourne; Trinity Coll., Melbourne. BSc 1953; DiplEd(Hons) 1954; ThL(Hons) 1959; BEd 1960; MEd 1969; FACE 1990. Mathematics Master: Melbourne High School, 1954–56; University High School, 1957–58; Tutor in Physics, Secondary Teachers' Coll., 1957; Assistant Curate: All Saints, East St Kilda, Melbourne, 1960–61; S Andrew's, Brighton, Melbourne, 1962–63; Asst Priest, S James, King Street, Sydney, 1963–67; Chaplain, Sydney Hosp., 1963–67; Rector, Christ Church, St Lucia, Brisbane, 1967–82; Residentiary Canon, S John's Cathedral, Brisbane, 1973–82; Archdeacon of Lilley, Brisbane, 1976–82. GCSJ 1979; KStJ 1981; OMLJ 2004. *Publications:* Body Search, 1993; A Pocket Lent Book, 1996. *Recreations:* education, music (classical and light opera), singing, choral conducting, wine making, travel, cricket (spectator), tennis (occasional game). *Address:* 4 Howley Court, Howrah, Tas 7018, Australia. *T:* (3) 6247 1706.

**NEWELL, Dame (Priscilla) Jane, (Lady Cuckney),** DBE 2013 (OBE 1997); Chair, John Lewis Partnership Pensions Trust, since 2013 (Trustee, since 2012); *b* London, 13 April 1944; *d* of Arthur Ronald Watts and Sylvia Margaret Watts (née McNabb); *m* 1st, 1977, Prof. Kenneth Wyatt Newell (*d* 1990); 2nd, 2007, Baron Cuckney (*d* 2008). *Educ:* Merrow Grange Convent, Guildford; Victoria Univ. of Wellington, NZ (BA French and English). Sen. Schol. 1980; BA 1st Cl. Hons Linguistics; Postgrad. Schol. 1981). Internat. CS, WHO, 1965–77; Sch. Adminr, Liverpool Sch. of Tropical Medicine, 1984–92; Assessor: Recruitment and Assessment Services, Cabinet Office, 1994–97; Assessment Consultancy Unit, Home Office, 1994–2006. Non-executive Director: Royal Liverpool Univ. Hosp. Trust, 1992–95; United Utilities plc, 1996–2006; Synesis Life Ltd, 2007–08. Chair: United Utilities Pension Scheme, 1998–2005; Electricity Supply Pension Scheme (UU Gp), 1998–2005; Royal Mail Pension Plan, 2005–12; Royal Mail Defined Contribn Pension Plan, 2009–12. Dir, Liverpool Associates in Tropical Health Ltd, 1994–98. Chair, 1995–97, Vice Pres., 1997–2014, now Emeritus Vice Pres., Liverpool Sch. of Tropical Medicine; Pro-Chancellor and Chair, Bd of Govs, London South Bank Univ., 1999–2007. Vice Pres., Pensions Archive Trust, 2009–; Trustee: Maxwell Pensioners Trust, 1992–97 (Chair, 1995–97); GlaxoSmithKline Pension Plan, 1994–2004; Dixons Gp Pension Scheme (UU Gp), 1998–2005; Common Purpose Charitable Trust, 1999–2015; Age UK, 2009–15. Patron, Hillcroft Coll., 2011–. Gov., Pensions Policy Inst., 2009–. JP: Liverpool, 1993–95; S Western Magistrates' Court, 1995–2013. Hon. LLD London South Bank, 2008. *Recreations:* gardening, cooking, music, walking. *E:* pjnonline@gmail.com. *Club:* Athenæum (Trustee, 2016–).

**NEWELL, Robert Fraser,** CVO 2011 (LVO 2000); Director-General, Royal Over-Seas League, 1991–2011; *b* 3 May 1943; *s* of late Horace and Henrietta Newell; *m* 1969, Shahnaz Bakhtiar; two *d. Educ:* University Coll. Sch. FIH (MHCIMA 1986, FHCIMA 1997). Hotel mgt positions in London, Iran and Kenya, 1965–75; Dir of Admin, Kenya Utalii Coll., Nairobi, 1975–79; Gen. Manager, Royal Over-Seas League, 1979–91. Vis. Lectr in Hotel Financial Mgt, Ecole Hôtelière de Lausanne, 1983–2001. Chm., Assoc. of London Clubs, 1992–95; Member: Club Secs and Managers Assoc., 1982–2011; Council of Commonwealth Socs Cttee (formerly Jt Commonwealth Socs Council), 1991–2011; Cttee, Eur. Atlantic Gp, 1993–2010; Cttee, Kenya Soc., 1996–; Council, Mayfair St James's Assoc., 2001–11. Mem., Adv. Bd, Spirit of Remembrance, 2011–. Volunteer, Chain of Hope, 2001–; Trustee, Bridge of Hope, 2012– (Chm. Trustees, 2013–). Fellow, Brit. Assoc. Hotel Accountants, 1997; FCMI (FIMgt 1983). *Recreations:* tennis, music, walking, grandchildren, Alpine-walking. *Address:* Pichlhofstrasse 6 - Top 8, Kaprun 5710, Austria. *Club:* Royal Over-Seas League (Hon.).

**NEWENS, (Arthur) Stanley**; b 4 Feb. 1930; s of Arthur Ernest and Celia Jenny Newens, Bethnal Green; m 1st, 1954, Ann (d 1962), d of J. B. Sherratt, Stoke-on-Trent; two d; 2nd, 1966, Sandra Christina, d of J. A. Frith, Chingford; one s two d. Educ: Buckhurst Hill County High Sch.; University Coll., London (BA Hons History); Westminster Training Coll. (Post-Graduate Certificate of Education). Coal face worker in N Staffs mines, 1952–55. Secondary Sch. Teacher, 1956–65, 1970–74. MP (Lab) Epping, 1964–70 (NUT sponsored); MP (Lab and Co-op) Harlow, Feb. 1974–1983; contested (Lab) Harlow, 1983 and 1987; MEP (Lab and Co-op) London Central, 1984–99. Chairman: Eastern Area Gp of Lab. MPs, 1974–83; Tribune Gp of MPs, 1982–83 (Vice-Chm., 1981–82); PLP Foreign Affairs Gp, 1982–83 (Vice-Chm., 1976–77); Dep. Leader, British Lab. Gp of MEPs, 1988–89 (Chm., 1985–87); Pres., EP Central Amer. and Mexico Delegn, 1994–96; Vice-Chm., Labour Action for Peace. Active Member: Labour Party, holding numerous offices, 1949–; NUM, 1952–55; NUT, 1956–. Pres., Liberation (Movement for Colonial Freedom), 1992– (Chm., 1967–92). Dir, London Co-operative Soc., 1971–77 (Pres., 1977–81); Mem., Central Exec., Co-op. Union, 1974–80. Sec., Harlow Council for Voluntary Service, 1983–84. Mem., Harlow Health Centres Trust, 1984–. Chairman: Harlow Civic Soc., 1999–; Gibberd Garden Trust, 1999–; President: Waltham Abbey Historical Soc., 1998–; Socialist History Soc., 2013– (Vice-Pres., 2005–13); Vice-Pres., Friends of Historic Essex, 1982–; Member: Adv. Bd, Modern Record Centre, 1974–85, 1999–2008; Council, London Record Soc., 2001–05; Council, Essex Soc. for Archaeol. and Hist., 2002– (Pres., 2005–08); Trustee, 2012–15; Vice Pres., 2016–). Publications: The Case Against NATO (pamphlet), 1972; Nicolae Ceausescu, 1972; Third World: change or chaos, 1977; A History of North Weald Bassett and its People, 1985; A Short History of the London Co-op Society Political Committee, 1988; (with Ron Bill) Leah Manning, 1991; The Kurds, 1994; Pathfinders, 1998; A Brief History of 100 Years of the Labour Party in the Eastern Region, 2000; Chris Morris: a landworker's struggle, 2003; A History of Struggle: 50th anniversary of Liberation (Movement for Colonial Freedom), 2004; (ed) A. E. Newens, The Memoirs of an Old East-Ender, 2006; Arthur Morrison: the novelist of realism in East London and Essex, 2008; In Quest of a Fairer Society: my life and politics, 2013; (ed) The John Collins Story, 2015; pamphlets and articles. Recreations: local historical research, family, reading, gardening. Address: The Leys, 18 Park Hill, Harlow, Essex CM17 0AE. T: (01279) 420108. E: stannewens@hotmail.com.

**NEWEY, Brian**; see Newey, S. B.

**NEWEY, Rev. Canon Edmund James**; Residentiary Canon and Sub-Dean, Christ Church, Oxford, since 2013; b Reading, 23 Sept. 1971; s of (Sidney) Brian Newey, qv; m 2003, Emma Rose Helen Wagstaff; one s one d. Educ: Abingdon Sch.; Lincoln Coll., Oxford (BA Modern Langs 1995); Emmanuel Coll., Cambridge (BA Theol. 1999); Westcott House; Manchester Univ. (PhD 2008). Lang. Asst, Akademisches Gymnasium and Wirtschaftkundliches Realgymnasium der Ursulinen, Innsbruck, 1992–93; Asst Master, Bolton Sch. (Boys Div.), 1994–97; ordained deacon, 2000, priest, 2001; Asst Curate, Birch with Fallowfield, Manchester, 2000–03; Rector, St Mary, Newmarket and St Agnes, Exning, 2003–07; Vicar, St Andrew, Handsworth, 2007–13; Area Dean of Handsworth, 2011–13. Vice-Chair, Govs, Christ Church Cathedral Sch., 2013–; Gov., Portsmouth GS, 2016–. Publications: Children of God: the child as source of theological anthropology, 2012; contribs to bks and learned jls. Recreations: walking and running on the fells, family and friends. Address: Christ Church, Oxford OX1 1DP. T: (01865) 276150. E: edmund.newey@lincoln.oxon.org. Club: Mercia Fell Runners.

**NEWEY, Rt Hon. Sir Guy (Richard)**, Kt 2010; PC 2017; **Rt Hon. Lord Justice Newey**; a Lord Justice of Appeal, since 2017; b 21 Jan. 1959; s of His Honour John Henry Richard Newey, QC and of Mollie Patricia Newey (née Chalk); m 1986, Angela Clare Neilson; one s three d. Educ: Tonbridge Sch.; Queens' Coll., Cambridge (MA 1st Cl., LLM 1st Cl.); Council of Legal Educn (1st Cl. in Bar Exams). Called to the Bar, Middle Temple, 1982, Bencher, 2010; in practice at Chancery Bar, 1983–2010; QC 2001; a Dep. High Ct Judge, 2006–10; Jun. Counsel to the Crown, Chancery, and A Panel, 1990–2001; Jun. Counsel to Charity Comrs, 1991–2001; a Judge of the High Court of Justice, Chancery Div., 2010–17; Chancery Supervising Judge for Midland, Wales and Western Circuits, 2014–17. Inspector into affairs of MG Rover, 2005–09. An Acting Deemster, 2003–09, Deemster, 2009–11, Isle of Man. Gov., New Beacon Educnl Trust Ltd, 2001–09. Publications: (contrib.) Directors' Disqualification, 2nd edn 1998; (contrib.) Civil Court Service, 1999; (contrib.) Equity and Administration, 2016. Address: Royal Courts of Justice, Strand, WC2A 2LL.

*See also M. C. Newey.*

**NEWEY, Michael Clive**, FRICS; Chief Executive, Broadland Housing Group, since 2003; President, Royal Institution of Chartered Surveyors, 2013–14; b Farnborough, Kent, 9 June 1963; s of His Honour John Henry Richard Newey, QC, and of Mollie Patricia Newey (née Chalk); m 1987, Catherine Louise Hern; one s one d. Educ: Tonbridge Sch., Kent; Portsmouth Poly. (BSc Urban Land Admin). FRICS 1996. Surveyor: Porter Cobb & Prall, later GA Property Services, 1986–88; Prudential Property Services, 1988; Principal Surveyor, Richard Ellis, 1988–94; Associate Dir, Savills, 1994–97; Develt Dir, Flagship Housing Gp, 1997–2000; Exec. Dir, Anglia Housing Gp, 2000–03; sabbatical on secondment as Special Advr on Community Housing, to Dept of Human Services, Govt of Victoria, 2008–09. Vis. Fellow, Royal Agricl Univ., 2013–. Member: Flats over Shops Steering Gp, DoE, 1991–94; Capital Investment Adv. Bd, DIT (formerly Adv. Bd, Regeneration Investment Orgn, UKTI), 2013–17; Steering Gp, Homes for Cathy, 2016–; Professional Mem., Global Regulatory Bd, RICS, 2017–. Royal Institution of Chartered Surveyors: Chairman: Jun. Orgn, 1992–93; Residential Policy, 1999–2003; Eur. Housing Forum, 2002–05; Public Affairs, 2003–07; Ind. Housing Commn, 2012–13; Dep. Chm., Mgt Bd, 2006–10. Chm., Broadland St Benedicts Ltd, 2011–. Chair, Develt Bd, 2015–16, Mem., Adv. Bd, 2015–16, UK Housing Centre, ESRC. Chm., Norwich Theatre Royal Services Ltd, 2015–. FCIH 2010; FRSA 2015. Mem., Australasian Housing Inst., 2009–. Hon. DSc Portsmouth, 2015. Recreations: holidays with family, golf, Norwich City Football Club, reading, theatre, housing policy. Address: Broadland Housing Group, Jarrold Stand, Norwich City Football Club, Carrow Road, Norwich NR1 1HU. T: (01603) 750292. E: michael.newey@broadlandgroup.org. Clubs: 1913 Wilderness; Victory Services; 1947 Surveyors (Newcastle).

*See also Rt Hon. Sir G. R. Newey.*

**NEWEY, (Sidney) Brian**; consultant in transport; Assistant to Chief Executive, Railways, British Rail, 1990–93, retired; b 8 Jan. 1937; s of Sidney Frank Newey and Edith Mary Newey; m 1967, Margaret Mary Stevens (d 1996); one s. Educ: Burton upon Trent Grammar Sch.; Worcester Coll., Oxford (MA Mod. History). British Rail: Traffic apprentice, Western Region, 1960; Stationmaster, Southall, Middx, 1964; Freight Marketing Manager, Western Region, 1971; Divl Manager, Birmingham, 1978; Dep. General Manager, London Midland Region, 1980; Gen. Manager, Western Region, 1985–87; Director, Provincial, 1987–90. Chm., Oxford Diocesan Bd of Finance, 2001–13. Member: Governing Body, Whitelands Coll., Roehampton, 2006–; Council, Univ. of Roehampton, 2011–19. Recreations: fell walking, history, reading, village and church affairs. Address: Chestnut Cottage, The Green South, Warborough, Oxon OX10 7DN. T: (01865) 858322.

*See also Rev. Canon E. J. Newey.*

**NEWHAM, Prof. Dianne Jane**, PhD; FCSP; Professor of Physiotherapy, King's College London, 1993–2016, now Emeritus; b 31 July 1949; d of Geoffrey Newham and Denise Millicent Newham; partner, Terry N. Williams; one s. Educ: Nairobi Convent Sch., Kenya; Ockbrook Moravian Sch.; Prince of Wales Sch. of Physiotherapy (MCSP, SRP 1976); UCL (MPhil 1982); North London Poly. (PhD 1985). FCSP 2007. Lab. Asst, Boots Co. Ltd, 1967–70; VSO, Nigeria, 1970–72; University College London: Physiotherapist, 1976–79; Res. Physiotherapist, Dept of Medicine, 1979–82; Associate Res. Fellow, Medicine and Surgery, 1985–87; Lectr in Physiology, 1987–89; King's College, London: Reader, 1989–93; Hd of Physiotherapy, 1989–2000; Dir, Div. of Applied Biomedical Res., 2000–12. Mem., Working Gp on establt of UK Acad. of Med. Scis, 1996–98. Publications: chapters on human muscle pain, skeletal muscle function and fatigue; original research papers in jls of physiology, physiotherapy and rehabilitation. Recreations: travel, gardening, food and wine. Address: Centre for Human and Applied Physiological Sciences, King's College London, Shepherd's House, Guy's Campus, SE1 1UL. T: (020) 7848 6320.

**NEWHOUSE, Jonathan Edward**; Chairman, Condé Nast, since 2019 (Chairman and Chief Executive, Condé Nast International, 1991–2019); b New York, 30 March 1952; s of Norman Newhouse and Alice Newhouse; m 1995, Ronnie Cooke; two d. Educ: Isidore Newman Sch.; Yale Univ. Exec. Vice Pres., New Yorker mag., 1985–88; Publisher, Details mag., 1988–89; Pres., Condé Nast Internat., 1989–2012. Non-exec. Dir, Farfetch, 2017–19. Mem. Bd, Condé Nast US, 2011–. Officier, Ordre des Arts et des Lettres (France), 2008. Address: Condé Nast International, The Adelphi, 1–11 John Adam Street, WC2N 6HT. T: (020) 7851 1802. E: jonathan.newhouse@advance.com. Club: Yale.

**NEWISS, Hilary Jane**; Chair, National Voices, since 2014; b Keighley, 16 April 1956; d of Reginald Stewart Newiss and Winifred Newiss; m 1985, Sir Peter Lytton Bazalgette, qv; one s one d. Educ: Harrogate Coll.; Somerville Coll., Oxford (BA Hons PPP 1977). Articled Clerk, Herbert Smith, 1979–81; admitted as solicitor, 1981; Solicitor: Clifford Chance, 1981–88; Theodore Goddard, 1988–90; Partner, Denton Hall, 1990–99. Fee-paid Judge, First-tier Tribunals Service, 2011–16. Member: Human Genetics Commn, 2000–06; Intellectual Property Adv. Cttee, 2001–05; Nat. Information Governance Bd, 2007–13; Adv. Panel for Public Sector Information, 2007–15. Trustee and non-executive Director, Roslin Foundn, 2006–; Charleston, 2006–15; Francis Crick Inst., 2011–15; Trustee, Natural Hist. Mus., 2015–; non-exec. Dir, Cell and Gene Therapy Catapult, 2018–. Publications: (ed and contrib.) International Intellectual Property Litigation (loose-leaf), 1997. Recreations: tennis, opera, theatre, art and design. Address: National Voices, 1st Floor, Bride House, 18–20 Bride Lane, EC4Y 8EE. E: vikki@newbaz.com.

**NEWLAND, Prof. Adrian Charles**, CBE 2010; FRCP, FRCPath; Professor of Haematology, Barts and the London School of Medicine and Dentistry, Queen Mary (formerly St Bartholomew's and Royal London School of Medicine and Dentistry, Queen Mary and Westfield College), University of London, since 1992; b 26 Aug. 1949; m 1973, Joanna Mary Shaw; one s one d. Educ: City of Norwich Sch.; Downing Coll., Cambridge (MA 1975); London Hospital Med. Coll. (MB BCh 1975). MRCP 1976, FRCP 1992; FRCPath 1992. Hon. Consultant, Barts Health (formerly Royal Hosps, then Barts and the London) NHS Trust, 1981–; Dir of R and D, Barts and the London NHS Trust, 1997–2001; Dir, NE Thames Cancer Network, 2001–13; Dir of Pathology, Barts Health (formerly Barts and the London) NHS Trust, 2004–15. Chairman: NICE Diagnostic Assessment Prog., 2010–; Healthcare Forum, UK Accreditation Service, 2013–; Dep. Chm., Chemotherapy Clinical Reference Panel, 2013–; Cancer Advr, Cancer Service Transformation Team, London, NHS England, 2013–. President: British Soc. for Haematology, 1998–99; RCPath, 2005–08; Internat. Soc. of Hematology, 2014–. Hon. Sec., Acad. of Medical Royal Colleges, 2007–10. Ed. in Chief, Hematology, 1995–. Publications: (jtly) Pocket Consultant Haematology, 1986; (ed jtly) Cambridge Medical Reviews, vols 14, 1991; numerous contribs in field of haematology incl. chapters in books; over 250 papers in learned jls. Recreations: good literature, fine wine, walking, foreign travel. Address: Department of Haematology, The Royal London Hospital, Whitechapel, E1 1BB. T: (020) 3246 0338, Fax: (020) 3246 0351. E: a.c.newland@qmul.ac.uk; Flat 109, Waterdale Manor House, 20 Harewood Avenue, NW1 6JX. Clubs: Athenæum, MCC.

**NEWLAND, Prof. David Edward**, MA; ScD; FREng, FIMechE, FIET; Professor of Engineering (1875), 1976–2003, now Emeritus, Head, Engineering Department, 1996–2002, and a Deputy Vice-Chancellor, 1999–2003, University of Cambridge; Fellow, Selwyn College, Cambridge, since 1976; consulting engineer; b 8 May 1936; s of late Robert W. Newland and Marion A. Newland (née Dearman); m 1959, Patricia Frances Mayne; two s. Educ: Alleyne's Sch., Stevenage; Selwyn Coll., Cambridge (Lyttelton Scholar, 1956; Mech. Sciences Tripos: Rex Moir Prize, 1956, Ricardo Prize, 1957; MA 1961; ScD 1990); Massachusetts Inst. of Technol. (ScD thesis on nonlinear vibrations, 1963). English Electric Co., 1957–61; Instr and Asst Prof. of Mech. Engrg, MIT, 1961–64; Lectr and Sen. Lectr, Imperial Coll. of Science and Technol., 1964–67; Prof. of Mech. Engrg, Sheffield Univ., 1967–76. Mem., Royal Commn on Envmtl Pollution, 1984–89. Visitor, Transport and Road Res. Lab., 1990–92; non-exec. Dir, Cambridge-MIT Inst., 2000–02. Past or present mem., cttees of IMechE, DTI, BSI, SERC, Design Council, Engrg Council and Royal Academy (formerly Fellowship) of Engineering, including: Mem., Editorial Panel, 1968–82 and Consultant Editor, 1983–87, Jl Mech. Engrg Sci., Proc. IMechE, Part C; Engrg Awards Panel, Design Council, 1977–79; Council, Fellowship of Engrg, 1985–88; Working Party on Engineers and Risk Issues, Engrg Council, 1990–94; Member: SRC Transport Cttee, 1969–72; Mech. Engrg and Machine Tools Requirements Bd, 1977, 1978; Chm., BSI Tech. Cttee on bellows expansion jts, 1976–85; Founding Vice-Pres., Internat. Inst. of Acoustics and Vibration, 1993 (Hon. Fellow, 2005). Technical witness, Flixborough Inquiry, 1974–75, and other engrg and patents cases; investigations following Piper Alpha, Potters Bar and other accidents; Engrg Advr, London Millennium Bridge Trust, 2000–01. Pres., Selwyn Coll. Alumni Assoc., 2013–14. Governor, St Paul's Schs, 1978–93. Freeman, City of London, 2000; Liveryman, Engrs' Co., 2001. Churchwarden, Ickleton, 1979–87. Distinguished Alumni Lectr, MIT, 1999. FREng (FEng 1982). Hon. DEng Sheffield, 1997. Charles S. Lake award, 1975, and T. Bernard Hall prize, IMechE, 1991, for papers in IMechE Procs; Applied Mechanics Award for dist. contribs, ASME, 2002. Publications: An Introduction to Random Vibrations and Spectral Analysis, 1975, 3rd edn, as Random Vibrations, Spectral and Wavelet Analysis, 1993; Mechanical Vibration Analysis and Computation, 1989; Discover Butterflies in Britain, 2006; Britain's Butterflies, 2002, 3rd edn 2015; Britain's Day-flying Moths, 2013, 2nd edn 2019; technical papers, mostly in British and Amer. engrg jls. Recreations: nature photography, entomology, walking, music. Address: Selwyn College, Cambridge CB3 9DQ. Club: Athenæum.

**NEWLAND, Martin**; media and strategic communications consultant; b 26 Oct. 1961; s of Edward and Elena Newland; m 1987, Bénédicte Smets; three s one d. Educ: Downside Sch.; Goldsmiths Coll., London Univ. (BA Hons (Hist.) 1984); Heythrop Coll., London Univ.

(MTh 1986). News Editor, Catholic Herald, 1986–88; Daily Telegraph: reporter, 1989–93; Home Ed., 1993–98; Dep. Ed. and Launch Ed., National Post, Canada, 1998–2003; Ed., The Daily Telegraph, 2003–05; Ed. and Launch Ed., The National, Abu Dhabi, 2008–09; Editl Dir, 2009–11, Chief Publishing Officer, 2011–14, Advr, 2014–15, Abu Dhabi Media; Consultant, Internat. Media Investments, Abu Dhabi, 2016–17. *Recreations:* walking, reading.

**NEWLANDS, David Baxter;** Chairman: Paypoint plc, 1998–2014; HellermannTyton plc, 2013–16; Touchstone Innovations plc, 2016–17; *b* 13 Sept. 1946; *s* of George Frederick Newlands and Helen Frederica Newlands; *m* 1973, Susan Helena Milne; two *s* two *d*. *Educ:* Edinburgh Acad. FCA 1969. Deloitte & Touche, 1963–86, Partner, 1977–86; Gp Finance Director: Saatchi & Saatchi, 1986–89; General Electric Co. plc, 1989–97. Non-executive Director: Weir Gp, 1997–2003; Global Software Services, 1998–2004; Tomkins plc, 1999–2010 (Chm., 2000–10); Standard Life Assce Co., 1999–2006 (Dep. Chm., 2004–06); London Regl Transport, 1999–2001; Britax Internat. plc, 1999–2001 (Chm., 2000–01); Chairman: Prospect Investment Mgt, 1999–2014; KESA Electricals, later Darty plc, 2003–12; OB10 (formerly Oxford Business Exchange), 2004–11; Impress Coöperative UA, 2007–10. Chm., Raeburn Place Foundn, 2014–. Chm. Trustees, SeeAbility, 2001–07. *Recreations:* golf, Rugby, bridge. *Address:* Lane End, Chucks Lane, Walton-on-the-Hill, Surrey KT20 7UB. *T:* (01737) 812582. *Clubs:* Caledonian, Royal Automobile; Walton Heath Golf (Dir, 2001–); Sutton and Epsom Rugby (Cheam); Golf House (Elie); Royal and Ancient Golf (St Andrews).

**NEWLANDS, Gavin Andrew Stuart;** MP (SNP) Paisley and Renfrewshire North, since 2015; *b* Paisley, 2 Feb. 1980; *s* of Gordon Newlands and Isabel Newlands; *m* 2008, Lynn Single; two *d*. *Educ:* Trinity High Sch., Renfrew. Business Analyst, McDonald's Restaurants Ltd, 2005–07; Asst Manager, then Business Analyst, later Business Manager, AG Restaurants Ltd, 2007–15. SNP spokesperson for Sport, 2017–; SNP spokesperson for NI and Wales, 2018–. Mem., Justice Cttee, 2017–. *Recreations:* spending time with family, walking, Rugby, football (watching), golf. *Address:* (office) 6 Porterfield Road, Renfrew PA4 8HG. *T:* (0141) 378 0600. *E:* gavin.newlands.mp@parliament.uk. *Club:* Paisley Rugby.

**NEWLANDS, Rev. Prof. George McLeod,** PhD, DLitt; FRSE; Professor of Divinity, University of Glasgow, 1986–2008, Hon. Professorial Research Fellow, 2008–17; Principal, Trinity College, Glasgow, 1991–97 and 2002–07; *b* 12 July 1941; *s* of George and Mary Newlands; *m* 1967, Mary Elizabeth Wallace; three *s*. *Educ:* Perth Acad.; Univ. of Edinburgh (MA 1st Cl. Classics (Vans Dunlop Scholar, 1963); BD 1st Cl. Eccles. Hist. (Cunningham Fellow, 1966); PhD 1970; DLitt 2005); Univ. of Heidelberg; Univ. of Zürich; Churchill Coll., Cambridge (MA). Ordained minister, C of S, 1970, and priest, C of E, 1982. Asst Minister, Muirhouse, Edinburgh, 1969–70; Lectr in Divinity, Univ. of Glasgow, 1969–73; Cambridge University: Lectr in Divinity, 1973–86; Fellow, Wolfson Coll., 1975–82; Fellow and Dean, Trinity Hall, 1982–86; Glasgow University: Dean, Faculty of Divinity, 1988–90; Dir, Centre for Theol., Lit. and the Arts, 1999–2002. Hensley Henson Lectr, Oxford, 1995. Vis. Prof., Univ. of Mainz, 1999; Vis. Scholar: Claremont Sch. of Theol., Calif, 2002; Princeton Theol Seminary, 2005, 2009. Hon. Fellow, Sch. of Divinity, Univ. of Edinburgh, 2010. Member: Doctrine Commn, C of E, 1983–86; Doctrine Cttee, Scottish Episcopal Ch, 2008–11; Convener, Panel on Doctrine, C of S, 1995–99. Member: Eur. Cttee, World Alliance of Reformed Churches, 1987–95; Church and Nation Cttee, C of S, 1992–96; Unity, Faith and Order Commn, Action for Churches Together in Scotland, 1995–; Scottish Churches Initiative for Unity, 1995–2003; HEFCE RAE Panel for Theology and Religious Studies, 1996, 2001, 2008 (Chm.); Center of Theol Inquiry, Princeton, 1998; Netherlands RAE Panel, 1999. Founder Mem., Affirmation Scotland, 2006–17. Pres., Soc. for Study of Theology, 2013–14. FRSA 2005; FRSE 2008. Member, Editorial Board: Theology in Scotland, 1996–2016; Conversations in Religion and Theol., 2007–11; Modern Believing, 2011–. *Publications:* Hilary of Poitiers, 1978; Theology of the Love of God, 1980; (ed) Explorations in Theology 8, 1981; The Church of God, 1984; Making Christian Decisions, 1985; God in Christian Perspective, 1994; Generosity and the Christian Future, 1997; (ed jtly) Scottish Christianity in the Modern World, 2000; John and Donald Baillie: transatlantic theology, 2002; The Transformative Imagination, 2004; (ed jtly) Fifty Key Christian Thinkers, 2004; (ed jtly) Believing in the Text, 2004; Traces of Liberality, 2006; Christ and Human Rights, 2006; (jtly) Faith and Human Rights, 2008; (jtly) Hospitable God, 2010; Spirit of Liberality, 2014; *festschrift:* The God of Love and Human Dignity: essays for George Newlands, by P. Middleton, 2007; contribs to theol pubns. *Recreations:* music, walking. *Address:* 49 Highsett, Cambridge CB2 1NZ. *Club:* New (Edinburgh).

**NEWLING, Caro,** OBE 2018; Joint Founder and Director, Neal Street Productions Ltd, since 2003; *b* London, 12 April 1957; adopted *d* of John and Evelyn Newling; partner, Gary Hamilton Powell. *Educ:* Brighton and Hove High Sch.; Roedean Sch.; Warwick Univ. (BA Hons Th. Studies); Webber-Douglas Acad. of Dramatic Art. Sen. Press Officer, RSC, 1986–91; Co-Founder and Exec. Producer, Donmar Warehouse Th., 1992–2002; over 70 prodns for Donmar Warehouse, W End and NY; prodns for Neal Street Productions, London and NY, incl. The Bridge Project, Shrek The Musical, Charlie and the Chocolate Factory, The Moderate Soprano, The Lehman Trilogy, The Ferryman, This House. Chair, Paines Plough, 2011–; Member: Bd, National Th., 2002–10; Bd of Mgt, Soc. of London Theatre, 2008– (Pres., 2014–17). Chair, Linbury Biennial Prize for Stage Design, 2010–. Hon. FRWCMD, 2017. *Recreation:* walking the Sussex Downs and the Scottish hills with friends and dogs. *Address:* Neal Street Productions Ltd, 26–28 Neal Street, First Floor, Covent Garden, WC2H 9QQ. *T:* (020) 7240 8890. *E:* post@nealstreetproductions.com.

**NEWLOVE,** family name of **Baroness Newlove.**

**NEWLOVE, Baroness** *cr* 2010 (Life Peer), of Warrington in the County of Cheshire; **Helen Margaret Newlove;** community reform campaigner; Victims' Commissioner, 2012–19; *b* Salford, 28 Dec. 1961; *m* 1986, Garry Newlove (*d* 2007); three *d*; *m* 2012, Paul Shacklady. Campaigner against anti-social behaviour. Founder, Newlove Warrington, 2008. Mem. Bd, Centre for Contemp. Coronial Law, Univ. of Bolton. *Publications:* It Could Happen to You, 2013. *Address:* House of Lords, SW1A 0PW.

**NEWMAN, Rt Rev. Adrian;** Area Bishop of Stepney, 2011–18; *b* 21 Dec. 1958; *s* of John Henry Newman and Ruth Doreen Newman; *m* 1981, Gillian Ann Hayes; three *s*. *Educ:* Univ. of Bristol (BSc (Econ.) 1980); Trinity Theol Coll., Bristol (DipHE (Theol.) 1985; MPhil (Theol.) 1989). Ordained deacon, 1985, priest, 1986; Curate, St Mark's, Forest Gate, 1985–89; Vicar, Hillsborough and Wadsley Bridge, Sheffield, 1989–96; Rector, St Martin in the Bull Ring, Birmingham, 1996–2004; Dean of Rochester, 2005–11. *Recreations:* sport, music, reading.

**NEWMAN, Andrew William;** Chief Executive, Spelthorne Community Television, since 2015; *b* Plymouth, 4 Nov. 1969; *s* of Alastair John Newman and Geraldine Newman; *m* 2002, Terry Louise Burgess; two *s*. *Educ:* St Paul's Sch., London; University Coll. London (BSc Psychol.). Researcher, 1992–93, Asst Producer, 1993–95, Big Breakfast and The Word, Planet 24 Prodns; Asst Producer and writer, Brasseye, Talkback Prodns, 1995–96; Producer: Big Breakfast, Planet 24 Prodns, 1996–97; The Sunday Show, BBC TV, 1997; The 11 O'Clock Show and Ali G, Talkback Prodns, 1998; Commng Editor, Channel 4, 1999–2000; Hd of Progs, E4, 2000–01; Controller of Entertainment, Channel Five, 2001–03; Hd of Entertainment, 2003–05, Hd of Entertainment and Comedy, 2005–09, Channel 4; Chief Creative Officer, 2009–11, Chief Exec., 2011–15, Objective Productions. Exec. Prod., TV series, Who Is America, 2018. Chm., TV Cttee, BAFTA, 2011– (Dep. Chm., 2009–11). Member: BAFTA; Magic Circle. *Recreations:* watching television, collecting vintage Vivienne Westwood clothes, entertaining children, loving and hating contemporary art, buying books on Francis Bacon, magic, photography, arguing, occasional journalism, going for lunch, watching more television. *Address:* 49 Star Street, W2 1QA. *T:* (020) 7262 7707. *E:* andrewnewman@spelthornecommunitytv.com. *Clubs:* Soho House, Ivy.

**NEWMAN, Catherine Mary;** QC 1995; a Recorder, since 2000; a Deputy High Court Judge, since 2008; Lieutenant-Bailiff (Judge) of the Royal Court of Guernsey, 2001–14; *b* 7 Feb. 1954; *d* of Dr Ernest Newman and Josephine (*née* McLaughlin); one *s* one *d*. *Educ:* University Coll. London (LLB 1st Cl. Hons 1978). Called to the Bar, Middle Temple, 1979 (Harmsworth Schol.), Bencher, 2002; admitted to courts of Dubai Internat. Financial Centre, 2010; called to the Bar, BVI, 2011; in practice in business and commercial fields, Chancery Div., 1980–; Dep. Registrar in Bankruptcy, 1991–2000; an Asst Recorder, 1998–2000. Member: Bar Council, 1987–90; Public Interest Adv. Panel, Legal Services Commn, 2000–04; Council, UCL, 2008–11. Chm., Inns of Ct and Bar Educnl Trust, 2005–13. Mem. (formerly Foundn) Trustee, CAFOD, 2009–. *Publications:* Bar Finals Guide, 1980, 3rd edn 1987; Insolvency Issues, 1999; (Consulting Ed.) French on Winding Up, 2nd edn, 2008. *Recreation:* eating with friends. *Address:* Maitland Chambers, 7 Stone Buildings, Lincoln's Inn, WC2A 3SZ. *T:* (020) 7406 1200.

**NEWMAN, Cathy;** presenter, Channel 4 News, since 2011; *b* Guildford, 14 July 1974; *d* of David Newman and Julia Newman; *m* 2001, John O'Connell; two *d*. *Educ:* Lady Margaret Hall, Oxford (BA 1st Cl. Hons English 1995). Researcher/trainee writer, The Independent, 1995–96; reporter, Media Week, 1996–97; contrib., Book Pages, Daily Telegraph, 1996–97; Media Business Reporter, The Independent, 1997; Financial Times: Media Corresp., 1998–99; Political Corresp., 1999–2002; Chief Political Corresp., 2002–06; Political Corresp., Channel 4 News, 2006–11. Presenter, Sunday Prog., GMTV, 2000–05. Regular blogger, Daily Telegraph, 2012–. Judge, Baileys Women's Prize for Fiction, 2015. Laurence Stern Fellow, Washington Post, 2000. Patron, Kids, 2016–. *Publications:* Bloody Brilliant Women: the pioneers, revolutionaries and geniuses your history teachers forgot to mention, 2018. *Recreations:* playing the violin, gardening, watching Agatha Christie adaptations, matchmaking (unsuccessful), walking on Exmoor. *Address:* Channel 4 News, ITN, 200 Gray's Inn Road, WC1X 8XZ. *T:* (020) 7833 3000. *E:* cathy.newman@itn.co.uk. *Club:* Soho House.

**NEWMAN, Charles William Frank;** a District Judge, 1991–2018; *b* 30 May 1946; *s* of John Leonard Newman and Enid Mary Newman; *m* 1st, 1970, Clare Willatt (decd); one *d*; 2nd, 1986, Anna Elizabeth Meacock; two *s*. *Educ:* Hawthorne Road Primary Sch., Kettering; Kimbolton Sch.; Queen Mary Coll., London (LLB Hons 1968). Admitted solicitor, 1972; Registrar of Co. Court, 1987. Mem., Judicial Appts Commn, 2006–12. Gov., Queen's Sch., Chester, 2003–09. *Recreations:* cooking, wine, reading, walking in the Lakes. *Club:* Army and Navy.

**NEWMAN, Ven. David Maurice Frederick;** Warden, Launde Abbey, since 2017; *b* Woking, 23 Aug. 1954; *s* of Frederick Newman and Peggy Newman; *m* 1982, Rev. Canon Helen Greet; one *s* two *d*. *Educ:* Hertford Coll., Oxford (MA 1979); St John's Coll., Nottingham (DipTh 1977). Ordained deacon, 1979, priest, 1980; Assistant Curate: Christ Church, Orpington, 1979–83; St Mary's, Bushbury, W Midlands, 1983–86; Vicar, All Saints, Ockbrook, and St Stephens, Borrowash, Derbyshire, 1986–97; Team Rector, Emmanuel, Loughborough and St Mary-in-Charnwood, 1997–2009; Rural Dean, Akeley E, Loughborough, 1999–2006; Archdeacon of Loughborough, 2009–17. Hon. Canon, Leicester Cathedral, 2006–. *Publications:* What Are We About to Receive?, 1982; (ed) Taking on Faith in the City, 1986; Growing Up into the Children of God, 2019. *Recreations:* walking, sport, theatre. *Address:* Launde Abbey, East Norton, Leics LE7 9XB. *T:* (01572) 717254. *E:* dmfnewman@gmail.com.

**NEWMAN, Edward;** Member (Lab), Manchester City Council, 1979–85 and since 2002; *b* 14 May 1953; *m* (decd); three *c*. Formerly in light engineering, cable making; postal worker, Manchester. Manchester City Council: Exec. Mem. for Housing, then Neighbourhood Services, 2004–08; Chair: Health Scrutiny (formerly Health and Wellbeing) Cttee, 2011–15; Manchester and Trafford Jt Health Scrutiny Cttee, 2013–17; Dep. Lord Mayor, 2016–17; Lord Mayor, 2017–18. MEP (Lab) Greater Manchester Central, 1984–99. Mem. Bd, Willow Park Housing Trust, Wythenshawe, Manchester, 2004–13 (Chm., 2008–11); Chm. Bd, Wythenshawe Community Housing Gp, 2013–16. *Publications:* (contrib.) The European Ombudsman: origins, establishment, evolution, 2005. *Address:* 234 Ryebank Road, Chorlton cum Hardy, Manchester M21 9LU.

**NEWMAN, Sir Francis (Hugh Cecil),** 4th Bt *cr* 1912, of Cecil Lodge, Newmarket; *b* 12 June 1963; *s* of Sir Gerard Robert Henry Sigismund Newman, 3rd Bt and of Caroline Philippa, *d* of late Brig. Alfred Geoffrey Neville, CBE, MC; *S* father, 1987; *m* 1990, Katharine, *d* of Timothy Edwards; three *s* one *d*. *Educ:* Eton; Univ. of Pennsylvania (BA Econs). *Recreations:* family, collecting, sport. *Heir:* s Thomas Ralph Gerard Newman, *b* 7 Jan. 1993. *Address:* Burloes Hall, Royston, Herts SG8 9NE. *Clubs:* Pratt's, Turf; Eton Vikings.

**NEWMAN, Sir Geoffrey (Robert),** 6th Bt *cr* 1836; Director, Blackpool Sands (Devon) Utilities Co. Ltd, since 1970; *b* 2 June 1947; *s* of Sir Ralph Alured Newman, 5th Bt, and Hon. Ann Rosemary Hope, *d* of late Hon. Claude Hope-Morley; *S* father, 1968; *m* 1980, Mary, *y d* of Colonel Sir Martin St John Valentine Gibbs, KCVO, CB, DSO, TD; one *s* three *d*. *Educ:* Heatherdown, Ascot; Kelly Coll., Tavistock. 1st Bn, Grenadier Guards, 1967–70; Lt, T&AVR, until 1979. Daniel Greenaway & Sons Ltd, 1973–75; Mem., Transglobe Expedition, 1977–79; Prodn Controller, Wadlow Grosvenor Internat., 1980–90. Vice Chm. and Dir, Dartmouth Tourist Inf. Centre, 1995–2003; Mem., Devon Assoc. of Tourist Attractions, 1995–. Chm., Dartmouth Outdoor Swimming Pool, 1999–2013. Walk Leader/Guide, The Wayfarers, 1990–2005. Pres., Dartmouth and Kingswear Soc., 2001–; Chm., Marine Conservation Soc., 2002–10. Vice Pres., Dartmouth Rugby Football Club, 2005–; Trustee, Britannia Mus., Britannia RNC, 2007–; Chm., Dartmouth and Dist Indoor Pool Trust, 2008–. FRGS. *Recreations:* sub-aqua, sailing, all sports. *Heir:* s Robert Melvil Newman, *b* 4 Oct. 1985.

**NEWMAN, Jeremy Steven,** FCA; Chairman, Optionis (formerly Arkarius) Group Ltd, since 2014; *b* 30 Sept. 1959; *s* of Harold and Marilyn Newman; *m* 1987, Judi Levy; one *s* one *d*. *Educ:* Haberdashers' Aske's Sch., Elstree; City of London Poly. (Dip. Accountancy with Dist.); Harvard Business Sch. (AMP; ISMP). FCA 1982. Stoy Hayward & Co., then BDO Stoy Hayward LLP, later BDO LLP, 1978–2011; Partner, 1986; Man. Partner, 2001–08; CEO, BDO Internat., 2008–11; Chm., Audit Commn, 2012–15; Chm., Single Source Regulations Office, 2014–16. Member: Murray Cttee on Audit Firm Governance, 2008–09; Internat. Integrated Reporting Cttee, 2009–11; Panel, CMA, 2017–; non-exec. Bd Mem. and Chm., Audit and Risk Cttee, CPS, 2012–18; Lead non-exec. Bd Mem., Dep.

Chm., and Chm., Audit and Risk Cttee, Govt Law Dept (formerly Treasury Solicitor's Dept), 2013–18. Non-executive Director: Social Investment Business, 2013–; Social and Sustainable Capital, 2017–. Chair, Workforce Develt Trust (formerly Skills for Health and Justice), 2017–. Trustee, Social Investment Business Foundn, 2013–. Hon. Treasurer: British ORT, 1986–95; Community Security Trust, 2000–09; Labour Friends of Israel, 2004–05; Trustee, various charitable trusts; Trustee, Frontline, 2018– (Chair, Finance, Audit and Risk Cttee, 2018–); Chm. of Trustees, Sacks Morasha (formerly Morasha) Jewish Primary Sch., 2007–; Founder Mem. and Gov., Leigh City Technology Coll., 1990–2008; Gov. and Chair, Audit Cttee, N Herts Coll. Hart Learning Gp, 2016–18. Mem. Council and Finance Cttee, Open Univ., 2014–17. Hon. Vis. Prof., Cass Business Sch., 2013–. *Recreations:* opera, cinema, reading, spending time with my wife and children, foreign travel. *E:* jeremysnewman@hotmail.com.

**NEWMAN, John Arthur,** FSA; Reader, Courtauld Institute of Art, University of London, 1987–2001; *b* 14 Dec. 1936; *s* of late Arthur Charles Cecil Newman and Wynifred Kate Newman (*née* Owles); *m* 1965, Margaret Banner; two d. *Educ:* Dulwich Coll.; University Coll., Oxford (MA); Courtauld Inst. of Art, London Univ. (Academic Dip. 1965). Lectr, Courtauld Inst. of Art, 1966–87. Mem., Historic Buildings Council for England, 1977–84; Comr, English Heritage, 1986–89; Chm., Adv. Bd for Redundant Churches, 2000–05; Mem., Royal Commn on Ancient and Historical Monuments of Wales, 2000–10. Pres., Soc. of Architectural Historians of GB, 1988–92. *Publications:* Buildings of England series: Kent (2 vols), 1969, rev. edns as: vol. I, Kent: West and the Weald, 2012, vol. II, Kent: North East and East, 2013; (with Nikolaus Pevsner) Dorset, 1972; Shropshire, 2nd edn 2006; (contrib.) The History of the King's Works, vol. V, 1975; (ed with Howard Colvin) Roger North on Architecture, 1981; (contrib.) The History of the University of Oxford, vol. III, 1986, vol. IV, 1997; Buildings of Wales series: Glamorgan, 1995; Gwent/Monmouthshire, 2000. *Address:* 29 Scotton Street, Wye, Ashford, Kent TN25 5BU.

**NEWMAN, Prof. Judith Alice,** OBE 2012; PhD; Professor of American Studies, University of Nottingham, 2000–15, now Emeritus; *b* 9 May 1950; *d* of Ellis Edward Newman and Alice Dorothy Elizabeth Newman (*née* Herringshaw); *m* 1978, Ian Revie (marr. diss. 1999); one s, and one step s. *Educ:* Univ. of Edinburgh (MA English, MA French); Clare Coll., Cambridge (PhD 1982). University of Newcastle upon Tyne: Lectr, 1976–91; Reader, 1991–95; Prof. of American and Postcolonial Literature, 1995–2000. Chairman: British Assoc. for American Studies, 1995–98 (Sec., 1993–95; Hon. Fellow, 2018); American Studies Panel, 2001 RAE; Main Panel L, 2008 RAE; Member: AHRC Res. Panel for English, 2004–07 (Convenor, 2007–09); AHRC Peer Review Coll., 2004. Founding FEA 1999; AcSS 2000. *Publications:* Saul Bellow and History, 1984; John Updike, 1988; Nadine Gordimer, 1988, reprinted 2014 (trans. Spanish 1997); (ed) Dred: a tale of the Great Dismal Swamp, 1992, 2nd edn 1998; The Ballistic Bard, 1995; Alison Lurie, 2000; Nadine Gordimer's Burger's Daughter (critical essays), 2003; Fictions of America, 2007; (ed with Celeste-Marie Bernier) Public Art, Memorials and Atlantic Slavery, 2009; Utopia and Terror in Contemporary American Fiction, 2013; (ed jtly) Edinburgh Companion to Nineteenth-Century American Letters and Letter-Writing, 2016; 110 scholarly essays in learned jls and collections. *Recreations:* family, gardening, genealogy, trips home to Caithness, learning Spanish, University of the Third Age. *Address:* School of American and Canadian Studies, University of Nottingham, University Park, Nottingham NG7 2RD. *T:* (0115) 921 3722. *E:* Judith.Newman@nottingham.ac.uk.

**NEWMAN, Kevin;** Senior Executive Vice President, 2003–15, and Head of Retail Banking and Wealth Management, 2014–15, HSBC Bank USA; *b* 28 June 1957; *s* of John and Valerie Newman; *m* 1983, Catherine Stewart-Murray; two s one d. *Educ:* Keele Univ. (BA Amer. Studies and Politics); Essex Univ. (US Govt and Politics). Mars Gp Services, 1981–85; Inf. Centre Manager, Business Systems Manager and Management Inf. Systems Dir, Woolworth, 1985–89; First Direct: joined 1989; Ops Dir, 1990; Chief Exec., 1991–97; Global Delivery Dir, Citibank, 1997–2000; Hd, HSBC.com, 2001–03; Hd, Personal Financial Services, HSBC USA, 2003–09; Hd, One HSBC Prog., 2009–11; Gp Hd, Retail Banking, HSBC, 2011–14. *Recreations:* squash, tennis, ski-ing, golf, gym workout, American football, family.

**NEWMAN, Malcolm,** CPFA; Director, Pragmatics, since 2006; *b* 2 April 1946; *s* of John George and Elizabeth Newman; *m* 1980, Marilyn Wilson; one s one d. *Educ:* Jarrow Grammar Sch. Clerk, Hebburn UDC, 1962–66; Newcastle upon Tyne City Council: various positions, 1966–71; Sen. Audit Asst, 1971–72; Sen. Management Accountant, 1972–73; Chief Accountant, 1973–77; Asst City Treas. (Accounting), 1977–79; Man. (Cons.) and Gen. Man., Wilson Johnson, 1979–80; Asst Finance Officer (Audit and Tech.), Sefton MDC, 1980–82; Hd of Financial Services 1982–85, Bor. Treas. 1985–87, London Borough of Southwark; City Treas., 1987–97, Dep. Chief Exec., 1990–97, Sheffield City Council; Dir, John Carlisle Partnerships, 1997–2006. Director: Hallamshire Investments plc, 1988–97; Northern Gen. Hosp. NHS Trust, 1997; Chm., START Fedn, 1994. Governor: Sheffield Hallam Univ. (formerly Sheffield Poly.), 1989–94; Silverdale Sch., 1993–97. *Recreations:* outdoors, jogging, Newcastle United, learning about myself.

**NEWMAN, Nanette, (Mrs Bryan Forbes);** actress and writer; *b* 29 May 1934; *d* of Sidney and Ruby Newman; *m* 1955, Bryan Forbes, CBE (d 2013); two d. *Educ:* Sternhold Coll., London; Italia Conti Stage Sch.; RADA. Appeared as a child in various films for Children's Film Foundn; other film appearances include: The L-Shaped Room, 1962; The Wrong Arm of the Law, 1962; Seance on a Wet Afternoon, 1963; The Wrong Box, 1965; The Whisperers, 1966; Deadfall, 1967; The Madwoman of Chaillot, 1968; The Raging Moon, 1971 (Variety Club Best Film Actress Award); The Stepford Wives, 1974; International Velvet, 1978 (Evening News Best Film Actress Award); The Mystery of Edwin Drood, 1992; *television:* Call My Bluff, What's My Line, London Scene, Stay with me till Morning, Jessie (title role), Let There Be Love, A Breath of Fresh Air, Late Expectations, The Endless Game, The Mixer; own series: The Fun Food Factory, 1977; Newman Meets, 2000–01; Celebrations, 2001; Patten on a Plate, 2001. *Publications:* God Bless Love, 1972 (repr. 16 times); Lots of Love, 1973 (repr. 7 times); Vote for Love, 1976 (repr. 4 times); All Our Love, 1978; Fun Food Factory, 1976 (repr. twice); Fun Food Feasts, 1978; The Root Children, 1978; The Pig Who Never Was, 1979; Amy Rainbow, 1980; The Facts of Love, 1980; That Dog, 1980, reissued 2011; Reflections, 1981; The Dog Lover's Coffee Table Book, 1982; The Cat Lover's Coffee Table Book, 1983; My Granny was a Frightful Bore, 1983, repr. 2003; A Cat and Mouse Love Story, 1984; Nanette Newman's Christmas Cook Book, 1984; Pigalev, 1985; The Best of Love, 1985; The Summer Cookbook, 1986; Archie, 1986; Small Beginnings, 1987; Bad Baby, 1988; Entertaining with Nanette Newman and her Daughters Sarah and Emma, 1988; Sharing, 1989; Charlie the Noisy Caterpillar, 1989; ABC, 1990; 123, 1991; Cooking for Friends, 1991; Spider the Horrible Cat, 1992; There's a Bear in the Bath, 1993; There's a Bear in the Classroom, 1996; The Importance of Being Ernest the Earwig, 1996; Take 3 Cooks, 1996; Up to the Sky and Down Again, 1999; To You With Love, 1999; Bedtime Stories, 2002; Good Baby, Bad Baby, 2003; Small Talk, 2004; Ben's Book, 2005; Eating In, 2005; What Will You Be, Grandma?, 2011. *Recreation:* painting. *Address:* c/o Lloyds Private Banking, 50 Grosvenor Street, W1K 3LF. *Fax:* (01344) 845174.

**NEWMAN, Paul Lance;** QC 2009; *b* London, 30 Nov. 1966; *s* of Philip Newman and Valerie Elizabeth Newman (*née* Da Costa); *m* 2015, Emily Charlotte Campbell; three s by a previous marriage. *Educ:* Downing Coll., Cambridge (BA 1989); Harvard Law Sch. (LLM). Hardwicke and Kennedy Schol., Lincoln's Inn, 1989; called to the Bar, Lincoln's Inn, 1991; in practice as barrister, 1992–. *Publications:* contribs to legal jls. *Recreations:* sport (particularly cricket and football), history, music. *Address:* Wilberforce Chambers, 8 New Square, Lincoln's Inn, WC1A 3QP. *T:* (020) 7306 0102, *Fax:* (020) 7306 0095. *E:* pnewman@wilberforce.co.uk. *Clubs:* Bentley Cricket (Vice-Pres.); Southgate Hockey (Oakwood).

**NEWMAN, Vice Adm. Sir Roy (Thomas),** KCB 1992 (CB 1991); JP; DL; Flag Officer Plymouth, and Commander Central Sub Area Eastern Atlantic, 1992–96; *b* 8 Sept. 1936; *s* of Mr and Mrs T. U. Newman; *m* 1960, Heather (née Macleod); four s. *Educ:* Queen Elizabeth's Grammar Sch., Barnet, Herts; Open Univ. (BA). Joined RN, 1954; specialised in anti-submarine warfare, 1963; joined Submarine Service, 1966; Comdr 1971, Captain 1979; commanded: HMS Onyx, 1970–71; HMS Naiad, 1978–79; First Submarine Sqn and HMS Dolphin, 1981–83; Seventh Frigate Sqn and HMS Cleopatra, 1984–85; Dir of Naval Warfare, 1986–88; Flag Officer Sea Trng, 1988–89; COS to C-in-C Fleet and Dep. Comdr Fleet, 1990–92. Pres., Royal Naval Assoc., 1996–2001 (Vice Patron, 2001–). Chm., Trustees, RN Submarine Mus., 1998–2005. Younger Brother, Trinity House, 1997. Freeman, Shipwrights' Co., 1996. JP SE Hants, 1996; DL Hants, 2001. *Recreations:* cricket, golf, music, art.

**NEWMAN TAYLOR, Sir Anthony (John),** Kt 2008; CBE 2003 (OBE 1992); FRCP; FFOM, FMedSci; Professor of Occupational and Environmental Medicine, Imperial College London, since 1992; *b* 11 Dec. 1943; *s* of Reginald John Newman Taylor and Violet Anne (*née* Hilliard); *m* 1st, 1968, Gillian Frances Crick (marr. diss.); two s one d; 2nd, 1986, Frances Victoria Costley; one s. *Educ:* Radley Coll.; St Bartholomew's Hosp. Med. Coll. (MB BS 1970; MSc 1979). FRCP 1986; FFOM 1987; FMedSci 1999. Postgrad. trng, St Bartholomew's and Brompton Hosps, 1970–77; Royal Brompton Hospital: Consultant Physician, 1977–2010; Med. Dir, 1994–2005; Dir of Research, 1997–2006; Acting Chief Exec., 1996, July–Oct. 2002 and June 2004–March 2005; Dep. Chief Exec., 2003–06; Faculty of Medicine, Imperial College London: Hd, 2006–08, Dir, R&D, 2012–18, Nat. Heart and Lung Inst.; Dep. Principal, 2008–10; Principal, 2010–12; President's Envoy for Health, 2012–. Non-exec. Dir, Imperial Coll. London Healthcare NHS Trust, 2012–16. Civilian Advr in Chest Medicine to RAF, 1983–2010. Chairman: Industrial Injuries Adv. Council, 1996–2008 (Mem., 1983–2008; Chm., Res. Wkg Gp, 1984–96); Ind. Medical Expert Gp, Armed Forces Compensation Scheme, 2010–; HSE Workplace Health Expert Cttee, 2015–; Adv. Bd for Nat. Centre for Mesothelioma Res., 2017–. Member: MRC Cttee on toxic hazards in envmt and workplace, 1982–90; Bevan Commn, 2008–; Ind. Scrutiny Gp Armed Forces Compensation Scheme Rev., 2010–11; Central Adv. Cttee on Pensions and Compensation, MoD, 2011–; Adv. Bd, Centre for Blast Injuries Studies, RBL, 2012–. Advr in occupational medicine, Nat. Asthma Campaign, subseq. Asthma UK, 1994–2010. WHO Advr to Minister of Health, India on long term consequences of methyl isocyanate exposure to population of Bhopal, 1985; Advr to Dept of Health, Valencia on epidemic of lung disease in textile spray workers, 1994. Mem., Health Honours Cttee, 2005–12. Chm., Coronary Artery Disease Res. Assoc., 1998–2009 (Trustee, 2009–14). non-executive Director: Royal Brompton and Harefield Trust, subseq. Foundn Trust, 2006–12; Imperial Coll. Healthcare NHS Trust, 2012–. Gov., Chislehurst C of E Primary Sch., 1995–99. *Publications:* (Sen. Ed.) Parkes Occupational Lung Disorders, 4th edn 2016; chapters in textbooks on respiratory disease and occupational and environmental lung disease; papers in Lancet, BMJ, Thorax, Amer. Jl of Respiratory Disease and Critical Care Medicine; Jl of Allergy and Clinical Immunology, etc. *Recreations:* history and politics, cricket. *Address:* 11 Waldegrave Road, Bickley, Kent BR1 2JP. *Clubs:* Athenæum, MCC.

**NEWMARK, Brooks Phillip Victor;** Research Associate, Department of Politics and International Relations, University of Oxford, since 2015; *b* 8 May 1958; *s* of late Howard Newmark and of Gilda Newmark (now Gourlay); *m* 1985, Lucy Keegan; four s one d. *Educ:* Bedford Sch.; Harvard Coll. (AB); Worcester Coll., Oxford (DPhil); Harvard Business Sch. (MBA); St Antony's Coll., Oxford (MSc). Vice Pres., Shearson Lehman Brothers Inc., 1984–87; Director: Newmark Brothers Ltd, 1987–92; Stellican Ltd, 1992–98; Partner, Apollo Mgt LP, 1998–2005. Contested (C): Newcastle Central, 1997; Braintree, 2001. MP (C) Braintree, 2005–15. Opposition Whip, HM Treasury, 2007–08, Foreign Affairs, 2009–10; a Lord Comr of HM Treasury (Govt Whip), 2010–12; Parly Sec., Cabinet Office, 2014. Mem., Treasury Select Cttee, 2006–07, 2012–14. Mem., Adv. Panel on Rough Sleeping, 2018–. Founder and Co-Chm., Women2win, 2005–14; Founder: A Partner in Educn, 2009–; Million Jobs Campaign, 2012–14. Bd Dir, Harvard Univ. Alumni Assoc., 2005–15. Chm., United and Cecil Club, 2010–14. *Recreations:* football (Newcastle United supporter), running, ski-ing. *Clubs:* Beefsteak, Boodle's, White's; St Moritz Tobogganing.

**NEWPORT, Viscount;** Alexander Michael Orlando Bridgeman; *b* 6 Sept. 1980; *s* and heir of 7th Earl of Bradford, *qv*.

**NEWPORT, Dean of;** see Tonge, Very Rev. L.

**NEWRY AND MORNE, Viscount; Robert Francis John Needham;** Managing Director, Arctic Shores Ltd, since 2014; Principal Consultant, NewAtlantic Ltd, since 2014 (Managing Director, 2013–14); *b* 30 May 1966; *s* and heir to Earl of Kilmorey, *qv*; *m* 1991, Laura Mary, o *d* of Michael Tregaskis; one s one d. *Educ:* Sherborne Prep. School; Eton College; Lady Margaret Hall, Oxford (BA); Imperial Coll., London (MBA 1993). Management trainee, Benjamin Priest, 1988–90; Sales Man., Lewmar Marine Ltd, 1991–92; Asst Man., Business Develt, Inchcape Pacific Ltd, 1994–95; Business Develt Manager, Inchcape NRG, 1995–97; Dir, Ops, Inchcape NRG HK, 1998–2000; Exec. Dir, NRG Solutions, 1997–2000; Dir, Morne Consultancy Ltd, 2000; Associate Dir, Ricoh UK Ltd, 2001–03; Director: Collabra Net Solutions Ltd, 2000; Newfield Inf. Technol., 2003–13. Non-exec. Dir, Fenix Media Ltd, 2001–04. *Recreations:* running, conservation. *Heir:* s Hon. Thomas Francis Michael Needham, *b* 25 Sept. 1998.

**NEWSAM, Malcolm,** CBE 2017; Commissioner for Children's Services, Northamptonshire Council, since 2018; *b* Derby, 27 April 1955; *s* of Malcolm and Audrey Newsam; *m* 2007, Caroline Beddoe; two step s. *Educ:* Bemrose Grammar Sch.; Keble Coll., Oxford (BA Modern Hist. 1976); Leicester Univ. (MA Social Work 1982). Social worker, 1982–84, Social Services Manager, 1984–96, Derbyshire CC; Asst Dir, Derby CC, 1996–2002; Asst Rev. Dir, Audit Commn, 2002–03; Dir, Social Services, 2004–06, Dir, Children's Services, 2006–09, Beds CC; Interim Corporate Dir, Children's Services, Thurrock BC, 2009; Interim Exec. Dir, Schs, Children and Families, Essex CC, 2009–10; Interim Corporate Dir, Families and Social Care, Kent CC, 2011; Interim Dir of Children's Services, Peterborough CC, 2011–12, Improvement Consultant, Doncaster MBC, 2013; Associate Consultant, iMPOWER Consulting, 2013–14; Improvement Consultant, Haringey LBC, 2014–16; Project Dir, Doncaster MBC, 2013–14; Comr for Children's Social Care, Rotherham MBC, 2014–16; Ind. Chair, Improvement Bd, Knowsley BC, 2014–17; Comr for Children's Services, Sandwell Council, 2016–18. *Recreations:* cinema, travel, restaurants, hill walking, Eastern religions and meditation. *Address:* Imprana Ltd, 59 Union Street, Dunstable, Beds LU6 1EX. *T:* (01908) 281590. *E:* malcolm.newsam@live.co.uk.

**NEWSAM, Sir Peter (Anthony),** Kt 1987; Chairman, Central London Connexions Board, 2002–05; Director, University of London Institute of Education, 1989–94; *b* 2 Nov. 1928; *s* of late W. O. Newsam and of Mrs D. E. Newsam; *m* 1st, 1953, Elizabeth Joy Greg (marr. diss. 1987; she *d* 2012); four *s* one *d*; 2nd, 1988, Sue Addinell (marr. diss. 2017); one *d*; 3rd, 2017, Sarah King. *Educ:* Clifton Coll.; Queen's Coll., Oxford (MA, DipEd). Asst Principal, BoT, 1952–55; teacher, 1955–63; Asst Educn Officer, N Riding of Yorks, 1963–66; Asst Dir of Educn, Cumberland, 1966–70; Dep. Educn Officer: W Riding of Yorks, 1970–72; ILEA, 1972–76; Educn Officer, ILEA, 1977–82; Chm., CRE, 1982–87; Sec., ACC, 1987–89; Dep. Vice-Chancellor, Univ. of London, 1992–94; Chief Adjudicator, Sch. Orgn and Admissions, 1998–2002. Advr to Educn Select Cttee, 2002–05. *Address:* Greenlea, Church Lane, Thornton le Dale, Pickering, N Yorks YO18 7QL.

**NEWSON, Prof. Linda Ann,** OBE 2015; PhD; FBA 2000; Professor of Geography, King's College London, 1994–2011, now Emeritus; Director, Institute of Latin American Studies (formerly for the Study of the Americas), University of London, since 2012; *b* 2 Aug. 1946; *d* of Donald George Newson and Evelyn Maud Newson (*née* Lee). *Educ:* Grey Coat Hosp., Westminster; University Coll. London (BA 1967; PhD 1972). King's College, London: Lectr, 1971–87; Reader, 1987–94; Hd, Sch. of Humanities, 1997–2000; FKC 2001. Vis. Prof., Univ. of Calif. Berkeley, 1989. Fellow, Newberry Liby, Chicago, 1985 and 2000. Leverhulme Emeritus Fellow, 2011–13. Mem. Council, British Acad., 2007–10. Trustee: Latin America Bureau, 2014–; Canning House, 2015– (Liby Bd, 2017–). C. O. Sauer Award, Conf. of Latin Americanist Geographers, USA, 1992; Back Award, RGS, 1993; Preston James Lifetime Achievement Award, Conf. Latin Americanist Geographers, USA, 2017. *Publications:* Aboriginal and Spanish Colonial Trinidad: a study in culture contact, 1976; The Cost of Conquest: Indian societies in Honduras under Spanish rule, 1986; Indian Survival in Colonial Nicaragua, 1987; Patterns of Life and Death in Early Colonial Ecuador, 1995; (with S. Minchin) From Capture to Sale: the Portuguese slave trade to Spanish America in the early seventeenth century, 2007; Conquest and Pestilence in the Early Spanish Philippines, 2009; (ed with John P. King) Mexico City through History and Culture, 2009; Making Medicines in Early Colonial Lima, Peru: apothecaries, science and society, 2017. *Address:* Institute of Latin American Studies, School of Advanced Study, University of London, Malet Street, WC1E 7HU. *T:* (020) 7862 8868.

**NEWSON, Marc Andrew,** CBE 2012; RDI 2006; designer; *b* Sydney, Australia, 20 Oct. 1963; *s* of Carol Conomos; *m* 2008, Charlotte Stockdale; two *d*. *Educ:* Sydney Coll. of the Arts. Solo exhibitions include: Design Works, Powerhouse Mus., Sydney, 2001; Kelvin 40, Fondation Cartier pour l'art contemporain, Paris, 2004; Groningen Mus., Netherlands, 2004; Design Mus., London, 2004–05; Gagosian Gall., NY, 2007, 2010, 2019, London, 2008; Philadelphia Mus. of Art, 2013–14; group exhibitions include: Conrad Foundn Collection, Design Mus., London, 1996, (guest curator), 2001; Review Gall., Design Mus., London, 1998–99; Milan in a Van, V&A Mus., 2002; Somewhere Totally Else, Design Mus., London, 2003–04; Design Real, Serpentine Gall., 2009; Out of Hand, Mus. of Art and Design, NY, 2014; Design is a State of Mind, Serpentine Gall., 2014. Designer for Special Projects, Apple, 2014–19. Adjunct Professor in Design: Hong Kong Poly. Univ., 2007; Sydney Coll. of the Arts, 2007. Designer of Year Award, Design Miami, 2006; London Design Medal, London Design Fest., 2008. Hon. Dr Visual Arts Sydney. *Address:* Marc Newson Ltd, 7 Howick Place, SW1P 1BB. *T:* (020) 7932 0990, *Fax:* (020) 7630 6017. *E:* pod@marc-newson.com. *Clubs:* George, Groucho.

**NEWSON-SMITH, Sir Peter (Frank Graham),** 3rd Bt *cr* 1944, of Totteridge, co. Hertford; Director of Music, Claysemore Preparatory School, 1979–2003; *b* 8 May 1947; *s* of Sir John Newson-Smith, 2nd Bt and of Vera, Lady Newson-Smith; *S* father, 1997; *m* 1974, Mary Ann Owens (*née* Collins); one *s* one *d*, and two step *s*. *Educ:* Dover Coll.; Trinity Coll. of Music, London. GTCL; LT (MusEd). Asst Dir of Music, Dover Coll. Jun. Sch., 1969–73; Director of Music: Westbourne House, Chichester, 1973–78; Hazelwood, Limpsfield, 1978–79. Hon. Treas., Music Masters' Assoc., 2002–06. Chm., Young Musicians of Muscat, 2002–07. Freeman, City of London, 1969; Liveryman, Musicians' Co., 1969–. *Recreations:* travel, DIY, gardening. *Heir: s* Oliver Nicholas Peter Newson-Smith, *b* 12 Nov. 1975. *Address:* Old Beech House, Burton Street, Marnhull, Dorset DT10 1PP.

**NEWSUM, Jeremy Henry Moore;** DL; FRICS; Trustee, Grosvenor Estate, since 1993 (Executive Trustee, 1993–2016); Group Chief Executive, Grosvenor (formerly Chief Executive, Grosvenor Estate Holdings), 1989–2008 (non-executive Director, 2008–16); *b* 4 April 1955; *s* of late Neill Henry Hillas Newsum and Jane Ridsdale Newsum (*née* Moore); *m* 1979, Gillian Lucy Ratcliff; three *d*. *Educ:* Rugby; Reading Univ. (BSc Estate Mgt). With: Grosvenor Estate Holdings, 1976–78; Savills, 1979–85; London Partner, Bidwells, 1985–87; with Grosvenor (formerly Grosvenor Estate Hldgs), 1987–2016. Non-exec. Dir, TR Property Investment Trust, 2002–08. Pres., British Property Fedn, 2001–02; Chm., Urban Land Inst., 2009–11. Chm., Cambridge Ahead, 2013–14, now Hon. Vice Chm. A Church Comr, 1993–2000. Mem. Council, Imperial Coll. London, 2004–16. DL Cambs, 2014. *Recreation:* oil painting. *Address:* Priory House, Swavesey, Cambs CB24 4QJ. *T:* (01954) 232084.

**NEWTON,** 5th Baron *cr* 1892, of Newton-in-Makerfield, Co. Lancaster; **Richard Thomas Legh;** *b* 11 Jan. 1950; *er s* of 4th Baron Newton and Priscilla Egerton-Warburton; *S* father, 1992; *m* 1978, Rosemary Whitfoot, *yr d* of Herbert Clarke; one *s* one *d*. *Educ:* Eton; Christ Church, Oxford (MA). Solicitor, May May & Merrimans, 1976–79. General Comr for Income Tax, 1983–. Mem., Wealden DC, 1987–99. Mem., Sussex Downs Conservation Bd, 1992–95, 1997–98. *Recreation:* bridge. *Heir: s* Hon. Piers Richard Legh, *b* 25 Oct. 1979. *Address:* Laughton Park Farm, Laughton, Lewes, East Sussex BN8 6BU. *T:* (01825) 840627. *Clubs:* Pratt's, MCC.

**NEWTON, Air Vice-Marshal Barry Hamilton,** CB 1988; CVO 2006; OBE 1975; an Extra Gentleman Usher to the Queen, since 2002 (a Gentleman Usher, 1989–2002); *b* 1 April 1932; *m* 1959, Constance Lavinia Aitken (*d* 2016); one *s* one *d*. *Educ:* Highgate. RAF Coll. Cranwell, 1951; commnd 1953; 109 (Pathfinder) Sqn; 76 (cloud sampling) Sqn (nuclear weapon trials, Australia and Christmas Island, 1955–58); Flying Instructor, RAF Coll. Cranwell, 1959; Sqn Comdr, FTS, 1961; Personal Staff Officer to C-in-C RAF Germany/Comdr 2 ATAF, 1967; OC Ops Wing, RAF Cottesmore, 1969; Defence Policy Staff, 1972, ndc 1974; Cabinet Office, 1975–79; Air Cdre Flying Trng, HQ Support Comd, 1979–82; ADC to the Queen, 1982–83; Sen. RAF Mem., RCDS, 1983–85; Comdt, JSDC, 1986–88. Vice-Chm., Council of TAVRAs, 1989–99; (First) Hon. Air Cdre, 606 (Chiltern) Sqn, 1996–2007, Hon. Inspector-Gen., 2000–09, RAuxAF; Pres., UK Reserve Forces Assoc., 2005–13. Vice-Pres., Not Forgotten Assoc., 2016–. Hon. Freeman, Lightmongers' Co., 2002; Freeman, City of London, 2002; Liveryman, Hon. Co. of Air Pilots (formerly GAPAN), 2007–. *Recreations:* military history, walking, philately. *Address:* c/o National Westminster Bank, Blue Boar Row, Salisbury, Wilts SP1 1DF. *Club:* Royal Air Force.

**NEWTON, Clive Richard;** QC 2002; *s* of Henry Newton and Winifred Newton; *m* 1986, Robin Jeanne Williams (marr. diss. 1999); two *s*. *Educ:* Harrow Co. Grammar Sch. for Boys; Wadham Coll., Oxford (maj. schol.; BA First Cl. Hons; MA; BCL). Called to the Bar, Middle Temple, 1968 (Major Harmsworth Entrance Exhibnr; Astbury Law Schol.; Archibald Safford Prizeman; (jtly) Criminal Law Prize, 1967), Bencher, 2012; *ad eundem* Lincoln's Inn, 1978, Inner Temple, 1984; Lecturer: Wadham Coll., Oxford, 1969–76 and 1980–82; Oriel Coll., Oxford, 1985–. Mem., Anglo-American Real Property Institute, 1992–2005. *Publications:* General Principles of Law, 1972, 3rd edn 1983; (with R. S. Parker) Cases and Statutes on General Principles of Law, 1980; (ed jtly) Jackson's Matrimonial Finance and Taxation, 5th edn 1992 to 9th edn 2012. *Recreations:* walking, swimming, cricket, theatre. *Address:* 1 King's Bench Walk, Temple, EC4Y 7DB. *T:* (020) 7936 1500, *Fax:* (020) 7936 1590. *E:* cnewton@1kbw.co.uk.

**NEWTON, Derek Henry;** Chairman, C. E. Heath plc, 1984–87; *b* 14 March 1933; *s* of Sidney Wellington Newton and Sylvia May Newton (*née* Peacock); *m* 1st, 1957, Judith Ann (*d* 1995), *d* of Roland Hart, Kingston, Surrey; two *d*; 2nd, 2012, Angela Mary, *d* of Sir George Robert Edwards, OM, CBE, FRS. *Educ:* Emanuel School. FCII. Commissioned Royal Artillery, 1952–54 (Lieut). Clerical, Medical & General Life Assurance Society, 1954–58; C. E. Heath Urquhart (Life & Pensions), 1958–83, Chm., 1971–84; Dir, C. E. Heath, 1975, Dep. Chm., 1983–84; Director: Glaxo Insurance (Bermuda), 1980–93; Glaxo Trustees, 1980–92; Clarges Pharmaceutical Trustees, 1985–92. Governor, BUPA Med. R&D, 1981–94. *Recreations:* cricket, golf. *Address:* Pantiles, Meadway, Oxshott, Surrey KT22 0LZ. *T:* (01372) 842273. *E:* derekhnewton@hotmail.com. *Clubs:* Royal Automobile, MCC; Surrey County Cricket (Chm., 1979–94; Pres., 2004).

**NEWTON, Rev. Canon Sir George (Peter Howgill),** 4th Bt *cr* 1900, of The Wood, Sydenham Hill; Vicar, Holy Trinity, Aldershot, since 2003 (Priest-in-charge, 1999–2003); *b* 26 March 1962; *s* of Sir (Harry) Michael (Rex) Newton, 3rd Bt and Pauline Jane Newton; *S* father, 2008; *m* 1988, Jane Louise Rymer; two *d*. *Educ:* Sherborne; Pembroke Coll., Cambridge (MA Maths; Sen. Optimae); Oak Hill Coll. (BA Theol and Pastoral Studies 1993). Ordained deacon, 1993, priest, 1994. Curate, St Thomas', Blackpool, 1993–99; Rural Dean, Aldershot, 2012–18. Hon. Canon, Guildford Cathedral, 2018–. Liveryman, Girdlers' Co. (Master, 2016–17). *Recreations:* cricket, bridge. *Heir: uncle* Rev. Canon Christopher Wynne Newton [*b* 23 July 1925; *m* 1950, Margaret Ormerod; two *s*]. *Address:* 2 Cranmore Lane, Aldershot, Hants GU11 3AS. *T:* (01252) 320618. *E:* vicar@htca.org.uk.

**NEWTON, Gillian Mary,** CBE 2009; Chief Executive, Fire Service College, Department for Communities and Local Government (formerly Office of the Deputy Prime Minister), 2004–08; *b* 13 Oct. 1952; *d* of late Thomas Frank Newton and Florence Elizabeth Newton (*née* Johnston). *Educ:* Trinity Grammar Sch., Northampton; Univ. of Hull; St Thomas' Hosp., London (RGN 1975); South Bank Poly., London (DipEd 1984); Univ. of Surrey (MSc Educnl Studies 1988). Various posts incl. Ward Sister, and Asst Dir of Nurse Educn, NHS, 1975–93; Dir, Professional Develt, Frances Harrison Coll., Guildford, 1991–93; Head: Sch. of Health Studies, Univ. of Portsmouth, 1993–95; Educn, NHS Exec., DoH, 1995–2000; Trng and Develt, HM Prison Service, 2000–04. Member: Northants Police Authy, 2008–12; Northants Police Audit Cttee, 2012–14. Non-exec. Dir, E Midlands Ambulance Service NHS Trust, 2011–14. Trustee, Age UK (formerly Age Concern) Northants, 2009–12; Assoc. Visitor, MND Assoc., 2016–. *Publications:* (with C. Andrewes) Medical Nursing, 1984.

**NEWTON, Ian;** *see* Newton, R. E. I.

**NEWTON, Prof. Ian,** OBE 1999; FRS 1993; FRSE; Head, Avian (formerly Vertebrate) Ecology Section, NERC Institute of Terrestrial Ecology, 1989–99, now Emeritus Fellow, NERC Centre for Ecology and Hydrology; *b* 17 Jan. 1940; *s* of Haydn Edwin Newton and Nellie Newton (*née* Stubbs); *m* 1962, Halina Teresa Bialkowska; two *s* one *d*. *Educ:* Bristol Univ. (BSc Zoology 1961); Worcester Coll., Oxford (DPhil Ornithology 1964; DSc 1982). FRSE 1994. Dept of Zoology, Oxford, 1964–67; Nature Conservancy, Edinburgh, 1967–73; Institute of Terrestrial Ecology, Natural Environment Research Council: Edinburgh, 1973–79; Huntingdon, 1979–99; research on avian population ecology, incl. finches, waterfowl, birds of prey, impact of pesticides. President: BOU, 1999–2003 (Vice-Pres., 1989–93); British Ecological Soc., 1994–95; Chairman: Council, RSPB, 2003–08; Bd, Peregrine Fund, 2005–08; British Trust for Ornithol., 2009–13; Trustee, Jl British Birds, 2009–. Hon. Fellow, Amer. Ornith. Union, 1983. Hon. DSc Sheffield, 2001. Union Medal, BOU, 1988; President's Medal, British Ecological Soc., 1989; Gold Medal, RSPB, 1991; Elliott Coues Award, Amer. Ornith. Union, 1995; Marsh Award in Conservation Biology, Zool Soc. of London, 1995; Sarkis Acopian Award, Hawk Mountain Sanctuary, USA, 2007; Godman-Salvin Medal, BOU, 2010; Salim Ali Internat. Award for Nature Conservation, Bombay Natural History Soc., 2014. *Publications:* Finches, 1972; Population Ecology of Raptors, 1979; The Sparrowhawk, 1986; (ed) Lifetime Reproduction in Birds, 1989; Population Limitation in Birds, 1998; The Speciation and Biogeography of Birds, 2003; The Ecology of Bird Migration, 2008; Bird Migration, 2010; Bird Populations, 2013 (Marsh Award for best ecol. book, British Ecol Soc., 2014); Farming and Birds, 2017; papers in sci. jls. *Recreations:* apple growing, walking. *T:* (01529) 497255.

**NEWTON, Jeremy;** Vice Principal and Director of Advancement, Guildhall School of Music and Drama, since 2018; *b* 14 June 1955; *s* of Arthur James Newton and Dorothy Burton Newton; *m* 1978, Mary Rose Colleran; one *s* one *d*. *Educ:* Manchester GS; St John's Coll., Cambridge (MA Hons Mod. and Medieval Langs). FCA 1989. Audit Supervisor, Coopers & Lybrand, 1976–80; Dep. Dir, 1980–84, Dir, 1984–90, Chief Exec., 1990–94, Eastern Arts Assoc., then Eastern Arts Bd; Nat. Lottery Dir, Arts Council of England, 1994–98; Chief Exec., NESTA, 1998–2005; Dir, Louise T. Blouin Foundn, 2005–07; Man. Dir, RADA, 2007–08; Chief Exec., Prince's Foundn for Children and the Arts, later Children & the Arts, 2008–18. Chair: Youth Dance England, 2005–09; Nat. Assoc. of Youth Theatres, 2013–18. Fellow, Judge Business Sch., Univ. of Cambridge, 2009–. Trustee, Geffrye Mus., 2014–; Mem. Bd, Cambridge Live, 2015–18. DUniv Loughborough, 2006. *Recreations:* theatre, cinema, chess, lacrosse, stand-up comedy. *E:* jeremy.newton@gsmd.ac.uk.

**NEWTON, Sir John Garnar,** 4th Bt *cr* 1924, of Beckenham Kent; *b* 10 July 1945; *s* of Sir Kenneth Garnar Newton, 3rd Bt, OBE, TD and Margaret Isabel, *d* of Rev. Dr George Blair, Dundee; *S* father, 2008; *m* 1972, Jacynth Anne Kay Miller; three *s* (incl. twins). *Educ:* Reed's Sch., Cobham. Master, Leathersellers' Co., 2005–06. *Heir: er twin s* Timothy Garnar Newton [*b* 4 Sept. 1973; *m* 2004, Sarah Jane Howat].

**NEWTON, Prof. (John) Michael,** DSc; Professor of Pharmaceutics, School of Pharmacy, University of London, 1984–2001, now Emeritus (Fellow, School of Pharmacy, 2000); Hon. Professor, Department of Mechanical Engineering, University College London, since 2001; *b* 26 Dec. 1935; *s* of Richard and Dora Newton; *m* 1st, 1959, Janet Hinninghan (marr. diss. 1986); one *s* two *d*; 2nd, 2003, Fridrun Podczeck (*d* 2016). *Educ:* Leigh Grammar Sch., Lancs; Sch. of Pharmacy, Univ. of London (BPharm; DSc 1990); Univ. of Nottingham (PhD). FRPharmS. Apprentice pharmacist, Royal Albert Edward Infirmary, Wigan, 1953–55; Demonstrator, Univ. of Nottingham, 1958–62; Sen. Lectr, Sunderland Polytechnic, 1962–64; Lectr, Univ. of Manchester, 1964–67; Sen. Scientist, Lilly Research

Centre Ltd, 1968–71; Lectr, Univ. of Nottingham, 1972–78; Prof. of Pharmaceutics, Univ. of London, at Chelsea College, 1978–83. Mem., Medicines Commn, 1996–2000. Dist. Lectr, Nagai Foundn, Tokyo, 1997. Hon. Dr: Uppsala, 1995; Coimbra, 2013. Harrison Meml Medal, RPSGB, 1996. *Publications*: over 450 peer-reviewed pubns in sci. jls associated with pharmaceutical technology and engineering. *Recreations*: fell walking, long distance running (Belgrave Harriers), gardening.

**NEWTON, (John) Nigel;** Founder, and Chief Executive, Bloomsbury Publishing Plc, since 1986 (Chairman, 1986–2007); *b* 16 June 1955; *s* of late Peter Leigh Newton and Anne St Aubyn Newton; *m* 1981, Joanna Elizabeth Hastings-Trew; one *s* two *d*. *Educ*: Deerfield, Mass; Selwyn Coll., Cambridge (BA 1976; MA). Asst to Sales Dir, Macmillan Ltd, 1976–78; Dep. Man. Dir, Sidgwick & Jackson Ltd, 1978–86. Chm., World Book Day, 2006; Pres., Book Aid Internat., 2008–. Chairman: Charleston Trust, 2010–16; British Library Trust, 2012–. Trustee, IISS, 2012–. Former Mem. Council, Publishers Assoc. Mem., Visiting Cttee, Cambridge Univ. Library. Campaign mem., Rescue The Cuckmere Valley, 2002–. *Recreations*: walking, great views. *Address*: (office) 50 Bedford Square, WC1B 3DP. *T*: (020) 7631 5600. *E*: nigel.newton@bloomsbury.com. *Clubs*: Garrick, Beefsteak, MCC, Hurlingham.

**NEWTON, Prof. John Norman,** FRCP; FFPH; Director of Health Improvement (formerly Chief Knowledge Officer), Public Health England, since 2013; *b* Birmingham, 7 Jan. 1959; *s* of Eric and Eileen Newton; *m* 1987, Eva Stevens; one *d*. *Educ*: Shrewsbury Sch.; Trinity Coll., Oxford (MA); King's Coll. London (MB BS); London Sch. of Hygiene and Tropical Medicine (MSc). FRCP 1998; FFPH 2000. Consultant Epidemiologist, Univ. of Oxford, 1992–2003; Chief Exec., UK Biobank Ltd, 2003–05; Regl Dir, Public Health, NHS S Central, 2007–13. Associate, Eden Project, 2019–. Hon. Professor of Public Health: Univ. of Manchester, 2004–; Univ. of Exeter, 2016–; Professorial Fellow, RSPH, 2012–; Garden Fellow, RCP, 2012–. Vice-Pres., FPH, 2019–. *Publications*: contrib. papers on epidemiol. to jls incl. Lancet. *Recreation*: mountaineering. *Address*: Public Health England, Wellington House, 133–155 Waterloo Road, SE1 8UG. *T*: (020) 3682 0135. *E*: john.newton@phe.gov.uk.

**NEWTON, Julia Carolyn;** a District Judge (Magistrates' Courts), since 2010; *b* Morecambe, Lancs, 23 July 1955; *d* of Geoffrey Newton and Maureen Newton (*née* Wilkinson); *m* 1986, Mark Lanyon Hindley; three *d*. *Educ*: Univ. of Southampton (LLB 1976); Coll. of Law, Lancaster Gate. Admitted solicitor, 1979; a Dep. Dist Judge (Magistrates' Courts), 2003–10. *Address*: Highbury Corner Magistrates' Court, 51–53 Holloway Road, N7 8JA.

**NEWTON, Rt Rev. Mgr Keith;** First Ordinary, Personal Ordinariate of Our Lady of Walsingham, since 2011; *b* 10 April 1952; *s* of James Henry and Eva Newton; *m* 1973, Gillian Irene Newton (*née* Donnison); two *s* one *d*. *Educ*: Alsop High Sch., Liverpool; KCL (BD, AKC 1973); Christchurch Coll., Canterbury (PGCE 1974); St Augustine's Coll., Canterbury. Ordained deacon, 1975, priest, 1976; Curate, St Mary's, Gt Ilford, 1975–78; Vicar, i/c St Matthews, Wimbledon Team Ministry, 1978–85; Rector, St Paul's, Blantyre, Dio. Southern Malaŵi, 1985–86; Dean of Blantyre, 1986–91; Priest i/c, 1991–93, Vicar, 1993–2002, Holy Nativity, Knowle; Priest i/c, All Hallows, Easton, 1997–2002; Bishop Suffragan of Richborough, 2002–10; Provincial Episcopal Visitor, Canterbury, 2002–10. RD, Brislington, 1995–99; Area Dean, Bristol S, 1999–2001. Hon. Canon: Southern Malaŵi, 1986–2011; Bristol Cathedral, 2000–02. Ordained priest (RC), 2011; Protonotary Apostolic, 2011. *Recreations*: travel, theatre. *Address*: 24 Golden Square, W1F 9JR.

**NEWTON, Lesley; Her Honour Judge Newton;** a Circuit Judge, since 2001; a Senior Circuit Judge and Designated Family Judge, since 2014; *b* 4 April 1955; *d* of Archie Newton and Joan Newton (*née* Robinson); *m* 1987, David Anthony Hernandez, *qv*; one *s* one *d*. *Educ*: Univ. of Manchester (LLB 1976). Called to the Bar, Middle Temple, 1977, Bencher, 2019; barrister on N Circuit, 1979–2001; Head, Young Street Chambers, Manchester, 1997–2001; Asst Recorder, 1995–99; Recorder, 1999–2001. Mem., Family Justice Council, 2004–11; Pres., Council of HM Circuit Judges, 2016. Mem. Bd, Nuffield Family Justice Observatory, 2019–. Course Dir for Family Law, Judicial Coll., 2011–17. *Address*: Manchester Family Court, The Civil Justice Centre, 1 Bridge Street West, Manchester M60 9DJ. *T*: (0161) 240 5000.

**NEWTON, Michael;** *see* Newton, J. M.

**NEWTON, Nigel;** *see* Newton, J. N.

**NEWTON, Lt Gen. Sir Paul (Raymond),** KBE 2012 (CBE 2003); Professor of Security and Strategy Studies, and Director, Strategy and Security Institute, University of Exeter, since 2012; *b* 29 June 1956; *s* of Maj. Raymond Newton and Gladys Newton (*née* Nash); *m* 1985, Jan Eardley; two *s* one *d*. *Educ*: Pembroke Coll., Cambridge (MPhil 1993); Army Staff Coll., Camberley. CO 2nd Bn Princess of Wales's Royal Regt, 1994–97; HCSC 1999; Comdr, 8 Inf. Bde, 2000–03; rcds 2003; CDS's Liaison Officer to US Jt Staff, 2003; Dep., Strategic Planning, HQ Multi-Nat. Force Iraq, 2004; ACOS Intelligence, UK PJHQ, 2005–06; Comdr, Force Strategic Engagement Cell, HQ Multi-Nat. Force Iraq, 2007; ACDS, Develt, Concepts and Doctrine, 2008–10; Comdr, Force Develt and Trng, 2010–12. Col Comdt, Queen's Div., 2010–. Founder, Paul Newton Consultants Ltd (formerly Paul Newton Strategic Consultancy), 2011–; Strategic Advr and Chm., Internat. Adv. Bd (Defence and Security), Babcock Ltd, 2012–. Sen. Associate Fellow, RUSI, 2010–. Honorary Colonel: Southampton Univ. OTC, 2008–12; 15 Psychol Ops Gp, 2010–14; Small Arms Sch. Corps, 2010–14. Officer, Legion of Merit (USA), 2004; First Oak Leaf Cluster (USA), 2007. *Recreations*: sailing, ski-ing, international relations, history. *Clubs*: Army and Navy; New Forest Workmen's.

**NEWTON, (Robert Edward) Ian;** school inspector and educational consultant, since 1995; *b* 4 Aug. 1946; *o s* of John Newton and Ethel Albiston; *m* 1969, Rev. Canon Fiona Olive Pallant; one *s* one *d*. *Educ*: Dulwich Coll.; Oriel Coll., Oxford (BA Hons Nat. Sci. (Physics) 1967; MA 1973); Inst. of Education, London Univ. (Postgrad. CertEd 1968); Univ. of the Highlands and Islands (MLitt Island Studies 2015). Rugby School: Physics Teacher, 1968; Sixth Form girls' housemaster, 1976; Head of Physics, 1991; Headmaster, Bedales Sch., 1992–94. Admin. Officer, HMC/GSA Wkg Party on Univ. Admission, 1996–98; Charter Mark Award assessor, 1996–97; Reporting Inspector, Ind. Schs Inspectorate, 2000–. Qualified Yachtmaster Ocean, 2000–. Chm., Edward Barnsley Educnl Trust and Workshop Co., 1997–2000. Governor: Coventry Sch. Foundn, 1999–2003; Laxfield Sch., 2005–13. FRGS 2001. CFM 1983. *Publications*: Wave Physics, 1990. *Recreations*: sailing, playing the bassoon, walking. *Address*: Manor Farm Cottage, 67 Langham Road, Field Dalling, Holt NR25 7LG. *Club*: Royal Naval Sailing Association.

**NEWTON, Hon. Sir Roderick Brian,** Kt 2014; **Hon. Mr Justice Newton;** a Judge of the High Court of Justice, Family Division, since 2014; *b* 15 April 1958; *s* of late Brian Newton and June Newton; *m* 1978, Clare Augusta Swanzy; two *s* two *d*. *Educ*: Bishop's Stortford Coll.; City of London Poly. (BA Hons 1980). Called to the Bar, Middle Temple, 1982; Asst Recorder, 1998–2000; Recorder, 2000–05; Circuit Judge, 2005–14. Tutor, Judicial Coll., 2010–. *Recreations*: gardening, horses, livestock, classical music, natural history. *Address*: Royal Courts of Justice, Strand, WC2A 2LL.

**NEWTON, Sarah;** MP (C) Truro and Falmouth, since 2010; *m* Alan Newton; one *s* two *d*. *Educ*: Falmouth Sch.; King's Coll. London (BA Hist.); Grad. Sch. of Internat. Studies, USA. Formerly: Mktg Officer for IBIS, then Citibank; Director: American Express; Age Concern England; Internat. Longevity Centre. Former Mem. (C) Merton LBC. An Asst Govt Whip, 2015–16; Parly Under-Sec. of State, Home Office, 2016–17; Minister of State (Minister for Disabled People, Health and Work), DWP, 2017–19. Member: Admin Select Cttee, 2010–12; Welfare Reform Bill Cttee, 2011; Sci. and Technol. Select Cttee, 2012–15; Care Bill Cttee, 2014; Ecclesiastical Cttee, 2014–15. Dep. Chm., Cons. Party, 2012–15. FRSA. *Address*: House of Commons, SW1A 0AA.

**NEWTON DUNN, William Francis;** Member (Lib Dem), Richmond London Borough Council, since 2018; Member (Lib Dem) East Midlands Region, European Parliament, since 2019; *b* 3 Oct. 1941; *s* of late Lt-Col Owen Newton Dunn, OBE, and Barbara (*née* Brooke); *m* 1970, Anna Terez Arki; one *s* one *d*. *Educ*: Marlborough Coll. (scholar); Gonville and Caius Coll., Cambridge (MA); INSEAD Business Sch., Fontainebleau (MBA). With Fisons Ltd (Fertiliser Division), 1974–79. MEP (C) Lincolnshire, 1979–94; contested (C) Lincolnshire and Humberside S, 1994; MEP for E Midlands Reg., 1999–2014 (C, 1999–2000; Lib Dem, 2000–14); contested (Lib Dem) E Midlands Reg., 2014. European Parliament: Cons. Spokesman: on Transport, 1984–87; on Rules of Procedure, 1987–89; on Political Affairs, 1989–91; Chm., 1979 Cttee (Cons. backbench MEPs), 1983–88; Mem. Bureau, Cons. MEP Gp, 1988–94; Dep. Leader, EDG, 1991–93; Chm. and Jt Leader, British Cons. MEP Sect., EPP, 1993–94; Chm., 2000–04; Whip, 2004–07, Lib Dem MEPs; Quaestor, 2009–12; Member: Envmt Cttee, 2009–10; Develt Cttee, 2009–14; Organised Crime Cttee, 2012–14. Contested: (C) Carmarthen, Feb. 1974, Cardiff W, Oct. 1974; (Lib Dem) Hayes and Harlington, 2017. *Publications*: Greater in Europe, 1986; Big Wing: biography of Air Chief Marshal Sir Trafford Leigh-Mallory, 1992; The Man Who Was John Bull: biography of Theodore Hook, 1996; The Devil Knew Not (novel), 2000; Europe Needs an FBI, 2004; What Do MEPs Do, 2014; pamphlet on the EU's Democratic Deficit, 1986. *Recreations*: grandchildren, writing. *Address*: 29 Old Palace Lane, Richmond TW9 1PQ. *T*: (020) 8948 0614. *E*: newtondunnbill@gmail.com.

**NEWTON-PRICE, James Edward;** QC 2018; Head, Criminal and Regulatory Team, Pump Court Chambers, since 2010; a Recorder, since 2018; *b* Isleworth, 26 Nov. 1965; *s* of Richard and Elizabeth Newton-Price; *m* 1996, Alison; one *s* one *d* (twins). *Educ*: Priory Sch., Lewes; Hertford Coll., Oxford (BA Hist. 1988); City Univ., London (DipLaw 1991); Inns of Court Sch. of Law. Called to the Bar, Middle Temple, 1992; in practice as barrister, 1994–. Legal Assessor, Health and Care Professions Tribunal, 2016; Legally Qualified Chair, Med. Practitioners Tribunal, 2017. *Recreations*: family, walking, fiction, history, art, season ticket holder at Fulham FC. *Address*: 3 Pump Court, Temple, EC4Y 7AJ. *T*: (020) 353 0711, (01962) 868161. *E*: jnp@pumpcourtchambers.com.

**NEWTON-SMITH, Rain;** Chief Economist (formerly Director of Economics), Confederation of British Industry, since 2014; *b* Oxford, 21 June 1975; *d* of Dr William Newton-Smith and Dorris Heffron; *m* 2007, Andrew Goodwin; four *d*. *Educ*: Univ. of Toronto Schs; Trinity Coll., Oxford (BA PPE); London Sch. of Econs and Pol Sci. (MSc Econs). Economist, Bank of England, 1999–2008; Advr to UK Exec. Dir, IMF, 2004–06; Sen. Economist, 2008–10, Hd, Emerging Mkts, 2010–14, Oxford Economics. Dir, Eynsham Partnership Acad., 2018–. Co-Chair, Circular Economy Awards. Member: Council, REconS, 2018–; Soc. of Professional Economists. Young Global Leader, WEF, 2012. *Recreations*: wild swimming, triathlons, raising four independent girls, bringing our community together. *Clubs*: Eynsham Roadrunners, City of Oxford Swimming.

**NEY, Dame Mary,** DBE 2019; consultant in local government, since 2015; Government Commissioner, Rotherham Metropolitan Borough Council, 2015–18 (Lead Commissioner, 2017–18); Associate, Cratus, since 2017; *b* London, 30 Aug. 1949; *d* of John Joseph Ney and Lena Emily Ney. *Educ*: Notre Dame High Sch., Southwark; London Univ. (BSc Maths 1970; MSc Maths 1971); Regent St Poly. (Postgrad. Dip. Mgt Studies 1975). Deptl Develt Officer, 1979–80, Asst Dir, Social Services (Finance, Strategy and Policy), 1980–92, London Bor. of Southwark; Dir, Social Services and Housing, London Bor. of Harrow, 1992–2000; Chief Exec., Royal Bor. of Greenwich, 2000–14. Non-exec. Dir, MHCLG (formerly DCLG), 2016–. Trustee: CAFOD, 2007–; RCAOS, 2017–. *Recreations*: travel, theatre. *E*: mary.ney@btinternet.com.

**NEYROUD, Peter William,** CBE 2011; QPM 2004; Chief Constable and Chief Executive, National Policing Improvement Agency, 2007–10 (Chief Constable and Chief Executive designate, 2006–07); Lecturer in Evidence-based Policing, Institute of Criminology, University of Cambridge, since 2016 (Affiliated Lecturer and Resident Scholar, Jerry Lee Centre for Experimental Criminology, 2012–16); Research Associate, Centre for Criminology, Oxford, since 2011; Director, Peter Neyroud Research Associates Ltd, since 2011; *b* 12 Aug. 1959; *s* of John Arthur Lucien Neyroud and Penelope Mary Anne (*née* Edwards); *m* 1986, Sarah Longman; two *s* two *d*. *Educ*: Winchester Coll.; Oriel Coll., Oxford (MA Mod. Hist.); Portsmouth Univ. (MSc Prof. Studies); Wolfson Coll., Cambridge (Dip Applied Criminology; PhD Criminology). Joined as Constable, Hampshire Constabulary, 1980; Sergeant, Southampton and Basingstoke, 1984–86; Inspector, Southampton, 1987–91; Chief Inspector, E Hampshire, 1991–93; Staff to Pres., ACPO, 1993–95; Detective Supt and Dir of Intelligence, 1995–97; West Mercia Constabulary: Asst Chief Constable (Support), 1998–2000; Dep. Chief Constable, 2000–02; Chief Constable, Thames Valley Police, 2002–06. Member: Sentencing Guidelines Council, 2004–10; Ind. Review Panel, Parole Bd, 2006–11. Visiting Fellow: Nuffield Coll., Oxford, 2008–16; Teesside Univ., 2011–; Bucks New Univ., 2014–; Leon Radzinowicz Vis. Fellow, Cambridge Univ., 2008–09; Visiting Professor: Chester Univ., 2011–; Edgehill Univ., 2014–. Trustee, Internet Watch Foundn, 2012– (Vice-Chair, 2015–). Hon. LLD Portsmouth, 2006. *Publications*: Policing, Ethics and Human Rights, 2001; Participation in Policing, 2001; Police Ethics for the 21st Century, 2003; Dictionary of Policing, 2008; Science and Policing, 2011; Policing, Ethics and Values, 2012; Cambridge Crime Harm Index, 2016. *Recreations*: running, reading, writing, gardening, four children. *Address*: c/o Institute of Criminology, University of Cambridge, Sidgwick Avenue, Cambridge CB3 9DA. *E*: pwn22@cam.ac.uk.

**NÉZET-SÉGUIN, Yannick,** CC 2012; Artistic Director and Principal Conductor, Orchestre Métropolitain, Montreal, since 2000; Music Director, Philadelphia Orchestra, since 2012; Jeanette Lerman-Neubauer Music Director, Metropolitan Opera, New York, since 2018; *b* Montreal, 6 March 1975. *Educ*: Conservatoire de musique du Québec (piano, conducting, composition, choir and chamber music); Westminster Coll., Princeton (choral conducting). Music Dir, Rotterdam Philharmonic Orch., 2012–18. Hon. Dr: Quebec, 2011; McGill, 2017; DMus: Curtis Inst., 2014; Westminster Choir Coll., Rider Univ., 2015. Royal Philharmonic Soc. Award, 2008; Canada Nat. Arts Centre Award, 2010; Prix Denise Pelletier, Les Prix du Québec, 2011; Artist of Year, Musical America, 2016. *Address*: c/o Askonas Holt, 15 Fetter Lane, EC4A 1BW. *T*: (020) 7400 1700. *E*: info@askonasholt.co.uk.

**NG, Jern-Fei;** QC 2018; *b* Petaling, Jaya, Malaysia, 6 Aug. 1979; *m* 2009, Mei Jean Soong; one *s* one *d*. *Educ*: La Salle Secondary Sch., Petaling, Jaya, Malaysia; Cambridge Tutor's Coll., Croydon; Trinity Coll., Cambridge (BA Hons Law; MA). Called to the Bar,

Lincoln's Inn, 2002; in practice as barrister and arbitrator, 2004–. Chm., Foreign Lawyers Chapter, and Mem., Professional Affairs Cttee, Singapore Acad. of Law, 2017–. Mem., Hon. Bd, Cambridge Law Rev., 2018–. *Address:* Essex Court Chambers, 24 Lincoln's Inn Fields, WC2A 3EG. *T:* (020) 7813 8000. *E:* jfng@essexcourt.net.

**NGUYEN-VAN-TAM, Prof. Jonathan Stafford,** MBE (Mil.) 1997; DM; FFPH, FRSPH; FRSB, FRCPath; Professor of Health Protection, University of Nottingham, since 2007; Deputy Chief Medical Officer, Department of Health and Social Care (on secondment), since 2017; *b* Boston, Lincs, 2 Feb. 1964; *s* of Paul and Elizabeth Nguyen-Van-Tam. *Educ:* Hawthorn Tree Corner Primary Sch., Boston; Boston Grammar Sch.; Sch. of Medicine, Univ. of Nottingham (BMedSci 1984; BM BS 1987; DM 2001). MFPH 1996, FFPH 2006; FRSPH 2007; FRSB 2013; FRCPath 2014. Lectr in Public Health, 1991–97, Sen. Lectr in Public Health, 1997–99, Univ. of Nottingham; Associate Dir, SmithKline Beecham plc, 2000–01; Hd, Med. Affairs, Roche Products Ltd, 2001–02; Med. Dir, Aventis Pasteur MSD Ltd, 2001–04; Consultant Epidemiologist, HPA, 2004–07. Cadet Forces MO, (Major) RAMC TA, 1988–2000. Hon. FFPM 2015. *Publications:* Introduction to Pandemic Influenza, 2010, 2nd edn 2012; contrib. articles to learned jls. *Recreations:* family, running, mountain walking, fishing, Boston United FC (season ticket holder). *Address:* Department of Health and Social Care, 39 Victoria Street, SW1H 0EU. *Club:* Victory Services.

**NGUYEN VAN THAO;** Ambassador of Vietnam to the Court of St James's, 2014–17; *b* Vietnam, 1964; *m* Nguyen Minh Hien; two *d. Educ:* Acad. of Finance, Vietnam (BA). Dep. Sec. Gen., Vietnam Chamber of Commerce and Industry, 1997–2007; CEO, APEC CEO Summit, Vietnam, 2006; Dir Gen., Dept of Admin and Finance, 2007–11; Asst Minister, Min. of Foreign Affairs, 2011–14. Permanent Member: Vietnam-US Soc.; Assoc. for Liaison with Overseas Vietnamese; Vice Pres., Vietnam Business and Software Assoc. *Recreation:* golf.

**NGWENYA, Marjorie;** consultant; Executive Director, School of Insurance, Africa Leadership University, since 2017; *b* Coventry, 3 Dec. 1979; *d* of Ben Ngwenya and Mercy Ngwenya. *Educ:* London Business Sch. (MSc Leadership and Strategy 2013). FIA 2006. Consultant, Deloitte, 1999–2002; Business Develt Manager, Gen Re, 2002–04; Manager, Deloitte, 2004–07; Sen. Risk Actuary and Vice Pres., Swiss Re, UK, 2007–09; freelance contractor, 2009–10; Dir, Mazars LLP, 2010–13; Chief Risk Officer, African Ops, Old Mutual, 2012–16; Gp Exec., Strategy, Liberty Gp, S Africa, 2016–17. Non-exec. Dir, Bidvest Life Ltd (SA). Editor, The Actuary mag., 2009–11; Mem. Council, Inst. and Faculty of Actuaries, 2011– (Pres., 2017–18). Mem. Bd, Legal Resources Trust, SA, 2013–. Vis. Lectr, Actuarial Sci., Cass Business Sch., 2013–. *Publications:* articles in The Actuary mag. *Recreations:* singing, swimming, friends and family, Formula 1, travelling, tutoring. *Address:* PostNet Suite 21, Oubaai, Private Bag X6528, George 6530, South Africa. *T:* (27) 714536430. *E:* marj.home@icloud.com.

**NIBLETT, His Honour Anthony Ian;** a Circuit Judge, 2002–19; *b* 11 June 1954; *s* of late A. W. Niblett and of J. A. Niblett (*née* McMickan); *m* 1991, Valerie Ann Ranger; one *s* one *d. Educ:* Varndean Grammar Sch., Brighton; Univ. of Birmingham (LLB Hons); Coll. of Law. Called to the Bar, Inner Temple, 1976; Barrister, SE Circuit, 1977–2002; Asst Recorder, 1993–98; a Recorder, 1998–2002. Member: Professional Conduct Cttee, Bar Council, 1993–97; S Eastern Circuit Cttee, 1995–98 and 2000–02; Sussex Probation Bd, 2007–10. Jun. (Sec.), Sussex Bar Mess, 1986–95. Gov., Varndean Coll., Brighton, 1997–2003. *Recreations:* reading history, theatre, gardening.

**NIBLETT, Robin Christian Howard,** CMG 2015; DPhil; Director, Royal Institute of International Affairs (Chatham House), since 2007; *b* 20 Aug. 1961; *s* of Alan and Christine Niblett; *m* 1990, Trisha de Borchgrave; two *d. Educ:* Cottesmore Sch.; Charterhouse; New Coll., Oxford (BA Mod. Langs 1984; MPhil 1993; DPhil Internat. Relns 1995). Musician, 1985–87; Center for Strategic and International Studies, Washington, DC: Res. Associate, 1988–91; Eur. Rep., 1992–97; Dir, Strategic Planning, 1997–2000; Exec. Vice Pres. and Chief Operating Officer, 2001–06. Special Advr, Foreign Affairs Cttee, H of C, 2015–. Chairman: WEF Global Agenda on Europe, 2012–13; Experts Gp, 2014 NATO Summit. Non-exec. Dir, Fidelity Eur. Values Investment Trust, 2010–. Mem. Council, ODI, 2010–14. *Publications:* (ed with W. Wallace) Rethinking European Order: West European responses, 1989–97, 2001; (ed) America and a Changed World: a question of leadership, 2010. *Recreations:* tae kwon do, tennis, electric guitar. *Address:* Royal Institute of International Affairs, Chatham House, 10 St James's Square, SW1Y 4LE. *T:* (020) 7957 5702.

**NICE, Sir Geoffrey,** Kt 2007; QC 1990; a Recorder, since 1987; Vice Chairman, Bar Standards Board, 2009–13; *b* 21 Oct. 1945; *s* of William Charles Nice and Mahala Anne Nice (*née* Tarryer); *m* 1974, Philippa Mary Gross; three *d. Educ:* St Dunstan's College, Catford; Keble College, Oxford. Called to the Bar, Inner Temple, 1971, Bencher, 1996. Member: CICB, 1995–2002; Bd, Indict, 2001–04. Sen. Trial Attorney, 1998–2001, Principal Trial Attorney, Milosevic prosecution, 2002–06, Internat. Criminal Tribunal for Former Yugoslavia; Comr, Royal Court, Jersey, 2006–07. Gresham Prof. of Law, Gresham Coll., 2012–16; Professorial Res. Fellow, Univ. of Buckingham, 2014–16. Mem., Internat. Steering Gp and Chm. Trustees, Iran Tribunal, 2011–. Mem., Adv. Bd, Weidenfeld Scholars, 2012–16. Co-founder, Geoffrey Nice Foundn, 2014–. Patron, Prisoners of Conscience, 2012–. Contested (SDP/Liberal Alliance) Dover, 1983, 1987. Hon. LLD Kent, 2005. *Publications:* Justice for All and How to Achieve It: citizens, lawyers and the law in the age of human rights, 2017. *Address:* 1 Temple Garden Chambers, 1 Harcourt Buildings, Temple, EC4Y 9DA. *T:* (020) 7583 1315. *Club:* Reform.

**Ní CHIONNA, Orna, (Lady Turner of Ecchinswell);** Deputy Chairman, National Trust, since 2014 (Member of Council, since 2013; Trustee, since 2014); *b* Dublin, 21 Feb. 1956; *d* of Eoin Ó Cionna and Eibhlín Uí Chionna; *m* 1985, (Jonathan) Adair Turner (*see* Baron Turner of Ecchinswell); two *d. Educ:* Scoil Lorcáin, Dublin; Sion Hill, Dublin; University Coll., Dublin (BE Electronics 1977); University Coll., Cork (MEngSc Microelectronics 1980); Harvard Business Sch. (MBA with Dist. 1983). Stagiaire, EC, Brussels, 1978; Mktg Engr, Lake Electronics Ltd, Dublin, 1980–81; with McKinsey & Co., 1983–2001, Partner, 1990–2001. Non-executive Director: Northern Foods plc, 2002–11 (Chm., Remuneration Cttee, 2005–10; Sen. Ind. Dir, 2005–11); Bupa, 2003–08 (Sen. Ind. Dir, 2007–08); Bank of Ireland UK Hldgs plc, 2002–07; Royal Mail Gp (formerly Royal Mail Hldgs), 2010–19 (Chm. Remuneration Cttee, 2011–19; Sen. Ind. Dir, 2011–19); Saga plc, 2014– (Sen. Ind. Dir, 2017–; Chm., Risk Cttee, 2015–); Chm., Remuneration Cttee, 2010–13, Sen. Ind. Dir, 2011–13, HMV plc; Chm., Remuneration Cttee, Burberry plc, 2018–; Chm., Adv. Bd, Eden McCallum Ltd, 2009–14; Mem., UK Retail and Consumer Adv. Bd, Apax Partners LLP, 2005–08. Mem., Soil Assoc., 2007–13 (Trustee, 2002–15). Mem., 2010–16, Chair, 2013–16, Business Adv. Council, and Mem., Bd of Govs, 2013–16, Saïd Business Sch., Oxford Univ. Non-exec. Dir, Greenham Common Community Trust, 2005–13. Trustee: Bristol & West Pension Fund, 2002–07; Sir John Soane Museum, 2012–. *Recreations:* garden design, music, languages. *Address:* c/o Eden McCallum LLP, Orion House, 5 Upper St Martin's Lane, WC2H 9EA. *T:* (020) 7361 7000. *E:* orna.nichionna@edenmccallum.com.

**NICHOL, Sir Duncan (Kirkbride),** Kt 1993; CBE 1989; Chairman, HM Courts Service Board, 2008–11; Hon. Professorial Fellow, Manchester Centre for Healthcare Management, University of Manchester, 1999–2004 (Professor and Director, Health Services Management Unit, 1994–98); *b* 30 May 1941; *s* of James and Mabel Nichol; *m* 1972, Elizabeth Wilkinson; one *s* one *d. Educ:* Bradford Grammar Sch.; St Andrews Univ. (MA Hons). FHSM 1987; Hon. FFPHM 1991. Asst Gp Sec. and Hosp. Sec. to Manchester Royal Infirmary, 1969–73; Dep. Gp Sec. and Actg Gp Sec., Univ. Hosp. Management Cttee of S Manchester, 1973–74; Dist Administrator, Manchester S Dist, 1974–77; Area Administrator, Salford AHA(T), 1977–81; Regional Administrator, 1981–84, Regional Gen. Manager, 1984–89, Mersey RHA; Chief Exec., NHS Management Executive, 1989–94. Chairman: Parole Bd of England and Wales, 2004–08; QC Selection Panel, 2005–08; Skills for Justice, 2010–15. Comr for Judicial Appts, 2001–06. Non-executive Director: HM Prisons Bd/Correctional Services Strategy Bd, 1994–2005; BUPA, 1994–2002; Primary Group, 2001–08; Deltex Medical, 2004–; Christie Hospital NHS Trust, 2008–12; UK Accreditation Service Ltd, 2009– (Chm., Clinical Pathology Accreditation (UK) Ltd, 2000–09); Chairman: B Plan Information Systems, 1999–2001; Synergy Health (formerly Synergy Healthcare), 2012–15 (Dir, 2002–15); Acad. for Healthcare Science, 2012–15; Countess of Chester Hosp. NHS Foundn Trust, 2012–. Member: Central Health Services Council, 1980–81; NHS Training Authy, 1983–85; Chm., Jt Prison and Probation Services Accreditation Panel for Offending Behaviour Progs, 1999–2005. Pres., Inst. of Health Services Management, 1984–85; Chm., Educn Cttee, King Edward's Hosp. Fund for London, 1987–94. Hon. DLitt Salford, 1990. *Publications:* contributed: Health Care in the United Kingdom, 1982; Management for Clinicians, 1982; Working with People, 1983; Managers as Strategists, 1987. *Recreations:* walking, golf. *Club:* Athenæum.

**NICHOLAS, Sir David,** Kt 1989; CBE 1982; Editor and Chief Executive, 1977–89, Chairman, 1989–91, Independent Television News; *b* 25 Jan. 1930; *m* 1952, Juliet Davies (*d* 2013); one *s* one *d. Educ:* Neath Grammar School; University Coll. of Wales, Aberystwyth. BA (Hons) English. National Service, 1951–53. Journalist with Yorkshire Post, Daily Telegraph, Observer; joined ITN, 1960; Deputy Editor, 1963–77. Produced ITN General Election Results, Apollo Moon landing coverage, and ITN special programmes. Dir, Channel Four TV, 1992–97. Chm., Sports News TV, 1996–2003. Visiting Editor: Graduate Sch. of Journalism, Berkeley, Calif, 1993; Sch. of Journalism, Univ. of Boulder, Colorado, 1994. Chm., Deptford Challenge Trust, 1996–2005. Mem. Council, Goldsmiths Coll., 1996–2003 (Hon. Fellow, 2004). FRTS 1980. Fellow, UC Aberystwyth, 1990. Hon. LLD Wales, 1990; Hon. DHL Southern Illinois, 2000. Producers' Guild Award 1967, on return of Sir Francis Chichester; Cyril Bennett Award, RTS, 1985; Judges' Award, RTS, 1991; News World Lifetime Achievement Award, 2001; Lifetime Achievement Award, RTS, 2012. *Recreation:* walking. *Club:* Reform (Chm., Media Gp, 1998–2003).

**NICHOLAS, Prof. David,** PhD; Founder and Director, CIBER Research Ltd, since 2012; *b* 14 March 1947; *s* of Roy and Rita Nicholas; *m* 1976, Kay Reeves; one *s* one *d. Educ:* Huish's Grammar Sch., Taunton; Poly. of N London (MPhil 1986); PhD City Univ. 1995. MCLIP (ALA 1968). Asst Librarian, Hackney Public Libraries, 1971; Librarian, Middleton St George Coll. of Educn, Co. Durham, 1972; Res. Fellow, Univ. of Bath and Poly. of N London, 1973–76; Res./Inf. Asst, Time-Life International, 1976–77; Poly., later Univ. of N London, 1978–97, Sen. Res. Tutor, 1990–97; Hd, Dept of Inf. Sci., City Univ., 1998–2004; Dir, Dept of Inf. Studies (formerly Sch. of Liby, Archive and Inf. Studies), 2004–11, Centre for Publishing, 2005–11, UCL; Prof. of Inf. Sci., Northumbria Univ., 2013–15. Adjunct Prof., Univ. of Tennessee, 2012–; Prof., Tomsk State Univ., Russia, 2014–; Guest Prof., Wuhan Univ., China, 2018–. Hon DSc W London, 2010. *Publications:* Immunology: an information profile, 1985; Online Searching: its impact on information users, 1987; Assessing Information Needs, 2000; Digital Consumers, 2008; Information Science: critical concepts in political science, 2014. *Recreations:* cycling, gardening, travelling by train. *Address:* CIBER Research Ltd, 1 Westwood Farmhouse, Greenham, Newbury RG14 7RU. *E:* Dave.Nicholas@ciber-research.eu.

**NICHOLAS, Garvin Edward Timothy;** barrister and attorney-at-law; *b* Trinidad, 24 Jan. 1967; *s* of Edward and Simona Nicholas; *m* Dr Nicola Alcalá; one *s. Educ:* Trinity Coll., Trinidad; Oxford Brookes Univ. (LLB); Inns of Court Sch. of Law, City Univ. Postgrad. DipLS; City, Univ. of London (LLM Maritime). Local Govt Councillor, 1992–96. Chm., F and GP Cttee, Diego Martin Regl Corp., 1992–96; called to the Bar, Inner Temple, 2001; in practice as barrister, 2001–; Legal Counsel to Leader of the Opposition, Trinidad and Tobago, 2003; Temp. Senator, Upper Hse of Parlt, 2003–04; Leader, Movt for Nat. Develt, 2007–10; Press Sec., Office of Prime Minister, 2010; High Comr for Trinidad and Tobago in the UK, 2010–14; Attorney Gen. of Trinidad and Tobago, 2015; Hd, Odysseus Chambers, 2017–. *Recreations:* golf, debating, politics, travel, charity. *E:* gnicholas@odysseuschambers.com. *Club:* Rotary (Port of Spain W) (Past Pres.).

**NICHOLAS, Mark Charles Jefford;** presenter and commentator on cricket; *b* 29 Sept. 1959; *s* of late Peter Jefford Nicholas and of Anne Evelyn Nicholas (stage name Loxley; she later *m* Brian Widlake). *Educ:* Bradfield Coll. Professional cricketer, Hampshire CCC, 1977–95: county cap, 1982; captain, 1984–95; winning team: John Player Sunday League, 1986; Benson & Hedges Cup, 1988, 1992; NatWest Trophy, 1992. Advertising dept, The Observer, 1980; PR consultant, Hill & Knowlton (UK) Ltd, 1987–88; TV and radio commentator; presenter and commentator: Sky TV, 1999; Channel 4 cricket, 1999–2005; Cricket On Five, Channel 5 (formerly Channel 5, then Five), 2006. Former journalist, Daily Telegraph. Sports Presenter of the Year, RTS, 2006. *Publications:* A Beautiful Game: my love affair with cricket, 2016.

**NICHOLAS, Michael Bernard,** FRCO; organist, choral director and composer; *b* 31 Aug. 1938; *s* of Bernard Victor Herbert Nicholas and Dorothy (*née* Gilfillan); *m* 1975, Heather Grant Rowdon; two *s. Educ:* City of London Sch.; Trinity Coll. of Music (Jun. Exhibitioner); Jesus Coll., Oxford (MA). FRCO 1958 (CHM 1964). Organist and Choirmaster: Louth Parish Church, Lincs, 1960–64; St Matthew's Ch, Northampton, 1965–71; Organist and Master of Choristers, Norwich Cathedral, 1971–94 (Organist Emeritus, 2005); (part-time) Lectr in Music, UEA, 1971–94; Chief Exec., RCO, 1994–97. Conductor: Louth Choral and Orchestral Soc., 1960–64; Northampton Bach Choir and Orch., 1965–71; Norwich Philharmonic Chorus, 1972–94; Co-Founder and Co-Artistic Dir, Norwich Fest. of Contemporary Church Music, 1981–92; Musical Dir, Allegri Singers, 1994–2000; Organist and Dir of Music, All Saints' Church, Blackheath, 1995–99; Dir of Music, St Mary-le-Tower, Ipswich, 1999–2013; Founder and Conductor, Tower Chamber Choir, 2001–13. Member: Council, RSCM, 1978–87; Council, RCO, 1980–94 and 1998–2004; Council, 1995–2015, Academic Bd, 1995–, Guild of Church Musicians. Pres., Tower Chamber Choir, 2013–; a Vice-President: Organ Club, 1995–; Church Music Soc., 2002–; an Hon. Patron, Beccles Choral Soc., 2016–. Mem., Cathedral Organists' Assoc., 1971– (Pres., 1975–77). Hon. FGCM 1995; FRSCM 2018. Hon. DMus UEA, 1995. *Publications:* Sightsinging, 1966; Muse at St Matthew's, 1968; various choral and organ compositions. *Recreations:* bridge, walking, reading. *Club:* Athenæum.

**NICHOLAS, Shān;** Director: Taprobane Management Services Ltd, 2007–17; Lasting Transformation Ltd, since 2011; *b* 24 Oct. 1952; *d* of Kenneth Nicholas and Jane Nicholas (*née* Selliah); one *d* with Pal Luthra. *Educ:* London Sch. of Econs and Pol Sci. (BSc Econ 1974); London Sch. of Hygiene and Tropical Medicine (MSc Med. Demography 1977). Asst Dir, Runnymede Trust, 1978–85; Hd, Human Resource Develt, London Bor. of Hackney, 1986–94; Exec. Dir Corp. Develt and Co. Secretary, Stonham Housing, 1998–2005; Chief Exec., Princess Royal Trust for Carers, 2005–07; Interim Chief Executive: YWCA (England and Wales), 2007–08; Brook London, 2008–09; Interim Develt Dir, Criminal Justice, and Vice Chair, T2A Alliance, Barrow Cadbury Trust, 2009–10; Interim Chief Exec., Child Poverty Action Gp, 2010; Interim Dir, British Inst. of Human Rights, 2010; Consultant, Coll. of Social Work, 2011; Interim Chief Executive: Children's Soc., 2011–12; Refugee Council, 2012–13; British Assoc. for Adoption and Fostering, 2013; United Response, 2014–15; Swanswell, 2016; Toynbee Hall, 2017; Brandon Trust, 2018; Independent Age, 2019. *Publications:* (contrib.) Britain's Black Population, 1980; articles for British and French jls on race and immigration. *Recreations:* arts, theatre, music, reading. *E:* shan.nicholas1@btopenworld.com.

**NICHOLL, His Honour Anthony John David;** a Circuit Judge, 1988–2003; *b* 3 May 1935; *s* of late Brig. and Mrs D. W. D. Nicholl; *m* 1961, Hermione Mary (*née* Landon); two *d* (one *s* decd). *Educ:* Eton; Pembroke Coll., Oxford; Wycliffe Hall, Oxford (DBTS). Called to Bar, Lincoln's Inn, 1958. Practised in London, 1958–61, in Birmingham, 1961–88; Head of Chambers, 1976–87; Chm., Fountain Court Chambers (Birmingham) Ltd, 1984–88. A Recorder, 1978–88. Reader, Coventry Dio., 1962–64, 2003–18, now Reader Emeritus. *Recreations:* history, theology, music, gardening, choral singing, walking.

**NICHOLL, Prof. Jonathan Paul,** CBE 2015; DSc; Professor of Health Services Research, University of Sheffield, since 1994; *b* Bristol, 15 April 1953; *s* of late Capt. Jack Nicholl and Berry Nicholl; partner, Joanna Saunders; one *s* two *d*. *Educ:* Abingdon Sch.; Univ. of Bristol (BA Philos.); Univ. of North London (MSc Stats); Univ. of Sheffield (DSc Health Services Res. 2009). CStat 1998. Res. Associate, Transport Studies Gp, UCL, 1977–81; University of Sheffield: Statistician, 1981–93, Dir, 1993–2010, Medical Care Res. Unit; Dean, Sch. of Health and Related Res., 2010–17; Dir, NIHR Sch. for Public Health Res., 2012–17. *Publications:* 200 res. articles, mainly in gen. med. jls. *Recreations:* cricket, gardening, antique silver. *Address:* School of Health and Related Research, University of Sheffield, 30 Regent Street, Sheffield S1 4DA. *E:* j.nicholl@sheffield.ac.uk.

See also Air Vice Marshal S. M. Nicholl.

**NICHOLL, Air Vice-Marshal Steven Mark,** CB 2001; CBE 1991; AFC 1981; FRAeS; Director, Military Requirements, Military Air and Information, BAE SYSTEMS, 2002–11; *b* 15 Nov. 1946; *s* of late Capt. Jack Nicholl and Berry Nicholl; *m* 1974, Suzanne Tucker; two *s* one *d*. *Educ:* Abingdon Sch.; Pembroke Coll., Oxford (BA Eng.). FRAeS 1993. RAF university cadetship, 1965; flying/staff duties, 1970–88; Gp Capt. Plans, HQ RAF Germany, 1989–91; OC RAF Leuchars, 1992–93; rcds 1994; Dir Air Ops, Dir Air Plans, 1995–98, ACDS OR Air, subseq. Capability Manager (Strike), 1998–2001, MoD; Dir, Military Requirements, MASS, BAE SYSTEMS, 2002–11. *Recreations:* golf, ski-ing, dog agility, reading. *Address:* 1 Tythe Close, Stewkley, Bucks LU7 0HD. *Clubs:* Royal Air Force; Leighton Buzzard Golf.

See also J. P. Nicholl.

**NICHOLLS,** family name of **Baron Nicholls of Birkenhead.**

**NICHOLLS OF BIRKENHEAD,** Baron *cr* 1994 (Life Peer), of Stoke D'Abernon in the County of Surrey; **Donald James Nicholls,** Kt 1983; PC 1986; a Lord of Appeal in Ordinary, 1994–2007; Second Senior Lord of Appeal, 2002–07; *b* 25 Jan. 1933; *yr s* of late William Greenwow Nicholls and Eleanor Jane; *m* 1960, Jennifer Mary, *yr d* of late W. E. C. Thomas, MB, BCh, MRCOG, JP; two *s* one *d*. *Educ:* Birkenhead Sch.; Liverpool Univ. (LLB 1st cl. hons); Trinity Hall, Cambridge (Foundn Schol.; BA 1st cl. hons with dist., Pt II Law Tripos, LLB 1st cl. hons with dist.; Hon. Fellow, 1986). 2nd Lieut, RAPC, 1951–53. Certif. of Honour, Bar Final, 1958; called to Bar, Middle Temple, 1958, Bencher, 1981, Treas., 1997; in practice, Chancery Bar, 1958–83; QC 1974; Judge of High Court of Justice, Chancery Div., 1983–86; a Lord Justice of Appeal, 1986–91; Vice-Chancellor, Supreme Court, 1991–94; a Non-permanent Judge, Hong Kong Court of Final Appeal, 1998–2004. Mem., H of L, 1994–2017. Chairman: Lord Chancellor's Adv. Cttee on Legal Educn and Conduct, 1996–97; Jt Parly Cttee on Parly Privilege, 1997–99. Mem., Senate of Inns of Court and the Bar, 1974–76. Patron, Cayman Is Law Sch., 1994–2006. Pres., Birkenhead Sch., 1986–2016. Visitor, Clare Hall, Cambridge, 1991–94. Hon. LLD Liverpool, 1987. *Publications:* Let Equity Prevail: recollections and reflections, 2015. *Club:* Athenæum (Trustee, 1998–2011).

See also Hon. J. P. Nicholls.

**NICHOLLS, Brian;** Director, John Brown Engineering, 1979–91; *b* 21 Sept. 1928; *s* of late Ralph and Kathleen Nicholls; *m* 1961, Mary Elizabeth Harley; one *s* two *d*. *Educ:* Haberdashers' Aske's Sch., Hampstead; London Univ. (BSc Econ); Harvard Business Sch. George Wimpey & Co., 1951–55; Constructors John Brown Ltd, 1955–75; Director: CJB Projects Ltd, 1972–75; CJB Pipelines Ltd, 1974–75; Dep. Chm., CJB Mohandessi Iran Ltd, 1974–75; Industrial Adviser, Dept of Trade, 1975–78; Director: John Brown Engrg Gas Turbines, 1979–91; Rugby Power Co., 1990–91; Vice Pres., John Brown Power Ltd, 1987–90; consultant, Scottish Enterprise, 1991–98. Member: Council, British Rly Industry Export Gp, 1976–78; Overseas Projects Bd, 1976–78; BOTB, 1978. Member: Council, British Chemical Engineering Contractors Assoc., 1973–75; Trade and Industry Cttee, British Algerian Soc., 1974–75; Scottish Council (Develt and Industry), 1983–98 (Vice Pres., 1991–98; Fellow 1998). Columnist, Jazz Jl, 1952–58; Ed., Jazz News, 1957–59. Dep. Chm., Nat. Jazz Fedn, 1954–59; Dir, Scottish Opera, 1993–99. Freeman Mem., Incorp. of Coopers of Glasgow, 1991; Mem., Trades House of Glasgow, 1990. *Recreations:* travel, walking, music. *Address:* Willow Cottage, 2 Redcliffe Street, Cheddar, Somerset BS27 3ND.

**NICHOLLS, Christine Stephanie,** DPhil; writer; *b* 23 Jan. 1943; *d* of Christopher James Metcalfe, Mombasa, Kenya, and Olive Metcalfe (*née* Kennedy); *m* 1966, Anthony James Nicholls, *s* of Ernest Alfred Nicholls, Carshalton; one *s* two *d*. *Educ:* Kenya High School; Lady Margaret Hall, Oxford (BA); St Antony's Coll., Oxford (MA, DPhil). Henry Charles Chapman Res. Fellow, Inst. of Commonwealth Studies, London Univ., 1968–69; freelance writer for BBC, 1970–74; res. asst, 1975–76; Jt Editor, 1977–89, Editor, 1989–95, DNB; Editor, Sutton Pocket Biographies, 1996–2000. Writer, monthly historical blog for Old Africa Mag., 2011–. *Publications:* The Swahili Coast, 1971; (with Philip Awdry) Cataract, 1985; Power: a political history of the 20th Century, 1990; The Dictionary of National Biography: 1961–70, 1981; 1971–80, 1986; 1981–85, 1990; Missing Persons, 1993; 1986–90, 1996; (ed) The Hutchinson Encyclopedia of Biography, 1996; David Livingstone, 1998; The History of St Antony's College, Oxford, 1950–2000, 2000; Elspeth Huxley: a biography, 2002; Red Strangers: the white tribe of Kenya, 2005; A Kenya Childhood, 2011. *Recreations:* reading novels, playing the flute. *Address:* 27 Davenant Road, Oxford OX2 8BU. *T:* (01865) 511320.

**NICHOLLS, Colin Alfred Arthur;** QC 1981; a Recorder, 1984–99; *b* 29 Aug. 1932; twin *s* of late Alfred Charles Victor Nicholls and of Lilian Mary (*née* May); *m* 1976, Clarissa Allison Spenlove, *d* of late Clive and of Theo Dixon; two *s*. *Educ:* Brighton Coll.; Trinity Coll., Dublin. MA, LLB. Called to the Bar, Gray's Inn, 1957 (Albion Richardson Schol.), Bencher, 1989. Mem., Commonwealth Expert Gp on Rule of Law, 2011; Chairman: Commonwealth Working Gp on Cybercrime, 2012–; Commonwealth Working Gp on Virtual Currencies, 2015–; Commonwealth Expert Gp on Review of Commonwealth Computer and Computer Related Crime Model Law, 2016–. Auditor, 1956, and Hon. Mem., 1958–, TCD Historical Soc. Commonwealth Lawyers Association: Mem. Council, 1987–90; a Vice Pres., 1990–96; Hon. Treas., 1996–; Hon. Sec., 1999–2003; Pres., 2003–05; Hon. Life Pres., 2007. Fellow, Soc. of Advanced Legal Studies, 1998. Gov., FBA, 2001–07. Trustee: Commonwealth Human Rights Initiative, 1998–2007; Commonwealth Law Conf. Foundn, 2003–07. *Publications:* (jtly) Corruption and Misuse of Public Office, 2006, 3rd edn 2017. *Recreation:* painting (exhib. RHA, ROI and NEAC). *Address:* 3 Raymond Buildings, Gray's Inn, WC1R 5BH. *T:* (020) 7400 6400. *Club:* Garrick.

**NICHOLLS, David Alan,** CB 1989; CMG 1984; Senior Political-Military Associate, Institute for Foreign Policy Analysis, Cambridge, Mass, USA, 1991–2014; *b* 28 Aug. 1931; *s* of Thomas Edward and Beatrice Winifred Nicholls; *m* 1955, Margaret (*née* Lewis); two *d*. *Educ:* Cheshunt Grammar School; St John's Coll., Cambridge (Schol., Wright's Prizeman 1952, 1953; BA Hons 1954; MA 1989). Served RAF (Flying Officer), 1950–51. Admiralty, 1954–64; Private Sec., 1954; Private Sec. to Parliamentary Sec., 1958–59; Principal, 1959; MoD, 1964–75; Private Sec. to Minister of Defence for Admin, 1968–69; Asst Sec., 1969; Cabinet Office, 1975–77; Asst Under-Sec. of State, MoD, 1977–80; Asst Sec., Gen. for Defence Planning and Policy, NATO, 1980–84; Dep. Under Sec. of State (Policy), MoD, 1984–89. Vis. Fellow, Magdalene Coll., Cambridge, 1989–90; Associate Fellow, RIIA, 1990–93; Hon. Fellow, Graduate Sch. of Internat. Studies, Univ. of Birmingham, 1992–98. Chm., Defence and Security Cttee, London Chamber of Commerce and Industry, 1994–2004 (Mem., 1991–). Chm., Soc. for Italic Handwriting, 1987–97. Mem., Visiting Cttee, RCA, 1991–92. *Recreations:* sketching, printmaking. *Address:* c/o HSBC, Shrewsbury, Shropshire SY1 1SL. *Club:* National Liberal.

**NICHOLLS, David Alan;** novelist, screenwriter; *b* Southampton, 30 Nov. 1966; *s* of late Alan Nicholls and of Ann Nicholls; partner, Hannah Weaver; one *s* one *d*. *Educ:* Toynbee Comprehensive Sch.; Barton Peveril Coll.; Univ. of Bristol (BA). Actor (stage-name, David Holdaway), 1991–98; script ed., 1996–2000; writer, 1999–: *television:* I Saw You, 2000 and 2002; Cold Feet, 2000 (British Acad. TV Craft Award for Best New Writer); Rescue Me, 2002; Much Ado About Nothing (Shakespeare Re-told Series), 2005; Aftersun, 2006; (screenplay) Tess of the D'Urbervilles, 2008; The 7:39, 2014; Patrick Melrose, 2018 (British Acad. TV Craft Award for Best Drama Writer, BAFTA, 2019); *film screenplays:* Simpatico, 1999; Starter for 10, 2006; And When Did You Last See Your Father?, 2007; One Day, 2011; Great Expectations, 2012; Far from the Madding Crowd, 2015; *theatre:* Aftersun, Old Vic, 2006. UK Author of the Year, Nat. Book Awards, 2014. Hon. DLitt: Edinburgh, 2015; Bristol, 2016. *Publications:* Starter for 10, 2003; The Understudy, 2005; One Day, 2009 (Popular Fiction Book of Year, Galaxy Nat. Book Awards, 2010); Us, 2014; Sweet Sorrow, 2019. *Address:* c/o Jonny Geller, Curtis Brown, 28 Haymarket, SW1Y 4SP. *T:* (020) 7393 4400.

**NICHOLLS, Dr (Jill) Nicola,** LVO 2012; non-executive Director, Buro Happold Engineering Ltd, 2014–17; *b* Epping, Essex, 13 Feb. 1958; *d* of Alan and Barbara Keep; one *s* one *d*. *Educ:* Univ. of Bristol (BSc 1st Cl. Hons Chem.); Gonville and Caius Coll., Cambridge (PhD Inorganic Chem. 1982). Res. Fellow, Gonville and Caius Coll., Cambridge, 1982–85; with Charterhouse Bank, then a Dir, Charterhouse Develt Capital, 1985–2003. Non-executive Director: Cambridge Enterprise Ltd, 2006–11; BPP Univ. (formerly BPP University Coll. of Professional Studies), 2008–. Mem., Adv. Bd, Judge Business Sch., Univ. of Cambridge, 2004–13. Lead, Governance Rev. for Law Soc., 2016. Trustee, then Chair, Green-Works, 2002–10; Chair, Woodland Trust, 2010–16 (Trustee, 2005–16); Trustee, Landmark Trust, 2013–14. *Publications:* contribs to scientific jls. *Recreations:* dance (mostly watching), woods and trees, local issues. *E:* nicola.nicholls@blueyonder.co.uk.

**NICHOLLS, Rt Rev. John;** Bishop of Sheffield, 1997–2008; an Honorary Assistant Bishop: Diocese of Derby, since 2008; Diocese of Manchester, since 2012; *b* 16 July 1943; *s* of late James William and Nellie Nicholls; *m* 1969, Judith Dagnall; two *s* two *d*. *Educ:* Bacup and Rawtenstall Grammar School; King's Coll., London (AKC); St Boniface Coll., Warminster. Curate, St Clement with St Cyprian, Salford, 1967–69; Curate, 1969–72, Vicar 1972–78, All Saints and Martyrs, Langley, Manchester; Dir of Pastoral Studies, Coll. of the Resurrection, Mirfield, 1978–83; Canon Residentiary of Manchester Cathedral, 1983–90; Suffragan Bishop of Lancaster, 1990–97. Hon. Fellow, Univ. of Central Lancashire, 1997. DUniv Sheffield Hallam, 2007; Hon. LittD Sheffield, 2009. BGCStJ, 2007 (Prelate, 2007–15). *Publications:* (jtly) A Faith Worth Sharing? A Church Worth Joining?, 1995. *Recreations:* music (listening and singing), reading, films. *Address:* 75 Rowton Grange Road, Chapel-en-le-Frith, High Peak SK23 0LD. *T:* (01298) 938249. *E:* jnseraphim@gmx.com.

**NICHOLLS, John;** see Nicholls, R. J.

**NICHOLLS, Prof. John Graham,** FRS 1988; Professor of Neurobiology, International School for Advanced Studies, Trieste, 1998; *b* 19 Dec. 1929; *s* of late Dr Nicolai and of Charlotte Nicholls; *m* (marr. diss.); two *s*. *Educ:* Berkhamsted Sch.; Charing Cross Hosp.; King's Coll. and University Coll., London. BSc (1st cl. Hons); PhD; MB, BS. Research and teaching in Neurobiology at: Oxford, 1962; Harvard, 1962–65; Yale, 1965–68; Harvard, 1968–73; Stanford, 1973–83; Biocenter, Basel, 1983–98. *Publications:* From Neuron to Brain (with S. Kuffler), 1976, 5th edn (with A. R. Martin, P. Fuchs, D. Brown, M. Diamond and D. Weisblat), 2012; The Search for Connections, 1987; Pioneers of Neurobiology: my brilliant eccentric heroes, 2015. *Recreations:* Latin American history, music. *Address:* Scuola Internazionale Superiore di Studi Avanzati, via Bonomea 265, Trieste 34136, Italy.

**NICHOLLS, Hon. John (Peter);** QC 2006; barrister; *b* 30 Nov. 1963; *s* of Baron Nicholls of Birkenhead, *qv*; *m* 1991, Divya Bhatia, *d* of late Captain and Mrs Rajindar Bhatia; one *s* one *d*. *Educ:* Winchester Coll.; Trinity Hall, Cambridge (BA 1st Cl. Law 1985). Called to the Bar, Middle Temple, 1986; in practice as a barrister, specialising in business and commercial fields, Maitland Chambers, 1987. *Recreations:* sport, travel. *Clubs:* Aula; Hawks (Cambridge); Lensbury; Bombay Gymkhana.

**NICHOLLS, Jonathan William Nicholas,** PhD; University Secretary, Open University, since 2018; *b* Chelmsford, 16 June 1956; *s* of Arthur John Nicholas Nicholls and Cecily Mary Nicholls (*née* Cosgrove); *m* 1998, Susan Catherine Rasmussen; one step *s* one step *d*. *Educ:* Univ. of Bristol (BA 1st Cl. Hons Eng. 1978); Emmanuel Coll., Cambridge (PhD 1984); Harvard Univ. (Herchel Smith Scholar, 1981–82). University of Warwick: Admin. Officer, 1982–86; Asst Registrar, 1986–89; Sen. Asst Registrar, 1989–92; Academic Registrar, 1992–99; Registrar, 1999–2003; Registrar and Sec., Univ. of Birmingham, 2004–07; Registrary, Univ. of Cambridge, 2007–16; Fellow of Emmanuel College,

Cambridge, 2007, now Emeritus; Dir, Strategic and Policy Services (Educn), Shakespeare Martineau LLP, 2017–18. Director: Cambridge Univ. Health Partners Ltd, 2008; Cambridge Ahead Ltd, 2013. Gov., Cambridge Univ. Hosps NHS Foundn Trust, 2007. Chm., Assoc. of Heads of Univ. Admin, 2013–16 (Dep. Chm., 2006–12). Governor: Hills Rd Sixth Form Coll., 2010–14; Univ. of Cambridge Primary Sch., 2015. Trustee, Storey's Field Community Trust, 2013. *Publications:* The Matter of Courtesy: medieval courtesy books and the Gawain-poet, 1984. *Recreations:* cycling, running, watching football and cricket, birds, books, music, grandchildren. *Club:* Oxford and Cambridge.

**NICHOLLS, Most Rev. Linda Carol;** *see* Canada, Primate of the Anglican Church of.

**NICHOLLS, Michael John Gadsby;** QC 2006; barrister and author; *b* 29 April 1948; *s* of late Ronald Harry Nicholls and Betty Jean Nicholls (*née* Gadsby); *m* 1st, 1970, Marian Howe (marr. diss. 2006); 2nd, 2007, Debbie Taylor. *Educ:* Whitley Abbey Sch., Coventry; BRNC, Dartmouth; Inns of Court Sch. of Law. Served RN, 1967–72 (specialist in hydrographic survey), Lieut 1971. Called to the Bar, Middle Temple, 1975; Army Legal Services, 1975–80, Major 1979; Dep. Dir, Army Legal Services, BAOR (GSO2), 1979; admitted solicitor, 1980, and in private practice, 1980–83; on staff of Official Solicitor to Supreme Court and Head of UK Child Abduction Unit, 1983–98; returned to private practice, 1998; in practice England, Wales and Western Australia, specialising in internat. family law and medical ethics, incl. jurisdiction, recognition and enforcement, conflicts of laws, children's cases incl. status, surrogacy, abduction and relocation, and medical treatment disputes. Consultant to Family Law Cttee, Council of Europe. Vis. Lectr, Acad. of Eur. Law, Trier. Member: Internat. Family Law Cttee, Family Justice Council; Mental Health Tribunal (formerly Review Bd) of WA. *Publications:* (contrib.) Principles and Practice of Forensic Psychiatry, 1990; (jtly) The Human Rights Act 1998: a special bulletin, 1998; (contrib.) The Legal Aspects of Munchausen's Syndrome by Proxy, 2001; (jtly) International Movement of Children: law, practice and procedure, 2004, 2nd edn 2016; (jtly) The New Brussels II Regulation, 2005; (jtly) The 1996 Hague Convention on the Protection of Children, 2012; contribs on internat. family law and medical ethics to learned jls. *Recreations:* walking on the beach, painting, fly-fishing. *Address:* 1 Hare Court, Temple, EC4Y 7BE. *T:* (020) 7797 7070; Francis Burt Chambers, Allendale Square, 77 St Georges Terrace, Perth, WA 6000, Australia. *T:* (8) 92200597. *Clubs:* Special Forces; Honourable Artillery Company Saddle; Weld (Perth, WA).

**NICHOLLS, Nicola;** *see* Nicholls, J. N.

**NICHOLLS, Patrick Charles Martyn;** Consultant, Dunn & Baker, solicitors, 1987–2001; *b* 14 Nov. 1948; *s* of late Douglas Charles Martyn Nicholls and Margaret Josephine Nicholls; *m* 1976, Bridget Elizabeth Fergus Owens; one *s* two *d*. *Educ:* Redrice Sch., Andover. Qualified solicitor, 1974; Partner, Dunn & Baker, 1976–87. Mem., E Devon District Council, 1980–84. MP (C) Teignbridge, 1983–2001; contested (C) same seat, 2001. PPS to Ministers of State: Home Office, 1984–86; MAFF, 1986–87; Parliamentary Under-Secretary of State: Dept of Employment, 1987–90; DoE, 1990; Opposition spokesman on health, 1997–98, on agric., 1998–99. Vice Chm., Social Security Select Cttee, 1990–93. Vice-Chm., Cons. Party, 1993–94. Vice Chm., Soc. of Cons. Lawyers, 1986–87. Steward, British Boxing Bd of Control, 1985–87. Columnist, Western Morning News, 2002–. Lectr on Anglo-American relns and British constitution, incl. for Educnl Cultural Exchanges Ltd, Anglo-American Inst. and ESU. MCIJ 2004. Freeman, City of London, 1996. *Recreations:* theatre, opera, historical research, ski-ing. *Address:* Whitehall Manor, Whitehall, Hemyock, Devon EX15 3UQ. *T:* (01823) 680100. *Clubs:* Carlton; Newport Yacht.

**NICHOLLS, Paul Richard;** QC 2012; *b* Chelmsford, 27 Nov. 1967; *s* of Michael Arthur Nicholls and Ann Nicholls; *m* 1994, Claire Hollinghurst; one *s* two *d*. *Educ:* Latymer Sch., Edmonton; Sheffield Univ. (LLB); Worcester Coll., Oxford (BCL). Called to the Bar, Inner Temple, 1992; in practice as a barrister, specialising in employment, public and commercial law, 1992–. *Publications:* (contrib.) Halsbury's Laws of England, Administrative Law, 4th edn 2001; (contrib.) Tolley's Employment Law Handbook. *Recreations:* country walks, real ale, cricket. *Address:* Matrix Chambers, Gray's Inn, WC1R 5LN. *T:* (020) 7404 3447, *Fax:* (020) 7404 3448. *E:* paulnicholls@matrixlaw.co.uk.

**NICHOLLS, Prof. (Ralph) John;** Consultant Surgeon, St Mark's Hospital, London, 1978–2006, now Emeritus; Hon. Professor of Colorectal Surgery, Imperial College London, since 1997; *b* 20 May 1943; *s* of Clifton Wilson Nicholls and Muriel Morten Nicholls (*née* Heathcote); *m* 1966, Stella Mary McBride; two *s* one *d* (and one *d* decd). *Educ:* Felsted Sch., Essex; Gonville and Caius Coll., Cambridge (BA 1964; MB 1968, BChir 1967, MChir 1978; MA 1999); London Hosp. Med. Coll. London Hosp. trng posts, 1966–78; MRC Res. Fellow, 1971–72; Alexander von Humboldt Fellow, 1976–77; Consultant Surgeon, St Thomas' Hosp., 1982–93; Clin. Dir, St Mark's Hosp., London, 1997–2001; Associate Med. Dir, NW London Hosps NHS Trust, 2005–06. Hon. Civilian Consultant in Surgery to RAF, 1999–2008; Consultant, Policlinico de Monza, Italy, 2006–. Chm. Trustees, Northwick Park Inst. for Medical Res., 2007–14. Ed., Colorectal Disease, 1999–2014. Mem., Specialist Adv. Cttee in Gen. Surgery, Jt Cttee for Higher Surgical Trng, 1997–2003. President: Assoc. of Coloproctology of GB and Ireland, 1999–2000; Eur. Assoc. of Coloproctology, 2004; Sec., Div. of Coloproctology, Sect. of Surgery, Union Européene des Médecins Spécialistes, 1997–2003. Hon. FRCPSGlas 1992; Hon. FRCSE 2007; Hon. FRCP 2008; Hon. FRCSI 2018; Hon. Fellow: Brazilian Soc. Surgery, 1982; Swiss Soc. Gastroenterol., 1990; Canadian Soc. of Colon and Rectal Surgery, 1995; Amer. Soc. Colon and Rectal Surgeons, 2008; Amer. Coll. of Surgeons, 2010; Australian Soc. of Coloproctology, 2018. Membre d'Honneur: Assoc. Française de Chirurgie, 1997; Academie Nationale de Chirurgie, 2005; Hon. Member, Society of Surgery: of Yugoslavia, 2002; of Chile, 2003; of Spain, 2004; Fellow: Società Italiana di Chirurgia Colorettale, 2004; Polish Assoc. of Surgeons, 2016; Hon. Member: Colorectal Soc. of Australia, 2007; Argentine Soc. of Coloproctology, 2007; British Soc. of Gastroenterol., 2011; Austrian Soc. of Surgeons, 2018. Médaille de l'Académie Nationale de Chirurgie (France), 2016. *Publications:* (ed jtly) Restorative Proctocolectomy, 1993; (ed with R. R. Dozois) Colorectal Surgery, 1997; (Associate Ed.) Corman's Colon and Rectal Surgery, 6th edn 2012; contribs to learned jls incl. Lancet, BMJ, British Jl Surgery, Annals of Surgery, Gut, Diseases of the Colon and Rectum, Colorectal Disease. *Recreations:* languages, travel, history, viola, vegetable growing, bridge. *Address:* 24 St Mark's Crescent, NW1 7TU. *T:* (020) 7267 4433. *Clubs:* Athenæum; St Alban's.

**NICHOLLS, Robert Michael,** CBE 1995; Chairman, Intensive Care National Audit and Research Centre, 2016–19; *b* 28 July 1939; *s* of late Herbert Edgar Nicholls and Bennetta L'Estrange (*née* Burges); *m* 1961, Dr Deírín Deirdre (*née* O'Sullivan); four *s*. *Educ:* Hampton Sch.; University Coll. of Wales (BA 1961); Univ. of Manchester (DSA 1962). FHSM (AHA 1963; FHA 1993). Asst Sec., Torbay Hosp., 1964; House Governor, St Stephen's Hosp., Chelsea, 1966; Asst Clerk to the Governors, St Thomas' Hosp., 1968; Dep. Gp Sec., Southampton Univ. Hosp. Management Cttee, 1972; Dist Administrator, Southampton and SW Hampshire Health Dist, 1974; Area Administrator, Newcastle upon Tyne AHA(T), 1977; Regl Administrator, SW RHA, 1981; Dist Gen. Man., Southmead DHA, 1985; Regl Gen. Man., later Chief Exec., Oxford RHA, 1988–93; Exec. Dir, London Implementation Gp, NHS Mgt Exec., 1993–96; health care mgt consultant, 1996–2005; Chm., Nat. Clinical Assessment Authy, 2003–05; Regl Health Comr, London, Appts Commn, 2005–08 (Dep. Chair, 2007–08). Chm., Gen. Pharmaceutical Council, 2009–14. Vis. Prof. of Society and Health, Bucks New Univ., 2014–17. Co-Chair, Prescribing for Excellence Ref. Gp, Scottish Govt, 2014–17. Non-exec. Dir, Nestor Healthcare Gp plc, 1997–2003 (Sen. non-exec. Dir, 2001–03). Health Sector Reform Advr, British Council, 1997–2003. Member: Health Educn Council, 1984–87; CMO's Med. Educn Wkg Pty, 1992–93; GMC, 1996–2005 (Chm., Preliminary Proceedings Cttee, 2000–03); All Party Pharmaceutical Gp, 2009–14; Bd, Medical Educn England, 2010–12. Member: Clinical Adv. Bd, Oxford Univ. Med. Sch., 2001–08; Bd, Modernising Pharmacy Careers, 2010–13; Oxford A Res. Ethics Cttee, 2015–17. National Council, Inst. of Health Service Management (formerly IHA): Mem., 1976–86; Pres., 1983–84. Associate Fellow, Templeton Coll., Oxford, 1996–2001. *Publications:* (contrib.) Resources in Medicine, 1970; (contrib.) Working with People, 1983; (contrib.) Rationing of Healthcare in Medicine, 1993; (contrib.) Doctors in Society, 2005. *Recreations:* bird-watching, choral singing, jazz, opera, sport. *Address:* Thame, Oxon.

**NICHOLLS, Stephen John;** a District Judge (Magistrates' Courts), since 2011; *b* Bournemouth, 12 Dec. 1956; *s* of Deryck John Nicholls and Geraldine Mary Nicholls; *m* 1991, Lynne Brien; one *s* one *d*. *Educ:* St Peter's Sch., Southbourne; Dorset Inst. of Higher Educn (BA Hons). Admitted as solicitor, 1981; articled clerk, 1979–81, solicitor, 1979–91, J. W. Miller & Sons; Andrews McQueen, 1991–98; Law Chambers, 2001–11. Lectr (pt-time), Open Univ., 1998–2003. Asst Coroner, Dorset, 2009–. *Recreations:* cricket, photography, films. *Address:* Poole Magistrates' Court, The Law Courts, Park Road, Poole BH15 2NS. *T:* (01202) 502800, *Fax:* (01273) 811770.

**NICHOLS, Rt Rev. Anthony Howard,** PhD; Dean of Students and Lecturer in Biblical Studies, Trinity Theological College, Perth, 2003–13, now Honorary Lecturer; *b* 29 March 1938; *m* 1968, Judith Margaret Ross; two *s* two *d*. *Educ:* Univ. of Sydney (BA; MEd); Univ. of London (BD Hons); Macquarie Univ. (MA Hons); Moore Coll., ACT (Theol. scholar); PhD Univ. of Sheffield 1997. Latin and history teacher, 1960–63. Assistant Curate: St Paul's Chatswood, 1966; St Bede's, Drummoyne, 1967; Lectr, Biblical Studies, Moore Coll., Sydney, 1968–72; Lectr, Biblical Studies and Educn, 1972–81, Dean of Faculty of Theology, 1977–81, Satya Wacana Christian Univ., Salatiga, Indonesia; Principal: Nungalinya Coll., Darwin (Training Coll. for Aboriginal theol students), 1982–87; St Andrew's Hall, Melbourne (CMS Training Coll.), 1988–91; Bishop of NW Australia, 1992–2003. Vice-Pres., Church Missionary Soc. of Australia, 1994–; Vis. Lectr, Anglican Inst., Bandung, Indonesia, 2004–; Vis. Prof., Sabah Theological Seminary, Malaysia, 2012; Vis. Lectr, Satya Wacana Christian Univ., Salatiga, Indonesia, 2019. Stephen Bayne Scholar, Univ. of Sheffield, 1985–86. *Publications:* Mission of the Soul: studies in the Psalms, 1996; Jesus in All the Scriptures, 2007; jl articles on Bible translation, missiology, Indonesian religions, Aboriginal culture, and philosophy of educn. *Address:* 62/60 Kalinda Drive, City Beach, WA 6015, Australia.

**NICHOLS, Prof. Colin Graham,** PhD; FRS 2014; Carl Cori Professor, since 2006, and Director, Center for Investigation of Membrane Excitability Diseases, since 2010, Washington University, St Louis; *b* Leicester, 27 Aug. 1960; *s* of Graham P. Nichols and Margaret A. Nichols (*née* Warner); *m* 1992, Diana L. (*née* Coleman); two *s*. *Educ:* Kingswood Sch., Corby; Royal Grammar Sch., Worcester; Leeds Univ. (BSc 1982; PhD 1985). Postdoctoral Fellow, Univ. of Maryland, 1985–91; Washington University, St Louis: Asst Prof., 1991–96; Associate Prof., 1996–2000; Prof., 2000–. *Recreations:* travel, theatre. *Address:* 6975 Dartmouth Avenue, St Louis, MO 63130, USA. *T:* (314) 3626630. *E:* cnichols@wustl.edu.

**NICHOLS, Dinah Alison,** CB 1995; Director, Pennon Group plc, 2003–13; a Crown Estate Counsellor, 2011–13 (Commissioner, 2003–11); *b* 28 Sept. 1943; *d* of late Sydney Hirst Nichols and Freda Nichols. *Educ:* Wyggeston Girls' Grammar Sch., Leicester; Bedford Coll., Univ. of London (Reid Arts Schol., BA Hons History, 1965; Hon. Fellow, RHBNC, 1997). Ministry of Transport: Asst Principal, 1965–69; Asst Private Sec. to Minister, 1969–70; Principal, 1970–74; Cabinet Office, 1974–77; Asst Sec., DoE, 1978–83; Principal Private Sec. to Sec. of State for Transport, 1983–85; Under Sec., DoE, 1985–91; Dep. Sec., DoE, later DETR, then DEFRA, 1991–2002; Dir Gen., Envmt, 1996–2002. Director: John Laing ETE, 1987–90; Anglian Water plc, 1992–95; Shires Smaller Companies plc, 1999–2012. Sec. of State for the Envmt's Rep., Commonwealth War Graves Commn, 1993–97. Dir, Cities in Schs, 1996–2000; Mem. Bd, Toynbee Housing Assoc., 1996–2007; Chairman: Toynbee Partnership Housing Assoc., 2002–07; Groundwork N London (formerly Groundwork Camden & Islington), 2003–10; National Forest Co., 2005–11; Member: Green Alliance, 2003–; Aldersgate Gp, 2007–; Policy Cttee, CPRE, 2009–13; Ind. Mem., Governance Community, Nat. Trust, 2013–18. Trustee: Travel Foundn, 2003–09; Keep Britain Tidy (formerly Envmtl Campaigns (ENCAMS)), 2005–16 (Chm., 2012–16); Groundwork London, 2008–10; Land Trust, 2010–; SW Lakes Trust, 2014–. Gov., Plymouth Univ., 2017–. Winston Churchill Meml Fellow, 1969. Life FRSA. Liveryman, Water Conservators' Co., 2009–; Liveryman, Musicians' Co., 2016–. Mem., Goldsmiths Choral Union. *Recreations:* fell walking, choral singing (Goldsmiths Choral Union), classical music, theatre, history, countryside. *Club:* Swiss Alpine (Assoc. of British Members).

**NICHOLS, Jeremy Gareth Lane,** MA; Headmaster, Stowe School, 1989–2003; Interim Headmaster, Aiglon College, Switzerland, 2007; *b* 20 May 1943; *yr s* of late Derek Aplin Douglas Lane Nichols and of Ruth Anne Baiss (formerly Nichols); *m* 1972, Patricia Anne, *d* of Cdre Alan Swanton, DSO, DFC and bar, RN; one *s* three *d*. *Educ:* Lancing Coll., Sussex; Fitzwilliam Coll., Cambridge (BA English Lit. 1966; MA); Perugia Univ. Assistant Master: Livorno Naval Acad., 1965; Rugby Sch., 1966–67; Eton Coll., 1967–89, House Master, 1981–89; Gilman Sch., Baltimore, USA, 1979–80. Chm., Assoc. of Educnl Guardians for Internat. Students, 1995–2002. Founding Mem. Bd and Pres., Model EP, 1994–2000. Advr Trustee, Manor Charitable Trust, 1989–2003. Mem. Council, Univ. of Buckingham, 2010–14. Governor: Wellesley House Sch., 1985–2004; Papplewick Sch., 1988–2003; Aysgarth Sch., 1990–2004; Truro High Sch., 2004–15; West Buckland Sch., 2004–14. FCT (FCollP 1997); FRSA. *Recreations:* outdoor pursuits, sport, music, old cars. *Address:* Tresithick House, St Erme, Truro, Cornwall TR4 9AU. *Clubs:* Hawks (Cambridge); I Zingari, Free Foresters, Corinthian Casuals.

**NICHOLS, John Roland;** Director of Global Business Development, Chartered Institute for Securities and Investment (formerly Securities and Investments Institute), 2009–10; *b* 13 Nov. 1951; *s* of Richard Alan Nichols and Katherine Louisa Nichols (*née* Barham); *m* 1983, Suzanne, *d* of James Harry Davies, MBE, RA retd, and Helen Christine Davies, JP (*née* Berry); one *s* one *d*. *Educ:* Latymer Upper Sch., Hammersmith; Univ. of Surrey (BSc Hons). Admitted as solicitor, 1977; entered FCO, 1977: First Secretary: Budapest, 1979–82; FCO, 1982–85; Brasilia, 1985–89; FCO, 1989–93; Counsellor and Dep. High Comr, Dhaka, 1993–95; Consul-Gen., Geneva, 1995–97; Dep. Hd of Mission, Dir of Trade Promotion and Consul-Gen., Berne, 1997–2000; Dep. Chief Exec., and Dir of Communications, Internat. Financial Services, London (on secondment), 2000–03; Ambassador to Hungary, 2003–07; Ambassador to Switzerland and (non-resident) to Liechtenstein, 2008–09. Freeman, City of London, 2006; Freeman, 2008, Liveryman, 2013, Musicians' Co. (Ct

Asst, 2014–; Chm., Yeoman Coordination Cttee, 2014–17; Sen. Warden, 2018–19). Mem. Cttee, Guildford Art Soc., 2010–. Trustee, London Arts Orch., 2014–. *Recreations:* trying hard to be more than a Sunday painter, travel, cycling, gardening, opera, music (in the Musicians' Co., former Chm. of extensive programme of outreach into London schools to introduce children to classical music, bringing live music to children with special needs and disabilities, and to people with Alzheimer's and dementia, organising performance opportunities for outstanding young artists), theatre.

**NICHOLS, Judith Elaine;** *see* Coello, J. E.

**NICHOLS, His Eminence Cardinal Vincent Gerard;** *see* Westminster, Archbishop of, (R.C).

**NICHOLSON OF WINTERBOURNE,** Baroness *cr* 1997 (Life Peer), of Winterbourne in the Royal County of Berkshire; **Emma Harriet Nicholson;** *b* 16 Oct. 1941; *d* of Sir Godfrey Nicholson, 1st Bt and late Lady Katharine Constance Lindsay, 5th *d* of 27th Earl of Crawford; *m* 1987, Sir Michael Harris Caine (*d* 1999); one adopted *s* one step *c* (and one step *c* decd). *Educ:* St Mary's School, Wantage; Royal Academy of Music. LRAM, ARCM. Computer Programmer, Programming Instructor, Systems Analyst, ICL, 1962–66; Computer Consultant, John Tyzack & Partners, 1967–69; Gen. Management Consultant and Computer Consultant, McLintock Mann and Whinney Murray, 1969–74; joined Save the Children Fund, 1974, Dir of Fund Raising, 1977–85, Pres., Hatherleigh Dist Br.; Founder and Bd Mem., Stichting Redt de Kinderen, Netherlands, 1982–88; Founder and Mem., Comité d'Honneur Sauvez Les Enfants, France, 1983; Consultant, 1985–87: World Assoc. of Girl Guides and Girl Scouts; The Duke of Edinburgh's Award Scheme; Foster Parents Plan UK; Westminster Children's Hosp. Contested (C) Blyth Valley, 1979. MP Devon West and Torridge (C, 1987–95, Lib Dem, 1995–97). PPS to Minister of State, Home Office, 1992–93, MAFF, 1993–95, to Financial Sec. to HM Treasury, 1995; Lib Dem spokesperson on Overseas Develt and Human Rights, 1996–97. Prime Minister's Trade Envoy to Azerbaijan, Kazakhstan, Turkmenistan and Iraq, 2015–. Mem., Select Cttee on Employment, 1990–91; Founder and Jt Chm., All Party Parly Gp for Romanian Children; Chairman: All Party Parly Gp for Oman, for Kuwait, for UNA Adv. Gp; and Founder, All Party Parly Gp on Euro Inf. Mkt Gp; All Party Parly Gp on Foreign Affairs, 2010, 2016–17; All Party Parly Gp on Prevention of Sexual Violence in Conflict, 2016–17; Co-Dep. Chm., British-Iranian All Party Parly Gp; Vice Chm., All Party Parly Gp on Penal Affairs, 1992, on Human Trafficking, 2010, on European Reform, 2010, for Georgia, 2010, for Jordan, 2014; Mem., All Party Parly Gp for Bulgaria, for Moldova, for Romania, for Saudi Arabia (Treas.), on Tackling Terrorism, on Transatlantic and Internat. Security, for Trinidad and Tobago, for UN, for Ahmadiyya Muslim community, on British-Iraq (Chm., 2009); Treasurer: All Party Parly Gp for Islamic Finance; All Party Parly Gp for Positive Eur. Gp, for British Caribbean; Sec., All Party Parly Gp on Syria, for Human Rights; Mem., Parly Panel, RCN, 1990–92; Sec. then Chm., Cons. Backbench Envmt Cttee, 1990–91; Vice-Chm., Cons. Party, 1983–87; Mem., Cons. Muslim Forum, 2017—. Alternate Mem., UK Delegn to WEU and Council of Europe, 1990–92. House of Lords: front bench spokesman on Data Protection, 1998; Prime Minister's Trade Envoy to Iraq, 2014; Mem., Select Cttee on Soft Power and the UK's Influence, 2013–14; Chm., H of L *ad hoc* Select Cttee on Prevention of Sexual Violence in Conflict, 2015–16. MEP (Lib Dem) SE Region, 1999–2009. European Parliament: Vice-Chairman: Cttee on For. Affairs (Vice-Pres., 2007–09), Human Rights, Common Defence and Security Policy; Pres., Delegn for Relns with Iraq; Member: Cttee on Women's Rights and Equal Opportunities; For. Affairs Cttee; Subcttee for Human Rights; Euro-Mediterranean Parly Assembly (Vice-Pres., Cttee on Women's Rights); Delegns to Mashreq countries and Gulf States, and to Euro-Mediterranean Partnership; Delegn for Relns with Iran; Stability Pact for SE Europe Parly Gp: Substitute Member: Cttee on Budgets; Parly Co-op Cttee for Kazakhstan, for Kyrgyzstan, for Uzbekistan, for Tajikistan, for Turkmenistan, for Mongolia; Agriculture and Rural Develt Cttee; EP/Romania Jt Parly Cttee; Delegn for Relns with the Mashreq Countries; Rapporteur for Iraq, for Romania, for Kashmir; Shadow Rapporteur for Iraq, for EU-India Free Trade Agreement, for a Special Place for Children in EU Ext. Action; Member, EU Election Observation Missions to: Palestine, 2005; Lebanon, 2005, 2009; Afghanistan, 2005; Azerbaijan, 2005; Armenia, 2007; Pakistan, 2008; Chief Observer, EU Election Observation, Yemen, 2006; Member: UN Election Observation Missions, Iraq, 2005; Eur. Parlt Delegn, OSCE Internat. Election Observation Mission, Moldova, 2009; Council of Europe Delegn to OSCE Election Observation Mission, Kazakhstan, 2011; UK Delegn to Parly Assembly of Council of Europe and Eur. Security and Defence Assembly, 2010–; former Co-Chm., High Level Gps for Romanian Children and for Moldovan children; High Rep. of Pres. of Rep. of Molodova for Children, 2007–10; High Rep. of Prime Minister of Romania for Children, 2009. Fellow, Industry and Parlt Trust. Vis. Parly Fellow, St Antony's Coll., Oxford, 1995–96 (Sen. Associate Mem., 1997–98, 1998–99, 2001–). WHO Envoy for Health, Peace and Develt, E Mediterranean Reg., 2002. Hon. Advr to PM of Iraq in the field of health, 2008–14. Board Member: Middle East and N Africa Council, Amer. Bar Assoc.; Foundn for Dialogue Among Civilisations, 2007–13; Founder and Exec. Chm., Iraq Britain Business Council, 2009–15 (Pres., 2015–); Board Member: Global Warming Policy Foundn, 2009–; Durham Global Security Inst. Strategic Adv. Bd, 2011–; Architecture Develt Agency, 2014–. Vice-Moderator, Movement for Ordination of Women, 1991–93. Founder and Pres., Caine Prize for African Writing; Founder and Mem., Parly Appeal for Romanian Children, until 2009; Trustee: Africa '95; Booker Prize Foundn; Chm., Booker Prize for Russian Fiction, 1999–. Dir, Shelter; Founder and Chm., AMAR Internat. Charitable Foundn (formerly AMAR Appeal), 1991–; Founder and Pres. Asociatia Children's High Level Gp, 2006–; Member: Exec. Bd, UNICEF UK; MRC; Mgt Bd, European Movement (Vice-Chm.); POW Adv. Trust on Disability; Council, PITCOM; Centre for Policy Studies; RIIA; Adv. Bd, Women of Tomorrow Awards; Adv. Bd Mem. and Judge, Franklin D. Roosevelt Internat. Disability Rights Award, 2011–13; RAM Appeal Cttee; Courts of Reading, Southampton, Exeter and Sussex Univs; Editl Panel, 300 Gp Newsletter. Vice President: Small Farmers' Assoc.; ADC; ADAPT (Founder and Chm.); Methodist Homes for the Aged; LEPRA; Farms for City Children; Local Govt Gp for Europe. Deputy Chairman: Duke of Edinburgh's Award 30th Anniv. Tribute Project, 1986–88; Duke of Edinburgh's Internat. Project '87, 1987–88. President: Plymouth and W Devon Cassette, Talking Newspaper; W Regl Assoc. for the Deaf; Vice Pres., Little Foundn; Co-Patron, Manningford Trust; Patron: Hospice Care Trust, N Devon; CRUSAID; Devon Care Trust; Wilsford Trust; Relatives and Residents Assoc. (former Mem., Mgt Bd); Vice Patron, Blind in Business (Patron, 1993–95); Chm. Adv. Cttee, Carnegie UK Trust Venues Improvement Programmes. Mem., Co. of Inf. Technologists. Non-exec. Dir, Jt Leasing Co., 2013– (Chm., Supervisory Bd, 2013–). Chm., Internat. Year of the Disabled, UNESCO, 1981; former Co-Chm., UNA Adv. Gp, UNESCO; Former Vice-President: Assoc. of District Councils; British Tinnitus Assoc.; Nat. Assoc. for Maternal and Child Welfare; Child Psychotherapy Trust; The Missing Persons Hotline; former Member, Council: Howard League for Penal Reform; Media Soc.; Industry Churches Forum; former Member: Mgt Bd, European Movement; Guild of Mgt Consultants; Forum UK; Inst. of Economic Affairs; Council for Arab British Understanding; Prince of Wales Adv. Trust on Disability; Adv. Council, Justis Legal Databases; Develt Cttee, Exeter Univ.; British Romanian Assoc.; London Business Women's Network; Adv. Council, United World Foundn; Adv. Council, Centre for Adoptive Identity Studies, Univ. of East London; former Patron: Cities in Schs; Internat. Cttee for a Free Iraq; Ecaterina Iliescu Meml Lect.; British Deaf Accord; Nat. Deaf Blind and Rubella Assoc.; AMANA; Soc. for Freedom of the City of London Municipality; Freedom Council; Reading Industrial Therapy Orgn; Women into IT Foundn; Women's Engineering Soc.; Women's Business Assoc.; Sense South West; Opera South West; PHAB South West; Devon Daycare Trust; Deaf Educn through Listening and Talking; Nat. Music and Disability Inf. Service; former Trustee: Covent Garden Cancer Res. Trust; Motor Neurone Disease Assoc.; World Meml Fund for Disaster Relief. FRSA. Hon. Dr: N London, 1998; Victor Babes Univ., Timisoara, Romania, 2002; Acad. of Econ. Studies, Bucharest; Univ. of Birmingham, 2004; Dimitrie Cantemir Christian Univ., Bucharest, 2006; Oklahoma City Univ., USA, 2010; Kingston Univ., 2014. *Publications:* Why does the West forget?, 1993; Secret Society, 1996; (ed jtly) The Iraqi Marshlands, 2002; (ed) The Southern Mesopotamian Marshlands, 2012; contrib. various periodicals. *Recreations:* music, chess, reading, walking. *Address:* House of Lords, SW1A 0PW. *Club:* Reform.

**NICHOLSON, Dr Anthony Andrew,** FRCR; Consultant Interventional Radiologist, Leeds Teaching Hospitals, since 2003; *b* Liverpool, 5 April 1950; *s* of William Bell Nicholson and Marguerita Fleming Nicholson; *m* 1975, Lesley Oxendale; one *s* three *d*. *Educ:* Hillfoot Hey High Sch., Liverpool; Univ. of Wales, Swansea (BSc Hons 1972); Gonville and Caius Coll., Cambridge (MSc 1974); Univ. of Sheffield (MB ChB Hons 1983). FRCR 1988. Consultant Interventional Radiologist, Hull and E Yorks Hosps, 1990–2003. Pres., British Soc. of Interventional Radiol., 1999–2001; Dean and Vice Pres., RCR, 2008–11. Co-Founder and active supporter, Families for Individual Needs and Dignity, 1992–. Hon. FRCSI 2010; Dist. Fellow, Cardiovascular and Interventional Soc. of Eur., 2010. *Publications:* Textbook of Endovascular Procedures, 2000; 15 book chapters; over 200 articles in jls. *Recreations:* cycling, Rugby Union, Everton Football Club, music, theatre, travel, gardening. *Address:* 75 Southfield, Hessle, East Yorks HU13 0EX. *T:* (0113) 392 2860. *E:* tonynick60@gmail.com.

**NICHOLSON, Air Vice-Marshal Antony Angus,** CBE 1997; LVO 1980; FRAeS; defence and security consultant, since 2004; *b* 27 June 1946; *s* of late Air Cdre Angus Archibald Norman Nicholson, CBE, AE and Joan Mary, *d* of Ernest Beaumont, MRCVS, DVSM; *m* 1980, Fenella Janet Fraser; one *s* one *d*, and one step *s*. *Educ:* Eton Coll.; Churchill Coll., Cambridge (MA). FRAeS 1998. Joined RAF, 1968: helicopter pilot, 28 Sqn (Hong Kong), 3 Sqn SOAF (Oman), and 230 Sqn (UK), 1970–75; OC 3 Sqn SOAF, 1975–77; Equerry to HRH Duke of Edinburgh, 1978–80; OC 72 Sqn, 1981–83; MoD, 1984–86; RAF Instr, Army Staff Coll., 1986–88; Stn Comdr, RAF Shawbury, 1988–90; rcds 1991; Air Cdre Flying Trng, 1993–96; Dir, Operational Requirements (Air), 1996–98; Dir Gen. Air Systems 1, Defence Procurement Agency, 1998–2000. Eurofighter Internat. Ltd, 2000–01; Director: Babcock Defence, 2001–04; Primeguild Ltd, 2006–. Trustee, Hants and IoW Air Ambulance, 2010–16; Gov., S Central Ambulance Service NHS Foundn Trust, 2018–. DSM (Oman), 1977. *Recreations:* squash, hill walking, Gloucester RFC. *Club:* Army and Navy.

**NICHOLSON, Dr Brian Andrew,** CEng, Eur Ing; QC 2019; *b* Wells, Som, 14 Feb. 1974; *s* of David Sydney Nicholson and June Veronica Nicholson; *m* 2017, Ricky John Watson. *Educ:* Blue Sch., Wells; Univ. of Bath (BSc 1st Cl. Hons Electrical and Electronic Engrg 1995; PhD 1998); City Univ. (DipLaw 1999); Inns of Court Sch. of Law (DipLS 2000). MIET 1995; MIEEE 1995; CEng 2006; Eur Ing 2007. Called to the Bar, Lincoln's Inn, 2000 (Hardwicke Schol., 1999; Cassel Schol., 2000); in practice as barrister, specialising in intellectual property, 2000–; Standing Counsel to Comptroller Gen. of Patents, Designs and Trade Marks, 2014–19. MACM 2001; MBCS 2006. FRSA 2009. Freeman, City of London, 2001; Liveryman, Poulters' Co., 2007–. *Recreations:* electronic and mechanical engineering, technical diving. *Address:* 11 South Square, Gray's Inn, WC1R 5EY. *T:* (020) 7405 1222. *E:* bnicholson@11southsquare.com. *Club:* House of St Barnabas.

**NICHOLSON, Sir Bryan (Hubert),** GBE 2005; Kt 1987; Chairman, Financial Reporting Council, 2001–05 (Director and Deputy Chairman, 1993–96; Member, 1996–98); Senior Advisor, Penfida Partners LLP, since 2006; *b* 6 June 1932; *s* of late Reginald Hubert and Clara Nicholson; *m* 1956, Mary Elizabeth, *er d* of A. C. Harrison of Oxford; one *s* one *d* (and one *s* decd). *Educ:* Palmers School, Grays, Essex; Oriel College, Oxford (MA PPE; Hon. Fellow, 1989). 2nd Lieut, RASC, 1950–52; Unilever Management Trainee, 1955–58; Dist. Manager, Van den Berghs, 1958–59; Sales Manager, Three Hands/Jeyes Group, 1960–64; Sperry Rand: Sales Dir, UK, Remington Div., 1964–66; Gen. Manager, Australia, Remington Div., 1966–69; Managing Dir, UK and France, Remington Div., 1969–72; Dir, Ops, Rank Xerox (UK), 1972–76; Dir, Overseas Subsidiaries, Rank Xerox, 1976; Exec. Main Bd Dir, Rank Xerox, 1976–84; Chm., Rank Xerox (UK) and Chm., Rank Xerox GmbH, 1979–84; Chm., MSC, 1984–87; Chm. and Chief Exec., PO, 1987–92; Chairman: Girobank, 1987–89; BUPA, 1992–2001 (Vice Pres., 2001–05; Pres., 2005–); Varity Hldgs, later Varity Europe Ltd, 1993–96; Cookson Gp, 1998–2003; Accountancy Foundn, 2003–04 (Dir, 2000–03). Non-executive Director: Rank Xerox, 1984–87; Baker Perkins Holdings, 1982–84; Evode, 1981–84; Internat. Post Corp. SA, 1988–92; GKN, 1991–2000 (Sen. Ind. Dir, 1996–2000); Varity Corp., USA, 1993–96; LucasVarity, 1996–99; Equitas Hldgs Ltd, 1996–2005; Action Centre for Europe Ltd, 1996–2004; Newsquest plc, 1997–99; Victoria plc, 2012 (Sen. Ind.); non-executive Chairman: GOAL plc, 2001–02; EDI plc, 2004–06 (Dep. Chm., 2002–04; Sen. Ind. Dir, 2006–11); Member: Adv. Bd, Active Internat., 2001–; Eur. Adv. Bd, Proudfoot Consulting, 2006–09. Confederation of British Industry: Mem. Council, 1987–2002; Mem., President's Cttee, 1990–98; Dep. Pres., 1993–94, 1996–97; Pres., 1994–96; Chairman: Task Force on Vocational Educn and Training, 1988–89; Educn and Training Affairs Cttee, 1990–93; Global Counsellor, Conf. Bd, 1994–2007 (Emeritus, 2007); Chairman: CNAA, 1988–91; NICG, 1988–90; NCVQ, 1990–93; Interchange Panel, 1996–97; Pres., N of England Educn Conf., 1996. Department of Employment: Member: Adv. Cttee on Women's Employment, 1985–87; Women's Issues Wkg Gp, 1992–93; Race Relns Adv. Gp, 1985–87. Member: NEDC, 1985–92; Council, Inst. of Manpower Studies, 1985–93; Governing Council, Business in the Community, 1985–93; Council, Prince's Youth Business Trust, 1986–2002; Council, Industrial Soc., 1988–2002 (Chm., 1990–93); Adv. Council, Economic and Regional Analysis, 1998–2010; Prime Minister's Adv. Cttee on Business Appointments, 1998–2009; Editl Bd, European Business Jl, 1988–2005; Adv. Bd, Britain in Europe, 1999–2004; Council, Atlantic Coll., 1999–2002; Adv. Gp, Higher Educn Policy Inst., 2002–05. President: Involvement and Participation Assoc., 1990–94; ACFHE, 1992–93; AFC, 1993–94; Nat. Centre for Young People with Epilepsy, 2005–11, now Life Vice Pres., Young Epilepsy; Vice President: Re-Solv (Soc. for Prevention of Solvent Abuse), 1985–; NCH Action for Children (formerly Nat. Children's Home), 1989–2002; SRHE, 1992–2010. Observer, 2006–08, Mem., 2008–13, Public Interest Oversight Bd, Internat. Fedn of Accountants. Chancellor, Sheffield Hallam Univ., 1992–2001; Pro Chancellor and Chm. Council, Open Univ., 1996–2004. President: Oriel Soc., 1988–92; Open Univ. Foundn, 2004–12. Patron: Rathbone Community Industry (formerly Rathbone Soc.), 1987–2016; Inst. of Financial Accountants, 2012–16; Vice Pres., Industrial Trust, 1999–2010; Mem., Exec. Cttee, Pilgrims Soc., 2016– (Chm., Nominations Cttee, 2017–). Trustee: Babson Coll., Mass, USA, 1990–96; Buxton Fest. Foundn, 2003–09; Internat. Accounting Standards Cttee Foundn, 2006–12. President:

Wakefield Trinity Wildcats, 2000–11; Nomad Th., E Horsley, 2002–. UK Hon. Rep. for W Berlin, 1983–84. CCMI (CBIM 1985); Hon. CIPD 1994. FCGI (CGIA 1988); FCIM 1990; FRSA 1985. Freeman, City of London, 1988. Hon. Fellow: Manchester Metropolitan Univ. (formerly Polytechnic), 1990; SCOTVEC, 1994; Scottish Qualifications Authy, 1997; Open Univ., 2006; Hon. FCA, ICAEW, 2011. Hon. DEd CNAA, 1992; DUniv: Open, 1994; Sheffield Hallam, 2001; Hon. DLitt Glasgow Caledonian, 2000. *Recreations:* tennis, bridge, opera, political history. *Club:* Oxford and Cambridge (Chm., 1995–97).

**NICHOLSON, Sir Charles (Christian),** 3rd Bt *cr* 1912, of Harrington Gardens, Royal Borough of Kensington; *b* 15 Dec. 1941; *s* of Sir John Norris Nicholson, 2nd Bt, KBE, CIE and Vittoria Vivien (*d* 1991), *y d* of Percy Trewhella; *S* father, 1993; *m* 1975, Martha Don, *d* of Stuart Warren Don and *widow* of Niall Anstruther-Gough-Calthorpe; one step *s* one step *d*. *Educ*: Ampleforth; Magdalen Coll., Oxford. KM. *Heir: b* James Richard Nicholson [*b* 24 Oct. 1947; *m* 1980, Sarah Hazel, *d* of Richard Alan Budgett; one *s* one *d*]. *Address:* Turners Green Farm, Elvetham, Hartley Wintney, Hants RG27 8BE. *Clubs:* Brooks's, Pratt's; Royal Yacht Squadron.
*See also Sir E. H. Anstruther-Gough-Calthorpe, Bt.*

**NICHOLSON, Rev. David;** Vicar, St John's, Cudworth, since 1997; a Chaplain to the Queen, since 2014; *b* Batley, W Yorks, 8 Oct. 1957; *s* of late Percy and Winifred Nicholson. *Educ:* Batley Grammar Sch.; Salisbury and Wells Theol Coll. Ordained deacon, 1983, priest, 1984; Curate: Trevethin, Pontypool, 1983–85; Ebbw Vale, 1985–87; Vicar: St Stephen's, Newport, 1987–95; Abertillery, Cwmtillery and Six Bells, 1995–97. Hon. Chaplain, Mission to Seafarers, 1987–95. Mem. of Council, Additional Curates' Soc., 1994–2016. Governor: Churchfield Primary Sch., Cudworth, 1997–2017; Birkwood Primary Sch., Cudworth, 2002–; Cherry Dale Primary Sch., Cudworth, 2002–; Shafton Primary Acad., Shafton, 2015–. Priest Associate, Our Lady Walsingham, 1984. Mem., SSC, 1987–. *Recreations:* travel, cooking, history, music, family and friends. *Address:* The Vicarage, St John's Road, Cudworth, Barnsley, S Yorks S72 8DE. *T:* (01226) 710279. *E:* FrNicholson@aol.com.

**NICHOLSON, David John;** public affairs consultant, Butler-Kelly Ltd, 1998–2012; *b* 17 Aug. 1944; *s* of late John Francis Nicholson and Lucy Warburton Nicholson (*née* Battrum); *m* 1981, Frances Mary, *d* of late Brig. T. E. H. Helby, MC; two *s* one *d*. *Educ:* Queen Elizabeth's Grammar School, Blackburn; Christ Church, Oxford (MA Hons Mod. Hist.). Dept of Employment, 1966; Research Fellow, Inst. of Historical Res., 1970; Cons. Res. Dept, 1972 (Head, Political Section, 1974–82); Assoc. of British Chambers of Commerce, 1982–87 (Dep. Dir-Gen., 1986–87). Contested (C) Walsall S, 1983; MP (C) Taunton, 1987–97; contested (C) same seat, 1997. PPS to Minister for Overseas Develt, 1990–92. Member: Select Cttee on Parly Comr for Admin, 1992–97; Public Accounts Cttee, 1992–94; Select Cttee on Employment, 1994–96; Select Cttee on Educn and Employment, 1996–97; Jt Sec., All-Party Parly Gp for Population and Develt, 1990–94; Treasurer: All-Party Parly Gp on Water, 1993–97; All-Party Parly Gp on Waste Management, 1995–97; Sec., Cons. Backbench Social Services Cttee, 1988–90; Chm., Cons. W Country Mems Cttee, 1994–95 (Vice-Chm., 1992–93); Sec., Cons. Backbench Agriculture Cttee, 1995–97. Pres., Taunton Horticultural and Floricultural Soc., 1992–. Mem., Central Council, 2013–, Exec. Cttee, 2016–, Royal Over-Seas League. *Publications:* (ed with John Barnes) The Diaries of L. S. Amery: vol. I, 1896–1929, 1980; vol. II, The Empire at Bay, 1929–45, 1988; (contrib.) International Encyclopedia of Military History (2 vols), 2006; Crisis of the British Empire: turning points after 1880, 2017. *Recreations:* travel, gardening, music, old buildings. *Address:* Allshire, East Anstey, Tiverton, Devon EX16 9JG.

**NICHOLSON, Frank;** DL; Managing Director, Vaux Breweries Ltd, 1984–99; Director, Swallow Group plc (formerly Vaux Group), 1987–99; *b* 11 Feb. 1954; 5th *s* of late Douglas Nicholson, TD and Pauline Nicholson; *m* 1986, Lavinia Stourton; three *s*. *Educ:* Harrow Sch.; Magdalene Coll., Cambridge (MA). FRICS 1977. Assistant, Debenham, Tewson and Chinnocks, 1976–81; Tied Trade Dir, Vaux Breweries Ltd, 1981–84. Dir, Washington Develt Corp., 1985–88; Chairman: Sunderland Youth Enterprise Trust, 1986–2012; Wearside Opportunity, 1988–92; City of Sunderland Partnership, 1992–99. Dep. Chm., Sunderland Univ. (formerly Poly.), 1991–2002 (Hon. Fellow, 1991). Gov., Durham Sch., 1999–2016. DL 1995, High Sheriff, 1999–2000, Co. Durham. Prince of Wales Community Ambassador's Award, 1995; Queen's Award for Enterprise Promotion, 2010. *Recreations:* walking the dogs, supporting Sunderland Association Football Club. *Address:* Cocken House, Chester-le-Street, Co. Durham DH3 4EN. *T:* (0191) 388 0505. *Clubs:* Royal Automobile; Northern Counties (Newcastle); Chilton and Windlestone Workingmen's (Co. Durham).
*See also Sir P. D. Nicholson.*

**NICHOLSON, Graham Beattie;** Chief Legal Adviser and Adviser to the Governor, Bank of England, 2009–15; *b* Lowestoft, 22 Feb. 1949; *s* of John Arthur and Ena Patricia Nicholson; one *d*. *Educ:* Bloxham Sch., Banbury; Trinity Hall, Cambridge (BA Law 1971). Admitted as solicitor, 1974; Freshfields, later Freshfields Bruckhaus Deringer LLP, 1971–2008: Partner, 1980–2008; Hd, Co. Dept, 1986–90; Man. Partner, 1990–93. Director: City of London Sinfonia, 2002–10; Barbican Centre Trust, 2009–13. *Recreations:* chamber music, sailing, literature, wine, gardening. *Address:* Hoo Hall, Hoo, Woodbridge, Suffolk IP13 7QT. *T:* (01473) 737623. *E:* graham.nicholson1@btinternet.com. *Clubs:* Athenæum; Aldeburgh Yacht.

**NICHOLSON, Jack;** American film actor, director and producer; *b* 22 April 1937; *s* of John and Ethel May Nicholson; *m* 1961, Sandra Knight (marr. diss. 1966); one *d*. *Films include:* Cry-Baby Killer, 1958; Studs Lonigan, 1960; The Shooting (also produced); Easy Rider, 1969; Five Easy Pieces, 1970; The Last Detail, 1973; Chinatown, 1974; One Flew Over the Cuckoo's Nest, 1975 (Acad. Award for Best Actor, 1976); The Passenger, 1975; The Shining, 1980; The Postman Always Rings Twice, 1981; Reds, 1981; Terms of Endearment (Acad. Award for Best Supporting Actor), 1984; Prizzi's Honor, 1985; Heartburn, 1986; The Witches of Eastwick, 1986; Ironweed, 1987; Batman, 1988; The Two Jakes, 1991 (also dir.); A Few Good Men, 1992; Man Trouble, 1993; Hoffa, 1993; Wolf, 1994; The Crossing Guard, 1996; Mars Attacks!, 1997; Blood & Wine, 1997; As Good as it Gets (Acad. Award for Best Actor), 1998; The Pledge, 2001; About Schmidt, 2003; Anger Management, 2003; Something's Gotta Give, 2004; The Departed, 2006; The Bucket List, 2008; How Do You Know, 2011. *Address:* c/o Bresler Kelly & Associates, 11500 West Olympic Boulevard, Suite 510, Los Angeles, CA 90064–1529, USA.

**NICHOLSON, James Frederick;** farmer; Member for Northern Ireland, European Parliament, 1989–2019 (OUP, 1989–94; UU, 1994–2009; UCUNF, 2009–14; UU, 2014–19); *b* 29 Jan. 1945; *s* of Thomas and Matilda Nicholson; *m* 1968, Elizabeth Gibson; six *s* one *d*. *Educ:* Aghavilly Primary Sch. Member: Armagh Dist Council, 1975–97 (Chm., 1994–95; Mayor of Armagh, March–June 1995); Southern Health and Social Services Bd, 1977–. Mem. (OU) Newry and Armagh, NI Assembly, 1982–86. Contested (OUP) Newry and Armagh, 1987. MP (OU) Newry and Armagh, 1983–85.

**NICHOLSON, Rt Hon. Sir (James) Michael (Anthony),** Kt 1988; PC 1995; a Lord Justice of Appeal, Supreme Court of Judicature, Northern Ireland, 1995–2007; *b* 4 Feb. 1933; *s* of late Cyril Nicholson, QC, DL and late Eleanor Nicholson (*née* Caffrey); *m* 1973, Augusta Mary Ada, *d* of late Thomas F. Doyle and Mrs Elizabeth Doyle, Co. Cork; one *s* two *d*. *Educ:* Downside; Trinity College, Cambridge (MA). Called to the Bar of N Ireland, 1956; to English Bar, Gray's Inn, 1963 (Hon. Bencher, 1995); to Bar of Ireland, 1975; QC (NI), 1971; Bencher, Inn of Court of NI, 1978; Chm., Exec. Council of Inn of Court of NI and of Bar Council, 1983–85; High Court Judge, NI, 1986–95. Chm., Mental Health Review Tribunal (NI), 1973–76; Mem., Standing Adv. Commn for Human Rights (NI), 1976–78. High Sheriff, Co. Londonderry, 1972. President: Irish Cricket Union, 1978; NW ICU, 1986–93. *Recreations:* cricket, chess. *Address:* 19 Ballyalloly Road, Comber, Newtownards, Co. Down BT23 5PN. *E:* jmanicholson@gmail.com. *Club:* MCC.

**NICHOLSON, Prof. Jeremy Kirk,** PhD; FRCPath, FMedSci; CBiol, FRSB, CChem, FRSC; Professor of Biological Chemistry, Imperial College London, 1998–2018, now Emeritus; Professor of Medicine, Director, Australian National Phenome Centre and Pro Vice-Chancellor for Health Sciences, Murdoch University, since 2018; *b* Lytham St Annes, Lancs, 19 Aug. 1956; *s* of late James Nicholson and of Mavis Nicholson (*née* Kirkland). *Educ:* Univ. of Liverpool (BSc Hons 1977); St Thomas's Hosp. Med. Sch., London (PhD 1980). CBiol 1982; MIBiol 1982, FRSB (FIBiol 2002); MRCPath 1992, FRCPath 1999; CChem 1993; FRSC 1993. RTZ Post Doctoral Res. Fellow, Dept of Chem., 1980–81, Lectr in Chem., 1981–82, Birkbeck Coll., Univ. of London; Lectr in Experimental Pathol. and Toxicol., Sch. of Pharmacy, Univ. of London, 1982–85; Birkbeck College, University of London: Lectr in Chem., 1985–89; Reader in Biol Chem., 1989–92; Prof. of Biol Chem., 1992–98; Imperial College London: Hd, Biol Chem., Biomedical Scis Div., Faculty of Medicine, 1998–2007; Hd, Dept of Biomolecular Medicine, Div. of Surgery, Oncol., Reproductive Biol. and Anaesthetics, Faculty of Medicine, 2007–09; Hd, Dept of Surgery and Cancer, 2009–18; Dir, Centre for Gut and Digestive Health, Inst. of Global Health Innovation, 2010–18; Dir, MRC-NIHR Nat. Phenome Centre, 2012–18. Honorary Professor: of Molecular Systems Biol., Shanghai Jiao Tong Univ., 2005; of Analytical Chem., Inst. of Chemical Phys, Chinese Acad. of Scis, Dalian, 2005; Dept of Chem., Tsinghua Univ., Beijing, 2005; of Medicine, Zhe-Jaing Univ., Hongzhou, 2005; of Systems Biol., Shanghai Univ. of Traditional Chinese Medicine, 2005; of Biol Spectroscopy, State Key Lab. of Magnetic Resonance and Molecular and Atomic Phys, Chinese Acad. of Scis, Wuhan, 2006; Univ. of NSW, 2015; Einstein Hon. Prof., Chinese Acad. of Scis, 2014; Honorary Director: Metabonomics Res. Centre, Inst. of Chem. Phys, Chinese Acad. of Scis, Dalian, 2006; Wuhan Key State Lab. of Magnetic Resonance Res., Chinese Acad. of Scis, Wuhan, 2006; Vis. Prof., Nanyang Technical Univ., Singapore, 2012. Fellow, British Toxicol Soc., 2006; FMedSci 2010. Hon. Member: Nat. Magnetic Resonance Soc., India, 2009; Soc. of Toxicology, USA, 2013; Hon. Fellow, Metabolomics Soc., USA, 2013; Hon. FRCP 2018. Hon. DSc HK Baptist, 2019. Lectures: Theophilus Redwood, RSC, 2007; NIH Stars in Cancer and Nutrition Dist., 2010; Robert E. Stowell, Univ. of Calif, Davis, 2014. SAC Silver Medal, 1992, SAC Gold Medal, 1997, Silver Medal for Chemical Biol., 2003, Interdisciplinary Prize, 2008, RSC; Jubilee Silver Medal, British Chromatographic Soc., 1994; Pfizer Internat. Acad. Innovation Award for Chemical and Medicinal Technol., 2002; Pfizer Global Discovery Chem. Discipline Prize, 2006; Thompson-Reuters ISI Highly Cited Researcher (Pharmacol. and Toxicol.), 2014, 2015; Clarivate Highly Cited Researcher (Pharmacol. and Toxicol.), 2018. *Publications:* over 800 articles in major internat. jls on metabolic NMR spectroscopy and mass spectrometry, disease diagnosis and systems medicine. *Recreations:* scuba diving, off-road driving. *Address:* Department of Surgery and Cancer, Sir Alexander Fleming Building, Faculty of Medicine, Imperial College London, Exhibition Road, SW7 2AZ. *T:* (020) 7594 3195. *E:* j.nicholson@imperial.ac.uk, jeremy.nicholson@murdoch.edu.au.

**NICHOLSON, Jeremy Mark;** QC 2000; FCIArb; *b* 21 March 1955; *s* of Eric Day Nicholson and Joy Nicholson; *m* 1987, Elizabeth Brooke-Smith; two *s*. *Educ:* Rugby Sch.; Trinity Hall, Cambridge (MA); Coll. of Law. Called to the Bar, Middle Temple, 1977 (Harmsworth Schol.), Bencher, 2017; in practice at the Bar, 1978– ; arbitrator, 2011– ; adjudicator and mediator, 2018–. FCIArb 2011. *Recreations:* sailing, travelling, architecture, pursuing superficial interests. *Address:* 4 Pump Court, Temple, EC4Y 7AN. *T:* (020) 7842 5555. *Club:* Royal Automobile.

**NICHOLSON, Prof. Keith,** PhD; Chief Executive Officer, Skaill Advisory Services, since 2000; Executive Chairman, Cyber Security Scotland, since 2016; *b* Lochinver; *m* Angela. *Educ:* Kelvin Hall Sch., Hull; Univ. of Manchester (BSc Hons; MSc); Univ. of Strathclyde (PhD 1983). CChem 1986; FRSC 1986. Certified Inf. Security Manager 2003; Certified Inf. Systems Auditor 2004. Consultant, Geoconsultancy Services, Glasgow, 1983–85; Lectr, Univ. of Papua New Guinea, 1986–87; Asst Prof., Geothermal Energy Inst., Univ. of Auckland, 1987–90; Prof. of Energy and the Envmt, Robert Gordon Univ. (formerly Inst. of Technol.), Aberdeen, 1991–99; Prof. of Energy and Envmtl Engrg, Univ. of Aalborg, 1999–2000. Chief Executive Officer: Envirosurveys, Auckland, 1987–90; TP Gp, 1991–2000. Technol. Advr, Scottish Govt, 2008–; Mem., Scottish Govt Cyber Security Adv. Bd, 2011–. Chm., Revenue Scotland, 2015–; non-executive Board Member: Scottish Natural Heritage, 2010–16 (Chm., Audit and Risk Cttee, 2010–16); SEPA, 2011–18 (Mem., Audit Cttee, 2011–18); SFC, 2012–18 (Member: Audit Cttee, 2012–18; Res. and Knowledge Exchange Cttee, 2012–18); Visit Scotland, 2018– (Mem., Audit Cttee, 2018–). Vis. Prof. of Cyber Security, UHI, 2019–. Hon. Fellow, Univ. of Paisley, 2002–07. Fellow, Assoc. of Applied Geochemists, 1986. MInstD 2001. *Publications:* (ed) Geothermal Energy, 1987; (ed) Geothermal Energy, 1989; Doing Business on the Internet, 1993; Geothermal Fluids: chemistry and exploration techniques, 1993, 2nd edn 2011; (jtly) Skye: the complete visitor's guide, 1994; (ed) Manganese Mineralisation, 1997; (ed) Energy and the Environment, 1999; over 150 scientific papers and reports. *Recreations:* wildlife, hill-walking, photography, golf, archaeology, antiquarian books, malt whisky. *E:* knicholson@knicholson.co.uk.

**NICHOLSON, Lindsay,** MBE 2018; FRAS; writer and life coach; Editorial Director, Good Housekeeping, 2008–17; *b* 7 Aug. 1956; *d* of late Anthony Cuthbertson-Nicholson and of Sheila (*née* Pigram); *m* 1981, John Merritt (*d* 1992); one *d* (and one *d* decd). *Educ:* University Coll. London (BSc Hons Astronomy and Physics); Martha Beck Inst. (life coach trng). Editl trng scheme, Mirror Gp Newspapers, 1978–80; worked on magazines: Woman's Own, 1981–83; Honey, 1983–84; Living, 1984–85; Best, 1987–89; Woman, 1992–95; Editor-in-Chief: Prima (incl. Launch of Prima Baby and Your Home), 1995–99; Good Housekeeping mag., 1999–2006; Editl Dir, National Magazine Co., 2006–08. Chairman: BSME, 1997; Women in Journalism, 2002–04; Editl Trng Cttee, PPA, 2002–05; Press Complaints Comr, 2008–14. Ext. Mem. Council, UCL, 2014–. Advr, Maths Action, 2017–. Trustee, Home-Start, 2000–08; Patron, The Way (Widowed and Young) Foundn, 2007–13. FRAS 2003. Hon. Vis. Prof., City Univ., 2007–. Churchwarden, St Bride's, Fleet St, 2012–13. Editor of Year, 1999, 2015, Chairman's Award, 2005, PPA; Mark Boxer Award, BSME, 2007. *Publications:* Living on the Seabed, 2005. *Recreations:* horse-riding, power walking. *Address:* Wild and Precious Ltd, 2 Bank Mill Wharf, Berkhamsted HP2 2NT. *T:* 07973 672082. *Club:* University Women's.

**NICHOLSON, Margaret Anne Windham;** *see* Heffernan, M. A. W.

**NICHOLSON, Maria Bernadette**; see Maguire, M. B.

**NICHOLSON, Martin Buchanan**, CMG 1997; HM Diplomatic Service, retired; Associate Fellow, Royal Institute of International Affairs, 1999–2002; *b* 12 Aug. 1937; 2nd *s* of late Carroll and Nancy Nicholson; *m* 1964, Raili Tellervo Laaksonen; one *s* one *d*. *Educ*: Oundle Sch.; St Catharine's Coll., Cambridge (BA 1961; MA 1964); Moscow Univ. (Post-grad.). Entered Foreign Office, 1963; served Moscow, 1965–68 and 1971; Prague, 1972–75; Research Dept, FCO, 1975–78 and 1981–86; Minister, UK Delegn to MBFR, Vienna, 1978–81; Advr on Soviet, later Russian, Affairs, Cabinet Office (on secondment), 1987–94; Minister-Counsellor, Moscow, 1994–97. Res. Associate, IISS, 1998–99. *Publications*: Towards a Russia of the Regions, 1999; Memories of Childhood, 2008; On the Fringes of Europe: student years, 2011; Activities Incompatible: memoirs of a Kremlinologist and a family man, 2013; Twitching the Iron Curtain in Central Europe and London: memoirs 1972–1984, 2017; articles on Soviet and Russian affairs in The World Today and Internat. Affairs. *Recreations*: memoirs, family history, walking, gardening. *Address*: 13 Riverdale Gardens, Twickenham TW1 2BX. *T*: (020) 8892 8214.

*See also* Sir R. B. *Nicholson*.

**NICHOLSON, Rt Hon. Sir Michael**; see Nicholson, Rt Hon. Sir J. M. A.

**NICHOLSON, Prof. Nigel**, PhD; FBPsS; Professor of Organisational Behaviour, London Business School, 1990–2018, now Emeritus; *b* Banbury, 1 June 1944; *s* of Hubert Nicholson and Barbara Nicholson (*née* Collard); two *s* two *d* by former marriages; *m* 2002, Adèle Nsengiyumva; one *s*. *Educ*: University Coll., Cardiff (BA Hons Psychol. 1975; PhD 1975). Sen. Res. Fellow, MRC/ESRC Social and Applied Psychol. Res. Unit, Univ. of Sheffield, 1972–90. FBAM 1994; Fellow, Internat. Assoc. of Applied Psychol., 1998; FFFI; CCMI. *Publications*: Steel Strike, 1983; Managerial Job Change, 1988; Managing the Human Animal, 2000; (ed) Blackwell Encyclopedic Dictionary of Organisational Behaviour, 2004; Traders: risks, decisions and management in financial markets, 2005; Family Wars, 2008; The 'I' of Leadership, 2013; over 200 articles. *Recreations*: being a dad, playing jazz flute, tennis, reading, writing, music, advancing understanding of evolution on modern life and business. *Address*: 8 The Squirrels, Pinner, Middx HA5 3BD. *E*: nnicholson@london.edu.

**NICHOLSON, Sir Paul (Douglas)**, KCVO 2011; Kt 1993; Chairman, Vaux Group, 1976–99 (Managing Director, 1971–92); Lord-Lieutenant, County Durham, 1997–2013; *b* 7 March 1938; *s* of late Douglas Nicholson, TD and Pauline Nicholson; *m* 1970, Sarah, *y d* of Sir Edmund Bacon, Bt, KG, KBE, TD; one *d*. *Educ*: Harrow; Clare College, Cambridge (MA). FCA. Lieut, Coldstream Guards, 1956–58; joined Vaux Breweries, 1965. Chm., Northern Investors Co., 1984–89; Director: Tyne Tees Television, then Yorkshire-Tyne Tees Television Hldgs, 1981–97; Northern Development Co., 1986–2000; Northern Electric, 1990–97; Scottish Investment Trust plc, 1998–2005; Steelite International plc, 2000–02. Chm., Urban Develt Corp. for Tyne and Wear, 1987–98. Chm., N Region, CBI, 1977–79; Chm., N Regional Bd, British Technology Group, 1979–84. Chm., Brewers and Licensed Retailers Assoc. (formerly Brewers' Soc.), 1994–96; Pres., NE Chamber of Commerce, 1995–96. High Sheriff, Co. Durham, 1980–81; DL Co. Durham, 1980. *Publications*: Brewer At Large (memoirs), 2003. *Recreations*: deerstalking, riding and driving horses (winner, Liverpool Foxhunters' Steeplechase, 1963 and 1965; Pres., Coaching Club, 1990–97). *Address*: Goodwell Farm, Brancepeth, Durham DH7 8DN. *T*: (0191) 378 0275. *Clubs*: Boodle's, Pratt's; Northern Counties (Newcastle upon Tyne).

*See also* F. *Nicholson*.

**NICHOLSON, Paul James**, OBE 2006; FRCP; occupational physician; Associate Medical Director, Global Medical Operations, Procter & Gamble, 2011–16; *s* of James and Margaret Nicholson. *Educ*: Univ. of Newcastle upon Tyne (MB BS 1981). MRCGP 1986; AFOM 1986, MFOM 1992, FFOM 1998; DAvMed 1990; MIOSH 1994, FIOSH 1999; FRCP 2000. MO, RAF, 1981–91 (Sqdn Leader). Occupational Physician, ICI Chemicals & Polymers Ltd, Teesside, 1991–93; Sen. Corporate Med. Advr, Procter & Gamble UK and Ireland, 1993–2005; Associate Med. Dir, Procter & Gamble Beauty Care, EMEA, 2000–11. Faculty of Occupational Medicine: Mem. Bd, 1996–99, 1999–2000 and 2006–08; Mem., Fellowship Cttee, 1999–2003; Clin. Lead, Occupational Health Standards and Accreditation, 2008–11; Society of Occupational Medicine: Hon. Asst Ed., 1991–2001; Mem. Council, 1993–95, 1999–2002; Pres., 2000–01; British Medical Association: Mem., Occupational Medicine Cttee, 1996–2005, 2006–; Chair, 2008–; Fellow, 2015; British Occupational Health Research Foundation: Vice Chm., 2003–04, Chm., 2008–10, Occupational Asthma Res. Wkg Gp; Chm., Occupational Contact Dermatitis Res. Wkg Gp, 2008–10; Mem., Res. Cttee, 2008–11. *Publications*: (contrib.) BASICS Monographs on Immediate Care, 1986, 2nd edn 1990; Occupational Asthma: prevention, identification and management: systematic review and recommendations, 2010; Occupational Contact Dermatitis & Urticaria: prevention, identification and management: systematic review and recommendations, 2010; Occupational Health Service Standards for Accreditation, 2010; contrib. papers to jls on aeromedical helicopters, gender and pilots, unemployment, aging workers, cyanide antidotes, shiftwork, occupational asthma, occupational contact dermatitis, health risk communication, occupational health services, systematic reviews, alcohol, drugs and the workplace, cognitive enhancing drugs and the workplace, ageing and the workplace and occupational health - the value proposition. *Address*: 16 North Block, County Hall Apartments, SE1 7PJ. *E*: pjnicholson@doctors.org.uk.

**NICHOLSON, Robin Alaster**, CBE 1999; Partner, Cullinan Studio (formerly Edward Cullinan Architects), since 1980 (Director, 1989–2016); *b* 27 July 1944; *s* of late Gerald Hugh Nicholson and Margaret Evelyn Nicholson (*née* Hanbury); *m* 1969, Fiona Mary Bird; two *s* (and one *s* decd). *Educ*: Eton Coll.; Magdalene Coll., Cambridge (MA); University Coll. London (MSc 1969). RIBA 1989. Architect: Evan Walker Associates, Toronto, 1966; James Stirling, Chartered Architects, 1969–76; Boza Lührs Muzard, Santiago, Chile, 1973; Tutor in Architecture: UCL, 1974–76; Poly of N London, 1976–79. Vis. Fellow, Univ. of Wales, 1984; Hon. Prof., Univ. of Nottingham, 2013–. 9th Happold Medal Lect., Construction Industry Council, 2013. Dir, RIBA Journals Ltd, 1993–97. Mem. Council, 1991–97, Vice Pres., 1992–94, RIBA; Chm., Construction Industry Council, 1998–2000; Mem. Bd, Movement for Innovation, 1998–2002; Mem., DETR, subseq. DTLR, then ODPM, Urban Sounding Bd, 2001–03; Comr, Commn for Architecture and the Built Envmt, 2002–10; Dir, NHBC, 2007–13. Chm., Cambs Quality Panel, 2010–. FRSA 1995. Hon. FIStructE 2002; Hon. FCIBSE 2013. *Recreations*: gardening, making things. *Address*: (office) 5 Baldwin Terrace, N1 7RU. *T*: (020) 7704 1975. *Club*: The Edge.

**NICHOLSON, Sir Robin (Buchanan)**, Kt 1985; PhD; FRS 1978; FREng; *b* 12 Aug. 1934; *s* of late Carroll and Nancy Nicholson; *m* 1st, 1958, Elizabeth Mary Caffyn (*d* 1988); one *s* two *d*; 2nd, 1991, Yvonne, *d* of late Arthur and Gwendoline Appleby. *Educ*: Oundle Sch.; St Catharine's Coll., Cambridge (BA 1956; PhD 1959; MA 1960). FIMMM; MInstP; FREng (FEng 1980). University of Cambridge: Demonstrator in Metallurgy, 1960; Lectr in Metallurgy, 1964; Fellow of Christ's Coll., 1962–66, Hon. Fellow 1984; Prof. of Metallurgy, Univ. of Manchester, 1966. Inco Europe Ltd: Dir of Research Lab., 1972; Dir, 1975; Man. Dir, 1976–81; Co-Chm., Biogen NV, 1979–81. Chief Scientific Advr to Cabinet Office, 1981–85 (Central Policy Review Staff, 1981–83). Director: Pilkington Brothers, then Pilkington, plc, 1986–96; Rolls-Royce plc, 1986–2005; BP plc, 1987–2005. Chairman: CEST, 1987–90; ACOST, 1990–93. Member: SERC (formerly SRC), 1978–81; Council for Sci. and Technol., 1993–2000. Mem. Council: Royal Soc., 1983–85; Fellowship of Engrg, 1986–89; Gov., Exeter Univ., 2005–16. Pres., Inst. of Materials, 1997–98. Foreign Associate, Nat. Acad. of Engrg, USA, 1983. CCMI. Founder MAE 1988. Hon. FIChemE; Hon. Fellow UMIST, 1988. Hon. DSc: Cranfield, 1983; Aston, 1983; Manchester, 1985; Exeter, 2018; Hon. DMet Sheffield, 1984; Hon. DEng Birmingham, 1986; DUniv Open, 1987. Rosenhain Medallist, Inst. of Metals, 1971; Platinum Medal, Metals Soc., 1982. *Publications*: Precipitation Hardening (with A. Kelly), 1962; (jtly) Electron Microscopy of Thin Crystals, 1965; (ed and contrib. with A. Kelly) Strengthening Methods in Crystals, 1971; numerous papers to learned jls. *Recreations*: family life, gardening, music. *Club*: MCC.

*See also* M. B. *Nicholson*.

**NICHOLSON, Sarah-Jane, (Lady Nicholson)**; see Marsh, S.-J.

**Ní CHUILÍN, Carál**; Member (SF) Belfast North, Northern Ireland Assembly, since 2007; *b* New Lodge, Belfast. *Educ*: Open Univ. (BSc Social Scis 1994). Imprisoned on explosives charges, 1989; released, 1993. Co-ordinator, Tar Anall, support services for political ex-prisoners and families. Mem. (SF) Belfast CC, 2005–07. Formerly Co-chair: N Belfast Partnership Bd; Urban II. *Address*: Northern Ireland Assembly, Parliament Buildings, Stormont, Belfast BT4 3XX.

**NICKELL, Sir Stephen (John)**, Kt 2015; CBE 2007; FBA 1993; Warden, Nuffield College, Oxford, 2006–12; *b* 25 April 1944; *s* of John Edward Hilary Nickell and Phyllis Nickell; *m* 1976, Susan Elizabeth (*née* Pegden); one *s* one *d*. *Educ*: Merchant Taylors' Sch.; Pembroke Coll., Cambridge (BA; Hon. Fellow 2006); LSE (MSc). Maths teacher, Hendon County Sch., 1965–68; London School of Economics: Lectr, 1970–77; Reader, 1977–79; Prof. of Economics, 1979–84; Dir, Inst. of Econs and Stats, Prof. of Econs, and Fellow of Nuffield Coll., Oxford Univ., 1984–98; Sch. Prof. of Econs, LSE, 1998–2005. Member: Academic Panel, HM Treasury, 1981–89; ESRC, 1990–94; Monetary Policy Cttee, Bank of England, 2000–06; Bd, UK Statistics Authy, 2008–10; UK Budget Responsibility Cttee, 2010–16; Chairman: Nat. Housing and Planning Advice Unit, 2006–09; Adv. Cttee on Civil Costs, 2007–10. President: Eur. Assoc. of Labour Economists, 1999–2002; REconS, 2001–04 (Mem. Council, 1984–94). Fellow, Econometric Soc., 1980. Hon. Member: Amer. Economic Assoc., 1997; Amer. Acad. Arts and Scis, 2006. Hon. Fellow, Nuffield Coll., Oxford, 2003. Hon. DSc Warwick, 2008. IZA Prize in Labor Econs, 2008. *Publications*: The Investment Decisions of Firms, 1978; (with R. Layard and R. Dornbusch) The Performance of the British Economy, 1988; (with R. Jackman and R. Layard) Unemployment, 1991; (with R. Jackman and R. Layard) The Unemployment Crisis, 1994; The Performance of Companies, 1995; articles in learned jls. *Recreations*: reading, cricket, cooking. *E*: steve.nickell@nuffield.ox.ac.uk.

**NICKERSON, Jane Mary**; Chief Executive Officer, Swim England (Amateur Swimming Association), since 2017; *b* Coventry, 25 Jan. 1956; *d* of William and Gladys, (Pat), Nickerson. *Educ*: Blackdown Sch., St Joseph's Coll., Morlaix, Brittany; St Paul's Coll., Newbold Revel (BEd Hons; Cert Ed). Associate CIPD. House Manager, Birmingham Metropole Hotel, 1977–97; Chief Operating Officer, 1997–2017, Interim CEO, 2016–17, Amateur Swimming Assoc.; Manager, GB and England Swimming Team, 1992–97. Director: Badminton GB, 2012–; British Swimming Bd, 2018–. Chm., Swim Gp, 2016–; Mem. Bd, Swimsafe, 2016–. Treas., Sec. and listening volunteer, Coventry and Dist Samaritans, 2009–. *Recreations*: swimming, walking, reading, wildlife travel and photography, theatre. *Address*: The Squirrels, 9 Daleway Road, Finham, Coventry CV3 6JF. *T*: 07771 814302. *E*: jane.nickerson@swimming.org.

**NICKERSON, Rachel**; see Campbell-Johnston, R.

**NICKLAUS, Jack William**; professional golfer, 1961–2000; *b* 21 Jan. 1940; *s* of Louis Charles Nicklaus and Helen (*née* Schoener); *m* 1960, Barbara Jean Bash; four *s* one *d*. *Educ*: Upper Arlington High Sch.; Ohio State Univ. Won US Amateur golf championship, 1959, 1961; became professional golfer, 1961; designs golf courses in USA, Europe, and Far East; Chm., Golden Bear Internat. Inc. Captained US team which won 25th Ryder Cup, 1983. Major wins include: US Open, 1962, 1967, 1972, 1980; US Masters, 1963, 1965, 1966, 1972, 1975, 1986; US Professional Golfers' Assoc., 1963, 1971, 1973, 1975, 1980; British Open, 1966, 1970, 1978, and many other championships in USA, Europe, Australia and Far East. Hon. Dr Athletic Arts Ohio State, 1972; Hon. LLD St Andrews, 1984. Presidential Medal of Freedom (USA), 2005. *Publications*: My 55 Ways to Lower Your Golf Score, 1962; Take a Tip from Me, 1964; The Greatest Game of All, 1969 (autobiog.); Lesson Tee, 1972; Golf My Way, 1974; The Best Way to Better Your Golf, vols 1–3, 1974; Jack Nicklaus' Playing Lessons, 1976; Total Golf Techniques, 1977; On and Off the Fairway, 1979 (autobiog.); The Full Swing, 1982; My Most Memorable Shots in the Majors, 1988; Jack Nicklaus: my story, 1997. *Address*: (office) 11780 US Highway #1, North Palm Beach, FL 33408, USA.

**NICKLESS, Edmund Francis Paul**, MBE 2017; CSci, CGeol, FGS; Executive Secretary, Geological Society of London, 1997–2015; *b* 25 Jan. 1947; *e s* of Philip Wilfred Nickless and Gabrielle Frances Nickless (*née* Hughes); *m* 1970, Elisabeth Deborah Pickard; two *d*. *Educ*: Salvatorian Coll., Harrow; Queen Mary Coll., Univ. of London (BSc). FGS 1971; CGeol 1990; EurGeol 2002; CSci 2004. Various posts with British Geol Survey, London and Edinburgh, 1968–83; Sec., Earth Scis Directorate, NERC, Swindon, 1983–89; Envmtl Advr, Sci. and Technol. Secretariat, Cabinet Office, 1989–91; Asst Dir, British Geol Survey, 1991–97. Fellow, Geological Soc. of America, 2012. *Publications*: various papers on geology in learned jls and official pubns of British Geol Survey. *Recreations*: listening to music, gardening, walking. *Address*: Ringrose House, Main Street, Belton-in-Rutland LE15 9LB. *T*: (01572) 717324. *Club*: Athenæum.

**NICKLIN, Hon. Sir Matthew (James)**, Kt 2017; **Hon. Mr Justice Nicklin**; a Judge of the High Court, Queen's Bench Division, since 2017; *b* Oxford, 1970; *s* of Hugh David James Nicklin and Gillian Gawith Nicklin. *Educ*: Tasker-Milward Sch., Haverfordwest; Newcastle Univ. (LLB (Hons) 1st Cl. 1992). Called to the Bar, Lincoln's Inn, 1993, Bencher 2015; in practice as barrister, specialising in defamation and privacy law, 1996–2017; a Recorder, 2009–17; QC 2013; Jt Hd of Chambers, 5RB, 2014–17. Barrister Mem., Bar Standards Bd, 2007–13. FRSA 2010. *Publications*: The Law of Privacy and the Media, 2002, 3rd edn 2016. *Recreations*: scuba diving, travel. *Address*: Royal Courts of Justice, Strand, WC2A 2LL. *Clubs*: Century, Rushmore, Ivy.

**NICKLIN, Susanna**; Chief Executive Officer, MILD Group (Marsh Agency Ltd, since 2013; Dulwich Books Ltd, since 2015; Live Lit, since 2016; Indigo Press, since 2017); *b* 26 June 1964; *d* of Philip and Hilary Nicklin; *m* 1997, Paul Marsh (*d* 2009); one *s* one *d*. *Educ*: Exeter Coll., Oxford (MA). Literary Agent, 1987–2002; Dir, English PEN, 2002–05; Dir, Literature, British Council, 2005–13. Trustee, English Assoc. *Recreations*: gardening, walking, music, family, friends, France. *Address*: c/o Marsh Agency Ltd, 50 Albermarle Street, W1S 4BD. *T*: (020) 7493 7361.

**NICKOLDS, Paula Margaret**; Managing Director, John Lewis, since 2017; *b* Bromley, Kent, 3 Feb. 1973; *d* of Clive and Sheila Nickolds; *m* 2003, David Morley. *Educ*: St Helen's Sch., Northwood; Southampton Univ. (BA Hons 1994). With John Lewis, 1994–: Buying

Dir, Home, 2009–13; Buying and Brand Dir, 2013–15; Commercial Dir, 2015–16. Trustee: John Lewis Foundn, 2012–16; GDST, 2013–16. *Recreations:* family, walking, theatre, travel. *Address:* John Lewis Partnership, 171 Victoria Street, SW1E 5NN. *T:* (020) 7828 1000. *E:* paula.nickolds@johnlewis.co.uk.

**NICKSON,** family name of **Baron Nickson.**

**NICKSON,** Baron *cr* 1994 (Life Peer), of Renagour in the District of Stirling; **David Wigley Nickson,** KBE 1987 (CBE 1981); FRSE; Vice Lord-Lieutenant of Stirling and Falkirk, 1997–2005; *b* 27 Nov. 1929; *s* of late Geoffrey Wigley Nickson and Janet Mary Nickson; *m* 1st, 1952, Helen Louise Cockcraft (*d* 2012); three *d*; 2nd, 2013, Mrs Eira Drysdale (*née* Govett). *Educ:* Eton; RMA, Sandhurst. Commnd Coldstream Guards, 1949–54. Joined Wm Collins, 1954; Dir, 1961–85; Jt Man. Dir, 1967; Vice Chm., 1976–83; Gp Man. Dir, 1979–82; Chm., Pan Books, 1982. Director: Scottish United Investors plc, 1970–83; General Accident plc, 1971–98 (Dep. Chm., 1993–98); Scottish & Newcastle (formerly Scottish & Newcastle Breweries) plc, 1981–95 (Dep. Chm., 1982–83; Chm., 1983–89); Clydesdale Bank, 1981–89 (Dep. Chm., 1990–91; Chm., 1991–98); Radio Clyde PLC, 1982–85; Edinburgh Investment Trust plc, 1983–94; Hambro's PLC, 1989–98; National Australia Bank Ltd, 1991–96. Mem., H of L, 1994–2015. Chm., Top Salaries, then Sen. Salaries, Rev. Body, 1989–95; Chairman: SDA, 1989–90, Scottish Enterprise, 1990–93; CBI in Scotland, 1979–81; Pres., CBI, 1986–88 (Dep. Pres., 1985–86). Member: Scottish Indust. Develt Adv. Bd, 1975–80; Scottish Econ. Council, 1980–94; NEDC, 1985–88; Scottish Cttee, Design Council, 1978–81; Nat. Trng Task Force, 1989–91. Chairman: Countryside Commn for Scotland, 1983–85; Scottish Adv. Cttee, ICRF, 1994–2001; Atlantic Salmon Trust, 1989–96 (Mem., Council of Management, 1982–; Vice-Pres., 1996–2005); Conon Dist Salmon Fishery Bd, 1994–2005; Sec. of State for Scotland's Atlantic Salmon Task Force, 1996; Pres., Assoc. of Scottish Dist Salmon Fishery Bds, 1996–2011 (Vice Chm., 1989–92); Dir, Countryside Alliance, 1998–2000. Chairman: Cromarty Firth Fisheries Trust, 1999–2012; Loch Lomond Shores Trust, 1999–2002. Trustee: Game Conservancy, 1988–91; Prince's Youth Business Trust, 1987–90; Princess Royal's Trust for Carers, 1990–94. Chancellor, Glasgow Caledonian Univ., 1993–2002. Capt., Queen's Body Guard for Scotland, Royal Co. of Archers. Freeman, City of London, 1999; Hon. Freeman, Fishmongers' Co., 1999. DL Stirling and Falkirk, 1982. CCMI (CBIM 1980); FRSE 1987. Hon. Fellow, Paisley Coll., subseq. Univ. of Paisley, 1992. DUniv Stirling, 1986; Hon. DBA Napier Polytechnic, 1990; DUniv Glasgow Caledonian, 1993. *Recreations:* fishing, shooting, bird watching, the countryside. *Address:* The River House, Doune, Perthshire FK16 6DA. *T:* (01786) 841614. *Clubs:* Boodle's, Flyfishers'.

*See also* M. A. Campbell.

**NICKSON, John Denis;** author, mentor and philanthropy campaigner; *b* Lytham St Annes, Lancs, 10 April 1947; *s* of Denis and Joan Nickson; *m* 2005, Simon Rew. *Educ:* Giggleswick Sch.; University Coll. London (BA Hons Anthropol. 1968). Actor and th. producer, 1968–75; fundraiser, London Samaritans, 1975–76; Dir, Information and Sponsorship, British Council, 1977–89; Dir of Develt, ENO, 1989–96; Director: RA Trust, Royal Acad. of Arts, 1996–2005; Tate Foundn, Tate, 2005–11. Gov., Atlantic Council, 1997–2010; Mem., Governing Council, RCM, 2012–. Trustee: London Music Masters, 2013–; Opera Rara, 2013–; UK Community Foundns, 2015–. *Publications:* Giving is Good for You: why Britain should be bothered and give more, 2013; Our Common Good: if the state provides less, who will provide more?, 2017. *Recreations:* music, visual arts, reading, walking, talking, the weather. *T:* 07817 140540. *E:* johndnickson@gmail.com.

**NICOL, Hon. Sir Andrew (George Lindsay),** Kt 2009; **Hon. Mr Justice Nicol;** a Judge of the High Court of Justice, Queen's Bench Division, since 2009; *b* 9 May 1951; *s* of late Duncan Rennie Nicol and Margaret (*née* Mason); *m* 2005, Camilla Palmer; two *s*. *Educ:* Selwyn Coll., Cambridge (BA, LLB); Harvard Law Sch. (LLM). Harkness Fellow, 1973–75; Special Assistant: to Dir of Housing and Community Develt, California, 1975–76; Allen Allen and Hemsley, solicitors, Sydney, NSW, 1976–77; Lectr in Law, LSE, 1977–87; called to the Bar, Middle Temple, 1978, Bencher, 2004; barrister, 1979–2009; QC 1995; Asst Recorder, 1998–2000; Recorder, 2000–09; Dep. High Court Judge, 2003–09; Presiding Judge, SE Circuit, 2011–14. Dep. Chm., Boundary Commn for England, 2017–. Chm., Immigration Law Practitioners' Assoc., 1997–2000. *Publications:* (with G. Robertson) Media Law, 1984, 5th edn 2007; (with A. Dummett) Subjects, Citizens, Aliens and Others, 1990; (with G. Millar and A. Sharland) Media Law and Human Rights, 2001, 2nd edn 2009. *Recreations:* family, sailing, walking. *Address:* Royal Courts of Justice, Strand, WC2A 2LL.

**NICOL, (Andrew) William;** JP; BSc; FICE, FIMechE, FIET; Chairman, 1987–93, and Chief Executive, 1990–93, South Western Electricity plc; *b* 29 April 1933; *s* of Arthur Edward Nicol and Ethel Isabel Gladstone Nicol (*née* Fairley); *m* 1960, Jane Gillian Margaret Mann; one *s*. *Educ:* King's College School, Wimbledon; Durham Univ. (BSc). W. S. Atkins & Partners, 1960–67; Electricity Council, 1967–69; London Electricity Board, 1969–81; Dep. Chm., SE Electricity Board, 1981–87. Chairman: Trustees, NICEIC Pension Fund, 1986–93; South Western Enterprises, 1992–93. JP Surrey 1976. *Recreation:* Honourable Artillery Company. *Club:* Caledonian.

**NICOL, Karen,** RDI 2015; designer and artist, since 1975; *b* Rotherham, 27 May 1952; *d* of Peter and Kit Nicol; *m* 1981, Peter Clark; two *d*. *Educ:* Harrogate Coll.; Manchester Metropolitan Univ. (BA Hons); Royal Coll. of Art (MA(RCA)). Mixed media and embroidery textile artist and designer working in fashion, interiors and art, 1975–. Royal College of Art: Sen. Lectr, 1990–2005; Res. Fellow, 2006–08; Vis. Prof., 2008–12. Hon. FRCA 2014. FRSA. *Publications:* Embellished New Vintage, 2012. *Recreation:* hunting through flea markets and car boot sales for unexpected beauty and inspiration. *Address:* 18 St Mary's Road, East Molesey, Surrey KT8 0ST. *T:* (020) 8979 4593, 07740 375136. *E:* karen@karennicol.com. *W:* www.karennicol.com, www.instagram.com/karennicol1.

**NICOL, Dr Richard Charles,** FREng, FIET; Director and Chief Executive Officer, Fynntek Ltd, research consulting, 2001–14; *b* 14 July 1948; *s* of George Nicol and Alice (*née* Ardley); *m* 1974, Rosemary Jane Greaves; one *s* one *d*. *Educ:* University Coll. London (BSc Eng; PhD 1976). FIET (FIEE 1994). Joined Post Office Res., 1970; British Telecommunications, 1976–88; Manager, Univ. Res. Prog., 1988–92; BT Laboratories, then BTexact Technologies: Divl Manager, Visual Telecomms, 1992–95; Hd, Centre for Human Communications, 1995–98; Hd of Res., 1998–2001. Chm., ICT (formerly Digital Communications) KTN, 2007–14. Dir, Suffolk Develt Agency, 2000–09; Mem. Bd, Suffolk Learning and Skills Council, 2001–08. Chairman: of Corp., Suffolk New Coll. (formerly Suffolk Coll.), 2009–13; Suffolk New Acads Trust, 2013–14; Mem. Council, Univ. of Essex, 2006–11. FREng 2000. *Recreations:* sailing, walking. *Club:* Ipswich and Suffolk.

**NICOL, William;** *see* Nicol, A. W.

**NICOLI, Eric Luciano,** CBE 2006; Chairman: Yo! Sushi, since 2015; Centtrip, since 2015; *b* 5 Aug. 1950; *s* of Virgilio and Ida Nicoli; *m* 1977, Rosalind West (marr. diss. 2005); one *s* one *d*; *m* 2005, Lucy Caldwell; two *d*. *Educ:* Diss Grammar Sch.; King's College London

(BSc Hons 1st class Physics). Marketing, Rowntree Mackintosh, 1972–80; United Biscuits: Marketing, 1980–83; Business Planning, 1984; Managing Dir, Frozen Food Div., 1985, Biscuit and Confectionery Div., 1986–88; Chief Exec., Europe, 1989–90; Gp Chief Exec., 1991–99; Chm. HMV Gp plc, 2001–04 (Dir, 2000–04); Exec. Chm., Thorn EMI plc, then EMI Gp plc, 1999–2007 (Dir, 1993–2007; CEO, 2007); Chairman: Tussauds Gp, 2001–07 (Dir, 1999–2007); Vue Entertainment Ltd, 2006–10; uSwitch Ltd, 2013–15; Sen. Partner, Sunningdale Capital LLP, 2010–14. Dir, Akazoo (formerly R&R Music) Ltd, 2008–. Non-exec. Dir, Greencore Gp plc, 2010–17; Sen. Ind. Dir, PGA European Tour, 2019–. Dep. Chm., BITC, 1991–2003. Chm., Per Cent Club, 1995–2007. Trustee, Comic Relief, 1999–2004; Chm., EMI Music Sound Foundn, 2003–09 (Trustee, 2001). *Recreations:* music, sport, food.

**NICOLL, Alison Jane;** *see* Watt, A. J.

**NICOLL, Prof. Angus Gordon,** CBE 2002; FRCP, FRCPCH, FFPH; Head, Influenza and Other Respiratory Viruses Programme, European Centre for Disease Prevention and Control, 2011–13 (on secondment as National Expert, 2005–11); *b* 5 Aug. 1950; *s* of James Nicoll and Mary Laugharne; *m* 1982, Mary Grizel Braham; one *s* two *d*. *Educ:* Trinity Coll., Cambridge (MA; BChir 1976, MB 1977); Middlesex Hosp., LSHTM (MSc Epidemiol. 1985). Paediatric trng, London, Scotland and Nottingham; trng in public health, London and Africa; Sen. Lectr in HIV Epidemiol., LSHTM and in E Africa, 1987–91; Consultant, 1991–2011, Dir, Communicable Disease Surveillance Centre, 2000–05, HPA. Hon. Sen. Lectr, Inst. of Child Health, London, 1996–; Hon. Prof., LSHTM, 2001–. *Publications:* (ed jtly) Manual of Childhood Infections, 1987, 2001. *Recreations:* family, running and other outdoor pursuits, theatre, social history. *Clubs:* John Snow Society; St Albans Striders.

**NICOLLE, Frederick Villeneuve,** FRCSCan; Consultant Plastic Surgeon, Hammersmith Hospital, 1970–97; Senior Lecturer, University of London and Royal Postgraduate Medical School, 1970–97; *b* 11 March 1931; *s* of Arthur Nicolle and Alice Nicolle (*née* Cobbold); *m* 1957, Helia Immaculata Stuart-Walker; one *s* two *d*. *Educ:* Eton; Trinity Coll., Cambridge (BA; MB BChir 1956; MChir 1970). FRCSCan 1963. McLaughlin Travelling Fellow, Canada, 1964; Consultant Plastic Surgeon, Montreal Gen. Hosp. and Montreal Children's Hosp., 1964–69; Lectr, McGill Univ., 1964–69; returned to UK, 1970; in private practice in aesthetic and reconstructive plastic surgery, 1970–97. Vis. Prof. in Plastic Surgery, China, Syria, S America, SA, Australia, NZ and guest lectr in many countries; Hon. Prof., Singapore Assoc. of Plastic Surgeons, 1980. President: Brit. Assoc. Aesthetic Plastic Surgery, 1984–86 (Hon. Mem.); Chelsea Clinical Soc., 1986; Internat. Alpine Surgical Soc., 1996, 1997; Treas., Internat. Soc. Aesthetic Plastic Surgery, 1986–94 (Trustee, 1992–94); Member: Brit. Assoc. Plastic Surgery, 1966; Internat. Soc. Plastic Surgery, 1971; Amer. Soc. Aesthetic Plastic Surgery, 1982. *Publications:* The Care of the Rheumatoid Hand, 1975; Aesthetic Rhinoplasty, 1996; chaps in numerous text books of plastic and reconstructive surgery; contrib. British Jl Plastic Surgery and Jl Aesthetic Surgery. *Recreations:* painting, ski-ing, shooting, fishing, tennis. *Address:* East Wing, Chippenham Park, Ely, Cambs CB5 7PT. *Club:* White's.

**NICOLLE, Stéphanie Claire;** QC (Jersey) 1995; HM Solicitor General for Jersey, 1994–2008; *b* 11 March 1948; *d* of Walter Arthur Nicolle and Madeleine Claire Nicolle (*née* Vitel). *Educ:* Convent of the Faithful Companions of Jesus, Jersey; St Aidan's Coll., Univ. of Durham. Called to the Bar, Gray's Inn, 1976; called to the Jersey Bar, 1978; Crown Advocate, 1986–94. Adjunct Prof. of Immovable Property, Inst. of Law, Jersey, 2009–12. *Publications:* (with P. Matthews) The Jersey Law of Property, 1991; The Origin and Development of Jersey Law, 1998. *Address:* 11 Parade Road, St Helier, Jersey, Channel Islands JE2 3PL.

**NICOLSON,** family name of **Baron Carnock.**

**NICOLSON, Adam;** *see* Carnock, 5th Baron.

**NICOLSON, John MacKenzie;** media consultant, freelance journalist and broadcaster, since 2017; *b* Glasgow, 1961; *s* of John Donald Nicolson and Marion (*née* Stant); partner, Juliano Zini. *Educ:* Univ. of Glasgow (MA Hons); Harvard Univ. (Harkness Fellow; Kennedy Schol.); Scottish and World Student Debating Champion, winner of Observer Mace, 1983). Speech writer, US Senate, 1985–87; freelance journalist and broadcaster, 1987–2015: reporter for Newsnight, Assignment, Public Eye, Panorama, On the Record; presenter: News 24; BBC Breakfast; ITV News; TalkRadio; contrib. The Times, Sunday Times, Observer, Sunday Telegraph, Guardian. MP (SNP) Dunbartonshire E, 2015–17; contested (SNP) same seat, 2017. Mem., DCMS Select Cttee, 2015–17. SNP spokesperson on Culture, Media and Sport, 2015–17. *Recreations:* travel, reading, music, cooking, art, exploring derelict buildings. *E:* johnnynicolson@aol.com.

**NICOLSON, Juliet;** writer; *b* Bransgore, Hants, 9 June 1954; *d* of Nigel Nicolson, OBE, author, and Philippa Janet, *d* of Sir (Eustace) Gervais Tennyson d'Eyncourt, 2nd Bt; *m* 1977, James Macmillan-Scott (marr. diss. 1995); two *d*; *m* 2009, Charles Vernon Anson, *qv*. *Educ:* Benenden Sch.; Westminster Tutors; St Hugh's Coll., Oxford (BA English Lit. 1976; MA). With Hamish Hamilton, 1976–81; Chatto & Windus, 1981–83; Atlantic Monthly Press/ Grove Press, 1983–94; Ed Victor Ltd, Literary Agency, 1996–2000; writer and journalist, 2000–. *Publications:* The Perfect Summer: dancing into shadow in 1911, 2006; The Great Silence 1918–1920: living in the shadow of the Great War, 2009; Abdication, 2012; A House Full of Daughters (memoir), 2016. *Recreations:* talking, walking, cooking. *Address:* c/o Curtis Brown, Haymarket House, 28–29 Haymarket, SW1Y 4SP. *T:* (020) 7393 4400.
*See also* Baron Carnock.

**NICOLSON, Margaret Mary;** *see* Appleton, M. M.

**NICOLSON, Roy Macdonald;** Chief Executive, Scottish Amicable Life plc, 1997–2000; *b* 12 June 1944; *s* of Alan Neil Nicolson and Mary Nicolson; *m* 1972, Jennifer Margaret Miller; one *s* one *d*. *Educ:* Paisley Grammar School. FFA. Joined Scottish Amicable, 1960; Asst London Secretary, 1971; Asst Actuary, 1973; Pensions Manager (Operations), 1976; Asst Gen. Manager (Pensions), 1982; Gen. Manager (Systems), 1985; Dep. Chief Gen. Manager, then Man. Dir, 1990. Director: J. Rothschild Assurance Hldgs, 1991–99; St James's Place Capital, 1997–2000; Prudential Assurance Co., 1997–2000; Nat. Australia WM (Europe), 2001–04; Nat. Australia WM Hldgs, 2003–04; Nat. Australia Gp (Europe), 2004–12; Chairman: Advice First Ltd, 2002–04; BDO Stoy Hayward Wealth Mgt, 2004–10. *Recreations:* golf, bridge. *Address:* Ardgarten, Doune Road, Dunblane, Perthshire FK15 9HR. *T:* (01786) 823849.

**NIEDUSZYŃSKI, Anthony John;** Secretary to Monopolies and Mergers Commission, 1993–96; *b* 7 Jan. 1939; *er s* of Tadeusz Adolf Antoni Nieduszyński, LLD and Madeleine Gladys Lilian (*née* Huggler); *m* 1980, Frances, *yr d* of Wing Comdr Max Oxford, OBE; one *d*. *Educ:* St Paul's School (Foundation Scholar); Merton College, Oxford (Postmaster; 1st cl. Hon. Mods 1959; 1st cl. Lit Hum 1961; MA). Board of Trade, 1964; Private Sec. to Pres. of BoT, 1967–68; Principal Private Sec. to Minister for Trade and Consumer Affairs, 1972–74 and to Sec. of State for Trade, 1974; Asst Sec., Dept of Prices and Consumer Protection, 1974, Dept of Industry, 1977, Home Office, 1982; Under Sec., DTI, 1985–93; Head: of Radiocommunications Div., 1985; of Air Div., 1988; of Business Task Forces Div.

2, 1990; of Aerospace Div., 1992. *Recreations:* Gregorian chant, growing olives in Tuscany, language, opera, grandchildren. *Address:* Clarendon House, 33 Strand, Topsham, Exeter, Devon EX3 0AY. *Clubs:* Farmers, Polish Hearth.

**NIELSEN, Anne Hedensted;** *see* Steffensen, A. H.

**NIELSON, Poul;** Member, European Commission, 1999–2004; *b* 11 April 1943; *s* of Svend and Esther Nielson; *m* 1967, Anne-Marie Jørgensen; one *s* two *d. Educ:* Århus Univ. (Masters degree in Political Sci. 1972). Nat. Chm., Social Democratic Student Movt, 1966–67; Chm., Foreign Affairs Cttee, SDP, 1974–79, 2009–; Mem., UN Sec. Gen.'s Adv. Bd on Water and Sanitation, 2004–15. MP (SDP) Denmark, 1971–73, 1977–84, 1986–99; Minister of Energy, 1979–82; Minister for Develt Co-operation, 1994–99. Head of Section, Min. of Foreign Affairs, 1974–79, 1984–85; Cons. in Public Mgt, Danish Admin. Sch., 1985–86; Investment Cons., Danish Wage Earner Pensions Fund, 1985–88; Man. Dir, LD Energi A/S, 1988–94; Mem., Bd of Dirs, Denerco, Danop, Vestas and other cos, 1986–94. Adjunct Prof., Aalborg Univ., 2005–. Special Advr, Nordic Council of Ministers, 2015–16. Polio Eradication Champion Award, Rotary Internat., 1999. *Publications:* Power Play and Security, 1968; The Company Act and the Wage Earners, 1974; Politicians and Civil Servants, 1987; En hel Nielson (memoirs), 2011. *Recreations:* photography, literature, music, gardening, table tennis.

**NIEMAN, Sandra;** *see* Horley, S.

**NIENOW, Prof. Alvin William,** FREng; Professor of Biochemical Engineering, University of Birmingham, 1989–2004, now Emeritus; *b* 19 June 1937; *o s* of late Alvin William Nienow and Mary May Nienow (*née* Hawthorn); *m* 1959, Helen Mary Sparkes; two *s* one *d. Educ:* St Clement Danes Grammar Sch.; University Coll. London (BSc Eng, 1st Cl. Hons; PhD; DSc Eng). FIChemE; CEng, FREng (FEng 1985); CSci 2003. Industry, 1958–61; Lectr and Sen. Lectr, 1963–80, Hon. Res. Fellow, 1980–, Dept of Chem. and Biochem. Engineering, UCL; University of Birmingham: Prof. of Chem. Engineering, 1980–89; Dir, SERC, later BBSRC, Centre for Biochem. Engrg, 1989–2000. Chm., Scientific Cttee, Biochem. Engrg Course, Eur. Soc. of Biochem. Engrg Scis, 2003–. Vis. Prof., Fellow and Lectr, China and Japan; Vis. Prof. of Biochem. Engrg, Loughborough Univ., 2009–; Vis. Prof., Sch. of Life and Health Scis, Aston Univ., 2015–. Eminent Speaker, Chemical Coll., IEAust, 1999; Plenary Lectr, Pharmaceutical Section, AIChE, 2009. Member: AFRC, 1987–90; Biotechnol. Directorate, SERC, 1990–93; Engrg Bd, SERC, then EPSRC, 1991–94; Planning and Resources Bd, BBSRC, 1994–96; Council, IChemE, 1984–89; Scientific Adv. Cttee, EFCE, 1987–94; Standing Cttee for Engrg, Royal Acad. of Engrg, 1996–98; Internat. Adv. Bd, Inst. of Chemical Process Fundamentals, Acad. of Scis, Czech Republic, 1996–; Peer Review Coll., Danish Council for Strategic Res., 2008–; numerous other scientific and engrg bodies. Consultant: BHR Gp Fluid Mixing Processes, 1985–; Rhône-Poulenc Conseil Technologique, 1988–2000 (Pres., 1998–2000). Mem., Governing Body, Silsoe Res. Inst., 1996–98. Hon. Mem., Czech Soc. of Chemical Engrg, 2008. Ed. (Europe and Africa), Jl Chem. Engrg, Japan, 2001–05. Dr *hc* W Pomeranian Univ. of Technol., 2010; Hon. DSc Loughborough, 2012. Moulton Medal, 1984, Donald Medal, 2000, IChemE; Jan E. Purkyne Medal, Czech Acad. of Science, 1993; Lifetime Contribution Award, Eur. Fedn of Chemical Engrg Wkg Party on Mixing, 2003; Special Contributions Medal, Szczecin Univ. of Technol., 2008; Peter Dunnill Award, BioIndustry Assoc., 2018. *Publications:* (jtly) Mixing in the Process Industries, 1985, 2nd edn revised 1997; (ed) 3rd International Conference on Bioreactor and Bioprocess Fluid Dynamics, 1993, 4th International Conference, 1997; (jtly) Biochemical Engineering Principles, 2005; numerous papers on mixing, fluidisation and biochem. engrg in learned jls. *Recreations:* sport, travel, dancing, music, real ale, ski-ing (Escapade Medal, Trois Vallées, 2012, 2015). *Address:* Department of Chemical Engineering, University of Birmingham, Edgbaston, Birmingham B15 2TT. *Clubs:* MCC; Edgbaston Priory (Vice Pres., 2016–), Reading Cricket and Hockey (Vice Pres., 1982–).

**NIGGLI, Olivier;** Director General, World Anti-Doping Agency, since 2016; *b* La Chaux-de-Fonds, Switzerland, 3 May 1970; *s* of Luc Niggli and Josiane Niggli (*née* Tercier); partner, Mona Lacombe; one *s. Educ:* Univ. of Lausanne (LLB); London Sch. of Econs and Pol Sci. (LLM); McGill Univ. (MBA). Associate Lawyer, Carrard & Associés (formerly Kellerhals Carrard), 1997–2001; Chief Financial Officer and Dir, Legal Affairs, World Anti-Doping Agency, 2001–11; Partner, Carrard & Associés (formerly Kellerhals Carrard), 2011–14; Chief Operating Officer, World Anti-Doping Agency, 2014–15. *Publications:* Substantial Assistance in the Fight Against Doping, 2012; contribs to Patent Rights, Lawyer Rev., Brussels Observer, JusLetter, SBA/CAS Conf. papers. *Recreations:* ski-ing, sailing. *Address:* World Anti-Doping Agency, Stock Exchange Tower, Suite 1700, Montreal, QC H4Z 1B7, Canada. *T:* (314) 9049232. *E:* olivier.niggli@wada-ama.org.

**NIGHTINGALE, Anne,** MBE 2000; presenter, BBC Radio 1, since 1970; guest presenter, BBC Radio 2; *b* Osterley, W London; one *s* one *d. Educ:* Lady Eleanor Holles Sch., Hampton; Poly. of Central London (Dip. Journalism). Columnist, Cosmopolitan, 1975–78; Presenter, The Old Grey Whistle Test, BBC TV, 1978–82; regular broadcaster on BBC Radio 4; regular appearances as DJ at major music festivals, UK, Europe, USA and Asia. Music albums: Annie on One, 1995; y4K Presents: Annie Nightingale, 2007; Masterpiece Ministry of Sound, 2015. Hon. DLitt Westminster, 2012. *Publications:* How to Form a Beat Group, 1965; Chase the Fade (autobiog.), 1982; Wicked Speed (autobiog.), 2000; contrib. The Guardian, The Times, Punch, Radio Times, etc. *Recreation:* studying architecture and tall buildings. *Address:* BBC Radio 1, W1W 6AJ. *E:* annienightingale@gmail.com.

**NIGHTINGALE, Anthony John Liddell,** CMG 2012; JP; Director, Jardine Matheson Holdings Ltd, since 1994; Managing Director, Jardine Matheson Group, 2006–12; *b* Huddersfield, 8 Nov. 1947; *s* of William John Nightingale and Rosemary Mabel Nightingale; *m* 1973, Christina Philomena de Souza; one *s* one *d. Educ:* Uppingham Sch.; Peterhouse, Cambridge (BA Hons Classics 1969). Joined Jardine Matheson Gp, 1969; various roles in Japan, Saudi Arabia and Hong Kong; Director: Jardine Cycle & Carriage Ltd, 1993– (Chm., 2002–12); Jardine Strategic Hldgs Ltd, 2006–; Dairy Farm Internat. Hldgs Ltd, 2006–; Hongkong Land Hldgs Ltd, 2006–; Mandarin Oriental Internat. Ltd, 2006–. Non-executive Director: Schindler Hldg AG, 2013–; Prudential plc, 2013–; Independent non-executive Director: China Xintiandi Ltd, 2013–15; Vitasoy Internat. Hldgs Ltd, 2015–; Shui On Land Ltd, 2016–. Chm., Hong Kong General Chamber of Commerce, 2003–05; Member: Hong Kong Port Develt Bd, 1991–98; Hong Kong Trade Develt Council, 2005–09; (Non-Official) Commn on Strategic Develt, 2006–17; Cttee on Strategic Enhancement of Hong Kong as an Internat. Financial Centre, 2010–17; Cttee on Real Estate Investment Trusts, Securities and Futures Commn, 2011–17; Adv. Council, Hong Kong Univ. of Sci. and Technol., 2013–; Council of Advisers on Innovation and Strategic Develt, HKSAR, 2018–. Hong Kong Rep., APEC Business Adv. Council, 2005–17; Hong Kong Rep., APEC Vision Gp, 2018–; Chm., Hong Kong-APEC Trade Policy Study Gp Ltd, 2010–17. Vice Pres., Real Estate Developers Assoc. of Hong Kong, 2007–13. Chm., 1995–2005, Patron, 2012–, Hong Kong Tennis Foundn; Chair, Sailors Home and Missions to Seafarers (formerly Sailors Home and Missions to Seamen), 2006–. Mem., Chongqing Mayor's Internat. Adv. Council, 2010–12; Dir, UK ASEAN Business Council, 2012–18. Hon. Prof., Hong Kong Baptist Univ., 2012–. Chm., Friends of Uppingham Sch. Ltd, 2017–. JP Hong Kong, 2005. Silver Bauhinia Star (Hong Kong), 2007. *Recreations:* climbing, hiking, tennis, ski-ing, golf, poster and woodblock art. *Address:* Jardine Matheson Holdings Ltd, 9th Floor, One Exchange Square, Central, Hong Kong. *T:* 28438207, *Fax:* 28435393. *E:* ajn@jardines.com. *Clubs:* Hong Kong, Hong Kong Country, Shek O Country, Mariners', Hong Kong Jockey (Hon. Voting Mem.), China (Hong Kong).

**NIGHTINGALE, Benedict;** *see* Nightingale, W. B. H.

**NIGHTINGALE, Caroline Ann;** *see* Slocock, C. A.

**NIGHTINGALE, Sir Charles (Manners Gamaliel),** 17th Bt *cr* 1628; Grade 7, Department of Health, 1996–2007; *b* 21 Feb. 1947; *s* of Sir Charles Athelstan Nightingale, 16th Bt, and Evelyn Nadine Frances (*d* 1995), *d* of late Charles Arthur Diggens; *S* father, 1977. *Educ:* St Paul's School. BA Hons Open Univ., 1990. Entered DHSS as Executive Officer, 1969; Higher Executive Officer, 1977; Sen. Exec. Officer, DoH, 1989. *Heir:* cousin Edward Lacy George Nightingale, *b* 11 May 1938. *Address:* 16 Unity Grove, Harrogate HG1 2AQ.

**NIGHTINGALE, Mary Louise;** Newsreader; Presenter, ITV Evening News, since 2000; *b* 26 May 1963; *d* of late David Trewyn Nightingale and Jennifer Constance Mary Nightingale (*née* Tetley); *m* 2000, Paul Fenwick; one *s* one *d. Educ:* Oakdene Sch., Beaconsfield; St Margaret Sch., Exeter; King Edward VI Sch., Totnes; Bedford Coll. London (BA Hons English 1985). Presenter: World Business Satellite, TV Tokyo, 1990–94; World Business Report, BBC World Service TV, 1991–93; London Tonight and London Today, ITV, 1993–99; Reuters Financial Television, 1994; BBC Radio Five Live, 1994–97; Rugby World Cup, ITV, 1995; Newscaster, ITN World News, 1995; newsreader, Lunchtime News 2001–17, News at Ten, 2001–15, ITV News; Presenter: Ski Sunday, BBC, 1996; Holiday, BBC, 1997–98; Wish You Were Here?, ITV, 1999–2001. Patron: Willow Foundn; Rainbow Trust; Mariposa Trust; Action for Children; Ambassador, Prince's Trust; Duchenne Children's Trust; Charlie Waller Meml Trust. Newscaster of the Year, TRIC, 2002, 2004. *Recreations:* travel, ski-ing, friends and family, pottering around on the River Dart. *Address:* c/o ITN, 200 Gray's Inn Road, WC1X 8XZ. *Club:* Royal Dart Yacht.

**NIGHTINGALE, Neil;** Creative Director, BBC Earth, 2009–18; *b* 6 Feb. 1960; *s* of Ivor and Ann Nightingale; *m. Educ:* Wadham Coll., Oxford (BA (Zool.) 1982; MA). Freelance journalist; BBC: researcher; producer, 1989–95, credits include: The Natural World; Wildlife on One; Lost Worlds Vanished Lives; The Private Life of Plants; The Restless Year; One Life; Great Barrier Reef; Editor: The Natural World, 1995–2001; The Wildlife Specials, 1997–2001; Director: Walking with Dinosaurs 3D, 2013; Prehistoric Planet 3D, 2014; Director and Producer: Enchanted Kingdom 3D, 2014; Wild Africa 3D, 2015; Executive Producer, 2001–03: Wild Africa; Wild Down Under; Congo; Wild New World; Wild Battlefields; Head, 2003–09, Exec. Producer, 2009–11, BBC Natural History Unit; Executive Producer: Tiny Giants 3D, 2014; Earthflight 3D and Predators 3D, 2016; Earth - One Amazing Day, 2017; Producer, Oceans: Our Blue Planet, 2018. *Publications:* New Guinea: an island apart, 1992; Wild Down Under, 2003. *Recreations:* sailing, diving, wildlife, travel.

**NIGHTINGALE, Nicholas John;** Secretary General, World Alliance of YMCAs, 1999–2002; *b* 29 Aug. 1942; *s* of late Christopher, (Toby), and of Muriel, (Buster), Nightingale; *m* 1968, Sue Lyth (Rev. Dr Sue Nightingale); one *s* two *d* (and one *d* decd). *Educ:* Brighton, Hove and Sussex GS; Trinity Coll., Dublin (BA, LLB 1964); Harvard Business Sch. (AMP 1983). Qualified as solicitor, 1968; Solicitor, Slaughter & May, 1970–74; Partner, Patterson Glenton & Stracey, 1974; Solicitor and Co. Sec., Rowntree Mackintosh, 1975–85; Exec. Dir, Rowntree plc, 1985–89; Co. Sec., Tate & Lyle, 1989–93; Nat. Sec., YMCA England (formerly Nat. Council, YMCAs), 1993–98. Director: Tom Smith Crackers, 1983–85; Original Cookie Co., 1985–89; Cookie Jar, 1989–98; Ellis Patents, 1990–. Chm., Service 9, Bristol Council of Social Service, 1966–70; Treas., YMCA Metropolitan Reg., 1992–93. Vice Chm., Yorks Rural Community Council, 1985–89. Member: Ecumenical Advocacy Cttee, Ecumenical Advocacy Alliance, 2000–02; Council, Assoc. for Prevention of Torture, 2001–08. Mem., York Merchant Adventurers, 1986– (Gov., 2011–12). Chm., Yorks Churches Fair and Just Trade Proj. (formerly Yorks Churches Trade Justice Campaign), 2004–10. Trustee, Nat. Centre for Early Music, 2010–. Chm. Govs, Easingwold Sch., 2004–10. *Recreations:* family life, walking, singing, opera, croquet, churchwarden. *Address:* 27 East Mount Road, York YO24 1BD. *T:* (01904) 689742.

**NIGHTINGALE, Roger Daniel;** economist and strategist; *b* 5 June 1945; *s* of Douglas Daniel John Nightingale and Edna Kathleen Vincent; one *s* four *d. Educ:* Welwyn Garden City Grammar Sch.; Keele Univ. (BA double hons Maths and Econs); University Coll. London (MSc Stats). Economist, Hoare & Co., 1968; Datastream, 1972, Dir, 1975; Hoare Govett, 1976, Dir, 1980; Head of Economics and Strategy Dept, Smith New Court, 1988–90; founded Roger Nightingale & Associates Ltd, consultancy firm, 1990. *Publications:* articles in financial magazines and newspapers. *Recreations:* snooker, collecting dictionaries, European history. *Club:* Reform.

**NIGHTINGALE, (William) Benedict (Herbert);** theatre critic, The Times, 1990–2010; *b* 14 May 1939; *s* of late Ronald Nightingale and Hon. Evelyn Nightingale, *d* of 1st Baron Burghclere; *m* 1964, Anne Bryan Redmon; two *s* one *d. Educ:* Charterhouse Sch.; Magdalene College, Cambridge (BA Hons); Univ. of Pennsylvania. General writer and northern drama critic, The Guardian, 1963–66; Literary Editor, New Society, 1966–68; theatre critic, New Statesman, 1968–86; Sunday theatre critic, New York Times, 1983–84; Prof. of English, Theatre and Drama, Univ. of Michigan, 1986–89. Mem., Drama Panel, and New Writing Cttee, Arts Council, 1975–80. Gov., Goldsmiths' Coll., 1978–81. *Publications:* Charities, 1973; Fifty Modern British Plays, 1981; Fifth Row Center, 1985; The Future of the Theatre, 1998; What's So Flinking Bunny?, 2010; Great Moments in the Theatre, 2012; (with Martyn Palmer) Les Misérables: from stage to screen, 2013. *Address:* 40 Broomhouse Road, SW6 3QX. *Club:* Garrick.

**NIGHY, William Francis, (Bill);** actor; *b* 12 Dec. 1949; *s* of Alfred Martin Nighy and Catherine Josephine (*née* Whittaker); partner, Diana Quick; one *d. Educ:* St Francis of Assisi Primary Sch., Caterham; John Fisher Grammar Sch., Purley; Guildford Sch. of Dance and Drama. *Theatre includes:* acting debut in The Milk Train Doesn't Stop Here Anymore, Watermill Th., Newbury; Everyman Th., Liverpool, 1972–75; Landscape, Silence, Gateway Th., Chester; The Warp, ICA, 1979; Betrayal, Almeida, 1991; A Kind of Alaska, Donmar Warehouse, 1998; The Vertical Hour, NY, 2006; National Theatre: Illuminatus!, 1977; A Map of the World, 1984; Pravda, 1985; King Lear, 1986; Mean Tears, 1987; Arcadia, 1993; The Seagull, 1994; Skylight, 1997; Blue/Orange, 2000–01; *television includes:* Easter 2016, 1982; The Last Place on Earth, 1985; Antonia and Jane, The Men's Room, 1991; The Maitlands, 1993; Longitude, 2000; Auf Wiedersehen, Pet (series 3), 2002; State of Play (Best Actor award, BAFTA, 2004), The Lost Prince, The Canterbury Tales, Ready When You are Mr McGill, The Young Visiters, 2003; He Knew He Was Right, 2004; The Girl in the Café, 2005; Gideon's Daughter, 2006 (Golden Globe for Best Performance by an Actor in a Mini-Series, 2007); Page Eight, 2011; Turks & Caicos, Salting the Battlefield,

2014; Ordeal by Innocence, 2018; extensive work on BBC radio, inc. Lord of the Rings; *films include:* Fairy Tale, 1997; Still Crazy, 1998 (Peter Sellers Comedy Award, Evening Standard British Film Awards); Blow Dry, The Lawless Heart, Lucky Break, 2001; AKA, 2002; I Capture the Castle, Underworld, Love Actually, 2003 (Best Supporting Actor awards: Los Angeles Film Critics, 2003; BAFTA, and London Film Critics' Circle, 2004; Peter Sellers Comedy Award, Evening Standard British Film Awards, 2004); Shaun of the Dead, Enduring Love, 2004; The Hitchhiker's Guide to the Galaxy, The Constant Gardener, 2005; Pirates of the Caribbean: Dead Man's Chest, Stormbreaker, 2006; Notes on a Scandal, 2007; Valkyrie, The Boat that Rocked, Glorious 39, 2009; Astro Boy, Harry Potter and the Deathly Hallows, Pt 1, 2010; Chalet Girl, 2011; The Best Exotic Marigold Hotel, 2012; Jack the Giant Slayer, About Time, 2013; I, Frankenstein, Pride, 2014; The Second Best Exotic Marigold Hotel, 2015; Dad's Army, 2016; Their Finest, The Limehouse Golem, 2017; The Bookshop, 2018; Sometimes Always Never, Pokémon Detective Pikachu, 2019. *Recreations:* reading, rhythm and blues, walking the dog. *Address:* c/o Markham, Froggatt & Irwin Ltd, 4 Windmill Street, W1T 2HZ. *Club:* Garrick.

**NIKOLAJEVA, Prof. Maria,** PhD; Professor of Education, since 2008, and Director, Centre for Children's Literature, since 2010, University of Cambridge; *b* Moscow, 16 May 1952; *d* of Alexei Nikolajev and Natalia Nikolajeva (*née* Tiain); *m* 1981, Staffan Skott; two *s* one *d*. *Educ:* Moscow Linguistic Univ. (MA 1973); Stockholm Univ. (PhD 1988). Jun. Researcher, Film Research Inst., Moscow, 1974–81; Stockholm University: Post-doctoral Researcher, 1991–94; Sen. Lectr, 1994; Associate Prof., 1995–99; Prof., 1999–2008; Associate Prof., Åbo Akademi Univ., 1997– (Vis. Prof., 1998–99). Visiting Professor: Univ. of Massachusetts, Amherst, 1993; San Diego State Univ., 1999–2001; Hon. Prof., Univ. of Worcester, 2007. FEA 2013. *Publications:* Den förlorade tiden och andra fantastiska berättelser, 1985; Masjas ryska kokbok, 1986; (with Bo Dellensten) Upptäck datorn!, 1987; The Magic Code: the use of magical patterns in fantasy for children, 1988; Selma Lagerlöf ur ryskt perspektiv, 1991; (ed) Modern litteraturteori och metod i barnlitteraturforskningen, 1992; (ed) Voices from Far Away: current trends in international children's literature research, 1995; (ed) Aspects and Issues in the History of Children's Literature, 1995; (ed) Återkommande mönster i Selma Lagerlöfs författarskap, 1995; När Sverige erövrade Ryssland: en studie i kulturernas samspel, 1996; Children's Literature Comes of Age: toward a new aesthetic, 1998; Barnbokens byggklossar, 1998, 3rd edn, 2017; (with Ulla Bergstrand) Läckergommarnas kungarike, 1999; From Mythic to Linear: time in children's literature, 2000; Bilderbokens pusselbitar, 2000 (trans. Danish); (with Carole Scott) How Picturebooks Work, 2001; The Rhetoric of Character in Children's Literature, 2002; The Aesthetic Approach to Children's Literature, 2005; (ed with Sandra Beckett) Beyond Babar: the European tradition in children's literature, 2006; Power, Voice and Subjectivity in Literature for Young People, 2009; Om hur jag växte upp under diktaturen (memoir), 2010; Reading for Learning: cognitive approaches to children's literature, 2014; (ed with Clementine Beauvais) The Edinburgh Companion to Children's Literature, 2017; *fiction:* Var är solen?, 1987 (trans. Finnish, Danish, Dutch); Vem sa det först?, 1989; Nedräkningen, 1993 (trans. Danish, Lithuanian); Det finns inga kungar, 1994; contribs to essay collections; articles in academic jls incl. Children's Lit. Assoc. Qly, Children's Lit. in Educn, The Lion and the Unicorn, Canadian Children's Lit., Marvels & Tales, Papers, Style, Para★doxa, Compar(a)ison, Neohelikon. *Recreations:* travel, nature, animal and bird watching, gardening, papermaking, doll-house decoration. *Address:* University of Cambridge, Faculty of Education, 184 Hills Road, Cambridge CB2 8PQ. *T:* (01223) 767600. *E:* mn351@cam.ac.uk.

**NIKOLAYEVA-TERESHKOVA, Valentina Vladimirovna;** *see* Tereshkova.

**NIMMO, Very Rev. Dr Alexander Emsley;** Rector, St Margaret's, Aberdeen, since 1990; *b* Glasgow, 28 Feb. 1953; *s* of Alexander Emsley Nimmo and Christina Agnes Nimmo (*née* Roff). *Educ:* Univ. of Aberdeen (BD 1976; PhD 1997); Univ. of Edinburgh (MPhil 1983). FSA (Scot.) 1993. RNR. Edinburgh Theol Coll., 1976–78; ordained deacon, 1978, priest 1979; Precentor, Inverness Cathedral, 1978–81; Priest-in-Charge, 1981–83, Rector, 1984, St Peter's, Stornoway; Rector, St Michael and All Saints, Edinburgh, 1984–90; Dean of Aberdeen and Orkney, 2008–17, now Dean Emeritus. Canon, St Andrew's Cathedral, Aberdeen, 1996; Synod Clerk, 2001. Chaplain: Saughton Prison, Edinburgh, 1987–90; HM Theatre, Aberdeen, 1990–; Episcopal Vis. Chaplain, Peterhead Prison, 2004–07. Mem., 1745 Assoc. (Chm., 2011–14). Hon. Canon, Christ Church Cathedral, Hartford, Conn, 2016–19. *Publications:* (contrib.) Dictionary of Scottish Church History and Theology, 1993; (contrib.) After Columba - after Calvin, 1999; (contrib.) Sir Thomas Urquhart of Cromarty, 2011; (contrib.) Living with Jacobitism 1690–1788, 2014. *Recreations:* music, hill-walking, cooking, gardening, languages. *Address:* The Clergy House, St Margaret of Scotland, Gallowgate, Aberdeen AB25 1EA. *T:* (01224) 644969. *E:* alexander306@btinternet.com. *Club:* Aberdeenshire Theological.

**NIMMO SMITH, Rt Hon. Lord; William Austin Nimmo Smith;** PC 2005; a Senator of the College of Justice in Scotland, 1996–2009; *b* 6 Nov. 1942; *s* of late Dr Robert Hermann Nimmo Smith and Mrs Ann Nimmo Smith; *m* 1968, Jennifer Main; one *s* one *d*. *Educ:* Eton Coll. (King's Scholar, 1956); Balliol Coll., Oxford (BA Hons Lit. Hum. 1965); Edinburgh Univ. (LLB 1967). Admitted to Faculty of Advocates, 1969; Standing Junior Counsel to Dept of Employment, 1977–82; QC (Scot.) 1982; Advocate-Depute, 1983–86; Temp. Judge, Court of Session, 1995–96; Insolvency Judge, 1997–2005; Intellectual Property Judge, 1998–2005; Judge, Lands Valuation Appeal Court, 2002–09; Mem., First Div., Inner House of Court of Session, 2005–09. Chairman: Medical Appeal Tribunals, 1986–91; Vaccine Damage Tribunals, 1986–91; Mem. (part-time), Scottish Law Commn, 1988–96. Chm. Council, Cockburn Assoc. (Edinburgh Civic Trust), 1996–2001. *Recreations:* mountaineering, music. *Address:* c/o Parliament House, Parliament Square, Edinburgh EH1 1RQ.

**NISBET, Andrew;** Director, Key West Holdings Ltd, since 2014; *b* Bristol, 21 Aug. 1960; *s* of Peter and Mary Nisbet; *m* 1985, Anne Marie West; one *s* one *d*. *Educ:* King's Coll., Taunton. With Peter Nisbet & Co. Ltd, 1978–83, Nisbets plc, 1983– (Chm., 1983–). Trustee: Nisbet Trust, 2014–; Bristol Music Trust, 2014–. Mem., Soc. of Merchant Venturers, 2002–. High Sheriff, City of Bristol, 2012–13. *Address:* 22 Clifton Road, Clifton, Bristol BS8 1AQ.

**NISBET, Douglas;** *see* Nisbet, J. D.

**NISBET, Prof. Hugh Barr,** LittD; Professor of Modern Languages, University of Cambridge, 1982–2007, now Emeritus; Fellow, Sidney Sussex College, since 1982; *b* 24 Aug. 1940; *s* of Thomas Nisbet and Lucy Mary Hainsworth; *m* 1st, 1962, Monika Luise Ingeborg Uecker (marr. diss. 1981); two *s*; 2nd, 1995, Angela Maureen Parker (*née* Chapman). *Educ:* Dollar Acad.; Univ. of Edinburgh (MA, PhD 1965); Univ. of Cambridge (LittD 2009). University of Bristol: Asst Lectr in German, 1965–67; Lectr, 1967–72; Reader, 1972–73; Prof. of German Lang. and Lit., Univ. of St Andrews, 1974–81. Mem., Gen. Teaching Council for Scotland, 1978–81. President: British Soc. for Eighteenth Century Studies, 1986–88; MHRA, 2010. Governor, Dollar Acad., 1978–81. Jt Editor, Cambridge Studies in German, 1983–2008; Germanic Editor, 1973–80, Gen. Editor, 1981–84, Modern Language Rev. *Publications:* Herder and the Philosophy and History of Science, 1970; (ed with Hans Reiss) Goethe's Die Wahlverwandtschaften, 1971; Goethe and the Scientific Tradition, 1972; (ed) German Aesthetic and Literary Criticism: Winckelmann to Goethe, 1985; (ed with Claude Rawson) Cambridge History of Literary Criticism, 9 vols, 1989–2013; (ed with John Hibberd) Texte, Motive und Gestalten der Goethezeit, 1989; (ed with D. E. D. Beales) Sidney Sussex College, Cambridge: historical essays, 1996; (ed with Laurence Dickey) Hegel's Political Writings, 1999; Lessing: Eine Biographie, 2008 (Hamann-Forschungspreis, 2010; Einhard Prize for Biography, 2011), rev. and updated English edn as Gotthold Ephraim Lessing: his life, works and thought, 2013; *translations:* Kant, Political Writings, 1970, 2nd edn 1991; Hegel, Lectures on the Philosophy of World History, 1975, 2nd edn 1980; Hegel, Elements of the Philosophy of Right, 1991; Hegel, Political Writings, 1999; (and ed) Lessing, Philosophical and Theological Writings, 2005; articles and reviews on German literature and thought. *Recreations:* music, art history. *Address:* Sidney Sussex College, Cambridge CB2 3HU. *T:* (01223) 338877.

**NISBET, (James) Douglas;** Senior Partner, Glasgow, Ernst & Young, since 2002; President, Institute of Chartered Accountants of Scotland, 2009–10; *b* Glasgow, 2 June 1959; *s* of James Nisbet and Sybil Nisbet; *m* 1994, Lesley; one *s* five *d*. *Educ:* Univ. of Strathclyde (BA Accountancy and Operational Res. 1980). Chartered Accountant, 1983. Arthur Young McLelland Moores, later Ernst & Young: joined, 1980; Man. Partner, Scotland, 2002–07. Jun. Vice Pres., 2007–08, Sen. Vice Pres., 2008–09, ICAS. Mem. Council, CBI Scotland, 2003–09 and 2012–. *Recreations:* golf, football, keep fit. *Address:* Ernst & Young LLP, G1, 5 George Square, Glasgow G2 1DY. *T:* (0141) 226 9000, *Fax:* (0141) 226 9001. *E:* dnisbet@uk.ey.com.

**NISBET-SMITH, Dugal,** CBE 1996; Director, Newspaper Society, 1983–97; *b* 6 March 1935; *s* of David and Margaret Homeward Nisbet-Smith; *m* 1959, Dr Ann Patricia Taylor; one *s* two *d*. *Educ:* Southland Boys' High Sch., Invercargill, NZ. Journalist on Southland Daily News, NZ, 1952–56; Features writer and reporter, Beaverbrook Newspapers, London, 1956–60; variously Asst Editor, Gen. Manager and Man. Dir, Barbados Advocate Co., Barbados, WI, Gen. Manager, Sierra Leone Daily Mail Ltd, W Africa, Dep. Gen. Manager, Trinidad Mirror Co., 1960–66; Sen. Industrial Relations Manager, Mirror Gp Newspapers, London, 1966–68; Develt Manager, 1969–71, Production Dir, 1971–73, Man. Dir, 1974–78, Scottish Daily Record and Sunday Mail Ltd, Glasgow; joined Bd, Mirror Gp Newspapers, 1976; Dir/General Manager, 1978–80, Man. Dir, 1980–81, Times Newspapers Ltd; Publishing Advr to HH the Aga Khan, Aiglemont, France, 1981–83. *Recreations:* travel, sculpture, painting. *Address:* 2 Middleton Place, Langham Street, W1W 7TA. *T:* (020) 7636 6403.

**NISH, David Thomas;** Chief Executive, Standard Life plc, 2010–15; *b* Barrhead, 5 May 1960; *s* of Thomas Nish and Jean C. M. Nish (*née* Scott); *m* 1983, Caroline Smith; one *s* one *d*. *Educ:* Univ. of Glasgow (BAcc); ICAS. Joined Price Waterhouse, 1981, Partner, 1993–97; Scottish Power plc: Dep. Finance Dir, 1997–99; Finance Dir, 1999–2005; Exec. Dir, Infrastructure Div., 2005; Finance Dir, Standard Life plc, 2006–09. Non-executive Director: Green Investment Bank plc, 2012–16; London Stock Exchange Gp plc, 2015–18; Vodafone Gp plc, 2016–; HSBC, 2016–; Zurich Insce Gp, 2016–19. Dep. Chm., ABI, 2012–15. *Recreations:* travel, cycling, ski-ing, trekking, watching Rugby.

**NISSAN, Gwyneth;** *see* Williams, Gwyneth.

**NISSEN, Alexander David;** QC 2006; a Recorder, since 2007; a Deputy High Court Judge, since 2013; *b* 30 Aug. 1963; *s* of Charles Nissen and Jillian Nissen (*née* Moss); *m* 1995, Sally Daniel. *Educ:* Mill Hill Sch.; Manchester Univ. (LLB Hons 1984). Called to the Bar, Middle Temple, 1985, Bencher, 2019; in practice as barrister, specialising in construction and engrg law and related professional negligence disputes, 1989–. FCIArb 2000; Chartered Arbitrator, 2003. *Publications:* (contrib.) Keating on Building Contracts, later Keating on Construction Contracts, 5th edn 1991 to 10th edn 2016; contrib. articles in Construction Jl. *Recreations:* theatre, escaping exercise, Coronation Street, dreaming about good food. *Address:* Keating Chambers, 15 Essex Street, WC2R 3AA. *T:* (020) 7544 2600, *Fax:* (020) 7544 2700. *E:* anissen@keatingchambers.com.

**NISSEN, David Edgar Joseph,** CB 1999; Solicitor and Director General Legal Services, Department of Trade and Industry, 1997–2002; *b* 27 Nov. 1942; *s* of Tunnock Edgar Nissen and Elsie Nissen (*née* Thorne); *m* 1969, Pauline Jennifer (*née* Meaden); two *d*. *Educ:* King's School, Chester; University College London (LLB). Solicitor, admitted 1969. Asst Solicitor, W Midlands Gas Board, 1969–70; Prosecuting Solicitor, Sussex Police Authority, 1970–73; HM Customs and Excise, 1973–90: Asst Solicitor, 1983–87; Principal Asst Solicitor, 1987–90; Legal Advr to Dept of Energy (Principal Asst Treasury Solicitor), 1990–92; Solicitor to HM Customs and Excise, 1992–95; Legal Advr to Home Office, 1995–97. *Recreations:* photography, music, gardening.

**NISSEN, George Maitland,** CBE 1987; Chairman, Chiswick House Friends, 2001–17; *b* 29 March 1930; *s* of Col Peter Norman Nissen, DSO, and Lauretta Maitland; *m* 1956, Jane Edmunds, *d* of late S. Curtis Bird, New York; two *s* two *d*. *Educ:* Eton; Trinity Coll., Cambridge (MA). National Service, KRRC, 1949–50, 2/Lieut. Sen. Partner, Pember & Boyle, Stockbrokers, 1982–86; Chairman: Foreign & Colonial Emerging Markets Trust (formerly CDFC Trust) plc, 1987–99; Liberty Syndicate Management Ltd, 1997–2002; Director: Morgan Grenfell Gp, 1984–87 (Advr, 1987–92); Festiniog Rlwy, 1993–2003; Ffestiniog Travel (formerly Festiniog Rlwy Hldgs), 1993–. Mem., Stock Exchange, 1956–92 (Dep. Chm., 1978–81; Mem. Council, 1973–91); Chairman: Gilt-Edged Market Makers Assoc., 1986–92; IMRO, 1989–92; Dir, The Securities Assoc., 1986–89; Mem., Inflation Accounting Steering Gp, 1976–80. Non-exec. Dir, Ealing, Hammersmith and Hounslow HA, 1993–96. Mem. Council, GDST (formerly GPDST), 1993–2008. Gov., Godolphin and Latymer School, Hammersmith, 1987–97; Trustee, Lucy Cavendish Coll., Cambridge, 1994–97; Pres., Reed's Sch., Cobham, 1995–. Chm. of Holding Trustees, CPRW, 1991–; Trustee, Chiswick House and Gardens Trust, 2005–. Chm., Book Guild, 1993–2010. Hon. FRAM 1994. *Recreations:* railways, music. *Address:* Swan House, Chiswick Mall, W4 2PS. *T:* (020) 8995 8306. *E:* g.nissen@talk21.com.

**NITTVE, (Arvid) Lars (Olov);** museum adviser, since 2016; Executive Director, M+, Hong Kong, 2011–16; *b* 17 Sept. 1953; *s* of Bengt and Ulla Nittve; *m* 1st, 1988, Anna Olsson (marr. diss. 1999); one *s*; 2nd, 2005, Shideh Shaygan. *Educ:* Stockholm Univ. (MA 1978). Res. Asst and Lectr, Dept of Art History, Stockholm Univ., 1978–85; Art Critic, Svenska Dagbladet, Stockholm, 1979–85; Sen. Curator, Moderna Museet, Stockholm, 1986–90; Director: Rooseum-Center for Contemporary Art, Malmö, 1990–95; Louisiana Mus. of Modern Art, Humlebæk, Denmark, 1995–98; Tate Gall. of Modern Art, subseq. Tate Modern, 1998–2001; Dir, Moderna Museet, Stockholm, 2001–10. Prof., Umea Univ., Sweden, 2010. Hon. Dr Umea, 2009. *Publications* include: Svenska Valaffischer, 1979; Ola Billgren, 1985; Jan Håfström: grammaticus, 1990; Ulrik Samuelson: exit, 1987; Landskapet i nytt ljus, 1987; The Sublime - Walter De Maria, 1992; Truls Melin, 1992; Rolf Hanson, 1995; Sunshine & Noir: art in LA 1960–1996, 1997; Fashination, 2004. *Address:* Nittve Information Ltd, Byvägen 32, 83795 Undersåker, Sweden.

**NIVEN, Alastair Neil Robertson**, LVO 2012; OBE 2001; PhD; Associate Director, Iraq Britain Business Council, 2013–17; *b* 25 Feb. 1944; *s* of late Harold Robertson Niven and Elizabeth Isobel Robertson Niven (*née* Mair); *m* 1970, Helen Margaret Trow; one *s* one *d*. *Educ*: Dulwich Coll.; Gonville and Caius Coll., Cambridge (MA); Univ. of Ghana (Commonwealth Schol.; MA); Univ. of Leeds (PhD). Lecturer in English: Univ. of Ghana, 1968–69; Univ. of Leeds, 1969–70; Lectr in English Studies, Univ. of Stirling, 1970–78; Dir Gen., Africa Centre, London, 1978–84; Chapman Fellow 1984–85, Hon. Fellow 1985, Inst. of Commonwealth Studies; Special Asst to Sec. Gen., ACU, 1985–87; Lit. Dir, Arts Council of GB, then of England, 1987–97; Dir of Literature, British Council, 1997–2001; Principal, King George VI and Queen Elizabeth Foundn of St Catharine's, Cumberland Lodge, 2001–13. Visiting Professor: Univ. of Aarhus, 1975–76; Sheffield Hallam Univ., 1998–2002; Vis. Fellow, Aust. Studies Centre, Univ. of London, 1985; Hon. Lectr, SOAS, 1979–85; Hon. Fellow: Univ. of Warwick, 1988; Harris Manchester Coll., Oxford, 2012–. Editor, Jl of Commonwealth Literature, 1979–92. Chairman: Public Schools Debating Assoc. of Eng. and Wales, 1961–62; Literature Panel, GLAA, 1981–84; Welfare Policy Cttee, 1983–87, Exec. Cttee, 1987–92, UK Council for Overseas Student Affairs; Southern Africa Book Develt Educn Trust, 1997–2003; Soc. of Bookmen, 2003–04; Bd, Border Crossings, 2013–; Commonwealth Scholarship and Fellowship Plan Support Gp, 2013–; Sec. and Treas., Assoc. for Commonwealth Lit. and Lang. Studies, 1986–89; Member: Public Affairs Cttee, Royal Commonwealth Soc., 1979–99; Laurence Olivier Awards Theatre Panel, 1989–91; British Library Adv. Cttee for the Centre for the Book, 1990–97; Home Office Standing Cttee on Arts in Prisons, 1995–97. Trustee: Millennium Liby Trust, 1998–2008; Council for Educn in the Commonwealth, 2013–. President: Windsor WEA, 2003–13; English PEN, 2003–07. Judge: Booker Prize, 1994, Man Booker Prize, 2014; Forward Poetry Prizes, 1996; David Cohen British Literature Prize, 2000 (deviser of Prize, 1992); The Independent Foreign Fiction Prize, 2001; DSC Prize for South Asian Literature, 2012 (Mem., Mgt Cttee, 2012–14); Chairman of Judges: Eurasia Reg., 1994, 1995, Adv. Cttee, 1996–2006, Commonwealth Writers' Prize; Stakis Prize for Scottish Writer of Year, 1998; ESU Marsh Prize for Biography, 1999–2011; Saif Ghobash Banipal Prize for Arabic Literary Translation, 2017; Mem. Council, Caine Prize for African Writing, 2000– (Chm., 2019–). Chm. of Govs, Royal Sch., Windsor, 2004–08. Mem. Editorial Bd, Annual Register, 1988– (Chm., 2013–). *Publications*: The Commonwealth Writer Overseas (ed), 1976; D. H. Lawrence: the novels, 1978; The Yoke of Pity: the fiction of Mulk Raj Anand, 1978; D. H. Lawrence: the writer and his work, 1980; (with Sir Hugh W. Springer) The Commonwealth of Universities, 1987; (ed) Under Another Sky: the Commonwealth Poetry Prize anthology, 1987; (ed jtly) Enigmas and Arrivals: an anthology of Commonwealth writing, 1997; articles in Afr. Affairs, Ariel, Brit. Book News, Jl of Commonwealth Lit., Jl of Indian Writing in English, Jl of RSA, Lit. Half-Yearly, Poetry Review, TES, THES, World Lit. Written in English, etc; study guides on Elechi Amadi, Wm Golding, R. K. Narayan, Raja Rao. *Recreations*: theatre, travel, lists. *Address*: 51 Hanover Gardens, SE11 5TN. *Club*: Athenæum.

See also C. H. R. Niven.

**NIVEN, Dr Colin Harold Robertson**, OBE 2007; Founding Principal: Sherborne Qatar, 2009; St George's British Connection School, Tbilisi, Georgia, 2012–13; Master of Schools (Shanghai, Beijing, Suzhou), for Dulwich College International, China, 2003–06; *b* 29 Sept. 1941; *s* of late Harold Robertson Niven and Elizabeth Isobel Robertson Niven (*née* Mair). *Educ*: Dulwich Coll. (Capt. of School); Gonville and Caius Coll., Cambridge (MA); Brasenose Coll., Oxford (DipEd); Nancy Univ. (LèsL); Lille Univ. (Dr de l'Univ.). Lycée Mixte, Châlons-sur-Marne, 1963–64; Samuel Pepys Comprehensive Sch., 1964; Sedbergh Sch., 1964; Fettes Coll., 1965–73 (Housemaster, 1971–73); Head of Mod. Langs, Sherborne Sch., 1973–83; Principal: Island Sch., Hong Kong, 1983–87; St George's English Sch., Rome, 1988–91; Vis. Fellow, Westminster Coll., Oxford, 1991; Dir of Internat. Liaison, Sherborne Internat. Study Centre, 1992; Headmaster, Alleyn's Sch., Dulwich, 1992–2002; Master, Dulwich Coll. Internat. Sch., Shanghai, 2003–05. Hon. Res. Fellow, Exeter Univ., 1981–83. Dir, West Heath Ltd, 2003–. Chm., European Div., 1990–91, Chm., London Div., 1998, HMC. Sen. Consultant, CfA (Charity Fundraising Appts), 2002–06. Pres., Marlowe Soc., 1996–2003; Chm., Friends of E. H. Shepard, 2002–08. Trustee, Dulwich Picture Gall., 1996–99. Vice-Pres., Rugby Fives Assoc., 2001–. Judge: Marsh Biography Awards, 2000–11, Children's Lit. in Translation Awards, 2008–; Duke of Edinburgh's Eng. Lang. Book Prize, 2004–13. Governor: Portsmouth GS, 1999–2003; Sherborne Sch. Internat. Coll., 2001–; Blackheath Nursery and Prep. Sch., 2006–; St Lawrence Coll., Ramsgate, 2008–13 (Vice-Pres., 2013–18); ESU, 2011–; Chm. of Govs, Gavà Sch., Barcelona, 2015; Trustee, Campion Sch., Athens, 2002–12; Member: Council, King's Coll., Madrid, 1999–2004 and 2006–17; Educn Cttee, 1999–2009, Cttee, London Branch, 2006–, ESU; Council, British Sch. of Latvia, 2017–. Patron, Ind. Schs MLA, 1998–2008. President: Edward Alleyn Club, 2005–06 (Vice-Pres., 2003); Dulwich Soc., 2011–; Alleyn Club, 2013–14 (Vice Pres., 2012–13). FRSA. Freeman, City of London, 1999. CCF Medal 1983. Officier, Ordre des Palmes Académiques (France), 2002. *Publications*: Voltaire's Candide, 1978; Thomas Mann's Tonio Kröger, 1980; Vailland's Un jeune homme seul (critical edn), 1983; Island School: the first twenty years, 1987. *Recreations*: theatre, sport, foreign travel, cats, opera (Mem. choir, Dorset Opera, 1978–91). *Address*: 9 Oakfield Gardens, Dulwich Wood Avenue, SE19 1HF. *T*: (020) 8670 6957. *E*: niven.dulwich@yahoo.com. *Clubs*: Athenæum, Royal Over-Seas League, English-Speaking Union.

See also A. N. R. Niven.

**NIVISON**, family name of **Baron Glendyne**.

**NIXON, Dr Anthony;** motivational public speaker, since 1982; Business, Management and Marketing Consultant, A. & M. Nixon Enterprises, 1992–2018; *s* of late David and Mariam Nixon; *m* 1975, Marion Audrey Farr (*d* 2012); one *s* four *d*. *Educ*: Univ. of Peshawar (BA 1955); Univ. of Karachi (DipM 1959; MA Econ. 1960); Massachusetts Inst. of Technol. (Postgrad. Business and Mgt 1960); UCW, Aberystwyth (MSc Pol Econ. 1986); Leeds Poly. (Dip. Liby and Inf. Sci., 1966); Salford Univ.; Manchester Univ.; DipEd ACP 1958; Concordia Coll. and Univ., Delaware (PhD 2013); Concordia Univ. (PhD Mental Health and Alzheimer's Disease 2017). Chartered Librarian 1970. Local Govt Officer, Lancs CC, 1968–71; Chief College Librarian and Lectr, Burnley Coll. of Further and Higher Educn, 1972–93 (Mem., Acad. Bd and Bd Cttees); Chairman and Managing Director: A. & M. Nixon Enterprises Ltd, 1990–91; Costcutter Nixon Supermkt, 1993–96. Columnist, New Life (London weekly mag.), 1987–88. Probation Officer Volunteer and Exec. Cttee Mem., Rossendale Probation and Aftercare Service, 1975–81; Chairman: NHS Exec. Complaints Procedure, NW Reg., DoH, 1999–2003; Complaints Procedure, Cumbria and Lancs NHS Strategic HA, 2003; East Lancashire Hospitals NHS Trust: Mem., Patient and Public Involvement Forum, 2005–07; Mem., Develt Cttee for Rossendale, 2006–; Gov., 2009–; Gov. to Council of Govs, 2011; Patient-led Inspections, 2013–; Gov., Blackpool Teaching Hosps NHS Foundn Trust, 2014–17; Gov., Manchester Univ. NHS Foundn Trust, 2017–18. Lancashire Probation Board: Mem., 2001–07; Chairman: Audit and Assessment Cttee, 2002–04 (Mem., 2001–02); Complaints Appeal Panel, 2002–; Member: Performance Cttee, 2003–04; Information Security Gp, 2003–05; Risk Mgt Cttee, 2003–. Lay Assessor, Lancs Reg., Nat. Care Standards Commn (formerly Inspection Unit, Social Services, Lancs CC), 2000–06; Member: Local Involvement Network (LINKS), NHS Health & Social Care, Lancs CC, 2007–; Regl Adv. Cttee on Clinical Excellence Awards to Consultants, NHS Adv. Cttee on Clinical Excellence Awards, DoH, 2008–17. Mem., Community Relns Council, 1980–92, Chm., Employment Panel, 1987–88, Hyndburn and Rossendale. Rossendale Borough Council: Ind. Mem., Ethics Cttee, 2004–; Standards Cttee, 2006–10; Mem., Rossendale Strategic Partnership Cttee, 2004–06. Dir, Exec. Trustee and Sec., Bd of Dirs, BHAF Ltd, Manchester, 1998–2001 (Chm., Finance Cttee); non-exec. Dir and Trustee, Burnley, Pendle and Rossendale Crossroads Ltd, 2005–06. Mem., Lancs Healthwatch, 2012–15. Cttee Mem., Rossendale Dist, CPRE, 2005–. Business Advr and Mentor, Prince's Business Trust, 1999–. Chm., E Lancs Reg., CS Fellowship, 2002–. Mem. Ct, Univ. of Manchester, 2002–04. Gov., Lancashire County Sch., Rossendale, 1980–93, 2004–. Mem., Univ. of Third Age, Padiham. Travelled extensively in Russian Fedn and Republics of Latvia, Estonia and Lithuania and met prominent govt and religious leaders, industrialists, trade union officials, etc in order to promote goodwill between Britain and former Soviet Union, 1987; organised exchange visits between British and Soviet families for first time during Soviet rule, 1987–91. Consultant: Collective Farm, Piraviena, Rumsiskes, Lithuania, 1988–90; Pedagogical Univ., Vilnius, Lithuania, 1997. Has given talks on local radio in Lancs and on various Russian, Lithuanian, Estonian and Latvian radio and TV stations. Gold Medal, Public Speaking and Presentational Skills, LAMDA, 1969. *Publications*: South Asia: detente and co-operation or confrontation?, 1982; (contrib.) Day of Peace 1917–87, 1987; Meeting People through Russia to the Baltics, 1990; No Life Without You, 2016; contrib. articles to Sunday Times, New Scientist, Educa, Satellite Technol. and British and foreign jls. *Recreations*: discussing politics and philosophising on national and international economic and social issues; travelling, reading, country walks, picnics, futurologist, creative writing, cooking, swimming, gym, gardening. *Address*: Rose Bungalow, 7 Flax Close, Helmshore, Rossendale, Lancs BB4 4JL. *E*: anthonynixon96@yahoo.co.uk. *Club*: Inter-Varsity (Manchester).

**NIXON, David A.,** OBE 2010; Artistic Director, Northern Ballet, since 2001; *b* Windsor, Ont; *s* of David Nixon and Alice Nixon (*née* Charvel); *m* 1985, Yoko Ichino. *Educ*: National Ballet Sch. of Canada. Principal Dancer: Deutsche Oper Berlin, 1985–90; Nat. Ballet of Canada, 1989–91; Ballet Master, Deutsche Oper Berlin, 1994–95; Dir, BalletMet, Columbus, Ohio, 1994–2001. Guest artist: Birmingham Royal Ballet; Bayerisches Staatsoper, Munich; Hamburg Ballet; Royal Winnipeg; Japan Fest. Best Male Performance, 1987; Dir of Year, Dance Europe mag., 2003, 2006.

**NIXON, Prof. John Forster**, FRS 1994; Research Professor of Chemistry, 2003–11, now Emeritus, University of Sussex (Professor of Chemistry, 1986–2003); *b* 27 Jan. 1937; *s* of late Supt Edward Forster Nixon, MBE and Mary Nixon (*née* Lytton); *m* 1960, Dorothy Joan (Kim) Smith; one *s* one *d*. *Educ*: Univ. of Manchester (BSc 1st Cl. Hons Chem. 1957, MSc 1958; PhD 1960; DSc 1973). Research Associate in Chem., Univ. of Southern Calif., LA, 1960–62; ICI Fellow, Inorganic Chem. Dept, Univ. of Cambridge, 1962–64; Lectr in Inorganic Chem., Univ. of St Andrews, 1964–66; University of Sussex: Lectr in Chem., 1966–76; Reader, 1976–86; Subject Chm. in Chem., 1981–84; Dean, Sch. of Chem. and Molecular Scis, 1989–92. Vis. Associate Prof. in Chem., Univ. of Victoria, BC, Canada, 1970–71; Visiting Professor: Simon Fraser Univ., BC, 1976; IIT, Bangalore, 2005; IISER, Trivandrum, 2010; Vis. Fellow, ANU, 2004. Mem., Editl Bd, Phosphorus, Sulfur and Silicon, 1989–2006. Mem. Bd of Dirs, Internat. Council for Main Gp Chem., 2000–06. Member: Internat. Cttee on Phosphorus Chem., 1983, 2000–; IUPAC Commn on Inorganic Nomenclature, 1985–87; Inorganic Chem. Panel, SERC Cttee, 1986–89; EPSRC Cttee, 1997–98. Royal Soc. Leverhulme Trust Sen. Res. Fellow, 1993. Mem. Council, Dalton Div., RSC, 1994–99. Corday-Morgan Medal and Prize, Chem. Soc., 1973; Main Gp Element Medal, 1985, Tilden Lectr and Medal, 1992, Ludwig Mond Lectr and Medal, 2003, RSC; Geza Zemplen Medal, Budapest Technical Inst., 2003; Alexander von Humboldt Prize, 2004; Alexander von Humboldt Res. Award, 2009. FRSA 1992. *Publications*: (jtly) Phosphorus: the carbon copy, 1998; approx. 400 papers in various learned jls. *Recreations*: walking, watching cricket, theatre. *Address*: Department of Chemistry and Biochemistry, School of Life Sciences, University of Sussex, Brighton, Sussex BN1 9RQ. *T*: (01273) 678536.

**NIXON, Prof. Patrick**, PhD; FBCS; Vice-Chancellor, University of Ulster, since 2015; *b* Liverpool, 9 Sept. 1967; *s* of late Alan Nixon and of Margaret Nixon (*née* Mulligan); two *s* one *d*; *m* 2015, Vanessa Gstrein; one step *s* one step *d*. *Educ*: Univ. of Liverpool (BSc Hons Computer Sci. 1990); Univ. of Sheffield (PhD Computer Engrg 1994); Trinity Coll. Dublin (MA *jure officii* 1999). Community worker, Congregation of Christian Brothers, Liverpool, 1986–87; Lectr, TCD, 1994–2000; Prof. of Computer Sci., Univ. of Strathclyde, 2000–05; University College Dublin: Sci. Foundn Ireland Prof. in Distributed Systems, 2005–10; Acad. Dir, INTEL's Ind. Living and Digital Health Centre, 2005–10; Vice Principal (Res.), Faculty of Engrg, Maths and Physical Scis, 2005–10; Dep. Vice-Chancellor (Res.), Univ. of Tasmania, 2010–15. FBCS 2017; FRSA 2017. *Publications*: edited jointly: Directions in Software Engineering for Parallel Systems, 1995; Transputer Applications and Systems, vol. 1, 1995; Managing Interactions in Smart Environments, 2000; Software Engineering for Parallel and Distributed Systems, 2000; Trust Management, Volume 2692 of Lecture Notes in Computer Science, 2003; Middleware for Pervasive and Ad-hoc Computing, 2004; Pervasive Computing, Volume 3968 of Lecture Notes in Computer Science, 2006; Proceedings of 11th International Conference on Ubiquitous Computing, 2010; (ed) Transputer and Occam Developments, 1995; contribs to jls and conferences. *Address*: University of Ulster, Cromore Road, Coleraine, Co. Londonderry BT52 1SA. *T*: (028) 7012 4329. *E*: vice-chancellor@ulster.ac.uk, paddy.nixon@ulster.ac.uk. *Clubs*: Ulster Reform (Belfast); Tasmanian (Hobart).

**NIXON, Patrick Michael**, CMG 1989; OBE 1984; HM Diplomatic Service, retired; Regional Coordinator for Coalition Provisional Authority, Southern Iraq, 2004; *b* 1 Aug. 1944; *s* of late John Moylett Gerard Nixon and Hilary Mary (*née* Paterson); *m* 1968, Elizabeth Rose Carlton; four *s*. *Educ*: Downside; Magdalene Coll., Cambridge. Joined HM Diplomatic Service, 1965; MECAS, Lebanon, 1966; Cairo, 1968; Lima, 1970; FCO, 1973; Tripoli, Libya, 1977; British Inf. Services, New York, 1980; Asst, later Hd, Near East and N Africa Dept, FCO, 1983; Ambassador and Consul-Gen. at Doha, Qatar, 1987–90; Counsellor, FCO, 1990–93; High Comr to Zambia, 1994–97; Dir, FCO, 1997–98; Ambassador to UAE, 1998–2003. Governor: All Hallows Sch., Cranmore Hall, 2003–12 (Chm., 2005–12); Downside, 2005–12. *Address*: The Old Vicarage, Church Street, Maiden Bradley, Warminster, Wilts BA12 7HN. *E*: patricknixon82@gmail.com.

**NIXON, Rev. Rosemary Ann;** Vicar of Cleadon, 1999–2007; Pastor to the Community of Durham Cathedral, since 2011; *b* 25 May 1945; *d* of Edwin Nixon and Dorothy Hall. *Educ*: Bishop Grosseteste Coll. of Educn (CertEd); Trinity Coll., Bristol (DipTh (London); BD Hons (London)); Durham Univ. (MA); Edinburgh Univ. (MTh). School teacher, Denton, Manchester, 1966–69; Parish Worker, St Luke's, West Hampstead, 1973–75; Tutor, St John's Coll., Durham and Dir of St John's Coll. Extension Prog., 1975–89; ordained deacon, 1987, priest, 1994; Team Vicar and Dir of the Urban Studies Unit, Parish of Gateshead, 1990–92; Staff Mem., Edinburgh Theol Coll., 1992–95; Principal, Theol Inst., Scottish Episcopal Church, 1995–99. Hon. Canon, St Mary's Cathedral, Edinburgh, and Pantonian Prof. of Theol., Edinburgh, 1996–99; Hon. Minor Canon Emeritus,

Durham Cathedral, 2015. Mem., SOTS, 1981–. *Publications:* Who's the Greatest?: Sunday schools today, 1984; Jonah: working with the word, 1986; The Message of Jonah, 2003; articles in theol dictionaries and periodicals. *Recreations:* music, hill walking, photography, friends, art. *Address:* Charisholme, 6 Wearside Drive, Durham DH1 1LE. *T:* (0191) 384 6558.

NIXON, Sir Simon (Michael Christopher), 5th Bt *cr* 1906; *b* 20 June 1954; *s* of Major Cecil Dominic Henry Joseph Nixon, MC (*d* 1994), and of Brenda Nixon (*née* Lewis); *S* uncle, 1997; *m* 2002, Pauline Julia Jones. *Heir: b* Michael David Hugh Nixon, *b* 19 May 1957.

NIZAMI, Farhan Ahmad, CBE 2007; DPhil; Founder Director, Oxford Centre for Islamic Studies (formerly Islamic Trust), since 1985; Prince of Wales Fellow, Magdalen College, Oxford, since 1997; *b* 25 Dec. 1956; *s* of late Prof. Khaliq Nizami and Razia Nizami; *m* 1983, Farah Deba Ahmad; one *s* one *d*. *Educ:* Aligarh Muslim Univ., India (BA Hons History, 1st cl., 1977; Univ. Medal, 1977; Begam Khursheed Nurul Hasan Gold Medal, 1977; Nat. Schol., 1977–79; MA, 1st cl., 1979; Univ. Medal, 1979); Wadham Coll., Oxford (Oxford Overseas Schol.; Frere Exhibnr; DPhil 1983). Rothman's Fellow in Muslim Hist., 1983–85, Fellow, 1985–97, Emeritus Fellow, 1997, St Cross Coll., Oxford. Secretary: Bd of Trustees, Oxford Centre for Islamic Studies (formerly Islamic Trust), 1985–; Bd of Dirs, Oxford Trust for Islamic Studies, 1998–2013; Dir, Oxford Inspires, 2002–03; Chm., Oxford Endeavours Ltd, 2003–. Scholar Consultant to Christian-Muslim Forum, 2005–09. Member: Council, Al-Falah Prog., Univ. of Calif, Berkeley, 1997–2004; Adv. Council, Wilton Park, 2000–04 (Chm., 2004–09); Court, Oxford Brookes Univ., 2000–09; Adv. Bd, Dialogues Project, New School Univ., NY, 2003–15; Internat. Adv. Panel, Universiti Teknologi, Malaysia, 2013–; Internat. Adv. Bd, Universiti Tun Abdul Razak, 2013–18; Internat. Adv. Bd, Doha Center for Interfaith Dialogue, 2014–. Member: Archbp of Canterbury's Ref. Gp for Christian-Muslim Relations, 2001–04; Academic Consultative Cttee, Cumberland Lodge, 2003–12; Steering Cttee C-100, World Econ. Forum, Davos, 2003–07; Internat. Adv. Panel, World Islamic Econ. Forum (formerly Business Forum, Organisation of the Islamic Conf.), Malaysia, 2004–08; Internat. Jury, Sharjah Prize for Arab Culture, UNESCO, 2012–17; Adv. Council, UN Alliance of Civilizations, 2015–. Hon. Vice Pres., Christian Muslim Forum, 2012–. Gov., Magdalen Coll. Sch., Oxford, 2005–10. Patron, Oxford Amnesty Lectures, 2003–. Founder Editor, Jl of Islamic Studies, 1990–; Series Editor, Makers of Islamic Civilization, 2004–. Class IV, Order of Crown (Brunei), 1992. *Recreations:* reading, cricket. *Address:* Oxford Centre for Islamic Studies, Marston Road, Oxford OX3 0EE. *T:* (01865) 278731.

NOAKES, Baroness *cr* 2000 (Life Peer), of Goudhurst in the co. of Kent; Sheila Valerie Noakes, DBE 1996; company director; *d* of Albert Frederick Masters and Iris Sheila Masters (*née* Ratcliffe); *m* 1985, Colin Barry Noakes. *Educ:* Eltham Hill Grammar Sch.; Univ. of Bristol (LLB). FCA. Joined Peat Marwick Mitchell & Co., 1970; seconded to HM Treasury, 1979–81; seconded to Dept of Health as Dir of Finance, NHS Management Exec., 1988–91; Partner, Peat Marwick Mitchell & Co., subseq. KPMG Peat Marwick, then KPMG, 1983–2000; a Dir, Bank of England, 1994–2001 (Chm., Cttee of non-exec. Dirs, 1998–2001). Opposition spokesman, H of L, on work and pensions, 2001–10, on health, 2001–03, on HM Treasury, 2003–10. Non-executive Director: Hanson plc, 2001–07; Carpetright plc, 2001–14 (Dep. Chm., 2012–14); SThree (formerly Solutions in Staffing and Software) plc, 2001–07; John Laing plc, 2002–04; ICI plc, 2004–08; Severn Trent plc, 2008–14; Royal Bank of Scotland Gp plc, 2011–. Comr, Public Works Loan Bd, 1995–2001; Dep. Chm., Ofcom, 2014–18. Member: Council, ICAEW, 1987–2002 (Pres., 1999–2000); Inland Revenue Management Bd, 1992–99; NHS Policy Bd, 1992–95; Chancellor of Exchequer's Private Panel, 1993–97; Bd of Governors, Inst. of Mgt, 1997–2002; Public Services Productivity Panel, 1998–2000; Adv. Council, Inst. of Business Ethics, 1998–2003. Trustee, Thomson Reuters (formerly Reuters) Founders Share Co., 1998–2013. Mem. Bd, ENO, 2000–08. Governor: London Business Sch., 1998–2001; Eastbourne Coll., 2000–04; Marlborough Coll., 2000–02. Hon. DBA London Guildhall, 1999; Hon. LLD Bristol, 2000; Hon. DSc Buckingham, 2001. *Recreations:* ski-ing, horse racing, opera, early classical music. *Address:* House of Lords, SW1A 0PW. *T:* (020) 7219 5230. *Club:* Farmers.

NOAKES, John Edward, OBE 1993; FRCGP; Partner, group medical practice in Harrow, 1961–99; *b* 27 April 1935; *s* of Edward and Mary Noakes; *m* 1960, Margaret Ann Jenner; two *s* one *d*. *Educ:* Wanstead County High Sch.; Charing Cross Hospital Medical Sch. (MB BS); DObstRCOG. Trainer, Gen. Practice Vocational Trng Scheme, Northwick Park Hosp., 1974–82. Member: Brent Harrow Local Med. Cttee, 1972–97; Harrow HA, 1982–90; CMO's Wkg Gp on Health of Nation, 1990–98; Chm., Brent Harrow Med. Audit Adv. Gp, 1992–95. Non-exec. Director: HEA, 1995–2000; HDA, 2000–03. Mem. Council, RCGP, 1989–94 (Vice-Chm., 1990–92; Chairman: NW London Faculty, 1989–91; Maternity Care Task Gp, 1994). *Recreations:* music (mainly opera), horticulture (Alpine plants), exploring Britain's canal system in own Narrow Boat. *Address:* Old Church Cottage, Chapel Lane, Long Marston, Herts HP23 4QT.

NOBAY, Prof. (Avelino) Robert, PhD; Senior Research Associate, Financial Markets Group, London School of Economics and Political Science, 1996–2014; Brunner Professor of Economic Science, University of Liverpool, 1980–96; *b* 11 July 1942; *s* of Theodore Anastasio Nobay and Anna Gracia D'Silva; *m* 1st, 1965; two *s*; 2nd, 1987, Carole Ann McPhee. *Educ:* Univ. of Leicester (BA); Univ. of Chicago; PhD Southampton. Jun. Economist, Electricity Council, London, 1964–66; Res. Officer, NIESR, 1966–70; Sen. Lectr, Univ. of Southampton, 1970–80. Vis. Associate Prof., Univ. of Chicago, 1977–79; Adjunct Prof., Centre for Internat. Econ. Studies, Univ. of Adelaide, 2001–03. *Publications:* (with H. G. Johnson) The Current Inflation; (with H. G. Johnson) Issues in Monetary Economics. *Recreations:* sailing, golf, music.

NOBES, (Charles) Patrick; retired Headmaster and teacher of English; *b* 17 March 1933; *oc* of Alderman Alfred Robert Nobes, OBE, JP, and Marguerite Violet Vivian (*née* Fathers), Gosport, Hants; *m* 1958, Patricia Jean (*née* Brand) (marr. diss. 2004); three *s*. *Educ:* Price's Sch., Fareham, Hants; University Coll., Oxford. MA. With The Times, reporting and editorial, 1956–57; Head of English Dept, King Edward VI Grammar Sch., Bury St Edmunds, 1959–64; Head of English and General Studies and Sixth Form Master, Ashlyns Comprehensive Sch., Berkhamsted, 1964–69; Headmaster: The Ward Freman Sch., Buntingford, Herts, 1969–74; Bedales Sch., 1974–81; Weymouth Grammar Sch., 1981–85, later The Budmouth Sch., 1985–86; St Francis' Coll., Letchworth, 1986–87. Chairman: HMC Co-ed Schs Gp, 1976–80; Soc. of Headmasters of Independent Schs, 1978–80; Mem., SHA Council, 1985–86. Pres., Soc. of Old Priceans, 1999–. General Editor and adapter, Bulls-Eye Books (series for adults and young adults with reading difficulties), 1972–. Churchwarden, Yare Valley Churches, 2018–. *Publications:* Eighteen to Eighty (poems), 2012. *Recreations:* writing, cricket and hockey, King Arthur, Hampshire, music, First World War, Salisbury Cathedral.

NOBLE, Adam; *see* Noble, R. A.

NOBLE, Adrian Keith; freelance director; Artistic Director, Royal Shakespeare Company, 1991–2003; *b* 19 July 1950; *s* of late William John Noble and Violet Ena (*née* Wells); *m* 1991, Joanne Elizabeth Pearce; one *s* one *d*. *Educ:* Chichester High Sch. for Boys; Bristol Univ. (BA); Drama Centre, London. Associate Dir, Bristol Old Vic, 1976–79; Resident Dir, RSC, 1980–82; Guest Dir, Royal Exchange Theatre, Manchester, 1980–81; Associate Dir, RSC, 1982–90. Artistic Dir, Shakespeare Festival, San Diego, 2010–13; Mellon Vis. Artist and Thinker, Columbia Univ., 2014. *Stage productions include:* Ubu Rex, A Man's A Man, 1977; A View from the Bridge, Titus Andronicus, The Changeling, 1978; Love for Love, Timon of Athens, Recruiting Officer (Edinburgh Fest.), 1979; Duchess of Malfi, 1980, Paris 1981 (Critics Award for Best Dir, 1982); Dr Faustus, The Forest, A Doll's House, 1981 (Critics Awards for Best Dir and Best Revival, 1982); King Lear, Antony and Cleopatra, 1982; A New Way to Pay Old Debts, Comedy of Errors, Measure for Measure, 1983; Henry V, The Winter's Tale, The Desert Air, 1984; As You Like It, 1985; Mephisto, The Art of Success (and NY, 1989), Macbeth, 1986; Kiss Me Kate, 1987; The Plantagenets, 1988; The Master Builder, 1989; The Three Sisters, 1990; Henry IV, parts 1 and 2, 1991; The Thebans, 1991; Hamlet, Winter's Tale (Globe Award for Best Dir, 1994), 1992; King Lear, Travesties, Macbeth, 1993; A Midsummer Night's Dream, 1994; Romeo and Juliet, The Cherry Orchard, 1995; Little Eyolf, 1996; Cymbeline, Twelfth Night, 1997; The Tempest, The Lion, the Witch and the Wardrobe, 1998; The Family Reunion, 1999; The Seagull, The Secret Garden, 2000; Chitty Chitty Bang Bang (also NY, 2005), Pericles, 2002; Brand, A Woman of No Importance, 2003; The Home Place, Gate, Dublin, 2005; Summer and Smoke, 2006, Kean, 2007, Apollo; Hamlet, Stratford Fest., Canada, 2008; Hedda Gabler, Th. Royal, Bath, 2010, Hong Kong Fest., 2014; The King's Speech, Yvonne Arnaud, Guildford, Wyndham's and tour, 2012; The Tempest, Th. Royal, Bath, 2012; The Captain of Köpenick, NT, 2013; Who's Afraid of Virginia Woolf, Th. Royal, Bath, 2014; Before the Dawn (Kate Bush), Apollo Hammersmith, 2014; The Importance of Being Earnest, Vaudeville, 2015; Ross, Chichester Fest. Th., 2016; A Room with a View, Th. Royal, Bath, 2016; Sousatzka, Toronto, 2017; *opera:* Don Giovanni, Kent Opera, 1983, Lyon, 2009; The Fairy Queen (Grand Prix des Critiques), 1989, Il Ritorno d'Ulisse in Patria (Grand Prix des Critiques), 2000, Aix-en-Provence Fest.; The Magic Flute, Glyndebourne, 2004; Falstaff, Gothenburg, 2005; Così fan Tutti, 2006, Marriage of Figaro, 2007, Lyon; Macbeth, Metropolitan Opera, 2007; Carmen, Opéra Comique, Paris, 2008; Alcina, Wiener Staatsoper, 2010; Xerxes, Theater an der Wien, 2011; Simon Bocanegra, Rome, 2012; Don Carlo, Bolshoi, Moscow, 2013; Hansel und Gretel, Staatsoper, Vienna, 2015; Otello, Staatsoper, Vienna, 2019; *films:* A Midsummer Night's Dream, 1996; Mrs Lowry and Son, 2019; *television:* Triple Sensation, CBC, 2008–09. Vis. Prof., Univ. of the Arts London (formerly London Inst.), 2001–. Hon. Bencher, Middle Temple, 2001. Hon. FGS. Hon. DLitt: Birmingham, 1994; Bristol, 1996; Exeter, 1999; Warwick, 2001. *Publications:* How to do Shakespeare, 2010. *Address:* c/o Duncan Heath, Independent Talent Group Ltd, 40 Whitfield Street, W1T 2RH.

NOBLE, Alison; *see* Noble, J. A.

NOBLE, Alistair William; Sheriff of Lothian and Borders at Edinburgh, since 2008; *b* 10 Jan. 1954; *s* of late William Alexander Noble and Alexanderina Noble (*née* Fraser); *m* 1986, Olga Helena Marr Wojtas. *Educ:* Aberdeen Grammar Sch.; Aberdeen Univ. (LLB). Admitted Advocate, 1978; Temporary Sheriff, 1986; Sheriff of N Strathclyde at Dunoon, 1992–99; Sheriff of Glasgow and Strathkelvin, 1999–2008. *Recreation:* reading. *Address:* Sheriff Court House, 27 Chambers Street, Edinburgh EH1 1LB. *T:* (0131) 225 2525.

NOBLE, Amelia Anne Doris, (Mrs S. Manchipp); graphic designer; Founder and Director, Amelia Noble & Partners, 2009; *b* 5 May 1973; *d* of David and Antonia Noble; *m* 2000, Simon Manchipp; one *s* one *d*. *Educ:* Bedgebury Sch., Goudhurst; London Guildhall Univ. (Foundn Course in Art and Design); Central St Martin's Coll. of Art and Design (BA Hons); Royal Coll. of Art (MA). Partner, Co-founder and Dir, Kerr/Noble, 1997–2008. Visiting Lecturer: Central St Martins Coll. of Art and Design, 1997–2002; Sch. of Communication, RCA, 2017–. Clients include Liberty, V&A Mus., Shakespeare's Globe Th., British Council, Design Mus., Tate Modern, Grafik Mag., Charities Adv. Trust, RCA and Phaidon. Ext. Examr for BA Graphic Design and Illustration course, Cambridge Sch. of Visual and Performing Arts, 2012–15. Mem., Sounding Bd, Design Council, 2014–. Freeman, Fishmongers' Co., 2004. *Recreations:* the arts, choir, understanding telegraphic speech and enforced herpetology. *Address:* Amelia Noble & Partners, 44 Champion Hill, SE5 8BS. *T:* 07976 939859. *E:* mail@amelianoble.com. *Club:* Typographic Circle.

NOBLE, Andrew James, LVO 1995; HM Diplomatic Service; Ambassador to Romania, since 2018; *b* 22 April 1960; *s* of Kenneth John Noble and late Rosemary Noble; *m* 1992, Helen Natalie Pugh; two *s* two *d*. *Educ:* Honley High Sch., Huddersfield; Gonville and Caius Coll., Cambridge (BA Hons Modern and Medieval Langs 1982). Entered HM Diplomatic Service, 1982; Third Sec., Bucharest, 1983–86; Federal Foreign Ministry, Bonn, 1986–87 (on secondment); Second Sec., Bonn, 1987–89; FCO, 1989–94; First Sec., Cape Town/Pretoria, 1994–98; Dep. Hd, Security Policy Dept, FCO, 1998–2001; Dep. Hd of Mission and Consul Gen., Athens, 2001–05; Hd, Security Strategy Unit, later Security Dir, then Dir, Security and Estates, FCO, 2005–09; Minister and Consul Gen., Berlin, 2010–14; Ambassador to Algeria, 2014–17. *Recreations:* choral singing, cooking, my family. *Address:* c/o Foreign and Commonwealth Office, King Charles Street, SW1A 2AH. *E:* Andrew.Noble@fco.gov.uk.

NOBLE, Rt Rev. Brian Michael; Bishop of Shrewsbury, (RC), 1995–2010, now Emeritus; *b* 11 April 1936; *s* of Thomas Joseph and Cecelia Noble. *Educ:* Ushaw Coll., Durham. Ordained priest for RC Diocese of Lancaster, 1960; parish appts, 1960–72; Chaplain, Lancaster Univ., 1972–80; Lectr, Pontificio Collegio Beda, Rome, 1980–87; Parish Priest, St Benedict's, Whitehaven, and Dean of West Cumbria, 1987–95. Canon of Lancaster Cath. Chapter, 1994; Ecumenical Canon, Chester Cathedral, 2003–15. Hon. DTheol Chester, 2010. *Recreations:* music, poetry, natural history, walking. *Address:* Laburnum Cottage, 97 Barnston Road, Barnston, Heswall, Wirral CH61 1BW.

NOBLE, David, CBE 1989; Under Secretary and Head of Administrative Division, Medical Research Council, 1981–89, retired; *b* 12 June 1929; *s* of late William Ernest Noble and Maggie (*née* Watt); *m* 1st, 1969, Margaret Patricia Segal (*d* 2009); 2nd, 2012, Betty Price. *Educ:* Buckhurst Hill County High Sch., Essex; University Coll., Oxford (BA Hons English, 1952). Admin. Assistant, UCH, 1952–58; Mem., Operational Res. Unit, Nuffield Provincial Hosps Trust, 1958–61; Project Sec., Northwick Park Hosp. and Clinical Res. Centre, NW Thames RHA and MRC, 1961–68; Medical Research Council: Principal, 1968–72; Asst Sec., 1972–81. Member: Nat. Biological Standards Bd, 1983–90; PHLS Bd, 1990–97 (Dep. Chm., 1996–97). *Publications:* contribs to literature on operation and design of hosps and res. labs. *Recreations:* music, reading, travel. *Address:* Wild Strawberries, The Street, Brightwell cum Sotwell, Wallingford OX10 0RP. *T:* (01491) 837553.

NOBLE, Sir David (Brunel), 6th Bt *cr* 1902, of Ardmore and Ardadan Noble, Cardross, Co. Dunbarton; sales consultant, Allied Maples Group Ltd, 1989–97; *b* 25 Dec. 1961; *s* of Sir Marc Brunel Noble, 5th Bt, CBE and Jennifer Lorna, *d* of late John Mein-Austin; *S* father, 1991; *m* 1st, 1987, Virginia Ann (marr. diss. 1993), *yr d* of late Roderick Wetherall; two *s*; 2nd, 1993, Stephanie (*née* Digby); two *s* one *d* (and one *s* decd). *Educ:* Eton Coll.; Cambridge Tutors, Croydon; Canterbury Coll.; Greenwich Univ. (BA). Sales Exec.,

Gabriel Communications Ltd, 1986–88. Patron, Special Needs Children, 1997–. *Recreations:* golf, photography, gardening. *Heir:* s Roderick Lancaster Brunel Noble, b 12 Dec. 1988. *Address:* Meridian Court, 4 Wheelers Lane, Linton, Maidstone, Kent ME17 4BL. *Club:* HAC.

**NOBLE, David Clive**; Finance Director (formerly Director General, Finance), Defence Equipment and Support, Ministry of Defence, 2007–12; b 11 Nov. 1955; s of Keith and Dorothy Noble; m 1982, Jennifer Bainbridge; two s one d. *Educ:* King Edward VI Sch., Southampton; Queen's Coll., Oxford (BA 1978). ACMA 1986. Finance Director: Rolls-Royce and Associates, 1995–98; Rolls-Royce Energy Ops, 1998–2001; Gp Finance Dir, Nedalo, 2002–03; Finance Dir, Defence Procurement Agency, 2003–07. Non-exec. Dir, Northampton Gen. Hosp. NHS Trust, 2013–. Mem., Audit Cttee, STFC, 2013–. Chm. Govs, Yelvertoft Primary Sch.

**NOBLE, David Jonathan**; Chief Parliamentary Counsel and Chief Executive, Parliamentary Counsel Office, New Zealand, 2013–16 (Chief Parliamentary Counsel and Compiler of Statutes (on secondment from Treasury Solicitor's Department), 2007–11); b 19 April 1955; s of late Kevin Charles Noble and Dr Prudence Mary Noble (née Proudlove); m 1986, Diana Stuart Jeffery; one s one d. *Educ:* Wallington Grammar Sch. for Boys, Surrey; Univ. of Birmingham (MSocSc); Univ. of Warwick (LLB Hons; Lord Rootes Scholar). Res. Asst, Faculty of Laws, UCL, 1978–81; called to the Bar, Gray's Inn, 1981; Sen. Asst Solicitor, London Bor. of Camden, 1983–86; Solicitor, Nabarro Nathanson, 1986; Principal Solicitor, London Bor. of Camden, 1986–87; Sen. Principal Legal Asst, DoE, 1987–91; Nat. Expert, DG XI, EC, 1991–94; Asst Solicitor, DoE, 1994–96; Sen. Principal Jurist, DG XI, EC, 1996–98; Principal Estabt Officer, Legal Secretariat to Law Officers, 1998–2000; Dir of Legal Services, Food Standards Agency, 2000–01; Dep. Legal Advr, Home Office, 2001–04; Legal Advr, DFES, later DCSF, 2004–07; Dir, Central Adv. Div., Treasury Solicitor's Dept, 2011–13. Trustee: Migrant Help UK, 2017– (Vice-Chair, 2019–); NAM Pubns Ltd and Aidsmap, 2017–; Salisbury Sixth Form Coll., 2017–18. Mem. Adv. Bd, Environmental Law Rev., 2001–. *Publications:* (contrib.) Discretion and Welfare, 1981; (contrib.) Protecting the European Environment: enforcing EC environmental law, 1996; (contrib.) Perspectivas de Derecho Comunitario Ambiental, 1997; articles pubd in Urban Law and Policy and Jl of Planning and Environmental Law. *Club:* Royal Over-Seas League.

**NOBLE, Prof. Denis**, CBE 1998; FMedSci; FRS 1979; Burdon Sanderson Professor of Cardiovascular Physiology, Oxford University, 1984–2004, now Professor Emeritus; Tutorial Fellow, 1963–84, Professorial Fellow, 1984–2004, now Emeritus, Balliol College, Oxford; b 16 Nov. 1936; s of George and Ethel Noble; m 1965, Susan Jennifer Barfield, BSc, BA, DPhil; one s one d. *Educ:* Emanuel Sch., London; University Coll. London (BSc, MA, PhD; Fellow 1985). Asst Lectr, UCL, 1961–63; Tutor in Physiology, Balliol Coll., and Univ. Lectr, Oxford Univ., 1963–84; Praefectus of Holywell Manor (Balliol Graduate Centre), 1971–89; Vice-Master, Balliol Coll., 1983–85. Founder Dir, Physiome Scis Inc., 1994–2003. Visiting Professor: Alberta, 1969–70; Univs of BC, Calgary, Edmonton, and SUNY at Stonybrook, 1990; Univ. of Auckland, 1990; Osaka Univ., 2005; Adjunct Prof., Xian Jiaotong Univ., China, 2003–07. Lectures: Darwin, British Assoc., 1966; Nahum, Yale, 1977; Bottazzi, Pisa, 1985; Ueda, Tokyo, 1985; Lloyd Roberts, London Med. Soc., 1987; Allerdale Wyld, Northern Industrial and Technical Soc., 1988; Bowden, UMIST, 1988; Annual, Internat. Science Policy Foundn, 1993; Rijlant, Internat. Congress of Electrocardiology, Japan, 1994; Frank May, Leicester Univ., 1996; Conf. Claude Bernard, Soc. de Physiologie, Lille, 1996; Stevenson, Univ. of Western Ontario, 1996; Larmor, Belfast, 2003; Magnes, Jerusalem, 2003; Conway, UCD, 2004. Chm., Jt Dental Cttee (MRC, SERC, Depts of Health), 1985–90. Hon. Sec., 1974–80, Foreign Sec., 1986–92, Hon. Mem., 1997, Physiol Soc.; Founder Mem., Save British Science; Pres., Med. Section, BAAS, 1991–92; Sec. Gen., IUPS, 1994–2001 (Pres., 2009–17; Chm., IUPS Congress, Glasgow, 1993); Pres., Virtual Physiological Human Inst., 2012–. Member: Partnership Korea, DTI, 1995–2000; Korea Adv. Gp, UK Trade & Investment (formerly Trade Partners UK), DTI, 2000–06. Editor, Progress in Biophysics, 1967–; Cons. Ed., Jl of Experimental Physiology, 2004–; Chief Ed., Disease Models, 2004–07; Head, Physiol. Faculty, Faculty of 1000, 2004–. Founder FMedSci 1998; Hon. MRCP 1988; Hon. FRCP 1994; Hon. FIPEM 2001. MAE 1989; Hon. Member: Amer. Physiol. Soc., 1996; Japanese Physiol Soc., 1998; Hon. Foreign Mem., Acad. Royale de Médecine de Belgique, 1993. Hon. DSc: Sheffield, 2004; Bordeaux 2, 2005; Warwick, 2008. Scientific Medal, Zool Soc., 1970; Gold Medal, British Heart Foundn, 1985; Pierre Rijlant Prize, Belgian Royal Acad., 1991; Baly Medal, RCP, 1993; Hodgkin-Huxley-Katz Prize, Physiol Soc., 2004; Mackenzie Prize, British Cardiac Soc., 2005. *Publications:* Initiation of the Heartbeat, 1975, 2nd edn, 1979; Electric Current Flow in Excitable Cells, 1975; Electrophysiology of Single Cardiac Cells, 1987; Goals, No Goals and Own Goals, 1989; Sodium-Calcium Exchange, 1989; Ionic Channels and the Effect of Taurine on the Heart, 1993; The Logic of Life, 1993; (ed with J.-D. Vincent) Ethics of Life, 1997 (trans. French 1998); The Music of Life, 2006 (trans. French 2007, Spanish 2008, Italian, Japanese, Korean, 2009, Chinese, Slovenian, 2010); Selected Papers of Denis Noble: a journey in physiology towards enlightenment, 2012; Dance to the Tune of Life: biological relativity, 2016; papers mostly in Jl of Physiology; contribs on sci. res. and funding to New Scientist, nat. press, radio and TV. *Recreations:* Indian and French cooking, Occitan language and music, classical guitar. *Address:* 49 Old Road, Oxford OX3 7JZ. *T:* (office) (01865) 272528.

**NOBLE, Gillian Mae**, CB 1999; Director (formerly Deputy Director) (Law and Order, Health and Local Government), HM Treasury, 1995–2001; b Edinburgh, 18 Nov. 1947; d of John Noble and Jessie Mae Noble (née Bonnington). *Educ:* Aberdeen Univ. (MA Hons Econ. Sci. 1969); University Coll. London (MSc Public Sector Econs 1974). Joined MoT, subseq. DoE, as econ., 1969; transf. to HM Treasury, 1976; various posts dealing with: planning and control of public expenditure, 1976–84; pensions and social security, 1984–87; Asst Sec., 1986; Head: Banking Div., 1987–92; Educn Sci. and Nat. Heritage Div., 1992; Under Sec., 1993; Hd, Health, Social Services and Territorial Depts Gp, 1993–95. Lay Mem., Nat. Biol Standards Bd, 2002–09. Trustee: Meningitis Trust, 1996–2014; St George's Hospital Charity (formerly Charitable Foundn), 2001–09 (Chm., 2002–09); Trustee and Chm., CSIS Charity Fund, 2007–19. *Recreations:* listening to music, visiting heritage properties.

**NOBLE, Rt Rev. John Ashley**; Bishop of North Queensland, 2002–07; Vicar, St Andrews with St Luke's, Clifton Hill, North Fitzroy, 2007–11; b 30 March 1944; s of Mowbray Lloyd Noble and Norma June (née Shucksmith); m 1969, Lorene May Christine Wardrop; one s one d. *Educ:* St Francis Theological Coll., Brisbane (ThL 1965); Univ. of Queensland (BA 1973); Mt Gravatt Teachers' Coll., Brisbane (Cert. in Teaching, Secondary 1973). Deacon 1965, priest 1968; Asst Curacies, 1965–69; History Subject Master, Queensland Dept of Educn, 1974–78; Asst Chaplain, St Peter's Coll., Adelaide, 1979–81; Chaplain, St Paul's Sch., Brisbane, 1981–82; Diocese of Brisbane: Rector, St John's, Dalby, 1982–84; Rector, St Barnabas', Sunnybank, 1984–88; Lectr, St Francis Theol Coll., 1989–93; an East Bishop, 1993–2002; Bishop of the Northern Region, 1993–99; Dir, Ministries Develt and Theol Educn, 1999–2002. *Recreations:* reading, music, computers. *Address:* 139 Aspinall Street, Golden Square, Vic 3555, Australia.

**NOBLE, Prof. (Julia) Alison**, OBE 2013; DPhil; FRS 2017; CEng; FREng, FIET; Technikos Professor of Biomedical Engineering, University of Oxford, since 2011; Fellow of St Hilda's College, Oxford, since 2011; b Nottingham, 28 Jan. 1965; d of James Bryan Noble and Patricia Ann Noble; m 2001, Mark Louis Durand; two d. *Educ:* St Hugh's Coll., Oxford (BA Hons 1st Cl. Engrg Sci. 1986; DPhil Engrg Sci. 1989). CEng 1995; FIET 2001; FREng 2008. Res. Scientist, GE Corporate R&D Center, Schenectady, NY, 1989–94; University of Oxford: Lectr, 1995–2000, Reader, 2000–02, in Engrg Sci.; Prof. of Engrg Sci., 2002–11; Dir, Inst. of Biomed. Engrg, 2012–16; Fellow, Wolfson Coll., Oxford, 2005–11. Sen. MIEEE 2006. *Publications:* articles in professional jls. *Recreations:* pilates, attending live concerts and sports events. *Address:* Institute of Biomedical Engineering, Department of Engineering Science, University of Oxford, Old Road Campus Research Building, off Roosevelt Drive, Headington, Oxford OX3 7DQ. *T:* (01865) 617690. *E:* alison.noble@eng.ox.ac.uk.

**NOBLE, (Richard) Adam**; Teacher, Blake Church of England Primary School, Witney, since 2016; b 9 June 1962; s of late John Alfred Noble and Susan Vera Noble (née Thornton); m 1994, Katrina Johnson (marr. diss. 2010); two s. *Educ:* Bolton Sch. (Boys' Div.); SSEES, Univ. of London (BA Hons); Moscow State Univ.; St Antony's Coll., Oxford (MPhil). Joined FCO, 1987; Third, then Second Sec. (Chancery), Moscow, 1987–89; Second, then First Sec., FCO, 1989–93; First Sec., The Hague, 1993–95; FCO, 1995–98; First Sec. (Political) New Delhi, 1998–2001; Hd, Res. Analysts, FCO, 2001–02; Dep. Consul-Gen. and Dep. Hd of Mission, Hong Kong, 2004–06; Chief Exec., Wilton Park, 2006–07; Hd, Res. Analysts, FCO, 2007–08. Teacher: Crawford Primary Sch., Camberwell, 2012–14; Cumnor House Sch., 2014–16.

**NOBLE, Roy**, OBE 2001; broadcaster, BBC Wales and S4C, since 1985 (part-time, 1980–85); Vice Lord-Lieutenant of Mid Glamorgan, 2012–17; b Brynaman, Carmarthenshire, 8 Nov. 1942; s of Ivor Henry Noble and Sarah Hannah Noble (née Jones); m 1968, Elaine Evans; one s. *Educ:* Amman Valley Grammar Sch.; Cardiff Training Coll. (Teacher's Cert. 1964); University Coll., Cardiff (BEd (Hons) 1980). LCP 1979. Teacher, Bath, 1964–66, Glamorgan, 1966–74; Headteacher: Ysgol Thomas Stephens, Pontneddfechan, 1974–81; Llangattock Ch in Wales Primary Sch., Crickhowell, 1981–85; presenter: radio incl. daily and Sunday progs, BBC Radio Wales, 1985–; television: series incl. Noble Trails, Noble Guides, Common Ground; Welsh lang. broadcaster (pt-time), S4C. Chm., Wales Youth Agency, 1998–2001; Member: Welsh Assembly Partnership Forum for the Older Person, 2005–08; Wales Tourism Adv. Bd, 2014; President: Curiad Calon; Rhondda Cynon Taff Alzheimer's Soc.; former Pres., Llangollen Internat. Musical Eisteddfod; Vice-President: Age Cymru; Velindre Hosp. Cancer Res. Appeals; St Davids Foundn Hospice, Newport; Cynon Valley Cancer Support Gp; LATCH; Noah's Ark Appeal. Trustee, Order of St John Cymru Wales, 2008–. Pres., Tenby Male Choir; Vice-President: Cwmbach Male Choir; Cor Bro Ogwr; Morriston Orpheus Male Choir; Hon. Mem., Treorchy Male Choir. Vice Pres., Aberdare RFC; Patron, Brynamman RFC. Mem., S Wales Br., ESU (former Vice Chm.). DL Mid Glamorgan, 2007. Hon. Fellow, UWIC, 2002. Paul Harris Fellow, Rotary Internat., 2009. RVS (formerly WRVS) Champion in Wales, 2012–. Accepted into Gorsedd y Beirdd, Nat. Eisteddfod of Wales, 2008. Chancellor's Medal, Univ. of Glamorgan, 2009. KStJ 2016; Comdr, St John Cymru Wales, 2011– (Trustee, 2011–15). *Publications:* Noble Expressions, 1992; Roy Noble's Book of Nicknames, 1997; Roy Noble's Wales, 1999; Y Bachan Noble (autobiog., Welsh), 2001; Noble Thoughts, 2002; Noble Ways: lay-bys in my life (autobiog.), 2010; Down the Road and Round the Bend, 2018; articles in mags and nat. press. *Recreations:* travelling by car (touring), whisky, factual books, watching Rugby football, buses (qualified bus driver), battlefields (visited many in Britain, Europe and America). *Address:* Llys Aman, Lle Hyfryd, Llwydcoed, Aberdare, Rhondda Cynon Taff CF44 0UN. *T:* (01685) 874076. *E:* nobleroy@talktalk.net.

**NOBLE, Sir Timothy (Peter)**, 4th Bt cr 1923, of Ardkinglas, co. Argyll; b Gerrard's Cross, 21 Dec. 1943; yr s of Sir Andrew Napier Noble, 2nd Bt, KCMG and Sigrid, 2nd d of Johan Michelet; S brother, 2010; m 1976, Elizabeth Mary, d of late Alexander Wallace Aitken; two s one d. *Educ:* Eton Coll.; University Coll., Oxford (BA 1965; MA); INSEAD, Fontainebleau (MBA 1970). Called to the Bar, Gray's Inn, 1969. Chief Exec., 1982–2000, Chm., 2000–07, Noble Group Ltd. Chairman: Business Archives Council of Scotland, 1986–95; Royal Scottish Nat. Opera Endowment Trust, 1994–2001; British Ski Acad., 1997–2003; Dir, British Snowsport Fedn, 1993–98. Hon. Consul for Luxembourg, 2000–13. *Publications:* Noble Blood, 2007. *Recreations:* ski-ing, tennis, golf, bridge, history, astronomy, wine, poetry. *Heir:* s Lorne Andrew Wallace Noble [b 13 July 1980; m 2009, Verity Anne Bertram]. *Address:* Ardnahane, Barnton Avenue, Edinburgh EH4 6JJ. *Clubs:* Bruntsfield Golf (Edinburgh); Summit (Scotland).

**NOBLETT, Ven. William Alexander**, CBE 2012; Chaplain-General and Archdeacon to HM Prisons, 2001–11; Chaplain to the Queen, since 2005; b Dublin, 16 April 1953; s of Joseph Henry and Hilda Florence Noblett; m 1986, Margaret Armour; one s. *Educ:* High Sch., Dublin; Salisbury and Wells Theol Coll.; Univ. of Southampton (BTh 1978); MTh Oxford 1999. Ordained deacon, 1978, priest, 1979; Curate, Sholing, Southampton, 1978–80; Rector, Ardamine Union, 1980–82; Chaplain, RAF, 1982–84; Vicar, Middlesbrough St Thomas, 1984–87; Chaplain of HM Prison: Wakefield, 1987–93; Norwich, 1993–97; Full Sutton, 1997–2001. Canon and Prebend, York Minster, 2001–12, now Canon Emeritus. Hon. Canon, Liverpool Cathedral, 2009–12. *Publications:* Prayers for People in Prison, 1998; Inside Faith: praying for people in prison, 2009. *Recreations:* reading, music. *Address:* 155 Hawksbill Way, Peterborough, Cambs PE2 8NS.

**NOBRÉ, Prof. Anna Christina de Ozório, (Kia)**, PhD; FBA 2015; Professor of Translational Cognitive Neuroscience, since 2014, and Director, Oxford Centre for Human Brain Activity, University of Oxford; Fellow, St Catherine's College, Oxford, since 2014. *Educ:* Williams Coll. (BA); Yale Univ. (MS; MPhil; PhD 1993). Postdoctoral res., Yale Univ.; Instructor, Behavioral Neurol. Unit, Beth Israel Hosp., Harvard Med. Sch.; University of Oxford: McDonnell-Pew Lectr in Cognitive Neurosci., 1994–96; Lectr, 1996–2002, Reader, 2002–06, Prof., 2006–14, Dept of Exptl Psychol.; Jun. Res. Fellow, 1994–96, Tutorial Fellow, 1996–2014, New Coll., Oxford. Adjunct Prof., Northwestern Univ., Chicago. MAE. *Publications:* (ed jtly) The Oxford Handbook of Attention, 2013; contribs to learned jls. *Address:* St Catherine's College, Manor Road, Oxford OX1 3UJ.

**NOCKLES, Gillian**; see Moore, G.

**NODDER, Timothy Edward**, CB 1982; Deputy Secretary, Department of Health and Social Security, 1978–84; b 18 June 1930; s of Edward Nodder; m 1952, Sylvia Broadhurst; two s two d. *Educ:* St Paul's Sch.; Christ's Coll., Cambridge. Under-Sec., DHSS, 1972. *Recreation:* natural history. *Address:* 83 Oakley Street, SW3 5NP.

See also L. A. McLaughlin.

**NOE, Prof. Thomas Harold**, PhD; Ernest Butten Professor of Management Studies, Saïd Business School, University of Oxford, since 2008; Fellow of Balliol College, Oxford, since 2008; b Whittier, Calif, 24 Aug. 1957; s of Harold Noe and Mary Noe; m 1997, Dr Debrah Pozsonyi; one s. *Educ:* Whittier Coll. (BA Philos. and Hist. 1979); Univ. of Texas, Austin (PhD Finance 1987); Univ. of Oxford (MA 2008). Asst Prof., Georgia Inst. of Technol.,

1988–91; Prof., Georgia State Univ., 1992–97; A. B. Freeman Prof. of Finance, Tulane Univ., 1997–2007. Associate Editor: Rev. of Financial Studies, 2003–06; Rev. of Corporate Finance Studies, 2010–16; Jl Banking and Finance, 2016–; Co-Editor, Jl of Econs and Mgt Strategy, 2007–. *Publications:* many articles in learned jls incl. Amer. Econ. Rev., Jl of Political Econ., Review of Econ. Studies, Jl of Financial Econs, Jl of Finance, Rev. of Financial Studies, etc. *Recreations:* weightlifting, book collecting (neo-Latin). *Address:* Balliol College, Broad Street, Oxford OX1 3BJ. *T:* (01865) 288933. *E:* thomas.noe@sbs.ox.ac.uk.

**NOEL,** family name of **Earl of Gainsborough.**

**NOEL, Lynton Cosmas;** barrister, retired 1994; *b* 25 Oct. 1928; *m* 1962, Teresa Angela Diamonda; one *s* one *d.* *Educ:* St Joseph's RC Sch., Grenada; Polytechnic/Holborn Coll. of Law, Languages and Commerce; Inns of Court Sch. of Law (LLB). Called to the Bar, Lincoln's Inn, 1976. Asst Head Teacher, 1956–60; Telephone Engr, GPO, 1960–67; practised law, 1976–84; Lectr in Law, Coll. of Law Studies, 1984; 1st Sec., Grenada High Commn, London, 1984–85; Chargé d'Affaires, Caracas, 1985–90; High Comr for Grenada in London, 1990–92; returned to practice at the Bar, 1992. *Recreations:* music, chess.

**NOEL, Robert John Baptist;** Lancaster Herald of Arms, since 1999; *b* 15 Oct. 1962; *s* of late Hon. Gerard Eyre Wriothesley Noel; *m* 2013, Rowena Hale; one *s* one *d.* *Educ:* Ampleforth; Exeter Coll., Oxford (MA Hebrew); St Edmund's Coll., Cambridge (MPhil Internat. Relns). Baltic Exchange, 1984–85; Christie's, 1988–91; Bluemantle Pursuivant, 1992–99. Vice-Chm., White Lion Soc., 1998–. Fellow, Purchase Soc., 1998. Officer of Arms Attendant, Imperial Soc. of Kts Bach., 2001–. *Address:* College of Arms, 130 Queen Victoria Street, EC4V 4BT. *T:* (020) 7332 0414, *Fax:* (020) 7248 6448. *Clubs:* Garrick, Pratt's, Chelsea Arts, Royal Automobile.

**NOEL, Robert Montague;** Chief Executive, Land Securities Group PLC, since 2012; *b* Bradford, 12 June 1964; *s* of Henry Noel and Elizabeth Noel; *m* 1992, Sophie Bourdaire; one *s* two *d.* *Educ:* Marlborough Coll.; Univ. of Reading (BSc 1986). FRICS 1989. Director: Nelson Bakewell Ltd, 1992–2002; Great Portland Estates plc, 2002–09; Man. Dir, London Portfolio, Land Securities Gp PLC, 2010–12. Dir, New West End Co., 2004–12. Chm., Westminster Property Assoc., 2009–11. Trustee, LandAid, 2010–16. Mem. Bd, Natural Hist. Mus., 2016–; Mem. Bd, British Property Fedn, 2016– (Pres., 2018–19). *Address:* Land Securities Group PLC, 100 Victoria Street, SW1E 5JL. *T:* (020) 7413 9000.

**NOEL-BUXTON,** family name of **Baron Noel-Buxton.**

**NOEL-BUXTON,** 4th Baron *cr* 1930, of Aylsham, Norfolk; **Charles Connal Noel-Buxton;** *b* Kingston-upon-Thames, 17 April 1975; *s* of 3rd Baron Noel-Buxton and of Sarah Margaret Surridge Noel-Buxton (*née* Barrett, now Adam); S father, 2013. *Educ:* Eton Coll. *Heir:* uncle Hon. Simon Campden Buxton [*b* 9 April 1943; *m* 1981, Alison Dorothy Liddle; one *s* one *d*]. *Club:* MCC.

**NOEL-PATON, Hon. (Frederick) Ranald;** Chairman, Murray Global Return plc, 2000–05 (Director, 1998–2005); *b* 7 Nov. 1938; *s* of Baron Ferrier, ED and Joane Mary, *d* of Sir Gilbert Wiles, KCIE, CSI; *m* 1973, Patricia Anne Stirling; four *d.* *Educ:* Rugby School; Haverford Coll.; McGill Univ. (BA 1962). Various posts, British United Airways, 1965–70; various sen. exec. posts, British Caledonian Airways, 1970–86; John Menzies Plc: Gp Man. Dir, 1986–97; Dep. Chm., 1997–98. Dir, 1986–98, Chm., 1998–2004, Pacific Assets Trust plc; Director: General Accident plc, 1987–98; Macallan-Glenlivet plc, 1990–96; Royal Bank of Scotland Gp, 1991–93. Hon. DBA Napier, 1992. *Recreations:* fishing, walking, golf, gardening, bird watching, the arts. *Address:* Pitcurran House, Abernethy, Perthshire PH2 9LH. *Clubs:* Royal Perth Golfing Soc. and County and City (Perth); Royal and Ancient Golf (St Andrews); Hong Kong, Shek O Country (Hong Kong).

**NOEST, Peter John,** FRICS; Managing Director, P. H. Gillingham (Investments) Ltd, since 1987; Chairman, P. H. Gillingham Group Ltd, since 2003; *b* 12 June 1948; *s* of late Major A. J. F. Noest and Mrs M. Noest-Gerbrands; *m* 1st, 1972, Lisabeth Penelope Moody (marr. diss. 1993); one *s* one *d*; 2nd, 1993, Jocelyn Claire (*d* 2003), *yr d* of late A. D. Spencer; one *s.* *Educ:* St George's Coll., Weybridge; Royal Agricl Coll., Cirencester (MRAC 1971). FRICS 1978 (ARICS 1973). Joined Knight Frank & Rutley, 1971; Partner i/c Dutch office, Amsterdam, 1972; London Partner, 1977; full equity Partner, 1981; Consultant, 1983, full equity Partner, 1984, Man. Partner, 1985, Hampton & Sons; Dir, Hampton & Sons Holdings, 1987 (subseq. merged with Lambert Smith to form Lambert Smith Hampton); Dir, Lambert Smith Hampton, 1988–92. Man. Dir, then CEO, Capital Consultancy Gp Ltd, 1993–2013; Consultant, Fortis MeesPierson, 1993–2009. Ambassador, New Barn Th., Cirencester, 2018. *Publications:* (contrib.) Office Development, ed by Paul Marber, 1985. *Recreations:* hunting, shooting, travel, photography, country life, wines and food, Gascony, garden design, arboriculture, business pelmanism, creating synergy, mentoring and brainstorming with the young. *Address:* Bedwell House, London Road, Northleach, Cheltenham, Glos GL54 3LU.

**NOGAMI, Yoshiji,** Hon. CBE 2017; Executive Adviser, Mizuho Bank, since 2008; *b* 19 June 1942; *s* of Hiroshi Nogami and Masako Nogami; *m* 1978, Geraldine Ann Woods McDermott; three *s.* *Educ:* Univ. of Tokyo (BA American Studies). Joined Min. of Foreign Affairs, Japan, 1966; Econ. Counsellor, Washington, 1985–88; Actg Dir, Japan Inst. for Internat. Affairs, Tokyo, 1988–91; Deputy Director-General: ME and African Affairs Bureau, 1991–93, Foreign Policy Bureau, 1993–94, Min. of Foreign Affairs; Consul Gen., Hong Kong, 1994–96; Dir Gen., Econ. Affairs Bureau, Min. of Foreign Affairs, 1996–97; Ambassador to OECD, 1997–99; Dep. Minister for Foreign Affairs, 1999–2001; Vice-Minister for Foreign Affairs, 2001–02; Sen. Vis. Fellow, RIIA, 2002–04; Ambassador of Japan to Court of St James's, 2004–08. Pres., Japan Inst. for Internat. Affairs, 2008–18. Officier de la Légion d'Honneur (France), 2001. *Recreations:* golf, cookery. *Address:* c/o Mizuho Bank, 1–5–5 Otemachi, Chiyoda-ku, Tokyo 100–8176, Japan.

**NOKES, Rt Hon. Caroline;** PC 2018; MP for Romsey and Southampton North, since 2010 (C, 2010–19; Ind, since 2019); *b* Lyndhurst, 26 June 1972; *d* of Roy James Perry, *qv*; one *d.* *Educ:* La Sagesse Convent, Romsey; Peter Symonds Coll.; Univ. of Sussex (BA Hons). Researcher for Roy Perry, MEP, 1994–2004; Chief Exec., Nat. Pony Soc., 2008–09. Mem. (C) Test Valley BC, 1999–2011 (Exec. Mem. for Leisure, 2001–10). Parly Under-Sec. of State, DWP, 2016–17, Cabinet Office, 2017–18; Minister of State, Home Office, 2018–19. *Recreations:* riding, cookery. *Address:* House of Commons, SW1A 0AA. *T:* (020) 7219 1468. *E:* caroline.nokes.mp@parliament.uk.

**NOKES, Stephen Anthony;** Senior Advisor, RSAcademics, since 2016; Headmaster, John Hampden Grammar School, High Wycombe, 2000–16; *b* Portsmouth, 31 Aug. 1952; *s* of Alan and Sheila Nokes; *m* 1984, Diana Rose; two *s.* *Educ:* St John's Coll., Southsea; University Coll. Swansea (MA); St John's Coll., Oxford (PGCE 1978); Univ. of Hertfordshire (AdvDip 1982). Teacher of Hist., Chiswick Sch., 1978–86; Hd of Hist. and Pols, Chesham High Sch., 1986–89; Hd of Humanities, 1989–92, Sen. Teacher, 1992–96, Dep. Hd, 1996–99, Beaconsfield High Sch. Dir, Sheldon Erskine Ltd, appt consultants, 2008–. Chm., Bucks Sch. Forum, 2008–10; founder Mem., Grammar Sch. Heads Assoc. (formerly Professional Assoc. of Selective Schs), 2007–16 (Vice Chm., 2011–15; Chm., 2015–16); Member: High Achieving Sports Schs, 2007–16; Internat. Boys' Schs Coalition, 2007–16; Boys' Assoc. Selective Schs, 2010–16. Chm., Thames Valley Politics Assoc., 1997–2000. Governor: Davenies Sch., Beaconsfield, 2005–18; Westfield Sch., Bourne End, 2005–09; Aldenham Sch., Herts, 2009–18; St Piran's Sch., 2013–17; Watford GS for Boys, 2015– (Chair, Bd of Govs, 2018–); Dr Challoner's GS, Amersham, 2016–; Bedales Sch., 2018– (Chair, Educn Cttee, 2018–). Patron, Old Hampdians, 2013–16. Trustee, Causeway Foundn, 2014–. Freeman, Educators' Co., 2010–17. *Publications:* (jtly) Guide to First World War Battlefield Sites, 1987. *Recreations:* watching, analysing, discussing sport especially Rugby; theatre, ballet and travel (with wife); collecting and driving sports and classic cars (with sons); watching movies, playing with techno gadgets (middle-aged male); shooting (clay). *E:* stevenokes@mac.com. *Club:* Lansdowne.

**NOLAN, Benjamin;** QC 1992; a Recorder, since 1989; a Deputy High Court Judge; *b* 19 July 1948; *s* of Benjamin Nolan and Jane Nolan (*née* Mercer); two *d.* *Educ:* St Joseph's Coll., Blackpool; Newcastle upon Tyne Polytechnic; LLB London, 1970. Called to the Bar, Middle Temple, 1971, Bencher, 2004. *Recreations:* travel, cooking, walking, swimming, gardening. *Address:* Dere Street Chambers, 33 Broad Chare, Newcastle upon Tyne NE1 3DQ. *T:* (0191) 232 0541.

**NOLAN, Christopher Edward,** CBE 2019; film director, screenwriter and producer; *b* London, 30 July 1970; *m* 1997, Emma Thomas; four *c.* *Educ:* Haileybury; University Coll. London (BA English Lit. 1993). *Films* include: Following, 1998; Memento, 2000; Insomnia, 2002; Batman Begins, 2005; The Prestige, 2006; The Dark Knight, 2008; Inception, 2010; The Dark Knight Rises, 2012; Man of Steel, 2013; Interstellar, 2014; Dunkirk, 2017. *Address:* c/o William Morris Endeavor Entertainment, 9601 Wilshire Boulevard, Beverly Hills, CA 90210, USA.

**NOLAN, Dominic Thomas;** QC 2006; a Recorder, since 2005; *b* 16 Jan. 1963; *s* of late Dennis Nolan and of Patricia Nolan; *m* 1988, Catherine Lucy, (Kate), Allen; three *s.* *Educ:* St Teresa's Jun. Boys' Sch., Norris Green; St Edward's Coll., Liverpool; Univ. of Nottingham (LLB Hons 1984). Called to the Bar, Lincoln's Inn, 1985 (Hardwicke Scholar, Buchanan Prizeman, Student of the Yr, 1985), Bencher, 2013; Head, Ropewalk Chambers, 2009–12. Special Lectr, 2003–09, Hon. Prof. (formerly Special Prof.), 2009–, Sch. of Law, Univ. of Nottingham. *Recreations:* family, friends, music, National Hunt racing, cycling. *Address:* Hailsham Chambers, 4 Paper Buildings, Temple, EC4Y 7EX. *T:* (020) 7643 5000.

**NOLAN, Dr Jeremy Paul,** FRCA, FRCP, FFICM; Consultant in Anaesthesia and Intensive Care Medicine, Royal United Hospitals Bath NHS Foundation Trust (formerly Royal United Hospital NHS Trust), since 1994; *b* Sudbury, Suffolk, 14 Oct. 1959; *s* of Michael Nolan and Marlene Nolan; *m* 1991, Sandra Tapley; two *s.* *Educ:* Kimbolton Sch.; Univ. of Bristol (MB ChB 1983). FRCA 1989; FRCP 2009; FFICM 2011. Trng in anaesthesia and medicine, Plymouth Gen. Hosp., 1983–86; Registrar in Anaesthesia, Bristol hosps, 1987–89; Attending Anesthesiologist, Shock Trauma Center, Baltimore, 1990–91; Sen. Registrar in Anaesthesia, Royal United Hosp., Bath and Southampton Gen. Hosp., 1991–94. Hon. Prof. of Resuscitation Medicine, Univ. of Bristol, 2015–; Prof. of Resuscitation Medicine, Univ. of Warwick, 2018–. Chairman: Resuscitation Council, 2006–09; Eur. Resuscitation Council, 2016–. Hon. FRCEM 2005. Editor-in-Chief, Resuscitation Jl, 2008–. *Publications:* Advanced Life Support, 2001, 7th edn 2016; (ed jtly) Emergency Airway Management, 2008, 2nd edn 2015; (ed jtly) Oxford Handbook of Anaesthesia for Emergency Care, 2012; papers in jls. *Recreation:* running. *Address:* Department of Anaesthesia, Royal United Hospitals Bath NHS Foundation Trust, Combe Park, Bath BA1 3NG. *T:* (01225) 825056, *Fax:* (01225) 825061. *E:* jerry.nolan@nhs.net.

**NOLAN, Hon. Michael Alfred Anthony;** QC 2015; *b* Bexhill, 17 June 1955; *s* of Baron Nolan, PC and Margaret Nolan; *m* 1984, Adeline Oh; two *s* one *d.* *Educ:* Ampleforth Coll., Yorks; St Benet's Hall, Oxford (MA); City Univ. (DipLaw). Called to the Bar, Middle Temple, 1981. Mem., Exec. Cttee, Commercial Bar Assoc., 1998–2001. *Publications:* (contrib.) Butterworth's Commercial Court and Arbitration Pleadings, 2005. *Recreations:* ski-ing, tennis, opera, theatre, cricket. *Address:* Quadrant Chambers, 10 Fleet Street, EC4Y 1AU. *T:* (020) 7583 4444, *Fax:* (020) 7583 4455. *Clubs:* Hurlingham, MCC.

**NOLAN, Prof. Peter Hugh,** CBE 2009; PhD; Chong Hua Professor of Chinese Development, 2012–16, now Professor Emeritus, and Founding Director, Centre of Development Studies, 2012–17, and Research Professor, 2016–19, Department of Politics and International Studies, University of Cambridge; Fellow, since 1979, and Director, China Centre, since 2017, Jesus College, Cambridge; *b* 28 April 1949; *s* of Charles Patrick Nolan and Barbara Vere Nolan; *m* 1975, Siobáin Suzanne Mulligan; one *s* one *d.* *Educ:* St Boniface's Coll., Plymouth; Fitzwilliam Coll., Cambridge (Open Schol.; BA 1970); SOAS, Univ. of London (MSc 1971; PhD 1981). Res. Fellow, Contemporary China Inst., SOAS, Univ. of London, 1971–75; Lectr, Dept of Economic History, Univ. of NSW, 1976–78; Res. Officer, Inst. of Commonwealth Studies, Oxford Univ., 1978–79; Cambridge University: Asst Lectr, 1979–84, Lectr, 1984–97, Faculty of Econs and Politics; Dir of Studies in Econs, Jesus Coll., 1980–97; Chair, Develt Studies Cttee, 1995–2011; Sinyi Prof. of Chinese Mgt, Judge Inst. of Mgt Studies, subseq. Judge Business Sch., 1997–2012. Hon. Dr Copenhagen Business Sch., 2009. *Publications:* (jtly) Inequality: India and China compared 1950–1970, 1976; Growth Processes and Distributional Change in a South Chinese Province: the case of Guangdong, 1983; (ed jtly) Re-thinking Socialist Economics, 1986; The Political Economy of Collective Farms: an analysis of China's post-Mao rural economic reforms, 1988; (ed jtly) Market Forces in China: competition and small business—the Wenzhou debate, 1989; (ed jtly) The Chinese Economy and Its Future, 1990; State and Market in the Chinese Economy: essays on controversial issues, 1993; (ed jtly) China's Economic Reforms in the 1980s: the costs and benefits of incrementalism, 1994; (ed jtly) The Transformation of the Communist Economies: against the mainstream, 1995; China's Rise, Russia's Fall: politics and economics in the transition from Stalinism, 1995; Indigenous Large Firms in China's Economic Reforms: the case of Shougang Iron and Steel Corporation, 1998; Coca-Cola and the Global Business Revolution, 1999; China and the Global Economy, 2001; China and the Global Business Revolution, 2001; (in Chinese) Looking at China's Enterprises, 2002; China at the Crossroads, 2003; Transforming China, 2003; (jtly) The Global Business Revolution and the Cascade Effect, 2007; Integrating China, 2007; Capitalism and Freedom: the contradictory character of globalisation, 2007; Crossroads: the end of wild capitalism, 2009; Is China Buying the World?, 2012; Chinese Firms, Global Firms: industrial policy in the age of globalisation, 2014; Re-balancing China, 2014; Understanding China: the Silk Road and the Communist Manifesto, 2016; China and the West: crossroads of civilisation, 2018. *Recreations:* swimming, music, playing recorder. *Address:* Jesus College, Cambridge CB5 8BL. *T:* (01223) 339477.

**NOLAN, Philip Michael Gerard,** PhD; Chairman, Associated British Ports plc, since 2017; *b* 15 Oct. 1953; *m* 1978, Josephine Monaghan; two *c.* *Educ:* Queen's Univ., Belfast (BSc Geol. 1976; PhD 1980); London Business Sch. (MBA 1991). Lectr in Geol., Ulster Poly., 1979–81; joined BP, 1981: geologist, holding posts in exploration, appraisal and develt, in UK, US and Australia, 1981–87; BP Exploration, London: commercial and planning posts, Head Office, 1987–93; Manager, Acquisitions and Disposals, 1993–95; on secondment as Man. Dir, Interconnector (UK) Ltd, 1995–96; joined BG, 1996: Dir, East Area, 1996–97, Man. Dir, 1997–99, Chief Exec., 1999–2001, Transco; Dir, BG,

1999–2000; Chief Executive: Lattice Gp plc, 2000–01; eircom Ltd, 2002–06. Chairman: Infinis Ltd, 2007–10; John Laing plc, 2010–18; Ulster Bank, 2013–17; Affinity Water, 2013–18; non-exec. Dir, De La Rue plc, 2000–09. *Recreations:* golf, watching football and Rugby, walking, listening to music, reading.

**NOLAN, Rt Rev. William;** *see* Galloway, Bishop of, (RC).

**NOLLENT, Prof. Andrea;** Professor of Law, since 2012, and Vice Chancellor and Chief Executive Officer, since 2015, University of Law; *b* England, 9 Sept. 1962; *d* of Orr James Mill and Patricia Carol Sugden; *m* 1988, Serge Nollent (marr. diss. 2012); one *s* one *d*; *m* 2018, Patrick Sherwell. *Educ:* Ackworth Quaker Sch.; Univ. of Dundee (LLB Hons 1985); Univ. of Huddersfield (Cert Ed); Univ. of Durham (MJur 1995). Lectr in Law of the EU, 1990–2003, Dean, 2003–10, Sheffield Hallam Univ.; Dean, Nottingham Law Sch., 2010–14; Provost, Univ. of Law, 2014–15. Vis. Prof., Univ. of Paris Est, 2011–. *Publications:* contribs to Law Teacher. *Recreation:* hill walking on the Isle of Skye. *Address:* University of Law, 2 Bunhill Row, Moorgate, EC1Y 8HQ. *E:* andrea.nollent@law.ac.uk.

**NOON, Paul Thomas,** OBE 2013; General Secretary, Prospect, 2002–12 (Joint General Secretary, 2001–02); *b* 1 Dec. 1952; *s* of Thomas Noon and Barbara Noon (*née* Grocott); *m* 1977, Eileen Elizabeth Smith; two *d.* MoD, 1971–74; Institution of Professional Civil Servants: Asst Negotiations Officer, 1974–77; Negotiations Officer, 1977–81; Asst Sec., 1981–89; Asst Gen. Sec., 1989–99; Gen. Sec., Instn of Professionals, Managers and Specialists, 1999–2001. Mem., Gen. Council, 2001–12, Exec. Cttee, 2002–12, TUC. Board Member: Unions Today, 1999–2002; Trade Union Fund Managers, 2001– (Dep. Chm., 2012–); Chairman: CCSU, 2001–03, 2009–11; Civil Service Housing Assoc., (Vice-Chm., 1999–2002); non-exec. Dir, Unity Trust Bank, 2012–16. Mem. Bd, ETM Placements, 2006–07. Member: Green Economy Council, 2011–12; Central Arbitration Cttee, 2016–. Trustee, Skills for Growth, 2014–17. Coordinator, Trade Unionists for Safe Nuclear Energy, 2016–18. *Recreations:* reading, politics, family. *Address:* 3 Warwick Close, Bexley, Kent DA5 3NL. *T:* 07446 834162. *E:* noon.p@sky.com.

**NOONAN, Michael;** Member of the Dáil (TD) (FG), since 1981; Minister for Finance, Ireland, 2011–17; *b* Limerick, 22 May 1943; widower; three *s* two *d. Educ:* St Patrick's Teacher Training Coll., Dublin; University Coll. Dublin. Minister: for Justice, 1982–86; for Industry, Commerce and Trade, 1986; for Energy, 1987; for Health, 1994–97. Chm., Public Accounts Cttee. Leader, Fine Gael Party, 2001–02. *Address:* Dáil Éireann, Leinster House, Kildare Street, Dublin 2, Ireland.

**NOONEY, David Matthew;** Director, Civil Justice and Legal Services, Department for Constitutional Affairs, 2003–04; *b* 2 Aug. 1945; *m* 1973, Maureen Georgina Revell; one adopted *d. Educ:* St Joseph's Acad., Blackheath. FICMA. HM Treasury, 1965–86; on loan to Lord Chancellor's Dept as Management Accounting Advr, 1986–88, transf. to the Dept, 1989; Head, Resources Div., 1988–91; Head, Civil Business, 1991–93; Head, Legal Services and Agencies Div., 1993; Prin. Estabt and Finance Officer, then Dir, Corporate Services, CPS, 1993–98; on secondment to Welsh Office, 1998–99; Dir, Modernising Govt Prog., LCD, 1999–2003. *Recreations:* sport, theatre, crosswords, poetry.

**NOORDHOF, Hon. Dame Jennifer Jane;** *see* Eady, Hon. Dame J. J.

**NORBROOK, Prof. David Gordon Ellis;** Merton Professor of English Literature, University of Oxford, 2002–14, now Emeritus; Fellow of Merton College, Oxford, 2002–14, now Emeritus; *b* 1 June 1950. *Educ:* Univ. of Aberdeen (MA 1972); Balliol Coll., Oxford; Magdalen Coll., Oxford (Prize Fellow 1975; DPhil 1978). Oxford University: Lectr in English, 1978–98; Fellow and Tutor in English, Magdalen Coll., 1978–98, Emeritus Fellow, 1999; Prof. of English, Univ. of Maryland, 1999–2002. Visiting Professor: Graduate Center, CUNY, 1989; École des Hautes Études en Scis Sociales, Paris, 2009; Washington Univ., St Louis, 2016. *Publications:* Poetry and Politics in the English Renaissance, 1984, 2nd edn 2002; (with Henry Woudhuysen) The Penguin Book of Renaissance Verse, 1992; Writing the English Republic: poetry, rhetoric and politics 1627–1660, 1999 (James Holly Hanford Prize, Milton Soc. of America, 2000); (ed) Lucy Hutchinson's Order and Disorder, 2001; (ed jtly) The Works of Lucy Hutchinson, vol. 1: Translation of Lucretius, 2012, vol. 2: Theological Writings and Translations, 2018; (ed Jtly) Lucretius and the Early Modern, 2016; numerous articles and reviews. *Recreation:* (armchair) travel. *Address:* Merton College, Oxford OX1 4JD.

**NORBURN, Prof. David,** PhD; Founding Director, The Management School, Imperial College of Science, Technology and Medicine, and Professor of Management, University of London, 1987–2003; *b* 18 Feb. 1941; *s* of late Richard Greville and Constance Elizabeth Norburn; *m* 1st, 1962, Veronica Ellis (marr. diss. 1975); one *s* one *d*; 2nd, 1975, Prof. Susan Joyce Birley, *qv. Educ:* Bolton Sch.; LSE (BSc); City Univ. (PhD); Harvard Business Sch. (Internat. Teachers Prog.). Salesman, Burroughs Corp., 1962–66; Management Consultant, Price Waterhouse, 1966–67; Sen. Lectr, Regent Street Polytechnic, 1967–70; Sen. Res. Fellow, City Univ., 1970–72; Lectr, Sen. Lectr, Dir, MBA programme, London Business Sch., 1972–82; Inaugural Chairholder, Franklin D. Schurz Prof. in Strategic Management, Univ. of Notre Dame, Indiana, 1982–85; Prof. of Strategic Management, Cranfield Inst. of Technology, 1985–87. Director: Newchurch & Co., 1985–97; Whurr Publishing Co. Ltd, 1994–2002; Com. Medica Ltd, 1999–2003; Management Diagnostics Ltd, 2001–08; Mainstream Hldgs US), 2005–08. Director: Strategic Mgt Soc., 1993–2002; Bd of Companions, Inst. of Mgt, 1994–97. Freeman, Clockmakers' Co. CCMI (Chartered FSMS; FRSA. Editor, European Business Journal, 1988–2003. *Publications:* British Business Policy (with D. Channon and J. Stopford), 1975; (jtly) Globalisation of Telecommunications, 1994; (jtly) Fusion in Home Automation, 1994; (with Sir William Nicoll and R. Schoenberg) Perspectives on European Business, 1995; articles in professional jls. *Recreations:* antiquarian horology, competitive tennis, carpentry. *Address:* Beech House, Forest Grange, Horsham RH13 6HX.

**NORBURN, Susan Joyce, (Mrs David Norburn);** *see* Birley, S. J.

**NORBURY, 7th Earl of,** *cr* 1827 (Ire.); **Richard James Graham-Toler;** Baron Norwood 1797; Baron Norbury 1800; Viscount Glandine 1827; *b* 5 March 1967; *o s* of 6th Earl of Norbury and of Anne, *d* of Francis Mathew; *S* father, 2000.

**NORBURY, Caroline,** MBE 2012; Founder and Chief Executive, Creative England, since 2011; *b* Kluang, Malaysia, 24 July 1966; *d* of Robert and Doreen Norbury; *m* 1986, Ed Barker; one *s* one *d. Educ:* Univ. of Essex (BA Govt 1988); City Univ., London (MA Cultural Leadership 2009). Dir, Signals Media, 1990–97; Chief Executive Officer: First Take Films, 1998–2001; South West Screen, 2001–11. *Address:* Creative England, 1st Floor, College House, 32–36 College Green, Bristol BS1 5SP. *T:* (0117) 933 8920. *E:* ceomail@creativeengland.co.uk.

**NORBURY, Hugh Robert;** QC 2012; *b* Edinburgh, 6 April 1970; *s* of Robert and late Jane Norbury; *m* 1997, Cecilia Ivimy; two *s. Educ:* Eton Coll.; Worcester Coll., Oxford (BA PPE); City Univ. (CPE); King's Coll. London (LLM). Called to the Bar, Lincoln's Inn, 1995; in practice as barrister, specialising in chancery and commercial, especially fraud.

*Recreations:* spending time with family and friends, running, ski-ing, tennis, wine, trees. *Address:* Serle Court, 6 New Square, Lincoln's Inn, WC2A 3QS. *T:* (020) 7242 6105. *E:* clerks@serlecourt.co.uk.

**NORDMANN, François;** Swiss Ambassador to France, 2002–07, and to Monaco, 2006–07; *b* 13 May 1942; *s* of Jean and Bluette Nordmann; *m* 1980, Miriam Bohadana. *Educ:* Univ. de Fribourg (licencié en droit). Private Sec. to Foreign Minister, Switzerland, 1975–80; Counsellor and Perm. Observer, Mission to UN, NY, 1980–84; Ambassador to Guatemala, El Salvador, Honduras, Nicaragua, Costa Rica and Panama, 1984–87; Ambassador and Head of Swiss Perm. Delegn to UNESCO, Paris, 1987–92; Ambassador and Dir, Directorate of Internat. Orgns, Swiss Foreign Min., Berne, 1992–94; Ambassador to UK, 1994–99; Mission to Internat. Orgns, Geneva, 2000–02. Pres., Assoc. du Fest. Internat. de Films de Fribourg, 2015–. Officier de la Légion d'Honneur (France), 2013. *Recreations:* reading, theatre, walking, golf. *Club:* Cercle de l'Union Interalliée (Paris).

**NORFOLK, 18th Duke of,** *cr* 1483; **Edward William Fitzalan-Howard;** DL; Earl of Arundel, 1139; Baron Beaumont, 1309; Baron Maltravers, 1330; Earl of Surrey, 1483; Baron FitzAlan, Clun, and Oswaldstre, 1627; Earl of Norfolk, 1644; Baron Howard of Glossop, 1869; Earl Marshal and Hereditary Marshal and Chief Butler of England; Premier Duke and Earl; *b* 2 Dec. 1956; *er s* of 17th Duke of Norfolk, KG, GCVO, CB, CBE, MC and Anne Mary Teresa, CBE (*née* Constable-Maxwell); *S* father, 2002; *m* 1987, Georgina, *y d* of Jack and Serena Gore; three *s* two *d. Educ:* Ampleforth Coll., Yorks; Lincoln Coll., Oxford. Chairman: Sigas Ltd, 1979–88; Parkwood Group Ltd, 1989–2002. DL W Sussex, 2002. *Recreations:* ski-ing, motor-racing, shooting. *Heir: s* Earl of Arundel and Surrey, *qv. Address:* Arundel Castle, West Sussex BN18 9AB. *T:* (01903) 883400. *Club:* British Racing Drivers' (Silverstone).

**NORFOLK, Archdeacon of;** *see* Betts, Ven. S. J.

**NORFOLK, Lawrence William;** writer, since 1988; *b* 1 Oct. 1963; *s* of Michael Norfolk and Shirley Kathleen (*née* Blake); *m* 1994, Vineeta Rayan; two *s. Educ:* KCL (BA Hons (English) 1986; AKC 1986). *Publications:* Lemprière's Dictionary, 1991 (Somerset Maugham Award, 1992); The Pope's Rhinoceros, 1996; In the Shape of a Boar, 2001; (with Neal White) Ott's Sneeze, 2002; John Saturnall's Feast, 2012. *Recreations:* swimming, skydiving, reading. *Address:* c/o Blake Friedmann Literary Agency, Ground Floor, 15 Highbury Place, N5 1QP.

**NORGROVE, Sir David (Ronald),** Kt 2016; Chairman, UK Statistics Authority, since 2017; *b* 23 Jan. 1948; *s* of Douglas and Ann Norgrove; *m* 1977, Jenny Stoker; one *s* two *d. Educ:* Christ's Hosp.; Exeter Coll., Oxford (BA; Hon. Fellow, 2018); Emmanuel Coll., Cambridge (DipEcon); London Sch. of Econs (MSc). HM Treasury, 1972–78 and 1980–85; First Nat. Bank of Chicago, 1978–80; Private Sec. to the Prime Minister, 1985–88; Marks and Spencer, 1988–2004, Exec. Dir, 2000–04; Chairman: The Pensions Regulator, 2005–10; Low Pay Commn, 2009–16; Pensions First Gp LLP, 2011–14. Non-exec. Dir, Strategic Rail Authy, 2002–04. Chairman: Rev. of Family Justice System, 2010–11; Family Justice Bd, 2012–16. Trustee, BM, 2004–12 (Dep. Chm. of Trustees, 2010–12; Chmn., Audit Cttee, 2005–12; Chm., British Mus. Co., 2004–05; Chm., Friends of BM, 2008–12). Chm., Amnesty Internat. Charitable Trust, 2009–14; Trustee: Hanover Trust, 1993–2003; Media Trust, 1998–2003; Mencap, 2000–03; British Mus. Trust, 2016–. Mem. Council, Univ. of Oxford, 2014–18 (Dep. Chair, 2016–18). *Recreations:* music, walking, ski-ing, Arsenal.

**NORGROVE, Michael William,** CBE 2009; Director of Excise, Customs, Stamps and Money Laundering, HM Revenue and Customs, 2009–12; *b* 16 Dec. 1952; *s* of Walter and Nellie Norgrove; *m* 1977, Lalita (*née* Shiner); one *s* one *d. Educ:* Palmer's Boys' Sch., Grays, Essex; Bedford Coll., London (BA 1974); King's Coll. London (MA 1975); St John's Coll., Oxford (PGCE 1978). Joined HM Customs and Excise as Exec. Officer, 1978, Admin. trainee, 1981; seconded to HM Treasury, 1985–87; Principal, 1986; seconded to UK Permanent Repn, Brussels, 1988–93; Asst Sec., 1992; Head, Financial Mgt Div., 1993–98; apptd Comr, HM Bd of Customs and Excise, 1998; Comr, Ops (Compliance), 1998–2001; Dir, Large Business Gp, 2001–02; Exec. Dir, Intelligence, HM Customs and Excise, subseq. HMRC, 2002–06; Dir, Central Compliance, 2006–08, Excise, Stamps and Money, 2008–09, HMRC. *Recreations:* Real tennis, bird watching, jazz.

**NORKUS, Renatas;** Ambassador of the Republic of Lithuania to the Court of St James's, since 2017, and, (non-resident) to Portugal and to Oman, since 2018; *b* Plungė, Lithuania, 7 Aug. 1967; *m* Sandra Smaidrytė; two *s* one *d. Educ:* Vilnius Univ. (LLM); Grad. Inst. of Internat. Studies, Geneva (Internat. Security Policy course, 1994). Joined Diplomatic Service of Lithuania, 1991; Third Sec., Central and Eastern Europe Div., 1991–92, Second Sec., Eur. Security and Co-operation Div., 1992, Min. of Foreign Affairs; Mem., Delegn to OSCE Forum for Security Co-operation, Vienna, 1992–93; Dir, Defence Policy and Progs Dept, Min. of Nat. Defence (on secondment), 1994–98; Hd, Americas Div., Political Dept, Min. of Foreign Affairs, 1998–99; Counsellor and Dep. Hd of Mission to NATO and WEU, 1999–2001; Minister-Counsellor (Congressional Affairs), 2001–03, Dep. Chief of Mission, 2003–04, Washington; Dep. Security Policy Dir, Min. of Foreign Affairs, 2004; Undersec., Min. of Nat. Defence, 2004–08; Ambassador and Perm. Rep. to UN, OSCE and other internat. orgns, Vienna, 2008–10; Ambassador and Perm. Rep. to OSCE, 2010; Ambassador and Chm., OSCE Perm. Council, 2011; Ambassador and Perm. Rep. to OSCE, 2012; Ambassador to Russian Fedn, 2012–14; Ambassador-at-Large, 2014–15, Dir, 2015–17, Transatlantic Cooperation and Security Policy Dept, Min. of Foreign Affairs. Scholar-in-residence, Inst. of Internat. Affairs, Rome, 1996. *Address:* Embassy of Lithuania, Lithuania House, 2 Bessborough Gardens, SW1V 2JF. *T:* (020) 7592 2840, *Fax:* (020) 7592 2864. *E:* amb.uk@urm.lt.

**NORLAND, Otto Realf;** Director, Northern Navigation International Ltd, USA, 1991–2006; London representative, Deutsche Schiffsbank (formerly Deutsche Schiffahrtsbank) AG, 1984–2000; Chairman, Otto Norland Ltd, 1984–2000; *b* 24 Feb. 1930; *s* of Realph I. O. Norland and Aasta S. Sæther; *m* 1955, Gerd Ellen Andenæs; two *d* (one *s* decd). *Educ:* Norwegian University College of Economics and Business Administration, Bergen. ACIB 1956, FCIB 1970. Hambros Bank Ltd, 1953–84, Dir, 1964–84, Exec. Dir, Banking Div., 1970–78. Director: Alcoa of Great Britain Ltd, 1968–84 (Chm., 1978–84); Banque Paribas Norge A/S, Oslo, 1986–88. Dir, Aluminium Fedn Ltd, 1979–84 (Pres., 1982). FRGS 1982. Freeman, City of London, 2005; Liveryman, Shipwrights' Co., 2006. *Recreations:* travel, stamps, books (polar explorations). *Clubs:* Naval and Military, Den Norske; Norske Selskab, Bibliofilklubben.

**NORMAN, (Alexander) Jesse;** MP (C) Hereford and South Herefordshire, since 2010; Financial Secretary to the Treasury, since 2019; *b* London, 23 June 1962; *s* of Sir Torquil (Patrick Alexander) Norman, *qv; m* 1992, Kate, *d* of Baron Bingham of Cornhill (Life Peer), KG, PC; two *s* one *d. Educ:* Eton Coll.; Merton Coll., Oxford (Open Exhibnr; BA Classics); University Coll. London (MPhil; PhD Philosophy 2003). Project Dir, Sabre Foundn, 1989–91; Manager, then Asst Dir, 1991–97, Dir, 1997, BZW; Teaching Fellow and Lectr, UCL, 1998–2003; Lectr, Birkbeck Coll., London, 2003; Exec. Dir, Policy Exchange, 2005–06. Hon. Res. Fellow, UCL, 2005–10. Director: Classical Opera Co., 2004–15;

Roundhouse, 2007–14. Trustee: Kindle Centre, 2007–10; Hay Fest., 2008–17. Parly Under-Sec. of State, BEIS, 2016–17; Parly Under-Sec. of State, 2017–18, Minister of State, 2018–19, DfT; Paymaster Gen., 2019. Chm., Select Cttee on Culture, Media and Sport, 2015–17. Patron: Herefordshire Riding for Disabled, 2009–; No 1 Ledbury Rd, 2010–; Music Pool, 2010–; Herefords Mind, 2011–. Pres., Hereford Hosp. Radio, 2011–; Vice President: Ross Horticl Soc., 2011–; Herefords and Glos Canal Trust, 2011–. *Publications*: The Achievement of Michael Oakeshott, 1992; Breaking the Habits of a Lifetime: Poland's first steps to the market, 1992; After Euclid: visual reasoning and the epistemology of diagrams, 2006; Compassionate Conservatism, 2006; Compassionate Economics, 2008; Churchill's Legacy, 2009; The Big Society, 2010; Edmund Burke: philosopher, politician, prophet, 2013; Adam Smith: what he thought, and why it matters, 2018; pamphlets, essays, journalism and academic articles. *Recreations*: music, especially jazz and opera, hill-walking, sports, cinema. *Address*: House of Commons, SW1A 0AA; Suite 2A, Penn House, Broad Street, Hereford HR4 9AP. *E*: jesse.norman.mp@parliament.uk. *Club*: Westfields Football.

**NORMAN, Rev. Canon Andrew;** Director of Ministry and Mission, Diocese of Leeds, since 2017; *b* Cuckfield, W Sussex, 26 Jan. 1963; *s* of John Warden Norman and Anna Louise Norman; *m* 1991, Amanda Cullen; two *d*. *Educ*: University Coll., Oxford (MA PPE); Ridley Hall, Cambridge and Virginia Theol Seminary (Cert. in Theol. and Ministry 1995); Selwyn Coll., Cambridge (MA Theol. 1999); Newcastle Poly. (Postgrad. Dip. in Mgt Studies; Intermediate Dip. in French); Univ. of Birmingham (MPhil Missiology 2007). Lay Asst, St Luke's-in-the-City, Liverpool, 1986; Thomas De La Rue and Co. Ltd: Mgt Trainee, 1986–87; Production Controller, 1987–88; Project Manager, 1989; Sales Admin. Manager, 1990–92; ordained deacon, 1995, priest, 1996; Asst Chaplain, St Michael's, Paris, 1995–99; Associate Vicar, Christ Church, Clifton, Bristol, 2000–02; Archbishop of Canterbury's Asst Sec. for Anglican Communion & Ecumenism, 2002–04, Principal Sec. for Internat., Ecumenical and Anglican Communion Affairs, 2005–08; Principal, Ridley Hall Theol Coll., Cambridge, 2009–17. Hon. Provincial Canon, Canterbury Cathedral, 2005–; Honorary Canon: Ely Cathedral, 2012–17; Wakefield Cathedral, 2017–. *Publications*: Anglican Mission en France, 1995; A Church Observed: being Anglican as times change, 2018. *Recreations*: current affairs, travel and related reading, savouring France. *Address*: Church House, 17–19 York Place, Leeds LS1 2EX. *T*: (0113) 353 0280. *E*: andrew.norman@leeds.anglican.org.

**NORMAN, Rear-Adm. Anthony Mansfeldt,** CB 1989; Bursar and Fellow, St Catharine's College, Cambridge, 1989–97; *b* 16 Dec. 1934; *s* of Cecil and Jean Norman; *m* 1961, Judith Pye; one *s* one *d*. *Educ*: Royal Naval Coll., Dartmouth. MA Cantab 1992. Graduate ndc. Various sea/shore appts, 1952–73; Staff of Dir Underwater Weapons, 1973–74; student ndc, 1974–75; CO HM Ships Argonaut and Mohawk, 1975–76; Fleet Anti-Submarine Warfare Officer, 1976–78; CO (Captain), HMS Broadsword, 1978–80; Asst Dir Naval Plans, MoD, 1980–83; Captain: 2nd Frigate Sqdn, HMS Broadsword, 1983–85; Sch. of Maritime Ops, HMS Dryad, 1985–86; Dir Gen., Naval Personal Services, MoD (Navy), 1986–89. *Recreations*: tennis, hill walking, travel. *Address*: c/o National Westminster Bank, 208 Piccadilly, W1A 2DG. *Club*: Army and Navy.

**NORMAN, Archibald John;** Chairman: Lazard London, 2013–19; Marks & Spencer plc, since 2017; *b* 1 May 1954; *s* of late Dr Archibald Percy Norman, MBE and Aleida Elisabeth Norman; *m* 1983, Vanessa Mary Peet; one *d*. *Educ*: Univ. of Minnesota; Emmanuel Coll., Cambridge (BA Hons Econs, MA); Harvard Business Sch. (MBA 1979). Citibank NA, 1975–77; McKinsey & Co. Inc., 1979–86, Principal 1984; Gp Finance Dir, Woolworth Holdings plc, later Kingfisher plc, 1986–91; Gp Chief Exec., 1991–96, Chm., 1996–99, Asda Group plc. Chairman: Chartwell Land plc, 1987–91; Energis plc, 2002–05; Aurigo Mgt, then Aurigo Mgt Partners LLP, 2006–10; HSS, 2007–12; ITV plc, 2010–16; Hobbycraft Ltd, 2013–18; non-exec. Chm., French plc, 1999–2001; non-exec. Dir, Target plc, 1988–91; Director: Coles, Australia, 2007–; Target Ltd, Australia, 2013–19; Member: British Railways Bd, 1992–94; Railtrack Gp Bd, 1994–2000; Advr, Wesfarmers, Australia, 2007–19. Sen. Advr, Lazard & Co., 2004–13. Member: DTI Deregulation Taskforce, 1993–97; Anglo-German Deregulation Taskforce, 1995. MP (C) Tunbridge Wells, 1997–2005. Chief Exec. and Dep. Chm., Cons. Party, 1998–99 (a Vice-Chm., 1997–98); Opposition front bench spokesman on the envmt, transport and the regions, 2000–01. Lead non-exec. Dir, BEIS, 2016–. Gov., NIESR, 1997–. Trustee, Cystic Fibrosis Trust, 2009–12. Fellow, Marketing Soc. Hon. Dr: Leeds Metropolitan, 1995; York, 2012. Yorkshire Business Man of the Year, 1995; NatWest Retailer of the Year, 1996; Special Award, Inst. for Turnaround, 2010. *Recreations*: farming, horses, tennis, opera, football.

**NORMAN, David Mark;** Chairman, Norlan Resources Ltd, since 1998; *b* 30 Jan. 1941; *s* of late Mark Richard Norman, CBE and of Helen Norman (*née* Bryan); *m* 1966, Diana Sheffield; one *s* three *d*. *Educ*: Eton Coll.; McGill Univ. (BA); Harvard Business Sch. (MBA). Norcros Ltd, 1967–77, Dir of Ops and Main Bd Dir, 1975–77; Russell Reynolds Associates Inc., 1977–82: Exec. Dir, 1977–78; Man. Dir, 1978–82; Chairman: Norman Resources Ltd, 1982–83; Norman Broadbent Internat. Ltd, 1983–98; Chm. and Chief Exec., 1987–97, non-exec. Chm., 1997–98, BNB Resources plc. Chm., Royal Ballet Sch., 2000–09; Gov., Royal Ballet, 1996–2009. Trustee, Royal Botanic Gardens, Kew, 2002–07. Pres., Tennis and Rackets Assoc., 2011– (Chm., 1982–97). *Recreations*: golf, tennis, rackets, classical music, opera, ballet. *Address*: Burkham House, Alton, Hants GU34 5RS. *T*: (01256) 381437. *E*: dmnorman2@aol.com. *Clubs*: Boodle's; Queen's (Dir, 2007–; Chm., 2011), All England Lawn Tennis.

**NORMAN, Duncan Charles,** MBE 2000; HM Diplomatic Service; Ambassador to Albania, since 2016; *b* Chertsey, 12 Oct. 1971; *s* of Roy Edwin Norman and Margaret Rosina Norman; *m* 1997, Kerry Jones; one *d*. *Educ*: Ryde Sch., IoW. Entered FCO, 1990; Vice Consul, Riyadh, 1994–97; Dep. Hd of Mission, Yerevan, 1998–2000; Desk Officer, then Hd, Gulf Sect., ME Dept, FCO, 2000–03; Hd, Governor's Office, BVI, 2004–06; Dep. High Comr, Dhaka, 2006–10; Hd, HR Services Unit, HR Dept, FCO, 2010–13; Hd, Afghanistan Unit, FCO, 2013–16. *Recreations*: reading, music, cycling. *Address*: c/o Foreign and Commonwealth Office, King Charles Street, SW1A 2AH. *T*: (020) 7270 3000.

**NORMAN, Rev. Dr Edward Robert Michael;** Canon Residentiary, 1995–2004, and Chancellor, 1999–2004, York Minster; *b* 22 Nov. 1938; *o s* of Ernest Edward Norman and Yvonne Louise Norman. *Educ*: Chatham House Sch.; Monoux Sch.; Selwyn Coll., Cambridge (MA, PhD, DD). FRHistS. Lincoln Theological Coll., 1965. Deacon, 1965; Priest, 1971. Asst Master, Beaconsfield Sec. Mod. Sch., Walthamstow, 1957–58; Fellow of Selwyn Coll., Cambridge, 1962–64; Fellow of Jesus Coll., Cambridge, 1964–71; Lectr in History, Univ. of Cambridge, 1965–88; Dean of Peterhouse, Cambridge, 1971–88 (Emeritus Fellow); Dean of Chapel, Christ Church Coll., Canterbury, 1988–95. Wilkinson Prof. of Church History, Wycliffe Coll., Univ. of Toronto, 1981–82; Associated Schol., Ethics and Public Policy Center, Washington, 1986–; Hon. Prof., Univ. of York, 1996–2004. NATO Res. Fellow, 1966–68. Asst Chaplain, Addenbrooke's Hosp., Cambridge, 1971–78. Hon. Curate, St Andrew-by-the-Wardrobe, and St James Garlickhythe, City of London, 2005–12. Ordinariate of Our Lady of Walsingham, 2012–. Lectures: Reith, 1978; Prideaux, 1980; Suntory-Toyota, LSE, 1984. Six Preacher in Canterbury Cathedral, 1984–90. FRSA. *Publications*: The Catholic Church and Ireland, 1965; The Conscience of the State in North America, 1968; Anti-Catholicism in Victorian England, 1968; The Early Development of Irish Society, 1969; A History of Modern Ireland, 1971; Church and Society in Modern England, 1976; Christianity and the World Order, 1979; Christianity in the Southern Hemisphere, 1981; The English Catholic Church in the Nineteenth Century, 1983; Roman Catholicism in England, 1985; The Victorian Christian Socialists, 1987; The House of God: church architecture, style and history, 1990; Entering the Darkness: Christianity and its modern substitutes, 1991; An Anglican Catechism, 2001; Out of the Depths, 2001; Secularisation, 2002; Anglican Difficulties, 2004; The Mercy of God's Humility, 2004; The Roman Catholic Church, 2007. *Recreation*: watching television. *Address*: Flat 7, Oakland Court, Kings Road, Herne Bay, Kent CT6 5RL. *T*: (01227) 742400.

**NORMAN, Ven. Garth;** Archdeacon of Bromley and Bexley (formerly Bromley), 1994–2003, now Emeritus; *b* 26 Nov. 1938; *s* of Harry and Freda Norman; *m* 1977, Jacqueline Elisabeth (*née* Yunge-Bateman); one *s*. *Educ*: Henry Mellish Grammar Sch., Nottingham; Univ. of Durham (BA Hons Theol., DipTh, MA); Univ. of East Anglia (MEd); Univ. of Cambridge (PGCE). Deacon 1963, priest 1964; Curate, St Anne's, Wandsworth, 1963–66; Team Vicar, Trunch, Norfolk, 1966–71; Rector of Gimingham, 1971–77; Team Rector of Trunch, 1977–83; RD, Repps, 1975–83; Principal, Chiltern Christian Trng Scheme, Dio. of Oxford, 1983–88; Dir of Training, Dio. of Rochester, 1988–94; Hon. Canon of Rochester Cathedral, 1991–2003. *Recreations*: walking, music, cycling. *Address*: 12 Scotsdowne Road, Trumpington, Cambridge CB2 9HU. *T*: (01223) 844303.

**NORMAN, George Alfred B.;** *see* Bathurst Norman.

**NORMAN, Geraldine Lucia,** OBE 2011; Advisor to Director, State Hermitage Museum, St Petersburg, since 2012 (UK Representative, 2001–12); Director, Hermitage Foundation UK, since 2014 (Secretary, then Chief Executive, Friends of The Hermitage, subseq. Hermitage Foundation UK, 2003–12); *b* 13 May 1940; *d* of Harold Hugh Keen and Catherine Eleanor Lyle Keen (*née* Cummins); *m* 1971, Frank Norman (*d* 1980). *Educ*: St Mary's Sch., Calne; St Anne's Coll., Oxford (MA). Teaching Asst, UCLA, 1961–62; Statistician, The Times, 1962–66; Econ. Writer, FAO, Rome, 1966–67; Sale Room Corresp., The Times, 1969–87; Art Market Corresp., The Independent, 1987–95. Exec. Dir, Hermitage Develt Trust, 1999–2001; Exec. Ed., Hermitage Mag., 2003–05. Medal in memory of 300 years of St Petersburg (Russian Fedn), 2005. News Reporter of Year, British Press Awards, 1976. *Publications*: (as Geraldine Keen) The Sale of Works of Art, 1971; Nineteenth Century Painters and Painting: a dictionary, 1977; (with Tom Keating and Frank Norman) The Fake's Progress, 1977; (as Florence Place) Mrs Harper's Niece, 1982; Biedermeier Painting, 1987; (with Natsuo Miyashita) Top Collectors of the World, 1993; The Hermitage: the biography of a great museum, 1997; (ed) Bob Hecht, by Bob Hecht, 2014; Dynastic Rule: Mikhail Piotrovsky and the Hermitage, 2016. *Recreations*: transcendental meditation, reading detective stories. *Address*: 5 Seaford Court, 220 Great Portland Street, W1W 5QR. *T*: (020) 7387 6067.

**NORMAN, Gregory John,** AO 1999 (AM 1987); golfer; Chairman and Chief Executive Officer, Great White Shark Enterprises LLC; *b* 10 Feb. 1955; *s* of M. Norman; *m* 1st, 1981, Laura Andrassy (marr. diss. 2007); one *s* one *d*; 2nd, 2008, Christine Marie Evert, *qv* (marr. diss. 2009). *Educ*: Townsville Grammar Sch.; High Sch., Aspley, Queensland. Professional golfer, 1976–; tournament wins include: Open, Turnberry, 1986; Open, Royal St George's, 1993; Australian Open, 1980, 1985, 1987, 1995, 1996; US PGA, 1993, 1994; Players' Championship, 1994; numerous awards and other wins in Australia, S Africa, USA. *Publications*: My Story, 1983; Shark Attack, 1988; Greg Norman's Better Golf, 1994; The Way of the Shark, 2006. *Address*: Great White Shark Enterprises LLC, 2041 Vista Parkway, Level 2, West Palm Beach, FL 33411, USA.

**NORMAN, (Herbert) John (La French),** FISOB; writer and organ consultant; *b* 15 Jan. 1932; *s* of late Herbert La French Norman, Hon. RCO, FRSA, and Hilda Caroline (*née* West); *m* 1956, Jill Frances Sharp; one *s* two *d*. *Educ*: Tollington Sch.; Imperial Coll., London (BSc 1953). ARCS 1953. Wm Hill & Son and Norman & Beard Ltd (organbuilders by appt to HM Queen), 1953–74; Dir, 1960–74; Man. Dir, 1970–74; Exec., IBM UK Ltd, 1974–90. Work on organs in cathedrals in Gloucester, Norwich, Lichfield, Southwell Minster, Chelmsford and Brisbane, Australia; also Bath Abbey and RCO. Organ Advr, Dio. London, 1975–; Organ Consultant to: Harrow Sch.; Lancing Coll.; Mill Hill Sch.; English and American Ch, Den Haag; Gibraltar Cathedral; Liberal Jewish Synagogue, St John's Wood; St Margaret's, Westminster; St Mary's Pro-cathedral, Dublin; St Helen's, Bishopsgate; St Mary's, Twickenham; Chapel of St Mary Undercroft, Houses of Parliament; Mullingar Cathedral, Ireland; St Lawrence, Whitchurch (Handel organ); Parish Churches of Oakham, Westbourne, Ashton-on-Ribble, Baldock, Bolton, Farnham, Coulsdon and Donaghadee (NI); Armenian Ch, Kensington; St Botolph, Aldersgate; Worcester Cathedral; St Mary-le-Bow, City of London; St Mary, Rye; St Peter, Notting Hill; St Swithun, Worcester; Edington Priory Ch; St John, Notting Hill; Holy Trinity, Bramley; Prichard-Jones Hall, Univ. of Bangor; Great Hall, QMUL; OBE Chapel, St Paul's Cathedral; St Michael, Sutton Court, Chiswick; West Wittering Parish Ch; St Mary, Finedon; St Boniface Anglican Ch, Antwerp, Belgium; Liverpool Anglican Cathedral; All Saints', Fulham; St Paul, Oldham; St Thomas, Salisbury; St Dunstan, Bellingham; St John, Watford; St Mary, Ewell; St Mark, Surbiton; St Peter and St Paul, Fressingfield. Founding Editor: Musical Instrument Technol., 1969–2002; The Organbuilder, 1983–2000; In Sight, 1991–95; Columnist, Organists' Rev., 1980–. Member: St Albans Diocesan Synod, 1980–86; Organs Cttee, Council for Care of Churches, 1987–2001; London DAC for Care of Churches, 1989–; Cathedrals Fabric Commn for England, 1991–2001. Chm., British Inst. of Organ Studies, 2006–11 (Hon. Life Mem., 2017); Past Pres., Inst. of Musical Instrument Technol. Freeman, City of London; Liveryman, Musicians' Co., 1972–. Hon. FIMIT. *Publications*: (with Herbert Norman) The Organ Today, 1966, 2nd edn 1980; The Organs of Britain, 1984; (with Jim Berrow) Sounds Good, 2002; The Box of Whistles, 2007; Organ Works, 2019. *Recreations*: writing, music, architecture, travel. *Address*: 15 Baxendale, Whetstone, N20 0EG. *T*: (020) 8445 0801. *W*: www.jnorman.me.uk.

**NORMAN, Prof. Jane Elizabeth,** MD; Professor of Maternal and Fetal Health, and Director, Tommy's Centre for Maternal and Fetal Health Research, since 2008, and Vice Principal, People and Culture, since 2015, University of Edinburgh; Hon. Consultant Obstetrician and Gynaecologist, Edinburgh Royal Infirmary, since 2008; *b* England, 1963. *Educ*: Edinburgh Univ. (MB ChB 1986; MD 1992). MRCOG 1992. Trng in obstetrics and gynaecol., Univ. of Edinburgh, 1986–92; University of Glasgow: Clin. Lectr, 1993; Personal Chair, 2006–07; Regius Prof. of Obstetrics and Gynaecol., 2007–08. FMedSci 2012; FRSE 2017. *Publications*: (with D. Hart) Gynaecology Illustrated, 5th edn, 2000; (ed with I. Greer) Preterm Labour: managing the risk in clinical practice, 2005; chapters in: Gynaecology by Ten Teachers, 17th edn 2000 and 18th edn 2006; Preterm Birth, 2004; Preterm Birth: Mechanisms, Mediators, 2007; Dewhurst's Textbook of Obstetrics and Gynaecology, 2012; contrib. articles to jls incl. BMJ, PLOS Medicine, Lancet, British Jl Obstetrics and Gynaecol., Obstetrics and Gynaecol., Jl Reproductive Immunol., Amer. Jl Obstetrics and Gynaecol., Jl Clin. Endocrinol. and Metabolism. *Address*: MRC Centre for Reproductive Health, Queen's Medical Research Institute, 47 Little France Crescent, Edinburgh EH16 4TJ. *T*: (0131) 242 6623. *E*: jane.norman@ed.ac.uk.

**NORMAN, Jesse**; see Norman, (Alexander) Jesse.

**NORMAN, Jessye**; soprano, concert and opera singer; b Augusta, Ga, USA, 15 Sept. 1945; d of late Silas Norman Sr and Janie King Norman. Educ: Howard Univ., Washington, DC (BM cum laude). Peabody Conservatory, 1967; Univ. of Michigan, 1967–68 (MMus). Operatic début, Deutsche Oper, Berlin, 1969; La Scala, Milan, 1972; Royal Opera House, Covent Garden, 1972; NY Metropolitan Opera, 1983; American début, Hollywood Bowl, 1972; Lincoln Centre, NYC, 1973. Tours include North and South America, Europe, Middle East, Australia, Israel, Japan. Many international festivals, including Aix-en-Provence, Aldeburgh, Berlin, Edinburgh, Flanders, Helsinki, Lucerne, Salzburg, Tanglewood, Spoleto, Hollywood, Ravinia. Hon. Fellow: Newnham Coll., Cambridge, 1989; Jesus Coll., Cambridge, 1989. Hon. DMus: Howard Univ., 1982; Univ. of the South, Sewanee, 1984; Boston Conservatory, 1984; Univ. of Michigan and Brandeis Univ., Mass, 1987; Harvard Univ., 1988; Cambridge, 1989; Hon. DHL Amer. Univ. of Paris, 1989. Hon. RAM 1987. Musician of the Year, Musical America, 1982; prizes include: Grand Prix du Disque (Acad. du Disque Français), 1973, 1976, 1977, 1982, 1984; Grand Prix du Disque (Acad. Charles Cros), 1983; Deutscher Schallplattenpreis, 1975, 1981; Cigale d'Or, Aix-en-Provence Fest., 1977; IRCAM record award, 1982; Grammy, 1984, 1988. Commandeur de l'Ordre des Arts et des Lettres, France, 1984. Publications: Stand Up Straight and Sing! (memoir), 2014.

**NORMAN, John**; see Norman, H. J. La F.

**NORMAN, Jonathan Charles A.**; see Ashley-Norman.

**NORMAN, Prof. Kenneth Roy**, FBA 1985; Professor of Indian Studies, University of Cambridge, 1990–92, Emeritus Professor 1992; b 21 July 1925; s of Clement and Peggy Norman; m 1953, Pamela Raymont; one s one d. Educ: Taunton School; Downing College, Cambridge (MA 1954). Fellow and Tutor, Downing College, Cambridge, 1952–64; Lectr in Indian Studies (Prakrit), 1955–78, Reader, 1978–90, Univ. of Cambridge. Foreign Mem., Royal Danish Acad. of Sciences and Letters, 1983. Publications: Elders' Verses I (Theragāthā), 1969; Elders' Verses II (Therīgāthā), 1971; (trans.) Jain Cosmology, 1981; Pāli Literature, 1983; The Group of Discourses (Sutta-nipāta), Vol. I, 1984, Vol. II, 1992, 2nd edn 2001; Collected Papers: Vol. I, 1990, Vol. II, 1991, Vol. III, 1992, Vol. IV, 1993, Vol. V, 1994, Vol. VI, 1996, Vol. VII, 2001, Vol. VIII, 2007; Poems of Early Buddhist Monks, 1997; The Word of the Doctrine (Dhammapada), 1997; A Philological Approach to Buddhism, 1997; (with W. Pruitt) The Pātimokkha, 2001; (with W. Pruitt) Kaṅkhāvitaraṇī, 2003; (ed) Pāli Tipitakam Concordance, Vol. II 4–9, 1963–73; (ed) Critical Pāli Dictionary Vol. II 11–17, 1981–90. Recreations: pottery, reading. Address: 43 Blenheim Close, Shepreth, Royston, Herts SG8 6PT. T: (01763) 262900.

**NORMAN, Lisa Marie**; see Harker, L. M.

**NORMAN, Sir Nigel (James)**, 4th Bt cr 1915 of Honeyhanger, Shottermill, co. Surrey; b 5 Feb. 1956; er s of Sir Mark Annesley Norman, 3rd Bt and Joanna Camilla (née Kilgour); S father, 2013; m 1st, 1985, Joanna Naylor-Leyland (marr. diss 1989); 2nd, 1994, Mrs Juliet Clare Louise Marriott (née Baxendale); three s one d. Heir: s Antony Richard St Valery Norman, b 10 March 1995.

**NORMAN, Philip Frank William**; author and journalist; b 13 April 1943; s of Clive and Irene Norman; m 1990, Sue Summers; one d. Educ: Ryde Sch., Isle of Wight. Trainee reporter, Hunts Post, Huntingdon, 1961–64; Reporter: Cambridge News, 1965; Northern Despatch, 1965; Northern Echo, 1965–66; Feature Writer, Sunday Times Mag., 1966–75; Atticus Columnist and Feature Writer, Sunday Times, 1976–82. Writer of musicals: This is Elvis: Viva Las Vegas, 2006 (2 national tours), revived 2018; Laughter in the Rain: the Neil Sedaka Story, 2010. Publications: Slip on a Fat Lady, 1970; Plumridge, 1971; Wild Thing, 1972; The Skaters' Waltz, 1979 (one of 20 Best Young British Novelists, 1983); Shout!: the true story of the Beatles, 1981, 4th edn 2003; The Road Goes on For Ever, 1982; The Stones, 1984, 6th edn 2012; Tilt the Hourglass and Begin Again, 1985; Your Walrus Hurt the One You Love, 1985; Awful Moments, 1986; Pieces of Hate, 1987; The Life and Good Times of the Rolling Stones, 1989; Words of Love, 1989; Days in the Life: John Lennon remembered, 1990; The Age of Parody, 1990; Elton, 1991, 3rd edn, as Sir Elton, 2000, reissued 2019; Everyone's Gone to the Moon, 1995; Buddy: the biography, 1996; Babycham Night, 2003; John Lennon: the life, 2008; Mick Jagger, 2012; Paul McCartney: the biography, 2016; Slowhand: the life and music of Eric Clapton, 2018; contrib. Times, Guardian, Daily Mail, New York Times, Vanity Fair, Playboy, Cosmopolitan, GQ, Spectator, New Statesman, Rolling Stone etc. Recreations: literature, cinema, learning French. Address: c/o Peters, Fraser and Dunlop, 55 New Oxford Street, WC1A 1BS. E: philip@philipnorman.com. Clubs: Groucho, Ivy.

**NORMAN, Sir Ronald**, Kt 1995; OBE 1987; DL; CEng; Chairman, Priority Sites, 1997–2001; b 29 April 1937; s of Leonard William Norman and Elsie Louise Norman (née Cooke); m 1st, 1961, Jennifer Mansfield (marr. diss. 1972); two s one d; 2nd, 1973, Joyce Lyon. Educ: Dulwich Coll.; King's Coll., London (BSc Eng.). CE; CEng, MICE 1966. Man. Dir, then Chm., Cecil M. Yuill Ltd, Developers, Hartlepool, 1965–86; Chm., R. Norman Ltd, Developers, Durham, 1986–93. Chm., Teesside Develt Corp., 1987–98. Pres., Cleveland Community Foundn, 1998–; Vice-Pres., Trincomalee Trust, 1998–. Pres., Durham Co. Scouts Assoc., 2006–. DL Cleveland, 1996. Hon. Freeman, Hartlepool, 2014. Publications: The Odd Man Out in the Alps, 2008. Recreations: mountain climbing (has climbed all the Munros in Scotland), book collecting, restoring antique books. Address: Sparrow Hall, Dalton-Piercy, Cleveland TS27 3HY. T: (01429) 273857.

**NORMAN, Russell**; food writer, broadcaster, restaurateur; Founder, Polpo Ltd, since 2009; b London, 9 Dec. 1965; s of Ernest Clifford Norman and Carole Julia Norman (née Giddy, now Beadle); m 2004, Jules McNally; one s two d. Educ: Heathland Sch., Hounslow; Sunderland Poly. (BA English); Inst. of Educn, Univ. of London (PGCE English and Drama). Maitre d', Joe Allen Restaurant, 1990–99; Hd of Drama, Bentley Wood High Sch., 1995–98; General Manager: Circus Restaurant, 1999–2002; Zuma Restaurant, 2002–06; Ops Dir, Caprice Hldgs Ltd, 2006–09. Presenter, BBC TV series, The Restaurant Man, 2014. Columnist, Esquire Mag., 2015–. Publications: Polpo: a Venetian cookbook (of sorts), 2012; Spuntino: comfort food (New York style), 2015; Venice: four seasons of home cooking, 2018. Recreations: travelling to Venice, growing radicchio, puntarelle and cicoria in my garden in Kent, riding, playing Scrabble, cooking, and generally mucking around. Address: c/o Cathryn Summerhayes, Curtis Brown, 28–29 Haymarket, SW1Y 4SP. T: (020) 7393 4282. E: cathryn.summerhayes@curtisbrown.co.uk. Club: Groucho.

**NORMAN, Susan Elizabeth, (Mrs J. C. Sheridan)**, OBE 2014; Chief Executive and Registrar, United Kingdom Central Council for Nursing, Midwifery and Health Visiting, 1995–2002; b 9 Aug. 1946; d of late Dr J. M. Norman and Betty Norman (née Colyer); m 1983, John Christopher Sheridan. Educ: St Nicholas Sch., Fleet, Hants; Dartington Hall, Devon; St Thomas' Hosp. (RGN); Bedford Coll., London (RNT); South Bank Univ. (BEd Hons). Student nurse, St Thomas' Hosp., 1965–69; Dist Nurse, RBK&C, 1969–71; Staff Nurse, Royal Marsden Hosp., 1972; Nursing Officer (Dist Nursing), Kensington and Chelsea, 1972–73; Staff Nurse, Montreal Gen. Hosp., 1974–75; Tutor Student, London Univ., 1975–77; Tutor and Sen. Tutor, Nightingale Sch., 1977–87; Principal Nursing Officer (Asst Sec.), DoH, London and Leeds, 1988–95. Vis. Prof., London South Bank (formerly S Bank) Univ., 2002–. President: Nat. Assoc. of Theatre Nurses, 2002–04; Nightingale Fellowship, 2007–16; Chair: in touch Support, 2006–10; Florence Nightingale Mus. Trust, 2012–16. FRSA 1997. Hon. DSc Plymouth, 2002. Publications: Nursing Practice and Health Care, 1989, 5th edn 2008. Recreations: music (singing and opera), walking, UK and France, eating out.

**NORMAN, Sir Torquil (Patrick Alexander)**, Kt 2007; CBE 2002; Chairman, Roundhouse Trust, 1996–2007; b 1933; s of Sir Henry Nigel St Valery Norman, 2nd Bt, CBE and Patricia Moyra Norman; m 1961, Lady (Elizabeth) Anne (d 2005), d of Alexander Victor Edward Paulet Montagu; three s two d. Educ: Eton; Trinity Coll., Cambridge (BA 1957). Served RAF. Investment banker, NY; Man. Dir, Berwick Timpo, toy co., until 1979; former Chm., Bluebird Toys. Set up Norman Trust; bought Roundhouse, 1996, re-launched as arts venue, 2006. Publications: Kick the Tyres, Light the Fires, 2012.
See also A. J. Norman.

**NORMANBY, 5th Marquis of**, cr 1838; **Constantine Edmund Walter Phipps**; Baron Mulgrave (Ire.) 1767; Baron Mulgrave (GB) 1794; Earl of Mulgrave and Viscount Normanby 1812; b 24 Feb. 1954; e s of 4th Marquis of Normanby KG, CBE and Hon. Grania Guinness (OBE 2000), d of 1st Baron Moyne; S father, 1994; one d by Ms Sophie McCormick; m 1990, Mrs Nicola St Aubyn (see Marchioness of Normanby); two s one d. Educ: Eton; Worcester Coll., Oxford; City Univ. Publications: as Constantine Phipps: Careful with the Sharks, 1985; Among the Thin Ghosts, 1989; What You Want, 2014. Heir: s Hon. John Samuel Constantine Phipps, b 26 Nov. 1994. Address: Mulgrave Castle, Whitby, N Yorks YO21 3RJ. Club: Garrick.

**NORMANBY, Marchioness of; Nicola Phipps**; journalist, author; b 15 Feb. 1960; d of late Milton Shulman and of Drusilla Beyfus, qv; m 1st, 1987, Edward St Aubyn (marr. diss. 1990); 2nd, 1990, Earl of Mulgrave (see Marquis of Normanby); two s one d. Educ: St Paul's Girls' Sch.; Corpus Christi Coll., Oxford (BA Hons). Trustee: Nat. Gall., 2004–12; Garden Mus., Lambeth, 2013– (Curator, exhibn, Fashion and Gardens, 2014. Publications: (as Nicola Shulman): A Rage for Rock Gardening, 2002, 3rd edn 2004; Graven with Diamonds: the many lives of Thomas Wyatt, 2011, 3rd edn 2014; Spring/Summer - Autumn/Winter: fashion and gardens, 2014. Recreations: singing, Latin, gardening. Address: Mulgrave Castle, Whitby, N Yorks YO21 3RJ.
See also A. Shulman.

**NORMAND, Andrew Christie**, CB 2001; SSC; FSAScot; Sheriff at Glasgow, 2006–15; b 7 Feb. 1948; m 1975, Barbara Jean Smith; two d. Educ: George Watson's Coll., Edinburgh; Univ. of Edinburgh (MA 1968; LLB 1970); Queen's Univ., Kingston, Ont (LLM 1972). Admitted solicitor, 1974. Crown Office: Legal Asst, Edinburgh, 1974–76, 1977; seconded to Scottish Law Commn, 1976; Sen. Legal Asst, Edinburgh, 1977–78, Perth, 1978–81; Asst Solicitor, 1981–87; Procurator Fiscal, Airdrie, 1987–88; Dep. Crown Agent for Scotland, 1988–90; Regl Procurator Fiscal, Glasgow, 1990–96; Crown Agent for Scotland, 1996–2003; an all-Scotland Sheriff, 2003–06.

**NORMANTON, 7th Earl of**, cr 1806; **James Shaun Christian Welbore Ellis Agar**; Baron Mendip, 1794; Baron Somerton, 1795; Viscount Somerton, 1800; Baron Somerton (UK), 1873; b 7 Sept. 1982; s of 6th Earl of Normanton and Victoria Susan (née Beard); S father, 2019; m 2012, Lady Lucy Caroline Alexander, yr d of Earl Alexander of Tunis, qv; two s one d. Educ: Harrow Sch.; Santa Clara Univ., Calif; RAC Cirencester. Heir: s Viscount Somerton, qv. Address: Somerley, Ringwood, Hants BH24 3PL.

**NORMINGTON, Sir David (John)**, GCB 2011 (KCB 2005; CB 2000); First Civil Service Commissioner and Commissioner for Public Appointments, 2011–16; b 18 Oct. 1951; s of late Ronald Normington and of Kathleen Normington (née Towler); m 1985, Winifred Anne Charlotte Harris, qv. Educ: Bradford Grammar Sch.; Corpus Christi College, Oxford (BA Hons Mod. Hist.). Department of Employment, subseq. Department for Education and Employment: joined 1973; Private Sec. to Perm. Sec., 1976–77; Principal Private Sec. to Sec. of State for Employment, 1984–85; Employment Service Regional Dir for London and SE Region, 1987–89; Hd of Strategy and Employment Policy Div., 1990–92; Dir of Personnel and Develt, 1992–95, of Personnel and Support Services, 1995–97; Dir Gen., Strategy, Internat. and Analytical Services, 1997–98; Dir Gen. for Schs, 1998–2001; Permanent Secretary: DfEE, then DfES, 2001–05; Home Office, 2006–10. Mem. Council, Univ. of Warwick, 2011– (Chm., 2017–). Trustee, NSPCC, 2012–18 (Vice Chm., 2013–18); Gov., Royal Ballet, 2016– (Chm., Birmingham Royal Ballet, 2018–). Mem., Council of Reference, Westminster Abbey, 2014–. Recreations: gardening, ballet, walking, cricket.

**NORMINGTON, Winifred Anne Charlotte, (Lady Normington)**; see Harris, W. A. C.

**NORREY, Philip Julian**, PhD; Chief Executive, Devon County Council, since 2006; b 9 July 1963; s of Harold and Dorothy Norrey; m 2003, Stephanie Ann Sloman. Educ: Colchester Royal Grammar Sch.; Univ. of Bristol (BA Hons Hist. 1984; PhD Hist. 1988). Audit Examiner, District Audit, 1989; graduate trainee, Somerset CC, 1990; Asst Dir of Educn, N Somerset DC, 1996–98; Dep. Dir, 1998–2003, Dir, 2003–06, of Educn, Devon CC. Chm., Assoc. of County Chief Execs, 2011–12. Hon. Fellow, Univ. of Exeter, 2003. Publications: contrib. Parliamentary Jl. Recreations: cycling, food and wine, historical research, Burnley Football Club, railways, classical music, 70s and 80s TV drama. Address: c/o Devon County Council, County Hall, Topsham Road, Exeter EX2 4QD. T: (01392) 383201. E: phil.norrey@devon.gov.uk.

**NORREYS, Lord; Henry Mark Willoughby Bertie**; b 6 June 1958; s and heir of the Earl of Lindsey (14th) and Abingdon (9th), qv; m 1989, Lucinda, d of Christopher Moorsom; two s. Educ: Eton; Univ. of Edinburgh. Kt of Honour and Devotion, SMO Malta, 1995; Kt of Justice, Constantinian Order of St George, 1998; Kt, Order of St Maurice and St Lazarus, 1999. Heir: s Hon. Willoughby Henry Constantine St Maur Bertie, b 15 Jan. 1996. Address: The Old Dairy, Gilmilnscroft, Sorn, Mauchline, Ayrshire KA5 6ND. Clubs: Pratt's; Puffin's (Edinburgh).

**NORRIE, family name of Baron Norrie**.

**NORRIE, 2nd Baron** cr 1957; **George Willoughby Moke Norrie**; b 27 April 1936; s of 1st Baron Norrie, GCMG, GCVO, CB, DSO, MC, and Jocelyn Helen (d 1938), d of late R. H. Gosling; S father, 1977; m 1st, 1964, Celia Marguerite, JP (marr. diss. 1997), d of John Pelham Mann, MC; one s two d; 2nd, 1997, Mrs Pamela Ann McCaffry, d of Sir Arthur Ralph Wilmot, 7th Bt. Educ: Eton College; RMA Sandhurst. Commissioned 11th Hussars (PAO), 1956; ADC to C-in-C Middle East Comd, 1960–61; GSO 3 (Int.) 4th Guards Brigade, 1967–69; retired, 1970. Underwriting Mem. of Lloyd's, 1977–97. Director: Fairfield Nurseries (Hermitage) Ltd, 1976–89; International Garden Centre (British Gp) Ltd, 1984–86; Conservation Practice Ltd, 1989–91; Hilliers (Fairfield) Ltd, 1989–97; Advisor to: S Grundon (Waste) Ltd, 1991–2001; CH2M Hill Ltd (London), 1994–96. Non-exec. Dir, Philip T. English Internat. Financial Services Ltd, 2007–12. Mem., EC Cttee, Sub Cttee F (Environment), H of L, 1988–92. President: The Conservation

Volunteers (formerly British Trust for Conservation Volunteers), 1987–2014; Internat. Cultural Exchange, 1988–2000; The Salespeople's Charity (formerly Commercial Travellers Benevolent Instn), 1992–; Royal British Legion (Newbury Branch), 1971–96; Nat. Kidney Fedn, 1994–2001; Vice President: Tree Council, 1990–2001; Council for Nat. Parks, 1990–. Member, Council: Winston Churchill Meml Trust, 1993–2010; Royal Scottish Forestry Soc., 2012–17. Patron: Age Resource, 1991–2004; Faure-Alderson Romanian Appeal, 1993–2001; Janki Foundn, 1997–; Galloway Nat. Park Assoc., 2017–; UK Patron, RLSS, 1994–2018 (Mem., Commonwealth Council, 1999–2018). Gov., Dunstan Park Sch., Thatcham, 1989–94. Mem., British Soc. of Dowsers, 1999–. Sponsored: Swimming and Water Safety Bill, 1993 (enacted under statutory order, 1994); Nat. Parks Bill, 1993 (incorp. in Envmt Act, 1995). Freeman, City of London, 1999. Green Ribbon Political Award for services to the envmt, H of L, 1993. *Publications:* Portals of Discovery (memoir), 2016. *Recreations:* fishing, golf. *Heir: s* Hon. Mark Willoughby John Norrie [*b* 31 March 1972; *m* 1st, 1998, Carol (marr. diss. 2012), *e d* of Michael Stockdale; two *s*; 2nd, 2014, Penelope Menzel; one *s*]. *Address:* Holehouse, Penpont, Thornhill, Dumfriesshire DG3 4AP. *T:* (01848) 600243. *Clubs:* Cavalry and Guards, MCC.

**NORRIE, Prof. Alan William,** PhD; FBA 2011; Professor of Law, University of Warwick, since 2009 (Head, School of Law, 2011–15); *b* Arbroath, Scotland, 14 Nov. 1953; *s of* Tom Norrie and Gertrude Norrie; *m* 1978, Gwendoline Chapman; two *s. Educ:* Bishop's Stortford Coll.; Methodist Coll., Belfast; Univ. of Edinburgh (LLB 1975); Univ. of Sheffield (MA Criminol. 1976); Univ. of Dundee (PhD 1985). Lectr, Univ. of Dundee, 1977–86; Lectr, 1987–91, Sen. Lectr, 1991–94, Univ. of Warwick; Drapers' Prof. of Law, QMW, 1994–97; Edmund-Davies Prof. of Criminal Law and Criminal Justice, KCL, 1997–2009. Leverhulme Major Res. Fellow, 2015–18. *Publications:* Law, Ideology and Punishment, 1991; Crime, Reason and History, 1993, 3rd edn 2014; Punishment, Responsibility and Justice, 2000; Law and the Beautiful Soul, 2005; Dialectic and Difference, 2010; Justice and the Slaughter Bench, 2017. *Recreations:* reading, music, film, theatre, art, football, gardening. *Address:* School of Law, University of Warwick, Coventry CV4 7AL. *T:* (024) 7615 1107. *E:* A.W.Norrie@warwick.ac.uk.

**NORRIE, Her Honour Marian Farrow, (Mrs W. G. Walker);** a Circuit Judge, 1986–2012; *b* 25 April 1940; *d of* Arthur and Edith Jackson; *m* 1st, 1964; two *d*; 2nd, 1983, (William) Guy Walker, CBE (*d* 2007); one step *s* two step *d. Educ:* Manchester High Sch. for Girls; Nottingham Univ. (LLB). Admitted Solicitor of Supreme Court, 1965; a Recorder, 1979–86. Consultant, Norrie, Bowler & Wrigley, Solicitors, Sheffield, 1983–86 (Sen. Partner, 1968–83). Member: Parole Bd, 1983–85; Appts Commn, Press Council, 1985.

**NORRINGTON, Humphrey Thomas,** OBE 2001; Vice Chairman, Barclays Bank, 1991–93; *b* 8 May 1936; *s of* Sir Arthur Norrington and Edith Joyce, *d of* William Moberly Carver; *m* 1963, Frances Guenn Bateson (*d* 2018); two *s* two *d. Educ:* Dragon School, Oxford; Winchester; Worcester College, Oxford (MA). Barclays Bank: joined, 1960; general management, 1978–87; Dir, 1985–93; Exec Dir, Overseas Ops, 1987–91. Chm., Exec. Cttee, British Bankers' Assoc., 1990–91. Chm., Southwark Cathedral Develt Trust, 1986–93; Director: City Arts Trust, 1988–93; Mildmay Mission Hosp., 1992–2007 (Vice Pres., 2007–); World Vision UK, 1991–2005. Member, Archbishops' Commission: on Rural Areas, 1988–90; on Orgn of the C of E, 1994–95. Chm., Premier Christian Media Trust, 1999–2011; Trustee: Lambeth Trust (formerly Lambeth Fund), 1991–2014; Stewards' Trust, 2007–. Hon. Treas., RSPB, 1996–2003; Hon. Treas., 1997–2004, Vice Pres., 2005–, RCM. *Recreations:* music, countryside. *Address:* Hill House, Frithsden Copse, Berkhamsted, Herts HP4 2RQ. *T:* (01442) 871855. *Club:* Oxford and Cambridge.

*See also* Sir R. A. C. Norrington.

**NORRINGTON, Sir Roger (Arthur Carver),** Kt 1997; CBE 1990 (OBE 1980); Chief Conductor: Zurich Chamber Orchestra, 2011–16, now Conductor Laureate; Camerata Academica Salzburg, 1997–2006, now Conductor Laureate; *b* 16 March 1934; *s of* late Sir Arthur Norrington and Edith Joyce, *d of* William Moberly Carver; *m* 1st, 1964, Susan Elizabeth McLean May (marr. diss. 1982); one *s* one *d*; 2nd, 1986, Karalyn Mary Lawrence; one *s. Educ:* Dragon Sch., Oxford; Westminster; Clare Coll., Cambridge (BA; Hon. Fellow, 1991); Royal Coll. of Music. Freelance singer, 1962–72. Principal Conductor: Kent Opera, 1966–84; Bournemouth Sinfonietta, 1985–89; Music Director: Orch. of St Luke's, NY, 1990–94; Schütz Choir of London, 1962–82; London Classical Players, 1978–98; Chief Conductor, Radio Sinfonie Orchester Stuttgart, 1998–2011. Prince Consort Prof., RCM, 1997. Guest conducts many British, European and American orchestras, appears at Covent Garden, Coliseum, Proms and festivals; broadcasts regularly at home and abroad. Débuts: British, 1962; BBC Radio, 1964; TV 1967; Germany, Austria, Denmark, Finland, 1966; Portugal, 1970; Italy, 1971; France and Belgium, 1972; USA, 1974; Holland, 1975; Switzerland, 1976. Many gramophone recordings. Hon. RAM 1988. FRCM 1992. DUniv York, 1991; Hon. DMus Kent, 1994. Cavaliere, Orden al Merito (Italy), 1981; Ehrenkreuz, 1st cl. (Austria), 1999; Bundesdienstkreuz (Germany), 2012. *Publications:* occasional articles in various musical journals. *Recreations:* gardening, reading, walking.

*See also* H. T. Norrington.

**NORRIS, Brig. His Honour (Alaric) Philip,** OBE 1982; a Circuit Judge, 1995–2008; *b* 20 Sept. 1942; *yr s of* late Charles Henry Norris and Maud Frances Norris (*née* Neild); *m* 1967, Pamela Margaret Parker; three *s. Educ:* Sir William Turner's Sch., Coatham, Redcar; Queens' Coll., Cambridge (MA); Dip. in Law and Amer. Studies, Univ. of Virginia, USA, 1979. Admitted Solicitor, 1968; commnd Army Legal Services, 1970; served MoD, SHAPE, BAOR, Berlin, NEARELF, NI, UKLF/Land Comd, USA and Geneva; retired, in rank of Brig., 1995. Asst Recorder, 1988–92, Recorder of the Crown Court, 1992–95. Liveryman, Fruiterers' Co., 2005–. *Recreations:* a bit of all sorts, but not golf. *Address:* c/o Woolwich Crown Court, 2 Belmarsh Road, SE28 0EY.

**NORRIS, Hon. Sir Alastair Hubert,** Kt 2007; FCIArb; **Hon. Mr Justice Norris;** a Judge of the High Court, Chancery Division, since 2007; Vice-Chancellor, County Palatine of Leicester, 2013–17; *b* 17 Dec. 1950; *s of* Hubert John Norris and Margaret Murray (*née* Savage); *m* 1982, Patricia Lesley Rachel White; one *s* two *d. Educ:* Pate's Grammar Sch., Cheltenham; St John's Coll., Cambridge (MA). FCIArb 1991. Called to the Bar, Lincoln's Inn, 1973, Bencher, 2005; QC 1997; an Asst Recorder, 1998–2000; a Recorder, 2000–01; a Circuit Judge, 2001–07. *Recreation:* sailing. *Address:* Royal Courts of Justice, 7 Rolls Building, Fetter Lane, EC4A 1NL. *Clubs:* Gloucestershire County Cricket; Marlow Sailing, Teifi Boating.

**NORRIS, Alexander James Jordan;** MP (Lab Co-op) Nottingham North, since 2017; *b* Manchester, 4 Feb. 1984; *s of* Peter and Carole Norris; *m* 2017, Emma Foody. *Educ:* Manchester Grammar Sch.; Univ. of Nottingham (BA Hons Hist. and Politics). Area Organiser, UNISON, 2015–17. Mem. (Lab), Nottingham CC, 2011–17 (Mem. Cabinet, 2011–17). *Recreations:* season ticket holder at Manchester City Football Club, runner, border collie owner. *Address:* House of Commons, SW1A 0AA. *T:* (020) 7219 3899. *E:* alex.norris.mp@parliament.uk.

**NORRIS, Dan;** *b* 28 Jan. 1960; *s of* David Norris and June Norris (*née* Allen). *Educ:* Chipping Sodbury Comprehensive Sch.; Univ. of Sussex (MSW). Researcher and author. Member (Lab): Bristol CC, 1989–92, 1995–97; Avon CC, 1994–96. Contested (Lab): Northavon, 1987; Wansdyke, 1992. MP (Lab) Wansdyke, 1997–2010; contested (Lab) NE Somerset, 2010. Member: Lab. Leadership Campaign Team, 1998–2000; Lab. Party Campaign Team, 2000–01. An Asst Govt Whip, 2001–03; PPS to Sec. of State for NI, 2005–07, to Sec. of State for Foreign and Commonwealth Affairs, 2007–09; Parly Under-Sec. of State, DEFRA, 2009–10. Founder, Kidscape SW, 2000. Hon. Fellow, Sch. of Cultural and Community Studies, Univ. of Sussex, 1989. Mem., USDAW. Ed., Liberal Demolition (qly jl), 2000. *Publications:* Violence Against Social Workers: the implications for practice, 1990; contribs to learned jls and newspaper articles. *Recreation:* photography. *E:* dan.norris@me.com.

**NORRIS, David O.;** *see* Owen Norris.

**NORRIS, Geoffrey;** Chief Music Critic, Daily Telegraph, 1995–2009; *b* 19 Sept. 1947; *s* of Leslie and Vera Norris. *Educ:* Univ. of Durham (BA); Inst. Teatra, Muzyki i Kinematografii, Leningrad; Univ. of Liverpool. ARCM 1967. Lectr in Music History, RNCM, 1975–77; Commning Editor, Scholarly Music Books, OUP, 1977–83; Music Critic: The Times, 1983; Daily Telegraph, 1983–95. Prof., Rachmaninoff Music Inst., Tambov, 2005–. Mem., Critics' Circle. *Publications:* Rakhmaninov, 1976, 2nd edn, Rachmaninoff, 1993; (with Robert Threlfall) A Catalogue of the Compositions of S. Rachmaninoff, 1982; contribs to New Grove Dictionary of Music and Musicians, Oxford Companion to Music. *Recreation:* Italy. *Club:* Arts.

**NORRIS, John Robert,** CBE 1991; PhD, DSc; Director, Group Research, Cadbury Schweppes Ltd, 1979–90; *b* 4 March 1932; *s of* Albert Norris and Winifred May Perry; *m* 1st, 1956, Barbara Jean Pinder (*d* 1994); one *s* one *d* (and two *s* decd); 2nd, 1998, Pauline Mary Corrigan. *Educ:* Depts of Bacteriology and Agriculture, Univ. of Leeds (BSc 1st Cl. Hons 1954, PhD 1957, DSc 1987). Lectr in Bacteriology, Univ. of Glasgow, 1957–63; Microbiologist, Shell Research Ltd, 1963–73 (Dir, Borden Microbiol Lab., 1970–73); Dir, Meat Res. Inst., ARC, 1973–79. Editor, Methods in Microbiology, 1969–92. *Publications:* papers in microbiol jls. *Recreations:* walking, wood carving, Yoga, photography. *Address:* Langlands, 10 Langley Road, Bingley, West Yorks BD16 4AB. *T:* (01274) 406973.

**NORRIS, Prof. Kenneth John,** DPhil; Director, Science, Zoological Society of London, since 2014; *b* Birmingham, 17 Nov. 1963; *s of* John Norris and Barbara Norris; *m* 1989, Tracy Evans; one *s* one *d. Educ:* University Coll. of Wales, Aberystwyth (BSc Envmtl Biol. 1985); St Cross Coll., Oxford (DPhil 1989). Postdoctoral Researcher, Univ. of Oxford, 1989–92; Res. Biologist, RSPB, 1993–97; University of Reading: Lectr, 1997–2003; Reader in Applied Ecol., 2003–04; Prof. of Agro-ecol., 2005–14; Dir, Centre for Agri-Envmtl Res., 2005–14. *Publications:* over 100 scientific papers. *Recreations:* cycling, reading, rock music. *Address:* Institute of Zoology, Zoological Society of London, Regent's Park, NW1 4RY. *T:* (020) 7449 6244. *E:* ken.norris@ioz.ac.uk.

**NORRIS, Margaret Jane;** Founder, Chief Executive Officer and Artistic Director, The Big House, since 2013; *b* Birmingham, 4 Dec. 1958; *d of* Brian Norris and Lois Norris (*née* Powell); two *d* by James Duke. *Educ:* Hermann Francke Schule, Halle, GDR; Bolton Co. Grammar Sch.; Roehampton Inst. of Higher Educn (BHum Hons 1980). Tech. crew, Royal Exchange Th., Manchester, 1980–82; TV and theatre actress, 1982–2012; *theatre* includes: appearances at Library Th., Manchester, Oldham Coliseum, Royal Exchange Th., Manchester, Salisbury Playhouse, W Yorks Playhouse, Bolton Octagon, Live Th., Newcastle, Theatre Royal, Windsor and Soho Th.; Aspern Papers, Theatre Royal, Haymarket, 1984; Court in the Act, 1986; *television* includes: Coronation St, 1996–97; director: Daisy Pulls It Off, Teachers, Duke's Playhouse, Lancaster, 1991–92; Josephine, Battersea Arts Centre, 1993 and nat. tour, 1994; The Bodies, Live Th., Newcastle, 1995; Bad Girls: The Musical, W Yorks Playhouse, 2006, transf. Garrick, 2007; Any Which Way, Only Connect Th. and Pentonville Prison, 2008; Badman Christmas (performed by serving prisoners in Wormwood Scrubs), 2009; His Teeth, Only Connect Th., 2011; Family Matters, Only Connect Th., 2012; productions directed at The Big House: Phoenix, Baby/Lon, The Realness, Politrix, Electric, Knife Edge (transf. Royal Court), 2016; Phoenix Rising (performed in car park underneath Smithfield Meat Market), 2017; Bullet Tongue, 2018; Bullet Tongue Reloaded, 2019; producer, film, Mrs Ratcliffe's Revolution, 2007; playwright: Long Division - the Israel/Palestine Conflict, 1988; Ladies Night (revisions and adaptation), 1989; Hold Tight (musical), 1991; Hot Stuff (musical), 1993; Ferry Cross the Mersey (musical), 1996. Artistic Dir, Only Connect, 2007–12. *Recreation:* finding secret hiding places. *Address:* The Big House, 151 Englefield Road, N1 3LH. *T:* 07939 539708. *E:* tbhartisticdirector@gmail.com.

**NORRIS, Philip;** *see* Norris, Brig. His Honour A. P.

**NORRIS, Rufus;** theatre director; Director, National Theatre, since 2015 (Associate Director, 2012–15); *b* 16 Jan. 1965; *s of* Malcolm and Lauriston Norris; *m* 1994, Tanya Ronder; two *s. Educ:* North Bromsgrove High Sch.; Kidderminster Coll. of Further Educn; RADA (Dip.). Actor, 1989–92; director, 1992–; Artistic Dir, Arts Threshold, 1992–95; Asst Dir, Royal Court Th., 1996–97; Associate Dir, Young Vic Th., 2002–. Director: Afore Night Come, 2001, Sleeping Beauty, 2002, Young Vic; Festen, Lyric, 2004; Tintin, Barbican, 2005, Playhouse, 2007; Cabaret, Lyric, 2006; Vernon God Little, Young Vic, 2007; The Country Girl, Apollo, 2010; Don Giovanni, ENO, 2010; Dr Dee, Manchester Internat. Fest., 2011, ENO, 2012; Feast, Young Vic, 2013; National Theatre: Death and the King's Horseman, 2009; London Road, 2011; Table, The Amen Corner, 2013; Behind the Beautiful Forevers, 2014; Everyman, wonder.land, 2015; The Threepenny Opera, 2016; Mosquitoes, My Country: A Work in Progress, 2017; Macbeth, 2018; Small Island, 2019; films: King Bastard, 2009; Broken, 2009; London Road, 2015. Arts Foundn Fellow, 2001. *Address:* c/o Nick Marston, Curtis Brown, Haymarket House, 28–29 Haymarket, SW1Y 4SP.

**NORRIS, Stephen Anthony;** film producer and media consultant; *b* 14 June 1959; *s of* Roy Anthony Norris and Brenda Winifred Norris; *m* 1986, Susan Jennifer Boyle; two *s* one *d. Educ:* St Nicholas Grammar Sch. Warner Bros Productions, London, 1979–82; European Production, Warner Bros, LA, 1982–84; Dir of Ops, Enigma Productions, 1984–86; Sen. Vice Pres., Columbia Pictures, LA, 1986–88; Man. Dir, Enigma Productions Ltd, 1989–97; British Film Comr, 1998–2006; Man. Dir, Film, Framestore (formerly Framestore CFC), 2006–10; Chief Exec., Apollo Prodns, 2010–; Exec. Prod., Pinewood Films, 2011–. Dir, British Film and TV Producers Assoc., 1989–91; Vice Chm., Producers Alliance for Cinema and TV, 1991–93; Council Member: British Screen Adv. Council, 1998–2006; BAFTA, 1999–2005; Chm., UK Screen, 2010–. Associate Producer/Producer: Memphis Belle, 1990; Being Human, 1993; War of the Buttons, 1994; Le Confessional (Best Film, Canadian Acad., 1995); My Life So Far, 1998; Producer/Executive Producer: Triangle, 2009; Harry Brown, 2009; Me and Orson Welles, 2009; Heartless, 2010; A Fantastic Fear of Everything, 2012; Last Passenger, Dom Hemingway, Powder Room, 2013; Belle, The Riot Club, 2014; Robot Overlords, Kill Your Friends, 2015. *Recreations:* cinema, Rugby, my family, golf. *Address:* 160 Great Portland Street, W1W 5QA.

**NORRIS, Steven John,** FRICS, FCILT, FCIHT; Chairman: Soho Estates Ltd, since 2011; London Resort Company Holdings, since 2014; Driver Group plc, since 2015; This Land, since 2018; Partner, Norris McDonough LLP, since 2013; *b* 24 May 1945; *s* of John Francis Birkett Norris and Eileen Winifred (*née* Walsh); *m* 1969, Peta Veronica Cecil-Gibson (marr. diss.); two *s*; *m* 2000, Emma Courtney; one *s*. *Educ:* Liverpool Institute; Worcester College, Oxford. MA. Private company posts, 1967–90; Dir-Gen., Road Haulage Assoc., 1997–2000; Sen. Partner, Park Place Communications, 2001–13; Chairman: Jarvis plc, 2003–10; AMT-Sybex Gp Ltd, 2005–12; Saferoad BLG, 2007–13; Internet Corp., 2008–17; Base Communications, 2011–18. Sen. Advr, BNP Paribas Real Estate UK, 2017–19 (Chm., 2013–17). Non-executive Director: initiate Consulting Ltd, 2003–14; Optare, 2014–; Sen. Ind. Dir, ITIS Hldgs Ltd, 1998–2011. Board Member: Transport for London, 2000–01 and 2008–12; London Develt Agency, 2008–12; Chairman: Council, Nat. Infrastructure Planning Assoc., 2013–; Highways UK, 2015–. Mem., Berks CC, 1977–85. Mem., Berks AHA, 1979–82; Vice-Chm., W Berks District HA, 1982–85. Contested (C) Oxford E, 1987. MP (C): Oxford E, 1983–87; Epping Forest, Dec. 1988–1997. PPS to Hon. William Waldegrave, MP, Minister of State, DoE, 1985–87, to Rt Hon. Nicholas Ridley, Sec. of State for Trade and Industry, 1990, to Rt Hon. Kenneth Baker, Home Sec., 1991–92; Parly Under-Sec. of State, Dept of Transport, 1992–96. Vice Chm., Cons. Party, 2000–01. Chairman: Grant Maintained Schools Trust, 1988–89; Crime Concern Trust, 1988–91; Alcohol and Drug Addiction Prevention and Treatment, 1990–92; Prince Michael Road Safety Awards Scheme, 1997–2004; Urology Foundn, 2004–14; London Action Trust, 2006–11; East Side Young Leaders Acad., 2006–11. Vice-Pres., RNID/Action on Hearing Loss, 2015–. FCILT (FCIT 1997); FCIHT (FIHT 1997); FRICS 2013; Hon. CompICE 1996; Hon. Fellow, Assoc. for Project Mgt (Hon. Fellow, Assoc. of Project Managers, 2012). Freeman, City of London, 1985; Liveryman: Coachmakers' and Coach Harness Makers' Co., 1985–; Watermen and Lightermen's Co., 1997–; Co. of Carmen, 1998–. Hon. LLD E London, 2015. *Publications:* Changing Trains, 1996. *Recreations:* reading, politics. *Address:* Norris McDonough LLP, 5–8 The Sanctuary, Westminster, SW1P 3JS. *Clubs:* Brooks's, Royal Automobile, Garrick, Arts.

**NORRIS, William John;** QC 1997; *b* 3 Oct. 1951; *s* of late Dr John Phillips Norris, QGM and Dr Joan Hattersley Norris; *m* 1987, Lesley Jacqueline Osborne; two *d*. *Educ:* Sherborne Sch.; New Coll., Oxford (MA). Called to the Bar, Middle Temple, 1974 (Benefactors' Scholarship). Chm., Personal Injury Bar Assoc., 2006–08. Mem., panel of chairmen, Sport Resolutions UK, 2005–; Legal Mem., Nat. Anti-Doping Panel, 2011–; Mem., panel of chairmen, Judicial Panels: British Horseracing Authy, 2018–; FA, 2018–; IAAF, 2019–. Trustee, Injured Jockeys Fund, 2006–. Gen. Ed., Kemp and Kemp, The Quantum of Damages, 2004–. *Publications:* Perhaps It Will Brighten Up Later, 2004; 100 Years—Still Counting, 2011. *Recreations:* sailing (former Class Captain, XOD), shooting, racing, writing. *Address:* 39 Essex Chambers, 81 Chancery Lane, WC2A 1DD. *T:* (020) 7832 1111. *Clubs:* Royal Cruising, Royal Lymington Yacht.

**NORRISS, Air Marshal Sir Peter (Coulson),** KBE 2000; CB 1996; AFC 1977; defence consultant, retired; *b* 22 April 1944; *s* of Arthur Kenworthy Norriss and Marjorie Evelyn Norriss; *m* 1971, Lesley Jean McColl; two *s* one *d*. *Educ:* Beverley Grammar Sch.; Magdalene Coll., Cambridge (MA 1970); Harvard Business Sch. Joined RAF, 1966; Flying Instructor RAF Coll., Cranwell, 1969–71; Buccaneer Pilot, 1972–76; RAF Staff Coll., 1977; on Staff of RAF Minister, 1977–79; OC, No 16 Sqn, 1980–83; Head, RAF Presentation Team, 1984; Station Comdr, RAF Marham, 1985–87; ADC to the Queen, 1985–87; Higher Comd and Staff Course, 1988; on Staff, Operational Requirements, 1988–91; Dir Gen. Aircraft 2, 1991–95; Dir Gen. Air Systems 1, MoD (PE), 1995–98; Controller Aircraft, 1996–2000, and Dep. Chief of Defence Procurement (Ops), 1998–2000, MoD (PE, subseq. Defence Procurement Agency). Non-executive Director: DERA, 1998–2000; Turbomeca UK Ltd (formerly Microturbo Ltd), 2002–08 (Chm., 2002–07); Chemring Gp plc, 2004–13. Member, Advisory Board: Tickets for Troops, 2010–; Services Sound and Vision Corp., 2019–. Pres., RAeS, 2003–04. *Recreations:* golf, ski-ing. *Club:* Royal Air Force.

**NORTH,** family name of Earl of Guilford.

**NORTH, Lord; Frederick Edward George North;** *b* 24 June 2002; *s* and *heir* of Earl of Guilford, *qv*.

**NORTH, Alan;** *see* North, R. A.

**NORTH, Air Marshal Sir Barry Mark, (Air Marshal Sir Baz),** KCB 2015; OBE 2002 (MBE 1996); FRAeS; Deputy Commander for Capability and Personnel, Headquarters Air Command, 2013–16; President, Royal Air Forces Association, since 2017; *b* Clatterbridge, Cheshire, 13 Sept. 1959; *s* of Robert and Doreen North; *m* 1985, Fiona Jane Walker; two *d*. *Educ:* Carre's Grammar Sch., Sleaford, Lincs; Trent Poly., Nottingham (HND Business Studies); King's Coll. London (MA Defence Studies). ADC to CDS, 1988–91; Officer Commanding: 78 Sqdn, 1991; Special Forces Flight 7 Sqdn, 1992–96; Personal Staff Officer to AOC 1 Gp, 1996–98; Wing Comdr, Ops, HQ Strike Comd, 1998–99; OC 33 Sqdn, 1999–2002; Dep. Asst COS, J1/5/6 and Hd, Jt Helicopter Comd, 2002–04; Station Comdr, RAF Aldergrove and Sen. RAF Officer, NI, 2004–06; Air Component Comdr and AOC 83 Expeditionary Air Gp, 2006; Dir, Air Resources and Plans, MoD, 2007–09; AOC, 22 Gp, RAF and COS Trng, HQ Air Comd, 2009–10; Asst Chief of the Air Staff, 2010–13. Non-exec. Dir, CAA, 2010–13. Trustee, Nuffield Trust for Armed Forces, 2017–; Vice-Patron, Gallantry Medalists' League, 2018–; Vice-Pres., Officers' Assoc., 2018–. Mem., Adv. Bd, Nottingham Business Sch., 2017–. Hon. Air Cdre, 2503 (Co. Lincoln) Sqdn, RAuxAF, 2016–. Liveryman, Gold and Silver Wyre Drawers' Co., 2003–; Upper Freeman, 2010, Liveryman, 2015, Hon. Co. of Air Pilots (formerly GAPAN). QCVS 2006. FRAeS 2014. Alumnus of the Year, Nottingham Trent Univ., 2011; Hon. Dr Nottingham Trent, 2018. *Recreations:* frightening the rough of the occasional golf course, pottering in the garden. *Club:* Royal Air Force.

**NORTH, Sir Jeremy William Francis,** 3rd Bt *cr* 1920; *b* 5 May 1965; *s* of Sir (William) Jonathan (Frederick) North, 2nd Bt and Sara Virginia North (*née* Hardman); *S* father, 2018, but his name does not appear on the Official Roll of the Baronetage; *m* 1986, Lucy, *d* of G. A. van der Meulen; two *s* two *d*. *Heir: s* Jocelyn Montagu Dudley North, *b* 23 March 1989.

**NORTH, Lloyd Wayne Frazer; His Honour Judge North;** a Circuit Judge, since 2018; *b* Chester, 3 Nov. 1964; *s* of Christopher and Sylvia North; *m* 1993, Janet Breese; one *d*. *Educ:* St Mary's Coll., Colwyn Bay; Queen Mary Coll., Univ. of London (LLB Hons 1986); Coll. of Law, Chester. Admitted as solicitor, 1989; Sparlings Solicitors: staff solicitor, 1989–91; Salaried Partner, 1992–94; Equity Partner, 1994–2014; Solicitor Advocate (Civil), 2005; a Dist Judge, 2014–18. *Recreations:* aikido martial arts instructor (3rd Dan), theatre, dog walking, weight training. *Address:* Norwich Combined Court Centre, The Law Courts, Bishopsgate, Norwich NR3 1UR.

**NORTH, Sir Peter (Machin),** Kt 1998; KBE 1989; DCL; FBA 1990; Principal of Jesus College, Oxford, 1984–2005; Pro-Vice-Chancellor, University of Oxford, 1988–93, and 1997–2005 (Vice-Chancellor, 1993–97); *b* Nottingham, 30 Aug. 1936; *o s* of late Geoffrey Machin North and Freda Brunt (*née* Smith); *m* 1960, Stephanie Mary (OBE 2000; JP, DL), *e d* of T. L. Chadwick; two *s* one *d*. *Educ:* Humberstone Foundn Sch., Cleethorpes; Oakham Sch.; Keble Coll., Oxford (BA 1959, BCL 1960, MA 1963, DCL 1976; Hon. Fellow, 1984). National Service, Royal Leics Regt, 2nd Lieut, 1954–56. Teaching Associate, Northwestern Univ. Sch. of Law, Chicago, 1960–61; Lecturer: University Coll. of Wales, Aberystwyth, 1961–63; Univ. of Nottingham, 1963–65; Tutor in Law, 1965–76, Fellow, 1965–84, Keble Coll., Oxford. Mem., Hebdomadal Council, 1985–99. A Law Comr, 1976–84; called to the Bar, Inner Temple, 1992 (Hon. Bencher, 1987). Vis. Professor: Univ. of Auckland, 1969; Univ. of BC, 1975–76; Dir of Studies, Hague Acad. of Internat. Law, 1970 (general course in private internat. law, 1990); Lectures: Hague Acad. of Internat. Law, 1980; Horace Read Meml, Dalhousie Univ., 1980; Colston, Bristol Univ., 1984; Frances Moran Meml, TCD, 1984; Philip James, Leeds Univ., 1985; James Smart, 1988; MacDermott, QUB, 1991; Graveson, KCL, 1992; Douglas McK. Brown, Univ. of BC, 1998; F. A. Mann, 2000. Chairman: Road Traffic Law Review, 1985–88; Conciliation Project Adv. Cttee, 1985–88; Management Cttee, Oxford CAB, 1985–88; Appeal Cttee, Assoc. of Certified Accountants, 1990–93 (Mem., 1987–93); Ind. Review of Parades and Marches in NI, 1996–97; Standing Adv. Cttee on Private Internat. Law, 1998–2009; Ind. Cttee for Supervision of Standards of Telephone Inf. Services, 1999–2006; Review of Drink and Drug Driving Law, 2009–10; Member: Lord Chancellor's Adv. Cttee on Legal Educn, 1973–75; Social Scis and the Law Cttee, ESRC (formerly SSRC), 1982–85; Govt and Law Cttee, ESRC, 1985–87; Adv. Develt Council, Nat. Fisheries Mus., 1996–2000; Sen. Salaries Review Body, 2004–12; Accountancy Investigation and Disciplinary Bd Tribunal, 2005–13. Council Member: British Inst. of Internat. and Comparative Law, 1986–2005 (Chm., Private Internat. Law Section, Adv. Bd, 1986–92); Univ. of Reading, 1986–89; British Acad., 1996–99. Oxford University Press: Delegate, 1993–2008; Chm., Finance Cttee, 2005–08 (Mem., 1993–2005); Vice-Chm., Visitors, Ashmolean Mus., Oxford, 2006–07 (Visitor, 2004–07). Pres., Oxford Inst. of Legal Practice, 1999–2010; Mem., Inst. of Internat. Law, 1985; Mem., Internat. Acad. of Comparative Law, 1990. Hon. QC 1993. Hon. Fellow: UCNW, Bangor, 1988; Trinity Coll., Carmarthen, 1995; Univ. of Wales, Aberystwyth, 1996; Jesus Coll., Oxford, 2005. Hon. LLD: Reading, 1992; Nottingham, 1996; Aberdeen, 1997; New Brunswick, 2002; DHL Arizona, 2005. Mem., Editorial Cttee, British Yearbook of Internat. Law, 1983–; General Editor, Oxford Jl of Legal Studies, 1987–92. *Publications:* Cheshire, Private International Law, 8th edn 1970 to 14th edn as Cheshire and North's Private International Law (cons. ed.), 2008; (ed jtly) Chitty on Contracts, 23rd edn 1968 to 26th edn 1989; Occupiers' Liability, 1971, 2nd edn 2014; The Modern Law of Animals, 1972; Private International Law of Matrimonial Causes, 1977; Contract Conflicts, 1982; (with J. H. C. Morris) Cases and Materials on Private International Law, 1984; Private International Law Problems in Common Law Jurisdictions, 1993; Essays in Private International Law, 1993; Civil Liability for Animals, 2012; articles and notes in legal jls. *Recreations:* children, grandchildren, gardening, cricket. *Address:* 34 Woodstock Close, Oxford OX2 8DB. *T:* (01865) 557011; 5 Coln Manor, Coln St Aldwyns, Cirencester, Glos GL7 5AD. *T:* (01285) 750400.

**NORTH, Rt Rev. Philip John;** *see* Burnley, Bishop Suffragan of.

**NORTH, Prof. (Richard) Alan,** PhD; FRS 1995; Professor, University of Manchester, 2004–13, now Emeritus (Vice-President, 2004–11); *b* 20 May 1944; *s* of Douglas Abram North and Constance (*née* Ramsden); *m* 1st, 1969, Jean Valerie Aitken Hall (marr. diss. 1982); two *d*; 2nd, 1991, Annmarie Surprenant; two *s*. *Educ:* Univ. of Aberdeen (BSc; MB, ChB 1969; PhD 1973). Asst and Associate Prof., Dept of Pharmacol., Loyola Univ., Chicago, 1975–81; Massachusetts Institute of Technology: Associate Prof., Dept of Nutrition and Food Sci., 1981–84; Prof. of Neuropharmacol., Dept of Applied Biol Scis, 1984–86; Sen. Scientist, Vollum Inst., Oregon Health Scis Univ., Portland, 1987–93; Prin. Scientist, Geneva Biomedical Res. Inst., Glaxo Wellcome R&D (formerly Glaxo Inst. for Molecular Biol.), 1993–98; Prof. of Molecular Physiol., Inst. of Molecular Physiol., Univ. of Sheffield, 1998–2004; Dean, Faculty of Life Scis, 2004–08, Dean, Faculty of Med. and Human Scis, 2006–11, Univ. of Manchester; Dir, Manchester Academic Health Sci. Centre, 2008–10. Visiting Professor: Flinders Univ., 1983; Bogomoletz Inst., 1984; Frankfurt Univ., 1988; Univ. of Melbourne, 1991. Gaddum Lecture, British Pharmacol Soc., 1988. Mem., MRC, 2001–06. Pres., Physiol Soc., 2003–06. Ed.-in-Chief, British Jl of Pharmacol., 2000–04. FMedSci 2004. *Publications:* original res. papers in jls of physiol., pharmacol., neuroscience and biochem. *Recreation:* mountaineering. *Address:* University of Manchester, Michael Smith Building, Oxford Road, Manchester M13 9PT. *T:* (0161) 275 1499, *Fax:* (0161) 275 1498. *E:* r.a.north@manchester.ac.uk.

**NORTH, Richard Conway;** Chairman, Majid Al Futtaim Properties LLC, 2016–17 (non-executive Director, 2009; Deputy Chairman, 2014–16); *b* 20 Jan. 1950; *s* of John and Megan North; *m* 1978, Lindsay Jean Buchanan; three *d*. *Educ:* Marlborough Coll.; Sidney Sussex Coll., Cambridge (BA 1971; MA 1974). FCA 1976; FCT 1993. Coopers & Lybrand, 1971–91: qualified as accountant, 1974; seconded to: NY, 1976–78; Midland Bank, 1981–82; Partner, 1983–91; Group Finance Director: Burton Gp plc, 1991–94; Bass, subseq. Six Continents, plc, 1994–2003; CEO, Hotel Div., Six Continents, subseq. InterContinental Hotels Gp plc, 2002–04; Chairman: Britvic Soft Drinks, 1996–2004; Woolworths Gp plc, 2007–08 (non-exec. Dir, 2006–07). Non-executive Director: ASDA Gp plc, 1997–99; Bristol Hotel Company Inc., 1997–98; Leeds United plc, 1998–2002; Felcor Lodging Trust Inc., 1998–2004; LogicaCMG (formerly Logica) plc, 2002–04; Majid Al Futtaim Gp LLC, 2006–09; Mecom plc, 2007–09. Chm., Payments Council, 2010–14. Member: Cttee, 100 Gp, 1996–2000; Exec. Cttee, World Travel and Tourism Council, 2004. Mem. Senate, ICAEW, 1991–2000. *Recreations:* golf, soccer, rock 'n' roll, history. *Clubs:* Athenæum, Hurlingham; Huntercombe Golf; Berkshire Golf.

**NORTH, Prof. Robert, (Robert North Dodson);** freelance choreographer; Professor and Director, Ballett Akademie, Munich, Germany, 2007–10; Ballet Director, Krefeld and Mönchengladbach Theatres, Germany, since 2007; *b* 1 June 1945; *s* of Charles Dodson and Elizabeth Thompson; *m* 1st, 1978, Janet Smith (marr. diss.); 2nd, 1999, Sheri Cook. *Educ:* Pierrepont Sch. (A levels in Maths, Physics and Art); Central Sch. of Art; Royal Ballet Sch. Dancer and choreographer, London Contemporary Dance Co., 1966–81 (Jt Artistic Dir, 1980–81); seasons with Martha Graham Dance Co., 1967 and 1968; Teacher of Modern Dance, Royal Ballet Sch., 1979–81; Artistic Dir, Ballet Rambert, 1981–86; freelance work, Europe and USA, 1986–90; Ballet Dir, Teatro Regio, Turin, 1990–91; Artistic Dir, Gothenburg Ballet, 1991–96; Dir, Corps de Ballet, Arena di Verona, 1997–99; Artistic Dir, Scottish Ballet, 1999–2002. Has choreographed ballets for dance companies throughout the world, including: Royal Ballet; English National Ballet; Dance Theatre of Harlem; Royal Danish Ballet; San Francisco Ballet; Oakland Ballet; Finnish Nat. Ballet; Batsheva; Janet Smith and Dancers; La Scala, Milan; Rome Opera; Staatsoper Dresden; Györ Ballett; *ballets choreographed* include: Troy Game; Death and the Maiden; The Annunciation; A Stranger I Came; Running Figures; Pribaoutki; Colour Moves; Entre dos Aguas; full-length ballets: Carmen; Elvira Madigan; Romeo & Juliet; Living in America; Prince Rama and the Demons; Life, Love & Death; The Russian Story; The Snowman; The Cradle Will Rock; Eva; Ragazzi Selvaggi; Orlando; Carmina Burana; Bach; Wie Ihr's Wollt; Tschaikowskys Träume; Casanova; Fado/Bolero; Lost Children; Pictures from the New World; Pinocchio; Rhapsody; Petrushka; Offenbach; Souvenirs aus West und Ost; also choreography for films, television (incl. Lonely Town, Lonely Street, and For My Daughter (Golden Prague Award, 1983)), theatre, musicals and opera (Carmen, Royal Albert Hall). *Address:* c/o D. Scrimgeour, Apartado 905, 41080 Sevilla, Spain.

**NORTHAM, Jeremy Philip;** actor; *b* 1 Dec. 1961; *s* of late Prof. John and Rachel Northam; *m* 2005, Elizabeth L. Moro (marr. diss.). *Educ:* King's Coll. Sch., Cambridge; Bristol Grammar Sch.; Bedford Coll., London (BA Hons English); Bristol Old Vic Theatre Sch. *Theatre* includes: National Theatre, 1989–91: Hamlet, School for Scandal, The Voysey Inheritance (Olivier Award for Outstanding Newcomer); Royal Shakespeare Co., 1992–94: Loves Labour's Lost, The Country Wife, The Gift of the Gorgon; Old Times, Donmar Warehouse, 2004; Hay Fever, Noël Coward Th., 2012; *television* includes: Journey's End, Piece of Cake, 1988; Martin of Lewis, 2003; The Tudors, 2007; Fiona's Story, 2008; Miami Medical (USA), 2010; White Heat, 2012; New Worlds, 2014; The Crown, 2016, 2017; *films* include: Wuthering Heights, Soft Top Hard Shoulder, 1992; Carrington, The Net, Voices, 1995; Emma, 1996; Mimic, Amistad, 1997; The Misadventures of Margaret, 1998; Gloria, The Winslow Boy, An Ideal Husband, Happy Texas, 1999; The Golden Bowl, 2000; Enigma, Gosford Park, 2001; Possession, 2002; Cypher, The Singing Detective, 2003; The Statement, Stroke of Genius, 2004; Guy X, 2005; A Cock and Bull Story, 2006; Dean Spanley, 2008; Glorious 39, 2009; Creation, 2009; Eye in the Sky, The Man Who Knew Infinity, Our Kind of Traitor, 2016. Best Actor, Evening Standard Awards, 2000; Best Film Actor, Variety Club, 2000; Best British Actor, Critics Circle Award, 2000. *Address:* c/o Curtis Brown, 5th Floor, Haymarket House, 28–29 Haymarket, SW1Y 4SP.

**NORTHAMPTON, 7th Marquess of,** *cr* 1812; **Spencer Douglas David Compton;** DL; Earl of Northampton, 1618; Earl Compton, Baron Wilmington, 1812; *b* 2 April 1946; *s* of 6th Marquess of Northampton, DSO, and Virginia (*d* 1997), *d* of Lt-Col David Heaton, DSO; *S* father, 1978; *m* 1st, 1967, Henriette Luisa Maria (marr. diss. 1973), *o d* of late Baron Bentinck; one *s* one *d*; 2nd, 1974, Annette Marie (marr. diss. 1977), *er d* of C. A. R. Smallwood; 3rd, 1977, Hon. Mrs Rosemary Dawson-Damer (marr. diss. 1983); one *d*; 4th, 1985, Hon. Mrs Michael Pearson (marr. diss. 1988); one *d*; 5th, 1990, Pamela Martina Raphaela Kyprios (marr. diss. 2013); 6th, 2013, Tracy Goodman. *Educ:* Eton. DL Northants 1979. *Recreation:* freemasonry (Pro Grand Master, United Grand Lodge of England, 2001–09). *Heir: s* Earl Compton, *qv. Address:* Compton Wynyates, Tysoe, Warwicks CV35 0UD. *Club:* Turf.

**NORTHAMPTON, Bishop of, (RC),** since 2005; **Rt Rev. Peter John Haworth Doyle;** *b* 3 May 1944; *s* of John Robert Doyle and Alice Gertrude Doyle (*née* Haworth). *Educ:* St Ignatius Coll., Stamford Hill; Allen Hall Seminary. Ordained priest, 1968; Asst Priest, Portsmouth and Windsor, 1968–75; Adminr, St John's Cathedral, Portsmouth, 1975–87; Parish Priest: St Joseph's, Maidenhead, 1987–91; St Peter's, Winchester, 1991–2005. Canon, Portsmouth Cathedral, 1983–2005; VG, Dio. Portsmouth, (RC), 2001–05. Mem., Old Brotherhood, 1994–2005. *Recreations:* Rugby (played for Windsor and Portsmouth RFCs, now a spectator), golf, ski-ing. *Address:* Bishop's House, Marriott Street, Northampton NN2 6AW. *T:* (01604) 715635, *Fax:* (01604) 792186. *E:* admin@northamptondiocese.com.

**NORTHAMPTON, Archdeacon of;** *see* Ormston, Ven. R. J.

**NORTHBOURNE, 6th Baron** *cr* 1884; **Charles Walter Henri James;** *b* 14 June 1960; *s* of 5th Baron Northbourne and Aliki Louise Hélène Marie Sygne (*née* Claudel); *S* father, 2019; *m* 1987, Catherine Lucy, *d* of Ralph Burrows; two *s* one *d*. *Heir: s* Hon. Henry Christopher William James, *b* 3 Dec. 1988.

**NORTHBROOK, 6th Baron** *cr* 1866; **Francis Thomas Baring;** Bt 1793; Trustee, Fortune Forum, since 2006; *b* 21 Feb. 1954; *s* of 5th Baron Northbrook and of Rowena Margaret, 2nd *d* of Brig.-Gen. Sir William Manning, GCMG, KBE, CB; *S* father, 1990; *m* 1st, 1987, Amelia Sarah Elizabeth (marr. diss. 2006), *er d* of Dr Reginald Taylor; three *d*; 2nd, 2013, Charlotte Lee, *d* of Thomas W. Pike. *Educ:* Winchester Coll.; Bristol Univ. (BA Hons 1976). FRGS 1986. Trainee accountant, Dixon Wilson & Co., 1976–80; Baring Brothers and Co. Ltd, 1981–89; Sen. Investment Man., Taylor Young Investment Management Ltd, 1990–93; Investment Man., Smith and Williamson Securities, 1993–95; Dir, Mars Asset Mgt Ltd, 1996–2006. Chm., Dido Films Ltd, 2002–07. Elected Mem., H of L, 1999; an Opposition Whip, 1999–2000. Trustee: Khetri Trust, India, 1987–; Winchester Medical Trust, 1991–96. Mem. Adv. Bd, Iman Foundn, 2016–. Mem., Gunmakers' Co., 2011–. *Heir:* (to baronetcy) *kinsman* Peter Baring [*b* 12 Sept. 1939; *m* 1973, Rose, *d* of George Nigel Adams; one *s*]. *Address:* House of Lords, SW1A 0PW. *Clubs:* White's, Pratt's, Beefsteak.

**NORTHCOTE,** family name of **Earl of Iddesleigh**.

**NORTHERN, Richard James,** MBE 1982; HM Diplomatic Service, retired; consultant, since 2011; Director, RN4 Consultancy Ltd, since 2011; *b* 2 Nov. 1954; *s* of late James Wilfred Northern and Margaret Northern (*née* Lammie); *m* 1981, Linda Denise Gadd; two *s* one *d*. *Educ:* Bedford Sch.; Jesus Coll., Cambridge (BA 1976; MA 1980). Joined HM Diplomatic Service, 1976: FCO, 1976–78; MECAS, Beirut and London, 1978–80; Third Sec. and Vice Consul, Riyadh, 1980–83; Second, later First, Sec. (Political/Inf.), Rome, 1983–87; First Secretary: FCO, 1987–92; (Economic), Ottawa, 1992–94; Dep. Consul Gen. and Dep. Dir for Trade and Investment, Toronto, 1994–97; Counsellor (Econ./Commercial), Riyadh, 1997–2000; Counsellor, FCO, 2000–01; Dir Gen. for Trade and Investment in Italy, and Consul Gen., Milan, 2001–06; Asst Dir, Human Resources, FCO, 2006–10; Ambassador to Libya, 2010–11. Sen. Consultant, Internat. Hosps Gp, 2011–18; Sen. Advr, G4S, 2011–12; Sensitivity Reviewer, FCO Services, 2014–. Chm., British-Italian Soc., 2015–. Mem., Governing Council, Old Bedfordians' Club, 2016–. *Recreations:* tennis, music, languages, wine, football. *Address:* c/o Baldwins, 9 Thorney Leys Park, Witney OX28 4GE. *E:* richard@rn4consultancy.co.uk. *Clubs:* Oxford and Cambridge; Luton Town Football.

**NORTHERN TERRITORY (AUSTRALIA), Bishop of the,** since 2015; **Rt Rev. Dr Gregory David Anderson;** *b* Sydney, 1 Oct. 1961; *s* of Roger Barry Anderson and Shirley Mirrette Anderson (*née* Owen); *m* 1988, Annette Lorraine Eriksson; two *s* two *d*. *Educ:* James Ruse Agricultural High Sch.; Sydney Univ. (BA Hons; PhD); Moore Theol Coll. (BTh; DipMin; MA Theol.); Deakin Univ. (Master of Professional Educn and Trng). GAICD 2016. Lectr, Nungalinya Coll., Darwin, 1995–2001; ordained deacon, 2001, priest, 2002; Aboriginal Ministry Develt Officer, Dio. of the Northern Territory, 2001–06; Hd, Dept of Mission, Moore Theol Coll., 2007–14. *Recreations:* squash, singing, crosswords, gardening. *Address:* GPO Box 2950, Darwin, NT 0801, Australia. *T:* (8) 89417440, *Fax:* (8) 89417446. *E:* bishop@ntanglican.org.au.

**NORTHESK, 15th Earl of,** *cr* 1647; **Patrick Charles Carnegy,** PhD; Lord Lour 1639; Lord Rosehill and Eglismauldie 1647; writer, lecturer and broadcaster; *b* 23 Sept. 1940; *s* of Canon Patrick Charles Carnegy and Joyce Eleanor (*née* Townsley); *S* kinsman, 2010; *m* 2010, Jill Gomez, *qv. Educ:* Rugby; Trinity Hall, Cambridge (BA 1963; MA 1967; PhD 2008). Journalist, TES, 1964–69; Asst Ed., TLS, 1969–78; Ed., Faber & Faber Ltd, 1978–88; Dir, Faber Music Ltd, 1979–88; Dramaturg, ROH, 1988–92. Stratford-upon-Avon theatre critic, The Spectator, 1998–2013. Leverhulme Res. Fellow, 1994–96. Mem., BBC Gen. Adv. Council, 1990–96. *Publications:* Faust as Musician: a study of Thomas Mann's novel Doctor Faustus, 1973; (ed) Christianity Revalued, 1974; Wagner and the Art of the Theatre, 2006 (Special Jury Prize, George Freedley Meml Award, 2006; Royal Philharmonic Soc. Award, 2007); (ed) John Harris: artist about Cambridge, 2018. *Heir: b* Colin David Carnegy [*b* 16 Aug. 1942; *m* 1973, Rosemary Frances Deschamps (*née* Chamier); three *s* one *d*]. *E:* patrick.carnegy@btopenworld.com.

**NORTHESK, Countess of;** *see* Gomez, J.

**NORTHLAND, Viscount; Adam Harry Knox;** *b* 7 Dec. 1994; *s* and *heir* of Earl of Ranfurly, *qv.*

**NORTHOLT, Archdeacon of;** *no new appointment at time of going to press.*

**NORTHOVER,** Baroness *cr* 2000 (Life Peer), of Cissbury in the co. of West Sussex; **Lindsay Patricia Northover,** PhD; PC 2015; *b* 21 Aug. 1954; *d* of Maurice Charles Colin Granshaw and Patricia Winifred Granshaw (*née* Jackson); *m* 1988, Prof. John Martin Alban Northover, *qv* (marr. diss. 2017); two *s* one *d*. *Educ:* Brighton and Hove High Sch.; St Anne's Coll., Oxford (exhibitioner; MA Modern History); Bryn Mawr Coll. (ESU schol.); Univ. of Pennsylvania (MA History and Philosophy of Sci. 1978; PhD 1981). Res. Fellow, UCL and St Mark's Hosp., 1980–83; Fellow, St Thomas's Hosp. Med. Sch., 1983–84; Lectr, Wellcome Inst. for the History of Medicine and UCL, 1984–91. Mem., cttee negotiating Liberal and SDP merger, 1987–88; Chair: SDP Health and Welfare Assoc., 1987–88; SDP Parly Cands' Assoc., 1987–88; Lib Dem Parly Cands' Assoc., 1988–91; Chair, Women Liberal Democrats, 1992–95. House of Lords: Lib Dem spokesperson on health, 2001–02, on internat. develt, 2002–10, 2015–16, on foreign and commonwealth affairs, 2016–; govt spokesman on health, internat. develt and justice, and for women and equalities, 2010–12, on health, internat. develt, women and equalities, DCMS and DEFRA, 2012–13, on educn, internat. develt, women and equalities, and DEFRA, 2013–14; lead govt spokesperson for DFID, 2011–14; a Baroness in Waiting (Govt Whip), 2010–14; Parly Under-Sec. of State, DFID, 2014–15; Prime Minister's Trade Envoy to Angola, 2016–, to Zambia, 2017–. Member: Select Cttee on Embryonic Stem Cell Res., 2001–02; Sub-Cttee on Foreign Affairs, Defence and Internat. Develt, 2003–04, on Economic and Financial Affairs and Internat. Trade, 2008–10, Select Cttee on EU. Sec., All-Party Gp on Overseas Develt, 2003–10. President: Liberal Democrat Women, 2014–; Liberal Internat. British Gp, 2017–. Member: Council, Overseas Develt Inst., 2005–10; Adv. Council, Wilton Park, 2016–; Council, Royal African Soc., 2018–. Mem. Exec., CPA, 2006–10 (Vice-Chair, 2008–10). Contested: (SDP/Alliance) Welwyn, Hatfield, 1983 and 1987; (Lib Dem) Basildon, 1997. Hon. Associate Prof., Inst. of Global Health Innovation, Imperial Coll. London, 2015–. Trustee: Tropical Health and Educn Trust, 2007–10; UNICEF UK, 2009–10; Liberal Democrats, 2009–11; Malaria Consortium, 2016–18. Patron, Breast Cancer Campaign, 2002–09. Trustee, Bryn Mawr Coll. Assoc. (GB). *Publications:* academic books and contribs to learned jls. *Address:* House of Lords, SW1A 0PW.

**NORTHOVER, Prof. John Martin Alban;** Honorary Professor of Intestinal Surgery, Imperial College, London, since 2001; Senior Surgeon, St Mark's Hospital for Intestinal and Colorectal Disorders, London, 2005–12 (Consultant Surgeon, 1984–2005); Consultant Surgeon, The London Clinic, 1988–2016; *b* 17 June 1947; *s* of William Joseph Northover and Peggy Vesta Northover (*née* Jacobs); *m* 1st, 1974, Sheila Ann Scott (marr. diss. 1987); two *s*; 2nd, 1988, Lindsay Patricia Granshaw (*see* Baroness Northover) (marr. diss. 2017); two *s* one *d*. *Educ:* Southern Grammar Sch., Portsmouth; King's Coll. Hosp., London (MB BS Hons 1970; MS 1980). KCH and Middlesex Hosp. trng posts, 1970–84; Dir, Colorectal Cancer Unit, CRUK (formerly ICRF), 1985–2005. Res. Fellow, Univ. of Cape Town, 1976–77. Arris and Gale Lectr, RCS, 1979. Hon. Civilian Consultant Advr in Colorectal Surgery to the Army, 1998–2014; Official Prison Visitor, HMP Pentonville, 2016–. Chm., MRC Colorectal Cancer Trials Data Monitoring and Ethics Cttee, 1995–2008; Member: Adv. Cttee on Distinction Awards, NW London, 2001–03; NHS Bowel Screening Adv. Cttee, 2008–16. Pres., Assoc. of Coloproctology of GB and Ireland, 2007–08; Vice-Pres., Internat. Soc. of Univ. Colon and Rectal Surgeons, 1998–99; Member: James IV Assoc. of Surgeons, 2001–11; Soc. of Pelvic Surgeons, 2004–10; Corresp. Mem., Surgical Res. Soc. of Southern Africa, 1989; Hon. Mem., Sect. of Colon and Rectal Surgery, RACS, 1992. *Publications:* (ed jtly) Pocket Examiner in Surgery, 1984, 2nd edn 1992; (ed with J. Kettner) Bowel Cancer: the facts, 1992; (ed with R. Phillips) Modern Coloproctology, 1993; (ed jtly) Current Surgical Practice, Vol. 8, 1998; (ed with W. Longo) Re-operative Colon and Rectal Surgery, 2003; Your Guide to Bowel Cancer, 2007; book chapters; numerous contribs to learned jls incl. Lancet, BMJ, British Jl Surgery, British Jl Cancer. *Address:* 116 Harley Street, W1G 7JL. *T:* (020) 7486 1008, *Fax:* (020) 7486 0665; 340 Princess Park Manor, Royal Drive, N11 3GX. *T:* (020) 8368 7439.

**NORTHUMBERLAND, 12th Duke of,** *cr* 1766; **Ralph George Algernon Percy;** DL; Bt 1660; Earl of Northumberland, Baron Warkworth 1749; Earl Percy 1766; Earl of Beverley 1790; Lord Lovaine, Baron of Alnwick 1784; Chairman, since 1992, and President, since 1995, Northumberland Estates; *b* 16 Nov. 1956; 2nd *s* of 10th Duke of Northumberland, KG, GCVO, TD, PC, FRS and Lady Elizabeth Diana Montagu-Douglas-Scott (*d* 2012), *er d* of 8th Duke of Buccleuch and Queensberry, KT, GCVO, PC; *S brother,* 1995; *m* 1979, Isobel Jane Richard (*see* Duchess of Northumberland); two *s* two *d*. *Educ:* Eton; Oxford Univ. MRICS (ARICS 1986). Land Agent with: Cluttons, 1979–82; Humberts, 1982–86; Northumberland Estates, 1986–96. DL Northumberland, 1997. *Recreations:* tennis, fishing, shooting, painting. *Heir: s* Earl Percy, *qv. Address:* Alnwick Castle, Alnwick, Northumberland NE66 1NG. *T:* (01665) 602456; Syon House, Brentford, Middlesex TW8 8JF. *T:* (020) 8560 2353.

**NORTHUMBERLAND, Duchess of; (Isobel) Jane Percy;** Lord-Lieutenant of Northumberland, since 2009; *d* of John Walter Maxwell Miller Richard; *m* 1979, Ralph George Algernon Percy (*see* Duke of Northumberland); two *s* two *d*. Trustee, Alnwick Garden Trust. *Address:* Alnwick Castle, Alnwick, Northumberland NE66 1NG.

**NORTHWAY, Eileen Mary,** CBE 1990; RRC 1982 (ARRC 1969); Principal Nursing Officer and Matron-in-Chief, Queen Alexandra's Royal Naval Nursing Service, 1986–90, retired; *b* 22 July 1931; *d* of Ernest and Margaret Northway. *Educ:* St Michael's Convent, Newton Abbot. SRN 1952, SCM 1954; joined QARNNS 1956. QHNS, 1986–90. OStJ 1985. *Recreations:* gardening, reading.

**NORTON,** family name of **Barons Grantley** and **Rathcreedan**.

**NORTON, 8th Baron** *cr* 1878; **James Nigel Arden Adderley;** *b* 2 June 1947; *er s* of 7th Baron Norton, OBE and Betty Margaret, *o d* of James McKee Hannah; *S* father, 1993; *m* (marr. diss.); one *s* one *d*; *m* 1997, Frances Elizabeth Prioleau, *yr d* of George Frederick Rothwell; one *d*. *Educ:* Downside. FCA 1970. *Heir: s* Hon. Edward James Arden Adderley [*b* 19 Oct. 1982; *m* 2010, Sarah Jane Wilkinson]. *Address:* Chalet Petrus, rue de Patier 24, 1936 Verbier, Switzerland.

**NORTON OF LOUTH,** Baron *cr* 1998 (Life Peer), of Louth in the co. of Lincolnshire; **Philip Norton,** PhD; Professor of Government, since 1986, Director, Centre for Legislative Studies, since 1992, and Head, Department of Politics and International Studies, 2002–07, University of Hull; *b* 5 March 1951; *y s* of late George E. Norton and Ena D. Norton. *Educ:* Univ. of Sheffield (BA 1st cl. Hons; Nalgo Prize 1972; PhD); Univ. of Pennsylvania (MA; Thouron Scholar). Lectr, 1977–82, Sen. Lectr, 1982–84, Reader, 1984–86, Univ. of Hull. Member: Exec. Cttee, Study of Parlt Gp, 1981–93, 2012– (Acad. Sec., 1981–85); Exec. Cttee, British Politics Gp (USA), 1982–95, 2009–11 (Pres., 1988–90); Exec. Cttee, Political Studies Assoc. of UK, 1983–89; Society and Politics Res. Develt Gp, ESRC, 1987–90; Council, Hansard Soc., 1997– (Dir of Studies, 2002–). Chm., H of L Select Cttee on the Constitution, 2001–04; Co-Chair, Parly Univ. Gp, 2009–; Chair, All Party Parly Gp on Constitution, 2010–15; Pres., Study of Parlt Gp, 2019–. Chairman: Cons. Pty Commn to Strengthen Parlt, 1999–2000; Standards Cttee, Kingston-upon-Hull City Council, 1999–2003. Co-Chm., Res. Cttee of Legislative Specialists, Internat. Political Sci. Assoc., 1994–2003. Pres., Politics Assoc., 1993–2008; Vice-Pres., Political Studies Assoc., 2002–. Trustee, Hist. of Parlt Trust, 1999–. Chair, Higher Educn Commn, 2014– (Co-Chair, 2012–14). Governor, King Edward VI Grammar Sch., Louth, 1988– (Warden, 1990–93). FRSA 1995; FAcSS (AcSS 2001); FRHistS 2018. Assoc. Ed., Political Studies, 1987–93; Ed., Jl of Legislative Studies, 1995–. Hon. LLD Lincoln, 2011. Freeman, Kingston-upon-Hull, 2016. *Publications:* Dissension in the House of Commons 1945–74, 1975; Conservative Dissidents, 1978; Dissension in the House of Commons 1974–79, 1980; The Commons in Perspective, 1981; (jtly) Conservatives and Conservatism, 1981; The Constitution in Flux, 1982; The British Polity, 1984, 5th edn 2010; Law and Order and British Politics, 1984; (ed) Parliament in the 1980s, 1985; (ed jtly) The Political Science of British Politics, 1986; (ed) Legislatures, 1990; (ed) Parliaments in Western Europe, 1990; (ed) New Directions in British Politics, 1991; (jtly) Politics UK, 1991, 9th edn 2018; (ed jtly) Parliamentary Questions, 1993; (jtly) Back from Westminster, 1993; Does Parliament Matter?, 1993; (ed) National Parliaments and the European Union, 1996; (ed jtly) The New Parliaments of Central and Eastern Europe, 1996; (ed) The Conservative Party, 1996; (ed) Legislatures and Legislators, 1998; (ed) Parliaments and Governments in Western Europe, 1998; (ed) Parliaments and Pressure Groups in Western Europe, 1999; (ed jtly) Parliaments in Asia, 1999; (ed) Parliaments and Citizens in Western Europe, 2002; Parliament in British Politics, 2005, 2nd edn 2013; (ed jtly) Post-Communist and Post-Soviet Parliaments: the initial decade, 2007; (ed jtly) The Internet and Parliamentary Democracy in Europe, 2008; (ed) A Century of Constitutional Reform, 2011; (ed) Eminent Parliamentarians, 2012; The Voice of the Backbenchers, 2013; Reform of the House of Lords, 2017. *Recreations:* table-tennis, walking. *Address:* School of Law and Politics, University of Hull, Hull, East Yorkshire HU6 7RX. *T:* (01482) 465863. *Club:* Royal Over-Seas League.

**NORTON, Sir Barry (John),** Kt 2015; Member (C), 1983–2016, and Leader, 2001–16, West Oxfordshire District Council; *b* Oxford, 31 Jan. 1946; *s* of Robert Vernon and Gladys Eveline Norton; *m* 1969, Maureen Lydia Hazell; one *s* one *d*. *Educ:* Witney Grammar Sch. Co. Dir, construction gp, 1969–85; recruitment consultant, 1986–94; Constituency Agent, W Oxon Cons. Assoc., 1995–2014. Mem. (C), N Leigh Parish Council, 1973–2016. Gov., N Leigh C of E Primary Sch., 2002–14. Sec., then Chm., N Leigh FC, 1969–95. *Recreation:* ardent sports fan. *Address:* 15 Perrott Close, North Leigh, Witney, Oxon OX29 6RU. *T:* (01993) 881777. *E:* barryjohnnorton@gmail.com.

**NORTON, Lt Gen. Sir George (Pemberton Ross),** KCVO 2013; CBE 2008 (MBE 1998); UK Military Representative to NATO and European Union, since 2016; *b* London, 27 Nov. 1962; *s* of late Richard Glover Norton and Philippa Margaret Norton (*née* Fisher); *m* 1990, Alexandrine Freiin von Lüninck; three *d*. *Educ:* Summer Fields; Radley; St John's Coll., Cambridge (BA 1984; MA); RMA Sandhurst; German Armed Forces Staff Coll., Hamburg. Commnd Grenadier Guards, 1985; regtl duty, 1985–93; MA to COS ARRC, 1995–97; Capt., Queen's Co., 1997–2000; Directing Staff, Staff Coll., 2000–02; CO 1st Bn Grenadier Guards, 2002–04; Dir Policy and Plans, Combined Forces Comd, Afghanistan, 2004; Sec. to Chiefs of Staff Cttee, MoD, 2005–06; HCSC 2006; Dep. Comdr, Task Force Helmand, Afghanistan, 2007; Comdr 38 (Irish) Bde, 2007–10; Dep. Comdr I Marine Expeditionary Force (Forward) and Regl Comd (SW), Afghanistan, 2010–11; GOC London Dist and Maj. Gen. Comdg Household Div., 2011–13; Dep. Comdr, NATO Rapid Deployable Corps - Italy, 2013–16. Regtl Lt Col, Grenadier Guards, 2012–17 (Regtl Trustee, 2017–). QCVS 2011. Mil. Patron, Style for Soldiers. Freeman, Ironmongers' Co., 2014. Bronze Star Medal (USA), 2004; Meritorious Honor Award (USA), 2011. *Recreations:* ski-ing, cricket, red wine. *Address:* UK Joint Delegation, HQ NATO, BFPO 49. *Clubs:* Cavalry and Guards, MCC, Pratt's, Pitt, Buck's.

**NORTON, Heather Sophia; Her Honour Judge Norton;** a Circuit Judge, since 2012; Resident Judge, Reading Crown Court, since 2018; *b* Thatcham, 24 Nov. 1966; *d* of Doris Norton; *m* 1996, Very Rev. Nicholas Charles Papadopulos, *qv*; one *s* one *d*. *Educ:* Chichester High Sch. for Girls; Millfield Sch.; Birmingham Univ. (LLB Hons). Called to the Bar, Middle Temple, 1988; a Recorder, 2007–12; Resident Judge, Canterbury Combined Court, 2016–18. Chm., Bishops Disciplinary Tribunals, 2018–. Hon. Recorder of Canterbury, 2017–18. Mem. Council, Univ. of Kent, 2015–18. *Publications:* (jtly) Pace: a practical guide to the Police and Criminal Evidence Act 1984, 2006, 5th edn 2019; (jtly) Vulnerable People and the Criminal Justice System, 2017. *Recreations:* music, history, walking (occasionally running), women's equality. *Address:* Reading Crown Court, Old Shire Hall, The Forbury, Reading RG1 3EH. *E:* HHJ.Heather.Norton@ejudiciary.net.

**NORTON, Dame Hilary Sharon Braverman;** *see* Blume, Dame H. S. B.

**NORTON, Jim;** *see* Norton, M. J.

**NORTON, John Lindsey;** Chairman, National Society for Prevention of Cruelty to Children, 1995–2001 (Hon. Treasurer, 1991–95); *b* 21 May 1935; *s* of Frederick Raymond Norton and Doris Ann Norton; *m* 1959, Judith Ann Bird; three *d*. *Educ:* Winchester College; Cambridge Univ. (MA). Blackburn Robson Coates & Co., 1959–63; BDO Binder Hamlyn, later Binder Hamlyn, 1963–96: Nat. Man. Partner, 1983–88; Chm., BDO Binder, 1988–92; Sen. Partner, Binder Hamlyn, 1993–96. Chairman: Barking Power Ltd, 1995–2011; Thames Valley Power Ltd, 1995–2011 (Dir, 1995–2011). *Recreations:* walking, gardening, golf. *Address:* Knowle Cottage, 1 Shorts Lane, Beaminster, Dorset DT8 3BD.

**NORTON, Michael Aslan,** OBE 1998; social entrepreneur; author; *s* of Richard and Helene Norton; *m* 1977, Hilary Sharon Braverman Blume (*see* Dame H. S. B. Blume); one *d*, and two step *s*. *Educ:* Charterhouse; King's Coll., Cambridge (MA Natural Scis). Investment Manager, Samuel Montagu & Co., 1964–67; Exec., New Enterprises, IPC, 1968; Publishing Exec., BPC Publishing, 1969–71; freelance writer, lectr, OU tutor and activist, 1971–75; Founder and Director: Directory of Social Change, 1975–94; Centre for Innovation in Voluntary Action, 1995–; Founder and Chm., Spring Impact (formerly Internat. Centre for Social Franchising), 2012–. Creator of first lang. teaching prog. in UK for non-English speaking immigrant families and children, 1965–70; Co-ordinator, Save Piccadilly Campaign, 1972–74; Co-Founder: Soho Housing Assoc., 1974; Changemakers, 1994 (Chm., 1994–); UnLtd, the Foundn for Social Entrepreneurs, 2001; UnLtd India, 2007; UnLtd SA, 2010; Buzzbnk (formerly BuzzBank), 2010 (Chm., 2010–); Founder: Books for Change, 1996; YouthBank, 1998; Booksline (India), 2000; Young Achievers Trust, 2006; Otesha Proj. UK, 2007; SmallWorks, 2011; Co-Founder, Internat. Centre for Social Franchising, 2012; Sponsor, Children's Develt Bank prog. for street banking in S Asia, 2004; Initiator: MyBnk children's banking and financial literacy prog. in UK, 2006; youth volunteering prog., 2009–; reclaiming unused food, 2019–; FoodCycle (formerly FoodWorks). Adjunct Prof., Univ. of Cape Town Graduate Sch. of Business, 2011–16; Prof., China Global Philanthropy Inst. (formerly China Philanthropy Res. Inst., Beijing Normal Univ.), 2015–. Hon. DLitt Wolverhampton, 2009. Karmaveer Award, Indian Confedn of NGOs, 2012; Beacon Fellow, 2013; UK Charity Award (Outstanding Achievement), 2014. *Publications:* The Community Newspaper Kit, 1975; The Mural Kit, 1976; Colour in your Environment, 1979; A Guide to the Benefits of Charitable Status, 1981; A Guide to Company Giving, 1984; The WorldWide Fundraisers Handbook, 1996, 3rd edn 2009; The Non-Profit Sector in India, 1997; Getting Started in Fundraising (India), 2000; (with Nina Botting) The Complete Fundraising Handbook, 4th edn 2001 to 5th edn 2007; Getting Started in Communication (India), 2003; 365 Ways to Change the World, 2005; Need to Know? Fundraising, 2007; The Everyday Activist, 2007; Writing Better Fundraising Applications, 1992, 4th edn (with M. Eastwood) 2010; Click2Change, 2012. *Recreations:* cycling, bridge, crosswords, dreaming up ideas to change the world, mentoring and supporting emerging social entrepreneurs.

**NORTON, Michael James, (Jim),** OBE 2019; FREng; independent director and consulting engineer; *b* 15 Dec. 1952; *s* of Christopher Stephen Norton and Lilian Ivy Norton; *m* 1976, Barbara Foster; one *s*. *Educ:* Roan Sch., Blackheath; Sheffield Univ. (BEng Hons (Electronic Engrg) 1974; Mappin Medal, 1974). AMIEE 1974, FIET (FIEE 1997); FREng 2011. Post Office (Telecommunications), later British Telecommunications, 1970–87 (lastly, Sen. Man., Internat. Business); Practice Dir, Butler Cox plc, 1987–90; Marketing Dir, Cable & Wireless (Europe), 1990–93; Chief Exec., Radiocoms Agency, DTI, 1993–98; Dir, Electronic Commerce Team, Performance and Innovation Unit, Cabinet Office, 1999; Institute of Directors: Hd of Electronic Business Policy, 1999–2001; Sen. Policy Advr, e-Business and e-Govt, 2004–08; Ext. Examr, IoD Cert. in Co. Direction, 2008–14; Chm., Deutsche Telekom Ltd, 2001–02. Non-executive Director: Securicor plc, 2000–02; 3i European Technology Trust, 2000–04; Zetex (formerly Telemetrix) plc, 2000–08 (Sen. Ind. Dir, 2003–08); F & C Capital & Income (formerly F & C PEP & ISA) Trust plc, 2001–14; Applegate Marketplace Ltd, 2015–; Canada-UK Council, 2016–. Chm., UK Spectrum Policy Forum, 2013–15. Mem., Commn on Nat. Security in 21st Century, IPPR, 2007–09. Mem., Ind. Rev. of UEA Climatic Res. Unit, 2010. Mem., Audit and Risk Cttee, RAEng, 2017– (Mem., Engrg Policy Cttee, 2014–17; Mem., Finance Cttee, 2014–17). Ext. Bd Mem., POST, 2001–18; Strategic Stakeholder Gp Mem., Nat. Hi-Tech Crime Unit, 2005–06; Council Mem., PICTFOR (formerly PITCOM), 2005–12 (Chm., Prog. Cttee, 2009–12). British Computer Society: Trustee, 2008–13; Vice Pres., 2008–11; Pres., 2011–12; Trustee Dir, BCS L&D Ltd, 2014–15. Vis. Prof. of Electronic Engrg, Univ. of Sheffield, 1998–. Coventry University: Gov., 2012–18; Chm., Audit and Risk Cttee, 2014–18; Chm., Serious Games Internat. Ltd, 2016–18; Pro-Chancellor, 2018–. FRSA 1993; FInstD 2001. Hon. DEng Sheffield, 2003; Hon. LLD Bath, 2012. *Recreations:* reading, music, amateur radio. *Address:* 179b Kimbolton Road, Bedford MK41 8DR. *W:* www.profjimnorton.com.

**NORTON, Hon. Sir Nicholas John H.;** *see* Hill-Norton.

**NORTON, Maj. Peter Allen,** GC 2006; CEng; Principal Consultant, IMSL, in counter-drone, counter-threat, ordnance, munitions and explosives, since 2016; Member, Directing Staff and Lecturer in Explosive Ordnance Engineering and Counter-IED Technologies, Defence Academy College of Management and Technology, 2008–13; *b* 10 Dec. 1962; *m* 1st, 1994, Susan Ann Chapman (marr. diss. 2009); two *s*; 2nd, 2013, Dr Katherine Jane Eburn Hewins; two *d*. *Educ:* Cranfield Univ. (MSc Explosive Ordnance Engrg, 2008). CEng 2011. Enlisted RAOC, 1983; trained as Ammunition Technician; Instr, Improvised Explosive Device Disposal, Army Sch. of Ammunition, 1993–95; loan service, Royal Army of Oman, 1995–98; Royal Logistics Corps: Sen. Ammunition Technician, 1998; Conductor, 2002; commnd, 2002; 2nd i/c Combined Explosives Exploitation Cell, Iraq, 2005 (GC for outstanding bravery and leadership). Private consultant in counter-threat, ordnance, munitions and explosives, 2015–16. Mem., Nat. Council, IExpE, 2010–14 (Chm., Tech. Cttee, 2011–14). Dir, Help for Heroes Recovery, 2011–16; Trustee, Help for Heroes, 2016–18; Chm., VC and GC Assoc., 2014– (Vice Chm., 2013–14); Trustee, VC and GC Benevolent Fund, 2007–15. MIExpE 1991, FIExpE 2012; MCGI 2010. Hon. Dr Canterbury Christ Church, 2017. FBI Star, 2009; US Army Commendation Medal, 2009. *Recreations:* spending time with his family, photography.

**NORTON, Sally;** *see* Harrison, S.

**NORTON-GRIFFITHS, Sir Michael,** 4th Bt *cr* 1922; consultant on conservation and land use economics, Nairobi, since 1998; *b* Boston, USA, 11 Jan. 1941; *s* of Sir Peter Norton-Griffiths, 2nd Bt and Kathryn, *e d* of late George F. Schrafft; *S* brother, 2017; *m* 1965, Ann, *o d* of late Group Captain Blair Alexander Fraser; one *s*. *Educ:* Eton; Keble Coll., Oxford (BA Zoology; DPhil Ethology). Serengeti Res. Inst., 1969–73; Man. Dir, EcoSystems Ltd, Nairobi, 1977–87; Hd, Eastern Sahel Univ., World Conservation Union, 1988; Consultant, Global Envmt Monitoring System, UN Envmt Prog., 1989–92; Vis. Scientist, Harvard Inst. for Internat. Develt, 1992; Vis. Res. Fellow, Centre for Social and Econ. Res. on Global Envmt, UCL, 1993–96. Crew mem., winning yacht Aerial, Clipper '96 round the world yacht race, 1996–97. Aerial Census Consultant: Frankfurt Zoological Soc., Kazakhstan, 2007; WWF, Mongolia, 2009–10; Rio Tinto, Mongolia, 2013; Lone Pine Fellow, Property and Envmtl Res. Centre, Bozeman, Montana, 2007; Vis. Res. Fellow, Inst. of Econ. Affairs and Internat. Policy Network, London, 2009; Sen. Res. Fellow, World Agroforestry Centre, Nairobi, 2011–13. *Heir: s* Alastair Norton-Griffiths, *b* 23 Feb. 1976.

**NORWICH, 3rd Viscount** *cr* 1952, of Aldwick; **Jason Charles Duff Bede Cooper;** *b* 27 Oct. 1959; *s* of 2nd Viscount Norwich, CVO and Anne Frances May Cooper (*née* Clifford); *S* father, 2018. *Heir:* none.

**NORWICH, Bishop of,** since 2019; **Rt Rev. Graham Barham Usher;** *b* York, 11 Sept. 1970; *s* of Michael Usher and Fionna Usher; *m* 1996, Rachel Margaret Sarah Thomson; one *s* one *d*. *Educ:* Pocklington Sch.; Univ. of Edinburgh (BSc); Corpus Christi Coll., Cambridge (MA). Ordained deacon, 1996, priest, 1997; Asst Curate, St Mary's, Nunthorpe, Middlesbrough, 1996–99; Vicar, Holy Trinity, N Ormesby, Middlesbrough, 1999–2004; Rector and Lectr, Hexham Abbey, 2004–14; Area Dean of Hexham, 2006–11; Bishop Suffragan of Dudley, 2014–19. Hon. Canon, St Cyprian's Cathedral, Kumasi, Ghana, 2007–14. Mem., Internat. Commn for Anglican Orthodox Theological Dialogue, 2017–. Sec. of State appointee, Northumberland Nat. Park Authy, 2009–13; Chm., Adv. Cttee, NE Region, Forestry Commn, 2009–14; Lay Mem., Access and Governance Cttee, Newcastle Biomedicine Biobank, 2012–14; Mem., Human Tissue Authy, 2016–. Chm., Churches' Housing Assoc. of Dudley and Dist, 2014–. Ind. Person, Dudley MBC, 2017–. *Publications:* Places of Enchantment: meeting God in landscapes,

2012. *Recreations:* wild lonely places, painting and drawing, reading, beekeeping, the company of friends. *Address:* Bishop's House, Norwich NR3 1SB. *T:* (01603) 629001. *E:* bishop@dioceseofnorwich.org.

**NORWICH, Dean of;** *see* Hedges, Very Rev. J. B.

**NORWICH, Archdeacon of;** *see* Hutchinson, Ven. K. E.

**NORWOOD, Mandi, (Mrs M. Norwood-Kelly);** publishing consultant; Editorial Director and Senior Vice President, 2011–18, Chief Editorial and Creative Director, 2015–18, Modern Luxury Publishing (formerly Niche Media, then GreenGale Publishing), New York; *b* 9 Oct. 1963; *m* 1995, Martin Kelly; two *d.* Sub-editor, Look Now, 1983–84; Features Editor, Clothes Show, 1986; Dep. Editor, More!, 1986–90; Editor: Looks, 1989–90; Company, 1990–95; Cosmopolitan, 1995–2000; Editor-in-Chief: Mademoiselle, 2000–01; Shop Etc, 2004–06; Founding Partner, Trampoline Gp, Leadership and Mgt Consultancy, 2008–11. Ed. of Year, British Press Awards, 1993. *Publications:* Girls Just Want to Have Fun (short stories), 1999; How to be Number One in Your Own World, 2000; Sex and the Married Girl, 2003; The Hitched Chick's Guide to Modern Marriage, 2004; Rock Star Momma, 2007; Michelle Style, 2009. *Club:* Groucho.

**NORWOOD, Her Honour Suzanne Freda, (Mrs John Lexden Stewart);** a Circuit Judge, 1973–95; *b* 24 March 1926; *d* of late Frederic Francis Norwood and Marianne Freda Norwood (*née* Thomas); *m* 1954, John Lexden Stewart (*d* 1972); one *s. Educ:* Lowther Coll., Bodelwyddan; St Andrews Univ. MA English, MA Hons History. Called to Bar, Gray's Inn, 1951; practised at Bar, SE Circuit. Member: Parole Bd, 1976–78; Mental Health Review Tribunal, 1983–98 (Chm., Oxford and Anglia Area, 1994–98). Member: Greenwich and Bexley AHA, 1979–82; Greenwich DHA, 1982–85; Bexley DHA, 1985–90. Pres., Medico-Legal Soc., 1990–92. Hon. LLD St Andrews, 1996. *Recreations:* walking, housekeeping, opera. *Address:* 69 Lee Road, SE3 9EN.

**NORWOOD-KELLY, Mandi;** *see* Norwood, M.

**NOSS, Dame Celia Mary;** *see* Hoyles, Dame C. M.

**NOSS, John Bramble;** HM Diplomatic Service, retired; *b* 20 Dec. 1935; *s* of John Noss and Vera Ethel (*née* Mattingly); *m* 1957, Shirley May Andrews; two *s* one *d. Educ:* Portsmouth Grammar School. Foreign Office, 1954; RAF, 1955–57; served FO, Beirut, Copenhagen, FCO; Russian language training, 1965; Moscow, 1965–68; Santiago, 1968–70; FCO, 1970–73; First Sec. (Economic), Pretoria, 1974–77; First Sec. (Commercial), Moscow, 1977–78; FCO, 1978–81; Consul (Inward Investment), New York, 1981–85; High Comr, Solomon Is, 1986–88; Dep. Hd of Mission and Commercial Counsellor, Helsinki, 1988–91; Consul-Gen., Perth, 1991–93; Internat. Advr, Primary Aluminium Inst., 1994–97 (Dep. Sec. Gen., 1996–97). *Recreations:* family, reading, golf. *Address:* 8 Hither Chantlers, Langton Green, Tunbridge Wells, Kent TN3 0BJ. *T:* (01892) 862157.

**NOSSAL, Sir Gustav (Joseph Victor),** AC 1989; Kt 1977; CBE 1970; FRS 1982; FAA; Director, The Walter and Eliza Hall Institute of Medical Research, Melbourne, 1965–96; Professor of Medical Biology, University of Melbourne, 1965–96, now Professor Emeritus; *b* Austria, 4 June 1931; *m* 1955, Lyn B. Dunnicliff; two *s* two *d. Educ:* Sydney Univ. (1st Cl. Hons BScMed (Bacteriology), 1952; 1st Cl. Hons MB, BS 1954 (Mills Prize)); Melbourne Univ. (PhD 1960). FAA 1967; FRACP 1967; Hon. FRCPA 1971; FRACMA 1971; FRCP 1980; FTS 1981; Hon. FRSE 1983. Jun., then Sen. Resident Officer, Royal Prince Alfred Hosp., Sydney, 1955–56; Res. Fellow, Walter and Eliza Hall Inst. of Med. Res., 1957–59; Asst Prof., Dept of Genetics, Stanford Univ. Sch. of Medicine, Calif, 1959–61; Dep. Dir (Immunology), Walter and Eliza Hall Inst. of Med. Res., 1961–65. Vis. scientist and vis. professor to several univs and res. insts; has given many lectures to learned societies, assocs and univs. Dir, CRA Ltd, 1977–97. World Health Organisation: Member: Expert Adv. Panel on Immunology, 1967; Adv. Cttee Med. Res., 1973–80; Special Consultant, Tropical Disease Res. Prog., 1976; Chm., Global Programme for Vaccines and Immunization, 1993–2002. Chm., West Pac Adv. Co. Med. Res., 1976–80; Member: Aust. Science and Technol. Council, 1975–83; Bd, CSIRO, 1987–94; Prime Minister's Sci. and Engrg Council, 1989–98. Chairman: Felton Bequests' Cttee, 1977–; Vic Health Promotion Foundn, 1987–96; Bill and Melinda Gates Foundn Vaccine Prog., 1998–2003. President: Internat. Union of Immunological Socs, 1986–89; Australian Acad. of Science, 1994–98. Mem., Aust. Soc. of Immunology; Hon. Mem., Amer. (1975), French (1979), Indian (1976), Soc. of Immunology; Foreign Hon. Mem., Amer. Acad. of Arts and Scis, 1974. For. Associate, US Nat. Acad. of Scis, 1979; Fellow, New York Acad. of Scis, 1977; For. Fellow, Indian Nat. Sci. Acad., 1980. Hon. MD Johannes Gutenberg Univ., Mainz, 1981. Emil von Behring Prize, Philipps Univ., Marburg, Germany, 1971; Rabbi Shai Shacknai Memorial Prize, Univ. of Jerusalem, 1973; Ciba Foundn Gold Medal, 1978; Burnet Medal, Aust. Acad. of Sci., 1979; Robert Koch Gold Medal, Univ. of Bonn, 1996; Peter Wills Medal, Research Australia Awards, 2012. Mem. Editorial Bd of several med. jls. *Publications:* Antibodies & Immunity, 1968, rev. edn 1977; Antigens Lymphoid Cells & The Immune Response, 1971; Medical Science & Human Goals, 1975; Nature's Defences (Boyer Lectures), 1978; Reshaping Life: key issues in genetic engineering, 1984; Diversity and Discovery, 2007. *Recreations:* golf, literature. *Address:* Department of Pathology, University of Melbourne, Parkville, Vic 3010, Australia. *T:* (3) 98538256. *Club:* Melbourne (Melbourne).

**NOTLEY, Maj.-Gen. Charles Roland Sykes,** CB 1994; CBE 1991; President of the Ordnance Board, 1992–94; *b* 5 May 1939; *s* of late Major Henry Sykes Notley, 3rd Carabiniers, and Mrs Stephanie Paterson-Morgan; *m* 1965, Katherine Sonia Bethell; two *d. Educ:* Winchester Coll. Commnd 3rd Carabiniers, 1959; Command, Royal Scots Dragoon Guards, 1979–82; Dir, Op. Requirements (Land), MoD, 1986–89; Dir, Logistic Ops (Army), MoD, 1989–90; Vice-Pres., Ordnance Board, 1991–92. *Recreations:* equitation, sailing. *Address:* c/o Royal Bank of Scotland, 62 Threadneedle Street, EC2R 8LA. *Clubs:* Royal Ocean Racing; Royal Yacht Squadron (Cowes); Royal Cruising.

**NOTT, Emma Catherine; Her Honour Judge Nott;** a Circuit Judge, since 2018; *b* Hitchin, Herts, 25 Sept. 1972; *d* of Clive and Jill Nott; one *s* two *d. Educ:* Hitchin Girls' Comprehensive Sch.; Selwyn Coll., Cambridge (BA 1994). Called to the Bar, Gray's Inn, 1995. Chm., Police Misconduct Panel, 2015–18. Mem., Equality, Diversity and Social Mobility Cttee, Bar Council, 2016–18. Dir, Hope for Hypothalmic Hamartomas, 2009–. *Recreations:* sun, sea, sand, snow, ski, après-ski. *Address:* Reading Crown Court, Old Shire Hall, The Forbury, Reading RG1 3EH.

**NOTT, Rt Hon. Sir John (William Frederic),** KCB 1983; PC 1979; farmer, Trewinnard Manor, St Erth, Cornwall; *b* 1 Feb. 1932; *s* of late Richard Nott, Bideford, Devon, and Phyllis (*née* Francis); *m* 1959, Miloska Sekol Vlahovic, Maribor, Slovenia (OBE 2012); two *s* one *d. Educ:* King's Mead, Seaford; Bradfield Coll.; Trinity Coll., Cambridge. Lieut, 2nd Gurkha Rifles (regular officer), Malayan emergency, 1952–56; Trinity Coll., Cambridge, 1957–59 (BA Hons Law and Econs); Pres., Cambridge Union, 1959; called to the Bar, Inner Temple, 1959; Gen. Manager, S. G. Warburg & Co. Ltd, Merchant Bankers, 1959–66. MP (C) Cornwall, St Ives, 1966–83; Minister of State, HM Treasury, 1972–74; Cons. front bench spokesman on: Treasury and Economic Affairs, 1974–76; Trade, 1976–79; Sec. of State for Trade, 1979–81; Sec. of State for Defence, 1981–83. Chm. and Chief Executive, Lazard Brothers & Co. Ltd, 1985–90 (Dir, 1983–90); Chm., Hillsdown Hldgs plc, 1993–99 (Dir, 1991–99). Chairman: Etam plc, 1991–95; Maple Leaf Foods Inc., Canada, 1993–95; Dep. Chm., Royal Insurance PLC, 1986–91 (Dir, 1985–91); Director: AMEC plc, 1991–93; Apax Partners & Co. Capital Ltd, 1996–; Altium Capital Hldgs, 1996–; Chiswell Associates Ltd, 1999–2002; 30 St James Square Investments, 2001–; Adviser: Apax Partners, 1990–98; Freshfields, 1991–95. *Publications:* Here Today, Gone Tomorrow (autobiog.), 2002; Mr Wonderful Takes a Cruise, 2004; Haven't We Been Here Before? Afghanistan to the Falklands: a personal connection, 2007; Trewinnard—A Cornish History, 2013; Mr Wonderful seeks Immortality, 2014; Memorable Encounters, 2018. *Recreations:* farming, fishing. *Address:* 31 Walpole Street, SW3 4QS. *T:* (020) 7730 2351. *E:* johnnott@btopenworld.com. *Clubs:* Pratt's, Beefsteak, Buck's.
*See also* Rt Hon. Sir H. G. W. Swire.

**NOTT, Roger Charles L.;** *see* Lane-Nott.

**NOTTINGHAM, Bishop of, (RC),** since 2015; **Rt Rev. Patrick Joseph McKinney;** *b* 30 April 1954; *s* of Patrick and Bridget McKinney. *Educ:* St Mary's Coll., Oscott; Gregorian Pontifical Univ., Rome (LTh). Ordained priest, 1978; Asst Priest, Our Lady of Lourdes, Yardley Wood, Birmingham, 1978–82; Chaplain, St Thomas Aquinas Secondary Sch., Kings Norton, 1979–82; Teacher, Fundamental Theology, 1984–89, Rector and Lectr in Ecclesiology, 1989–98, St Mary's Coll., Oscott; Parish Priest, St John's, Great Haywood, 1998–2001; Episcopal Vicar, Archdiocese of Birmingham, 1998–2006; Parish Priest, Our Lady and All Saints, Stourbridge and Dean, Dudley Deanery, 2006–15. Chair, Ecumenical Commn, Archdiocese of Birmingham, 1986–89. Mem., Met. Chapter of St Chad, 1992–2015. Prelate of Honour, 1990. *Recreations:* walking, reading, watching football, going to the theatre and cinema. *Address:* Bishop's House, 27 Cavendish Road East, The Park, Nottingham NG7 1BB. *T:* (0115) 947 4786. *E:* bishop.secretary@nrcdt.org.uk.

**NOURRY, Arnaud;** Chairman and Chief Executive Officer, Hachette Livre, since 2003; *b* 7 Jan. 1961; *s* of Claude Nourry and Marie Paule Nourry (*née* Boiron); *m* 1996, Danielle Belforti; two *s* one *d. Educ:* Ecole Supérieure de Commerce, Paris (MBA 1982); Paris Univ. (3rd degree Sociology 1983). Consultant, Mensia, 1986–90; Hachette Livre: Project Manager, 1990–95; Dep. Finance Officer, 1995–97; Gen. Manager, Hatier textbook div., 1998–2002. Ordre National du Mérite (France); Chevalier de la Légion d'Honneur (France). *Recreations:* classical music, tennis, wine. *Address:* Hachette Livre, 58 Rue Jean Bleuzen, CS 70007, 92178 Vanves Cedex, France. *T:* (1) 43923543, *Fax:* (1) 43923532. *E:* crault@hachette-livre.fr.

**NOURSE, Christopher Stuart;** Executive Director, Frederick Ashton Foundation, since 2011; *b* Salisbury, 13 Aug. 1946; *s* of late Rev. John Nourse and Helen Nourse (*née* Allison); *m* 2008, Charles Shu Ming Chan. *Educ:* Hurstpierpoint Coll., Sussex; Edinburgh Univ. (LLB); Inns of Court Sch. of Law. Life Offices' Assoc., 1970–72; various managerial positions with Royal Opera Hse, English Opera Gp and Royal Ballet New Gp, 1972–76; Gen. Manager, 1976–86, Admin. Dir, 1986–91, Sadler's Wells Royal Ballet, later Birmingham Royal Ballet; Asst to Gen. Dir, Royal Opera Hse, 1991–96; Admin. Dir, Royal Opera Hse Trust, 1996–97; Exec. Dir, Rambert Dance Co., 1997–2001; Man. Dir, English Nat. Ballet, 2001–03; freelance arts project manager, 2004–10. Projects include: project manager, Appeal launch for A Statue for Oscar Wilde, NPG, 1997; Adminr, Nat. Dance Awards, 2004–10; project manager, Dance Proms, Royal Albert Hall, 2011–14. Non-executive Director: London Dance Network, 1998–2000 (Vice-Chm.); Dancers' Pension Scheme, 2006–15 (Chm., 2010–15); Candoco Dance Co., 2008–14. Chm., Dame Margot Fonteyn Scholarship Fund, 2007–; Trustee: Nat. Youth Dance Trust, 2002–04; Youth Dance England, 2004–16; Cecchetti Soc., 2009–. Gov., Royal Ballet, 2008–. Mem., Strategic Develt and Fundraising Cttee (formerly Develt Panel), RAD, 2015–. Hon. Steward, Westminster Abbey, 2004–. FRSA. *Recreations:* music, the performing and visual arts, ballroom dancing, the countryside, the Orient. *Address:* 278 Earl's Court Road, SW5 9AS. *Club:* Travellers.

**NOURSE, Edmund Alexander Martin;** QC 2015; *b* UK, 27 Jan. 1970; *s* of Dr Christopher Henry Nourse and late Victoria Helen Mary Phillips; *m* 2005, Susan Julians; two *d. Educ:* Magdalen Coll., Oxford (BA 1st Cl. Hons Modern Hist.); City Univ. (DipLaw). Called to the Bar, Lincoln's Inn, 1994; in practice as barrister, specialising in commercial law, 1995–. *Recreations:* cricket, cooking, travel, photography. *Address:* One Essex Court, Temple, EC4Y 9AR.

**NOUSS, Hunada,** FCA; Chief Operating Officer, Children's Investment Fund Foundation, 2013–18; *b* 19 Jan. 1959. *Educ:* Lady Margaret Hall, Oxford (BA Hons PPE, MA). FCA 1984; ATII 1985. Arthur Andersen, 1980–90; Dir of Tax and Treasury, Lowe Gp plc, 1990–92; Dir, Financial Planning, Diageo plc, and other roles, 1993–2001; Finance Dir, Burger King, 2001–05; Dir-Gen., Finance and Corporate Services, DCLG, 2007–10; Dir-Gen., Finance, and Chief Financial Officer, DWP, 2010–12. Non-exec. Dir, Gentoo Gp Ltd, 2013–17. Non-exec. Dir, Met Office, 2018–; Mem. Bd, Educn and Skills Funding Agency, 2018–. Trustee, Breast Cancer Campaign, 2009–15. Mem. Council, City Univ. London, 2011–. *Recreations:* photography, travel.

**NOUVEL, Jean Henri;** architect, since 1966; *b* 12 Aug. 1945; *s* of Roger Nouvel and Renée Nouvel (*née* Barlangue); *m* 1992, Catherine Richard; one *d*; two *s* by Odile Fillion. *Educ:* Ecole Nationale Supérieure des Beaux Arts, Paris. Founder: Jean Nouvel and Associates, 1984–89; Jean Nouvel and Emmanuel Cattani, 1989–94; Ateliers Jean Nouvel, 1994–. Projects include: residential, educational, office and retail buildings in France; Institut du Monde Arabe, Paris, 1987; Hôtel de Saint-James, Bordeaux; Lyon Opera House, 1993; Fondation Cartier, Paris, 1994; Palais de Justice, Nantes, 2000; Cultural and Congress Centre, Lucerne, 2000; Gasometer, Vienna, 2001; Andel, Prague, 2001; Reina Sofia Mus. extension, Madrid, 2005; Guthrie Theater, Minneapolis, 2006; Musée du quai Branly, Paris, 2006; Pavilion B, Genoa Exhibition Centre, 2009; Copenhagen Concert Hall, 2009; Serpentine Gall. Summer Pavilion, 2010; One New Change, Cheapside, 2010; Baku Mus. of Modern Art, Azerbaijan, 2010; Montpelier City Hall, 2011; Tower, Doha, 2012; One Central Park, Sydney, 2014; Paris Philharmonie, 2015; White Walls, Nicosia, 2015; Louvre Abu Dhabi, 2017. Silver Medal, 1983, Gold Medal, 1998, French Acad. of Architecture; Grand Prix National d'Architecture, France, 1987; Praemium Imperiale, Japan Art Assoc., 2001; Royal Gold Medal, RIBA, 2001; Pritzker Architecture Prize, 2008. Commandeur, Ordre des Arts et des Lettres (France), 1997 (Chevalier, 1983); Officier: Ordre du Mérite (France), 2006 (Chevalier, 1987); Légion d'Honneur (France), 2010 (Chevalier, 2002). *Address:* Ateliers Jean Nouvel, 10 Cité d'Angoulême, 75011 Paris, France.

**NOUY, Danièle Marcelle Blanche;** Chevalier de la Légion d'Honneur 2008; Officier de l'Ordre du Mérite 2011; Chair, Supervisory Board, Single Supervisory Mechanism, 2014–18; *b* Rennes, France, 30 July 1950; *d* of Georges Police and Marcelle Police (*née* Pensec); *m* 1972, Jean-Yves Nouy; two *d. Educ:* Inst. d'Études Politiques, Paris (degree in Pol Sci. and Public Admin 1971); Panthéon-Assas Univ., Paris (Postgrad. Cert. Law (Civil and Admin. Law) 1972). Banque de France: Supervisor of French credit instns, French

Banking Supervision Commn, 1974–84; Rep. in NY, 1985–86; Policy Expert on Euromkts, Foreign Dept, 1986–87; Commission Bancaire: Hd, Res. Dept, 1987–90; Dir, Hd of supervision of French banks, 1990–94; Dir, Associate to Sec. Gen., 1994–96; Dep. Sec. Gen., 1996–98, Sec. Gen., 1998–2003, Basel Cttee on Banking Supervision; Secretary General: Commn Bancaire, 2003–10; French Prudential Supervision and Resolution Authy, 2010–13. Chair, Cttee of Eur. Banking Supervisors, 2006–08. *Publications:* (contrib.) Financial Supervision in the 21st Century, 2013; contrib. papers to Rev. d'Economie Financière, Rev. Banque, Financial Stability Rev., Jl Financial Stability, Risk, Débats Economiques et Financiers.

**NOVA SCOTIA AND PRINCE EDWARD ISLAND, Archbishop of,** and Metropolitan of the Ecclesiastical Province of Canada; since 2017; **Most Rev. Ronald Wayne Cutler;** Bishop of Nova Scotia and Prince Edward Island, since 2014; *b* Montreal, 30 Oct. 1958; *s* of Victor Cutler and Rita Cutler; *m* 1984, Marianne Elizabeth Blair; one *s* one *d*. *Educ:* McGill Univ. (BTh 1983). Rector: Parish of Twillingate, 1981–86; Parish of Smith's Sound, 1986–91; Parish of Sydney Mines and Baddeck, 1991–96; Regl Dean of Cape Breton, 1993–96; Rector, Parish of St John the Evangelist, Sackville, 1996–2008; Regl Dean of Fort Sackville, 2002–03; Archdeacon of Fort Sackville, 2003–08; Suffragan Bishop of Nova Scotia and Prince Edward Island, 2008–14. DD *hc* Univ. of King's Coll., Halifax, 2012. *Recreations:* golf, woodworking, walking, social dance. *Address:* 1340 Cathedral Lane, Halifax, NS B3H 2Z1, Canada. *T:* (902) 4200717, *Fax:* (902) 4250717. *E:* rcutler@nspeidiocese.ca.

**NOVOSELOV, Sir Konstantin S.,** Kt 2012; PhD; FRS 2011; Royal Society Research Fellow, since 2007, and Professor of Physics, since 2010, University of Manchester; *b* Nizhnii Tagil, Russia, 23 Aug. 1974; *s* of Sergey Novoselov and Tatiana Novoselova; *m* Irina Barbolina; two *d*. *Educ:* Moscow Inst. of Physics and Technol. (MSc *cum laude* 1997); Univ. of Nijmegen (PhD 2004). Researcher: Inst. for Microelectronics Technol., Chernogolovka, 1997–99; High Magnetic Field Lab., Univ. of Nijmegen, 1999–2001; Researcher, 2001–05, Leverhulme Res. Fellow, 2005–06, Univ. of Manchester. Special Prof., Radboud Univ. Nijmegen, 2013–. Hon. FRSC 2011; Hon. FInstP 2011. Hon. DSc Manchester, 2011. Europhysics Prize, Eur. Physics Soc. Condensed Matter Div., 2008; (jtly) Nobel Prize in Physics, 2010; Leverhulme Medal, Royal Soc., 2013. *Publications:* contrib. res. papers to jls incl. Nature, Science, Nature Materials, Nature Physics, Nature Nanotechnol., Rev. of Modern Physics, Physical Rev. Letters, Procs of NAS. *Address:* School of Physics and Astronomy, University of Manchester, Oxford Road, Manchester M13 9PL.

**NOWAK, Paul;** Deputy General Secretary, Trades Union Congress, since 2016 (Assistant General Secretary, 2013–16); *b* Birkenhead, 18 May 1972; *s* of John and Ann Novak; *m* 1998, Vicky Mason; two *s* one *d*. *Educ:* Wirral Grammar Sch. for Boys; Liverpool John Moores Univ. (BA Hons Urban Studies). Clerical Asst, Cheshire CC, 1996–97; Trades Union Congress: Policy and Campaigns Officer, 1998–2000; Regl Sec., Northern, 2000–02; Nat. Organiser, 2002–11; Hd, Orgn and Services, 2011–13. Mem. Council, ACAS, 2011–. Trustee, People's History Mus., 2017–. *Publications:* (contrib.) Union Organization and Activity, 2004; (contrib.) Union Revitalisation in Advanced Economies: assessing the contribution of Union organising, 2009. *Recreations:* family, playing guitar and ukelele (badly), Everton FC. *Address:* Trades Union Congress, Congress House, Great Russell Street, WC1B 3LS. *T:* (020) 7467 1231. *E:* pnowak@tuc.org.uk.

**NOYER, Christian;** Governor, Banque de France, 2003–15, now Hon. Governor; Chairman, Bank for International Settlements, 2010–15; *b* 6 Oct. 1950. *Educ:* Univ. of Rennes (lic. en droit 1971); Univ. of Paris (DèS droit 1972); Inst d'Etudes Politiques, Paris (Dip. 1972); Ecole Nat. d'Admin. Mil. service, Naval Officer, 1972. Entered Treasury, Min. of Finance, France, 1976; Financial Attaché, Perm. Repn to EEC, Brussels, 1980–82; French Treasury: Chief of Banking Office and of Export Credit Office, 1982–85; Advr to Minister for Econ. Affairs and Finance, 1986–88; Dep. Dir in charge of internat. multilateral issues, 1988–90; Dep. Dir in charge of debt mgt, monetary and banking issues, 1990–92; Dir responsible for public hldgs and public financing, 1992–93; Chief of Staff, Minister for Economic Affairs, 1993; Dir, Treasury, 1993–95; Chief of Staff to Minister for Econ. Affairs and Finance, 1995–97; Dir, Min. of Econ. Affairs, Finance and Industry, 1997–98; Vice-Pres., European Central Bank, 1998–2002; Special Advr, Min. of Economy, Finance and Industry, France, 2002–03. Pres., Autorité de contrôle prudentiel, subseq. de contrôle prudentiel et de résolution, France, 2010–15. Member: European Monetary Cttee, 1993–95, 1998 (Alternate Mem., 1988–90); Econ. and Financial Cttee, 1999–2002; OECD Working Party, 1993–95; Alternate Mem., G7 and G10, 1993–95. Alternate Gov., IMF and World Bank, 1993–95. Non-exec. Dir, Power Corp of Canada, 2016–. Mem. Council, Lloyds of London, 2018–. Chm., Paris Club of Creditor Countries, 1993–97. Chevalier, Ordre Nat. du Mérite (France), 1994; Commandeur, Légion d'Honneur (France), 2012 (Chevalier, 1998; Officier, 2007); Commandeur, Ordre des Arts et des Lettres (France), 2011; Comdr, Ordre Nat. du Lion (Senegal), 1995; Grand Cross, Order of Civil Merit (Spain), 2002; Officier, Ordre Nat. de Valeur (Cameroon), 2007; Gold and Silver Star, Order of Rising Sun (Japan), 2016. *Publications:* Banks: the rules of the game, 1990; articles in jls. *Address:* c/o Banque de France, 9 rue de Valois, 75001 Paris, France.

**NOYES, Dr Peter,** CPsychol; Director, Noyes Consulting Ltd, since 2013; Vice Chancellor, University of Wales, Newport, 2007–12; *b* 4 Aug. 1956; *s* of Alfred and Nora Noyes; *m* 1980, Prof. Janet Martin (marr. diss. 2016); two *s* one *d*. *Educ:* Loughborough Univ. (BSc Hons Social Psychol. 1977; PGCE Primary Educn 1981); PhD Educnl Psychol. London Univ. 1989. CPsychol 1989. Child Care Officer, Marchant-Holliday Sch., 1981–82; teacher: Wadebridge Jun. Sch., 1982–83; Saltash Jun. Sch., 1983–86; Res. Associate, Univ. of Bristol, 1986–88; Cheltenham and Gloucester College of Higher Education: Hd, Dept of Community and Social Studies, Res. Dir and Hd of Psychol., 1988–92; Dean: Educn and Health, 1992–93; Business and Social Studies, 1993–96; University of Wales College, Newport, subsequently University of Wales, Newport: Dean, Educn, Humanities and Sci., 1996–97; Asst Principal, 1997–99; Dep. Vice Chancellor, 1999–2006. Mem., Student Experience and Teaching Quality Cttee, HEFCW, 2008–12; Chairman: Welsh Internat. Consortium, 2010–12; Univs Assoc. for Lifelong Learning, 2010–12; Dep. Chm., Higher Educn Wales, 2011–12. Mem. Council, Univ. of Wales, 2005–11. Member: Assoc. Sci. Educn, 1986–; British Educnl Res. Assoc., 1986–. Mem. Council, CBI, 2006–11. Gov., Olveston C of E Prim. Sch., 2013–. FRSA 2002. *Publications:* articles in educn and psychol. jls. *Recreations:* supporter of Brighton and Hove Albion FC, supporter of Bristol Rugby Club, horse racing, theatre. *Address:* Orchard House, Quaperlake Street, Bruton, Somerset BA10 0HG. *T:* 07775 684598. *E:* noyes1956@hotmail.co.uk.

**NOYORI, Prof. Ryoji,** DEng; Fellow, RIKEN, since 2015 (President, 2003–15); University Professor, Nagoya University, since 2003; Director-General, Centre for Research and Development Strategy, Japan Science and Technology Agency, since 2015; *b* Kobe, Japan, 3 Sept. 1938; *s* of Kaneki and Suzuko Noyori; *m* 1972, Hiroko Oshima; two *s*. *Educ:* Univ. of Kyoto (BSc 1961; MSc 1963; DEng 1967); Harvard Univ. Res. Associate, Dept of Industrial Chemistry, Univ. of Kyoto, 1963–68; Nagoya University: Associate Prof. of Chemistry, 1968–72; Prof. of Chemistry, 1972–2003; Dir, Chemical Instrument Centre, 1979–91; Dean, Graduate Sch. of Sci., 1997–99; Dir, Res. Centre for Materials Sci., 2000. Sci. Advr, 1992–96, Mem., Scientific Council, 1996–2015, Min. of Educn, Sci. and Culture, subseq. Educn, Culture, Sports, Sci. and Technol., Japan. Dir, Sci. Mus., Japan Science Foundn, 2015–. For. Mem., Royal Soc., 2005. Numerous awards, incl. (jtly) Nobel Prize for Chemistry, 2001. *Publications:* Asymmetric Catalysis in Organic Synthesis, 1994; articles in scientific jls. *Address:* RIKEN, 2–1 Hirosawa, Wako, Saitama 351–0198, Japan; Department of Chemistry, Graduate School of Science, Nagoya University, Chikusa, Nagoya, Aichi 464–8602, Japan.

**NSUGBE, Oba Eric;** QC 2002; a Recorder, since 1999; Senior Advocate, Nigeria, 2005; *b* 23 Dec. 1962; *s* of Philip O. Nsugbe and Patricia Nsugbe; *m* 1994, Ambereen Laila (*née* Salamat); one *s* one *d*. *Educ:* St Edward's Sch., Oxford; Univ. of Hull (LLB Hons); Inns of Court Sch. of Law; Nigerian Law Sch. Called to the Bar, Gray's Inn, 1985, Bencher, 2005; Jt Hd of Chambers, 3 Pump Court, 2007–; barrister and solicitor, Nigeria, 1986. Mem., Judicial Studies Bd of England and Wales, 1996–2002. Bar Council: Member: Professional Conduct Cttee, 2001–; Pupillage and Trng Cttee, 2000–02; Response Cttee on Carter Reform of Legal Aid, 2006–07. Member: Glidewell Cttee on Judicial Appts and Silk, 2002–03; Cttee on reform of Silk, DCA, 2004–05. Gray's Inn Advocacy Trainer, 2004–07. Vis. Prof. of Law, City Univ., 2008–. FRSA 2006. *Recreations:* squash, football, jazz, travel, African art. *Address:* (chambers) 3 Pump Court, Temple, EC4Y 7AJ. *T:* (020) 7353 0711, *Fax:* (020) 7353 3319. *E:* oba.nsugbe@hotmail.co.uk.

**NTAGALI, Most Rev. Stanley;** *see* Uganda, Archbishop of.

**NUGEE, Hon. Sir Christopher (George),** Kt 2013; **Hon. Mr Justice Nugee;** a Judge of the High Court of Justice, Chancery Division, since 2013; *b* 23 Jan. 1959; *s* of late Edward George Nugee, TD, QC and Rachel Elizabeth Nugee; *m* 1991, Emily Thornberry (*see* Rt Hon. E. Thornberry); two *s* one *d*. *Educ:* Radley Coll.; Corpus Christi Coll., Oxford (BA 1st Cl. Hons Lit. Hum 1981); City Univ. (Dip. Law (Distinction) 1982). Called to the Bar, Inner Temple, 1983 (Queen Elizabeth Schol., 1983; Eldon Law Schol., 1984), Bencher, 2003; in practice at the Bar, 1984–2013; QC 1998; a Recorder, 2002–13; a Dep. High Ct Judge, 2003–13; a Judge of the Cts of Appeal of Jersey and Guernsey, 2011–13. Member: Bar Council, 1991–93 (Mem., Professional Conduct Cttee, 1992–96); Cttee, Assoc. of Pension Lawyers, 1998–2002. *Recreations:* Tideway sculling, cycling, my family. *Address:* Royal Courts of Justice, Rolls Building, 7 Rolls Buildings, Fetter Lane, EC4A 1NL.
*See also* Lt Gen. R. E. Nugee.

**NUGEE, Emily;** *see* Thornberry, Rt Hon. E.

**NUGEE, Lt Gen. Richard Edward,** CVO 2016; CBE 2012 (MBE 1998); FRGS; Chief of Defence People, since 2016; *b* Hampstead, 3 June 1963; *s* of late Edward George Nugee, TD, QC and Rachel Elizabeth Nugee; *m* 1990, Frances Renee Isabelle Bernard; two *s*. *Educ:* Radley Coll.; Durham Univ. (BA Hons Anthropol. 1985); City and Guilds Inst. 1994; King's Coll. London (MA Mil. Affairs 1995). Army Scholar, 1979; Cadet, 1982; commnd 1985; acsc 1995; JSCSC 2001; Comdr, 40 Regt (Lowland Gunners), RA, 2003; COS, Project Hyperion, 2005; HCSC 2006; Chief Jt Fires and Influence HQ, ARRC, 2006; Dir Manning (Army), 2009–12; Dir Gen. Personnel, Army, 2012–13; COS ISAF Jt Comd, 2013–15; ACDS (Personnel Capability) and Defence Services Sec., 2015–16. Member: Commonwealth War Graves Commn, 2015–16; Veterans Gateway Steering Gp, 2017–; Governing Body, Women in Defence, 2019–; Chair, Conflict Wound Res. Strategy Gp, 2018–. Commodore: British Kiel Yacht Club, 2008–09; RA Yacht Club, 2011–13 (Adm., 2019–); Chm., Thorney Island Water Sports Centre, 2011–13. Trustee: Forces Trust, 2004– (Chm., 2012–); Nugee Foundn, 2007–; Scar Free Foundn, 2016–; Patron: KCL to King's Sierra Leone Partnership Fundraising Expedition, 2018; AJEX. Hon. Mem., Faculty of Public Health, 2018–. CCMI 2016 (Mem., Companions Bd, 2017–). Inaugural Internat. Data Governance Award, DebTech Internat. LLC, Data Admin Newsletter and Wilshire Conferences Inc., 2010. Legion of Merit (USA), 2015. *Publications:* contribs to magazines incl. British Army Rev., RA Jl, HR Dir. *Recreations:* family, offshore sailing, cycling, singing, theatre. *E:* richard@nugee.com.
*See also* Hon. Sir C. G. Nugee.

**NUGENT,** family name of **Earl of Westmeath**.

**NUGENT, Sir Christopher George Ridley,** 6th Bt *cr* 1806, of Waddesdon, Berks; *b* 5 Oct. 1949; *er s* of Sir Robin George Colborne Nugent, 5th Bt and of Ursula Mary, *d* of Lt-Gen. Sir Herbert Fothergill Cooke, KCB, KBE, CSI, DSO; *S* father, 2006, but his name does not appear on the Official Roll of the Baronetage; *m* 1985, Jacqueline Vagba; three *s*. *Educ:* Eton; Univ. of East Anglia. *Heir: s* Terence Nugent, *b* 1 March 1986.

**NUGENT, Adm. Sir James Michael B.;** *see* Burnell-Nugent.

**NUGENT, Sir Nicholas (Myles John),** 8th Bt *cr* 1795, of Ballinlough, co. Westmeath; *b* London, 17 Feb. 1967; *o s* of Sir John Edwin Lavallin Nugent, 7th Bt and of Penelope Anne, *d* of late Brig. Richard Nigel Hanbury, CBE, TD; *S* father, 2009; *m* 1999, Alice Mary, *d* of Peter Player; two *d* (and one *d* decd). *Educ:* Eton. Dir, Robert J. Goff & Co. plc, 2007–; non-exec. Dir, Kilcarn Stud Ltd. *Heir: cousin* Charles Rupert Nugent [*b* 24 Jan. 1962; *m* 1989, Louise Victoria Nixon; two *s* one *d*]. *Address:* Ballinlough Castle, Co. Westmeath.

**NUGENT, Sir (Walter) Richard (Middleton),** 6th Bt *cr* 1831, of Donore, Co. Westmeath; *b* 15 Nov. 1947; *er s* of Sir Peter Walter James Nugent, 5th Bt and of Anne Judith, *o d* of Major Robert Smyth, Gaybrook, Co. Westmeath; *S* father, 2002; *m* 1985, Kayoko Okabe. *Educ:* Headfort; Downside. FCA 1970. Deloitte, Plender, Griffiths & Co., 1967–74; Gp Tax Mgr, Europe, Carrier Corp., 1974–76; Chief Accountant, Swire Pacific Ship Mgt, 1977–79; Corporate Accountant, Asia Pacific, Everett Steamship Corp., SA, 1980–84; Dir of Finance, IMS Japan KK, 1986–2003. *Heir:* none. *Address:* 61–6 Yaguchi-dai, Naka-ku, Yokohama-shi 231–0831, Kanagawa-ken, Japan. *T:* (45) 6219283.

**NUNBURNHOLME,** 6th Baron *cr* 1906; **Stephen Charles Wilson;** *b* 29 Nov. 1973; *o s* of 5th Baron Nunburnholme and of Linda Kay (*née* Stephens); *S* father, 2000; *m* 2002, Chie Mannami, MA (RCA); two *s*. *Educ:* Univ. of Westminster. *Heir: s* Hon. Charles Taiyo Christobal Wilson, *b* 14 Sept. 2002.

**NUNES, Prof. Terezinha,** PhD; Professor of Educational Studies, 2005–17, now Emeritus, and Course Director for Masters in Child Development and Education, 2009–14, University of Oxford; Fellow, Harris Manchester College, Oxford, 2005–17; *b* 3 Oct. 1947; *d* of Luiz Conzaga Nunes and Semíramis Oliveira Nunes; *m* 1st, 1973, David W. Carraher (marr. diss. 1990); one *s* one *d*; 2nd, 1995, Prof. Peter Elwood Bryant, *qv*. *Educ:* Univ. Federal de Minas Gerais (BS Psychol); City Univ. of New York (MA Psychol. 1975; PhD 1976). Accredited Psychologist. Res. asst, NY Infant Day Care Study, 1973–75; Adjunct Lectr, Dept of Psychol., Brooklyn Coll., NY, 1975; Hd, Inst. of Child Develt, Belo Horizonte, Brazil, 1976–77; Associate Prof., 1976–78, and Hd, Centre of Applied Psychol., 1977, Dept of Psychol., Univ. Federal de Minas Gerais; University of Pernambuco: Associate Prof. and Course Tutor, Masters prog. in Psychol., 1978–90; Hd, Pedagogical Centre, 1981–84; Res. Fellow, Sch. of Educn, Open Univ., 1990–91; Institute of Education, University of London: Lectr, 1991–93; Sen. Lectr, 1993–96;

Course Tutor for Masters in Child Develt, 1993–98; Prof. of Educn, Child Develt and Learning, 1996–2000; Res. Tutor and Hd, Child Develt and Learning Acad. Gp, 1998–2000; Prof. of Psychol. and Hd of Dept, Oxford Brookes Univ., 2000–05. Fulbright Fellow, 1971–76; Vis. Fellow, Wolfson Coll., Oxford, 1988–89; British Acad. Res. Reader, 2003–04; Vis. Prof., Univ. Bandeirantes, São Paulo, Brazil, 2012. Hon. Dr Szeged, 2018. Hans Freudenthal Medal, Internat. Union of Maths Educn, 2017. *Publications*: as Terezinha Carraher: O Método Clínico: usando os exames de Piaget, 1982; (jtly) Na Vida, Dez; Na Escola, Zero: os contextos culturais da aprendizagem de matemática, 1988; Sociedade e Inteligência, 1989; as Terezinha Nunes: (jtly) Dificuldades de aprendizagem da leitura: teoria e prática, 1992; (jtly) Street Mathematics and School Mathematics, 1993; (with P. E. Bryant) Children Doing Mathematics, 1996 (trans. Portuguese, Spanish and Greek); Developing Children's Minds Through Literacy and Numeracy: an inaugural lecture, 1998; (jtly) Introdução a Educacao Matemática: os números e as operações numéricas, 2001, 2nd edn 2005; Teaching Mathematics to Deaf Children, 2004 (trans. Greek, 2012); (with P. E. Bryant) Improving Literacy Through Teaching Morphemes, 2006; (with P. E. Bryant) Children's Reading and Spelling: beyond the first steps, 2009; (with P. E. Bryant) Leitura e Escrita: além dos primeiros passos, 2014; (jtly) Teaching and Learning About Whole Numbers in Primary School, 2018; papers in acad. jls on research on child develt, maths educn, literacy learning, working memory and deaf children's learning. *Recreations*: travelling, reading, cooking. *Address*: Department of Education, University of Oxford, 15 Norham Gardens, Oxford OX2 6PY. *T*: (01865) 284892, *Fax*: (01865) 274027. *E*: terezinha.nunes@education.ox.ac.uk.

**NUNN, Very Rev. Andrew Peter;** Dean of Southwark, since 2012; *b* Leicester, 30 July 1957; *s* of Peter Nunn and Jill Nunn (*née* Upton). *Educ*: Bushloe High Sch., Wigston; Guthlaxton Upper Sch., Wigston; Leicester Poly. (BA Hons Public Admin. 1979); Leeds Univ. (BA Hons Theol. and Religious Studies 1982); Coll. of the Resurrection, Mirfield. Ordained deacon, 1983, priest, 1984; Asst Curate, St James, Manston, 1983–87; Curate-in-charge, 1987–91, Vicar, 1991–95, St Hilda, Richmond Hill; Chaplain and PA to Bishop of Southwark, 1995–99; Southwark Cathedral: Priest Vicar, 1995–99; Vice Provost and Precentor, 1999–2000; Sub Dean and Precentor, 2000–10; Acting Dean of Southwark, 2010–11. Proctor in Convocation, Gen. Synod, 2005–10, 2010–15, 2015– (Chaplain, 2011–12; Mem., Panel of Chairs, 2016–); Sen. Selector and Bishop's Selection Advr (Vocation), 2006–12. Member: Liturgical Commn, 2011–12; Crown Nominations Commn, 2011–17. Delegate from Archbishop's Council, TEAM Conf., S Africa, 2007. Chaplain, Agnes Stewart C of E High Sch., Leeds, 1987–95. Trustee, Fellowship of the Maple Leaf, 2017–. Hon. Chaplain and Hon. Liveryman, Co. of Launderers, 2000–; Hon. Liveryman, Co. of Glaziers and Painters of Glass, 2012–; Hon. Chaplain: Whitsters Club, 2007–; Innholders' Co., 2014– (Freeman, 2018–). *Publications*: Lift Up Your Hearts, 2011. *Recreations*: reading, theatre, music, travelling, driving, friends. *Address*: Southwark Cathedral, London Bridge, SE1 9DA. *T*: (020) 7367 6700, *Fax*: (020) 7367 6725. *E*: andrew.nunn@southwark.anglican.org.

**NUNN, Catherine Amelia;** Chief Executive, Lakeland Ltd, since 2016; *b* Banbury, 7 Jan. 1970; *d* of Robert and Rosanne Randle; *m* 2013, Roger Nunn; one *s* one *d*. *Educ*: Univ. of Hull (BSc Hons Chem. 1990); Ecole Européenne des Affaires (Master in Eur. Mgt 1994; Diplom. Kauffrau 1994; Dip. de Grande Ecole 1994). Mgt consultant, Radermacher & Partner, 1994–96; Retail Territory Manager, Deutsche BP AG, 1996–99; Performance Manager, BP Global Special Projects, 1999–2002; Sen. Retail Strategy Analyst, 2002–03, Global Prog. Manager, Retail, 2003–06; BP plc; Bereichsleiterin Tankstellen, Aral AG, 2006–10; Principal Auditor, Downstream, 2010–11, UK Retail Dir, 2011–16, BP plc. Mem. Bd, Assoc. of Convenience Stores, 2011–16. *Recreations*: food, wine, family, travel, books, forklift truck driving (novice). *Address*: Lakeland, Alexandra Buildings, Windermere, Cumbria LA23 1BQ. *T*: (01539) 488200, *Fax*: (01539) 488300. *E*: catherine.nunn@lakeland.co.uk.

**NUNN, Imogen Mary, (Lady Nunn);** *see* Stubbs, I. M.

**NUNN, John Francis,** PhD, DSc, MD; FRCS, FRCA; FGS; Head of Division of Anaesthesia, Medical Research Council Clinical Research Centre, 1968–91; *b* 7 Nov. 1925; *s* of late Francis Nunn, Colwyn Bay; *m* 1949, Sheila, *d* of late E. C. Doubleday; one *s* two *d*. *Educ*: Wrekin Coll.; Birmingham Univ. (MD (Hons) 1970; PhD 1959; DSc 1992). FRCA (FFARCS 1955); FRCS 1983. MO, Birmingham Univ. Spitzbergen Expedition, 1948; Colonial Med. Service, Malaya, 1949–53; University Research Fellow, Birmingham, 1955–56; Leverhulme Research Fellow, RCS, 1957–64; Part-time Lectr, Postgrad. Med. Sch., Univ. of London, 1959–64; Consultant Anaesth., Hammersmith Hosp., 1959–64; Prof. of Anaesthesia, Univ. of Leeds, 1964–68. Member: Council, RCS, 1977–82 (Mem. Board, Faculty of Anaesthetists, Vice-Dean, 1977–79, Dean, 1979–82); Council, Assoc. of Anaesthetists, 1973–76 (Vice Pres., 1988–90); Pres., Sect. Anaesthesia, RSM, 1984–85. Hunterian Professor, RCS, 1960; Visiting Professor, various American Universities, 1960–98; British Council Lecturer: Switzerland, 1962; USSR, 1963; Czechoslovakia, 1969; China, 1974. Joseph Clover Lectr, RCS, 1968. Mem., Egypt Exploration Soc. FGS 2001. Hon. FFARCSI 1985; Hon. FRSocMed 1992; Hon. FANZCA 1993 (Hon. FFARACS); Hon. FRCA 1993. Hon. Dr: Turin, 1993; Uppsala, 1996. (1st) Sir Ivan Magill Gold Medal, Assoc. of Anaesthetists of GB and Ireland, 1988; Richardson Award, Geologists' Assoc., 1999. *Publications*: Applied Respiratory Physiology, 1969, 4th edn as Nunn's Applied Respiratory Physiology, 1993, (contrib.) 5th edn 2000 to 7th edn 2010; (ed jtly) General Anaesthesia, 3rd edn 1971, 5th edn 1989; Ancient Egyptian Medicine, 1996; (jtly) The Tale of Peter Rabbit (in ancient Egyptian hieroglyphs), 2005; several chapters in medical text-books, and publications in Journal Appl. Physiol., Lancet, Nature, British Journal Anæsth., etc. *Recreations*: Egyptology, model engineering. *Address*: 3A Dene Road, Northwood, Middx HA6 2AE. *T*: (01923) 826363.

**NUNN, Sir Trevor (Robert),** Kt 2002; CBE 1978; director; Artistic Director, Royal National Theatre, 1997–2003; *b* 14 Jan. 1940; *s* of late Robert Alexander Nunn and of Dorothy May (*née* Piper); *m* 1st, 1969, Janet Suzman (*see* Dame J. Suzman) (marr. diss. 1986); one *s*; 2nd, 1986, Sharon Lee Hill (marr. diss. 1991); two *d*; 3rd, 1994, Imogen Stubbs, *qv* (marr. diss. 2011); one *s* one *d*. *Educ*: Northgate Grammar Sch., Ipswich; Downing Coll., Cambridge (BA). Producer, Belgrade Theatre, Coventry; Royal Shakespeare Company: Chief Exec., 1968–86; Artistic Dir, 1968–78; Jt Artistic Dir, 1978–86; Dir Emeritus, 1986–. Major productions include: *theatre*: The Life and Adventures of Nicholas Nickleby, Aldwych, 1980, transf. NY, 1981–82 and 1986; Cats, New London, 1981, NY 1982, London revival 2014, NY revival, 2016; Starlight Express, Apollo Victoria, 1984, NY 1987; Les Miserables, Queen's, 1985–2019, NY 1987–2003 and revival, 2006; Chess, Prince Edward, 1986, NY 1988 and 2003; Aspects of Love, Prince of Wales, 1989, NY 1990, Menier Chocolate Factory, 2010; Sunset Boulevard, Adelphi, 1993, NY 1994; Oklahoma!, RNT, 1998, NY 2002; My Fair Lady, RNT, then transf. Th. Royal, Drury Lane, 2001; South Pacific, RNT, 2001; Anything Goes, RNT, 2002, transf. Th. Royal, Drury Lane, 2003; The Woman in White, Palace, 2004, NY 2005; Acorn Antiques: the musical, Th. Royal, Haymarket, 2005; Porgy and Bess, Savoy, 2006; The Seagull, King Lear, RSC, 2007; Gone with the Wind, New London, 2008; Inherit the Wind, Old Vic, 2009; A Little Night Music, Garrick, 2009, NY 2009; Cyrano de Bergerac, Chichester, 2009; Birdsong, Comedy, 2010; Flare Path, Rosencrantz and Guildenstern Are Dead, The Tempest, The Lion in Winter, Th. Royal, Haymarket, 2011; Kiss Me, Kate, Chichester Fest., 2012, transf. Old Vic, 2012; All That Fall, Jermyn Street Th., A Chorus of Disapproval, Harold Pinter Th., 2012; Relative Values, Th. Royal, Bath, 2013, transf. Harold Pinter Th., 2014; Scenes from a Marriage, St James Th., 2013; Fatal Attraction, Th. Royal Haymarket, 2014; Volpone, Swan Th., Stratford, 2015; The Wars of the Roses, Rose Th., Kingston, 2015; King John, Rose Th., Kingston, 2016; A Midsummer Night's Dream, New Wolsey Th., Ipswich, 2016; Love in Idleness, Lettice and Lovage, Menier Chocolate Factory, 2017; Dessert, Southwark Playhouse, 2017; Agnes Colander, Th. Royal, Bath, 2018, transf. Jermyn Street Th., 2019; Fiddler on the Roof, Menier Chocolate Factory, 2018; The Bridges of Madison County, Menier Chocolate Factory, 2019; *films*: Hedda, 1976; Lady Jane, 1986; Twelfth Night, 1996; Red Joan, 2019. Mem., Arts Council of England, 1994–96. Hon. MA: Newcastle upon Tyne, 1982; Warwick.

**NUNNELEY, Sir Charles (Kenneth Roylance),** Kt 2003; CA; Chairman: Nationwide Building Society, 1996–2002 (Director, 1994–2002; Deputy Chairman, 1995–96); National Trust, 1996–2003; *b* 3 April 1936; *s* of late Robin Michael Charles Nunneley and Patricia Mary (*née* Roylance); *m* 1961, Catherine Elizabeth Armstrong Buckley; one *s* three *d*. *Educ*: Eton Coll. CA 1961. Robert Fleming (merchant bankers), 1962–96: Dir, 1968–96, Dep. Chm., 1986–96; Chairman: Save & Prosper Gp, 1989–96; JP Morgan Income & Capital Investment Trust (formerly Fleming, then JP Morgan Fleming, Income & Capital Investment Trust) plc, 1992–2007; IMRO Ltd, 1992–97 (Dir, 1986–97); Monks Investment Trust plc, 1996–2005 (Dir, 1977–2005); Edinburgh Fund Managers Gp plc, 2003; Dep. Chm., Clerical Medical & General Life Assurance Soc., 1978–96 (Dir, 1974–96); Dir, Macmillan Ltd, 1982–96. Chm., Instnl Fund Managers' Assoc., 1989–92. National Trust: Member: Council, 1992–2003; Exec. Cttee, 1991–2003; Chm., Finance Cttee, 1991–96. Chm. Council, N Wessex Downs Area of Outstanding Natural Beauty, 2004–10. Mem., Adv. Bd, Aberdeen Select Charity Funds, 2011–19. Mem. Court, Grocers' Co., 1975– (Master, 1982–83). Governor, Oundle Schs, 1975–99. *Recreations*: walking, theatre, photography. *Address*: 116 Rivermead Court, Ranelagh Gardens, SW6 3SD.

**NURSAW, Sir James,** KCB 1992 (CB 1983); QC 1988; HM Procurator General and Treasury Solicitor, 1988–92; *b* 18 Oct. 1932; *s* of William George Nursaw (*d* 1994); *m* 1959, Eira (*d* 2018), yr *d* of late E. W. Caryl-Thomas, MD, BSc, Barrister-at-law; two *d*. *Educ*: Bancroft's School; Christ's Coll., Cambridge (Schol.; MA, LLB). Called to Bar, Middle Temple, 1955 (Blackstone Entrance Schol. and Prize, Harmsworth Schol.), Bencher, 1989. Senior Research Officer, Cambridge Univ. Dept of Criminal Science, 1958. Joined Legal Adviser's Branch, Home Office, 1959; Principal Asst Legal Advr, HO and NI Office, 1977–80; Legal Secretary, Law Officers' Dept, 1980–83; Legal Adviser, Home Office and NI Office, 1983–88. Counsel to Chm. of Cttees, H of L, 1993–2002. Liveryman, Loriners' Co. *Clubs*: Oxford and Cambridge, MCC.

**NURSE, Sir Paul (Maxime),** Kt 1999; PhD; FRS 1989; President, Royal Society, 2010–15; Director, Francis Crick Institute (formerly UK Centre for Medical Research and Innovation), since 2011; *b* 25 Jan. 1949; *s* of Miriam Nurse; *m* 1971, Anne Teresa (*née* Talbott); two *d*. *Educ*: Harrow County Grammar Sch.; Univ. of Birmingham (BSc); Univ. of East Anglia (PhD). Research Fellow, Univ. of Edinburgh, 1973–79; SERC Advanced Fellow and MRC Sen. Fellow, Univ. of Sussex, 1979–84; Hd of Cell Cycle Control Laboratory, Imp. Cancer Res. Fund, London, 1984–87; Oxford University: Fellow, 1987–93, Hon. Fellow, 1993–, Linacre Coll.; Iveagh Prof. of Microbiology, 1987–91; Royal Soc. Napier Res. Prof., 1991–93; Dir of Lab. Res., 1993–96, Dir Gen., 1996–2002, ICRF; Chief Exec., Cancer Res. UK, 2002–03; Pres., Rockefeller Univ., NY, 2003–10. Trustee, British Mus., 2012–. Chancellor, Bristol Univ., 2017–. MAE 1992; Foreign Associate US NAS, 1995. Fleming Lectr, 1984, Marjory Stephenson Lectr, 1990, Soc. of Gen. Microbiology; Florey Lectr, Royal Soc., 1990; Wenner-Gren Lectr, Stockholm, 1993; Dunham Lectr, Harvard, 1994. President: Genetical Soc., 1990–94; British Sci. Assoc., 2014–15. Founder FMedSci 1998. Hon. FBA 2016. Ciba Medal, Biochemical Soc., 1991; Feldberg Foundn Prize, 1991; (jtly) Louis Jeantet Prize for Medicine, Geneva, 1992; Gairdner Foundn Internat. Jt Award, 1992; Royal Soc. Wellcome Medal, 1993; Jimenez Diaz Meml Award, Madrid, 1993; Rosenstiel Award, Brandeis Univ., 1993; Pezcoller Award for Oncology Res., Trento, 1995; Royal Soc. Royal Medal, 1995; Dr Josef Steiner Prize, Steiner Cancer Foundn, Bern, 1996; Dr H. P. Heineken Prize, Netherlands, 1996; Alfred P. Sloan Jr Prize and Medal, General Motors Cancer Res. Foundn, 1997; Judd Award, Meml Sloan-Kettering Cancer Center, NY, 1998; Lasker Award, Albert and Mary Lasker Foundn, NY, 1998; (jtly) Nobel Prize for Physiology or Medicine, 2001. Hon. FREng 2012. Officer, Légion d'Honneur (France), 2002; Order of the Rising Sun, Gold and Silver Star (Japan), 2018. *Publications*: numerous, in sci. jls, concerned with cell and molecular biology. *Recreations*: gliding, astronomy, talking. *Address*: Francis Crick Institute, 1 Midland Road, NW1 1AT.

**NUSSBAUM, David Simon Matthew;** Chief Executive, The Elders Foundation, since 2016; *b* Stoke on Trent, 13 July 1958; *s* of Gerald and Enid Nussbaum; *m* 1983, Kathleen Kinderman; two *s* two *d*. *Educ*: Queens' Coll., Cambridge (BA Theol. 1980; MA); Univ. of Edinburgh (MTh 1981); Heriot-Watt Univ. (Dip. Accounting (Distn) 1982); London Business Sch. (MSc Finance (Distn) 1998). CA 1985; CTA 1985. Audit Sen./Asst, 1982–86, Asst Manager, 1986–87, Price Waterhouse; Investment Controller, 3i plc, 1987–90; Commercial and Business Develt Manager, Reedpack Ltd, 1990–91; Corporate Develt Dir, 1991–92, Finance Dir, 1992–97, Field Group plc; Dir, Finance, Inf. and Planning, and a Dep. Chief Exec., Oxfam, 1997–2002; Transparency International: Man. Dir, 2002–03; Chief Exec., 2003–07; Chief Exec., WWF-UK, 2007–16. Chm., Transparency International UK, 2012–17 (non-exec. Dir, 2008–17); non-executive Director: Traidcraft plc, 1991–2006 (Chm., 1999–2006); Shared Interest, 2006–14 (Vice-Chair, 2013–14); Low Carbon Accelerator, 2006–13; Internat. Integrated Reporting Council, 2015– (Dep. Chair, 2017–); Drax Gp plc, 2017– (Sen. Ind. Dir, 2019–). Mem., Ethical Investment Adv. Gp, C of E, 2019–. FRSA. MInstD. Hon. DCL Newcastle, 2011. *Publications*: (contrib.) Christianity and the Culture of Economics, 2001; (contrib.) Charities, Governance and the Law: the way forward, 2003. *Recreation*: Post-Christendom orthopraxis. *Address*: The Elders Foundation, 3 Tilney Street, W1K 1BJ. *T*: (020) 7013 4641. *E*: David.Nussbaum@TheElders.org.

**NÜSSLEIN-VOLHARD, Christiane,** PhD; Director, Max Planck Institute for Developmental Biology, 1985–2014, now Director Emeritus (Director of Department of Genetics, 1990); *b* 20 Oct. 1942; *d* of Rolf Volhard and Brigitte Volhard (*née* Haas). *Educ*: Univ. of Tübingen (PhD Genetics 1973). Res. Associate, Max Planck Institute for Virus Research, 1972–74; EMBO Fellow: Biozentrum Basel Lab., 1975–76; Univ. of Freiberg, 1977; Head of Gp, European Molecular Biology Lab., Heidelberg, 1978–80; Max Planck Gesellschaft: Gp Leader, Friedrich Miescher Lab., 1981–85; Scientific Mem., 1985–90; Dir, Friedrich Miescher Lab., 2005–12. Mem., Sci. Council, ERC, 2005–12. (Jtly) Nobel Prize for Physiology or Medicine, 1995. *Publications*: Coming to Life: how genes drive development, 2006; articles in learned jls. *Address*: Max-Planck-Institut für Entwicklungsbiologie, Spemannstraße 35/III, 72076 Tübingen, Germany.

**NUTBEAM, Prof. Donald**, PhD; FFPH; Professor of Public Health, University of Sydney, since 2016; Principal Senior Advisor, Sax Institute, Sydney, since 2018 (Senior Advisor, 2016–18); Senior Advisor, Sydney Health Partners, since 2016; *b* 18 May 1955; *s* of late Walter Charles Nutbeam and Ada Rose Nutbeam; *m* 1978, Sarah Choules; one *s* one *d*. *Educ*: St Bartholomew's Grammar Sch., Newbury; Univ. of Southampton (MA; PhD 1988). FFPH 2003. Health Educn Officer, Portsmouth Health Dist, 1978–81; Res. Assistant, Wessex RHA, 1981–83; Res. Fellow in Health Promotion, Southampton Univ., 1983–85; Hd of Res., Welsh Heart Prog., Univ. of Wales Coll. of Medicine, 1985–88; Dir, Res. and Policy, Health Promotion Authy, Wales, 1988–90; University of Sydney, Australia: Prof. of Public Health, 1990–2000; Hd, Dept of Public Health and Community Medicine, 1997–2000; Associate Dean of Medicine, 1999–2000; Hd of Public Health, DoH, 2000–03; University of Sydney, Australia: Pro-Vice-Chancellor, 2003–06; Provost and Dep. Vice-Chancellor, 2006–09; Vis. Prof., 2009–16; Vice-Chancellor, Univ. of Southampton, 2009–15. Visiting Professor: LSHTM, 2001–06; Nanjing Univ., 2010–15; Southampton Univ., 2015–. Ed.-in-Chief, Public Health Res. and Practice, 2016–. FAAHMS 2018. *Publications*: numerous contribs to scientific jls and texts. *Recreations*: sport, gardening, travel. *Address*: School of Public Health, University of Sydney, NSW 2006, Australia. *Club*: Athenæum.

**NUTT, Prof. David John**, DM; FRCP, FRCPsych, FMedSci; Edmond J. Safra Professor of Neuropsychopharmacology and Head, Centre for Neuropsychopharmacology (formerly Department of Neuropsychopharmacology and Molecular Imaging), Imperial College London, since 2008; *b* 16 April 1951; *s* of R. J. (Jack) Nutt and Eileen M. (*née* Baber); *m* 1979, Diana Margaret Sliney; two *s* two *d*. *Educ*: Bristol GS; Downing Coll., Cambridge (MB BChir); Guy's Hosp.; Lincoln Coll., Oxford (DM 1983). MRCP 1977, FRCP 2002; MRCPsych 1983, FRCPsych 1994; FMedSci 2002; FRSB (FSB 2012). Oxford University: Clinical Scientist, MRC Clinical Pharmacology Unit, 1978–82; Lectr, Dept of Psychiatry, 1982–84; Wellcome Sen. Fellow in Clinical Sci., 1985–86; Head, Section of Clinical Sci., Nat. Inst. of Alcohol Abuse and Alcoholism, NIH, 1986–88; Bristol University: Dir, Psychopharmacology Unit, 1988–2008; Prof. of Psychopharmacology, 1994–2009; Head: Div. of Psychiatry, 1995–97; Dept of Clinical Medicine, 1997–2003; Community Based Medicine, 2004–09; Dean of Clinical Medicine and Dentistry, 1999–2003. Chairman: Adv. Council on the Misuse of Drugs, 2008–09 (Chm., Technical Cttee, 2000–08); Ind. Scientific Cttee on Drugs, 2010–; Member: Ind. Inquiry into Misuse of Drugs Act 1971, 1997–2000 (reported, 2000); Cttee on the Safety of Medicines, 2001–; Lead Scientist, DTI Foresight Prog., Brain Science Addiction and Drugs, 2005–06. FMedSci 2002. John Maddox Prize for Standing up for Science, Sense about Science, 2013. *Publications*: Inverse Agonists, 1994; jointly: Hypnotics and Anxiolytics, 1995; Depression, Anxiety and the Mixed Conditions, 1997; Panic Disorder: clinical diagnosis, management and mechanisms, 1998; Generalized anxiety disorder: diagnosis, treatment and its relationship to other anxiety disorders, 1998; Atlas of Psychiatric Pharmacotherapy, 1999, rev. edn 2006, 2nd edn 2007; Milestones in Drug Therapy: anxiolytics, 2000; Post Traumatic Stress Disorder: diagnosis, management and treatment, 2000, 2nd edn 2009; Clinician's Manual on Anxiety Disorder and Comorbid Depression, 2000; Anxiety Disorders: an introduction to clinical management and research, 2001; Mood and Anxiety Disorders in Children and Adolescents, 2001; Anxiety Disorders Comorbid with Depression: panic disorder and agoraphobia, 2002; Generalised Anxiety Disorder: symptomatology, pathogenesis and management, 2002; Anxiety Disorders, 2003; Calming the Brain, 2003; (jtly) Treating Depression Effectively, 2004, 2nd edn 2007; (jtly) Drugs and the Future: brain science, 2006; (jtly) Serotonin and Sleep: molecular, functional and clinical aspects, 2007; (jtly) Handbook of Fear and Anxiety, 2008; (jtly) Addiction, 2008; (with S. J. Wilson) Sleep Disorders, 2008; (jtly) The Neurobiology of Addiction, 2010; Drugs: without the hot air, 2012; (jtly) Substance Abuse, 2013. *Recreations*: gardening, grandchildren, swimming. *Address*: Burlington-Danes Building, Hammersmith Hospital, Du Cane Road, W12 0NN. *T*: (020) 7594 6628.

**NUTTALL, Christopher Peter**; Director of Research and Statistics, Home Office, 1989–99; *b* 20 April 1939; *s* of Barbara Goodwin and David Nuttall; *m* 1966, Caryn Thomas; two *s*; partner, Joy Louise Hutcheon, qv. *Educ*: Queen Elizabeth Grammar Sch., Wakefield; Univ. of Keele (BA); Univ. of California at Berkeley (MA). Home Office Res. Unit, 1963–75 (Principal Res. Officer, 1971–75); Dir of Res., 1975–80, Dir Gen., Res. and Stats, 1980–82, Min. of Solicitor Gen., Ottawa; Asst Dep. Solicitor Gen. of Canada, 1982–89; Asst Under-Sec. of State, Home Office, 1989. Consultant to Govt of Barbados on criminal justice res., inf. and policy, 2000–03. UN Human Rights Fellow, 1967–68. *Publications*: Parole in England and Wales, 1977; The Barbados Crime Survey, 2002; Sentencing in Barbados, 2003; Handbook for Crime Prevention in Southern Africa and the Caribbean, 2008; articles on parole, deterrence, crime prevention and imprisonment. *Recreations*: The United States, photography, taking baths, books. *Address*: 2, The Cottage, The Hill, Polstead, Suffolk CO6 5AH.

**NUTTALL, David John**; *b* Sheffield, 25 March 1962; *s* of Roy Nuttall and Kathleen Nuttall; *m* 2004, Susan Smith (*née* Finn). *Educ*: Aston Comp. Sch., Rotherham; Univ. of London (LLB ext.). Admitted solicitor, 1990, NP, 1998; Taylor Son & Co., later Taylors, solicitors: trainee legal exec., 1980–88; Legal Exec. and Articled Clerk, 1988–90; Partner, 1990–98; Sen. Partner, 1998–2006; NP, Nuttall's Notaries, 2006–10. Contested (C): Sheffield Hillsborough, 1997; Morecambe and Lunesdale, 2001; Bury N, 2005; Yorkshire and the Humber, EP, 1999. MP (C) Bury N, 2010–17; contested (C) same seat, 2017. *Recreations*: walking, watching sport, bird watching. *E*: dnuttall@aol.com.

**NUTTALL, Rev. Derek**, MBE 1990; Minister, United Reformed Church, Windsor, 1990–2003; *b* 23 Sept. 1937; *s* of Charles William Nuttall and Doris Nuttall; *m* 1965, Margaret Hathaway Brown (*d* 1993); two *s* one *d*; *m* 2000, Doreen Margaret Fox. *Educ*: Ironville Sch.; Somercotes Sch.; Overdale Coll., Selly Oak (Diploma). Semi-skilled worker in industry, 1953–60; office clerk, 1960–61; college, 1961–65; ministry in Falkirk, 1965–67; Vice Chm., Central Scotland Br., The Samaritans, 1966–67; ordained, 1967; ministry and community work in Aberfan, 1967–74: Gen. Sec., Community Assoc.; mem., church and community cttees; Nat. Organiser, 1974–78, Dir, 1978–90, Cruse—the Nat. Orgn for the widowed and their children, subseq. Cruse—Bereavement Care. Member: Exec., Internat. Fedn of Widow/Widower Orgns, 1980–90; Internat. Workgroup on Death and Dying, 1980–90; Internat. Liaison Gp on Disasters, 1986–90; Sec., Wkg Party on Social and Psychological Aspects of Disasters, 1989–91. Chm., Churches Together in Windsor, 1992–95; Convenor, Reading and Oxford Dist URC Pastoral Cttee, 1995–98. Chaplain: King Edward VII Hosp., Windsor, 1991–2003; Thames Valley Hospice, Windsor, 1993–2003. *Publications*: The Early Days of Grieving, 1986, rev. and expanded edn 2006; (contrib.) Interpreting Death, 1997; To Everything a Season: an exploration of loss and grief in the bible, 2010; articles and papers on bereavement and on needs of widows, widowers and bereaved children. *Recreations*: music, reading, writing, keeping up with the family's activities, enjoying East Sussex. *Address*: Lymewood, Tilsmore Road, Heathfield, East Sussex TN21 0XT. *T*: (01435) 866026.

**NUTTALL, Elizabeth McColgan**; *see* McColgan-Nuttall.

**NUTTALL, Graeme John**, OBE 2014; Partner, Fieldfisher LLP (formerly Field Fisher & Martineau, then Field Fisher Waterhouse LLP), since 1988; *b* Bury, Lancs, 29 Dec. 1959; *s* of Geoffrey Nuttall and Anne Nuttall; *m* 1985, Elizabeth Jane; two *s*. *Educ*: Price's Grammar Sch., and Price's VI Form Coll., Fareham; Peterhouse, Cambridge (BA 1981). CTA. Field Fisher & Martineau: articled clerk, 1982–84; Solicitor, 1984–88. Chairman: Parfetts Employee Trust Ltd, 2008–; MJP Trustee Ltd, 2010–; Central Surrey Health Trustee Ltd, 2011–; PB Design Employee Trustee Ltd, 2014–; Tibbalds Employee Trustee Ltd, 2016–; PG Employee Trustee Ltd, 2016–; Allford Hall Monaghan Morris Employee Ownership Trustee Ltd, 2017–; Director: Piccadilly Trustee Ltd, 2015–; Net Efficiency Ltd, 2015–; PAYE Employee Trustee Ltd, 2018–. Trustee, Inst. for Future of Work, 2018–. Exec. Fellow, Inst. for Study of Employee Ownership and Profit Sharing, 2018–. Govt's Independent Advr on Employee Ownership (pt-time), 2012 (report, Sharing Success: the Nuttall Review of Employee Ownership, 2012). *Publications*: Employee Ownership: legal and tax aspects, 1987; Nelson-Jones and Nuttall's Tax Tables, 1988, 5th edn 1992; Nuttall's Tax Tables 1994–95, 1994; (jtly) Sponsorship, Endorsement and Merchandising, 2nd edn 1998. *Recreations*: art, horse racing. *Address*: Fieldfisher LLP, Riverbank House, 2 Swan Lane, EC4R 3TT. *T*: (020) 7861 4000, *Fax*: (020) 7488 0084. *E*: graeme.nuttall@fieldfisher.com.

**NUTTALL, Sir Harry**, 4th Bt *cr* 1922, of Chasefield, Bowdon, Chester; *b* 2 Jan. 1963; *s* of Sir Nicholas Keith Lillington Nuttall, 3rd Bt and Rosemary Caroline (*née* York); *S* father, 2007; *m* 1st, 1996, Kelly Marie Allen (marr. diss. 1999); 2nd, 2002, Dalit, *o d* of late Isaac Cohen, Stockholm; one *s* one *d*. *Heir*: *s* James Isaac Nuttall, *b* 2 Nov. 2005. *Clubs*: White's; British Racing Drivers'.

**NUTTALL, Rt Rev. Michael**; Bishop of Natal, 1982–2000; *b* 3 April 1934; *s* of Neville and Lucy Nuttall; *m* 1959, Dorris Marion Meyer; two *s* one *d*. *Educ*: Maritzburg Coll. (matric. 1951); Univ. of Natal (BA 1955); Rhodes Univ. (BA Hons in History 1956); MA (Cantab); MA, DipEd (Oxon); BD Hons (London). Teacher at Westville High Sch., Natal, 1958; Lectr in History, Rhodes Univ., 1959–62; Theological Student, St Paul's Coll., Grahamstown, 1963–64; ordained deacon, 1964, priest, 1965; Assistant Priest, Cathedral of St Michael and St George, Grahamstown, 1965–68; Lectr in Ecclesiastical History, Rhodes Univ., 1969–74; Dean of Grahamstown, 1975; Bishop of Pretoria, 1976–81. Pemberton Fellow, University Coll. Durham, 2001. Hon. DTheol Western Cape, 1998; Hon. DLitt Natal, 2000. *Publications*: Prayerfulness in the Spirit, 2002; Number Two to Tutu - a memoir, 2003; A Voice within Church and Society: a personal anthology, 2015; chapters in: Better Than They Knew, Volume 2 (ed R. M. de Villiers), 1974; Authority in the Anglican Communion (ed Stephen W. Sykes), 1987; Change and Challenge (ed J. Suggit and M. Goedhals), 1998; The Oxford Guide to the Book of Common Prayer (ed C. Hefling and C. Shattuck), 2006; articles in Dictionary of S African Biography. *Recreations*: walking, bird watching. *Address*: 362 Amber Valley, Private Bag X30, Howick, 3290, South Africa.

**NUTTALL, Prof. Patricia Anne**, OBE 2000; PhD; Professor of Arbovirology, Department of Zoology, University of Oxford, 2013–17, now Emeritus; Fellow of Wolfson College, Oxford, 1974–77 and since 1990; *b* 21 Jan. 1953; *m* 1984, Robert Warden Cragg; twin *d*. *Educ*: Univ. of Bristol (BSc 1974); Univ. of Reading (PhD 1978); MA Oxon 1995. Worked in Australia and Slovakia; joined NERC Inst. for Virology and Envmtl Microbiol., subseq. CEH Oxford, 1980; acting Dir, 1995–97; Site Dir, 1997–2001; Director: NERC Centre for Ecology & Hydrology, 2001–11; Nat. Capability Integration, 2011–12, Special Projects, 2012–13, NERC. Hon. Professor: University of Oxford, 1996–; Univ. of Nankia, China, 2008; Vis. Prof. of Drug Discovery, Univ. of Oxford, 2010–13. Chm., Partnership for Eur. Envmtl Res., 2008–10. Ivanovsky Medal for Virology, Russian Acad. of Scis, 1996; Harry Hoogstraal Medal, Amer. Soc. of Tropical Medicine and Hygiene, 2016. Chevalier, Ordre de Mérite Agricole (France), 2009. *Address*: Department of Zoology, University of Oxford, Oxford OX1 3SZ. *T*: (01865) 271167. *E*: pat.nuttall@zoo.ox.ac.uk.

**NUTTALL, Paul**; Member for North West, European Parliament, 2009–19 (UK Ind, 2009–18; Ind, 2018–19); *b* Liverpool, 30 Nov. 1976. *Educ*: Savio High Sch.; Hugh Baird Coll.; N Lincs Coll.; Edge Hill Univ. (BA Hist.); Liverpool Hope Univ. (MA). Formerly Lectr in History. Chm., 2008–10, Dep. Leader, 2010–16, Leader, 2016–17, UKIP. Contested (UK Ind): Bootle, 2015; Stoke-on-Trent Central, Feb. 2017; Boston and Skegness, 2017.

**NUTTALL, Simon James**; Visiting Professor, 1995–2006, and Member of the Academic Council, 1997–2006, College of Europe, Bruges; *b* 6 Oct. 1940; *s* of John C. Nuttall and Amy L. Nuttall. *Educ*: Glossop Grammar Sch.; St John's Coll., Oxford (MA). HM Diplomatic Service, 1963–71; Office of Clerk of the Assembly, Council of Europe, 1971–73; Eur. Commn, 1973–95. Vis. Fellow, 1995–97, Acad. Visitor, 2000–04, LSE. *Publications*: European Political Co-operation, 1992; European Foreign Policy, 2000; articles on European foreign policy. *Recreations*: reading, writing. *Address*: Duck House, South Street, Sherborne, Dorset DT9 3LT. *Club*: Oxford and Cambridge.

**NUTTING, Diane Patricia, (Lady Nutting)**, OBE 1998; Chairman: Georgian Group, 1999–2014; Prince of Wales's Drawing School, 2005–08; *b* 8 Sept. 1941; *d* of Duncan and Patricia Kirk; *m* 1st, 1959, 2nd Earl Beatty, DSC (*d* 1972); one *s* one *d*; 2nd, 1973, John Nutting (*see* Sir John Nutting, Bt); one *s* one *d*. *Educ*: Moira House, Eastbourne. Director: Anglia Television, 1980–95; Chiltern Radio, 1985–95. Member: Council, Nat. Trust, 1985–2000 (Chm., Thames and Chiltern Region, 1984–97; Mem., Properties Cttee, 1991–); Royal Fine Art Commn, 1985–2000; Cathedrals Fabric Commn, 1990–2000; St Albans Fabric Commn, 1993–; Churches Preservation Trust, 1997–. Trustee: Nat. Heritage Meml Fund and Heritage Lottery Fund, 1991–97; British Architectl Liby Trust, 2002–; Kelmarsh Hall Charitable Trust, 2002–; Wilts Historic Buildings Trust. Mem., Westminster CC, 1968–78 (Mem. Town Planning Cttee). JP Inner London, 1978. *Recreations*: history, architectural history. *Address*: The Manor House, Great Cheverell, Devizes, Wilts SN10 5YA; K3 Albany, Piccadilly, W1J 0AY. *Club*: Athenæum.

**NUTTING, Sir John (Grenfell)**, 4th Bt *cr* 1903, of St Helens, Booterstown, co. Dublin; QC 1995; a Recorder of the Crown Court, since 1986; a Judge, 1995–2014, Senior Judge, 2014, Courts of Appeal of Jersey and Guernsey; a Deputy High Court Judge, since 1998; *b* 28 Aug. 1942; *s* of Rt Hon. Sir Anthony Nutting, 3rd Bt, PC and of Gillian Leonora (*née* Strutt); *S* father, 1999; *m* 1973, Diane Patricia, Countess Beatty (*see* D. P. Nutting), one *s* one *d*, and one step *s* one step *d*. *Educ*: Eton Coll.; McGill Univ. (BA 1964). Called to the Bar, Middle Temple, 1968, Hon. Bencher 1991; Jun. Treasury Counsel, 1981–86; First Jun. Treasury Counsel, 1987–88; Sen. Treasury Counsel, 1988–93; First Sen. Treasury Counsel, 1993–95. Mem., Bar Council, 1976–80, 1986–87; Chm., Young Bar, 1978–79; Vice Chm., Criminal Bar Assoc., 1995. Member: Lord Chancellor's Adv. Cttee on Legal Educn and Conduct, 1977–99; Appts Panel, Ind. Supervisory Authy for Hunting, 2001–05; Commissioner: for Interception of Communications (Jersey and Guernsey), 1999–2004; for Regulation of Investigatory Powers (Jersey and Guernsey), 2004–14. Chm., Inquiry into Former Armed Service Personnel in Prison, Howard League for Penal Reform, 2009–11 (Report, 2011). Mem., Sec. of State for Justice's Rev. Cttee concerning former mems of Armed Forces and criminal justice system, 2013–14. Chm., Burghley Horse Trials Ltd,

2011–18. Chm., Helmsdale River Bd, and Helmsdale Dist Salmon Fishery Bd, 2001–17. Pres., NE Milton Keynes Conservative Assoc., 1990–93. A Patron, Philharmonia Orch., 2001–10. Chm. of Govs, Burghley House Preservation Trust, 2009–19; Trustee, Trust Hse Trust, 2010–; Mem., Provost's Appeals Panel, 2012–, Chm., Henry VI Soc., 2014–, Eton Coll. FRPSL 1970. *Recreations:* shooting, stalking, fishing. *Heir: s* James Edward Sebastian Nutting [*b* 12 Jan. 1977; *m* 2007, Antonia, *d* of Eugen von Boch; one *s* one *d*]. *Address:* The Manor House, Great Cheverell, Devizes, Wilts SN10 5YA; K3 Albany, Piccadilly, W1J 0AY; Achentoul, Kinbrace, Sutherland KW11 6UB. *Clubs:* White's (Chm., 2014–17), The Other.

**NUTTON, Prof. Vivian,** PhD; FBA 2008; Professor of the History of Medicine, University College London, 1993–2009, now Emeritus; *b* Halifax, Yorks, 21 Dec. 1943; *s* of Eli and Constance Nutton; *m* 1973, Christine Clements; one *s* two *d*. *Educ:* Elland C of E Prim. Sch.; Bradford Grammar Sch.; Selwyn Coll., Cambridge (BA 1965; PhD 1970; Hon. Fellow 2009). Res. Fellow, 1967–69, Fellow and Dir of Studies in Classics, 1969–77, Selwyn College, Cambridge; Historian (Ancient), Wellcome Inst., and Hon. Lectr, UCL, 1977–93. Visiting Professor: Johns Hopkins Univ., Baltimore, 1988; Russian People's Friendship Univ., Moscow, 1998; Vis. Fellow, Inst. for Advanced Study, Princeton, 2000; Hooker Dist. Vis. Prof., McMaster Univ., 2007; Hon. Prof., Dept of Classics and Centre for Hist. of Medicine, 2011–13, Prof., Dept of Classics, 2013–14, Univ. of Warwick; Prof. of Hist. of Medicine and Culture, First Moscow State Univ., 2015–. Corresp. Mem., Internat. Acad. of Hist. of Medicine, 1985; Member: Acad. Internat. d'Histoire des Scis, 1993; Academia Europaea, 2000; Deutsche Akademie der Wissenschaften (formerly Deutsche Akademie der Naturforscher Leopoldina), 2002; Fellow, Studio Firmano per la Storia della Medicina, 2003; correspondant étranger, Académie des Inscriptions et Belles-Lettres, 2016. Hon. FRCP 1999; Hon. Fellow, Faculty of the History and Philosophy of Medicine, Soc. of Apothecaries, 2014. *Publications:* Galen, On Prognosis: text, translation, commentary, 1979; (ed) Galen: problems and prospects, 1981; (ed jtly) Theories of Fever from Antiquity to the Enlightenment, 1981; John Caius and the Manuscripts of Galen, 1987; From Democedes to Harvey: studies in the history of medicine, 1988; (ed) Medicine at the Courts of Europe, 1500–1837, 1990; (jtly) The Western Medical Tradition, 800 BC to AD 1800, 1995 (Histoire de la lutte contre la maladie, 1999); (ed jtly) The History of Medical Education in Britain, 1995; Galen, On My Own Opinions: text, translation and commentary, 1999; (ed) The Unknown Galen, 2002; Ancient Medicine, 2004, 2nd edn 2012; (ed) Pestilential Complexities: understanding medieval plague, 2008; (trans. and ed) Girolamo Mercuriale, De arte gymnastica, 2008; (ed jtly) Girolamo Mercuriale: medicina e cultura nell'Europa del Cinquecento, 2008; Galen, On Problematical Movements, 2011; (trans. jtly) Galen, Psychological Writings, 2013; Rumbustious John: change and renewal in Victorian Sandridge, 2014; (ed) Principles of Anatomy according to the Opinion of Galen by Johann Guinter and Andreas Vesalius, 2017; (trans.) An Autobibliography by John Caius, 2018. *Recreations:* bellringing, singing, playing piano and organ. *Address:* Life Sciences Faculty, University College London, Gower Street, WC1E 6BT. *E:* ucgavnu@ucl.ac.uk.

**NUVOLONI, Stefano Vincenzo;** QC 2017; *b* Kampala, Uganda, 1970; *s* of Carlo Alberto Nuvoloni and Dr Maureen Nuvoloni; *m* 2001, Kirsty Wotherspoon; one *s*. *Educ:* Claires Court Sch.; Windsor Boys' Sch.; Queen Mary Coll., Univ. of London (LLB); King's Coll. London (MA). Called to the Bar, Inner Temple, 1994; in practice as a barrister, specialising in family law, 22 Old Bldgs, 1995–2002, St Ives Chambers, 2002–11, 5 Paper Buildings, 2011–12, No5 Chambers, 2012–. *Recreations:* all free time is taken up with the family's obsession with horses, but golf when time allows. *Address:* No5 Chambers, Fountain Court, Steelhouse Lane, Birmingham B4 6DR. *T:* 0845 210 5555, *Fax:* (0121) 606 1501. *E:* sn@no5.com.

**NYE,** Baroness *cr* 2010 (Life Peer), of Lambeth in the London Borough of Lambeth; **Susan Jane Nye;** Director, Government Relations, No 10 Downing Street, 2007–10; *b* London, 17 May 1955; *m* 1989, Gavyn Davies, *qv*; two *s* one *d*. *Educ:* Westcliff High Sch. for Girls. Sec., No 10 Downing St, 1976; Advr to Gordon Brown, MP, 1992–2007. *Address:* House of Lords, SW1A 0PW.

**NYE, Roderick Christopher, (Rick);** Managing Director, Populus, since 2013 (Director, 2003–13); *b* 28 Feb. 1967; *s* of late Bertram Edward Nye and Elsie Doreen Nye; *m* 1994, Diana Grace, *d* of John and Priscilla Douglas. *Educ:* Norton Knatchbull Sch., Ashford; American Univ., Washington; Univ. of Leeds (BA Hons 1989). Policy Advr to David Owen, 1989–90; Journalist, VNU Business Publications, 1990–92; Dep. Dir, 1992–95, Dir, 1995–99, Social Market Foundn; Dir, Cons. Res. Dept, 1999–2003. Mem. (C), Westminster CC, 1998–2002. *Publications:* Welfare to Work: the 'America Works' experience, 1996; (ed) The Future of Welfare, 1997. *Recreations:* United States, reading, sport (watching), Chelsea FC. *Address:* (office) 10 Northburgh Street, EC1V 0AT. *Club:* Sam's.

**NYE, Simon Beresford;** writer; *b* 29 July 1958; *s* of Dennis Beresford Nye and Sheila Elizabeth Nye; *m* 2011, Claudia Stumpfl; two *s* two *d*. *Educ:* Collyer's Sch., Horsham; Bedford Coll., London (BA French and German 1980). Writer: *television series:* Men Behaving Badly, 1992–99; Frank Stubbs Promotes, 1993–95; Is It Legal?, 1995–98; My Wonderful Life, 1997–98; How Do You Want Me?, 1998–99; Beast, 2000–01; The Savages, 2001; Wild West, 2002–03; Hardware, 2003–04; Carrie and Barry, 2004–05; Reggie Perrin, 2009–10; Just William, 2010; Warren United, 2014; The Durrells, 2016–19; Urban Myths: the Sex Pistols v Bill Grundy, 2018; Scrambled Eggs, 2019; *television films:* True Love, 1996; The Railway Children, 2000; Pollyanna, 2003; Pride, 2004; Beauty, 2004; Tunnel of Love, 2004; Open Wide, 2005; My Family and Other Animals, 2005; Catwalk Dogs, 2007; Tommy Cooper: not like that, like this, 2014; 4 ITV pantomimes, 1998–2002; *translations* of plays: Don Juan, 2002; Accidental Death of an Anarchist, 2003. *Publications:* Men Behaving Badly, 1989; Wideboy, 1991; The Best of Men Behaving Badly, 2000; various translations. *Recreation:* sitting in cafés. *Address:* c/o Knight Hall Agency, Lower Ground Floor, 7 Mallow Street, EC1Y 8RQ. *T:* (020) 3397 2901.

**NYE, William James,** LVO 2015; Secretary-General, Archbishop's Council and General Synod of the Church of England, since 2015; *b* Amersham, 28 March 1966; *s* of Lt Col Ralph Nye and Barbara Nye; *m* 2006, Dr Katherine Bartlett; one *d*. *Educ:* Christ's Hosp.; Clare Coll., Cambridge (BA 1987); Yale Univ. (MA 1989). HM Treasury, 1990–98; DCMS, 1998–2000; HM Treasury, 2001–02; Home Office: Finance Dir, 2002–05; Dir, Counter-Terrorism and Intelligence, 2005–07; Dir in Office for Security and Counter-Terrorism, 2007–08; Dir, Nat. Security Secretariat, later Dir, Strategy and Counter-terrorism, Nat. Security Secretariat, Cabinet Office, 2008–11; Principal Private Sec. to the Prince of Wales and the Duchess of Cornwall, 2011–15. *Address:* Church House, Great Smith Street, SW1P 3AZ. *Club:* Sussex County Cricket.

**NYMAN, Bernard Martin;** Sole Principal, BM Nyman & Co., solicitors and publishing lawyers, since 1999; *b* London, 27 Feb. 1954; *s* of Raymond Nyman and Jean Nyman; *m* 1986, Carole Stern; two *d*. *Educ:* Royal Liberty Sch.; Univ. of Sheffield (BA Hons Law 1975). Admitted solicitor, 1979; Solicitor, 1979–83, Partner, 1983–94, Rubinstein Callingham; Partner, Manches & Co., 1994–98. Trustee: Enid Blyton Trust for Children, 2000–08; Cleft Lip and Palate Assoc., 2003–14. *Publications:* The Encyclopaedia of Forms and Precedents, vol. 21 (pt 2), Copyright, 1991 to 2015; (contrib.) Character Merchandising, 2nd edn 1996; (contrib.) Copinger and Skone James on Copyright, 14th edn 1999 to 16th edn 2013. *Recreations:* jazz, cricket, football, reading, films, family, meditating, cuddling cats. *Address:* BM Nyman & Co., 25 Limes Avenue, N12 8QN. *T:* (020) 3601 4163, *Fax:* (020) 8445 2852. *E:* bernie@bmnyman.co.uk.

**NYMAN, Michael,** CBE 2008; composer; *b* 23 March 1944; *s* of Mark and Jeanette Nyman; *m* 1970; two *d*. *Educ:* Royal Academy of Music; King's College London (BMus); Conservatorul Ciprian Porumbescu, Bucharest. FRAM 1991. Music critic, Spectator, New Statesman, The Listener, 1968–78; formed: Michael Nyman Band, 1977; MN Records, 2005. *Film scores include:* The Draughtsman's Contract, 1982; Drowning by Numbers, 1988; The Cook, The Thief, His Wife and Her Lover, 1989; Monsieur Hire, 1989; The Hairdresser's Husband, 1990; Prospero's Books, 1991; The Piano, 1992; Carrington, 1994; The Diary of Anne Frank, 1995; The Ogre, 1996; Gattaca, 1997; Ravenous, 1998; Wonderland, The End of the Affair, 1999; Act Without Words, 2000; The Claim, 2001; 24 Hours in The Life of a Woman, The Actors, 2002; Natalie, 2003; Detroit: Ruin of a City, 9 Songs, A Cock and Bull Story, The Libertine, 2005; Man on Wire, 2008; Everyday, 2012; McQueen, 2018; *other compositions:* A Broken Set of Rules, Royal Ballet, 1983; The Man Who Mistook his Wife for a Hat (opera), 1986; String Quartets, 1985, 1988, 1990, 1995; Six Celan Songs, 1990–91; Noises, Sounds and Sweet Airs (opera), 1991; Where the Bee Dances, for saxophone and orch., 1991; Songs for Tony, 1993; The Piano Concerto, 1993; MGV (Musique à Grand Vitesse), 1993; Harpsichord Concerto, 1995; Trombone Concerto, 1995; After Extra Time, 1996; Double Concerto for Saxophone and Cello, 1997; Cycle of Disquietude, 1998; The Commissar Vanishes, 1999; Facing Goya (opera), 2000, revised 2002; Concerto for Saxophone Quartet and Orch., 2001; a dance he little thinks of, for orch., 2001; Violin Concerto, 2003; Man and Boy: Dada (opera), For John Peel (trio), Acts of Beauty (chamber ensemble), 2004; Love Counts (opera), Melody Waves, 2005; 11th Symphony: Hillsborough Memorial, 2014; War Work (also dir), 2015; ballet scores. *Video art:* Videofile, 2009; Images Were Introduced, 2013. Ivor Novello Classical Music Award, 2011. *Publications:* Experimental Music: Cage and Beyond, 1974, 2nd edn 1999; Sublime, 2008. *Recreation:* QPR. *Club:* Groucho.

**NZIMBI, Most Rev. Benjamin Mwanzia;** Archbishop of Kenya, 2002–09; Bishop of All Saints Cathedral Diocese, 2002–09; *b* 17 Oct. 1945; *s* of Paul Nzimbi Munuve and Martha Nditi Nzimbi; *m* 1974, Alice Kavula Nzimbi; three *s* two *d*. *Educ:* Univ. of Nairobi (BA Religious Studies and Philos. 1974); Trinity Coll., Nairobi; Hamline Univ., St Paul, USA (MA Mgt for Non-Profit 1999). Taught in secondary sch. and teachers' colls, 1974–84. Ordained, deacon, 1978, priest, 1979; Curate, All Souls Parish, Machakos, and Chaplain, Machakos Teachers' Coll., 1978–84; Vicar, St Francis Parish, Karen, Nairobi, 1984–85; Bishop: Machakos Dio., 1985–95; Kitui Dio., 1995–2002. Ombudsman, Jomo Kenyatta Univ. of Agriculture and Technol., 2013. *Address:* c/o Anglican Church of Kenya, PO Box 40502, 00100 Nairobi, Kenya.

# O

**OAKDEN, Edward Anthony,** CMG 2006; HM Diplomatic Service; Ambassador to Jordan, since 2015; *b* 3 Nov. 1959; *s* of Richard Ralph Oakden and Patricia Jeanne Oakden; three *d*; *m* Dr Florence Eid. *Educ:* Repton Sch.; Cambridge Univ. (BA Hons Hist.). Entered FCO 1981; Second Secretary: Baghdad, 1984–85; Khartoum, 1985–88; Private Sec. to Ambassador and First Sec., Washington, 1988–92; Deputy Head: EU Dept (Ext.), 1992–94; Eastern Adriatic Dept, 1994; Private Sec. to Prime Minister, 1995–97; Deputy Head: EU Dept (Internal), 1994–98; of Mission, Madrid, 1998–2002; Hd, Security Policy Dept, 2002; Dir, Internat. Security, 2002–04; Dir, Defence and Strategic Threats, and Ambassador for Counter-terrorism, 2004–06; Ambassador to UAE, 2006–10; Man. Dir, UKTI, 2010–13 (on secondment); Dir, Middle East and North Africa, FCO, 2013–15. *Recreations:* family, running, swimming, history, classical music. *Address:* c/o Foreign and Commonwealth Office, King Charles Street, SW1A 2AH.

**OAKELEY, Sir Robert (John Atholl),** 9th Bt *cr* 1790, of Shrewsbury; Managing Director, Picador plc, since 1995; *b* Fareham, 13 Aug. 1963; *s* of Sir John Digby Atholl Oakeley, 8th Bt and Maureen Frances Oakeley; *S* father, 2016; *m* 1989, Amanda, *d* of late William Knowles; one *s* one *d*. *Educ:* West Hill Park Sch.; Gregg Sch. Director: Rowles Ltd, 1999–; Rowles Picador Ltd, 1999–; Pat's Garage Ltd, 2012–; Hawkers Lodge Properties Ltd, 2013–. *Recreations:* sailing, cycling. *Heir: s* William Oakeley, *b* 13 Oct. 1995. *Address:* Picador plc, Portsmouth Road, Sholing, Southampton SO19 9RP. *T:* (023) 8025 5432. *E:* robert.oakeley@picadorplc.co.uk.

**OAKES, Sir Christopher,** 3rd Bt *cr* 1939, of Nassau, Bahama Islands; *b* 10 July 1949; *s* of Sir Sydney Oakes, 2nd Bt, and Greta (*d* 1977), *yr d* of Gunnar Victor Hartmann, Copenhagen, Denmark; *S* father, 1966; *m* 1978, Julie Dawn, *d* of Donovan Franklin Cowan, Regina, Canada; one *s* one *d*. *Educ:* Bredon, Tewkesbury; Georgia Mil. Acad., USA. *Heir: s* Victor Oakes, *b* 6 March 1983.

**OAKES, (William) John,** MA; Headmaster, Dartford Grammar School, since 2009; *b* Hindley, 17 Jan. 1956; *s* of Norman and Marion Oakes; *m* 1987, Amanda Percival; one *s* one *d*. *Educ:* Bishop Vesey's Grammar Sch.; Goldsmiths' Coll., Univ. of London (BSc; PGCE); Univ. of Greenwich (MA Outdoor Educn). NPQH. Langley Park School for Boys: Hd of Geology, 1978–2001; Hd of Outdoor Educn, 1981–2001; Sen. Teacher, 1989–2001; Dartford Grammar School: Asst Headteacher, 2001–04; Dep. Headteacher, 2004–06; Hd of Sch. and Acting Headteacher, 2007–09. Member and Director, Head Teacher Group: Internat. Baccalaureate Schs and Colls Assoc., 2009–; Kent and Medway Trng, 2009–; Confucius Classrooms, 2009– (Chm., Head Teacher Steering Gp, 2015–). Nat. Leader of Educn. *Recreations:* outdoor pursuits, Rugby, gardening, travel. *Address:* Dartford Grammar School, West Hill, Dartford, Kent DA1 2HW. *T:* (01322) 223039. *E:* head@dartfordgrammarschool.org.uk.

**OAKESHOTT,** family name of **Baron Oakeshott of Seagrove Bay**.

**OAKESHOTT OF SEAGROVE BAY,** Baron *cr* 2000 (Life Peer), of Seagrove Bay in the co. of Isle of Wight; **Matthew Alan Oakeshott;** Chairman, OLIM Property Ltd, since 2012; Joint Managing Director, Value and Income Trust plc, since 1986; *b* 10 Jan. 1947; *o s* of Keith Robertson Oakeshott, CMG and of Jill Oakeshott; *m* 1976, Dr Pippa Poulton; two *s* one *d*. *Educ:* Charterhouse (Sen. Foundn Scholar); University Coll. and Nuffield Coll., Oxford (BA 1st cl. Hons PPE). ODI/Nuffield Fellow, Kenya Ministry of Finance and Planning, 1968–70; Special Advr to Rt Hon. Roy Jenkins, MP, 1972–76; Investment Mgr, then Dir, Warburg Investment Management, 1976–81; Investment Mgr, Courtaulds Pension Fund, 1981–85; founder and Jt Man. Dir, OLIM Ltd (Independent Investment Managers), 1986–2012. Mem. (Lab) Oxford City Council, 1972–76. Member: SDP Nat. Cttee, 1981–82; SDP Nat. Economic Policy Cttee, 1981–83. Contested: (Lab) Horsham and Crawley, Oct. 1974; (SDP/Alliance) Cambridge, 1983. A Lib Dem spokesman on Treasury, 2001–11, and on Work and Pensions, 2003–10, H of L; Mem., Select Cttee on Economic Affairs, H of L, 2001–08; Chm., Business Adv. Gp, BIS, 2010–11. Gov., NIESR, 2010–. *Publications:* (contrib.) By-Elections in British Politics, 1973. *Recreations:* music, elections, Arsenal FC. *Address:* c/o House of Lords, SW1A 1AA.

**OAKHAM, Archdeacon of;** *see* Steele, Ven. G. J.

**OAKLEY, Christopher John,** CBE 1999; Chief Executive, MEF Holdings, since 2016 (Chief Executive, MEF Comm V (formerly Comm VA MEF), 2003–14); *b* 11 Nov. 1941; *s* of late Ronald Oakley and Joyce Oakley; *m* 1st, 1962, Linda Margaret Viney (marr. diss. 1986); one *s* two *d*; 2nd, 1990, Moira Jean Martingale (marr. diss. 2003); one *s*, and two adopted *d*; 3rd, 2004, Lisa Hanson; one step *d*. *Educ:* Skinners' School, Tunbridge Wells. Kent and Sussex Courier, 1959; Bromley and Kentish Times, 1963; Kent and Sussex Courier, 1963; Evening Argus, Brighton, 1966; Evening Echo, Basildon, 1969; Evening Post, Leeds, 1970; Dep. Editor, Yorkshire Post, 1976; Editor, Lancashire Evening Post, 1981; Dir, Lancashire Evening Post, 1981–83; Editor, Liverpool Echo, 1983–89; Dir, Liverpool Daily Post and Echo Ltd, 1984–89; Editor-in-Chief, 1989–91, Man. Dir, 1990–93, Chm., 1993–97, Birmingham Post & Mail; Gp Chief Exec., Midland Ind. Newspapers plc, 1991–97; Man. Dir, Mirror Regl Newspapers, 1997–98; Chief Exec., Regl Ind. Media, 1998–2002; Exec. Chm., HRM Partnership Ltd, 2002–03. Chairman: Coventry Newspapers, 1991–97; Midland Weekly Media, 1997; Newsco Insider Ltd, 2002–14; Chapter Eight Ltd, 2009–14; Royal Armouries Trading and Enterprises Ltd, 2010–12. Pres., Newspaper Soc., 1997–98; Hon. Vice Pres., Soc. of Editors. Nat. Appeals Chm., Newspaper Press Fund, 2000–01. Trustee: Royal Armouries, 2002–10; Television Trust for the Envmt, 2010–19. Hon. Fellow, Univ. of Central Lancashire, 1998. *Address:* MEF Holdings, Dreve des Pins 40, 1420 Braine-l'Alleud, Belgium.

**OAKLEY, Deborah Clare Judge;** Investment Manager, Veritas Investment Management, since 2010; *b* Liverpool, 12 Aug. 1964; *d* of Joseph and Jean Judge; *m* 2001, Oliver Oakley; two *s*. *Educ:* Brighthelmston Sch., Southport; Southport Tech. Coll. (BEC Dip. Business Studies 1982); Univ. of Manchester Inst. of Sci. and Technol. (BSc Hons Mgt Scis 1985). Dir and Investment Manager, Newton Investment Mgt, 1986–2006. Non-executive Director: NHS Camden, 2007–11 (Chair, Audit Cttee, 2008–11); HPA, 2009–13 (Chair, Biol Medicines Tech. Cttee, 2011–12); Royal Free London NHS Foundn Trust, 2011–17 (Chair, Audit Cttee, 2011–17); Medicines and Healthcare Products Regulatory Agency, 2012–18 (Chair, Audit and Risk Assce Cttee, 2015–18); NHS Digital, 2018– (Chair, Audit and Risk Cttee, 2018–). Mem., CFA (ASIP 1988). Chair, Brookfield Sch. PTA, Camden, 2009–14; William Ellis Sch. Parent Assoc., Camden, 2016–. Volunteer: C4WS, Kentish Town, 2005–; Sanktus, Kentish Town, 2019–. Mem. Kenwood Ladies Pond Assoc. *Recreations:* cycling, outdoor swimming (all year round), choral singing, running, drinking coffee. *Address:* c/o Veritas Investment Management, 90 Long Acre, WC2E 9RA.

**OAKLEY, Rev. Canon Mark David;** Dean, St John's College, Cambridge, since 2018; Deputy Priest in Ordinary to the Queen, since 1996; *b* 28 Sept. 1968; *s* of David Oakley and Sheila (*née* Cupples). *Educ:* Shrewsbury Sch.; King's Coll., London (BD 1st cl. 1990; AKC 1990); St Stephen's House, Oxford. Ordained deacon, 1993, priest, 1994; Asst Curate, St John's Wood Ch, 1993–96; Chaplain to the Bp of London, 1996–2000; Priest-in-charge, subseq. Rector, St Paul's, Covent Garden, 2000–05; Archdeacon of Germany and Northern Europe, and Chaplain of St Alban's, Copenhagen, 2005–08; Canon Emeritus, Holy Trinity Pro-Cathedral, Brussels, 2008–; Priest-in-charge, Grosvenor Chapel, Mayfair, 2008–10; Canon Res. and Treasurer, 2010–12, Canon Chancellor, 2012–18, St Paul's Cathedral. Area Dean, Westminster St Margaret, 2004–05. Eric Abbott Meml Lectr, Eric Abbott Meml Trust, Westminster Abbey and Keble Coll., Oxford, 2002; Vis. Lectr, Dept of Theol. and Religious Studies, KCL, 2014–; Vis. Lectr, Nat. Gall., 2015–; Vis. Scholar, Sarum Coll., 2017–. Hon. Chaplain, Vintners' Co., 2011–. Univ. Sermon, Oxford, 2014, 2018; Lect., Guntrip Trust, 2018. Governor: St Clement Danes Sch., 2000–05; City Literary Inst., 2002–05. Trustee: Civil Liberties Trust, 2014–; King's Theological Trust, 2015–. Mem. Bd, RS Thomas and ME Eldridge Soc., 2017–. Vice Pres., Radius, 2011–; Patron, Tell MAMA, 2013–; Ambassador, StopHate UK, 2015–. Pres., Shrops Horticl Soc., 2014–15. Freeman, City of London, 1999. Judge, Ted Hughes Award, 2018. Community Volunteer Upstander Award, Nat. Hate Crime Awards, 2016. *Publications:* The Collage of God, 2001, 2nd edn 2012; (ed) John Donne: selected poetry and prose, 2004; (ed) Readings for Weddings, 2004, 2nd edn 2013; (ed) Readings for Funerals, 2015; The Splash of Words: believing in poetry, 2016 (Michael Ramsey Prize, 2019); (ed) A Good Year, 2016; By Way of the Heart, 2019; My Sour Sweet Days: George Herbert poems through Lent, 2019. *Recreations:* poetry, theatre, dog-walking, reading in the bath, Radio 4. *Address:* St John's College, Cambridge CB2 1TP. *E:* mdo26@cam.ac.uk. *Club:* Garrick.

**OAKLEY, Robin Francis Leigh,** OBE 2001; Contributing Political Analyst, CNN, since 2009 (European Political Editor, 2000–09); *b* 20 Aug. 1941; *s* of Joseph Henry Oakley, civil engineer and Alice Barbara Oakley; *m* 1966, Carolyn Susan Germaine Rumball; one *s* one *d*. *Educ:* Wellington College; Brasenose College, Oxford (MA). Liverpool Daily Post, 1964–70; Sunday Express, 1970–79; Assistant Editor: Now! magazine, 1979–81; Daily Mail, 1981–86; Political Editor: The Times, 1986–92; BBC, 1992–2000. Presenter, The Week in Westminster, BBC Radio, 1987–92, 2000–05. Turf columnist: Spectator, 1995–; FT, 2003–06. Trustee, Thomson Foundn, 2001–14. *Publications:* Valley of the Racehorse: a year in the life of Lambourn, 2000; Inside Track: the political correspondent's life, 2001; Frankincense and More: the Barry Hills biography, 2010; The Cheltenham Festival: a centenary history, 2011; Clive Brittain: the smiling pioneer, 2012; Britain and Ireland's Top Racehorses of All Time, 2012; Tales from the Turf, 2013; (with Edward Gillespie) Sixty Years of Jump Racing: from Arkle to McCoy, 2017. *Recreations:* theatre, horse racing, sports, bird watching. *Address:* 24 Bridge End, Dorchester-on-Thames, Wallingford, Oxon OX10 7JP. *Club:* Royal Automobile.

*See also* B. M. G. Elkington.

**OAKLEY, Prof. Stephen Phelps,** PhD; FBA 2008; Kennedy Professor of Latin, and Fellow of Emmanuel College, University of Cambridge, since 2007; *b* 20 Nov. 1958; *s* of Julian Oakley and Jillian Oakley (now Marshallsay); *m* 1998, Ruth Mary Otway; two *s*. *Educ:* Bradfield Coll., Berks; Queens' Coll., Cambridge (BA Hons Classics 1980; MA 1983; PhD 1985). Res. Fellow, 1984–86, Official Fellow, 1986–98, Emmanuel Coll., Cambridge; Reader in Classics, 1998–2002, Prof. of Latin, 2002–07, Univ. of Reading. MAE 2012. Mem., Pontifical Acad. of Latin, 2014. *Publications:* The Hill Forts of the Samnites, 1995; A Commentary on Livy, books 6–10, Vol. 1 1997, Vol. 2 1998, Vol. 3 2005, Vol. 4 2005; contrib. learned jls. *Recreations:* gardening, exploring Dorset. *Address:* Emmanuel College, Cambridge CB2 3AP. *T:* (01223) 334200. *E:* spo23@cam.ac.uk.

**OAKLEY, Dame Susan (Elizabeth Anne);** *see* Devoy, Dame S. E. A.

**OAKS, Agnes,** CBE 2010; former freelance ballerina; Ballet Teacher, Tallinn Ballet School, since 2018; freelance guest teacher, since 2018; *b* 29 May 1970; *d* of Juhan Oks and Valentina Oks; *m* 1990, Thomas Edur, *qv*; one *d*. *Educ:* Estonian State Ballet Sch.; Bolshoi Ballet Sch., Moscow; Royal Ballet Sch. (PDTC 2007). Principal Ballerina with: Estonian Opera Ballet, 1989–90; English Nat. Ballet, 1990–96; Birmingham Royal Ballet, 1996–97; Resident Guest Artist with English National Ballet, 1997–2009; has danced most classical ballets, inc. Swan Lake, Cinderella, Sleeping Beauty, The Nutcracker, Giselle, Coppélia, Romeo and Juliet, Don Quixote, and many others; Asst to Artistic Dir, 2009–16, Repetiteur, 2016–17, Estonian Nat. Ballet. Patron (with Thomas Edur): British Ballet Orgn, 2004–; English Nat. Ballet Sch., 2008–. 2001 Year Award, Achievements in Dance, Estonia, 2002; Unique Partnership Award (with Thomas Edur), Critics' Circle, 2003; Olivier Award, Achievements in Dance (with Thomas Edur), 2004; Best Female Dancer Award, Critics' Circle, 2008. Third Class Order of the White Star (Estonia), 2001. *Address:* c/o Tallinn Ballet School, Toom-Kooli 11, Tallinn 10130, Estonia.

**OAKSHOTT, Sir Thomas Hendrie,** 4th Bt *cr* 1959, of Bebington, co. Palatine of Chester; *b* Nairobi, 12 June 1959; *e s* of Hon. Sir Michael Arthur John Oakshott, 3rd Bt and Christina Rose Methuen Oakshott (*née* Banks) (*d* 1985); *S* father, 2014. *Educ:* Rugby Sch.; Edinburgh Univ. (BMus 1983). FRCO; LRAM. *Heir: b* Charles Michael Oakshott [*b* 21 May 1961; *m* 1989, Anne Stapleton; one *s* two *d*]. *Address:* Warre House Cottage, Common Lane, Eton College, Windsor, Berks SL4 6DU.

**OATEN, Mark;** Chief Executive, International Fur Trade Federation, since 2011; *b* 8 March 1964; *s* of Ivor Condell Oaten and Audrey Oaten; *m* 1992, Belinda Fordham (marr. diss.); two *d*. *Educ:* Hatfield Poly. (BA Hons 1986); Hertfordshire Coll. of FE, Watford (Dip in Public Relns 1989). Consultant, Shandwick Public Affairs, 1990–92; Consultant, 1992–95, Man. Dir, 1995–97, Westminster Public Relations. Dir, Oasis Radio, 1995–96. Mem. (Lib Dem) Watford BC, 1986–94. Contested (Lib Dem) Watford, 1992. MP (Lib Dem) Winchester, 1997–2010. PPS to Leader of Liberal Democrat Party, 1999–2001. Lib Dem spokesman: on disabilities, 1997–99; on foreign affairs and defence, 1999–2001; on Cabinet Office, 2001–02; on home affairs, 2003–10. Mem., Select Cttee on Public Admin, 1999–2001. Chm., All-Pty Prisoners of War Gp, 1998–2000; Sec., All-Pty EU Accession Gp, 2000–05; Co-Chm., All-Pty Adoption Gp, 2000–05; Treas., All-Pty Human Rights Gp, 2000–05. Chm., Lib Dem Parly Pty, 2001–03. Mem., Council of Europe, 2008–10. Director: British Healthcare Trades Assoc., 2008–11; Unlock, 2008. *Publications:* Coalition, 2007; Screwing Up, 2009. *Recreations:* gardening, cinema, swimming, football.

**OATES,** Baron *cr* 2015 (Life Peer), of Denby Grange in the County of West Yorkshire; **Jonathan Oates;** Senior Adviser, Children's Investment Fund Foundation, since 2017; *b* London, 1969; *s* of Rev. Canon John Oates, *qv*; civil partnership 2006, David Hill. *Educ:* Marlborough Coll.; Exeter Univ. (BA Hons Politics). Actg Dep. Head, St James' Secondary Sch., Zongoro, Zimbabwe, 1988; Political Consultant, Westminster Strategy, 1993–98; Parly Advr, Parliament of S Africa, 1999–2001; Policy Advr to Youth Justice Bd, 2001–02; Associate, Mark Bolland Associates Ltd, 2002–04; Dir, Bell Pottinger, 2004–07 and 2008–09; Dir of Communications, Lib Dems, 2007–08 and 2009–10; COS to Dep. Prime Minister, 2010–15. Election Agent to: Edward Davey, 1997; Jenny Tonge, 2001; Campaign Manager for Jeremy Browne, 2005. Mem., Royal Bor. of Kingston Council, 1994–98 (Dep. Leader, 1997–98). *Recreations:* running, poetry, politics, swimming.

**OATES, Joan Louise,** PhD; FBA 2004; Fellow, Girton College, Cambridge, 1971–95, Life Fellow, since 1995; Senior Fellow, McDonald Institute for Archaeological Research, Cambridge, since 1995; *b* 6 May 1928; *d* of Harold Burdette Lines and Beatrice Naomi Lines; *m* 1956, (Edward Ernest) David (Michael) Oates, FBA (*d* 2004); one *s* two *d*. *Educ:* Syracuse Univ., Syracuse, NY (BA 1950); Girton Coll., Cambridge (Fulbright Schol., Wenner-Gren Schol.; PhD 1953). Asst Curator, Metropolitan Mus. of Art, NYC, 1954–56; Lectr in Hist. and Archaeol. of Ancient Near East, Univ. of Cambridge, 1989–95. Guggenheim Fellow, 1966–67. Arents Medal, Syracuse Univ., 1991; John Coles Medal, British Acad., 2014. *Publications:* Babylon, 1976 (trans. German, Italian, Spanish, Polish, Lithuanian, Turkish, Hungarian, Arabic), rev. edn 2005; (ed jtly) Of Pots and Plans, 2002; with David Oates: The Rise of Civilization, 1976 (trans. Japanese, Hungarian, Arabic); Nimrud: an Assyrian City revealed, 2001, 2nd edn 2004; Excavations at Tell al Rimah: the pottery, 2001; Excavations at Tell Brak, vol. 1, Mitanni and Old Babylonian, 1997, vol. 2, Nagar in the 3rd Millennium BC, 2001; over 120 papers in jls and chapters in books. *Recreations:* snorkelling, walking, bird watching, painting. *Address:* 86 High Street, Barton, Cambridge CB23 7BG. *T:* (01223) 262273.

**OATES, Rev. Canon John;** Rector of St Bride's Church, Fleet Street, 1984–2000; Prebendary, St Paul's Cathedral, 1997–2001, now Prebendary Emeritus; *b* 14 May 1930; *s* of John and Ethel Oates; *m* 1962, Sylvia Mary (*d* 2018), *d* of Herbert Charles and Ada Harris; three *s* one *d*. *Educ:* Queen Elizabeth School, Wakefield; SSM, Kelham. Curate, Eton College Mission, Hackney Wick, 1957–60, Founder, 59 Club, 1959; Development Officer, C of E Youth Council and mem. staff, Bd of Education, 1960–64; Development Sec., C of E Council for Commonwealth Settlement, 1964–65, Gen. Sec. 1965–70; Sec., C of E Cttee on Migration and Internat. Affairs, Bd for Social Responsibility, 1968–71; Vicar of Richmond, Surrey, 1970–84; RD, Richmond and Barnes, 1979–84; Area Dean, City of London, 1997–2000; permission to officiate, dios of London and Southwark, 2000–. Commissary: of Archbishop of Perth and Bishop of NW Australia, 1968–2000; to Archbishop of Jerusalem, 1969–75; to Bishop of Bunbury, 1969–. Hon. Canon, Bunbury, 1969–. Mem., Unilever Central Ethical Compliance Gp, 1991–97; Consultant, Creative Visions, USA, 2001–. Chapter Clerk, London City Deanery, 1994–97; Mem., Coll. of Canons, St Paul's Cathedral, 2001–. Chaplain: Inst. of Journalists, 1984–2000 (Life FCIJ 1995); Inst. of Public Relations, 1984–2000; Publicity Club of London, 1984–2000; London Press Club, 1984–2000; Co. of Marketors, 1984–2000; Co. of Stationers and Newspapermakers, 1989–2000; Co. of Turners, 1995–2001; Guild of St Bride, 2000–; Hon. Asst, St Cyprian's, Clarence Gate, 2001–. Freeman, City of London, 1985; Hon. Liveryman: Marketors' Co., 1999–; Turners' Co., 2000–. *Recreations:* broadcasting, walking, exploring. *Address:* 27 York Court, The Albany, Albany Park Road, Kingston upon Thames KT2 5ST. *T:* 07481 684248. *E:* john@oates.co.uk. *Club:* Garrick.
*See also Baron Oates.*

**OATES, (John) Keith;** Deputy Chairman, 1994–99 and Managing Director, 1991–99, Marks and Spencer plc; Forestry Commissioner for England, 2013–16 (non-executive Director, English Committee, 2007–13, Member, GB Board of Forestry Commissioners, 2013–16, Forestry Commission); independent consultant, since 2016; *b* 3 July 1942; *s* of late John Alfred Oates and Katherine Mary (*née* Hole); *m* 1968, Helen Mary (*née* Blake) (*d* 2015); one *s* three *d*. *Educ:* King's Sch., Chester; Arnold Sch., Blackpool; London School of Economics (BScEcon); Univ. of Manchester Inst. of Sci. and Technology (DipTech Industrial Admin); Bristol Univ. (MSc Management Accounting). FCT 1982. Work Study trainee, Reed Paper Gp, 1965–66; Budgets and Planning Man., IBM (UK) Ltd, 1966–73; Gp Financial Controller, Rolls Royce (1971) Ltd, 1973–74; Controller, Black and Decker Europe, 1974–78; Vice Pres., Finance, Thyssen Bornemisza NV, 1978–84; Finance Dir, Marks and Spencer plc, 1984–91 (Founder Chm., Marks and Spencer Financial Services). Chm., Phaunos Timber Fund Ltd, 2006–12; non-executive Director: John Laing plc, 1987–89; British Telecom, 1994–2000; Guinness, 1995–97; MCI Communications Corp., 1996–97; Diageo, 1997–2004; FSA, 1998–2001; Coutts Bank, Monaco, 2002–05. Gov., BBC, 1988–93. Member: Council, CBI, 1988–2000; Bd, London First, 1993–96; Sports Council of GB, 1993–97; English Sports Council, 1997–99; Public Mem., Network Rail, 2012–15. Chm., Quality, Efficiency and Standards Team, 1999–2000. Chm., Eur. Council of Financial Execs, 1984; Mem., 100 Gp Chartered Accountants, 1985–93. Pres., UMIST Assoc., 1996–97. Mem. Council, Wycombe Abbey Sch., 1995–2016. Patron: Campaign for Resource, Bristol Univ., 1996–2002; London Christies Against Cancer, 1999–2001. DTI Innovation Lecture, 1997. CCMI (CIMgt 1992). FRSA 1993. Hon. LLD Bristol, 1998; Hon. DSc UMIST, 1998. *Recreations:* music, travel, fly fishing, ski-ing, ancestry, gardening, comedy, spectator sports (esp. Association Football, athletics and cricket), supporter of Blackpool FC, AS Monaco and Lancashire CCC. *Club:* MCC.

**OATES, Laurence Campbell,** CB 2006; Official Solicitor to the Supreme Court, 1999–2006; Public Trustee, 2001–06; *b* 14 May 1946; *s* of late Stanley Oates and Norah Christine Oates (*née* Meek); *m* 1968, Brenda Lilian Hardwick; one *s* one *d*. *Educ:* Beckenham and Penge Grammar School; Bristol Univ. (LLB 1967). Called to the Bar, Middle Temple, 1968; Dept of Employment, 1976–80; Law Officers' Dept, 1980–83; Asst Treasury Solicitor, Dept of Transport, 1983–88; Lord Chancellor's Department: Under Sec. and Hd of Legislation Gp, 1988–92; Circuit Administrator, Midland and Oxford Circuit, 1992–94; Assoc. Head of Policy Gp, 1995–96; Dir, Magistrates' Courts' Gp, 1996–99. Lay Advr, RCPCH, 2007–15. Trustee: Royal Hosp. for Neuro-disability, 2007–18 (Mem., Ethics Cttee, 2010–); Grange Centre, 2007–17; Just Advocacy, 2007–16; Woking CAB, 2014–; Citizens Advice Surrey, 2014–. Gov., Woking Coll., 2007–17. Dir, Healthwatch Surrey, 2015–. *Recreations:* music, golf. *Address:* 5 Ashwood Place, Ashwood Road, Woking, Surrey GU22 7JR.

**OATES, Matthew Radcliffe;** author, broadcaster and poet; specialist on nature and wildlife, National Trust, 1991–2018; *b* Yeovil, Som, 7 Aug. 1953; *s* of Robert and Helen Oates; *m* 1979, Sally Enticknap; one *s* three *d*. *Educ:* Christ's Hosp. Sch., Horsham; MA English 1975. Naturalist and nature conservationist; specialist on butterflies, habitat mgt, grazing ecol., rewilding and people's relationships with the natural world. Columnist, Nature Notebook, The Times, 2014–. *Publications:* In Pursuit of Butterflies, 2015; Beyond Spring, 2017; His Imperial Majesty: a natural history of the Purple Emperor butterfly, 2020. *Recreations:* domesticated cats, red ball cricket and Test Match Special, nature. *T:* 07771 971488. *E:* matthew@matthew-oates.co.uk.

**OATES, Seamus Michael,** CBE 2017; Chief Executive Officer and Executive Headteacher, Tri-borough Alternative Provision Multi Academy Trust, since 2011; *b* Bristol, 7 July 1964; *s* of Tom and Jenny Oates; *m* 1992, Joanna; one *s* one *d*. *Educ:* Nailsea Sch.; Southampton Univ. (BSc Hons); Manchester Univ. (PGCE 1987). NPQH 2005. Hd of ICT in Schs and Libraries, RBKC, 1998–2002; Dir, Kingwood City Learning Centre, 2002–03; Headteacher, Bridge Acad., 2003–. Mem., Youth Justice Bd, 2013–17. Headteacher Bd Mem., NW London and S Central England, 2016–18. *Publications:* contrib. to TES. *Recreations:* kitesurfing, gardening, antiques. *Address:* TBAP Multi Academy Trust, c/o Bridge AP Academy, Finlay Street, SW6 6HB. *T:* 07809 611744. *E:* head@tbap.org.uk.

**OATLEY, Brian;** Chairman, Invicta Community Care NHS Trust, 1997–2001; *b* 1 June 1935; *s* of Arnold and Vivian Oatley. *Educ:* Bolton School; King's College, Cambridge (BA, PGCE). Teacher, North Manchester Grammar School, 1959–64; Assistant, Senior Assistant and Deputy County Education Officer, Kent County Council, 1964–84, County Educn Officer, 1984–88. Chm., Maidstone Priority Care NHS Trust, 1991–97. Member: RHS; Kent Trust for Nature Conservation; Camden Choir. Gov., Kent Inst. of Art and Design, 1989–98. *Recreations:* music, travel, gardening, painting. *Address:* 6A Arundel Square, N7 8AT.

**OATLEY, Michael Charles,** CMG 1991; OBE 1975; international intelligence consultant, retired; *b* 18 Oct. 1935; *s* of Sir Charles Oatley, OBE, FRS and Lady Oatley (*née* Enid West); *m* 1st, Pippa Howden; two *s* one *d*; 2nd, Mary Jane Laurens; one *s*. *Educ:* The Leys Sch.; Trinity Coll., Cambridge. Served RN, 1953–55. HM Foreign, later Diplomatic, Service, 1959–91; a Man. Dir, Kroll Associates, 1991–94; Man. Dir, 1994–98, Chm., 1998–2001, Ciex Ltd. Dir, Ovag Ltd, 2002–09; private consultancy, 2009–16. *Address:* Castlebrook House, Nunney, Frome, Somerset BA11 4LN. *Clubs:* Chelsea Arts, Naval.

**OBAMA, Barack Hussein, Jr,** JD; President of the United States of America, 2009–16; *b* Honolulu, 4 Aug. 1961; *s* of late Barack Obama and Ann Dunham; *m* 1992, Michelle Robinson; two *d*. *Educ:* Columbia Univ. (BA Pol Sci. 1983); Harvard Univ. (JD *magna cum laude* 1991). Ed.-in-Chief, Harvard Law Review. Writer and financial analyst, Business Internat. Corp., 1984–85; Dir, Developing Communities Project, Chicago, 1985–88; Exec. Dir, Project Vote, Illinois, 1992; Associate, Miner, Barnhill & Galland, PC, Chicago, 1993–96, Of Counsel, 1996–2004; Sen. Lectr, Law Sch., Univ. of Chicago, 1993–2004. Mem., Illinois Senate, Dist 13, Springfield, 1997–2005; US Senator (Democrat) from Illinois, 2005–08; US Senate: Member: Envmt and Public Works Cttee, 2005–06; Foreign Relns Cttee; Veterans' Affairs Cttee. Nobel Peace Prize, 2009. *Publications:* Dreams from My Father: a story of race and inheritance, 1995; Audacity of Hope: thoughts on reclaiming the American dream, 2006; Change We Can Believe In: Barack Obama's plan to renew America's promise, 2008; Of Thee I Sing: a letter to my daughters (for children), 2010. *Address:* c/o The White House, Washington, DC 20500, USA.

**OBAN (St John's Cathedral), Provost of;** *see* Campbell, Very Rev. Canon M. R.

**OBASANJO, Gen. Olusegun;** President of Nigeria, 1999–2007; Nigerian Head of State, Head of the Federal Military Government and Commander-in-Chief of the Armed Forces, Nigeria, 1976–79; Member, Advisory Council of State, 1979–2007; farmer; *b* Abeokuta, Ogun State, Nigeria, 5 March 1937; *m*; two *s* three *d*. *Educ:* Abeokuta Baptist High Sch.; Mons Officers' Cadet Sch., England. Entered Nigerian Army, 1958; commission, 1959; served in Zaire (then, the Congo), 1960. Comdr, Engrg Corps, 1963; Comdr of 2nd (Rear) Div. at Ibadan; GOC 3rd Inf. Div., 1969; Comdr, 3rd Marine Commando Div.; took surrender of forces of Biafra, in Nigerian Civil War, 1969–70; Comdr Engrg Corps, 1970–75. Political post as Federal Comr for Works and Housing, Jan.–July 1975. Chief of Staff, Supreme HQ, July 1975–Feb. 1976. Mem., Internat. Ind. Commn on Disarmament and Security; Mem., Africa Progress Panel, 2006–. Part-time Associate, Univ. of Ibadan. *Publications:* My Command (autobiog.), 1980; Africa in Perspective: myths and realities, 1987; Nzeognu, 1987; Africa Embattled, 1988; Constitution for National Integration and Development, 1989; Not My Will, 1990; Challenge of Leadership in African Development, 1990; Impact of Europe in 1992 on West Africa, 1990; Leadership Challenge of Economic Reforms in Africa, 1991; Challenge of Agricultural Production and Food Security in Africa, 1992. *Recreations:* squash, table tennis, billiards, snooker.

**O'BEIRNE RANELAGH, John,** (John Ranelagh), PhD; Director, Nordic Media, since 2015; *b* 3 Nov. 1947; *o s* of late James O'Beirne Ranelagh and Elaine Lambert O'Beirne Ranelagh; *m* 1974, Elizabeth Grenville, *y d* of Prof. Sir William Rede Hawthorne, CBE, FRS. *Educ:* St Christopher's Sch.; Cambridgeshire Coll. of Arts and Technology; Christ Church, Oxford (MA); Eliot Coll., Univ. of Kent (PhD). Chase Manhattan Bank, 1970; Campaign Dir, Outset Housing Assoc., 1971; Univ. of Kent Studentship, 1972–74; BBC TV, 1974; Conservative Res. Dept, 1975–79; Associate Producer, Ireland: a television history, BBC TV, 1979–81; Commissioning Editor, Channel Four TV Co., 1981–88 (Sec. to the Bd, 1981–83); Dep. Chief Exec. and Dir of Programmes, TV2 Denmark, 1988; Exec. Producer and writer, CIA, BBC TV/NRK/Primetime, 1989–92; Associate, Hydra Associates, 1989–91; Consultant, TVI Portugal, 1992–94; Director: Kanal Kaks, Estonia, 1995–97; TMS Ltd, 1999–2002; Barnimagen, 2000–01; Nordic World, 2006–14 (Exec. Chm., 2006–08); Vizrt, 2008–11 (Dep. Chm., 2009–11). Consultant, TV 2 Norway, 1991–2014. Mem., Ind. Television Commn, 1994–99. Exec. Producer, Lykkelandet, 2003–04 (Gullruten Prize winner). Dir, Broadcasting Research Unit, 1988–90 (Mem., Exec. Cttee, 1984–87). Mem., Political Cttee, UNA, 1978–90. Governor, Dansford Sch., 1977–81. Convener, Univ. of Cambridge Intelligence Seminar, 2018–. Kt 1st Cl., Royal Order of Merit (Norway), 2013. *Publications:* Science, Education and Industry, 1978; (with Richard Luce) Human Rights and Foreign Policy, 1978; Ireland: an illustrated history, 1981; A Short History of Ireland, 1983, 3rd edn 2012; The Agency: the rise and decline of the CIA, 1986 (Nat. Intelligence Book Award, and New York Times Notable Book of the Year, 1987); (contrib.) Freedom of Information, ed by Julia Neuberger, 1987; (contrib.) The Revolution in Ireland 1879–1923, ed D. G. Boyce, 1988; Den Anden Kanal, 1989;

Thatcher's People, 1991; CIA: a history, 1992; (contrib.) In the Name of Intelligence: essays in honor of Walter Pforzheimer, 1994. *Recreations:* Bentley motor cars, reading. *Address:* The Garner Cottages, Mill Way, Grantchester, Cambridge CB3 9NB. *Clubs:* Travellers, Chelsea Arts, Groucho; Metropolitan (Washington).

**OBORNE, Peter Alan;** Political Columnist, Daily Mail, since 2015; Columnist, Middle East Eye, since 2015; *b* 11 July 1957; *s* of Brig. John Oborne and Margaret Oborne; *m* 1986, Martine Karmock; two *s* three *d. Educ:* Sherborne Sch.; Christ's Coll., Cambridge (BA Hist. 1978). N. M. Rothschild & Sons Ltd, 1981–84; Financial Weekly, 1985–86; Daily Telegraph, 1986; Reporter, Evening Standard, 1987–96; Asst Ed., Sunday Express, 1996–2001; Political Ed., Spectator, 2001–06 (Contrib. Ed., 2006–); Political Columnist, Daily Mail, 2006–10; Chief Political Commentator, Daily Telegraph, 2010–15. Presenter, films (all for Channel 4) including: Mugabe's Secret Famine, 2003; Afghanistan: here's one we invaded earlier, 2003; Dirty Race for the White House, 2004; Iraq: the reckoning, 2005; Spinning Terror, 2006; Waiting for the Taliban, 2009; Holy Warriors, 2009; Inside the Pro-Israel Lobby, 2009; Wonderful World of Tony Blair, 2011; Unreported World: Vlad's Army, 2011. *Publications:* Alastair Campbell: New Labour and the rise of the media class, 1999, revd edn (with Simon Walters), 2004; Basil D'Oliveira: cricket and conspiracy, 2004; The Rise of Political Lying, 2005; The Use and Abuse of Terror, 2006; The Triumph of the Political Class, 2007; (with James Jones) Muslims Under Siege, 2008; (with Jesse Norman) Churchill's Legacy: the Conservative case for the Human Rights Act, 2009; (with Frances Weaver) Guilty Men, 2011; (with David Morrison) A Desperate Delusion: why the West is wrong about nuclear Iran, 2013; Wounded Tiger: a history of cricket in Pakistan, 2014; (with Richard Heller) White on Green: celebrating the drama of Pakistan cricket, 2016; Not the Chilcot Report, 2017; (with Tom Roberts) How Trump Thinks, 2017. *Recreations:* reading, cricket (Captain, White City All Stars CC), horse-racing. *Address:* 60 Elmwood Road, W4 3DZ. *E:* peter.oborne@btinternet.com.

**O'BOYLE, Fionnuala Mary J.;** *see* Jay-O'Boyle, F. M.

**O'BRIEN,** family name of **Baron Inchiquin**.

**O'BRIEN, Anthony John;** Director, Western Balkans, British Council, 2012–15; *b* 17 Jan. 1951; *s* of Padraig and Sheila O'Brien; *m* 1975, Yolanda Lange; three *d. Educ:* Jesus Coll., Cambridge (BA Law 1971); Univ. of Manchester (DipTEO, PGCE 1975); Inst. of Educn, London (MA Educn 1986). Volunteer teacher of English, VSO, Aswan, Egypt, 1971–73; Lectr in ESP, Univ. of Tabriz, Iran, 1975–77; British Council: Dir of Studies, Morocco, 1978–82; Consultant, London, 1982–85; Dir, English Language Centre, Singapore, 1986–90, Hong Kong, 1990–94; Dir, Morocco, 1994–97; Dir, English Lang. Teaching, London, 1997–2002; Dir, Sri Lanka, 2002–06; Dir, Poland, 2006–11; Dir, Serbia, 2011–12. Chm., Adv. Bd, Creative Mentorship, Serbia, 2013– (Mentor, 2012–; Mem. Bd, 2013–). Trustee and Dir, Well Christian Healing Centre, Leamington Spa, 2016– (Chair, 2017–). Dir, St Gabriel's C of E Acad., Rugby, 2016–. *Publications:* Nucleus: medicine, 1980; Teacher Development: evaluation and teacher profiles in TESOL, 1984; numerous articles for professional jls. *Recreations:* learning more of other cultures, travel (visiting family and friends), walking. *Address:* 2 Seymour Grove, Warwick CV34 6LS.

**O'BRIEN, Asma;** *see* Khalil, A.

**O'BRIEN, Barry John;** Chairman, European Mergers and Acquisitions, Jefferies International Ltd, since 2014; *b* Cardiff, 27 Oct. 1952; *s* of John, (Jack) and Patricia O'Brien; *m* 1984, Susan Bond; two *s* one *d. Educ:* St Illtyd's Coll., Cardiff; University Coll. London (LLB; Hon. Fellow, 2013). Admitted as solicitor, 1978; Articled Clerk, then Associate, Slaughter and May, 1976–84; with Freshfields, later Freshfields Bruckhaus Deringer LLP, 1984–2014, Partner, 1986–2014. Mem., Educn Leadership Team, Business in the Community, 2005–13. Dir, England and Wales Cricket Bd, 2018–. Vice Chm. Govs, 2003–14, Chm. Govs, 2014–18, Arnold Hse Sch.; Chm. Govs, Haggerston Girls' Sch., 2008–18; Mem., Arnold Foundn Bd, 2007–, Gov., 2012–, Rugby Sch. Liveryman, Solicitors' Co., 2013–. *Publications:* contribs to legal pubns. *Recreations:* family, sport (Welsh Rugby, Glamorgan cricket, Arsenal, and golf), opera, contemporary art. *Address:* Jefferies International Ltd, Vintners Place, 68 Upper Thames Street, EC4V 3BJ. *T:* (020) 7029 8558. *E:* bobrien@jefferies.com. *Clubs:* Athenæum, Walbrook, Ivy, MCC; Glamorgan County Cricket (Mem. Cttee, 2008–; Chm., 2011–18); Loch Lomond (Dir, 2018–); Highgate Golf.

**O'BRIEN, Basil Godwin,** CMG 1996; High Commissioner of the Bahamas to the United Kingdom, 1999–2007, and Ambassador to the European Union, Belgium, France, Germany and Italy, 1999–2008; *b* 5 Dec. 1940; *s* of late Cyril O'Brien and Kathleen O'Brien (*née* Brownrigg); *m* 1967, Marlene Devika Chand; two *s. Educ:* St John's Coll., Nassau; Univ. Tutorial Coll., London; London Inst. of World Affairs (Dip. Internat. Affairs, London Univ.). HEO, Min. of Ext. Affairs, Bahamas, 1969–70; Asst Sec., later Dep. Perm. Sec., Cabinet Office, 1970–78; Permanent Secretary: Min. of Tourism, 1978–86; Min. of Foreign Affairs, 1986–89; Min. of Agriculture, Trade and Ind., 1989–93; Min. of Educn, 1993–94; Sec. to Cabinet and Hd, Public Service, 1994–99. Permanent Representative: to IMO, London; to Internat. Orgn for Migration and WTO, Geneva; to Bureau of Internat. Expositions, Paris. Director: Source River Hldgs Co. Ltd; Source River Ltd; formerly: Director: Bahamas Hotel Trng Coll.; Bahamasair Hldgs Co. Past Chm., Bd of Govs, St John's Coll., Nassau. Past Mem., Anglican Central Educn Authy. Mem., La Chaîne des Rôtisseurs. *Recreations:* walking, swimming, gardening. *Clubs:* Royal Automobile, Royal Over-Seas League; Skal.

**O'BRIEN, Most Rev. Brendan Michael;** Archbishop of Kingston (Ontario), (RC), 2007–19, now Archbishop Emeritus; *b* Ottawa, 28 Sept. 1943; *s* of Redmond and Margaret O'Brien (*née* Foran). *Educ:* Univ. of Ottawa (BA); St Paul Univ., Ottawa (BTh); Lateran Univ., Rome (Dr Moral Theology). Ordained priest, 1968; Pastor in several Ottawa parishes; ordained bishop, 1987; Auxiliary Bishop of Ottawa, 1987–93; Bishop of Pembroke, 1993–2000; Archbishop of St John's, 2000–07. *Address:* c/o 390 Palace Road, Kingston, ON K7L 4T3, Canada. *T:* (613) 5484461, *Fax:* (613) 5484744. *E:* obrien@romancatholic.kingston.on.ca.

**O'BRIEN, Brian Murrough Fergus;** Deputy Special Commissioner of Income Tax, 1991–2006; *b* 18 July 1931; *s* of late Charles Murrough O'Brien, MB, BCh and Elizabeth Joyce O'Brien (*née* Peacocke). *Educ:* Bedford Sch.; University Coll., Oxford (BA 1954, MA 1959). Nat. Service, Royal Inniskilling Fusiliers, 1950–51. Called to the Bar, Lincoln's Inn, 1955; Office of Solicitor of Inland Revenue, 1956–70; Asst Solicitor, Law Commn, 1970–80; Secretary, Law Commn, 1980–81. Special Comr of Income Tax, 1981–91. Mem., Senate of Inns of Court and Bar Council, 1977–80; Hon. Gen. Sec., 1962–67 and Chm., 1974–76, CS Legal Soc.; Chm., Assoc. of First Div. Civil Servants, 1979–81. Lay Chm., Westminster (St Margaret's) Deanery Synod, 1978–82. Trustee, St Mary's, Bourne St, 1968–2005. *Recreations:* music, travel. *Address:* 14 Marshall Court, Northampton Road, Market Harborough, Leics LE16 9HZ. *T:* (01858) 463832. *Club:* Reform.

**O'BRIEN, Dr Carl Michael,** CBE 2017; CStat, CSci; Chief Fisheries Science Adviser, Department for Environment, Food and Rural Affairs and Centre for Environment, Fisheries and Agriculture Science, since 2010; *b* Stevenage, 15 May 1959; *s* of Michael O'Brien and Jean O'Brien (*née* Austin, later Lavery); *m* 1991, Maria Joaquina Pinheiro Pires; one step *d. Educ:* University Coll. London (BSc Stats 1980; MSc Stats 1981; PhD Statistical Sci. 1983). CStat 1994; CSci 2009. Post-doctoral Res. Associate, UCL, 1983–85; Computational Statistician, 1985–87, Statistical Knowledge Engr, 1987–89, Numerical Algorithms Gp; Statistical Computing Consultant, Univ. of London, 1989–91; Vis. Researcher, Museu Paraense Emílio Goeldi/Nat. Council for Scientific and Technol. Develt, 1991–94; Vis. Prof., Faculdade de Ciências Agrárias, Brazil, 1993–95; Sen. Scientist, 1995–98, Principal Scientist, 1998–2005, Science Leader, 2005–07, Dir, Fisheries Div., 2007–10, Cefas. Buckland Prof., Buckland Foundn, 2015. International Council for Exploration of the Sea: UK Delegate, 2012–; Chm., Awards Cttee, 2017–; Vice-Pres., 2018–. Mem., Mutford Parish Council, 1997– (Chair, 2015–). FLS 2000. *Publications:* Ecologia e Modelamento de Florestas Tropicais, 1995; Management of Shared Stocks, 2004; contribs to Nature. *Recreations:* cycling, walking. *Address:* Centre for Environment, Fisheries and Agriculture Science, Lowestoft Laboratory, Pakefield Road, Lowestoft, Suffolk NR33 0HT. *T:* (01502) 524256, 07786 800193. *E:* carl.obrien@cefas.co.uk.

**O'BRIEN, David P.,** OC 2008; Chairman: EnCana Corporation, 2002–13 (Director, 1990); Royal Bank of Canada, 2004–14 (Director, 1996–2014); *b* 9 Sept. 1941; *s* of John L. O'Brien and Ethel; *m* 1968, Gail Baxter Corneil; one *s* two *d. Educ:* Loyola Coll. (BA Hons Econs 1962); McGill Univ. (BCL 1965). Associate and Partner, Ogilvy Renault (law firm), 1967–77; various mgt posts, 1978–85, Exec. Vice Pres., 1985–89, Petro-Canada; Pres. and CEO, Noverco Inc., 1989; Dir, 1990, Chm., 1992, PanCanadian Petroleum Ltd (Pres. and CEO, 1990–95); Dir, 1995–2001, Pres. and Chief Operating Officer, 1995–96, Chm., Pres. and CEO, 1996–2001, Canadian Pacific Ltd; Chm. and CEO PanCanadian Energy Corp., 2001–02. Director: TransCanada Pipelines Ltd, 2001–12; Molson Inc., 2002–12; Enerplus Resources Fund, 2008. *Recreations:* tennis, biking, golf. *Clubs:* Calgary Petroleum, Calgary Golf and Country, Glencoe Golf and Country (Calgary).

**O'BRIEN, Prof. Denis Patrick,** FBA 1988; Professor of Economics, University of Durham, 1972–97, now Emeritus; *b* Knebworth, Herts, 24 May 1939; *s* of Patrick Kevin O'Brien and Dorothy Elizabeth Crisp; *m* 1st, 1961, Eileen Patricia O'Brien (*d* 1985); one *s* two *d*; 2nd, 1993, Julia Stapleton; one *d. Educ:* Douai Sch.; University Coll. London (BSc (Econ) 1960); PhD Queen's Univ., Belfast, 1969. In industry, 1960–62; Queen's University, Belfast: Asst Lectr, 1963–65; Lectr, 1965–70; Reader, 1970–72. Dist. Fellow, History of Econs Soc., 2003. *Publications:* (with D. Swann) Information Agreements, 1969; J. R. McCulloch, 1970; Correspondence of Lord Overstone, 3 vols, 1971; (jtly) Competition in British Industry, 1974; (ed) J. R. McCulloch: Treatise on Taxation, 1975; The Classical Economists, 1975; Competition Policy, Profitability and Growth, 1979; (with J. Presley) Pioneers of Modern Economics in Britain, 1981; (with A. C. Darnell) Authorship Puzzles in the History of Economics, 1982; (with J. Creedy) Economic Analysis in Historical Perspective, 1984; Lionel Robbins, 1988; Thomas Joplin and Classical Macroeconomics, 1993; Methodology, Money and the Firm, 2 vols, 1994; The Classical Economists Revisited, 2004; History of Economic Thought as an Intellectual Discipline, 2007; The Development of Monetary Economics, 2007; (ed with J. Creedy) G. W. Norman: taxation and the promotion of human happiness, 2009; (ed with J. Creedy) Darwin's Clever Neighbour: George Warde Norman and his circle, 2010. *Recreation:* the violin.

**O'BRIEN, Dermod Patrick;** QC 1983; a Recorder of the Crown Court, 1978–2005; *b* 23 Nov. 1939; *s* of Lieut D. D. O'Brien, RN, and Mrs O'Brien (*née* O'Connor); *m* 1974, Zoë Susan Norris (marr. diss. 2003); two *s. Educ:* Ampleforth Coll., York; St Catherine's Coll., Oxford. BA (Jurisprudence); MA. Called to Bar, Inner Temple, 1962, Bencher, 1993; joined Western Circuit, 1963; in practice as a barrister, 2 Temple Gardens, 1963–2010, Head of Chambers, 1999–2003. Governor, Milton Abbey Sch., 1992–2012. *Recreations:* fishing, shooting, ski-ing, gardening. *Address:* Rodwell Manor, West Lambrook, Kingsbury Episcopi, Somerset TA13 5HA. *Clubs:* Boodle's; Piscatorial.

**O'BRIEN, Edna Josephine,** Hon. DBE 2017; writer; *b* Ireland, 1930; marr. diss.; two *s. Educ:* Irish convents; Pharmaceutical Coll. of Ireland. Yorkshire Post Novel Award, 1971; Ulysses Medal, UCD, 2006; Lifetime Achievement Award, Irish Booksellers, 2009; PEN/Nabokov Achievement in International Literature Award, PEN American Centre, 2018. *Publications:* The Country Girls, 1960 (screenplay for film, 1983; play, 2012); The Lonely Girl, 1962; Girls in Their Married Bliss, 1963; August is a Wicked Month, 1964; Casualties of Peace, 1966; The Love Object, 1968; A Pagan Place, 1970; A Pagan Place (play), 1971; Night, 1972; A Scandalous Woman (short stories), 1974; Mother Ireland, 1976; Johnnie I hardly knew you, 1977; Mrs Reinhardt and other stories, 1978; Virginia (play), 1979; The Dazzle, 1981; Returning, 1982; A Christmas Treat, 1982; A Fanatic Heart (selected stories), 1985; Tales for the Telling, 1986; Flesh and Blood (play), 1987; Madame Bovary (play), 1987; The High Road, 1988; Lantern Slides (short stories), (Los Angeles Times Award) 1990; Time and Tide, 1992 (Writers' Guild Award, 1993); House of Splendid Isolation, 1994; Down by the River, 1997; James Joyce, 1999; Wild Decembers, 1999; In The Forest, 2002; Iphigenia (play), 2003; Triptych (play), 2003; The Light of Evening, 2006; Byron in Love, 2009; Haunted (play), 2010; Saints and Sinners, 2011; Country Girl (memoir), 2012; The Love Object (short stories), 2013; The Little Red Chairs, 2015; Girl, 2019. *Recreations:* reading, theatre, film. *Address:* c/o Caroline Michel, Peter Fraser Dunlop, 55 New Oxford Street, WC1A 1BS. *T:* (020) 7344 1000; (theatre) c/o Angharad Wood, Tavistock Wood, 45 Conduit Street, W1S 2YN. *T:* (020) 7494 4767.

**O'BRIEN, John Gerard;** Chief Executive, London Councils, since 2007; *b* 18 Jan. 1960; *s* of Patrick and Bridget O'Brien; *m* 1990, Anne-Marie Boyce; one *s. Educ:* St Martin's Sch., Brentwood; Univ. of Warwick (BA Hons Hist. and Politics 1982). Grad. trainee, Basildon DC, 1982–84; Principal Asst, Westminster CC, 1984–88; Mgt Consultant, KPMG, 1988–99; Dir (Solutions), Improvement and Develt Agency for Local Govt, 1999–2003; Dir, Local Govt Perf. and Practice, ODPM, subseq. DCLG, 2003–06; Dir, Ind. Commn, LGA (on secondment), 2006–07. Chair, SOLACE Foundn, 2011–14. *Publications:* (with K. Ennals) The Enabling Role of Local Authorities, 1990. *Recreations:* family, friends, sport. *Address:* London Councils, 59½ Southwark Street, SE1 0AL. *Club:* Essex County Cricket.

**O'BRIEN, Prof. Kevin Donald,** PhD; Professor of Orthodontics, since 1996, and Director, Manchester Clinical Trials Unit, since 2016, University of Manchester; *b* Edinburgh, 2 Feb. 1957; *s* of Frances Pagett; *m* 1979, Janet Miller; one *s* two *d. Educ:* King Edward VI Sch., Stourbridge; Univ. of Manchester (BDS 1979; MSc 1986; PhD 1991). FDSRCPSGlas 1984; DOrthRCS 1986; FDS RCS 2011. Gen. Dental Practitioner, 1979–84; hosp. trainee, 1984–87; MRC Fellow, 1987–91; Asst Prof., Univ. of Pittsburgh, 1991–92; University of Manchester: Sen. Lectr, 1992–96; Dean, Dental Sch., 2004–07; Associate Dean, Faculty of Med. and Human Sci., 2007–10. Member: Council, British Orthodontic Soc., 1998–2004; Dental Schs Council, 2004–07; Gen. Dental Council, 2009–13 (Chm., 2011–13); Dental Prog. Bd, Health Educn England, 2011–13. Ed., Jl of Orthodontics, 2001–04. *Publications:* articles in Amer. Jl of Orthodontics, Eur. Jl of Orthodontics. *Recreations:* football spectator, walking, gardening. *Address:* Manchester Clinical Trials Unit, Room 1.315, Jean McFarlane Building, University of Manchester, Manchester M15 6FH. *T:* (0161) 275 6620. *E:* kevin.obrien@manchester.ac.uk.

**O'BRIEN, Prof. Lucy Frances**, DPhil; Professor of Philosophy, University College London, since 2014; *b* Hassan, S India, 9 June 1964; *d* of Gerald Patrick O'Brien and Frances Huband de Savoye O'Brien; *m* 1992, Mark Daniel Sacks (*d* 2008); one *s* one *d*; partner, Peter James Breen. *Educ*: Addison Primary Sch.; Godolphin and Latymer Sch. for Girls; Sheffield Univ. (BA Pure Maths and Philosophy; MPhil Philosophy); New Coll., Oxford (DPhil Philosophy 1993). Res. Asst, Centre of Philosophy, KCL, 1991; Lectr in Philosophy, 1992–2004, Reader, 2004–14, UCL. Dir, Aristotelian Soc., 2008–14. Co-Ed., Mind, 2015–. Vice-Pres., Royal Inst. of Philosophy, 2016–. *Publications*: Self-Knowing Agents, 2007; (ed with M. Soterion) Mental Actions, 2009; contrib. articles to jls incl. Now, Eur. Jl Philosophy, Philosophical and Phenomenological Res., Analysis, Philosophical Issues. *Recreations*: walking and talking, mainly on Hampstead Heath, watching and cheering Rugby, mainly on Hampstead Heath, theatre, reading, television box sets, boating and mackerel fishing in Co. Kerry, Eire. *Address*: Department of Philosophy, University College London, Gower Street, WC1E 6BT. *T*: (020) 7679 3073. *E*: l.obrien@ucl.ac.uk. *Club*: Hampstead Rugby (Hon. Mem.).

**O'BRIEN, Margaret Anne**; Senior Lecturer in Public Health, University of East London, since 2018; Senior Teaching Fellow, University of Southampton, since 2018; *b* 18 March 1955; *d* of late Eric James Hues and of Enid Dorothy Hues; *m* 1st, 1977, Malcolm Richard Elliott (marr. diss. 2006); one *s*; 2nd, 2007, Jarrard Michael O'Brien (marr. diss. 2018). *Educ*: Steyning Grammar Sch. Registered Nurse, 1976; Registered Midwife, 1979. Midwife, Southlands Hosp., Shoreham, 1979–95; Regl Officer, Royal Coll. of Midwives, 1995–97; Hd of Midwifery, Southampton Gen. Hosp., 1997–2000; Dir of Midwifery, 2000–08, and Gen. Manager, 2002–08, Queen Charlotte's and Chelsea Hosp., London; Dir of Midwifery and Hd of Nursing, Imperial Coll. NHS Healthcare Trust, 2008–11; Dir of Midwifery, Auckland Dist Health Bd, NZ, 2011–16; Clinical Lead, Staff Experience, Waitemata Dist Health Bd, NZ, 2016–17. Pres., Royal Coll. of Midwives, 2004–08 (Hon. Fellow, 2009). *Recreation*: travel and exploring different cultures.

**O'BRIEN, Rt Hon. Michael**; PC 2009; QC 2005; barrister; *b* Worcester, 19 June 1954; *s* of Timothy Thomas and Mary O'Brien; *m* 1987, Alison Munro; two *d*. *Educ*: BA Hons Hist. and Pol. Lectr in Law, Colchester Inst., 1981–87; solicitor, 1987–2011; called to the Bar, Middle Temple, 2011; barrister, specialising in court of protection and judicial reviews, No5 Chambers, Birmingham, 2011–. MP (Lab) N Warwicks, 1992–2010; contested (Lab) same seat, 2010, 2015. Opposition spokesperson: HM Treasury, 1995–96; City, 1996–97; Parly Under-Sec. of State, Home Office, 1997–2001, FCO, 2002–03; Minister of State: (Minister for Trade, Investment and Foreign Affairs), FCO and DTI, 2003–04; (Minister for Energy, e-Commerce and Postal Services), DTI, 2004–05; Solicitor General, 2005–07; Minister of State: DWP, 2007–08; DECC, 2008–09; (Minister for Health Services), DoH, 2009–10. Member: Home Affairs Select Cttee, 1992–94; Treasury Select Cttee, 1994–95. Chm., Lab. Home Affairs Cttee, 1995–96. Parly Advr, Police Fedn, 1993–96. *E*: mob@no5.com.

**O'BRIEN, Neil John**, OBE 2016; MP (C) Harborough, since 2017; *b* Huddersfield, 6 Nov. 1978; *m* 2012, Jemma; one *d*. *Educ*: All Saints High Sch., Huddersfield; Greenmead Coll., Huddersfield; Christ Church, Oxford. Director: Open Europe, 2005–08; Policy Exchange, 2008–12; Special Advisor: HM Treasury, 2012–16; to Prime Minister, 2016–17. Mem., Sci. and Technol. Cttee, H of C, 2017–. *Publications*: The Renewal of Government, 2010. *Address*: House of Commons, SW1A 0AA. *T*: (020) 7219 3000.

**O'BRIEN, Prof. Patrick Karl**, DPhil; FBA 1990; Professor of Economic History, University of London, 1990–98; Professor of Global Economic History, London School of Economics, 2009–14; *b* 12 Aug. 1932; *s* of William O'Brien and Elizabeth Stockhausen; *m* 1959, Cassy Cobham; one *s* two *d*. *Educ*: London Sch. of Economics (Lilian Knowles Schol.; BSc 1958); Nuffield Coll., Oxford (DPhil). London University: Res. Fellow, 1960–63; Lectr, 1963–70; Reader in Econs and Econ. Hist., 1967–70; Oxford University: Univ. Lectr in Econ. Hist., 1970–84; Reader, 1984–90; Faculty Fellow, 1970–84, Professorial Fellow, 1984–90, Emeritus Fellow, 1991, St Antony's Coll.; Dir, Inst. of Historical Res., Univ. of London, 1990–98; Centennial Prof. of Econ. Hist., LSE, 1999–2009. Convenor: Eur. Res. Prog. on Regimes for Prodn, Develt and Diffusion of Useful and Reliable Knowledge in E and W from Accession of the Ming Dynasty 1368 to the Industrial Revolution 1756–1846, 2009–13; Leverhulme Trust Funded Network on Economic Outcomes Flowing from the Revolution and Napoleonic Wars 1793–1815, LSE, 2015–17. Pres., Econ. Hist. Soc., 1999–2001. MAE 2002. Hon. Foreign Fellow, Amer. Historical Assoc., 2013. Hon. Dr: Carlos III, Madrid, 1998; Uppsala, 1999. *Publications*: The Revolution in Egypt's Economic System, 1966; The New Economic History of the Railways, 1977; (with C. Keyder) Economic Growth in Britain and France 1780–1914, 1978; (ed jtly) Productivity in the Economies of Europe in the 19th and 20th Centuries, 1983; (ed) Railways and the Economic Development of Western Europe 1830–1914, 1983; (ed) International Productivity Comparisons 1750–1939, 1986; The Economic Effects of the Civil War, 1988; (ed jtly) The Industrial Revolution and British Society, 1993; (ed) Industrialization: perspectives on the international economy, 1998; (ed) Philips Atlas of World History, 2000; Imperialism and Industrialization of Britain and Europe, 2000; (ed jtly) Urban Achievement in Early Modern Europe, 2001; (ed) The Political Economy of British Historical Experience, 2002; (ed) Two Hegemonies: Britain 1846–1914 and the United States 1941–2001, 2002; contribs to many learned jls. *Recreations*: Western art, walking. *Address*: 13 Woodstock Close, Oxford OX2 8DB. *T*: (01865) 512004.
*See also H. V. Calcraft.*

**O'BRIEN, Prof. (Patrick Michael) Shaughn**, DSc; MD; FRCOG; Foundation Professor of Obstetrics and Gynaecology, Keele University Medical School, 1989, now Emeritus; Consultant Obstetrician and Gynaecologist, since 1989, and Clinical Director, Obstetrics and Gynaecology, 2012–15, Royal Stoke University Hospital (formerly University Hospital North Staffordshire); *b* 1 April 1948; *s* of late Patrick O'Brien and Joan O'Brien (*née* Edleston); *m* 1985, Sandie Louise Norman; one *s* one *d*. *Educ*: Boys' Grammar Sch., Pontypridd; Welsh Nat. Sch. of Medicine, Univ. of Wales (MB BCh 1972; MD 1979); DSc Keele, 2008. MRCOG 1979, FRCOG 1991. Res. Fellow, Univ. of Nottingham, 1974–76; Sen. House Officer, John Radcliffe Hosp., Oxford, 1976–77; Registrar: Brighton Sussex Co. Hosp., 1977–78; Middlesex Hosp., 1978–79; Clin. Lectr and Sen. Registrar, Univ. of Nottingham, 1979–84; Sen. Lectr and Consultant, Royal Free Hosp. Med. Sch., 1984–89. Postgrad. Clin. Tutor, N Staffs Hosp., 1996–2000; Chm., N Staffs Med. Inst., 2002–05; Specialty Gp Lead Reproductive Health West Midlands (North) Comprehensive Local Res. Network, 2012–14; Clinical Lead, W Midlands (N) Comprehensive Local Res. Network, Reproductive Health and Childbirth, 2012. Chm., N Staffs Med. Inst., 2015–. Mem., Council of Govs, Shrewsbury and Telford NHS Trust, 2012–14. Internat. Fellow, Council, RCOG, 2015– (Vice Pres., 2004–07); Chm. and Founder, Internat. Soc. for Premenstrual Disorders, 2008–; Chm., British Soc. of Psychosomatic Obstetrics and Gynaecol., 2011–14. Pres., Birmingham and Midlands Obstetric and Gynaecol Soc., 2015–. FRSocMed. Mem., Bd of Govs, Shrewsbury Girls' High Sch., GDST, 2012–. Founder and Foundn Editor-in-Chief, The Obstetrician and Gynaecologist, 1998–2004; Editor-in-Chief, Map of Medicine (Obstetrics and Gynaecol.), 2008–13. Co-inventor: Menstrual Pictogram, 2013; PreMentricS app to diagnose premenstrual syndrome, 2014. Student of sculpture, Heatherley Sch. of Fine Art, Chelsea. *Publications*: Premenstrual Syndrome, 1987; The Year Book of Obstetrics and Gynaecology, vol. 5, 1997, vol. 6, 1998, vol. 7, 1999, vol. 8, 2000; Problems of Early Pregnancy, 1997; Evidence Based Fertility, 1998; Gene Identification, Manipulation and Therapy, 1998; Fetal Programming, 1999; Hormones and Cancer, 1999; Introduction to Research Methodology, 1999, 2nd edn 2007; Placenta, 2000; Disorders of the Menstrual Cycle, 2000; Psychological Disorders in Obstetrics and Gynaecology, 2006; The Premenstrual Syndromes: PMS and PMDD, 2007; Introduction to Research Methodology for Specialists and Trainees, 2017; Biopsychosocial Factors in Obstetrics and Gynaecology, 2017; over 300 pubns inc. 40 chapters and numerous orig. res. papers, abstracts and revs on premenstrual syndrome, menopause, menstrual disorders, pre-eclampsia, GnRH analogues, gynaecological endocrinology. *Recreations*: classical music, jazz, play clarinet and saxophone, travel, ski-ing, sailing holidays, sculptures (exhibited: Granary Gallery, Weston Park Nat. Fine Art Competition, 2013, 2014, 2016; Shrewsbury Open Studios Exhibn, 2017; Annual Med. Art Soc. Exhibn, RSocMed, 2017, 2018; Heatherley Sch. of Fine Art Diploma Show, Chelsea, 2019). *Address*: Cardington House, Shrewsbury SY1 1ES. *T*: (01782) 672382.

**O'BRIEN, His Honour Patrick William**; a Circuit Judge, 1991–2014; a Deputy Circuit Judge, since 2014; *b* 20 June 1945; *s* of William C. O'Brien and Ethel M. O'Brien; *m* 1970, Antoinette Wattebot; one *s* two *d*. *Educ*: St Joseph's Academy, Blackheath; Queens' College, Cambridge (MA, LLM). Called to the Bar, Lincoln's Inn, 1968, Bencher, 2003; practised SE Circuit; a Recorder, 1987. *Publications*: (contrib. jtly) Great Oxford: essays on the life and work of Edward de Vere, 17th Earl of Oxford, 2004. *Recreations*: cricket, choral singing, musical theatre. *Address*: Armigers, Thaxted, Dunmow, Essex CM6 2NN. *Clubs*: MCC; Norfolk (Norwich).

**O'BRIEN, Air Vice-Marshal Robert Peter**, CB 1997; OBE 1983; Air Secretary, 1994–97, and Chief Executive, RAF Personnel Management Agency, 1997–98; *b* 1 Nov. 1941; *s* of Major Thomas Joseph O'Brien, MC, RE and Doris Winifred O'Brien; *m* 1964, Carole Evelyn Anne Wallace; two *s*. *Educ*: Salesian College, Farnborough; RAF College, Cranwell. BA (External) London 1962. Commissioned 1962; Pilot 31 Sqn (Canberras), 1963–66; Central Flying Sch./4FTS (Gnats), 1966–67; ADC to AOC 38 Gp, 1967–70; Flt Comdr, 15 Sqn (Buccaneers), 1970–73; Army Staff Coll., 1974; HQ RAF Germany, 1975–77; OC London UAS (Bulldogs), 1977–79; Chief Instr/TTTE (Tornados), 1980–83; Stn Comdr, RAF Marham, 1983–85; Air Staff, MoD, 1985–87; Dep. Comdr/COS HQ BF Cyprus, 1988–91; Dir of Infrastructure (RAF), MoD, 1991–92; Comdt, JSDC, 1992–94. ADC to the Queen, 1983–85. *Address*: c/o Lloyds, Cox's and King's Branch, PO Box 1190, 7 Pall Mall, SW1Y 5NA. *Club*: Royal Air Force.

**O'BRIEN, Sir (Robert) Stephen**, Kt 2013; CBE 1987; Chairman: Barts Health NHS Trust (formerly Barts and the London NHS Trust), 2010–15; International Health Partners, 2005–14; *b* 14 Aug. 1936; *s* of Robert Henry and Clare Winifred O'Brien; *m* 1st, 1958, Zoë T. O'Brien (marr. diss. 1989); two *s* two *d*; 2nd, 1989, Meriel Barclay. *Educ*: Sherborne Sch., Dorset. Joined Charles Fulton & Co. Ltd, 1956; Dir, 1964; Chm., 1973–82; Chief Exec., 1983–92, Vice-Chm., 1992–2003, Vice Pres., 2003–, BITC. Chm., Cranstoun, 1969–83 (Pres., 1983–88); Dir, Kirkland-Whittaker Co. Ltd, 1980–82. Chief Exec., London Forum, 1993–94; Vice-Chm., 1993–2005, Chief Exec., 1995–99, London First Centre, subseq. Think London; London First: Chief Exec., 1992–2002; Chm., 2002–05; Jt Pres., 2005. Chairman: Foreign Exchange and Currency Deposit Brokers Assoc., 1968–72; Project Fullemploy, 1973–91; Home Sec.'s Adv. Bd on Community Radio, 1985–86; Unitas Communications, 2007–13; London Works, 2013–. Ordained Deacon, 1971; Hon. Curate, St Lawrence Jewry, 1973–80; Chm., Christian Action, 1976–88. Vice-Chm., Church Urban Fund, 1994–2002. Pres., Esher Assoc. for Prevention of Addiction, 1979–90. Chm., UK 2000, 1988–92 (Mem. Bd, 1986–92); Director: Cities in Schools, 1989–95; Prince of Wales' Business Leaders Forum, subseq. Internat. Business Leaders Forum, 1990–2010; Member: Admin. Council, Royal Jubilee Trusts, 1984–89; Mgt Cttee, Action Resource Centre, 1986–91; Council, RSA, 1987–91; Trustee: Learning from Experience Trust, 1986–94; Immigrants Aid Trust, 1997–2007; PYBT, 1987–99; Mayor's Fund for London, 2008–17; High St Fund, 2011–13; Barts Health Charity, 2012–18; Foundn for Future London, 2015–; Chairman: Prince's Trust Regl Council for London, 2000–06; Tower Hamlets Primary Care Trust, 2005–10; Lord Mayor's Appeal Cttee, 2010–11; Taskforce on Mental Health and Society, 2013–. Chm., Unicorn Children's Th., 2006–09. Chm. Govs, UEL, 1999–2005. Hon. Fellow, QMUL, 2012. Hon. LLD Liverpool, 1994; Hon DSc City, 2000; DUniv: Middx, 2001; UEL 2005. *Recreations*: classical music, gardening, cooking. *Address*: Woodhouse, Compasses Road, Pattiswick, Essex CM77 8BB.

**O'BRIEN, Prof. Sean Patrick**, FRSL; freelance writer, since 1989; Professor of Creative Writing, Newcastle University, since 2006 (Visiting Professor, 2003–06); *b* 19 Dec. 1952; *s* of Patrick Francis O'Brien and Mary Irene O'Brien; partner, Ms Gerry Wardle. *Educ*: Selwyn Coll., Cambridge (BA 1974); Birmingham Univ. (MA 1977); Leeds Univ. (PGCE 1981). Teacher of English, Beacon Community Coll., Crowborough, 1981–89; Fellow in Creative Writing, Univ. of Dundee, 1989–91; Northern Arts Literary Fellow, Univs of Durham and Newcastle upon Tyne, 1992–94; Lectr on Writing (MA course), 1998, and Prof. of Poetry, 2003–06, Sheffield Hallam Univ. British Council Visiting Writer: Univ. of Odense, 1996; Hokudai Univ., Sapporo, 1997; Writer in Residence: South Bank Centre Poetry Internat., 1998; Univ. of Leeds, 1999; (with Julia Darling) Live Theatre Newcastle, 2001–03; Weidenfeld Vis. Prof. of Comparative European Literature, St Anne's Coll., Oxford, 2017. External Examiner: MLitt, Univ. of St Andrews, 2003–06; MSc, Univ. of Edinburgh, 2006–10; MA, BA, Univ. of Manchester, 2007–10; BA, Univ. of Warwick, 2011–14; BA, Univ. of Lancaster, 2012–16. Specialist Advr to Scottish Arts Council, 2003–05. Vice Pres., Poetry Soc., 2006–11. Mem., Newcastle Lit. and Philosophical Soc., 1990. Mem., Vujonistas. FRSL 2007. Hon. DCL Northumbria, 2003; Hon. DLitt: Hull, 2009; Roehampton, 2018. Gregory Award, 1979; Somerset Maugham Award, 1984; Cholmondeley Award, 1988; E. M. Forster Award, AAAL, 1993; Northern Writer of the Year, Northern Arts and New Writing North, 2001; Northern Rock Foundn Award, 2007. *Publications*: The Indoor Park, 1983; The Frighteners, 1987; HMS Glasshouse, 1991; Ghost Train (Forward Prize for Best Collection), 1995; (jtly) Penguin Modern Poets 5, 1995; The Deregulated Muse: essays on contemporary poetry in Britain and Ireland, 1998; (ed) The Firebox: poetry in Britain and Ireland after 1945, 1998; Downriver (Forward Prize for Best Collection), 2001; Cousin Coat: selected poems 1976–2001, 2002; The Birds, 2002; (jtly) Rivers, 2002; Keepers of the Flame, 2003; Laughter When We're Dead, in Live Theatre: six plays from the North East, 2003; (ed jtly) Ten Hallam Poets, 2005; (contrib.) Ellipsis 1 (short stories), 2005; The Inferno, a New Verse Version, 2006; The Drowned Book, 2007 (Forward Prize for Best Collection, 2007; T. S. Eliot Prize, 2007); The Silence Room (short stories), 2008; Afterlife (novel), 2009; (jtly) Night Train, 2009; November, 2011; Collected Poems, 2012; (ed jtly) Train Songs, 2013; The River Road, 2014; The Beautiful Librarians, 2015 (Roehampton Poetry Prize (jtly), 2015); (trans. with D. Hahn) Selected Poems of Corsino Fortes, 2015; Once Again Assembled Here (novel), 2016; Hammersmith, 2016;

The Railwayman (graphic novel), 2016; Quartier Perdu (short stories), 2018; Europa, 2018. *Recreations:* reading, listening to music, walking the dog. *Address:* School of English Language, Literature and Linguistics, Percy Building, Newcastle upon Tyne NE1 7RU. *T:* (0191) 222 3875. *E:* sean.o'brien@newcastle.ac.uk.

**O'BRIEN, Shaughn;** *see* O'Brien, P. M. S.

**O'BRIEN, Sir Stephen;** *see* O'Brien, Sir R. S.

**O'BRIEN, Rt Hon. Sir Stephen (Rothwell),** KBE 2017; PC 2013; Under-Secretary-General for Humanitarian Affairs and Emergency Relief Coordinator, United Nations, 2015–17; *b* Tanzania, 1 April 1957; *s* of David and Rothy O'Brien; *m* 1986, Gemma Townshend; two *s* one *d*. *Educ:* Sedbergh Sch.; Emmanuel Coll., Cambridge (MA); Chester Coll. of Law. Solicitor, Freshfields, 1981–88; Gp Internat. Dir and Gp Sec., Redland plc, 1988–98. MP (C) Eddisbury, July 1999–2015. PPS to Opposition spokesman on foreign affairs, 2000, to Chm. of Cons. Pty, 2000–01; an Opposition Whip, 2001–02; Shadow Financial Sec. to the Treasury, 2002; Shadow Paymaster Gen., 2002–03; Shadow Sec. of State for Industry, 2003–05; Shadow Minister for Skills and Higher Educn, 2005; Shadow Minister for Health, 2005–10; Parly Under-Sec. of State, DFID, 2010–12; Prime Minister's Envoy and Special Rep. for the Sahel, 2012–15. Member, Select Committee: on Educn and Employment, 1999–2001; on Envmt, Food and Rural Affairs, 2001. All Party Groups: Chairman: Malaria and Neglected Tropical Diseases; Tanzania; Classical Music; Primary Headache Disorders; Roofing; Jt Chm., Minerals; Vice-Chairman: Aid, Trade and Debt; Member: Africa; British-American; Hong Kong. Introduced Private Members Bill on Honesty in Food Labelling, 2001 and 2003. Mem., Cons. Nat. Membership Cttee, 1999–2001; Secretary: Cons. Trade and Industry Cttee, 1999–2001; Cons. NI Cttee, 1999–2001. Associate Mem., British-Irish Inter-Parly Body, 2000–10. Mem., Internat. Investment Panel and SE Regl Council, CBI, 1995–98. UK Building Materials Producers, then Construction Products Association: Chm., Public and Parly Affairs Cttee, 1995–99; Member: Cttee of Mgt; Pres.'s Strategy Cttee; Econ. and Market Forecasting Panel, 1989–95; Parly Advr, Manufg Technologies Assoc., 2005–10. Mem. Bd, DIT, 2019–. FCIS 1997 (Parly Advr, 2000–10). Chm., Motability Operations Gp, 2019–; Vice Chair, Savannah Petroleum plc, 2017–. Internat. Business Consultant, Observe Ltd, 2014–. Director: Cambridge Univ. Careers Service, 1992–99; City of London Sinfonia, 2001–15; Small Business Res. Trust, 2006–07. Chm., Malaria Consortium, 2006–10; Global Advocate, Roll Back Malaria Partnership, WHO, 2013–15; Patron, Malaria No More UK, 2014–15. Trustee, Bd, Liverpool Sch. of Tropical Medicine, 2006–10, 2013–15 (Vice Chm.); Dir/Trustee, Innovative Vector Control Consortium, 2008–10, 2015– (Chm., 2017–). Chm., Chichester Cons. Assoc., 1998–99 (Vice-Pres., 1999–). Global Champions Award for Action on Malaria Control and Advocacy, 2014. *Recreations:* music (piano, conducting), fell-walking, historic vehicles. *Clubs:* Winsford Constitutional and Conservative; Cheshire Pitt.

**O'BRIEN, Susan Joyce;** QC (Scot.) 1998; FCIArb; *b* 13 Aug. 1952; *d* of Sir Frederick William Fitzgerald O'Brien, QC (Scot.) and Audrey Muriel O'Brien (*née* Owen); *m* 1978, Peter Ross, Professor of Evolutionary Computing, Napier Univ., now Emeritus; two *d*. *Educ:* St George's Sch., Edinburgh; Univ. of York (BA Hons 1973; BPhil 1976); Univ. of Edinburgh (LLB 1978); Univ. of Aberdeen (Dip. in Internat. Arbitration Law and Practice, 2018). Admitted Solicitor, Scotland, 1980; Asst Solicitor, Shepherd & Wedderburn WS, 1980–86; WS 1983; admitted to Faculty of Advocates, 1987; Standing Junior Counsel to: Registrar Gen., 1991; Home Office, 1992–97; Temp. Sheriff, 1995–99. Chair: Caleb Ness Inquiry for Edinburgh and the Lothians Child Protection Cttee, report pub. 2003; Scottish Child Abuse (formerly Historical Child Abuse) Inquiry, 2015–16. Member: Investigatory Powers Tribunal, 2009–; Pensions Appeal Tribunals (Scotland), 2012–15. Fee paid Employment Judge (formerly Chm., Employment Tribunal), 2000–15. Mem., Panel of Legal Assessors for Gen. Teaching Council for Scotland, 2005–10. Reporter, Scottish Legal Aid Bd, 1999–2005. Chm., Faculty Services Ltd, 2005–07. Gov., Heriot-Watt Univ., 2013–16. FCIArb 2018. *Address:* Advocates' Library, Parliament Square, Edinburgh EH1 1RF.

**O'BRIEN, Timothy Brian,** RDI 1991; designer; Hon. Associate Artist, Royal Shakespeare Company, since 1988 (Associate Artist, 1966–88); *b* 8 March 1929; *s* of Brian Palliser Tiegue O'Brien and Elinor Laura (*née* Mackenzie); *m* 1997, Jenny Jones. *Educ:* Wellington Coll.; Corpus Christi, Cambridge (MA); Yale Univ. Design Dept, BBC TV, 1954; Designer, Associated Rediffusion, 1955–56; Head of Design, ABC Television, 1956–65 (The Flying Dutchman, 1958); partnership in stage design with Tazeena Firth, 1974–79; output incl.: The Bartered Bride, The Girl of the Golden West, 1962; West End prodns of new plays, 1963–64; London scene of Shakespeare Exhibn, 1964; Tango, Days in the Trees, Staircase, RSC, and Trafalgar at Madame Tussaud's, 1966; All's Well that Ends Well, As You Like It, Romeo and Juliet, RSC, 1967; The Merry Wives of Windsor, Troilus and Cressida (also Nat. Theatre, 1976), The Latent Heterosexual, RSC, 1968; Pericles (also Comédie Française, 1974), Women Beware Women, Bartholomew Fair, RSC, 1969; 1970: Measure for Measure, RSC; Madame Tussaud's in Amsterdam; The Knot Garden, Royal Opera; 1971: Enemies, Man of Mode, Merchant of Venice, RSC; 1972: La Cenerentola, Oslo; Lower Depths, The Island of the Mighty, RSC; As You Like It, OCSC; 1973: Richard II, Love's Labour's Lost, RSC; 1974: Next of Kin, NT; Summerfolk, RSC; The Bassarids, ENO; 1975: John Gabriel Borkman, NT; Peter Grimes, Royal Opera (later in Göteborg, Paris); The Marrying of Ann Leete, RSC; 1976: Wozzeck, Adelaide Fest.; The Zykovs, RSC; The Force of Habit, NT; 1977: Tales from the Vienna Woods, Bedroom Farce, NT; Falstaff, Berlin Opera; 1978: The Cunning Little Vixen, Göteborg; Evita, London (later in Australia, Austria, USA, S Africa); A Midsummer Night's Dream, Sydney Opera House; 1979: The Rake's Progress, Royal Opera; 1981: Lulu, Royal Opera; 1982: La Ronde, RSC; Le Grand Macabre, ENO; 1983: Turandot, Vienna State Opera; 1984: The Mastersingers of Nuremberg, ENO; Tannhäuser, Royal Opera; 1985: Samson, Royal Opera; Sicilian Vespers, Grande Théatre, Geneva; Old Times, Haymarket; Lucia di Lammermoor, Köln Opera; 1986: The Threepenny Opera, NT; Die Meistersinger von Nürnberg, Netherlands Opera; The American Clock, NT; 1987: Otello, and Die Entführung aus dem Serail, Royal Opera; 1988: Three Sisters, RSC; 1989: Cymbeline, RSC; Exclusive, Strand; 1990: King, Piccadilly; Love's Labours Lost, RSC; 1991: Twelfth Night, Tartuffe, Playhouse; War and Peace, Kirov, Leningrad; Beauty and the Beast, City of Birmingham Touring Opera; 1992: Christopher Columbus, RSC; 1993: Eugene Onegin, Royal Opera; Misha's Party, RSC; 1994: On Approval, Playhouse; The Clandestine Marriage, Queen's; 1995: The Merry Wives of Windsor, NT; The Merry Wives of Windsor, Oslo; 1996: Outis, La Scala, Milan; 1997: A Christmas Carol, Clwyd; 1998: Evita, US tour; 1999: Twelfth Night, Macbeth, Clwyd; 2001: Bedroom Farce, Clwyd; 2002: Romeo and Juliet, Clwyd; 2004: Werther, Lisbon; 2005: Ulysses Comes Home, Birmingham Opera Co.; 2006: Das Rheingold, Lisbon; 2007: Die Walküre, Lisbon; 2008: Siegfried, Lisbon, 2008; Macbeth, Clwyd, 2008; Götterdämmerung, Lisbon, 2009. Jt Artistic Dir and Co-Designer, redevelt of site of New Place, Stratford upon Avon, 2014–16. Chm., Soc. of British Theatre Designers, 1984–91; Master, Faculty of RDI, 1999–2001. Trustee, Useful Simple Trust, 2008. (Jtly) Gold Medal for Set Design, Prague Quadriennale, 1975; (jtly) Golden Triga, for Best Nat. Exhibit, Prague Quadriennale, 1991. *Address:* The Level, Blackbridge Road, Freshwater Bay, Isle of Wight PO40 9QP. *E:* all@highwaterjones.com.

**O'BRIEN, Sir Timothy John,** 7th Bt *cr* 1849; *b* 6 July 1958; *s* of John David O'Brien (*d* 1980) and of Sheila Winifred, *o d* of Sir Charles Arland Maitland Freake, 4th Bt; *S* grandfather, 1982, but his name does not appear on the Official Roll of the Baronetage; *m* 2000, Susannah, *yr d* of Bryan Farr; three *d*. *Educ:* Millfield; Univ. of Hartford, Conn. *Heir:* *b* James Patrick Arland O'Brien [*b* 22 Dec. 1964; *m* 1992, Lianna Mace; two *s* one *d*].

**O'BRIEN, Dame Una,** DCB 2015 (CB 2011); Permanent Secretary, Department of Health, 2010–16; *b* Solihull, 23 Dec. 1957; *d* of Patrick O'Brien and Margaret O'Brien. *Educ:* Convent HCJ, Birmingham; St Anne's Coll., Oxford (BA Hons Modern Hist.); Harvard Univ. (Kennedy Schol.); London Sch. of Econs (MSc Econ Internat. Relns). Parly res. asst to Lab. frontbench spokesmen on NI, 1980–82; Res. Officer, Inst. of Educn, Univ. of London, 1984–86; Corporate Services Manager, London Lighthouse, 1987–90; Department of Health, 1990–2016: Policy Manager, for people with physical disability, 1990–92; Performance Manager, NHS W Midlands, NHS Mgt Exec., 1992–93; Private Sec., Minister of State for Health, 1993–94; Principal Private Sec., Sec. of State for Transport, 1994–95; Dep. Dir, Prime Minister's Efficiency Unit, Cabinet Office, 1996–98; Sec., Public Inquiry into Paediatric Cardiac Surgery in Bristol (Kennedy Inquiry), 1998–2001; on secondment to NHS as Dir, Develt and Clin. Governance, UCL NHS Foundn Trust, 2002–05; Dir, Provider Reform, Policy, 2005–07; Dir Gen., Policy and Strategy, 2007–10. Mem. Panel, Public Inq. into the Renewable Heat Incentive Scheme, NI, 2017–. Trustee, Macmillan Cancer Support, 2018–. Member, Council: Univ. of Birmingham, 2016–; LSHTM, 2018–. Mem., Bd of Visitors, Ashmolean Mus., 2019–. *Recreations:* travel, theatre, walking, the River Thames.

**O'BRIEN, Sir William,** Kt 2010; JP; *b* 25 Jan. 1929; *m* Jean; three *d*. *Educ:* St Joseph's Sch., Castleford; Leeds Univ. (BEd 1978). Coalminer, 1945–83. Member: Knottingley UDC, 1952 (Chm., Housing Cttee, 1954–56; Chm., Finance Cttee, 1960–74; Leader of Council, 1964–74); West Riding CC, 1964–68; Wakefield DC, 1973–83 (Dep. Leader and Chm., Finance and Gen. Purposes Cttee). Mem., NUM, 1945–; Local Branch Official, 1956–83. MP (Lab) Normanton, 1983–2005. Opposition front bench spokesman on the Environment, 1987–92, for Northern Ireland, 1992–96. Member: Public Accounts Cttee, 1983–88; Energy Select Cttee, 1986–88; Envmt, Transport and Regions Select Cttee, 1997–2005; Public Accounts Commn, 1997–2005. Chm., Dr Jackson Cancer Fund, Pontefract, 1996–; Sec., Pontefract Groups Together, 2006–15; Mem., Pontefract Town Centre Partnership, 2008–; Friend, Pontefract Castle Gp, 2009–; Pres., Pontefract Magna Carta Gp, 2017– (Sec., 2013–17, 2018–). Governor: Carleton Community High Sch., 2006–; Orchard Head Primary Sch., 2007–. JP Wakefield, 1979. *Recreations:* reading, organising, gardening, community interests. *Address:* 29 Limetrees, Ferrybridge Road, Pontefract WF8 2QB.

**O'BRIEN QUINN, James Aiden;** *see* Quinn.

**OBRIST, Hans Ulrich;** Co-Director, Exhibitions and Programmes, and Director, International Projects, Serpentine Gallery, since 2006; *b* Zurich, 21 May 1968; *s* of Fritz Obrist and Ella Obrist (*née* Bernegger). *Educ:* Univ. of St Gallen (Economy and Soc. Scis). Curator in Residence, Cartier Foundn, Paris, 1991; Founder and Head, Migrateurs prog., 1993–2006, Curator, 2000–06, Musée d'Art Moderne de la Ville de Paris; Curator, Museum in Progress, Vienna, 1993–2000. Lectr, Univ. of Lüneburg, 1993–2000; Prof., Univ. of Venice, 2000. Founder and Ed. in Chief, Point d'Ironie, 1997–. Has curated over 250 exhibitions. *Publications:* (ed) Gerhard Richter's Sils, 1992; (ed) Gerhard Richter's Text: schriften und interviews, 1993; (ed) Paul-Armand Gette's Nymphaeum, 1993; (ed) Bertrand Lavier's Argo, 1994; (ed) Christian Boltanski's Les Vacances à Berck-Plage (About 1975), 1995; (ed) Annette Messager's Nos Témoignages, 1995; (ed) Gerhard Richter's The Daily Practice of Painting: writings and interviews 1962–93, 1995; Do It, 1995; (ed) Gilbert & George's Oh, the Grand Old Duke of York, 1996; (ed jtly) The Words of Gilbert & George, with Portraits of the Artists from 1968 to 1997, 1997; (ed jtly) Unbuilt Roads, 107 Unrealised Projects, 1997; (ed jtly) Sogni/Dreams, 1999; (ed jtly) Weltwissen Wissenwelt: Das globale Netz von Text und Bild, 2000; (ed jtly) Interarchive: archival practices and sites in the contemporary art field, 2002; (ed jtly) Bridge the Gap?, 2002; Hans Ulrich Obrist: interviews, vol. 1, 2003; (ed) Do It, 2004; (ed jtly) Prefaces by Hans Ulrich Obrist 1989–2005, 2005; (ed jtly) Smithson Time: a dialogue, 2005; (ed jtly) Matthew Barney: drawing restraint 1987–2002 v.1, 2006; (jtly) Anri Sala, 2006; (with Pedro Reyes) El Aire Es Azul/The Air is Blue, 2006; (jtly) donsstopdontstopdontstopdontstop, 2006; (with Robert Violette) The Words of Gilbert & George, 2006; (ed jtly) Barry Flanagan: sculpture 1965–2005, 2006; Hans Ulrich Obrist: everything you always wanted to know about curating but were afraid to ask, 2007; (with Nicolas Trembley) The Secret Files of Gilbert and George, 2007; (with Pedro Reyes) The Air is Blue—Art Meets Architecture: Luis Barragan revisited, 2007; The Future Will Be…, 2007; (jtly) Ryan Gander: intellectual colours, 2007; (with Adrian Notz) Merz World: processing the complicated order, 2007; (ed jtly) Rirkrit Tiravanija—A Retrospective, 2007; (jtly) Olafur Eliasson: the Goose Lake Trail (Southern Route), 2007; (jtly) Thomas Bayrle: 40 years of Chinese rock 'n' roll, 2007; Formulas for Now, 2008; (jtly) Susan Hefuna: Pars Pro Toto, 2008; (jtly) Victor Man, 2008; (with Dietmar Elger) Gerhard Richter: text, writings, interviews and letters, 2009; (ed) Susan Hefuna: Pars Pro Toto II, 2009; (jtly) Ways Beyond Art: Ai Weiwei, 2009; Hans Ulrich Obrist: interviews, vol. 2, 2010; (ed) London a Portrait of a City: Serpentine Gallery 24-hour interview marathon, 2010; (jtly) Marianne Heske: a doll's house, 2011; Ways of Curating, 2014; The Conversation Series: Rem Koolhaas, 2007; Yona Friedman, 2007; Wolfgang Tillmans, 2007; Gilbert and George, 2007; Zaha Hadid, 2007; Thomas Demand, 2007; John Chamberlain, 2007; Konrad Klapheck, 2007; Robert Crumb, 2007; Olafur Eliasson, 2008; Nancy Spero, 2008; Philippe Parreno, 2008; Dominique Gonzalez-Foerster, 2008; Christian Boltanski, 2009; Gustav Metzger, 2009; Enzo Mari, 2009; Ken Adam and Katharina Fritsch, 2009; John Baldessari, 2009; Yoko Ono, 2010; Hens-Peter Feldmann, 2010; Rosemarie Trockel, 2010; Jeff Koons, 2010; Cedric Price, 2010; Marina Abramovic, 2010; Lucien Hervé, 2011; Rirkrit Tiravanija, 2011; Cerith Wyn Evans, 2011; Dan Graham, 2012; Kazuyo Sejima, 2012; Claude Parent, 2012; Edouard Glissant, 2012; Lives of the Artists, Lives of the Architects, 2015; contributing editor for internat. art magazines incl. Artforum, Atlantica, Flash Art Internat., der Freund, Paradis Mag., Numero d and Trans. *Address:* Serpentine Gallery, Kensington Gardens, W2 3XA. *T:* (020) 7402 6075, *Fax:* (020) 7402 4103. *E:* information@serpentinegallery.org.

**OBUNGE, Rev. Onimim Loloba, (Nims),** MBE 2008; DL; Minister in Charge, Freedom's Ark Church, Tottenham, since 1993; Founder and Chief Executive, Peace Alliance, since 2001; *b* London, 2 Jan. 1965; *s* of late Ambassador Daye Dagogo Obunge and of Lady Emma Sokari Obunge; *m* 1996, Edosa Jacqueline Arthur; one *s* one *d*. *Educ:* Univ. of Jos, Nigeria (BSc Politics and Internat. Law 1986); Hampstead Bible Sch. Ordained Minister, 1990; Associate Pastor, Victory Ch, Finchley, then Sen. Pastor, Victory Ch, Tottenham, 1990–93. Chm., ind. adv. gp, London Criminal Justice Partnership, 2007–. Mem., Roundtable for Gun Crime, 2002–, Stop and Search Action Team, 2005–, Home

Office. Member: London Adv. Bd, CRE, 2004–07; Adv. Bd, London Crime Stoppers, 2005–. Metropolitan Police Authority: Member: Trident Ind. Adv. Gp, 2002–; Stop and Search Security Panel, 2003; Ind. Adv. Gp, Operation Blunt, 2005–07. Borough of Haringey: Member: Local Strategic Partnership, 2005–; Crime Disorder Reduction Partnership, 2005–; Chm., Other Violent Crime Partnership Bd, 2006–. Mem. Bd, Spring Harvest, 2007–09. Ecumenical Bor. Dean, 2000–. Police Chaplain, Haringey Police, 2000–. Founder and Mem., Haringey Multifaith Forum (Chm., 2002–05); Founder, Haringey and London Week of Peace, 2001–. DL Greater London, 2009. *Recreations:* swimming, table tennis, lawn tennis. *Address:* The Peace Alliance/Freedom's Ark, Tottenham Town Hall, Town Hall Approach, N15 4RY. *T:* (020) 8808 9439, (020) 8493 0050, *Fax:* (020) 8493 0058. *E:* info@peacealliance.org.uk.

**O'BYRNE, Andrew John Martin;** QC 2006; *b* 23 April 1950; *s* of late Andrew John O'Byrne and Winifred O'Byrne; *m* 1977, Anne Victoria Roby; two *s. Educ:* St Joseph's Coll., Blackpool; Univ. of Liverpool (LLB). Called to the Bar, Gray's Inn, 1978, Bencher, 2014; in practice, specialising in criminal law, incl. serious fraud. Mem., Bar Council, 2013–16. Leader, Northern Circuit, 2014–16. *Recreations:* family, reading, good wine, good company. *Address:* St Johns Buildings, 24a–28 St John Street, Manchester M3 4DJ. *T:* (0161) 214 1500, *Fax:* (0161) 835 3929.

**O'CALLAGHAN, James Dominic,** FREng; Co-Founder and Director, Eckersley O'Callaghan, since 2004; *b* Bedford, 1 March 1971; *s* of Rodney Norman John O'Callaghan and Cheryl Joy O'Callaghan; *m* 2008, Amy Slatter; two *s* one *d. Educ:* Tring Sch.; Univ. of Manchester (BEng Hons Civil Engrg). CEng 1995; FIStructE 2018; FREng 2018. Dewhurst Macfarlane and Partners, 1995–2004. Prof. of Architectural Glass, Delft Univ. of Technol., 2019. *Recreation:* sailing. *Address:* Eckersley O'Callaghan Ltd, 236 Gray's Inn Road, WC1X 8HB. *T:* (020) 7354 5402. *E:* james@eocengineers.com. *Club:* Hayling Island Sailing.

**O'CARROLL, Derek;** Sheriff of South Strathclyde, Dumfries and Galloway at Airdrie, since 2014; *b* Herts, 20 Jan. 1960; *s* of Maurice and Ita O'Carroll. *Educ:* Cults Acad., Aberdeen; Edinburgh Univ. (LLB Hons; DipLP). Solicitor, 1991–99; called to the Scottish Bar, 2000; Chairman: Social Security Tribunal, 1999–2007; Rent Assessment Cttee, 2002–07; Private Rented Housing Panel, 2002–07; Convener, Mental Health Tribunal, 2005–10; Sheriff (pt-time), 2006–10; All-Scotland Floating Sheriff, 2010–14. Mem., Scottish Legal Aid Bd, 1998–2002. Dir, Faculty Services Ltd, 2003–07; Mem., Faculty of Advocates, 2000– (Mem. Council, 2005–08); Hon. Sec. Sheriffs' Assoc., 2015– (Mem. Council, 2011–14). *Publications:* contrib. articles and pubns on legal topics especially landlord and tenant/housing law, public law, employment/discrimination law. *Recreations:* travel, swimming, pool, keeping fit, good food and drink. *Address:* Sheriff Court House, Graham Street, Airdrie ML6 6EE.

**O'CATHAIN,** Baroness *cr* 1991 (Life Peer), of The Barbican in the City of London; **Detta O'Cathain,** OBE 1983; Managing Director, Barbican Centre, 1990–95; *b* 3 Feb. 1938; *d* of late Caoimhghin O'Cathain and Margaret O'Cathain; *m* 1968, William Bishop (*d* 2001). *Educ:* Laurel Hill, Limerick; University College, Dublin (BA). Aer Lingus, Dublin, 1961–66; Group Economist, Tarmac, 1966–69; Economic Advr, Rootes Motors, 1969–72; Sen. Economist, Carrington Vyella, 1972–73; Economic Advr, British Leyland, 1973–74; Dir, Market Planning, Leyland Cars, 1974–76; Corporate Planning Exec., Unigate, 1976–81; Milk Marketing Board: Head of Strategic Planning, 1981–83; Dir and Gen. Manager, 1984; Man. Dir Milk Marketing, 1985–88. Advr on Agricl Marketing to Minister of Agriculture, 1979–83. Member: British-Irish Parly Assembly, 2008–11; Council of Europe, 2009; WEU, 2009. Non-executive Director: Midland Bank, 1984–93; Channel 4, 1985–86; Tesco, 1985–2000; Sears, 1987–94; British Airways, 1993–2004; BET, 1994–96; BNP Paribas (formerly BNP) UK Holdings Ltd, 1995–2005; Thistle Hotels, 1996–2003; South East Water plc, 1998–2008; William Baird Plc, 2000–02; Allders plc, 2000–03. FCIM 1987 (Pres., 1998–2001); FRSA 1986. Hon. Fellow, Harris Manchester Coll., Oxford, 2008. Mem., Brooklands Mus. Trust, 2006–10 (Chm., Appeal Bd, 2007–10). Chm. Council, Chichester Cathedral, 2010–16; Mem. Council, St George's House, Windsor Castle, 2018–. Commander: Royal Norwegian Order, 1992; Order of the Lion (Finland), 1992; Mem., Order of Pres. of Azerbaijan, 2011. *Recreations:* music, reading, walking, gardening. *Address:* House of Lords, SW1A 0PW. *T:* (020) 7219 0662.

**O'CEALLAIGH, Dáithí;** Director General, Institute of International and European Affairs, Dublin, 2010–13; Chairman, Press Council of Ireland, 2010–16; *b* 24 Feb. 1945; *m* 1968, Antoinette Reilly; one *s* one *d. Educ:* University College Dublin (BA). Teacher, Zambia, 1968–71; entered Diplomatic Service, Ireland, 1973; Third Sec., 1973, First Sec., 1974, Dept of Foreign Affairs; First Sec., Moscow, 1975–77, London, 1977–82; First Sec., 1982–85, Counsellor, 1985, Anglo-Irish Div., Dublin; Counsellor, Anglo-Irish Secretariat, Maryfield, 1985–87; Consul General, New York, 1987–93; Ambassador, Finland and Estonia, 1993–98; Asst Sec., Admin Div., 1998–2000; Second Sec. General, Anglo-Irish Div., 2000–01, Dublin; Ambassador: to UK, 2001–07; to UN, Geneva, 2007–09. Hon. Prof., Inst. of Irish Studies, Univ. of Liverpool, 2008. MRIA 2019. Hon. Dr Geneva Sch. of Diplomacy and Internat. Relns, 2010; Hon. DPhil Ulster, 2017. Comdr, First Class, Order of White Rose of Finland, 2004. *Publications:* (ed jtly) Britain and Europe: the endgame, an Irish perspective, 2015. *Recreations:* bird-watching, cinema, history, theatre, jazz, vintage cars. *Address:* 1 Vesey Place, Dun Laoghaire, Co. Dublin, Ireland.

**OCEAN, Humphrey;** *see* Butler-Bowdon, H. A. E.

**OCKELTON, (Christopher) Mark (Glyn);** Vice President, Upper Tribunal (Immigration and Asylum Chamber) (formerly Deputy President, Immigration Appeal Tribunal, later Asylum and Immigration Tribunal), since 2000; a Recorder, since 2003; a Deputy High Court Judge, since 2008; *b* 11 July 1955; *s* of Denis William Ockelton and Elvire Mabel Louise Jeanne (*née* May); *m* 1992, Brigid Joan Oates; one step *s* one step *d. Educ:* Winchester Coll.; Peterhouse, Cambridge (BA 1976; MA 1980); BD London 1989. Called to the Bar, Lincoln's Inn, 1977 (Mansfield Scholar), Bencher, 2001; Lectr in Law, 1979–93, Sen. Lectr, 1993–96, Hon. Fellow, 1996–2003, Vis. Fellow, 2003–, Univ. of Leeds; Immigration Adjudicator, 1992–96; Chm., 1996–2000, Vice-Pres., Jan.–May 2000, Immigration Appeal Tribunal; Actg Sen. Judge for Sovereign Base Areas, 2014–. Dep. Internat. Course Dir, Judicial Coll., 2014–17. Vis. Prof. of Law, Univ. of Louisville, 1984–85; Vis. Lectr, Univ. du Maine, France, 1989. Parish Clerk: St Mary's Ch, Whitby, 1994–2017; St Mary's Ch, Rotherhithe, 2004–. Dep. Chancellor, Dio. of Hereford, 2010–; Chancellor, Dio. of Southwell and Nottingham, 2016–. Mem., Ancient Soc. of Coll. Youths, 1974–; Parish Clerks' Co., 2005–. Hon. Col, Commonwealth of Ky, 1985. *Publications:* The Tower, Bells and Ringers of Great St Mary's, Cambridge, 1981; Trusts for Accountants, 1987; Heydon and Ockelton's Evidence: cases and materials, 3rd edn 1991, 4th edn 1996; contrib. articles and reviews in legal, philosophical, antiquarian and campanological jls. *Recreations:* books, bells, buildings. *Address:* Upper Tribunal (Immigration and Asylum Chamber), Field House, 15–25 Bream's Buildings, EC4A 1DZ. *Club:* Athenæum.

**OCKENDON, Prof. John Richard,** FRS 1999; Professor of Mathematics, University of Oxford, 2008–10, now Emeritus; Fellow, St Catherine's College, Oxford, 1965–2010, now Emeritus; *b* 13 Oct. 1940; *s* of George and Doris Ockendon; *m* 1967, Hilary Mason; one *d. Educ:* Dulwich Coll.; St John's Coll., Oxford (MA; DPhil 1965). Lectr, Christ Church, Oxford, 1963–65; University of Oxford: Lectr in Applicable Maths, 1975–2008; Res. Dir, Oxford Centre for Industrial and Applied Maths, 1989–2009; Dir, Oxford Centre for Collaborative Applied Maths, 2008–10. Adv. Prof., Fudan Univ., Shanghai, 1999; Adjunct Prof., Univ. Teknologi Malaysia, 2014. Chair, Scientific Cttee, Smith Inst. Knowledge Transfer Network, 2001–08; Chief Mathematician and Tech. Dir, Smith Inst. for Industrial Maths and System Engrg, 2014–17. SIAM Fellow, 2009. Gold Medal, IMA, 2006. *Publications:* (with C. Elliott) Free Boundary Problems, 1981; (with H. Ockendon) Viscous Flow, 1997; (jtly) Applied Partial Differential Equations, 1999; (with H. Ockendon) Waves and Compressible Flow, 2003; (jtly) Applied Solid Mechanics, 2008. *Recreations:* bird watching, Hornby-Dublo, old sports cars. *Address:* Mathematical Institute, University of Oxford, Andrew Wiles Building, Radcliffe Observatory Quarter, Woodstock Road, Oxford OX2 6GG. *T:* (01865) 270513.

**OCONE, Prof. Raffaella,** OBE 2019; PhD; FIChemE; CEng, FREng; FRSE; FRSC; Professor of Chemical Engineering, Heriot-Watt University, since 1999; *b* Morcone, Italy, 14 Jan. 1960; *d* of Giuseppe Ocone and Franca Ocone (*née* Lombardi). *Educ:* Univ. di Napoli, Federico II (Laurea, Chem. Engrg); Princeton Univ. (MA 1989; PhD 1992). FIChemE 2003; CEng 2003; CSci 2005; FRSC 2009; FREng 2013. Lectr, Univ. di Napoli, Federico I, 1991–95; Reader, Univ. of Nottingham, 1995–99. Visiting Professor: Louisiana State Univ., 1992–93; Univ. Claude Bérnard, Lyon, 1994–95; Caroline Herschel Vis. Prof., Ruhr Univ., Bochum, Germany, 2017. FRSE 2006; FRSA 2009. Cavaliere, Ordine della Stella della Solidarietà (Italy), 2006. *Publications:* (with G. Astarita) Special Topics in Transport Phenomena, 2002; contribs to scientific pubns. *Recreations:* reading, classical music, opera, fiction, gym, playing the piano badly; does not own a TV. *Address:* Chemical Engineering, School of Engineering and Physical Sciences, Heriot-Watt University, Edinburgh EH14 4AS. *T:* (0131) 451 3129. *E:* r.ocone@hw.ac.uk.

**O'CONNELL, Sir Bernard,** Kt 2004; management consultant, 2004–08; Principal and Chief Executive Officer, Runshaw College, Lancashire, 1984–2004; *b* 16 April 1945; *s* of Richard and Brigid O'Connell; *m* 1966, Jane; one *s* one *d. Educ:* London Univ. (BSc Econ.); Liverpool Univ. (MA, MEd); Manchester Univ. (Teacher's Cert.). Millbank Coll. of Commerce, 1968–79; Vice-Principal, Old Swan Tech. Coll., 1979–84. *Publications:* Creating an Outstanding College, 2005; college manuals. *Recreations:* watching Liverpool FC, travel, reading. *Address:* 28 Magazine Brow, Wallasey, Merseyside CH45 1HP. *T:* (0151) 639 1556. *E:* oconnellbernard@yahoo.co.uk.

**O'CONNELL, Cathy;** *see* Newman, C.

**O'CONNELL, Enda;** *see* O'Connell, P. E.

**O'CONNELL, Sir Maurice (James Donagh MacCarthy),** 7th Bt *cr* 1869, of Lakeview, Killarney and Ballybeggan, Tralee; *b* 10 June 1958; *s* of Sir Morgan Donal Conail O'Connell, 6th Bt and of Elizabeth, *o d* of late Major John MacCarthy O'Leary; *S* father, 1989; *m* 1993, Francesca, *d* of late Clive Raleigh; one *s. Heir: s* Morgan Daniel Clive MacCarthy O'Connell, *b* 17 Nov. 2003. *Address:* Lakeview House, Killarney, Co. Kerry, Ireland.

**O'CONNELL, Prof. (Patrick) Enda,** PhD; CEng, FREng; FICE; Professor of Water Resources Engineering, Newcastle University (formerly University of Newcastle upon Tyne), since 1984; *b* 3 April 1945; *s* of Patrick and Cecilia O'Connell; *m* 1974, Jane Rosemary; one *s* two *d. Educ:* University Coll., Galway (BEng 1st Cl. Hons (Civil)); Imperial Coll., London (DIC; PhD). Asst Lectr, 1968–69, Lectr, 1969–76, Dept of Civil Engrg, Imperial Coll., London; Section/Div. Hd, NERC Inst. of Hydrol., 1976–84; Dir, Water Resource Systems Res. Lab., Sch. of Civil Engrg and Geoscis, 1984–2009, Earth Systems Engrg, 2003–09, Univ. of Newcastle upon Tyne, later Newcastle Univ. FREng 2005. *Publications:* contrib. internat. jls incl. Jl Hydrol., Hydrological Processes, Hydrological Scis, Hydrol., Earth Systems Scis, Sci. of the Total Envmt, Water Resources Mgt, Water Resources Res. *Recreations:* walking in the Yorkshire Dales, ski-ing, salmon angling in the West of Ireland (Mem., Irish Internat. Trout Angling Team, 1967–69), enjoying the food and wines of Tuscany. *Address:* School of Civil Engineering and Geosciences, Newcastle University, Newcastle upon Tyne NE1 7RU. *T:* (0191) 222 6405, *Fax:* (0191) 222 6669. *E:* enda.oconnell@ncl.ac.uk.

**O'CONNELL, Ruairi;** HM Diplomatic Service; Ambassador to Kosovo, 2015–19; *b* 22 Feb. 1977; *s* of Capt. Frederick Michael O'Connell and Dora Ann O'Connell (*née* Mahon); *m* 2010, Elida Lawton; one *s* two *d. Educ:* Downside Sch., Somerset; Univ. of Oxford (BA Hons PPE 1999); University Coll. London (MA Politics, Security and Integration 2000). Entered FCO, 2001; Yugoslavia Desk Officer, FCO, 2001–02; Second Sec. (Pol), 2004–05, Dep. Hd of Mission, 2004–08, Pristina; Advr, then Chef de Cabinet for Foreign Sec.'s Special Rep. on Climate Change, FCO, 2008–10; Dep. Hd of Dept, Finance Directorate, FCO, 2010–11; Dep. Dir, London 2012 and GREAT Campaign, 2012–13; Hd, Illegal Wildlife Trade Campaign, FCO, 2013; Dep. Dir, Directorate for Defence and Internat. Security, 2013–14. Chair, Kosovo Property Agency Bd, 2014–. *Recreations:* Rugby (esp. Saracens), football (Everton), science fiction. *Address:* c/o Foreign and Commonwealth Office, King Charles Street, SW1A 2AH.

**O'CONNELL, Stephen John;** Member (C) Croydon and Sutton, London Assembly, Greater London Authority, since 2008; *b* Dulwich, 19 Sept. 1956; *s* of Ronald John and Phyllis Jean O'Connell; two *s. Educ:* Brockley Co. Grammar Sch. CeMAP 2000; CeFA 2001. Barclays Bank, 1976–2005. Mem. (C) Croydon Council, 2002– (Cabinet Member: Safety and Cohesion, 2006–08; Regeneration and Econ. Develt, 2008–10; Community Safety, 2010–11; Finance and Performance, 2011–14; Safety and Community, 2011–14; Dep. Leader, 2006–08; Shadow Spokesman on Finance, 2014–15, on Safety and Justice, 2015–19). Mem., Metropolitan Police Authy, 2008–12 (Chm., Finance Cttee, 2008–11); non-exec. Advr, Mayor's Office for Policing and Crime, 2013–16; Chm., Police and Crime Cttee, London Assembly, 2016–19. Chm., Surrey Br., RSPCA, 2016–. Trustee: Crystal Palace FC Foundn, 2013–; Kenley Meml Hall, 2017–; RAFA, Kenley, 2018–. FRSA. *Recreations:* dog walking, real ale, political literature, Crystal Palace Football Club. *Address:* Greater London Authority, City Hall, The Queen's Walk, SE1 2AA. *T:* (020) 7983 4405, *Fax:* (020) 7983 4419. *E:* Steve.O'Connell@london.gov.uk. *W:* www.twitter.com/steveo_connell.

**O'CONNOR, Biddie;** *see* O'Connor, B. A.

**O'CONNOR, Rev. Canon (Brian) Michael (McDougal);** Dean of Auckland, New Zealand, 1997–2000; *b* 20 June 1942; *s* of Brian McDougal O'Connor and Beryl O'Connor; *m* 1968, Alison Margaret Tibbutt (marr. diss. 2004); two *s. Educ:* Lancing Coll.; St Catharine's Coll., Cambridge (BA, MA); Cuddesdon Coll., Oxford. Admitted Solicitor, 1964; Asst Curate, St Andrew, Headington, 1969–72; Sec., Oxford Dio. Pastoral Cttee, 1972–79; Vicar, Rainham, Kent, 1979–97; Rural Dean of Gillingham, 1981–88; Priest-in-charge, Little Missenden, 2002–04. Hon. Canon: of Rochester Cathedral, 1988–97; of

Auckland Cathedral, 2000–. Church Comr, 1995–97. Member: General Synod, 1975–90 (Mem., Standing Cttee, 1985–90); Crown Appointments Commn, 1987–90; ACC, 1988–92. Deleg., WCC Assembly, Canberra, 1991. Commissary for Bishop: of Auckland, NZ, 1996–97; of Newcastle, NSW, 1996–. Exec. Officer, Ecclesiastical Law Soc., 2001–07. *Address*: The Lawn, 64 Fore Street, Otterton, Budleigh Salterton, Devon EX9 7HB. *T*: (01395) 488898. *E*: canonmichaeloc@aol.com.

**O'CONNOR, Bridget Anne, (Biddie);** Headmistress, Haberdashers' Aske's School for Girls, Elstree, 2011–19; *b* Chesterfield, 28 April 1958; *d* of John O'Connor and Joan O'Connor (née Mears); *m* 1982, Simon Salem; one *d*. *Educ*: St Helena's Sch., Chesterfield; St Hugh's Coll., Oxford (BA Lit.Hum. 1980); Sidney Sussex Coll., Cambridge (PGCE 1981). Asst Classics Teacher and Form Tutor, Clarence Gate, Francis Holland Sch., 1981–84; Asst Classics Teacher, then Hd of Dept, Old Palace Sch., Croydon, 1984–91; Haberdashers' Aske's School for Girls, Elstree: Hd of Classics, 1991–97; Hd of Sixth Form, 1993–98; Dep. Headmistress, 1998–2002; Headmistress, Loughborough High Sch., 2002–11. *Recreations*: reading, cooking, art, gardening, walking.

**O'CONNOR, Christopher;** Director, Chris O'Connor & Associates Ltd, since 2013; *b* Poynton, 21 April 1966; *s* of Patrick O'Connor and Veronica O'Connor; partner, Susan Chennell; one *d*. *Educ*: Salford Univ. (BEng Hons Electronic Engrg); Manchester Business Sch. (MBA). Design Engr, British Aerospace, 1989–91; Programme Manager: Hewlett-Packard, 1991–2000; Agilent Technologies, 2000–06; Dir, Bradford-i Business Transformation Prog., City of Bradford MDC, 2006–07; Dir, 2008–10, Chief Exec., Shared Services, 2010–13, DfT. *Recreations*: all forms of motorsport (watching), rallying (competing). *Address*: Chris O'Connor & Associates Ltd, Common Lodge, Moss Lane, St Michaels, Preston PR3 0TY. *T*: (01995) 679396. *E*: chris.oconnor@coassociates.co.uk.

**O'CONNOR, Christopher Paul,** OBE 2012; HM Diplomatic Service; Consul-General, Los Angeles, 2013–17; *b* Epsom, 18 Dec. 1968; *m* Martha Dorothy Nelems; two *d*. *Educ*: Fitzwilliam Coll., Cambridge (BA Hons 1991); Durham Univ. (MA 1993). Entered FCO, 1993; Southern Eur. Dept, FCO, 1993–94; UN/Internat. Orgns Res. Gp, London, 1994–95; Attaché, Cairo, 1995–96; Second Sec., Riyadh, 1996–99; First Sec., UK Delegn to NATO, 1999; Sen. Policy Advr, Canadian Dept for Foreign Affairs, 1999–2000 (on secondment); Head: Political Section, Ottawa, 2000–03; ME Peace Process Team, FCO, 2003–05; Dep. Hd of Mission, Beirut, 2006–08; Ambassador to Tunisia, 2008–13. *Recreations*: learning languages, being a father.

**O'CONNOR, Hon. Deirdre Frances;** Judge, Federal Court of Australia, 1990–2002; President, Administrative Appeals Tribunal, 1990–94 and 1999–2002; *b* 5 Feb. 1941; *d* of D. A. Buff; *m* 1974, Michael John Joseph, SC; four *s* (and one *s* decd). *Educ*: Bethlehem Coll., Ashfield; Sydney Univ. (BA 1961; LLB 1st Cl. Hons 1974); DipEd New England 1963. Teacher of hist., various high schs and tech. colls, 1963–74; Lectr in Law, Univ. of NSW, 1974–75; Sen. Lectr in Law, Macquarie Univ., 1975–78; part-time Lectr on media and law, Aust. Film and TV Sch., 1975–80; admitted NSW Bar, 1980; Comr, NSW Law Reform Commn, 1983–85; Chm., Aust. Broadcasting Tribunal, 1986–90. President: Nat. Native Title Tribunal, 1993–94; Aust. Industrial Relns Commn, 1994–97. Mediator, NSW Workers Compensation Commn, 2002; Judicial Mem., NSW Parole Authy (formerly Parole Bd), 2003– (Alternate Chm.). Chm., Telephone Information Services Standards Council, 2010–. Mem., Aust. Inst. Judicial Admin, 1992–. Trustee, Internat. Inst. of Communications, 1989–92. Member, Council: Order of Australia, 1990–96; Univ. of Canberra, 1992–95. *Recreations*: reading, antiques.

**O'CONNOR, Sir Denis (Francis),** Kt 2010; CBE 2002; QPM 1996; HM Chief Inspector of Constabulary, 2009–12; *b* 21 May 1949; *m* 1972, Louise (née Harvey); one *s* two *d*. *Educ*: La Sainte Union Coll.; Southampton Univ. (BEd Hons 1974); Cranfield Inst. of Technol. (MSc 1985). Chief Supt, Notting Hill, 1990; Asst Chief Constable, Surrey Police, 1991; Dep. Chief Constable, Kent Constabulary, 1993; Asst Comr, SW Area, later S London, Metropolitan Police, 1997–2000; Chief Constable, Surrey Police, 2000–04; HM Inspector of Constabulary, 2004–09. Former Member: Criminal Justice Wkg Gp, Adv. Council on Misuse of Drugs; DoH Task Force on Effectiveness of Drug Services; Mem., Ind. Inquiry into the Misuse of Drugs Act 1971, 1997–2000. Vice-Pres., ACPO, 2002–04. Radzinowicz Fellow and Lectr, Inst. of Criminology, Univ. of Cambridge, 2013–. Non-exec. Dir, Coll. of Policing, 2013–17. Chm., Surrey Care Trust, 2017–. Hon. DLaws Wolverhampton, 2012. *Publications*: Developing a Partnership Approach for Drugs Education, 1992; Management by Objectives on Trial, 1992; Community Policing: are good intentions enough?, 1994; Increasing Community Safety from Drug Related Crime, 1995; Criminal Justice: what works?, 1995; Drugs: partnerships for policy, prevention and education, 1998; Performance from the Outside-In, 2010; (contrib.) Police Leadership: rising to the top, 2015; article in Criminal Justice Jl. *Recreations*: reading, walking, gardening.

**O'CONNOR, Desmond Bernard, (Des),** CBE 2008; entertainer and singer; *b* 12 Jan. 1932; *m* 1st, Phyllis; one *d*; 2nd, Gillian Vaughan; two *d*; 3rd, Jay; one *d*; 4th, Jodie Brooke Wilson; one *s*. Served RAF. Former Butlin's Red Coat, Filey; professional début, Palace Theatre, Newcastle upon Tyne, 1953; one-man shows, UK, Canada, USA and Australia, 1980–; Royal Variety Show appearances, incl. compère, 1997; Des O'Connor and Jimmy Tarbuck Live on Stage, London Palladium, 2015, UK tour, 2016, 2017, 2018, 2019; The Ultimate Des O'Connor, UK tour, 2016, 2017; musicals: Dreamboats and Petticoats, Playhouse, London, 2011–12; Wizard of Oz, London Palladium, 2012. Television includes: Spot the Tune, 1958; Sunday Night at the London Palladium; Take Your Pick, 1992, 1994, 1996; Pot of Gold, 1993, 1995; Countdown, 2007–08; own shows: The Des O'Connor Show, 1963 and 1970–76; Kraft Music Hall Presents: The Des O'Connor Show, 1970–71 (USA); Des O'Connor Tonight, 1977–2003; Des O'Connor Now, 1985; Fame in the Family, 2000–; Today with Des and Mel, 2002–06. Has made over 1,000 appearances at the London Palladium. No 1 single, I Pretend, 1968. Male TV Personality, TV Times, annually 1969–73; Lifetime Achievement Award, Nat. TV Awards, 2001; Grand Order of Water Rats Lifetime Achievement Award, 2012. *Publications*: Bananas Can't Fly (autobiog.), 2001; Laughter Lines: comic verse to celebrate life's little moments, 2014. *Address*: c/o Lake-Smith Associates, Ashdown House, The Nightingales, Biddenden, Kent TN27 8HN. *E*: Pat@lakesmith.co.uk. *W*: www.officialdesoconnor.com.

**O'CONNOR, Gillian Denise;** *see* Brasse, G. D.

**O'CONNOR, Rev. Canon Michael;** *see* O'Connor, Rev. Canon B. M. McD.

**O'CONNOR, Michael,** CBE 2000; Chief Executive, StepChange, 2014–17; Interim Chief Executive, Action on Hearing Loss, 2018; *b* London, 15 Dec. 1956; *s* of John and Kathleen O'Connor; *m* 2019, Elizabeth Owen. *Educ*: Univ. of Keele (BSc Hons Physics and Geol. 1979); Imperial Coll. London (MSc Social and Envmtl Aspects of Sci. and Technol. 1980; DIC). Civil Servant, DoH, HM Treasury and Cabinet Office, 1982–89; Dir, Coronary Prevention Gp, 1989–92; Consultant on public health policy, 1992–93; Dir for Developed Economies, Consumers Internat., 1993–96; Chief Executive: Millennium Commn, 1996–2006; Olympic Lottery Distributor, 2006–10; Consumer Futures (formerly Consumer Focus), 2010–14. Non-exec. Mem., Customer Fairness Cttee, British Gas, 2013–16; Mem., Advertising Adv. Cttee, Broadcast Advertising Code, 2018–. Founding Mem., Coll. of Fellows, Keele Univ., 2013–. Trustee: ASH, 1993–95; Mental Health Foundn, 2003–09; London Irish Centre Charity, 2017–. *Recreations*: art, walking, music, poetry. *E*: moconnorcf@gmail.com.

**O'CONNOR, Michael Thomas;** freelance costume designer, since 1992; *b* London, 27 Oct. 1965; *s* of Thomas Patrick O'Connor and Patricia Theresa O'Connor (née Fraser); partner, John Phillip Usher. *Educ*: Slade Sch. of Fine Art (Fine Art foundn). Costumier, Bermans and Nathans, 1986–92. Member: Acad. of Motion Picture Arts and Scis, 2009–; BAFTA, 2009–. *Films include*: Assistant Costume Designer: Oscar and Lucinda, 1998; Topsy Turvy, 2000; Quills, 2001; Costume Designer: The Last King of Scotland, 2006; Brick Lane, 2007; The Duchess, 2008 (Academy Award, BAFTA Award, Costume Designers Guild Award, Phoenix Film Critics Soc. Award, Satellite Award, for Costume Design, 2009); Miss Pettigrew Lives For a Day, 2008; The Eagle, Jane Eyre, 2011; Invisible Woman, 2014; Suite Française, 2015; All Is True, A Private War, 2019.

**O'CONNOR, Neil Brendan,** CBE 2016; Director, Ministry for Housing, Communities and Local Government (formerly Department for Communities and Local Government), 2009–18; *b* Hackney, 4 May 1963; *s* of John O'Connor and Eleanor, (Judy), O'Connor; *m* 2006, Juliet Mountford; three *s* one *d*. *Educ*: Finchley Catholic High Sch. Transport clerk, W H Malcolm Ltd, 1980; Clerical Officer, PSA, 1980–83; Department of the Environment: Clerical Officer, 1983–85; EO, 1985–90; HEO, 1990–97; Principal Officer (Grade 7), 1997–2002; Deputy Director: ODPM, 2002–06; Home Office, 2006–07; DCSF, 2007; Cabinet Office, 2007–08; Dep. Dir, DCLG, 2008–09. *Recreations*: classic minis (Mem., Mini Cooper Register), northern soul, football. *Club*: West Ham United Football.

**O'CONNOR, Patrick Michael Joseph;** QC 1993; *b* 7 Aug. 1949; *s* of Denis Bellew O'Connor and Ingelore Biegel; *m* 1986, Gillian Denise Brasse, qv; two *d*. *Educ*: St Francis Xavier's Grammar Sch., Liverpool; UCL (LLB Hons). Called to the Bar, Inner Temple, 1970, Bencher, 2008. *Publications*: articles in Criminal Law Review and other academic and professional jls. *Address*: Doughty Street Chambers, 53–54 Doughty Street, WC1N 2LS. *T*: (020) 7404 1313.

**O'CONNOR, Ronald;** Education Advisor, Abu Dhabi Education Council; *b* 1 Dec. 1950; *s* of John O'Connor and Mary O'Connor (née McDermott); *m* 1992, Marie Harvey Milne; one *s*. *Educ*: Stirling Univ. (BA (Hons), Dip Ed). Teacher, modern langs, Belmont Acad., Ayr, 1977–81; Principal Teacher, modern langs, 1981–83, Asst Head, 1983–88, Garnock Acad.; Educn Officer, 1988–93, Asst Dir of Educn, 1993–95, Strathclyde Regl Council; Glasgow City Council: Sen. Depute Dir of Educn, 1995–99; Dir of Social Work Services, 1999–2002; Dir of Educn Services, 2002–04; Exec. Dir (Educn, Training and Young People), 2004–07. *Recreations*: golf, football, reading.

**O'CONNOR, Sandra Day;** Associate Justice of the Supreme Court of the United States, 1981–2006; *b* 26 March 1930; *d* of Harry and Ada Mae Day; *m* 1952, John Jay O'Connor III (*d* 2009); three *s*. *Educ*: Stanford Univ. (BA 1950; LLB 1952). Legal appts in Calif and Frankfurt, 1952–57; in private practice, 1959–60; Asst Attorney-Gen., Arizona, 1965–69; Judge: Maricopa County Superior Ct, 1975–79; Arizona Ct of Appeals, 1979–81. Mem. Senate, Arizona, 1969–75 (majority leader, 1972–75). Director: Nat. Bank of Arizona, Phoenix, 1971–74; Blue Cross/Blue Shield, Arizona, 1975–79. American Bar Association: Member: Exec. Bd, Central Eur. and Eurasian Law Initiative, 1990–; Exec. Cttee, Mus. of Law, 2000–; Adv. Commn, Standing Cttee on Law Library of Congress, 2002–; Commn on Civic Educn and Separation of Powers, 2005–; Mem., Adv. Cttee, Judicial, Amer. Soc. of Internat. Law, 2001–; Hon. Mem., Adv. Cttee for Judiciary Leadership Develt Council. Chm., Maricopa County Juvenile Detention Home, 1963–64; Pres., Heard Museum, Phoenix, 1968–74, 1976–81; Member: Nat. Bd, Smithsonian Assocs, 1981: Selection Cttee, Oklahoma City Nat. Meml and Mus., 2005–; Adv. Bd, Stanford Center on Ethics, 2005–; Adv. Bd, Smithsonian Nat. Mus. of Natural History, 2006–; Bd of Trustees, Rockefeller Foundn, 2006–; Co-Chm., Nat. Adv. Council, Campaign for Civic Mission of Schs, 2005–. Founder and Chair, iCivics Inc., 2009–. Trustee, Stanford Univ., 1976–81; Chancellor, Coll. of William and Mary, 2005–11. Hon. Bencher, Gray's Inn, 1982. *Publications*: Lazy B: growing up on a cattle ranch in the American Southwest, 2002; The Majesty of the Law: reflections of a Supreme Court Justice, 2003; (for children): Chico, 2005; Finding Susie, 2009.

**O'CONNOR, Sean Michael;** producer, director and writer for film, theatre, television and radio; Executive Producer, Eastenders, BBC 1, 2016–17; *b* Bromborough, 11 Feb. 1968; *s* of Alan James O'Connor and Anne O'Connor; partner, 2007, R. H. Haywood. *Educ*: St Anselm's Coll., Birkenhead; University Coll. London (BA Hons Eng. Lang. and Lit.). Regl Theatre Young Director Scheme, Lyric Hammersmith, Queen's Th., Hornchurch, 1989–92; freelance theatre dir, 1992–99; TV producer, Eastenders, Footballers' Wives, Hollyoaks, Family Affairs, Minder, 1999–2009; film producer, Camberwell Prodns, 2010–; Editor, The Archers, BBC Radio, 2013–16. Producer, film, The Deep Blue Sea, 2011; dir, The Entertainer, Curve Th., Leicester and tour, 2019. Mem., BAFTA, 2004–. Trustee, Estate of Sir Terence Rattigan, 2017–. *Publications*: Straight Acting, 1998; (with Tom Morris) Juliet and her Romeo (adaptation), 2010; Handsome Brute, 2013; The Fatal Passion of Alma Rattenbury, 2019. *Recreations*: theatre, opera.

**ODDIE, William Edgar, (Bill),** OBE 2003; writer, actor and broadcaster; *b* 7 July 1941; *m* 1st, Jean Hart (marr. diss.); two *d*; 2nd, Laura Beaumont; one *d*. *Educ*: Halesowen Grammar Sch.; King Edward's Sch., Birmingham; Pembroke Coll., Cambridge (BA 1963; MA 1967). Mem. Council, RSPB (Vice-Pres.). *Theatre* includes: writer and performer, Cambridge Circus (revue), Cambridge Footlights, transf. London, then NZ and Australia; performer: Tommy; Mikado, Coliseum, 1988; The Ghost Train, Lyric, Hammersmith, 1992; *television* includes: joint writer: Doctor in the House; Doctor at Large; Astronauts; writer and actor: TW3; BBC3; The Goodies (eight series), 1970–81; presenter: Ask Oddie; Who Do You Think You Are? (one prog. of series), 2004; The Truth About Killer Dinosaurs, 2005; wildlife programmes incl. Birding With Bill Oddie (three series); Bill Oddie Goes Wild; Britain Goes Wild; Springwatch (series), 2005, 2006, 2007 and 2008; Autumnwatch (series), 2006, 2007 and 2008; Bill Oddie: Back in the USA, 2007; Bill Oddie's Wild Side (series), 2008; Bill Oddie's Top 10 Frights and Delights, 2010; *radio* includes: jt writer, I'm Sorry I'll Read That Again; presenter, Breakaway. *Publications*: Little Black Bird Book, 1982; Gone Birding, 1983; (jtly) Big Bird Race, 1983; (jtly) The Toilet Book, 1986; Bird Watching with Bill Oddie, 1988; Bird Watching for Under Tens; Bill Oddie's Colouring Guides, 1991–92; Follow That Bird!, 1994; (jtly) Bird in the Nest, 1995; (jtly) Birding With Bill Oddie, 1997; Bill Oddie's Gripping Yarns: tales of birds & birding, 2000; One Flew into the Cuckoo's Egg, 2008; Bill Oddie Unplucked: columns, blogs and musings, 2015; articles in jls.

**ODDIE, Dr William John Muir;** Editor, Catholic Herald, 1998–2004; *b* 1 June 1939; *s* of John Male and Irene Oddie; *m* 1968, Cornelia; one *s* two *d*. *Educ*: Silcoates Sch., Yorks; Trinity Coll., Dublin (BA 1964; MA 1980); Leicester Univ. (PhD 1970); St Stephen's House, Oxford (MA Oxon 1981). Sec., Ancient Monuments Soc., 1970–72; ordained deacon, 1977, priest 1978; Asst Curate, Holy Trinity, Westbury on Trym, Bristol, 1978–80; Bp's Chaplain to Graduates, Oxford Univ., 1980–85; Librarian, Pusey House, Oxford,

1980–85; Fellow, St Cross Coll., Oxford, 1981–85; Rector, St Andrew's, Romford, 1985–87; received into RC Church, 1991; freelance journalist, Sunday Telegraph, Daily Telegraph, Daily Mail, Sunday Times, etc, 1987–98. Chm., G. K. Chesterton Soc., 2008–16. *Publications:* Dickens and Carlyle: the question of influence, 1972; What will Happen to God? feminism and the reconstruction of Christian belief, 1984; After the Deluge: essays towards the desecularisation of the Church, 1987; The Crockford's File: Gareth Bennett and the death of the Anglican mind, 1989; The Roman Option: crisis and the realignment of English-speaking Christianity, 1996; John Paul the Great: maker of the post-conciliar Church, 2003; Chesterton and the Romance of Orthodoxy: the making of GKC, 1874–1908, 2008; The Holiness of G. K. Chesterton, 2010. *Recreations:* reading, music, travel, domestic pursuits. *Address:* 10 Fane Road, Old Marston, Oxford OX3 0SA. *T:* (01865) 247450.

**ODDSSON, Hon. Davíd**, Hon. KBE 1990; Editor, Morgunbladid, since 2009; *b* 17 Jan. 1948; *s* of Oddur Ólafsson and Ingibjörg Kristín Lúdvíksdóttir; *m* 1970, Ástridur Thorarensen; one *s*. *Educ:* Univ. of Iceland (grad. Lawyer). Reykjavík Theatre Co., 1970–72; Morgunbladid Daily, 1973–74; Almenna Bókafélagið Publishing House, 1975–76; Office Manager, 1976–78, Man. Dir, 1978–82, Reykjavík Health Fund; Mayor of Reykjavík, 1982–91; MP (Ind) Reykjavik, 1991–2005; Prime Minister of Iceland, 1991–2004; Foreign Minister, 2004–05; Chm., Bd of Govs, Central Bank of Iceland, 2005–09. Leader, Independent Party, 1991–2005. Hon. LLD Manitoba, 2000. Grand Cross, Order of Merit (Luxembourg). *Publications:* (trans.) Estonia: a study of imperialism, by Anders Küng, 1973; Róbert Elíasson Returns from Abroad (TV drama), 1977; A Policy of 27 Independence, 1981; Stains on the White Collar (TV drama), 1981; Everything's Fine (TV drama), 1991; A Couple of Days without Gudny (short stories), 1997; Stolen from the Author of the Alphabet (short stories), 2002. *Recreations:* bridge, forestry, angling.

**ODDY, (William) Andrew**, OBE 2002; DSc; FSA; Keeper of Conservation, British Museum, 1985–2002; *b* 6 Jan. 1942; *s* of late William T. Oddy and Hilda F. Oddy (*née* Dalby); *m* 1965, Patricia Anne Whitaker; one *s* one *d*. *Educ:* Bradford Grammar Sch.; New Coll., Oxford (BA 1964; BSc 1965; MA 1969; DSc 1994). FSA 1973; FIIC 1974. Joined British Museum Research Lab., 1966, research into conservation and ancient technology; Head of Conservation, 1981. Member: Scientific Cttee, Internat. Congress on Deterioration and Preservation of Stone, 1976–91; Dept of Transport Adv. Cttee on Historic Wrecks, 1981–91; Council, Textile Conservation Centre, 1985–99; Cons. Cttee, Council for Care of Churches, 1985–90; Cons. Cttee, Cons. Unit, Mus. and Gall. Commn, 1987–92; Science-based Archaeol. Cttee, SERC, 1990–93; Council, Internat. Inst. for Conservation of Historic and Artistic Works, 1990–96 (Pres., 2001–07); Fabric Adv. Cttee, Cathedral and Abbey Church of St Alban, 1991–2010. Member: Council, RNS, 1975–78 and 2007–12 (Vice Pres., 2009–12; Hon. FRNS 2018); Res. Cttee, Soc. of Antiquaries of London, 2001–05. Trustee: Anna Plowden Trust, 1998–2006; Gabo Trust, 2002–10; Mercian Regiment Mus. (Worcs), 2012–15 (Editor, Friends' Newsletter, 2013–15). Hon. Res. Fellow, UCL, 1992–2001. Lectures: Chester Beatty, RSA, 1982; Leventritt, Harvard Univ. Art Mus., 1996; Forbes Prize, Internat. Inst. for Conservation, 1996. Freeman, Goldsmiths' Co., 1986. *Publications:* editor: Problems in the Conservation of Waterlogged Wood, 1975; Aspects of Early Metallurgy, 1980; Scientific Studies in Numismatics, 1980; Metallurgy in Numismatics II, 1988; The Art of the Conservator, 1992; Restoration: is it acceptable?, 1994; joint editor: Conservation in Museums and Galleries, 1975; Metallurgy in Numismatics I, 1980; Aspects of Tibetan Metallurgy, 1981; A Survey of Numismatic Research 1978–1984, 1986; Metallurgy in Numismatics IV, 1998; Reversibility: does it exist?, 1999; Past Practice – Future Prospects, 2001; (jtly) Romanesque Metalwork: copper alloys and their decoration, 1986; (ed) Coinage and History in the Seventh Century Near East 2, 2010; (ed jtly) Coinage and History in the Seventh Century Near East 4, 2015; papers in learned jls. *Recreations:* family history, early Islamic coinage and history. *Address:* 5 Albany Terrace, Worcester WR1 3DU.

**O'DELL, Mrs June Patricia**, OBE 1990; equality campaigner; Chair and Board Member, Probus Women's Housing Society Ltd, 1996–2005; *b* 9 June 1929; *d* of Leonard Vickery, RN and Myra Vickery; *m* 1951 (marr. diss. 1963); one *s* two *d*. *Educ:* Edgehill Girls College; Plymouth Technical College. Estate Agent; Sen. Partner, Chesney's, Estate Agents, 1965–88; Dir, Eachdale Developments Ltd, 1988–98. Nat. Pres., Fedn of Business and Professional Women, 1983–85; Chm., Employment Cttee, Internat. Fedn of Business Professional Women, 1983–87; Dep. Chm., EOC, 1986–90; Member: Women's Nat. Commn, 1983–85; European Adv. Cttee for Equal Treatment between Women and Men, 1986–90; Authorised Conveyancing Practitioners Bd, 1991–95; Legal Aid Adv. Cttee, 1993–94. Non-exec. Dir, Aylesbury Vale Community Healthcare NHS Trust, 1991–98. Gov., Sir William Ramsay Sch., 2002–05. FRSA 1986 (Mem. Council, 1992–97). *Recreations:* music, particularly opera and choral; writing, literature, the countryside, equestrian events. *Address:* Gable End, High Street, Great Missenden, Bucks HP16 9AA.

**ODELL, Sir Stanley (John)**, Kt 1986; *b* 20 Nov. 1929; *s* of George Frederick Odell and Florence May Odell; *m* 1952, Eileen Grace Stuart; four *d*. *Educ:* Bedford Modern School. Chairman: Mid Beds Young Conservatives, 1953–59; Mid Beds Cons. Assoc., 1964–69 (Pres., 1991–2005); Beds Cons. European Constituency Council, 1979; E of England Provincial Council, Cons. Party, 1983–86 (Pres., 1991–93); Nat. Union of Cons. and Unionist Assocs, 1989–90 (Vice Chm., 1986–89); Pres., Bedford & Kempston Cons. Assoc., 2005–12. Chairman: S Beds Community Health Care NHS Trust, 1994–99; Beds and Luton Community Health Care NHS Trust, 1999–2001; Mary Seacole Homes for the Homeless in Luton, 1999–2012. Chm., Anglo-American Cttee, RAF Chicksands, 1987–96. Member of Court: Bedfordshire (formerly Luton) Univ., 1994–; Intelligence Corps, 2002–11. Chm., Biggleswade and Dist Young Farmers' Club, 1949–51; Founder Playing Mem., Biggleswade Rugby Club, 1949. Patron: Friends of Chicksands Priory, 1983–2008; Camphill, Beds, 1998–; John Bunyan Museum, Bedford, 1999–; Churchwarden, Campton Parish Church, 1978–91. Hon. Fellow, Univ. of Beds (Hon. Fellow, Luton Univ., 2002). *Recreations:* politics, shooting. *Address:* Woodhall Farm, Campton, Shefford, Beds SG17 5PB. *T:* (01462) 813230.

**ODGERS, Anthony Louis**; Chief Financial Officer, University of Cambridge, since 2017; *b* 28 Sept. 1967; *s* of Ian and Juliet Odgers; *m* 1996, Tara Usher; two *s* two *d*. *Educ:* King's Sch., Canterbury; Gonville and Caius Coll., Cambridge (BA Natural Scis 1989; MA 1993); INSEAD (MBA). Deutsche Morgan Grenfell: Graduate Trainee, then Exec., Project Finance Advisory, 1989–93; Exec., then Asst Dir, Corporate Finance, 1995–99; Lehman Brothers: Sen. Vice Pres., UK and Communications M&A, 1999–2002; Man. Dir and Hd of Communications M&A, 2002–07; Deutsche Bank: Chief Operating Officer, Adv. Business, 2007–09; Hd, Restructuring Adv. (EMEA), 2009–10; Hd of Portfolio, Shareholder Exec., BIS, 2010–14; Dep. Chief Exec. and Dir, Corporate Finance Practice, UK Govt Investments, HM Treasury (formerly Shareholder Exec., BIS), 2014–17. *Recreations:* swimming, table tennis, cricket (watching), cinema, traditional North London over-parenting. *Address:* University of Cambridge, The Old Schools, Trinity Lane, Cambridge CB2 1TN.

**ODGERS, Sir Graeme (David William)**, Kt 1997; DL; Chairman, Kent Economic Board (formerly Kent and Medway Economic Board), 2001–09; *b* 10 March 1934; *s* of late William Arthur Odgers and Elizabeth Minty (*née* Rennie); *m* 1st, 1957, Diana Patricia Berge (*d* 2012); one *s* two *d* (and one *d* decd); 2nd, 2014, Susan Tait. *Educ:* St John's Coll., Johannesburg; Gonville and Caius Coll., Cambridge (Mech. Scis Tripos); Harvard Business Sch. (MBA, Baker Scholar). Investment Officer, Internat. Finance Corp., Washington DC, 1959–62; Management Consultant, Urwick Orr and Partners Ltd, 1962–64; Investment Executive, Hambros Bank Ltd, 1964–65; Director: Keith Shipton and Co. Ltd, 1965–72; C. T. Bowring (Insurance) Holdings Ltd, 1972–74; Chm., Odgers and Co. Ltd (Management Consultants), 1970–74; Dir, Industrial Develt Unit, DoI, 1974–77; Assoc. Dir (Finance), General Electric Co., 1977–78; Gp Finance Dir, 1979–86, Gp Man. Dir, 1983–86, Tarmac; British Telecommunications: pt-time Mem. Bd, 1983–86; Govt Dir, 1984–86; Dep. Chm. and Chief Finance Officer, 1986–87; Gp Man. Dir, 1987–90; Chief Exec., Alfred McAlpine plc, 1990–93; Chm., Monopolies and Mergers Commn, 1993–97. Non-executive Director: Dalgety, 1987–93; Nat. & Provincial Bldg Soc., 1990–93; Scottish and Southern Energy, 1998–2004. Chm., Locate in Kent, 1998–2006; Dep. Chm., Kent Partnership, 2001–09. Pres., New Marlowe Th. Develt Trust, 2009–11 (Chm., 2007–09; Trustee, 2011–). Mem., Kent Ambassadors, 1998–. DL Kent, 2002. Freedom, City of Canterbury, 2015. Hon. Fellow, Canterbury Christchurch Univ., 2010. Hon. DLaws Greenwich, 2004; Hon. DCL Kent, 2005. Kent Invicta Award, 2009. *Recreation:* golf. *Address:* Cramond House, Harnet Street, Sandwich CT13 9ES. *Club:* Royal Cinque Ports Golf.

**ODITAH, Dr Fidelis Hilary Izuka**; QC 2003; Senior Advocate of Nigeria, since 2004; *b* 27 March 1964; *s* of Augustine and Vera Oditah; *m* 1992, Precilla Osondu; two *s* two *d*. *Educ:* Univ. of Lagos (LLB); Magdalen Coll., Oxford (MA, BCL; DPhil 1989). Called to the Bar, Lincoln's Inn, 1992, Bencher, 2010; Fellow and Tutor in Law, Merton Coll., Oxford, and Travers Smith Braithwaite Lectr in Corporate Finance Law, Univ. of Oxford, 1989–97. Vis. Prof., Univ. of Oxford, 2000–. *Publications:* Legal Aspects of Receivables Financing, 1991; The Future for the Global Securities Markets, 1996; Insolvency of Banks, 1996; contrib. learned jls. *Recreations:* golf, tennis, music, reading. *Address:* 3–4 South Square, Gray's Inn, WC1R 5HP. *T:* (020) 7696 9900, *Fax:* (020) 7696 9911. *E:* fidelisoditah@southsquare.com.

**ODLING-SMEE, John Charles**, CMG 2005; Director, European II Department, International Monetary Fund, 1992–2003; *b* 13 April 1943; *s* of late Rev. Charles William Odling-Smee and Katharine Hamilton Odling-Smee (*née* Aitchison); *m* 1996, Carmela Veneroso. *Educ:* Durham School; St John's College, Cambridge (BA 1964); MA Oxon 1966. Junior Research Officer, Dept of Applied Economics, Cambridge, 1964–65; Asst Research Officer, Inst. of Economics and Statistics, Oxford, 1965–66; Fellow in Economics, Oriel College, Oxford, 1966–70; Research Officer, Inst. of Economics and Statistics, Oxford, 1968–71 and 1972–73; Economic Research Officer, Govt of Ghana, 1971–72; Senior Research Officer, Centre for Urban Economics, LSE, 1973–75; Economic Adviser, Central Policy Review Staff, Cabinet Office, 1975–77; Senior Economic Adviser, HM Treasury, 1977–80; Senior Economist, IMF, 1981–82; Under-Sec., HM Treasury, 1982–89; Dep. Chief Economic Advr, HM Treasury, 1989–90; Sen. Advr, IMF, 1990–91. *Publications:* (with A. Grey and N. P. Hepworth) Housing Rents, Costs and Subsidies, 1978, 2nd edn 1981; (with R. C. O. Matthews and C. H. Feinstein) British Economic Growth 1856–1973, 1982; articles in books and learned jls. *Address:* 3506 Garfield Street NW, Washington, DC 20007, USA. *T:* (202) 3383471. *E:* jodlingsmee@juno.com.

**O'DOHERTY, Patrick**; Principal, Lumen Christi College, Derry, 2003–15 (Vice Principal, 1997–2003); *b* Londonderry, 10 Nov. 1956; *s* of Gerard and Agnes O'Doherty; *m* 1977, Darina; two *d*. *Educ:* St Columb's Coll., Derry; Queen's Univ., Belfast (BEd 1979); Univ. of Ulster (MSc Educn Mgt 1996). Professional Qual. for Headship NI 2001. St Columb's College: Teacher of English, 1979–82; Hd of Latin, 1982–88; Hd of English, 1988–97. *Recreations:* visiting Italy, classical civilizations.

**ODONE, Cristina**; writer and broadcaster; Founder and Chair, Parenting Circle (formerly National Parenting Trust), since 2017; *b* 11 Nov. 1960; *d* of late Augusto and Ulla Odone; *m* 2005, Edward Lucas, *s* of John Randolph Lucas, *qv*; one *d*. *Educ:* Worcester Coll., Oxford (MA). Freelance journalist, 1983–84; journalist: Catholic Herald, 1985–86; The Times diary, 1987; Vice-Pres., Odone Associates, Washington, 1988–92; Editor, The Catholic Herald, 1992–96 (Mem., Bd of Dirs, 2007–19); Dep. Ed., New Statesman, 1998–2004; television reviewer, 1996–98, columnist, 2010–16, The Daily Telegraph; columnist, Observer, 2001–08. Res. Fellow, Centre for Policy Studies, 2009–. Mem., Ext. Adv. Panel, Faculty of Theology and Religion, Oxford Univ. Member: Adv. Bd, Citizens' Service Scheme, 1995–; Bd of Dirs, Longford Trust, 2003–. FRSA 1996. *Publications:* novels: The Shrine, 1996; A Perfect Wife, 1997; The Dilemmas of Harriet Carew, 2008; The Good Divorce Guide, 2009; non-fiction: In Bad Faith, 2008; What Real Women Want, 2009; Assisted Suicide, 2010; Concentrated Parenting: 7 key moments in the lives of children, 2017. *Recreations:* walking, travelling. *Address:* c/o Curtis Brown Ltd, 5th Floor, Haymarket House, 28–29 Haymarket, SW1Y 4SP.

**O'DONNELL**, family name of **Baron O'Donnell**.

**O'DONNELL, Baron** *cr* 2012 (Life Peer), of Clapham in the London Borough of Wandsworth; **Augustine Thomas, (Gus), O'Donnell**, GCB 2011 (KCB 2005; CB 1994); Secretary of the Cabinet and Head of the Home Civil Service, 2005–11; *b* 1 Oct. 1952; *s* of Helen O'Donnell (*née* McClean) and James O'Donnell; *m* 1979, Melanie Joan Elizabeth Timmis; one *d*. *Educ:* Univ. of Warwick (BA Hons); Nuffield Coll., Oxford (MPhil). Lectr, Dept of Political Economy, Univ. of Glasgow, 1974–79; Economist, HM Treasury, 1979–85; First Sec. (Econ.), British Embassy, Washington, 1985–88; Sen. Economic Adviser, 1988–89, Press Sec., 1989–90, HM Treasury; Press Sec. to Prime Minister, 1990–94; Under Sec., Monetary Gp, 1994–95, Dep. Dir, Macroeconomic Policy and Prospects Directorate, 1995–96, HM Treasury; Minister (Economic), British Embassy, Washington, and UK Exec. Dir, IMF and World Bank, 1997–98; HM Treasury: Dir, Macroeconomic Policy and Prospects Directorate, 1998–2000; Man. Dir, Macroeconomic Policy and Internat. Finance, 2000–02; Hd of Govt Econ. Service, 1998–2003; Permanent Sec., 2002–05. Advr to CEO, TD Bank, 2012–; Sen. Advr, 2012–13, Chm., 2013–, Frontier Economics; non-exec. Dir and Strategic Advr, Brookfield Asset Mgt, 2013–; Chair, Bd of Trustees, Pro Bono Economics, 2016–; Mem., Brexit Adv. Panel, techUK, 2017–. Mem., Economist Trust, 2013–; Trustee, The Tablet newspaper, 2005–. Pres., IFS, 2016–. Mem. Cttee, AELTC, 2015–. Visiting Professor: LSE, 2013–; UCL, 2013–. Hon. FBA 2014. *Publications:* articles in economic jls. *Recreations:* football, cricket, golf, tennis. *Address:* House of Lords, SW1A 0PW. *Club:* All England Lawn Tennis.

**O'DONNELL, Prof. Barry**, FRCS, FRCSI; President, Royal College of Surgeons of Ireland, 1998–2000; Professor of Paediatric Surgery, Royal College of Surgeons in Ireland, 1986–93, now Professor Emeritus; Consultant Paediatric Surgeon, Our Lady's Hospital for Sick Children, Dublin, 1957–93; *b* 6 Sept. 1926; *e s* of Michael J. O'Donnell and Kathleen O'Donnell (*née* Barry); *m* 1959, Mary Leydon, BA, BComm, BL, *d* of John Leydon, LLD, KCSG; three *s* one *d*. *Educ:* Christian Brothers College, Cork; Castleknock College, Dublin; University College, Cork (MB Hons 1949). MCh NUI, 1954. FRCS 1953,

FRCSI 1953; FRCSEd ad hominem 1992; FRCPSGlas qua surgeon 1999. Ainsworth Travelling Scholar, Boston (Lahey Clinic and Boston Floating Hosp., 1955–56); Sen. Registrar, Hosp. for Sick Children, London, 1956–57. Vis. Prof. at many US univs, incl. Harvard, Columbia, Johns Hopkins, Michigan, Pennsylvania; Hunterian Prof., RCS, 1986. Jt Pres., British, Canadian and Irish Med. Assocs, 1976–77; President: British Assoc. of Paediatric Surgeons, 1980–82; Surgical Sect., Royal Acad. of Medicine of Ireland, 1990–92; Mem. Council, RCSI, 1972–77 and 1993–96 (Vice Pres., 1996–98); Chm., Jl Cttee, BMA, 1982–88. Director: Standard Chartered Bank, Ireland, 1977–90; West Deutsche Landesbank, 1990–96. Vicary Lect., RCS, 2013. Hon. FRCS 2007. Hon. Fellow: Amer. Acad. of Pediatrics, 1974; New England Surgical Assoc., 1996; Amer. Surgical Assoc., 1998; Coll. of Medicine of S Africa, 2001; Faculty of Nursing, RCPI, 2013; Hon. FACS 1999; Hon. Mem., Boston Surgical Soc., 2000. Silver Jubilee Medal, 1977; People of the Year Award, New Ireland Insce Co., 1984; Denis Browne Gold Medal, British Assoc. of Paediatric Surgeons, 1989; Urology Medal, American Acad. of Pediatrics, 2003; Dist. Alumnus Award, UC, Cork, 2004; Lifetime Achievement Award, Irish Medical Times, 2014. *Publications:* Essentials of Paediatric Surgery, 1961, 4th edn 1992; Abdominal Pain in Children, 1985; (ed jtly) Paediatric Urology, 3rd edn 1997; Terence Millin, 2003; Irish Surgeons and Surgery in the Twentieth Century, 2008. *Recreations:* repeating myself, incompetent golf. *Address:* 28 Merlyn Road, Ballsbridge, Dublin 4, Ireland. *T:* and *Fax:* 2694000. *E:* bodonnell6926@gmail.com. *Club:* Portmarnock Golf.

**O'DONNELL, Sir Christopher (John),** Kt 2003; Chair of Council, University of York, 2008–17; *b* 30 Oct. 1946; *s* of Anthony John O'Donnell and Joan Millicent O'Donnell; *m* 1971, Maria Antonia Wallis; three *s* one *d*. *Educ:* Imperial Coll., London (BSc Eng Hons); London Business Sch. (MSc Econ). Man. Dir, Vickers Ltd Medical Engineering, 1974–79; Area Vice Pres., Europe, C. R. Bard, Inc., 1979–88; Man. Dir, Smith & Nephew Medical Ltd, 1988–93; Gp Dir, 1993–97, Chief Exec., 1997–2007, Smith & Nephew plc. Non-exec. Dir, BOC Gp, 2001–06. *Recreations:* flying, golf. *Address:* Wetherby, W Yorks.

**O'DONNELL, Donal Gerard;** Hon. Mr Justice O'Donnell; a Judge of the Supreme Court of Ireland, since 2010; *b* Belfast, 25 Oct. 1957; *s* of late Rt Hon. Turlough O'Donnell and Eileen O'Donnell (*née* McKinley); *m* 1985, Mary Rose Binchy; two *s* two *d*. *Educ:* St Mary's, Belfast; University Coll., Dublin (BCL 1980); King's Inns (BL 1982); Univ. of Virginia (LLM 1983). Called to Irish Bar, 1982, Bar of NI, 1989; Sen. Counsel, 1995. Mem. (pt-time), Law Reform Commn, 2005–12. *Recreations:* golf, reading, walking. *Address:* The Supreme Court, Four Courts, Dublin 7, Ireland.

**O'DONNELL, Fiona;** Member (Lab), East Lothian Council, since 2017; *b* Nanaimo, Vancouver Is., Canada, 27 Jan. 1960; *d* of Pat Kenny and Gladys Kenny (*née* Miners); three *s* one *d*. *Educ:* Lochaber High Sch.; Glasgow Univ. Project manager, Stonham Housing Assoc.; Asst Manager, Capability Scotland, Upper Springland; Constituency Asst to Douglas Alexander, MP; researcher for Hugh Henry, MSP and Trish Goodman, MSP; researcher and PA, Mackay Hannah; organiser, then Develt Officer, Scottish Labour Party. MP (Lab) E Lothian, 2010–15; contested (Lab) same seat, 2015. Non-exec. Dir, NHS Lothian, 2017–. Member: Co-op Party; GMB; Amnesty Internat. *Recreations:* swimming, food and wine with friends, housework.

**O'DONNELL, Hugh Bede Butler;** Member (Lib Dem) Scotland Central, Scottish Parliament, 2007–11; *b* 1 May 1952; *s* of late Hugh O'Donnell and Christina O'Donnell; *m* (separated); one *s* one *d*. *Educ:* Queen Margaret Coll., Edinburgh (BA Hons 1996); Southern Connecticut State Univ. Civil Servant, 1969–72; manager, Tesco Plc, 1972–85; agent, Prudential Portfolio Managers, 1985–95; support worker, Quarriers, 1995–99; Parly Aide to Donald Gorrie, MSP, 1999–2007. Non-exec. Dir, Social Enterprise, RECAP, 2003–10. Election Supervisor, UN Mission to Kosovo, 2001. *Recreations:* relaxing on island of Kos, failing to learn Greek, TV crime fiction, bad DIY, olive picking, the life of Alexander the Great, reading historical fiction, raging at the world.

**O'DONNELL, Ian Francis George;** Executive Director of Corporate Resources, London Borough of Ealing, 2009–19; *b* London, 22 Jan. 1962; *s* of Bernard Francis O'Donnell and Joan Alice O'Donnell; *m* 1992, Jacquie Louise Duckworth; one *s* one *d*. *Educ:* Kent Coll., Canterbury; University Coll., London (BSc Econs). CIPFA 2000. Credit Controller, Ind Coope Ltd, 1984–85; Accts and Rechargeable Works Manager, London Bor. of Barnet, 1985–87; Credit Manager, Hay Mgt Consultants, Sydney, 1987–88; London Borough of Camden: Community Charge Manager, 1988–90; Local Revenues Manager, 1990–92; Hd of Exchequer, 1992–99; Hd, Client Financial Services, 1999–2003; Asst Dir of Finance, London Bor. of Lambeth, 2003–06; Dir of Finance, London Bor. of Waltham Forest, 2006–09. Expert Advr, on Debt, to Cabinet Office, 2011–12; Treas., W London Waste Authy, 2012–. Chm. Bd, Fighting Fraud Locally, 2012–16. Trustee, Public Concern at Work, 2012–16. Hon. Treas., Comics Creators' Guild, 1997–2002. Pres., Soc. of London Treasurers, 2016. Freedom, City of London, 2012. *Recreations:* golf, game and sport angling, Arsenal FC, the arts.

**O'DONNELL, James Anthony;** Organist and Master of the Choristers, Westminster Abbey, since 2000; *b* 15 Aug. 1961; *s* of late Dr (James Joseph) Gerard O'Donnell and of Dr Gillian Anne O'Donnell (now Womersley). *Educ:* Westcliff High Sch., Essex; Jesus Coll., Cambridge (Organ Scholar and Open Scholar in Music; BA 1982, MA; Hon. Fellow, 2011). Westminster Cathedral: Asst Master of Music, 1982–88; Master of Music, 1988–99. Prof. of Organ, 1997–2004, Vis. Prof. of Organ, 2004–, Vis. Prof. Choral Conducting, 2013–, RAM; Vis. Performance Fellow, Univ. of Aberdeen, 2013–. FRCO 1983 (Performer of the Year, 1987; Mem. Council, 1989–2003; Pres., 2011–13). Hon. FRSCM 2000; Hon. RAM 2001; Hon. FGCM 2001; Hon. FRCM 2009. Has made many recordings with Westminster Cathedral Choir and Choir of Westminster Abbey. Hon. DMus Aberdeen, 2013. Gramophone Record of the Year and Best Choral Recording awards, 1998 for masses by Martin and Pizzetti; Royal Philharmonic Soc. award, 1999. KCSG 1999. *Recreations:* opera, food, wine. *Address:* c/o The Chapter Office, 20 Dean's Yard, Westminster Abbey, SW1P 3PA. *Clubs:* Athenæum, Chelsea Arts.

**O'DONNELL BOURKE, Patrick Francis John;** Group Finance Director, John Laing Group plc, 2011–19; *b* 22 March 1957; *m* 1992, Jane; three *s*. *Educ:* Stonyhurst Coll.; Trinity Coll., Cambridge (BA 1979). ACA 1983. KPMG, 1979–86; Hill Samuel, 1986–87; Barclays de Zoete Wedd, 1987–95; Powergen: Hd of M&A, 1995–98; Gp Treas., 1998–2000; Gp Finance Dir, Viridian Gp, 2000–07; Gp Chief Exec., Viridian Gp Ltd, 2007–11.

**O'DONOGHUE, Denise,** OBE 1999; non-executive Director, ITV Studios UK, since 2014 (Managing Director, 2010–14); *b* 13 April 1955; *d* of late Micheal O'Donoghue and Maura O'Donoghue; *m* 1987, James Mulville, *qv* (marr. diss. 1998); *m* 2006, Michael Holland. *Educ:* St Dominic's Girls' Sch.; York Univ. (BA Hons). Coopers & Lybrand, 1979–81; Dir, IPPA, 1981–83; Holmes Associates, 1983–86; Managing Director: Hat Trick Films, 1995–2006; Hat Trick Hldgs, 2003–06. Non-exec. Dir, Big Talk Productions, 2013–. FRTS 1998; CCMI (CIMgt 1998). Awards from RTS, BAFTA, and Broadcasting Press Guild; Emmy Awards.

**O'DONOGHUE, Gary Neil;** Washington Correspondent, BBC News, since 2014; *b* London, 13 Feb. 1968; *s* of Francis O'Hagan O'Donoghue and Constance Lilian O'Donoghue (*née* Hoddy); partner, Sarah Lewthwaite; one *d*. *Educ:* Worcester Coll. for the Blind; Christ Church, Oxford (BA Philos. and Mod. Langs; MA). BBC: reporter and occasional presenter, In Touch, BBC Radio 4, 1992–; Political Reporter, BBC Westminster, 1992–94; presenter and reporter, From The Edge, BBC TV, 1994–99; reporter, The World Tonight, 1994–95, The Today Prog., 1995–2000, BBC Radio 4; Presenter (British News), News Reporter and Political Reporter, BBC World Service News, 2000–04; Political Corresp., BBC News, 2004–13; Chief Political Corresp., BBC Radio 4, 2011–12 and 2013–14. *E:* gary.odonoghue@bbc.co.uk.

**O'DONOGHUE, Hughie,** RA 2009; artist; *b* Manchester, 5 July 1953; *s* of Daniel O'Donoghue and Sabina, (Sheila), O'Donoghue; *m* 1974, Clare Reynolds; two *s* one *d*. *Educ:* St Augustine's Grammar Sch., Manchester; Trinity and All Saints Coll., Leeds; Goldsmith's Coll., Univ. of London (MA). Artist in Residence: Nat. Gall., 1984–85; St John's Coll., Oxford, 2000; Eton Coll., 2013; solo exhibitions include: Haus der Kunst, Munich, 1997; Irish Mus. of Modern Art, Dublin, 1998–99, 2009; RHA Gall., Dublin, 1999; Fitzwilliam Mus., Cambridge and tour, 2001–03; Imperial War Mus., London and Manchester, 2003–04; Gemeentemuseum, The Hague; Centre Culturel Irlandais, Paris; Leeds Art Gall., 2009; DOX Mus., Prague, 2011; RA, 2012; Abbot Hall, Kendal, 2012; Leighton House Mus., London, 2016; created stained glass windows for Henry VII Lady Chapel, Westminster Abbey, 2013; designed window for Cloister of Canterbury Cathedral, 2018; created painting for Imperial Society of Knights Bachelor chapel, St Paul's Cathedral, 2018. Mem., Aosdána, 2013–. Hon. LLD NUI, Cork, 2005. *Recreations:* walking the Atlantic coastline of County Mayo, following trials and tribulations of Manchester United. *Address:* c/o Marlborough Fine Art, 6 Albermarle Street, W1S 4BY. *T:* (020) 7629 5161. *E:* mfa@marlboroughfineart.com, odon@iol.ie. *Clubs:* Arts, Academicians' Room.

**O'DONOGHUE, Gen. Sir Kevin,** KCB 2005; CBE 1996; Chief of Defence Materiel, Ministry of Defence, 2007–10; Master General of Logistics, 2009–12; *b* 9 Dec. 1947; *s* of late Phillip James O'Donoghue and Winifred Mary O'Donoghue; *m* 1973, Jean Monkman; three *d*. *Educ:* Eastbourne Coll.; UMIST (BSc 1st Cl. Hons). Commnd RE, 1969; 23 Engr Regt, BAOR; Adjt 21 Engr Regt, 1974; Instructor, RMA Sandhurst, 1976; Staff Coll., Canada, 1978; Mil. Ops, MoD, 1979; MA to CGS, 1980; OC 4 Field Sqdn, 1982; Directing Staff, Staff Coll., Camberley, 1984; Comdr, 25 Engr Regt, BAOR, 1986–88; Dep. ACOS, HQ UKLF, 1988; Higher Comd and Staff Course, 1990; Comdr Corps RE, 1 (BR) Corps, 1990; Comd Engr, ACE Rapid Reaction Corps, 1992; NATO Defence Coll., 1993; Dir, Staff Ops, SHAPE, 1993; COS HQ QMG, 1996–99; ACGS, 1999–2001; UK Mil. Rep. to NATO and EU, 2001–02; DCDS (Health), 2002–04, Chief of Defence Logistics, 2004–07, MoD; Chief Royal Engr, 2004–09. Col, Royal Glos, Berks and Wilts Regt, 2001–07; Col Comdt, RE, 2002–09. Hon. Col Comdt, RLC, 2008–12. Chm., SSAFA (formerly SSAFA Forces Help), 2010–17. Gentleman Usher to the Sword of State, 2013–18. Chm. Govs, Eastbourne Coll., 2013–17. Liveryman, Masons' Co., 2010–. Hon. DSc Cranfield, 2007. *Recreations:* military history, furniture restoration, gardening. *Club:* Army and Navy.

**O'DONOGHUE, (Michael) Peter (Desmond);** York Herald, College of Arms, since 2012; *b* Sevenoaks, Kent; *s* of Michael John O'Donoghue and Elizabeth Anne Hawkins O'Donoghue (*née* Borley); *m* 2002, Catherine Ann Wolfe, PhD; one *s* one *d*. *Educ:* Dulwich Coll.; Gonville and Caius Coll., Cambridge (BA 1994). Independent genealogist, historian and archivist, 1994–2003; College of Arms: Res. Asst, 1994–2005; Bluemantle Pursuivant of Arms, 2005–12. Vice Pres., Assoc. of Genealogists and Researchers in Archives, 2011–; Pres., St John Ambulance Gtr London, 2016–. Patron, Guild of One Name Studies, 2017–. Freeman, City of London, 2005–; Liveryman, Armourers and Brasiers' Co., 2010–. Jt Editor, Coat of Arms, 2004–16. FSA 2015. *Publications:* The Electrical Contractors' Association 1901–2001, 2001; various articles in heraldic and genealogical jls and magazines. *Address:* College of Arms, Queen Victoria Street, EC4V 4BT. *T:* (020) 7332 0776. *E:* york@college-of-arms.gov.uk.

**O'DONOGHUE, Most Rev. Patrick;** Bishop of Lancaster, (RC), 2001–09, now Emeritus; *b* 4 May 1934; *s* of Daniel O'Donoghue and Sheila O'Donoghue (*née* Twomey). *Educ:* St Edmund's Coll., Ware, Herts. Ordained priest, 1967; Asst priest, Willesden, 1967–70; Mem., Diocesan Mission Team, Westminster, 1970–73; Pastoral Dir, Allen Hall, 1973–78; Asst Administrator, Westminster Cathedral, 1978–85; Rector, Allen Hall, 1985–91; Administrator, Westminster Cathedral, 1991–93; Auxiliary Bishop of Westminster (Bishop in W London), 1993–2001. *Recreations:* football, theatre, country walking, the Arts. *Address:* Nazareth House, Drommahane, Mallow, Co. Cork, Ireland.

**O'DONOGHUE, Peter;** see O'Donoghue, M. P. D.

**O'DONOHOE, Nicholas Peter;** Chief Executive Officer, CDC Group, since 2017; *b* Liverpool, 10 April 1957; *s* of Niall O'Donohoe and Barbara O'Donohoe; *m* 2003, Stephenie Nicola Barwise, *qv*; one *s* one *d*, and two *d* by a previous marriage. *Educ:* Trinity Coll., Dublin (BA Hons); Wharton Sch., Univ. of Pennsylvania (MBA). Goldman Sachs, 1981–96: Resident Manager, Zurich, 1988–91; Exec. Dir, Equity Capital Mkts, 1991–93; Hd of Internat. Mktg, Goldman Sachs Asset Mgt, 1991–96; JP Morgan: Hd, Eur. Equity Sales and Res., 1996–99; Hd, Eur. Equity, 1999–2002; Global Hd of Res., 2003–10; Mem., Investment Bank Global Mgt Cttee, 2004–11; Mem., Exec. Cttee, JP Morgan Chase, 2007–11; CEO, Big Society Capital, 2011–15; Sen. Advr, Bill and Melinda Gates Foundn, 2016–17. Chm., UK Dormant Assets Commn, 2016–17. Member: Adv. Bd, Bridges Ventures, 2011–; Investment Cttee, Women's World Banking Global Microfinance Fund, 2011–17; Bd, Mustard Seed Investment, 2017–. Mem. Bd, Global Impact Investing Network, 2009–; Chm., Social Innovation Council, WEF, 2013–16; Dep. Chm., Global Steering Cttee on Social Impact Investment, 2015–. *Recreations:* tennis, cycling, ski-ing. *Address:* CDC Group, 123 Victoria Street, SW1E 6DE. *E:* nickodonohoe@gmail.com. *Clubs:* Queen's, Royal Automobile.

**O'DONOHOE, Stephanie Nicola;** see Barwise, S. N.

**O'DONOVAN, Kathleen Anne;** Member of Court, Bank of England, 1999–2005 (Chairman, Audit Committee); *b* Warwicks, 23 May 1957. *Educ:* University Coll. London (BSc Econs). Joined Turquands Barton Mayhew, subseq. Ernst & Young, 1975; Partner, 1989–91; Finance Dir, BTR, then BTR Siebe, subseq. Invensys plc, 1991–2002. Co-founder, Bird & Co. Gp, 1981. Non-executive Director: EMI Gp, 1997–2007 (Chm., Audit Cttee, 1999–2007); Prudential plc, 2003–12 (Chm. Audit Cttee, 2006–12); Great Portland Estates plc, 2003–09; O$_2$, 2005–07; ARM Hldgs plc, 2006–15; Trinity Mirror plc, 2007–13; DS Smith plc, 2012–.

**O'DONOVAN, Michael;** Chief Executive, Multiple Sclerosis Society, 2002–06; *b* 26 Sept. 1946; *s* of James and Mary O'Donovan; *m* 1969, Susan Mary (*née* O'Brien); three *s*. *Educ:* St Ignatius Coll., N15; Durham Univ. (BA Hons Mod. Hist.). Beecham Group: Gen. Manager, then Man. Dir, Toiletries and Household Div., 1981–85; Regl Man. Dir, Far East, 1985–89; SmithKline Beecham, subseq. GlaxoSmithKline: Vice-Pres., Over-the-Counter Medicine Develt, 1990–92; Vice-Pres., Strategic Planning, 1993–2001. Non-exec. Dir, Adler Europe, 2005–07; Treasurer: Eur. Patients' Forum, 2006–10; Exec. Cttee, Eur. MS Platform, 2006–12. Vice-Chm., Neurol Alliance, 2003–06 (Mem., 2003–06); Co-Chair, National Voices, service user alliance, 2008–09 (Trustee, 2009–12). Chairman: Central London Community Healthcare NHS, 2009–12; Heatherwood and Wexham Park NHS Foundn Trust, 2012–14; non-exec. Dir, Frimley Health NHS Foundn Trust, 2014–. Member: Adv. Cttee, Inst. of Complex Neurodisability, 2003–10; Bd, European Medicines Agency, 2009–12. Trustee: Long Term Conditions (formerly Medical Conditions) Alliance, 2005–08 (Chm., 2008); South Hill Park Arts Centre, 2018–. *Recreations:* keeping fit, modern history. *Club:* Royal Scots (Edinburgh).

**O'DONOVAN, Rev. Canon Oliver Michael Timothy**, DPhil; FBA 2000; FRSE; Professor of Christian Ethics and Practical Theology, University of Edinburgh, 2006–12, now Emeritus; *b* 28 June 1945; *s* of Michael and Joan M. O'Donovan; *m* 1978, Joan Elizabeth Lockwood; two *s*. *Educ:* University Coll. Sch., Hampstead; Balliol Coll., Oxford (MA, DPhil); Wycliffe Hall, Oxford; Princeton Univ. Ordained deacon 1972, priest 1973, dio. of Oxford. Tutor, Wycliffe Hall, Oxford, 1972–77; Prof. of Systematic Theology, Wycliffe Coll., Toronto, 1977–82; Regius Prof. of Moral and Pastoral Theology, Univ. of Oxford, 1982–2006; Canon of Christ Church, Oxford, 1982–2006. McCarthy Vis. Prof., Gregorian Univ., Rome, 2001; Hon. Prof., Sch. of Divinity, Univ. of St Andrews, 2013–. Member: C of E Bd for Social Responsibility, 1976–77, 1982–85; ARCIC, 1985–90; Anglican-Orthodox Jt Doctrinal Discussions, 1982–84; Gen. Synod of C of E, 2005–06; C of E Faith and Order Commn, 2010–16; Chm., Archbishops' Rev. of Crown Nominations Commn, 2016–17. Pres., Soc. for the Study of Christian Ethics, 1997–2000. Hulsean Lectr, Cambridge Univ., 1993–94; Bampton Lectr, Oxford Univ., 2003. Canon Provincial and Provincial Theologian, Dio. York, 2015–. FRSE 2009. Hon. DD Wycliffe Coll., Toronto, 2002. *Publications:* The Problem of Self-Love in Saint Augustine, 1980; Begotten or Made?, 1984; Resurrection and Moral Order, 1986; On the Thirty Nine Articles, 1986, 2nd edn, 2011; Peace and Certainty, 1989; The Desire of the Nations, 1996; (with Joan Lockwood O'Donovan) From Irenaeus to Grotius, 1999; Common Objects of Love, 2002; The Just War Revisited, 2003; (with Joan Lockwood O'Donovan) Bonds of Imperfection, 2004; The Ways of Judgment, 2005; The Word in Small Boats: sermons from Oxford, 2010; Self, World and Time, 2013; Finding and Seeking, 2014; Entering into Rest, 2017; contrib. Jl of Theol Studies, Jl of Religious Ethics, Ethique, Studies in Christian Ethics, and Political Theol. *Address:* 6a Comely Park, Dunfermline KY12 7HU.

**O'DONOVAN, Prof. Peter Joseph**, FRCS, FRCOG; Consultant Gynaecologist, Bradford Teaching Hospitals NHS Trust, 1990–2016 (Lead Gynaecological Cancer, 2006–16; Lead Intellectual Property, 2007–12); Professor of Medical Innovation, since 2003, Director, Institute of Pharmaceutical Innovation, since 2008, University of Bradford; *b* 13 Dec. 1954; *s* of Patrick Joseph O'Donovan and Sheila Doreen O'Donovan; *m* 1988, Carmel Beirne; two *s* two *d*. *Educ:* Presentation Brothers' Coll., Cork; UC Cork, Nat. Univ. Ireland (MB BCh BAO). FRCS 1982; MRCOG 1986, FRCOG 1998. Bradford Teaching Hospitals NHS Trust: Dir, Post Grad. Med. Educn, 1997–2003; Dir, Merit Centre, 1997–2016. Mem., Medical Devices Agency, DoH, 2001–09. Dir, Medipex (NHS Innovation), 2004–16. Dir, Eur. Acad. Gynaecol Surgery, 2007–. Pres., British Soc. for Gynaecological Endoscopy, 2002–04; Dir, Eur. Soc. Gynaecol Endoscopy, 2016– (Treas., 2006–12; Vice Pres., 2012–14; Pres., 2014–16). Ed. in Chief, Reviews in Gynaecological Practice, 2001–05; Ed., Gynecol Surgery, 2003–06. *Publications:* Recent Advances in Gynaecological Surgery, 2002; Conservative Surgery for Menorrhagia, 2003; Preserving Your Womb: alternatives to hysterectomy, 2005; Ambulatory Gynaecological Surgery, 2006; Complications in Gynaecological Surgery, 2008; Conservative Surgery for Abnormal Uterine Bleeding, 2007; Modern Management of Abnormal Uterine Bleeding, 2008; Hysteroscopy, 2015; Alternatives to Hysterectomy, 2018. *Recreations:* food, walking, tennis, Rugby Union (as spectator), reading tabloid newspapers, writing, travel. *Address:* Glandore, 3A Creskeld Crescent, Bramhope, Leeds LS16 9EH. *T:* (0113) 261 4259, (office) (01274) 550851. *E:* podonovan@hotmail.com.

**O'DOWD, Sir David (Joseph)**, Kt 1999; CBE 1995; QPM 1988; DL; law enforcement consultant, 2002–10; HM Chief Inspector of Constabulary, 1996–2001; *b* 20 Feb. 1942; *s* of late Michael Joseph O'Dowd and Helen (*née* Merrin); *m* 1963, Carole Ann Watson; one *s* one *d*. *Educ:* Gartree High Sch.; Oadby, Leics; Univ. of Leicester (Dip. Social Studies); Open Univ. (BA); Univ. of Aston (MSc); FBI Nat. Acad., USA. Sgt, Inspector and Chief Inspector, CID, Leicester City Police, 1961–77; Supt, W Midlands Police, Coventry and Birmingham, 1977–84; Hd, Traffic Policing, Dir, Complaints and Discipline Investigation Bureau and Hd, Strategic Planning and Policy Analysis Unit, Metropolitan Police, 1984–86; Chief Constable, Northants Police, 1986–93; HM Inspector of Constabulary, 1993–96. British Chief Constables' Rep., Nat. Exec. Inst., FBI Acad., Washington, 1988. Nat. Dir, Police Graduate and Extended Interview Scheme, 1992–93. Vis. Teaching Fellow, Mgt Centre, Univ. of Aston, Birmingham, 1988; Vis. Prof., UWE, 2002. Fellow, 1994, Gov., 2002–10, Univ. of Northampton (formerly Nene Coll., then UC Northampton). CCMI (CIMgt 1988). Freedom, City of London, 2008. DL 2002, High Sheriff, 2006–07, Northants. Hon. DSc Aston, 2003. OStJ 1999. *Recreation:* golf. *Clubs:* Northampton Golf (Harlestone, Northants), PGA National Cyprus (Paphos, Cyprus) (Captain, 2015).

**O'DOWD, John Fitzgerald;** Member (SF) Upper Bann, Northern Ireland Assembly, since 2003; *b* Banbridge, Co. Down, 10 May 1967; *s* of Vincent and Bridie O'Dowd; *m* 1998, Mary; three *c*. *Educ:* Lismore Comp. Sch. Mem., Craigavon Council, 1997–2010. Minister of Educn, NI, 2011–16. Contested (SF) Upper Bann, 2010, 2017. *Address:* 57 Church Place, Lurgan, Co. Armagh BT66 6HD. *T:* (028) 3834 9675.

**O'DRISCOLL, Most Rev. Percival Richard;** Archbishop of Huron and Metropolitan of Ontario, 1993–2000; Bishop of Huron, 1990–2000; *b* 4 Oct. 1938; *s* of T. J. O'Driscoll and Annie O'Driscoll (*née* Copley); *m* 1965, Suzanne Gertrude Savignac; one *s* one *d*. *Educ:* Bishop's Univ., Lennoxville, Quebec (BA, STB); Huron Coll., London, Ont. (DD). Ordained deacon 1964, priest 1966; Assistant Curate: St Matthias, Ottawa, 1965–67; St John Evan, Kitchener, 1967–70; Religious Educn Dir, St Paul's Cathedral and Bishop Cronyn Memorial, London, 1970; Rector: St Michael & All Angels, London, 1970–75; St Bartholomew's, Sarnia, 1975–80; Rector, St Paul's Cathedral, and Dean of Huron, 1980–87; Suffragan Bishop of Huron, 1987–89; Coadjutor Bishop, 1989–90. *Recreations:* camping, hiking, photography. *Address:* 4–1241 Beaverbrook Avenue, London, Ontario, N6H 5P1, Canada. *Club:* London (Ontario).

**O'DWYER, Martin Patrick; His Honour Judge O'Dwyer;** a Circuit Judge, since 2007; *b* Wallasey, 24 Dec. 1955; *s* of Patrick O'Dwyer and Norah O'Dwyer (*née* Winterton). *Educ:* Merton Coll., Oxford (BA). Called to the Bar, Middle Temple, 1978; a Recorder, 1998–2007. *Recreations:* Dandie Dinmont terriers, gardening.

**ŌE, Kenzaburo;** Japanese writer; *b* 31 Jan. 1935; *m* 1960, Yukari Itami; two *s* one *d*. *Educ:* Tokyo Univ. (BA French Lit. 1959). Visited Russia and Western Europe to research and write series of essays on Youth in the West, 1961. Shinchosa Lit. Prize, 1964; Tanizaka Prize, 1967; Nobel Prize for Literature, 1994. *Publications:* The Catch, 1958 (Akutagawa Prize); Nip the Buds, Shoot the Kids, 1958; Our Age, 1959; Screams, 1962; The Perverts, 1963; Hiroshima Notes, 1963; Adventures in Daily Life, 1964; A Personal Matter, 1964; The Silent Cry (original title, Football in the First Year of the Man'en Era), 1967; Teach us to Outgrow our Madness: four short novels, 1978; (ed) Fire from the Ashes: short stories about Hiroshima and Nagasaki, 1985; The Treatment Tower, 1990; Japan, the Ambiguous and Myself (lectures), 1995; A Quiet Life, 1998; Rouse Up O Young Men of the New Age!, 2002; Somersault, 2003; A Healing Family (biog. and autobiog.), 2007; The Changling, 2010; Death By Water, 2016. *Address:* Atlantic Books, Ormond House, 26–27 Boswell Street, WC1N 3JZ; 585 Seijo-Machi, Setagaya-Ku, Tokyo, Japan.

**OEHLERS, Maj.-Gen. Gordon Richard,** CB 1987; Director, Corps of Commissionaires, 1994–99; *b* 19 April 1933; *s* of late Dr Roderic Clarke Oehlers and Hazel Ethne Oehlers (*née* Van Geyzel); *m* 1956, Doreen, (Rosie), Gallant (*d* 2015); one *s* one *d*. *Educ:* St Andrew's School, Singapore. CEng, FIET. Commissioned Royal Corps of Signals, 1958; UK and Middle East, 1958–64; Adjutant, 4th Div. Signals Regt, 1964–66; Instructor, School of Signals, 1966–68; OC 7th Armd Bde HQ and Signals Sqdn, 1968–70; GSO2 (Weapons), 1970–72; CO 7th Signal Regt, 1973–76; Commander Corps Royal Signals, 1st (British) Corps, 1977–79; Dir, Op. Requirements 4 (Army), 1979–84; ACDS (Comd Control, Communications and Inf. Systems), 1984–87. Dir of Security and Investigation, British Telecom, 1987–94. Col Comdt, RCS, 1987–93; Hon. Col 31st (Greater London) Signal Regt (Volunteers), 1988–94. Chm., Royal Signals Instn, 1990–93. Pres., British Wireless Dinner Club, 1986–87. *Recreations:* interested in all games esp. badminton (Captain Warwicks County Badminton Team, 1954–56), lawn tennis (Chm., Army Lawn Tennis Assoc., 1980–86), golf. *Address:* c/o National Westminster Bank, 4 High Street, Petersfield, Hants GU32 3JF. *Club:* Liphook Golf (Captain, 1998–99; Pres., 2017–20).

**OESTERHELT, Dr Jürgen;** Ambassador of Germany to the Holy See, 1997–2000; *b* 19 Aug. 1935; *s* of Dr Egon Oesterhelt and Trude (*née* Pfohl); *m* 1963, Katharina Galeiski; one *s* one *d*. *Educ:* Munich Univ. (LLD 1959); State Bar Exam. 1962; Columbia Univ., NY (Master of Comparative Law 1963). Internat. lawyer in Paris, 1963–64; joined German Diplomatic Service, 1964; Moscow, 1964–65; German Foreign Office, 1965–67; UN, NY, 1967–71; Sofia, 1971–74; German Foreign Office, 1974–77; Athens, 1977–80; Foreign Office: Hd of Div., Legal Dept, 1980–85; Dir, Political Dept, 1985–86; Dir Gen., Legal Dept and Legal Advr to Foreign Minister, 1986–92; Ambassador to Turkey, 1992–95; Ambassador to the UK, 1995–97. Mem., Bd of Trustees, Anglo-German Foundn, 2003–09. Commander's Cross: Order of Merit (Germany), 1997 (Cross, 1988); Order of Phoenix (Greece), 1982; Order of White Rose (Finland), 1989; Grand Cross: Order of Merit (Austria), 1990; Order of Pius IX, 2000. *Recreations:* music, reading. *Address:* Auf der Königsbitze 4, 53639 Königswinter, Germany. *E:* juergen@oesterhelt.de.

**OESTREICHER, Rev. Canon Dr Paul;** Hon. Consultant, Centre for International Reconciliation, Coventry Cathedral, 1997–2005 (Director of the International Ministry of Coventry Cathedral, 1986–97); Canon Residentiary of Coventry Cathedral, 1986–97, now Canon Emeritus; Member of the Society of Friends (Quakers), since 1982; Quaker Chaplain to the University of Sussex, 2004–10, now Chaplain Emeritus; journalist; *b* Meiningen, Germany, 29 Sept. 1931; *s* of Paul Oestreicher and Emma (*née* Schnaus); *m* 1st, 1958, Lore Feind (*d* 2000); one *s* two *d* (and one adopted *s* decd); 2nd, 2002, Prof. Barbara Einhorn; two step *s* (one adopted step *d* decd). *Educ:* King's High Sch., Dunedin; Univ. of Otago (BA Pol Sci. and German 1953); Victoria Univ., NZ (MA Hons Pol Sci. 1955); Lincoln Theol Coll. Fled to NZ with refugee parents, 1939; Editor, Critic (Otago Univ. newspaper), 1952–53; subseq. free-lance journalist and broadcaster; returned to Europe, 1955. Humboldt Res. Fellow, Bonn Univ., 1955–56, Free Univ. of Berlin, 1992–93; fraternal worker with German Lutheran Church at Rüsselsheim, trng in problems of industrial soc. (Opel, Gen. Motors), 1958–59; ordained 1959; Curate, Dalston, E London, 1959–61; Producer, Relig. Dept, BBC Radio, 1961–64; Assoc. Sec., Dept of Internat. Affairs, Brit. Council of Churches with special resp. for East-West Relations, 1964–69; Vicar, Church of the Ascension, Blackheath, 1968–81; Asst Gen. Sec. and Sec. for Internat. Affairs, BCC, 1981–86; Dir of (Lay) Trng, Dio. Southwark, 1969–72; Hon. Chaplain to Bp of Southwark, 1975–81; Public Preacher in Dio. Southwark, 1981–86; Hon. Canon of Southwark Cathedral, 1978–83, Canon Emeritus 1983–86. Vis. Fellow, 2010, Res. Associate, 2011–, Nat. Centre for Peace and Conflict Studies, Univ. of Otago. Member: Gen. Synod of C of E, 1970–86, 1996–97; Internat. Affairs Cttee, C of E, 1965–2001. Member: Brit. Council of Churches working parties on Southern Africa and Eastern Europe; Anglican Pacifist Fellowship, 1960– (Counsellor, 1998–); Exec. Cttee, Christian Peace Conf., Prague, 1964–68; Exec. Mem., Christian Concern for Southern Africa, 1978–81; Chm. of Trustees, Christian Inst. (of Southern Africa) Fund, 1984–95; Chairman: British Section, Amnesty International, 1974–79; Christians Aware, 1999–2000; Pres., Action by Christians against Torture, 2005–. Mem. Council, Keston Coll. (Centre for the Study of Religion and Communism), 1976–82. Vice-Chm., 1980–81, Vice-Pres. 1983–, Campaign for Nuclear Disarmament; Mem. Alternative Defence Commn, 1981–87; Vice-Chm., Ecumenical Commn for Church and Society in W Europe (Brussels), 1982–86. Trustee, Dresden Trust, 1993–2005. Companion, Community of the Cross of Nails, 2007–. Shelley Lectr, Radio NZ, 1987; Keynote speaker, WCC Internat. Ecumenical Peace Convocation, Kingston, Jamaica, 2011. Launched Oestreicher Leadership Prog., King's High Sch., Dunedin, 2013. Freeman, Meiningen, Germany, 1995. Hon. DLitt Coventry Polytechnic, 1991; Hon. LLD Sussex, 2005; DD Lambeth 2008; Hon. DD Otago, 2009. Prize for Promotion of European Unity, Wartburg Foundn, 1997; Award of Merit, City of Coventry, 2002. Cross of Merit, 1st Cl. (Germany), 1995; Cross of Merit, Free State of Saxony, 2004. *Publications:* (ed English edn) Helmut Gollwitzer, The Demands of Freedom, 1965; (trans.) H. J. Schultz, Conversion to the World, 1967; (ed, with J. Klugmann) What Kind of Revolution: A Christian-Communist Dialogue, 1968; (ed) The Christian Marxist Dialogue, 1969; (jtly) The Church and the Bomb, 1983; The Double Cross, 1986 (rev. German edn, Aufs Kreuz Gelegt, 1994). *Recreations:* addicted to newsprint, active and passive, Mozart, Bach, Johann Strauss, Father and Son and the cry of seagulls. *Address:* 97 Furze Croft, Furze Hill, Hove, E Sussex BN3 1PE. *T:* (01273) 728033. *E:* paul.oestreicher.nz@gmail.com; 42/8 Leeds Street, Te Aro, Wellington 6011, New Zealand.

**O'FARRELL, Hon. Barry Robert;** Chief Executive, Racing Australia, since 2017; *b* Melbourne, 24 May 1959; *m* 1992, Rosemary Kent Cowan; two *s*. *Educ:* Australian National Univ. (BA 1979). State Dir, NSW Liberal Party, 1992–95. MP (L): Northcott, 1995–99; Ku-ring-gai, 1999–2015. New South Wales Government: Shadow Minister, 1998–2007; Dep. Leader of the Opposition, 1999–2002, 2003–07; Leader of the Opposition, 2007–11; Premier of NSW, 2011–14; Minister for Western Sydney, 2011–14. Leader, NSW Liberal Party, 2007–14. Dep. Chm., Australia-India Council, 2015–; Pres. and Ind. Chair, Diabetes Australia, 2019–; Chair, West Tigers RLFC, 2019–. Hon. Dr Holy Spirit Univ., Kaslik, Lebanon, 2012. *Recreations:* bushwalking, reading, family. *Address:* PO Box 1372, Wahroonga, NSW 2076, Australia.

**O'FARRELL, Declan Gerard,** CBE 2000; Chairman, Castletown Corporation Limited, since 2008 (Chief Executive Officer, 2003–08); *b* 10 Feb. 1949; *s* of Bartholomew and Mary Carmel O'Farrell; *m* 1971, Jennie; one *s* three *d*. *Educ:* Finchley Catholic Grammar Sch. FCCA 1973–2009. With British Tissues, 1967–81 (mgt trainee to Gp Mgt Accountant); financial analyst, Express Dairies, 1981; various financial posts with Express Foods Gp (Financial Controller, Distribn Div., until 1986); joined LT bus operations, 1986; Dir, 1989–2004, Man. Dir, 1989–94, Chief Exec., 1994–2003, Metroline (new bus co. subsid.), subseq. Metroline plc. Dir, NW London TEC, 1990–2001 (Chm., 1993–96); Founder Mem., London TEC Council. Chm., Business Link London, 1997–2001. Chairman: West Herts Coll., 2004–11; Herts Community NHS Trust (formerly Herts Community Health Services, NHS), 2010–. *Recreations:* gardening, golf, vintage bus.

**O'FARRELL, Hon. Dame Finola (Mary Lucy), (Hon. Dame Finola Andrews),** DBE 2016; Hon. Mrs Justice O'Farrell; a Judge of the High Court of Justice, Queen's Bench Division, since 2016; *b* 15 Dec. 1960; *d* of John Stephen O'Farrell and Rosaleen Mary O'Farrell; *m* 1993, Stuart Andrews (*d* 2010); one *d. Educ:* St Philomena's Sch., Carshalton; Durham Univ. (BA Hons). Called to the Bar, Inner Temple, 1983; in practice, specialising in construction law; QC 2002; a Recorder, 2006–16. Mem., editl team, Keating on Building Contracts, 5th edn 1991, 6th edn 1995; Jt Ed., Construction Law Yearbook, 4th edn, 1999; Consulting Ed., Construction Law Reports, 2007–. *Publications:* (contrib.) Engineers' Dispute Resolution Handbook, 2006, 2nd edn 2011; (contrib.) ICE Manual of Construction Law, 2010. *Recreations:* travelling, ballet, literature. *Address:* Royal Courts of Justice, Strand, WC2A 2LL.

**O'FARRELL, Margaret Helen, (Maggie);** author; *b* Coleraine, NI, 27 May 1972; *m* William Sutcliffe; one *s* two *d. Educ:* North Berwick High Sch.; Brynteg Comp. Sch.; New Hall Coll., Cambridge (BA Hons Eng. Lit. 1993). Editl Asst, Asst Arts Ed., then Dep. Literary Ed., Independent on Sunday, 1996–2000. *Publications:* After You'd Gone, 2000 (Betty Trask Award, 2001); My Lover's Lover, 2002; The Distance Between Us, 2004 (Somerset Maugham Award, 2005); The Vanishing Act of Esme Lennox, 2006; The Hand that First Held Mine (Costa Novel Award), 2010; Instructions for a Heatwave, 2013; This Must be the Place, 2016; I Am, I Am, I Am (memoir), 2017. *Address:* c/o A. M. Heath and Co., 6 Warwick Court, WC1R 5DJ.

**O'FERRALL, Rev. Patrick Charles Kenneth,** OBE 1989; Hon. Assistant Priest: St Andrew's, Farnham, since 2012; St Tomas on the Bourne, Farnham, since 2018; *b* 27 May 1934; *s* of late Rev. Kenneth John Spence O'Ferrall and Isoult May O'Ferrall; *m* 1st, 1960, Mary Dorothea (*d* 1997), 4th *d* of late Maj. C. E. Lugard and Mrs K. I. B. Lugard; one *s* two *d;* 2nd, 1999, Wendy Elizabeth Barnett (*née* Gilmore). *Educ:* Pilgrims Sch., Winchester (Cathedral Chorister); Winchester Coll. (Scholar); New Coll., Oxford (BA Lit.Hum. 1958; MA); Harvard Business Sch. (AMP 1983). Nat. Service, 1952–54, 2nd Lieut, Royal Fusiliers. Iraq Petroleum and associated cos, 1958–70; BP, 1971–73; Total CFP Paris (Total Moyen Orient), 1974–77; Total Oil Marine, London: Commercial Manager, 1977–82; Dir, Gas Gathering Pipelines (N Sea) Ltd, 1977–78; Project Co-ordination Manager, Alwyn N, 1983–85; Projects Co-ordination Manager, 1985–90; Dep. Chm., 1991–93, Chm., 1993–99, Lloyd's Register of Shipping. Mem., Offshore Industry Adv. Bd, 1992–94. Chm., City of London Outward Bound Assoc., 1993–97. Mem., Court of Common Council, Corp. of London, 1996–2001. Liveryman, Co. of Shipwrights, 1992–; Master, Coachmakers' and Coach Harness Makers' Co., 1993–94. FRSA 1993; CCMI (CIMgt 1994). Hon. FREng 2001. Lay Reader, 1961–2000; ordained deacon, 2000, priest, 2001; Curate (Ordained Local Minister), 2000–07, Hon. Asst Priest, 2007–12, SS Peter and Paul, Godalming. Hon. Chaplain: Aldgate Ward Club, 2001–15; Baltic Exchange, 2001–16. *Recreations:* music (playing violin and singing), tennis, golf, wine, crosswords, travel. *Address:* Pear Tree House, 66 Firgrove Hill, Farnham, Surrey GU9 8LW. *T:* (01252) 724498. *E:* patrickoferrall@gmail.com. *Club:* MCC.

**OFFER, Prof. Avner,** DPhil; FBA 2000; Chichele Professor of Economic History, University of Oxford, 2000–11; Fellow, All Souls College, Oxford, 2000–11, now Emeritus; *b* 15 May 1944; *s* of Zvi and Ivriyah Offer; *m* 1966, Leah Koshet; one *s* one *d. Educ:* Western Valley Sch., Yif'at, Israel; Hebrew Univ. (BA 1973); St Antony's Coll., Oxford; Merton Coll., Oxford (MA 1976; DPhil 1979). Mil. service, Israel, 1962–65; Kibbutz mem., 1965–67; Conservation Officer, Israel, 1967–69; Jun. Res. Fellow, Merton Coll., Oxford, 1976–78; Lectr in Econ. and Social Hist., 1978–90, Reader, 1990–91, Univ. of York; Reader in Recent Social and Econ. Hist., Univ. of Oxford, and Fellow, Nuffield Coll., 1992–2000. Hartley Fellow, Univ. of Southampton, 1981–82; Vis. Associate, Clare Hall, Cambridge, 1984; Res. Fellow, Inst. Advanced Study, ANU, 1985–88; Sen. Fellow, Rutgers Univ., 1991–92; Sen. Vis. Fellow, Remarque Inst., NY Univ., 1999; Leverhulme Major Res. Fellow, 2008–11; Principal Investigator, Inst. for New Econ. Thinking project on Nobel Prize in Econs, 2011–13. FAcSS (AcSS 2003). *Publications:* Property and Politics 1870–1914: landownership, law, ideology and urban development in England, 1981; The First World War: an agrarian interpretation, 1989; (ed) In Pursuit of the Quality of Life, 1996; The Challenge of Affluence: self-control and well-being in the United States and Britain since 1950, 2006; (ed) Insecurity, Inequality and Obesity in Affluent Societies, 2012; The Nobel Factor, 2016; articles on land, law, empire, consumption and quality of life. *Recreations:* literature, classical music, visual arts. *Address:* 15 Hamilton Road, Oxford OX2 7PY. *T:* (01865) 553380.

**OFFER, Ven. Clifford Jocelyn;** Archdeacon of Norwich and Canon Residentiary (Canon Librarian) of Norwich Cathedral, 1994–2008, now Archdeacon Emeritus; *b* 10 Aug. 1943; *s* of late Rev. Canon Clifford Jesse Offer and Jocelyn Mary Offer; *m* 1980, Dr Catherine Mary Lloyd; two *d. Educ:* King's Sch., Canterbury; St Peter's Coll., Oxford (sent down); Exeter Univ. (BA 1967). Westcott House, Cambridge. Ordained deacon, 1969, priest, 1970; Curate, St Peter and St Paul, Bromley, 1969–74; Team Vicar, Southampton City Centre, 1974–83; Team Rector, Hitchin, 1983–94. Vice Chm., then Chm., St Albans ABM, 1989–94; Chairman: Norwich Diocesan Adv. Bd for Mission and Ministry (formerly ABM), 1994–99, 2000–03; Norwich Course Mgt Cttee, 1999–2003; Norwich Bd of Ministry, 2003–08; Warden of Readers, Dio. Norwich, 1994–2008; Bishops' Advr (formerly Bishops' Selector), 1995–2014; Mem., Gen. Synod of C of E, 1999–2005. Mem., Council for E Anglia Studies, 2000–08. FRSA 1997. *Publications:* King Offa in Hitchin, 1992; In Search of Clofesho, 2002. *Recreations:* collecting naval buttons, ship-modelling, growing chrysanthemums, bell-ringing. *Address:* Chase House, Peterstow, Herefordshire HR9 6JX. *T:* (01989) 567874.

**OFFMANN, Karl Auguste;** President, Republic of Mauritius, 2002–03; *b* 25 Nov. 1940; *s* of Laurent Wilford Offmann and Liliane Armoorgum; *m* 1969, Marie-Rose Danielle Moutou; two *s. Educ:* Mech. Engrg Apprenticeship Scholar 1956; Claver House, London (Dip. Social and Political Sci. 1975). Plant and Personnel Manager, L'Express, daily newspaper, 1963–79. Leader, Internat. Young Christian Workers Movement, 1957–79; politician, 1976–2002 (full-time, 1982–2002). Founder Mem., Africa Forum, 2006–. Grand Commander, Order of Star and Key of the Indian Ocean (Republic of Mauritius); Grand Croix 1st class, l'Ordre National à Madagascar. *Address:* P18 Cité Jules Koenig–Vuilleminn, Beau–Bassin, Mauritius. *T:* 454 2880, *Fax:* 454 9634. *E:* offmann@intnet.mu.

**OFFORD, Dr Matthew James,** FRGS; MP (C) Hendon, since 2010; *b* Alton, Hants, 3 Sept. 1969; *s* of Christopher and Hilda Offord; *m* 2010, Claire Michelle Rowles. *Educ:* Amery Hill Sch., Alton; Nottingham Trent Univ. (BA Hons); Lancaster Univ. (MA); King's Coll. London (PhD 2011). FRGS 2005. Political analyst, BBC, 2001–10. Mem. (C) Barnet BC, 2002–10 (Dep. Leader, 2006–09). Mem., Envmtl Audit Cttee, 2012–15, 2016–. Chm., Hendon Cons. Assoc., 2004–07. Contested (C) Barnsley E and Mexborough, 2001. *Recreations:* scuba diving, sailing, swimming, reading, travel, wine. *Address:* House of Commons, SW1A 0AA. *T:* (020) 7219 7083. *E:* matthew.offord.mp@parliament.uk.

**OFIELD-KERR, Prof. Simon Douglas,** PhD; Deputy Vice-Chancellor (Academic), University of the Arts London, since 2017; *b* Newton Abbott, 28 Jan. 1966; *s* of late Derek Malcolm Ofield and of Patricia Ofield; civil partnership 2006, Anton Kerr; one *s. Educ:* Bishopshalt Sch., Hillingdon; Exeter Coll. of Art and Design (BA Hons Fine Art 1990); Univ. of Leeds (MA Social Hist. of Art 1992; PhD Hist. of Art 1997). Academic Gp Chair for Art, Philosophy and Visual Culture, Middlesex Univ., 1996–2006; Dean, Faculty of Art, Design and Architecture, Kingston Univ., 2006–11; Vice-Chancellor, Univ. for the Creative Arts, 2011–16. Member, Executive Group: UK Arts and Design Instns Assoc., 2011–; GuildHE, 2013–16. Trustee, Turner Contemporary, Margate, 2017–. Gov., Kingston Grammar Sch., 2010–16. FRSA 2006. Mem. Bd and Founder Ed., Jl of Visual Culture, 2002–. *Publications:* articles in Art History, Jl of Visual Culture, Oxford Art Jl, Visual Culture in Britain. *Address:* University of the Arts London, 272 High Holborn, WC1V 7EY. *T:* (020) 7514 6060. *E:* s.ofieldkerr@arts.ac.uk.

**OFILI, Christopher,** CBE 2017; artist; *b* Manchester, 1968. *Educ:* Tameside Coll. of Technol.; Chelsea Sch. of Art (Christopher Head Drawing Scholarship 1989; BA); Hochschule der Künste, Berlin; Royal Coll. of Art (MA). British Council Travel Scholarship, Zimbabwe, 1992. Solo exhibitions include: Kepler Gall., London, 1991; Victoria Miro Gall., London, 1996, 2000, 2002, 2012; Contemporary Fine Arts, Berlin, 1997, 2005; Southampton City Art Gall., 1998; Serpentine Gall., London, 1998; Whitworth Art Gall., Manchester, 1998–99; Gavin Brown's Enterprise, NY, 1999; Gall. Side 2, Japan, 2001; (as GB rep.) Venice Biennale, 2003; Studio Mus., Harlem, 2005; Tate Britain, 2005–07, 2010 (retrospective); kestnergesellschaft, Hanover, 2006; David Zwirner, NY, 2007, 2009, 2017; Arts Club of Chicago, 2010; New Mus., NY, 2014–15; Aspen Art Mus., 2015; Nat. Gall., 2017; Victoria Miro Venice, 2017, ICA, Miami, 2017–19; David Zwirner Gall., NY, 2019. Group exhibitions include: Cornerhouse Gall., Manchester, 1993; MOMA, Oxford, 1995; ICA, 1997; Mus. of Contemp. Art, Sydney, 1997; RA, 1997; Walker Art Gall., Liverpool, 1997; British Council touring exhibn, incl. Finland, Sweden and Czech Republic, 1997–2000; Tate Gall., 1998–99; 6th Internat. Biennale, Istanbul, 1999; Carnegie Mus. of Art, Pittsburgh, 1999–2000; Brooklyn Mus. of Art, NY, 1999; Saatchi Gall., 2000; South Bank Centre, 2000; Mus. of Contemp. Art, LA, 2001; Bronx Mus. of the Arts, NY, 2002 (and touring); Santa Monica Mus. of Art, Calif, 2002; MOMA, NY, 2002; Nat. Gall. and UK tour, 2003; Joslyn Art Mus., Omaha, 2004; Palais de Tokyo, Paris, 2005; ICA, Boston, 2005; MOMA, NY, 2005; MOMA, NY, V&A, Hayward Gall., London, 2006; MIMA, Middlesbrough, Gary Tatinsian Gall., Moscow, 2007; Whitechapel Gall., London, 2009; Metamorphosis: Titian, ROH and Nat. Gall., London, 2012; White Cube, London, 2015; Venice Biennale, 2015; Art Gall. of Southern Australia, 2017; David Zwirner Gall., NY, 2018; Studio Mus., Harlem, 2019. Other projects, commissions for: Folkestone Liby, 2002, Nobel Peace Centre, Oslo, 2005, Stephen Lawrence Centre, London, 2007 (in collaboration with David Adjaye); Sampling the Myth, ROH, London, 2014; Mus. of Contemporary Art, Chicago, 2017. Trustee, Tate, 2000–05. Hon. Fellow, Univ. of the Arts, London, 2004. Turner Prize, 1998; Southbank Award, Visual Arts, London, 2004. *Address:* c/o Victoria Miro Gallery, 16 Wharf Road, N1 7RW.

**O'FLAHERTY, Prof. Coleman Anthony,** AM 1999; Deputy Vice-Chancellor, University of Tasmania, Australia, 1991–93, Professor Emeritus 1993; *b* 8 Feb. 1933; *s* of Michael and Agnes O'Flaherty; *m* 1957, Nuala Rose Silke (*d* 1999). *Educ:* Nat. Univ. of Ireland (BE); Iowa State Univ. (MS, PhD). FICE, FIEI; FIE(Aust); FCIHT. Engineer: Galway Co. Council, Ireland, 1954–55; Canadian Pacific Railway Co., Montreal, 1955–56; M. W. Kellogg Co., USA, 1956–57; Asst Prof., Iowa State Univ., 1957–62; Leeds University: Lectr, 1962–66; Prof. of Transport Engineering, Inst. for Transport Studies and Dept of Civil Engineering, 1966–74; First Asst Comr (Engineering), Nat. Capital Develt Commn, Canberra, 1974–78; Dir and Principal, Tasmanian Coll. of Advanced Educn, subseq. Tasmanian State Inst. of Technology, 1978–90. Vis. Prof., Univ. of Melbourne, 1973. Chairman: Tasmanian Liby Adv. Bd, 1997–2006; Tasmania State Liby and Archives Trust, 1997–2006. Trustee, Tasmanian Mus. and Art Gall., 1993–2000. Dep. Nat. Pres., Assoc. Independent Retirees, 2007–10 (Pres., Tasmanian Div., 2005–07). Hon. LLD Tasmania, 1994. *Publications:* Highways, 1967, vol. I of 4th edn (Transport Planning and Traffic Engineering), 1997, vol. II of 4th edn (Highway Engineering), 2001, 5th edn as (The Location, Planning, Design, Construction and Maintenance of Road Pavements), 2015; (jtly) Passenger Conveyors, 1972; (jtly) Introduction to Hovercraft and Hoverports, 1975; contribs to professional jls. *Recreation:* bush walking. *Address:* 22 Beach Road, Legana, Tasmania 7277, Australia. *T:* and *Fax:* (3) 63301990. *Club:* Launceston.

**O'FLAHERTY, Stephen John,** CMG 2003; Managing Director, Goldman Sachs International, since 2005; *b* 15 May 1951; *s* of late Brig. Denis O'Flaherty, CBE, DSO and of Jill O'Flaherty; *m* 1975, (Sarah) Louise Gray; one *s* two *d. Educ:* Douai Sch.; Jesus Coll., Oxford (BA). HM Diplomatic Service, 1975–2004: entered FCO, 1975; Second Sec., New Delhi, 1977–80; First Secretary: FCO, 1980–81; Prague, 1981–84; FCO, 1984–88; Vienna, 1988–92; Counsellor, FCO, 1992–2004. *Address:* (office) Plumtree Court, 25 Shoe Lane, EC4A 4AU.

**O'FLYNN, Patrick James;** Member for Eastern Region, European Parliament, 2014–19 (UK Ind, 2014–18; Ind, 2018–19); *b* Cambridge, 29 Aug. 1965; *m* Carol Ann Rice; two *c. Educ:* Parkside Community Coll., Cambridge; Long Road Sixth Form Coll., Cambridge; King's Coll., Cambridge (BA Econs 1987); City Univ., London (Dip. Journalism). Reporter, Hull Daily Mail, 1989–92; reporter, 1992–93, political corresp., 1993–96, Birmingham Post; Dep. Political Ed., Sunday Express, 1996–98; Chief Political Commentator, 1998–2000, Political Ed., 2000–14, Daily Express. Dir of Communications, then Econs spokesman, UKIP, 2014–15. Contested (UK Ind) Cambridge, 2015.

**of MAR,** family name of **Countess of Mar**.

**O'GARRA, Dr Anne,** FRS 2008; Group Leader, Immunoregulation and Infection, and Associate Research Director, Francis Crick Institute, since 2015; Adjunct Professor, National Heart and Lung Institute, Imperial College London, since 2012; *b* Gibraltar, 4 Nov. 1954; *d* of late Louis O'Garra and Teresa O'Garra (*née* Azzopardi); *m* Dr Paulo Julio de Miranda Vieira. *Educ:* Chelsea Coll., Univ. of London (BSc 1st Cl. Hons Microbiol. and Biochem. 1980); Nat. Inst. for Med. Res. (PhD 1983). Postdoctoral Fellow, Div. of Immunol., NIMR, 1983–87; DNAX Research Institute, Palo Alto, California: Postdoctoral Fellow, 1987–89; Sen. Res. Associate, 1989–93; Staff Scientist, then Sen. Staff Scientist, 1993–98; Principal Staff Scientist, 1999–2001; Head, Div. of Immunoregulation, MRC Nat. Inst. for Med. Res., 2001–15. Mem., EMBO, 2009. FMedSci 2005; FAAAS 2006. *Publications:* contribs to scientific jls incl. Nature, Eur. Jl Immunol., Jl Exptl Medicine, Immunol., Immunity. *Address:* Francis Crick Institute, 1 Midland Road, NW1 1AT.

**OGATA, Prof. Sadako,** Hon. DCMG 2011; Special Advisor to President, Japan International Cooperation Agency (President, 2003–12); Co-Chair, Commission on Human Security, 2001–03; Chair, Advisory Board on Human Security, 2003–11, now Hon. Chair; *b* 16 Sept. 1927; *m*; one *s* one *d*. *Educ*: Univ. of the Sacred Heart, Tokyo (BA); Georgetown Univ. (MA); PhD California (Berkeley). Prof., 1980–90, Director of Internat. Relations, 1987–88, Dean, Faculty of Foreign Studies, 1989–90, Sophia Univ., Japan, now Prof. Emeritus. Minister, Perm. Mission of Japan to UN, 1976–78; Chm. Exec. Bd, UNICEF, Japanese Rep. to UN Commn on Human Rights, 1982–85; UN High Comr for Refugees, 1991–2000. Special Advr to Minister of Foreign Affairs, Japan, 2012–. Hon. DCL Oxon, 1998; Hon. LLD Cantab, 1999. *Publications*: Defiance in Manchuria: the making of Japanese foreign policy 1931–1932, 1964; The Turbulent Decade: confronting the refugee crisis of the 1990s, 2005. *Address*: c/o Japan International Cooperation Agency, Nibancho Center Building, 5–25 Niban-cho, Chiyoda-ku, Tokyo 102–8012, Japan.

**OGBORN, Prof. Miles,** PhD; FBA 2012; Professor of Geography, Queen Mary, University of London. Formerly at St David's UC, Lampeter. Philip Leverhulme Prize, Leverhulme Trust, 2001; Dist. Histl Geographer, Assoc. of Amer. Geographers, 2009. *Publications*: Spaces of Modernity: London's geographies 1680–1780, 1998; (contrib.) Introducing Cultural Studies, 1999, 2nd edn 2008; (ed jtly) Cultural Geography in Practice, 2003; (ed with C. W. J. Withers) Georgian Geographies: essays on space, place and landscape in the Eighteenth Century, 2004; Indian Ink: script and print in the making of the English East India Company, 2007; Global Lives: Britain and the world, 1550–1800, 2008; (ed with C. W. J. Withers) Geographies of the Book, 2010; contribs to jls incl. Jl Histl Geog., Trans IBG, Hist. of Sci. *Address*: School of Geography, Queen Mary, University of London, Mile End Road, E1 4NS.

**OGDEN, Sir Peter (James),** Kt 2005; Founder and Chairman, The Ogden Trust, since 1994; *b* 26 May 1947; *s* of late James Platt Ogden and Frances Ogden (*née* Simmonds); *m* 1970, Catherine Rose Blincoe; two *s* one *d*. *Educ*: Rochdale Grammar Sch.; Univ. of Durham (BSc 1968; PhD 1971); Harvard Business Sch. (MBA 1973); Hughes Hall, Cambridge (MA 2002). Man. Dir, Morgan Stanley & Co., 1985; Chairman: Computacenter Ltd, 1985–97 (non-exec. Dir, 1997–); Dealogic Ltd, 1985–2018. Hon. FInstP 2010. Hon. DCL Durham, 2002; Hon. DSc Warwick, 2009. *Recreation*: sailing. *Address*: The Ogden Trust, Unit 3C, Phoenix Brewery, 13 Bramley Road, W10 6SP. *T*: (020) 8634 7470. *E*: office@ogdentrust.com. *Club*: Royal Yacht Squadron (Cowes).

**OGDEN, Prof. Raymond William,** PhD; FRS 2006; George Sinclair Professor of Mathematics, University of Glasgow, 1984–2010 and since 2012; *b* 19 Sept. 1943; *s* of Arthur and Norah Ogden; *m* 1969, Susanne Thomas; two *s* two *d*. *Educ*: Gonville and Caius Coll., Cambridge (BA 1966; PhD 1970). SRC Postdoctoral Res. Fellow, UEA, 1970–72; Lectr, 1972–76, Reader, 1976–80, in Maths, Univ. of Bath; Prof. of Maths, Brunel Univ., 1981–84; 6th Century Chair in Engrg, Univ. of Aberdeen, 2010–12. *Publications*: Non-linear Elastic Deformations, 1984, 2nd edn 1997; (jtly) Nonlinear Theory of Electroelastic and Magnetoelastic Interactions, 2014; more than 200 articles in internat. scientific jls. *Recreations*: music, wine, learning languages, absorbing the sun in the Mediterranean. *Address*: School of Mathematics and Statistics, Mathematics and Statistics Building, University of Glasgow, University Place, Glasgow G12 8SQ. *E*: Raymond.Ogden@glasgow.ac.uk.

**OGDEN, Dr Vanessa Jane;** Chief Executive Officer, Mulberry Schools Trust, and Headteacher, Mulberry School for Girls, since 2006; *b* London, 2 Nov. 1966; *d* of Dr David Ogden and Judith Hocking; *m* 1997, Dr Jonathan Roberts. *Educ*: Manchester Univ. (BA Hons Theol. and Religious Studies 1989); Institute of Education, Univ. of London (PGCE Religious Studies 1993; MA Educn 1998; NPQH 2002; DEd 2012 (BELMAS Prize)). Hd of Dept, Walford High Sch., Northolt, 1993–98; Hurlingham and Chelsea School, Hammersmith and Fulham: Hd of Faculty, 1998–99; Asst Headteacher, 1999–2000; Acting Dep. Headteacher, 2000–01; Dep. Headteacher, Stationers' Crown Woods Acad., Greenwich, 2001–06. Nat. Leader for Educn, 2011. Acad. Fellow, Inst. of Educn, UCL (formerly Univ. of London), 2012–. Chair, Nat. Forum of Headteachers (Teach First), 2016– (Trustee, Teach First, 2009–16). Mem., Nat. RE Commn, 2016–18. Mem., Adv. Gp on personal, social, health and econ. educn to Sec. of State for Educn, 2015–16. Advr, Centre for Social Justice Educn Policy Gp, 2012–14. Mem. Bd, Leadership Res. Council, Foundn for Leadership in Educn, 2017–19. Chm. Bd, Somerset Challenge, 2013–16. Trustee: Haberdashers' Aske Fedn Trust, 2014–; WOW Foundn, 2019–; Trustee and Chair, Fair Educn Alliance, 2019–. Sir Halley Stewart Fellow, 1996–97. *Publications*: contributor: Learning to Teach RE in the Secondary, 2000; Perspectives on SMSC, 2000; (jtly) School Subject Teaching: the history and future of the curriculum, 2000; Successful System Leadership: the London Challenge, 2015. *Recreations*: ballet, opera, music, cooking, gardening. *Address*: Mulberry School for Girls, Richard Street, Commercial Road, E1 2JP. *T*: (020) 7790 6327, *Fax*: (020) 7265 9882. *E*: sjameson@mulberryschoolstrust.org.

**OGG, Derek Andrew;** QC (Scot.) 1999; Senior Advocate Depute, 2007–11; Head, National Sexual Crimes Unit, Crown Office, Edinburgh, 2009–11; *b* 19 Sept. 1954; *s* of Alec and Elsie Ogg. *Educ*: Edinburgh Univ. (LLB 1978). Dip. in Master Advocacy, Nat. Inst. for Trial Advocacy, USA, 1996. Asst Solicitor, Ross & Connel Solicitors, Dunfermline, 1978–80; Partner and Founder, Hunter Burns & Ogg Solicitors, Edinburgh, Perth and Dunfermline, 1980–89; Standing Jun. Counsel, Scottish Office, 1983–88; called to the Scottish Bar, 1989; Jun. Counsel, 1989–99; Reserve Counsel, UN *Ad Hoc* Tribunal for War Crimes in Former Republic of Yugoslavia, The Hague, 1998–2004. Chm. (*ad hoc*), Discipline Tribunal, ICAS, 2001–. Chm., Faculty of Advocates Criminal Bar Assoc., 2003–05. Founder and Chm., Scottish Aids Monitor, 1983–93; Trustee, Nat. Aids Trust, 1987–90. Mem., Royal Philosophical Soc., Glasgow. Founding Fellow (FFCS) 2002, Hon. Fellow, 2004, Inst. for Contemporary Scotland. *Recreations*: hill-walking in Scotland, collecting and competing classic cars, supporter of Celtic Football Club, reading history, occasional broadcaster and commentator on public affairs on TV and radio in Scotland. *Address*: Rawcliffe House, 10 Rawcliffe Gardens, Mansionhouse Road, Glasgow G41 3DA. *E*: derekandrewogg@hotmail.com.

**OGILVIE, (Dame) Bridget (Margaret), (Dr Bridget Ogilvie),** AC 2007; DBE 1997; FRCPath, FMedSci; FRS 2003; FAA; FRSB; Director: Wellcome Trust, 1991–98; AstraZeneca (formerly Zeneca Group plc), 1996; High Steward of University of Cambridge, 2001–09; *b* 24 March 1938; *er d* of late John Mylne Ogilvie and Margaret Beryl (*née* McRae). *Educ*: New England Girls' Sch., Armidale, NSW; Univ. of New England, Armidale (BRurSc 1960; Distinguished Alumni Award, 1994); PhD 1964, ScD 1981, Cambridge. FRSB (FIBiol 1985); FRCPath 1992. Parasitology Div., Nat. Inst. for Med. Res., London, 1963–81; Ian McMaster Fellow, CSIRO Div. of Animal Health, Australia, 1971–72; with Wellcome Trust, 1979–98: Co-ordinator, Tropical Med. Prog., 1979–81; Dep. Sec. and Asst Dir, 1981–84; Dep. Dir, Science, 1984–89; Dir, Science Progs, 1989–91. Director: Lloyds Bank, 1995; Lloyds TSB Gp, 1996–2000. Visiting Professor: Dept of Biology, Imperial Coll., London, 1985–93; UCL, 1998–. Member: Council for Science and Technol., 1993–2000; Commonwealth Scholarship Commn, 1993–2000; Adv. Council for Chemistry, Univ. of Oxford, 1997–2001; Australian Health and Med. Res. Strategic Review, 1998–99; Chairman: COPUS, 1998–2002; AstraZeneca Sci. Teaching Trust, 1998–2006; Medicines for Malaria Venture, 1999–2006; Adv. Cttee for Sci., Technol., Business, British Liby, 2000–02. Non-executive Director: Scottish Sci. Trust, 1999–2002; Manchester Technol. Fund, 1999–2004. Chm., Assoc. of Med. Res. Charities, 2002–07. Trustee: Sci. Mus., London, 1992–2003; RCVS Trust Fund, 1998–2001; NESTA, 1998–2002; Cancer Res. UK (formerly CRC), 2001–10; Sense about Science, 2002–; Centre of the Cell, UK, 2005–14. Chairman, Governing Body: Inst. for Animal Health, 1997–2003; Lister Inst., 2002–11. Hon. Patron, Illawarra Health and Med. Res. Inst., Univ. of Wollongong, 2016–. Founder FMedSci 1998; FAA 2008. Hon. Member: British Soc. for Parasitology, 1990; Amer. Soc. of Parasitologists, 1992; BVA, 1998; BAAS, 2005; British Soc. of Immunology, 2017; Hon. FRCP 1996 (Hon. MRCP 1992); Hon. FRACP 1998; Hon. ARCVS 1993. Hon. Fellow: UCL, 1993; Girton Coll., Cambridge, 1993; St Edmund's Coll., Cambridge, 1999; Mansfield Coll., Oxford, 2010; Hon. FRVC 1994; Hon. FIBiol 1998; Hon. FRSocMed 1999. Hon. DSc: Nottingham, Salford, Westminster, 1994; Glasgow, Bristol, ANU, 1995; Buckingham, Dublin, Trent, Oxford Brookes, 1996; Greenwich, 1997; Auckland, NZ, Durham, Kent, 1998; Exeter, Imperial Coll., London, 1999; Leicester, 2000; Manchester, St Andrews, 2001; Wollongong, 2005; New England, Melbourne, 2015; Warwick, 2017; Hon. LLD: TCD, 1996; Dundee, 1998; Hon. MD Newcastle, 1996; Dr *hc* Edinburgh, 1997. Lloyd of Kilgerran Prize, Foundn for Sci. and Technology, 1994; Wooldridge Meml Medal, BVA, 1998; Australian Soc. for Medical Res. Medal, 2000; Kilby Award, Kilby Awards Foundn, USA, 2003; Duncan Davies Meml Medal, Res. and Develt Soc., 2004; Ralph Doherty Meml Medal, Qld Inst. of Medical Res., 2006. *Publications*: contrib. scientific papers to parasitological and immunological jls. *Recreations*: the company of friends, looking at landscapes, music, gardening. *Address*: 79 Brondesbury Road, NW6 6BB. *Clubs*: Reform; Oxford and Cambridge; Queen's (Sydney).

**OGILVIE, Ven. Gordon;** Archdeacon of Nottingham, 1996–2006; *b* 22 Aug. 1942; *s* of late Gordon and Eliza J. Ogilvie (*née* Cullen); *m* 1967, Sylvia Margaret, *d* of late Rankin and Jessie Weir; one *s* one *d*. *Educ*: Hillhead High Sch., Glasgow; Glasgow Univ. (MA 1964); London Coll. of Divinity (Associate, 1966; ext. BD London Univ., 1967). Ordained deacon, 1967, priest, 1968; Asst Curate, Ashtead, 1967–72; Vicar, St James, New Barnet, 1972–80; Dir, Pastoral Studies, Wycliffe Hall, Oxford, 1980–87; Priest-in-charge, 1987–89, Team Rector, 1989–96, Harlow Town Centre with Little Parndon; Chaplain, Princess Alexandra Hosp., Harlow, 1988–96. Hon. Canon, Chelmsford Cathedral, 1993–96. Bishop's warrant to officiate, United Dio. of St Andrews, Dunkeld and Dunblane, 2007–. *Recreations*: sport in general, piano, photography. *Address*: 49 Argyle Street, St Andrews, Fife KY16 9BX. *T*: (01334) 470185. *E*: gordon.ogilvie@virgin.net.

**OGILVIE, Prof. Sheilagh Catheren,** PhD; FBA 2004; Professor of Economic History, University of Cambridge, since 2004; *b* 7 Oct. 1958; *d* of Robert Townley Ogilvie and Sheilagh Stuart Ogilvie. *Educ*: Queen Elizabeth Sch.; Univ. of St Andrews (MA 1st cl. Hons 1979); Trinity Coll., Cambridge (PhD 1985); Univ. of Chicago (MA 1992). Res. Fellow, Trinity Coll., Cambridge, 1984–88; Univ. Asst Lectr, 1989–92, Univ. Lectr, 1992–99, Reader in Econ. History, 1999–2004, Faculty of Econs, Univ. of Cambridge. *Publications*: The Park Buffalo: the history of the conservation of the North American bison, 1979; (ed) Proto-Industrialization in Europe, 1993; (ed with Markus Cerman) Protoindustrialisierung in Europa: Industrielle Produktion vor dem Fabrikszeitalter, 1994; Germany: a new social and economic history, (ed) vol. 2, 1630–1800, 1996, (ed with Richard Overy) vol. 3, Since 1800, 2003; (ed with Markus Cerman) European Proto-Industrialization, 1996; State Corporatism and Proto-Industry: the Württemberg Black Forest 1590–1797, 1997; A Bitter Living: women, markets and social capital in Early Modern Germany, 2003; Institutions and European Trade: merchant guilds, 1000–1800, 2011; (ed jtly) Revolution des Fleißes, Revolution des Konsums?, 2015; The European Guilds: an economic analysis, 2019; articles in Amer. Historical Rev., Bohemia, Český časopis historický, Comparative Studies in Soc. and Hist., Continuity and Change, Early Modern Women, Econ. Hist. Rev., Explorations in Econ. Hist., Histoire sociale/Social History, Histoires et sociétés rurales, Historical Jl, Historická Demografie, Jahrbuch für Wirtschaftsgeschichte, Jahrbuch für Regionalgeschichte, Jl of Econ. Hist., Jl of Econ. Perspectives, The History of the Family, Past & Present, Revue d'Allemagne et des pays de langue allemande, Social Hist. and Trans of RHistS, Zeitschrift für Agrargeschichte und Agrarsoziologie, Zeitschrift für württembergische Landesgeschichte. *Recreations*: indiscriminate reading, walking in Central European mountains, thinking, talking, counting. *Address*: Faculty of Economics, University of Cambridge, Sidgwick Avenue, Cambridge CB3 9DD. *T*: (01223) 335222, *Fax*: (01223) 335475. *E*: sco2@econ.cam.ac.uk.

**OGILVIE-GRANT,** family name of **Earl of Seafield**.

**OGILVIE THOMPSON, Julian;** Director: De Beers Consolidated Mines Ltd, 1966–2006 (Deputy Chairman, 1982–85 and 1998–2001; Chairman, 1985–97); De Beers SA, 2002–08; *b* 27 Jan. 1934; *s* of late Hon. N. Ogilvie Thompson, formerly Chief Justice of S Africa, and of Eve Ogilvie Thompson; *m* 1956, Hon. Tessa Mary Brand, *yr* surv. *d* of 4th Viscount Hampden, CMG and Leila, Viscountess Hampden; two *s* two *d*. *Educ*: Diocesan Coll., Rondebosch; Univ. of Cape Town; Worcester Coll., Oxford. MA. Diocesan Coll. Rhodes Scholar, 1953. Joined Anglo American Corp. of SA Ltd, 1956; Dir, 1970; Exec. Dir, 1971–82; Dep. Chm., 1983–90; Chm., 1990–2002; Anglo American plc: Chief Exec., 1999–2000; Chm., 1999–2002; Chairman: Anglo American Gold Investment Co. Ltd, 1976–90; Minorco SA (formerly Minerals and Resources Corp. Ltd), 1982–99; Vice Chairman: First Nat. Bank Ltd, 1977–90; Urban Foundn, 1986–95. Rhodes Trustee, 2002–15; Trustee, Mandela Rhodes Foundn, 2003–. Hon. LLD Rhodes, 1986. Comdr, Order of the Crown (Belgium), 1993; Grand Official, Order of Bernardo O'Higgins (Chile), 1996; Presidential Order of Honour (Botswana), 1997. *Recreations*: bird shooting, golf. *Address*: Froome, 114 Froome Street, Athol Extension 3, Sandton, 2196, S Africa. *T*: (11) 8843925. *Club*: White's.

**OGILVY,** family name of **Earl of Airlie**.

**OGILVY, Lord; David John Ogilvy;** *b* 9 March 1958; *s* and *heir* of 13th Earl of Airlie, *qv*; *m* 1st, 1981, Hon. Geraldine Harmsworth (marr. diss. 1991), *d* of 3rd Viscount Rothermere; one *d*; 2nd, 1991, Tarka Kings; three *s*. *Educ*: Eton and Oxford (MA). Man. Dir, Richard L. Feigen UK Ltd, art dealers, 1982–2002. Trustee: Macmillan Trust, 2006–; Rothschild Foundn, 2013–. *Heir*: *s* Master of Ogilvy, *qv*. *Address*: Airlie Castle, Kirriemuir, Angus DD8 5NG.

**OGILVY, Master of; David Huxley Ogilvy;** *b* 11 Dec. 1991; *s* and *heir* of Lord Ogilvy, *qv*.

**OGILVY, Sir Francis (Gilbert Arthur),** 14th Bt *cr* 1626 (NS), of Inverquharity, Forfarshire; Chartered Surveyor; Proprietor, Ogilvy Chalmers (formerly Chalmers & Co.), Haddington, since 1999; *b* 22 April 1969; *s* of Sir David John Wilfrid Ogilvy, 13th Bt and of Penelope Mary Ursula, *d* of Captain Arthur Lafone Frank Hills, OBE; *S* father, 1992; *m* 1996, Dorothy, *e d* of Rev. Jock Stein and Rev. Margaret Stein; three *s* one *d*. *Educ*: Edinburgh Acad.; Glenalmond; RAC, Cirencester (BSc Hons). MRICS. *Heir*: *s* Robert David Ogilvy, *b* 8 July 1999. *Address*: Winton Castle, Pencaitland, E Lothian EH34 5AT.

**OGILVY, Hon. James (Donald Diarmid)**; Chairman, Foreign & Colonial Management Ltd, 1998–99 (Chief Executive, 1988–97); *b* 28 June 1934; *y s* of 12th Earl of Airlie, KT, GCVO, MC and Lady Alexandra Marie Bridget Coke, *d* of 3rd Earl of Leicester, GCVO, CMG; *m* 1st, 1959, June Ducas (marr. diss. 1978; she *d* 2001); two *s* two *d*; 2nd, 1980, Lady Caroline (*née* Child-Villiers), *d* of 9th Earl of Jersey. *Educ:* Eton Coll. Served 1st Bn, Scots Guards, Egypt, 1953–55 (2nd Lieut). Partner, Rowe & Pitman, 1959–86; Vice Chm., Mercury Asset Management plc, 1986–88. Chairman: Sutherlands (Holdings), 1998–2000; Off Plan Fund, 2004–05. Director: Foreign and Colonial Investment Trust, 1990–97; Foreign & Colonial Emerging Markets, 1995–98; Berkshire Capital Corp. UK, 1998–2006; Lord North Street Holdings Ltd, 2005–08; Black Sea Fund, 2005–06. Dir, 1974–76, Chm., 1976–83, Inst. for Obstetrics and Gynaecology; Gov., Queen Charlotte's and Chelsea Hosp. for Women, 1974–80. Trustee: Gascoyne Cecil Estates, 1974–; Milton Peterborough Estates, 1987–2007; Belvoir Estate, 2000–06. Chm., Garden Museum (formerly Museum of Garden History), 2002–11. A Page of Honour to King George VI, 1947–51. Mem., Queen's Body Guard for Scotland, Royal Co. of Archers. Grand Official, Nat. Order of the Southern Cross (Brazil), 1993. *Recreations:* shooting, golf. *Address:* Sedgebrook Manor, Sedgebrook, Grantham, Lincs NG32 2EU. *T:* (01949) 842337; Flat 20, Stack House, Cundy Street, SW1W 9JS. *Clubs:* White's, Pratt's, Turf, Boodle's Ladies.

**OGILVY-WEDDERBURN, Sir Andrew John Alexander**, 7th Bt *cr* 1803, of Balindean, Perthshire (13th Bt *cr* 1704 but for the attainder, 1746); *b* 4 Aug. 1952; *s* of Sir (John) Peter Ogilvy-Wedderburn, 12th and 6th Bt, and late Elizabeth Katharine, *e d* of John A. Cox, Drumkilbo; *S* father, 1977; *m* 1st, 1984, Gillian Meade (marr. diss. 2014), *yr d* of Richard Adderley, Pickering, N Yorks; two *s* (twins) one *d* (and one *s* decd); 2nd, 2014, Fiona Margaret Anne, *d* of William Beaton, Earls Mill, Moray. *Educ:* Gordonstoun. Served Black Watch (RHR), 1970–2003; Comdr 1st Bn, 1993–95, retired as Lt Col. QCVS 1996. *Heir: s* Peter Robert Alexander Ogilvy-Wedderburn, *b* 20 April 1987. *Address:* Silvie House, Alyth, Perthshire PH11 8NA.

**OGLE, Very Rev. Catherine**; Dean of Winchester, since 2017; *b* Upminster, 12 May 1961; *d* of Henry Charles Ogle and Josephine Ogle (*née* Bathard); *m* 1990, Robin Goater; one *s*. *Educ:* Perse Sch. for Girls, Cambridge; Univ. of Leeds (BA 1982; MPhil 1985; MA 1991); Westcott House, Cambridge; Fitzwilliam Coll., Cambridge (BA 1987). Ordained deacon, 1988; Asst Curate, St Mary, Middleton, Leeds, 1988–91; Religious Progs Ed., BBC Radio Leeds, 1991–95; NSM, St Margaret and All Hallows, Leeds, 1991–95; ordained priest, 1994; Priest-in-charge, Woolley with W Bretton, 1995–2001; Vicar of Huddersfield, 2001–10; Chaplain, Univ. of Huddersfield, 2003–06; Dean of Birmingham, 2010–17. Mem. Council, Coll. of the Resurrection, Mirfield, 2008–10. Hon. Canon, Wakefield Cathedral, 2008–10. Hon. DLitt Aston, 2014. *Recreations:* painting, reading, theatre, walking, cooking, fashion, Radio 4. *Address:* Cathedral Office, 9 The Close, Winchester SO23 9LS. *E:* dean@winchester-cathedral.org.uk.

**OGLESBY, Michael John**, CBE 2011; Vice Lord-Lieutenant, Greater Manchester, 2008–14; Chairman, Bruntwood Ltd, since 2000; *b* Scunthorpe, 5 June 1939; *s* of George Oglesby and Alice Oglesby; *m* 1964, Jean Davies McLauchlan (CBE 2016); one *s* one *d*. *Educ:* De Aston Sch., Market Rasen; Aston Univ., Birmingham (BSc Building). Founder, 1978, CEO, 1980–2000, Bruntwood Estates Ltd. Chairman: MIDAS, 2004–; RNCM, 2004–12; Steering Bd, MCRC, 2005–. Chm., Oglesby Charitable Trust, 1993–. Member, Board: Global Leadership Bd, Manchester Univ., 2007–; Paterson Bldg Redevelt Bd, Christie Hosp., 2018–. Feoffee, Chetham's Sch. of Music, 2007–. DL 2005, High Sheriff 2007, Gtr Manchester. Hon. LLD Manchester, 2006; Hon. DSc Aston, 2007. Prince of Wales Medal for Arts Philanthropy, 2011. *Recreations:* sailing, ski-ing, theatre, music. *Address:* Bruntwood Ltd, Lowry House, 17 Marble Street, Manchester M2 3AW.

**OGLEY, William David**; Chief Executive, States of Jersey, 2003–11; *b* 26 May 1955; *s* of Thomas William and Olive Ogley; *m* 1976, Anne Dolores Walker; two *d*. *Educ:* Manchester Univ. (BA Hons Physics and Psych.); CIPFA (prize winner). Derbyshire CC, 1976–83 (to Principal Accountant, 1980–83); Group Accountant, Oxfordshire CC, 1983–85; Hertfordshire County Council: Sen. Asst County Treasurer, 1985–88 (Educn and Social Services); Dep. County Treasurer, 1988–90; Dir, Inf. Systems, 1990–91; Dir of Finance, 1991–93; Dep. Controller and Dir of Resources, Audit Commn, 1993–96; Chief Exec., 1996–2003. *Recreations:* tennis, gardening, sailing, family, reading.

**OGMORE**, 3rd Baron *cr* 1950, of Bridgend; **Morgan Rees-Williams**; *b* 19 Dec. 1937; *s* of 1st Baron Ogmore, PC, TD and (Alice Alexandra) Constance Rees-Williams (*née* Wills); *S* brother, 2004; *m* 1990, Beata Ewa Solska; two *s*. *Educ:* Mill Hill Sch. Lieut, The Welch Regt, 1956–58. *Heir: s* Hon. Tudor David Rees-Williams, *b* 11 Dec. 1991. *Address:* 50 Novello Street, SW6 4JB. *T:* (020) 7736 2734.

**OGNALL, Hon. Sir Harry Henry**, Kt 1986; DL; a Judge of the High Court of Justice, Queen's Bench Division, 1986–2000; *b* 9 Jan. 1934; *s* of Leo and Cecilia Ognall; *m* 1977, Elizabeth Young; two step *s* and two *s* one *d* of former marriage. *Educ:* Leeds Grammar Sch.; Lincoln Coll., Oxford (MA (Hons)); Univ. of Virginia, USA (LLM; Fulbright Scholar, 1956). Called to Bar (Gray's Inn), 1958; Bencher, 1983. Joined NE Circuit; a Recorder, 1972–86; QC 1973. Member: Criminal Injuries Compensation Bd, 1976; Planning Cttee, Senate of Inns of Court and Bar, 1980–83; Professional Conduct Cttee, 1985; Judicial Studies Bd (Chm., Criminal Cttee), 1986–89; Parole Bd, 1989–91 (Vice-Chm., 1990–91; Chm., Life Sentence Rev. Cttee, 1990–91); a Judicial Mem., Proscribed Orgns Appeal Commn, 2001–09. Arbitrator, Motor Insurers' Bureau Agreement, 1979–85. Trustee, Martin House Hospice, 2002–10. DL W Yorks, 2000. *Publications:* A Life of Crime: memoirs of a high court judge, 2017. *Recreations:* photography, bridge, grandchildren. *Club:* Ilkley Bowling.

**O'GORMAN, Michelle Jane**; *see* Corbett, M. J.

**O'GRADY, Frances Lorraine Maria**; General Secretary, Trades Union Congress, since 2012 (Deputy General Secretary, 2003–12); *b* 9 Nov. 1959; *d* of James and Margaret O'Grady; one *s* one *d*. *Educ:* Milham Ford Comprehensive Sch., Oxford; Manchester Univ. (BA Pols and Mod. Hist.); Middlesex Polytechnic (Dip Ind Relns and Trade Union Studies). Employment Rights Officer, Women and Employment Project, 1982–87; Health and Safety Officer, City Centre, London, 1987–88; Campaigns Officer, Health Rights, 1988–89; Sen. Researcher, TGWU, 1989–94; Trades Union Congress: Campaigns Officer, 1994–96; Dir, New Unionism, 1996–98; Hd, Orgn, 1998–2003. Non-exec. Dir, Court, Bank of England, 2019–. Member: Unite (TGWU); NUJ. *Publications:* (with Heather Wakefield) Women, Work and Maternity: the inside story, 1989. *Recreations:* labour history, cinema, Arsenal FC. *Address:* Trades Union Congress, Congress House, Great Russell Street, WC1B 3LS. *T:* (020) 7636 4030. *E:* fogrady@tuc.org.uk.

**O'GRADY, Jeremy Robert**; Founding Editor, since 1995, and Editor in Chief, since 2003, The Week magazine; *b* Wüppertal, Germany, 12 July 1953; *s* of Major Robert Hardress Standish O'Grady, MC and Hon. Joan O'Grady; *m* 2005, Hon. (Juliana) Caroline (Matilda) Law, *d* of Baron Coleraine, *qv*; three *s* one *d*. *Educ:* Ampleforth Coll.; Trinity Coll., Cambridge (BA Social and Pol Scis 1975); Cornell Univ. (MA Govt). Res. Officer, Child Welfare, London Bor. of Redbridge, 1979–82; Researcher, Inst. of Community Studies, 1982–84; Film Censor, BBFC, 1984–94. Res. Fellow, London Business Sch., 1991–93. Co-Founder, Intelligence Squared, 2002–. *Publications:* New Ways of Delivering Local Services, 1985. *Recreations:* arguing, hiking. *Address:* 2 Sterndale Road, W14 0HS. *E:* jeremy_ogrady@theweek.co.uk.

**O'GRADY, Michael Gerard**; QC (Scot.) 1999; Sheriff of Lothian and Borders at Edinburgh, since 2007; Temporary Judge, since 2004; Appeal Court Sheriff, since 2015; *b* 19 Aug. 1954; *s* of Thomas Anthony O'Grady and Margaret Imelda O'Grady (*née* King); *m*. *Educ:* Univ. of Glasgow (MA, LLB). Solicitor in private practice, 1977–88; admitted to Faculty of Advocates, 1988; Advocate Depute, 1993–97; Standing Junior to FCO, 1997–98; Chm., Advocates' Criminal Law Gp, 1999–2000; Floating Sheriff of Glasgow and Strathkelvin, 2000–07. Examiner, Glasgow Graduate Law Sch., 2002–. *Recreations:* guitar, travel, reading, art. *Address:* Sheriff Court House, 27 Chambers Street, Edinburgh EH1 1LB. *Club:* Scottish Arts (Edinburgh).

**O'GRADY, Paul James**, MBE 2008; drag queen, entertainer, television and radio presenter, author and actor; *b* Birkenhead, 14 June 1955; *s* of late Patrick O'Grady and Mary, (Molly), O'Grady; one *d*; *m* 2017, Andre Portasio. *Educ:* Redcourt St Anselm's; Corpus Christi High Sch., Birkenhead. Television series: The Lily Savage Show, 1997; Lily Savage's Blankety Blank, 1998–2002; Lily Live, 2000–01; Paul O'Grady's Orient, 2000; Paul O'Grady's America, 2001; Eyes Down, 2003; The Paul O'Grady Show, 2004–05, 2013–14; The New Paul O'Grady Show, 2006; Paul O'Grady Live, 2010–11; Paul O'Grady's For the Love of Dogs, 2012–18; Paul O'Grady's Working Class, 2013; Paul O'Grady's Animal Orphans, 2014–16; The Paul O'Grady Show, 2015; The Sally Army and Me, 2016; For the Love of Animals, 2017; Blind Date, 2017–; Paul O'Grady's Hollywood, 2017; Paul O'Grady's Little Heroes, 2018; other television includes: Playhouse Presents: Nellie and Melba (co-writer), 2012; Little Crackers: Boo (writer), 2012; radio: presenter, Radio 2, 2009–; theatre: Prisoner Cell Block H – the Musical, 1995; Annie, 1998; Snow White; Aladdin; Child Catcher in Chitty Chitty Bang Bang, 2002; Cinderella, 2015. Hon. Fellow, Liverpool John Moores Univ., 2005. Hon. DArts De Montfort, 2010. *Publications:* At My Mother's Knee… and other low joints, 2008; The Devil Rides Out, 2010; Still Standing: the Savage years, 2012; Open the Cage, Murphy!, 2015; Paul O'Grady's Country Life, 2017. *Recreations:* fire eating, smallholder, conservationist, gay activist.

**OGSTON, Prof. Derek**, CBE 1995; MD, PhD, DSc; FRCP; FRSE 1982; Professor of Medicine, 1983–97, and Vice Principal, 1987–97, University of Aberdeen; *b* 31 May 1932; *s* of Frederick John Ogston and Ellen Mary Ogston; *m* 1963, Cecilia Marie Clark; one *s* two *d*. *Educ:* King's Coll. Sch., Wimbledon; Univ. of Aberdeen (MA, PhD 1962; MD 1969; DSc 1975; MLitt 1999; BTh 2005). FRCP Edin. 1973; FRCP 1977; FRSB (FIBiol 1987). University of Aberdeen: Res. Fellow, 1959–62; Lectr in Medicine, 1962–69; Sen. Lectr in Med., 1969–75; Reader in Med., 1975–76; Regius Prof. of Physiology, 1977–83; Dean, Faculty of Medicine, 1984–87. MRC Trav. Fellow, 1967–68. Vice-Chm., Grampian Health Bd, 1993–97 (Mem., 1991–97); Mem., GMC, 1984–94. Member: Governing Body, Rowett Res. Inst., 1977–92; Court, Univ. of Aberdeen, 1998–2002. Hon. LLD Aberdeen, 2007. *Publications:* Physiology of Hemostasis, 1983; Antifibrinolytic Drugs, 1984; Venous Thrombosis, 1987; The Life and Work of George Smith, RSA, 2000; George Leslie Hunter 1877–1931, 2002; Working Children, 2003; Leslie Hunter: drawings and paintings of France and Italy, 2004; Children at School, 2005; (jtly) King's College, Aberdeen, 2009; (jtly) Stichill Parish: past and present, 2010; (jtly) Trees and Woodlands of Stichill Parish, 2016; (jtly) Butterflies and Moths in the Scottish Borders Parish of Stichill, 2017; (jtly) A History of Music in the University of Aberdeen, 2017; scientific papers on haemostasis. *Recreations:* music, travel, wildlife. *Address:* 64 Rubislaw Den South, Aberdeen AB15 4AY. *T:* (01224) 316587.

**OGUNDEHIN, Michelle Aramide Janet**; writer, editor, television presenter and consultant; *b* Salford, 5 Nov. 1967; *d* of Aderemi and Barbara Ogundehin; *m* 1996, Eamonn Dunne (marr. diss. 1998); one *s* by a former partner. *Educ:* Bartlett Sch. of Architecture, University Coll. London (BSc Hons Architecture 1989; DipArch 1992). Asst Ed., Blueprint, 1995–96; Sen. Ed., Blueprint Mag., 1996; Elle Decoration UK: Features Dir, 1997–98; Dep. Ed., 1998–99; Ed.-at-Large, 1999–2004; Editor-in-Chief: Real Homes, 2007–08; Elle Decoration UK, 2004–17; Elle Decoration Country, 2011–17. Dir, MO:Studio Ltd, 2002–. Trustee, V&A Mus., 2008–15; Dir, V&A Enterprises Bd, 2009–15. Dir, South Coast Design Forum, 2008–13. TV presenter: Grand Designs House of the Year, 2015–; Inside Out Homes, 2016; Interior Design Masters, 2019. FRSA 2009. *Publications:* (with P. Murray) Understanding Plans, 1997; Bringing Architecture Home, 2003; (contrib.) LA Lofts, 2006; Swarovski Crystal Palace, 2010; (contrib.) House of Hoppen: 40 years of Kelly Hoppen, 2016; Happy Inside, 2020. *Recreations:* Basset Hounds, Italy, good design, film, friends, family, food. *W:* www.michelleogundehin.com, www.twitter.com/MOgundehin, www.instagram.com/michelleogundehin.

**OGUNTADE, George Adesola**, CFR 2010; CON 2005; High Commissioner of Nigeria in the United Kingdom, since 2017; *b* Ijebu-Ode, Western Nigeria, 10 March 1940; *s* of S. A. Oguntade; *m* 2002, Modupeola Adewemimo; three *s*. *Educ:* Ijebu-Ode Grammar Sch.; Holborn Coll. of Law, Univ. of London (LLB Hons 1964); Nigerian Law Sch. Called to the Nigerian Bar, 1966; Judge, Lagos State High Court, 1980; Judge, Court of Appeal, Nigeria, 1988–2004; Judge, Supreme Court of Nigeria, 2004–10. Chancellor, Lagos State Univ., 2017–. Chancellor: Ch of Nigeria (Anglican Communion), 1992–99; Anglican Dio. Lagos, 1992–2017. *Recreations:* golf, travelling. *Address:* Nigeria High Commission, 9 Northumberland Avenue, WC2N 5BX. *T:* (020) 7839 2037, *Fax:* (020) 7839 7872. *E:* oguntade@nigeriahc.org.uk. *Clubs:* Rotary, Island (Lagos); Lagos Motor Boat.

**OGUS, Prof. Anthony Ian**, CBE 2002; FBA 2007; Professor of Law, University of Manchester, 1987–2008, now Emeritus; *b* 30 Aug. 1945; *s* of Samuel Joseph Ogus and Sadie Phyllis Ogus (*née* Green); *m* 1st, 1980, Catherine Klein (*d* 1998); 2nd, 2001, Helen Margaret Legard Owens. *Educ:* St Dunstan's Coll.; Magdalen Coll., Oxford (BA 1966; BCL 1967; MA 1970). Asst Lectr in Law, Univ. of Leicester, 1967–69; Tutorial Fellow in Law, Mansfield Coll., Oxford, 1969–75; Sen. Res. Fellow, Centre for Socio-Legal Studies, Wolfson Coll., Oxford, 1975–78; Prof. of Law, Univ. of Newcastle, 1978–87. Res. Prof., Univ. of Maastricht, 1997–2008; Erasmus Prof. of Private Law, Univ. of Rotterdam, 2008–11. Mem., Social Security Adv. Cttee, 1994–2008. Columnist, Opera Now, 2015–. *Publications:* Law of Damages, 1973; (jtly) Law of Social Security, 1978, 5th edn 2002; (jtly) Policing Pollution, 1983; (jtly) Readings in the Economics of Law and Regulation, 1984; Regulation: legal form and economic theory, 1994; (jtly) Controlling the Regulators, 1998; (jtly) Economie du droit: le cas français, 2002; Costs and Cautionary Tales: economic insights for the law, 2006; Travels with my Opera Glasses, 2013; articles in legal periodicals and Opera Now. *Recreations:* theatre, opera, concerts, cycling, reading, internet chess. *Address:* Gowland Court, Ogleforth, York YO1 7JG. *T:* (01904) 801804. *W:* www.anthonyogus.co.uk. *Club:* Oxford and Cambridge.

**O'HAGAN**, 4th Baron *cr* 1870; **Charles Towneley Strachey**; *b* 6 Sept. 1945; *s* of Hon. Thomas Anthony Edward Towneley Strachey (*d* 1955; having assumed by deed poll, 1938, the additional Christian name of Towneley, and his mother's maiden name of Strachey, in lieu of his patronymic) and Lady Mary (who *m* 1981, St John Gore, CBE, FSA; she *d* 2000), *d* of 3rd Earl of Selborne, PC, CH; *S* grandfather, 1961; *m* 1995, Mrs Elizabeth Lesley Eve

Macnamara (née Smith); two d from previous marriages. *Educ:* Eton; (Exhibitioner) New College, Oxford. Page to HM the Queen, 1959–62. Independent Member, European Parliament, 1973–75; Junior Opposition Whip, House of Lords, 1977–79; MEP (C) Devon, 1979–94. *Heir: b* Hon. Richard Towneley Strachey, *b* 29 Dec. 1950. *Address:* The Granary, Beaford, Winkleigh, Devon EX19 8AB.

**O'HAGAN, Dr Dara;** Member (SF) Upper Bann, Northern Ireland Assembly, 1998–2003; *b* 29 Aug. 1964; *d* of Joseph and Bernadette O'Hagan. *Educ:* Univ. of Ulster (BA Hons Hist. and Politics 1991); Queen's Univ., Belfast (MSSc 1994; PhD 1998). Contested (SF) Upper Bann, 2001.

**O'HAGAN, Leonard John Patrick,** CBE 2012; DL; Chairman, Northern Ireland Water, since 2015; *b* Newry, Co. Down, 15 May 1954; *s* of late Leonard O'Hagan and of Ruby O'Hagan; *m* 1981, Maureen Dalzell; one *s* one *d*. *Educ:* St Colman's Coll., Newry; Queen's Univ., Belfast (BSc Econ). Jefferson Smurfit Group: PA to Sir Michael Smurfit, 1985–88; Man. Dir, Print and Distribution Div., 1988–90; Chief Operating Officer, Fitzwilton plc, 1990–99; CEO, Fitzwilton Ltd, 1999–2002. Chairman: Safeway Ireland, 1996–2000; Resource Services Gp, 2011–14; non-executive Director: Waterford Wedgwood UK plc, 1999–2002; Independent News and Media, 2012–. Chm., Belfast Harbour Comrs, 2007–14. CEO, RCPI, 2013–15; Chm., All-island Congenital Heart Disease Network, 2015–. Mem. Council, CBI, 1993–2000; Chm., CBI/IBEC Business Cttee, 1997–2001; Vice Pres., Ireland-US Business Council, 2008–. Chm., Metropolitan Arts Centre, 2010. FInstD 2002. DL Co. Down, 2010. Hon. DSc Ulster, 2011; Hon. DSc Econs QUB, 2013. *Recreations:* sailing, ski-ing, golf, art. *Clubs:* Royal North of Ireland Yacht, Royal St George Yacht.

**O'HANLON, Prof. Michael David Peter,** PhD; Director, Pitt Rivers Museum, Oxford, 1998–2015; Professor, University of Oxford, 2014; Professorial Fellow, Linacre College, Oxford, 1998–2015, now Emeritus; *b* 2 July 1950; *s* of late Michael Charles O'Hanlon and Rosemary Alice O'Hanlon, Kitale, Kenya; *m* 1981, Linda Helga Elizabeth, *d* of (Anthony) Noble Frankland, *qv*; one *d*. *Educ:* Kenya; Plymouth Coll., Devon; Pembroke Coll., Cambridge (MA); University Coll. London (PhD 1985). Field res., Wahgi Valley, PNG Highlands, 1979–81; Curator, Pacific collections, Ethnography Dept, BM, 1983–98. Visitor: Mus. of Hist. of Sci., Oxford Univ., 1998–2015; Oxford Univ. Mus. of Nat. Hist., 2002–15; Mem., Cttee to Visit, Peabody Mus., Harvard, 2003–13; Trustee, Horniman Mus., 2010–14. Mem. Council, 1994–97, Hon. Sec., 1997–98, RAI. Reviews Editor, MAN, 1988–90; Mem., Editl Bd, Jl Material Culture, 1996–2015. *Publications:* Reading the Skin, 1989; Paradise: portraying the New Guinea Highlands, 1993; (ed with E. Hirsch) The Anthropology of Landscape, 1995; (ed with Robert L. Welsch) Hunting the Gatherers: ethnographic collectors, agents and agency in Melanesia 1870s–1930s, 2000; (ed with E. Ewart) Body Arts and Modernity, 2007; The Pitt Rivers Museum: a world within, 2014; contrib. articles and reviews in professional jls.

**O'HARA, Brendan;** MP (SNP) Argyll and Bute, since 2015; *b* Glasgow, 27 April 1963; *m* Catherine; two *d*. *Educ:* St Andrew's Secondary Sch., Carntyne; Univ. of Strathclyde (BA Econ. Hist. and Modern Hist. 1992). Work with Glasgow DC; television producer, STV, Sky Sports, BBC; TV programmes include: Comedy Connections; Movie Connections; The Football Years; Scotland's Greatest Album; Road to Referendum. SNP spokesperson for culture and media, 2017–18. Mem., DCMS Select Cttee, 2017–. Contested (SNP): Glasgow Springburn, 1987; Glasgow Central, 1992. *Address:* House of Commons, SW1A 0AA.

**O'HARA, Joanne Lesley;** Chief Executive and Chief Forester, Scottish Forestry, since 2019; *b* Hendon, 31 Dec. 1966; *d* of William Patrick Michael O'Hara and Lucy Josephine O'Hara; *m* 1999, Dr Andrew Robert Kerr; two *d*. *Educ:* Goffs Comprehensive Sch.; Univ. of Edinburgh (BSc Hons Agric., Forestry and Rural Econ.). MICFor 2015. Dist Forester, Kielder Forest Dist, Forestry Commn, 1991–96; Head: Planning, Forest Enterprise GB, 1996–2002; Corporate and Forest Planning, Forest Enterprise England, 2002–07; Natural Heritage Mgt, Scottish Govt, 2007–13; Dep. Dir, 2013–15, Head, 2015–19, Forestry Commn Scotland; a Forestry Comr, 2015–19. *Recreations:* hill walking, mountain biking, film, theatre, music, food. *Address:* Scottish Forestry, Silvan House, 231 Corstorphine Road, Edinburgh EH12 7AT. *T:* (0131) 370 5232. *E:* jo.ohara@forestry.gov.scot.

**O'HARE, John Edward;** Master of Senior Courts Costs Office (formerly Supreme Court Taxing, later Costs, Office), 1995–2016; Deputy Costs Judge, 2017–19; *b* 26 Feb. 1949; *s* of Kevin Mark Plunkett O'Hare and Kathleen Mary O'Hare; *m* 1st, 1970, Vivien Eleanor Harwood; one *s*; 2nd, 1993, Alison Jane Springett; one *s*. *Educ:* Bromley Boys' GS; Leicester Univ. (LLB). Called to the Bar, Lincoln's Inn, 1972; College of Law: Lectr, 1974–78; Sen. Lectr, 1978–85; Principal Lectr, 1985–95. *Publications:* Civil Litigation, 1980, 19th edn 2019; (ed) White Book Service, 1999–2020. *Recreations:* bridge, cycling.

**O'HARE, Kevin Patrick,** CBE 2018; Director, Royal Ballet, since 2012; *b* Hull, 14 Sept. 1965; *s* of Michael O'Hare and Anne Veronica O'Hare (née O'Callaghan). *Educ:* Royal Ballet Sch. Sadler's Wells Royal Ballet, subseq. Birmingham Royal Ballet: Dancer, 1984–90; Principal Dancer, 1990–2000; Company Manager, 2001–04; Royal Ballet: Company Manager, 2004–09; Admin. Dir, 2009–12. Mem., Bd of Dirs, Northern Ballet, 2015–; Mem. Bd, Dance UK, 2013–. Gov., Royal Ballet Sch., 2000–09, 2012. Major roles as dancer incl. Siegfried, Florimund, Albrecht, Romeo, Amynta in Sylvia; performed in works by Ashton, Balanchine, Cranko, MacMillan, Van Manen, Tharp and Tudor. Hon. DA Hull, 2014. *Address:* Royal Opera House, Covent Garden, WC2E 9DD. *T:* (020) 7212 9685. *E:* kevin.ohare@roh.org.uk. *Club:* Soho House.

**O'HARE, Prof. Peter,** PhD; Professor of Virology, Department of Medicine, Imperial College London, since 2010; *b* 9 Dec. 1956; *s* of Eugene and Sinéad O'Hare; *m* 1983, Jane Hillier; two *d*. *Educ:* St Columb's Coll., Derry; Sheffield Univ. (BSc 1978); NIMR, London (PhD 1981). Res. Fellow, NIMR, London, 1981–83; Damon-Runyon Res. Fellow, Johns Hopkins Univ. Medical Sch., 1983–86; Gp Leader, 1986–2010, Dir, 2002–10, Marie Curie Research Inst. Chm., Scientific Adv. Bd, Pancreatic Cancer UK, 2012–. MAE 2008. *Publications:* numerous articles on molecular and cell biology, virology and field of gene delivery, in learned jls, Nature, Cell etc. *Recreations:* passionate (though untalented) photographer, hiking, canoeing, vociferous supporter of Irish Rugby, history of science. *Address:* Department of Medicine, Imperial College London, St Mary's Campus, Norfolk Place, W2 1PG.

**O'HEAR, Prof. Anthony,** OBE 2018; PhD; Professor of Philosophy (formerly Garfield Weston Professor of Philosophy), University of Buckingham, since 2003 (Head, Department of Education, 2003–09); Director, Royal Institute of Philosophy, 1994–2019; *b* 14 Jan. 1942; *s* of Hugo O'Hear and Ann Margery Hester O'Hear (née Gompertz); *m* 1981, Patricia Catherine Mary Patterson (Patricia Linton, in ballet); one *s* two *d*. *Educ:* St Ignatius Coll., Tottenham; Heythrop Coll.; Warwick Univ. (MA 1968; PhD 1971). Lecturer in Philosophy: Univ. of Hull, 1971–75; Univ. of Surrey, 1975–84; Prof. of Philosophy, Univ. of Bradford, 1985–2003. Vis. Res. Fellow, LSE, 2002–12; Calouste Gulbenkian Vis. Prof., Catholic Univ. of Portugal, 2004–05; Vis. Scholar, Social Philosophy and Policy Center, Bowling Green State Univ., Ohio, 2010. Member: CATE, 1990–94; SCAA, 1993–97; TTA, 1994–97; Teachers' Standards Review Gp, 2011–12; Initial Teacher Trng Framework Gp, 2015–16. Dir, Cuckoo Hall Academies Trust, 2012–; Gov., Heron Hall Free Sch., Edmonton, 2013–. Ed., Philosophy, 1995–2019. Fellow, Royal Inst. of Philosophy, 2018. *Publications:* Karl Popper, 1980; Education, Society and Human Nature, 1981; Experience, Explanation and Faith, 1984; What Philosophy Is, 1985; The Element of Fire, 1988; Introduction to the Philosophy of Science, 1989; Jesus for Beginners, 1993; Beyond Evolution, 1997; After Progress, 1999; Philosophy in the New Century, 2001; Plato's Children, 2006; The Great Books, 2007; The Landscape of Humanity, 2008; (with Mark Sidwell) The School of Freedom, 2009; (with N. O'Hear) Picturing the Apocalypse: the Book of Revelation in the arts over two millennia, 2015 (Art and Christianity Enquiry/Mercers' International Book Award, 2017). *Recreations:* music, visual arts, ski-ing, tennis. *Address:* University of Buckingham, Hunter Street, Buckingham MK18 1EG. *T:* (01280) 820219. *E:* anthony.ohear@buckingham.ac.uk. *Club:* Athenæum.

**O'HIGGINS, Michael;** Chair, Local Pensions Partnership, since 2015; *b* Dublin, 1 Aug. 1954; *s* of William and Bridget Higgins; *m* 2011, Patricia Brown (née Swinfen). *Educ:* Trinity Coll. Dublin (BA Econs 1975); London Sch. of Econs and Pol Sci. (MSc Social Policy 1976). Reader in Social Policy, Univ. of Bath, 1978–87; Principal Adminr, OECD, Paris, 1987–88; Partner, Price Waterhouse Mgt Consultancy, 1989–96; Man. Partner, PA Consulting Gp, 1997–2006; Chair: Audit Commn, 2006–12; Pensions Regulator, 2011–14; NHS Confedn, 2012–15; Jersey Competition Regulatory Authy, 2016–; Guernsey Competition Regulatory Authy, 2016–. Specialist Advr, H of C Select Cttee on Social Services, 1980–88. Chm., Investec Structured Products, Calculus VCT, plc, 2010–19; non-executive Director: HM Treasury, 2008–14 (Chair, Audit Cttee, 2008–14); Oxford Med. Diagnostics, 2010–12; Network Rail, 2012–18 (Chair, Remuneration Cttee, 2013–18). Visiting Fellow: Harvard Univ., 1984–85; ANU, 1986; Visiting Professor: LSE, 1992–98; Univ. of Bath, 2009–12. Chair, Centrepoint, 2004–11. *Publications:* (ed jtly) The Future of Welfare, 1986; (ed jtly) Poverty, Inequality and Income Distribution in Comparative Perspective: the Luxembourg Income Study, 1987; contrib. papers to jls incl. Rev. of Income and Wealth, Jl Social Policy, Public Admin, Political Qly, Policy & Politics, British Tax Rev. *Recreations:* sport, classical jazz music, cooking, wine, travel, modern art. *Address:* Local Pensions Partnership, 2nd Floor, 169 Union Street, SE1 0LL. *E:* chair@localpensionspartnership.org.uk.

**OHLSON, Dawn Elizabeth;** Engineering Director, Thales Avionics UK, since 2017; *b* Farnborough, 10 April 1972; *d* of Gordon Ohlson and Kathleen Ohlson; *m* 2007, Richard Castle; two *d*. *Educ:* Somerville Coll., Oxford (MEng Engrg and Computer Sci. 1994). CEng 1999; FIET 2008. Racal Avionics, then Thales Avionics UK Ltd: Engr, 1994–2000; Product Strategy Mgt and Tech. Directorate roles, 2000–05, incl. secondment to Thales Avionics, Valence; Dir, Educnl Affairs, HQ, Thales UK plc, 2005–09; Res. and Develt Job Family Dir, HQ, Thales Gp, Neuilly-sur-Seine, Paris, 2009–15; UK Dir of Systems, HQ, Thales UK plc, 2015–17. Mem. Bd, Engrg Council, 2007–14. Mem. Bd, STEMNET, 2006–12. Vice Pres., IET, 2019–. Mem., Basketmakers Assoc. First Woman Award for Engrg, 2015; WISE Excellence Award, 2006. *Recreations:* creative arts, weaving with willow and hedgerow materials, walking with family (downgraded from trekking until little legs get longer). *Address:* Thales Avionics UK, Manor Royal, Crawley, W Sussex RH10 9HA. *T:* (01293) 580000. *E:* dawn.ohlson@uk.thalesgroup.com.

**OHLSON, Sir Peter (Michael),** 4th Bt *cr* 1920; *b* Scarborough, 18 May 1939; *s* of Sir Eric James Ohlson, 2nd Bt, and Marjorie Joan, *d* of C. H. Roosmale-Cocq; *S* brother, 2017; *m* 1968, Sarah, *o d* of Maj.-Gen. Thomas Brodie, CB, CBE, DSO; two *d*. *Educ:* Harrow Sch.; Trinity Coll., Cambridge (BA Law 1962; MA). Express Dairy Co., 1974–84: Dir, 1976–84; Man. Dir, Foods Div., 1976–81; Chief Exec., Express Dairy UK, 1981–84; Partner, Tyzack & Partners, 1985–98, Sen. Partner, 1995–98. Hon. Chm., Royal Tennis Court, Hampton Court, 2007–10. *Recreations:* horse racing, Real tennis. *Heir: cousin* Christopher Mark Ohlson [*b* 3 June 1944; *m* 2008, Finna Jane Ayres]. *Address:* 33 The Avenue, Kew, Richmond, Surrey TW9 2AL. *E:* peterohlson@btinternet.com. *Clubs:* Royal Tennis Court, Jesters.

**OISTRAKH, Igor Davidovich;** violinist, violist and conductor; Professor, Royal Conservatoire, Brussels, since 1996; *b* Odessa, 27 April 1931; *s* of late David Oistrakh; *m* 1960, Natalia Nikolaevna Zertsalova, pianist, Hon. Artist of Russia; one *s*. *Educ:* Music Sch. and State Conservatoire, Moscow. FRCM. Many foreign tours (USSR, Europe, the Americas, Japan, Aust.); Prof., Internat. Summer Acad., Belgium, 1997–. Many gramophone recordings. Mem. jury of major violin competitions. Hon. President: César Franck Soc., Liège; Russian Br., Eur. String Teachers Assoc.; Hon. Member: Beethoven Soc., Bonn; Ysaye Foundn, Liège; Wieniawski Soc., Poznan; Heifetz Soc., USA; Mendelssohn and Schumann Foundns, Leipzig. 1st prize: Violin Competition, Budapest, 1949; Wieniawski Competition, Poznan, 1952; Igor Oistrakh internat. violin competition estabd Iserlohn, Germany, 1993. People's Artist of USSR, 1989.

**OJHA, Anupam,** OBE 2014; Director, National Space Academy, since 2008; *b* Crawley, 26 Sept. 1968; *s* of Sushil Ojha and Vidushi Chaudhary; *m* 2013, Dilveer Kaur Brach; one *s*. *Educ:* St Anne's Coll., Oxford (MA Physics 1992); Univ. of East Anglia (PGCE 1995). FRAS 2008. Teacher of Physics, Costessey High Sch., Norwich, 1995–99; Hd of Physics, King Richard Sch., Cyprus, 1999–2001; Hd of Sci., Flegg High Sch., 2001–03; Advanced Skills Teacher, Cardinal Newman Sch., Coventry, 2003–06; Asst Headteacher, Great Barr Sch., 2006–08. Hon. Prof., Dept of Phys and Astronomy, Univ. of Leicester, 2016–. Mem., STFC, 2018–. Member: Human Spaceflight and Exploration Sci. Adv. Cttee, ESA, 2018–; Space Exploration Adv. Cttee, UK Space Agency, 2018–; Global Space Congress Adv. Bd, UAE Space Agency, 2018–. Advanced Skills Teacher status, 2003. Mem., British Parachute Assoc. *Recreations:* skydiving (FAI 'D' licence holder), freediving, scuba diving, triathlon, astronomy. *Address:* National Space Centre, Exploration Drive, Leicester LE4 5NS. *T:* (0116) 258 2133. *E:* anuo@spacecentre.co.uk, ao224@leicester.ac.uk.

**OKA, Prof. Takeshi,** PhD; FRS 1984; FRSC 1977; Professor of Chemistry, Astronomy and Astrophysics, 1981–2003, and Robert A. Millikan Distinguished Service Professor, 1989–2003, University of Chicago, now Emeritus Professor; *b* 10 June 1932; *s* of Shumpei and Chiyoko Oka; *m* 1960, Keiko Nukui; two *s* two *d*. *Educ:* University of Tokyo. BSc, PhD. Fellow, Japanese Soc. for Promotion of Science, 1960–63; National Research Council of Canada: Postdoctorate Fellow, 1963–65; Asst Research Physicist, 1965–68; Associate Research Physicist, 1968–71; Senior Research Physicist, 1971–75; Herzberg Inst. of Astrophysics, 1975–81. Centenary Lectr, Royal Soc., 1982; Chancellor's Distinguished Lectr, Univ. of California, 1985–86. Fellow, Amer. Acad. of Arts and Scis, 1987. Hon. DSc: Waterloo, 2001; UCL, 2004. Steacie Prize, Steacie Fund, NRSC, 1972; Earle K. Plyler Prize, Amer. Physical Soc., 1982; William F. Meggers Award, 1997, Ellis R. Lippincott Award, 1998, Optical Soc. of America; E. Bright Wilson Award in Spectroscopy, ACS, 2002; Davy Medal, Royal Soc., 2004. *Address:* Department of Chemistry, University of Chicago, 5735 S Ellis Avenue, Chicago, IL 60637, USA.

**OKALIK, Paul**; MLA for Iqaluit-Sinaa, Nunavut, 2013–17; Minister of Justice, 2013–16, and Minister of Health and for Immigration, 2014–16, Nunavut, Canada; *b* 26 May 1964; one *s* two *d*. *Educ*: Iqaluit High Sch.; Carleton Univ. (BA); Univ. of Ottawa (LLB 1997). Called to the Bar, 1999. MLA for Iqaluit W, 1999–2011. Nunavut, Canada: Premier and Minister of Exec. and Intergovtl Affairs, 1999–2008; Minister of Justice, 2000–08; Speaker, 2010–11; Minister of Culture and Heritage, 2013–14; of Languages, 2013–14.

**O'KANE, Michael Colin**; Senior Partner, Peters & Peters Solicitors LLP, since 2016; *b* London, 4 May 1969; *s* of Michael and Kathleen O'Kane; *m* 1998, Emma Margaret Collins Lowry; one *s* one *d*. *Educ*: St Columb's Coll., Derry; Manchester Metropolitan Univ. (LLB Hons 1992); Inns of Court Sch. of Law (BVC 1993). Senior Crown Prosecutor: CPS, 1994–99; CPS HQ, 1999–2002; Partner, 2004–, Hd, Business Crime, 2009–16, Peters & Peters Solicitors. *Publications*: The Law of Criminal Cartels, 2009; (contrib.) Research Handbook on Institutional Competition Law, 2012; contribs to Jl American Foreign Antitrust and Trade Regulation. *Recreations*: following Liverpool and Fulham football clubs, fossicking in Donegal. *Address*: Peters & Peters Solicitors LLP, 15 Fetter Lane, EC4A 1BW. *T*: (020) 7822 7777. *E*: mokane@petersandpeters.com. *Club*: Garrick.

**OKASHA, Prof. Samir**, DPhil; FBA 2018; Professor of Philosophy of Science, University of Bristol, since 2003; *b* Norwich, 9 Oct. 1971; *s* of Ahmed Yousri Kamel Okasha and Elizabeth Okasha; *m* 2007, Havi Carel; two *s*. *Educ*: St Anne's Coll., New Coll. and Balliol Coll., Oxford (BA Philos. and Econs 1992; MA; BPhil Philos. 1995; DPhil Philos. 1998). Jacobsen Res. Fellow, LSE, 1998–2000; Lectr in Philosophy, Univ. of York, 2000–03. *Publications*: Philosophy of Science: a very short introduction, 2002, 2nd edn 2015; Evolution and the Levels of Selection, 2006; Agents and Goals in Evolution, 2018. *Recreations*: cycling, cooking, reading, travelling. *Address*: Department of Philosophy, University of Bristol, Cotham House, Bristol BS6 6JL. *T*: (0117) 331 0697. *E*: samir.okasha@bristol.ac.uk.

**O'KELLY, Helen W.**; see Watanabe-O'Kelly.

**OKEOVER, Sir Andrew Peter Monro W.**; see Walker-Okeover.

**OKINE, Most Rev. Robert Garshong Allotey**; Archbishop of West Africa, 1993–2003; Bishop of Koforidua-Ho, Ghana, 1981–2003; *b* 12 July 1937; *s* of late Robert Cudjoe Okine and Miriam Naadjah Decker; *m* 1967, Juliana Sakai (*née* Nerquaye-Tetteh); two *s* two *d*. *Educ*: Anglican Church schs, Gold Coast and Gambia; Methodist Boys' High Sch., Bathurst, The Gambia; Adisadel Coll., Cape Coast, Ghana; Theol Coll., SSM, Kelham (GOE 1964); Inst. of Pastoral Educn, London, Ont. (CertCPE 1972); Huron Coll., Univ. of W Ontario, Canada (BMin 1973); Vanderbilt Univ., Nashville, USA (MA 1975); George Peabody Coll. for Teachers, Nashville, USA (EdS 1975); Haggai Inst. for Advanced Leadership Trng, Singapore (Cert. Completion 1990). Ordained deacon 1964, priest 1965; Asst Curate, St Andrew's, Sekondi, 1964–66; Chaplain and teacher, Adisadel Coll., Cape Coast, 1966–68; Rector: St James, Agona-Swedru, 1968–69; Bishop Aglionby Meml Parish, Tamale, 1969–71; Assistant Priest: St Anne's, Byron, and St George's, London, Ont., Canada, 1971–73; Holy Trinity Episcopal Church, Nashville, USA, 1973–75; Christ Church Parish, Cape Coast, 1975–81; Headmaster, Acad. of Christ the King, 1976–81; Principal, St Nicholas Theol Coll., 1976–81; Archdeacon of Koforidua and Rector, St Peter's, Koforidua, Feb.–Oct. 1981. Hon. Canon, Cathedral Church of Most Holy Trinity, Accra, 1979–81. Chairman: Provincial Liturgical Commn, 1984–2003; Bd of Educn, Anglican Educn Unit, 1991–2003; Human Resources Develt Desk, Jt Anglican Diocesan Council, 1991–2003; Council, Anglican Provinces of Africa, 1999–2003; Mem., Anglican Peace and Justice Network, Global Anglican Consultative Council, 1996–2002. Founder, Kwabeng Anglican Secondary Technical Sch., 1983; Gov., Adisadel Coll., 1987–97. Patron, YMCA (Eastern), 1984–2003. DD *jure dignitatis* W Ontario, 1982. Lanfranc Award for Education and Scholarship, Abp of Canterbury, 2018. Order of the Volta (Ghana), 2008. *Recreations*: entertaining, watching good movies, listening to all brands of music. *Address*: 10 Lizam Road (off ECOMOG), Haatso, Accra, Ghana.

**OKKENHAUG, Prof. Klaus**, PhD; Professor of Immunology, University of Cambridge, since 2017; *b* Montreal, 19 March 1970; *s* of Ragnvald Okkenhaug and Lee Haviland; *m* 2000, Hanneke de Ridder; two *s*. *Educ*: Univ. of Victoria, BC (BSc 1993); Univ. of Toronto (PhD 1999). Postdoctoral Fellow, Ludwig Inst. for Cancer Res., UCL, 1999–2002; Gp Leader, Babraham Inst., 2003–17. *Recreations*: running, ski-ing, pining for the fjords. *Address*: Department of Pathology, University of Cambridge, Tennis Court Road, Cambridge CB2 1QP. *E*: ko256@cam.ac.uk.

**OKOGIE, His Eminence Cardinal Anthony Olubunmi**, CON 1999; DD; Archbishop of Lagos, (RC), 1973–2012, now Archbishop Emeritus; *b* Lagos, 16 June 1936. *Educ*: St Gregory's Coll., Lagos; St Theresa's Minor Seminary, Ibadan; St Peter and St Paul's Seminary, Ibadan; Urban Univ., Rome. Priest, 1966; appointments include: Acting Parish Priest, St Patrick's Church, Idumagbo, 1967–71; Asst Priest, and Master of Ceremonies, Holy Cross Cathedral, Lagos, 1967–71; Religious Instructor, King's Coll., Lagos, 1967–71; Director of Vocations, Archdiocese of Lagos, 1968–71; Manager, Holy Cross Group of Schools, Lagos, 1969–71; Auxiliary Bishop of Oyo, 1971–72; Auxiliary Bishop to Apostolic Administrator, Archdiocese of Lagos, 1972–73. Cardinal, 2003. Vice-Pres., 1983–88, Pres., 1988–94, Catholic Bishops Conf. of Nigeria; Roman Catholic Trustee of Christian Assoc. of Nigeria, 1974–; Member: State Community Relns Cttee, 1984–; Prerogative of Mercy, 1986–; Adv. Council on Religious Affairs, 1987–; Pontifical Council for Social Communications, 2003–; Congregation for the Evangelization of Peoples, 2003–; Council of Cardinals for Study of Organizational and Econ. Questions of Holy See, 2006–14. Special Envoy of HH Pope Benedict XVI, Nat. Eucharistic Congress, Ghana, 2005. Chm., Christian Assoc. of Nigeria, 1989–97. *Address*: c/o 19 Catholic Mission Street, PO Box 8, Lagos, Nigeria.

**OKORO, Sandie**; Senior Vice President and Group General Counsel, World Bank, since 2017; *b* London, 16 Oct. 1964; *d* of Sunday and Pamela Okoro; one *s* one *d*. *Educ*: Putney High Sch.; Univ. of Birmingham (LLB); Inns of Court Sch. of Law. Called to the Bar, Lincoln's Inn, 1987; in practice as barrister, 1987–91; admitted as solicitor, 1991; joined Coopers & Lybrand, 1987, trainee solicitor, 1989–91, Hd of Legal for Corporate Services, 1991–2007; Gen. Counsel, Baring Asset Mgt, 2007–14; Global Gen. Counsel, HSBC Asset Mgt, 2014–17. Mem. Council, Justice, 2013–17. Gov. and non-exec. Dir, RSC, 2015–. Dir, Powerlist Foundn, 2008–14; Dir and Mem., Panel of Experts, P.R.I.M.E. Finance Foundn, 2011–17. Pres., Internat. Lawyers for Africa, 2008–14. Trustee, Laworks, 2009–12. MInstD 2008. Freedom, City of London, 2018. Hon. Bencher, Middle Temple, 2017. Hon. LLD City, 2014. *Recreations*: theatre, ballet, film, literature, cooking, travel. *Address*: World Bank, 1818 H Street NW, Washington, DC 20433, USA.

**OKRI, Ben**, OBE 2001; FRSL; novelist and poet; *b* 15 March 1959; *s* of Silver and Grace Okri. *Educ*: Univ. of Essex. Poetry Editor, West Africa, 1983–86; broadcaster and presenter, BBC, 1983–85; Fellow Commoner in Creative Arts, Trinity Coll., Cambridge, 1991–93. Vis. Prof., Sch. of English, Univ. of Leicester, 2012–14. Mem. Bd, RNT, 1999–2006. Play (adapted), The Outsider, Print Room, 2018. Member: Soc. of Authors, 1986–; Council, RSL, 1999–2004. FRSL 1998; FRSA 2003. Hon. DLitt: Westminster, 1997; Essex, 2002; Exeter, 2004; London, 2010; Hon. Dr of Utopia, Univ. voor het Algemeen Belang, Belgium, 2009; Hon. DArts Bedfordshire, 2010. Crystal Award, World Econ. Forum, Switzerland, 1995; Grinzane Prize for Africa, 2008; Internat. Literary Award of Novi Sad, 2008. *Publications*: Flowers and Shadows, 1980; The Landscapes Within, 1982; Incidents at the Shrine, 1986 (Commonwealth Prize for Africa, 1987; Paris Review Aga Khan Prize for fiction, 1987); Stars of the New Curfew, 1988; The Famished Road, 1991 (Booker Prize, 1991; Premio Letterario Internazionale Chianti-Ruffino-Antico Fattore, 1993; Premio Grinzane Cavour, 1994); An African Elegy, 1992; Songs of Enchantment, 1993; Astonishing the Gods, 1995; Birds of Heaven, 1995; Dangerous Love, 1996 (Premio Palmi, 2000); A Way of Being Free, 1997; Infinite Riches, 1998; Mental Fight, 1999; In Arcadia, 2002; Starbook, 2007; Tales of Freedom, 2009; A Time for New Dreams, 2011, Wild, 2012; The Age of Magic, 2014; The Magic Lamp: dreams of our age, 2017; (ed) Rise Like Lions: poetry for the many, 2018; The Freedom Artist, 2019. *Recreations*: music, chess, theatre, art, good conversation, walking, silence. *Address*: c/o The Marsh Agency Ltd, 50 Albemarle Street, W1S 4BD. *Club*: PEN International (Vice-Pres., English Centre, 1997).

**OLAZÁBAL, José María**; golfer; *b* Fuenterrabia, Spain, 5 Feb. 1966; *s* of Gaspar and Julia Olazábal. Professional golfer, 1985–; wins include: European Masters, 1986; Benson and Hedges Internat. Open, 1990, 2000; NE+-C World Series, 1990, 1994; The Internat. (USA), 1991; Grand Prix of Europe, 1991; Mediterranean Open, 1992, 1994; Volvo PGA Championship, 1994; US Masters, 1994, 1999; Dubai Desert Classic, 1998; French Open, 2001; Buick Invitational, 2002; Member: European Ryder Cup Team, 1987, 1989, 1991, 1993, 1997, 1999, 2006, 2008 (Vice-Captain), 2012 (Captain), 2014 (Vice-Captain); Spanish Team, Alfred Dunhill Cup, 1999, 2000; Continental Europe Team, Seve Trophy, 2013 (Captain); European Team, Royal Trophy, 2013 (Captain). *Address*: c/o 112 PGA Tour Boulevard, Ponte Vedra Beach, FL 32082, USA.

**OLCAYTO, Rory Erol**; Chief Executive, Open City and Open House London, since 2016; *b* Taplow, 11 May 1972; *s* of Ender Olcayto and Joan Olcayto (*née* St John); one *d*. *Educ*: Colgrain Primary Sch., Helensburgh; Hermitage Acad., Helensburgh; Univ. of Strathclyde (BSc Hons Architectural Studies; MSc Computer Aided Building Design). Architectural asst, HD, Mimarlik, Istanbul, 1991; Dir, Strathclyde Winterschool 1994, 1993–94; architectural assistant: Quaternaire, Liege, 1994; Hamilton DC, 1994–95; lead artist, Inner Workings (videogames), 1997–99; 1st year studio leader, Dept of Arch. and Building Sci., Univ. of Strathclyde, 2000–02; architectural asst, Gordon Murray + Alan Dunlop Architects, 2001–03; Asst Ed., Project Scotland, 2003–06; Dep. Ed., Construction Manager, 2006–07; Sen. Reporter, Building Design, 2007–08; Architects' Journal: Features Ed., 2008–09; Dep. Ed., 2010–14; Actg Ed., 2014–15; Ed., 2015–16. FRSA. *Publications*: The Architecture of Rogers Stirk Harbour + Partners: British Museum World Conservation and Exhibitions Centre, 2014; (ed) Sinan: the first starchitect, 2016. *Recreations*: towns and cities on foot, forests and coastlines on bike, meze at home with family and friends, sketching and drawing with thick black pens; and these things: cinema, theatre, galleries, bookshops, swimming, tennis, late night telly, art, technology, history, magic, pop, politics, satire, lists. *Address*: College Place, London. *E*: rolcayto@yahoo.co.uk.

**OLDENBURG, Claes Thure**; artist; *b* Stockholm, 28 Jan. 1929; *s* of Gösta Oldenburg and Sigrid Elisabeth (*née* Lindfors); *m* 1st, 1960, Pat Muschinski (marr. diss. 1970); 2nd, 1977, Coosje van Bruggen (*d* 2009). *Educ*: Yale Univ. (BA 1951); Art Inst. Chicago. Apprentice reporter, City News Bureau, Chicago, 1950–52; became American citizen, 1953. First gp exhibn at Club St Elmo, Chicago, 1953; subseq. at local shows, Chicago and Evanston, 1953–56; moved to NY, 1956; has participated in numerous gp exhibns of contemp. art in USA and Europe, including: Dallas Mus. Contemp. Art, 1961, 1962; ICA, 1963; Mus. Mod. Art, NY, 1963, 1988, 1990, 1991; Washington Gall. Mod. Art, 1963; Tate Gall., 1964; Metropolitan Mus. Art, NY, 1969; Whitney Mus. of American Art, NY, 2010, 2012; Mus. of Fine Arts, Boston, Kettles Yard, Cambridge, 2010; Gagosian Gall., London, 2010, 2011; Pace Gall., NY, 2011, 2012, 2014, 2017; Gagosian Gall., Paris, 2012; Nat. Art Centre, Tokyo, Hauser & Wirth, London, Barbican Art Gall., London, 2013; Pace London, 2014; one-man shows in USA and Europe, including: Reuben Gall., NY, 1960; Sidney Janis Gall., NY, 1964–70; Art Inst. of Chicago, 1971; Margo Leavin Gall., LA, 1975, 1976, 1978, 1998; Guggenheim Mus., NY, 1995; Paula Cooper Gall., NY, 2002; Zwirner & Wirth, NY, 2005; Honor Fraser, LA, 2006; Craig F. Starr Gall., NY, 2008; Mus. Moderne, Vienna, Neue Nationalgalerie, Berlin, Guggenheim Mus., Bilbao, 2012; Walker Art Center, Minneapolis, 2013; travelling exhibitions: Tate Gall. and other European galls, 1970; Musée d'Art Moderne, Paris, 1977; Nat. Gall. of Art, Washington, 1995; Solomon R. Guggenheim Mus., NY, and galls in London, LA and Bonn, 1995–96; numerous commnd works in permanent collections in USA and Europe, incl. Centre Georges Pompidou, Paris, Museums of Contemp. Art, Chicago and LA, Tate Gall.; numerous outdoor works in corporate and private collections. Member: AAIL, 1975; Amer. Acad. Arts and Scis, 1978. Awards include: Brandeis Award for Sculpture, 1971; Medal, Amer. Inst. Architects, 1977; Wilhelm-Lehmbruck Sculpture Award, Duisburg, 1981; Wolf Foundn Prize, Israel, 1989; Lifetime Achievement Award, Internat. Sculpture Centre, 1994. *Publications*: Spicy Ray Gun, 1960; Ray Gun Poems, 1960; More Ray Gun Poems, 1960, 2nd edn 1973; Injun and Other Histories, 1960; Store Days, 1967; Notes, 1968; Constructions, Models and Drawings, 1969; Notes in Hand, 1971; Raw Notes, 1973; Log, May 1974–August 1976, 1976; (jtly) Il Corso del Coltello: Menu, 1985 (trans. Italian 1985); (jtly) Sketches and Blottings toward the European Desktop, 1990 (trans. Italian 1990); Multiples in Retrospect, 1991; (with Coosje van Bruggen) Large-Scale Projects, 1994; exhibn catalogues; contribs to books and jls. *Address*: c/o Pace Gallery, 32 E 57th Street, New York, NY 10022–2513, USA.

*See also* R. E. Oldenburg.

**OLDENBURG, Richard Erik**; Consultant, Sotheby's North and South America, since 2006 (Chairman, 1995–2000; Hon. Chairman, 2000–06); *b* 21 Sept. 1933; *s* of Gösta Oldenburg and Sigrid Elisabeth (*née* Lindforss); *m* 1st, 1960, Harriet Lisa Turnure (*d* 1998); 2nd, 2003, Mary Ellen Meehan. *Educ*: Harvard Coll. (AB 1954). Manager, Design Dept, Doubleday & Co., NYC, 1958–61; Man. Editor, Trade Div., Macmillan Co., NYC, 1961–69; Dir, Publications, 1969–72, Dir, 1972–94, Museum of Modern Art, NYC. *Address*: c/o Sotheby's, 1334 York Avenue, New York, NY 10021, USA.

*See also* C. T. Oldenburg.

**OLDFATHER, Irene**; Director, Health and Social Care Alliance Scotland, since 2012; *b* 6 Aug. 1954; *d* of Campbell and Margaret Hamilton; *m* 1978, Rodrick Oldfather; one *s* one *d*. *Educ*: Univ. of Strathclyde (BA Hons Politics 1976; MSc Res. 1983). Lectr in US Politics, Univ. of Arizona, 1978–79; Policy Planner, Glasgow CC, 1980–90; Political Researcher, MEP, 1990–97; freelance journalist, European affairs, 1994–98; part-time Lectr, Paisley Univ., 1996–98. Lead Consultant, Dementia, Big Lottery Life Changes Trust, 2011–12. MSP (Lab) Cunninghame S, 1999–2011. Scottish Parliament: Convenor: Cross Party Gp on Tobacco Control; Cross Party Gp on Alzheimer's and Dementia, 2007–11 (produced Charter of Rights for People with Dementia and Main Carers, 2009); Member: Eur. Cttee, 1999–2011 (Convenor, 2001–03, 2007–11; Vice-Convenor, 2003–07); Health and Community Care Cttee, 1999–2001. Contested (Lab) Cunninghame S, Scottish Parlt, 2011. Member: European Cttee of Regions, 1997–2011 (Vice Pres., Socialist Gp, 2001–11); European Econ. and Social Cttee, 2016–. Member, Board: Scottish Health

Council, 2015–; Scottish Ambulance Service, 2018–. Mem. (Lab) N Ayrshire Council, 2012–17. *Publications:* Path to Active Ageing, 2012; In Good Faith, 2013; Digital Health and Technology: giving you choice and control, 2014; res. paper for Scotland Europa; articles on Brexit in The Times and Scotsman. *Recreations:* going to ballet, reading, children, pets, travel (especially to Catalonia). *E:* iro_07@hotmail.com.

**OLDFIELD, (Anne) Belinda,** FICE; General Manager, Revenue and Risk, Scottish Water, since 2014; *b* Ballymena, 5 June 1963; *d* of David and Mattie Gillen; *m* 1993, Andrew John Oldfield; two *s*. *Educ:* Ulster Univ. (HND Civil Engrg 1983); Abertay Univ. (BEng Hons Civil Engrg 1988); Open Univ. (MBA 1997). FICE 2015. Civil/Structural Engineer: Montgomery Smith & Partners, 1987–90; Building Design Partnership, 1990–93; Civil Engr, Water and Drainage Dept, Central Regl Council, 1993–98; East of Scotland Water: Capital Investment Manager, 1998–2000; Hd, Econ. and Quality Regulation, 2000–02; Strategic Planning Lead, Scottish Water Merger Team, 2001–02; Gen. Manager Regulation, Scottish Water, 2002–14. Non-exec. Dir, Highlands and Islands Enterprise, 2016–. Pres., Scottish Area, Inst. of Water, 2016–17. Panel Mem., Saltire Awards, 2017–. *Recreations:* family, cinema, ski-ing, reading, walking. *Address:* Scottish Water, Castle House, 6 Castle Drive, Carnegie Campus, Dunfermline KY11 8GG. *T:* (01383) 848430, 07875 879262. *E:* belinda.oldfield@scottishwater.co.uk. *Club:* Scottish Ski.

**OLDFIELD, Bruce,** OBE 1990; designer; *b* 14 July 1950; parents unknown; brought up by Dr Barnardo's, Ripon, Yorks. *Educ:* Ripon Grammar School; Sheffield City Polytechnic (Hon. Fellow 1987); Ravensbourne College of Art; St Martin's College of Art. Established fashion house, 1975; produced designer collections of high fashion clothes for UK and overseas; began exporting clothes worldwide, 1975; began making couture clothes for individual clients, 1981; opened first Bruce Oldfield retail shop, selling ready to wear and couture to international clientèle, 1984; opened addnl premises focusing on weddings, 2009; launched signature fragrance, 2011. Exhibitor: British Design Exhibn, Vienna, 1986; Australian Bicentennial Fashion Show, Sydney Opera House, 1988. Lectures: Fashion Inst., NY, 1977; Los Angeles County Museum, 1983; Internat. Design Conf., Aspen, Colorado, 1986 (Speaker and show). Vice Pres., Barnardo's. Trustee, Royal Acad., 2000–02. Gov., London Inst., 2000–02. Hon. Fellow RCA, 1990. Hon. DCL Northumbria at Newcastle, 2001; DUniv UCE, 2005; Hon. DLitt Hull, 2009. Designed for films: Jackpot, 1974; The Sentinel, 1976. *Publications:* (with Georgina Howell) Bruce Oldfield's Season, 1987; Bruce Oldfield: Rootless: an autobiography, 2004. *Recreations:* music, reading, driving, working. *Address:* 27 Beauchamp Place, SW3 1NJ. *T:* (020) 7584 1363. *E:* hq@bruceoldfield.com. *W:* www.bruceoldfield.com.

**OLDFIELD, Michael Gordon, (Mike);** musician and composer; *b* 15 May 1953; *s* of Dr Raymond Henry Oldfield and Maureen Bernadine Liston; four *s* two *d* (and one *s* decd). *Educ:* St Edward's, Reading; Presentation Coll., Reading. Records include: Tubular Bells, 1973 (over 16 million copies sold to date); Hergest Ridge; Ommadawn; Incantations; Platinum; QE2, 1980; Five Miles Out, 1982; Crises, 1983; Discovery, 1984; The Killing Fields (film sound track), 1984; Islands, 1987; The Wind Chimes (video album), 1988; Earthmoving, 1989; Amarok, 1990; Heaven's Open, 1991; Tubular Bells II, 1992; The Songs of Distant Earth, 1994; Voyager, 1996; Tubular Bells III, 1998; Music of the Spheres, 2008; Man on the Rocks, 2014; Return to Ommadawn, 2017. Extensive world wide concert tours, 1979–. Mem., Assoc. of Professional Composers. Freeman, City of London, 1982. Hon. Pict. *Publications:* Changeling (autobiog.), 2007. *Recreations:* helicopter pilot, squash, ski-ing, cricket. *Club:* Jacobs Larder (Ealing).

**OLDFIELD, Richard John,** OBE 2018; Chairman, Oldfield Partners LLP, since 2005; Vice Lord-Lieutenant of Kent, since 2011; *b* London, 11 Oct. 1955; *s* of Christopher Charles Bayley Oldfield and Bridget Ruth Pearl Oldfield (*née* Craigie); *m* 1st, 1982, Hon. Alexandra Frances Margaret (*d* 1995), *d* of 2nd Viscount Davidson; two *s* one *d*; 2nd, 1997, Amicia de Moubray; one *s*. *Educ:* Eton Coll.; New Coll., Oxford (BA Modern Hist.). With S. G. Warburg, then Mercury Asset Mgt, 1977–96, Dir, 1990–96; Chief Exec., Alta Advisers, 1997–2005. Non-executive Director: Keystone Investment Trust, 2001–10 (Chm., 2002–10); Witan Investment Trust plc, 2011–; Shepherd Neame Ltd, 2016– (Chm., Oct. 2020–). Chm., Oxford Univ. Endowment Mgt Ltd, 2007–14. Wykeham Fellow, New Coll., Oxford, 2015. Pres., Demelza Hospice Care for Children, 2005– (Chm., 2000–02; Trustee, 2000–05); Trustee: Leeds Castle Foundn, 2001–11; Canterbury Cathedral Trust, 2009–; Royal Marsden Cancer Charity, 2011–; Clore Duffield Foundn, 2013–; Amber Foundn, 2016–; Prince's Trust, 2018–. Seneschal, Canterbury Cathedral, 2014–. High Sheriff, 2008–09, DL, 2011, Kent. Hon. Dr Kent, 2018. *Publications:* Simple But Not Easy, 2007. *Address:* Doddington Place, Sittingbourne, Kent ME9 0BB. *E:* rjo@oldfieldpartners.com. *Clubs:* White's, Beefsteak.

**OLDHAM, Gavin David Redvers,** OBE 2018; Founder, and Chairman, since 2014, Share plc (formerly The Share Centre (Holdings) Ltd) (Chief Executive, 1994–2013); Founder and Chairman, The Share Centre, since 1990 (Chief Executive, 1990–2013); *b* London, 5 May 1949; *s* of David George Redvers Oldham and Penelope Barbara Oldham (*née* Royle); *m* 1975, Virginia Russell; four *d*. *Educ:* Eton Coll.; Trinity Coll., Cambridge (BA 1971). FCSI. CSE Aircraft Services Ltd, 1971–76; Wedd Durlacher Mordaunt, later Barclays de Zoete Wedd, 1976–86: Partner, 1984–86; Secretariat, 1984–86; Founder and Chief Exec., 1986–89, Chm., 1989–90, Barclayshare. Lay Mem., Oxford Dio., Gen. Synod, 1995–; Church Comr, 1998–2013 and 2015–18 (Dep. Chm., Assets Cttee, 2013); Dioceses Commn, 2019–. Trustee, Personal Finance Educn Gp, 2003–14; Founder and Chm., Share Foundn, 2005–; Founder and Man. Dir, Share Radio, 2014–. MInstD 1988. *Recreations:* sailing, family tree, philosophical/theological discussion. *Address:* c/o Share plc, Oxford House, Oxford Road, Aylesbury, Bucks HP21 8SZ. *T:* (01296) 439100, *Fax:* (01296) 414410. *E:* gdro@btconnect.com, gavin.oldham@share.co.uk, gavin.oldham@shareradio.co.uk, gavin.oldham@sharefound.org. *Clubs:* Leander, Royal Motor Yacht.

**OLDHAM, Sir John,** Kt 2003; OBE 2001; FRCGP; Chairman, Independent Commission on Whole Person Care, 2013–15; Adjunct Professor, Global Health Innovation, Imperial College London, since 2014; *b* 17 Aug. 1953; *s* of Kenneth and Marian Oldham; *m* 1987, Julia Robinson. *Educ:* Manchester Univ. (MB ChB 1977); Manchester Business Sch. (MBA Dist. 1992); DCH London 1980. FRCGP 2002. House Officer, Manchester Royal Infirmary, 1978–79; SHO, Royal Manchester Children's Hosp., 1979–80; GP trainee, Darbishire House, Manchester, 1980–81; SHO, St Mary's Hosp., Manchester, 1981–84; Principal GP, Manor Hse Surgery, Glossop, 1984– (Sen. Partner, 1987–2010). Exec. Chm., Quest4Quality Ltd, 2007–10. Hd, Nat. Primary Care Develt Team, 2000–06; Founder and Chm., Improvement Foundn, 2006–07; Advisor (part-time): Mersey RHA, 1989–91; Primary Care Div., DoH, 1996–99; Med. Advr (pt-time), Derbys FHSA and N Derbys HA, 1990–96. Non-exec. Bd Mem., School Food Trust, 2005–09; non-exec. Dir, Internat. Soc. for Quality and Accreditation, 2008–12 (Treas., 2010–12); Mem., Nat. Quality Bd, NHS, 2009–14; Nat. Clinical Lead for Quality and Productivity, DoH, 2010–13; Mem. Bd, Care Quality Commn, 2018–. *Publications:* Sic Evenit Ratio Ut Componitur: the small book about large system change, 2004; contribs to BMJ. *Recreations:* hiking, cooking, blues music. *Address:* 2 Crofton Avenue, Chiswick, W4 3EW. *E:* john.oldham@quest4quality.co.uk.

**OLDHAM, Peter Robert;** QC 2010; *b* London, 2 April 1963; *s* of Alexander and Gillian Oldham; *m* 1990, Jane; one *s* one *d*. *Educ:* Corpus Christi Coll., Cambridge (BA Hist. 1984). Called to the Bar, Gray's Inn, 1990.

**OLDLAND, Andrew Richard;** QC 2011; a Recorder, since 2004; Senior Partner, Michelmores LLP, since 2017 (Partner, since 2011); *b* Newbury, 11 May 1965; *s* of Michael and Alison Oldland; *m* 1997, Gretchen Holtz; one *s* two *d*. *Educ:* Bradfield Coll.; London Sch. of Econs and Pol Sci. (BSc Econ); City Univ. (DipLaw). Called to the Bar, Inner Temple, 1990, in practice as barrister, specialising in regulatory offences and financial crime; Standing Counsel, HMRC, 2008–11; A List Counsel, Serious Fraud Office, 2009–11. *Recreations:* sailing, walking, pole-vaulting. *E:* andrew.oldland@michelmores.com.

**OLDMAN, Dr Crystal Elizabeth,** CBE 2017; Chief Executive, Queen's Nursing Institute, since 2012; *b* Tunbridge Wells, 29 March 1959; foster *d* of John Skae and Gwyn Skae; *m* 1986, Gary Oldman, OBE; two *s*. *Educ:* Weald of Kent Sch. for Girls; Brunel Univ.; Buckinghamshire New Univ. (MA); Univ. of Surrey (MSc; PGCE); Oxford Brookes Univ. (PGDip); Open Univ. (EdD). RN 1980; RHV 1983; RNT 1998. RN, 1977–80; Staff Nurse, UCH, 1980–82; Health Visitor, W London, 1983–94; Buckinghamshire College of Higher Education, then Buckinghamshire Chiltern University College, later Buckinghamshire New University: Sen. Lectr, 1994–99; Principal Lectr, 1999–2001; Hd, Dept of Community, Mental Health and Learning Disability Nursing, 2001–03; Hd, Sch. of Social Work, Psychol., Community and Educn, 2003–08; Associate Dean, 2008–09; Dean, 2009–12. Hon. Prof., London South Bank Univ., 2018–. Chair, UCH London Nurses' Charity, 2013–18. Winston Churchill Fellow, 2017. *Recreations:* family, theatre, cinema, garden, history of nursing and public health. *Address:* Queen's Nursing Institute, 1A Henrietta Place, W1G 0LZ. *T:* (020) 7549 1400.

**OLDMAN, Gary;** actor; *b* 21 March 1958; *m* 1st, 1988, Lesley Manville, *qv* (marr. diss. 1990); one *s*; 2nd, 1991, Uma Thurman (marr. diss. 1993); 3rd, Donya Fiorentino (marr. diss. 2001); two *s*; 4th, 2008, Alexandra Edenborough (marr. diss. 2015); 5th, 2017, Gisele Schmidt. *Educ:* South East London Sch. for Boys; Rose Bruford Coll. of Speech and Drama (BA Theatre Arts 1979). *Theatre* includes: Greenwich Young People's Theatre; Theatre Royal, York; Glasgow Citizens' Theatre: Massacre at Paris, A Waste of Time, Desperado Corner, Chinchilla, 1980 (toured Europe and S America); Royal Court Theatre: Rat in the Skull, 1984; The Pope's Wedding, 1984; Women Beware Women, 1986; Serious Money, 1987; Royal Shakespeare Company: The Desert Air, 1985; The War Plays, 1985; Real Dreams, 1986; The Country Wife, Royal Exchange, Manchester, 1986; Entertaining Mr Sloane, Oldham Rep. Co., 1987; *films* include: Sid and Nancy, 1986; Prick Up Your Ears, 1987; Track 29, 1988; Paris By Night, 1989; State of Grace, 1990; JFK, Chattahoochee, 1991; Bram Stoker's Dracula, 1992; True Romance, 1993; Romeo is Bleeding, Immortal Beloved, The Professional, 1994; Murder in the First, The Scarlet Letter, 1995; The Fifth Element, Air Force One, 1997; Lost in Space, Nil By Mouth, 1998 (writer and dir; BAFTA Award for best original screenplay); Hannibal, The Contender, 2001; Harry Potter and the Prisoner of Azkaban, 2004; Batman Begins, Harry Potter and the Goblet of Fire, 2005; Backwoods, 2006; Harry Potter and the Order of the Phoenix, 2007; The Dark Knight, 2008; The Unborn, A Christmas Carol, 2009; The Book of Eli, 2010; Red Riding Hood, Harry Potter and the Deathly Hallows, Pt 2, Tinker, Tailor, Soldier, Spy, 2011; Lawless, The Dark Knight Rises, 2012; RoboCop, Dawn of the Planet of the Apes, 2014; Child 44, 2015; Criminal, 2016; Darkest Hour (Best Actor, Golden Globe Awards, Screen Actors Guild, BAFTA, Academy Awards, 2018), Hunter Killer, 2018; Killers Anonymous, 2019; *television* includes: Remembrance, 1982; Meantime, 1984; Heading Home, 1991; Fallen Angels: dead end for Delia, 1993.

**O'LEARY, Catherine Elizabeth; Her Honour Judge O'Leary;** a Circuit Judge, since 2009; *b* Manchester, 1957; *d* of Cornelius Rapheal O'Leary and Hannah Elizabeth Dennehy O'Leary (*née* Neville); *m* 2015, Benedict Gordon Charles Mandry; three *s* by a previous marriage. *Educ:* Hollies Convent Grammar Sch.; Liverpool Univ. (LLB 1978). Called to the Bar, Gray's Inn, 1979; Dep. District Judge, 1992–98; District Judge, 1998–2009; Recorder, 2002–09. Mem., Women in Literature Book Club. *Recreations:* cooking, theatre, reading. *Address:* Liverpool Civil and Family Courts, 35 Vernon Street, Derby Square, Liverpool L2 2BX. *T:* (0151) 296 2200, *Fax:* (0151) 296 2201.

**O'LEARY, Rt Hon. Elizabeth Mary;** *see* Truss, Rt Hon. E. M.

**O'LEARY, (Michael) John;** Editor, Policy Review Magazine, 2008–11; *b* 11 Dec. 1951; *s* of Captain Daniel Joseph O'Leary, RN, and Sylvia Jane O'Leary; *m* 1977, Susan Berenice Whittingham; two *s* one *d*. *Educ:* Taunton Sch.; Sheffield Univ. (BA Politics 1973; Pres., Students' Union, 1973–74). Reporter, Evening Chronicle, Newcastle upon Tyne, 1975–78; Reporter/news editor, 1978–85, Dep. Editor, 1985–90, THES; Educn Corresp., 1990–93, Educn Editor, 1993–2002, The Times; Editor, THES, 2002–07. Mem., Govt Inquiry into Primary Sch. Test Standards, 1999. Mem., Adv. Bd, Quacquerelli Symonds World Univ. Rankings, 2010–. *Publications:* (ed) The Times Good University Guide, annually 1993–2016. *Recreations:* squash, tennis, travel, watching Arsenal. *Club:* Woodford Wells (Woodford).

**O'LEARY, Maj. Gen. William Joseph,** TD 1997; DL; Deputy Commander Field Army, 2018–March 2020; *b* Dagenham, 12 March 1960; *s* of Patrick John O'Leary and Helena May O'Leary; *m* 2009, Anita Fiona Marina Newcourt. *Educ:* TS Indefatigable, Anglesey. Served RN, 1976–79. Product Design Engr, Ford Motor Co., 1979–92; Engrg and Sales Consultant, Combined Technologies Ltd, 1992–2006; Global Business Develt Manager, Akwel Automotive, 2006–. Commnd REME TA, 1988; Second in Comd, 100 Regt RA Light Aid Detachment, 1988–90; OC, 36 Signal Regt Light Aid Detachment, 1990–91; Second in Comd, 209 Support Workshop, REME, 1991–92; Officer Commanding: 100 Regt RA Regtl Workshop, 1992–96; 150 Recovery Co., 103 Bn REME, 1996–98; Second in Comd, 1998–99, Commanding Officer, 1999–2002, 103 Bn REME; TA Colonel: Regl Forces, 2002–05; Recruiting Gp, 2005–09; Dep. Comdr, 145 (S) Bde, 2009–12; Asst Comdr, Force Troops Comd, 2012–15; ADC to HM the Queen, 2012–15; Asst Dep. Mil. Sec., 2015–18. Col Comdt, REME, 2019–. Vice Patron, Oasis Trust, 2016–. Mem., Ct of Assts, Turners' Co., 2015–. DL Bucks, 2013. Chm., Army Reserves Golf, 2005–; Pres., REME Golf, 2017–; Vice Pres., Army Football, 2018–. QVRM 2015. *Recreations:* golf, Rugby, motorsport. *Address:* Headquarters Field Army, IDL 435, Zone 7, Ramillies Building, Marlborough Lines, Monxton Road, Andover, Hants SP11 8HJ. *T:* (01264) 381587. *E:* William.OLeary281@mod.gov.uk.

**OLIPHANT, Tuelonyana Rosemary D.;** *see* Ditlhabi Oliphant.

**OLISA, Sir Kenneth Aphunezi,** Kt 2018; OBE 2010; Chairman, Restoration Partners, since 2006; Lord-Lieutenant of Greater London, since 2015; *b* Nottingham, 13 Oct. 1951; *s* of Charles Harry Olisa and Barbara Enid Olisa (*née* Blaskey); *m* 1976, Julia Berenice Sherwood; two *d*. *Educ:* High Pavement Grammar Sch., Nottingham; Fitzwilliam Coll., Cambridge (BA 1974; MA 1981; Hon. Fellow 2018). FBCS 2006. IBM: Systems Engr, 1974–76; Salesman, 1976–78; Series/1 Product Mktg Manager, 1978–80; Wang Labs Inc.: Product Mktg Dir, 1981–82; Sales Manager, 1982–84; Mktg Dir EMEA, 1984–86; Vice Pres., US and Worldwide Mktg, 1986–90; Sen. Vice Pres., EMEA, 1990–92; Chairman:

Interregnum plc, 1992–2006; Metapraxis, 1993–2005; VossNet plc, 1994–97; DMATEK plc, 1996–98; GeoConference, 1996–2000; Callcentric, 1997–2000; Catalyst Solution, 1999–2000; Independent Audit, 2007–; Outsourcery, 2013–16. Non-executive Director: Open Text Corp., 1998–2008; uDate.com, 2000–03; Eurasian Natural Resources Corp., 2007–10; Reuters Gp, 2004–08; Thomson Reuters Corp., 2008–18. Dir, Thames Reach, 1992–2016 (Chm., 1994–2016; Pres., 2016–). Mem., Postal Services Commn, 2000–04. Mem. Bd, Ind. Parly Standards Authy, 2009–13. Mem., Women's Enterprise Taskforce, BERR, 2006–09; Dir, W Lambeth NHS Healthcare Trust, 1995–99. Founding Chm., Aleto Foundn (formerly Powerlist Foundn), 2010–. Dir, Inst. of Dirs, 2013–18 (Dep. Chm., 2016–18). Chm., Shaw Trust, 2013–; Trustee: Thomson Reuters (formerly Reuters Foundn), 2005–18; BCS, Chartered Inst. for IT, 2007–14 (Chairman: Strategic Panels, 2007–10; Policy and Public Affairs Bd, 2010–12; BCS Learning and Develt, 2012–14); Gov., Peabody Trust, 1998–2007. Pres., London Youth, 2019–. 1869 Benefactor Fellow, Fitzwilliam Coll., Cambridge, 2012. Liveryman, Information Technologists' Co., 1993– (Master, 2010–11). Life Vice Pres., Fitzwilliam Soc., 2011; Mem., Guild of Cambridge Benefactors, 2012. DUniv: Nottingham Trent, 2018; Kingston, 2018. CStJ 2017. *Recreations:* golf, ski-ing. *Address:* Restoration Partners, Linen Hall, 162–168 Regent Street, W1B 5TD. *Clubs:* Oxford and Cambridge, Walbrook; Bladen Social.

**OLIVARES, Sara Jean Mary;** *see* Chandler, S. J. M.

**OLIVER, Prof. Alexander Duncan,** LittD; Professor of Philosophy, University of Cambridge, since 2012; Fellow, Gonville and Caius College, Cambridge, since 2004; *b* Bristol, 24 Aug. 1966; *s* of Michael John Oliver and Suzanne Nesta Newman; *m* 1988, Catrin Margaret Clare Hutton (*d* 2017); one *s* one *d. Educ:* Bristol Grammar Sch.; Clare Coll., Cambridge (BA 1988; MA; PhD 1994; LittD 2014); Yale Univ. (Mellon Fellow) MA; MPhil 1990). Res. Fellow, Gonville and Caius Coll., Cambridge, 1993–94; University of Cambridge: Temp. Asst Lectr in Philosophy, 1994–95; Asst Lectr, 1995–97; Lectr, 1998–2000; Sen. Lectr, 2000–05; Reader, 2005–12; Director of Studies in Philosophy: Sidney Sussex Coll., 1993–97; Trinity Hall, 1995–98; Queens' Coll., 1996–2002; Gonville and Caius Coll., 2004–15; Dir, Grad. Studies, 1999, 2000, Chm., 2008–09, Faculty of Philosophy; Fellow: Gonville and Caius Coll., 1994–96; Queens' Coll., 1996–2004; Judge Business Sch., 2009–16. Leverhulme Trust Maj. Res. Fellow, 2002–04; Mind Assoc. Sen. Res. Fellow, 2012–13. Mem., Knowledge Transfer Panel, AHRC, 2007–09. Mem., Analysis Trust Cttee, 1996–2016 (Sec., 1996–2000). Gov. The Perse Sch., 2019–. *Publications:* (ed with D. H. Mellor) Properties, 1997; (ed with J. Lear) The Force of Argument, 2010; (with T. Smiley) Plural Logic, 2013, 2nd edn 2016; contrib. articles to philosophical jls. *Recreations:* beer, Italy, labrador retrievers, reggae. *Address:* Gonville and Caius College, Cambridge CB2 1TA. *Clubs:* Athenæum; Elizabethan (Yale).

**OLIVER, Prof. (Ann) Dawn (Harrison),** PhD, LLD; FBA 2005; Professor of Constitutional Law, University College London, 1993–2008, now Emeritus; *b* 7 June 1942; *d* of Gordon and Mieke Taylor; *m* 1967, Stephen John Lindsay Oliver (*see* Sir S. J. L. Oliver); one *s* two *d. Educ:* Newnham Coll., Cambridge (BA 1964; MA 1967; PhD 1993; Associate Fellow, 1996–99); LLD Cantab 2011. Called to the Bar, Middle Temple, 1965 (Harmsworth Schol.; Bencher, 1996; Treas., 2011); in practice at the Bar, 1965–69; Consultant, Legal Action Gp, 1971–76; University College London: Lectr in Law, 1976–87; Sen. Lectr, 1987–90; Reader in Public Law, 1990–93; Head of Law Dept, 1993–98; Dean, Faculty of Laws, 1993–98 and 2007; Hon. Fellow, 2001. Hon. Fellow, Soc. of Advanced Legal Studies, 1997–. Member: Wkg Party on Noise, DoE, 1990–91; Animal Procedures Cttee, Home Office, 2003–11. Member: Commn on Election Campaigns, Hansard Soc., 1990–91; Study of Parlt Gp, 1991–2018 (Pres., 2010–15); Labour and Liberal Democrats Jt Consultative Cttee on Constitutional Reform, 1996–97; Royal Commn on Reform of the H of L, 1999; Fabian Soc. Commn on the future of the Monarchy, 2002–03; Convenor, UK Constitutional Law Gp, 2006–10. Bar Standards Board: Mem., Bar Vocational Course Rev., 2008; Chm., Bar Transfer Test Rev., 2012. Chm., Advertising Adv. Cttee, ITC, 1999–2003. Mem., Exec. Cttee, Internat. Assoc. of Constitutional Law, 2007–10. Trustee: Citizenship Foundn, 1990–94; British Inst. of Internat. and Comparative Law, 2012–17; Law for Life, 2017–. Hon. QC 2012. Editor, Public Law, 1993–2001. *Publications:* (ed jtly) The Changing Constitution, 1985, 8th edn 2015; (ed jtly) New Directions in Judicial Review, 1988; (ed jtly) Economical with the Truth: the press in a democratic society, 1990; Government in the United Kingdom: the search for accountability, effectiveness and citizenship, 1991; (jtly) The Foundations of Citizenship, 1994; (jtly) Public Service Reform: issues of accountability and public law, 1996; (ed jtly) Halsbury's Laws of England on Constitutional Law and Human Rights, 1996; (ed jtly) The Law and Parliament, 1998; Common Values and the Public-Private Divide, 1999; Constitutional Reform in the UK, 2003; (ed jtly) Human Rights and the Private Sphere, 2008; Justice, Legality and the Rule of Law: lessons from the Pitcairn prosecutions, 2009; (ed jtly) The Regulatory State: constitutional implications, 2010; (ed jtly) How Constitutions Change, 2011; (ed jtly) Parliament and the Law, 2013; Constitutional Guardians: the House of Lords, 2015; (jtly) The Constitutional Standards of the House of Lords Select Committee on the Constitution, 2nd edn 2015; articles and book chapters on constitutional and admin. law and on law and politics. *Recreations:* walking, London, Aldeburgh, travel. *Address:* 3 Lloyds Place, SE3 0QE.

**OLIVER, Caroline Rosemary;** *see* Carberry, C. R.

**OLIVER, Sir Craig (Stewart),** Kt 2016; Principal, Teneo (formerly Teneo Blue Rubicon), since 2016; *b* Nottingham, 15 May 1969; *s* of Ian Thomas Oliver and Elsie Oliver; three *d. Educ:* Stirling High Sch.; Univ. of St Andrews (MA); Cardiff Sch. of Journalism (Postgrad. Dip. Journalism). Exec. Editor, ITV News, 2004–06; Editor, BBC News at Six and BBC News at Ten, 2006–10; Controller of English Services, BBC Global News (World Service), 2010–11; Dir, Politics and Communications, No 10 Downing St, 2011–16. *Publications:* Unleashing Demons: the inside story of Brexit, 2016. *Address:* 133 Duke Road, W4 2BX. *E:* craigoliver2013@gmail.com.

**OLIVER, Prof. David,** MD; FRCP; FRSocMed; Consultant Physician, Geriatric and General Internal Medicine, Royal Berkshire NHS Foundation Trust, since 2004; Visiting Professor of Medicine for Older People, City, University of London (formerly City University London), since 2009; Senior Visiting Fellow, King's Fund, since 2013; *b* Manchester, 13 Jan. 1966; *s* of Dr Fred Oliver and Marlene Oliver; *m* 1992, Anne Sowdon. *Educ:* Manchester Grammar Sch.; Queen's Coll., Oxford (BA Physiol Scis 1987); Trinity Hall, Cambridge (MB BChir 1989); Univ. of London (MHM 1997; MD 2000; Dip. Med. Educn 2000); Univ. of Middlesex (MSc Health and Social Care Leadership 2004); Univ. of Manchester (MA Health Care Ethics and Law 2007). Dip. Geriatric Medicine. FRCP 2001. Trng posts, Newcastle Royal Victoria Infirmary, Epping Hosp., Manchester Royal Infirmary, Guy's Hosp., St George's Hosp., Conquest Hosp., Hastings, Kent, Canterbury Hosp. and St Thomas' Hosp., 1989–98; Consultant Physician, Clin. Dir and Lead Clinician, Queen Mary's Hosp., Sidcup, 1998–2004; Sen. Lectr, Sch. of Health and Social Care, Univ. of Reading, 2004–09; Clin. Dir, Royal Berks NHS Foundn Trust, 2004–10 (Lead Clinician, 2004–09); Specialist Clin. Advr to DoH, 2009–10; Nat. Clin. Dir for Older Peoples Services (England), DoH, 2009–13; Specialist Clinical Advr, NHS Emergency Care Improvement Partnership, 2013–16. Vis. Prof., Univ. of Surrey, 2014–. Vice Pres. (Clinical), RCP, 2016–19 (former Chm., Speciality Cttee for Geriatric Medicine). Pres., British Geriatrics Soc., 2014–16. FRSocMed. Mem., Old Mancunians Assoc. Columnist, BMJ, 2015–. *Publications:* (jtly) Making Health Care Systems Fit for an Ageing Population, 2014; over 100 book chapters; contrib. original papers, rev. articles, editls and commentary pieces to jls, incl. Health Service Jl; regular blogs for King's Fund and British Geriatrics Soc. *Recreations:* supporting Manchester City FC and the England cricket team, playing village cricket, theatre, travel, walking, angling, canoeing. *Address:* Royal Berkshire NHS Foundation Trust, Reading RG1 7AN. *E:* david.oliver@royalberkshire.nhs.uk; Royal College of Physicians, 11 St Andrews Place, Regent's Park, NW1 4LE. *E:* david.oliver@rcplondon.ac.uk; King's Fund, 11–13 Cavendish Square, W1G 0AN. *E:* d.oliver@kingsfund.org.uk. *Club:* Royal Society of Medicine.

**OLIVER, Hon. David Keightley Rideal;** QC 1986; *b* 4 June 1949; *o s* of Baron Oliver of Aylmerton, PC; *m* 1st, 1972, Marisa Mirasierras (marr. diss. 1987); two *s*; 2nd, 1988, Judith Britannia Caroline Powell (marr. diss. 2004); two *s. Educ:* Westminster School; Trinity Hall, Cambridge; Institut d'Etudes Européennes, Brussels. Called to the Bar, Lincoln's Inn, 1972, Bencher, 1994; Junior Counsel to Dir-Gen. of Fair Trading, 1980–86. *Recreations:* gardening, bird watching, shooting.

**OLIVER, Dawn, (Lady Oliver);** *see* Oliver, A. D. H.

**OLIVER, Dame Gillian (Frances),** DBE 1998; FRCN; Independent Consultant and Advisor for Nursing and Allied Health Professionals, Macmillan Cancer Relief, 2004–06 (Director of Service Development, 2000–04); *b* 10 Oct. 1943; *d* of Frank Joseph Power and Ethel Mary Power; *m* 1966, Martin Jeremy Oliver; three *d. Educ:* Brentwood County High Sch., Essex; Middlesex Hosp., London (RN); Open Univ. (BA 1979). FRCN 1998. Night Sister and Ward Sister, Clatterbridge Centre for Oncology, 1978–87; Advr in Oncology Nursing, RCN, 1987–89; Regl Nurse, Cancer Services, Mersey RHA, 1989–90; Dir of Patient Services, Clatterbridge Centre for Oncology, 1990–2000. Hon. Fellow, Liverpool John Moores Univ., 2006. *Recreations:* travel, music, literature. *Address:* 1 Well Close, Ness, Neston, Cheshire CH64 4EE.

**OLIVER, Comdr James Arnold,** RN; Trust Manager, God's House in Ewelme, and Clerk to the Governors, Ewelme Exhibition Endowment, since 2006; *b* 10 Aug. 1941; *s* of Capt. Philip Daniel Oliver, CBE, RN and Audrey Mary Oliver (*née* Taylor); *m* 1973, Anne Elise de Burgh Sidley. *Educ:* Sedbergh Sch.; BRNC. Joined RN, 1959; seaman officer, 1959–88; navigation specialist, 1969; Divl Officer, Dartmouth, 1971–73; served in minesweepers, frigates and HM Ships Ark Royal, 1973–74, Sheffield, 1976–78, and Fearless, 1984–86; CO, Barbados Coastguard, 1981–83. Dep. Clerk, 1989–90, Clerk, 1990–2005, Ironmongers' Co. (Mem. Court, 2006–). FCMI (FIMgt 1994). *Recreations:* cruising under sail, country life, carriage driving, late medieval history.

*See also* Sir S. J. L. Oliver.

**OLIVER, Sir (James) Michael (Yorrick),** Kt 2003; DL; Chairman: Helios Underwriting plc (formerly Hampden Underwriting plc), 2007–17; Zirax plc, 2005–10; Europa Oil & Gas, 2004–10; Director, Hampden Capital plc, 2005–11; Lord Mayor of London, 2001–02; *b* 13 July 1940; *s* of George Leonard Jack Oliver and Patricia Rosamund Oliver (*née* Douglas); *m* 1963, Sally Elizabeth Honor Exner; two *d. Educ:* Brunswick Sch.; Wellington Coll. FCSI (MSI 1992). Rediffusion Ltd, 1959–63; Manager, Helios Ltd, 1965–70; Kitcat & Aitken, 1970–86 (Partner, 1977–86); Dir, Kitcat & Aitken & Co., 1986–90; Man. Dir, Carr Kitcat & Aitken, 1990–93; Dir, Lloyds Investment Managers Ltd, 1994–96; Dir, Investment Funds, Hill Samuel Asset Management Ltd, subseq. Scottish Widows Investment Partnership, 1996–2001. Director: Garbhaig Hydro Power Co., 1988–2010; German Investment Trust, 1994–97; German Smaller Cos Investment Trust, 1994–2001; Euro Spain Fund Ltd, 1996–2005; Portugal Growth Fund, 1996–2000; Hill Samuel UK Emerging Cos Investment Trust plc, 1996–2000; European Growth Fund, 2001–08; Chm., Central and Eastern European Fund Ltd, 2003–10. Dir, Centrepoint Soho, 1992–96. Trustee: UK Growth & Income Fund; Income Plus Fund, 1992–2004. Chm., St John Ambulance, City of London Centre, 1998–99, 2003–. Governor: Bishopsgate Foundn, 1983–2010 (Chm., 1985–88); King Edward's Sch., Witley, 1992–2007; Univ. of East London, 1999–2003; Chancellor, City Univ., 2001–02. Chm., Steering Cttee for Mus. of Port of London and Docklands, 1993–2009 (Chm., Trustees, 1996–98); Mem., Mus. of London Develt Council, 1991–96; Trustee: Geffrye Mus., 1992–97; Mus. of London, 2003–10. Gov., Hon. the Irish Soc. and Vice Adm. of the North, 2007–09. Common Councilman, City of London Corp., 1980–87; Alderman, Ward of Bishopsgate, 1987–2009; Sheriff, City of London, 1997–98. Liveryman, Ironmongers' Co., 1962– (Master, 1991–92). JP City of London, 1987; DL Cambs, 2004. FRGS 1962. Hon. LLD UEL, 1999; Hon. DLitt City, 2001. KStJ 2001. *Recreations:* archaeology, travel. *Address:* Paradise Barns, Bucks Lane, Little Eversden, Cambridge CB23 1HL. *T:* (01223) 263303. *Clubs:* City of London, East India.

**OLIVER, Jamie Trevor,** MBE 2003; chef; *b* May 1975; *s* of Trevor and Sally Oliver; *m* 2000, Juliette Norton; two *s* three *d. Educ:* Westminster Catering Coll. Began cooking at parents' pub, The Cricketers, Clavering, Essex; worked in France; head pastry chef, The Neal Street Restaurant, London; sous chef, River Café, London; consultant chef, Monte's, London, until 2002; established restaurants: Fifteen, London, 2002; Fifteen, Amsterdam, 2004; Fifteen, Cornwall, 2006; Jamie's Italian, 2008; Barbecoa, 2010; established: Recipease shops, Clapham Junction and Brighton, 2009; Jamie magazine, 2009; Jamie at Home party planning, 2009; Jamie Oliver's Fabulous Feasts event catering, 2010; Jamie's Wood Fired Ovens, 2010. Presenter, TV series: The Naked Chef (3 series), 1999–2001; Jamie's Kitchen, 2002; Return to Jamie's Kitchen, 2003; Jamie's School Dinners, 2005; Jamie's Great Escape, 2005; Jamie's Return to School Dinners, 2006; Jamie's Chef, 2007; Jamie at Home, 2007, 2008; Jamie's Ministry of Food, 2008; Jamie's American Road Trip, 2009; Jamie's Family Christmas, 2009; Jamie Does…, 2010; Jamie Oliver's Food Revolution (USA), 2010, 2011; Jamie's 30 Minute Meals, 2010; Jamie's Dream School, 2011; Jamie Cooks Summer, 2011; Jamie's Great Britain, 2011; Jamie's Summer Food Rave Up, 2012; Jamie's 15 Minute Meals, 2012; Jamie's Money Saving Meals, 2013, 2014; Jamie and Jimmy's Friday Night Feast, 2014–; Jamie's Comfort Food, 2014; Jamie's Cracking Christmas, 2014; Jamie's Sugar Rush, 2015; Jamie's Super Food, 2015, 2016; Jamie's Night Before Christmas, 2015; Jamie's Quick & Easy Food, 2017, 2018, 2019; Jamie Cooks Italy, 2018. *Publications:* The Naked Chef, 1999; The Return of the Naked Chef, 2000; Happy Days with the Naked Chef, 2001; Jamie's Kitchen, 2002; Jamie's Dinners, 2004; Jamie's Italy, 2005; Cook with Jamie: my guide to making you a better cook, 2006; Jamie at Home: cook your way to the good life, 2007; Jamie's Ministry of Food: anyone can learn to cook in 24 hours, 2008; Jamie's America, 2009; Jamie Does…, 2010; Jamie's 30 Minute Meals, 2010; Jamie's Great Britain, 2011; Jamie's 15 Minute Meals, 2012; Save with Jamie: shop smart, cook clever, waste less, 2013; Jamie's Comfort Food, 2014; Everyday Super Food, 2015; Super Food Family Classics, 2016; Jamie Oliver's Christmas Cookbook, 2016; Five Ingredients Quick & Easy Food, 2017; Jamie Cooks Italy, 2018; Veg, 2019. *Address:* Jamie Oliver Enterprises Ltd, Benwell House, 15–21 Benwell Road, N7 7BL.

**OLIVER, Rt Rev. John Keith**; Bishop of Hereford, 1990–2003; Hon. Assistant Bishop, diocese of Swansea and Brecon, since 2004; *b* 14 April 1935; *s* of Walter Keith and Ivy Oliver; *m* 1961, Meriel Moore (*d* 2014); two *s* (one *d* decd). *Educ*: Westminster Sch. (Fellow 2003); Gonville and Caius Coll., Cambridge (MA, MLitt); Westcott House. Asst Curate, Hilborough Group of Parishes, Norfolk, 1964–68; Chaplain and Asst Master, Eton College, 1968–72; Team Rector: South Molton Group of Parishes, Devon, 1973–82; Parish of Central Exeter, 1982–85; Archdeacon of Sherborne, 1985–90. Chm., ABM, 1993–98. Chaplain, 2003–13, Trustee, 2005–13, RABI; Trustee, Marches Energy Agency, 2004–13; President: Nat. Farm Attractions Network, 2009–13; Auto-Cycle Union, 2009–17. Mem., Billy Wright Inquiry, Banbridge, NI, 2005–10. FRAgS 2012 (ARAgS 2007). Freeman, City of Hereford, 2002. *Publications*: The Church and Social Order, 1968; contribs to Theology, Crucible. *Recreations*: railways, music, architecture, motorcycling. *Address*: The Old Vicarage, Glascwm, Powys LD1 5SE. *Clubs*: Farmers, Oxford and Cambridge.

**OLIVER, Ven. John Michael**; Archdeacon of Leeds, 1992–2005; *b* 7 Sept. 1939; *s* of Frederick and Mary Oliver; *m* 1964, Anne Elizabeth Barlow; three *d*. *Educ*: Ripon Grammar Sch.; St David's Coll., Lampeter (BA 1962); Ripon Hall, Oxford. Ordained deacon, 1964, priest 1965; Asst Curate, St Peter, Harrogate, 1964–67; Senior Curate, Bramley, Leeds, 1967–72; Vicar: St Mary, Harrogate, 1972–78; St Mary with St David, Beeston, Leeds, 1978–92. Ecumenical Officer for Leeds, 1980–86; Rural Dean of Armley, 1986–92; Hon. Canon of Ripon, 1987–92. *Recreations*: cricket, theatre, cooking, a reluctant gardener. *Address*: 42A Chapel Lane, Barwick in Elmet, Leeds LS15 4EJ. *T*: (0113) 393 5019. *E*: olivers42@talktalk.net.

**OLIVER, Jonathan Barnaby Larson**; Group Communications Director and Member, Group Executive Committee, Prudential plc, since 2015 (Group Director of Media Relations, 2013–15); *b* Burton upon Trent, 18 April 1973; *s* of John and Hilary Oliver; *m* 2006, Caroline Rosemary Carberry, *qv*; one *s* two *d*. *Educ*: Repton Sch., Derbys; Peterhouse, Cambridge (BA Hons Hist. 1994). Reporter, Leicester Mercury, 1995–96; Business corresp., Daily Express, 1996–2000; Dep. Political Ed., Mail on Sunday, 2000–08; Political Ed., Sunday Times, 2008–10; Dir, Media Relns, TLG Communications, 2010–12. *Recreations*: reading history, spending time with family. *Address*: (office) 12 Arthur Street, EC4R 9AQ. *E*: jonathan.oliver@prudential.co.uk.

**OLIVER, Kaye Wight**, CMG 2001; OBE 1994; HM Diplomatic Service, retired; High Commissioner to Lesotho, 1999–2002; *b* 10 Aug. 1943. Joined Dept of Customs and Excise, 1962; entered Diplomatic Service, 1965; served FCO, Kuala Lumpur, Lilongwe and Paris; First Sec., Nairobi, 1983–84; Head of Chancery and Consul, Yaoundé, 1984–87; FCO, 1987–90; Consul and Dep. Head of Mission, later Chargé d'Affaires, Kinshasa, Burundi and Rwanda, 1990–94; on secondment to ODA, 1994–95; Ambassador to Rwanda, 1995–98 and (non-resident) to Burundi, 1996–98. Member, Commonwealth Election Observer Group: to Kenya, 2002; to Nigeria, 2007; to Swaziland, 2008; to Rwanda, 2010; to Kenya, 2013. *Address*: 7 Elliott Road, Chiswick, W4 1PF.

**OLIVER, Sir Michael**; see Oliver, Sir J. M. Y.

**OLIVER, Neil Paterson**; author and broadcaster, since 2000; *b* Renfrew, Scotland, 21 Feb. 1967; *s* of Archibald Paterson Oliver and Norma Agnes Cameron Oliver (*née* Neill); *m* 2009, Trudi Alexandria Wallace; two *s* one *d*. *Educ*: Univ. of Glasgow (MA Hons Archaeol.); Napier Univ., Edinburgh (Dip. Journalism); Queen Margaret Coll., Edinburgh (Dip. Public Relns). Freelance field archaeologist, 1988–91; reporter, Dumfriesshire Newspapers Gp, 1991–94; Dep. Ed., E Lothian Courier, 1994–95; Press Officer, 1995–98, Internet Ed., 1998–2000, BT. Presenter, television series: Two Men in a Trench, 2002–03; Coast, 2005– ; The Face of Britain, 2006; Scotland's History: the Top Ten, 2006; The History Detectives, 2007; A History of Scotland, 2008–09; A History of Ancient Britain, 2011; A History of Celtic Britain, 2011; Vikings, 2012; Sacred Wonders of Britain, 2013; Coast Australia, 2013; The Search for Bannockburn, 2014; The Memorial: beyond the Anzac legend, 2014; The Celts, 2015; Coast New Zealand, 2016; Britain's Ancient Capital: Secrets of Orkney, 2017; Rise of the Clans, 2018. Pres., Nat. Trust Scotland, 2017–. Patron, Assoc. of Lighthouse Keepers, 2008–; Ambassador, Combat Stress, 2017–. Hon. DLitt Abertay Dundee, 2011; Hon. PhD Glasgow, 2015. *Publications*: (with A. Pollard) Two Men in a Trench I, 2002; (with A. Pollard) Two Men in a Trench II, 2003; Not Forgotten, 2005; Coast From the Air, 2007; Amazing Tales for Making Men Out of Boys, 2008; A History of Scotland, 2009; A History of Ancient Britain, 2011; Vikings: a history, 2012; Master of Shadows, 2015. *Recreations*: drinking tea, drinking wine, fantasising about one day moving the whole family to a small holding.

**OLIVER, Maj.-Gen. Richard Arthur**, CB 1999; OBE 1986; Chief of Staff Headquarters Adjutant General (Personnel and Training Command), 1996–99; *b* 16 July 1944; *s* of late Arthur R. L. and Betty Oliver; *m* 1972, Julia Newsum; three *s*. *Educ*: Repton Sch.; RMA, Sandhurst; RMCS (psc†). GSO2, Exercise Planning Staff, HQ BAOR, 1977–79; OC, 25 Field Sqdn Regt, 1979–81; GSO2, Exercise Planning Staff, HQ 3rd Armoured Div., 1981; Chief Logistic Plans, HQ 1st (Br.) Corps, 1982–83; CO, 36 Engr Regt, 1983–85; Col, Army Staff Duties 2, MoD (Army), 1985–88; hcsc, Army Staff Coll., 1988; Comdr, Berlin Infantry Bde, 1988–90; rcds 1991; Brig., AQ, HQ 1st (Br.) Corps, 1992; Deputy Chief of Staff: G1/G4 HQ Allied Comd Europe, Rapid Reaction Corps, 1992–94; HQ Land Comd, 1994–96. Business Develt Advr, Granada Food Services, 1999–2000; Chief Exec., Year Out Gp, 2000–14. Member: Nat. Bd, Race for Opportunity, BITC, 1998–99; Bd of Trustees (formerly Council), Cranstoun Drug Services, 2000–15 (Chm., 2001–15); Pilot Bd, Young Volunteer Challenge, DfES, 2003–05; Travel Advice Review Gp, FCO, 2004–06; Consular Stakeholders Panel, FCO, 2007–11; BS8848 Rev. Panel, BSI, 2007–16 (Chm., 2013–16). FInstD 1998–2015. *Publications*: (contrib.) The British Army and the Operational Level of War, 1989; articles in RUSI Jl, Wilts Beekeeping Assoc. mag. and various educnl and travel mags. *Recreations*: gardening, game sports, water colours, reading, qualified beekeeper (Educn Officer, Wilts Beekeeping Assoc., 2017–). *Address*: Queensfield, 28 Kings Road, Easterton, Devizes, Wilts SN10 4PX. *T*: (01380) 812368. *Club*: Army and Navy.

**OLIVER, Dr Ronald Martin**, CB 1989; RD 1973; FRCP; Deputy Chief Medical Officer (Deputy Secretary), Department of Health and Social Security, 1985–89, retired; *b* 28 May 1929; *s* of late Cuthbert Hanson Oliver and Cecilia Oliver; *m* 1957, Susanna Treves Blackwell; three *s* one *d*. *Educ*: King's Coll. Sch., Wimbledon; King's Coll., London; St George's Hosp. Med. Sch. (MB, BS 1952). MRCS, LRCP 1952; DCH 1954; DPH 1960; DIH 1961; MD London 1965; MFOM 1978; FRCP 1998 (MRCP 1987); MFCM 1987. Served RNR: Surg. Lieut, 1953–55; Surg. Lt-Comdr, retd 1974. St George's Hosp., London: House Surgeon and Physician, 1952–53; Resident Clin. Pathologist, 1955–56; trainee asst, gen. practice, 1956–57; Asst County MO, Surrey CC, 1957–59; MO, London Transport Exec., 1959–62; MO, later SMO, Treasury Med. Service (later CS Med. Adv. Service), 1962–74; seconded Diplomatic Service as Physician, British Embassy, Moscow, 1964–66; SMO, 1974–79, SPMO, 1979–85, DHSS; Chief Med. Advr, ODA, 1983–85. Gov., Manor House Sch., Little Bookham, 1991–99 (Chm., 1995–99). *Publications*: papers in med. jls on epidemiology of heart disease, public health, toxicology, and health service admin. *Recreations*: golf, travelling. *Address*: 4 Hawks Hill House, Guildford Road, Leatherhead, Surrey KT22 9GS. *T*: (01372) 362323. *Club*: Effingham Golf.

**OLIVER, Simon Jonathan; His Honour Judge Oliver**; a Circuit Judge, since 2010; *b* Reading, 9 May 1958; *s* of John Michael Oliver and Shirley Mary Oliver; *m* 1983, Melanie Louise Joanna Stevens; two *s*. *Educ*: Reading Sch.; Univ. of Exeter (LLB 1980; MPhil 1998). Called to the Bar, Inner Temple, 1981; *ad eundem* Lincoln's Inn, 1984; in practice as barrister, specialising in family and educn law, 1981–2007; Recorder, 2003–10; a Designated Family Judge for Berks, 2012–17. Chair: (pt-time) Special Educnl Needs and Disability Tribunal, 1994–2007 (Actg Pres., 2008–09); Care Standards Tribunal, 2000–07 (Dep. Pres., 2007–10). Member: Stewards' Enclosure, Henley Royal Regatta, 1982– ; Glyndebourne Fest. Soc., 2009–. Liveryman, Co. of Founders, 1985 (Mem., Ct of Assts, 2009–18). FRSA. *Publications*: Special Educational Needs and the Law, 1996, 2nd edn 2007; Enforcing Family Finance Orders, 1999, 2nd edn 2012. *Recreations*: ski-ing, gardening, opera, making chutneys and piccalilli. *Address*: Central Family Court, 42–49 High Holborn, WC1V 6NP. *Clubs*: Leander (Henley-on-Thames); Surrey County Cricket.

**OLIVER, Prof. Stephen George**, PhD; FMedSci; Professor of Systems Biology and Biochemistry and Director, Cambridge Systems Biology Centre, University of Cambridge, 2007–17, now Emeritus Professor; Fellow, Wolfson College, Cambridge, 2009–17, now Emeritus; *b* 3 Nov. 1949; *s* of late Anthony George Oliver and Ivy Florence Oliver (*née* Simmons); *m* 1st, 1972, Rowena Philpott (marr. diss. 2008); one *d*; 2nd, 2009, Elaine Fenn. *Educ*: Univ. of Bristol (BSc Hons Microbiol. 1971); Nat. Inst. for Medical Research (PhD 1974). SRC Res. Fellow, Univ. of Calif, Irvine, 1974–77; Lectr in Microbiol., Univ. of Kent, Canterbury, 1977–81; Sen. Lectr in Applied Molecular Biol., 1981–87, Prof. of Biotechnol., 1987–99, UMIST; Prof. of Genomics, Univ. of Manchester, 1999–2007. Ed.-in-Chief, Yeast, 1985–. Chairman: MRC Bioinformatics and Mathematical Biol. Fellowships Panel, 2001–04; Wellcome Trust Molecules, Genes and Cells Funding Cttee, 2004–08. FMedSci 2002; FRSB 2018. Fellow, Amer. Acad. for Microbiol., 2000; FAAAS 2008; Mem. EMBO 2004. Hon. Member: Hungarian Acad. of Scis, 1998; British Mycol Soc., 2008. Kathleen Barton-Wright Meml Prize, Inst. of Biology, 1996; Astra-Zeneca Award, Biochem. Soc., 2001; Marjory Stephenson Prize, Microbiol. Soc., 2016; Lifetime Achievement Award, Yeast Genetics Meeting, Genetics Soc. of Amer., 2018. *Publications*: (ed with K. Gull) The Fungal Nucleus, 1981; (with T. A. Brown) Microbial Extrachromosomal Inheritance, 1985; (with J. M. Ward) A Dictionary of Genetic Engineering, 1985; (ed with M. F. Tuite) Biotechnology Handbooks—Saccharomyces, 1991; (jtly) The Eukaryotic Genome: organisation and regulation, 1997; (ed jtly) Encyclopedia of Microbiology, vols 1–4, 2000; (ed with J. I. Castrillo) Yeast Systems Biology, 2003; (ed with J. I. Castrillo) Systems Biology of Alzheimer's Disease, 2015; articles in scientific jls. *Recreations*: music, the outdoors, searching for hills to walk or bike up in East Anglia. *Address*: Cambridge Systems Biology Centre and Department of Biochemistry, University of Cambridge, Cambridge CB2 1GA.

**OLIVER, Rt Rev. Stephen John**; Area Bishop of Stepney, 2003–10; *b* 7 Jan. 1948; *s* of John Oliver and Nora Oliver (*née* Greenhalgh); *m* 1st, 1969, Hilary Joan Barkham (*d* 2010); two *s*; 2nd, 2017, Kathryn Mary Davies. *Educ*: St Augustine's Coll., Canterbury; King's Coll. London (AKC 1970). Ordained deacon, 1971, priest, 1972; Asst Curate, Clifton, Nottingham, 1970; Vicar, Christ Church, Newark on Trent, 1975; Rector, St Mary Plumtree, Nottingham, 1979; Producer, Religious Programmes, BBC, 1985, Chief Producer, 1987; Rector of Leeds, 1991–97; Canon Residentiary, St Paul's Cathedral, 1997–2003. Mem., Liturgical Commn, Gen. Synod of C of E, 1991–2001. Hon. Canon, Ripon Cathedral, 1996. Chm., Praxis, 1997–2001; Member: Elida Gibbs Ethics Cttee, 1994–96; W Yorks Playhouse Community and Educn Cttee, 1991–96; Leeds Common Purpose Adv. Gp, 1994–96; Unilever Central Ethical Compliance Gp, 1997–2003. Trustee, More Than Gold, 2008–10. Chairman, Governors: Leeds Girls' High Sch., 1993–96; Agnes Stewart High Sch., 1993–96. Pres., Leeds Church Inst., 1991–96. *Publications*: Why Pray?, 1993; (ed) Pastoral Prayers, 1996; (contrib.) New SCM Dictionary of Liturgy and Worship, 2002; Guiding Stars, 2005; (ed) Inside Grief, 2013. *Recreations*: reading, theatre, flying, ski-ing. *Address*: 6 Riverside, Southwell, Notts NG25 0HA.

**OLIVER, Sir Stephen (John Lindsay)**, Kt 2007; QC 1980; President of First-tier Tax Chamber and Vice-President (Tax) of Upper Tribunal, 2009–11; Vice President (Finance) of Upper Tribunal, 2010–11 (Presiding Special Commissioner, and President, VAT and Duties (formerly Value Added Tax) Tribunals, 1992–2009); a fee-paid Judge of Upper Tribunal, 2011–13; *b* 14 Nov. 1938; *s* of late Philip Daniel Oliver and Audrey Mary Oliver; *m* 1967, Ann Dawn Harrison Taylor (*see* A. D. H. Oliver); one *s* two *d*. *Educ*: Rugby Sch.; Oriel Coll., Oxford (MA Jurisprudence). National Service, RN, 1957–59: served submarines; Temp. Sub-Lieut. Called to the Bar, Middle Temple, 1963; Bencher, 1987; a Recorder, 1989–91; Circuit Judge, 1991–92. Mediator, Pump Court Tax Chambers, 2012–. President: Financial Services and Mkts Tribunal, 2001–10; Pensions Regulator Tribunal, 2005–10. Asst Boundary Comr, Parly Boundary Commn, 1977. Chm., Blackheath Concert Halls Charity, 1986–92; Mem. Council, London Sinfonietta, 1993–2014. Trustee: Britten-Pears Foundn, 2001–09; TaxAid, 2007–13. *Recreations*: music, films, golf. *T*: (020) 7414 8080.
See also J. A. Oliver.

**OLIVER-JONES, His Honour Stephen**; QC 1996; a Circuit Judge, 2000–15; *b* 6 July 1947; *s* of Arthur William Jones and Kathleen Jones; *m* 1972, Margaret Anne Richardson; one *s* one *d*. *Educ*: Marling Sch., Stroud; UC, Durham Univ. (BA Hons). Lectr in Law, Durham Tech. Coll., 1968–70. Called to the Bar, Inner Temple, 1970, Bencher, 2010; Mem., Oxford, later Midland and Oxford, Circuit; an Asst Recorder, 1988–93; a Recorder, 1993–2000; Designated Civil Judge for W Midlands and Warwicks, 2002–09. Legal Mem., Mental Health Tribunal (formerly Pres., Mental Health Rev. Tribunal), 1997–. Mem., Civil Procedure Rule Cttee, 2002–08. *Publications*: Laurie Lee 1914–1997: a bibliography, 2018. *Recreations*: fly fishing, book collecting. *E*: soliverjones@msn.com. *Club*: East India.

**OLIVIER, Lady**; see Plowright, Dame J. A.

**OLIVIER, Joan Sheila Ross**; Headmistress, Lady Margaret School, Parsons Green, 1984–2006; *b* 30 April 1941; *m* 1966, John Eric Hordern Olivier; one *s*. *Educ*: Queen Mary Coll., Univ. of London (BA Hons); Hughes Hall, Cambridge (PGCE). Hd of History, Camden Sch. for Girls, 1965–73; Dep. Hd, Lady Margaret Sch., 1973–84. Chm., Wimbledon Br., NADFAS, 2012–15. JP Wimbledon, 1993–2011. *Recreations*: bridge, quilters.

**OLIVIERI, René**; Chairman, The Wildlife Trusts, 2012–17; *b* 1 May 1953; *m* Dr Anne Luetcke; one *s* one *d*. *Educ*: Univ. of Oregon, Eugene (BA Political Scis); Johns Hopkins Univ. (MA Internat. Relns). Blackwell Publishers: Publisher, 1980–83; Editl and Mktg Dir, 1983–85; Dep. Man. Dir, 1985–88; Man. Dir, 1988–2000; CEO, 2000–07; Chief Operating Officer, Wiley-Blackwell, 2007–08; Chm., Tubney Charitable Trust, 2008–12. Chairman: InfoSource Inc., 1990–2000; NCC Blackwell, 1992–96; Polity Press, 1995–2000; Marston Book Services, 1998–2000; Track Record Global, 2016–. Sen. mgt mentoring and trng on innovation and new business models, 2015–; Sen. Ind. Dir and Chair of Finances, Staff and Resources, Heritage Fund. Non-exec. Dir, IOP Publishing, 2014–. Member: Bd, HEFCE, 2008–14; Council, RSPCA, 2019–; Trustee, Board: HLF, then NLHF, 2018– (Chm., Finance, Staffing and Resources Cttee, 2018–); NHMF, 2018–. Chairman: Belgrade Th., 2011–12; Blikbook, 2011–15. Mem., Chancellor's Ct of Benefactors, Oxford Univ., 2015–. *Publications:* peer-reviewed articles in scientific and professional jls, and popular articles in mags and newspapers. *Recreations:* theatre, horse riding, tennis, ski-ing, scuba diving, early music. *E:* rene.olivieri@mhcom.co.uk.

**OLLERENSHAW, Eric,** OBE 1991; *b* 26 March 1950; *s* of Eric and Barbara Ollerenshaw. *Educ:* London Sch. of Economics and Political Science (BSc Econs). History teacher, Northumberland Park Sch., Tottenham, Hendon Sch., Barnet, and Tom Hood Sch., Leytonstone, 1973–2000. Member (C): ILEA, 1986–90 (Leader, Cons. Gp, 1988–90); Hackney LBC, 1990–2007 (Leader, Cons. Gp, 1996); London Assembly, GLA, 2000–04 (Dep. Leader, 2000–02, Leader, 2002–04, Cons. Gp). MP (C) Lancaster and Fleetwood, 2010–15; contested (C) same seat, 2015, 2017. PPS to Baroness Warsi, 2010–15. Hd of Cities and Diversity, Cons. Party, 2005–10. Mem. Bd, London Develt Agency, 2004–08. Chair, Ind. Review of Local Council Tax Schemes, 2015–16. *Recreations:* reading, listening to music.

**OLLEY, (John) Brian;** HM Diplomatic Service; Ambassador to Lithuania, since 2019; *b* Moshi, Tanzania, 14 Feb. 1957; *s* of Bill Olley and Stella Olley; *m* 1989, Pascale Abadie; two *s* one *d*. *Educ:* King's Sch., Canterbury; Univ. of Nottingham (BSc 1st Cl. 1978; MSc 1984); Royal Mil. Acad. Sandhurst. Joined Army, 1980; Queen's Gurkha Engrs, 1980–83; various postings, Hong Kong, Nepal, Germany, London; sc 1990; CO 1RSME Regt, 1998–2000; joined FCO, 2001; Pol Officer and Hd, Security Sector Reform Section, Afghanistan Unit, Kabul and London, 2002–03; Hd, Pol and Public Affairs, Helsinki, 2004–08; Dep. High Comr, Cyprus, 2008–13; High Comr, Cameroon, and Ambassador to Gabon, Chad and Equatorial Guinea, 2013–17. *Recreations:* tennis, golf, family. *Address:* c/o Foreign and Commonwealth Office, King Charles Street, SW1A 2AH. *E:* brian.olley@fco.gov.uk.

**OLLILA, Jorma Jaakko,** Hon. CBE 2007; Chairman, Board of Directors, Nokia Corporation, 2006–12 (Chief Executive Officer, 1992–2006, and Chairman, Group Executive Board, 1999–2006); Advisory Partner, Perella Weinberg Partners, since 2014; *b* Seinäjoki, Finland, 15 Aug. 1950; *m* Liisa Annikki Metsola; two *s* one *d*. *Educ:* Univ. of Helsinki (MSc Political Sci. 1976); LSE (MSc Econ 1978); Helsinki Univ. of Technology (MSc Eng 1981). Citibank: Account Manager, Corporate Bank, Citibank NA, London, 1978–80; Account Officer, 1980–82, Mem. Bd of Mgt, 1983–85, Citibank Oy; Nokia: Mem., Gp Exec. Bd, 1985–2006; Vice-Pres., Internat. Operations, 1985–86; Sen. Vice-Pres., Finance, 1986–89; Dep. Mem., Bd of Dirs, 1989–90; President: Nokia Mobile Phones, 1990–92; Nokia, 1992–99. Chairman: Bd, MTV Oy, 1993–97; Royal Dutch Shell, 2006–15; Outokumpu, 2013; Member Board: ICL plc, 1992–2000; Otava Books and Magazines Gp Ltd, 1996–; UPM-Kymmene, 1997–2008 (Vice-Chm., 2004–08); Ford Motor Co., 2000–08; Tetra Laval Gp, 2013–; Member Supervisory Board: Tietotehdas Oy, 1992–95; Pohjola Insurance Co. Ltd, 1992–97; NKF Holding NV, 1992–99; Oy Rastor Ab, 1992–93; Sampo Insurance Co. Ltd, 1993–2000; Merita Bank Ltd, 1994–2000. Chm. Supervisory Bd, Finnish Foreign Trade Assoc., 1993–98; Vice Chm. Bd, Finnish Sect., ICC, 1993–97; Member: Planning Bd for Defence Economy, 1992–96; Technol. Delegn, Ministry of Trade and Industry, 1992–95; Bd and Exec. Cttee, Confedn of Finnish Industry and Employers, 1992–2002 (Dep. Chm. Bd, 1995–2002); Council, State Technical Res. Centre, 1992–93; Bd, Econ. Inf. Bureau, 1993–97; Council, Centre for Finnish Business and Policy Studies, 1993–2001; Supervisory Bd, Foundn for Pediatric Res., 1993–98; Sci. and Technology Policy Council of Finland, 1993–2002; Council of Supervisors, Res. Inst. of Finnish Economy, 1993–2000; Exec. Bd, Assoc. for Finnish Cultural Foundn, 1993–99; Delegn, Finnish-Swedish Chamber of Commerce, 1993–99; Supervisory Bd, WWF Finland, 1995–97; Competitiveness Adv. Gp, EC, 1995–96; European Round Table of Industrialists, 1997– (Chm., 2005–09); GBDe Business Steering Cttee, 1999–. Overseas Adv. Trustee, American-Scandinavian Foundn, 1994–. Chm. Adv. Cttee, Helsinki Univ. of Technology, 1996– (Vice-Chm., 1993–95); Member: Council, Helsinki Sch. of Econs and Business Admin, 1993–98; Dean's Council, John F. Kennedy Sch. of Govt, Harvard, 1995–; Internat. Bd, United World Colls, 1995–; Bd of Dirs, Univ. of Helsinki, 2009–. Hon. PhD Helsinki, 1995; Hon. DSc Helsinki Univ. of Technol., 1998. Comdr 1st Cl., Order of White Rose (Finland), 1996; Order of White Star (Estonia), 1995; Comdr, Order of Orange (Nassau), 1995; Officer's Cross, Order of Merit (Hungarian Republic), 1996; Commander's Cross, Order of Merit, Germany, 1997, Poland, 1999. *Publications:* (with Harri Saukkomaa) Mahdoton menestys: kasvun paikkana Nokia (autobiog.), 2013.

**OLMERT, Ehud;** Prime Minister of Israel, 2006–09 (Acting, Jan.–April 2006, Interim Prime Minister, April–May 2006); Member, Knesset, 1973–98 and 2003–09; *b* Nahlat Jabotinsky, Binyamina, 30 Sept. 1945; *s* of Mordechai and Bella Olmert; *m* Aliza Richter; two *s* two *d*. *Educ:* Hebrew Univ. of Jerusalem (BA Psychol. and Philos. 1968; BA Law 1973). Military service, 1963, 13th Regt, Golani Bde, wounded, completed service at Hamahane newspaper, 1971. Started practising law, private law firm, 1975; Sen. Partner, Ehud Olmert and Associates Law Firm, 1978. Volunteer, Israel Defence Forces, 1979–82, completed officers' course, volunteered for reserve service in Lebanon. Knesset: Member, 1981–88: For. Affairs and Defence Cttee; Finance Cttee; Educn and Culture Cttee; Defence Budget Cttee; Minister: of Minority Affairs, 1988–90; of Health, 1990–92; of Industry, Trade and Labour, 2003–06; of Communications, 2003–05; of Finance, 2005 and 2007; of Welfare and Social Services, 2006–07; Vice Prime Minister, 2003. Mayor of Jerusalem, 1993–2003.

**OLNER, William John;** *b* 9 May 1942; *s* of Charles William Olner, miner and Lillian Olner; *m* 1962, Gillian Everitt. *Educ:* Atherstone Secondary Modern Sch.; North Warwicks Tech. Coll. Engineer, Rolls Royce, 1957–92. Nuneaton and Bedworth Borough Council: Cllr, 1972–92; Leader, 1982–87; Mayor, 1987–88; Chm. Envmtl Health Cttee, 1990–92. MP (Lab) Nuneaton, 1992–2010. Member: Envmt, Transport and the Regions (formerly Envmt) Select Cttee, 1995–2001; Foreign Affairs Select Cttee, 2001–05; DCLG (formerly ODPM) Select Cttee, 2005–10. Chm., Industry and Parlt Trust, 2007–10. Mem. (Lab) Warwicks CC, 2013– (Chair, Regulatory Cttee, 2013–). *Recreations:* hospice movement, walking, current affairs. *Address:* 6 Cotswold Crescent, Nuneaton, Warwicks CV10 8PL.

**O'LOAN,** family name of **Baroness O'Loan**.

**O'LOAN, Baroness** *cr* 2009 (Life Peer), of Kirkinriola in the County of Antrim; **Nuala Patricia O'Loan,** DBE 2008; MRIA; Chair: Governing Authority, National University of Maynooth, since 2011; Daniel Morgan Independent Panel, since 2014; Catholic Council for Independent Inquiry into Child Sexual Abuse, since 2015; *b* 20 Dec. 1951; *m* 1975, Declan O'Loan, *qv*; five *s*. *Educ:* King's College, London (LLB Hons); Coll. of Law. Solicitor of Supreme Ct of England and Wales. Articled Clerk, Stephenson Harwood, London, 1974–76; Law Lectr, Ulster Poly., 1976–80; University of Ulster: Law Lectr, 1985–92; Sen. Lectr, 1992–2000; Jean Monnet Chair in European Law, 1992–99; Police Ombudsman for NI, 2000–07. Special Comr, CRE, 2004–05. Chm., Formal Investigation into Human Rights, Equality and Human Rights Commn, 2008–09; Member: Ind. Gp for Dialogue and Peace, 2007–10; Ind. Rev. of Outsourcing Abuse, UK Border Agency, for Home Sec., 2009–10; Ind. Rev. Panel for Police Service of NI Investigation into matters arising out of Report of Police Ombudsman for NI into circumstances surrounding death of Raymond McCord, Jr and related matters, 2010–; Internat. Contact Gp for the Basque country, 2011–; Internat. Steering Gp, Operation Kenova. Roving Ambassador and Special Envoy for Conflict Resolution, Ireland, 2008–11; Special Envoy on UN Security Council Resolution 1325 on Women, Peace and Security, 2009–11. Lay Visitor, RUC Stations, 1991–97; Chm., NI Consumer Council for Electricity, 1997–2000; Member: Gen. Consumer Council for NI, 1991–96 (Convenor, Energy and Transport Gp, 1994–96); UK Domestic Coal Consumers' Council, 1992–95; Ministerial Working Gp on Green Economy, 1993–95; Northern HSS Bd, 1993–97 (Convenor for Complaints, 1996–97); Police Authy for NI, 1997–99; Legal Expert Mem., EC Consumers' Consultative Council, 1994–95. Mem., Club de Madrid NetPLUSS, 2011–. MRIA 2012. *Publications:* articles on European law, policing and consumer law, and faith issues. *Recreations:* music, reading. *Address:* 48 Old Park Avenue, Ballymena, Northern Ireland BT42 1AX. *T:* (028) 2564 9636. *E:* oloann@parliament.uk.

**O'LOAN, Declan;** Member (SDLP) North Antrim, Northern Ireland Assembly, 2007–11; *b* Ballymena, 5 Aug. 1951; *s* of Charles and Elizabeth O'Loan; *m* 1975, Nuala Patricia (see Baroness O'Loan); five *s*. *Educ:* Imperial Coll., London (BSc 1973); Fitzwilliam Coll., Cambridge (PGCE 1974); Univ. of Ulster (MBA 1989). Teacher of Maths: Ramsden Sch. for Boys, 1974–76; Rainey Endowed Sch., Magherafelt, Co. Derry, 1976–80; St Mary's Yala, Kenya, 1980–82; St Patrick's Iten, Kenya, 1982–83; Methodist Coll., Belfast, 1983–87; Teacher of Maths, 1987–2005, Hd of Maths, 1990–2005, St Louis Grammar Sch., Ballymena. Member (SDLP): Ballymena BC, 1993–2015 (Dep. Mayor, 2008–09; Chm., Audit and Scrutiny Cttee, 2011–12); Mid and E Antrim BC (formerly DC), 2014–19 (Chairman: Audit and Scrutiny Cttee, 2016–17; Jt Cttee, arc21, 2016–19). Northern Ireland Assembly: Member: Finance and Personnel Cttee, 2007–11; Cttee on Procedures, 2007–10; Assembly and Exec. Rev. Cttee, 2010; Chm., Cttee on Standards and Privileges, 2009–11; Dep. Chm., Culture, Arts and Leisure Cttee, 2010–11. Member: NI Community Relns Council, 2001–08; Indep. Panel of Victims and Survivors Service, NI, 2012–19. Member: Bd, NI Assembly and Business Trust, 2007–11; Exec. Cttee, NI Assembly Br., CPA, 2009–11. Contested (SDLP): N Antrim, 2010, 2015, 2017; N Antrim, NI Assembly, 2011. Chm., Ballymena District Policing Partnership, 2010–12; Mem., Ballymena Policing and Community Safety Partnership, 2012–15. Hon. Consul for Romania in NI, 2010–18. *E:* declanoloan@gmail.com.

**O'LOGHLEN, (Sir) Michael,** (7th Bt *cr* 1838, of Drumconora, Ennis); QC (Vic) 1991; *b* Melbourne, 21 May 1945; *e s* of Sir Colman Michael O'Loghlen, 6th Bt and of Margaret O'Loghlen (*née* O'Halloran); *S* father, 2014, but his name does not yet appear on the Official Roll of the Baronetage; *m* 1st, 1967, Elizabeth Mary Clarke (marr. diss. 1988); three *s*; 2nd, 1989, Elizabeth Margaret Heslop (marr. diss. 2003); one step *s* one step *d*. *Educ:* Xavier Coll., Kew; Univ. of Melbourne (LLB). In practice, Victorian Bar, 1970–2010. Hon. Life Mem., Vic Compensation Bar Assoc., 2010 (former Chm.). *Heir: s* Hugh O'Loghlen, *b* 6 Dec. 1968. *Address:* PO Box 280, Apollo Bay, Vic 3233, Australia.

**O'LONE, Sir Marcus James,** KCVO 2018 (CVO 2013; LVO 2003); Agent to the Queen, Sandringham, 1998–2018; *b* Belfast, 18 Nov. 1953; *s* of late Col Robert John O'Lone, DSO, OBE and Charmian O'Lone; *m* 1981, Elizabeth Mary Foster; one *s* two *d*. *Educ:* Wellington Coll., Crowthorne; Royal Agricultural Coll., Cirencester. FAAV 1980; FRICS 1986. Agent to the Marquess of Salisbury, 1977–95; Dep. Ranger, Windsor Great Park, 1995–98. Pres., NW Norfolk Scouts, 1998–2018; Vice Pres., Norfolk Scouts, 2005–18. *Recreations:* shooting, fishing, golf. *Address:* The Bell House, Church Street, Bowerchalke, Salisbury, Wilts SP5 5BE. *T:* (01722) 781048. *Club:* Farmers.

**OLSEN, Hon. John Wayne,** AO 2007; Chairman, since 2016, and Chief Executive Officer, since 2010, American Australian Association Ltd (Deputy Chairman, 2010–16); *b* 7 June 1945; *s* of S. J. Olsen; *m* 1968, Julie, *d* of G. M. Abbott; two *s* one *d*. *Educ:* Kadina Memorial High Sch.; Sch. of Business Studies, SA. Managing Dir, J. R. Olsen & Sons Pty Ltd, 1968–79. Pres., S Australia Liberal Party, 1976–79; South Australia Government: MP (L): Rocky River, 1979–85; Custance, 1985–90; Kavel, 1992–2002; Chief Sec. and Minister of Fisheries, 1982; Leader of the Opposition, 1982–90; Senator for SA, 1990–92; Shadow Minister of Industry, Trade, Regl Develt, Public Works and Small Business, 1992–93; Minister for Industry, Manufg, Small Business, Regl Develt and Minister for Infrastructure, 1993–96; Minister for State Develt, and for Multicultural and Ethnic, then Multicultural, Affairs, 1996–2001; Premier of SA, 1996–2001; Consul General for Australia: in LA, 2002–06; in NY, 2006–09. Chairman: SA Football Commn, 2010–; Adelaide Oval Stadium Mgt Authy, 2014–; Perth US Asia Centre, 2016–. Fellow, Nat. Inst. of Accts. *Recreation:* barefoot water ski-ing. *Address:* PO Box 133, Glenelg, SA 5045, Australia. *Club:* West Adelaide Football.

**OLSSON, Curt Gunnar;** Chairman, Skandinaviska Enskilda Banken, 1984–96; *b* 20 Aug. 1927; *s* of N. E. and Anna Olsson; *m* 1954, Asta Engblom; two *d*. *Educ:* Stockholm Sch. of Econs (BSc Econs 1950). Managing Director, Stockholm Group: Skandinaviska Banken, 1970–72; Skandinaviska Enskilda Banken, 1972–76; Man. Dir and Chief Exec., Head Office, 1976–82, and first Dep. Chm., 1982–84, Skandinaviska Enskilda Banken. Hon. Consul Gen. for Finland, 1989–99. Hon. DEcon, Stockholm, 1992. Kt Order of Vasa, Sweden, 1976; King Carl XVI Gustaf's Gold Medal, Sweden, 1982; Comdr, Royal Norwegian Order of Merit, 1985; Comdr, Order of the Lion, Finland, 1986.

**OLSWANG, Simon Myers;** Senior Partner, 1981–98, Chairman, 1998–2002, Olswang, solicitors (formerly Simon Olswang & Co.); non-executive company director and executive film producer; *b* 13 Dec. 1943; *s* of Simon Alfred Olswang and Amelia Olga Olswang; *m* 1969, Susan Jane Simon; one *s* two *d*. *Educ:* Bootham Sch., York; Newcastle upon Tyne Univ. (BAEcon). Admitted solicitor, 1968; Attorney at Law, California State Bar, 1978. Trainee, Asst Solicitor, then Partner, Brecher & Co., 1966–81; Founder, Simon Olswang & Co., 1981. Member: Entertainments Symposium Adv. Bd, UCLA, 1982–88; British Screen Adv. Council, 1985–2010 (Chm., Wkg Party on Convergence, 1994–99); non-exec. Director: Press Assoc., 1995–97; Amdocs Ltd, 2004–18; DIC Entertainment Inc., 2005–08; Amiad Filtration Systems Ltd, 2009–18; Mem., Adv. Bd, Palamon Capital Partners, 2002–. Member: Council, BFI, 1998–99; Bd, BL, 2001–08; Bd, Intellectual Property Inst., 2004–06. Chm. Govs and Trustee, Langdon Coll. of Further (Special) Educn, 1992–2009; Overseas Mem., Bd of Trustees, Council of Christians and Jews, 2006–12; Mem., Bd of Trustees, Tel Hai Academic Coll., 2012–. Executive Producer: Peter and the Wolf, 2008; The Flying Machine, 2011; Zaytoun, 2012. Blog, http://simonolswang.wordpress.com. *Publications:* (contrib.) Accessright: an evolutionary path for copyright into the digital era, 1995; (contrib.) Masters of the Wired World, 1988. *Recreations:* family, friends, sailing, theatre, cinema, travel, fruit-farming. *Address:* 1 Fordington Road, N6 4TD. *Clubs:* Garrick; Royal Motor Yacht (Poole).

**OLVER, Sir Richard (Lake),** Kt 2013; FREng; Partner, Edgewater Energy LLC, since 2009; Senior Advisor: C,D&R LLP, since 2008; HSBC Bank plc, since 2011; Chairman, Sand Hill Petroleum, since 2016; *b* 2 Jan. 1947; *s* of Graham Lake Olver and Constance Evelyn Olver; *m* 1968, Pamela Kathleen Larkin; two *d*. *Educ:* City Univ. (BSc 1st Cl., Civil

Eng); Univ. of Virginia Business Sch. FREng 2005; FICE 2010. British Petroleum: joined Engineering Dept, 1973, UK and overseas; Vice-Pres., BP Pipeline Inc., 1979; Divl Manager, New Technology, 1983; Divl Manager, Corporate Planning, 1985; Man. Dir, Central North Sea Pipelines, 1988; Gen. Manager, BP Gas Europe, 1988; Chief of Staff, BP, and Head, Corporate Strategy, 1990; Chief Exec., BP Exploration, USA, and Exec. Vice-Pres., BP America, 1992; Dep. CEO, 1995, CEO, 1998, BP Exploration; Chm., BP Amer. Adv. Bd, 1998; Man. Dir, BP Exploration and Production, 1998–2003; Dep. Gp Chief Exec., BP plc, 2003–04; Dep. Chm., TNK-BP (Russia), 2004–06; Chm., BAE SYSTEMS, 2004–14. Mem., Trilateral Commn, 2005–14. UK Business Ambassador, 2008–. Member: PM's Business Adv. Gp, 2010–15; India-UK CEO Forum, 2010–14. Dir, EdgeMarc LLC, 2012–16. Non-exec. Dir, Thomson-Reuters (formerly Reuters), 1997–2009. Hon. DSc: City, 2004; Cranfield, 2006. Non-exec. Dir of the Year, Sunday Times, 2011; President's Medal, RAE, 2015. *Recreations:* sailing, downhill ski-ing, ballet, fine art. *Address:* C,D&R LLP, Cleveland House, 33 King Street, SW1Y 4AR. *E:* dick@sirrichardolver.com.

O'MAHONY, Patrick James Martin; His Honour Judge O'Mahony; a Circuit Judge, since 2004; *b* 18 April 1951; *s* of Patrick Noel and Elizabeth Nora O'Mahony; *m* 1979, Jane Tayler; one *s* two *d*. *Educ:* Stonyhurst Coll.; UCL (LLB (Laws) 1972). Called to the Bar, Inner Temple, 1973; in practice as barrister, London, 1973–83 and 1988–2004; Sen. Crown Counsel, Attorney Gen.'s Chambers, Hong Kong, 1983–88. Hon. Recorder of Margate, 2002–. *Recreations:* long distance running, horse racing, literary criticism. *Address:* c/o Canterbury Crown Court, Chaucer Road, Canterbury, Kent CT1 1ZA. *Clubs:* Hong Kong Football; Red and Yellow Racing (Broadstairs).

O'MALLEY, His Honour Stephen Keppel; DL; a Circuit Judge, 1989–2010; *b* 21 July 1940; *s* of late D. K. C. O'Malley and Mrs R. O'Malley; *m* 1963, Frances Mary, *e d* of late James Stewart Ryan; four *s* two *d*. *Educ:* Ampleforth Coll.; Wadham Coll., Oxford (MA). Called to Bar, Inner Temple, 1962; Mem. Bar Council, 1968–72; Co-Founder, Bar European Gp, 1977; a Recorder, Western Circuit, 1978–89. Wine Treasurer, Western Circuit, 1986–89. DL Somerset, 1998. *Publications:* Legal London, a Pictorial History, 1971; European Civil Practice, 1989. *Address:* Maypole Knapp House, West End, Somerton, Somerset TA11 6RH.

OMAND, Sir David (Bruce), GCB 2004 (KCB 2000); Visiting Professor: King's College London, since 2006; Paris School of International Affairs, Sciences Po, Paris, since 2014; Security and Intelligence Co-ordinator and Permanent Secretary, Cabinet Office, 2002–05; *b* 15 April 1947; *s* of late J. Bruce Omand, JP, and of Esther Omand; *m* 1971, Elizabeth, *er d* of late Geoffrey Wales, RE, ARCA; one *s* one *d*. *Educ:* Glasgow Acad.; Corpus Christi Coll., Cambridge (BAEcon; MAEcon; Hon. Fellow, 2010); Open Univ. (BSc Maths/Physics 2007). Ministry of Defence: Asst Principal, 1970; Private Sec. to Chief Exec. (PE), 1973; Asst Private Sec. to Sec. of State, 1973–75, 1979–80; Principal, 1975; Asst Sec., 1981; Private Sec. to Sec. of State, 1981–82; on loan to FCO as Defence Counsellor, UK Delegn to NATO, Brussels, 1985–88; Asst Under Sec. of State (Management Strategy), 1988–91 (Programmes), 1991–92; Dep. Under Sec. of State (Policy), MoD, 1992–96; Dir, GCHQ, 1996–97; Permanent Under-Sec. of State, Home Office, 1998–2001; Chm., Centre for Mgt and Policy Studies, Cabinet Office, 2001–02. Non-exec. Dir, Finmeccanica UK Ltd, 2008–14; Sen. Ind. Dir, Babcock International plc, 2012– (non-exec. Dir, 2009–12); Mem., Sen. Adv. Bd, Paladin Capital, 2016–. Mem., Global Commn on Internet Governance, 2014–16. Trustee, Natural History Mus., 2006–14. Hon. PhD: Birmingham, 2008; Glasgow 2019. *Publications:* Securing the State, 2010; (with Mark Phythian) Principled Spying: the ethics of secret intelligence, 2018. *Recreations:* opera, hill-walking. *Club:* Reform.

O'MARA, Jared; MP for Sheffield Hallam, since 2017 (Lab, 2017–18; Ind, since 2018); *b* Sheffield, 1981. *Educ:* Tapton 6th Form Coll.; Staffordshire Univ. (BA 1st Cl. Journalism). Campaigns Officer, British Council of Disabled People; proprietor and event organiser, West Street Live. Mem., Women and Equalities Cttee, H of C, 2017. Gov. and Trustee, Paces (sch. and community resource for disabled people). *Address:* House of Commons, SW1A 0AA.

O'MARA, Margaret; Director, Human Resources, National Offender Management Service, Home Office, 2006–07; *b* 10 May 1951; *d* of Thomas Patrick and Madge O'Mara. *Educ:* St Hilda's Coll., Oxford (1st Cl. Hons Lit.Hum.); University Coll. London (MSc Econs of Public Policy). Entered HM Treasury, 1973; Private Sec. to Chancellor of Exchequer, 1982–85; Head: Economic Briefing Div., 1985–87; Monetary Policy Div., 1987–90; Public Expenditure Div., monitoring Dept of Employment, 1990–92; Arts Gp, then Libraries, Museums and Galls Gp, Dept of Nat. Heritage, 1992–95; Dir, Personnel and Support, then Personnel, HM Treasury, 1995–2000; Associate Dir, Policing and Security, NIO, 2000–03; Director: Organised Crime, 2003–04, Crime Reduction, 2004–06, Home Office. Mem., Exec., Assoc. of Grace Baptist Churches (SE), 2007–. Trustee, Particular Baptist Fund, 2008–17, 2018–; Dir, Grace Baptist Charities Ltd, 2009–. *Recreations:* walking, cooking, Irish history.

O'MORCHOE, David Nial Creagh, CB 1979; CBE 2007 (MBE 1967); (The O'Morchoe); Chief of O'Morchoe; *b* 17 May 1928; *s* of Nial Creagh O'Morchoe and Jessie Elizabeth, *d* of late Charles Jasper Joly, FRS, FRIS, MRIA, Astronomer Royal of Ireland; *S* father as Chief of the Name (O'Morchoe, formerly of Oularleigh and Monamolin), 1970; *m* 1954, Margaret Jane, 3rd *d* of George Francis Brewitt, Cork; two *s* one *d*. *Educ:* St Columba's Coll., Dublin (Fellow 1983–2007); Chm. of Fellows, 1989–99); RMA Sandhurst. Commissioned Royal Irish Fusiliers, 1948; served in Egypt, Jordan, Gibraltar, Germany, Kenya, Cyprus, Oman; psc 1958, jssc 1966; CO 1st Bn RIrF, later 3rd Bn Royal Irish Rangers, 1967–68; Directing Staff, Staff Coll., Camberley, 1969–71; RCDS 1972; Brigade Comdr, 1973–75; Brig. GS, BAOR, 1975–76; Maj.-Gen. 1977; Comdr, Sultan of Oman's Land Forces, 1977–79, retired. Dep. Col, 1971–76, Col 1977–79, The Royal Irish Rangers. Pres., Republic of Ireland Dist, RBL, 1999–; SSAFA (formerly SSAFA/Forces Help Society, then SSAFA Forces Help): Chm., 1987–2010, Pres., 2010–, Rep. of Ireland Br.; Council Mem., 2002–10; Hon. Life Mem., 2010; Mem. Council, Concern, Dublin, 1984–2004 (Sec., 1989–98). Member: Church of Ireland Gen. Synod, 1993–2005; Rep. Church Body, 1994–2004. Founder Mem., Standing Council of Irish Chiefs and Chieftains, 1992 (Chm., 1994–98). Mem., Order of Friendly Brothers of St Patrick, 1980– (Grand Pres., 2002–08). KLJ 2010. *Recreation:* active interest in international sports competitions. *Heir:* s Dermot Arthur O'Morchoe, *b* 11 Aug. 1956. *Address:* c/o Bank of Ireland, Gorey, Co. Wexford, Ireland. *Clubs:* Friendly Brothers (Dublin); Irish Cruising.

OMRANI, Samantha Jane; *see* Knights, S. J.

ÖNAÇ, Aydin; Headmaster, St Olave's Grammar School, 2010–17; *b* Derbyshire, 21 Dec. 1951; *s* of Yusuf Önaç and Muriel Önaç (*née* Hallam); *m* 1st, 1976, Tahera Khakoo (marr. diss. 1990); one *s* one *d*; 2nd, 2013, Saima Malik. *Educ:* Lady Manners Grammar Sch., Bakewell (Head Boy); Royal Coll. of Music (BMus; ARCM); University Coll. London (BSc 1st Cl. Hons Maths 1981). Concert pianist, 1973–; pupil of Cyril Smith; performances with LSO, LPO, with conductors incl. Sir Charles Groves; plays all Rachmaninov piano concertos. Teacher of Maths, Hemel Hempstead Sch., 1982–84; Hd, Maths, Bridgnorth Endowed Sch., 1984–90; Dep. Hd, The Chase, Malvern, 1990–2002; Headteacher: Tewkesbury Sch., 2002–06; Fortismere, Muswell Hill, 2006–10. Consultancy work for National Coll., 2007–09. FRSA 2008. *Recreations:* Rugby, squash, chess, rock climbing (incl. Kilimanjaro), travel, foreign languages, reading, charity, passionate about maths and music, favourite cities are London, Istanbul and Florence.

ONASANYA, Fiona; *b* Cambridge. *Educ:* Univ. of Hertfordshire (LLB Hons). Solicitor: Nockolds LLP Solicitors, 2010–12; Eversheds, 2013–16; Howes Percival, 2016; DC Law, 2016–17. Mem. (Lab) Cambs CC, 2013–16. MP for Peterborough, 2017–May 2019 (Lab, 2017–18; Ind, 2018–19). Mem., Communities and Local Govt Cttee, H of C, 2017–18.

OÑATE LABORDE, Santiago; Coordinator, Investigation and Identification Team, Organisation for Prohibition of Chemical Weapons, since 2018; *b* 24 May 1949; *s* of Santiago Oñate and Clara Laborde; *m* 1981, Laura Madrazo; three *d*. *Educ:* Universidad Nacional Autónoma de México (LLB 1972); postgrad. studies at Università degli Studi di Pavia, LSE and Univ. of Wisconsin-Madison. Prof. of Law, Universidad Autónoma Metropolitana-Azcapotzalco, Mexico, 1976–81; Vis. Prof., Law Sch., Univ. of Wisconsin-Madison, 1981–82. Mem. Congress, Chamber of Deputies, Mexico, 1985–88; Mem., Representative Assembly of Federal Dist, Mexico, 1988–91; Ambassador, Permanent Rep. to OAS, Washington, 1991–92; Attorney Gen. for Protection of Envmt, 1992–94; COS, President's Office, 1994; Sec. of State for Labour, 1994–95; Pres., Nat. Exec. Cttee, Partido Revolucionario Institucional, 1995–96; Ambassador for Mexico: to UK, 1997–2001; to the Netherlands, 2001–03; Legal Advr, OPCW, 2004–13; Permanent Observer of Mexico to Council of Europe, 2013–18. UN Audiovisual Lecture series, The Chemical Weapons Convention: an overview, 2009. *Publications:* La Acción Procesal en la Doctrina y el Derecho Positivo Mexicano, 1972; El Estado y el Derecho, 1977; Legal Aid in Mexico, 1979; Los Trabajadores Migratorios Frente a la Justicia Norteamericana, 1983; articles in Voz y Voto on Europe's migration crisis. *Recreations:* theatre, music, walking, nature protection. *Address:* (office) Johan de Wittlaan 32, 2517 JR, The Hague, Netherlands. *Club:* University (Mexico).

ONDAATJE, Sir Christopher; *see* Ondaatje, Sir P. C.

ONDAATJE, Michael; *see* Ondaatje, P. M.

ONDAATJE, Sir (Philip) Christopher, OC 1993; Kt 2003; CBE 2000; President, Ondaatje Foundation, since 1975; *b* 22 Feb. 1933; *s* of Philip Mervyn Ondaatje and Enid Doris Gratiaen; *m* 1959, Valda Bulins; one *s* two *d*. *Educ:* Blundell's Sch., Tiverton; LSE. National and Grindlays Bank, London, 1951–55; Burns Bros, & Denton, Toronto, 1955–56; Montrealer Mag. and Canada Month Mag., 1956–57; Maclean-Hunter Publishing Co. Ltd, Montreal, 1957–62; Financial Post, Toronto, 1963–65; Pitfield Mackay, Ross & Co. Ltd, Toronto, 1965–69; Founder: Pagurian Corp. Ltd, 1967–89; Loewen, Ondaatje, McCutcheon & Co. Ltd, 1970–88. Mem. Adv. Bd, Royal Soc. of Portrait Painters, 1998–; Mem. Council, RGS, 2001–05. Trustee, Nat. Portrait Gall., 2002–09. Mem., Canada's Olympic Bob-Sled Team, 1964. FRGS 1992. Hon. LLD Dalhousie, 1994; Hon. DLitt: Buckingham, 2002; Exeter, 2003; Macquarie, 2011. *Publications:* Olympic Victory, 1964; The Prime Ministers of Canada (1867–1967), 1967, rev. edn (1867–1985), 1985; Leopard in the Afternoon, 1989; The Man-Eater of Punanai, 1992; Sindh Revisited: a journey in the footsteps of Sir Richard Francis Burton, 1996; Journey to the Source of the Nile, 1998; Hemingway in Africa, 2003; The Power of Paper, 2007; The Glenthorne Cat, 2008; The Last Colonial, 2012. *Recreations:* tennis, golf, adventure, photography. *Address:* Glenthorne, Countisbury, near Lynton, N Devon EX35 6NQ. *Clubs:* Travellers, MCC; Somerset County Cricket (Life Mem.); Chester Golf; Lyford Cay (Bahamas).
*See also* M. Ondaatje.

ONDAATJE, (Philip) Michael, CC 2017 (OC 1988); writer; *b* 12 Sept. 1943; *s* of Philip Mervyn Ondaatje and Enid Doris Gratiaen. *Educ:* Dulwich Coll.; Univ. of Toronto; Queen's Univ., Canada. Prof., Dept of English, Glendon Coll., York Univ., 1971–. *Publications: poetry:* The Dainty Monsters, 1967; The Man with Seven Toes, 1968; There's a Trick I'm Learning to Do, 1979; Secular Love, 1984; The Cinnamon Peeler, 1991; (ed) The Long Poem Anthology, 1979; Handwriting, 1998; *prose:* Leonard Cohen (criticism), 1968; The Collected Works of Billy the Kid (poetry and prose), 1970; (ed) The Broken Ark, 1971; How to Train a Bassett, 1971; Rat Jelly, 1973; Coming Through Slaughter, 1976; Running in the Family (autobiog.), 1982; In the Skin of a Lion, 1987 (Trillium Award, 1987); (ed) From Ink Lake: an anthology of Canadian stories, 1990; Elimination Dance, 1991 (trans. French); The English Patient, 1992 (jt winner, Booker Prize, 1992; Trillium Award, 1992; Golden Man Booker Prize, 2018; filmed, 1997); Anil's Ghost, 2000; The Conversations: Walter Murch and the art of editing film, 2002; Divisadero, 2007 (Governor General's Award, Canada Council for Arts, 2007); The Cat's Table, 2011; Warlight, 2018.
*See also* Sir P. C. Ondaatje.

O'NEIL, H. James, (Jim); Co-Head, Corporate and Investment Banking, Europe, Middle East and Africa, Bank of America (formerly Bank of America Merill Lynch), since 2017; *b* New York, 1966; *s* of Henry O'Neil and Doris O'Neil. *Educ:* Univ. of Virginia (BS); Univ. of Chicago (MBA High Hons). Merrill Lynch & Co., subseq. Bank of America Merrill Lynch, 1993–2010, latterly Hd, Internat. Corporate Finance; Hd, Mkt Investments, 2010–12, Chief Exec., 2012–13, UK Financial Investments Ltd; Co-Hd, 2013–14, Hd, 2014–17, Global Financial Instns Gp, Bank of America Merrill Lynch. *Address:* Bank of America, Financial Centre, 2 King Edward Street, EC1A 1HQ.

O'NEIL, Roger; Member, Advisory Board, Nevastar Finance Ltd, since 2009; *b* 22 Feb. 1938; *s* of James William O'Neil and Claire Kathryn (*née* Williams); *m* 1976, Joan Mathewson; one *s* one *d*. *Educ:* Univ. of Notre Dame (BS Chemical Engrg, 1959); Cornell Univ. (MBA 1961). Joined Mobil Corp., New York, 1961; Various staff and exec. positions in Japan, Hong Kong, Australia, Paris, Cyprus, London and New York, 1963–73; Chm., Mobil cos in SE Asia, Singapore, 1973–78; Manager, Planning, Mobil Europe Inc., London, 1978–81; Manager, Corporate Econs and Planning, Mobil Corp., New York, 1981–82; Gp Vice Pres., Container Corp. of America, Chicago, 1982–84; Pres., Mobil Oil Italiana SpA, Rome, 1984–87; Chm. and Chief Exec., Mobil Oil Co., London, 1987–91; Dir and Vice Pres., Mobil Europe, 1991–92; Exec. Vice Pres. and Mem. Exec. Cttee, Statoil, 1992–97. Sen. Oil and Gas Advr, Dresdner Kleinwort Benson, 1997–2003. Non-exec. Bd Mem., Enterprise Oil plc, 1997–2002. Vice-Pres., Inst. of Petroleum, 1989–93 (FInstPet 1988). Mem., Adv. Bd, Johnson Business Sch., 1990–, Mem. Council, 2016–, Cornell Univ. FRSA 1988. *Publications:* Along the Way: a story of places, people and the international oil business, 2011. *Recreations:* archæology, squash, golf. *Address:* 3 Ormonde Gate, SW3 4EU. *Clubs:* Royal Automobile, Hurlingham; Royal Mid-Surrey Golf.

O'NEIL, William Andrew; CM 1995; CMG 2004; Secretary-General, International Maritime Organization, 1990–2003, now Emeritus; *b* Ottawa, 6 June 1927; *s* of Thomas Wilson and Margaret O'Neil (*née* Swan); *m* 1950, Dorothy Muir (decd); one *s* two *d*; *m* 2007, Olga Bosquez. *Educ:* Carleton Univ.; Univ. of Toronto (BASc Civil Engrg 1949). Engrg posts with Fed. Dept of Transport, 1949–55; Div. Engr, Regl Dir and Dir of

Construction, St Lawrence Seaway Authy, 1955–71; Federal Department of Transport: Dep. Administrator, Marine Services, 1971–80; also Comr, Canadian Coast Guard, 1975–80; St Lawrence Seaway Authority, 1980–90: Pres. and Chief Exec. Officer; Dir, Canarctic Shipping Co.; Pres., Seaway Internat. Bridge Corp. Council of International Maritime Organization: Canadian Rep., 1972–90; Chm., 1980–90. Chairman: Canadian Cttee, Lloyd's Register of Shipping, 1987–88; Adv. Bd, Panama Canal Authy, 1999–. Dir, Tsakos Energy Navigation, 2004–14. Mem. Bd, Internat. Maritime Bureau, 1991–. Chm., Governing Bd, Internat. Maritime Law Inst., Malta, 1991–2003. Chancellor, World Maritime Univ., 1991–2003. Member: Assoc. of Professional Engrs of Ont; ASCE; Engrg Alumni Hall of Dist., Univ. of Toronto, 1996. Hon. Freeman, Shipwrights' Co., 2002. FILT (FCIT 1994); FRSA 1992; Foreign Mem., Royal Acad. of Engrg, 1994. Hon. Titulary Mem., Comité Maritime Internat., 2001. Hon. LLD: Univ. of Malta, 1993; Meml Univ. of Newfoundland, Canada, 1996; Korea Maritime, 2002; Hon. DSc Nottingham Trent, 1994. Engrg Medal, 1972, Gold Medal, 1995, Assoc. of Professional Engrs of Ont; Distinguished Public Service Award, USA, 1980; Admirals' Medal, Admirals' Medal Foundn, Canada, 1994; NUMAST Award, 1995; Seatrade Personality of the Year Award, 1995; Silver Bell Award, Seamen's Church Inst., NY, 1997; Cdre Award, Conn Maritime Assoc., USA, 1998; Dioscuri Prize, Italian Naval League, 1998; Vice-Adm. Jerry Land Medal, Soc. of Naval Architects and Marine Engrs, USA, 1999; Halert C. Shepheard Award, Chamber of Shipping of America, 2000; Dist. Servs Medal, Directorate Gen. for Maritime Affairs, Colombia, 2001; Lifetime Achievement Award, Communications and IT in Shipping, 2002; 15 Nov. 1817 Medal, Uruguay, 2002. Ordre Nat. des Cèdres (Lebanon), 1995; Grand Cross, Order of Vasco Núñez de Balboa (Panama), 1998; Golden Jubilee Medal, 2002.

**O'NEILL**, family name of **Barons O'Neill, O'Neill of Clackmannan, O'Neill of Gatley** and **Rathcavan**.

**O'NEILL**, 4th Baron *cr* 1868; **Raymond Arthur Clanaboy O'Neill**, KCVO 2009; TD 1970; Lord-Lieutenant of County Antrim, 1994–2008; *b* 1 Sept. 1933; *s* of 3rd Baron and Anne Geraldine (she *m* 2nd, 1945, 2nd Viscount Rothermere, and 3rd, 1952, late Ian Fleming, and *d* 1981), *e* of Hon. Guy Charteris; *S* father, 1944; *m* 1963, Georgina Mary (*d* 2017), *er d* of Lord George Montagu Douglas Scott; three *s*. *Educ:* Eton; Royal Agricultural Coll. 2nd Lieut, 11th Hussars, Prince Albert's Own; Major, North Irish Horse, AVR; Lt-Col, RARO; Hon. Colonel: NI Horse Sqn, RYR, 1986–91; 69 Signal Sqn, NI Horse, 1988–93. Chairman: Ulster Countryside Cttee, 1971–75; NI Museums Council, 1993–98; Vice-Chm., Ulster Folk and Transport Mus., 1987–90 (Trustee, 1969–90); Member: NI Tourist Bd, 1973–80 (Chm., 1975–80); NI Nat. Trust Cttee, 1980–91 (Chm., 1981–91); Museums and Galleries Commn, 1987–94; President: Youth Action (formerly NI Assoc. of Youth Clubs), 1965–2010; Royal Ulster Agricl Soc., 1984–86 (Chm. Finance Cttee, 1974–83). DL Co. Antrim, 1967. *Recreations:* vintage motoring, railways, gardening. *Heir: s* Hon. Shane Sebastian Clanaboy O'Neill [*b* 25 July 1965; *m* 1997, Celia, *e d* of Peter Hickman; three *s*]. *Address:* Shanes Castle, Antrim, N Ireland BT41 4NE. *T:* (028) 9446 3264. *Club:* Turf.

**O'NEILL OF BENGARVE**, Baroness *cr* 1999 (Life Peer), of The Braid in the County of Antrim; **Onora Sylvia O'Neill**, CH 2014; CBE 1995; PhD; FBA 1993; FMedSci; *b* 23 Aug. 1941; *d* of Hon. Sir Con O'Neill, GCMG and Rosemary Margaret (*née* Pritchard) (later Lady Garvey); *m* 1963, Edward John Nell (marr. diss. 1976); two *s*. *Educ:* St Paul's Girls' Sch.; Somerville Coll., Oxford (BA, MA; Hon. Fellow, 1993); Harvard Univ. (PhD). Asst, then Associate Prof., Barnard Coll., Columbia Univ., 1970–77; University of Essex: Lectr, 1977–78; Sen. Lectr, 1978–83; Reader, 1983–87; Prof. of Philosophy, 1987–92; Principal, Newnham Coll., Cambridge, 1992–2006. Hon. Prof. of Ethics and Political Philos., Faculty of Philos., Univ. of Cambridge, 2003. Member: Animal Procedures Cttee, 1990–94; Nuffield Council on Bioethics, 1991–98 (Chm., 1996–98); Human Genetics Adv. Commn, 1996–99; MRC, 2012–18; Chm., Equality and Human Rights Commn, 2012–16. Chm., Nuffield Foundn, 1998–2010 (a Trustee, 1997–2010). Fellow, Wissenschaftskolleg, Berlin, 1989–90. President: Aristotelian Soc., 1988–89; Mind Assoc., 2003–04; British Acad., 2005–09. FMedSci 2002; Fellow, Austrian Acad. Sci., 2003. Mem., Amer. Philos. Soc., 2003. Foreign Hon. Mem., Amer. Acad. of Arts and Scis, 1993; Hon. FRS 2007; Hon. MRIA 2003. Hon. Bencher, Gray's Inn, 2002. Hon. DLitt: UEA, 1995; Dublin, 2002; Ulster, 2003; Bath, 2004; QUB, 2005; Edinburgh, 2007; UCL, 2012; Sussex, 2012; Reading, 2018; DU Essex, 1996; Hon. LLD: Nottingham, 1999; Aberdeen, 2001; Harvard, 2010; Glasgow, 2010; NUI, 2011; Leeds, 2012; Tulane, 2015; Hon. DLit London, 2003; Hon. DCL: Oxford, 2003; Newcastle, 2008; DUniv: Stirling, 2005; Heriot-Watt, 2007; York, 2010; Hon. DLaw Cambridge, 2007; Hon. Dr Ludwig Maximilian Univ., Munich, 2006; Hon. DSc Imperial Coll. London, 2014. Pour le Mérite, 2015; Kant Preis, Kantgesellschaft, 2015; Bundesverdienstkreuz, 2016; Holberg Prize (Norway), 2017; Berggruen Prize for Philos. and Culture, Berggruen Inst., 2017. *Publications:* Acting on Principle, 1976; Faces of Hunger, 1986; Constructions of Reason, 1989; Towards Justice and Virtue, 1996; Bounds of Justice, 2000; Autonomy and Trust in Bioethics, 2002; A Question of Trust, 2002; (with N. Manson) Rethinking Informed Consent in Bioethics, 2007; Constructing Authorities: reason, politics and interpretation in Kant's philosophy, 2016; Justice Across Boundaries: whose obligations?, 2016; Speech Rights and Speech Wrongs, 2016; From Principles to Practice: normativity and judgement in ethics and politics, 2018; numerous articles on philosophy, esp. political philosophy and ethics in learned jls. *Recreations:* walking, talking. *Address:* House of Lords, SW1A 0PW.

**O'NEILL OF CLACKMANNAN**, Baron *cr* 2005 (Life Peer), of Clackmannan in Clackmannanshire; **Martin John O'Neill**; *b* 6 Jan. 1945; *s* of John and Minnie O'Neill; *m* 1973, Elaine Marjorie Samuel; two *s*. *Educ:* Trinity Academy, Edinburgh; Heriot-Watt Univ. (BA Econ.); Moray House Coll. of Education, Edinburgh. Insurance Clerk, Scottish Widows Fund, 1963–67; Asst Examiner, Estate Duty Office of Scotland, 1971–73; Teacher of Modern Studies: Boroughmuir High School, Edinburgh, 1974–77; Craigmount High School, Edinburgh, 1977–79; Social Science Tutor, Open Univ., 1976–79. MP (Lab): Stirlingshire E and Clackmannan, 1979–83; Clackmannan, 1983–97; Ochil, 1997–2005. Opposition spokesman on Scottish affairs, 1980–84, on defence matters, 1984–88, on energy, 1992–95; chief opposition spokesman on defence, 1988–92. Mem., Select Cttee, Scottish Affairs, 1979–80; Chm., Select Cttee on Trade and Industry, 1995–2005. Hon. Dr Heriot-Watt, 2011. *Recreations:* watching football, reading, listening to jazz, the cinema. *Address:* House of Lords, SW1A 0PW.

**O'NEILL OF GATLEY**, Baron *cr* 2015 (Life Peer), of Gatley in the County of Greater Manchester; **Terence James (Jim) O'Neill**; Visiting Research Fellow, Breugel, since 2013; *b* Manchester, 17 March 1957; *s* of late Terence and Kathleen O'Neill; two *c*. *Educ:* Burnage High Sch., Manchester; Univ. of Sheffield (BA Econs 1978; MA 1979); Univ. of Surrey (PhD 1983). Economist: Bank of America, 1982–83; Internal Treasury Mgt, Marine Midland Bank, 1983–88; Swiss Bank Corp., 1988–95 (Hd of Global Res., 1991–95); Goldman Sachs: Economist and Partner, 1995–2013; Co-Hd, Global Econs Res. and Chief Currency Economist, 1995–2001; Hd, Global Econs Res., 2001–08; Chief Economist, 2001–10; Hd of Global Econs, Commodities and Strategy Res., 2008–10; Chm., Goldman Sachs Asset Mgt, 2010–13. Creator of acronym, BRICs (Brazil, Russia, India and China as the growth opportunities of the future), 2001. Chm., City Growth Commn, 2013–14. Commercial Sec., HM Treasury, 2015–16. Non-exec. Dir, DFE, 2013–. Chm., RIIA, 2018–. Hon. DLitt Sheffield, 2014. *Publications:* The Growth Map: economic opportunity in the BRICs and beyond, 2011; The BRIC Road to Growth, 2013. *Recreations:* sport, tennis, running, football, travel. *Address:* House of Lords, SW1A 0PW.

**O'NEILL, Aidan Mark Sebastian**; QC 2017; QC (Scot.) 1999; *b* 27 Jan. 1961; *s* of John Joseph, (Jack), O'Neill and Teresa Josephine O'Neill (*née* Birt); civil partnership 2006, Douglas Edington, *s* of late Capt. J. A. R., (Jock), Edington and Mrs H. A. L. C. Edington. *Educ:* St Francis Xavier Coll., Coatbridge; Holy Cross High Sch., Hamilton; Langside Coll., Glasgow; Univ. of Edinburgh (LLB Hons 1st cl. 1982); Univ. of Sydney (LLM Hons 1st cl. 1987); European Univ. Inst., Florence (LLM 1993); Univ. of Edinburgh (LLD 2013). Admitted Faculty of Advocates, 1987; called to the Bar, Inner Temple, 1996; Standing Jun. Counsel to Educn Dept, Scottish Office, 1997–99; Associate Mem., 2000, Mem., 2010–, Matrix Chambers, Gray's Inn. Inaugural Univ. Center for Values, Law and Public Affairs Fellow in Law and Normative Inquiry, Princeton Univ., 2007–08; Chair, Edinburgh Centre for Constitutional Law, 2009–; Hon. Fellow, Sch. of Law, Univ. of Edinburgh, 2009. *Publications:* (jtly) EU Law for UK Lawyers: the domestic impact of EU law within the UK, 1994, 2nd edn 2011; Decisions of the European Court of Justice and their Constitutional Implications, 1994; Judicial Review in Scotland: a practitioner's guide, 1999; articles in jls incl. Modern Law Rev., European Human Rights Law Rev., Juridical Rev., Judicial Rev., Common Knowledge, Public Law, Northern Ireland Legal Qly, Edinburgh Law Rev., Legal Studies, Common Market Law Rev., Scots Law Times, The Tablet. *Address:* Matrix Chambers, Gray's Inn, WC1R 5LN. *T:* (020) 7404 3447, *Fax:* (020) 7404 3448.

**O'NEILL, Prof. Alan,** PhD; Professor of Meteorology, University of Reading, 1993–2015, now Emeritus; Visiting Professor, Cavendish Laboratory, University of Cambridge, since 2015; Life Member, Clare Hall, Cambridge, 2015; *b* Merthyr Tydfil, 23 Sept. 1950; *s* of Bernard and Irene O'Neill; *m* 1973, Angela Portlock; one *s* one *d*. *Educ:* County Grammar Sch., Merthyr Tydfil; St Nicholas Grammar Sch., Northwood; Oriel Coll., Oxford (MA Physics); Open Univ. (MSc Maths); Univ. of Reading (PhD Meteorol. 1979). Hd, Stratospheric Res., Meteorological Office, 1974–93; SPSO (Individual Merit), 1990–93; University of Reading: Dir, Nat. Centre for Earth Observation, 2008–13; Dir of Res., Sch. of Math. and Phys. Scis, 2014–15. *Publications:* contrib. papers to Qly Jl RMetS. *Recreations:* reading history, walking, music, theatre. *Address:* Department of Meteorology, University of Reading, Berks RG6 6BB. *E:* a.oneill@reading.ac.uk. *Club:* Meteorological.

**O'NEILL, Alan Dennis**; Chairman, Hertfordshire Learning and Skills Council, 2003–08; *b* 2 March 1945; *s* of Dennis O'Neill and Audrey Florence O'Neill; *m* 1969, Susan Fearnley; one *s* two *d*. *Educ:* King George V Sch., Southport; Bishopshalt Sch., Hillingdon; Univ. of Birmingham (BSc Hons Physics 1966). Joined Kodak Ltd as res. scientist, 1966; Dir and Manager, Manufacturing Ops, 1991–96; Vice-Pres. and Chief Purchasing Officer, Eastman Kodak Co., 1996–98; Chm. and Man. Dir, Kodak Ltd, 1998–2001. *Recreations:* beekeeping, skiing, gardening, golf. *Address:* St Michael's Croft, Woodcock Hill, Berkhamsted, Herts HP4 3TR.

**O'NEILL, Brendan Richard,** PhD; FCMA; Chief Executive, ICI plc, 1999–2003 (Chief Operating Officer, 1998–99; Director, 1998–2003); *b* 6 Dec. 1948; *s* of John Christopher O'Neill and Doris O'Neill (*née* Monk); *m* 1979, Margaret Maude; one *s* two *d*. *Educ:* West Park GS, St Helens; Churchill Coll., Cambridge (MA Nat. Sci. 1972); Univ. of East Anglia (PhD Chemistry 1973). FCMA (FCIMA 1983). Ford Motor Co., 1973–75; British Leyland, 1975–81; BICC plc, 1981–83; Gp Financial Controller, Midland Bank, 1983–87; Guinness plc: Dir of Financial Control, 1987; Finance Dir, 1988–90, Man. Dir, Internat. Reg., 1990–92, United Distillers; Man. Dir, Guinness Brewing Worldwide, 1993–97; Chief Exec., Guinness, Diageo plc, 1997–98. Director: Guinness plc, 1993–97; EMAP plc, 1995–2002; Diageo plc, 1997–98; Tyco International, 2003–16; Rank Gp plc, 2004–07; Endurance Specialty Hldgs Ltd, 2004–14; Willis Towers Watson (formerly Watson Wyatt, then Towers Watson), 2006–; Informa plc, 2008–17. Mem. Council, 2000–07, Finance Cttee, 1994–2000, Cancer Res. UK (formerly ICRF). Trustee, Inst. of Cancer Research, 2015– (Hon. Treas., 2015–). *Recreations:* music, reading, family.

**O'NEILL, Brian Patrick**; QC 2010; a Recorder, 2002–19; *b* Dungannon, Co. Tyrone, 29 Nov. 1962; *s* of Patrick O'Neill and Bernadette O'Neill; *m* 2001, Charmaine Silveira; two *s* one *d*. *Educ:* St Patrick's Acad., Dungannon; Brunel Univ. (LLB Hons). Called to the Bar, Gray's Inn, 1987. *Recreations:* walking our lovely labradoodle (Storm), watching and coaching football, cooking and eating out with friends, encouraging my teenage children to get out of bed in the morning and switch off their screens at night. *Address:* 2 Hare Court, Temple, EC4Y 7BH. *T:* (020) 7353 5324. *E:* brianoneillqc@2harecourt.com. *Clubs:* Arsenal Football; Broomwood Football (Wandsworth).

**O'NEILL, Dennis James,** CBE 2000; operatic tenor; Director, Wales International Academy of Voice, University of Wales Trinity St David, since 2011; *b* 25 Feb. 1948; *s* of late Dr William P. O'Neill and Eva A. O'Neill (*née* Rees); *m* 1st, 1970, Ruth Collins (marr. diss. 1987); one *s* one *d*; 2nd, 1988, Ellen Folkestad. *Educ:* Gowerton Boys' Grammar Sch. FTCL 1969; ARCM 1971. Specialist in Italian repertoire and works of Verdi in particular; Début: Royal Opera House, Covent Garden, 1979; Vienna State Opera, 1981; Hamburg State Opera, 1981; San Francisco Opera, 1984; Chicago Lyric Opera, 1985; Paris Opera, 1986; Metropolitan Opera, NY, 1986; Bayerische Staatsoper, Munich, 1992; has performed worldwide in opera and concerts. Many recordings. Presenter, Dennis O'Neill, BBC TV, 1987, 1988, 1989. Vis. Prof., RAM, 2005 (Hon. RAM 2006). Dir, Wexford Fest. Artists Develt prog., 2005–; Dir (and Founder), Cardiff Internat. Acad. of Voice, Cardiff Univ., 2007–10. Fellow, 2010, Prof. of Practice, 2016, Univ. of Wales Trinity St David. FLSW 2014. Hon. Fellow, Univ. of Cardiff, 1997; Hon. FRWCMD (Hon. FWCMD, 1993). Hon. DMus Glamorgan, 2003. Verdi medal, Amici di Verdi, 2005; Golden Jubilee Award, Welsh Music Guild, 2005. OStJ 2008 (SBStJ 2006). *Recreations:* dinner parties, Verdi. *Address:* Wales International Academy of Voice, 42 The Parade, Roath, Cardiff CF24 3AD.

**O'NEILL, Prof. Hugh St Clair,** PhD; FRS 2012; FAA; Laureate Professor, Research School of Earth Sciences, Australian National University, since 2014; *b* Farnborough, Hants, 5 Sept. 1953; *s* of Captain Barry O'Neill and Barbara O'Neill; *m* 1985, Marlene Quincey; one *s* one *d*. *Educ:* Wellington Coll.; St Edmund Hall, Oxford (BA 1975); Univ. of Manchester (PhD 1978). Res. Fellow, Res. Sch. of Earth Scis, ANU, 1981–86; Staff Scientist, Bayerisches Geoinstitut, Univ. of Bayreuth, Germany, 1987–94; Research School of Earth Sciences, Australian National University: Sen. Fellow, 1994–2004; Prof., 2004–12; Associate Dir, 2006–13; Distinguished Prof., 2012–14. FAA 2008; Australian Laureate Fellow, 2013. *Publications:* contrib. papers to learned scientific jls. *Recreations:* field work, walking, theatre, popular history.

**O'NEILL, Jim;** *see* Baron O'Neill of Gatley.

**O'NEILL, John;** Rector, The High School of Glasgow, since 2015; *b* Coatbridge, 13 Feb. 1965; *s* of Thomas and Jean O'Neill; *m* 1993, Maureen Jackson; one *s*. *Educ:* St Ambrose High Sch., Coatbridge; Univ. of Glasgow (MA Hons Medieval and Modern Hist. 1987); St Andrew's Coll. of Educn (PGCE Dist. 1988). Teacher of History, Politics and Religion,

St Thomas More Sch., Wood Green, 1988–89; Teacher of History and Modern Studies, Glasgow and N Lanarks DC, 1989–92; Teacher of History, Politics and Modern Studies, and Sen. Tutor, Merchiston Castle Sch., 1992–97; Teacher of History and Modern Studies, and Asst Housemaster, Glasgow Acad., 1997–2000; Hd of Sixth Form and Housemaster, Merchiston Castle Sch., 2000–04; Sen. Dep. Rector, High Sch. of Glasgow, 2004–15. *Recreations:* history, poetry, road cycling, family. *Address:* 2 Sella Road, Bishopbriggs, Glasgow G64 1UZ. *E:* rector@hsog.co.uk.

**O'NEILL, John Joseph, (Jonjo);** racehorse trainer, since 1987; *b* 13 April 1952; *s of* Thomas and Margaret O'Neill; *m* 1997, Jacqueline (*née* Bellamy); three *s* two *d*. *Educ:* Castletownroache Nat. Sch. National Hunt Jockey, 1969–87: winner, 901 races; Champion Jockey, 1977–78, 1979–80; broke record for number of winners in one season, 149 in 1977–78; winner: Cheltenham Gold Cup: 1979 on Alverton; 1986 on Dawn Run; Champion Hurdle: 1986 on Sea Pigeon; 1984 on Dawn Run; has trained over 2,000 winners including: Gipsy Fiddler, Windsor Castle Stakes, Royal Ascot; Well Sharp, Ascot Stakes, Royal Ascot; Tominator, Northumberland Plate; Mini Sensation, Coral Welsh National, 2002; Synchronised, Coral Welsh National, 2011, Betfred Cheltenham Gold Cup, 2012; Butler's Cabin, Irish Grand National, 2007; Don't Push It, Grand National, 2010; Taquin de Seuil, Challow Novices' Hurdle, 2012, BetVictor Gold Cup, Cheltenham, 2016; also 26 winners at Cheltenham National Hunt Fest., 19 winners at Aintree Fest. and 3 winners at Punchestown Fest. Ireland's People of Year Award, 1986. *Address:* Jackdaws Castle, Temple Guiting, Cheltenham, Glos GL54 5XU. *T:* (01386) 584209, *Fax:* (01386) 584219. *E:* reception@jonjooneillracing.com. *W:* www.jonjooneillracing.com.

**O'NEILL, Prof. Luke Anthony John,** PhD; FRS 2016; Professor of Biochemistry, Trinity College Dublin, since 2009; *b* Dublin, 17 June 1964; *s of* Kevin O'Neill and Carmel O'Neill (*née* Sherry); *m* 1993, Margaret Worrall; two *s*. *Educ:* St Peter's Sch., Bray, Co. Wicklow; Presentation Coll., Bray; Trinity Coll. Dublin (BA Hons Natural Scis); Royal Coll. of Surgeons, Univ. of London (PhD Pharmacol.). MRC Postdoctoral Fellow, Strangeways Res. Lab., Cambridge, 1988–91; Lectr in Biochem., 1991–99, Associate Prof., 1999–2007, TCD. MRIA 1996. FTCD 1996. *Publications:* contribs to scientific jls; Humanology: a scientist's guide to our amazing existence, 2018; The Great Irish Science Book, 2019. *Recreations:* music, boating. *Address:* 4A Burdett Avenue, Sandy Cove, Co. Dublin, Ireland. *E:* laoneill@tcd.ie.

**O'NEILL, Mark William Robert,** PhD; Associate Professor, College of Arts, and Museum Consultant, University of Glasgow, 2016; *b* 10 Nov. 1956; *s of* Michael O'Neill and Greta (*née* Desmond). *Educ:* University Coll., Cork (BA Hons 1976; HDipEd 1977); Leicester Univ. (Grad. Cert. Mus. Studies 1985); Getty Leadership Inst. (Mus. Mgt Inst. 1993); City of London Univ. (PhD 2011). Curator, Springburn Mus., 1985–90; Glasgow Museums, 1990–2005: Keeper of Social Hist., 1990–92; Sen. Curator of Hist., 1992–97; Hd, Curatorial Services, 1997–98; Head, 1998–2005; Hd, Glasgow Arts and Mus, 2005–09; Dir of Policy and Research, Glasgow Life, 2009–16. Expert Advr, Event Communication, 2017–. Judge, Eur. Mus. of Year Award, 2016–. FMA 1997. *Publications:* contrib. articles on philosophy and practice of museums, cities, culture and regeneration. *Recreations:* classical music, fiction, psychology.

**O'NEILL, Martin Hugh Michael,** OBE 2004 (MBE 1983); Manager, Nottingham Forest Football Club, 2019; *b* Kilrea, NI, 1 March 1952; *m* Geraldine; two *d*. Professional footballer: Nottingham Forest, 1971–81 (League Champions, 1978; European Cup winners, 1979 and 1980); Norwich City, 1981, 1982–83; Manchester City, 1981–82; Notts Co., 1983–85; Mem., NI team, 1971–84 (64 caps); Manager: Grantham Town, 1987–89; Shepshed Charterhouse, 1989; Wycombe Wanderers, 1990–95 (Vauxhall Conf. winners, promoted to Football League, 1992–93); Norwich City, 1995; Leicester City, 1995–2000; Celtic, 2000–05; Aston Villa, 2006–10; Sunderland, 2011–13; Republic of Ireland nat. football team, 2013–18.

**O'NEILL, Michael Angus,** CMG 2012; HM Diplomatic Service, retired; Assistant Secretary-General, United Nations, and Assistant Administrator for External Relations and Advocacy, United Nations Development Programme, 2014–18; *b* 25 May 1965; *s of* Capt. Shane O'Neill and Jean O'Neill (*née* Macintosh Mayer); *m* 1991, Claire Naomi, *d* of Sir David (Gordon) Bannerman, *qv*; three *s* one *d*. *Educ:* Manchester Grammar Sch.; Brasenose Coll., Oxford (MA); LSE (MSc). MoD, 1988–91; Second Sec., UK Delegn to NATO, 1991–94; joined HM Diplomatic Service, 1994; Second, later First, Sec., FCO, 1994–98; Vis. Fellow, Inst. for Nat. Security Studies, Washington, DC, 1998–99; First Sec., Washington, 1999–2002; Counsellor, UK Mission to UN, NY, 2002–06; Counsellor, UK Perm. Repn to EU, Brussels, 2006–07; UK Special Rep. for Sudan, FCO, 2007–10; UK Sen. Rep., Southern Afghanistan and Head of Mission, Helmand Provincial Reconstruction Team, 2010–12; Ambassador to Qatar, 2012–13; Dir, Cabinet Office Nat. Security Secretariat, 2013–14. *Recreations:* travel, watching films and football, walking a chocolate labrador. *Address:* Canterbury, Kent.

**O'NEILL, Michelle;** Member (SF) Mid-Ulster, Northern Ireland Assembly, since 2007; Leader, Sinn Féin, since 2017; *m* Paddy O'Neill; one *s* one *d*. Pol Advr to Francie Molloy, NI Assembly, 1998–2005. Mem. (SF) Dungannon and S Tyrone BC, 2005–15 (Mayor, 2010–11). Minister of Agriculture and Rural Develt, 2011–16, of Health, 2016–17, NI. Formerly Member: Bd, E Tyrone Comhairle Ceantair; Mid Ulster Dáil Ceantair. *Address:* Northern Ireland Assembly, Parliament Buildings, Stormont, Belfast BT4 3XX.

**O'NEILL, Paul Henry;** Senior Advisor, The Blackstone Group, 2003–11; Chairman (non-executive), Value Capture LLC, since 2005; *b* 4 Dec. 1935; *m* 1955, Nancy Jo Wolfe; one *s* three *d*. *Educ:* Fresno State Coll., Calif (BA Econs); Indiana Univ. (MPA). Computer analyst, Veterans Admin, 1961–66; Asst Dir, Associate Dir and Dep. Dir, Office of Mgt and Budget, 1967–77; Vice-Pres., 1977–85, Pres., 1985–87, Internat. Paper Co.; Chm. and CEO, 1987–99, Chm., 1999–2000, Alcoa; Sec., US Treasury, 2001–02. Director: Eastman Kodak, 2003–06; TRW Automotive Hldgs, 2003–14; Nalco Co., 2003–07; Qcept, 2004–; Celanese Corp., 2004–13. Director: Peterson Inst. for Internat. Econs (formerly Inst. for Internat. Econs), 2003–12; Center for Global Develt, 2004–10. Mem. Bd of Trustees, RAND Corp., 2003–13 (formerly Chm.). *Recreation:* painting. *Address:* Suite 100, One North Shore Center, 12 Federal Street, Pittsburgh, PA 15212, USA.

**O'NEILL, Robert James,** CMG 1978; HM Diplomatic Service, retired; *b* 17 June 1932; *m* 1958, Helen Juniper; one *s* two *d*. *Educ:* King Edward VI Sch., Chelmsford; Trinity Coll., Cambridge (Schol.; 1st cl. English Tripos Pts I and II). Entered HM Foreign (now Diplomatic) Service, 1955; FO, 1955–57; British Embassy, Ankara, 1957–60; Dakar, 1961–63; FO, 1963–68, Private Sec. to Chancellor of Duchy of Lancaster, 1966, and to Minister of State for Foreign Affairs, 1967–68; British Embassy, Bonn, 1968–72; Counsellor Diplomatic Service, 1972; seconded to Cabinet Office as Asst Sec., 1972–75; FCO, 1975–78; Dep. Governor, Gibraltar, 1978–81; Under Sec., Cabinet Office and Mem., Jt Intelligence Cttee, 1981–84; Asst Under-Sec. of State, FCO, 1984–86; Ambassador to Austria, and concurrently Head of UK Delegn, MBFR, Vienna, 1986–89; Ambassador to Belgium, 1989–92; EC Presidency Rep. for Macedonia, 1992. EU Rep., OSCE Bosnia elections Task Force, 1995. Chm., Anglo-Austrian Soc., 2014–19. *Publications:* (with N. Weaver) Edward Bawden in the Middle East, 2008. *Recreations:* diplomatic history, hill-walking. *Address:* 4 Castle Street, Saffron Walden, Essex CB10 1BP. *T:* (01799) 520291. *Club:* Travellers.

**O'NEILL, Prof. Robert John,** AO 1988; FASSA; Director, Lowy Institute for International Policy, 2003–12; Chairman, Australian Strategic Policy Institute, Canberra, 1999–2005; Chichele Professor of the History of War, and Fellow of All Souls College, University of Oxford, 1987–2001, now Emeritus Fellow; *b* 5 Nov. 1936; *s of* Joseph Henry and Janet Gibbon O'Neill; *m* 1965, Sally Margaret Burnard; two *d*. *Educ:* Scotch Coll., Melbourne; Royal Military Coll. of Australia; Univ. of Melbourne (BE); Brasenose Coll., Oxford (MA, DPhil 1965; Hon. Fellow, 1990). FASSA 1977 (Jubilee Fellow, 2018); FIE(Aust) 1981–96; FRHistS 1990–2004. Served Australian Army, 1955–68; Rhodes Scholar, Vic, 1961; Fifth Bn Royal Australian Regt, Vietnam, 1966–67 (mentioned in despatches); Major 1967; resigned 1968. Sen. Lectr in History, Royal Military Coll. of Australia, 1968–69; Australian National University: Sen. Fellow in Internat. Relations, 1969–77, Professorial Fellow, 1977–82; Head, Strategic and Defence Studies Centre, 1971–82 (Adjunct Prof., 2001–); Dir, IISS, 1982–87; Dir of Graduate Studies, Modern History Faculty, Univ. of Oxford, 1990–92. Dep. Chm. Bd, Graduate Sch. of Govt, 2003–05, Chm., Internat. Academic Adv. Bd, US Studies Centre, 2009–11, Univ. of Sydney. Official Australian Historian for the Korean War, 1969–82. Dir, Shell Transport and Trading, 1992–2002. Chairman: Management Cttee, Sir Robert Menzies Centre for Australian Studies, Univ. of London, 1990–95; Bd, Centre for Defence Studies, KCL, 1990–95; Chm. Council, IISS, 1996–2001 (Mem. Council, 1977–82, 1992–94, Vice-Chm. Council, 1994–96). Governor: Ditchley Foundn, 1989–2001; Internat. Peace Acad., 1990–2001; Salzburg Seminar, 1992–97; Trustee: Imperial War Museum, 1990–98 (Chm. Trustees, 1998–2001); Commonwealth War Graves Commn, 1991–2001; Mem., Rhodes Trust, 1995–2001. Mem., Adv. Bd, Investment Co. of America, 1988–2010, and Dir, two other mutual funds, Capital Group, LA, 1992–2013. Pres., Rylstone and Dist Historical Soc., 2003–07; Mem. Exec. Cttee, Blackheath History Forum, 2009–. Chm., Round Table Moot, 1986–92. Hon. Col 5th (Volunteer) Royal Green Jackets, 1993–99. Foundn Fellow, Australian Inst. of Internat. Affairs, 2009. Hon. DLitt ANU, 2001. Centenary Medal (Australia), 2003; Nat. Volunteer Award (Australia), 2012. *Publications:* The German Army and the Nazi Party 1933–1939, 1966; Vietnam Task, 1968; General Giap: politician and strategist, 1969; (ed) The Strategic Nuclear Balance, 1975; (ed) The Defence of Australia: fundamental new aspects, 1977; (ed) Insecurity: the spread of weapons in the Indian and Pacific Oceans, 1978; (ed jtly) Australian Dictionary of Biography, Vols 7–14, 1979–97; (ed with David Horner) New Directions in Strategic Thinking, 1981; Australia in the Korean War 1950–1953, Vol. 1, Strategy and Diplomacy, 1981, Vol. II, Combat Operations, 1985; (ed with David Horner) Australian Defence Policy for the 1980s, 1982; (ed) Security in East Asia, 1984; (ed) The Conduct of East-West Relations in the 1980s, 1985; (ed) New Technology and Western Security Policy, 1985; (ed) Doctrine, the Alliance and Arms Control, 1986; (ed) East Asia, the West and International Security, 1987; (ed) Security in the Mediterranean, 1989; (ed with R. J. Vincent) The West and the Third World, 1990; (ed with Beatrice Heuser) Securing Peace in Europe 1945–62, 1992; (ed jtly) War, Strategy and International Politics, 1992; (ed with John Baylis) Alternative Nuclear Futures, 1999; (ed) Essential Histories, 78 vols, 2000–14; (ed) Paving the Way, 2019; articles in many learned jls. *Recreations:* local history, walking.

**O'NEILL, Sally Jane;** QC 1997; a Recorder, since 2000; *b* 30 Sept. 1953; *d* of late Maj. John O'Neill, RA retd and Frances Agnes O'Neill (*née* Riley); *m* 1986, David Bloss Kingsbury. *Educ:* St Joseph's Convent, Stafford; Alleyne's Grammar Sch., Uttoxeter; Mid-Essex Technical Coll. (LLB 1975). Called to the Bar, Gray's Inn, 1976, Bencher, 2002; in practice at the Bar, 1976–. An Asst Recorder, 1997–2000. Chm., Criminal Bar Assoc., 2007–08. *Recreations:* gardening, tennis, ski-ing, sailing, bull dogs, P. G. Wodehouse. *Address:* Furnival Chambers, 32 Furnival Street, EC4A 1JQ. *T:* (020) 7405 3232.

**O'NEILL, Susan Janet;** *see* Watts, S. J.

**O'NEILL, William Alan;** Executive Vice President, News Corporation, 1990–2002; Director, News International plc, 1995–2002; *b* 22 May 1936; *s of* John O'Neill and Martha O'Neill (*née* Kitson); *m* 1962, Alene Joy Brown (*d* 2018); one *d* (one *s* decd). *Educ:* Sydney Tech. Coll. Gp Employee Relns Manager, News Ltd (Australia), 1977–80; Gen. Manager, 1981, Dir, 1981–90, Times Newspapers Ltd; Vice-Pres. (Personnel), News America Publishing, 1984–85; Exec. Vice-Pres., and Gen. Manager, New York Post, 1985–86, and Vice-Pres. (Human Resources), News Corp., 1986; Man. Dir, News Internat. Newspapers, 1987–90; Director: News Corp., 1987–90; News Gp Newspapers Ltd, 1987–90; Director and Executive Vice-President: News America Inc., 1990–2002; News America Publishing Inc., 1990–2002; CEO, News Internat. plc, 1995. Chm., Convoys Ltd, 1987–89; Dep. Chm., Townsend Hook, 1987–89; Director: Sky TV; Eric Bemrose Ltd. Life Mem., American-Australian Assoc. *Recreations:* travelling, genealogy. *Address:* 31 Wolfeton Way, San Antonio, TX 78218–6035, USA. *T:* (210) 8058871.

**ONG, Colin Yee Cheng,** FCIArb; QC 2017; *s of* Ong Pang Ting and Teresa Liew; *m* 1967, Lim Hui Min; three *s* one *d*. *Educ:* Univ. of Sheffield (LLB Hons 1990); Queen Mary and Westfield Coll., Univ. of London (LLM 1992; PhD 1995); Dip. Internat. Commercial Arbitration 2003; FCIArb 2003; Chartered Arbitrator 2004. Called to the Bar, Inner Temple, 1991, Bencher 2010; in practice as barrister, 1991–, specialising in commercial law and internat. arbitration; Advocate and Solicitor: Brunei, 1998; Singapore, 2012. Adjunct Associate Prof., Nat. Univ. of Singapore, 2004–13; Adjunct Prof., Univ. Kebangsaan Malaysia, 2007–11; Visiting Professor: KCL, 2007–10; Univ. of Malaya, 2009–10; of Law, Univ. of Indonesia, 2014–; Univ. of Hong Kong, 2014–; Univ. Padjadjaran Indonesia, 2014–; Vis. Professorial Fellow, QMUL (formerly QMW), 1996–2013. Prin. Legal Consultant, ASEAN Centre for Energy, 2002–03; Panel Mem., ASEAN Protocol on Enhanced Dispute Settlement Mechanism, 2008–11; Mem., Adv. Cttee, China-ASEAN Legal Res. Centre, 2010–. Vice Chairman: Arbitration Cttee, Inter-Pacific Bar Assoc., 1996–; Arbitration Cttee, Internat. Bar Assoc., 2009–11; Vice President: Asia Pacific Regl Arbitration Gp, 2009–; Asia Pacific Users Council, London Court of Internat. Arbitration, 2010–12; President: Adv. Governing Council, Indonesian Nat. Bd of Arbitration, 2003–; Appointing Council, Cambodian Nat. Commercial Arbitration Cttee, 2012–; Vice Pres., Appointing Council, Thailand Arbitration Centre, 2016–. Pres., Arbitration Assoc. Brunei Darussalam, 2008–. Fellow: Malaysian Inst. Arbitrators, 2004; Singapore Inst. Arbitrators, 2005. *Publications:* Cross Border Litigation within ASEAN, 1997; Trade Mark Laws of Brunei, 2003; (with O'Reilly) Costs in International Arbitration, 2013; (ed with L. Newman) Interim Measures in International Arbitration, 2014; Dispute Resolution Provisions, 1999 FIDIC Form, 2015; *contributor:* Attachment of Assets, 2005; Enforcement of Money Judgements, 2005; Foreign Judgements, 2005; Leading Asian Arbitrators Handbook, 2007; (with Hwang) Take the Witness: cross-examination in international arbitration, 2010; ASEAN World Arbitration Reporter, 2nd edn 2010; Asia Arbitration Handbook, 2011; International Arbitration Review, 6th edn 2015; Investment Treaty Arbitration Review, 2016. *Recreations:* reading, classical music, cooking, travelling. *Address:* 36 Stone, 4 Field Court, WC1R 5EF. *T:* (020) 7440 6900. *E:* colin.ong@36stone.co.uk.

**ONIONS, Jeffery Peter**; QC 1998; *b* 22 Aug. 1957; *s* of late Derrick and Violet Onions; *m* 1987, Sally Louise Hine; one *d*. *Educ*: St Albans Sch.; St John's Coll., Cambridge (BA 1979, MA 1983; LLM (LLB 1980); hockey blue 1977–79). Called to the Bar, Middle Temple, 1981 (Astbury Schol.), Bencher, 2010; in practice at the Bar, 1981–. Mem., Bar Council, 1987–89. *Recreations*: cricket, wine, opera. *Address*: 1 Essex Court, Temple, EC4Y 9AR. *T*: (020) 7583 2000. *Clubs*: Reform; MCC, Middlesex CC, Surrey CC; Hawks (Cambridge); 1890.

**O'NIONS, Sir (Robert) Keith**, Kt 1999; PhD; FRS 1983; Rector, 2010–14, and President, 2013–14, Imperial College London; Chairman: Cambridge Enterprise, University of Cambridge, since 2014; British Geological Survey, since 2017; *b* 26 Sept. 1944; *s* of William Henry O'Nions and Eva O'Nions; *m* 1967, Rita Margaret Bill; three *d*. *Educ*: Univ. of Nottingham (BSc 1966); Univ. of Alberta (PhD 1969). Post-doctoral Fellow, Oslo Univ., 1970; Demonstr in Petrology, Oxford Univ., 1971–72, Lectr in Geochem., 1972–75; Associate Prof., then Prof., Columbia Univ., NY, 1975–79; Royal Soc. Res. Prof., 1979–95, and Fellow, Clare Hall, 1980–95, Cambridge Univ. (Hon. Fellow, 1995); Oxford University: Prof. of Physics and Chemistry of Minerals, 1995–2004 (on leave of absence, 2000–04); Head, Dept of Earth Scis, 1995–99; Fellow, St Hugh's Coll., 1995–2004, now Hon. Fellow; Fellow, Wolfson Coll., 2004–10; Chief Scientific Advr, MoD, 2000–04; Dir Gen. of Res. Councils, Office of Sci. and Technol., later Dir Gen., Sci. and Innovation, DTI, subseq. DIUS, 2004–08; Dir, Inst. for Security Sci. and Technol., Imperial Coll. London, 2008–10. Vis. Prof., Univ. of Oxford, 2004–05. Non-exec. Dir, Finmeccanica UK, 2008–10; Dir, Nu Instruments Ltd, 2012–16. Mem. Bd, Agency for Sci., Technol. and Res., Singapore, 2013–. Trustee: Natural History Mus., 1996–2006 (Chm., 2003–06); Nanyang Tech. Univ., Singapore, 2010–18; Defence Nat. Rehabilitation Centre, 2016–19. Hon. FREng 2005. Hon. Fellow, Indian Acad. of Scis, 1998; For. Fellow, Nat. Indian Sci. Acad., 2000; Mem., Norwegian Acad. of Sciences, 1980. Hon. doctorates from Univs of Abertay, Alberta, Cardiff, Edinburgh, Glasgow, Heriot-Watt, Paris, RHBNC, Loughborough, Nottingham and Birmingham; Hon. Dr Imperial Coll. London, 2018. Macelwane Award, Amer. Geophys. Union, 1979; Bigsby Medal, Geol Soc. London, 1983; Holmes Medal, Eur. Union of Geosciences, 1995; Lyell Medal, Geol Soc. of London, 1995; Urey Medal, Eur. Assoc. Geochemistry, 2001. *Publications*: contrib. to jls related to earth and planetary sciences. *E*: keith.onions@enterprise.cam.ac.uk.

**ONIONS, His Honour Robin William**; a Circuit Judge, 2000–16; *b* 12 April 1948; *s* of late Ernest Onions, DFC, and Edith Margaret Onions; *m* 1970, Catherine Anne Graham; two *s*. *Educ*: Prestfelde Sch., Shrewsbury; Priory Grammar Sch., Shrewsbury; London Sch. of Econs (LLB 1970). Articled clerk, Royal Borough of Kingston upon Thames, 1971–73; admitted solicitor, 1973; J. C. H. Bowdler & Sons, Shrewsbury, subsequently Lanyon Bowdler: solicitor, 1974–76; Partner, 1977–2000; Sen. Partner, 1993–2000. A Recorder, 1991–2000; Resident Judge, Shrewsbury Crown Court, 2005–14. Mem., Parole Bd, 2010–15. *Recreations*: football, cricket, travel, gardening, keeping fit?

**ONN, Melanie**; MP (Lab) Great Grimsby, since 2015; *b* Great Grimsby, 19 June 1979; *d* of Jacqueline Jagger; *m* 2014, Christopher Jenkinson; one *s*. *Educ*: Healing Comprehensive Sch., Grimsby; Franklin Coll., Grimsby; Middlesex Univ. (BA Hons Politics, Philosophy and Internat. Studies 2000). Labour Party: Facilities Adminr, 2000–03; Communications Officer to Gen. Sec., 2003–06; Compliance Officer, 2006–10; Hd of Compliance, 2010; Regl Organiser, Yorks and Humber, Unison, 2010–15. Shadow Dep. Leader of H of C, 2015–16; Shadow Minister for Housing, 2017–19. Mem., Procedure Cttee, H of C, 2016–. *Address*: House of Commons, SW1A 0AA. *T*: (020) 7219 6282; (office) 112 Cleethorpe Road, Grimsby, NE Lincs DN31 3HW. *T*: (01472) 359584. *E*: melanie.onn.mp@parliament.uk.

**ONSLOW**, family name of **Earl of Onslow**.

**ONSLOW, 8th Earl of**, *cr* 1801; **Rupert Charles William Bullard Onslow**; Bt 1660; Baron Onslow 1716; Baron Cranley 1776; Viscount Cranley 1801; *b* 16 June 1967; *s* of 7th Earl of Onslow and of Robin Lindsay Onslow (*née* Bullard); *S* father, 2011; *m* 1999, Leigh, *d* of late E. Jones-Fenleigh, one *d*. *Educ*: Eton; Western Kentucky Univ., USA. *Recreations*: photography, riding, shooting. *Heir*: *kinsman* Anthony Ernest Edward Onslow, *b* 30 May 1955. *Address*: Temple Court, Clandon Park, Guildford, Surrey GU4 7RQ.

**ONSLOW, Andrew George**; QC 2002; *b* 10 Feb. 1957; *s* of late John Onslow and of Susan Margaret Ursula Onslow; *m* 1991, Elizabeth Jane Owen; three *s* two *d*. *Educ*: Lancing Coll.; Corpus Christi Coll., Oxford (Open Schol.; BA 1st Cl. Hons Lit.Hum. 1979); City Univ. (Dip. Law 1981). Called to the Bar, Middle Temple, 1982, Bencher, 2019; in practice, specialising in commercial law. *Address*: 3 Verulam Buildings, Gray's Inn, WC1R 5NT. *T*: (020) 7831 8441, *Fax*: (020) 7831 8479. *E*: aonslow@3vb.com.

**ONSLOW, Sir Richard (Paul Atherton)**, 9th Bt *cr* 1797, of Althain, Lancashire; *b* Bournemouth, 16 Sept. 1958; *o s* of Sir John Roger Wilmot Onslow, 8th Bt and of Catherine Zoia (*née* Greenway, now Keefe); *S* father, 2009; *m* 1st, 1984, Josephine Anne Dean (marr. diss. 2003); one *s* one *d*; 2nd, 2014, Carol Anne, *y d* of late Harold Hillary. *Educ*: Cheltenham Coll.; Univ. of Leicester (BSc Hons). *Heir*: *s* Harry Alexander John Onslow, *b* 7 Oct. 1986.

**ONTARIO, Bishop of**, since 2011; **Rt Rev. Michael Douglas Oulton**; *b* Sackville, NB, 21 Dec. 1959; *s* of C. Robert Oulton and Lucy L. Oulton (*née* Sharpe); *m* 1980, Rev. Jeanie Lee Vautour; two *s* one *d*. *Educ*: Tantramor Regl High Sch., Sackville; Mt Allison Univ., Sackville (BA); Univ. of New Brunswick, Fredericton (LLB); Univ. of Toronto (Wycliffe Coll.) (MDiv). Associate Lawyer: Hicks Le Moine, Amherst, NS; Ove B. Samuelson, Sackville; ordained deacon, 1992, priest, 1993; Rector: Parish of Alberton, PEI, 1992–97; Parish of St Peter, Kingston, Ont, 1997–2004; Parish of Christ Ch, Belleville, Ont, 2004–11. *Recreations*: time with my family, hockey, golf. *Address*: Diocese of Ontario, 165 Ontario Street, PO Box 490 Kingston Main, Kingston, ON K7L 4W5, Canada. *T*: (613) 5444774, *Fax*: (613) 5473745. *E*: moulton@ontario.anglican.ca.

**ONWURAH, Chinyelu Susan, (Chi)**; MP (Lab) Newcastle upon Tyne Central, since 2010; *b* Wallsend, 12 April 1965. *Educ*: Kenton Sch.; Imperial Coll. London (BEng Electrical Engrg 1987); Manchester Business Sch. (MBA 2002). CEng 2003; FIET 2012; FCGI 2017. With Nortel, 1987–95; Cable & Wireless, 1995–99; Director: product strategy, Global Telesystems UK, 1999–2000; mkt develt, Teligent, 2000–01; Partner, Hammatan Ventures, 2001–04; Hd, telecoms technol., Ofcom, 2004–10. Shadow Minister: for innovation and sci., BIS, 2010–13; Cabinet Office, 2013–15; Industrial Strategy, Sci. and Innovation, 2016–. *Address*: House of Commons, SW1A 0AA.

**OPENSHAW, Dame Caroline Jane, (Lady Openshaw)**; *see* Swift, Dame C. J.

**OPENSHAW, Hon. Sir (Charles) Peter (Lawford)**, Kt 2005; DL; a Judge of the High Court of Justice, Queen's Bench Division, 2005–17; *b* 21 Dec. 1947; *s* of late Judge William Harrison Openshaw and Elisabeth Joyce Emily Openshaw; *m* 1979, Caroline Jane Swift (*see* Dame C. J. Swift); one *s* one *d*. *Educ*: Harrow; St Catharine's College, Cambridge (MA). Called to the Bar, Inner Temple, 1970, Bencher, 2003; practised on Northern Circuit, Junior 1973; Assistant Recorder, 1985; a Recorder, 1988–99; QC 1991; Hon. Recorder of Preston, 1999–2005; a Sen. Circuit Judge, 1999–2005; a Presiding Judge, N Eastern Circuit, 2009–12. Dir, Criminal Trng, Judicial Coll., 2013. Mem., Criminal Procedure Rules Cttee, 2005–17. Hon. Canon, Blackburn Cathedral, 2008–18. DL Lancs, 2000. *Recreations*: fishing, gardening, village life.

**OPENSHAW, Prof. Peter John Morland**, PhD; FRCP; FMedSci; Professor of Experimental Medicine, since 1997, College Consul (Clinical), since 2016, and Senior Consul, since 2019, Imperial College London; *b* Glastonbury, 11 Nov. 1954; *s* of William Arthur Openshaw and Susan Elizabeth (*née* Scott Stokes); *m* 1st, 1979, Clare Patricia Vaughan (*d* 1996); two *s* one *d*; 2nd, 2001, Evelyn Samuels Welch; one step *s* two step *d*. *Educ*: Sidcot and Bootham Quaker Schs; Guy's Hosp., Univ. of London (BSc 1976; Paediatric Prize, 1978; MB BS 1979; Gold Medal in Medicine 1979); PhD NIMR 1988. MRCP 1982, FRCP 1994. SHO, Brompton Hosp., 1981–82; Medical Registrar and Lectr, RPMS, 1983–85; Wellcome Trust Sen. Fellow in Clin. Sci., 1988–98; Hon. Physician, St Mary's Hosp., 1990–; Hd, Sect. of Respiratory Infections, Nat. Heart and Lung Inst., Imperial Coll. London, 2018–. Croonian Lect. on influenza, RCP, 2013; NIHR Sen. Investigator, 2014–19. Member: European Scientific Working Gp on Influenza, 2008– (Vice-Pres., 2008–14); Scientific Adv. Gp on Emergencies, 2009–10. Director: Mechanisms of Severe Acute Influenza Consortium, 2009–14; HIC-Vac, 2017–. Mem., various Wellcome Trust funding panels, 1997–2010. President: British Soc. for Immunol., 2014–18; RSV Soc., 2017–. FMedSci 1999. Mem., Med. Res. Club, 1989– (Sec., 2004–09). Robert M. Chanock Lifetime Achievement Award, Internat. RSV Symposium, 2012; Eur. Fedn of Immunol Socs Medal, 2014. *Publications*: contrib. papers on viral immunology and respiratory medicine to jls incl. Nature Medicine, Jl Exptl Medicine. *Recreations*: fresh air, odd music, tying knots. *Address*: Respiratory Medicine, St Mary's Campus, Imperial College, Norfolk Place, Paddington, W2 1PG. *T*: (020) 7594 3854, *Fax*: (020) 7262 8913. *E*: p.openshaw@imperial.ac.uk.

**OPIE, Alan John**, OBE 2013; baritone; *b* 22 March 1945; *s* of Jack and Doris Winifred Opie; *m* 1970, Kathleen Ann Smales; one *s* one *d*. *Educ*: Truro Sch.; Guildhall Sch. of Music (AGSM); London Opera Centre. Principal rôles include: Papageno in The Magic Flute, Sadler's Wells Opera, 1969; Tony in the Globolinks, Santa Fe Opera, 1970; Officer in the Barber of Seville, Covent Garden, 1971; Don Giovanni, Kent Opera, and Demetrius, English Opera Gp, 1972; Prin. Baritone with ENO, 1973–96; *English National Opera*: Figaro; Papageno; Guglielmo; Beckmesser; Valentin; Lescaut in Manon; Eisenstein and Falke in Die Fledermaus; Danilo; Silvio; Junius in Rape of Lucretia; Cecil in Gloriana; Faninal in Der Rosenkavalier; Germont in La Traviata; Marcello and Schaunard in La Bohème; Kovalyov in The Nose; Strephon in Iolanthe; Grosvenor in Patience; Tomsky in Queen of Spades; Paolo in Simon Boccanegra; Harlequin in Ariadne auf Naxos; Dr Faust by Busoni; Sharpless in Madame Butterfly; Fiddler in Königskinder; Sancho in Don Quixote, 1994; Alfonso in Così fan Tutte, 1997; Falstaff, 1997 and 2004; Don Carlo in Ernani, 2000; title rôle in Rigoletto, 2003; Leon Klinghoffer in The Death of Klinghoffer, 2012; Jack the Ripper: the women of Whitechapel, 2019; *Royal Opera, Covent Garden*: Hector in King Priam, 1985; Ping in Turandot, 1986; Mangus in The Knot Garden, 1988; Falke in Die Fledermaus, 1989; Paolo in Simon Boccanegra; rôles in Death in Venice, 1992; Sharpless in Madama Butterfly, 1993; Faninal in Der Rosenkavalier, 1995; Germont in La Traviata, 2001, 2002; Balstrode in Peter Grimes, 2004; Sulpice in La Fille du Regiment, 2012; *Glyndebourne Festival Opera*: Sid in Albert Herring, 1985, 1990; rôles in Death in Venice, 1989; Figaro in Le Nozze di Figaro, 1991; Balstrode in Peter Grimes, 1992; Dr Falke in Die Fledermaus, 2006; Vicar in Albert Herring, 2008; *Scottish Opera*: Baron in La Vie Parisienne, 1985; Storch in Intermezzo, 1986; Forester in Cunning Little Vixen, 1991; *Opera North*: Diomede in Troilus and Cressida, 1995; *Metropolitan Opera, NY*: Balstrode in Peter Grimes, 1994; Sharpless in Madama Butterfly, 1997; Fieramosca in Benvenuto Cellini, 2003; Forester in Cunning Little Vixen with NY Philharmonic Orch., 2011; *Welsh National Opera*: Frank in Die Fledermaus, 2011; Sharpless in Madama Butterfly, 2013; *La Scala, Milan*: title role, Outis, by Berio, world première 1996; Forester in Cunning Little Vixen, 2003; Kolenaty in The Makropoulos Case, 2008; Germont in La Traviata, Berlin, 2001, Toronto, 2007; Balstrode in Peter Grimes, Florence, Japan, Paris Bastille, 2002; Sharpless in Madama Butterfly, China, 2002, Los Angeles, 2004; Mao in Madame Mao (world première), Santa Fe, 2003; Rigoletto, Philadelphia, 2007, for Australian Opera, 2010; Panglos in Candide, Naples, 2007; Scarpia in Tosca, Toronto, 2008; Falstaff, Strasbourg and Washington, 2009; Germont in Traviata, San Diego, 2010; Golaud in Pelleas and Melisande, 2010; Gianni Schicchi, 2012, Opera Holland Park; has also appeared at Bayreuth Fest., Berlin (Unter den Linden, Berlin Staatsoper, 1990) and in Amsterdam and Munich (rôles include Beckmesser), and at Buxton Fest. and in Brussels, Chicago, Vienna, Paris, Strasbourg, Dallas, Toronto and Sydney. Has made numerous recordings, esp. of operas of Benjamin Britten. Grammy Awards for recordings of Peter Grimes, 1996, and Die Meistersinger, 1997. *Address*: Chartwood Lodge, Punchbowl Lane, Dorking, Surrey RH5 4ED.

**OPIE, Geoffrey James**; freelance lecturer on 19th and 20th century art and design, 1989–2005, now retired; *b* 10 July 1939; *s* of Basil Irwin Opie and Florence Mabel Opie (*née* May); *m* 1st, 1964, Pamela Green; one *s* one *d*; 2nd, 1980, Jennifer Hawkins; one *s*. *Educ*: Humphry Davy Grammar School, Penzance; Falmouth Sch. of Art (NDD); Goldsmiths' Coll., London (ATC). Asst Designer, Leacock & Co., 1961; Curator, Nat. Mus. of Antiquities of Scotland, 1963; Designer, Leacock & Co., 1967; Curator, Victoria and Albert Mus., 1969, Educn Dept, 1978–89, Head of Educn Services, 1983–89. *Publications*: The Wireless Cabinet 1930–1956, 1979; (contrib.) Encyclopedia of Interior Design, 1997; contribs to various jls. *Recreations*: painting, literature, music, motorcycling.

**OPIE, Julian Gilbert**; artist; *b* 12 Dec. 1958; *s* of Roger and Norma Opie. *Educ*: Magdalen Coll. Sch., Oxford; Chelsea Coll. of Art; Goldsmiths' Sch. of Art. Trustee, Tate Gall., 2002–06. *Solo exhibitions include*: Lisson Gall., London, 1983, 1985, 1986, 2001, 2004, 2008, 2012; Hayward Gall., 1993; Ikon Gall., Birmingham, 2001; Galerie Barbara Thumm, Berlin, 2002, 2007; Barbara Krakow Gall., Boston, 2002, 2007, 2010, 2013; K21, Dusseldorf, 2003; Neues Mus., Nuremberg, 2003; MCA, Chicago, 2003; ICA, Boston, 2005; Scai The Bathhouse, Tokyo, 2005; Alan Cristea Gall., London, 2006, 2008, 2011, 2013, 2015; Centro de Arte Contemporáneo, Malaga, 2006; Arts Council of Indianapolis, 2006; Walking on the Vltava, Mus. Kampa, Prague, 2007; MAK, Vienna, 2008; Krobath Wimmer, Vienna, 2008; Art Tower, Mito, 2008; Krobath Gall., Vienna, 2013, Berlin, 2014; Valentina Bonomo Gall., Rome, 2013; Patrick de Brock, Knokke, 2013; Gerhardsen Gerner, Oslo, 2013, 2015, Berlin, 2014; Kukje Gall., Seoul, 2014; Mus. of Contemp. Art, Krakow, 2014; Holburne Mus. and Bowes Mus., 2014; Channing Sch. for Girls and ARK Gall., 2014; Mario Sequeira, Braga, 2015; Taidehalli, Helsinki, 2015; NPG, London, 2017; Fosun Foundn, Shanghai, 2017; Suwon Ipark Mus. of Art, South Korea, 2017; F1963, Busan, 2018; Nat. Gall. of Vic, Melbourne, 2018; numerous group exhibitions; *works in collections include*: British Council, Contemp. Arts Soc., Tate Gall., Cincinnati Mus. of Modern Art, Stedelijk Mus., Amsterdam; *commissions include*: perimeter wall paintings, HM Prison Wormwood Scrubs, 1994; Imagine You Are Moving, Heathrow Airport, 1997; outdoor installation, Public Art Fund, City Hall Park, NYC, 2004; Infra (ballet), Royal Opera House, 2009; NPG, 2011; Promenade, Calgary, 2012; La Jolla Community Foundn,

San Diego, 2013; Citizen M. Hotel, Paris and New York, 2014; PKZ, Zurich, 2014; Arendt and Medernach, Luxembourg, 2015; Citizen M Tower Hill, London, 2015; Takamatsu City, 2015; Carnaby St, London, 2016; Tower 535, Causeway Bay, Hong Kong, 2016; Jut Land Develt Corp., Taipei, 2016. *Publications:* (jtly) Julian Opie Portraits, 2003; Julian Opie: editions (catalogue raisonné), vol. 1, 1984–2011, 2011, vol. 2, 2012–2015, 2015. *Address:* c/o Lisson Gallery, 67 Lisson Street, NW1 5DA.

**OPIE, Lisa Moreen;** Managing Director Factual, BBC Studios, since 2016; *b* 27 Feb. 1960; *d* of Ivan and Lucille Opie; *m* 1991, Julian Meres; one *s* one *d*. *Educ:* Welsh Coll. of Music and Drama; Univ. of Wales (Grad. Dip.); Indiana Univ. Actress, various theatre cos, 1982–88; Researcher Presenter, BBC Radio Wales, 1988–90; Flextech, 1993–2006: a Promotions Producer, 1993–94, Dep. Hd of Programming, 1994–97, Children's Channel; Hd of Programming, Trouble, 1997–99; Exec. Vice Pres., Flextech Channels, 1999–2003; Man. Dir, Flextech Television, 2003–06; Man. Dir Content, Channel Five, 2006–08; Dir, Umbrella Media, 2008–10; Man. Dir, Twofour Digital and Rocket Sci. Gp, 2011–12; Controller, Business, Knowledge and Daytime, BBC, 2012–16. Chm., EM Media, 2009–13. Gov., Nat. Film and TV Sch., 2007–09. Mem., BAFTA. FRTS; FRSA. *Recreations:* pottery, ski-ing, music, cooking, reading. *Address:* BBC, Broadcasting House, Portland Place, W1A 1AA.

**ÖPIK, Lembit;** author; broadcaster; international training, public and political affairs practitioner; *b* 2 March 1965; *s* of Uno and Liivi Öpik. *Educ:* Royal Belfast Academical Instn; Bristol Univ. (BA Hons Philosophy). Pres., Univ. of Bristol Students' Union, 1985–86; Mem., Nat. Exec., NUS, 1987–88. Procter and Gamble Ltd, 1988–97: Brand Asst, 1988–89; Asst Brand Manager, 1989–91; Corporate Trng and Orgn Develt Manager, 1991–96; Global Human Resources Trng Manager, 1996–97. Mem., Newcastle upon Tyne CC, 1992–97. Mem., Lib Dem Federal Exec., 1997–2008. MP (Lib Dem) Montgomeryshire, 1997–2010; contested (Lib Dem) same seat, 2010. Lib Dem spokesman for Young People, 1997–2002, for NI, 1997–2007, for Wales, 2001–07, for Business, Enterprise and Regulatory Reform, 2007; for Housing, 2007–08; Mem., Welsh Affairs team, 1997–2007; Mem., Business and Enterprise Select Cttee, 2009–10. Leader, Welsh Liberal Democrats, 2001–07. Registrar, London Academy Business Sch., 2012–13. Music Gp Manager, ZY Records, 2013–; Dir of Commns and Public Affairs, Motorcycle Action Gp, 2013–. Broadcaster, BBC Radio Kent, 2014–. Chm. of Parlt, Asgardia, 2018–. FRAS 2002. *Publications:* (jtly) Xenophobe's Guide to Estonians, 2010; (jtly) The Alternative View: the way back for the Liberal Democrats, 2012; All at Sea, 2016. *Recreations:* aviation, astronomy, motorcycling, cinema.

**OPPENHEIM, Prof. Charles,** PhD, DSc; FCLIP; Professor of Information Science, Department of Information Science, Loughborough University, 1998–2009 (Head, Department of Information Science, 2006–09); *b* 25 April 1946; *s* of Georg Oppenheim and Eva Henrietta Oppenheim (*née* Stein); *m* 1st, 1968, Pauline Jeanette Kirwan (marr. diss. 1994); two *d*; 2nd, 1996, Adrienne Muir. *Educ:* Orange Hill Boys' Grammar Sch.; UMIST (BSc; PhD); City Univ. (Dip Inf. Sci.); London Univ. (Cert Ed); DSc Loughborough, 2006. FCLIP 1981, Hon. FCLIP 1995. Patent Inf. Officer, Glaxo Holdings, 1970–73; Lecturer: Plymouth Polytechnic, 1973–76; City Univ., 1976–80; Dir, R & D, Derwent Publications, 1980–84; Product Develt Manager, Pergamon Infoline, 1984–87; Business Develt Manager, Reuters, 1987–92; Prof. of Inf. Sci., Strathclyde Univ., 1992–96; Prof., De Montfort Univ., 1996–98. Vis. Prof., Univ. of Queensland, 2010–13; Hon. Vis. Prof., Faculty of Mgt, Cass Business Sch., 2013–; Prof., Aberdeen Business Sch., 2013–14; Vis. Scholar, Robert Gordon Univ., 2014–; Vis. Prof., Northampton Univ., 2014–17. Mem., Aberdeen Philatelic Soc. FRSA 2000; FRPSL 2019. *Publications:* The Legal and Regulatory Environment for Electronic Information, 1992, 4th edn 2001; The No Nonsense Guide to Legal Issues in Web 2.0 and Cloud Computing, 2012; more than 400 articles in jls. *Recreations:* chess, philately, collecting interesting T-shirts, visiting National Trust properties. *Address:* 2 Kirkbrae View, Cults, Aberdeen AB15 9RU. *T:* 07583 442915. *E:* c.oppenheim@btinternet.com. *Club:* Bon Accord Chess (Aberdeen).

**OPPENHEIM, Jeremy;** Director, Managing Together, Home Office, since 2017; *b* 6 June 1955; *s* of late Ian and of Doryene Oppenheim; *m* 1985, Karen J. Tanner; two *d*. *Educ:* Lancaster Univ. (BA Hons); London Univ. (CQSW; Dip. Social Work). Qualified Youth and Community Worker. Social Worker, Jewish Welfare Bd, 1977–79; part-time Detached Youth Worker, ILEA, 1978–81; Social Worker, 1982–85, Team Manager, 1985–89, Service Manager, 1989–93, Haringey; Asst Dir, Social Services, Barking and Dagenham, 1993–97; Dir, Social Services, Hackney, 1997–99; Chief Exec., Jewish Care, 1999–2003; Home Office: Dir, Nat. Asylum Support Service, 2004–06; Children's Champion, 2005–09; Dir, Social Policy, 2006–07; Dir, Regionalisation and Stakeholders, Border and Immigration Agency, 2007–08; UK Border Agency: Dir, Organisation Design and Develt Directorate, 2008; Regl Dir, NE, Yorks and the Humber Reg., Nat. Lead - Temp. Migration, 2008–11; Dir, Immigration and Settlement, 2011–13; Home Office: Dir, Growth and Engagement, 2013–15; Safeguarding, 2015–17. *Recreations:* family, friends, cooking, reading.

**OPPENHEIM, Hon. Phillip Anthony Charles Lawrence;** author, broadcaster; Managing Director, Cubana Ltd, since 2011; *b* 20 March 1956; *s* of late Henry Oppenheim and of Baroness Oppenheim-Barnes, *qv*; *m* 2003, Dr Susie Morris. *Educ:* Harrow; Oriel College, Oxford. BA Hons. MP (C) Amber Valley, 1983–97; contested (C) same seat, 1997. PPS to Sec. of State for Health, 1988–90, to Sec. of State for Educn and Sci., 1990–92, to Home Sec., 1992–93, to Chancellor of the Exchequer, 1993–94; Parliamentary Under-Secretary of State: Dept of Employment, 1994–95; DTI, 1995–96; Exchequer Sec. to HM Treasury, 1996–97. Co-editor, What to Buy for Business, 1980–85. Columnist, The Sunday Times, 1998–2000. *Publications:* A Handbook of New Office Technology, 1982; Telecommunications: a user's handbook, 1983; A Word Processing Handbook, 1984; The New Masters: can the West match Japan?, 1991; Trade Wars: Japan versus the West, 1992. *Recreations:* Rugby, tennis, travel, ski-ing, tropical plants. *Address:* 29 Redburn Street, SW3 4DA.

**OPPENHEIM-BARNES,** Baroness *cr* 1989 (Life Peer), of Gloucester in the county of Gloucestershire; **Sally Oppenheim-Barnes;** PC 1979; *b* 26 July 1930; *d* of Mark and Jeanette Viner; *m* 1st, 1949, Henry M. Oppenheim (*d* 1980); one *s* two *d*; 2nd, 1984, John Barnes (*d* 2004). *Educ:* Sheffield High Sch. Formerly: Exec. Dir, Industrial & Investment Services Ltd; Social Worker, School Care Dept, ILEA. Trustee, Clergy Rest House Trust. MP (C) Gloucester, 1970–87. Vice Chm., 1971–73, Chm., 1973–74, Cons. Party Parly Prices and Consumer Protection Cttee; Opposition Spokesman on Prices and Consumer Protection, 1974–79; Mem. Shadow Cabinet, 1975–79; Min. of State (Consumer Affairs), Dept of Trade, 1979–82. Mem., H of L, 1989–2019. Chairman: Nat. Consumer Council, 1987–89; Council of Management, Nat. Waterways Museums Trust, 1988–89. Non-executive Director: and Mem., Main Bd, Boots Co., 1982–93; Fleming High Income Trust, 1989–97; HFC Bank, 1989–98. *Recreations:* tennis, bridge.
*See also Hon. P. A. C. L. Oppenheim.*

**OPPENHEIMER, (Lætitia) Helen, (Lady Oppenheimer);** writer on moral and philosophical theology; *b* 30 Dec. 1926; *d* of Sir Hugh Lucas-Tooth (later Munro-Lucas-Tooth), 1st Bt and Lætitia Florence Lucas-Tooth, OBE, *d* of Sir John Findlay, 1st Bt; *m* 1947, Sir Michael Oppenheimer, Bt, *qv*; three *d*. *Educ:* Cheltenham Ladies' Coll.; Lady Margaret Hall, Oxford (Schol.; BPhil, MA). Lectr in Ethics, Cuddesdon Theological Coll., 1964–69. Served on: Archbp of Canterbury's Gp on the law of divorce (report, Putting Asunder, 1966); C of E Marriage Commn (report, Marriage, Divorce and the Church, 1971); Wkg Party, ACCM (report, Teaching Christian Ethics, 1974); C of E Wkg Party on Educn in Personal Relationships (Chm.), 1978–82; Inter-Anglican Theol and Doctrinal Commn (report, For the Sake of the Kingdom, 1986); General Synod Wkg Party on the law of marriage (report, An Honourable Estate, 1988). Pres., Soc. for the Study of Christian Ethics, 1989–91. Lectures: John Coffin Meml, London Univ., 1977; First Mary Sumner, Mothers' Union, 1978; Larkin-Stuart, Trinity Coll., Toronto, 1997; Fourth Leveson, Leveson Centre for the Study of Ageing, 2005; preached University Sermon, Oxford, 1979, Cambridge, 1983. DD Lambeth, 1993. *Publications:* Law and Love, 1962; The Character of Christian Morality, 1965, 2nd edn 1974; Incarnation and Immanence, 1973; The Marriage Bond, 1976; The Hope of Happiness: a sketch for a Christian humanism, 1983; Looking Before and After: The Archbishop of Canterbury's Lent Book for 1988; Marriage, 1990; Finding and Following, 1994; Making Good: creation, tragedy and hope, 2001; Profitable Wonders (anthology), 2003; What A Piece of Work: on being human, 2006; On Being Someone: a Christian point of view, 2011; Christian Faith for Handing On, 2014; contributor: New Dictionary of Christian Theology, 1983; New Dictionary of Christian Ethics, 1986; Companion Encyclopedia of Theology, 1996; Dictionary of Ethics, Theology and Society, 1996; articles in Theology, Religious Studies, Studies in Christian Ethics, etc, and in various collections of essays. *Address:* L'Aiguillon, Grouville, Jersey, Channel Islands JE3 9AP.

**OPPENHEIMER, His Honour Michael Anthony;** a Circuit Judge, 1991–2012; *b* 22 Sept. 1946; *s* of Felix Oppenheimer and Ingeborg Hanna Oppenheimer; *m* 1973, Nicola Anne Brotherton (*see* N. A. Oppenheimer); one *s* one *d*. *Educ:* Westminster Sch.; LSE (LLB). Called to the Bar, Middle Temple, 1970 (Blackstone Exhibnr 1970); Asst Recorder, 1985–89; Recorder, 1989–91. A Chm., Bar Disciplinary Tribunal, 1999–2006. *Recreations:* cinema, theatre, wine and food, bridge, playing, performing and listening to music. *Club:* Athenæum.

**OPPENHEIMER, Sir Michael (Bernard Grenville),** 3rd Bt *cr* 1921; *b* 27 May 1924; *s* of Sir Michael Oppenheimer, 2nd Bt, and Caroline Magdalen (who *m* 2nd, 1935, Sir Ernest Oppenheimer; she *d* 1972), *d* of Sir Robert G. Harvey, 2nd Bt; *S* father, 1933; *m* 1947, Lætitia Helen Lucas-Tooth (*see* L. H. Oppenheimer); three *d*. *Educ:* Charterhouse; Christ Church, Oxford (BLitt, MA). Served with South African Artillery, 1942–45. Lecturer in Politics: Lincoln Coll., Oxford, 1955–68; Magdalen Coll., Oxford, 1966–68. *Publications:* The Monuments of Italy, 6 vols, 2002. *Heir:* none. *Address:* L'Aiguillon, Grouville, Jersey, Channel Islands JE3 9AP.

**OPPENHEIMER, Nicholas Frank;** Chairman, De Beers Group, 1998–2012; *b* Johannesburg, 8 June 1945; *s* of late Harry Frederick Oppenheimer, and Bridget (*née* McCall); *m* 1968, Orcillia Lasch; one *s*. *Educ:* Harrow Sch.; Christ Church, Oxford (BA PPE, MA). Joined Anglo-American Corp., 1968; Dir, 1974; non-exec. Dir, Anglo-American plc, 1999–2011; Deputy Chairman: Anglo-American Corp. of SA Ltd, 1983–2001; De Beers Consolidated Mines Ltd, 1985–97; Dep. Chm., 1990, subseq. Chm., De Beers Centenary AG; Chairman: Central Selling Orgn, 1984; Anglogold, 1997–2000. Director: De Beers Hldgs Ltd, 1983–2012; De Beers Industrial Corp. Ltd; E. Oppenheimer & Son (Pty) Ltd. *Address:* PO Box 61631, Marshalltown 2107, South Africa.

**OPPENHEIMER, Nicola Anne;** Advisor, Odgers Berndtson (formerly Odgers Ray & Berndtson), since 2013 (Partner, 2001–13); *b* 30 Sept. 1950; *d* of Basil Vincent Brotherton and Joan Pamela Brotherton; *m* 1973, Michael Anthony Oppenheimer, *qv*; one *s* one *d*. *Educ:* St Margaret's Sch., Bushey; Queen's Coll., London; Queen Mary Coll., London Univ. (LLB). Called to the Bar, Middle Temple, 1972. Lord Chancellor's Department, 1973–96; Judicial Appts Div., 1985; Head of Personnel Management, 1987; Head of Legal Services and Agencies Div., 1991; Prin. Estabt and Finance Officer, 1993–96; Cabinet Office: Prin. Estabt and Finance Officer, 1996–2000; Fellow, Knowledge Mgt Centre for Mgt and Policy Studies, 2000–01. Chairman, Trustees: King's Consort, 1998–2000; Orchestra of St John, 2000–01; The English Concert, 2013–16 (Trustee, 2001–); Trustee: Classical Opera Co., 1999–2005; Early Opera Co., 2005–; Spitalfields Music, 2010–; Member, Development Board: RAM, 1996–2009; LAMDA, 1999–2007; Mem., Organising Cttee, Grove Park Music Fest., 2002–18. *Recreations:* early music, theatre, bridge, walking. *Address:* Odgers Berndtson, 20 Cannon Street, EC4M 6XD. *T:* (020) 7529 1111. *E:* nicky.oppenheimer@odgersberndtson.com.

**OPPENHEIMER, Peter Morris;** Student of Christ Church, Oxford, 1967–2008, now Emeritus; President, Oxford Centre for Hebrew and Jewish Studies, 2000–08, Emeritus Governor, since 2009; *b* 16 April 1938; *s* of late Friedrich Rudolf and Charlotte Oppenheimer; *m* 1964, Catherine, er *d* of late Dr Eliot Slater, CBE, FRCP, and Dr Lydia Pasternak; two *s* one *d*. *Educ:* Haberdashers' Aske's Sch.; The Queen's Coll., Oxford (BA 1961). National Service, RN, 1956–58. Bank for International Settlements, Basle, 1961–64; Research Fellow, Nuffield Coll., Oxford, 1964–67; Univ. Lectr in Econs, 1967–2000; on secondment as Chief Economist, Shell Internat. Petroleum Co., 1985–86. Vis. Prof., London Graduate Sch. of Business Studies, 1976–77; Temp. Econ. Attaché, British Embassy, Moscow, 1991. Mem., Gen. Bd of Faculties, Oxford Univ., 1989–97. Director: Panfida plc (formerly Investing in Success Equities Ltd), 1975–92; Target Hldgs, 1982–84; J. Rothschilds Investment Management, 1982–86; Jewish Chronicle Ltd, 1986–2006 (Chm., 2001–04); Delbanco, Meyer and Co. Ltd, 1986–2001; Dixons Group plc, 1987–93 (Chm., Audit Cttee, 1987–92); OAO Purneftegaz, Russia, 1998–2001; OAO Tomskneft of VNK, Russia, 1999; Far Eastern Shipping Co., Russia, 1999–2000; VSMPO, Russia, 1999–2001. Chm., Caminus Energy Ltd, 1991–93. Delegate, OUP, 1987–97 (Mem., Finance Cttee, 1989–97). Specialist Advr, H of C Expenditure Cttee, 1975–76. Mem., Royal Commn on Legal Services, 1976–79. Mem. Council, Trade Policy Research Centre, 1976–89, and co-Editor, The World Economy, 1977–89; Member: Editl Bd, International Affairs, 1989–2014; Bd, Jewish Policy Res. (formerly Inst. of Jewish Affairs), 1991–2001; Renewable Energy Adv. Gp, Dept of Energy, 1991–92; Academic Adv. Council, World ORT Union, 1992–2010; Spoliation Adv. Panel, DCMS, 2000–; Internat. Adv. Bd, Immanuel Kant Fed. Univ., Kaliningrad, Russia, 2018–. Former Mem., Internat. Econs Steering Gp, and Energy and Envmt Steering Gp, RIIA. Governor: St Edward's Sch., Oxford, 1979–2015; St Clare's, Oxford, 1985– (Chm., 1993–2006); Haberdashers' Monmouth Schs, 1987–2003. Hon. Freeman, Haberdashers' Co., 1987. Presenter: (BBC radio): File on 4, 1977–80; Third Opinion, 1983; Poles Apart, 1984; (BBC TV) Outlook, 1982–85; (Granada TV) Under Fire, 1988; (participant) Round Britain Quiz, Radio 4, 1979–96. *Publications:* (ed) Issues in International Economics, 1980; (ed with B. Granville and contrib.) Russia's Post-Communist Economy, 2001; contribs to symposia, conference procs, prof. jls, bank reviews, etc. *Recreations:* music, opera, amateur dramatics, swimming, ski-ing. *Address:* 6 Linton Road, Oxford OX2 6UG. *T:* (01865) 558226.

**OPPERMAN, Guy Thomas**; MP (C) Hexham, since 2010; Parliamentary Under-Secretary of State, Department for Work and Pensions, since 2017; *b* Marlborough, Wilts, 18 May 1965; *s* of Michael Opperman and Julia Opperman. *Educ:* Univ. of Lille (Dip. 1st Cl. 1984); Univ. of Buckingham (LLB 1986). Farmer, Africa, 1987; called to the Bar, Middle Temple, 1989; in practice as a barrister, 1989–2010. Dir, TD Chrome Ltd, family engrg business, until 2009. Mem. (C) Wilts CC, 1995–99. An Asst Govt Whip, 2015–16; a Lord Comr of HM Treasury (Govt Whip), 2016–17. Contested (C): N Swindon, 1997; Caernarfon, 2005. *Publications:* Doing Time: prisons in the 21st century; over 100 articles. *Recreation:* amateur steeplechase jockey. *Address:* House of Commons, SW1A 0AA; (constituency office) 1 Meal Market, Hexham NE46 1NF. *Club:* Albert Edward (Hexham).

**O'PREY, Prof. Paul Gerard**, CBE 2016; PhD; Vice-Chancellor and Professor of Modern Literature, Roehampton University, since 2004; *b* 2 April 1956; *s* of Desmond Alexander O'Prey and Ada Dorothy O'Prey (*née* Reid); *m* 1984, Maria del Pilar Garcia Navarro; one *s* one *d*. *Educ:* St George Sch., Southampton; King Edward VI Sch., Southampton; Keble Coll., Oxford; Univ. of Bristol (PhD). Sec. to Robert Graves, 1977–81; writer, translator and researcher, 1981–88; University of Bristol: Tutor in English, 1989–93; Warden of Goldney, 1989–2004; Sen. Warden, 1993–95; Director: Res. Develt, 1995–99; Res. and Enterprise Develt, 1999–2002; Academic Affairs, 2002–04. Chm., Longer Term Strategy Cttee, UUK, 2010– (Mem. Bd, 2010–18); Member: Academic Bd, Worldwide Univs Network, 2002–04; Strategic Adv. Cttee on Leadership Governance and Mgt, HEFCE, 2005–11; Bd, HE Careers Service Unit, 2006–13; Bd, London Higher, 2006–09, 2017–19. Pres., War Poets Assoc., 2007–12; Mem. Council, Friends of the Imperial War Mus., 2009–. Gov., Putney High Sch., 2004–09. Trustee: Froebel Trust, 2012–; Edward James Foundn (W Dean Coll. of Art and Conservation), 2016–. FEA 2018. Hon. DLaws Bristol, 2011; Hon. DLitt Manhattanville Coll., NY, 2011. *Publications:* In Broken Images: selected letters of Robert Graves 1914–1946, 1982; (ed) Joseph Conrad, Heart of Darkness, 1983; Between Moon and Moon: selected letters of Robert Graves 1946–1972, 1984; (ed) Robert Graves Selected Poems, 1986; The Reader's Guide to Graham Greene, 1988; (with Lucia Graves) Emilia Pardo Bazán, The House of Ulloa, 1990; (ed) Robert Graves: collected writings on poetry, 1995; (ed) First World War: poems from the Front, 2014; (ed) Mary Borden: poems of love and war, 2015; (ed) Laurence Binyon: poems of two wars, 2016; (ed) Counter-Wave: poetry of rescue in the First World War, 2018; chapters in books and articles in jls. *Address:* Roehampton University, Roehampton Lane, SW15 5PJ. *T:* (020) 8392 3101, *Fax:* (020) 8392 3029. *E:* vicechancellor@roehampton.ac.uk. *Club:* Athenæum.

**O'RAHILLY, Sir Stephen (Patrick)**, Kt 2013; MD; FRCP, FRCPI, FMedSci, FRCPath; FRS 2003; FRSB; Professor of Clinical Biochemistry and Medicine (formerly Professor of Metabolic Medicine), Departments of Medicine and Clinical Biochemistry, since 1996, Head, Clinical Biochemistry Department, since 2002, and Director, Institute of Metabolic Science, Metabolic Research Laboratories, since 2007, University of Cambridge; Fellow of Pembroke College, Cambridge, since 2007; Hon. Consultant Physician, Addenbrooke's Hospital, since 1994; Director, MRC Metabolic Diseases Unit (formerly MRC Centre for Obesity and Related Metabolic Diseases), since 2007; Scientific Director, NIHR Cambridge Biomedical Research Centre, since 2010; *b* 1 April 1958; *s* of Patrick Francis O'Rahilly and Emer (*née* Hyland); *m* 1st, 1990, Suzy Oakes (*d* 2011); 2nd, 2016, Philippa Lamb; one step *s*. *Educ:* Beneavin Coll., Finglas, Dublin; University Coll., Dublin (MB BCh BAO 1981; MD 1987; Hon. Fellow, Faculty of Medicine, 2000). FRCP 1996; FRCPI 1996; FRCPath 2002. House Officer, Mater Hosp., Dublin, 1981–82; Senior House Officer: St Bartholomew's Hosp., London, 1982–83; Hammersmith Hosp., 1983–84; Res. Fellow, Nuffield Dept of Medicine, Diabetes Res. Lab., Univ. of Oxford, 1984–87; Registrar in Diabetes and Endocrinology, Oxford HA, 1987–89; MRC Travelling Fellow, Harvard Med. Sch., Boston, 1989–91; Wellcome Trust Sen. Fellow in Clinical Sci., Univ. of Cambridge, 1991–96; Fellow, Churchill Coll., Cambridge, 1992–2006. British Diabetic Association: Redcliffe-Maud Fellow, 1986–87; R. D. Lawrence Lectr, 1996. Lectures: Clinical Endocrinology Trust, 1999; Rufus Cole, Rockefeller Univ., 2000; McCallum, Univ. of Toronto, 2000; Andrew Marble, Joslin Clinic, Boston, USA, 2001; Linacre, St John's Coll., Cambridge, 2004; H. C. Jacobaeus, Novo Nordic Foundn, 2005; Kroc, Univ. of Mass, 2007; Croonian, RCP, 2011; Sir Philip Randle, Biochemical Soc., 2011; Edward K. Dunham Lectr for Promotion of Med. Scis, Harvard Med. Sch., 2015; Harveian Orator, RCP, 2016. FMedSci 1999; FRSB (FSB 2010). Pres., Soc. for Endocrinology, 2014–16. Hon. Member: Assoc. of American Physicians, 2004; Assoc. of Physicians, 2004; German Soc. of Internal Medicine, 2011; Hon. MRIA, 2017; Foreign Associate, NAS, USA, 2011. Hon. DSc: UCD, 2008; Warwick, 2009; Buckingham, 2013; RCSI, 2018; Hon. LLD Dundee, 2012. Medal, 2000, Dale Medal, 2010, Soc. of Endocrinology; Graham Bull Prize, RCP, 2000; Novartis Award for diabetes research, 2001; European Jl of Endocrinology Prize, 2001; Heinrich Wieland Prize, 2002; Carl W. Gottschalk Award, Univ. of N Carolina, 2003; Rolf Luft Award, Karolinska Inst., 2005; Solomon Berson Award, Mt Sinai Med. Sch., NY, 2007; Clinical Investigator Award, Endocrine Soc., USA, 2007; Feldberg Prize, 2007; Res. Investigator Award, NIHR, 2008; Health Prize, InBev-Baillet Latour Fund, 2010; Ulysses Medal, University Coll., Dublin, 2013; Res. Achievement Award, Obesity Soc., 2013; K. J. Zülch Prize, Gertrud Reemtsma Foundn, Germany, 2014; Baly Medal, RCP, 2014; Debrecen Award for Molecular Medicine, Univ. of Debrecen, Hungary, 2014; Hormone Medal, Eur. Soc. of Endocrinology, 2015; EASD/Novo Nordisk Foundn Diabetes Prize for Excellence, 2015; Helmholz Diabetes Award, Helmholtz Zentrum München, 2016; Galen Medal, Apothecaries' Co., 2019; Banting Medal for Scientific Achievement, Amer. Diabetes Assoc., 2019. *Publications:* papers on: pathophysiol. and genetics of Type 2 diabetes; mechanism of insulin action; molecular and cell biol. of human fat cells; molecular basis for human obesity. *Recreations:* reading, travel, friends, food and wine, tennis (lawn and Real). *Address:* University of Cambridge, Institute of Metabolic Science, Box 289, Addenbrooke's Hospital, Hills Road, Cambridge CB2 0QQ.

**ORAMO, Sakari**, Hon. OBE 2009; Chief Conductor and Artistic Advisor, Royal Stockholm Philharmonic Orchestra, since 2008; Chief Conductor: BBC Symphony Orchestra, since 2013; Ostrobothnian Chamber Orchestra, since 2013; *b* Finland, 1965; *m* Anu Komsi, soprano; two *s*. *Educ:* musical training as violinist; Sibelius Acad., Helsinki (conducting, under Jorma Panula). Formerly violinist, Avanti! Chamber Orch.; Concert Master, 1992–94, Co-Principal Conductor, 1994, Finnish Radio SO (professional conducting début, 1993); Artistic Dir, Finland 75 SO, 1995–98; Principal Conductor and Artistic Adviser, 1998–99, Music Dir, 1999–2008, City of Birmingham SO; Chief Conductor, 2003–12, Hon. Conductor, 2012–, Finnish Radio SO; Principal Conductor, Kokkola Opera, 2006–. Débuts include: CBSO, 1995; Henry Wood Promenade Concert, 1999. Guest Conductor: LA Philharmonic Orch.; NY Philharmonic Orch.; Berlin Philharmonic; NHK SO, Japan; Oslo Philharmonic Orch. Elgar Soc. Medal, 2008; Confederation of Scandinavian Societies' Internat. Award, 2018. *Address:* c/o HarrisonParrott Ltd, The Ark, 201 Talgarth Road, W6 8BJ.

**ORANMORE and BROWNE**, 5th Baron *cr* 1836 (Ire.); **Dominick Geoffrey Thomas Browne**; Baron Mereworth (UK) 1926; *b* 1 July 1929; *e s* of 4th Baron Oranmore and Browne (*s* of 3rd Baron and Lady Verena Ponsonby, *d* of 8th Earl of Bessborough) and his 1st wife, Mildred Helen, *d* of Hon. Thomas Egerton (3rd *s* of 3rd Earl of Ellesmere and Lady Bertha Anson, *e d* of 3rd Earl of Lichfield); *S* father, 2002; *m* 1957, Sara Margaret Wright (marr. diss. 1974). Poet and playwright. *Heir: nephew* Shaun Dominick Browne [*b* 22 Jan. 1964; *m* 1990, Elizabeth Jane Bird; two *s* two *d*].

**ORBACH, Susie**, PhD; psychotherapist and psychoanalyst to individuals, couples and groups; broadcaster; lecturer; *b* London, 6 Nov. 1946; *d* of Maurice Orbach and Ruth Orbach (*née* Huebsch); one *s* one *d*; *m* 2015, Jeanette Winterson, *qv*. *Educ:* City Univ. of NY (BA (Highest Hons) Women's Studies 1972); Sch. of Soc. Welfare, State Univ. of NY, Stony Brook (MSW 1974); Psychoanalysis Unit, University Coll. London (PhD 2001). Co-Founder, Women's Therapy Centre, London, 1976–81; Co-Founder and Co-Dir, Women's Therapy Centre Inst., NY, 1981–84. Visiting Professor: Gender Inst., LSE, 1998–2002; Sociol., LSE, 2002–08; Vis. Scholar, New Sch. for Social Res., 2008–09. Convener, ANYBODY, 2002–17 (launched ENDANGERED BODIES, 2011). Hon. DLitt SUNY, Stony Brook, 2001; Hon. DSc: London Metropolitan, 2009; Westminster, 2016; DUniv Essex, 2004; Hon. DArts UEL, 2011. Lifetime Achievement Award, Brit. Psychoanalytic Council, 2018. *Publications:* Fat is a Feminist Issue, 1978, Fat is a Feminist Issue II, 1982, combined edn 1997, rev. edn 2016; (with L. Eichenbaum) Outside In Inside Out: a feminist and psychoanalytic approach to women's psychology, 1982, 2nd edn as Understanding Women: a feminist psychoanalytic approach, 1983; (with L. Eichenbaum) What Do Women Want?: exploding the myth of dependency, 1983; Hunger Strike: the anorectic's struggle as a metaphor for our time, 1986, 2nd edn 2005; (with L. Eichenbaum) Bittersweet: love, competition and envy in women's friendships, 1987, 2nd edn as Between Women, 1988; What's Really Going on Here?, 1995; Towards Emotional Literacy, 1999; The Impossibility of Sex, 1999, 2004; On Eating, 2002; Bodies, 2009 (Dist. Pubn Award, Assoc. for Women in Psychol., 2010), 2019; (ed jtly) Fifty Shades of Feminism, 2013; In Therapy, 2016; In Therapy: the unfolding story, 2018; articles in Government Equalities Office, Psychoanalytic Dialogues. *Recreations:* friends, cooking. *E:* susie@susieorbach.co.uk.

**ORCHARD, Prof. Andrew Philip McDowell**, PhD; FBA 2015; FRSC; Rawlinson and Bosworth Professor of Anglo-Saxon, University of Oxford, since 2013; Fellow, Pembroke College, Oxford, since 2013; *b* London, 27 Feb. 1964; *s* of Kenneth and Patricia Orchard; *m* 1991, Clare Brind; one *s* one *d*. *Educ:* University Coll. Sch.; Exeter Coll., Oxford (BA); Queens' Coll., Cambridge (PhD 1991). Fellow, St John's Coll., Oxford, 1990; Lectr, 1991–99, Reader, 1999–2000, Hd, 1999–2000, Dept of Anglo-Saxon, Norse and Celtic, Univ. of Cambridge; Fellow, Emmanuel Coll., Cambridge, 1991–2000; University of Toronto: Professor: of Engl. and Medieval Studies, 2000–13; Dir, Centre for Medieval Studies, 2004–07; Fellow, 2001–13, Provost and Vice-Chancellor, 2007–13, Trinity Coll. Principal Investigator, Consolidated Liby of Anglo-Saxon Poetry. Sir Israel Gollancz Meml Lectr, British Acad., 2019. Editor: Cambridge Studies in Anglo-Saxon England, 1997–2007; Toronto Old Norse-Icelandic Studies, 2003–; Notes and Queries, 2003–; Toronto Anglo-Saxon Studies, 2008–; Member, Editorial Board: Anglo-Saxon England, 1998–; Jl Medieval Latin, 2000–; Dumbarton Oaks Medieval Liby, 2008–. FRSC 2013. *Publications:* The Poetic Art of Aldhelm, 1994; Pride and Prodigies: studies in the monsters of the Beowulf-Manuscript, 1995, rev. edn 2003; The Cassell Dictionary of Norse Myth and Legend, 1997, 3rd edn 2002; A Critical Companion to Beowulf, 2003, rev. edn 2005; The Elder Edda: a book of Viking Lore, 2011; *Recreations:* books and beer, solitude and silence, wandering in Iceland. *Address:* Pembroke College, Oxford OX1 1DW. *T:* (01865) 276444, *Fax:* (01865) 276418. *E:* andy.orchard@ell.ox.ac.uk. *Club:* Athenæum.

**ORCHARD, Anthony Edward**; QC 2011; *b* England; *s* of Lawrence William Orchard, CBE and Elspeth Ada Orchard (*née* Campbell); *m* 2007, Jacqueline Amy Zoest. *Educ:* Oratory Sch., Woodcote; Southampton Univ. (LLB Hons 1990). Metropolitan Police Officer, 1981–86; called to the Bar, Inner Temple, 1991; in practice as barrister, specialising in criminal law, 1991–. Friend, Nat. Railway Mus. *Recreations:* golf, cricket, walking. *Address:* 5 King's Bench Walk, Temple, EC4Y 7DN. *T:* (020) 7353 5638. *E:* anthony.orchard@5kbw.co.uk. *Clubs:* Denham Golf; Grannies Cricket.

**ORCHARD, Rev. Prof. Stephen Charles**, PhD; Principal, Westminster College, Cambridge, 2001–07; Moderator, General Assembly of United Reformed Church, 2007–08; *b* 30 March 1942; *s* of Ronald and Evelyn Orchard; *m* 1965, Linda Irene Smith; one *s* two *d*. *Educ:* Derby Sch.; Trinity Coll., Cambridge (BA 1965; PhD 1969); Cheshunt Coll., Cambridge. Ordained, Congregational Ch, 1968; Minister: Abercarn, S Wales, 1968–70; Sutton, Surrey, 1970–77; Free Ch, Welwyn Gdn City, 1977–82; Asst Gen. Sec. (Community Affairs), BCC, 1982–86; Gen. Sec. and Dir, Christian Educn Movt, 1986–2001. Chair, British and Foreign Sch., 1996–2007. Associate Prof., Sch. of Educn, Brunel Univ., 1999; Sen. Mem., St Edmund's Coll., Cambridge, 2004–07. Ed., REToday, 1990–2001. Chm., RE Council of England and Wales, 1999–2001. Templeton Prize judge, 1996–99. Chm., URC Hist. Soc., 1997–2012 (Pres., 2012–18); Pres., Cambridge Theol Fedn, 2005–07. Chair: Alliance House Foundn, 2001–; Westhill Endowment Trust, 2006–13; Derbyshire Family History Soc., 2009–; Trustee, Dr Williams's Liby, 1999–. Hon. DHum Brunel, 2000. *Publications:* History of Cheshunt College, 1968; A Christian Appreciation of the Welfare State, 1985; Our Commonwealth: a Christian view of taxation, 1987; The Pursuit of Truth in Community: a Christian view of education, 1992; (with W. L. H. Smith) The History of the Post Office in Lewes, 1992; A Human Jesus, 2006; (ed) The Sunday School Movement, 2007; Nonconformity in Derbyshire, 1600–1800, 2009; Congregationalism and Catholicity, 2009; (contrib.) Religion and Change in Modern Britain, 2012; (contrib.) The Free Churches and Society, 2012; (contrib.) Companion to Nonconformity, 2013; (contrib.) The Oxford History of Protestant Dissenting Traditions, Vol. II, 2018; contrib. Oxford DNB, British Jl Religious Educn, Jl URC History Soc., Derbys Family Hist. Soc. *Recreations:* music, walking, gardening. *Address:* c/o Westminster College, Madingley Road, Cambridge CB3 0AA.

**ORCHARD, Stephen Michael**, CBE 1999; Chief Executive, 1989–2003, and Member, 1992–2003, Legal Services Commission (formerly Legal Aid Board); *b* 5 Aug. 1944; *s* of Stephen Henry Orchard and Ellen Frances Orchard; *m*; one *s* one *d*. *Educ:* Swanage Grammar School. Lord Chancellor's Dept, 1961–89. *Recreations:* walking, food and wine. *Address:* 28 Cow Lane, Wareham, Dorset BH20 4RE.

**ORCHARD, Susan Kathleen**; *see* Doughty, S. K.

**ORCHARD-LISLE, Brig. Paul David**, CBE 1988; TD 1961; DL; *b* 3 Aug. 1938; *s* of late Mervyn and Phyllis Orchard-Lisle. *Educ:* Marlborough College; Trinity Hall, Cambridge (MA; Hon. Fellow, 2007). FRICS. Nat. Service, RA, 1956–58. Joined Healey & Baker, 1961; Sen. Partner, 1988–99; Chm., Healey & Baker Investment Advisers Inc., 1999–2001. RA (TA), 1958–88; ADC (TA), 1985–87; Brig. (TA), UKLF, 1985; Chm., TAVRA Greater London, 1988–91. Pres., RICS, 1986–87; Chm., RICS Foundn, 2003–05. Chairman: Slough Estates plc, 2005–06 (non-exec. Dir, 1984–2006; Dep. Chm., 1993–2005); Apache Capital Partners LLP, 2008–11; Standard Life Investments Property Income Trust, 2011–14 (Dir, 2004–14); Stobart Property Operating Bd, 2011–17; Apache 2012 Ltd, 2014–15; Director: Europa Capital Partners, 2000–06; Trinity Capital plc, 2006–09; Stobart Gp plc, 2011–14 (Consultant, 2014–18); Woodhall Spa Golf Mgt Ltd, 2014–; Chesterfield House Mgt Ltd, 2015–16. Commonwealth War Graves Comr, 1998–2003. Chm., RA Mus., 2000–06 (Mem. Bd, 2009–13). Member Council: Union Jack Club, 1997–2010; SSAFA, 2001–07. Property Advr, RBL, 2007–16. Pres. of Council,

Reading Univ., 1994–2003 (Mem. Council, 1989–94); Member of Council: Marlborough Coll., 1991–2006 (Chm., 2001–06); RVC, 2008–13 (Dep. Chm., 2009–13; Hon. Fellow 2013); Governor: West Buckland Sch., 1986–2005 (Chm., 2000–05; Pres., 2006–17; Patron, 2017–); Harrow Sch., 1988–99; Nottingham Trent Univ., 1992–94. Trustee: Church Schs Foundn, 2001–11; Crafts Council, 2004–06. Chm., Crown Golf (UK), 2008–09; Dir, Powerleague, 2008–13. Hon. Fellow: Coll. of Estate Management, 1985; Chartered Assoc. of Bldg Engrs, 2008. Hon. DSc City, 1998; Hon. LLD Reading, 2003. DL Gtr London, 1987 (Representative DL Westminster, 2007–13). *Recreation:* golf. *Address:* Pitstone Copse, Golf Club Road, Little Gaddesden, Herts HP4 1LY. *T:* (01442) 843388. *Clubs:* Athenæum, Savile.

**ORD-SMITH, Robin Jeremy,** MVO 1998; HM Diplomatic Service; High Commissioner to Tonga, since 2019; *b* Ferndown, Dorset, 8 Oct. 1965; *s* of late Derek and Mary Ord-Smith; *m* 1998, Tania Vallis (marr. diss. 2013); two *s*; one *a*. *Educ:* Ferndown Upper Sch.; Univ. of Surrey (BSc Linguistic and Internat. Studies). Entered FCO, 1985; Vice Consul: Algeria, 1991; Romania, 1991–94; Third Sec. (Political and Press), 1994–98, Second Sec., State Visit, 1998, Kuala Lumpur; Legationsrat 1er Klasse, German Foreign Ministry, 1999; Dep. Hd, Indonesia and East Timor Section, FCO, 1999–2000; Japanese lang. trng, 2000–01; on secondment as Mktg Manager, BAE SYSTEMS Japan, 2001–02; First Sec. (Commercial), 2002–06, Dir, Trade Promotion, 2006–07, Tokyo; Asst Private Sec. to the Duke of York, 2007–10; Dir, UK Trade and Investment, Baghdad, 2011; Ambassador to Tajikistan, 2012–14; Ambassador to the Kyrgyz Republic, 2015–19. *Recreations:* golf, travel, photography, languages, history. *Address:* c/o Foreign and Commonwealth Office, King Charles Street, SW1A 2AH. *Clubs:* Travellers; Royal and Ancient Golf (St Andrews); Woking Golf; Lucifer Golfing Society.

**ORDE, His Honour Denis Alan;** author; a Circuit Judge, 1979–2001; *b* 28 Aug. 1932; *3rd s* of late John Orde, CBE, Littlehoughton Hall, Northumberland, and Charlotte Lilian Orde, County Alderman; *m* 1961, Jennifer Jane, *d* of late Dr John Longworth, Masham, Yorks; two *d*. *Educ:* independent private schs; Oxford Univ. (MA Hons). Served Army, 1950–52, 2nd Lieut 1951; TA, 1952–64 (RA), Capt. 1958. Pres., Oxford Univ. Conserv. Assoc., 1954; Mem. Cttee, Oxford Union, 1954–55; Vice-Chm., Fedn of Univ. Conserv. Assocs, 1955. Called to Bar, Inner Temple, 1956; Pupil Studentship, 1956; Profumo Prize, 1959; Bencher, 1998; Hd of Chambers, 1979. Assistant Recorder: Kingston upon Hull, 1970; Sheffield, 1970–71; a Recorder of the Crown Court, 1972–79; Liaison Judge to Magistrates, 1983–97; Dep. High Court Judge (Civil), 1983–2005; Resident Judge, Crown Court, 1986–2001; sat in NE and London. A Pres., Mental Health Review Tribunal (Restricted Cases), 2001–05. Chairman: Criminal Justice Liaison Cttee, Cos of Northumberland, Tyne and Wear and Durham, 1995–2000; Criminal Justice Strategy Cttee for Durham Co., 2000–01; Mem., Lord Chancellor's County Adv. Cttee, 1987–2001. Contested (C): Consett, 1959; Newcastle upon Tyne West, 1966; Sunderland South, 1970. Rep. for NE, Bow Gp, 1962–70. Mem., St Giles, Chollerton PCC, 1980–91. Life Vice-Pres., Northumberland LTA, 1982–. Gov., Christ's Hospital, Sherburn, 1993–98. *Publications:* Nelson's Mediterranean Command, 1997, repr. 2014; In the Shadow of Nelson: the life of Admiral Lord Collingwood, 2008, repr. 2019; contrib. Oxford DNB and to magazines. *Recreations:* writing naval history, cricket, family history, biography. *Address:* Chollerton Grange, Chollerton, near Hexham, Northumberland NE46 4TG; Aristotle Court, 75 Plater Drive, Oxford Waterside, Oxford OX2 6QU. *Club:* Northern Counties (Newcastle).

**ORDE, Sir Hugh (Stephen Roden),** Kt 2005; OBE 2001; QPM 2010; President, Association of Chief Police Officers of England, Wales and Northern Ireland, 2009–15; *b* 27 Aug. 1958; *s* of Thomas Henry Egil Orde and Stella Mary Orde; *m* 1st, 1985, Kathleen Helen (marr. diss. 2010); one *s*; 2nd, 2011, Denise Weston; one two *d*. *Educ:* Univ. of Kent at Canterbury (BA Hons Public Admin and Mgt). Joined Metropolitan Police, 1977; Sergeant, Brixton, 1982; Police Staff Coll., 1983; Inspector, Greenwich, 1984–90 (Bramshill Schol., 1984–87); Staff Officer to Dep. Asst Comr, SW London, as Chief Inspector, 1990; Chief Inspector, Hounslow, 1991–93; Superintendent, Territorial Support Gp, 1993–95; Detective Chief Superintendent, Major Crimes, SW Area, 1995–98; Comdr, Crime, S London, 1998; Dep. Asst Comr (Comr's Comd), 1999–2002; Chief Constable, Police Service of NI, 2002–09. Chm., UK Police Meml Trust, 2010–. *Publications:* (with Desmond Rea) Bear in Mind These Dead: the Omagh bombing and policing, 2016. *Recreations:* wine, gardening.

**ORDE, Sir John Simon Arthur Campbell-,** 7th Bt *cr* 1790, of Morpeth; JD; *b* 15 Aug. 1981; *s* of Sir John Alexander Campbell-Orde, 6th Bt and Lacy Ralls, *d* of Grady Gallant; *S* father, 2016, but his name does not appear on the Official Roll of the Baronetage; *m* 2006, Maura (marr. diss. 2009), *o d* of Philip McClelland. *Educ:* Univ. of Cincinnati. Admitted Attorney, Ohio, 2007; former Gen. Counsel, Professionals Guild of Ohio.

**ORDE-POWLETT,** family name of **Baron Bolton**.

**ORDIDGE, Prof. Roger John,** PhD; FMedSci; Professor of Imaging Science, and Director, Melbourne Brain Centre Imaging Unit, University of Melbourne, since 2011; *b* 22 Aug. 1956; *s* of John Ordidge and Margaret Ordidge; *m* 1978, Claire Page; one *s* two *d*. *Educ:* Univ. of Nottingham (BSc Phys 1977; PhD Phys 1981). Develt Scientist, 1982–83, Sen. Develt Scientist, 1983–86, Oxford Research Systems; Lectr in Phys, Univ. of Nottingham, 1986–89; Prof. of Phys, Oakland Univ., Mich, 1989–93; Co-Dir, MR Research Lab., Henry Ford Hosp., Detroit, 1989–93; Joel Prof. of Physics Applied to Medicine, 1994–2011, Vice Dean for Res., Faculty of Engrg Scis, 2006–10, UCL. Institute of Neurology: Hon. Sen. Fellow, 1996–2011; Dir, Wellcome Trust High Field MR Res. Lab., 1999–2011. Fellow, Internat. Soc. of Magnetic Resonance in Medicine, 2001–. FMedSci 2006. *Publications:* approx. 250 res. papers on MRI and its applications in learned jls; eight patents on design of MRI scanners, one patent on radio-frequency pulse design to improve MRI machines. *Recreations:* tennis, hiking, golf, exploring Australia, grandfather training (by grandchildren). *Address:* Melbourne Brain Centre, Kenneth Myer Building, 30 Royal Parade, University of Melbourne, Vic 3010, Australia. *T:* (3) 83441953. *E:* roger.ordidge@unimelb.edu.au.

**O'REGAN, Hon. Sir Mark (Andrew),** KNZM 2013; **Hon. Justice O'Regan;** a Judge, Supreme Court of New Zealand, since 2014; *b* Wellington, NZ, 30 Nov. 1953; *s* of Hon. Sir (John) Barry O'Regan and Cassie O'Regan; *m* 1985, Nicola Ann Saker; two *s* one *d*. *Educ:* St Patrick's Coll., Silverstream; Victoria Univ. of Wellington (BA 1974; LLM with distinction 1979). Admitted as barrister and solicitor of High Court, 1977; Station Manager, DHL Internat. SA, Paris, 1980–81; Solicitor, 1982–84, Partner, 1984–2000, Chapman Tripp, barristers and solicitors, Wellington; a Judge, High Court of NZ, Auckland, 2000–04; a Judge, 2004–14 and Pres., 2010–14, Court of Appeal of NZ. *Recreations:* cricket, walking, reading. *Address:* Supreme Court of New Zealand, 85 Lambton Quay, Wellington 6011, New Zealand. *Club:* Wellington (Wellington).

**O'REGAN, Sister Pauline Margaret,** DCNZM 2001; CBE 1990; writer; *b* 28 June 1922; *d* of John Joseph O'Regan and Mary Margaret O'Regan (*née* Barry). *Educ:* Cronadun Primary Sch., W Coast, NZ; St Mary's High Sch., Greymouth; Univ. of Canterbury, Christchurch (MA Hist.). Entered Order of Sisters of Mercy, 1942; professed as Sister of Mercy, 1944; teacher, St Mary's Coll., Christchurch, 1945–49; Principal: Villa Maria Coll., Christchurch, 1950–66; Mercy Coll., Timaru, 1967–68; teacher, Aranui High Sch., Christchurch, 1973–77; community worker, Aranui, 1978–. Winston Churchill Fellow, 1979. Mem., Winston Churchill Meml Trust Bd, NZ, 1985–90. *Publications:* A Changing Order, 1986, 2nd edn 1995; (jtly) Community, 1989; Aunts and Windmills, 1991; There is Hope for a Tree, 1995; (jtly) Parish: for the people in the pews, 2000; Miles to Go, 2004, 2nd edn 2007. *Recreations:* cryptic crosswords, films, reading. *Address:* Christchurch, New Zealand.

**O'REGAN, Sir Stephen Gerard, (Sir Tipene),** Kt 1994; Ngai Tahu tribal leader; company director; academic historian; *b* 23 Sept. 1939; *s* of Rolland O'Regan and Rena Ruhia O'Regan (*née* Bradshaw); *m* 1963, Sandra Ann McTaggart; one *s* four *d*. *Educ:* Marist Brothers Primary Sch.; St Patrick's Coll.; Victoria Univ. (BA (Hons) Pol Sci. and Hist.); Wellington Teachers' Coll. Sen. Lectr and Head of Dept of Social Studies and Maori, Wellington Teachers' Coll., 1968–83; founded Aoraki Consultant Services, 1983, now Principal Dir. Maori Fisheries Negotiator with Crown, 1987–92. Chairman: Mawhera Incorp., 1976–88; Sealord Group (formerly Sealord Products) Ltd, 1993–2002; Ngai Tahu Hldg Corp. Ltd, 1996–2000; Te Tapuae o Rehua Ltd, 1997–2005; Escorial Co. Ltd, 1999–2004; Clifford Bay Marine Farms Ltd, 2000–15; Dep. Chm., Transit NZ Authy, 2000–06; Director: Ngai Tahu Fisheries Ltd, 1986–90; Broadcasting Corp. of NZ, 1986–88; Television NZ Ltd, 1988–95; Whale Watch Kaikoura Ltd, 1988–2009; Moana Pacific Fisheries Ltd, 1990–95; Ngai Tahu Property Group Ltd, 1993–2000; Meridian Energy Ltd, 2000–05. Co-Chm., NZ Constitutional Adv. Panel, 2012–13. QEII Postgrad. Schol. in Maori, 1977–78; Lansdowne Fellow, Univ. of Victoria, BC, 1994; Canterbury University: Ngai Tahu Fellow (History), 1977–78; Vis. Lectr, NZ History, 1989–2000; Sen. Res. Fellow, 2001–04; Asst Vice-Chancellor (Maori), 2005–10; Adjunct Prof., 2011–; Vis. Fellow, Stanford Univ., 2009; Fellow, Univ. of Auckland, 2011 (Chm., Centre for Maori Research Excellence, 2006–15). Mem., Adv. Bd, Univ. of Otago Business Sch., 2003–15. Chairman: Ngai Tahu Maori Trust Bd, 1983–96 (Mem., 1974–96); Ngai Tahu Charitable Trust, 1983–97; Ngai Tahu Negotiating Gp, 1990–99; Maori Fisheries Commn, 1990–93; Treaty of Waitangi Fisheries Commn, 1993–2000; Dep. Chm., Fedn of Maori Authorities, 1986–88 (Exec. Mem., 1988–97); Member: Maori Adv. Cttee, NZ Historic Places Trust, 1977–90; NZ Geographic Bd, 1983–2013; Bd of Trustees, Nat. Mus. of NZ, 1984–94; NZ Conservation Authy, 1990–96; Bd, Law of the Sea Inst., 1995–2001; Bd of Trustees, Marine Stewardship Council, 2000–05; Trustee, Christchurch Arts Centre, 2010–13. Patron: Foundn for Res. on Marine Mammals, 2001; Christchurch Arts Fest., 1998–2015. Writer and presenter, Manawhenua: the Natural World of the Maori (TV documentary series), 1987. Dist. Fellow, Inst. of Dirs, NZ, 2001. Hon. DLitt Canterbury, 1992; Hon. DComm: Lincoln, 2004; Victoria, 2006. New Zealander of the Year, Nat. Business Review, 1993; Supreme Award, NZ Seafood Industry Council, 2002. *Publications:* New Myths and Old Politics, 2014; contribs to numerous books, articles in jls, reports, etc. *Address:* 342 Marine Parade, Christchurch 8061, New Zealand. *Clubs:* Royal Port Nicholson Yacht; Waikawa Boating.

**O'REILLY, Sir Anthony (John Francis),** Kt 2001; PhD; Chief Executive, Independent News & Media, 2004–09 (Executive Chairman, 2000–04); Chairman: Independent Newspapers PLC, 1980–2009; Waterford Wedgwood PLC, 1993–2009; *b* Dublin, 7 May 1936; *oc* of J. P. O'Reilly, former Inspector-General of Customs; *m* 1962, Susan (marr. diss.), *d* of Keith Cameron, Australia; three *s* three *d* (of whom two *s* one *d* are triplets); *m* 1991, Chryss Goulandris. *Educ:* Belvedere Coll., Dublin; University Coll., Dublin (BCL 1958); Bradford Univ. (PhD 1980). Admitted Solicitor, 1958. Industrial Consultant, Weston Evans UK, 1958–60; PA to Chm., Suttons Ltd, Cork, 1960–62; Chief Exec. Officer, Irish Dairy Bd, 1962–66; Man. Dir, Irish Sugar Bd, 1966–69; Man. Dir, Erin Foods Ltd, 1966–69; Jt Man. Dir, Heinz-Erin, 1967–70; Man. Dir, H. J. Heinz Co. Ltd, UK, 1969–71; H. J. Heinz Co.: Sen. Vice-Pres., N America and Pacific, 1971–72; Exec. Vice-Pres. and Chief Op. Off., 1972–73; Pres. and Chief Operating Officer, 1973–79; Pres., 1979–96; CEO, 1979–98; Chm., 1987–2000. Lectr in Business Management, UC Cork, 1960–62. Director: Robt McCowen & Sons Ltd, 1961–62; Agricl Credit Corp. Ltd, 1965–66; Nitrigin Eireann Teoranta, 1965–66; Allied Irish Investment Bank Ltd, 1968–71; Thyssen-Bornemisza Co., 1970–72; Independent Newspapers (Vice Chm., 1973–80); Nat. Mine Service Co., 1973–76; Mobil, 1979–88; Bankers Trust Co., 1980–90; Allegheny Internat. Inc., 1982–87; Washington Post, 1987–94; GEC, 1990–92; Chairman: Fitzwilliam Securities Ltd, 1971–77; Fitzwilton Ltd, 1978– (Dep. Chm., 1972–78); Atlantic Resources PLC, 1981. Member: Incorp. Law Soc.; Council, Irish Management Inst.; Hon. LLD: Wheeling Coll., 1974; Rollins Coll., 1978; Trinity Coll., 1978; Allegheny Coll., 1983. *Publications:* Prospect, 1962; Developing Creative Management, 1970; The Conservative Consumer, 1971; Food for Thought, 1972. *Recreations:* Rugby (played for Ireland 29 times), tennis. *Clubs:* Reform, Annabel's; Stephen's Green (Dublin); Duquesne, Allegheny, Fox Chapel, Pittsburgh Golf (Pittsburgh); Carlton (Chicago); Lyford Cay (Bahamas).

**O'REILLY, Most Rev. Colm;** Bishop of Ardagh and Clonmacnoise, (RC), 1983–2013, now Bishop Emeritus; *b* 11 Jan. 1935; *s* of John and Alicia O'Reilly. Ordained priest, 1960. *Address:* St Michael's, Longford, Ireland. *T:* (43) 46432.

**O'REILLY, Sir John (James),** Kt 2007; DSc, PhD; CEng, FREng; FRAeS; Chairman: NICC Standards Ltd, since 2008; ERA Foundation Ltd, 2016–19 (Director, since 2008); *b* 1 Dec. 1946; *s* of Patrick William and Dorothy Ann O'Reilly; one *s* one *d*. *Educ:* Brunel Univ. (BTech 1969; DSc 1991); Essex Univ. (PhD 1982). Student apprentice, RRE, Malvern, 1963–69; Lectr, then Sen. Lectr, Univ. of Essex, 1972–85; Prof. of Electronic Engrg, 1985–94, Hd, Sch. of Electronic Engrg and Computer Systems, 1985–93, UCNW, later Univ. of Wales, Bangor; Principal Res. Fellow, BT Labs, 1993–94; Prof. of Telecommunications, 1994–2001, Hd, Dept of Electronic and Electrical Engrg, 1997–2001, UCL; Chief Exec., EPSRC, 2001–06; Vice-Chancellor, Cranfield Univ., 2006–13; Dir Gen., Knowledge and Innovation, BIS, 2013–15. Chief Exec., IDB Ltd, 1986–94. Comr, Royal Commn for the Exhibn of 1851, 2011–. Mem. Bd, Agency for Sci., Technol. and Res., Singapore, 2011–; Chm., Sci. and Engrg Res. Council, Singapore, 2012–. Vis. Prof., UCL, 2015–; RAEng Industrial Vis. Prof., Huddersfield Univ. Member: Bd, Khalifa Univ., UAE, 2015–17; Council, Univ. of Exeter, 2015–. Pres., IEE, 2004–05 (Vice-Pres., 2000–02; Dep. Pres., 2002). Trustee, RAeS, 2013–. FREng 1993. Hon. FIChemE 2004; Hon. FIET 2011. Hon. Foreign Member: Acad. Hassan II des Scis et Techniques, 2006–; Lisbon Acad. of Scis, 2008–. *Publications:* Telecommunication Principles, 1984; Optimisation Methods in Electronics and Communications, 1984; (ed with K. W. Cattermole) Problems of Randomness in Communication Engineering, 1984; contrib. numerous jl and conf. papers. *Recreations:* music, theatre, gardening, cooking.

**O'REILLY, Most Rev. Leo,** STD; Bishop of Kilmore, (RC), 1998–2019; *b* 10 April 1944; *s* of Terence O'Reilly and Maureen (*née* Smith). *Educ:* St Patrick's Coll., Maynooth (BSc, BD, HDipEd); Gregorian Univ., Rome (STD 1982). Ordained priest, 1969; on staff: St Patrick's Coll., Cavan, 1969–76; Irish Coll., Rome, 1976–81; Chaplain, Bailieborough

Community Sch., 1981–88; missionary work, Nigeria: diocese of Minna, 1988–90; staff, St Paul's Seminary, Abuja, 1990–95; Parish Priest, Castletara, Cavan, 1995–97; Coadjutor Bishop of Kilmore, 1997–98. *Publications:* Word and Sign in the Acts of the Apostles: a study in Lucan theology, 1987. *Recreations:* walking, reading, golf.

**O'REILLY, Leo Columba Martin,** CB 2017; Permanent Secretary, Department for Communities, Northern Ireland, 2016–18; *b* Ballymena, Co. Antrim, 9 June 1955; *s* of Thomas O'Reilly and Catherine O'Reilly; *m* 1978, Jane McCallan; two *s* one *d*. *Educ:* St Mac Nissi's Coll., Garron Tower; Queen's Univ., Belfast (BA Hons Econ. and Social Hist. and Econs 1977); Univ. of Ulster (Dip. Mgt Studies 1982; MSc Public Policy 1987); Warwick Business Sch. (Dip. Public Finance and Leadership 2007). Dir, Prison Personnel, 1992–95, Dir, Prison Service Finance, 1995–97, NI Office; Department of Finance and Personnel, NI: Hd, Equal Opportunities and Appts Div., 1997–2000; Hd, Eur. Div., 2000–02; Budget Dir, 2002–07; Perm. Sec., 2007–09; Perm. Sec., Dept of Envmt, NI, 2009–16. Ind. Mem., Rev. of Intra-UK Allocation of Domestic Farm Support, 2019–. Trustee, Timoney Leadership Inst., Dublin, 2014–. Chm. Govs, Our Lady and St Patrick's Coll., Belfast, 2014–. *Recreations:* running, theatre, reading - political biography, gardening (damage control). *E:* leo.oreilly@btinternet.com.

**O'REILLY, Air Vice-Marshal Patrick John,** CB 1999; CEng, FIET, FRAeS; Director of Military Support, Claverham Ltd, 2000–06; *b* 26 April 1946; *s* of John Francis O'Reilly and Elizabeth O'Reilly (*née* Hammond); *m* 1974, Christine Adair Williamson; two *s*. *Educ:* Ryland Bedford Sch., Sutton Coldfield; Aston Univ. (BSc). Joined RAF 1969; numerous aircraft engrg appts in UK, Germany and the Falkland Is involving fast-jet and rotary aircraft; rcds 1991; Air Officer Wales, 1992–94; Dir Gen. Technical Services, and Pres. of Ordnance Bd, 1996–98, retd 1999. Pres., Wales, Midlands and SW Area, RAFA, 2008–15. Liveryman, Engineers' Co., 2004 (Master, 2015–16). *Recreation:* shooting. *Address:* Seend, Wilts. *Clubs:* Royal Air Force; Bath and County.

**O'REILLY, Peter Terence,** QFSM 2016; Chief Fire Officer and Chief Executive, Greater Manchester Fire and Rescue Service, 2015–18; *b* Belfast, NI, 21 Aug. 1966; *s* of Peter and Margaret O'Reilly; *m* 1987, Christine Cassidy; two *d*. *Educ:* St Mary's Grammar Sch., Belfast; Univ. of Ulster (MBA); Univ. of Warwick (Postgrad. Cert. Strategic Leadership). Northern Ireland Fire and Rescue Service: Firefighter, 1990–96; Leading Firefighter, 1996–2000; Sub Officer, 2000–01; Station Comdr, 2001–03; District Comdr, 2003–05; Gp Comdr, 2005–09; Area Comdr, 2009–11; Asst Chief Fire Officer, Gtr Manchester Fire and Rescue Service, 2011–15. Strategic Lead for Health, Chief Fire Officers Assoc., 2015–. *Publications:* contrib. articles to trade jls incl. Emergency Services Times, esp. on fire service being a health asset. *Recreations:* golf, watching Manchester United, physical fitness, reading. *T:* 07712 662815. *Club:* Swinton Park Golf.

**OREJA AGUIRRE, Marcelino,** Marqués de Oreja (Spain) *cr* 2010; Member, European Commission, 1994–99; President, Institute of European Studies, San Pablo-CEU University, since 2000; *b* 13 Feb. 1935; *m* 1967, Silvia Arburua; two *s*. *Educ:* Univ. of Madrid (LLD). Prof. of Internat. Affairs, Diplomatic Sch., Madrid, 1962–70; Dir of Internat. Service, Bank of Spain, 1970–74; Minister of Foreign Affairs, 1976–80; Governor-Gen., Basque Country, 1980–82; Sec. Gen., Council of Europe, 1984–89; Mem. (Partido Popular) European Parlt, 1989–94 (Chm., Institutional Affairs Cttee, 1989–94). *Address:* 81 Nunez de Balboa, 28006 Madrid, Spain. *T:* (1) 5759101.

**ORFORD, Julia Amanda;** *see* Dias, J. A.

**ORGAN, Bryan;** *see* Organ, H. B.

**ORGAN, Diana Mary;** Trustee, Gloucestershire Young Carers, since 2012 (Strategic Lead, 2010–12); *b* 21 Feb. 1952; *d* of Jack Stanley Pugh and Vera Lillian Pugh; *m* 1975, Richard Thomas Organ; two *d*. *Educ:* Church of England Coll., Edgbaston; St Hugh's Coll., Oxford (BA Hons 1973); Bath Univ. (CertEd 1974). Special Needs Teacher, High Heath Special Sch., 1975; Remedial Teacher, Cardiff, 1976; Special Needs Teacher, Plymouth, 1977–78; Dep. Head, St German's Primary Sch., 1978–79; Head, Special Needs Units, Shepton Mallet, 1979–82; special needs posts, Somerset, 1982–92; Lab Gp policy researcher, Oxfordshire CC, 1993–95. MP (Lab) Forest of Dean, 1997–2005. Chief Exec., Young Gloucestershire, 2006–10. Trustee: Glos Envmtl Trust Co., 2005–; Community Foster Care, 2005; UK Youth, 2006–. Trustee, Nat. Waterways Trust, 2009–12. *Recreations:* gardening, cinema, sailing, swimming. *Address:* Gloucestershire Young Carers, 7 Twigworth Court Business Centre, Twigworth GL2 9GG. *T:* (01452) 733060.

**ORGAN, (Harold) Bryan;** painter; *b* Leicester, 31 Aug. 1935; *oc* of late Harold Victor Organ and Helen Dorothy Organ; *m* (marr. diss. 1981); *m* 1982, Sandra Mary Mills. *Educ:* Wyggeston Sch., Leicester; Coll. of Art, Loughborough; Royal Academy Schs, London. Lectr in Drawing and Painting, Loughborough Coll. of Art, 1959–65. One-man exhibns: Leicester Museum and Art Gallery, 1959; Redfern Gallery, 1967, 1969, 1971, 1973, 1975, 1978, 1980; Leicester 1973, 1976; New York, 1976, 1977; Turin, 1981. Represented: Kunsthalle, Darmstadt, 1968; Mostra Mercato d'Arte Contemporanea, Florence, 1969; 3rd Internat. Exhibn of Drawing, Germany, 1970; São Paulo Museum of Art, Brazil; Baukunst Gallery, Cologne, 1977. Works in public and private collections worldwide. 16 portraits in National Portrait Gallery include: Dr Roy Strong, 1971; Lester Piggott, 1973; Harold Macmillan, 1980; Prince of Wales, 1981; Lady Diana Spencer, 1981; Lord Denning, 1982; Jim Callaghan, 1983; Duke of Edinburgh, 1983; other portraits include: Malcolm Muggeridge, 1966; Sir Michael Tippett, 1966; Mary Quant, 1969; Princess Margaret, 1970; Elton John, 1973; President Mitterrand, 1985; Richard Attenborough, 1985, 2003; Colin Cowdrey, 1996; Lord Woolf, 2002; Roy Jenkins, 2002; Martin Johnson, 2004; Lord Sugar, 2010; Sir David Attenborough, 2016. Hon. MA Loughborough, 1974; Hon. DLitt: Leicester, 1985; Loughborough, 1992. *Address:* c/o Redfern Gallery, 20 Cork Street, W1S 3HL. *T:* (020) 7734 1732.

**ORGILL, Richard Michael James;** Global Head of Corporate and Institutional Banking, HSBC Holdings plc, 1998–2001; *b* 14 Oct. 1938; *m* 1968, Anne Whitley; two *s* one *d*. *Educ:* Bryanston Sch. FCIB 1989. Gen. Manager and Chief Exec. Officer, Hongkong and Shanghai Banking Corp., Malaysia, 1985–89; Gen. Manager Internat., Hongkong and Shanghai Banking Corp., Hong Kong, 1989–90; Gen. Manager and Chief Exec. Officer, Hongkong Bank of Australia Ltd, 1990–93; Chief Operating Officer, 1993–94, Dir and Dep. Chief Exec., 1994–98, Midland Bank plc. Director: HSBC (formerly Midland) Bank plc, 1994–2001; Hongkong and Shanghai Banking Corp. Ltd, 1999–2001; HSBC Investment Bank Hldgs plc, 1999–2001; ICICI Bank UK Ltd, 2002–12.

**ORHNIAL, Anthony Joseph Henry,** CB 2007; Director, Personal Tax and Welfare Reform, HM Treasury, 2005–08; *b* 31 Oct. 1947; *s* of Antoine Orhnial and late Hilda Orhnial (later Mell); *m* 1982, Gertrud Wienecke; one *d*. *Educ:* St Edward's Coll., Malta; St Benedict's Sch., Ealing; London Sch. of Economics (BSc (Econ), MSc (Econ)). Research Asst, RTZ Services Ltd, 1970–71; Kingston Polytechnic, Kingston on Thames: Lectr, 1971–74; Sen. Lectr, 1974–84; Principal Lectr in Economics, 1984–88; Principal: Inland Revenue, 1988–91; HM Treasury, 1991–93; Asst Dir, 1993–2000, Dir, 2000–05, Personal Tax, Inland Revenue. Specialist Advr, Finance Bill Sub-Cttee, Econ. Affairs Cttee, H of L, 2010–18; Fiscal Expert, IMF, 2018–. Vis. Lectr in Economics, Konstanz Univ., Germany,
1979–80. Trustee, Child Poverty Action Gp, 2010–. *Publications:* Limited Liability and the Modern Corporation, 1982; articles in Economica, Jl of Accounting Research, British Review of Economics. *Recreations:* travel, reading, cookery, furniture restoration. *Address:* 32 Marjorie Grove, SW11 5SJ.

**O'RIORDAN, Rear-Adm. John Patrick Bruce,** CBE 1982; DL; Chief Executive, St Andrew's Group of Hospitals, Northampton, 1990–2000; *b* 15 Jan. 1936; *yr s* of Surgeon Captain Timothy Joseph O'Riordan, RN and Bertha Carson O'Riordan (*née* Young); *m* 1959, Jane, *e d* of John Alexander Mitchell; one *s* two *d*. *Educ:* Kelly College. Nat. Service and transfer to RN, 1954–59; served in submarines, Mediterranean, Home and Far East; HM Ships Porpoise (i/c) and Courageous, NDC, HMS Dreadnought (i/c), MoD, 1960–76; Captain (SM), Submarine Sea Training, 1976–78; RCDS, 1979; HMS Glasgow (i/c), 1980–81; ACOS (Policy), Saclant, USA, 1982–84; Dir, Naval Warfare, MoD, 1984–86; Mil. Dep. Comdt, NATO Defence Coll., Rome, 1986–89. Director: Workbridge Enterprises Ltd, 1990–2000; Ind. Healthcare Assoc., 1993–2000; NXD O'Riordan Bond, 1999–2008. Chairman: SSAFA Forces Help (formerly SSAFA) Northants, 1996–2000; SSAFA Forces Help, Dumfriesshire and the Stewartry, 2000–08 (Chm., Scottish Resources Cttee, 2006–08). Patron, John Paul Jones Birthplace and Mus., 2012–. JP Northants, 1991–2000; DL Northants, 1997. *Recreations:* sailing, Rugby football, stalking, fishing, painting. *Address:* Pineapple Cottage, Wills Lane, Cerne Abbas, Dorchester, Dorset DT2 7JY. *Clubs:* Army and Navy, Royal Navy of 1765 and 1785; Royal Yacht Squadron, Royal Naval Sailing Association.

*See also* Lt Gen. A. J. N. Graham.

**O'RIORDAN, Marie;** Editor-in-Chief, John Brown Media, since 2009; *b* 3 April 1960; *d* of Michael and Maura O'Riordan. *Educ:* University Coll. Dublin (BA English and Hist.; MA Modern English and American Lit.). More! magazine: Prodn Editor, 1990–92; Dep. Editor, 1992–94; Editor, 1994–96; Editor, Elle magazine, 1996–99; Gp Publishing Dir, EMAP Elan, 1999–2001; Ed., Marie Claire, 2001–08; Agony Aunt and Columnist, The Times, 2009–. EMAP Editor of Year, 1996; IPC Media Editor of Year, 2003 and 2005. *Recreations:* reading, movies, walking, travelling. *Clubs:* Soho House, Groucho.

**O'RIORDAN, Prof. Timothy,** OBE 2010; FBA 1999; Professor of Environmental Sciences, University of East Anglia, 1980–2006, now Emeritus; *b* 21 Feb. 1942; *s* of late Kevin Denis O'Riordan and Norah Joyce O'Riordan (*née* Lucas); *m* 1967, Ann Morison Philip (*d* 1992); two *d*. *Educ:* Univ. of Edinburgh (MA 1963); Cornell Univ. (MS 1965); Univ. of Cambridge (PhD 1967). Asst Prof. and Associate Prof., Dept of Geography, Simon Fraser Univ., Canada, 1967–74; Reader, Sch. of Environmental Scis, UEA, 1974–80. Chm., Envmt Cttee, Broads Authy, 1989–98; Mem., UK Sustainable Develt Commn, 2000–08; Adviser: Envmtl Res. Directorate, EC, 1996–97; Accounting for Sustainability Project, 2007; Member, Environmental Advisory Council: Dow Chemicals, 1992–98; Eastern Group plc, 1995–2000; Asda plc, 2004–12; Advr, Anglian Water, 2006–16. Pres., CPRE Norfolk, 2002–. Trustee, Norfolk Can Inspire, 2012–15. FRSA. DL Norfolk, 1998; Sheriff of Norwich, 2009–10. Gill Meml Award, RGS, 1982; Distinguished Friend of Oxford Univ., 2011. *Publications:* Environmentalism 1976, 2nd edn 1981; (jtly) Countryside Conflicts, 1986; (jtly) Sizewell B: an anatomy of the inquiry, 1987; (ed) Environmental Science for Environmental Management, 1994, 2nd edn 1999; (ed jtly) Interpreting the Precautionary Principle, 1994; (ed) The Politics of Climate Change in Europe, 1996; (ed) Ecotaxation, 1997; (ed jtly) The Transition to Sustainability, 1998; Globalism, Localism and Identity, 2000; (ed jtly) Reinterpreting the Precautionary Principle, 2001; (ed jtly) Biodiversity, Human Livelihoods, and Sustainability, 2002; Addressing Tipping Points for a Precarious Future, 2013. *Recreations:* swimming, bird watching, classical double bass playing. *Address:* Wheatlands, Hethersett Lane, Colney, Norwich NR4 7TT. *T:* (01603) 810534. *E:* t.oriordan@uea.ac.uk.

**ORITA, Masaki;** Professor of International Law, Chuo University, 2007–13; Chairman, Institute of International Affairs, since 2005; *b* 29 July 1942; *s* of Saburo Orita and Saeko Orita; *m* 1967, Masako Okami; one *s*. *Educ:* Univ. of Tokyo (LLB 1965); St Catherine's Coll., Oxford (Dip. Econ. and Pol Sci.). Entered Ministry of Foreign Affairs, Japan, 1965; First Secretary: USSR, 1975–77; Japanese Delegn to OECD, 1977–79; Dep. Budget Examiner, Min. of Finance, Tokyo, 1979–81; Dir, Treaties Div., Min. of Foreign Affairs, 1981–84; Pol Counsellor, USA, 1984–87; Dir, Overseas Estabts Div., Minister's Secretariat, 1987–89; Dep. Dir-Gen., ME and African Affairs Bureau, 1989; Exec. Asst to Prime Minister of Japan, 1989–91; Consul-Gen., Hong Kong, 1992–94; Dir-Gen., Treaties Bureau, 1994–95, N American Bureau, 1995–97, Min. of Foreign Affairs; Ambassador to Denmark (and concurrently to Lithuania), 1997–2001; Ambassador to UK, 2001–04; Sen. Advr to Minister of Foreign Affairs, 2005–06; Ambassador and Special Envoy for UN Reform, 2005–06. Comdr, Order of Orange Nassau (Netherlands), 1991; Grand Cross, Order of Dannebrog (Denmark), 1998; Gold and Silver Star, Order of Sacred Treasure (Japan), 2017. *Address:* 1–29–5–203 Daizawa, Setagaya-ku, Tokyo 155–0032, Japan. *Clubs:* Kojunsha, Tokyo (Tokyo).

**ORKNEY,** 9th Earl of, *cr* 1696; **Oliver Peter St John;** Lord Dechmont, Viscount Kirkwall, 1696; Professor of Political Studies, 1998, and Senior Scholar, since 1999, University of Manitoba (Associate Professor, 1972–98); *b* Victoria, BC, 27 Feb. 1938; *s* of Lt-Col Frederick Oliver St John, DSO, MC (*d* 1977; *g s* of 5th Earl of Orkney) and of Elizabeth, *d* of E. H. Pierce; *S* kinsman, 1998; *m* 1st, 1963, Mary Juliet (marr. diss. 1985), *d* of W. G. Scott-Brown, CVO, MD, FRCS, FRCSE; one *s* three *d*; 2nd, 1985, Mrs Mary Barbara Huck, *d* of late Dr David B. Albertson; one step *s* three step *d*. *Educ:* Woodbridge Sch.; Univ. of British Columbia (BA 1960); LSE (MSc 1963); PhD London Univ. 1972. Lecturer: UCL, 1963–64; Univ. of Manitoba, 1964–66; Asst Prof., Univ. of Manitoba, 1966–72. Visiting Professor: Carleton Univ., 1981–82; Canadian Armed Forces, W Germany, 1985 and 1990–91; Univ. of Victoria, 1986, 2002; USAF Special Ops Sch., Florida, 1993–2003. Partner, Heartland Associates Inc., 1998–. Patron: John Rae Soc. of Orkney, 2013; St Andrew's Soc. of Winnipeg, 2013. Member: RIIA, 1962–64; Canadian Inst. of Internat. Affairs, 1964–2014; Honorary Life Member: Intrepid Soc. of Manitoba, 2015; Royal Commonwealth Soc. of Manitoba, 2015. Fellow, Royal Military Inst. of Manitoba, 2007. Public lectures, Carriage House, 2008–. Regular radio and TV commentaries, Canada and USA. Outreach Award, Univ. of Manitoba, 1996; Stanton Award for Excellence in Teaching, 1997; Citizen of the Year award, St Andrew's Soc., Winnipeg, 2010, 2012. *Publications:* Fireproof House to Third Option, 1977; Mackenzie King to Philosopher King, 1984; Air Piracy, Airport Security and International Terrorism: winning the war against hijackers, 1991; (contrib.) Aviation Terrorism and Security, 1998; (ed and contrib.) From the Great War to the Global Village, 2005; numerous contribs to jls. *Recreations:* swimming, squash, tennis, photography, touring, farming. *Heir: s* Oliver Robert St John [*b* 19 July 1969; *m* 1997, Consuela Hazel Davies; one *s* one *d*]. *Address:* 597 Gertrude Avenue, Winnipeg, MB R3L 0M9, Canada. *E:* hrtland@mts.net.

**ORMAN, Stanley,** PhD; Chief Executive Officer, Orman Associates, Maryland, since 1996; *b* 6 Feb. 1935; *s* of Jacob and Ettie Orman; *m* 1960, Helen (*née* Hourman); two *s* two *d*. *Educ:* Hackney Downs Grammar School; King's College London. BSc (1st Cl. Hons) 1957; PhD (Organic Chem.) 1960. MICorr; FRIC 1969. Research Fellowship, Brandeis Univ., 1960–61; AWRE Aldermaston, research in corrosion and mechano-chemical corrosion, 1961–74, project work, 1974–78; Director Missiles, 1978–81, Chief Weapon System Engineer Polaris, 1981–82, MoD; Minister-Counsellor, Hd of Defence Equip. Staff, British Embassy, Washington, 1982–84; Dep. Dir, AWRE, MoD, 1984–86; Dir Gen., SDI Participation Office, MoD, 1986–90; Chief Exec. Officer, General Technology Systems Inc., 1990–95. Founder Chm., Reading Ratepayers' Assoc., 1974; Pres., Reading Hebrew Congregation, 1970–74. Jelf Medal, Faculty of Natural Sci., KCL. *Publications:* Faith in G.O.D.S.: stability in the nuclear age, 1991; An Uncivil Civil Servant, 2013; contrib. articles on free radical chemistry, materials science and mechano-chemical corrosion; over 300 articles on ballistic missile defence, nuclear warhead issues and defence policy in jls and other media. *Recreations:* sporting—originally athletics, now tennis; designing bow ties, embroidery. *Address:* 11420 Strand Drive #104, Rockville, MD 20852, USA. *E:* stanleyo11@verizon.net.

**ORME, Jeremy David,** FCA; accountant; *b* 27 Dec. 1943; 2nd *s* of John Samuel Orme, CB, OBE, and of Jean Esther (*née* Harris); *m* 2001, Jennifer Anne Page, *qv*; two *s* from former marriage. *Educ:* Winchester Coll.; Christ Church, Oxford (MA). Robson Rhodes, chartered accountants, 1966–87, Man. Partner, 1982–87; Asst Sec. (on secondment), Dept of Transport, 1979–81; SIB, 1987–98 (investigations and enforcement roles); FSA, 1998–2001 (various roles concerned with financial crime). Member: National Bus Co., 1984–86 (Dep. Chm. 1985–86); Audit Commn for Local Authorities and NHS in England and Wales, 1989–2000 (Dep. Chm., 1997–2000); Chm., Financial Fraud Information Network, 1997–2000.
*See also* B. J. Coles.

**ORME, Prof. Michael Christopher L'Estrange,** MD; FRCP; Chairman, European Association for Clinical Pharmacology and Therapeutics, 2003–07 (Secretary, 1991–2003); Professor of Pharmacology and Therapeutics, Liverpool University, 1984–2001, now Emeritus; *b* 13 June 1940; *s* of Christopher Robert L'Estrange Orme and Muriel Evelyn Janet Orme; *m* 1st, 1967, Joan Patricia Abbott (*d* 2013); one *s*; 2nd, 2015, Hilary Margaret Day. *Educ:* Sherborne Sch.; Sidney Sussex Coll., Cambridge (MB BChir 1964; MA 1965; MD 1975); King's Coll. Hosp. FRCP 1980; FFPM 1989; FFSRH (FFFP 1994); FFPH (FFPHM 2000). House Officer and Registrar posts, KCH, Hammersmith Hosp., Brompton Hosp. and St Mary's Hosp., 1965–69; Sen. Registrar, Hammersmith Hosp., 1970–73; Wellcome Fellowship, Karolinska Inst., Stockholm, 1973–74; Liverpool University: Sen. Lectr, 1975–81; Reader in Clinical Pharmacology, 1981–84; Dean, Faculty of Medicine, 1991–96. Hon. Consultant Physician, Royal Liverpool and Broadgreen Univ. Hosps NHS Trust, 1975–2001; Dir of Educn and Trng, NW Regl Office, NHS Exec., 1996–2001. Gov., Glos Hosp. NHS Foundn Trust, 2008–10. Secretary: Clin. Sect., British Pharmacol Soc., 1982–88; Clin. Sect., Internat. Union of Pharmacol., 1987–93. Pres., Liverpool Medical Inst., 1994–95; Chm., Specialist Adv. Cttee on Clin. Pharmacol. and Therapeutics, 1991–93; Member: Internat. Adv. Bd, World Conf. on Clin. Pharmacol. and Therapeutics, 1989, 1992, 1996, 2000; WHO Scientific Working Gp on Drugs in Breast Milk, and on Filariasis, 1981–96. Gov., Birkenhead Sch., Wirral, 1990–2005. Founder FMedSci 1998. Hon. FRCGP 1998; Hon. FBPhS 2015. Hon. Fellow, Univ. of Central Lancs, 2001. Hon. DSc Salford, 2000; Hon. MD: Internat. Med. Univ., Malaysia, 2004; Karolinska Inst., Stockholm, 2013. Paul Martini Prize, Paul Martini Stiftung, Germany, 1974. *Publications:* Self Help Guide to Medicine, 1988; (ed) Therapeutic Drugs, 1991; contribs to learned jls. *Recreations:* sailing, astronomy, cooking, walking. *Address:* 4 Bishton Drive, Pershore, Worcs WR10 3ED.

**ORME, Canon Prof. Nicholas Ian,** DPhil, DLitt, DD; FSA, FRHistS; Professor of History, University of Exeter, 1988–2007, now Emeritus; *b* 3 June 1941; *s* of late Edward and Kathleen Orme; *m* 1981, Rona Jane Monro; one *d*. *Educ:* Bristol Cathedral Sch.; Magdalen Coll., Oxford (MA 1966, DPhil 1969, DLitt 1986); DD Oxon 2008. FRHistS 1973; FSA 1982. Lectr, Univ. of Exeter, 1964–88. Research Fellow: Nuffield Foundn, 1991; Leverhulme Trust, 1993; British Acad., 1998; Vis. Res. Fellow, Merton Coll., Oxford, 1982; Vis. Scholar, St John's Coll., Oxford, 1997; Vis. Prof., Univ. of Minnesota, 1998; Vis. Lectr, Arizona State Univ., 2002. Chm. Council, 1996–2000, and Vice-Pres., 1996–, Devon and Cornwall Record Soc.; President: Somerset Archaeol Soc., 1997; Bristol and Glos Archaeol Soc., 2003; Devon History Soc., 2003–06; Devonshire Assoc., 2011–12. Licensed Reader, Church of England, 1993–; Lay Canon, Truro Cathedral, 2005–11, Emeritus Canon, 2011–. Corresp. Fellow, Medieval Acad. of America, 2003. *Publications:* English Schools in the Middle Ages, 1973; Education in the West of England 1066–1548, 1976; The Minor Clergy of Exeter Cathedral, 1980; Early British Swimming, 1983; From Childhood to Chivalry, 1984; Exeter Cathedral as it was 1050–1550, 1986; Education and Society in Medieval and Renaissance England, 1989; John Lydgate's Table Manners for Children, 1989; (ed) Unity and Variety: a history of the Church in Devon and Cornwall, 1991; (with M. Webster) The English Hospital: 1070 to 1570, 1995; White Bird Flying (children's stories), 1995; English Church Dedications, 1996; Education in Early Tudor England, 1998; The Saints of Cornwall, 2000; Medieval Children, 2001; (with David Lepine) Death and Memory in Medieval Exeter, 2003; (with John Chynoweth and Alexandra Walsham) Richard Carew's Survey of Cornwall, 2004; Medieval Schools, 2006; Cornish Wills 1342–1540, 2007; Cornwall and the Cross, 2007; The Cathedral Cat, 2008; Exeter Cathedral: the first thousand years, 2009 (Book of Yr, Devon Hist. Soc., 2011); Victoria County History of Cornwall, vol. 2, 2010; (with J. Cannon), Westbury-on-Trym: monastery, minister and college, 2010; Fleas, Flies and Friars: children's verse from Medieval England, 2011; The Church in Devon 400–1560, 2013; English School Exercises 1420–1530, 2013; The Churches of Medieval Exeter, 2014; The Kalendars: Bristol's oldest guild and public library, 2016; The History of England's Cathedrals, 2017; Medieval Pilgrimage, 2018. *Recreations:* exercising, cycling, church-crawling. *Address:* c/o Department of History, University of Exeter, Amory Building, Rennes Drive, Exeter EX4 4RJ.

**ORME, His Honour Robert Thomas Neil;** a Circuit Judge, 1992–2014; *b* 25 Jan. 1947; *s* of Thomas Elsmore Orme and Iris Marguerita Orme; *m* 1971, Angela Mary Stokes; one *s* one *d*. *Educ:* Denstone Coll., Staffs; University Coll. London (LLB Hons). Called to the Bar, Gray's Inn, 1970; Midland and Oxford Circuit; Asst Recorder, 1984–88; Recorder, 1988–92. W Midlands Probation Cttee, 1996–2001; W Midlands Probation Bd, 2001–12; a Judge (formerly Pres.), Mental Health Review Tribunals, 2001–. Gov., Denstone Coll. Staffs, 2000–16. Chm., Moseley Soc., 1993–2008; Trustee, Moseley Community Develt Trust, 2001–16. *Recreations:* opera, theatre, keen interest in conservation.

**ORMEROD, Prof. David Christopher;** Professor of Law, University College London, since 2015; a Law Commissioner for England and Wales (on secondment), since 2010; a Deputy High Court Judge, since 2018; *b* Ashton-under-Lyne, Lancs, 30 April 1966; *s* of Derek and Margaret Ormerod; *m* 2010, Olivia Florence Klevan; one *d*. *Educ:* Baines Grammar Sch.; Essex Univ. (LLB). Called to the Bar, Middle Temple, 2002, Bencher 2009; barrister specialising in criminal fraud. Lectr in Law, Nottingham Univ., 1989–2000; Professor of Law: Univ. of Hull, 2000–01; Univ. of Leeds, 2001–05; QMUL, 2005–15. General Editor: Blackstone's Criminal Practice, 2008–; Criminal Law Rev., 2012–. Hon. Life Mem., Criminal Bar Assoc., 2013; Hon. Mem., N Eastern Circuit, 2013; Hon. Bencher, NI Bar. Hon. QC 2013. *Publications:* Smith and Hogan's Criminal Law, 11th edn 2005 to 15th edn (with Karl Laird) 2018; (with David Huw Williams) Smith's Law of Theft, 9th edn 2007. *Address:* Law Commission, 52 Queen Anne's Gate, SW1H 9AG. *T:* (020) 3334 3594. *E:* david.ormerod@lawcommission.gsi.gov.uk.

**ORMEROD, Mark Edward,** CB 2007; Chief Executive, UK Supreme Court, since 2015; *b* 3 Aug. 1957; *s* of Dr Thomas Edward Ormerod and late Dr June Anne (*née* Vaux). *Educ:* Oundle Sch.; Leeds Univ. (BA); Univ. de Tours (MèsL). Trainee accountant, Whinney Murray, 1980–81; joined Lord Chancellor's Department, 1981: Inner London Crown Court, 1981–83; posts at HQ, 1983–93; Principal Private Sec. to Lord Chancellor, 1993–96; Head: of Magistrates' Courts Div., 1996–97; of Criminal Justice Div., 1997–99; Dir, Criminal Justice, 1999–2001; career break, 2001–02; Director: Criminal Law and Policy, Home Office, 2002–04; Family Justice, DCA, 2004–05; Civil and Family Justice and Customer Services, HMCS, DCA, subseq. MoJ, 2005–08; Dir, Access to Justice Policy, MoJ, 2008–09; Chief Exec., Law Commn of England and Wales, 2009–11; Chief Exec., Probation Assoc., 2011–14; Founder Dir, Probation Inst., 2014–15. Sec., Sir Hayden Phillips' review of honours system, Cabinet Office, 2004. Gov., Aylwin Girls' Sch., 2002–06. *Recreations:* sailing, gardening, singing. *Address:* c/o Supreme Court of the United Kingdom, Parliament Square, SW1P 3BD.

**ORMEROD, Pamela Catherine;** *see* Meadows, P. C.

**ORMEROD, Prof. Stephen James,** PhD; FIEEM; FLSW; FRSB; Professor of Ecology, Cardiff University, since 2001; *b* Burnley, Lancs, 24 Jan. 1958; *s* of Mathew Henry, (Harry), Ormerod and Marjorie Ormerod (*née* Crossley); *m* 2004, Dr Isabelle Durance; one *s*, and three step *s*. *Educ:* Burnley Grammar Sch.; Huddersfield Poly. (BSc 1st Cl. 1980); Univ. of Wales Inst. of Sci. and Technol. (MSc Applied Hydrobiol. 1981; PhD Freshwater Ecol. 1985). FIEEM 1987. University of Wales Institute of Science and Technology, then University of Wales College of Cardiff, later Cardiff University: Sen. Res. Associate, 1984–94; Lectr, 1994–95; Sen. Lectr, 1995–97; Reader in Ecol., 1997–2001. Vis. Prof., Univ. de Pau et des Pays de L'Adour, 1997–2001. Editor, 1999–2000, Chief Editor, 2000–04, Jl of Applied Ecol. Mem., Countryside Council for Wales, 1991–95; Dep. Chm., 2012–15, Chm., 2015–18, Envmt Panel, Welsh Water; Mem. Bd, UK Jt Nature Conservation Cttee, 2018–. Mem. Council, RSPB, 2003–17 (Chm. Council, 2012–17; Chm., Wales Adv. Cttee, 2007–12; Vice Pres., 2018–). Member, Council: Freshwater Biol Assoc., 2000–04; British Trust for Ornithol., 2011–12; Trustee: Assoc. of Rivers Trusts, subseq. Rivers Trust, 2008–12; Buglife, 2018– (Chm., 2018–). Pres., Inst. of Ecol. and Envmtl Mgt, 2007–10 (President's Medal, 2010). Fellow, Winston Churchill Meml Trust, 1987. FRSB (FSB 2013). FLSW 2013. Marsh Award for Marine and Freshwater Ecol., ZSL, 2011. *Publications:* The Dippers (with S. J. Tyler), 1994; over 280 scientific papers on river and wetland ecology. *Recreations:* family, outdoors (especially birds and wildlife), arts, travel. *Address:* Cardiff School of Biosciences, Cardiff University, Museum Avenue, Cardiff CF10 3AX. *E:* ormerod@cardiff.ac.uk.

**ORMOND, Richard Louis,** CBE 2001; Director, National Maritime Museum, 1986–2000 (Head of Picture Department, 1983–86); Director, John Singer Sargent catalogue raisonné project, since 1980; *b* 16 Jan. 1939; *s* of late Conrad Eric Ormond and Dorothea (*née* Gibbons); *m* 1963, Leonée Jasper; two *s*. *Educ:* Christ Church, Oxford (MA). Assistant Keeper, 1965–75, Dep. Director, 1975–83, Nat. Portrait Gallery. Kress Prof., Nat. Gall. of Art, Washington, 2001–02. Chm., Watts Gall., Compton, Surrey, 1985–. *Publications:* J. S. Sargent, 1970; Catalogue of Early Victorian Portraits in the National Portrait Gallery, 1973; Lord Leighton, 1975; Sir Edwin Landseer, 1982; The Great Age of Sail, 1986; F. X. Winterhalter and the Courts of Europe, 1987; (jtly) Frederic, Lord Leighton, 1996; (jtly) Sargent Abroad, 1997; (jtly) John Singer Sargent, vol. 1, the early portraits, 1998, vol. 2, portraits of the 1890s, 2002, vol, 3, the later portraits, 2003, vol. 4, figures and landscapes, 1874–1882, 2006, vol. 5, figures and landscapes, 1883–1899, 2010, vol. 6, Venetian figures and landscapes, 1898–1913, 2009, vol. 7, figures and landscapes, 1900–1907, 2012, vol. 8, figures and landscapes, 1908–1913, 2014, vol. 9, figures and landscapes, 1914–1925, 2016; (jtly) John Singer Sargent (catalogue of exhibn at Tate Gallery), 1998; The Monarch of the Glen: Landseer in the Highlands, 2005; (jtly) Sargent's Venice, 2006; Edwin Landseer: the private drawings, 2009; (jtly) Sargent and the Sea, 2009; (jtly) G. F. Watts: the hall of fame, 2012; (jtly) Sargent Portraits of Artists and Friends (catalogue of exhibn at NPG), 2015; (jtly) Sargent: the watercolours (catalogue of exhibn at Dulwich Picture Gall., 2017). *Recreations:* cycling, opera, theatre. *Address:* 8 Holly Terrace, N6 6LX. *T:* (020) 8340 4684. *Club:* Garrick.

**ORMONDROYD, Janet Eve Lynne;** Chief Executive, Bristol City Council, 2008–12; *b* Baildon, W Yorks, 4 Sept. 1954; *d* of Rowland and Elsie Briggs; *m* 1st, 1973, Chris Ormondroyd; one *s* one *d*; 2nd, 1999, Doug Greenwood (*d* 2012). *Educ:* Salt Grammar Sch., Shipley; Bradford-Ilkley Coll. (BA Hons); Bradford Univ. (MA Managing Change). Dir, Bradford Council, 1988–2003; Dir, Local Govt Practice, ODPM, 2003–04; Chief Exec., Suffolk Coastal DC, 2004–05; Dep. Chief Exec., Hull CC, 2005–08; Interim Chief Exec., Rotherham MBC, 2014–15. Mem. Bd, Centre for Cities, 2010–12. Gp Chair, InCommunities Housing, 2016–. Non-exec. Dir, Health and Social Care Inf. Centre, 2014. FRSA. *Recreations:* interior decorating, gardening, cooking, travelling, swimming.

**ORMROD, Prof. (William) Mark,** DPhil; FSA, FRHistS; Professor of Medieval History, 1995–2017, now Emeritus, and Dean, Faculty of Arts and Humanities, 2015–17, University of York; *b* 1 Nov. 1957; *s* of David F. Ormrod and Margaret S. Ormrod; partner, Richard M. Dobson. *Educ:* King's Coll., London (BA 1979; AKC 1979); Worcester Coll., Oxford (DPhil 1984). FRHistS 1990; FSA 2006. Lectr in Medieval Hist., Queen's Univ., Belfast, 1984–87; British Acad. Postdoctoral Res. Fellow, St Catharine's Coll., Cambridge, 1987–90; University of York: Lectr in Medieval Hist., 1990–95; Academic Co-ordinator for Arts and Humanities, 2010–15. Hon. Fellow, Historical Assoc., 2015. *Publications:* The Reign of Edward III, 1990, 2nd edn 2000; Political Life in Medieval England, 1995; (with Anthony Musson) The Evolution of English Justice, 1999; (ed) The Kings and Queens of England, 2001, 2nd edn 2004; (ed with Rosemary Horrox) A Social History of England, 2006; Edward III, 2011; (with Bart Lambert and Jonathan Mackman) Immigrant England, 1300–1550, 2019; contrib. to English Histl Rev., Speculum, etc. *Recreations:* music, theatre, literature, travel. *Address:* Department of History, University of York, York YO10 5DD. *T:* (01904) 426168. *E:* mark.ormrod@york.ac.uk.

**ORMSBY, Irena;** *see* Murray, Irena.

**ORMSBY GORE,** family name of **Baron Harlech.**

**ORMSTON, Ven. Richard Jeremy;** Archdeacon of Northampton, since 2014; *b* Sutton Coldfield, 17 Nov. 1961; *s* of Joseph and Mary Ormston; *m* 1988, Jacqueline Dakin; one *s* one *d*. *Educ:* Southlands Coll., London (BA 1983); Oak Hill Theol Coll. (BA 1987); Brunel Univ. (MTh 1998). Ordained deacon, 1987, priest, 1988; Asst Curate, St Mary, Rodbourne Cheney, 1987–91; Rector, Collingtree with Courteenhall and Milton Malsor, 1991–2001; Rural Dean, Wootton, 1996–2001; Rector, St Peter, Oundle, 2001–14; Rural Dean, Oundle, 2003–13. Hon. Canon, Peterborough Cathedral, 2003–. *Recreation:* supporting Northampton Saints RFC. *Address:* Westbrook, 11 The Drive, Northampton NN1 4RZ.

**OROMBI, Most Rev. Henry Luke;** Bishop of Kampala, 2003–12; Archbishop of Uganda, 2003–12; *b* 11 Oct. 1949; *s* of Luka Jalobo and Susan Jalobo; *m* 1972, Phoebe Orombi; two *s* one *d* (and one *d* decd). *Educ:* St John's Coll., Nottingham (BTh 1983). Ordained 1979; Diocesan Youth Pastor, Madi/W Nile, 1979–86; Archdeacon, Goli, 1987–93; Bishop of Nebbi, 1993–2003. *Recreations:* music, walking. *Address:* c/o PO Box 335, Nakasero, Kampala, Uganda. *T:* (41) 270218, *Fax:* (41) 251925. *E:* Orombih@yahoo.com.

**O'RORKE, His Honour Richard Charles Colomb;** a Circuit Judge, 1994–2010; *b* 4 June 1944; *s* of late Charles Howard Colomb O'Rorke and Jacqueline O'Rorke; *m* 1966, Jane Elizabeth Phoebe Harding; one *s* three *d*. *Educ:* Blundell's Sch.; Exeter Coll., Oxford. Called to the Bar, Inner Temple, 1968; Recorder, Midland and Oxford Circuit, 1987–94. Judicial Mem., Parole Bd, 2010–Sept. 2020. *Recreations:* Japanese martial arts, literature and culture, gardening. *Address:* c/o HM Courts and Tribunal Service, PO Box 8793, Leicester LE1 8BN.

**O'ROURKE, Andrew;** Ambassador of Ireland, retired; *b* 7 May 1931; *s* of Joseph O'Rourke and Elizabeth (*née* O'Farrell); *m* 1962, Hanne Stephensen; one *s* two *d*. *Educ:* Trinity Coll., Dublin (BA, BComm). Joined diplomatic service, 1957; Third Sec., Berne, 1960; First Sec., London, 1964; First Sec., later Counsellor, Dept of Foreign Affairs, Dublin, 1969–73; Counsellor, later Dep. Perm. Rep., Perm. Rep. of Ireland to EEC, 1973–78; Sec.-Gen., Dept of For. Affairs, 1978–81; Perm. Rep. to EEC, 1981–86; Ambassador to: France, OECD and UNESCO, 1986–87; UK, 1987–91; Denmark, Norway and Iceland, 1991–96. Grand Cross: Order of Civil Merit, Spain, 1985; OM, Luxembourg, 1986; OM, Portugal, 1987. *Recreations:* walking, golf, European affairs. *Address:* 2 Sorrento Lawn, Dalkey, Co. Dublin, Ireland. *Club:* Kildare Street and University (Dublin).

See also K. H. O'Rourke.

**O'ROURKE, Prof. Kevin Hjortshøj,** PhD; FBA 2013; FAcSS; MRIA; Professor of Economics, New York University Abu Dhabi, since 2019; *b* Bern, Switzerland, 25 March 1963; *s* of Andrew O'Rourke, *qv*; *m* 1993, Rosemary Byrne; two *s* two *d*. *Educ:* Trinity Coll., Dublin (BA); Harvard Univ. (AM; PhD 1989). Asst Prof., Columbia Univ., 1989–92; Lectr, then Sen. Lectr, UCD, 1992–2000; Prof. of Econs, TCD, 2000–11; Chichele Prof. of Econ. History, Univ. of Oxford, 2011–19; Fellow, All Souls Coll., Oxford, 2011–19. Res. Dir, Centre for Econ. Policy Res., 2014–18 (Dir, Econ. History Prog., 2011–13). Res. Vis. Associate Prof., Harvard Univ., 1989; Res. Associate, Nat. Bureau for Econ. Res., Cambridge, Mass, 2000–; Vis. Prof., Sciences Po, Paris, 2005. Pres., Eur. Historical Econs Soc., 2009–11; Vice Pres., Econ. Hist. Assoc., 2011–12. Econs Deleg., OUP, 2016–19. Mem., Municipal Council, Saint Pierre d'Entremont, 2008–. MRIA 2009. FAcSS 2019. *Publications:* (with J. Williamson) Globalization and History, 1999; (with R. Findlay) Power and Plenty, 2007; (ed with S. Broadberry) The Cambridge Economic History of Modern Europe, 2010; (ed with J. Williamson) The Spread of Modern Industry to the Periphery since 1870, 2017; A Short History of Brexit: from Brentry to Backstop, 2019. *Recreations:* family, walking, reading, Shamrock Rovers FC. *Address:* Social Science Building (A5), New York University Abu Dhabi, Saadiyat Campus, PO Box 129188, Abu Dhabi, United Arab Emirates.

**O'ROURKE, Patrick Jake;** journalist, since 1970; author; *b* 14 Nov. 1947; *s* of Clifford Bronson O'Rourke and Delphine O'Rourke (*née* Loy); *m* 1st, 1990, Amy Lumet (marr. diss.); 2nd, 1995, Christina Mallon; one *s* two *d*. *Educ:* Miami Univ. (BA); Johns Hopkins Univ. (MA). Free-lance writer and ed., miscellaneous small press publications, 1970–73; National Lampoon: writer/editor, 1973–75; Man. Editor, 1975–77; Editor-in-Chief, 1977–81; free-lance writer, 1981–85; Foreign Corresp., Rolling Stone, 1986–2001; Contributing Ed., Weekly Standard, 1996–2018; Corresp., Atlantic Monthly, 2001–06; columnist, The Daily Beast, 2014–16; Editor-in-Chief, American Consequences, 2017–. H. L. Mencken Res. Fellow, Cato Inst., 1993–. William Howard Russell Prize, The Times, 2016. *Publications:* Modern Manners, 1983; The Bachelor Home Companion, 1987; Republican Party Reptile, 1987; Holidays in Hell, 1988; Parliament of Whores, 1991; Give War a Chance, 1992; All the Trouble in the World, 1994; Age and Guile Beat Youth, Innocence and a Bad Haircut, 1995; Eat the Rich, 1998; The CEO of the Sofa, 2001; Peace Kills, 2004; On the Wealth of Nations, 2007; Driving Like Crazy, 2009; Don't Vote, It Just Encourages the Bastards, 2010; Holidays in Heck, 2011; The Baby Boom, 2014; Thrown Under the Omnibus, 2015; How the Hell Did This Happen?, 2017; None of My Business, 2018. *Address:* c/o Grove/Atlantic Press, 154 W 14th Street, New York, NY 10011, USA.

**O'ROURKE, Stephen Robb-Russell;** QC (Scot.) 2017; barrister; *b* Greenock, 17 May 1976; *s* of James and Patricia O'Rourke; *m* 2004, Joanna Allison Baird; one *d*. *Educ:* St John's Primary Sch., Port Glasgow; St Aloysius' Coll., Glasgow; Univ. of Edinburgh (LLB 1st Cl. Hons 1998; DipLP 1999); Univ. of Bologna. Associate MCIArb 2004, MCIArb 2018. Advocate, 2002; Advocate Depute, 2010–13; Accredited in Advocacy, Nat. Inst. for Trial Advocacy, Boulder, Colo, 2011; Accredited Mediator, Center for Understanding in Conflict, NY, 2013; Standing Jun. to Advocate Gen. for Scotland, 2013–17; called to the Bar, Middle Temple, 2018. Advocate Mem., Scottish Sentencing Council, 2015–; Legal Mem., Parole Bd for Scotland, 2017–. Mem., Scottish Mediation Network, 2016–. Mem., Centre for Commercial Law, Edinburgh Law Sch., 2008–. *Publications:* Green's Glossary of Scottish Legal Terms (1946), 4th edn 2004 to 6th edn 2014; The Crown Agent, 2019. *Recreations:* golf, fishing, writing. *Address:* Terra Firma Chambers, Parliament House, Parliament Square, Edinburgh EH1 1RF. *T:* (0131) 260 5830. *E:* stephen.orourke@advocates.org.uk. *Club:* New (Edinburgh).

**ORPEN, Prof. (Anthony) Guy,** PhD; Professor of Structural Chemistry, since 1994, and Deputy Vice-Chancellor and Provost, since 2014, University of Bristol; *b* Pointe-a-Piérre, Trinidad, 5 Oct. 1955; *s* of Christopher Martin Willson Orpen and Shirley Orpen (*née* Esselen); *m* 1984, Carrie Pooler; one *d*. *Educ:* Univ. of Cape Town (BSc (Dist.) Chem. and Physics 1975); Gonville and Caius Coll., Cambridge (PhD Chem. 1979). University of Bristol: Lectr in Inorganic Chem., 1979–90; Reader in Structural Chem., 1990–94; Hd, Sch. of Chem., 2001–06; Dean, Faculty of Sci., 2006–09; Pro Vice-Chancellor (Res. and Enterprise), 2009–14. Mem., NERC, 2014–18. Chair and Scientific Ed., Jl Chem. Soc., Dalton Trans, 1995–99. Non-exec. Dir, Univ. Hosps Bristol NHS Foundn Trust, 2012–. Chm., Bd of Trustees, Cambridge Crystallographic Data Centre, 2011–13. Royal Society of Chemistry: Meldola Medal and Prize, 1982; Corday-Morgan Medal and Prize, 1997; Tilden Lect., 1999–2000; Structural Chemistry Award, 2004; Nyholm Lect., 2007–08. *Publications:* contribs to internat. peer-reviewed jls. *Recreations:* family, cooking, supporting Tottenham Hotspur. *Address:* University of Bristol, Senate House, Tyndall Avenue, Bristol BS8 1TH. *T:* (0117) 928 8038. *E:* pa-dvc@bristol.ac.uk.

**ORR, Dr Andrew William,** FRCGP; author; Vice Lord-Lieutenant of Kincardineshire, since 2008; *b* London, 12 July 1946; *s* of Lt Col Harold Arthur Orr, RA and Joan Margaret Newland Orr (*née* Glossop); *m* 1971, Antonia Sybilla Atkinson; two *s* one *d*. *Educ:* Haileybury Coll.; St Bartholomew's Hosp. (MB BS 1971); DRCOG 1974; DCH 1977. MRCS 1971; LRCP 1971; MRCGP 1977, FRCGP 1999. RAMC, 1970–78, Regtl Med. Officer, Scots Guards; Capt. 1973; Major 1977; GP, Montrose, 1978–2006. Trainer and Tutor in Gen. Practice, Univ. of Dundee, 1984–2006; Exec., Angus Div. of Gen. Practice, 1987–2006; Member: E Scotland Postgrad. Cttee, 1989–2004; Scottish Intercollegiate Guidelines Network, 2001–03. Designer and Partner, Rank & File Stationery Products, 1987–97. Consultant to offshore petroleum trng industries, 1993–2000. Founder, Montrose Day Care Centre, 1984; Chm., Montrose Heritage Trust, 2011–; Pres., Montrose Soc., 2012–17. Mem., 1990–, Surgeon, 2010–, Queen's Bodyguard for Scotland (Royal Co. of Archers). Pres., TS Carron, Stonehaven Sea Cadets, 2012–. DL Kincardineshire, 2004. *Publications:* Sea Dog Bamse: World War II canine hero (with Angus Whitson), 2008; Skipshunden Bamse En Norsk Krigshelt, 2011; various med. res. and rev. articles. *Recreations:* collecting and conserving paintings and antiques, historical research and writing, field sports. *Address:* Creebank, Hillside, Montrose, Angus DD10 9HY. *E:* orrkirkside@btinternet.com.

**ORR, Prof. Christopher John,** MBE 2008; RA 1995; RE 1990; artist; Professor of Printmaking, and Director of Printmaking Department, Royal College of Art, 1998–2008, now Professor Emeritus; Treasurer, Royal Academy, 2014–18; *b* 8 April 1943; *s* of Ronald Orr and Violet (*née* Townley); *m* 1984, Catherine Terris; one *s* one *d*. *Educ:* Royal Coll. of Art (MA; RCA 1967). Artist and teacher, 1967–. One man touring exhibitions: The Complete Chris Orr, 1976; Many Mansions, 1990. Work in public collections: British Council; Arts Council; V&A Mus.; Science Mus.; Govt Art Collection; BM; NPG. *Publications:* Many Mansions, 1990; The Small Titanic, 1994; Happy Days, 1999; Semi-Antics, 2001; The Disguise Factory, 2003; Cities of Holy Dreams, 2007; The Multitude Diaries, 2008; Chris Orr, The Making of Things, 2013; The Miserable Lives of Fabulous Artists, 2018. *E:* chrisorr@aol.com. *W:* www.chrisorr-ra.com. *Club:* Chelsea Arts.

**ORR, Craig Wyndham;** QC 2006; barrister; *b* 8 Jan. 1962; *s* of late Joseph Leonard Orr and of Dawyne Orr; *m* 1998, Jane Lloyd-Sherlock; two *s* one *d*. *Educ:* St Andrew's Coll., Grahamstown, SA; Rugby Sch.; Downing Coll., Cambridge (BA Hons 1984); University Coll., Oxford (BCL 1985). Called to the Bar, Middle Temple, 1986 (Fox Scholar 1986); in practice as a barrister, 1988–, specialising in commercial litigation. *Publications:* (jtly) Fountain Court Chambers' Carriage by Air, 2001; (contrib.) Professional Negligence and Liability, 2006–. *Recreations:* travel, wine, food. *Address:* One Essex Court, Temple, EC4Y 9AR. *T:* (020) 7583 2000.

**ORR, David Campbell,** CBE 2018; Chief Executive Officer, National Housing Federation, 2005–18; *b* Kirkconnel, Scotland, 27 March 1955; *s* of Jack and Janet Orr; *m* 1979, Carol Massey; one *s* two *d*. *Educ:* Univ. of Dundee (MA 1976). Dep. Warden, Community House Glasgow, 1976–77; Co-ordinator, Centrepoint, 1977–86; Chief Executive Officer: Newlon Housing Trust, 1986–90; Scottish Fedn of Housing Assocs, 1990–2005. Chair, Reall, 2014–; Senior Independent Director: Housing Finance Corp., 2005–14; Affordable Housing Finance, 2014–; Board Member: My Home Finance, 2010–; Clarion Housing Gp., 2018–. Pres., Housing Europe, 2008–10. *Recreations:* cinema, theatre, squash, hill walking, Heart of Midlothian FC, singing, family.

**ORR, David Malcolm,** CBE 2018; FREng; independent consultant, since 2013; External Board Member, Houses of Parliament, since 2013; Chair, Independent Assurance Panel, HS2, since 2015; *b* 19 Aug. 1953; *s* of James and Mabel Orr; *m* 1975, Vyvienne McKay; one *s* one *d*. *Educ:* Belfast Royal Acad.; Queen's Univ., Belfast (BSc 1974, MSc 1978). FICE 2002; FIEI 2006; FIAE 2007; FREng 2009. Joined Roads Service, NI, 1974: Chartered Civil Engr, 1974–2008; Dir, Network Services, 2001–06; Dir, Dept of Finance and Personnel, 2006–11; Perm. Sec., Dept for Regl Develt, NI, 2011–12. Pres., ICE, 2007–08 (Vice Pres., 2004–07). Hon. DSc Ulster, 2017. *Recreations:* travel, cycling, local history.

**ORR, Deborah Jane;** newspaper columnist, The I-Paper, since 2018; *b* 23 Sept. 1962; *d* of John Scott Orr and Winifred Meta Orr; *m* 1997, William Woodard Self, *qv* (marr. diss. 2018); two *s*, and one step *s* one step *d*. *Educ:* St Andrews Univ. (MA 1983). Dep. Editor, City Limits Magazine, 1988–90; Editor, Guardian Weekend Magazine, 1993–98; columnist: The Independent, 1998–2009; The Guardian, 2009–18. Columnist of the Year, What the Papers Say Awards, 1999. *E:* Orr.Deborah.Jane@gmail.com.

**ORR, Iain Campbell;** HM Diplomatic Service, retired; Founder, BioDiplomacy consultancy, 2002; *b* 6 Dec. 1942; *s* of late Rev. David Campbell Orr and Hilda Dora Moore; *m* 1978, Susan Elizabeth Gunter; one *s* one *d*. *Educ:* Kirkcaldy High Sch.; St Andrews Univ. (MA); Linacre Coll., Oxford (BPhil). Asst Lectr, Dept of Politics, Glasgow Univ., 1967–68; entered HM Diplomatic Service, 1968; language student, Hong Kong, 1969–71; Second, later First Sec., Peking, 1971–74; FCO, 1974–78; Asst Political Adviser, Hong Kong, 1978–81; Dublin, 1981–84; FCO, 1984–87; Consul-Gen., Shanghai, 1987–90. Dep. High Comr, Wellington, 1991–94; Counsellor, FCO, 1994–98; Dep. High Comr, Ghana, 1998–2000. Co-founder, Global Islands Network; Member: Adv. Council, World Land Trust, 2003–; Council, UK Overseas Territories Conservation Forum, 2006–. *Recreations:* natural history, islands, anthologies, reading poetry.

**ORR, Prof. Jean Agnes,** CBE 2004; Professor of Nursing, and Head, School of Nursing and Midwifery, Queen's University of Belfast, 1991–2008, now Emeritus; Chairman, WAVE Trauma Centre, since 2013; *b* 10 Sept. 1943; *d* of E. Smyth; *m* 1968, I. Orr. *Educ:* Ulster Poly. (BA Hons Social Admin 1976); Manchester Univ. (MSc 1978). RN 1965; Registered Health Visitor 1971. Nursing Officer, Down and Lisburn Trust, NI, 1976–77; Lectr, Ulster Poly., 1978–81; Lectr, 1981–89, Sen. Lectr, 1989–91, Manchester Univ. Subject Specialist Reviewer, QAA, 1997–2002. Member: Council of Deans and Hds of UK Univ. Faculties for Nursing, Midwifery and Health Visiting, 1991–2008; Bd, IVINUR (Internat. Virtual Nursing Sch.), 2004; NMC, 2006; Council, Pharmaceutical Soc. of NI, 2006. Adjunct Faculty Mem., Univ. of Mass, 1995; Mem. Bd, Univ. of Mass/Ghana Health Care Consortia, 1995; Ext. Academic Advr, Univ. Teknologi MARA, Malaysia, 2006. Patron, WAVE Trauma Centre, NI, 2001; Trustee: Early Childhood Develt Prog., 1985; Marie Curie Cancer Care UK, 2000. *Publications:* Learning to Care in the Community, 1985, 2nd edn 1993; Health Visiting, 1985, 3rd edn 2012; Women's Health in the Community, 1987; A Community Health Profile, 1994; Nurses' Voices from the Northern Ireland Troubles, 2013. *Recreations:* travelling, music, good food.

**ORR, John Carmichael;** Chairman: Molins plc, 1991–99; Waddington plc, 1997–99; *b* 8 Aug. 1937; *s* of John Washington Orr and Nora Margaret Orr (*née* Carmichael); *m* 1967, Janet Sheila Grundy; one *s* one *d*. *Educ:* King Edward's Sch., Birmingham; Trinity Hall, Cambridge (MA). Industrial & Commercial Finance Corporation Ltd, 1960–68; S. G. Warburg & Co. Ltd, 1969–81 (Dir, 1972–81); Finance Dir, Grand Metropolitan plc, 1981–87; Man. Dir, Merrill Lynch Europe Ltd, 1987–90. Non-executive Director: Sketchley plc, 1990–99; Throgmorton Trust plc, 1990–2002; Marston, Thompson & Evershed plc, 1992–96; Govett Strategic Investment Trust plc, 1992–97; Granada plc, 1992–2004; W. H. Smith plc, 1993–2004; Lazard Brothers & Co. Ltd, 1993–2002. Emeritus Trustee, Foundn for Liver Res. (formerly Liver Res. Trust), 2011 (Trustee, 1999–2010; Chm., 2003–10). *Recreations:* tennis, golf, opera, theatre. *Address:* 7 Kitson Road, SW13 9HJ. *T:* (020) 8563 9616. *Clubs:* Roehampton; Royal Wimbledon.

**ORR, John Douglas,** CBE 2010; FRCSEd, FRCPEd; consulting paediatric surgeon with medico-legal and expert witness practice; Consultant Paediatric Surgeon, Royal Hospital for Sick Children, Edinburgh, 1984–2009; President, Royal College of Surgeons of Edinburgh, 2006–09; *b* 11 July 1945; *s* of Sir John Henry Orr, OBE, QPM and Isobel Margaret Orr; *m* 1971, Elizabeth Erica Yvonne Miklinska; two *s* one *d*. *Educ:* George

Heriot's Sch., Edinburgh; High Sch., Dundee; St Andrews Univ. (MB ChB 1969); Univ. of Stirling (MBA). FRCSEd 1975; FRCPEd; FRCPSGlas *ad eundem*. Sen. Surgical Registrar, Aberdeen Royal Infirmary, 1978–80; Sen. Paediatric Surgical Registrar, Edinburgh and Gt Ormond St Hosps, 1980–84; Med. Dir, Royal Hosp. for Sick Children, Edinburgh, 1996–2000; Associate Med. Dir, Lothian Univ. Hosps NHS Trust, 2000–05. Mem. Bd, NHS Quality Improvement Scotland, 2007–11. Hon. FRCSI; Hon. FRCS (Hong Kong); Hon. FRCS (Sri Lanka). *Recreations:* golf, gardening. *Address:* 428 Lanark Road, Edinburgh EH13 0LT. *Clubs:* Moynihan Chirurgical; Royal & Ancient Golf (St Andrews).

**ORR-EWING, Hon. Sir (Alistair) Simon,** 2nd Bt *cr* 1963, of Hendon, co. Middlesex; *b* 10 June 1940; *e s* of Baron Orr-Ewing, OBE and Joan Helen Veronica Orr-Ewing (*née* McMinnies); *S* to Btcy of father, 1999; *m* 1968, Victoria, *er d* of Keith Cameron; two *s* one *d*. *Educ:* Harrow; Grenoble Univ.; Trinity Coll., Oxford (BA Hons PPE). FRICS 1972. Trainee surveyor, 1968–72. Dir various private cos. Mem. (C), RBK&C Council, 1982–90 (Chm., Planning Cttee, 1986–88). *Recreations:* ski-ing, shooting, tennis. *Heir: s* Archie Cameron Orr-Ewing [*b* 29 March 1969; *m* 1999, Nicola de Selincourt; three *s*]. *Address:* Fifield House, Fifield, Chipping Norton, Oxon OX7 6HH. *T:* (01993) 830305. *Clubs:* Boodle's, MCC.

**ORR-EWING, Prof. Andrew John,** DPhil; FRS 2017; Professor of Chemistry, University of Bristol, since 2004; *b* Reigate, Surrey, 22 Dec. 1965; *s* of Ian Michael Orr-Ewing and Catherine Margaret Orr-Ewing. *Educ:* Dr Challoner's Grammar Sch., Amersham; Jesus Coll., Oxford (BA 1st Cl. Hons Chemistry 1988; DPhil 1991). Postdoctoral Res. Associate, Stanford Univ., USA, 1992–93; University of Bristol: Royal Soc. Elizabeth Challenor Res. Fellow, 1994–98; Lectr, 1999–2000, Reader, 2000–04, Sch. of Chemistry. *Publications:* contribs to jls incl. Science, Nature Chem. and physical chem. jls. *Recreations:* ski-ing, reading, fish keeping, opera, scuba diving, chess, cryptic crosswords. *Address:* School of Chemistry, University of Bristol, Cantock's Close, Bristol BS8 1TS. *T:* (0117) 928 7672. *E:* a.orr-ewing@bristol.ac.uk.

**ORR EWING, Sir Archibald Donald,** 6th Bt *cr* 1886, of Ballikinrain, Stirlingshire, and Lennoxbank, co. Dunbarton; *b* 20 Dec. 1938; *er s* of Major Sir Ronald Archibald Orr Ewing, 5th Bt and Marion Hester, *yr d* of Col Sir Donald Walter Cameron of Lochiel, KT, CMG; *S* father, 2002; *m* 1st, 1965, Venetia Elizabeth Turner (marr. diss. 1972); 2nd, 1972, Nicola Jean-Anne Black; one *s*. *Educ:* Gordonstoun; Trinity Coll., Dublin (MA). Grand Master Mason of Scotland, 1999–2004 and 2005–08. *Heir: s* Alistair Frederick Archibald Orr Ewing, *b* 26 May 1982. *Address:* Cardross House, Port of Menteith, Stirling FK8 3JY.

**ORR EWING, Major Edward Stuart,** CVO 2007; landowner and farmer, since 1969; Lord-Lieutenant of Wigtown, 1989–2006; *b* 28 Sept. 1931; *s* of late Captain David Orr Ewing, DSO, DL and of Mary Helen Stuart Orr Ewing (*née* Noaks); *m* 1st, 1958, Fiona Anne Bowman (*née* Farquhar) (marr. diss. 1981); one *s* two *d*; 2nd, 1981, Diana Mary Waters. *Educ:* Sherborne; Royal Military Coll. of Science. Regular soldier, The Black Watch, 1950–69. DL Wigtown, 1970. *Recreations:* country sports, painting. *Address:* Auchtriemakain, Portpatrick, Wigtownshire DG9 8TJ. *T:* (01776) 810219. *Club:* New (Edinburgh).

**ORR-EWING, Hon. Sir Simon;** see Orr-Ewing, Hon. Sir A. S.

**ORRELL, His Honour James Francis Freestone;** a Circuit Judge, 1989–2016; *b* 19 March 1944; *s* of late Francis Orrell and Marion Margaret Orrell; *m* 1970, Margaret Catherine Hawcroft; two *s*. *Educ:* Ratcliffe; Univ. of York (BA History). Called to the Bar, Gray's Inn, 1968; Recorder, Midland and Oxford Circuit, 1988. Judicial Mem., Parole Bd, 2018–.

**ORRELL-JONES, Keith;** Chairman, Smiths Group (formerly Smiths Industries) plc, 1998–2004; *b* 15 July 1937; *m* 1961, Hilary Kathleen Pegram; four *s*. *Educ:* Newcastle-under-Lyme High Sch.; St John's Coll., Cambridge (BA 1961; MA 1967). Tarmac Civil Engineering, 1961–64; RMC plc, 1964–70; Marley plc, 1970–72; Area Manager, ARC, 1972–81; Pres., ARC America, 1981–87; Chief Exec., ARC, 1987–89; Dir, Consolidated Gold Fields, 1989; Pres., Blue Circle America, and Dir, Blue Circle Industries plc, 1990–92; Gp Chief Exec., Blue Circle Industries, 1992–99; Chm., FKI plc, 1999–2004. Dir, Smiths Industries plc, 1992–98. FRSA 1989; CCMI (CIMgt 1992). *Address:* 6 Gerald Road, SW1W 9EQ. *Club:* Royal Automobile.

**ORWIN, Peter David,** OBE 1991; MC 1966; HM Diplomatic Service, retired; Director, Cyjax (formerly Welund Horizon) Ltd, since 2013; *b* 20 Dec. 1944; *s* of late John Antony Arnold Orwin and of Catherine Mary Orwin (*née* Rutherford); *m* 1977, Pamela Jane Heath; one *s* two *d*. *Educ:* Peter Symonds Sch.; RMA, Sandhurst. Commnd into Prince of Wales's Own Regt of Yorkshire, 1964; served Berlin, 1965; Aden, 1965–67; UK, 1968–69; Cyprus, 1969–70; UK/MoD, 1970–74; retd 1975; entered HM Diplomatic Service, 1975: First Secretary: Athens, 1977–84; Brasilia, 1984–87; FCO, 1987–89; First Sec., then Counsellor, Tel Aviv, 1989–93; Counsellor, FCO, 1993–96; Counsellor, The Hague, 1996–99. Security and Business Risks Advr, Syngenta (formerly Zeneca Agrochemicals), 1999–2009. Director: Drum-Cussac Ltd, 2001–02; PE-2 Ltd, 2004–06; Welund Report, later Papea Ltd, 2008–16. Associate MInstD. *Recreations:* country pursuits, travel, sailing. *Address:* 31 Molyneux Place, Tunbridge Wells TN4 8DQ.

**OSAMOR,** Baroness *cr* 2018 (Life Peer), of Tottenham in the London Borough of Haringey and of Asaba in the Republic of Nigeria; **Martha Otito Osamor;** *b* Delta State, Nigeria; *m* (*d* 1975); four *c*. Teacher in Nigeria, then London; Tottenham Law Centre, 1977–97. Mem. (Lab) Haringey Council, 1986–90. Co-founder, United Black Women's Action Gp; Dir, ALL Women's Welfare Assoc. Ltd; Chm. Trustees, Haringey Law Centre. *Address:* House of Lords, SW1A 0PW.

See also K. O. Osamor.

**OSAMOR, Kate Ofunne;** MP (Lab and Co-op) Edmonton, since 2015; *b* N London, 15 Aug. 1968. *Educ:* Creighton Comprehensive Sch.; Univ. of E London (BA Hons Third World Studies 2006). Big issue; NHS Exec. Asst, Camidoc GP Out of Hours, 2002–10; Black and Ethnic Minorities Labour, 2012–13; NHS Practice Manager: Sterndale Surgery, 2012–13; Park Lodge Med. Centre, 2013–15. Shadow Sec. of State for Internat. Develt, 2016–18. Member: Petitions Select Cttee, 2015–16; Educn Select Cttee, 2015–16. Mem., Nat. Exec., Labour Party, 2014–. *Address:* House of Commons, SW1A 0AA.

**OSBALDESTON, Prof. Michael David,** OBE 2008; Professor and Director, Cranfield School of Management, Cranfield University, 2003–09, now Professor Emeritus; *b* 12 Feb. 1949; *s* of Richard Grahame Osbaldeston and Betty Osbaldeston (*née* McKenzie); *m* 1974, Valerie Davies; one *s* one *d*. *Educ:* Bishop Vesey's Grammar Sch.; Liverpool Univ. (BSc Hons); Liverpool Univ. Business Sch. (MBA). Consultant, Merrett Cyriax Associates, 1971–73; Researcher, Ashridge Res. Unit, 1973–76; Ashridge Management College, 1976–2000: Programme Dir, 1977–81; Dir, Ext. Relns, 1982–84; Dir of Studies, 1985–87; Dean, 1988–90; Chief Exec., 1990–2000; Dir of Global Learning, Shell Internat. Ltd, 2000–02. Non-executive Director: Chartwell Ltd, 1997–2001; Univ. of Stellenbosch Business Sch.-Exec. Develt Ltd, 2000–; Internat. Develt Advr, Skema Business Sch., France, 2009–; Associate Dir, 2011–12, Dir, 2012–, Quality Services, Eur. Foundn for Mgt Develt (Vice-Pres., 1997–2000). Vice-Pres., Ashridge Bonar Law Meml Trust, 2009–. Gov., RAU (formerly RAC), 2009–17. Vice-Pres., Strategic Planning Soc., 1995–2000. FCIPD (FIPD 1985); CCMI (CIMgt 1991). *Publications:* The Way We Work: a European study of changing practice in job design, 1979; (contrib.) Redesigning Management Development in The New Europe, 1998; contrib. numerous articles and papers in mgt jls. *Recreations:* sailing, theatre, France, grandfathering. *Address:* Oak House, 1 Dairymede, Speen, Princes Risborough, Bucks HP27 0TD. *T:* (01494) 488754; Cranfield University, Cranfield, Bedford MK43 0AL. *T:* (01234) 754403. *Club:* Athenæum.

**OSBORN, Alec;** see Osborn, W. A.

**OSBORN, Prof. Denise Rae,** PhD; Secretary-General, Royal Economic Society, since 2015; Robert Ottley Professor of Econometrics, 1996–2013, Professor (part-time), 2013–15, University of Manchester, now Emeritus Professor; *b* Sydney, 23 Nov. 1948; *d* of Raymond Allen Osborn and Lillian Agnes Osborn; *m* 1978, Nicholas Robert Devereux Berman; one *s* one *d* (and one *s* decd). *Educ:* Univ. of Sydney (BEc 1st Cl. Hons and Univ. Medal 1970, MEc 1972); London Sch. of Econs and Political Sci. (PhD 1976). Res. Officer, NIESR, 1975–77; University of Manchester: Lectr, 1977–89; Sen. Lectr, 1989–92; Prof. of Econometrics, 1992–96. Vis. Prof., Univ. of Tasmania, 2013–16. *Publications:* (jtly) The Econometric Analysis of Seasonal Time Series, 2001; contribs to learned jls in econometrics, econs, statistics and criminol. *Recreations:* family, theatre and concerts, travel, country walking, gym. *Address:* Royal Economic Society, 2 Dean Trench Street, SW1P 3HE. *T:* (020) 3137 6301. *E:* denise.osborn@manchester.ac.uk.

**OSBORN, Frederic Adrian, (Derek),** CB 1991; Chairman, Cynnal Cymru—Sustain Wales; *b* 14 Jan. 1941; *s* of late Rev. George R. Osborn and E. M., (Betty), Osborn, MBE; *m* 1st, 1971, Caroline Niebuhr Tod (*d* 2003); one *d* one *s*; 2nd, 2009, Linda Pritchard. *Educ:* Leys School, Cambridge; Balliol College, Oxford (BA Maths 1963; BPhil 1965). Min. of Housing and Local Govt, 1965–75; Dept of Transport, 1975–77; Department of the Environment, 1977–95: Under Sec., Finance, 1982–86, Housing Gp, 1986–87; Dep. Sec., Local Govt and Finance, 1987–89; Dir Gen., Envmtl Protection, 1990–95. Chm., EEA, 1995–2000; Co-Chm., UN Special Session on sustainable develt, 1997; Bd Mem. for England and Wales, Envmt Agency, 1996–98; Special Advr, H of C Envmtl Audit Cttee, 1998–99, 2001–05; Chairman: UNED-UK, 1996–2002; Internat. Inst. for Envmt and Develt, 1998–2004 (Vice-Chm., 2004–06); UK Round Table on Sustainable Develt, 1999–2000; Member: Sustainable Develt Commn, 2000–06; Bd, Inst. of Eur. Envmt Policy, 2002–; Eur. Econ. and Social Cttee, 2006–10 (Chm., Sustainable Develt Observatory, 2006–10). Mem. Bd, Severn Trent Plc, 1998–2006; Chm., Jupiter Global Green Investment Trust, 2001–06. Vis. Fellow, Green Coll., Oxford, 1996–97; Vis. Prof., Sch. of Public Policy, UCL, 1998–. Trustee, Stakeholder Forum for a Sustainable Future, 2015– (Chm., 2002–07; Pres., 2007–15). *Publications:* Earth Summit II, 1998; contribs to Jl of Envmtl Law, Pol Qly. *Recreations:* walking, piano, reading, bridge.

**OSBORN, Rev. Canon Lionel Edwin;** Chair, Newcastle upon Tyne District of the Methodist Church, 2001–15; President, Methodist Conference, 2011–12; Ecumenical Canon, St Nicholas' Cathedral, Newcastle, since 2014; *b* Birmingham, 6 May 1952; *s* of John Edwin Osborn and Audrey Joan Osborn; *m* 1977, Charlotte Elizabeth Windows. *Educ:* Five Ways Grammar Sch., Birmingham; Wesley Coll., Bristol. Methodist Minister: Ripley, Derbyshire, 1976–81; Bury and Heywood, 1981–88; Bramhall, Cheshire, 1988–96; N Shields and Whitley Bay, 1996–2001; Stamford and Rutland, 2015–. Chaplain, Northern League Football, 1998–2015. *Publications:* Light from Light: saints along the way, 2014; contrib. articles to Methodist pubns. *Recreations:* football, cricket, walking, reading, classical music. *Address:* 2 Wensum Close, Oakham, Rutland LE15 6FU. *T:* (01572) 720721. *E:* lionel.osborn@methodist.org.uk.

**OSBORN, Sir Richard (Henry Danvers),** 9th Bt *cr* 1662, of Chicksands Priory, Co. Bedford; fine art consultant; *b* 12 Aug. 1958; surv. *s* of Sir Danvers Lionel Rouse Osborn, 8th Bt, and Constance Violette, JP, OStJ (*d* 1988), *d* of late Major Leonard Frank Rooke, KOSB and RFC; *S* father, 1983; *m* 2006, Belinda Mary Elworthy; one *d*. *Educ:* Eton. Christie's, 1978–83; Consultant to P & D Colnaghi Ltd, 1984–86. Dir, Paul Mitchell Ltd (antique frames and picture conservation), 1991–2002. *Recreations:* cricket, tennis, squash, horse racing, Real tennis, golf. *Address:* 48 Lessar Avenue, SW4 9HQ. *Clubs:* Pratt's, MCC, Turf, White's; New Zealand Golf.

**OSBORN, (Wilfred) Alec,** MBE 2005; CEng, FIMechE; President, Institution of Mechanical Engineers, 2006–07; *b* 16 May 1939; *s* of Fredrick Osborn and Annie Osborn (*née* Wade); *m* 1963, Mary Jane Flanders; three *d*. *Educ:* Grantham Coll. for Further Educn. CEng 1969; FIMechE 1991. Student apprentice, Rubery Owen & Co., 1955–60; Design Engr, British Racing Motors, 1960–69; Perkins Engines: Design Engr, 1969–75; Chief Engineer: Applications Engrg, 1975–77; Test Ops, 1977–82; Product Engrg, 1982–2002; Consultant, 2002–04. Lectr (pt time), Stamford Coll. for Further Educn, 1963–73. Institution of Mechanical Engineers: Chm., Combustion Engines Gp, 1994–97; Vice Pres., 2002–04; Dep. Pres., 2004–06; Chm., Technical Strat. Bd, 2004–06; Member: Risk and Audit Cttee, 2008–15; Investigating Panel, 2011–; Chm., Trustee Bd Awards Cttee, 2012–18 (Vice Chm., 2010–12). Member: Quality Audit Cttee, Engrg Council UK, 2003–06; Dewar Trophy Tech. Cttee, RAC, 2005–; Industrial Adv. Cttee, Univ. of Leeds, 2008–18. Freeman, City of London, 2002; Liveryman, Co. of Engineers, 2002–. Chairman: Govs, Deacon's Sch., Peterborough, 1997–2004; Interim Exec. Bd, Hereward Community Coll., Peterborough, 2002–04; Dir, Thomas Deacon City Acad., Peterborough, 2004–09; Gov., Grantham Coll., 2009–13. Trustee, Maudslay Scholarship Foundn, Pembroke Coll., Cambridge, 2007–. *Recreations:* golf, cricket, gardening, walking. *Clubs:* Farmers, MCC.

**OSBORNE, Rt Hon. Lord; Kenneth Hilton Osborne;** PC 2001; a Senator of the College of Justice in Scotland, 1990–2011; *b* 9 July 1937; *s* of Kenneth Osborne and Evelyn Alice (*née* Hilton); *m* 1964, Clare Ann Louise Lewis; one *s* one *d*. *Educ:* Larchfield Sch., Helensburgh; Merchiston Castle Sch., Edinburgh; Edinburgh Univ. (MA, LLB). Admitted to Faculty of Advocates in Scotland, 1962; QC (Scotland) 1976. Standing Junior Counsel to Min. of Defence (Navy) in Scotland, 1974–76; Advocate-Depute, 1982–84. Chairman: Disciplinary Cttee, Potato Marketing Bd, 1975–90; (part-time), VAT Tribunals, 1985–90; Medical Appeal Tribunals, 1987–90; Mem., Lands Tribunal for Scotland, 1985–87. Chm., Local Govt Boundary Commn for Scotland, 1990–2000. *Recreations:* ski-ing, fishing, gardening, music, cooking. *Address:* 42 India Street, Edinburgh EH3 6HB. *T:* (0131) 225 3094; Primrose Cottage, Bridgend of Lintrathen, by Kirriemuir, Angus. *T:* (01575) 560316. *Club:* New (Edinburgh).

**OSBORNE, Dr Basil Alfred Herbert Ernst;** Bishop of Amphipolis, 2006–09; Head of the Episcopal Vicariate of Orthodox Parishes of Russian Tradition in Great Britain and Ireland (Ecumenical Patriarchate), 2006–09; *b* Alexandria, Egypt, 12 April 1938; *s* of Alexander W. R. Osborne and Josephine Gerringer; *m* 1962, Rachel Vida Spitzer (*d* 1991); two *s* one *d*; *m* 2010, Jessica Mary, *widow* of John Aubrey Rose; one step *d*. *Educ:* State Univ. of New York at Buffalo (BA (Classics), 1963); Univ. of Cincinnati, Ohio (PhD (Classics), 1969). Ordained deacon, 1969, priest, 1973; consecrated bishop, 1993; Bishop of Sergievo, 1993–2006; Asst Bishop, 1993–2003, Administering Bishop, 2003–06, Russian Orthodox

Dio. of Sourozh; VG, 1997–2003. A Pres., Churches Together in England, 1993–98; Chm., Oxfordshire Ecumenical Council, 1997–98. Chm. Bd of Dirs, Inst. for Orthodox Christian Studies, Cambridge, 1999–2003. Rep. of Russian Orthodox Church, Internat. Commn on Anglican-Orthodox Theol Dialogue, 2001–06. Editor: Sourozh: A Journal of Orthodox Life and Thought, 1980–2006; The Messenger, 2006–09. Phi Beta Kappa, 1963. *Publications:* The Light of Christ, 1992, 2nd edn 1996; Speaking of the Kingdom, 1993; The Healing Word, 2008; Liturgy and Cosmology in the 364-day Calendar Tradition, 2019. *Address:* 68 Victoria Road, Oxford OX2 7QE. *T:* (01865) 557454.

**OSBORNE, Rev. Canon Brian Charles;** Vicar of Holy Trinity, Skirbeck, Boston, Lincolnshire, 1980–2003; Chaplain to the Queen, 1997–2008; *b* 17 May 1938; *s* of Walter and Gweneth Osborne; *m* 1968, Kathryn Ruth Grant; two *d*. *Educ:* St Andrews Univ. (MA Hons Classics); DipTh London Univ. 1980; Clifton Theol Coll. Ordained deacon, 1963, priest, 1964; Asst Curate, Holy Trinity, Boston, 1963–68; Priest-in-charge, 1968–71, Incumbent, 1971–75, St John's, New Clee, Grimsby; Vicar, St Augustine's, Derby, 1975–80. Pt-time Chaplain, Pilgrim Hosp., Boston, 1984–88. Rural Dean, Holland East, 1985–94; Hon. Canon of Lincoln, 1992–2006, now Canon Emeritus. Retired Clergy Advr, 2004–12. *Recreations:* reading, photography. *Address:* 3 Newlands Road, Haconby, Bourne, Lincs PE10 0UT. *T:* (01778) 570818.

**OSBORNE, Clive Maxwell Lawton;** JP; Legal Adviser, Serious Organised Crime Agency, 2005–11; *b* 20 July 1955; *s* of Raymond Peter Osborne and Eileen Mary Osborne (*née* Lawton); *m* 1985, Ursula Frances Amanda Futcher; one *s* one *d*. *Educ:* Newcastle High Sch.; Christ Church, Oxford (Open Exhibnr; MA). Called to the Bar, Gray's Inn, 1978 (Holker Sen. Schol.), Bencher, 2009 (Trustee, 2019); joined Home Office, 1980; Asst Legal Advr, 1991–97; Legal Dir, DTI, 1997–99; Asst Legal Advr, NI Office, 1999–2001; Dep. Legal Advr, Home Office and NI Office, 2001–05. UK Pres., Camden Asset Recovery Inter-Agency Network, 2007. Pres., Old Newcastilian Club, 2014–15. Hon. Steward, Westminster Abbey, 2014–15. JP Cheshire, 2014. Freeman, City of London, 2014; Liveryman, Glaziers' Co., 2014 (Steward, 2016–17; Ct Asst, 2018–). *E:* cmlosborne21@gmail.com. *Clubs:* Travellers, City Livery; Potters (Stoke-on-Trent).

**OSBORNE, David Allan;** HM Diplomatic Service, retired; Ambassador to Honduras, 1998–2002; *b* 31 Aug. 1942; *s* of Donald Stewart Osborne and Caroline Susie Osborne (*née* Stanbury); *m* 1966, Joan Marion Duck; two *d* (one *s* decd). *Educ:* St Albans Grammar Sch.; Central London Poly. (DMS). Joined Commonwealth Relations Office, 1961; Accra, 1963–65; FCO, 1966–68; Guatemala City, 1968–73; Bonn, 1973–74; Valletta, 1974–77; sabbatical, 1977–78; First Sec., FCO, 1978–79; Mexico City, 1979; San José (concurrently accredited to Managua and San Salvador), 1980–84; FCO, 1984–88; Dep. Consul Gen., São Paulo, 1988–91; EU Monitor, Croatia, 1991–92; FCO, 1992–94; Santiago, 1994–95; FCO, 1995–96; Chargé d'Affaires, Managua, 1997. Hon. Citizen of Honduras, 2002. EU Monitor Medal, 1992. *Recreations:* reading, walking, chess, indigenous cultures in Latin America, various sports. *Address:* Firlings, 54 Firle Road, Seaford, East Sussex BN25 2HU.

**OSBORNE, Douglas Leonard,** FCIS; Chief Executive, Leukaemia Research Fund, 1989–2007; *b* 19 Oct. 1940; *s* of Leonard Osborne and Gladys Ellen (*née* Ward); *m* 1969, Barbara Helen Bartrop; one *s* one *d*. *Educ:* Royal Masonic Sch. ACIS 1967, FCIS 1985. London Association for the Blind: Asst Sec., 1965–75; Asst Dir, 1975–79; Dir, 1979–83; Administrator, Leukaemia Res. Fund, 1983–89. Trustee: BlindAid (formerly Metropolitan Soc. for the Blind), 1979–2013; Alternative Hair Charitable Foundn, 2012–; Beefy's Charity Foundn, 2013–; Dir, Beefy's Enterprises Ltd, 2015–. *Publications:* (ed jtly) Charities Administration, 1986, and Supplements, 1987–. *Recreations:* listening to music, cooking, travel, swimming. *Address:* 360 Topsham Road, Exeter, Devon EX2 6HF.

**OSBORNE, Rt Hon. George (Gideon Oliver),** CH 2016; PC 2010; Editor, Evening Standard, since 2017; *b* 23 May 1971; *s* and *heir* of Sir Peter George Osborne, Bt, *qv*; *m* 1998, Hon. Frances Victoria, *d* of Baron Howell of Guildford, *qv*; one *s* one *d*. *Educ:* St Paul's Sch., London; Davidson Coll., N Carolina (Dean Rusk Schol.); Magdalen Coll., Oxford (MA Hons Mod. Hist.). Freelance journalist, 1993; Hd, Pol Sect., Cons. Res. Dept, 1994–95; Special Advr, MAFF, 1995–97; Pol Office, 10 Downing St, 1997; Pol Sec. to Leader of Opposition, 1997–2001; Sec. to Shadow Cabinet, 1997–2001. MP (C) Tatton, 2001–17. An Opposition Whip, 2003; Opposition frontbench spokesman on Treasury, 2003–04; Shadow Chief Sec. to HM Treasury, 2004–05; Shadow Chancellor of the Exchequer, 2005–10; Chancellor of the Exchequer, 2010–16; First Sec. of State, 2015–16. Member: Public Accounts Cttee, 2001–03, Public Accounts Commn, 2002–03, H of C; Select Cttee on Transport, 2003. Trustee, Arts and Business, 2006–10. Chm., Northern Powerhouse Partnership, 2016–. Sen. Advr, BlackRock Investment Inst., 2017–; Chm., Partners Council, Exor, 2018–. Hon. Prof. of Econs, Univ. of Manchester, 2017–; Distinguished Vis. Fellow, Hoover Instn, Stanford Univ., 2017–; Dean's Fellow, Graduate Sch. of Business, Stanford Univ., 2017–. *Address:* Evening Standard, 2 Derry Street, Kensington, W8 5EE. *T:* (020) 3615 2410.

**OSBORNE, Georgiana Louise,** CVO 2017; Lord-Lieutenant of Angus, 2001–19; *b* 24 Aug. 1944; *d* of Richard Douglas Moore and June Louise Moore (*née* Peachey); *m* 1968, James Carnegy Osborne; three *s* one *d*. *Educ:* Wellington Diocesan Sch. for Girls (Nga Tawa), Marton, NZ; Victoria Univ. of Wellington (BA); Lausanne Univ. (Philips Overseas Schol. 1964). Dep. Pres., Angus Br., 1991–98, Pres., Tayside Br., 1999–2004, BRCS. JP Angus, 2001–08. Patron, 2003, Trustee, 2004–12, Angus Coll.; Trustee, Queen Mother's Memorial Fund for Scotland, 2003–08. Pres., Angus, Perth and Kinross Br., 2006–09, Jt Pres., Dundee and Angus Br., 2010–, SSAFA; Hon. Vice Pres., Dundee and Angus Bn, Boys' Bde, 2012–19. Hon. Pres., Strathmore Assoc., 2013–; Hon. Pres., Tayside SO, 2018– (Hon. Vice Pres., 2013–18). Pres., Black Watch Assoc., 2005–19 (Vice Pres., 2001–05; Hon. Pres., Angus Br., 2019–). Patron, Dorward House, Montrose, 2006–. Badge of Honour for Distinguished Service, 1996, for Outstanding Service, 2004, BRCS. *Recreations:* music and the arts in general, tennis, golf. *Address:* Balmadies, Guthrie, Forfar, Angus DD8 2SH. *T:* and *Fax:* (01307) 818242.

**OSBORNE, Ven. Hayward John;** Archdeacon of Birmingham, 2001–18, now Archdeacon Emeritus; *b* 16 Sept. 1948; *s* of Ernest and Frances Joy Osborne; *m* 1973, Sandra Julie Hollander; two *s* three *d*. *Educ:* Sevenoaks Sch.; New Coll., Oxford (BA 1970, MA 1973); King's Coll., Cambridge (PGCE); Westcott House Theol Coll., Cambridge. Ordained deacon, 1973, priest, 1974; Curate, Bromley Parish Ch, 1973–77; Team Vicar, Halesowen, 1977–83; Team Rector, St Barnabas, Worcester, 1983–88; Vicar, St Mary, Moseley, Birmingham, 1988–2001; Area Dean, Moseley, 1994–2001; Priest-in-charge, Allens Cross, 2008–10. Mem., Gen. Synod of C of E, 1998–2015. Hon. Canon, Birmingham Cathedral, 2000–01. *Recreations:* music, theatre, computing, photography. *E:* hs.osborne@btinternet.com.
See also K. F. Colvin.

**OSBORNE, Jana;** General Secretary, National Federation of Women's Institutes, since 1996; *b* 11 Jan. 1953; *d* of Jan Koutny' and Miloslava Koutna'; *m* 1978, Graeme Stephen Osborne. *Educ:* Charles Univ., Prague (BA Hons Modern Langs 1978); Poly. of Central London (Postgrad. Personnel Mgt Course); Kingston Univ. (LLM Employment Law, 2003). MIPD 1989. Journalist and interpreter, Nihon Denpa News, Prague, 1974–79; Personnel Officer, Bowater Industrial plc, 1987–88; Office Manager, Thorpac Gp plc, 1988–89; National Federation of Women's Institutes: Personnel Officer, 1989–92; Head of Personnel, 1992–95; Gen. Manager, 1995–96. *Recreations:* cycling, walking, music, literature, gardening. *Address:* (office) 104 New Kings Road, SW6 4LY. *T:* (020) 7371 9300.

**OSBORNE, Rt Rev. June;** *see* Llandaff, Bishop of.

**OSBORNE, Kenneth Hilton;** *see* Osborne, Rt Hon. Lord.

**OSBORNE, Prof. Michael John,** FAHA; FAIM; Professor, Peking University, China, since 2003; Foundation Distinguished Professor, Institute for Advanced Study, La Trobe University, Australia, since 2006; Honorary Professor, University of Melbourne, since 2006; *b* 25 Jan. 1942; *s* of Samuel Osborne and Olive May Osborne (*née* Shove); *m* 1st, 1978, Dawn Brindle (marr. diss. 2005); 2nd, 2009, Liang Wenquan; one *s*. *Educ:* Eastbourne Grammar Sch.; Christ Church, Oxford (MA); Catholic Univ. of Leuven (DPhil and Lett.). Lectr, Dept of Classics, Bristol, 1966–67; Lectr, then Sen. Lectr, Dept of Classics and Archaeology, Univ. of Lancaster, 1967–82; University of Melbourne: Prof. and Chm., Dept of Classical and Near Eastern Studies, 1983–90, now Prof. Emeritus. Dep./Associate Dean, Faculty of Arts, 1985–89; Pro-Vice-Chancellor and Vice-Pres., Academic Bd, 1989; Vice-Chancellor and Pres., La Trobe Univ., 1990–2006. Mem., Inst. for Advanced Study, Princeton, 1978–; Visiting Professor: Maximilians Univ., Munich, 1973; Leuven, 1975, 1988; Vis. Fellow, other univs, 1972–85; Guest Prof., Hellenic Educn and Res. Centre, Athens, 2006–; Prof., Peking Foreign Studies Univ., China, 2008–; Hon. Professor: Yunnan Univ., China, 1994; Kunming Med. Coll., China, 1995; Yunnan Normal Univ., China, 1997; Yunnan Agricl Univ., China, 2001; Harbin Med. Univ., China, 2001; Sichuan Univ., China, 2002. Chm., Victorian Vice-Chancellors' Cttee, 1993–94; Member: Bd of Dirs, Australian Vice-Chancellors' Cttee, 1994–96 (Chm., Students and Scholarships Cttee, 1995–96; Chm., Standing Cttee for Internat. Affairs, 1996–2004; Leader, delegn to Hungary, Czech and Slovak Republics, 1993, to S Africa, 1994, to China, 1998–); Business/Higher Educn Round Table (Mem., Task Force on Higher Educn, 1996–; Mem. Bd of Dirs, 1996–2003); Res. Cttee, Cttee for Econ. Develt of Australia, 1993–96; Bd of Dirs, Internat. Develt Program, 1996–99; Bd of Dirs, Grad. Careers Council of Australia, 1996–98; Co-Chm. Planning Cttee, Australian Educn Internat., 2000–02. President: Univ. Mobility in Asia Pacific Scheme, 2000–02; Internat. Network of Univs, 2000–06; Co-Pres., Peking Univ.-La Trobe Univ.-Beijing Foreign Studies Univ. Centre for China Studies, 2005–08; Chm., Nat. Centre for Hellenic Studies and Res., 1997–2005; Mem., Governing Bd, World Heritage Trng and Res. Inst. for Asia and Pacific Region, 2007–. FAHA 1985; FAIM 2000. Laureate: Royal Acad. of Sci., Letters and Fine Arts, Belgium, 1980; Acad. of Institutions and Cultures, Thessaloniki, 2013; Alexander S. Onassis Public Benefit Foundn Res. Fellow, 2001; Hon. Fellow: Hungarian Acad. of Engrg, 1998; Greek Epigraphic Soc., 2013; Corresp. Mem., Acad. of Athens, 1998. Hon. DLitt: Athens, 2001; La Trobe, 2007. Aristotle Award, Greece, 1998; Hon. Distinction, Hellenic Republic of Cyprus, 2000; Centenary Medal, Australia, 2003; Niki Award, Australia, 2005; Gold Crown of World Congress of Greeks of the Diaspora, Greece, 2006. *Publications:* Naturalization in Athens, 4 vols, 1981–83; Lexicon of Greek Personal Names, vol. II: Attica, 1994; The Foreign Residents of Athens, Studia Hellenistica Vol. 33, 1995; Correspondence between China and Great Britain: vol. I, railways and mines, 2006, vol. II, education, 2007, vol. III, commerce and trade, 2008, vol. IV, protocol, 2009, vol. V, territorial and legal issues, 2009; Athens in the Third Century BC, 2010; Inscriptiones Graecae, vol. II/III (3) Attica 300–229 BC, 2015; numerous articles in learned jls on Greek history, Greek epigraphy and archaeology, higher educn policy; *festschrift:* Philathenaios, 2010. *Recreations:* tennis, travel, Australian Rules football, Rugby League. *Address:* Institute for Advanced Study, Michael J. Osborne Centre, La Trobe University, Melbourne, Vic 3086, Australia. *T:* (4) 88022880. *Club:* Essendon Football.

**OSBORNE, Prof. Nigel,** MBE 2003; composer; Reid Professor of Music, 1990–2012, now Emeritus and Co-Director, Institute for Music in Human and Social Development, 2007–12, Edinburgh University; *b* 1948. *Educ:* St Edmund Hall, Oxford; studied at Warsaw Acad. and Polish Radio Exptl Studio. FRCM 1996. Staff of Music Dept, Nottingham Univ., 1978; Co-Editor-in-Chief, Contemporary Music Review. Initiator of programme of rehabilitation for refugee children in Balkans and Caucasus, 1992–. Queen's Award, Edinburgh Univ., 1997. *Compositions include:* Seven Words, 1971 (Radio Suisse Romande Prize); Heaventree, 1973 (Gaudeamus Prize); Kinderkreuzzug, 1974; I am Goya, 1977 (Radcliffe Award); Orlando Furioso, 1978; In Camera, 1979; Sinfonia, 1982; Sinfonia II, 1983; Zansa, 1985; The Electrification of the Soviet Union (opera), 1987; Violin Concerto, 1990; Terrible Mouth, 1991; The Sun of Venice, 1993; Art of Fugue, 1993; Sarajevo (opera), 1994; Evropa (first opera of war in Sarajevo), 1995; Oboe Concerto, 1998; String Quartet no 1, 1999; Widows (opera), 2000; The Piano Tuner, 2004; Differences in Demolition (opera), 2007; orchestral, choral, instrumental, ballet and electronic music; numerous recordings.

**OSBORNE, Sir Peter (George),** 17th Bt *cr* 1629; Chairman and Managing Director, Osborne & Little plc (design company), since 1967; *b* 29 June 1943; *s* of Lt-Col Sir George Osborne, 16th Bt, MC, and Mary (Grace) (*d* 1987), *d* of C. Horn; *S* father, 1960; *m* 1968, Felicity Alexandra, *d* of Grantley Loxton-Peacock; four *s*. *Educ:* Wellington Coll., Berks; Christ Church Coll., Oxford. *Heir:* s Rt Hon. George Gideon Oliver Osborne, *qv*. *Address:* 1 St James's Gardens, W11 4RB. *Club:* White's.

**OSBORNE, Rachel Claire Elizabeth,** ACA; Chief Financial Officer, Debenhams plc, since 2018; *b* Sedgefield, Co. Durham, 2 March 1965; *d* of Stanley Osborne and Barbara Foster (*née* Roby); *m* 2012, Allan Bentley; two *s*. *Educ:* Joseph Rowntree Comp. Sch., York; St Peter's Sch., York; Christ's Coll., Cambridge (BA Vet. Medicine 1986; MA). ACA 1990. Audit Manager, KPMG, London, 1988–91; Haircare Analyst, UK Forecaster and Sen. Analyst, Procter and Gamble, 1991–94; UK Finance Dir, then Dir, Strategy and Planning, Europe, PepsiCo, 1994–2003; Dir, Business Performance, Kingfisher, 2003–09; Chief Financial Officer, UK and Ire., SODEXO, 2010–11; Finance Dir, John Lewis, 2011–15; Finance Dir, Commercial and Enterprise Gp, Vodafone Gp plc, 2015–16; Chief Financial Officer, Domino's Pizza, 2016–18. *Recreations:* gardening, cooking, my children. *Address:* Windsor. *E:* rachelosborne999@gmail.com.

**OSBORNE, Richard Ellerker;** author and music critic; *b* 22 Feb. 1943; *s* of late William Harold Osborne and Georgina Mary Osborne (*née* Farrow); *m* 1985, Hailz-Emily Wrigley; one *s*. *Educ:* Worksop Coll.; Univ. of Bristol (BA, MLitt). Asst Master, Bradfield Coll., 1967–88 (Head of Sixth Form Gen. Studies, 1978–88; Head of English, 1982–88); presenter and contrib., BBC Radio 3, 1969–; Music Critic, The Oldie, 1992–. Mem., Critics' Panel, Gramophone, 1974–; Chm., Music Section, Critics' Circle, 1984–87. *Publications:* Rossini, 1985, 2nd edn 2007; Conversations with Karajan, 1989; Herbert von Karajan: a life in music, 1998; Till I End My Song, 2002; Karajan: Mensch und Mythos, 2008; Garsington Opera: a celebration, 2011; Music and Musicians of Eton, 2012; The Grange, Hampshire, 2012; (ed and trans.) Ferdinand Hiller Conversations with Rossini, 2015; contribs to newspapers, jls, music dictionaries and guides. *Recreations:* hill-walking, food and wine, reading in the garden, watching cricket. *Address:* 2 Vaughan Copse, Eton, Berks SL4 6HL. *E:* reo1792@gmail.com.

**OSBORNE, Prof. Robin Grimsey**, PhD; FBA 2006; Professor of Ancient History, University of Cambridge, since 2001 (Director, Museum of Classical Archaeology, 2008–14); Fellow, King's College, Cambridge, since 2001; *b* 11 March 1957; *s* of John Leonard Osborne and Joyce Elizabeth Osborne (*née* Warner); *m* 1st, 1979, Catherine Joanna Rowett (marr. diss. 2013); two *d*; 2nd, 2014, Caroline Vout. *Educ*: Colchester Royal Grammar Sch.; King's Coll., Cambridge (BA 1979; PhD 1982; MA 1983). Jun. Res. Fellow, King's Coll., Cambridge, 1982–86; University of Oxford: Tutorial Fellow in Ancient Hist., Magdalen Coll., 1986–89; Univ. Lectr in Ancient Hist., 1989–96; Prof. of Ancient Hist., 1996–2001; Fellow and Tutor, 1989–2001, Emeritus Fellow, 2001–, Corpus Christi Coll. Chm., Council of Univ. Classical Depts, 2006–12. Chm., Sub-Panel 31, Classics and Byzantine Studies, REF 2014. President: Soc. for Promotion of Hellenic Studies, 2002–06; Classical Assoc., 2012–13. Vice Chair, Council, British Sch. of Athens, 2016–. Member, Editorial Board: Jl of Hellenic Studies; Jl of Mediterranean Archaeology; Omnibus; Past and Present; Cambridge Classical Jl; Jl of Greek Archaeology; Archaeology and Text; Cambridge Classical Studies; Classical Culture and Soc. *Publications*: Demos: the discovery of classical Attika, 1985; Classical Landscape with Figures: the ancient Greek city and its countryside, 1987; (ed jtly) Art and Text in Ancient Greek Culture, 1994; (ed jtly) Placing the Gods: sanctuaries and the sacred landscape of ancient Greece, 1994; (ed jtly) Ritual, Finance, Politics: Athenian democratic accounts presented to David Lewis, 1994; Greece in the Making 1200–479 BC, 1996 (trans. Spanish 1998, Greek 2000), 2nd edn 2009; Archaic and Classical Greek Art, 1998; (ed jtly) Performance Culture and Athenian Democracy, 1999; (ed) The Athenian Empire, 4th edn 2000; (ed) Classical Greece, vol. 1, Short Oxford History of Europe, 2000 (trans. Spanish 2001, Polish 2002); (ed jtly) Greek Historical Inscriptions 403–323 BC, 2003; (ed) Studies in Ancient Greek and Roman Society, 2004; Greek History, 2004 (trans. Japanese 2011), 2nd edn 2014; (ed) The Old Oligarch, 2nd edn 2004; (ed jtly) Mediterranean Urbanization 800–600 BC, 2005; (ed jtly) Poverty in the Roman World, 2006; (ed jtly) Rethinking Revolutions through Classical Greece, 2006; (ed jtly) Art's Agency and Art History, 2007; (ed jtly) Classical Archaeology, 2007, 2nd edn 2012; (ed) Debating the Athenian Cultural Revolution: art, literature, philosophy and politics 430–380 BC, 2007; Athens and Athenian Democracy, 2010; The History Written on the Classical Greek Body, 2011; Athenian Democracy, 2014; (ed jtly) Greek Historical Inscriptions 478–404 BC, 2017; The Transformation of Athens: painted pottery and the creation of classical Greece, 2018; numerous articles in learned jls. *Address*: King's College, Cambridge CB2 1ST. *E*: ro225@cam.ac.uk.

**OSBORNE, Roy Paul**; HM Diplomatic Service, retired; *b* 13 July 1951; *s* of Gilbert William Osborne and Jean Mary Osborne; *m* 1977, Vivienne Claire Gentry; two *d*. *Educ*: St Christopher's Junior Sch., Cowley; Magdalen Coll. Sch., Oxford. Entered FCO, 1970; served Oslo, Islamabad and Rome; FCO, 1981–85, Asst Private Sec. to Minister of State, 1983–85; Second Sec., Commercial/Aid, later First Sec., Head of Chancery and Consul, Yaoundé, 1985–89; First Sec., Press and Inf., Madrid, 1989–93; Section Head, Drugs and Internat. Crime, FCO, 1993–97; Ambassador to Nicaragua, 1997–2000; Dep. Hd, Overseas Territories Dept, 2001–04; Dir, Trade and Investment, Berne, 2005–09. *Recreations*: volunteer warden, Steart Marshes, Wildfowl and Wetlands Trust; member of Quantock Countryside Volunteers, gardening, wildlife conservation. *Address*: Pear Tree Farm, Over Stowey, Som TA5 1JB. *T*: (01278) 734604.

**OSBORNE, Sandra Currie**; *b* 23 Feb. 1956; *d* of Thomas Clark and Isabella Clark; *m* 1982, Alastair Osborne; two *d*. *Educ*: Camphill Sen. Secondary Sch., Paisley; Anniesland Coll.; Jordanhill Coll.; Strathclyde Univ. (MSc). Community Worker, Glasgow; Women's Aid. Mem. (Lab), S Ayrshire Council, 1991–97. MP (Lab) Ayr, 1997–2005, Ayr, Carrick and Cumnock, 2005–15; contested (Lab) same seat, 2015.

**OSBORNE, Steven**; classical pianist; *b* Broxburn, Scotland, 12 March 1971; *s* of Ian Osborne and Jean Osborne (*née* McNeil); *m* 2004, Jean Johnson. *Educ*: St Mary's Music Sch., Edinburgh; Univ. of Manchester (MusB 1st cl. Hons 1991); Royal Northern Coll. of Music (GRNCM 1992; Postgrad. Dip. 1993; MusM 1994). Orchestral collaborations include: CBSO, NHK Symphony Orch., BBC SO, BBC Scottish SO, Scottish Chamber Orch., Munich Philharmonic, Berlin SO, Australian Chamber Orch.; performances at venues including: Carnegie Hall, Kennedy Center, Suntory Hall, Philharmonie Berlin, Concertgebouw Amsterdam, Royal Albert Hall, Wigmore Hall. Recordings include works by Debussy, Rachmaninov, Beethoven, Alkan, Britten, Tippett, Messiaen, Shostakovich, Liszt and Kapustin. Clara Haskil Prize, 1991; (jtly) First Prize, Naumburg Internat. Piano Competition, 1997; Best Concerto Recording (Britten), Gramophone Awards, 2009; Best Instrumental Recording (Mussorgsky/Prokofiev), Gramophone Awards, 2013; Instrumentalist of the Year, Royal Philharmonic Soc. Awards, 2013. *Recreations*: hill walking, tennis, pool, reading, jazz. *Address*: c/o Sulivan Sweetland, 1 Hillgate Place, Balham Hill, SW12 9ER. *T*: (020) 8772 3470. *E*: es@sulivansweetland.co.uk.

**OSBORNE, Susan Edna**, CBE 2005; independent nursing and management consultant, 2009–14; *b* 7 Dec. 1952; *d* of late John Gilbertson Osborne and Edna Joan Osborne (*née* Boughen). *Educ*: Dame Alice Harpur Sch. for Girls, Bedford; University Coll. Hosp. (SRN 1974); Queen Charlotte's Hosp. for Women (SCM 1976); London Univ. (DipN); South Bank Univ. (MSc); King's Coll. London (MSc). Staff Nurse, Orthopaedic/Surgery, UCH, 1974–75; pupil midwife, Queen Charlotte's Hosp., 1975–76; Staff Nurse, Medicine, Radcliffe Infirmary, 1976–77; Night Sister, UCH, 1977–78; Sister, Intensive Therapy Unit, then Nursing Officer, Whittington Hosp., London, 1979–83; Sen. Nurse, Central Middx Hosp., 1983–86; Dep. Dir, Nursing Service, 1986–87, Acute Service Manager, 1987–89, Homerton Hosp.; Actg Regl Nurse, 1989–90, NHS Trust Develt Officer, 1990–91, NE Thames RHA; Chief Exec., Royal London Homeopathic Hosp. NHS Trust, 1991–94; mgt and nursing consultant, 1994–98; Dir, Nursing and Quality, Luton & Dunstable Hosp. NHS Trust, 1998–2000; Dir of Nursing Services, St Mary's NHS Trust, 2000–07; Dir of Nursing, Imperial Coll. Healthcare NHS Trust, 2007–08; Chief Nurse, NHS E of England, 2008–09. Non-exec. Dir, Homerton Univ. Hosp. NHS Foundn Trust, 2014–18. Chm., Safe Staffing Alliance, 2014–15. Trustee, Cavell Nurses' Trust (formerly NurseAid), 2010–. *Publications*: numerous contribs to nursing and health services jls, incl. Jl Advanced Nursing, Nursing Times, Jl Nursing Mgt, Health Services Jl, Nursing Standard. *Recreations*: general socialising, theatre, the Archers, cats, golf, enjoying life.

**OSBORNE, Trevor**, FRICS; Chairman, Trevor Osborne Property Group Ltd, since 1973; *b* 7 July 1943; *s* of Alfred Osborne and Annie Edmondson; *m* 1st, 1969, Pamela Ann Stephenson (marr. diss. 1998); one *s* one *d*; 2nd, 2003, Barbara Jane Fitzpatrick (marr. diss. 2014). *Educ*: Sunbury Grammar School. South Area Estate Manager, Middx County Council, 1960–65; Partner, A. P. C., 1966–67; Principal, Private Property Interests, 1967–73; Chm., 1973–93, Chief Exec., 1981–93, Speyhawk plc; Chairman: St George, 1985–96; Hawk Development Management, 1992–98; Lucknam Park Ltd, 1991–95; Building & Property Management Services, 1993–96; non-exec. Dir, Redland, 1989–92. Pres., British Property Fedn, 1991–92 (Mem. Council, 1985–92); BPF Vis. Fellow, Land Mgt, Reading Univ., 1987–90; Vis. Fellow, Architecture and Planning, Oxford Brookes Univ., 2003– (Mem. Court, 2008–14). Founder Mem. and Chm., POW Urban Villages Forum, 1992–99; Member: Royal Opera House Develt Bd, 1987–94 (Chm., ROH Development Ltd, 1994); Council of Advrs, Prince of Wales Inst. of Architecture (Trustee, 1991–93); Council, City Property Assoc., 1987–94; Royal Fine Art Commn, 1994–99 (Trustee, 2003–); Council Mem., Georgian Group, 2002–09; Chm., Adv. Bd, SE Excellence, 2006–09. Governor: Bournemouth Univ. Business Sch., 2008–11; Bath Spa Univ., 2013–. Formerly Mem., Wokingham DC (Leader, 1980–82); Trustee, Wokingham Cons. Assoc., 1982–91. Pres., Windsor Arts Centre; Chm., St Sebastian's Playing Field Trust; Director: London First, 1992–95; Buxton Fest., 2004–14; Bath Mozartfest Ltd, 2012–; Trustee, Holbourne Mus. Trust Co., 2008–14. Freeman, City of London; Liveryman, Chartered Surveyors' Co. Fellow, Duke of Edinburgh Award World Fellowship; FRSA. *Recreations*: travel, walking, art, theatre, opera, tennis. *Address*: Trevor Osborne Property Group Ltd, Rectory Lodge, Combe Hay, Bath BA2 7EG. *Club*: Athenæum.

**OSBOURN, Prof. Anne Elisabeth**, PhD; FRS 2019; FLS; Project Leader, John Innes Centre, since 2005; Director, Norwich Research Park Industrial Biotechnology Alliance, since 2013; *b* Shipley, W Yorks, 2 April 1961; *d* of Robert Vinden Osbourn and Barbara Osbourn; *m* 1987, Michael Crouch; two *d*. *Educ*: Bingley Grammar Sch.; Univ. of Durham (BSc 1st Cl. Botany 1982); Univ. of Birmingham (PhD 1985). Res. Associate, John Innes Inst., 1985–87; Res. Fellow, 1987–99, Gp Leader, 1999–2005, Sainsbury Lab.; John Innes Centre: Hd, Dept of Metabolic Biol., 2006–08; Inst. Strategic Prog. Leader, 2008–13; Associate Res. Dir, 2008–13. Hon. Prof., UEA, Norwich Res. Park, 2006–. Founder and Chair, SAW Trust, 2005–. NESTA Dream Time Fellow, 2004–05; Branco Weiss Sci. in Sci. Fellow, 2005–10. FLS 2018. Medal, Univ. of Helsinki, 2003. *Publications*: Mock Orange (poetry), 2019; over 170 scientific articles. *Recreations*: wild swimming, keeping fit, writing and reading poetry. *Address*: John Innes Centre, Norwich Research Park, Norwich NR4 7UH. *T*: (01603) 450407. *E*: anne.osbourn@jic.ac.uk.

**OSBOURNE, Lt Gen. Edward Alexander S.**; *see* Smyth-Osbourne.

**OSEI, Isaac**; Managing Director, Tema Oil Refinery, since 2017; *b* 29 March 1951; *s* of late Nana Osei Nkwantabisa I and of Eunice Rosina Osei; *m* 1980, Marian Fofo; two *s* two *d*. *Educ*: Achimota Sch.; Univ. of Ghana (BSc Hons Econs); Center for Develt Econs, Williams Coll., Mass (MA Develt Econs). Asst Econ. Planning Officer, Min. of Finance, Ghana, 1973–77; Chief, Commercial Ops, 1977–81, Projects, R&D, 1981–82, Ghana Tourist Develt Co.; Managing Consultant, Ghanexim Econ. Consultants, 1982–2000; High Comr for Ghana in UK, and Ambassador to Ireland, 2001–06; Chief Exec., Ghana Cocoa Bd, 2006–08. MP (New Patriotic Party), Subin Constituency, Ghana, 2009–16. Chair, Bd of Govs, Commonwealth Secretariat, 2002–04. Director: E. K. Osei & Co. (Civil Eng. and Gen. Bldg Contractors), 1982–95; Kas Products Ltd (Quarry Masters), 1982–99; Intravenous Infusions Ltd, 1988– (Man. Dir, 1999–2001; Chm., 2007–). *Recreations*: from a distance, football and American football, reading. *Address*: Tema Oil Refinery, PO Box Co 599, Tema, Ghana. *E*: ikeosei@email.com.

**OSGERBY, Jay**, OBE 2013; RDI 2007; designer; Founding Director: Barber & Osgerby Ltd, since 1996; Universal Design Studio Ltd, since 2001; Map Project Office Ltd, since 2012; *b* Oxford, 23 Oct. 1969; *s* of Paul Osgerby and Wendy Osgerby (*née* Hickman); *m* 2000, Helen Louise Smith; one *s* two *d*. *Educ*: Ravensbourne Coll. (BA 1st cl. Hons Furniture and Product Design; Fellow, 2013); Royal Coll. of Art (MA Arch.). Tutor: Oxford Brookes Univ., 1993–97; Ravensbourne Coll., 1996–2000. Vis. Tutor and Ext. Examiner, RCA, 2008–12. Clients include: Vitra, B&B Italia, Knoll, Louis Vuitton, Flos, Venini, Isokon and Cappellini; *commissions* include: furniture for De La Warr Pavilion, RIBA, Portsmouth Cathedral; torches for London 2012 Olympic and Paralympic Games; design of £2 coin for Royal Mint. *Exhibitions* at: V&A; Sotheby's; Haunch of Venison, London; Design Miami/Basel; MOMA, NY; Internat. Furniture Fair, NY; Musée de la Mode et du Textil, Paris; Design Mus.; Crafts Council; *work in permanent collections*: V&A; Metropolitan Mus. of Art, NY; Design Mus.; Art Inst. of Chicago; Indianopolis Mus. of Art. FRSA 2005. Hon. DA Oxford Brookes, 2012; Hon. Dr Middx, 2018. Best New Designer, ICFF, NY, 1998; Jerwood Applied Arts Prize (jtly), Jerwood Foundn, 2004; Designer of the Future, Design Miami/Basel, 2006; Designer of Year, Maison & Objet, 2013; Panerai Official London Design Medal, 2015; Elle Deco Internat. Design Award, 2016. *Publications*: (with Edward Barber) The Design Work of Edward Barber and Jay Osgerby, 2010; (with Edward Barber) One by One, 2015; (jtly) Barber Osgerby: projects, 2017. *Address*: Barber & Osgerby, 37–42 Charlotte Road, EC2A 3PG. *T*: (020) 7033 3884. *E*: info@barberosgerby.com.

**O'SHAUGHNESSY**, family name of **Baron O'Shaughnessy**.

**O'SHAUGHNESSY**, Baron *cr* 2015 (Life Peer), of Maidenhead in the Royal County of Berkshire; **James Richard O'Shaughnessy**; *b* Taplow, Bucks, 26 March 1976; *s* of Michael O'Shaughnessy and Veronica O'Shaughnessy; *m* 2005, Lucy Sheppard; one *s* two *d*. *Educ*: Wellington Coll.; St Hugh's Coll., Oxford (BA PPE 1998; MA). Special Advr, Conservative Res. Dept, 2001–03; Hd, Res., LLM Communications, 2003–04; Dep. Dir, Policy Exchange, 2004–07; Dir, Policy and Res., Conservative Party, 2007–10; Dir, Policy, Prime Minister's Office, 2010–11. Gp Hd of Strategy, Wellington Coll., 2012–14; Chief Policy Advr, Portland Communications, 2012–15; Man. Dir, Floreat Education, 2013–16 (Trustee, 2017–); Advr, Character Lab., USA, 2014–16. Dir, Mayforth Consulting, 2012–17. Chm., Internat. Positive Educn Network, 2014–16. A Lord in Waiting (Govt Whip), 2017; Parly Under-Sec. of State, DoH, then DHSC, 2017–18. Vis. Fellow, Policy Exchange, 2012–16. Hon. Sen. Res. Fellow, Sch. of Educn, Univ. of Birmingham, 2012–16. Chm. Govs, Garratt Park Sch., 2005–07; Gov., Lena Gardens Sch., 2013–16. *Publications*: More Good School Places (with Charlotte Leslie), 2005; (ed) The Leadership Effect: can headteachers make a difference, 2007; Competition Meets Collaboration: helping school chains address England's long tail of educational failure, 2012. *Recreations*: family, reading, football, AFC Wimbledon. *E*: james@oshaughnessy.co.uk.

**O'SHEA, Colette**; Managing Director, London Portfolio, since 2014, and Retail Portfolio, since 2019, Land Securities Group plc; *b* Essex, 1 April 1968; *d* of Bernard O'Shea and Teresa O'Shea. *Educ*: Univ. of Reading (BSc 1989). FRICS 2012. Hd, Estates, Mercers' Co., 1999–2003; Develt Manager, 2003–08, Hd, Develt, London Portfolio, 2008–14, Land Securities Group plc. Non-exec. Dir, Genesis Housing Assoc., 2011–. Pres., British Council for Offices, 2014–15. *Recreations*: walking, running, cycling, design. *Address*: Land Securities Group plc, 100 Victoria Street, SW1E 5JL. *T*: 07802 801569. *E*: colette.oshea@landsecurities.com.

**O'SHEA, Michael Kent**; Director, Export Control and Non-Proliferation, Department of Trade and Industry, 2002–04; *b* 12 March 1951; *s* of Donovan Henry Victor and Joan O'Shea; *m* 1988, Linda Beata Szpala (*d* 2005). *Educ*: Bristol Grammar Sch.; Corpus Christi Coll., Cambridge (BA 1st Cl. Hons History). Department of Trade and Industry, 1973–2004: Under Sec., Finance and Resource Mgt, 1992–96; Dir, Engrg Automotive and Metals, 1996–98; Dir, Engrg Industries, 1998–2002. *Recreations*: owning Theo's Charm, watching National Hunt racing and cricket, playing bridge, listening to Wagner, visiting Italy, walking, cooking, drinking good beer and wine. *Club*: Gloucestershire CC.

**O'SHEA, Prof. Michael Roland,** PhD; Professor of Neuroscience and Co-Director, Centre for Computational Neuroscience and Robotics (formerly Director, BBSRC Sussex Centre for Neuroscience), University of Sussex, 1991–2016, now Emeritus; *b* 5 April 1947; *s* of Capt. Jack Arthur O'Shea and Ellen O'Shea (*née* Hughes); *m* 1st, 1977, Barbara Moore (marr. diss. 1991); (one *d* decd); 2nd, 1997, Jennifer Rusted; one *s* and one adopted *d. Educ:* Forest Hill Sch., London; Univ. of Leicester (BSc 1st Cl. Hons Biol Scis 1968); Univ. of Southampton (PhD Neurobiol. 1971). University of California, Berkeley: NATO Fellow, 1971–73; NIH Fellow, 1973–75; SRC Fellow, Univ. of Cambridge, 1975–77; Asst Prof., Univ. of Southern Calif., LA, 1977–79; Associate Prof., Brain Research Inst., Univ. of Chicago, 1979–85; Professor of: Neurobiol., Univ. of Geneva, 1985–88; Molecular Cell Biol., RHBNC, Univ. of London, 1988–91. *Publications:* The Brain: a very short introduction, 2005; numerous papers on neuroscience in learned jls. *Recreations:* classical music, mountaineering, modern poetry, triathlons, restoration of classic Lotus. *Address:* 29 Eldred Avenue, Brighton BN1 5EB. *T:* (01273) 678508; Sussex Neuroscience, School of Biological Sciences, University of Sussex, Brighton BN1 9QG.

**O'SHEA, Sir Timothy (Michael Martin),** Kt 2008; PhD; FREng; Principal and Vice-Chancellor, and Professor of Informatics and Education, University of Edinburgh, 2002–18; *b* 28 March 1949; *s* of John Patrick O'Shea and Elisabeth Hedwig Oberhof; *m* 1982, Prof. Eileen Scanlon; two *s* two *d. Educ:* Royal Liberty Sch., Havering; Sussex Univ. (BSc); Leeds Univ. (PhD). FREng 2017. Postgrad. res., Univs of Texas at Austin and Edinburgh; Open University: founder, Computers and Learning Res. Gp, 1978; Lectr, 1978–82, Sen. Lectr, 1983–87, Inst. of Educnl Technol.; Prof. of IT and Educn, 1987–97; Pro-Vice-Chancellor for QA and Res., 1994–97; Vis. Prof. of Computer Supported Collaborative Learning, 1998–2001; Master of Birkbeck Coll., and Prof. of Inf. and Communication Technologies, 1998–2002, Pro-Vice-Chancellor, 2001–02, Union Laurel, 2002, Fellow, Birkbeck Coll., 2003, Univ. of London. Vis. Scientist, Xerox PARC Calif, and Vis. Schol., Univ. of Calif, Berkeley, 1986–87. Chm., NATO prog. on Advanced Educnl Technol., 1988–90. Member: Bd, China-Britain Business Council, 2008–10; Strategy Commn, German Govt Exzellenzinitiative, 2009–13; Dep. Pres., French Govt Initiatives d'Excellence en Formations Innovantes, 2011–12. Chairman: London Metropolitan Network Ltd, 1999–2002; HERO Ltd, 2000–02; Scottish Inst. for Enterprise, 2009–; Mem. Bd, Scottish Enterprise, 2006–10 (Chm., Proof of Concept Stakeholders, 2004–10). Universities Scotland: Convenor: Res. and Commercialisation Cttee, 2003–07; Res. and Knowledge Exchange Cttee, 2016–18; Vice Convenor, 2009–12. Director: Edexcel Foundn, 1998–2001 (Mem., Exec. Cttee, 1998–2001); Univs and Colls Staff Develt Agency, 1999–2000. Chm., Inf. Systems Sector Gp, CVCP, 1999. Member: HEFCE Cttee on Equal Opportunities, Access and Lifelong Learning, 1998; JISC, 2000–13 (Chm., 2008–13); Bd, UUK, 2001–04; Bd, British Council, 2003–09; Univ. Adv. Bd, Coursera, 2013–17 (Chair, 2016–17); Univ. Council, All-Party Parly Univ. Gp, 2013–18; Res. and Knowledge Exchange Cttee, Scottish Funding Council, 2016–. Scottish Government: Convenor, Further and Higher Educn Sector Oversight Bd for Info. and Technol., 2013–16; Member: Financial Services Adv. Bd, 2014–; Digital Services Sponsor Bd, 2015–17; Mem., Strategic Funding Gp, 2016–17. Pres., Psychol. Sect., BAAS, 1991–92; Chm., Artificial Intelligence Soc., 1979–82. Trustee, Eduserv, 1999–2000; Chm., Newbattle Abbey Coll. Trust, 2012–17. Curator, Sch. of Advanced Study, London Univ., 1999–2002; Provost, Gresham Coll., 2000–02; Mem. Council, RCM, 2001; Governor: City Lit. Inst., 1998–2000; SOAS, 1998–2002; St George's Med. Sch., London Univ., 2000–02; Mem. Governing Council, Confucius Inst. HQ, 2007–. Chm., Bd of Dirs, Edinburgh Fest. Fringe, 2012–. Fellow, European Co-ordinating Cttee for Artificial Intelligence, 1999; FRSE 2004; FAcSS (AcSS 2009). Presenter and author, The Learning Machine (TV series), 1985. DUniv: Heriot-Watt, 2008; Strathclyde, 2011; Hon. LLD McGill, 2012; Hon. Dr St Petersburg Univ. of Humanities and Social Scis, 2013. *Publications:* include: Self-improving teaching systems, 1979; (jtly) Learning and Teaching with Computers, 1983; (jtly) Artificial Intelligence: tools, techniques and applications, 1984; (ed) Advances in Artificial Intelligence, 1985; (ed jtly) Intelligent Knowledge-based Systems: an introduction, 1987; (ed jtly) Educational Computing, 1987; (ed jtly) New Directions in Educnl Technology, 1992; contrib. learned jls.

**OSHEROFF, Prof. Douglas Dean,** PhD; Professor of Physics and Applied Physics, 1987, now Emeritus, and J. G. Jackson and C. J. Wood Professor of Physics, 1992, now Emeritus, Stanford University (Chairman, Department of Physics, 1993–96 and 2001–04); *b* 1 Aug. 1945; *s* of William and Bessie Anne Osheroff; *m* 1970, Phyllis Shih-Kiang Liu. *Educ:* California Inst. of Technology (BSc Physics 1967); Cornell Univ. (PhD Physics 1973). AT&T Bell Laboratories: Mem., technical staff, 1972–81; Hd, Solid State and Low Temp. Physics Res., 1981–87. MNAS, 1987; Mem., Amer. Acad. Arts and Scis, 1982. Fellow, APS. Sir Francis Simon Meml Award, 1976; Oliver E. Buckley Condensed Matter Physics Prize, 1981; Macarthur Prize Fellow Award, 1981; (jtly) Nobel Prize for Physics, 1996. *Publications:* contrib. chapters in books; numerous papers and articles in jls incl. Phys Rev., Phys Rev. Letters, Jl Low Temp. Phys. *Recreations:* photography, hiking, travel, music. *Address:* Department of Physics, Stanford University, Stanford, CA 94305–4060, USA.

**OSIKENA, Josephine Onotseogboya;** Director, Foreign Policy Centre, 2010–17; *b* South Lambeth, London, 8 Feb. 1974; *d* of late Francis D. Osikena and Maria O. Osikena (*née* Odiodio). *Educ:* Lilian Baylis Sch., Kennington; London Guildhall Univ. (BA Hons French and Econs 1998); Sch. of Oriental and African Studies, Univ. of London (MSc Develt Studies 1999). British Council Lang. Asst, Academie de Créteil, France, 1996–97; various short-term co-ordinator roles including: BBC, 2000; Cendent Internat. Assignment Services, 2000–02; Land Securities Trillium, 2002–03; DEFRA, 2003; DfT, 2003; Cabinet Office, 2004; Healthcare Commn, 2004; Women's Nat. Commn, 2004; London Bor. of Tower Hamlets, 2005; Prog. Manager, 2005–08, Prog. Dir, 2008–10, Democracy and Internat. Develt, Foreign Policy Centre. French Interpreter (pt-time volunteer), Camden CAB, 2004–09; conservation volunteer, Nat. Trust, 2012. Mem., Clapham Soc., 2012–. *Publications:* (contrib.) US Strategy in Africa: AFRICOM, terrorism and security challenges, 2010; reports for Foreign Policy Centre. *Recreations:* international affairs, African political economy, local history - particularly social housing, jazz fusion, improvised music, fringe theatre, swimming, jogging and walking.

**OSLER, Douglas Alexander,** CB 2002; HM Senior Chief Inspector of Education (formerly of Schools), Scottish Executive (formerly Scottish Office), 1996–2002; *b* 11 Oct. 1942; *s* of Alexander Osler and Jane Brown; *m* 1973, Wendy Cochrane; one *s* one *d. Educ:* Univ. of Edinburgh (MA Hons Hist.); Moray House Coll. of Educn (Teaching Cert.). Teacher, Liberton High Sch., Edinburgh, 1965; Principal Teacher, History, Dunfermline High Sch., 1969; HM Inspector, Chief Inspector, Depute Sen. Chief Inspector of Schools, Scottish Office, 1974–95. Interim Scottish Prisons Complaints Comr, 2003; Reviewer, Parole Bd of Scotland, 2004; Ind. Reviewer, Scottish Courts Service, 2005. Chm., Inquiry into Child Abuse at Cabin Hill Sch., Belfast, 2004–05; Ind. Chm., Scottish Cons. Party Policy Adv. Gp, 2006; Chm. Comrs, S Eastern Educn and Liby Bd, NI, 2006–10; Ambassador, Scottish Adv. Cttee, Skillforce, 2014– (Vice-Chm., 2010–13). Chm., Assessment Bd, Caritas Awards, 2012–14. Chm., Royal Blind and Scottish War Blinded, 2008–14. ESU Fellowship, 1966; Internat. Leadership Fellowship, USA, 1989; Vis. Prof., Strathclyde Univ., 2003–05. Trustee, Scottish Schools Pipes and Drums Trust, 2014–. Book reviewer, Scotsman, 2011–15. KSG 2001. *Recreations:* gardening, reading, Rotary International.

**OSMOND, Prof. Charles Barry,** PhD; FAA; FRS 1984; ML; Professor of Plant Science, University of Wollongong, 2011–13, Hon. Visiting Professor, 2014–17; Hon. Visiting Fellow, Research School of Biology, Australian National University, 2004–17; *b* 20 Sept. 1939; *s* of Edmund Charles Osmond and Joyce Daphne (*née* Krauss); *m* 1st, 1962, Suzanne Alice Ward; one *s* one *d* (and two *s* decd); 2nd, 1983, Ulla Maria Cornelia Gauhl (*née* Büchen). *Educ:* Morisset Central Sch.; Wyong High Sch.; Univ. of New England, Armidale (University Medal in Botany, 1961; BSc 1961, MSc 1963); Univ. of Adelaide (PhD 1965). FAA 1978. Post-doctoral Res. Associate, Botanical Sciences Dept, Univ. of Calif, LA, 1965; Royal Commn for Exhibn of 1851 and CSIRO Fellow, Botany Sch., Cambridge Univ., 1966; successively Res. Fellow, Fellow and Sen. Fellow, Dept of Environmental Biol., ANU, Canberra, 1967–78, Prof. of Biology, 1978–87; Exec. Dir, Biol Sciences Center, Desert Res. Inst., Reno, 1982–86; Arts and Scis Prof., Duke Univ., USA, 1987–91; Prof., 1991–2001, and Dir, 1991–98, Res. Sch. of Biol Scis, ANU, Canberra; Pres. and Exec. Dir, Biosphere 2 Center, Columbia Univ., 2001–03. Fulbright Sen. Scholar, Univ. of Calif, Santa Cruz, 1973–74; Carnegie Instn Fellow (Plant Biol.), Stanford, 1973–74; Richard Mereton Guest Prof., Technical Univ., Munich, 1974; Overseas Fellow, Churchill Coll., Cambridge, 1980. Mem., German Nat. Acad. Leopoldina, 2001. Goldacre Award, Aust. Soc. of Plant Physiologists, 1972; Edgeworth David Medal, Royal Soc. of NSW, 1974; Forschungspreis, Alexander von Humboldt Foundn, 1997; Clarke Medal, Royal Soc. of NSW, 1998. *Publications:* (ed jtly) Photosynthesis and Photorespiration, 1971; (ed jtly) Photorespiration in Marine Plants, 1976; (jtly) Physiological Processes in Plant Ecology, 1980; (ed jtly) Encyclopedia of Plant Physiology, Vols 12 A-D, Physiological Plant Ecology, 1981–83; (ed jtly) Photoinhibition, 1987; (ed jtly) New Vistas in Measurement of Photosynthesis, 1989; (ed jtly) Plant Biology of the Basin and Range, 1990; (ed jtly) Water and Life, 1992; (ed jtly) Nurturing Creativity in Research, 1997; articles on plant metabolic biology and its ecological implications in learned jls, 1963–. *Recreation:* biological research. *Address:* PO Box 3252, Weston Creek, ACT 2611, Australia. *T:* (2) 62871487.

**OSMOND, Richard George;** Secretary, The Post Office, 1995–97; *b* 22 Jan. 1947; *s* of late Lt-Col Clifford George Osmond, OBE, RE and Florence Rose Osmond (*née* Baker). *Educ:* Merchant Taylors' Sch. (Exhibnr); Univ. of Exeter. FCIPD (FIPD 1988). Post Office, 1967–97: Dep. Sec., 1985; Controller, Corporate Personnel, 1986; Head of Community Affairs, 1989; Dir, Group Personnel, 1993. Dir, Headteachers into Industry, 1990–96; Mem., Adv. Bd, Centre for Educn and Industry, Univ. of Warwick, 1992–98, Hon. Associate Fellow, 1998–2001; Chm., Policy Adv. Cttee, Sch. Curriculum and Industry Partnership, 1995–97. Vis. Fellow, Inst. of Educn, London Univ., 1997–99. Diocesan Gov., Univ. of Winchester (formerly King Alfred's Coll., Winchester), 1999–2008; Chm. of Governors, Peter Symonds Coll., Winchester, 2000–04. Vice Pres., ACRE, 1997–2008. FRSA 1990 (Member: Early Learning Study, 1993–94; Educn Adv. Gp, 1996–2001). Member, Council: Friends of Cathedral Music, 1977–83, 2003–09; L'Amitié Henri Bosco, 2010–14. Freeman, City of London, 1989; Liveryman, Musicians' Co., 1990–. *Recreations:* church music, bird watching, bridge. *Address:* 10 Hazel Grove, Winchester SO22 4PQ. *T:* (01962) 850818. *Club:* Athenæum.

**OSMOTHERLY, Sir Edward (Benjamin Crofton),** Kt 2002; CB 1992; Clerk Adviser, European Scrutiny Committee, House of Commons, 2003–10; *b* 1 Aug. 1942; *s* of Crofton and Elsie Osmotherly; *m* 1970, Valerie (*née* Mustill); one *d* one *s. Educ:* East Ham Grammar School; Fitzwilliam College, Cambridge (MA). Asst Principal, Ministry of Housing and Local Govt, 1963–68 (Private Sec. to Parly Sec., 1966–67, to Minister of State, 1967–68); Principal, 1968–76; Harkness Fellow, 1972–73 (Guest Scholar, Brookings Instn, Washington DC; Exec. Fellow, Univ. of California at Berkeley); Asst Sec., DoE, 1976–79; seconded to British Railways Bd, 1979; Head of Machinery of Govt Div., CSD, 1980–81; Under Sec. (Railways), Dept of Transport, 1982–85; Under Sec., Dir of Personnel, Management and Training, Depts of the Environment and of Transport, 1985–89; Dep. Sec., Public Transport and Res. Dept, 1989–92, Prin. Establishment and Finance Officer, 1992–93, Dept of Transport; Local Govt Ombudsman, 1993–2001; Chm., Commn for Local Admin in England, 1994–2001; Mem., Adjudication Panel for England, 2002–03. Chm., Ind. Review of Govt Business Statistics, 1996. Chm., British and Irish Ombudsman Assoc., 1998–2001. *Recreation:* reading.

**OSOFSKY, Lisa Kate;** Director, Serious Fraud Office, since 2018; *b* New York, 18 Sept. 1961; *d* of Gilbert and Marcia Osofsky; *m* 1991, Marc D. Wassermann; one *s* one *d. Educ:* Amherst Coll. (BA 1983); Harvard Law Sch. (JD 1987). Law Clerk to US Dist Court Judge, Northern Dist of Illinois, Chicago, 1987–88; Associate, Dechert Price & Rhoads, Philadelphia, 1988–89; Asst US Attorney, Northern Dist of Illinois, 1989–92; Special Attorney, Fraud Section, Criminal Div., US Dept of Justice, stationed in London, 1992–93; Asset Confiscation Project, Home Office, London, 1993–94; Member, Middle Temple, 1994; Asst US Attorney, Northern Dist of Illinois, 1994–95; Associate Dir, Office of Internat. Affairs, US Dept of Justice, Washington, 1995–96; Dep. Gen. Counsel, FBI, Washington, 1996–2000; called to the Bar, 1997, Bencher, Middle Temple, 2019; pupil, 9–12 Bell Yard, London, 2001–02; Exec. Dir, Counsel and Money Laundering Reporting Officer, Goldman Sachs Internat., London, 2003–06; Regulatory Advr, Corporate Investigations Div., Control Risks, London, 2006–13; EMEA Regl Chair, Exiger, London, 2013–18. *Publications:* (contrib.) Butterworth's International Guide to Money Laundering Law, 1995; contribs to jls incl. Accountancy Age, Law Soc. Gazette, Insider Business, The Lawyer, The Times, Legal Week, Jl Internat. Banking Law. *Recreations:* travelling, opera. *Address:* Serious Fraud Office, 2–4 Cockspur Street, SW1Y 5BS. *T:* (020) 7239 7272. *E:* private.office@sfo.gov.uk. *Club:* Reform.

**OSÓRIO, Antonio Mota de Sousa H.;** *see* Horta-Osório.

**OSOWSKA, Francesca,** OBE 2015; Chief Executive, Scottish Natural Heritage, since 2017; *b* Whitehaven, Cumbria, 25 July 1970; *d* of Thomas Osowski and Barbara Osowska (*née* Matthews, later Davis). *Educ:* St Bees Sch.; Churchill Coll., Cambridge (BA Econs 1992); Coll. of Europe, Bruges (MSc Eur. Econs). Govt economist, Employment Dept Gp, later DfEE, 1993–2001; Scottish Executive, later Scottish Government: Sen. Civil Servant, 2001–07; Principal Private Sec. to the First Minister of Scotland, 2007–09; Director: Culture, Ext. Affairs and Tourism, 2009–10; Housing, Regeneration and Commonwealth Games, 2011–12; Commonwealth Games and Sport, 2013–14; Scotland Office, 2015–17. *Recreation:* triathlon (particularly in hot and sunny climes). *Address:* Scottish Natural Heritage, Great Glen House, Leachkin Road, Inverness IV3 8NW. *T:* (01463) 725001. *E:* ceo@snh.gov.uk. *Club:* Edinburgh Triathletes.

**OSTERLEY, Robin Marius;** Chief Executive, Charity Retail Association, since 2015; *b* 22 Feb. 1957; *s* of late Allan Osterley and of Barbara Dora Osterley; *m* Karen; two *s* two *d. Educ:* Monkton Combe Sch.; St Edmund Hall, Oxford (BA Hons 1979). Sen. Mktg Manager, ICL, 1982–93; Mktg Manager, Orch. of St John's, Smith Square, 1994; Man. Dir, Cala Records Ltd, 1994–96; Chief Exec., Making Music (formerly The National Federation of Music Societies), 1997–2013; Chief Exec., Supporters Direct, 2014–15.

Member: Exec. Cttee, Music Educn Council, 2001–13; Nat. Music Council, 2001–13 (Chm., 2001–09); Music Manifesto Partnerships and Advocacy Gp, 2009–11; Chair, Special Interest Gp for Arts and Heritage, 2008–13, Dir, 2011–13, ACEVO; Dir, Voluntary Arts, 2011–13. Chm., Superact! CIC, 2014. Music Director: Stevenage Choral Soc., 2001–; Alyth Choral Soc., 2014–. Chm. Govs, Hunsdon JMI Sch., 2005–15; Parent Gov. Rep., Oversight and Scrutiny Cttee, Herts CC, 2013–16. Chair, Hunsdon Village Hall, 2017–. *Recreations:* singing, conducting, bad piano playing, running slowly, never letting the grass grow under the feet. *E:* robinosterley@googlemail.com.

**OSTLER, Catherine Emma, (Mrs Albert Read);** author; Contributing Editor, Daily Mail, since 2011; *d* of late John R. Ostler and of Patricia Ann Ostler; *m* 2003, Albert Nathaniel Read, *qv*; one *s* two *d*. *Educ:* Cheltenham Ladies' Coll.; St Hilda's Coll., Oxford (BA English 1991; MA). Tatler, 1991–94, latterly Features Ed.; Features Writer, Mail on Sunday, 1994–96; Editor: Saturday Mag., Express, 1996–99; Times Weekend, 1999–2000; PeopleNews.com, 2000–01; ES Mag., 2002–09; Tatler, 2009–10. *Address:* Daily Mail, Northcliffe House, 2 Derry Street, W8 5TS.

**OSTLER, Dr Nicholas David MacLachlan;** Chairman, Foundation for Endangered Languages, since 1996; *b* Tunbridge Wells, Kent, 20 May 1952; *s* of Kenneth M. Ostler and Yvonne L. Ostler (*née* Jolly); *m* 1st, 1983, Olga M. Sarasti (marr. diss. 1988); one *d*; 2nd, 1997, Jane Dunn. *Educ:* Yardley Court Prep. Sch.; Tonbridge Sch.; Balliol Coll., Oxford (BA Classics Mods, PPE 1975; MA 1987); Massachusetts Inst. of Technol. (PhD Linguistics 1979). Foreign Lectr, Toyama Univ., Japan, 1979–81; Consultant, Logica Ltd, 1982–83; Principal Consultant, Scicon Ltd, London, 1983–87; Sen. Consultant, Touche Ross Mgt Consultants, 1987–91; Dir, Linguacubun Ltd, 1991–2001; ind. author, 2001–. Res. Associate, SOAS, 2007–16. Mem., Integration Panel, Internet Corp. for Assigned Names and Numbers, 2013–. Hon. Fellow (Linguistics), Lancaster Univ., 1999–; Academician, Russian Acad. Linguistics, 2004–. Ed., Ogmios, Foundn for Endangered Langs, 1995–2006. *Publications:* Empires of the World: a language history of the world, 2005; Ad Infinitum: a biography of Latin, 2007; The Last Lingua Franca: the rise and fall of world languages, 2010; Passwords to Paradise: how languages have re-invented world religions, 2016; contribs to Foundn for Endangered Langs procs. *Recreations:* whippets, using dead languages. *Address:* 129 High Street, Hungerford, Berks RG17 0DL. *T:* 07720 889319. *E:* n@ostler.net.

**OSTRIKER, Prof. Jeremiah Paul,** PhD; Professor of Astronomy, Columbia University, 2012–17; Senior Researcher, Princeton University, 2012–16; *b* 13 April 1937; *s* of Martin Ostriker and Jeanne (*née* Sumpf); *m* 1958, Alicia Suskin; one *s* two *d*. *Educ:* Harvard Univ. (AB Physics and Chem. 1959); Univ. of Chicago (PhD Astrophysics 1964). Postdoctoral Fellow, Univ. of Cambridge, 1964–65; Princeton University: Res. Associate and Lectr, 1965–66; Asst Prof., 1966–68; Associate Prof., 1968–71; Prof., Dept of Astrophysical Scis, 1971–2012; Chm., Dept of Astrophysical Scis, and Dir, Observatory, 1979–95; Charles A. Young Prof. of Astronomy, 1982–2002, Charles A. Young Professor Emeritus, 2012; Provost, 1995–2001; Dir, Princeton Inst. for Computational Sci. and Engrg, 2005–09; Plumian Prof. of Astronomy and Experimental Philosophy, Inst. of Astronomy, and Fellow of Clare Coll., Univ. of Cambridge, 2001–04. Treasurer, NAS, 2008–16. Mem., Editl Bd and Trustee, Princeton Univ. Press, 1982–84 and 1986. Trustee, 1997–2006, Hon. Trustee, 2007–, Amer. Mus. of Natural Hist. Mem., Amer. Philosophical Soc., 1994; Foreign Member: Royal Netherlands Acad. of Arts and Scis, 1999; Royal Soc., 2007. Hon. DSc Chicago, 1992. Henry Norris Russell Prize, AAS, 1980; Vainu Bappu Meml Award, INSA, 1993; Karl Schwarzschild Medal, Astronomische Ges., 1999; US Nat. Medal of Sci., 2000; Gold Medal for Astronomy, RAS, 2004; Catherine Wolfe Bruce Gold Medal, Astronomical Soc. of Pacific, 2011; James Craig Watson Medal, NAS, 2012; Open Science Champion of Change, The White House, 2013; Gruber Cosmology Prize, 2015. *Publications:* Development of Large-Scale Structure in the Universe, 1991; (ed with J. N. Bahcall) Unsolved Problems in Astrophysics, 1997; (ed with A. Dekel) Formation of Structure in the Universe, 1999; (with S. Mitton) Heart of Darkness: unravelling the mysteries of the invisible universe, 2013; contribs to Astrophysical Jl and Nature on topics in theoretical astrophysics. *Recreations:* squash, bicycling, photography. *Address:* Princeton University, 109 Peyton Hall, Ivy Lane, Princeton, NJ 08544–1001, USA. *E:* ostriker@princeton.edu; Department of Astronomy, Columbia University, Mail Code 5246, 550 West 120th Street, New York, NY 10027, USA.

**OSTROWSKI, Joan Lorraine;** *see* Walley, J. L.

**O'SULLIVAN, Alison Jane;** Director, Children and Young People (formerly Children's Services), Kirklees Council, 2006–16 (Director for Children and Adults, 2012–15); *b* 25 March 1955; *d* of Kenneth Attenborough and Hazel (*née* Wain, now Hart); *m* 1983, Patrick Joseph O'Sullivan; two *s*. *Educ:* John Port Comprehensive Sch., Etwall, Derbys; Univ. of Bradford (BA Hons (Applied Social Studies), CQSW, 1978); Huddersfield Poly. (DMS 1990). Bradford Social Services: social worker, Manningham area of Bradford, 1978–83; Team Manager, 1983–92; Sen. Manager, Children's Services, 1992–97; Assistant Director: Learning Disability, Physical Disability, and Sensory Impairment and Mental Health Services, 1997–99; Adult Services, 1999–2000; on secondment to Bradford AHA, as Jt Comr for Older People's Services, 2000–02; Dir of Social Services, Bradford CC, 2002–05. Pres., Assoc. of Dirs of Children's Services, 2015–16 (Vice Pres., 2014–15). Chair of Trustees, Nat. Children's Bureau, 2019–. Co-Chair, Expert Wkg Gp for Looked-After Children, 2016; Mem., Adv. Bd, Children's Comr, 2016–. *Recreations:* building extensions, gardening, narrowboating, watching romantic comedies, ski-ing.

**O'SULLIVAN, David;** Ambassador for the European Union to the United States of America, 2014–19; *b* 1 March 1953; *s* of late Gerald and Philomena O'Sullivan; *m* 1984, Agnes O'Hare; one *s* one *d*. *Educ:* St Mary's Coll., Rathmines, Dublin; Trinity Coll. Dublin (MA 1975); Coll. of Europe, Bruges. Irish Diplomatic Service, 1977–79; entered European Commission, 1979; First Sec., Delegn to Tokyo, 1981–84; Mem., Cabinet of Comr Peter Sutherland, 1985–89; Hd, Educn and Trng Unit, 1989–93; Dep. Hd, Cabinet of Comr Padraig Flynn, 1993–96; Dir, Eur. Social Fund, 1996–99; Dir-Gen., Educn, Trng and Youth, Feb.–May 1999; Hd, Cabinet of Pres. Romano Prodi, 1999–2000; Sec.-Gen., 2000–05; Dir Gen. for Trade, 2005–10; Dir Gen. for External Relns, 2010; Chief Operating Officer, Eur. External Action Service, 2011–14. Vis. Prof., European Coll., Parma, 2013–. Hon. DPhil Dublin Inst. of Technol., 2005. Transatlantic Business Award, American Chamber of Commerce to EU, 2014. *Recreations:* tennis, music, cinema.

**O'SULLIVAN, Derek Anthony;** QC 2016; *b* Oakham, Rutland, 30 Dec. 1964; *s* of Patrick and Veronica O'Sullivan; *m* 1997, Sophie; one *s*. *Educ:* Durham Univ. (BA); Inns of Court Sch. of Law. Called to the Bar, Lincoln's Inn, 1990. *Recreations:* Real tennis, golf. *Address:* 39 Essex Chambers, 81 Chancery Lane, WC2A 1DD. *T:* (020) 7832 1111. *E:* derek.osullivanqc@39essex.co.uk. *Clubs:* Lansdowne; Huntercombe Golf; Hardwick Real Tennis, Oratory Real Tennis, Holyport Real Tennis.

**O'SULLIVAN, Marie Louise;** *see* Kinsler, M. L.

**O'SULLIVAN, Michael Joseph,** CMG 2008; Director, O'Sullivan Education Consulting Ltd; *b* 21 Dec. 1958; *s* of late Patrick Joseph O'Sullivan and Mary Elizabeth O'Sullivan (*née* Herbert); *m* 1989, Moira Helen Grant; one *s* two *d*. *Educ:* Brasenose Coll., Oxford (BA Hons German and French); Wolfson Coll., Cambridge (MPhil Linguistics). VSO Teacher of English, Xiangtan, Hunan, China, 1982–84; joined British Council, 1985: E Europe and N Asia Dept, 1985–87; Asst Dir, China, 1987–90; UK planner, Corporate Affairs, 1991–93; Dir, S China (Hong Kong), 1993–95; Hd, Corporate Planning, 1995–97; Policy Dir, Asia Pacific, 1997–2000; Dir, China, 2000–05; Regl Dir, China, 2005–07; Sec. Gen., EU Chamber of Commerce, China, 2007–08; Dir, Cambridge Commonwealth Trust and Cambridge Overseas Trust, 2008–13; Chief Exec., Cambridge Internat. Exams, later Cambridge Assessment Internat. Educn, 2013–18. Fellow, Wolfson Coll., Cambridge, 2008–. *Recreations:* cycling, travel, music, rowing. *Address:* Wolfson College, Barton Road, Cambridge CB3 9BB.

**O'SULLIVAN, His Honour Michael Neil;** a Circuit Judge, 2004–13; *b* 5 Feb. 1943; *s* of Ernest George Patrick Sullivan (who changed family name to O'Sullivan by Deed Poll, 1967) and Dorothy Florence (*née* Piper); *m* 1972, Maria Colette Smith; one *s* two *d*. *Educ:* Beaumont Coll.; City of London Coll. Exporter, motor mechanic, asst works manager, advertiser, Co. Court Clerk and Trust Adminr, 1960–70; called to the Bar: Gray's Inn, 1970; King's Inns, Ireland, 1994. Asst Recorder, 1991–95, Recorder, 1995–2004. Member: Mental Health Tribunal, 2009–13; Parole Bd, 2010–15. *Recreations:* Rugby Union (player, coach, club and internat. spectator), wood-turning, fly-fishing, reading and writing poetry, walking between interesting public houses. *Club:* Folkestone Rugby Football (Pres., 2008–14).

**O'SULLIVAN, Prof. Patrick Edmund,** OBE 1988; PhD; CEng; FInstE; Haden-Pilkington Professor of Environmental Design and Engineering, University College London, 1999–2002, now Emeritus; *b* 28 March 1937; *s* of Daniel O'Sullivan and Margaret Cecilia (*née* Mansfield); *m* 1963, Diana Grimshaw; three *s* one *d*. *Educ:* Finchley Catholic Grammar Sch.; Leeds Univ. (BSc); Durham Univ. (PhD). FCIBSE 1975. University of Newcastle upon Tyne: DSIR Post-Doctoral Res. Fellow, 1963–64; Sen. Res. Fellow in Bldg Sci., 1964–66; Lectr, 1966–70; Sen. Lectr, 1970; Prof. of Architectural Sci., UWIST, 1970–89; Dean, Faculty of the Built Envmt, and Head, Bartlett Sch., UCL, 1989–99. Non-exec. Dir, Titon Hldgs, 2002–13. Chm., Bldg Regulation Adv. Cttee, DETR, 2000–01. Chm., Friendly Trust, 2009–14. Hon. FRIBA; Hon. FCIBSE 2000. MIOA 1975. Gold Medal, RSH, 1999. *Publications:* Insulation and Fenestration, 1967; articles in learned jls.

**O'SULLIVAN, Patrick Henry Pearse,** FCA; Chairman: ERS Syndicate Management Ltd, Lloyd's of London, since 2013; Saga plc, since 2018; *b* 15 April 1949; *s* of Cornelius J. O'Sullivan and Marie Slowey; *m* 1974, Evelyn Holohan; two *s* one *d*. *Educ:* Trinity Coll., Dublin (BBS 1971); London Sch. of Econs (MSc Accounting and Finance 1975). FCA 1985. Arthur Andersen & Co., 1971–74; with Bank of America, working in Germany, San Francisco, LA, Miami and London, 1975–87; Gen. Manager, BA Futures Inc., London, 1987–88; Exec. Dir and Financial Controller, Goldman Sachs, 1988–89; Man. Dir, Internat. Financial Guaranty Insce Co., 1990–93; Hd, Internat. Banking and Structured Finance, 1994–96, Chief Operating Officer, 1996–97, Barclays/BZW; Chief Exec., Eagle Star Insce Co. Ltd, 1997–2002; Gp Finance Dir, 2002–07, Vice Chm. and Chief Growth Officer, 2007–09, Zurich Financial Services. Chairman: Farmers Gp Inc., 2007–09; Old Mutual, 2010–18; Shareholder Exec., 2012–14; non-executive Director: Man Gp plc, 2007–13; Collins Stewart plc, 2007–09; COFRA Hldg AG, Switzerland, 2007–12; Bank of Ireland, 2009–15 (Dep. Gov., 2011–15). *Recreation:* golf. *Address:* Oak Gables, Daneshill, The Hockering, Woking, Surrey GU22 7HQ. *E:* patrick@o-sullivan.org. *Clubs:* Royal Automobile, Mark's; Wisley.

**O'SULLIVAN, Robert Michael;** QC 2012; *b* Solihull, 9 April 1966; *s* of Dermot O'Sullivan and Valerie O'Sullivan (*née* Wetton). *Educ:* Dauntsey's Sch., Wilts; King's Coll. London (LLB; AKC). Called to the Bar, Lincoln's Inn, 1988; in practice as barrister, specialising in crime. *Recreation:* all things cricket. *Address:* 5 Paper Buildings, Temple, EC4Y 7HB. *T:* (020) 7583 6117. *Clubs:* MCC, Royal Automobile.

**O'SULLIVAN, Ronnie,** OBE 2016; snooker player; *b* 5 Dec. 1975; *s* of Ronnie and Maria O'Sullivan. World Jun. Snooker Champion, Bangalore, 1991; turned professional, 1992; wins include: UK Championship, 1993 (youngest ever winner of a ranking event), 1997, 2001, 2007, 2014, 2017; British Open, 1994; Masters, 1995, 2005, 2007, 2009, 2014, 2016, 2017; Asian Classic, 1996; German Open, 1996; Regal Scottish Open, 1998, 2000; China Open, 1999, 2000; Regal Scottish Masters, 1998, 2000, 2002; Irish Masters, 2001, 2003, 2005, 2007; World Championship, 2001, 2004, 2008, 2012, 2013; Premier Snooker League, 1997, 2001, 2002, 2004, 2005, 2006, 2007, 2008, 2010; Welsh Open, 2004, 2005, 2014, 2016; Totesport Grand Prix, 2004; Shanghai Masters, 2009; Dafabet Masters, 2016; English Open, 2017; Coral Tour Championship, 2019. Player of the Year and Fans' Player of the Year, World Snooker, 2014. *Publications:* Ronnie: the autobiography of Ronnie O'Sullivan, 2004; Running, 2013; Framed (novel), 2016; Double Kiss (novel), 2017; The Break (novel), 2018; Top of Your Game: eating for mind and body, 2019. *Address:* c/o Grove Leisure, 4 Redwing Court, Ashton Road, Romford RM3 8QQ.

**O'SULLIVAN, Sally Angela;** Director, August Media, 2005–18; *b* 26 July 1949; *d* of late Lorraine and Joan Connell; *m* 1st, 1973, Thaddeus O'Sullivan (marr. diss.); 2nd, 1980, Charles Martin Wilson, *qv* (marr. diss. 2001); one *s* one *d*. *Educ:* Ancaster House Sch.; Trinity Coll., Dublin (BA). Dep. Editor, Woman's World, 1977–78; Women's Editor: Daily Record, 1980; Sunday Standard, 1981; Editor, Options, 1982–88; Launch Editor, Country Homes & Interiors, 1986; Editor: She, 1989; Harpers & Queen, 1989–91; Editor-in-Chief: Good Housekeeping, 1991–95; Ideal Home, Homes & Ideas, Woman & Home, Homes & Gardens, Country Homes & Interiors, Beautiful Homes, Living, etc, 1996–98; Chief Exec., Cabal Communications, 1998–2003; Gp Editorial Dir, Highbury House Communications, 2003–05. Non-executive Director: London Transport, 1995–2000; Anglian Water, 1996–2001. Member: Broadcasting Standards Council, 1994–2003; Foresight Retail and Consumer Services Panel, 1999–2001. Chm., Turn2Us (formerly Elizabeth Finn Care), 2018– (Trustee, 2010–13; Dep. Chm., 2013–18); non-exec. Dir, Elizabeth Finn Homes Ltd, 2015–. Trustee, Market Harborough Building Soc. Charitable Foundn, 2019–. Hon. Fellow, Univ. of Central Lancashire, 2012. Magazine Editor of the Year, 1986 and 1994. *Recreations:* family, horses, farming.

**O'SULLIVAN, (Thomas) Sean (Patrick);** QC 2014; a Recorder, since 2016; *b* Harrow, 19 Jan. 1974; *s* of Thomas and Christine O'Sullivan; *m* 2000, Samantha Goodhew; one *s* one *d*. *Educ:* Merchant Taylors' Sch., Northwood; Exeter Coll., Oxford (MA Mod. Hist.); City Univ. (CPE). Called to the Bar, Middle Temple, 1997; in practice as a barrister, specialising in commercial litigation, 4 Pump Court, 1997–. *Publications:* Civil Appeals, 2010, 2nd edn 2015. *Recreations:* tennis, golf, cricket, watching football. *Address:* 4 Pump Court, Temple, EC4Y 7AN. *T:* (020) 7842 5555. *Club:* Oxford and Cambridge.

**O'SULLIVAN, Hon. Victoria;** *see* Glendinning, Hon. Victoria.

**O'SULLIVAN, Zoë Siobhan**; QC 2015; b London, 16 Jan. 1968; d of T. R. O'Sullivan and Susan O'Sullivan; m 1999, Peter Thomas; three s. Educ: Lady Margaret Hall, Oxford (MA Hons English Lang. and Lit. 1991); City Univ., London (DipLaw 1992); Inns of Court Sch. of Law. Called to the Bar, Middle Temple, 1993, Bencher, 2018; in practice as barrister, specialising in commercial law, 1994–. Fellow, Westminster Abbey Inst., 2015–16. Recreations: singing (Member, Bach Choir), classical music, ballet, running, family, travelling the Greek islands. Address: Serle Court, 6 New Square, Lincoln's Inn, WC2A 3QS. T: (020) 7400 7135. E: zosullivan@serlecourt.co.uk.

**OSWALD, Prof. Andrew John**, DPhil; Professor of Economics and Behavioural Science, Warwick University, since 1996; b 27 Nov. 1953; s of late Ian Oswald and Joan Oswald (née Thomsett); m 1st, 1975, Coral Simpson (marr. diss. 2004); two d; 2nd, 2012, Amanda Goodall. Educ: Hollywood High Sch., Perth, Aust.; Currie High Sch., Edinburgh; Stirling Univ. (BA); Strathclyde Univ. (MSc); Nuffield Coll., Oxford (DPhil 1980). Lectr, Balliol Coll., Res. Officer at Inst. of Econs and Stats, and Jun. Res. Fellow, St John's Coll., Oxford Univ., 1979–82; Vis. Lectr, Princeton Univ., 1983–84; Jun. Res. Fellow, St John's Coll., Oxford, 1985–86; Sen. Res. Fellow, Centre for Lab Econs, LSE, 1987–98; De Walt Ankeny Prof. of Econs, Dartmouth Coll., USA, 1989–91; Sen. Res. Fellow, Centre for Econ. Performance, LSE, 1992–95; Jacob Wertheim Fellow, Harvard Univ., 2005; ESRC Professorial Fellow, 2006–09; Vis. Fellow, Cornell Univ., 2008; Vis. Prof., Univ. of Zurich, 2008. Acting Res. Dir, IZA Inst., Bonn, 2011–13. Mem., Bd of Editors, Science Jl, 2010–. Hon. Dr Basel, 2013. Tassie Medallion, Stirling Univ., 1975; Lester Prize, Princeton Univ., 1995; Medal, Univ. of Helsinki, 1996. Publications: (with A. Carruth) Pay Determination and Industrial Prosperity, 1989; (with D. Blanchflower) The Wage Curve, 1994; contrib. numerous articles to jls. Recreations: walking, racquet sports. Address: Economics Department, Warwick University, Coventry CV4 7AL. T: (024) 7652 3510.

**OSWALD, Lady Angela Mary Rose**, CVO 2001 (LVO 1993); Woman of the Bedchamber to HM Queen Elizabeth the Queen Mother, 1983–2002; b 21 May 1938; d of 6th Marquess of Exeter, KCMG, and Lady Mary Burghley, d of 7th Duke of Buccleuch, KT; m 1958, Sir (William Richard) Michael Oswald, qv; one s one d. Educ: Winceby House Sch., Bexhill. Extra Woman of the Bedchamber to HM Queen Elizabeth the Queen Mother, 1981–83. Freeman, City of London, 1995. Address: The Old Rectory, Weasenham, King's Lynn, Norfolk PE32 2TB. T: (01328) 838311.

**OSWALD, Kirsten Frances**; Chair and Business Convener, Scottish National Party, since 2018; b Dundee, 21 Dec. 1972; d of Ed and late Helen Oswald; m Davinder Bedi; two s. Educ: Carnoustie High Sch.; Univ. of Glasgow (MA Hons Hist. 2005). HR, Motherwell Coll., 1998–2002; Hd of HR, South Lanarks Coll., 2002–15. MP (SNP) E Renfrewshire, 2015–17; contested (SNP) same seat, 2017. SNP spokesperson on armed forces and veterans, 2015–17.

**OSWALD, Sir Michael**; see Oswald, Sir W. R. M.

**OSWALD, Richard Anthony**; Deputy Health Service Commissioner, 1989–96; b 12 Jan. 1941; s of late Denis Geoffrey Oswald and Dorothy Lettice Oswald (née Shaw); m 1963, Janet Iris Penticost; three s one d (and one d decd). Educ: The Leys School, Cambridge. DipHSM, MHSM, 1966. NHS admin. posts, 1961–77; Dist Administrator, Leeds West, 1977–84; Gen. Manager, Leeds Western HA, 1985–89. Trustee: CHASE Children's Hospice Service, 1998–2005 (Chm., 1999–2001); St Mary's Historic House and Gardens Charitable Trust, 2006–14. Churchwarden, St Peter's Henfield, 2014–17. Recreations: church, amateur theatre (Chm., Henfield Theatre Co., 2010–14), painting. Address: Croft Cottage, Nep Town Road, Henfield, W Sussex BN5 9DU. T: (01273) 492702.

**OSWALD, Sir (William Richard) Michael**, KCVO 1998 (CVO 1988 LVO 1979); National Hunt Advisor to the Queen, since 2003; Racing Manager for Queen Elizabeth the Queen Mother, 1970–2002; b 21 April 1934; s of Lt-Col William Alexander Hugh Oswald, ERD and Rose-Marie (née Leahy); m 1958, Lady Angela Mary Rose Cecil (see Lady A. M. R. Oswald); one s one d. Educ: Eton; King's College, Cambridge (MA). 2nd Lieut The King's Own Royal Regt, 1953; Captain, Royal Fusiliers (TA), 1957. Manager, Lordship and Egerton Studs, 1962–70; Manager, 1970–97, Dir, 1998–99, Royal Studs. Mem. Council, Thoroughbred Breeders' Assoc., 1964–2001 (Pres., 1996–2001); Chm., Bloodstock Industry Cttee, Animal Health Trust, 1989–2002; Trustee, British Equine Veterinary Assoc. Trust, 1998–2004. Mem., Jockey Club. Hon. Air Cdre, No 2620 (Co. of Norfolk) Sqdn, RAuxAF, 2001–16; Pres., 42F Squadron Air Cadets, 2014–. Hon. DSc De Montfort, 1997. Recreations: painting, military history. Address: The Old Rectory, Weasenham, King's Lynn, Norfolk PE32 2TB. T: (01328) 838311, Fax: (01328) 838264; The Royal Studs, Sandringham, Norfolk PE35 6EF. T: (01485) 540588. Clubs: Army and Navy, Royal Air Force.
See also Lt Col Sir A. F. Matheson of Matheson.

**OTAKA, Tadaaki**, Hon. CBE 1997; Music Director, Osaka Philharmonic Orchestra, since 2018 (Chief Conductor, 2017–18); Music Advisor and Principal Conductor, Kioi Sinfonietta, Tokyo, since 1995; b 8 Nov. 1947; s of Hisatada and Misaoko Otaka; m 1978, Yukiko. Educ: Toho Music Coll., Tokyo; Vienna Acad. Chief Conductor, Tokyo Philharmonic Orch., 1974–91, now Conductor Laureate; Conductor, Sapporo SO, 1981–86; Principal Conductor, BBC Nat. Orch. of Wales, 1987–95, now Conductor Laureate; Chief Conductor, Yomiuri Nippon SO, 1992–98; Dir, Britten Pears Orch., 1998–2001; Music Advr and Chief Conductor, Sapporo SO, 1998–2015, now Hon. Music Dir; Principal Guest Conductor, Melbourne SO, 2010–12; Perm. Conductor, NHK SO, and Artistic Dir, New Nat. Th., Tokyo, 2010–14. Suntory Award (Japan), 1992. Recreations: fishing, cooking, computer. Address: c/o Askonas Holt Ltd, 15 Fetter Lane, EC4A 1BW. T: (020) 7400 1700.

**OTAÑO, Marta**; see Andreasen, M.

**OTLEY, Prof. David Templeton**, PhD; Distinguished Professor of Accounting and Management, Lancaster University Management School, 2000–11, now Emeritus; b 10 June 1944; s of late Frank Otley and Catherine Otley; m 1971, Shelagh Elizabeth Gill; one s one d. Educ: Wellington Grammar Sch.; Churchill Coll., Cambridge (BA 1966, MA 1970); Brunel Univ. (MTech 1971); Manchester Business Sch. (PhD 1976). CDipAF 1980. OR Scientist, NCB, 1966–69; University of Lancaster: Lectr in Financial Control, 1972–83; Sen. Lectr, 1983–86; Prof. of Mgt Control, 1987–88; KPMG Prof. of Accounting, 1988–2000; Associate Dean, 2002–11. Non-exec. Dir, Lancaster HA, 1992–94. Vice-Chm., Business and Mgt Panel, 1996 RAE; Chairman: Accounting and Finance Panel, 2001 RAE; Main Panel I, 2008 RAE; Hong Kong Business, Accounting, Economics and Finance Panel, 2014, RAE. Mem. Mgt Bd, ICAEW Centre for Business Performance, 1999–2011; Sen. Moderator, ICAEW Advanced Stage Examinations, 2001–08; Member: ESRC Res. Grants Bd, 1996–2001; ESRC Audit Cttee, 2002–08. Chm., Mgt Control Assoc., 1983–88, 2005–09. Pres., Mgt Accounting Sect., AAA, 2009–10. Gen. Editor, British Jl of Mgt, 1989–98. Fellow, British Acad. of Mgt, 1994. Publications: (with C. R. Emmanuel) Accounting for Management Control, 1985, 2nd edn 1990; Accounting Control and Organizational Behaviour, 1987; (jtly) Accounting for the Human Factor, 1989; (jtly) Management Control: theories, issues and practices, 1995, 2nd edn 2005; (with K. Soin) Management Control and Uncertainty, 2014; numerous contribs to acad. and prof. jls. Address: Lancaster University Management School, Lancaster LA1 4YX. T: (01524) 593636, Fax: (01524) 847321. E: d.otley@lancs.ac.uk. Club: Oxford and Cambridge.

**O'TOOLE, Dr Barbara Maria, (Mo)**; Visiting Professor of Creativity and Innovation, Newcastle University Business School, since 2008; b 24 Feb. 1960. Educ: Convent of the Sacred Heart, Fenham, Newcastle upon Tyne; Newcastle upon Tyne Poly. (BA Hons 1983); Univ. of Newcastle upon Tyne (PhD 1994). Lecturer: Postgrad. Sch. for Advanced Urban Studies, Univ. of Bristol, 1991–94; in Politics, Univ. of Newcastle upon Tyne, 1994–97; Hd, Policy Promotion, Local Govt Internat. Bureau, 1997–99. MEP (Lab) NE Region, 1999–2004. Former Chm., Northern Film & Media; Man. Dir, MOPA Public Affairs, 2004–05; England Partnership Manager, NESTA, 2005–08. Publications: Prélèvement Obligatoire: a transitional comparison of European local taxation systems, 1991; Rebuilding the City: property led regeneration in the UK, 1992; An Evaluation of the Castlemilk Initiative for the Scottish Office, 1995; Regulation Theory and the British State, 1996.

**O'TOOLE, Liam Bernard**, PhD; Chief Executive Officer, Versus Arthritis (formerly Arthritis Research UK), since 2009; b Liverpool, 27 Nov. 1960; s of Bernard O'Toole and Anne O'Toole; m 1992, Sarah Davidson; two s one d. Educ: Tiffin Sch., Kingston upon Thames; University Coll. of North Wales, Bangor (BSc); Univ. of Sheffield (PhD 1988). Post-doctoral Res. Asst, Dept of Biol. and Pre-clinical Medicine, Univ. of St Andrews, 1987–89; Royal Soc./CNRS Exchange Fellow, Univ. of Nice, 1989; Res. Information Officer, British Diabetic Assoc., 1990–92; Medical Research Council: Res. Prog. Manager, Physiol Med. Infections Bd, 1992; Internat. Section Prog. Manager, 1992–94; Clin. Trials Manager, 1994–97; Prog. Manager, Molecular and Cellular Medicine Bd, 1997–2001; Admin. Dir, NCRI, 2001–04; CEO, UK Clinical Res. Collaboration, 2004–08; Hd, Office for Strategic Co-ordination of Health Res., 2007–09. Member, Committee: Adv. Bd to Wales Office for Res. and Develt for Health and Social Care, 2007–; User Panel, EPSRC, 2008–09; Mem., Exec. Council, AMRC, 2012–. Publications: contrib. articles to Clin. Oncol., Nature Reviews Cancer, Annals of Oncol., Eur. Jl of Cancer. Recreations: family, Rugby, scuba diving, tennis. Address: Versus Arthritis, Copeman House, St Mary's Court, St Mary's Gate, Chesterfield, Derbys S41 7TD. T: 0300 790 0400.

**O'TOOLE, Rt Rev. Mark Anthony**; see Plymouth, Bishop of, (RC).

**O'TOOLE, Mo**; see O'Toole, B. M.

**OTTAWA, Bishop of**, since 2007; **Rt Rev. John Holland Chapman**; b Ottawa, 19 Jan. 1954; s of Ven. William Donald Chapman and Jean Chapman (née Holland); m 1976, Catherine Elizabeth Brabazon; two s one d. Educ: Carleton Univ., Ottawa (BA 1975); Huron Coll., Univ. of Western Ontario (MDiv 1978); Univ. of the South, Sewanee (DMin 1984); Huron Univ. Coll. (DD 2008). Ordained deacon, 1978, priest, 1978; Asst Curate, St Matthias', Ottawa, 1978–79; Chaplain, Huron Coll., 1979–83; Lectr, Huron Univ. Coll., 1983–87; Rector, St Jude's, London, Ont, 1987–99; Prof. in Pastoral Theol., 1999–2001, Dean of Theol., 2001–07, Huron Coll. Address: Anglican Diocese of Ottawa, 71 Bronson Avenue, Ottawa, ON K1R 6G6, Canada.

**OTTAWAY, Rt Hon. Sir Richard (Geoffrey James)**; Kt 2014; PC 2013; b 24 May 1945; s of late Professor Christopher Ottaway, PhD, FRCVS and Grace Ottaway; m 1982, Nicola E. Kisch. Educ: Backwell Secondary Modern School, Somerset; Bristol University. LLB (Hons). Entered RN as an Artificer apprentice, 1961; commissioned and entered RNC, Dartmouth, 1966; served with Western Fleet, HM Ships Beechampton, Nubian and Eagle, 1967–70; Bristol Univ., 1971–74; articled to Norton Rose Botterell & Roche, 1974; admitted Solicitor, 1977; specialist in international, maritime and commercial law; Partner, William A. Crump & Son, 1981–87. Dir, Coastal Europe Ltd, 1988–95. MP (C) Nottingham N, 1983–87; contested (C) same seat, 1987; MP (C) Croydon S, 1992–2015. PPS to Ministers of State, FCO, 1985–87, to Pres. of BoT, 1992–95, to Dep. Prime Minister, 1995; an Asst Govt Whip, 1995–96; a Lord Comr of HM Treasury (Govt Whip), 1996–97; an Opposition Whip, 1997; Opposition front bench spokesman on: local govt and London, 1997–98; defence, 1999–2000; Treasury, 2000–01; the envmt, 2004–05. Chm., Foreign Affairs Select Cttee, 2010–15 (Mem., 2003–04); Member: Standards and Privileges Select Cttee, 2001–04; Parly Intelligence and Security Cttee, 2005–10. Vice-Chm., 1922 Cttee, 2005–10. Chm., All-Party Parly Gp on Population and Development, 1992–95. A Vice-Chm., 1998–99, Mem. Bd, 2006–10, Cons. Party. Chm., Margaret Pyke Trust, 2015–. Publications: (jtly) Road to Reform, 1987; (jtly) Privatisation 1979–1994, 1994; Has London lost its confidence?, 2002; papers on combating internat. maritime fraud, on financial matters and on the environment. Recreations: jazz, yacht racing. Clubs: Royal Thames Yacht, Royal Ocean Racing, Island Sailing.

**OTTER, Stephen**, QPM 2009; non-executive Director, Taunton and Somerset NHS Foundation Trust, since 2015; b Bethnal Green, 24 May 1962; s of Tony and Rosemary Otter; m 2005, Sophie Hamer; three s one d. Educ: London Sch. of Econs (MSc(Econ) Criminal Justice Studies); Fitzwilliam Coll., Cambridge (Postgrad. Dip. Applied Criminol.). Patrol Constable, Maidenhead, Thames Valley Police, 1982–85; Patrol Inspector, 1985–87, Detective Inspector, 1987–88, Tsim Sha Tsui, Royal Hong Kong Police; Metropolitan Police: Constable, 1989–91; Sergeant, 1991–93; Inspector, 1994–96; Chief Inspector, 1996–97; Superintendent, 1997–98; Bor. Comdr (Chief Superintendent), 1998–2001; Comdr, 2001–02; Asst Chief Constable, 2002–04, Dep. Chief Constable, 2004–07, Avon and Somerset Police; Chief Constable, Devon and Cornwall Constabulary, 2007–12; HM Inspector of Constabulary, 2012–16. Dir, Robus Solutions Ltd, 2016–; Chm., Pluss Ltd, 2016–19. FRSA. Recreations: yoga, rowing, reading, gardening. Club: Exeter Rowing.

**OTTOLENGHI, Yotam**; food writer; chef/patron of Ottolenghi and NOPI, London; b Jerusalem, 14 Dec. 1968; s of Michael and Ruth Ottolenghi; civil partnership 2011, Karl Allen; two s. Educ: Tel Aviv Univ. (MA Philosophy and Comparative Lit. 1997); Cordon Bleu Cookery Sch., London. Pastry chef, The Capital, Knightsbridge, 1997; pastry section, Kensington Place and Launceston Place, London, 1998; Hd Pastry Chef, Baker & Spice, London, 1999–2000; opened Ottolenghi Deli, Notting Hill, 2002, Islington, 2004, Kensington, 2005, Belgravia, 2007, Spitalfields, 2015; opened NOPI restaurant, 2011. Television series: Jerusalem on a Plate, 2011; Ottolenghi's Mediterranean Feasts, 2012; Ottolenghi's Mediterranean Island Feasts, 2013. Publications: Ottolenghi: The Cookbook, 2008; Plenty, 2010; (with Sam Tamimi) Jerusalem, 2012; Plenty More, 2014; (with Ramael Scully) NOPI, 2015; (with Helen Goh) Sweet, 2017; Simple, 2018. Recreations: pilates, eating out, travelling.

**OTTON, Sir Geoffrey (John)**, KCB 1981 (CB 1978); Second Permanent Secretary, Department of Health and Social Security, 1979–86, retired; b 10 June 1927; s of late John Alfred Otton and Constance Alma Otton; m 1952, Hazel Lomas (née White); one s one d. Educ: Christ's Hosp.; St John's Coll., Cambridge (MA). Home Office, 1950–71: (seconded to Cabinet Office, 1959–61; Principal Private Sec. to Home Sec., 1963–65); Dept of Health and Social Security, 1971–86. Recreation: music. Address: 45 Jenner Court, St Georges Road, Cheltenham GL50 3ER. T: (01242) 227390.

**OTTON, Rt Hon. Sir Philip (Howard),** Kt 1983; PC 1995; FCIArb; a Lord Justice of Appeal, 1995–2001; Judge of the Court of Appeal, Gibraltar, 2003–08; Judge of Civil and Commercial Court, Qatar, 2006–11; arbitrator and mediator, 2001–16; *b* 28 May 1933; *o s* of late Henry Albert Otton and Leah Otton, Kenilworth; *m* 1965, Helen Margaret, *d* of late P. W. Bates, Stourbridge; two *s* one *d*. *Educ:* Bablake School, Coventry; Birmingham Univ. (LLB 1954). Chartered Arbitrator 2007. 2nd Lieut, 3rd Dragoon Guards, 1955–57. Called to the Bar, Gray's Inn, 1955, Bencher 1983; QC 1975. Dep. Chm., Beds QS, 1970–72; Junior Counsel to the Treasury (Personal Injuries), 1970–75; a Recorder of the Crown Court, 1972–83; Judge of the High Court, QBD, 1983–95; Presiding Judge, Midland and Oxford Circuit, 1986–88; Judge in Charge of Official Referees Courts, 1991–95. Surveillance Comr, 2001–10; Appeals Adjudicator, Enemy Property Claims Assessment Panel Schemes, BEIS, 2011–19. Chairman: Royal Brompton and National Heart and Lung Hospitals SHA, 1991–94; Royal Brompton and Harefield (formerly Royal Brompton Hosp.) NHS Trust, 1994–2002; Nat. Heart and Lung Inst., 1991–95. Non-exec. Dir, Equitable Life Assurance Soc., 2001–03. President: Soc. of Construction Law, 1995–2004; Bar Disability Panel, 1996–2001; Professional Negligence Bar Assoc., 1997–2001; Personal Injury Bar Assoc., 2000–02. Mem., Middle Temple, 2007–. Mem., Transitional Med. Bd, Imperial Coll. Sch. of Medicine, 1995–2002. Governor, Nat. Heart and Chest Hosps, 1979–85. Trustee: Migraine Trust, 1992–98; Media Standards Trust, 2007–13. Pres., Holdsworth Club, Birmingham Univ., 2000–01. Visitor, Univ. of Essex, 2001–05. Hon. Legal Advr, OStJ, 2001–08. Convenor, FA Premier League, 2004–16; Mem., Disciplinary Panel, Formula 1 Internat. Court of Appeal, 2010–16. Fellow: Inst. of Advanced Legal Studies, 1999; Amer. Law Inst., 2000; Hon. Fellow, Inst. of Judicial Admin, Birmingham Univ., 1995. Hon. Mem., Amer. Bar Assoc. FCIArb (Mediation) 1994; FRSocMed 1998. Hon. LLD: Nottingham Trent, 1997; Birmingham, 2007; DU Essex, 2006. Award of Merit, City of Coventry, 2005. *Recreations:* theatre, opera, music, walking. *Address:* The Bell House, Taynton, near Burford, Oxon OX18 4UH. *Clubs:* Garrick, Pilgrims.

**OTTON-GOULDER, Catharine Anne;** QC 2000; a Recorder, since 2000; a Deputy High Court Judge, since 2008; a Deemster, Isle of Man, since 2008; *b* 9 April 1955; *e d* of late Prof. Michael Douglas Goulder, DD and Alison Clare (*née* Gardner). *Educ:* Somerville Coll., Oxford (BA 1st Cl. Hons Lit. Hum. 1977). Admitted as solicitor, 1980; called to the Bar, Lincoln's Inn, 1983; Mem., Brick Court Chambers, 1984–; Asst Recorder, 1997–2000. Reader, C of E, 1998–. *Address:* Brick Court Chambers, 7–8 Essex Street, WC2R 3LD.

**OTTOW, Prof. Annetje,** PhD; Professor of Public Economic Law, Europa Institute, since 2007, and Vice-President, Executive Board, since 2018, Utrecht University (Dean, Faculty of Law, Economics and Governance, 2014–18); *b* 10 Aug. 1965; *m* Ton Tekstra; one *s*. *Educ:* Leiden Univ. (LLM *cum laude* 1988); Queen Mary Coll., Univ. of London (LLM 1990); Univ. of Amsterdam (PhD 2006). Admitted to Bar of Netherlands, 1990; Attorney: De Brauw Blackstone Westbroek, The Hague, Rotterdam and Brussels, 1990–95; Houthoff Buruma, 1995–2001, Partner, Regulatory and Competition Div., 1997–2001; Sen. Researcher and Lectr, Inst. for Information Law, Univ. of Amsterdam, 2001–06. Visiting Professor: Florence Sch. of Regulation, Eur. Univ. Inst. of Florence, 2011; Competition Law Center, George Washington Univ., 2012; Chinese Univ. of Hong Kong, 2013. Founder, Tijdschrift voor Toezicht, 2010. Non-Govtl Advr to Internat. Competition Network, 2009. Mem. Bd, Ind. Post and Telecommunications Authy, Netherlands, 2006–13 (Vice Pres., 2012–13); Chm. (Internal), Strategy Cttee, Authority Consumer Mkts, Netherlands, 2012–13. Non-exec. Dir, CMA, 2013–18. Member, Supervisory Board: VU Univ. Amsterdam and VU Univ. Med. Center, 2013–16; Het Juridisch Loket, 2013–. *Publications:* (contrib.) EU Agencies in - and - the External Relations of the EU, 2014; (contrib. with C. A. Fonteijn) Mundi et Europae Civis: liber amicorum Jacques Steenbergen, 2014; Market and Competition Authorities: good agency principles, 2015; contribs to Jl Antitrust Enforcement, Eur. Contract Law, Utrecht Law Rev. *Recreations:* cycling, yoga. *Address:* Janskerkhof 3, 3512 BK Utrecht, Netherlands. *T:* 302537091. *E:* a.t.ottow@uu.nl.

**OTTY, Timothy John;** QC 2006; *b* 12 Aug. 1967; *s* of Neville and Jean Otty; *m* 1998, Gabriella Ricciardi; two *d*. *Educ:* Tower House Prep. Sch.; St Paul's Sch.; Trinity Coll., Cambridge (exhibnr, BA 1989, MA 1992); Inns of Court Sch. of Law. Volunteer worker: Mother Teresa's Home for destitute and dying, 1989; Royal Hosp. for Neurodisability, 1990–98. Called to the Bar, Lincoln's Inn, 1990 (Tancred Schol.; European Bursary Award); Virgin Islands, 2014. Stagiaire, Eur. Commn of Human Rights, 1993; Vice Chm., Bar Human Rights Cttee of England and Wales, 2005–10. Member: Attorney General's Treasury Panel, 2003–06; Exec. Cttee and Council, Commonwealth Lawyers' Assoc., 2005–; Exec. Cttee, Human Rights Lawyers Assoc., 2009–; Foreign Sec.'s Adv. Gp on Human Rights, 2010–15. UK Rep., Venice Commn, 2019–. Vis. Lecturer: LSE, 2006–14; Georgetown Univ., 2010; Visiting Fellow: Mansfield Coll., Oxford, 2009–10; King's Coll. London, 2016–. Trustee, British Inst. of Internat. and Comparative Law, 2011–13. Chm., Human Dignity Trust, 2011–16; Trustee, Irene Taylor Music in Prisons Trust, 2007–13. Mem., Editl Bd, Eur. Human Rights Law Rev., 2008–. Judges' Commendation, Bar Council Pro Bono Award, 2007; Liberty and Justice Human Rights Lawyer of the Year, 2008. *Publications:* (contrib.) Sweet & Maxwell's Human Rights Practice, 2001. *Recreations:* marathon running, golf, Liverpool FC, Italy, cinema, theatre, tennis. *Address:* Blackstone Chambers, Temple, EC4Y 9BW. *T:* (020) 7583 1770, *Fax:* (020) 7822 7350. *Clubs:* Athenæum; Serpentine Running.

**OUABDESSLAM, Gabrielle Helen Louise;** *see* Huddart, G. H. L.

**OUDKERK, Daniel Richard;** QC 2010; *b* 9 April 1969; *s* of Patrick Oudkerk and Ann Oudkerk; *m* 2001, Joanna Pollard; three *s*. *Educ:* Univ. of Bristol (LLB Hons). Called to the Bar, Inner Temple, 1992; in practice as barrister, specialising in commercial and employment law. *Recreations:* ski-ing, cycling, wild brown trout. *Address:* Essex Court Chambers, 24 Lincoln's Inn Fields, WC2A 3EG. *T:* (020) 7813 8000. *E:* doudkerk@essexcourt.net.

**OUELLET, Hon. André;** PC (Can.) 1972; QC (Can.) 1992; President and Chief Executive Officer, Canada Post Corporation, 1999–2004 (Chairman, 1996–99); *b* St Pascal, Quebec, 6 April 1939; *s* of Albert Ouellet and Rita Turgeon; *m* 1965, Édith Pagé; two *s* two *d*. *Educ:* Univ. of Ottawa (BA 1960); Univ. of Sherbrooke (LLL 1963). Called to the Bar. MP (L): Montreal-Papineau, 1967–88; Papineau-St-Michel, 1988–96; PMG, 1972–74; Minister: for Consumer and Corporate Affairs, 1974–76; of Urban Affairs, 1976–78; of Public Works, 1978–79; PMG 1980–84, and Minister for Consumer and Corporate Affairs, 1980–83; Minister of Labor, 1983–84; Minister of State for Regl Economic Develt, 1984; Pres., Privy Council and Govt Leader in H of C, 1984; Minister of Foreign Affairs, 1993–96. Hon. Dr Ottawa, 1995. *Recreations:* golf, reading, theatre. *Address:* 17 Chase Court, Ottawa, ON K1V 9Y6, Canada.

**OUELLET, His Eminence Cardinal Marc;** Prefect of the Congregation for Bishops, and President, Pontifical Commission for Latin America, since 2010, PSS; *b* 8 June 1944. *Educ:* Amos Teacher Training Coll., Quebec; Grand Séminaire de Montréal (LTh Univ. of Montreal 1968); St Thomas Aquinas Pontifical Univ., Rome (LPh 1976); Gregorian Univ., Rome (Dr Dogmatic Theol. 1983). Ordained priest, 1968; Curate, St Sauveur, Val d'Or, 1968–70; teacher of philosophy, Major Seminary, Bogota; Faculty Member and Professor: Major Seminary, Manizales, Columbia, 1974; Grand Séminaire de Montréal; Major Seminary, Cali, Columbia, 1983 (Rector, 1984–89); Rector: Grand Séminaire de Montréal, 1990; St Joseph's Seminary, Edmonton, 1994; Titular Chair of Dogmatic Theol., John Paul II Inst., Lateran Pontifical Univ., 1996–2002; Sec., Pontifical Council for the Promotion of Christian Unity, 2001–03; Titular Bp, Agropoli, 2001; Cardinal, 2003; Archbishop of Quebec, (RC), and Primate of Canada, 2003–10.

**OUGHTON, John Raymond Charles;** Second Permanent Secretary and Chief Executive, Office of Government Commerce, HM Treasury, 2004–07 (Deputy Chief Executive, 2003–04); *b* 21 Sept. 1952; *s* of late Peggy Oughton. *Educ:* Reading Sch.; University Coll., Oxford (BA Mod. Hist. 1974). Joined MoD, 1974; Mem. UK Delegn, UN Law of Sea Conf., 1978; Asst Pvte Sec. to Minister of State for Defence, 1978–80; on secondment to Canadian Govt, 1980–81; Sales Policy, 1981–83; Office of Personal Advr to Sec. of State for Defence, 1984; Pvte Sec. to Minister for the Armed Forces, 1984–86; Sen. Principal, Directorate of Procurement Policy, 1986–87; Asst Sec., Dir of Procurement Policy, 1988–89; Head of Resources and Plans (Navy), 1990–93; Office of Public Service, Cabinet Office: Under Sec. and Head, Govt Efficiency Unit, 1993–98; Dir, Efficiency and Effectiveness Gp, 1996–98; Ministry of Defence: Dep. Under-Sec. of State, 1998; Hd, Chief of Defence Logistics Implementation Team, 1998–99; Dep. Chief of Defence Logistics, 1999–2003. Interim Man. Dir, KMG Gp, 2008. FRSA; FCIPS. *Recreations:* squash, badminton, travel, watching cricket and football. *Address:* 1 Adderley Grove, SW11 6NA. *T:* (020) 7223 5793. *E:* johnoughton@yahoo.co.uk. *Clubs:* Oxford and Cambridge; Tottenham Hotspur Football, Middlesex CC.

**OULTON, Claire Marion,** MA; Head of Leadership Appointments, RSAcademics Ltd, since 2015; *b* 23 July 1961; *d* of Prof. L. Zisman and S. Zisman; *m* 1986, Nicholas Oulton; two *d*. *Educ:* Somerville Coll., Oxford (BA Hons History 1983; MA 1994); KCL (PGCE 1984). Teacher of History, Benenden Sch., 1984–88; Head of History, Charterhouse, 1988–94; Headmistress: St Catherine's Sch., Guildford, 1994–2000; Benenden Sch., 2000–13. Governor: Charterhouse, 2003; John Wallis Acad., Ashford, 2010–14. Trustee: 1851 Trust, 2014–; RYS Foundn.

**OULTON, Rt Rev. Michael Douglas;** *see* Ontario, Bishop of.

**OUNSTED, Deborah Clare, (Mrs Richard Walker-Arnott),** CBE 2014; non-executive Director: Funding Affordable Homes SICAV SIF, since 2015; Funding Affordable Homes Housing Association, since 2015; *b* Reading, 1 June 1951; *d* of John Ounsted and Irene Ounsted (*née* Newns); *m* 1988, Richard Walker-Arnott; one *s* one *d*. *Educ:* Abbey Sch., Reading; Girton Coll., Cambridge (MA Modern and Mediaeval Langs); Oxford Brookes Poly. (Postgrad. Dip. Publishing). Local govt officer, GLC and London Bor. of Islington, 1972–78; Area Manager, Circle 33 Housing Trust, 1978–83; Chief Executive: Habinteg Housing Association, 1983–92; Octavia Hill Housing Trust, 1992–2000. Chairman: Joseph Rowntree Housing Trust, 2006–11 (Trustee, 2002–11); Joseph Rowntree Foundn, 2006–11 (Trustee, 2002–11; Vice Chm., 2004–06). Mem. Council, Gresham Coll., 2015–. Governor: Thomas Telford Sch., 2009–18 (Vice Chm., 2012–18); Hammersmith Acad., 2011–19. Mem., Ct of Assts, Mercers' Co., 2008– (Master, 2014–15). *Publications:* Wheelchairs, No Handicap in Housing, 1987; Getting into Housing, 2001, 2nd edn 2003. *Recreation:* learning new things. *Address:* Flat 116, Dorset House, Gloucester Place, NW1 5AG.

**OUSELEY,** Baron *cr* 2001 (Life Peer), of Peckham Rye in the London Borough of Southwark; **Herman George Ouseley,** Kt 1997; President, Different Realities Partnership Ltd, 2006–10 (Managing Director, 2000–06); non-executive Director, Focus Consultancy Ltd, 2000–10; *b* 24 March 1945; *m* 1972, Margaret Neill; one *s* one *d*. Various public service posts, 1963–86; Race Relations Adviser: Lambeth BC, 1979–81; GLC, 1981–84; Dir of Educn, 1986–88, Chief Exec., 1988–90, ILEA; Chief Exec., London Borough of Lambeth, 1990–93; Chm., CRE, 1993–2000. Mem., H of L, 2001–19. Member: Council, Inst. of Race Relations, 1990–; Council, FA, 2008–13; Chair: Kick It Out, 1994–2019; Chandran Foundn (formerly PRESET Educn and Employment Charitable Trust), 1997–2019; Patron: Presentation Housing Assoc., 1990–2000; Daneford Trust, 1998–2018; Helena Kennedy Foundn, 2003–18; Reach Soc., 2014–19. Non-exec. Dir, Brooknight Security, 1995–2005, 2015–. Pres., LGA, 2001–04 (Vice Pres., 2010–19). Trustee, Manchester United Foundn, 2007–16. *Publications:* The System, 1981; pamphlets and articles on local government, public services, employment, training and race equality issues.

**OUSELEY, Hon. Sir Duncan (Brian Walter),** Kt 2000; a Judge of the High Court, Queen's Bench Division, 2000–19; *b* 24 Feb. 1950; *s* of late Maurice and Margaret Ouseley; *m* 1974, Suzannah Price; three *s*. *Educ:* Trinity Sch., Croydon; Fitzwilliam Coll., Cambridge (MA; Hon. Fellow, 2011); University Coll. London (LLM). Called to the Bar, Gray's Inn, 1973 (Atkin Scholar 1972); Bencher 2000; Junior Counsel to the Crown, Common Law, 1986–92; QC 1992; a Recorder, 1994–2000; QC (NI) 1997; Jt Hd of Chambers, 2000; Lead Judge, Admin. Court, 2010–15. Pres., Immigration Appeal Tribunal, 2003–05; Chm., Special Immigration Appeal Commn, 2003–06. Chairman, Examination in Public Shropshire Structure Plan, 1985, Hampshire Structure Plan, 1991. Vice-Chm. Planning and Envmt, Bar Assoc., 2000. *Recreations:* family, sport, music, wine. *Club:* Garrick.

**OUSTON, Hugh Anfield;** educational consultant, since 2014; Head, Robert Gordon's College, Aberdeen, 2004–14; Warden, Glenalmond College, 2019–April 2020; *b* Dundee, 4 April 1952; *s* of Philip and Elizabeth Ouston; *m* 1988, Yvonne Caroline Young; two *s* two *d*. *Educ:* Glenalmond Coll.; Christ Church, Univ. of Oxford (BA Hons); Univ. of Aberdeen (DipEd). Teacher of History, N Berwick High Sch., 1977–84; Hd of History, Beeslack High Sch., 1984–92; Asst Hd, Dunbar Grammar Sch., 1992–97; Dep. Principal, George Watson's Coll., Edinburgh, 1997–2004. *Recreations:* bird watching, gardening, hill walking.

**OUTHWAITE, Wendy Jane Tivnan;** QC 2009; producer of Ambriel English sparkling wine; *b* Taplow, Bucks, 11 July 1965; *d* of Ian and Carol Guthrie; *m* 1994, Charles Outhwaite; three *s* one *d*. *Educ:* Wycombe Abbey; St Hugh's Coll., Oxford (MA Juris.); Institut d'Etudes Européennes, Brussels (License special en droit Européen). Called to the Bar, Lincoln's Inn, 1990; barrister specialising in torts and judicial review, 1990–2012. *Publications:* The Civil Practitioner's Guide to the Human Rights Act, 2000; (contrib.) Healthcare Law: the impact of the Human Rights Act 1998, 2000; (contrib.) Burnett Hall on Environmental Law, 2nd edn 2008. *Recreations:* boxing, wine.

**OUTLAW, Nathan Daniel;** Chef Patron, Nathan Outlaw Restaurants Ltd, since 2009; *b* Maidstone, 7 March 1978; *s* of Clive and Sharon Outlaw; *m* 2001, Rachel Morris; one *s* one *d*. *Educ:* Holmesdale Sch., Snodland, Kent; Thanet Coll. Chef: Intercontinental Hotel, Hyde Park Corner, London, 1996–97; Chavot Restaurant, Fulham, 1997–98; 2nd chef, Seafood Restaurant, Padstow, Cornwall, 1998–99; sous chef, Lords of the Manor, Gloucester, 1999–2001; Head Chef, Vineyard at Stockcross, Berks, 2001–03; Chef/Proprietor, The Black Pig, Rock, Cornwall, 2003–04; Head Chef: St Ervan Manor, Padstow, 2005–06; Restaurant Nathan Outlaw, Marina Villa Hotel, Fowey, Cornwall,

2007–09; Proprietor/Chef: Restaurant Nathan Outlaw (formerly Nathan Outlaw Seafood Grill), St Enodoc Hotel, Rock, 2009–15 (2 Michelin Stars, 2010); Outlaw's Fish Kitchen, Port Isaac, Cornwall, 2013–; The Mariners Public House, Rock, Cornwall, 2014–19; Restaurant Nathan Outlaw, Port Isaac, Cornwall, 2015– (2 Michelin Stars, 2015); Consultant Chef, Outlaw's Seafood and Grill at The Capital Hotel, Knightsbridge, 2012–19 (1 Michelin Star, 2014); Consultant Chef, Siren at The Goring Hotel, Belgravia, 2019–. *Publications:* Nathan Outlaw's British Seafood, 2012; Nathan Outlaw's Fish Kitchen, 2014; Nathan Outlaw's Everyday Seafood, 2016; Nathan Outlaw's Home Kitchen, 2017; Restaurant Nathan Outlaw, 2019. *Recreations:* collecting cookery books, Star Wars, spending time with family. *Address:* Restaurant Nathan Outlaw, 6 New Road, Port Isaac, Cornwall PL29 3SB. *E:* RNO@nathan-outlaw.com.

**OUTRAM, Sir Alan James,** 5th Bt *cr* 1858; MA; *b* 15 May 1937; *s* of late James Ian Outram and late Evelyn Mary Littlehales; *S* great-uncle, 1945; *m* 1976, Victoria Jean, *d* of late George Dickson Paton, Bexhill-on-Sea; one *s* one *d*. *Educ:* Spyway, Langton Matravers, Swanage; Marlborough College, Wilts; St Edmund Hall, Oxford. Harrow School: Asst Master, 1961–98; Housemaster, 1979–91; Under Master, 1992–96. Lt-Col TAVR. Pres., Dorset LTA, 1995–2005, now Life Vice-Pres. *Recreations:* music, bridge, cycling. *Heir: s* Douglas Benjamin James Outram, *b* 15 March 1979. *Address:* 2 St Ann Street, Salisbury, Wilts SP1 2DN. *Club:* Vincent's (Oxford).

**OUYANG, Prof. Wen-Chin,** PhD; FBA 2018; Professor of Arabic and Comparative Literature, School of Oriental and African Studies, University of London, since 2013; *b* Taipei, Taiwan, 28 Sept. 1960; *d* of Chi-Chang Ouyang and Lin Yen-Fang Ouyang; *m* 2005, Lun-Yun Chang (*d* 2018). *Educ:* Univ. of al-Fatih, Tripoli (BA, BEd 1982); Columbia Univ., New York (MA 1986; MPhil 1987; PhD 1992). Asst Prof. of Arabic Lang. and Lit., 1991–97, Associate Prof., 1997, Univ. of Virginia; Lectr in Arabic, 1997–2005, Sen. Lectr in Arabic Lit., 2005–08, Reader in Arabic Lit., 2008–13, SOAS, Univ. of London. Vis. Prof. of Arabic, Nat. Cheng-Chi Univ., Taipei, 2010–11; Visiting Lecturer: Univ. of Chicago, 1993; in Arabic, Univ. of Cambridge, 2000; Fall Fellow, Centre for Study of Islam and Society, Univ. of Leiden, 2016. Interdisciplinary Mem., REF Main Panel D, 2018–. Member: Albert Hourani Annual Book Award Cttee, 2002–03; Judging Panel: Man Booker Internat. Prize for Fiction, 2013–15; Dryden Translation Prize, British Comparative Lit. Assoc., 2015–; Saif Ghobash Banipal Arabic Literary Translation Prize, 2016–17. Member: Exec. Cttee, British Comparative Lit. Assoc., 2013–20; Council, Soc. for Libyan Studies, 2015–19. Regl Ed., Bulletin of SOAS, 2003–13; Ed.-in-Chief, Middle Eastern Literatures, 2011–; Mem., Editl Bd, Jl Libyan Studies, 2014–; Co-Chair, Publications Cttee, Legenda Studies in Comparative Lit., British Comparative Lit. Assoc., 2017–. Founder and Series Co-Ed., Edinburgh Studies in Classical Arabic Lit., 2010–. *Publications:* Literary Criticism in Medieval Arabic Islamic Culture: the making of a tradition, 1997; (ed) New Perspectives on the Arabian Nights: ideological variations and narrative horizons, 2005; (ed with S. Hart) Companion to Magical Realism, 2005; Poetics of Love in the Arabic Novel: nation-state, modernity and tradition, 2012; Politics of Nostalgia in the Arabic Novel: nation-state, modernity and tradition, 2013; (ed) The Arabian Nights: an anthology of 19th century English translations, 2014; contribs to learned jls incl. Arabic Lit., Arabic and Middle Eastern Literatures, Middle Eastern Literatures, Jl Qur'anic Studies, Comparative Critical Studies, Modern Langs Qly, Oriente Moderno, Al-Masaq: Jl Medieval Mediterranean, Alif: a Jl Comparative Poetics, Bull. SOAS. *Recreations:* cinema, theatre, classical music, art, travel, world culinary cultures. *Address:* School of Oriental and African Studies, University of London, Thornhaugh Street, Russell Square, WC1H 0XG. *T:* (020) 7898 4348. *E:* wo@soas.ac.uk.

**OVENDEN, Rev. Canon John Anthony,** LVO 2007; Fellow and Dean of Chapel, Harris Manchester College, Oxford, 2012–15; Chaplain, Mansfield College, Oxford, since 2014; *b* 26 May 1945; *s* of Rev. Edward and Marjorie Ovenden; *m* 1974, Christine Ann Broadhurst; two *s* one *d*. *Educ:* St Paul's Cathedral Choir Sch.; Ardingly Coll.; Borough Rd Coll. of Educn; Southampton Univ. (DipTh 1974); Salisbury and Wells Theol Coll.; Open Univ. (BA Hons 1980, 1993); King's Coll. London (MA 1996); Univ. of Oxford (MA 2012). Ordained deacon, 1974, priest, 1975; Assistant Curate: Handsworth, Sheffield, 1974–77; Uckfield, and Priest in Charge of Isfield, Sussex, 1977–80; Precentor and Sacrist, Ely Cathedral, 1980–85; Vicar, St Mary's, Primrose Hill, 1985–98; Canon of Windsor, Chaplain in the Great Park and Chaplain, Cumberland Lodge, 1998–2012 (Fellow, 2014); Canon Chaplain, 1998–2012, Canon Precentor, 2007–12, Canon Emeritus, 2012–, St George's Chapel. Chaplain to the Queen, 2002–15. Golden Jubilee Medal, 2002; Diamond Jubilee Medal, 2012. *Publications:* (contrib.) Christians and Muslims in the Commonwealth: a dynamic role in the future, ed Anthony O'Mahony and Ataullah Siddiqui, 2001. *Recreations:* theatre-going and concert-going, music, walking, reading. *Address:* Little Croft, Great Rissington, Cheltenham, Glos GL54 2LN.

**OVENDEN, Richard,** OBE 2019; FSA; Bodley's Librarian, University of Oxford, since 2014; Fellow, Balliol College, Oxford, since 2014; *b* Deal, Kent, 25 March 1964; *s* of Stanley and Betty Doreen Ovenden; *m* 1994, Lyn Youngson; two *d*. *Educ:* Sir Roger Manwood's Sch.; Durham Univ. (BA Hons 1985); University Coll. London (DipLib 1987; MA 1987). Asst Librarian, H of L Liby, 1987–89; Curator, Nat. Liby of Scotland, 1989–99; Hd, Special Collections, Edinburgh Univ. Liby, 1999–2002; Dir of Collections, Edinburgh Univ., 2002–03; Bodleian Library: Keeper, Special Collections, 2003–12; Dep. Librarian, 2012–14. Mem. Bd, Council on Liby and Inf. Resources; Treas., Consortium of Eur. Res. Libraries; Pres., Digital Preservation Coalition. Mem. Council, Univ. of Oxford, 2017–. Mem., American Philosophical Soc., 2015. FSA 2007. FRSA 2006. Hon. Fellow, St Hugh's Coll., Oxford, 2014. *Publications:* John Thomson (1837–1921): photographer, 1997; (jtly) A Radical's Books, 1999; contribs to jls on book history, history of photography, information sci. *Recreations:* photography, art galleries, cooking, family life. *Address:* Bodleian Library, Broad Street, Oxford OX1 3BG. *T:* (01865) 277158. *E:* richard.ovenden@bodleian.ox.ac.uk. *Clubs:* Roxburghe; Grolier (New York).

**OVERBURY, Rupert Simon; His Honour Judge Overbury;** a Circuit Judge, since 2007; *b* Aldershot, 26 Dec. 1957; *s* of late (Henry) Colin (Barry) Overbury, CBE and of Dawn Rhodes Overbury (*née* Dade, now Boyd); *m* 1996, Claire Elizabeth Brett; two *s*. *Educ:* Framlingham Coll.; Central London Poly. (BA Hons Law). Called to the Bar, Middle Temple, 1984; barrister, 3 New Square, Lincoln's Inn, 1984–93, 18 Red Lion Court, 1993–2007; Recorder, 2003–07; Diversity and Community Relations Judge for Suffolk, 2015–. Chm., Trustee Bd, Saxmundham and Leiston CAB, 2006–13. Hon. Comdr, 48 Fighter Wing, USAF Judge Advocate Staff, 2015. *Recreations:* fly-fishing, shooting, travel, wood turning. *Address:* Ipswich Crown Court, 1 Russell Road, Ipswich, Suffolk IP1 2AG. *T:* (01473) 228585. *E:* hhj.rupert.overbury@ejudiciary.net.

**OVEREND, Sandra;** Training and Development Manager, Henry Brothers Ltd, since 2017; *b* Magherafelt, 11 May 1973; *d* of Billy and Glynis Armstrong; *m* 1997, Nigel Overend; two *s* one *d*. *Educ:* Cookstown High Sch.; Univ. of Ulster (BA Hons Business Studies). DipHE Accounting; Stonebridge Associated Colls PR. Asst accountant, 1996–98; Office Manager for Billy Armstrong, MLA, 1998–2011; Women's Develt Officer, UU Party, 2008–11. Mem. (UU) Mid-Ulster, NI Assembly, 2011–17; contested (UU) same seat, 2017. Contested (UU) Mid-Ulster, 2015. Chair, Bellaghy Primary Sch. Parents' Assoc., 2010–. Mem., Select Vestry, Ballyscullion Parish Ch. *Recreations:* cycling, reading.

**OVERY, Prof. Richard James,** PhD; FRHistS; FBA 2000; Professor of History, Exeter University, since 2004; *b* 23 Dec. 1947; *s* of James Herbert Overy and Margaret Grace Overy (*née* Sutherland); *m* 1992, Kim Turner (marr. diss. 2004); two *d*, and one *s* two *d* from previous marriage. *Educ:* Sexey's Grammar Sch., Som; Gonville and Caius Coll., Cambridge (BA 1969; MA 1972; PhD 1977). Cambridge University: Res. Fellow, Churchill Coll., 1972–73; Lectr, Queens' Coll., 1973–79; Asst Univ. Lectr, 1976–79; King's College, London: Lectr, 1980–88; Reader, 1988–92; Prof. of Modern Hist., 1992–2004; FKC 2003. Chm., RAF Mus. Research Bd, 2013–. Trustee, RAF Mus., 1999–2003. Mem., Eur. Acad. for Scis and Arts, 2013. FRHistS 1997; FRSA 2006. T. S. Ashton Prize, Econ. Hist. Soc., 1982; Cass Prize, Business Hist. Soc., 1987; Samuel Eliot Morison Prize, Soc., for Mil. Hist., 2001; James Doolittle Award, MIT, 2010. *Publications:* William Morris, Viscount Nuffield, 1976; The Air War 1939–45, 1980; The Nazi Economic Recovery, 1982, 2nd edn 1996; Goering: the Iron Man, 1984, 2nd edn 2000; The Origins of the Second World War, 1987, 2nd edn 1998; The Road to War, 1989, 3rd edn 2009; War and Economy in the Third Reich, 1994; The Interwar Crisis 1919–1939, 1994; Why the Allies Won, 1995; The Penguin Atlas of the Third Reich, 1996, 2nd edn 2000; The Times Atlas of the Twentieth Century, 1996, 2nd edn 1999; Bomber Command 1939–45, 1997; Russia's War, 1998; (Gen. Ed.) The Times History of the World, 1999, 9th edn 2015; The Battle, 2000; Interrogations: the Nazi elite in Allied hands 1945, 2001; The Dictators, 2004 (Wolfson History Prize, Hessell Tiltman Prize for History, 2005); The Morbid Age: Britain between the wars, 2009; 1939: countdown to war, 2009; The Third Reich: a chronicle, 2010; The Bombing War: Europe 1939–1945, 2013 (Cundill Award, 2014); A History of War in 100 Battles, 2014; (ed) Oxford Illustrated History of World War II, 2015; The Birth of the RAF, 1918, 2018; contrib. to Econ. Hist. Rev., Jl of Strategic Studies, Past and Present, English Histl Rev., etc. *Recreation:* opera. *Address:* Department of History, University of Exeter, Amory Building, Rennes Drive, Exeter EX4 4RJ. *E:* r.overy@ex.ac.uk. *Club:* Academy.

**OWADA, Hisashi;** a Judge, 2003–18, and President, 2009–12, International Court of Justice; *b* Niigata, Japan, 18 Sept. 1932; *s* of Takeo Owada and Shizuka Tamura; *m* 1962, Yumiko Egashira; three *d*. *Educ:* Univ. of Tokyo (BA 1955); Univ. of Cambridge (LLB 1956). Joined Foreign Service of Japan; Private Secretary: to Foreign Minister, 1971–72; to Prime Minister, 1976–78; Principal Legal Advr and Dir-Gen., Treaties Bureau, Foreign Ministry, 1984–87; Dep. Foreign Minister, 1989–91; Vice Foreign Minister, 1991–93; Advr to Foreign Minister, 1999–2003; Permanent Representative: to OECD, 1988–89; to UN, 1994–98 (Pres., Security Council, 1997, 1998). Sen. Advr to Pres., World Bank, 1998–2003. Judge, Perm. Court of Arbitration. Professor: Waseda Univ., Japan, 1999–2003; Leiden Univ.; Adjunct Professor: Tokyo Univ., 1963–88; Columbia Law Sch., 1994–98; Visiting Professor: Harvard Univ., 1979–81, 1987, 1989, 2000–02; NY Univ. Law Sch., 1994–98. Pres., Japan Inst. Internat. Affairs, 1999–2003. Mem., Institut de Droit Internat. (Pres., 2011–13). Hon. Fellow, Trinity Coll., Cambridge, 2002. Hon. Mem., Amer. Soc. of Internat. Law (Mem., Exec. Council). Bd Mem., UN Foundn; Lifetime Trustee, Aspen Inst.; Hon. Gov., Ditchley Foundn. Hon. LLD: Keiwa Coll., Japan, 2000; Banares Hindu, India, 2001; Waseda, Japan, 2004; Groningen, 2009; Cambridge, 2015. *Publications:* Practice of Japan in International Law, 1984; From Involvement to Engagement: a new direction for foreign policy of Japan, 1994; On Diplomacy, 1997; A Treatise on International Relations, 2003; In the Cause of Peace and Scholarship, 2008. *Recreations:* music, ski-ing, mountain walking.
*See also Emperor of Japan.*

**OWEN,** family name of **Baron Owen**.

**OWEN, Baron** *cr* 1992 (Life Peer), of the City of Plymouth; **David Anthony Llewellyn Owen,** CH 1994; PC 1976; European Union Co-Chairman, International Conference on Former Yugoslavia, 1992–95; *b* Plympton, South Devon, 2 July 1938; *s* of Dr John William Morris Owen and Mary Llewellyn; *m* 1968, Deborah Schabert; two *s* one *d*. *Educ:* Bradfield College; Sidney Sussex College, Cambridge (BA 1959; MB, BChir 1962; MA 1963; Hon. Fellow, 1977); St Thomas' Hospital. FRCP 2005. St Thomas' Hospital: house appts, 1962–64; Neurological and Psychiatric Registrar, 1964–66; Research Fellow, Medical Unit, 1966–68. Contested (Lab) Torrington, 1964; MP (Lab 1966–81, SDP, 1981–92) Plymouth Sutton, 1966–74, Plymouth Devonport, 1974–92. PPS to Minister of Defence, Administration, 1967; Parly Under-Sec. of State for Defence, for RN, 1968–70; Opposition Defence Spokesman, 1970–72, resigned over EEC, 1972; Parly Under-Sec. of State, DHSS, 1974; Minister of State: DHSS, 1974–76; FCO, 1976–77; Sec. of State for Foreign and Commonwealth Affairs, 1977–79; Opposition spokesman on energy, 1979–80. Sponsored 1973 Children's Bill; ministerially responsible for 1975 Children's Act. Co-founder, SDP, 1981; Chm., Parly Cttee, SDP, 1981–82; Dep. Leader, SDP, 1982–83; Leader, SDP, 1983–87, resigned over issue of merger with Liberal Party, re-elected, 1988–92. Co-founder: Social Market Foundn, 1989; Charter 2010, 2009–10. Chm., New Europe, 1999–2005. Chairman: Decision Technology Internat., 1970–72; Middlesex Hldgs, subseq. Global Natural Energy plc, 1995–2006; Yukos International, 2002–05; Europe Steel, 2002–15; Director: New Crane Publishing, 1992–2005; Coats Viyella plc, 1994–2001; Abbott Laboratories Inc., 1996–2011; Intelligent Energy, 2003–05; Hyperdynamics, 2009–14. Member: Ind. Commn on Disarmament and Security Issues, 1980–89; Ind. Commn on Internat. Humanitarian Issues, 1983–88; Carnegie Commn on Preventing Deadly Conflict, 1994–99; Eminent Persons Gp on Curbing Illicit Trafficking in Small Arms and Light Weapons, 1999–2003. Chm., Humanitas, 1990–2001. Governor, Charing Cross Hospital, 1966–68. Patron, Greenham Common Trust, 2004–15; Pres., Enham Trust, 2004–12; Chm., Daedalus Trust, 2011–17. President: Nat. Marine Aquarium, 2006–10; River Thames Soc., 2010–. Chancellor, Liverpool Univ., 1996–2009. *Publications:* (ed) A Unified Health Service, 1968; The Politics of Defence, 1972; In Sickness and in Health, 1976; Human Rights, 1978; Face the Future, 1981; A Future That Will Work, 1984; A United Kingdom, 1986; Personally Speaking to Kenneth Harris, 1987; Our NHS, 1988; Time to Declare (autobiog.), 1991; (ed) Seven Ages (anthology of poetry), 1992; Balkan Odyssey, 1995; The Hubris Syndrome, 2007, 2nd edn 2012; In Sickness and in Power, 2008, 4th edn 2016; Time to Declare: second innings (autobiog.), 2009; Nuclear Papers, 2009; Europe Restructured: the Eurozone crisis and its aftermath, 2012; Bosnia and Herzegovina: the Vance-Owen Peace Plan, 2013; The Hidden Perspective: the military conversations 1906–1914, 2014; The Health of the Nation: NHS in peril, 2014; Cabinet's Finest Hour: the hidden agenda of May 1940, 2016; British Foreign Policy After Brexit, 2017; Hubris—The Road to Donald Trump: power, populism, narcissism, 2018; articles in Lancet, Neurology, Clinical Science, Brain, Qly Jl Med., Foreign Affairs and Psychiatrist. *Recreation:* sailing. *Address:* 78 Narrow Street, Limehouse, E14 8BP. *T:* (020) 7987 5441, (office) (01442) 872617, *Fax:* (01442) 876108. *E:* davidowen@lorddavidowen.co.uk. *W:* www.lorddavidowen.co.uk.

**OWEN, Albert**; MP (Lab) Ynys Môn, since 2001; b 10 Aug. 1959; s of late William Owen and Doreen Owen (née Woods); m 1983, Angela Margaret Magee; two d. Educ: Holyhead Comprehensive Sch.; Coleg Harlech; Univ. of York (BA Hons Politics 1997). Merchant seafarer, 1975–92; full-time educn, 1992–97; Manager, Centre for the Unwaged (advice, trng and information centre), 1997–2001. Member: Welsh Affairs Cttee, 2001–10; Energy and Climate Change Cttee, 2010–15; Internat. Develt Cttee, 2015–17; Business, Energy and Industrial Strategy Cttee, 2016–; Panel of Chairs, 2010–. Recreations: travel by train, cooking, gardening, walking, running, cycling. Address: House of Commons, SW1A 0AA; (constituency office) Ty Cledwyn, 18a Thomas Street, Holyhead, Anglesey LL65 1RR. T: (01407) 765750.

**OWEN, (Alfred) David**, OBE 1997; Group Chairman, 1975–2010, Consultant, since 2010, Rubery Owen Holdings Ltd; b 26 Sept. 1936; m 1966, Ethne (née Sowman); two s one d. Educ: Brocksford Hall; Oundle; Emmanuel Coll., Cambridge Univ. (MA). Joined Rubery Owen Gp, 1960; Gen. Man., Rubery Owen Motor Div., 1962–67; Dep. Man. Dir, Rubery Owen & Co. Ltd, 1967; Gp Man. Dir, Rubery Owen Holdings Ltd, 1969–81; Director: Severn Valley Railways (Holdings) plc, 1984–2019; Blackwell Sci. Ltd, 1993–2003; Welconstruct Gp (formerly Grimmitt Hldgs) Ltd, 2001–07; Darlaston Housing Trust Ltd, 2004–10; Walsall Housing Regeneration Community Agency, 2005–11; Jt Patron, BRM Assoc., 2013–. Warden, Birmingham Assay Office, 1999–2005. Member: Council, Univ. of Aston, 1981–2001; Bd, British Library, 1982–90; Bd, Nat. Exhibn Centre, 1982–2006; Bd, Castle Vale Housing Action Trust, 1993–2000. President: Comité de Liaison Eur. de la Distribn Ind. de Pièces de rechange et équipements pour Autos, 1988–90; Comité de Liaison de la Construction de Carrosseries et de Remorques, 1998–99; Commercial Trailer Assoc., 1992–2004. Treas., SMMT, 2001–16. Chm., Charles Hayward Foundn, 2004–09. Dir, Library of Birmingham Trust, 2013–16. Mem., Develt Bd, Aston Univ., 2013–. Associate Gov., Walsall Coll., 2016–. Hon. DSc Aston, 1988; DUniv Central England, 2000. Recreations: photography, music, industrial archaeology, local history, collecting books, paintings, archive of the Black Country and Sutton Coldfield. Address: Mill Dam House, Mill Lane, Aldridge, Walsall, West Midlands WS9 0NB. T: (0121) 353 1221. Club: National.

**OWEN, Arthur Leslie, (Les)**; non-executive director and financial services professional; Group Chief Executive, AXA Asia Pacific Holdings, 2000–06 (Board Member, 1998–2006); b 6 Feb. 1949; s of Arthur Llewellyn Owen and Annie Louise Owen (née Hegarty); m 1972, Valerie Emmott; three d. Educ: Holt High Sch., Liverpool; Univ. of Manchester (BSc Hons Maths); Inst. for Mgt Develt, Lausanne. FIA 1975; FIAA 2004–10; FPMI. Joined Sun Life Corp., 1971: Chief Gen. Manager, 1992–95; Gp Man. Dir, 1995–97; Chief Exec., AXA Sun Life plc, 1997–99; Board Member: Sun Life & Provincial Hldgs plc, 1996–2000; AXA Nichidan, Japan, 1999–2002; Alliance Bernstein (formerly Alliance Capital Management) (Australia & NZ), 2000–06; AXA Minmetals, China, 2002–06; Computershare plc, 2007–; Football Fedn of Aust., 2007–11; Discovery Hldgs, 2007–; Royal Mail Gp, 2010–19 (Chm., 2018–19); Chm., AXA China Region, 2002–06; non-exec. Chm. Jelf Gp plc, 2010–15; non-executive Director: Just Retirement, 2010–14; CPP, 2010–15. Member Board: Western TEC, 1994–98; PIA, 1997–99. Recreations: sport, soccer, cricket, golf, gardening, reading. Address: Broadway Lea, Broadway, Shipham, Somerset BS25 1UE.

**OWEN, David**; see Owen, A. D.

**OWEN, David Christopher**; QC 2006; arbitrator and mediator; b 21 June 1958; s of late Kenneth and Barbara Owen; m 1985, Philippa Reid; one s one d. Educ: Marlborough Coll.; Merton Coll., Oxford (BA 1st Cl. Hons Hist.; MA). Administrator, Defence Procurement and Overseas Finance Divs, HM Treasury, 1979–81; called to the Bar, Middle Temple, 1983; Mediator Accreditation, CEDR, 2003. Member: Magic Circle, 1978–; Inner Magic Circle (Gold Star), 2019–. Founder and Chair, Breathe Arts Health Res., 2009–. Publications: (ed jtly) MacGillivray on Insurance Law, 9th edn 1997 to 11th edn 2008. Recreations: magic, music, travel. Address: 20 Essex Street, WC2R 3AL. T: (020) 7842 1200, Fax: (020) 7842 1270. E: clerks@20essexst.com.

**OWEN, David Harold Owen**, OBE 1998; Registrar of the Privy Council, 1983–98; b 24 May 1933; er twin s of late Lloyd Owen Owen and Margaret Glyn Owen, Machynlleth, Powys; m 1st, 1961, Ailsa Ransome Wallis (d 1993); three d; 2nd, 1995, Julia (née Beck) (d 2018), widow of W. M. Lowe. Educ: Harrow Sch.; Gonville and Caius Coll., Cambridge. Called to the Bar, Gray's Inn, 1958. Served Royal Welch Fusiliers, 1951–53 (2nd Lieut). Campbell's Soups Ltd, King's Lynn, 1958–68; Lord Chancellor's Dept, 1969–80 (Private Sec. to Lord Chancellor, 1971–75); Chief Clerk, Judicial Cttee of Privy Council, 1980–83. Recreations: music, travel. Address: Whitelea, Stoney Lane, Bovingdon, Herts HP3 0DP. Club: Reform.
  See also M. N. Gibbon.

**OWEN, Prof. (David) Roger (Jones)**, PhD, DSc; FRS 2009; FREng, FICE; Professor in Civil Engineering, Swansea University (formerly University of Wales, Swansea), 1983, Research Professor in Civil Engineering, since 2009; b Llanelli, 27 May 1942; s of Evan William Owen and Margaret Owen; m 1964, Janet Mary Pugh; two d. Educ: Univ. of Wales, Swansea (BSc 1963; MSc 1964); Northwestern Univ. (PhD 1967); Univ. of Wales (DSc 1983). FICE 1983; FREng 1996. Walter P. Murphy Res. Fellow, Northwestern Univ., 1966–67; Lectr, Sen. Lectr, then Reader, Univ. of Wales, Swansea, 1967–82. Founder and Chm., Rockfield Software Ltd, 1985–. Hon. DSc: Porto, 1996; Ecole normale supérieure, Cachan, 2008; Poly. Univ. of Catalonia, 2012; Split, 2016. Foreign Member: US Nat. Acad. of Engrg, 2011; Chinese Acad. of Scis, 2011. Computational Mechanics Award, 2002, Gauss-Newton Medal, 2004, Internat. Assoc. for Computational Mechanics; Warner T. Koiter Medal, Amer. Soc. of Mechanical Engrs, 2003; Gold Medal, Univ. of Split, 2004; Premier Medal, Spanish Soc. for Computational Mechanics, 2005; China Friendship Medal, 2016. Publications: (with E. Hinton) Finite Element Programming, 1977; (with E. Hinton) An Introduction to Finite Element Computations, 1979; (with E. Hinton) Finite Elements in Plasticity: theory and practice, 1980; (jtly) Computational Methods for Plasticity: theory and applications, 2008; over 400 articles in scientific jls. Recreations: tennis, flying, golf, walking. Address: 91 West Cross Lane, West Cross, Swansea SA3 5LU. T: (01792) 404935, Fax: (01792) 295676. E: d.r.j.owen@swansea.ac.uk.

**OWEN, Dr Diana Jane**, OBE 2018; Director General, Royal Over-Seas League, since 2017; b Assam, India, 23 Feb. 1957; d of Roy and Caroline Eastment; m 1986, Martin Owen; one s one d. Educ: Univ. of Leeds (BA 1st Cl. Hons Internat. Hist. and Politics 1978; PhD 1982). Product Manager, E. J. Arnold & Son Ltd, 1983–88; Property Manager and Area Manager, Nat. Trust, 1988–2007; Dir and Chief Exec., Shakespeare Birthplace Trust, 2007–17. Yamani Medal, Iqbal Acad., 2011. Publications: Petworth: the servants' quarters, 1997. Recreations: walking, gardening, yoga, theatre, ballet, family. Address: Royal Over-Seas League, Over-Seas House, Park Place, SW1A 1LR. T: (020) 7408 0214, Fax: (020) 7499 6738. E: dowen@rosl.org.uk.

**OWEN, Sir Geoffrey (David)**, Kt 1989; Head of Industrial Policy, Policy Exchange, since 2016; b 16 April 1934; s of late L. G. Owen and Violet Owen (née Chamberlain); m 1st, 1961, Dorothy Jane (d 1991); two s one d; 2nd, 1993, Miriam Marianna Gross, qv. Educ: Rugby Sch.; Balliol Coll., Oxford (MA). Joined Financial Times, 1958, feature writer, industrial correspondent; US Correspondent, 1961; Industrial Editor, 1967; Executive, Industrial Reorganisation Corp., 1967–69; Dir of Admin, Overseas Div., 1969, Dir of Personnel and Admin, 1972, British Leyland Internat.; Dep. Editor, 1974–80, Editor, 1981–90, Financial Times; London School of Economics and Political Science: Dir, Business Policy Prog., Centre for Econ. Performance, 1991–98; Sen. Fellow, 1998–2014, Vis. Prof. in Practice, 2014–, Dept of Mgt. Dir, Laird Gp, 2000–06. Chm., Wincott Foundn, 1998–2015. Publications: Industry in the USA, 1966; From Empire to Europe, 1999; The Rise and Fall of Great Companies: Courtaulds and the reshaping of the man-made fibres industry, 2010; (with M. M. Hopkins) Science, the State and the City: Britain's struggle to succeed in biotechnology, 2016.

**OWEN, Gordon Michael William**, CBE 1991; Chairman, NXT plc, 2001–05; b 9 Dec. 1937; s of late Christopher Owen and Mrs Margaret Joyce Milward (née Spencer); m 1963, Jennifer Pearl, (Jane), Bradford (marr. diss. 2001); one s one d; m 2001, Tina Elizabeth (née Davies). Educ: Cranbrook Sch. Cable & Wireless, 1954–91: Dir, 1986–91; Jt Man. Dir, 1987–88; Dep. Chief Exec., 1988–90; Gp Man. Dir, 1990–91; Chairman: Mercury Communications Ltd, 1990–91 (Man. Dir, 1984–90); Peterstar Communications, St Petersburg, 1992–94; Energis Communications Ltd, subseq. Energis plc, 1993–2002; Utility Cable plc, 1994–98; Acorn (formerly Acorn Computer) Group, 1996–98; Yeoman Gp plc, 1996–2004; Director: Portals Gp, 1988–95; London Electricity, 1989–97; Waste Gas Technology, 1993–2002; Olivetti SpA, 1996–2001. Chm., MacIntyre Care, 1993–2003. Chm., Acad. of St Martin in the Fields Orch., 2002–04 (Vice-Chm., 1994–2002). Chm. Bd of Govs, St Michael's Sch., Otford, 1994–2011. Recreations: beekeeping, stamp collecting, sailing, bad golf. Address: Sutton End House, Sutton, W Sussex RH20 1PY.

**OWEN, Sir Hugo Dudley C.**; see Cunliffe-Owen.

**OWEN, Ivor Henri**, CBE 1992; CEng, FIMechE; Director General, Design Council, 1988–93; b 14 Nov. 1930; s of Thomas and Anne Owen; m 1954, Jane Frances Graves; two s one d. Educ: Liverpool College of Technology; Manchester College of Science and Technology. Engineering apprentice, later design engineer, Craven Bros (Manchester), Stockport, 1947–57; Manufacturing Develt Engr, Steam Turbine Div., English Electric, Rugby, 1957–62; Manager, Netherton Works, English Electric, Bootle, 1962–66 (hydro electric plant, steam turbine components, condensers, nuclear equipment); Manager, English Electric Computers, Winsford, 1966–69; Manager, Winsford Kidsgrove Works, ICL, 1969–70; Man. Dir, RHP Bearings, 1970–81; Thorn EMI: Chief Exec., Gen. Engineering Div., 1981–83; Chm., Appliance and Lighting Group, 1984–87; Dir, 1984–87. Chm., Ball Roller Bearing Manufrs Assoc., 1978–80; Vice-Pres., Fedn European Bearing Manufrs Assoc., 1978–80. Royal Acad. of Engrg Vis. Prof., Univ. of Bath, 1994–97. FRSA. Recreations: theatre, reading, gardening.

**OWEN, Jane Caroline**; HM Diplomatic Service; Ambassador to Switzerland and (non-resident) to Liechtenstein, since 2018; b 15 April 1963; d of Thomas and Jeanne Owen; m 1998, David Donnelly; one s one d. Educ: Ellerslie Sch., Malvern; Trinity Coll., Cambridge (BA Hons 1986). English teacher, JET prog., Osaka, Japan, 1986; entered FCO, 1987; Mexico and Central American Dept, FCO, 1987; Japanese lang. trng, 1988–90; 2nd Sec., Commercial, Tokyo, 1990–93; Head: Exports to Japan Unit, DTI, 1993–96 (on secondment); Mediterranean and Asia Sect., EU Dept (External), FCO, 1996–98; Dep. Hd of Mission, Hanoi, 1998–2002; Dir of Trade Promotion, Tokyo, 2002–06; Counsellor, Climate, Science, Economy and Trade, 2006–08, Dir of Trade and Investment, 2008–10, New Delhi; Ambassador to Norway, 2010–14; Chief Operating Officer, UKTI, 2014–16. Recreations: travelling, scuba diving, ski-ing, spending time with my family. Address: c/o Foreign and Commonwealth Office, King Charles Street, SW1A 2AH.

**OWEN, Jennifer Ann**, CBE 2010; Deputy Chief Executive, 2010–12, and Executive Director, Adults, Health and Community Wellbeing (formerly Adult Social Care), 2004–12, Essex County Council; b 23 Aug. 1954; d of Col John Edward Owen and Jean Wardle Owen; m 2001, Jeff Jerome; one s. Educ: Sheffield Poly. (BA Hons Applied Soc. Studies; CQSW, CMS 1976). Regl Dir, Social Services Inspectorate, DoH, 2001–04. Non-executive Director: Royal Free London (formerly Hampstead) NHS Foundn Trust, 2010; Housing & Care 21, 2011–. Pres., Assoc. of Dirs of Adult Social Services, 2009–10 (Vice-Pres., 2008–09); Trustee, Bd, SCIE, 2007–13. Trustee, Alzheimer's Soc., 2014– (Vice Chair). Recreations: theatre, country walks, travelling, company of friends.

**OWEN, John Aubrey**; Senior Partner, Inside Advice, consultancy services, since 2001; b 1 Aug. 1945; s of late Prebendary Douglas Aubrey Owen and Patricia Joan Owen (née Griggs); m 1971, Julia Margaret Jones; one s one d. Educ: City of London Sch.; St Catharine's Coll., Cambridge (MA). Joined Min. of Transport, 1969; Asst Private Sec. to Minister for Transport Industries, 1972; DoE, 1973–75; Dept of Transport, 1975–78; seconded to Cambridgeshire CC, 1978–80; DoE, 1980–2001: Regional Dir, Northern Regional Office, Depts of the Environment and Transport, 1987–91; Dir, Personnel Management, 1991–95. Dir, Regeneration, then Skills, Educn and Regeneration, later Skills, Enterprise and Communities, Govt Office for London, 1995–2001. Chm., Mosaic (formerly New Islington and Hackney) Housing Assoc., 2002–06; Dep. Chm., Family Mosaic Housing Assoc., 2006–15. Recreations: gardening, reading, watching cricket, genealogy. Address: 33 Valley Road, Welwyn Garden City, Herts AL8 7DH. T: (01707) 321768. E: johna.owen@ntlworld.com. Club: Middlesex CC.

**OWEN, Prof. John Joseph Thomas**, FRS 1988; Sands Cox Professor and Head of Department of Anatomy, University of Birmingham, 1978–2001; b 7 Jan. 1934; s of Thomas and Alice Owen; m 1961, Barbara Schofield Forster (marr. diss. 1992); two s. Educ: Univ. of Liverpool (BSc, MD); MA Oxon 1963. Lecturer: Univ. of Liverpool, 1960–63; Univ. of Oxford, 1963–72; Fellow, St Cross Coll., Oxford, 1968–72; Sen. Scientist, Imperial Cancer Res. Fund's Tumour Immunology Unit, UCL, 1972–74; Prof. of Anatomy, Univ. of Newcastle upon Tyne 1974–78. Vis. Scholar, Stanford Univ., USA, 2000–01; Greenberg Scholar, Oklahoma Med. Res. Foundn, USA, 2001–02. Medical Research Council: Mem., Physiol Systems and Disorders Bd, 1978–83; Chm., Grants Cttee, B, 1980–83; Mem., Cell Bd, 1991–94; Member: Wellcome Trust's Biochemistry and Cell Biology Panel, 1987–90; Council, Nat. Kidney Res. Fund, 1987–90; Council, Royal Soc., 1991–93. Founder FMedSci 1998. Publications: numerous contribs to sci. literature. Recreations: road and track cycling, dancing, Japanese studies, helping with my grandchildren.

**OWEN, Prof. John Wyn**, CB 1994; FRSPH; FLSW; Member, Administrative Council, Madariaga - College of Europe Foundation, 2005–15; Professor, College of Medicine, Swansea University, since 2013; b 15 May 1942; s of late Idwal Wyn Owen and of Myfi Owen (née Hughes); m 1967, Elizabeth Ann (née MacFarlane); one s one d. Educ: Friars School, Bangor; St John's Coll., Cambridge (BA 1964, MA 1968); Hosp. Admin. Staff Coll. (DipHA 1967). Trainee, King Edward VII's Hosp. Fund for London, 1964–66; Dep. Hosp.

Sec., West Wales Gen. Hosp., Carmarthen, 1966–67; Hosp. Sec., Glantawe HMC, Swansea, 1967–70; Staff Training Officer, Welsh Hosp. Bd, Cardiff, 1968–70; Divl Administrator, Univ. of Wales, Cardiff, HMC, 1970–72; St Thomas' Hospital: Asst Clerk, and King's Fund Fellow, 1972–74; Dist Administrator, St Thomas' Health Dist, Teaching, 1974–79; Trustee, Refresh, 1976–78; Hon. Tutor, Med. Sch., 1974–79; Praeceptor, Sch. of Health Administration, Univ. of Minnesota, 1974–79; Exec. Dir, United Medical Enterprises, London, 1979–85; Dir, NHS Wales, Welsh Office, 1985–94; Chm., Welsh Health Common Services Authy, 1985–94; Dir Gen., NSW Health Dept, Sydney, 1994–97; Sec., Nuffield Trust, 1997–2005. Personal Chair, Univ. of Wales, 2012; Professorial Fellow, Royal Soc. Public Health, 2012. Chairman: Olympic Health and Med. Working Cttee, 1994–97; DoH Change Mgt Gp on Nurse Regulation, 1999–2001; Member: Strategic Planning and Evaluation Cttee, Nat. Health and MRC, 1994–97; Australian Health Ministers' Adv. Council, 1994–97 (Chm., 1995–97); Health Adv. Bd, 1994–97; Public Health Assoc., 1994; Mgt Cttee, Nat. Breast Cancer Centre, 1995–97. Mem., Bd, 2006–, Chair, Global Health Cttee, 2007–13, UK Health Protection Agency; Member: Wales Bd, Health Protection Cttee, 2006–13; Health Protection Adv. Cttee, Welsh Assembly Govt, then Welsh Govt, 2010– (Chm., 2014–); Global Council, Health Action Partnership Internat., 2010; Adv. Bd, Global Health Section, Internat. Studies Assoc., 2014–; Sen. Global Health Advr, InterAction Council, 2015–; Vice-Chm., Nat. Heart Forum, 2007–16. Sen. Associate, Judge Inst. of Mgt Studies, Univ. of Cambridge, 1997–2010; Adjunct Prof., Public Health, Univ. of Sydney, 2006–; Visiting Fellow: Univ. of NSW, 1979; LSE, 1997–2010. Trustee, RESEC, and Chair, RESEC Cymru/Wales, 2009–. Trustee, Florence Nightingale Museum Trust, 1983–90; Chm., Health Bldg Educn Gp, British Consultants' Bureau, 1983–85; Mem. Adv. Forum, Personnel Lead Body, 1992–94. Chm., Europe in the World, European Foundn Centre, 2004–05. Founder Mem., Med. Chapter, Australian Opera, 1995–97; Mem., NSW Cambridge Soc. Cttee, 1996–97; Sec., London Cambridge Soc., 1997–2004 (Chm., 2004–11); Chair, Wales Br., Britain Australia Soc., 2009–13. Chm., Canada UK Colloquium, 2013; Mem. Bd, Canada UK Council, 2014–. Chm., UWIC, 2005–11; Member: Court, Univ. of Wales, 1998–2011; Council, Univ. of Wales Coll. of Medicine, 1997–2005; Pres., Johnian Soc., St John's Coll., Cambridge, 2016–17. Member: Inst. of Medicine, NAS, USA, 1998; US Nat. Acad. of Medicine, 2016. FRGS 1968; FRSA 1998; FHSM 1992; FACHSE 1994; FRSocMed 1997; FRSPH 2013. CCMI 2005; Founding FLSW 2010 (Mem. Council, 2010–18; Treas., 2012–18). Hon. FFPHM 1991; Hon. MRCP 2002; Hon. FRCP 2015. Hon. Fellow: UCW, Aberystwyth, 1991; UCW, Bangor, 1992. Hon. Mem., Gorsedd of Bards, 2000. DUniv Glamorgan, 1999; Hon. DSc City, 2004. *Publications:* contribs to professional jls. *Recreations:* organ playing, opera, travel. *Address:* Newton Farm, Newton, Cowbridge CF71 7RZ. *T:* (01446) 775113. *Clubs:* Athenæum; Cardiff and County.

**OWEN, John Wynne,** CMG 1998; MBE 1979; DL; HM Diplomatic Service, retired; Chairman (non-executive): CLS Fabrication Ltd, 1989–2012; Autoport North America Inc., since 2004 (Director, since 2002); Iceman Capital Ltd, since 2006; Loriners' Investment Co. Ltd, 2008–16; Fidelity China Special Situations plc, 2010–16; *b* 25 April 1939; *s* of Thomas David Owen and Mair Eluned Owen; *m* 1st, 1962, Thelma Margaret Gunton (*d* 1987); one *s* two *d*; 2nd, 1988, Carol Edmunds; one step *d*. *Educ:* Gowerton Grammar Sch.; Westminster Coll., London. FO 1956; 2nd Lieut Royal Signals, 1958–60; served Djakarta, Saigon, Paris, San Salvador, to 1967; resigned 1967; business, 1967–70; reinstated 1970; FCO, 1970–73; Tehran, 1973–77; São Paulo, 1978–80; Peking, 1980–82; FCO, 1983; special leave, 1985; Chm., Gunham, Holdings Ltd, 1985–89; Counsellor, FCO, 1989–92; Consul Gen., Boston, 1992–95; Governor, Cayman Is, 1995–99. Non-executive Director: Scimitar Advrs, 1999–2015; Queensgate Bank and Trust Co. Ltd, 2006–10 and 2015– (non-exec. Dir, Queensgate Bank Ltd, 2010–15, Queensgate Trust Co. Ltd, 2010–15). Chairman: British Laminated Plastics Fabricators' Assoc., 1987–90; Isle of Wight Strategic Partnership, 2006–08; IoW Chamber of Commerce, Trade and Industry, 2008–15; IoW Business Ambassadors, 2018–; Adv. Bd, Kinetic Partnership, 2018–. Trustee: Grandparents Fedn, subseq. Grandparents Assoc., 2000–09 (Dep. Chm., 2002–09); Fidelity UK Foundn, 2006–; Fidelity Internat. Foundn, 2007–; LAMDA, 2017–. Chm., Friends of the Cayman Is, 2006–. Founding Mem., UK/China Business Leaders Club, 2016–. Fellow, Univ. of Wales, Aberystwyth, 2006. FCMI; FInstD. Freeman, City of London, 1978; Liveryman, Loriners' Co., 1978– (Mem., Ct of Assts, 1999–; Master, 2005). DL Isle of Wight, 2007. *Recreations:* walking, art, reading, fly-fishing.

**OWEN, Jonathan Robert,** OBE 2014; social entrepreneur and author, since 2001; *b* Eaglescliffe, 2 June 1958; *s* of Toby and Gaie Owen; *m* 1997, Hiromi Takahashi. *Educ:* Eton Coll.; Queens' Coll., Cambridge (BA Modern Hist. 1980; MA); London Business Sch. (MSc 1986). Brand mgt, Procter & Gamble, 1980–83; Hd of Res., SDP, 1983–84; Partner: Cap Gemini, Mac Gp, 1986–98; Accenture (formerly Andersen Consulting), 1998–2001; owner, Auvian Ltd, 2001–. Co-Founder and Trustee: Teach First, 2002–16; Start Up, 2005–16; Future Leaders, 2006–17; Teaching Leaders, 2008–17 (Chm., 2008–17); Achievement for All, 2011–16; Spark Inside, 2012–18 (Chm., 2012–16); Stir Educn, 2013– (Chm., 2013–); Right to Succeed, 2015– (Chm., 2015–); Trustee: Educn Develt Trust, 2016–18 (Internat. Chm., 2016–18); Bounce Forward, 2017– (Chm., 2017–); Chm., Educn Commn, 2018–. FRGS 1998; FRSA. *Publications:* Management Stripped Bare, 2002, 3rd edn 2012; Hardcore Management, 2004; How to Lead, 2005, 5th edn 2018; Leadership Skills Handbook, 2006, 4th edn 2017; How to Manage, 2006, 5th edn 2018; Power at Work, 2008; Tribal Business School, 2008; Death of Modern Management, 2009; How to Sell, 2010; How to Influence, 2010; Leadership Rules, 2011; Management Rules, 2011; Mobile MBA, 2011; How to Coach, 2013; Quantitative Easing: the wrong sort of money; 2013; Mindset of Success, 2015, 2nd edn 2018; Global Teams, 2017; Myths of Leadership, 2017; Resilience, 2019. *Recreations:* tribes, extreme jogging, chocolate, opera. *Address:* c/o Conduit Club, 40 Conduit Street, W1S 2YQ.

**OWEN, Les;** *see* Owen, A. L.

**OWEN, Lynette Isabel,** OBE 2009; copyright and rights consultant; Copyright Director, Pearson Education Ltd, 2002–13; *b* 29 June 1947; *d* of Warwick Jack Burgoyne Owen and Betty Isabel Owen (*née* Drummond). *Educ:* Bedford Coll., London (BA Hons (English) 1968). Rights Asst, CUP, 1968–73; Rights Manager, Pitman Publishing Ltd, 1973–75; N American Sales Manager, Marshall Cavendish, 1975–76; Rights Manager, 1976–87, Rights Dir, 1988–94, Longman Gp UK; Rights and Contracts Dir, Addison Wesley, 1994–98; Rights Dir, Pearson Educn Ltd, 1998–2001. Mem. Bd, Ind. Publishers Guild, 2014–. London Internat. Book Fair/British Council Lifetime Achievement Award for contribn to internat. publishing, 2003; (inaugural) Kim Scott Walwyn Prize, 2004; Ind. Publishers Guild Award for Services to Ind. Publishers, 2018. *Publications:* Selling Rights, 1991, 8th edn 2018; Clark's Publishing Agreements, contrib. 2nd and 3rd edns, gen. ed. and contrib. 4th edn 1993 to 10th edn 2017; handbooks on copyright and licensing for Eastern Europe, China, etc; numerous articles in Bookseller, Publishing News, Learned Publishing, etc. *Recreations:* theatre, music, art, reading. *Address:* 147B St Pancras Way, NW1 0SY. *T:* and *Fax:* (020) 7284 0470. *E:* lynetteowen@hotmail.co.uk.

**OWEN, Michael James;** football commentator, BT Sport, since 2013; former professional footballer; *b* 14 Dec. 1979; *s* of Terence Owen and Janette Owen; *m* 2005, Louise Bonsall; one *s* three *d*. *Educ:* Hawarden High Sch.; Idsall Sch.; Lilleshall Sch. of Excellence. Liverpool Football Club, 1996–2004: member, winning team: Worthington Cup, 2001; FA Cup 2001; UEFA Cup, 2001; Charity Shield, 2001; European Super Cup, 2001; player: Real Madrid, 2004–05; Newcastle Utd, 2005–09 (Captain, 2008–09); Manchester Utd, 2009–12; Stoke City, 2012–13. Mem., England Football Team, 1998–2008; Mem., World Cup team, 1998, 2002, 2006. Ambassador and Advr, Qipco British Champions' Series, Flat Racing, 2013–. Young Player of the Year, PFA, 1998; BBC Sports Personality of the Year, 1998; Ballon d'Or, France Football, 2001. *Publications:* (with Dave Harrison) Michael Owen: in person (autobiog.), 2000; Michael Owen's Soccer Skills, 2000; (with Paul Hayward) Michael Owen: off the record (autobiog.), 2004; Reboot: my life, my time (autobiog.), 2019. *Address:* c/o MOM Sports, MOM House, Shay Lane, Hampton, Malpas, Cheshire SY14 8AD.

**OWEN, Sir Michael (John),** Kt 2014; PhD; FRCPsych, FMedSci; FLSW; Professor of Psychological Medicine and Head, Institute of Psychological Medicine and Clinical Neuroscience (formerly Department of Psychological Medicine, then Department of Psychological Medicine and Neurology), since 1998, Director, MRC Centre for Neuropsychiatric Genetics and Genomics, since 2009, School of Medicine, Cardiff University (formerly University of Wales College of Medicine, Cardiff); *b* 24 Nov. 1955; *s* of Dr John Robson Owen and Mary Gillian Owen (*née* Dowsett); *m* 1985, Dr Deborah Cohen; two *s* one *d*. *Educ:* Univ. of Birmingham (BSc Anatomical Studies 1977; PhD Neurosci. 1982; MB ChB 1983). MRCPsych 1987, FRCPsych 1997. University of Wales College of Medicine, Cardiff, then School of Medicine, Cardiff University: Sen. Lectr, Dept of Psychological Medicine and Inst. of Med. Genetics, 1990–95; Prof. of Neuropsychiatric Genetics, 1995–98; Pro Vice-Chancellor for Res., 2001–04; Dep. Pro Vice-Chancellor for Res., 2005–13; Chm., Div. of Community Specialties, School of Medicine, Cardiff Univ., 2002–05. Hon. Consultant Psychiatrist, Cardiff and Vale NHS Trust, 1990–; Dir, Neurosci. and Mental Health Res. Inst., 2010–14. FMedSci 1999; FLSW 2011. Hon. MD Birmingham, 2018. Strömgren Medal, Erik Strömgren Foundn, 2011; Lieber Prize, Brain and Behavior Res. Foundn, 2012; William K. Warren Dist. Res. Award, Internat. Congress on Schizophrenia Res., 2013; Lifetime Achievement Award, Internat. Soc. of Psychiatric Genetics, 2015; Award for Outstanding Contribution to Neurosci., British Neurosci. Assoc., 2017. *Publications:* (jtly) Seminars in Psychiatric Genetics, 1994; (ed jtly) Psychiatric Genetics and Genomics, 2002; articles on psychiatric genetics and psychiatry. *Recreations:* walking, cycling, reading, sailing, fishing. *Address:* MRC Centre for Neuropsychiatric Genetics and Genomics, Hadyn Ellis Building, Cathays, Cardiff CF24 4HQ. *T:* (029) 2068 8320. *E:* owenmj@cardiff.ac.uk.

**OWEN, Dr Myrfyn;** Director General, Wildfowl and Wetlands Trust, 1992–97; ecological consultant, 1997–2009; *b* 8 April 1943; *s* of William Owen and Anne Mary Owen; *m* 1967, Lydia Marian Vaughan (*née* Rees); two *d*. *Educ:* Sir Hugh Owen Grammar Sch.; University Coll., Aberystwyth (BSc 1964); Univ. of Leeds (PhD 1967). Wildfowl Trust, later Wildfowl and Wetlands Trust: Ecologist, 1967; Conservation Res. Officer, 1974; Asst Dir (Res.), 1979; Head of Res., 1988; Dir, 1991–92. *Publications:* Wildfowl of Europe, 1976; Wild Geese of the World, 1980; Wildfowl in Great Britain, 1986; Waterfowl Ecology, 1990; numerous scientific papers. *Recreations:* gardening, cookery, cycling, wildlife. *Address:* Woodleigh House, 62 Woodmancote, Dursley, Glos GL11 4AQ. *T:* (01453) 543244.

**OWEN, Nicholas David Arundel;** Presenter: BBC News, 2007–19; Classic FM, since 2010; *b* 10 Feb. 1947; *m* 1983, Brenda (*née* Firth); two *s* two *d*. Newspaper journalist, 1964–81; BBC TV, 1981–83; Presenter, ITN, 1984–2007. *Publications:* The Brighton Belle, 1972; History of the British Trolleybus, 1974; Diana, The People's Princess, 1997; Days Like This, 2012. *Recreations:* railways, reading, walking, golf, bridge. *Address:* PO Box 57948, W4 2UJ.

**OWEN, Patricia, (Mrs Peter Owen);** *see* Hodge, P.

**OWEN, Peter Francis,** CB 1990; Secretary General, Institute of Chartered Accountants in England and Wales, 2002–03 (Executive Director, 1998–2002); Executive Director, Better Government Initiative, since 2013; *b* 4 Sept. 1940; *s* of Arthur Owen and Violet (*née* Morris); *m* 1963, Ann Preece; one *s* one *d*. *Educ:* The Liverpool Inst.; Liverpool Univ. (BA French). Joined MPBW, 1964; Cabinet Office, 1971–72; Private Sec. to successive Ministers of Housing and Construction, 1972–74; Asst Sec., Housing Policy Review, 1975–77, Local Govt Finance, 1977–80; Under Sec. and Regional Dir of Northern and Yorks and Humberside Regs, Depts of the Environment and of Transport, 1980–82; Under Secretary: Rural Affairs, DoE, 1983; Local Govt Finance Policy, DoE, 1984–86; Dep. Sec., Housing and Construction, DoE, 1986–90; Head of Econ. and Domestic Affairs Secretariat, Cabinet Office, 1990–94; Dep. Sec., Sch. Curriculum and Teachers, DFE, 1994–95; Dir Gen. for Schools, DfEE, 1995–98. *Recreations:* reading, gardening, French, classical guitar. *Address:* Oakmead, The Avenue, Hampton, Middlesex TW12 3RS.

**OWEN, Philip W.;** *see* Wynn Owen.

**OWEN, Prof. Richard John,** PhD; Professor of Innovation Governance, University of Bristol, since 2017; *b* Campbeltown, Scotland, 20 Oct. 1966; *s* of Gordon Owen and Maria Owen; *m* 1995, Therese Hassell; one *s* one *d*. *Educ:* Christ Coll., Brecon; Univ. of Wales (BSc; PhD 1997). Faculty Scientist, Bermuda Biological Station for Res., 1997–2003; Hd, Envmt and Human Health, Envmt Agency, 2003–08; Prof., Policy Studies Inst. and Univ. of Westminster, 2008–10; University of Exeter Business School: Prof. of Sci. and Innovation Governance and Chair, Responsible Innovation, 2010–17; Dir, Postgrad. Res., 2012–14; Associate Dean (Res.), 2014–16; Interim Pro-Vice Chancellor and Exec. Dean, 2016. Strategic Advr, EPSRC, 2011–16. Vis. Prof., Univ. Coll. of Oslo and Akershus, 2015–. FRSA 2010. *Publications:* Responsible Innovation: managing the responsible emergence of science and innovation in society, 2013; contribs to books and articles in scientific jls. *Recreations:* Norfolk Terriers, country walks, travel, theatre. *Address:* School of Economics, Finance and Management, University of Bristol, Priory Road Complex, Priory Road, Bristol BS8 1TU.

**OWEN, Richard Wilfred,** FCA; retired from Touche Ross, 1993; *b* 26 Oct. 1932; *s* of Wilfred Owen and Ivy (*née* Gamble); *m* 1966, Sheila Marie Kerrigan; three adopted *s* one adopted *d*, and one foster *s* one foster *d*. *Educ:* Gunnersbury Catholic Grammar Sch. Lloyds Bank, 1949–51; RAF Russian translator, 1951–53; accountancy articles, 1953–58; Thomson McLintock, 1958–62; Crompton Parkinson, 1962–64; Touche Ross & Co., 1964–93: admitted to Partnership, 1969; seconded to HM Treasury, 1971; Partner-in-Charge, Management Consultancy, 1974–87, Nat. Dir, Personnel, 1987–93; UK Chm., 1988–90; Eur. Dir, Management Consultancy, 1990–92. Pres., Management Consultancies Assoc., 1987. Chm., Cardinal Hume Centre, 1996–2002; Trustee, Isabel Hospice, 1994–2000. Chm., Salisbury Cathedral Close Preservation Soc., 2015–18. KSG 1997. *Recreation:* Salisbury Cathedral guide. *Address:* 26 The Close, Salisbury, Wilts SP1 2EJ.

**OWEN, Rob,** OBE 2015; FRGS; Chief Executive, St Giles Trust, since 2007; *b* Woking, 27 July 1965; *s* of late John Owen and of Sue Owen; *m* 2000, Cindy Yendell; one *s* one *d*. *Educ:* Univ. of Liverpool (BA Hons); Henley Business Sch. (MBA). Nomura, 1987–90; Schroders, 1991–98; ABN-Amro, 1998–2001. FRGS 1991. *Publications:* Sports Sponsorship: going for gold, 2006. *Recreations:* running, snow boarding, family. *Address:* St Giles Trust, Georgian House, 64–68 Camberwell Church Street, SE5 8JB. *E:* Rob.Owen@ StGilesTrust.org.uk. *Club:* Reform.

**OWEN, Robert Frank;** QC 1996; **His Honour Judge Owen;** a Circuit Judge, since 2009; a Deputy High Court Judge, since 2008; *b* 31 May 1953; *s* of Tudor Owen and Pat Owen; *m* 1980, Anna Shaw; three *s*. *Educ:* St Asaph Grammar Sch.; Poly. of Central London (LLB Hons). Called to the Bar, Gray's Inn, 1977, Bencher, 2007; Recorder, 2000–09. *Recreations:* coastal walking, sport. *Address:* Birmingham Civil Justice Centre, 33 Bull Street, Birmingham B4 6DS.

**OWEN, Robert John Richard;** Director, Stanhill Capital Ltd, since 2011; *b* 11 Feb. 1940; *s* of Richard Owen and Margaret Owen (*née* Fletcher); *m* (marr. diss.); two *s* one *d*; *m* Margaret Helen. *Educ:* Repton School; Oxford University. Foreign Office, 1961–68, incl. HM Embassy, Washington, 1965–68; HM Treasury, 1968–70; Morgan Grenfell & Co., 1970–79 (Dir, 1974); Lloyds Bank International, 1979–85 (Dir); Chm. and Chief Exec., Lloyds Merchant Bank, 1985–88; Comr for Securities, Hong Kong, 1988–89; Chm., Securities and Futures Commn, Hong Kong, 1989–92. Chairman: Techpacific Capital Ltd, 1999–2004; Internat. Securities Consultancy Ltd, 2000–; Crosby Asset Mgt Ltd (formerly Crosby Capital Partners Inc.), 2002–11; IB Daiwa Ltd, 2005–08; Repton Internat. Schs Ltd, 2013–; Sen. Advr, Nomura Internat. (Hong Kong) Ltd, 1993–2007; Dep. Chm., Nomura Asia Hldgs Ltd, 1994–97; Director: European Capital Co. Ltd, 1992–2001; Sunday Communications Ltd, 2000–07; Singapore Exchange Ltd, 2004–13; Citibank (Hong Kong) Ltd, 2004–; Repton Dubai Ltd, 2007–; Foremarke Dubai Ltd, 2013–; Repton Abu Dhabi Ltd, 2013–. Mem. Council and Mem. Regulatory Bd, Lloyd's of London, 1993–95; Bd Mem., Dubai Financial Services Authority, 2002–. Gov., Repton Sch., 1994–. *Recreations:* oriental paintings, mountain walking. *Address:* Mary Knoll House, Whitcliffe, Ludlow, Shropshire SY8 2HD.

**OWEN, Hon. Sir Robert (Michael),** Kt 2001; a Judge of the High Court, Queen's Bench Division, 2001–14; *b* 19 Sept. 1944; *s* of Gwynne Llewellyn Owen and Phoebe Constance Owen; *m* 1969, Sara Josephine Rumbold; two *s*. *Educ:* Durham Sch.; Exeter Univ. (LLB). Called to Bar, Inner Temple, 1968, Bencher, 1995; QC 1988. Judicial Mem., Transport Tribunal, 1985–97; Recorder, 1987–2000; Dep. High Court Judge, 1994–2000; Presiding Judge, Western Circuit, 2005–08. Chm., Litvinenko Inquiry, 2014–16. DTI Inspector, 1991–92; Mem., Ind. Parly Standards Authy, 2016–. Chairman: Gen. Council of the Bar, 1997; Civil Cttee, Judicial Studies Bd, 2004–08; Dir of Trng for Sen. Judiciary, 2010–12; Chm. Bd, Judicial Coll., 2011–12. Chm., London Common Law and Commercial Bar Assoc., 1994–95. Chairman: vCJD Trust, 2002–; Fowey Harbour Commn Consultative Gp, 2006–10; British Internat. 6m Assoc., 2014–17; Cornwall Garden Soc., 2017–; Pres., Internat. 6m Assoc., 2018–. Trustee: Pestalozzi Internat. Village Trust, 2014–18; Slynn Foundn, 2017–. Governor: Coll. of Law, 1998–2004; Truro and Penrith Coll., 2018–. Hon. LLD Exeter, 2007. *Clubs:* Les Six; Royal Yacht Squadron.

**OWEN, Robert Tudor Hooson;** Vice Lord-Lieutenant of Merseyside, since 2018; *b* Liverpool, 28 June 1949; *s* of Joseph Tudor Hooson Owen and May Owen; *m* 1973, Patricia Margaret Fawcett; one *s* one *d*. *Educ:* Quarry Bank High Sch., Liverpool; Liverpool Poly. (DipArch). Founding Partner, Owen Ellis Architects, 1980–2012. Chair: Youth Panel, Liverpool and Knowsley Magistrates Bench, 2004–09; Investigating Cttees, NMC, 2012–20. Chm. Trustees, Local Solutions, 2006–13; Mem., Merseyside Police and High Sheriff's Trust, 2006–17. Chm. Govs, Belvedere Sch., Liverpool, 1995–98. DL, 2012, High Sheriff, 2015, Merseyside; JP Liverpool and Knowsley, 1980–2019. *Recreations:* golf, woodwork, gardening, watercolour and acrylic painting, Liverpool FC. *Address:* 3 Golf Courtyard, School Lane, Woolton, Liverpool L25 7UA. *T:* (0151) 486 6990, 07775 530651. *E:* robertthowen@gmail.com. *Clubs:* Athenæum (Liverpool) (Pres., 2011–12); Woolton Golf (Pres., 2018–).

**OWEN, Roger;** *see* Owen, D. R. J.

**OWEN, Ruth Ellen,** CBE 2010; Partner, Advisory Services, EY Australia, since 2017; *b* Kingston upon Thames, 12 Oct. 1968; *d* of Michael Owen and Penny Owen. *Educ:* Epsom High Sch.; Queen Mary and Westfield Coll., Univ. of London (BA Hons Politics 1990). Joined DSS, 1990; Business Strategy Dir, 2005–08, Chief Operating Officer, 2008–11, Jobcentre Plus; Work Services Dir and Dep. Chief Operating Officer, DWP, 2011–12; Dir Gen. Customer Services (formerly Personal Tax), HMRC, 2012–17. *Recreation:* supporting Manchester City Football Club.

**OWEN, Dame Susan (Jane),** DCB 2018; CB 2010; Permanent Secretary, Department for Digital, Culture, Media and Sport (formerly Department for Culture, Media and Sport), 2013–19; Civil Service Diversity Champion, 2015–19; *b* 3 June 1955; *d* of Glyn and Diana Owen; *m* 1987, Prof. Martin C. Albrow; one *s*, and three step *s*. *Educ:* Lady Eleanor Holles Sch.; Newnham Coll., Cambridge (MA; Hon. Fellow 2018); University Coll. Cardiff (MSc Econ. 1977). Lectr, UC Cardiff, 1979–88; HM Treasury: Econ. Advr, 1989–95; Asst Sec./ Grade 5, EU Co-ordination, 1995–98; on secondment: Econ. Advr, Work/Family Balance Policy, No 10 Policy Unit, 1998–99; Econ. Counsellor, Washington, FCO, 1999–2002; Dir, EMU Policy, Euro Preparations and Debt Mgt, 2002–05; Dir of Ops, 2005; Dir Gen. for Corporate Performance, 2006–09, Actg Perm. Sec., 2008, DFID; Dir Gen. for Strategy (formerly Welfare and Wellbeing), DWP, 2009–13. Associate Fellow, Newnham Coll., Cambridge, 2011–14. Trustee: IFS, 2013–; NIESR, 2013–; Center for Global Develt, 2015–; Windsor Leadership Trust, 2016–. *Publications:* contrib. articles to jls incl. Fiscal Studies, Work, Employment and Society, Jl Labour Economics. *Recreations:* family, friends, sport, theatre, cooking, gardening. *Clubs:* Royal Automobile; Everton Football.

**OWEN, Tim Wynn;** QC 2000; a Recorder, since 2004; a Deputy High Court Judge, since 2010; *b* 11 Jan. 1958; *s* of Meurig Wynn Owen and Thelma Owen (*née* Parry); *m* 1992, Jemma Redgrave; two *s*. *Educ:* Atlantic Coll.; London Sch. of Economics (BA 1st Cl. Hons History 1979); PCL (Dip. Law 1982). Campaign Co-ordinator, Radical Alternatives to Prison, 1979–81; called to the Bar, Middle Temple, 1983 (Bencher, 2005); in practice at the Bar, 1984–; called to the Bar of Antigua and Barbuda, 1994. *Publications:* (jtly) Prison Law, 1993, 4th edn 2008. *Recreations:* film, travel. *Address:* Matrix Chambers, Griffin Building, Gray's Inn, WC1R 5LN. *T:* (020) 7404 3447.

**OWEN, His Honour Tudor Wyn,** FRAeS; a Circuit Judge, 2007–18; *b* Aberdare, Glamorgan, 16 May 1951; *s* of late Abel Rhys Owen and Mair Owen (*née* Jenkins); *m* 1978 (marr. diss.). *Educ:* Aberdare Boys Grammar Sch.; King's Coll. London (LLB Hons 1973); Council of Legal Educn. Called to the Bar, Gray's Inn, 1974; in practice on SE Circuit, 1975–2007; DTI Inspector, 1987; Asst Recorder, 1991–93; Recorder, 1993–2007. Mem., SE Circuit Cttee, 1993–96. General Council of the Bar: Mem., 1988–94; Member: Professional Conduct Cttee, 1989–91; Professional Standards Cttee, 1991–92; Gen. Mgt Cttee, 1992–94; Vice-Chm., Bar Cttee, 1992–93. Mem., Criminal Bar Assoc. Cttee, 1986–92 (Treas., 1989–92). Panel Mem., Bar Disciplinary Tribunals, 1995–2007. Mem., Parole Bd, 2010–; Judicial Mem., Mental Health Review Tribunal, 2010–. UK delegate to European Air Sports, 2005–06. FRAeS 2003. Freeman, City of London, 2004; Liveryman, Hon. Co. of Air Pilots (formerly GAPAN), 2005 (Asst to Court, 2007–09; Warden, 2009–12; Master, 2013–14). *Recreations:* flying helicopters and WWII aeroplanes, racing historic Formula 1 cars, travel. *Clubs:* Garrick, Royal Air Force; St Moritz Tobogganing.

**OWEN, Ursula Margaret,** OBE 2004; publisher and writer; *b* 21 Jan. 1937; *d* of Emma Sophie Sachs (*née* Boehm) and Werner Sachs; *m* 1960, Edward Roger John Owen (marr. diss.); one *d*. *Educ:* Putney High Sch.; St Hugh's Coll., Oxford (BA Hons Physiol.); Bedford Coll., London (Dip. Soc. Studies). Psychiatric social worker, Littlemore Hosp., Oxford 1960–62; Lectr, English Lang., Amer. Univ. in Cairo, 1962–63; research work in mental health and physical disabilities, 1964–67; Editor, Frank Cass, 1971–73; Sen. Editor, Barrie & Jenkins, 1973–75; Virago Press: Founder-dir, 1974; Editl Dir, 1974–90; Jt Man. Dir, 1982–90; Dir, Paul Hamlyn Fund, 1990–92. Cultural Policy Advr to Lab. Party, 1990–92; Ed. and Chief Exec., Index on Censorship, 1993–2006. Dir, New Statesman and Society, 1983–90. Chm., English Touring Opera, 2007–. Trustee: World Film Collective, 2009–15; Women for Refugee Women, 2009–11; Carcanet Press, 2011–; Ledbury Poetry Fest., 2015–. Governor: Parliament Hill School, 1991–93; South Bank Centre, 2003–15. *Publications:* (ed) Fathers: Reflections by Daughters, 1983; (ed with Mark Fisher) Whose Cities?, 1991. *Recreations:* music, reading, film, travel, spending time with my four grandchildren and one great grandchild. *Address:* 1c Spencer Rise, NW5 1AR.

**OWEN-JONES, His Honour David Roderic;** a Circuit Judge, 2011–19; *b* Bangor, N Wales, 16 March 1949; *s* of John Eryl Owen-Jones, CBE, DL and Mabel Clara Owen-Jones (*née* McIlvride). *Educ:* Llandovery Coll.; University Coll. London (LLB 1970; LLM 1971). Called to the Bar, Inner Temple, 1972, Lincoln's Inn ad eundem, 1986; a Recorder, 2001–11. Mem., Lord Chancellor's Adv. Cttee on Appointment of JPs for Inner London, 1984–90. Vice Chm., Assoc. of Liberal Lawyers, 1986–94. Gov., Internat. Students House, 1995–2010 (Trustee, 1981; Fellow, 2010). Trustee, Lord Edmund-Davies Legal Educn Trust, 2015–. Legal Advr to Hon. Soc. of Cymmrodorion, 2006–. Contested (Lib): Carmarthen, Feb. and Oct. 1974; Rugby and Kenilworth, 1983, 1987. FRSA 1984. Mem., Livery Co. of Wales, 2015. *Recreations:* theatre, travel, historical biography. *E:* dojesq@ gmail.com. *Clubs:* National Liberal (Trustee, 1990–), Reform.

**OWEN-JONES, Sir Lindsay Harwood,** KBE 2005 (CBE 2000); Honorary Chairman, L'Oréal, 2011–13 (Chairman and Chief Executive Officer, 1988–2006; non-executive Chairman, 2006–11); *b* 17 March 1946; *s* of Hugh A. Owen-Jones and Esmee Owen-Jones (*née* Lindsay); *m*; one *d*; *m* 1994, Cristina Furno. *Educ:* Worcester Coll., Oxford (BA; Hon. Fellow, 2006); European Inst. of Business Admin. Product Manager, L'Oréal, 1969; Head, Public Products Div., Belgium, 1971–74; Manager, SCAD (L'Oréal subsid.), Paris, 1974–76; Marketing Manager, Public Products Div., Paris, 1976–78; Gen. Manager, SAIPO (L'Oréal subsid.), Italy, 1978–81; Pres., 1981–83, Chm., 1991–2011, COSMAIR (L'Oréal agent), USA; Vice-Pres., L'Oréal Mgt Cttee and Mem. Bd of Dirs, 1984; Pres. and Chief Operating Officer, 1984–88. Director: Air Liquide, 1994–2009; Sanofi-aventis, 1999; Ferrari, 2005–14. Commandeur, Légion d'Honneur (France), 2005 (Officier, 1998). Hon. DSc Cranfield Sch. of Mgt, 2001. *Recreation:* private helicopter pilot.

**OWEN NORRIS, David,** FSA, FRAM, FRCO; composer, pianist and broadcaster; *b* 16 June 1953; *s* of Albert Norris and Margaret Norris (*née* Owen); two *s*. *Educ:* Royal Academy of Music (FRAM 1986); Keble Coll., Oxford (MA; Hon. Fellow, 2006). FRCO 1972. Repetiteur, Royal Opera House, 1977–80; Asst Mus. Dir, RSC, 1977–79; Prof., Royal Acad. of Music, 1977–89; Dir, Petworth Fest., 1986–92; Artistic Dir, Cardiff Fest., 1992–95; Gresham Prof. of Music, 1993–97; Prof., 1999–2007, Vis. Prof., 2007–, RCM; AHRC (formerly AHRB) Fellow in Performing Arts, 2000–04, Prof., 2007–, Southampton Univ. Chm., Steans Inst. for Singers, Chicago, 1992–98. Concerts world-wide; tours of Australia, USA, Canada; four appearances in BBC Proms; radio and TV progs in GB and N America incl. progs on Radio 3 and Radio 4, BBC2 films on Elgar, Britten, Vaughan Williams and Parry, and documentary, The Real Thing?. Gilmore Artist, 1991. Recordings include: concertos by Elgar, Lambert, Phillips and Horowitz; complete piano music of Elgar, Dyson and Quilter; complete chamber music of Grace Williams; viola music by Bax, Rawsthorne, McEwen, Leighton, Bridge; cello sonatas by Sherwood, Rawsthorne; songs by Elgar, Somervell, Quilter, Britten, Tippett, Trevor Hold, Mendelssohn and Schubert (incl. Kosegarten Liederspiel), complete Sterndale Bennett and Sullivan; 'The World's First Piano Concertos' on Square Piano; newly discovered items from Jane Austen's music collection; all Mendelssohn's Songs without Words; The Jupiter Project: 1820s Mozart arrangements. Compositions include: Think only this, 2002; Tomorrow nor Yesterday, 2005; Prayerbook, 2006; Piano Concerto in C, 2008; The Jolly Roger, 2008; Sterne, 2013; Symphony, 2013; Turning Points, 2015; HengeMusic, 2015; The Angels of Louth, 2019; Letters from Lear, 2019. FSA 2015.

**OWENS, Ann Rosemarie;** *see* Easter, A. R.

**OWENS, Prof. David Howard,** PhD; FREng; Professor of Control and Systems Engineering, and Head of Department, Automatic Control and Systems Engineering, University of Sheffield, 1999–2009, now Emeritus; Professor of Engineering, since 2016, and Principal Scientist, since 2017, Zhengzhou University, China; *b* 23 April 1948; *s* of Maurice Owens and Joan Owens; *m* 1969, Rosemary Frost; one *s* one *d*. *Educ:* Imperial Coll., London (BSc 1st Cl. Hons Phys 1969; PhD 1973). CEng 1976; FIET (FIEE 1976); FIMechE 2001; CMath 1979; FIMA 1979; FREng 2008. SO, UKAEA Winfrith, 1969–73; Lectr, Sen. Lectr, then Reader, Dept of Control Engrg, Univ. of Sheffield, 1973–84; Prof. of Engrg Maths, 1984–87, Prof. of Mechanical Engrg, 1987–90, Strathclyde Univ.; Prof. and Hd, Sch. of Engrg and Computer Sci., Univ. of Exeter, 1990–99; Dean of Engrg and Convener of Deans, Univ. of Sheffield, 2002–06. Dir and Chm., Exeter Enterprises Ltd, 1995–99; Dir, Iter8 Control Systems, 2007–14. Chm., UK Automatic Control Council, 1999–2002; Ind. Mem., Nuclear Safety Adv. Cttee, HSE, 1995–2006. Visiting Professor: Univ. of Southampton, 2011–; Univ. of Bournemouth, 2018–. Scientific Consultant, Italian Inst. of Technol., Genoa, 2012–16. Governor: Sheffield Teaching Hosps NHS Foundn Trust, 2012–15; Henry Fanshawe Foundn, 2014–18 (co-opted Mem., Governing Body, Dronfield Henry Fanshawe Sch., 2015–). Freeman, Co. of Cutlers in Hallamshire, 2007. *Publications:* Feedback and Multivariable Systems, 1979; Multivariable and Optimal Systems, 1981; Analysis and Control of Multipass Processes, 1982; Stability Analysis for Linear Repetitive Processes, 1992; Control Systems Theory and Applications for Linear Repetitive Processes, 2007; Iterative Learning Control: an optimization paradigm, 2016; over 500 technical articles in areas of control and systems engrg. *Recreations:* reading, guitar, sketching, entertaining. *Address:* Department of Automatic Control and Systems Engineering, University of Sheffield, Mappin Street, Sheffield S1 3JD. *T:* (0114) 222 5684, *Fax:* (0114) 222 5661. *E:* d.h.owens@sheffield.ac.uk.

**OWENS, Eleanor Jayne**; Her Honour Judge Owens; a Circuit Judge, since 2014; Lead Judge, South East Region Court of Protection, since 2015; *b* Norwich, 25 Aug. 1969; *d* of Peter Michael Slaughter and Veronica Audrey Slaughter. *Educ*: St Bede's Sch., Redhill; New Hall, Cambridge (BA 1991); Nottingham Trent Univ. (LLB Hons). Admitted solicitor, 1997; Legal Advr, Cumbria, 1991–96, Cambs, 1996–99; Legal Team Manager, Cambs, 1999–2013; Dep. Justices' Clerk, Cambs, 2013–14; a Recorder, 2009–14. *Recreations*: horse riding, gardening, reading, cinema, walking, opera. *Address*: Oxford Combined Court, St Aldates, Oxford OX1 1TL. *T*: (01865) 264246. *E*: hhj.eleanor.owens@ejudiciary.net.

**OWENS, Prof. Ian Peter Farrar**, PhD; Professor of Evolutionary Ecology, Imperial College London, since 2004; Director of Science, Natural History Museum, since 2011; *b* Sutton Coldfield, 1967; *s* of Peter and Sheila Owens; *m* 1992, Sally Ann Gibbins; two *s*. *Educ*: Univ. of Liverpool (BSc Zoology 1989); Univ. of Leicester (PhD Evolutionary Biol. 1992). Natural Hist. Mus. Scholar, Ornithological Section, Natural Hist. Mus., Tring, 1987; NERC Student, Univ. of Leicester, 1989–91; NERC Postdoctoral Res. Fellow, Inst. of Zool., Zool Soc. of London and UCL, 1992–95; Lectr in Ecol., 1995–98, Sen. Lectr in Ecol., 1998–2000, Univ. of Queensland; Imperial College London: Governors' Lectr in Biol., 2000–02; Reader in Evolutionary Ecol., Silwood Park, 2003–04; Dep. Dir, NERC Centre for Population Biol., 2004–10; Hd, Ecol. and Evolution Section, 2006–09; Hd, Div. of Biol., 2009–; Hd, Dept of Life Scis, 2007–11. Member: NERC Peer Rev. Coll., 2002–07; NERC Steering Panel on Post-genomics and proteomics, 2004–; DEFRA Peer Rev. Panel, 2006–. Ed., Behavioral Ecology, 2001–07; Member, Editorial Board: Jl of Evolutionary Biology, 2001–06; Series B Biol Scis, Procs of Royal Soc., 2002–08; Ecology Letters, 2003–06; BMC Evolutionary Biology, 2006–; BMC Ecology, 2006–; Mem. Council, Encyclopedia of Life, 2012–. Member: Bd of Trustees, Nat. Biodiversity Network, 2012–; Council, British Trust for Ornithol., 2012–. External Examiner: Univ. of Lancaster, 2005–08; UEA, 2007–09; Univ. of Cambridge, 2009–12. Hon. Res. Fellow, Inst. of Zool., Zool Soc. of London, 2004. Scientific Medal, Zool Soc. of London, 2005. *Publications*: Evolutionary Ecology of Birds: life histories, mating systems and extinction (with P. M. Bennett), 2002; approx. 100 articles in scientific jls on ecology, evolution, animal behaviour and biodiversity. *Recreations*: bird watching, natural history, walking, photography. *Address*: Natural History Museum, Cromwell Road, SW7 5BD. *T*: (020) 7942 5374, *Fax*: (020) 7942 5765. *E*: i.owens@nhm.ac.uk.

**OWENS, Jeffrey Phillip**, CMG 2012; Visiting Professor, Vienna University, since 2012; Senior Tax Policy Advisor, Ernst & Young, since 2012; *b* Swansea, 26 Jan. 1946; *s* of Granville Philip Owens and Megan James Owens; *m* 1989, Janice Callaghan; two *s* two *d*. *Educ*: Inst. of Mgt Accountants; Univ. of Wales, Cardiff (BSc Econs); Queens' Coll., Cambridge (PhD Econs 1973); Alliance Française (Dip. Langue Français). Commercial trainee, British Steel, 1962–64; cost accountant, Tube Investments UK, 1964–66; Economist, 1972–80, Sen. Economist, 1980–86, Hd of Division, 1986–2001, Dir, Center for Tax Policy and Admin, 2001–12, OECD, Paris. Advr to govts and orgns, incl. EC, 2012–14, World Bank, 2014–, EIB, 2016–, IADB; Sen. Advr, UNCTAD, 2015–. Robert Schuman Fellow, Eur. Univ. Inst., Florence, 2013. Chm., SMU-TA Adv. Panel, Singapore, 2015–. Mem., Franco-Welsh Soc. Internat. Tax Person of Year, Tax Notes jl, USA, 2011. *Publications*: Growth of Euro-Dollar Market, 1974; Local Government, 1991; Tax Systems in North Africa and European Countries, 1994; (contrib.) BRICS and the Emergence of International Tax Coordination, 2015; Tax Barriers to the BRI, 2018. *Recreations*: sailing, ski-ing, gardening, cooking, cinema, travel, family, good wine, reading. *Address*: 23 avenue Onze Novembre, Meudon 92190, France. *T*: 778671068. *E*: jeffrey.p.owens@gmail.com. *Club*: St Quentin Sailing.

**OWENS, Lynne Gillian**, CBE 2015; QPM 2009; Director General, National Crime Agency, since 2016; *b* 29 Jan. 1969; *m*; one *d*. *Educ*: Univ. of Exeter (MA 2008). Police constable, Metropolitan Police, 1989–93; Sergeant, later Detective Chief Inspector, Kent Police, 1993–2002; Detective Superintendent, later Dep. Chief Constable, Surrey Police, 2002–09; Dep. Asst Comr, then Asst Comr, Metropolitan Police, 2009–12; Chief Constable, Surrey Police, 2012–16. *Address*: National Crime Agency, Units 1–6 Citadel Place, Tinworth Street, SE11 5EF. *T*: (01207) 238 0229. *E*: Lynne.Owens@nca.gov.uk.

**OWENS, Matthew**, FRCO; conductor, composer and organist; Director of Music, St Anne's Cathedral, Belfast, since 2019; *b* 17 Jan. 1971; *s* of John Duncan Owens and Brenda Owens; *m* 2004, Alison Jane Darragh, PhD; two *s*. *Educ*: Chetham's Sch. of Music, Manchester; Queen's Coll., Oxford (BA Hons Music 1992; MA 1996); Royal Northern Coll. of Music (MusM 1994; PPRNCM 1994); Amsterdam Conservatorium. FRCO 1994. Sub organist, Manchester Cathedral, 1996–99; Organist and Master of Music, St Mary's Episcopal Cathedral, Edinburgh, 1999–2004; Organist and Master of Choristers, 2005–19, Preb., 2017–, Wells Cathedral. Asst and Associate Dir, Nat. Youth Choir, 1993–2000; Organist, Musical Dir and Singer, BBC Daily Service, 1994–99; Artistic Dir and Conductor, Exon Singers, 1997–2011; Conductor, Wells Cathedral Oratorio Soc., 2005–19; Founder and Artistic Director: Cathedral Commissions, 2006–; new music wells festival, 2008–; Founder and Dir, Cranmer Anthem Book, 2017–. Tutor in Organ Studies: Chetham's Sch. of Music, 1994–99; RNCM, 1995–2000; Wells Cathedral Sch., 2006–13. Mem., Cathedrals' Liturgy and Music Gp, Assoc. English Cathedrals, 2008–13. Pres., Cathedral Organists' Assoc., 2010–13. Hon. FGCM 2012. *Publications*: The Holly and the Ivy, 2012; St Matthew Passion, 2013; Crux fidelis, 2014; Holy Trinity Blessing, 2015; Joseph Fili David, 2015; Magnificat and Nunc Dimittis 'Fauxbourdon Service', 2015; This Joyful Eastertide, 2015; Lullay, my liking, 2016; Ut queant laxis, 2016; Lord of the Dance, 2016; Toccata on Good King Wenceslas, 2017; (contrib.) The Oxford Book of Choral Pedagogy; educational articles, and reviews in Organists' Rev., Choir and Organ, Cathedral Music. *Recreations*: reading, concerts, opera, cooking, travel, film, art, politics, horseracing, walking Elsie the dog. *Address*: Belfast Cathedral, Donegall Street, Belfast BT1 2HB.

**OWENS, Prof. Nicholas John Paul**, PhD; CBiol, FRSB; FRGS; FMBA; Professor of Marine Science, University of the Highlands and Islands, since 2015; Director, Scottish Association for Marine Science, since 2015; Chief Executive Officer: SAMS Group, since 2015; SAMS Research Services Ltd, since 2016; Principal, SAMS-UHI, since 2015; *b* 17 Jan. 1954; *s* of Michael John Joseph Benedict Owens and Christine Mary Theresa Owens; *m* 1982, Susan Mary Forster (*d* 2015); four *s*. *Educ*: Univ. of Liverpool (BSc 1976); Univ. of Dundee (PhD 1981). MIBiol, CBiol 1983; FRSB (FIBiol 2009); FRGS 2009. Res. Scientist, Inst. for Marine Envmtl Res., 1979–92; University of Newcastle: Prof. of Marine Sci., 1992–2000; Hd, Dept of Marine Scis and Coastal Mgt, 1993–99; Director: NERC Plymouth Marine Lab., 2000–07; British Antarctic Survey, 2007–12; Sir Alister Hardy Foundn for Ocean Sci., 2012–15; Prof. of Ocean Sci., Plymouth Univ., 2012–15. Non-exec. Dir, CEFAS, DEFRA, 2012–15 (Chm., Sci. Adv. Cttee, 2012–15); Chair, Partnership for Observation of Global Ocean, 2019–. Bd Dir, PML (formerly Plymouth Marine) Applications Ltd, 2001–07. Trustee: Nat. Marine Aquarium, 2002–09; Scottish Assoc. for Marine Sci., 2009–10. Hon. Prof., Univ. of Plymouth, 2006–12. FMBA 2015. *Publications*: over 100 articles in learned marine sci. jls. *Recreations*: game fishing, yachting, running, mountaineering, gardening. *Address*: Scottish Association for Marine Science, Scottish Marine Institute, Oban, Argyll PA37 1QA. *E*: nick.owens@sams.ac.uk. *W*: www.twitter.com/n1jpo. *Clubs*: Allen Valley Angling and Conservation; Oban Sailing; Clyde Cruising.

**OWENS, Prof. Susan Elizabeth**, OBE 1998; PhD; FBA 2011; Professor of Environment and Policy, University of Cambridge, 2004–16, now Emerita; Fellow of Newnham College, Cambridge, 1981–2016, now Emerita; *b* 24 Jan. 1954; *d* of Alfred Raymond Penrose and Patricia Mary Penrose (*née* Dorrell); *m* 1976. *Educ*: Stevenage Girls' Sch.; Univ. of East Anglia (BSc Hons, PhD). Res. Officer, Energy Panel, SSRC, 1979; Res. Fellow, Inst. of Planning Studies, Univ. of Nottingham, 1980–81; University of Cambridge: Asst Lectr in Geography, 1981–86; Lectr, 1986–2000; Reader in Envmt and Policy, 2000–04; Hd, Dept of Geography, 2010–13. King Carl XVI Gustaf Vis. Prof. of Envmtl Sci., Stockholm Resilience Centre and Royal Inst. of Technol., 2008–09; Hon. Prof., Univ. of Copenhagen, 2008–13. Global Envmtl Change Programme Res. Fellow, ESRC, 1993–94. Member: UK Round Table on Sustainable Develt, 1995–98; Countryside Commn, 1996–99; Govt Adv. Panel on Integrated Transport Policy, 1997–98; Royal Commn on Envmtl Pollution, 1998–2008 (Special Advr, 1992–94); Steering Panel for OST review of Sci. in DEFRA, 2005–06; Res. Cttee (formerly Strategic Res. Bd), ESRC, 2007–11; Hazardous Substances Adv. Cttee, 2013–; Science Adv. Council, Stockholm Envmt Inst., 2013– (Chair, 2015–); Social Sci. Expert Gp, DEFRA, 2016–; Making Sense of Sci. for Policy Wkg Gp, Sci. Advice for Policy by Eur. Acads, 2018–19; Chm., Governance Working Gp, European Envmtl and Sustainability Adv. Councils, 2003–06. Mem., sub-panel H31, Town and Country Planning, RAE 2008. Mem., Royal Soc. Sci. Policy Adv. Gp, 2008–13. Trustee, Miriam Rothschild and John Foster Human Rights Trust, 2007–10. FAcSS (AcSS 2002). Life Hon. MRTPI 2013 (Hon. MRTPI 2006). Hon. ScD: Royal Inst. Technol., Stockholm, 2012; UEA, 2015. Back Award, RGS (with IBG), 2000. *Publications*: Energy, Planning and Urban Form, 1986; (jtly) Environment, Resources and Conservation, 1990; (ed jtly) Britain's Changing Environment from the Air, 1991; (jtly) Land Use Planning Policy and Climate Change, 1992; (jtly) Land and Limits: interpreting sustainability in the planning process, 2002, 2nd edn 2011; Knowledge, Policy, and Expertise: the UK Royal Commission on Environmental Pollution 1970–2011, 2015; contrib. learned jls, incl. Trans Inst. of British Geographers, Land Use Policy, Town Planning Review, Political Qly, Jl of Risk Res., Envmt and Planning A, Govt and Policy (Envmt and Planning C), Envmtl Conservation, European Envmt, Global Envmtl Change, Jl Envmtl Law, Critical Policy Studies, Envmtl Sci. and Policy, Envmtl Res. Letters, Envmt Internat., Sci. and Public Policy. *Recreations*: walking, literature. *Address*: Department of Geography, University of Cambridge, Downing Place, Cambridge CB2 3EN. *T*: (01223) 333399.

**OWER, Dr David Cheyne**, TD 1975; Senior Principal Medical Officer, Department of Health and Social Security, 1976–87; *b* 29 July 1931; *s* of Ernest Ower and Helen Edith Cheyne (*née* Irvine); *m* 1954, June Harris; two *s* two *d*. *Educ*: King's Coll. Sch., Wimbledon; King's Coll., London; King's Coll. Hosp. Med. Sch. (MB, BS 1954). DObstRCOG 1959; FFPH (FFCM 1983; MFCM 1976). Jun. hosp. appts, King's Coll. Hosp. and Kingston Hosp., 1955; RAF Med. Br., 1956–58; gen. practice, 1959–64; DHSS (formerly Min. of Health) Med. Staff, 1965–87. T&AVR, and RAMC(V), 1962–; Lt-Col RAMC(V); CO 221 (Surrey) Field Amb., 1973–75. *Recreations*: music, bridge, thinking about playing golf. *Address*: Bonshaw, Winchester Road, Alresford, Hants SO24 9EZ. *T*: (01962) 735152.

**OWERS, Dame Anne (Elizabeth)**, DBE 2009 (CBE 2001); Chairman: Board, Clinks, since 2011; Board, Koestler Trust, since 2013; Independent Monitoring Boards, since 2017; *b* 23 June 1947; *d* of William Spark and Anne Smailes Spark (*née* Knox); *m* 1st, 1968 (marr. diss.); two *s* one *d*; 2nd, 2005, Edmund Stephen Cook. *Educ*: Washington Grammar Sch., Co. Durham; Girton Coll., Cambridge (BA Hons 1968). Research and teaching in Zambia, 1968–71; work at JCWI, 1981–92 (Gen. Sec., 1986–92); Dir, Justice, 1992–2001; HM Chief Inspector of Prisons for England and Wales, 2001–10. Mem., IPCC, 2012–17. Chm. Bd of Trustees, Refugee Legal Centre, 1994–98; Member: Lord Chancellor's Adv. Cttee on Legal Educn and Conduct, 1997–99; Home Office Task Force on Human Rights, 1999–2001; Legal Services Consultative Panel, 2000–01; non-exec. Dir, Criminal Cases Rev. Commn, 2010–14. Chm. Bd, Christian Aid, 2008–13. Hon. Fellow: South Bank Univ., 2005; Lucy Cavendish Coll., Cambridge, 2007. DUniv Essex, 2006; Hon. DCL Oxford, 2013. *Publications*: (ed jtly) Economic, Social and Cultural Rights, 1999; chapters and papers on immigration and nationality matters and on prisons. *Recreations*: music, walking, friends, family.

**OWUSU, Elsie Margaret Akua**, OBE 2003; RIBA; Founder and Principal, Elsie Owusu Architects, since 1989; Partner, Feilden & Mawson LLP, architects, 2006–16; Founder and Director: artistConstructor Ltd; archQuestra Ltd; *b* 9 Dec. 1953; *d* of Paul Kofi Owusu and Joyce Ophelia Owusu; one *d*. *Educ*: Demonstration Sch., Legon, Ghana; Streatham Hill and Clapham Girls' High Sch.; Architectural Association Sch. of Architecture; Chelsea Coll. of Art. RIBA 1989; Specialist Conservation Architect 2012. Design Team, Solon SE Housing Assoc., 1981–85; Women's Design Service, 1985–86; in private practice, Owusu and Teague, 1986–89. Lead architect: for Feilden & Mawson: interiors, UK Supreme Court, 2006–09; Green Park Underground Station (masterplan and conservation plan), 2008–09; for Elsie Owusu Architects: Lagos Bus Rapid Transit, 2008–10; pilot route of Accra Bus Rapid Transit, 2011–12; (with Sir Peter Blake) 60 Aden Grove, N16, 2012. Founder Member: Soc. of Black Architects, 1990 (first Chm., 1990–92); Black Internat. Construction Orgn, 1996–; Sec., Fedn of Black Housing Orgns, 1994–96 (Mem., Exec. Cttee, 1994–96); Member: Haringey Employment Commn, 1996–97; Trafalgar Square Plinth Cttee, 1999–2000; Building Regulations Adv. Cttee, 2001–03; Enabling Panel, CABE, 2002–08; Adv. Bd, Ayebia Clarke Publishing, 2010–; Council, Architectural Assoc., 2015–; Council, RIBA, 2015– (Mem., Educnl Vis. Bd, 1995–96; RIBA Role Model, 2015); Board Member: Arts Council of England, subseq. Arts Council England, 2002–09; Nat. Trust, 2002–04. Acting Chair, 2006–08, Chair, 2008–09, Aduna. Dir, JustGhana Ltd, 2007–. Vice-Pres., Women's Transport Seminar, 2005–07. Mem., Bd of Trustees, Royal African Soc., 2008–. Trustee, UK Supreme Court Arts Trust, 2016–. Vice-Chair and Trustee, London Sch. of Architecture, 2015–. Member: Bd of Governors, Middlesex Univ., 1996–2000; Corp., Coll. of NE London, 1996–2001. FRSA. *Recreations*: reading, walking, drawing, dreaming. *Address*: 30 Chalfont Court, Baker Street, NW1 5RS. *T*: (020) 7486 2188.

**OWUSU-ANKOMAH, Papa**; Companion, Order of the Volta, 2008; High Commissioner of the Republic of Ghana to the United Kingdom, since 2017; *b* Sekondi, Ghana, 27 April 1958; *s* of Yaw Owusu-Ankomah and Augustina Owusu-Ankomah; *m* 1984, Augustina Appiah; two *s* one *d*. *Educ*: Univ. of Ghana (LLB Hons 1979); Ghana Sch. of Law. Called to the Bar, Ghana, 1981. MP, Ghana, 1997–2017; Minister for Youth and Sports, 2001; Majority Leader in Parlt, Minister for Parly Affairs, 2001–03; Attorney-Gen. and Minister for Justice, 2003–05; Minister for Interior, 2005–06; for Educn, Sci. and Sports, 2006–07; for Trade, Industry and Private Sector Develt and Presidential Special Initiatives, 2007–08. Mem., United Grand Lodge of England. *Recreations*: reading, listening to music. *Address*: 41 Avenue Road, St John's Wood, NW8 6BS. *T*: (020) 7201 5944. *E*: papa.owusu-ankomah@ghc-uk.org.

**OXBURGH,** family name of **Baron Oxburgh.**

**OXBURGH, Baron** *cr* 1999 (Life Peer), of Liverpool in the county of Merseyside; **Ernest Ronald Oxburgh,** KBE 1992; PhD; FRS 1978; Chairman, 2OC, 2006–17; Rector, Imperial College of Science, Technology and Medicine, 1993–2001; *b* 2 Nov. 1934; *m* Ursula Mary Brown; one *s* two *d*. *Educ:* Liverpool Inst.; University Coll., Oxford (BA 1957, MA 1960); Univ. of Princeton (PhD 1960). Departmental Demonstrator, 1960–61, Lectr in Geology, 1962–78, Univ. of Oxford; Fellow of St Edmund Hall, Oxford, 1964–78, Emeritus Fellow, 1978, Hon. Fellow, 1986; University of Cambridge: Prof. of Mineralogy and Petrology, 1978–91; Hd of Dept of Earth Scis, 1980–88; Fellow of Trinity Hall, 1978–82, Hon. Fellow, 1988; Queens' College: Pres., 1982–89; Professorial Fellow, 1989–91; Hon. Fellow, 1992; Chief Scientific Advr, MoD, 1987–93. Chairman: Shell Transport & Trading plc, 2004–05; Falck Renewables, 2007–11; Green Energy Options, 2011–. Chm., SETNET, 2001–05. Visiting Professor: CIT, 1967–68; Stanford and Cornell Univs, 1973–74; Sherman Fairchild Distinguished Vis. Scholar, CIT, 1985–86. Trustee, Natural History Mus., 1993–2002 (Chm. Trustees, 1999–2002). Chm., H of L Select Cttee on Sci. and Technol., 2001–05. Member: SERC, 1988–93; Hong Kong UGC, 1988–2002; Nat. Cttee of Inquiry into Higher Educn (Dearing Cttee), 1996–97. President: Eur. Union of Geosciences, 1985–87 (Hon. Fellow 1993); BAAS, 1995–96; Carbon Capture and Storage Assoc., 2005–16; Inst. of Measurement and Control, 2012–15. FGS (Pres., 2000–02); Fellow: Geol. Soc. of America; Amer. Geophys. Union. Hon. Mem., Geologists' Assoc.; Foreign Corresp., Geologische Bundesanstalt, Austria and of Geological Soc. of Vienna; Foreign Member: Venezuelan Acad. of Scis, 1992; Deutsche Akad. der Naturforscher Leopoldina, 1994; Corresp. Mem., Australian Acad. of Sci., 1999; For. Associate, US Acad. of Scis, 2001. FIC 2003. Hon. FIMechE 1993; Hon. FCGI 1996; Hon FREng 2000. Hon. Fellow, Univ. Coll., Oxford, 1983. DSc (*hc*): Univ. of Paris, 1986; Leicester, 1990; Loughborough, 1991; Edinburgh, 1994; Birmingham, 1996; Liverpool, 1996; Southampton, 2003; Liverpool John Moores, 2006; Lingnan, Hong Kong, 2006; Newcastle upon Tyne, 2007; Leeds, 2009; Wyoming, 2011; Hon. DSc St Andrews, 2013. Bigsby Medal, Geol Soc., 1979; Sir George Thomson Gold Medal, Inst. of Measurement and Control, 2010; Public Service Medal, Singapore, 2010; Melchett Lectr and Medal, Inst. of Energy, 2014. Officier, Ordre des Palmes Académiques (France), 1995. *Publications:* contribs to Nature, Jl Geophys Res., Phil Trans Royal Soc., Annual Reviews, Science, Bull. Geol. Soc. America, Jl Fluid Mechanics, Jl Geol Soc. London. *Recreations:* mountaineering, orienteering, reading, theatre. *Address:* c/o House of Lords, SW1A 0PW.

**OXENBURY, Helen Gillian;** children's writer and illustrator; *b* Suffolk, 2 June 1938; *d* of Thomas Bernard Oxenbury and Muriel (*née* Taylor); *m* 1964, John Mackintosh Burningham (*d* 2019); one *s* two *d*. *Educ:* Ipswich Sch. of Art; Central Sch. of Art. Stage designer, Colchester, 1960, Tel-Aviv, 1961; TV designer, London, 1963. BookTrust Lifetime Achievement Award (jtly), 2018. *Publications: author and illustrator:* Number of Things, 1967; ABC of Things, 1971; Pig Tale, 1973; (with F. Maschler) A Child's Book of Manners: Verses, 1978; The Queen and Rosie Randall, 1979; 729 Curious Creatures, 1980; 729 Merry Mixips, 1980; 729 Puzzle People, 1980; 729 Animal Allsorts, 1980; Crazy Creatures, 1980; Assorted Animals, 1980; Bill and Stanley, 1981; Bedtime, 1982; Monkey See, Monkey Do, 1982; Holidays, 1982; Helping, 1982; Mother's Helper, 1982; Animals, 1982; Beach Day, 1982; Shopping Trip, 1982; Good Night, Good Morning, 1982; The Birthday Party, 1983; The Dancing Class, 1983; Eating Out, 1983; The Car Trip, 1983; The Drive, 1983; The Checkup, 1983; First Day of School, 1983; First Day at Playschool, 1983; Playschool, 1983; Grandma and Grandpa, 1984; Our Dog, 1984; The Important Visitor, 1984; Helen Oxenbury Nursery Story Book, 1985; Tom and Pippo Go Shopping, 1988; Tom and Pippo's Day, 1988; Tom and Pippo in the Garden, 1988; Tom and Pippo Go for a Walk, 1988; Tom and Pippo Make a Mess, 1988; Tom and Pippo Read a Story, 1988; Tom and Pippo See the Moon, 1988; Tom and Pippo and the Washing Machine, 1988; Pippo Gets Lost, 1989; Tom and Pippo and the Dog, 1989; Tom and Pippo in the Snow, 1989; Tom and Pippo Make a Friend, 1989; Tom and Pippo on the Beach, 1993; It's My Birthday, 1994; First Nursery Stories, 1994; *illustrator:* The Great Big Enormous Turnip, 1968; The Quangle-Wangle's Hat, 1969; Letters of Thanks, 1969; The Dragon of an Ordinary Family, 1969; The Hunting of the Snark, 1970; Meal One, 1971; Cakes and Custard: Children's Rhymes, 1974; Balooky Klujypop, 1975; Animal House, 1976; Tiny Tim: Verses for Children, 1981; We're Going on a Bear Hunt, 1989; Farmer Duck, 1992; The Three Little Wolves and The Big Bad Pig, 1993; So Much, 1994; Alice in Wonderland, 1999; Franny B. Kranny, 2001; Big Momma Makes the World, 2002; Alice Through the Looking Glass, 2005; The Growing Story, 2007; Ten Little Fingers Ten Little Toes, 2008; There's Going to be a Baby, 2010; King Jack and the Dragon, 2011; Charley's First Night, 2012; When Charley Met Grampa, 2013; Captain Jack and the Pirates, 2015; Time Now to Dream, 2016; The Giant Jumperee, 2017; Helen Oxenbury: a life in illustration, 2018. *Address:* c/o Greene and Heaton Ltd, 37 Goldhawk Road, W12 8QQ.

**OXENBURY, Dame Shirley (Ann),** DBE 1992 (OBE 1987); Personal Assistant to Rt Hon. Christopher Patten, 1997–2000; *b* 4 July 1936. *Educ:* Ensham County Sch., London, SW17. PA to Harold Fielding, 1965–70; Personal Assistant (at Conservative Central Office) to Chairman of the Conservative Party: Katharine Macmillan, Sara Morrison, Baroness Young, 1970–75; Lord Thorneycroft, 1975–81; Cecil Parkinson, 1981–83; John Gummer, 1983–85; Norman Tebbit, 1985–87; Peter Brooke, 1987–89; Kenneth Baker, 1989–90; Christopher Patten, 1990–92; Norman Fowler, 1992–94; Jeremy Hanley, 1994–95; Brian Mawhinney, 1995–97. Women's Transport Service (FANY), 1979–. *Recreations:* swimming, arts, learning languages. *T:* (020) 7798 8316.

**OXFORD, Bishop of,** since 2016; **Rt Rev. Dr Steven John Lindsey Croft;** *b* 29 May 1957; *s* of James and Marian Croft; *m* 1978, Ann Christine Baker; two *s* two *d*. *Educ:* Worcester Coll., Oxford (BA Hons 1980, MA 1983); St John's Coll., Durham (PhD 1984). Ordained deacon, 1983, priest, 1984; Curate, St Andrew's, Enfield, 1983–87; Vicar, St George's, Ovenden, Halifax, 1987–96; Mission Consultant, Dio. Wakefield, 1993–96; Priest-in-charge, St Augustine, Halifax, 1994–96; Warden, Cranmer Hall, St John's Coll., Durham, 1996–2004; Archbishop's Missioner, and Team Leader, Fresh Expressions, 2004–09; Bishop of Sheffield, 2009–16. Took seat in H of L, 2013. *Publications:* The Identity of the Individual in the Psalms, 1987; Growing New Christians, 1993; Making New Disciples, 1994; (jtly) Emmaus, The Way of Faith, vols 1–6, 1996, vols 7–8, 1998; Man to Man: friendship and faith, 1999; Ministry in Three Dimensions: ordination and leadership in the local church, 1999; (jtly) Travelling Well, 2000; The Lord is Risen, 2001; Missionary Journeys, Missionary Church, 2001; Transforming Communities: re-imagining the Church for the 21st century, 2002; (jtly) Learning for Ministry: making the most of study and training, 2005; Moving On in a Mission-Shaped Church, 2005; The Advent Calendar, 2006; (ed) The Future of the Parish System, 2006; (ed) Mission-shaped Questions, 2008; Jesus' People: what the church should do next, 2009; (ed) Fresh Expressions in the Sacramental Tradition, 2010; Exploring God's Mercy, 2010; Exploring God's Love, 2011; (jtly) Women and Men in Scripture and the Church: a guide to key issues, 2013; The Gift of Leadership: according to the scriptures, 2016; (ed) Rooted and Grounded: faith formation and the Christian tradition, 2019. *Recreations:* walking, cooking, films. *Address:* Church House Oxford, Langford Locks, Kidlington, Oxford OX5 1GF. *T:* (01865) 208200, *Fax:* (01865) 790470. *E:* bishop.oxford@oxford.anglican.org.

**OXFORD, Archdeacon of;** *see* Gorick, Ven. M. C. W.

**OXFORD AND ASQUITH,** 3rd Earl of, *cr* 1925; **Raymond Benedict Bartholomew Michael Asquith,** OBE 1992; Viscount Asquith 1925; Director: Zander Corporation Ltd, since 2002; Meteor Asset Management Ltd, since 2009; Hansa Trust, since 2013; *b* 24 Aug. 1952; *er s* of 2nd Earl of Oxford and Asquith, KCMG and Anne Mary Celestine (*née* Palairet); *S* father, 2011; *m* 1978, Mary Clare, *e d* of Francis Pollen; one *s* four *d*. *Educ:* Ampleforth; Balliol College, Oxford. HM Diplomatic Service, 1980–97: FCO, 1980–83; First Sec., Moscow, 1983–85; Cabinet Office and FCO, 1985–92; Counsellor, Kiev, 1992–97. Elected Mem., H of L, 2014. *Heir: s* Viscount Asquith, *qv. Address:* The Manor House, Mells, Frome, Somerset BA11 3PN.
*See also* Hon. Sir D. A. G. *Asquith.*

**OXFORD, Prof. John Sydney,** PhD; FRCPE, FRSB; Professor of Virology, Queen Mary (formerly Barts and the Royal London Hospitals), University of London, 1988–2014, now Emeritus; Founder, hVIVO (formerly Retroscreen Virology Ltd), since 1990; Founder and Director, Oxford Media and Medicine Ltd, since 2011; *b* 6 March 1942; *s* of Sydney and Edith Oxford; *m* 1965, Gillian Claire Mason; one *s* four *d*. *Educ:* Univ. of Reading (BSc Hons 1963; Lord Kitchener Meml Fund Scholar); Univ. of Sheffield (PhD 1966). FRCPE 2013; FRSB (FSB 2013). Lectr in Med. Microbiol., Univ. of Sheffield, 1966–70; Res. Fellow, John Curtin Sch. of Med. Res., ANU, 1970–73; Member, Scientific Staff: NIMR, Mill Hill, 1973–76; Nat. Inst. for Biol Standards and Control, S Mimms, 1976–88. Vis. Schol., Dept of Microbiol., Univ. of Melbourne, 1987–88. Chm., Global Hygiene Council, 2005–. Res. in location and analysis of lung samples from permafrost or lead coffin encased victims of 1918 Spanish influenza. Fellow, Strehlow Aboriginal Res. Foundn, Adelaide, 1990. MInstD 1993. Hon. DSc Kingston, 2011. *Publications:* (jtly) Influenza, the Viruses and the Disease, 1985; (jtly) Conquering Viral Disease, 1986; (jtly) Human Virology, 1993, 5th edn 2016; contrib. 300 scientific papers on influenza viruses with special emphasis on hygiene, antivirals and vaccines. *Recreations:* literature and poetry, historical analysis of World War I and emergence of Spanish influenza in 1916; travelling the world as regards prevention of bird flu H5N1 and making science films and pieces for BBC, Channel 4 and National Geographic; spending special time with my wife, five children, nine grandchildren and family. *Address:* Blizard Institute, Queen Mary College, 4 Newark Street, E1 2AT. *E:* j.oxford@qmul.ac.uk. *Club:* Athenæum.

**OXFUIRD,** 14th Viscount of, *cr* 1651; **Ian Arthur Alexander Makgill,** MA; Bt 1627 (NS); Lord Makgill of Cousland, 1651; Managing Director, Ticon UK Ltd, management consultancy; *b* 16 Oct. 1969; *s* of 13th Viscount of Oxfuird, CBE and of Alison Campbell, *e d* of Neils Max Jensen, Randers, Denmark; *S* father, 2003; *m* 2009, Ruth Mairo, *d* of Samuel Fripp; one *s* one *d*. *Educ:* Canford Sch., Wimborne; Univ. of Plymouth (BA Hons Media); Univ. of Middlesex (MA Design for Computer Media). Project manager for business to consumer IT projects for Axon and Tesco; started mgt consultancy firm for public sector, Ticon UK Ltd, 2003. *Recreations:* boxing, ski-ing, contemporary art. *Heir: s* Master of Oxfuird, *qv. E:* ian@spendnetwork.com.

**OXFUIRD, Master of;** Hon. **Max George Samuel Makgill;** *b* 24 Aug. 2012; *s* and heir of Viscount of Oxfuird, *qv*.

**OXLEY, Julian Christopher;** Director and Secretary, 1984–89, Director-General, 1989–96, Guide Dogs for the Blind Association; *b* 23 Nov. 1938; *s* of Horace Oxley and Lilian Oxley (*née* Harris); *m* 1979, Carol (*née* Heath) (*d* 2010); one *d*; *m* 2014, Catherine Margaret (*née* Follows-Smith); one *s* two *d* from previous marriage. *Educ:* Clifton Coll., Bristol; Oriel Coll., Oxford (Organ Scholar, MA). FCA. Dir and Sec., Williams & James plc, 1970–84. Chm., Internat. Fedn of Guide Dog Schs, 1990–97. Non-exec. Dir, Heatherwood and Wexham Park Hosps NHS Trust, 1999–2006. Mem. Council, Gloucester Civic Trust, 1972–75. Chm. of Govs, Selwyn Sch., Gloucester, 1980–84. Trustee, Nat. Confedn of PTAs, 2002–09 (Chm., 2004–09). Hon. Treas., CPRE Glos, 2015–. *Recreations:* music, old furniture, railway signalling and operation. *Address:* Cura, Main Road, Minsterworth, Gloucester GL2 8JH. *T:* (01452) 750797. *E:* julian.oxley@btinternet.com.

**OXMANTOWN, Lord;** Laurence Patrick Parsons; Founder, Oriental Parsons Consultants, Beijing; President, Citiarc Group; Executive Director, BC Developments, since 2014; China Representative, Battersea Power Station Development Co. Ltd, since 2014; *b* 31 March 1969; *s* and heir of Earl of Rosse, *qv; m* 2004, Anna, *d* of Qicai Lin; one *s* one *d*. *Educ:* Aiglon Coll., Switzerland; Univ. of Beijing Language Inst. Jones Lang Wootton, China, 1993–96; Vice Pres., Taihe Real Estate Gp, 1996–2001; Marketing Dir, Guohua Real Estate, 2002–04; Vice Pres., Zhongpu Real Estate, 2004–07; Man. Dir, China Horizon Real Estate Gp, Beijing, 2007–11; Partner and Mktg Dir, Daisy Capital Internat., 2012–14. *Heir: s* Hon. William Yufan Charles Parsons, *b* 28 June 2008. *Address:* Birr Castle, Rosse Row, Birr, County Offaly, R42 VO27, Ireland.

**OYELOWO, David Oyetokunbo,** OBE 2016; actor; *b* Oxford, 1 April 1976; *s* of Stephen Oyelowo; *m* 1998, Jessica Watson; four *c*. *Educ:* London Acad. of Music and Dramatic Art. *Films* include: The Last King of Scotland, 2006; Rise of the Planet of the Apes, 2011; The Paperboy, Lincoln, 2012; Interstellar, Selma, 2014; Queen of Katwe, A United Kingdom, 2016; Gringo, 2018; Don't Let Go, 2019; *television* includes: MI-5, 2004; Five Days, 2007; Star Wars Rebels, 2015–16; Les Misérables, 2018; *theatre* includes: Othello, New York Theatre Workshop, 2016. *Address:* c/o Hamilton Hodell, 20 Golden Square, W1F 9JL. *T:* (020) 7636 1221, *Fax:* (020) 7636 1226. *E:* info@hamiltonhodell.co.uk.

**OZAWA, Seiji;** Japanese conductor; Co-founder and Artistic Director, Tokyo Opera Nomori, since 2005; Music Director, Vienna State Opera, 2002–10; *b* Shenyang, China, 1 Sept. 1935; *m* 1st, Kyoko Edo; 2nd, Vera Ilyan; one *s* one *d*. *Educ:* Toho School of Music, Tokyo; studied with Hideo Saito, Eugène Bigot, Herbert von Karajan, Leonard Bernstein. Won Besançon Internat. Comp., 1959, Koussevitzky Meml Scholarship, 1960. Asst Conductor, NY Philharmonic Orch., 1961–62 and 1964–65; music dir, Ravinia Fest., Chicago, 1964–68; conductor, Toronto SO, 1965–69; music dir, San Francisco SO, 1970–76, music advisor, 1976–77; Artistic Advr, Tanglewood Fest., 1970–73; Music Dir, Boston SO, 1973–2002. Tours with Boston Symphony Orchestra: Europe, 1976, 1988, 1993; Japan, 1978; China (musical and cultural exchange), 1979; European music festivals, 1979, 1984, 1991; 14 USA cities (orchestra's hundredth birthday), 1982; Japan, 1982 and 1986; Far East, 1989, 1994; S America, 1992; tours with Vienna Philharmonic: Asia, 1993, 1996, 2000; Europe, 1997, 1998, 2000, 2001; Berlin Philharmonic: regular concerts; tours incl. US/Asia, 1993; Guest conductor with major orchestras in Canada, Europe, Far East and USA; Conductor: Saito Kinen Orch., Japan (European tours, 1987, 1989, 1991; Carnegie Hall, NY, 1991; Saito Kinen Fest., later Seiji Ozawa Matsumoto Fest., 1992–); Salzburg Fest. Opera highlights: La Scala, Milan; Covent Garden, London; Paris Opera (incl. world première of Messiaen's Saint François d'Assise); Vienna State Op. début, Eugene Onegin, 1988; many recordings (awards). Pres., Ozawa Internat. Chamber Music Acad., 2005–. Evening at Symphony, PBS television series with Boston Symphony Orch. (Emmy award). Hon. DMus: Univ. of Mass; New England Conservatory of Music;

Wheaton Coll., Norton, Mass. Seiji Ozawa Hall inaugurated at Tanglewood, Mass, 1994. Inouye Award (first), for lifetime achievement in the arts, Japan, 1994; Praemium Imperiale, 2011; Grammy Award for best opera recording, 2016. *Publications:* Owaranai Ongaku, 2014.

**OZDEMIROGLU, (Zehra) Ece;** Founder and Director, Economics for the Environment Consultancy, since 1992; *b* Istanbul, 1970; *d* of Taylan Ozdemiroglu and Tulin Zenel; *m* 2016, Neil McKeown. *Educ:* Istanbul Univ. (BA Econs 1991); University Coll. London (MSc Envmtl Econs and Natural Resource Mgt 1992). Founder, UK Network of Envmtl Economists, 2004–. Mem. Steering Gp, Natural Capital Initiative, 2012–; Economics Lead, Proj. Coordination Team, Valuing Nature Prog., 2014–; Mem., Adaptation Sub-Cttee, Cttee on Climate Change, 2016–. *Publications:* (ed jtly) Acid Rain in Europe, 1997; (jtly) The Price of Virtue, 2001; (with P. Hardisty) Economics of Groundwater Remediation and Protection, 2005; (ed jtly) Equivalency Methods for Environmental Liability: assessing damage and compensation under the European Environmental Liability Directive, 2018. *Recreations:* play writing, acting, swimming, voluntary work. *Address:* Economics for the Environment Consultancy, 4 City Road, EC1Y 2AA. *T:* (020) 7580 5383. *E:* ece@eftec.co.uk.

**OZGA, Prof. Jennifer,** PhD; FBA 2013; Professor of the Sociology of Education, University of Oxford, 2010–15, now Emerita; Fellow, Green Templeton College. *Educ:* Univ. of Aberdeen (MA; MEd); Open Univ. (PhD). NUT; author and mgt of courses on educn for Open Univ. until 1991; Dean, Faculty of Educn, Bristol Poly., subseq. UWE, 1991–93; Prof. of Educn Policy and Dean of Social Scis, Keele Univ., 1993–2000; Prof. of Educnl Res. and Dir, Centre for Educnl Sociol., Univ. of Edinburgh, 2000–10. Vis. Prof., Univ. of Umeå, Sweden; Vis. Schol., Helsinki Univ., Finland. FAcSS (AcSS). Hon. Dr Turku, Finland. *Publications:* (with M. Lawn) Teachers, Professionalism and Class, 1981; (ed) Policy-making in Education, 1985; (ed jtly) Curriculum Policy: a reader, 1990; (ed) Women in Educational Management, 1992; (ed jtly) Work and Identity in the Primary School, 1997; Policy Research in Educational Settings, 2000; (ed with R. Lingard) The RoutledgeFalmer Reader in Education Policy and Politics, 2007; (ed jtly) Social Capital, Professionalism and Diversity, 2009; (ed jtly) Fabricating Quality in Europe: data and education governance, 2011; contribs to learned jls incl. World Yearbook of Educn, Educnl Rev., Jl Educn Policy, Critical Studies in Educn, Res. Papers in Educn, British Jl Sociol. of Educn, Eur. Educnl Res. Jl. *Address:* Department of Education, University of Oxford, 15 Norham Gardens, Oxford OX2 6PY.

**OZIN, Paul David;** QC 2016; *b* London, 16 April 1964; *s* of Ronald Ozin and Evelyn Ozin (*née* Barnett); partner, Stephen Davies. *Educ:* Carmel Coll., Wallingford (Schol.); Balliol Coll., Oxford (Theobald Exhibnr Juris.; BA Hons Juris.). Called to the Bar, Middle Temple, 1987; Standing Counsel (Crime) to DTI, then BERR, later BIS, subseq. BEIS, 2008–16; Leader, Regulatory and Disciplinary Team, 23 Essex St Chambers, 2010–. Mem. Cttee, Assoc. of Regulatory and Disciplinary Lawyers, 2015– (Vice-Chm., 2018–). Mem., Corporate Crime Consulting Editl Bd, LexisNexis, 2016–. *Publications:* (jtly) PACE: a practical guide to the Police and Criminal Evidence Act 1984, 2010, 5th edn, 2019; (contrib.) The Regulation of Healthcare Professionals: law, principle and process, 2019; contribs on criminal law and regulatory and disciplinary law subjects. *Recreations:* reading, opera, theatre, ballet, cinema, visual arts (consuming and attempting), intermittent exercise and Tai Chi Chuan (Wu style). *Address:* 23 Essex Street, WC2R 3AA. *T:* (020) 7413 0353. *E:* clerks@23es.com.

# P

**PACEY, Stephen James;** an Upper Tribunal Judge (Administrative Appeals Chamber) (formerly a Social Security and Child Support Commissioner), 1996–2013; *b* 5 July 1949; *s* of Randall Brown Pacey and May Pacey (*née* Oldknow); *m* 1978, Jessica Susan Turley; one *s*. *Educ:* Kimberley County Secondary Modern Sch.; Beeston Coll.; Trent Poly. (LLB 1971); Univ. of Huddersfield (LLM Dist. 2008); Middlesex Univ. (DProf 2015). Admitted Solicitor, 1975 (Wolverhampton Law Soc. Centenary Prizeman, 1975). Directorate of Legal Affairs, CBI, 1971–72; Lectr in Law, Isleworth Poly., 1972–73; solicitor in private practice, 1975–87; consultant planning inspector, 1989–91; Chm., Independent Tribunal Service, 1991–96; Dep. Social Security and Child Support Comr, 1993–96. Chairman (part-time): Social Security Appeal Tribunals, 1984–91; Med. Appeal Tribunals, 1987–91; Industrial Tribunals, 1988–91; Registered Homes Appeal Tribunals, 1992–96; pt-time Immigration Judge, 1998. Freeman, City of London, 1984. *Recreations:* photography, literature, performing arts.

**PACINO, Alfredo James, (Al);** actor; *b* New York, 25 April 1940; *s* of Salvatore Pacino and late Rosa Pacino; one *d* by Jan Tarrant; twin *s* and *d* by Beverly D'Angelo. *Educ:* High Sch. of Performing Arts, NY; Actors Studio, NY. Has worked as mail delivery boy, messenger, cinema usher and bldg supt; actor, dir and writer, NY theatres; appeared in première of The Indian Wants the Bronx, Waterford, Conn, 1966, and NY, 1968; Broadway début, Does a Tiger Wear a Necktie?, 1969 (Tony Award, best supporting actor); film début, Me, Natalie, 1969; *theatre includes:* Camino Real, Lincoln Center Rep. Theater, 1970; The Basic Training of Pavlo Hummel, 1972, (title rôle) Richard III, 1973, Boston Theater Co.; Arturo Ui, 1975; Jungle of Cities, 1979; American Buffalo, 1981, transf. UK, 1984; Julius Caesar, 1988; Salome, 1992; Circle in the Square, 1992; Hughie (also dir), 1996; The Resistible Rise of Arturo Ui, Michael Schimmel Centre, NY, 2002; The Merchant of Venice, Delacorte Th., NY, 2010; Glengarry Glen Ross, Gerald Schoenfeld Th., NY, 2012; An Evening with Al Pacino, UK, 2013, 2015; China Doll, Gerald Schoenfeld Th., NY, 2015; *films include:* Panic in Needle Park, 1971; The Godfather, 1972 (Best Actor Award, Nat. Soc. of Film Critics, USA); Scarecrow, 1973; Serpico, The Godfather Part II, 1974; Dog Day Afternoon, 1975; Bobby Deerfield, 1977; And Justice for All, 1979; Cruising, 1980; Author! Author!, 1982; Scarface, 1983; Revolution, 1985; The Local Stigmatic, 1989 (also play, Actors Playhouse, NY, 1969); Sea of Love, The Godfather Part III, 1990; Frankie and Johnny, 1991; Glengarry Glen Ross, Scent of a Woman (Acad. Award for best actor, 1993), 1992; Carlito's Way, Two Bits, 1994; City Hall, Heat, 1995; Donny Brasco, Looking for Richard (also writer, prod. and dir), 1996; Devil's Advocate, 1997; Man of the People, 1999; Any Given Sunday, Insider, Chinese Coffee (also dir), 2000; Insomnia, Simone, 2002; The Recruit, 2003; People I Know, The Merchant of Venice, 2004; Two for the Money, 2006; Ocean's Thirteen, 2007; Righteous Kill, 2008; Stand Up Guys, 2013; Salomé (also dir), Wilde Salomé (documentary) (also writer and dir), 2014; The Humbling, 2014; Danny Collins, 2015; Manglehorn, 2015; Misconduct, 2016; The Pirates of Somalia, 2017; Once Upon a Time in Hollywood, 2019; The Irishman, 2019; *television includes:* Angels in America, 2004; You Don't Know Jack, 2010 (Golden Globe for Best Actor in TV mini-series, 2011); Phil Spector, 2013; Paterno, 2018. Co-artistic Dir, Actors Studio Inc., NY, 1982–83; Mem., Artistic Directorate, Globe Theatre, 1997–. Cecil B. DeMille award for lifetime achievement, Golden Globe Awards, 2001. Fellow, BFI, 2014. *Address:* c/o United Talent Agency, 9336 Civic Center Drive, Beverly Hills, Los Angeles, CA 90210, USA.

**PACK, Maj.-Gen. Simon James,** CB 1997; CBE 1994 (OBE 1990); Royal Marines, retired; International Teams Director, England and Wales Cricket Board, 1997–2001; Chief Operating Officer (formerly Partnership Secretary), Gill Jennings & Every LLP, 2002–11; *b* 10 July 1944; *s* of late Captain A. J. Pack, OBE, RN and Eloise Pack; *m* 1970, Rosemary-Anne Fuller; one *s* one *d*. *Educ:* Fernden Prep. Sch.; Hurstpierpoint Coll.; Ecole de Commerce, Switzerland (Dip. French). Commnd into RM, 1962; served 3 Cdo Bde, Malaya, Sarawak, 1963–66; HMS Zulu, 1966–68; ADC to Governor of Queensland, 1969–70; Adjt, 41 Cdo, NI and Malta, 1970–72; Instructor, Officers Tactics Wing, Warminster, 1972–75; Army Staff Coll., 1976; MoD, 1977–78; 42 Cdo, Norway, Hong Kong, 1978–79; Directorate of Naval Plans, MoD, 1979–81; Directing Staff, Army Staff Coll., 1981–83; MoD, 1984–87; CO 45 Cdo Gp, 1987–89; COS, HQ Cdo Forces, 1989–90; Dir, Defence Commitments Staff, MoD, 1990–94; Comdr, British Forces, Gibraltar and NATO Comdr, Western Mediterranean, 1994–97. ADC to the Queen, 1990–94. Non-exec. Dir, Maritime Services Mgt Ltd, 1997–99. Dir, Friends of Admiralty Heritage Soc., 2000–15. Gov., Oratory Sch., Reading, 1991–2000. FCMI (FIMgt 1997). *Recreations:* watching cricket, golf, gardening, family bridge, opera. *Address:* Littlecroft, Privett, Hants GU34 3NR; 13A Prince of Wales Mansions, Prince of Wales Drive, SW11 4BG.

**PACKER,** family name of **Baroness Neville-Rolfe**.

**PACKER, Christopher Jonathan;** Legislative Counsel to the General Synod, since 2014; *b* Amersham, 28 May 1970; *s* of William Packer and Annabel Packer; *m* 1999, Karen Fulton; one *s*. *Educ:* Dr Challoner's Grammar Sch., Amersham; Gonville and Caius Coll., Cambridge (BA Hons English 1992); Coll. of Law (CPE 1993; Legal Practice Course 1994). Admitted solicitor 1996; Mishcon de Reya Solicitors: Trainee Solicitor, 1994–96; Asst Solicitor, 1996–98; Grade 7 Lawyer, Treasury Solicitor's Dept, 1998–2000; Office of the Parliamentary Counsel: Asst Parly Counsel, 2000–04; Sen. Asst Parly Counsel, 2004–09; Deputy Parly Counsel, 2009–14. *Recreations:* the garden, the cat, books, records, running, cooking, art. *Address:* The Legal Office, Church House, Great Smith Street, SW1P 3AZ. *T:* (020) 7898 1799. *E:* chris.packer@churchofengland.org.

**PACKER, Rt Rev. John Richard;** Bishop of Ripon and Leeds, 2000–14; an Honorary Assistant Bishop, Diocese of Newcastle, since 2014; *b* 10 Oct. 1946; *s* of John and Muriel Packer; *m* 1971, Barbara Jack; two *s* one *d*. *Educ:* Manchester Grammar Sch.; Keble Coll., Oxford (MA); Ripon Hall, Oxford; York Univ. (DSA). Ordained deacon, 1970, priest, 1971; Curate, St Peter, St Helier, 1970–73; Director of Pastoral Studies: Ripon Hall, 1973–75; Ripon Coll., Cuddesdon, 1975–77; Chaplain, St Nicolas, Abingdon, 1973–77; Vicar, Wath Upon Dearne with Adwick Upon Dearne, 1977–86; Rural Dean of Wath, 1983–86; Rector, Sheffield Manor, 1986–91; Rural Dean of Attercliffe, 1990–91; Archdeacon of W Cumberland, 1991–96; Priest i/c of Bridekirk, 1995–96; Bp Suffragan of Warrington, 1996–2000; York Provincial Chaplain to Mothers' Union, 2019–. Mem., Gen. Synod of C of E, 1985–91, 1992–96 and 2000–14. *Recreations:* history, walking. *Address:* Devonshire House, Alma Place, Whitley Bay NE26 2EQ. *T:* (0191) 253 4321. *E:* bppacker@googlemail.com.

**PACKER, Prof. Kenneth John,** PhD; FRS 1991; CChem, FRSC; Research Professor in Chemistry, Nottingham University, 1993–2001, now Emeritus; *b* 18 May 1938; *s* of late Harry James Packer and Alice Ethel Packer (*née* Purse); *m* 1962, Christine Frances Hart; one *s* one *d*. *Educ:* Harvey Grammar Sch., Folkestone; Imperial Coll., London (BSc Hons Chemistry, 1st cl., 1959); Cambridge Univ. (PhD 1962). CChem 1985, FRSC 1985. Post-doctoral Res. Fellow, Central Res. Dept, E. I. duPont de Nemours, Wilmington, USA, 1962–63; University of East Anglia: SERC Res. Fellow, 1963–64; Lectr in Chemistry, 1964–71; Sen. Lectr, 1971–78; Reader, 1978–82; Prof., 1982–84; BP Research: Sen. Res. Associate, Spectroscopy, 1984–87; Prin. Res. Associate, 1987–90; Chief Res. Associate, Analytical Res. Div., 1990–92; Chief Scientist, Gp Res. and Engrg, BP Internat., 1992–93. Visiting Professor in Chemistry: Southampton Univ.; KCL; Imperial Coll., London, 1985–92; UEA, 2004–. Science and Engineering Research Council: Member: Physical Chem. Cttee, 1976–81; Chem. Cttee, 1979–82; Sci. Bd, 1988–91; Chm., Central Services Panel, 1980–82; Cttee Mem., Chm. and Sec., British Radiofrequency Spectroscopy Gp; Mem. Council, Faraday Div., 1988–91; Mem. Scientific Affairs Bd, 1992–, RSC; Hon. Sec., Royal Instn of GB, 1993–98. Gov., Hampton Sch., Hanworth, 1990–93. Ed., Molecular Physics, 1982–88. *Publications:* NMR Spectroscopy of Solid Polymers, 1993; contrib. approx. 150 papers on topics involving develt and application of NMR spectroscopy to internat. jls. *Recreations:* fly-fishing, skiing, gardening, music. *Address:* The Beeches, 68 Cawston Road, Aylsham, Norwich NR11 6ED. *T:* (01263) 731728.

**PACKER, Sir Richard (John),** KCB 2000; consultant; Permanent Secretary, Ministry of Agriculture, Fisheries and Food, 1993–2000; *b* 18 Aug. 1944; *s* of late George Charles Packer and Dorothy May Packer (*née* Reynolds); *m* 1st, Alison Mary Sellwood; two *s* one *d*; 2nd, Lucy Jeanne Blackett-Ord (*see* Baroness Neville-Rolfe); four *s*. *Educ:* City of London School; Manchester Univ. (BSc 1965, MSc 1966). Ministry of Agriculture, Fisheries and Food, 1967–2000: on secondment as 1st Sec., Office of Perm. Rep. to EEC, 1973–76; Principal Private Sec. to Minister, 1976–78; Asst Sec., 1979; Under Sec., 1985–89; Dep. Sec. (Agricl Commodities, Trade and Food Prodn), 1989–93. Non-exec. Dir, Express Dairies plc, subseq. Arla Foods (UK), 2002–07. *Publications:* The Politics of BSE, 2006; Life to 70, 2015. *Recreations:* ideas, sport. *Address:* 113 St George's Road, SE1 6HY.

**PACKER, William John;** painter and critic; art critic, Financial Times, 1974–2004; *b* 19 Aug. 1940; *o s* of late (Harold George Edward) Rex Packer and Evelyn Mary Packer (*née* Wornham); *m* 1965, Clare, *er d* of late Thomas Winn and Cecily Philip; three *d*. *Educ:* Windsor Grammar Sch.; Wimbledon Sch. of Art (NDD 1963); Brighton Coll. of Art (ATC 1964). Teaching art full-time, 1964–67, part-time in art schs, 1967–77; visitor and external assessor, art schs and colls, 1977–2000. London corresp., Art & Artists, 1969–74. First exhibited, RA, 1963 and continues to exhibit widely; one-man exhibn, Piers Feetham Gall., 1996, 2001, 2004, 2009, 2014, 2018, jt exhibn, 2005; jt exhibn, Chapel Row Gall., Bath, 2007. Member: Fine Art Board, CNAA, 1976–83; Cttee, Contemporary Art Soc., 1977–83; Adv. Cttee, Govt Art Collection, 1977–84; Crafts Council, 1980–87; Council, Artists' Gen. Benevolent Instn, 1983–; Cttee, Nat. Trust Foundn for Art, 1986–98; Governing Council, FBA, 2006–12; Trustee, Heatherley Sch. of Art, 2007–14. Sole selector, first British Art Show, 1979–80; jt selector for exhibns and prizes, incl. Liverpool John Moores Exhibn, Hunting Prize, Discerning Eye, Lynn Painter-Stainers Prize, Threadneedle Prize. Curator, Elizabeth Blackadder Retrospective, Scottish Arts Council, 1982. Inaugural Henry Moore Lectr, Florence, 1986. Ballinglen Artist Fellow, Ballinglen Foundn, Co. Mayo, 1995. Member: NEAC; Small Paintings Gp. Hon. FRCA, 1988; Hon. RBA 1992; Hon. RBS; Hon. Mem., PS. *Publications:* The Art of Vogue Covers, 1980; Fashion Drawing in Vogue, 1983; Henry Moore: a pictorial biography, 1985; Carl Erickson, 1989; René Bouët-Willaumez, 1989; John Houston, 2003; Tai-Shan Schierenberg, 2005; Sarah Raphael, 2013; Jack Milroy, 2016; (jtly) Mary Newcomb, 2018; contribs to magazines, newspapers and exhibn catalogues. *Recreation:* singing in a choir. *Address:* 60 Trinity Gardens, Brixton, SW9 8DR. *T:* (020) 7733 4012. *Clubs:* Garrick, Chelsea Arts, Soho Academy, London Sketch.

**PACKHAM, Christopher Gary,** CBE 2019; naturalist, author, and broadcaster; *b* 4 May 1961; *s* of Colin Harold Packham and Marion Rita Packham (*née* Smith); one step *d*. *Educ:* Bitterne Park Schs; Richard Taunton Coll.; Southampton Univ. (BSc Hons Zoology 1983). Freelance camera assistant, 1983–86; freelance cameraman and photographer, 1985–2016; wildlife presenter for TV, 1985–; programmes include: Really Wild Show, Go Wild, Watchout, X-Creatures, Postcards from the Wild; Inside Out; Hands on Nature; Nature's Calendar; Springwatch; Autumnwatch; How Nature Works; The Truth About Wildlife; The Animal's Guide to Britain; Secrets of our Living Planet; Nature's Weirdest Events; Inside the Animal Mind; Wildlife Jack; Hive Alive; Chris Packham's Natural Selection; Winterwatch; Cats v Dogs: which is best?; Me and My Dog: the ultimate contest; The British Garden; Autumnwatch: New England. Environmental campaigner: Ban Driven Grouse Shooting, 2014–; Malta/Cyprus – Massacre on Migration, 2014–; compiler, A People's Manifesto for Wildlife and organiser, People's Walk for Wildlife, Hyde Park, 2018; Dir, Wild Justice, 2019–. President: London Wildlife Trust, 1996–2013; Hants Ornithological Soc., 2000–; Bat Conservation Trust, 2006–; British Trust for Ornithology, 2012–; Vice-President: The Wildlife Trusts, 2005–13; Hants Wildlife Trust, 2005–13; Butterfly Conservation, 2006–; RSPB, 2007–; Trustee: Marwell Zoo Trust, 1998–2003; Herpetological Conservation Trust, 1998–2005; Wildfowl and Wetland Trust, 2000–04; Hawk Conservancy Trust, 2002–09 (Pres., 2011–). Dilys Breese Medal, British Trust for Ornithology, 2010; Wildscreen Panda Award, 2017. *Publications:* Chris Packham's Back Garden Nature Reserve, 2001; Chris Packham's Wild Side of Town, 2003; One Hundred Things that Caught my Eye, 2015;

Fingers in the Sparkle Jar: a memoir, 2016. *Recreations:* travelling to horrible places to see beautiful things and photographing them, having no time to do anything, berating my dogs for barking. *Address:* All Electric Productions, PO Box 1805, Andover, Hants SP10 3ZN. *T:* (01305) 259605. *E:* info@allelectricproductions.co.uk.

**PADDICK,** Baron *cr* 2013 (Life Peer), of Brixton in the London Borough of Lambeth; **Brian Leonard Paddick;** *b* 24 April 1958; *s* of late Anthony Henry James and Evelyn Paddick; *m* 1983, Mary Stone (marr. diss. 1988); *m* 2009 (in Norway), Petter Belsvik. *Educ:* Queen's Coll., Oxford (BA PPE 1986; MA); Warwick Business Sch. (MBA 1990); Fitzwilliam Coll., Cambridge (Dip. Applied Criminology and Policing 2000). Joined Metropolitan Police Service, 1976; Borough Comdr, Lambeth, 2001–03; Dep. Asst Comr, 2003–07. Vis. Fellow, Ashridge Business Sch., 2008–13. London Mayoral candidate (Lib Dem) 2008 and 2012. *Publications:* Line of Fire (autobiog.), 2008. *Address:* House of Lords, SW1A 0PW.

**PADDOCK, Very Rev. Dr John Allan Barnes;** Dean of Gibraltar, 2008–17; *b* Gloucester, 8 Aug. 1951; *s* of Thomas Paddock and Megan Paddock (*née* Barnes); *m* Jennifer. *Educ:* Crypt Sch., Gloucester; Liverpool Univ. (BA Hons 1974; MA); Manchester Univ. (PGCE 1975); Oxford Univ. (MA 1981); Glasgow Univ. (PhD 2005); Cardiff Univ. (LLM). Ordained deacon, 1980, priest, 1981; Curate, St Katharine, Matson, 1980–82; Chaplain: Lancaster Royal Grammar Sch., 1983–86; RAF, 1986–90; St Olave's Grammar Sch., Orpington, 1991–94; Royal Russell Sch., Croydon, 1997–2000; Vicar: St Peter's, Folkestone, 2000–03; St George's, Gloucester, 2003–08. FRSA. *Recreations:* music, literature, arts, theatre, Hispanic studies, canon and ecclesiastical law.

**PADEL, Prof. Ruth Sophia,** DPhil; FRSL; FZS; writer; Professor of Poetry, King's College London, since 2017; *b* London, 8 May 1946; *d* of late John Hunter Padel and Hilda Horatia Padel (*née* Barlow); *m* 1984, Myles Fredric Burnyeat, *qv* (marr. diss. 2000); one *d.* *Educ:* N London Collegiate Sch.; Lady Margaret Hall, Oxford (BA Lit.Hum. 1969; DPhil 1976). Lecturer in Ancient Greek: Wadham Coll. and Corpus Christi Coll., Oxford, 1973–77; King's Coll., Cambridge, 1977–78; Res. Fellow, Wolfson Coll., Oxford, 1977–80; Bowra Res. Fellow, Wadham Coll., Oxford, 1978–79; Lectr in Greek, Birkbeck Coll., Univ. of London, 1981–84; Lectr in Creative Writing, 2013–16, Reader in Poetry, 2016–17, KCL. Resident Poet, Henry Wood Promenade Concerts, 2002; Writer in Residence: Somerset Hse, 2008–09; Envmt Inst., UCL, 2010–11; Royal Opera Hse, Covent Gdn, 2014; Leverhulme Artist in Residence, Christ's Coll., Cambridge, 2009–10. Inaugurated Poetry Workshop, BBC Radio 4, 2011. Chair of Judges: Forward Poetry Prize, 2010; T. S. Eliot Prize, 2016; Judge, Internat. Man Booker Prize, 2016. FZS 1984; FRSL 1998. Patron, 21st Century Tiger, 2014–. Trustee: Zool Soc. of London, 2012–; New Networks for Nature, 2015–. Writers' Award, Arts Council England, 1994; First Prize, UK Nat. Poetry Competition, 1996; Cholmondeley Award, Soc. of Authors, 2000; Res. Award, Calouste Gulbenkian Foundn, 2003; Darwin Now Award, British Council, 2009. *Publications:* poetry: Alibi, 1985; Summer Snow, 1990; Angel, 1993; Fusewire, 1996; Rembrandt Would Have Loved You, 1998; Voodoo Shop, 2002; Soho Leopard, 2004; Darwin: a life in poems, 2009; The Mara Crossing, 2010; Learning to Make an Oud in Nazareth, 2014; Tidings: a Christmas journey, 2016; Emerald, 2018; Beethoven Variations, 2020; *fiction:* Where the Serpent Lives, 2010; *non-fiction:* In and Out of the Mind: Greek images of the tragic self, 1992; Whom Gods Destroy: elements of Greek and tragic madness, 1995; I'm a Man: sex, gods and rock 'n' roll, 2000; 52 Ways of Looking at a Poem, 2002; Tigers in Red Weather, 2005; The Poem and the Journey, 2006; (ed) Alfred Lord Tennyson, 2007; Silent Letters of the Alphabet, 2010; (ed) Walter Ralegh, Selected Poems, 2010; (ed) Gerard Manley Hopkins, 2011. *Recreations:* tiger-watching, singing 16th century music, playing chamber music (viola), watching the sea from Cretan kafeneia, conservation, walking. *Address:* English Department, King's College London, Virginia Woolf Building, 22 Kingsway, WC2B 6LE. *E:* ruth.padel@kcl.ac.uk.

**PADFIELD, Nicholas David;** QC 1991; a Recorder, since 1995; a Deputy High Court Judge, Queen's Bench Division and Administrative Court, since 2008; *b* 5 Aug. 1947; *s* of late David Padfield and Sushila, *d* of Sir Samuel Runganadhan; *m* 1st, 1978, Nayana Parekh (*d* 1983); one *d*; 2nd, 1986, Mary Barran, JP, *d* of Sir Edward Playfair, KCB; two *s. Educ:* Dragon Sch.; Charterhouse; University Coll., Oxford (Open Scholar, MA; hockey blue; England hockey internat.); Trinity Hall, Cambridge (LLM Internat. Law). FCIArb. Called to the Bar, Inner Temple, 1972, Bencher, 1993; called to various Commonwealth and other overseas Bars. Mem., Panel of Lloyd's Arbitrators, 1991–. Dep. Chm., Cons. Party Ethics and Integrity Cttee. Chairman: Commonwealth and Ethnic Barristers' Assoc., 2003–04; London br., CIArb, 2007–08. Council of Advisors: (also Trustee) Lord Slynn Eur. Law Foundn; Internat. Council for Capital Formation, 2005–. Cttee, London Oratory Appeal, 1990–95. Trustee and Mem. Cttee, Sudan Archaeol Soc. Mem., Working Party on Endangered Languages, UN Gp of Experts on Geographical Names. Freeman: City of London, 2003; Scriveners' Co., 2003. *Address:* Beauchamp House, Chapel Street, Bloxham, Oxon OX15 4NB. *T:* (01295) 720506. *E:* ndp@nicholaspadfieldqc.com. *Clubs:* Garrick, MCC; Vincent's, Frewen (Oxford); Jockey (Nevis).

**PADFIELD, Prof. Nicola Margaret;** Master, Fitzwilliam College, Cambridge, 2013–19 (Fellow, since 1991); Professor of Criminal and Penal Justice, University of Cambridge, since 2017; *b* Windlesham, Surrey, 16 May 1955; *d* of late Wing Comdr James Michael Helme, DFC, AFC and Diana Wentworth Helme (*née* Howitt), JP; *m* 1979, Dr Christopher Padfield; two *s* one *d. Educ:* St Anne's Coll., Oxford (BA 1976); Darwin Coll., Cambridge (Dip. Criminol. 1977); Univ. of Aix-Marseille (Diplôme d'Études Supérieures 1979). Called to the Bar, Middle Temple, 1978, Bencher, 2009; Recorder, 2002–14. University of Cambridge: Alumni Affairs Officer, 1990–91; Affiliated Lectr, 1992–96; Lectr, 1998–2002, Sen. Lectr, 2002–04, Inst. of Criminology; Univ. Lectr, 2004–05; Sen. Lectr, 2005–12; Reader in Criminal and Penal Justice, 2012–17. Member: Advocacy Trng Council, 2007–10; Derek Wood, QC's Review of Bar Vocational Course, 2008; Res. Adv. Gp, Howard League, 2009–; Expert Advr, Council for Penological Co-operation, Council of Europe, 2010. Hon. QC 2018. Editor: Commonwealth Judicial Jl, 1989–2004; Archbold Review, 1996–2013. *Publications:* The Criminal Justice Process: text and materials, 1995, 5th edn (with J. Bild) 2016; (with N. Walker) Sentencing: theory, law and practice, 1996; Criminal Law, 1998, 10th edn 2016; A Guide to the Crime and Disorder Act 1998, 1998; (jtly) A Guide to the Proceeds of Crime Act 2002, 2002; Beyond the Tariff: human rights and the release of life sentence prisoners, 2002; (ed jtly) Discretion: its uses in criminal justice and beyond, 2003; (ed) Who to Release?: parole, fairness and criminal justice, 2007; (ed jtly) Release from Prison: European policy and practice, 2010; chapters in books; articles in legal and criminol. jls. *Recreations:* my grandchildren, travel (particularly on the back of a tandem), singing and playing the violin (badly). *Address:* Fitzwilliam College, Cambridge CB3 0DG. *T:* (01223) 332000, *Fax:* (01223) 332082. *E:* nmp21@cam.ac.uk.
See also P. A. Helme.

**PADGETT, Prof. Miles John,** PhD; FRS 2014; FRSE; FInstP; Kelvin Chair of Natural Philosophy, since 2011, and Vice-Principal for Research, since 2014, Glasgow University; *b* 1 June 1963; *m* 2001, Helen Reid; one *d. Educ:* Univ. of Manchester; Univ. of York (BSc 1st Cl. Hons Exptl Physics 1984); Univ. of St Andrews (MSc (Dist.) Optoelectronic and Laser Devices 1985); Trinity Coll., Cambridge (PhD Laser Physics 1989). FInstP 2002.

Consultant, then Sen. Consultant, PA Technol., 1989–92; University of St Andrews: Teaching and Res. Fellow, 1992–93; RSE/BP Res. Fellow, 1993–95; Royal Soc. Univ. Res. Fellow, 1995–99; Royal Soc. Univ. Res. Fellow, 1999–2003, Prof. of Physics, 1999–2011, Glasgow Univ. Leverhulme Trust/Royal Soc. Sen. Res. Fellow, 2007–08; Royal Soc.-Wolfson Res. Merit Award, 2009. FRSE 2001; Fellow: Soc. of Photographic Instrumentation Engrs, USA, 2008; Optical Soc., 2011. Metrology Award, Nat. Physical Lab., 1994; Optics and Photonics Div. Prize, 2008, Young Medal and Prize, 2009, Inst. Physics; Kelvin Medal, RSE, 2014; Prize for Res. into Sci. of Light, Eur. Physical Soc., 2015. *Publications:* contribs to learned scientific jls incl. Science, Optica, Nature Communications. *Address:* School of Physics and Astronomy, Glasgow University, Kelvin Building, Glasgow G12 8QQ.

**PADMORE, Elaine Marguirite,** OBE 2012; opera consultant and lecturer, since 2012; Director of Opera, Royal Opera House, Covent Garden, 2000–11; *b* Haworth, Yorks, 3 Feb. 1947; *d* of Alfred and Florence Padmore. *Educ:* Newland High Sch., Hull; Arnold Sch., Blackpool; Birmingham Univ. (MA; BMus); Guildhall Sch. of Music; LTCL. Liberal Studies Lectr, Croydon and Kingston Colls of Art, 1968–70; Books Editor, OUP Music Dept, 1970–71; Producer, BBC Music Div., 1971–76; Announcer, Radio 3, 1982–90. Major BBC Radio 3 series include: Parade, Music of Tchaikovsky's Russia, England's Pleasant Land, Journal de mes Mélodies; Presenter of numerous programmes, incl. Festival Comment, Edinburgh Fest., 1973–81; Chief Producer, Opera, BBC Radio, 1976–83: series incl. complete operas of Richard Strauss and first performances of works by Delius and Havergal Brian; formerly active as professional singer (soprano), particularly of opera; Lectr in Opera, RAM, 1979–87; Artistic Director: Classical Prodns, London, 1990–92; Wexford Festival Opera, 1982–94; DGOS Opera Ireland, 1989–90 and 1991–93; Artistic Consultant, 1992 London Opera Fest.; Dir, Royal Danish Opera, Copenhagen, 1993–2000. Member: Adv. Council, Park Lane Gp, 2004–; Bd, British Youth Opera, 2013–; Trustee, Countess of Munster Musical Trust, 2008–. Hon. ARAM. Hon. FTCL; Hon. FRBC. Hon. DMus Birmingham, 2008. Hungarian Radio Pro Musica Award for prog. Summertime on Bredon, 1973; Prix Musical de Radio Brno for prog. The English Renaissance, 1974; Sunday Independent Award for services to music in Ireland, 1985. Kt, Order of Dannebrog (Denmark), 1994. *Publications:* Wagner (Great Composers' Series), 1970; Music in the Modern Age: chapter on Germany, 1973; (contrib). 100 Nights at the Opera: an anthology to celebrate the 40th anniversary of Wexford Festival Opera, 1991; contributor to: New Grove Dict. of Music, Proc. of Royal Musical Assoc., Music and Letters, The Listener. *Recreations:* gardening, travel, art exhibitions. *E:* elainepadmore@gmail.com.

**PADMORE, Elizabeth Jane;** Chairman: Hampshire Hospitals NHS Foundation Trust, since 2010; Housing Solutions, since 2018; *b* Harrogate, 1 Feb. 1955; *d* of John Austen Farmar Woolley and Mary Woolley; *m* 1984, Giles Padmore (marr. diss. 2001); one *s. Educ:* Bar Convent, York; Brasenose Coll., Oxford (BA PPE 1977; BA Juris. 1978). Tutor in Moral and Pol Philos., 1978–79; Man. Dir, Letterstream, 1980–86; Internat. Dir, Corp. Affairs, EDS, 1987–94; Partner and Global Dir Policy and Corporate Affairs, Accenture, 1995–2006. Director: Clydesdale Bank plc, 2009–12; Nat. Australia Gp Europe, 2009–12. Mem. Bd, IPSA, 2013–18. Member: Council and Exec. Cttee, Chatham House, 2003–09; Council of Mgt, Ditchley Foundn, 2005–13; Director and Trustee: Women for Women Internat., 2007–13; Youth Business Internat., 2008–; Dir, Global Bd, Enablis, 2010–. Barclay Fellow, Green Templeton Coll., Oxford, 2013–. *Recreations:* theatre, music, opera, fly fishing, walking, old roses, gardens, cricket, good food and wine with friends. *Address:* Hampshire Hospitals NHS Foundation Trust, Basingstoke and North Hampshire Hospital, Aldermaston Road, Basingstoke, Hants RG24 9NA. *T:* (01256) 313035, *Fax:* (01962) 825265. *E:* elizabeth.padmore@hhft.nhs.uk. *Club:* Home House.

**PADMORE, Mark Joseph,** CBE 2019; tenor; *b* 8 March 1961; *s* of Peter Francis Padmore and Sheila Mary (*née* Stoyles); *m* 1996, Josette Patricia Simon, *qv* (marr. diss. 2004); one *d. Educ:* Simon Langton Grammar Sch. for Boys; King's Coll., Cambridge (BA (Hons), MA). Has performed at major festivals, incl. Aix-en-Provence, Edinburgh, BBC Proms, Salzburg, Spoleto, Tanglewood, Glyndebourne, Aldeburgh, Mostly Mozart, NY; opera house débuts: Teatro Comunale, Florence, 1992; Opéra Comique, Paris, 1993; Théâtre du Châtelet, 1995; Royal Opera House, Covent Gdn, 1995; Scottish Opera, 1996; Opéra de Paris, 1996; ENO, 1999; has also performed with WNO and Opera de Lausanne; concert appearances include: LSO; City of Birmingham Orch.; RPO; Les Arts Florissants; English Baroque Soloists; Czech Philharmonic Orch.; Berlin Phil.; Vienna Phil.; NY Phil.; Philadelphia Orch.; Royal Concertgebouw Orchs; Freiburg Baroque; Orch. of the Age of Enlightenment; English Concert; has given recitals in Barcelona, Brussels, Copenhagen, Madrid, Milan, Moscow, NY and Paris; in Lieder has appeared at: Wigmore Hall; Cheltenham Fest.; Queen Elizabeth Hall; de Singel Hall, Antwerp; has made more than 60 recordings, incl. As Steals the Morn (Vocal Recording of the Year, BBC Music Magazine, 2008), La Clemenza di Tito, St John and St Matthew Passions, The Creation and Messiah, Winterreise (Vocal Solo Award, Gramophone Magazine, 2010). *Recreations:* cycling, theatre. *Address:* c/o Maxine Robertson Management, Shakespeare House, 168 Lavender Hill, SW11 5TG. *T:* (020) 7993 2917. *E:* info@maxinerobertson.com.

**PADOVAN, John Mario Faskally;** *b* 7 May 1938; *s* of Umberto Mario Padovan and Mary Nina Liddon Padovan; *m* 1964, Sally Kay (*née* Anderson); three *s. Educ:* St George's College, Weybridge; King's College London (LLB; FKC 2003); Keble College, Oxford (BCL). FCA. County Bank, 1970–84: Dir, 1971; Dep. Chief Exec., 1974; Chief Exec., 1976; Chm., 1984; Dep. Chm., Hambros Bank and Dir, Hambros, 1984–86; Chm., Merchant Banking Div., Barclays de Zoete Wedd Gp, 1986–91; Dep. Chm., Barclays de Zoete Wedd, 1989–91; Dep. Chm., 1992, Chm., 1993–95, AAH; Dir, 1989–91, Chm., 1991–95, Mabey Hldgs. Chairman: Gardner Merchant, 1993–95; Evans of Leeds, 1997–99 (Dir, 1994–97); Furniture Village, 1998–2001; Schroder Split Fund, 2000–05; Williams Lea Gp, 2000–04 (Dir, 1992–2000); Interserve Gp Pension Fund, 2003–14; Dawnay Day Property Finance Gp, 2004–08; Director: Tesco, 1982–94; Whitbread, 1992–2002; Interserve (formerly Tilbury Douglas), 1996–2005 (Dep. Chm., 2003–05); HFC Bank, 1997–2003. Mem. Court, Drapers' Co., 1991– (Master, 1999–2000). *Recreations:* golf, walking, contemporary art. *Address:* 15 Lord North Street, SW1P 3LD. *T:* (020) 7222 3261. *Clubs:* Royal St George's Golf; St Enedoc Golf.

**PAGE, Adrienne May;** QC 1999; *b* 14 July 1952; *d* of late Gwythian Lloyd Page and of Betty Page (*née* Spring); *m* 1983, Anthony Crichton Waldeck (marr. diss. 2007); one step *s* one step *d. Educ:* Godolphin Sch., Salisbury; Univ. of Kent at Canterbury (BA Social Sci.). Called to the Bar, Middle Temple, 1974, Bencher, 2003; Asst Recorder, 1995–99; Recorder, 1999–2004; Hd of Chambers, 2003–11. *Recreation:* gardening. *Address:* 5 Gray's Inn Square, Gray's Inn, WC1R 5AH. *T:* (020) 7242 2902. *Club:* Beaulieu River Sailing.

**PAGE, Andrew John Walter;** HM Diplomatic Service; Western Balkans Director, Foreign and Commonwealth Office, 2018; *b* Cuckfield, W Sussex, 17 Sept. 1965; *s* of late John Henry Page and of Carol Page. *Educ:* Lancing Coll., W Sussex; Jesus Coll., Cambridge (BA Classics 1987). Investment analyst, County NatWest, 1987–90; entered FCO, 1990; Desk Officer, Internat. Debt, Econ. Relns Dept, FCO, 1990–91; lang. trng (Russian and Ukrainian), FCO, 1992; Second Secretary: Kiev, 1993–96; News Dept, FCO, 1996–98; Hd, SA sect., Africa Dept (Southern), FCO, 1998–2000; First Sec., Paris, 2000–04; Dep.

Dir, Russia, S Caucasus and Central Asia Directorate, FCO, 2004–08; Ambassador to Slovenia, 2009–13; Sen. Advr on European Banking and Govt Relns, PricewaterhouseCoopers (on secondment), 2014–17; Western Balkans Summit Dir, FCO, 2017–18. *Recreations:* Real tennis, lawn tennis, squash, golf, crosswords, bridge, English, French and Russian literature, music, theatre. *Address:* c/o Foreign and Commonwealth Office, King Charles Street, SW1A 2AH. *Clubs:* Jesters, MCC, Queen's; Hawks (Cambridge); Petworth House Tennis; W Sussex Golf.

**PAGE, Anthony (Frederick Montague);** stage, film and television director; *b* India, 21 Sept. 1935; *s* of Brig. F. G. C. Page, DSO, OBE, and P. V. M. Page. *Educ:* Oakley Hall, Cirencester; Winchester Coll. (Schol.); Magdalen Coll., Oxford (Schol., BA); Neighborhood Playhouse Sch. of the Theater, NY. Asst, Royal Court Theatre, 1958: co-directed Live Like Pigs, directed The Room; Artistic Dir, Dundee Repertory Theatre, 1962; The Caretaker, Oxford and Salisbury; Women Beware Women, and Nil Carborundum, Royal Shakespeare Co., 1963; BBC Directors' Course, then several episodes of Z-Cars, Horror of Darkness and 1st TV prodn Stephen D; Jt Artistic Dir, Royal Court, 1964–65; directed Inadmissible Evidence (later Broadway and film), A Patriot for Me, 1st revival of Waiting for Godot, Cuckoo in the Nest; Diary of a Madman, Duchess, 1966; Artistic Dir, two seasons at Royal Court: Uncle Vanya, 1970; Alpha Beta (also film); Hedda Gabler; Krapp's Last Tape; Not I; Cromwell; other plays transf. from Royal Court to West End: Time Present; Hotel in Amsterdam; revival, Look Back in Anger; West of Suez; directed Hamlet, Nottingham, 1970; Rules of the Game, Nat. Theatre; King Lear, Amer. Shakespeare Fest., 1975; Cowardice, Ambassadors, 1983; Heartbreak House, Broadway, 1984 (televised); Mrs Warren's Profession, RNT, 1985; Three Tall Women, Wyndham's, 1994; Absolute Hell, RNT, 1995; The Doll's House, Playhouse, 1996, NY, 1997 (Tony Award); A Delicate Balance, Theatre Royal, Haymarket, 1997; The Forest, Sleep With Me, 1999; Finding the Sun, Marriage Play, 2001, RNT; Cat on a Hot Tin Roof, Lyric, 2001, NY, 2003; The Master Builder, Albery, 2003; The Goat, or Who is Sylvia, Almeida, transf. Apollo, 2004; Who's Afraid of Virginia Woolf?, NY, 2005, Apollo, 2006; revival, The Night of the Iguana, Lyric, 2005; The Lady From Dubuque, Theatre Royal, Haymarket, 2007; revival, Waiting for Godot, NY, 2009; Long Day's Journey Into Night, Richmond Th., transf. Apollo, 2012; *television:* The Parachute, 1968; Emlyn; Hotel in Amsterdam; Speaking of Murder; You're Free; The Changeling; Headmaster; Sheppey; Absolute Hell, 1991; Middlemarch, 1994; My Zinc Bed, 2008; in USA: Missiles of October; Pueblo Incident; FDR, the Last Year; Bill (starring Mickey Rooney) (Golden Globe Award); Johnny Belinda; Bill on His Own; The Nightmare Years; Patricia Neal Story; Murder by Reason of Insanity; Second Serve; Pack of Lies; Chernobyl: The Final Warning, 1990; Guests of the Emperor; The Human Bomb; *films:* Inadmissible Evidence; I Never Promised You a Rose Garden; Absolution; Forbidden. Directors' and Producers' Award for TV Dir of Year, 1966. *Recreations:* painting, reading, travelling.

**PAGE, (Arthur) Hugo (Micklem);** QC 2002; *b* 16 Sept. 1951; *s* of Sir (Arthur) John Page and of Anne Page (née Micklem); *m* 1992, Angélique, *d* of Marquis de Folin, Paris. *Educ:* Harrow Sch.; Magdalene Coll., Cambridge (MA). Called to the Bar, Inner Temple, 1977; in practice, specialising in commercial law. Contested (C) Pontefract and Castleford, Oct. 1978, 1979. *Publications:* (contrib.) Halsbury's Laws, 4th edn, 1991. *Recreations:* travel, book collecting. *Address:* 20 Brechin Place, SW7 4QA. *T:* (020) 7370 6826; Blackstone Chambers, Blackstone House, Temple, EC4Y 9BW. *T:* (020) 7583 1770, *Fax:* (020) 7822 7350. *E:* hugopage@blackstonechambers.com.

**PAGE, Ashley,** OBE 2006; freelance choreographer and opera director, since 2012; Artistic Director, Scottish Ballet, 2002–12; *b* 9 Aug. 1956; named Ashley John Laverty; *s* of John Henry Laverty and Sheila Rachel Laverty; *m* Nicola Roberts; one *s* one *d*. *Educ:* St Andrew's Sch., Rochester; Royal Ballet Schs. Joined Royal Ballet at Covent Garden, 1976; Soloist, 1980, Principal Dancer, and choreographer, 1984–2002. Works choreographed for: Royal Ballet, incl. Fearful Symmetries (Time Out Award, 1994; Olivier Award, 1995); Ballet Rambert, subseq. Rambert Dance Co.; Dutch Nat. Ballet; Dance Umbrella Fest.; San Francisco Ballet; Polish Nat. Ballet; Vienna State Ballet; Royal Ballet of Flanders; Joffrey Ballet, Chicago; Glyndebourne Opera and other cos in GB and abroad; for Scottish Ballet: The Nutcracker; Cinderella; The Sleeping Beauty; The Pump Room; Nightswimming into Day; Pennies from Heaven; Alice; for Scottish Opera, Eugene Onegin; director: La bohème, 2014, Carmen, 2015, Nevill Holt Opera; Orfeo ed Euridice, Scottish Opera, 2015. Hon. DDra Royal Conservatoire of Scotland, 2012. Herald Archangel Award, Edinburgh Internat. Fest., 2011; Critics' Circle Nat. Dance Award for Outstanding Achievement, 2012. *Recreations:* interest in all the arts, travel.

**PAGE, Benjamin Charles;** Chief Executive, Ipsos MORI UK and Ireland, since 2009; *b* Exeter, 9 Jan. 1965; *s* of Charles Page and Elizabeth Page (née Barrett); *m* (marr. diss.); one *s*. *Educ:* St John's Coll., Oxford (BA Hons Modern Hist.). Researcher: MIL (NOP), 1986–87; MORI, 1988–94; Dir, Social Research, 1994–2000; Chm., Ipsos MORI Social Research Inst., 2000–09. Mem., CABE, 2003–10. Dir, Involve, 2006–09. Commissioner: RSA 2020 Public Services Trust, 2009–11; Intergenerational Commn, Resolution Foundn, 2016–18. Trustee: Centre for London, 2014–; Centre for Ageing Better, 2018–; Tidy Britain Gp, 2019. Member: Adv. Bd, King's Fund, 2013–; London Regl Council, CBI, 2018–. Vis. Prof., KCL, 2019. *Publications:* Blair's Britain, 2007; contribs to Municipal Jl, Health Service Jl. *Recreations:* Italy, history, restaurants, skateboarding, insomnia. *Address:* Ipsos MORI, 3 Thomas More Square, E1W 1WY. *T:* (020) 3059 5000. *E:* ben.page@ipsos.com.

**PAGE, Bruce;** journalist; *b* 1 Dec. 1936; *s* of Roger and Beatrice Page; *m* 1969, Anne Louise Darnborough; one *s* one *d*. *Educ:* Melbourne High Sch.; Melbourne Univ. The Herald, Melbourne, 1956–60; Evening Standard, 1960–62; Daily Herald, 1962–64; Sunday Times, 1964–76; Daily Express, 1977; Editor, The New Statesman, 1978–82. Dir, Direct Image Systems and Communications Ltd, 1992–95. *Publications:* (jtly) Philby, 1968, 3rd edn 1977; (jtly) An American Melodrama, 1969; (jtly) Do You Sincerely Want to be Rich?, 1971, 2nd edn 2005; (jtly) Destination Disaster, 1976; contrib. Ulster, 1972; The Yom Kippur War, 1974; The British Press, 1978; The Murdoch Archipelago, 2003. *Recreations:* reading, writing. *Address:* 191 Cromwell Tower, Barbican, EC2Y 8DD.

**PAGE, Col (Charles) Timothy;** Commercial Director, Action on Hearing Loss, since 2019; *b* Boston, Lincs, 2 Dec. 1954; *s* of Geoffrey and Jean Page; *m* 2004, Christine Knight; two *s* three *d*. *Educ:* Bishops Stortford Coll.; Univ. of Exeter (BA Hons 1977). Royal Anglian Regt, 1974–93; CO, 1st Bn 22nd (Cheshire) Regt, 1993–96; Comdr, Old Coll., RMA, Sandhurst, 1996–98; ME Defence Specialist, 1998–99, a Dep. Dir, 2000–01, MoD. Nat. Dir, Emmaus UK, 2002–10; CEO, E Anglian Air Ambulance, 2011–14; Chief Exec., CAMRA, 2014–18. Liveryman, Drapers' Co., 1988– (Jun. Warden, 2018–19). *Recreations:* charity trustee, music, dance, sport, family, gardening, sailing. *Address:* Holly Cottage, 18 Church Street, Great Wilbraham, Cambs CB21 5JQ. *T:* (01223) 881738. *E:* tim21page@gmail.com.

**PAGE, Prof. Christopher Howard,** DPhil; FBA 2013; Senior Research Fellow, Sidney Sussex College, Cambridge, since 1985 (Vice-Master, 2008–11); Professor of Medieval Music and Literature, University of Cambridge, since 2011; Director, Gothic Voices, since 1982; *b* 8 April 1952; *s* of Ewart Lacey Page and Marie Victoria (née Graham); *m* 1st, 1975, Régine Fourcade (marr. diss. 2004); 2nd, 2004, Anne Dunan. *Educ:* Sir George Monoux Grammar Sch.; Balliol Coll., Oxford (BA English 1974; MA); Univ. of York (DPhil). Jun. Res. Fellow, Jesus Coll., Oxford, 1977–80; Lectr in English, New Coll., Oxford, 1980–85; Lectr in English, 1989–97, Reader in Medieval Music and Lit., 1997–2011, Univ. of Cambridge. Editor, Plainsong and Medieval Music, 1991–. Presenter, Spirit of the Age, Radio 3, 1992–97. Fellow, Fellowship of Makers and Restorers of Historical Instruments, 1982. Former Chm., Plainsong and Medieval Music Soc. FSA 2009. Dent Medal, Royal Musical Assoc., 1991. *Publications:* Voices and Instruments of the Middle Ages, 1987; The Owl and the Nightingale, 1989; the *Summa Musice*, 1991; Discarding Images, 1993; Songs of the Trouvères, 1995; Latin Poetry and Conductus Rhythm in Medieval France, 1997; The Christian West and its Singers: the first thousand years, 2010; The Guitar in Tudor England, 2015; The Guitar in Stuart England, 2017; articles in Early Music, Galpin Soc. Jl, Plainsong and Medieval Music, Musical Times, Jl of Amer. Musicological Soc. *Address:* Sidney Sussex College, Cambridge CB2 3HU. *T:* (01223) 338800.

**PAGE, Prof. Clive Peter,** OBE 2017; PhD; Professor of Pharmacology, and Director, Sackler Institute of Pulmonary Pharmacology, King's College London, since 1995; *b* 14 Oct. 1958; *s* of late Peter Page and of Edna Page; *m* 2004, Clare O'Leary; two *s* one *d*. *Educ:* Grovelands Primary Sch., Hailsham; Bexhill Grammar Sch.; Chelsea Coll., Univ. of London (BSc Hons Pharmacol.); Cardiothoracic Inst., Imperial Coll., London (PhD Pharmacol. 1984). Sandoz Ltd, Basel, 1984–86; Lectr, 1986–89, Reader, 1989–95, in Pharmacol., Jt Hd, Inst. of Pharmaceutical Sci., 2010–13, KCL. Chairman, Board: Verona Pharma Ltd, 2006–14; EpiEndo, Iceland, 2012– (Dir, 2012–); Immune Regulation (formerly Peptinnovate) Ltd, 2015–16, 2018–19 (Dir, 2014–); Director: Helperby Therapeutics plc, 2004–12; Babraham Biosciences Ltd, 2007–. Chm., Animal Scis Gp, Soc. of Biology (formerly Biosciences Fedn), 2004–12. Trustee, Babraham Inst., 2008–. Mem., Adv. Bd, Fraunhofer Inst. for Toxicol. and Experimental Medicine, 2019–. Hon. FBPhS 2018. *Publications:* (jtly) Integrated Pharmacology, 1997, 3rd edn 2006; over 200 scientific articles in learned jls. *Recreations:* travel, mountain walking, good food and wine. *Address:* Sackler Institute of Pulmonary Pharmacology, King's College London, Waterloo Campus, SE1 9NH. *T:* (020) 7848 4784/2, *Fax:* (020) 7848 4788. *E:* clive.page@kcl.ac.uk. *Club:* Athenæum.

**PAGE, David John,** FCCA; Deputy Chief Executive, Leeds City Council, 2001–09; *b* 24 Feb. 1954; *s* of Clifford Page and Evelyn Page (née Banks); *m* 1976, Carole Watson; one *s* one *d*. *Educ:* W Leeds Boys' High Sch.; Leeds Poly. FCCA 1976. Trainee accountant, CEGB, 1972–74; Leeds City Council, 1974–: Chief Accountant, 1985–88; Asst Dir of Finance, 1988–89; Sen. Asst Dir of Finance, 1989–92; Dir of Finance, 1992–99; Exec. Dir (Resources), 1999–2001. Chief Finance Officer, W Yorks PTA, 2000–09; non-exec. Dir, W Yorks PTE, 2000–09; Dir, Educn Leeds, 2001–09. Mem. Bd, Yorkshire CCC, 2006–09. *Recreations:* music, all sports, caravanning, quizzes. *Address:* 3 Stonegate, Ossett, Wakefield WF5 0JD. *E:* davejpage@btinternet.com. *Club:* Serra de Monchique Golf (Portugal).

**PAGE, David Michael;** Chairman: Fulham Shore plc, since 2012; Putney Beach plc, since 2015; *b* 20 June 1952; *s* of Edwin D. and N. M. E. Page; *m* (marr. diss. 2012); three *s* one *d*; *m* 2016, Andrea Pinnington. *Educ:* by Jesuits. Cartographer, 1970–71; primary sch. teacher, 1973–76; PizzaExpress: employee, 1976–81; franchisee, 1981–93; Chief Exec., 1993–98, 2000–03; Chm., 1998–2002; Chm., The Clapham House Group PLC, 2003–10. *Recreations:* none - always working. *T:* 07836 346934.

**PAGE, David Norman,** ARSA; RIBA; Senior Partner, Page\Park Architects, since 1981; *b* 4 Sept. 1957; *s* of Catherine and Bernard Page. *Educ:* Strathclyde Univ. (BSc; BArch). ARIAS 1982. Lectr, Dept of Architecture and Bldg Sci., Strathclyde Univ., 1982–94. Mem., Royal Fine Art Commn for Scotland, 1995. Projects include: Mus. of Scottish Country Life; Maggie's Highland Cancer Care Centre, Inverness (Best Bldg in Scotland, RIAS Award, 2006); Lighthouse Centre for Architecture and Design; Scottish NPG, 2011; Clyde Gateway, 2012; Glasgow Sch. of Art Mackintosh restoration, 2015; Saunders Centre, Sci. and Technol. Building, Glasgow Acad., 2015 (Doolan Award, RIAS, 2016). DUniv Strathclyde, 2004. *Publications:* (with Miles Glendinning) Clone City, 1999. *Recreation:* walking streets and landscapes. *Address:* Page\Park Architects, 20 James Morrison Street, Glasgow G1 5PE. *E:* d.page@pagepark.co.uk. *Club:* Adam Smith.

**PAGE, Prof. Edward Charles,** PhD; FBA 2001; Sidney and Beatrice Webb Professor of Public Policy, London School of Economics, since 2001; *b* London, 19 Oct. 1953; *s* of Edward Charles Page and Winifred Victoria Page; *m* 1975, Christine Mary Batty; one *s* two *d*. *Educ:* Kingston Poly. (BA (CNAA) German and Politics 1976); Univ. of Strathclyde (MSc Politics 1978; PhD Politics 1982). Lectr in Politics, Univ. of Strathclyde, 1978–81; University of Hull: Lectr, 1981–89; Sen. Lectr, 1989–92; Reader, 1992–95; Prof., 1995–2001. Vis. Associate Prof., Texas A&M Univ., 1986–87. Dir, ESRC Res. Prog. on Future Governance: Lessons from Comparative Public Policy, 1998–2003. Co-Ed., Eur. Jl Political Res., 2000–06; Associate Ed., Jl of Public Policy, 2006–11. *Publications:* (ed with R. Rose) Fiscal Stress in Cities, 1982; Political Authority and Bureaucratic Power, 1985, 2nd edn 1992; (ed with M. Goldsmith) Central and Local Government Relations: a comparative analysis of West European Unitary States, 1987; Centralism and Localism in Europe, 1992; (ed with J. Hayward) Governing the New Europe, 1995; People Who Run Europe, 1997; (ed with V. Wright) Bureaucratic Elites in Western Europe, 1999; Governing by Numbers: delegated legislation and everyday policy making, 2001; (jtly) Policy Bureaucracy: government with a cast of thousands, 2005; (ed with V. Wright) From the Active to the Enabling State, 2006; (ed with M. Goldsmith) Changing Government Relations in Europe, 2010; Policy without Politicians, 2012; contrib. to jls incl. British Jl Pol Sci., Eur. Jl Pol Res., Govt and Policy, W Eur. Politics, Jl Public Policy, Jl Theoretical Politics, Leviathan, Local Govt Studies, Pol Studies, Politique et Management Publique, Pouvoirs, Public Admin, Urban Affairs Qly. *Recreation:* jazz. *Address:* Department of Government, London School of Economics, Houghton Street, WC2A 2AE. *T:* (020) 7849 4629.

**PAGE, Ewan Stafford,** PhD, MA, BSc; Vice-Chancellor, University of Reading, 1979–93; *b* 17 Aug. 1928; *s* of late Joseph William Page and Lucy Quayle (née Stafford); *m* 1955, Sheila Margaret Smith; three *s* one *d*. *Educ:* Wyggeston Grammar Sch., Leicester; Christ's Coll., Cambridge (MA, PhD, Rayleigh Prize 1952); Univ. of London (BSc). Instr, RAF Techn. Coll., 1949–51; Lectr in Statistics, Durham Colls, 1954–57; Director: Durham Univ. Computing Lab., 1957–63; Newcastle Univ. Computing Lab., 1963–78; Visiting Prof., Univ. of N Carolina, Chapel Hill, USA, 1962–63; University of Newcastle upon Tyne: Prof. of Computing and Data Processing, 1965–78; Pro-Vice Chancellor, 1972–78 (Actg Vice-Chancellor, 1976–77). Member: Newcastle AHA, 1976–79; Berks AHA, 1980–82; Oxford RHA, 1982–84; West Berks DHA, 1984–93; Berks HA, 1993–96. Mem. Bd, Aycliffe and Peterlee Develt Corp., 1969–78. Chairman: Food Adv. Cttee, 1988–94; Univs' Authorities Panel, 1988–93. Pres., British Computer Soc., 1984–85 (Dep. Pres., 1983–84); Member: Gen. Optical Council, 1984–2001 (Vice-Chm., 1989–2001); Bd, Optical Consumer Complaints Service, 1999–2014; Vice-Pres., Assoc. of Optometrists, 2002–05; Hon. Treasurer, Royal Statistical Soc., 1983–89. CCMI (CBIM 1986); Hon. Fellow, Amer. Statistical Assoc., 1974; Hon. FBCS, 1976; Hon. Fellow, Northumbria

Univ. (formerly Newcastle upon Tyne Poly.), 1979. Hon. DSc Reading, 1993. Chevalier, l'Ordre des Palmes Académiques (France), 1991. *Publications:* (jtly) Information Representation and Manipulation in a Computer, 1973, 2nd edn 1978; (jtly) Introduction to Computational Combinatorics, 1978; papers in statistical and computing jls. *Recreations:* golf, music, reading, Freemasonry. *Address:* High View, Charlcombe Lane, Bath BA1 5TT.

**PAGE, Gordon Francis de Courcy,** CBE 2000; DL; Chairman: Cobham plc, 2001–08; AirTanker Holdings Ltd, since 2009; *b* 17 Nov. 1943; *s* of Sir Frederick William Page, CBE, FRS and late Kathleen (née de Courcy); *m* 1969, Judith Cecilia Mays (*d* 2018); two *s* two *d*. *Educ:* Moffats Prep. Sch.; Cheltenham Coll.; St Catharine's Coll., Cambridge (BA; MA 1970). With Rolls-Royce plc, 1962–89; Cobham plc, 1990–2008, Chief Exec., 1992–2001. Mem., 2000–08, Chm., 2004–08, Industrial Develt Adv. Bd, DTI. Mem., Dorset LSC, 2001–08; Pres., Dorset Chamber of Commerce and Industry, 2004–05; Mem., SW Innovation and Sci. Council, 2005–08; Chm., Dorset LEP, 2011–17. Chairman: FKI plc, 2004–07; Hamworthy plc, 2004–12; PH Warr plc, 2008–17. Non-exec. Dir, Bournemouth Council Trading Co. Ltd, 2014–. President: SBAC, 1997–98, 2002–03; Chartered Mgt Inst., 2003–04; Mem. Council, 2000–08, Pres., 2006–07, RAeS. Pro-Chancellor, Cranfield Univ., 2007–12. Gov., Canford Sch., 2003–12 (Dep. Chm., 2008; Chm., 2009–12). Trustee, Dorset Community Foundn, 2009–15. FInstD 1990. Hon. FRAeS 2009. DL Dorset, 2006. Hon. DSc Cranfield, 2003; Hon. DBA Bournemouth, 2009. *Recreations:* theatre, travel, classic cars. *Address:* Avon Reach, The Close, Avon Castle, Ringwood, Hants BH24 2BJ. *T:* (01425) 475365. *E:* gordonpage@outlook.com.

**PAGE, Howard William Barrett;** QC 1987; *b* 11 Feb. 1943; *s* of Leslie Herbert Barrett Page and Phyllis Elizabeth Page; *m* 1969, Helen Joanna Shotter (CVO 2011); two *s* one *d*. *Educ:* Radley Coll.; Trinity Hall, Cambridge (MA, LLB). Called to the Bar, Lincoln's Inn, 1967 (Mansfield Schol.); Bencher, 1994. Comr, Royal Ct of Jersey, 2000–15; Dep. Pres., Lloyd's Appeal Tribunal, 2000–10. *Recreations:* music, walking. *Address:* 6 New Square, Lincoln's Inn, WC2A 3QS.

**PAGE, Hugo;** *see* Page, A. H. M.

**PAGE, Jennifer Anne,** CBE 1994; Chief Executive, New Millennium Experience Company Ltd, 1997–2000; *b* 12 Nov. 1944; *d* of Edward and Olive Page; *m* 2001, Jeremy David Orme, *qv*. *Educ:* Barr's Hill Grammar School, Coventry; Royal Holloway College, Univ. of London (BA Hons). Entered Civil Service, 1968; Principal, DoE, 1974; Asst Sec., Dept of Transport, 1980; seconded BNOC, 1981; LDDC, 1983; Senior Vice-Pres., Pallas Invest SA, 1984–89; Chief Executive: English Heritage (Historic Buildings and Monuments Commn), 1989–95; Millennium Commn, 1995–97. Vice-Chair: Cathedrals Fabric Commn for England, 2006–16; Church Buildings Council, 2016–. Member, Board: Railtrack Group, 1994–2001; Equitable Life Assurance Soc., 1994–2001. Trustee, Nat. Churches Trust, 2008–18.

**PAGE, Prof. John Kenneth;** energy and environmental consultant; Professor of Building Science, University of Sheffield, 1960–84, now Emeritus; *b* 3 Nov. 1924; *s* of late Brig. E. K. Page, CBE, DSO, MC; *m* 1954, Anita Bell Lovell; two *s* two *d*. *Educ:* Haileybury College; Pembroke College, Cambridge. Served War of 1939–45, Royal Artillery, 1943–47. Asst Industrial Officer, Council of Industrial Design, 1950–51; taught Westminster School, 1952–53; Sen. Scientific Officer, Tropical Liaison Section, Building Research Station, 1953–56; Chief Research Officer, Nuffield Div. for Architectural Studies, 1956–57; Lecturer, Dept of Building Science, Univ. of Liverpool, 1957–60. Sen. Res. Fellow, Dept of Physics, UMIST, 2000–05; Hon. Fellow, Tyndall Centre for Climate Change, UMIST, subseq. Univ. of Manchester, 2002–08. Leverhulme Emeritus Fellow, 2006–08. Chm., Environmental Gp, and Mem., Econ. Planning Council, Yorks and Humberside Region, 1965–78; Regl Chm., Yorks and Humberside, CPRE, 2003–07. Founding Chm., UK Section, Internat. Solar Energy Soc.; Initiating Dir, Cambridge Interdisciplinary Envmtl Centre, 1990–92. Consultant author working with UN internat. agencies on energy use in Third World and on environmental health in tropical bldgs; working with WMO on revision of internat. technical note on building climatology, 2005–10. Farrington Daniels Internat. Award, for distinguished contribs to solar energy studies, 1989. *Publications:* 200 papers on Energy policy, Environmental Design and Planning, Environmental Management, Building Climatology and Solar Energy. *Address:* c/o 44 College Avenue, Maidenhead SL6 6AX.

**PAGE, Larissa;** *see* Joy, L.

**PAGE, Prof. Lesley Ann,** CBE 2014; PhD; President, Royal College of Midwives, 2012–17; *b* High Wycombe, 18 Jan. 1944; *d* of Leslie Edwin Page and Ivy Page; *m* 1986, Mark David Starr; two *s* one *d*. *Educ:* Orchard Sch., Slough; Open Univ. (BA 1977); Univ. of Edinburgh (MSc 1978); Univ. of Technol., Sydney (PhD 2005). RN 1965; RM 1966. Staff Nurse, St Bartholomew's Hosp., London, 1966–67; Night Sister, Royal Infirmary of Edinburgh, 1967–68; Ward Sister, Western Gen. Hosp., Edinburgh, 1968–72; Relief nurse and community work, Mills Meml Hosp., Terrace, BC, 1972–77; Lectr in Nursing, N Lothian Coll. of Nursing and Midwifery, Edinburgh, 1978; Lectr, Sch. of Nursing, UBC, 1979–80; Hd, Continuing Educn and Midwife Low Risk Proj., Grace Hosp., BC, 1980–86; Clin. Instructor, UBC Sch. of Medicine, 1984–86; Dir, Midwifery, John Radcliffe Hosp., Oxford, 1986–92; Queen Charlotte's Prof. of Midwifery, Thames Valley Univ. and Queen Charlotte's Hosp., 1994–2000; Head: Dept of Midwifery, Children and Women's Health Research Unit, 2000–01; Midwifery and Maternity Services, Royal Free NHS Trust, 2002–03; Midwifery and Nursing, Guy's and St Thomas' NHS Trust, 2003–06. Lectr, UBC Sch. of Nursing, 1995–98; Visiting Professor: Inst. of Obstetrics and Gynaecol., RPMS, Hammersmith Hosp., 1995–98; KCL, 2004–; Adjunct Professor: UTS, 2006–; Griffith Univ., 2015–; Hon. Res. Fellow, Oxford Brookes Univ., 2018. FRSocMed 2002. Hon. Fellow, Royal Coll. of Midwives, 2007. Hon. DSc W London, 2013. *Publications:* The New Midwifery: science and sensitivity in practice, 2000, 2nd edn (with R. McCandlish) 2006; over 200 articles in midwifery jls. *Recreations:* reading novels, walking, swimming, sailing incompetent crew. *Address:* 10 The Crescent, Rutherway, Oxford OX2 6QY. *T:* (07747 708630.

**PAGE, Peter R.;** *see* Randall-Page.

**PAGE, Piers John B.;** *see* Burton-Page.

**PAGE, Richard Lewis;** *b* 22 Feb. 1941; *s* of Victor Charles and Kathleen Page; *m* 1964, Madeleine Ann Brown; one *s* one *d*. *Educ:* Hurstpierpoint Coll.; Luton Technical Coll. Apprenticeship, Vauxhall Motors, 1959–64; HNC Mech. Engineering; Chm. of family co., 1964–95, 1997–2017. Young Conservatives, 1964–66; Councillor, Banstead UDC, 1968–71; contested (C) Workington, Feb. and Oct. 1974; MP (C): Workington, Nov. 1976–1979; Herts SW, Dec. 1979–2005; PPS to Sec. of State for Trade, 1981–82; to Leader of the House, 1982–87; Parly Under-Sec. of State, DTI, 1995–97; opposition front-bench spokesman on trade and industry, 2000–01. Mem., Public Accounts Cttee, 1987–95, 1997–2000; Vice-Chairman: Cons. Trade and Industry Cttee, 1988–95; All Party Engrg Gp, 1997–2005; All Party Chem. Gp, 1997–2005; Jt Chm., All Party Racing and Bloodstock Industries Cttee, 1998–2005; Chm., All Party Parly Scientific Cttee, 2003–05.

Chm., Internat. Office, Cons. Central Office, 1999–2000. Gov., Foundn for Western Democracy, 1998–2000. Chm. Investment Cttee, Leukaemia Res. Fund, 2005–09 (Hon. Treas., 1987–95); Chm., Keep Southwater Green, 2015–. Gov. and Trustee, Royal Masonic Sch., 1984–95, 1997–2014. Master, Pattenmakers' Co., 2012–13. *Recreations:* horse racing, shooting. *Address:* Marlpost, West Sussex.

**PAGE, Roy Malcolm;** Headmaster, Royal Grammar School, High Wycombe, 2006–15; *b* 24 June 1950; *s* of Alec John Page and Janet Selina Page; *m* 1973, Marilyn Rose Dawson; one *s* one *d*. *Educ:* Portsmouth Poly. (BSc Maths London Univ. 1971); Univ. of Reading (PGCE 1972); National Coll. for Sch. Leadership (NPQH 2001). Royal Grammar School, High Wycombe: Teacher of Maths, 1972–2015; Boarding Housemaster, 1982–84; Dep. Headmaster, 1989–2001; Sen. Dep. Headmaster, 2001–06. Nat. Leader of Educn, 2011. Chm., State Boarding Schs Assoc., 2012–14. Governor: Burnham Park E-ACT Acad., 2011–16 (Vice Chm., 2011–15; Chm., 2015–16); Bourne End Acad., 2015–18; Chalfont Community Coll., 2016– (Vice Chm., 2018–). *Recreations:* Rugby, cricket, golf, keeping fit, classic cars, bird watching, foreign travel. *Clubs:* Rotary (Princes Risborough); Whiteleaf Golf; Weston Turville Golf; MG Owners'.

**PAGE, Simon Richard;** District Judge (formerly Registrar), Guildford, Epsom and Reigate County Courts, and High Court of Justice, 1980–2000; a Recorder of the Crown Court, 1980–99; *b* 7 March 1934; *s* of Eric Rowland Page and Vera (née Fenton); *m* 1st, 1963 (marr. diss. 1977); three *s* one *d*; 2nd, 1984. *Educ:* Lancing; LSE (LLB External, 1956). Admitted solicitor (hons), 1957. National Service, Second Lieut RA, 1957–59. Private practice as solicitor, 1959–75; Pres., West Surrey Law Soc., 1972–73; Registrar, Croydon County Court, 1975–80; Pres., Assoc. of County Court and District Registrars, 1983–84. *Recreations:* golf, cricket, bridge. *Address:* c/o The Law Courts, Mary Road, Guildford GU1 4PS.

**PAGE, Stephen Alexander;** Chief Executive, Faber & Faber Ltd, since 2001 (Publisher, 2001–15); *b* 17 Feb. 1965; *s* of James and Frances Page; *m* 1993, Caroline Hird; two *s*. *Educ:* Bristol Univ. (BA Hons History). Bookseller, 1986–88; Marketing Exec./Manager, Longman, 1988–90; variety of roles at Transworld Publishers, 1990–94; 4th Estate: Sales Dir, 1994–95; Dep. Man. Dir, 1995–2000, Man. Dir, 2000; Gp Sales and Mktg Dir, HarperCollins Publishers, 2000–01. Non-exec. Dir, Bloomsbury Publishing plc, 2013–17. Member: Bd, Creative Skillset, 2011–18; Govt Adv. Panel on public library service in England, 2014–; Adv. Bd, ind. review of creative industries launched by New Labour, 2014; Bd, Clore Leadership Prog., 2017–; Creative Industries Council, 2019– (Chair, Cttee for implementation of Apprenticeship Levy in Creative Industries, 2016–17). Pres., Publishers Assoc., 2006–07. Trustee, Rathbones Folio Prize (formerly Folio Prize), 2013–. DUniv Derby, 2017. Most Inspiring Digital Publishing Person, FutureBook Awards, 2012. *Recreations:* music (listening and playing), film, reading, parenting, food, Brentford FC. *Address:* Faber & Faber Ltd, Bloomsbury House, 74–77 Great Russell Street, WC1B 3DA. *T:* (020) 7927 3800. *E:* stephen.page@faber.co.uk.

**PAGE, Stephen Dowland,** DPhil; business and IT strategist; photographer; *b* Welwyn Garden City, 4 Oct. 1961; *s* of Sidney Bedford Page and (Barbara) Honeywood Page; *m* 1998, Anthea Jane Morland; one *s*. *Educ:* Ironside State Sch., Brisbane; Church of England Grammar Sch., Brisbane; Univ. of Queensland (BMus Hons 1982); New Coll., Oxford (DPhil 1986; Commonwealth Schol.). Andersen Consulting, later Accenture: Business and Technol. Strategist, 1987–99; Partner, 2000–04; Man. Dir, 2004–07; Global Man. Dir, Strategic IT Effectiveness, 2007–08; Growth and Strategy Dir, Accenture Technol. Consulting, 2008–09. Capability Strategy Advr, MoD, 2004–10; non-executive Director: GCHQ, 2009–14; British Liby, 2011–19; Nat. Crime Agency, 2014–; BSI Gp, 2015–; TSB Bank plc, 2017–; Nominet UK, 2018–; Sen. Advr, PwC, 2013–. Assoc. Mem., Bupa, 2015–. Photographer, Fatkoala Images, 2009–. *Recreations:* classical music, travel, theatre. *Club:* Savile.

**PAGE, Timothy;** *see* Page, C. T.

**PAGE WOOD, Sir Anthony John,** 8th Bt *cr* 1837; *b* 6 Feb. 1951; *s* of Sir David (John Hatherley) Page Wood, 7th Bt and Evelyn Hazel Rosemary, *d* of late Captain George Ernest Bellville; *S* father, 1955. *Educ:* Harrow. Dir, Société Générale, London, 1988–2001. *Heir:* kinsman Mark William Evelyn Wood [*b* 1 Aug. 1940; *m* 1962, Mary June Miller; one *s* one *d*]. *Address:* 3 Montpelier Walk, Knightsbridge, SW7 1JL.

**PAGEL, Prof. Mark,** PhD; FRS 2011; Professor of Evolutionary Biology, University of Reading, since 1998; *b* Seattle, Washington, 5 June 1954; *s* of Lloyd and Elizabeth Pagel; partner, Prof. Ruth Mace, *qv*; two *s*. *Educ:* Univ. of Washington (BA Philosophy and Maths; PhD Mathematical Stats 1981). NSF Res. Fellow, 1986–88, Res. Fellow, 1988–91, Dept of Zool., Oxford Univ.; Res. Fellow, Univ. of London, 1992–93; Res. Fellow, Dept of Zool., Oxford Univ., 1994–98. Vis. Prof., Harvard Univ., 1991–92; Ext. Prof., Santa Fe Inst., USA, 2007–. *Publications:* (with P. Harvey) The Comparative Method in Evolutionary Biology, 1991; (Ed.-in-Chief) The Oxford Encyclopedia of Evolution, 2002; (ed with A. Pomiankowski) Evolutionary Genomics and Proteomics, 2008; Wired for Culture: the natural history of human co-operation, 2012. *Recreations:* cycling, walking. *Address:* School of Biological Sciences, Reading University, Reading, Berks RG6 6BX. *T:* (0118) 378 8900, *Fax:* (0118) 378 0180. *E:* m.pagel@reading.ac.uk.

**PAGET,** family name of **Marquess of Anglesey**.

**PAGET, His Honour David Christopher John;** QC 1994; a Circuit Judge, 1997–2012; a Permanent Judge, Central Criminal Court, 1998–2012; *b* 3 Feb. 1942; *s* of late Henry Paget and Dorothy Paget (née Colenutt), Johannesburg, S Africa; *m* 1968, Dallas Wendy (née Hill); two *d*. *Educ:* St John's Coll., Johannesburg; Inns of Court Sch. of Law. Called to Bar, Inner Temple, 1967, Bencher, 2003; Jun. Prosecuting Counsel to the Crown, 1982–89, Sen. Prosecuting Counsel, 1989–94, CCC; a Recorder, 1986–97. Freeman, City of London, 1999; Liveryman, Co. of Coopers, 1999–. *Recreations:* walking, bird watching, listening to music. *Club:* Garrick.

**PAGET, Sir Henry James,** 5th Bt *cr* 1871; *b* Wegberg, W Germany, 2 Feb. 1959; *s* of Lt-Col Sir Julian Tolver Paget, 4th Bt, CVO and Diana Frances Paget; *S* father, 2016; *m* 1993, Margrete Elizabeth Varvill (née Lynner); one *s* two *d*. *Educ:* Radley Coll. Commnd Coldstream Guards, 1979–82. J. Rothschild Assurance, later St James's Place, 1994–2016. *Recreations:* fishing, shooting, property renovation. *Heir:* *s* Bernard Halfdan Paget, *b* 4 July 1994. *Address:* Glenlivet House, Ballindalloch, Banffshire AB37 9DJ. *T:* (01807) 590376. *E:* henrypaget@sjpp.co.uk. *Club:* Cavalry and Guards.

**PAGET, Sir Richard (Herbert),** 4th Bt *cr* 1886, of Cranmore Hall, Co. Somerset; independent marketing consultant, since 2002; artisan food producer (Founder and Director, My Apple Juice, since 2010); *b* 17 Feb. 1957; *s* of Sir John Starr Paget, 3rd Bt and Nancy Mary, *d* of Lt-Col Francis Parish, DSO, MC; *S* father, 1992; *m* 1985, Richenda Rachel (marr. diss. 2013), *d* of Rev. Preb. J. T. C. B. Collins; three *d*. *Educ:* Eton Coll. City Business Machines, 1980–83; AES, 1983–87; Nixdorf Computers, 1987–88; Inforem plc, 1988–89; Sales Manager, SAS Inst., 1989–95; Outplacement Councillor, Encos, 1995–97; Empathy Audit Manager, Harding and Yorke Ltd, 1997–99; Business Development

Manager: VMTC, 1999–2001; Somersault Creative Marketing, 2001; non-exec. Dir, SFM Technol. Ltd, 1999–2002; Dir, Green Machine Computers Ltd, 2014–. Mem. Ct, Russia Co. Pres., Paget Gorman Signed Speech Soc. *Recreations:* pruning fruit trees, carriage driving, cricket, tennis. *Heir: b* David Vernon John Paget [*b* 26 March 1959; *m* 1990, Cluny Macpherson; one *s* two *d*]. *Address:* Marridge Hill House, Marridge, Ramsbury, Wilts SN8 2HG. *E:* richard@pagets.org.uk.

**PAGET-WILKES, Ven. Michael Jocelyn James;** Archdeacon of Warwick, 1990–2009; *b* 11 Dec. 1941; *s* of Arthur Hamilton Paget-Wilkes and Eleanor Bridget Paget-Wilkes; *m* 1969, Ruth Gillian Macnamara; one *s* two *d*. *Educ:* Harper Adams Agricultural Coll. (NDA); London Coll. of Divinity (ALCD). Agricultural Extension Officer, Tanzania, 1964–66; attended London Coll. of Divinity, 1966–69; Curate, All Saints', Wandsworth, 1969–74; Vicar: St James', Hatcham, New Cross, 1974–82; St Matthew's, Rugby, 1982–90. *Publications:* The Church and Rural Development, 1968; Poverty, Revolution and the Church, 1981. *Recreations:* squash, tennis, music, ski-ing, gardening. *Address:* 64 Tarlton, Cirencester, Glos GL7 6PA.

**PAGETT, Nicola Mary;** actress; *b* 15 June 1945; *d* of Barbara Scott and H. W. F. Scott; took stage name of Pagett; *m* 1977, Graham Swannell (marr. diss. 1999); one *d*. *Educ:* St Maur's Convent, Yokohama; The Beehive, Bexhill; RADA. *Stage:* Voyage Round My Father, Haymarket, 1971; Ophelia in Hamlet, Greenwich, 1974; Yahoo, Queen's, 1976; Taking Steps, Lyric, 1980; The Trojan War will not take place, NT, 1983; School for Scandal, Duke of York's, 1984; Aren't We All?, Haymarket, 1984; Old Times, Haymarket, 1985; The Light of Day, Hammersmith, 1987; The Rehearsal, Garrick, 1990; Party Time, Almeida, 1991; The Rules of the Game, Almeida, 1992; What the Butler Saw, NT, 1995; *films:* Seven Men at Daybreak, 1974; Oliver's Story, 1978; Privates on Parade, 1982; *television series:* Upstairs, Downstairs, 1972; Napoleon in Love, 1974; Anna Karenina, 1977; Scoop, 1987; A Bit of a Do, 1988–90; Ain't Misbehavin', 1994–95. *Publications:* Diamonds Behind My Eyes, 1997. *Address:* c/o Gavin Barker Associates, 2D Wimpole Street, W1G 0ED.

**PAGLIARI, Paul;** Lay Member: Employment Appeals Tribunal, since 2003; Professional Conduct Committee, Bar Standards Board, since 2012; Professional Standards Committee, Asset Based Finance Association, since 2013; *b* 31 March 1960; *s* of Luigi and Giovanna Pagliari. *Educ:* Univ. of Glasgow (MA 1981). FCIPD. Director of Human Resources: Scottish Power, 1999–2001; Scottish Water, 2002–05; Immigration and Nationality Directorate, Home Office, 2005–06; Dir, Change and Corporate Services, Scottish Exec., later Scottish Govt, 2006–08; UK Gp HR Dir, ISS UK Ltd, 2008–09. *Recreations:* ski-ing, tennis, socialising, reading, cinema. *E:* paul.pagliari@btinternet.com.

**PAGNAMENTA, Peter John;** television producer and writer; *b* 12 April 1941; *s* of late Charles Francis Pagnamenta, OBE and Daphne Pagnamenta; *m* 1966, Sybil Healy; one *s* one *d*. *Educ:* Shrewsbury; Trinity Hall, Cambridge (MA). Joined BBC, 1965; Prodn Asst, Tonight and 24 Hours, 1965–67; Asst Editor, 24 Hours, 1967; New York office, 1968–71 (Producer, US Election coverage and Apollo flights); Editor: 24 Hours, 1971; Midweek, 1972–75; Panorama, 1975–77; Dir of News and Current Affairs, Thames Television, 1977–80; Exec. Producer, All Our Working Lives (eleven part series), BBC2, 1984; Editor, Real Lives (documentary strand), BBC 1, 1984–85; Head of Current Affairs Gp, BBC TV, 1985–87; Exec. Producer, BBC TV Documentary Dept, 1981–85, 1987–97; Executive Producer: Nippon (eight parts), BBC 2, 1990; People's Century (26 parts), BBC 1, 1995–99; Pagnamenta Associates Ltd: Bubble Trouble (three parts), BBC 2, 2000. *Publications:* (with Richard Overy) All Our Working Lives, 1984; (ed) The Hidden Hall, 2005; (with Momoko Williams) Falling Blossom, 2006; (ed) Cambridge: an 800th anniversary portrait, 2008; Prairie Fever, 2012. *Address:* 6 Hamilton House, Vicarage Gate, W8 4HL.

**PAICE, Clifford,** FCILT; Member and Group Director, Economic Regulation, Civil Aviation Authority, 1989–97; *b* 26 Feb. 1938; *s* of Owen Edward and Dorothy Paice; *m* 1968, Elisabeth Marlin (*see* E. W. Paice); one *s* two *d*. *Educ:* Cambridgeshire High Sch.; LSE (BSc Econ.). FCILT (FCIT 1990). Joined Civil Service, 1959: War Office, 1959–61; MoD, 1962–65; Min. of Econ. Affairs, 1965–68; Treasury, 1968–72; Head, Econ. Divs, CAA, 1972–89. FRSA 1997. *Address:* 142 Cromwell Tower, Barbican, EC2Y 8DD. *T:* (020) 7628 5228.

**PAICE, Elisabeth Willemien,** OBE 2011; FRCP; FAcadMed; Dean Director, London Deanery (formerly Department of Postgraduate Medical and Dental Education), University of London, 2001–10; *b* 23 April 1945; *d* of Ervin Ross, (Spike), Marlin and Hilda van Stockum, HRHA; *m* 1968, Clifford Paice, *qv*; one *s* two *d*. *Educ:* Trinity Coll., Dublin (MB, BCh, BAO, MA); Dundee Univ. (Dip. Med. Ed.); Inst. of Leadership and Mgt (Level 7 Dip. Exec. Coaching and Leadership Mentoring). FRCP 1989. Clinical training, Westminster Hosp.; Senior Registrar in Rheumatology: Stoke Mandeville Hosp., 1977–79; UCH, 1979–82; Consultant Rheumatologist, Whittington Hosp. NHS Trust, 1982–95; Associate Dean, N Thames E, 1992–95, Dean Dir, N Thames, 1995–2000, Postgrad. Medicine, Univ. of London. Visiting Professor: Faculty of Clinical Scis, UCL, 2002–; Imperial Coll. London, 2010–. Chairman: Conf. of Postgrad. Med. Deans, 2006–08; NW London Integrated Care Pilot, 2011–; Case Cttee, Royal Med. Benevolent Fund, 2011–13. Non-exec. Dir, Hillingdon Hosps NHS Foundn Trust, 2014–. FAcadMed 2010. Outstanding Contribn Award for Leadership of Hosp. at Night, Skills for Health, 2009; Nat. Award for Professional Excellence, British Assoc. of Physicians of Indian Origin, 2010; NHS Mentor of the Year, NHS Leadership Awards, 2010. *Publications:* Delivering the New Doctor, 1998; New Coach: reflections from a learning journey, 2012; (with Sheila Marlin) A Grandparent's Survival Guide to Childcare, 2013; contrib. res. papers, editorials and book chapters on postgrad. med. educn. *Address:* 142 Cromwell Tower, Barbican, EC2Y 8DD. *T:* (020) 7628 5228.

**PAICE, Rt Hon. Sir James (Edward Thornton),** Kt 2012; PC 2010; DL; *b* 24 April 1949; *s* of late Edward Paice and Winifred Paice; *m* 1973, Ava Barbara Patterson; two *s*. *Educ:* Framlingham College, Suffolk; Writtle Agricultural College. Farm Manager, 1970–73; farmer, 1973–79; Framlingham Management and Training Services Ltd: Training Officer, 1979–82; Training Manager, 1982–85; Gen. Manager/Exec. Dir, 1985–87; non-exec. Dir, 1987–89; non-executive Director: United Framlingham Farmers, 1989–94; Camgrain Ltd, 2013–. MP (C) SE Cambridgeshire, 1987–2015. PPS to Minister of State, 1989–91, to Minister, 1991–93, MAFF, to Sec. of State for the Envmt, 1993–94; Parly Under-Sec. of State, DFE, then DFEE, 1994–97; opposition front bench spokesman on agriculture, 1997–2001, on home affairs, 2001–04; Shadow Minister for Agriculture and Rural Affairs, 2005–10 (Shadow Sec. of State, 2004–05); Minister of State, DEFRA, 2010–12. Mem., Select Cttee on Employment, 1987–89. Chm., All Party Racing and Bloodstock Cttee, 1992–94. Trustee: NIAB-TAG, 2014–17; Game and Wildlife Conservation Trust, 2014– (Chm., 2018–). Governor: Writtle Agricl Coll., 1991–94; King's Sch., Ely, 2014–. DL Cambs, 2013. *Recreations:* shooting, countryside issues.

**PAIGE, Deborah Penrose;** freelance director of theatre, film, television and radio drama; consultant and teacher in leading UK drama schools, since 2011; *b* 7 Feb. 1950; *d* of David and Barbara Dunhill; *m* 1969, John Paige (marr. diss. 1985); two *d*. *Educ:* Godalming County Grammar Sch.; Dartington Hall Sch.; Bristol Old Vic Theatre Sch. Actress, 1970–84; Asst Dir, Bristol Old Vic, 1986–87; Associate Dir, Soho Theatre Co., 1988–90; Artistic Director: Salisbury Playhouse, 1990–94, productions incl. A Midsummer Night's Dream, 1991, The Tempest, 1992, States of Shock (co-production with Nat. Th.), 1993, For Services Rendered (transf. Old Vic), 1993; Sheffield Theatres, 1995–2000, productions incl. The Merchant of Venice, 1996, King Lear, 1997, South Pacific, 1997, Brassed Off (transf. NT), 1999; Founder, Paigeworks, 2005; productions incl. Afterbirth, 2005, Into the Blue, 2010, Arcola Th.; freelance productions incl. The Daughter-in-Law, 2014, The Sugar Wife, 2015, RADA. Assoc. Teacher, RADA, 2003–; Hd of Recorded Drama, LAMDA, 2009–11; Interim Hd of Performance, Mountview Acad. of Theatre Arts, 2012; writer, BA in Acting and Performance, Univ. for Creative Arts, Farnham, 2014–15. Director: television: Eastenders, 2001–02; Casualty, 2003, 2005; Judge John Deed, 2004; Holby City, 2006–07; radio: (for BBC Woman's Hour) Only in London, The Farming of Bones, To The North. *Recreations:* walking, music, reading.

**PAIGE, Elaine,** OBE 1995; actress, singer and broadcaster; *b* 5 March 1948; *d* of Eric Bickerstaff and Irene Bickerstaff. *Educ:* Southaw Sch. for Girls, Barnet. *Theatre:* The Roar of the Greasepaint, the Smell of the Crowd, UK tour, 1964; Rock Carmen, Maybe That's Your Problem, Alexandra, Birmingham, 1966; Nuts, Stratford East, 1967; Maybe That's Your Problem, Roundhouse; West End début, Hair, Shaftesbury, 1968; Jesus Christ Superstar, Palace, 1971; Sandy in Grease, New London, 1973; Rita in Billy, Drury Lane, 1974; Eva Perón in Evita, Prince Edward, 1978 (Best Actress in a Musical, SWET, 1978); Grizabella in Cats, New London, 1981; Carabosse in Abbacadabra, Lyric Hammersmith, 1983; Florence Vassey in Chess, Prince Edward, 1986; Reno Sweeney in Anything Goes, Prince Edward, 1989 (co-producer); Edith Piaf in Piaf, Piccadilly, 1993; Norma Desmond in Sunset Boulevard, Adelphi, 1994 and 1995, NY, 1996; Célimène in The Misanthrope, Piccadilly, 1998; Anna in The King and I, London Palladium, 2000–01; Angèle in Where There's a Will, UK tour, 2003; Mrs Lovett in Sweeney Todd, NY, 2004; Beatrice Stockwell in The Drowsy Chaperone, Novello, 2007; Carlotta Campion in Follies, Washington, NY and Los Angeles, 2011–12; Queen Rat in Dick Whittington, London Palladium, 2017; has appeared in four Royal Variety Performances; *film:* A Closed Book, 2009; *television:* Phyllis Dixey, Ladykillers, 1980; Ladybirds, 1980; Elaine Paige in Concert, 1985; A View of Harry Clark (play), 1988; Showstoppers: In Concert at the White House, 1988; Unexplained Laughter (play), 1989; Elaine Paige in Concert, 1991; South Bank Show: the faces of Elaine Paige, 1996; Boston Pops Opening, 1997; Dora Bunner in A Murder is Announced, 2005; Where the Heart Is, 2005; The Elaine Paige Show, 2014; A Midsummer Night's Dream, 2016; Home from Home, 2018; *radio:* Elaine Paige on Sunday, BBC Radio 2, 2004–. Perf. at opening of Winter Olympic Games, Salt Lake City, 2002; concert tours in UK, Europe, ME, Australia, NZ and FE, 1984–; 40th Anniv. World Concert Tour, 2008; concert at Lincoln Center, NY, 2012; concert tour, USA and Scandinavia, 2013; 50th Anniv. World Tour, 2014–15 (filmed as I'm Still Here, 2015); Stripped Back tour, 2016, 2017, Australia and NZ, 2019; Music for Mercy concert, Rome, 2016. Has made numerous recordings (9 gold albums, incl. 4 multi-platinum). Mem., BAFTA. Hon. LittD UEA, 2012. Variety Club Awards: Showbusiness Personality of Year, 1978; Recording Artiste of Year, 1986; Best Actress, 1995; Gold Badge of Merit, BASCA, 1993; Lifetime Achievement Award, HMV, 1996; Lifetime Achievement Award, NODA, 1999; Special Award for 40 years on stage, Variety Club, 2009; Inspiration Award, Breakthrough Cancer, 2014; Lifetime Achievement Award, Variety Hall of Fame, 2016; Best Female Baddie, Great British Panto Awards, 2018. Pres., Dan Maskell Tennis Trust, 2010–. *Publications:* Memories, 2008. *Recreations:* ski-ing, tennis, clay pigeon shooting, painting. *Address:* E. P. Records Personal Management, c/o Nick Fiveash, 4 Baxendale Street, E2 7BY. *T:* 07971 240987. *E:* nickfiveash@me.com. *Clubs:* Mosimann's, Queen's, St James, h.

**PAIN, Barry Newton,** CBE 1979; QPM 1976; Commandant, Police Staff College, Bramshill, and HM Inspector of Constabulary, 1982–87, retired; *b* 25 Feb. 1931; *s* of Godfrey William Pain and Annie Newton; *m* 1st, 1952, Marguerite Agnes King (*d* 2009); one *s* one *d*; 2nd, 2010, Stella Gail Orme. *Educ:* Waverley Grammar Sch., Birmingham. Clerk to Prosecuting Solicitor, Birmingham, 1947–51; 2nd Lieut (Actg Captain) RASC, Kenya, 1949–51. Birmingham City Police, 1951–68; Staff Officer to HM Inspector of Constabulary, Birmingham, 1966–68; Asst Chief Constable, Staffordshire and Stoke-on-Trent Constabulary, 1968–74; Chief Constable of Kent, 1974–82; JSSC 1970. Adviser to Turkish Govt on Reorganization of Police, 1972. Pres., Assoc. of Chief Police Officers, 1981–82. *Recreations:* golf, shooting, boating.

**PAIN, Jacqualyn Christina Mary;** Headmistress, Northwood College, 2009–18; *b* 31 Aug. 1957; *d* of J. K. and J. W. Pain. *Educ:* Sch. of St Helen and St Katharine, Abingdon; St David's UC, Lampeter (MA); Birkbeck Coll., London Univ. (MA); Univ. of Leicester (MBA); NPQH 2001. Teacher: Tiffin Girls' Sch., 1981–83; Old Palace Sch., 1983–84; James Allen's Girls' Sch., 1984–96 (on secondment to Inst. of Educn, Univ. of London, 1992–94); Dep. Head, Northwood Coll., 1996–2000; Head, Henrietta Barnett Sch., 2000–05; Headmistress, St Albans High Sch., 2005–08. *Recreations:* running, woodwork, philosophy, cooking. *Clubs:* University Women's, International Rescue.

**PAIN, Rt Rev. Richard Edward;** Bishop of Monmouth, 2013–19; *b* 1956; *m* 1982, Juliet Morgan; two *s*. *Educ:* Bristol Univ. (BA 1979); Univ. of Wales, Cardiff (BD 1984); St Michael's Coll., Llandaff. Ordained deacon, 1984, priest, 1985; Curate, Caldicot, 1984–86; Priest-in-charge, 1986–88, Vicar, 1988–91, Cwmtillery; Vicar: Six Bells, 1988–91; Risca, 1991–98; Overmonnow with Wonastow and Michel Troy, 1998–2003; Monmouth with Overmonnow, 2003–08; Priest-in-charge, Mamhilad with Monkswood and Glascoed Chapel, 2008–13; Archdeacon of Monmouth, 2008–13. Warden of Ordinands, Dio. of Monmouth, 2001–06; Canon, St Woolos Cath., Newport, 2003.

**PAINE, Sir Christopher (Hammon),** Kt 1995; DM; FRCP, FRCR; Consultant in Radiotherapy and Oncology, Churchill Hospital, Oxford, 1970–95; President, British Medical Association, 2000–01; *b* 28 Aug. 1935; *s* of late Major John Hammon Paine and Hon. Mrs Joan Frances Shedden, MBE; *m* 1959, Susan Martin; two *s* two *d*. *Educ:* Eton Coll.; Merton Coll., Oxford (BM, BCh 1961; DM 1981); St Bartholomew's Hosp. Med. Sch. FRCP 1976; FRCR (FFR 1969). Junior med. posts, Oxford, London, Paris, 1962–70; Oxford University: Lectr in Radiotherapy and Oncology, 1972–95; Dir of Clinical Studies (clinical dean), 1982–85; Dist Gen. Manager, Oxfordshire HA, 1984–88; Chm., Oxford Med. Staff Council, 1991–92. Med. Dir, Adv. Cttee for Distinction Awards, 1994–99. Pres., British Oncological Assoc., 1989–91; Royal College of Radiologists: Dean, Faculty of Clinical Oncology, 1990–92; Vice-Pres., 1991–92; Pres., 1992–95. Pres., RSocMed, 1996–98. Mem., Adv. Bd, Weill Cornell Med. Coll., Qatar, 2001–13. Hon. Fellow: HK Coll. of Radiologists, 1995; Faculty of Radiologists, RCSI, 1995; Hon. FRCSE, 2005. *Publications:* papers on health services and cancer. *Recreation:* gardening. *Address:* Long Cottage, Ashendon, Aylesbury, Bucks HP18 0HB. *T:* (01296) 651961. *E:* northavenue@btinternet.com. *Club:* Farmers.

**PAINE, Surg. Rear Adm. Michael Patrick William Halden,** FRCS; Medical Director General (Naval), 1997–99; *b* 18 March 1939; *s* of Comdr Geoffrey W. W. H. Paine, RN and Eileen Paine (*née* Irwin); *m* 1972, Thayer Clark (*d* 2015). *Educ*: Downside Sch.; London Hosp. Med. Coll. (MB BS 1963); Southampton Univ.; Edinburgh Univ. FRCS 1976. Joined Royal Navy, 1963; HMS Plymouth, 1965–66; HMS Repulse (SSBN), 1967–68; surgical trainee, RN Hosp. Haslar, 1969–75; PMO, HMS Bulwark, 1975–76; RN Hosp. Plymouth, 1977–79; Orthopaedic Senior Registrar: Southampton Gen. and Lord Mayor Treloar's Hosps, 1979; RN Hosp. Haslar, 1980; Cons. Orth. Surg., RN Hosp. Plymouth, 1981–82; HMS Illustrious, 1982–84; Cons. Orth. Surg., RN Hosp. Haslar, 1984–88; RAMC Sen. Officers' Course (Course Medal), 1986; Defence Med. Services Directorate, MoD, 1988–90 (Mem., Thompson Rev. of Service Hosps); Fleet MO, 1990–92; ACOS (Med. and Dental), C-in-C Fleet, 1992–97. QHS 1994–99. *Recreation:* sailing. *Address:* 513 Canaan Street, Canaan, NH 03741, USA.

**PAINE, Roger Edward;** management coach and consultant, Vice President, Solace Enterprises Ltd, since 2001 (Executive Director, 1996–99; Managing Director, 1999–2001); Proprietor, Gate Associates Ltd, since 2009; *b* 20 Oct. 1943; *s* of Ethel May Jones and Edward Paine. *Educ*: Stockport Sch.; Univ. of Wales (BA Hons); Univ. of Manchester (part time; Dip TP); Univ. of Birmingham (MSocSci). Town Planner: Lancs CC, 1964–66; Stockport CB, 1966–68; Lancs CC, 1968–70; Salford City, 1970; Stockport Borough: Corporate Planner, 1971–73; Head of Corporate Planning, 1973–75; Co-ordinator of Central Units, 1975–77; Dep. Chief Exec., Camden, 1977–80; Chief Executive: Wrekin Council, 1980–88; Cardiff CC, 1988–94. Pres., Solace, 1992–93. Chairman: Coll. of Traditional Acupuncture, Leamington Spa, 2006–10; Winchcombe Business Forum, 2010–14. Director of Music: Evesham Parish Church, 2002–09; St Andrew's, Tywardreath, 2018–; Dir, Evesham Fest. of Music, 2007–12; Chm., Winchcombe Fest. of Music and Arts, 2011–14. *Recreations:* music, travel, sport, history. *Address:* Gardens Cottage, Prideaux, St Blazey, Par, Cornwall PL24 2SS.

**PAINES, Nicholas Paul Billot;** QC 1997; a Law Commissioner, since 2013; *b* 29 June 1955; *s* of late Anthony John Cooper Paines and of Anne Paines; *m* 1985, Alison Jane Sargent Roberts; one *s* three *d*. *Educ*: Downside Sch.; New Coll., Oxford (BA 1977; MA 1984); Université Libre de Bruxelles (Licence spéciale en droit européen). Called to the Bar, Gray's Inn, 1978, Bencher, 2016; in practice at the Bar, 1980–2013; called to the Bar, NI, 1996; Mem., Supplementary Panel of Jun. Counsel to the Crown (Common Law), 1993–97; a Recorder, 2002; a Dep. High Court Judge, 2010. A Dep. Upper Tribunal Judge (formerly a Dep. Social Security and Child Support Comr), 2001–. Mem., Bar Council, 1991–96; Treas., Bar European Gp, 2001–14 (Chm., 1996–98). Mem. Council, St Christopher's Fellowship, 1983–2002. Jt Editor, Common Market Law Reports, 1996–2010. *Publications: contributions to:* Halsbury's Laws of England, 3rd edn, 1986; Vaughan, Law of the European Communities, 1986; Bellamy and Child, Common Market Law of Competition, 4th edn, 1993; Value Added Tax: commentary and analysis, 2009. *Recreations:* family life, music, running moderate distances. *Address:* Law Commission, 1st Floor, Tower, 52 Queen Anne's Gate, SW1H 9AG.

**PAINTER, Anne Elizabeth;** *see* Curry, A. E.

**PAINTER, Ven. David Scott;** Archdeacon of Oakham, 2000–11, now Archdeacon Emeritus; Canon Residentiary of Peterborough Cathedral, 2000–11; *b* 3 Oct. 1944; *s* of Frank Painter and Winifred Ellen Painter (*née* Bibbings). *Educ*: Queen Elizabeth's Sch., Crediton; Trinity Coll. of Music (LTCL 1965); Worcester Coll., Oxford (BA 1968; MA 1972); Cuddesdon Theol Coll. Ordained deacon, 1970, priest, 1971; Curate, St Andrew, Plymouth, 1970–73; Chaplain, Plymouth Poly., 1971–73; Curate, All Saints, St Marylebone, 1973–76; Domestic Chaplain to Archbishop of Canterbury, 1976–80; Vicar, Holy Trinity, Roehampton, 1980–91; RD, Wandsworth, 1985–90; Canon Residentiary and Treas., Southwark Cathedral, and Dio. Dir of Ordinands, Southwark, 1991–2000. *Recreations:* music, country walking, crossword puzzles, bridge. *Club:* Oxford and Cambridge.

**PAINTER, Sophia Mary;** *see* Tickell, S. M.

**PAINTER, Terence James,** CB 1990; a Deputy Chairman and Director General, Board of Inland Revenue, 1986–93; *b* 28 Nov. 1935; *s* of late Edward Lawrence Painter and Ethel Violet (*née* Butler); *m* 1959, Margaret Janet Blackburn; two *s* two *d*. *Educ*: City of Norwich Sch.; Downing Coll., Cambridge (BA (History)). Nat. Service Commn, Royal Norfolk Regt, 1958–59. Entered Inland Revenue as Asst Principal, 1959; Principal, 1962; seconded to Civil Service Selection Bd, 1967–68; Asst Sec., 1969; seconded to HM Treasury, 1973–75; Under-Sec., 1975–86; Dep. Sec., 1986–93. *Recreations:* music, books, theatre, gardening. *Club:* Reform.

**PAISLEY,** family name of **Baroness Paisley of St George's.**

**PAISLEY OF ST GEORGE'S,** Baroness *cr* 2006 (Life Peer), of St George's in the County of Antrim; **Eileen Emily Paisley;** Vice-President, Democratic Unionist Party, since 1994; *m* 1956, Rev. Ian Richard Kyle Paisley (Baron Bannside, PC); twin *s* three *d*. Mem. (DemU) Belfast City Council, 1967–73. Member (DemU): East Belfast, NI Assembly, 1973–74; NI Constitutional Convention, 1975–76. Mem., H of L, 2006–17. Dir, Bannside Library Ltd. *Publications:* Take a Break, 2007.
*See also* Hon. I. R. K. Paisley.

**PAISLEY, Bishop of, (RC),** since 2014; **Rt Rev. John Keenan;** *b* Glasgow, 19 Dec. 1964. *Educ*: St Gregory's Primary, Wyndford, Glasgow; Shrigley Salesian Coll., Cheshire; Univ. of Glasgow (LLB 1988); Gregorian Univ., Rome (STB 1993; PhL 1995). Ordained priest, 1995; Asst Priest, Christ the King, Kingspark, 1995–2000; Chaplain: Holyrood, 1997–2000; Univ. of Glasgow, 2000–14; Parish Priest, St Patrick's, Anderston, 2013–14; Vocations Dir, Archdiocese of Glasgow, 2013–14. Lectr in Philosophy, Scotus Coll., 1995–2005. *Address:* Diocesan Offices, Cathedral Precincts, Incle Street, Paisley PA1 1HR.

**PAISLEY, Hon. Ian Richard Kyle;** MP (DemU) North Antrim, since 2010; *b* 12 Dec. 1966; *s* of Baron Bannside, PC and of Baroness Paisley of St George's, *qv*; *m* 1990, Fiona Margaret Elizabeth Currie; two *s* two *d*. *Educ*: Shaftesbury House Coll.; Methodist Coll.; Queen's Univ., Belfast (BA Hons Modern History; MSSc Irish Politics 1995). Res. Asst for Dr Ian Paisley, MP, H of C, 1989–2010. Member: NI Forum for Political Dialogue, 1996–98; NI Police Bd, 2001–10. Justice spokesman, DUP, 1992–2002. Mem. (DemU) Antrim N, NI Assembly, 1998–2010. Jun. Minister, Office of First Minister and Dep. First Minister, NI, 2007–08. DUP spokesperson on Envmt, Food and Rural Affairs, 2010–15, Work and Pensions, 2010–15, Energy and Climate Change, 2010–17, Communities and Local Govt, 2015–, Culture, Media and Sport, 2015–. Mem., NI Affairs Cttee, 2010–, Panel of Chairs, 2016–, H of C. Fellow, Sch. of Leadership, Maryland State Univ., 1997. Royal Humane Soc. Testimonial, 1999. *Publications:* Reasonable Doubt: the case for the UDR Four, 1991; Echoes: Protestant identity in Northern Ireland, 1994; Peace Deal?, 1998; Ian Paisley: a life in photographs, 2004; articles in jls. *Recreations:* my children, Chinese food, cinema, Rugby, motorcycling. *Address:* House of Commons, SW1A 0AA; 9–11 Church Street, Ballymena, Co. Antrim BT43 6DD.

**PAISNER, Harold Michael;** Senior Partner, Berwin Leighton Paisner LLP, 2001–15, now Senior Partner Emeritus; Senior Counsel, since 2018; *b* 4 June 1939; *s* of Leslie and Suzanne Paisner; *m* 1967, Judith Rechtman; two *s*. *Educ*: St Paul's Sch., London; University Coll., Oxford (BA Hons); Coll. of Law, London. Investment and merchant banking, 1963; admitted Solicitor, 1971; formerly registered with Paris Bar; former Sen. Partner, Paisner & Co. UK. Nat. Pres., Union Internat. des Avocats, 2006–11 (former Pres., Foreign Investment Cttee; Advr to Pres., 2015–); Chm., Internat. Issues Cttee, Law Soc., 2010–16; Member: Internat. Bar Assoc.; British Baltic Lawyers Assoc.; American Bar Assoc.; Hon. Mem., Lithuanian Bar. Non-executive Director: Lin Pac Gp Ltd, 1990–2003; Think London, 2002–11; FIBI Bank (UK) plc, 2005–12; Interface Inc., 2007–16; Puma High Income VCT plc, 2010–14; Chm., Puma VCT 11 plc, 2015–; Mem., Adv. Bd, Biotechpharma UAB, 2015–. Dir, Inst. of Jewish Policy Res., 1999–2015 (Chm., 2009–15; Vice-Pres., 2015–). Gov., Ben Gurion Univ. of the Negev. *Recreations:* music, reading history, biography and current affairs, ski-ing. *Address:* 16 Ilchester Place, W14 8AA. *T:* (office) (020) 3400 1000. *E:* harold.paisner@bclplaw.com. *Club:* Athenæum.

**PAISNER, Martin David,** CBE 2004; Partner, Bryan Cave Leighton Paisner (formerly Berwin Leighton Paisner) LLP; *b* Windsor, 1 Sept. 1943; *s* of Leslie and Suzanne Paisner; *m* 1978, Susan Sarah Spence; two *s* two *d*. *Educ*: St Paul's Sch., London; Worcester Coll., Oxford (MA); Univ. of Michigan, Ann Arbor (LLM). Admitted as solicitor, 1970; Partner, Paisner & Co., subseq. Berwin Leighton Paisner LLP, 1972–2003. Chairman: Myers-JDC-Brookdale Inst., Jerusalem, 2009–; Weizmann UK, 2010–. Trustee: BL Trust; Holocaust Educnl Trust; Woolf Inst.; Oxford Centre for Hebrew and Jewish Studies; Ovarian Cancer Action; Heart Cells Foundn; Stuart Young Foundn; Jerusalem Foundn; Peter Cruddas Foundn; Phillips & Rubens Charitable Trust; Wolfson Family Charitable Trust; Maurice Wohl Charitable Foundn; Maurice and Vivienne Wohl Philanthropic Foundn. *Recreations:* reading and collecting, principally 18th and 19th century English literature, travel posters, Victoriana, bronze and porcelain figures and walking sticks. *Address:* Bryan Cave Leighton Paisner LLP, Adelaide House, London Bridge, EC4R 9HA. *T:* (020) 3400 2356, *Fax:* (020) 3400 1111. *E:* martin.paisner@bclplaw.com. *Clubs:* Garrick, Reform.
*See also* H. M. Paisner.

**PAJACZKOWSKI, Kathryn;** *see* Firth, K.

**PAJARES, Ramón,** OBE 2000; Director and Advisor, Como Hotels and Investments Co. Ltd, 2000–05; *b* 6 July 1935; *s* of Juan Antonio Pajares Garcia and Rosario Salazar; *m* 1963, Jean Kathleen Porter; one *s* two *d*. *Educ*: Madrid Inst. of Hotel and Tourism Studies. Nat. Service, Spanish Navy, 1955–57. Hotel posts: Ritz, Barcelona, 1954–55; San Jorge, Playa de Aro, 1957; Pargue, Llavaneras, 1957–59; Mansion, Eastbourne, 1959–61; Kleiner Reisen, Koblenz, Germany, 1961; Feldbergerhof, Feldberg, 1961–62; Le Vieux Manoir, Morat, Switzerland, 1962; Reina Isabel, Canary Is, 1963–69; Food and Beverage Dir, Inn on the Park, London, 1969–71; Gen. Manager, San Antonio, Lanzarote, Canary Is, 1972–74; Gen. Manager and Vice-Pres., Inn on the Park, later Four Seasons, 1975–94; Man. Dir, Savoy Gp of Hotels and Restaurants, 1994–99. Non-exec. Dir, Macdonald Hotels, 2002–. Trustee, Savoy Educnl Trust, 1998– (Chm., 2012–17). Member: Assoc. Culinaire Française, 1971; Cookery and Food Assoc., 1973; Gov., Royal Acad. of Culinary Arts, 1998–. Pres., BHA, 2000–06. FIH (FHCIMA 1982). Freeman, City of London, 1988. Hon. DEd Bournemouth, 2000. Hotelier of Year Award, Brit. Hotel and Catering Ind., 1984; Personnalité de l'année for Hotel Ind., 1986; Catey Special Award, Caterer & Hotel Keeper Mag., 1997; Lifetime Achievement Award, Eur. Hotel Design and Develt Awards, 1998; British Travel Industry Hall of Fame, 1998; Hotelier of World, Hotels Mag., 1998; Spanish Govt Silver Medal, for services to tourism, 2000. Mérito Civil (Spain), 1984; Oficial de la Orden de Isabel la Católica (Spain), 1989. *Recreation:* classical music.

**PAKENHAM,** family name of **Earl of Longford.**

**PAKENHAM, Catherine Ruth, (Kate), (Mrs Christopher Spira);** Executive Producer, Donmar Warehouse, 2012–18; *b* London, 4 May 1975; *d* of Hon. Kevin Pakenham and Ruth Pakenham (*née* Jackson, now East); *m* 2006, Christopher Spira; one *s* one *d*. *Educ*: Godolphin and Latymer Sch., London; Gonville and Caius Coll., Cambridge (BA English Lit. 1996; MA). Producer and Dir for TV progs incl. Paddington Green, BBC, and What Will They Think of Next?, ITV, 1996–2001; Producer: Old Vic New Voices, 2001–07; Old Vic Th., 2007–12. *Recreations:* reading, writing, art, tennis, walking, ski-ing.

**PAKENHAM, Hon. Sir Michael (Aidan),** KBE 2003; CMG 1993; HM Diplomatic Service, retired; Senior Adviser, Access Industries, since 2004; *b* 3 Nov. 1943; *s* of 7th Earl of Longford, KG, PC, and Elizabeth, Countess of Longford, CBE; *m* 1980, Meta (Mimi) Landreth Doak, *d* of William Conway Doak of Maryland, USA; two *d* two step *d*. *Educ*: Ampleforth College (schol.); Trinity College, Cambridge (schol.; MA Classics); Rice University, Texas (exchange fellow). Reporter, Washington Post, 1965; Foreign Office, 1965; Nairobi, 1966; Warsaw, 1967; FCO, 1970; Asst Private Sec., later Private Sec. to Chancellor of Duchy of Lancaster (European Community Affairs), on secondment to Cabinet Office, 1971–74; Geneva (CSCE), 1974; New Delhi, 1974; Washington, 1978; Head of Arms Control and Disarmament Dept, FCO, 1983–87; Counsellor (External Relations), UK Perm. Rep. to EC, Brussels, 1987–91; Ambassador and Consul-Gen., Luxembourg, 1991–94; Minister, Paris, 1994–97; Cabinet Office (on secondment): Dep. Sec. (Overseas and Defence), 1997–99; Chm., Jt Intelligence Cttee, 1997–2000 and Intelligence Co-ordinator, 1999–2000; Ambassador to Poland, 2001–03. Chm., Pakenvest International Ltd, 2004–; Consultant, Thales International, 2004–06; Sen. Advr, Droege & Co., 2005–07; Mem., European Adv. Bd, Northrop Grumman, 2008–11; Dir, Westminster Gp, 2008–16. Trustee, Chevening House, 2005–17. Mem. Council, 2005–13, Vice-Chm., 2009–13, KCL; FKC 2012. Freeman of City of London, 1992. Distinguished Friend, Oxford Univ., 2016. *Recreations:* golf, reading history, museums, Arsenal FC. *Address:* Cope House, 15B Kensington Palace Gardens, W8 4QG. *T:* (020) 7908 9966. *Clubs:* Garrick, MCC; Swinley Forest Golf, High Post Golf.

**PAKENHAM, Thomas Frank Dermot;** writer; *b* 14 Aug. 1933; *e s* of 7th Earl of Longford, KG, PC, and Elizabeth, Countess of Longford, CBE; *S* father, 2001, but does not use the title; *m* 1964, Valerie, *d* of Major R. G. McNair Scott; two *s* two *d*. *Educ*: Dragon School, Oxford; Belvedere Coll., Dublin; Ampleforth Coll., York; Magdalen Coll., Oxford (BA Greats 1955). Travelled, Near East and Ethiopia, 1955–56 (discovered unrecorded medieval Ethiopian church at Bethlehem, Begemdir, 1956). Free-lance writing, 1956–58. Editorial staff: Times Educational Supplement, 1958–60; Sunday Telegraph, 1961; The Observer, 1961–64. Founder Mem. 1958, and Mem. Cttee, 1958–64, Victorian Soc.; Founder Mem., and Mem. Cttee, 1968–72, Historic Irish Tourist Houses and Gardens Assoc. (HITHA); Treas., 1972–2002, Chm., 2002–05, British-Irish Assoc.; Sec. (co-founder), Christopher Ewart-Biggs Memorial Trust, 1976–; Founder and Chm., Irish Tree Soc., 1990–. Chm., Ladbroke Assoc., 1988–91. Sen. Associate Mem., St Antony's Coll., Oxford, 1979–81. Hon. DLitt: Ulster, 1992; TCD, 2000; QUB, 2004. *Publications:* The Mountains of Rasselas: an Ethiopian adventure, 1959, 1998; The Year of Liberty: the story of the Great Irish Rebellion of 1798, 1969; The Boer War, 1979 (Cheltenham Prize, 1980); (selected and introd with Valerie Pakenham) Dublin: a travellers' companion, 1988; The Scramble for Africa, 1991 (W. H. Smith Prize, 1992; Alan Paton Meml Prize, 1992);

Meetings with Remarkable Trees, 1996; Remarkable Trees of the World, 2002; The Remarkable Baobab, 2004; In Search of Remarkable Trees: on safari in southern Africa, 2007; The Company of Trees: a year in a life-time's quest, 2015. *Recreation:* water. *Address:* Tullynally, Castlepollard, Westmeath, Ireland. *T:* (44) 9661159. *Club:* Beefsteak.

**PAKER, Adam David;** Associate, Saje Impact; *b* Monmouth, NJ, 19 Feb. 1971; *s* of Yakup Paker and Ruth Paker; *m* 2011, Jennifer Hepker; three *d. Educ:* Highgate Jun. Sch.; Westminster Sch.; Magdalen Coll., Oxford (BA Jt Hons Mod. Langs); INSEAD (MBA). Exec., Robert Fleming & Co. Ltd, 1993–99; Manager, ISL, 2000–01; Dir, FIFA, 2001–05; Hd, Global Sports, Virtual Marketing Services, 2005–07; Business Dir, Havas Sports, 2008–09; Consultant, Threshold Sports, 2009–10; Chief Executive: Commonwealth Games England, 2011–14; Amateur Swimming Assoc., 2014–16. *Recreations:* football, running, sub-aqua, following Arsenal and England national team, supporting Team GB and Team England.

**PAKINGTON,** family name of **Baron Hampton**.

**PALACIO VALLELERSUNDI, Ana;** Founding Partner, Palacio y Asociados, Madrid, 1985; Senior Strategic Counsel, Albright Stonebridge Group, Washington, DC, since 2010; Elective Member, Council of State, Spain, 2012–18; *b* Madrid, 22 July 1948. *Educ:* French Lycée, Madrid; Univ. Complutense, Madrid (degrees in Law, Pol Sci., Sociol.). Lectr. MEP, 1994–2002 (Chm., Legal Affairs and Internal Market Cttee, 1999–2002); Mem. for Toledo, Congress of Deputies, Spain, 2002–06; Minister of Foreign Affairs, 2002–04; Sen. Vice-Pres. and Gen. Counsel, World Bank, 2006–08. Mem. Bd Governors, Law Soc. of Madrid; Dep. Chm. Council, European Law Socs; Pres. Exec. Council, Europäische Rechtsakademie (Acad. of European Law), Trier. Mem. Editorial Bd, Revue du Droit de l'Union Européenne. Vis. Prof., Edmund F. Walsh Sch. of Foreign Service, Georgetown Univ., 2014–. Hon. Mem., Law Soc. of England and Wales; Mem., Inner Temple. Cruz de San Raimundo de Peñafort; Banda, Orden del Águila Azteca (Mexico), 2002; Orden de Stara Planina (Bulgaria), 2003; Gran Cruz: Orden Piana (Vatican), 2002; Placa de Plata de la Orden Nacional José Matias Delgado (El Salvador), 2003; del Sol (Brazil), 2003; Orden del Mérito de Duarte (Dominican Republic), 2003; Orden de Carlos III (Spain), 2004; Orden al Mérito (Chile), 2004; Sandra Day O'Connor Justice Prize, 2016.

**PALCA, Julia Charlotte;** Chair of Council, City, University of London, since 2018 (Member, since 2017); *b* Guildford, 25 March 1956; *d* of Henry Palca and Edith, (Vicky), Palca; *m* 1985, Nicolas Stevenson; three *s. Educ:* Queen Anne's Sch., Caversham; Durham Univ. (BA Law and Pols 1977). Trainee and Solicitor, Oswald Hickson Collier & Co., 1978–81; Solicitor, Lovell, White & King, 1981–85; In-house Counsel, Mirror Gp Newspapers Ltd, 1985–86; Partner, 1986–2009, Consultant, 2009–12, Olswang LLP. Employment Judge (pt-time), 2001–. Dir, Inst. of Employment Studies, 2000–08. Mem. Bd, City of London Law Soc., 2005–12. Trustee: Community Self Build, 1998–2001; Cancer Link, 1999–2001; Macmillan Cancer Support, 2001–19 (Chm., 2010–19); Royal Free Charity, 2005–18 (Chm., 2010–18); Koestler Trust, 2013–15; CMS (formerly Olswang) Foundn, 2014–; Nuffield Trust, 2015–; Special Advr, Prison Reform Trust, 2001–15; Mem., Patient Information Adv. Gp, 2001–04. *Publications:* Employment Law Checklists, 1993, 4th edn 2009; (ed jtly) Yearbook of Media and Entertainment Law, 2nd edn 1996 to 4th edn 1999; (jtly) Blackstone's Employment Law Checklists, 2006, 7th edn 2012; (jtly) Goulding on Employee Competition, 2007. *Recreations:* theatre, art, dancing. *Address:* City, University of London, Northampton Square, Clerkenwell, EC1V 0HB. *T:* (020) 7040 3466. *E:* julia.palca@city.ac.uk.

**PALEY, Maureen;** Founder and Director, Maureen Paley (formerly Interim Art), since 1984; *b* New York, 17 Sept. 1959; *d* of Alfred and Sylvia Paley. *Educ:* Sarah Lawrence Coll., Bronxville, NY; Brown Univ. (BA); Royal Coll. of Art (MA). Worked in photography and film, 1980–84; Lecturer: Bournemouth and Poole Coll. of Art, 1981–83; AA, 1981–82; curator: Antidotes to Madness?, Riverside Studios, London, 1986; Photography as Performance, Photographer's Gall., London, 1986; Wall Works, Cornerhouse, Manchester, 1987; Symptoms of Interference, Conditions of Possibility: Ad Reinhardt, Joseph Kosuth, Felix Gonzalez-Torres, Camden Art Centre, 1994; Wall to Wall, Serpentine Gall., Southampton City Art Gall., Leeds City Art Gall., 1995; The Cauldron, Henry Moore Sculpture Trust, Halifax. Vis. Lectr, RCA, Chelsea Coll. of Art and Design. Mem., Soc. of London Art Dealers; Benefactor: Artangel; Camden Arts Centre; Chisenhale Gall.; Creative Industries Fedn; ICA; Michael Clark Co.; Open Sch. East; Serpentine Galls; South London Gall.; Studio Voltaire; Tate; The Showroom; Whitechapel Gall.; Nottingham Contemporary; Artists Space, Swiss Inst., The Kitchen, White Columns (NY). *Publications:* Technique Anglaise, 1991; Gillian Wearing—Signs…, 1997; Art London, 1999, 2nd edn 2000; Peter Hujar/Paul P.—When Ghost Meets Ghost, 2008; exhibition catalogues. *Address:* Maureen Paley, 21 Herald Street, E2 6JT. *T:* (020) 7729 4112, *Fax:* (020) 7729 4113. *E:* info@maureenpaley.com. *Clubs:* Annabel's, Groucho, Soho House.

**PALIN, Sir Michael (Edward),** KCMG 2019; CBE 2000; actor, writer and traveller; President, Royal Geographical Society, 2009–12; *b* 5 May 1943; *s* of late Edward and Mary Palin; *m* 1966, Helen M. Gibbins; two *s* one *d. Educ:* Birkdale Sch., Sheffield; Shrewsbury; Brasenose Coll., Oxford (BA 2nd Cl. Hons Mod. Hist.; Hon. Fellow, 2006). Pres., Campaign for Better Transport (formerly Transport 2000), 1987–. *Television:* actor and writer: Monty Python's Flying Circus, 1969–74; Ripping Yarns, 1976–80; actor: Three Men in a Boat, 1975; GBH, 1991; The Wipers Times, 2013; Remember Me, 2014; Vanity Fair, 2018; writer: East of Ipswich, 1987; Number 27, 1988; *stage play:* The Weekend, Strand, 1994. *Films:* actor and jt author: And Now for Something Completely Different, 1970; Monty Python and the Holy Grail, 1974; Monty Python's Life of Brian, 1978; Time Bandits, 1980; Monty Python's "The Meaning of Life", 1982; American Friends, 1991; actor, writer and co-producer: The Missionary, 1982; actor: Jabberwocky, 1976; A Private Function, 1984; Brazil, 1985; A Fish Called Wanda, 1988 (Best Supporting Film Actor, BAFTA Award, 1988); Fierce Creatures, 1997; The Death of Stalin, 2017. *Television* series: contributor, Great Railway Journeys of the World, 1980, 1994; writer and presenter: Around the World in Eighty Days, 1989; Pole to Pole, 1992; Palin's Column, 1994; Full Circle, 1995–96; Michael Palin's Hemingway Adventure, 1999; Sahara With Michael Palin, 2002; Himalaya, 2004 (Best Presenter Award, RTS, 2005); Michael Palin's New Europe, 2007; Around the World in 20 Years, 2008; Brazil with Michael Palin, 2012; presenter: Palin on Redpath, 1997; The Bright Side of Life, 2000; The Ladies who Loved Matisse, 2003; Michael Palin and the Mystery of Hammershoi, 2005; Timewatch: the last day of WW1, 2008; Michael Palin in Wyeth's World, 2013; Michael Palin's Quest for Artemisia, 2015; Michael Palin meets Jan Morris, 2016; Michael Palin in North Korea, 2018; narrator, Clangers, children's series, 2015. *Live shows:* Monty Python Live (Mostly), O2 Arena, 2014; Travelling to Work (tour), 2014; Michael Palin - Live on Stage, Australia, 2015, 2018; The Thirty Years Tour, 2019; Michael Palin: Erebus, Python and other stories, 2019. Hon. Fellow, SOAS, 2008. Hon. DLitt: Sheffield, 1992; Edinburgh, 2007; Hon. DLit QUB, 2000; Hon. DSc St Andrews, 2017. Ness Award, RGS, 1998; Lifetime Achievement Award, British Comedy Awards, 2002; Special Award, BAFTA, 2005; Fellow, BAFTA, 2013. *Publications:* Monty Python's Big Red Book, 1970; Monty Python's Brand New Bok, 1973; Dr Fegg's Encyclopeadia of All World Knowledge, 1984; Limericks, 1985; Around the World in Eighty Days, 1989; Pole to Pole, 1992 (Travel Writer of the Year, British Book Awards, 1993); Hemingway's Chair (novel), 1995; Full Circle, 1997; Hemingway Adventure, 1999; Sahara, 2002; (jtly) The Pythons Autobiography by The Pythons, 2003; Himalaya, 2004 (TV and Film Book of the Year, British Book Awards, 2005); Diaries: the Python years 1969–1979, 2006; New Europe, 2007; Diaries: halfway to Hollywood 1980–1988, 2009; The Truth (novel), 2012; Brazil, 2012; Diaries: travelling to work, 1988–1998, 2014; Erebus: the story of a ship, 2018; North Korea Journal, 2019; *for children:* Small Harry and the Toothache Pills, 1981; (with R. W. Seymour and Alan Lee) The Mirrorstone, 1986; The Cyril Stories, 1986. *Recreations:* reading, running, railways—preferably all three in a foreign country. *Address:* (office) Mayday Management PS Ltd, PO Box 74642, W6 6JT. *E:* paulbird@maydaymgt.co.uk. *Club:* Athenæum.

**PALIN, Air Chief Marshal Sir Roger Hewlett,** KCB 1989; OBE 1978; Controller, Royal Air Force Benevolent Fund, 1993–98; *b* 8 July 1938; *m* 1967, Kathryn Elizabeth Pye; two *d. Educ:* Canford Sch.; St John's Coll., Cambridge (BA 1967; MA 1979; Hon. Fellow, 2007); psc. FRAeS; FIPD. Commnd KRRC, 1958; served 3 Para. Bn, 1958–59, 10 Para. Bn (TA), 1959–62; Flight Lieut, 1964; Sqn Leader, 1970; Wing Comdr, 1975; Group Captain, 1980; ADC to the Queen, 1981–82; Air Cdre, 1984; Dir of Defence Policy, MoD, 1984–85; Air Vice-Marshal, 1986; ACDS (Progs), 1986–87; AOC No 11 Gp, 1987–89; Air Marshal, 1989; C-in-C, RAF Germany and Comdr Second Allied Tactical Air Force, 1989–91; Air Chief Marshal, 1991; Air Mem. for Personnel, 1991–93; Air ADC to the Queen, 1991–93; retired 1993. Guest Schol., Woodrow Wilson Internat. Center for Scholars, Washington, 1980; Res. Associate, IISS, 1993. *Recreations:* sport, travel, international relations, defence studies.

**PALING, Her Honour Helen Elizabeth, (Mrs W. J. S. Kershaw);** a Circuit Judge, 1985–2000; *b* 25 April 1933; *o d* of A. Dale Paling and Mabel Eleanor Thomas; *m* 1961, William John Stanley Kershaw, PhD; one *s* three *d. Educ:* Prince Henry's Grammar Sch., Otley; London Sch. of Economics. LLB London 1954. Called to Bar, Lincoln's Inn, 1955; a Recorder, 1972–85. *Address:* c/o Quayside Law Courts, Newcastle upon Tyne NE1 2LA. *T:* (0191) 201 2000.

**PALIOS, Markos;** corporate turnaround specialist; Co-owner and Executive Chairman, Tranmere Rovers FC, since 2014; *b* 9 Nov. 1952; five *d*, and two step *s*; *m* 2009, Nicola Claire Coulson. *Educ:* St Anselm's Coll., Birkenhead; Manchester Univ. (BSc Psychol.). FCA 1995. Professional footballer, Tranmere Rovers FC, and Crewe Alexandra FC, 1973–86; Partner, Arthur Young, 1986–89; Partner, 1989–2003, UK Leader for Business Regeneration, 1997–2003, Coopers & Lybrand, then PricewaterhouseCoopers; Chief Exec., Football Assoc., 2003–04; European Leader, FTI Palladium Partners, 2005–06. Dir, British Judo Assoc., 2012–16 (co-author, Elite Performance System Review, 2012; Chm., Finance, Risk and Governance); Mem., Audit Cttee, Surrey CCC, 2011– (Mem., Audit, Risk and Governance Cttee). Media commentator on football, 2010–. *Recreations:* family, sport, history, politics.

**PALLEY, Dr Claire Dorothea Taylor,** OBE 1998; Constitutional Adviser, 1980–94, 1999–2004 and 2005–07, Consultant to Attorney-General, since 2008, Republic of Cyprus; Principal of St Anne's College, Oxford, 1984–91, Hon. Fellow, 1992; *b* 17 Feb. 1931; *d* of Arthur Aubrey Swait, Durban; *m* 1952, Ahrn Palley (marr. diss. 1985; he *d* 1993); five *s. Educ:* Durban Girls' Coll.; Univs of Cape Town and London. BA 1950, LLB 1952, Cape Town; PhD London 1965; MA Oxon 1984. Called to Bar, Middle Temple. Queen's University, Belfast: Lectr, 1966–67; Reader, 1967–70; Prof. of Public Law, 1970–73; Dean of Faculty of Law, 1971–73; Prof. of Law, 1973–84, and Master of Darwin Coll., 1974–82, Univ. of Kent. Member: Council, Minority Rights Group, 1975–94; UN Sub-Commn on Prevention of Discrimination and Protection of Minorities, 1988–98. Hon. LLD: QUB, 1991; Cape Town, 2008. *Publications:* The Constitutional History and Law of Southern Rhodesia, 1966; The United Kingdom and Human Rights, 1991; An International Relations Debacle: the UN Secretary-General's Mission of Good Offices in Cyprus 1999–2004, 2005; contrib. learned jls. *Address:* 13 Nikou Sophocleous Avenue, Pachna, 4700 Limassol, Cyprus.

**PALLISTER, Hon. Brian William;** MLA (PC) Fort Whyte, since 2012; Premier of Manitoba, Canada, since 2016; *b* Portage la Prairie, Manitoba, 6 July 1954; *s* of Bill Pallister and Anne Pallister; *m* 1989, Esther; two *d. Educ:* Brandon Univ. (BA, BEd). Teacher, William Morton Collegiate, 1976–79; Founder, Pallister Financial, 1980–. MLA (PC) Portage la Prairie, 1992–97; Minister of Govt Services, Manitoba, 1995–97; MP Portage-Lisgar, 2000–08; Leader of Official Opposition, Manitoba, 2012–16. *Recreations:* hiking, biking, playing piano and singing. *Address:* Office of the Premier, 450 Broadway, Winnipeg, MB R3C 0V8, Canada. *T:* (204) 9453714. *E:* premier@leg.gov.mb.ca.

**PALLISTER, (Rufina) Aswini;** *see* Weeeratne, R. A.

**PALLOT, Prof. Judith,** PhD; Professor of the Human Geography of Russia, University of Oxford, 2008–17, now Emeritus; Official Student of Christ Church, Oxford, 1979–2017, now Emeritus Student; *b* Maidenhead, 25 July 1949; *d* of Arthur Keith Pallot, CB, CMG and Marjorie Pallot (*née* Smith); *m* 2003, Jeremy Charles Thomas Fairbank; one *d. Educ:* Lynton House Sch. for Girls; Maidenhead High Sch.; Univ. of Leeds (BA 1st Cl.); University Coll. London (PhD 1977); MA Oxon. Lectr, Univ. of Leeds, 1973–79; Lectr, 1979–, Sen. Proctor, 1996–97, Univ. of Oxford; Jun., then Sen. Censor, Christ Church, Oxford, 2001–05. Pres., British Assoc. for Slavonic and E Eur. Studies, 2016–. *Publications:* (with D. J. B. Shaw) Planning in the Soviet Union, 1981; (with D. J. B. Shaw) Landscape and Settlement in Romanov Russia, 1990; (ed) Transforming Peasants: society, state and the peasantry, 1861–1930, 1998; Land Reform in Russia 1906–17: peasant responses to Stolypin's project of rural transformation, 1999; (with T. Nefedova) Russia's Unknown Agriculture: household production in post-socialist Russia, 2007; (with L. Piacetini) Gender, Geography and Punishment: the experience of women in Carceral Russia, 2012; (with E. Katz) Waiting at the Prison Gate: women, identity and the Russian prison system, 2017. *Recreations:* opera and ballet, horse riding. *Address:* Christ Church, Oxford OX1 1DP. *T:* (01865) 276222. *E:* judith.pallot@chch.ox.ac.uk.

**PALMA, Kamela;** High Commissioner for Belize in London, 2008–12; *b* Belize City, 7 Jan. 1952; *d* of late Carton Fairweather and Isabel Palm, RN (nurse); one *d. Educ:* St John's Coll., Belize; Viterbo Univ., Wisconsin; Inst. of Educn, London. Headteacher, St Peter Claver Coll., Punta Gorda, Belize; Lectr, Belize Teachers' Trng Coll.; Dir, Regl Lang. Centre, Univ. of Belize, 2000–01; CEO and Perm. Sec., Govt of Belize, 2001–03; Dep. Ambassador, Guatemala, 2004. Mem., Bd of Govs, Commonwealth Secretariat, 2009–11 (Mem., Exec. Cttee, 2008–12). Chm., Nat. Council on Ageing, 2003–08; Member, Board of Directors: Toledo Inst. for Develt and Envmt, 2001–; Belize Council for Visually Impaired, 2005–. Founder and Chair, Nurse Isabel Palma Foundn, 2013–. *Recreations:* dancing, reading, opera, travel, walking. *Address:* Buena Vista, One Mile San Antonio Road, Punta Gorda, Belize.

**PALMER,** family name of **Earl of Selborne** and **Barons Lucas of Crudwell, Palmer** and **Palmer of Childs Hill**.

**PALMER,** 4th Baron *cr* 1933, of Reading; **Adrian Bailie Nottage Palmer;** Bt 1916; *b* 8 Oct. 1951; *s* of Col the Hon. Sir Gordon Palmer, KCVO, OBE, TD, MA, FRCM and the Hon. Lady Palmer, DL; *S* uncle, 1990; *m* 1st, 1977, Cornelia Dorothy Katherine (marr. diss. 2004), *d* of R. N. Wadham, DFC, Exning, Newmarket; two *s* one *d*; 2nd, 2006, Loraine (marr. diss. 2013), *d* of Jim McMurrey, Texas, USA. *Educ:* Eton; Edinburgh Univ. Mem., Exec. Council, HHA, 1981–99; Chm., HHA for Scotland, 1994–99 (Mem., Exec. Council, 1980–99; Vice Chm., 1993). Elected Mem., H of L, 1999. Mem., Queen's Body Guard for Scotland (Royal Company of Archers), 1992–96. Sec., Scottish Peers Assoc., 2006–18. Scottish Rep. to European Landowning Orgn, 1986–92. Pres., British Assoc. for Biofuels and Oils, 2000–. Sec., The Royal Caledonian Hunt, 1989–2005. *Recreation:* gardening. *Heir:* s Hon. Hugo Bailie Rohan Palmer [*b* 5 Dec. 1980; *m* 2015, Vanessa, *y d* of Peter Webb, NSW, Australia]. *Address:* Manderston, Duns, Berwickshire TD11 3PP. *T:* (01361) 883450. *Clubs:* Pratt's; New (Edinburgh).

**PALMER OF CHILDS HILL,** Baron *cr* 2011 (Life Peer), of Childs Hill in the London Borough of Barnet; **Monroe Edward Palmer,** OBE 1982; FCA; chartered accountant; *b* 30 Nov. 1938; *s* of William and Sybil Polikoff; *m* 1962, Susette Sandra (*née* Cardash); two *s* one *d*. *Educ:* Orange Hill Grammar Sch. FCA 1963. Chm., Hendon CAB, 1981–83; Vice-Chm., Barnet CAB, 1986–88; Treasurer: Disablement Assoc., London Borough of Barnet, 1971–88; Liberal Parly Party, 1977–83; Jt Treasurer, Liberal Party, 1977–83; Pres., Lib Dem Friends of Israel, 2015– (Chm., 1987–2010). Councillor (L, then Lib Dem) London Borough of Barnet, 1986–94 and 1998–2014 (Leader, Lib Dem Gp, 1999–2008). Contested: (L) Hendon South, 1979, 1983, 1987; (Lib Dem) Hastings and Rye, 1992, 1997. House of Lords: Lib Dem lead spokesman on Taxation, 2013–15; a Dep. Speaker, 2018–. Treas., London Reg., Lib Dems, 2008–09. Dir, Barnet Homes, 1994–2009. Chm. Adv. Council, Property Redress Scheme, 2014–. Vice Pres., Jewish Leadership Council, 2017–. *Recreations:* politics, fishing, horse riding. *Address:* 31 The Vale, NW11 8SE. *T:* (020) 8455 5140. *Club:* National Liberal.

**PALMER, Adrian Oliver;** QC 1992; a Recorder, since 1992; *b* 20 Aug. 1950; *s* of late Richard Gilbert Palmer and Patricia Mary Palmer; *m* 1974, Rosemary Shaw; one *s* one *d*. *Educ:* Clifton Coll., Bristol; St John's Coll., Cambridge (MA); Bristol Univ. (LLM). Called to the Bar, Middle Temple, 1972, Bencher, 2003; Dep. High Court Judge, 2000–). *Recreations:* gardens, sheep, walking. *Address:* Guildhall Chambers, 23 Broad Street, Bristol BS1 2HG. *T:* (0117) 930 9000.

**PALMER, Dr Andrew Charles,** CMG 2014; CEng, FREng, FIMechE; Chief Executive Officer, Aston Martin, since 2014; *b* Birmingham, 30 June 1963; *s* of Brian M. Palmer and Mary C. Palmer (*née* Henshaw); *m* 2004, Hitomi Kamiomachi; one *s* three *d*. *Educ:* Coventry Univ. (Dip. Mgt 1987); Warwick Univ. (MSc Design Engrg 1990); London Business Sch. (Accelerated Develt Prog. 2002); Cranfield Univ. (PhD Engrg Mgt 2004). CEng 2003; FIMechE 2003; CMgr 2004; FREng 2017. Tech. apprentice, 1973–83, project engr, 1983–86, Automotive Products Ltd; Chief Engr, Manual Transmission, Rover Gp, 1986–91; Nissan Motor Corporation: business admin manager, 1991–2001; Dep. Man. Dir, Nissan Euro Tech. Centre, 2001–02; Prog. Dir and Corporate Vice Pres. for Light Commercial Vehicles, 2002; Pres., Motor Light Truck Co., 2003; Chm., Infiniti Co. Ltd, 2009; Senior Vice President: Global Planning and IS/IT, 2009–13; Global Mktg and Communications, 2011–13; Global Sales, 2013; Chief Planning Officer and Exec. Vice Pres., 2013–14. Vis. Prof., Tokyo Univ. of Agric. and Technol., 2009. Hon. DTech Coventry, 2010. *Recreations:* motor racing (competition licence), motor cycling, reading, listening to rock music. *Address:* Aston Martin Lagonda Ltd, Banbury Road, Gaydon, Warwicks CV35 0DB.

**PALMER, Prof. Andrew Clennel,** PhD; FRS 1994; FREng, FICE; Professor, Department of Civil and Environmental Engineering (formerly of Civil Engineering), National University of Singapore, 2007–15 (Keppel Professor, 2008–12); Fellow, Churchill College, Cambridge, since 1996; *b* 26 May 1938; *s* of Gerald Basil Coote Palmer and Muriel Gertrude Palmer (*née* Howes); *m* 1963, Jane Rhiannon Evans; one *d*. *Educ:* Pembroke Coll., Cambridge (BA, MA); Brown Univ. (PhD). FICE 1985; FREng (FEng 1990). Lectr, Liverpool Univ., 1965–67; Cambridge University: Sen. Asst in Res., 1967–68; Lectr, 1968–75; Fellow, Churchill Coll., 1967–75; Chief Engr, R. J. Brown and Associates, 1975–79; Prof. of Civil Engrg, UMIST, 1979–82; Vice-Pres. Engrg, R. J. Brown and Associates, 1982–85; Man. Dir, Andrew Palmer and Associates, 1985–93; Technical Dir, SAIC Ltd, 1993–96; Jafar Res. Prof. of Petroleum Engineering, Cambridge Univ., 1996–2005. Visiting Professor: Harvard Univ., 2002–03; Nat. Univ. of Singapore, 2006–07. Managing Director: Bold Is Engrg Ltd, 2005–09 (Co. Sec., 2009–15); Bold Island Engrg (Singapore) Pte Ltd, 2014. Pres., Pipeline Industries Guild, 1998–2000. Trustee, Amer. Univ., Sharjah, 2014–. Hon. DSc Clarkson, 2007. *Publications:* Structural Mechanics, 1976; Subsea Pipeline Engineering, 2004; Dimensional Analysis, 2008; Arctic Offshore Engineering, 2012; articles and papers in scientific and engrg jls. *Recreations:* travel, glass-blowing, cooking, languages. *Club:* Athenæum.

**PALMER, Andrew Eustace,** CMG 1987; CVO 1981; HM Diplomatic Service, retired; an Extra Equerry to the Duke of Kent, since 1996; *b* 30 Sept. 1937; *s* of late Lt-Col Rodney Howell Palmer, MC, and of Mrs Frances Pauline Ainsworth (*née* Gordon-Duff); *m* 1962, Davina, *d* of Sir Roderick Barclay, GCVO, KCMG; two *s* one *d*. *Educ:* Winchester Coll.; Pembroke Coll., Cambridge (MA). Second Lieut, Rifle Bde, 1956–58. Joined HM Foreign (later Diplomatic) Service, 1961; American Dept, FO, 1962–63; Third, later Second, Secretary (Commercial), La Paz, 1963–65; Second Sec., Ottawa, 1965–67; Treasury Centre for Administrative Studies, 1967–68; Central Dept, FO, later Southern European Dept, FCO, 1968–72; First Sec. (Information), Paris, 1972–76; Asst Head of Defence Dept, FCO, 1976–77; RCDS 1978; Counsellor, Head of Chancery and Consul-Gen., Oslo, 1979–82; Hd, Falkland Is Dept, FCO, 1982–85; Fellow, Harvard Center for Internat. Affairs, 1985–86; Ambassador to Cuba, 1986–88; seconded as Pvte Sec. to the Duke and Duchess of Kent, 1988–90; Ambassador to the Holy See, 1991–95. Local organiser, Bilderberg Conf., Turnberry, 1998. Mem. Council, 1996–2008, Vis. Fellow, Politics and Internat. Relns, 2008–, Reading Univ.; Chm., Friends of Univ. of Reading, 2005–17. Hon. DLitt Reading, 2016. Comdr, Order of St Olav (Norway), 1981. *Publications:* A Diplomat and his Birds, 2005. *Recreations:* fishing, following most sports, photography, ornithology. *Address:* Peasemore Manor, Newbury, Berks RG20 7JF. *Clubs:* Brooks's, MCC.

*See also Viscount Garmoyle.*

**PALMER, Andrew Richard Alexander;** Group Chief Executive Officer, Learndirect, since 2016; *b* Harrow, 28 Jan. 1976; *s* of Dr Neil Ingamells Palmer and Catherine Mary Palmer; *m* 2009, Sarah Meredith (marr. diss. 2018); two *d*. *Educ:* Nottingham High Sch.; Univ. of Leeds (BSc Hons Zoology 1998). Consultant, PSD Gp, 1998–2000; Dir, Ops, e-skills UK, 2000–07; Dir, Educn and Skills, BT, 2007–12; Managing Director: Skillnet Ltd, 2012–13; Aspire Achieve Advance Ltd, 2013–15. Member: Bd, OFSTED, 2011–15; Skills Commn, 2011–14. Mem., Educn and Skills Cttee, CBI, 2008–12. Trustee, Dagfa Sch., Nottingham, 2011–14. FRSA 2017. *Recreations:* trying to be a good dad, enjoying English countryside, Rugby Union (watching and occasionally refereeing). *Address:* Edwalton, Nottinghamshire. *E:* andy.r.a.palmer@me.com.

**PALMER, Angela Silver, (Mrs J. D. F. Palmer);** artist; journalist; *b* 27 March 1957; *m* 1988, Jeremy David Fletcher Palmer, *er s* of Maj.-Gen. Sir (Joseph) Michael Palmer, KCVO; two *s* one *d*. *Educ:* George Watson's Ladies' Coll., Edinburgh; Ruskin Sch. of Drawing and Fine Art, Oxford (BA 2005); RCA (MA 2007). Trainee, Evening News, Edinburgh, 1979–82; Peterborough Column, Daily Telegraph, 1982–84; Editor, PHS, The Times, 1984–86; News Editor, Observer, 1986–88; Editor: Observer Mag., 1988–92; Elle, 1992–93. Commissions: Wellcome Trust; Aberdeen Univ.; Pembroke Coll., Oxford; Exeter Coll., Oxford; Ashmolean Mus., Oxford; exhibtd RA Summer Exhibn, 2005; Ghost Forest, installation of African rainforest trees, Trafalgar Square, London, and Thorvaldsens Plads, Copenhagen, 2009, Oxford Univ. Mus. of Nat. Hist. and Pitt Rivers Mus., Oxford, 2010–12; solo exhibitions: Waterhouse and Dodd Gall., London, 2008, 2012; Wellcome Trust, London, 2009; Fine Art Soc., 2014; work in permanent collection: Ashmolean Mus., Oxford (Egyptian Galls); RCP; Royal Papworth Hosp., Cambridge; Scottish Nat. Portrait Gall.; Smithsonian Air and Space Mus. FRSA 2003. Journalist of the Year, Scotland, 1980; Waugh Scholarship and Fitzgerald Prize, Exeter Coll., Univ. of Oxford, 2003; Polly Campbell Award, Jerwood Space, 2007; RCA Soc. and Thames and Hudson Award, 2007. *Recreation:* family. *Address:* 20 Highbury Terrace, N5 1UP.

**PALMER, Lt-Gen. Anthony Malcolm Douglas,** CB 2005; CBE 1995; non-executive Chairman: Shoreditch Bar Group, since 2012; Eden Logistics, since 2016; *b* 13 March 1949; *s* of late Lt-Col A. G. D. Palmer and Joan Palmer (*née* Wintour); *m* 1972, Harriet Ann Jardine; two *s* one *d*. *Educ:* Woodcote House; Winchester Coll. Commnd RGJ, 1969; despatches, 1972, 1990; BAOR, 1969–70; NI, 1970–71; Shorncliffe, 1971–73; Catterick, 1973–74; Warminster, 1974–76; 2nd Bn RGJ, 1976, Ops Officer, 1978–80; Trng Co. Comdr, Winchester, 1980–81; Staff Coll., Pakistan, 1981; Co. Comdr, 3rd Bn RGJ, 1983–85; MoD, 1985–87; Directing Staff, Camberley, 1987–89; CO, 2nd Bn RGJ, 1989–91; Col, MoD, 1991; Comdr, 8 Inf. Bde, 1993; rcds 1995; Dir, Army Plans, 1996–99; Chief Exec., Army Trng and Recruiting Agency, 1999–2002; Dep. Chief of Defence Staff (Personnel), 2002–05. Chm., Warrior Prog., 2008–16. Chairman: Silicon CPV plc, 2008–09; Adv. Bd, Pax Mondial, 2009–14; Adv. Bd, Pyreco, 2011–; Antheda, 2011–. Chm., Pakistan Soc., 2006–12. Gov., Hazlegrove Sch. and King's Sch., Bruton, 2014– (Chm. Govs, 2015–). *Recreations:* music, bridge, golf, tennis, fishing. *Clubs:* Army and Navy, Royal Green Jackets.

**PALMER, Anthony Thomas Richard;** *see* Palmer, Tony.

**PALMER, Caroline Ann, (Cally),** CBE 2006; Chief Executive, Royal Marsden NHS Foundation Trust (formerly NHS Trust), since 1998; National Cancer Director, NHS England (on secondment), since 2015; *d* of Christopher and Ann Palmer; *m* 2004, Phil Yeates; two *s* one *d* by a previous marriage. *Educ:* Woking Girls Grammar Sch.; Westfield Coll., London Univ. (BA 1979); London Business Sch. (MSc 1995). MHSM, DipHSM 1983. Gen. mgt trng scheme, 1980–83; Asst Unit Admnr, St Luke's Hosp., 1983–85; Royal Free Hospital, subseq. Royal Free Hampstead NHS Trust: Associate Unit Admnr, 1985–87; Dep. Manager, 1987–90; Gen. Manager, 1990–94; Dep. CEO, 1994–98. *Recreations:* history of art, ballet. *Address:* Royal Marsden NHS Trust, Fulham Road, SW3 6JJ.

**PALMER, Sir (Charles) Mark,** 5th Bt *cr* 1886; *b* 21 Nov. 1941; *s* of Sir Anthony Frederick Mark Palmer, 4th Bt, and Henriette Alice (later Lady Abel Smith, DCVO); *S* father, 1941; *m* 1976, Hon. Catherine Elizabeth Tennant, *y d* of 2nd Baron Glenconner; one *s* one *d*. *Heir: s* Arthur Morris Palmer, *b* 9 March 1981. *Address:* Mill Hill Farm, Sherborne, Northleach, Glos GL54 3DU. *T:* (01451) 844395.

**PALMER, Cdre Christopher Laurence,** CBE 2010; RN; Chief Executive, Corporation of the Church House, since 2010; Gentleman Usher to the Queen, since 2011; *b* Mablethorpe, 5 April 1954; *s* of Flt Lt Laurence George Palmer, DFC, RAF and Sheila Palmer (*née* Dingle); *m* 1979, Janet Elizabeth Hughes; one *s* one *d*. *Educ:* King Edward VI Sch.; Sudbury Grammar Sch.; Univ. of Southampton (BSc Hons 1975); BRNC. Qualified Helicopter Observer, 1977; 820 Sqn, HMS Blake, 1978; 819 Sqn, HMS Gannet, 1978–80; 815 Sqn, HMS Arrow, Falklands, 1980–82 (mentioned in despatches, 1982); 702 Sqn, HMS Osprey, 1982–84; Flying Instructor to Prince Andrew, 1983–84; HMS Battleaxe, 1984–85; RNSC, 1985; HMS Southampton, 1986–87; HMS Cumberland, 1988–90; CO 702 Sqn, 1990–91; XO HMS Fearless, 1991–93; MoD, 1993–95; Comdr BRNC, 1995–98; MoD, 1998–2002; Fleet HQ, 2002–05; CO RNAS Yeovilton, 2005–09. Trustee, Fleet Air Arm Meml Ch, 2012–. Liveryman, Hon. Co. of Air Pilots (formerly GAPAN), 2006. FCMI 2007; FRAeS 2010. *Recreations:* sailing, powerboats, motorcycling, flying, theatre, saxophone. *Address:* c/o Corporation of the Church House, 27 Great Smith Street, SW1P 3AZ. *T:* (020) 7898 1310. *E:* chris.palmer@churchofengland.org. *Clubs:* Fleet Air Arm Squadron, Army and Navy; Emsworth Sailing.

**PALMER, Clare Mary;** *see* Murray, C. M.

**PALMER, David Erroll Prior,** CBE 2003; Chairman, UK Hydrographic Office, 2005–09; *b* 20 Feb. 1941; *s* of Sir Otho Prior-Palmer, DSO, and Sheila Peers (*née* Weller-Poley), OBE; *m* 1974, Elizabeth Helen Young; two *s* one *d*. *Educ:* Eton; Christ Church, Oxford (MA PPE). Joined Financial Times, 1964: New York Correspondent, 1967; Management Editor, 1970; News Editor, 1972; Foreign Editor, 1979; Dep. Editor, 1981; Gen. Manager and Dir, 1983; Dep. Chief Exec., 1989; Chief Exec., 1990–93; Independent Newspapers (Ireland): Man. Dir, 1994–98; Chm., 1999–2002; Chairman: South-West Sussex Radio, 1995–2004; Dedalo Grupo Gráfico, 2004–06; ToxiMet, 2010–16; Dir, Polestar Gp, 2003–06. Chm., Barts and E London Healthcare Merger Project, 2010–11. Dir, The Mary Rose Trust, 2004–16 (Dep. Chm., 2016–). First British finisher, seventh over-all, Observer Singlehanded Transatlantic Race, 1976; Nat. Dragon Champion, Edinburgh Cup, 2007. *Publications:* The Atlantic Challenge, 1977. *Recreations:* sailing, travelling. *Address:* Dairy Cottage, Hunters Race, Chichester, W Sussex PO19 3BZ. *Clubs:* Garrick; Royal Yacht Squadron (Cowes); Itchenor Sailing (near Chichester).

**PALMER, Dame Felicity (Joan),** DBE 2011 (CBE 1993); mezzo-soprano. *Educ:* Erith Grammar Sch.; Guildhall Sch. of Music and Drama. AGSM (Teacher/Performer), FGS. Kathleen Ferrier Meml Prize, 1970; major appearances at concerts in Britain, America, Belgium, France, Germany, Italy, Russia and Spain, firstly as soprano and then as mezzo-soprano; début as soprano, Dido in Dido and Aeneas, Kent Opera, 1972; début in USA, Marriage of Figaro, Houston, 1973; soprano roles included: Pamina in The Magic Flute, ENO, 1975; Cleopatra in Julius Caesar, Herrenhausen Hanover, and Frankfurt Opera, 1978; title role, Alcina, Bern Opera, 1978; Elektra in Idomeneo, Zurich Opera, 1980; the Countess in The Marriage of Figaro, ENO; Elvira in Don Giovanni, Scottish Opera and ENO; Marguerite in Damnation of Faust, ENO; mezzo-soprano roles include: ENO: Tristan und Isolde, 1981; Rienzi, 1983; Mazeppa, 1984; Herodias in Salome, and The Witch in Hansel and Gretel, 1987; Orfeo, Opera North, 1984; King Priam, Royal Opera, 1985; Albert Herring, Glyndebourne, 1985; Tamburlaine, Opera North, 1985; Katya Kabanova, Chicago Lyric Opera, 1986; début at La Scala, Milan, as Marguerita in world première of Riccardo III by Flavio Testi, 1987; Last Night of the Proms, 1987; début, Netherlands Opera, as Kabanicha in Katya Kabanova, 1988, same role, Glyndebourne, 1988; Mistress Quickly in Falstaff, 1988 and 1990, Marcellina in The Marriage of Figaro,

1989, Glyndebourne; world première of Tippett's New Year, Houston, USA, 1989; The Marriage of Figaro and The Gambler (Prokofiev), Chicago, 1991; Klytemnestra in Elektra, WNO, 1992, La Scala, Milan and Japan, 1995, Royal Opera, 2005, Netherlands Opera, 2006; Orlando, Aix-en-Provence, 1993; Dialogue des Carmélites, Geneva, 1993, Metropolitan, NY, 2002; La Fille du Régiment, San Francisco, 1993, Royal Opera, 2007; Ariodante, WNO, 1994; The Rake's Progress, Chicago, 1994; Ballo in Maschera, Catania, 1995; Countess in The Queen of Spades, Glyndebourne, 1995, ENO, 2015, Royal Opera, 2019; Juno/Ino in Semele, Royal Opera, 1996; Mahagonny, Paris, 1997, Chicago, 1998; Fricka in The Ring, Munich, 1997 and 1999, Canaries, 1999, Met. Opera House, NY, 2000; Sweeney Todd, Royal Opera, 2003; The Yeomen of the Guard, Royal Albert Hall, 2012; Peter Grimes, ENO, 2014; recitals in Amsterdam, Paris, Vienna, 1976–77, Tokyo, 1991; concert tours with BBC SO, Europe, 1973, 1977 and 1984, Australasia, Far East and Eastern Europe, 1977–; ABC tour of Australia, 1978. Recordings include: Poèmes pour Mi, with Pierre Boulez; Holst Choral Symphony, with Sir Adrian Boult; title role in Gluck's Armide; Elektra in Idomeneo, with Nikolaus Harnoncourt; Klytemnestra in Elektra, with Semyon Bychkov, Christoph von Dohnányi, James Levine and Valery Gergiev; The Music Makers; Sea Pictures; Britten's Phaedra; recitals, with John Constable, of songs by Poulenc, Ravel and Fauré, and of Victorian ballads. *Address:* c/o Intermusica, Crystal Wharf, 9 Kingsway, WC2B 6XF.

**PALMER, Prof. Frank Robert,** FBA 1975; Professor and Head of Department of Linguistic Science, University of Reading, 1965–87; *b* 9 April 1922; *s* of George Samuel Palmer and Gertrude Lilian (*née* Newman); *m* 1948, Jean Elisabeth Moore; three *s* two *d*. *Educ:* Bristol Grammar Sch.; New Coll., Oxford (Ella Stephens Schol., State Schol.) 1942–43 and 1945–48; Merton Coll., Oxford (Harmsworth Sen. Schol.) 1948–49; MA Oxon 1948; Craven Fellow, 1948. Served war, E Africa, 1943–45. Lectr in Linguistics, Sch. of Oriental and African Studies, Univ. of London, 1950–60 (study leave in Ethiopia, 1952–53); Prof. of Linguistics, University Coll. of N Wales, Bangor, 1960–65; Dean of Faculty of Letters and Social Sciences, Univ. of Reading, 1969–72. Linguistic Soc. of America Prof., Buffalo, 1971; Distinguished Visiting Professor: Foreign Languages Inst., Beijing, 1981; Univ. of Delaware, 1983. Professional visits to Canada, USA, Mexico, Venezuela, Peru, Chile, Argentina, Uruguay, Brazil, India, Japan, China, Indonesia, Morocco, Tunisia, Uganda, Kuwait and most countries of Europe. MAE 1991. Hon. DLitt Reading, 1996. *Publications:* The Morphology of the Tigre Noun, 1962; A Linguistic Study of the English Verb, 1965; (ed) Selected Papers of J. R. Firth, 1968; (ed) Prosodic Analysis, 1970; Grammar, 1971, 2nd edn 1984; The English Verb, 1974, 2nd edn 1987; Semantics, 1976, 2nd edn 1981; Modality and the English Modals, 1979, 2nd edn 1990; Mood and Modality, 1986, 2nd edn 2001; (ed jtly) Studies in the History of Western Linguistics, 1986; Grammatical Roles and Relations, 1994; (ed) Grammar and Meaning, 1995; (ed jtly) Modality in Contemporary English, 2003; (ed jtly) English Modality in Perspective: genre analysis and cultural studies, 2004; articles and reviews on Ethiopian langs, English and linguistic theory, in learned jls. *Recreations:* gardening, crosswords. *Address:* Whitethorns, Roundabout Lane, Winnersh, Wokingham, Berks RG41 5AD. *T:* (0118) 978 6214.

**PALMER, Sir Geoff;** *see* Palmer, Sir G. H. O.

**PALMER, Geoffrey,** OBE 2005; actor; *b* 4 June 1927; *m* 1963, Sally Green; one *s* one *d*. *Educ:* Highgate Sch. *Theatre* includes: Difference of Opinion, Garrick; West of Suez, Royal Court, 1971; Private Lives, Globe, 1973; Eden End, NT, 1974; St Joan, Old Vic, 1977; Tishoo, Wyndham's, 1979; Kafka's Dick, Royal Court, 1986; Piano, NT, 1990; *television* includes: The Fall and Rise of Reginald Perrin, 1976–78; Butterflies; The Last Song; Absurd Person Singular, 1984; Insurance Man, 1985; Fairly Secret Army, 1985; Seasons Greetings, 1986; As Time Goes By, 1992–2002; The Savages, 2001; He Knew He Was Right, 2004; Bert and Dickie, Parade's End, 2012; *films* include: O Lucky Man!, 1973; The Honorary Consul, 1982; A Zed and Two Noughts, 1985; Clockwise, 1986; A Fish Called Wanda, 1988; The Madness of King George, 1994; Mrs Brown, 1997; Tomorrow Never Dies, 1998; Anna and the King, 1999; Peter Pan, 2002; Piccadilly Jim, 2003; Pink Panther II, 2007; W. E., 2010; Paddington, 2013.

**PALMER, Sir Geoffrey (Christopher John),** 12th Bt *cr* 1660; *b* 30 June 1936; *er s* of Lt-Col Sir Geoffrey Frederick Neill Palmer, 11th Bt, and Cicely Katherine (who *m* 1952, Robert W. B. Newton; she *d* 1989), *o d* of late Arthur Radmall, Clifton, nr Watford; *S* father, 1951; *m* 1957, Clarissa Mary, *er d* of Stephen Villiers-Smith, Knockholt, Kent; four *d*. *Educ:* Eton. Agent for Burberry, Norway, Sweden, Finland, 1971–94. *Recreations:* golf, crossword puzzles, shooting. *Heir: b* Jeremy Charles Palmer [*b* 16 May 1939; *m* 1968, Antonia (marr. diss. 2009), *d* of late Ashley Dutton; two *s*]. *Address:* Carlton Curlieu Hall, Leicestershire LE8 0PH. *T:* (0116) 259 2656. *Clubs:* MCC, I Zingari, Free Foresters, Eton Ramblers, Butterflies, Gentlemen of Leicestershire, Lincolnshire Gentlemen's Cricket, Derbyshire Friars, XL, Frogs, Old Etonian Golfing Society, Old Etonian Racquets and Tennis, Northants Amateurs' CC.

**PALMER, Rt Hon. Sir Geoffrey (Winston Russell),** AC 1991; KCMG 1991; PC 1986; QC (NZ) (SC 2008); barrister; Professor of Law, Victoria University of Wellington, New Zealand, 1974–79 and 1991–94, Distinguished Fellow, Faculty of Law, since 2010; *b* 21 April 1942; *s* of Leonard Russell and Jessie Patricia Palmer; *m* 1963, Margaret Eleanor Hinchcliff; one *s* one *d*. *Educ:* Nelson Coll.; Victoria Univ. of Wellington (BA; LLB); Univ. of Chicago (JD). Barrister and Solicitor, High Court of New Zealand. Prof. of Law, Univ. of Iowa, 1969–73, and 1991–95. Vis. Prof. of Law, Univ. of Virginia, 1972–73; Global Affiliated Prof. of Law, Univ. of Iowa, 2015–; Vis. Prof., QMUL, 2015–16. MP (Lab) Christchurch Central, NZ, 1979–90; Dep. Prime Minister, 1984–89; Attorney-Gen., 1984–89; Minister of Justice, 1984–89; Minister for the Environment, 1987–90; Prime Minister, 1989–90. Partner, Chen Palmer & Partners (formerly Chen & Palmer), barristers and solicitors, Wellington, 1995–2004; Pres., Law Commn, NZ, 2005–10; Chm., UN Sec. Gen.'s Panel on Gaza flotilla incident, 2010–11; Mem., Govt Inquiry into Operation Burnham, NZ Defence Force in Afghanistan, 2018–19. Bencher, Middle Temple, 2016. *Publications:* Unbridled Power?—an interpretation of New Zealand's constitution and government, 1979, 2nd edn 1987; Compensation for Incapacity—a study of law and social change in Australia and New Zealand, 1979; Environmental Politics—a greenprint for New Zealand, 1990; New Zealand's Constitution in Crisis, 1992; Environment—the international challenge, 1995; Bridled Power, 1997, 4th edn 2004; Constitutional Conversations, 2002; (with J. Carlson and B. Weston) International Environmental Law and World Order, 3rd edn 2012; Reform: a memoir, 2013; (with A. Butler) A Constitution for Aotearoa New Zealand, 2016; (with A. Butler) Towards Democratic Renewal, 2018. *Recreations:* cricket, golf, playing the trumpet. *Address:* 63 Roxburgh Street, Mount Victoria, Wellington, New Zealand. *T:* (4) 8015185; Harbour Chambers, 111 The Terrace, Wellington, New Zealand.

**PALMER, Sir Godfrey Henry Oliver, (Sir Geoff),** Kt 2014; OBE 2003; PhD, DSc; Professor of Biological Sciences, Heriot-Watt University, 1992–2005, now Emeritus; *b* St Elizabeth, Jamaica, 9 April 1940; *s* of Aubrey and Ivy Georgina Palmer; *m* 1969, Margaret Anne Wood; one *s* two *d*. *Educ:* North Street and Kingston Sen. Schs, Jamaica; Shelbourne Secondary Modern Sch., London; Highbury Co. Sch., London; Leicester Univ. (BSc); Univ. of Edinburgh (PhD 1968); Heriot-Watt Univ. (DSc 1985). Jun. lab. technician, Queen Elizabeth Coll., London, 1958–61; Sen. Scientist, Brewing Res. Foundn, 1968–77; Lectr, then Sen. Lectr, 1977–88, Reader, 1988–92, Heriot-Watt Univ. Hon. President: Edinburgh and Lothians Regl Equality Council, 1977; Assoc. of Jamaicans, Birmingham, 2003. Hon DSc: Abertay, 2009; Open, 2010; Heriot-Watt, 2015. *Publications:* Cereal Science and Technology, 1989; Mr White and the Ravens (novel), 2005; The Enlightenment Abolished (novel), 2007. *Recreations:* community service, Scottish-Caribbean history, TV, reading, sports. *Address:* 23 Waulkmill Drive, Penicuick, Midlothian EH26 8LA. *T:* (01968) 675148, 07906 178073.

**PALMER, Horace Anthony, (Tony);** Chairman, Meyer International, 1997–99 (Director, 1995–99); *b* 20 Feb. 1937; *s* of Horace Charles and Violet Victoria Palmer; *m* 1961, Beryl Eileen Freakley; two *d*. *Educ:* Pinner County Grammar School; Hammersmith Sch. of Building. FRICS; FCIOB. Trainee Quantity Surveyor, 1954; joined Taylor Woodrow, 1954; Contracts Manager, 1970; Subsidiary Dir, 1974; Subsidiary Man. Dir, 1987; Man. Dir, 1989; Chief Exec., 1990–97. Chairman: High Point Rendel Gp plc, 1997–2003; Monacon Hldgs Ltd, 1997–2001; Parker Plant Ltd, 1997–2001; Pilkington Tiles, 1998; Galliford, subseq. Galliford Try, 1999–2005; non-exec. Dir, Berkeley Gp, 1997–2007. *Recreations:* sports, reading biography.

**PALMER, Howard William Arthur;** QC 1999; a Recorder, since 2006; *b* 24 June 1954; *s* of William Alexander Palmer, CBE, DL and Cherry Anne Palmer (*née* Gibbs); *m* 1983, Catherine Margaret Jackson; one *s* three *d*. *Educ:* Eton Coll.; University Coll., Oxford (MA Juris). Called to the Bar, Inner Temple, 1977; Lectr, KCL, 1977–78; barrister in private practice, 1978–. Mem. Council, Univ. of Reading, 2008–17. *Recreations:* cricket, golf, fieldsports, theatre, hedgelaying, enjoying the countryside. *Address:* 2 Temple Gardens, EC4Y 9AY. *T:* (020) 7822 1200. *Clubs:* MCC; Berkshire County Cricket.

**PALMER, James Edwin;** Chair and Senior Partner, Herbert Smith Freehills LLP, since 2015; *s* of late Malcolm John Frederick Palmer and of Rachel Mary Palmer; *m* 1990, Nicola Jane Lister White; three *s*. *Educ:* Winchester Coll.; Queens' Coll., Cambridge (BA 1985). Herbert Smith, later Herbert Smith Freehills: joined, 1986; admitted solicitor, 1988; Partner, 1994–; Mem., Partnership Council, 2002–06; Global Head: Equity Capital Mkts, 2005–10; Corporate, 2010–12. Chairman: Company Law Sub-Cttee, City of London Law Soc., 2002–06; Law Soc./City of London Law Soc. Takeovers Jt Wkg Party, 2002–15; Mem., Listing Authority Adv. Cttee, FSA, 2008–13 (Chm., 2012–13); Chm., Listing Authority Adv. Panel, 2013–16, Mem., Mkts Practitioner Panel, 2013–, Financial Conduct Authy. Chm., Legal Services Gp, TheCityUK, 2016–. Trustee, Reform Res. Trust, 2010–. *Publications:* (contrib.) Butterworths Takeovers: law and practice, 2005, 2nd edn (ed jtly), 2015; (contrib.) Hannigan and Prentice: the Companies Act 2006—a commentary, 2007; (contrib.) Buckley on the Companies Acts, 2007–11. *Recreations:* fly fishing, reading. *Address:* Herbert Smith Freehills LLP, Exchange House, Primrose Street, EC2A 2EG. *T:* (020) 7374 8000. *E:* james.palmer@hsf.com.

**PALMER, John,** CB 1986; Chairman, European Passenger Services, British Rail, 1990–94; *b* 13 Nov. 1928; 2nd *s* of late William Nathaniel Palmer and Grace Dorothy May Palmer (*née* Procter); *m* 1958, Lyliane Marthe Jeanjean; two *d*. *Educ:* Heath Grammar Sch., Halifax; The Queen's Coll., Oxford (Lit.Hum.) (MA). Entered Min. of Housing and Local Govt, 1952; Cabinet Office, 1963–65; Asst Sec., 1965; Under Secretary: DoE, 1971; Dept of Transport, 1976–82; Dep. Sec., Dept of Transport, 1982–89. Liveryman, Carmen's Co., 1987 (Freeman, 2014). *Address:* 72 College Road, SE21 7LY. *Club:* Oxford and Cambridge.

**PALMER, Judith Mary;** Director, Poetry Society, since 2008; *b* Epping, 14 Dec. 1965; adopted *d* of Thomas William Palmer and Mary Elizabeth Palmer (*née* Charlier). *Educ:* Brigidine Convent, Windsor; Univ. of Bristol (BA Hons English 1986). Hd, Educn Dept, W&G Foyle Booksellers, 1986–87; Mktg Asst, Macmillan Press, 1987–88; Publicity Officer, A & C Black Publishers, 1988–90; Publicity Manager, The Women's Press, 1990–91; freelance arts producer, newspaper feature writer and radio broadcaster, 1991–2008; Sen. Res. Fellow, Manchester Metropolitan Univ., 2006–07; Public Prog. Manager, The Women's Liby, London Metropolitan Univ., 2007–08. Judge, Commonwealth Writers Prize, 2002. Mem., Humanities External Adv. Bd, Univ. of Oxford, 2016–. Trustee: Poetry Soc., 1998–2001 (Chair); Poetry Sch., 2002–05 (Chair); Keats Foundn, 2010–. *Publications:* Private Views: artists working today, 2004; contributor: Oxford Companion to English Literature, 1999; Zero Gravity: a cultural user's guide, 2005; A Record of Fear, 2006; Sitting Room, 2006; Earth, Air, Sky and Water, 2006; Andrew Bracey, 2007; Lorna Graves, 2008; The Pity, 2014; contribs to exhibn catalogues and jls. *Recreations:* botany, pataphysics, art, long walks. *Address:* The Poetry Society, 22 Betterton Street, WC2H 9BX. *T:* (020) 7420 9880. *E:* info@poetrysociety.org.uk.

**PALMER, Keith Francis,** OBE 2010; Chairman, AgDevCo, since 2009; *b* Cardiff, 27 July 1947; *s* of Frank Palmer and Gwenda Palmer; *m* 1974, Penny McDonagh; four *d*. *Educ:* Howardian High Sch., Cardiff; Univ. of Birmingham (BSc Hons 1st Cl. 1968; PhD 1971); Churchill Coll., Cambridge (Dip. Develt Econs 1974). Asst Sec., Finance Ministry, PNG, 1974–78; Economist, Fiscal Affairs Dept, IMF, 1978–79; Sen. Economist, Energy Dept, World Bank, 1979–84; N. M. Rothschild & Sons Ltd, 1984–2008: Dir, 1987; Man. Dir, 1992; Co-Chief Exec., 1997–98; Exec. Vice-Chm., 1998–2002; non-exec. Vice-Chm., 2002–08. Chairman: InfraCo Africa, 2004–14; InfraCo Asia Investments Ltd, 2014–18. Non-exec. Chm., Emerging Africa Infrastructure Fund, 2002–07. *Recreations:* classical music, geology.

**PALMER, Prof. Marilyn,** MBE 2015; PhD; FSA 1991; Professor of Industrial Archaeology, Leicester University, 2000–08, now Emeritus; *b* 30 April 1943; *d* of Joseph Henry Allum and Mary Winifred Allum; *m* 1965, David Palmer (marr. diss. 1991). *Educ:* St Anne's Coll., Oxford (BA Hons Modern History 1965; MA 1969); Leicester Univ. (PGCE (Distinction) 1966; Postgrad. Cert. in British Archaeol. (Distinction) 1973; PhD 1976). History Teacher, Loughborough High Sch., 1966–69; Lectr, 1969–72, Sen. Lectr, 1972–77, Loughborough Coll. of Educn; Loughborough University: Lectr, 1977–80; Sen. Lectr, 1980–83; Head, History Dept, 1983–88; Leicester University: Sen. Lectr in History, 1988–98; Reader in Industrial Archaeol., and Hd, Archaeol. Div., 1998–2000; Head, Sch. of Archaeol. and Ancient Hist., 2000–06; adult educn lectr on indust. archaeology, 1973–. Gilder Lehrman Fellow, Colonial Williamsburg Foundn, 2006; Vis. Fellow, All Souls Coll., Oxford, 2007; Leverhulme Emeritus Fellow, 2009–12. Vice Pres., HA, 1986–93; Mem., Royal Commn on Historical Monuments of England, 1993–99; National Trust: Member: Industrial Archaeology Adv. Gp, 1993–99 (Chm., 1999–2001); Archaeol. Panel, 2001–14; Midlands Regl Adv. Bd (formerly E Midlands Regl Cttee), 2008–14; Specialist Advr, Historic Envmt Panel, 2017–; Mem., Industrial Archaeol. Adv. Panel, English Heritage, 2001–14 (Mem., Ancient Monuments Adv. Cttee, 1999–2001); Chm., Assoc. for Indust. Archaeology, 2004–08 (Mem. Council, 1980–2004; Pres., 1986–89, 2010–); Council for British Archaeology: Vice-Pres., 2008–16, Chm., 2016–17; Chm., E Midlands Region, 2012–. Chm., Charnwood Br., U3A, 2012–16. Jt Editor, 1984–2002, Book Review Editor, 2002–, Industrial Archaeology Review. *Publications:* (with P. A. Neaverson) Industrial Landscapes of the East Midlands, 1992; Industry in the Landscape, 1994; Industrial Archaeology: principles and practice, 1998; South-West Textile Industry: a social archaeology, 2005; (with David Gwyn) Understanding the Workplace: a research framework for industrial archaeology in Britain, 2005; (with P. S. Barnwell) Post-Medieval

Landscapes: landscape history after Hoskins, 2007; (with A. J. Horning) Crossing Paths or Sharing Tracks: future directions in the archaeological study of post-1550 Britain and Ireland, 2007; (with Michael Nevell and Mark Sissons) Industrial Archaeology: a practical handbook, 2012; (with P. S. Barnwell) Country House Technology, 2012; (with Ian West) Technology in the Country House, 2016; articles in jls. *Recreations:* hill walking, travelling—and industrial archaeology! *Address:* School of Archaeology and Ancient History, University of Leicester, Leicester LE1 7RH. *T:* (0116) 252 2821.

**PALMER, Sir Mark;** *see* Palmer, Sir C. M.

**PALMER, Martin Giles;** Secretary General, Alliance of Religions and Conservation, since 1995; Director, International Consultancy on Religion, Education and Culture, since 1984; *b* Bristol, 14 Oct. 1953; *s* of Rev. Canon Derek George Palmer and Cecile June Palmer (*née* Goddard); *m* 1st, 1973, Sandra Ann Fischer (marr. diss.); one *s* one *d*; 2nd, 2006, Victoria Elisabeth Strathern Finlay. *Educ:* Hartcliffe Comprehensive Sch., Bristol; Commonweal Comprehensive Sch., Swindon; Selwyn Coll., Cambridge (BA 1976; MA 1979). Regl Sec., Christian Educn Movement, NW England, 1977–79; Chair, Hong Kong Res. Gp, 1977–84; Dir, Centre for Study of Religion and Educn in Inner City, 1979–84. Religious Advr to WWF Internat., 1988–95. Vis. Prof. on Religion, History and Nature, Univ. of Winchester. Fellow, Club of Rome, 2012. *Publications:* Worlds of Difference, 1985; Faith and Nature, 1987; Tao Te Ching, 1993; Living Christianity, 1993; I Ching, 1995; Travels Through Sacred China, 1996; Chuang Tzu, 1996; Sacred Britain, 1997; Kuan Yin, 1998; The Jesus Sutras, 2001; The Times Atlas of World Religions, 2002; The Sacred History of Britain, 2002; Faith in Conservation, 2003; Religions of the World, 2005; The Atlas of Religion, 2007; Sacred Land, 2012; Shangsu: the most venerable book, 2014; Faith and Finance, 2017; The Romance of the Three Kingdoms, 2018. *Recreations:* anything old, especially churches, temples, cities, coins and brasses, cooking, all things Chinese, moderately long walks. *Address:* Alliance of Religions and Conservation, 6 Gay Street, Bath BA1 2PH. *T:* (01225) 758004, *Fax:* (01225) 442962. *E:* Martinp@arcworld.org. *Clubs:* Babington House; Foreign Correspondents' (Hong Kong).

**PALMER, Nicholas Douglas;** Head, Compassion in World Farming UK, since 2018 (Head of Policy, 2017–18); *b* 5 Feb. 1950; *s* of late Reginald Palmer and Irina Palmer (*née* Markin); *m* 2000, Fiona Hunter. *Educ:* Copenhagen Univ. (MSc equivalent); Birkbeck Coll., London (PhD Maths 1975). Computer scientist: Ciba-Geigy, Switzerland, 1977–82 and 1985–97; MRC London, 1982–85. MP (Lab) Broxtowe, 1997–2010; contested (Lab) same seat, 2010, 2015. PPS to DEFRA Ministerial team, 2003–05, to Energy Minister, DTI, 2005–07, to Sci. Minister, DTI, 2007, to Minister for Energy, BERR, 2007–08. Member: European Scrutiny Select Cttee, 1998–99; NI Select Cttee, 1999–2001; HM Treasury Select Cttee, 2001–03; Justice Select Cttee, 2008–10. Dir, Policy, Cruelty Free Internat. (formerly British Union for Abolition of Vivisection), 2011–16; freelance consultant on Parly and EU affairs, 2016–17. Contested (Lab): Chelsea, 1983; E Sussex and S Kent, EP elecn, 1994. Dir, Internat. and Corporate Affairs, British Union for Abolition of Vivisection, 2010. *Publications:* The Comprehensive Guide to Board Wargaming, 1973; The Best of Board Wargaming, 1980; Beyond the Arcade, 1985. *Recreation:* computer games. *E:* NickMP1@aol.com.

**PALMER, Prof. Nigel Fenton,** DPhil; FBA 1997; Professor of German Medieval and Linguistic Studies, University of Oxford, 1992–2012, now Emeritus; Professorial Fellow, St Edmund Hall, Oxford, 1992–2012, now Emeritus; *b* 28 Oct. 1946; *s* of James Terence Palmer and Constance May Palmer (*née* Fenton); *m* 1974, Susan Patricia Aldred; one *s* one *d*. *Educ:* Hyde County Grammar Sch.; Worcester Coll., Oxford (MA, DPhil). Lectr in German, Durham Univ., 1970–76; University of Oxford: Univ. Lectr in Medieval German, 1976–90; Reader in German, 1990–92; Fellow, Oriel Coll., 1976–92. Corresponding Fellow: Medieval Acad. of America, 2008; Akademie der Wissenschaften zu Göttingen, 2010. Fellow, 1982, Humboldt Res. Prize, 2007, Alexander von Humboldt Foundn. Dr phil *hc* Bern, 2013. *Publications:* Visio Tnugdali, 1976; Tondolus der Ritter, 1980; (with K. Speckenbach) Träume und Kräuter, 1990; Die Blockbücher der Berlin-Breslauer Sammelbandes, 1992; German Literary Culture in the Twelfth and Thirteenth Centuries, 1993; Zisterzienser und ihre Bücher, 1998; Bibelübersetzung und Heilsgeschichte, 2007; (with J. F. Hamburger) The Prayer Book of Ursula Begerin, 2015. *Address:* St Edmund Hall, Oxford OX1 4AR. *T:* (01865) 510487.

**PALMER, Penelope Jane;** *see* Dash, P. J.

**PALMER, Richard William,** CBE 2006 (OBE 1987); Executive Vice President, British Olympic Association, since 1997; *b* 13 April 1933; *s* of late Richard Victor Palmer and Mary Ellen Palmer (*née* Sambrook). *Educ:* Haverfordwest Grammar Sch.; Trinity Coll., Carmarthen; The College, Chester (Dip PE); Univ. of Leicester (MEd). Head, PE Dept, Windsor Grammar Sch., 1961–64; Sec., UAU, 1964–69; Gen. Sec., British Univs Sports Fedn, 1969–74; Dep. Sec. Gen., 1975–77, Sec. Gen., 1977–97, British Olympic Assoc. Vice Pres., European Olympic Cttees, 1993–97; Pres., British Inst. of Sports Administrators, 1997–2003; Chm., Confedn of British Sport, 1998–99; Mem., Sports Council of Wales, 2005–12. Gen. Sec., Commonwealth Games Council for England, 1977–86; Dep. Chef de Mission, GB, 1976, Chef de Mission, GB, 1980, 1984, 1988, 1992, 1996, Olympic Games and Olympic Winter Games; Gen. Team Manager, England, Commonwealth Games, 1978, 1982, 1986. Technical Dir, London's 2012 Olympic Bid, 2004–05; Internat. Advr, Glasgow's 2014 Commonwealth Games Bid, 2006–07. Dir, Sports Coach UK, 1998–2012. FRSA 1998. Freeman of Pembroke, 1990. Prix de Merit, Assoc. of Nat. Olympic Cttees, 1990; J. L. Manning Award, Sports Writers' Assoc., 1996; Olympic Order, IOC, 1998; Emlyn Jones Award, British Inst. of Sports Admin, 2003. *Recreations:* golf, sailing, Rugby Union, gardening, fishing. *Address:* British Olympic Association, 101 Cavendish Street, W1W 6XH. *T:* (020) 7842 5700. *Clubs:* Scribes, East India; Haverfordwest and Fulwell Golf.

**PALMER, Sir Robert John Hudson,** 9th Bt *cr* 1791; *b* 20 Dec. 1960; *s* of Sir John Edward Somerset Palmer, 8th Bt and of Dione Catharine Palmer (*née* Skinner); *S* father, 2019; *m* 1990, Lucinda Margaret Barker; one *s* one *d*. *Heir: s* Charles Palmer, *b* 1992.

**PALMER, Rory;** Member (Lab) East Midlands Region, European Parliament, since 2017; *b* Worksop, 19 Nov. 1981; *s* of Kenneth Palmer and Glenys Palmer (*née* Hope, later Watson); *m* 2015, Rowan Walker; two *d*. *Educ:* Univ. of York (BA Hons Social Policy). Policy Researcher, 2004; Political Advr, 2004–09. Mem. (Lab), Leicester CC, 2007–17 (Dep. Mayor, 2011–17). Vice-Pres., LGA, 2018–. Mem. Bd, Special Olympics Nat. Summer Games, 2009. Gov., Regent Coll., Leicester, 2008–14. Regl Bd Mem., E Midlands Lab Party, 2017–. Contested (Lab) Bosworth, 2010. *Recreations:* tennis, golf, horse-racing, country walking, cookery. *Address:* (office) Harold Wilson House, 23 Barratt Lane, Nottingham NG9 6AD. *T:* (0115) 922 9717. *E:* mail@rorypalmer.org.

**PALMER, Roy Newberry;** HM Coroner, Greater London (South District), 2001–14; Assistant Coroner (formerly Deputy Coroner), City of London, since 2002; *b* Peterborough, 2 Aug. 1944; *s* of late George Joseph Palmer and Muriel Joyce Palmer (*née* Clarke); *m* 1967, Dr Celia Mountford; two *d*. *Educ:* St George's Coll., Salisbury, Southern Rhodesia; Mt St Mary's Coll., Spinkhill, Derbys; London Hosp. Med. Coll., Univ. of London (MB BS 1968); LLB London 1974. MRCS 1967; LRCP 1968; DObstRCOG 1970; FFFLM 2005. Called to the Bar, Middle Temple, 1977. GP, Sawbridgeworth, Herts, 1970–73; Medical Protection Society: Asst Sec., 1973–85; Dep. Sec., 1985–89; Sec. and Med. Dir, 1989–98; Dep. Coroner, Gtr London (W Dist), 2000–01. Vis. Sen. Res. Fellow, Sch. of Law (Centre of Med. Law and Ethics), 1999–2002. Gov., Expert Witness Inst., 2000–06 (Chm., Professional Bodies Adv. Gp, 1999–2006). President: Medico-Legal Soc., 2000–02; Sect. of Clin. Forensic and Legal Medicine, RSocMed, 2001–03; SE England Coroners' Soc., 2004–05 (Vice-Pres., 2003–04); British Acad. of Forensic Scis, 2009–11 (Mem., Exec. Council, 2004–06); Med. Sec., Coroners' Soc. of England and Wales, 2009–13 (Mem. Council, 2003–13); Mem. Bd, Faculty of Forensic and Legal Medicine, RCP, 2006 (Mem., Fellowship Cttee). Pres., Soc. for Relief of Widows and Orphans of Medical Men, 1997–2015, Pres. Emeritus, 2016. Medical Society of London: Hon. Sec., 2005–07; Vice-Pres., 2007–09 and 2013–16; Pres., 2012; Trustee, 2013– (Chm., 2018–). Trustee, Coroners' Courts Support Service, 2011–13 (Chm., Mgt Cttee, 2011–13). Hon. Warden, Queen's Chapel of the Savoy, 1987–2011. Freeman, City of London, 1998; Juror, Guildable Manor of Southwark, City of London, 2016; Liveryman: Apothecaries' Soc., 1998 (Hon. Sec., 2003–05; Chm., Livery Cttee, 2007–09; Mem., Ct of Assts, 2009–; Master, 2015–16); Barbers' Co., 2012. Hon. FRCPath 2013. *Publications:* (consultant ed.) Jervis on the Office and Duties of Coroners, 13th edn 2014, (contrib.) 14th edn 2019; contrib. chapters on medico-legal topics in textbooks. *Recreations:* classical music, opera, theatre, art galleries, food and wine, walking. *Address:* City of London Coroner's Court, Walbrook Wharf, 78–83 Upper Thames Street, EC4R 3TD. *T:* (020) 7332 1598, *Fax:* (020) 7332 1800. *E:* RoyNPalmer@gmail.com. *Club:* Garrick.

**PALMER, Prof. Sarah Rosalind, (Mrs G. Williams),** PhD; FRHistS; Director, Greenwich Maritime Institute, 1998–2010, and Professor of Maritime History, 1999–2010, now Emeritus, University of Greenwich; *b* 16 Sept. 1943; *d* of Arthur Montague Frank Palmer and Marian Ethel Francis, (Jill), Palmer; *m* 1st, 1969, William David Walburn (marr. diss. 1978); one *s* one *d*. 2nd, 1979, Glyndwr Williams. *Educ:* Wimbledon High Sch. (GPDST); Univ. of Durham (BA); Univ. of Indiana (MA); London Sch. of Econs and Pol Sci. (PhD 1979). FRHistS 1980. Res. Asst, LSE, 1967–68; Queen Mary College, London: Lectr, then Sen. Lectr in Econ. Hist., 1969–98; Hd, Dept of Hist., 1994–98. Chm., British Commn for Maritime Hist., 2003–09. Trustee, Nat. Mus, Liverpool, 2000–08. Member (Lab): Maidstone BC, 1970–73; Kent CC, 1985–93. Contested (Lab and Co-op): Weston-super-Mare, 1970; Bristol NW, 1983. Treas., Labour Party, Tonbridge and Malling, 2014–. Vice Pres., Marine Soc. and Sea Cadets, 2004–. Sen. Res. Fellow, Bahria Univ., Pakistan, 2008–10. Chair, Greenwich Forum, 2009–. Gov., Mereworth Community Primary Sch., 2010–. FRSA 1996; Fellow, Soc. for Nautical Res., 2015. *Publications:* Shipping, Politics and the Repeal of the Navigation Laws, 1990; contrib. learned jls. *Recreations:* gardening, walking, cooking. *Address:* Russet Barn, 281 Broadwater Road, W Malling, Kent ME19 6HT.

**PALMER, Simon Erroll P.;** *see* Prior-Palmer.

**PALMER, Dr Stephen Charles;** Priest-in-charge, St Congan's, Turriff, Aberdeenshire, 2010–14; Chaplain to the Queen, 2008–14; *b* Lowestoft, 13 May 1947; *s* of Thomas Clement Palmer and Joanna Edith Barbara Palmer (*née* Stoy); *m* 1968, Christine, *d* of Alan Tranah and Masie Tranah (*née* Owen); one *s* one *d*. *Educ:* RN Weapons Electrical Sch. (HMS Collingwood); Oak Hill Theol Coll. (Dip. Pastoral Studies 1974); Portsmouth Univ. (PhD 2004). FRGS 1998; FLS 2001. Served Royal Navy, 1963–71: RN Wireless Station Suara, Singapore, 1964; HMS Whitby, 1966; HMS Blake, 1969; ordained deacon, 1974, priest, 1975; Curate, Crofton Parish, 1974; Bishop of Portsmouth's Domestic Chaplain, 1977; Rector: Brighstone, Brook and Mottistone, IoW, 1980–91; Falkland Islands, 1991–96; Vicar: Christchurch Portsdown Hill, 1996–2002; Newport Minster and Newport St John, IoW, 2002–09. Rural Dean, W Wight, 1986–91; Hon. Canon, Portsmouth Cathedral, 1991–2009, then Canon Emeritus; Bishop of Portsmouth's Advr on Envmt, 1998–2006. Chaplain: RN Reserve, 1979–91; IoW Council, 2003–09. Member: Council, Royal Nat. Mission to Deep Sea Fisherman, 1998–2007; Exec. Council, British Beekeepers Assoc., 2003–09; Exec. Cttee, Scottish Beekeepers Assoc., 2012; Trustee, S Georgia Whaling Mus., 1992–96. *Publications:* (contrib.) The Falkland Islands Dictionary of Biography, 2008; numerous articles in Falkland Islands Jl, 1995–2010. *Recreations:* beekeeping, postal history, amateur radio. *Club:* Union Jack.

**PALMER, Prof. Stuart Beaumont,** PhD; FREng; FLSW; Professor of Experimental Physics, University of Warwick, 1987–2011, now Emeritus; Secretary-General, International Union of Pure and Applied Physics, 2012–14; *b* 6 May 1943; *s* of Frank Beaumont Palmer and Florence Beryl Palmer (*née* Wilkinson); *m* 1966, Susan Mary Clay; two *s* one *d*. *Educ:* Ilkeston Grammar Sch.; Sheffield Univ. (BSc 1964; PhD 1968; DSc 1986). CPhys, FInstP, 1981; FInstNDT 1989; CEng, FIET (FIEE 1992). University of Hull: Asst Lectr, 1967–70; Lectr, 1970–78; Sen. Lectr, 1978–83; Reader, 1983–87; University of Warwick: Chair, Physics Dept, 1989–2001; Pro-Vice-Chancellor, 1995–99; Sen. Pro-Vice-Chancellor, 1999–2000; Actg Vice-Chancellor, 2001; Dep. Vice-Chancellor, 2001–09; Interim Chair, Sch. of Life Scis, 2009–10; Trustee, Pension Fund, 2008–. Vis. Prof., Univ. of Grenoble, 1982–83; Vis. Scientist, Queen's Univ., Kingston, Canada, 1986; Adjunct Prof., Queensland Univ. of Technol., Brisbane, 2012–. Chm., Standing Conf. of Profs of Physics, 2001–03; chm. and mem., various SERC and EPSRC cttees and working gps. Chm., Nat. Transparent Approach to Costing Develt Gp, HEFCE, 2008–16. Member: Council, Cardiff Univ., 2014– (Chm., 2016–); UCEA, 2017–. Hon. Sec., Inst. of Physics, 2009–17; Chm. Bd, Inst. of Physics Publishing 2011–17; Trustee: Science Council, 2014–17; Univs Superannuation Scheme, 2016–19. FREng 2000; FLSW. Hon. DSc Warwick, 2011. *Publications:* (with M. Rogalski) Advanced University Physics, 1995, 2nd edn 2005; (with M. Rogalski) Quantum Physics, 1999; (with M. Rogalski) Solid State Physics, 2000; over 250 contribs to learned scientific jls in magnetism, ultrasound and non destructive testing. *Recreations:* tennis, sailing, flying, ski-ing. *Address:* University of Warwick, Coventry CV4 7AL. *T:* (024) 7657 4004; Max Gate, Forrest Road, Kenilworth CV8 1LT. *Clubs:* Athenæum; Hull Sailing; Warwick Boat; Coventry Flying.

**PALMER, Sue;** educational writer, speaker and childhood campaigner; *b* Manchester, 25 Nov. 1948; *d* of John and Pauline Hall; *m* 1st (marr. diss.); 2nd (marr. diss.); one *d*. *Educ:* Moray Hse Coll., Edinburgh (Primary Teaching Dip. 1974); Univ. of Manchester (MEd 1985). Teacher, Coniston Primary Sch., 1975–82; Headteacher, Caddonfoot Primary Sch., 1982–84; writer and teacher of dyslexic children, 1986–90; Gen. Ed., Longman Book Project, 1990–94; freelance writer, travelling player (The Language Live Roadshow), consultant and speaker on literacy, 1994– (speaker on child develt in modern world, 2005–). Chair: Scottish Play Commn, 2009–13; Scottish Play Policy Forum, 2009–13; Mem., Scottish Early Years Task Force, 2011–13. Organiser: Balance campaign about literacy teaching, 1990; Time to Teach campaign, 2002; Member, Steering Group: Open EYE campaign for early years educn, 2009–; Save Childhood, 2011–14; Early Childhood Action, 2011–; Founder and Chair, Upstart Scotland, 2015–. Contribs to TV progs on literacy teaching, 1995–2005. Pres., Montessori AMI UK, 2009–13. Trustee, Play Scotland, 2010–13; Patron: English Speaking Bd, 2007–; Children's Football Alliance, 2009–; Carefree Kids, 2010–; Children's Wood, 2013–; Ringsfield Trust, 2014–. *Publications:* over 200 books on literacy, literacy teaching and child development, including: Toxic

Childhood: how the modern world is damaging our children and what we can do about it, 2006, 2nd edn 2015; Detoxing Childhood, 2007; 21st Century Boys, 2009; 21st Century Girls, 2013; Upstart: the case for raising the school starting age and providing what the under-sevens really need, 2016; contrib. articles to educnl and nat. press and to acad. jls. *Recreations:* books, films, conversation, ranting about forward-facing pushchairs. *Address:* c/o LBA Literacy Agency, 91 Great Russell Street, WC1B 3PS. *T:* (020) 7637 1234, *Fax:* (020) 7637 2111. *E:* sue@suepalmer.co.uk.

**PALMER, Prof. Timothy Noel**, CBE 2015; DPhil, DSc; FRS 2003; Royal Society 2010 Anniversary Research Professor of Atmospheric Oceanic and Planetary Physics, Clarendon Laboratory, University of Oxford, since 2010; Fellow, Jesus College, Oxford, since 2010; Senior Scientist, since 2011, and Fellow, since 2014, European Centre for Medium-Range Weather Forecasts (Head, Predictability and Seasonal Forecast Division, 2002–10); *b* 31 Dec. 1952; *s* of Alfred Henry Palmer and Anne Josephine Palmer; *m* 1978, Gill Dyer; three *s*. *Educ:* Wimbledon Coll.; Bristol Univ. (BSc 1974); Wolfson Coll., Oxford (DPhil 1977; DSc 1999). Vis. Scientist, Univ. of Washington, 1981; PSO, Meteorological Office, 1982–2002. Lead author, Third Assessment Report, Intergovtl Panel on Climate Change, 2001. Chm., Monsoon Numerical Experimentation Gp, UN WMO, 1989–96; Co-ordinator, EU Vth Framework Project: Development of a Multi-model Ensemble System for Interannual Prediction, 1999–2003; Co-Chm., World Climate Res. Prog. Climate Variability and Predictability Scientific Steering Gp, UN WMO, 2004–. Rothschild Dist. Vis. Prof., Isaac Newton Inst. for Mathematical Scis, Univ. of Cambridge, 2010. Pres., RMetS, 2011–12. Foreign Member: Amer. Philosophical Soc., 2015; Accademia dei Lincei, 2017. Hon. Member: Amer. Meteorol Soc., 2019; Amer. Acad. of Arts and Scis, 2019. Hon. DSc Bristol, 2016. *Publications:* contrib. to learned jls. *Recreations:* golf, cycling, ski-ing, playing guitar (folk, blues, rock and roll). *Address:* Atmospheric Oceanic and Planetary Physics, Clarendon Laboratory, Oxford OX1 3PU. *T:* (01865) 272897. *E:* tim.palmer@physics.ox.ac.uk.

**PALMER, Tony;** *see* Palmer, H. A.

**PALMER, Tony;** film, television and theatre director; author; brought up by godparents, late Bert Spencer (railway engineer) and Elsie Spencer; *m* 2001, Michela Antonello; two *s* one *d*. *Educ:* Lowestoft Grammar Sch. Presenter, Night Waves, R3, 1994–98 (Sony Award, 1996). Prof. of Ukrainian Cultural Studies, Lesya Ukrainka Univ., 2016–. FRGS 1993. *Films:* over 100, including: All My Loving, 1968; Farewell Cream, 1968 (Platinum Record); 200 Motels, 1971 (Gold Record); Rory Gallagher Irish Tour, 1974 (Platinum Record); All This & World War Two, 1976 (Gold Record), rev. edn as The Beatles and World War II, 2016; All You Need is Love, 1977; A Time There Was, 1979 (Italia Prize); The Space Movie (music by Mike Oldfield), 1979, rev. 2016 (Gold Medal, NY Film Fest. 2016); Death in Venice (Britten opera), 1979 (Gold Medal, NY Film Fest., 1980); At the Haunted End of the Day, 1980 (Italia Prize); Once at a Border, 1981 (Special Jury Prize, San Francisco); Wagner, 1982 (Best Drama, NY Film and TV Fest.); Puccini, 1984; God Rot Tunbridge Wells, 1985 (Best Drama, NY); Callas, 1986 (Gold Medal, NY); Testimony, 1987 (Fellini Prize); The Children, 1989 (Best Director, NY); Menuhin, 1990 (Grand Award, NY); The Symphony of Sorrowful Songs, 1993 (platinum CD; Jury Prize, Chicago Film Fest.); England, My England, 1995 (Best Dir, NY); Parsifal, 1998 (1st prize, Casta Diva, Moscow; Golden Mask, Russia); The Harvest of Sorrow, 1999; Ladies and Gentlemen, Miss Renée Fleming, 2001; Hero - the Bobby Moore Story, 2002; Toward the Unknown Region - Malcolm Arnold, 2003 (Preis der Deutschen Schallplatten Kritik, 2009); John Osborne and the Gift of Friendship, 2004; Margot, 2005; The Salzburg Festival, 2006; O Thou Transcendent: the life of Ralph Vaughan Williams, 2008; O Fortuna! Carl Orff, 2009; Vangelis and the Journey to Ithaka, 2009 (Outstanding Achievement Award, Sofia Film Fest., 2010); The Wagner Family, 2010; Bird on a Wire, 2010 (filmed 1972, then lost; rediscovered 2009; Special Jury Prize, Jerusalem Film Fest., 2010); Grierson Prize, 2011; World Medal, NY Film and TV Fest., 2012); Holst - In the Bleak Midwinter, 2011; Falls The Shadow - Athol Fugard, 2012 (Gold Medal, NY Film and TV Fest., 2013); Nocturne - Benjamin Britten, 2013 (World Medal, NY Film and TV Fest., 2014); Hindemith - A Pilgrim's Progress, 2014 (World Medal, NY Film Fest., 2014); The Pursuit of Happiness, 2015; *theatre:* Billy Connolly's Great Northern Welly Boot Show, 1972; John Osborne's Deja Vu, Comedy, 1992; dir operas, Berlin, Karlsruhe, Munich, Hamburg, Zürich, Augsburg, St Petersburg, Savonlinna, Moscow, Ravello, Helsinki, Bonn. Hon. DLitt: Winchester, 2011; West London, 2012. Numerous BAFTA and Emmy awards. Gold Medal, Bulgarian Min. of Culture, 2016; Lifetime Achievement Award, Toronto, Toronto Hot-Docs Fest., 2017. *Publications:* Born Under a Bad Sign, 1970, new edn 2012; Trials of Oz, 1971, new edn 2011; Electric Revolution, 1972; Biography of Liberace, 1976, new edn 2012; All You Need is Love, 1976; Charles II, 1979; A Life on the Road (biog. of Julian Bream), 1982, 2nd edn 2010; Menuhin: a family portrait, 1991, new edn 2016. *Recreation:* walking. *Address:* Nanjizal, St Levan, Cornwall TR19 6JJ. *Club:* Garrick.

**PALMER-WHITE, Jack Edwin;** Anglican Communion Permanent Representative to the United Nations Institutions, Geneva, since 2017; *b* Brighton, 6 April 1988; *s* of Alastair Palmer and Rev. Betsy Blatchley; *m* 2016, Rosanne. *Educ:* Christ's Hospital; Univ. of Surrey (BA Hons 1st cl. Internat. Politics); London Sch. of Econs and Pol Sci. (MSc (Dist.) Religion in the Contemporary World). Commns Associate, Sojourners, Washington, DC, 2011–12; Parly Asst, 2012–15, Social and Public Affairs Advr, 2015–17, Archbishop of Canterbury. *Recreations:* rowing, running, cinema, learning French. *Address:* Anglican Communion Office, St Andrew's House, 16 Tavistock Crescent, W11 1AP. *E:* un.rep@anglicancommunion.org.

**PÁLSSON, Thorsteinn;** Editor-in-Chief, Fréttablaðið, 2006–09; Chairman, Kvika (formerly MP Bank), Iceland, 2011; *b* 29 Oct. 1947; *s* of Pall Sigurdsson and Ingigerdur Thorsteinsdottir; *m* 1973, Ingibjörg Rafnar; one *s* two *d*. *Educ:* Commercial Coll., Reykjavik; Univ. of Iceland (law degree). Journalist, Morgunbladid, 1974–75; Editor-in-Chief, Visir, 1975–79; Admin. Dir, Confedn of Icelandic Employers, 1979–83; MP (Independence) Southland, Iceland, 1983–99; Minister of Finance, 1985–87; of Industry, 1987; Prime Minister, 1987–88; Minister of Fisheries, 1991–99; of Justice and Ecclesiastical Affairs, 1991–99; Ambassador: to UK, 1999–2002; to Denmark, 2003–05. Chm., Independence Party, 1983–91.

**PALTROW, Gwyneth;** actress; *b* Los Angeles, 29 Sept. 1973; *d* of late Bruce W. Paltrow and of Blythe Katharine Danner; *m* 1st, 2003, Christopher Anthony John Martin, *qv* (marr. diss. 2016); one *s* one *d*; 2nd, 2018, Brad Falchuk. *Educ:* Spence Sch., New York; Univ. of Calif, Santa Barbara. Williamstown Theater, Mass. Acting début, Picnic (with Blythe Danner), 1989; Rosalind, in As You Like It, 1999; Proof, Donmar Warehouse, 2002; other plays include: The Adventures of Huck Finn; Sweet Bye and Bye; The Seagull. Film début, Shout, 1991; films include: Moonlight and Valentino; Se7en, 1995; Emma, 1996; Great Expectations, Sliding Doors (Best Actress, Golden Globe Awards, 1999), Hush, A Perfect Murder, 1998; Shakespeare in Love (Academy Award for Best Actress, 1999), The Talented Mr Ripley, 1999; Duets, 2000; Bounce, 2001; Shallow Hal, The Royal Tenenbaums, Possession, 2002; Sylvia, Sky Captain and the World of Tomorrow, 2004; Proof, Infamous, 2006; Running with Scissors, 2007; The Good Night, Iron Man, Two Lovers, 2008; Iron Man 2, 2010; Country Strong, Contagion, 2011; Avengers, 2012; Iron Man 3, Thanks for Sharing, 2013; Mortdecai, 2015; Captain America: Civil War, 2016; Spiderman: Homecoming, 2017; Avengers: Infinity War, 2018; Avengers: Endgame, 2019; *television includes:* The Politician, 2019. Founded lifestyle website Goop, 2008. *Publications:* My Father's Daughter, 2011; (jtly) It's All Good, 2013; (jtly) It's All Easy, 2016. *Address:* c/o CAA, 2000 Avenue of the Stars, Los Angeles, CA 90067, USA.

**PALUMBO,** family name of **Baron Palumbo** and **Baron Palumbo of Southwark**.

**PALUMBO, Baron** *cr* 1991 (Life Peer), of Walbrook in the City of London; **Peter Garth Palumbo,** MA; Chairman, Arts Council of Great Britain, 1989–94; *b* 20 July 1935; *s* of late Rudolph and of Elsie Palumbo; *m* 1st, 1959, Denia (*d* 1986), *d* of late Major Lionel Wigram; one *s* two *d*; 2nd, 1986, Hayat, *er d* of late Kamel Morowa; one *s* two *d*. *Educ:* Eton College; Worcester College, Oxford. MA Hons Law. Mem., H of L, 1991–2019. Governor, London School of Economics and Political Science, 1976–94; Chairman: Tate Gallery Foundn, 1986–87; Painshill Park Trust Appeal, 1986–96; Serpentine Gall., 1994–2014, now Chm. Emeritus; Bd Mem. and Dir, Andy Warhol Foundn for the Visual Arts, 1994–97; Trustee: Mies van der Rohe Archive, 1977–; Tate Gallery, 1978–85; Whitechapel Art Gallery Foundation, 1981–87; Natural History Mus., 1994–2004; Design Mus., 1995–2005; Trustee and Hon. Treas., Writers and Scholars Educnl Trust, 1984–99; Mem. Council, Royal Albert Hall, 1995–99. Chm., Jury, Pritzker Architecture Prize, 2004–16. Chancellor, Portsmouth Univ., 1992–2007; Gov., Whitgift Sch., 2002–10 (Advr Emeritus to Bd of Govs, 2010–). Liveryman, Salters' Co., 1965–. Hon. FRIBA 1986; Hon. FFB 1994; Hon. FIStructE 1994. Hon. DLitt Portsmouth, 1993. Patronage of the Arts Award, Cranbrook Acad. of Arts, Detroit, 2002. Nat. Order of Southern Cross (Brazil), 1993. *Recreations:* music, travel, gardening, reading. *Address:* 2 Astell Street, SW3 3RU. *T:* (020) 7351 7371. *Clubs:* White's, Pratt's, Garrick.

*See also* Lord Lovat.

**PALUMBO OF SOUTHWARK, Baron** *cr* 2013 (Life Peer), of Southwark in the London Borough of Southwark; **James Rudolph Palumbo;** Co-Founder, 1991, Chief Executive, 1991–2008 and Chairman, 2008–16, Ministry of Sound Group Ltd (formerly Ministry of Sound); *b* London, 6 June 1963; *s* of Baron Palumbo, *qv* and Denia (*née* Wigram) (*d* 1986); one *s* by Atoosa Hariri. *Educ:* Eton; Worcester Coll., Oxford (BA Hist.). Former posts with Merrill Lynch and Morgan Grenfell & Co. *Publications:* Tomas, 2009; Tancredi, 2011.

**PAMPLIN, Elizabeth Ann;** human resources and corporate ethics consultant, since 1999; Chief Executive, Liberal Democrats, 1998–99; *b* 13 April 1940; *d* of Richard Thomas Webb and Hilda Ethel Webb (*née* Teague); *m* 1969, Terence Michael Pamplin (*d* 2004); twin *d*. *Educ:* Rosebery GS; St Hugh's Coll., Oxford (BA PPE 1962; DPSA 1963). Chartered FCIPD (FIPD 1991). Clarks Ltd, 1963–66; Industrial Trng Service, 1966–71; Sen. Lectr, Personnel Mgt and Trng, Slough Coll. of HE, 1973–75; human resource management and consultancy: MSC, 1975–77; Petroleum Industry Trng Bd, 1977–82; RBK&C, 1983–91; P & L Associates, 1991–93; DoT, 1993–96; Cabinet Office, 1996–97. Examr in personnel mgt, PCL, then Univ. of Westminster, 1985–98; Nat. Examr, IPD, subseq. CIPD, 1996–2004. Governor: Lord Mayor Treloar Sch., 2000–10, Treloar Sch. and Coll., 2010–12; Wavell Sch., 2006–10; Abbey Sch., 2006–. Contested (SDP), 1983, (SDP/L Alliance), 1987, Reigate. Freeman, City of London, 1997; Liveryman, Co. of Musicians, 1997–. FRGS 2000. *Publications:* reports and articles. *Recreations:* music, early dance, walking, countryside conservation. *Address:* Little Critchmere, Manor Crescent, Haslemere, Surrey GU27 1PB.

**PAMUK, Orhan;** writer; Robert Yik-Fong Tam Professor of Humanities, Columbia University, New York; *b* Istanbul, 7 June 1952; *m* 1982, Aylin Türegün (marr. diss. 2002); one *d*. *Educ:* private schs in Istanbul. Vis. Scholar, Columbia Univ., 1985–88. Founder, Masumiyet Müzesi (Museum of Innocence), Istanbul, 2012. Hon. Dr: St Petersburg, 2017; Accademia di Bella Arti di Brera, 2017. Nobel Prize in Literature, 2006; Budapest Grand Prize, Budapest Internat. Book Fest., 2017. *Publications:* Cevdet Bey Ve Oğulları (Cevdet Bey and His Sons), 1982; Sessiz Ev, 1983 (Silent House, 2012); Beyaz Kale, 1985 (The White Castle, 1991); Kara Kitap, 1990 (The Black Book, 1994); Gizli Yüz: Senaryo (Secret Face), 1992; Yeni Hayat, 1994 (The New Life, 1997); Benim Adım Kırmızı, 1998 (My Name is Red, 2001); Öteki Renkler: Seçme Yazılar Ve Bir Hikâye, 1999 (Other Colours: essays and a story, 2007); Kar, 2002 (Snow, 2004); İstanbul: Hatıralar Ve Şehir, 2003 (Istanbul: memories and the city, 2005); Babamın Bavulu (My Father's Suitcase), 2007; Masumiyet Müzesi, 2008 (Museum of Innocence, 2009); Manzaradan Parçalar: Hayat, Sokaklar, Edibayat (Fragments of the Landscape), 2010; Saf ve Düsüceli Romanci (The Naive and the Sentimental Novelist: understanding what happens when we write and read novels) (Norton Lectures), 2011; Kafamda Bir Tuhaflık (A Strangeness in My Mind), 2015; Kirmizi Saçli Kadin (The Red-Haired Woman), 2016.

**PANAYI, Pavlos;** QC 2014; *b* Harrow, 25 Feb. 1973; *s* of Costas Panayi and Myrophora Panayi; *m* 2004, Gabrielle Turner (separated); three *s* one *d*. *Educ:* Whitmore High Sch. Harrow; Queen Mary Coll., Univ. of London (LLB 1994). Called to the Bar, Gray's Inn, 1995; in practice as barrister, specialising in fraud and financial crime. *Recreations:* cycling, cooking, scuba-diving, backgammon. *Address:* 7BR, 7 Bedford Row, WC1R 4BS. *E:* ppanayi@7br.co.uk.

**PANAYIDES CHRISTOU, Tasos,** Hon. GCVO 1990; Chairman, ENESEL (formerly AVRA) Shipmanagement SA, 1997–2011; *b* 9 April 1934; *s* of Christos Panayides and Efrosini Panayides; *m* 1969, Pandora Constantinides; two *s* one *d*. *Educ:* Paphos Gymnasium; Teachers' Training Coll.; Univ. of London (Diploma in Education); Univ. of Indiana, USA (MA Political Science, Diploma in Public Administration). Teacher, 1954–59; First sec. to Pres., 1960–63; Director, President's Office, 1963–69; Ambassador of Cyprus to Federal Republic of Germany, Austria, and Atomic Energy organisation, Vienna, 1969–78; High Comr in UK, and Ambassador to Sweden, Norway, Denmark and Iceland, 1979–90; Doyen of the Diplomatic Corps in London and Sen. High Comr, 1988–90; Permanent Sec., Min. of Foreign Affairs, Cyprus, 1990–94; Ambassador to Sweden, Finland, Norway, Denmark, Latvia, Lithuania and Estonia, 1994–96. Rep., Exec. Cttee, Union of Greek Shipowners, 1997–2003; Vice-Pres., Cypriot Union of Shipowners, 2004–08 (Cllr Mem., Exec. Steering Cttee, 2009). Chairman: Commonwealth Foundn Grants Cttee, 1985–88; Commonwealth Fund Tech. Co-operation Bd of Reps, 1986–89; Commonwealth Steering Cttee of Sen. Officials, 1994–95. Hon. Fellow, Ealing Coll. of Higher Educn, 1983. Freeman, City of London, 1984. Hon. LLD Birmingham, 1991. 1st Cl., Grand Order and Grand Cross with Star and Sash, Federal Republic of Germany, 1978; Grand Cross in Gold with Star and Sash, Austria, 1979; Golden Cross of the Archdiocese of Thyateira and Great Britain, 1981; Grand Cross in Gold of Patriarchate of Antioch, 1984. *Publications:* articles in newspapers and magazines. *Recreations:* swimming, reading books.

**PANCHO, Cassa,** MBE 2013; Founder and Artistic Director, Ballet Black, since 2001; *b* London, 23 Aug. 1978; *d* of Winston and Patricia Pancho; *m* 2009, Richard Bolton. *Educ:* Acton High Sch.; Durham Univ. (BA Classical Ballet); Royal Acad. of Dance (LRAD). Estabd Ballet Black Jun. Sch., Shepherd's Bush, 2002; started BB Associate Prog., 2004.

Work commnd from choreographers incl. Christopher Hampson, Will Tuckett, Richard Alston, Javier de Frutos, Arthur Pita and Annabelle Lopez Ochoa. Patron, Central Sch. of Ballet, 2015; Vice Pres., London Ballet Circle, 2016–. Freeman, City of London, 2018. *E*: admin@balletblack.co.uk.

**PANK, Dorian Christopher L.;** *see* Lovell-Pank.

**PANKE, Ceredwin Mary;** *see* Roberts, C. M.

**PANKHURST, Dr Helen Sylvia Tarik,** CBE 2019; Senior Advisor, CARE International, since 2006; Chancellor, University of Suffolk, since 2018; *b* Addis Ababa, Ethiopia, 8 May 1964; *d* of Richard and Rita Pankhurst; *gd* of Sylvia Pankhurst and *ggd* of Emmeline Pankhurst; one *s* one *d*. *Educ:* Lycée Guébré-Mariam; Lycée Français Charles de Gaulle; United World Coll. of the Atlantic; Univ. of Sussex (BA); Univ. of Edinburgh (PhD 1990). Audit and financial mgt trainee, KPMG Peat Marwick, Cambridge, 1991–93; Asst, then Regl Prog. Officer, Horn of Africa, ACORD, 1993–98; Hd, Internat. Dept, Womankind Worldwide, 1998–2003; Country Rep., WaterAid Ethiopia, 2003–06. Convenor: Gtr Manchester focused GM4Women2028, 2018–; Centenary Action Gp, 2018–. Trustee: WaterAid, 2006–13; Farm Africa, 2006–13; Water and Sanitation for the Urban Poor, 2015–18; ActionAid, 2016–. Supporter, then Patron, Pankhurst Centre, 1980–; Patron: Our Emmeline statue, 2016; Sylvia Pankhurst statue, 2017; Friends of Sophia Goulden Soc., 2018–. Hon. PhD Edge Hill, 2014. Volunteer, London Olympic Opening Ceremony, 2012; support and cameo rôle in film, Suffragette, 2015. *Publications:* Gender Development and Identity: an Ethiopian study, 1992; Deeds not Words: the story of women's rights, then and now, 2018. *Recreations:* reading, walking. *Address:* Office of the Chancellor, University of Suffolk, Waterfront Building, 19 Neptune Quay, Ipswich, Suffolk IP4 1QJ. *E*: chancellor@uos.ac.uk; CARE International UK, 9th Floor, 89 Albert Embankment, SE1 7TP. *E*: Helen.Pankhurst@care.org.

**PANKHURST, Julie Kathryn;** Co-founder, Friendsreunited, 2000–05; *b* 16 Jan. 1967; *d* of John Victor Hill and Patricia May Hill; *m* 1998, Stephen Pankhurst, *qv*; two *d*. *Educ:* Queen Elizabeth's Girls' Sch., Barnet; Dehavilland Coll., Borehamwood; Luton Coll. of Higher Educn (HNC); Middlesex Poly. (HND Dist.). Software engr, GEC Avionics Ltd, 1985–88; Sen. Analyst Programmer, MFI Furniture Centres Ltd, 1988–2000. Patron, Plan UK, 2005–12; Trustee, Happy Charitable Trust, 2006–. *Recreations:* philanthropy, travelling, photography, walking, jewellery making, sewing.

**PANKHURST, Stephen;** Director and Co-founder, Friendsreunited, 2000–05; *b* 4 Jan. 1964; *s* of Nigil Frederick Pankhurst and Irene Pankhurst; *m* 1998, Julie Kathryn Hill (*see* J. K. Pankhurst); two *d*. *Educ:* Orange Hill Sch.; Imperial Coll., London (BSc Hons Maths). Software engr, GEC Avionics Ltd, 1985–87; developer, ITL, 1987–90; Develt Manager, Bovis Construction, 1990–93; freelance software consultant, 1993–2000; Dir/Co-founder, Happygroup, 2000–05. *Recreations:* football, cinema, walking, comic collecting, playing with my children. *E*: steve@scruffybeggars.co.uk.

**PANNICK,** family name of **Baron Pannick**.

**PANNICK, Baron** *cr* 2008 (Life Peer), of Radlett in the county of Hertfordshire; **David Philip Pannick;** QC 1992; Fellow of All Souls College, Oxford, since 1978; a Recorder, 1995–2005; *b* 7 March 1956; *s* of late Maurice Pannick and Rita Pannick; *m* 1st, 1978, Denise Sloam (*d* 1998); two *s* one *d*; 2nd, 2003, Nathalie Trager-Lewis; one *s* two *d*. *Educ:* Bancroft's Sch., Woodford Green, Essex; Hertford Coll., Oxford (MA, BCL; Hon. Fellow, 2004). Called to the Bar, Gray's Inn, 1979, Bencher, 1998. Jun. Counsel to the Crown (Common Law), 1988–92; Dep. High Court Judge, 1998–2005. Mem., Select Cttee on the Constitution, H of L, 2009–13 and 2016–. Columnist, The Times, 1991–. Mem., Editl Bd, Public Law, 1990–2014. Gov., Hebrew Univ., Jerusalem, 2016– (Hon. Fellow, 2013). Hon. LLD Hertfordshire, 1998. *Publications:* Judicial Review of the Death Penalty, 1982; Sex Discrimination Law, 1985; Judges, 1987; Advocates, 1992; (ed with Lord Lester of Herne Hill) Human Rights Law and Practice, 1999, 3rd edn 2009; I Have to Move My Car, 2008. *Recreations:* travel, supporting Arsenal FC, musicals. *Address:* Blackstone Chambers, Blackstone House, Temple, EC4Y 9BW. *T*: (020) 7583 1770.

**PANNONE, Rodger John;** DL; Senior Partner, Pannone & Partners (formerly Pannone March Pearson), Solicitors, 1993–2003 (Consultant, 2003–09); President of the Law Society of England and Wales, 1993–94; *b* 20 April 1943; *s* of late Cyril John Alfred Pannone and Violet Maud (*née* Weeks); *m* 1966, Patricia Jane Todd; two *s* one *d*. *Educ:* St Brendan's Coll., Bristol; Coll. of Law, London; Law Sch., Manchester. Articled to Casson & Co., Salford, 1966–69; Asst Solicitor and Partner, W. H. Thompson, 1969–73; Partner, Pannone March Pearson, subseq. Pannone & Partners, 1973–2003; Chm., Renovo PLC, 2006–11; Dir, Co-operative Legal Services Ltd, 2006–12. Chm., Forensic Sci. Service, 1994–2003. Member: Lord Chancellor's Adv. Cttee on Civil Justice, 1986–89; Council, Law Soc., 1979–96 (Vice-Pres., 1992–93). Gov., Univ. of Law (formerly Coll. of Law), 1990– (Chm., 1999–2005); Mem. Council, Manchester Univ., 1996– (Chm., 2000–04). Chm., Standards Cttee, Tameside MBC, 2001–11. Vice-Pres., British Acad. of Experts, 1994–. Chm., Manchester Concert Hall Ltd, 1993–2007. Regl Chm., Emmaus North West, 2005–10. FRSA 1992. DL Greater Manchester, 1999. Hon. Life Mem., Canadian Bar, 1993. Hon. Fellow: Manchester Metropolitan Univ., 1994; Birmingham Univ., 1998. Hon. DLitt Salford, 1997; Hon. LLD: Nottingham Trent, 1993; College of Law, 2009; Hon. LittD Manchester, 2004. *Publications:* numerous legal pubns. *Recreations:* the Lake District, walking slowly, food and wine. *Address:* 17 Ballbrook Avenue, Didsbury, Manchester M20 6AB. *T*: (0161) 445 4342. *Clubs:* St James's (Manchester); Wyresdale Anglers.

**PANTER, Sir Howard (Hugh),** Kt 2013; Joint Chief Executive Officer and Creative Director, Trafalgar Entertainment Group, since 2017; *b* 25 May 1949; *s* of late Hugh Panter and Hilary Panter (*née* Robinson); *m* 1994, Rosemary Anne Squire (*see* Dame R. A. Squire); one *d*, and one step *s* one step *d*. *Educ:* Claysmore Sch.; London Acad. of Music and Dramatic Art (Dip. Prodn and Stage Mgt). Producer: Knightsbridge Prodns, 1975–79; SRO Prodns, 1979–80; Man. Dir, Freedman Panter Prodns, 1980–86; Man. Dir, Turnstyle Gp Ltd, 1987–2000; Jt Chief Exec. and Creative Dir, Ambassador Th. Gp, 2000–16. Chm., Rambert Dance Company, 2009–. *Recreations:* opera, contemporary dance, visual arts, cricket. *Address:* Trafalgar Entertainment, 8th Floor, 55 The Strand, WC2N 5LR. *Club:* Garrick.

**PANTER, Ven. Richard James Graham, (Ricky);** Archdeacon of Liverpool, 2002–17; Vicar, St John and St James, Orrell Hey, Bootle, 1996–2011; *b* 18 Sept. 1948; *s* of Rev. Ernest Downes Panter and Marjorie (*née* Lea); *m* 1974, Jane Christine Wilson; two *s* two *d*. *Educ:* Monkton Combe Sch., Bath; Worcester Coll. of Educn (Cert. Ed.); Oak Hill Theol Coll. Teacher, RE, Chatham Tech. High Sch. for Boys, 1970–71; Primary Teacher, St John's Boscombe C of E Primary Sch., 1971–73. Ordained deacon, 1976, priest, 1977; Curate, Holy Trinity, Rusholme, 1976–80; Asst Vicar, St Cyprian with Christchurch, Edge Hill, 1980–85; Vicar, St Andrews, Clubmoor, 1985–96; Area Dean of Bootle, 1999–2002. *Recreations:* singing (Royal Liverpool Phil. Choir), walking, caravanning. *Address:* 115 Papillon Drive, Liverpool L9 9HL. *E*: rickypanter@gmail.com.

**PANTER, Dame Rosemary Anne, (Lady Panter);** *see* Squire, Dame R. A.

**PANTLING, Mary Fitzgerald;** *see* Allen, M. F.

**PANTON, (Elizabeth) Jane;** Headmistress, Bolton School Girls' Division, 1994–2005, and Chairman of Executive Committee, Bolton School, 2002–05; *b* 20 June 1947; *d* of Richard Henry Panton and Constance Doreen Panton. *Educ:* Clayton Hall Grammar Sch., Newcastle; Merchant Taylors' Sch. for Girls, Liverpool; St Hugh's Coll., Oxford (MA Hons History); West Midlands Coll. of Educn, Walsall (PGCE). Teacher, Moreton Hall, near Oswestry, 1972–73; Third Mistress, Shrewsbury High Sch., 1973–83; Head of History and of Sixth Form, Clifton High Sch., Bristol, 1983–88; Headmistress, Merchant Taylors' Sch. for Girls, Crosby, Liverpool, 1988–94. Member: ISC (formerly HMC/GSA) Assisted Places Working Party, 1992–2000; GSA Professional Develt Cttee, 1992–96; ISIS North Cttee, 1993–99 (Chm., 1997–99); Chm., GSA NW, 2000–02. Mem., Sefton FHSA, 1990–92. Mem. Council, Liverpool Univ., 1990–94. Member, Management Committee: Landscape Trust, 2007–12; Lake District Summer Music, 2007–13. Mem., Yealand Conyers Parish Council, 2007–. Trustee, Lakeland Sinfonia, 2017–. Governor: Westholme Sch., Blackburn, 2006–12; Casterton Sch., Kirkby Lonsdale, 2010–13; Sedbergh Sch., 2013–; Yealand C of E Primary Sch., 2017–; Cartmel Priory C of E Sch., 2017–. *Recreations:* fell walking, UK and abroad, birdwatching, foreign travel, music, art, reading.

**PANUFNIK, Roxanna;** composer of classical music; *b* 24 April 1968; *d* of Sir Andrzej Panufnik and Camilla Panufnik (*née* Jessel); *m* 2001, Stephen Macklow-Smith; one *s* two *d*. *Educ:* Royal Acad. of Music (GRSM Hons 1989; LRAM 1989; ARAM 1998). Associate Composer, London Mozart Players, 2012–. Major *compositions:* Westminster Mass, 1998; The Music Programme (opera), 1999; Powers and Dominions (harp concerto), 2001; LEDA (ballet), 2003; Abraham (violin concerto), 2004; Love Abide (choir and orch.), 2006; Three Paths to Peace, 2008; The Audience (narrator and string quartet), 2009; Schola Missa de Angelis (choir and brass octet or strings), 2010; Dance of Life: Tallinn Mass (soprano soloist, narrator, upper voice choir, double mixed choir and orchestra), 2011; Four World Seasons, 2011; The Song of Names (Jewish oratorio), 2012; Orchestrapædia (chamber orchestra), 2013; Two Composers, Four Hands (double string orchestra), 2013; Memories of my Father (string quartet), 2013; Since We Parted, 2014; Silver Birch (opera), 2016; Unending Love (choir and Asian instrument ensemble), 2017; Songs of Darkness, Dreams of Light (for Last Night of the Proms, 2018); Faithful Journey—a Mass for Poland, 2018; Across the Line of Dreams, 2018–19; major recordings: Dance of Life: Tallinn Mass; Dreamscape; Love Abide; Westminster Mass; Angels Sing; The Upside Down Sailor; Beastly Tales; Padre Pio (Stay with Me, Prayer); Spirit of the Saints; 99 Words; Celestial Bird. *Recreations:* food (eating and cooking), reading, family time, cycling. *Address:* c/o Peters Edition Ltd, 2–6 Baches Street, N1 6DN. *T*: (020) 7553 4000. *E*: katie.tearle@editionpeters.com. *W*: www.roxannapanufnik.com.

**PAPADEMOS, Lucas,** PhD; Senior Fellow, Center for Financial Studies, Goethe University, Frankfurt, since 2014; Prime Minister of Greece, 2011–12; *b* Athens, 11 Oct. 1947. *Educ:* Athens Coll.; Massachusetts Inst. of Technol. (BSc Physics 1970; MSc Electrical Engrg 1972; PhD Econs 1977). Res. Asst and Teaching Fellow, MIT, 1973–75; Lectr in Econs, 1975–77, Asst and Associate Prof. of Econs, 1977–84, Columbia Univ., NY; Sen. Economist, Federal Reserve Bank of Boston, 1980; Vis. Prof. of Econs, Athens Sch. of Econs and Business, 1984–85; Bank of Greece: Econ. Counsellor (Chief Economist), 1985–93; Dep. Gov., 1993–94; Gov., 1994–2002; Prof. of Econs, Univ. of Athens, 1988–2014. Gov., IMF for Greece, 1994–2002; Member: Monetary Cttee, EC, 1985–88, 1990; Gen. Council, 1999–2010, Governing Council, 2001–10, European Central Bank (Vice Pres., 2002–10); Committee of EC Central Bank Governors, subseq. Council of EMI: Mem., 1985–93, Chm., 1989, Cttee of Alternates; Chm., Monetary Policy Sub-Cttee, 1992–94; Council Mem., 1994–98. Chm., Adv. Bd, Hellenic Observatory, Eur. Inst., LSE, 1998–. Pres., Acad. of Athens (Mem., 2006–; Vice Pres., Section of Ethical and Political Scis). Grand Comdr, Order of Honour (Greece), 1999. *Publications:* (jtly) Efficiency, Stability and Equity: a strategy for the evolution of the economic system of the European Community, 1987; (jtly) Stabilisation and Recovery of the Greek Economy, 1990; (with P. De Grauwe) The European Monetary System in the 1990s, 1990; (jtly) External Constraints on Macroeconomic Policy: the European experience, 1991; contrib. numerous articles and essays to books and learned jls, incl. Greek Econ. Rev., Eur. Econ. Rev. and Econ. Bulletin.

**PAPADOPULOS, Heather Sophia;** *see* Norton, H. S.

**PAPADOPULOS, Very Rev. Nicholas Charles;** Dean of Salisbury, since 2018; *b* Longfield, Kent, 23 July 1966; *s* of Michael and Jennifer Papadopulos; *m* 1996, Heather Sophia Norton, *qv*; one *s* one *d*. *Educ:* King's Sch., Rochester; Gonville and Caius Coll., Cambridge (BA 1988); Ripon Coll., Cuddesdon. Called to the Bar, Middle Temple, 1990. Ordained deacon, 1999, priest, 2000; Vicar, St Peter's, Eaton Square, London, 1997–2013; Canon Treasurer, Canterbury Cathedral, 2013–18. *Publications:* God's Transforming Work, 2011. *Address:* The Dean's Office, 6 The Close, Salisbury SP1 2EG. *T*: (01722) 555110. *E*: thedean@salcath.co.uk.

**PAPALOIZOU, Prof. John Christopher Baillie,** DPhil; FRS 2003; Professor of Mathematical Physics, University of Cambridge, 2005–14, now Emeritus; *b* 4 May 1947; *s* of Michael and Sarah Papaloizou; *m* 1978, Elaine Joseph; one *s*. *Educ:* UCL (BSc 1st cl. Hons 1965); Univ. of Sussex (DPhil 1972). Research Fellow: Univ. of Sussex, 1971–73; Univ. of Oxford, 1973–74; Res. Associate, Culham Lab., 1974–76; Res. Fellow, Cambridge Univ., 1976–80; Queen Mary College, London University: Lectr, 1980–86; Reader, 1986–88; Prof. of Mathematics and Astronomy, 1988–2004. *Publications:* monthly notices of RAS and papers in Astronomy and Astrophysics and Astrophysical Jl. *Club:* Royal Astronomical Society Dining.

**PAPANDREOU, George Andreas;** Prime Minister and Minister of Foreign Affairs, Greece, 2009–11; President: Panhellenic Socialist Movement, 2004–12; Socialist International, since 2006; Movement of Democratic Socialists, since 2015; *b* St Paul, Minn, 16 June 1952; *m* 1989, Ada Papanou; one *s* one *d*. *Educ:* King City Secondary Sch., Toronto; Amherst Coll., Massachusetts (BA Sociol.); Stockholm Univ. (undergrad. studies Sociol.); LSE (MSc Sociol. and Develt). Member of Parliament: Achaia (Patras) Dist, 1981–96; 1st Dist, Athens, 1996–2004; 1st Dist, Salonika, 2004–07; Achaia, 2007–09; Attica, 2012–14. Under Sec. for Cultural Affairs, Ministry of Culture, 1985–87; Minister of Educn and Religious Affairs, 1988–89, 1994–96; Dep. Minister of Foreign Affairs, 1993–94; Alternate Minister of Foreign Affairs, 1996–99; Minister of Foreign Affairs, 1999–2004. Chm., Parly Cttee of Educn, 1981–85; Vice-Chm., cross-party Parly Cttee for Free Radio, 1987; in charge, Parly Cttee for Culture and Educn, 1989–93; Panhellenic Socialist Movement: Member: Central Cttee, 1984–2015; Exec. Office, 1987–88, 1996–2015; Pol Bureau, 1996–2015; Sec., Cttee on Greek Diaspora, 1990–93. Founding Member: Helsinki Citizens Assembly, Prague, 1990; Lagonisi Initiative on Co-operation in Balkans, 1994; Member Board: Foundn of Mediterranean Studies (Mem., Res. Teams); Foundn for Res. and Self-Educn. Fellow, Center for Internat. Affairs, Harvard Univ., 1992–93. Hon. Dr Law Amherst Coll., 2002. Botsis's Foundn for the Promotion of Journalism Award, 1988; SOS against Racism, and Affiliated Orgns Cttee Award, 1996; Abdi Ipekci Special Award for Peace and Friendship, 1997; (jtly) Statesman of the Year, Peace Building Awards, Eastwest Inst., 2000. Comdr, Order of Yaroslav (Ukraine), 1996; Grand Commander: Order of Polish Republic (Poland), 1996; Order of Merit (Hungary),

2003; Grand Cross: Order of the Lion (Finland), 1996; Order of Civil Merit (Spain), 1998; Order of Polar Star (Sweden), 1999; Order of White Star (Estonia), 1999; Order of Honour, first class (Austria), 1999; Order of Merit, first class (Germany), 2000; Order of Isabella the Catholic (Spain), 2001; Order of the Crown (Belgium), 2001; Order of Infante Dom Henrique (Portugal), 2002; Order of Pius IX (Vatican), 2002; Order of Merit (Italy), 2003; Order of El Sol (Peru), 2003.

**PAPANDREOU, Vassiliki, (Vasso)**, PhD; MP (Pasok) Athens, 1985–89 and 1993–2012; *d* of Andreas and Anastasia Papandreou. *Educ:* Athens Economic Univ. (BSc 1969; Special Hon. Distinction, 1991); London Univ. (MSc 1971); Reading Univ. (PhD 1980). Economics Tutor, Exeter Univ., 1971–73; Res. Asst, Oxford Univ., 1973–74; Lectr, High Business and Econs Sch., Athens, 1981–85; Dep. Minister, 1985–86; Alternate Minister: for Industry, Energy and Technology, 1986–87; for Trade, 1988–89; Minister: of Develt, 1996–99; of the Interior, Public Admin and Decentralisation, 1999–2001; of the Envmt, Physical Planning and Public Works, 2001–04. Mem. for Social Affairs, Employment, Industrial Relns and Educn, CEC, 1989–93. Vice President: Parly Assembly, Council of Europe, 1995–96; Parly Assembly, WEU, 1995–96. Panhellenic Socialist Movement: Mem., Central Cttee, 1974–; Mem., Exec. Bureau of Central Cttee, 1984–88, 1996–2006. Dir, Hellenic Orgn for Small and Medium Size Firms, 1981–85. Mem., Bd of Dirs, Commercial Bank of Greece, 1982–85. Hon. DEd CNAA, 1992; Hon. DLitt Sheffield, 1992; Dr *hc* Paul Sabatier Univ., Toulouse, 1993. Chevalier, Legion of Honour (France), 1993; Grand Cross, Order of Leopold II (Belgium), 1993; Great Cross, Order of North Star (Sweden), 1999; Insignia of Patriarch Cross, Order A Patriarch of Ierosolyma, 1999. *Publications:* Multinational Companies and Less Developed Countries: the case of Greece, 1981; numerous papers and articles. *Address:* (office) Akadimias 28, 10671 Athens, Greece.

**PAPHIDES, Catherine Elizabeth, (Caitlin);** *see* Moran, C. E.

**PAPOULIAS, Dr Karolos;** President of the Hellenic Republic, 2005–15; *b* 4 June 1929; *s* of Maj. Gen. Grigoris Papoulias and Vassilikh Papoulias; *m* May Panou; three *d*. *Educ:* Univ. of Athens (law degree); Univ. of Milan (Master of Law (Civil Law)); Univ. of Cologne (PhD Private Internat. Law). Sec., Socialist Democratic Union, 1967–74; Member: Central Cttee, PASOK, 1974– (Sec., Internat. Relns Cttee, 1975–85); Co-ordination Council, 1974–2004; Exec. Bureau, 1974–2004; Political Secretariat, 1974–2004; Co-ordinating Cttee, Socialist and Progressive Parties of Mediterranean, 1975–85. MP (PASOK) Ioanina, 1977–2004; Under-Sec., 1981–85; Dep. Minister of Foreign Affairs, 1981–85; Minister of Foreign Affairs, 1985–89; Dep. Minister of Defence, 1989–90; Minister of Foreign Affairs, 1993–96; Hd, Parly Delegn to OSCE, 1997–2003; Pres., Standing Cttee for Defence and Foreign Affairs, 1998–2004. Awarded numerous foreign decorations, including: Grand Cross, Order of Merit (Cyprus), 1984; Grand Cross, 1988, Grand Collar, 2005, Order of Makarios III (Cyprus); Grand Cross, Order of Redeemer (Hellenic Republic), 2005; Grand Cross, 1994, Collar, 2006, Order of Merit (Italy). *Publications:* monograph on the Greek Resistance 1941–1944; contrib. studies and articles to European newspapers and mags. *Recreations:* athletics, gardening, theatre, art, literature. *Clubs:* Athenian, Hellenic Language Heritage; Ethnicos Gymnastikos Syllogos.

**PAPOUTSIS, Christos;** economist; Advisor to Executive Director for Greece, World Bank Group, since 2013; *b* 11 April 1953; *m* Lia Taliouri; one *d*. *Educ:* Univ. of Athens Sch. of Law (Econs). Special Advr, Min. of Presidency, Greek Govt, 1981–84; European Parliament: Mem., 1984–95; Vice Pres., Socialist Gp, 1987–94; Mem. Cttees on Foreign Affairs, Security and Defence, Budgets and Budgetary Control, 1989–94; Mem., EC (Comr for Energy and Eurotom, Enterprise Policy, Commerce, Tourism and Social Economy), 1995–99; MP (Pasok) Athens, 2000–12; Minister of Mercantile Marine, 1999–2001, of Citizen Protection, 2010–12, Greece. *Publications:* European Destinations, 1994; The Colour of the Future, 1998; For Europe in the 21st Century, 1999. *Address:* (office) Lykavittou 5, 10672 Athens, Greece.

**PAPP, Helen Richenda;** *see* Wallace, H. R.

**PAPPANO, Sir Antonio,** Kt 2012; conductor and pianist; Music Director, Royal Opera House, Covent Garden, since 2002; Principal Conductor, Academia Nazionale di Santa Cecilia, Rome, since 2005; *b* London, 30 Dec. 1959; *m* 1995, Pamela Bullock. *Educ:* studied under Norma Verrilli, Arnold Franchetti and Gustav Meier, USA. Has worked as pianist and assistant conductor with: NY City Opera; Gran Teatro del Liceo, Barcelona; Frankfurt Opera; Lyric Opera of Chicago; Bayreuth Fest.; Music Dir, Norwegian Opera, 1990–92; Music Dir, Th. Royal de la Monnaie, Brussels, 1992–2002. Principal Guest Conductor, Israel Philharmonic Orch., 1997–2000. Has conducted world-class orchestras in Europe and the USA, incl. Boston SO, Chicago SO, Cleveland Orch., LA Philharmonic, LSO, Berlin Philharmonic, Concertgebouw Orch., Orch. de Paris and Vienna Philharmonic Orch.; has also conducted at Metropolitan Opera and Bayreuth Fest. Recordings include: La Rondine; Il Trittico; Werther; The Turn of the Screw; Manon; Tosca; Don Carlos; Tristan und Isolde; Tchaikovsky Symphonies 4, 5, 6; Respighi's Roman Trilogy; Guillaume Tell; Aida; Verdi Requiem and Rossini Petite Messe Solennelle. Cavaliere, Gran Croce dell'Ordine al Merito (Italy), 2012. *Address:* c/o IMG Artists, Capital Tower, 91 Waterloo Road, SE1 8RT. *T:* (020) 7957 5800.

**PAPPENHEIM, Karin;** Executive Director (formerly General Manager), Association of Anaesthetists of Great Britain and Ireland, since 2011; *b* 11 Dec. 1954; *d* of Wolfgang and Joy Pappenheim; one *s* one *d*. *Educ:* St Paul's Girls' Sch.; Sussex Univ. (BA Hons Intellectual Hist.); London Coll. of Printing; Université de Toulouse; Goldsmiths' Coll. (Post grad. dip. in communcns). Weidenfeld & Nicolson, Publishers, 1977–79; Camden Social Services, 1980–82; Greater London Assoc. for Disabled People, 1982–84; Alcohol Concern, 1984–89; FPA, 1989–95; Dir, Nat. Council for One Parent Families, 1995–97; Chief Executive: Haemophilia Soc., 1998–2004; Employment Opportunities for People with Disabilities, 2004–09; Dir, Work and Independence, Shaw Trust, 2009–10; Interim Chief Exec., Vital Regeneration, 2010–11. Trustee: Terrence Higgins Trust, 1998–2003; NCVO, 1999–2005; Woman's Trust, 2010–13. *Recreations:* family and friends, travel in France.
*See also* M. Pappenheim.

**PAPPENHEIM, Katharine;** *see* Tearle, K.

**PAPPENHEIM, Mark;** writer and editor; *b* 25 May 1956; *s* of Wolfgang and Joy Pappenheim; *m* 1988, Katharine Tearle, *qv*; two *s*. *Educ:* St Paul's Boys' Sch.; Merton Coll., Oxford (BA Hons Lit. Hum., MA); City Univ., London (Cert. Arts Admin). Box-office manager, Buxton Fest. and Opera Hse, 1979–80; Asst Hd of Educn, WNO, 1980–81; Fest. Administrator, Vale of Glamorgan Fest., 1982; Asst Administrator, Live Music Now, 1982–83; Pubns Ed., Opera North, 1983–84; Radio Ed., Radio Times, 1984–90; with The Independent, 1990–2016: Arts Editor, 1996–98; Classical Music Reviews Ed., 1998–2008; Opera Critic, The Daily Express, 1998–2002. Classical Music Reviewer, Radio Times, 2018–. Artistic Assessor, Arts Council England, 2011. Editor: BBC Proms programmes, 1998–2005; BBC Proms Guide, 2000–06; BBC Proms interactive television notes, 2006–08; London (formerly Lufthansa) Festival of Baroque Music Programmes, 2008–17; Hallé Programmes, 2011–. *Publications:* numerous articles; essays; programme notes, incl. BBC Proms, Edinburgh Internat. Fest., Royal Opera, Glyndebourne Fest. Opera, South Bank Centre, EMI Records, Decca Classics, Warner Classics; contrib. BBC Music Mag., Opera Mag., Radio Times. *Recreations:* beekeeping (newsletter editor, 2006–09, County Representative, 2009–10, Sussex Beekeepers' Assoc., Brighton & Lewes Div.), sourdough bread-making (Mem., Real Bread Campaign), running (Run Leader, Lewes Athletic Club). *Address:* 42 Ferrers Road, Lewes, E Sussex BN7 1PZ. *T:* (01273) 483546.
*See also* K. Pappenheim.

**PAPPS, Alastair Harkness,** CB 2002; Associate Director, Centre for Management and Policy Studies, Cabinet Office (on secondment from HM Prison Service), 1999–2002; *b* 28 April 1942; *s* of Osborne Stephen Papps and Helen Papps (*née* Harkness); *m* 1963, Marian Caroline Clayton; two *s* one *d*. *Educ:* King Edward's Sch., Birmingham; St Catharine's Coll., Cambridge (MA); Univ. of Newcastle upon Tyne (Dip. in Applied Social Studies 1970). Joined HM Prison Service, 1965; Prison Service Staff Coll., Wakefield, 1965–66; Asst Gov., Huntercombe Borstal, 1966–69; Tutor, Prison Service Staff Coll., Wakefield, 1970–73; Asst Gov., 1973–75, Dep. Gov., 1975–77, Wakefield Prison; Personnel Div., Prison Service HQ, 1977–80; Governor: Acklington Prison, 1980–83; Durham Prison, 1983–87; Frankland Prison, 1987–89; Dep. Dir, subseq. Dir, North Regl Office, 1989–90; Area Manager, North East, 1990–95; Dir of Ops-North, and Mem., Prisons Bd, 1995–99. Ed., Prison Service Jl, 1987–89. Vice-Chm., Standards Cttee, Rutland CC, 2006–12. Chm., NICRO UK Trust for a Safer S Africa, 2000–09; Expert Advr, Zahid Mubarek public judicial inquiry, 2004–06. Trustee, Prisons Video Trust, 2007– (Chm., 2018–). Lay Member: Professional Conduct Bd, BPsS, 2007–08; Disciplinary and Regulatory Cttees, ACCA, 2011–; Lay Rep., E Midlands Healthcare Workforce Deanery, 2009–13. *Publications:* articles in jls. *Recreations:* reading, theatre, cinema, travel, observing politics. *Address:* 1 Lauriston Road, Wimbledon, SW19 4TJ. *Club:* Nottingham.

**PAQUET, Dr Jean-Guy,** CC 1994 (OC 1984); GOQ 2005 (OQ 1992); FRSC; Corporate Director, National Optics Institute (President and Chief Executive Officer, 1994–2005; Chairman of Board, 2005–18); *b* Montmagny, Qué, 5 Jan. 1938; *s* of Laurent W. Paquet and Louisianne Coulombe. *Educ:* Université Laval (BSc Engrg Physics, 1959; DSc Elec. Engrg, 1963); Ecole Nat. Sup. de l'Aéronautique, Paris (MSc Aeronautics, 1960). FRSC 1978; FAAAS 1981. Université Laval: Asst Prof. of Elec. Engrg, 1962; Associate Prof., 1967; Head, Elec. Engrg Dept, 1967–69; Vice-Dean (Research), Faculty of Science, 1969–72; Prof. of Elec. Engrg, 1971; Vice-Rector (Academic), 1972–77; Rector, 1977–87; Pres., La Laurentienne Vie Inc., 1987–94. Fellowships: French Govt, 1959; NATO, 1962; Nat. Science Foundn, 1964; Québec Govt, 1965. Def. Res. Bd of Canada Grant, 1965–76. National Research Council of Canada: Fellowship, 1961; Grant, 1964–77; Mem., Associate Cttee on Automatic Control, 1964–70; Special Asst to Vice-Pres. (Scientific), 1971–72. Pres., Conf. of Rectors and Principals of Univs of Prov. of Québec, 1979–81. Member: Council, Univs of Prov. of Qué, 1973–77; Bd, Assoc. of Scientific, Engrg and Technol Community of Canada, 1970–77 (Pres., 1975–76); Bd, French Canadian Assoc. for Advancement of Science, 1969–71; Canadian Assoc. of Univ. Res. Administrators; Special Task Force on Res. and Develt, Science Council of Canada, 1976; Order of Engrs, Qué; Amer. Soc. for Engrg Educn; Amer. Management Assoc., 1980; Soc. for Res. Administrators. Member Board: Interamerican Univs Assoc., 1980–87; Assoc. des universités partiellement ou entièrement de langue française, 1981–87 (Vice-Pres., 1983); Assoc. of Commonwealth Univs, 1981–87; Founding Mem., Corporate Higher Educn Forum. Pres., Selection Cttee, Outstanding Achievement Awards, Canada, 1984 (Mem., 1983). DSc *hc*: McGill Univ., 1982; Technical Univ., Nova Scotia, 1987; Sherbrooke, 2002; DLaw *hc*, York Univ., 1983; Dr *hc*: Montreal, 2004; Quebec, 2016. Légion d'Honneur (France), 2017. *Publications:* (with P. A. Roy) Rapport d'études bibliographiques: l'automation dans la production et la distribution de l'énergie électrique, 1968; (with J. F. Le Maître) Méthodes pratiques d'étude des oscillations non-linéaires: application aux systèmes par plus-ou-moins, 1970; more than fifty pubns in scientific jls, on control systems engrg; articles on research, develt and scientific policy. *Recreations:* jogging, travels, golf. *Address:* National Optics Institute, 2740 rue Einstein, Sainte-Foy, Québec, QC G1P 4S4, Canada. *T:* (418) 6577006, *Fax:* (418) 6577088. *Clubs:* Cercle de la Garnison de Québec, Golf Royal Québec (Québec).

**PARASKEVA, Rt Hon. Dame Janet,** DBE 2010; PC 2010; Chair: Jersey Appointments Commission, since 2014; Council for Licensed Conveyancers; *b* 28 May 1946; *d* of Antonis Paraskeva and Doris Amanda Paraskeva (*née* Fowler); *m* 1967, Alan Richard Derek Hunt (marr. diss. 1983); two *d*, and two step *s*; civil partnership 2007. *Educ:* Open Univ. (BA Social Scis 1983). HM Inspector of Schs, DES, 1983–88; Dir, Nat. Youth Bureau, 1988–91; Chief Exec., Nat. Youth Agency, 1991–95; Dir, England, Nat. Lotteries Charities Bd, 1995–2000; Chief Exec., Law Soc., 2000–06; First Civil Service Comr, 2006–10. Chair: Olympic Lottery Distributor, 2006–13; Child Maintenance and Enforcement Commn, 2008–12 (Chm. designate, 2007–08); Plan (Internat.) UK, 2009–16. Member: Nat. Bd for Crime Prevention, 1993–95; Youth Justice Bd, 1998–2000; Council, Competition Commn, 2012–14. Ind. Auditor of Commitment to Good Regulation, ASA, 2017. Non-executive Director: Fosse Community NHS Trust, 1992–99; Serious Organised Crime Agency, 2005–13; Assets Recovery Agency, 2007–08; Herts Partnership NHS Foundn Trust. Ind. Mem., Consumer Council for Water, 2005–08; Mem. Panel, Detainee Inquiry, 2010–13. Gov., Ryde Acad., IoW, 2013–17. JP City of Leicester, 1993–2000. Hon. LLD Brighton, 2006; Hon. MLitt Worcester, 2009. *Publications:* articles in youth, educn and law jls and periodicals and in TES. *Recreations:* gardening, reading, singing.

**PARAYRE, Jean-Paul Christophe;** Commandeur de la Légion d'Honneur; Commandeur, l'Ordre National du Mérite, 1991; Chairman, Vallourec, 2000–13 (Member, Supervisory Board, 1989–2013); Member, Supervisory Board, Peugeot SA, 1984–2014; *b* Lorient, 5 July 1937; *s* of Louis Parayre and Jehanne Malarde; *m* 1962, Marie-Françoise Chaufour; two *s* two *d*. *Educ:* Lycées in Casablanca and Versailles; Ecole Polytechnique, Paris; Ecole Nationale des Ponts et Chaussées. Engr, Dept of Highways, 1963–67; Technical Adviser: Min. of Social Affairs, 1967; Min. of Economy and Finance, 1968; Dir of Mech. Industries, Min. of Industry and Res., 1970–74; Manager of Planning, Automobile Div. of Peugeot, 1975; Manager, Automobile Div., Peugeot-Citroën, 1976; Chm. and CEO, Peugeot SA, 1977–88; Mem., Supervisory Bd, 1977–84, Dir-Gen., 1984–88, Chm. and Chief Exec. Officer, 1988–90, Dumez SA; Vice-Chm. and Chief Operating Officer, Bolloré, 1994–99 (Dir, 1994–2000); Chm. and CEO, Saga, 1996–99. Chm., GIE Trans-Manche Construction, 1986–92; Vice-Chm., Lyonnaise des Eaux-Dumez, 1990–92; Mem., Board of Directors: Crédit National, then Natexis, 1978–97; Valeo, 1986–91; GTM, 1986–92; LVMH, 1987–89; Jean Lefebvre, 1988–92; McAlpine, 1990–92; Inchcape plc, 1991–94; Indosuez, 1991–94; Bolloré (formerly Albatros) Investissement, 1994; Coflexip, 1995–2000; Delmas, 1995–99; Stena International BV, 1995–2006; Tarmac plc, 1995–99; Sea Invest France, 1999–2004; Stena UK, 1999–2003; Carillion plc, 1999–2004; SNEF, 1999–; Stena Line, 2001–05; Stena Internat. Sarl, 2006–13. *Recreations:* tennis, golf. *Address:* 203 avenue Molière, 1050 Brussels, Belgium. *Clubs:* Polo de Paris, Golf de Morfontaine; Golf de Sotogrande.

**PARDOE, His Honour Alan Douglas William**; QC 1988; a Circuit Judge, 2003–13; First-tier Tribunal Judge (formerly a Chairman), Mental Health Review Tribunals (Restricted), 2005–12; *b* 16 Aug. 1943; *s* of William Pardoe and Dr Grace Pardoe, FRSC. *Educ:* Oldbury Grammar Sch.; St Catharine's Coll., Cambridge (MA, LLB). Called to the Bar, Lincoln's Inn, 1971, Bencher, 1998. Lecturer in Law: Univ. of Exeter, 1965–70; Univ. of Auckland, NZ, 1970; Univ. of Sussex, 1970–74; in practice at the Bar, 1973–2003. A Recorder, 1990–2003. Judicial Mem., Parole Bd, 2010–17. *Publications:* A Practical Guide to the Industrial Relations Act 1971, 1972; articles in legal periodicals. *Recreations:* the company of friends, living in London. *E:* alan.pardoe3@btinternet.com. *Clubs:* Travellers, Oxford and Cambridge.

**PARDOE, John Wentworth**; Chairman, Sight and Sound Education Ltd, 1979–89; *b* 27 July 1934; *s* of Cuthbert B. Pardoe and Marjorie E. W. (*née* Taylor); *m* 1958, Joyce R. Peerman; two *s* one *d*. *Educ:* Sherborne; Corpus Christi Coll., Cambridge (MA). Television Audience Measurement Ltd, 1958–60; Osborne Peacock Co. Ltd, 1960–61; Liberal News, 1961–66. MP (L) Cornwall N, 1966–79; Treasurer of the Liberal Party, 1968–69. Presenter, Look Here, LWT, 1979–81. Sen. Res. Fellow, PSI, 1979–81. Consultant to Nat. Assoc. of Schoolmasters, 1967–73. Director: William Schlackman Ltd, 1968–71; Gerald Metals, 1972–83; Mem. London Metal Exchange, 1973–83. Mem., Youth Trng Bd, 1985–89. *Recreations:* walking, reading, music, carpentry. *Address:* 18 New End Square, NW3 1LN.

**PAREKH**, family name of **Baron Parekh**.

**PAREKH**, Baron *cr* 2000 (Life Peer), of Kingston upon Hull, in the East Riding of Yorkshire; **Bhikhu Chhotalal Parekh**, FBA 2003; Professor of Political Philosophy, University of Westminster, 2001–09, now Emeritus; Professor of Political Theory, University of Hull, 1982–2001, now Emeritus; *b* 4 Jan. 1935; *s* of Chhotalal Parekh and Gajaraben Parekh; *m* 1959, Pramila (*née* Dalal); three *s*. *Educ:* Univ. of Bombay (BA 1954, MA 1956); Univ. of London (PhD 1966). Tutor, LSE, 1962–63; Asst Lectr, Univ. of Glasgow, 1963–64; Lectr, Sen. Lectr and Reader, Hull Univ., 1964–82. Vice-Chancellor, Univ. of Baroda, 1981–84. Visiting Professor: Univ. of BC, 1967–68; Concordia Univ., 1974–75; McGill Univ., 1976–77; Harvard Univ., 1996; Inst. of Advanced Study, Vienna, 1997; Univ. of Pompeu Fabra, Barcelona, 1997; Univ. of Pennsylvania, 1998; Ecole des Hautes Etudes en Sciences Sociales, Paris, 2000; Centennial Prof., LSE, 2001–03. Mem., Rampton/Swann Cttee of Inquiry into Educnl Problems of Ethnic Minority Children, 1978–82; Mem. Council, PSI, 1985–90; Vice Pres., UK Council for Overseas Students Affairs, 1989–94; Chm., British Assoc. of S Asia Scholars, 1989–91, 2004–07. Dep. Chm., CRE, 1985–90; Member: Commn on Rise of Neo-Fascism in Europe, 1992–93; Nat. Commn on Equal Opportunities, CVCP, 1994–99; Chm., Commn on Future of Multi-Ethnic Britain, 1998–2000. Trustee: Runnymede Trust, 1986–2008; Inst. for Public Policy Res., 1988–95; Gandhi Foundn, 1988– (Pres., 2012–); Anne Frank Educnl Trust, 1992–. AcSS 1999 (Pres., 2003–08); FRSA 1988; Fellow, Asiatic Soc., Bombay, 2004. Holds 17 hon. doctorates. British Asian of the Year, Asian Who's Who, 1991; Special Lifetime Achievement Award for Asians, BBC, 1999; Sir Isaiah Berlin Prize, Pol Studies Assoc., 2003. Saraswat Gaurav Award, Gujarat, 2004; Pravasi Bharatiya Samman Award, India, 2005; Pride of India Award, India Internat. Foundn, London, 2006; Distinguished Global Thinker Award, India Internat. Centre, New Delhi, 2006; Sardar Patel Vishva Pratibha Award, Ahmedabad, 2012. Padma Bhushan (India), 2007. *Publications:* Politics and Experience, 1968; Dissent and Disorder, 1971; The Morality of Politics, 1972; Knowledge and Belief in Politics, 1973; Bentham's Political Thought, 1973; Colour, Culture and Consciousness, 1974; Jeremy Bentham: ten critical essays, 1974; The Concept of Socialism, 1975; Hannah Arendt and the Search for a New Political Philosophy, 1981; Karl Marx's Theory of Ideology, 1982; Contemporary Political Thinkers, 1982; Political Discourse, 1986; Gandhi's Political Philosophy, 1989; Colonialism, Tradition and Reform, 1989; Jeremy Bentham: critical assessments (4 vols), 1993; The Decolonisation of Imagination, 1995; Crisis and Change in Contemporary India, 1995; Gandhi, 1997; Rethinking Multiculturalism, 2000; A New Politics of Identity, 2008; Talking Politics, 2011; Debating India, 2015; articles in learned jls incl. Political Studies, British Jl of Political Science, Social Research, Jl of History of Ideas, Indian Jl of Social Science, Ethics, Hist. of Pol Thought, TLS, Canadian Jl of Philosophy, Radical Philosophy, THES, Transit, Les Temps Modernes, Constellations, Dialegs, Rev. of Internat. Studies, Internat. Relations. *Recreations:* reading, music, walking. *Address:* 211 Victoria Avenue, Hull HU5 3EF.
See also Hon. A. B. Parekh.

**PAREKH, Prof. the Hon. Anant Bhikhu**, DPhil; FRS 2019; FMedSci; Professor of Physiology, University of Oxford, since 2002; Fellow, Merton College, Oxford, since 2016; *b* Hull; *s* of Baron Parekh, *qv*; *m* 1998, Prof. Maike Glitsch; one *s*. *Educ:* Hymers Coll., Hull; University Coll., Oxford (BA Med. Scis; DPhil 1991). University of Oxford: Wellcome Trust Career Develt Fellow, 1996–2000; Fellow, Keble Coll., 1996–2002; Sen. Res. Fellow, Lister Inst., 2000–05; Monsanto Sen. Res. Fellow, Exeter Coll., 2002–03; Fellow, Lady Margaret Hall, 2002–15. *Publications:* contrib. scientific articles to jls incl. Nature, Cell. *Recreations:* cricket, music, reading. *Address:* Department of Physiology, Anatomy and Genetics, University of Oxford, Parks Road, Oxford OX1 3PT. *T:* (01865) 282174. *E:* anant.parekh@dpag.ox.ac.uk.

**PARFITT, Andrew John**; Director, Enlightened Leadership, since 2013; *b* 24 Sept. 1958; *s* of John Raymond Parfitt and Jeanne Parfitt; *m* 1996, Laura Druce; two *d*. *Educ:* Bristol Old Vic Theatre Sch.; Wharton Business Sch. Asst stage manager, Bristol Arts Centre, 1978; studio manager, BBC, 1979–84; programme presenter, British Forces Broadcasting Service, 1984; BBC: educn producer, 1985; producer, features and magazines, Radio 4, 1986–91; Breakfast Show Editor, Radio 5, 1991–93; Radio 1: Editor, 1993–95; Managing Editor, 1995–98; Controller: BBC Radio 1, 1998–2011; BBC 1Xtra, 2002–11; BBC Switch, 2006–10; BBC Asian Network, 2008–11; BBC Popular Music, 2008–11; Dir, Exec. Talent, EMEA, Saatchi & Saatchi Fallon Gp, 2011–13. Chm., Nat. Foundn for Youth Music, 2013–17; Trustee, Services Sound and Vision Corp., 2013–. *Recreations:* running, painting, music, presenting radio programmes.

**PARFITT, David John**; film producer; Director: Renaissance Theatre Company, since 1987; Trademark Films, since 1999; *b* 8 July 1958; *s* of late William Arnold Parfitt and Maureen Parfitt (*née* Collinson); *m* 1st, 1988, Susan Coates (marr. diss. 1993); one *s*; 2nd, 1996, Elizabeth Barron; two *s*. *Educ:* Bede Grammar Sch., Sunderland; Barbara Speake Stage Sch., London. Actor, 1970–88; producer, 1985–: productions include: *theatre*: Tell Me Honestly, 1985, John Sessions at the 11th Hour, 1986, Donmar Warehouse; Romeo and Juliet, 1986, Public Enemy, 1987, Lyric Hammersmith; Napoleon, Albery, 1987; Much Ado About Nothing, As You Like It, and Hamlet, Phoenix, 1988; Look Back in Anger, Lyric, 1989; A Midsummer Night's Dream, King Lear, Dominion, 1990; Scenes from a Marriage, Wyndhams, 1990; Travelling Tales, Haymarket, 1991; Uncle Vanya, Lyric Hammersmith, 1991; Coriolanus, Chichester Fest. Th., 1992; Les Liaisons Dangereuses, Playhouse, 2004; Elling, Bush, 2007; A Bunch of Amateurs, 2014, The Wipers Times, 2016–18, Watermill Newbury, touring and transf. Arts Th., 2018; Trial by Laughter, Watermill Newbury and tour, 2018–19; *television*: Twelfth Night, 1988; Look Back in Anger, 1989; Parade's End, 2012; The Wipers Times, 2013; Glyndebourne: the untold history, 2014; Birth of an Opera, 2016; *films*: Henry V, 1988; Peter's Friends, 1992; Swan Song, 1992; Much Ado About Nothing, 1993; Mary Shelley's Frankenstein, 1994; The Madness of King George, 1995; Twelfth Night, 1996; The Wings of the Dove, 1997; Shakespeare in Love, 1998; (consultant) Gangs of New York, 2002; I Capture the Castle, 2003; Chasing Liberty, 2004; (exec. prod.) Dean Spanley, 2008; A Bunch of Amateurs, 2008; My Week with Marilyn, 2011; (exec. prod.) Loving Vincent, 2017; Red Joan, 2018. BAFTA: Mem. Bd of Trustees, 2000–11 (Chm.), 2008–10); Chm., Film Cttee, 2004–07; Chm., Film London, 2011–17. Trustee, Chicken Shed Th. Co., 1997–2012; Patron, Royalty Th., Sunderland, 1999–. Gov., Dulwich Coll., 2018–. Hon. DA Sunderland, 1999; Hon. Dr Drama RSAMD, 2001. *Address:* Trademark Films Ltd, 14a Goodwin's Court, WC2N 4LL. *T:* (020) 3322 8900. *E:* mail@trademarkfilms.co.uk.

**PARFITT, Nicholas John; His Honour Judge Parfitt**; a Circuit Judge, since 2016; *b* Blandford Forum, 3 Feb. 1967; *s* of John Parfitt and Jennifer Parfitt; partner, Gillian Parrott; one *s*. *Educ:* Sherborne Sch.; Univ. of Bristol (BA 1989). Called to the Bar, Middle Temple, 1993; a District Judge, 2010–16. *Recreations:* cycling, music, theatre, cricket, reading.

**PARGETER, Catherine Jane**; *see* Brunner, C. J.

**PARGETER, Rt Rev. Philip**; Auxiliary Bishop of Birmingham, (RC), and Titular Bishop of Valentiniana, 1989–2009, now Emeritus; *b* 13 June 1933; *s* of Philip William Henry Pargeter and Ellen Pargeter. *Educ:* St Bede's Coll., Manchester; Oscott Coll., Sutton Coldfield. Priest, 1959; on staff of Cotton College, 1959–85; Administrator, St Chad's Cathedral, Birmingham, 1985–90; Canon, 1986. *Recreations:* reading, listening to music, walking.

**PARHAM, Prof. Peter Robert**, PhD; FRS 2008; Professor of Structural Biology, Stanford University, since 1992; scientist and immunogeneticist, since 1977; *b* Stanmore, Middx, 15 Aug. 1950; *s* of Ronald and Hilda Parham; *m* 1978, Frances Brodsky. *Educ:* Stanburn Prim. Sch., Stanmore; Haberdashers' Aske's Sch., Elstree; St John's Coll., Cambridge (BA Natural Scis 1972); Harvard Univ. (PhD Biochem. and Molecular Biol.). Jun. Fellow, Soc. of Fellows, Harvard Univ., 1977–80; Asst Prof., 1980–88, Associate Prof., 1988–92, Stanford Univ. FMedSci 2016. *Publications:* The Immune System, 2000, 3rd edn 2009. *Recreations:* seaside swimming, landmarks, watching bad birds. *Address:* Department of Structural Biology, 299 Campus Drive West, Stanford University, Stanford, CA 94305-5126, USA. *T:* (650) 7237456, *Fax:* (650) 4248912. *E:* peropa@stanford.edu.

**PARHAM, Philip John**, CMG 2015; HM Diplomatic Service; UK Commonwealth Envoy, since 2018; *b* 14 Aug. 1960; *s* of John Carey Parham and Christian Mary Parham (*née* Fitzherbert); *m* 1985, Anna Catherine Astrid Louise, (Kasia), Giedroyć; five *s* two *d*. *Educ:* Eton Coll.; Christ Church, Oxford (MA Lit.Hum.). Morgan Grenfell, 1983–89 (Sen. Asst Dir, 1988); Barclays de Zoete Wedd Ltd, 1989–93 (Dir, 1993); joined FCO, 1993; FCO, 1993–96 (Private Sec. to Parly Under-Sec. of State, 1995); First Sec. (Chancery), Washington, 1996–2000; Dir, Trade and Investment Promotion, Saudi Arabia, 2000–03; FCO, 2003–04; Hd, Counter Terrorism Policy Dept, FCO, 2004–06; High Comr to Tanzania, 2006–09; Dep. Perm. Rep., UK Mission to UN, NY, 2009–13; Ambassador to UAE, 2014–18. Liveryman, Skinners' Co. Hon. Fellow, Harris Manchester Coll., Oxford, 2014. *Recreations:* children, theology, gardening, researching the parentage of Mary Anne Smythe. *Address:* c/o Foreign and Commonwealth Office, King Charles Street, SW1A 2AH.

**PARHAM, Richard David**; Chairman: Dixi & Associates, 2001–10; Coventry and Warwickshire Connexions, 2001–11; *b* 17 Nov. 1944; *s* of James Parham and Lily Elizabeth Parham; *m* 1967, Janet Burton; one *s* one *d*. *Educ:* Royal Liberty Sch., Romford; Barking Coll. of Technol. Ford Motor Co., 1961–67; Rootes Motors, 1967–69; Chrysler UK, then Chrysler UK/Talbot Motor Co., 1969–81: Profit Analysis Manager, then Finance Manager, Hills Precision Ltd, 1969–72; Manager, Product and Pricing Analysis, then Pricing and Investment, 1972–76; Co. Comptroller, 1976–77; Dir of Finance, 1977–80; Asst Man. Dir, 1981–94, Man. Dir, 1994–99, Peugeot Talbot, subseq. Peugeot, Motor Co. Chairman: Coventry, Solihull and Warwicks Partnerships, 2000–08; Coventry and Warwicks Regeneration Zone, 2001–08. Mem. Council, Coventry and Warwicks LLSC. Chm. Bd of Govs, 2002–08, Pro Chancellor, 2009–11, Coventry Univ.; Mem. Ct, Warwick Univ., 1998–2009. Hon. DBA Coventry 1999. *Recreations:* Rugby, cricket, music, reading, golf.

**PARIS, Archbishop of, (RC)**, since 2018; **Most Rev. Michel Christian Alain Aupetit**; *b* Versailles, 23 March 1951; *s* of André Aupetit and Louise Aupetit (*née* Bâty). *Educ:* Lycée Hoche, Versailles; Bichat Med. Sch., Univ. of Paris (DMed 1978); Univ. Paris-Est Créteil (Dip. in Med. Ethics 1994); Seminary of Paris (BTh). Dr of Gen. Medicine, Colombes, Paris, 1979–90; ordained priest, 1995; Vicar, Church of Saint-Louis-en-l'Île, 1995–98; Lectr in Medical Ethics, Henri Mondor Hospital, Créteil, 1997–2006; Vicar, Saint-Paul-Saint-Louis, 1998–2001; Parish Priest, Église Notre-Dame-de-l'Arche-d'Alliance, and Dean, Pasteur-Vaugirard, 2004–06; Vicar Gen., Archdio. of Paris, 2006–13; Aux. Bishop of Paris and Titular Bishop of Massita, 2013–14; Bishop of Nanterre, 2014–17. Pres., Council of Family and Soc., French Episcopal Conf., 2017–18. Member: Congregation for Bishops, 2018; Congregation for Oriental Churches, 2019; Congregation for the Clergy, 2019. Sch. and Coll. Chaplain, Marais, 1995–2001. *Publications:* Contraception: the answer of the Church, 1999; Discovering Christ, 2005; The Embryo: what's the issue?, 2008; Death, and After?, 2009, Man, Sex and God, 2011; Are We Building a Human or Inhuman Society, 2016. *Address:* Diocese de Paris, 10 rue du Cloître-Notre-Dame, 75004 Paris, France. *W:* www.twitter.com/michelaupetit, www.facebook.com/mgrmichelaupetit, www.instagram.com/mgrmichaelaupetit.

**PARIS, Andrew Martin Ingledew**, FRCS; Consultant Urological Surgeon, The Royal London Hospital, 1976–2005, and St Bartholomew's Hospital, 1994–2005, now Emeritus Consulting Urological Surgeon; *b* 27 Nov. 1940; *s* of Vernon Patrick Paris and Heather Constance Ingledew Paris (*née* Dear); *m* 1975, Susan Philippa, *d* of Perys Goodwin Jenkins; one *d*. *Educ:* London Hosp. Med. Coll., Univ. of London (MB BS 1964). MRCS 1964, FRCS 1971; LRCP 1964; DObstRCOG 1967. Clinical Dir of Surgery and Urology, Royal London Hosp., then Barts and the London NHS Trust, 1979–2002; Consultant Paediatric Urological Surgeon, Newham Gen. Hosp., 1995–2005. Hon. Urological Surgeon, Italian Hosp., London, 1979–90. Regl Advr on Urology, NE Thames, 1982–87. Examr in Dental Surgery, RCS, 1983–89. Founder Mem., St John Ambulance Air Wing, Hon. Surgeon, 1971–92; Trustee, St John Travelling Fellowships in Transplantation, 1992–. FRSocMed (Vice Pres., Section of Urology, 1983–84). Sen. Mem., British Assoc. of Urological Surgeons, 2005. Trustee: Marie Celeste Samaritan Soc., 1996– (Chm., 2006–); Long Shop Mus., 2004–18. Freeman, City of London, 1984; Liveryman, Soc. of Apothecaries, 1967– (Chm. Livery Cttee, 1992–93; Mem. Ct of Assts, 1994–; Master, 2007–08). OStJ 1985. *Publications:* contribs on urology and transplantation to med. jls. *Recreations:* croquet, ski-ing, sailing. *Address:* The Old Vicarage, Aldringham cum Thorpe, Suffolk IP16 4QF. *T:* (01728) 833673. *E:* andrewparis@tiscali.co.uk. *Clubs:* Athenæum; Aldeburgh Yacht; Thorpeness Croquet.

**PARIS, Prof. Jeffrey Bruce**, PhD; FBA 1999; Professor of Mathematics, Manchester University, 1984–2017, now Emeritus; *b* 15 Nov. 1944; *s* of George William and Marie Eileen Paris; *m* 1st, 1967, Malvyn Loraine Blackburn (marr. diss. 1983); two *d*; 2nd, 1983, Alena Vencovská; three *s* one *d*. *Educ:* Manchester Univ. (BSc 1st Cl. Maths 1966; PhD Mathematical Logic 1969). Manchester University: Lectr, Dept of Maths, 1969–74; Reader, 1974–84. Junior Whitehead Prize, London Mathematical Soc., 1983. *Publications:* The Uncertain Reasoner's Companion, 1994; Pure Inductive Logic, 2015; numerous research papers in learned jls. *Recreations:* angling, painting. *Address:* School of Mathematics, The University of Manchester, Manchester M13 9PL. *T:* (0161) 275 5800.

**PARISH, Neil Quentin Gordon**; MP (C) Tiverton and Honiton, since 2010; *b* 26 May 1956; *s* of Reginald Thomas Parish and Kathleen Susan Mary Parish; *m* 1981, Susan Gail; one *s* one *d*. *Educ:* Brymore Sch., Somerset. Left sch. at 16 to run farm of 100 acres; farm increased to 300 acres, dairy and arable, 1990. Member (C): Sedgemoor DC, 1983–95 (Dep. Leader, 1989–95); Somerset CC, 1989–93; Parish Council, 1985–. European Parliament: Mem. (C) SW Region, England, 1999–2009; spokesman on agriculture and on fisheries; Chairman: Agric. and Rural Develt Cttee, 1999–2009; Animal Welfare Intergroup, 2007–09; Member: Envmt Cttee, 2001–09; Fisheries Cttee, 2002–09; Chm., Select Cttee on Envmt, Food and Rural Affairs, 2015–. Mem., EU Australian and NZ delegn. Contested (C) Torfaen, 1997. *Recreations:* swimming, walking. *Address:* House of Commons, SW1A 0AA.

**PARISH, Prof. Richard**, CBE 2014; CBiol; FFPH; FRSPH; FRSB; Chief Executive: Royal Society for Public Health, 2008–13 (Chief Executive: Royal Society of Health, 2005–08; Royal Institute of Public Health, 2008); Institute of Healthcare Management, 2012–13; *b* 11 Oct. 1951; *s* of Leslie Thomas Parish, FCCA and Winifred Alice Parish; *m* 1976, Joan Margaret Shepherd; one *s* one *d*. *Educ:* Univ. of London (BSc ext. 1975); South Bank Poly. (PDipHEd 1978); Huddersfield Univ. (MEd). CBiol 1989; MSB (MIBiol 1989), FRSB (FSB (by distinction) 2011); Hon. MFPHM 2001; FRIPH 2006; FRSocMed 2013. Dir of Health Promotion, Stockport HA, 1980–85; Head of Progs, 'Heartbeat Wales' and Sen. Lectr, Welsh Nat. Sch. of Medicine, 1985–87; Dir of Ops, Health Promotion Authy for Wales, 1987–90; Principal and Chief Exec., Humberside Coll. of Health, 1990–96; Dir, Health and Community Studies, and Prof. of Public Health, Sheffield Hallam Univ., 1996–97; Hd, Health Studies, and Prof., Univ. of York, 1997–99; Regl Dir, Educn and Trng, NHS Eastern Reg., 1999; Chief Exec., HDA, 2000–03; Consultant, WHO, 2003–05. Chm., Pharmacy and Public Health Forum, 2011–; non-exec. Dir, Public Health England, 2013–; Mem. Bd, UK Public Health Register, 2013–. Prof. of Health Develt, Univ. of Chester, 2014–; Visiting Professor: Anglia Ruskin (formerly Anglia Poly.) Univ., 2003–; Staffordshire Univ., 2008–13; Brunel Univ., 2008–; UCL 2014–; Robert Gordon Univ., 2014–. Hon. Consultant, NE Essex PCT, 2008–13. Chm., Nat. No-Smoking Day, 2005–12. Exec. Bd Mem., Nat. Health Forum (formerly Nat. Heart Forum), 2000–13; Vice Pres. for Europe, Internat. Union for Health Promotion and Educn, 2014–15. Gov., Moggerhanger Primary Sch., 2005–09. FRSPH (FRSH 1988), Hon. FRSPH 2013; MCIPR (MIPR 1989); Foundation Fellow, Inst. of Health Visiting, 2012. Hon. Mem., APHA, 2006; Hon. FRPharmS 2013. Hon DSc Brunel, 2014. *Publications:* contribs on health promotion and health policy, incl. for WHO. *Recreations:* photography, rambling, cycling, Inland Waterways, boating. *Address:* Cop Rise, 21 Moor View, Meltham, Holmfirth, W Yorks HD9 5RT. *T:* (01484) 311783.

**PARISH, Stephen William**; Chairman, Norton Rose Fulbright LLP (formerly Norton Rose LLP), 2009–18 (Group Chairman, Norton Rose, 2009–12); *b* Worthing, 4 Sept. 1951; *s* of Alexander Leonard Stephen Parish and Sheila Margaret Parish; *m* 1980, Joyce Smith; two *s* one *d*. *Educ:* Worthing High Sch.; Univ. of Birmingham (LLB 1973). Admitted solicitor, 1976; Norton Rose Botterell & Roche, then Norton Rose, then Norton Rose LLP, later Norton Rose Fulbright LLP, 1976–2018: Admin Partner, 1997–2000; Global Hd of Banking, 2006–09. *Recreations:* travel, family, theatre, ballet, opera. *Club:* MCC.

**PARISOT, Pierre Louis André**; Chevalier de l'Ordre du Mérite; Chevalier de la Légion d'Honneur; Chairman: Aquiris, 2001–10; Transorco, 2009–13; *b* Ambacourt, France, 9 Jan. 1940; *s* of Louis Parisot and Marie (née Boye); *m* 1963, Evelyne Treilhou; two *s* two *d*. *Educ:* Ecole Polytechnique; Ecole Nationale des Ponts et Chaussées; Institut d'Etudes Politiques de Paris. Assistant to the Director, Civil Works Department: Réunion Island, 1966–72; Morbihan, Brittany, 1973–76; Dep. Dir, Personnel Policy and Mod. Management Methods, Min. of Civil Works, Transport and Envmt, 1976–77; Technical Advr, French Home Office Cabinet, 1977–80; Internat. Dir, St Gobain subsid., SOBEA, 1980–84; Dir Gen., SOGEA (Gp Générale des Eaux), 1985–90; Chm., Supervisory Bd, Société des Tuyaux Bonna (Gp Générale des Eaux, subseq. Vivendi), 1990–; Dep. Man. Dir, Société Générale d'Entreprises, 1991–97; Vice-Pres., Strategic Sourcing and Purchasing, Veolia Environnement, 2002–08; Chm., Transmanche-Link (TML), 1991–2006; Chairman and Chief Executive: Consortium Stade de France SA, 1995–98; Omnium de Traitement et de Valorisation, 1997–2001. *Recreations:* sailing, ski-ing. *Address:* 34 rue Rieussec, 78220 Viroflay, France. *T:* (1) 30245445.

**PARK, Hon. Sir Andrew (Edward Wilson)**, Kt 1997; a Judge of the High Court of Justice, Chancery Division, 1997–2006; *b* 27 Jan. 1939; *m* 1962, Ann Margaret Woodhead; two *s* one *d* (and one *s* decd). *Educ:* Leeds Grammar Sch.; University Coll., Oxford. Winter Williams Law Schol., 1959; BA (Jurisp.) 1960, MA 1964. FTII 1990. Various academic posts in UK and abroad, 1960–68. Called to the Bar, Lincoln's Inn, 1964, Bencher, 1986; QC 1978; QC (NI) 1992; a Recorder, 1989–94; practice at Revenue Bar, 1965–97. Chairman: Taxation and Retirement Benefits Cttee of the Bar Council, 1978–82; Revenue Bar Assoc., 1987–92; Treasurer, Senate of the Inns of Court and Bar, 1982–85. Hon. Pres., London Br., 2001–, Hon. Fellow, 2008, Chartered Inst. of Taxation. *Publications:* The Sources of Nigerian Law, 1963; various articles, notes and reviews in legal periodicals, mainly concerning taxation. *Recreations:* tennis, golf, watching Rugby League. *Address:* 10 New Road, Esher, Surrey KT10 9PG.

**PARK, David**; *see* Park, W. D.

**PARK, Gilbert Richard**, TD 1985; freelance journalist, since 2012; Consultant in Critical Care Medicine, North Middlesex University Hospital, 2009–12; specialist photographer, podcaster and videographer in medically related areas, since 2009; Secretary General, World Federation of Societies of Intensive and Critical Care Medicine, 2001–05; *b* 17 May 1950; *s* of Whyrill Heslop and Czeslawa Park; one *s* one *d*. *Educ:* Edinburgh Univ. (BSc; MB ChB; MD); MA Cantab; Anglia Ruskin Univ. (FdA 2010). FRCA 1976. Training posts in Edinburgh, 1974–83; Associate Lectr, Univ. of Cambridge, 1984–2010; Consultant in Anaesthesia and Intensive Care, 1983–2010, Dir, Intensive Care, 1985–2000, Addenbrooke's Hosp., Cambridge; Consultant in Anaesthesia and Resuscitation, RAMC, 1985–92. Hunterian Prof., RCS, 1986; Vis. Prof., Duke Univ., 1992. Non-exec. Dir, UK Transplant, 2001–05. Hon. Mem. Bulgarian Soc. of Anaesthetists, 2001; Academician, European Acad. of Anesthesiology, 2001. Hon. Dr of Med. Sci. Pleven, 1995. Freelance journalist on sailing and power boating. *Publications: jointly:* Intensive Care: a handbook, 1988; Anaesthesia and Intensive Care Information, 1989, 2nd edn 1995; The Management of Acute Pain, 1991, 2nd edn 2001; Sedation and Analgesia in the Critically Ill Patient, 1993; A Colour Atlas of Intensive Care, 1995; Fighting for Life, 1996; A Pocket Book of Pharmacology in the Critically Ill, 1996; Algorithms for Rational Prescribing in the Critically Ill, 1997; Handbook of drugs in intensive care: an A–Z guide, 2000; Anaesthesia and Intensive Care Information: key facts in anaesthesia and intensive care, 2002; (ed) Liver Disease, 1993; *edited jointly:* Anaesthesia and Intensive Care for Patients with Liver Disease, 1995; Sedation and Analgesia in the Critically Ill, 1995; Tricks and Traps, 1997; Sepsis in the Critically Ill, 1999; Beginners Guide to Fluid and Electrolyte Balance, 2000; Pharmacology in the Critically Ill, 2001; Top Tips in Intensive Care, 2001; 150 papers in learned jls; specialised educnl calendars; contrib. articles to sailing press. *Recreations:* landscape photography, hill walking, powerboating. *Address:* 2 Harbour Way, Emsworth, Hants PO10 7BE.

**PARK, Graham**; *see* Park, J. G.

**PARK, Ian Grahame**, CBE 1995; Chairman, Northcliffe Newspapers Group Ltd, 1995–2003 (Managing Director, 1982–95); Director, Daily Mail and General Trust plc, 1994–2009; *b* 15 May 1935; *s* of William Park and Christina (née Scott); *m* 1965, Anne Turner; one *s*. *Educ:* Lancaster Royal Grammar Sch.; Queens' Coll., Cambridge. 1st Bn Manchester Regt, Berlin (Nat. Service Commn), 1954–56. Trainee Journalist, Press and Journal, Aberdeen, 1959; Asst Lit. Editor, Sunday Times, 1960–63; various management posts, Thomson Newspapers, 1963–65; Liverpool Daily Post and Echo, 1965–82, Man. Dir and Editor in Chief, 1972–82; Dir, Associated Newspaper Holdings Ltd, 1983–95. Mem. Council, Newspaper Soc., 1967–95 (Pres., 1980–81); Dir, Press Assoc., 1973–83 (Chm., 1978–79 and 1979–80); Dir, Reuters, 1978–82, 1988–94. Mem. Newspaper Panel, Monopolies and Mergers Commn, 1986–95. Dir, Radio City (Sound of Merseyside Ltd), 1973–82; Dir, Liverpool Playhouse, 1973–80; Trustee, Blue Coat Soc. of Arts, Liverpool, 1973–82. FRSA. Gov. and Trustee, Dr Johnson's House Trust, 1996–2016. *Recreations:* eighteenth-century English pottery, twentieth-century English pictures. *Address:* c/o Daily Mail and General Trust plc, 2 Derry Street, W8 5TT. *Club:* Reform.

**PARK, (James) Graham**, CBE 1995; Consultant, H. L. F. Berry & Co. Solicitors, 2004–07 (Senior Partner, 1983–2003); Compliance Officer, Conservative Party, 1999–2006; *b* 27 April 1941; *s* of late Alderman James Park, OBE and Joan Park (née Sharp); *m* 1969, Susan Don; one *s*. *Educ:* Malvern Coll., Worcs; Manchester Univ. (LLB Hons). Articled, 1965; admitted as solicitor, 1968; Partner, H. L. F. Berry & Co. Solicitors, 1969–83. Mem., Parole Bd, 1996–2002 and 2003–10 (Appraiser, 2010–15); a Judge of First-tier Tribunal: Criminal Injuries Compensation (formerly Mem., Criminal Injuries Compensation Appeals Panel), 2000–11; Mental Health (formerly Mem., Mental Health Rev. Tribunal), 2003–12. Chm., Fitness to Practise Panel, NMC, 2012–. Chairman, Constituency Conservative Association: Knutsford, 1982–83; Altrincham and Sale, 1983–87; Chm., NW Area Cons. Assoc., 1992–95; Vice-Pres., 1996–98, Pres., 1998, Nat. Union of Cons. and Unionist Assocs; Pres., Nat. Cons. Convention and Mem., Bd of Mgt, 1998–99, Chm., Constitutional Cttee, 2000–06, Cons. Party; Chm., Cons. Party Conf., 1998. Chm., Financial Trustees, Cons. Agents' Benevolent Assoc., 2016–. Contested (C): Crewe, Feb. and Oct. 1974; Middleton and Prestwich, 1979. Mem. Court, Salford Univ., 1989–97. *Recreations:* cricket, motor-racing, cycling. *Address:* (office) 758 Oldham Road, Failsworth, Manchester M35 9XB. *T:* (0161) 681 4005.

**PARK, John William**; Public Policy, Amazon, since 2017; *b* 14 Sept. 1973; *s* of George and Elizabeth Park; two *d*. Electrical fitter, 1989–98, trade union convenor, 1998–2001, Rosyth Dockyard; Res. Officer, 2001–02, Nat. Industrial Campaigns Officer, 2002–03, AEEU, then Amicus; Hd, Employee Relns, Babcock Naval Services, 2003–04; Asst Sec., Scottish TUC, 2004–07. MSP (Lab) Mid Scotland and Fife, 2007–Dec. 2012. Policy and Strategy Dir, 2012–17, Asst Gen. Sec., 2013–17, Community.

**PARK, Dame Merle (Florence), (Dame Merle Bloch)**, DBE 1986 (CBE 1974); Principal, Royal Ballet, 1959–83; Director, Royal Ballet School, 1983–98; *b* Salisbury, S Rhodesia, 8 Oct. 1937; *d* of P. J. Park, Eastlea, Salisbury, S Rhodesia, C Africa; *m* 1st, 1965, James Monahan, CBE (marr. diss. 1970; he *d* 1985); one *s*; 2nd, 1971, Sidney Bloch (*d* 2000). *Educ:* Elmhurst Ballet Sch. Founder, Ballet Sch., St Peter's Sq., W6, 1977–83. Joined Sadler's Wells Ballet, 1955; first rôle, a Mouse (Sleeping Beauty prologue); first solo, Milkmaid (Façcze); principal soloist, 1959. First danced: Blue Bird (Act III, Sleeping Beauty), 1956; Swanhilda (Coppelia), Mamzelle Angot (Mamzelle Angot), 1958; Lise (Fille Mal Gardée), 1960; Cinderella, 1962; Juliet (Romeo and Juliet), 1965; Giselle, Celestial (Shadow Play), 1967; Clara (Nutcracker), Aurora (Sleeping Beauty), 1968; Odette (Swan Lake), 1971; A Walk to Paradise Garden, 1972; Firebird, Odette/Odile (Swan Lake), Dances at a Gathering, 1973; Manon, Emilia (The Moor's Pavane), Aureole, Terpsichore (Apollo), Elite Syncopations, 1974; Lulu, 1976; Kate (The Taming of the Shrew), La Bayadère, Tuesday's Child (Jazz Calendar), Triad, Symphonic Variations, Waltzes of Spring (in Royal Opera Fledermaus), Le Papillon, 1977; Countess Larisch (Mayerling), 1978; La Fin du Jour, 1979; Mary Vetsera (Mayerling), Natalia (A Month in the Country), Adieu, 1980; Chloë (Daphnis and Chloë), Isadora, 1981; Raymonda, 1983. Queen Elizabeth Award, Royal Acad. of Dancing, 1982. *Recreations:* gardening, coaching professionals, reading. *Address:* c/o Royal Ballet School, 46 Floral Street, Covent Garden, WC2E 9DA.

**PARK, Nicholas Wulstan**, CBE 1997; RDI 2006; director and animator of stop motion films; Partner, Aardman Animations Ltd, since 1995; *b* 6 Dec. 1958. *Educ:* Sheffield Poly., Faculty of Art and Design; National Film and TV Sch. Films include: A Grand Day Out, 1989 (BAFTA award for Best Animated Short, 1990); Creature Comforts, 1990 (Acad. Award for Best Animated Short, 1990); The Wrong Trousers, 1993 (Acad. Award and BAFTA award for Best Animated Short Film, 1993); A Close Shave, 1995 (Acad. Award and BAFTA award for Best Animated Film, 1995; Emmy for Best Popular Arts Programme, 1996); Chicken Run, 2000; Cracking Contraptions, 2002; Wallace and Gromit: the Curse of the Were-Rabbit, 2005 (Acad. Award and BAFTA Alexander Korda award, 2006); Wallace and Gromit: A Matter of Loaf and Death, 2008 (BAFTA award for Best Animated Short Film, 2009); (exec. prod.) Shaun the Sheep Movie, 2015; Early Man, 2018; TV series: Shaun the Sheep, BBC1, 2007–10. *Address:* Aardman Animations Ltd, 1410 Aztec West Business Park, Almondsbury, Bristol BS32 4RT. *T:* (01454) 859000.

**PARK, Stephen**, FCA, FCT; Managing Director, Park Consulting Ltd, since 2016; *b* 7 Aug. 1952; *m* Linda Susan; three *s* one *d*. FCA 1977; FCT 1992. Exec. coach and finance mentor, 2015–. *E:* Park.Stephen@btinternet.com.

**PARK, Prof. (William) David**, FSA; FIIC; Professor, Courtauld Institute of Art, London, 2008–18, now Emeritus (Director, Conservation of Wall Painting Department, 1985–2018; Director, Robert H. N. Ho Family Foundation Centre for Buddhist Art and Conservation, 2013–18); *b* 23 May 1952; *s* of late Bill and Elizabeth Park; *m* 1984, Leslie Ross (marr. diss. 1985). *Educ:* Dorking County Grammar Sch.; Univ. of Manchester (BA 1973, MA 1974); Corpus Christi Coll., Cambridge. FSA 1986. Leverhulme Res. Fellow, Courtauld Inst., London, 1980–85. Co-ordinator, Nat. Survey of Medieval Wall Painting, 1980–; Mem. Council, British Archaeol. Assoc., 1993–96; Chm., Paintings Cttee, Council for the Care of Churches, 1996–2006. Vis. Prof., Univ. Paris 1, Panthéon-Sorbonne, 2001. FIIC 2010. *Publications:* (ed with C. Norton) Cistercian Art and Architecture in the British Isles, 1986; (with C. Norton and P. Binski) Dominican Painting in East Anglia: the Thornham Parva

Retable and the Musée de Cluny Frontal, 1987; (ed with S. Cather and P. Williamson) Early Medieval Wall Painting and Painted Sculpture in England, 1990; (with S. Boldrick and P. Williamson) Wonder: painted sculpture from Medieval England, 2002; (ed with R. Griffith-Jones) The Temple Church in London: history, architecture, art, 2010; (jtly) Wall Paintings of Eton, 2012; (ed jtly) Art of Merit: studies in Buddhist art and its conservation, 2013; contrib. learned jls. *Recreation:* Paris. *Address:* The Clock House, Kirklees Hall, Clifton, Huddersfield HD6 4HD.

**PARKER,** family name of **Earls of Macclesfield** and **Morley**.

**PARKER, Sir Alan,** Kt 2014; Founder and Chairman, Brunswick Group LLP, since 2004 (Senior Partner, 1987–2004); UK Business Ambassador, since 2010; *b* 3 May 1956; *s* of Sir Peter Parker, KBE, LVO; *m* 1st, 1977, Caroline Louise (marr. diss. 2006), *d* of Thaddeus Gordon; one *s* three *d*; 2nd, 2007, Jane Hardman; three *s* one *d*. Dep. Man. Dir, Broad St Associates, 1982–87. Chairman: UK Now, 2011–; Duke of Edinburgh Commonwealth Study Conference, 2011–; Save the Children UK, 2008–15; Save the Children, 2016–18; Vice Chairman: China Now, 2008; Employment Opportunities; Trustee: Business Commitment to Envmt Leadership Awards scheme, 2007–; House of Illustration, 2007–; Queen Elizabeth Diamond Jubilee Trust, 2012–17. Mem. Council, Temenos Acad.; Bd Dir, FilmClub, 2008–; Mem., Adv. Bd, Videre, 2009–. Gov., SOAS, 2007–09 (Global Ambassador, 2011–). *Recreation:* friends. *Address:* Brunswick Group LLP, 16 Lincoln's Inn Fields, WC2A 3ED. *T:* (020) 7404 5959, *Fax:* (020) 7831 2823.

**PARKER, Alan Charles,** CBE 2008; private investor; non-executive Chairman, Mothercare, 2011–18 (Executive Chairman, 2011–12); *b* 25 Nov. 1946; *s* of Charles and Kathleen Parker; *m* 1st, 1974, Pauline Howell (*d* 2010); one *s* one *d*; 2nd, 2016, Susan Hooper. *Educ:* West Buckland Sch.; Univ. of Surrey (BSc Hotel Mgt); Harvard Business Sch. (AMP). Sales and Mktg Dir, Thistle Hotels, 1974–82; Sales and Mktg Dir, 1982–85, Man. Dir Europe, 1985–87, Crest Hotels; Sen. Vice Pres. for Europe, ME and Africa, Holiday Inn, 1987–92; Man. Dir, Whitbread Hotel Co., 1992–2004; Chief Exec., Whitbread plc, 2004–10. Chairman: Darty plc, 2012–16; Parkdean Resorts (formerly Park Resorts), 2014–17; non-executive Director: Jumeirah Group LLC, 2007–12; Restaurant Brands International (formerly Burger King Worldwide), 2012–16. Chm., British Hospitality Assoc., 2011–14 (Pres., 2014–18); Dir, World Travel and Tourism Council, 2003–10; Mem. Bd, VisitBritain, 2003–10. Vis. Prof., Univ. of Surrey, 2000. Trustee, West Buckland Sch., 2005–14 (Chm., Govs, 2011–14). FIH (FHCIMA 1992). Business Leader of the Year, 2003, Individual of the Year, 2009, Hotel Report Awards; inducted into British Travel Industry Hall of Fame, 2007; Lifetime Achievement Awards: Catey, 2010; Internat. Hotel Investment Forum, 2010. *Recreations:* sailing, Rugby, opera, ballet, Arsenal FC.

**PARKER, Alan Frank Neil;** charity trustee and education consultant; *b* 24 July 1953; *s* of Frank Parker, ISO and Joan Parker; *m* 1983, Valerie Shawcross, *qv* (marr. diss. 2002). *Educ:* Leicester Poly. (BA Hons 1977); Inst. of Education, London Univ. (MA Educn 1984). UK Council for Overseas Student Affairs, 1977–83; Sen. Adminr (Educn), ACC, 1984–85; Principal Officer (Colls), Surrey CC, 1986–89; Asst Sec. (Educn), 1990–92, Educn Officer, 1992–97, AMA; Dir of Educn, London Borough of Ealing, 1997–2002. Schools Adjudicator, 2004–12. Member, Examination Procedures Review Panel: Ofqual, 2013–; Qualifications Wales, 2017–. Vice-Pres., 2001, Pres., 2002, ConfEd (formerly Soc. of Educn Officers); Mem. Council, Assoc. of Dirs of Children's Services, 2007–08; Dir, Educn Law Assoc., 2018–. Dir and Trustee, NFER, 2002–17; Trustee, AEC Trust, 2015– (Chair, 2018–). FRSA 1996. MInstLM 2008. *Publications:* (contrib.) Visions of Post-Compulsory Education, 1992; (contrib. jtly) The Promises and Perils Facing Today's School Superintendent, 2002; Education and Inspections Act 2006: the essential guide, 2007; (contrib.) What's Next for Education?, 2015; pamphlets. *Recreations:* outdoor activities, visual and performing arts. *Address:* c/o AEC Trust, Brown Shipley, Founders Court, Lothbury, EC2R 7HE. *E:* alan.parker@blueyonder.co.uk.

**PARKER, Sir Alan (William),** Kt 2002; CBE 1995; film director and writer; Chairman, Film Council, 1999–2004; *b* 14 Feb. 1944; *s* of William and Elsie Parker; *m* 1st, 1966, Annie Inglis (marr. diss. 1992); three *s* one *d*; 2nd, 2001, Lisa Moran; one *s*. *Educ:* Owen's Sch., Islington. Advertising Copywriter, 1965–67; Television Commercials Director, 1968–78. Wrote screenplay, Melody, 1969; wrote and directed: No Hard Feelings, 1972; Our Cissy, 1973; Footsteps, 1973; Bugsy Malone, 1975; A Turnip Head's Guide to the British Cinema, 1985; Angel Heart, 1987; Come See the Paradise, 1990; The Road to Wellville, 1995; Evita, 1996; Angela's Ashes, 2000; directed: The Evacuees, 1974; Midnight Express, 1977; Fame, 1979; Shoot the Moon, 1981; The Wall, 1982; Birdy, 1984; Mississippi Burning, 1989; The Commitments, 1991; The Life of David Gale, 2003. Vice-Chm., Directors Guild of Great Britain, 1982–86; Chm., BFI, 1998–99. Pres., Eur. Fedn of Film Dirs, 2013–. Fellow, BAFTA, 2013. Hon. DLitt UEA, 1998; Hon. DArts: Sunderland, 2005; Southampton Solent, 2012. BAFTA Michael Balcon Award for Outstanding Contribution to British Film, 1985. Officier, Ordre des Arts et des Lettres (France), 2005. *Publications:* novels: Bugsy Malone, 1976; Puddles in the Lane, 1977; The Sucker's Kiss, 2003; cartoons: Hares in the Gate, 1983; Making Movies, 1998; Will Write and Direct For Food, 2005; non-fiction: The Making of Evita, 1997.

**PARKER, Sir Andrew,** KCB 2019; Director General, Security Service, since 2013. *Educ:* Univ. of Cambridge (BA Natural Scis). Security Service, 1983–: Dep. Dir Gen., 2007–13. *Address:* Security Service, PO Box 3255, SW1P 1AE.

**PARKER, Ann;** *see* Burdus, J. A.

**PARKER, Anne Mary,** CBE 1990; Chair, National Care Standards Commission, 2001–04; *b* 11 Oct. 1939; *d* of Daniel Morley and Mary Morley (*née* Waters); *m* 1968, Dr Andrew Parker (marr. diss. 2000). *Educ:* Notre Dame Grammar Sch., Blackburn; Univ. of Keele (BA Hons); Univ. of Manchester (AdvDip Social Admin; Hon. Fellow 1996). Berkshire County Council: Asst Co. Welfare Services Officer, 1967–71; Asst Dir, 1971–74, Dep. Dir, 1974–80, Dir, 1980–94, Social Services; Simon Fellow, Manchester Univ., 1994–95; freelance consultant, 1996–97; Ind. Case Examr, CSA, 1997–2001. Non-executive Director: Nestor Health Care, 1999–2001; Wirral Univ. Teaching Hosp. NHS Foundn Trust, 2005–13; Riverside Care and Support (formerly English Churches Housing Gp, then Riverside English Churches Housing Gp), 2008–17. Chairman: Complaints Panel, Audit Commn, 2004–07; Fitness to Practise Panel, NMC, 2012–13; Member: Health Educn Council, 1984–91; Criminal Injuries Compensation Appeals Panel, 2000–09; Ext. Reviewer, Office of Parly and Health Service Ombudsman, 2005–08. Board Member: Centre for Policy in Ageing, 1991–97 (Vice-Chm.); Carers Nat. Assoc., then Carers UK, 1995–2002 (Chm., 1998–2002). Hon. Sec., Assoc. of Dirs of Social Services, 1986–89. Mem. Bd, NISW, 1990–98 (Life Fellow, 1998). Mem. Bd, Anchor Trust, 1996–99; Trustee: Lloyds TSB Foundn, 2004–10; Church Homeless Trust (formerly Church Housing Trust), 2016–. *Address:* 50 Riverside Gardens, Romsey, Hants SO51 8HN. *T:* (01794) 518656. *E:* anne@annep1.plus.com.

**PARKER, Dr Becky,** MBE 2008; FRAS; Director, Institute for Research in Schools, since 2016; *b* Hitchin, Herts, 24 Oct. 1960; *d* of John and Kathleen Parker; *m* 2000, Peter Atkin; one *d*. *Educ:* Univ. of Sussex (BSc 1st Cl. Hons 1984); Univ. of Chicago. Teacher and Hd of Educn, Inst. of Physics, 1988–90; Sen. Lectr, Sch. of Physical Scis, Univ. of Kent, 2004–05; Hd of Physics, 2005–12, Dir, Langton Star Centre, 2008–16, Simon Langton Grammar Sch. for Boys. Acad. Visitor, Imperial Coll. London. Hon. FInstP 2014. Patrick Moore Medal, RAS, 2013; Kavli Educn Medal, Royal Soc., 2016. *Recreations:* playing the bassoon, swimming, walking, supporting my daughter in sailing. *Address:* Institute for Research in Schools, Wellcome Wolfson Building, 165 Queen's Gate, SW7 5HD.

**PARKER, Cameron Holdsworth,** CVO 2007; OBE 1993; JP; Lord-Lieutenant of Renfrewshire, 1998–2007; Vice-Chairman, Lithgows Ltd, 1991–97 (Managing Director, 1984–92); *b* 14 April 1932; *s* of George Cameron Parker and Mary Stevenson Parker; *m* 1st, 1957, Elizabeth Margaret Thomson (*d* 1985); three *s*; 2nd, 1986, Marlyne Honeyman, JP, FSI (*d* 2009). *Educ:* Morrison's Acad., Crieff; Glasgow Univ. (BSc Hons). John G. Kincaid & Co. Ltd, Greenock: Asst Manager, 1958; Asst Gen. Man., 1961; Dir, 1963; Man. Dir, 1967; Chm., 1976; Chm. and Chief Exec., Scott Lithgow Ltd, Port Glasgow, 1980–83. Bd Mem., British Shipbuilders, 1977–80, 1981–83. Director, 1984–94 (Chairman, 1984–92): Campbeltown Shipyard Ltd; J. Fleming Engrg Ltd; Glasgow Iron & Steel Co. Ltd; Landcatch Ltd; Lithgow Electronics Ltd; Malakoff & Wm Moore Ltd; McKinlay & Blair Ltd; Prosper Engrg Ltd; Director: Lithgows Pty Ltd, 1984–94; Scottish Homes, 1992–96; Clyde Shaw Ltd, 1992–94. Mem. Scottish Council, CBI, 1986–92. Mem., Argyll and Clyde Health Bd, 1991–95. Pres., SSAFA, Renfrewshire, 1998–2007. Hon. Pres., Accord Hospice, Paisley, 1998–2007. Freeman, City of London, 1981; Liveryman, Co. of Shipwrights, 1981–. DL 1993, JP 1998, Renfrewshire. DUniv Paisley, 2003. *Recreation:* golf. *Address:* Heath House, Rowantreehill Road, Kilmacolm, Renfrewshire PA13 4PE. *T:* (01505) 873197.

**PARKER, Charles Herbert;** Chief Executive, Baker Dearing Educational Trust, 2012–19 (Director of Operations, 2010–12); *b* 26 July 1953; *e s* of late Capt. Herbert Blake Parker, RN and of Diana Katharine Parker (*née* Barnwell); *m* 1977, Victoria Kathleen Scott (*d* 2017); two *s* one *d* (and one *d* decd). *Educ:* Winchester Coll.; Trinity Coll., Oxford (MA 1979); Insead (MBA 1982). Commercial Dir, Charter plc, 1990–96; Clerk to Mercers' Co., 1998–2008; Academies Advr, Partnerships for Schs, 2008–10. Director: Johnson Matthey plc, 1990–93; Cape plc, 1990–96; Faber Music Ltd, 2010–12. Gov., Royal Ballet Sch., 2000–09; Dir, Birmingham Royal Ballet, 2009–17. Governor: Thomas Telford Sch., 2002–08; Walsall Acad., 2003–08; Sandwell Acad., 2006–08. *Recreations:* shooting, classical ballet, cycling. *Address:* 147 Marsham Court, Marsham Street, SW1P 4LB. *Club:* Boodle's.
*See also* E. B. *Parker,* Gen. Sir N. R. *Parker.*

**PARKER, Charles Lucian Henry;** Chief Executive and Head of Public Service, States of Jersey, since 2018; *b* Kampala, Uganda, 3 April 1961; *s* of Malcolm and Bridget Parker; one *s* one *d*. *Educ:* Christ's Hosp. Sch.; Warwick Univ. (BA Hons). Dept of Employment, 1982–87; Thamesdown BC, 1987–90; Hd, Inner Cities, Manchester CC, 1990–95; Liverpool City Council: Dir, Speke-Garston Partnership, 1995–99; Exec. Dir, Regeneration, 1999–2006; Director: Enterprise plc, 2006–07; Investment, Finance and Performance, English Partnership, 2007–08; Chief Executive: Oldham MBC, 2008–14; Westminster CC, 2014–18. *Recreations:* swimming, cycling, walking, sailing, music, film, watching live sport and Manchester City FC. *Address:* States of Jersey, PO Box 140, 19–21 Broad Street, St Helier, Jersey JE2 3RR.

**PARKER, Christopher James Francis;** QC 2006; **His Honour Judge Christopher Parker;** a Circuit Judge, since 2012; *b* 22 June 1958; *s* of Bernard James and Peta Jocelyn Parker; *m* 1988, Stevie Jenkinson; one *s* one *d*. *Educ:* Ampleforth; Univ. of Exeter (LLB 1979). RN, 1980–88. Called to the Bar, Gray's Inn, 1986. *Address:* The Crown Court at Southampton, London Road, Southampton, Hants SO15 2XQ.

**PARKER, Christopher Roy;** QC 2008; *b* Leeds, 13 Oct. 1958; *s* of Roy and Margaret Parker; *m* 2000, Caroline Wilkinson; two *s*. *Educ:* Univ. of Oxford (MA, BCL); Univ. of Illinois (LLM); Harvard Univ. (LLM). Called to the Bar: Lincoln's Inn, 1984; BVI, 2006; in practice as barrister specialising in company law, insolvency, commercial fraud and trusts. *Recreations:* sailing, football, tennis. *Address:* Maitland Chambers, 7 Stone Buildings, Lincoln's Inn, WC2A 3SZ. *T:* (020) 7406 1200, *Fax:* (020) 7406 1300. *E:* cparker@maitlandchambers.com. *Clubs:* Chelsea Football; Royal Dart Yacht (Dartmouth).

**PARKER, Christopher Stuart,** CBE 1999; Headmaster, Nottingham High School, 1995–2007; *b* 16 Feb. 1947; *s* of late Gerald Stuart Parker and Brenda Mary Parker (*née* Briggs); *m* 1969, Margaret, *er d* of late Charles Godfrey Hannant and Frances Hannant; two *s*. *Educ:* Windsor Grammar Sch.; Bristol Univ. (BA 1968); St Catharine's Coll., Cambridge (PGCE 1969). Asst Master, Bedford Modern Sch., 1969–72; Head of Geography, Bradford Grammar Sch., 1972–78; Dep. Head, Goffs Sch., 1978–86; Headmaster, Batley Grammar Sch., 1986–95. HMC-OFSTED Lead Inspr, 1995–98; Member: Admiralty Interview Bd, 1990–97; Assisted Places Cttee, 1995–2004 (Chm., 2002–04); Jt Chair, HMC/GSA/Ind. Schs Bursars' Assoc. Assisted Places Wkg Party, 1996–98; Chairman: Assisted Places Cttee, 1996–2004, Bridges and Partnerships Cttee, 1998–99, HMC; Govt Adv. Gp on Independent/State Sch. Partnerships, 1997–2002; Jt Chm., LGA/ISC Cttee, 2001–04; Mem., Permanent Forum on Independent/State Sch. Partnerships, 2002–04 (Chm., Evaluation Cttee, 2002–04). Mem., Norfolk Wildlife Trust, 2009–; Friend, Sculthorpe Moor, Hawk and Owl Trust, 2010–; Mem., Friends of Horsey Seals, 2015–. Governor: Nottingham Trent Univ., 1996–99; Bedford Modern Sch., 2007–10; Trustee, Seckford Foundn, 2007–10. FRSA 1994. *Publications:* articles in American Jl of Geography, Envmt and Planning. *Recreations:* watching sport, travel, wildlife photography. *Address:* Mill End, 19 Mill Lane, Briston, Melton Constable, Norfolk NR24 2JG.
*See also* N. D. *Parker.*

**PARKER, Cornelia Ann,** OBE 2010; RA 2009; sculptor and installation artist; *b* Cheshire, 1956; *m* Jeff McMillan; one *d*. *Educ:* Glos Coll. of Art and Design; Wolverhampton Poly. (BA Hons 1978); Reading Univ. (MFA 1982). Sen. Fellow in Fine Art, Cardiff Inst., 1992–95; Prof. of Conceptual Art, Eur. Grad. Sch., Saas-Fee, Switzerland. *Works* include: Cold Dark Matter: An Exploded View, 1991; The Maybe, 1995; Hanging Fire (Suspected Arson), 1999; Shirt Burnt by a meteorite, 1997; Edge of England, 1999; Blue Shift, 2001; Subconscious of a Monument, 2002; The Distance (A Kiss with String Attached), 2003; Brontëan Abstracts, 2006; Never Endings, 2007, 2008; Chomskian Abstracts, 2008; Magna Carta, 2015; One More Time, 2015; *solo exhibitions* include: Stoke City Art Gall. and Mus., Stoke-on-Trent, 1980; Ikon Gall., Birmingham, 1988, 2007, 2014; Cornerhouse, Manchester, 1989; Chisenhale Gall., 1991; Whitechapel Gall., 1991, 2008, 2011; Gall. 102, 1993; Serpentine Gall., 1995, 1998; Chapter Arts Centre, Cardiff, 1996; Casa Masaccio, Italy, 1997; ArtPace, San Antonio, Deitch Projects, 1998; Frith Street Gall., 1999, 2002, 2008, 2013; Sci. Mus., Warburg Inst., 1999; ICA, Boston, ICA, Philadelphia, Aspen Art Mus., Arts Club, Chicago, 2000; Gall. Civica D'Arte Moderna, Turin, 2001; Finesilver Gall., 2003; Galerie Guy Bartschi, Geneva, 2003, 2008, 2014; D'Amelio Terras, NY, 2003, 2005, 2010; Galerie Carles Tache, Barcelona, 2004, 2008, 2013; Mus. and Art Gall., Norwich, Norwich Castle, 2004; RIBA, Modern Art Mus., Fort Worth, Texas, Württembergischer Kunstverein, Yerba Buena Center for Arts, San Francisco, 2005; Mus.

de Arte, Lima, 2008; Artland, Edinburgh, 2009; Baltic Centre for Contemp. Art, Two Rooms, NZ, 2010; York St Mary's, 2011; Whitworth Art Gall., Manchester, 2014, 2015, 2017; BL, Bodleian Liby, Univ. of Oxford, 2015; MOMA, NY, Metropolitan Mus. of Art, NY, Terrace Wires, St Pancras Internat., 2016; *group exhibitions* include: Ikon Gall., Birmingham, 1983; Whitechapel Gall., 1985, 1990, 1992, 2011, 2017; Kettle's Yard, Cambridge, 1990, 1991, 1998, 2001; Frith St Gall., 1995, 1997, 1999, 2001, 2002, 2006, 2010, 2014, 2017; Tate Gall., 1997; V&A Mus., 1998; Tate Modern, 2000; Tate Britain, 2003; Barbican Art Gall., 2008; Tate Liverpool, 2009, 2014; BM, 2009; MOMA, NY, 2010; RA Summer Exhibn, 2011, 2012, 2013, 2014, 2015, 2016, 2017; Wallace Collection, 2013; Holden Gall., Manchester Sch. of Art, 2013; Nitra Gall., Slovakia, 2013; Guggenheim Bilbao Mus., 2014; Gwangju Biennale, 2014; Jerwood Gall., Hastings, 2014; Dunedin Public Art Gall., 2015; Compton Verney, 2015; City Art Centre, 2016; Henry Moore Inst., 2016; *work in public collections* including: Arts Council of GB; British Council; BM; Fundacio La Caixa, Barcelona; Henry Moore Foundn; ICA, Boston; MOMA, NY; Musée d'Art Moderne/Centre Pompidou; Metropolitan Mus. of Art, NY; Tate Gall.; Royal Collection; V&A; curated exhibn, Foundling Mus., 2016. Hogarth Fellow, Foundling Mus., 2014. Vis. Fellow, LMH, Oxford, 2016–19. Hon. Dr: Wolverhampton, 2000; Birmingham, 2005; Gloucestershire, 2008. *Address*: c/o Frith Street Gallery, 17–18 Golden Square, W1F 9JJ.

**PARKER, Prof. David**, DPhil; FRS 2002; CChem, FRSC; Professor of Chemistry, Durham University, since 1992; *b* 30 July 1956; 2nd *s* of late Joseph William Parker and Mary Parker (*née* Hill); *m* 1979, Fiona Mary MacEwan; one *s* two *d*. *Educ*: Durham Johnston Sch.; King Edward VI Grammar Sch., Stafford; Christ Church, Oxford (BA, MA); Hertford Coll., Oxford (DPhil 1980). CChem 1989; FRSC 1992. NATO post-doctoral Fellow, Univ. Louis Pasteur, Strasbourg, 1980–81; Durham University: Lectr, 1982–89; Sen. Lectr, 1989–92; Hd, Dept of Chemistry, 1995–98 and 2003–06. Visiting Professor: Strasbourg, 1994; Monash, 1998 and 2006; Recognising Inspiration in Sci. and Engrg Fellow, EPSRC, 2014. Lectures: Iddles, Univ. of New Hampshire, 2003; Vielberth, Regensburg, 2004; Chem. Soc. Inaugural, UCD, 2006. Royal Society of Chemistry: Hickinbottom Fellowship, 1988–89; Tilden Lectr, 2003–04; Corday-Morgan Medal, 1987; Interdisciplinary Award, 1995; Supramolecular Chem. Award, 2002; Ludwig Mond Award, 2011; ICI Prize in Organic Chem., 1991; IBC Supramolecular Sci. and Technol. Award, 2000; Wolfson Res. Merit Award, Royal Soc., 2004–08; Lecoq de Boisbaudran Award, European Rare Earth Soc., 2012. *Publications*: Macrocycle Synthesis, 1996; patents; contrib. numerous papers, res. and rev. articles to learned jls. *Recreations*: cricket, golf, hill-walking, soccer. *Address*: Department of Chemistry, University of Durham, South Road, Durham DH1 3LE. *T*: (0191) 334 2033, *Fax*: (0191) 384 4737. *E*: david.parker@dur.ac.uk. *Club*: Durham City Cricket.

**PARKER, Rev. Prof. David Charles**, OBE 2015; DTh; FBA 2012; FSA; Professor of Digital Philology, Institute for Textual Scholarship and Electronic Editing, University of Birmingham, since 2017; *b* Boston, Lincs, 4 July 1953; *s* of Thomas Henry Louis and Mary Parker; *m* 1976, Karen Beaumont; two *s* two *d*. *Educ*: Univ. of St Andrews (MTh 1975); Emmanuel Coll., Cambridge (DipTh 1976); Rijksuniversiteit of Leiden (DTh 1990). Curate: St Paul's Ch, Mill Hill, London, 1977–80; Bladon with Woodstock, Dio. Oxford, 1980–85; Tutor in Biblical Studies, Queens' Coll., Birmingham, 1985–93; University of Birmingham: Lectr, 1993–96; Sen. Lectr, 1996–98; Reader, 1998–2001; Professor of New Testament Textual Criticism and Palaeography, 2001–05; Edward Cadbury Prof. of Theology, 2005–17. FSA 2009. Soc. of Royal Cumberland Youths, 2010. *Publications*: Paul's Letter to the Colossians by Philip Melanchthon, 1989; The New Testament in Greek IV, vol. 1, 1995, vol. 2, 2007; The Living Text of the Gospels, 1997; John Calvin, Commentarius in Epistolam Pauli ad Romanos, 1999; An Introduction to the New Testament Manuscripts and their Texts, 2008; Manuscripts, Texts, Theology: collected papers 1997–2007, 2009; Codex Sinaiticus: the story of the world's oldest Bible, 2010; Textual Scholarship and the Making of the New Testament, 2012. *Recreations*: bell-ringing, gardening. *Address*: Institute for Textual Scholarship and Electronic Editing, 3 Elms Road, University of Birmingham, Birmingham B15 2TT. *T*: (0121) 415 8341. *E*: d.c.parker@bham.ac.uk.

**PARKER, Diana Clare**; Partner, Withers LLP, since 1987; *b* Newcastle upon Tyne, 30 Oct. 1957; *m* 1991, Dr John Maxwell Landers, *qv*. *Educ*: Churchill Coll., Cambridge (BA 1979; MPhil 1980). Arbitrator 2012; MCIArb 2012. Admitted solicitor, 1983; Withers LLP, 1981–, specialising in family law, Chm., 1999–2007. Co-Founder, Family Mediators Assoc., 1985. *Recreation*: allotments. *Address*: Withers LLP, 20 Old Bailey, EC4M 7AN. *T*: (020) 7597 6198, *Fax*: (020) 7597 6543. *E*: diana.parker@withersworldwide.com.

**PARKER, (Diana) Jean**, CBE 1989; Director, Goldsborough Healthcare plc, 1994–97; *b* 7 June 1932; *d* of Lewis William Reeve Morley and Amy (*née* Southwood); *m* 1959, Dudley Frost Parker (*d* 1971); one *s* one *d*. *Educ*: Kesteven and Grantham Girls' Sch.; Birmingham Univ. (BCom). Director: Vacu-Lug Traction Tyres Ltd, 1957–2018; Central Independent Television Plc, 1982–97; British Steel (Industry) Ltd, 1986–90; Grantham and Dist Hosp. NHS Trust, 1995–98; Chm., Middle England Fine Food Ltd, 1995–2004. Mem. Bd, E Midlands Electricity, 1983–90; Mem., E Midlands, later Eastern Adv. Bd, National Westminster Bank, 1985–92. Chairman: Lincs Jt Develt Cttee, 1983–97; Chm., CBI Smaller Firms Council, 1986–88. Chm., N Lincs HA, 1987–90; non-exec. Dir, Lincs Ambulance and Health Service Trust, 1991–92; Chm., Lincs Community Council, 2000–03.

**PARKER, Edward Barnwell**; Co-Founder and Chief Executive, Walking with the Wounded, since 2010; *b* Petersfield, Hants, 13 Oct. 1965; *s* of late Capt. Herbert Blake Parker, RN and of Diana Katharine Parker (*née* Barnwell); *m* 1992, Harriet Douglas-Bate; three *c*. *Educ*: Winchester Coll.; RMA Sandhurst. Served Army, Royal Green Jackets, 1984–92; Cazenove & Co., 1992–95; Man. Dir, Salomon Bros, then Citigroup, 1995–2003; Edward Parker Wines, 2003–12. Advr, EEF Expeditions Ltd, 2013–. Ambassador, SkillForce, 2011–. Mem. Adv. Bd, Endeavour Fund, 2012–. *Recreations*: theatre, walking, cinema, sailing, family holidays, Norwich City Football Club, successfully skied to North Pole in 2011 and South Pole in 2013, completed Marathon des Sables, 2016. *Address*: Walking with the Wounded, Stody Hall Barns, Stody, Melton Constable, Norfolk NR24 2ED. *T*: (01263) 863900. *E*: edward@wwtw.org.uk.

*See also* C. H. Parker, Gen. Sir N. R. Parker.

**PARKER, Frederick John, (Jack)**, FICE, FIStructE, FCIHT; Chief Highway Engineer (Under Secretary), Department of Transport, 1988–91; *b* 6 Sept. 1927; *s* of Charles Fred Parker and Eleanor Emily (*née* Wright); *m* 1955, Ann Shirley Newnham; three *d*. *Educ*: Shene Grammar School; Univ. of Liverpool (BEng 1948; MEng 1951). Engineer with Scott, Wilson, Kirkpatrick & Partners in London, Hong Kong and elsewhere, 1952–65; Sen. Engineer, then Partner, with Husband & Co., 1965–78; Director, W. S. Atkins & Partners, 1978–88. Institution of Highways and Transportation: Chm., Greater London Br., 1975–77; Vice-Pres., 1985; Pres., 1988. Vice-Chm., Brit. Nat. Cttee of Permanent Internat. Assoc. of Road Congresses, 1988–91. *Publications*: professional papers in engineering jls. *Recreations*: athletics (Olympics 1952 and 1956, European silver medallist 1954); local affairs, music. *Address*: 83A Temple Sheen Road, East Sheen, SW14 7RS. *T*: (020) 8876 1059. *Clubs*: South London Harriers (Pres., 2016–18); Probus (Barnes, Sheen and Mortlake) (Pres., 2011–).

**PARKER, Air Vice-Marshal Gavin Douglas Anthony**, CB 2019; OBE 2009; Defence Attaché and Head of the British Defence Staff, Washington DC, since 2017; *b* Harare, 22 Feb. 1969; *s* of late John Anthony Grindal Parker and Elizabeth Agnes Hope Parker; *m* 2013, Lucy Rose; one *s* five *d*. *Educ*: Newcastle Univ. (BSc Hons Physics 1990); MA Defence Studies. Commnd RAF, 1990; completed fast jet pilot trng, 1993; AO Scotland, 2011–13; ACOS PJHQ J5, 2013–15; AOC No 2 Gp, 2015–17. *Address*: British Embassy, 3100 Massachusetts Avenue NW, Washington, DC 20008–3600, USA. *T*: (202) 5886703. *E*: Gavin.Parker542@mod.gov.uk.

**PARKER, Geoffrey**; *see* Parker, N. G.

**PARKER, Prof. Geoffrey Alan**, FRS 1989; Derby Professor of Zoology, School of Biological Sciences, University of Liverpool, 1996–2009, now Emeritus; *b* 24 May 1944; *s* of late Dr Alan Parker and G. Ethel Parker (*née* Hill); *m* 1st, 1967, Susan Mary Wallis (*d* 1994); one *s* one *d*; 2nd, 1997, Carol Elizabeth Emmett; one step *d*. *Educ*: Stockton Heath Primary Sch.; Lymm Grammar Sch.; Univ. of Bristol (BSc (1st Cl. Hons Zoology; Rose Bracher Prize for Biology); PhD); Univ. of Cambridge (MA). University of Liverpool: Asst Lectr, 1968–69; Lectr, 1969–76; Sen. Lectr, 1976–80; Reader, 1980–89; Prof. in Dept of Envmtl and Evolutionary Biol., 1989–96. Fellow of King's Coll., Cambridge, 1978–79; Nuffield Sci. Res. Fellow, 1982–83; BBSRC (formerly SERC) Sen. Res. Fellow, 1990–95. Lectures: Niko Tinbergen, Assoc. for Study of Animal Behaviour, 1995; Hamilton, Internat. Soc. for Behavioural Ecology, 2006; 13th Immlemann, Univ. of Bielefeld, 2014; Annual Chris Barnard, Univ. of Nottingham, 2016. Hon. FRES 2012. Hon. DSc: Bristol, 2011; Memorial Univ. of Newfoundland, 2018. Medal, Assoc. for Study of Animal Behaviour, 2002; Dist. Animal Behaviorist Award, Animal Behavior Soc., 2003; Spallanzani Medal, 8th Biology of Spermatozoa Conf., 2005; Frink Medal, Zool Soc. of London, 2005; Dist. Zoologist Award, Benelux Congress of Zoology, 2007; Darwin Medal, Royal Soc., 2008. *Publications*: (jtly) Evolution of Sibling Rivalry, 1997; over 200 papers in learned jls. *Recreations*: playing Dixieland and Mainstream jazz in local bands (clarinet and tenor saxophone); breeding, showing and judging exhibition bantams (Hon. Sec./Treasurer, 1987–94, Pres., 2002–, Partridge & Pencilled Wyandotte Club; Mem. Council, 1986–90, 2004–08, Pres., 2003–06, Poultry Club; Vice-Pres., Plymouth Rock Club, 2002–05; Supreme Champion, Nat. Poultry Club GB Show, 1997; Championship Judge, Nat. Fedn Poultry Clubs Show, 2011). *Address*: Saunton, The Runnel, Neston, South Wirral, Cheshire CH64 3TG. *T*: (0151) 336 4202.

**PARKER, Geoffrey John**, CBE 1985; Deputy Chairman, Maritime Transport Services Ltd, 1997–98 (Chief Executive, 1989–97); Chairman, Thamesport (London) Ltd, 1997–98; *b* 20 March 1937; *s* of Stanley John Parker and Alice Ellen Parker; *m* 1957, Hazel Mary Miall; two *s* two *d*. *Educ*: County Grammar Sch., Hendon. Commercial Dir, Townsend Car Ferries Ltd, 1972–74; Man. Dir, Atlantic Steam Navigation Co., 1974–87; Man. Dir, 1976–87, Chm., 1983–87, Felixstowe Dock & Rly Co.; Chairman: Larne Harbour Bd, 1983–87; European Ferries PLC, 1986–87; Chief Exec., Highland Participants, 1987–89. Mem., Nat. Bus Co., 1980–87. FCIT 1982. *Recreation*: golf. *Address*: 101 Valley Road, Ipswich, Suffolk IP1 4NF. *T*: (01473) 216003. *Clubs*: Ipswich and Suffolk (Ipswich); Ipswich Golf (Purdis Heath, Ipswich).

**PARKER, George William**; Political Editor, Financial Times, since 2007; *b* Guildford, 19 Jan. 1966; *s* of John Parker and Margaret Parker; *m* 1992, Gabrielle O'Neill; one *s* two *d*. *Educ*: Tiverton Comp. Sch.; Queen Mary Coll., Univ. of London (BA Geog.); City Univ. (Dip. Newspaper Journalism). Western Morning News: North Devon reporter, 1988–89; industrial corresp., 1989–90; political corresp., 1990–95; Financial Times: political corresp., 1995–99; UK News Editor, 1999–2002; Bureau Chief, Brussels, 2002–07. Presenter, Week in Westminster, 2010–, What the Papers Say, 2010–, BBC Radio 4. *Recreations*: cycling, football, cricket. *Address*: 15 Defoe Avenue, Richmond, Surrey TW9 4DL. *T*: 07872 156468. *E*: george.parker@ft.com.

**PARKER, Guy**; Chief Executive, Advertising Standards Authority, since 2009; *b* London, 4 Dec. 1969; *s* of late Jonathan and Nicola Parker; *m* 2002, Camilla Dexter; two *s* one *d*. *Educ*: Wellington Coll., Berks; Univ. of Kent, Canterbury (BA Politics and Internat. Relns); Watford Coll. (Dip. Advertising). Investigations Exec., ASA; Committee of Advertising Practice: Copy Advice Exec., 1994–97; Copy Advice Manager, 1997–99; Asst Sec., 1999–2001; Sec., 2001–04; Dir, Complaints and Investigations, 2004–09, Dep. Dir Gen., 2008–09, Advertising Standards Authy. Mem. Bd and Exec. Cttee, 2007–, Chm., 2013–16, Eur. Advertising Standards Alliance; Mem. Bd and Exec. Cttee, 2015–, Vice Pres., 2019–, Internat. Council for Advertising Self-Regulation. *Recreations*: family, history, science, walking, cricket. *Address*: Advertising Standards Authority, Mid City Place, 71 High Holborn, WC1V 6QT. *E*: guyp@asa.org.uk.

**PARKER, Rear Adm. Henry Hardyman**, CB 2016; Director (Ships Acquisition), since 2014; (retired RN 2016); Head, Royal Corps of Naval Constructors, since 2017; *b* Cheltenham, 20 Dec. 1963; *s* of William John Parker and Sidsel Annette Parker; *m* 1999, Dr Katherine Bristol; three *s* one *d*. *Educ*: Cheltenham Coll., Pembroke Coll., Cambridge (BA Engrg 1986); Open Univ. (PhD Evolutionary Ecol. 1995). Joined RN, 1983; Weapon Engrg Officer, HMS Invincible, 2000–01; Mil. Asst to Chief of Defence Staff, 2001–03; seconded to BAE Systems, Barrow, 2003–05; Asst Naval Attaché, Washington, DC, 2005–07; Chief Engr, Successor Prog., 2007–11; Dir (Precision Attack) and Controller of the Navy, 2012–13; Dir (Carrier Strike), 2013–14. *Publications*: three papers on landlocked Arctic Charr. *Recreations*: fishing, sailing, walking, choir, heavy duty gardening. *Address*: c/o Naval Secretary, Leech Building, Fleet Headquarters, Whale Island, Portsmouth PO2 8BY. *Club*: Leander.

**PARKER, Prof. Ian**, PhD; FRS 2008; Professor of Neurobiology and Behavior, since 1995, and Professor of Physiology and Biophysics, since 2006, University of California, Irvine; *b* 6 Jan. 1951. *Educ*: University Coll. London (BSc Physiol. 1972; PhD Physiol. 1984). Res. Asst, Dept of Biophysics, UCL, 1975–84; University of California, Irvine: Asst Prof., 1984–90, Associate Prof., 1990–95, Dept of Psychobiol.; Co-Dir, Imaging Core Centre for Hearing Res., 2007–. Vis. Prof., Dept of Physiol., Univ. of Maryland Sch. of Medicine, 1995–96. Member, Editorial Board: Jl Gen. Physiol., 1998–; Biophysical Jl, 2006–. Mem., Internat. Jt Projects Cttee, Royal Soc., 2009–13. FAAAS 2009. *Publications*: (contrib.) Handbook of Nonlinear Optical Spectroscopy, 2008; contribs to jls incl. Biophysical Jl, Jl Cell Biol., Jl Gen. Physiol., Cell Calcium, Immunol., Science. *Address*: Department of Neurobiology and Behavior, University of California, Irvine, CA 92697–4550, USA.

**PARKER, Jack**; *see* Parker, F. J.

**PARKER, James Frederick Somerville;** Vice Lord-Lieutenant, Stirling and Falkirk, 2011–17; *b* Campsie Glen, Stirlingshire, 10 July 1941; *s* of George Coats Parker and Helena Bettys Adelaide Somerville (*née* Buckmaster); *m* 1968, Rosemary Janice Skelton; two *s* one *d*. *Educ*: Winchester Coll.; Univ. of Newcastle upon Tyne (BA Econ. Studies). Mitsubishi Heavy Industries, 1966; Elliott Automation Ltd, 1967–69; Hawker Siddeley Dynamics Ltd, 1970–72; J & J Denholm Ltd, 1972–2012. DL Stirling and Falkirk, 1991. *Recreations*: shooting, stalking, fishing, gardening. *Address*: The Moss, Killearn, Stirlingshire G63 9LJ. *T*: (01360) 550053. *E*: themoss@freeuk.com. *Club*: Western (Glasgow).

**PARKER, Dr James Gordon,** OBE 2002; Co-ordinator, International Public Lending Right Network, since 1995; Head of Public Lending Right, 2013–14 (Registrar, 1991–2013); *b* 1 June 1952; *s* of James Frank Taylor Parker and Mary Hutchison Gordon; *m* 1975, Catherine Ann Hyndman; one *s* one *d*. *Educ*: Stranraer High Sch.; Edinburgh Univ. (MA 1st Cl. Hons History 1974; PhD 1977). Vans Dunlop Res. Schol., Edinburgh Univ., 1974–77; Carnegie Travelling Schol. to India, 1976; Royal Commission on Historical Manuscripts: Res. Asst, 1977–87; Asst Keeper, resp. for Nat. Register of Archives, 1987–91. Mem., Adv. Cttee, 1991–2006, Chm., Mgt Bd, 2009–13, PLR. Patron, Laser Foundn, 2001–07. Trustee, William Hall Trust, 2019–. Benson Medal, RSL, 2004; Medalha de Honra, Sociedade Portuguesa de Autores, 2009. *Publications*: (contrib.) The Scots Abroad, 1985; Bibliographies of British Statesmen No 5 (Lord Curzon), 1991; (contrib.) International Directory of Company Histories, vol. 4, 1991; (ed) Proceedings of the First International Conference on Authors' Lending Right, 1996; (ed) Whose Loan is it Anyway?: essays in celebration of PLR's 20th anniversary, 1999; Public Lending Right: an introductory guide, 2016; contrib. New DNB; reviews and contribs to learned jls. *Recreations*: golf, gardening, family. *Address*: 14 Ash Grove, Kirklevington, Yarm, Stockton-on-Tees TS15 9NQ. *T*: (01642) 791445. *E*: parker-j20@sky.com.

**PARKER, James Mavin, (Jim Parker);** composer and conductor; *b* Hartlepool, 18 Dec. 1934; *s* of James Robertson Parker and Margaret Mavin; *m* 1969, Pauline George; two *d*; one *d* by a previous marriage. *Educ*: various grammar schools; Guildhall Sch. of Music (AGSM 1959; Silver Medal; Hon. GSM 1986). LRAM 1959. Professional oboeist, 1959; joined the Barrow Poets, 1963. Wrote musical settings of Sir John Betjeman's poems, Banana Blush, 1973 (recorded these and subsequent settings with Sir John as speaker); wrote music for Chichester Theatre, 1974–77; music for television and films, 1977–, includes: Credo; Another Six English Towns; Good Behaviour; Wynne and Penkovsky; Mapp and Lucia; Time After Time; Betjeman's Britain; Late Flowering Love; The Miser; España Viva; The Blot (silent film made in 1921); Girl Shy (Harold Lloyd silent film); Wish Me Luck; House of Cards; Parnell and the Englishwoman; The House of Eliott; Soldier Soldier; Body and Soul; To Play the King (BAFTA award for best TV music, 1993); Goggle Eyes; Late Flowering Lust; Moll Flanders (BAFTA award, 1996); Tom Jones (BAFTA award, 1997); A Rather English Marriage (BAFTA award, 1998); The Midsomer Murders; Born and Bred; Foyle's War. *Compositions* include: with William Bealby-Wright: Moonshine Rock, 1972; Mister Skillicorn Dances, 1974; with Cicely Herbert: Mayhew's London, 1978; La Comédie Humaine, 1986; (with John Betjeman) Poems (ballet), 1981; In The Gold Room (words by Oscar Wilde), 1983; (with Jeremy Lloyd) The Woodland Gospels, 1984; (with John Edmunds) Pelican Five, 1986. Recordings with Barrow Poets, Keith Michell, Peter Sellers, Harry Secombe, Twiggy, etc. *Publications*: (with Wally K. Daly) Follow the Star, 1975; (with Jeremy Lloyd) Captain Beaky, 1977; with Tom Stanier: The Shepherd King, 1979; The Burning Bush, 1980; All Aboard, 1983; Blast Off, 1986; A Londoner in New York (suite for brass), 1986; (with Tom Stanier and Chris Ellis) Babylon Times, 1988; English Towns (for flute and piano), 1988; Mississippi Five (woodwind quintet), 1991; Lullingstone (for concert band), 1986; The Golden Section (brass quintet), 1993; Concerto for clarinet and strings, 1994; (with Alan Platt) The Happy Prince (one act opera), 1995; Light Fantastic (for string sextet or ten brass), 2002; Boulevard (for woodwind quintet), 2006; Mexican Wildlife (for brass quintet), 2006; Fat Tuesday in New Orleans (for concert wind band), 2007; Bonjour M Grappelli (string quartet), 2013; A South American Journey (for recorder and harpsichord), 2014; Hoofers (sonata for oboe and piano), 2015; Paean, 2016. *Recreations*: literature, 20th Century art. *Address*: 16 Laurel Road, Barnes, SW13 0EE. *T*: (020) 8876 8442.

**PARKER, Jean;** *see* Parker, D. J.

**PARKER, Sir John;** *see* Parker, Sir T. J.

**PARKER, Prof. John Stewart,** DPhil; FLS; VMH; Director, Botanic Garden, and Professor of Plant Cytogenetics, 1996–2010, Curator, Herbarium, 2001–10, University of Cambridge; Fellow, Clare Hall, Cambridge, 2007–15, now Emeritus (Vice-President, 2013–15); *b* 12 July 1945; *s* of George Parker and Helen Parker (*née* Teare); *m* 1970, Iris Veronica Berry (marr. diss.); two *s*; *m* 1999, Mary Elizabeth Edmunds. *Educ*: Birkenhead Sch.; Christ Church, Oxford (BA 1966; MA 1970; DPhil 1971). Lectr, 1969–90, Reader, 1990–92, QMC; Prof. of Botany, Univ. of Reading, 1992–96; Fellow, St Catharine's Coll., Cambridge, 1997–2007. Dir, NIAB, 2004–09 (Mem. Council, 1998–2001). Mem. Council, RHS, 1998–99. Trustee: Royal Botanic Gardens, Kew, 1996–2002; Brogdale Horticultural Trust, 1999–2004; Science and Plants for Schs, 1998–2008; Sci. Cttee, Mendel Mus., Brno, 2002–04 (Advr and Designer, Genetic Gdn). Reina Victoria Eugenia Chair, Complutense Univ., Madrid, 2007–08; Advr, Dean of Biol Scis, Univ. of Vienna, 2010–14. Mem. Bd, Darwin Correspondence Project Adv. Bd, 2014–. Hon. Res. Fellow, Natural History Mus., 1995–2005. FLS 1998. VMH 2012. *Publications*: (jtly) The Sainsbury Laboratory: science, architecture, art, 2012; numerous papers in scientific jls. *Recreations*: church architecture, bird watching, landscape history, gardening, apples and cheese. *Address*: Clare Hall, University of Cambridge, Herschel Road, Cambridge CB3 9AL.

**PARKER, Rt Hon. Sir Jonathan (Frederic),** Kt 1991; PC 2000; a Lord Justice of Appeal, 2000–07; a Justice of Appeal, Gibraltar, 2010–15; *b* 8 Dec. 1937; *s* of late Sir (Walter) Edmund Parker, CBE and late Elizabeth Mary Butterfield; *m* 1967, Maria-Belen Burns; three *s* one *d*. *Educ*: Winchester College; Magdalene College, Cambridge (MA). Called to Bar, Inner Temple, 1962, Bencher, 1985; practising member of the Bar, 1962–91; QC 1979; a Recorder, 1989–91; Attorney Gen. of Duchy of Lancaster, 1989–91; Judge of the High Court of Justice, Chancery Div., 1991–2000; Vice Chancellor, Co. Palatine of Lancaster, 1994–98. *Recreations*: painting, reading. *Address*: The Grange, Radwinter, Saffron Walden, Essex CB10 2TF. *Club*: Garrick.

**PARKER, Hon. Dame Judith Mary Frances,** DBE 2008; a Judge of the High Court, Family Division, 2008–19; *b* 19 June 1950. *Educ*: Univ. of Oxford (BA Juris. 1972). Called to the Bar, Middle Temple, 1973, Bencher, 2000 (Autumn Reader, 2013; Co-Master of the Garden); QC 1991; Asst Recorder, 1998–2000; Recorder, 2000–08.

**PARKER, Hon. Sir Kenneth (Blades),** Kt 2009; a Judge of the High Court of Justice, Queen's Bench Division, 2009–15; *b* 20 Nov. 1945; *s* of Rudolph Parker, Capt., Argyll and Sutherland Highlanders and Catherine (*née* Boyd); *m* 1967, Margaretha Constance Beyerman; three *s* one *d*. *Educ*: Kettering Grammar Sch.; Exeter Coll., Oxford (Class. Schol.; 1st cl. Lit. Hum. 1968; 1st cl. BCL 1973; Vinerian Schol.). Lectr in Law, Univ. of Oxford and Fellow, Exeter Coll., Oxford, 1973–76; called to the Bar, Gray's Inn, 1975, Bencher, 2002; QC 1992; Recorder, 2000–09; Dep. High Ct Judge, 2006–09; a Law Comr, 2000–09. Judicial Comr, Office of Investigatory Powers Comr, 2017–. Specialist Advr, H of C Select Cttee for Trade and Ind., 1991. Mem., Information Tribunal, 2002–10. *Publications*: (Asst Ed.) Chitty on Contracts, 23rd edn, 1972; (contrib.) Common Market Law of Competition, 1987. *Recreations*: tennis, ski-ing.

**PARKER, Lyn;** Chef de Cabinet, President of the International Criminal Court, 2011–16; *b* 25 Nov. 1952; *s* of Ronald Arthur Parker and Tjardina Torrenga; *m* 1991, Jane Elizabeth Walker; two *d*. *Educ*: King's Sch., Canterbury; Magdalen Coll., Oxford (BA Jurisprudence); Manchester Univ. (MA European Community Studies). Lectr in Law, Manchester Univ., 1975–78; joined HM Diplomatic Service, 1978; Second, later First, Sec., Athens, 1980–84; FCO, 1984–88; Cabinet Office, 1989–91; Head of Chancery and Political Counsellor, New Delhi, 1992–95; Counsellor (Political), UK Perm. Repn to EU, Brussels, 1995–99; Hd, Whitehall Liaison Dept, FCO, 1999–2001; High Comr to Cyprus, 2001–05; Ambassador to the Netherlands, 2005–09. *Recreations*: music, sailing, cycling.

**PARKER, (Lynda) Tanya;** a Deputy Upper Tribunal Judge (formerly a Deputy Social Security and Child Support Commissioner), 2008–16; *d* of Sidney Sansom and Olive May (*née* Hudson); *m* 1968, Prof. David Francis Parker; two *c*. *Educ*: Manchester Univ. (LLB); Univ. of Calif, Berkeley (LLM). Called to the Bar, Gray's Inn, 1966; Associate WS, 2002. Lecturer: Nottingham Univ., 1966–73; Univ. of WI, 1970–72 (on secondment). Regl Chm., Appeals Service, 1991–2000; Social Security and Child Support Comr, 2000–08; a Dep. First-tier Tribunal Judge, War Pensions and Armed Forces Compensation Chamber (formerly Chm., Pensions Appeal Tribunal), 2001–13; Dep. Social Security Comr for NI, 2006–11. *Recreations*: friends, travel, performing and visual arts. *Club*: Royal Over-Seas League.

**PARKER, Margaret Lucille Jeanne, (Margot);** Member (UK Ind) East Midlands Region, European Parliament, 2014–19; *b* Grantham, 24 July 1943; *m*; two *s*. Gp buyer, S American lingerie co., 1989–95; Sales Dir, Itelsa Inc., 1996–2003; Sales Dir, bespoke fragrance co., 2003–08; Dir and Hd of Communications, Eur. Promotional Products Assoc., 2003–07; Dir and Eur. spokesman, British Promotional Merchandise Assoc., 1996– (Sword of Honour and Fellow, 2007). Contested (UK Ind): Sherwood, 2010; Corby and E Northants, Nov. 2012.

**PARKER, Ven. Matthew John;** Archdeacon of Stoke-upon-Trent, since 2013; *b* Manchester, 1 June 1963; *s* of Michael and Carol Parker; *m* 1988, Sarah Pym; one *s* two *d*. *Educ*: Bishop Wand Sch., Sunbury-on-Thames; Univ. of Manchester (BA English Lit. 1985); Sidney Sussex Coll., Cambridge (BA 1988); Ridley Hall, Cambridge. Ordained deacon, 1988, priest, 1989; Assistant Curate: St Mary's, Twickenham, 1988–91; St George's, Stockport, 1991–94; Team Vicar, Stockport SW Team, 1993–2000; Team Rector, Leek and Meerbrook Team, 2000–13; Rural Dean, Leek, 2007–13. Hon. Canon, Lichfield Cathedral, 2013–. Chair, Moorlands Together Local Strategic Partnership, 2004–07. Chaplain, Stockport Grammar Sch., 1991–94. *Recreations*: theatre, book club, music, family, Staffordshire bull terrier. *Address*: 39 The Brackens, Newcastle under Lyme, Staffs ST5 4JL. *T*: (01782) 663066. *E*: archdeacon.stoke@lichfield.anglican.org.

**PARKER, Major Sir Michael (John),** KCVO 2000 (CVO 1991); CBE 1996 (MBE (mil.) 1968); Producer: Royal Tournament, 1974–99; Edinburgh Tattoo, 1991–94; 320 royal and national celebrations around the world, 1965–2010; *b* 21 Sept. 1941; *s* of Capt. S. J. Wilkins and V. S. M. Wilkins (*née* Parker); name changed by Deed Poll, 1959; *m* 2005, Emma Bagwell Purefoy (*née* Gilroy). *Educ*: Dulwich Coll. Prep. Sch.; Hereford Cathedral Sch.; RMA Sandhurst. Captain, Queen's Own Hussars, 1961–71 (produced Berlin Tattoo, 1965, 1967 and 1971), Major, TA, Special List, attached QOH, 1973–2003. Producer of 320 royal, nat. celebrations and international events, 1972–2010: Berlin Tattoo, 1972–88, Bandanza, 1990; Last Tattoo, 1992; Aldershot Army Display, 1974–83; Queen's Bonfire, Windsor and others, Queen's Silver Jubilee, 1977; Wembley Musical Pageant, 1969, 1979, 1981, 1985; Great Children's Party for Internat. Year of the Child, 1979; Carols for the Queen, 1979; Royal Fireworks (Prince of Wales's wedding), 1981; Heart of the Nation, son et lumière, Horse Guards, 1983, 1985; Royal Ball for America's Cup, Newport, 1983; Great St John Party (180,000 children), Hyde Park, 1985; King Hussein of Jordan's 50th Birthday Celebration, 1985; Finale, Christmas Horse Show, Olympia, 1986–2004; SSAFA, Queen's Shilling, Royal Albert Hall, 1987; Jordanian Royal Wedding, 1987 (of Prince Feisal); Coronation Anniversary Celebration, Jordan, 1988; Joy to the World, Royal Albert Hall, 1988–97; Royal Equestrian Day, Oman, 1990; Fortress Fantasia, Gibraltar, 1990; Queen Mother's 90th Birthday Celebration, Horse Guards, 1990; Opening Ceremony, World Equestrian Games, Stockholm, 1990; Economic Summit Spectacular, Buckingham Palace, 1991; British Nat. Day Expo '92, Seville, 1992; The Queen's 40th Anniversary Celebration, 1992; Memphis in May Internat. Tattoo, 1992–94; King Hussein of Jordan's 40th Anniversary Celebrations, Unveiling of Queen Elizabeth Gate in Hyde Park, 1993; Jordanian Royal Wedding, 1993 (of Prince Abdullah); Channel Tunnel Gala Fireworks Display, D-Day Celebrations in Portsmouth, Normandy Veterans, RAH, Army Benevolent Fund, Drumhead Service, Royal Hosp. Chelsea, (opening and finale) Pavarotti, Internat. Horse Show Modena Italy, P&O ship naming, China, 1994; P&O ship naming, Portsmouth, VE Day 50th Anniversary Celebrations in Hyde Park and Buckingham Palace, VJ 50th Anniversary Celebrations on Horse Guards, Jersey Liberation Fireworks, Horse Show in Santa Barbara, 1995; Tri Service Massed Bands, Horse Guards, 1995; Oriana Gala, Sydney, 1996; Dawn Princess Naming, Fort Lauderdale, and The Countryside Rally, Hyde Park, 1997; Grand Princess Gala Naming, NY, 1998; Fireworks, Royal Windsor Horse Show, 1998–2004; re-opening of Albert Memorial, Hyde Park, 1998; Centenary Celebrations for King Abdul Aziz al Saud, Saudi Arabia, 1999; Royal Mil. Tattoo, Horse Guards, 2000; Queen Mother's 100th birthday celebrations, Horse Guards, 2000; All The Queen's Horses, Windsor, 2002; London Golden Jubilee Weekend Fest., June 2002, incl. nat. beacon, fireworks and nat. processions; Opening of Meml Gates, Constitution Hill, 2002; opening of Memphis SO, Canon Performing Arts Center, 2003; Minerva II ship naming, Port of London, 2003; Centenary Celebration, Royal Welsh Agricl Show, 2004; Music on Fire!, RMA Sandhurst, 2004, 2006, 2008; 60th Anniv. Liberation Celebrations, Jersey, 2005; RYS Trafalgar 200th Anniv. Fireworks, 2005; Central Sch. of Speech and Drama Centenary, Old Vic, 2006; Not Forgotten Assoc. for Wounded and Disabled Service Personnel concert, Tower of London, and Christmas celebration, St James's Palace, 2006, Debt of Honour, 2007, 90th birthday celebration, Buckingham Palace, 2010. Vice-President: Morrison Orpheus Choir, 1972–; Queen Elizabeth the Queen Mother's Meml Fund, 2001–; Support for Africa, 2002–; CiB, 2002–; Patron: Chicken Shed Theatre Co., 2002–; Brooklands SLD Sch., 2002–; Trustee, ABF The Soldier's Charity, 2003–13. Evening Standard Ambassador for London, 1995; Walpole Gold Medal for Excellence, and Walpole Award for Best Cultural Achievement, 2002; CiB Communicator of the Year Award, 2002; SPAM Lifetime Achievement Award 2002; Derek Harper Technol. Award, RTS, 2003. KStJ 1985 (OStJ 1982). Grand Officer, Order of al Istiqlal (Jordan), 1987. *Publications*: The Awful Troop Leaders Gunnery Crib, 1969; It's All Going Terribly Wrong, 2012; Images of the Royal Tournament 1974–99, 2017; Images of 'Joy to the World' 1988–97, 2018. *Recreations*: painting, antiques, giving parties. *Club*: Cavalry and Guards.

**PARKER, (Michael) Miles,** OBE 2013; PhD; Deputy Chief Scientific Adviser and Director of Strategic Evidence and Analysis (formerly of Science, then for the Evidence Programme), Department for Environment, Food and Rural Affairs, 2002–12; Visiting Research Fellow, Centre for Science and Policy, University of Cambridge, since 2013 (Associate Fellow, since 2010); *b* 20 Nov. 1948; *s* of late Michael Rowton Parker and of Anne Margaret Bodkin; *m* 1991, Claire Christine Nihoul; two *s*, and two step *d*. *Educ:* Ampleforth Coll., York; Trinity Coll., Dublin Univ. (BA Mod.; PhD). CBiol 2002. FRSB (FSB 2000). Asst Inspector of Fisheries, Dept for Agric. and Fisheries, Ireland, 1975–83; Ministry of Agriculture, Fisheries and Food: PSO, Directorate of Fisheries Res., 1983–87; Principal, Food Contamination and Safety Policy, 1987–89; Sci. Liaison Officer, Chief Scientist's Gp, 1989–92; Grade 6, Cabinet Office Sci. Secretariat, 1992; Hd, Sci. Div., MAFF, 1992–98; Dir of Food Res., Central Sci. Lab., 1998; Dir, Internat., OST, 1998–2002. Non-exec. Dir, Cadbury Ltd, 1993–95. Chm., Marine Pollution Working Gp, Internat. Council for Exploration of the Sea, 1983–85. *Publications:* (ed with P. Tett) Exceptional Plankton Blooms, 1987; articles on science policy, marine ecol. and marine pollution in scientific jls. *Recreations:* omnicuriosity, Irish poetry and literature of 20th and 21st centuries. *Address:* Fairhaven, Long Lane, Fowlmere, Cambs SG8 7TG. *T:* (01763) 209066.

**PARKER, Michael St J.;** *see* St John Parker.

**PARKER, Miles;** *see* Parker, Michael M.

**PARKER, Nathaniel;** actor; *b* London, 5 May 1962; *s* of Sir Peter Parker, KBE, LVO and Gillian Parker; *m* 1992, Anna Patrick; two *d*. *Educ:* Leighton Park Sch.; London Acad. of Music and Dramatic Art. *Theatre:* Claw and the Recruiting Officer, Mold, 1985; Romeo and Juliet, Young Vic, 1986; Everyman in his Humour, The Winter's Tale, The Rover, Richard II, A Midsummer Night's Dream, The Storm, RSC, 1989–90; Merchant of Venice, Phoenix, transf. NY, 1989–90; 50 Revolutions, Whitehall, 1999; Speed the Plow, Duke of York's, 2000; Quartermain's Terms, tour, 2008; The Audience, Gielgud, 2013; Wolf Hall and Bring up the Bodies, Stratford, Aldwych, transf. NY, 2013–15; This House, Chichester, transf. Garrick, 2016; An Ideal Husband, Vaudeville, 2018; *television* includes: Piece of cake, 1988; Never Come Back, 1989; Heroes II: The Return, The War that Never Ends, 1991; Dancing Queen, 1993; David, Into Thin Air, Far From the Madding Crowd, 1997; Vanity Fair, 1998; Trust, 1999; The Inspector Linley Mysteries, 2001–07; The Private Life of Samuel Pepys, 2003; Pretending to be Judith, 2004; Bleak House, 2005; November: Nazis on Trial, 2006; Land Girls, 2009; Injustice, Merlin, 2011; The Proxy, Me and Mrs Jones, 2012; Still Life, 2013; The Outcast, 2015; Of Kings and Prophets, 2016; *films* include: War Requiem, 1987; Hamlet, 1991; The Bodyguard, 1992; Wide Sargasso Sea, 1993; A Warrior's Tale, 1994; Othello, 1995; Beverly Hills Ninja, 1997; Lover's Prayer, 1999; Haunted Mansion, 2003; Stardust, Flawless, Fade to Black, 2007; Perfect Host, 2009; The Domino Effect, Sergeant Slaughter, 2011; Don't Miss the Cup, 2013. Mem., BAFTA, 2005–. *Recreations:* getting home!, gardening, horse racing and riding, watching most sport and most films, walking our whippets. *Address:* Independent Talent Agency Group Ltd, 40 Whitfield Street, W1T 2RH. *E:* nathanielparker@mac.com.

**PARKER, Nicholas Duncan,** FCA; Tax Partner, RSM UK, since 1985 (Tax Manager, 1983–85); President, Institute of Chartered Accountants of England and Wales, 2017–18; *b* Newquay, 25 June 1955; *s* of Gerald Stuart Parker and Brenda Mary Parker (*née* Briggs); *m* 1979, Janice Holden; two *s*. *Educ:* Windsor Grammar Sch. ACA 1978, FCA 1988; CTA 1980. ACA student, Oury & Co., 1974–79; Tax Manager, Touche Ross, 1979–83. Mem., Soc. of Trust and Estate Practitioners. *Recreations:* mountain climbing (Mt Everest Base Camp, Mt Meru, Mt Aconcagua, 1995); sailed BT Global Challenge, 2004–05; ran London Marathon, 1994; held Private Pilot Licence. *Address:* Brambles, Crawley Hill, West Wellow, Romsey, Hants SO51 6AP. *T:* 07747 698666. *E:* ndparker@aol.com.
*See also C. S. Parker.*

**PARKER, Gen. Sir Nicholas Ralph, (Sir Nick),** KCB 2009; CBE 2002; Chairman: Step Up To Serve, since 2014; Team Rubicon UK, since 2015; *b* 13 Oct. 1954; *s* of late Capt. Herbert Blake Parker, RN and of Diana Katharine Parker (*née* Barnwell); *m* 1979, Rebecca Clare Wellings; two *s*. *Educ:* Sherborne Sch.; RMA Sandhurst. CO, 2nd Bn Royal Green Jackets, 1994–95; Comdr, 20 Armoured Bde, 1997–2000; Comdr, Jt Task Force, Sierra Leone, 2001; GOC 3rd Div., and Gov., Edinburgh Castle, 2002–04; Comdt, Jt Services Comd and Staff Coll., 2004–05; Dep. Comdg Gen., Multinat. Corps, Iraq, 2005–06; GOC NI, 2006–07; Comdr Regl Forces, Land Forces Comd, 2007–09; Dep. Comdr ISAF—Afghanistan, and Sen. British Military Rep. (Afghanistan), later UK Nat. Contingent Comdr, 2009–10; Jt Comdr, Mil. Security Op. in Support of 2012 London Olympics, 2011–12; Comdr (formerly C-in-C) Land Forces, 2010–13; ADC Gen. to the Queen, 2010–13. Mem., Defence Reform Adv. Bd, Min. of Defence, Ukraine, 2016–19. Dir, Military Mutual, 2014–; Chm., Coote Capital, 2014–. Mem. Bd, Invictus Games CIC, 2014; Dir, Team Rubicon Global, 2015–. Sen. Associate Fellow, RUSI, 2013–. Pres., Fovant Badges Soc., 2014–. Author, Independent Review of ACPO (report publd 2013). Officer, Legion of Merit (USA), 2007. *Recreations:* fishing, drawing, Coronation Street, gardening. *Club:* Cavalry and Guards.
*See also C. H. Parker, E. B. Parker.*

**PARKER, Prof. (Noel) Geoffrey,** PhD, LittD; FBA 1984; Andreas Dorpalen Professor of European History and Associate, Mershon Center, since 1997, and Distinguished University Professor, since 2007, Ohio State University; *b* 25 Dec. 1943; *s* of late Derek Geoffrey Parker and Kathleen Betsy Symon; *m* 1st, Angela Maureen Chapman; one *s* one *d*; 2nd, Jane Helen Ohlmeyer; two *s*. *Educ:* Nottingham High Sch.; Christ's Coll., Cambridge (BA 1965; MA; PhD 1968; LittD 1981). Fellow of Christ's Coll., Cambridge, 1968–72; Lectr in Mod. Hist., 1972–78, Reader in Mod. Hist., 1978–82, and Prof. of Early Mod. Hist., 1982–86, St Andrews Univ. Charles E. Nowell Dist. Prof. of History, Univ. of Illinois at Urbana-Champaign, 1986–93 (Dept Chair, 1989–91); Robert A. Lovett Prof. of Military and Naval Hist., Yale Univ., 1993–96. British Acad. Exchange Fellow, Newberry Library, Chicago, 1981, Japan Acad., Tokyo, 2010; J. S. Guggenheim Foundn Fellow, 2001–02; H. F. Guggenheim Sen. Fellow, 2002–03; Fellow, Real Academia Hispano-Americana de Ciencias, Artes y Letras, Cádiz, 2004. Visiting Professor: Vrije Universiteit, Brussels, 1975 (Dr phil and letters *hc*, 1990); Univ. of BC, Vancouver, Canada, 1979–80; Keio Univ., Tokyo, 1984; Oxford Univ., 2004; Affiliate Prof., Centro de Información y Docencia Económicas, Mexico, 2016–. Lees Knowles Lectr in Mil. Hist., Univ. of Cambridge, 1984. Television scripts and broadcasts. For. Mem., Royal Netherlands Acad. of Arts and Scis, 2005. Corresp. Fellow, Spanish Royal Acad. of History, 1988–; Corresp. FRSE, 2016; Fellow, Amer. Acad. of Arts and Sci., 2017. Hon. Dr Letters: Vrije Univ., Brussels, 1990; Katholieke Univ., Brussels, 2005; Burgos Univ., 2010. Samuel E. Morison Prize, Soc. for Mil. Hist., 1990; Alumni Assoc. Award for Distinguished Teaching, Ohio State Univ., 2006; A. H. Heineken Foundn Prize for Hist., Royal Dutch Acad. of Scis, 2012. Order of Isabel the Catholic (Spain), Kt Grand Cross, 1992 (Encomienda, 1988); Order of Alfonso the Wise (Spain), Kt Grand Cross, 1984. *Publications:* The Army of Flanders and the Spanish Road 1567–1659, 1972, 4th edn 2004; The Dutch Revolt, 1977, 3rd edn 1985; Philip II, 1978, 4th edn 2001; Europe in Crisis 1598–1648, 1979, 2nd edn 2001; Spain and the Netherlands 1559–1659, 1979, 2nd edn 1990; The Thirty Years' War, 1984, 2nd edn 1996; (ed) The World: an illustrated history, 1986, 3rd edn 1995; The Military Revolution: military innovation and the rise of the West 1500–1800, 1988, 3rd edn 1996 (Dexter Prize, 1987–90; Soc. of Military History Dist. Book Prize for non-US Military History, 1988); (with Colin Martin) The Spanish Armada, 1988, 3rd edn 1999, rev. and expanded edn as La Gran Armada, 2011, 2nd edn 2013; (ed) Cambridge Illustrated History of Warfare, 1995, 2nd edn 2008; (ed) The Times Compact Atlas of World History, 1995, 5th edn 2008; (ed with Robert C. Cowley) The Reader's Companion to Military History, 1996; The Grand Strategy of Philip II, 1998; Success is Never Final: Empire, war and faith in early modern Europe, 2002, 2nd edn 2003; Felipe II: la biografía definitiva, 2010; Global Crisis: war, climate change and catastrophe in the seventeenth century, 2013 (Sunday Times Book of Yr, 2013; Soc. of Military History Dist. Book Prize for non-US Military History, 2013; British Acad. Medal, 2014); Imprudent King: a new life of Philip II, 2014; Emperor: a new life of Charles V, 2019; works trans. into many langs; edited numerous other works; articles and reviews. *Recreations:* reading, archaeology. *Address:* History Department, Ohio State University, 230 Annie and John Glenn Avenue, Columbus, OH 43210-1367, USA. *T:* (614) 2926721, *Fax:* (614) 2922282.

**PARKER, Sir Peter;** *see* Parker, Sir W. P. B.

**PARKER, Peter Joseph Jacques,** PhD; FMedSci; FRS 2006; Senior Group Leader, Francis Crick Institute, since 2015; Professor of Cancer Cell Biology, and Head, Division of Cancer Studies, King's College London, since 2006; *b* 30 Sept. 1954; *s* of Philip Joseph Jacques Parker and late Phyllis Joyce Eileen Jacques Parker; *m* 1976, Jennifer Jean Cave; one *s*. *Educ:* Brasenose Coll., Oxford (BA 1976; PhD 1979). Gp Leader, ICRF, 1985–86; Lab. Hd, Ludwig Inst., London, 1986–90; Principal Scientist, ICRF, then Cancer Res. UK, 1990–2015. Hon. Prof., UCL, 1997–. *Publications:* over 300 res. and review articles in learned jls. *Recreations:* tennis, walking, sculpture, theatre, pottery. *Address:* Protein Phosphorylation Laboratory, Francis Crick Institute, 1 Midland Road, NW1 1AT. *E:* Peter.Parker@crick.ac.uk; CRUK KHP Centre, King's College London, New Hunt's House, Guy's Hospital, St Thomas Street, SE1 1UL. *T:* (020) 7848 6616, *Fax:* (020) 7848 6435. *E:* peter.parker@kcl.ac.uk.

**PARKER, His Honour Philip Laurence,** QC 2000; a Circuit Judge, 2008–19; *b* 10 Aug. 1953; *s* of late Robert Bernard Parker and Barbara Doherty Parker; *m* 1980 (marr. diss. 2002); three *d*. *Educ:* Prior Park Coll., Bath; King Edward's Sch., Birmingham; Matthew Boulton Tech. Coll., Birmingham; Univ. of Birmingham (LLB). Called to the Bar, Middle Temple, 1976. *Recreations:* golf, ski-ing.

**PARKER, Richard Jonathan,** CBE 2013; FREng; special advisor to companies and agencies, since 2016; Director of Research and Technology, Rolls-Royce plc, 2001–16; *b* Scunthorpe, 30 Jan. 1954; *s* of Harold Colin Parker and Margaret Mavis Parker; *m* 1985, Jeanette Carol Kofler; two *d*. *Educ:* Scunthorpe Grammar Sch.; High Ridge Comprehensive Sch., Scunthorpe; John Leggott VI Form Coll., Scunthorpe; Imperial Coll. London (BSc Physics 1976); Loughborough Univ. (MBA Dist. 1992). FREng 2004. CASE Res. Student, Imperial Coll. London and Nat. Physical Lab., 1975–78; Rolls-Royce: Res. Scientist, then Sen. Res. Scientist, 1978–90, Gp Leader, Optical Scis, Applied Sci. Lab, 1990–92; Chief of Composites and Ceramics, 1992–94; Chief of Compressor Engrg, Design and Mech. Technol., 1994–97; Gen. Manager, Compressor Engrg, 1997–98; Engrg Dir and Dep. Man. Dir, Compressor Systems, 1998–2000; Man. Dir, Compressor Systems Operating Business Unit, 2000–01; Dir, Engrg and Technol., Civil Aerospace, 2004–05. Visiting Professor: Aerospace Engrg, Loughborough Univ., 2007–; Mech. Engrg, Imperial Coll. London, 2016–; Hon. Prof., Materials Engrg, Birmingham Univ., 2010–; Dist. Visitor, Nat. Physical Lab., 2016–. Chm. Bd, Clean Sky Jt Undertaking, Brussels, 2012–. Hon. DEng: Pusan Nat., Korea, 2009; Sheffield, 2010; Nanyang Technol., Singapore, 2013; Loughborough, 2013; Imperial Coll. London, 2017; Hon. DSc Heriot Watt, 2011. Gold Medal, RAeS, 2015. *Recreations:* walking, films, music, fine dining. *E:* ric.parker@btinternet.com.

**PARKER, Sir Richard (William) Hyde,** 12th Bt *cr* 1681; DL; *b* 5 April 1937; *o s* of Sir William Stephen Hyde Parker, 11th Bt, and Ulla Ditlef (*d* 1998), *o d* of C. Ditlef Nielsen, PhD, Copenhagen; *S* father, 1951; *m* 1972, Jean, *d* of late Sir Lindores Leslie, 9th Bt; one *s* three *d* (incl. twin *d*). *Educ:* Millfield; Royal Agricultural College. High Sheriff and DL, Suffolk, 1995. *Heir: s* William John Hyde Parker, *b* 10 June 1983. *Address:* Melford Hall, Long Melford, Suffolk CO10 9AA.

**PARKER, Robert Christopher Towneley,** FBA 1998; Wykeham Professor of Ancient History, University of Oxford, 1996–2016, now Emeritus; Fellow of New College, Oxford, 1996–2016, now Emeritus; *b* 19 Oct. 1950; *s* of Geoffrey Parker and Janet Parker (*née* Chidley); *m* 1979, Joanna Hilary Martindale; one *d*. *Educ:* St Paul's Sch., London; New Coll., Oxford (MA, DPhil). CUF Lectr in Greek and Latin Languages and Literature, Oxford Univ., and Fellow of Oriel Coll., Oxford, 1976–96. Townsend Vis. Prof., Cornell Univ., 2008; Sather Prof. of Classical Lit., Univ. of Calif, Berkeley, 2013. Foreign Mem., Royal Danish Acad., 2007; MAE 2011; Corresp. Mem., German Archaeol Inst., 2016. For. Fellow, Acad. of Athens, 2017. Officier, Ordre des Palmes Académiques (France), 2010. *Publications:* Miasma, 1983; Athenian Religion: a history, 1996; Polytheism and Society in Athens, 2005 (Criticos Prize, London Hellenic Soc.); On Greek Religion, 2011; Greek Gods Abroad, 2017. *Recreation:* gardening. *Address:* New College, Oxford OX1 3BN.

**PARKER, Dr Robert John,** CSci, CChem; FRSC; Chief Executive, Royal Society of Chemistry, since 2011; *b* Palmers Green, London, 29 Oct. 1958; *s* of Claude Albert Parker and Mary Agnes Parker (*née* O'Shea); *m* 1983, Rosemary Jane Maxey; one *s* two *d*. *Educ:* St Ignatius Coll., Enfield; King's Coll. London (BSc Chem. 1981; PhD Chem. 1985). CChem 1990; FRSC 1998; CSci 2004. Royal Society of Chemistry: Asst Ed., 1985–88; Staff Ed., 1988; Editl Manager, 1988–95; Publisher, 1995–98; Gen. Manager, Journals and Reviews, 1998–2003; Editl Dir, 2003–07; Man. Dir, Publishing, 2007–11. Mem., Adv. Cttee, Chem. Weapons Convention, 2016–. Chm., Assoc. of Learned and Professional Soc. Publishers, 2009–10. Mem., Adv. Bd, Sci. Mus., 2016–. Trustee and Mem. Bd, Sci. Council, 2011–16; Mem. Bd, Eur. Assoc. for Chemical and Molecular Scis, 2011–. *Recreations:* motorcycling, art history, embarrassing my children, eating canapés for the RSC. *Address:* Royal Society of Chemistry, Burlington House, Piccadilly, W1J 0BA. *E:* parkerr@rsc.org.

**PARKER, Robert Stewart,** CB 1998; Parliamentary Counsel, 1992–2010; Sir Thomas Pope Fellow, Trinity College, Oxford, since 2010; *b* 13 Jan. 1949; *o s* of Robert Arnold Parker and Edna Parker (*née* Baines). *Educ:* Brentwood School; Trinity College, Oxford (Scholar; First in Mods; MA 1974). Called to the Bar, Middle Temple, 1975 (Harmsworth Exhibnr; Astbury Senior Law Scholarship); Lincoln's Inn *ad eundem*, 1977. Classics Master, Brentwood School, 1971–74; in practice at the Bar, 1975–80; Office of Parly Counsel, 1980; Law Commn, 1985–87; Dep. Parly Counsel, 1987–92. Freeman, City of London, 1984; Liveryman, Wheelwrights' Co., 1984. Member: Horatian Soc.; City of London Br., Royal Soc. of St George; Kipling Soc.; Edinburgh Walter Scott Club; Hopkins Soc.; Friends of Classics, 2000–; Oxford Univ. Philological Soc., 2011–; Egypt Exploration Soc., 2012–; Herculaneum Soc., 2012–; Oxford Univ. Soc. of Bibliophiles, 2013–; U3A, Oxford Br., 2014–; Bd of Patrons, Cambridge Humanities Rev., 2017; Chm., Trinity Soc.,

2012–16. Life Friend, Bodleian Liby, 2009. MCMI (MBIM 1984); MRI 2018; FRSA 2000; FSA 2015. *Publications:* Cases and Statutes on General Principles of Law (with C. R. Newton), 1980; (contrib.) The Best of Days? (Brentwood School Millennium book), 2000. *Recreations:* the Livery, classical and English literature, biblical Hebrew, papyrology, palaeography, theatre, books, music. *Address:* 9 Southall Way, Brentwood CM14 5LS. *Clubs:* Athenæum, City Livery, Langbourn Ward, Civil Service.
See also E. Blackburn.

**PARKER, Prof. Roger Leslie,** PhD; FBA 2008; Thurston Dart Professor of Music, King's College London, since 2007; *b* 2 Aug. 1951; *m* 1972, Lynden Cranham; two *s* one *d*. *Educ:* Goldsmiths' Coll., London (BMus 1973); King's Coll., London (MMus 1975; PhD 1981). Associate Prof., Cornell Univ., 1982–93; Oxford University: Lectr in Music, 1994–97; Prof. of Music, 1997–99; Fellow, St Hugh's Coll., 1994–99; Prof. of Music, Cambridge Univ., 1999–2006; Fellow, St John's Coll., Cambridge, 1999–2006. Jt Gen. Ed., Donizetti Critical Edn, 1987–. Premio Giuseppe Verdi, Istituto nazionale di studi verdiani, 1985; Dent Medal, Royal Musical Assoc., 1991. *Publications:* (ed jtly) Reading Opera, 1988; (ed) Oxford Illustrated History of Opera, 1994; Leonora's Last Act, 1997; Remaking the Song, 2006; (with Carolyn Abbate) A History of Opera: the last 400 years, 2012. *Address:* Department of Music, King's College London, Strand, WC2R 2LS.

**PARKER, Stephen,** CBE 2009; Legal Adviser to HM Treasury, 2003–17; *b* 3 Oct. 1957; *s* of late Fernley and Ann Parker; *m* 1987, Philippa Casimir-Mrowczynska; three *s*. *Educ:* Stockport Grammar Sch.; Emmanuel Coll., Cambridge (MA, LLB). Called to the Bar, Lincoln's Inn, 1982; Legal Asst, then Sen. Legal Asst and Lawyer, DTI, 1984–87; Law Officers' Dept, 1987–88; Lawyer: DTI, 1988–94; Home Office, 1994–2000; Dir, Legal Services A, DEFRA, 2001–03. *Recreations:* mineralogy, natural history, history. *Club:* Oxford and Cambridge.

**PARKER, Steven Nigel; His Honour Judge Steven Parker;** a Circuit Judge, since 2013; *b* Newent, Glos, 4 Dec. 1964; *s* of Brian Parker and Sylvia Parker; *m* 1988, Jane Ridgway; two *s* one *d*. *Educ:* Haberdashers' Monmouth Sch.; Lanchester Poly. (LLB Hons); Inns of Court Sch. of Law (BVC). Called to the Bar, Gray's Inn, 1987; a Dep. District Judge, 2000; a Recorder, 2008–13. *Recreations:* sport, theatre. *Address:* Liverpool Civil and Family Court, 35 Vernon Street, Liverpool L2 2BX.

**PARKER, Tanya;** see Parker, L. T.

**PARKER, Sir (Thomas) John,** GBE 2012; Kt 2001; DSc; FREng; Chairman: Pennon Group plc, since 2015; Laing O'Rourke, since 2017; Vice Chairman, DP World (Dubai), since 2006; President, Royal Academy of Engineering, 2011–14; *b* 8 April 1942; *s* of Robert Parker and Margaret Elizabeth Parker (*née* Bell); *m* 1967, Emma Elizabeth (*née* Blair); one *s* one *d*. *Educ:* Belfast Coll. of Technology; Queen's Univ. Belfast (DSc (Eng)). FREng (FEng 1983); FRINA; FIMarE. Harland & Wolff, Belfast: Student Apprentice Naval Architect, 1958–63; Ship Design Staff, 1963–69 (Nat. Physical Lab. (Ship Hydrodynamics), 1964); Numerical Applications Manager, 1969–71; Prodn Drawing Office Manager, 1971–72; Gen. Manager, Sales and Projects, 1972–74; Man. Dir, Austin-Pickersgill Ltd, Sunderland, 1974–78; British Shipbuilders: Dir of Marketing, 1977–78; Bd Mem. for Shipbuilding, 1978–83; Dep. Chief Exec., 1980–83; Chm. and Chief Exec., Harland and Wolff, 1983–93; Dep. Chm. and Chief Exec., 1993–94, Chm., 1994–2000, Babcock Internat. Gp. Mem., British Coal Corp., 1986–93; Chairman: Lattice Gp plc, 2000–02; Firth Rixson, 2001–03; RMC Gp plc, 2002–05; Nat. Grid (formerly Nat. Grid Transco) plc, 2002–12; Peninsular and Oriental Steam Navigation Co., 2005–06; Anglo American plc, 2009–17; Advanced Plasma Power, 2017–; Jt Chm., Mondi plc and Mondi Ltd, 2007–09; non-executive Director: GKN, 1993–2002; BG plc, 1997–2000; P&O Princess Cruises, 2000–03 (Dep. Chm., 2001–03); Brambles Industries, 2001–03; Carnival plc, 2003–; Carnival Inc., 2003–; Airbus Gp (formerly EADS), 2007–. Non-exec. Dir, 2004–09, Sen. non-exec. Dir, 2005–09, Bank of England; Lead non-exec. Dir, Cabinet Office, 2017–. Chancellor, Univ. of Southampton, 2006–11. Member: Council, RINA, 1978–80, 1982– (Pres., 1996–99); Bd of Governors, Sunderland Polytechnic, 1976–81; Internat. Cttee, Bureau Veritas, Paris, 1979–83; Gen. Cttee, Lloyd's Register of Shipping, 1983– (Chm. Tech. Cttee, 1996–2001); Industrial Develt Bd of NI, 1983–87. Hon. ScD Trinity Coll. Dublin, 1986; Hon. DSc: Ulster, 1992; Abertay Dundee, 1997; Southampton, 2006; Aston, 2012; DUniv Surrey, 2001; Hon DEng Plymouth, 2011; Hon Dr Imperial Coll. London, 2013. *Publications:* papers to Trans IES, RINA, RAEng. *Recreations:* reading, ships, sailing, music.

**PARKER, Timothy Charles;** Chairman: British Pathe Ltd, since 2007; Samsonite Corporation, since 2008 (Chief Executive Officer, 2008–14); National Trust, since 2014; Post Office Ltd, since 2015; HM Courts and Tribunals Service, since 2018; *b* 19 June 1955; *s* of Clifford and Eileen Parker; *m* 1984, Thérèse Moralis; two *s* two *d*. *Educ:* Pembroke Coll., Oxford (MA); London Business School (MSc). Chief Executive: Kenwood Appliances plc, 1986–95; C. & J. Clark Ltd, 1996–2002; CEO, 2002–04, Dep. Chm., 2004–, Kwik-Fit; Chief Exec., AA, 2004–07. Director: Kleeneze plc, 1998–2002; CDC Capital Partners, then CDC Gp plc, 2001–04; Legal & Gen. plc, 2002–04; Boots plc, 2004–07; Compass Group plc, 2007–08 and 2009–10; non-exec. Dir, Nine Entertainment Gp (formerly PBL Media), 2007–11 (Chm., 2008–11); Chm., Autobar Gp, 2010–14. Chm., Emerging Africa Infrastructure Fund, 2007–08. Mem., Adv. Bd, 2004–07, Industrial Advr, 2008–15, Mem., UK Adv. Bd, 2015–, CVC Capital Partners. First Dep. Mayor of London, 2008; Chief Exec., GLA Gp, 2008. Board Member: SW Regl Develt Agency, 1998–2001; Audit Commn, 2006–07. Vis. Fellow, Oxford Univ. Centre for Corporate Reputation, 2008–11. Trustee: RAM, 2016–; Grange Fest., 2017–. Gov., Bedales Sch. FRSA 1990. *Address:* National Trust, 20 Grosvenor Gardens, SW1W 0DH. *Clubs:* Garrick, Travellers.

**PARKER, Sir (William) Peter (Brian),** 5th Bt *cr* 1844, of Shenstone Lodge, Staffordshire; FCA; Partner, Stephenson Nuttall & Co., chartered accountants, Newark, since 1988; *b* 30 Nov. 1950; *s* of Sir (William) Alan Parker, 4th Bt and Sheelagh Mary, *o d* of late Dr Sinclair Stevenson; *S* father, 1990; *m* 1976, Patricia Ann, *d* of R. Filtness and Mrs D. Filtness; one *d* (one *s* decd). *Educ:* Eton. FCA 1974. *Heir: cousin* Timothy John Parker, *b* 17 May 1959. *Address:* Lazy Acre, Byards Leap, Cranwell, Sleaford NG34 8EZ.

**PARKER BOWLES, Thomas Henry Charles;** Food Editor, Esquire, since 2010; Restaurant Critic, Mail on Sunday, since 2015; *b* London, 18 Dec. 1974; *s* of Brig. Andrew Parker Bowles, OBE and Camilla Parker Bowles (now HRH Duchess of Cornwall) (*see under* Royal Family); *m* 2005, Sara Buys; one *s* one *d*. *Educ:* Eton Coll., Windsor; Worcester Coll., Oxford (MA Engl. 1997). Publicist, DDA, 1997–99; Co-Founder, Quintessentially, 2000; food columnist, Tatler, 2000–09; writer, GQ, 2009–10; co-presenter, Market Kitchen, 2007–10; Contributing Ed., Condé Nast Traveller, 2011–; Co-Creative Dir, London Food Monthly, 2017–. Judge: The Hotplate, 2015, Family Food Fight, 2017–, Channel 9; Masterchef, 2017–. *Publications:* E is for Eating: an alphabet of greed, 2004; The Year of Eating Dangerously, 2007; Full English, 2009; Let's Eat, 2012; Let's Eat Meat, 2014; The Fortnum & Mason Cookbook, 2016; Fortnum & Mason Christmas and Other Winter Feasts, 2018. *Recreations:* eating, drinking, dawdling. *Address:* c/o Factual Management, 14 Vernon Street, W14 0RJ. *T:* (020) 3735 9470. *Clubs:* White's, Groucho, Quo Vadis.

**PARKER-BROWN, Hazel Christine;** Executive Director for Corporate Services, Legal Services Commission, 2008–11; *m* 1978, Alexander Parker-Brown (*d* 2012); two *s* one *d*. *Educ:* Convent of the Holy Child Jesus, Combe Bank; Walthamstow Hall, Sevenoaks; Salford Univ.; Coll. of Law (Chester). Admin trainee, DoE, 1976; various posts in historic bldgs, road safety, energy and envmt, 1976–90, incl. Asst Private Sec. to Minister for Housing and Construction, 1979–81; Head, Finance Policy (formerly Public Expenditure) Div., 1990–94, Head, Finance, Strategy and Audit Div., 1994–95, PSA; Head, Office Services Div., DoE, 1995–97; Dir, Human Resource Services, Highways Agency, DETR, 1998–99; Dir, Human Resources, DETR, then DTLR, subseq. Dir of Human Resources and Corporate Services, DfT, 1999–2002; Dir, Business Delivery Services, DfT, 2002–04; Dir of Corporate Services, Commn for Social Care Inspection, 2004–08. Chm., Free Trade Wharf Residents' Assoc., 2013–. Trustee, St Anne's Limehouse PCC, 2015– (Treas., 2015–19); Sec. and Trustee, Care for St Anne's, 2016–.

**PARKER PEARSON, Prof. Michael George,** PhD; FBA 2015; FSA, FSAScot; Professor of British Later Prehistory, Institute of Archaeology, University College London, since 2012; *b* Wantage, 26 June 1957; *s* of George Parker Pearson and Patricia Parker Pearson; *m* 2000, Karen Godden. *Educ:* Taunton Sch.; Univ. of Southampton (BA Archaeol. 1979); King's Coll., Cambridge (PhD Archaeol. 1985). MCIfA (MIFA 1989); FSA 1991; FSAScot 1996. Inspector of Ancient Monuments, English Heritage, 1984–90; University of Sheffield: Lectr, 1990–99, Reader, 1999–2005, in Archaeol.; Prof. of Archaeol., 2005–12. Mem. Council, 1999–2005, Vice-Pres., 2006–09, Prehistoric Soc. *Publications:* Bronze Age Britain, 1993, 2nd edn 2005; Looking at the Land, 1994; Architecture and Order, 1994; Between Land and Sea, 1999; The Archaeology of Death and Burial, 1999; Earthly Remains, 2001; In Search of the Red Slave, 2002; Food, Culture and Identity in the Neolithic and Early Bronze Age, 2003; South Uist, 2004; Fiskerton, 2004; Warfare, Violence and Slavery in Prehistory, 2005; From Stonehenge to the Baltic, 2007; Pastoralists, Warriors and Colonists, 2010; From Machair to Mountains, 2012; Stonehenge, 2012; articles in Antiquity, Jl of Material Culture, Jl of Archaeol Sci., Procs of Royal Soc., Nature, Antiquaries Jl, Procs of Prehistoric Soc. *Recreations:* cats, parties, pig roasts. *Address:* Institute of Archaeology, 31–34 Gordon Square, University College London, WC1H 0PY. *T:* (020) 7679 4767. *E:* m.parker-pearson@ucl.ac.uk.

**PARKER-SMITH, Jane Caroline Rebecca;** international concert organist and recording artist, since 1970; *b* 20 May 1950; *m* 1996, John Gadney (*d* 2012). *Educ:* Barton Peveril Grammar Sch., Eastleigh; Royal Coll. of Music, London (ARCM 1966); postgrad. study with Nicolas Kynaston, London, and Jean Langlais, Paris. LTCL 1969. Concerts include: Westminster Cathedral, 1970; RFH, 1975, 2003, 2014, 2016; BBC Prom. Concerts, 1972; Jyvaskyla Fest., Finland, 1977; Stockholm Concert Hall, 1980; Hong Kong Arts Fest., 1988; Roy Thomson Hall, Toronto, 1989; City of London Fest., 1992; Fest. Paris Quartier d'Été, 1995; Centennial Convention, NY, 1996, Nat. Convention, Philadelphia, 2002, American Guild of Organists; Cube Concert Hall, Shiroishi, Japan, 2000; Sejong Cultural Centre, Seoul, 2004; Westminster Abbey, 2005; Birmingham Symphony Hall, 2005; Esplanade Concert Hall, Singapore, 2005; Philharmonie Essen, 2006; Walt Disney Concert Hall, LA, 2006, 2019; Lahti Organ Fest., Finland, 2006; Monaco Cathedral, 2009; Verizon Hall, Philadelphia, 2009; Auditorium Maximum der Ruhruniv. Bochum, 2011; Davies Symphony Hall, San Francisco, 2011; Mariinsky Concert Hall, St Petersburg, 2011; ZK Matthews Hall, Univ. of S Africa, Pretoria, 2011; American Guild of Organists Nat. Convention, Nashville, 2012; Lotte Concert Hall, Seoul, 2019. Mem., ISM, 1995–. Hon. FGMS 1996; Hon. FNMSM 1997. *Recreations:* cooking, antiques, travel, Daily Telegraph cryptic crossword, Formula One racing, horse racing. *Address:* 174 The Quadrangle Tower, Cambridge Square, W2 2PJ. *T:* and *Fax:* (020) 7262 9259. *E:* janeparkersmith@btconnect.com. *W:* www.janeparkersmith.com.

**PARKES, Rt Rev. (Anthony) John;** see Wangaratta, Bishop of.

**PARKES, Sir Edward (Walter),** Kt 1983; DL; FREng; Vice-Chancellor, University of Leeds, 1983–91; Chairman, Committee of Vice-Chancellors and Principals of the Universities of the United Kingdom, 1989–91 (Vice-Chairman, 1985–89); *b* 19 May 1926; *o s* of Walter Frederick Parkes; *m* 1950, Margaret Parr, CBE (*d* 2007); one *s* one *d*. *Educ:* King Edward's, Birmingham; St John's College, Cambridge; Scholar; 1st cl. hons Mech. Sci. Tripos, 1945; MA, PhD, ScD; FIMechE. At RAE and in the aircraft industry, 1945–48; research student and subsequently Univ. Lecturer, Cambridge, 1948–59; Fellow and Tutor of Gonville and Caius College; Vis. Prof., Stanford Univ., 1959–60; Head of the Department of Engineering, Univ. of Leicester, 1960–65; Prof. of Mechanics, Cambridge, and Professorial Fellow, Gonville and Caius Coll., 1965–74 (Mem. Gen. Bd, Dep. head of Dept of Engineering); Vice-Chancellor, City Univ., 1974–78; Chm., UGC, 1978–83. Member: Brynmor Jones Cttee, 1964–65; Adv. Bd for Res. Councils, 1974–83; University and Polytechnic Grants Cttee for Hong Kong, 1974–96; Chairman: Clinical Academic Staff Salaries Cttee, 1985–90; Academic Adv. Bd, Asian Univ. of Sci. and Technology, Thailand, 1994–98. Chm., Adv. Panel on Limestone Workings in the W Midlands, 1983–95. DL W Yorks, 1990. Hon. FIMechE 1992. Hon. DTech Loughborough, 1984; Hon. DSc: Leicester, 1984; City, 1988; Hon. LLD Wales, 1984. Silver Bauhinia Star (Hong Kong), 1999. *Publications:* Braced Frameworks, 1965, 2nd edn 1974; papers on elasticity, dynamic plasticity or thermal effects on structures in Proc. and Phil. Trans. Royal Society and other jls. *Address:* The Cottage, Headington Hill, Oxford OX3 0BT. *Club:* Athenæum.

**PARKES, Rt Rev. John;** see Parkes, Rt Rev. A. J.

**PARKES, John;** see Parkes, R. J.

**PARKES, John Alan,** CBE 1996; Chief Executive, Humberside County Council, and Clerk to Humberside Lieutenancy, 1988–96; Director, EMIH Ltd, 1996–98; *b* 18 Jan. 1939; *s* of Arthur and Alice Parkes; *m* 1963, Margaret Jill (*née* Clayton); two *d*. *Educ:* Nottingham High Sch.; Oriel Coll., Oxford (MA). IPFA 1965 (Gold Medal, 1965). Various posts from graduate traineeship, Council Finance, Derbyshire, 1961–68; Asst County Treasurer, Glos, 1968–71; Dep., then County Treasurer, Lindsey, 1971–74; Dir of Finance, Humberside, 1974–88. Member: Phildrew Ventures Adv. Cttee, 1986–96; Financial Reporting Council, 1990–95. Advr, ACC, 1976–96; Sec., 1980–86, Pres., 1987–88, Soc. of County Treasurers; Dir, Humberside TEC, 1990–96. A Public Works Loan Comr, 1996–2013 (Dep. Chm., 2002–05; Chm., 2005–13). Mem., ER and Hull HA, 2000–02. Mem. Council, Univ. of Hull, 1996–2007 (Treas. and Pro-Chancellor, 2001–07, Pro-Chancellor Emeritus, 2007). Freeman, City of London, 1988. Hon. Fellow, Univ. of Humberside, 1991. DUniv Hull, 2009. DL E Riding of Yorks, 1996. *Publications:* articles on local govt finance in prof. jls. *Recreations:* walking, cars, railways. *Address:* Cedarwood, St Edward's Drive, Stow on the Wold GL54 1AW. *T:* (01451) 831933.

**PARKES, Richard John Byerley;** QC 2003; **His Honour Judge Parkes;** a Circuit Judge, since 2009; *b* 8 June 1950; *s* of Richard Byerley Parkes and Margaret Elizabeth Parkes (*née* Service); *m* 1981, Janet Oliver (marr. diss. 2006); three *s*. *Educ:* Westminster Sch.; Peterhouse, Cambridge. Taught Latin and Greek, 1972–76; called to the Bar, Gray's Inn, 1977, Bencher, 2006; Asst Recorder, 1998–2000; Recorder, 2000–09; a Dep. High Court Judge, 2007–. A Pres., Restricted Patients Panel, Mental Health Review Tribunal, 2007–.

*Publications:* (contrib. and ed) Gatley on Libel and Slander, 9th edn 1997 to 11th edn 2009, Jt Gen. Ed., 2010–; (contrib.) The Law of Privacy and the Media, 2002, 3rd edn 2016; (Jt Ed.) Entertainment and Media Law Reports, 2009–. *Address:* Winchester Combined Court Centre, Winchester SO23 9EL. *T:* (01962) 814100. *Clubs:* Garrick, MCC.

**PARKES, Prof. (Ronald) John,** PhD; FRS 2011; FLSW; FRSB; Professor of Geomicrobiology and Distinguished Research Professor, Cardiff University, 2003, now Emeritus (Head, School of Earth and Ocean Sciences, 2009–14); *b* 21 Nov. 1950; *m* 1975, Hilary; two *s*. *Educ:* Birmingham Univ. (BEd Hons 1974); Aberdeen Univ. (PhD 1978). FRSB (FSB 2011). PDRA, UWIST, 1977–80; Sen. Scientific Officer, 1980–85, Principal Scientific Officer, 1985–89, Scottish Marine Biol Assoc.; University of Bristol: Sen. Lectr, 1989–94; Reader 1994–96; Dir, Biogeochemistry Centre, 1995; Prof., Dept of Earth Scis, 1996–2003. FLSW 2011; Fellow, Amer. Acad. of Microbiol., 2013. *Publications:* contribs to scientific jls incl. FEMS Microbiol. Ecol., Applied and Envmtl Microbiol., Nature, Science. *Address:* School of Earth and Ocean Sciences, Cardiff University, Main Building, Park Place, Cardiff CF10 3AT.

**PARKHILL, Prof. Julian,** PhD; FRS 2014; FMedSci; Marks and Spencer Professor of Farm Animal Health, Food Science and Safety, University of Cambridge, since 2019; *b* Leigh-on-Sea, 23 Sept. 1964; *s* of Gordon and Margaret Parkhill. *Educ:* Westcliff High Sch. for Boys; Univ. of Birmingham (BSc Biol Scis 1986); Univ. of Bristol (PhD 1991). Sanger Centre, later Wellcome Trust Sanger Inst., 1997–2019, Sen. Investigator, 2003–19. Vis. Prof., Univ. of Oxford, 2003–; Hon. Professor: LSHTM, 2012–; Univ. of Cambridge, 2013–. FMedSci 2009. *Address:* Department of Veterinary Medicine, University of Cambridge, Madingley Road, Cambridge CB3 0ES. *T:* (01223) 337701. *E:* jp369@cam.ac.uk.

**PARKHOUSE, Nicholas,** DM; FRCS; Consultant Plastic Surgeon, King Edward VII Hospital Sister Agnes (formerly King Edward VII Hospital for Officers), since 1998; *b* 7 Aug. 1957; *s* of late David Parkhouse and of Eileen Croxford, 'cellist; *m* 1986, Helen (*d* 2010), *d* of late Austin and of Margaret Fitzmaurice; two *s*; 2nd *m*, 2019, Alison Elizabeth Toovey, *d* of Richard and Elizabeth Dean. *Educ:* St Paul's Sch.; Oriel Coll., Oxford (Open Exhibnr; BA 1978); Middx Hosp. Med. Sch. (MB BS 1981); DM 1990, MCh 1991, Oxon. FRCS 1985. Surgical trng at John Radcliffe Hosp., Oxford, Wexham Park, Orsett and Basildon Hosp., E Grinstead, Mt Vernon and UCH, 1982–91; Consultant Plastic Surgeon: Mt Vernon Hosp., 1991–94; Queen Victoria Hosp., E Grinstead, 1994–2006. Director: Rainsford Burn Centre, 1991–94; McIndoe Burns Centre, E Grinstead, 1994–97; McIndoe Surgical Centre Ltd, 2002–. Hunterian Prof., RCS, 1989; Visiting Professor: USC, 2001; Mayo Clinic, Minn, 2001. Ed., British Jl Plastic Surgery, 1997–2002. Mem. Council, British Assoc. Plastic Surgeons, 1997–2002, 2005–11. Plastic Surgery Advr to NICE, 2002–11. Fellow, Amer. Assoc. of Plastic Surgeons, 2004. Freeman, City of London, 1998; Liveryman, Hon. Co. of Air Pilots (formerly GAPAN), 1998. De Havilland Trophy, 1990. *Publications:* contrib. chapters on burn injury; contrib. scientific jls on reconstructive surgery and restoration of function. *Recreations:* flying, fishing, family. *Address:* King Edward VII Hospital Sister Agnes, Beaumont Street, W1G 6AA; The McIndoe Surgical Centre, E Grinstead, W Sussex RH19 3EB. *T:* (01825) 741100; Chelworth House, Chelwood Gate, W Sussex RH17 7JZ. *T:* (01825) 740615. *Clubs:* Royal Air Squadron, Queen's; Garrick; White's; Vincent's (Oxford); Leander (Henley); Houghton (Stockbridge).

**PARKHOUSE, Peter;** Chairman, Severn NHS Trust, 1992–95; *b* 22 July 1927; *s* of late William Richard Parkhouse, MBE, and Alice Vera Parkhouse (*née* Clarke); *m* 1st, 1950, Mary Alison Holland (*d* 1987); one *s* one *d*; 2nd, 1994, Sally Isabel Squires. *Educ:* Blundell's Sch.; Peterhouse, Cambridge (coll. organist, 1944–45; BA 1947; MA 1951). Instr Lieut, RN, 1947–50; Cologne Univ., 1950–51; Asst Master, Uppingham Sch., 1951–52; Asst Principal, Min. of Food, 1952; transf. to MAFF, 1955; served in private office of successive Ministers and Parly Secs, 1954–58; Principal 1958; Principal Private Sec. to Minister, 1966–67; Asst Sec. 1967; Under-Sec. 1973; Dir in Directorate-Gen. for Agriculture, Commn of European Communities, 1973–79; Under-Sec., MAFF, 1979–84. Mem., EDC for Agriculture, 1982–84. Mem., Mgt Cttee, Cheltenham Internat. Fest. of Music, 1992–95. Mem., Tetbury Hosp. Action Gp, 1989–92; Trustee, Tetbury Hosp. Trust Ltd, 1992–93 and 1996–2004; Gov., Barnwood House Trust, 1996–2004. Vice-Pres., Nat. Star Coll. (formerly Nat. Star Centre, Coll. of Further Educn), Cheltenham, 2002–07 (Dir, 1997–2002). *Recreations:* music (organist emeritus of Tetbury Parish Church and Beverston Church), fishing. *Address:* Stafford House, 14 The Chipping, Tetbury, Glos GL8 8ET. *T:* (01666) 502540. *Club:* Oxford and Cambridge.

**PARKIN, Bernard Maurice Walcroft;** artist and photographer; Racing Photographer to the Queen, since 2002 (Racing Photographer to Queen Elizabeth the Queen Mother, 1961–2002) (Royal Warrant, since 1993); Official Photographer to Cheltenham Racecourse, 1972–2007; *b* 7 Jan. 1930; *s* of Horace Parkin and Dorothy Jane Parkin; *m* 1955, Pamela Edith Humphreys; one *s* one *d*. *Educ:* Cheltenham Dunalley; Cheltenham Central Boys' Sch.; Cheltenham Sch. of Art. Garrison cartographer, RA, Malta, 1948–49; estabd own business of photography, design artwork, calligraphy and cartooning, specialising in horseracing, 1953–; Spirax-Sarco Ltd: company artist, 1960–91; Ed. and Producer, Spirax News (worldwide engrg monthly), 1980–91. Press Officer, Stratford-upon-Avon Racecourse, 1968–75; Artist: to Jockeys Assoc. of GB, 1969–2007; to Stable Lads Welfare Trust, 1989–2000. Has compiled large liby of own racing photos, 1953–. Mem., Horserace Writers and Photographers Assoc., 1975–. Life Mem., Royal Artillery Assoc., 2009. Hon. Life Mem., Cheltenham Racecourse, 2007. Founder Mem., Cleeve Hill Round Table, 1965. Racing Photographer of the Year, Stud and Stable mag., 1971, Bonusprint/Channel 4, 1990. *Publications:* In The Shadow of Cleeve Hill: the autobiography of Bernard Parkin, royal racing photographer, 2019; many books illustrated with technical drawings, cartoons, caricatures or photographs including: Steam Trapping and Air Venting, by Lionel Northcroft, 1968; The History of Royal Ascot, by Dorothy Laird, 1974; Great Horsemen of the World, by Guy Wathen, 1990; The Book of Derby Quotations, by Laurie Brannan, 2004; by Stewart Peters: Festival Gold, 2004; Grand National, 2005; The Hennessy Gold Cup, 2006. *Recreations:* gardening, illustrated short story and letter writing, composing poetry. *Address:* Beldon House, Bushcombe Lane, Woodmancote, Cheltenham GL52 9QQ. *T:* (01242) 672784. *Club:* Stratford-upon-Avon Race (Hon. Life Mem. 1976; Chm., Entertainments Cttee, 1976–83).

**PARKIN, Prof. David John,** PhD; FBA 1993; Professor of Social Anthropology, Oxford University, 1996–2008, now Emeritus; Fellow of All Souls College, Oxford, 1996–2008, now Emeritus; *b* 5 Nov. 1940; *s* of Cecil Joseph Parkin and Rose May Parkin (*née* Johnson); *m* 1st, 1962, Monica Ann Lacey (marr. diss. 1998); two *s* one *d*; 2nd, 2003, Vibha Joshi; one *s*. *Educ:* London Univ. (BA 1st cl. Hons African Studies 1962); SOAS (PhD Social Anthropol. 1965). FRAI 1966. Res. Associate, E African Inst. of Social Res., Makerere Univ. Coll., Kampala, Uganda, 1962–64 and 1966–67; School of Oriental and African Studies, University of London: Asst Lectr, 1964–65; Lectr, 1965–71; Lecturer: Sussex Univ., 1971–72; SOAS, 1972–76; Reader in Anthropol., 1976–81, Prof. of Anthropology with ref. to Africa, 1981–96, SOAS (Hon. Fellow, 2009; Emeritus Life Fellow, 2009). University of Nairobi: Sen. Res. Fellow, Lang. Survey Unit, 1968–69; Sen. Res. Associate, 1977–78; Vis. Prof., Univ. of Calif, Berkeley, 1980; Directeur d'études Associé, Ecole des Hautes Etudes en Sciences Sociales, Paris, 1986, 1987 and 1993; Chercheur Associé, CNRS, Paris, 1992–93; Professorial Res. Fellow, Max Planck Inst. for Religious and Ethnic Diversity, Goettingen, 2010–11; Peking Univ. Global Fellowship, 2016. Hon. Dir, Internat. African Inst., 1992–95. Chm., Assoc. of Social Anthropologists of GB and Commonwealth, 1989–93. MAE 1993. Rivers Meml Medal, RAI, 1985; Pres.'s Lifetime Achievement Award, RAI, 2018. *Publications:* Neighbours and Nationals in an African City Ward, 1969; Palms, Wine and Witnesses, 1972; (ed) Town and Country in Central and Eastern Africa, 1975; The Cultural Definition of Political Response, 1978; The Sacred Void, 1991; (contrib.) Holistic Anthropology, 2007; (contrib.) The Body in Balance: humoral medicines in practice, 2013; edited: Semantic Anthropology, 1982; The Anthropology of Evil, 1985; Swahili Language and Society, 1985; Transformations of African Marriage, 1987; Social Stratification in Swahili Society, 1989; Bush, Base, Forest, Farm, 1992; Continuity and Autonomy in Swahili Communities, 1994; The Politics of Cultural Performance, 1996; Autorité et Pouvoir chez les Swahili, 1998; Islamic Prayer Across the Indian Ocean, 2000; Anthropologists in a Wider World, 2000; (contrib.) Language and Superdiversity, 2015; Shenchu Dangdai Shijie de Renleixue: sige jiangzuo (Anthropology Situated in the Contemporary World: four lectures), 2017; contrib. jls. *Recreations:* music, voyaging. *Address:* All Souls College, Oxford OX1 4AL.

**PARKIN, Jonathan;** Regional Employment Judge, North West, since 2017 (South West, 2011–17); *b* Buxton, 3 June 1955; *s* of Michael and Sheila Parkin; *m* 1983, Catherine Vickerman; two *d*. *Educ:* Manchester Grammar Sch.; Clare Coll., Cambridge (BA Law 1977; MA 1981). Called to the Bar, Middle Temple, 1978; barrister in private practice, 1979–2000; Chm. (pt-time), Industrial Tribunals, 1997–2000; Employment Judge, 2000–11; a Recorder, 2000–10. *Publications:* (with C. Goodier) Employment Tribunals: the complete guide to procedure, 3rd edn 2005 to 6th edn 2011. *Recreations:* walking, theatre, watching Manchester City FC. *Address:* Manchester Employment Tribunal, Alexandra House, 14–22 The Parsonage, Manchester M3 2JA. *T:* (0161) 833 6100.

**PARKIN, Prof. Robert,** PhD; CEng, FREng, FIMechE; Pro Vice Chancellor for Research and Knowledge Transfer, University of Bradford, 2014–17, now Emeritus Professor; *b* Leicester, 22 April 1953; *s* of Geoffrey and Betty Parkin; *m* 1990, Marilyn Anne Southall; one *s* one *d*. *Educ:* City of Leicester Boys' Sch.; Univ. of Leicester (BSc Hons Engrg and Sci. 1976); Leicester Poly. (PhD 1980). CEng 1980; FIMechE 1980; FIET (FIEE 1984); FREng 2015. Res. engr, Rank Taylor Hobson, 1981–83; Lectr, 1983–87, Sen. Lectr, 1987–93, Prof. of Mechatronics, 1993, De Montfort Univ.; Prof. of Mechatronics, 1994–2007, Dean, Wolfson Sch. of Mech. and Manufrg Engrg, 2007–14, Loughborough Univ. SMIEE 1994. FRSA. *Publications:* contrib. jl and conf. papers in field of mechatronics. *Recreations:* art, theatre, cinema, walking, travel, saxophone. *Address:* Room D26, Richmond Building, University of Bradford, Bradford, W Yorks BD7 1DP. *T:* (01274) 233210. *E:* r.m.parkin@bradford.ac.uk.

**PARKIN, Sara Lamb,** OBE 2001; Principal Associate, Sustainability Literacy Project, since 2016; *b* 9 April 1946; *d* of late Dr George Lamb McEwan and Marie Munro Rankin; *m* 1969, Dr Donald Maxwell Parkin; two *s*. *Educ:* Barr's Hill School, Coventry; Edinburgh Royal Infirmary (RGN). Ward Sister, Royal Infirmary, Edinburgh, and Res. Asst, Nursing Res. Unit, Univ. of Edinburgh, 1973–74; Council Mem., Brook Adv. Centre, 1974–76; Family Planning Nurse, Leeds AHA, 1976–80. Green Party, UK: Internat. Liaison Sec., 1983–90; Speaker, 1989–92; Chair, Executive, 1992; Co-Sec., European Green Co-ordination, 1985–90. Founder Dir, 1994–2016, Trustee, 2006–18, Forum for the Future. Member: Bd, Envmt Agency, 2000–06; NERC, 2003–09; Sci. in Society Adv. Panel, Res. Councils UK, 2008–09; EU Expert, Governing Bd, European Trng Foundn, 2009–15. Founding Associate, Engrg Council (UK), 2011–. Member: Bd, Leadership Foundn for Higher Educn, 2003–09; Sci. in Soc. Adv. Gp, Living with Envmtl Change Res. Prog., 2009–12; Higher Educn Acad., 2014–18; Advr, NUS, 2014–19; Trustee: Friends of the Earth Trust, 1995–2002; Carnegie Trust for Univs in Scotland, 2016–; Students Organising for Sustainability, 2019–. Chm., Richard Sandbrook Trust, 2010–. Patron: Population Matters; Mus. of Islay Life. CompICE 1996; CompInstE 2002. Hon. FSE 2006; Hon. FIEnvSc 2011. *Publications:* Green Parties: an international guide, 1989; Green Futures: agenda for the twenty first century, 1991; Green Light on Europe, 1991; The Life and Death of Petra Kelly, 1994; The Positive Deviant: sustainability leadership in a perverse world, 2010. *Recreations:* long-distance walking, birdwatching, gardening, music, theatre, film. *Address:* Sustainability Literacy Project, 173 Hoxton Street, N1 6PJ. *T:* (020) 7739 5263. *W:* www.saraparkin.org.

**PARKIN, Prof. Stuart Stephen Papworth,** PhD; FRS 2000; FInstP; Director, Max Planck Institute of Microstructure Physics, Halle, Germany, since 2014; Alexander von Humboldt Professor, Martin Luther University Halle-Wittenberg, Germany, since 2014 (International Award for Research, 2013); *b* 9 Dec. 1955. *Educ:* Edinburgh Acad.; Trinity Coll., Cambridge (BA 1977; PhD 1980; Hon. Fellow, 2014). Res. Fellow, Trinity Coll., Cambridge, 1979. FIEEE 2003; FAAAS 2003; FInstP. Manager, Magnetoelectronics Gp, IBM Almaden Res. Centre, San Jose, Calif, 1983–2015; IBM Fellow, 1999; Dir, IBM-Stanford Spintronic Sci. and Applications Center, 2004–15. Vis. Prof., Nat. Taiwan Univ., 2006–; Dist. Res. Chair Prof., Nat. Yunlin Univ. of Sci. and Technol., Taiwan, 2007–; Distinguished Visiting Professor: Nat. Univ. of Singapore, 2007–; Eindhoven Univ. of Technol., 2008–; World Class Univ. Prog., KAIST, Korea, 2008–11; Hon. Prof., UCL, 2009. Member: NAS, 2008; NAE, 2009; German NAS, Leopoldina, 2015. Fellow: APS; American Acad. of Arts and Scis, 2009; Materials Res. Soc. Hon. Fellow, Indian Acad. of Scis, 2012; Fellow, World Acad. of Scis, 2012; Corresp. FRSE, 2016. Hon. Dr: RWTH Aachen, 2007; Einhoven Univ. of Technol., 2008; Regensburg, 2011; Technische Universität Kaiserslautern, 2013. C. V. Boys Prize, Inst. of Physics, 1991; Internat. Prize for new materials, American Physical Soc., 1994; Europhysics Prize, Hewlett Packard, 1997; IBM Master Inventor, 1997; Prize for Industrial Applications of Physics, American Inst. of Physics, 1999; Innovator of the Year, R&D Mag., 2001; Humboldt Res. Award for US Senior Scientists, 2004; Johannes Gutenberg Researcher Award, 2008; Daniel E. Noble Award, IEEE, 2008; Magnetism Prize and Neel Medal, IUPAP, 2009; David Adler Lectureship Award, APS, 2012; Von Hippel Award, Materials Res. Soc., 2012; Swan Medal, IoP, 2013; Millennium Technol. Prize, Technol. Acad. Finland, 2014; Eur. Res. Council Advance Grant - Spin Orbitronics for Electronic Technologies, 2015. *Address:* Max Planck Institute of Microstructure Physics, Weinberg 2, 06120 Halle (Saale), Germany. *E:* stuart.parkin@icloud.com, stuart.parkin@mpi-halle.mpg.de.

**PARKINS, Graham Charles;** QC 1990; a Recorder, 1989–2006; *b* 11 Nov. 1942; *s* of John Charles Parkins and Nellie Elizabeth Parkins; *m* 1st, 1964, Carole Ann Rowe (marr. diss. 1977); two *s* one *d*; 2nd, 1977, Susan Ann Poole (*d* 1994); two *d*; 3rd, 1995, Linda Smith. *Educ:* Harwich County High Sch.; Mid-Essex Coll. of Law; LLB Hons London. Called to the Bar, Inner Temple, 1972; an Asst Recorder, 1986–89. Mem., FB Soc., Norwich. *Recreations:* golf, relaxing. *Address:* 6 Harold Collins Place, Colchester CO1 2GQ. *Club:* North Countryman's (Colchester).

**PARKINSON, Andrew David Gibson;** Chief Executive, British Rowing, since 2015; *b* London, 20 May 1969; *s* of John Parkinson and Margaret Parkinson (*née* Gibson); *m* 2003, Annette Darby; one *s. Educ:* Highgate Sch.; Nottingham Trent Univ. (BSc Sport (Admin and Sci.)). Movt Educn Instructor, Focus 2000 Ltd, 1996–98; Nat. Co-ordinator, Sailability NZ, 1997–98; Supervisor, NZ CCS Ltd, 1998–99; Manager, Sport Services, Paralympics NZ, 1999–2003; Med. and Scientific Dir, Internat. Paralympic Cttee, 2003–06; Hd of Ops, 2006–08, Dir, 2008–09, Drug-Free Sport, UK Sport; Chief Exec., UK Anti-Doping, 2009–14. Chairman: Ad-Hoc Eur. Cttee, World Anti-Doping Agency, 2012–15; Taskforce for Russian Paralympic Cttee reinstatement, Internat. Paralympic Cttee, 2016–19; Mem. Bd, Cycling Anti-Doping Foundn, 2018–. Pres., NZ Wheelchair Rugby, 1999–2001. *Recreations:* sport, family, reading, skateboarding. *Address:* British Rowing, 6 Lower Mall, Hammersmith, W6 9DJ. *T:* (020) 8237 6700. *E:* andy.parkinson@britishrowing.org.

**PARKINSON, Howard,** CVO 1998; HM Diplomatic Service, retired; High Commissioner, Republic of Mozambique, 2003–07; *b* 29 March 1948; *s* of Ronald Parkinson and Doris (*née* Kenyon); *m* 1974, Linda Wood; one *s* one *d. Educ:* Openshaw Tech. High Sch., Manchester. BoT, 1967–69; joined HM Diplomatic Service, 1969; Latin American Floater, 1972–74; Vice Consul: Tegucigalpa, 1974–75; Buenos Aires, 1975–78; Second Sec., Maputo, 1978–81; Second, later First Sec., FCO, 1981–85; First Sec. (Commercial), Lisbon, 1985–89; on loan to British Gas, 1989–91; Asst Hd, Migration and Visa Dept, FCO, 1991–94; Consul Gen., Washington, 1994–96; Commercial and Econ. Counsellor, Kuala Lumpur, 1997–2000; Dep. High Comr, Mumbai (Bombay), 2001–03. *Recreations:* travel, music, reading. *E:* howardparkinson@hotmail.com.

**PARKINSON, Katherine;** actress; *b* Isleworth, 8 July 1977; *d* of Alan Parkinson and Janet Parkinson; *m* 2009, Harry Peacock; two *d. Educ:* Tiffin Girls' Sch.; St Hilda's Coll., Oxford (BA Lit.Hum.). Theatre: The Seagull, Royal Court, 2007; Season's Greetings, RNT, 2010; Absent Friends, Harold Pinter, 2012; Dead Funny, Vaudeville, 2016; Home, I'm Darling, NT, transf. Duke of York's, 2018; Uncle Vanya, Th. Royal, Bath, 2019; television: Doc Martin, 2005–09; The IT Crowd, 2006–13 (BAFTA, 2014); The Bleak Old Shop of Stuff, 2011–12; The Honourable Woman, 2014; In the Club, 2014–16; The Kennedys, 2015; Humans, 2015–18; Hang Ups, 2018; Defending the Guilty, 2019; film, The Guernsey Literary and Potato Peel Pie Society, 2018.

**PARKINSON, Dr Martin Lee,** AC 2017; Secretary, Department of the Prime Minister and Cabinet, Australia, since 2016; *b* Stawell, Vic, 26 Sept. 1958; *m* 1st, 1979, Suzanne Thomson (marr. diss. 2004); one *s* one *d*; 2nd, 2011, Heather Smith. *Educ:* Univ. of Adelaide (BEc Hons I); Australian Nat. Univ. (MEc); Princeton Univ. (MA; PhD 1990). Treasury, Australia, 1981–97; IMF, 1997–2000; Deputy Secretary: Treasury, 2001–07; Climate Change, Dept of the Prime Minister and Cabinet, 2007; Sec., Dept of Climate and Energy Efficiency, 2007–11; Sec. to the Treasury, Dept of the Treasury, 2011–14. Director: Orica Ltd, 2015; O'Connell Street Associates, 2015; German-Aust. Chamber of Industry and Commerce, 2015. Hd of Secretariat, Prime Minister's Task Gp on Emissions Trading, 2006–07; Chm., Prime Minister's Task Gp on Energy Efficiency, 2010. Member: Bd of Taxation, 2011–14; Infrastructure Australia, 2011–14; Council of Financial Regulators, 2011–14; Chm., Adv. Bd, Aust. Office of Financial Mgt, 2011–14. Mem. Bd, Reserve Bank of Australia, 2011–14. Mem., Public Policy Cttee, Grattan Inst., 2015. Mem., Male Champions of Change, 2012–. Life Mem., Aust. Business Economists. DUniv Adelaide, 2015. Fellow, Acad. of Social Scis Australia. Public Service Medal, 2008; ANZSOG Inst. of Governance Public Sector Excellence Award, 2013; Alumnus of the Year, ANU, 2013. *Address:* Department of the Prime Minister and Cabinet, PO Box 6500, Canberra, ACT 2600, Australia. *T:* (2) 62715111, *Fax:* (2) 62715414. *E:* martin.parkinson@pmc.gov.au.

**PARKINSON, Sir Michael,** Kt 2008; CBE 2000; interviewer, television presenter, writer; *b* 28 March 1935; *m* 1959, Mary Heneghan; three *s. Educ:* Barnsley Grammar School. Journalist on local paper; The Guardian; Daily Express; radio work; has written for Punch, The Listener, New Statesman; Columnist: Sunday Times, 1965–; Daily Mirror, 1986–90; Daily Telegraph, 1991; Radio Times, 2009–; Producer and interviewer: Granada's Scene at 6.30; Granada in the North; World in Action; What the Papers Say; reporter on 24 Hours (BBC); Exec. producer and presenter, London Weekend Television, 1968; Presenter: Cinema, 1969–70; Tea Break, Where in the World, The Movie Quiz, 1971; host of own chat show, Parkinson, 1971–82 and 1998–2007 (Most Popular Talk Show, Nat. TV Awards, 1998, 1999, 2000, 2001); TV-am, 1983–84; Parkinson in Australia, 1979–84; The Boys of '66, 1981 (documentary); Give Us a Clue, 1984–92; All Star Secrets, 1984–86; The Skag Kids, 1985; Parkinson One-to-One, 1987–88; Desert Island Discs, BBC Radio 4, 1986–88; LBC Radio, 1990; Help Squad, 1991–92; Ghostwatch, 1992; Surprise Party, 1993; A League Apart: 100 years of Rugby League, BBC2, 1995; Going for a Song, BBC1, 1995–99; Parkinson on Sport, R5, 1994–97; Parkinson's Sunday Supplement, R2, 1996–2007; Michael Parkinson's Greatest Entertainers', ITV, 2006; My Favourite Things, R2, 2011–; Parkinson: Masterclass, Sky Arts, 2012–. An Evening with Sir Michael Parkinson, theatre show tour, 2016–. Founder-Director, Pavilion Books, 1980–97. Chancellor, Nottingham Trent Univ., 2008–14. Fellow, BFI, 1998. Hon. Dr: Lincs, 1999; Humberside, 1999; Sheffield Hallam, 2018; Hon. DLitt Huddersfield, 2008. Sports Feature Writer of the Year, British Sports Journalism Awards, 1995; Sony Radio Award, 1998; Sports Writer of the Year, British Press Awards, 1998; Media Personality of the Year, Variety Club, 1998; Best Light Entertainment, BAFTA, 1999; Media Soc. annual award, 2000. *Publications:* Football Daft, 1968; Cricket Mad, 1969; (with Clyde Jeavons) Pictorial History of Westerns, 1972; Sporting Fever, 1974; (with Willis Hall) Football Classified, 1974; George Best: an intimate biography, 1975; (with Willis Hall) A-Z of Soccer, 1975; Bats in the Pavilion, 1977; The Woofits, 1980; Parkinson's Lore, 1981; The Best of Parkinson, 1982; Sporting Lives, 1992; Sporting Profiles, 1995; Michael Parkinson on Golf, 1999; Michael Parkinson on Football, 2001; Michael Parkinson on Cricket, 2002; Parky: my autobiography, 2008; Parky's People, 2010; Muhammad Ali: a memoir, 2016; George Best: a memoir, 2018. *Address:* c/o Parkinson Productions, PO Box 4825, Maidenhead, Berks SL60 1JP.

**PARKINSON, Prof. Michael Henry,** CBE 2007; PhD; Associate Pro Vice Chancellor (Civic Engagement), University of Liverpool, since 2015 (Adviser to Vice Chancellor, 2014–15); *b* 11 Aug. 1944; *s* of John Parkinson and Margaret Parkinson (*née* Corrin); *m* 1966, Fran Anderson; one *s* one *d. Educ:* Univ. of Liverpool (BA); Univ. of Manchester (MA (Econ) with Dist.); Liverpool John Moores Univ. (PhD 2002). Prof. of Political Sci., 1972–73, Dir, Urban Studies Prog., 1976–79, Washington Univ. in St Louis; Liverpool Univ., 1979–92; Liverpool John Moores University: Prof. of Urban Affairs and Dir, Eur. Inst. for Urban Affairs, 1992–2014; Advr on Civic Engagement to Vice Chancellor, 2012–13. Director: CITIES Prog., ESRC, 2000–03; State of English Cities Prog., ODPM, 2004–06; Neighbourhoods, Cities and Regions Panel, DCLG, then MHCLG, 2007–. City Advr, Birmingham CC, 2006–. Dir, Merseyside Develt Corp., 1992–97. Mem. Bd, Prime Minister's Regeneration Investment Orgn, 2013–. Adviser to: EC; DCLG; ODPM; H of C Select Cttee; OECD; EUROCITIES; Core Cities; LGA. Mem., Living Landmarks Cttee, Big Lottery. Trustee: Centre for Cities, 2011–17; Alternative Futures Gp, 2014–; Procure Plus Hldgs, 2016–. Gov., Merseyside Further Educn Coll. and Special Sch. Citizen of Honour, Liverpool, 2016. *Publications:* Liverpool on the Brink, 1985; Reshaping Local Government, 1987; Regenerating the Cities, 1988; Leadership and Urban Regeneration, 1990; Cultural Policy and Urban Regeneration, 1994; European Cities Towards 2000, 1994; Competitive European Cities, 2004; Liverpool Beyond the Brink, 2019. *Recreations:* celebrating with Liverpool FC, exploring Crete, looking after our Joey. *E:* michael.parkinson@liverpool.ac.uk.

**PARKINSON, Prof. Richard Bruce,** DPhil; Professor of Egyptology, University of Oxford, since 2013 (Director, Griffith Institute, 2014–16); Fellow of Queen's College, Oxford, since 2013; *b* Darlington, 25 May 1963; *o s* of Harold Parkinson and Jessie Rae Parkinson; civil partnership 2005, *m* 2014, Timothy Griffiths Reid. *Educ:* Barnard Castle Sch.; Queen's Coll., Oxford (BA 1985; DPhil 1988). Lady Wallis Budge Jun. Res. Fellow, University Coll., Oxford, 1990–91; Asst Keeper, Dept of Ancient Egypt and Sudan, BM, 1992–2013. Visiting Lecturer: Georg-August-Universität, Göttingen, 2006; Universität zu Köln, 2007–; Guest Researcher: Univ. of Copenhagen, 2009, 2013; Johannes Gutenberg-Universität, Mainz, 2011. Hon. Dr New Bulgarian, 2006. *Publications:* The Tale of the Eloquent Peasant, 1991, rev. edn 2005; Voices from Ancient Egypt: an anthology of Middle Kingdom writings, 1991; (with M. Bierbrier) Hieroglyphic Texts 12, 1993; (with S. Quirke) Papyrus, 1995 (French edn 2010); The Tale of Sinuhe and Other Ancient Egyptian Poems 1940–1640 BC, 1997, rev. edn 1999; Cracking Codes: the Rosetta Stone and decipherment, 1999; Poetry and Culture in Middle Kingdom Egypt: a dark side to perfection, 2002, rev. edn 2010; Pocket Guide to Egyptian Hieroglyphs, 2003; (with J. Nunn) The Tale of Peter Rabbit: hieroglyph edition, 2003; The Rosetta Stone, 2005; The Painted Tomb-Chapel of Nebamun, 2008; Reading Ancient Egyptian Poetry: among other histories, 2009; Hunefer and His Book of the Dead, 2010; The Book of the Dead of Hunefer: a pull-out papyrus, 2010; The Ramesseum Papyri, 2012; The Tale of the Eloquent Peasant: a reader's commentary, 2012; (with L. Baylis) Four 12th Dynasty Literary Papyri (Pap. Berlin P. 3022–5): a photographic record, 2012; A Little Gay History: desire and diversity across the world, 2013 (French edn 2013); consultant and illustrator for books by Meredith Hooper: The Tomb of Nebamun, 1997; Who Built the Pyramid?, 2000; The Tomb of Nebamun: explore an Ancient Egyptian tomb, 2008; articles in specialist jls. *Recreations:* English and French literature, music, opera, walking. *Address:* Oriental Institute, University of Oxford, Pusey Lane, Oxford OX1 2LE. *E:* richard.parkinson@orinst.ox.ac.uk.

**PARKINSON, Stephen Lindsay;** Partner, since 2005, and Senior Partner, since 2018, Kingsley Napley LLP (Head of Criminal and Regulatory Litigation Department, later Group, then of Criminal Litigation, 2006–18); *b* 15 June 1957; *s* of late Rev. Edward James Parkinson and Dr Mary Vere Parkinson (*née* Young); *m* 1982, Penelope Jane Venvell; one *s* two *d. Educ:* Hampton Grammar Sch.; Chippenham Sch.; University Coll. London (LLB 1979). Called to the Bar, Lincoln's Inn, 1980; admitted to Bar, Turks and Caicos Is, 2009, 2011, 2013; admitted solicitor, 2005; pupillage, 1980–82; sub-editor, Butterworths Legal Publishers, 1982–84; Legal Asst, Dept of DPP, 1984–86; Sen. Crown Prosecutor, then Asst Br. Crown Prosecutor, CPS, 1986–88; Law Officers' Dept, 1988–91; Hd, Internat. Co-operation Unit, CPS, 1991–92; Asst Solicitor, DTI, 1992–96; Hd, Company/Chancery Litigation Gp, Treasury Solicitor's Dept, 1996–99; Dep. Legal Sec. to Law Officers, 1999–2003; barrister, seconded to Kingsley Napley, 2003–05. Member: Adv. Bd, Centre for Criminal Law, UCL, 2009–; Times Law Panel, 2009–. *Publications:* (with David Corker) Disclosure in Criminal Proceedings, 2009; articles in national press. *Recreations:* life of Churchill, gym, walking, running. *Address:* Kingsley Napley LLP, Knight's Quarter, 14 St John's Lane, EC1M 4AJ.

**PARKS, Prof. Rowan Wesley,** MD; FRCSEd, FRCSI; Professor of Surgical Sciences, University of Edinburgh, since 2010; Honorary Consultant Surgeon, Royal Infirmary of Edinburgh, since 1999; *b* Belfast, 5 March 1966; *s* of George Parks and Elisabeth Parks; *m* 1990, Janet McLuckie; two *s* two *d. Educ:* Royal Belfast Academical Instn; Queen's Univ., Belfast (MB BCh BAO 1989; MD 1997). FRCSI 1993; FRCSEd 2001; FFSTEd 2014. Pre-Registration House Officer, Belfast, 1989–90; Surgical Trainee, NI, 1990–98; Fellow in Hepato-Pancreato-Biliary Surgery, 1998–99, Sen. Lectr in Surgery, 1999–2006, Reader in Surgery, 2006–10, Univ. of Edinburgh. Dep. Dir, Medicine, NHS Educn for Scotland, 2012–. Vice Pres., RCSEd, 2018–. Pres., Assoc. of Surgeons of GB and Ireland, 2017–18 (Mem. 1996–). Member: Internat. Hepato-Pancreato-Biliary Assoc., 1996–; Eur. and African Hepato-Pancreato-Biliary Assoc., 1996–; Assoc. of Upper Gastrointestinal Surgeons, 1996–; Internat. Soc. of Surgery, 2000–; Eur. Surgical Assoc., 2003–; James IV Assoc., 2008–. *Publications:* Surgery in Focus, 2005; Principles and Practice of Surgery, 5th edn 2007 to 7th edn 2018; Hepatobiliary and Pancreatic Surgery, 5th edn 2013 to 6th edn 2019. *Recreations:* boating and sailing, travel, family. *Address:* Department of Clinical Surgery, Royal Infirmary of Edinburgh, 51 Little France Crescent, Edinburgh EH16 4SA. *T:* (0131) 242 3614. *E:* r.w.parks@ed.ac.uk.

**PARKS, Timothy Harold;** author, translator; *b* 19 Dec. 1954; *s* of late Harold James Parks and Joan Elizabeth Parks (*née* MacDowell); *m* 1979, Rita Maria Baldassarre (marr. diss. 2017); one *s* two *d. Educ:* Westminster City Sch.; Downing Coll., Cambridge (BA 1977); Harvard Univ. Mktg Exec., Tek Translation and Internat. Print, 1979–80; freelance teacher and translator, Verona, 1981–85; Lectr, Univ. of Verona, 1985–92. Vis. Lectr, 1992, Assoc. Prof., 2015–19, Istituto Universitario di Lingue Moderne, Milan. Mem., Soc. of Authors, 1986–. *Publications: fiction:* Tongues of Flames, 1985 (Somerset Maugham Award, Betty Trask Award); Loving Roger, 1986 (John Llewellyn Rhys Award); Home Thoughts, 1987; Family Planning, 1989; Goodness, 1991; Shear, 1993; Mimi's Ghost, 1995; Europa, 1997; Destiny, 1999; Judge Savage, 2003; Rapids, 2005; Cleaver, 2006; Dreams of Rivers and Seas, 2008; The Server, 2012; Painting Death, 2014; Thomas and Mary: a love story, 2016; In Extremis, 2017; as John MacDowell: Cara Massimina, 1990; *essays:* Adultery and Other Diversions, 1998; Hell and Back, 2001; The Fighter, 2007; Sex is Forbidden, 2013; Where I'm Reading From: the changing world of books, 2014; *non-fiction:* Italian Neighbours, 1992; An Italian Education; Translating Style, 1997; A Season with Verona, 2002; Medici Money: banking, metaphysics and art in 15th-century Florence, 2005; Teach us to Sit Still: a sceptic's search for health and healing, 2010; Italian Ways: on and off the rails from Milan to Palermo, 2013; A Literary Tour of Italy, 2015; The Novel: a survival skill, 2015; Life and Work: writers, readers and the conversations between them, 2016; Out of My Head: on the trail of consciousness, 2018; translations from Italian of books by several authors, incl. Calasso, Calvino, Machiavelli, Moravia, Tabucchi, Leopardi and Jaeggy; contribs to short story and essay collections, conf. proceedings and jls. *Address:* c/o United Agents, 12–26 Lexington Street, W1F 0LE.

**PARLY, Florence;** Minister for the Armed Forces, France, since 2017; *b* Boulogne-Billancourt, 8 May 1963. *Educ:* Inst. d'études politiques de Paris (Dip.); L'École nat. d'admin (Dip.). Civil Servant, Budget Directorate, France, 1987–91; Jun. Advr, Min. of Public Service, then Min. of Housing and Equipment and Ministry of Interior, 1991–93; Budget Directorate: Head: Protection and Social Security Office, 1993–94; housing, equipment, city and urban planning, 1994–95; culture and audiovisual matters, 1995–97; Advr for budget affairs, Prime Minister's Office, 1997–2000; Sec. of State for Budget, 2000–02; Mission Head, France Trésor Agency, 2003–04; Chm. Bd, Regl Develt Agency,

Ile-de-France, 2004–06; Air France: Dir for Investment Strategy, 2006–08; Dep. Dir Gen., Cargo, 2008–12, short-haul activities (Orly and Escales France), 2013–14; Asst Dir Gen., SNCF, 2014–16; Dir Gen., SNCF Voyageurs, 2016–17. *Address:* Ministère des Armées, 14 rue St-Dominique, 75007 Paris, France.

**PARMINTER**, Baroness *cr* 2010 (Life Peer), of Godalming in the County of Surrey; **Kathryn Jane, (Kate), Parminter;** Chief Executive, Campaign to Protect Rural England (formerly Director, Council for the Protection of Rural England), 1998–2004; *b* 24 June 1964; *d* of James Henry Parminter and June Rose Parminter; *m* 1994, Neil Roger Sherlock, *qv*; two *d*. *Educ*: Millais Sch.; Collyer's Sixth Form Coll., Horsham; Lady Margaret Hall, Oxford (MA Theol.). Graduate trainee, Nestlé Co., 1986–88; Parly researcher for Simon Hughes, MP, 1988–89; Sen. Account Exec., Juliette Hellman Public Relns, 1989–90; Royal Society for the Prevention of Cruelty to Animals: Public Relations Officer, 1990–92; Head: Campaigns and Events, 1992–95; Public Affairs, 1995–96; Press and Public Affairs, 1996–98; a Vice-Pres., 2010–. Mem., Commn into Public Services, 2003–04, Adv. Bd, 2004–10, NCC. Mem. (Lib Dem), Horsham DC, 1987–95. Member: Lib Dem Policy Review Gp, 2005–07; Lib Dem Reform Commn, 2008; Lib Dem Federal Exec., 2008–10. Trustee, IPPR, 2007–18. Chm., Campaign for Protection of Hunted Animals, 1997–98. Patron, Meath Epilepsy Trust, 2010. *Publications:* (contrib.) Working For and Against Government, in Pressure Group Politics in Modern Britain, 1996; (contrib.) The Progressive Century: the future of the Centre Left in Britain, 2001. *Recreations:* pre-Raphaelite paintings, walking. *Club:* National Liberal.

**PARMLEY, Sir Andrew (Charles),** Kt 2018; PhD; FRCO(CHM); Principal, Harrodian School, since 2014 (Head of Senior School, 2001–14); Lord Mayor of London, 2016–17; *b* Manchester, 17 Oct. 1956; *s* of Granville and Betty Parmley; *m* 1980, Wendy Davina Calder Hodgson. *Educ*: Blackpool Grammar Sch.; Royal Acad. of Music (BMus); Manchester Univ. (MusM); Royal Holloway Coll., London (PhD 1987); Jesus Coll., Cambridge. FRCO (CHM) 1976; FTCL 1977. Director of Music: Forest Sch., 1983–92; S Hampstead High Sch., 1992–96; Grey Coat Hosp., Westminster, 1996–2001; St James' Garlickhythe, 1982–. Examr, adjudicator, composer, broadcaster, conductor, editor and writer. Chairman of Governors: City of London Sch. for Girls, 2001–03; GSMD, 2003–06 (Vis. Prof., 2016–). Chm., Montessori St Nicholas Charity, 2007–14; Patron: London Docklands Singers, 1992–; Marcel Sinfonia, 1995–; Thames Chamber Choir, 1999–; English Chamber Choir, 2015–; Jonas Foundn (Geneva), 2015–; London Youth Choir, 2015–; Internat. Ambassador, LSO, 2016–. Gov., Hon. Irish Soc., 2018–. Hon. Bencher, Middle Temple, 2016. Hon. VCM 1985; Hon. FGS (Hon. FGSM 2005); Hon. FRAM 2017. Mem., Common Council, Vintry Ward, 1992–2001, Alderman, 2001; Liveryman: Parish Clerks' Co., 1989– (Master, 2006–07); Musicians' Co., 1994– (Master, 2011–12); Glass Sellers' Co., 2002– (Master, 2013–14); Vintners' Co., 2004– (Master, 2017–18); Blacksmiths' Co., 2014– (Ct Asst, 2015); Hon. Liveryman: Joiners' Co., 2002– (Ct Asst, 2007); Horners' Co., 2003– (Ct Asst, 2014); Water Conservators' Co., 2005–; Educators' Co., 2011– (Ct Asst, 2015); Clockmakers' Co., 2015; Constructors' Co., 2015–; Builders' Merchants' Co., 2015; Tobacco Pipe Makers' Co., 2016–; Security Professionals' Co., 2016–; Management Consultants' Co., 2016–; Painter-Stainers' Co., 2016; Hon. Freeman, Envmtl Cleaners' Co., 2016; Steering Alderman, Guild of Nurses, 2016; Pres., Guild of Young Freemen, 2016; Sheriff, City of London, 2014–15. Hon. PhD: City, 2017; Strathclyde, 2018. Comité d'Honneur, Les Editions des Abbesses. KStJ 2016 (SBStJ 2014). *Recreations:* fundraising for organ restoration, Leukaemia and Lymphoma Research, etc, fundraising for 2012 Diamond Jubilee Ring of Bells for Royal Flotilla on Thames, fishing (Captain, Corp. of London Members' Fishing Team), marathons - running and walking. *Address:* 120 Marsham Court, Marsham Street, SW1P 4LB. *E:* andrew.parmley@outlook.com. *Clubs:* Reform, Guildhall.

**PARMOOR**, 5th Baron *cr* 1914, of Frieth, co. Bucks; **(Michael Leonard) Seddon Cripps;** a Circuit Judge, 1998–2012; Resident Judge, Aylesbury Crown Court, 2011–12; Recorder of Amersham, 2011–12; *b* 18 June 1942; *s* of (Matthew) Anthony Leonard Cripps, CBE, DSO, TD, QC and Dorothea Margaret Cripps; *S* cousin, 2008; *m* 1971, Elizabeth Anne Millward Shennan; one *s* one *d* (and one *s* decd). *Educ*: Eton Coll. Called to the Bar, Middle Temple, 1965; Member *ad eundem*, Lincoln's Inn, 1969, Inner Temple, 1984; a Recorder, 1986–98; Standing Counsel to HM Customs and Excise, 1989–98. Chairman, Disciplinary Committee: Milk Mktg Bd, 1979–90; Potato Mktg Bd, 1979–90. Legal Mem., Immigration Appeal Tribunal, 1998–2000; Pres., Immigration Services Tribunal, 2000–10; a Judge of First-tier Tribunal, and a Dep. Judge, Upper Tribunal, 2010–11. Liveryman, Fuellers' Co., 1985; Freeman, City of London, 1986; Hon. Lt Col, Alabama State Militia, 1975. *Recreations:* family, walking slowly. *Heir: s* Hon. Henry William Anthony Cripps [*b* 2 Sept. 1976; *m* 2003, Katherine Helen, *d* of Sir Michael Terence Wogan, KBE; one *s* one *d*]. *Address:* Bessemers, Moor Wood, Lane End, High Wycombe, Bucks HP14 3HZ.

**PARNELL**, family name of **Baron Congleton**.

**PARNELL, Rowena;** *see* Arshad, Rowena.

**PARR, Martin;** photographer, curator, editor and film-maker; *b* 23 May 1952; *s* of Donald Parr and Joyce Parr (*née* Watts); *m* 1980, Susan P. Mitchell; one *d*. *Educ*: Manchester Poly. (1st cl. Creative Photography 1973). Freelance photographer, 1973–; Mem., Magnum, photo co-operative, 1994–; freelance TV film-maker, 1996–; Vis. Prof. of Photography, Univ. of Industrial Arts, Helsinki, 1990–92; Visiting Lecturer: Nat. Coll. of Art and Design, Dublin, and Chelsea Sch. of Art, 1975–82; Sch. of Documentary Photography, Newport, 1982–84; W Surrey Coll. of Art and Design, 1983–. Exhibitions worldwide, including: Photographer's Gall., 1977, 1981, 1982, 1987, 1995; Whitechapel Art Gall., 1978; Hayward Gall., 1979; Serpentine Gall., 1986; Nat. Centre of Photography, Paris, 1987, 1995; RA, 1989; RPS, 1989; Janet Borden Gall., NY, 1991, 1992, 1996; Nat. Mus. of Photography, Bradford, 1998; Hepworth Wakefield, 2016; Nat. Maritime Mus., 2018; NPG, 2019; retrospective exhibn, Barbican Gall., 2002. Work in permanent collections incl. V&A Mus., MOMA, NY, Walker Art Gall., Liverpool. Arts Council of GB Photography Award, 1975, 1976, 1979. *Publications:* Bad Weather, 1982; A Fair Day, 1984; (with Ian Walker) The Last Resort: photographs of New Brighton, 1986, 2nd edn 1998; (jtly) The Actual Boot: the photographic postcard 1900–1920, 1986; The Cost of Living, 1989; Signs of the Times, 1992; Home and Abroad, 1993; From A to B, 1994; Small World, 1995; West Bay, 1997; Flowers, 1999; Common Sense, 1999; Boring Postcards, 1999; Auto Portrait, 2000; Think of England, 2000; Boring Postcards USA, 2000; Boring Postcards Germany, 2001; Martin Parr Retrospective, 2002; Phone Book, 2002; Bliss, 2003; 7 Communist Still Lives, 2003; Fashion Magazine, 2005; Mexico, 2006; Parking Spaces, 2007; Objects & Postcards, 2008; Luxury, 2009; Playas, 2009; Japan, 2010; Life's a Beach, 2012; Up and Down Peachtree, 2012; Non Conformists, 2013; Paris, 2014; We Love Britain, 2014; Hong Kong, 2014; Voewood, 2014; Autoportrait, 2015; Real Food, 2016; Think of Scotland, 2017; Oxford, 2017; Conventional Photography, 2017; Beach Therapy, 2018; Only Human, 2019; Return to Manchester, 2019. *Recreation:* working! *Address:* c/o Magnum, 63 Gee Street, EC1V 3RS. *T:* (020) 7490 1771. *Club:* Clifton Poker.

**PARR, Rear Adm. Matthew John,** CB 2014; HM Inspector of Constabulary, since 2016 and of Fire and Rescue Services, since 2017; *b* Coventry, 20 Aug. 1962; *s* of John and Margaret Parr; *m* 1992, Marianne Hendry; three *d*. *Educ*: Addey and Stanhope Sch.; Durham Univ. (BSc Hons 1983); Royal Naval Coll., Dartmouth. Joined RN, 1984; HMS Splendid (submarine), 1985; Navigating Officer, HMS Conqueror, Resolution and Repulse; Exec. Officer, HMS Triumph, 1993; Ops Officer, staff of Comdr, Task Force 311, 1995–97; CO, HMS Trafalgar, 1997–99; 6th Frigate Sqdn and HMS Montrose, 2001–03; Dep. Flag Officer, Sea Trng, Plymouth; Comdr, British Forces, Gibraltar, 2007–09; Dir, Operational Capability, then Principal SO to CDS, MoD; ACNS, 2011–13; Comdr Ops and Rear Adm., Submarines, 2013–15. Younger Brother, Trinity House, 2011–. Chm. Trustees, RN Rugby Union, 2017–. *Address:* HM Inspectorate of Constabulary and Fire and Rescue Services, Globe House, 89 Eccleston Square, SW1V 1PN. *T:* (020) 3513 0512. *E:* matt.parr@hmicfrs.gov.uk. *Clubs:* Royal Navy of 1765 and 1785; St Moritz Tobogganing.

**PARRIS, Matthew Francis;** author, journalist and broadcaster; *b* 7 Aug. 1949; *s* of late Leslie Francis Parris and of Theresa Eunice Parris (*née* Littler); civil partnership 2006, Julian Glover. *Educ*: Waterford School, Swaziland; Clare Coll., Cambridge (BA Hons; Hon. Fellow, 2006); Yale Univ., USA (Paul Mellon Fellowship). Foreign Office, 1974–76; Conservative Research Dept, 1976–79; MP (C) West Derbyshire, 1979–86; Presenter: Weekend World, LWT, 1986–88; various series on BBC Radio 4 incl. Great Lives, 2006–. Occasional columnist, various pubns, 1986–88; Reviewer, Sunday Times, 1986–88; Parly Sketch Writer, 1988–2001, Columnist, 1988–, The Times; Columnist, The Spectator, 1996–. Mem., Broadcasting Standards Council, 1992–97. Various journalistic awards incl. Political Journalist of the Year, Press Awards, 2014. *Publications:* Inca-Kola: a traveller's tale of Peru, 1990; So Far So Good, 1991; Look Behind You!, 1993; (ed) Scorn, 1994; (jtly) Great Parliamentary Scandals, 1995, 2004; (ed) Scorn with Added Vitriol, 1995; (ed jtly) Read My Lips: a treasury of things politicians wish they hadn't said, 1996; I Couldn't Possibly Comment: parliamentary sketches, 1997; The Great Unfrocked: two thousand years of church scandal, 1998; (ed) Scorn with Extra Bile, 1999; Off-Message, 2001; Chance Witness: an outsider's life in politics (autobiog.), 2002; Castle in Spain: a mountain ruin, an impossible dream, 2005; (ed jtly) Mission Accomplished!: a treasury of things politicians wish they hadn't said, 2008; (ed) Scorn: updated for a new century, 2008; (ed) Parting Shots: undiplomatic diplomats—the ambassadors' letters you were never meant to see, 2010; (ed) The Spanish Ambassador's Suitcase, and other stories, 2012; (ed) Scorn: the wittiest and wickedest insults in human history, 2016. *Address:* c/o The Times, 1 London Bridge Street, SE1 9GF.

**PARRITT, Clive Anthony,** FCA, CF, FIIA; Consultant, Audiotronix Ltd, since 2016 (Group Chief Finance Officer, 2007–16); *b* London, 11 April 1943; *s* of Allan and Peta Parritt; *m* 1st, 1968, Valerie Sears (marr. diss. 1983); two *s*; 2nd, 1985, Deborah Jones; two *s*. *Educ*: FCA 1966; FIIA 1976; CF 2009. Partner, Fuller Jenks Beecroft, later Touche Ross & Co., 1973–82; Partner, 1982–2001, Man. Partner, 1986–96, Chm., 1996–2001, Baker Tilly; Chief Exec., Business Exchange plc, 2001–03. Chm., BG Training Ltd, 2004–; non-executive Director: Baronsmead Venture Trust plc, 1998–2016; Harvard Managed Offices Ltd, 2001–; London & Associated Properties plc, 2006–; Baronsmead Aim VCT plc, 2006–10; Jupiter US Smaller Cos plc (formerly F&C US Smaller Cos plc), 2007–; Industrial Pipefreezing Services Ltd, 2007–. Pres., London Soc. of Chartered Accountants, 1982–83; Mem. Council, ICAEW, 1983–2014 (Vice-Pres., 2009–10; Dep. Pres., 2010–11; Pres., 2011–12). Ind. Mem., Performance, Audit and Risk Cttee, Arts Council England, 2018–. Mem., Chartered Accountants' Co., 1992– (Master, 2017–18). Mem., BAFTA. Gov., Arnold Hse Sch., 2003–10. *Recreations:* theatre, travel, food. *Address:* 34 Eton Avenue, NW3 3HL. *T:* (020) 7794 2443, 07713 621274. *E:* clive@parritt.com.

**PARROTT, Andrew Haden;** conductor and musicologist; Music Director: London Mozart Players, 2000–06; New York Collegium, 2002–09; *b* 10 March 1947. *Educ*: Merton Coll., Oxford (schol.; BA 1969). Dir of Music, Merton Coll., Oxford, 1969–71; sometime musical assistant to Sir Michael Tippett. Founded Taverner Choir, 1973, then Taverner Consort and Taverner Players, for performance of music ranging from medieval to late 18th century. Débuts: BBC Prom. concerts, 1977; EBU, 1979; La Scala, 1985; Salzburg, 1987; Guest Conductor worldwide of symphony and chamber orchs, period-instrument orchs, choirs, opera and contemporary music. Some 60 recordings. Hon. Sen. Res. Fellow, Univ. of Birmingham, 2000–. *Publications:* (ed jtly) New Oxford Book of Carols, 1992; The Essential Bach Choir, 2000, German edn 2003; contrib. learned jls. *Address:* c/o Rayfield Allied, Studio 26 China Works, 100 Black Prince Road, SE1 7SJ.

**PARROTT, Brian Robert;** consultant in social care, health and local government, since 2001; Independent Chairman, London Borough of Barking and Dagenham Adults' Safeguarding Board, since 2017; *b* 24 Sept. 1949; *s* of late Derek Parrott and Lilian Parrott (*née* Thoy); *m* 1974, Pamela Elizabeth Rigby; two *s*. *Educ*: Bedford Modern Sch.; Downing Coll., Cambridge (BA 1971); Univ. of Kent (CQSW 1973). Social Worker, Camden LBC, 1973–76; Sen. Social Worker, Notts CC, 1976–81; Area Officer, Haringey LBC, 1981–85; Asst Dir, 1985–90, First Asst Dir, 1990–95, Social Services, Suffolk CC; Dir of Social Services, Surrey CC, 1995–2001. Chm., Central Suffolk NHS PCT, 2002–05. Dir, Verita (The Inquiry Consultancy), 2002–06; Mem. Bd, Nat. Develt Team for Inclusion, 2011–14; Chm., Suffolk Family Carers, 2006–12; Independent Chairman: London Bor. of Tower Hamlets Children's Safeguarding Bd, 2010–12; London Bor. of Tower Hamlets Adults' Safeguarding Board, 2010–16; London Bor. of Richmond Adults' Safeguarding Bd, 2014–17; non-exec. Dir, Norfolk and Suffolk NHS Foundn Trust, 2012–17. Chm., Resources Cttee, Assoc. of Dirs of Social Services, 2000–01; Jt Chm., Assoc. of Dirs of Adult Social Services Associates Network, 2008–14; Trustee, Assoc. of Dirs of Adult Social Services, 2018–. Trustee: In Control, 2008–11; Community Action Suffolk, 2017–; Suffolk User Forum, 2017–. Vis. Fellow, UEA, 2002–05, 2009–11. FRSA 1999; FRGS 2012. *Publications:* (jtly) A Unitary Approach to Social Work: application in practice, 1981; contribs to social work and local govt publications and jls. *Recreations:* world affairs, politics, travel, mountains, sport, Ipswich Town FC. *Address:* 3 Jervis Close, Holbrook, Ipswich, Suffolk IP9 2RR. *T:* (01473) 328056.

**PARROTT, Eluned Siân;** Director: Parrott Communications, since 2016; Unite Foundation, since 2018; *b* Abergavenny, 14 Aug. 1974; *d* of Ian Clive Jenkins and Carole Ann Jenkins; *m* 1996, Daniel David Parrott; one *s* one *d*. *Educ*: St Peter's Collegiate Sch., Wolverhampton; Cardiff Univ. (BMus Hons); Chartered Inst. of Mktg (Cert., Adv. Cert., PGDip). Press Officer, Techniquest Sci. Discovery Centre, Cardiff, 1995–97; Mkt and Develt officer, Nat. Youth Arts Wales, 1997–2000; Hd, Public Engagement, Cardiff Univ., 2000–11. Mem. (Lib Dem) S Wales Central, Nat. Assembly for Wales, July 2011–2016. *Recreations:* music, sport (particularly football and cricket). *E:* Eluned@Parrott.Wales.

**PARROTT, Jasper William;** Director, since 1969, and Executive Chairman, since 2013, HarrisonParrott Ltd (Chairman and Managing Director, 1987–2012); *b* 8 Sept. 1944; *s* of Sir Cecil Parrott, KCMG, OBE and of Lady (Ellen) Parrott; *m* 1974, Cristina Ortiz, pianist; two *d*. *Educ*: Tonbridge Sch.; Peterhouse, Cambridge (MA). With Ibbs and Tillett, concert mgt, 1965–69. Chm., 1983–84, Pres., 1986–89, British Assoc. of Concert Agents. Dir, The

Japan Festival UK, 1991; Internat. Consultant and Advr, Sakip Sabanci Mus., Istanbul, 2005–07; Consultant, Reykjavik Concert and Conf. Centre, 2007–. Hon. Trustee, Royal Botanical Gardens, Kew, 1995–. *Publications:* Beyond Frontiers, 1984 (trans. German, Japanese, French, Russian, Norwegian, Finnish and Icelandic). *Recreations:* books, tennis, languages, gardens. *Address:* c/o HarrisonParrott Ltd, The Ark, 201 Talgarth Road, W6 8BJ. *T:* (020) 7229 9166.

**PARROY, Michael Picton**; QC 1991; a Recorder, 1990–2019; *b* 22 Oct. 1946; *s* of Gerard May and Elizabeth Mary Parroy; *m* 1978, Susan Patricia Blades (*née* Winter). *Educ:* Malvern College; Brasenose College, Oxford (MA). Called to the Bar, Middle Temple, 1969, Bencher, 2001; Head of Chambers, 3 Paper Bldgs, 1995–2004. Trustee, Wincanton Recreational Trust, 2000–17. *Publications:* Road Traffic, in Halsbury's Laws of England, 4th edn, vol. 40, 1983. *Recreations:* gardening, food and wine, stone carving.

**PARRY**; *see* Jones Parry and Jones-Parry.

**PARRY, Ambrose**; *see* Brookmyre, C. J.

**PARRY, Bryn St Pierre**, OBE 2010; Co-Founder and Chief Executive, Help for Heroes, 2007–16; *b* Salisbury, 22 Sept. 1956; *s* of Lt Col Robin Parry, MC and Doreen Painter; *m* 1981, Emma Christina Ponsonby (*see* E. C. Parry); one *s* two *d*. *Educ:* Wellington Coll.; RMA, Sandhurst. Served Army, RGJ, 1975–85 (retd as Captain). Cartoonist, sculptor, designer, artist and author, 1985–2007. *Publications:* Mad Dogs and Englishmen, 2001; (with E. C. Parry) Home on the Range, 2002; (with Giles Catchpole) Shooting Types, 2003; (with Giles Catchpole) Horses for Courses, 2004; 101 Shooting Excuses, 2005; Sex in the Countryside, 2005; Dog Training with Mr Perks, 2006; Shooting Top Tips, 2007; (with Giles Catchpole) Shooting Types: second barrel, 2011. *Recreations:* shooting, walking in the hills, fly fishing, cycling, cooking, vegetable gardening. *Address:* Stable Cottage, Wick Lane, Downton, Wilts SP5 3NH. *Club:* Rifles.

**PARRY, Rear Adm. Christopher John**, CBE 2004; PhD; Managing Director (formerly Director), Merl House Ltd, since 2008; *b* 29 Nov. 1953; *s* of Comdr John Jenkyn Parry, OBE, PhD, RN and Joan Elizabeth Parry (*née* Axford); *m* 1989, Jacqueline Margaret Nicholson; one *s* one *d*. *Educ:* Portsmouth Grammar Sch.; Jesus Coll., Oxford (BA 1975, MA 1980); Univ. of Reading (PhD 2017). HMS London, 1977–78; aviation appts in FAA, 1978–88; 826 Naval Air Sqdn, HMS Antrim, incl. Falklands War (despatches); HMS Hermione and Brazen; Staff of FO Sea Trng; Exec. Officer, HMS York, 1988–89; Central Staff, MoD, 1989–92; Staff of C-in-C Fleet, 1992–93; CO, HMS Gloucester, 1994–96; Captain, Maritime Warfare Centre, 1996–98; rcds 1999; CO, HMS Fearless, 2000–01; Dir, Operational Capability, MoD, 2001–03; Comdr, UK/Netherlands Amphibious Task Gp, 2003–05; Dir-Gen., Jt Doctrine and Concepts, subseq. Developments, Concepts and Doctrine, MoD, 2005–08. Chm., Marine Mgt Orgn, 2009–10. Non-exec. Dir, SVGC Ltd, 2012–. President: Combined Services and RN Rugby Leagues, 2001–08; Portsmouth Navy Seahawks, Rugby League Club, 2009–. FCMI; FInstD; FRUSI. *Publications:* (with J. M. Parry) The Isle of Wight, 2000, 7th edn 2017; (with J. M. Parry) The Best of Hampshire, 2009; (with J. M. Parry) The Best of Sussex, 2010; Down South: a Falklands war diary, 2012; Super Highway: seapower in the 21st century, 2014; numerous anonymous and occupational contribs to successive Govt Reviews, pubns and papers; numerous strategic trends, future forecasting, defence and security articles and studies in various pubns. *Recreations:* Shakespeare, hill walking, medieval and military history, being in Wales, thinking. *Clubs:* Royal Air Force; Vincent's (Oxford).

**PARRY, His Honour David Johnston**; a Circuit Judge, 1995–2002; a Deputy Circuit Judge, 2002–07; *b* 26 Aug. 1941; *s* of Kenneth Johnston Parry and Joyce Isobel Cooper (formerly Parry); *m* Mary Harmer; one *s* three *d*. *Educ:* Merchant Taylors' Sch., Northwood; St Catharine's Coll., Cambridge (MA Hons). Admitted Solicitor, 1969; Partner, later Jt Sen. Partner, Dixon Ward, Richmond, 1969–95; Asst Recorder, 1986–91; Recorder, 1991–95. Co-Chm., Richmond Legal Advice Service, 1969–95; Administrator, Richmond Duty Solicitors' Scheme, 1990–95; part-time Chm., Independent Tribunal Service, 1993–96; a part-time Chm., Lord Chancellor's Adv. Cttee for SW London, 2006–12. Member: Law Society; London Criminal Courts Solicitors' Assoc. Liveryman, Merchant Taylors' Co., 2001–. *Recreations:* family activities, reading, music, television, DIY, sport, travel, light gardening, bridge. *Address:* c/o Court Service, 2nd Floor, Rose Court, 2 Southwark Bridge, SE1 9HS. *Clubs:* Old Merchant Taylors'; Nothing (Richmond-upon-Thames).

**PARRY, Sir Eldryd (Hugh Owen)**, KCMG 2011; OBE 1982; MD, FRCP; Joint Founder and Chairman, Tropical Health and Education Trust, 1989–2007; *b* 28 Nov. 1930; *s* of Dr Owen Parry and Dr Constance Parry (*née* Griffiths); *m* 1960, Helen Madeline, *d* of Humphry and Madeline House; one *s* three *d*. *Educ:* Shrewsbury; Emmanuel Coll., Cambridge (Hon. Fellow 2013); Welsh Nat. Sch. of Medicine (BChir 1955; MA; MD). FWACP. Junior posts, Cardiff Royal Infirmary, Nat. Heart Hosp., Hammersmith Hosp., 1956–65; seconded to UCH, Ibadan, 1960–63; Associate Prof., Haile Selassie I Univ., Addis Ababa, 1966–69; Prof. of Medicine, Ahmadu Bello Univ., 1969–77; Foundn Dean, Faculty of Health Sciences, Univ. of Ilorin, Nigeria, 1977–80; Dean and Prof. of Medicine, Sch. of Med. Scis, Kumasi, 1980–85; Dir, Wellcome Tropical Inst., 1985–90; Sen. Res. Fellow, 1990–95, Vis. Prof., 1996–, Hon. Fellow, 1997, LSHTM. Special Prof., Dept of Med., Univ. of Nottingham, 1997–2015. Albert Cook Meml Lectr, Kampala, 1974. Member: Med. and Dental Council, Ghana, 1980–85; Council, All Nations Christian Coll., 1986–99; Founding Mem., Amoud Univ. Med. Faculty, Somaliland, 2006. Hon. FRSTM&H 1983 (Donald Mackay Medal, 1998); Hon. FRCS 2008; Hon. Fellow: Ghana Coll. of Physicians and Surgeons, 2003; UWCM, 2004. Hon. DSc Kwame Nkrumah Univ. of Sci. and Technol., Kumasi, Ghana, 2003. Frederick Murgatroyd Prize, RCP, 1973; Centenary Lifetime Achievement Medal, RSTM&H, 2007. *Publications:* Principles of Medicine in Africa, 1976, 4th edn 2013 (RSM/Soc. of Authors prize, 2004; BMA first prize public health, 2005); papers on medicine in the tropics in med. jls. *Recreations:* allotment, Ceredigion, violin. *Address:* 21 Edenhurst Avenue, SW6 3PD.

**PARRY, Emma Christina**, OBE 2010; Co-Founder, Help for Heroes, 2007; Director, Bryn Parry Studios, 1985–2009 and since 2016; *b* Rustington, Sussex, 29 Oct. 1959; *d* of Myles and Anne Ponsonby; *m* 1981, Bryn St Pierre Parry, *qv*; one *s* two *d*. *Educ:* New Hall Sch. Man. Dir, 2007–12, Exec. Vice Chm., 2012–16, Help for Heroes Trading Ltd. *Publications:* (with Bryn Parry) Home on the Range, 2002. *Recreations:* walking, cycling, baking, ballet. *Address:* Stable Cottage, Wick Lane, Downton, Salisbury, Wilts SP5 3NH. *T:* (01725) 510220. *E:* emma@brynparry.com.
*See also* Air Vice Marshal J. M. M. Ponsonby.

**PARRY, Isabel Clare; Her Honour Judge Parry**; a Circuit Judge, since 2002; a Designated Family Judge, Cardiff, since 2012; *b* 29 Jan. 1957; *d* of Elwyn James Griffith Parry and Joyce McLean Parry (*née* Edwards); *m* 1983, Gareth Richard Llewellyn George; one *s* one *d*. *Educ:* St Clare's Convent Grammar Sch., Porthcawl; Girton Coll., Cambridge (MA); Inns of Court Sch. of Law. Called to the Bar, Gray's Inn, 1979; Asst Recorder, 1996–2000; a Recorder, 2000–02. *Recreations:* music, theatre, cooking.

**PARRY, Jann Peta Olwen**; writer; *b* 12 Feb. 1942; *d* of John Hywel Parry and Evelyn Florence Upton; *m* 1994, Richard Ruegg Kershaw (*d* 2014). *Educ:* Univ. of Cape Town (BA); Girton Coll., Cambridge (BA Hons 1965). Producer/writer, BBC World Service, 1970–89; Dance Critic: Listener, 1981; Spectator, 1982, 1995–96; writer and dance critic, The Observer, 1983–2006; contrib., Dance Tabs website, 2012–. Member: Dance Panel, Arts Council, 1988–90; Exec. Cttee, Dance UK, 1991–2001. Mem., Critics' Circle, 1983–. *Publications:* Different Drummer: the life of Kenneth MacMillan, 2009 (Theatre Book Prize, Soc. for Theatre Res., 2009); contrib. to Dance Now, Dance Mag. (US), Dancing Times, Dance & Dancers, About the House mag., Royal Acad. of Dance Gazette, Playbill (US). *Recreations:* research, ballet classes, volunteer at Battersea Dogs and Cats Home. *Address:* 82 Prince of Wales Mansions, Prince of Wales Drive, SW11 4BL. *T:* (020) 7738 8732.

**PARRY, Johanna Elizabeth Martin**; *see* Parry, J. E. M.

**PARRY, Prof. Jonathan Patrick**, PhD; FBA 2001; Professor of Anthropology, London School of Economics and Political Science, 1993–2009, now Emeritus; *b* 10 Sept. 1943; *s* of Dennis Arthur Parry and Kathleen Aroma Parry (*née* Forbes); *m* 1972, Margaret Dickinson; one *s* one *d*. *Educ:* King's Coll., Cambridge (BA 1965; PhD 1971). Lectr, Dept of Social Anthropol., Univ. of Edinburgh, 1971–74; Lectr, 1974–84, Sen. Lectr, 1984–86, Reader, 1986–93, Dept of Social Anthropol., subseq. Dept of Anthropol., LSE. *Publications:* Caste and Kinship in Kangra, 1979; (ed with M. Bloch) Death and the Regeneration of Life, 1982; (ed with M. Bloch) Money and the Morality of Exchange, 1989; Death in Banaras, 1994; (ed with J. Breman) The World of Indian Industrial Labour, 1999; (ed with R. Guha) Institutions and Inequalities, 1999. *Recreations:* reading novels, cinema. *Address:* Department of Anthropology, London School of Economics and Political Science, Houghton Street, WC2A 2AE.

**PARRY, Kevin Allen Huw**, OBE 2018; Chairman, Royal London Mutual Insurance Society Ltd, since 2019; *b* Swansea, 29 Jan. 1962; *s* of Hubert Llewelyn Parry and Florence Eileen Parry; *m* 2013, Catherine Brock; three *c*. *Educ:* Olchfa Sch., Swansea; Robinson Coll., Cambridge (BA 1983). FCA 1986. KPMG, 1983–99, Man. Partner; CEO, Management Consulting Gp plc, 2000–08; Chief Financial Officer, Schroders plc, 2009–13 (non-exec. Dir, 2002–08). Chm., Intermediate Capital Gp plc, 2016– (non-exec. Dir, 2009–); non-executive Director: Knight Frank LLP, 2004–07; Daily Mail and General Trust plc, 2014–; Standard Life Aberdeen plc, 2014–18; Nationwide Building Soc., 2016–. Mem. Bd, Homes and Communities Agency, 2014–17 (interim Chm., 2016). Chm., Royal Nat. Children's Springboard Foundn, 1995–2019. Liveryman, Chartered Accountants' Co., 2005 (Mem. Ct, 2005–). *Recreations:* shooting, watching sport. *Address:* c/o Royal London Mutual Insurance Society Ltd, 55 Gracechurch Street, EC3V 0RL. *T:* (020) 3272 5454. *Clubs:* Oxford and Cambridge, Walbrook.

**PARRY, Rev. Canon Marilyn Marie**, PhD; Canon Residentiary of Christ Church, Oxford and Diocesan Director of Ordinands, Oxford, 2001–11, now Canon Emeritus; *b* 24 Aug. 1946; *d* of Robert Warren Fortey and Jane Carolyn (*née* Turner); *m* 1969, Rev. David Thomas Newton Parry; one *s* one *d*. *Educ:* Western Coll., Oxford, Ohio (BA Maths, Theol. and Philos. 1968); Univ. of Manchester (MA Theol. 1977, PhD 2000); Gilmore Scheme (IDC 1978). Diocese of Manchester: Accredited Lay Worker, 1978; ordained deaconess, 1979, deacon, 1987, priest, 1994; Curate, St Peter, Westleigh, 1978–85 and C of E Chaplain, Leigh Infirmary, 1983–85; Chaplain's Asst, N Manchester Gen. Hosp., 1985–90 and Chaplaincy Team Leader, Booth Hall Children's Hosp., 1989–90; Northern Ordination Course: New Testament Tutor, 1990–97; Dir of Studies, 1991–97; Nat. Advr for Pre-Theol Educn and Selection Sec., Ministry Div., Archbishops' Council, 1997–2001. Select Preacher, Oxford Univ., 2003–04. *Recreations:* making music with friends, allotment gardening, good conversation. *Address:* 32 Barry Road, Pontypridd CF37 1HY.

**PARRY, Prof. Martin Lewis**, OBE 1998; PhD; Visiting Professor, Centre for Environmental Policy and Visiting Research Fellow, Grantham Institute, Imperial College London, 2008; *b* 12 Dec. 1945; *s* of John Fyson Parry and Frances Joan (*née* Stewart); *m* 1968, Cynthia Jane Mueller; two *d*. *Educ:* Univ. of Durham (BA Hons); Univ. of West Indies (MSc); Univ. of Edinburgh (PhD). Lectr, Univ. of Edinburgh, 1972–73; University of Birmingham: Lectr, 1973–86; Sen. Lectr, 1986–88; Reader, 1988–89; Prof. of Envmtl Management, 1989–91; Prof. of Envmtl Management, and IBM Dir, Envmtl Change Unit, Oxford Univ., 1991–94; Prof. of Envmtl Mgt, Dept of Geography, UCL, 1996–99; Dir, Jackson Envmt Inst., UCL, subseq. at UEA, 1996–2003; Prof. of Envmtl Scis, UEA, 1999–2003. Chairman: Working Gp II, Intergovtl Panel on Climate Change, 2003–08; Scientific Steering Cttee, Prog. of Res. on Vulnerability, Impacts and Adaptation, 2010–. Ed., Global Envmtl Change, 1992–2005. Hon. FRS 1997. Peek Award, RGS, 1991; Gerbier-Mumm Internat. Award, WMO, 1993. *Publications:* Climatic Change, Agriculture and Settlement, 1976; (jtly) The Impact of Climatic Variations on Agriculture, Vol. 1 1988, Vol. 2 1989; Climate Change and World Agriculture, 1990; (jtly) Economic Implications of Climate Change in Britain, 1995; (jtly) Climate Impact and Adaptation Assessment, 1998; (ed jtly) Climate Change 2007: impacts, adaptation and vulnerability, 2007; (jtly) Assessing the Costs of Adaptation to Climate Change, 2009; (jtly) Climate Change and Hunger, 2010; (jtly) Climate Adaptation Futures, 2013; (jtly) Plant Genetic Resources and Climate Change, 2013. *Recreations:* sailing, scuba.

**PARRY, Philip Christopher; His Honour Judge Philip Parry**; a Circuit Judge, since 2016; *b* Salford, 23 June 1973; *s* of John Parry and Christine Parry (*née* Marshall); *m* 2003, Carol Doughty; one *s* one *d*. *Educ:* Sheffield Hallam Univ. (LLB Hons 1994); Inns of Court Sch. of Law. Called to the Bar, Lincoln's Inn, 1995; with Russell & Russell, Solicitors, 1996–2000; admitted as solicitor, 1998; with DLA Piper, Solicitors, Manchester, 2000–03 (resigned from Roll of Solicitors, 2003); in practice as barrister, Manchester, 2003–16; a Recorder (Crime), 2012–16. *Recreations:* golf, Bolton Golf Club. *Address:* Preston Combined Court Centre, Openshaw Place, Ringway, Preston PR1 2LL. *E:* hhj.philip.parry@ejudiciary.net.

**PARRY, Richard Hawley Grey**, PhD, ScD; FICE; author; civil engineering lecturer and consultant, 1967–2010; Secretary General, International Society for Soil Mechanics and Geotechnical Engineering, 1981–99; *b* 27 April 1930; *s* of late Joseph Grey Parry and Ena Rachel (*née* Hawley); *m* 1954, Frances Irene McPherson; three *s* one *d*. *Educ:* Swinburne Technical Coll.; Melbourne Univ. (BCE 1951; MEngSc 1954; MEng 1963); Imperial Coll., London (PhD 1957); MA 1967, ScD 1983, Cantab. Res. Student and Sen. Demonstrator, Melbourne Univ., 1952–54; Shell Res. Student, Imperial Coll., London, 1954–56; Engr, Soil Mechanics Ltd, 1956–57; Res. Officer, CSIRO, 1957–60; Dir, Foundation Engineering (Aust.) Pty Ltd, 1960–67; Colombo Plan consultant on bridge sites, Sarawak, 1963–64; Lectr, Engrg Dept, Cambridge Univ., 1967–90; Fellow, Pembroke Coll., Cambridge, 1970–90, now Fellow Emeritus. MASCE (Life Mem.). British Geotech. Soc. Prize, 1978 (Skempton Gold Medal, British Geotech. Soc., 1999. *Publications:* (ed) Stress-Strain Behaviour of Soils, 1971; Mohr Circles, Stress Paths and Geotechnics, 1995, 2nd edn 2004; Engineering the Pyramids, 2004; Engineering the Ancient World, 2005; Engineering the Pre-Industrial Age, 2013; The Pilbara Contract, 2017; technical papers in learned jls and proceedings. *Recreations:* archaeology, history of civil engineering, allotment, family history, reading, table tennis, golf, bridge, short mat bowls. *Address:* 5 Farm Rise, Whittlesford, Cambridge CB22 4LZ. *T:* (01223) 832024.

**PARRY, Richard James;** Corporate Director (Education) and Lead Director for Children and Young People (formerly Director, then Strategic Director, of Education), City and County of Swansea, 1998–2012; *b* 4 Oct. 1953; *s* of John and Margaret Parry; *m* 1st, 1981, Barbara Parish; one *s* one *d*; 2nd, 1991, Gwyneth Selby; one *d*. *Educ:* Emmanuel Coll., Cambridge (BA, MA). Teacher, 1976–88: Head of Maths, Hatfield Sch., 1979–82; Head of Maths, Fearnhill Sch., Letchworth, 1983–88; Maths Adv. Teacher, Herts, 1985–88; Maths Advr, 1988–93, Chief Advr, 1993–96, W Glam; Asst Dir of Educn, 1996–97, acting Chief Educn Officer, 1997–98, City and County of Swansea. *Recreations:* golf, distance running, sport generally.

**PARRY, Roger George,** CBE 2014; Chairman: YouGov plc, since 2007; MSQ Partners Ltd, since 2011; Oxford Metrics plc, since 2017; *b* 4 June 1953; *s* of George Parry and Margarita (*née* Mitchell); *m* 1990, Johanna Elizabeth Martin Waterous, *qv*; one *s*. *Educ:* Sutton Grammar Sch.; Bristol Univ. (BSc Hons); Jesus Coll., Oxford (MLitt). With Saatchi & Saatchi, 1976; freelance reporter: and producer, BBC, 1977–85; LBC, 1979–83; Thames TV, 1979–83; consultant, McKinsey & Co., 1985–88; Director: WCRS Gp plc, 1988–90; Aegis Gp plc, 1990–94; Advr, KPMG, 1993–95; Vice-Pres., Carat N America, 1995–98; CEO, More Gp plc, 1995–98; Chief Exec., 1998–2004, Chm., 2004–06, Clear Channel Internat. Chairman: Johnston Press plc, 2001–09; Future Network plc, subseq. Future plc, 2001–11; Mobile Streams plc, 2006–17. Director: Jazz FM plc, 1995–2002; iTouch plc 2000–05. Chm., Local Media Alliance, 2009–10. Non-exec. Dir, Uber UK, 2018–. Vis. Fellow, Oxford Univ., 2009–. Trustee: Shakespeare's Globe, 1987–2013 (Chm., 2005–13); Liver Foundn, 2004–12. *Publications:* People Businesses: managing professional service firms, 1991; Enterprise, 2003; Making Cities Work, 2003; Creating Viable Local Media Companies, 2009; The Ascent of Media: from Gilgamesh to Google via Gutenberg, 2011; Developing the Neural Nudge, 2013; Beyond Digital: the marketing renaissance, 2018. *Recreations:* ski-ing, squash, sailing, tennis, croquet, backgammon, fishing, swimming, cinema, NY Times crossword. *Clubs:* Garrick, MCC; Ocean (Bahamas).

**PARRY, Victor Thomas Henry,** MA Oxon; FCLIP; Director of Central Library Services and Goldsmiths' Librarian, University of London, 1983–88; *b* 20 Nov. 1927; *s* of Thomas and Daisy Parry; *m* 1959, Mavis K. Russull; two *s* one *d*. *Educ:* St Julian's High Sch., Newport; St Edmund Hall, Oxford (MA); University College, London (DipLib). FCLIP (FLA 1959). Manchester Public Libraries, 1950–56; Colonial Office and CRO Library, 1956–60; Librarian, Nature Conservancy, 1960–63; British Museum (Natural History), 1963–74; Chief Librarian and Archivist, Royal Botanic Gdns, Kew, 1974–78; Librarian, SOAS, Univ. of London, 1978–83. Sen. Examiner, LA, 1959–68. Chm., Circle of State Librarians, 1966–68; Mem., Adv. Cttee, British Library Dept of Humanities and Social Scis (formerly Reference Div.), 1983–90; Council Member: Sir Anthony Panizzi Foundn, 1983–89; London Soc., 1984–88. Chm., Friends of Univ. of London Liby, 1998–2000. FRAS 1981; FRSA 1985. *Publications:* contrib. prof. books and jls. *Recreations:* ball games, books, bridge, railways. *Address:* 69 Redway Drive, Twickenham TW2 7NN. *T:* (020) 8894 0742. *Club:* Surrey CC.

**PARRY, Vivienne Mary Hunt, (Mrs Tim Joss),** OBE 2011; writer and broadcaster; *b* 4 June 1956; *d* of late Michael Mills and Mary Mills; *m* 1st, 1978, Paul Parry (marr. diss. 2007); two *s*; 2nd, 2012, Tim Joss. *Educ:* St Swithun's Sch., Winchester; Bedford Coll., London; University Coll. London (BSc Hons Zoology). Nat. Organiser, Birthright, 1979–94; Presenter, Tomorrow's World, 1994–97; Reporter, Panorama, How Safe is Beef?, and Test Tube Bodies, 1996; Presenter, Morning Surgery, 1997; Columnist: News of the World, 1998–2002; Guardian, 2004–05; Body & Soul supplement, The Times, 2005–09; Presenter, Radio 4: Inside the Ethics Committee (3 series), 2005, 2006, 2007; Am I Normal? (8 series), 2006–10; Just So Science, 2013, 2014. Member: MRC, 2009–16; Organ Donor Taskforce, 2006–; Bd, UK Res. and Innovation, 2017–; Hd of Engagement, Genomics England, 2014–; Bd, Governing Body, Nuffield Council on Bioethics, 2017–. Facilitator, G8 Dementia Summit, 2013. Administrator, GUS Charitable Trust, 1997–2007; Trustee, Diana Meml Fund, 1998. Mem. Council, UCL, 2005–15 (Vice Chair, 2009–15). Member, Advisory Board: Sci. Media Centre, 2003–12; Cheltenham Sci. Fest., 2004– (Chair, 2017–); Trustee, Cheltenham Festivals, 2017–. *Publications:* The Real Pregnancy Guide, 1996; The Truth About Hormones, 2005. *Recreations:* gardening, swimming, walking. *Address:* Lingermans, Burford Road, near Brize Norton, Oxon OX18 3NZ.

**PARRY-EVANS, Air Chief Marshal Sir David,** GCB 1991 (KCB 1985); CBE 1978; Royal Air Force, retired; *b* 19 July 1935; *s* of late Group Captain John Parry-Evans, MRCS, LRCP, DLO, and Dorothy Parry-Evans; *m* 1960, Ann, 2nd *d* of late Charles Reynolds and Gertrude Reynolds; two *s*. *Educ:* Berkhamsted School. Joined RAF, 1956; served FEAF, Coastal Command, United States Navy, RN Staff Coll., 1958–70; Headquarters Strike Command, 1970–74; OC 214 Sqn, 1974–75; OC RAF Marham, 1975–77; MoD, 1977–81 (Director of Defence Policy, 1979–81); Comdt, RAF Staff Coll., 1981–82; AOC Nos 1 and 38 Groups, RAF Strike Comd, 1982–85; C-in-C RAF Germany, and Comdr, Second ATAF, 1985–87; Dep. Chief of Defence Staff (Progs and Personnel), 1987–89; Air Mem. for Personnel, 1989–91. Gov., Royal Star and Garter Home, 1991–99 (Chm., 1996–99). Chief Comdr, St John Ambulance, 1992–98. KStJ 1992. *Address:* c/o National Westminster Bank, 26 Spring Street, W2 1JA. *Club:* Royal Air Force.

**PARRY EVANS, Mary Alethea, (Lady Hallinan);** a Recorder of the Crown Court, 1978–97; *b* 31 Oct. 1929; *oc* of Dr Evan Parry Evans, MD, JP, and Dr Lilian Evans; *m* 1955, Sir (Adrian) Lincoln Hallinan (*d* 1997); two *s* two *d*. *Educ:* Malvern Girls' Coll.; Somerville Coll., Oxford (BCL, MA). Called to Bar, Inner Temple, 1953; Wales and Chester Circuit. Member: Cardiff City Council, 1961–70; S Glamorgan CC, 1972–81; S Glamorgan Health Authority, 1977–81. Lady Mayoress of Cardiff, 1969–70. *Address:* Cotham Lodge, West Street, Newport, Pembrokeshire SA42 0TD.

**PARRY JONES, Terence Graham;** *see* Jones, Terry.

**PARSLEY, Paula Jane;** *see* Bradshaw, P. J.

**PARSLOE, Prof. Phyllida;** Chairman, North Bristol NHS Trust, 1999–2003; Professor of Social Work, Bristol University, 1978–96, now Emeritus Professor; *b* 25 Dec. 1930; *d* of late Charles Guy Parsloe and Mary Zirphie (*née* Munro). *Educ:* Bristol Univ. (BA, PhD); London Univ. (Cert. in Mental Health). Probation Officer, Devon CC, 1954–59; Psychiatric Social Worker, St George's Hospital, 1959–65; Lectr, London Sch. of Economics, 1965–70; Associate Prof., Sch. of Law, Indiana Univ., 1970–73; Prof. of Social Work, Univ. of Aberdeen, 1973–78; Pro-Vice Chancellor, 1988–91, Warden of Wills Hall, 1991–97, Bristol Univ. Member: Central Council for Educn and Training in Social Work, 1986–92; Commonwealth Scholarships Commn. Mem. Bd, Ammerdown Centre, 1993–; Trustee, Winterbourne Mediaeval Barn Trust, 2009–. Mem., Thornbury Town Council, 2004 (Mayor, 2009–10 and 2012–13). Chair: Thornbury Community Building Trust, 2006–; Camphill Communities Thornbury, 2007–; Thornbury Arts Fest., 2007–; WEA Thornbury, 2009–; Thornbury Community Assoc. *Publications:* The Work of the Probation and After Care Officer, 1967; Juvenile Justice in Britain and America, 1978; (with Prof. O. Stevenson) Social Service Teams: the practitioner's view, 1978; Social Service Area Teams, 1981; report to the Sec. of State for Scotland on Social Work in Prisons, 1987; (with S. Macara *et al*) Data Protection in Health and Social Services, 1988; Aiming for Partnership, 1990; (ed) Risk Assessment in Social Care and Social Work, 1999; contribs to: British Jl of Social Work, Community Care, Social Work Today, British Jl Criminology. *Recreations:* hill walking, crafts, gardening. *Address:* Lion House, 9 Castle Street, Thornbury, S Glos BS35 1HA.

**PARSON, Prof. Simon Henry,** PhD; FAS; Regius Professor of Anatomy, University of Aberdeen, since 2018 (Professor of Anatomy, 2013–18); President, Anatomical Society, since 2019; *b* Leeds, 23 May 1966; *s* of Stuart Henry Parson and June Anne Parson; *m* 2015, Jessica Louise Dickson; one *s*. *Educ:* Woodhouse Grove Sch.; Durham Univ. (BSc Hons Zool. 1987); Univ. of Edinburgh (PhD Neurosci. 1991). Lectr in Anatomy, Univ. of Leeds, 1994–2005; Sen. Lectr in Anatomy, Univ. of Edinburgh, 2005–13. FAS 2012. *Recreations:* mountaineering, ski-ing, cycling, classic and vintage car rallying. *Address:* Anatomy, University of Aberdeen, Suttie Centre, Foresterhill, Aberdeen AB25 2ZD. *T:* (01224) 274328. *E:* simon.parson@abdn.ac.uk. *Clubs:* Historic Rally Car Register, Vintage Sports Car.

**PARSONS,** family name of **Earl of Rosse**.

**PARSONS, Adrian;** *see* Parsons, C. A. H.

**PARSONS, Andy;** writer, actor and stand-up comedian; *b* 15 Oct. 1967. *Educ:* Helston Comp. Sch.; Churston Grammar Sch.; Christ's Coll., Cambridge (BA Hons Law 1988). *Television* includes: lead writer: Weekending; Spitting Image; writer and performer: Smith & Jones; The Lenny Henry Show; The Stand-Up Show (4 series); The Comedy Store Series; Saturday Live; Live at the Apollo; regular on Mock the Week (12 series); Live Floor Show; radio includes: Parsons and Naylor's Pullout Sections, Scrooby Trevithick, The PMQ Show; national tours: Citizens!, 2009; Gruntled, 2011; I've Got a Shed, 2013; Peak Bulls**t, 2017; also tours of Australia and New Zealand. Comedy Award, Time Out, 2002. *Recreation:* relaxing in shed. *E:* andy@andyparsons.co.uk.

**PARSONS, Prof. Barry Eaton,** PhD; Professor of Geodesy and Geophysics, University of Oxford, 2003–18, now Emeritus; Fellow of St Cross College, Oxford, 1986–2015, now Emeritus; *b* 24 May 1948; *s* of Ernest Harold Parsons and Olive Parsons (*née* Eaton). *Educ:* Downing Coll., Cambridge (BA Natural Scis 1969; PhD 1973). Res. Asst, Principal Res. Scientist and Associate Prof., Dept of Earth and Planetary Scis, MIT, 1973–86; Reader in Geodesy, Univ. of Oxford, 1986–; Dir, Centre for Observation and Modelling of Earthquakes, Volcanoes and Tectonics (formerly Centre for Observation and Modelling of Earthquakes and Tectonics), 2002–13. Fellow, Amer. Geophys. Union, 2011. Augustus Love Medal, Eur. Geoscis Union, 2017. *Publications:* articles in Geophysical Jl Internat., Geophysical Res. Letters, Jl of Geophysical Res., Nature, Science, Earth and Planetary Science Letters. *Address:* Department of Earth Sciences, University of Oxford, South Parks Road, Oxford OX1 3AN.

**PARSONS, (Charles) Adrian (Haythorne);** consultant to solicitors on charity matters; *b* 15 June 1929; *s* of Dr R. A. Parsons and Mrs W. S. Parsons (*née* Haythorne); *m* 1951, Hilary Sharpe; one *d*. *Educ:* Bembridge Sch.; Wadham Coll., Oxford. Called to Bar, Gray's Inn, 1964. Coutts & Co., Bankers, 1952–64; joined Charity Commn, 1964; Dep. Comr, 1972; Comr, 1974–89; Head of Legal Staff, 1981; Unit Trust Ombudsman, 1989–90; National Solicitors Network Ombudsman, 1989–94. Complaints Convenor, Retained Organs Commn, 2003–04. *Address:* 6 Garrick Close, The Green, Richmond, Surrey TW9 1PF. *T:* (020) 8940 3731. *Club:* Oxford and Cambridge.

**PARSONS, (Christopher) Nicholas,** CBE 2014 (OBE 2004); actor, presenter and solo performer; *b* 10 Oct. 1923; *s* of late Dr Paul Frederick Nigel Parsons and Nell Louise Parsons (*née* Maggs); *m* 1st, 1954, Denise Pauline Rosalie Bryer (marr. diss. 1989); one *s* one *d*; 2nd, 1995, Ann Reynolds. *Educ:* St Paul's Sch.; Univ. of Glasgow. Engrg apprentice, Clydebank; amateur theatre actor. *Theatre* includes: The Hasty Heart, Aldwych, 1945; Charley's Aunt, Palace, 1947; Arsenic and Old Lace (tour); in rep., Bromley, Kent, 1949–51; cabaret incl. Quaglino's, Ciros, The Colony, Society, Café de Paris, 1951–65; comedian, Windmill Th., 1952, Watergate Revue, Lyric Revue, 1954; Swing Along with Arthur Haynes, Palladium, 1963; Boeing Boeing, Duchess, 1967; Say Who You Are, Vaudeville, 1968; Uproar in the House, Whitehall, 1968; Charlie Girl, Victoria Palace and tour, 1986–87; Into the Woods, Phoenix, 1990; Rocky Horror Show, Duke of York's, 1994 and 1995 (tours 1996, 1998–99 and 2000); numerous pantomimes and one-man shows incl. Nicholas Parsons' Happy Hour, Edinburgh Fringe, 1999–; Just a Laugh a Minute and The Life and Work of Edward Lear, UK festivals, tours and regular cruises; *television* includes: comedy partnership with Arthur Haynes, 1956–66; Last Train to Surbiton (series), 1966; Benny Hill Show, 1968–70; host: Sale of the Century, 1971–84; The All New Alphabet Game, 1988; Laughlines, 1990; Just a Minute, 1994, 1995, 1999 and 2012; participant, Comedy World Cup, 2012; *films* include: Brothers-in-Law, Carlton-Browne at the FO, Happy is the Bride, Upstairs Downstairs, Too Many Crooks, Eyewitness, Carry on Regardless; Don't Raise the Bridge, Lower the River; radio includes: host, Just a Minute, 1967–; Listen to This Space, 1967–73. Rector, St Andrews Univ., 1988–91. Barker, Variety Club of GB, 1975–; Member: Lord's Taverners, 1965– (Pres., 1998–2000); Grand Order of Water Rats, 1996– (King Rat, 2019); Gov., NSPCC, 1977; Ambassador: ChildLine, 2004–; Silverline, 2015–. Hon. LLD: St Andrews, 1991, Leicester, 2016; Hon. DA Lincoln, 2007. Radio Personality of Year, Variety Club, 1967; Lifetime Achievement Award: Sony, 2010; Broadcasting Press Guild, 2019. *Publications:* Egg on the Face, 1985; The Straight Man; my life in comedy, 1994; Nicholas Parsons With Just a Touch of Hesitation, Repetition and Deviation—My Life in Comedy (memoirs), 2010; Welcome to Just a Minute, 2014. *Recreations:* gardening, photography. *Address:* (agent) Jean Diamond, 31 Percy Street, W1T 2DA. *T:* (020) 7631 0400, *Fax:* (020) 7631 0500. *E:* jd@diman.co.uk.

**PARSONS, Colin James,** FCA; Chairman, Trow Engineering (Canada), 2003–10 (Director, 1999–2003); *b* Neath, Wales, 15 Jan. 1934; *m* 1960, Alice McAuley; two *s*. *Educ:* Haverfordwest and Neath Grammar Schs. CA 1955; FCA 1991. Peat Marwick Mitchell, Toronto, 1957–59; Monarch Development Corp., 1959–99: Pres., 1977–92; Chm., 1992–99; Taylor Woodrow plc: Dir, 1987–; Gp Chm., 1992–99; Chief Exec., 1997–98. Pres. and Chm., London Chamber of Commerce and Industry, 1998–2000; Pres., Canada-UK Chamber of Commerce, 1998–99. Dir, Foundn for Canadian Studies in UK, 1997–2000. *Recreations:* tennis, golf. *Address:* 154 Valley Road, Toronto, ON M2L 1G4, Canada. *Clubs:* Brooks's; Albany, Granite, Donalda (Toronto).

**PARSONS, David;** *see* Parsons, J. D.

**PARSONS, David Huw;** a District Judge (Magistrates' Courts), since 2004; *b* 11 May 1957; *s* of Dr D. Ll. Parsons and Margaret P. G. Parsons (*née* Lumley); three *d*. *Educ:* Duffryn High Sch., Newport; University Coll. of Wales, Aberystwyth (LLB Hons); Coll. of Law, Guildford. Admitted solicitor, 1981; Sen. Partner and Founding Partner, Hodson, Parsons Solicitors, Newport, S Wales, 1983–2004; Actg Stipendiary Magistrate, 2000–01; Dep. Dist Judge (Magistrates' Courts), 2001–04; Immigration Adjudicator, 2001–04. *Recreations:* reading, Royal Navy, motorcycling, hill walking, cooking, ski-ing, Pembrokeshire, travel. *Address:* c/o Bristol Magistrates' Court, Marlborough Street, Bristol BS1 3NU. *T:* (0117) 943 5117. *Club:* Oriental.

**PARSONS, David Robert**, CBE 2009; Member (C), 1991–2013, and Leader, 2003–12, Leicestershire County Council; *b* Bristol, 1950; *s* of Robert Donald Probert-Parsons and Beryl Maureen Probert-Parsons (*née* Higgins); *m* 1977, Elizabeth Dolby; two *s* one *d*. *Educ*: Cotham Grammar Sch., Bristol; Salford Univ. (BSc Hons 1972); St John's Coll., Oxford (BA 1976); Bristol Poly. (Dip. Educn Mgt 1982). Pres., Students' Union, Univ. of Oxford, 1975–76. Sci. Teacher, Castle Sch., Thornbury, St Mary Redcliffe and Temple Sch., Bristol and Mangotsfield Sch., 1977–90. Mem. (C), Bristol CC, 1979–91; Leader, Blaby DC, 2001–03. Chairman: E Midlands Regl Assembly, 2002–10; E Midlands Councils, 2010–12. Mem., Cttee of the Regions, EU, 2005–13. Dep. Chm., LGA, 2008–12 (Chm., Improvement Bd, 2008–15); Mem., Regl Econ. Council, 2008–10; Chm., Local Govt Develt Agency, 2010–12. Contested (UK Ind) S Holland and The Deepings, 2015. *Recreations*: farming, cartography.

**PARSONS, Sir John (Christopher)**, KCVO 2002 (CVO 1998; LVO 1992); Deputy Keeper of the Privy Purse and Deputy Treasurer to the Queen, 1988–2002; an Extra Equerry to the Queen, since 2002; *b* 21 May 1946; *s* of late Arthur Christopher Parsons and of Veronica Parsons; *m* 1982, Hon. Anne Manningham-Buller, *d* of 1st Viscount Dilhorne, PC; two *s* one *d*. *Educ*: Harrow; Trinity College, Cambridge (MA Mech. Scis). FCA; FIC. Dowty Group Ltd, 1968–72; Peat, Marwick, Mitchell & Co., 1972–85; Asst Treas. to the Queen, 1985–87; Dep. Dir (Finance), Royal Collection, 1992–93. Lay Mem., Chapter, 2001–14, Treas., 2004–14, Lay Canon, 2014–16, now Emeritus, Peterborough Cathedral. Trustee and Treas., Music in Country Churches, 2006–; Trustee, Country Houses Foundn, 2006–. Mem. Council and Treas., Internat. Dendrology Soc., 2009–. Gov., Elstree Sch., 1987–2014 (Vice-Chm., 2002–09; Chm., 2009–14). *Address*: The Old Rectory, Eydon, Daventry, Northants NN11 3QE. *Clubs*: Brooks's, Pratt's.

**PARSONS, Prof. (John) David**, DSc; FREng, FIET; independent consultant, since 1998; David Jardine Professor of Electrical Engineering, 1982–98, and Head, Department of Electrical Engineering and Electronics, 1983–86 and 1996–98, University of Liverpool; *b* 8 July 1935; *s* of Oswald Parsons and Doris Anita (*née* Roberts); *m* 1969, Mary Winifred Stella Tate (*d* 2010). *Educ*: University College of Wales, Cardiff (BSc); King's College London (MSc (Eng), DSc (Eng)). FIET (FIEE 1986); FREng (FEng 1988). GEC Applied Electronics Labs, 1959–62; Regent Street Poly., 1962–66; City of Birmingham Poly., 1966–68; Lectr, Sen. Lectr and Reader in Electronic Engrg, Univ. of Birmingham, 1969–82; University of Liverpool: Dean, Faculty of Engrg, 1986–89; Pro-Vice-Chancellor, 1990–96. Vis. Prof., Univ. of Auckland, 1982; Vis. Res. Engr, NTT, Japan, 1987. UN Expert in India, 1977; Hon. SPSO, RSRE, Malvern, 1978–82. Member Council: IERE, 1985–88; IEE, 1988–89. *Publications*: Electronic and Switching Circuits, 1975; Mobile Communication Systems, 1989; The Mobile Radio Propagation Channel, 1992, 2nd edn 2000; many papers on radio communication systems and radio propagation in learned jls. *Recreations*: golf, bridge, playing banjo and ukulele, classic cars. *Address*: 5 Norcote Lodge, Old Town Lane, Formby, Merseyside L37 3HP.

**PARSONS, Kathryn**, MBE 2017; Co-Founder, and Chief Executive Officer, Decoded, since 2011; *b* London, 1981; *d* of James and Marie Parsons. *Educ*: Channing Sch. for Girls, London; Downing Coll., Cambridge (MA Classics). Non-exec. Dir, BEIS, 2017–. *Recreations*: cryptography, cartography, cartwheels.

**PARSONS, Loretta Caroline Rose**; see Minghella, L. C. R.

**PARSONS, Luke Arthur**; QC 2003; *b* 3 March 1962; *s* of John Andrew Parsons and Frances Patricia Parsons; *m* 1989, Isabelle Jane Munro; five *s*. *Educ*: John Fisher Sch., Purley; Bristol Univ. (LLB 1984). Called to the Bar, Inner Temple, 1985; practising commercial barrister, 1986–; Hd of Quadrant Chambers, 2012–. Gov., Linacre Centre on Bioethics, 2002–07. *Publications*: (jtly) Admiralty and Commercial Forms and Precedents, 1991. *Recreations*: history, classical music, theatre. *Address*: Quadrant Chambers, Quadrant House, 10 Fleet Street, EC4Y 1AU. *T*: (020) 7583 4444, *Fax*: (020) 7583 4455. *E*: luke.parsons@quadrantchambers.com.

**PARSONS, Michael John**; Director General, Government Property, Cabinet Office, since 2017; *b* St Albans, 1 Sept. 1965; *s* of John Parsons and Geraldine Parsons. *Educ*: Churston Grammar Sch.; Christ's Coll., Cambridge (BA Nat. Scis and Computer Sci. 1986). CPFA 1989. Cambridgeshire County Council, 1986–2009: various accountancy roles; Asst Dir, Resources; Dir, Resources; Dep. Chief Exec., Corp. Services; Dir, Resources and Performance, Herts CC, 2009–13; Dir, Resource and Orgnl Develt, UK Border Agency, 2013; Chief Operating Officer, then Dir Gen., Capabilities and Resources, Home Office, 2013–17. *Recreations*: running, walking, sailing, cinema. *Address*: Cabinet Office, 70 Whitehall, SW1A 2AS. *T*: (020) 7276 3573. *E*: michael.parsons@cabinetoffice.gov.uk.

**PARSONS, Nicholas**; see Parsons, C. N.

**PARSONS, Prof. Peter John**, FBA 1977; Regius Professor of Greek, University of Oxford, 1989–2003; Student of Christ Church, Oxford, 1964–2003; *b* 24 Sept. 1936; *s* of Robert John Parsons and Ethel Ada (*née* Frary); *m* 2006, Barbara Montagna Macleod (*d* 2006). *Educ*: Raynes Park County Grammar Sch.; Christ Church, Oxford (MA 1961). Oxford University: Craven Scholar, 1955; 1st Cl. Hons Mods and de Paravicini Scholar, 1956; Chancellor's Prize for Latin Verse and Gaisford Prize for Greek Verse, 1st Cl. Lit. Hum., Derby Scholar, Dixon and Sen. Scholar of Christ Church, 1958; Passmore Edwards Scholar, 1959; Lectr in Documentary Papyrology, 1960–65; Lectr in Papyrology, 1965–89. J. H. Gray Lectr, Univ. of Cambridge, 1982; Heller Lectr, Univ. of Calif, Berkeley, 1988. Hon. PhD: Bern, 1985; Athens, 1995; Hon. DLitt Milan, 1994. *Publications*: (jtly) The Oxyrhynchus Papyri XXXI, 1966, XXXIII and XXXIV, 1968, LIV, 1987, LIX, 1992, LX, 1994, LXVI, 1999, LXVIII, 2003, LXXI, 2007, LXXVIII, 2012, LXXIX, 2013, LXXXIII, 2018; The Oxyrhynchus Papyri XLI, 1973; (with H. Lloyd-Jones) Supplementum Hellenisticum, 1983; City of the Sharp-Nosed Fish: Greek lives in Roman Egypt, 2007; (jtly) The Vienna Epigrams Papyrus, 2015; articles in learned jls. *Recreations*: music, film, gardening, cooking and eating. *Address*: Christ Church, Oxford OX1 1DP. *T*: (01865) 422132.

**PÄRT, Arvo**; free-lance composer, since 1967; *b* Estonia, 11 Sept. 1935; *s* of August Pärt and Linda Anette Pärt (*née* Mäll); *m* 1st, 1959, Hille Aasmäe (marr. diss.); one *d*; one *b* by Marina Nestieva; 2nd, 1972, Nora Supina; two *s*. *Educ*: composition studies with Heino Eller, Conservatory of Music, Tallinn, Estonia. Sound Engr, Estonian broadcasting station, Tallinn, 1958–67; free-lance composer, Tallinn, 1967–80; emigrated to Vienna, 1980; became Austrian citizen, 1981; Scholar, Deutscher Akademischer Austauschdienst, Berlin, 1981; in Berlin, 1981–2010, in Estonia, 2010–. Hon. Member: Amer. Acad. of Arts and Letters, 1996; Royal Sch. of Church Music, UK, 2003; Accad. Nazionale di Santa Cecilia, Rome, 2004; Internat. Soc. for Contemporary Music, 2014; Associate Mem., Royal Acad. of Sci and Fine Arts, Belgium, 2001; Mem., Pontifical Council for Culture, Vatican, 2011–. Mem., Estonian Acad. of Scis, Academician for Music, 2011. Hon. PhD: Acad. of Music and Th., Tallinn, 1989; Royal Swedish Music Acad., 1991; Hon. DMus: Sydney, 1996; Durham, 2002; Fryderyk Chopin Univ. of Music, Poland, 2018; Hon. Dr: Univ. of Tartu, Estonia, 1998; Univ. Nacional de Gen. San Martin Escuela de Humanidades, Argentina, 2003; Freiburg, 2007; Liège, 2009; St Andrews, 2010; Pontifical Inst. for Sacred Music, Vatican, 2011; Lugano, 2012; Oxford, 2016; St Vladimir's Orthodox Theol Seminary, USA, 2014. Triumph award, Russia, 1997; Culture Prize, Estonia, 1998; Herder Award, Germany, 2000; Composition Trophy C. A. Seghizzi, Gorizia, Italy, 2003; Borderland Award, Sejny, Poland, 2003; Classic Brit Award, 2003, 2011; Composer of the Year, Musical America, 2005; Eur. Award of Sacred Music, Germany, 2005; Internat. Brückepreis, Görlitz/Zgorzelec, Germany/Poland, 2007; Baltic Star Prize, St Petersburg, 2007; Sonning Music Prize, Denmark, 2008; Lifelong Achievement Award, Republic of Estonia, 2009; Lifelong Achievement Award, Internat. Istanbul Music Fest., 2010; Hommage, Konrad Adenauer Fund, Germany, 2011; Praemium Imperiale, Japan, 2014; Medal of Pontifical Council for Culture, Per Arte ad Deum, Poland, 2016; Ratzinger Prize, Vatican, 2017; Honoured Artist of Music, Internat. Assoc. of People in Music, Russia, 2017; German Music Authors' Prize, 2019. Order of the Nat. Coat of Arms (Estonia), 2nd class 1998, 1st class 2006; Commandeur de l'Ordre des Arts et des Lettres (France), 2001; Cross of Honour for Sci. and Art, 1st class (Austria), 2008; Chevalier, Légion d'Honneur (France), 2011; Decoration for Sci. and Art (Austria), 2015; Cultural Merit Order (Music Category) (Romania), 2016; Cross of Recognition, 2nd class (Latvia), 2019. *Compositions* include: Sinfonie No 1, 1963; Sinfonie No 2, 1966; Pro et contra (cello concerto), 1966; Credo, 1968; Sinfonie No 3, 1971; Fratres (variations for ensembles, orchestra and various instruments), 1977–2009; Tabula Rasa (double violin concerto), 1977; Sarah was Ninety Years Old, 1976, 1989; Spiegel im Spiegel, 1978–2011; Passio, 1982; Stabat Mater, 1985; Te Deum, 1985; Sieben Magnificat-Antiphonen (choir a capella), 1988; Miserere, 1989; Berliner Messe (choir, soloists and organ), 1990; Berliner Messe (choir, soloists and string orch.), 1991; Litany (soloists, choir and orch.), 1994; Kanon Pokajanen (choir a cappella), 1997; Como cierva sedienta (solo soprano and orch.), 1998; Cantique des Degrés (choir and orch.), 1999; Orient & Occident (string orch.), 2000 (Classical Brit Contemp. Music Award, 2003); Cecilia, Vergine Romana (choir and orch.), 2000; My Heart's in the Highlands (voice and organ), 2000, (voice, violin, viola, violoncello and piano), 2013; Salve Regina (choir and organ), 2001; Lamentate (piano and orch.), 2002; In Principio (choir and orch.), 2003; Passacaglia (violin and piano), 2003; L'Abbé Agathon (soprano and 8 celli), 2004; Da Pacem Domine (choir and instruments), 2004–10 (Grammy Award, Best Choral Recording, 2007); Vater Unser (voice and piano), 2005, (voice and string orchestra or string quintet), 2013; La Sindone (orch.), 2005; Für Lennart (orch.), 2006; Passacaglia (violin or two violins and orch.), 2007; These Words… (string orch.), 2008; Symphony No 4 Los Angeles, 2008 (Classical Brit Award for Composer of the Yr, 2011); O-Antiphonen (cello octet), 2008; Stabat Mater (choir and string orch.), 2008; Silhouette (string orch. and percussion), 2009; Adam's Lament (choir and string orch.), 2010; In Spe (woodwind, horn and string orch.), 2010; Salve Regina (choir, celesta and string orch.), 2011; Virgencita, 2012–13; Swansong: Littlemore Tractus (orch.), 2013; Greater Antiphons, 2015; Kleine Litanei (mixed choir a cappella), 2015; And I heard a voice…/Ja ma kuulsin hääle… (mixed choir a cappella), 2017. *Address*: c/o Universal Edition, Bösendorferstr. 12, 1010 Vienna, Austria.

**PARTASIDES, Constantine**; QC 2014; Partner, Three Crowns LLP, since 2014; *b* Nicosia, Cyprus, 5 Dec. 1969; *s* of Doros and Vera Partasides; *m* 2000, Dr Patricia Cabredo Hofherr; two *d*. *Educ*: Haberdasher's Aske's Sch. for Boys, Elstree; King's Coll. London (BA Hons Modern Hist.); Peterhouse, Cambridge (MPhil Internat. Relns 1993). Admitted as Solicitor, 1996, Solicitor Advocate, 2008; with Freshfields, subseq. Freshfields Bruckhaus Deringer, 1994–2014, Partner, 2004–14. *Publications*: (jtly) Redfern & Hunter on International Arbitration, 5th edn 2009, 6th edn 2015. *Recreations*: history, politics, football. *T*: 07872 156814. *E*: constantine.partasides@threecrownsllp.com.

**PARTHIER, Prof. Benno**; Director, Institut für Pflanzenbiochemie, Halle, 1990–98, now Emeritus; President, Deutsche Akademie der Naturforscher Leopoldina, 1990–2003; *b* 21 Aug. 1932; *s* of Hermann and Helene Parthier; *m* 1967, Christiane Luecke; one *s* two *d*. *Educ*: Martin Luther Univ., Halle-Wittenberg (Dip. Biol. 1958; Dr rer. nat. 1961; Dr habil. 1967). Asst, Botanical Inst., Univ. Halle, 1958–65; Head, Dept of Molecular Biol., Inst. of Plant Biochemistry, Acad. of Scis, GDR, 1967–90. Mem., learned socs, Germany and overseas. Hon. Dr Würzburg, 2003. *Publications*: (with R. Wollgiehn) Von der Zelle zum Molekül, 1971 (Polish edn 1976); (with L. Nover and M. Luckner) Zell differenzierung, Molekulare Grundlagen und Probleme, 1978 (English edn 1982); numerous papers in sci. jls; Editor and co-Editor 10 sci. jls. *Recreations*: gardening, travelling. *Address*: c/o Deutsche Akademie der Naturforscher Leopoldina, Postfach 110543, 06109 Halle, Germany. *T*: (345) 4723915.

**PARTINGTON, Adrian Frederick**, FRCO; Director of Music, Gloucester Cathedral, since 2008; Artistic Director, BBC National Chorus of Wales, since 2000; *b* Nottingham, 1 Oct. 1958; *s* of Kendrick and Mary Partington; *m* 1981, Clare Diana Crane; four *s* one *d*. *Educ*: King's Sch., Worcester; Royal Coll. of Music; King's Coll., Cambridge (BA 1981; MA). FRCO 1978. Organ Scholar: St George's Chapel, Windsor, 1976–78; King's Coll., Cambridge, 1978–81; Asst Organist, Worcester Cathedral, 1981–91; Dir of Music, Sch. of St Mary and St Anne, Abbots Bromley, 1991–95; Lectr, RWCMD, 1995–2011. Conductor: City of Birmingham Symphony Youth Chorus, 1995–2000; Bristol Choral Soc., 2000–13. Jt Artistic Dir, Three Choirs Fest., 2008–. *Address*: 7 Millers Green, Gloucester GL1 2BN. *T*: (01452) 524764. *E*: adrian.partington@gloucestercathedral.org.uk.

**PARTINGTON, Ven. Brian Harold**, OBE 2002; Archdeacon of Man, 1996–2005, now Emeritus; Vicar of St George's, Douglas, 1996–2004; *b* 31 Dec. 1936; *s* of Harold Partington and Edith (*née* Hall); *m* 1962, Valerie Nurton; two *s* one *d*. *Educ*: Burnage Grammar Sch., Manchester; St Aidan's Coll., Birkenhead. Nat. Service, RAF, 1955–57; local govt officer, Manchester Corp., 1953–59. Ordained deacon, 1963, priest, 1964; Assistant Curate: Emmanuel Church, Didsbury, Manchester, 1963–66; St Mary's, Deane, Bolton, 1966–68; Vicar: Kirk Patrick, Sodor and Man, 1968–96; Foxdale, 1977–96; St John's, 1977–96. Bishop's Youth Officer, 1968–77; Rural Dean of Peel, 1976–96; Canon of St Patrick, St German's Cathedral, 1985–96. Pres., Hospice Isle of Man (formerly Hospice Care), 2008– (Chm., 1988–96; Vice Pres., 1996–2008). Exec. Chm., IOM Sports Council, 1990–2002; Chm., Internat. Island Games Orgn, 2005–07 (Vice-Chm., 2001–05; Hon. Life Mem., 2007); President: IOM Hockey Assoc., 1997–2006; IOM Cricket Assoc., 1998–2006; Pres., IOM Golf Union, 2010–12. *Recreations*: cricket, golf, travel, sailing. *Address*: Brambles, Kirk Patrick, Isle of Man IM5 3AH. *T*: (01624) 844173. *Clubs*: St John's Cricket; Peel Golf (Capt., 2006; Pres., 2016); IOM Yacht (Principal, RYA Trng Centre, 2006–16).

**PARTINGTON, Gillian Doreen, (Mrs W. D. Partington)**; see Ruaux, Her Honour G. D.

**PARTINGTON, Prof. (Thomas) Martin**, CBE 2002; Professor of Law, 1987–2006, now Emeritus, and Senior Research Fellow, since 2009, Bristol University; Special Consultant to the Law Commission, 2006–07 (a Law Commissioner, 2001–05); *b* 5 March 1944; *s* of Thomas Paulett Partington and Alice Emily Mary Partington; *m* 1st, 1970, Marcia Carol Leavey (marr. diss.); one *s*; 2nd, 1978, Daphne Isobel Scharenguivel; one *s* one *d*. *Educ*: King's Sch., Canterbury; Peterhouse, Cambridge (BA 1965; LLB 1966). Called to the Bar, Middle Temple, 1984, Bencher, 2006. Asst Lectr, Bristol Univ., 1966–69; Lectr, Warwick Univ., 1969–73; LSE, 1973–80; Prof. of Law, Brunel Univ., 1980–87 (Dean,

Faculty of Soc. Scis, 1985–87); Dean, Faculty of Law, 1988–92, Pro-Vice-Chancellor, 1995–99, Bristol Univ. Visiting Professor: Osgoode Hall Law Sch., Canada, 1976; Univ. of NSW, 1983; Vis. Sen. Res. Fellow, Inst. of Advanced Legal Studies, 2006–10. Academic Advr, Univ. (formerly Coll.) of Law, 2006–14. Chm., Cttee of Heads of Univ. Law Schools, 1990–92. Vice-Chm., Legal Action Gp, 1982–83; Member: Lord Chancellor's Adv. Cttee on Legal Aid, 1988–91; Law Society's Trng Cttee, 1989–92; Law Society's Academic Consultative Cttee, 1989–92; Judicial Studies Bd, 1992–95 (Mem., Tribunals Cttee, 1988–95); Trng Cttee, Ind. Tribunal Service, 1990–94; Council on Tribunals, 1994–2000; Civil Justice Council, 1998–2005; Bd, United Bristol Healthcare NHS Trust, 1998–2001; Adv. Cttee, Leverhulme Trust Res. Awards, 1999–2006; External Adviser, Educn and Trng Cttee, Inst. of Housing, 1985–89. Chm., Council, 2009–10, Bd, 2010–, Dispute Service; Specialist Advr, Public Admin Select Cttee, 2012; Consultant, Qatar Financial Centre Authy, 2012–14; External Reviewer, Hong Kong Res. Grants Council, 2012–; Chm., Review of Inst. of Advanced Legal Studies, Univ. of London, 2012. Part time Chairman: Soc. Security Appeals Tribunal, 1990–94; Med. Appeals Tribunal, 1992–94; Disability Appeals Tribunal, 1992–94. Expert Consultant: Leggatt Review of Tribunals, 2000–01; Employment Tribunals Taskforce, 2001–02. Barrister, Chambers of A. Arden, QC, 1993–2010. Chm., Socio-Legal Studies Assoc., 1993–95. Gen. Editor, Anglo-American Law, now Common Law World, Review, 1984–2003; Mem., Editl Cttee, Tribunals Jl. FRSA 1999; FAcSS 2015. Hon. Fellow, Soc. of Advanced Legal Studies, 2001. Hon. QC 2008. Lifetime Achievement Award, Socio-Legal Studies Assoc., 2016. *Publications:* Landlord and Tenant, 1975; Claim in Time, 1978; (with A. Arden) Housing Law, 1983; (with P. O'Higgins) Bibliography of Social Security Law, 1986; Secretary of State's Powers of Adjudication in Social Security Law, 1990; (with J. Hill) Housing Law: cases, materials and commentary, 1991; United Kingdom: Social Security Law, 1998, 3rd edn, 2009; (with M. Harris) Administrative Justice in the 21st Century, 1999; Introduction to the English Legal System, 2000, 14th edn 2019; Consulting Ed., Halsbury's Laws of England, vol. 65, Legal Aid; articles on public law, housing law, social security law, legal educn, law reform, Legal Aid and Legal Services. *Recreations:* listening to music, reading fiction, cooking. *Address:* First Floor Flat, 8/9 Clifton Hill, Bristol BS8 1BN. *T:* (0117) 973 6294.

**PARTRIDGE, David John Gratiaen,** RIBA; Managing Partner, Argent LLP, since 2012; Joint Chief Executive Officer, Argent Related Partnership, since 2016; *b* Hatton, Sri Lanka, 2 Aug. 1958; *s* of John and Wendy Partridge; *m* 1988, Rebecca Lee; one *s* one *d*. *Educ:* King's Sch., Canterbury; Christ's Coll., Cambridge (BA 1979; DipArch). RIBA 1983. Partner, Gebler Tooth Partridge, 1983–90; Argent Group, 1990–2012: Bd Dir, 1997–2012; Jt CEO, 2006–12. Chm., CityCo Manchester Ltd, 2006–10. Pres., British Council for Offices, 2015–16. Chair, UK Green Bldg Council, 2017–. *Recreations:* Ibiza, diving, watching sport and the arts. *Address:* Argent LLP, 4 Stable Street, N1C 4AB. *T:* (020) 3664 0226. *E:* david.partridge@argentllp.co.uk.

**PARTRIDGE, Derek William,** CMG 1987; HM Diplomatic Service, retired; *b* 15 May 1931; *o s* of late Ernest and Ethel Elizabeth Partridge (*née* Buckingham), Wembley. *Educ:* Preston Manor County Grammar Sch., Wembley. Entered Foreign Service (later Diplomatic Service), 1949. Royal Air Force, 1949–51. Served: Foreign Office, 1951–54; Oslo, 1954–56; Jedda, 1956; Khartoum, 1957–60; Sofia, 1960–62; Bangkok, 1962; Manila, 1962–65; Djakarta, 1965–67; FCO, 1967–70; Diplomatic Service Inspectorate, 1970–72; British Consul-General, Brisbane, 1972–74; First Sec. (Economic and Commercial), Colombo, 1974–77; FCO, 1977–86: Counsellor and Head of Migration and Visa Dept 1981–83; Counsellor and Head of Nationality and Treaty Dept, 1983–86; High Comr, Sierra Leone, 1986–91. Mem. (Lib Dem) Southwark BC, 1994–2002. Chm., Pumphouse Educnl Trust, 2002–12. Gov., St George's Primary Sch., Southwark, 1996–2002. Recipient of Maundy Money from HM the Queen, 2016. *Address:* 16 Wolfe Crescent, Rotherhithe, SE16 6SF. *T:* (020) 7231 2759. *Club:* National Liberal (Vice Pres., 2017–).

**PARTRIDGE, Ian Harold,** CBE 1992; full-time concert singer (tenor), 1963–2008; Professor, Royal Academy of Music, since 1996; *b* 12 June 1938; *s* of late Harold Partridge and Ena Stinson; *m* 1959, Ann Glover; two *s*. *Educ:* New Coll., Oxford (chorister); Clifton Coll. (music scholar); Royal Coll. of Music; Guildhall Sch. of Music (LGSM, singing and teaching). Began as piano accompanist, although sang tenor in Westminster Cath. Choir, 1958–62; performed in England and all over the world, both in recitals (with sister Jennifer) and in concerts; has worked with many leading conductors, incl. Stokowski, Boult, Giulini, Boulez and Colin Davis. Opera debut at Covent Garden as Iopas in Berlioz, Les Troyens, 1969. Title role, Britten's St Nicolas, Thames Television (Prix Italia, 1977). Over 150 records, *including:* Bach, St John Passion; Handel, Chandos Anthems, and Esther; Schubert, Die Schöne Müllerin, Die Winterreise; Schumann, Dichterliebe; Beethoven, An die ferne Geliebte; Vaughan-Williams, On Wenlock Edge; Warlock, The Curlew; Fauré and Duparc Songs; Britten, Serenade and Winter Words; Lord Berners, Complete Songs; as conductor (of Pro Cantione Antiqua), The Triumphs of Oriana. Innumerable radio broadcasts, many TV appearances. Chm., Royal Soc. of Musicians, 1999–2001 (Gov., 1995–99 and 2005–); Pres., ISM, 1996–97; Dir, Performing Artists' Media Rights Assoc., 1996–2002. Governor, Clifton Coll., 1981–. Sir Charles Santley Meml Gift, Musicians' Co., 1992. Hon. RAM 1996. Harriet Cohen Award, 1967. *Recreations:* bridge, horse racing, theatre, cricket. *Address:* 127 Pepys Road, SW20 8NP. *Clubs:* Garrick, Royal Over-Seas League.

**PARTRIDGE, James Richard John,** OBE 2002; Founder and Director, Face Equality International, since 2018; *b* Chipping Sodbury, 30 Oct. 1952; *s* of Sir (Ernest) John Partridge, KBE and Joan Emily, (Johnnie), Partridge, MBE; *m* 1978, Caroline Judith Schofield; one *s* two *d*. *Educ:* Clifton Coll.; University Coll., Oxford (MA Hons PPE); London Sch. of Hygiene and Tropical Medicine (MSc Med. Demography). Asst Health Economist at St Thomas' Hosp., 1976–78; Res. Fellow, Unit for Study of Health Policy, Guy's Hosp., 1978–79; dairy farmer, St Andrews, Guernsey, 1979–92; econs teacher, Ladies' Coll., Guernsey, 1986–92; Founder and Chief Exec., Changing Faces, 1992–2017. Dir, Dining with a Difference, 2001–. Mem., Appraisal Cttee, NICE, 1999–2004; Association Mem., Bupa, 2013–; Lay Mem., Ind. Reconfiguration Panel, DoH, then DHSC, 2017–. Mem., States of Guernsey Agricl and Milk Mktg Bd, 1988–92. Associate, Business Disability Forum, 1992–. Trustee and Dir, Guernsey Community Foundn, 2010–. Hon. FRCSEd 2005. Hon. DSc: West of England, 1999; Bristol, 2005. *Publications:* Changing Faces: the challenge of facial disfigurement, 1990, 7th edn 2017. *Recreations:* family, organic vegetable growing, golf, reading, writing and researching. *Address:* Moulière, La Banquette, Albecq, Guernsey, Channel Islands GY5 7EQ. *T:* 07785 508402. *E:* james.partridge@faceequalityinternational.com. *Club:* Royal Guernsey Golf.

**PARTRIDGE, Dame Linda,** DBE 2009 (CBE 2003); FMedSci; FRS 1996; FRSE; Weldon Professor of Biometry, since 1994, and Director, Institute of Healthy Ageing, since 2007, University College London; *b* 18 March 1950; *d* of George and Ida Partridge; *m* 1st, 1983, Dr V. K. French (marr. diss. 1992); 2nd, 1996, Prof. Michael John Morgan, *qv*. *Educ:* Convent of the Sacred Heart, Tunbridge Wells; St Anne's Coll., Oxford (MA); Wolfson Coll., Oxford (DPhil 1974). Post-doctoral Fellow, York Univ., 1974–76; Edinburgh University: Lectr, 1976–87; Reader in Zoology, 1987–92; Prof. of Evolutionary Biol., 1992–93; NERC Res. Prof., 1997–2002, BBSRC Professorial Fellow, 2002–07, UCL. Founder Dir, Max Planck Inst. for Biol. of Ageing, Cologne, 2008–. Hon. Prof., Faculty of Maths and Natural Scis, Univ. of Cologne, 2011–. Croonian Prize Lect., Royal Soc., 2009. Mem. Council, BBSRC, 1998–2001. Trustee, Natural Hist. Mus., 2000–08. President: Internat. Soc. for Behavioural Ecology, 1990–92; Assoc. for Study of Animal Behaviour, 1995–97; Genetical Soc., 1999–2003. Member: Eur. Acad. of Scis, 2004; EMBO, 2005. FRSE 1992; FMedSci 2004. Hon. DSc: St Andrews, 2004; Oxford, 2011; Bath, 2011; Brighton, 2012. Frink Medal, Zool Soc. of London, 2000; Sewall Wright Award, Amer. Soc. of Naturalists, 2002; Fondation IPSEN Longevity Prize, 2004; Lord Cohen Medal, British Soc. for Res. on Ageing, 2004; Medal, Assoc. for Study of Animal Behaviour, 2005; Living Legend, Help the Aged, 2006; Thomassen a Thuessink Medal, Univ. of Groningen, Netherlands, 2008; Darwin-Wallace Medal, Linnean Soc., 2009; Women of Outstanding Achievement Award for Sci. Discovery, Innovation and Entrepreneurship, UK Resource Centre for Women in Sci., Engrg and Technol., 2009. *Publications:* on ageing and evolutionary biology in scientific jls. *Recreations:* birdwatching, tennis, hill walking, gardening. *Address:* Institute of Healthy Ageing, Department of Genetics, Evolution and Environment, University College London, Darwin Building, Gower Street, WC1E 6BT.

**PARTRIDGE, Sir Michael (John Anthony),** KCB 1990 (CB 1983); Permanent Secretary, Department of Social Security, 1988–95; *b* 29 Sept. 1935; *s* of late Dr John Henry Partridge, DSc, PhD, and Ethel Green; *m* 1968, Joan Elizabeth Hughes; two *s* one *d*. *Educ:* Merchant Taylors'; St John's Coll., Oxford (BA (1st Cl. Hons Mods and Lit Hum) 1960, MA 1963; Hon. Fellow, 1991). Entered Home Civil Service (Min. of Pensions and Nat. Insce), 1960; Private Sec. to Permanent Sec., 1962–64; Principal, 1964–71 (MPNI, Min. of Social Security and DHSS); DHSS: Asst Sec., 1971–76; Under Sec., 1976–81; Dep. Sec., 1981–83; Dep. Under-Sec. of State, Home Office, 1983–87; Second Permanent Sec., DHSS, 1987–88. Non-executive Director: Norwich Union, 1996–2000; Epworth Investment Mgt Ltd, 1996–2011; The Stationery Office, 1997–99; Aviva (formerly CGNU), 2000–03; Magdi Yacoub Inst. (formerly Harefield Res. Foundn), 2001–14 (Vice-Chm., 2003–14); Chm., The Stationery Office Pension Scheme, 2003–. Senior Treasurer, Methodist Ch Finance Div., 1980–96; Mem., Central Finance Bd and Council, Methodist Ch, 1980–2011. Trustee: Harefield Hosp. Heart Transplant Trust, 1991–2003; Methodist Ministers' Pensions Trust, 1993–2011. Member: Court, Univ. of York, 1991–95; Council, Univ. of Sheffield, 2001–03. Governor: Middlesex Univ., 1992–2014 (Chm., 1997–2001; Pro-Chancellor, 2002–); Merchant Taylors' Sch., 1992–99; Chm. of Govs, Heathfield Sch., 2004–11. Pres., Old Merchant Taylor's Soc., 2002–03. CCMI (CBIM 1988). Liveryman, Merchant Taylors' Co., 1987. DUniv Middlesex, 2015. *Publications:* (ed jtly) Serta Scissorum, 2012. *Recreations:* Do-it-Yourself, classical sites, reading, ski-ing. *Address:* 27 High View, Pinner, Middlesex HA5 3NZ. *T:* (020) 8868 0657. *Club:* Oxford and Cambridge.

**PARTRIDGE, Sir Nicholas (Wyndham), (Sir Nick),** Kt 2009; OBE 1999; Chief Executive, Terrence Higgins Trust, 1991–2013; *b* Rickmansworth, 28 Aug. 1955; *s* of Miles and Patricia Partridge; civil partnership 2008, Simon Vearnals. *Educ:* W Somerset Sch., Minehead; Keele Univ. (BA Hons Internat. Relns 1978). Thorn EMI, 1978–80; Rank Xerox, 1980–82; Amsterdam, 1982–84; with Terrence Higgins Trust, 1985–2013. Chair, Involve, 1998–2011. Mem., Commn for Health Improvement, 1999–2004; Vice-Chair, Expert Adv. Gp on AIDS, 2001–12; Deputy Chair: Healthcare Commn, 2004–09; UK Clin. Res. Collaboration, 2005–; Health and Social Care Inf. Centre, subseq. NHS Digital, 2013–17; Mem., Health Honours Cttee, 2012–18; Chm., Clinical Priorities Adv. Gp, NHS England, 2013–. Hon. DLitt Keele, 2008; Hon. DSc De Montfort, 2011. *Recreations:* cooking, travel, 20th century music.

**PASCALE, Lorraine;** television chef and cookery writer; *b* 17 Nov. *Educ:* Leith's Sch. of Food and Wine (Dip. Food and Wine); Univ. of W London (BSc 1st Cl. Culinary Arts Mgt 2011). Model, NY; worked in kitchens of hotels, restaurants, incl. Petrus, Mandarin Oriental, Gilgamesh, The Wolseley, London; opened shop, Ella's Bakehouse, Covent Gdn, 2009. Presenter, TV series: Baking Made Easy, 2011; Home Cooking Made Easy, 2011; Lorraine's Fast, Fresh and Easy Food, 2012; My Kitchen Rules, 2014; How To Be A Better Cook, 2014. Ambassador, Prince's Trust, 2012–; Govt Fostering Ambassador, 2014–. *Publications:* Home Cooking Made Easy, 2011; Baking Made Easy, 2011; Fast, Fresh and Easy Food, 2012; A Light Way To Bake, 2013; How To Be A Better Cook, 2014; Eating Well Made Easy, 2015; Bake, 2017.

**PASCALL, David Lewis,** CBE 1993; Managing Director, Pascall Associates, European business and financial consultancy, since 2008; *b* 5 Feb. 1949; *s* of Robert Lewis Pascall and Dorothy Pascall (*née* Smith); *m* 1980, Carolyn Judith White; one *s* two *d*. *Educ:* Queen Mary's Grammar Sch., Basingstoke; Univ. of Birmingham (BSc 1st Cl. Hons Chem. Engrg 1970); INSEAD, Fontainebleau (MBA Dist. 1979). With British Petroleum Co. plc, 1967–93: posts in oil refining, trading, finance and business management in UK and, 1974–79, Germany and France; Divl Manager, BP Finance Internat., 1986–89; Manager: BP Share Sale, 1987; Project 1990 (cultural change prog.), 1989–93; Finance Dir, 1993–94, Chief Exec., Asia Pacific, 1994–95, MAI plc; Finance Dir to Hon. Sir Rocco Forte, 1996–98; Eur. Transaction Dir, Prin. Finance Gp, Nomura Internat., 2000–02; Man. Dir, Terra Firma Capital Partners Ltd, 2002–07. On secondment to: Central Policy Rev. Staff, Cabinet Office, 1982–83; No 10 Policy Unit, 1983–84. Chairman: Bio Products Laboratory Ltd, 2010–12; DCI Biologicals Inc., 2011–12; Enercoutim Gp, Portugal, 2016–. Non-executive Director: Colt Gp Ltd, 1999–2000; Deutsche Annington Regl Supervisory Bds, 2001–11; Airports Internat., 2008–09; Royal Free NHS Trust, 2009–10. Advr, MoD Defence Costs Review, 1994. Mem., 1990–91, Chm., 1991–93, Nat. Curriculum Council; Mem. Exec. Cttee, Field Studies Council, 1993–99. Mem., Develt Adv. Council, Univ. of Birmingham, 2005–09. Chm., Newham Partnership Working Ltd, 2013–14. Foundn Gov., Sir John Cass and Redcoat Comprehensive Sch., Stepney, 1995–2001, 2008– (Chm., 2009–15). Chm., Mind in Haringey, 2015–; Dep. Chm., Pathway, 2010–18. Mem., Nat. Soc., 1994–2000. FRSA 1993. *Recreations:* my family, current affairs, golf. *Address:* 31 Lanchester Road, N6 4SX. *T:* (020) 8883 8740. *E:* david@pascallassociates.co.uk. *Clubs:* Highgate Golf, Trevose Golf.

**PASCO, Adam Gerhold;** Managing Director, Adam Pasco Media, since 2012; Editor: BBC Gardeners' World magazine, 1991–2012; Waitrose Garden Magazine, 2016–17; Garden Editor, Waitrose Weekend, since 2018; *b* 11 Jan. 1957; *s* of Cecil Filmer Pasco and Sheila Mary Pasco (*née* Gerhold); *m* 1992, Jayne Petra Fisher; one *s* one *d*. *Educ:* North East Surrey Coll. of Technol. (HND Applied Biology 1977); Univ. of Nottingham (BSc Horticulture 1982). Technical Editor, 1982–84, Editor, 1984–88, Garden Answers magazine; Editor, Garden News, 1988–90. Gardening Correspondent, Daily Telegraph, 1995–2000; Ed., then Editl Dir, BBC Easy Gardening magazine, 2002–06; Editl Dir, BBC Magazines' Gardening Gp, 2003–11; weekly blog column on gardenersworld.com, 2007–12; presenter, World Radio Gardening, 2013–15, and blogger, https://worldradiogardening.wordpress.com, 2015–16. *Publications:* Collins Complete Garden Manual, 1998; Greenfingers Book, 1999; Collins Gardeners' Calendar, 2000. *Recreations:* gardening, cookery, photography, writing, walking, guitar, ukulele, travel, family life.

**PASCOE, Alan Peter,** MBE 1975; Executive Chairman, The Partnership Consultancy, since 2014; *b* 11 Oct. 1947; *s* of late Ernest George Frank Pascoe and of Joan Rosina Pascoe; *m* 1970, Della Patricia (*née* James); one *s* one *d*. *Educ*: Portsmouth Southern Grammar Sch.; Borough Road Coll. (Cert. in Educn); London Univ. (BEd Hons). Master, Dulwich Coll., 1971–74; Lectr in Physical Educn, Borough Road Coll., Isleworth, 1974–76. Dir, 1976–83, Man. Dir, 1983, Chm., 1985–98, CEO, 1994–98, Alan Pascoe Associates Ltd, then API Gp of Cos; Chm., Carat Sponsorship, 1987–92; Dir, WCRS, then Aegis Gp, 1986–92; Chm., Fast Track, 1998–2012; Pres., CSM Sport & Entertainment (formerly Chime Sports and Events Div.), 2013–14 (Chm., 2010–13). Vice Chm., London 2012 Olympic Bid, 2003–05. Member: Sports Council, 1974–80; Minister for Sport's Working Party on Centres of Sporting Excellence; BBC Adv. Council, 1975–79. Trustee: Torch Trophy Trust, 2006–12; Young Enterprise Trust, 2008–12; Sported, 2013–. European Indoor Champion, 50m Hurdles, 1969; Eur. Games Silver Medallist, 110m Hurdles, 1971; Silver Medal, Olympic Games, Munich, 4×400m Relay, 1972; Europa Cup Gold Medallist, 400m Hurdles, 1973; Commonwealth Games Gold Medal, 400m Hurdles, and Silver Medal, 4×400m Relay, 1974; Eur. Champion and Gold Medallist in both 400m Hurdles and 4×400m Relay, 1974; Europa Cup Gold Medallist, 400m Hurdles, 1975; Olympic Finalist (injured), Montreal, 1976; Europe's Rep., World Cup, 1977. Fellow, Mktg Soc., 2014. Mem. Bd, London Marathon Events Ltd, 2017–. Trustee, London Manhattan Charitable Trust, 2015–. DUniv Brunel, 1997. Hollis Sponsorship Personality of the Year, Hollis Publications, 2004; Outstanding Achievement Award, UK Sponsorship Awards, 2014; Lifetime Achievement Award, Sports Industry Awards, 2014. *Publications*: An Autobiography, 1979. *Recreations*: theatre, sport, travel.

**PASCOE, Martin Michael;** QC 2002; *b* 1953; *s* of late Michael Raymond Pascoe and Dorothy Agnes Pascoe. *Educ*: Christ Church, Oxford (BA Juris. 1976, BCL 1977). Called to the Bar, Lincoln's Inn, 1977, Bencher, 2011; in practice, specialising in corporate and internat. insolvency law. *Address*: 3–4 South Square, Gray's Inn, WC1R 5HP. *T*: (020) 7696 9900, *Fax*: (020) 7696 9911. *E*: martinpascoe@southsquare.com.

**PASCOE, Dr Michael William;** Head of Science, Camberwell College of Arts (formerly Camberwell School of Arts and Crafts), 1981–90; *b* 16 June 1930; *s* of Canon W. J. T. Pascoe and Mrs D. Pascoe; *m* 1st, 1956, Janet Clark (marr. diss. 1977); three *d*; 2nd, 1977, Brenda Hale Reed; one *d*. *Educ*: St John's, Leatherhead; Selwyn Coll., Cambridge (BA, PhD). MInstP. Res. Student (Tribology), Cambridge, 1951–55; Physicist: Mount Vernon Hosp., Northwood, 1956–57; British Nylon Spinners Ltd, 1957–60; Chemist/Physicist, ICI Paints Div., 1960–67; Lectr (Polymer Science), Brunel Univ., 1967–77; Principal Scientific Officer, 1976–79, Keeper of Conservation and Technical Services, 1979–81, British Museum. Tutor and Counsellor, Open Univ., 1971–76. Occasional Lecturer: West Dean Coll., 1989–90; Camberwell Coll. of Arts; ICCROM; Vis. Lectr in Materials, Univ. of Brunel, 1995 and 1999. Consultant to: Historic Wrecks Cttee, Dept of Trade (Marine), 1979–81; Royal Acad. of Arts (Great Japan exhibn), 1982; Mary Rose Trust, 1978–83; Council for the Care of Churches, 1980–91; Public Record Office (Domesday exhibn), 1986; Science Museum, 1988; Crafts Council; States of Jersey; Parliament of Guyana, 1991; Univ. of Stirling, 1991–92; and advr on conservation facilities, Portsmouth CC; Govt and cultural instns of Guatemala on conservation matters, 1996; Conservation Advr, Winchester Coll. FRSA. *Publications*: contrib. to books on polymer tribol. and technol.; articles in scientific, engrg and conservation jls on tribol., materials technol., history of adhesives and on conservation methods. *Recreations*: painting and drawing, theatre, active in University of the Third Age, lecturing in gen. sci., history and contemporary topics, *inter alia*.

**PASCOE, Nigel Spencer Knight;** QC 1988; Legal Assessor; a Recorder of the Crown Court, 1979; *b* 18 Aug. 1940; *er s* of late Ernest Sydney Pascoe and of Cynthia Pascoe; *m* 1964, Elizabeth Anne Walter; two *s* four *d*. *Educ*: Epsom Coll. Called to the Bar, Inner Temple, 1966, Bencher, 1996; Leader, Western Circuit, 1995–98; a Pres., Mental Health Review Tribunal, 2002. Chm., Bar Public Affairs Cttee, 1996–98. County Councillor for Lyndhurst, Hants, 1979–84. Founder and Editor, All England Qly Law Cassettes, 1976–85; Chm., Editl Bd, Counsel mag., 2000–07. *Publications*: The Trial of Penn and Mead, 1985; The Nearly Man, 1994; Pro Patria, 1996; Who Killed William Rufus?, 2000; Without Consent, 2004; To Encourage the Others, 2006; Last Call to San Giorgio, 2014; Sleeping Dogs, 2015; Sweet Reason, 2015; My Country Right or Wrong, 2015; Made in Cornwall, 2016; Innocent 2017; Flying Solo, 2019; articles in legal jls. *Recreations*: theatre, devising and presenting with Elizabeth Pascoe legal anthologies, after-dinner speaking, play writing, broadcasting. *Address*: Pump Court Chambers, Temple, EC4Y 7AJ. *T*: (020) 7353 0711. *Club*: Garrick.

**PASCOE, Gen. Sir Robert (Alan),** KCB 1985; MBE 1968; Adjutant General, 1988–90; Aide de Camp General to the Queen, 1989–91, retired; *b* 21 Feb. 1932; *er s* of late Clarence and Edith Mary Pascoe; *m* 1st, 1955, Pauline (*née* Myers) (*d* 2013); one *s* three *d*; 2nd, 2016, Alison Mary Masters (*née* Miller). *Educ*: Tavistock Grammar Sch.; RMA, Sandhurst. rcds, psc; Middle East Centre for Arab Studies, Shemlan. Commissioned Oxford and Bucks LI, 1952; served with 1 Oxf. Bucks, 1 DLI and 4 Oxf. Bucks (TA), 1953–57; Middle East Centre for Arab Studies, Lebanon, 1958–59; 1st Cl. Interpretership (Arabic); GSO2 Land Forces Persian Gulf, 1960–62; sc Camberley, 1963; Co. Comd 2RGJ, UK and Malaysia, 1964–66 (despatches (Borneo) 1966); GSO2 HQ 2 Div. BAOR, 1967–68; Co. Comd 1RGJ, UK and UNFICYP, 1968–69; Second in Comd 2RGJ, BAOR, 1969; MA to QMG, 1970–71; Comd 1RGJ, 1971–74, BAOR and NI (despatches (NI) 1974); Col General Staff HQ UKLF, 1974–76; Comd 5 Field Force BAOR, 1976–79; rcds 1979; Army Rep. on Staff of Security Co-ordinator, NI, 1979–80; Asst Chief of Gen. Staff (Operational Requirements), MoD, 1981–83; Chief of Staff, HQ, UKLF, 1983–85; GOC Northern Ireland, 1985–88. Rep. Col Comdt, RGJ, 1988–90; Colonel Commandant: 1st Bn Royal Green Jackets, 1986–91; Army Legal Corps, 1988–90. Hon. Col, Oxfordshire ACF, 1991–2002; Vice Pres., Oxfordshire ACF League, 2002–19. Mem. Adv. Bd, The Rifles, 2007–12. Chm., Belautruche (UK) plc, 1997–2000; non-exec. Dir, Belautruche NV, 1997–2000. Chairman of Governors: Royal Sch., Bath, 1988–96 (Governor, 1981–96); Royal High Sch., Bath, 1996–2006. Gov., King Edward VII's Hosp., London, 2006–15 (Mem. of Council 1995–2006). President: Army LTA, 1986–91; Army Boxing Assoc., 1989–90; RGJ Golf Soc., 1999–2005; Reg. Forces Employment Assoc., 1997–99 (Chm., 1994–97); Potterne Br., RBL, 2006–18; Veterans Charity (formerly Project 65), 2007–18; Chm., Ex-Services Resettlement Gp, 1994–98. Mem. and Vice Pres., Royal Patriotic Fund Corp., 1992–2011; Patron: Retired Officers Assoc., 1991–2001; NI Veterans' Assoc., 2017–. Chairman: 43rd and 52nd Club, 1992–2002; Oxford and Bucks LI Mus. Trustees, 1992–2002. Hon. Associate, Girls' Day Sch. Trust, 2007. Freeman, City of London, 1992; Hon. Liveryman, Fruiterers' Co., 1992. *Recreations*: gardening, golf, fishing, tennis, ski-ing. *Club*: Cavalry and Guards.

**PASCOE-WATSON, George William;** Senior Partner, Portland Communications, since 2015 (Partner, since 2009); *b* Edinburgh, 21 Aug. 1966; *s* of John and Margaret Pascoe-Watson; *m* 2011, Natalie Jane Kirby; two *s*. *Educ*: George Heriot's Sch., Edinburgh; Royal High Sch., Edinburgh; Napier Coll., Edinburgh. The Sun: reporter, 1988–94; political corresp., 1994–96; Dep. Political Ed., 1996–2006; Political Ed., 2006–10. *Recreation*: golf. *Address*: Portland, 1 Red Lion Court, EC4A 3EB. *E*: gpw@portland-communications.com. *Club*: Richmond Golf.

**PASLEY, Sir Robert Killigrew Sabine,** 6th Bt *cr* 1794, of Craig, Dumfriesshire; chartered accountant; Chief Strategy Officer, Cell C (Pty) Ltd, South Africa; *b* 23 Oct. 1965; *s* of Sir Malcolm Pasley, 5th Bt, FBA and of Virginia Killigrew (*née* Wait); *S* father, 2004; *m* 2002, Katja Antoinette Jozefina Arnoldina Hermans; one *s* three *d*. *Educ*: Univ. of Exeter (BSc Hons Theoretical Physics 1987). ACA 1990. Formerly Strategy Dir, Vodacom Gp, SA. *Heir*: *s* Henry Malcolm Sabine Pasley, *b* 8 Sept. 2009.

**PASSI, Nitin;** Founder and Chief Executive Officer, Missguided Ltd, since 2009; *b* Manchester, 22 Nov. 1982; *s* of Rajib and Neera Passi. *Educ*: Cranleigh Sch., Surrey; Newcastle Univ. (BA Business 2005). *E*: nitin@missguided.com.

**PASSINGHAM, Prof. Richard Edward,** PhD; FRS 2009; Professor of Cognitive Neuroscience, University of Oxford, 1997–2008; Fellow, Wadham College, Oxford, 1976–2008, now Emeritus; *b* London, 16 Aug. 1943; *s* of Bernard and Margaret Passingham; *m* 1971, Clare Darlington; one *s* one *d*. *Educ*: Shrewsbury Sch.; Balliol Coll., Oxford (BA 1966); Inst. of Psychiatry, Univ. of London (MSc Clin. Psychol. 1967); PhD London 1971. University of Oxford: Lectr, Dept of Exptl Psychol., 1976–93; Reader *ad hominem*, 1993–97; Hon. Sen. Lectr, MRC Cyclotron Unit, Hammersmith Hosp., 1991; Hon. Principal, Wellcome Centre for Neuroimaging, UCL, 1994. Fellow, Assoc. for Psychol Sci., 2010. *Publications*: The Human Primate, 1982; The Frontal Lobes and Voluntary Action, 1993; What is Special About the Human Brain?, 2008; The Neurobiology of the Prefrontal Cortex, 2012; A Short Guide to Brain Imaging, 2015; A Very Short Introduction to Cognitive Neuroscience, 2016; (ed) Computational Theories and Their Implementation in the Brain, 2017. *Recreations*: playing the piano, listening to classical music, reading novels, biographies, history. *Address*: 16 Ambleside Drive, Oxford OX3 0AG. *T*: 07811 345104. *E*: dick.passingham@psy.ox.ac.uk.

**PASSLEY, Patrick Derek,** LVO 2013; Founder, and Principal (formerly Managing Director), London College of Law (formerly Paralegal Charity), since 1994; *b* London, 10 Oct. 1965; *s* of Ivan Augustus Passley and Lurline Isamanda Passley; *m* 1991, Jean Francis; two *d*. *Educ*: Poly. of E London (LLB Hons); Middlesex Univ. (CertEd; Assessors Trainers Award Cert.). Law Lectr, Barnet Coll., 1991–2002. Commission for Racial Equality: Mem., 1999–2003; Chm., Nat. Sports Cttee, 2001; Official Observer on Disability Rights Commn, 2000–03; Special Advr to Trevor Philips, 2003–04; nominated CRE Comr for the Formal Investigation into CPS, 2000–01, and into Prison Service, 2000–03; UK Delegate, Consultative Commn on Industrial Change, Eur. and Econ. Social Cttee, Brussels, 2004–12. Member Council: Prince's Trust, 2001–12 (Mem. Adv. Bd, 2013–); King George's Jubilee Trust, 2001. Member: Equity Sub-gp, Sport England, 2000–03; Mgt Cttee, Sporting Equals, CRE/Sport England, 2005–08; Communications Cttee, FA, 2003–04; Adult Learning Cttee, Nat. LSC, 2000–04 and 2005; London E Local LSC, 2001–03. Sec., African and Caribbean Finance Forum, 2001–03; Trustee, African Caribbean Leadership Council, 2007–. Jt Council for Anglo-Caribbean Churches, 2003. *Recreations*: amateur boxing (former Nat. Amateur Boxing Champion and Commonwealth Rep. for England at Super Heavyweight, 1989–90), movies, current affairs, sport.

**PASSMORE, Colin John;** Senior Partner, Simmons & Simmons LLP, since 2011; *b* Grays, Essex, 25 Jan. 1959; *s* of Roger and Dorothy Passmore; *m* 1985, Julie Braithwaite (*d* 2009); three *d*. *Educ*: Palmer's Endowed Sch. for Boys, Grays; Southampton Univ. (LLB 1981); Coll. of Law, Guildford. Admitted as solicitor, 1984, as solicitor-advocate (civil), 1999. Coward Chance: articled clerk, 1982–84; qualified lawyer, 1984–86; Simmons & Simmons LLP: Associate, Hong Kong, 1988; Partner, 1990; Sen. Litigation Partner, 2005–11. Freeman: City of London; Solicitors' Co. *Publications*: Privilege, 1998, 4th edn 2019; (contrib.) Fraud, ed Ormerod and Montgomery, 2007. *Recreations*: the law, travel, political history, horse riding, seeking to make a small difference. *Address*: Simmons & Simmons LLP, City Point, One Ropemaker Street, EC2Y 9SS. *T*: (020) 7628 2020, *Fax*: (020) 7628 2070. *E*: colin.passmore@simmons-simmons.com.

**PASSMORE, George,** RA 2017; artist; *b* Plymouth, Devon, 1942. *Educ*: Dartington Hall Coll. of Art; Oxford Sch. of Art; St Martin's Sch. of Art. Collaboration with Gilbert Proesch, *qv*, as Gilbert and George. Gallery exhibitions include: Modern Fears, 1980, The Believing World, 1983, New Pictures, 1987, Worlds & Windows, 1990, New Democratic Pictures, 1992, Anthony d'Offay Gall.; The Rudimentary Pictures, Milton Keynes Gall., 2000; New Horny Pictures, White Cube$^2$, 2001; Perversive Pictures, NY, 2004; Jack Freak Pictures, White Cube, 2009, European mus. tour, 2010; The Banners, White Cube, 2015; Gilbert and George: the beard pictures and their f***osophy, White Cube, 2017; museum exhibitions include: The Paintings, 1971, Photo-Pieces 1971–80, 1981, Whitechapel Art Gall.; Pictures 1982 to 85, Hayward Gall., 1987; Enclosed and Enchanted, MOMA, Oxford, 2000; The Dirty Words Pictures (retrospective), Serpentine Gall., 2002; Gilbert & George: major exhibition (retrospective), Tate Modern, 2007, US mus. tour, 2008; London Pictures, White Cube, 2012; living sculpture includes: The Red Sculpture; Underneath the Arches; The Singing Sculpture; Our New Sculpture. Work in permanent collections incl. Nat. Portrait Gall., Tate Modern and San Francisco Mus. of Modern Art. Represented GB, Venice Biennale, 2005. (Jtly) Turner Prize, 1986. *Publications*: (as George), with Gilbert Proesch: Lost Day; Oh, the Grand Old Duke of York; What Our Art Means. *Address*: c/o White Cube$^2$, 144–152 Bermondsey Street, SE1 3TQ.

**PASSMORE, John William;** QC 2015; *b* Guildford, 23 Aug. 1969; *s* of Arthur Peter Roy Passmore and Ethel Rosemarie Anne Passmore (*née* Glanville); *m* 2011, Claire Rosalind Wood; one *s* one *d*. *Educ*: Weydon Sch., Farnham; Univ. of Bristol (LLB Hons); Inns of Court Sch. of Law. Called to the Bar: Lincoln's Inn, 1992; NI, 2003; in practice as a barrister, specialising in commercial and Admiralty law, 1993–. Member: Bar Pro-Bono Unit, 1998–; Equality and Diversity Cttee, Bar Council, 2012–. *Recreations*: running, cinema, ballet, opera, music, travelling, food and drink. *Address*: Quadrant Chambers, 10 Fleet Street, EC4Y 1AU. *T*: (020) 7583 4444. *E*: john.passmore@quadrantchambers.com.

**PASTON-BEDINGFELD, Sir Henry Edgar;** *see* Bedingfeld.

**PATAKI, George Elmer;** Principal, Pataki-Cahill Group LLC, since 2007; Senior Counsel, Norton Rose Fulbright, since 2017; Governor, New York State, 1995–2006; *b* 24 June 1945; *s* of Louis Pataki and Margaret Pataki; *m* Elizabeth (Libby) Rowland; two *s* two *d*. *Educ*: Peekskill High Sch.; Yale Univ. (BA 1967); Columbia Univ. Sch. of Law (JD 1970). Associate, Dewey, Ballantine, Bushby, Palmer and Wood, 1970–74; Partner, Plunkett & Jaffe, 1974–89; Of Counsel, Chadbourne and Parke LLP, 2007–17. Mem., State Assembly 91st AD, 1985–92; Ranking Minority Member: Assembly Envmtl Conservation Cttee, 1987–90; Assembly Educn Cttee, 1991–92; Mem., State Senate 37th SD, 1993–95; Chm., State Ethics Cttee, 1993–95. Mayor, Peekskill, Westchester City, 1982–84. Co-proprietor, Pataki Farm, Peekskill, NY. *Recreations*: hiking in the woods, ski-ing, basketball, working on the family farm.

**PATE, Prof. John Stewart,** FRS 1985; FAA 1980; FLS; Professor of Botany, University of Western Australia, 1974–2000, now Emeritus Professor and Honorary Research Fellow, since 2001; *b* 15 Jan. 1932; *s* of Henry Stewart Pate and Muriel Margaret Pate; *m* 1959, Elizabeth Lyons Sloan, BSc (*d* 2004); three *s*. *Educ*: Campbell College; Queen's Univ., Belfast (BSc, MSc, PhD, DSc). FLS 1990. Lectr, Sydney Univ., 1956–60; Lectr, Reader,

Personal Chair in Plant Physiology, Queen's Univ. Belfast, 1960–73. Vis. Fellow, Univ. of Cape Town, 1973. Hon. DSc UWA 2006. *Publications:* (ed with J. F. Sutcliffe) Physiology of the Garden Pea, 1977; (ed with A. J. McComb) Biology of Australian Plants, 1981; (with K. W. Dixon) Tuberous, Cormous and Bulbous Plants, 1983; (ed with J. S. Beard) Kwongan: plant life of the sandplain, 1984; (ed with K. A. Meney) Australian Rushes: biology, identification and conservation of Restionaceae and allied families, 1999; (ed jtly and contrib.) Agriculture as a Mimic of Natural Ecosystems, 1999; reviews on carbon nitrogen metabolism and biology of Australian flora and on understanding how plants can bioengineer soil profiles (three key reviews 2001, 2006, 2012). *Recreations:* music, writing books on nature study, hobby farming, academic contact. *Address:* School of Plant Biology, University of Western Australia, 35 Stirling Highway, Crawley, WA 6009, Australia; 681 Mount Shadforth Road, Denmark, WA 6333, Australia.

**PATEL,** family name of **Barons Patel** and **Patel of Bradford**.

**PATEL,** Baron *cr* 1999 (Life Peer), of Dunkeld in Perth and Kinross; **Narendra Babubhai Patel,** KT 2009; Kt 1997; Consultant Obstetrician, Tayside Teaching Hospitals NHS Trust, Dundee, 1974–2003, now Hon. Consultant; Hon. Professor, University of Dundee, 1974–2003; *b* 11 May 1938; *m* 1970, Dr Helen Dally; twin *s* one *d. Educ:* Univ. of St Andrews (MB, ChB 1964). MRCOG 1969, FRCOG 1988; FRSE 1999; FMedSci. Chairman: Acad. of Med. Royal Colls, Scotland, 1994–95; Acad. of Med. Royal Colls, UK, 1996–98; Specialist Trng Authority, 1998–2001; Clinical Standards Bd for Scotland, 1999–2003; NHS Quality Improvement, Scotland, 2002–06; Member: Council, GMC, 1998–2003; Armed Forces Pay Review Bd, 2000–06; MRC, 2008–12. Chm., Stem Cell Steering Cttee, 2003–; Vice-Pres., All Party Parly Gp on Maternity Services, 2002–, on Infertility Services, 2003–; Mem., Sci. and Technol. Cttee, H of L, 2000, 2004, 2005–08, 2010–15, 2017–. Pres., RCOG, 1995–98 (Hon. Sec., 1987–92; Vice-Pres., 1992–95); Vice Pres., FIGO, 2000–03. Chancellor, Dundee Univ., 2006–17. Founder FMedSci 1998. Hon. Fellowships: FACOG 1996; FSOGC 1997; FSACOG 1997; FICOG 1997; FRCPE 1997; FRCSE 1997; FRCPGlas 1998; FRCS 1998; FSLCOG 1998; FRANZCOG 1998; FRCA 1998; FRCPI 2000; FFPH 2003; FRCGP 2004; FRCPsych 2005; Eur. Soc. of Perinatal Medicine, 2002. Hon. Mem., German, Finnish, Argentinian, Chilean and Italian Socs of Obstetrics and Gynaecology. Hon. DSc: Napier, 1996; Aberdeen, 2001; St Andrews, 2001; Hon. MD: Stellenbosch, 2001; Hon. Dr: Athens, 2004; London, 2008; Hon. LLD Dundee, 2004. *Publications:* books and articles on pre-term labour, foetal monitoring, birth handicap, obstetrics, etc. *Recreations:* occasional golf, walking. *Address:* University of Dundee, Nethergate, Dundee DD1 4HN.

**PATEL OF BRADFORD,** Baron *cr* 2006 (Life Peer), of Bradford, in the County of West Yorkshire; **Kamlesh Kumar Patel,** OBE 1999; Professor, since 2000, and Head, International School of Communities, Rights and Inclusion, since 2008, University of Central Lancashire; University Director of Strategic Partnerships, and Senior Advisor to the Vice Chancellor, University of East London, since 2010; *b* 28 Sept. 1960; *s* of Sudhindra Kumar Patel and Savita Devi Patel; *m* 1998, Yasmin Saloojee; two *s*, and two step *d. Educ:* Univ. of Huddersfield (DipSW; CQSW). Ambulance man, 1981–83; social worker, 1983–87; Specialist Case Worker, Bradford Social Services, 1987–89; Manager, The Bridge Project (voluntary orgn for substance abuse/mental health), 1987–95; University of Central Lancashire: Sen. Lectr, 1995–98, Principal Lectr in Health and Social Care Policy, 1998–2000; Hd, Centre for Ethnicity and Health, 2000–08; Prof. and Sen. Mgt Team, De Montfort Univ., 2010. Nat. Strategic Dir, Nat. Inst. for Mental Health in England, 2003–04 (on secondment); Nat. Dir, Black and Minority Ethnic Mental Health Prog., DoH, 2004–07; Expert Ministerial Advr to Sec. of State for DCLG, 2008–09. A Lord in Waiting (Govt Whip), 2008–09. Chm., All Party Parly Gp on Men's Health, 2010–. Hon. Lectr, Univs of Huddersfield, Lancaster, Salford and Northumbria, 1991–95. Chm., Mental Health Act Commn, 2002–08 (Mem., 1995–2001; Vice-Chm., 2001–02); Member: Commn for Healthcare Audit and Inspection, 2003–06; (and Trustee) UK Drug Policy Commn, 2007–09. Chm., Nat. Prison Drug Treatment Review Gp, 2008–10 (reported 2010); Member: Adv. Council on Misuse of Drugs, 1990–96; Nat. Treatment Agency, 2001–09; Global Task Force, UNICEF, 2006–; Chairman: Integrated Equality and Human Rights Cttee, Leics, Leicester and Rutland, 2010–; Internat. Deaf Foundn, 2010–; Community Innovations Enterprise and Internat. Forum for Community Innovations, 2011–; Bradford Teaching Hosps NHS Foundn Trust, 2014–16. Patron: Men's Health Forum, 2006–; Sharing Voices Bradford, 2006–; Bridge Proj., Bradford, 2008–; Equality Partnerships, 2009–; Westminster Health Forum, 2009–; British Muslim Heritage Centre, 2009–; Bradford Cyrenians, 2010–; Awazz, Nottingham, 2012–; Engaged Communities, 2012–; Mental Health First Aid, 2012–. Pres., Bradford Magistrates Chaplaincy Service, 2008–. Hon. DLitt Manchester Metropolitan, 2007; Hon. DCL Huddersfield, 2008. Plaque of Recognition (India), 1999; Award of Achievements (Educn), India Internat. Foundn, 2008; Glory of India Award, 2009. *Publications:* numerous contribs to books, jls, Home Office and DoH Reports on drugs, alcohol, mental health, community engagement, research, black and minority ethnic health and social care. *Recreations:* cricket, cricket coach. *Address:* 3 Old School, 23 James Street, Thornton, Bradford BD13 3NR; House of Lords, SW1A 0PW. *E:* patelkk@parliament.uk, kkpatel@ucl.ac.uk.

**PATEL, Bhikhu Chhotabhai;** Co-Chairman, Waymade Plc, Atnahs Group and associated companies; *b* Kenya, 1 Aug. 1947; *s* of late Chhotabhai and of Shantaben Patel; *m* 1975, Shashikala Naranbhai Patel; one *s* two *d. Educ:* Univ. of Bristol (BA Arch.; DipArch.). RIBA 1978. (With V. C. K. Patel) co-founded: Waymade Healthcare plc, 1984; Amdipharm, 2002. CCMI 2002. Mem., Lions Clubs Internat. (Melvin Jones Fellow; Recognition of Distinguished Leadership Award, 2004). Hon. LLD Bristol, 2006; Hon. DSc Anglia Ruskin, 2008. (Jtly) UK Entrepreneur of the Year, 2001. *Recreations:* swimming, walking, travelling, reading.
*See also* V. C. K. Patel.

**PATEL, Chaitania,** CBE 1999; FRCP; Founder and Chairman: Court Cavendish Group, since 2007; HC-One, since 2011; *b* 14 Sept. 1954; *s* of Bhupendra and Ashru Patel; *m*; three *d. Educ:* Southampton Univ. (BM 1979). MRCP 1982, FRCP 1999. MRC Res. Fellow, Pembroke Coll., Oxford, 1985; Investment Banker, Merrill Lynch and Lehman Brothers, 1985–89; founded Court Cavendish plc, 1989, subseq. Care First plc; Chief Exec., Westminster Health Care Ltd, 1999–2002; CEO, Priory Gp, 2002–07. Chm. and Founder Partner, Elysian Capital, 2008–; Chm., Integrated Pharmaceutical Services Ltd, 2010–14; Dep. Chm., Care Mgt Gp, 2008–. Member: Better Regulation Task Force, 1997–2002; DoH Task Force for Older People, 1997–2002; Dir, Acute Bd, Independent Healthcare Assoc., 2003–05. Mem. Adv. Bd, Bridges Community Ventures, 2009–13. Trustee: Help the Aged, 2000–02; IPPR, 2000–09 (Sec., 2000–07); Windsor Leadership Trust, 2001–11. Patron: British Olympics Team 2012 Appeal, 2009; Policy Res. Inst. on Ageing and Ethnicity, 2004–10; The Infant Trust; Rwandan Meml Project. FRSA. DUniv Open, 2002. *Recreations:* golf, music, theatre, travelling, films, photography. *E:* chai@courtcavendish.com. *Clubs:* Royal Automobile, Mosimann's, Soho House, Arts, Harry's Bar, Eden; Beaverbrook Golf.

**PATEL, Dame Indira,** DBE 2011 (OBE 1998); National Council of Women Great Britain Representative on United Nations Non-Governmental Organisation Committee on Status of Women, New York, since 2003; *b* Kenya, 27 March 1946; *d* of Ishwerbhai Patel and Dahiben Patel; *m* 1964, Bhanu Patel; two *s* (one *d* decd). *Educ:* Bondeni Girls Primary Sch., Mombasa; Coast Girls High Sch., Mombasa; High Ridge Teachers Trng Coll., Nairobi. Primary sch. teacher, Nairobi, Kenya, 1965–75; asst, sub post office, 1976–82; Liaison Officer (pt-time), Visits Section, FCO, 1998; newsagent retail business, 1982–87; property mgt, 1982. Chm., UK Asian Women's Conf., 1987–93; Chair, Women's Nat. Commn Task force on World Conf. on Racism, Durban, 2000, on Female Genital Mutilation for UN Commn on Status of Women, 2000. Mem. Cttee, UN Develt Fund, 2000–03; Comr, Women's Nat. Commn, 2003–07; Mem., Organising Cttee, Commn on Status of Women, NY, 2003–10; Co-Chm., morning briefings, UN NGO Cttee on Status of Women, NY, 2003–09. Fellow, Internat. Fedn of Business and Professional Women, 1996–. Internat. speaker on human rights of women, and oppression of women in name of culture, religion and traditions incl. forced and early marriages, traditions of dowries, trafficking in women and girls, harmful traditional practices affecting women - rights of widows, crimes in name of honour, sexual and reproductive rights, 1985–; Patron, UN Decade of Culture of Peace. *Recreations:* organising holidays and travelling, cooking, interior designing, swimming. *E:* dameindirapatel@gmail.com.

**PATEL, Prof. Ketan Jayakrishna,** PhD; FRS 2015; FMedSci; Professor of Molecular Medicine and Stem Cell Genomics, University of Cambridge, since 2017; Senior Member of Scientific Staff, MRC Laboratory of Molecular Biology, Cambridge, since 1999; Fellow, Gonville and Caius College, Cambridge, since 1995; *b* Nairobi, Kenya, 23 Dec. 1961; *s* of Jayakrishna and Manjula Patel; partner, Dr Fanni Gergely; one *d. Educ:* Banda Sch., Nairobi; Marlborough Coll.; Royal Free Hosp., Univ. of London (MB BS); Cambridge Univ. (PhD 1995). MRCP 1988. Hse Officer, Royal Free Hosp., 1985–86; SHO, Northwick Park Hosp., 1986–88; MRC Fellow, MRC Lab. of Molecular Biol., 1989–93; Registrar in Medicine, Royal Free Hosp., 1993–95; MRC Clinician Scientist, MRC Lab. of Molecular Biol., 1994–99; Res. Fellow, GCCC, 1995–99; MRC Sen. Clin. Fellow, Cambridge Univ. Sch. of Medicine, 1999–2004. Mem., EMBO, 2013. FMedSci 2013. *Publications:* contribs to scientific jls. *Recreations:* opera, oolong teas of China, fine wine. *Address:* MRC Laboratory of Molecular Biology, Francis Crick Avenue, Cambridge CB2 0QH. *E:* kjp@mrc-lmb.cam.ac.uk; 29 Kingfisher Gardens, Trumpington, Cambridge CB2 9AP.

**PATEL, Praful Raojibhai Chaturbhai;** company director; investment adviser in UK, since 1962; Chairman, Asia Fund Ltd, 1984–2011; *b* Jinja, Uganda, 7 March 1939; *s* of Raojibhai Chaturbhai Patel, Sojitra, Gujarat, India, and Maniben Jivabhai Lalaji Patel, Dharmaj, Gujarat; unmarried. *Educ:* Government Sec. Sch., Jinja, Uganda; London Inst. of World Affairs, attached to University Coll., London (Extra Mural Dept). Queen's Scout, 1956. Sec., Uganda Students Union, 1956–58; Deleg. to Internat. Youth Assembly, New Delhi, 1958; awarded two travel bursaries for visits to E, Central and S Africa, and Middle East, to study and lecture on politics and economics; arrived in Britain as student, then commenced commercial activities, 1962; increasingly involved in industrial, cultural and educational projects affecting immigrants in Britain. Spokesman for Asians in UK following restriction of immigration resulting from Commonwealth Immigrants Act 1968; Hon. Sec., All Party Parly Cttee on UK Citizenship, 1968–82; Founder and Council Mem., UK Immigration Advisory Service, 1970–82; Mem., Uganda Resettlement Bd, 1972–74; Hon. Secretary, Uganda Evacuees Resettlement Advisory Trust, 1974–2000; Mem., Indian Govt Consultative Cttee on non-resident Indian investments, 1986–91; Pres., Nava Kala India Socio-Cultural Centre, London, 1962–75; Chm. Bd of Trustees, Swaminarayan Hindu Mission, UK, 1970–76 (Advr to HH Pramukh Swami Maharaj); Jt Convener, Asian Action Cttee, 1976; Director: Shree Ganesh Foundn, 1999–; Indo-British Cultural Exchange, 2002– (Hon. Sec., 1980–82); Chm. and Trustee, Manava Trust, 1979–; Trustee: Charutar Arogya Mandal Trust, 1980–2017; India Overseas Trust, 2002–; Kailas Manasarovar Trust, 2002–. Gen. Sec., Internat. Ayurveda Foundn, 2003–; Hon. Sec., Biomedical Foundn of India, 2010–. Contested (Lab) Brent North, 1987. Producer: ballet, Nritya Natika Ramayana, 1982; film, Kailas Manasarovar Yatra, 1997. Asian Times Award, 1986; Neasden Swaminarayan Mandir Award. *Publications:* articles in newspapers and journals regarding immigration and race relations, natural health issues, politics and business. *Recreations:* cricket, campaigning and lobbying, current affairs, promoting traditional Ayurveda medicines and inter-faith co-operation, collection of 3000 Ganesh Murtis and Hindu artefacts donated to Shree Ganesh Foundation. *Address:* 60 Bedford Court Mansions, Bedford Avenue, WC1B 3AD. *T:* (020) 7580 0897, *Fax:* (020) 7436 2418; Praful Patel Associates, 3rd Floor, Readymoney Mansion, 43 Veer Nariman Road, Bombay 400023, India. *T:* (22) 2049248. *E:* prcp@prafulpatel.co.in.

**PATEL, Rt Hon. Priti;** PC 2015; MP (C) Witham, since 2010; Secretary of State for the Home Department, since 2019; *b* London, 29 March 1972; *d* of Sushil K. Patel and Anjana Patel; *m* 2004, Alex Sawyer; one *s. Educ:* Westfield Girls' Sch., Watford; Keele Univ. (BA Econs); Univ. of Essex (Dip. British Govt). Dep. Press Sec. to Rt Hon. William Hague, MP, 1997–2000; Associate Dir, Shandwick, 2000–03; Corporate Relns Manager, Diageo plc, 2003–07; Dir, Corporate Communications, Weber Shandwick, 2007–10. Exchequer Sec., HM Treasury, 2014–15; Minister of State (Minister for Employment), DWP, 2015–16; Sec. of State for Internat. Develt, 2016–17. *Recreations:* cricket, horseracing, travel. *Address:* House of Commons, SW1A 0AA. *T:* (020) 7219 3000. *E:* WithamMP@parliament.uk.

**PATEL, Rashmita;** *see* Shukla, R.

**PATEL, Sandip;** QC 2014; *b* Kampala, Uganda; *s* of Suryakant and Savita Patel; *m* 1996, Sophie Ramsay; one *s* one *d. Educ:* Rooks Heath Sch.; Essex Univ. (LLB Hons). Called to the Bar, Middle Temple, 1991; in practice as a barrister, 1992–. *Publications:* (contrib.) Electronic Evidence, 3rd edn. *Recreations:* cricket, walking the dog, music. *Address:* Furnival Chambers, 30–32 Furnival Street, EC4A 1JQ.

**PATEL, Sarika;** Partner, Zeus Caps, 2012–18; *b* Bombay, 10 Aug. 1965; *d* of Jagdish Sharma and Usha Sharma; *m* 1991, Bijendra Patel; one *s. Educ:* Univ. of Bombay (BCom 1985; LLB 1988); Univ. of Paisley (Postgrad. Dip. Business 2002). Chartered Accountant 1988; Chartered Marketer 1996. C. M. Shah and Co. Chartered Accts, 1985–88; Audit Officer, Pricewaterhouse, 1988–89; Product Manager—Water Purifiers, and Financial Analyst and Manager Budgets, Eureka Forbes Ltd, India, 1989–94; Business Advr, North Ayrshire Council, 1996–2000; Innovation Manager, Univ. of Paisley, 2000–02; Dir, Innovation and Sectors, London Develt Agency, 2002–05; Hd, Technol., Grant Thornton UK, 2005–08; Gp Dir, MW Corp., 2008–12, and CEO, Klopman Europe, 2008–11. Non-exec. Dir, Imperial NHS Trust, 2013–18. Member: Gambling Commn, 2016–; Bd, Office for Nuclear Regulation, 2017–. Trustee, Royal Instn of GB, 2013–. Non-exec. Vice Chm., Centrepoint, 2007–16; Chm., Action for Children, 2019–. Mem. Court, Univ. of Greenwich, 2010–13. *Recreations:* reading, walking, tennis, cooking, theatre, family. *Address:* 4 Thames Crescent, W4 2RU. *T:* (020) 8995 2422. *E:* sarika.sharmapatel@gmail.com.

**PATEL, Vijaykumar Chhotabhai Kalidas,** OBE 2019; principal Co-founder, 1984, and Chief Executive Officer, since 1989, Waymade Healthcare plc and associated companies; *b* Kenya, 10 Nov. 1949; *s* of late Chhotabhai and of Shantaben Patel; *m* 1975, Smita Kanaiyalal Patel; two *s. Educ:* Leicester Sch. of Pharmacy (BSc Pharm.). MRPS 1973. Opened first pharmacy, Leigh-on-Sea, Essex, 1975, subseq. expanded to chain of pharmacies, then supplier of pharmaceuticals; (with B. C. Patel) co-founded: Waymade Healthcare plc, 1984; Amdipharm, 2002; Atnahs Pharma, 2013; Invest and Develop property co., 2013; owner, Driven Worldwide, 2013. CCMI 2002; FRSA. Mem., Lions Clubs Internat. (Melvin Jones Fellow). Mem., Bd of Govs, De Montfort Univ., 2014–. Hon. DSc: Anglia Ruskin, 2008; De Montfort, 2010. (Jtly) UK Entrepreneur of the Year, 2001; Alumnus of Yr, De Montfort Univ., 2012. *Recreations:* collector of watches and clocks, cars, keep fit, travelling, swimming, hill-walking, public speaking.
*See also B. C. Patel.*

**PATEMAN, Prof. Carole,** DPhil; FBA 2007; FLSW; Professor of Political Science, University of California, Los Angeles, 1990–2011, now Distinguished Professor Emeritus; Hon. Professor, University of Cardiff, 2008–18; *b* Maresfield, Sussex; *d* of Ronald and Beatrice Bennett. *Educ:* Lewes Grammar Sch.; Ruskin Coll., Oxford (Dip. Pol Sci. and Econs (Dist.) 1965); Lady Margaret Hall, Oxford (BA PPE 1967; DPhil 1971). Jun. Res. Fellow, Somerville Coll., Oxford, 1970–72; Reader in Govt, Univ. of Sydney, 1980–89. Vis. Prof. of Pol Sci., Stanford Univ., 1980; Vis. Prof. of Politics, Princeton Univ., 1985–86; Kirsten Hesselgren Prof., Swedish Council for Res. in Humanities and Social Scis, 1988–90; Adjunct Prof., Res. Sch. of Social Scis, ANU, 1993–2000; Vis. Prof., UBC, 1996; Res. Prof., Sch. of Eur. Studies, Cardiff Univ., 2006–08. President: Internat. Pol Sci. Assoc., 1991–94; Amer. Pol Sci. Assoc., 2010–11. Fellow, Univ. of Manchester, 1997. FASSA 1980; Fellow, Amer. Acad. Arts and Scis 1996; FAcSS (AcSS 2010); FLSW 2015. Hon. DLitt: ANU, 1998; NUI 2005; Hon. DSSc Helsinki, 2006. Lifetime Achievement Award, 2004, Special Recognition Award 2013, UK Pol Studies Assoc.; Johan Skytte Prize in Pol Sci., Skytte Foundn, 2012. *Publications:* Participation and Democratic Theory, 1970 (trans. Japanese, Portuguese, Chinese); The Problem of Political Obligation, 1979, 2nd edn 1985; (ed jtly) Women, Social Science and Public Policy, 1985; (ed jtly) Feminist Challenges: social and political theory, 1986, 2013; The Sexual Contract, 1988 (Victoria Schuck Award, 1989, Benjamin Lippincott Award, 2005, Amer. Pol Assoc.) (trans. French, Spanish, Portuguese, Italian, Serbian, Slovak, Croatian, Korean, Chinese); The Disorder of Women, 1989 (trans. Croatian, Japanese); (ed jtly) Feminist Interpretations and Political Theory, 1991; (ed jtly) Justice and Democracy, 2004; (with C. Mills) Contract and Domination, 2007; (ed with Matthew Murray) Basic Income Worldwide: horizons of reform, 2012. *Relevant publications:* (ed jtly) Illusions of Consent: engaging with Carole Pateman, 2008; (ed jtly) Carole Pateman: democracy, feminism and welfare, 2011. *Address:* 90 Adventurers Quay, Cardiff CF10 4NQ.

**PATEMAN-JONES, Alan John;** rare breed farmer, Poole Batten Farm; *b* Ilford, Essex, 20 Sept. 1958; *s* of Edward and Violet Jones; *m* 2006, Jacqueline; two *s. Educ:* Westminster City Sch.; King's Coll., London (BA Hons Geog. 1984). Joined Army 1978; Officer Cadet, RMA Sandhurst, 1978–80; Young Officers' Course, RSME, 1980; Troop Comdr, 24 Field Sqdn, 1981, 10 Field Sqdn, 1984–86; OC 4 Field Sqdn, 21 Engr Regt, 1986–88, RE; Paymasters' Course, RAPC, 1988; 29 Commando Regt, RA, 1988–89; 4th/7th Dragoon Guards, 1989–90. National Westminster Bank: Holborn Circus and City Regl Office, 1991–92; Change Mgt, NatWest Tower, 1992–93; Exec. Asst, Business Develt Dir, 1993–94; Customer Service Design Team, 1994–95; Sen. Manager, Mgt Consultancy Services, Retail Banking Team, Coopers & Lybrand, 1995–97; Exec. Consultant and Partner, Mgt Consultancy Services, Retail Banking Team, Ernst & Young, 1997–2000; Lloyds TSB: Dir, Affluent Sector, Wealth Div., 2000–01; Chief Exec., UK Wealth Mgt, 2001–02; Man. Dir, Customer and Staff Offers and Chm., UK Wealth Mgt, 2002–04; Partner, Mgt Consultancy Services and Hd, Retail Banking, 2004–06, Man. Partner, Financial Services, N Europe, Middle East, India and Africa, 2006–08, Ernst & Young; Dir Gen., Commonwealth War Graves Commn, 2010–14. Non-exec. Chm., Nolan Redsham Ltd, 2014–. Co-opted Mem., Action for Children, 2009–19 (Trustee, Pension Fund, 2011–14); Trustee, English Heritage Foundn, 2014–15. *Recreations:* fell walking, reading, Private Pilot's Licence (H), four border collies, rare pig breeding. *Address:* Poole Batten Farm, Burrington, Umberleigh, Devon EX37 9NG.

**PATERSON, Alasdair Talbert;** Librarian, 1994–2006, also Director of Information Services, 2006, University of Exeter; *b* 22 Oct. 1947; *s* of Talbert Robertson Paterson and Alys Morton Paterson (*née* Campbell); *m* 1st, 1967, Corinne Brenda Norton (marr. diss. 1975); one *s*; 2nd, 1976, Ann Mary Cecilia Mulheirn (*d* 2015); one *s* one *d. Educ:* Leith Acad.; Royal High Sch., Edinburgh; Univ. of Edinburgh (MA 1st cl. Hons 1970); Univ. of Sheffield (MA 1972). ALAI 1990. Asst Librarian, Univ. of Liverpool, 1972–86; Deputy Librarian: UC Cork, 1986–89; Univ. of Sheffield, 1989–94. Mem., Devon and Exeter Instn, 1994–. Eric Gregory Award, Soc. of Authors, 1975. *Publications:* Bibliography of Studies in Regional Industrial Development, 1978; The Floating World, 1984; Brief Lives, 1987; On the Governing of Empires, 2010; Elsewhere or Thereabouts, 2014; articles in prof. jls. *Recreations:* literature, the arts, travel, gardening, walking, watching sport, boules. *Address:* Taddyforde House North, New North Road, Exeter EX4 4AT. *T:* (01392) 430498. *Club:* Isca Pétanque (Exeter).

**PATERSON, Alexander Craig, (Alastair),** CBE 1987; FREng; Senior Partner, Bullen and Partners, Consulting Engineers, 1969–88, retired (Partner 1960–69); *b* 15 Jan. 1924; *s* of Duncan McKellar Paterson and Lavinia (*née* Craig); *m* 1947, Betty Hannah Burley (*d* 2008); two *s* two *d. Educ:* Glasgow High Sch.; Royal Coll. of Science and Technol. (ARCST); Glasgow Univ. (BSc). FICE 1963; FIMechE 1964; FIStructE 1970; FREng (FEng 1983); FCIArb 1968. Commnd REME, 1944; served India and Burma, attached Indian Army, 1944–47. Engineer: with Merz and McLellan, 1947–58; with Taylor Woodrow, 1958–60. Mem., Overseas Projects Bd, 1984–87. Institution of Structural Engineers: Mem. Council, 1976–89; Vice Pres., 1981–84; Pres., 1984–85; Institution of Civil Engineers: Mem. Council, 1978–81 and 1982–91; Vice-Pres., 1985–88; Pres., 1988–89. Pres., British Section, Société des Ingénieurs et Scientifiques de France, 1980; Chm., British Consultants Bureau, 1978–80; Member: Council, British Bd of Agrément, 1982–95; Engrg Council, 1987–90. Mem. Court, Cranfield Inst. of Technol., 1970–80. Hon. DSc Strathclyde, 1989. *Publications:* professional and technical papers in engrg jls. *Recreation:* gardening. *Address:* Willows, The Byeway, West Wittering, Chichester, West Sussex PO20 8LJ. *T:* (01243) 514199. *Club:* Caledonian.

**PATERSON, Bill;** see Paterson, W. T.

**PATERSON, Clare;** freelance television executive and consultant, since 2018; Commissioning Editor (formerly Commissioning Executive), BBC Documentaries, 2009–17; *b* Kent, 14 June 1957; *d* of Peter Paterson and Beryl Paterson (*née* Johnson); *m* 1995, John Wyver; two *s* one *d. Educ:* Sydenham High Sch.; St Anne's Coll., Oxford (BA Classics and Modern Langs). Trainee with EU, 1978–79; Researcher/Asst Producer, BBC, 1979–83; in-house producer, Channel 4 Television, 1983–86; Dir/Exec. Producer, 1986–89, Exec. Producer, 1989–2004, BBC; Hd of Documentaries, RDF TV, 2004–09. Trustee: Horniman Mus. and Dir, Horniman Mus. Enterprises, 2002–16; Refugee Council, 2018–. Gov., Graveney Sch., 2011–. *Publications:* Grow Up: 101 things your child needs to know before leaving home, 2005. *Recreations:* painting, crime fiction, my children, cold water swimming. *E:* clare@clarepaterson.com.

**PATERSON, Douglas McCallum,** CBE 2006; Chief Executive, Aberdeen City Council, 1995–2008; *b* 20 Nov. 1949; *s* of Douglas James Paterson and Violet Joan Paterson (*née* McCallum); *m* 1971, Isobel Stewart Beaton; two *d. Educ:* Aberdeen Univ. (MA Hons Econs 1971; DipEd 1976; MEd Hons 1981); Aberdeen Coll. of Educn (PGCE Dist. 1976); Robert Gordon Univ. (Dip Mgt 1990, DipM 1990). Manager, John Wood Gp, 1971–75; Grampian Regional Council: teacher, then head teacher, 1976–86; Advr in Educn, 1986–90; Depute Dir of Educn, 1990–92; Sen. Depute Dir of Educn, 1992–94; Dir of Educn, 1994–95. Hon. LLD Aberdeen, 2005. *Recreations:* walking, theatre, local history and culture, music, D-I-Y, spending time with my grandchildren.

**PATERSON, Francis, (Frank),** MBE 2013; FCILT; General Manager, Eastern Region, British Rail, York, 1978–85; Member, British Railways (Eastern) Board, 1978–85; Chairman, North Yorkshire Family Practitioner Committee, 1987–91; *b* 5 April 1930; *s* of Francis William Paterson and Cecilia Eliza Reid Brownie; *m* 1950, Grace Robertson (*d* 1996); two *s* two *d. Educ:* Robert Gordon's Coll., Aberdeen. Joined LNER as Junior Clerk, 1946; clerical and supervisory positions in NE Scotland; management training, Scotland, 1956–59; various man-management, operating and marketing posts, Scotland, Lincs and Yorks, 1960–66; Operating Supt, Glasgow North, 1967–68; Sales Manager, Edinburgh, 1968; Asst Divl Manager, S Wales, 1968–70; Dir, United Welsh Transport, 1968–70; Harbour Comr, Newport Harbour, 1968–70; Divl Manager, Central Div., Southern Region, 1970–75; Director: Southdown Motor Services Ltd, 1970–73; Brighton, Hove & District Omnibus Co., 1970–73; Dep. Gen. Man., Southern Region, 1975–77; Chief Freight Manager, British Railways Bd, 1977–78. Dir, N Yorks Moors Rly plc, 1993–2000. Vice-Chm., Nat. Railway Mus. Adv. Bd, 1984–2012 (Mem., 1978–2012); Member: CBI Southern Regional Council, 1975–77; CBI Transport Policy Cttee, 1977–78; BBC NE Adv. Council, 1987–91; Chm., BBC Local Radio Adv. Council, Radio York, 1987–91. Vice Chm., York and Selby CPRE, 2002–. President: St Andrews Soc. of York, 1989–90; Rotary Club of York, 2002–03. Trustee: Friends of Nat. Railway Museum, 1988–2012 (Chm., 2002–12; Pres., 2017–); York Civic Trust, 2004–10. Mem. Court, Univ. of York, 1981–92. FCILT (FCIT 1978 (Mem. Council, CIT, 1979–84); FILT 1999). OStJ 1980. *Publications:* papers to transport societies. *Recreations:* transport, travel, hill walking, country pursuits, Scottish culture, enjoying grandchildren. *Address:* Alligin, 97 Main Street, Askham Bryan, York YO23 3QS. *T:* (01904) 708478. *E:* fpater30@gmail.com.

**PATERSON, Gil(bert);** Member (SNP) Clydebank and Milngavie, Scottish Parliament, since 2011 (Scotland West, 2007–11); Proprietor, Gil's Motor Factors, since 1973; *b* 11 Nov. 1942; *m* (marr. diss.); one *s. Educ:* Possilpark Secondary Sch. Company owner and director. Mem., Strathclyde Regl Council, 1975–78. Mem. (SNP) Central Scotland, Scottish Parlt, 1999–2003; Member: Equal Opportunities Cttee, 2001–03; Procedures Cttee, 2003; Convener, Cross-Party Gp on Men's Violence against Women and Children, 1999–2003. Contested (SNP): Glasgow Central, June 1980; Strathkelvin and Bearsden, 1987; Airdrie and Shotts, Scottish Parlt, 2003. Mem. Nat. Exec., 1995–98, Vice Convenor Fundraising, 2003–, SNP. Mem. Bd, Rape Crisis, 2003–14. *Recreations:* reading, climbing, motorcycling, ski-ing, snowboarding, researching oriental ceramics. *Address:* Scottish Parliament, Edinburgh EH99 1SP.

**PATERSON, Prof. Ian,** PhD; FRS 2005; FRSE; FRSC; Professor of Organic Chemistry, University of Cambridge, since 2001; Fellow, Jesus College, Cambridge, since 1983; *b* 4 May 1954; *s* of Angus and Violet Paterson; *m* 1977, Nina Kuan. *Educ:* Kirkton High Sch., Dundee; Univ. of St Andrews (BSc 1976); Christ's Coll., Cambridge (PhD 1979). Res. Fellow, Christ's Coll., Cambridge, 1978–79; NATO/SERC Postdoctoral Res. Fellow, Columbia Univ., NY, 1979–80; Lectr in Chemistry, UCL, 1980–83; University of Cambridge: Univ. Lectr in Chemistry, 1983–97; Reader in Organic Chemistry, 1997–2001. Lectures: Organic Reactions, USA, 1992; Sandoz, Basel, 1994; Merck, McGill Univ., 2001; Wyeth-Ayerst, MIT, 2002; H. C. Brown, Purdue Univ., 2004; Novartis, Basel, 2006; Bristol-Myers Squibb, UC Irvine, 2007; Gilead Sciences, Stanford, 2008; AstraZeneca, Univ. of Alberta, 2008; Gassman, Univ. of Minnesota, 2009; Abbott, Univ. of Illinois, 2010; Wilson Baker, Univ. of Bristol, 2014; Inaugural Gilbert Stork, Univ. of Wisconsin-Madison, 2014, Univ. of Pennsylvania, 2015; Novartis Central Europe, 2014. FRSE 2010; FRSC 2015. Wilsmore Fellow, Univ. of Melbourne, 2010. Royal Society of Chemistry: Meldola Medal and Prize, 1983; Hickinbottom Res. Fellowship, 1989; Bader Prize, 1996; Synthetic Organic Chemistry Award, 2001; Robert Robinson Award, 2004; Tilden Prize, 2009; Natural Product Chemistry Award, 2014; Pfizer Award in Chemistry, 1990, 1993; ICI (AstraZeneca) Award in Organic Chemistry, 1990. *Publications:* extensive articles in jls incl. Angewandte Chemie, Organic Letters, Jl of ACS, Tetrahedron Letters, Chemical Communications. *Recreations:* gardening, travel. *Address:* Department of Chemistry, University of Cambridge, Lensfield Road, Cambridge CB2 1EW.

**PATERSON, James Rupert;** HM Diplomatic Service, retired; *b* 7 Aug. 1932; *s* of late Major Robert Paterson, MC, Seaforth Highlanders and Mrs Josephine Paterson; *m* 1956, Kay Dineen (*d* 2018); two *s* two *d. Educ:* Nautical Coll., Pangbourne; RMA, Sandhurst. Commnd RA, 1953 (Tombs Meml Prize); Staff Coll., Camberley, 1963; retd from Army with rank of Major, 1970; joined FCO, 1970; First Sec., Pakistan, 1972; Dep. High Comr, Trinidad and Tobago, 1975; Ambassador to the Mongolian People's Republic, 1982; Consul-General, Istanbul, 1985, Geneva, 1989–92. *Recreations:* reading, travel, golf. *Address:* c/o Barclays Bank, Deal, Kent CT14 6EP.

**PATERSON, Janet Lynn,** OBE 2019 (MBE 2014); Chief Executive Officer, British Olympic Foundation, since 2000; *b* Lethbridge, Canada, 21 Aug. 1965; *d* of Gordon Paterson and Beverley Paterson; *m* 1999, Andrew Hibbert. Dir, Olympic Relns, British Olympic Assoc., 2009; Chef de Mission, Youth Olympic Games, Singapore 2010; Dep. Chef de Mission, Team GB, London 2012; Chef de Mission, Team England, Commonwealth Games, Glasgow 2014. Member, Board: Internat. Inspiration, 2009–15; Spirit of 2012, 2013–15. Hon. LLD Bath, 2014. *Address:* British Olympic Foundation, 101 New Cavendish Street, W1W 6XH. *E:* jan.paterson@teamgb.com.

**PATERSON, Most Rev. John Campbell;** Bishop of Auckland, 1995–2010; Primate and Presiding Bishop of the Anglican Church in Aotearoa, New Zealand and Polynesia, 1998–2004; Archbishop Emeritus, since 2015; *b* 4 Jan. 1945; *s* of Thomas Paterson and Lucy Mary Paterson; *m* 1968, Marion Reid Anderson; two *d. Educ:* King's Coll., Auckland; Auckland Univ. (BA); St John's Coll., Auckland (LTh (Hons)); Dip. Public Speaking (NZ Speech Bd), 1969. Ordained, deacon, 1969, priest, 1970; Assistant Curate, Whangarei, 1969–71; Vicar, Waimate North Maori Pastorate, 1971–76; Co-Missioner, Auckland Maori Mission, 1976; Chaplain, Queen Victoria Sch., 1976–82; TF Chaplain, 1976–84; Sec., Te Pihopatanga o Aotearoa, 1978–86; Provincial Sec., Church of the Province of NZ, 1986–92; Gen. Sec., Anglican Church in Aotearoa, NZ and Polynesia, 1992–95. Priest in

Charge: Parish of Whangarei, 2013; Parish of Takapuna, 2014; Parish of St Aidan, Remuera, 2016. Chm., ACC, 2002–09 (Mem., 1990–96; Vice-Chm., 1996–2002). *Publications:* (ed) He Toenga Whatiwhatinga, 1983. *Recreations:* music, sport, literature. *Address:* c/o PO Box 87 255, Meadowbank, Auckland 1742, New Zealand.

**PATERSON, Lea;** Executive Director, Human Resources, Bank of England, since 2017; *b* Chester, 21 Oct. 1972; *d* of Ian James Paterson and Louise Anne Paterson (*née* Howlett); *m* 2000, Simon Trussler; one *s* two *d*. *Educ:* Winstanley Coll., Wigan; London Sch. of Econs and Pol Sci. (BSc Econs; MSc Econs). Consultant, London Economics, 1994–97; Econs Corresp., Independent, 1997–99; Econs Corresp., 1999–2000, Econs Ed., 2000–04, The Times; Bank of England: Sen. Manager, 2004–12; Hd of Div., 2012–14; Dir, Ind. Evaluation Office, 2014–17. *Recreation:* family and friends.

**PATERSON, Prof. Lindsay John,** PhD; FBA 2013; FRSE; Professor of Education Policy, University of Edinburgh, since 1998; *b* Hamilton, Scotland, 6 June 1956; *m*; one *s*. *Educ:* Tain Royal Acad.; Univ. of Aberdeen (MA 1978); Univ. of Edinburgh (PhD 1981). Higher SO, 1981–84, Sen. SO, 1984–85, Unit of Statistics, Agricl Res. Council; Lectr in Statistics, Heriot-Watt Univ., 1985–89; Res. Fellow, Centre for Educnl Sociol., Univ. of Edinburgh, 1989–95; Prof. of Educn Policy, Heriot-Watt Univ., 1995–98. FRSE 2004. *Publications:* The Autonomy of Modern Scotland, 1994; (jtly) Politics and Society in Scotland, 1996, 2nd edn 1998; A Diverse Assembly: the debate on a Scottish Parliament, 1998; (jtly) The Scottish Electorate: the 1997 General Election and beyond, 1999; (with F. Bechhofer) Principles of Research Design in the Social Sciences, 2000; Crisis in the Classroom: the exam debacle and the way ahead for Scottish education, 2000; Education and the Scottish Parliament, 2000; (jtly) New Scotland, New Politics?, 2001; Scottish Education in the Twentieth Century, 2003; (jtly) Living in Scotland: social and economic change since 1980, 2004; Social Radicalism and Liberal Education, 2015; chapters in scholarly books, 1991–; articles in jls incl. Biometrika, British Educnl Res. Jl, British Jl of Sociol., Internat. Statistical Rev., Jl of Royal Statistical Soc., Oxford Rev. of Educn, Political Qly, Regl and Federal Studies, Scot. Histl Rev., Sociol. of Educn, Sociol Res. Online, Sociol Rev. *Recreations:* conversation, reading, listening to music. *Address:* School of Social and Political Science, University of Edinburgh, Chrystal Macmillan Building, 15A George Square, Edinburgh EH8 9LD. *T:* (0131) 651 6380. *E:* lindsay.paterson@ed.ac.uk.

**PATERSON, Prof. Michael Stewart,** PhD; FRS 2001; Professor of Computer Science, University of Warwick, 1979–2009, now Emeritus; *b* 13 Sept. 1942. *Educ:* Trinity Coll., Cambridge (BA 1964; PhD 1968). Lectr, 1971–74, Reader, 1974–79, in Computer Sci., Univ. of Warwick. *Address:* Department of Computer Science, University of Warwick, Coventry CV4 7AL.

**PATERSON, Rt Hon. Owen (William);** PC 2010; MP (C) North Shropshire, since 1997; *b* 24 June 1956; *s* of late Alfred Paterson and Cynthia Paterson (*née* Owen); *m* 1980, Hon. Rose Emily Ridley (*see* Hon. R. E. Paterson); two *s* one *d*. *Educ:* Radley Coll.; Corpus Christi Coll., Cambridge (MA Hist.). British Leather Co.: Sales Dir, 1980; Man. Dir, 1993–97. Pres., European Tanners' Confedn, 1996–97. Contested (C) Wrexham, 1992. Opposition Whip, 2000–01; PPS to Leader of Opposition, 2001–03; Shadow Minster for DEFRA, 2003–05; Shadow Minister of State for Transport, 2005–07; Shadow Sec. of State for NI, 2007–10; Secretary of State: for NI, 2010–12; for Envmt, Food and Rural Affairs, 2012–14. *Recreations:* travel, history, trees, riding, hunting, racing, poultry. *Address:* House of Commons, SW1A 0AA.

**PATERSON, Peter,** WS; Sheriff of Lothian and Borders at Selkirk, since 2013; *b* 11 Oct. 1954; *s* of Dr Robert Craig Paterson and Margaret Paterson; *m* 1993, Dorothy Taylor; one step *d*. *Educ:* Cumnock Acad.; Heriot-Watt Univ. (BA); Univ. of Edinburgh (LLB); Nottingham Law Sch., Nottingham Trent Univ. (LLM). WS 1998. Partner: Skene Edwards WS, 1986–2000; Tods Murray LLP, 2000–12; pt-time Chm., Employment Tribunals, 1993–2000; temp. Sheriff, 1993–2005; pt-time Sheriff, 2005–12; All-Scotland Floating Sheriff, 2012–13. *Recreation:* running. *Address:* 448 Lanark Road, Edinburgh EH14 5BB. *T:* (0131) 441 3617. *E:* sheriffpaterson@me.com.

**PATERSON, Rt Rev. Robert Mar Erskine;** Bishop of Sodor and Man, 2008–16; an Honorary Assistant Bishop: Diocese of Hereford, since 2017; Diocese of Worcester, since 2017; *b* Cardiff, 27 Feb. 1949; *s* of David Donaldson Paterson and Letitia Paterson; *m* 1971, Pauline Anne Laing; one *s* two *d*. *Educ:* St John's Coll., Univ. of Durham (BA 1971; Van Mildert Scholar 1971; DipTh 1972); MA Dunelm 1982. Ordained deacon, 1972, priest, 1973; Assistant Curate: Harpurhey, Manchester, 1972–73; Sketty, Swansea, 1973–78; Rector, Llangattock and Llangynidr, 1978–83; Vicar, Gabalfa, Cardiff, 1983–94; Team Rector, Cowbridge, 1994–2000; Principal Officer, Council for Mission and Ministry, Church in Wales, 2000–06; Chaplain to Archbishop of York, 2006–08; Dean, Cathedral Church of St German, Peel, 2008–11. Chm., Central Readers' Council, 2009–16; Vice-Chairman: Theol Educn for the Anglican Communion, 2002–09; Liturgical Commn, 2008–16; Vice-Chair and Mem. Bd, Fresh Expressions, 2009–13. *Publications:* Short, Sharp and Off the Point: a guide to good and bad preaching, 1987; The Monarch Book of Christian Wisdom, 1997; (contrib.) Common Worship Today, 2000; (contrib.) The Book of Common Prayer Worldwide, 2006; Making Christ Visible, 2018. *Recreations:* early music, walking, cycling, theatre, reading. *Address:* Cedar House, 63 Greenhill, Evesham, Worcs WR11 4LX.

**PATERSON, Hon. Rose Emily;** DL; Chairman: Aintree Racecourse, since 2014 (Director, 2005–14); Weston Park Foundation, since 2015 (Trustee, since 2002); *b* Newcastle-upon-Tyne, 13 Aug. 1956; *d* of 4th Viscount Ridley, KG, GCVO, TD and Anne Ridley; *m* 1980, Rt Hon. Owen William Paterson, *qv*; two *s* one *d*. *Educ:* New Hall, Cambridge (BA Hist. 1978; MA 1982). With Sotheby's, 1979–2001; Hd, Paintings Dept, Sotheby's Chester, 1980–86; Paintings Specialist and Consultant, 1986–2001; Art Corresp., Daily Telegraph, 1985–95. Member: Council, Ellesmere Coll., 2012–15; Adv. Bd, University Coll., Shrewsbury, 2014–. Trustee, Develt Fund, Nat. Museums of Merseyside, 1992–95. Mem., Jockey Club, 2013– (Steward, 2019). DL Shropshire, 2014. *Recreations:* racing, hunting, gardening, medieval history. *Address:* Shellbrook Hill, Ellesmere, Shropshire SY12 9EW. *T:* (01978) 710266. *E:* rose@repaterson.co.uk.

**PATERSON, Air Vice-Marshal Ross,** CB 2014; OBE 2001; DL; Air Officer Scotland, since 2014; Aide-de-Camp to the Queen, since 2016; *b* Stockton-on-Tees, 1 June 1961; *s* of late Graham Paterson and Pauline Hope Paterson (*née* Thursz); *m* 1984, Dr Helen Mary Martindale; two *s*. *Educ:* Kimbolton Sch.; Portsmouth Poly. (BSc Biol. 1982); Univ. of Surrey (PGCE Chem. 1983). Initial officer trng, RAF, 1983; various trng and HR delivery and policy appts, 1984–98; OC Admin. Wing, RAF Leuchars, 1998–2000; Dep. Dir Defence Housing and Tri-Service Act Rev. Teams, 2000–03; CO, RAF Brampton, RAF Wyton and RAF Henlow, 2003–04; Dep. Dir, RAF Personnel Mgt Agency (Remuneration and Benefits), MoD, 2004–05; Dir Service Personnel Policy (Pay and Allowances), MoD, 2006–09; Prime Minister's Strategy Unit, Cabinet Office, 2009; Dir Personnel Policy (RAF), HQ Air Comd, 2009–11; Hd, Financial/Non-Financial Conditions of Service Rev., MoD, 2011; Chief Exec., Service Personnel and Veterans Agency, later Defence Business Services, 2011–14. Chartered FCIPD 2011. DL Fife, 2017. *Recreations:* family, hill walking and ski-ing (ex RAF Mountain Rescue Service), smallholding, beekeeping, reading and the arts, shooting, Scottish country life. *Address:* (office) 25 Learmonth Terrace, Edinburgh EH4 1NZ.

**PATERSON, Steven;** *b* Stirling, 25 April 1975. *Educ:* Cambusbarron Prim. Sch.; Stirling High Sch.; Univ. of Stirling (BA Hons Hist. and Politics). Visitor Attraction Asst, Argyll, The Isles, Loch Lomond, Stirling and the Trossachs, Scottish Tourist Bd, then VisitScotland, 1997–2006; Media and Communications Manager for Bruce Crawford, MSP, 2006–15. Mem. (SNP), Stirling Council, 2007–15. MP (SNP) Stirling, 2015–17; contested (SNP) same seat, 2017.

**PATERSON, Dame Vicki (Ann),** DBE 2013; Executive Head, Federation of Brindishe Schools, Lewisham, 2011–18; Executive Headteacher, Brindishe Lee and Brindishe Green Schools, 2007–18, and Brindishe Manor School, 2011–18; *b* Coventry, 1956; *d* of Ronald and Rose Paterson; partner, Gerlinde Achenbach; one *s* one *d*. *Educ:* Univ. of Birmingham (BEd Hons); Inst. of Educn, Univ. of London (DipEd Hons); London South Bank Univ. (MBA (Ed)). Primary sch. teacher, Bexley, 1978–85; Advr for Sci., Bexley Sch. Improvement Team, 1985–89; Headteacher, Brindishe Sch., Lewisham, 1989–2007. Nat. Leader in Educn, 2011–18. Sen. Partner, 2012–16, Trustee, 2016–, ChallengePartners.org. *Recreation:* walking and cycling alongside the Thames and all around London. *Address:* 58 Eversley Road, SE7 7LD. *E:* vickiapaterson@gmail.com.

**PATERSON, William Alexander;** *see* Alexander, Bill.

**PATERSON, Prof. William Edgar,** OBE 1999; PhD; FRSE, FAcSS; Professor of German and European Politics, 1994–2008, now Emeritus, and Director, Institute for German Studies, 1994–2005 and 2006–08, now Emeritus, University of Birmingham; Honorary Professor of European and German Politics, Aston Centre for Europe, School of Languages and Social Sciences, Aston University, 2009–18; *b* Blair Atholl, Perthshire, 26 Sept. 1941; *s* of late William Paterson, FRICS, FLAS, Land Agent, and Winnie Paterson (*née* McIntyre); *m* 1st, 1964, Jacqueline Cramb (*d* 1974); two *s*; 2nd, 1979, Phyllis MacDowell; one *d*, and one step *s* one step *d*. *Educ:* Morrison's Acad.; Univ. of St Andrews (MA, Class Medallist); London Sch. of Econs (S. H. Bailey Schol.; MSc, PhD 1973). FRSE 1994. Lectr in Internat. Relns, Univ. of Aberdeen, 1967–70; University of Warwick: Volkswagen Lectr in German Politics, 1970–75; Sen. Lectr, 1975–82; Reader, 1982–89; Prof. and Chm. of Dept, 1989–90; Salvesen Prof. of Eur. Insts, and Dir, Europa Inst., Univ. of Edinburgh, 1990–94. Vis. Prof., Univ., of Freiburg, 1999. Jt Ed., German Politics, 1991–2001; Member, Editorial Board: Jl Common Mkt Studies, 1991–2003 (Co-Ed., 2003–08); Internat. Affairs, 1993–2015; Comparative European Politics, 2000–; Perspectives on European Politics and Society, 2004–; Co-Editor: Palgrave European Union Studies, 1992–; New Perspectives in German Studies, 1998–2008; Palgrave Studies in European Union Politics, 2005–; New Perspectives in German Political Studies, 2009–. Mem., ESRC Res. Priorities Bd, 1995–99; Chm., One Europe or Several? prog. for ESRC, 2001–03. Mem., Königswinter Conf. Steering Cttee, 1994–. Chairman: Assoc. for Study of German Politics, 1974–76 (Hon. Vice Pres., 2000); Univ. Assoc. for Contemporary Eur. Studies, 1989–94; Chm., German-British Forum, 2005–13 (Vice-Chm., 1999–2005). Member: Wissenschaftliches Direktorium, Institut für Europäische Politik, Berlin, 1980–; Lothian Lectures Cttee, 1991–94; Adv. Bd, Centre for British Studies, Humboldt Univ., Berlin, 1999–; Kuratorium, Allianz Kulturstiftung, 2000–04. Associate Fellow, RIIA, 1994; FAcSS (AcSS 2000). FRSA 1998. Participant, Queen's Coll., Dundee team, University Challenge, 1963. Mem., Malt Whisky Soc. Lifetime Achievement Award: Assoc. for Study of German Politics, 2004; Univ. Assoc. for Contemporary European Studies, 2007; Special Recognition Award, Political Studies Assoc., 2011. Officer's Cross, Order of Merit (FRG), 1999. *Publications:* The SPD and European Integration, 1974; *jointly:* Social Democracy in Post-War Europe, 1974; The Federal Republic of Germany and the European Community, 1987; Government and the Chemical Industry, 1988; Governing Germany, 1991; A History of Social Democracy in Post-War Europe, 1991; The Kohl Chancellorship, 1998; The Future of the German Economy, 2000; Germany's European Diplomacy, 2000; *edited jointly:* Social and Political Movements in Western Europe, 1976; Social Democratic Parties in Western Europe, 1977; Foreign Policy Making in Western Europe, 1978; Sozialdemokratische Parteien in Europa, 1978; The West German Model, 1981; The Future of Social Democracy, 1986; Developments in West German Politics, 1989; Politics in Western Europe Today, 1990; El Futuro de la Social Democracia, 1992; Developments in German Politics, 1992; Rethinking Social Democracy in Western Europe, 1993; Developments in German Politics 2, 1996; Developments in German Politics 3, 2003; Governance in Contemporary Germany, 2005; The German Crisis, 2009; Research Agendas in European Union Studies, 2009; Developments in German Politics 4, 2013; The European Union in Crisis, 2017; Germany and the European Union: Europe's reluctant hegemon?, 2018; contrib. over 100 articles to edited collections and learned jls. *Recreations:* walking, visiting galleries, collecting 20th century Scottish painting. *Address:* 220 Myton Road, Warwick CV34 6PS. *T:* (01926) 492492. *E:* w.paterson@aston.ac.uk. *Club:* Reform.

**PATERSON, William Tulloch, (Bill);** actor, since 1968; *b* 3 June 1945; *s* of late John Paris Paterson and of Ann Tulloch Paterson; *m* 1984, Hildegard Bechtler; one *s* one *d*. *Educ:* Whitehill Sen. Secondary Sch., Glasgow; RSAMD (FRCS (FRSAMD 2005)). First professional engagement, Glasgow Citizens' Theatre, 1968; Asst Dir, Citizens' Theatre for Youth, 1970–72; Founder Mem., 7:84 (Scotland) Theatre Co. *Stage:* The Cheviot, the Stag and the Black Black Oil, 1973; Writer's Cramp, 1977; Whose Life is it Anyway?, Savoy, 1978; Guys and Dolls, NT, 1982; Schweyk, NT, 1983; Death and the Maiden, Royal Court, 1992; Misery, Criterion, 1993; Mongrel's Heart, Edinburgh, 1994; Ivanov, Almeida, 1997; Marriage Play, RNT, 2001; Earthquakes in London, RNT, 2010; And No More Shall We Part, Traverse, 2012; The Low Road, Jerwood, Royal Court, 2013; The Vote, Donmar, 2015; Waiting for Godot, Royal Lyceum, Edinburgh, 2015; *films:* Comfort and Joy, The Killing Fields, 1984; Defence of the Realm, 1985; A Private Function, 1986; The Adventures of Baron Munchausen, 1987; The Witches, 1989; Truly Madly Deeply, 1991; Chaplin, 1992; Richard III, 1996; Hilary and Jackie, 1998; Complicity, 2000; Crush, 2001; Bright Young Things, 2003; Rag Tale, 2005; Amazing Grace, 2006; Miss Potter, 2007; Into the Storm, 2009; Creation, 2009; Dad's Army, 2016; Happy New Year, Colin Burstead, 2018; *television:* Smiley's People, 1981; Auf Wiedersehen Pet, 1986; The Singing Detective, 1987; Traffik, 1989; Tell Tale Hearts, 1992; Hard Times, 1993; The Writing on the Wall, 1995; The Crow Road, 1996; Wives and Daughters, 1999; The Whistleblower, 2001; Zhivago, 2002; Danielle Cable Eye Witness, 2003; Sea of Souls, 2004–07; Criminal Justice, 2008; Little Dorrit, 2008; Law and Order UK, 2009–10; Spanish Flu: the Forgotten Fallen, 2009; Dr Who, 2010; 37 Days, 2014; Outlander, 2015; Churchill's Secret, 2016; Fleabag, 2016, 2019; The Rebel, 2016–17; The Mysterious Case of Agatha Christie, 2018; Good Omens, 2019. *Publications:* Tales from the Backgreen, 2008. *Address:* c/o Gordon and French, 12–13 Poland Street, W1F 8QB.

**PATERSON HESFORD, Irene;** *see* Findlay, I.

**PATEY, Sir William (Charters)**, KCMG 2009 (CMG 2005); HM Diplomatic Service, retired; Ambassador to Afghanistan, 2010–12; *b* 11 July 1953; *s* of William Maurice Patey and Christina Kinnell Patey; *m* 1978, Vanessa Carol Morrell; two *s*. *Educ*: Trinity Acad., Edinburgh; Univ. of Dundee (MA Hons). Joined FCO, 1975; MECAS, 1977–78; Commercial Attaché, Abu Dhabi, 1978–81; Second Sec., Tripoli, 1981–84; FCO, 1984–88; First Sec. (Political), Canberra, 1988–92; Dep. Head, UN Dept, 1992–93, Inspector, 1994–95, FCO; Dep. Head of Mission and Consul-Gen., Riyadh, 1995–98; Hd, Middle East Dept, FCO, 1999–2002; Ambassador: to Sudan, 2002–05; to Iraq, 2005–06; to Saudi Arabia, 2007–10. Internat. Affairs Advr, Control Risks, 2012–; Mem. Bd, HSBC Bank Middle East, 2012–; Sen. Advr, AECOM, 2017–. Pres., Khartoum Cheshire Home, 2002–05. Hon. Pres., St Margaret's Film Soc., 1996. Patron: Kids for Kids Charity, 2002– (Trustee, 2002–10); Together for Sudan, 2003–; Trustee, Turquoise Mountain Foundn, 2012–. Chm., Swindon Town FC, 2012–13. Hon. Fellow: New Westminster Coll., Vancouver, 2012; Univ. of Exeter, 2013. Hon LLD Dundee, 2016. Chevalier d'Honneur, Chaîne des Rôtisseurs, 2009. *Recreations*: tennis, theatre, golf.

**PATHAK, Kirit Kumar**, OBE 1997; Chairman, AB World Foods Ltd, since 2007 (Chairman and Chief Executive, Patak's Foods Ltd, 1990–2007); *b* 12 Sept. 1952; *s* of late Laxmishanker Gopalji and Shanta Gaury Pathak; *m* 1976, Meena Desai (*see* M. Pathak); two *s* one *d*. *Educ*: Banbury Technical Coll.; Lancaster Poly. Joined Patak's (family Indian food business) at age 17. Member: NW Industrial Develt Bd, 1998–; UKTI, 1999–2016. Mem. Council, Food From Britain, 1998–2003; Vice-Pres., FDF, 2003. Corporate Hon. Fellow, Liverpool John Moores Univ., 2002. Hon. Dr Business Management UCE Birmingham, 1996. *Recreations*: meditation, football, tennis, ski-ing, trekking, horse riding, swimming, cooking, DIY. *Address*: AB World Foods Ltd, Kiriana House, Kiribati Way, Leigh, Lancs WN7 5RS. *T*: (01942) 267000, *Fax*: (01942) 267070. *E*: info@pataksfoods.co.uk.

**PATHAK, Meena**, OBE 2001; Director, 1981–2007, and Deputy Chairperson, 2000–07, Patak's Foods Ltd; *b* 12 Aug. 1956; *d* of Col Naishad Desai and Dr Hansa Desai; *m* 1976, Kirit Kumar Pathak, *qv*; two *s* one *d*. *Educ*: Bombay Internat. Sch.; hotel mgt and food technol. Bd Mem., Univ. of Central Lancashire, 2000–. Hon. Fellow, Bolton Inst., 2002. Hon. Dr Central Lancashire, 1992. *Publications*: The Flavours of India, 2002; Indian Cooking for Family and Friends, 2003; Meena Pathak Celebrates Indian Cooking, 2007. *Recreations*: meditation, music, arts, reading, sports (cricket). *Address*: Patak's Foods Ltd, AB World Foods Ltd, Kiriana House, Kiribati Way, Leigh, Lancs WN7 5RS. *T*: (01942) 267000, *Fax*: (01942) 267070.

**PATIENCE, Adèle**; *see* Williams, J. A.

**PATIENCE, His Honour Andrew**; QC 1990; a Circuit Judge, 1999–2011; *b* 28 April 1941; *s* of late William Edmund John Patience and Louise Mary Patience; *m* 1975, Jean Adèle Williams, *qv*; one *s* one *d*. *Educ*: Whitgift School, Croydon; St John's College, Oxford (MA). Called to the Bar, Gray's Inn, 1966; a Recorder, 1986–99; Resident Judge, Maidstone Crown Court, 2000–10; Hon. Recorder of Dover, 2001–. Kent Ambassador, 2011–. Patron, Chatham Dockyard Historical Soc., 2012–; Ambassador, Chatham Historic Dockyard Trust, 2015–. Pres., British Red Cross, Kent, 2012–. *Recreations*: mimicry, complaining, horse racing. *Club*: Oxford and Cambridge.

**PATIL, Pratibha Devisingh**; President of India, 2007–12; *b* Maharashtra, 19 Dec. 1934; *d* of Narayan Rao; *m* 1965, Dr Devisingh Ramsingh Shekhawat; one *s* one *d*. *Educ*: Mooljee Jetha Coll., Jalgaon (MA Pol Sci. and Econs); Govt Law Coll., Bombay (LLB). Formerly in practice as a lawyer, Jalgaon District Court. Mem., Maharashtra Legislative Assembly, 1962–85; Dep. Minister, Public Health, Prohibition, Tourism, Housing and Parly Affairs, 1967–72; Minister: Social Welfare, 1972–74; Public Health and Social Welfare, 1974–75; Prohibition, Rehabilitation and Cultural Affairs, 1975–76; Educn, 1977–78; Leader of the Opposition, 1979–80; Minister: Urban Develt and Housing, 1982–83; Civil Supplies and Social Welfare, 1983–85. Member: Rajya Sabha, 1985–90 (Dep. Chm., 1986–88; Chm., July–Sept. 1987); Lok Sabha, 1991–96. Gov., Rajasthan, 2004–07. Pres., Maharashtra Pradesh Congress Cttee, 1988–90. *Address*: c/o Office of the President, Rashtrapati Bhavan, New Delhi 110 004, India.

**PATNICK, Julietta**, CBE 2005; Visiting Professor of Cancer Screening, University of Oxford, since 2008; *b* 10 June 1957; *d* of Barry Freeman and Shirley (*née* Samuels); *m* 1978, Michael Patnick; one *s* one *d*. *Educ*: Univ. of Sheffield (BA Hons Ancient Hist. and Classical Civilisation 1978). FFPH 2002. Co-ordinator, Breast Screening, Trent Regl HA, 1987–90; Nat. Co-ordinator, NHS Breast Screening Prog., 1990–94; Dir, NHS Cancer Screening Progs, 1995–2015. Member: Care Record Develt Bd, 2004–07; Medicines for Women's Health Expert Working Gp, 2006–13. Trustee, Cavendish Cancer Care, 2006–12. Gov., Sheffield Hallam Univ., 2017–. Hon. Fellow in Public Health, Univ. of Oxford, 2004. Hon. Mem., RCR, 2009. Hon. FRCSEd 2015; Hon. FRCPath, 2016. DUniv Sheffield Hallam, 2011; Hon. MD Sheffield, 2011; Hon. DSc Loughborough, 2012. *Recreations*: family, travel, food. *Address*: Cancer Epidemiology Unit, University of Oxford, Richard Doll Building, Roosevelt Drive, Oxford OX3 7LF. *E*: julietta.patnick@ndph.ox.ac.uk.

**PATON, Rt Hon. Lady; Ann Paton**; PC 2007; a Senator of the College of Justice in Scotland, since 2000; Chair, Scottish Law Commission, since 2019; *d* of James McCargow and Ann Dunlop or McCargow; *m* 1974, Dr James Y. Paton; no *c*. *Educ*: Laurel Bank Sch.; Univ. of Glasgow (MA 1972; LLB 1974). Admitted to the Scottish Bar, 1977. Standing Junior Counsel: to the Queen's and Lord Treasurer's Remembrancer (excluding *Ultimus Haeres*), 1979; in Scotland to Office of Fair Trading, 1981; QC (Scot.) 1990; Advocate Depute, 1992–94. Member: Criminal Injuries Compensation Bd, 1995–2000; Parole Bd, 2003–07. Dir, Scottish Council of Law Reporting, 1995–2000. Mem. Governing Body, Queen Margaret UC, 2001–04. Hon. LLD Glasgow, 2013. *Publications*: Map of Sheriffdoms and Sheriff Court Districts in Scotland, 1977, 2nd edn 1980; (Jt Asst Editor) Gloag and Henderson, Law of Scotland, 8th edn 1980, to 10th edn 1995; (with R. G. McEwan) A Casebook on Damages in Scotland, 1983, 2nd edn as Damages in Scotland (sole author), 1989, re-titled Damages for Personal Injuries in Scotland, 1997; Faculty Digest Supplement 1971–1980, 1995; contrib. Scottish Current Law Statutes, Session Cases, Scots Law Times, Green's Reparation Bulletin, and Judicial Studies in Scotland Equal Treatment Bench Bk. *Recreations*: sailing, hill-walking, music, art.

**PATON, Alasdair Chalmers**; Chief Executive, Scottish Environment Protection Agency, 1995–2000; *b* Paisley, 28 Nov. 1944; *o s* of David Paton and Margaret Elizabeth Paton (*née* Chalmers); *m* 1969, Zona Gertrude Gill; one *s* one *d*. *Educ*: John Neilson Instn, Paisley; Univ. of Glasgow (BSc). Assistant Engineer: Clyde Port Authy, 1967–71; Dept of Agric. and Fisheries for Scotland, 1971–72; Sen. Engineer, Scottish Develt Dept, 1972–77; Engineer, Public Works Dept, Hong Kong Govt, 1977–80; Scottish Development Department: Sen. Engineer, 1980–84; Principal Engineer, 1984–87; Dep. Chief Engineer, 1987–91; Dir and Chief Engineer, Water and Waste Directorate, Scottish Office Envmt Dept, 1991–95. *Recreations*: Rotary, sailing, golf. *Address*: Oriel House, Academy Square, Limekilns, Fife KY11 3HN. *Club*: Royal Scots (Edinburgh).

**PATON, Alexander Charles, (Charlie)**, RDI 2012; Director, Seawater Greenhouse Ltd, since 2000; *b* Camberley, Surrey, 27 June 1950; *s* of Eric Giles and Joan Paton; *m* 1984, Marlene McKibbin; two *s* one *d*. *Educ*: Bryanston Sch.; Central Sch. of Art and Design. Founder and Director: Smallworks, 1974–; Light Works Ltd, 1979–. Liveryman, Gardeners' Co., 2008–. *Recreations*: forestry, gardening. *Address*: 2a Greenwood Road, E8 1AB.

**PATON, Ann**; *see* Paton, Rt Hon. Lady.

**PATON, Charlie**; *see* Paton, A. C.

**PATON, Douglas Shaw F.**; *see* Forrester-Paton.

**PATON, Hon. (Frederick) Ranald N.**; *see* Noel-Paton.

**PATON, Rt Rev. Ian James**; *see* St Andrews, Dunkeld and Dunblane, Bishop of.

**PATON, William**; Director, TÜV Süddeutschland, 2001–04; *b* 29 Nov. 1941; *s* of Matthew Paton and Elizabeth Paton (*née* Shearer); *m* 1964, Elizabeth Anne Marr; two *s*. *Educ*: Douglas Ewart Sch., Newton Stewart; Univ. of Glasgow (BSc Hons Physics). Seismologist, SSL Ltd, 1964; Mgt Trainee, Colvilles Ltd, 1965; National Engineering Laboratory: scientific posts, 1965–80; Dir of Ops, 1990–95; Dir, 1995–97; Chief Exec., TÜV Product Service Ltd, 1997–2001. Dir and Sen. Exec., Nat. Engrg Assessment Gp, 1997–. Patents relating to improvements in carbon fibre processing technol., engrg designs and sports equipment. *Publications*: various articles in technical jls. *Recreations*: golf, travel, bridge. *Address*: 2 Wester Balrymonth, St Andrews, Fife KY16 8NN. *T*: (01334) 472131.

**PATON WALSH, Jill**, CBE 1996; self-employed author, since 1966; *b* 29 April 1937; *d* of John Llewelyn Bliss and Patricia Paula DuBern; *m* 1st, 1961, Antony Paton Walsh (separated; he *d* 2003); one *s* two *d*; 2nd, 2004, John Rowe Townsend (*d* 2014). *Educ*: St Michael's Convent, Finchley; St Anne's Coll., Oxford (BA English; MA; DipEd). Schoolteacher, Enfield Girls' Grammar Sch., 1959–62. Arts Council Creative Writing Fellowship, Brighton Poly., 1976–77, 1977–78; Gertrude Clark Whitall Meml Lectr, Library of Congress, 1978; vis. faculty mem., Center for Children's Lit., Simmons Coll., Boston, Mass, 1978–86. A Judge, Whitbread Lit. Award, 1984; Chm., Cambridge Book Assoc., 1987–89; Mem. Council, Soc. of Authors, 1999– (Mem., Mgt Cttee, 1986–88); Member: Cttee, Children's Writers' and Illustrators' Gp; Adjunct British Bd, Children's Literature New England. Pres., The Dorothy L. Sayers Soc., 2015–. FRSL 1996. *Publications*: *fiction*: Farewell, Great King, 1972; Lapsing, 1986; A School for Lovers, 1989; The Wyndham Case, 1993; Knowledge of Angels, 1994; A Piece of Justice, 1995; The Serpentine Cave, 1997; Thrones, Dominations (completion of novel by Dorothy L. Sayers), 1998; A Desert in Bohemia, 2000; Presumption of Death (with material by Dorothy L. Sayers), 2002; Debts of Dishonour, 2006; The Bad Quarto, 2007; The Attenbury Emeralds, 2010, The Late Scholar, 2013 (based on the characters of Dorothy L. Sayers); *for children*: The Island Sunrise: pre-historic Britain, 1975; *fiction*: Hengest's Tale, 1966; The Dolphin Crossing, 1967; (with Kevin Crossley-Holland) Wordhoard, 1969; Fireweed (Book World Fest. Award), 1970; Goldengrove, 1972; Toolmaker, 1973; The Dawnstone, 1973; The Emperor's Winding Sheet (jtly, Whitbread Prize), 1974; The Butty Boy, 1975 (US edn as The Huffler); Unleaving (Boston Globe/Horn Book Award), 1976; Crossing to Salamis, The Walls of Athens, and Persian Gold, 1977–78 (US combined edn as Children of the Fox, 1978); A Chance Child, 1978; The Green Book, 1981 (re-issued as Shine, 1988); Babylon, 1982; Lost & Found, 1984; A Parcel of Patterns (Universe Prize), 1984; Gaffer Samson's Luck, 1985 (Smarties Prize Grand Prix, 1984); Five Tides, 1986; Torch, 1987; Birdy and the Ghosties, 1989; Grace, 1991; When Grandma Came, 1992; Matthew and the Sea-Singer, 1992; Pepi and the Secret Names, 1994; When I Was Little Like You, 1997. *Recreations*: photography, gardening, reading. *Address*: c/o David Higham Associates, 7th Floor, Waverley House, 7–12 Noel Street, W1F 8GQ.

**PATRIARCA, Stephen Richard**; adviser to students in Vienna applying to UK universities, since 2013; Vice President, Society for Information Competence and Information Infrastructure, since 2018; *b* 3 May 1953; *s* of late Ronald and Maureen Patriarca. *Educ*: Sweyne Sch., Rayleigh; UC of Swansea (BA Hons 1975). Asst English Master, 1978–95, Hd of Sixth Form, 1988–95 (first piloted new Philosophy A Level and worked with Royal Inst. of Philosophy to encourage the subject in schs), Dep. Headmaster, 1995–2000, Hulme GS, Oldham; Headmaster, later Principal, William Hulme's GS, Manchester, 2000–08 (city acad. from 2007). Internat. educnl leadership and mgt consultant for ind. English-medium schs and specialised support for UK private schs seeking academy status, 2008–13; Associate Dir, 2008–09, Advr, 2009–13, Danube Internat. Sch., Vienna; Advr and Consultant to Batley Grammar Sch., 2011. Trustee, Anglo Austrian Soc., 2002–09. *Recreations*: Vienna coffee houses, Heurigen, lakes and mountains, music, art, cooking, wine, revaluing Habsburg Austria, Austrian Wine and campaigning for recognition of the Ukrainian Holodomor, preparing audiobooks of classic English literature. *W*: www.stevepatriarca.at. *Club*: East India.

**PATRICK, Andrew**; HM Diplomatic Service; Adviser, Department for Digital, Culture, Media and Sport, since 2018; *b* 28 Feb. 1966; *s* of Henry Patrick and Carol Patrick (*née* Biddle). *Educ*: Poltair Sch., Cornwall; Univ. of Bristol (BSc Hons Maths 1987); City Univ., London (Dip. in Law 1988). Joined FCO, 1988; Third, later Second Sec., Nicosia, 1991–95; First Sec., NATO, Brussels, 1995–96; Asst Private Sec. to Sec. of State, FCO, 1997–2000; Dep. Hd, News Dept, FCO, 2001–04; Dep. High Comr, S Africa, 2004–07; Dep. Hd of Mission, Afghanistan, 2007–09; Additional Dir S Asia, FCO, 2009–12; Ambassador to Burma, 2013–18. *Address*: c/o Foreign and Commonwealth Office, King Charles Street, SW1A 2AH.

**PATRICK, Gail**; *see* Patrick, L. G.

**PATRICK, Graham McIntosh**, CMG 1968; CVO 1981; DSC 1943; Under Secretary, Department of the Environment, 1971–81, retired; *b* 17 Oct. 1921; *m* 1945, Barbara Worboys (*d* 2013); two *s*. *Educ*: Dundee High Sch.; St Andrews Univ. RNVR (Air Branch), 1940–46. Entered Ministry of Works, 1946; Regional Director: Middle East Region, 1965–67; South West Region, DoE, 1971–75; Chm., South West Economic Planning Bd, 1971–75; Dir, Scottish Services, PSA, 1975–81. *Address*: 69 Swallows Court, Pool Close, Spalding PE11 1GZ.

**PATRICK, Rev. James Harry Johnson; His Honour Judge Patrick**; a Circuit Judge, since 2010; *b* Tiverton, Devon, 14 March 1967; *s* of late John Churchill Patrick and of Sally Patrick (*née* Johnson, now Mrs Peter Ward-Enticott). *Educ*: Blundell's Sch.; City of Birmingham Poly. (LLB Hons); Inns of Court Sch. of Law; Southern Theol Educn and Trng Scheme (DipHE); St Stephen's House, Oxford. Called to the Bar, Inner Temple, 1989, Bencher, 2015; Recorder, 2004–10. Ordained deacon, 1999, priest, 2000; Hon. Asst Curate, All Saints with St John, Clifton, Bristol, 1999–2010; ordained deacon (RC Ordinariate of Our Lady of Walsingham), 2011; Deacon, N London Ordinariate Gp at Our Lady of Mt Carmel and St George, Enfield, 2011–13; Parish Deacon, Our Lady of the Assumption and St Gregory, Warwick St, Soho, 2013–15; Deacon, Bristol Ordinariate Gp and Clifton Cathedral, 2016– (Gp Pastor, 2018–). Wine Treas., Western Circuit, 1995–2000. Hon. Legal Advr to Bp of Ebbsfleet, 2001–10; Hon. Chaplain to High Sheriff of Bristol, 2004–05. *Recreations:* fun, friends, laughter, travel, collecting pictures. *Address:* Bristol Crown Court, Small Street, Bristol BS1 1DA. *T:* (0117) 976 3030. *Club:* East India.

**PATRICK, (Lilian) Gail;** Sheriff of Tayside, Central and Fife at Kirkcaldy, 1991–2001; part-time Sheriff, since 2001; *b* 24 Dec. 1941; *d* of Alexander Findlay McFadzean, MA, LLB and Elizabeth Fullerton McFadzean (*née* Fenton); *m* 1967, Spencer Francis Rodger, LLB, WS, *s* of Francis and Isabel Patrick; one *s* three *d*. *Educ:* Radleigh Sch., Glasgow; Marr Coll., Troon; St Andrews Univ. (MA); Edinburgh Univ. (LLB). Enrolled as solicitor, 1966; pt-time practice, 1967–79; Lecturer and Tutor: Glasgow Univ., 1967–82; Edinburgh Univ., 1980–82, 1985–90; pt-time Procurator Fiscal Depute, 1979–80; admitted to Faculty of Advocates, 1981; Standing Jun. Counsel, Scottish Educn Dept, 1986–91; Chm., Social Security Appeal Tribunal, 1986–91; Reporter, Scottish Legal Aid Bd, 1986–91; Temp. Sheriff, 1988–91; called to the Bar, Lincoln's Inn, 1990. *Recreations:* golf, cycling, bridge, music. *Clubs:* Murrayfield Golf (Edinburgh), Elie and Earlsferry Golf.

**PATRICK, Simon John,** OBE 2017; a Principal Clerk, Committee Office, House of Commons, 2013–16; *b* 13 Oct. 1956; *s* of John Patrick and Mary Patrick (*née* Ansell). *Educ:* Merchant Taylors' Sch.; Pembroke Coll., Cambridge (BA Maths 1978, MA 1982). House of Commons: a clerk, 1978–2016: Clerk: Cttee of Public Accts, 1986–89; Employment Cttee, 1989–91; Table Office, 1991–95; Nat. Heritage Cttee, 1995–97; Treasury Cttee, 1998–2001; Jl Office, 2001–05; Eur. Scrutiny Cttee, 2005–06; Delegated Legislation, 2006–09; of Bills, 2009–13. *Publications:* (an Asst Ed) Erskine May's Parliamentary Practice, 23rd edn 2004, 24th edn 2011; (contrib.) Essays on the History of Parliamentary Procedure in honour of Thomas Erskine May, 2017. *Recreations:* classical music, typography, computing. *E:* simon.patrick@cantab.net.

**PATRICK, Stuart Leslie,** CBE 2019; Chief Executive, Glasgow Chamber of Commerce, since 2009; *b* Greenock, 20 May 1962; *s* of Alexander James Patrick and Jenny Irene Patrick; one *s*. *Educ:* Greenock Acad.; Univ. of Glasgow (BAcc (Hons) 1984); Univ. of Strathclyde (MBA 1992). CA 1988. Auditor and Business Advr, Ernst & Young, 1984–89; Co. Sec., Govan Initiative Ltd, 1989–92; Scottish Enterprise Glasgow: Hd, Strategy, 1992–99; Dir, Finance and Strategy, 1999–2006; Ops Dir, 2006–08; Sen. Commercial Dir, Scottish Enterprise, 2008–09. Non-exec. Chm., Wise Gp, 2013–; non-executive Director: Ashton Properties Ltd, 1996–2013; Clyde Gateway Urban Regeneration Co., 2014–; Scottish Opera, 2014–; City of Glasgow Coll., 2016–. Director: Four Acres Charitable Trust, 1985– (Chair, 2018–); Arches Th. Co., 2004–18; Glasgow Sci. Centre, 2006–. *Recreations:* theatre, tennis, travel, Germanophile and Sinophile. *Address:* Glasgow Chamber of Commerce, 30 George Square, Glasgow G2 1EQ. *T:* (0141) 204 2121. *E:* chamber@glasgowchamberofcommerce.com.

**PATRICKSON, David G.;** *see* Gallagher Patrickson, D.

**PATTEN,** family name of **Barons Patten** and **Patten of Barnes**.

**PATTEN, Baron** *cr* 1997 (Life Peer), of Wincanton in the co. of Somerset; **John Haggitt Charles Patten;** PC 1990; Senior Advisor, Charterhouse Capital Partners LLP (formerly Charterhouse Development Capital Ltd), since 2001; *b* 17 July 1945; *s* of late Jack Patten and Maria Olga (*née* Sikora); *m* 1978, Louise Alexandra Virginia Charlotte Rowe (*see* Lady Patten); one *d*. *Educ:* Wimbledon Coll.; Sidney Sussex Coll., Cambridge (PhD 1972). University Lectr, 1969–79, Fellow, Hertford Coll., 1972–94, Univ. of Oxford. Oxford City Councillor, 1973–76. MP (C) City of Oxford, 1979–83; Oxford W and Abingdon, 1983–97. PPS to the Ministers of State at the Home Office, 1980–81; Parliamentary Under-Secretary of State: NI Office, 1981–83; DHSS, 1983–85; Minister of State for Housing, Urban Affairs and Construction, DoE, 1985–87; Minister of State, Home Office, 1987–92; Sec. of State for Educn, 1992–94. Advr, 1996–2000, non-exec. Dep. Chm., 2000–01, Charterhouse plc; non-executive Director: Lockheed Martin UK Ltd, 1999–2003; Lockheed Martin UK Holdings Ltd, 2003–16. Advr, Lockheed Martin International (formerly Lockheed Martin Overseas Corp.), 1997–2016; Advr, Thomas Goode & Co. Ltd, 1997–. Hon. Fellow, Harris Manchester Coll., Oxford, 1996. *Publications:* The Conservative Opportunity (with Lord Blake), 1976; English Towns, 1500–1700, 1978; (ed) Pre-Industrial England, 1979; (ed) The Expanding City, 1983; (with Paul Coones) The Penguin Guide to the Landscape of England and Wales, 1986; Things to Come: the Tories in the 21st Century, 1995. *Recreation:* talking with my wife and daughter. *Address:* House of Lords, SW1A 0PW.

**PATTEN OF BARNES, Baron** *cr* 2005 (Life Peer), of Barnes in the London Borough of Richmond; **Christopher Francis Patten,** CH 1998; PC 1989; Chancellor, University of Oxford, since 2003; Chairman, BBC Trust, 2011–14; *b* 12 May 1944; *s* of late Francis Joseph Patten and Joan McCarthy; *m* 1971, Mary Lavender St Leger Thornton; three *d*. *Educ:* St Benedict's School, Ealing; Balliol College, Oxford (Hon. Fellow, 1990). Conservative Research Dept, 1966–70; Cabinet Office, 1970–72; Home Office, 1972; Personal Asst to Chairman of Conservative Party, 1972–74; Director, Conservative Research Dept, 1974–79. Governor and C-in-C, Hong Kong, 1992–97; Chm., Ind. Commn on Policing for NI, 1998–99. MP (C) Bath, 1979–92; contested (C) same seat, 1992. PPS to Chancellor of Duchy of Lancaster and Leader of House of Commons, 1979–81, to Secretary of State for Social Services, 1981; Parly Under-Sec. of State, NI Office, 1983–85; Minister of State, DES, 1985–86; Minister of State (Minister for Overseas Develt), FCO, 1986–89; Sec. of State for the Envmt, 1989–90; Chancellor of Duchy of Lancaster, 1990–92; Chm. of Cons. Party, 1990–92. Vice Chm., Cons. Parly Finance Cttee, 1981–83; Mem., Select Cttees on Defence and Procedure, 1982–83. Mem., Eur. Commn, 1999–2004. Co-Chm., Internat. Crisis Gp, 2004–11. Director: Independent Newspapers, 1998–99; Cadbury plc, 2005–10; Russell Reynolds, 2008–. Chancellor, Univ. of Newcastle, 1999–2009. Hon. FRCPE 1994. Hon. Fellow, St Antony's Coll., Oxford, 2003. Hon. DJur: Massachusetts, 1999; Birmingham, 2001; Bath, 2003; Hon. DCL: Newcastle, 1999; Oxford 2003; Hon. DLitt: Sydney, 2001; Exeter, 2002; Ulster, 2004; DUniv: Keele, 2002; Stettin, 2004; Hon. DBA Kingston, 2003; Hon. DSc SE Europe, Rep. of Macedonia, 2009. Commandeur, Légion d'Honneur (France), 2016. *Publications:* The Tory Case, 1983; East and West, 1998; Not Quite the Diplomat, 2005; What Next? Surviving the 21st Century, 2008; First Confession: a sort of memoir, 2017. *Recreations:* reading, tennis, gardening. *Address:* House of Lords, SW1A 0PW. *Clubs:* Athenæum, Royal Automobile, Oxford and Cambridge; All England Lawn Tennis.

**PATTEN, Lady;** Louise Alexandra Virginia Charlotte Patten; Senior Adviser, Bain & Co. Inc., since 1997; *b* 2 Feb. 1954; *m* 1978, John Haggitt Charles Patten (*see* Baron Patten); one *d*. *Educ:* St Paul's Girls' Sch., Hammersmith; St Hugh's Coll., Oxford (MA Hons). Manager, Citibank NA, 1977–81; Resident Vice Pres., Wells Fargo Bank NA, 1981–85; Partner: PA Consulting Gp, 1985–93; Bain & Co. Inc., 1994–97. Non-executive Director: Hilton Gp plc, 1993–2003; Harveys Furnishings plc, 1993–2000; GUS (formerly Gt Universal Stores) plc, 1997–2006; Somerfield plc, 1998–2005 (Actg Chm., 1999–2000); Brixton plc, 2001–10 (Chm., 2003–10); UK Asset Resolution Ltd (formerly Bradford & Bingley plc), 2003–13; Marks & Spencer plc, 2006–11; Northern Rock (Asset Mgt) plc, 2010–14; Intu Properties plc (formerly Capital Shopping Centres), 2011–; Control Risks Gp Hldgs Ltd, 2011–14; Abcam plc, 2014–; Gallagher, 2016–. *Publications:* Bad Money, 2009; Good As Gold, 2010. *Address:* c/o Bain & Co. Inc., 40 Strand, WC2N 5HZ. *T:* (020) 7969 6000.

**PATTEN, Benedict Joseph;** QC 2010; *b* Belfast, 12 March 1962; *s* of James and Patricia Patten; *m* 1998, Celia Grace; three *s*. *Educ:* Stonyhurst Coll.; New Coll., Oxford (BA); City Univ. (Dip. Law). Called to the Bar, Middle Temple, 1986. *Recreations:* tennis, reading, theatre. *Address:* 4 New Square, Lincoln's Inn, WC2A 3RJ.

**PATTEN, Brian;** poet; *b* 7 Feb. 1946. Regents Lectr, Univ. of Calif (San Diego), 1985. FRSL 2003. Freedom, City of Liverpool, 2001. Hon. Fellow, Liverpool John Moores Univ., 2002. Hon LittD Liverpool, 2006; DUniv Open, 2013. Cholmondeley Award for Poetry, 2002. *Publications: poetry:* Penguin Modern Poets, 1967; Little Johnny's Confession, 1967; Notes to the Hurrying Man, 1969; The Irrelevant Song, 1971; The Unreliable Nightingale, 1973; Vanishing Trick, 1976; The Shabby Angel, 1978; Grave Gossip, 1979; Love Poems, 1981; Clare's Countryside: a book on John Clare, 1982; New Volume, 1983; Storm Damage, 1988; Grinning Jack (Selected Poems), 1990; Armada, 1996; The Blue and Green Ark, 1999; New Selected Poems, 2007; Collected Love Poems, 2008; View from the Boathouse Window, 2010; *novel:* Mr Moon's Last Case, 1975 (Mystery Writers of Amer. Special Award, 1976); *for younger readers:* The Elephant and the Flower, 1969; Jumping Mouse; 1971; Emma's Doll, 1976; The Sly Cormorant and the Fish: adaptations of The Aesop Fables, 1977; (ed) Gangsters, Ghosts and Dragonflies, 1981; Gargling with Jelly, 1985; Jimmy Tag-along, 1988; Thawing Frozen Frogs, 1990; (ed) The Puffin Book of Twentieth Century Children's Verse, 1991; Grizzelda Frizzle, 1992; The Magic Bicycle, 1993; Impossible Parents, 1994; The Utter Nutters, 1994; (ed) The Puffin Book of Utterly Brilliant Poetry, 1998; Beowulf and the Monster, 1999; Juggling with Gerbils, 2000; Little Hotchpotch, 2000; Impossible Parents Go Green, 2000; The Story Giant, 2001 (and play, 2014, 2016); Ben's Magic Telescope, 2003; (with Roger McGough) The Monsters' Guide to Choosing a Pet, 2004; Puffin Book of Modern Children's Verse, 2006; The Big Snuggle-up, 2011; Can I Come Too?, 2013; Monster Slayer, 2016; *plays:* The Pig And The Junkle, 1975; (with Roger McGough) The Mouth Trap, 1982; Blind Love, 1983; Gargling with Jelly, 1989; *recordings:* Brian Patten Reading His Own Poetry, 1969; British Poets Of Our Time, 1974; Vanishing Trick, 1976; The Sly Cormorant, 1977; Grizzelda Frizzle and other stories, 1995; The Mersey Sound, 1997. *Address:* c/o Rogers, Coleridge and White, 20 Powis Mews, W11 1JN. *Club:* Chelsea Arts.

**PATTEN, Louise Alexandra Virginia Charlotte;** *see* Lady Patten.

**PATTEN, Rt Hon. Sir Nicholas (John),** Kt 2000; PC 2009; **Rt Hon. Lord Justice Patten;** a Lord Justice of Appeal, since 2009; *b* 7 Aug. 1950; *s* of late Peter Grenville Patten and Dorothy Patten (*née* Davenport); *m* 1984, Veronica Mary Schoeneich (marr. diss. 1998); two *s* one *d*. *Educ:* Tulse Hill Sch.; Christ Church, Oxford (Open Schol.; MA; BCL (1st Cl. Hons Jurisprudence)). Called to the Bar, Lincoln's Inn, 1974, Bencher, 1997 (Treas., 2018); QC 1988; a Dep. High Court Judge, 1998–2000; a Judge of the High Court of Justice, Chancery Div., 2000–09. Vice-Chancellor, Co. Palatine of Lancaster, 2005–08. Chm., Chancery Bar Assoc., 1997–99. *Recreation:* gardening. *Address:* Royal Courts of Justice, Strand, WC2A 2LL. *Club:* Athenæum.

**PATTENDEN, Prof. Gerald,** FRS 1991; Sir Jesse Boot Professor of Organic Chemistry, Nottingham University, 1988–2005, Emeritus Professor of Chemistry, 2009 (Pro-Vice-Chancellor, 1997–2003); *b* 4 March 1940; *s* of Albert James and Violet Eugenia Pattenden; *m* 1969, Christine Frances Doherty; three *d*. *Educ:* Brunel Univ. (BSc); Queen Mary College London (PhD, DSc; Hon. Fellow, 2000). FRSC. Lectr, UC, Cardiff, 1966–72; Nottingham University: Lectr, 1972–75; Reader, 1975–80; Prof., 1980–88; Hd of Dept of Chem., 1988–96; Res. Prof. of Organic Chem., 2005–09. Chm., Org. Chem. Cttee, SERC, 1992–94. Mem. Council, Royal Soc., 2001–03. Royal Society of Chemistry: Pres., Perkin Div., 1995–97 (Scientific Ed., Perkin Trans); Corday-Morgan Medal and Prize, 1975; Simonsen Lect. and Medal, 1987; Tilden Lect. and Medal, 1991; Award for Synthetic Organic Chem., 1992; Pedler Lect. and Medal, 1993; Award for Heterocyclic Chem., 1994; Award for Natural Product Chemistry, 1997; Hugo Müller Lect. and Medal, 2001; Robert Robinson Lect., 2007; Merck Award Lect. and Medal, 2009. Hon. DLaws Nottingham, 2015. *Publications:* editor of several books; over 490 contribs to internat. jls of chemistry. *Recreations:* sport, DIY, gardening. *Address:* School of Chemistry, University of Nottingham, University Park, Nottingham NG7 2RD. *T:* (0115) 951 3530. *E:* gp@nottingham.ac.uk.

**PATTERSON, Ben;** *see* Patterson, G. B.

**PATTERSON, (Constance) Marie, (Mrs Barrie Devney),** CBE 1978 (OBE 1973); National Officer, Transport and General Workers' Union, 1976–84 (National Women's Officer, 1963–76); Member of General Council of TUC, 1963–84 (Chairman, 1974–75 and 1977); *b* 1 April 1934; *d* of Dr Richard Swanton Abraham; *m* 1st, 1960, Thomas Michael Valentine Patterson (marr. diss. 1976); 2nd, 1984, Barrie Devney. *Educ:* Pendleton High Sch.; Bedford Coll., Univ. of London (BA). Member: Exec., Confedn of Shipbuilding and Engrg Unions, 1966–84 (Pres., 1977–78); Hotel and Catering Trng Bd, 1966–87; Equal Opportunities Commn, 1975–84; Central Arbitration Commn, 1976–94; Legal Aid Adv. Cttee, 1988–90; Council, Office of Banking Ombudsman, 1992–2001. Dir of Remploy, 1966–87. Lay Mem., Press Council, 1964–70. Chm. Council, Queen's Coll., Harley St, 1994–2000; Mem. Court, LSE, 1984–2005 (Mem. Council, 2000–02). Chm., Galleon Trust, 1998–2005. FRSA 2000. Hon. DSc Salford, 1975. *Recreations:* sight-seeing, jig-saws.

**PATTERSON, Eric,** MBE 1970; HM Diplomatic Service, retired; Consul-General, 1982–88 and Counsellor (Commercial), 1986–88, Auckland; *b* 2 May 1930; *s* of Richard and Elizabeth Patterson; *m* 1st, 1953, Doris Mason (*d* 1999); two *s*; 2nd, 2001, Charlotte Pellizzaro (*née* Bathurst). *Educ:* Hookergate Grammar Sch., Co. Durham. Served Royal Signals, 1948–50. Local govt service, 1947–50; Lord Chancellor's Dept, 1950–52; BoT, 1952–62; Asst Trade Comr, Halifax, NS, 1962–67; Second Sec. (Commercial), Khartoum, 1967–70; First Sec. (Commercial), The Hague, 1970–74; FCO, 1974–76; First Sec. (Commercial), Warsaw, 1976–80; FCO, 1980–82. *Recreations:* golf, photography, bowls. *Address:* 1/35 Howe Street, Howick, Auckland 2014, New Zealand.

**PATTERSON, Gareth Thomas;** QC 2017; *b* Comber, Co. Down, 5 Nov. 1969; *s* of James Stirling Patterson and Ellen Houston Patterson (*née* Chambers); *m* 2010, Miranda Clifton Grove; one *s* three *d*. *Educ:* Royal Belfast Academical Instn; Queens' Coll., Cambridge (BA Hons Law 1991). Called to the Bar, Gray's Inn, 1995. *Recreations:* family, walking, fishing, reading, opera. *Address:* 6KBW College Hill, 21 College Hill, EC4R 2RP. *T:* (020) 3301 0910.

**PATTERSON, Gavin Echlin;** Chairman, Europe, Middle East and Africa, Salesforce Ltd, since 2019; *b* Altrincham, 6 Sept. 1967; *s* of William Echlin Patterson and Christine Anne Patterson; *m* 1997, Karen Lacovara; one *s* three *d*. *Educ:* Emmanuel Coll., Cambridge (BA 1989; MA; MEng 1990). Procter and Gamble, 1990–99, mktg roles incl. Eur. Mktg Dir, Haircare, 1999; Man. Dir, Consumer, Telewest Communications plc, 1999–2003; BT

Group plc: Man. Dir, Consumer, 2004–08; Exec. Dir, 2008–19; Chief Exec., BT Retail, 2008–13; Chief Exec., 2013–19. Non-executive Director: Johnston Press plc, 2008–09; British Airways plc, 2011–. Member: Internat. Business Council, WEF, 2014–19; Internat. Adv. Bd, British American Business, 2017–19. Board Member: Movement to Work, 2014–19; Productivity Leadership Gp, 2017–19. Pres., Advertising Assoc., 2011–14; Mem., BAFTA, 2012–; Vice-Pres., RTS, 2016–. Mem., Adv. Bd, Judge Business Sch., Univ. of Cambridge, 2011–13. Trustee, BM, 2012–. *Recreations:* supporting Liverpool FC, live music, collecting movie posters, cooking, fine wine.

**PATTERSON, George Benjamin, (Ben);** Director, CJA Consultants Ltd, since 2004; *b* 21 April 1939; *s* of late Eric James Patterson and Ethel Patterson; *m* 1970, Felicity Barbara Anne Raybould; one *s* one *d*. *Educ:* Westminster Sch.; Trinity Coll., Cambridge (MA); London Sch. of Economics. Lecturer, Swinton Conservative Coll., 1961–65; Editor (at Conservative Political Centre), CPC Monthly Report, 1965–74; Dep. Head, London Office of European Parlt, 1974–79. MEP (C) Kent W, 1979–94; contested (C) Kent W, Eur. Parly elecns, 1994. Prin. Administrator, Internal Market, then Econ. and Monetary Affairs Div., DG for Res., EP, 1994–2004. Mem (C), Hammersmith LBC, 1968–71. Contested (C) Wrexham, 1970. Chm., Cons. Party, Kent Area, 2010–13. MInstD. *Publications:* The Character of Conservatism, 1973; Direct Elections to the European Parliament, 1974; Europe and Employment, 1984; Vredeling and All That, 1984; VAT: the zero rate issue, 1988; A Guide to EMU, 1990; A European Currency, 1994; Options for a Definitive VAT System, 1995; The Co-ordination of National Fiscal Policies, 1996; The Consequences of Abolishing Duty Free Within the EU, 1997; Adjusting to Asymmetric Shocks, 1998; The Feasibility of a Tobin Tax, 1999; The Determination of Interest Rates, 1999; Exchange Rates and Monetary Policy, 2000; Tax Co-ordination in the European Union, 2002; Background to the Euro, 2002; Taxation in Europe: recent developments, 2003; Understanding the EU Budget, 2011; The Conservative Party and Europe, 2011; An Exercise in Causality, 2014. *Recreations:* reading science fiction, walking. *Address:* 38 Le Village, 09300 Montségur, France. *T:* (5) 61640119, 07582 068693; 33 Brunswick House, Fulham Reach, W6 9LH.

**PATTERSON, Harry;** novelist; *b* 27 July 1929; *s* of Henry Patterson and Rita Higgins Bell; *m* 1st, 1958, Amy Margaret Hewitt (marr. diss. 1984); one *s* three *d*; 2nd, 1985, Denise Lesley Anne Palmer. *Educ:* Roundhay Sch., Leeds; Beckett Park Coll. for Teachers; London Sch. of Economics as external student (BSc(Hons) Sociology). FRSA. NCO, The Blues, 1947–50. 1950–58: tried everything from being a clerk to a circus tent-hand; 1958–72: variously a schoolmaster, Lectr in Liberal Studies, Leeds Polytechnic, Sen. Lectr in Education, James Graham Coll. and Tutor in Sch. Practice, Leeds Univ.; since age of 41, engaged in full-time writing career. Dual citizenship, British/Irish. DUniv Leeds Metropolitan, 1995; Hon. DLitt London, 2014. *Publications:* (as Jack Higgins) Prayer for the Dying, 1973 (filmed 1985); The Eagle has Landed, 1975 (filmed 1976); Storm Warning, 1976; Day of Judgement, 1978; Solo, 1980; Luciano's Luck, 1981; Touch the Devil, 1982; Exocet, 1983; Confessional, 1985 (filmed 1985); Night of the Fox, 1986 (filmed 1989); A Season in Hell, 1989; Cold Harbour, 1990; The Eagle Has Flown, 1990; Angel of Death, 1995; Drink with the Devil, 1996; Day of Reckoning, 2000; Edge of Danger, 2001; Bad Company, 2003; Dark Justice, 2004; Wolf at the Door, 2009; The Judas Gate, 2010; (as Harry Patterson): The Valhalla Exchange, 1978; To Catch a King, 1979 (filmed 1983); Dillinger, 1983; Walking Wounded (stage play), 1987; and many others (including The Violent Enemy, filmed 1969, and The Wrath of God, filmed 1972) under pseudonyms (Martin Fallon, Hugh Marlowe, Henry Patterson); some books trans. into 60 languages. *Recreations:* tennis, old movies. *Address:* c/o Sophie Hicks Agency, 60 Gray's Inn Road, WC1X 8AQ.

**PATTERSON, Dr Karalyn Eve,** FBA 2010; FRS 2014; FMedSci; Senior Scientist, now Visiting Scientist, MRC Cognition and Brain Sciences Unit, University of Cambridge; Emeritus Fellow, Darwin College, Cambridge. *Educ:* MA Cantab 1995. PhD. FMedSci 2003. *Publications:* (ed jtly) Memory, 1998; articles in learned jls. *Address:* MRC Cognition and Brain Sciences Unit, 15 Chaucer Road, Cambridge CB2 7EF.

**PATTERSON, Prof. Laurence Hylton,** PhD; CChem, FRSC; Professor of Drug Discovery, and Director, Institute of Cancer Therapeutics, University of Bradford, 2005–16, part-time Professor of Drug Discovery, since 2016; *b* Ilford, 22 June 1952; *s* of late George Patterson and Olive Patterson; *m* 1st, 1974, Susan Doyle (marr. diss. 2000); one *s* one *d*; 2nd, 2002, Samantha Orr; three *s*. *Educ:* West Hatch Tech. High Sch., Chigwell; Hatfield Poly. (BSc Hons 1974); King's Coll. London (PhD 1977). FRSC 2004; CChem 2004. Sen. Scientist, Fisons Pharmaceuticals, 1977–80; Prof. of Pharmacy, De Montfort Univ., 1980–99; Prof. of Medicinal Chemistry and Hd, Dept of Pharmaceutical and Biol Chem., Sch. of Pharmacy, Univ. of London, 1999–2004. Founder Dir and Shareholder, Biostatus Ltd, 2003–; Founder Shareholder, Icanthera Ltd, 2012–; Chair, SAB Oncotherics Ltd, 2014–. Hon. Professor: Third Military Medical Univ., Chongqing, 2008; Southwestern Univ., Beibei, 2011; Vis. Prof., Shanghai Inst. of Materia Medica, Chinese Acad. of Sci., 2008. Hon. MRPharmS 2007. *Publications:* over 200 scientific articles, patents and scientific reviews. *Recreation:* keeping up physically and mentally with three lively boys (eldest at Giggleswick). *Address:* Institute of Cancer Therapeutics, University of Bradford, W Yorks BD7 1DP. *T:* (01274) 233226. *E:* l.h.patterson@bradford.ac.uk. *Club:* Athenæum.

**PATTERSON, Dr Linda Joyce,** OBE 2000; FRCP, FRCPE; health service consultant, since 2010; Clinical Vice President, Royal College of Physicians, 2010–13; *b* Liverpool, 12 April 1951; *d* of Thomas William Matthew Patterson and Mary Frances Patterson (née Ollerhead); partner, Christopher Stephen Green. *Educ:* Liverpool Institute High Sch. for Girls; Middlesex Hosp. Med. Sch., Univ. of London (MB BS 1975). FRCPE 1991; FRCP 1993. Consultant physician, East Lancashire, 1986–2011. Medical Director: Burnley NHS Trust, 1995–2000; Commn for Health Improvement, 2000–04. Non-executive Director: Nat. Patient Safety Agency, 2006–12; Calderdale and Huddersfield NHS Foundn Trust, 2013–. Trustee: White Ribbon Campaign, 2008–14; Alzheimer's Soc., 2010–13. *Publications:* (jtly) Health Care for Older People: practitioner perspective in a changing society, 1998. *Recreations:* playing piano, opera, politics, feminism. *Club:* Royal Society of Medicine.

**PATTERSON, Lindy Ann;** QC (Scot.) 2010; FCIArb, FRICS, FCInstCES; arbitrator and adjudicator; *b* Berwick-on-Tweed, 12 Sept. 1958. *Educ:* Univ. of Edinburgh (LLB Hons). WS 2001. FCInstCES 2011; FCIArb 2012. Admitted solicitor, Scotland, 1981, England and Wales, 2009; Solicitor Advocate, Scotland, 1993, England and Wales, 2016; called to the Bar, Middle Temple, 2017. Partner: Bird Semple, 1988–98; MacRoberts, 1998–2003; Dundas & Wilson, then CMS Cameron McKenna LLP, 2003–17. Pt-time Lectr and Tutor, DipLP, Univ. of Edinburgh, 2008–. Mem., London Court of Internat. Arbitration, 2015–; Chair, Domestic Appts Sub-Cttee, Scottish Arbitration Centre, 2017–. Accredited Adjudicator, Technol. and Construction Solicitors' Assoc., 2000. Mem., Internat. Panel of Adjudicators, FIDIC, 2012–; Pres., Dispute Resolution Bd Fedn (Region 2), 2018– (Dir, 2013–17); Mem., ICC Commn on Arbitration and ADR, 2018–. Mem., ARBRIX, 2009. Vice-Chair, Cttee, Shelter Scotland, 2011–17. Freeman, Arbitrators' Co., 2008. *Recreations:* dogs, hill walking, reading, singing. *Address:* 39 Essex Chambers, 81 Chancery Lane, WC2A 1DD. *E:* lindy.patterson@39.essex.com.

**PATTERSON, Dr Margaret Florence,** OBE 2014; food safety consultant; Principal Scientific Officer, Agri-Food and Biosciences Institute, Belfast, 1995–2015; *b* Belfast, 26 Feb. 1959; *d* of David John and Mary Elizabeth Patterson. *Educ:* Carolan Grammar Sch., Belfast; Queen's Univ. Belfast (BSc Hons Food Sci.; MSc (Dist.) Orgn and Mgt; PhD Food Microbiol. 1984). CSci (Food Sci.) 2004. Res. Fellow, QUB, 1984–86; SSO, Dept of Agric. and Rural Develt, NI, 1986–95; on secondment as Food Safety Consultant, IAEA, 1995; Lectr, 1987–95, Reader, 1995–2011, Dept of Food Sci., QUB, now Hon. Prof. President: Soc. for Applied Microbiol., 2005–08; Inst. of Food Sci. and Technol., 2013–15. FIFST 1992. *Publications:* contribs to scientific pubns on food sci. and food safety. *Recreations:* travelling, gardening, walking. *Address:* Carryduff, Belfast.

**PATTERSON, Marie;** *see* Patterson, C. M.

**PATTERSON, Dr Mark Jonathan Lister;** Hon. Consultant Haematologist, Manchester Royal Infirmary, 1997–2007; Consultant Haematologist, Mid Cheshire NHS Trust, 1996–2007; *b* 2 March 1934; *s* of Alfred Patterson and Frederica Georgina Mary Lister Nicholson; *m* 1958, Jane Teresa Mary Scott Stokes; one *s* two *d*. *Educ:* privately; St Bartholomew's Hosp. Med. Coll., Univ. of London (MB 1959). MRCP. Jun. hosp. appts at St Bartholomew's Hosp., Royal Postgrad. Med. Sch., and MRC Exptl Haematol. Unit; Consultant Haematologist to Nat. Heart and Chest Hosps, 1967–84. Mem., GLC, 1970–73 and 1977–81; contested (C) Ealing N, Feb. 1974. Chm., Covent Gdn Develt Cttee, 1977–82. *Recreations:* medicine, politics, conservation and restoration of important buildings, organising concerts of all genres. *Address:* Wolverton Manor, Shorwell, Newport, Isle of Wight PO30 3JS. *T:* (01983) 740609, 07831 444149. *E:* markpatterson@wolvertonmanor.co.uk.

**PATTERSON, Paul Leslie;** composer; Manson Professor of Composition, Royal Academy of Music, since 1997; Artistic Director, Park Lane Group Young Composer Forum, since 1998; formed: Manson Ensemble, 1968; The Patterson Quintet, 1982; *b* 15 June 1947; *s* of Leslie and Lilian Patterson; *m* 1981, Hazel Wilson; one *s* one *d*. *Educ:* Royal Academy of Music. FRAM 1980; FRNCM 2007. Freelance composer, 1968–; Arts Council Composer in Association, English Sinfonia, 1969–70; Director, Contemporary Music, Warwick Univ., 1974–80; Prof. of Composition, and Hd of Composition and Twentieth Century Music, RAM, 1985–97; Composer in Residence: SE Arts Assoc., 1980–82; Bedford School, 1984–85; Southwark Fest., 1989–91; James Allen School, Dulwich, 1990–91; Three Spires Fest., Truro, 1992–94; NYO, 1997–; Guest Prof., Yale Univ., 1989–90; Vis. Prof. of Composition, Univ. of Canterbury, Christchurch, 2000–; Vis. Composition Tutor, RNCM, 2002–. Artistic Dir, Exeter Fest., 1991–97; Artistic Advr, N Devon Fest., 1999–. Chm., Mendelssohn Scholarship, Royal Schs of Music, 1997–. Member: Exec. Cttee, Composers Guild, 1972–75; Council, SPNM, 1975–81, 1985–; Adv. Council, BBC Radio London, 1986–; Adv. Cttee, Arts Council's Recordings Panel, 1986–94; Artistic Director of RAM Festivals: Lutosławski, 1984; Penderecki, 1986; Messiaen, 1987; Henze, 1988; Berio, 1989, 2004; Carter, 1990; Da Capo, 1993; Schnittke, 1994; Ligeti, 1995; film music, 1996; Birtwistle, 1997; Donatoni, 1998; Russian, 1999; Pärt, 2000; Kagel, 2001. Featured Composer at: Three Choirs Fest., Patterson at South Bank Fest., 1988; Cheltenham Fest., 1988, 1990; Peterborough Fest., 1989; Exeter Fest., 1991; Presteigne Fest., 2001; Sounds New, 2007; Hampstead and Highgate Fest., 2007. Performances world wide by leading orchestras and soloists and ensembles; also film and TV music. Numerous recordings. Pres., RAM Club, 1993–94. FRSA 1989. Hon. FLCM 1997. Lesley Boosey Award, Royal Philharmonic Soc., 1996. OM, 1987, Gold Medal, 2009, Polish Ministry of Culture. *Publications:* Rebecca, 1968; Trumpet Concerto, 1969; Time Piece, 1972; Kyrie, 1972; Comedy for Five Winds, 1973; Requiem, 1974; Fluorescences, 1974; Clarinet Concerto, 1976; Cracowian Counterpoints, 1977; Voices of Sleep, 1979; Concerto for Orchestra, 1981; Canterbury Psalms, 1981; Sinfonia, 1982; Mass of the Sea, 1983; Deception Pass, 1983; Duologue, 1984; Mean Time, 1984; Europhony, 1985; Missa Brevis, 1985; Stabat Mater, 1986; String Quartet, 1986; Magnificat and Nunc Dimittis, 1986; Propositions, 1987; Trombone Quartet, 1987; Suite for Cello, 1987; Sorriest Cow, 1987; Tides of Mananan, 1988; Te Deum, 1988; Tunnel of Time, 1989; White Shadows, 1989; Symphony, 1990; The End, 1990; Mighty Voice, 1991; Violin Concerto, 1992; Little Red Riding Hood, 1992; Magnificat, 1993; Music for Opening Channel Tunnel, 1994; Overture: Songs of the West, 1995; Soliloquy, 1996; Rustic Sketches, 1997; Hell Angels, 1998; Gloria, 1999; Western Winds, 1999; Millennium Mass, 2000; Deviations, 2001; Cello Concerto, 2002; Jubilee Dances, 2002; Three Little Pigs, 2003; Bug for Solo Harp, 2003; Harpo Maniac, 2004; Fifth Continent, 2005; Orchestra on Parade, 2005; Allusions, 2007; Viola Concerto, 2008; Phoenix Concerto, 2009; Two Grooves, 2009; Avians Harp Quartet, 2010; Lizards for Solo Harp, 2012; Serenade for Violin and Orchestra, 2013; Spirals for Solo Harp, 2013; Fantasia for Harp and Orchestra, 2014; Spiders Web, Harp and String Quartet, 2014. *Recreations:* sailing, croquet, swimming, computing. *Address:* 31 Cromwell Avenue, Highgate, N6 5HN. *T:* (020) 8348 3711.

**PATTERSON, Most Hon. Percival (Noel James),** ON 2002; PC 1992; QC 1983; Prime Minister of Jamaica, 1992–2006; *b* 10 April 1935; *s* of Henry Patterson and Ina James; *m* (marr. diss.); one *s* one *d*. *Educ:* Somerton Primary, St James; Calabar High Sch., Kingston; Univ. of the West Indies (BA Hons English 1958); LSE (LLB 1963). Called to the Bar, Middle Temple, 1963; admitted to Jamaican Bar, 1963; private legal practice, Kingston. Senator, Leader of Opposition Business, 1969–70; MP (PNP) SE, then Eastern, Westmoreland, Jamaica, 1972–80 and 1989–2006; Minister of Industry, Trade and Tourism, 1972–77; Dep. Prime Minister, 1978–80, 1989–91; Minister: of Foreign Affairs and Foreign Trade, 1978–80; of Develt Planning and Production, 1989–90; of Finance and Planning, 1990–91; of Defence, 1992–2006. People's National Party: Mem. Exec. Council, 1964; Vice-Pres., 1969; Chm., 1983–92; Pres. and Leader, 1992–2006; Member: Global Leadership Foundn, 2006–; Club de Madrid, 2007–; Council, InterAction, 2007–; Bd. of Trustees, African Union Foundn, 2013–; Chm., Tech. Cttee, Caribbean Cricket Premier League, 2013–. Agricola Medal, FAO, 2001; Golden Star Award, Caribbean and Latin Amer. Action Gp, 2002; Chancellor's Medal, Univ. of W Indies, 2006. Order of Francisco Morazán, Gran Cruz Placa de Oro (Honduras), 1990; Order of Águila Azteca (Mexico), 1990; Order of Liberator Simon Bolivar (Venezuela), 1st Class, 1992; Order of San Martin (Argentina), 1992; Order of Gran Cruz Gonzalo Jiménez de Quesada (Colombia), 1994; Order of Jose Marti (Cuba), 1997; Order of the Volta (Ghana), 1999; Gran Cruz Placa de Orode Juan Mora Fernández (Costa Rica), 2001; Grand Cross, Nat. Order of Civil Merit (Spain), 2006; Order of Belize, 2006; Grand Cross, Order of Southern Cross (Brazil), 2006; Order of Excellence (Guyana), 2006; OCC 2009; Supreme Companion, Order of the Companions of O. R. Tambo (Gold) (South Africa), 2013. *Recreations:* music, sports (cricket, boxing, track and field, tennis). *Address:* Heisconsults, R. Danny Williams Building, 10th Floor, 28–48 Barbados Avenue, Kingston 5, Jamaica.

**PATTERSON, Simon Iain;** a Managing Director, Silver Lake, since 2012; *b* Birmingham, 4 May 1973; *s* of Timothy John Patterson and Cherry Patterson; *m* 2002, Harriet Jo Bell; two *s* one *d*. *Educ:* King's Coll., Cambridge (BA 1995); Stanford Univ. (MBA 2005). Business Analyst, McKinsey, 1995–97; Dir, Financial Times, 1997–99; Sen. Vice Pres., GF-X, 1999–2003; Silver Lake, 2005–. Non-executive Director: N Brown Gp plc, 2013–16; Tesco plc, 2016–. Mem., Adv. Bd, Prince's Trust, 2013–16 (Chm., Internet and Media Leadership Gp, 2010–13); Trustee: Natural History Mus., 2015–; Royal Foundn of the Duke and Duchess of Cambridge (formerly the Duke and Duchess of Cambridge and Prince Harry, then the Duke and Duchess of Sussex), 2016–. *Recreations:* sailing, golf. *Clubs:* Athenæum; Itchenor Sailing.

**PATTERSON, Vilma Hazel Ann,** MBE 2004; Chairman, Probation Board for Northern Ireland, 2012–18 (Member, 2009–12); *b* Belfast, 5 Feb. 1957; *d* of John G. Duff and Hazel Duff; *m* 1981, Geoffrey Patterson; one *s* one *d*. *Educ:* Victoria Coll., Belfast; St Godric's Coll., Hampstead. Sportsground and Landscape Mgt Analyst, 1976–2005, Dir, 1985–2005, John G. Duff (Annadale) Ltd. Mem., Independent Monitoring Bd, 1996–2008 (Chm., 1998–2001); Chm., Assoc. of Independent Monitoring Bd Members, 2003–08. Member: Parades Commn for NI, 2005–10; Prison Service Pay Rev. Body, 2011–13; Armed Forces Pay Review Body, 2014–20; Boundary Commn for NI, 2019–; a Civil Service Comr for NI, 2009–15; non-exec. Mem., Audit Cttee, Office of Police Ombudsman, 2010–15. Chm., Women in Business Network, 2001–04; Dir, Women on the Move, 2009–15. *Recreations:* striving for peace and harmony, gardening, craft, art, theatre, museums. *Club:* Belvoir Park Golf.

**PATTIE, Rt Hon. Sir Geoffrey (Edwin),** Kt 1987; PC 1987; Senior Partner, Terrington Management LLP, 1999–2015; Chairman, GEC-Marconi, 1996–99 (Joint Chairman, 1991–96); *b* 17 Jan. 1936; *s* of late Alfred Edwin Pattie, LDS, and Ada Olive (*née* Carr); *m* 1960, Tuëma Caroline (*née* Eyre-Maunsell); one *s* (one *d* decd). *Educ:* Durham Sch.; St Catharine's Coll., Cambridge (BA 1959, MA; Fellow Commoner, 2005; Hon. Fellow, 2007). Called to Bar, Gray's Inn, 1964. Served: Queen Victoria's Rifles (TA), 1959–61; (on amalgamation) Queen's Royal Rifles (TA), then 4th Royal Green Jackets, later 7th (TA) Battalion, The Rifles, 1961–65; Captain, 1964, Hon. Col, 1996–99, Dep. Col Comdt (TA and Cadets), 1999–2007. Mem. GLC, Lambeth, 1967–70; Chm. ILEA Finance Cttee, 1968–70. Marketing Dir, 1997–98, Dir of Communications, 1998–99, GEC. Contested (C) Barking, 1966 and 1970. MP (C) Chertsey and Walton, Feb. 1974–1997. Parly Under Sec. of State for Defence for the RAF, 1979–81, for Defence Procurement, 1981–83; Minister of State: for Defence Procurement, 1983–84; DTI (Minister for IT), 1984–87; Vice-Chm., Cons. Party, 1990–97. Sec., Cons. Parly Aviation Cttee, 1974–75, 1975–76, Vice Chm., 1976–77, 1977–78; Jt Sec., Cons. Parly Defence Cttee, 1975–76, 1976–77, 1977–78, Vice Chm., 1978–79; Mem., Cttee of Public Accounts, 1976–79; Vice-Chm., All Party Cttee on Mental Health, 1977–79. Mem. General Synod of Church of England, 1970–75. Chm., Intellectual Property Inst., 1994–99. Chm. of Governors, London Coll. of Printing, 1968–69. Trustee, Excalibur Scholarship Scheme, 1992–. FRSA 1990. Hon. LLD Sheffield, 1996. *Publications:* Towards a New Defence Policy, 1976; (with James Bellini) A New World Role for the Medium Power: the British Opportunity, 1977; One of our Delegations is Missing, 2002. *Recreations:* opera, theatre, following Middlesbrough Football Club. *Club:* Reform.

**PATTINSON, Kristina;** *see* Harrison, K.

**PATTINSON, Timothy John Hull;** a District Judge (Magistrates' Courts), since 2009; *b* Winchester, 15 March 1956; *s* of John Pattinson and Mary Grace Pattinson (*née* Hull); *m* 2003, Juliet Elizabeth Winsor. *Educ:* Winchester Coll.; University Coll. London (BA Hons English Lit.). Trainee solicitor, Lawrence Graham, London, 1980–83; admitted as solicitor, 1983; English Teacher, 1984; Assistant Solicitor: Thomas Coombs, Dorchester, 1985–86; Dutton Gregory, Winchester, 1987–89; sole practitioner, Winchester, 1989–2001; Consultant, Talbot Walker, Andover, 2001–09; Dep. Dist Judge (Magistrates' Courts), 1999–2009. *Recreations:* walking, cycling, browsing through books, walking in Italy, cross-country ski-ing. *Address:* Basingstoke Magistrates' Court, London Road, Basingstoke RG21 4AB.

**PATTISON, David Arnold,** PhD; Best Value Inspector, Audit Commission, 2000–06; *b* 9 Feb. 1941; *s* of David Pattison and Christina Russell Bone; *m* 1967, Anne Ross Wilson; two *s* one *d*. *Educ:* Glasgow Univ. (BSc 1st Cl. Hons, PhD). Planning Assistant, Dunbarton County Council, 1966–67; Lecturer, Strathclyde Univ., 1967–70; Head of Tourism Division, Highlands and Islands Development Board, 1970–81; Chief Exec., Scottish Tourist Board, 1981–85; Dir of Leisure and Tourism Consulting, Arthur Young Group, 1985–90; Principal Associate: Cobham Resource Consultants, 1990–96; Scott Wilson Resource Consultants, 1996–98; Dir, David A. Pattison Associates, 1998–2000. Hon. Pres., Scottish YHA, 1995–. *Publications:* Tourism Development Plans for: Argyll, Bute, Ayrshire, Burgh of Ayr, Ulster. *Recreations:* reading, watching soccer and Rugby, golf, gardening. *Address:* 4 Braefoot Grove, Dalgety Bay, Fife KY11 9YS.

**PATTISON, Rev. Prof. George Linsley,** DD; 1640 Professor of Divinity, University of Glasgow, since 2013; *b* 25 May 1950; *s* of George William Pattison and Jean Pattison; *m* 1971, Hilary Christine Cochrane; one *s* two *d*. *Educ:* Perse Sch., Cambridge; Edinburgh Univ. (MA, BD); Durham Univ. (PhD 1983, DD 2004). Ordained deacon, 1977, priest, 1978; Curate, St James' Church, Benwell, Newcastle upon Tyne, 1977–80; Priest-in-charge, St Philip and St James' Church, Kimblesworth, Co. Durham, 1980–83; Res. Student, Durham Univ., 1980–83; Rector, Badwell Ash, Great Ashfield, Hunston and Stowlangtoft with Langham, Suffolk, 1983–91; Dean of Chapel, King's Coll., Cambridge, 1991–2001; Associate Prof. of Theol., 2002–03, Vis. Prof. of Theol., 2005–11, Univ. of Aarhus, Denmark; Lady Margaret Prof. of Divinity, Univ. of Oxford 2004–13; Canon of Christ Church, Oxford, 2004–13. Montgomery Fellow, Dartmouth Coll., 2013; Fellow, Max Weber Centre for Advanced Cultural and Social Studies, 2017–18. Vis. Res. Prof., 1997, 2000, Vis. Prof. of Theol., 2011–, Univ. of Copenhagen. Vice-Pres., Modern Churchpeople's Union, 1999–2008. Has broadcast on BBC Radio 3, Radio 4 and World Service on subjects of art and religion. Editor, Modern Believing, 1994–98. *Publications:* Art, Modernity and Faith, 1991, 2nd edn 1998; Kierkegaard: the aesthetic and the religious, 1992, 2nd edn 1999; (ed) Kierkegaard on Art and Communication, 1993; (with Sister Wendy Beckett) Pains of Glass, 1995; (with S. Platten) Spirit and Tradition, 1996; Agnosis: theology in the void, 1996; Kierkegaard and the Crisis of Faith, 1997; (ed with S. Shakespeare) Kierkegaard: the self in society, 1998; The End of Theology and the Task of Thinking About God, 1998; Poor Paris!, 1998; Anxious Angels, 1999; The Later Heidegger, 2000; A Short Course in the Philosophy of Religion, 2001; Kierkegaard's Upbuilding Discourses, 2002; Kierkegaard, Religion and the Nineteenth Century Crisis of Culture, 2002; A Short Course in Christian Doctrine, 2005; The Philosophy of Kierkegaard, 2005; Thinking About God in an Age of Technology, 2005; Crucifixions and Resurrections of the Image, 2009; God and Being, 2011; Kierkegaard and the Theology of the Nineteenth Century, 2012; Kierkegaard and the Quest for Unambiguous Life, 2013; Heidegger and Death, 2013; The Heart Cold Never Speak, 2013; (ed with J. Lippitt) The Oxford Handbook of Kierkegaard, 2013; (ed jtly) The Oxford Handbook of Theology and Modern European Thought, 2013; Paul Tillich's Philosophical Theology: a fifty year reappraisal, 2015; Eternal God/Saving Time, 2015; A Phenomenology of the Devout Life, 2018; (with Kate Kirkpatrick) The Mystical Sources of Existentialist Thought: being, nothingness, love, 2019; articles on theology, philosophy of religion and the arts in specialist and non-specialist jls. *Recreations:* family life, music, films, theatre, visiting cities, walking. *Address:* Theology and Religious Studies, University of Glasgow, Glasgow G12 8QQ.

**PATTISON, Sir John (Ridley),** Kt 1998; DM; FRCPath, FMedSci; Professor of Medical Microbiology, University College London, 1984–2004, now Emeritus; *b* 1 Aug. 1942; *s* of Tom Frederick and Elizabeth Pattison; *m* 1965, Pauline Evans; one *s* two *d*. *Educ:* Barnard Castle Sch.; University Coll., Oxford (BSc, MA; BM, BCh 1968; DM 1975); Middlesex Hosp. Med. Sch. FRCPath 1985. Asst Lectr in Pathology, then Lectr in Virology, Middx Hosp. Med. Sch., 1970–75; Lectr, then Sen. Lectr in Virology, St Bartholomew's and London Hosp. Med. Colls, 1976–77; Prof. of Medical Microbiol., KCH Med. Sch., 1977–84; Dean, UCL Med. Sch., 1990–98; Vice-Provost, UCL, 1994–99; Dir of R&D, DoH and NHS, 1999–2004 (on secondment). Hon. NHS Consultant, UCH, subseq. UCL Hosps NHS Trust, 1984–2004; Hon. Consultant, PHLS, 1980–2003 (Board Mem., 1989–95); Sen. Med. Advr, MRC, 1996–99. Mem., MRC, 1992–95, 1999–2004 (Mem., Grants Cttee, 1985–87, Systems Bd, 1988–92; Chm., Physiol Medicine and Infection Bd, 1992–95); Chm., Spongiform Encephalopathy Adv. Cttee, 1995–99 (Mem., 1994–95). Mem. Council, Soc. of Gen. Microbiol., 1981–87. Member of Board: LSHTM, 1989–92; Inst. of Child Health, 1992–96; Inst. of Neurology, 1995–97. Member: Mgt Cttee, King's Fund, 1993–99 (Dep. Chm., 1994–99); King's Fund London Commn, 1994–95. Editor-in-Chief, Epidemiology & Infection, 1980–94; Mem. Council, Internat. Jl Exptl Pathology, 1979–. Founder FMedSci 1998. *Publications:* (ed jtly) Principles & Practice of Clinical Virology, 1987, 5th edn 2004; (ed jtly) Practical Guide to Clinical Virology, 1989; (ed jtly) Practical Guide to Clinical Bacteriology, 1995; papers and reviews on aspects of medical virology, esp. rubella virus and parvovirus infections. *Recreations:* family, windsurfing, books. *Address:* 17 Broadwater Lane, Towcester, Northants NN12 6YF. *T:* (01327) 352116. *E:* portsea200@btopenworld.com.

**PATTISON, Lindsay;** Worldwide Chief Transformation Officer, Group M and WPP Global, since 2017; *b* Chipping Norton, 17 April 1973; *d* of late Desmond James and of Christine James (*née* Houlton); *m* 2011, David Pattison. *Educ:* Univ. of Stirling (BA Hons Eng. Lit.). Media Manager, Team Y&R, 1998–2001; Brand Manager, Sony Ericsson, 1998–2001; Man. Partner, PHD, 2003–09; UK CEO and Global Chief Strategy Officer, 2009–14, Worldwide CEO, 2014–17, Maxus. Vice Chair, WEF Global Agenda Council, 2014–15. Mem., WACL, 2008– (Pres., 2014–15). *Publications:* blogs and articles. *Recreations:* music, theatre, swimming, tennis, fashion. *Address:* Group M, 26 Red Lion Square, WC1R 4HQ.

**PATTISON, Michael Ambrose,** CBE 1996; Director, Sainsbury Family Charitable Trusts, 1995–2006; *b* 14 July 1946; *s* of late Osmond John Pattison and Eileen Susanna Pattison (*née* Cullen); *m* 1975, Beverley Jean, *d* of late Hugh E. Webber, II and Dr Genevieve Webber Rhines (*née* Downes), Florida, USA; one *d*. *Educ:* Sedbergh School; University of Sussex (BA Hons 1968). Min. of Overseas Develt, 1968; Asst Private Sec. to Minister, 1970; seconded to HM Diplomatic Service as First Sec., Perm. Mission to UN, New York, 1974; ODA, 1977; Private Sec. to successive Prime Ministers, 1979–82; ODA, 1982, Establishment Officer, 1983–85; Chief Exec. and Sec. Gen., RICS, 1985–95; Dir, Surveyors Holdings Ltd, 1985–95. Mem. Council, British Consultants Bureau, 1985–95. Non-exec. Dir, Ordnance Survey, 1997–2001. Trustee: Battersea Arts Centre Trust, 1988–94; Sedbergh Sch. Foundn, 2007–14; Cedars Castle Hill, Shaftesbury, 2007–. Member: Cambridge Univ. Careers Service Syndicate, 1989–93; HEFCE Appeals Panel, 1999–2018; Gov., Thames Poly., subseq. Greenwich Univ., 1989–97 (Pro-Chancellor, 1994–97). Vis. Fellow, City Univ., 1990. FRSA 1990. *Recreations:* tennis, golf, cricket, Real tennis, local history in UK and USA, countryside. *Address:* 8 Bimport, Shaftesbury, Dorset SP7 8AX. *T:* (01747) 852017. *Clubs:* Athenæum; Warwickshire CC; Atlantic Beach and Tennis (Florida).

**PATTISON, Scott;** Floating Sheriff of South Strathclyde, Dumfries and Galloway at Hamilton, since 2015 (at Ayr, 2012–15); *b* Motherwell, 18 Sept. 1969; *s* of Samuel Pattison and Jean Pattison (*née* Campbell); *m* 1992, Aileen Beggan; one *d*. *Educ:* Dalziel High Sch., Motherwell; Univ. of Glasgow (MA; LLB; DipLP). Trainee solicitor, Crown Office and Procurator Fiscal Service, 1993–94; Procurator Fiscal Depute, Hamilton, 1994–98; Principal Procurator Fiscal Depute: specialising in human rights, 1998–99; Crown Office Appeals Unit, 1999–2001; Race Equality and Diversity, Crown Office Policy Gp, 2001–02; Divl Procurator Fiscal, Glasgow, 2002–04; Hd, Policy Gp, Crown Office, 2005–06; Procurator Fiscal, Paisley, 2006–08; Dir of Ops, Crown Office, 2008–11; Floating Sheriff, Grampian, Highlands and Islands at Aberdeen, 2011–12. *Recreations:* music, songwriting, running. *Address:* Sheriff Court House, 4 Beckford Street, Hamilton ML3 0BT. *E:* sheriffspattison@scotcourts.gov.uk.

**PATTISON, Rev. Stephen Bewley,** DLitt; H. G. Wood Professor of Theology, University of Birmingham, 2010–19 (Professor of Religion, Ethics and Practice, 2007–10); *b* 14 Sept. 1953; *s* of Theodore Pattison and Rosamund Audrey Pattison (*née* Greening); *m* 2003, Charmian Beer. *Educ:* Bootham Sch., York; Selwyn Coll., Cambridge (BA 1976); Edinburgh Theol Coll. (Dip. in Pastoral Studies 1978); Univ. of Edinburgh 1982; DLitt 2001); Univ. of Birmingham (MSocSc 1991). Ordained deacon, 1978, priest, 1980; Asst Curate, All Saints' Ch, Gosforth, 1978–79; Chaplain, Edinburgh Theol Coll., 1982–83; Lectr, Dept of Theol., Univ. of Birmingham, 1983–88; Chief Officer, Central Birmingham CHC, 1988–90; Lectr, then Sen. Lectr, Sch. of Health and Social Welfare, Open Univ., 1990–98; Dist. Res. Fellow, 1998–2000, Prof. and Head, 2000–07, Sch. of Religious and Theol Studies, Cardiff Univ. Vis. Sen. Res. Fellow, Jesus Coll., Oxford, 2004–05; Hon. Prof., Sch. of Medicine and Health, Durham Univ., 2011–17. Gifford Lectr, Aberdeen Univ., 2007. Hon. FRCGP 2013. *Publications:* A Critique of Pastoral Care, 1987, 3rd edn 2000; Alive and Kicking: towards a practical theology of healing and illness, 1988; Pastoral Care and Liberation Theology, 1994; The Faith of the Managers, 1997; Shame: theory, therapy, theology, 2000; (ed jtly) The Blackwell Reader in Pastoral and Practical Theology, 2000; (ed jtly) Values in Professional Practice, 2004; The Challenge of Practical Theology, 2007; Seeing Things: deepening relations with visual artefacts, 2007; (ed jtly) Emerging Values in Health Care, 2010; Saving Face, 2013; (jtly) Values in Health and Social Care, 2017; (jtly) Invitation to Research in Practical Theology, 2018. *Recreation:* growing things. *Address:* 11A Salisbury Road, Moseley, Birmingham B13 8JS. *T:* 07951 145989. *E:* sbpattison@hotmail.com.

**PATTISON, Stephen Dexter,** CMG 2003; DPhil; HM Diplomatic Service, retired; Vice President, Public Affairs, ARM Ltd, since 2012; *b* 24 Dec. 1953; *s* of George Stanley and May Elizabeth Pattison; *m* 1987, Helen Chaoushis; one *d*. *Educ:* Sir George Monoux Sch.; Queens' Coll., Cambridge (BA 1976); Wadham Coll., Oxford (DPhil 1980). Joined FCO, 1981: Second Sec., Nicosia, 1983–86; FCO, 1986–89; First Sec., Washington, 1989–94; Dep. Hd, Non-Proliferation Dept, FCO, 1994–96; Dir of Trade Promotion and Consul-Gen., Warsaw, 1997–2000; Hd, UN Dept, FCO, 2000–03; Fellow, Harvard Univ., 2003–04; Dir, Internat. Security, FCO, 2004–07; Head, Internat. Business Develt, Dyson,

2008–11; CEO, Internat. Chamber of Commerce (UK), 2011–12. Chairman: Micro:bit Educnl Foundn, 2018–; IoT Security Foundn, 2019–. Trustee Bd Mem., BCS, 2017–. *Recreations:* the arts, cricket. *Address:* c/o ARM Ltd, 110 Fulbourn Road, Cambridge CB1 9NJ.

**PATTRICK, Prof. Richard Annandale Douglas,** PhD; Professor of Earth Science, University of Manchester, 2001–17, now Emeritus; *b* 31 March 1953; *s* of Dr Francis Gilson Pattrick and Hope Annandale Pattrick; *m* 1979, Sheila Margaret Murdoch; two *s* one *d*. *Educ:* Univ. of St Andrews (BSc Hons Geol.); Univ. of Strathclyde (PhD Applied Geol. 1980). University of Manchester: Lectr in Geol., 1979–98; Reader in Mineralogy, 1998–2001; Hd, Grad. Sch., 2001–03; Hd, Sch. of Earth, Atmospheric and Envmtl Sci., 2003–07; Associate Dean, Grad. Educn, 2007–08. Chm., Diamond Light Source Sci. Adv. Cttee, 2015–17 (Mem., 2011–13; Vice Chm., 2013–15); Mem., Sci. Adv. Cttee, Max IV Lab. (Sweden), 2017–19. Vice Pres., 1988–92, Pres., 2010–11, Mineralogical Soc. of GB and Ireland. *Publications:* (with D. A. Polya) Mineralisation in the British Isles, 1993; (ed with D. J. Vaughan) Mineral Surfaces, 1995; 160 contribs on metallogenesis, applied mineralogy and envmtl geosci. in peer reviewed jls. *Recreations:* sport: tennis (county level, student international), hockey (student international), supporter of Macclesfield Town FC, live internet and radio commentator, golf. *Address:* University of Manchester, Manchester M13 9PL. *E:* richard.pattrick@manchester.ac.uk. *Clubs:* Macclesfield Town Football; Buxton High Peak Golf.

**PATTULLO, Sir (David) Bruce,** Kt 1995; CBE 1989; Governor, Bank of Scotland, 1991–98 (Group Chief Executive, 1988–96); *b* 2 Jan. 1938; *s* of late Colin Arthur Pattullo and Elizabeth Mary Bruce; *m* 1962, Fiona Jane Nicholson; three *s* one *d*. *Educ:* Rugby Sch.; Hertford Coll., Oxford (BA). FCIBS. Commnd Royal Scots and seconded to Queen's Own Nigeria Regt. Gen. Man., Bank of Scotland Finance Co. Ltd, 1973–77; Chief Exec., British Linen Bank Ltd, 1977–78 (Dir, 1977–98); Bank of Scotland: Dep. Treas., 1978; Treas. and Gen. Manager (Chief Exec.), 1979–88; Dir, 1980–98; Dep. Governor, 1988–91. Director: Melville Street Investments, 1973–90; Bank of Wales, 1986–98; NWS Bank plc, 1986–98; Standard Life Assurance Co., 1985–96. Chm., Cttee, Scottish Clearing Bankers, 1981–83, 1987–89; Pres., Inst. of Bankers in Scotland, 1990–92 (a Vice-Pres., 1977–90). First Prizeman (Bilsland Prize), Inst. of Bankers in Scotland, 1964. FRSE 1990. Hon. LLD Aberdeen, 1995; DUniv Stirling, 1996; Hon. DBA Strathclyde, 1998. *Recreations:* tennis, hill walking. *Address:* 6 Cammo Road, Edinburgh EH4 8EB. *Club:* New (Edinburgh).

**PAUFFLEY, Hon. Dame Anna (Evelyn Hamilton),** DBE 2003; a Judge of the High Court of Justice, Family Division, 2003–17; *b* 13 Jan. 1956; *d* of late Donald Eric Hamilton Pauffley and Josephine Sybil Pauffley; *m* 2001, Frank Harris; one step *s* two step *d*. *Educ:* Godolphin Sch., Salisbury; London Univ. (BA Hons). Called to the Bar, Middle Temple, 1979, Bencher 2003; QC 1995; a Recorder, 1998–2003. Hon. LLD City, 2005. Family Div. Liaison Judge, London and Thames Valley, 2004–17; Sen. Family Liaison Judge, 2013–17.

**PAUK, György;** Order of the Hungarian Republic, 1998; international concert violinist; Professor: Guildhall School of Music and Drama; Royal Academy of Music, since 1987; Professor Emeritus, Franz Liszt Academy of Music, Budapest, since 2006; *b* 26 Oct. 1936; *s* of Imre and Magda Pauk; *m* 1959, Susanne Mautner; one *s* one *d*. *Educ:* Franz Liszt Acad. of Music, Budapest. Toured E Europe while still a student; won three internat. violin competitions, Genoa 1956, Munich 1957, Paris 1959; soon after leaving Hungary, settled in London, 1961, and became a British citizen. London début, 1961; seasonal appearances there and in the provinces, with orchestra, in recital and chamber music; also plays at Bath, Cheltenham and Edinburgh Fests and London Promenade Concerts; performs in major European music venues; US début, under Sir George Solti, with Chicago Symph. Orch., 1970, followed by further visits to USA and Canada to appear with major orchs; holds master classes in many US univs, major music schs in Japan and Internat. Mozart Acad., Prague; Vis. Prof., Winterthur Conservatorium, Switzerland, 1996; plays regularly in Hungary following return in 1973; overseas tours to Australia, NZ, S America, S Africa, Middle and Far East; many performances for BBC, incl. Berg and Bartók concertos, with Boulez. As conductor/soloist, has worked with the English, Scottish and Franz Liszt chamber orchs and London Mozart Players; guest dir, Acad. of St Martin-in-the-Fields; with Peter Frankl and Ralph Kirshbaum, formed chamber music trio, 1973; performances at major fests; public concerts in GB have incl. complete Brahms and Beethoven Cycles; the trio has also made many broadcasts for the BBC. First performances: Penderecki's Violin Concerto, Japan, 1979, UK, 1980; Tippett's Triple Concerto, London, 1980; Lutosawski's Chain 2, with composer conducting, Britain, The Netherlands and Hungary, 1986–87; Sir Peter Maxwell Davies' Violin Concerto, Switzerland, 1988; William Mathias' Violin Concerto, Manchester, 1991. Has made many recordings including: Bartok Sonatas (among top records in US, 1982), and Bartók's music for solo violin, with piano, for two violins and violin concertos; Tippett Concerto (Best Gramophone Record Award, 1983); Berg Concerto (Caecilia Prize, Belgium, 1983); complete sonatas for violin and harpsichord by Handel; all violin concertos and orch. works by Mozart; Brahms Sonatas. Has given master classes in USA (Juilliard Sch., Cleveland Inst. of Music, USC, Oberlin Coll., Manhattan Sch. of Music), in Japan (Tokyo Univ. of the Arts, Geidai, Tokyo Sch. of Music), in China (Beijing and Shanghai Univs) and in Europe. Hon. GSM 1980. Hon. RAM 1990. Hon DMus Royal Acad. of Music, Univ. of London, 2016. Bartók Pásztory Prize, Hungary, 2008. *Publications:* Négy Húron Pendülök: nyolcvan év emlékei (autobiog.), 2016.

**PAUL,** family name of **Baron Paul**.

**PAUL,** Baron *cr* 1996 (Life Peer), of Marylebone in the City of Westminster; **Swraj Paul;** PC 2009; Padma Bhushan; Chairman: Caparo Group Ltd, since 1978; Caparo Bull Moose Inc., since 1988; *b* 18 Feb. 1931; *s* of Payare and Mongwati Paul; *m* 1956, Aruna Vij; two *s* one *d* (and one *s* one *d* decd). *Educ:* Punjab Univ. (BSc); Mass Inst. of Technol. (BSc, MSc (Mech. Engrg)). Began work as Partner in family-owned Apeejay Surrendra Gp, India, 1953; came to UK in 1966 and estabd first business, Natural Gas Tubes Ltd; Caparo Group Ltd formed in 1978 as holding co. for UK businesses involved in engrg, hotel and property develt, investment; Caparo Industries Plc (engrg, metals) formed in 1981. Founder Chm., Indo-British Assoc., 1975–2000. Chancellor: Univ. of Wolverhampton, 1999–; Univ. of Westminster, 2006–14; Pro-Chancellor, 1997–2000, Chancellor, 2000–01, Thames Valley Univ. Dep. Speaker, H of L, 2008–10. FRSA. Padma Bhushan (equivalent to British Peerage), 1983. Hon. PhD Amer. Coll. of Switzerland, Leysin, 1986; Hon. DSc: (Econ) Hull, 1992; Buckingham, 1999; DUniv: Bradford, 1997; Central England, 1999; Hon. DLitt Westminster, 1997. Corporate Leadership Award, MIT, 1987. Freeman, City of London, 1998. *Publications:* Indira Gandhi, 1984, 2nd edn 1985; Beyond Boundaries (autobiog.), 1998. *Address:* Caparo House, 103 Baker Street, W1U 6LN. *T:* (020) 7486 1417. *Clubs:* MCC; Royal Calcutta Turf, Royal Calcutta Golf (Calcutta); Cricket of India (Bombay).

**PAUL, Alan Roderick,** CMG 1997; Founder and Managing Director, Alan Paul Partners Ltd (formerly Sirius Search Ltd), Hong Kong, since 2010; Chairman, Glasford International, since 2014; *b* 13 May 1950; *s* of late Roderick Ernest Paul and Hilda May Paul (*née* Choules); *m* 1979, Rosana Yuen-Ling Tam; one *s* one *d*. *Educ:* Wallington High Sch. for Boys; Christ Church, Oxford (Scholar; MA Modern Langs, 1st class Hons). HM Diplomatic Service, 1972–2001: FCO, 1972–73; language training, Univs of Cambridge and Hong Kong, 1973–75; FCO, 1975–77; Peking, 1977–80; FCO, 1980–84; Head of Chancery, The Hague, 1984–87; Asst Head, 1987–89, Head, 1989–91, Hong Kong Dept, FCO; Counsellor and Dep. Sen. Rep., 1991–97, Sen. Rep. (with personal rank of Ambassador), 1997–2000, Sino-British Jt Liaison Gp, Hong Kong; FCO, 2000–01. Dir, 2001–04, Partner, 2004–10, Executive Access Ltd, Hong Kong. *Recreations:* reading, music, chess, gym. *Address:* Alan Paul Partners, Level 16, Hong Kong Club Building, 3A Chater Road, Central, Hong Kong.

**PAUL, Prof. Douglas John,** PhD; Professor of Semiconductor Devices, Department of Electronics and Electrical Engineering, University of Glasgow, since 2007 (Director, James Watt Nanofabrication Centre, 2010–15); *b* Greenock, 25 Feb. 1969; *s* of John Stuart Paul and Margaret Paul; *m* 2011, Amy Jane Lloyd. *Educ:* Greenock Acad.; Churchill Coll., Cambridge (BA Phys and Theoretical Phys 1990; PhD 1994). CPhys 1999; FInstP 2007; CEng 2015. Cavendish Laboratory, University of Cambridge: Res. Associate, 1994–98; EPSRC Advanced Res. Fellow, 1998–2003; Sen. Res. Associate, 2003–07; Res. Fellow, 1994–98, Fellow, 1998–2007, St Edmund's Coll., Cambridge. EPSRC Quantum Technol. Fellow, 2015–June 2020. Member: Chem., Biol Physics Panel, NATO Sci. Cttee, 2004–08; Chem., Biol, Radiol and Nuclear Scientific Adv. Cttee, Home Office, 2004–; DSAC, 2010–13; High Impact Threats Expert Adv. Gp, 2013, Scientific Adv. Gp for Emergencies, 2014, Cabinet Office; DSEC, 2018–. Mem., Sci. Bd, Inst. of Phys, 2004–10. Mem., Enhancing Value: getting the most out of UK res. Task Force, Nat. Centre for Univs and Business (formerly Council for Industry and Higher Educn), 2011–. SMIEEE 2003; FHEA 2009; FRSE 2011. President's Medal, Inst. of Phys, 2014. *Publications:* (ed with L. W. Molenkamp) Technology Roadmap for European Nanoelectronics, 1999, 2nd edn 2000; (with E. Kasper) Silicon Quantum Information Circuits, 2005; articles in Nature, Nano Letters, Applied Phys Letters, Phys. Rev. and IEEE jls. *Recreations:* wine tasting, cooking, cycling, singing, piano. *Address:* Rankine Building, School of Engineering, University of Glasgow, Oakfield Avenue, Glasgow G12 8LT. *T:* (0141) 330 5219. *E:* Douglas.Paul@glasgow.ac.uk.

**PAUL, Geoffrey David,** OBE 1991; freelance editorial consultant; *b* 26 March 1929; *s* of Reuben Goldstein and Anne Goldstein; *m* 1st, 1952, Joy Stirling (marr. diss. 1972); one *d*; 2nd, 1974, Rachel Mann; one *s*. *Educ:* Liverpool, Kendal, Dublin. Weekly newspaper and news agency reporter, 1947–57; asst editor, Jewish Observer and Middle East Review, 1957–62; Jewish Chronicle, 1962–96: successively sub-editor, foreign editor, Israel corresp., deputy editor; Editor, 1977–90; US Affairs Editor, 1991–96; Consultant, Sternberg Foundn, 1996–2012. Dir, Anglo-Israel Assoc., 2001–03. FRSA 1993. *Publications:* Living in Jerusalem, 1981. *Address:* 1 Carlton Close, West Heath Road, NW3 7UA.

**PAUL, George William;** DL; Chairman, Suffolk Horse Society, 2012–15 and since 2017 (Company Secretary, 2015–17); *b* 25 Feb. 1940; *s* of William Stuart Hamilton Paul and Diana Violet Anne Martin; *m* 1st, 1963, Mary Annette Mitchell (*d* 1989); two *s* one *d*; 2nd, Margaret J. Kilgour (*née* Hedges). *Educ:* Harrow; Wye Coll., Univ. of London (BSc Agric. Hons). Pauls & Whites Foods: Marketing Dir, 1968; Managing Dir, 1972; Pauls & Whites: Dir, 1972; Group Managing Dir, 1982; Chm., Pauls, 1985; Harrisons & Crosfield: Dir, 1985; Jt Chief Exec., 1986; Chief Exec., 1987–94; Chm., 1994–97; Norwich Union: Dir, 1990–2000; Vice-Chm., 1992–94; Chm., 1994–2000; Dep. Chm., CGNU, then Aviva, 2000–05. Chairman: Agricolas Holdings Ltd, 1998–2000; Agricola Gp Ltd, 2000–12; J. P. Morgan Fleming Overseas Investment Trust, 2001–10; Notcutts Ltd, 2006–10 (Dir, 1998–2010). Mem., Jockey Club; Chm., Jockey Club Estates Ltd, 1991–2005. Chm. Trustees, Nat. Horseracing Mus., 2008–12. Pres., Suffolk Agricultural Assoc., 1984, 2010. Chm., Essex and Suffolk Foxhounds, 1974–77, 1993–2013 (Jt Master and Huntsman, 1977–85). High Sheriff, 1990, DL, 1991, Suffolk. *Recreations:* theatre, the arts, country sports, sailing. *Clubs:* Boodle's, Farmers.

**PAUL, Air Marshal Sir Ronald Ian S.;** *see* Stuart-Paul.

**PAUL, Wesley Irwin;** Founding Partner, Tellus Matrix Group, since 2016; *b* Georgetown, Guyana, 1957. JP Morgan & Co., 1975–2000: a Man. Dir; Global Hd of Fixed Income, Foreign Exchange, Emerging Mkts, Econ. Res.; Global Hd of Investments; Mem., Global Mgt Cttee, London and NY; former Chief Exec., Edgeworth Capital, Lehman Brothers JV Hedge Fund. Chm., Firsthaven Partners LLP, 2010–15. Chm., Bd of Trustees, Royal Armouries, 2012–15. Non-exec. Dir, Harbour Capital LLP, Hong Kong, 2010–. Member: Adv. Bd, Durham Univ. Global Security Inst., 2012–; Adv. Council, RUSI, 2013–. *Recreations:* human development, international security and geopolitics, arms and armour, history, museums, fishing, shooting, theatre, books, arts. *E:* wesleyipaul@gmail.com.

**PAUL-CHOUDHURY, Sumit;** Strategy Director and Editor Emeritus, New Scientist, since 2017 (Editor-in-Chief, 2016–17); *b* London; *s* of Sukhendu Paul-Choudhury and Mandira Paul-Choudhury; *m* 1st, 2001, Kathryn Oates (*d* 2005); 2nd, 2009, Lucia Graves. *Educ:* Imperial Coll. London (BSc Hons Physics 1992); Queen Mary and Westfield Coll., Univ. of London (MSc Maths 1994). ARCS 1992. Technical Editor, Risk Magazine, 1994–99; Vice Pres., ERisk, 2000–02; Man. Dir, Risk Communications, 2003–05; Online Editor, New Scientist, 2008–11; Editor-in-Chief, Arc, 2012–15; Ed., New Scientist, 2011–16; Creative Dir, New Scientist Live, London, 2016. *Recreations:* electronic music, theatrical production, writing fiction, London, archaeology, travel, dancing. *Address:* c/o New Scientist, 25 Bedford Street, WC2E 9ES. *T:* (020) 7611 1202.

**PAULET,** family name of **Marquess of Winchester**.

**PAULIN, Oswyn George,** CB 2013; Head, Government Legal Service for Northern Ireland, and Departmental Solicitor, 2007–15; *b* Leeds, 16 July 1951; *s* of Douglas Paulin and Mary Paulin (*née* Robertson); *m* 1987, Romaine Gail Hamilton; four *s* one *d*. *Educ:* Rosetta Primary Sch., Belfast; Annadale Grammar Sch., Belfast; Queen's Univ., Belfast (LLB). Articled clerk, Elliott Duffy Garrett, 1973–76; admitted as solicitor, 1976; Professional Asst, Crown Solicitor's Office, 1976–85; Sen. Legal Asst, NI Office, 1985–89; Crown Solicitor's Office: Sen. Legal Asst, 1989–92; Asst Crown Solicitor, 1992–2002; Crown Solicitor, 2002–07. Mem. Bd, Praxis Care, 2016–. Pres., Belfast Literary Soc., 2010–11. Mem., Gen. Synod, C of I, 2012–. Gov., Wellington Coll. Belfast.
*See also* T. N. Paulin.

**PAULIN, Prof. Roger Cole,** Dr phil, LittD; Schröder Professor of German, University of Cambridge, 1989–2005, now Emeritus; Fellow, Trinity College, Cambridge since 1989; *b* 18 Dec. 1937; *s* of Thomas Gerald Paulin and Paulina (*née* Duff); *m* 1966, Traute Fielitz; one *s* one *d*. *Educ:* Otago Boys' High Sch., Dunedin, NZ; Univ. of Otago (MA); Heidelberg Univ. (Dr phil); MA, LittD (Cantab). Asst Lectr, Univ. of Birmingham, 1963–64; Lectr, Univ. of Bristol, 1965–73; Fellow and Coll. Lectr in German, Trinity Coll., Cambridge, 1974–87; Univ. Lectr, Univ. of Cambridge, 1975–87; Henry Simon Prof. of German, Univ. of Manchester, 1987–89. Mem., Editl Bd, Literatur-Lexikon, 1988–93. Bundesverdienstkreuz, 2011. *Publications:* Ludwig Tieck: a literary biography, 1985, 2nd

**PAULIN, Thomas Neilson**; poet and critic; G. M. Young Lecturer in English, University of Oxford, 1994–2010; Fellow, Hertford College, Oxford, 1994–2010, now Emeritus; b 25 Jan. 1949; s of Douglas and Mary Paulin (née Robinson); m 1973, Munjiet Kaur Khosa; two s. Educ: Hull Univ. (BA); Lincoln Coll., Oxford (BLitt). English Department, University of Nottingham: Lectr, 1972–89; Reader in Poetry, 1989–94; Prof. of Poetry, 1994. NESTA Fellow, 2000–03. Hon. DLitt: Saskatchewan, 1987; Stafford, 1995; Hull, 2000. Publications: Thomas Hardy: the poetry of perception, 1975; A State of Justice, 1977 (Eric Gregory Award, 1976, Somerset Maugham Award, 1978); The Strange Museum, 1980 (Geoffrey Faber Meml Award, 1982); Liberty Tree, 1983; The Riot Act, 1985; Ireland and the English Crisis, 1985; (ed) The Faber Book of Political Verse, 1986; The Hillsborough Script, 1987; Fivemiletown, 1987; Seize the Fire, 1989; (ed) The Faber Book of Vernacular Verse, 1990; Minotaur: poetry and the nation state, 1992; Walking a Line, 1994; Writing to the Moment: selected critical essays, 1996; The Day-Star of Liberty: William Hazlitt's radical style, 1998; The Wind Dog, 1999; The Invasion Handbook, 2002; The Road to Inver, 2004; Crusoe's Secret: the aesthetics of dissent (essays), 2005; The Secret Life of Poems, 2008; Euripides' Medea, 2010; Love's Bonfire, 2012. Address: c/o Faber & Faber, Bloomsbury House, 74–77 Great Russell Street, WC1B 3DA.

**PAULSON, Prof. Lawrence Charles**, PhD; FRS 2017; Professor of Computational Logic, University of Cambridge, since 2002; Fellow, Clare College, Cambridge, since 1987; b Philadelphia, 20 Sept. 1955; s of late Michael Steele Paulson and Mae Paulson; m 1st, 1985, Susan Mary Hills (d 2010); one s one d; 2nd, 2012, Elena Tchougounova. Educ: Calif Inst. of Technol. (BS Maths 1977); Stanford Univ. (PhD Computer Sci. 1981). Res. Asst, Univ. of Edinburgh, 1982–83; University of Cambridge: Asst Dir of Res., 1983–93; Lectr, 1993–98; Reader in Computational Logic, 1998–2002. Dist. Affiliated Prof., Dept of Informatics, Tech. Univ. of Munich, 2006–. FACM 2008. Publications: Logic and Computation: interactive proof with Cambridge LCF, 1987; ML for the Working Programmer, 1991, 2nd edn 1996; Isabelle: a generic theorem prover, 1994; (jtly) Isabelle/HOL: a proof assistant for higher-order logic, 2002; contribs to refereed jls and conf. papers. Recreations: ballroom dancing, theatre, et cetera. Address: Computer Laboratory, William Gates Building, University of Cambridge, 15 JJ Thomson Avenue, Cambridge CB3 0FD. T: (01223) 334623. E: lp15@cam.ac.uk.

**PAUNCEFORT-DUNCOMBE, Sir David (Philip Henry)**, 5th Bt cr 1859, of Great Brickhill, Bucks; b Aldershot, Hants, 21 May 1956; s of Sir Philip Digby Pauncefort-Duncombe, 4th Bt and of Rachel Moyra Pauncefort-Duncombe (née Aylmer); S father, 2011; m 1987, Sarah Ann Battrum; one s one d. Educ: Gordonstoun; RAC Cirencester. Estate manager. Recreation: fly fishing. Heir: s Henry Digby Pauncefort-Duncombe, b 16 Dec. 1988. Address: Great Brickhill Manor, Milton Keynes, Bucks MK17 9BE.

**PAVEY, Joanne Marie**, MBE 2015; professional athlete (distance runner), since 1997; b Honiton, Devon, 20 Sept. 1973; d of Robert and Linda Davis; m 1995, Gavin Pavey; one s one d. Educ: Feniton Primary Sch.; King's Sch., Ottery St Mary, Devon; Exeter Coll.; Avon and Gloucester Coll. of Health (BSc Hons Physiotherapy). MCSP. World Cup, Bronze, 2002, Commonwealth Games, Silver, 2006, 5,000m; World Championship, Bronze, 2007, Eur. Championship, Silver, 2012, 10,000m; Continental/World Cup, Bronze, 2014, Commonwealth Games, Bronze, 2014, 5,000m; Eur. Champion, 10,000m, 2014. Competed in Olympic Games: Sydney, 2000; Athens, 2004; Beijing, 2008; London, 2012; Rio de Janeiro, 2016. Publications: This Mum Runs, 2016. Recreation: running. Address: c/o MTC (UK) Ltd, 71 Gloucester Place, W1U 8JW. T: (020) 7935 8000, Fax: (020) 7935 8066. E: office@mtc-uk.com, info@jopavey.com. Club: Exeter Harriers Athletics.

**PAVEY, Martin Christopher**; Headmaster, Cranbrook School, 1981–88; b 2 Dec. 1940; s of Archibald Lindsay Pavey and Margaret Alice Pavey (née Salsbury); m 1969, Louise Margaret (née Bird); two s. Educ: Magdalen College Sch., Oxford; University Coll., London (Hons English); Nottingham Univ. (MA English); Univ. of Cambridge (Dip. Educn). Wigglesworth & Co., London and E. Africa (Shipping and Finance), 1956–62; Assistant Master: King's Sch., Ely, 1962–64; Lancing Coll., 1968–71; Fairham Comprehensive School, Nottingham: Head of English, 1971–75; Dep. Headmaster, 1975–76; Headmaster, 1976–81; Headmaster, Latymer Upper School, Hammersmith, 1988–91. Chm., AgeCare, RSAS, 2002–08. Recreations: art, architecture, cinema. Address: 5 Vineyards, Bath BA1 5NA.

**PAVLOPOULOS, Prof. Prokopis**, PhD; President of the Hellenic Republic, since 2015; b Kalamata, 10 July 1950; s of Vasilis and Maria Pavlopoulou; m Viassia Peltsemi; one s two d. Educ: 4th Elementary Sch., Kalamata; Paralia High Sch., Kalamata; Law Sch., Univ. of Athens (degree with dist. 1973); Univ. of Paris II (Master of Advanced Studies in Public Law 1974; PhD 1977). University of Athens Law School: Asst Prof., 1983–85; Associate Prof., 1985–89; Prof. of Public Law, 1989, now Prof. Emeritus. Vis. Prof., Univ. of Paris II, 1986. Sec. to first (interim) Pres. of Greece, 1974–75; Dep. Minister of Presidency responsible for Media, and Govt Spokesman, Nat. Unity Govt, 1989–90; Dir, Presidency Legal Office, 1990–95; Spokesman, New Democracy pol party, 1995–96; State MP (New Democracy), 1996–2000; Hd, Public Admin, Public Order and Justice Dept, 1996–2000; MP (New Democracy) Athens, 2000–14; Parly Spokesman for New Democracy Party, 2000–04; Minister: of Interior, Public Admin and Decentralization, 2004–07; of Interior, 2007–09. Member: Standing Cttees on Public Admin, Public Order and Justice; special Standing Cttee on Instns and Transparency; Cttee for Revision of Constitution. Officier, Légion d'Honneur (France), 2010; Grand Cross, Order of Redeemer, 2015, Grand Collar, Order of Makarios III, 2015 (Hellenic Republic). Publications: La directive en droit administrative, 1978; (with Dr G. Timagenis) The Law and Practice Relating to Pollution Control in Greece, 1982; The Constitutional Guarantee of the Writ of Annulment: a contemporary viewpoint of the rule of law, 1982; Courses in Administrative Science, 1983; The Civil Liability of the State, vol. I, 1986, vol. II, 1989; Guarantees of the Right to Judicial Protection in European Community Law, 1993; The Public Works Contract, 1997; Articles, 1987–2003, 2003; Constitutional Reform, Looked at from the Parliamentary Experience, 2010; The Twilight of Political Leaderships: cause or effect of the economic crisis?, 2011; Public Law at the Time of Economic Crisis, vol. I, 2nd edn 2014; (jtly) Public Law, 3rd edn 2015. Address: Presidential Mansion, Vassileos Georgiou B' 2 Avenue, 10028 Athens, Greece. T: 2107283211, 2107283251, Fax: 2108821165. E: secretariat@presidency.gr.

**PAVORD, Anna, (Mrs T. D. O. Ware)**; Gardening Correspondent, The Independent, 1986–2016; b 20 Sept. 1940; d of Arthur Vincent Pavord and Christabel Frances (née Lewis); m 1966, Trevor David Oliver Ware; three d. Educ: Univ. of Leicester (BA Hons English). PA/Dir, Line Up, BBC2, 1963–70; contributor, Observer Mag., 1970–92; writer and presenter, Flowering Passions, Channel 4 TV, 1991–92. Associate Editor, Gardens Illustrated, 1993–2008. Member: NT Gardens Panel, 1996–2006 (Chm., 2002–06); English Heritage Parks and Gardens Panel, 2001–10. Hon. DLitt Leicester, 2005. Veitch Meml Gold Medal, 2001. Publications: Foliage, 1990; The Flowering Year, 1991; Gardening Companion, 1992; Hidcote, 1993; The Border Book, 1994; The New Kitchen Garden, 1996; The Tulip, 1999; Plant Partners, 2001; The Naming of Names, 2005; Bulb, 2009; The Curious Gardener, 2010; Landskipping, 2016. Recreations: sailing, walking, gardening, visiting Sikkim. Address: c/o Caradoc King, United Agents, 12–26 Lexington Street, W1F 0LE. T: (020) 3214 0971.

**PAVORD, Prof. Ian Douglas**, DM; FRCP; FMedSci; Professor of Respiratory Medicine, University of Oxford, since 2013; Hon. Consultant Physician, Oxford University Hospitals NHS Trust, since 2013; NIHR Senior Investigator, 2011–19, now Emeritus; b Abergavenny, 3 July 1961; s of Antony and Jenny Pavord; m 1989, Sue Harris; two s one d (incl. twin s and d). Educ: King Henry VIII Comprehensive Sch.; University Coll. London and Westminster Hosp. (MB BS 1984); Univ. of Nottingham (DM 1992); Univ. of Oxford (MA 2013). MRCP 1987, FRCP 2000. House Officer, Westminster and Rochford Hosps, 1984–85; SHO in Medicine, Taunton and Somerset Hosps, 1985–87; Registrar in Gen. Medicine, Peterborough and Leicester Hosps, 1987–90; Res. Fellow in Respiratory Medicine, 1990–92, Lectr in Respiratory Medicine, 1992–95, Nottingham City Hosp.; Consultant Physician, Glenfield Hosp., Leicester, 1995–2013. Vis. Fellow, St Joseph's Hosp.-McMaster Univ., Canada, 1995; Hon. Prof., Inst. for Lung Health, 2005–13. Med. Dir, Asthma UK, 2008–14. British Thoracic Society: Co-Chm., cough guidelines gp, 2004–06; Chm., BTS/SIGN asthma diagnosis and monitoring guidelines gp, 2007–14; Mem., scientific meetings cttee, 2004–07. Mem., MRC Coll. of Experts. FERS 2014; FMedSci 2015. Associate Ed., Amer. Jl Respiratory and Critical Care Medicine, 2005–10; Jt Ed., Thorax, 2010–15. Publications: contributor: Current Diagnosis and Therapy, 1995; Handbook of Respiratory Medicine, 2001; Clinical Respiratory Medicine, 2004; Allergy and Allergic Diseases, 2nd edn, 2008; Handbook of Experimental Pharmacology, 2009; contribs to scientific jls incl. Lancet, BMJ, Thorax, Chest, Cough, Internat. Jl Cardiol., Eur. Respiratory Jl, Jl RCP, Clin. Exptl Allergy, New England Jl of Medicine. Recreation: golf. Address: Nuffield Department of Medicine Research Building, University of Oxford, Roosevelt Drive, Oxford OX3 7FZ.

**PAWLAK, His Honour Witold Expedyt**; a Circuit Judge, 2004–17; a Deputy Circuit Judge, since 2017; b 1947; s of Felicjan and Jolanta Pawlak; m 1971, Susan Dimsdale; one s one d. Educ: Trinity Coll., Cambridge (BA 1969; MA). Called to the Bar, Inner Temple, 1970; in practice, 1970–2004; a Recorder, 1995–2004. Address: Wood Green Crown Court, Woodhall House, Lordship Lane, Wood Green, N22 5LF.

**PAWLE, Oliver John Woodforde**; Chairman: FTI Consulting (formerly Financial Dynamics), since 2005; Board Services, Korn/Ferry Whitehead Mann, since 2009; Founder and Chairman of Trustees, New Entrepreneurs Foundation, since 2011; b Ndola, Northern Rhodesia, 24 June 1950; s of Roger and Nan Pawle; m 1983, Emma Mary Frances Birtwistle; one s two d. Educ: Downside Sch.; Nottingham Univ. (BA Industrial Econs). Accountant, Price Waterhouse, 1971–76; Baring Brothers, 1976–84, Dir, 1980–84; Dir, County NatWest, 1984–97; Vice Chm., UBS Investment Bank, 1997–2007. Dir, Adv. Bd, Delancey plc, 2007–. Director: Reform, 2007–; Develt Bd, CAFOD, 2010–; Adv. Bd, Nat. Theatre, 2005–; Gov., Goodenough Trust, 1998–2015. Recreations: theatre, politics, opera, golf, cricket, horse-racing. Address: 33 Blenkarne Road, SW11 6HZ. T: 07836 337179. E: oliver.pawle@kornferry.com. Clubs: Boodle's, Hurlingham, MCC; Berkshire; St Enodoc Golf.

**PAWLEY, Prof. (Godfrey) Stuart**, PhD; FRS 1992; FRSE; Professor of Computational Physics, University of Edinburgh, 1985–2002, now Emeritus; b 22 June 1937; s of George Charles Pawley and Winifred Mary (née Wardle); m 1961, Anthea Jean Miller; two s one d. Educ: Bolton Sch.; Corpus Christi Coll., Cambridge (MA, PhD 1962). FRSE 1975. Chem. Dept, Harvard Univ., 1962–64; University of Edinburgh: Lect, 1964–69; Reader, 1970–85. Guest Prof., Chem. Dept, Århus Univ., Denmark, 1969–70. Publications: (contrib.) An Introduction to OCCAM 2 programming, 2nd edn, 1989; (as Godefridus) Killer Sudoku and Other Puzzles, 2017; numerous scientific papers. Recreations: choral singing, mountain walking, rock gardening. Address: 29 Fulford Park, Fulford, York YO10 4QE.

**PAWLEY, (Robert) John**; Director of Professional Services, Valuation Office Agency, 1995–99; b 10 Sept. 1939; s of Frederick Clifford and Marjorie Pawley; m 1965, Simone Elizabeth Tayar; two s. Educ: Plymouth Coll.; Exeter Univ. (BA). Private practice, Plymouth, 1962–71; joined Valuation Office, 1972; Dist Valuer, Waltham Forest, 1977, Haringey, 1978–81; Suptg Valuer, Chief Valuer's Office, London, 1981–84, Cambridge, 1984–87; Asst Chief Valuer, 1987–88; Dep. Chief Valuer, Inland Revenue Valuation Office, later Dep. Chief Exec. (Technical), Valuation Office Agency, 1989–95. Recreations: 18th century English naval history and exploration, period model boats, antiques.

**PAWLEY, Stuart**; see Pawley, G. S.

**PAWSEY, James Francis**; Director: Shilton Consultants LLP, 2006–09; Alavan Consulting Ltd 2003–05; b 21 Aug. 1933; s of William Pawsey and Mary Mumford; m 1956, Cynthia Margaret Francis; six s (including twins twice). Educ: Coventry Tech. School; Coventry Tech. Coll. Chief Exec., Autobar Machine Div., 1970–80; Dir, Autobar Gp, 1980–2006; non-exec. Dir, St Martins Hosps, 1989–2004; Director: Love Lane Investments, 1995–2008; Keyturn Solutions, 1997–2004. MP (C) Rugby, 1979–83, Rugby and Kenilworth, 1983–97; contested (C) Rugby and Kenilworth, 1997. Parliamentary Private Secretary: DES, 1982–83; DHSS, 1983–84; to Minister of State for NI, 1984–86. Member: Parly Scientific Cttee, 1982–97; Select Cttee of Parly Comr for Admin, 1983–97 (Chm., 1993); Select Cttee on Standing Orders, 1987–97; Exec., 1922 Cttee, 1989–97; Liaison Cttee, 1993–97; Ct of Referees, 1993–97; Chm., Cons. Parly Educn Cttee, 1985–97; Mem. Exec., IPU, 1984–97 (Vice-Chm., 1994–96); Chm., W Midlands Gp of Cons. MPs, 1993–97; Pres., Rugby Constituency Cons. Assoc., 2013–16. Member: Rugby RDC, 1965–73; Rugby Borough Council, 1973–75; Warwickshire CC, 1974–79; former Chm. and Pres., Warwickshire Assoc. of Parish Councils. Founder Mem., Snakes and Ladders Dining Club, H of C. KLJ. Publications: The Tringo Phenomenon, 1983. Address: 38 Shilton Lane, Bulkington, Warwickshire CV12 9JP.
See also M. Pawsey.

**PAWSEY, Mark**; MP (C) Rugby, since 2010; b Meriden, 16 Jan. 1957; s of James Francis Pawsey, qv; m 1984, Tracy Harris; two s two d. Educ: Reading Univ. (BSc Estate Mgt 1978). Trainee Surveyor, Strutt & Parker, 1978–79; Account Manager, Autobar Vending Supplied Ltd, 1979–82; Founder and Man. Dir, Central Catering Supplies, 1982–2008. Member: Communities and Local Govt Select Cttee, 2010–15; Business, Energy and Industrial Strategy Cttee, 2017–. Contested (C) Nuneaton, 2005. Recreations: Rugby football, planting woodland, cooking. Address: House of Commons, SW1A 0AA. E: mark.pawsey.mp@parliament.uk.

**PAWSON, Anthony John Dalby**; Head of Defence Export Services, Ministry of Defence, 2007–09; b 14 Oct. 1946; s of Donald Pawson and Kathleen (née Goodwin); m 1969, Kathleen Chisholm (d 2004); one s one d. Educ: Kent Coll., Canterbury; City Univ. (BSc 1st Class Hons Computer Science). MoD 1967; Private Sec. to Chief of Air Staff, 1978–80; First Sec., UK Delegn to NATO, Brussels, 1981–83; Private Sec. to Sec. of State for NI,

1990–92; RCDS 1992; Asst Under-Sec. of State (Fleet Support), MoD, 1993–95; Under-Sec. (Overseas and Defence), Cabinet Office, 1995–97; Ministry of Defence: Dir Gen. Marketing, 1997–98; Dir Gen. Defence Export Services, 1998–2003; Dir Gen. of Corp. Communication, 2003–04; Dep. Chief of Defence Intelligence, 2004–07. *Recreations:* Rugby, cricket. *Clubs:* Civil Service; Tunbridge Wells Rugby Football; Borderers' Cricket.

**PAWSON, John Ward,** CBE 2019; RDI 2005; architectural designer; *b* 6 May 1949; *s* of James Stoddart Pawson and Winifred Mary Pawson (*née* Ward); *m* 1989, Catherine Mary Clare Berning; one *s*; one *s* by Hester van Roijen. *Educ:* Eton; Architectural Assoc. Sch. Dir, W. L. Pawson and Son Ltd, Halifax, 1967–73; Lectr, Nagoya Univ. of Commerce, 1974–77. *Architectural projects* include: van Roijen Apt, London, 1981; Bruce Chatwin Apt, London, 1982; Waddington Galls, London, 1983; Neuendorf House, Mallorca, 1989; Calvin Klein Store, NY, 1995; Cathay Pacific Lounges, Hong Kong, 1998; Pawson House, London, 1999; Monastery of Our Lady of Novy Dvur, Bohemia, 2004; Sackler Crossing, Royal Botanic Gardens, Kew, 2006; 50 Gramercy Park North, NY, 2006; Montemaggio Estate, Tuscany, 2007; Martyrs Pavilion, St Edward's Sch., Oxford, 2009; Schrager Apartment, NY, 2009; Bel Air House, LA, 2009; Casa delle Bottere, Treviso, 2011; Syukou Fujisawa Gall. and Café, Okinawa, 2012; St Tropez Houses, Provence, 2012; Palmgren House, Stockholm, 2013; Picornell House, Mallorca, 2013; Montauk House, Long Island, NY, 2013; Christopher Kane Store, London, 2015; Life House, Llanbister, Wales, 2016; Paros House I and II, Greece, 2016; Okinawa House, Japan, 2016; Design Mus., Kensington, 2016; Feuerle Collection, Berlin, 2016; Life House, 2016; Farini Bakery and Café, Milan, 2017; Jaffa Hotel and Residences, Tel Aviv, 2018; Jil Sander Store, Tokyo, 2018; Wooden Chapel, Unterliezheim, Germany, 2018; Kitzbühel House, Austria, 2018; Home Farm, Oxfordshire, 2018; Valextra Store, Milan, 2019; *set design:* Chroma, Royal Opera House, 2006; L'Anatomie de la Sensation, Opéra Bastille, Paris, 2011; Wayne McGregor tribute, Royal Opera House, 2016; *interiors:* B60 Sloop, Kiel, 2007; Baracuda Ketch, Viareggio, 2008; *interior renovations:* Basilica, Archabbey of Pannonhalma, 2012; St Moritz Ch, Augsburg, 2013; (installation) Perspectives, St Paul's Cathedral, 2011, Basilica di San Giorgio Maggiore, Venice, 2013. *Publications:* Minimum, 1996; Mini-Minimum, 1998; Barn (photography by Fi McGhee), 1999; (ed) Architecture of Truth, by Lucien Hervé, 2000; (with Annie Bell) Living and Eating, 2001; Themes and Projects, 2002; Leçons du Thoronet, 2006; A Visual Inventory, John Pawson, 2012; Spectrum, John Pawson, 2017; *relevant publications:* John Pawson, 1992; Critic, 1995; John Pawson Works, by Deyan Sudjic, 2000, rev. edn 2005; John Pawson Plain Space, by Alison Morris, 2010; John Pawson Katalog, by Winifred Nerdinger, Alison Morris, 2012; John Pawson, Anatomy of Minimum, by Alison Morris, 2019. *Address:* Unit B, 70–78 York Way, N1 9AG. *T:* (020) 7837 2929. *E:* email@johnpawson.com.

**PAWSON, Robert Edward Cruickshank; His Honour Judge Pawson;** a Circuit Judge, since 2017; Resident Judge, Swindon Combined Court, since 2017; *b* London, 5 Nov. 1964; *s* of Michael Pawson and Carolyn Pawson; *m* 1998, Hon. Alicia Crossley; two *s* one *d*. *Educ:* Sch. of Oriental and African Studies, Univ. of London (BA 1987; MA 1988). Called to the Bar, Inner Temple, 1994; a Recorder, 2012–17. Vice Chm., Wilts Magistrates' Assoc., 2018–. *Recreations:* family, fish, walking, watching other people engaging in sport. *Address:* The Law Courts, Islington Street, Swindon, Wilts SN1 2HG. *Clubs:* Woodgrave Cricket; Henley Royal Regatta.

**PAXMAN, Giles;** *see* Paxman, T. G.

**PAXMAN, Jeremy Dickson;** journalist, author and broadcaster; *b* 11 May 1950; *s* of late Arthur Keith Paxman and Joan McKay Dickson. *Educ:* Malvern College; St Catharine's College, Cambridge (Exhibnr; Hon. Fellow, 2000). Reporter: N Ireland, 1974–77; BBC TV Tonight, 1977–79; Panorama, 1979–85; The Bear Next Door; presenter: Breakfast Time, 1986–89; Newsnight, 1989–2014; Did You See?, 1991–93; You Decide—with Paxman, 1995–96; Start The Week, R4, 1998–2002; Churchill: the nation's farewell, 2015; Chairman: University Challenge, 1994–; Times Past, Times Present, R4, 1996; writer and presenter: The Victorians, 2009; Empire, 2012; Britain's Great War (series), 2014; Rivers with Jeremy Paxman (series), 2017. Vice Pres., London Library, 2015–. Contributing Editor, Financial Times, 2014–. Hon. Fellow, St Edmund Hall, Oxford, 2000. Hon. LLD Leeds, 1999; Hon. DLitt: Bradford, 1999; Buckingham, 2016; DUniv Open, 2006; Hon Dr: Northumbria, 2015; Exeter, 2016. Award for Internat. Current Affairs, RTS, 1985; Award for best personal contribution to television, Voice of Viewer and Listener, 1993, 1998, 2006; Richard Dimbleby Award, BAFTA, 1996, 2000; Interview of the Year, RTS, 1997 and 1998; BPG Award, 1998; Variety Club Media Personality of the Year, 1999; Presenter of the Year, RTS, 2001, 2007. *Publications:* (jtly) A Higher Form of Killing: the secret story of gas and germ warfare, 1982; Through the Volcanoes: a Central American journey, 1985; Friends in High Places: who runs Britain?, 1990; Fish, Fishing and the Meaning of Life, 1994; The Compleat Angler, 1996; The English: a portrait of a people, 1998; The Political Animal, 2002; On Royalty, 2006; The Victorians: Britain through the paintings of the age, 2009; Empire: what ruling the world did to the British, 2011; Great Britain's Great War, 2013; A Life in Questions (memoirs), 2016. *Recreations:* food, books, fishing. *Address:* c/o Anita Land Ltd, 10 Wyndham Place, W1H 2PU. *Clubs:* Beefsteak, Garrick, Chelsea Arts; Piscatorial Society.

*See also* T. G. Paxman.

**PAXMAN, (Timothy) Giles,** CMG 2013; LVO 1989; HM Diplomatic Service, retired; government and international relations consultant, since 2014; *b* 15 Nov. 1951; *s* of late Arthur Keith Paxman and Joan McKay Paxman (*née* Dickson); *m* 1980, Segolene Claude Marie Cayol; three *d*. *Educ:* Malvern Coll.; New Coll., Oxford; Ecole Nat. d'Admin, Paris. DoE, 1974–76; Dept of Transport, 1976–78; joined FCO, 1980: 1st Secretary: UK Perm. Rep. to EC, 1980–84; FCO, 1984–88; Head of Chancery, Singapore, 1988–92; on secondment to Cabinet Office, 1992–94; Counsellor (Econ. and Commercial), Rome, 1994–98; Counsellor (Pol Affairs), UK Perm. Repn to EU, Brussels, 1999–2002; Minister and Dep. Hd of Mission, Paris, 2002–05; Ambassador to Mexico, 2005–09; Ambassador to Spain and concurrently (non-resident) to Andorra, 2009–13. *Recreations:* sailing, ski-ing, jazz and blues music, cinema, golf.

*See also* J. D. Paxman.

**PAXTON, (Peter) Robin;** Associate Director, Criticaleye, since 2008; *b* 14 April 1951; *s* of late Richard Gordon Paxton and of Marion Paxton; *m* 1987, Linda Jane French; two *s*. *Educ:* Leighton Park Sch.; Sussex Univ. (BA Hons); LSE (MScEcon); Nuffield Coll., Oxford. Joined London Weekend Television, 1977; Managing Director: LWT Broadcasting Ltd, 1993–94; Carlton Television (India), 1995–97; Walt Disney TV Internat. (Asia-Pacific), 1997–2001; Discovery Networks, EMEA, 2002–07. Chm., YoYo Media Ltd, 2008–11. Ind. non-exec. Dir, Nimbus Communications Ltd, 2007–16. Chairman: Tourette Syndrome Assoc., 2009–; Headlong Theatre Company, 2009–. Trustee Dir, ITV Pension Scheme Ltd, 2012–.

**PAY, Jill Patricia;** Serjeant at Arms, House of Commons, 2008–12; management consultant, since 2013; *b* Anerley, London, 16 Jan. 1946; *d* of late William and Joan Arnold; *m* 1967, John Pay; two *d*. *Educ:* Croydon High Sch. for Girls; Croydon Coll. (Business Studies). Exec. Asst to Creative Dir, Ogilvy & Mather, 1963–72; Business Manager, private med. practice, 1978–87; Croydon TVEI Project, Dept of Employment, 1987–94; House of Commons, 1994–2012: Hd Office Keeper, 1994; Accommodation Rationalisation Manager, 1999–2001; Exec. Officer to Serjeant at Arms, 2001–04; Asst Serjeant at Arms, 2004–08. Chm. Govs, Edenham High Sch., 1987–94. Trustee: Coram Beanstalk (formerly Beanstalk), literacy charity, 2013– (Dep. Chm., 2017–19; Chm., 2019–); Coram Gp 2019–. Chm., Senate, Pink Shoe, 2013–. *Recreations:* performing arts, travel, food (eating and cooking), reading, family and friends. *E:* jillypay@gmail.com.

**PAYE, Jean-Claude;** Chevalier de la Légion d'Honneur; Commandeur de l'Ordre National du Mérite; Chevalier de l'Ordre National du Mérite agricole; Croix de la Valeur militaire; Attorney at Law, Cabinet Gide Loyrette Nouel, Paris, 2001–09; *b* 26 Aug. 1934; *s* of late Lucien Paye and of Suzanne Paye (*née* Guignard); *m* 1963, Laurence Hélène Marianne Jeanneney; two *s* two *d*. *Educ:* Lycée Bugeaud, Algiers; Lycée Carnot, Tunis; Faculté de droit, Tunis; Institut d'Etudes Politiques, Paris; Ecole Nationale d'Administration. Government service, 1961–64; Technical Advr to Sec. of State for Scientific Research, 1965; Advr to Minister of Social Affairs, 1966; Chief Advr to Vice-Pres., EEC, 1967–73; Advr, Embassy, Bonn, 1973; Asst Principal Private Sec. to Minister of Foreign Affairs, 1974–76; Diplomatic Advr to Prime Minister, 1976–79; Head of Economic and Financial Affairs, Ministry of Foreign Affairs, 1979–84; Sec.-Gen., OECD, 1984–96 (Pres., Exec. Cttee in special Session, 1980–84); Mem., Conseil d'Etat, France, 1996–2000. Bd Mem., Renault SA, 1997–2009. Board Member: Transparence International—France, 1996–2016; Fondation Nationale des Sciences Politiques, 1996–2016; Fondation pour l'innovation politique, 2005–16. *Address:* 1 Place A. Deville, 75006 Paris, France.

**PAYKEL, Prof. Eugene Stern,** MD; FRCP, FRCPsych; FMedSci; Professor of Psychiatry, University of Cambridge, 1985–2001, now Emeritus Professor (Head of Department, 1985–2000); Professorial Fellow, Gonville and Caius College, Cambridge, 1985–2001, now Emeritus Fellow; *b* 9 Sept. 1934; *s* of late Joshua Paykel and Eva Paykel; *m* 1969, Margaret, *d* of late John Melrose and Joan Melrose; two *s*. *Educ:* Auckland Grammar Sch.; Univ. of Otago (MB ChB, MD; Stuart Prize, Joseph Pullar Schol., 1956); DPM London. Maudsley Hosp., 1962–65; Asst Prof. of Psychiatry and Co-Dir/Dir, Depression Res. Unit, Yale Univ., 1966–71; Consultant and Sen. Lectr, 1971–75, Reader, 1975–77, Prof. of Psychiatry, 1977–85, St George's Hosp. Med. Sch., Univ. of London. Chief Scientist's Adviser and Mem., Mental Illness Res. Liaison Gp, DHSS, 1984–88; Chm., Jt Cttee on Higher Psychiatric Trng, 1990–95. Previously examiner Univs of Edinburgh, Nottingham, Manchester, London, and RCPsych. Mem., Neurosciences Bd, MRC, 1981–85, 1995–99. Mem., Bethlem Royal and Maudsley Hosp. SHA, 1990–94. Vice Pres., RCPsych, 1994–96 (Chm., Social and Community Psych. Sect., 1984–88); Zonal Rep., World Psychiatric Assoc., 1993–99 (Chm., Pharmaco-psychiatry Sect., 1993–98); Hon. Mem., British Assoc. for Psychopharmacology, 1991 (Pres., 1982–84); President: Marcé Soc., 1992–94; Collegium Internat. Neuropsychopharmacologicum, 2000–02. Trustee, Mental Health Foundn, 1988–95. Founder FMedSci 1998; Hon. FRCPsych 2001 (MRCPsych 1971, FRCPsych 1977). Hon. Mem., Assoc. of Eur. Psychiatrists, 2007. Foundations Fund Prize for Res. in Psychiatry, 1978; BMA Film Competition Bronze Award, 1981; Anna Monika Stiftung 2nd Prize, 1985; Eur. Coll. of Neuropsychopharmacol.-Lilly Award for Clin. Neurosci., 2001. Jt Editor, Jl of Affective Disorders, 1979–93; Editor, Psychological Medicine, 1994–2006; Mem., Editl Bd, Jl of Affective Disorders, etc. *Publications:* The Depressed Woman, 1974; Psychopharmacology of Affective Disorders, 1979; Monoamine Oxidase Inhibitors: the state of the art, 1981; Handbook of Affective Disorders, 1982, 2nd edn 1992; Community Psychiatric Nursing for Neurotic Patients, 1983; papers on depression, psychopharmacology, social psychiatry, life events, evaluation of treatment. *Recreations:* opera, music, theatre. *Address:* Department of Psychiatry, University of Cambridge, Box 189, Level E4, Addenbrooke's Hospital, Hills Road, Cambridge CB2 2QQ.

**PAYNE, Alan Jeffrey,** CMG 1988; HM Diplomatic Service, retired; *b* 11 May 1933; *s* of Sydney Ellis Payne and Lydia Payne; *m* 1959, Letitia Freeman; three *s*. *Educ:* Enfield Grammar Sch.; Queens' Coll., Cambridge (Exhibnr). FIL 1962. RN, 1955–57. EMI, London, later Paris, 1957–62; Secretariat, NATO, Paris, 1962–64; joined Diplomatic Service, 1965; Commonwealth Relations Office (later FCO), 1965–67; British High Commn, Kuala Lumpur, 1967–70; FCO, 1970–72; British Embassy, Budapest, 1972–75; Counsellor, Mexico City, 1975–79; FCO, 1979–82; Consul-General, Lyons, 1982–87; High Comr, Jamaica, and Ambassador (non-resident) to Haiti, 1987–89. Sec. Gen., Internat. Primary Aluminium Inst., 1989–97. *Recreations:* music, theatre, growing trees, restoring old cars. *Club:* Royal Automobile.

**PAYNE, (Andrew John) Sebastian,** MW; Buyer, International Exhibition Co-operative Wine Society, since 2012 (Chief Buyer, 1985–2012); *b* 3 April 1947; *s* of John Laurence Payne and Dorothy Gwendoline Payne (*née* Attenborough); *m* 1973, Frances Elizabeth Harrison; two *d*. *Educ:* Tonbridge Sch. (Schol.); Trinity Coll., Oxford (BA Lit.Hum. and Med. and Mod. Greek 1970; MA 1973). MW 1977. F. & E. May, wine shippers, 1970–73; IEC Wine Soc., 1973–. Mem., Govt Wine Adv. Cttee, 1993–. Chm., Inst. of Masters of Wine, 1995–96. Chevalier, Ordre Nat. du Mérite Agricole (France), 1999. *Address:* International Exhibition Co-operative Wine Society, Gunnelswood Road, Stevenage SG1 2BT. *T:* (01438) 761283. *Club:* Travellers.

*See also* G. J. N. Payne.

**PAYNE, Anthony Edward;** freelance composer and writer; *b* 2 Aug. 1936; *s* of Edward Alexander Payne and Muriel Margaret Elsie Payne (*née* Stroud); *m* 1966, Jane Marian Manning, *qv*. *Educ:* Dulwich Coll.; Durham Univ. (BA Hons Music 1961). Composition Tutor: London Coll. of Music, 1983–85; Sydney Conservatorium, 1986; Univ. of W Australia, 1996; Vis. Milhaud Prof., Mills Coll., Calif, 1983; Vis. Professorial Fellow in composition, UEA, 2012–13. Scripted talks, reviews, interviews and series presentations, BBC, 1963–. Contributor: Daily Telegraph, 1964–; Times, 1964–; Independent, 1986–; Country Life, 1995–. FRCM 2005. Hon. DMus: Birmingham, 2001; Kingston, 2002; Durham, 2007. Elgar Medal, Elgar Soc., 2011. *Compositions:* principal works include: Paraphrases and Cadenzas, 1969; Paean, 1971; Sonatas and Ricercas, 1971; Phoenix Mass, 1972; Concerto for Orchestra, 1974; The World's Winter, 1976; String Quartet, 1978; The Stones and Lonely Places Sing, 1979; Song of the Clouds, 1980; Springs Shining Wake, 1981; A Day in the Life of a Mayfly, 1981; Evening Land, 1981; Songs and Seascapes, 1984; The Spirit's Harvest, 1985; The Song Streams in the Firmament, 1986; Half Heard in the Stillness, 1987; Consort Music, 1988; Sea Change, 1988; The Enchantress Plays, 1990; Time's Arrow, 1990; Symphonies of Wind and Rain, 1991; A Hidden Music, 1992; Orchestral Variations, 1994; Empty Landscape, 1995; completion of Elgar's Third Symphony, 1997; Piano Trio, 1998; Scenes from the Woodlanders, 1999; Of Knots and Skeins, 2000; Visions and Journeys, 2002; Poems of Edward Thomas, 2003; Storm Chorale for Solo Violin, 2004; Horn Trio, 2004; completion of Elgar's Sixth Pomp and Circumstance March, 2005; Windows on Eternity, 2006; Piano Quintet, 2007; Out of the Depths Comes Song, 2008; From a Mouthful of Air, 2008; The Period of Cosmographie, 2009; Second String Quartet, 2010; Undiscover'd Country, 2012; Piano Quartet, 2013; Of Land, Sea and Sky, 2016; Third String Quartet, 2018; *arrangements:* for chamber ensemble of Bruckner's Second Symphony, 2011; for orchestra of Vaughan Williams' Four Last Songs, 2013; for orchestra of Vaughan Williams' Two Nocturnes, 2014. *Publications:*

Schoenberg, 1968; Frank Bridge—Radical and Conservative, 1976, 2nd edn 1984; Elgar's Third Symphony: the story of the reconstruction, 1998; articles in learned jls, incl. Musical Times, Tempo, Listener, etc, 1962–. *Recreations:* cinema, English countryside. *Address:* 2 Wilton Square, N1 3DL. *T:* (020) 7359 1593. *E:* paynecomp@googlemail.com.

**PAYNE, Christine Grace;** General Secretary, Equity, since 2005; *b* 30 Dec. 1956; *d* of Jeffrey and Shirley Brass; *m* 1981, Terry Payne; one *d*. *Educ:* Loughborough Univ. (BSc Hons Psychol.); Middlesex Poly. (Dip. Industrial Relns and Trade Union Studies). Joined Equity, 1979: TV Commercials Orgnr, 1981–91; Asst Sec., recorded perfs, 1991–99; Asst Gen. Sec., live perfs, 1999–2005. Mem., Gen. Council and Exec. Cttee, TUC. *Address:* c/o Equity, Guild House, Upper St Martin's Lane, WC2H 9EG. *T:* (020) 7379 6000. *E:* cpayne@equity.org.uk.

**PAYNE, Dr Christopher Charles,** OBE 1997; researcher and writer, since 2011; *b* 15 May 1946; *s* of Rupert George Payne and Evelyn Violet (née Abbott); *m* 1969, Margaret Susan Street; one *s* one *d*. *Educ:* Wadham Coll., Oxford (MA, DPhil). Post-Doctoral Fellow, Univ. of Otago, NZ, 1972; SSO, NERC, Oxford, 1973–77; PSO, 1977–83, Head, Entomology Dept, 1983–86, Glasshouse Crops Res. Inst., Littlehampton; Head, Crop Protection Div., Inst. of Horticultural Res., E Malling, 1987–90; Chief Exec., Horticulture Research Internat., 1990–99; Prof. of Horticulture and Landscape, Univ. of Reading, 1999–2003; self-employed consultant in biol sci., 2003–11. Vis. Prof. of Plant Scis, Univ. of Reading, 2003–07. Hon. Professor: Univ. of Warwick, 1991–99; Univ. of Birmingham, 1995–99. President: Soc. for Invertebrate Pathology, 1993–94; Assoc. of Applied Biologists, 1995–96. Chm., Assured Produce Scheme, 2001–06; Dir, Assured Food Standards, 2003–06; Sen. Exec., Nat. Horticultural Forum, 2004–05; Chm., Tech. Cttee, Horticultural Trades Assoc., 2007–11. Trustee, Royal Botanic Gdns, Kew, 1997–2003. Member: Western Front Assoc., 2009– (Chm., Cumbria Br., 2015–17); Police Hist. Soc., 2010–; CWA, 2011–. Editor in Chief, Biocontrol Science and Technology, 1991–2000. *Publications:* (with R. Hull and F. Brown) Virology: directory and dictionary of animal, bacterial and plant viruses, 1989; The Chieftain: Victorian true crime through the eyes of a Scotland Yard detective, 2011; numerous contribs to books and learned jls. *Recreations:* gardening, walking, history of the London Metropolitan Police (1840–78) and of the First World War. *Address:* The Outlook, Back Lane, Arnside, Cumbria LA5 0BS. *T:* (01524) 761418. *E:* oldthatch@btinternet.com. *W:* chrispaynebooks.com.

**PAYNE, Sir David Neil,** Kt 2013; CBE 2004; FRS 1992; FREng; Director, Optoelectronics Research Centre, since 1995 (Deputy Director, 1989–95), and Professor of Photonics, since 1991, University of Southampton; *b* 13 Aug. 1944; *s* of Raymond and Maisie Payne. *Educ:* Univ. of Southampton (BSc, PhD). FREng 2005; FIET (FIEE 2005). Commissioning Engineer, English Electric Co., 1962; University of Southampton: Research Asst, 1969; Jun. Res. Fellow, 1971; Pirelli Res. Fellow, 1972, Sen. Res. Fellow, 1978, Principal Res. Fellow, 1981; Pirelli Reader, 1984. Chm., SPI Optics Inc., 2000–05 (Dir, 2005–). Fellow, Optical Soc. of America, 1995; Foreign Member: Norwegian Acad. of Scis, 2004; Russian Acad. of Scis, 2006. Awards include: Rank Prize for Optoelectronics, 1991; IEEE/OSA John Tyndall Award, 1991; Computers and Communications Prize, Foundn for Computer and Communications Promotion in Japan, 1993; Franklin Medal, Franklin Inst., 1998; Edward Rhein Foundn Basic Res. Award, Germany, 2000; Mountbatten Medal, IEE, 2001; Kelvin Medal (jt award of 8 engrg socs), 2004; Microptics Award, Optical Soc. of Japan, 2005. *Publications:* numerous contribs to learned jls. *Recreations:* cooking, motorcycling, gardening. *Address:* Optoelectronics Research Centre, University of Southampton, Highfield, Southampton SO17 1BJ. *T:* (023) 8059 3583.

**PAYNE, (Geoffrey John) Nicholas;** Director, Opera Europa, since 2003; *b* 4 Jan. 1945; *s* of John Laurence Payne and Dorothy Gwendoline Payne (née Attenborough); *m* 1986, Linda Jane Adamson; two *s*. *Educ:* Eton Coll. (King's Schol.); Trinity Coll., Cambridge (BA Eng Lit). Finance Assistant, Royal Opera House, 1968–70; Subsidy Officer, Arts Council, 1970–76; Financial Controller, Welsh National Opera, 1976–82; Gen. Adminr, Opera North, 1982–93; Dir, Royal Opera, Covent Garden, 1993–98; Gen. Dir, ENO, 1998–2002. *E:* nicholas.payne@opera-europa.org.
See also A. J. S. Payne.

**PAYNE, Jane Marian, (Mrs A. E. Payne);** see Manning, J. M.

**PAYNE, Keith,** VC 1969; AM 2015 (OAM 2006); *b* 30 Aug. 1933; *s* of Henry Thomas Payne and Remilda Payne (née Hussey); *m* 1954, Florence Catherine Payne (née Plaw); five *s*. *Educ:* State School, Ingham, North Queensland. Soldier, Department of Army, Aug. 1951–75; 1 RAR, Korea, 1952–53; 3 RAR, Malaya, 1963–65; Aust. Army Trng Team, Vietnam, 1969 (Warrant Officer; awarded VC after deliberately exposing himself to enemy fire while trying to cover his outnumbered men); WO Instructor: RMC, Duntroon, ACT, 1970–72; 42 Bn, Royal Qld Regt, Mackay, 1973–75; Captain, Oman Army, 1975–76. Member: VC and GC Assoc.; Legion of Valour, USA; Aust. Army Training Team Vietnam Assoc.; Life Member: and Qld State Patron, Totally and Permanently Disabled Soldiers' Assoc. (Mackay Centre); Korea & SE Asia Forces Assoc.; Special Operations Assoc., USA; RSL (also Sarina Sub Br.). Patron: TRY-Sponsored Aust. Cadet Corps Units (Victoria); Mackay Legacy; Nat. Vice Patron, Australian Bravery Assoc. Life Gov., TRY and Community Services, Vic. Mem. Cttee (overseas), Victoria Cross and George Cross Assoc. Freeman City of Brisbane and of Shire of Hinchinbrook. Vietnamese Cross of Gallantry, with bronze star, 1969; US Meritorious Unit Citation; Vietnamese Unit Citation Cross of Gallantry with Palm; DSC (US); SSM (US). *Recreations:* football, fishing, hunting. *Address:* 1 Forest Court, Andergrove, Mackay, Qld 4740, Australia. *T:* (7) 49552794.

**PAYNE, Leonard Sidney,** CBE 1983; Director, J. Sainsbury Ltd, 1974–86; Adviser on Distribution and Retailing, Coopers & Lybrand, since 1986; *b* 16 Dec. 1925; *s* of Leonard Sydney Payne and Lillian May Leggatt; *m* 1944, Marjorie Vincent (decd); two *s*. *Educ:* Woodhouse Grammar School. FCCA, FCILT. Asst Accountant, Peek Frean & Co. Ltd, 1949–52; Chief Accountant, Administrator of various factory units, head office appts, Philips Electrical Industries, 1952–62; Dep. Gp Comptroller, Morgan Crucible Co. Ltd, 1962–64; British Road Services Ltd: Finance Dir, 1964–67; Asst Man. Dir, 1967–69; Man. Dir, 1969–71; Dir of Techn. Services and Develt, Nat. Freight Corp., 1971–74, Vice-Chm. Executive 1974. President: Freight Transport Assoc., 1980–82; Chartered Inst. of Transport, 1983–84. Chm., CBI Transport Policy Cttee, 1980–86. CCMI. *Recreations:* gardening, swimming, squash, chess. *Address:* Apartment 5, Evenholme, Green Walk, Bowdon, Altrincham, Cheshire WA14 2SL.

**PAYNE, Prof. Michael Christopher,** PhD; FRS 2008; Professor of Computational Physics, University of Cambridge, since 2000; Fellow, Pembroke College, Cambridge, since 1984; *b* 1960. *Educ:* Pembroke Coll., Cambridge (BA 1981; PhD 1985). Lectr in Physics, until 1998, Reader in Computational Physics, 1998–2000, Univ. of Cambridge. Institute of Physics: Hon. Fellow; Maxwell Medal and Prize, 1996; Mott Lect., 1998. Swan Medal, Inst. of Physics, 2014. *Address:* Theory of Condensed Matter Group, Cavendish Laboratory, University of Cambridge, JJ Thomson Avenue, Cambridge CB3 0HE.

**PAYNE, Michael Robert;** international strategic advisor to sports and entertainment industry; advisor and board member to International Olympic Committee, Formula One, international sports federations, governments and industry, since 2004; *b* 25 March 1958; *s* of Robert Gilmore Payne and Sheila Brennan Savory; *m* Marta Salsas; two *s* one *d*. *Educ:* St Anthony's Prep. Sch., London; Highgate Sch., London. Mem., British Ski Team, 1974–78; British Professional Freestyle Ski Champion, 1977, 1978. West Nally Sports Mktg Agency, London, 1979–83; ISL Agency, Switzerland and Korea, 1983–88; Global Marketing and TV Rights Dir, IOC, 1983–2004, later Adv. Dir, Montreux Jazz Fest. Mem. Adv. Bd, Imperial Coll., London. Contributor on sports business issues, FT, BBC, CNN, Fortune, Japan Yomiuri Shimbun. *Publications:* Olympic Turnaround, 2005 (trans. Chinese, Japanese, Korean, Spanish, German, Greek, Italian, Russian, Bulgarian, Portuguese, Turkish, Slovak). *Recreation:* ski-ing. *Address:* 74 Boulevard d'Italie, MC 98000, Monaco. *T:* (6) 80867976. *E:* michael@michaelrpayne.com. *W:* www.michaelrpayne.com, www.twitter.com/michaelrpayne1.

**PAYNE, Nicholas;** see Payne, G. J. N.

**PAYNE, Nicholas Kevin,** FCCA; Finance and Operations Director, Government Legal Department (formerly Treasury Solicitor's Department), since 2014; *b* Isleworth, 21 Jan. 1966; *s* of Michael Charles and Kay Payne; *m* 2011, Carolyn Marie Mackay. *Educ:* Teddington Boys' Sch.; Richmond upon Thames Coll. of Further Educn; Open Univ. (BSc Hons; MBA). FCCA 1999. Customer Accounting Asst, 1984–85, Customer Accounting Supervisor, 1985–86, SE Electricity Bd; London Electricity Board, then London Electricity plc: Systems Accounting Asst, 1986–87; Bought Ledger Supervisor, 1987–88; Internal Auditor, 1988–89; Sen. Internal Auditor, 1989–90; Area Accounting Unit Manager (Western), 1990–91; Finance Officer (Engrg Resource Mgt System), 1991–93; Budgets and Forecast Officer (Engrg), 1993–94; Financial Planning Manager (Network Services), 1994–97; Chief Accountant, RAF Logistics Comd, 1997–2000; Financial Controller, Defence Logistics Orgn (Air), 2000–01; Director of Finance: Cambs Constabulary, 2001–05; Centre Top Level Budget, MoD, 2006–07; Financial Controller, 2007–09, Dir, Commercial and Financial Control, 2009–10, BERR; Hd, Commercial Scrutiny, 2010–12, Commercial Strategy and Industrial Policy Dir, 2012–14, MoD; rcds 2011–12. MCIPS 2011. FCMA 2000. *Recreations:* ballet, cinema, theatre, walking, member of MENSA; UK, European and world championship medallist for Team GB in Tang Soo Do. *Address:* Government Legal Department, 102 Petty France, SW1H 9AJ. *T:* 07825 420772.

**PAYNE, Peter Charles John,** PhD; MSc(AgrEng); farmer, 1975–2000; *b* 8 Feb. 1928; *s* of late C. J. Payne, China Clay Merchant, and Mrs F. M. Payne; *m* 1961, Margaret Grover; two *s* one *d*. *Educ:* Plymouth Coll.; Teignmouth Grammar School; Reading University. BSc Reading 1948; Min. of Agriculture Scholar, Durham Univ., MSc(AgrEng) 1950; Scientific Officer, Nat. Institute of Agricultural Engineering, 1950–55; PhD Reading 1954; Lecturer in Farm Mechanisation, Wye College, London Univ., 1955–60; Lecturer in Agricultural Engineering, Durham Univ., 1960–61; Principal, Nat. Coll. of Agricultural Engineering, Silsoe, 1962–75 (Hon. Fellow, 1980); Visiting Professor: Univ. of Reading, 1969–75; Cranfield Inst. of Technology, 1975–80. Chm., Agricl Panel, Intermed. Technol. Develt Gp, 1979–86. Vice-Pres., Section III, Commn Internationale du Génie Rural, 1969. FIAgrE 1968; FRAgS 1971; CEng 1980. *Publications:* various papers in agricultural and engineering journals. *Recreation:* sailing. *Address:* 5 Mulberry Quay, Market Strand, Falmouth TR11 3HD. *T:* (01326) 318880.

**PAYNE, (Sadeqa) Shaheen;** see Rahman, S. S.

**PAYNE, Sebastian;** see Payne, A. J. S.

**PAYNE, Most Rev. (Sidney) Stewart;** Metropolitan of the Ecclesiastical Province of Canada and Archbishop of Western Newfoundland, 1990–97, retired; *b* 6 June 1932; *s* of Albert and Hilda Payne; *m* 1962, Selma Carlson Penney, St Anthony, Newfoundland; two *s* two *d*. *Educ:* Elementary and High School, Fogo, Newfoundland; Memorial Univ. of Newfoundland (BA); Queen's Coll., Newfoundland (LTh); BD (General Synod). Incumbent of Mission of Happy Valley, 1957–65; Rector, Parish of Bay Roberts, 1965–70; Rector, Parish of St Anthony, 1970–78; Bishop of Western Newfoundland, 1978–97. DD *hc*: Univ. of King's Coll., Halifax, NS, 1981; Queen's Coll., St John's, NL, 2006. *Address:* 101A East Valley Road, Corner Brook, NL A2H 2L4, Canada.

**PAYNE, Stephen Michael,** OBE 2004; RDI 2006; CEng; FRINA; FREng; independent consultant, since 2011; President, Royal Institution of Naval Architects, 2007–10; *b* 28 Jan. 1960; *s* of Michael John Robert Payne and Pauline Patricia Payne. *Educ:* Univ. of Southampton (BSc Eng (Hons) Ship Sci. 1984). CEng 2002; FRINA 2002; FREng 2008. Naval architect, Marconi Radar Systems, Chelmsford, 1984–85; Jun. Naval Architect, 1985–87, Naval Architect, 1987–92, Sen. Naval Architect, 1992–95, Technical Marine Planning Ltd, London; Carnival Corporation, 1995–: Sen. Naval Architect, 1995; Project Manager: MS Rotterdam (VI), 1995–97; MS Costa Atlantica, 1997–98; Chief Designer, then Proj. Manager, RMS Queen Mary 2, 1998; Dir, Proj. Mgt, 2000–04, Vice Pres. and Chief Naval Architect, 2004–10, Carnival Corporate Shipbuilding. Mem. Council, 2005–, Exec. Cttee, 2006–, RINA. Co-founder, Future Engineers 2008, in assoc. with RAEng; Awards Cttee, RAEng, 2009–11. Dir/Trustee, Southampton Cultural Develt Trust, 2010–15; Trustee, Webb Inst., Glen Cove, NY, 2011–. Gov., Quilley Sch. of Engrg, Eastleigh, 2009–15. Freeman, City of London, 2004; Liveryman, Co. of Shipwrights, 2005– (Freeman, 2004). Hon. FIED 2009. Hon. DSc: Southampton, 2007; Winchester, 2015. Bronze Medal, RINA, 1988; Special Achievement Award, RAEng, 2006; MN Medal, 2006; Admiral Land Medal, SNAME, 2011. *Publications:* Grande Dame: Holland America Line and the SS Rotterdam, 1990; MS Statendam, 1993; contribs to Naval Architects, Ships Monthly, Steamboat Bill, Designs, Cruise Industry News. *Recreations:* public speaking, model-ship making, writing, cooking, airships, history of passenger ships. *Address:* c/o Royal Institution of Naval Architects, 8–9 Northumberland Street, WC2N 5DA.

**PAYNE, Most Rev. Stewart;** see Payne, Most Rev. S. S.

**PAYNTER, Alan Guy Hadley;** Commissioner, 1997–2000, and Director, Corporate Services, 1999–2000, HM Customs and Excise; *b* 5 Nov. 1941; *s* of Leslie Alan Paynter and Dorothy Victoria Paynter (née Voak); *m* 1964, Mary Teresa Houghton; two *d*. *Educ:* East Ham Grammar Sch.; Central London Poly. (Post-grad. DMS 1972). EO, then HEO, MPBW, 1960–72 (Asst Private Sec. to Minister of Public Bldg and Works, 1968–71); HM Customs and Excise: Sen. Exec. Officer, 1972; Principal, 1978; on secondment to Overseas Containers Ltd, 1981–83; Sen. Principal, Computer Services, 1983–87; Asst Sec., 1987; Head, 1989–93, Dir, 1993–99, Information Systems; Mem. of Board, 1993–2000. Hon. Treas., Thorpe Bay Bowling Club, 2006–10. Trustee, 2007–15, Chm. of Trustees, 2007–11, Havens Hospices; Dir, Havens Hospices Develt Co., 2015–18. *Recreations:* golf, bowling, theatre, gardening.

**PAYTON, Michael Andrew Hartland;** Chairman, Clyde & Co., Solicitors, since 2013 (Senior Partner, 1984–2013); *b* Llandrindod Wells, 8 June 1944; *oc* of late Geoffrey Hartland Payton and Pamela Payton (née Miller Kerr); *m* 1978, Sally Ann, *d* of late Dick and Pamela Farmer; two *d* and two step *s*. *Educ:* Felsted Sch. (Schol.). Articled, Hunt & Wrigley,

Northallerton, 1962–66; admitted solicitor, 1966; Asst Solicitor, 1967–71, Partner, 1971–, Clyde & Co., specialising in shipping, then insurance. Chairman: Solicitors' Indemnity Mutual Insce Assoc., 1984–2000; Exec., British Maritime Law Assoc., 1986–; Novae Insce Co. Ltd, 2005–09; Internat. Dispute Resolution Centre, 2011–; Dir, London Authorities Mutual Ltd, 2007–09. Freeman, City of London, 2007–; Liveryman: Solicitors' Co., 2002– (Addnl Asst to Ct, 2014–16); Shipwrights' Co., 2010–. Hon. QC 2012; Hon. Bencher, Inner Temple, 2012. *Publications:* contribs to learned jls on insce, arbitration and mediation. *Recreations:* horse racing, my wife, Normandy. *Address:* 30 Bisham Gardens, N6 6DD. *T:* (020) 8340 8986. *E:* michael.payton@clydeco.com. *Clubs:* Garrick, MCC.

**PEACE, Elizabeth Ann,** CBE 2008; Chief Executive, British Property Federation, 2002–14; Chairman, Shadow Sponsor Body, Restoration and Renewal Programme, Palace of Westminster, since 2018; *b* Birmingham, 5 Dec. 1952; *d* of Herbert Powers and Gwendoline Powers (*née* Burbridge); *m* 1978, Nigel David Peace; two *s*. *Educ:* King Edward VI Camp Hill Grammar Sch. for Girls, Birmingham; Royal Holloway Coll., Univ. of London (BA Hons Hist.). Admin. trainee, then Grade 7, MoD, 1974–91; Dir, Corporate Affairs and Co. Sec., QinetiQ plc (formerly DERA), 1991–2002. Pres., Farnborough Aerospace Consortium, 1996–2002. Non-executive Director: Planning Inspectorate, 2005–08; Turley Assocs, 2008–13; Redrow plc, 2014–17; Howard de Walden Estates, 2014–; Member, Board: Peabody Housing Assoc., 2009–17; Morgan Sindall plc, 2012–17. Chairman: Eur. Property Fedn, 2004–11; Shadow Bd, Curzon Regeneration Co., 2015–17; Shadow Property Agency, then Government Property Agency, 2017–; Old Oak and Park Royal Develt Corp., 2017–. Comr, CABE, 2008–11. Mem., Standards Cttee, Westminster CC, 2008–11. Chm., Centre for London, 2016–; Mem., Mayor of London's Homes for Londoners Bd, 2016–. Trustee: LandAid Charitable Trust, 2005–19 (Chm., 2015–19); Inst. for Sustainability, 2009–12; Churches Conservation Trust, 2013–; Architectural Heritage Fund, 2014– (Chm., 2015–). Pres., Property Litigation Assoc., 2016–; Hon. Vice Pres., Cambridge Univ. Land Soc., 2011–. Hon. Fellow, Coll. of Estate Mgt, 2008; Hon. FRIBA, 2010. Liveryman, Chartered Surveyors' Co., 2007. Hon. DLitt Westminster, 2011. *Recreations:* opera, reading, gardening and conservation, keeping age at bay, hounding offspring and shopping. *Address:* c/o Old Oak and Park Royal Development Corporation, 169 Union Street, SE1 0LL. *E:* liz@lizpeace.co.uk.

**PEACE, Sir John (Wilfred),** Kt 2011; Lord-Lieutenant for Nottinghamshire, since 2012; *b* 2 March 1949; *m* 1971, Christine Blakemore; three *d*. *Educ:* Sandhurst. Experian (formerly CCN): Founding Dir, 1980; Man. Dir, 1991–96; Chief Exec., 1996–2000; Chm., 2006–14; Chief Exec., Great Universal Stores, later GUS, plc, 2000–06. Chm., Burberry, 2002–18; Dep. Chm., 2007–09, Chm., 2009–16, Standard Chartered Bank, then Standard Chartered plc. Chancellor, Nottingham Trent Univ., 2017–. High Sheriff, Notts, 2011–12. *Recreations:* horse riding, golf.

**PEACH, Air Chief Marshal Sir Stuart (William),** GBE 2016 (CBE 2001); KCB 2009; DL; Chairman, Military Committee, North Atlantic Treaty Organisation, since 2018; *b* Staffordshire, 22 Feb. 1956; *s* of Clifford Peach and Jean Mary Peach; *m* 1986, Brigitte Ender; one *s* one *d*. *Educ:* Sheffield Univ. (BA 1977); Downing Coll., Cambridge (MPhil 1997; Hon. Fellow 2013). Joined RAF, 1974; 13 Sqdn, 1979–81; IX (B) Sqdn, 1982–84; 31 Sqdn, 1984–89; RAF Staff Coll., 1990; HQ RAF Germany, 1991–93; OC IX (Bomber) Sqdn, 1993–96; Dir, Defence Studies, 1997–99; Comdr British Forces (Air) Italy, 1999–2000; Air Comdr (Forward) Kosovo, 2000; Comdt, Air Warfare Centre, 2000–03; Dir Gen., Intelligence Collection, 2003–06; Chief, Defence Intelligence, 2006–09; Chief of Jt Ops, 2009–11; Comdr Jt Forces Comd, 2011–13; Vice Chief of the Defence Staff, 2013–16; Chief of the Defence Staff, 2016–18. Hon. Col, Royal Logistics Corps (Army). Trustee, Imperial War Mus., 2012– (Chm. 2016–). Hon. DTech: Kingston, 2003, Loughborough, 2014; Hon. DLitt Sheffield, 2007. DL Lincs, 2014. *Publications:* Perspectives on Air Power, 1998; service manuals; articles in defence jls on air power and ops. *Recreations:* military history, cooking, sport. *Club:* Royal Air Force.

**PEACOCK, Dame Alison (Margaret),** DBE 2014; DL; Chief Executive, Chartered College of Teaching, since 2017; *b* London, 17 Oct. 1959; *d* of Leslie and Patricia Mann; *m* 1983, Jonathan Peacock; two *d*. *Educ:* Univ. of London (BA Hons); Univ. of Warwick (PGCE); Queens' Coll., Cambridge (MEd 1997; Hon. Fellow, 2018). Headteacher, Wroxham Sch., Potters Bar, 2003–16. Visiting Professor: Univ. of Hertfordshire, 2016–; Wrexham Glyndwr Univ., 2017–. Hon. DLitt Brighton, 2014; Hon. DEd Bath Spa, 2019. DL Herts, 2015. *Publications:* (jtly) Creating Learning Without Limits, 2012. *Address:* Chartered College of Teaching, 9–11 Endsleigh Gardens, WC1H 0EH.

**PEACOCK, Hon. Andrew (Sharp),** AC 1997; GCL 2006; Chairman, Amadeus Energy Ltd, 2007–09; *b* 13 Feb. 1939; *s* of late A. S. Peacock and Iris Peacock. *Educ:* Scotch Coll., Melbourne, Vic; Melbourne Univ. (LLB). Former Partner, Rigby & Fielding, Solicitors; Chm., Peacock and Smith Pty Ltd, 1962–69. Army Reserve (Captain), 1966–94. Pres., Victorian Liberal Party, 1965–66; MP (L) Kooyong, Australia, 1966–94; Minister for Army and Minister assisting Prime Minister, 1969–71; Minister for Army and Minister asstg Treasurer, 1971–72; Minister for External Territories, Feb.–Dec. 1972; Mem., Opposition Exec., 1973–75; Oppos. Shadow Minister for For. Affairs, 1973–75, 1985–87; Minister for: the Envmt, 1975; Foreign Affairs, 1975–80; Industrial Relns, 1980–81; Industry and Commerce, 1982–83; Leader of the Parly Liberal Party, and of the Opposition, 1983–85; Dep. Leader, Liberal Party and Dep. Leader, Opposition, 1987–89; Leader, Parly Liberal Party, and of the Opposition, 1989–90; Shadow Attorney-Gen. and Shadow Minister for Justice, 1990–92; Shadow Minister: for Trade, 1992–93; for Foreign Affairs, 1993–94; Australian Ambassador to the USA, 1997–2000. Pres., Boeing Australia, 2002–07; Chm., MFS Ltd, 2007–08. Chm. Internat. Democrat Union, 1989–92. Mem., Business Council of Australia, 2003–07. Mem., Internat. Adv. Panel, Graduate Sch. of Govt, Univ. of Sydney, 2003–. *Recreations:* horse racing, sailboarding, Australian Rules football. *Clubs:* Australian (Sydney); Melbourne, Melbourne Cricket, Victoria Racing, Melbourne Racing (Melbourne); Moonee Valley Racing.

**PEACOCK, Dr Christabel Phyllis,** CBE 2014; FRSB; FRAgS; Chairman and Founder, Sidai Africa Ltd, since 2011; *b* Bristol, 27 Feb. 1958; *d* of late Prof. Joseph Henry Peacock and Dr Gillian Frances Peacock. *Educ:* St Mary's Calne; Univ. of Reading (BSc Hons 1980; PhD 1984). FRSB (FSB 2009). Vis. Scientist, Internat. Livestock Centre of Africa, 1980–84; CSIRO Advr to Govt of Indonesia, 1985–86; Agricl Systems Specialist, UNFAO and Asst Prof., Asian Inst. of Technol., Bangkok, 1986–88; Project Co-ordinator, Ethiopia, 1988–96; Farm Africa: Regl Goat Develt Dir, 1995–96; Dep. Dir, 1996–99; CEO, 1999–2010. Mem., Editl Bd, World Agric. Mem., Global Develt website Adv. Panel, Guardian. Founding Mem., All Party Parly Gp for Agric. and Food for Develt; Mem., Ind. Adv. Gp on Zoonoses and Emerging Livestock Systems, BBSRC. Mem. Bd, Internat. Goat Assoc., 2004–12. FRAgS 2009. Hon. DSc Reading, 2011. Charity Principal of Year, UK Charity Awards, 2003; Ashoka Fellow, 2011; Outstanding Social Entrepreneur of Year, Schwab Foundn, 2015. *Publications:* Improving Goat Production in the Tropics: a manual for development workers, 1996; Goat Types of Ethiopia and Eritrea,

1996; contrib. scientific papers and book chapters. *Recreations:* scuba diving, watching the England cricket team beat Australia, walking, gardening, travelling. *Address:* Glebe Cottage, Bryants Bottom, Great Missenden, Bucks HP16 0JS. *T:* (01494) 488399. *E:* christie.peacock@sidai.com. *Club:* MCC.

**PEACOCK, Elizabeth Joan;** JP; DL; *b* 4 Sept. 1937; *d* of late John and Dorothy Gates; *m* 1963, Brian David Peacock; two *s*. *Educ:* St Monica's Convent, Skipton. Asst to Exec. Dir, York Community Council, 1979–83; Administrator, four charitable trusts, York, 1979–83. County Councillor, N Yorks, 1981–84. MP (C) Batley and Spen, 1983–97; contested (C) same seat, 1997, 2001. PPS to Minister of State, Home Office, 1991–92, to Minister for Social Security and disabled people, 1992. Mem., Select Cttee on Employment, 1983–87. Chairman: All Party Trans Pennine Gp, 1988–94; All Party Wool Textile Gp, 1989–97. Hon. Sec., Yorks Cons. MPs, 1983–88; Vice Chm., Cons. Back-bench Party Organisation Cttee, 1985–87; Mem. Exec. Cttee, 1922 Cttee, 1987–91; Mem. Exec., CPA, 1987–92. Mem., BBC Gen. Adv. Council, 1987–93; Chm., BBC Yorkshire Regl Audience Council (formerly Local Regl Cttee, Yorks), 2006–10. Vice Pres., Yorks Area Young Conservatives, 1984–87; Pres., Yorks Area Cons. Trade Unionists, 1991–98 (Vice Pres., 1987–91). Chm., Assoc. of Former Members of Parlt, 2015–. FRSA 1990–2010 (Chm., Yorks Reg., 2003–06). JP Macclesfield, 1975–79, Bulmer East 1983; DL W Yorks, 1998. Spectator Campaigner of Year, 1992; Yorkshire Woman of Year, 1993; Yorkshire Woman of Achievement, 1993. *Publications:* A Yorkshire Lass at the Court of Thatcher, 2013. *Recreations:* reading, motoring. *Address:* Spen House, George Lane, Notton, Wakefield, W Yorks WF4 2NQ.

*See also* J. D. Peacock, N. C. Peacock.

**PEACOCK, Eric;** *see* Peacock, W. E.

**PEACOCK, Geraldine,** CBE 2001; Chair, Charity Commission for England and Wales, 2004–06; freelance facilitator, since 2007; *b* 26 Jan. 1948; *d* of late Peter Davies and of Joyce Davies (*née* Pullin); *m* 1971, Harry Peacock (marr. diss. 1988); three *s*. *Educ:* Redland High Sch., Bristol; Durham Univ. (BA Hons Sociology 1969); Univ. of California; Univ. of Newcastle upon Tyne (CQSW 1981; post-grad. dip. in Applied Social Work Studies 1981). Teaching Asst, Univ. of California, and Heroin Addiction Counsellor, San Bernardino State Prison, 1969–70; Med. Social Worker, Durham Hosp. Bd, 1970–72; Lectr in Criminology, Teesside Poly., 1972–75; Social Worker: Thalidomide Children's Trust, 1975–85; Lady Hoare Trust for Handicapped Children, 1975–79; Course Co-ordinator, Open Univ., 1975–82; Lectr in Social Work, Queen's Coll., Glasgow, 1982–86; Dep. Dir, London Boroughs Training Cttee, 1986–89; Chief Executive: Nat. Autistic Soc., 1989–97; Guide Dogs for the Blind Assoc., 1997–2003. Associate Fellow, Skoll Centre for Social Entrepreneurship, Saïd Business Sch., Oxford Univ., 2006–; Vis. Fellow, Centre for Charity Effectiveness, Cass Business Sch., London, 2007–. A Civil Service Comr, 2001–04; Comr and Bd Mem., Commn on Unclaimed Assets, 2006–. HM Treasury: Mem., Social Investment Taskforces, 2000–06; Chm., Futurebuilders Taskforce, 2003–04; Member: Strategy Unit Adv. Panel on Charity Law and Regulation, Cabinet Office, 2002–06; Action Community Unit Adv. Panel, Home Office, 2002–06. Columnist: Third Sector mag., 1999–, and other charity mags. Lectr, Stanford and Berkeley Univs, 2009–. Member: Exec. Cttee, ACEVO (formerly ACENVO), 1994–2006 (Chm., 1996–2000); Council, Industrial Soc., 1996–2001; Exec. Cttee, NCVO, 2000–03 (Trustee, 1999–2006). Vice-Chm., Internat. Fedn of Guide Dog Schs for the Blind, 2001–03; Vice Pres., Parkinson's Disease Soc., 2006–. Member: Social Enterprise Initiative Adv. Bd, Harvard Business Sch., 2003–; Business Adv. Forum, Saïd Business Sch., Oxford Univ., 2006–; Trustee, Rainbow Trust, 2007–; Patron: Movers and Shakers, 2005–; CDFA, 2004–. Hon. LLD Teesside, 2005. *Publications:* (jtly) Social Work and Received Ideas, 1988; (ed jtly) The Haunt of Misery: essays in helping and caring, 1989; Appraising the Chief Executive, 1996; The Magic Roundabout: a guide to social investment for charities, 2004. *Recreations:* theatre, cinema, art, literature, family. *Address:* White Lion House, 5 New Street, Wells, Somerset BA5 2LA. *T:* (01749) 672926. *E:* gerpea@gmail.com.

**PEACOCK, Ian Douglas,** OBE 1998; Chief Executive, Lawn Tennis Association, 1986–96; *b* 9 April 1934; *s* of Andrew Inglis Peacock and Minnie Maria (*née* King); *m* 1st, 1962, Joanna Hepburn MacGregor (marr. diss. 2007); one *s* one *d*; 2nd, 2008, Philippa Katharine Bland. *Educ:* Sevenoaks Sch. Pilot Officer, RAF, 1953–54. Slazengers Ltd, 1955–83, Man. Dir 1976–83; Sports Marketing Surveys Ltd, 1984–85. President: British Sports & Allied Industry Fedn, 1984–85; UK Tennis Industry Assoc., 2008–18 (Life Pres., 2018). Director: Golf Foundn, 1982– (Chm., 1996–2003); Vice Pres., 2003–; Chm., Golf Ball Cttee, 1976–96); LTA Trust, 1988–96; Queen's Club Ltd, 1993–96; Wembley Nat. Stadium Ltd, 1998–2002; Tennis Foundn (formerly British Tennis Foundn), 1998–2010. Trustee: Torch Trophy Trust, 1993– (Chm., 1998–2006; Vice Pres., 2006–); Dan Maskell Tennis Trust, 1997–; English Nat. Stadium Trust, 1998–2009. *Recreations:* golf, painting. *Address:* 135 More Close, St Paul's Court, West Kensington, W14 9BW. *Clubs:* Royal Air Force, All England Lawn Tennis and Croquet, Queen's; Royal Ashdown Forest Golf (Forest Row).

**PEACOCK, (Ian) Michael,** OBE 2005; Chairman, UBC Media Group plc (formerly Unique Broadcasting Co. Ltd), 1989–2005; *b* 14 Sept. 1929; *e s* of Norman Henry and Sara Barbara Peacock; *m* 1956, Daphne Lee; two *s* one *d*. *Educ:* Kimball Union Academy, USA; Welwyn Garden City Grammar School; London School of Economics (BSc Econ.). BBC Television: Producer, 1952–56; Producer Panorama, 1955–58; Asst Head of Television Outside Broadcasts, 1958–59; Editor, Panorama, 1959–61; Editor, BBC Television News, 1961–63; Chief of Programmes, BBC 2, 1963–65; Controller, BBC 1, BBC Television Service, 1965–67; Managing Dir, London Weekend Television Ltd, 1967–69; Chm., Monitor Enterprises Ltd, 1970–89; Man. Dir, Warner Bros TV Ltd, 1972–74; Exec. Vice-Pres., Warner Bros Television Inc., 1974–76. Dir, Video Arts Ltd, 1972–89; Pres., Video Arts Inc., 1976–78; Man. Dir, Dumbarton Films Ltd (formerly Video Arts Television), 1978–87; Chairman: Video Answers, 1989–90; Publishing Projects plc, 1990–92. Dep. Chm., Piccadilly Radio, 1988–89; Man. Dir, Truly Classic Yachts Ltd, 1994–2002. Chm., Michael Peacock Charitable Foundn, 1990–2010. IPPA: First Chm., 1981–82; Mem. Council, 1983–88. Mem., Ct of Governors, LSE, 1982–2009, now Emeritus Gov. (Chm., Campaign for the LSE, 2001–04). Hon. FTCL 2003; Hon. Fellow, LSE 2004. *Address:* 21 Woodlands Road, Barnes, SW13 0JZ. *T:* (020) 8876 2025. *Club:* Savile.

**PEACOCK, Ian Rex;** Chairman: Mothercare plc, 2002–11; MFI Furniture Group plc, 2000–06; Housing Finance Corporation, since 2013 (non-executive Director, since 2013); *b* 5 July 1947; *s* of late Mervyn (George) and Evelyn (Joyce) Peacock; *m* 1973, Alyanee Chya-Rochana; one *s*. *Educ:* Kingswood Grammar Sch.; Trinity Coll., Cambridge (MA). Open Univ. (MA). Economist: Unilever Plc, 1968–73; Cripps Warburg Ltd, 1973–75; Kleinwort Benson Gp, 1975–94 (Gp Dir, 1990–94); Co-Hd, Merchant Banking Div., USA, 1994–97, Chief Operating Officer, Investment Banking, 1997–98, BZW Ltd; Special Advr, Bank of England, 1998–2000. Non-executive Director: Norwich & Peterborough Bldg Soc., 1997–2005; C. Hoare & Co., 2010–17 (Consultant to Bd, 2008–10); Director: Lombard Risk Mgt, 2000–10 (Dep. Chm., 2004–10); i-documentsystems, 2000–03. Chm.,

Family Mosaic Housing Assoc., 2007–13. Trustee: WRVS, 2001–07; PHG Foundn, 2007–; Chiswick House and Gardens Trust, 2011–. Quondam Fellow, Hughes Hall, Cambridge, 2012– (City Fellow, 2009–12). *Recreations:* music, particularly opera, squash, gardening, travel. *E:* ianrpeacock@hotmail.com. *Club:* Athenæum.

PEACOCK, James; *see* Peacock, W. J.

PEACOCK, Prof. John Andrew, PhD; FRS 2007; FRSE; Professor of Cosmology, University of Edinburgh, since 1998; *b* 27 March 1956; *s* of Arthur John Peacock and Isobel Watson Peacock (*née* Moir); *m* 1982, Catherine Heather Lewis; one *s* two *d*. *Educ:* Jesus Coll., Cambridge (BA 1977; PhD 1981). Res. astronomer, 1983–92, Hd of Res., 1992–98, Royal Observatory, Edinburgh. FRSE 2006. Shaw Prize in Astronomy, 2014. *Publications:* Cosmological Physics, 1999. *Recreations:* playing classical clarinet, hill walking. *Address:* Institute for Astronomy, University of Edinburgh, Royal Observatory, Blackford Hill, Edinburgh EH9 3HJ. *T:* (0131) 668 8100, *Fax:* (0131) 668 8416. *E:* jap@roe.ac.uk.

PEACOCK, Jonathan David; QC 2001; *b* 21 April 1964; *s* of Brian David Peacock and Elizabeth Joan Peacock, *qv*; *m* 1997, Charlotte Ann Cole; one *s* one *d*. *Educ:* King's Sch., Macclesfield; Nunthorpe Grammar Sch., York; Corpus Christi Coll., Oxford (MA Juris 1st Cl.). Called to the Bar, Middle Temple, 1987 (Sen. Schol.). *Recreations:* cricket, sailing. *Address:* 11 New Square, Lincoln's Inn, WC2A 3QB. *T:* (020) 7242 4017. *Club:* United and Cecil.
*See also* N. C. Peacock.

PEACOCK, Michael; *see* Peacock, I. M.

PEACOCK, Nicholas Christopher; QC 2009; *b* Keighley, W Yorks; *s* of Brian David Peacock and Elizabeth Joan Peacock, *qv*; *m* 1995, Susan; two *d*. *Educ:* Nunthorpe Grammar Sch., York; St Edmund Hall, Oxford (BA Juris.). Called to the Bar, Middle Temple, 1989. *Recreations:* cycling, Land Rovers. *Address:* Maitland Chambers, 7 Stone Buildings, Lincoln's Inn, WC2A 3SZ. *T:* (020) 7406 1200, *Fax:* (020) 7406 1300. *E:* npeacock@maitlandchambers.com.

PEACOCK, Peter James, CBE 1998; Member (Lab) Highland and Islands, Scottish Parliament, 1999–2011; *b* 27 Feb. 1952; *s* of James and Doreen Peacock; *m* 1973, Shona Pearson; two *s*. *Educ:* Hawick High Sch.; Jordanhill Coll. of Educn (Dip. Youth Work and Community Studies 1973). Community Educn Officer, Orkney CC, 1973–75; Area Officer for Highland, Grampian, Tayside, Orkney, Shetland and Western Isles, and Central Policy Advr, Scottish Assoc. of CABx, 1975–87; Partner, The Apt Partnership, 1987–96. Member: Highland Regl Council (Dep. Leader; Chm. Finance Cttee), 1982–96; (Lab) Highland Council, 1995–99 (Leader/Convenor; Chm., Policy and Resources Cttee). Scottish Executive: Dep. Minister for Children and Educn, 1999–2000, for Finance and Local Govt, then for Finance and Public Services, 2000–03; Minister for Educn and Young People, 2003–06. Vice Pres., COSLA. Chm., Customer Forum for Water in Scotland, 2011–; Policy Dir, Community Land Scotland, 2011–. Mem., Ofcom Adv. Cttee for Scotland, 2012–. Former Member: Bd, Scottish Natural Heritage; European Cttee of Regions; Scottish Economic Council; Bd, Scottish Post Office; Bd, Cairngorm Partnership. Chm., Scottish Library and Information Council, 1991–94; former Chairman: Moray Firth Community Radio; Community Work North; former Member: Scottish Valuation Adv. Council; Centres for Highlands and Islands Policy Studies. *E:* peter.peacock@btinternet.com.

PEACOCK, Prof. Sharon Jayne, CBE 2015; PhD; Professor of Public Health and Microbiology, University of Cambridge, since 2019; Interim Director, National Infection Service, Public Health England, since 2019; *b* Margate, Kent, 24 March 1959; *d* of Francis and Mary Hardstaffe; *m* 1983, Peter Peacock; one *s* two *d*. *Educ:* Southampton Univ. (BM 1988); Open Univ. (PhD 2003). MRCP 1991; MRCPath 1997. Postgrad. med. trng, Southampton, Brighton and Oxford, 1988–95; Wellcome Trust Res. Trng Fellow in Microbiol., Univ. of Oxford and Trinity Coll. Dublin, 1995–99; Sen. Lectr in Microbiol., Univ. of Oxford, 1998–2002; Hd, Bacterial Diseases Res., Mahidol-Oxford Tropical Medicine Res. Unit, Mahidol Univ., Bangkok, 2002–09; Prof. of Clinical Microbiol., Dept of Medicine, Univ. of Cambridge, 2009–15; Prof. of Clinical Microbiology, LSHTM, 2015–19; Founding Dir, Bloomsbury Res. Inst., 2015–19. Sen. Investigator, NIHR, 2017–. Mem., EMBO, 2015. FMedSci 2013; Fellow, American Acad. of Microbiol., 2014. *Publications:* 420 scientific articles incl. 21 book chapters. *Recreations:* classical music, kettlebell, running. *E:* sjp97@medschl.cam.ac.uk.

PEACOCK, Stephanie; MP (Lab) Barnsley East, since 2017; *b* Birmingham. *Educ:* Queen Mary, Univ. of London (BA Modern and Contemp. Hist. 2010); Canterbury Christ Ch Univ. (PGCE 2011); Inst. of Educn, Univ. of London (MA 2013). Parly Asst, H of C, 2005–10; Teacher of History and Politics, Teach First, 2010–12; Trng Officer, Usdaw, 2012–13; Political Officer, Birmingham and W Midlands Reg., GMB, 2013–17. Contested (Lab) Halesowen and Rowley Regis, 2015. *Address:* House of Commons, SW1A 0AA.

PEACOCK, (William) Eric, CMG 2003; DBA; DL; non-executive Director, Exemplas Holdings Ltd (Chief Executive, 1996); Chief Executive, Business Link Hertfordshire, 1996–2006; *b* 22 Sept. 1944; *s* of Robert and Violet Peacock; *m* 1988, Carole Nicholls; one *s*. *Educ:* Bellahouston Acad.; Queen's Univ. Belfast (MBA 1974, DBA 1976). Barbour Ltd, 1960–79, Man. Dir, 1974–79; Managing Director: Hollis Gp plc, 1979–83; Hartsford Dales Ltd, 1983–93; Chm. and CEO, Babygro plc, 1983–88; Man. Dir, Missenden Abbey Management Develt Centre, 1993–96. Chairman: Cafe Slim Ltd, 2002–; What If, 2002–; Stevenage Packaging Ltd, 2003–; Eupac Ltd, 2003–06; 4 Less Finance Plc, 2004–; Silent Edge Ltd, 2004–06; Rialto Gp Ltd, 2004–. Non-executive Director: Hertfordshire Univ. Business Sch., 2002–; FCO, 2003; DTI, later BERR; ECGD, 2011–. Gp Chm., Acad. for Chief Execs Ltd, 1997–. Chm., Peacock Foundn, 1987–. DL Herts 2003. *Recreations:* enthusiast and alchemist. *Address:* Green Fallow House, Bury Rise, Bovingdon, Herts HP3 0DN. *T:* (01442) 832154.

PEACOCK, Dr (William) James, AC 1994; BSc, PhD; FRS 1982; FAA; Chief, Division of Plant Industry, 1978–2003, Fellow, since 2004, Commonwealth Scientific and Industrial Research Organization; Chief Scientist, Australian Government, 2006–08; *b* 14 Dec. 1937; *m* 1961, Margaret Woodward; one *s* two *d*. *Educ:* Katoomba High Sch.; Univ. of Sydney (BSc, PhD). FAA 1976. CSIRO Postdoctoral Fellow, 1963 and Vis. Associate Prof. of Biology, 1964–65, Univ. of Oregon; Res. Consultant, Oak Ridge National Lab., USA, 1965; res. staff, Div. of Plant Industry, CSIRO, 1965–. Adjunct Prof. of Biology, Univ. of Calif, San Diego, 1969; Vis. Prof. of Biochem., Stanford Univ., 1970; Vis. Distinguished Prof. of Molecular Biol., Univ. of Calif, LA, 1977; Distinguished Prof., UTS, 2011–. Pres., Aust. Academy of Sci., 2002–06. For. Associate, US Nat. Acad. of Scis, 1990; For. Fellow, Indian Nat. Science Acad., 1990. FTSE (FTS 1988); FAIAST (FAIAS 1989). Hon. DSc: Charles Sturt, 1996; Ghent, 2004; NSW, 2008; Univ. of Technol., Sydney, 2014; Hon. DAgrSc Sydney, 2002. Edgeworth David Medal, Royal Soc. of NSW, 1967; Lemberg Medal, Aust. Biochem. Soc., 1978; BHP Bicentennial Prize for Pursuit of Excellence in Science and Technol., 1988; CSIRO Medal for Leadership of Div. of Plant Industry, 1989; Burnet Medal, Aust. Acad. of Sci., 1989; (jtly) Prime Minister's Prize for Science (inaugural winner), 2000; CSIRO Lifetime Achievement Award, 2005; Radobank Leadership Award, 2012; ACT Sen. Australian of the Yr, 2013. *Publications:* editor of 5 books on genetics and molecular biology; approx. 350 papers. *Recreations:* cultivation of native plants, bushwalking. *Address:* 16 Brassey Street, Deakin, ACT 2600, Australia. *T:* (home) (2) 62814485.

PEACOCKE, Prof. Christopher Arthur Bruce, FBA 1990; Professor of Philosophy, since 2004, Johnsonian Professor of Philosophy, since 2013, and Chair, Department of Philosophy, since 2013, Columbia University; Collaborative Fellow, Institute of Philosophy, School of Advanced Study, University of London, since 2016; *b* 22 May 1950; *s* of late Rev. Dr Arthur Robert Peacocke, MBE; *m* 1980, Teresa Anne Rosen; one *s* one *d*. *Educ:* Magdalen College Sch., Oxford; Exeter Coll., Oxford (MA, BPhil, DPhil; Hon. Fellow, 2017). Kennedy Schol., Harvard Univ., 1971; Sen. Schol., Merton Coll., Oxford, 1972; Jun. Res. Fellow, Queen's Coll., Oxford, 1973; Prize Fellow, All Souls Coll., Oxford, 1975; Fellow and Tutor, New Coll., Oxford, and CUF Lectr in Philosophy, 1979–85; Susan Stebbing Prof. of Philosophy, KCL, 1985–88; Waynflete Prof. of Metaphysical Philosophy, Univ. of Oxford and Fellow of Magdalen Coll., Oxford, 1989–2000; Prof. of Philosophy, New York Univ., 2000–04; Richard Wollheim Prof. of Philosophy, UCL, 2007–15; Chm., Promotions and Tenure Cttee, Faculty of Arts and Scis, Columbia Univ., 2011–13. Visiting Professor: Berkeley, 1975; Ann Arbor, 1978; UCLA, 1981; Maryland, 1987; NY Univ., 1996–99; Vis. Fellow, ANU, 1981; Fellow, Center for Advanced Study in the Behavioral Sciences, Stanford, 1983; Vis. Res. Associate, Center for Study of Language and Information, Stanford, 1984; Leverhulme Personal Res. Professorship, 1996–2000. Lectures: Whitehead, Harvard, 2001; Immanuel Kant, Stanford, 2003; Content and Context, Institut Jean Nicod, Paris, 2010; Gareth Evans Meml, Oxford, 2010; Kohut, Chicago, 2011; Master-Seminar, Fribourg Univ., 2015; Sainsbury, KCL, 2018. Pres., Mind Assoc., 1986; Member, Steering Committee: European Soc. for Philosophy and Psychology, 1991–95; Presidential Scholars in Society and Neurosci., Columbia Univ., 2014–. Fellow, Amer. Acad. of Arts and Scis, 2010. Hon. DLitt Warwick, 2007. *Publications:* Holistic Explanation: action, space, interpretation, 1979; Sense and Content, 1983; Thoughts: an essay on content, 1986; A Study of Concepts, 1992; Being Known, 1999; The Realm of Reason, 2004; Truly Understood, 2008; The Mirror of the World: subjects, consciousness, and self-consciousness, 2014; The Primacy of Metaphysics, 2019; papers on philosophy of mind and language, metaphysics and epistemology, and the perception of music, in Jl of Philosophy, Philosophical Rev., etc. *Recreations:* music, visual arts. *Address:* Department of Philosophy, Columbia University, 1150 Amsterdam Avenue, 708 Philosophy Hall, MC 4971, New York, NY 10027, USA. *T:* (212) 8543384.

PEAKE, John Fordyce; consultant; Associate Director (Scientific Development), Natural History Museum, 1989–92; *b* 4 June 1933; *s* of late William Joseph Peake and of Helena (*née* Fordyce); *m* 1963, Pamela Joyce Hollis; two *d*. *Educ:* City of Norwich Grammar Sch.; University Coll. London (BSc). National Trust, 1955–56; Norwich Technical Coll., 1956–58; Nature Conservancy Studentship, 1958–59; British Museum (Natural History): Research Fellow, 1959–61; Sen. Scientific Officer, 1961–69; PSO, 1969–71; Dep. Keeper, 1971–85; Keeper of Zoology, 1985–89. Hon. Research Associate, Bernice P. Bishop Mus., Honolulu, 1972. Royal Society: Member: Aldabra Research Cttee, 1972–77; Southern Zones Cttee, 1982–86; Unitas Malacologica: Treas. 1962–63, Mem. Council, 1963–75; Vice Pres., Malacological Soc. of London, 1976–78; Council Mem., Zoological Soc. of London, 1985–88. *Publications:* (editor and contributor with Dr V. Fretter) Pulmonates, 3 vols, 1975–79; papers on taxonomy, biogeography and ecology of terrestrial molluscs in sci. jls. *Recreations:* gardening, local history. *Address:* Crows Nest, Back Lane, Blakeney, Holt, Norfolk NR25 7NP. *T:* (01263) 740388.

PEAKE, John Morris, CBE 1986; Managing Director, Baker Perkins Holdings, 1980–85; *b* 26 Aug. 1924; *s* of late Albert Edward Peake and Ruby Peake (*née* Morris); *m* 1953, Elizabeth Rought (*d* 2018); one *s* one *d*. *Educ:* Repton School; Clare College, Cambridge (Mech. Scis Tripos; MA 1949); Royal Naval College, Greenwich (Dip. Naval Arch.). CEng, FIMechE; CMath, FIMA. Royal Corps of Naval Constructors, 1944–50; Personnel Administration Ltd, 1950–51; Baker Perkins (BP): joined 1951; Dir, parent co., 1956; Jt Man. Dir, BP Ltd, 1963–66; Man. Dir, BP Pty, 1969–74, in Australia; Pres., BP Inc., 1975–77, in USA; Dep. Man. Dir, BP Holdings, 1978–79; Chm., Baker Perkins plc, 1984–87. Chairman: Cambridgeshire Careers Guidance Ltd, 1995–98; Careers Services Nat. Assoc., 1997–98. Member: Council, CBI, 1980–89 (Chairman: Overseas Schols Bd, 1981–87; Educn and Trng Cttee, 1986–88); Council, BTEC, 1986–89 (Chm., Bd for Engineering, 1985–91); MSC, subseq. Trng Commn, 1986–88; RSA Examinations Bd, 1987–93 (Chm., 1989–93); RSA Council, 1989–93; Design Council, 1991–93 (Chm. Educn Cttee, 1990–94); Chm., Greater Peterborough Partnership, 1994–95; Vice Chm., Gtr Peterborough TEC, 1990–94. Chm., Nene Park Trust, 1988–93. Hockey Silver Medal, London Olympics, 1948. CCMI. Hon. DTech CNAA, 1986. *Recreations:* sport, travel. *Address:* 14 Beech Court, 33B Arterberry Road, Wimbledon, SW20 8AG. *T:* (020) 3105 6256. *Clubs:* East India; Hawks (Cambridge).

PEAKE, Joseph Anthony; educational consultant, Independent Schools Teacher Induction Panel, since 2016; *b* Manchester, 13 March 1954; *s* of Patrick and Margaret Peake; *m* 1981, Julie Foster; two *s* one *d*. *Educ:* St Cuthbert's RC Sch., Bolton; Queen's Coll., Oxford (MA Chem.; PGCE). VSO, Ghana, 1976–78; Asst Master, Manchester GS, 1979–84; Hd of Chemistry and Dir of Curriculum, Millfield Sch., 1984–94; Headmaster, St George's Coll., Weybridge, 1995–2016. Chief Examr, A-Level Chem., 1990–95. Mem., Ind. Schs Inspectorate Cttee, 1999–2003. Mem., Soc. of Heads, 2005 (Chm., Educn Cttee, 1998–2003). Mem., Ind. Schs Governing Council, 2006–09. Chm., Catholic Ind. Schs Conf., 2009–15. Governor: New Hall Sch., 2016– (Vice Chm., 2018–); King's Ely, 2017–. *Publications:* Chemistry for Senior Secondary Schools, 1990. *Recreations:* music, walking, Bolton Wanderers. *Address:* Easter House, The Street, Horringer, Suffolk IP29 5SJ. *Club:* East India.

PEAKE, Timothy Nigel, CMG 2016; FRAeS; astronaut, European Space Agency, since 2009; *b* Chichester, 7 April 1972; *s* of Nigel and Angela Peake; *m* Rebecca; two *s*. *Educ:* Chichester High Sch. for Boys; RMA, Sandhurst; Portsmouth Univ. (BSc Hons Flight Dynamics 2005). Commnd AAC, 1992; qualified as helicopter pilot, 1994; Instructor, 1998; Test Pilot, 2005–09 (retired as Major, 2009); Sen. Test Pilot, AugustaWestland Helicopters, 2009. Principia mission, long-duration flight to Internat. Space Station, 2015–16. Mem., Defence Innovation Adv. Panel, MoD, 2017–. FBIS. Mem., Soc. of Exptl Test Pilots. *Publications:* Hello, is this planet Earth?, 2016; Ask an Astronaut: my guide to life in space, 2017; The Astronaut Selection Test, 2018. *Recreations:* diving, ski-ing, flying, family. *Address:* European Astronaut Centre, Linder Höhe, 51147 Cologne, Germany. *T:* 22036001224. *E:* astrocom@esa.int.

PEAKER, Prof. Malcolm, DSc, PhD; FRS 1996; FZS, FRSE; Director, Hannah Research Institute, Ayr, 1981–2003; Hannah Professor, University of Glasgow, 1981–2003; *b* 21 Aug. 1943; *s* of Ronald Smith Peaker and Marian (*née* Tomasin); *m* 1965, Stephanie Jane Large; three *s*. *Educ:* Henry Mellish Grammar Sch., Nottingham; Univ. of Sheffield (BSc Zoology; DSc); Univ. of Hong Kong (SRC NATO Scholar; PhD). FZS 1969; FRSB (FIBiol 1979); FRSE 1983. Inst. of Animal Physiology, ARC, 1968–78; Head, Dept of Physiol., Hannah Res. Inst., 1978–81. Chm. Bd, London Zoo, 1992–93; Vice-Pres., Council, Zoological

Soc. of London, 1992–94; Mem. Council, RSE, 1999–2002. Mem., Rank Prize Funds Adv. Cttee on Nutrition, 1997–. Scientific Governor, British Nutrition Foundn, 1997– (Chm., 2002–04). Non-exec. Dir, Edinburgh Instruments Ltd, 2004–11. Raine Distinguished Visitor, Univ. of WA, 1998. Munro Kerr Lecture, Munro Kerr Soc., 1997; Annual Lecture, Edinburgh Centre for Rural Res./RSE/Inst. of Biol., 2000; Dist. Lectr, Univ. of Hong Kong, 2000. Hon. DSc Hong Kong, 2000. Mem. Editorial Board: Jl of Dairy Science, 1975–78; Internat. Zoo Yearbook, 1978–82; Jl of Endocrinology, 1981–91; Procs of RSE, 1989–92; Mammary Gland Biology and Neoplasia, 1993–2000; Editor, British Jl of Herpetology, 1977–81. *Publications:* Salt Glands in Birds and Reptiles, 1975; (ed) Avian Physiology, 1975; (ed) Comparative Aspects of Lactation, 1977; (ed jtly) Physiological Strategies in Lactation, 1984; (ed jtly) Intercellular Signalling in the Mammary Gland, 1995; (ed jtly) Biological Signalling and the Mammary Gland, 1997; papers in physiol, endocrinol, zool, biochem., vet. and agricl science jls. *Recreations:* vertebrate zoology, natural history, photography (video and still), golf, grumbling about bureaucrats. *Address:* Rushmere, 13 Upper Crofts, Alloway, Ayr KA7 4QX. *Club:* Royal Troon Golf.

**PEARCE, Prof. Alastair Tom Parslow**, PhD; President, LASALLE College of Arts, Singapore, 2008–12; *b* 9 Dec. 1953; *s* of Tom and Florence Pearce; *m* Dr Maureen Cleary. *Educ:* Royal Acad. of Music (LRAM); King's Coll., London (BMus, MMus; PhD). Nat. Advr for Computing in the Arts, Univ. of Oxford, 1979–82; University of Central England: Vice-Principal, Birmingham Conservatoire, 1994–98; Dean, Fac. of Educn, 1998–2001; Principal, Rose Bruford Coll., 2001–08. *Publications:* contribs to music jls and articles on managing performing arts higher educn. *Recreations:* fine wine, cooking, writing.

**PEARCE, Andrew John**, OBE 2013; HM Diplomatic Service; Governor of Montserrat, since 2018; *b* 7 Oct. 1960; *s* of Edward Peter Pearce and Renee Joyce Pearce; *m* 1986, Pornpun Pathumvivatana; one *s* one *d*. *Educ:* St Catherine's Coll., Oxford (MA 1st Cl. Hons Chemistry 1983). Joined FCO, 1983; Third Sec., Nr East and N Africa Dept, FCO, 1983–84; lang. trng, SOAS, London, 1984–85; Second Sec. (Pol), Bangkok, 1985–88; Head: Chemical Weapons Sect., Arms Control and Disarmament Dept, FCO, 1988–90; Iberian Sec., S European Dept, FCO, 1990–92; First Secretary: Pol and Public Affairs, Tel Aviv, 1992–96; Econ. Affairs, Pretoria, 1996–2000; Counsellor and Deputy Head of Mission: Bucharest, 2001–03; Bangkok, 2004–08; Hd of Security, FCO, 2009–15; Dir, FCO Services, 2015–16; Chargé d'Affaires, Lithuania, 2017. *Recreations:* tennis, long-distance walking, exploring, cat rearing, wildlife spotting, gardening. *Address:* c/o Foreign and Commonwealth Office, King Charles Street, SW1A 2AH. *E:* andy.pearce@fco.gov.uk.

**PEARCE, Brian**; *see* Pearce, J. B.

**PEARCE, Christopher Donovan James**; non-executive Chairman, Proteome Sciences (formerly Electrophoretics International) plc, since 2016 (Chief Executive Officer, then Executive Chairman, 1991–2016); *b* 1 March 1953; *m* 1981, Sandra Lynette Jenkins; two *s* one *d* (and one *d* decd). *Educ:* St John's Coll., Hurstpierpoint. CFA (AIIMR 1977). Partner, Scott Goff Hancock & Co., 1971, acquired by Smith New Court Securities plc, 1986, Dir, 1986–90; Exec. Chm. and Jt Founder, Fitness First, 1992–2003; non-exec. Dir, Fitness First Hldgs Ltd, 2003–05. Mem., London Stock Exchange, 1978–90; MSI (Dip) 1990. *Recreations:* theatre, ballet, opera, Rugby, golf, tennis. *Address:* Proteome Sciences plc, Hamilton House, Mabledon Place, WC1H 9BB. *Club:* Burhill Golf.

**PEARCE, Sir (Daniel Norton) Idris**, Kt 1990; CBE 1982; TD 1972; DL; Deputy Chairman, English Partnerships, 1993–2001; *b* 28 Nov. 1933; *s* of late Lemuel George Douglas Pearce and Evelyn Mary Pearce; *m* 1963, Ursula Helene Langley (marr. diss. 1997); two *d*. *Educ:* West Buckland Sch.; College of Estate Management. FRICS. Commnd RE, 1958; comd 135 Field Survey Sqdn, RE(TA), 1970–73. Joined Richard Ellis, 1959: Partner, 1961–92; Man. Partner, 1981–87; Consultant, 1992–2000. Chairman: English Estates, 1989–94; Flexit Cos, 1993–98; Varsity Funding, 1995–2000; Redburgh Ltd, 1996–2000; Director: The Phoenix Initiative, 1991; ITC, 1992–94; Nat. Mortgage Bank, 1992–97; Swan Hill (formerly Higgs & Hill), 1993–2002; Dusco UK Ltd, 1993–2002; Innisfree, 1996–2006; Millennium & Copthorne Hotels, 1996–2006; Regalian, 1998–2001; Resolution, 1998–2002. Royal Instn of Chartered Surveyors: Member: Gen. Council, 1980–94; Management Bd, 1984–91; Chm., Parly and Public Affairs Cttee, 1984–89; Vice Pres., 1986–90; Pres., 1990–91. Chm., Internat. Assets Valuation Standards Cttee, 1981–86. Member: Adv. Panel for Instnl Finance in New Towns, 1974–80; Sec. of State for Health and Social Security Inquiry into Surplus Land in the NHS, 1982; PSA Adv. Bd, 1981–86; FCO Adv. Panel on Diplomatic Estate, 1985–97; Financial Reporting Review Panel, 1991–93; Bd, London Forum, 1993–2001; Property Advr, NHS Management Bd, 1985–90; Dep. Chm., Urban Regeneration Agency, 1993–2001; Dir, London First Centre, 1995–2001. Chm., Higher Educn Funding Council for Wales, 1992–96; Member: UFC, 1991–93; HEFCE, 1992–96. Vice Chm., Greater London TA&VRA, 1991–94 (Mem., 1970–98; Chm., Works and Bldgs Sub-Cttee, 1983–90). Chm. Develt Bd, Nat. Art-Collections Fund, 1988–92. Dir, English Courtyard Assoc., 2007–09. Member: Court, City Univ., 1987–2000; Council, Univ. of Surrey, 1993–2004 (Pro-Chancellor, 1994–2004, now Emeritus, Chm., 1998–2001); Council, Reading Univ., 1997–2000; Comr, Royal Hosp., 1995–2001. Chairman: Governors, Stanway Sch., Dorking, 1982–85; W Buckland Sch. Foundn, 2002–07. Trustee, Rochester Bridge Trust, 1991–94. Governor: Peabody Trust, 1992–2003; RCA, 1997–2012 (Sen. Fellow 2012). Contested (C) Neath, 1959. DL Greater London, 1986. Hon. Fellow: Coll. of Estate Management, 1987; Univ. of Wales Cardiff, 1997; Centenary Fellow, Thames Poly., 1991; Companion, De Montfort Univ., 1992. Hon. Col, 135 Ind. Topographic Sqn, RE(V), TA, 1989–94. FRSA 1989. Hon. DSc: City, 1990; Oxford Poly., 1991; Salford Univ., 1991; Hon. DEng West of England, 1994; Hon. DTech E London, 1999; DUniv: Surrey, 2004; Glamorgan, 2010. Royal Engineers Gold Medal, 2011. *Publications:* A Call to Talent, 1993; various articles on valuation and property matters. *Recreations:* reading, opera, ballet, travel. *Club:* Brooks's.

**PEARCE, Fred**; *see* Pearce, L. F.

**PEARCE, Gareth David**, FCA; Chairman, Smith & Williamson, 2000–13; *b* 13 Aug. 1953; *s* of late Howard Spencer Pearce and Enid Norma Pearce (*née* Richards); *m* 1984, Virginia Louise Miller; four *d*. *Educ:* Abingdon Sch.; Balliol Coll., Oxford (MA). FCA 1997 (ACA 1979). Peat Marwick Mitchell & Co., 1975–81; Electra Investment Trust plc, 1982–86, Dir, Electra Mgt plc, 1984–86; Smith & Williamson, Chartered Accountants: Dir, 1986–2013; Hd, Corporate Finance Dept, 1986–95; Man. Dir, 1995–2000. Chm., Nexia Internat., 2000–08. Dir, Nat. Mutual Life Assce Soc., 1997–2002 (Dep. Chm., 1999–2002). *Recreations:* chess, fishing, reading, travelling. *Address:* Bewley Court, Lacock, Wilts SN15 2PG. *T:* (01249) 730573. *Club:* Hurlingham.

**PEARCE, Geoffrey John**; Director of Finance and Resources, London Borough of Redbridge, 1999–2015; *b* Edgware, 7 Oct. 1951; *s* of Ridley and Peggy Pearce; *m* 1982, Janet McIntyre; one *s* one *d*. *Educ:* Wembley Co. Grammar Sch.; Nottingham Univ. (BA Hons Philosophy 1973). CIPFA 1977. Accountancy Asst, London Borough of Barnet, 1973–74; Sen. Accountancy Asst, Royal Borough of Kensington and Chelsea, 1974–76; Senior Accountant: London Borough of Brent, 1976–80; City of London, 1980–83; Gp Accountant, London Borough of Brent, 1983–85; London Borough of Redbridge: Chief Accountant, 1985–88; Chief Payments and Benefits Officer, 1988–99; Finance Dir, E London Waste Authy, 1999–2015. Advr to govt and professional wkg gps on London finance, schools funding, housing finance and public sector auditing. Pres., 2006, Sec., 2008–15, Soc. of London Treasurers. Freeman, City of London, 1981. *Publications:* contrib. articles to local govt and IT/computer jls. *Recreations:* music, gym, hoping Spurs win a trophy. *E:* Geoff.PearceServices@gmail.com.

**PEARCE, Howard John Stredder**, CVO 1993; HM Diplomatic Service, retired; Governor of the Falkland Islands and Commissioner, South Georgia and the South Sandwich Islands, 2002–06; *b* 13 April 1949; *s* of late Ernest Victor Pearce and Ida (*née* Booth); *m* 2004, Caroline Thomée; one *d*. *Educ:* City of London Sch.; Pembroke Coll., Cambridge (MA, LLB). Joined HM Diplomatic Service, 1972; FCO, 1972–74; Third Sec., Buenos Aires, 1975–78; FCO, 1978–83; First Sec. and Hd of Chancery, Nairobi, 1983–87; FCO, 1987–90; Sen. Associate Mem., St Antony's Coll., Oxford, 1990–91; Dep. Hd of Mission, Budapest, 1991–94; Fellow, Center for Internat. Affairs, Harvard Univ., 1994–95; Hd, Central European Dept, FCO, 1996–99; High Comr, Malta, 1999–2002. Mem., Exec. Cttee, VSO, 1988–90. Chairman: S Georgia Heritage Trust, 2006–16; Exhibiting Socs of Scottish Artists, 2008–17; Fortingall Art, 2012–17; Scottish Trust for Underwater Archaeol., 2013–19; Develt Trust and Campaign Bd, Perth Coll., 2016–18; MyParkScotland, 2016–18; Black Mountains Chamber Music Trust, 2019–; Dep. Chm., Greenspace Scotland, 2009–15. Trustee, New Island Conservation Trust, 2008–. Officer's Cross (Republic of Hungary), 1999. *Recreations:* classical music, opera, reading, travel.

**PEARCE, Sir Idris**; *see* Pearce, Sir D. N. I.

**PEARCE, Jessica Mary**; *see* Hand, J. M.

**PEARCE, (John) Brian**, OBE 2000; Director, The Inter Faith Network for the United Kingdom, 1987–2007; *b* 25 Sept. 1935; *s* of late George Frederic Pearce and Constance Josephine Pearce; *m* 1960, Michelle Etcheverry; four *s*. *Educ:* Queen Elizabeth Grammar Sch., Wakefield; Brasenose Coll., Oxford (BA). Asst Principal: Min. of Power, 1959; Colonial Office, 1960; Private Sec. to Parly Under-Sec. of State, 1963; Principal: Colonial Office, 1964; Dept of Economic Affairs, 1967; Principal Private Sec. to Sec. of State for Economic Affairs, 1968–69; Asst Sec., Civil Service Dept, 1969, Under-Sec., 1976; Under-Sec., HM Treasury, 1981–86, retd. MLitt Lambeth, 1993; Hon. DLaws Warwick, 2009; Hon. DD Heythrop Coll., Univ. of London. *Recreations:* comparative theology, philosophy, music, travel. *Address:* 1B Allison Grove, Dulwich, SE21 7ER.

**PEARCE, Prof. John Martindale**, DPhil; FRS 2006; FLSW; Professor of Psychology, Cardiff University, 1992–2017; *b* 6 Dec. 1947; *s* of Jack and Mavis Pearce; *m* 1976, Victoria Anne Bradley; one *s* two *d*. *Educ:* Univ. of Leeds (BSc Hons); Univ. of Sussex (DPhil). Lectr, Sch. of Psychol., Cardiff Univ., 1980–92. Vis. Prof., Dept of Psychol., Duke Univ., 1987–88; Vis. Fellow, Inst. of Advanced Study, Indiana Univ., Bloomington, 1999; Vis. Erskine Fellow, Univ. of Canterbury, Christchurch, 2001; Humboldt Res. Fellow, Philipps Univ., Marburg, 2010–11. Ed., Qly Jl of Experimental Psychology: Comparative and Physiological Psychology, 1997–2000. Pres., Exptl Psychol. Soc., 2012–14. FLSW 2010. *Publications:* Introduction to Animal Cognition, 1987, 3rd edn as Animal Learning and Cognition: an introduction, 2008. *Recreations:* music, travelling in remote places. *Address:* School of Psychology, Cardiff University, Cardiff CF10 3YG. *T:* (029) 2087 4483, *Fax:* (029) 2087 4848. *E:* pearcejm@cf.ac.uk.

**PEARCE, Laurence Frederick, (Fred)**; freelance author and journalist, since 1989; *b* Faversham, Kent, 30 Dec. 1951; *s* of Kenneth and Sheila Pearce; *m* 1979, Sarah Willis; two *d* (one *s* decd). *Educ:* Maidstone Grammar Sch.; Sidney Sussex Coll., Cambridge. Ed., Bacus student newspaper, 1975–76; Dep. Ed., What's Brewing?, Campaign for Real Ale, 1977–78; Press Officer, Price Commn, 1978–79; reporter, Municipal Engrg, 1979–81; News Ed., 1982–89, Envmtl Consultant, 1992–, New Scientist. Mem., NUJ. *Publications:* Watershed, 1982; Acid Rain, 1986; Turning Up the Heat, 1989; Green Warriors, 1990; (with Ian Winton) Ian and Fred's Big Green Book, 1992, 2nd edn 2010; The Dammed, 1992; Heinz Guide to British Beaches, 1994; (with P. Harrison) AAAS Atlas of Population and Environment, 2000; Global Warning: essential science, 2002; Keepers of the Spring, 2004; Deep Jungle, 2005; When the Rivers Run Dry, 2006, 2nd edn 2019; The Last Generation, 2007; Confessions of an Ecosinner, 2008; The Climate Files, 2010; Peoplequake, 2010; Earth: then and now, 2010; The Landgrabbers, 2012; The New Wild, 2015; Fallout, 2018; (jtly) Our Planet, 2019. *Address:* 40 Crieff Road, SW18 2EA. *E:* pearcefred1@hotmail.co.uk.

**PEARCE, Rev. Neville John Lewis**; Priest-in-charge, Swainswick/Woolley, Diocese of Bath and Wells, 1993–98; Chief Executive, Avon County Council, 1982–89; *b* 27 Feb. 1933; *s* of John and Ethel Pearce; *m* 1958, Eileen Frances Potter (*d* 2014); two *d*. *Educ:* Queen Elizabeth's Hosp., Bristol; Silcoates Sch., Wakefield; Univ. of Leeds (LLB Hons 1953, LLM 1954); Trinity Theol Coll., Bristol. Asst Solicitor: Wakefield CBC, 1957–59; Darlington CBC, 1959–61; Chief Asst Solicitor, Grimsby CBC, 1961–63, Dep. Town Clerk, 1963–65; Dep. Town Clerk, Blackpool CBC, 1965–66; Town Clerk, Bath CBC, 1967–73; Dir of Admin and County Solicitor, Avon CC, 1973–82. Ordained (C of E), 1991; Asst Curate, St Swithin, Walcot, Bath, 1991–93. *Recreations:* family and friends, ministering to local churches. *Address:* Penshurst, Weston Lane, Bath BA1 4AB. *T:* (01225) 426925.

**PEARCE, Prof. Nicholas John**, FSA; Sir John Richmond Professor of Fine Art, University of Glasgow, since 2012; *b* 7 Nov. 1956; *s* of late Dennis William Pearce and of Audrey Joyce Pearce (*née* Bray); partner, Sarah Louise Foskett; two *d*. *Educ:* Huddersfield Poly. (BA Politics and Oriental Studies); Sch. of Oriental and African Studies, Univ. of London (MA Chinese Art and Archaeol). Curatorial Asst, V&A Mus., 1983–87; Curator, Eastern Art and Design, Burrell Collection, Glasgow Mus. 1987–96 (Hon. Curator, 1998–); Dep. Keeper (pt-time), Oriental Mus., Univ. of Durham, 1994–96; University of Glasgow: Lectr, then Sen. Lectr, 1997–2006; Hd, Hist. of Art, 1998–2003 and 2008–10; Prof., 2007–12; Hd, Sch. of Culture and Creative Arts, 2010–14. Exchange Prof., Hist. of Decorative Arts Prog., 2012–15, Fellow, Smithsonian Provenance Res. Initiative, 2014–15, Smithsonian Res. Associate, 2017–, Smithsonian Instn, Washington. Hon. Res. Associate, Dept of Hist. and Applied Art, Nat. Mus of Scotland, 1998–2005. Trustee: Textile Conservation Foundn, 2012–; Nat. Galls of Scotland, 2014–; Sir William Burrell Trust, 2014–. FSA 2011; FRSA 2002. Hon. Fellow, Faculty of Arts, Univ. of Edinburgh, 1991–93. *Publications:* (jtly) Chinese Export Art and Design, 1987; (jtly) Mingei - The Living Tradition in Japanese Arts, 1991; (with J. Wilkinson) Harmony and Contrast: a journey through East Asian art, 1996; Photographs of Peking, China 1861–1908: through Peking with a camera, 2005; (with J. Steuber) Original Intentions: essays on production, reproduction and interpretation in the arts of China, 2012; (ed jtly) William Hunter's World: William Hunter and the art and science of eighteenth century collecting, 2015; (contrib.) Imagining Qianlong, Louis XV's Chinese Emperor Tapestries and Battle Scene Prints at the Imperial Court in Beijing, 2017; (contrib.) Collecting and Displaying China's

'Summer Palace' in the West: the Yuanmingyuan in Britain and France, 2018; contrib. to books and jls. *Recreations:* music, painting and decorating, an attempt at gardening. *Address:* School of Culture and Creative Arts, University of Glasgow, 8 University Gardens, Glasgow G12 8QH. *T:* (0141) 330 3826. *E:* nick.pearce@glasgow.ac.uk.

**PEARCE, Prof. Nicholas Robin,** FAcSS; Professor of Public Policy and Director, Institute for Policy Research, University of Bath, since 2015; *b* 24 May 1968; *s* of late Peter Bailes Pearce and of Lynda Margaret Pearce; *m* 2000, Rebecca Asher; one *s* one *d*. *Educ:* Univ. of Manchester (BA Hons); Balliol Coll., Oxford (MPhil Politics). Res. Asst to Bryan Davies, MP, 1993–97; Res. Fellow in Educn, IPPR, 1997; Special Advr to Leader of H of C, 1998; Sen. Res. Fellow in Educn, IPPR, 1998–99; Advr (pt-time), Social Exclusion Unit, 1998–99; Special Adviser: to Sec. of State for Educn and Employment, 1999–2001; to Home Sec., 2001–03; Dir, IPPR, 2004–07 and 2010–15; Hd, Strategic Policy, Prime Minister's Office, 2007–08; Hd, Prime Minister's Policy Unit, 2008–10. Mem., UK/India Roundtable, 2006–. Chm., Council of Trustees, Tavistock Inst. of Med. Psychol., 2014–; Member, Board: British Archtl Trust Bd (formerly RIBA Trust), 2008–14; RIBA, 2014–17. Founder Scholar, British Psychoanalytical Council, 2019. FAcSS 2018. Hon. FRIBA 2014. *Publications:* (with J. Hillman) Wasted Youth, 1998; (ed with J. Hallgarten) Tomorrow's Citizens, 2000; (ed with W. Paxton) Social Justice: building a fairer Britain, 2005; (jtly) Freedom's Orphans, 2006; (ed with J. Margo) Politics for a New Generation, 2007; (jtly) The Condition of Britain, 2014; (with M. Kenny) Shadows of Empire: the Anglosphere in British politics, 2018; (ed with G. Kelly) Britain Beyond Brexit, 2019. *Recreations:* twentieth century architecture, travel in South America. *Address:* Institute for Policy Research, University of Bath, Bath BA2 7AY. *E:* nicholasrpearce@googlemail.com.

**PEARCE, Peter Huxley;** Director, Mary Roxburghe Trust, since 2016; *b* 16 May 1956; *s* of Dr Alan John Pearce and Marion Joyce (*née* Wright); *m* 1983, Christina Zalichi; two *s*. *Educ:* Reading Univ. (BSc Hons Rural Estate Mgt). FRICS 1981. National Trust: Man. Land Agent, E Midlands Reg., 1982–87, Southern Reg., 1988–95; Dir, Uppark Repair Project, 1989–95; Dir, Landmark Trust, 1995–2012; Chief Exec., Edward James Foundn, 2012–15. Trustee, Edward James Foundn, 2008–11. *Recreations:* historic buildings, music, fishing, landscape and conservation, family life.

**PEARCE, Richard William; His Honour Judge Pearce;** a Circuit Judge, since 2015; Specialist Civil Circuit Judge, Manchester Civil Justice Centre, since 2018; *b* Brereton, Cheshire, 21 Jan. 1963; *s* of Raymond and Muriel Pearce; *m* 1986, Teresa Reape; two *s* one *d*. *Educ:* Abbot Beyne Sch., Burton-on-Trent; Trinity Coll., Cambridge (BA 1984). Called to the Bar, Middle Temple, 1985; in practice as barrister, specialising in clin. negligence and personal injury work, Manchester, 1985–2015; a Recorder, 2008–15. *Recreations:* music (especially choral singing), theatre, literature, ski-ing, allotmenteering. *Address:* Manchester Civil Justice Centre, 1 Bridge Street West, Manchester M60 9DJ.

**PEARCE, Prof. Robert Alasdair;** Professor in Law, University of Buckingham, 2010–16, now Emeritus; Professor Emeritus, University of Wales, Trinity St David, since 2008; *b* 28 Nov. 1951; *s* of Walter Charles Pearce and Dorothy Kate Pearce. *Educ:* George Dixon's Grammar Sch.; Cotham Grammar Sch.; Sir Thomas Rich's Sch.; Pembroke Coll., Oxford (BA Hons (Jurisprudence) 1973; BCL 1974; MA 1978). Lectr in Law: Univ. of Newcastle upon Tyne, 1974–79; Univ. of Lancaster, 1979–80; Lectr, then Statutory Lectr, UC, Cork, NUI, 1981–89; University of Buckingham: Sen. Lectr in Law, 1989–90; Prof. of Law of Property and Equity, 1990–2003; Dean, Acad. Affairs, 1993–94; Pro-Vice-Chancellor, 1994–2002; Actg Vice-Chancellor, 2000–01; Vice-Chancellor, Univ. of Wales, Lampeter, 2003–08. Welsh Supernumerary Fellow, Jesus Coll., Oxford, 2007–08. Vis. Prof., Univ. of Glos, 2010–. Auditor, HEQC, then QAA, 1993–2003; Mem., Adv. Cttee on Degree Awarding Powers, QAA, 2003–08; Chm., Postgrad. Internat. Assessment Bd, Irish Res. Council for Humanities and Social Scis, 2006–07 (Bd Mem., 2004–05). Chairman: Oxford Univ. Law Course Adv. Cttee, 1971–72; Univs Assoc. for Lifelong Learning Cymru, 2004–08. Mem., Future Skills Wales, 2003–06. Parkside Housing Group, Windsor: Dir, 1998–2003; Vice-Chm., 2000–02; Chm., 2002–03. Mem., Cttee of Mgt, Rockboro Sch. Assoc., 1983–87; Governor: Pebble Brook Sch., Aylesbury, 1997–2000; Rycotewood Coll., Thame, 2000–03 (Vice-Chm., 2001–03). Hon. LLD Buckingham, 2007. *Publications:* A Commentary on the Succession Act 1965, 2nd revd edn 1986; (with I. J. Dawson) Licences Relating to the Occupation or Use of Land, 1979; Land Law (of the Republic of Ireland and Northern Ireland), 1985, 3rd edn (with Dr John Mee) 2011; (with A. J. Stevens) The Law of Trusts and Equitable Obligations, 1995, 7th edn (with W. Barr) 2018; (with A. J. Stevens) Land Law, 1997, 5th edn 2013. *Recreation:* gardening.

**PEARCE, Robert Edgar;** QC 2006; *b* 22 June 1953; *s* of Edgar Pearce and Stella Mary Louise Pearce (*née* Dimock); *m* 1984, Janice Linscott; two *d*. *Educ:* Whitgift Sch.; Christ Church, Oxford (BA 1st Cl. Jurisprudence 1975; BCL 1976). Called to the Bar, Middle Temple, 1977; in practice at Chancery bar, 1978–; Bencher, Lincoln's Inn, 2013. Standing Counsel to the Charity Commn, 2001–06; Mem., Legal Adv. Commn, C of E, 2016–. *Publications:* (contrib. ed.) Butterworths Civil Court Practice, annually 1997–; (consultant ed.) Halsbury's Laws of England, vol. on Charities; various articles. *Recreations:* music, ski-ing. *Address:* Radcliffe Chambers, 11 New Square, Lincoln's Inn, WC2A 3QB. *T:* (020) 7831 0081, *Fax:* (020) 7405 2560. *E:* rpearce@radcliffechambers.com.

**PEARCE, Dame Shirley (Anne),** DBE 2014 (CBE 2005); PhD; Vice-Chancellor, Loughborough University, 2006–12; *b* 19 Feb. 1954; *m* 2012, Sir John Christopher Gains, *qv*. *Educ:* Norwich High Sch.; St Anne's Coll., Oxford (BA PPP 1975); Inst. of Psychiatry, Univ. of London (MPhil Clin. Psychol. 1977; PhD Psychol. 1986). Clin. psychologist, St Mary's Hosp., Paddington, 1977–81; Lectr, then Sen. Lectr in Psychol., UCL, 1981–94; University of East Anglia: Prof. of Health Psychol., 1994–2006; Dir, Sch. of Health Policy and Practice, 1994; Dean, Schs of Health, 1997–2000; Pro Vice-Chancellor, Health and Professional Schs, 2000–06. Mem. and Dep. Chair, Healthcare Commn, 2004–07; Mem., Cttee on Standards in Public Life, 2018–. Chair, Coll. of Policing, 2013–. Mem. Bd, HEFCE, 2009–15. Ext. Mem., Quality Assce Framework, Min. of Educn, Singapore, 2014–19. Trustee and Mem. Council, Univ. of Cambridge; Chm. of Court and Council, LSE, 2017–. *Publications:* (ed jtly) The Practice of Behavioural Medicine, 1989; (contrib.) Psychological Factors in Measurement in Pain, 2000; contribs to learned jls. *Recreations:* running, gardening.

**PEARCE, Teresa;** MP (Lab) Erith and Thamesmead, since 2010; *b* Southport, 1 Feb. 1955; *d* of Arthur and Josephine Farrington; two *d*. *Educ:* St Thomas More RC Sch., Eltham. Inland Revenue, 1975–79; Knox Cropper, 1989–99; Sen. Manager, PricewaterhouseCoopers, 1999–2009. Mem. (Lab) Bexley LBC, 1998–2002. Shadow Minister for Housing and Planning, 2015–16; Shadow Sec. of State for Communities and Local Govt, 2016–17. Mem., Erith Slopes Socialist Book Club. *Recreations:* cinema, reading, travel. *Address:* House of Commons, SW1A 0AA. *T:* (020) 7210 6936. *E:* teresa.pearce.mp@parliament.uk. *W:* www.teresapearce.org.uk.

**PEARCE, Trevor William,** CBE 2014; QPM 2006; Chairman, UK Anti-Doping, since 2017 (Board Member, 2016–17); *b* Bounds Green, North London, 29 Oct. 1956; *s* of David Pearce and Margaret Pearce (*née* Leitch); *m* 1980, Helen Jones; one *s* one *d*. *Educ:* Open Univ. (BA 1989); City Univ. (MPhil 1992). Constable to Detective Superintendent, Kent Co. Constabulary, 1975–98; National Crime Squad: Detective Superintendent to Dep. Dir Gen., 1998–2004; Dir Gen., 2004–06; Exec. Dir, 2006–10, Dir Gen., 2010–13, SOCA; Dir, Nat. Crime Agency, 2013–15. Mem., Gambling Commn, 2015–. Trustee: Canterbury Oast Trust, 2015–; Stop the Traffik, 2016–. *Publications:* contribs to jls on policing and risk. *Recreations:* Rugby, folk music, walking, working in allotment. *Address:* UK Anti-Doping, Fleetbank House, 2–6 Salisbury Square, EC4Y 8AG. *T:* (020) 3161 5013. *E:* trevor.pearce@ukad.org.uk. *Club:* Reform.

**PEARCE-HIGGINS, Daniel John;** QC 1998; **His Honour Judge Pearce-Higgins;** a Circuit Judge, since 2004; Designated Civil Judge, Worcester Combined Court, since 2009; *b* 26 Dec. 1949; *m*. *Educ:* St Paul's Sch., London; Univ. of Bristol (BSc Philosophy and Politics). Called to the Bar, Middle Temple, 1973, Bencher, 2009; an Asst Recorder, 1995–99; a Recorder, 1999–2004. Hon. Recorder, City of Hereford, 2016–. Mem., Mental Health Review Tribunal, 2000–. CEDR accredited mediator, 1999–2004. FCIArb 1999–2004. Mem., Prog. Adv. Cttee, Cumberland Lodge, 2007–15; Gov., Hereford Cathedral Perpetual Trust, 2014–. *Address:* c/o Worcester Combined Court Centre, Shirehall, Foregate Street, Worcester WR1 1EQ.

**PEARCEY, Oliver Henry James;** historic environment consultant, since 2006; Special Projects Director, English Heritage, 2004–06; *b* 13 June 1951; *s* of late Lawrence Henry Victor Pearcey and Gladys Winifred Pearcey (*née* Bond); *m* 1979, Elizabeth Platts; two *d*. *Educ:* Westminster Sch.; Univ. of Sussex (BSc Biochem). Department of the Environment: Admin. trainee, 1972–78; Principal, 1978–85; on secondment to GLC, 1981–83; English Heritage: Team Leader, 1985–88, Head, 1988–91, Historic Bldgs Div.; Dir, Conservation, Midlands Reg., 1991–94; Dep. Dir, 1994–97, Dir, 1997–2002, Conservation; Designation Dir, 2002–04. Mem., IHBC, 1998. *Recreations:* industrial archaeology, English salt-glaze stoneware, reading voraciously. *Address:* 125B Dalling Road, W6 0ET. *T:* (020) 8222 8468.

**PEAREY, David Dacre;** HM Diplomatic Service, retired; Governor, British Virgin Islands, 2006–10; *b* 15 July 1948; *s* of William Pearey and Dorothy Pearey; *m* 1996, Susan Anne (*née* Knowles); one *d*. *Educ:* Oundle Sch.; Bristol Univ. (BSc Hons Econs). Joined MoD as trainee, 1971; Pvte Sec. to Parly Under Sec. of State for Defence (RAF), 1974–76; joined FCO, 1979; First Secretary: Ankara, 1979–82; Energy and Policy Planning Depts, FCO, 1983–87; Dep. High Comr, Kampala, 1987–90; Southern European and Inspectorate Depts, FCO, 1990–95; Counsellor, Lagos, 1995–99; Dep. High Comr, Karachi, 2000–04; High Comr, Malawi, 2004–06. Mem., Glyndebourne Fest. Soc., 1998–. FRGS 1993. *Recreations:* travel, mountains, opera, walking, reading. *E:* dandspearey@aol.com. *Clubs:* Travellers, Hurlingham.

**PEARL, His Honour David Stephen,** PhD; a Circuit Judge, 1994–2012; a Deputy High Court Judge, 2008–12; an Upper Tribunal Judge (Administrative Appeals Chamber), 2008–12; National Chair, Medical Practitioners Tribunal Service, 2012–16; *b* 11 Aug. 1944; *s* of late Chaim Pearl and Anita Pearl (*née* Newman); *m* 1st, 1967, Susan Roer (marr. diss.); three *s*; 2nd, 1985, Gillian Furr (*née* Maciejewska); one step *s* one step *d*. *Educ:* George Dixon Grammar Sch., Birmingham; Westminster City Sch.; Birmingham Univ. (LLB); Queens' Coll., Cambridge (Sen. Scholar; LLM, MA, PhD). Called to the Bar, Gray's Inn, 1968, Bencher, 2002; Cambridge University: Asst Lectr in Law, 1967–72; Lectr, 1972–89; Res. Fellow, Queens' Coll., 1967–69; Fellow and Dir of Studies in Law, Fitzwilliam Coll., Cambridge, 1969–89 (Life Fellow, 1989); Prof. of Law and Dean, Sch. of Law, UEA, 1989–94, Hon. Prof., 1995–; a Recorder, 1992–94. Immigration Appeals Adjudicator, 1980–92; Chm., 1992–97, Pres., 1998–99, Immigration Appeal Tribunal; Chief Immigration Adjudicator, 1994–98; Pres., Care Standards Tribunal, 2002–08; Chm., Restricted Patients Panel, 2009–15. Mem., Judicial Appts Commn, 2006–12. Judicial Studies Board: Member: Civil and Family Cttee, 1994–96; Tribunals Cttee, 1996–99, 2004–11; Dir of Studies, 1999–2001. Vice-Pres., Internat. Soc. for Family Law, 1991–97. Ind. Mem., Standards Cttee, Uttlesford DC, 2015–; Dep. Ind. Mem., Civic Affairs Cttee, Cambridge CC, 2018–. Yorke Prize, Cambridge, 1972; Shaw Prize, Boston Coll. Law Sch., 1985; Van Heyden de Lancy Prize, Cambridge, 1991. *Publications:* A Textbook on Muslim Law, 1979, 3rd edn as Muslim Family Law (with W. Menski), 1998; Interpersonal Conflict of Laws in India, Pakistan and Bangladesh, 1980; (with K. Gray) Social Welfare Law, 1980; (jtly) Family Law and Society, 1983, 6th edn 2008; Family Law and Immigrant Communities, 1986; (with A. Grubb) Blood Testing AIDS and DNA Profiling, 1990; (jtly) Butterworth's Immigration Law Service, 1991–2007; (ed jtly) Clarke, Hall and Morrison on Children, 2004–14. *Recreations:* very amateur dramatics, Toastmasters Speakers Club. *Address:* c/o Littleton Chambers, 3 Kings Bench Walk, Temple, EC4Y 7HR. *T:* (020) 7797 8600.

**PEARL, Prof. Laurence Harris,** PhD; FRS 2008; Professor of Structural Biology, Genome Damage and Stability Centre, University of Sussex, since 2009; Head, Division of Structural Biology, Institute of Cancer Research, since 2017; *b* Manchester, 18 June 1956; *s* of Monty and Carole Pearl; *m* 1994, Frances M. G.; two *s* one *d*. Prof. of Structural Biol., UCL, 1996–99; Prof. of Protein Crystallography and Section Chm., Inst. of Cancer Res., 1999–2009; Hd, Sch. of Life Scis, Univ. of Sussex, 2009–17. Wellcome Trust Sen. Investigator, 2011–18. Mem., EMBO, 2005; MAE 2012. FMedSci 2007. Translational Cancer Res. Prize, Cancer Res. UK, 2013; Novartis Medal and Prize, Biochemical Soc., 2018. *Publications:* contrib. scientific jls. *Recreations:* feeding my family, juggling, computer animation, canoeing and river boating. *Address:* Genome Damage and Stability Centre, Science Park Road, University of Sussex, Falmer, Brighton, E Sussex BN1 9RQ. *E:* Laurence.Pearl@sussex.ac.uk.

**PEARL, Her Honour Patricia;** a Circuit Judge, 2006–18; *b* Derby, 5 June 1953; *d* of Thomas Andrew Smallwood and Eva May Smallwood; *m* 1975; one *d*; partner, Ian S. Hilton. *Educ:* Parkfield Cedars Grammar Sch., Derby; Rugby High Sch. for Girls; Lady Margaret Hall, Oxford (BA Hons Geog. 1974). Admitted solicitor, 1977; a District Judge, 1998–2006. Chm., Restricted Patients Panel, Tribunals Service Mental Health, 2009–15. *Publications:* Small Claims Procedure: a practical guide, 1999, 6th edn 2014; (contrib. ed) Civil Procedure (The White Book), 2001–16. *Recreations:* photography, walking the long-distance footpaths of Britain.

**PEARLMAN, Natasha Genia;** Consultant Editor, Glamour, since 2018; *b* London, 31 May 1982; *d* of Joseph Gershon Pearlman and Barbara Pearlman; *m* 2012, Ben Clerkin; two *d*. *Educ:* N London Collegiate Sch.; Univ. of Bristol (BA English 2004). Commng Ed., Daily Mail, 2006–10; Features Ed., News of the World, 2011; Deputy Editor: Fabulous mag., 2011–12; Elle UK, 2012–15; Ed., Grazia magazine, 2015–18. *Recreations:* cooking, obsessively attempting to recreate Ben's cookies at home, avid G2 and T2 puzzler.

**PEARLMAN, Her Honour Valerie Anne,** CBE 2008; a Circuit Judge, 1985–2008; Designated Family Circuit Judge, 1991–2008 (a Senior Circuit Judge, 2003–08); *b* 6 Aug. 1936; *d* of late Sidney and Marjorie Pearlman; *m* 1972; one *s* one *d*. *Educ:* Wycombe Abbey Sch. Called to the Bar, Lincoln's Inn, 1958, Bencher, 2002; a Recorder, 1982–85. Member: Parole Bd, 1989–94; Civil and Family Cttee, Judicial Studies Bd, 1992–97; Chm., Home Sec's Adv. Bd on Restricted Patients, 1991–98; Mem., Cttee on Mentally Disordered Offenders, Mental Health Foundn, 1992–95. Mem., Council of Circuit Judges, 1998–2001;

Vice-Pres., Inner London Magistrates' Assoc., 1999–. Patron, Children UK (formerly British Juvenile and Family Courts Soc.), 2000–. Member: Council, Marlborough Coll., 1989–97; Governing Body, Godolphin and and Latymer Sch., 1998–2003. Patron, Suzy Lamplugh Trust, 1987–. *Recreations:* gardening, reading.

**PEARMAN, Hugh Geoffrey,** MBE 2019; architecture and design critic; Editor, RIBA Journal, since 2006; *b* 29 May 1955; *s* of late Douglas Pearman and Tegwyn Pearman (*née* Jones); *m* 2005, Kate Hobson; two *s* two *d*. *Educ*: Skinners' Sch., Tunbridge Wells; St Chad's Coll., Durham Univ. (BA Hons Eng. Lang. and Lit.). Asst Editor, Building Design Magazine, 1978–82; Communications Editor, BDP, 1982–86; architecture and design critic, Sunday Times, 1986–2016. Member: Envmtl and Arts Panel, South Bank Employers' Gp, 1990–2000; Architectl Adv. Panel, Arts Council of GB, then of England, 1992–95; Council, RSA, 2004–06 (Chm., Art for Architecture Adv. Panel, 2000–04); Croydon Place Rev. Panel, 2017–. Curator, British Council internat. touring exhibn, 12 for 2000: Building for the Millennium, 1998–2000. Vis. teacher in architecture, Univ. of Greenwich, 1999–2000; Vis. Prof. in Architecture, RCA, 2015. Trustee and Dir, 2012–16, Vice Pres., 2014–16, AA. Founder and Juror, Stirling Prize for Architecture, 1996–98; judge, various architecture competitions; Mem. Nat. Panel, Civic Trust Awards, 2014–16. FRSA 1990. Hon. FRSS (Hon. FRBS 1996); Hon. FRIBA 2001. Contributor to television and radio. *Publications:* Excellent Accommodation, 1984; Rick Mather: urban approaches, 1992; The Ark, London, 1993; Contemporary World Architecture, 1998; Equilibrium: the work of Nicholas Grimshaw and Partners, 2000; (introd.) Ten Years, Ten Cities: Terry Farrell and Partners 1991–2001, 2002; (introd.) 30 Bridges, 2002; The Deep, 2002; The Architecture of Eden, 2003; Airports: a century of architecture, 2004; (contrib.) The Brits Who Built the Modern World, 2014; articles in newspapers, magazines and periodicals. *Recreations:* walking, looking, photographing. *Address:* 29 Nelson Road, N8 9RX. *T:* (020) 8374 5454. *E:* hughpearman@blueyonder.co.uk.

**PEARS, Dr Iain George;** author; *b* 8 Aug. 1955; *s* of George Derrick Pears and Betty Mitchell Pears (*née* Proudfoot); *m* 1985, Prof. Ruth Harris, *qv*; two *s*. *Educ*: Wadham Coll., Oxford (BA, MA); Wolfson Coll., Oxford (DPhil). Correspondent for Reuters: Italy, 1983–84; London, 1984–87; USA, 1987–89; France, 1989–90. *Publications:* The Discovery of Painting, 1988; The Raphael Affair, 1990; The Titian Committee, 1991; The Bernini Bust, 1992; The Last Judgement, 1993; Giotto's Hand, 1994; Death and Restoration, 1995; An Instance of the Fingerpost, 1997; The Immaculate Deception, 1999; The Dream of Scipio, 2002; The Portrait, 2005; Stone's Fall, 2009; Arcadia, 2015. *Recreation:* print collecting. *E:* iainpears@hotmail.com.

**PEARS, Mary Madeline;** *see* Chapman, M. M.

**PEARS, Ruth;** *see* Harris, R.

**PEARS, Tim(othy);** novelist; *b* 15 Nov. 1956; *s* of William Steuart Pears and Jill (*née* Charles-Edwards); *m* 1998, Hania Porucznik; one *s* one *d*. *Educ*: Exeter Sch.; National Film and Television Sch. (Directing course 1993). Various jobs, including building labourer, farm worker, night porter, teacher, museum gall. manager, etc. *Publications:* In the Place of Fallen Leaves, 1993 (Ruth Hadden Meml Award, 1993; Hawthornden Prize, 1994); In a Land of Plenty, 1997 (televised, 2001); A Revolution of the Sun, 2000; Wake Up, 2002; Blenheim Orchard, 2007; Landed, 2010; Disputed Land, 2011; In the Light of Morning, 2014; The Horseman, 2017; The Wanderers, 2018; The Redeemed, 2019. *Recreations:* football coaching, urban exploring, rural wandering. *Address:* 462 Banbury Road, Oxford OX2 7RG. *T:* (01865) 552605. *E:* pearznik@yahoo.co.uk. *W:* www.timpears.com.

**PEARS, Sir Trevor (Steven),** Kt 2017; CMG 2011; Executive Chairman, Pears Foundation, since 2000; Director, William Pears Group, since 1986; *b* London, 18 June 1964; *s* of Clive and Clarice Pears; *m* 1993, Daniela; one *s* two *d*. *Educ*: City of London Sch.; City of London Poly. (BA Hons Business Law). *Recreations:* golf, swimming, salsa dancing.

**PEARSE, Barbara Mary Frances, (Mrs M. S. Bretscher),** PhD; FRS 1988; Staff Scientist, Medical Research Council Laboratory of Molecular Biology, Cambridge, 1981–2005; *b* 24 March 1948; *d* of Reginald William Blake Pearse and Enid Alice (*née* Mitchell); *m* 1978, Mark Steven Bretscher, *qv*; one *s* one *d*. *Educ*: The Lady Eleanor Holles Sch., Hampton, Middx; University Coll. London (BSc Biochemistry, PhD; Fellow, 1996). MRC Res. Fellowship, 1972–74; Beit Meml Fellowship, 1974–77; SRC Advanced Fellowship, 1977–82; CRC Internat. Fellowship Vis. Prof., Stanford Med. Centre, USA, 1984–85. Mem., EMBO, 1982–. EMBO Medal, 1987. *Publications:* contribs to sci. jls. *Recreations:* wild flowers, planting trees, fresh landscapes. *Address:* Ram Cottage, 63 Commercial End, Swaffham Bulbeck, Cambridge CB25 0ND. *T:* (01223) 811276.

**PEARSE, Sir Brian (Gerald),** Kt 1994; FCIB; Deputy Chairman, Britannic Assurance Plc, 1997–2002; Chief Executive, Midland Bank, 1991–94; *b* 23 Aug. 1933; *s* of Francis and Eileen Pearse; *m* 1959, Patricia M. Callaghan; one *s* two *d*. *Educ*: St Edward's Coll., Liverpool. Martin's Bank Ltd, 1950; Barclays Bank, 1969–91: Local Dir, Birmingham, 1972; Gen. Man., 1977; Chief Exec. Officer, N America, 1983; Finance Dir, 1987–91; Dir, Midland Bank, 1994–95. Chm., Lucas Industries, later LucasVarity, PLC, 1994–98; non-executive Director: Smith & Nephew, 1993–2002; HSBC plc, 1992–94. Chm., Assoc. for Payments Clearing Services, 1987–91. Director: British American Chamber of Commerce, 1987–98; Private Finance Panel, 1993–95; BOTB, 1994–97; Charities Aid Foundn Bank, 1998–92. Chairman: Young Enterprise, 1992–95; British Invisibles, 1994–97; Housing Corp., 1994–97; Dep. Chm., Tor Homes, 1998–2003. Chm. Council, Centre for Study of Financial Innovation, 1998–2013. Member: Council for Industry of Higher Educn, 1994–98; City Promotion Panel, 1995–97; Bd of Banking Supervision, 1998–2001. Treas., KCL, 1992–99 (FKC 1996). Pres., CIB, 1993–94. Trustee, Charities Aid Foundn, 1995–99. Gov., Univ. of Plymouth, 1997–2006 (Univ. Govs, 2002–06). Trustee, 2007–, Chm., Trustees, 2013–, Dio. of Plymouth (Chm., Finance Cttee, 2006–12); Chm., Plymouth Catholic and Anglican Acad. Trust, 2013–16. Hon. DLaws Plymouth, 2006. *Recreations:* Rugby football, opera. *Address:* Coach House, Modbury, Ivybridge PL21 0TE. *Club:* Royal Automobile.

**PEARSE, Charlotte Louisa;** *see* May, C. L.

**PEARSON,** family name of **Viscount Cowdray** and **Baron Pearson of Rannoch.**

**PEARSON OF RANNOCH,** Baron *cr* 1990 (Life Peer), of Bridge of Gaur in the district of Perth and Kinross; **Malcolm Everard MacLaren Pearson;** *b* 20 July 1942; *s* of Col John MacLaren Pearson; *m* 1st, 1965, Francesca Frua De Angeli (marr. diss. 1970); one *d*; 2nd, 1977, Hon. Mary (marr. diss. 1995), *d* of Baron Charteris of Amisfield, GCB, GCVO, QSO, OBE, PC; two *d*; 3rd, 1998, Caroline, *d* of Major Hugh Launcelot St Vincent Rose. *Educ:* Eton. Founded Pearson Webb Springbett, later PWS gp of reinsurance brokers, 1964, Chm., 1970–2008. Member: H of L Select Cttee on Eur. Communities, 1992–96; Sub-cttee C on Envmt and Social Affairs, 1992–95. Founded Rannoch Trust, 1984 (Exec. Trustee). Mem., Council for Nat. Academic Awards, 1983–93 (Hon. Treas., 1986–93).

Patron: Nat. Soc. for Mentally Handicapped People in Residential Care (Rescare), 1994–; British Register of Chinese Herbal Medicine, 1998–. *Recreations:* stalking, fishing, golf. *Address:* House of Lords, SW1A 0PW. *Clubs:* White's; Swinley Forest Golf.
*See also* Sir P. A. Le Marchant, Bt.

**PEARSON, Prof. Andrew David John,** MD; FRCP, FRCPCH; Cancer Research UK Professor of Paediatric Oncology and Head, Paediatric Section, Institute of Cancer Research, University of London, 2005–14; Head, Children's Unit, and Hon. Consultant Paediatric Oncologist, Royal Marsden Hospital Foundation NHS Trust, 2005–14; *b* 2 March 1955; *s* of John and Jean Pearson; *m*; two *s* three *d*; *m* 2006, Gaby Charlton; one *d*. *Educ:* Univ. of Newcastle upon Tyne (MB BS 1st Cl. Hons 1977); DCH 1980; MD 1989. MRCP 1979, FRCP 1992; FRCPCH 1996. MRC Lilly Internat. Travelling Fellow, Dept of Paediatrics, Univ. of Minnesota, 1983–84; Sen. Registrar in Paediatric Oncology, 1984, Hon. Sen. Registrar, 1985–89, Royal Victoria Inf., Newcastle upon Tyne; Hon. Consultant Paediatrician, Newcastle HA, 1989–94; Hd, Dept of Paediatric Oncology, Children's Services Directorate, 1992–2005, and Hon. Consultant Paediatric Oncologist, 1994–2005, Newcastle upon Tyne Hosps NHS Trust; University of Newcastle upon Tyne: Lectr, 1985–89, Sen. Lectr, 1989–94, in Paediatric Oncology, Dept of Child Health; Prof. of Paediatric Oncology, Sch. of Clinical Med. Scis, 1994–2005; Postgrad. Sub-Dean, 1998–2002, Dean of Postgrad. Studies, 2002–05, Fac. of Med. Scis. Trustee, Inst. of Cancer Res., 2005–11. United Kingdom Cancer Study Group: Chm., Neuroblastoma Wkg Gp, 1991–95; Chm., Biol Studies Cttee, 1996–2002; Hd, Div. of Therapeutics, 1999–; Co-Chm., UKCCSG/Childhood Leukaemia Wkg Party Clin. Res. Governance Gp, 2003–06; Chm., 2003–06. Chairman: Eur. Neuroblastoma Study Gp, 1994–99; Europe Neuroblastoma (SIOPEN), Internat. Soc. of Paediatric Oncology, 1998–2001 (Founding Chm.), 2005–07; Co-Chm., Internat. Neuroblastoma Risk Gp Strategy Cttee, 2004–. Chm., Scientific Adv. Bd, Solving Kids' Cancer, 2017–. Lifetime Achievement Award, Advances in Neuroblastoma Res., 2016. *Publications:* over 370 articles on children's cancer res., particularly neuroblastoma, drug develt and pharmacol. *Recreation:* walking. *Address:* c/o Institute of Cancer Research, 15 Cotswold Road, Sutton, Surrey SM2 5NG.

**PEARSON, Anthony James,** CBE 2002; Director of Security, Prison Service, 1993–99; *b* 2 Nov. 1939; 2nd *s* of Leslie Pearson and Winifred Pearson (*née* Busby); *m* 1964, Sandra Lowe; two *d*. *Educ:* Saltley Grammar Sch., Birmingham; Exeter Univ. (BA Hons 1961); Oxford Univ. (Dip. Soc. and Public Admin 1962). Assistant Prison Governor: Maidstone, 1963–67; Albany, 1967–69; Parkhurst, 1970–72; Dep. Governor, Wandsworth Prison, 1972–73; Prison Service HQ, 1973–77; Prison Governor: Gartree, 1977–81; Brixton, 1981–85; HM Dep. Chief Inspector of Prisons, 1985–87; Prison Service Headquarters: Hd of Div., 1987–89; Hd, Directorate of Telecommunications, 1989–91; Area Manager, 1991–93. Trustee: Centre for Crime & Justice Studies, 1998–2010 (Chm., 2002–10); Butler Trust, 1999–2014 (Dep. Chm., 2001–10; Chm., 2010–14); Langley House Trust, 2001–12. *Recreations:* Rugby, cricket (armchair expert).

**PEARSON, Rev. Canon Brian William;** Associate Director of Vocations, Diocese of Bath and Wells, 2011–16; freelance consultant on Anglican Ministry, 2016–19; *b* 18 Aug. 1949; *s* of Victor William Charles Pearson and Florence Irene (*née* Webster); *m* 1974, Althea Mary Stride; two *s*. *Educ:* Roan Sch. for Boys, Blackheath; Brighton Polytechnic (BSc Hons); City Univ. (MSc); Ordination Training (Southwark Ordination Course); MTh Oxford 1994. Systems Engineer: IBM UK, 1967–71; Rohm and Haas UK, 1971–72; Lectr, Thames Polytechnic, 1972–81; College Head of Dept, Northbrook Coll., W Sussex, 1981–88; Bishop's Research Officer and Communications Officer, Bath and Wells, 1988–91; Archbishop's Officer for Mission and Evangelism and Tait Missioner, dio. of Canterbury, 1991–97; Hon. Canon, Canterbury Cathedral, 1992; Gen. Dir, CPAS, 1997–2000; Dir of Studies for Ordained Local Ministry, and Priest i/c, Leek Wootton, diocese of Coventry, 2000–06. Ministerial Trng Advr, Bath and Wells Dio., 2007–11; Assisting Minister, Langport Team Ministry, 2008–18; Lectr (pt-time), Strode Coll., 2006–09; Archdeacon's Visitor to St Andrew's, Compton Dundon, Bath and Wells, 2010–13. Trustee, Christians in Sport, 1996–2001. Partner, Woodspring Psychological Services, 2006–14. Non-executive Director: Trinity Coll., Bristol, 1997–2000; Christian Research, 2000–03; 2K Plus Internat. Sports Media, 2004–09, 2011–13. Regl Rep., Over The Wall Orgn, 2002–06. Hon. Chaplain: Warwicks Police HQ, 2000–06; Centrex Police Trng Centre, Ryton, 2002–06; Avon and Somerset Police, 2007–. Chairman: Som Seniors Cricket Assoc., 2017–; Somerton/Ilchester Patient Participation Gp, 2018–. Fellow, Coll. of Preachers, 1995. *Publications:* Yes Manager: Management in the local church, 1986; (with George Carey) My Journey, Your Journey, 1996; How to Guide: managing change, 1996; (contrib.) A Preacher's Companion, 2004; A Sporting Month with 2K Plus, 2012. *Recreations:* cricket player (Som Over-60s/70s), ECB umpire and coach, theatre, discerning more about contemporary life gleaned through the insights of two highly perceptive sons, biblical history and applied theology, travel associated with family history research, arts centre volunteer, lawn bowls. *Address:* Woodspring, Northfield, Somerton, Som TA11 6SL.

**PEARSON, Daniel John,** RDI 2012; landscape designer, journalist and writer; Principal, Dan Pearson Studio, since 1987; *b* Windsor, 9 April 1964; *s* of Raymond and Sheila Pearson; partner, Dafydd Huw Morgan. *Educ:* RHS Wisley (Cert. Hons); Royal Botanic Garden, Kew (Dip. Hons). Columnist: Sunday Times, 1994–2003; Daily Telegraph, 2003–06; Observer Magazine, 2006–16. Projects include: Althorp House, 1997; Millennium Dome, 1999; Tokachi Millennium Forest, Hokkaido, 2002; Maggie's Cancer Caring Centre, London, 2005; Lowther Castle, 2007; King's Cross Central, 2014; Chatsworth, 2015. Mem., Soc. of Garden Designers, 2006–. Hon. FRIBA 2011. Grand Award, 2012, Historic Garden Award, 2014, Soc. of Garden Designers; Gold Medal and Best Show Garden, Chelsea Flower Show, 2015. *Publications:* (with Steve Bradley) Garden Doctors, 1996; (with Terence Conran) The Essential Garden Book, 1998; The Garden: a year at Home Farm, 2001; Spirit: garden inspiration, 2009; Home Ground: sanctuary in the city, 2011. *Recreations:* gardening, listening to music, natural landscapes (travel). *Address:* The Nursery, The Chandlery, 50 Westminster Bridge Road, SE1 7QY. *T:* (020) 7928 3800, *Fax:* (020) 7928 3854. *E:* dan@danpearsonstudio.com.

**PEARSON, David Compton Froome;** Deputy Chairman, Robert Fleming Holdings Ltd, 1986–90 (Director, 1974–90); *b* 28 July 1931; *s* of late Compton Edwin Pearson, OBE and of Marjorie (*née* Froome); *m* 1st, 1966, Venetia Jane Lynn (marr. diss. 1994); two *d*; 2nd, 1997, Mrs Bridget Thomson. *Educ:* Haileybury; Downing Coll., Cambridge (MA). Linklaters & Paines, Solicitors, 1957–69 (Partner, 1961–69); Dir, Robert Fleming & Co. Ltd, 1969–90; Chairman: The Fleming Property Unit Trust, 1971–90; Gill & Duffus Group Plc, 1982–85 (Dir, 1973–85); Robert Fleming Securities, 1985–90; River & Mercantile Investment Management Ltd, 1994–96; Dep. Chm., Austin Reed Group Plc, 1977–96 (Dir, 1971–96); Director: Blue Circle Industries Plc, 1972–87; Lane Fox and Partners Ltd, 1987–91; Fleming Income & Growth Investment Trust plc (formerly River & Mercantile Trust Plc), 1994–2001; Chesterton International Plc, 1994–98. Mem., Finance Act 1960 Tribunal, 1978–84. Mem., Wessex Regl Cttee, NT, 1995–2004. *Recreations:* gardening, walking. *Address:* The Manor, Berwick St John, Shaftesbury, Dorset SP7 0EX. *T:* (01747) 828363. *Clubs:* Brooks's, Army and Navy.

**PEARSON, David Robert Stanley,** FSA; FCLIP; Research Fellow, Institute of English Studies, University of London, since 2017; *b* 7 May 1955; *s* of Robert Edward Orlando Pearson and Gladys Pearson (*née* Goldsworthy); *m* 1987, Lynne Wallace; one *s*. *Educ*: St Bees Sch., Cumbria; Sidney Sussex Coll., Cambridge (BA 1977; PhD 2009); Loughborough Univ. (DipLib). FCLIP 2001; FSA 2005. Curator, Eighteenth-century Short Title Catalogue, BL, 1986–92; Hd, Collection Develt, Nat. Art Liby, 1992–96; Librarian, Wellcome Trust, 1996–2004; Dir, Res. Liby Services, Univ. of London, 2004–09; Dir, Culture, Heritage and Libraries (formerly Libraries, Archives and Guildhall Art Gallery), City of London, 2009–17; Lyell Reader in Bibliography, Univ. of Oxford, 2017–18. Hon. Sen. Res. Associate, Dept of Inf. Studies, UCL, 2016–. Pres., Bibliographical Soc., 2010–12 (Hon. Sec., 1994–2002; Vice-Pres., 1995–2010). Freeman of the City of London, 2010; Liveryman, Stationers' and Newspaper Makers' Co., 2010–. *Publications*: Provenance Research in Book History, 1994, new edn 2019; Oxford Bookbinding 1500–1640, 2000; (ed) For the Love of the Binding: studies in bookbinding history, 2000; English Bookbinding Styles 1450–1800, 2005; Books as History, 2008; (ed) London 1000 Years, 2011. *Recreations*: bibliography, walking by the sea. *Address*: The Old Vicarage, 10 Copperfields, Royston, Herts SG8 5BH. *T*: (01763) 241379. *E*: david@drspearson.plus.com.

**PEARSON, (Edward) John (David);** Hon. Director General, European Commission, since 2001; *b* 1 March 1938; *s* of Sydney Pearson and Hilda Beaumont; *m* 1963, Hilary Stuttard; two *s* two *d* (and one *s* decd). *Educ*: Huddersfield Coll.; Emmanuel Coll., Cambridge (Sen. Scholar; MA). Admin. Trainee, London Transport Exec., 1959; Asst Principal, MoT, 1960, Principal 1965; Sen. Principal, 1971, Asst Sec., 1973, DoE; European Commission: Head of Div., Transport Directorate-Gen., 1973–81; Dir, Fisheries Directorate-Gen., 1981–91; Dir, Regl Policy and Cohesion Directorate-Gen., 1991–98; Dep. Financial Controller, EC, 1999–2001 (Acting Financial Controller, July–Aug. 2000). Co. Sec., Arthur Ransome Soc., 2017–. *Recreations*: orienteering (Pres., Belgian Orienteering Assoc., 1982–87; Chm., Develt and Promotion Cttee, 1986–88, Mem. Council, 1988–94, Pin of Honour, 1994, Internat. Orienteering Fedn; Chm., Languedoc-Roussillon Orienteering Assoc., 2015–17), hill-walking (Pyrenees High Level Route from Atlantic to Mediterranean in 43 days, 2006; climbed the 283 Scottish Munros between 1964 and 2011; completed Annapurna Circuit, Nepal, 2011), writing (magazine articles published on ornithology, Hungarian history and language, mountaineering, Arthur Ransome). *Address*: Mas d'en Clarimon, Route de Paloll à la Selva, 66400 Céret, France. *T*: (4) 68833458. *E*: hilaryandjohnpearson@hotmail.com.

**PEARSON, Sir (Francis) Nicholas (Fraser),** 2nd Bt *cr* 1964, of Gressingham, Co. Palatine of Lancaster; *b* 28 Aug. 1943; *s* of Sir Francis Fenwick Pearson, 1st Bt, MBE and of Katharine Mary, *d* of Rev. D. Denholm Fraser; *S* father, 1991; *m* 1978, Henrietta Elizabeth, *d* of Comdr Henry Pasley-Tyler, CBE and Haroldine Lucas. *Educ*: Radley Coll. Commnd The Rifle Brigade, 1961; ADC to: Army Comdr, Far East, 1967; C-in-C, Far East, 1968. Dir, Hill & Delamain Ltd, 1970–75; Dep. Chm., Claughton Manor Brickworks, 1978; Chm., Turner Gp Ltd, 1979; Director: Intercontinental Hotel Group Ltd, 1989–92; Virgin Atlantic Airlines, 1989–92; Saison Hldgs BV, 1990–93. Psychotherapist, 2005–18. Chm., Pure Gym Ltd. Trustee: Ruskin Foundn; Temenos Foundn. Prospective Parly Cand. (C), Oldham West, 1976–79. *Recreations*: poetry, music, gardening. *Heir*: none. *Address*: c/o HSBC Private Bank, 69 Pall Mall, SW1Y 5EY.

**PEARSON, Rt Rev. Geoffrey Seagrave;** Bishop Suffragan of Lancaster, 2006–17; Associate Priest, Ellel with Shireshead, Forton, 2008–17; an Honorary Assistant Bishop, Diocese of Liverpool, since 2018; *b* 18 July 1951; *m* 1973, Jean Richardson; one *s* two *d*. *Educ*: St John's Coll., Durham (BA 1972); Cranmer Hall, Durham. Ordained deacon, 1974, priest, 1975; Asst Curate, Kirkheaton, 1974–77; Curate-in-charge, 1977–82, Incumbent, 1982–85, Ch of the Redeemer, Blackburn; Asst Home Sec., Gen. Synod Bd for Mission and Unity, and Hon. Curate, Forty Hill, 1985–89; Vicar, Roby, 1989–2006. Exec. Sec., BCC Evangelism Cttee, 1986–89; Area Dean, Huyton, 2002–06; Hon. Canon, Liverpool Cathedral, 2003–06. *Address*: 10 Elderswood, Rainhill, Prescot L35 4QY.

**PEARSON, Dr Graham Scott,** CB 1990; CChem, FRSC; Hon. Visiting Professor of International Security, Division of Peace Studies, University of Bradford, 1996–2016; Director General, Chemical and Biological Defence Establishment (formerly Director, Chemical Defence Establishment), Porton Down, 1984–95; *b* 20 July 1935; *s* of Ernest Reginald Pearson and Alice (*née* Maclachlan); *m* 1960, Susan Elizabeth Meriton Benn; two *s*. *Educ*: Woodhouse Grove Sch., Bradford; St Salvator's Coll., Univ. of St Andrews (BSc 1st Cl. Hons Chemistry, 1957; PhD 1960). Postdoctoral Fellow, Univ. of Rochester, NY, USA, 1960–62; joined Scientific Civil Service, 1962; Rocket Propulsion Estab., 1962–69; Def. Res. and Develt Staff, Washington, DC, 1969–72; PSO to Dir Gen. Res. Weapons, 1972–73; Asst Dir, Naval Ordnance Services/Scientific, 1973–76; Technical Adviser/Explosives, Materials and Safety (Polaris), 1976–79; Principal Supt, Propellants Explosives and Rocket Motor Estab., Westcott, 1979–80; Dep. Dir 1, 1980–82 and Dep. Dir 2, 1982–83, RARDE, Fort Halstead; Dir Gen., ROF (Res. and Develt) 1983–84; Asst Chief Scientific Advr (Non-Proliferation), MoD, 1995. Archivist, Hidcote Manor Garden, 2002–; Ed., Hidcote Life, 2016–. Fellow, IUPAC, 2004. DUniv Bradford, 2018. *Publications*: (ed jtly) Key Points for the Fourth Review Conference, 1996; The UNSCOM Saga: chemical and biological weapons non-proliferation, 1999; (ed jtly) Key Points for the Fifth Review Conference, 2001; (ed jtly) Scientific and Technical Means of Distinguishing Between Natural and Other Outbreaks of Disease, 2001; (ed jtly) Maximizing the Security and Development Benefits from the Biological and Toxin Weapons Convention, 2002; (ed jtly) The Implementation of Legally Binding Measures to Strengthen the Biological and Toxin Weapons Convention, 2004; The Search for Iraq's Weapons of Mass Destruction: inspection, verification and non-proliferation, 2005; (ed jtly) Key Points for the Sixth Review Conference, 2006; Hidcote: the garden and Lawrence Johnston, 2007, 3rd edn 2013; Lawrence Johnston: the creator of Hidcote, 2010, 3rd edn 2015; (ed jtly) Key Points for the Seventh Review Conference, 2011; (ed jtly) BioWeapons Monitor, 2014; (ed jtly) Key Points for the Eighth Review Conference, 2016; contributor to: Advances in Photochemistry, vol. 3, 1964; Advances in Inorganic and Radio Chemistry, vol. 8, 1966; Oxidation and Combustion Reviews, vol. 3, 1968 and vol. 4, 1969; Biological Weapons: Weapons of the Future?, 1993; Non-Conventional Weapons Proliferation in the Middle East, 1993; Verification after the Cold War, 1994; Weapons Proliferation in the 1990s, 1995; Verification 1997, 1997; Biological Weapons: limiting the threat, 1999; Biological Warfare: modern offense and defense, 2000; Encyclopedia of Bioterrorism Defense, 2005; Deadly Cultures: biological weapons since 1945, 2006; Terrorism, War or Disease? Unraveling the Use of Biological Weapons, 2008; Encyclopedia of Bioterrorism Defense, 2nd edn 2011; Turning International Obligations into Effective National Action: the 2007–2010 Intersessional Process of the Biological Weapons Convention, 2011; The BTWC Seventh Review Conference: a modest outcome, 2012; Moving Towards Enhanced Assurance of Compliance with the Biological and Toxin in Weapons Convention, 2013; Moving Towards Consensus, 2014; Reviving the Intersessional Process: achieving effective action, 2015; Preventing Biological Threats: what can you do?, 2015; Effective Biosecurity Education Implementation: the vital importance of a co-ordinated approach, 2016; An Effective Intersessional Process and Implementation Support Unit, 2016; The BTWC Eighth Review Conference: a disappointing outcome, 2017; articles on combustion, and on chemical and biological defence and arms control, in scientific jls, and on Hidcote and Lawrence Johnston in horticultural jls; official reports. *Recreations*: photography, reading, archival research, gardening.

**PEARSON, His Honour Ian Howard;** a Circuit Judge, 2004–17; *b* 30 May 1949; *s* of Harry Seabourn and Elsie Margaret Pearson; *m* 1971, Sian Williams; two *d*. *Educ*: Farnham Grammar Sch.; Univ. of Leicester (LLB Hons); Coll. of Law, Guildford. Admitted as solicitor, 1973; Partner, Tanner & Taylor, Solicitors, Hants and Surrey, 1975–94; a Judge Advocate (pt time), 1992; Dep. Judge Advocate, 1994–95; Asst JAG, 1995–2004; Vice JAG, 2004; Asst Recorder, 1999–2000; a Recorder, 2000–04. Mem. (Lab), Rushmoor BC, 1986–94. Contested (Lab) Aldershot, 1987. *Recreations*: travel, literature, visual arts, food and wine, sport, avoiding watching opera.

**PEARSON, Ian Phares,** PhD; Chief Executive, IPP Associates, since 2010; Chairman, Code Investing (formerly CrowdBnk Ltd), since 2013; *b* 5 April 1959; *m* 1988, Annette Pearson (marr. diss. 2009); one *s* two *d*. *Educ*: Brierley Hill GS; Balliol Coll., Oxford (BA Hons PPE); Warwick Univ. (MA, PhD). Mem. (Lab) Dudley MBC, 1984–87. Local Govt Policy Res. Officer, Lab. Party, 1985–87; Dep. Dir, Urban Trust, 1987–88; business and economic develt consultant, 1988–91; Jt Chief Exec., W Midlands Enterprise Bd, 1991–94. MP (Lab) Dudley W, Dec. 1994–1997, Dudley S, 1997–2010. An Asst Govt Whip, 2001–02; a Lord Comr of HM Treasury (Govt Whip), 2002–03; Parly Under-Sec. of State, NI Office, 2002–05; Minister of State (Minister for Trade), FCO and DTI, 2005–06; Minister of State, DEFRA, 2006–07; Minister of State (Minister for Sci. and Innovation), DIUS, 2007–08; Econ. Sec., BERR, 2008–09; Econ. Sec. to HM Treasury, 2008–10. Chm., Octopus VCT2 plc, 2011–16; non-executive Director: Thames Water Utilities Ltd, 2014–; Apollo VCT, 2016–17.

**PEARSON, Prof. Jeremy David,** PhD; FMedSci; Professor of Vascular Biology, King's College London, 1991–2010, now Emeritus; Associate Medical Director (Research), British Heart Foundation, since 2002; *b* Upminster, Essex, 24 Dec. 1947; *s* of Kenneth and Margot Pearson; *m* 1974, Jane McCarthy; two *s*. *Educ*: Hertford Grammar Sch.; Queens' Coll., Cambridge (BA Natural Scis 1968; MA 1972; PhD 1975); St Cross Coll., Oxford (MA 1974). IBM Res. Fellow, Univ. of Oxford, 1974–76; SSO, then PSO, Babraham Inst., 1976–83; Sen. Scientist, then Hd, Section of Vascular Biol., MRC Clin. Res. Centre, Harrow, 1983–91. President: British Soc. for Haemostasis and Thrombosis, 1997–98; British Microcirculation Soc., 2002–05; Secretary: British Atherosclerosis Soc., 1998–2003; Eur. Vascular Biol. Orgn, 2000–10; Chairman: Strategy Cttee, Eur. Soc. for Microcirculation, 1998–2004; Council, Understanding Animal Res., 2017–; Mem., Basic Sci. Council, Eur. Soc. Cardiol., 2004– (Chm., 2016–18). Trustee: William Harvey Res. Foundn, 2003–14 (Chm. Bd, 2005–14); Scleroderma & Raynaud's UK (formerly Raynaud's and Scleroderma Assoc.), 2007– (Chm. Bd, 2014–). FMedSci 2004; Fellow, Eur. Soc. Cardiol. 2013. Hon. FRCP 2006; Hon. FBPhS 2016. *Publications*: contrib. scientific papers and reviews in field of endothelial cell biol. *Recreations*: walking, fine wine, good food, modern classical music. *Address*: British Heart Foundation, Greater London House, 180 Hampstead Road, NW1 7AW. *T*: (020) 7554 0344. *E*: pearsonj@bhf.org.uk.

**PEARSON, John;** *see* Pearson, E. J. D.

**PEARSON, John Anthony;** HM Diplomatic Service; Ambassador to Laos, since 2019; *b* Solihull, 28 April 1968; *s* of Anthony Kenneth Pearson and Antoinette Pearson; *m* 2002, Leyla Werleigh-Pearson; three *s*. *Educ*: S Island Sch., Hong Kong; Whitgift Sch., Croydon; Univ. of Nottingham (BSc Geog. 1990); King's Coll. London (MA Internat. Peace and Security 2002). Entered FCO, 1990; Desk Officer, Non-Proliferation and Defence Dept, FCO, 1990–92; Second Sec., Madrid, 1992–94; Desk Officer, Republic of Ireland Dept, 1994–96; Second Sec., Brasilia, 1996–99; Hd, Envmtl Security Team, Envmtl Policy Dept, FCO, 2000–01; Hd, UN Reform Team, UN Dept, FCO, 2002–05; Dep. Hd of Mission, Montevideo, 2005–08; Head: SE Asia Climate Change Network, Singapore, 2008–12; Trade and Investment, Mexico City, 2012–14; China Dept, FCO, 2014–19. *Recreations*: running, walking, music.

**PEARSON, Prof. John Richard Anthony,** PhD, ScD; FRS 2005; Scientific Consultant, Schlumberger Cambridge Research, 1996–2019 (Scientific Adviser, 1982–95); Chairman, Pearson Publishing Group, 1993–2018; *b* Cairo, 18 Sept. 1930; *s* of Charles Robert Pearson and Olive Pearson (*née* Nock); *m* 1954, Emma Margaret Anderson; three *s* one *d*. *Educ*: English Sch., Cairo; Bedford Modern Sch.; Trinity Coll., Cambridge (BA 1953; PhD 1958; ScD 1975); Harvard Univ. (AM 1954). CEng 1970; FIMMM; MIChemE 1957–. Nat. Service, 2nd Lieut, Royal Signals, 1948–50; Tech. Officer, ICI Ltd, 1957–59; Res. Scientist, Metal Box Co., 1959–60; Asst Dir Res., Dept of Chemical Engrg, Univ. of Cambridge, 1960–73; Dir of Studies in Maths and Fellow, Trinity Hall, Cambridge, 1961–73; Prof. of Chemical Engrg, Imperial Coll., London Univ., 1973–82. Visiting Professor: Princeton Univ., 1967; Univ. of Wisconsin, 1967; Rice Univ., 1969; MIT, 1973–76; Univ. of Sydney, 1982; Univ. of Louvain, 1994–95; D. A. Katz Lectr, Univ. of Michigan, 1975; Fairchild Schol., CIT, 1978–79, 1981; MTS Prof., Univ. of Minnesota, 2004. Hon. Professorial Fellow: Univ. of Wales, 1984–2012; Univ. of Birmingham, 1995–2013. Member and Chairman: UNIDO Tech. Assistance Cttee, Planta Piloto de Ingenieria Quimica, Argentina, 1973–79; Yucca Mountain Peer Rev. Cttee, US Dept of Energy, 2002–03; Mem., Internat. Geomechanics Commn, Govt of France, 1996–99. Pres., British Soc. of Rheology, 1980–82 (Gold Medal, 1986). Foreign Mem., NAE, 1980. Hon. DSc Minnesota, 2002. *Publications*: Mechanical Principles of Polymer Melt Processing, 1966; Polymer Melt Processing, 1985; papers on engrg sci. in scientific jls. *Recreations*: travel, opera, wine. *Address*: Pearson Publishing Group, Chesterton Mill, French's Road, Cambridge CB4 3NP. *E*: jrap@pearson.co.uk. *Clubs*: MCC; Cambridge University Real Tennis.

**PEARSON, Keith Philip,** MA; FRSE; Headmaster, George Heriot's School, Edinburgh, 1983–97; *b* 5 Aug. 1941; *s* of Fred G. and Phyllis Pearson; *m* 1965, Dorothy (*née* Atkinson); two *d*. *Educ*: Madrid Univ. (Dip. de Estudios Hispánicos); Univ. of Cambridge (MA; Cert. of Educn). FRSE 1995. Teacher, Rossall Sch., 1964–72 (Head of Mod. Langs, 1968–72); George Watson's College: Head of Mod. Langs, 1972–79; Dep. Principal, 1979–83. *Recreations*: sport, mountains, music, DIY.

**PEARSON, Sir Keith (Samuel),** Kt 2010; JP; DL; Chair, Health Education England, 2012–18; *b* Fulwood, Lancs, 6 April 1947. Gen. mgt, BUPA UK, 1976–89; Chief Executive Officer: BUPA Hong Kong, 1989–93; AON Thailand and Singapore, 1993–97; Summerlands Consultants Ltd, 1997–2004; Chair: NHS S Somerset PCG and PCT, 1998–2004; Norfolk, Suffolk and Cambs SHA, 2004–06; E of England SHA, 2006–10; NHS Confederation, 2010–12. Chm., Nat. Adv. Gp on Health in Criminal Justice, DoH and MoJ, 2009–; former Co-Chair, NHS State of Readiness Gp. Chm., Revalidation Implementation Adv. Bd (formerly Med. Revalidation Prog.), GMC, 2009–. Chm., Tallaght Hosp., 2011–. JP Peterborough, 1999; DL Cambs, 2011. *Publications*: Children in Her Shadow (novel), 2011; Reflections from Her Shadow (novel), 2014.

**PEARSON, Rt Rev. Kevin;** *see* Argyll and the Isles, Bishop of.

**PEARSON, Prof. Margaret Anne,** PhD; Pro-Vice-Chancellor (Public Benefit) and Executive Dean, College of Health and Social Care, University of Salford, 2013–15; *b* 13 Oct. 1952; *d* of late Charles Yorke and of Betty Yorke; one *s* one *d*; *m* 2012, Matthew Maisey. *Educ*: Newnham Coll., Cambridge (BA Hons Geog. 1975; MA 1977); RGN 1978; Liverpool Univ. (PhD Geog. 1985). Student Nurse, 1975–78, Staff Nurse, 1978–79, Sheffield AHA; Res. Officer, then Dir, Centre for Ethnic Minorities Health, Bradford Univ., 1982–84; Lectr in Health Policy, Nuffield Inst. for Health Services Studies, Leeds Univ., 1983–85; University of Liverpool: Lectr, then Sen. Lectr, in Med. Sociology, 1985–93; Prof. of Health and Community Care, 1993–96; Regl Dir of R&D, DoH/NHS Exec. NW, 1996–2001; Dep. Dir, NHS Human Resources, DoH, 2001–04; Dep. Vice-Chancellor, Keele Univ., 2004–07; Dir, Maggie Pearson Solutions, 2007–10; Academic Dir, Office of CSO, DoH, 2008–13. Member: UK Commn on Human Medicines, 2005–; Bd, UK Sector Skills Develt Agency, 2006–08. Chm., Main Panel C (Nursing and Midwifery, Dentistry, Pharmacy and Allied Health Professions and Subjects), 2008 RAE. Non-executive Director: Bridgewater Community NHS Foundn Trust, 2015–19; Aspire, 2016–. Trustee, Sefton Park Palm House Preservation Trust, 2016–. Hon. MFPH 1995. *Recreations*: family, music (flute player), reading, textile art. *E*: maggie.pearson1@btinternet.com.

**PEARSON, Michael;** *see* Pearson, T. M.

**PEARSON, Prof. Michael George,** FRCP; Professor of Clinical Evaluation, University of Liverpool, 2006–11, now Hon. Professor (Professor of Medicine, 2003–06); Consultant Physician, University Hospital, Aintree, Liverpool, since 1984; *b* 11 Jan. 1950; *s* of Dr C. Andrew Pearson, OBE and Jean M. Pearson; *m* 1973, Diane Kay Park; three *d*. *Educ*: Culford Sch., Bury St Edmunds; Gonville and Caius Coll., Cambridge (MA; MB BChir 1975); Liverpool Univ. Med. Sch. FRCP 1991. Royal College of Physicians: Associate Dir, 1997–98, Dir, 1998–2006, Clinical Effectiveness and Evaluation Unit; Dir, Clinical Standards, 2005–07. Trustee Dir, Respiratory Educn Training (formerly Resource) Centres, 1998–2015; Dir, Nat. Collaborating Centre for Chronic Conditions, 2000–04. Hon. Prof., Dept of Biol Scis, Salford Univ., 1991–2006. Theme Lead, NW Coast Collaboration for Leadership in Applied Health Res. and Care, 2013–16; Clinical Lead, Connected Health Cities, NW Coast, 2016–; Chief Medical Officer, AIMES Ltd (formerly AIMES Grid Services), 2017–. Dir, Lung Health Ltd, 2010–. Non-exec. Dir, Health and Social Care Inf. Centre, 2005–14. Mem. Exec., British Thoracic Soc., 1995–99. *Publications*: Questions in Respiratory Medicine, 1994; Controversies in Chronic Obstructive Pulmonary Diseases, 2003; contrib. numerous papers to scientific jls. *Recreations*: gardening, music. *Address*: 12 Willow Hey, Maghull, Liverpool L31 3DL. *E*: michael.pearson@liverpool.ac.uk.

**PEARSON, Michael George P.;** *see* Parker Pearson.

**PEARSON, Sir Nicholas;** *see* Pearson, Sir F. N. F.

**PEARSON, Lt Gen. Peter Thomas Clayton,** CB 2010; CBE 2000; strategy and leadership consultant, since 2010; *b* Hong Kong, 22 Oct. 1954; *s* of Robert Pearson and Irene Pearson; *m* 1979, Francesca Beill; two *s* one *d*. *Educ*: St Edward's, Oxford; Royal Military Acad. Sandhurst; Army Staff Coll. Platoon Commander: 10th Princess Mary's Own Gurkha Rifles, Hong Kong, 1976–77; 1st Bn, Argyll and Sutherland Highlanders, 1977–78; Intelligence Officer, 10th PMO Gurkha Rifles, Brunei, 1978–79; Instructor, Platoon Comdrs Div., Sch. of Infantry, Warminster, 1979–81; Adjutant, 10th PMO Gurkha Rifles, Hong Kong, 1981–83; OC Support Co., 10th PMO Gurkha Rifles, 5 Airborne Bde, Aldershot, 1983–85; Staff Coll., Camberley, 1986; COS 20 Armoured Bde, 1986–88; OC D Co., 10th PMO Gurkha Rifles, Brunei, 1989–90; Mil. Asst to C-in-C, 1990–93; Commanding Officer: 10th PMO Gurkha Rifles, 1993–94; 3rd Bn The Royal Gurkha Rifles, 1994–95; HCSC, 1996; Comdr 19 Mechanized Bde, 1997–2000; COS to Comdr Field Army, 2000–02; Dep. Comdr Ops, Stabilisation Force Bosnia, 2002–03; Comdr British Forces and Adminr Sovereign Base Areas Cyprus, 2003–06; Comdt, RMA Sandhurst, 2006–07; Dep. Comdr Allied Jt Force Comd, Naples, 2007–09. Exec. Dir, British Schs Exploring Soc., then British Exploring Soc., 2010–14 (Fellow, 2018). Col of Regt, The Royal Gurkha Rifles, 1999–2009. Lieut, Tower of London, 2010–15. Governor: Corps of Commissionaires, 2010–15; Mil. Knights of Windsor, 2012–. Trustee, British Forces Foundn, 2006–; Pres., Berks Br., SSAFA, 2014–. *Publications*: Bugle and Kukri, vol. 3: the story of the 10th Princess Mary's Own Gurkha Rifles, 2000. *Recreations*: fly fishing, Rugby Union (watching).

**PEARSON, Rebecca Astley;** *see* Clarke, R. A.

**PEARSON, Prof. Roger Anthony George,** DPhil; FBA 2009; Professor of French, University of Oxford, 1997–2016, now Emeritus; Fellow and Praelector in French, Queen's College, Oxford, 1977–2016, now Emeritus; *b* Belfast, 7 April 1949; *s* of Philip Arnold Pearson and Barbara Mary Pearson (*née* McKee); *m* 1981, Vivienne Gregory; one *s* one *d*. *Educ*: Harrow Sch.; Exeter Coll., Oxford (BA Hons 1971; DPhil 1976). Lectr in French, Queen's Coll., Oxford, 1973–77; Lectr, Univ. of Oxford, 1977–97. Leverhulme Maj. Res. Fellow, 2009–11. Officier, Ordre des Palmes Académiques (France), 2005. *Publications*: Stendhal's Violin: a novelist and his reader, 1988; The Fables of Reason: a study of Voltaire's contes philosophiques, 1993; Unfolding Mallarmé: the development of a poetic art, 1996; Mallarmé and Circumstance: the translation of silence, 2004; Voltaire Almighty: a life in pursuit of freedom, 2005; Stéphane Mallarmé, 2010; Unacknowledged Legislators: the poet as lawgiver in post-revolutionary France, 2016; *literary translations*: Voltaire, Candide and Other Stories, 1990, new edn 2006; Zola, La Bête humaine, 1996; Maupassant, A Life, 1999; Zola, Germinal, 2004. *Address*: Queen's College, Oxford OX1 4AW. *T*: (01865) 279120, *Fax*: (01865) 790819. *E*: roger.pearson@queens.ox.ac.uk.

**PEARSON, Siobhan Mary;** *see* Kenny, S. M.

**PEARSON, Sybil Angela Margaret, (Mrs Michael Pearson);** *see* Jones, S. A. M.

**PEARSON, Gen. Sir Thomas (Cecil Hook),** KCB 1967 (CB 1964); CBE 1959 (OBE 1953); DSO 1940, and Bar, 1943; DL; retired 1974; *b* 1 July 1914; *s* of late Vice-Admiral J. L. Pearson, CMG; *m* 1947, Aud (*d* 2013), *d* of late Alf Skjelkvale, Oslo; two *s*. *Educ*: Charterhouse; Sandhurst. 2nd Lieutenant Rifle Bde, 1934. Served War of 1939–45, M East and Europe; CO 2nd Bn The Rifle Bde, 1942; Dep. Comdr 2nd Independent Parachute Bde Gp 1944; Dep. Comdr 1st Air-landing Bde 1945; GSO1 1st Airborne Div. 1945; CO 1st Bn The Parachute Regt 1946; CO 7th Bn The Parachute Regt 1947; GSO1 (Land Air Warfare), WO, 1948; JSSC, GSO1, HQ Malaya, 1950; GSO1 (Plans), FARELF, 1951; Directing Staff, JSSC, 1953; Comdr 45 Parachute Bde TA 1955; Nat. Defence Coll., Canada, 1956; Comdr 16 Ind. Parachute Bde 1957; Chief of Staff to Dir of Ops Cyprus, 1960; Head of Brit. Mil. Mission to Soviet Zone of Germany, 1960; Major-General Commanding 1st Division, BAOR, 1961–63; Chief of Staff, Northern Army Group, 1963–67; Comdr, FARELF, 1967–68; Military Sec., MoD, 1968–72; C-in-C, Allied Forces, Northern Europe, 1972–74; psc 1942; jssc 1950; ndc Canada 1957. ADC Gen. to the Queen, 1974. Col Comdt, the Royal Green Jackets, 1973–77. Fisheries Mem., Welsh Water Authy, 1980–83. DL Hereford and Worcester, 1983. Haakon VII Liberty Cross, 1948; Medal of Honour, Norwegian Defence Assoc., 1973. Chevalier, Legion d'Honneur (France), 2015. *Recreations*: field sports, yachting. *Clubs*: Naval and Military; Kongelig Norsk Seilforenning.

**PEARSON, (Thomas) Michael,** MBE 2007; Member, Board of Trustees, Cruse Bereavement Care, 2015–17 (Trustee and Member Council, 1986–2015; Hon. Officer, since 1987; Chair, 1992–2005; Human Resources Adviser, since 2007); human resources adviser in private and charity/voluntary sectors, since 2001; *b* 23 Dec. 1941; *s* of Harold Hird Pearson and Mary Anderson Pearson (*née* Preston); *m* 1967, Margaret Green; one *s* one *d*. *Educ*: Lancaster Royal Grammar Sch.; Univ. of Liverpool (BA Hons Soc. Studies 1966); Univ. of Kent (BA Hons Archaeol Studies 2007). Chartered CCIPD (CIPM 1990). Career in personnel mgt/human resources: Glaxo Gp, 1966–85; Smiths Industries Group, 1985–2000: Dir of Personnel, Healthcare Gp, 1987–94, Personnel Dir, then Human Resources Dir, Portex Ltd, 1994–2000. Mem., Employment Tribunals, 1995–2011. Vice-Pres., IPM, 1990–92. Governor, Chichester Coll., W Sussex, 1986–2004 (Vice-Chm., Governing Body, 1992–2003). Trustee: Kent Refugee Action Network, 2016–17; Studying History and Archaeology in Lympne, 2017–. Volunteer HR Advr, Cranfield Trust, 2010–. *Recreations*: archaeology, visiting historic places and gardens. *Address*: Rose Cottage, Belcaire Close, Lympne, Hythe, Kent CT21 4JR. *T*: (01303) 269557. *E*: margaretandmike.pearson@gmail.com.

**PEART, Icah Delano Everard;** QC 2002; a Recorder, since 2000; *b* 19 Jan. 1956; *s* of Everard Leopold Peart and Doreen Mildred Peart; partner, Linda Torpey; two *s* one *d*. *Educ*: Ashmead Boys' Secondary Sch., Reading; London Sch. of Econs (LLB Hons); Coll. of Law. Called to the Bar, Middle Temple, 1978, Bencher, 2005; in practice specialising in criminal law; Asst Recorder, 1997–2000. Volunteer, Internat. Sen. Lawyers Project, 2010–. Appeal Steward, British Boxing Bd of Control, 2012–. *Recreations*: reading, cinema, watching Reading FC (Mem. Supporters' Club), my children, gym, cycling. *Address*: Garden Court Chambers, 57–60 Lincoln's Inn Fields, WC2A 3LS. *T*: (020) 7993 7600, *Fax*: (020) 7993 7700. *E*: icahp@gclaw.co.uk.

**PEASE,** family name of **Baron Gainford**.

**PEASE, George;** *S* brother, 2013 as 4th Baron Gainford, but does not use the title.

**PEASE, Sir (Joseph) Gurney,** 5th Bt *cr* 1882, of Hutton Lowcross and Pinchinthorpe, co. York; hotelier; *b* Guisborough, N Yorkshire, 16 Nov. 1927; *s* of Sir Alfred Edward Pease, 2nd Bt, and his 3rd wife, Emily Elizabeth Pease; *S* brother, 2008; *m* 1953, Shelagh Munro, *d* of Cyril Gounod Bulman; one *s* one *d*. *Educ*: Bootham Sch., York. Mem., Guisborough UDC, 1950–53. Contested (L): Bishop Auckland, 1959; Darlington, 1964; Westmorland, 1970; Penrith and the Border, 1974. Council Mem., Liberal Party, 1969; President: NE Young Liberal Fedn, 1961; NW Regl Liberal Party, 1970, 1971. *Publications*: A Wealth of Happiness and Many Bitter Trials, 1992. *Recreations*: fell-walking, writing, reading, family. *Heir*: *s* Charles Edward Gurney Pease, *b* 17 July 1955. *E*: gurneypease@btinternet.com.
See also C. C. Bright.

**PEASE, Sir Richard Thorn,** 3rd Bt *cr* 1920; Chairman, Yorkshire Bank, 1986–90 (Director, 1977; Deputy Chairman, 1981–86); *b* 20 May 1922; *s* of Sir Richard Arthur Pease, 2nd Bt, and Jeannette Thorn (*d* 1957), *d* of late Gustav Edward Kissel, New York; *S* father, 1969; *m* 1956, Anne, *d* of late Lt-Col Reginald Francis Heyworth; one *s* two *d*. *Educ*: Eton. Served with 60th Rifles, Middle East, Italy and Greece, 1941–46 (Captain). Director: Owners of the Middlesbrough Estate Ltd, 1954–86; Barclays Bank, 1964–89; Bank of Scotland, 1977–85; Grainger Trust PLC, 1986–94; Vice-Chairman: Barclays Bank Ltd, 1970–82; Barclays Bank UK Management, 1971–82; Chm., Foreign and Colonial High Income Trust, 1990–92. DL Northumberland, 1990. *Heir*: *s* Richard Peter Pease [*b* 4 Sept. 1958; *m* T. C. C., (Cecilie), (marr. diss. 1999), *d* of P. H. Tholstrup; one *s* by Kate Chubb].

**PEASE, Rosamund Dorothy Benson;** Under Secretary, Department of Health, 1989–95; *b* 20 March 1935; *d* of Helen Bowen (*née* Wedgwood) and Michael Stewart Pease; one *s*. *Educ*: Chester Sch., Nova Scotia; Perse Sch., Cambridge; Mount Sch., York; Newnham Coll., Cambridge (BA Classical Tripos). Asst Principal, Min. of Health, 1958; Principal, 1965; Asst Sec., Pay Board, 1973; Office of Manpower Economics, 1974; Cabinet Office, 1975–76; DHSS, 1976; Office of Population Censuses and Surveys, 1983; Under Sec., NI Office, 1985. *Recreations*: music, gardening, family.

**PEASGOOD, Clare;** *see* Morrow, C.

**PEAT, Sir Gerrard (Charles),** KCVO 1988; FCA; Partner, Peat Marwick Mitchell & Co., Chartered Accountants, 1956–87; Auditor to the Queen's Privy Purse, 1980–88 (Assistant Auditor, 1969–80); *b* 14 June 1920; *s* of Charles Urie Peat, MC, FCA, sometime MP and Ruth (*née* Pulley); *m* 1949, Margaret Josephine Collingwood; one *s* one *d*. *Educ*: Sedbergh Sch. FCA 1961. Served War, RAF and ATA (pilot), 1940–45 (Service Medals; Badge of Honour for services in ATA in WWII, 2008); Pilot, 600 City of London Auxiliary Sqdn, 1948–51. Underwriting Mem. of Lloyd's, 1973–; Member: Cttee, Assoc. of Lloyd's Members, 1983–89; Council of Lloyd's, 1989–92. Member: Corp. of City of London, 1973–78; Worshipful Co. of Turners, 1977–. Hon. Treasurer, Assoc. of Conservative Clubs, 1971–78. Jubilee Medal, 1977. *Recreations*: travel, fishing, golf. *Address*: Flat 10, 35 Pont Street, SW1X 0BB. *T*: (020) 7245 9736. *Clubs*: Boodle's, MCC.

**PEAT, Jeremy Alastair,** OBE 2012; Visiting Professor, International Public Policy Institute, University of Strathclyde, 2014; *b* 20 March 1945; *s* of John Scott Grainger Peat and Pamela Mary Peat (*née* Stephany); *m* 1972, Philippa Ann Jones; two *d*. *Educ*: Univ. of Bristol (BA Hons 1968); University College London (MSc 1977). Govt Econ. Service, 1969–80; Hd, Employment Policy Unit, Govt of Botswana, 1980–84; HM Treasury, 1984–85; Sen. Econ. Advr, Scottish Office, 1985–93; Gp Chief Economist, Royal Bank of Scotland, 1993–2005. Mem., Competition Commn, 2005–14. Dir, David Hume Inst., 2005–14. Board Member: Signet Accreditation Co. Ltd, 2007–15; Scottish Enterprise, 2011–17. Mem., Competition and Markets Authy, 2014–16. Co-Chair, Carnegie Working Gp on Affordable Credit, 2015–16. Hon. Prof., Heriot-Watt Univ., 1994. Vice Chm., SHEFC, 1999–2005. Mem., Lay Cttee, RCPE, 2012 (Hon. Fellow, 2015). Trustee: BBC, 2006–10 (a Gov., 2005–06; Chm., BBC Pension Trust, 2005–11); RZSScot, 2010– (Vice Chm., 2011–12; Chm., 2012–). Columnist, The Herald, 2005–. FCIBS 1999; FRSE 2005; FRSA. Hon. LLD Aberdeen, 1997; Hon. DLitt Heriot-Watt, 2010. *Publications*: (with Stephen Boyle) An Illustrated Guide to the Scottish Economy, 1999; (ed jtly) Scotland in a Global Economy: the 20:20 vision, 2002. *Recreations*: golf, reading, films, watching TV, walking dogs. *Address*: Croft Dyke, Roslin Glen, Midlothian EH25 9PX. *T*: (0131) 440 2247.

**PEAT, Sir Michael (Charles Gerrard),** GCVO 2011 (KCVO 1998; CVO 1994); FCA; Director, since 2014, and Chairman, since 2017, CQS Management Ltd; *b* 16 Nov. 1949; *m* 1976, Deborah Sage (*née* Wood); one *s* two *d* (and one *s* decd). *Educ*: Eton; Trinity Coll., Oxford (MA; Hon. Fellow, 2004); INSEAD, Fontainebleau (MBA). FCA 1975. KPMG Peat Marwick, 1972–93; Dir, Finance and Property Services, HM Household, 1990–96; Keeper of the Privy Purse, Treas. to the Queen, and Receiver-Gen., Duchy of Lancaster,

1996–2002; Private Sec. to the Prince of Wales, 2002–05; Principal Private Sec. to the Prince of Wales and the Duchess of Cornwall, 2005–11. Sen. Advr, CQS Gp, 2011–14; non-executive Director: Arbuthnot Banking Gp, 2007–10; Tamar Energy Ltd, 2012–16 (Chm., 2015–16); Arbuthnot Latham Ltd, 2015–; M&C Saatchi plc, 2016–; Sen. Ind. non-exec. Dir, Evraz plc, 2011–; Ind. Bd Mem., Deloitte LLP, 2011–19; Advr to Mr Wafic Rida Saïd, 2011–; Mem., UK Adv. Bd, Barclays Wealth and Investment Mgt, 2011–13; Chairman: Adv. Bd, GEMS UK, 2013–14; Adv. Bd, Bellaziz Hldgs Ltd, 2013–; GEMS MENASA Hldgs Ltd, 2017–.

**PEATTIE, Catherine;** Member (Lab) Falkirk East, Scottish Parliament, 1999–2011; *b* 24 Nov. 1951; *d* of late Ian Roxburgh and Catherine Cheape (*née* Menzies); *m* 1969, Ian Peattie; two *d. Educ:* Moray Secondary Sch., Grangemouth. Shop worker, 1966–68; factory worker, 1968–69; Trng Supervisor, 1970–75; Field Worker and Trng Officer, SPPA, 1980–86; Develt worker, Volunteer Network, Falkirk, 1986–90; Community Develt worker, Langlees Community Flat, Falkirk, 1990–91; Manager, Community Outreach, 1991–93; Dir, Falkirk Voluntary Action Resource Centre, 1993–99. Scottish Parliament: Convener, Equal Opportunities Cttee, 2003–07; Dep. Convener, Transport, Infrastructure and Climate Change Cttee, 2007–11; Mem., Scottish Commn for Public Audit, 2003–07. Contested (Lab) Falkirk E, Scottish Parlt, 2011. *E:* CathyPeattie@gmail.com.
*See also* C. L. Hilton.

**PEATTIE, Charles William Davidson,** MBE 2003; freelance cartoonist, since 1985; *b* 3 April 1958; *s* of Richard Peattie and Frances Peattie; *m* 1st, 1988, Siobhan Clark (marr. diss.); two *d*; 2nd, 2005, Claudia Granados; two *s. Educ:* Charterhouse; St Martin's Sch. of Art (BA Fine Art). Portrait painter, 1980–85; artist: Alex cartoon (written with Russell Taylor) in: London Daily News, 1987; The Independent, 1987–91; Daily Telegraph, 1992–; Celeb cartoon (written with Mark Warren and Russell Taylor) in Private Eye, 1987–. *Television:* co-writer: Lenny Henry in Pieces (series), 1991; Passion Killers, 1999; Celeb (series), 2002; *radio:* Alex Presents, 2012. Writer, producer, animator, Alex (stage play), Arts Th., 2007, toured UK and abroad, 2008; animator, The Song of Lunch (stage play), Pleasance Courtyard, Edinburgh, 2018. *Publications:* (with Mark Warren) Dick, 1987; Celeb, 1991; (co-designed with Phil Healey) Incredible Model Dinosaurs, 1994; The Original Celeb Gary Bloke, 2002; with Russell Taylor, Alex Year Books, 1987–: Alex, 1987; The Unabashed Alex, 1988; Alex II: Magnum Force, 1989; Alex III: Son of Alex, 1990; Alex IV: The Man with the Golden Handshake, 1991; Alex V: For the Love of Alex, 1992; Alex Calls the Shots, 1993; Alex Plays the Game, 1994; Alex Knows the Score, 1995; Alex Sweeps the Board, 1996; Alex Feels the Pinch, 1997; The Full Alex, 1998; The Alex Technique, 1999; The Best of Alex 1998–2001, 2001; The Best of Alex, annually 2002–14. *Address:* 29A Queens Avenue, Muswell Hill, N10 3PE. *T:* (020) 8374 1225. *Clubs:* Groucho, Soho House, Every House.

**PEATTIE, David Keith;** Chief Executive Officer, Nuclear Decommissioning Authority, since 2017; *b* Blackpool, 6 Aug. 1954; *s* of Thomas Richard Peattie and Dorothy Peattie; *m* 1982, Carol Rothwell; one *s* one *d. Educ:* Arnold Sch., Blackpool; Univ. of Dundee (BSc Hons Mech. Engr and Econs). CEng. British Petroleum, subseq. BP Amoco, then BP plc: Petroleum Engr, 1979–80; Commercial Analyst, BP Exploration, 1986–90; Exec. Asst to Gp CEO, 1990–92; M&A, BP Finance, 1992–95; Business Hd, Algeria, 1995–97; Exec. Asst to Gp CEO, 1997–99; Hd, Investor Relns, 1999–2002; Commercial Dir, BP Chemicals, 2002–05; Gp Vice Pres., 2005–07; Dep. CEO, 2007–09, Exploration and Prodn; Hd, BP Russia, 2009–13; CEO, Fairfield Energy, 2013–16. *Recreations:* hillwalking, Arsenal FC, sport. *Address:* Greenlands, Holmrook, Cumbria CA19 1UL. *E:* dkpeattie@gmail.com. *Club:* Royal Automobile.

**PEAY, Prof. Jill Valerie,** PhD; Professor of Law, London School of Economics, since 2005; *b* Kingston-upon-Thames, 11 June 1955; *d* of Kenneth Ernest Peay and Audrey Jean Peay (*née* Udall); partner, Alastair Partington. *Educ:* Tiffin Girls' Sch.; Birmingham Univ. (BSc; PhD 1980); Oxford Brookes Univ. (CPE (exemptions)); Inns of Court Sch. of Law. Called to the Bar, Gray's Inn, 1991. Res. Officer, 1980–82, Fellow, 1982–88, Centre for Criminological Res., Univ. of Oxford; Lectr, 1988–95, Sen. Lectr, 1995–96, Brunel Univ.; Sen. Lectr, 1996–2000, Reader, 2000–05, Law Dept, LSE; Associate Tenant, Doughty St Chambers, 1994–. Member: Richardson Cttee (Expert Adv. Cttee on mental health law reform), 1998–99; Res. Ethics Cttee, MoD, 2002–13. Mem., Wkg Party on Dementia: Ethical Issues, Nuffield Council on Bioethics, 2007–09. Jt Gen. Ed., Clarendon Studies in Criminology Series, OUP, 2014–16. *Publications:* (with G. Mansfield) The Director of Public Prosecutions: principles and practices for the Crown Prosecutor, 1987; Tribunals on Trial: a study of decision-making under the Mental Health Act 1983, 1989; Inquiries after Homicide, 1996; Criminal Justice and the Mentally Disordered, 1998; (with N. Eastman) Law without Enforcement: integrating mental health and justice, 1999; Decisions and Dilemmas: working with mental health law, 2003; Seminal Issues in Mental Health Law, 2005; Mental Health and Crime, 2010; (with T. Newburn) Policing: politics, culture and control, 2012. *Recreations:* friends, Scilly, paddling in the back seat of a kayak. *Address:* Department of Law, London School of Economics, Houghton Street, WC2A 2AE. *T:* (020) 7955 6391. *E:* j.peay@lse.ac.uk.

**PÉBEREAU, Michel,** Grand Officier de la Légion d'honneur, 2008 (Commandeur, 2004); Commandeur de l'Ordre National du Mérite; Chairman, BNP Paribas, 2000–12, now Honorary Chairman (Chief Executive Officer, 2000–03); *b* 23 Jan. 1942; *m* 1962, Agnès Faure; two *s* two *d. Educ:* Ecole Polytechnique; Ecole Nationale d'Administration. Inspecteur Général des Finances honoraire. Inspecteur des Finances, 1967–70; Rep., later Tech. Advr, Cabinet of Minister of Econ. and Finance, 1970–74; Rep., Sub-Dir, Asst Dir and Hd of Service, Treasury Directorate, Ministry of Econ. and Finances, 1971–82; Dir, then Rep., Cabinet of Minister of Econ., 1978–81; Crédit Commercial de France: Man. Dir, 1982–87; Chm. and Chief Exec. Officer, 1987–93; Chm. and CEO, Banque Nationale de Paris, 1993–2000; Chm., Banque Paribas, 1999–2000. Chairman: French Banking Fedn, 2002–03 (Chm., Mkt and Investment Banking Commn, 2000–); French Banking Assoc., 2002–04; European Banking Fedn, 2004; Bd, Institut de l'Entreprise, 2005; Supervisory Bd, French Aspen Inst., 2005; IIEB, 2006. Director: BNP Paribas UK Ltd; Lafarge; Saint-Gobain; Total; Société Anonyme des Galeries Lafayette; Mem., Supervisory Bd, AXA. Institute of Political Studies, Paris: Sen. Lectr, 1967–78; Prof., 1980–2000; Mem., 1984, Chm., 1988, Mgt Cttee; Sen. Lectr, Nat. Sch. of Statistics and Econ. Admin, 1968–79. Mem., Acad. des Scis Morales et Politiques. Dep. Chm., Commn of Control for Film Industry, 1981–85; Chm., Commn for Selective Assistance for Film Distribn, 1987–89. *Publications:* La Politique Economique de France, 3 Vols; science fiction book reviews for La Recherche, 1983–2002, for Le Journal du Dimanche, 2003–. *Address:* c/o BNP Paribas, 3 rue d'Antin, 75002 Paris, France.

**PECK, David Arthur;** Clerk to Merchant Taylors' Company, 1995–2006; *b* 3 May 1940; *s* of late Frank Archibald Peck and Molly Peck (*née* Eyels); *m* 1968, Jennifer Mary Still; one *s* two *d. Educ:* Wellingborough Sch.; St John's Coll., Cambridge (MA). Admitted Solicitor, 1966; Partner, Birkbeck Julius Coburn & Broad, 1967; Sen. Partner, Birkbeck Montagu's, 1985–91; Partner, Penningtons, 1991–95. Mem. Council, Radley Coll., 1993–2013. *Recreations:* golf, walking, cinema. *Address:* 45 Homefeld Road, W4 2LW. *Clubs:* MCC (Cttee, 1998–2001; Foundn Trustee, 2010–); Hawks (Cambridge).
*See also Maj.-Gen. R. L. Peck.*

**PECK, Donald MacInnes,** DPhil; social investor; Co-Founder, Lok Capital and Lok Foundation, Delhi, India, since 2006; Treasurer, Institute for Public Policy Research, since 2008; *b* Pembury, Kent, 28 May 1952; *s* of Sir Edward Heywood Peck, GCMG and Alison Mary Peck (*née* MacInnes); *m* 1979, Lucy Veronica Macnair; two *s. Educ:* Winchester Coll.; Wadham Coll., Oxford (BA Mod. Hist. 1973); St Antony's Coll., Oxford (DPhil Latin Amer. Studies 1977). Asst Dir, Morgan Grenfell & Co., 1978–81; Dir, Lloyds Merchant Bank, 1981–87; Sen. Investment Officer, Internat. Finance Corp., Washington, DC, 1988–91; Commonwealth Development Corporation, later Actis LLP, 1991–2008: Dir, 1999–2004; Partner, New Delhi, 2004–08. Advr, India Prog. Cttee, Paul Hamlyn Foundn, 2009–. Trustee: Foundn Rachel and Pamela Schiele, 1994– (Chm., 2010–); Think Ahead Orgn, 2016–; Organic Res. Centre, 2017–. *Recreations:* walking amid mountains, classical music, tennis, agrarian history, history of Argentina. *Address:* The Old Post Office, Combe, Hungerford, W Berks RG17 9EH. *T:* (01488) 668518.

**PECK, Prof. Edward William,** PhD; Vice-Chancellor, Nottingham Trent University, since 2014; *b* Ormskirk, 10 May 1959; *s* of Edward and Vera Peck; *m* 1989, Ingrid Barker; two *d. Educ:* Ormskirk Grammar Sch.; Univ. of Bristol (BA Philosophy 1981); Univ. of Nottingham (MA Social Policy and Admin 1986); Univ. of Newcastle upon Tyne (PhD 1996). NHS Mgt Trainee, Wessex RHA, 1982–84; Community Mental Health Team Manager, Nottingham HA, 1984–86; Gen. Manager, Mental Health Services, Newcastle HA, 1986–92; Sen. Consultant, 1992–94, Dir, 1994–2002, Centre for Mental Health Services Develt, KCL; University of Birmingham: Dir, Health Services Mgt Centre, 2002–08; Pro-Vice-Chancellor and Hd, Coll. of Social Sci., 2008–14. Non-exec. Dir, Heart of England Foundn NHS Trust, 2012–14. Mem., Ind. Panel for Govt Rev. of Funding Post-18 Educn, 2018–19. Trustee, UCAS, 2018–. Non-exec. Dir, Notts Co. FC, 2017–18. *Publications:* (jtly) Managing Networks of Twenty-first Century Organisations, 2006; (with Perri 6) Beyond Delivery: policy implementation as sense-making and settlement, 2006; (with H. Dickinson) Leading and Managing in Inter-Agency Settings, 2008; (with H. Dickinson) Performing Leadership, 2009; book chapters; contribs to peer-reviewed jls. *Recreations:* enduring Everton, walking Hilda, driving tractor, strumming guitar. *Address:* Nottingham Trent University, Burton Street, Nottingham NG1 4BU. *T:* (0115) 848 6561. *E:* edward.peck@ntu.ac.uk.

**PECK, Heather Lydia;** Chair, Lantra, since 2017; *b* Stoke-on-Trent, 13 April 1954; *d* of Thomas Cotton and Doreen Goodwin; *m* 2013, Adrian Michael Peck; one step *s* one step *d. Educ:* Congleton Grammar Sch.; Queen Mary Coll., Univ. of London (BSc Hons Zool. with Physiol.); CIPD Cert. Psychol. of Mgt 2017. MAFF, then DEFRA, 1975–2008; Dir, 2008–11, Chm., 2011–14, Cambs Community Services NHS Trust; Dep. Chm. and Sen. Ind. Dir, Norfolk Community Health and Care NHS Trust, 2015–. Asst Boundary Comr, 2011–13. Non-exec. Dir, Food Standards Agency, 2014–17. Mem. Bd, Oxford Farming Conf., 2007–09 (Chm., 2010). Sec., Adv. Council, Welfare Issues of Dog Breeding, 2010–14. Chm., Dog Welfare Trust, 2015–; Trustee, Norfolk Citizens Advice, 2018–. FCIPD 1993. *Recreations:* walking the dogs, sailing the Norfolk Broads, creative writing. *Address:* Lantra, Lantra House, Stoneleigh Park, Coventry CV8 2LG. *E:* heather@drydraytonestate.com. *Club:* Farmers.

**PECK, Maj.-Gen. Richard Leslie,** CB 1991; FRGS; CEng, FICE; Director, The Churches Conservation Trust (formerly Redundant Churches Fund), 1992–97; *b* 27 May 1937; *s* of late Frank Archibald Peck and Molly Peck (*née* Eyels); *m* 1962, Elizabeth Ann, *d* of late Major Denis James Bradley and Barbara Edith Amy Bradley (*née* Metcalfe); two *s* one *d. Educ:* Wellingborough Sch.; Royal Mil. Acad., Sandhurst; Royal Mil. Coll. of Science, Shrivenham. BScEng. Commnd RE, 1957; served Cyprus, Libya, Germany, UK; psc 1969; Bde Major 5 Inf. Bde, 1969–71; Sqn Comd BAOR, 1972–73; Directing Staff, Staff Coll., 1973–77; CO 21 Engr Regt, 1977–79; Asst Mil. Sec., 1979–81; Comd 19 Inf. Bde, 1981–83; RCDS 1984; Dir Army Service Conditions, MoD, 1985; Dir Personnel, Staff of CDS, 1985–87; Engr-in-Chief (Army), 1988–91. Trustee and Mem. Council, 1992–2013, Treas., 1999–2013, Vice-Pres., 2014–, Lord Kitchener Nat. Meml Fund. Col Comdt, RE, 1991–97; Col, Queen's Gurkha Engineers, 1991–96. Pres., London South-West Br., SSAFA (formerly SSAFA Forces Help), 2008–. Freeman, City of London, 1991; Mem., Engineers' Co., 1990–. *Recreations:* Association football, cricket, golf, shooting, ski-ing, Rugby football. *Clubs:* MCC; I Zingari, Free Foresters, Cryptics; Royal Mid-Surrey Golf.
*See also D. A. Peck.*

**PECKFORD, Hon. (Alfred) Brian;** PC (Can.) 1982; Premier of the Province of Newfoundland and Labrador, 1979–89; *b* Whitbourne, Newfoundland, 27 Aug. 1942; *s* of Ewart Peckford and Allison (*née* Young), St John's; *m* 1st, 1969, Marina Dicks; three *d*; 2nd, 1986, Carol Ellsworth; one *s. Educ:* Lewisporte High Sch.; Memorial Univ. of Newfoundland (BAEd). Schoolmaster, 1962–63 and 1966–72. MHA (Progressive C) Green Bay, 1972–89; Special Asst to Premier, 1973; Minister: of Dept of Municipal Affairs and Housing, 1974; of Mines and Energy, 1976, also of Rural Development, 1978. Leader of Progressive Cons. Party, Newfoundland and Labrador, 1979–89. Pres., Peckford Consulting Ltd (formerly Peckford Inc.), 1989–. Conducted inquiries for Govts of Canada and British Columbia. Served on boards of Canadian Broadcasting Corp., and several Canadian junior mining cos. Chancellor, Acsenda Sch. of Mgt (formerly Sprott Shaw Degree Coll.), 2007–16. Hon. LLD Meml Univ. of Newfoundland, 1986. Vanier Award, 1982; Outstanding Service Award, Newfoundland and Labrador Oil and Gas Industries Assoc., 2001. *Publications:* The Past in the Present, 1982; Some Day the Sun Will Shine and Have Not Will be No More, 2012. *Recreations:* bicycling, walking, writing and reading. *Address:* PO Box 41056, RPO Woodgrove, Nanaimo, BC V9T 6M7, Canada.

**PECKHAM, Prof. Catherine Stevenson,** CBE 1998; MD, FRCP, FRCOG, FRCPath, FFPH, FMedSci; Professor of Paediatric Epidemiology, since 1985, and former Head, Centre for Paediatric Epidemiology and Biostatistics, Institute of Child Health, University of London; Hon. Consultant, Hospital for Sick Children, Great Ormond Street, 1985–2002; *b* 7 March 1937; *d* of late Alexander King, CMG, CBE; *m* 1958, Sir Michael John Peckham, *qv*; three *s. Educ:* St Paul's Girls' Sch.; University Coll., London (MB BS, MD). FFPH (FFPM 1980); FRCP 1988; FRCPath 1991; FRCOG 1994. Reader in Community Medicine and Head of Dept, Charing Cross Hosp. Med. Sch., 1980–85. Dir, Infections in Pregnancy Screening Prog. in England, 2008–. Member: Standing Med. Adv. Cttee, DoH, 1992–2001; Health Adv. Cttee, British Council, 1992–95; Bd, PHLS, 1989–92; Children Nationwide, Scientific Adv. Cttee, 1994–; Chairman: Steering Cttee on Epidemiol Res., Surveillance and Forecasting, WHO Global Prog. on AIDS, 1991–93; Exec. Cttee, British Paediatric Surveillance Unit, 1993–2002; Adv. Cttee on Dangerous Pathogens, DoH, 1999–2002; London Children's Taskforce, 2001–03; Military Health Res. Adv. Gp, 2001–; Confidential Enquiries Adv. Cttee, NICE, 2002–; Medical Foundn for AIDS Res. & Sexual Health, 2002–. Member: Fulbright Commn, 1987–95; Bd of Govs, St Paul's Sch., 1992– (Dep. Chm., 2001–06); Nuffield Council of Bioethics, 2000–06 (Vice-Chm., 2003–06); Council, Inst. of Educn, 2001–05; ASA, 1993–99. Chair, Positive

Action for Children Fund, 2010–. Founder FMedSci 1998; Founder FRCPCH. Harding Award, Action Research, 1993; James Spence Medal, RCPCH, 2003. *Publications:* The Peckham Report: national immunization study, 1989; chapters and papers on infections in pregnancy and early childhood, national cohort studies and epidemiology of common childhood conditions. *Recreation:* flute.

**PECKHAM, Sir Michael (John),** Kt 1995; FRCP, FRCS, FRCR, FRCPath; artist; oncologist; Founder and Director, School of Public Policy, University College London, 1996–2000; *b* 2 Aug. 1935; *s* of William Stuart Peckham and Gladys Mary Peckham; *m* 1958, Catherine Stevenson King (*see Prof. C. S. Peckham*); three *s*. *Educ:* St Catharine's Coll., Cambridge (MA; Hon. Fellow, 1998); University College Hosp. Med. Sch., London (MD). MRC Clin. Res. Schol., Inst. Gustav Roussy, Paris, 1965–67; Institute of Cancer Research, London: Lectr, 1967–71; Sen. Lectr, 1971–74; Prof. of Radiotherapy, 1974–86; Dean, 1984–86; Dir, BPMF, 1986–90; Dir, R&D, DoH, 1991–95. Consultant: Royal Marsden Hosp., 1971–86; to Royal Navy, 1974–86. Mem., MRC, 1991–95; Mem., MRC Cell Biology and Disorders Bd, 1977–81. Member, Special Health Authority: Gt Ormond St Hosp., 1988–90; Brompton Nat. Heart and London Chest Hosps, 1986–90; Hammersmith and Queen Charlotte's Hosps, 1989–90. President: European Soc. of Therapeutic Radiology and Oncology, 1983–85; British Oncological Assoc., 1986–88; Fedn of European Cancer Socs, 1989–91; Mem., British Council Scientific Adv. Cttee, 1988–92. Vice-Chm., Council, ICRF, 1988–91. Chairman: BUPA Foundn, 1996–2004; Nat. Educn Res. Forum, 1999–2006; OST Foresight, Future of Healthcare, 1999–2000; Develt Forum, 2000–05; MS Soc. Sci. and Develt Bd, 2001–06; Macmillan Cancer Support Observatory, 2003–07. Founder: Bob Champion Cancer Trust, 1983; British Oncological Assoc., 1985; Co-founder, European Soc. of Therapeutic Radiology and Oncology, 1988. Mem., Inst. of Medicine, Nat. Acad. of Scis, Washington, 1995. Pres., Internat. Adv. Cttee, Canadian Inst. of Health Res., 2000–05. Trustee: Louise Buchanan Meml Trust, 1973–99; Guy's and St Thomas' Charitable Foundn, 1996–2000. Editor-in-Chief, European Jl of Cancer, 1989–95. Artist: first show, Bangor Univ., 1962; solo exhibitions: Bear Lane Gall., Oxford, 1964; Woodstock Gall., London, 1970; Upper Street Gall., London, 1976; Consort Gall., London, 1982; Christopher Hull Gall., London, 1983, 1989, 1992, 1997; Richard Demarco Gall., Edinburgh, 1989; Millinery Works Gall., London, 2001; ICH Gall., London, 2004; Tryon Street Gall., London, 2013; Millinery Works Gall., 2017; group exhibition: Treatments, RA Summer Exhibn, 2004 (drawings in clin. notes of his patients). Fellow: UCL, 1995; UCL Hosps, 1998; Inst. of Cancer Res., 1999. Founder FMedSci 1998. Dr *hc*: Univ. de Franche-Comté at Besançon, 1991; Catholic Univ. of Louvain, 1993; Hon. DSc: Loughborough, 1992; Exeter, 1996; London, 2007. *Publications:* Management of Testicular Tumours, 1981; (jtly) The Biological Basis of Radiotherapy, 1983; (jtly) Primary Management of Early Breast Cancer, 1985; (jt sen. editor) Oxford Textbook of Oncology, 1995; (with M. Marinker) Clinical Futures, 1998; A Model for Health: innovation and the future of health services, 1999.

**PEDDER, William Arthur;** Director, Corporate Affairs, Hutchison Whampoa (Europe) Ltd, 2006–11; *b* 20 Sept. 1950; *s* of Vice Adm. Sir Arthur Reid Pedder, KBE, CB, and Dulcie, *d* of O. L. Bickford; *m* 1983, Rosemarie Ghazaros; one *s* one *d*. *Educ:* Winchester Coll.; Merton Coll., Oxford (BA). Lieut, RN, 1972–79. Hogg Robinson Insce Gp, 1979–82; Manager, Lazard Bros, 1982–85; Dir, Dresdner Kleinwort Wasserstein, 1987–2001; Chief Exec., Invest·UK, subseq. Inward Investment, UK Trade & Investment, 2001–06. *Recreations:* sailing, theatre, ski-ing, tennis, shooting.

**PEDDIE, Hon. Ian James Crofton;** QC 1992; a Recorder, 1997–2019; *b* 17 Dec. 1945; *s* of Baron Peddie, MBE, JP, LLD and Hilda Mary Alice (*née* Bull), (Lady Peddie); *m* 1976, Susan Renée Howes; two *s* two *d*. *Educ:* Gordonstoun Sch.; University Coll. London (LLB Hons). Called to the Bar, Inner Temple, 1971; Asst Recorder, 1992–97. Member: SE Circuit, 1971–; Family Law Bar Assoc., 1980–; Exec. Cttee, Assoc. of Lawyers for Children, 2010–15; Vice Chair, Legal Services Cttee, Bar Council, 2010–. *Recreations:* family life, classic cars. *Address:* Garden Court Chambers, 57–60 Lincoln's Inn Fields, WC2A 3LS. *T:* (020) 7993 7600, *Fax:* (020) 7993 7700.

**PEDDLE, Gen. Brian;** General of The Salvation Army, since 2018; *b* Markland, Newfoundland, Canada, 8 Aug. 1957; *s* of Thomas and Gladys Peddle; *m* 1978, Rosalie Rowe; two *d*. Salvation Army: various appts, Canada and Bermuda Territory, 1997–2007; Divnl Comdr, NZ, Fiji and Tonga Territory, 2007–09; Chief Sec., UK with Republic of Ireland Territory, 2009–11; Territorial Comdr, Canada and Bermuda Territory, 2011–14; Internat. Sec. for Americas and Caribbean, 2014–15, COS, 2015–18, Internat. HQ. *Recreations:* hiking, kayaking, cycling, fishing. *Address:* The Salvation Army International Headquarters, 101 Queen Victoria Street, EC4V 4EH. *T:* (020) 7332 0101. *E:* ihq-theGeneral@salvationarmy.org.

**PEDERSEN, Prof. (Knud) George,** OC 1993; OOnt 1994; OBC 2002; PhD; FCCT, FRSA; Professor, The University of Western Ontario, 1985–96, now Emeritus (President and Vice-Chancellor, 1985–94); Chancellor, University of Northern British Columbia, 1998–2004; *b* 13 June 1931; *s* of Hjalmar Nielsen Pedersen and Anna (*née* Jensen); *m* 1st, 1953, Joan Elaine Vanderwarker (*d* 1988); one *s* one *d*; 2nd, 1988, Penny Ann Jones. *Educ:* Vancouver Normal Sch. (Dip. in Teaching 1952); Univ. of BC (BA History and Geography, 1959); Univ. of Washington (MA 1964); Univ. of Chicago (PhD 1969). FCCT 1977; FRSA 1983. Schools in North Vancouver: Teacher, Highlands Elem. Sch., 1952–56; Vice-Principal, North Star Elem. Sch., 1956–59; Principal, Carisbrooke Elem. Sch., 1959–61; Vice-Principal, Handsworth Sec. Sch., 1961–63; Principal, Balmoral Sec. Sch., 1963–65; Univ. of Chicago: Teaching Intern, 1966; Staff Associate, Midwest Admin Center, 1965–66, Res. Associate (Asst Prof.), 1966–68; Asst Prof., Ontario Inst. for Studies in Educn and Univ. of Toronto, 1968–70; Asst Prof. and Associate Dir, Midwest Admin Center, Div. of Social Sciences, Univ. of Chicago, 1970–72; Faculty of Educn, Univ. of Victoria: Associate Prof., 1972–75; Dean, 1972–75; Vice-Pres. (Academic), and Prof., Univ. of Victoria, 1975–79; President and Professor: Simon Fraser Univ., 1979–83; Univ. of British Columbia, 1983–85; Interim Pres., Univ. of Northern BC, 1995; Pres., Royal Roads Univ., 1995–96. Universities Council of British Columbia: Mem., Prog. Co-ordinating Cttee, 1975–78; Mem., Business Affairs Cttee, 1975–78; Mem., Long-range Planning Cttee, 1979–85; Mem. Council, Ontario Univ., 1985–94 (Chm.). Chm., Adv. Cttee on Educnl Planning, Min. of Educn (Prov. of BC), 1977–78; Member: Jt Bd of Teacher Educn, Prov. of BC, 1972–75; BC Council for Leadership in Educn, 1973–80; Interior Univ. Progs Bd, Min. of Educn, 1977–78. Member, Board of Directors: Assoc. of Univs and Colls of Canada, 1979–84 (Mem., Adv. Cttee, Office of Internat. Develt, 1979–83; Chm., 1989–91); Public Employers' Council of BC, 1979–84; Vancouver Bd of Trade, 1983–85; Pulp and Paper Res. Inst. of Canada, 1983–85; Corporate and Higher Educn Forum, 1988–94; President: N Vancouver Teachers' Assoc., 1962–63; N Vancouver Principals' and Vice-Principals' Assoc., 1963–64; Vice-Pres., Inter-American Orgn for Higher Educn, 1991–93 (Mem. Bd of Dirs, 1979–85; Vice-Pres., N America, 1985–89); Sec.-Treasurer, Canadian Assoc. of Deans and Directors of Educn, 1972–73 and 1973–74; Mem., Exec. Bd, ACU, 1991–94. Member: BoT, Vancouver, 1983–85; Nat. Council, Canadian Human Rights Foundn, 1984–94. Mem., Bd of Dirs, MacMillan Bloedel Ltd, 1984–86. Chm., Bd of Govs, Emily Carr Univ. of Art and Design, 2004–10; Member, Board of Governors: Arts, Sciences and Technol. Centre, 1980–85; Leon and Thea Koerner Foundn, 1981–85; Member: Bd of Trustees, Discovery Foundn, 1980–85; Bd, Bill Reid Foundn, 2000–07 (Pres., 2000–02). Consultant, Salzburg Seminar, Austria, 1987–99. Hon. LLD: McMaster, 1996; Simon Fraser 2003; Northern BC, 2005; Hon. DLitt: Emily Carr Inst. of Art and Design, 2003; Fraser Valley Univ. Coll., 2007. Confedn of Canada 125th Anniversary Medal 1992; Golden Jubilee Medal, 2003; Diamond Jubilee Medal, 2012. *Publications:* The Itinerant Schoolmaster: a socio-economic analysis of teacher turnover, 1973; chapters in books on educn; articles in Administrator's Notebook (Univ. of Chicago), selected articles for Elem. Sch. Principals, Res. in Educn, Educn and Urban Soc., Educn Canada, Teacher Educn, Resources in Educn, Elem. Sch. Jl, Jl of Educnl Admin, Canadian Jl of Univ. Continuing Educn, and Book of the States; book reviews; proc. of confs and symposia; governmental and institutional studies and reports. *Address:* 2232 Spruce Street, Vancouver, BC V6H 2P3, Canada. *T:* (604) 7332400. *E:* pgpedersen@telus.net. *Club:* University Golf (Vancouver).

**PEDERSEN, Prof. Roger Arnold,** PhD; FRSB; Adjunct Professor and Senior Research Scientist, Stanford University School of Medicine, since 2018; *b* 1 Aug. 1944; *s* of Viggo Bernhardt Pedersen and Emily Anita Pedersen. *Educ:* Stanford Univ. (AB with Dist. 1965); Yale Univ. (PhD 1970). FRSB (FSB 2011). Postdoctoral Fellow, Johns Hopkins Univ., 1970–71; University of California, San Francisco: Asst Prof., 1971–79; Associate Prof., 1980–84; Prof., 1985–2001; University of Cambridge, 2001–11: Prof. of Regenerative Medicine, 2002–11, now Emeritus; Dir, Anne McLaren Lab. for Regenerative Medicine, 2008–11; Dir of Res., Lab. for Regenerative Medicine and Dept of Surgery, Sch. of Clin. Medicine, 2011; Fellow, Churchill Coll., Cambridge, 2006–18. Mem., Internat. Soc. for Stem Cell Res. *Publications:* (ed jtly) Experimental Approaches to Mammalian Embryonic Development, 1986; (ed jtly) Animal Applications of Research in Mammalian Development, 1991; (ed jtly) Current Topics in Developmental Biology, Vols 30–48, 1995–2000; (ed jtly) Handbook of Stem Cells, Vol. 1, Embryonic Stem Cells, 2004; (ed jtly) Human Embryonic Stem Cells, 2005; (ed jtly) Essentials of Stem Cell Biology, 2006; over 100 peer-reviewed articles in scientific jls, 1971–. *Recreations:* violin playing and making, flying (single engine airplanes).

**PEDLEY, Rt Rev. (Geoffrey) Stephen;** Bishop Suffragan of Lancaster, 1998–2005; an Honorary Assistant Bishop, Diocese of Newcastle, since 2005; *b* 13 Sept. 1940; *s* of Geoffrey Heber Knight and Muriel Pedley; *m* 1970, Mary Frances Macdonald; two *s* one *d*. *Educ:* Marlborough College; Queens' College, Cambridge (MA); Cuddesdon Theological College. Curate: Liverpool Parish Church, 1966; Holy Trinity, Coventry, 1969; Rector of Kitwe, Zambia, 1971–77; Vicar of St Peter's, Stockton, 1977–88; Rector, Whickham, 1988–93; Residentiary Canon, Durham Cathedral, 1993–98. Chaplain to the Queen, 1984–98. *Recreations:* architecture, English literature, travel. *Address:* The Blue House, Newbrough, Northumberland NE47 5AN.

**PEDLEY, Prof. Timothy John,** PhD, ScD; FRS 1995; G. I. Taylor Professor of Fluid Mechanics, 1996–2009, now Emeritus, and Head of Department of Applied Mathematics and Theoretical Physics, 2000–05, University of Cambridge; Fellow of Gonville and Caius College, Cambridge, 1973–89 and since 1996; *b* 23 March 1942; *s* of Richard Roman Pedley and Jean Mary Mudie Pedley (*née* Evans); *m* 1965, Avril Jennifer Martin Uden; two *s*. *Educ:* Rugby Sch.; Trinity Coll., Cambridge (BA 1963; MA, PhD 1967; ScD 1982). Post-doctoral Fellow, Johns Hopkins Univ., 1966–68; Res. Associate, then Lectr, Physiol. Flow Studies Unit and Dept of Maths, Imperial Coll. London, 1968–73; Department of Applied Mathematics and Theoretical Physics, University of Cambridge: Asst Dir of Res., 1973–77; Lectr, 1977–89; Reader in Biolog. Fluid Dynamics, 1989; Prof. of Applied Maths, Univ. of Leeds, 1990–96. EPSRC Sen. Res. Fellow, 1995–2000. Chairman: Math. Scis Section, BAAS, 1996–97; World Council for Biomechanics, 2002–06; RAE Applied Maths sub-panel 2007, 2005–08; President: IMA, 2004–05; Cambridge Philosophical Soc., 2006–07; IUTAM, 2008–12; Member, Council: EPSRC, 2009–13; Royal Soc., 2012–14; Mem., Royal Soc./RAEng Adv. Cttee for NPL, 2012–14. Lectures: Midwest Mechanics, 1995–96; G. I. Taylor, Univ. of Cambridge, 1998; Clifford, Tulane Univ., 2003; Rutherford Meml, NZ, 2003; Talbot, Univ. of Illinois, 2004; Ludwig Prandtl Meml, Zurich, 2007; Ascher H. Shapiro, MIT, 2010; Hassan Aref Meml, Virginia Tech., 2015. C.V. Raman Chair, Indian Acad. of Scis, 2016. MAE 2011. Foreign Associate, US NAE, 1999; Fellow: Amer. Inst. of Med. and Biol Engrg, 2001; Amer. Phys. Soc., 2005; Foreign Fellow, Nat. Acad. of Sci., India, 2007. Editor, Jl of Fluid Mechanics, 2000–06. Hon. DSc Imperial Coll. London, 2013. Adams Prize, Faculty of Maths, Cambridge Univ., 1977. Gold Medal, IMA, 2008. *Publications:* (ed) Scale Effects in Animal Locomotion, 1977; (jtly) The Mechanics of the Circulation, 1978; The Fluid Mechanics of Large Blood Vessels, 1980; (ed with C. P. Ellington) Biological Fluid Dynamics, 1995; (ed with P. W. Carpenter) Flow in collapsible tubes and past other highly compliant boundaries, 2003; numerous articles in fluid mechanics and biomechanics jls. *Recreations:* bird-watching, reading, crosswords. *Address:* 47 Derwent Close, Cambridge CB1 8DY; Department of Applied Mathematics and Theoretical Physics, Centre for Mathematical Sciences, Wilberforce Road, Cambridge CB3 0WA. *T:* (01223) 339842.

**PEEBLES, Iain Alexander Scott;** *see* Bannatyne, Hon. Lord.

**PEEBLES, Prof. Phillip James Edwin,** FRS 1982; Professor of Physics, 1965, and Albert Einstein Professor of Science, 1984, Princeton University, now Professor Emeritus; *b* Winnipeg, 25 April 1935; *s* of Andrew Charles Peebles and Ada Marian (*née* Green); *m* 1958, Jean Alison Peebles; three *d*. *Educ:* Univ. of Manitoba (BSc 1958); Princeton Univ. (MA 1959; PhD 1962). Member: Amer. Phys. Soc.; Amer. Astron. Soc.; AAAS; Internat. Astron. Union; Fellow: Amer. Physical Soc.; Amer. Acad. of Arts and Scis; Royal Soc. of Canada. Hon. DSc: Univ. of Toronto, 1986; Univ. of Chicago, 1986; McMaster Univ., 1989; Univ. of Manitoba, 1989. Dirac Medal, Abdus Salam Internat. Centre for Theoretical Physics, 2013. *Publications:* Physical Cosmology, 1971; The Large Scale Structure of the Universe, 1979; (ed jtly) Objects of High Redshift, 1980; Quantum Mechanics, 1992; Principles of Physical Cosmology, 1993. *Address:* 24 Markham Road, Princeton, NJ 08540, USA; Joseph Henry Laboratory, Princeton University, Princeton, NJ 08544, USA.

**PEEK, Bruno Mark,** LVO 2012 (MVO 2002); OBE 2000; Pageantmaster, organiser and co-ordinator, national and international events, since 1981; Chairman, Beacon Millennium Ltd; *b* 12 Sept. 1951; adopted *s* of George and Mildred Peek; one *d*; *m* 1st (marr. diss.); 2nd (marr. diss. 1999); one step *d*. *Educ:* Alderman Leach Secondary Sch., Gorleston, Great Yarmouth. Event organiser and consultant, English Tourist Bd (Mem., England Entertains Exec. Cttee, 1984); Develt Dir, Sparks Creative Services, 1989–92. Major nat. and internat. events include: Operation Sea Fire (chain of beacon fires), 1981; Great Armada Pageant, 1987–88; Fire over England (beacon signal fires), 1988; Beacon Europe (beacon signal fires), 1992; 50th Anniv. Celebrations, VE Day, 1995; Great British Poppy Chain for 75th Anniv. of RBL, 1996; Beacon Millennium, Millennium Flame, 1999–2000; Nelson Returns to England for Great Yarmouth Pageant, 2000; Golden Jubilee Summer Party, Golden Jubilee Summer Party Torch Relay, Golden Jubilee Dinner, 2002; Nelson's Farewell to Norfolk, Royal Nelson Show, 2005; VC and GC Dinner for 60th Anniv. Celebrations, end of World War II, 2005; Trafalgar Weekend, 2005; Rededication of Nelson's Monument, Great Yarmouth, 2007; Grand Tour of 50 English cities of the Loving Cup of England, 2007; Nat. St George's Day Banquet, Banqueting House, Whitehall, 2007; Service of

Commemoration of Falkland Islands conflict and Heroes' Dinner, Old Royal Naval Coll., Greenwich, 2007; Celebration Dinner and Ball, Diamond Wedding Anniversary of the Queen and Duke of Edinburgh, 2007; official visit of Loving Cup of England to Malta, 2008; St George's Day Reception, Westminster Hall, 2008; Millennium Flame handover to Variety Club GB, 2008; Queen's Birthday Dinner, 2009; Trafalgar Night Dinner, 2009; Royal Wedding Dinner, 2011; Great Poppy Party Weekend (England, Wales and NI) for 90th Anniv. of RBL, 2011; Queen's Diamond Jubilee Beacons, 2012; Olympic Games Dinner at Ritz Hotel, London, 2012; Fly a Flag for the Commonwealth, 2014–18; VE Day Beacons, 2015; Fly the Red Ensign for Merchant Navy Day, 2015; The Queen's 90th Birthday Beacons, 2016; Battle's Over: a nation's tribute, 11 Nov. 2018; Merchant Navy 100 Gala Dinner, Nautical Inst., 2019; VE Day 75 Commemoration and Celebrations, 2019–20; VC and GC Dinner, 2020. Coordinator: Enjoy England Celebrate St George's Day campaign, 2008; Fly the Flag, 2008; Fly a Flag for Our Armed Forces, 2009. Trustee, 1998–, and Internat. Co-ordinator, 2000–, Covenant Home Ministries (Kisumu) Kenya. Freedom of the City of London, 1989. Order of Polonia Restituta, 1988. *Recreations:* walking, gardening. *Address:* Pageantmasters House, 110 Lowestoft Road, Gorleston-on-Sea, Great Yarmouth, Norfolk NR31 6NB. *T:* 07737 262913.

**PEEK, Sir Richard Grenville,** 6th Bt *cr* 1874, of Rousdon, Devon; *b* 3 Feb. 1955; *s* of Sir William Grenville Peek, 5th Bt and Lucy Jane Peek (*née* Dorrien-Smith); *S* father, 2004; *m* 1983, Melanie Jane Waterson; three *s*. *Educ:* Eton. *Heir: s* Timothy Grenville Peek, *b* 21 Nov. 1989.

**PEEL,** family name of **Earl Peel.**

**PEEL, 3rd Earl** *cr* 1929; **William James Robert Peel,** GCVO 2006; PC 2006; DL; Bt 1800; Viscount Peel, 1895; Viscount Clanfield, 1929; Lord Chamberlain of HM Household, since 2006; *b* 3 Oct. 1947; *s* of 2nd Earl Peel and Kathleen (*d* 1972), *d* of Michael McGrath; *S* father, 1969; *m* 1st, 1973, Veronica Naomi Livingston (marr. diss. 1987), *d* of Alastair Timpson; one *s* one *d*; 2nd, 1989, Hon. Mrs Charlotte Hambro, *yr d* of Baron Soames, PC, GCMG, GCVO, CH, CBE and Lady Soames, LG, DBE; one *d*. *Educ:* Ampleforth; University of Tours; Cirencester Agric. Coll. Duchy of Cornwall: Mem., Prince's Council, 1993–96; Lord Warden of the Stannaries and Keeper of the Privy Seal, 1994–2006. Mem., Nature Conservancy Council for England, then English Nature, 1991–96; Chm., 1994–2000, Pres., 2000–08, Game and Wildlife Conservation Trust (formerly Game Conservancy Trust); former Mem. Cttee, Yorkshire Dales Nat. Park. President: Yorks Wildlife Trust, 1989–96; Gun Trade Assoc., 1993–99; Chm., Standing Conf. on Country Sports, 2001–06. Elected Mem., H of L 1999–; Mem., Sub-Cttee D, H of L Select Cttee on EU (Envmt and Agric.), 2004–. DL N Yorks, 1998. *Heir: s* Viscount Clanfield, *qv*. *Address:* Eelmire, Masham, Ripon, N Yorks HG4 4PF.

**PEEL, Catherine Anne;** *see* Mackintosh, C. A.

**PEEL, David Alexander Robert;** Inquiry Manager (formerly Reference Secretary, then Inquiry Secretary), Competition (formerly Monopolies and Mergers) Commission, 1996–2011; *b* 12 Nov. 1940; *s* of late Maj. Robert Edmund Peel and Sheila Mary (*née* Slattery); *m* 1971, Patricia Muriel Essery; two *s*. *Educ:* St Edmund's Coll., Ware; University Coll., Oxford. Building labourer, New Scotland Yard develt, 1963; joined MoT, 1964; Private Sec. to Minister of State, 1967; Principal, 1968; DoE, 1970; First Sec., UK Perm. Repn to EC, Brussels, 1972; Private Sec. to Minister for Transport, 1975; Asst Sec., Depts of Transport and the Environment, 1976–90: Nat. Roads Prog. and Highway Policy, 1982; Okehampton Bypass (Confirmation of Orders) Act, 1985; Interdeptl Review on Using Private Enterprise in Govt, 1986; Office Services, 1987–90; Under Sec., Dir of Admin. Resources, DoE, 1990–96. *Recreations:* allotment gardening, ballet, baroque architecture.

**PEEL, Robert Edmund Guy,** FIH; Chairman, Peel Hotels plc, since 1998; *b* 13 March 1947; *s* of John and Joanna Peel. *Educ:* Eton Coll. FIH (FHCIMA 1985). Various hotel appts, Europe, 1964–66; Queen Anne's Hotels & Properties, then Trust Houses Ltd, later Trust House Forte plc, 1966–76; Dir, 1976–98, Chief Exec., 1977–97, Mount Charlotte Investments, later Thistle Hotels plc. Director: Brierley Investments Ltd, 1992–96; Ivory & Sime Discovery Trust, 1994–2005. Dir, London Tourist Bd, 1994–98. *Recreations:* deep sea fishing, marine biology, tennis, gardening. *Address:* (office) 19 Warwick Avenue, Maida Vale, W9 2PS. *Club:* White's.

**PEEL, Robert Roger;** QC 2010; a Recorder, since 2011; a Deputy High Court Judge, since 2016; *b* Singapore, 29 Jan. 1966; *s* of Geoffrey Peel and Joan Peel; *m* 1993, Victoria Williams; two *s* one *d*. *Educ:* Eton Coll.; Brasenose Coll., Oxford (BA Mod. Langs); City Univ. (DipLaw). Called to the Bar, Middle Temple, 1990. *Recreations:* Real tennis, cricket, National Hunt. *Address:* 29 Bedford Row, WC1R 4HE. *Clubs:* MCC; Strollers Cricket; Holyport Real Tennis; Jesters.

**PEEL, Yana;** Chief Executive Officer, Serpentine Galleries, 2016–19; *b* St Petersburg, Russia, 1974; *d* of Yuri and Jane Mirkin; *m* 1999, Stephen Peel; one *s* one *d*. *Educ:* McGill Univ. (BA Hons Russian Studies); London Sch. of Econs and Pol Studies (DipEcon); Univ. of Cambridge (Harvard Kennedy Exec. Educn Module); Blavatnik Sch. of Mgt, Oxford Univ. (Leadership Prog.). Exec. Dir, Goldman Sachs, 1997–2003; Co-Founder and Co-Dir, Outset Contemp. Art Fund, 2003–10; Co-Founder and Dir of Intelligence, Squared Asia, 2009–; CEO, 2012–16, Chm., 2016–, Intelligence Squared Gp. Henry Crown Fellow; Young Global Leader, WEF. Hon. FRIBA 2019. *Publications:* Art for Baby, Art for Baby Colour, Art for Baby Faces, 2008. *Address:* 1 Hyde Park Gardens, W2 2LT. *T:* (020) 7298 1534.

**PEERS, Most Rev. Michael Geoffrey;** Primate of the Anglican Church of Canada, 1986–2004; *b* 31 July 1934; *s* of Geoffrey Hugh Peers and Dorothy Enid Mantle; *m* 1963, Dorothy Elizabeth Bradley; two *s* one *d*. *Educ:* University of British Columbia (BA Hons); Universität Heidelberg (Zert. Dolm.-Interpreter's Certificate); Trinity Coll., Toronto (LTh). Ordained deacon 1959, priest 1960; Curate: St Thomas', Ottawa, 1959–61; Trinity, Ottawa, 1961–65; University Chaplain, Diocese of Ottawa, 1961–66; Rector: St Bede's, Winnipeg, 1966–72; St Martin's, Winnipeg, with St Paul's Middlechurch, 1972–74; Archdeacon of Winnipeg, 1969–74; Rector, St Paul's Cathedral, Regina, 1974–77; Dean of Qu'Appelle, 1974–77; Bishop of Qu'Appelle, 1977–82; Archbishop of Qu'Appelle and Metropolitan of Rupert's Land, 1982–86. Ecumenist-in-Residence, Toronto Sch. of Theol., Univ. of Toronto, 2004–06. Sen. Res. Associate, Trinity Coll., Toronto, 2008–. Hon. DD: Trinity Coll., Toronto, 1978; St John's Coll., Winnipeg, 1981; Wycliffe Coll., Toronto, 1987; Univ. of Kent, 1988; Montreal Dio. Coll., 1989; Coll. of Emmanuel and St Chad, Saskatoon, 1990; Thorneloe Univ., 1991; Univ. of Huron Coll., 1998; Lutheran Theol Seminary, Saskatoon, 2001; Vancouver Sch. of Theol., 2003; Episcopal Divinity Sch., Cambridge, Mass, 2004; Gen. Theol Seminary, NY, 2007; Hon. DCL Bishop's Univ., Lennoxville, 1993. *Publications:* Grace Notes: journeying with the Primate 1995–2004, 2005; The Anglican Episcopate in Canada, vol. 4, 2009.

**PEET, Ronald Hugh,** CBE 1974; Chief Executive, Legal & General Group plc, 1972–84; *b* 12 July 1925; *s* of Henry Leonard and Stella Peet; *m* 1st, 1949, Winifred Joy Adamson (*d* 1979); two *s* two *d*; 2nd, 1981, Lynette Judy Burgess Kinsella. *Educ:* Doncaster Grammar Sch.; Queen's Coll., Oxford (MA). Served in HM Forces, Captain RA, 1944–47. Legal and General Assurance Society Limited: joined 1952; emigrated to Australia, 1955; Sec., Australian Branch, 1955–59; Asst Life Manager, 1959–65; Manager and Actuary for Australia, 1965–69; returned to UK as General Manager (Ops), 1969; Dir, 1969–84; Chm., 1980–84. Chairman: Aviation & General Insurance Co. Ltd, 1978–80; Stockley Plc, 1984–87; PWS Holdings plc, 1987–88; Director: AMEC Plc, 1984–96; Howard Gp plc, 1985–86; Independent Insurance Group plc, 1988–99. Director: City Arts Trust Ltd, 1976–90 (Chm., 1980–87); Royal Philharmonic Orchestra Ltd, 1977–88; English National Opera, 1978–84, 1985–95. Chm., British Insurance Assoc., 1978–79. FIA. *Recreations:* music, opera. *Address:* 9 Marlowe Court, Petyward, SW3 3PD. *Club:* Hurlingham.

**PEET, Sara Elizabeth;** *see* Staite, S. E.

**PEGDEN, Jeffrey Vincent;** QC 1996; **His Honour Judge Pegden;** a Circuit Judge, since 2007; a Circuit Judge, Court of Appeal Criminal Division, since 2015; *b* 24 June 1950; *s* of late George Vincent Pegden and Stella Blanche Kathleen Pegden; *m* 1981, Delia Mary Coonan; one *s* one *d*. *Educ:* Univ. of Hull (LLB Hons 1972). Called to the Bar, Inner Temple, 1973, Bencher, 2002; a Recorder, 1996–2007. Mem., Crown Court Rules Cttee, 2001–07. Judicial Coll. Course Dir, Criminal Seminars, 2010–16. FRSA. *Recreations:* reading, music, gardening, walking, films, theatre, travel.

**PEGGIE, Robert Galloway Emslie,** CBE 1986; Commissioner for Local Administration (Ombudsman) in Scotland, 1986–94; Chairman, Scottish Local Government Staff Commission, 1994–97; *b* 5 Jan. 1929; *s* of John and Euphemia Peggie; *m* 1st, 1955, Christine Jeanette Simpson (*d* 2000); one *s* one *d*; 2nd, 2001, Janice Helen Renton. *Educ:* Lasswade High Sch. Certified accountant; Accountancy apprenticeship, 1946–52; Accountant in industry, 1952–57; Public Service, Edinburgh City, 1957–74; Chief Exec., Lothian Regl Council, 1974–86. Trustee, Lloyds TSB Foundn, 1995–98. Mem., Gen. Convocation and Court, Heriot-Watt Univ., 1988–97 (Convener, Finance Cttee, 1989–97); Governor, Edinburgh Coll. of Art, 1989–99 (Vice-Chm., 1995–97; Chm., 1998–99). DUniv Heriot-Watt, 1998. *Recreation:* golf. *Address:* 9A Napier Road, Edinburgh EH10 5AZ. *T:* (0131) 229 6775.

**PEIRCE, Rev. Canon (John) Martin;** Canon Residentiary of Christ Church, Oxford, 1987–2001, now Canon Emeritus, and Oxford Diocesan Director of Ordinands, 1985–2001; *b* 9 July 1936; *s* of Martin Westley and Winifred Mary Peirce; *m* 1968, Rosemary Susan Milne; two *s*. *Educ:* Brentwood Sch.; Jesus Coll., Cambridge (MA); Westcott House, Cambridge. Served Royal Air Force, 1954–56. Teacher, St Stephen's Coll., Hong Kong, 1960–64; Curate, St John Baptist, Croydon, 1966–70; Team Vicar, St Columba, Fareham, 1970–76; Team Rector, Langley, Slough, 1976–85. *Recreations:* walking, gardening. *Address:* 8 Burwell Meadow, Witney, Oxon OX28 5JQ. *T:* (01993) 200103.

**PEIRCE, Robert Nigel;** HM Diplomatic Service, retired; Co-founder, Voice Technology Solutions, since 2014; *b* 18 March 1955; *s* of Kenneth Frank Peirce and Margaret Peirce. *Educ:* Taunton Sch.; St Catherine's Coll., Oxford (MA); Faculty of Oriental Studies, Univ. of Cambridge. Joined FCO, 1977; Hong Kong, 1979–80; Peking, 1980–83; FCO, 1983–85; Cabinet Office, 1985–86; Dep. Political Advr, Hong Kong, 1986–88; Private Sec. to Sec. of State for Foreign and Commonwealth Affairs, 1988–90; UK Mission to UN, 1990–93; Political Advr to Governor, Hong Kong, 1993–97; RCDS, 1998; Sec., Ind. Commn on Policing for NI, 1998–99; Counsellor, Washington, 1999–2004; Consul-Gen., Los Angeles, 2005–09. Advr to Commn on Future of Policing in Ireland, 2017–18. Chm., Britweek Inc., 2007–17. Senior Vice President: Abraxis Bioscience Inc., 2009–10; All About Advanced Health Proj., 2010–11; NantWorks LLC, 2011–12; Pres., RN Peirce Intl Inc., 2013–. Trustee, Education Develt Center, 2012–. *Recreations:* family, friends, travel. *Address:* 12403 Macao Court, Oak Hill, VA 20171, USA. *Club:* Hong Kong (Hong Kong).

**PEIRE, Fernando Javier;** Director, The Ivy and The Ivy Club, since 2007; *b* Gibraltar, 25 Sept. 1959; *s* of Emilio Herbert Peire and Maria de Los Angeles Perez Torrilla. *Educ:* Latymer Sch.; Victoria Univ. of Manchester (BA Hons French Studies 1983). Manager, S & K Restaurant, Didsbury, 1983–87; Manager, The Left Bank Restaurant, 1987–90; Maître d', The Ivy Restaurant, 1990–98; Dir, Quo Vadis Restaurant, 1999–2001; Consultant, Morton's Club, Halcyon Hotel, Villa Nova, Barbados, 2001–04; Dir, Frontline Club, 2004–05. Originator and presenter: Restaurant Inspector, series 1, 2011, series 2, 2012; The Ivy documentary, 2015. *Publications:* The Ivy Now, 2017. *Address:* The Ivy, 1–5 West Street, WC2H 0HU. *T:* (020) 7836 4751. *E:* fernando.j.peire@gmail.com, fpeire@the-ivy.co.uk. *Clubs:* Academy, Soho House.

**PEIRIS, Prof. (Joseph Sriyal) Malik,** DPhil; FRCPath; FRS 2006; Professor of Virology and Tam Wah-Ching Professor in Medical Science, University of Hong Kong; Scientific Director, HKU-Pasteur Research Centre, since 2007; *b* Sri Lanka. *Educ:* Univ. of Ceylon (MB BS 1972); Univ. of Oxford (DPhil 1981). Dept of Microbiol., Univ. of Peradeniya, 1982–88; virologist, Royal Victoria Infirmary, Newcastle upon Tyne, 1988–95; Univ. of Hong Kong, 1995–: former Prof., Dept of Microbiol.; Dir, Sch. of Public Health, 2013–17. Pres., Asia Pacific Soc. of Medical Virology. Chevalier, Légion d'Honneur (France), 2007. *Publications:* articles in jls and chapters in books. *Address:* School of Public Health, University of Hong Kong, 5–6/F Laboratory Block, 21 Sassoon Road, Hong Kong.

**PEIRSE, Sir Henry Njerš de la Poer B.;** *see* Beresford-Peirse.

**PELHAM,** family name of **Earls of Chichester** and **Yarborough.**

**PELHAM, Clare Elizabeth;** Chief Executive, Epilepsy Society, since 2016; *m* 1983, Prof. David Barr (marr. diss.); one *s* one *d*. *Educ:* London Sch. of Econs (BSc Econ). Home Office: Principal, 1987–93; Hd, Efficiency and Consultancy, 1993–95; Hd, Police Strategy, 1995–97; Customer Satisfaction Mgr, IBM, 1997–98; Dir of Corporate Affairs, HM Prison Service, 1998–2001; Dir, Cabinet Office, 2001–02; Dir, Coca-Cola Co., GB and Ire., 2002–03; Sen. Dir, Rev. of Immigration Enforcement, Home Office, 2004; Dir, DCA, 2004–06; Chief Executive: Judicial Appts Commn, 2006–10; Leonard Cheshire Disability, 2010–16. Mem., Charity Tax Commn, 2017–. Chm., Voluntary Organisations Disability Gp, 2013–15. Hon. Dr Open, 2017. *Recreations:* cake, conversation, changing the world. *Address:* Epilepsy Society, Chesham Lane, Chalfont St Peter, Bucks SL9 0RJ. *T:* (01494) 601302. *E:* clare.pelham@epilepsysociety.org.uk. *Club:* Athenæum.

**PELHAM, Sir Hugh (Reginald Brentnall),** Kt 2011; PhD; FRS 1988; Member, scientific staff, Medical Research Council Laboratory of Molecular Biology, Cambridge, 1981–2019 (Deputy Director, 1996–2006; Director, 2006–18); *b* 26 Aug. 1954; *s* of late Reginald A. and Pauline M. Pelham; *m* 1st, 1976, Alison Slowe (marr. diss. 1989); 2nd, 1996, Mariann Bienz, *qv*; one *s* one *d*. *Educ:* Marlborough Coll., Wiltshire; Christ's Coll., Cambridge (MA, PhD; Hon. Fellow, 2010). Research Fellow, Christ's Coll., 1978–84; Dept of Embryology, Carnegie Instn of Washington Baltimore, Md, 1979–81; Hd, Cell Biol. Div., MRC Lab. of Molecular Biol., Cambridge, 1992–2006. Hon. Prof. of Molecular Biol., Univ. of Cambridge, 2015. Visitor, Univ. of Zürich, 1987–88. Mem., EMBO, 1985. Founder

FMedSci 1998. Colworth Medal, Biochemical Soc., 1988; EMBO medal, 1989; Louis Jeantet Prize for Medicine, 1991; King Faisal Internat. Prize for Sci., 1996; Croonian Lecture and Medal, Royal Soc., 1999. *Publications:* papers in sci. jls on molecular and cell biology.

**PELHAM, Mariann, (Lady Pelham);** see Bienz, M.

**PELHAM BURN, Angus Maitland,** MBE 2019; DL; Vice Lord-Lieutenant for Kincardineshire, 1978–2000; Director, Bank of Scotland, 1977–2000 (Director, 1973–2001, Chairman, 1977–2001, North Local Board); *b* 13 Dec. 1931; *s* of late Brig. Gen. H. Pelham Burn, CMG, DSO, and late Mrs K. E. S. Pelham Burn; *m* 1959, Anne R. Pelham Burn (*née* Forbes-Leith); four d. *Educ:* Harrow; N of Scotland Coll. of Agriculture. Hudson's Bay Co., 1951–58; Wolf Bounty Officer, Ont, 1955. Director: Aberdeen and Northern Marts Ltd, 1970–86 (Chm., 1974–86); Jessfield Ltd, 1970–88; Aberdeen Meat Marketing Co. Ltd, 1973–86 (Chm., 1974–86); Prime Space Design (Scotland) Ltd, 1981–87; Status Timber Systems, 1986–90; Skeendale Ltd, 1987–88; Abtrust Scotland Investment Co., 1989–96; Dana Petroleum plc, 1999–2008; Chairman and Director: MacRobert Farms (Douneside) Ltd, 1970–87; Pelett Administration Ltd, 1973–94; Taw Meat Co., 1984–86; Oilcats Ltd, 2006–07; Chairman: Aberdeen Asset Mgt (formerly Aberdeen Trust) plc, 1993–2000; Scottish Provident Instn, 1995–98 (Dir, 1975–98; Dep. Chm., 1991–95). Chm., Aberdeen Airport Consultative Cttee, 1986–2006; Mem., Accounts Commn, 1980–94 (Dep. Chm., 1992–94). Chm., Global Philanthropic Internat. Ltd, 2002–; Dir, Global Philanthropic Ops Pty Ltd, 2004–11. Mem. Council, Winston Churchill Meml Trust, 1984–93; Dir, Aberdeen Assoc. for Prevention of Cruelty to Animals, 1975–95 (Chm., 1984–89). Pres., Aberdeen Br., Inst. of Marketing, 1987–90. Member: Kincardine CC, 1967–75 (Vice Convener, 1973–75); Grampian Regional Council, 1974–94. Patron, Knockando Woolmill Trust, 2012–. Member, Queen's Body Guard for Scotland (Royal Co. of Archers), 1968–2010. Hon. FInstM. JP Kincardine and Deeside, 1984–2005; DL Kincardineshire 1978. LlD Robert Gordon Univ., 1996. CStJ 1995 (OStJ 1978). *Recreations:* photography esp. wildlife, vegetable gardening. *Address:* Kennels Cottage, Dess, Aboyne, Aberdeenshire AB34 5AY. *T:* (013398) 84445, *Fax:* (013398) 84430. *E:* snow.bunting2@gmail.com.

**PELL, Emma Laetitia;** see Squire, E. L.

**PELL, His Eminence Cardinal George,** AC 2005; DD, DPhil; Prefect, Secretariat for the Economy, Vatican, 2014–19, now Prefect Emeritus; *b* 8 June 1941; *s* of G. A. and M. L. Pell. *Educ:* St Patrick's Coll., Vic; Corpus Christi Coll., Vic; Urban Univ., Rome (STB, STL); Campion Hall, Oxford Univ. (DPhil); Monash Univ. (MEd). FACE. Episcopal Vicar for Educn, Dio. of Ballarat, 1973–84; Principal, Inst. for Catholic Educn, 1981–84; Rector, Corpus Christi Coll., Clayton, 1985–87; Auxiliary Bishop, Archdio. of Melbourne, 1987–96; Archbishop of Melbourne, 1996–2001; Archbishop of Sydney, 2001–14. Cardinal, 2003. Nat. Chaplain, Order of St Lazarus, 2001–07; Grand Prior, NSW Lieutenancy of the Equestrian Order of the Holy Sepulchre of Jerusalem, 2001–14; Conventual Chaplain ad honorem, SMO Malta, 2007–. Member: Vatican Council for Justice and Peace, 1990–95, 2002–17; Vatican Congregation for the Doctrine of the Faith, 1990–2000; Vatican Council, Synod of Bishops, 2001–08, 2012–19; Presidential Cttee, Vatican Council for the Family, 2003–17; Vatican Congregation for Divine Worship, 2005–17; Vatican Supreme Cttee, Pontifical Missions Socs, 2005–19; Vatican Council of Cardinals on Orgnl and Econ. Problems of the Holy See, 2007–14; Pontifical Council for Pastoral Assistance to Healthcare Workers, 2010–17, for Promoting the New Evangelisation, 2010; Vatican Congregation for Bishops, 2012–19; Adv. Gp of Cardinals to Pope Francis, 2013–18; Pres., Vatican *Vox Clara* Cttee, 2001–19. Cardinal Elector in Papal Conclave, 2005 and 2013. Chm., Australian Catholic Relief, 1989–97; Mem., Gov. Cttee, Internat. Catholic Migration Commn, 2008–14. Foundn Pres., John Paul II Institute for Marriage and the Family, Melbourne, 2000–01. Foundn Pro-Chancellor, Australian Catholic Univ., 1990–95 (Pres., then 1994–2014). Apostolic Visitor, Seminaries of NZ, 1994, PNG, and Solomon Is, 1995, Pacific, 1996, Irian Jaya, and Sulawesi, 1998. Hon. Fellow, St Edmund's Coll., Cambridge, 2003. LHD *hc* Christendom Coll., Va, 2006; Hon. DLaws: Notre Dame, Australia, 2010; Australian Catholic Univ., 2014. Honour of the Pallium, Rome, 1997, 2001; GCLJ 1998; KGCHS 2002; Bailiff Grand Cross: of Honour and Devotion, SMO Malta, 2008; of Justice, Sacred Mil. Constantinian Order of St George, 2009. *Publications:* The Sisters of St Joseph in Swan Hill 1922–72, 1972; Catholicism in Australia, 1988; Rerum Novarum: one hundred years later, 1992; Issues of Faith and Morals, 1996; Catholicism and the Architecture of Freedom, 1999; Be Not Afraid, 2004; God and Caesar, 2007; Freedom for All: negotiating freedom in a world of individuals, 2009; Test Everything: hold fast to what is good, 2010; One Christian Perspective on Climate Change, 2011; Contemplating Christ with Luke, 2012. *Clubs:* Oxford and Cambridge; Melbourne, Australian (Sydney); Richmond Football (Vic).

**PELLEW,** family name of **Viscount Exmouth**.

**PELLEW, Dr Jill Hosford,** FRHistS; Senior Research Fellow, Institute of Historical Research, School of Advanced Study, University of London, since 2009; *b* 29 April 1942; *d* of late Prof. Frank Thistlethwaite, CBE and Jane (*née* Hosford); *m* 1965, Mark Edward Pellew, *qv*; two *s. Educ:* Cambs High Sch. for Girls; St Hilda's Coll., Oxford (BA 1964; MA 1968); Queen Mary Coll., London (MA 1970); PhD London 1976. FRHistS 2015. MoD, 1964–66; part-time univ. teaching, Univ. of Saigon, Univ. of Sussex, Hollins Coll., Va, American Univ., Washington, DC, 1967–89; Exec. Sec., Chatham Hse Foundn, Washington, DC, 1984–89; Develt Officer, St Hilda's Coll., Oxford, 1989–90; Dir of Develt, Imperial Coll. of Science, Technology and Medicine, London, 1991–94; Dir, Develt Office, Univ. of Oxford, 1994–99; Fellow, Trinity Coll., Oxford, 1995–99; Vice-Pres., Grenzebach Glier Europe, 2000–07. Mem., Council, British Sch. at Rome, 2003–09; Trustee: Council for Advancement and Support of Educn (Europe), 1996–99; Estorick Foundn, 1999–2009; Schola Cantorum of Oxford, 2003–17; Inst. of Historical Res., Univ. of London, 2005– (Mem., Adv. Council, 2005–12); Victoria Co. History of Oxon, 2005–; Young Classical Artists Trust, 2012–18; 21st Century Trust, 2018–. *Publications:* The Home Office 1848–1914: from clerks to bureaucrats, 1982; (ed with S. Cassese) The Comparative History of Public Administration: the merit system, 1987; (ed with D. Cannadine) History and Philanthropy: past, present, future, 2008; (ed with L. Goldman) Dethroning Historical Reputations: universities, museums and the commemoration of benefactors, 2018; articles in learned jls on admin. hist. and hist. of universities and philanthropy. *Recreations:* reading, listening to music, entertaining family and friends. *Address:* 30 Taynton, Burford, Oxon OX14 4UH. *Club:* Reform.

**PELLEW, Mark Edward,** CVO 2000 (LVO 1980); HM Diplomatic Service, retired; Chief Executive to the Secretary General, Anglican Communion, 2002–05; *b* 28 Aug. 1942; *e s* of late Comdr Anthony Pownoll Pellew, RN retd, and Margaret Julia Critchley (*née* Cookson); *m* 1965, Jill Hosford Thistlethwaite (*see* J. H. Pellew); two *s. Educ:* Winchester; Trinity Coll., Oxford (BA). Entered HM Diplomatic Service, 1965; FO, 1965–67; Third Sec., Singapore, 1967–69; Second Sec., Saigon, 1969–70; FCO, 1970–76; First Sec., Rome, 1976–80; Asst Head of Personnel Ops Dept, FCO, 1981–83; Counsellor: Washington, 1983–89; on secondment to Hambros Bank, 1989–91; Head of N America Dept, FCO, 1991–96; Ambassador to the Holy See, 1998–2002. Chairman: Hosting for Overseas Students, 2005–; Friends of Diocese in Europe, 2010–. *Recreations:* singing, playing the horn. *Address:* 51 St George's Square, SW1V 3QN. *Club:* Hurlingham.
See also R. A. Pellew.

**PELLEW, Robin Anthony,** OBE 2006; PhD; Chief Executive, National Trust for Scotland, 2001–07; *b* 27 Sept. 1945; *s* of late Comdr Anthony Pownoll Pellew, RN and Margaret Julia Critchley (*née* Cookson); *m* 1974, Pamela Daphne Gibson MacLellan; one *s* one *d. Educ:* Marlborough Coll.; Edinburgh Univ. (BSc 1968); University College London (MSc 1972; PhD 1981). Sen. Res. Scientist, Serengeti Res. Inst., Tanzania, 1973–78; BBC Natural History Unit, 1978–79; Res. Fellow, Physiology Lab., Cambridge, 1979–82; Cambridge University Press: Sen. Editor, 1982–86; Editorial Manager, 1986–87; Dir, Conservation Monitoring Centre, IUCN, 1987–88; Dir, World Conservation Monitoring Centre, Cambridge, 1988–93; Dir and Chief Exec., WWF-World Wide Fund for Nature, 1994–99; Chief Exec., Animal Health Trust, 1999–2001. Non-exec. Dir, Nat. Forest Co., 2007–14. Member: Envmt Cttee, RSA, 1993–98; UK Round Table on Sustainable Develt, 1995–99; Conservation and Science Cttee, 1997–2001, Inst. of Zool. Cttee, 1997–2001, Zool. Soc. of London. Trustee, Cambridge Past, Present & Future, 2008–16 (Chm., 2008–16). *Publications:* numerous scientific papers on wild life management and conservation in professional jls. *Recreations:* travel, watching wild life. *Address:* 32 Selwyn Gardens, Cambridge CB3 9AY.
See also M. E. Pellew.

**PELLING, Andrew John;** Contributing Editor, insidecroydon.com, since 2011; Member (Lab), Croydon Borough Council, since 2014 (Chair, Pension Committee, 2016–17 and since 2018); *b* 1959; *s* of Anthony Adair Pelling, *qv*; *m* Sanae (marr. diss.); one *s* two *d*; *m* 2006, Lucy (marr. diss.); one *d. Educ:* Trinity Sch., Croydon; New Coll., Oxford (MA PPE; Sec. and Librarian, Oxford Union Soc., 1979–80; Pres., Cons. Assoc., 1980). Head of Debt Syndicate: Samuel Montagu & Co. Ltd, 1981–82; Nikko Europe, 1982–84; Citicorp, 1984–86; Namura Internat. plc, 1986–94; NatWest Markets, 1994–97; Hd of Debt Capital Markets, UFJ Internat. plc, 1997–2005; Hd of Origination, Tokai Tokyo Securities Europe Ltd, 2007–12. Croydon Borough Council: Mem. (C), 1982–2006; Chm., Educn, 1988–94; Dep. Opposition Leader, 1996–2002, Opposition Leader, 2002–05, Cons. Gp. Greater London Authority: Mem. (C) Croydon and Sutton, London Assembly, 2000–08; Cons. spokesman on London business, 2000–04; Bd Mem., LDA, 2000–04 (Chm., Audit Panel, 2001–04); Mem., Private Investment Commn, 2002–04; London Assembly: Chairman: Graffiti Investigative Cttee, 2001–02; Public Services Cttee, 2002–04; Budget Cttee, 2004–05, 2007; Audit Panel, 2004–07. MP Croydon Central, 2005–10 (C, 2005–07, Ind, 2007–10); contested (Ind) same seat, 2010. Member: Croydon Police Consultative Cttee, 2000–10; LSC, London S, 2001–04; Educn Select Cttee, 2006–08; Children, Schools and Families Select Cttee, 2008–10. Chm., London Road Safety Panel Exec., 2015–18 (Vice-Chm., 2018–). Mem., CATE, 1990–94. Mem., S Wandle Valley Partnership, 2001–05. Presenter, Croydon Radio, 2012–14. Dir, Croydon Carers Centre, 2008–11; Vice Chm., Croydon FC, 2011–13. Treas., Croydon Co-op. Party, 2013–17. *E:* puttingcroydonfirst@gmail.com.

**PELLING, Anthony Adair;** Lecturer: Osher Institute, University of Richmond, since 2015; Shepherd's Center U3A, since 2015; Science Museum, Virginia, since 2019; *b* 3 May 1934; *s* of Brian and Alice Pelling; *m* 1st, 1958, Margaret Lightfoot (*d* 1986); one *s* one *d*; 2nd, 1989, Virginia Glen-Calvert. *Educ:* Purley Grammar Sch.; London Sch. of Economics (BSc Econ); Gen. Sec., Students' Union); Wolverhampton Coll. of Technol. MIPM. Nat. Service, RAOC, Sgt, 1955–57. National Coal Board, 1957–67; entered MPBW as Principal, 1967; Asst Sec., 1970, Under Sec., 1981, DoE; seconded as Dep. Dir, Business in the Community, 1981–83; Dept of Transport, 1983–85; Dir, Construction Industry, and Dir, Sports and Recreation Div., DoE, 1985–87; London Regional Dir, DoE, 1987–91; Dir, Construction Policy, DoE, 1991–93. Dir, GJW Government Relations Ltd, London and Washington, 1993–95. President: ESU, Richmond, 1998–2000; Byrd Theatre Foundn, Richmond, 2002–08; Chm., Region IV, and Mem. Nat. Bd, US ESU, 2000–02, 2007–09; Mem. Bd, Guardian Foundn, United Methodist Family Services, VA, 2006–08. *Recreations:* theatre, Torch Club. *Address:* 70 West Square Drive, Richmond, VA 23238–6158, USA. *E:* gjw1995pel@aol.com. *Clubs:* Reform; Kiwanis (Richmond, VA) (Mem. Bd, 2014–16).
See also A. J. Pelling.

**PELLING, Prof. Christopher Brendan Reginald,** DPhil; FBA 2009; FLSW; Regius Professor of Greek, University of Oxford, 2003–15, now Emeritus; Student of Christ Church, Oxford, 2003–15; *b* 14 Dec. 1947; *s* of Reginald Charles Pelling and (Frances Lilian) Brenda Pelling; *m* 1973, Margaret Ann Giddy; one *s* one *d* (and one *s* decd). *Educ:* Balliol Coll., Oxford (BA 1970); Christ Church, Oxford (DPhil 1975). Res. Fellow, Peterhouse, Cambridge, 1972–74; Lectr, 1974–75, McConnell Laing Fellow and Praelector in Classics, 1975–2003, University Coll., Oxford. Adjunct Prof. of Hist., Utah State Univ. 1998–; Visiting Professor: Washington and Lee Univ., Lexington, Va, 1986, 1989, 1997, 2000; Univ. of N Carolina, Chapel Hill, 2002. FLSW 2011. Hon. Fellow, University Coll., Oxford, 2012. *Publications:* Plutarch: life of Antony, 1988; (ed) Characterization and Individuality in Greek Literature, 1990; (ed) Greek Tragedy and the Historian, 1997; Literary Texts and the Greek Historian, 2000; Plutarch and History, 2002; Rome in Crisis, 2010; Plutarch: life of Caesar, 2011; (with Maria Wyke) Twelve Voices from Greece and Rome: ancient ideas for modern times, 2014; (with Simon Hornblower) Herodotus 6, 2017; Herodotus and the Question Way, 2019; articles in learned jls. *Recreations:* cricket, golf, music, conviviality. *Address:* Christ Church, Oxford OX1 1DP. *T:* (01865) 276204, *Fax:* (01865) 276150. *E:* chris.pelling@chch.ox.ac.uk. *Club:* MCC.

**PELLING, (Philip) Mark;** QC 2003; **His Honour Judge Pelling;** a Specialist Chancery Senior Circuit Judge, since 2006; *b* 27 June 1956; *s* of Philip Clive and Jean Rosemary Pelling; *m* 1986, Charlotte Jones; one *s* one *d. Educ:* Bancroft's Sch., Woodford Green; King's Coll., London (LLB; AKC). Called to the Bar, Middle Temple, 1979, Bencher, 2011; Accredited Mediator, CEDR, 2000; a Recorder, 2004–06. Hon. Bencher, King's Inns, Dublin, 2019. Board of Governors, Ravensbourne College of Design and Communication, London: Mem., 1992–2000; Chm., Audit Cttee, 1994–95; Chm., Standing Cttee, 1995–97; Chm., 1997–2000. *Publications:* (with R. A. Purdie) Matrimonial and Domestic Injunctions, 1982, 2nd edn 1987. *Recreations:* sailing, flying, shooting. *Address:* London Circuit Commercial Court, Rolls Building, Fetter Lane, EC4A 1NL. *Clubs:* Royal Automobile, Royal Ocean Racing; Royal Western Yacht.

**PELLING, Rowan Dorothy;** Editor, The Amorist, since 2017; Founding Editor, Erotic Review, 1996–2004; *b* 17 Jan. 1968; *d* of Ronald and Hazel Pelling; *m* 1995, Angus MacKinnon; two *s. Educ:* Walthamstow Hall, Sevenoaks; St Hugh's Coll., Oxford. Columnist: Independent on Sunday, 2000–08; Daily Telegraph, 2008–; Daily Mail, 2009–. Consultant, Dedalus Ltd. Judge, Man Booker Prize, 2004. Fellow, British American Project, 2004. *Publications:* The Erotic Review Bedside Companion, 2000; (ed) The Decadent Handbook, 2006; Debrett's: a modern Royal marriage, 2011. *Recreations:* racy novels, red wine, TV detective dramas, Maine Coon cats, Vivienne Westwood frocks, skinny-dipping at Newnham Riverbank club. *E:* rowan@pelling.demon.co.uk. *Clubs:* Chelsea Arts, Academy, Blacks.

**PELLY, Deborah Susan;** see Mattinson, D. S.

**PELLY, Laurent;** freelance opera and theatre director; Director, Pel-Mel Groupe, since 2018; *b* Fontenay sous Bois, France, 14 Jan. 1962; *s* of Jacques Pelly and Jeanine Pelly (*née* Loiseau). Founder and Artistic Dir, Compagnie Théâtre du Pélican, 1980; Dir, Centre Dramatique National des Alpes, Grenoble, 1997–2007; Co-Dir, Théâtre nat. de Toulouse Midi-Pyrénées, 2007–17. Freelance opera and theatre projects at opera houses including: Royal Opera Hse, Covent Garden; Glyndebourne Fest.; Metropolitan Opera, NY; Vienna State Opera; Theater an der Wien; San Francisco Opera; Santa Fe Opera; Opera Nat. de Paris; Opera de Lyon; La Scala, Milan; Teatro Regio, Turin; Th. Royal de la Monnaie, Brussels; Teatro del Liceu, Barcelona; Teatro Royal, Madrid; Opera Philadelphia; Chicago Lyric Opera; Deutsche Oper, Berlin; *productions include:* Orphée aux enfers, 1999; La Belle Hélène, 2001; Platée, 2002; Les contes d'Hoffmann, 2003, 2018; La grande duchesse, 2004; L'élisir d'amore, 2006; La vie parisienne, 2007; La fille du régiment, 2007; Cunning Little Vixen, 2008; Hänsel und Gretel, 2008; Pelléas et Mélisande, 2009; La traviata, 2009; Manon, 2010; Cendrillon, 2011; L'heure espagnole/L'enfant et les sortilèges, 2012; Robert le Diable, 2012; L'étoile, 2014; Le Comte Ory, 2014; Don Pasquale, 2014, 2018, 2019; Le Roi Carotte, 2015, 2019; Le Médecin Malgré Lui, 2016; Béatrice et Bénédict, 2016; Le Coq d'Or, 2016, 2017; Viva la mamma!, 2017, 2018; Il Barbiere di Siviglia, 2017, 2018; Candide, 2018; Lucia, 2018, 2019; Falstaff, 2019; Barbe Bleu, 2019. *Address:* c/o Maestro Arts, 1 Eastfields Avenue, SW18 1FQ. *T:* (020) 3637 2789. *E:* sally@maestroarts.com.

**PELLY, Sir Richard (John),** 7th Bt *cr* 1840, of Upton, Essex; farmer, since 1991; *b* 10 April 1951; *s* of Richard Heywood Pelly, 2nd *s* of Sir Alwyne Pelly, 5th Bt, MC and of Mary Elizabeth Pelly (*née* Luscombe); *S* uncle, 1993; *m* 1983, Clare Gemma Dove; three *s*. *Educ:* Wellington Coll., Berks; Wadham Coll., Oxford (BA Agriculture and Forestry Science). ACA 1978–82. Price Waterhouse, London, 1974–78; Birds Eye Foods Ltd, 1978–81; New Century Software Ltd, 1981–99. *Heir: s* Anthony Alwyne Pelly, *b* 30 Oct. 1984. *Address:* The Manor House, Preshaw, Upham, Southampton SO32 1HP. *T:* (01962) 771757.

**PEMBER, Susan Alison,** OBE 2000; Director of Policy, Holex, since 2015; *b* 23 Dec. 1954; *d* of Bernard Pember and Muriel Pember; one *s*; *m* 1996, Brian Hudgell. *Educ:* Glamorgan Coll. of Educn (Cert Ed); Poly. of Wales, Pontypridd (BEd Univ. of Wales). Lectr, Redbridge Coll., 1977–83; Sen. Lectr, Southgate Coll., 1983–86; Educn Officer, 1986–87, Sen. Educn Officer, 1987–91, London Bor. of Enfield; Principal, Canterbury Coll., 1991–2000; Dir, Adult Basic Skills Strategy Gp, then Apprenticeships and Skills for Life, later Further Educn and Learning and Skills Perf. Gp, DFES, later DIUS, 2000–09; Dir, Learning and Skills Council Transition to Skills Funding Agency, DIUS, later BIS, 2009–10; Dir, Further Educn and Skills Investment, BIS, 2010–13. *Recreations:* textiles, ski-ing, gardening.

**PEMBERTHY, Sacha;** see Romanovitch, S.

**PEMBERTON, (Christopher) Mark,** OBE 2012; heritage consultant; *b* Much Wenlock, Shropshire, 24 Oct. 1952; *s* of Frank and Freda May Pemberton. *Educ:* Abraham Darby Sch., Telford; Fitzwilliam Coll., Cambridge (BA 1975). Ironbridge Gorge Museum Trust: mus. asst, 1975–80; Gen. Manager, 1980–85; Dep. Dir, 1985–87; Science Museum, London: Mktg Dir, 1987–91; Asst Dir and Hd, Public Affairs, 1991–2000; English Heritage: Business Dir, 2000–05; Dir, Properties and Educn, 2005–10; Dir of Nat. Collections, 2010–15; House Dir, Castle Howard, 2015–18. Chm., RCGP Enterprises Ltd, 2014–. Chm., Waltham Abbey Royal Gunpowder Mills Charitable Foundn, 2011–; Dir, Ops, Nat. Mus. of the RN, 2019–. Trustee, St Bartholomew's Heritage, 2018–. FMA 1987. *Address:* 117B Dartmouth Road, NW2 4ES. *T:* (020) 8450 4613. *Club:* Athenæum.

**PEMBERTON, Gary Milton,** AC 1999; Chairman, Racing NSW, 2004–08; *s* of Eric Pemberton; *m* Margaret Whitford; four *c*. *Educ:* Fort Street High Sch. Australian Wool Bd, 1961–72; joined Brambles Industries Ltd, 1972: Chief Exec., 1982–93; Dep. Chm. 1994–96; Chairman: Qantas Airways Ltd, 1993–2000; TAB Ltd, 1997–2002; Billabong International, 2002–06; Director: Commonwealth Bank, 1989–93; John Fairfax Hldgs Ltd, 1992–93; CSR Ltd, 1993–94. Chief Exec. Officer, 1994–95, Pres., 1995–96, Sydney Organising Cttee of the Olympic Games.

**PEMBERTON, Jessica Louise Chantall; Her Honour Judge Pemberton;** a Circuit Judge, since 2014; *b* Sheffield, 10 Aug. 1968; *d* of Adam and Brigitte Pemberton; *m* 1991, David; two *s*. *Educ:* Keele Univ. (BA Jt Hons Law and Sociol. 1991); Coll. of Law, Guildford. Admitted Solicitor, 1992; in practice as solicitor, 1994–2007; called to the Bar, Inner Temple, 2007; a Recorder, 2012–14. *Recreations:* singing, travel, theatre. *Address:* Sheffield Family Hearing Court, 50 West Bar, Sheffield S3 8PH.

**PEMBERTON, Mark;** see Pemberton, C. M.

**PEMBERTON, Steven James;** actor and writer, since 1995; *b* Blackburn, 1 Sept. 1967; *s* of Derek and Margaret Pemberton; partner, Alison Rowles; two *s* one *d*. *Educ:* Bretton Hall Coll. (BA Hons Th. Arts). Artistic Dir, 606 Th. Co., 1991–95; Asst Ed., Variety Internat. Film Guide, 1991–96. *Television:* co-writer, creator and actor: The League of Gentlemen, 1999–2002, 2017; Psychoville, 2009–11; Inside No 9, 2014–; Mapp and Lucia, 2014; actor: Gormenghast, 2000; Blackpool, 2004; Shameless, 2004; Lassie, 2005; The Old Curiosity Shop, 2007; Benidorm, 2007–15; Doctor Who, 2008; Whitechapel, 2009–13; Happy Valley, 2014; *films:* Death on the Nile, 2004; Mr Bean's Holiday, 2007; *theatre:* The 25th Annual Putnam County Spelling Bee, Donmar, 2011; She Stoops to Conquer, NT, 2012; Dead Funny, Vaudeville, 2016; The League of Gentlemen (also writer), nat. tour, 2018. Hon. DLitt Huddersfield, 2013. *Recreations:* theatre, cinema, crosswords, family, travel. *Address:* c/o PBJ Management, 22 Rathbone Street, W1T 1LG. *T:* (020) 7287 1112. *E:* chiggy@pbjmgt.co.uk.

**PEMBROKE,** 18th Earl of, *cr* 1551, **AND MONTGOMERY,** 15th Earl of, *cr* 1605; **William Alexander Sidney Herbert;** Baron Herbert of Cardiff, 1551; Baron Herbert of Shurland, 1605; Baron Herbert of Lea (UK); *b* 18 May 1978; *s* of 17th Earl of Pembroke and Montgomery, and Claire Rose Herbert (*née* Pelly); *S* father, 2003; *m* 2010, Victoria, *d* of Michael Bullough, Perth; one *s* one *d*. *Educ:* Bryanston Sch.; Sheffield Hallam Univ. (1st cl. Hons Industrial Design). Two years as product designer, Conran & Partners. Runs Wilton Estate. *Recreations:* scuba diving, ski-ing. *Heir: s* Lord Herbert, *qv*.

**PEMSEL, David Skipwith;** Chief Executive Officer, Guardian Media Group, 2015–20; Chief Executive, Premier League, since 2020; *b* London, 31 March 1968; *s* of Christopher John Pemsel and Heather Sonia Pemsel (*née* Leslie); *m* 2001, Katharine Stanners; one *s*. *Educ:* East Sheen Sch. Gp Account Dir, Ogilvy & Mather, 1994–96; Man. Partner, St Lukes Communications, 1996–2000; Partner, Shine, 2000–02; Gp Mktg Dir, ITV, 2005–10; Guardian News and Media: Chief Mktg Officer, 2011–12; Chief Commercial Officer, 2012–13; Dep. CEO, 2013–15. Member: Council, Mktg Gp of GB, 2009–; Bd, Scott Trust, 2015–. Non-exec. Dir, British Fashion Council, 2015–. Mem., BAFTA, 2006–. *Recreations:* tennis, cycling. *Address:* Guardian Media Group, Kings Place, 90 York Way, N1 9GU. *T:* (020) 3353 3969. *E:* david.pemsel@theguardian.com. *Clubs:* Soho House, Ivy, Thirty.

**PEÑA, Paco;** musician; flamenco guitar player, since 1954; Professor of Flamenco, Rotterdam Conservatory, since 1985; *b* 1 June 1942; *s* of Antonio Peña and Rosario Perez; *m* 1982, Karin Vaessen; two *d*. *Educ:* Córdoba, Spain. London début, 1968; New York début, 1983; founded: Paco Peña Flamenco Co., 1970; Centro Flamenco Paco Peña, Córdoba, 1981; composed Misa Flamenca, 1991, Requiem for the Earth, 2004; Quimeras, 2010; produced: Musa Gitana, 1999; Voces y Ecos, 2002; A Compás, 2006; Flamenco sin Fronteras, 2010; Flamencura, 2015; Patrias, 2016. Ramón Montoya Prize, 1983; Gold Medal in Arts, John F. Kennedy Center for Performing Arts, 2012. Officer, Order of Merit (Spain), 1997. *Address:* c/o MPM London, 4th Floor, 11 Denmark Street, WC2H 8LS; c/o Karin Vaessen, 4 Boscastle Road, NW5 1EG. *Fax:* (020) 7485 2320.

**PENBERTHY, Rt Rev. Joanna Susan;** see St Davids, Bishop of.

**PENDER,** 4th Baron *cr* 1937; **Henry John Richard Denison-Pender;** *b* 19 March 1968; *s* of 3rd Baron Pender and Julia (*née* Cannon); *S* father, 2016; *m* 1st, 1994, Vanessa Jane (marr. diss. 2012), *d* of John Eley; one *s* one *d*; 2nd, 2015, Georgina Sheila, *d* of David Pearman. *Heir: s* Hon. Miles John Cuthbert Denison-Pender, *b* 10 Dec. 2000.

**PENDER, David James;** Sheriff of North Strathclyde, since 1995; *b* 7 Sept. 1949; *s* of James and Isa Pender; *m* 1974, Elizabeth Jean McKillop; two *s* two *d*. *Educ:* Queen's Park Sen. Secondary Sch., Glasgow; Edinburgh Univ. (LLB Hons). Qualified as Solicitor, 1973; Partner, MacArthur Stewart, Solicitors, Oban, 1977–95. Sec., Oban Faculty of Solicitors, 1977–95. *Recreations:* travel, bridge, reading. *Address:* Sheriff's Chambers, Paisley Sheriff Court, St James Street, Paisley PA3 2HW. *T:* (0141) 887 5291.

**PENDER, Prof. Gareth,** PhD; FREng; FRSE; Professor of Environmental Engineering, since 2000, and Deputy Principal (Research and Innovation), since 2016, Heriot-Watt University; *b* Helensburgh, 24 Jan. 1960; *s* of Blair and Gweneth Pender; *m* 1984, Isobel McNaught Connell; one *s* two *d*. *Educ:* Strathclyde Univ. (BSc Civil Engrg 1981; PhD 1985). FREng 2013. Engr, Crouch & Hogg, 1984–89; Lectr, Univ. of Glasgow, 1989–2000; Hd, Sch. of Built Envmt, then Sch. of Energy, Geosci., Infrastructure and Society, Heriot-Watt Univ., 2008–16. FRSE 2007. *Recreations:* golf, ski-ing, walking. *Address:* George Heriot Wing, Heriot-Watt University, Edinburgh EH14 4AS. *T:* (0131) 451 3312. *E:* g.pender@hw.ac.uk.

**PENDER, Simon Charles;** Sheriff of North Strathclyde at Dumbarton, 2004–19; *b* 23 June 1953; *s* of Robert R. E. Pender and Jean Elisabeth (*née* Haddow); *m* 1984, Linda Jeanne Miller; two *s* two *d*. *Educ:* Trinity Coll., Glenalmond; Univ. of Heidelberg; Univ. of Edinburgh (LLB). Solicitor, 1976–99: Partner: Breeze Paterson & Chapman, 1980–95; Dundas & Wilson, CS, 1995–99. Temp. Sheriff, 1995–99; Sheriff of S Strathclyde, Dumfries and Galloway at Hamilton, 1999–2004. Mem., Royal Scottish Pipers' Soc. *Recreations:* sailing, playing the great Highland bagpipe, ski-ing and various other sports, including golf, shooting and cycling, studying the Gaelic language. *Clubs:* Glasgow Highland; Cardross Golf; Royal Northern and Clyde Yacht, Mudhook Yacht, Clyde Cruising.

**PENDERECKI, Krzysztof;** Rector, State Academy of Music, Kraków, 1972–87; Professor of Composition, School of Music, Yale University, New Haven, Conn, 1973–78; *b* Debica, Poland, 23 Nov. 1933; *s* of Tadeusz Penderecki and Zofia Penderecki; *m* 1965, Elzbieta Solecka; one *s* one *d*. *Educ:* State Acad. of Music, Kraków, Poland (Graduate 1958). Compositions include: Threnody to the Victims of Hiroshima, 1960 (52 strings); Passion According to St Luke, 1965–66 (oratorio); Dies irae, 1967; Utrenja, 1969–71 (oratorio); Devils of Loudon, 1969 (opera); Cello Concerto No 1, 1971–72; First Symphony, 1972; Magnificat, 1974 (oratorio); Awakening of Jacob, 1974 (orchestra); Paradise Lost, 1976–78 (rappresentazione for Chicago Lyric Opera; Milton libretto, Christopher Fry); Violin Concerto, 1977; Te Deum, 1979–80; (Christmas) Symphony No 2, 1980; Lacrimosa, 1980; Agnus Dei (for chorus a cappella), 1981; Cello Concerto No 2, 1982 (Grammy Award, Nat. Acad. of Recording Arts and Scis, 1988); Viola Concerto, 1983; Polish Requiem, 1983–84; Die schwarze Maske, 1986 (opera); Veni creator and Song of Cherubin (for chorus a cappella), 1987; Das unterbrochene Gedanke (for string quartet), 1988; Symphony No 3, 1988–95; Symphony No 4, 1989; Ubu Rex, 1991 (opera); Symphony No 5, 1991–92; Sinfonietta per archi, 1992; Flute Concerto, 1992–93; Quartet for clarinet and string trio, 1993; Violin Concerto No 2, 1995 (Grammy Award, 1999); Seven Gates of Jerusalem (oratorio), 1997; Credo (oratorio), 1998 (Grammy Award, 2001); Sextett, 2000; Concerto grosso per tre violocelli, 2000; Concerto per pianoforte e orch., 2001; Largo per violoncello ed orchestra, 2003; Concerto grosso No 2 per 5 clarinetti, 2004; Symphony No 8, Lieder der Vergänglichkeit, 2005–07; Concerto per corno, 2008; Quartetto per archi No 3, 2008; Kadisz, 2009; Missa brevis, 2012; Concerto Doppio, 2012; Dies Illa, 2014; Concertino per tramoba ed orchestra, 2015; Polonaise pour orchestre, 2015; Symphony No 6, Chinese Songs, 2017; Fanfara, 2018; Katyn (film score), 2007 (Best Film Score, Polish Film Awards, 2008). Hon. Professor: Moscow Tchaikovsky Conservatory, 1997; Beijing Conservatory, 1998; Komitas State Conservatory, Yerevan, 2008. Hon. Dr: Univ. of Rochester, NY; St Olaf Coll., Northfield, Minn; Katholieke Univ., Leuven; Univ. of Bordeaux; Georgetown Univ., Washington; Univ. of Belgrade; Universidad Autónoma, Madrid; Adam Mickiewicz Univ.; Warsaw Univ.; Acad. of Music, Cracow and Warsaw; Univ. of Glasgow; Duquesne Univ., Pittsburgh. Member: RAM (Hon.); Akad. der Künste, Berlin (Extraordinary); Akad. der Künste der DDR, Berlin (Corresp.); Kungl. Musikaliska Akad., Stockholm; Accad. Nazionale di Santa Cecilia, Rome (Hon.); Acad. Nacional de Bellas Artes, Buenos Aires (Corresp.); Royal Acad. of Music, Dublin (Hon.); Akad. der schönen Künste, Munich (Corresp.); Composers Union of Armenia (Hon.); Musikverein Graz (Hon.); Hon. Foreign Mem.: Amer. Acad. Arts and Letters. Grosser Kunstpreis, 1966, Staatspreis, 2002, des Landes Nordrhein-Westfalen; Prix Italia, 1967/68; Gottfried von Herder Preis der Stiftung FvS zu Hamburg, 1977; Prix Arthur Honegger, 1977; Sibelius Prize, Wihouri Foundn, 1983; Premio Lorenzo Magnifico, 1985; Wolf Prize, 1987; Manuel de Falla Gold Medal, Accademia de Bellas Artes, Granada, 1989; Grawemeyer Award, Univ. of Louisville, 1992; Internat. Music Council/UNESCO Prize for Music, 1993; Prime Time Emmy Award, Acad. of Television Arts and Scis, 1995 and 1996; Crystall Award, Econ. Forum, Davos, 1997; Music Award, City of Duisburg, 1999; Cannes Classical Award, 2000; Prince of Asturios Award, 2001; Eduardo Martínez Torner Medal, Conservatorio Superior de Música, Oviedo, 2003; Romano Guardini Prize, Catholic Acad., Bavaria, 2002; Praemium Imperiale, 2004; Super Wiktor Award, Polish Wiktory TV Acad., 2011; Glocal Hero Award, Transatlantyk Film and Music Fest., Poznan, 2012; Lifetime Achievement Award, Internat. Classical Music Awards, 2014; Viadrina Prize, Europa-Universität, Frankfurt an der Oder, 2012; Per Artem ad Deum Medal, Pontifical Council of Culture, 2015. Das Grosse Verdienstkreuz des Verdienstordens (Germany), 1990; Order of White Eagle, 2005; Commander, Three Star Order, Riga, 2006; Order of Honour, Armenia, 2009; Order of Cross, Terra Mariana, Estonia, 2014. Hon. Citizen, Krakow, 2013. *Publications:* all works published. *Recreations:* dendrology, gardening. *Address:* Schott Musik International, Concert Opera Media Division, Weihergarten 5, 55116 Mainz, Germany. *T:* (6131) 2460, *Fax:* (6131) 246250.

**PENDLEBURY, Graham**; Director, Local Transport, Department for Transport, 2013–19; *b* 7 Oct. 1958; *s* of Alan Pendlebury and late Margaret Elizabeth Pendlebury (*née* Moore); *m* 1991, Jill Amanda Thatcher; one *s*. *Educ*: Bolton Sch. (Boys' Div.); Sidney Sussex Coll., Cambridge (MA Hons Hist. 1981). Entered Civil Service, 1984; grad. trainee, 1986–90; Grade 7, Cabinet Office, then Dept of Transport, then DETR, 1990–99; Hd, Policy Strategy Integration Div., DETR, then DTLR, 1999–2001; Hd, Aviation Envmtl Div., DTLR, then DfT, 2001–04; Dir, Road and Vehicle Safety and Standards, 2004–07, Dir, Envmt and Internat., 2007–10, Dir, Greener Transport and Internat., 2010–13, DfT. Policy Fellow, Centre for Sci. and Policy, Univ. of Cambridge, 2011–13, 2016–19. FCIHT 2018. *Publications*: Aspects of the English Civil War in Bolton and its Neighbourhood 1640–1660, 1983. *Recreations*: history, reading, walking, family, Bolton Wanderers FC.

**PENDRED, Piers Loughnan**; Director General, International Psychoanalytical Association, 2000–07; *b* 24 Aug. 1943; *s* of Loughnan Wildig Pendred and Dulcie Treen Hall; *m* 1973, Carol Ann Haslam; one *s* one *d*. *Educ*: Ardingly College; Trinity Hall, Cambridge (MA Fine Arts and Architecture). VSO teacher, S India, 1965–67; British Council, 1967–99: Television Officer, Sudan, 1967–69, Ethiopia, 1969–71; TV Training Officer, London, 1972–76; Head of Production, 1976–81; Dir, Design, Production and Publishing, 1981–84; Dir, Press and Inf., 1984–87; Controller, later Dir of Finance, 1987–94; Special Asst to Dir-Gen., 1994–95; Asst Dir-Gen., 1996–99. Sen. Exec. Programme, London Business Sch., 1987. Trustee, Centre for Internat. Briefing, 1996–99.

**PENDRY**, family name of **Baron Pendry**.

**PENDRY, Baron** *cr* 2001 (Life Peer), of Stalybridge in the County of Greater Manchester; **Thomas Pendry**; PC 2000; *b* 10 June 1934; *m* 1966, Moira Anne Smith (separated 1983, she *d* 2019); one *s* one *d*. *Educ*: St Augustine's, Ramsgate; Oxford Univ. RAF, 1955–57. Full time official, Nat. Union of Public Employees, 1960–70; Mem., Paddington Borough Council, 1962–65; Chm., Derby Labour Party, 1966. MP (Lab) Stalybridge and Hyde, 1970–2001. An Opposition Whip, 1971–74; a Lord Comr of the Treasury and Govt Whip, 1974; resigned 1977; Parly Under-Sec. of State, NI Office, 1978–79; Opposition spokesman on NI, 1979–81, on overseas development, 1981, on regional affairs and devolution, 1981–83, on sport and tourism, 1992–97. Member: Select Cttee on Envmt, 1987–92; Select Cttee on Members' Interests, 1987–92. Founder Mem., and Chm., 1980–92, All Party Football Gp. Member: Speaker's Conf., 1973; UK delegn to WEU and Council of Europe, 1973–75. Pres., Football Foundn, 2003– (Chm., 1999–2003); Chm., Football Trust, 1997–99. Steward, British Boxing Bd of Control, 1987–98. President: Stalybridge Public Band; Stalybridge Labour Club; Patron, Nat. Fedn of Football Supporters, 1998–. Freeman, Bor. of Tameside and Lordship of Mottram in Longendale, 1995. *Publications*: Taking it on the Chin (memoirs), 2016. *Recreations*: sport; football, cricket, boxing (sometime Middleweight Champion, Hong Kong; boxed for Oxford Univ.). *Address*: House of Lords, SW1A 0PW. *Clubs*: Garrick, Royal Air Force, MCC, Lord's Taverners; Vincent's (Oxford); Stalybridge Labour.

**PENDRY, Sir John (Brian)**, Kt 2004; PhD; FRS 1984; Professor of Theoretical Solid State Physics, Department of Physics, Imperial College London (formerly Imperial College of Science, Technology and Medicine, University of London), since 1981 (Head, Department of Physics, 1998–2001); Dean, Royal College of Science, 1993–96; *b* 4 July 1943; *s* of Frank Johnson Pendry and Kathleen (*née* Shaw); *m* 1977, Patricia Gard. *Educ*: Downing Coll., Cambridge (MA; PhD 1969; Hon. Fellow, 2005). Res. Fellow in Physics, Downing Coll., Cambridge, 1969–72; Mem. of Technical Staff, Bell Labs, USA, 1972–73; Sen. Asst in Res., Cavendish Lab., Cambridge Univ., and Fellow in Physics and Praelector, Downing Coll., 1973–75; SPSO and Head of Theory Gp, Daresbury Lab., 1975–81. Mem., PPARC, 1998–2002. Foreign Associate, US NAS, 2013; Foreign Mem., Norwegian Acad. of Sci. and Letters, 2014. *Publications*: Low Energy Electron Diffraction, 1974; Surface Crystallographic Information Service, 1987; scientific papers. *Recreations*: music, gardening, photography. *Address*: The Blackett Laboratory, Imperial College London, SW7 2AZ. *T*: (020) 7594 7606. *Clubs*: Athenæum, Oxford and Cambridge.

**PENFOLD, Peter Alfred**, CMG 1995; OBE 1986; international consultant; formerly HM Diplomatic Service; *b* 27 Feb. 1944; *s* of Alfred Penfold and Florence (*née* Green); *m* 1st, 1972, Margaret Quigley (marr. diss. 1983); 2nd, 1992, Celia Dolores Koenig. *Educ*: Sutton Co. Grammar Sch. Joined Foreign Service, 1963; Bonn, 1965–68; Kaduna, 1968–70; Latin American Floater, 1970–72; Canberra, 1972; FCO, 1972–75; Second Secretary: Addis Ababa, 1975–78; Port of Spain, 1978–81; First Sec., FCO, 1981–84; Dep. High Comr, Kampala, 1984–87; First Sec., FCO, 1987–91; Gov., BVI, 1991–95; Special Advr on Drugs in the Caribbean, 1995–96; High Comr, Sierra Leone, 1997–2000; Sen. Conflict Advr, DFID, 2001. Pres., UK Assoc. for Schs for the Blind, Sierra Leone, 2010–; Patron: Dorothy Springer Trust, 2010–; Hastings Sierra Leone Link, 2010–. *Publications*: Atrocities, Diamonds and Diplomacy, 2012. *Recreations*: travel, reading. *Address*: Fisherman's Wharf, Abingdon, Oxfordshire OX14 5RX.

**PENFORD, Adam**; Artistic Director, Nottingham Playhouse, since 2018; *b* Nottingham, 1 March 1980; *s* of Gregory and Inge Penford. *Educ*: Liverpool Inst. for Performing Arts (BA 1st Cl. Hons Performing Arts). Director: The Hostage, Southwark Playhouse, 2010; Stepping Out, 2012, Deathtrap, 2016, Salisbury Playhouse; Ghost the Musical, English Th. Frankfurt, 2014; Watership Down, Watermill, 2016; Platinum, Hampstead, 2016–17; Committee, Donmar Warehouse, 2017; The Boys in the Band, 2017; National Theatre: Island, 2012; One Man, Two Guvnors (revival), 2014; A Small Family Business, 2014; Nottingham Playhouse: Wonderland, 2018; Holes, 2018; The Madness of George III, 2018; Coram Boy, 2019; An Enemy of the People, 2019.

**PENGELLY, Emma L.**; *see* Little-Pengelly.

**PENGELLY, Richard Anthony**; Under Secretary, Welsh Office, 1977–85; *b* 18 Aug. 1925; *s* of Richard Francis Pengelly and Ivy Mildred Pengelly; *m* 1st, 1952, Phyllis Mary Rippon; one *s*; 2nd, 1972, Margaret Ruth Crossley; two *s* one *d*. *Educ*: Plymouth Coll.; School of Oriental and African Studies; London Sch. of Economics and Political Science (BScEcon). Served War: Monmouthshire Regt and Intell. Corps, 1943–47. Joined Min. of Supply as Asst Principal, 1950, Principal, 1954; NATO Defence Coll., 1960–61; Asst Sec., Min. of Aviation, 1964; RCDS 1971; Min. of Defence, 1972. *Recreation*: golf. *Address*: Byways, 8 Wern Goch Road, Cyncoed, Cardiff, S Wales CF23 6SD. *T*: (029) 2076 4418.

**PENHALIGON, Dame Annette**, DBE 1993; Member (Lib Dem): Restormel Borough Council, Cornwall, 2003–09; Cornwall County Council, 2005–09; *b* 9 Feb. 1946; *d* of late Owen Bennett Lidgey and Mabel Lidgey; *m* 1968, David Charles Penhaligon, MP (*d* 1986); one *s* one *d*; *m* 1994, Robert William Egerton. *Educ*: Truro Girls' Grammar Sch. Subpostmistress, Chacewater PO, 1967–79; Sec. to husband, David Penhaligon, MP (L) Truro, 1974–86. Mem. (L, then Lib Dem), Carrick DC, Cornwall, 1987–94. Non-exec. Dir, Cornwall Independent Radio, 1992–2002. Patron, Penhaligon's Friends. *Publications*: Penhaligon, 1989. *Recreation*: supporting charities helping people with learning disabilities. *Address*: Trevillick House, Fore Street, Grampound, Truro, Cornwall TR2 4RS. *T*: (01726) 884451.

**PENMAN, Ian Dalgleish**, CB 1987; Deputy Secretary, Central Services, Scottish Office, 1984–91; *b* 1 Aug. 1931; *s* of late John B. Penman and Dorothy Dalgleish; *m* 1963, Elisabeth Stewart Strachan; three *s*. *Educ*: High Sch., Glasgow; Glasgow Univ. (MA Classics); Balliol Coll., Oxford (MA Lit.Hum.; Snell Exhibnr and Ferguson Scholar). National Service, RAF, 1955–57 (Educn Br.). Asst Principal, HM Treasury, 1957–58; Scottish Office, 1958–91; Private Sec. to Parly Under-Sec. of State, 1960–62; Principal, Scottish Develt Dept, 1962–69; Asst Sec., Estab. Div., 1970–72; Asst Sec., Scottish Home and Health Dept, 1972–78; Under-Sec., Scottish Develt Dept, 1978–84. Member: Chm.'s Panel, CSSB, 1991–95; Sec. of State's Panel of Inquiry Reporters, 1992–94; Council on Tribunals, 1994–2001 (Mem., Scottish Cttee, 1994–2001); Church of Scotland Cttee on Probationers, 1994–97; C of S Bd of Ministry, 1997–2003. Chm., Viewpoint Housing Assoc., 1991–95; Chief Exec., Scottish Homes, April–Oct. 1991. *Recreations*: walking, music, travel. *Address*: 54/5 Newbattle Terrace, Edinburgh EH10 4RX.

**PENN, Charles Richard**, TD 1990; PhD; consultant and adviser on antimicrobial resistance; *b* 12 June 1957; *s* of Lt Col Charles Edward Penn and Mary Elizabeth Penn; *m* 1980, Elizabeth Jane Dawson; two *d*. *Educ*: Christ Church, Oxford (MA 1979); Wolfson Coll., Cambridge (PhD 1982). Res. Fellow, Wolfson Coll., Cambridge, 1982–84; SSO, Inst. for Animal Health, 1984–88; Sen. Res. Associate, Glaxo R&D, 1988–95; Sen. Med. Strategy Hd, Glaxo Wellcome, 1995–98; Dir for R&D, Centre for Applied Microbiol. and Res., subseq. HPA Porton Down, 1998–2005; Founder and Chief Develt Officer, Syntaxin, 2005–08; Scientist, 2009–11, Coordinator for Antimicrobial Resistance and Chm., Guidelines Review Cttee, 2011–15, WHO. Vis. Professorial Fellow, Univ. of Bath, 1999–2005. Mem., NICE Public Health Adv. Cttee, 2015–18. TAVR (RE), 1975–92. Co-inventor on patent, oxathiolane nucleoside analogues (treatment for AIDS/HIV). Chm., Winterbourne Parish Council, 2017–. *Publications*: papers in professional jls, inc. Nature. *Recreations*: hiking, fishing, gardening.

**PENN, Jeremy John Harley**; Chief Executive, Baltic Exchange, 2004–16; *b* 11 March 1959; *s* of late Comdr Geoffrey Briscoe Penn and of Barbara Penn (*née* Beverley Robinson); marr. diss.; one *s* one *d*; *m* 2016, Philippa Soden. *Educ*: Warwick Sch., Warwick; Corpus Christi Coll., Oxford (MA 1981); Harvard Business Sch. (AMP 1999). Reuters Gp plc, 1981–2001: Man. Dir, Reuters Asia, 1997–99; Dep. CEO, Reuterspace Div., 1999–2001; ind. consultant, 2002–03; Baltic Exchange, 2003–16. Director: Maritime London, 2004–; Maritime UK, 2010–. Trustee, Royal Museums Greenwich, 2015–. *Recreations*: theatre, skiing, golf, joinery. *Clubs*: Tanglin (Singapore); Wildernesse Golf (Kent).

**PENN, Richard**; consultant, since 2000; Senior Associate, Local Government Association, since 2000; *b* 4 Oct. 1945; *s* of George Stanley Penn; *m* 1968, Jillian Mary Elias; three *s* one *d*. *Educ*: Canton High Sch., Cardiff; University Coll., Cardiff (BSc Econs Jt Hons); University Coll., Swansea (DipEd). MBPS. Lectr, University Coll., Cardiff, 1968–70; Glamorgan, then W Glamorgan, CC, 1970–76; Asst Chief Exec., Cleveland CC, 1976–78; Dep. Chief Exec., W Midlands CC, 1978–81; Chief Executive: Knowsley Metropolitan Council, 1981–89; City of Bradford Metropolitan Council, 1989–99. Comr for Standards, Nat. Assembly for Wales, 2000–10; Chairman: S Wales Probation Bd, 2001–07; Ind. Remuneration Panel for Wales, 2008–15; Member: EOC, 1997–2002; Legal Services Commn, 2000–03. Gen. Manager, Caldicot and Wentlooge Levels Internal Drainage Bd, 2011–15. FCMI; FRSA. *Recreations*: family, Rugby Union, theatre, good food.

**PENN, Sean Justin**; actor, director and writer; *b* Burbank, Calif, 17 Aug. 1960; *s* of Leo Penn and Eileen Penn (*née* Ryan); *m* 1st, 1985, Madonna Louise Veronica Ciccone, *qv* (marr. diss. 1989); 2nd, 1996, Robin Wright (marr. diss. 2010); one *s* one *d*. *Educ*: Santa Monica High Sch.; studied acting with Peggy Feury. Joined LA Gp Repertory Theater (backstage work; dir, Terrible Jim Fitch (one-act play)); moved to NYC, 1980; *theatre includes*: Earthworms, 1980; Heartland, 1981; Slab Boys, 1983; Hurlyburly, 1988; The Late Henry Moss, 2000. *Films include*: Taps, 1981; Fast Times at Ridgemont High, 1982; Summerspell, Bad Boys, 1983; Crackers, Racing with the Moon, 1984; The Falcon and the Snowman, 1985; At Close Range, Shanghai Surprise, 1986; Colors, Judgement in Berlin, Cool Blue, 1988; Casualties of War, We're No Angels, 1989; State of Grace, 1990; The Last Party, Carlito's Way, 1993; Dead Man Walking, 1996; U-Turn, She's So Lovely (also prod.), The Game, Hugo Pool, 1997; As I Lay Dying (also prod.), Loved (also prod.), The Thin Red Line, Hurlyburly, Sweet and Lowdown, Being John Malkovich, 1999; Up at the Villa, The Weight of Water, 2000; Before Night Falls, 2001; I Am Sam, 2002; Mystic River (Academy Award for best actor), 2003; It's All About Love, 21 Grams, 2004; The Interpreter, The Assassination of Richard Nixon, 2005; All the King's Men, 2006; Milk (Academy Award for best actor), 2009; Fair Game, 2010; The Tree of Life, 2011; This Must be the Place, 2012; Gangster Squad, The Secret Life of Walter Mitty, 2013; The Gunman, 2015; *television includes*: The First, 2018; *director*: The Pledge, 2001; The Last Face, 2016; *director and writer*: The Indian Runner, 1991; The Crossing Guard, 1995; Into the Wild, 2007. *Publications*: Bob Honey Who Just Do Stuff, 2018.

**PENNA, Her Honour Jai**; a Circuit Judge, 2010–18; *b* Glasgow, 16 Jan. 1961; *née* Jacqueline Anne; *d* of Jeffery Warne Penna and Vivienne Aldcroft Penna (*née* Carrier); partner, Paula Margot Tyler, *qv*. *Educ*: Redland High Sch., Bristol; Trinity Coll., Cambridge (BA Hons Classics 1983); Manchester Poly. (CPE). Admitted as solicitor, 1989; a Recorder, 2002–10. *Publications*: (contrib.) Civil Court Practice, 2006; (contrib.) Child Case Management Practice, 2009; (contrib.) Children and Same Sex Families, 2012. *Recreations*: ski-ing, Italian language, travel.

**PENNANT**; *see* Douglas-Pennant.

**PENNANT-REA, Rupert Lascelles**; Chairman: The Economist Group, 2009–18 (non-executive Director, 2006–18); Royal London Group, 2013–18; *b* 23 Jan. 1948; *s* of late Peter Athelwold Pennant-Rea and Pauline Elizabeth Pennant-Rea; two *s* one *d*; *m* 2011, Cinzia De Santis; one step *d*. *Educ*: Peterhouse, Zimbabwe; Trinity Coll., Dublin (BA); Manchester Univ. (MA). Confedn of Irish Industry, 1970–71; Gen. and Municipal Workers Union, 1972–73; Bank of England, 1973–77; The Economist, 1977–93, Editor, 1986–93; Dep. Gov., Bank of England, 1993–95; Chairman: The Stationery Office, 1996–2005; PGI Gp Ltd (formerly Plantation & Gen. Investments, then PGI plc), 1997–; Security Printing and Systems, 1999–2006; Acuity Growth VCT (formerly Electra Kingsway VCT), 2002–11; Henderson Gp, 2005–13. Non-executive Director: British American Tobacco, 1995–2007; Sherritt Internat. Inc., 1995–2007; First Quantum Minerals, 2001–; Gold Fields, 2002–13; Go Ahead Gp, 2002–13; Times Newspapers, 2003–; Hochschild Mining plc, 2012–13. Trustee: Action Med. Res., 2000–07; Wincott Foundn, 2000–; Marjorie Deane Financial Journalism Foundn, 1998–; Speakers Trust, 2015–. Chm., Shakespeare Schs Fest., 2001–15. Gov., Peterhouse, Zimbabwe, 1994–. *Publications*: Gold Foil, 1979; (jtly) Who Runs the Economy?, 1980; (jtly) The Pocket Economist, 1983; (jtly) The Economist Economics, 1986. *Recreations*: music, golf, fishing, family. *Clubs*: MCC, Reform; Harare (Zimbabwe).

**PENNECK, Stephen John**, CStat, FSS; Director General, Office for National Statistics, 2009–12; *b* 25 June 1951; *s* of Norman James Penneck and Rose Esther Penneck; *m* 1979, Pauline Ann Tunnell; two *d*. *Educ*: Southampton Univ. (BSc Social Sc 1972); Birmingham Univ. (MSocSc 1973). Cadet statistician, CSO, 1972–73; Asst and Sen. Asst Statistician,

1973–78, Statistician, 1978–85, DTI; OFT, 1985–91; CSO, 1991–93; Chief Statistician, Hd of Profession, DTI, 1993–96; Office for National Statistics: Director: Nat. Accounts Div., 1997–2000; Nat. Stats and Policy Div., 2000–03; Statistical Outputs Gp, 2003–05; Exec. Dir, Surveys and Admin. Sources, 2005–08; Exec. Dir, Methodology, 2008–09. Pres., Internat. Assoc. for Official Statistics, 2011–13; Mem. Council, Royal Statistical Soc., 2014– (Hon. Officer for Official Statistics, 2018–). Mem., ISI, 2010 (Chm., Adv. Bd on Ethics, 2013–; Vice Pres., 2016–19; Pres.-elect, 2019–). Mem. (Lib Dem), Sutton LBC, 1983–94 and 2014– (Chm., Educn Cttee, 1986–91; Dep. Leader, 1988–94). Governor: Greenshaw High Sch., 1983–2004; All Saints (Benhilton) Primary Sch., 1986–2006. *Publications:* contrib. articles to Econ. Trends, Statistical News, Jl of Official Statistics, Statistical Jl of IAOS and conf. proceedings. *Recreations:* gardening, walking, travel, music. *Address:* 13 Worcester Road, Sutton, Surrey SM2 6PQ. *E:* stephen.penneck@gmail.com.

**PENNEFATHER, Maj.-Gen. David Anthony Somerset,** CB 1996; OBE 1991; Commandant General, Royal Marines, 1996–98; *b* 17 May 1945; *s* of late Capt. R. R. S. Pennefather, RN and Rachael Ann Pennefather (*née* Fawcitt); *m* 1972, Sheila Elizabeth Blacklee (*d* 2002); one *s* one *d*. *Educ:* Wellington Coll. Entered RM, 1963; commando service incl. US Marine Corps exchange, 1965–76; Army Staff Coll., 1977 (psc(m)); commando service and MoD, 1978–85; DS, Army Staff Coll., 1986–88; CO, 42 Commando, 1988–90; rcds 1991; hcsc 1992; Comdr, 3rd Commando Bde, 1992–94; Dir of Operations for Bosnia, JHQ Wilton, 1994; COS to CGRM, 1995; Comdr, Rapid Reaction Force Ops Staff, Bosnia, 1995; Sen. DS (Navy), RCDS, 2000 and 2002. Chm. Trustees, Royal Marines Mus., 2007–12. Sec., Royal Humane Soc., 2004–06. Soc. Liveryman, Co. of Clockmakers, 1973– (Mem., Ct of Assts, 1998–; Master, 2006–07). Comdr, Legion of Merit (USA), 1997. *Recreations:* forestry, woodland and land management, dendrology. *Club:* Army and Navy.

**PENNEY, Jennifer Beverly;** Senior Principal, Royal Ballet, retired 1988; *b* 5 April 1946; *d* of Beverley Guy Penney and Gwen Penney. *Educ:* in Canada (grades 1–12). Entered Royal Ballet Sch., 1962; joined Royal Ballet, 1963; became soloist during 1967, principal dancer during 1970, and senior principal dancer during 1974. Evening Standard Award, 1980. *Recreation:* painting (water-colours). *Address:* 36.258 Lower Ganges Road, Saltspring Island, BC V8K 1S7, Canada.

**PENNEY, John Anthony,** CMG 2000; translator, since 2000; *b* 30 Oct. 1940; *s* of late William Welch Penney and of Lily Penney; *m* 1st, 1968, Mary Hurley; 2nd, 1995, Miriam Franchini. *Educ:* Madrid Univ. (Dip. of Hispanic Studies 1960); St Catharine's Coll., Cambridge (BA (Hons) Mod. Langs, 1963; MA 1966); Nat. Autonomous Univ. of Mexico; Univ. of Paris IX, Ecole Supérieure d'Interprètes et de Traducteurs. HM Diplomatic Service, 1966–99: Jt Res./Analysis Dept, FCO, 1966–68; Lima, 1968–72; Hd, Americas Unit, FCO Res. & Analysis Dept, 1973–95; 1st Sec., Political Cttee, CSCE, UKMIS to UN, Geneva, 1974–75; Central Amer. and Caribbean Dept, FCO, 1977–78; Havana, 1978; Mexico and Central Amer. Dept, FCO, 1981–82; Paris, 1984–86; Santiago de Chile, 1988; Chief FCO Interpreter (Spanish), 1986–99; Antarctic Treaty UK Inspection Team, 1989; Minister-Counsellor, Consul-Gen., Dep. Hd of Mission, Brasilia, 1995–99. *Recreation:* music. *Address:* SMDB, Conj 4, Lote 3, Casa A, Lago Sul, Brasilia 71680–040, Brazil. *T:* (61) 33665344. *E:* penneyjohn@gmail.com.

**PENNEY, Robert Charles H.;** *see* Hughes-Penney.

**PENNICOTT, Maj.-Gen. Brian Thomas,** CVO 1994; Extra Gentleman Usher to the Queen, since 2008 (Gentleman Usher, 1995–2007); management consultant, 1998–2001; *b* 15 Feb. 1938; *s* of Thomas Edward Pennicott and Vera Ethel (*née* Gale); *m* 1962, Patricia Anne Chilcott (*d* 2010); two *s* three *d*. *Educ:* Portsmouth Northern Grammar Sch.; RMA, Sandhurst. Commnd, RA, 1957; RMCS, Shrivenham, 1969–70; Staff Coll., Camberley, 1971; GSO2 (W), Project Management Team 155mm Systems, 1972–73; NDC, Latimer, 1976–77; CO 29 Commando Regt, RA, 1977–80; SO1 Mil. Sec.'s Br. 6, MoD, 1980–82; Comdr Artillery, Falkland Is, 1982; Asst Mil. Attaché, Washington, 1982–83; Comdr Artillery, 1 Armd Div., 1983–86; NDC, Canada, 1986–87; Dep. Mil. Sec. (A), 1987–89; Dir, RA, 1989–91; Defence Services Sec., 1991–94 and ACDS (Personnel and Reserves), 1992–94. Gp Security Advr, 1994–95, Gp Personnel Manager, later Gp Human Resources Manager, 1995–96, Sun Alliance Gp; Gp Human Resources Manager, Royal & Sun Alliance Insurance Gp, 1996–98. Chm., Inksane (formerly BrandGuardian) Ltd (Hong Kong), 1999–2002. Chm., Simplyhealth Gp Ltd (formerly Hospital Saving Assoc., subseq. HSA Gp Ltd), 1999–2008. Col Comdt, RA, 1991–96; Hon. Col, 289 Commando Battery, RA(V), 1991–99. Chm., Army FA, 1991–94. *Recreations:* watching sport, bridge. *Address:* c/o Lloyds, Cox's & King's Branch, 39 Piccadilly, W1V 0AA.

**PENNICOTT, Ian;** QC 2003; SC (Hong Kong) 2014; *b* 5 Sept. 1958; *s* of Roy Stephen Pennicott and Patricia Dorothy Pennicott; *m* 1991, Andrea Clare (*née* Whitlock); two *d*. *Educ:* Kingston Poly. (BA Hons); Corpus Christi Coll., Cambridge (LLM). Called to the Bar: Middle Temple, 1982, Bencher, 2018; Hong Kong, 1984; in practice, specialising in building and engineering law, and construction related professional negligence. MCIArb. *Publications:* (contrib.) Keating on Building Contracts, 5th edn 1991 to 8th edn 2006; (contrib.) Halsbury's Laws of England, Vol. 4 (3), Building Contractors, Architects, Engineers, Valuers and Surveyors, reissue 2002; consultant editor: Halsbury's Laws of England, Vols 19 (1) and (2), Fuel and Energy, reissue 2007, Vol. 39 (14), Cross-Country Pipelines, reissue 2008; Halsbury's Laws of England, Vol. 6, Building Contracts, 5th edn 2011; Halsbury's Laws of England, Vols 19 (1) and (2), Energy and Climate Change, 5th edn 2011. *Recreations:* golf, Southampton Football Club. *Address:* Keating Chambers, 15 Essex Street, WC2R 3AU. *T:* (020) 7544 2600, *Fax:* (020) 7240 7722. *E:* ipennicott@keatingchambers.com; Des Voeux Chambers, 38/F Gloucester Tower, The Landmark, Central, Hong Kong. *E:* ianpennicott@dvc.com.hk. *Clubs:* Royal Automobile; Frilford Heath Golf (Oxon); Foreign Correspondents' (Hong Kong).

**PENNIE, Simone Sharon;** Finance Director, Angus Kyloe Partners Ltd, since 2015; *b* London, 1965; *d* of Thomas Cameron Hall and Hilary Victoria Hall; *m* 1998, Raymond George Pennie. *Educ:* Oxford Brookes Univ. (BA Hons Accountancy and Finance and Law 1987). ACA 1991. KPMG, 1988–94; P&O Nedlloyd, 1994–96; BBC Worldwide, 1996–2005; Finance Dir, BBC World News, 2005–11. Non-exec. Dir, Wye Valley NHS Trust, 2011–15. Mem., Gambling Commn, 2016–. Member: Ind. Audit Cttee, Univ. of Bath, 2011–17; Ind. Audit and Risk Cttee, Ofcom, 2012–15; Ind. Audit Cttee, Nat. Police Chiefs Council, 2015–16. Gov., Westonbirt Sch., 2012–15. Treas., Minchinhampton Commoners Cttee, 2013–. *Recreations:* sport, gardening, travel.

**PENNING, Rt Hon. Sir Michael (Allan);** Kt 2017; PC 2014; MP (C) Hemel Hempstead, since 2005; *b* 28 Sept. 1957; *s* of Brian and Freda Penning; *m* 1988, Angela Louden; two *d*. *Educ:* Appleton Comp. Sch., Benfleet; King Edmund Comp. Sch., Rochford. Served Grenadier Guards, 1974–79; RAMC, 1979–81; Essex Fire and Rescue Service, 1981–88; freelance media consultant, 1999–2000; Dep. Hd, News and Media, Conservative Party, 2000–04. Parly Under-Sec. of State, DfT, 2010–12; Minister of State: NI Office, 2012–13; DWP, 2013–14; Home Office and MoJ, 2014–16; Minister of State (Minister for the Armed Forces), MoD, 2016–17. Contested (C) Thurrock, 2001. GSM 1976. *Recreations:* keen angler, passionate Rugby Union supporter. *Address:* House of Commons, SW1A 0AA. *T:* (020) 7219 3000. *E:* penningm@parliament.uk.

**PENNING-ROWSELL, Prof. Edmund Charles,** OBE 2006; FRGS; Professor of Geography, since 1984, and Pro Vice-Chancellor (Research), since 1997, Middlesex University (formerly Middlesex Polytechnic) (Head, Flood Hazard Research Centre, 1970–2010); *b* 1 May 1946; *s* of late Edmund Lionel Penning-Rowsell and Margaret Penning-Rowsell; *m* 1968, Jacqueline Pritchett; two *d*. *Educ:* Chipping Norton Grammar Sch.; Sidcot Friends Sch.: University Coll. London (BSc 1967; PhD 1970; MA 1986). Lectr, Enfield Coll. of Technol., 1970–84; Dean of Social Sci., Middx Poly., then Middx Univ., 1984–97. FRGS 2000. Back Award, RGS, 2011. *Publications:* (with J. Chatterton) The Benefits of Flood Alleviation: a manual of assessment techniques, 1977; (with D. J. Parker) Water Planning in Britain, 1980; (jtly) Floods and Drainage: British policies for hazard reduction, agricultural improvement and wetland conservation, 1986; (jtly) The Economics of Coastal Management: a manual of benefit assessment techniques, 1992; (jtly) The Benefits of Flood and Coastal Risk Management: a manual of assessment techniques, 2005; (jtly) Flood and Coastal Erosion Risk Management: a manual for economic appraisal, 2013. *Recreations:* wine, gardening. *E:* Edmund@Penningrowsell.com.

**PENNINGTON, Hugh;** *see* Pennington, T. H.

**PENNINGTON, Michael Vivian Fyfe;** freelance actor and writer; *b* 7 June 1943; *s* of late Vivian Maynard Cecil Pennington and Euphemia Willock (*née* Fyfe); *m* Katharine Ann Letitia Barker (marr. diss.); one *s*. *Educ:* Marlborough Coll.: Trinity Coll., Cambridge (BA English). RSC, 1964–65; BBC, ITV, Woodfall Films Ltd, West End Theatre, Royal Court Theatre, etc, 1966–74; RSC, 1974–81: roles included Berowne, Angelo and Hamlet; Crime and Punishment, Lyric Hammersmith, 1983; National Theatre: Strider, 1984; Venice Preserv'd, 1984; Anton Chekhov, 1984; The Real Thing, Strand, 1985; Jt Artistic Dir, English Shakespeare Co., 1986–93: three world tours playing Henry V, Richard II, Coriolanus, Leontes, Macbeth, and Dir, Twelfth Night; Playing with Trains, RSC, 1989; Vershinin, The Three Sisters, Gate, Dublin, 1990; The Gift of the Gorgon, Barbican, 1992, Wyndham's, 1993; Dir, Twelfth Night, Tokyo, 1993; Hamlet, Gielgud, 1994; Taking Sides, Chichester, transf. Criterion, 1995; Dir, Twelfth Night, Chicago, 1996; The Entertainer, Hampstead, 1996; Waste, The Seagull, The Provok'd Wife, Anton Chekhov, Old Vic, 1997; The Misanthrope, Filumena, Major Barbara, Piccadilly, 1998; Gross Indecency, Gielgud, 1999; Timon of Athens, RSC, 1999; The Guardsman, Albery, 2000; What the Butler Saw, nat. tour, 2001; The Shawl, Sheffield Crucible, 2001; The Front Page, Chichester, 2002; John Gabriel Borkman, English Touring Th., 2003; Dir, A Midsummer Night's Dream, Regent's Park, 2003; The Seagull, Edinburgh Fest., 2003; The Madness of George III, W Yorks Playhouse, 2003; When the Night Begins, Hampstead, 2004; Colder Than Here, Soho, 2005; The Cosmonaut's Last Message, Donmar, 2005; Nathan the Wise, Hampstead, 2005; The Best of Friends, Hampstead and nat. tour, 2006; The Bargain, nat. tour, 2007; Little Nell, Th. Royal, Bath, 2007; Sweet William (solo Shakespeare show), NT, nat. and internat. tour and W End, 2007–09; Taking Sides, Collaboration, Chichester and W End, 2008–09; Love is My Sin, US and Eur. Tour, 2009–10; A Jubilee for Anton Chekhov, Hampstead, 2010; The Master Builder, Chichester, 2010; The Syndicate, Chichester, 2011; Judgement Day, Print Room, 2011; Antony and Cleopatra, Chichester, 2012; Dances of Death, Gate, 2013; Richard II, RSC, 2013; King Lear, NY, 2014, UK tour, 2016; Single Spies, Rose Th., Kingston, 2014; She Stoops to Conquer, Th. Royal Bath, 2015; The Winter's Tale, Garrick, 2015; The Resistible Rise of Arturo Ui, Donmar, 2017; Fanny and Alexander, Old Vic, 2018; *film:* The Iron Lady, 2011; *television* includes: Oedipus the King, 1985; Return of Sherlock Holmes, 1986; Dr Terrible's House of Horrible, 2001; Trial and Retribution, 2007; Endeavour, 2016. *Publications:* Rossya—A Journey Through Siberia, 1977; The English Shakespeare Company, 1990; Hamlet: a user's guide, 1995; Twelfth Night: a user's guide, 1999; Are You There, Crocodile: inventing Anton Chekhov, 2002; A Midsummer Night's Dream: a user's guide, 2005; Sweet William: twenty thousand hours with Shakespeare, 2012; Let Me Play the Lion Too, 2015; King Lear in Brooklyn, 2016. *Recreations:* music, literature. *Address:* c/o Diamond Management, 31 Percy Street, W1T 2DD.

**PENNINGTON, Prof. (Thomas) Hugh,** CBE 2013; PhD; FRCPath, FRCPE, FMedSci; FRSE; Professor of Bacteriology, University of Aberdeen, 1979–2003, now Emeritus (Dean, Faculty of Medicine, 1987–92); *b* 19 April 1938; *s* of Thomas Wearing Pennington and Dorothy Pennington; *m* 1965, Carolyn Ingram Beattie; two *d*. *Educ:* Lancaster Royal Grammar Sch.; St Thomas's Hosp. Med. Sch. (MB BS (Hons), Clutton Medal, Bristowe Medal, Beaney Scholarship; PhD). FRCPath 1990. House appts, St Thomas's Hosp., 1962–63; Asst Lectr, 1963–66, Lectr, 1966–67, Dept of Med. Microbiology, St Thomas's Hosp. Med. Sch.; Postdoctoral Fellow, Univ. of Wisconsin, 1967–69; Mem. Scientific Staff, 1969–70, Lectr, 1970–75, Sen. Lectr, 1975–79, MRC Virology Unit and Dept of Virology, Univ. of Glasgow. Chairman: Expert Gp on 1996 E.coli O157 outbreak in Central Scotland, 1996–97; Public Inquiry into 2005 Welsh E.coli O157 outbreak, 2006–09; Member: Scottish Food Adv. Cttee, Food Standards Agency, Scotland, 2000–05; Broadcasting Council for Scotland, 2000–05 (Vice Chair, 2003–05); BBC Rural Affairs Adv. Cttee, 2000–09; World Food Prog. Tech. Adv. Gp, 2002–07. Gov., Rowett Res. Inst., 1980–88, 1995–2004; Mem., Bd of Dirs, Moredun Res. Inst., 2003–06. Pres., Soc. for Gen. Microbiology, 2003–07. Lectures: Pumphandle, John Snow Soc., 1997; Appleyard, BVA, 1997; Col Stock, APHA, 1999; Frank May, Leicester Univ., 2001; Victor Horsley, BMA, 2003; Sampson Gamgee, Birmingham Med. Inst., 2004; Al-Hammadi, RCPE, 2007; Haldane Tait, Scottish Soc. of History of Medicine, 2010. Hon. Vice-Pres., Inst. of Food Sci. and Technol., 2010. Founder FMedSci 1998; FRES 1957; FRSA 1997; FRSE 1997; FRCPE 1998. Hon. DSc: Lancaster, 1999; Strathclyde, 2001; Aberdeen, 2003; Hull, 2004; Harper Adams, 2015. Caroline Walker Award, 1997; John Kershaw Meml Prize, RIPH&H, 1998; Silver Medal, Royal Scottish Soc. of Arts, 1999; Thomas Graham Medal, Royal Glasgow Philosophical Soc., 2001; 25th Anniv. Award for Achievement, Soc. of Food Hygiene Technol., 2004; Joseph Lister Medal, Soc. of Chemical Industry, 2009; Award for Meritorious Endeavours in Envmtl Health, Royal Envmtl Health Inst. of Scotland, 2010. *Publications:* (with D. A. Ritchie) Molecular Virology, 1975; When Food Kills, 2003; Have Bacteria Won?, 2016; papers on molecular virology, molecular epidemiology and systematics of pathogenic bacteria; contrib. London Review of Books. *Recreations:* collecting books, dipterology. *Address:* 13 Carlton Place, Aberdeen AB15 4BR. *T:* (01224) 645136.

**PENNY,** family name of **Viscount Marchwood.**

**PENNY, Gareth Peter Herbert;** Chairman: MMC Norilsk Nickel, since 2013; Edcon, since 2017; Investec Asset Management, since 2019; *b* Cape Town, SA, 24 Dec. 1962; *s* of Peter Penny and Shirley Penny; *m* 1994, Kate Halsted; one *s* one *d*. *Educ:* Bishops Diocesan Coll., Cape Town; Eton Coll.; Univ. of Oxford (Rhodes Schol.; MA PPE). Various positions, Anglo American Corp., Johannesburg, 1988–91; De Beers: various positions, 1991–2001; Exec. Dir, Sales and Mktg, 2001–04, Man. Dir, 2004–06, Diamond Trading

Co.; Gp CEO, De Beers, 2006–10; CEO, AMG Mining, 2011–12; Exec. Chm., New World Resources plc, 2012–16. Dir, Julius Baer Gp Ltd, 2007–19. *Recreations:* walking, cycling, sailing, reading. *Address:* Norilsk Nickel, 40 Queen Street, EC4R 1DD. *T:* (020) 7246 2533. *E:* janet.collins@nornickel.net. *Club:* Royal Automobile.

PENNY, Sir Nicholas (Beaver), Kt 2015; MA, PhD; FBA 2010; FSA; Director, National Gallery, 2008–15; *b* 21 Dec. 1949; *s* of Joseph Noel Bailey Penny, QC; *m* 1st, 1971, Anne Philomel Udy (marr. diss.); two *d*; 2nd, 1994, Mary Agnes Wall, now Crettier (*née* Crettier). *Educ:* Shrewsbury Sch.; St Catharine's Coll., Cambridge (BA, MA; Hon. Fellow, 2009); Courtauld Inst., Univ. of London (MA, PhD). Leverhulme Fellow in the History of Western Art, Clare Hall, Cambridge, 1973–75; Lectr, History of Art Dept, Univ. of Manchester, 1975–82; Sen. Res. Fellow, History of Western Art, King's Coll., Cambridge, 1982–84; Keeper of Western Art, Ashmolean Mus., Oxford, and Professorial Fellow, Balliol Coll., Oxford, 1984–89; Clore Curator of Renaissance Painting, 1990–2002, Keeper, 1998–2002, Nat. Gall.; Sen. Curator of Sculpture and Decorative Arts, Nat. Gall. of Art, Washington, 2002–08. Slade Prof. of Fine Art, Univ. of Oxford, 1980–81; Mellon Prof. at Center for Advanced Study in the Visual Arts, Nat. Gall. of Art, Washington, 2000–02; Prof. of Art Hist., Advanced Sch. of Art and Humanities, Nat. Acad. of Art Hangzhou, China, 2018–Dec. 2020; Thaw Sen. Fellow, Morgan Liby, NY, 2018. Mem., Amer. Acad. Arts and Scis, 2007. FSA 2003; Fellow, Swedish Acad. of Art, 2014. Hon. FKC 2013; Hon. Fellow, Balliol Coll., Oxford, 2014. DUniv St Andrews, 2014; Hon. DLitt School of Advanced Studies, Univ. of London, 2015. Cavaliere nell'Ordine al merito della Repubblica Italiana, 1990. *Publications:* Church Monuments in Romantic England, 1977; Piranesi, 1978; (with Francis Haskell) Taste and the Antique, 1981; Mourning, 1981; (ed jtly) The Arrogant Connoisseur, 1982; (with Roger Jones) Raphael, 1983; (ed) Reynolds, 1986; Alfred and Winifred Turner, 1988; (with Robert Flynn Johnson) Lucian Freud, Works on Paper, 1988; Ruskin's Drawings, 1988; (jtly) From Giotto to Dürer, 1991; Catalogue of European Sculpture in the Ashmolean Museum: 1540 to the present day, 3 vols, 1992; The Materials of Sculpture, 1993; Picture Frames, 1997; (jtly) From Dürer to Veronese, 1999; The Sixteenth Century Italian Paintings in the National Gallery, vol. 1, 2004, vol. 2, 2008, vol. 3 (with Giorgia Mancini), 2016; (with A. Radcliffe) Art of the Renaissance Bronze, 2004; Director's Choice, 2011; (jtly) The Sansovino Frame, 2015; A Closer Look: pictorial space, 2017; reviews for London Review of Books; articles in Apollo, Burlington Magazine, Connoisseur, Jl of Warburg and Courtauld Insts, Past and Present, and elsewhere.

PENNY, Patricia Joyce; *see* Longdon, P. J.

PENNYCOOK, Matthew Thomas; MP (Lab) Greenwich and Woolwich, since 2015; *b* 29 Oct. 1982; *m* Joanna Otterburn. *Educ:* London Sch. of Econs and Pol Sci. (BA 1st Cl. Hons Internat. Relns and Hist.); Balliol Coll., Oxford (Schol.; MPhil Internat. Relns (Dist.)). Volunteer, Child Poverty Action Gp; sen. roles in charity and voluntary sectors, incl. Fair Pay Network; Sen. Res. and Policy Analyst, Resolution Foundn. Shadow Minister for Brexit, 2016–. Mem., Energy and Climate Change Select Cttee, 2015–16. Mem. (Lab) Greenwich LBC, 2010–15. *Address:* House of Commons, SW1A 0AA.

PENNYCOOK, Richard John; Chairman, Fenwick Ltd, since 2017; *b* Salisbury, 26 Feb. 1964; *s* of late Gerald Douglas Pennycook and of Margaret Gladys Pennycook; *m* 1995, Suzanne Beal; two *d*. *Educ:* Univ. of Bristol (BSc 1985). ACA 1987, FCA 1997. Arthur Andersen, 1985–90; Alldders plc, 1990–95; Finance Dir, JD Wetherspoon plc, 1995–98; Chief Exec., Welcome Break Hldgs plc, 1998–2002; Finance Director: RAC plc, 2003–05; Wm Morrison Supermarkets plc, 2005–13; Chief Financial Officer, 2013–14, CEO, 2014–17, Co-operative Gp. Non-executive Director: Persimmon plc, 2008–16; Hut Gp Ltd, 2012–18 (Chm., 2013–18); Howden Joinery Gp plc, 2013– (Chm., 2016–). Chm., British Retail Consortium, 2018–. Lead non-exec. Bd Mem., DfE, 2017–. *Address:* Fenwick Ltd, 63 New Bond Street, W1S 1RQ.

PENNYCUICK, Prof. Colin James, FRS 1990; Senior Research Fellow, University of Bristol, 1997 (Research Professor in Zoology, 1993); *b* 11 June 1933; *s* of Brig. James Alexander Charles Pennycuick, DSO and Marjorie Pennycuick; *m* Sandy; one *s*. *Educ:* Wellington College; Merton College, Oxford (MA); Peterhouse, Cambridge (PhD). Lectr in Zoology, 1964–75, Reader, 1975–83, Bristol Univ.; seconded as Lectr in Zoology, Univ. of Nairobi, 1968–71, as Dep. Dir, Serengeti Res. Inst., 1971–73; Maytag Prof. of Ornithology, Univ. of Miami, 1983–92. *Publications:* Animal Flight, 1972; Bird Flight Performance, 1989; Newton Rules Biology, 1992; Modelling the Flying Bird, 2008; (jtly) Birds Never Get Lost, 2016. *Recreation:* astronomy. *Address:* School of Biological Sciences, University of Bristol, Woodland Road, Bristol BS8 1TQ.

PENRHYN, 7th Baron *cr* 1866; Simon Douglas-Pennant; *b* 28 June 1938; *s* of late Hon. Nigel Douglas-Pennant and Margaret Dorothy Douglas-Pennant (*née* Kirkham); *S* uncle, 2003; *m* 1963, Josephine Maxwell, *yr d* of Robert Upcott; two *s* two *d*. *Educ:* Eton Coll.; Clare Coll., Cambridge (BA Hons). Dir, Brintons Ltd, Kidderminster, 1990–98. *Recreations:* sport (golf, tennis), music, travelling. *Heir:* *s* Hon. Edward Sholto Douglas-Pennant, *b* 6 June 1966. *Address:* The Old Vicarage, Church Road, Castlemorton, Malvern, Worcs WR13 6BQ. *T:* (01684) 833513. *E:* simon.penrhyn@gmail.com. *Club:* MCC.

PENROSE, family name of Baroness Harding of Winscombe.

PENROSE, Rt Hon. Lord; George William Penrose; PC 2001; a Senator of the College of Justice in Scotland, 1990–2005; *b* 2 June 1938; *s* of late George W. Penrose and Janet L. Penrose; *m* 1st, 1964, Wendy Margaret Cooper (*d* 2013); one *s* two *d*; 2nd, 2017, Elizabeth Jean Steven (*née* Rae). *Educ:* Glasgow Univ. (MA, LLB). CA. Advocate, 1964; QC 1978; Advocate Depute, 1986; Home Advocate Depute, 1988. Procurator to Gen. Assembly of Ch of Scotland, 1984–90. Pres., Scottish procs of Aircraft and Shipbuilding Industries Arbitration Tribunal, 1977–83; Mem., panel of Chairmen, Financial Services Tribunal, 1988–90. Leader, Equitable Life Inquiry, 2001–04. Reporter, Penrose Inquiry, 2009–16. Chm. Court, Heriot-Watt Univ., 2008–15. FRSE 2010. Hon. LLD Glasgow, 2000; DUniv: Stirling, 2001; Heriot-Watt, 2015. *Recreation:* walking. *Address:* c/o Court of Session, Parliament House, Edinburgh EH1 1RQ.

PENROSE, Anne Josephine, (Mrs J. Penrose); *see* Robinson, A. J.

PENROSE, George William; *see* Penrose, Rt Hon. Lord.

PENROSE, John David; MP (C) Weston-super-Mare, since 2005; *b* 22 June 1964; *s* of late David Goronwe Penrose and of Anna Jill Penrose (who *m* 1995, Tom Lawrie); *m* 1995, Hon. Diana Mary Harding (*see* Baroness Harding of Winscombe); two *d*. *Educ:* Ipswich Sch.; Downing Coll., Cambridge (BA Hons 1986); Columbia Univ., NY (MBA 1991). J. P. Morgan, 1986–90; McKinsey & Co., 1992–94; Commercial Dir, Academic Books Div., Thomson Publishing, 1995–96; Man. Dir, Longman sch. textbooks for UK and Africa, Pearson plc, 1996–2000; Chm., Logotron, 2001–08. Contested (C): Ealing Southall, 1997; Weston-super-Mare, 2001. PPS to Chm., Cons. Policy Rev., 2006–08; Shadow Minister for Business, 2009–10; Parly Under-Sec. of State, DCMS, 2010–12; an Asst Govt Whip, 2013–14; a Lord Comr of HM Treasury (Govt Whip), 2014–16; Parly Sec., Cabinet Office, 2015–16; Minister of State, NI Office, 2018–19. Mem., Amnesty Internat. Mem., Blagdon and Dist Beekeeping Club. *Recreations:* fishing, beekeeping, listening to other people's opinions. *Address:* House of Commons, SW1A 0AA. *Clubs:* Weston-super-Mare Conservative; Weston-super-Mare Constitutional.

PENROSE, Prof. Oliver, FRS 1987; FRSE; Professor of Mathematics, Heriot-Watt University, 1986–94, now Professor Emeritus; *b* 6 June 1929; *s* of Lionel S. Penrose, FRS, and Margaret Penrose, *d* of John Beresford Leathes, FRS; *m* 1953, Joan Lomas Dilley (*d* 2014); two *s* one *d* (and one *s* decd). *Educ:* Central Collegiate Inst., London, Ont; University Coll. London (BSc 1949); Cambridge Univ. (PhD 1953). FRSE 1989. Mathematical Physicist, English Electric Co., Luton, 1952–55; Res. Asst, Yale Univ., 1955–56; Lectr, then Reader, in Mathematics, Imperial Coll., London 1956–69; Prof. of Mathematics, Open Univ., 1969–86. *Publications:* Foundations of Statistical Mechanics, 1970, repr. 2005; about 90 papers in physics and maths jls; various book reviews and book chapters. *Recreations:* making music, chess. *Address:* Fir Trees, Doctors Commons Road, Berkhamsted, Herts HP4 3DW. *T:* (01442) 862427. *W:* www.macs.hw.ac.uk/~oliver, www.openrose.me.uk.
*See also* Sir R. Penrose.

PENROSE, Sir Roger, OM 2000; Kt 1994; FRS 1972; Rouse Ball Professor of Mathematics, University of Oxford, 1973–98, now Emeritus; Fellow of Wadham College, Oxford, 1973–98, now Emeritus; *b* Colchester, Essex, 8 Aug. 1931; *s* of Lionel Sharples Penrose, FRS; *m* 1959, Joan Isabel Wedge (marr. diss. 1981); three *s*; *m* 1988, Vanessa Dee Thomas; one *s*. *Educ:* University Coll. Sch.; University Coll., Univ. of London (BSc spec. 1st cl. Mathematics), Fellow 1975; St John's Coll., Cambridge (PhD; Hon. Fellow, 1987). NRDC (temp. post, Feb.–Aug. 1956); Asst Lectr (Pure Mathematics), Bedford Coll., London, 1956–57; Research Fellow, St John's Coll., Cambridge, 1957–60; NATO Research Fellow, Princeton Univ. and Syracuse Univ., 1959–61; Research Associate King's Coll., London, 1961–63; Visiting Associate Prof., Univ. of Texas, Austin, Texas, 1963–64; Reader, 1964–66, Prof. of Applied Mathematics, 1966–73, Birkbeck Coll., London. Visiting Prof., Yeshiva, Princeton, Cornell, 1966–67 and 1969; Lovett Prof., Rice Univ., Houston, 1983–87; Distinguished Prof. of Physics and Maths, Syracuse Univ., NY, 1987–. Member: London Mathematical Soc.; Cambridge Philosophical Soc.; Inst. for Mathematics and its Applications; International Soc. for General Relativity and Gravitation. Adams Prize (Cambridge Univ.), 1966–67; Dannie Heineman Prize (Amer. Phys. Soc. and Amer. Inst. Physics), 1971; Eddington Medal (with S. W. Hawking), RAS, 1975; Royal Medal, Royal Soc., 1985; Wolf Foundn Prize for Physics (with S. W. Hawking), 1988; Dirac Medal and Prize, Inst. of Physics, 1989; Einstein Medal, 1990; Copley Medal, Royal Soc., 2008. *Publications:* Techniques of Differential Topology in Relativity, 1973; (with W. Rindler) Spinors and Space-time, Vol. 1, 1984, Vol. 2, 1986; The Emperor's New Mind, 1989 (Science Book Prize, 1990); Shadows of the Mind, 1994; (jtly) The Large, the Small and the Human Mind, 1997; The Road to Reality, 2004; many articles in scientific jls. *Recreations:* 3 dimensional puzzles, doodling at the piano. *Address:* Mathematical Institute, University of Oxford, Andrew Wiles Building, Radcliffe Observatory Quarter, Woodstock Road, Oxford OX2 6GG. *T:* (01865) 273538.

PENSLAR, Prof. Derek Jonathan, PhD; FRSC 2011; William Lee Frost Professor of Modern Jewish History, Harvard University, since 2018; *b* Los Angeles, 12 Aug. 1958; *s* of Bruce David Penslar and Alice Natalie Penslar (now Krone Harnell); *m* 1983, Robin Levin; one *s* one *d*. *Educ:* Stanford Univ. (BA with Dist. Hist. 1979); Univ. of Calif, Berkeley (MA Hist. 1980; PhD Hist. 1987). Asst Prof. of Hist. and Jewish Studies, 1987–93, Associate Prof., 1993–98, Indiana Univ., Bloomington; Associate Prof. of Jewish Hist., 1998–2001, Samuel Zacks Prof. of Jewish History, 2001–19, Dir, Centre for Jewish Studies, 2002–08, Univ. of Toronto; Stanley Lewis Prof. of Israel Studies, Univ. of Oxford, 2012–16; Fellow, St Anne's Coll., Oxford, 2012–16, now Hon. Fellow. Nachshon Vis. Prof. of Israel Studies, Harvard Univ., 2006; Visiting Professor: of Israel Studies, Columbia Univ., 2009; of Israel Studies, Univ. of Oxford, 2016–17; of History, Harvard Univ., 2016–18. Pres., Amer. Acad. for Jewish Res., 2018–. *Publications:* Zionism and Technocracy: the engineering of Jewish settlement in Palestine, 1870–1918, 1991 (trans. Hebrew, 2001); (ed with M. Brenner) In Search of Jewish Community: Jewish identity in Germany and Austria, 1918–1933, 1998; Shylock's Children: economics and Jewish identity in modern Europe, 2001; (ed with A. Shapira) Israeli Historical Revisionism: from left to right, 2002; (ed with I. Kalmar) Orientalism and the Jews, 2004; (ed jtly) Contemporary Antisemitism: Canada and the World, 2005; Israel in History: the Jewish State in comparative perspective, 2007; (ed jtly) A New Jewish Time: Jewish culture in an era of secularization, 5 vols in Hebrew, 2007; (with E. Kaplan) The Origins of Modern Israel: a documentary history, 2011; Jews and the Military: a history, 2013; chapters in books including: Purchasing Power: the economic dimensions of modern Jewish life, 2015; What Ifs of Jewish History: from Abraham to Zionism, 2016; Colonialism and the Jews, 2017; The Cambridge History of Judaism, vol. VIII, 2017; Theodor Herzl: the charismatic leader, 2020; contribs to Annales, Cathedra, German Hist., Hist. & Memory, Israel Studies, Jewish Social Studies, Jewish Hist., Jl Contemp. Hist., Jl Israel Hist., Jl Modern Jewish Studies, Leo Baeck Inst. Year Book, Tsiyon, Yisra'el, Jl Hist. Eur. Ideas, Jl Levantine Studies, Jl of Genocide Res. and Amer. Jewish Hist. *Recreations:* travel, hiking, music, literature, cinema. *Address:* Center for European Studies, Harvard University, 27 Kirkland Street, Cambridge, MA 02138, USA.

PENTLAND, Hon. Lord; Paul Benedict Cullen; a Senator of the College of Justice in Scotland, since 2008; Chairman, Scottish Law Commission, 2014–18; *b* 11 March 1957; *s* of James Finbarr Cullen and Ann Evaline Black or Cullen; *m* 1983, Joyce Nicol; two *s* one *d*. *Educ:* St Augustine's High Sch., Edinburgh; Edinburgh Univ. (LLB Hons). Admitted to Faculty of Advocates, 1982 (Clerk of Faculty, 1986–90); Standing Jun. Counsel to DoE in Scotland, 1988–91; Advocate Depute, 1992–95; QC (Scot.) 1995; Solicitor Gen. for Scotland, 1995–97. Chairman: Police Appeals Tribunal, 2003–08; Chm., Appeal Cttee, ICAS, 2005–08; a Judge of Upper Tax Tribunal, 2010–14; an Intellectual Property Judge of Court of Session, 2011–14. Scottish Cons. spokesman on home and legal affairs, 1997–98; Chm. Disciplinary Panel, Scottish Cons. Party, 2000–08. Cons. rep. on Scottish Office consultative steering gp on Scottish Parlt, 1998–99. Chm., Gilmerton Limestone Emergency inquiry, 2001–02. Vice Pres., Edinburgh S Cons. & Unionist Assoc., 1997–2008. Contested (C) Eastwood, 1997. *Recreations:* tennis, bridge, the Turf. *Address:* Court of Session, Parliament House, Edinburgh EH1 1RQ. *T:* (0131) 225 2595. *Clubs:* New (Edinburgh); Braid Lawn Tennis.

PENTLAND, Ven. Raymond Jackson, CB 2013; Archdeacon, 2006–14, and Director General Chaplaincy Services Headquarters Air Command and Chaplain-in-Chief, 2009–14, Royal Air Force; *b* 14 July 1957; *s* of Adam Jackson Pentland and Edith Henderson Pentland; *m* 1979, Christine Ann Lyth; one *s* one *d*. *Educ:* Cowdenknowes High Sch.; William Booth Meml Coll.; St John's Coll., Nottingham (DPS 1988); Open Univ. (BA 1990); Westminster Coll., Oxford (MTh 2002; Farmington Fellow, 2004). Salvation Army Officer, 1979–86; ordained deacon, 1988, priest, 1989; Asst Curate, St Jude's, Nottingham, 1988–90; Chaplain, 1990–2005, Comd Chaplain, 2005–06, RAF. QHC 2006–14. Mem., Gen. Synod, 2005–14. Hon. Canon, Lincoln Cathedral, 2014, now Canon Emeritus; Hon. Asst Curate, St Andrew by the Wardrobe and St James Garlickhythe, 2015–18; Associate Minister, Holy Trinity, Aylesbury, 2019–. Permission to officiate, Oxford and London, 2015–19. Hon. Chaplain: Coachmakers' and Coach Harness Makers' Co., 2010–; Battle of Britain Fighter Assoc., 2011–; Hon. Co. of Air Pilots, 2014–; Hon. Vice Pres., 101 Sqn Assoc., 2014–. Officer, RAuxAF, 2014– (Mem., Defence Bd Service Complaints Panel, 2014–; Air Vice-Marshal, Personnel Support Br., 2014–). Pres., Friends of St Clement Danes Church, 2013–; Patron, RAF Widows Assoc., 2014–; Trustee, Battle of Britain Meml Trust, 2015–. Battle Field Tour leader, 2014–. *Publications*: contrib. Contact Mag., Political Theol. *Recreations*: gourmet cuisine, travel, modern military history, Battle Field tours. *Address*: 16 Nicholas Charles Crescent, Aylesbury HP18 0GU. *T*: (01296) 323213. *E*: ray.pentland929@gmail.com. *Club*: Royal Air Force.

**PENTREATH, Rear Adm. Jonathan Patrick,** CB 2019; OBE 2012; Commander Joint Helicopter Command, since 2017; *b* Plymstock, 2 March 1966; *s* of late Capt. David Pentreath, CBE, DSO and Judith Pentreath; *m* 1994, Laura Thompson; one *s* three *d*. *Educ*: Haileybury Coll.; City Univ. (BSc). BRNC Dartmouth, 1984; 845 Naval Air Sqdn, 846 Naval Air Sqdn, 815 Naval Air Sqdn, 1992–99; Jt Helicopter Comd, 1999–2001; CO 845 Naval Air Sqdn, 2001–03; MoD, 2003–06; HMS Ocean, 2007–08; CO Cdo Helicopter Force, 2009–11; Capability Dir, Jt Helicopter Comd, 2012–14; rcds, 2014–15; CO RNAS Yeovilton, 2015–17. Chm., RN Winter Sports Assoc., 2015–19. QCVS 2003. *Recreations*: sailing, ski-ing, tennis, walking. *Address*: c/o Naval Secretary, Navy Command Headquarters, Whale Island, Portsmouth PO2 8BY.

**PENTREATH, Prof. Richard John, (Jan),** DSc, PhD; CBiol, FRSB; CRadP; FSRP; Research Professor, Environmental Systems Science Centre, University of Reading, 2000–07, now Professor Emeritus; *b* 28 Dec. 1943; *s* of John Alistair Dudley Pentreath and Mary Lena (*née* Gendall); *m* 1965, Elisabeth Amanda Leach; two *d*. *Educ*: Humphry Davy Grammar Sch.; QMC, London (BSc (Special)); DSc London; Univ. of Auckland (PhD). FRSB (FIBiol 1980); CBiol 1984; FSRP 1989 (Hon. FSRP 2018); CRadP 2008. Commonwealth Schol., 1966–68; SRC Fellow, 1969; Fisheries Radiobiol. Lab., MAFF, 1969–89: Hd, Aquatic Envmtl Protection Div. and Dep. Dir, Fisheries Res., 1988–89; Chief Scientist, and Dir Water Quality, NRA, 1989–95; Chief Scientist, and Dir, Envmtl Strategy, EA, 1995–2000. Member: NERC, 1992–98; Adv. Bd, Centre for Social and Econ. Res. on Global Envmt, 1994–2005; Res. Assessment Panel, HEFC, 1995–96, 1999–2001; Council, Marine Biol Assoc. of UK, 1997–2000; Council, Assoc. for Schs Science Engrg and Technol., 1998–2000; Internat. Commn on Radiol Protection, 2003–13, now Emeritus Mem. (Chm., Cttee 5, Envmtl Protection, 2005–13); Trustee, SAHFOS, 2001–16; Ind. Mem., JNCC, 2000–06. Res. Fellow, Plymouth Marine Lab., 2009–; Emeritus Res. Fellow, Centre for Envmt, Fisheries and Aquaculture Sci., 2014–. Pres., Cornwall Sustainable Bldg Trust, 2005–11. Non-exec. Dir, Research Sites Restoration Ltd, 2009–16. Hon. Prof., UEA, 1996–2008; Vis. Prof., ICSTM, 1997–2003. President: Cornwall Wildlife Trust, 2003–18; Restronguet Greek Soc., 2014–. Hon. DSc: Hertfordshire, 1998; UWE, 1999; Plymouth, 2002. *Publications*: Nuclear Power, Man and the Environment, 1980; contrib. numerous scientific papers. *Recreations*: Cornish history, crewing tall ships, visual arts. *Address*: Camelot House, Ropewalk, Penpol, Truro, Cornwall TR3 6NA. *T*: (01872) 862838.

**PENTY, Prof. Richard Vincent,** PhD; FREng; Professor of Photonics, since 2002, and Head, Centre for Photonic Systems, since 2019, Department of Engineering, University of Cambridge; Fellow, since 2002, and Master, since 2013, Sidney Sussex College, Cambridge; *b* Nottingham, 9 Sept. 1964; *s* of Peter Richard Penty and (Patricia) Janet Penty; *m* 1992, Victoria Frances Mary Eve; two *s* one *d*. *Educ*: Repton Sch.; Sidney Sussex Coll., Cambridge (BA Engrg and Electrical Sci. 1986; MA 1990; PhD Engrg 1990). SMIEE 2010; FIET 2012; FREng 2012. SERC IT Res. Fellow, Dept of Engrg, Univ. of Cambridge, 1989–90; Maudslay Res. Fellow, Pembroke Coll., Cambridge, 1989–90; Lectr, Sch. of Phys, Univ. of Bath, 1990–95; University of Bristol: Lectr in Electronic Engrg, 1995–98; Reader in Optical Communications, 1998–2001; Prof. of Photonics, 2001; Asst Dir of Res., Dept of Engrg, Univ. of Cambridge, 2001–02; Vice Master, 2008, 2011–12, Actg Master, 2012–13, Sidney Sussex Coll., Cambridge. Founder and Dir, PervasID Ltd, 2011–16 (Mem., Tech. Adv. Bd, 2016–). Chair, Strategic Adv. Bd, Future Compound Semiconductor Manufg Hub, 2017–. Mem., Bd of Dirs, Tyndall Nat. Inst., Cork, 2017–. Mem. Council, Univ. of Cambridge, 2019–. Editor-in-Chief, IET Optoelectronics Jl, 2006–19. *Recreations*: reading, running, sleeping. *Address*: The Master's Lodge, Sidney Sussex College, Cambridge CB2 3HU. *T*: (01223) 330868. *E*: master@sid.cam.ac.uk.

**PENZER, Dr Geoffrey Ronald,** FRSC; Partner, Penzer Allen, 1992; *b* 15 Nov. 1943; *s* of Ronald and Dora Penzer; *m* 1966, Sylvia Elaine (*née* Smith) (*d* 2016); one *s* one *d*. *Educ*: Merchant Taylors' Sch.; St John's Coll., Oxford (MA; DPhil 1969). CChem, FRSC 1979. Jun. Res. Fellow, Merton Coll., Oxford, 1967–69; Res. Chemist, Univ. of Calif, 1969–70; Lectr in Biol Chem., Univ. of York, 1970–75; British Council: Science Officer, Cairo, 1975–80; Science Officer, Mexico, 1980–84; Dir, Technical Co-operation Training Dept, 1984–87; Dir, Management Div., and Manager, HQ Location Project, 1987–91. Dir, Penzer Allen Ltd, 1993–. Mem., Ind. Monitoring Bd, HMP Belmarsh, 2009–12; Mem., Ind. Monitoring Bd, HMP Thameside, 2012–19 (Chm., 2012–15); Mem. for Gtr London, Nat. Council for Ind. Monitoring Bds, 2015–18; Mem., Professional Conduct Panel, Teaching Regulation Agency (formerly Teaching Agency, then Nat. Coll. for Teaching and Leadership), 2012–. Trustee: Outset, 1994–2002; bss Ltd, 2001–09. *Publications*: contrib. scientific books and jls. *Recreations*: music, landscapes, walking. *Address*: 62 Oakhill Road, Sevenoaks, Kent TN13 1NT.

**PENZIAS, Dr Arno Allan;** Venture Advisor, New Enterprise Associates (Venture Partner, 1998); *b* 26 April 1933; *s* of Karl and Justine Penzias; *m*; one *s* two *d*; *m* 1996, Sherry Levit Penzias. *Educ*: City Coll. of New York (BS Physics, 1954); Columbia Univ. (MA Physics, 1958; PhD Physics, 1962). Bell Laboratories: Mem., Technical Staff, 1961–72; Head, Radio Physics Res., 1972–76; Dir, Radio Res. Lab., 1976–79; Exec. Dir, Research, Communications Sciences, 1979–81; Vice-Pres., Research, 1981–95; Vice-Pres. and Chief Scientist, AT&T Bell Laboratories, 1995–96; Lucent Technologies, Bell Labs Innovations: Vice-Pres. and Chief Scientist, 1996–98; Sen. Tech. Advr, 1998–2000. Lectr, Princeton Univ., 1967–72, Vis. Prof., Astrophysical Scis Dept, 1972–85; Res. Associate, Harvard Univ., 1968–80; Adjunct Prof., State Univ. of NY, Stony Brook, 1974–84; Lee Kuan Yew Dist. Vis., Nat. Univ. of Singapore, 1991. Lectures: Kompfner, Stanford Univ., 1979; Gamow, Colorado Univ., 1980; Jansky, NRAO, 1983; Michelson Meml, Dept US Navy, 1985; Tanner, Southern Utah State Coll., 1987; Klopsteg, Northwestern Univ., 1987; NSF Distinguished, 1987; Regent's, Univ. of Calif., Berkeley, 1990; Einstein, Princeton, 1996. Member: Sch. of Engrg and Applied Science (Bd Overseers), Univ. Pennsylvania, 1983–86; Union Councils for Soviet Jews Adv. Bd, 1983–95; NSF Industrial Panel on Science and Technology, 1982–92; CIT Vis. Cttee, 1977–79; NSF Astronomy Adv. Panel, 1978–79; MNAS, 1975–; Wissenschaftliche Fachbeirat, Max-Planck Inst., Bonn, 1978–85 (Chm., 1981–83); Technology Adv. Council, EarthLink Network Inc., 1996–98; Board of Directors: IMNET, 1986–92; A. D. Little, 1992–2001; Duracell, 1995–96; LCC, 1996–2001; Warpspeed, 1996–2001. Vice-Chm., Cttee of Concerned Scientists, 1976– (Mem., 1975–). Mem., National Acad. of Engrg, 1990. Hon. MIEEE, 1990. Trustee, Trenton State Coll., 1977–79. Hon. degrees: Paris Observatory, 1976; Wilkes Coll., City Coll. of NY, Yeshiva Univ., and Rutgers Univ., 1979; Bar Ilan Univ., 1983; Monmouth Coll., 1984; Technion-Israel Inst. of Technology, Pittsburgh Univ., Ball State Univ., Kean Coll., 1986; Ohio State Univ., Iona Coll., 1988; Drew Univ., 1989; Lafayette Coll., 1990; Columbia Univ., 1990; George Washington Univ., 1992; Rensselaer Polytechnic Inst., 1992; Pennsylvania Univ., 1992; Bloomfield Coll., 1994; Ranken Tech. Coll., 1997; Hebrew Union Coll., 1997; Oxford, 2002. Henry Draper Medal, National Acad. of Sciences, 1977; Herschel Medal, RAS, 1977; (jtly) Nobel Prize for Physics, 1978; Townsend Harris Medal, City Coll. NY, 1979; Newman Award, City Coll. NY, 1983; Joseph Handleman Prize in the Scis, 1983; Grad. Faculties Alumni Award, 1984; Big Brothers Inc. of NY, City Achievement in Science Award, 1985; Priestly Award, Dickinson Coll., 1989; Pake Prize, APS, 1990; NJ Literary Hall of Fame, 1991; Pender Award, Pennsylvania Univ., 1992; NJ Science/Technology Medal, R&D Council of NJ, 1996; Industrial Res. Inst. Medalist, 1998. Mem. Editorial Bd, Annual Revs of Astronomy and Astrophysics, 1974–78; Associate Editor, Astrophysical Jl Letters, 1978–82. *Publications*: Ideas and Information: managing in a high-tech world, 1989; Harmony: business, technology & life after paperwork, 1995; 100 published articles, principally in Astrophysical Jl. *Address*: 2855 Sand Hill Road, Menlo Park, CA 94025, USA.

**PEPINSTER, Catherine;** journalist, author and broadcaster; *b* 7 June 1959; *d* of late Michel Joseph Pepinster and Winifred Pepinster (*née* Jones); *m* 2003, Kevin Charles Morley. *Educ*: Manchester Univ. (BA (Econ. and Soc. Sci.) 1980); City Univ., London (Postgrad. Dip. Journalism 1981); Heythrop Coll., Univ. of London (MA (Philos. and Religion) 2002). Local newspaper reporter, Manchester and London, 1981–85; Property Correspondent, Sheffield Morning Telegraph, 1985–86; Chief Reporter, Estates Times, 1986; News Ed., Building, 1987–89; reporter, The Observer, 1989–90; News Ed., Time Out, 1990–94; Asst News Ed., The Independent, 1994–95; Dep. News Ed., 1995–97, News Ed., 1997–98, Independent on Sunday; Features Ed., The Independent, 1998; Asst Ed., 1999–2002, Exec. Ed., 2002–04, Independent on Sunday; Ed., The Tablet, 2004–16. UK Develt Officer, Anglican Centre in Rome, 2017–. Res. Consultant, St George's House, Windsor, 2017–. Regular contributor, Thought for the Day, BBC Radio 4; contribs to other radio and TV. Vis. Scholar, St Benet's Hall, Oxford, 2014–15; Vis. Fellow, Residential Res. Library, Univ. of Durham, 2018. Dir, Kaleidoscope, 2010–. Trustee: Bible Soc., 2014–; Nat. Churches Trust, 2018–. *Publications*: (ed) John Paul II: reflections from The Tablet, 2005; (contrib.) Religion and the News, 2012; (contrib.) Religion, Society and God: public theology in action, 2013; The Keys and the Kingdom: the British and the Papacy from John Paul II to Francis, 2017. *Recreations*: walking, reading, architecture, the Belgian culture and lunch. *T*: 07970 740854. *E*: cpepinster@icloud.com. *Club*: Reform.

**PEPPÉ, Comdr William Lawrence Tosco,** OBE 1987; Vice Lord-Lieutenant of Ross and Cromarty, 2005–12; *b* 25 Nov. 1937; *s* of Lt-Col William Tosco Hill Peppé, DSO, OBE, MC and Alison Mary (*née* Johnson); *m* 1966, Deirdre Eva Preston Wakefield; three *s*. *Educ*: Wellington Coll.; King's Coll., Cambridge. Joined RN, 1955; Commanding Officer: 892 Naval Air Sqn, 1974–76; HMS Diomede, 1980–81; retd 1991. Chm., Skye and Lochalsh Access Forum, 2007–10. JP Skye and Lochalsh, 1992–2007; DL Ross and Cromarty, Skye and Lochalsh, 1996–2012. Hon. Sheriff, Portree and Lochmaddy, 2007. *Recreation*: country. *Address*: Glendrynoch Lodge, Carbost, Isle of Skye IV47 8SX.

**PEPPER, Sir David (Edwin),** KCMG 2005; DPhil; Chairman, Defence Science and Technology Laboratory, 2014–19; *b* 8 Feb. 1948; *s* of Samuel Edwin Pepper and Rose Pepper (*née* Pell); *m* 1970, Margaret Meehan; two *s*. *Educ*: Chigwell Sch.; St John's Coll., Oxford (MA, DPhil 1972). Joined Government Communications Headquarters, 1972: Principal, 1979; Grade 5, 1984; RCDS 1991; Dir of Admin, 1995–98; on loan to Home Office as Dir, Corporate Develt, 1998–2000; Dir, Policy and Resources, 2000–03; Dir, GCHQ, 2003–08. Mem., UK Adv. Bd, Thales, 2009–13; Advr, Deloitte, 2011–14. Trustee, Glos Wildlife Trust, 2015–. *Recreations*: walking, music, reading, cooking, family history.

**PEPPER, Prof. Gordon Terry,** CBE 1990; Hon. Visiting Professor, Sir John Cass Business School, City of London (formerly City University Business School), 1987–90 and 1998–2011 (Director, Centre for Financial Markets, 1988–97 and Professor, 1991–97); Director, Lombard Street Research Ltd, 1998–2015 (Chairman, 2000–09); *b* 2 June 1934; *s* of Harold Terry Pepper and Jean Margaret Gordon Pepper (*née* Furness); *m* 1958, Gillian Clare Huelin; three *s* one *d*. *Educ*: Repton; Trinity College, Cambridge (MA); FIA, FSIP. Equity & Law Life Assurance Soc., 1957–60; W. Greenwell & Co.: Partner, 1962; Joint Senior Partner, 1980–86; Chairman, Greenwell Montagu & Co., 1986–87; Dir and Sen. Advr, Midland Montagu, 1985–90; Chm., Payton Pepper & Sons Ltd, 1987–97. Member: Cttee on Industry and Finance, NEDC, 1988–90; ESRC, 1989–93; Adv. Cttee, Dept of Applied Econs, Cambridge Univ., 1992–97; Shadow Monetary Policy Cttee, 1997–2011; Council of Econ. Advrs to Opposition front bench, 1999–2006. *Publications*: Money, Credit and Inflation, 1990; Money, Credit and Asset Prices, 1994; Inside Thatcher's Monetarist Revolution, 1998; (with M. Oliver) Monetarism under Thatcher – Lessons for the Future, 2001; Liquidity Theory of Asset Prices, 2006; papers to Jl of Inst. of Actuaries. *Recreations*: sailing, family. *Address*: Durnsford Mill, Mildenhall, Marlborough, Wilts SN8 2NG. *T*: (01672) 511073. *E*: gordonpepper55@gmail.com. *Club*: Reform.

**PEPPER, Prof. John Robert,** OBE 2015; FRCS; Professor of Cardiothoracic Surgery, National Heart and Lung Institute, Imperial College London, since 1999; Consultant Cardiothoracic Surgeon, Royal Brompton Hospital, since 1990; *b* Plymouth, 8 March 1948; *s* of Donald and Maureen Pepper; *m* 1973, Hilary; two *s*. *Educ*: Clare Coll., Cambridge (BA 1968; MB BChir 1971; MChir); Guy's Hosp. Med. Sch. Sen Surgeon, 1971–72, SHO, Cardiothoracic Unit, 1972–73, Guy's Hosp.; Registrar: Gen. Surgery, St James' Hosp., Leeds, 1973–75; Cardiothoracic Surgery, Nat. Heart Hosp., London Chest Hosp. and Guy's Hosp., 1975–79; Consultant Cardiothoracic Surgeon: London Chest Hosp. and Southend Hosp., 1980–82; St George's Hosp. and St Helier Hosp., 1982–90. Mem., Soc. of Apothecaries. *Publications*: chapters to med. textbooks and contribs to scientific jls. *Recreations*: sailing, photography. *Address*: Royal Brompton Hospital, Sydney Street, SW3 6NP. *T*: (020) 7351 8530. *E*: j.pepper@rbht.nhs.uk.

**PEPPER, Sir Michael,** Kt 2006; FRS 1983; FREng; Pender Professor of Nanoelectronics, University College London, since 2009; Fellow of Trinity College, Cambridge, since 1982 (Senior Research Fellow, 1982–87; Professorial Fellow, 1987–2009); *b* 10 Aug. 1942; *s* of Morris and Ruby Pepper; *m* 1973, Jeannette Denise Josse, MB, BS, FRCPsych; two *d*. *Educ*: St Marylebone Grammar Sch.; Reading Univ. (BSc Physics, 1963; PhD Physics, 1967); MA 1987, ScD 1989, Cantab. FInstP 1991, Hon. FInstP 2012; FREng 2009. Res. Physicist, Mullard Ltd, 1967–69; res. in solid state physics, The Plessey Co., Allen Clark Res. Centre, 1969–73; Cavendish Lab., 1973–2009 (in association with The Plessey Co., 1973–82); Warren Res. Fellow of Royal Soc., Cavendish Lab., 1978–86; Principal Res. Fellow, GEC plc, Hirst Res. Centre, 1982–87; Prof. of Physics, Univ. of Cambridge, 1987–2009, now Emeritus. Jt Man. Dir, 1991–2007, Sen. Adviser, 2007–, Toshiba Res. Europe Ltd (formerly Toshiba Cambridge Res. Centre Ltd); Jt Founder and Dir, TeraView Ltd, 2001–. Mem., Univ. Council, 1993–97, 2000, Gen. Bd of Faculties, 1995–99, and various cttees of Council and Bd, 1993–99, Cambridge. Visiting Professor: Bar-Ilan Univ., Israel, 1984; in Physical Scis and Engrg, Univ. of Oxford, 2010–; Hon. Prof. of Pharmaceutical Sci., Univ. of Otago, NZ, 2005–10. Lectures: Inaugural Mott, Inst. of

Physics, 1985; Royal Soc. Review, 1987; Rankin, Liverpool Univ., 1987; G. I. Taylor, Cambridge Philosophical Soc., 1988; Resnick, Bar-Ilan Univ., 1995; Mountbatten Meml, IEE, 2003; Bakerian, Royal Soc., 2004; Saha Meml, Kolkata, 2008; Cherwell-Simon Meml, Oxford, 2010; C. V. Raman Meml, Indian Inst. of Sci., Bangalore, 2010; Inst. of Physics Prestige Speaker, Hereford and Worcester, 2010; Waterloo Inst. of Nanotechnol. Dist. Lectr, 2010; Inst. of Physics Cockroft-Walton Lectr, India, 2013; Srinivasan Meml Lectr, Indian Inst. of Sci., Bangalore, 2013; Fr Verstraeten Meml, St Xavier, Kolkata, 2013; Dirac, Univ. of NSW, 2013; Gustave Eiffel, ICE, 2014; Kelvin, IET, 2015. Past and present mem. of various cttees and panels of Inst. of Physics (Editl Bd, Jl of Physics, Condensed Matter, 1991–96; Sci. Adv. Ctee, Inst. of Physics Publishing, 2005–), Royal Soc. (Associate Editor, 1983–89; Mem. Council, 1999–2001; Editor, 2008–10, Mem. Editl Bd, 2010–13, Phil. Trans A), Rutherford Meml Cttee, 1987–91, DTI and SERC (Cttees on Solid State Devices, Semiconductors, 1984–89), Amer. Physical Soc. (Divl Associate Ed., Physical Review Letters, 1998–2001; Mem. Editl Bd, Physical Review B, 2005–11); Mem., Council for Industry and Higher Educn, 2005–08. Trustee, Wolfson Foundn, 2011–. Fellow, Amer. Physical Soc., 1992; MAE 2012. Hon. DSc: Bar-Ilan, 1993; Linköping, 1997; NSW, 2013; Leeds, 2019. Guthrie Prize and Medal, 1985, Mott Prize and Medal, 2000, Business and Innovation Medal (Gold), 2010, Isaac Newton Medal and Prize, 2019, Inst. of Physics; Hewlett-Packard Prize, European Physical Soc., 1985; Hughes Medal, 1987, Royal Medal, 2005, Royal Soc.; Faraday Medal, IET, 2013; Silver Dirac Medal, Australian Inst. of Physics, 2013. *Publications:* papers on semiconductors and solid state physics in jls. *Recreations:* whisky tasting, reading, travel, music. *Address:* Department of Electronic and Electrical Engineering, University College London, Torrington Place, WC1E 7JE. *E:* michael.pepper@ucl.ac.uk, mp10000@cam.ac.uk. *Clubs:* Athenæum; Arsenal Football.

**PEPPER, Michael Peter Gregory,** PhD; independent international statistical consultant, since 2004; *b* 2 June 1945; *s* of Arthur Pepper and Anne (née Panian); *m* 1st; two *s*; 2nd; one step *d*; 3rd, 2013, Ruth Lewis; two step *d*. *Educ:* Dr Challoner's Grammar Sch., Amersham; London Univ. (BSc Maths (Ext.)); Essex Univ. (MSc); PhD Bath. Res. Fellow, Univ. of Bath, 1970–74; Statistician, Dept of Energy, 1974–79; Sen. Statistician, Govt of Botswana, 1979–81; Statistician, Dept of Energy, 1981–86; Chief Statistician and Dir of Stats, Welsh Office, 1986–93; Hd of Price and Business Statistics Gp, CSO, subseq. ONS, 1993–2002; Exec. Dir, Business Transformation, ONS, 2002–04. *Recreations:* travel, gardening, choral music. *Address:* 2 Wetherell Place, Bristol BS8 1AR.

**PEPPER, Terence,** OBE 2002; Curator of Photographs and Exhibitions Organiser, 1978–2014, Senior Special Adviser on Photographs, since 2014, National Portrait Gallery; Senior Special Adviser on Photographs, Fashion and Textile Museum, since 2016; *b* 2 Jan. 1949; *s* of (Herbert Walter) Trevor Pepper and (Catherine) Rosemary (née Earle); partner, Rosalind Crowe. *Educ:* Epsom Coll.; Queen Mary Coll., Univ. of London (LLB); Council of Legal Educn; Sch. of Librarianship, Ealing Tech. Coll. ALA 1977. Asst Librarian, 1975, Librarian, 1976–78, NPG. Mem. Council, John Kobal Foundn, 1992–. Hon. FRPS 2002. *Publications:* exhibition catalogues: Monday's Children: fair and famous of the 1920s and 1930s, 1977; Camera Portraits by E. O. Hoppe, 1978; Photographs by Norman Parkinson: fifty years of portraits and fashion, 1981; Howard Coster's Celebrity Portraits, 1985; (contrib. with D. Mellor) Cecil Beaton, 1986; Portraits Helmut Newton, 1988; Lewis Morley: photographer of the sixties, 1989; (with J. Kobal) The Man Who Shot Garbo: the photographs of Clarence Sinclair Bull, 1989; Dorothy Wilding: the pursuit of perfection, 1991; The Lure of the Limelight: James Abbe, photographer of cinema and stage, 1995; High Society: photographs 1897–1914, 1998; (curated with P. Hoare) Icons of Pop, 1999; Horst Portraits, 2001; Cecil Beaton: portraits, 2004 (German edn 2005); Angus McBean: portraits, 2006; (curated with D. Friend) Vanity Fair Portraits: photographs 1913–2008, 2008 (Curator/Exhibn of the Year (jtly), Lucie Awards, 2008); Beatles to Bowie: the 60s exposed, 2009 (German edn 2009); Twiggy: a life in photographs, 2009; (with P. Prodger) Hoppe Portraits: society, studio and street, 2011; Man Ray Portraits, 2013; (with H. Trompeteler) Audrey Hepburn: portraits of an icon, 2015; (with M. Pell) 1920s Jazz Age: fashion and photographs, 2016. *Recreations:* swimming, cinema, reading Sunday newspapers, pop music.

**PEPPERALL, Hon. Sir Edward (Brian),** Kt 2018; **Hon. Mr Justice Pepperall;** a Judge of the High Court, Queen's Bench Division, since 2018; Justice of the Court of Appeal of Falkland Islands, South Georgia and South Sandwich Islands, since 2017; Presiding Judge, Midland Circuit, from Jan. 2020; *b* Bristol, 27 Dec. 1966; *s* of late Brian Robert Pepperall and of Marcia Louise Pepperall (née Gurden); *m* 2003, Sarah Josephine Fardell; one *s* two *d*. *Educ:* Queen Elizabeth's Hospital, Bristol; Univ. of Birmingham (LLB Law Hons 1988); Inns of Court Sch. of Law. MCIArb 2014. Called to the Bar, Lincoln's Inn, 1989, Bencher, 2015; in practice as a barrister, specialising in commercial and employment law; 2 Fountain Court, Birmingham, 1989–98; St Philips Chambers, Birmingham and London, 1998–2018 (Dep. Hd of Chambers, 2014–17); 2 Temple Gardens, London, 2011–13; a Recorder, 2009–18; QC 2013; a Dep. High Court Judge, Chancery and QBD, 2016–18. Mem., Civil Procedure Rule Cttee, 2010–16; Chm., Midland Chancery and Commercial Bar Assoc., 2016–. *Publications:* (Contrib. Ed.) The White Book, 2015–; contrib. to legal jls. *Recreations:* tennis, theatre, Manchester City FC, weekend taxi driver for my children's sporting interests. *Address:* Royal Courts of Justice, Rolls Building, Fetter Lane, EC4A 1NL.

**PEPPITT, His Honour John Raymond;** QC 1976; a Circuit Judge, 1991–2000; *b* 22 Sept. 1931; *s* of late Reginald Peppitt and Phyllis Claire Peppitt; *m* 1960, Judith Penelope James; three *s*. *Educ:* St Paul's Sch.; Jesus Coll., Cambridge (BA Classical Tripos). Called to the Bar, Gray's Inn, 1958, Bencher, 1982; a Recorder, 1976–91. *Recreation:* collecting water-colours. *Address:* The Old Rectory, Snargate, Romney Marsh, Kent TN29 0EW.

**PEPYS,** family name of **Earl of Cottenham.**

**PEPYS, Sir Mark (Brian),** Kt 2012; MD, PhD; FRS 1998; FRCP, FRCPath, FMedSci; Director, Wolfson Drug Discovery Unit, University College London, since 2011; Hon. Consultant Physician, Royal Free Hospital, since 1999; *b* 18 Sept. 1944; *s* of Prof. Jack Pepys, MD, FRCP, FRCPE, FRCPath, and Rhoda Gertrude Pepys (née Kussel); *m* 1971, Dr Elizabeth Olga Winternitz; one *s* one *d*. *Educ:* Trinity Coll., Cambridge (BA, MA; MD 1982; PhD 1973; Hon. Fellow, 2014); UCH Med. Sch., London. FRCP 1981; FRCPath 1991. Sen. Schol., 1964–65, Res. Schol., 1970–73, Fellow, 1973–79, Trinity Coll., Cambridge; MRC Trng Fellow, Dept of Pathology, Univ. of Cambridge, 1970–73; Registrar, then Sen. Registrar and Asst Lectr in Medicine, Hammersmith Hosp., 1973–75; Sen. Lectr, Hd of Immunology and Hon. Consultant Physician, Royal Free Hosp. Sch. of Medicine, 1975–77; Sen. Lectr in Medicine, 1977–80, Hon. Consultant Physician, 1977–99, Reader, 1980–84, Prof. of Immunol Medicine, 1984–99, RPMS, then ICSM, Hammersmith Hosp.; Prof. of Medicine and Hd, Div. of Medicine, Royal Free Campus, UCL Med. Sch. (formerly Royal Free and University Coll. Med. Sch.), 1999–2011, now Emeritus Prof.; Founder and Hd, NHS Nat. Amyloidosis Centre, 1999–2011. Member: Scientific Adv. Ctee, Lister Inst., 2006–11; Sci. and Med. Panel, Wolfson Foundn, 2007–; Scientific Council, Cardiothoracic Centre of Monaco, 2008–; Chair, Temp. Nominating Gp for Clinical Science, Royal Soc., 2013–15. Goulstonian Lectr, 1982, Lumleian Lectr, 1998, Harveian Orator, 2007, RCP; Sir Arthur Sims Travelling Prof., RCS, 1991; Kohn Lectr, RCPath, 1991; Chandos Lectr, Renal Assoc., 2000; Heberden Orator and Medallist, British Soc. for Rheumatology, 2002; Richard Kovacs Lectr, RSM, 2009; Michael Feiwel Meml Lectr, RSM, 2010; Gordon Cumming Meml Lectr, Med. Res. Soc., 2010; Adam Neville Lectr, Univ. of Dundee, 2010; Enno Mandema Meml Lectr, Internat. Soc. for Amyloidosis, 2012; Claude Amiel Lectr, ISN World Congress of Nephrology, 2017; McFadzean Vis. Prof. and McFadzean Dist. Lect., Univ. of Hong Kong, 2018; Burt Glazard Meml Lect., Brigham and Women's Hosp., Harvard Univ., 2019. Member Council: Royal Soc., 2003–05; Acad. of Med. Scis, 2003–06. Hon. Mem., Assoc. of Physicians of GB and Ireland, 1998. Founder FMedSci 1998. Fellow: UCL, 2003; Faculty of Medicine, Imperial Coll. London, 2004. Moxon Trust Medal, RCP, 1999; Glaxo Smith Kline Prize and Lect., Royal Soc., 2007; Ernst Chain Prize, Imperial Coll. London, 2008. *Publications:* international patents on drug design and novel therapies; contrib. articles on immunology, acute phase proteins, amyloidosis, drug discovery and develt in learned jls. *Recreations:* biking, wine. *Address:* 22 Wildwood Road, NW11 6TE. *T:* (020) 8455 9387. *Club:* Hurlingham.

**PERAHIA, Murray,** Hon. KBE 2004; FRCM; pianist and conductor; Principal Guest Conductor, Academy of St Martin-in-the-Fields, since 2001; *b* New York, 19 April 1947; *s* of David and Flora Perahia; *m* 1980, Naomi Shohet (Ninette); two *s*. *Educ:* High Sch. of Performing Arts; Mannes College (MS); studied piano with Jeanette Haien, M. Horszowski, Arthur Balsam. FRCM 1987; FRAM 1994. Co-Artistic Dir, Aldeburgh Fest., 1981–89; Hon. Dir, Britten-Pears Sch. for Advanced Musical Studies, 1981–. Won Kosciuszko Chopin Prize, 1965; début Carnegie Recital Hall, 1966; won Leeds Internat. Piano Festival, 1972; Avery Fisher Award, 1975; regular tours of Europe, Asia, USA; numerous recordings include complete Mozart Piano Concertos (as dir and soloist with English Chamber Orch.), complete Beethoven Piano Concertos (with Bernard Haitink and Royal Concertgebouw), Bartók Sonata for Two Pianos and Percussion (Grammy Award, 1989); Gramophone award for Handel and Scarlatti recording, 1997; Gramophone award for Bach English Suites recording, 1999; Chopin Études (Grammy Award, 2002). Hon. Fellow, Jesus Coll., Cambridge, 2007. *Address:* c/o IMG Artists-Europe, Capital Tower, 91 Waterloo Road, SE1 8RT.

**PERCEVAL, Michael;** HM Diplomatic Service, retired; Consul-General, Barcelona, 1992–96; *b* 27 April 1936; *o s* of late Hugh Perceval and Guida Brind; *m* 1968, Alessandra Grandis; one *s* one *d*. *Educ:* Downside Sch.; Christ Church, Oxford (Schol.; 2nd Cl. Hons English Lit.). Served Royal Air Force, Nicosia, 1956–60; film production asst, Athens, 1960; freelance correspondent, Madrid, 1961–69; joined FCO, 1970; First Sec. (Press), UK Rep. to EC, Brussels, 1972–74; First Sec. and subseq. Head of Chancery, British High Commission, Nicosia, 1974–78; Asst Head of Mexico and Caribbean Dept, FCO, 1978–79; Counsellor, Havana, 1980–82; Counsellor (Political and Economic) and Consul-Gen., Brasilia, 1982–85; Counsellor (Commercial), Rome, 1985–89; Consul-General, São Paulo, 1990–92. *Publications:* The Spaniards, 1969, 2nd edn 1972; The Mikipedia Memoirs (autobiog.), 2016; The Fiction of Ramón del Valle-Inclán (4 vols) (English trans.), 2017. *Recreations:* music, walking, the Mediterranean.

**PERCHARD, Colin William,** CVO 1997; OBE 1984; Minister (Cultural Affairs), India, British Council, 1993–2000; *b* 19 Oct. 1940; *m* 1970, Elisabeth Penelope Glynis, *d* of Sir Glyn Jones, GCMG, MBE; three *s*. *Educ:* Victoria Coll., Jersey; Liverpool Univ. (BA Hons History); Internat. Inst. for Educnl Planning, UNESCO, Paris (DipEd Planning and Admin). British Council: Asst Rep., Blantyre, Malawi, 1964–68; Regional Officer, Africa S of the Sahara, 1968–71: Asst Rep., Calcutta, 1971–72; Officer i/c Dhaka, 1972; Rep., Seoul, 1973–76; Dir, Technical Co-operation Trng Dept, 1976–79; Internat. Inst. for Educnl Planning, Paris, 1979–80; Rep., Harare, 1980–86; Controller, Africa Div., 1986–90; Dir and Cultural Counsellor, Turkey, 1990–93. Chm., Jersey Arts Trust, 2001–10; Pres., Société Jersiaise, 2016–19. Patron, Jersey Architects Assoc., 2003–. *Recreations:* theatre, music, cooking. *Address:* La Source, Rue de la Vignette, St Martin, Jersey JE3 6HY.

**PERCHE, Neisha;** see Crosland, N.

**PERCIVAL, (Catherine) Eve;** see Poole, C. E.

**PERCIVAL, Prof. Ian Colin,** PhD; FRS 1985; Professor of Theoretical Physics, 1991–96, Research Professor in Physics, 2000, now Professor Emeritus, Queen Mary University of London (formerly Queen Mary College, then Queen Mary and Westfield College, University of London); *b* 27 July 1931; *m* 1955, Jill Cuff (née Herbert) (*d* 1999); two *s* one *d*. *Educ:* Ealing County Grammar Sch.; UCL (BSc, PhD; Fellow, 1986). FRAS. Lectr in Physics, UCL, 1957–61; Reader in Applied Maths, QMC, 1961–67; Prof. of Theoret. Physics, Univ. of Stirling, 1967–74; Prof. of Applied Maths, QMC, 1974–91. Naylor Prize, London Mathematical Soc., 1985; Alexander von Humboldt Foundn Award, 1993; Dirac Medal and Prize, Inst. of Physics, 1999. *Publications:* (with Derek Richards) Introduction to Dynamics, 1983; (with Owen Greene and Irene Ridge) Nuclear Winter, 1985; Quantum State Diffusion, 1998; papers in learned jls on scattering theory, atomic and molecular theory, statistical mechanics, classical dynamics and theory of chaos and foundations of quantum theory. *Address:* Queen Mary University of London, Mile End Road, E1 4NS. *T:* (020) 7882 5555. *E:* i.c.percival@qmul.ac.uk.

**PERCY,** family name of **Duke of Northumberland.**

**PERCY, Earl; George Dominic Percy;** Chief Executive Officer, Hotspur Geothermal (formerly Cluff Geothermal) Ltd, since 2010; *b* 4 May 1984; *e s* and *heir* of Duke of Northumberland, *qv*. *Educ:* Eton; Univ. of Edinburgh (MA 2007); Univ. of Damascus. A Page of Honour to the Queen, 1996–98. *Address:* Alnwick Castle, Alnwick, Northumberland NE66 1NG.

**PERCY, Algernon Eustace Hugh H.;** see Heber-Percy.

**PERCY, Andrew,** MP (C) Brigg and Goole, since 2010; *b* Hull, 1977. *Educ:* York Univ. (BA Hons); Leeds Univ. (PGCE). History teacher in schs in E Yorks and N Lincs; MP's researcher; pt-time primary sch. teacher. Mem. (C) Hull CC, 2000–10. Contested (C) Normanton, 2005. Parly Under-Sec. of State, DCLG, 2016–17. Member, Select Committee: on Procedure, 2010–11; on Regulatory Reform, 2010–17; on Standing Orders, 2011–15; on Health, 2012–16; on NI Affairs, 2012–15; Panel of Chairs, 2015–16. *Address:* House of Commons, SW1A 0AA.

**PERCY, John Pitkeathly, (Ian),** CBE 1997; CA; Chairman, John Menzies plc Pension Fund, since 2007; *b* 16 Jan. 1942; *s* of John Percy and Helen Glass Percy (née Pitkeathly); *m* 1965, Sheila Isobel Horn; two *d*. *Educ:* Edinburgh Acad. Qualified as a Chartered Accountant with Graham Smart & Annan, Edinburgh, 1967; Grant Thornton: Partner, Edinburgh, 1970–78; London, 1978–91; Managing Partner, 1981–88; Sen. Partner, 1988–93; Chairman: Accounts Commn for Scotland, 1992–2000; Audit Scotland, 1998–2000; Companies House, 2002–06; UCEA, 2007–10. Director: William Wilson (Holdings), 1993–2005; Weir Gp plc, 1996–2010 (Dep. Chm., 2005–10); Kiln plc, 1998–2005 (Chm., 2002–05); Ricardo plc, 2000–08 (Dep. Chm., 2005–08); Cala Gp Ltd, 2000–12 (Chm., 2009–11); Chairman: Caledonian Bank, 1991–99; Deutsche Scotland (formerly Morgan Grenfell), 1992–2001; Cala Pension Fund, 2001–14; Wolseley Gp

Pension Fund, 2005–19; Romanes Media Pension Fund, 2007–17. Dir, Scottish Legal Aid Bd, 2000–05 (Dep. Chm., 1996–2002); Member: Auditing Practices Bd, 1992–2002; Internat. Auditing Practices Cttee, 1995–2000. Hon. Prof. of Accounting and Auditing, Aberdeen Univ., 1988– . Pres., Inst. of Chartered Accountants of Scotland, 1990–91 (Sen. Vice-Pres., 1989–91). Dep. Chm., Nat. Trust for Scotland, 2011–15. Chm. Court, Queen Margaret Univ., Edinburgh, 2004–10. Freeman, City of London, 1983; Liveryman, Painter Stainers' Co., 1983. FRSA 1989. Hon. LLD Aberdeen, 1999; DUniv Queen Margaret, Edinburgh, 2012. *Recreations:* golf, fishing. *Address:* 4 Westbank, Easter Park Drive, Edinburgh EH4 6SL. *T:* (0131) 312 6446. *Clubs:* Royal Automobile; New (Edinburgh); Royal & Ancient (St Andrews), Hon. Company of Edinburgh Golfers; Gairloch Golf, Bruntisfield Golfing Society, Luffness New Golf.

**PERCY, Very Rev. Canon Prof. Martyn William,** PhD; Dean of Christ Church, Oxford, since 2014; Professor of Theological Education, King's College London, since 2004; Professorial Research Fellow, Heythrop College, University of London, 2010–18; *b* 31 July 1962; *s* of Roy Percy and Sylvia Percy (*née* Owens); *m* 1989, Emma Bray; two *s*. *Educ:* Merchant Taylors' Sch., Northwood; Univ. of Bristol (BA Hons 1984); Univ. of Durham (Cert. Counselling 1990); King's Coll. London (PhD 1993); Univ. of Sheffield (MEd 2003); Univ. of Oxford (MA 2004). Publisher, 1984–88; ordained deacon, 1990, priest, 1991; Curate, St Andrew's, Bedford, 1990–94; Chaplain and Dir of Theol. and Religious Studies, Christ's Coll., Cambridge, 1994–97; Dir of Studies, Sidney Sussex Coll., Cambridge, 1995–97; Dir, Lincoln Theol Inst. for Study of Religion and Society, 1997–2004; Sen. Lectr, 1997–2000, Reader, 2000–03, Univ. of Sheffield; Reader, Univ. of Manchester, 2003–04; Principal, Ripon Coll. Cuddesdon, 2004–14, and Oxford Ministry Course, Oxford, 2006–14. Prof. of Theol. and Ministry, Hartford Seminary, Conn, USA, 2002–08; Tutor, 2015– , Fellow, 2016– , Saïd Business Sch., Univ. of Oxford. Vis. Fellow, Regent's Park Coll., Oxford, 2006–14; Vis. Prof., Values Studies Inst., Univ. of Winchester, 2017– ; Founding Fellow, Center for Theologically Engaged Anthropology, Univ. of Georgia, 2017– . Hon. Canon, 1997–2004, Canon Theologian, 2004–10, Sheffield Cathedral; Hon. Canon, Salisbury Cathedral, 2009–14, now Emeritus. Mem. Council and Dir, ASA, 2000–06; Member: Faith and Order Adv. Gp, 1998–2006; HEFCE RAE Panel (Humanities), 2005–08; Ind. Complaints Panel, Portman Gp, 2006–11; BBC Standing Cttee on Religion and Belief, 2009–14. Comr, Direct Mktg Authy, 2008–14; Advr, BBFC, 2010– . Founder and Co-Chair, Soc. for Study of Anglicanism, 2003– . Chair: Cliff Coll. Council, 2002–06; Cuddesdon and Denton Parish Council, 2007–14. Hon. Life Fellow, Harris Manchester Coll., Oxford, 2018; Hon. FKC 2018. Chair and Trustee, Ovalhouse Th., London, 2014– ; Trustee: William Temple Foundn, 2002–14; Gladstone's Library, Hawarden, 2014– ; Grubb Inst., 2015– ; Li Tim-Oi Foundn, 2015– . Patron, St Francis Children's Soc., 1997. Vice Pres., Modern Church Union, 2014– . Governor: Westminster Sch., 2014– ; St Edward's Sch., Oxford, 2015– . Ed., *Modern Believing*, 1997–2005. Freeman: City of London, 1989; Merchant Taylors' Co., 1989; Barbers' Co., 2015. *Publications:* Words, Wonders and Power: understanding contemporary Christian fundamentalism and revivalism, 1996; (ed) Intimate Affairs: spirituality and sexuality in perspective, 1997; Power and the Church: ecclesiology in an age of transition, 1998; Richard Hooker: an introduction, 1999; (ed) Previous Convictions: studies in religious conversion, 2000; (ed with G. R. Evans) Managing the Church?: order and organisation in a secular age, 2000; (ed) Calling Time: religion, society and change at the turn of the millennium, 2000; (ed with A. Walker) Restoring the Image: essays in honour of David Martin, 2001; (ed jtly) Darkness Yielding, 2001, 3rd edn 2009; Salt of the Earth: religious resilience in a secular age, 2002; (ed with I. Jones) Fundamentalism, Church and Society, 2002; (ed with S. Lowe) The Character of Wisdom: essays in honour of Wesley Carr, 2004; Engaging Theology: Christianity and contemporary culture, 2005; Clergy: the origin of species, 2006; (ed with I. Markham) Why Liberal Churches are Growing, 2006; (with L. Nelstrop) Evaluating Fresh Expressions, 2008; (jtly) Christ and Culture: essays after Lambeth, 2010; (ed with Christina Rees) Transfiguring Episcope: women and Church leadership, 2010; Shaping the Church: the promise of implicit theology, 2010; (ed jtly) Worship-Shaped Life: liturgical formation and the people of God, 2010; The Ecclesial Canopy: Faith, Hope, Charity, 2012; (ed with Robert Slocum) A Point of Balance, 2012; Anglicanism: confidence, commitment and communion, 2013; Thirty-Nine New Articles: preaching and proclaiming Anglican faith, 2013; (ed with Pete Ward) The Wisdom of the Spirit, 2014; (ed jtly) The Bright Field, 2014; (jtly) Curacies and How to Survive Them, 2015; (ed jtly) The Oxford Handbook of Anglican Studies, 2015; The Future Shapes of Anglicanism: charts, currents and contours, 2016; (ed) Clergy, Culture and Ministry: the dynamics of roles and relations in church and society, 2017; (ed jtly) SPCK Handbook: study of Ministry, 2017; (jtly) Untamed Gospel: poems, prose and protests, 2017; (ed jtly) Reasonable Radical? Reading the Writings of Martyn Percy, 2017. *Recreations:* reading, cinema, listening to jazz, running, squash. *Address:* The Deanery, Christ Church, Oxford OX1 1DP. *T:* (01865) 276150. *E:* dean@chch.ox.ac.uk. *Clubs:* Athenæum, Oxford and Cambridge; Cowley Workers Social.

**PERCY, Tulip;** *see* Siddiq, T.

**PEREIRA GRAY, Prof. Sir Denis (John),** Kt 1999; OBE 1981; FRCP, FRCGP, FMedSci; General Medical Practitioner, 1962–2000; Professor of General Practice, University of Exeter, 1986–2001, now Emeritus (Director of Postgraduate Medical School, 1987–97); President, Royal College of General Practitioners, 1997–2000; *b* 2 Oct. 1935; *s* of late Dr Sydney Joseph Pereira Gray and Alice Evelyn Gray; forename Pereira changed to surname by deed poll; *m* 1962, Jill Margaret Hoyte; one *s* three *d*. *Educ:* Exeter Sch.; St John's Coll., Cambridge (MA); St Bartholomew's Hosp. Med. Sch. MB BChir. FRCGP 1973; FRCP 1999. Sen. Lectr in Charge, Univ. of Exeter, 1973–86. Regional Adviser in Gen. Practice, 1975–2000; Consultant Adviser in Gen. Practice to Chief MO, DHSS, 1984–87. Mem., GMC, 1994–2003; Chm., Jt Cttee on Postgrad. Trng for Gen. Practice, 1994–97. Trustee, The Nuffield Trust (formerly Nuffield Provincial Hosps Trust), 1994–2006 (Chm., 2003–06). Chm. Council, RCGP, 1987–90 Hon. Editor, Journal, 1972–80, Publications, 1976–2000); Vice-Chm., 1998–2000, Chm., 2000–02, Acad. of Medical Royal Colls. Vice-Chm., Ethics and Confidentiality Cttee, Nat. Information Governance Bd, 2009–11. Editor, Medical Annual, 1983–87. Pres., What About the Children?, 2007– ; Patron, Nat. Assoc. for Patient Participation, 2003– . Honorary Professor: Peninsula Coll. of Medicine and Dentistry, 2010; Univ. of Exeter Med. Sch., 2013– . Lectures: James Mackenzie, RCGP, 1977; Pfizer, N England Faculty, RCGP, Gale Meml, SW England Faculty, RCGP, 1979; Eli Lilly, Haliburton Hume Meml, Newcastle upon Tyne and Northern Counties Med. Soc., Northcott Meml, Barnstaple, Harvard Davis, Denbigh, McConaghey Meml, Lifton, 1988; Murray Scott Meml, Aberdeen, 1990; Harben Meml, London, 1994; Sally Irvine, Ashridge Mgt Coll., 1995; Albert Wander, RSocMed, 1998; Andrew Smith, Durham, 1998; David Bruce, London, 1999; Frans Huygen, Nijmegen, Netherlands, 2001; Long Fox, Bristol, 2002; Deakin, Australia, 2002; Goodman, What About the Children?, 2013; Barbara Starfield, Univ. of Exeter, 2015. Internat. Mem., Nat. Acad. of Medicine (Mem., Inst. of Medicine, USA, 2000). Founder FMedSci 1998. Hon. FRSPH (Hon. FRSH 1997); Hon. FFPH 1997; Hon. FIHM 2000 (FHSM 1997); Hon. FRCPI 2001; Hon. FFGDP 2003; Hon FAcadMed 2013; Hon. Fellow, QMC, Univ. of London, 2000. Hon. DSc: De Montfort, 1997; Exeter, 2009; Hon. DM Nottingham, 2003. Gold Medal, Hunterian Soc., 1966, 1969; Sir Charles Hastings Prize, BMA, 1967, 1970; George Abercrombie Award, RCGP, 1978; Foundn Council Award, RCGP, 1980; Sir Harry Platt Prize, Modern Medicine Jl, 1981; Silver Medal, SIMG, 1989; Gold Medal, RIPH&H, 1999. *Publications:* Running a Practice (jtly), 1978, 3rd edn 1981; Training for General Practice, 1981; Forty Years On: the story of the first forty years of the RCGP, 1992; articles in Lancet, BMJ, Jl RCGP, British Jl Gen. Pract. *Recreation:* reading. *Address:* Alford House, 9 Marlborough Road, Exeter EX2 4TJ. *T:* (01392) 218080.

*See also* P. J. Pereira Gray.

**PEREIRA GRAY, Peter John,** FRICS; Managing Partner and Chief Executive Officer, Investment Division, Wellcome Trust, since 2001; *b* Exeter, 1963; *s* of Prof. Sir Denis (John) Pereira Gray, *qv*; *m* 1986, Sarah Mary Chamberlain; three *d*. *Educ:* Exeter Sch.; Trent Poly. (BA Urban Estate Surveying); Coll. of Estate Mgt (Dip. Property Investment). FRICS 2012. Sen. Surveyor, Drivers Jonas, 1986–88; Develt Manager, 1988–92, Dir, and Dep. Life Fund Manager, 1992–2001, Prudential Portfolio Managers; Wellcome Trust: Hd, Property Investment, 2001–05; Co-Hd, Portfolio Mgt, 2005–07; Dep. Chief Investment Officer, 2007–16. Advr, HRobotics Ltd, 2017– . Non-exec. Dir, iQSA, 2016; Chairman: FarmCare Ltd, 2014– ; Premier Marinas Ltd, 2015– ; XPG Estates Ltd, 2017– . Mem. Adv. Bd, Global Projects Center, Stanford Univ., 2017– . Co-Chm., Institutional Investors Roundtable, 2018– . Hon. Vice Pres., Cambridge Univ. Land Soc., 2012– . FRSA. Hon. FICPD 2011. *Publications:* Developing Property as an Asset Class, 2013; contrib. The Times. *Recreations:* tennis, walking in Devon and North Cornwall. *Address:* Wellcome Trust, 215 Euston Road, NW1 2BE. *T:* (020) 7611 8621.

**PERETZ, David Lindsay Corbett,** CB 1996; independent consultant on international financial issues, since 1999; *b* 29 May 1943; *s* of Michael and April Peretz; *m* 1966, Jane Wildman; one *s* one *d*. *Educ:* The Leys Sch., Cambridge; Exeter Coll., Oxford (MA). Asst Principal, Min. of Technol., 1965–69; Head of Public Policy and Institutional Studies, IBRO, 1969–76; HM Treasury: Principal, 1976–80; Asst Sec., External Finance, 1980–84; Principal Pvte Sec. to Chancellor of Exchequer, 1984–85; Under-Secretary: Home Finance, 1985–86; Monetary Gp, Public Finance, 1986–90; UK Exec. Dir, IMF and World Bank, and Economic Minister, Washington, 1990–94; Dep. Dir, Internat. Finance, HM Treasury, 1994–99. Chair, Ind. Adv. Cttee on Develt Impact, DFID, 2007–10; Chair, Bermuda Fiscal Responsibility Panel, 2015– . *Recreations:* walking, gardening, listening to music, sailing. *E:* dlcperetz@yahoo.co.uk.

*See also* G. M. J. Peretz.

**PERETZ, George Michael John;** QC 2015; *b* London, 1967; *s* of David Lindsay Corbett Peretz, *qv*; *m* 1995, Mandy Brown; one *d*. *Educ:* William Ellis Sch., Highgate; Exeter Coll., Oxford (BA Hons PPE); City Univ. (DipLaw). Called to the Bar, Middle Temple, 1990; in practice as barrister specialising in competition, state aid, VAT and customs, EU law, agriculture and medicines regulation; Legal Advr, OFT, 1992–97; Judge (pt-time), First-tier Tribunal (Social Entitlement Chamber), 2011– ; Mem., Attorney Gen.'s Panel of Jun. Counsel, 2002–15. Co-Chair, Jt Wkg Party of UK Bars and Law Socs on competition law, 2018– . Founder Mem., UK Trade Policy Forum, 2017– . Co-Chair, UK State Aid Law Assoc., 2012– . Gen. Rapporteur, Ligue Internationale du Droit de la Concurrence, 2017– (Dep. Gen. Rapporteur, 2015). *Recreations:* music (clarinet and piano), opera, France, walking, cycling, ancient Greece and Rome, history. *Address:* Monckton Chambers, 1–2 Raymond Buildings, Gray's Inn, WC1R 5NR. *T:* (020) 7405 7211. *E:* gperetz@monckton.com.

**PÉREZ DE CUÉLLAR, Javier,** Hon. GCMG 1992; Ambassador of Peru to France, 2001–04; holds personal rank of Ambassador; *b* 19 Jan. 1920; *m* Marcela (*née* Temple); one *s* one *d*. *Educ:* Law Faculty, Catholic Univ., Lima, Peru. Joined Peruvian Foreign Ministry, 1940; Diplomatic Service, 1944; Sec., Peruvian Embassies in France, UK, Bolivia and Brazil and Counsellor, Embassy, Brazil, 1944–60; Mem., Peruvian Delegn to First Session of Gen. Assembly, UN, 1946; Dir, Legal, Personnel, Admin, Protocol and Political Affairs Depts, Min. of Foreign Affairs, Peru, 1961–63; Peruvian Ambassador to Switzerland, 1964–66; Perm. Under-Sec. and Sec.-Gen. of Foreign Office, 1966–69; Ambassador of Peru to USSR and to Poland, 1969–71; Perm. Rep. of Peru to UN, 1971–75 (Rep. to UN Security Council, 1973–74); Special Rep. of UN Sec.-Gen. in Cyprus, 1975–77; Ambassador of Peru to Venezuela, 1978; UN Under-Sec.-Gen. for Special Political Affairs, 1979–81; Sec.-Gen., UN, 1982–91. Prime Minister and Foreign Minister, Peru, 2000–01. Pres., World Commn on Culture and Develt, UN/UNESCO, 1992– ; Chm. Emeritus, Inter-Amer. Dialogue, 1992– . Former Professor: of Diplomatic Law, Academia Diplomática del Perú; of Internat. Relations, Academia de Guerra Aérea del Perú. LLD *hc*: Univ. of Nice, France, 1983; Carleton Univ., Ottawa, 1985; Osnabruck Univ., 1986; Coimbra Univ., 1986; Oxford, 1993; other hon. degrees include: Jagiellonian Univ., Poland, 1984; Charles Univ. Czechoslovakia, 1984; Sofia Univ., Bulgaria, 1984; Universidad Nacional Mayor de San Marcos, Perú, 1984; Vrije Universiteit Brussel, Belgium, 1984; Sorbonne Univ., Paris, 1985; Cambridge Univ., 1989; Univ. of Salamanca, 1991; Oxford Univ., 1993. Various internat. awards including: Prince of Asturias Prize, 1987; Olof Palme Prize, 1989; Jawaharlal Nehru Award, 1989. Grand Cross, Order of El Sol (Peru); foreign decorations include: US Medal of Freedom; Grand Cross, Legion of Honour (France). *Publications:* Manual de Derecho Diplomático, 1964; Anarchy or Order, 1992; Pilgrimage for Peace, 1997. *Address:* Avenida Aurelio Miró Quesada 1071, Lima 27, Perú. *Clubs:* Travellers (Paris); Nacional, Ecuestre Huachipa, Jockey (Lima, Peru).

**PÉREZ ESQUIVEL, Adolfo;** sculptor; Hon. President: Servicio Paz y Justicia en América Latina, since 1986; Servicio Paz y Justicia Argentina, since 1973; President, International League for the Rights and Liberation of Peoples, since 1987; *b* 26 Nov. 1931; *m* 1956, Amanda Guerreño; three *s*. *Educ:* Nat. Sch. of Fine Arts, Buenos Aires. Prof. of Art, Manuel Belgrano Nat. Sch. of Fine Arts, Buenos Aires, 1956–76; Prof., Faculty of Architecture and Urban Studies, Univ. Nacional de la Plata, 1969–73; Gen. Co-ordinator, Servicio Paz y Justicia en América Latina, 1974–86. Work in permanent collections: Buenos Aires Mus. of Modern Art; Mus. of Fine Arts, Córdoba; Fine Arts Mus., Rosario. Joined group dedicated to principles of militant non-violence, and engaged in projects to promote self-sufficiency in urban areas, 1971; founded Paz y Justicia magazine, 1973. Co-founder, Ecumenical Movement for Human Rights, Argentina; Pres., Permanent Assembly for Human Rights. Premio la Nación de Escultura; Pope John XXIII prize, Pax Christi Orgn, 1977; Nobel Peace Prize, 1980. *Publications:* Resistir en la Esperanza, 2011. *Address:* Servicio Paz y Justicia, Piedras 730, CP 1070, Buenos Aires, Argentina.

**PERFECT, Fiona Elizabeth;** *see* Rae, F. E.

**PERFECT, Henry George,** FICE; Chairman: Babtie Group Ltd, 1996–2002; British Water, 2000–02; *b* 31 March 1944; *s* of George Hunter Perfect and Constance Mary Perfect (*née* Holland); *m* 1971, Kathleen Margaret Lilian Bain; two *s* one *d*. *Educ:* West Bridgford Grammar Sch., Nottingham; Birmingham Univ. (BSc Civil Engrg); Glasgow Univ. (MEng Foundn Engrg). FICE 1987. Asst Engr, C. H. Dobbie & Partners, 1965–69; Babtie Shaw & Morton, subseq. Babtie Group: Engr (projects incl. Kielder Water Scheme, and numerous reservoir, water and sewerage projects), 1969–83; Associate, 1983–86; Partner, 1987–93; Man. Dir, Water Business, 1994–95. *Publications:* several papers on civil and water engrg. *Recreations:* hill walking, cycling and tennis. *Address:* 28 Colquhoun Drive, Bearsden, Glasgow G61 4NQ.

**PERHAM, Linda**; Chair, Thames Water Trust Fund, since 2009; Director and Trustee, Vision Redbridge Culture and Leisure, since 2011; *b* 29 June 1947; *d* of late George Sidney Conroy and Edith Louisa Conroy (*née* Overton); *m* 1972, Raymond John Perham; two *d*. *Educ*: Mary Datchelor Girls' Sch.; Univ. of Leicester (BA Special Hons Classics); Ealing Tech. Coll. Postgrad. Dip. Liby Assoc.; MCLIP (ALA 1972). Library Asst, London Borough of Southwark, 1966; Inf. Officer, GLC Research Liby, 1970–72; City of London Polytechnic: Archives and Publications Librarian, 1972–76; Staff Develt Librarian, 1976–78; Cataloguer, Fawcett Liby, 1981–92; Bibliographical Librarian, Epping Forest Coll., 1992–97. MP (Lab) Ilford N, 1997–2005; contested (Lab) same seat, 2005. Mem., Select Cttee on Trade and Industry, 1998–2005; Chairman: All Party Gp on Libraries, 1998–2005; All Party Gp on Crossrail, 2003–05; Vice Chairman: All Party Gp on Male Cancers, 1998–2005; All Party Gp on Men's Health, 2001–05; Labour Friends of Israel, 2001–05; Hon. Secretary: All Party Gp on Ageing and Older People, 1998–2005; British-Israel Party Gp, 1998–2005; All Party Parly Gp on Corporate Social Responsibility, 2001–05; All Party Gp on Patient and Public Involvement in Health, 2004–05. London Borough of Redbridge: Councillor, 1989–97; Mayor, 1994–95; Chm., Highways Cttee, 1995–96, Leisure Cttee, 1996–97. Mem., Consumer Council for Water, London & SE (formerly Thames), 2005–11; Consumer Dir, TrustMark, 2006–11. Chair, East Living housing assoc., 2006–11; Vice Chair, London Voluntary Service Council, 2005–08; Board Member: East Thames Gp, 2006–11; Housing and Community Assoc., 2006–08. Mem. Ct, Univ. of Leicester, 2010–. Trustee, Friends of the Women's Library, 2005–09. Patron, Anxiety Care, Ilford, 1998–. Pres., Hainault Forest Community Assoc., 1997–. Lay Visitor, Eur. Care Gp, 2011–12. FRSA 2005. Hon. FCLIP 2003. JP: Redbridge, 1990; Newham, 2006; Redbridge, 2007–17. *Publications*: Directory of GLC Library Resources, 1970, 2nd edn 1971; Greater London Council Publications 1965–71, 1972; Libraries of London, 1973; How to Find Out in French, 1977. *Recreations*: travel, arts, cinema, theatre, sudoku, watching tennis. *E*: lindaperham@hotmail.com.

**PERHAM, Nancy Jane;** *see* Lane, N. J.

**PERKINS, Alice Elizabeth,** CB 2002; executive coach and board consultant; Partner and Executive Coach, JCA Group, 2006; *b* 24 May 1949; *d* of Derrick Leslie John Perkins and Elsa Rose Perkins, CBE (*née* Rink); *m* 1978, John Whitaker Straw, *qv*; one *s* one *d*. *Educ*: North London Collegiate Sch. for Girls; St Anne's Coll., Oxford (BA Hons Modern Hist. 1971; Hon. Fellow 2008). Joined CS, DHSS, 1971; Principal, 1976–84; Asst Sec., DHSS, then DSS, 1984–90; Dir of Personnel, DSS, 1990–93; Under Sec., Defence Policy and Materiel Gp, HM Treasury, 1993–95; Dep. Dir, Public Spending, HM Treasury, 1995–98; Dir, Corporate Mgt, DoH, 1998–2000; Hd of Civil Service Corporate Mgt, then Dir Gen., Corporate Develt Gp, Cabinet Office, 2000–05. Chm., Post Office Ltd, 2011–15. Non-executive Director: Littlewoods Orgn, 1997–2000; Taylor Nelson Sofres, 2005–08; BAA, 2006; BBC, 2014–17. Ext. Mem. Council, Oxford Univ., 2006–14; Faculty Mem., Meyler Campbell, 2009–. *Recreations*: gardening, looking at paintings.

**PERKINS, Brian Temple;** newsreader, BBC Radio 4, 1965–69 and 1978–2003; freelance broadcaster, since 2003; *b* 11 Sept. 1943; *s* of Ray and Laurel Perkins; *m* 1964, Joan Russell; one *s* two *d*. *Educ*: Wanganui and Wellington, NZ. Broadcaster: NZ Broadcasting Co., 1962–64; BBC, 1965–69; double bass player, NZBC SO, 1970–75; broadcaster: Radio NZ, 1975–78; BBC, 1978–2003. *Recreations*: music, fell-walking, France. *T*: (01483) 233919.

**PERKINS, Crispian G. S.;** *see* Steele-Perkins.

**PERKINS, Prof. Donald Hill,** CBE 1991; FRS 1966; Professor of Elementary Particle Physics, 1965–93, and Fellow of St Catherine's College, since 1965, Oxford University; *b* 15 Oct. 1925; *s* of George W. and Gertrude Perkins; *m* 1955, Dorothy Mary (*née* Maloney); two *d*. *Educ*: Malet Lambert High School, Hull. BSc London 1945; PhD London 1948; 1851 Senior Scholar, 1948–51. G. A. Wills Research Associate in Physics, Univ. of Bristol, 1951–55; Lawrence Radiation Lab., Univ. of California, 1955–56; Lectr in Physics, 1956–60, Reader in Physics, 1960–65, Univ. of Bristol. Mem., SERC, 1985–89. Hon. DSc: Sheffield, 1982; Bristol, 1995. Guthrie Medal, Inst. of Physics, 1979; Holweck Medal and Prize, Société Française de Physique, 1992; Royal Medal, Royal Soc., 1997; High Energy Physics Prize, Eur. Physical Soc., 2001. *Publications*: The Study of Elementary Particles by the Photographic Method (with C. F. Powell and P. H. Fowler), 1959; Introduction to High Energy Physics, 1972, 4th edn 2000; Particle Astrophysics, 2003; over 50 papers and review articles in Nature, Physical Review, Philosophical Magazine, Physics Letters, Proc. Royal Soc., Nuovo Cimento, etc. *Recreations*: gardening, reading. *Address*: 4A Brookside, Oxford OX3 7PJ.

**PERKINS, Douglas John David;** Co-founder, Co-owner and Managing Director, Specsavers Optical Group Ltd, since 1984; *b* Llanelli, 2 April 1943; *s* of Philip Denzil Perkins and Muriel Ester Perkins (*née* Thomas); *m* 1967, Mary Lesley Bebbington (*see* Dame M. L. Perkins); one *s* two *d*. *Educ*: Advanced Technology Coll. of Wales, Cardiff; British Optical Assoc. (Dip. Contact Lens Practice). FCOptom. Co-owner and optometrist, Bebbington and Perkins Gp, 1966–80. Liveryman, Spectacle Makers' Co. Hon. Fellow: Cardiff Univ., 2005; Swansea Inst., 2006. Hon. Dr: Anglia Ruskin, 2006; Plymouth, 2012; Glasgow Caledonian, 2017. *Recreations*: walking, yoga, grandchildren, watching Rugby and cricket. *Address*: Hautes Falaises, Fort George, St Peter Port, Guernsey GY1 2SR. *T*: (01481) 725901, *Fax*: (01481) 725968. *E*: doug.perkins@specsavers.com.

**PERKINS, Prof. Edwin Arend,** PhD; FRS 2007; FRSC; Professor of Mathematics, since 1989, and Canada Research Chair in Probability, since 2001, University of British Columbia; *b* 31 Aug. 1953; *s* of John Albert Perkins and Karin Brita (*née* Kunst); *m* 1974, Karen Marie Woitak; one *s* two *d*. *Educ*: Univ. of Toronto (BSc 1975); Univ. of Illinois (PhD 1979). University of British Columbia: Postdoctoral Fellow, 1979–80; NSERC Univ. Res. Fellow, 1980–81; Asst Prof. of Maths, 1982–85; Associate Prof. of Maths, 1985–89. Prof. Associé, Univ. of Strasbourg, 1984; SERC Res. Fellow, Cambridge Univ., 1986–87; Vis. Prof., Univ. of Wisconsin, 2000–01. FRSC 1988. *Publications*: Dawson-Watanabe Superprocesses and Measure-valued Diffusions, 1999; contribs to Memoirs Amer. Maths Soc. *Recreations*: hiking, cross-country ski-ing, canoeing. *Address*: Department of Mathematics, University of British Columbia, Vancouver, BC V6T 1Z2, Canada. *T*: (604) 8226670, *Fax*: (604) 8226074. *E*: perkins@math.ubc.ca.

**PERKINS, Prof. John Douglas,** CBE 2007; PhD; FIChemE, FIMA; CEng, CMath, CSci, FREng, FIET; Director, JP2 Consulting Ltd, since 2015; *b* 18 March 1950; *s* of late Douglas Herbert and of Isobel Mary Perkins; *m* 1st, 1975, Chantal Marie Lestavel (marr. diss. 1992); one *s*; 2nd, 2009, Jennifer Anne Chambers. *Educ*: Imperial Coll., London (BSc Eng; PhD 1976; DIC). ACGI 1971, FCGI 1996; FIChemE 1986; CEng 1986; CMath 1992; FIMA 1992; FREng 1993; CSci 2004; FIET 2015. Demonstrator in Chem. Engrg, Univ. of Cambridge, 1973–77; Lectr in Chem. Engrg, 1977–83, Sen. Lectr, 1983–85, Imperial Coll., London; ICI Prof. of Process Systems Engrg, Univ. of Sydney, Aust., 1985–88; Imperial College, University of London: Prof. of Chem. Engrg, 1988–99; Dir, Centre for Process Systems Engrg, 1992–98; Hd, Dept of Chem. Engrg and Chem. Technol., 1996–2001; Courtaulds Prof. of Chem. Engrg, 2000–04; Principal, Faculty of Engrg, 2001–04; Vice Pres. and Dean of Engrg and Phys. Scis, Univ. of Manchester, 2004–09; Provost, MASDAR Inst. of Sci. and Technol., Abu Dhabi, 2009–10. Vis. Prof., Imperial Coll. London, 2004–07, 2012–; Hon. Prof., Univ. of Manchester, 2009–. Chief Scientific Advr, BIS, 2012–15; Member: EPSRC, 2012–15; Council, IMA, 2015–16. UK Delegate, Governing Bd, EU Jt Res. Centre, 2012–15. Pres., IChemE, 2000–01 (Dep. Pres., 1999–2000; Mem. Council, 1997–2002); Vice Pres., RAEng, 2007–10 (Mem. Council, 2004–10). Mem. Ct, Heriot-Watt Univ., 2016–. FRSA 2004. Hon. DEng Brunel, 2018; Hon. DSc Kingston, 2018. *Recreations*: cinema, theatre, gastronomy, reading.

**PERKINS, John Vernon;** District Judge (Magistrates' Courts) (formerly Metropolitan Stipendiary Magistrate), 1999–2015; *b* 13 June 1950; *s* of late Sidney and Lilian Florence Perkins; *m* 1975, Margaret Craig; one *s* one *d*. *Educ*: Tottenham Grammar Sch. Admitted Solicitor, 1971; Articled Clerk, 1970–75, Asst Solicitor, 1975–80, Partner, 1980–99 (Sen. Partner, 1988–99), J. B. Wheatley & Co. Mem., London Criminal Courts Solicitors' Assoc., 1975–99 (Hon. Mem. 1999). *Recreations*: walking, swimming, gardening.

**PERKINS, Jonathan David;** a Judge of the Upper Tribunal (Immigration and Asylum Chamber) (formerly a Vice President, Immigration Appeal Tribunal, later a Senior Immigration Judge, Asylum and Immigration Tribunal), since 2003; *b* 15 Feb. 1958; *s* of Thomas Edward Perkins and Constance Perkins; *m* 1991, Margaret Anne Jackson; one *s* one *d*. *Educ*: Brierley Hill Grammar Sch.; University Coll. Cardiff (LLB Wales). Called to the Bar, Middle Temple, 1980; barrister, Midland and Oxford Circuit, 1981–99; Immigration Appeals Adjudicator, pt-time, 1993–99, full-time, 1999–2003. Methodist local preacher, 1988–. *Recreations*: church work, model making. *Address*: Upper Tribunal (Immigration and Asylum Chamber), Field House, Breams Building, Chancery Lane, EC4A 1DZ. *T*: (020) 7073 4200. *E*: perkins.family@btinternet.com.

**PERKINS, Dame Mary (Lesley),** DBE 2007; Co-founder and Director, Specsavers Optical Group Ltd, 1984; *b* 14 Feb. 1944; *d* of late (George) Leslie Bebbington and of Eileen Hilda Constance Bebbington (*née* Mawditt); *m* 1967, Douglas John David Perkins, *qv*; one *s* two *d*. *Educ*: Fairfield Grammar Sch., Bristol; Advanced Technol. Coll. of Wales, Cardiff. FBOA 1965. Co-owner and optometrist, Bebbington and Perkins, 1966–80. Freeman, City of London, 2001; Liveryman, Spectacle Makers' Co., 2008. Pres., Age Concern Guernsey, 1999–; Patron: Everywoman Ltd, 2006–; British Citizen Awards, 2015. Hon. CDir 2012. Hon. Fellow, Cardiff Univ., 2005; Hon. Graduate, Assoc. of Dispensing Opticians, 2014. Hon. Dr: Plymouth, 2012; Stirling, 2014; Bradford, 2016; Cardiff Metropolitan, 2016; Glasgow Caledonian, 2017. OStJ 2015. Lifetime Achievement Award, Ernst & Young, 2017. *Address*: Specsavers Optical Group Ltd, La Villiaze, St Andrews, Guernsey GY6 8YP.

**PERKINS, (Matthew) Toby;** MP (Lab) Chesterfield, since 2010; *b* 12 Aug. 1970; *s* of Victor F. Perkins and late Teresa Perkins; *m* 1996, Susan Beverley Francis; one *s* one *d*. *Educ*: Trinity Sch., Leamington Spa; Silverdale Sch., Sheffield. Telephone sales, CCS Media, 1991–95; Prime Time Recruitment: Recruitment Consultant, 1995–97; Branch Manager, 1997–99; Area Manager, 2000–02; estabd Club Rugby, 2005–10; Dir, Birdholme Children's Centre Nursery, 2007–10. Mem. (Lab) Chesterfield BC, 2003–11. Shadow Educn Minister, 2010–11; Shadow Business Minister, 2011–15; Shadow Minister for Defence, 2015–16. Member: Communities and Local Govt Select Cttee, 2010; Jt Cttee on Statutory Instruments, 2010–15; Internat. Trade Cttee, 2016–17. Former player, Chesterfield, Sheffield Tigers and Derbys Rugby Union; qualified Rugby coach, 2006. *Address*: House of Commons, SW1A 0AA.

**PERKS, David Michael;** Principal, East London Science School, since 2013; *b* Hemel Hempstead, 2 Sept. 1962; *s* of Brian Perks and Audrey Perks; *m* 2004, Jennifer Davey; one *s* one *d*. *Educ*: Robert Smythe Sch., Market Harborough; Magdalen Coll., Oxford (BA Hons Physics; PGCE). Teacher of Physics: Benfield Community Coll., Newcastle upon Tyne, 1986–91; Rossett High Sch., Harrogate, 1991–97; Hd of Physics, Graveney Sch., 1997–2012. Dir, Physics Factory, 2008–. Founder, 2003, and Advr, Debating Matters, sixth form debating competition, 2004–. *Publications*: (contrib.) The Routledge Falmer Guide to Key Debates in Education, 2004; What is Science Education For?, 2006; The Corruption of the Curriculum, 2007. *Recreations*: theatre, cricket, politics, technology. *Address*: East London Science School, The Clock Mill, Three Mill Lane, E3 3DU. *T*: 07795 323862. *E*: mail@davidperks.com.

**PERL, Alfredo;** pianist; Music Director, Detmold Chamber Orchestra, since 2009; *b* Chile, 25 June 1965. *Educ*: German Sch., Santiago; Univ. de Chile, Santiago; Cologne Conservatoire; with Maria Curcio in London. First performance at age of 9; début in Internat. Piano Series, Queen Elizabeth Hall, 1992; first recital at Wigmore Hall, 1994, and performed complete Beethoven Sonata cycle, 1996–97; UK recital appearances include: BBC Manchester and Scotland; Bridgewater Hall; St John's Smith Sq. Concert Series; has performed worldwide, including: Vienna Musikverein; London Barbican; Rudolfinum, Prague; Munich Herkulessaal; Izumi Hall, Osaka; Teatro Colón, Buenos Aires; Sydney Town Hall; Nat. Arts Centre, Ottawa; Great Hall, Moscow Conservatoire; orchestral appearances include: LSO; BBC SO; RPO; Hague Residentie; Florida Philharmonic; Leipzig Radio; Adelaide SO; Melbourne SO; Mozarteum Orch.; Orch. de la Suisse Romande; MDR Leipzig; début at BBC Prom. Concerts, with BBC Philharmonic Orch., 1997. Has made numerous recordings, incl. complete Beethoven Sonatas.

**PERLMAN, Itzhak;** violinist and conductor; *b* Tel Aviv, 31 Aug. 1945; *s* of Chaim and Shoshana Perlman; *m* 1967, Toby Lynn Friedlander; two *s* three *d*. *Educ*: Studied at Tel Aviv Acad. of Music with Ryvka Goldgart, and at Juilliard Sch., NY, under Dorothy Delay and Ivan Galamian. First solo recital at age of 10 in Israel; New York début, 1958. Leventritt Meml Award, NY, 1964. Tours extensively in USA and plays with all major American symphony orchestras; has conducted major orchestras worldwide incl. NY, Chicago, LA, Boston and Berlin Philharmonic Orchestras, LPO, Amsterdam Concertgebouw; recital tours of Canada, South America, Europe, Israel, Far East and Australia; Principal Guest Conductor, Detroit SO, 2001–05; Music Advr, St Louis SO, 2003–05. Has recorded numerous works for violin. Teacher, Juilliard Sch. and Perlman Music Prog. Has received many Grammy Awards. Hon. degrees: Harvard; Yale; Brandeis. *Recreation*: cooking. *Address*: c/o Primo Artists, 244 Fifth Avenue, Suite B222, New York, NY 10001, USA.

**PERLMUTTER, Prof. Saul,** PhD; Franklin W. and Karen Weber Dabby Professor, Physics Department, University of California, Berkeley; astrophysicist, Lawrence Berkeley National Laboratory; *b* 1959; *s* of Prof. Daniel D. Perlmutter and Prof. Felice Perlmutter (*née* Davidson); *m* Laura Nelson; one *d*. *Educ*: Germantown Friends Sch.; Harvard Univ. (AB Physics *magna cum laude* 1981); Univ. of Calif, Berkeley (PhD Physics 1986). University of California, Berkeley: postdoctoral res., 1986; Prof. of Physics, 2004–. Co-founder, 1988, Leader, 1992–, Internat. Supernova Cosmology Project. Mem., NAS. FAAAS 2003. Henri Chrétien Award, Amer. Astronomical Soc., 1996; (jtly) Shaw Prize in Astronomy, Shaw Foundn, 2006; (jtly) Gruber Prize in Cosmol., Gruber Foundn, 2007; (jtly) Einstein Medal, Albert Einstein Soc., 2011; (jtly) Nobel Prize in Physics, 2011. *Address*: Lawrence Berkeley National Laboratory, University of California, Berkeley, CA 94720, USA.

**PERMAN, Raymond John**, FRSE; Director, David Hume Institute, 2014–17; Chairman, James Hutton Institute, 2011–17 (Fellow, since 2017); *b* 22 Aug. 1947; *s* of late Leonard Perman and Gladys Perman (*née* Rockingham); *m* 1974, Fay Young, writer and editor; three *s*. *Educ*: Univ. of St Andrews; BA Hons Open Univ.; Univ. of Edinburgh (MBA 1987). Journalist: Westminster Press, 1969–71; The Times, 1971–75; Financial Times, 1976–81; Dep. Editor, Sunday Standard, 1981–83; Man. Dir, Insider Publications Ltd, 1983–94; Director: Caledonian Publishing plc, 1994–96; GJWS, 1997–98; Chief Exec., Scottish Financial Enterprise, 1999–2003. Chairman: Social Investment Scotland, 2002–09; Good Practice Ltd, 2005–11; Small Business Investment Taskforce, then Access to Finance Expert Gp, DTI, then BERR, later BIS, 2005–13; Mem. Bd, Scottish Enterprise, 2004–09. Chm., Scottish Adv. Council, WWF, 2004–07; Trustee, WWF UK, 2001–04. Mem. Court, Heriot-Watt Univ., 2003–09. FRSE 2017. *Publications*: The Man Who Gave Away His Island: a biography of John Lorne Campbell of Canna, 2010; HUBRIS: how HBOS wrecked the best bank in Britain, 2012; (ed jtly) Scotland's Decision, 2014; (ed) Alan Peacock Dissenting, 2015; (ed jtly) Britain's Decision, 2016; The Rise and Fall of the City of Money: a financial history of Edinburgh, 2019; numerous newspaper and magazine articles. *Recreations*: forestry, painting.

**PERMANAND, Rabindranath**; High Commissioner in London for Trinidad and Tobago, 1993–96; *b* 17 July 1935; *s* of late Ram Narais Permanand and of Kalawatee Permanand (*née* Capildeo); *m* 1969, Ursel Edda Schmid; one *s* one *d*. *Educ*: Queen's Royal Coll., Trinidad; Univ. of Calcutta (BA Hons); Univ. of Delhi (MA); Univ. of West Indies (Dip. Internat. Relations). History Teacher, Queen's Royal Coll., 1959–66; joined Min. of Foreign Affairs, 1966; Dep. High Comr, Georgetown, Guyana, 1966–69; First Sec., Ottawa, 1969–72; Chief of Protocol, 1973–77; Counsellor and Minister Counsellor, Brussels, 1977–81; Consul-Gen., Toronto, 1981–84; Head, Political Div., 1984–88; Ambassador and Perm. Rep. to UN, Geneva, 1988–93. *Recreations*: reading, music, cricket.

**PEROLLS, Graham Keith**, CMG 2014; OBE 1999; Founder and Executive Director, Hospices of Hope, 2000–17; *b* Dartford, 21 Sept. 1950; *s* of late Norman Grahame Perolls and Ellen Clara Perolls; *m* 1982, Carolyn Angela Eames; one *s* four *d*. *Educ*: Dartford Grammar Sch.; North West Kent Coll.; Univ. of Lund (Associate Inst. of Linguists). Dir, K.T. Coachworks Ltd, 1972–2008. Founder, Ellenor Foundn, 1985–2004; Pres., Hospice Casa Sperantei Romania, 1992–. *Recreations*: music, gardening, church.

**PEROWNE, Rear-Adm. (Benjamin) Brian**, CB 2001; DL; Chief Executive, Hft (formerly Home Farm Trust), 2001–11; *b* 24 July 1947; *s* of Rear-Adm. Benjamin Cubitt Perowne, CB and Phyllis Marjorie Perowne (*née* Peel); *m* 1975, Honora Rose Mary Wykes-Sneyd; two *s*. *Educ*: Gresham's Sch., Holt; BRNC, Dartmouth. FCIPD; CDipAF. Joined RN, 1965; RN Staff Coll., 1977; HM Yacht Britannia, 1980–82; CO, HMS Alacrity, 1982–83; Staff, CBNS Washington, 1986–88; CO, HMS Brazen, 1988–89; Asst Dir (Strategic Systems), MoD, 1989–90; Chief Naval Signals Officer, MoD, 1990–92; rcds 1993; Commodore Clyde and Naval Base Comdr, 1994–96; Dir Gen., Fleet Support (Ops and Plans), 1996–99; Chief Exec., Naval Bases and Supply Agency, 1999–2001, and Chief of Fleet Support, 2000–01. ADC to the Queen, 1994–96. Non-exec. Dir, Musgrove Park Hosp., 2013–. Trustee: Bletchley Park Trust, 2000–08; Assoc. for Real Change, 2001–09; Voluntary Orgn Disability Gp, 2008–11; Greenwich Foundn, 2010–18; Somerset Sight, 2011–. DL Somerset, 2012. *Recreations*: family, people, country and maritime, most sports. *Address*: Sticklynch Manor, West Pennard, Glastonbury, Som BA6 8NA. *Club*: Army and Navy.

**PEROWNE, Adm. Sir James (Francis)**, KBE 2000 (OBE 1983); Constable and Governor, Windsor Castle, since 2014; *b* 29 July 1947; *s* of late Lt Comdr John Herbert Francis Perowne and Mary Joy Perowne (*née* Dibb); *m* 1st, 1971, Susan Anne Holloway (marr. diss. 1990); four *s*; 2nd, 1992, Caroline Nicola Grimson. *Educ*: Sherborne Sch.; BRNC Dartmouth. CO, HMS Opportune, 1976–77; CO, HMS Superb, 1981–83; Staff of CBNS Washington, 1983–86; CO, HMS Boxer, 1986–88; Asst Dir, Naval Warfare, 1988–90; Captain, Second Submarine Sqdn, 1990–92; Captain, Sixth Frigate Sqdn and CO, HMS Norfolk, 1992–94; Sen. Naval Member, RCDS, 1995–96; Flag Officer Submarines, 1996–98; Comdr Submarines (NATO), Eastern Atlantic and Northwest Europe, 1996–98; COS (Ops) to C-in-C Fleet, 1996–98; Dep. SACLANT, 1998–2002. Chm., Central and Eastern (formerly Central, subseq. Midland) Region Cttee, Consumer Council for Water (formerly Watervoice), 2002–10. Non-executive Director: S Staffs Water plc, 2011–17 (Chm., 2017–); Cambridge Water Co., 2012–13. Member: MoJ (formerly DCA) Judiciary Review Bd, 2006–12; GMC Fitness to Practise Panel, 2006–08; GMC Interim Orders Panel, 2008–12; MPTS Interim Orders Panel, 2012–14. Pres., Submariners Assoc., 2002–16; Chairman: Submarine Officers' Life Members Assoc., 2002–16; Leics and Rutland Br., SSAFA (formerly SSAFA Forces Help), 2011–14. Pres., Assoc. of RN Officers and Royal Naval Benevolent Soc. for Officers, 2003–14; Chairman: British Red Cross Queen Mother Meml Fund, 2003–06; The James Caird Soc., 2006–17; Trustee, British Forces Foundn, 2002–. Patron, HMS Protector Assoc., 2007–. *Recreations*: boating, gardening, family. *Address*: c/o ARNO, 70 Porchester Terrace, W2 3TP. *E*: jamesperowne@aol.com. *Club*: Royal Navy of 1765 and 1785.

**PERRETT, Prof. David Ian**, DPhil; FBA 2005; FRSE; Professor of Psychology and Wardlaw Professor, University of St Andrews; *b* 11 April 1954. *Educ*: Univ. of St Andrews (BSc 1976); Univ. of Oxford (DPhil 1981). FRSE 1999. Lectr, then Reader in Psychol., Univ. of St Andrews. British Acad. Wolfson Res. Prof., 2009–12; Vis. Prof., Dalian Univ. of Technol., China, 2018–. President's Award, BPsS, 2000; Golden Brain Award, Minerva Foundn, 2002. *Publications*: In Your Face: the new science of human attraction, 2010; articles in learned jls. *Address*: School of Psychology and Neuroscience, University of St Andrews, Westburn Lane, St Andrews, Fife KY16 9JP.

**PERRICONE, Guido Roberto, (Guy)**; Chief Executive and Under Treasurer, Honourable Society of Middle Temple, since 2013; *b* Palermo, Italy, 3 July 1962; *s* of Mario and Lucille Perricone; *m* 1994, Nathalie Anne Françoise Guimard; one *s* one *d*. *Educ*: Westminster Sch., London; Trinity Coll., Cambridge (BA 1983); Coll. of Law, London. Admitted as solicitor, 1987. Solicitor, Linklaters & Paines, 1985–88; Vice Pres., Salomon Bros Internat., 1988–92; Asst Dir, S. G. Warburg Securities, 1992–93; Partner and Man. Dir, MeesPierson EurAmerica, 1993–97; Man. Dir, ABN Amro Bank, 1997–2005; Man. Dir, ICA, 2005–09; Chief Exec., Associated Bd of Royal Schs of Music, 2009–13. Treas. and Chm., Christ's Hosp. Sch. Foundn, 2013–18; Chm., Royal Acad. of Dance, 2015–; Trustee: Nat. Army Museum, 2017–; Gabrieli Choir and Consort, 2019–. *Recreations*: dance, music, travel, good food, football. *Address*: Honourable Society of the Middle Temple, Ashley Building, Middle Temple Lane, EC4Y 9BT. *T*: (020) 7427 4800. *E*: g.perricone@middletemple.org.uk. *Clubs*: Oxford and Cambridge, Hurlingham.

**PERRIN, Charles John**, CBE 2004; Deputy Chairman, Hambros Bank Ltd, 1986–98 (Chief Executive, 1995–98); *b* 1 May 1940; *s* of late Sir Michael Perrin, CBE, and Nancy May, *d* of late Rt Rev. C. E. Curzon; *m* 1966, Gillian Margaret, *d* of late Rev. M. Hughes-Thomas; two *d*. *Educ*: Winchester; New Coll., Oxford (Schol.; MA; Hon. Fellow, 1999). Called to the Bar, Inner Temple, 1965. Joined Hambros Bank, 1963, Dir, 1973–98; Chm., Hambro Pacific, Hong Kong, 1983–94; Dir, Hambros PLC, 1985–98. Non-exec. Dir, Harland and Wolff, 1984–89. Chairman: Retroscreen Virology, 1993–2011; MRC Pension Trust, 2004–10. Mem., Royal Brompton Nat. Heart and Lung Hosps SHA, 1993–94; non-exec. Dir, Royal Brompton Hosp. NHS Trust, 1994–98; Vice Chm., Royal Brompton & Harefield NHS Trust, 1998–2007. Mem. Council, 1994–2008, Trustee, 2008–10, Univ. of London (Hon. Fellow, 2016); Mem. Council 1997, Treas., 1999–2009, QMUL (formerly QMW) (Hon. Fellow, 2010); Gov., Royal Central Sch. of Speech and Drama (formerly Central Sch. of Speech and Drama), 2006–18. Hon. Treas., RVC, 2010–16 (Betts Prize, 2016). Vice-Chm., UK Cttee for UNICEF, 1972–91. Governor: Queen Anne's Sch., Caversham, 1981–2006; London Hosp. Med. Coll., 1991–95. Trustee: Med. Res. Foundn, 2006–15 (Chm., 2008–15); Nuffield Trust, 2006–14; RCP, 2007–11; Hampstead Wells and Campden Trust, 2011–. Liveryman, Shipwrights' Co., 1991. Hon. FRCP 2009. Quincentennial Award, RCP, 2018. *Recreation*: sailing. *Address*: 4 Holford Road, Hampstead, NW3 1AD. *T*: (020) 7435 8103. *Club*: Athenæum.

**PERRIN, Nicola Kathryn**; *see* Pollitt, N. K.

**PERRIN, Air Vice-Marshal Norman Arthur**; Secretary General, ECTEL (European Conference of Telecommunications Industry Associations), 1991–97; *b* 30 Sept. 1930; *s* of late Albert Arthur and Mona Victoria (*née* Stacey); *m* 1956, Marie (*née* Bannon) (*d* 2014), *d* of late Peter and Lucy Bannon; one *s*. *Educ*: Liverpool Collegiate School; Hertford College, Oxford; RAF Technical College. BA. Nat. Service commn, Airfield Construction Branch, RAF, Suez Canal Zone, 1951–53; perm. commn, Tech. Branch, 1953; Advanced GW course, 1956–57; Air Ministry, 1958–61; HQ 11 Group, 1961–62; Staff Coll., 1963; 390 Maintenance Unit, FEAF, 1964–65; OC Eng Wing, RAF Seletar, 1966–67; JSSC 1967; Op. Requirements, SAGW, 1967–70; Chief Instructor, Systems Engineering, RAF Coll., 1970–72; Group Captain Plans, HQ Maintenance Comd, 1972–75; C. Mech. Eng., HQ Strike Comd, 1975–78; RCDS 1979; Dir Air GW MoD (PE), 1980–83; Vice-Pres. (Air), Ordnance Board, 1983; Pres., Ordnance Board, 1984–86. Dir, TEMA, 1987–91. *Recreations*: bridge, crosswords, Liverpool FC watching, choral singing. *Address*: c/o Barclays Bank, 10 High Street, Marlow, Bucks SL7 1AR. *Club*: Royal Air Force.

**PERRING, Sir John (Raymond)**, 2nd Bt *cr* 1963, of Frensham Manor, Surrey; TD 1965; Chairman, Perrings Finance Ltd, 1987–2008; *b* 7 July 1931; *e s* of Sir Ralph Perring, 1st Bt and Ethel Mary (*d* 1991); *S* father, 1998; *m* 1961, Ella Christine (*d* 2019), *e d* of late Tony and Ann Pelham; two *s* two *d*. *Educ*: Stowe School. Nat. Service, then TA, RA, 1949–60; Royal Fusiliers (City of London), 1960–65. Joined family business, Perring Furnishings, 1951, Dir 1957, Jt Man. Dir 1964, Vice-Chm., 1972, Chm., 1981–88. Nat. Pres., Nat. Assoc. of Retail Furnishers, 1971–73; Mem. Council, Retail Consortium, 1972–91 (Chm., non-food policy cttee, 1987–91); Mem. EDC (Distributive Trades), 1974–78. City of London: Sheriff, 1991–92; One of HM Lieutenants, 1963–; Assistant, Merchant Taylors' Co., 1980, Master, 1988, 1994; Master, Furniture Makers' Co., 1978. Trustee, Ranyard Meml Charitable Trust, 1983–2004 (Chm., 1990–2001); Chm., Wimbledon DFAS, 1998–2002. Gov., Bishopsgate Foundn, 1993–2002. President: Bishopsgate Ward Club, 1997–98; Old Stoic Soc., 2002–03. OStJ 1986. *Recreations*: outdoor pursuits, Masia in Madremanya, Gerona. *Heir*: *s* John Simon Pelham Perring, *b* 20 July 1962. *Clubs*: Royal Automobile; Royal Wimbledon Golf; Bembridge Sailing.

**PERRINGS, Prof. Charles Aubrey**, PhD; Professor of Environmental Economics, Arizona State University, since 2005; *b* 7 July 1949; *s* of Aubrey and Noelle Perrings; *m* 2005, Ann Kinzig. *Educ*: SOAS, Univ. of London (BA Hons 1973, PhD 1976). Lectr in Econs, Nat. Univ. of Lesotho, 1976–78; Lectr, Sen. Lectr, then Associate Prof. of Econs, Univ. of Auckland, 1979–90; Prof. of Econs, Univ. of Calif, Riverside, 1991–92; Prof. of Envmtl Economics, Univ. of York, 1992–2005. Vis. Prof. of Econs, Univ. of Botswana, 1987–89. Ed., Envmt and Develt Econs, 1995–2005. Fellow, Beijer Inst., Royal Swedish Acad. of Scis, 1996–. *Publications*: Economy and Environment: a theoretical essay on the interdependence of economic and environmental systems, 1987 (trans. Italian 1992); (ed jtly) Biodiversity Conservation: problems and policies, 1994; (ed jtly) Biological Diversity: economic and ecological issues, 1995; Sustainable Development and Poverty Alleviation in Sub-Saharan Africa: the case of Botswana, 1996; (ed jtly) The Development of Ecological Economics, 1997; Economics of Ecological Resources: selected essays, 1997; (ed jtly) The Economics of Biodiversity Conservation in Sub-Saharan Africa: mending the Ark, 2000; (ed jtly) The Economics of Biological Invasions, 2000; (ed jtly) Natural Resource Accounting and Economic Development, 2003; (ed) Ecological Economics: origins and development, 2008; (ed jtly) Bioinvasions and Globalization: ecology, economics, management and policy, 2009; (ed jtly) Biodiversity, Ecosystem Functioning and Human Wellbeing: an ecological and economic perspective, 2009; (ed jtly) Bioinvasions and Globalization: ecology, economics, management, and policy, 2010; Our Uncommon Heritage: biodiversity, ecosystem services and human wellbeing, 2014; numerous papers in jls. *Recreations*: music, reading, walking. *Address*: School of Life Sciences, Arizona State University, Box 874501, Tempe, AZ 85287–4501, USA.

**PERRINS, Angela Margaret Mary**; *see* Rafferty, A. M. M.

**PERRINS, Prof. Christopher Miles**, LVO 1987; DPhil; FRS 1997; Director, Edward Grey Institute of Field Ornithology, 1974–2002, Professor of Ornithology, 1992–2002, Leverhulme Emeritus Fellow, 2002–04, Oxford University; Fellow, Wolfson College, Oxford, 1970–2002, now Emeritus; *b* 11 May 1935; *s* of Leslie Howard Perrins and Violet Amy (*née* Moore); *m* 1963, Mary Ceresole Carslake; two *s*. *Educ*: Charterhouse; QMC (BSc Hons Zool.; Hon. Fellow, QMW, 1996); Oxford Univ. (DPhil). Edward Grey Institute of Field Ornithology, University of Oxford: Research Officer, 1963–66; Sen. Res. Officer, 1966–84; Reader, 1984–92. Mem., General Bd of Faculties, Oxford Univ., 1983–91, 1995–99 (Chm., Bldgs Cttee, 1995–99); Delegate, OUP, 1994–2002. The Queen's Swan Warden, 1993–. President: Internat. Ornithol Congress, 1990–94; European Ornithologists' Union, 1997–99; BOU, 2003–07; Hon. Corresp. Mem. 1976–83, Hon. Fellow 1983–, Amer. Ornithologists' Union; Hon. Corresp. Mem. 1991–2002, Hon. Fellow 2002, German Ornithologists' Union; Hon. Fellow: Netherlands Ornithologists' Union, 1992; Spanish Ornithologists' Union, 2004. Godman-Salvin Medal, 1988, Union Medal, 2016, British Ornithologists' Union; Conservation Medal, RSPB, 1992. *Publications*: (ed with B. Stonehouse) Evolutionary Ecology, 1977; British Tits, 1979; (with T. R. Birkhead) Avian Ecology, 1983; (ed with A. L. A. Middleton) The Encyclopaedia of Birds, 1985; (with M. E. Birkhead) The Mute Swan, 1986; New Generation Guide: Birds, 1987; (ed with J. D. Lebreton and G. J. M. Hirons) Bird Population Studies, 1991; (Senior Ed.) Birds of the Western Palearctic, vol. VII, 1993, vols VIII and IX, 1994; (ed with D. W. Snow) The Birds of the Western Palearctic, concise edn, 2 vols, 1998; (ed) The New Encyclopedia of Birds, 2003; (ed jtly) Wytham Woods, 2010. *Recreations*: photography, walking. *Address*: Edward Grey Institute of Field Ornithology, Department of Zoology, University of Oxford, South Parks Road, Oxford OX1 3PS. *T*: (01865) 271169.

**PERRINS, Gregory Lloyd; His Honour Judge Perrins**; a Circuit Judge, since 2016; *b* Telford, Shropshire, 2 July 1974; *s* of Roy and Valerie Perrins; *m* 2004, Angela Margaret Mary Rafferty, *qv*; two *d*. *Educ*: Abraham Darby Sch., Telford; Univ. of Nottingham (LLB Hons; LLM Internat. Law). Called to the Bar, Inner Temple, 1997; in practice as barrister, 1997–2016; a Recorder, 2012–16. Chm., Police Appeals Tribunal, 2015–16.

**PERROTT, John Gayford**; HM Diplomatic Service, retired; British High Commissioner, The Gambia, 2000–02; *b* 5 July 1943; *s* of Dr Charles Hardy Perrott and Dr Phylis Perrott (*née* Dearns); *m* 1964, (Joan) Wendy Lewis; one *s* one *d. Educ*: Newport High Sch. Joined CRO, later FCO, 1962; Karachi, 1966–69; Ankara, 1970–72; Calcutta, 1973–76; Kathmandu, 1979–84; Istanbul, 1984–88; St Helena, 1993–97. *Recreations*: walking, golf.

**PERRY**, family name of **Baroness Perry of Southwark**.

**PERRY OF SOUTHWARK**, Baroness *cr* 1991 (Life Peer), of Charlbury in the County of Oxfordshire; **Pauline Perry**; President, Lucy Cavendish College, Cambridge University, 1994–2001; a Conservative Party Whip, House of Lords, 2011–16; *b* 15 Oct. 1931; *d* of John George Embleton Welch and Elizabeth Welch; *m* 1952, George Walter Perry (*d* 2008); three *s* one *d. Educ*: Girton Coll., Cambridge (MA; Hon. Fellow 1995). Teacher in English Secondary Sch., Canadian and American High Schs, 1953–54 and 1959–61; High School Evaluator, New England, USA, 1959–61; Research Fellow, Univ. of Manitoba, 1956–57; Lecturer in Philosophy: Univ. of Manitoba, 1957–59; Univ. of Massachusetts at Salem, 1960–62; Lectr in Education (part-time), Univ. of Exeter, 1962–66; Tutor for In-Service Trng, Berks, 1966–70; Part-time Lectr in Educn, Dept of Educational Studies, Oxford Univ., 1966–70; HM Inspector of Schools, 1970–86; Staff Inspector, 1975; Chief Inspector, 1981. Dir, S Bank Poly., 1987–92; Vice-Chancellor, S Bank Univ., 1992–93. Alexander Stone Lectr in Rhetoric, Glasgow, 1999. Member: Cttee on Internat. Co-operation in Higher Educn, British Council, 1987–97; ESRC, 1988–91; Governing Body, Institute of Develt Studies, Sussex Univ., 1987–94; Bd, South Bank Centre, 1992–94; NI Higher Educn Council, 1992–94; Nat. Adv. Council on Educn and Training Targets, 1992–95; Prime Minister's Adv. Panel on Citizen's Charter, 1993–97; Overseas Project Bd, 1993–98; Royal Soc. Project Sci. Bd of Patrons, 1995–2003; Bd, British Univ. in Egypt, 2018–. Mem., H of L, 1991–2016; Member, H of L Select Committee: on Science and Technol., 1992–95, 1997–2005, 2008–10, 2010–14 (Chair, Inquiry into Energy Efficiency, 2004–05); on Scrutiny of Delegated Powers, 1994–98; on relationships between local and central govt, 1995–96; on Stem Cell Research, 2001–02; on Religious Offences, 2002–03; Jt Select Cttee of Commons and Lords on Human Rights, 2000–03; Ecclesiastical Cttee, 2002–16; Chm., All-Party Parly Univs Gp, 1996–2009. Chairman: DTI Export Gp for Educn and Trng Sector, 1993–98; Judges Panel on Citizen's Charter, 1997–2004; C of E Rev. Gp on Operation of Crown Appts Commn, 1999–2001; Inquiry into Animals in Scientific Experiments, Nuffield Council on Bio-Ethics, 2003–05; Cttee on Quality and Standards, C&G, 2005–10; Advr on Police Trng to Home Office, 1991–93. Co-Chm., Policy Gp on Public Services, Cons. Party, 2006–07. President: Westminster & City Br., Chartered Mgt Inst. (formerly Inst. of Mgt), 2000–14; Higher Educn Foundn, 2002–06. Rector's Warden, Southwark Cath., 1990–94; Chair, Friends of Southwark Cath., 1994–2002. MInstD; CCMI (CIMgt 1993). Mem. Court, Univ. of Bath, 1991–99; Trustee: Bacon's City Technol. Coll., 1991–2009; Cambridge Univ. Foundn, 1997–2006; Pro-Chancellor, Univ. of Surrey, 2001–06; Vice-Pres., C&G, 1994–99; Pres., CIFE, 2000–13; Chm., Council, Roehampton Univ. (formerly Roehampton Inst.), 2001–06; Chair: Wandsworth Free Schs and Acads Commn, 2011–; Governing Body, Kaplan Coll., 2014–15. Governor: Gresham's Sch., 2000–06; Abbey Schs, 2012–14. Patron: British Friends of Neve Shalom-Wahat al Salaam, 2005–; St Mark's Coll., Limpopo, SA, 1991–; British Youth Opera, 1992–; Nat. Conf. of University Profs, 2016–; Council for Educn Econs, 2018– (Mem. Bd, 2017–18). Mem., Editl Bd, I-Mag., 2012–. Freeman, City of London, 1992; Liveryman, Bakers' Co., 1992–; Hon. Freeman, Fishmongers' Co., 2006. FRSA 1988. Hon. FCollP 1987; Hon. FCGI 2000. Hon. Fellow: Sunderland Polytechnic, 1990; Sunderland Univ., 1993; Northampton Univ., 1993; Lucy Cavendish Coll., 2001; Roehampton Univ., 2005. Hon. LLD: Bath, 1991; Aberdeen, 1994; Hon. DLitt: Sussex, 1992; South Bank, 1994; City, 2000; DUniv Surrey, 1995; Hon. DEd Wolverhampton, 1994; Hon. Dr, Mercy Coll., NY, 2014. Mem., Pedagogical Acad., Swedish Acad. of Sci., 1992. *Publications*: Case Studies in Teaching, 1969; Case Studies in Adolescence, 1970; Your Guide to the Opposite Sex, 1970; The Womb in Which I Lay, 2003; *contributions to*: Advances in Teacher Education, 1989; Women in Education Management, 1992; Public Accountability and Quality Control in Higher Education, 1990; The Future of Higher Education, 1991; Technology: the challenge to education, 1992; What is Quality in Higher Education?, 1993; Education in the Age of Information, 1993; School Inspection, 1995; Women and Higher Education, 1996; Against the Tide: women leaders in American and British higher education, 1996; Higher Education Reform, 2000; Diversity and Excellence, 2001; Creative Church Leadership, 2004; articles in various educnl jls; freelance journalism for radio and TV. *Recreations*: music, walking, cooking.

**PERRY, Alan Joseph**; Director, Whitehall Strategic Management Consultants Ltd, 1992–95; *b* 17 Jan. 1930; *s* of late Joseph and Elsie Perry; *m* 1961, Vivien Anne Ball; two *s. Educ*: John Bright Grammar Sch., Llandudno; Dartford Grammar Sch. Served RE, 1948–50. HM Treasury, 1951–68 and 1970–78; CSD, 1968–70; Principal 1968, Asst Sec. 1976; Counsellor (Economic), Washington, 1978–80; HM Treasury, 1980–86; Advr on Govt Affairs, Ernst & Whinney, 1986–88; Dir, Public Sector Services, Ernst & Young, 1989–92. Chm., Review of BBC External Services, 1984.

**PERRY, Charlotte**; *see* Moore, C.

**PERRY, His Honour (Christopher) Grenville**; a Circuit Judge, 2012–19; a Deputy Circuit Judge, since 2019; a Deputy Upper Tribunal Judge (Health, Education and Social Care Chamber), since 2019; *b* Plymouth, 17 Oct. 1953; *s* of Gerald Perry and Gaynor Perry; *m* 1987, Carolynne Holland; two *s. Educ*: Nantwich and Acton Grammar Sch.; Univ. of Nottingham (LLB Hons 1975). Admitted solicitor, 1978; solicitor, private practice, 1980–82; Lectr, 1982–84; Sen. Lectr, 1984–89, Principal Lectr, 1989–94, Coll. of Law, Chester; a District Judge, 1994–2012; a Recorder, 2001–12; Designated Family Judge for Staffs, 2014–19; a Judge of the Court of Protection, 2016–19; a Judge of the Mental Health Tribunal, 2017–19. Course Dir, Dep. District Judge Trng, Judicial Coll., 2009–12. Trustee: Nantwich Parish Church Preservation Fund, 2000–18; Greyhound Rescue West of England, 2002–08. *Recreations*: spending time in North Norfolk, walking retired greyhounds, pub quizzes, watching Crewe Alexandra FC. *Club*: Royal Over-Seas League.

**PERRY, Rt Hon. Claire (Louise)**; PC 2018; MP (C) Devizes, since 2010; *b* Bromsgrove, 3 April 1964; *d* of David Richens and Joanna Richens; *m* 1st, 1996, Clayton Perry (marr. diss. 2014); one *s* two *d*; 2nd, 2018, Prof. Bill O'Neill. *Educ*: Brasenose Coll., Oxford (BA Hons Geog. 1985); Harvard Business Sch. (MBA 1990). Vice Pres., Bank of America, 1985–88; Engagement Manager, McKinsey & Co., 1990–94; Dir and Hd of Equities E-commerce, Credit Suisse, 1994–2000. PPS to Sec. of State for Defence, 2011–12; an Asst Govt Whip, 2013–14; Parly Under-Sec. of State, DfT, 2014–16; Minister of State, BEIS, 2017–19. Adviser to Prime Minister on preventing the commercialisation and sexualisation of childhood, 2012–14. *Recreations*: gardening, cycling, reading. *Address*: House of Commons, SW1A 0AA. *T*: (020) 7219 7050. *E*: claire.perry.mp@parliament.uk.

**PERRY, Sir David (Howard)**, KCB 1986; Chief of Defence Equipment Collaboration, Ministry of Defence, 1985–87, retired; *b* 13 April 1931; *s* of Howard Dace Perry and Annie Evelyn Perry; *m* 1961, Rosemary Grigg; one *s* two *d. Educ*: Berkhamsted Sch.; Pembroke Coll., Cambridge (MA). CEng, FRAeS. Joined Aero Dept, RAE, 1954; Aero Flt Div., 1954–66; Aero Projs Div., 1966–71; Head of Dynamics Div., 1971–73; RCDS, 1974; Head of Systems Assessment Dept, RAE, 1975–77; Ministry of Defence (Procurement Executive): Dir-Gen. Future Projects, 1978–80; Dir-Gen. Aircraft 1, 1980–81; Dep. Controller of Aircraft, 1981–82, Controller of Aircraft 1982; Chief of Defence Procurement, 1983–85. *Recreations*: gardening, painting. *Address*: 23 Rectory Road, Farnborough, Hants GU14 7BU.

**PERRY, Grayson**, CBE 2013; RA 2011; artist in ceramics, print and textiles; occasional broadcaster and journalist; *b* 24 March 1960; *m* 1992, Philippa Fairclough; one *d. Educ*: King Edward VI Grammar Sch., Chelmsford; Braintree Coll. of Further Educn; Portsmouth Poly. (BA Fine Art). Chancellor, Univ. of the Arts, London, 2015–. Trustee, British Mus., 2015–. Patron: Art Room, 2014–; Grierson Trust, 2015–. *Solo exhibitions include*: James Birch Gall., London, 1984, 1985; The Minories, Colchester, 1986; Birch & Conran, London, 1987, 1988, 1990; Garth Clark Gall., NY, 1991; David Gill Gall., London, 1991–92; Clara Scremini Gall., Paris, 1994; Anthony d'Offay Gall., London, 1994, 1996–97; Laurent Delaye Gall., London, 2000; fig-1, London, 2000; Guerilla Tactics, Stedelijk Mus., Amsterdam and Barbican Art Gall., 2002; Tate St Ives, 2004; Victoria Miro Gall., London, 2004, 2006, 2012, 2019; Gall. Il Capricorno, Venice, 2005; Andy Warhol Mus., Pittsburgh, 2006; The Collection, Lincoln, 2006; Mus. of 21st Century Contemp. Art, Kanazawa, Japan, 2007; The Tomb of the Unknown Craftsman, British Mus., 2011–12; Who are You?, NPG, 2014–15; Provincial Punk (retrospective), Turner Contemporary, Margate, 2015; My Pretty Little Art Career, Mus. of Contemp. Art, Sydney, 2015–16; Hold Your Beliefs Lightly, Bonnefanten Mus., Maastricht, 2016, ARoS, Aarhus, 2016; The Most Popular Art Exhibition Ever!, Serpentine Gall., 2017; Vanity, Identity, Sexuality, Monnaie de Paris, 2018; Julie Cope's Grand Tour, Dovecot Studios, Edinburgh, then touring, 2019; *group exhibitions* include: ICA, 1981–82; Garth Clark Gall., NY, 1990, 1999; Whitechapel Gall., 1996, 2000; Crafts Council and Amer. Crafts Mus. NY, 1997–98; Richard Salmon Gall., London and Kettle's Yard, Cambridge, 1997–98; Stedelijk Mus., Amsterdam, Hydra Foundn, Greece, 1999; Laurent Delaye Gall., Saatchi Gall., 2001; Courtauld Inst., 2001–03; Blue Gall., London, Vancouver Art Gall., 2003; Tate Liverpool, 2004; Auckland Art Gall., NZ, 2005; MOMA, NY, 2006; British Mus., 2011; *work in public collections* including British Council, Crafts Council, Saatchi Collection, Pottery Mus., Stoke-on-Trent, MOMA, Glasgow, Stedelijk Mus., Amsterdam and Hydra Foundn, Greece; A House for Essex, Wrabness, 2015. *Television*: Channel 4: All in the Best Possible Taste, 2012; Who are You?, 2014; Dream House, 2015; Grayson Perry: all man, 2016; Grayson Perry: Divided Britain, 2017; Grayson Perry: rites of passage, 2018. Reith Lectr, BBC Radio 4, 2013. Hon. FRIBA 2016. Turner Prize, 2003. *Publications*: Cycle of Violence, 1992; (with W. Jones) Portrait of the Artist as a Young Girl, 2006; Playing to the Gallery, 2014; The Descent of Man, 2016. *Address*: c/o Victoria Miro Gallery, 16 Wharf Road, N1 7RW.

**PERRY, Grenville**; *see* Perry, C. G.

**PERRY, Hugh**; *see* Perry, V. H.

**PERRY, Jacqueline Anne, (Mrs V. Levene)**; QC 2006; barrister; attorney at law; *b* 7 March 1952; *d* of late Clarence and Diana Perry; *m* 1980, Victor Levene; one *s. Educ*: Copthall Co. Grammar Sch. for Girls; Lady Margaret Hall, Oxford (BA 1973, MA 1977). Called to the Bar, Gray's Inn, 1975, Bencher, 2005; practising as barrister, 1975–, specialising in personal injury, and clinical and professional negligence; admitted to Bar, California, 2001; Associate: Schuler & Brown, Van Nuys, Calif, 2006–10; Rufus-Isaacs, Acland & Grantham, Beverly Hills, Calif, 2010–16; Partner, Perry Fraser LLP, 2016–. Mediator and Mem., ADR (UK) Ltd, 2000. Grade A Advocacy Teacher, Master of Students, 2010–, Gray's Inn. Mem., UK Editl Cttee, Medicine, Sci. and Law, 2011–. Internat. Fellow, Internat. Acad. of Trial Lawyers, 2008. Broadcaster, as Nicola Charles: Granada TV, 1989–94; BBC Radio, 1990–96. *Publications*: (as Nicola Charles) with Janice James: Rights of Woman, 1990; Know Your Law, 1995. *Recreations*: cinema, theatre, motor cruising, cooking, reading (both high and low brow). *Address*: 2 Temple Gardens, Temple, EC4Y 9AY. *T*: (020) 7822 1200, *Fax*: (020) 7822 1300. *E*: jperry@2tg.co.uk.

**PERRY, John**; *see* Perry, R. J.

**PERRY, Rt Rev. John Freeman**; Bishop of Chelmsford, 1996–2003; an Assistant Bishop, Diocese of Bath and Wells, since 2011; *b* 15 June 1935; *s* of Richard and Elsie Perry; *m* 1st, 1959, Gay Valerie Brown (*d* 2009); three *s* two *d*; 2nd, 2011, Marilyn Eve Sertin; two step *s* two step *d. Educ*: Mill Hill School; London College of Divinity (ALCD); LTh St John's Coll., Nottingham, 1974; MPhil Westminster Coll., Oxford, 1986. Royal Signals, 1953–55; Assistant Curate: Christ Church, Woking, 1959–62; Christ Church, Chorleywood, 1962–63; Vicar, St Andrew's, Chorleywood, 1963–77; RD of Rickmansworth, 1972–77; Warden, Lee Abbey, Lynton, Devon, 1977–89; RD of Shirwell, 1980–84; Suffragan Bishop of Southampton, 1989–96. Hon. Canon, Winchester Cathedral, 1989–96. Took seat in H of L, 2000. Member: C of E Bd of Ministry, 1989–2002; Bd, Christian Solidarity Worldwide, 2004–13 (Chm., 2010–13); Chm., Cttee for Ministry of and among Deaf and Disabled, 1989–2001. Chm., Burrswood, 1989–2003; Pres., Fellowship of Christ the Healer, 2000–16; Vice-Pres., Lee Abbey Movt, 2010– (Chm., 2004–10). Vice-Pres., Univ. of Glos, 2004–. Gov., Monkton Combe Sch., Bath, 2004–10. Hon. Dr Anglia Poly. Univ., 2000. *Publications*: Effective Christian Leadership, 1983; (contrib.) Celebrating Community, 2006. *Recreations*: a large family, walking, sport, travel, watercolour painting, films. *Address*: 8 The Firs, Combe Down, Bath BA2 5ED.

**PERRY, John Scott, (Jack)**, CBE 2010; DL; Chief Executive, Scottish Enterprise, 2004–09; Chairman: Hospice Developments Ltd, since 2012; ICG-Longbow Senior Secured UK Property Debt Investments Ltd, since 2012; European Assets Trust plc (formerly European Assets Trust NV), since 2015; *b* 23 Nov. 1954; *s* of George Michael Perry, CBE and Madalynn Heber; *m* 1977, Lydia; one *s* two *d. Educ*: Glasgow Univ. (BSc (Pure Sci.) 1975); Strathclyde Univ. (Postgrad. Dip. Accountancy 1976). CA (ICAS) 1979; Certified Public Accountant (USA) 1985; CCIM 2004. Ernst & Young, 1976–2003: Managing Partner, Glasgow, 1995–2003; Regl Industry Leader, Technol. Communications and Entertainment, Scotland and NI, 1999–2003. Non-executive Director: Robert Wiseman Dairies plc, 2010–12; Capital for Enterprise Ltd, 2013–14; Silent Herdsman Hldgs Ltd, 2013–15; Witan Investment Trust plc, 2017– (Chm., Audit Cttee, 2018–); Mem., Adv. Cttee, Barclays UK and Ireland Private Bank, Barclays Wealth, 2010–13. Chm., CBI Scotland, 2001–03 (Mem. Council, 1996–2004, 2011–); Chm., Regl Chairmen, Mem., President's Cttee, CBI. Chm., TMRI Ltd, 2007–09. Chm., Scottish Aquaculture Innovation Centre, 2014–17. Former Mem., Ministerial Task Force on Econ. Forums. Member: Financial Services Adv. Bd, 2005–09; Adv. Bd, Asia Scotland Inst., 2013–14. Former Chm. Bd of Dirs, Craigholme Sch.; Vis. Tutor, Leadership Trust. FInstD 2010. Mem. Court, 2010–17, Treas., 2011–17, Univ. of Strathclyde; Mem., Adv. Bd, Univ. of Edinburgh Business Sch., 2010–16. DL Renfrewshire, 2011. Hon. DBA: Edinburgh Napier, 2010; Abertay Dundee, 2011; DUniv Strathclyde, 2018. *Recreations*: golf, ski-ing, reading, current affairs. *Address*: c/o European Assets Trust plc, F&C Asset Management plc, Quartermile 4, 7A Nightingale Way, Edinburgh EH3 9EG. *Clubs*: Glasgow Academical; Royal and Ancient Golf, Western Gailes Golf (Captain, 2011).

**PERRY, John William**; Chairman, Trace Computers, 1996–2001 (non-executive Director, 1994–96 and 2001–04); b 23 Sept. 1938; s of John and Cecilia Perry; m 1961, Gillian Margaret (d 2007); two d. Educ: Wallington Grammar Sch.; Brasenose Coll., Oxford (MA). Burroughs: Dir of Marketing, UK, 1967–71, Europe Africa Div., 1977–78; Group Dir, Internat. Marketing, 1978–80; Vice-President: Strategic Planning, 1981; Financial Systems Gp, 1983; Central USA, 1985–86; Man. Dir, Burroughs UK, 1986; Chm. and Man. Dir, Unisys, 1987–94; Corporate Officer, 1990, Pres., Financial Services, 1993–94, Unisys Corp.; Director, 1987–94: Sperry; Burroughs Machines; BMX Information Systems; BMX Holdings; Unisys Holdings; Convergent Technologies (UK). Mem., Nat. Task Force, Business in the Community, 1988–94. Trustee, Information Age Project, 1989. Mem., Bd of Governors, Polytechnic of East London, 1989. Recreations: gardening, reading, music. Address: The Great Barn, Sandpit Lane, Bledlow, Bucks HP27 9QQ.

**PERRY, Jonathan Peter Langman**; Chairman, Paragon Group of Companies PLC (formerly National Home Loans Holdings), 1992–2007; b 6 Sept. 1939; s of Thomas Charles Perry and Kathleen Mary Perry; m 1965, Sheila Johnson; two s one d. Educ: Peter Symonds Sch., Winchester. FCA. Butler Viney Childs, 1956–62; Cooper Brothers, 1962–66; Morgan Grenfell & Co., 1966–88 (Dir, 1973–88); Principal, Perry Associates, 1988–90; Chm. and Chief Exec., Ogilvie Adams & Rinehart, 1990–92; Vice-Chm., HSBC Investment Banking, 1997–99. Recreations: sailboat racing, golf, music. Clubs: Brooks's; Royal Yacht Squadron, Itchenor Sailing; West Sussex Golf.

**PERRY, Prof. Malcolm John**, PhD, ScD; Professor of Theoretical Physics, University of Cambridge, since 2005; Fellow and Lecturer in Mathematics, Trinity College, Cambridge, since 1986; b Birmingham, 13 Nov. 1951; s of John and Joan Perry; partner, Anna Nikola Żytkow. Educ: King Edward's Sch., Birmingham; St John's Coll., Oxford (BA Phys 1973); King's Coll., Cambridge (MA 1977; PhD 1978; ScD 1999). Res. Fellow, King's Coll., Cambridge, 1977–81; Mem., Inst. for Advanced Study, Princeton, 1978–79; Asst Prof., Princeton Univ., 1979–86; University of Cambridge: Royal Soc. Univ. Res. Fellow, Dept of Applied Maths and Theoretical Phys, 1986–93; Newton Lectr, 1994–98; Asst Dir of Res., 1999–2000; Reader in Theoretical Phys, 2000–05. Distinguished Res. Prof., Perimeter Inst., Waterloo, Ont, 2009–12. William Golay Knafel Fellow, Radcliffe Inst. for Advanced Study, Harvard Univ., 2017–18. Trustee, Stephen Hawking Foundn, 2015–. Publications: articles in professional jls. Recreations: early and classical music, mountaineering. Address: Trinity College, Cambridge CB2 1TQ. T: (01223) 338400. E: mjp1@cam.ac.uk.

**PERRY, Sir Michael (Sydney)**, GBE 2002 (CBE 1990; OBE 1978); Kt 1994; Chairman, Centrica plc, 1997–2004; b 26 Feb. 1934; s of Sydney Albert Perry and Jessie Kate (née Brooker); m 1958, Joan Mary Stallard; one s two d. Educ: King William's Coll., IoM; St John's Coll., Oxford (MA; Hon. Fellow 2005). Unilever, 1957–96: Chm., Lever Brothers (Thailand) Ltd, 1973–77; Pres., Lever y Asociados SACIF, Argentina, 1977–81; Chm., Nippon Lever KK, 1981–83; Jt Man. Dir, UAC Internat., 1983–85, Chm., 1985–87; Dir, Unilever plc and Unilever NV, 1985–96; Personal Products Co-ordinator, 1987–91; Vice-Chm., 1991–92, Chm., 1992–96, Unilever plc; Vice Chm., Unilever NV, 1992–96. Non-executive Director: Bass plc, 1991–2001 (Dep. Chm., 1996–2001); British Gas plc, 1994–97; Marks and Spencer plc, 1996–2001; Royal Ahold BV, 1997–2004; non-exec. Chm., Dunlop Slazenger Gp Ltd, 1996–2001; Chm., Chairmen's Counsel Ltd, 2006–12. Mem., BOTB, 1986–92; Jt Chm., Netherlands British Chamber of Commerce, 1989–93; Chairman: Japan Trade Gp, 1991–99; Sen. Salaries Rev. Body, 1995–2002; Marketing Council, 1996–99. Pres., Advertising Assoc., 1993–96. Pres., Liverpool Sch. of Trop. Med., 1997–2002 (Vice-Pres., 1991–97, 2002–19); Trustee, IPPR, 2004–08; Member Council: Cheltenham Coll., 1995–2000; Alice Ottley Sch., Worcester, 2001–08. Chairman: Shakespeare Globe Trust, 1993–2006; Three Choirs Foundn, 2014–18; Trustee: Leverhulme Trust, 1991–2008 (Chm., 2008–13); Glyndebourne Arts Trust, 1996–2004; Dyson Perrins Mus. Trust, 2000– (Chm., 2017–); Daiwa Foundn, 2008–15; Three Choirs Fest. Assoc., 2007–18. CCMI (CBIM 1992). FRSA 1992. Hon. LLD South Bank, 1995; DUniv Brunel, 1995; Hon. DSc Cranfield, 1995; Hon. DLit Worcester, 2013. Recreations: music (choral), walking. Clubs: Oriental, Sloane.

**PERRY, Nicholas Proctor**, CB 2018; Permanent Secretary, Department of Justice, Northern Ireland, 2010–18; b 24 May 1958; s of Very Rev. Thomas Perry and Joyce Perry (née Proctor); m 1988, Belinda Jane Neill (marr. diss. 1998); one s one d. Educ: St Columba's Coll., Dublin; Trinity Coll., Dublin (BA Hons 1980). Joined HM Customs and Excise, 1981; MoD, 1984–91 (Private Sec. to Parly Under-Sec., Defence Procurement, 1987–89); Northern Ireland Office, 1991–2018: Asst Sec., 1994; Principal Private Sec. to Sec. of State for NI, 1998–2000; Associate Dir, 2003–04, Dir Gen., 2004–08, Policing and Security; Dir Gen., Criminal Justice and Policing, 2008–10. Publications: (ed) Major General Oliver Nugent and the Ulster Division 1915-1918, 2007; (contrib.) Oxford DNB; contrib. books and jls on military history. Recreations: cricket, military history.

**PERRY, Norman Henry**, PhD; Chairman, Pension Board, Westminster City Council, 2017–18 (Vice Chairman, 2015–17); b 5 March 1944; s of late Charles and Josephine Perry; m 1970, Barbara Ann Marsden; two s. Educ: Quintin Sch., NW8; University Coll. London (BA 1965; PhD 1969). Lectr in Geography, UCL, 1965–69; Sen. Res. Officer, GLC, 1969–73; Sen. Res. Fellow, SSRC Survey Unit, 1973–75; joined DoE, 1975; Principal, London and Birmingham, 1975–80; Asst Sec., W Midlands Regl Office, 1980–86; Head of Inner Cities Unit (G4), Dept of Employment, then DTI, 1986–88; Under Sec., and Dir W Midlands, DTI, 1988–90; Chief Exec. and Policy Co-ordinator, Wolverhampton MBC, 1990–95; Chief Executive: Solihull MBC, 1995–2000; Housing Corp., 2000–04. Chm., Public Services Gp, HBJ Gateley Wareing LLP, 2007–12. Non-executive Director: English Partnerships, 2002–04; THFC plc, 2003–04; Merlion Gp plc, 2004–07. Dir, Wolverhampton TEC, 1990–95; Gov., Univ. of Wolverhampton, 1993–95; Mem., Adv. Bd, Inst. of Public Mgt, Warwick Univ., 2005–. Company Sec., Solihull Business Partnership Ltd, 1996–2000; Dir, Central Careers Ltd, 1996–99. Sec., Soc. of Metropolitan Chief Execs, 1998–2000; Chm., Assoc. of Local Authority Chief Execs, 1995–96. Mem., Adv. Body, Almshouse Assoc., 2005–16. FCMI (FIMgt 1983); FRSA 1996. Hon. CIPFA 2003. Publications: (contrib.) European Glossary of Legal and Administrative Terminology, 1974, 1979, 1988; contribs to books and learned jls in fields of geography, planning, organisational sociology and urban policy. Address: The Beeches, Howe Road, Watlington, Oxon OX49 5EL.

**PERRY, Roy James**; Member (C) South East Region, England, European Parliament, 1999–2004 (Wight and Hampshire South, 1994–99); b 12 Feb. 1943; s of George and Dora Perry; m 1968, Veronica Haswell; two d. Educ: Tottenham County Grammar Sch.; Exeter Univ. Lectr in Govt and Politics, 1966–75, Sen. Lectr, 1975–94, Southampton Tech. Coll. Leader, Test Valley Borough Council, 1985–94. Cons. spokesman on educn, culture and media, EP, 1994–2004; EPP co-ordinator, Petitions Cttee, 1999–2004 (Vice-Pres., 1999–2004). Mem. (C), Hants CC, 2005– (Dep. Leader, 2008–13; Leader, 2013–19; Exec. Lead Mem. for Children's Services; Exec. Mem., Ext. Affairs). Chm., SE England Councils, 2018–. Vice Chm., Children and Young People Bd, LGA, 2016–. Chairman: Test Valley Arts Foundn, 2005–10 (Trustee, 2004–); Hampshire Strategic Crime and Disorder Partnership, 2007. Trustee: Hampshire Museums Trust, 1998–2004; Hampshire Cultural Trust, 2014–. Recreations: bridge, French travel and food.
See also Rt Hon. C. Nokes.

**PERRY, (Rudolph) John**; QC 1989; b 20 Feb. 1936; s of late Rudolph Perry and Beatrice (née Tingling, subseq. Robertson); m; two s (one d decd). Educ: Ruseas High Sch., Lucea, Jamaica; Southgate Technical Coll.; London Sch. of Economics (LLB (Hons), LLM); Univ. of Warwick (MA (Industrial Relations)). Lectr (part-time), LSE, 1970–78; Lectr, 1971, Sen. Lectr, 1974–78, City of London Poly. Called to the Bar, Middle Temple, 1975; in practice, 1976; an Asst Recorder, 1988, Recorder, 1992–2002. Mem. Panel of Chairmen, Police Disciplinary Appeals Tribunals, 1997–2011. Recreations: watching cricket, travel, cinema. Address: 58c Mill Street, Old Kidlington, Oxon OX5 2EF.

**PERRY, Dr Sarah Grace**; writer, since 2006; b Chelmsford, 28 Nov. 1979; d of David and Maureen Butler; m 2000, Robert Perry. Educ: Chelmsford Co. High Sch. for Girls; Anglia Poly. Univ. (BA Hons English 2001); Royal Holloway, Univ. of London (MA Creative Writing 2006; PhD Creative Writing/the Gothic 2012). Civil servant, DWP and ODPM, 2002–07; Sec., Advocacy Trng Council, Council of Inns of Court, 2008–12; freelance legal journalist, 2012–16. Lectr, Royal Holloway, Univ. of London, 2009; Writer-in-Residence, Gladstone's Liby, 2013; UNESCO City of Lit. Writer-in-Residence for Prague, 2016. FRSL 2018. Publications: After Me Comes the Flood, 2014; The Essex Serpent, 2016 (Overall Book of Year Award, British Book Awards, 2017); Melmoth, 2018; contribs to Guardian, Independent, FT, Spectator. Recreations: Sherlock Holmes, Twitter, dressmaking, opera, wound anecdotes, pointing out that I was into Hilary Mantel first. Address: c/o Jenny Hewson, Rogers, Coleridge & White, 20 Powis Mews, W11 1JN.

**PERRY, Rev. Dr Simon**; Chaplain, Robinson College, University of Cambridge, since 2011; b 10 Sept. 1969; s of Bill and Joan Perry; m 1994, Rachel Olyott (marr. diss. 2008); three s one d. Educ: Regent's Park Coll., Oxford (BTh 1998); Bristol Univ. (PhD 2005). Data Analyst, Special Reaction Force, RAF, 1987–94; Minister, Fivehead Baptist Church, Somerset, 1998–2003; Chaplain, Fitzwilliam Coll., Cambridge, 2003–06; Jt Minister, Bloomsbury Central Baptist Ch, 2006–11. Publications: All Who Came Before, 2011; Resurrecting Interpretation, 2012; Atheism After Christendom, 2015. Recreations: rowing, running, guitar, conning clever people into thinking I'm one of them. Address: Robinson College, Grange Road, Cambridge CB3 9AN. E: revslammer@googlemail.com.

**PERRY, Prof. (Victor) Hugh**, DPhil; Professor of Experimental Neuropathology, University of Southampton, 1998–2018, now Emeritus; Hon. Consultant and Theme Lead in Neuroinflammation, Dementia Research Institute, University College London, since 2018; b 18 April 1952; s of Eric and Marie Perry; m 1992, Jessica Duxbury; one s one d. Educ: Magdalen Coll., Oxford (BA Hons 1974; MA; DPhil 1977). University of Oxford: Royal Soc. Locke Res. Fellow, 1982–86; Wellcome Trust Sen. Res. Fellow, 1986–95; Prof. of Exptl Neuropathology, 1996–98; Dir, Southampton Neurosci. Gp, 2001–08. Vis. Prof., Coll. of Medicine and Veterinary Medicine, Univ. of Edinburgh, 2011–. Mem., Nuffield Council on Bioethics, 2006–12. FMedSci 2005. Corresp. Mem., Brazilian Acad. of Scis, 2014. Publications: Macrophages and the Nervous System, 1994; over 300 papers and 55 reviews in scientific jls. Recreations: reading, walking, sailing, gardening. Address: Centre for Biological Sciences, University of Southampton, Mailpoint 840, LD80B, Southampton General Hospital, Hants SO16 6YD. T: (023) 8125 6103, Fax: (023) 8079 5332. E: vhp@soton.ac.uk.

**PERRY, William Arthur**; Command Secretary (Adjutant General, Personnel and Training Command), Ministry of Defence, 1994–97; b 5 Aug. 1937; s of Arthur Perry and Elizabeth Grace (née Geller); m 1962, Anne Rosemary Dight; two d. Educ: St Dunstan's Coll.; Kellogg Coll., Oxford (MSc 2004). Min. of Aviation, 1960–61; Second Sec. (Defence Supply), Bonn, 1964–66; Min. of Technology, then MoD, 1966–74; First Sec., UK Delegn to NATO, 1974–77; Head, Defence Secretariat 8, MoD, 1978–80; Counsellor (Defence Supply), Bonn, 1980–84; Regl Marketing Dir, Defence Exports Services Orgn, 1984–88; Asst Sec., MoD (PE), 1988–92; Dir (Finance and Secretariat), Air 1, MoD (PE), 1992–94. Mem., Royal Patriotic Fund Corp., 1994–97. Trustee: Wilts Archaeological and Natural History Soc. and Wilts Mus. (formerly Wilts Heritage Mus.), 2001–18 (Chm., 2004–10); Wilts Victoria County History Trust, 2014–. Recreations: opera, gardening, genealogy.

**PERRY, Dr William James**, Hon. KBE 1998; Michael and Barbara Berberian Professor, Freeman Spogli Institute for International Studies and School of Engineering, Stanford University, 1997, now Emeritus; Secretary of Defense, United States of America, 1994–97; b Pa, 11 Oct. 1927; m Lee; three s two d. Educ: Butler High Sch., Butler, Pa; Carnegie Tech.; Stanford Univ. (BS Maths, MS); Penn State Univ. (PhD Maths). Served US Army: Fort Belvoir, Japan and Okinawa, 1946–47; Army Reserves, 1950–55. Dir, Electronic Defense Labs, Sylvania/General Telephone; Exec. Vice Pres., Hambrecht and Quist Inc.; Founder, ESL Inc., 1964, Pres., 1964–77; Under-Sec. of Defense for Res. and Engrg, 1977–81; Stanford University: Co-Dir, Center for Internat. Security and Arms Control, 1988–93; Chm., Technol. Strategies & Alliances, 1985–93; Dep. Sec. of Defense, 1993–94. Mem., Nat. Acad. Engrg; Fellow, Amer. Acad. Arts and Scis. Distinguished Public Service Medal, Dept of Defense, 1980 and 1981; Distinguished Service Medal, NASA, 1981; Medal of Achievement, Amer. Electronics Assoc., 1980; US Presidential Medal of Freedom, 1997. Address: Stanford University, CA 94305, USA.

**PERSAUD, Dr Rajendra Dhwarka**, FRCPsych; consultant psychiatrist in private practice, Harley Street, since 2008; b 13 May 1963; s of late Prof. Bishnudat Persaud and of Dr Lakshmi Seeteram; m 1994, Maria Francesca Cordeiro; one s one d. Educ: Haberdashers' Aske's Sch., Elstree; University Coll. London (BSc 1st Cl. Hons Psychol.; MB BS Medicine; MSc; Fellow 2002); Birkbeck Coll., London (Dip Phil); Inst. of Psychiatry, London (MPhil). MRCPsych 1991, FRCPsych 2005; DHMSA 1992. HO, UCH, 1986–87; SHO, Maudsley Hosp., 1987–90; Research Fellow: Johns Hopkins Med. Sch., Baltimore, 1990–91; Inst. of Neurol., 1991–93; Lectr, 1993–2000, Sen. Lectr, 2000, Inst. of Psychiatry; Consultant Psychiatrist: Maudsley Hosp., 1994–2008; Surrey and Borders NHS Partnership Trust, 2008–10; practising privileges, Wellington Hosp., 2015–. Vis. Gresham Prof. of Psychiatry, 2004–07, now Emeritus; Vis. Lectr, Univ. of Buckingham, 2018–. Presenter, All in the Mind, BBC Radio 4; writer and presenter of TV series, incl. Psychology of Hostage Negotiation. Podcast Ed., RCPsych, 2015– (Jt Podcast Ed., 2014–15). Member: Med. Soc. of London, 2003; Ind. Doctor's Fedn, 2004. Denis Hill Prize, Royal Maudsley Hosp., 1990; Res. Prize and Medal, 1994, Morris Markowe Prize, 2005, RCPsych. Publications: Staying Sane: how to make your mind work for you, 1999; From the Edge of the Couch: bizarre psychiatric cases and what they teach us about ourselves, 2003; The Motivated Mind, 2005; Simply Irresistible, 2007; The Mind: a user's guide, 2008; Can't Get You Out of My Head (novel), 2016; The Streetwise Person's Guide to Mental Health Care, 2018; contrib. papers to BMJ, The Lancet, British Jl Psychiatry, New England Jl Medicine; contrib. Huffington Post, Project Syndicate, The I Newspaper, City AM. Recreations: poker, tennis, golf, theatre, shooting, Real tennis, beach tennis, chess. Address: 10 Harley Street, W1G 6AT. Clubs: Athenæum, Royal Automobile, Reform, Queen's.

**PERSEY, Lionel Edward**; QC 1997; a Recorder, since 2002; a Deputy High Court Judge, since 2010; *b* 19 Jan. 1958; *s* of Dr Paul Ronald Persey and Irene Persey; *m* 1984, Lynn Mear; one *s*. *Educ*: Haberdashers' Aske's Sch., Elstree; Birmingham Univ. (LLB Hons 1980). Called to the Bar, Gray's Inn, 1981; in practice as commercial and maritime barrister, 1982–; Jt Hd, Quadrant Chambers, 2006–12. Mem., Supplementary Panel, Jun. Treasury Counsel, 1992–97. Lloyd's Arbitrator, 2009–. *Recreations*: classical music, opera, reading, gardening. *Address*: Quadrant Chambers, Quadrant House, 10 Fleet Street, EC4Y 1AU. *T*: (020) 7583 4444, *Fax*: (020) 7583 4455. *E*: lionel.persey@quadrantchambers.com. *Club*: Reform.

**PERSSON, Göran**; Senior Advisor, JKL Group, Stockholm, since 2007; Prime Minister of Sweden, 1996–2006; *b* 20 Jan. 1949; *m* Annika Persson (marr. diss. 2002); *m* 2003, Anitra Steen; two *d* from a previous marriage. *Educ*: Orebro Univ. Organising Sec., 1971, Mem. of Bd, 1972–75, Swedish Social Democratic Youth League; mil. service, 1973–74; Sec., Workers' Educn Assoc., Sörmland, 1974–76; Chairman: Katrineholm Educn Authy, 1977–79; Bd of Educn, Södermanland Co., 1982–89. Mem., Riksdag (MP), 1979–84, 1991–94; Municipal Comr, Katrineholm, 1985–89; Minister for Schs and Educn, 1989–91; Minister of Finance, 1994–96. Chm., Swedish Social Democratic Party, 1996–2007. Vice-Chm., Oppunda Savings Bank, 1976–89; Chm., Södermanland Co-op. Soc., 1976–89; Nat. Auditor, Swedish Co-op. Wholesale Soc., 1988–89. Vice-Chm., Nordic Mus., 1983–89. Chm., Sveaskog Förvaltning AB, 2008–15. *Address*: JKL Group, Box 1405, Sveavägen 24–26, 111 84 Stockholm, Sweden.

**PERSSON, Rt Rev. William Michael Dermot**; Suffragan Bishop of Doncaster, 1982–92; an Assistant Bishop, Diocese of Bath and Wells, since 1994; *b* 27 Sept. 1927; *s* of Leslie Charles Grenville Alan and Elizabeth Mercer Persson; *m* 1957, Ann Davey; two *s* one *d*. *Educ*: Monkton Combe School; Oriel Coll., Oxford (MA); Wycliffe Hall Theological Coll. National service, Army, 1945–48; commissioned, Royal Signals. Deacon 1953, priest 1954; Curate: Emmanuel, South Croydon, 1953–55; St John, Tunbridge Wells, 1955–58; Vicar, Christ Church, Barnet, 1958–67; Rector, Bebington, Cheshire, 1967–79; Vicar, Knutsford with Toft, 1979–82. General Synod: Mem., House of Clergy, 1975–82, House of Bishops, 1985–92; Chm., Council for Christian Unity, 1991–92. *Recreations*: gardening, writing poetry. *Address*: Ryall's Cottage, Burton Street, Marnhull, Sturminster Newton, Dorset DT10 1PS.

**PERT, Prof. Geoffrey James**, PhD; FRS 1995; FInstP; Professor of Computational Physics, University of York, 1987–2007, now Emeritus Professor of Physics; *b* 15 Aug. 1941; *s* of Norman James Pert and Grace Winifred Pert (*née* Barnes); *m* 1967, Janice Ann Alexander; one *d*. *Educ*: Norwich Sch.; Imperial Coll., Univ. of London (BSc; PhD 1966). FInstP 1979. University of Alberta: Fellow, 1967–68; Asst Prof., 1968–70; University of Hull: Lectr, 1970–74; Sen. Lectr, 1974–78; Reader, 1978–82; Prof., 1982–87. *Publications*: Introductory Fluid Mechanics for Physicists and Mathematicians, 2013; papers in learned scientific jls. *Recreations*: hill-walking, gardening. *Address*: York Plasma Institute, Department of Physics, University of York, York YO10 5DD. *T*: (01904) 324910.

**PERT, His Honour Michael**; QC 1992; a Circuit Judge, 2004–15; Resident Judge for Leicester, 2006–14; *b* 17 May 1947; *s* of Lieut Henry McKay Pert (RN, retd) and Noreen (*née* Murphy); *m* 1971, Vivien Victoria Braithwaite (marr. diss. 1993); one *s* two *d*. *Educ*: St Boniface's Coll., Plymouth; Manchester Univ. (LLB Hons). Called to the Bar, Gray's Inn, 1970. A Recorder, 1988–2004. *Recreations*: beekeeping, sailing.

**PERTH, 18th Earl of**, *cr* 1605; **John Eric Drummond**; Baron Drummond of Cargill, 1488; Baron Maderty, 1609; Baron Drummond, 1686; Lord Drummond of Gilston, 1685; Lord Drummond of Rickertoun and Castlemaine, 1686; Viscount Strathallan, 1686; Hereditary Thane of Lennox and Hereditary Steward of Menteith and Strathearn; *b* 7 July 1935; *e s* of 17th Earl of Perth, PC and Nancy Seymour, *d* of Reginald Fincke, NYC; *S* father, 2002; *m* 1963, Margaret Ann (marr. diss. 1972), *o d* of Robin Gordon; two *s*; *m* 1988, Mrs Marion Elliot. *Educ*: Trinity Coll., Cambridge; Harvard Univ. (MBA). *Heir*: *s* Viscount Strathallan, *qv*.

**PERTH (Australia), Archbishop of**, and Metropolitan of Western Australia, since 2018; **Most Rev. Kay Maree Goldsworthy**, AO 2017; *b* Melbourne, 18 Aug. 1956; *d* of George Raymond Goldsworthy and Esther Gertrude Goldsworthy (*née* Holt); *m* 1988, Benjamin James; two *s*. *Educ*: CPE (Basic) Instep 1983; Alfred Hosp. (CPE 1984; Melbourne Coll. of Divinity, Trinity Coll., Melbourne (BTh 1985); CPE (Advanced) Instep 1987. Ordained deaconess, 1984, deacon, 1986, priest, 1992; Asst Deaconess, Thomastown/Epping, Melbourne, 1984–85; Asst Deaconess, 1985–86, Asst Curate, 1986–88, St Alban's Deer Park, Keilor; Chaplain, Perth Coll., 1988–95; Rector, Parish of Applecross, 1995–2007; Archdeacon: Fremantle, 1998–99; Southern Region, 1999–2003; Archdeacon of Perth and Registrar, 2007–08; Asst Bishop, Dio. of Perth, WA, 2008–15; Bishop of Gippsland, 2015–18. Administrator, Dio. of Perth, 2006–13. Canon, St George's Cathedral, Perth, 1994–98. *Address*: Anglican Diocese of Perth, GPO Box W2067, Perth, WA 6846, Australia. *E*: archbishop@perth.anglican.org.

**PERTH, (St Ninian's Cathedral), Provost of;** *see* Farquharson, Very Rev. H. B.

**PERUMBALATH, Rt Rev. John;** *see* Bradwell, Area Bishop of.

**PERUŠKO, Patrick; His Honour Judge Peruško;** a Circuit Judge, since 2016; *b* Pula, Croatia, 1 June 1963; *s* of Anton and Gillian Peruško; *m* 2000, Claire Lovell; one *s* one *d*. *Educ*: Leon Sch., Milton Keynes; Newcastle Poly. (LLB Hons). Admitted as solicitor, 1987; Dep. Dist Judge, 1997–2008; Dist Judge, 2008–16. *Recreations*: avoiding independent thought, supporting Chelsea Football Club, lead singer in rock band Time Flies, chief chauffeur for children, musical theatre.

**PERUTZ, Prof. Robin Noel**, PhD; FRS 2010; Professor of Chemistry, University of York, since 1991; *b* Dec. 1949; *s* of Max Ferdinand Perutz, OM, CH, CBE, FRS. *Educ*: Pembroke Coll., Cambridge (BA 1968); Univ. of Newcastle upon Tyne (PhD 1974). Posts in Muelheim, Edinburgh and Oxford; University of York: Lectr, 1983–89; Reader, 1989–91; Hd, Dept of Chem., 2000–04. Pres., Dalton Div., RSC, 2007–10. Nyholm Medal and Lect., RSC, 2005; Luigi Sacconi Medal, Italian Chemical Soc., 2008. *Address*: Department of Chemistry, University of York, Heslington, York YO10 5DD.

**PERVEZ, Sir (Mohammed) Anwar**, Kt 1999; OBE 1992; HPk 2000; Chairman, Bestway Group, since 2004 (Managing Director, 1975–2004); *b* 15 March 1935. *Educ*: Jhelum, Pakistan. Chairman: Batleys Ltd, 2005–; Well Pharmacy, 2014–. Founder, Bestway Foundn Charitable Trust. Hon. DLaws: Forman Christian Coll., Lahore, 2011; Bradford, 2012. *Address*: Bestway Group, 2 Abbey Road, Park Royal, NW10 7BW. *T*: (020) 8453 1234.

**PERY**, family name of **Earl of Limerick**.

**PERY, Viscount; Felix Edmund Pery**; *b* 16 Nov. 1991; *s* and *heir* of Earl of Limerick, *qv*. *Educ*: Latymer Upper Sch.; Ardingly Coll.

**PESARAN, Prof. (Mohammad) Hashem**, FBA 1998; PhD; Professor of Economics, Cambridge University, 1988–2012, now Emeritus; Fellow of Trinity College, Cambridge, since 1988; John Elliot Professor of Economics, since 2005, Distinguished Professor, since 2013, Director, Centre for Applied Financial Economics, since 2012, and Director, Dornsife Institute of New Economic Thinking, since 2014, University of Southern California; *b* 30 March 1946; *s* of Jamal and Effat Pesaran; *m* 1969, Marian Fay Swainston; three *s* two *d*. *Educ*: Salford Univ. (BSc 1968); Cambridge Univ. (PhD 1972; MA 2003). Jun. Res. Officer, Dept of Applied Econs, Cambridge Univ., and Lektor, Trinity Coll., Cambridge, 1971–73; Asst to Vice-Governor, 1973–74, and Head of Econ. Res. Dept, 1974–76, Central Bank of Iran; Under-Sec., Min. of Educn, Iran, 1977–78; Teaching Fellow, and Dir of Studies in Econs, Trinity Coll., Cambridge, 1979–88; Lectr in Econs, 1979–85, and Reader in Econs, 1985–88, Cambridge Univ. Prof. of Econs, and Dir, Program in Applied Econometrics, UCLA, 1989–93; Research Fellow: Inst. for Study of Labour, Bonn, 1999–; CESifo (Center for Economic Studies and Ifo Institute for Econ. Res.) Res. Network, Munich, 2000–. Visiting Lecturer: Harvard Univ., 1982; Dutch Network for Quantitative Econs, Groningen, 1985; Vis. Fellow, ANU, 1984 and 1988; Visiting Professor: Univ. of Rome, 1986; Univ. of Calif, LA, 1987–88; Univ. of Pennsylvania, 1993; Univ. of S Calif, 1995, 1997, 1999 and 2003. Director: Camfit Data Ltd, 1986–2009; Acorn Investment Trust, 1987–89 and 1991–93; Cambridge Econometrics, 1985, 1988–89 and 1992–96 (Hon. Pres., 1996–2005); (non-exec.), Chiltern Gp plc, 1999–2003; Partner, GSA Capital, 2006–09; Vice Pres., Tudor Investment Corp., 2000–02. Member: HM Treasury Academic Panel, 1993–; Academic Econometric Panel, ONS, 1997–2002; Outside Mem., Meteorol Office, 1994–97. Member: Bd of Trustees, Econ. Res. Forum of Arab Countries, Iran and Turkey, 1996–2001 (Mem. Adv. Bd and Res. Fellow, 1993–96); World Bank Council for the Middle East and N Africa region, 1996–2000; Bd of Trustees, British Iranian Trust, 1997–; Charter Mem., Oliver Wyman Inst., 1997–2000. Mem. Council, Royal Econ. Soc., 2007–. Fellow: Econometric Soc., 1989; Jl of Econometrics, 1990; Life Fellow, Econ. Res. Forum, Middle East, 2009. Founding Ed., Jl of Applied Econometrics, 1985–2014. Hon. Fellow, Grad. Sch. of Business and Econs, Maastricht Univ., 2013. Hon. DLitt Salford, 1993; Hon. Dr rer. pol. Goethe, Frankfurt, 2008; Hon. Dr Maastricht, 2013; Dr Oeconomiae hc, Univ. of Econs, Prague, 2016. Royal Econ. Soc. Prize, 1992. *Publications*: World Economic Prospects and the Iranian Economy—a short term view, 1974 (also Persian); (with L. J. Slater) Dynamic Regression: theory and algorithms, 1980 (trans. Russian 1984); (ed with T. Lawson) Keynes' Economics: methodological issues, 1985; The Limits to Rational Expectations, 1987; (with B. Pesaran) Data-FIT: an interactive software econometric package, 1987 (paperback edn, as Microfit, 1989); (ed with T. Barker) Disaggregation in Economic Modelling, 1990; (with B. Pesaran) Microfit 3.0, 1991, Microfit 4.0, 1997, Microfit 4.1, 2001, Time Series Econometrics using Microfit 5, 2009; (ed with S. Potter) Non-Linear Dynamics, Chaos and Econometrics, 1993; Handbook of Applied Econometrics, Vol. I (ed with M. Wickens), 1995, Vol. II (ed with P. Schmidt), 1997; (jtly) Energy Demand in Asian Developing Economies, 1998; (ed jtly) Analysis of Panels and Limited Dependent Variables, 1999; (jtly) Global and National Macroeconometric Modelling: a long-run structural approach, 2006; (ed with J. Nugent) Explaining Growth in the Middle East, 2007; (ed with F. di Mauro) The GVAR Handbook, 2013; Time Series and Panel Data Econometrics, 2015; scientific papers in econ. and econometric jls (Best Paper award 2002–04, Econometric Reviews; Best Paper Award 2004–05, Internat. Jl of Forecasting; Multa Scripsit Award, Jl of Econometric Theory, 2008). *Recreations*: basketball (half-blue, Cambridge University), squash, swimming. *Address*: Trinity College, Cambridge CB2 1TQ. *T*: (01223) 335216. *E*: mhp1@cam.ac.uk.

**PESCOD, Prof. Mainwaring Bainbridge**, OBE 1977; CEng, FICE, FCIWEM, FCIWM; Senior Environmental Consultant, Cundall, Johnston and Partners LLP, 2008–10; Tyne and Wear Professor of Environmental Control Engineering, 1976–98, now Emeritus, and Head of Department of Civil Engineering, 1983–98, University of Newcastle upon Tyne; *b* 6 Jan. 1933; *s* of Bainbridge and Elizabeth Pescod; *m* 1957, Mary Lorenza (*née* Coyle); two *s*. *Educ*: Stanley Grammar Sch., Co. Durham; King's Coll., Univ. of Durham (BSc); MIT (SM). CEng 1973, FICE 1980; FCIWEM (FIPHE 1971; FIWES 1983; FIWEM 1987; MIWPC 1967); FCIWM (FIWM 1997; MInstWM 1985). Lectr in Engrg, Fourah Bay Coll., Freetown, Sierra Leone, 1957–61; Asst Engr, Babtie, Shaw & Morton, CCE, Glasgow, 1961–64; Asst and Associate Prof. of Environmental Engrg, 1964–72, Prof. and Head of Div. of Environmental Engrg, 1972–76, Asian Inst. of Technol., Bangkok, Thailand. Chm. and Man. Dir, Envmtl Technology Consultants, 1988–2003; Corporate Fellow, SEC Ltd, 2003–08. Mem., Northumbrian Water Authority, 1986–89; Director: Northumbrian Water Group, 1989–97; Motherwell Bridge Envirotec, 1991–95; Chm., MB Technology (Malaysia) Sdn Bhd, 1996–2002. *Publications*: (ed with D. A. Okun) Water Supply and Wastewater Disposal in Developing Countries, 1971; (ed. with A. Arar) Treatment and Use of Sewage Effluent for Irrigation, 1988; (ed) Urban Solid Waste Management, 1991; pubns on water supply, wastewater treatment, environmental pollution control and management in learned jls and conf. proc. *Recreations*: golf, reading. *Address*: Tall Trees, High Horse Close Wood, Rowlands Gill, Tyne and Wear NE39 1AN. *T*: (01207) 542104. *Clubs*: British, Royal Bangkok Sports (Bangkok, Thailand).

**PEŠEK, Libor**, Hon. KBE 1996; Music Director, 1987–97, Conductor Laureate, since 1997, Royal Liverpool Philharmonic Society and Orchestra; Principal Guest Conductor, Prague Symphony Orchestra; *b* 22 June 1933. *Educ*: Academy of Musical Arts, Prague (studied conducting, piano, 'cello, trombone). Worked at Pilsen and Prague Opera Houses; Founder Director, Prague Chamber Harmony, 1958–64; Chief Conductor, Slovak Philharmonic, 1980–81; Conductor in residence, Czech Philharmonic, 1982– (tours and fests, Europe, Russia, Far East); guest conductor: Los Angeles Philharmonic, St Louis Symphony and other US orchestras; The Philharmonia, LSO, Orchestre Nat. de France, and other European orchestras; numerous recordings incl. much Czech repertoire. Pres., Prague Spring Fest., 1994. Hon. DMus Liverpool Polytechnic, 1989. *Recreations*: physics, Eastern philosophy and literature, particularly Kafka, Dostoyevsky and Tolstoy. *Address*: c/o IMG Artists (Europe), Capital Tower, 91 Waterloo Road, SE1 8RT.

**PESHAWAR, Bishop of;** *see* Rumalshah, Rt Rev. M. K.

**PESKIN, Richard Martin**; Chairman, Great Portland Estates plc, 1986–2009; *b* 21 May 1944; *s* of Leslie and Hazel Peskin; *m* 1979, Penelope Howard Triebner; one *s* two *d*. *Educ*: Charterhouse; Queens' Coll., Cambridge (MA, LLM). Great Portland Estates, 1967–2009: Dir, 1968; Asst Man. Dir, 1972–78; Jt Man. Dir, 1978–84; Man. Dir, 1984–2000. Chm., Internos Global Investors (formerly Internos Real Investors LLP), 2009–18; Mem., London Bd, Royal & Sun Alliance, 1990–2009. Consultant: Farrer & Co., 2010–13; Catalyst Capital, 2018–. FRSA 1989; FRICS 2010. CCMI (CBIM 1989). *Recreations*: crosswords, sudokus, fast walking, summer golf. *Address*: 41 Circus Road, NW8 9JH. *T*: (020) 7289 0492. *Clubs*: MCC (Mem., Estates Cttee, 1999–2005), Royal Automobile.

**PESSINA, Stefano**; Executive Vice Chairman and Chief Executive Officer, Walgreens Boots Alliance, since 2015; *b* 4 June 1941; *s* of Oreste Pessina and Elena Fusco Pessina; *m* (marr. diss.); one *s* one *d*. Various academic posts; independent business consultant, in pharmaceutical wholesaling, 1976–; Founder, Alliance Santé Gp, merged with UniChem plc, 1997, to form Alliance UniChem Gp; Chief Exec., 2001–04, Exec. Dep. Chm.,

2004–06, Alliance UniChem plc; merged with Boots Gp, 2006, to form Alliance Boots; Exec. Dep. Chm., 2006–07, Exec. Chm., 2007–15, Alliance Boots; merged with Walgreens, 2015, to form Walgreens Boots Alliance. Exec. Dir, Walgreens, 2012–15. *Recreations:* yachting, art. *Address:* Walgreens Boots Alliance, 108 Wilmot Road, Deerfield, IL 60016, USA. *E:* stefano.pessina@wba.com.

**PESTELL, John Edmund;** Partnership Secretary, Linklaters & Paines, 1990–94; *b* 8 Dec. 1930; *s* of late Edmund Pestell and Isabella (*née* Sangster); *m* 1958, Muriel Ada (*née* Whitby) (*d* 2015); three *s*. *Educ:* Roundhay Sch.; New Coll., Oxford (State Scholar; MA). National Service, 1949–50. Jt Intell. Bureau, 1953–57; Asst Principal, WO, 1957–60; Private Sec. to Parly Under Sec. of State for War, 1958–60; Principal, WO and MoD, 1960–70; Admin. Staff Coll., Henley, 1963; Private Sec. to Minister of Defence (Equipment), 1969–70; Asst Sec., MoD, 1970–72; Press Sec. (Co-ordination), Prime Minister's Office, 1972–74; Asst Sec., CSD, 1974–76, Under Sec., 1976–81; Under Sec., HM Treasury, 1981–84; Asst Under-Sec. of State, MoD, 1984–88; Resident Chm., CSSB, 1988–90. Mem., CS Pay Res. Unit Bd, 1978–80. Governor, Cranleigh Sch., 1975–95. *Address:* 42 Oatley House, Cote Lane, Bristol BS9 3TN. *T:* (0117) 962 5768. *Club:* Athenæum.

**PESTON, Robert James Kenneth;** Political Editor, ITV, since 2016; Presenter, Peston (formerly Peston on Sunday), ITV, since 2016; *b* 25 April 1960; *s* of Baron Peston; *m* 1998, Siân E. Busby (*d* 2012); one *s*, and one step *s*. *Educ:* Highgate Wood Comp. Sch.; Balliol Coll., Oxford (BA PPE 1982). City Editor, Independent on Sunday, 1991–92; Financial Times: Banking Editor, 1992–93; Hd of Investigations, 1993–95; Political Editor, 1995–2000; Financial Editor and Asst Editor, 2000; Editl Dir, CSQuest.com, 2000–02; Associate Editor, Spectator, 2000–01; City Ed. and Asst Ed., Sunday Telegraph, 2002–06; Business Editor, 2006–14, Econs Editor, 2014–15, BBC News. Columnist: New Statesman, 2001–02; Sunday Times, 2001–02. Writer and Presenter: TV documentaries: Super-Rich: the greed game, 2008; Britain's Banks: too big to save?, 2011; How China Fooled the World, 2014; Scotland: for richer or poorer?, 2014; Quelle Catastrophe! France, with Robert Peston, 2015; The Great Chinese Crash?, with Robert Peston, 2016; Europe - In or Out, 2016; Will Brexit Fix Britain, 2018; TV series: On the Money with Robert Peston, 2010; The Party's Over - How the West Went Bust, 2011; Robert Peston Goes Shopping, 2013; film, The Great Euro Crash, BBC2, 2012; radio, The Robert Peston Interview Show (with Eddie Mair), 2015. Member: Bd, Media Standards Trust, 2006–11; Council, ICA, 2012–13. Trustee, Educn and Employers Taskforce, 2011–17. Founder and Trustee, Speakers for Schools, 2011–; Chm. Trustees, Hospice UK, 2018–. Patron: Pro Bono Econs, 2009–; Nat. Citizen Service, 2017–. Hon. Fellow: Aberystwyth Univ., 2011; QMUL, 2017. Hon. DLit Heriot-Watt, 2010. Investigative Journalist of the Year, What the Papers Say awards, 1993; Sen. Financial Journalist of the Year, 2005, Online Media Award and Broadcaster of the Year, 2008, Harold Wincott awards; Scoop of the Year, 2005, Business Journalist of the Year, 2009, London Press Club; Scoop of the Year, 2007, 2008, Television Journalist of the Year and Specialist Journalist of the Year, 2008, RTS TV Journalism Awards; Business News/Current Affairs Prog. of the Year, Wincott Foundn, 2007; Journalist of the Year, 2007, 2008, Scoop of the Year, 2007, 2008, 2009, Business Journalist of Year Awards; Documentary of the Year, 2007, Broadcast News Journalist of the Year, 2007, 2008, Online Journalist Award, 2008, Work Foundn Workworld Media Awards; Private Equity and Venture Capital Digital Journalist of the Year, 2007; Best Performer in Non-acting Role, Broadcasting Press Guild, 2009; Broadcaster of the Year, Headline Money Awards, 2009; Political Journalist of the Year, Political Studies Assoc., 2009; Business and Finance Journalist of the Year, Press Gazette, 2009; Mainstream Media Blogger Award, Editl Intelligence Comment Awards, 2011; Financial/Econ. Story of Year Award, Foreign Press Assoc., 2012; Lung Cancer Journalism Award, Global Lung Cancer Coalition, 2014. *Publications:* Brown's Britain, 2005; Who Runs Britain?, 2008; How Do We Fix This Mess?, 2012; WTF: What have we done? Why did it Happen? How do we take back control?, 2017. *Recreations:* Arsenal, dance/ballet. *Address:* ITV News Westminster, Press Gallery, House of Commons, SW1A 0AA. *E:* peston@gmail.com.

**PETCH, Barry Irvine,** FCA; General Manager, IBM Financing International Ltd, 1989–93; *b* 12 Oct. 1933; *s* of Charles Reginald Petch and Anne (*née* Fryer); *m* 1966, Anne Elisabeth (*née* Johannessen); two *s* one *d*. *Educ:* Doncaster Grammar Sch.; Kingston Univ. (MA 1998). FCA 1967. IBM United Kingdom Ltd, 1959–80; Controller, IBM Europe, 1981–83; Vice-Pres., Finance, IBM Europe, 1983–89. Part-time Mem., Price Commn, 1973–77. Director: Pathfinder NHS Trust, 1995–99; IBM UK Pensions Trust Ltd, 1997–2000. Hon. Treas., RNID, 1998–2001. *Recreations:* tennis, golf, sailing. *Club:* Reform.

**PETCHEY, Sir Jack,** Kt 2016; CBE 2011 (OBE 2004); Chairman, Petchey Group of Companies; Founder, Jack Petchey Foundation for Young People, since 1999; *b* London, 19 July 1925; *s* of Stanley and Dorothy Petchey; *m* 2016, Frances Segelman; three *d* (one *s* decd). *Educ:* Monega Rd Sch., London. Director: West Ham Utd FC, 1972–90; Watford FC, 1990–96. Hon. Fellow: UEL, 2003; QMUL, 2006; UEA, 2008. *Publications:* 50/50 Man: the Jack Petchey story, 2006, 2013. *Recreations:* bridge, football. *Address:* Jack Petchey Foundation, Dockmaster's House, 1 Hertsmere Road, E14 8JJ.

**PETCHEY, Philip Neil;** barrister; Chancellor, Diocese of Southwark, since 2010; *b* Barking, 2 Sept. 1953; *s* of Joyce and Ronald Petchey; *m* 1995, Helen Lawford. *Educ:* Barking Abbey School; Oriel Coll., Oxford (BA 1975). Called to the Bar, Middle Temple, 1976; barrister in private practice, 1977–. Chm., London Br., Elgar Soc., 2014–. *Publications:* articles in legal jls. *Recreations:* walking, bell-ringing, reading, listening to music. *Address:* Francis Taylor Building, Inner Temple, EC4Y 7BY. *T:* (020) 7353 8415, *Fax:* (020) 7353 7622. *E:* philip.petchey@ftb.eu.com. *Club:* Oxford and Cambridge.

**PETERBOROUGH, Bishop of,** since 2010; **Rt Rev. Donald Spargo Allister;** Assistant Bishop, Diocese of Ely, since 2011; *b* 27 Aug. 1952; *s* of Charles and Barbara Allister; *m* 1976, Janice Reynolds; one *s* two *d*. *Educ:* Birkenhead Sch.; Peterhouse, Cambridge (BA 1974, MA 1977); Trinity Coll., Bristol. Ordained deacon, 1976, priest, 1977; Curate: St George's, Hyde, 1976–79; St Nicholas', Sevenoaks, 1979–83; Vicar, Christ Church, Birkenhead, 1983–89; Rector, St Mary's, Cheadle, 1989–2002; Archdeacon of Chester, 2002–10. Took seat in H of L, 2014. Chaplain, Arrowe Park Hosp., 1983–86; RD, Cheadle, 1999–2002. Chm., Church Soc., 1995–2000; Member: Gen. Synod, 2005–; Council for Christian Unity, 2006–18 (Chm., 2013–18). Hon. DTh Chester, 2011. Consultant Ed., C of E Newspaper, 1981–83. *Publications:* numerous articles in church and theol jls. *Recreations:* hill-walking, science fiction, medical ethics. *Address:* Bishop's Lodging, The Palace, Minster Precincts, Peterborough PE1 1YA. *E:* bishop@peterborough-diocese.org.uk. *Club:* Farmers.

**PETERBOROUGH, Dean of;** *see* Dalliston, Very Rev. C. C.

**PETERKEN, Dr Alexander Laurence Raynal;** Headmaster, Charterhouse, since 2018; *b* Guildford, 4 June 1974; *s* of Laurence Edwin Peterken, *qv*; *m* 1st, 2000, Clare Sophia Guthrie (*d* 2011); one *s* two *d*; 2nd, 2012, Henrietta Ruth Ford; one *s* two *d*. *Educ:* Eton Coll. (Music Exhibnr); Univ. of Durham (Choral Schol.; BA Theol. 1996); Inst. of Educn, Univ. of London (MA Educnl Mgt 2002); Univ. of Surrey (EdD 2008). Charterhouse School: Asst Master, 1997–99; Hd, Higher Educn and Careers, 1999–2001; Housemaster, Saunderites, 2002–08; Dep. Headmaster, 2008–10, Headmaster, 2010–17, Cheltenham Coll. Mem., Ind. Schs Exam Bd, 2011– (Vice Chm., 2015–). Governor: St Mark's Sch., Godalming, 2006–08; Pinewood Prep. Sch., Shrivenham, 2010–17; Lambrook Sch., 2018–; Brambletye Sch., 2018; Charterhouse-in-Southwark Bd, 2018–. *Recreations:* family, singing, Cornish walks, church architecture. *Address:* Charterhouse, Godalming, Surrey GU7 2DX. *Club:* Lansdowne.

**PETERKEN, Laurence Edwin,** CBE 1990; consultant, since 1996; Special Projects Director, NHS in Scotland, 1993–96; *b* 2 Oct. 1931; *s* of Edwin James Peterken and Constance Fanny (*née* Giffin); *m* 1st, 1955, Hanne Birgithe Von Der Recke (decd); one *s* one *d*; 2nd, 1970, Margaret Raynal Blair; one *s* one *d*. *Educ:* Harrow Sch. (Scholar); Peterhouse, Cambridge (Scholar); MA. Pilot Officer, RAF Regt, Adjt No 20 LAA Sqdn, 1950–52. Service Div. Manager, Hotpoint Ltd, 1961–63, Commercial Dir, 1963–66; Man. Dir, British Domestic Appliances Ltd, 1966–68; Dir, British Printing Corporation Ltd, 1969–73; Debenhams Ltd: Man. Dir, Fashion Multiple Div., 1974–76; Management Auditor, 1976–77; Controller, Operational Services, GLC, 1977–85; Acting Dir, Royal Festival Hall, 1985–88, to implement open foyer policy; Gen. Man., 1986–93, Dir, 1989–93, Gtr Glasgow Health Bd. Chairman: Working Party on Disposal of Clinical Waste in London, 1982–83; GLC Chief Officers' Guild, 1983–85; Member: Scottish Health Management Efficiency Gp, 1986–95; Scottish Health Clinical Resources and Audit Gp, 1989–93; Scottish Health Service Adv. Council, 1989–93; Criminal Injuries Compensation Appeal Panel, 1997–2006; Lay Member, Professional Conduct Committee: NMC, 2004–08; CIMA, 2005–08. Lay Chm., Conduct and Competence Cttee, NMC, 2008–13. Vice Chm., RIPA, W of Scotland, 1991–93. Trustee: Rodolfus Choir, 1998–2008; Council for Music in Hosps, 2004–08 (Mem., Scottish Cttee, 1997–2008). Churchwarden, Haslemere Parish Church, 1985–86. *Recreations:* music, memoirs. *Address:* Daltons, Hinton St Mary, Sturminster Newton, Dorset DT10 1NA. *Club:* Athenæum.
*See also* A. L. R. Peterken.

**PETERKIN, Maj. Gen. (Anthony) Peter G.;** *see* Grant Peterkin.

**PETERS, Prof. (Adrien) Michael,** MD, DSc; FMedSci; Professor of Applied Physiology, Brighton and Sussex Medical School, 2004, now Emeritus; *b* 17 May 1945; *s* of Adrien John Peters and Barbara Muriel Peters; *m* 1st; one *s*; 2nd, 1980, Rosemary Cox; two *s* one *d*. *Educ:* St Mary's Hosp. Med. Sch., Univ. of London (BSc, MSc); Univ. of Liverpool (MB ChB, MD 1970; DSc 2009). FRCR 1995; FRCPath 1996; FRCP 1997. GP, NSW, Australia, 1974–78, Liverpool, 1978–79; Res. Fellow, RPMS, 1979–82; Res. Physician, Glaxo Gp Res. Ltd, 1982–84; Sen. Lectr in Diagnostic Radiol., 1984–89, Reader in Nuclear Medicine, 1989–95, RPMS; Prof. of Diagnostic Radiol., RPMS, then ICSM, 1995–99; Prof. of Nuclear Medicine, Univ. of Cambridge, 1999–2004. Consultant in Paediatric Radiol., 1984–88, Hon. Consultant, 1988–93 and 1996–2001, Hosp. for Sick Children, Gt Ormond St; Hon. Consultant: Hammersmith Hosp., 1984–99; Addenbrooke's Hosp., 1999–2004; in Nuclear Medicine, Brighton and Sussex Univ. Hosps NHS Trust, 2004. Sen. Vis. Res. Fellow, Univ. of Cambridge, 2004–; Hon. Professor of Nuclear Medicine: UCL; KCL. FMedSci 2002. *Publications:* Physiological Measurement with Radionuclides in Clinical Practice, 1998; (ed) Nuclear Medicine in Radiological Diagnosis, 2003; numerous contribs to learned jls. *Address:* Brighton and Sussex Medical School, Eastern Road, Brighton BN2 5BE. *T:* (01273) 523360.

**PETERS, Most Rev. Arthur Gordon;** Archbishop of Nova Scotia and Metropolitan of the Ecclesiastical Province of Canada, 1997–2002 (Bishop of Nova Scotia, 1984–2002); *b* 21 Dec. 1935; *s* of William Peters and Charlotte Peters (*née* Symes); *m* 1962, Elizabeth Baert; one *s* two *d*. *Educ:* High School, North Sydney, NS; Univ. of King's College, Halifax, NS (BA 1960, BST 1963, BD 1973). Student, Parish of Waverley, 1961–63; deacon 1962, priest 1963, Nova Scotia; Morris Scholar, 1963, at Canterbury (Eng.), Geneva, Jerusalem, Norton (dio. Durham, Eng.); Rector: Weymouth, NS, 1964–68; Annapolis-Granville, NS, 1968–73; Christ Church, Sydney, NS, 1973–82; Bishop Coadjutor of Nova Scotia, 1982–84. Hon. DD Univ. of King's College, 1982. *Recreations:* swimming, ski-ing, reading, skating, photography. *Address:* 1101–5881 Spring Garden Road, Halifax, NS B3H 4S3, Canada.

**PETERS, (Boris) Kai (Georg);** Pro Vice-Chancellor, Coventry University, since 2017; *b* 26 Sept. 1962; *s* of late Gerhard Peters and Hilla Westerhold Peters. *Educ:* Glendon Coll.; York Univ., Toronto; Univ. of Quebec at Chicoutimi; Erasmus Univ., Rotterdam. Man. Dir, Westerhold, 1989–; Rotterdam School of Management: Dir, MBA Progs, 1994–99; Dean, 2000–03; Chief Exec., Ashridge, 2003–17; Chief Academic Officer, Hult Internat. Business Sch., 2015–17. Member, Board: Graduate Mgt Admissions Council, USA, 2002–04, 2006–11 (Chm., 2009–10); Assoc. of Business Schs, 2008–. Mem., Supervisory Bd, GAIA AG, Germany, 2002– (Chm., 2015–). Mem. Bd, Centrepoint, 2007–16. *Publications:* books and articles about strategy, leadership and mgt educn. *Recreations:* food, travel, commuting against the flow from London. *Address:* Coventry University, Priory Street, Coventry CV1 5FB.

**PETERS, Sir (David) Keith,** GBE 2018; Kt 1993; FRCP; FRS 1995; FMedSci; FLSW; Regius Professor of Physic, University of Cambridge, 1987–2005, now Emeritus; Fellow, Christ's College, Cambridge, 1987–2005, now Hon. Fellow; *b* 26 July 1938; *s* of Herbert Lionel and Olive Peters; *m* 1st, 1961, Jean Mair Garfield (marr. diss. 1978); one *s* one *d*; 2nd, 1979, Pamela Wilson Ewan, *qv*; two *s* one *d*; one *d* by Dr Elizabeth Warburton. *Educ:* Welsh National Sch. of Medicine (MB BCh 1961). MRCP 1964, FRCP 1975; FRCPath 1991; FRCPE 1995. Junior posts in United Cardiff Hosps, 1961–65; Med. Research Council, Clinical Res. Fellowship, 1965–68; Lectr in Med., Welsh Nat. Sch. of Med., 1968–69; Royal Postgraduate Medical School: Lectr, 1969; Sen. Lectr, 1974; Reader in Med., 1975; Prof. of Medicine and Dir, Dept of Medicine, 1977–87; Consultant Physician, Hammersmith Hosp., 1969–87. Interim Dir, MRC NIMR, 2006–08. Member: MRC, 1984–88 (Chm., MRC Physiological Systems Bd, 1986–88); ACOST, 1987–90; Council for Sci. and Technol., 2004–09 (Jt Chm., 2004–07); Chairman: NRPB, 1994–98; Council of Hds of Med. Schs and Deans of UK Faculties of Medicine, 1996–97; Global Med. Excellence Cluster, 2009–12. Chairman: Nat. Kidney Res. Fund, 1980–86 (Trustee, 2000–01); BHF, 1998–2002. Gov. and Mem., PPP Foundation, 1998–2002 (Chm., 2002). Member: Bd, Amersham Plc, 2000–04 (Mem., Sci. Adv. Bd, 1989– (Chm., 2001–04)); Chm., Sci. Adv. Bd, GE Healthcare Technologies, 2005–07; Sen. Advr in R & D, GlaxoSmithKline, 2005–16; Consultant, Francis Crick Inst., 2012–. Mem. Council, Royal Soc., 1999–2001. Hon. Council, Cardiff Univ., 2004–11. Foreign Mem., Amer. Philos. Soc., 1999. Founder FMedSci 1998 (Pres., 2002–06); FLSW 2010. Friend of Singapore, 2011. Hon. Fellow: Univ. of Wales Coll. of Medicine, 1997; ICSM, 1999; Cardiff Univ., 2001; Univ. of Wales, Swansea, 2001; Clare Hall, Cambridge, 2004. Hon. MD: Wales, 1987; Nottingham, 1996; Paris, 1996; Birmingham, 1998; Bristol, 2005; St Andrews, 2006; Edinburgh, 2007; Warwick, 2012; Hon. DSc: Aberdeen, 1994; Leicester, 1999; Glasgow, 2001; Sussex, 2004; Keele, 2006; KCL, 2010; UCL, 2011; Imperial Coll. London, 2014. Hon. Dr Cardiff, 2012; Hon. DMedSci Cambridge, 2016. *Publications:* (ed jtly) Clinical Aspects of Immunology, 4th edn 1982, 5th edn 1993; in various jls on immunology of renal and vascular disease. *Club:* Garrick.

**PETERS, Emma Kate**; Her Honour Judge Emma Peters; a Circuit Judge, since 2016; *b* Edinburgh, 10 June 1969; *d* of G. R. V. Gillespie and Patricia Jardine Gillespie; *m* 1996, Adrian Peters; two *d*. *Educ:* Poly. of Wolverhampton (LLB Hons 1990); Inns of Court Sch. of Law; RMA, Sandhurst. Called to the Bar, Lincoln's Inn, 1991; Legal Officer, Army Legal Services, 1992–2008; retd as Lt Col, 2008. Admitted to Faculty of Advocates, 2009; pt-time Legal Chm., Pensions Appeal Tribunal (Scotland), 2009; Asst Judge Advocate Gen., 2010–; a Recorder, 2012–15; Resident Judge, British Forces Germany, 2013–15. Trustee, Walking with the Wounded, 2016–. *Recreations:* family, cycling, walking. *Address:* Chelmsford Crown Court, PO Box 9, New Street, Chelmsford, Essex CM1 1EL.

**PETERS, Kai;** *see* Peters, B. K. G.

**PETERS, Sir Keith;** *see* Peters, Sir D. K.

**PETERS, Martin Trevor**, CB 1991; CEng, FRAeS; Technical Planning Director, British Aerospace plc, 1992–94; *b* 23 Dec. 1936; *s* of Reginald Thomas Peters and Catherine Mary Peters (*née* Ings); *m* 1958, Vera Joan Horton (*d* 2004); one *s*. *Educ:* Aylesbury Grammar Sch.; Watford Tech. Coll.; High Wycombe Coll. of Further Educn. MIMechE, CEng 1968; FRAeS 1988. Airtech, 1953–55; RAF, 1955–57; Airtech, 1957–59; RPE Westcott, 1959–64; NGTE Pyestock, 1964–71; MoD, 1971–77; Supt of Engineering, A&AEE Boscombe Down, 1977–79; NAMMA, Munich, 1979–81; Dir, Aircraft Post Design Services, MoD (PE), 1981–83; RCDS, 1984; Dir-Gen. Aircraft, 1984–87; Dep. Controller Aircraft, 1987–89; Dir, RAE, 1989–91; Tech. Dir, BAe Commercial Aircraft Ltd, 1991–92. *Recreations:* walking, music, 18th century ship modelling. *Address:* 144 Badger Road, Thornbury, S Glos BS35 1AD.

**PETERS, Lady Mary (Elizabeth)**, LG 2019; CH 2015; DBE 2000 (CBE 1990; MBE 1973); Lord-Lieutenant, County Borough of Belfast, 2009–14; Managing Director, Mary Peters Sports Ltd, 1977; *b* 6 July 1939; *d* of Arthur Henry Peters and Hilda Mary Peters. *Educ:* Portadown Coll., Co. Armagh; Belfast Coll. of Domestic Science (DipDomSc). Represented Great Britain: Olympic Games: 4th place, Pentathlon, 1964; 1st, Pentathlon (world record), 1972; Commonwealth Games: 2nd, Shot, 1966; 1st, Shot, 1st Pentathlon, 1970; 1st, Pentathlon, 1974. Member: Sports Council, 1974–80, 1987–94; NI Sports Council, 1974–93 (Vice-Chm., 1977–81); Ulster Games Foundn, 1984–93; NI BBC Broadcasting Council, 1981–84; NI Tourist Bd, 1993–2002. Dir, Churchill Foundn Fellowship Scholarship, Calif, 1972. Asst Sec., Multiple Sclerosis Soc., 1974–78. President: NI WAAA, 1985–87; British Athletic Fedn, 1996–98; Mary Peters Trust (formerly Ulster Sports and Recreation Trust), 1996– (Trustee, 1972); Mem., Women's Cttee, IAAF, 1995–97. Hon. Senior Athletic Coach, 1975–; BAAB Pentathlon Coach, 1976; Team Manager: GB women's athletic team, European Cup, 1979; GB women's athletic team, Moscow, 1980 and Los Angeles, 1984. President: OAPs' Coal and Grocery Fund; Lady Taverners, NI; Vice-President: Assoc. of Youth Clubs; NI Assoc. of Youth Clubs; Riding for the Disabled; Driving for the Disabled; Action Cancer; Patron: NIAAA, 1981–; Friends of Royal Victoria Hosp., Belfast, 1988–96. Freeman: Lisburn, 1998; Belfast, 2013. Hon. Captain, RNR, 2012. Awards: BBC Sports personality, 1972; Athletic Writers', 1972; Sports Writers', 1972; Elizabeth Arden Visible Difference, 1976; Athletics, Dublin (Texaco), 1970 and 1972; British Airways Tourist Endeavour, 1981; Living Action, 1985; Evian Health, 1985. Hon. DSc New Univ. of Ulster, 1974; DUniv QUB, 1998; Hon. DLitt Loughborough, 1999; Hon. DArts Leeds Beckett, 2004; Hon. DLaw Trinity Coll. Dublin, 2004; Hon. DLaw St Andrews, 2010; Hon. DUniv Open, 2012. DStJ 2017. Ron Pickering Meml Trophy for Services to Athletics, British Athletics Writers' Assoc., 2017. *Publications:* Mary P., an autobiography, 1974. *Address:* Willowtree Cottage, River Road, Dunmurry, Belfast, N Ireland BT17 9DP.

**PETERS, Michael;** *see* Peters, A. M.

**PETERS, Nigel Melvin;** QC 1997; His Honour Judge Peters; a Circuit Judge, since 2012; *b* 14 Nov. 1952; *s* of Sidney Peters and Maisie Peters (*née* Pepper). *Educ:* Hasmonean GS; Leicester Univ. (LLB 1975). Called to the Bar, Lincoln's Inn, 1976 (Mansfield Schol.; Bencher, 2006); Asst Recorder, 1994–98; Recorder, 1998–2012. *Recreations:* cricket, Real tennis, travel, food, wine. *Address:* Snaresbrook Crown Court, 75 Hollybush Hill, E11 1QW. *Clubs:* Garrick, MCC (Mem. Cttee, 1999– ).

**PETERS, Air Vice-Marshal Robert Geoffrey**, CB 1992; Clerk to the Guild of Air Pilots and Air Navigators, 1998–2000; *b* 22 Aug. 1940; *s* of Geoffrey Ridgway Peters and Henriette Catharine Peters; *m* 1966, Mary Elizabeth (*née* Fletcher) (*d* 2013); one *d* three *s*. *Educ:* St Paul's Sch., London; RAF Coll., Cranwell (Gen. Duties/Pilot). Beverley C Mk1 Pilot Nos 34 and 47 Sqdns, Singapore and UK, 1961–66; Flt Comdr, No 46 Sqdn (Andovers), RAF Abingdon, 1967–68; MoD Central Staffs (Asst MA to Chief Adviser Personnel and Logistics), 1968–69; OC Flying Trng Sqdn, Air Electronics and Air Engr Trng Sch., RAF Topcliffe, 1970–72; RAF Staff Coll., Bracknell, 1973; Air Sec.'s Dept, MoD, 1974–76; OC 10 Sqdn (VC10), RAF Brize Norton, 1977–78; Directorate of Forward Policy (RAF), MoD, 1979–81; PSO to Dep. SACEUR(UK), SHAPE, Belgium, 1981–83; OC RAF St Mawgan, 1984–85; RCDS 1986; Comdr, RAF Staff and Air Attaché, Washington, 1987–90; Comdt, RAF Staff Coll., Bracknell, 1990–93; Dir of Welfare, RAF Benevolent Fund, 1993–97. President: RAF Fencing Union, 1986–93; Combined Services Fencing Assoc., 1988–97. Freeman, City of London, 1977; Liveryman, Co. of Coachmakers and Coach Harness Makers, 1977; Upper Freeman, GAPAN, 1997–2000. QCVSA 1973. *Recreations:* golf, bridge, bell ringing. *Club:* Naunton Downs Golf.

**PETERS, Roger;** Regional Employment Judge (formerly Regional Chairman of Employment Tribunals), Southampton, 2004–11, fee-paid Judge, 2011–14; *b* 25 April 1945; *s* of Frederick James and Lilian Ivy Peters; *m* 1973, Isobel Susan Bell Briggs; three *s*. *Educ:* Reading Blue Coat Sch.; Coll. of Law. Admitted solicitor, 1968; Solicitor, Blandy & Blandy, Reading, 1968–71; Asst Chief Legal Officer, Redditch Develt Corp., 1971–76; Principal Legal Officer, S Yorks CC, 1976–81; Chief Solicitor, Leeds Perm. Bldg Soc., 1981–87; Partner, Staffurth & Bray, Bognor Regis, 1987–94; Chairman, Employment Tribunals: Manchester, 1995–96; London, 1997–2003; Chm., Reinstatement Cttee and Reserve Forces Tribunal, 2010–11. Legal corresp., Hospitality mag., 1987–95. *Publications:* Essential Law for Catering Students, 1992, 2nd edn 1995; (jt author and ed.) Health and Safety: liability and litigation, 1995; articles in Solicitors' Jl. *Recreations:* listening to classical music, motor boating.

**PETERS, Siobhan,** CMG 2007; Chief Financial Officer, Mayor's Office of Policing and Crime, since 2017; *b* Welwyn Garden City, 27 June 1970; *d* of Susan Peters; one *s* one *d*. *Educ:* Wadham Coll., Oxford (BA Hons Oriental Studies 1991); Open Univ. (MA Envmt Policy 2004). Auditor, Touche Ross, 1992–96; Desk Officer, FCO, London and Beijing, 1997–2004; Hd, G8 Climate Change Unit, DEFRA, 2004–05; Hd, Review Team, Stern Review of the Econs of Climate Change, HM Treasury, 2005–07; Team Leader, Energy, Envmt and Agriculture, HM Treasury, 2007–10; Dir, Strategy and Change, Home Office, 2010–17. *Recreation:* family life. *Address:* City Hall, Queen's Walk, SE1 2AA.

**PETERS, Prof. Timothy James,** PhD; CStat; FMedSci; Professor of Primary Care Health Services Research, since 2002, and Research Director, Faculty of Health Sciences, since 2017, University of Bristol; *b* London, 8 June 1958; *s* of Eric and Pauline Peters; *m* 1984, Janet Mary Taylor. *Educ:* Bognor Regis Comprehensive Sch.; Univ. of Exeter (BSc Hons Math. Stats and Operational Res. 1979; PhD Stats 1985); Wolfson Coll., Oxford (MSc Applied Stats 1980). FSS 1986; CStat 1993. Res. Asst, Univ. of Bristol, 1982–86; Lectr in Med. Stats, UWCM, 1986–92; University of Bristol: Sen. Lectr, 1992–97; Reader in Med. Stats, 1997–2001; Res. Dir, Faculty of Medicine and Dentistry, 2006–09; Hd, Dept of Community Based Medicine, 2008–10; Hd, Sch. of Clinical Scis, 2010–17; Associate Dean, Faculty of Medicine and Dentistry, 2012–15. Sen. Investigator, NIHR, 2008–16, now Emeritus. Co-Ed., Paediatric and Perinatal Epidemiol., 1987–2012. Chair: Res. Design Services Panel, 2007–09, 2012–13, Pre-doctoral Fellowships Selection Cttee, 2019–, NIHR; Methodology Res. Prog. Panel, MRC/NIHR, 2007–14 (Chair, Methodology Res. Prog. Adv. Gp. 2018–); Econ. Impact Panel, MRC, 2012–15; Definitive Intervention and Feasibility Awards Expert Panel, Health Res. Bd, Ireland, 2016, 2018–; Sectional Cttee Six, Acad. of Med. Scis, 2018– (Mem., 2015–18). Health and Care Research Wales (formerly National Institute for Social Care and Health Research): Chair: Sen. Fac. Mems Selection Panel, 2012–13; Health Res. Awards Bd, 2012–; Sen. Res. Leaders Selection Panel, 2015–19; Co-Dep. Chair, All Wales Prioritisation Panel, 2015–. Marie Curie (formerly Marie Curie Cancer Care): Chair, Res. Funding Cttee, 2014–19 (Mem., 2013–14); Chair, Res. Strategic Adv. Panel, 2020– (Mem., 2013–14; Dep. Chair, 2014–19); Member: Adv. Bd, Dimbleby Cancer Care, 2005–; Res. Adv. Panel, Macmillan Cancer Support, 2017–; REF 2021 sub-panel 2, public health, health services and primary care, UK HE Funding Councils, 2018–. Gov., University Hosps Bristol, 2011–17. FHEA 2002; FFPH 2002; FMedSci 2014. Hon. FRCSLT 2003; Hon. FRCGP 2007. *Publications:* (ed jtly) When to Screen in Obstetrics and Gynaecology, 1996, 2nd edn 2006; (ed with W. Hamilton) Cancer Diagnosis in Primary Care, 2007; contribs to internat. peer-reviewed jls. *Recreations:* horse riding and ownership, care of horses and ponies, cryptic crosswords. *Address:* Bristol Medical School, University of Bristol, Learning and Research, Southmead Hospital, Bristol BS10 5NB. *T:* (0117) 414 7839. *E:* tim.peters@bristol.ac.uk. *Club:* Wye Valley Riding.

**PETERS, Prof. Timothy John,** PhD, DSc; FRCP; Professor of Clinical Biochemistry, King's College, London, 1988–2004; Hon. Consultant Physician and Chemical Pathologist, King's College Hospital, 1988–2004; Researcher and Member, Academic and Curatorial Committee (formerly Hon. Senior Research Fellow), Ironbridge International Institute for Cultural Heritage (formerly Institute of Archaeology and Antiquity), University of Birmingham, since 2007; *b* 10 May 1939; *s* of Stanley and Paula Peters; *m* 1965, Judith Mary Bacon; one *s* two *d*. *Educ:* King Edward VI Sch., Macclesfield; Univ. of St Andrews (MB ChB (Hons) 1964; MSc 1966; DSc 1986); RPMS, Univ. of London (PhD 1970); Univ. of Birmingham (MA 2006). MRCPE 1969, FRCPE 1986; MRCP 1970, FRCP 1976; MRCPath 1983, FRCPath 1988. MRC Trng Fellow, RPMS, 1967–70; MRC Travelling Fellow, Rockefeller Univ., NY, 1970–72; Lectr, Sen. Lectr, then Reader, RPMS, and Hon. Cons. Physician, Hammersmith Hosp., 1972–79; Head, Div. of Clin. Cell Biology, MRC Clin. Res. Centre, and Hon. Cons. Physician, Northwick Park Hosp., 1979–88; Head, Dept of Clin. Biochemistry, 1988–2004, Sub-Dean for Postgrads and Higher Degree, Sch. of Medicine, 1988–2000, KCL; Associate Dean, London and SE Region, London Univ., 2000–04. Foundation Ed., Addiction Biology, 1995–2003. *Publications:* (ed) Alcohol Misuse: a European perspective, 1996; (ed jtly) International Handbook of Alcohol Dependence and Problems, 2001; (ed jtly) Skeletal Muscle: pathology, diagnosis and management of disease, 2002; over 500 articles on subcellular fractionation, alcohol misuse and toxicology, porphyria and iron metabolism, absorption and toxicology. *Recreations:* industrial archaeology, esp. of British inland waterways and wrought iron and concrete boats, and medical history, esp. of Stuart and Hanoverian monarchs and their relatives; contribs to Hist. of Psychiatry on nature of madness of King George III and related topics; use of computer diagnostics and handwriting analysis on historical figures. *Address:* Iron Lock Cottage, Beeston Brook, Tiverton, Tarporley, Cheshire CW6 9NH.

**PETERS, Rt Hon. Winston (Raymond);** PC 1998; Deputy Prime Minister and Minister of Foreign Affairs, New Zealand, since 2017; Leader, New Zealand First Party, since 1993; *b* 11 April 1945; *s* of Len Peters and Joan (*née* McInnes); *m* 1973; one *s* one *d*. *Educ:* Auckland Univ. (BA 1969; LLB 1973). With Russell, McVeagh, lawyers, 1974–75, Davenports, 1976–78; estabd own legal practice, Howick, 1982. MP: (Nat.) Hunua, 1979–81; Tauranga, 1984–2005 (Nat., 1984–93, NZ First, 1993–2005); (NZ First), 2005–08, 2011–15; (NZ First) Northland, 2015–; Minister of Maori Affairs and i/c of Iwi Transition Agency, 1990–93; Dep. Prime Minister and Treasurer, NZ, 1996–98; Minister of Foreign Affairs and Trade, 2005–08.

**PETERSEN, Prof. Ole Holger,** CBE 2008; MD; FRCP; FRS 2000; Professor, since 2010, and Academic Director, Academia Europea's Knowledge Hub, since 2016, Cardiff University (Director, Cardiff School of Biosciences, 2010–15); *b* 3 March 1943; *s* of Rear Adm. Joergen Petersen, Royal Danish Navy, and Elisabeth Klein, pianist; *m* 1st, 1968, Nina Bratting Jensen (marr. diss. 1995); two *s*; 2nd, 1995, Nina Burdakova. *Educ:* Univ. of Copenhagen Med. Sch. (MB ChB 1969; MD 1972). FRCP 2001. Lectr, 1969–73, Sen. Lectr, 1973–75, Inst. of Med. Physiology, Univ. of Copenhagen; Wellcome-Carlsberg Travelling Res. Fellow, Dept of Pharmacology, Univ. of Cambridge, 1971–72; Symers Prof. of Physiology, Univ. of Dundee, 1975–81; George Holt Prof. of Physiology, 1981–2009, and MRC Res. Prof., 1998–2009, Univ. of Liverpool. Vis. Prof., Stellenbosch Univ., 2000; Hon. Prof., Coll. of Medicine, Jinan Nat. Univ., Guangzhou, 2011–. Morton Grossman Meml Lectr, UCLA, 1985; Halliburton Lectr, KCL, 1986; Jacobaeus Prize Lectr, Nordic Insulin Foundn, 1994; Keynote Lectr, Gordon Res. Conf. on Calcium Signaling, Mass, USA, 2003, on Salivary Glands and Exocrine Secretion, Calif, USA, 2005; IUPS Lectr, FEPS Congress, Bratislava, 2007; State-of-the-Art Lectr, Amer. Gastroenterol. Assoc., Chicago, 2009; Horace W. Davenport Dist. Lectr, Exptl Biology, Amer. Physiological Soc., Boston, 2013; Hon. Pres. and Keynote Lectr, 37th Internat. Congress of Physiol Scis, Birmingham, 2013; Plenary Lect., Annual Congress, Brazilian Soc. of Physiol., 2013. Chairman: Starting Grant Panel for Physiol., Pathophysiol. and Endocrinol., Eur. Res. Council, 2009–11; Biol Scis Panel, HEFCE REF, 2010–14; Member: Sci. Adv. Council for Wales, 2010–19; Bioscis Steering Panel, Eur. Academies Sci. Adv. Council, 2013–19; Bd, Sci. Advice for Policy by Eur. Acads Consortium, EC, 2016–; Champion for Wales, Acad. of Med. Sci., 2014–19. President: FEPS, 2001–03; Physiological Soc. (UK), 2006–08 (Hon. Mem., 2015); Sec.-Gen., IUPS, 2001–10; Member Council: Bioscis Fedn, 2004–08; Royal Soc., 2004–06 (Vice-Pres., 2005–06); Mem. Exec. Bd, Academia Europaea, 2009– (Chm., Biomed. and Life Scis Class, 2014–; Vice-Pres., 2016–); Vice Pres. (Sci., Technol. and Medicine), Learned Soc. of Wales, 2014–18. Chm., Eur. Editl Bd, Physiological Reviews, 2003–11; Sen. Reviews Ed., Jl of Physiology, 2016–. MAE 1988; Mem., German Nat. Acad. of Scis Leopoldina, 2010; Foreign Mem., Royal Danish Acad. of Scis and Letters, 1988; Hon. Member: Polish Physiological Soc., 1993 (Czubalski Medal, 1993); Hungarian Physiological Soc., 2002; Hungarian Acad. of Sci., 2004; German Soc. for Gastroenterol., Digestive and Metabolic Diseases, 2017. FMedSci 1998; FLSW 2011. Jubilee Medal, Charles Univ., Prague, 1998; Purkyne Medal, Czech Acad. of Scis, 2003; Lifetime Achievement Award, Eur. Pancreatic Club, 2010; Walter B. Cannon Meml

Award and Cannon Award Lect., Amer. Physiol Soc., 2018. *Publications*: The Electrophysiology of Gland Cells, 1980; (jtly) Landmarks in Intracellular Signalling, 1997; Measuring Calcium and Calmodulin Inside and Outside Cells, 2001; Human Physiology, 2007; more than 400 articles in scientific jls on intracellular signalling mechanisms, including many articles in Jl of Physiology, Cell, Nature and PNAS. *Recreation*: classical music. *Address*: Cardiff School of Biosciences, Cardiff University, Sir Martin Evans Building, Museum Avenue, Cardiff CF10 3AX. *T*: (029) 2068 8249. *E*: PetersenOH@cardiff.ac.uk.

**PETERSHAM, Viscount; William Henry Leicester Stanhope**; *b* 14 Oct. 1967; *s* and heir of Earl of Harrington, *qv*; *m* 2001, Candida Sophia, *e d* of Ian Bond; one *s* one *d*. *Educ*: Aysgarth; Aiglon Coll.; Lansdowne Coll. Property develt. Patron, Save the Rhino Internat. FRGS. *Recreations*: mountaineering, wildlife conservation, shooting. *Heir: s* Hon. Augustus Henry Leicester Stanhope, *b* 26 Sept. 2005. *Address*: Crimonmogate, Lonmay, Fraserburgh, Aberdeenshire AB43 8SE. *Club*: Pratt's.

**PETERSON, Rev. David Gilbert**, PhD; Research Fellow, Moore Theological College, Sydney, 2007–12, now Emeritus Faculty Member; Principal, Oak Hill Theological College, 1996–2007; *b* 29 Oct. 1944; *s* of Gilbert Samuel and Marie Jean Peterson; *m* 1970, Lesley Victoria (*née* Stock); three *s*. *Educ*: Univ. of Sydney (MA); Moore Theol Coll., Sydney (BD (Lond.)); Univ. of Manchester (PhD 1978). Ordained deacon, 1968, priest, 1969; St Matthew's, Manly, dio. of Sydney, 1968–71; Lectr, Moore Theol. Coll., 1971–75, 1978–79, 1984–96; Post-grad. study, Univ. of Manchester and Sunday Asst, St Mary's, Cheadle, dio. of Chester, 1975–78; Rector and Sen. Canon, St Michael's, Provisional Cathedral, Wollongong, dio. of Sydney, 1980–83. Hon. Vis. Prof., Middlesex Univ., 2004–09. *Publications*: Hebrews and Perfection, 1982; Engaging with God, 1992; Possessed by God, 1995; The Book of Acts and its Theology, 1996; Where Wrath and Mercy Meet: proclaiming the atonement today, 2001; The Word Made Flesh: evangelicals and the incarnation, 2003; Christ and His People in the Book of Isaiah, 2003; Holiness and Sexuality, 2004; The Acts of the Apostles, 2009; Transformed by God: new covenant life and ministry, 2012; Encountering God Together: biblical patterns for ministry and worship, 2013; Commentary on Romans, 2017. *Recreations*: golf, swimming, music. *Address*: 1 Vista Street, Belrose, NSW 2085, Australia.

**PETERSON, Hon. David Robert**; PC (Can.) 1992; QC (Can.) 1980; Senior Partner, since 1991, and Chairman, 1998, now Chairman Emeritus, Cassels Brock & Blackwell LLP; *b* 28 Dec. 1943; *s* of Clarence Marwin Peterson and Laura Marie (*née* Scott); *m* 1974, Shelley Christine Matthews; two *s* one *d*. *Educ*: Univ. of Western Ontario (BA Phil./PolSci); Univ. of Toronto (LLB). Called to Bar, Ontario, 1969. Chm. and Pres., C. M. Peterson Co. Ltd, 1969–75; MLA for London Centre, Ontario, 1975–90; Leader, Liberal Party of Ontario, 1982–90; Leader of the Opposition, 1982–85; Premier of Ontario, 1985–90. Chm. and Dir of public cos. CStJ 1987. Chevalier, Légion d'Honneur (France), 1994. *Recreations*: theatre, riding, jogging, ski-ing, tennis, scuba diving, golf, reading, gardening. *Address*: Cassels Brock & Blackwell LLP, Suite 2100, Scotia Plaza, 40 King Street West, Toronto, ON M5H 3C2, Canada. *Club*: London (Ontario) Hunt.

**PETERSON, Gilles**, MBE 2004; broadcaster, producer and DJ; *b* Caen, France, 28 Sept. 1964; *s* of Armin and Michelle Moehrle; *m* Atsuko Hirai; two *s*. *Educ*: John Fisher Sch., Purley; Greenshaw Sch., Sutton. Work on pirate radio stations: Radio Invicta; K Jazz; Solar Radio; Horizon Radio; presenter: Radio London, 1986–87; Jazz FM, 1990–91; Kiss FM, 1991–98; Radio 1, 1998–2012; BBC 6Music, 2012–; Founder: record labels: Hardback; BGP; Acid Jazz, 1988; Talkin' Loud, 1989; Brownswood Recordings, 2006; publishing co, Omakase Music. *Publications*: Freedom Rhythm and Sound, 2009. *Address*: Brownswood Recordings, 29A Brownswood Road, N4 2HP. *T*: (020) 8802 4981. *E*: simon@brownswoodrecordings.com. *W*: www.gillespetersonworldwide.com

**PETERSON, Rev. Canon John Louis**, ThD; Canon for Global Justice and Reconciliation, Diocese of Washington, since 2005; *b* 17 Dec. 1942; *s* of J. Harold Peterson and Edythe V. Peterson; *m* 1966, Kirsten Ruth Bratlie; two *d*. *Educ*: Concordia Coll. (BA 1965); Harvard Divinity Sch. (STB 1968); Chicago Inst. for Advanced Theol Studies (ThD 1976). Instr, OT and Syro-Palestinian Archaeol., Seabury-Western Theol Seminary, Evanston, 1968–76; Canon Theologian and Admin. Asst to Bishop, dio. of Western Michigan, 1976–82; Vicar, St Stephen's Plainwell, Mich, 1976–82; Dean of St George's Coll., and Canon Residentiary, St George's Cathedral, Jerusalem, 1982–94, Hon. Canon, 1995–; Sec. Gen., Anglican Consultative Council, 1995–2004. Hon. Canon: Cathedral Ch of Christ the King, Kalamazoo, Mich, 1982–2007; Cathedral Church of Christ, Canterbury, 1995–2004; St George's Cathedral, Jerusalem, 1995–; St Michael's Cathedral, Kaduna, Nigeria, 1999–; St Paul's Cathedral, 2000–05; All Saints Cathedral, Mpwapwa, Tanzania, 2002–; St Dunstan's Cathedral, Benoni, SA, 2004–; Cathedral of St Peter and St Paul, Washington DC, 2005–; St Stephen's Cathedral, Harrisburg, Pennsylvania, 2008–. Senior Adviser to the Archbishop in Jerusalem, 2009–. Board Member: Spafford Children's Center, Jerusalem, 1994– (Chair, 1994–2009); Anglican Communion Compass Rose Soc., 2010– (Pres., 2013–15; Vice Pres., 2015–). Hon. DD: Virginia Theol Seminary, 1993; Univ. of South (Sewanee), 1996; Seabury-Western Theol Seminary, 1997; Seminary of the SW, 2015. *Publications*: A Walk in Jerusalem, 1998; contrib. Anchor Bible Dictionary, 1992. *Address*: 1001 Red Oak Drive, Hendersonville, NC 28791, USA.

**PETERSON, Will**; *see* Billingham, M. P. D.

**PETFORD, Prof. Nicholas**; DL; PhD, DSc; FGS; Vice Chancellor and Chief Executive Officer, University of Northampton, since 2010; *b* London, 27 May 1961; *s* of Brian Petford and Shirley Petford; *m* 1998, Gina Cherrett; one *s* two *d*. *Educ*: Mountbatten Sch., Southampton; Eastleigh Tech. Coll. (City and Guilds); Southwark Coll. (Access Course); Goldsmiths Coll. (BSc Geology 1987); Univ. of Liverpool (PhD 1991; DSc 2009); Harvard Business Sch. (Gen. Mgt Program 17). FGS 1986. Royal Soc. Res. Fellow, Univ. of Liverpool, 1990–93; Res. Fellow, Churchill Coll., Cambridge, 1991–94; Kingston University: Sen. Lectr, then Reader, 1995–2003, e-HR/Mktg, BP, 2001 (on sabbatical); Prof., 2003–06; Pro-Vice Chancellor, Bournemouth Univ., 2006–10. Vis. Researcher, Univ. of Michigan, 1991; Visiting Professor: Univ. of Vermont, 2004; Macquarie Univ., 2005, 2010–12; Open Univ., 2010–13. Vice Pres., Mineralogical Soc. of GB and Ireland, 2002–04. FRSA. DL Northants, 2019. *Publications*: (ed jtly) Hydrocarbons in Crystalline Rocks, 2003; (ed jtly) Physical Geology of High-Level Magmatic Systems, 2004; (ed jtly) Structure and Emplacement of High-Level Magmatic Systems, 2008; (jtly) The Field Description of Igneous Rocks, 2nd edn, 2011. *Recreations*: astronomy, sailing, Chelsea FC, crowdsurfing. *Address*: University of Northampton, Park Campus, Boughton Green Road, Northampton NN2 7AL. *T*: (01604) 892001. *E*: nick.petford@northampton.ac.uk. *Club*: Athenæum.

**PETHERBRIDGE, Edward**; actor and director; *b* 3 Aug. 1936; *s* of late William and Hannah Petherbridge; *m* 1st, 1957, Louise Harris (marr. diss. 1980); one *s*; 2nd, 1981, Emily Richard, actress; one *s* one *d*. *Educ*: Grange Grammar Sch., Bradford; Northern Theatre Sch. Early experience in repertory and on tour; London début, Dumain in Love's Labours Lost and Demetrius in A Midsummer Night's Dream, Regent's Park Open Air Theatre, 1962; All in Good Time, Mermaid, and Phoenix, 1963; with Nat. Theatre Co. at Old Vic, 1964–70, chief appearances in: Trelawny of the Wells, Rosencrantz and Guildenstern are Dead, A Flea in her Ear, Love for Love, Volpone, The Advertisement, The Way of the World, The White Devil; Alceste in The Misanthrope, Nottingham, Lulu, Royal Court, and Apollo, 1970; John Bull's Other Island, Mermaid, Swansong, opening of Crucible, Sheffield, 1971; Founder Mem., Actors' Co., 1972; chief appearances at Edinburgh Fests, NY, and on tour, 1972–75: 'Tis Pity she's a Whore, Rooling the Roost, The Way of the World, Tartuffe, King Lear; also devised, dir. and appeared in Knots (from R. D. Laing's book), The Beanstalk, a wordless pantomime, and dir. The Bacchae; RSC tour of Australia and NZ, 1976; dir. Uncle Vanya, Cambridge Theatre Co., 1977; Chasuble in The Importance of Being Earnest, and dir., devised and appeared in Do You Love Me (from R. D. Laing's book), Actors' Co. tour and Round House, 1977; Crucifer of Blood, Haymarket, 1979; Royal Shakespeare Company: tour, 1978, Twelfth Night; Three Sisters, 1979; Suicide, Newman Noggs in Nicholas Nickleby (Best Supporting Actor, London Drama Critics' Award, 1981), No Limits to Love, 1980; Nicholas Nickleby, Broadway, 1981; Twelfth Night, British Council tour (Philippines, Singapore, Malaysia, China and Japan), followed by season at Warehouse, London, 1982; Peter Pan, Barbican, 1983; The Rivals, NT, 1983; Strange Interlude, Duke of York's, 1984, Broadway, 1985 (Olivier Award, 1984); Love's Labours Lost, Stratford, 1984; Co-Dir, McKellen Petherbridge Co. at NT, 1984–86, acting in Duchess of Malfi, The Cherry Orchard, The Real Inspector Hound, and The Critic, 1985, company appeared at Internat. Theatre Fests, Paris and Chicago, 1986; Busman's Honeymoon, Lyric, Hammersmith, 1988; The Eight O'Clock Muse, one-man show, Riverside Studios, 1989; Alceste in The Misanthrope, co-prodn with Bristol Old Vic, 1989; The Power and the Glory, Chichester, 1990; Cyrano de Bergerac (title rôle), Greenwich, 1990; Point Valaine, and Valentine's Day (musical, from Shaw's You Never Can Tell), Chichester, 1991; Noël & Gertie, Duke of York's, 1991; The Seagull, RNT, 1994; Twelfth Night, Barbican, 1996; The Merry Wives of Windsor, Stratford, 1996; Cymbeline, Hamlet, Krapp's Last Tape, Stratford, 1997, transf. Barbican, NY, Washington and Edinburgh, 1997–98, Arts Th., 1999; The Accused, Haymarket Theatre Royal, 2000; The Relapse, RNT, 2001; The Woman in White, Palace Th., 2004; Donkeys' Years, Comedy, 2006; Office Suite, Chichester, 2007; The Importance of Being Earnest (musical), Riverside Studios, 2011; (and co-writer) My Perfect Mind, Plymouth Th. Royal, transf. Young Vic, 2013, Birmingham Repertory Th., Birmingham, 2014. Numerous television appearances include: Vershinin in Three Sisters (from RSC prod.); Lytton Strachey in No Need to Lie; Newman Noggs in Nicholas Nickleby (from RSC prod.); Gower in Pericles; Lord Peter Wimsey; Marsden in Strange Interlude; Uncle in Journey's End; No Strings. Hon. DLitt Bradford, 1989. *Publications*: Slim Chances and Unscheduled Appearances, 2011. *Recreations*: listening to music, photography, theatre history. *Address*: c/o United Agents, 12–26 Lexington Street, W1F 0LE.

**PETHICA, Sir John Bernard**, Kt 2014; PhD; FRS 1999; FREng; SFI Research Professor, since 2001, and Professor of Physics, Trinity College, Dublin; Chief Scientific Adviser, National Physical Laboratory, Teddington, 2007–17; Fellow of St Cross College, Oxford, 1986–2014 (Hon. Fellow, 2014). *Educ*: Trinity Hall, Cambridge (BA 1974; PhD 1978); MA Oxon. Lectr, Dept of Materials, 1987, Prof. of Materials Sci., 1996–2001, Vis. Prof., 2001–, Univ. of Oxford; Sony Corp. R&D Prof. (on leave of absence), Japan, 1993–94; Founding Dir, Centre for Res. on Adaptive Nanostructures and Nanodevices, Trinity Coll., Dublin, 2002–05. Dir, Nano Instruments Inc., Knoxville, Tenn, 1985–98. Physical Scis Sec. and Vice Pres., Royal Soc., 2009–14. Mem. Council, Royal Soc., 2004–06. FREng 2013. Rosenhain Medal and Prize, Inst. of Materials, 1997; Hughes Medal, Royal Soc., 2001; Holweck Medal, Soc. Française de Physique, 2002. *Publications*: contribs to jls. *Address*: Department of Physics, Trinity College Dublin, Dublin 2, Ireland.

**PETIT, Sir Dinshaw Manockjee**, 5th Bt *cr* 1890, of Petit Hall, Bombay; *b* 21 Jan. 1965; *er s* of Sir Dinshaw Manockjee Petit, 4th Bt and of his 1st wife, Nirmala Nanavatty; *S* father, 1998; *m* 1994, Laila, *d* of Homi Commissariat; one *s* one *d*. President: N. M. Petit Charities, 1998–; Sir D. M. Petit Charities, 1998–; F. D. Petit Sanatorium, 1998–; Persian Zoroastrian Amelioration Fund, 1998–; Petit Girls' Orphanage, 1998–; D. M. Petit Gymnasium, 1998–; Native Gen. Dispensary, 1998–; Bai Avabai F. Petit Residuary Estate Trust, 1998–; Two Account Trust, 1998; J. N. Petit Inst., 2004–. Trustee: Soc. for Prevention of Cruelty to Animals, 1998–; Concern India, 2005–17; J. B. Petit High Sch. for Girls, 2007–. Member: Exec. Cttee, B. D. Petit Parsi Gen. Hospital, 1998–; Mgt Cttee, Garib Zarthostiona Rehethan Fund, 2003–; Governing Body, K. R. Cama Oriental Inst., 2008–. Gov., Veermata Jijabai Tech. Inst., 1998–2015. Founder Mem., Nat. Centre for Performing Arts, 2008–. Chevalier, Ordre National du Mérite (France), 2005. *Heir: s* Rehan Jehangir Petit, *b* 4 May 1995. *Address*: Petit Hall, 66 Nepean Sea Road, Bombay 400006, India.

**PETITGAS, Franck R. M.**; Head, International, Morgan Stanley & Co., since 2018; *b* Nantes, 25 Feb. 1961; *s* of Victor and Denise Petitgas; *m* 1985, Catherine Gex; one *s*. *Educ*: Ecole Supérieure de Commerce, Paris. With S. G. Warburg & Co. Ltd, London and NY, 1986–93; Morgan Stanley & Co., NY, 1993; Morgan Stanley & Co.: Man. Dir and Hd, Global Capital Markets, Europe, until 2005; Co-Hd, Global Capital Mkts, 2005–07; Global Hd, Investment Banking, 2007–18. Trustee: Tate, 2008–15; Chichester Harbour Trust; Glyndebourne Prodns Ltd, 2016–; Mem. Council, Serpentine Gall.; Chm., Tate Foundn, 2011–. Conseiller du Commerce Extérieur, UK. Chevalier, Ordre de la Légion d'Honneur (France). *Recreations*: yachting, philosophy, arts. *E*: franck.petitgas@ms.com. *Clubs*: Royal Ocean Racing; Bosham Sailing.

**PETLEY, Vanessa Jane**; *see* Ward, V. J.

**PETO, Anthony Nicholas George**; QC 2009; *b* Salisbury, 21 Sept. 1960; *s* of Stefan and Johanna Peto; *m* 1991, Gloria Davenport; three *s* one *d*. *Educ*: Bishop Wordsworth's Sch., Salisbury; Brasenose Coll., Oxford (BA, BCL). Called to the Bar, Middle Temple, 1985; in private practice, Blackstone Chambers, Temple, specialising in commercial law, public law, civil fraud and asset recovery, 1985–; Co-Hd, Blackstone Chambers, 2012–. Counsel to Crown on Attorney Gen.'s A-Panel, 2008–09. *Recreations*: chamber music, keen amateur pianist. *Address*: Blackstone Chambers, Temple, EC4Y 9BW. *T*: (020) 7583 1770, *Fax*: (020) 7822 7350. *E*: tonypeto@blackstonechambers.com.

**PETO, Sir Francis (Michael Morton)**, 5th Bt *cr* 1855, of Somerleyton Hall, Suffolk; *b* 11 Jan. 1949; *er s* of Sir Henry George Morton Peto, 4th Bt, and Frances Jacqueline, *d* of Ralph Haldane Evers; *S* father, 2010; *m* 1974, Felicity Margaret, *d* of late Lt-Col John Alan Burns; two *s*. *Educ*: Sherborne; Leeds Univ. *Heir: s* David James Morton Peto [*b* 25 Aug. 1978; *m* 2008, Aika Yukino, *d* of Karl Engels; one *s* one *d*].

**PETO, Sir Henry (Christopher Morton Bampfylde)**, 5th Bt *cr* 1927, of Barnstaple, co. Devon; *b* 8 April 1967; *s* of Sir Michael Henry Basil Peto, 4th Bt and Sarah Susan, *y d* of Major Sir Dennis Stucley, 5th Bt; *S* father, 2008; *m* 1998, Louise Imogen, *y d* of Christopher Balck-Foote; one *s* two *d*. *Educ*: Eton; Oxford Brookes Univ. MRICS. *Heir: s* Jake Christopher Bampfylde Peto, *b* 11 Oct. 2004.

**PETO, Sir Richard**, Kt 1999; FRS 1989; Professor of Medical Statistics and Epidemiology, University of Oxford, since 1992; Fellow of Green Templeton College (formerly Green College), Oxford, since 1979; *b* 14 May 1943; *s* of Leonard Huntley Peto and Carrie Clarinda Peto; *m* 1970, Sallie Messum (marr. diss.); two *s*, and two *s* by Gale Mead (*d* 2001). *Educ*: Trinity Coll., Cambridge (MA Natural Sci.); Imperial Coll., London (MSc Statistics).

Research Officer: MRC, 1967–69; Univ. of Oxford, 1969–72; Lectr, Dept of Regius Prof. of Medicine, 1972–75, Reader in Cancer Studies, 1975–92, Univ. of Oxford. Founder FMedSci 1998. *Publications:* Natural History of Chronic Bronchitis and Emphysema, 1976; Quantification of Occupational Cancer, 1981; The Causes of Cancer, 1983; Diet, Lifestyle and Mortality in China, 1990, 2nd edn 2006; (jtly) Mortality from Smoking in Developed Countries 1950–2000, 1994, 2nd edn 2006. *Recreations:* science, children. *Address:* Richard Doll Building, Old Road Campus, Roosevelt Drive, Oxford OX3 7LF. *T:* (01865) 552830/743801.

**PETO, Prof. Timothy Edward Alexander,** DPhil; FRCP, FRCPath; Professor of Medicine, University of Oxford, since 1999; Consultant Physician in Infectious Diseases and General Medicine, John Radcliffe Hospital, since 1988; *b* London, 10 March 1950; *s* of late Stephen Peto and Johanna, (Hanni), Peto (*née* Stadlen); *m* 1974, Verity Robertson Cottrill; three *d* (and one *d* decd). *Educ:* Bishop Wordsworth's Sch., Salisbury; Brasenose Coll., Oxford (Hulme Schol.; BA 1st Cl. Animal Physiol. 1971; DPhil Neurophysiol. 1974); Oxford Med. Sch. (Hobson Meml Schol.; BM BCh 1977). MRCP 1979, FRCP 1992; FRCPath 2000. MRC Trng Fellow, 1979–82; Wellcome Res. Fellow, 1982–83; Clin. Lectr, 1982–88, Reader in Medicine, 1996–99, Univ. of Oxford. Co-Dir, Infection Theme, Oxford Biomed. Centre, 2007–; NIHR Sen. Investigator, 2009–. Scientific Sec., MRC AIDS Therapeutic Trials Cttee, 1987–2003. Hon. Scientist, MRC Clin. Trials Unit, 2000–12; Hon. Consultant, PHE, 2018–. *Publications:* contrib. articles to scientific jls on clin. trials and epidemiol. of HIV and tropical medicine, and characterization of transmission and bacterial resistance of bacterial infections using whole genome sequencing. *Recreations:* family, talking, thinking about mathematics. *Address:* Nuffield Department of Medicine, John Radcliffe Hospital, Oxford OX3 9DU. *T:* (01865) 741166. *E:* tim.peto@ndm.ox.ac.uk.

**PETRAEUS, Gen. David Howell;** Chairman, KKR Global Institute, since 2013; *b* Cornwall-on-Hudson, NY, 7 Nov. 1952; *s* of Sixtus Petraeus and Miriam Petraeus (*née* Howell); *m* 1974, Hollister Knowlton; one *s* one *d. Educ:* US Military Acad., West Point (BS 1974); US Army Command and General Staff Coll., Fort Leavenworth; Princeton Univ. (MPA 1985; PhD Internat. Relns 1987). Mil. Asst to Gen. John Galvin, SACEUR, 1987–89; Aide and Asst Exec. Officer to US Army Chief of Staff, 1989–91; Comdr, 3rd Bn, 187th Infantry Regt, 101st Airborne Div., 1991–93; ACOS for Plans, Ops and Trng, 101st Airborne Div., 1993–94; Chief of Ops, UN Force, Haiti, 1995; Comdr, 1st Bde, 82nd Airborne Div., 1995–97; Exec. Asst to Chm., Jt Chiefs, 1997–99; Asst Div. Comdr, 82nd Airborne Div., 1999–2000; COS, XVIII Airborne Corps, 2000–01; ACOS for Ops and Dep. Comdr, US Jt Interagency Counter-Terrorism Task Force, Bosnia, 2001–02; Commanding Gen., 101st Airborne Div., 2002–04 (incl. Operation Iraqi Freedom, 2003–04); Comdr, Multi-National Security Transition Command Iraq and NATO Trng Mission Iraq, 2004–05; Commanding General: Combined Arms Center, Fort Leavenworth, 2005–07; Multi-National Force—Iraq, 2007–08; Commander: US Central Command, 2008–10; NATO Internat. Security Assistance Force, and US Forces—Afghanistan, 2010–11; Dir, CIA, USA, 2011–12. Member: 82nd Airborne Div. Assoc.; 101st Airborne Div. Assoc. Defense Distinguished Service Medal (4 awards); Army Distinguished Service Medal (3 awards); Defense Superior Service Medal (2 awards); Bronze Star Medal with 'V'; State Dept Sec.'s Distinguished Service Award; NATO Meritorious Service Medal (2 awards). Officer, Order of Australia; Meritorious Service Cross (Canada); Cross of Merit of Minister of Defense (Czech Republic); Comdr, Légion d'Honneur (France); Comdr, Order of Merit (Poland); Knight Comdr's Cross (Germany); Knight Grand Cross, Order of Orange-Nassau (Netherlands); Gold Cross of Merit of the Carabinieri (Italy); Gold Award, Order of the Date Palm, (Iraq); Tong-il Security Medal (Korea); Chief of Defense Honor Emblem (Romania); Mil. Merit Order, First Cl. (UAE). *Publications:* Lessons of History and Lessons of Vietnam, 1987; (jtly) The US Army/Marine Corps Counterinsurgency Manual, 2007; articles in Washington Institute for Near East Policy, insights, Amer. Interest Mag., Parameters, Global Policy, Army Mag., Policy Options, Military Rev., Military Affairs, Army Jl, Armed Forces Jl Internat., Armed Forces and Soc., Infantry Mag., Field Artillery. *Recreations:* running, cycling, reading. *Clubs:* Cosmos (Washington, DC); Army Navy Country (Va).

**PETRE,** family name of **Baron Petre.**

**PETRE, 18th Baron** *cr* 1603; **John Patrick Lionel Petre,** KCVO 2016; Lord-Lieutenant of Essex, 2002–17; *b* 4 Aug. 1942; *s* of 17th Baron Petre and Marguerite Eileen, *d* of late Ion Wentworth Hamilton; *S* father, 1989; *m* 1965, Marcia Gwendolyn, *d* of Alfred Plumpton; two *s* one *d. Educ:* Eton; Trinity College, Oxford (MA). DL Essex, 1991. KStJ 2003. **Heir:** *s* Hon. Dominic William Petre [*b* 9 Aug. 1966; *m* 1998, Marisa Verna, *o d* of Anthony J. Perry; one *s* one *d*]. *Address:* Writtle Park, Highwood, Chelmsford, Essex CM1 3QF.

**PETRIDES, Prof. Michael,** PhD; FRS 2012; FRSC 2011; Professor, Department of Neurology and Neurosurgery and Department of Psychology, Director, Cognitive Neuroscience Unit, Montreal Neurological Institute and Hospital, since 1990, and James McGill Professor, since 2001, McGill University. *Educ:* Univ. of London; Christ's Coll., Cambridge (PhD). McGill University: Postdoctoral Fellow, 1977–79; Montreal Neurol Inst. and Hosp., 1979–. Killam Schol., 2002–07. James S. McDonnell 21st Century Scientist Award, 2001. *Publications:* (contrib.) Neuroscience of Rule-Guided Behavior, 2008; (contrib.) Neuropsychological Research: a review, 2008; Atlas of the Morphology of the Human Cerebral Cortex on the Average MNI Brain, 2018; contribs to Jl Neurosurgery, Neurosci. *Address:* Montreal Neurological Institute and Hospital, 3801 University Street, Montreal, QC H3A 2B4, Canada.

**PETRIE, Sir Peter (Charles),** 5th Bt *cr* 1918, of Carrowcarden; CMG 1980; Adviser on European and Parliamentary Affairs to Governor of Bank of England, 1989–2003; HM Diplomatic Service, retired; *b* 7 March 1932; *s* of Sir Charles Petrie, 3rd Bt, CBE, FRHistS and Jessie Cecilia (*d* 1987), *d* of Frederick James George Mason; *S* half-brother, 1988; *m* 1958, Countess Lydwine Maria Fortunata v. Oberndorff, *d* of Count v. Oberndorff, The Hague and Paris; two *s* one *d. Educ:* Westminster; Christ Church, Oxford. BA Lit. Hum., MA. 2nd Lieut Grenadier Guards, 1954–56. Entered HM Foreign Service, 1956; served in UK Delegn to NATO, Paris 1958–61; UK High Commn, New Delhi (seconded CRO), 1961–64; Chargé d'Affaires, Katmandu, 1963; Cabinet Office, 1965–67; UK Mission to UN, NY, 1969–73; Counsellor (Head of Chancery), Bonn, 1973–76; Head of European Integration Dept (Internal), FCO, 1976–79; Minister, Paris, 1979–85; Ambassador to Belgium, 1985–89. Member: Franco-British Council, 1994–2002 (Chm., British section, 1997–2002); Inst de l'Euro, Lyon, 1995–99; Acad. de Comptabilité, 1997–. Mem. Council, City Univ., 1997–2002. Chevalier, Légion d'Honneur (France), 2006. *Recreation:* country pursuits. **Heir:** *s* Charles James Petrie (OBE 2014) [*b* 16 Sept. 1959; *m* 1981, France de Hautecloque; three *s* (one *d* decd)]. *Address:* 16A Cambridge Street, SW1V 4QH; 40 rue Lauriston, 75116 Paris, France; Le Hameau du Jardin, Lestre, 50310 Montebourg, France. *E:* lydwinepo@aol.fr. *Clubs:* Brooks's, Jockey (Paris).

**PETROW, Judith Caroline;** *see* Bingham, J. C.

**PETT, Maj.-Gen. Raymond Austin,** CB 1995; MBE 1976; Chairman: Coventry and Rugby Hospital Co. plc, 2002–11; Derby Healthcare plc, 2005–07; Central Nottinghamshire Hospitals plc, 2006–07; Walsall Hospital Co. plc, 2007–11; *b* 23 Sept. 1941; *s* of late Richard John Austin Pett and Jessie Lyle Pett (*née* Adamson); *m* 1965, (Joan) Marie McGrath Price, *d* of FO Bernard Christopher McGrath, RAFVR (killed in action 1943) and of Mrs Robert Henry Benbow Price; one *s* one *d. Educ:* Christ's Coll., Finchley; RMA Sandhurst; rcds, psc. Commnd Lancashire Regt (Prince of Wales's Vols), 1961; regtl service in GB, BAOR, Swaziland and Cyprus; seconded 2nd Bn 6th QEO Gurkha Rifles, Malaysia and Hong Kong, 1967–69; Instr, RMA Sandhurst, 1969–72; 1st Bn, King's Regt, 1972; Staff Coll., 1972–73; DAA&QMG, HQ 48 Gurkha Inf. Bde, 1974–75; 1st Bn, Queen's Lancashire Regt, 1976–78; GSO2 ASD 3, MoD, 1978–80; CO, 1st Bn King's Own Royal Border Regt, 1980–82; Staff Coll. (HQ and Directing Staff), 1983–84; Col ASD 2, MoD, 1984; Col Army Plans, MoD, 1985; Comd Gurkha Field Force, 1985–86, and Comd 48 Gurkha Inf. Bde, 1986–87, Hong Kong; RCDS 1988; Dir, Army Staff Duties, MoD, 1989–91; DCS and Sen. British Officer, HQ AFNORTH, 1991–94; Dir of Infantry, 1994–96. Dir of Capital Develts, Royal Hosps NHS Trust, 1996–97; Chief Exec., Barts and the London NHS Trust, 1997–2000; Managing Director: HCP (Bidding) Ltd, 2004–06; HCP Defence Projects Ltd, 2001–04; Director: HCP (Holdings) Ltd, 2001–06; Healthcare Projects Ltd, 2001–06. Col, 6th QEO Gurkha Rifles, 1988–94; Col Comdt, King's Div., 1994–96. Trustee: Gurkha Welfare Trust, 1988–2007 (Chm., 1995–2011, Pres., 2012–, Western Br.); Somerset ACF Trust, 2008–16 (Chm., 2010–16). Chm., Army Mountaineering Assoc., 1994–96. President: Mid-Somerset Agricl Soc., 1996 (Vice-Pres., 1997–); Shepton Mallet Br., RBL, 1996–; League of Friends, Shepton Mallet Community Hosp., 2011–. Life FRSA 1997. Freeman, City of London, 2000; Liveryman, Painter Stainers' Co., 2000–. DL Somerset, 2007. *Recreations:* the arts, house restoration, cross-country ski-ing. *Clubs:* Army and Navy, Ronnie Scott's.

**PETTEGREE, Prof. Andrew David Mark,** DPhil; Professor of Modern History, University of St Andrews, since 1998; *b* 16 Sept. 1957; *s* of Kenneth William Pettegree and Jean Dorcas Pettegree; *m* 1995, Jane Karen Ryan; two *d. Educ:* Oundle Sch.; Merton Coll., Oxford (BA 1979; MA, DPhil 1983). Hanseatic Sch., Hamburg, 1982–84; Res. Fellow, Peterhouse, Cambridge, 1984–86; University of St Andrews: Lectr, 1986–94; Reader, 1994–98; Founding Dir, St Andrews Reformation Studies Inst., 1993–2004. Dir, Universal Short Title Catalogue, 2011–. FRHistS 1986 (Literary Dir, 1998–2003; Vice-Pres., 2012–14). *Publications:* Foreign Protestant Communities in Sixteenth Century London, 1986; Emden and the Dutch Revolt, 1992; The Early Reformation in Europe, 1992; Marian Protestantism, 1996; Reformation World, 2000; Europe in the Sixteenth Century, 2002; Reformation and the Culture of Persuasion, 2005; The Book in the Renaissance, 2010 (Phyllis Goodhart Gordon Prize, Renaissance Soc. of America, 2011); The Invention of News, 2014; (ed jtly) Lost Books: reconstructing the print world of pre-industrial Europe, 2014; Brand Luther, 2015. *Recreations:* golf, tennis. *Address:* School of History, University of St Andrews, St Andrews, Fife KY16 9AL. *E:* admp@St-And.ac.uk. *Club:* MCC.

**PETTIFER, Julian,** OBE 2010; freelance writer and broadcaster; *b* 21 July 1935; *s* of Stephen Henry Pettifer and Diana Mary (*née* Burton); unmarried. *Educ:* Marlborough; St John's Coll., Cambridge. Television reporter, writer and presenter: Southern TV, 1958–62; Tonight, BBC, 1962–64; 24 Hours, BBC, 1964–69; Panorama, BBC, 1969–75; Presenter, Cuba—25 years of revolution (series), ITV, 1984; Host, Busman's Holiday, ITV, 1985–86. Numerous television documentaries, including: Vietnam, War without End, 1970; The World About Us, 1976; The Spirit of '76, 1976; Diamonds in the Sky, 1979; Nature Watch, 1981–82, 1985–86, 1988, 1990, 1992; Automania, 1984; The Living Isles, 1986; Missionaries, 1990; See for Yourself, 1991; Assignment, 1991; Nature, 1992; The Culling Fields, 1999; Warnings from the Wild, 2000, 2001; radio broadcasts include: Asia File, 1995–, and Crossing Continents, 1999–, BBC Radio 4; The Sixties, BBC Radio 2, 2000. Trustee, Royal Botanic Gdns, Kew, 1993–96. President: Berks, Bucks and Oxfordshire Naturalists Trust, 1990–2009; RSPB, 1995–2001 and 2004–09; Vice-Pres., RSNC, 1992–. Reporter of the Year Award, Guild of Television Directors and Producers, 1968; Cherry Kearton Award for Contribution to Wildlife Films, RGS, 1990; Mungo Park Medal, RSGS, 1998. *Publications:* (jtly) Diamonds in the Sky: a social history of air travel, 1979; (jtly) Nature Watch, 1981; (jtly) Automania, 1984; (jtly) Missionaries, 1990; (jtly) Nature Watch, 1994. *Recreations:* gardening, sport, cinema. *Address:* c/o Bryony Kinnear, Apartment 1, 72 Courtfield Gardens, SW5 0NL.

**PETTIFER, Dr Richard Edward William,** MBE 2008; meteorological consultant, 1998–2016; General Secretary, PRIMET, 2007–16; *b* 19 Sept. 1941; *s* of Reginald Charles Edward Pettifer and Irene May Pettifer (*née* Bradley); *m* 1st, 1965, Colleen Rosemary Adams (*d* 1984); one *s* two *d*; 2nd, 1986, Maureen Eileen Macartney (*née* McCullough); one step *d. Educ:* Ealing County Grammar Sch. for Boys; London Polytechnic; Queen's Univ., Belfast (BSc 1st cl. Physics 1969; PhD Laser and Atmos. Physics 1975). FRMetS 1979; CMet 1994–2018. Asst Dir, Meteorological Office, 1980–85; Managing Director: Vaisala (UK) Ltd, 1985–98; Scientific and Technical Mgt Ltd, 1998–2005. Exec. Dir, RMetS, 1998–2006. Chairman: COST Project 43, 1978–84; LINK/Seasense, 1994–2001. Vice Pres., CIMO, 1980–84. *Publications:* over 100 papers, book contribs, public reports, etc on meteorological/oceanographic instrumentation and measurements, commercial meteorological mkt in Europe and the case for open data in meteorology. *Recreations:* gardening, golf, bee keeping, cricket, community support projects. *Address:* West Oaks, 4 Cranes Road, Sherborne St John, Hants RG24 9JD. *T:* 07739 212227. *E:* pettifer190@btinternet.com. *Clubs:* Meteorological; Weybrook Park Golf; Eversley Cricket; The Hambledon.

**PETTIGREW, Prof. Andrew Marshall,** OBE 2009; PhD; FBA 2003; Professor of Strategy and Organisation: Saïd Business School, University of Oxford, 2008–15, now Emeritus; Birkbeck, University of London; *b* 11 June 1944; *s* of late George Pettigrew and Martha (*née* Marshall); *m* 1967, Mary Ethna Veronica Moores (marr. diss. 2009); three *s* (one *d* decd); *m* 2009, Emma Clare Bennett. *Educ:* Corby Grammar Sch.; Liverpool Univ. (BA 1965; Dip. Ind. Admin 1967); Manchester Univ. (PhD Bus. Admin 1970). Res. Associate, Manchester Business Sch., 1966–69; Vis. Asst Prof., Yale Univ., 1969–71; Lectr, London Business Sch., 1971–76; Warwick Business School, University of Warwick: Prof. of Organisational Behaviour, 1976–85; Dir, Centre for Corporate Strategy and Change, 1985–95; Prof. of Strategy and Orgn, 1995–2003; Associate Dean of Res., 2002–03; Dean of Mgt Sch. and Prof. of Strategy and Orgn, Univ. of Bath, 2003–08. Sen. Golding Fellow, Brasenose Coll., Oxford, 2009–. Vis. Schol., 1981, Vis. Prof., 2001, Harvard Business Sch.; Vis. Schol., Stanford Univ., 1982. Member: Industry and Employment Cttee, ESRC, 1984–87; Jt Cttee, ESRC and SERC, 1988–91; Council, ESRC, 2005–10; Bd, Eur. Foundn for Mgt Develt, 2006–09 (Vice Pres., 2008–09; Chm., R & D Cttee, 2010–); Dep. Chm., Mgt Studies Panel, RAE, UFC, 1992. Fellow: British Acad. of Mgt, 1996 (Chm., 1986–90; Pres., 1990–93); Acad. of Mgt, 1997; SMS, 2005; AcSS 1999. Hon. Dr Linköping, 1989; Hon. LLD Liverpool, 2010; Dr *hc* Copenhagen Business Sch., 2010. *Publications:* The Politics of Organisational Decision Making, 1973; (with E. Mumford) Implementing Strategic Decisions, 1975; The Awakening Giant: continuity and change in ICI, 1985; The Management of Strategic Change, 1987; (with R. Whipp) Managing

Change for Competitive Success, 1991; (jtly) Shaping Strategic Change: making change in the NHS, 1992; (jtly) The New Public Management in Action, 1996; (with E. Fenton) The Innovating Organisation, 2000; (jtly) The Handbook of Strategy and Management, 2002; (jtly) Innovative Forms of Organising, 2003; (jtly) The Institutional Development of Business Schools, 2014; articles in professional jls. *Recreations:* antiquarian horology, military history, Herefordshire. *Address:* Saïd Business School, University of Oxford, Park End Street, Oxford OX1 1HP. *E:* andrew.pettigrew@sbs.ox.ac.uk.

**PETTIGREW, Colin William;** Sheriff of North Strathclyde at Paisley, since 2010 (Floating Sheriff, 2002–10); *b* 19 June 1957; *s* of Thomas Whitelaw Pettigrew and Mary Macrae Pettigrew (*née* Muir); *m* 1981, Linda McGill; one *s* one *d*. *Educ:* High Sch. of Glasgow; Glasgow Univ. (LLB Hons 1978). Admitted as solicitor, 1980. Trainee solicitor, 1978–80, Asst Solicitor, 1980–82, McClure Naismith Brodie & Co., Glasgow; Asst Solicitor, 1982–83, Partner, 1983–2002, Borland Johnson & Orr, subseq. Borland Montgomerie Keyden, Glasgow and T. J. & W. A. Dykes, Hamilton. Pres., Sheriffs' Assoc., 2015–17. Clerk to Congregational Bd, Uddington Old Parish Ch, Church of Scotland, 2013–18 (Elder, 1983–). *Recreations:* golf, gardening, travel. *Address:* Paisley Sheriff Court House, St James Street, Paisley PA3 2HW. *T:* (0141) 887 5291.

**PETTIGREW, James Neilson;** Chairman: Clydesdale Bank plc, since 2014; RBC Europe Ltd, since 2009; Scottish Financial Enterprise, since 2016; BlueBay Asset Management, since 2017; Miton Group plc, since 2017; Virgin Money plc, since 2018; *b* Dundee; *s* of James Pettigrew and Sheila Pettigrew; *m* 1984, Dr Joanna Lawson. *Educ:* Aberdeen Univ. (LLB); Univ. of Glasgow (Dip. Accountancy). FCT 1994. CA trainee, Arthur Young McCleland Moores & Co., 1980–84; Chief Accountant, J. Fleming & Co. Ltd, 1985–87; Divl Financial Dir, 1988–92, Gp Treas., 1993–98, Sedgwick Gp plc; Chief Finance Officer, ICAP plc, 1999–2006; Chief Operating Officer and Chief Finance Officer, Ashmore Gp plc, 2006–07; CEO, CMC Markets plc, 2007–09. Chm., Edinburgh Investment Trust plc, 2011–17. Non-exec. Dir, Aberdeen Asset Mgt plc, 2010–16; Senior Independent Director: Crest Nicholson plc, 2013–17; Rathbone Brothers plc, 2017– (Mem., Audit, Remuneration, Risk and Nomination Cttees, 2017–). Member: Foundn Bd, PS Waverley; Friends of TS Queen Mary; Adv. Bd, TheCityUK. Pres., ICAS, 2015–16 (Dep. Pres., 2014–15). Co-Chm., Scottish Financial Services Adv. Bd, 2016–. FRSA. *Recreations:* golf, gardening. *Club:* Caledonian.

**PETTIGREW, John Mark;** Chief Executive, National Grid, since 2016; *b* Pontypridd, Wales, 26 Oct. 1968; *s* of John and Patricia Pettigrew; *m* 1996, Lesley Davies; two *d*. *Educ:* University Coll. Cardiff, later Univ. of Wales Coll. of Cardiff (BSc Econs; MSc Internat. Econs and Banking); Harvard Univ. (AMP). Joined National Grid, 1991; Dir of Engrg, 2003–07; Chief Operating Officer and Exec. Vice Pres. for US Electricity Distribution and Generation, 2007–10; Chief Operating Officer, 2010–14; UK Exec. Dir, 2014–16. *Recreations:* Rugby, walking, running, golf, cooking. *Address:* National Grid plc, 1–3 The Strand, WC2N 5EH. *T:* (020) 7004 3000.

**PETTIGREW, Hon. Pierre Stewart;** PC (Canada) 1996; Executive Advisor, International, Deloitte & Touche, Toronto, since 2006; Member, Advisory Board, Forbes Manhattan, Toronto, since 2006; *b* 18 April 1951. *Educ:* Univ. du Québec à Trois Rivières (BA Philos.); Balliol Coll., Oxford (MPhil Internat. Relns 1976). Dir, Pol Cttee, NATO Assembly, Brussels, 1976–78; Exec. Asst to Leader of Quebec Liberal Party, 1978–81; Foreign Policy Advr to Prime Minister, 1981–84; Vice Pres., Samson Bélair Deloitte & Touche Internat. (Montreal), 1985–95. MP (L) Papineau, Quebec, 1996–2006. Minister: for Internat. Co-operation, 1996; responsible for La Francophonie, 1996; of Human Resources Develt, 1996–99; for Internat. Trade, 1999–2003; of Health, of Intergovtl Affairs, and responsible for Official Langs, 2003–04; of Foreign Affairs, 2004–06. Bd Mem., Inter Amer. Dialogue, Washington, 2010–. Hon. LLD Warwick, 2008. *Publications:* Pour une politique de la confiance, 1999. *E:* ppettigrew@deloitte.ca.

**PETTINI, Prof. Max,** PhD; FRS 2010; Professor of Observational Astronomy, University of Cambridge, 2002–16, now Emeritus; *b* 15 June 1949. *Educ:* University Coll. London (PhD Astrophysics 1978; Hon. Fellow 2011). Royal Greenwich Observatory; Anglo-Australian Observatory; UWA. *Publications:* articles in jls. *Address:* Institute of Astronomy, University of Cambridge, Madingley Road, Cambridge CB3 0HA.

**PETTITT, Adam Sven,** MA; Head, Highgate School, since 2006; *b* 5 Feb. 1966; *s* of Robin Garth Pettitt and Elizabeth Margaret Pettitt (*née* Jenkins); *m* 1997, Barbara Sauron; two *s* one *d*. *Educ:* Hailsham Sch.; Eastbourne Sixth Form Coll.; New Coll., Oxford (BA Mod and Medieval Langs 1988; MA 1995). Eton Coll., 1988–92; Hd of German, Oundle Sch., 1992–94; Hd of Mod. Langs, Abingdon Sch., 1994–98; Second Master, Norwich Sch., 1998–2006. Governor: Havelock Acad., Grimsby, 2006–11; Brighton Coll., 2007–; The Hall, Hampstead, 2008–17; London Acad. of Excellence Stratford, 2012–; Dep. Chm. Govs, London Acad. of Excellence Tottenham, 2017–. *Recreations:* cross-country running, reading, old buildings. *Address:* Highgate School, North Road, N6 4AY. *T:* (020) 8347 3576, *Fax:* (020) 8340 7674. *Club:* Athenæum.

**PETTITT, Gordon Charles,** OBE 1991; transport management consultant, 1993–2000; Managing Director, Regional Railways, British Rail, 1991–92; *b* 12 April 1934; *s* of Charles and Annie Pettitt; *m* 1956, Ursula Margareta Agnes Hokamp; three *d*. *Educ:* St Columba's Coll., St Albans; Pitman's Coll., London. FCILT. British Rail, 1950–92: Freight Sales Manager, Eastern Reg., 1976; Chief Passenger Manager, Western Reg., 1978; Divl Manager, Liverpool Street, Eastern Reg., 1979; Dep. Gen. Manager, 1983, Gen. Manager, 1985, Southern Reg.; Dir, Provincial, 1990–91. Director: Connex Rail Ltd, 1997–98; Heathrow Express Operating Co. Ltd, 1997–99; Network Rail Property Adv. Bd, 2003–06. Pres., Instn of Railway Operators, 2000–02 (Fellow, 2002). Governor, Middlesex Univ. (formerly Polytechnic), 1989–95. President: Bluebell Railway Preservation Soc., 2014–; Woking Homes, 2017–. *Recreations:* walking, foreign travel, Victorian art. *Address:* Beeches Green, 539 Woodham Lane, Woking, Surrey GU21 5SP.

**PETTS, Prof. Judith Irene,** CBE 2012; PhD; Vice-Chancellor, University of Plymouth, since 2016; *b* 7 Jan. 1954; *d* of Alexander and Rene Armitt; *m* 1977, Prof. Geoffrey Eric Petts (*d* 2018). *Educ:* Univ. of Exeter (BA Hons (Geog.) 1975); Loughborough Univ. (PhD 1996). MCIWM 2002–16. Loughborough University: Lectr, Centre for Extension Studies, 1987–95; Sen. Lectr, 1995–97, Dir, 1997–99, Centre for Hazard and Risk Mgt; University of Birmingham: Prof. of Envmtl Risk Mgt, 1999–2010; Hd, Sch. of Geog., Earth and Envmtl Scis, 2001–07; Pro-Vice-Chancellor (Res. and Knowledge Transfer), 2007–10; University of Southampton: Prof. of Envmtl Risk Mgt, 2010–16; Dean, Faculty of Social and Human Scis, 2010–13; Pro-Vice-Chancellor (Res. and Enterprise), 2014–16. Member: Council, NERC, 2000–06; Royal Commn on Envmtl Pollution, 2005–11; EPSRC Societal Issues Panel, 2006–11; EPSRC Strategic Adv. Network, 2011–13; Science Adv. Council, DEFRA, 2011–16; Council, BBSRC, 2014–18; Innovation Adv. Bd, NERC, 2015–18; Bd, Heart of SW LEP, 2016–; Council, Marine Biological Assoc., 2018–. FRGS 1999; FRSA 2003; FAcSS (AcSS 2007). *Publications:* (with G. Eduljee) Environmental Impact Assessment for Waste Treatment and Disposal Facilities, 1994; (jtly) Risk-based Contaminated Land Investigation and Assessment, 1997; (ed) Handbook of Environmental Impact Assessment, 1999. *Recreations:* travelling to remote places (particularly the Arctic), walking. *Address:* University of Plymouth, Drake Circus, Plymouth, Devon PL4 8AA.

**PETTS, Timothy David; His Honour Judge Petts;** a Circuit Judge, since 2018; *b* Gravesend, 1973; *s* of Dr David Petts and Pamela Petts; *m* 2004, Dr Sara Elin Roberts; two *s*. *Educ:* King Edward VI Sch., Chelmsford; Jesus Coll., Oxford (Organ Schol.; MA Juris.; MJur Eur. and Comparative Law); Inns of Court Sch. of Law. Called to the Bar, Inner Temple, 1996; in practice as barrister, 12 King's Bench Walk, 1997–2018; a Recorder, 2008–18. Contributing Ed., 2005–17, Gen. Ed., 2017–, Kemp & Kemp: Personal Injury Law, Practice and Procedure. *Recreations:* organ and choral music, improving my Welsh. *Address:* Cardiff Civil and Family Justice Centre, 2 Park Street, Cardiff CF10 1ET.

**PETTY, Prof. Michael Charles,** PhD, DSc; Professor of Engineering, University of Durham, 1994–2017, now Emeritus; Co-Director, Durham Centre for Molecular and Nanoscale Electronics (formerly for Molecular Electronics), 1987–2013; *b* 30 Dec. 1950; *s* of John Leonard Petty and Doreen Rosemary Petty (*née* Bellarby); *m* 1998, Anne Mathers Brawley (*d* 2017); one step *d*. *Educ:* Sussex Univ. (BSc 1st Cl. Hons Electronics 1972; DSc 1994); Imperial Coll., London (PhD 1976). University of Durham: Lectr in Applied Physics, 1976–88; Sen. Lectr, Sch. of Engrg, 1988–94; Chm., Sch. of Engrg, 1997–2000; Sir James Knott Res. Fellow, 2000–01; Chm. Council, St Mary's Coll., 2002–09. Non-exec. Dir, Centre of Excellence for Nanotechnol., Micro and Photonic Systems, 2004–06. *Publications:* Langmuir-Blodgett Films, 1995; Introduction to Molecular Electronics, 1996; Molecular Electronics, 2007; The Professor's Book of Whimsy, 2018; Organic and Molecular Electronics, 2019; numerous contribs on molecular electronics and nanoelectronics to scientific jls. *Recreations:* art, photography, gardening, wandering in the Yorkshire Dales, supporter of Middlesbrough and Crystal Palace FCs. *Address:* Department of Engineering, University of Durham, South Road, Durham DH1 3LE. *T:* (0191) 334 2419.

**PETTY-FITZMAURICE,** family name of Marquess of Lansdowne.

**PEYTON, Kathleen Wendy,** MBE 2014; writer (as K. M. Peyton); *b* 2 Aug. 1929; *d* of William Joseph Herald and Ivy Kathleen Herald; *m* 1950, Michael Peyton; two *d*. *Educ:* Wimbledon High Sch.; Manchester Sch. of Art (ATD). Taught art at Northampton High Sch., 1953–55; started writing seriously after birth of first child, although had already had 4 books published. *Publications:* as Kathleen Herald: Sabre, the Horse from the Sea, 1947, USA 1963; The Mandrake, 1949; Crab the Roan, 1953; as K. M. Peyton: North to Adventure, 1959, USA 1965; Stormcock Meets Trouble, 1961; The Hard Way Home, 1962; Windfall, 1963, USA (as Sea Fever), 1963; Brownsea Silver, 1964; The Maplin Bird, 1964, USA 1965 (New York Herald Tribune Award, 1965); The Plan for Birdsmarsh, 1965, USA 1966? Thunder in the Sky, 1966, USA 1967; Flambards Trilogy (Guardian Award, 1970; televised, 1977): Flambards, 1967, USA 1968; The Edge of the Cloud, 1969, USA 1969 (Carnegie Medal, 1969); Flambards in Summer, 1969, USA 1970; Fly-by-Night, 1968, USA 1969; Pennington's Seventeenth Summer, 1970, USA (as Pennington's Last Term), 1971; The Beethoven Medal, 1971, USA 1972; The Pattern of Roses, 1972, USA 1973 (televised); Pennington's Heir, 1973, USA 1974; The Team, 1975; The Right-Hand Man, 1977; Prove Yourself a Hero, 1977, USA 1978; A Midsummer Night's Death, 1978, USA 1979; Marion's Angels, 1979, USA 1979; Flambards Divided, 1981; Dear Fred, 1981, USA 1981; Going Home, 1983, USA 1983; Who, Sir? Me, Sir?, 1983 (televised); The Last Ditch, 1984, USA (as Free Rein), 1983; Froggett's Revenge, 1985; The Sound of Distant Cheering, 1986; Downhill All the Way, 1988; Darkling, 1989, USA 1990; Skylark, 1989; No Roses Round the Door, 1990; Poor Badger, 1991, USA 1991; Late to Smile, 1992; The Boy Who Wasn't There, 1992, USA 1992; The Wild Boy, 1993; Snowfall, 1994, USA 1998; The Swallow Tale, 1995; Swallow Summer, 1996; Swallow the Star, 1997; Unquiet Spirits, 1997; Firehead, 1998; Blind Beauty, 1999; Small Gains, 2003; Greater Gains, 2005; Blue Skies and Gunfire, 2006; Minna's Quest, 2007; No Turning Back, 2008; A Long Way from Home, 2009; Paradise House, 2011; When the Siren Sounded, 2013; All that Glitters, 2014; Wild Lily, 2015. *Recreations:* walking, gardening. *Address:* Rookery Cottage, North Fambridge, Chelmsford, Essex CM3 6LP.

**PEYTON, Rt Rev. Dr Nigel;** JP; Bishop of Brechin, 2011–17; Honorary Assistant Bishop, Diocese of Lincoln, since 2017; permission to officiate, Diocese of Southwell and Nottingham, since 2018; *b* 5 Feb. 1951; *s* of Hubert Peyton and Irene Louise Peyton (*née* Ellis); *m* 1981, Anne Marie Thérèse (*née* McQuillan), widow of Colin Campbell; one *s* one *d* (and one *d* decd). *Educ:* Latymer Upper Sch.; Univ. of Edinburgh (MA 1973; BD 1976); Edinburgh Theol Coll.; Union Theol Seminary, NY (Scottish Fellow, 1976; STM 1977); Univ. of Lancaster (PhD 2009). Deacon 1976, priest 1977; Chaplain, St Paul's Cathedral, Dundee, 1976–82; Dio. Youth Chaplain, Brechin, 1976–85; Priest-in-charge, All Souls, Invergowrie, 1979–85; Vicar, All Saints, Nottingham, 1985–91; Priest-in-charge, Lambley, 1991–99; Dio. Ministry Develt Advr, Southwell, 1991–99; Archdeacon of Newark, 1999–2011. Hon. Canon: Southwell Minster, 1999–2011; Des Moines, Iowa, 2012–. Chaplain: University Hosp., Dundee, 1982–85; Nottingham Bluecoat Sch., 1990–92; Bishop, Mission to Seafarers Scotland, 2013–17. Bishops' Selector, 1992–2000, Sen. Vocational Selector, 2001–11. Proctor in Convocation, 1995–2010. Dir, Ecclesiastical Insce Gp, 2005–12. Gov., Abertay Univ. (formerly Univ. of Abertay, Dundee), 2013–17; Gov., Bishop Grosseteste Univ., Lincoln, 2018–. Hon. Teaching Fellow, Univ. of Lancaster, 2010–18; Hon. Schol., Univ. of Liverpool, 2018. Columnist, Dundee Courier, 2012–17. JP Nottingham, 1987. *Publications:* Dual Role Ministry, 1998; (jtly) Managing Clergy Lives, 2013. *Recreations:* grandparenting, music, reading, gardening, walking, real ale. *Address:* 8 Bishops Place, Welton, Lincoln LN2 3FR. *T:* (01673) 862174, 07974 402449. *E:* nigel@peytons.org. *Clubs:* Royal Scots (Edinburgh); Nottingham Forest Football.

**PEYTON, Oliver,** Hon. OBE 2012; Founder and Chairman, Peyton and Byrne (formerly Gruppo Ltd); *b* 26 Sept. 1961; *s* of Patrick Peyton; *m* 1999, Charlotte Polizzi; two *s* one *d*. *Educ:* Leicester Poly. (Textiles course 1979). Founder, The Can night club, Brighton, 1981; owner, import business, 1985–92; owner, Gruppo Ltd, 1993; proprietor of restaurants: Atlantic Bar and Grill, Regent Palace Hotel, London, 1994–2005; Coast, Mayfair, 1995–2000 (Best Restaurant, The Times; Restaurant of Year, Time Out, 1998); Mash, Oxford Circus, 1998; Isola, subseq. Iso-bar, Knightsbridge, 1999–2004; The Admiralty, Somerset House, 2000–02 (Best New Restaurant, Time Out); Inn the Park, St James's Park, 2004; National Dining Rooms and National Café, Nat. Gall., 2006–; Wallace Restaurant, Wallace Collection, 2006–; Meals Café and Bakery, Heal's, Tottenham Ct Rd, 2006; Food From Kew, Royal Botanic Gardens; Restaurant at the Royal Academy, 2011; Peyton & Byrne bakeries.

**PEYTON-JONES, Dame Julia,** DBE 2016 (OBE 2003); Director, Serpentine Gallery, 1991–2016, and Co-Director, Exhibitions and Programmes; Professor, University of the Arts, London, since 2008; Senior Global Director, Galerie Thaddaeus Ropac, since 2017; *b* 18 Feb. 1952; *d* of late Jeremy Norman Peyton-Jones and Rhona Gertrude Jean (*née* Wood); *m* 1975, Prosper Riley-Smith (marr. diss. 1985); one *d*. *Educ:* Tudor Hall; Byam Shaw Sch. of Drawing and Painting (Dip BSD; LCAD); Royal Coll. of Art (MA; Sen. Fellow, 2008). LWT/Byam Shaw Bursary, 1973–74, 1974–75; John Minton Travelling

Schol., 1978. Started 20th century Picture Dept, Phillips, auctioneers, 1974–75; Lectr, Painting and Humanities Depts, Edinburgh Sch. of Art, 1978–79; Organiser: Atlantis Gall. London, 1980–81; Wapping Artists' Open Studios Exhibn, 1981–82; Tolly Cobbold Eastern Arts 4th Nat. Exhibn, Cambridge and tour, 1982–84; Raoul Dufy 1877–1953 exhibn, Hayward Gall., 1983–84; Linbury Prize for Stage Design (selection and exhibn), 1986–87 (Mem., Exec. Cttee, 1988–96); Sponsorship Officer, Arts Council and S Bank Bd, 1984–87; Curator, Hayward Gall., 1988–91. Arts Council: Collection Purchaser, 1989–90; Mem., Visual Arts Projects Cttee, 1991–93; Mem., Visual Arts, Photography and Architecture Panel, 1994–96. Member: Westminster Public Art Adv. Panel, 1996–; Artists' Film and Video Adv. Panel, 1997–99. Jury Member: Citibank Private Banking Photography Prize, 1997; BP Portrait Award, NPG, 1997–99; Turner Prize, 2000. Trustee: Public Art Develt Trust, 1987–88; Chisenhale Trust, 1987–89; New Contemporaries Exhibn, 1988–90; The Place, 2002. Painter, 1974–87; exhibitions include: Riverside Studios (individual), 1978; ICA, 1973; John Moores, Liverpool, 1978; Royal Scottish Acad., 1979. Mem. Ct of Govs, London Inst., 1998–2002. Hon. FRIBA 2003; Hon. FRCA 1997. Lifetime Achievement Award, Women of the World Festival, 2016. *Recreations:* contemporary arts in general, visual arts in particular.

**PFEIFFER, Michelle;** actress; *b* Santa Ana, Calif, 29 April 1958; *d* of late Dick Pfeiffer and of Donna Pfeiffer; *m* 1st, 1981, Peter Horton (marr. diss.); 2nd, 1993, David E. Kelley; one *s*; one adopted *d*. *Educ:* Fountain High Valley Sch., Calif. Co-owner, Via Rosa (production co.), 1989–2001. *Theatre:* Playground in the Fall, LA, 1981; Twelfth Night, NY 1989. *Films include:* Falling in Love Again, 1980; Grease 2, 1982; Scarface, 1983; Into the Night, Ladyhawke, 1985; Sweet Liberty, 1986; Amazon Women on the Moon, The Witches of Eastwick, 1987; Married to the Mob, 1988; Tequila Sunrise, Dangerous Liaisons, The Fabulous Baker Boys (Best Actress, Golden Globe Awards, 1990), 1989; The Russia House, 1990; Frankie and Johnny, 1991; Batman Returns, 1992; Love Field, 1993; The Age of Innocence, Wolf, My Posse Don't Do Homework, 1994; Dangerous Minds, Up Close and Personal, To Gillian on her 37th Birthday, 1996; One Fine Day (also exec. prod.), Privacy, 1997; A Thousand Acres (also prod.), 1998; The Deep End of the Ocean, A Midsummer Night's Dream, 1999; The Story of Us, What Lies Beneath, 2000; I Am Sam, 2002; White Oleander, 2003; Hairspray, Stardust, 2007; Chéri, Personal Effects, 2009; Dark Shadows, 2012; The Family, 2013; Murder on the Orient Express, 2017; Ant-Man and the Wasp, 2018; Avengers: Endgame, 2019. *Television includes:* Delta House, The Solitary Man, 1979; B. A. D. Cats, 1980; Collie and Son, Splendour in the Grass, The Children Nobody Wanted, 1981; One Too Many, 1983; Power, Passion and Murder, Natica Jackson, 1987. *Address:* c/o CAA, 2000 Avenue of the Stars, Los Angeles, CA 90067, USA.

**PFIRTER, Rogelio (Francisco Emilio);** Ambassador of Argentina to the Holy See, since 2016; *b* 25 Aug. 1948; *s* of Rogelio and Amanda Pfirter von Mayenfisch; *m* 1980, Isabel Serantes Braun. *Educ:* Colegio Inmaculada SJ, Argentina; Universidad del Litoral (grad as lawyer); Inst. of Foreign Service, Argentina. Third Sec., S America Dept, 1974; Second, then First Sec., Perm. Mission to UN, 1975–80; Counsellor: Undersecretariat of Foreign Affairs, 1980–81; London, 1982; Minister Counsellor, then Minister Plenipotentiary, Perm. Mission to UN, 1982–90; Alternate Perm. Rep. to UN, 1989; Dep. Hd, Foreign Minister's Cabinet, 1990–91; Dir, Internat. Security, Nuclear and Space Affairs, 1991; Under-Sec. of Foreign Affairs, 1992–95; Mem., Posting and Promotion Bd, 1993–95; Argentine Ambassador to UK, 1995–2000; Pres., Argentine Delegn, River Plate Commn, 2000–02; Under-Sec. of Foreign Affairs, 2002; Dir-Gen., Technical Secretariat, OPCW, 2002–10. Mem., Bd of Dirs, Argentine Nat. Commn for Space Activities, 1994–95. Pres., General Assembly, IMO, 1993–97; Member: UN Adv. Bd on Disarmament Matters, 1993–96; Consulting Bd, G8 Global Partnership's Internat. Working Gp, 2011–12; IISS, 2012–; Vice Chm., Global Agenda Council on Nuclear, Biol and Chemical Weapons, World Econ. Forum, 2010–12. Laurea ad hon. in Industrial Chem., Bologna, 2010. Interfaith Award, Internat. Council of Christians and Jews, 1998; City Council Medal, City of Ieper, Belgium; Consagración Prize, Argentine Nat. Acad. of Scis, 2017. Order of Merit, Cavaliere di Gran Croce (Italy), 1992; Order of Isabel la Católica (Spain), 1994; Nat. Order of Merit in the Great Cross (Colombia), 2005; Sigillum of the Alma Mater Studiorum (Bologna), 2006; Medal of Honour of Pope Benedict XVI, 2006; Order of Duke Branimira (Croatia), 2006; Grand Cross: Order of Merit (Chile), 2010; Order of Merit (Germany), 2010; Officier, Légion d'Honneur (France), 2010; Commander, Order of Orange-Nassau (Netherlands), 2010. *Publications:* (jtly) Cuentos Originales, 1965; articles on policy. *Address:* Vía della Conciliazione, 22, 00193 Rome, Italy. *Clubs:* White's; Círculo de Armas (Buenos Aires); Circolo della Caccia (Rome).

**PHAROAH, Prof. Peter Oswald Derrick,** MD; FRCP, FRCPCH, FFPHM; Professor of Public Health (formerly of Community Health), University of Liverpool, 1979–97, now Professor Emeritus; *b* 19 May 1934; *s* of Oswald Higgins Pharoah and Phyllis Christine Gahan; *m* 1960, Margaret Rose McMinn; three *s* one *d*. *Educ:* Lawrence Memorial Royal Military School, Lovedale, India; Palmers School, Grays, Essex; St Mary's Hospital Medical School. MD, MSc. Graduated, 1958; Med. House Officer and Med. Registrar appointments at various London Hosps, 1958–63; MO and Research MO, Dept of Public Health, Papua New Guinea, 1963–74; Sen. Lectr in Community Health, London School of Hygiene and Tropical Medicine, 1974–79. *Publications:* Endemic Cretinism, 1971. *Recreations:* walking, philately. *Address:* 11 Fawley Road, Liverpool L18 9TE. *T:* (0151) 724 4896.

**PHELAN, Sean Patrick;** Founder, 1995, and Chairman, 1995–2007, Multimap.com (sold to Microsoft, 2007); *b* 8 April 1958; *s* of Anthony Michael Phelan and Gwendoline Theresa Phelan (*née* Stock); partner, Audrey Mandela. *Educ:* St Ignatius Coll., Enfield; Univ. of Sussex (BSc Electronic Engrg); Institute Theseus, Sophia Antipolis, France (MBA). With Geac Computers, 1982–89; Principal Analyst, Yankee Gp Europe, 1991–95; Principal Consultant, Telecommunications and Media Convergence Practice, KPMG, 1995. Active early-stage investor through two angel networks, Cambridge Angels and London Business Sch.'s E100. *Recreations:* sailing, travel. *Address:* 2 Hampstead Hill Gardens, NW3 2PL.

**PHELPS, Annamarie,** CBE 2016; Vice Chairman, British Olympic Association, since 2017; Chairman, British Horseracing Authority, since 2019; *b* London, 24 May 1966; *d* of Vincent Stapleton and Ethna Stapleton; *m* 1997, Richard Charles Phelps; two *s* one *d*. *Educ:* Watford Grammar Sch. for Girls; Loreto Coll., St Albans; St John's Coll., Cambridge (BA Geog. 1987; Hon. Fellow, 2019). Rowing: World Championships: Silver Medal, lightweight coxless four, Vienna 1991, Montreal 1992, Indianapolis 1994; Gold Medal, lightweight coxless four, Prague 1993; Bronze, lightweight coxless 4, Commonwealth Regatta, London Ont 1994; Indoor Rowing World Championships: World Champion, lightweight women, 1992–94; world record holder, lightweight women, 1992–95. Fine Art Society, London: Decorative Arts Dir, 1994–2002; non-exec. Dir, 2002–; independent decorative arts specialist, 2002–. Editor, Decorative Art Soc. Jl, 2007–12. Director: British Rowing (formerly Amateur Rowing Assoc.), 1996–2018 (Chm., 2013–18); British Olympic Assoc., 2015–; Trustee, British Paralympic Assoc., 2008–18 (Vice Chm., 2013–18); Commonwealth Liaison, World Rowing Fedn, 2016–; Member, Board: European Rowing, 2017–; Head of Charles Regatta Inc., Boston, USA, 2018–. Chair, Cycling Ind. Rev., 2016–17. Chm., Cambridge Univ. Women's Boat Club, 2010–14; Dir, Boat Race Co. Ltd, 2012–14. Steward, Henley Royal Regatta, 2002–. Mem., Bd of Govs, Latymer Foundn at Hammersmith, 2016–. Freeman: City of London, 2006; Watermen and Lightermen's Co., 2012; Goldsmiths' Co., 2006 (Liveryman, 2012). DUniv York, 2017. *Publications:* as Annamarie Stapleton: (jtly) Austerity to Affluence: British art and design 1945–1962, 1997; John Moyr Smith, 1839–1912: a Victorian designer, 2002; (jtly) Artists' Textiles 1945–1970, 2002; (jtly) Jacqueline Groag: Wiener Werkstatte to American Modern, 2009; (jtly) Artists' Textiles in Britain and America 1940–1976, 2012; (contrib.) The Ambassador Magazine, 2012; (jtly) Pop!: design culture fashion, 2012; contrib. articles to Country Life, Decorative Art Soc. Jl, Rowing and Regatta Mag. *Address:* British Olympic Association, 101 Cavendish Street, W1W 6XH. *Clubs:* Chelsea Arts; Thames Rowing; Cambridge Univ. Women's Boat; Hillingdon Rowing (Hon. Mem.).

**PHELPS, Prof. Edmund Strother,** PhD; McVickar Professor of Political Economy, since 1982, and Director, Center on Capitalism and Society, since 2001, Columbia University, New York; Dean, New Huadu Business School, Minjiang University, 2010–16, now Hon. Dean; *b* 26 July 1933; *s* of Edmund Strother Phelps and Florence Esther Phelps (*née* Stone); *m* 1974, Viviana Regina Montdor. *Educ:* Amherst Coll., (BA 1955); Yale Univ. (PhD 1959). Economist, RAND Corp., 1959–60; Asst Prof., 1960–62, Associate Prof., 1963–66, Yale Univ.; Professor of Economics: Univ. of Pennsylvania, 1966–71; Columbia Univ., 1971–78, 1979–82; New York Univ., 1978–79. Nobel Prize in Economics, 2006. *Publications:* Fiscal Neutrality Toward Economic Growth, 1965; Golden Rules of Economic Growth, 1966; (jtly) Microeconomic Foundations of Employment and Inflation Theory, 1970; Inflation Policy and Unemployment Theory, 1972; Studies in Macroeconomic Theory, vol. 1, 1979, vol. 2, 1980; Political Economy, 1985; (jtly) The Slump in Europe, 1988; Structural Slumps, 1994 (trans. Chinese, 2003); Rewarding Work, 1997; Enterprise and Inclusion in the Italian Economy, 2002; Mass Flourishing, 2013; articles in learned jls. *Address:* Department of Economics, Columbia University, 1126 International Affairs Building, 420 West 118th Street, Mail Code 3334, New York, NY 10027, USA; (home) 45 East 89th Street, New York, NY 10128–1251, USA.

**PHELPS, Maurice Arthur;** human resource consultant, since 1989; Managing Director, Maurice Phelps Associates, since 1989; Managing Partner, E. P. First, since 2001 (Managing Partner, Emslie Phelps Consultancy Group, 1990–2001); *b* 17 May 1935; *s* of H. T. Phelps; *m* 1960, Elizabeth Anne Hurley (*d* 2017); two *s* one *d*. *Educ:* Wandsworth School; Corpus Christi College, Oxford Univ. BA Hons Modern History. Shell Chemical Co. Ltd, 1959–68; Group Personnel Planning Adviser, Pilkington Bros Ltd, 1968–70; Group Personnel Dir, Unicorn Industries Ltd, 1970–72; Dir of Labour and Staff Relations, W Midland Passenger Transport Exec., 1973–77; Dir of Personnel, Heavy Vehicle Div., Leyland Vehicles Ltd, 1977–80; Bd Mem. for Personnel and Industrial Relations, 1980–87, non-exec. Bd Mem., 1987–90, British Shipbuilders; Dir, British Ferries, and Dep. Chm. and HR Dir, Sealink UK Ltd, 1987–89. Jt Founding Partner, Emslie Phelps Associates, subseq. Emslie Phelps First, 1989–2003; Human Resource Consultant: Value Through People Ltd, 1991–; Saratoga (Europe), 1993–. Freeman: City of London, 1995; Co. of Watermen and Lightermen, 1995. *Publications:* The People Policy Audit, 1999; Human Resources Benchmarking, 2002; A Thameside Family, 2007; The Adventures of Mr Golly, 2007; The Phelps Dynasty, 2012. *Address:* Abbotsfield, Goring Heath, S Oxon RG8 7SA.

**PHELPS, Rosalind Jayne;** QC 2016; *b* Oxford, 19 May 1974; *d* of Dr Peter D. Phelps and Dr Susan Phelps; *m* 2005, Orlando John Gledhill, *qv*; three *s*. *Educ:* King Henry VIII Sch., Coventry; Univ. of Paris II, Panthéon-Assas (Dip. French Law 1995); Pembroke Coll., Oxford (BA Hons Law and French Law 1996; BCL 1997). Called to the Bar, Lincoln's Inn, 1998; in practice as barrister, specialising in commercial law, 1998–. *Publications:* (contrib.) Carriage by Air, 2000; (contrib.) The Law of Privilege, 2006, 3rd edn 2018. *Address:* Fountain Court Chambers, Temple, EC4Y 9DH. *T:* (020) 7583 3335.

**PHILBIN, Margaret Elizabeth, (Maggie),** OBE 2017; science and technology broadcaster, since 1982; Chief Executive Officer, TeenTech, since 2008; *b* Manchester, 23 June 1955; *d* of Thomas Martin Philbin and Betty Philbin (*née* Lowden); *m* 1982, Keith Chegwin (marr. diss 1992; he *d* 2017); one *d*. *Educ:* Evington Hall Grammar Sch., Leicester; Univ. of Manchester (BA Hons). BBC: presenter, Multi-Coloured Swap Shop, 1978–82; reporter: Tomorrow's World, 1982–89; Hospital Watch, 1986–92; BBC, 2000–13; Bang Goes the Theory, 2013–15. Pres., IED, 2014–18. Hon. Fellow, QMUL, 2015. Hon. DTech: De Montfort, 2012; Solent, 2017; Hon. DSc: Bath, 2015; Huddersfield, 2016; Leicester, 2018. *Recreations:* film, food, hiking, reading, talking! *E:* maggie@teentechevent.com.

**PHILIP, Rt Hon. Lord; Alexander Morrison Philip;** PC 2005; a Senator of the College of Justice in Scotland, 1996–2007; *b* 3 Aug. 1942; *s* of late Alexander Philip, OBE and Isobel Thomson Morrison; *m* 1971, Shona Mary Macrae (marr. diss.); three *s*. *Educ:* High School of Glasgow; St Andrews University (MA 1963); Glasgow University (LLB 1965). Solicitor, 1967–72; Advocate 1973; Advocate-Depute, 1982–85; QC (Scotland), 1984; Chm., Scottish Land Court, 1993–96; Pres., Lands Tribunal for Scotland, 1993–96. Chm., Medical Appeal Tribunals, 1988–92. Chm., Mull of Kintyre Rev., 2010–11. *Publications:* contrib. Oxford DNB. *Recreations:* golf, piping (Hon. Pipe-Major, Royal Scottish Pipers Soc., 2011–13). *Clubs:* Royal Scottish Pipers' Society (Edinburgh); Hon. Co. of Edinburgh Golfers; New (Edinburgh).

**PHILIP, Alexander Morrison;** see Philip, Rt Hon. Lord.

**PHILIPPE, André J.,** Hon. GCVO 1972; Dr-en-Droit; Luxembourg Ambassador to the United States of America, 1987–91; *b* Luxembourg City, 28 June 1926. Barrister-at-Law, Luxembourg, 1951–52. Joined Luxembourg Diplomatic Service, 1952; Dep. to Dir of Pol Affairs, Min. of Foreign Affairs, 1952–54; Dep. Perm. Rep. to NATO, 1954–61 and to OECD, 1959–61; Dir of Protocol and Legal Adviser, Min. of For. Affairs, 1961–68; Ambassador and Perm. Rep. to UN and Consul-Gen., New York, 1968–72 (Vice-Pres., 24th Session of Gen. Assembly of UN, 1969); Ambassador to UK, Perm. Rep. to Council of WEU, and concurrently Ambassador to Ireland and Iceland, 1972–78; Ambassador to France, 1978–84; Ambassador to UN, NY, 1984–87. Commander: Order of Adolphe Nassau (Luxembourg); Légion d'Honneur (France); Grand Officer: Order of Merit (Luxembourg), 1983; Order of Oaken Crown (Luxembourg), 1988.

**PHILIPPS,** family name of **Viscount St Davids** and **Baron Milford**.

**PHILIPPS, Charles Edward Laurence;** Chief Executive, Amlin plc, 1999–2018; *b* 20 Jan. 1959; *s* of Peter Anthony Philipps and Suzannah Margaret Philipps; *m* 1984, Fiona Land (marr. diss. 2011); one *s* two *d*. *Educ:* Eton Coll. Chartered Accountant, 1983. Binder Hamlyn, 1979–83; County Bank, subseq. NatWest Markets Corporate Finance, 1983–97 (Dir, 1993–97); Finance Dir, Angerstein Underwriting Trust plc, 1997–99. Non-exec. Dir, Great Portland Estates plc, 2014–. Pres., Insce Inst. of London, 2009–10. Trustee, Outward Bound Trust, 2011– (Chm., 2018–). *Recreations:* country pursuits, golf. *Address:* The Old Rectory, Dalham, Newmarket CB8 8TE. *Clubs:* Boodle's; Jockey Club Rooms (Newmarket); Royal St George's Golf, Royal Worlington and Newmarket Golf.

**PHILIPPS, Nicola Jane**; artist, predominantly portraiture, since 1988; *b* London, 27 Aug. 1964; *d* of Jeremy and Susan Philipps. *Educ:* St Mary's Sch., Wantage; Queensgate Sch., London; City & Guilds Art Sch.; Studio Cecil Graves, Florence. *Solo exhibitions:* Malcolm Innes Gall., Bury St James's, 1997; Arndean Gall., 2001, 2003, 2007; *group exhibitions* include: Malcolm Innes Gall., Knightsbridge, 1994; Bury St James's, 1995; Fine Art Commns, Art London, 2002–08; Internat. Art Fair, Palm Beach, 2008, Duke St, 2013; BP Portrait Exhibn, NPG, 2005, 2009. Commissions include: Judge Michael Boudin, commnd by US Court of Appeals for First Circuit, Boston, 2009; Hugh Bonneville, 2009; Princes William and Henry of Wales, commnd by NPG, 2010; Princes William and Henry of Wales, commnd by Eton Coll., 2010; Duke and Duchess of Northumberland, 2011; Duchess of Cambridge, commnd by the Prince of Wales, 2012; Hon. Louis B. Susman, commnd by American Embassy, London, 2012; The Queen, commnd by Royal Mail, 2013, commnd by Royal Co. of Archers, Queen's Bodyguard for Scotland, 2016, commnd by Royal Collection, 2018; Dean of Westminster, 2014; Fiona Bruce, 2014; Simon Weston, commnd by NPG, 2014; Baron George; Baron Richardson of Duntisbourne. *Publications:* Philipps: a family of artists at Picton, 2010. *Recreations:* riding, ski-ing, bridge. *Address:* c/o Fine Art Commissions Ltd, 19 Ryder Street, St James's, SW1Y 6PX. *E:* nicky@nickyphilipps.com. *Club:* Chelsea Arts.

**PHILIPS, Dalton;** *see* Philips, T. D. D.

**PHILIPS, Justin Robin Drew;** District Judge (Magistrates' Courts) (formerly Metropolitan Stipendiary Magistrate), 1989–2012; Lead Judge, Dedicated Drug Court, London, 2005–12; *b* 18 July 1948; *s* of late Albert Lewis Philips, Solicitor, and Henrietta Philips (*née* Woolfson). *Educ:* John Lyon School, Harrow; College of Law, London. Called to the Bar, Gray's Inn, 1969; practised criminal bar, 1970–89; Chm., Youth Court, 1993–98; an Asst Recorder, 1994–99; a Recorder, 1999–2006. Mem., Adv. Council on Misuse of Drugs, 2008–12; Seminar Leader, MSc Adolescent Addiction, Keele Univ., 2009. Hon. Sec., Hendon Reform Synagogue, 1990–94 (Mem. Council, 1979–90). Trustee, Tzedek Charity, 1993–2008; Patron: DrugFam, 2008–; Kids Count, 2010–; Drugsline, 2011–12. Mem., Va'ad Fuchsberg Center, Jerusalem, 2017–. *Recreations:* music, Judaic studies, attempting to keep fit. *Address:* Lev Yerushalayim, PO Box 71156, Jerusalem 9426201, Israel.

**PHILIPS, (Timothy David) Dalton;** Chief Executive Officer, Dublin Airport Authority, since 2017; *b* Dublin; *s* of Tim Philips and Susan Philips; *m* 1998, Penny; two *s* one *d*. *Educ:* St Gerard's Sch., Bray; St Columba's Sch., Dublin; Stowe Sch.; University Coll., Dublin (BA Hons 1991); Harvard Business Sch. (MBA 1998). Jardine Matheson, Hong Kong, 1993–96; Wal-Mart, 1998–2005; CEO, Brown Thomas Gp, Ire., 2005–07; Chief Operating Officer, Loblaw Cos Ltd, Canada, 2007–10; CEO, Wm Morrison Supermarkets plc, 2010–15. Chairman: Ridgeons Gp, 2016–; Byron, 2017–; non-executive Director: Social Innovation Fund, Ireland, 2016–; One51 plc, 2016–; Wilkinson Hardware Stores Ltd, 2016–; Sen. Advr, Boston Consulting Gp, 2016–. *Recreations:* marathon running, church affairs, wine and food. *Address:* Ballinacoola, Glenealy, Wicklow, Ireland.

**PHILIPSON-STOW, Sir (Robert) Matthew**, 6th Bt *cr* 1907, of Cape Town, Colony of Cape of Good Hope, and Blackdown House, Lodsworth, Co. Sussex; professional engineer with MacViro Consultants Inc., 1989–2006; *b* 29 Aug. 1953; *s* of Sir Christopher Philipson-Stow, 5th Bt, DFC and Elizabeth Nairn Philipson-Stow (*née* Trees); *S* father, 2005, but his name does not appear on the Official Roll of the Baronetage; *m* 2001, Wendy Bracken (*née* Harrel); one step *d*. *Educ:* Univ. of Waterloo (BASc 1978). PEng. MacLaren Engineers Inc., 1978–89. *Recreations:* cabinetry, sailing, reading, lawn bowling, walking. *Heir: b* Rowland Frederick Philipson-Stow [*b* 2 Sept. 1954; *m* 1979, Mary Susan (*née* Stroud); one *s* one *d*]. *Address:* 3760 Crestview Road, Victoria, BC V8P 5C6, Canada. *E:* stowmatthew@gmail.com.

**PHILIPSZ, Susan Mary,** OBE 2014; artist; *b* Glasgow, 21 Nov. 1965; *d* of John Philipsz and Susan Philipsz; *m* 2009, Eoghan McTigue. *Educ:* Duncan of Jordanstone Coll., Dundee (BA Fine Art); Univ. of Ulster, Belfast (MA Fine Art 1995). Mem., Mgt Cttee, Catalyst Arts, Belfast, 1996–98; Founder, Grassy Knoll Prodns, Belfast, 1998–. Artist in residence: Internat. Studio Prog., MoMA PS1, NY, 2000–01; Residency Prog., Kunst Werke eV, Berlin, 2001–02. *Solo exhibitions* include: Part File Score, Hamburger Bahnhof, Berlin, 2014; War Damaged Musical Instruments, Tate Britain, 2015; Night and Fog, Kunsthaus Bregenz, 2016; A Single Voice, Baltic Centre for Contemporary Art, Gateshead, 2017; Separated Strings, Staatliche Kunstsammlung, Dresden, 2018; *group exhibitions* include: Skulptur Projekte Münster 07, Münster, 2007; Solomon R. Guggenheim Mus., NY, 2010; dOCUMENTA (13), Kassel, 2012; Mus. of Modern Art, NY, 2013. Turner Prize, 2010. Hon. LLD Dundee, 2017. *Publications:* Susan Philipsz: there is nothing left here, 2008; Susan Philipsz: you are not alone, 2014. *Address:* Starnberger Strasse 2, 10781 Berlin, Germany.

**PHILLIMORE,** family name of **Baron Phillimore**.

**PHILLIMORE,** 5th Baron *cr* 1918, of Shiplake, Oxfordshire; **Francis Stephen Phillimore;** Bt 1881; land manager; *b* 25 Nov. 1944; *o s* of 4th Baron Phillimore and Anne Elizabeth Phillimore (*d* 1995), *e d* of Major Arthur Algernon Dorrien Smith, DSO; *S* father, 1994; *m* 1971, Nathalie Berthe Louisa Pequin; two *s* one *d*. *Educ:* Eton Coll.; Trinity Coll., Cambridge (BA). Called to the Bar, Middle Temple, 1972; in practice as barrister, 1972–2002. Member: Shiplake Parish Council, 1995–2011 (Chm., 1998–2003); Eye and Dunsden Parish Council, 2003–15. Mem., Ct of Assistants, Fishmongers' Co., 2001–. Trustee, Venice in Peril Fund, 1996–2013. Steward, Hurlingham Polo Assoc., 1998–2016. Mem., Garden Soc.; Founder Fellow, RHS. *Recreations:* polo, sailing, the arts, shooting, Venetian rowing, travel. *Heir: er s* Hon. Tristan Anthony Stephen Phillimore [*b* 18 Aug. 1977; *m* 2013, Jemma Tuomey; two *d*]. *Address:* 23 Phillimore Gardens, W8 7QG. *Clubs:* Brooks's, Pratt's, City Barge; Royal Yacht Squadron.

**PHILLIMORE, (John) Roger (Broughton);** Chairman, Lonmin plc, 2009–14; *b* Johannesburg, 21 June 1949; *s* of Michael and Felicity Phillimore; *m* 1981, Virginia Anne Crookshank. *Educ:* St Aidan's Coll., Grahamstown, SA; Univ. of Witwatersrand (BA Hons Applied Econs). Joined Anglo American, 1972; Divl Manager, Gold Div., 1978; Sec. to Exec. Cttee, 1978–81; Jt Man. Dir, Minorco, 1981–92. Dir, Harry Winston Diamond Corp., 1994–2012. *Recreations:* art, music, golf, equestrian. *Address:* Little Bentley Farm, Mottisfont, Romsey, Hants SO51 0LT. *Clubs:* Boodle's; Rand; Gassin Golf.

**PHILLIPS,** family name of **Barons Phillips of Sudbury** and **Phillips of Worth Matravers**.

**PHILLIPS OF SUDBURY,** Baron *cr* 1998 (Life Peer), of Sudbury in the co. of Suffolk; **Andrew Wyndham Phillips,** OBE 1996; founding Partner, Bates, Wells & Braithwaite, solicitors, London, 1970; freelance journalist; *b* 15 March 1939; *s* of late Alan Clifford Phillips and Dorothy Alice Phillips (*née* Wyndham); *m* 1968, Penelope Ann Bennett; one *s* two *d*. *Educ:* Uppingham; Trinity Hall, Cambridge (BA 1962). Qualified solicitor, 1964. Co-founder, 1971 and first Chm., Legal Action Gp; founder and first Chm., 1989–2000, first Pres., 2000–, Citizenship Foundn (Young Citizens); Initiator and First Pres., Solicitors' Pro Bono Gp (Law Works), 1997–; Mem., Nat. Lottery Charities Bd, 1994–96. Mem., H of L, 1998–2015. Trustee, Scott Trust (Guardian/Observer), 1994–2004. Pres., British-Iranian Chamber of Commerce, 2002–15. Pres., Trustee and Patron of various charities. Vice-Pres., Gainsborough's House, 2015– (Trustee, 1975–2015). Presenter, London Programme, LWT and Anglia TV, 1980–81; regular broadcaster, incl. Legal Eagle, Jimmy Young Show, BBC Radio Two, 1979–2001. Lectures incl. Hibbert, BBC Radio, 1988, Hinton Nevo, 2014. Chancellor, Univ. of Essex, 2003–13. Contested: (Lab) Harwich, 1970; (L) Saffron Walden, July 1977 and 1979; (L/Alliance) Gainsborough and Horncastle, 1983; (L) NE Essex, European Parlt, 1979. Lifetime Achievement Award, Third Sector, 2009. *Publications:* The Living Law; Charitable Status: a practical handbook, 1980, 6th edn 2008; (jtly) Charity Investment: law and practice. *Recreations:* the arts, local history, architecture, golf, walking. *Address:* River House, The Croft, Sudbury, Suffolk CO10 1HW. *T:* (01787) 882151. *E:* andrew_w_phillips@yahoo.com.

**PHILLIPS OF WORTH MATRAVERS,** Baron *cr* 1999 (Life Peer), of Belsize Park in the London Borough of Camden; **Nicholas Addison Phillips,** KG 2011; Kt 1987; PC 1995; President: of the Supreme Court of the United Kingdom, 2009–12 (Senior Lord of Appeal in Ordinary, 2008–09); Qatar International Court and Dispute Resolution Centre, 2012–18; non-permanent Judge, Court of Final Appeal, Hong Kong, since 2013; *b* 21 Jan. 1938; *m* 1972, Christylle Marie-Thérèse Rouffiac (*née* Doreau); two *d*, and one step *s* one step *d*. *Educ:* Bryanston Sch.; King's Coll., Cambridge (MA; Hon. Fellow, 2004). Nat. Service with RN; commnd RNVR, 1956–58. Called to Bar, Middle Temple (Harmsworth Scholar), 1962, Bencher, 1984. In practice at Bar, 1962–87; Jun. Counsel to Minister of Defence and to Treasury in Admiralty matters, 1973–78; QC 1978; a Recorder, 1982–87; a Judge of High Court of Justice, QBD, 1987–95; a Lord Justice of Appeal, 1995–98; a Lord of Appeal in Ordinary, 1999–2000; Master of the Rolls, 2000–05; Hd of Civil Justice, 2000–05; Lord Chief Justice, 2005–08. Mem., Panel of Wreck Comrs, 1979–87. Chairman: Law Adv. Cttee, British Council, 1991–97; Council of Legal Educn, 1992–97; BSE Inquiry, 1998–2000; Lord Chancellor's Adv. Cttee on Public Records, 2000–05; European Maritime Law Orgn, 2012–; Member: Adv. Council, Inst. of Eur. and Comparative Law, 1999–2007; Adv. Council, Inst. of Global Law, 2000–; President: British Maritime Law Assoc., 2005– (Vice Pres., 1993–2005); Network of Presidents of Supreme Cts of EC, 2006–08; British Inst. of Internat. and Comparative Law, 2016– (Mem., Council of Mgt, 1999–). Patron, CIArb, 2011–14. Trustee, Magna Carta Trust, 2000–05. Governor, Bryanston Sch., 1975–2008 (Chm. of Governors, 1981–2008); Visitor: Nuffield Coll., Oxford, 2000–05; UCL, 2000–05; Darwin Coll., Cambridge, 2005–08; Chancellor, Bournemouth Univ., 2009–18; Visiting Fellow: Dixon Poon Sch. of Law, KCL, 2013–; Oxford Inst. of Islamic Studies and Mansfield Coll., Oxford, 2013–; Vis. Prof., Law Faculty, Univ. of Oxford, 2014–16. Liveryman: Drapers' Co., 2005–; Shipwrights' Co., 2007–. Hon. Fellow: Soc. of Advanced Legal Studies, 1999–; UCL, 2006; Hughes Hall, Cambridge, 2012. Hon. Bencher, Gray's Inn, 2009. Hon. LLD: Exeter, 1998; Birmingham, 2003; London, 2004; Wolverhampton, 2009; Washington and Lee, Lexington, Va, 2009; Wake Forest, 2010; Hon. DCL City, 2003; Hon. LLD: Internat. Inst. of Maritime Law, 2007; BPP Univ., 2014. Officier, Légion d'Honneur (France), 2018. *Recreations:* sea, mountains. *Address:* House of Lords, SW1A 0PW. *Clubs:* Brooks's, Garrick.

**PHILLIPS, Adam;** psychoanalyst in private practice; writer; *b* 19 Sept. 1954; *s* of Eric and Jacqueline Phillips; partner, Judith Clark; two *d* one *s*. *Educ:* Clifton Coll., Bristol; St John's Coll., Oxford. Principal Child Psychotherapist, Charing Cross Hosp., 1990–97. Vis. Prof., English Dept, Univ. of York, 2006–. Gen. Ed., New Penguin Freud, 2003–. *Publications:* Winnicott, 1988; On Kissing, Tickling and Being Bored, 1992; On Flirtation, 1994; Terrors and Experts, 1995; Monogamy, 1996; The Beast in the Nursery, 1997; Darwin's Worms, 1999; Promises, Promises, 2000; Houdini's Box, 2001; Equals, 2002; Going Sane, 2005; Side-Effects, 2007; (with L. Bersani) Intimacies, 2008; (with B. Taylor) On Kindness, 2009; (with J. Clark) The Concise Dictionary of Dress, 2010; On Balance, 2010; Missing Out: in praise of the unlived life, 2012; Becoming Freud: the making of a psychoanalyst, 2014; Unforbidden Pleasures, 2015; In Writing, 2017.

**PHILLIPS, Adrian Alexander Christian,** CBE 1998; freelance environmental consultant; *b* 11 Jan. 1940; *s* of Eric Lawrance Phillips, CMG and Phyllis Phillips (*née* Bray); *m* 1963, Cassandra Frances Elaïs Hubback, MA Oxon, *d* of D. F. Hubback, CB; two *s*. *Educ:* The Hall, Hampstead; Westminster Sch.; Christ Church, Oxford (1st Cl. Hons MA Geography); University Coll. London (DipT&CP). MRTPI 1966; FRGS 1984. Planning Services, Min. of Housing and Local Govt, 1962–68; Sen. Research Officer and Asst Director, Countryside Commission, 1968–74; Special Asst, Executive Director, United Nations Environment Programme (UNEP), Nairobi, Kenya, 1974–75; Head, Programme Coordination Unit, UNEP, Nairobi, 1975–78; Director of Programmes, IUCN, Switzerland, 1978–81; Dir, then Dir Gen., Countryside Commn, 1981–92; Prof. of Countryside and Envmtl Planning, City and Regl Planning Dept, UWCC, 1992–2001. Chairman: Commn on Nat. Parks and Protected Areas, IUCN, 1994–96 (Dep. Chm., 1988–94); World Commn on Protected Areas, IUCN, 1996–2000; Sen. Advr on World Heritage, IUCN, 2000–04; Chm., Policy Cttee, CPRE, 2001–06. Chm., Cttee for Wales, RSPB, 1992–98. Trustee: WWF UK, 1997–2003; Woodland Trust, 2004–08; National Trust, 2005–12 (Mem., SW Regl Adv. Bd, 2013–); Chairman: Glos Envmtl Trust, 2001–09; Glos Nature Partnership, 2015–18; Sec. of State Appointee, Cotswold Conservation Bd, 2005–15. FRSA 1983. Hon. FLI. *Publications:* (ed jtly) Countryside Planning, 2004; articles and chapters on envmtl and conservation topics. *Recreations:* walking, stroking the cat. *Address:* 30 Painswick Road, Cheltenham, Glos GL50 2HA. *T:* 07881 620035.

**PHILLIPS, Alan;** *see* Phillips, His Honour D. A.

**PHILLIPS, Alan David John,** CMG 1999; international adviser on human and minority rights; Executive Director, Minority Rights Group, 1989–2000; *b* 4 April 1947; *s* of Reginald and Irene Phillips; *m* 1970, Hilary Siddell; one *s* two *d*. *Educ:* Brighton Coll.; Warwick Univ. (BSc Hons Physics; Physics Prize; Pres., Students' Union, 1968–69). Systems Auditor, Rank Xerox, 1970–73; Gen. Sec., World Univ. Service (UK), 1973–81; Dep. Dir, British Refugee Council, 1982–89. NGO Expert to UK and EC delegns at intergovtl Human Rights fora, 1991–; UK nominated ind. expert, 1998–, Vice Pres., 1999–2002, Pres., 2006–10, Council of Europe Adv. Cttee, Framework Convention on Nat. Minorities (contrib., Review, 2012). Internat. Lectr on Minority Rights, 2011–. Advr to Prime Minister of Kosovo, 2004–06. Mem., Cttee, Council for Assisting Refugee Academics, 1998–2005. Advr on Roma integration to EU, OSCE and Council of Europe, 2003–; Strategy Advr, Roma Educn Fund, 2016–; Advr, Refugee Res. Project. Chairman: Brighton and Hove Organic Gardening, 2001–16; Seedy Sunday, 2011–13; Brighton and Hove Allotment Fedn, 2013–14. Hon. LLD Warwick, 2005. Caballero Comandante, Orden B. O'Higgins (Chile), 2010. *Publications:* British Aid for Overseas Students, 1980; UN Minority Rights Declaration, 1993; Universal Minority Rights, 1995; (contrib.) World Directory of Minorities, 1997; Ethnicity, Pluralism and Human Rights, 2003; (contrib.) Mechanisms for the Implementation of Minority Rights, 2004. *Recreations:* family, organic gardening, walking, swimming. *E:* alan@alanphillips.org. *Club:* Brighton and Hove Allotment Soc.

**PHILLIPS, Alice Mary**; Headteacher, St Catherine's School, Bramley, since 2000; *b* 1 Aug. 1960; *d* of David and Lesley Alban; *m* 1986, Simon John Phillips; one *d*. *Educ*: Kendal High Sch.; Newnham Coll., Cambridge (BA 1982). Teacher of English, 1983–93, Hd, Dept of English, 1989–93, Royal Masonic Sch., Rickmansworth; Dep. Hd, Tormead Sch., 1993–99. Mem. Council, GSA, 2008–16 (Pres., 2014); Vice-Chm., ISC, 2016. *Recreations*: gardening, singing, cooking, music, ballet. *Address*: St Catherine's School, Bramley, Surrey GU5 0DF. *T*: (01483) 899605. *E*: headmistress@stcatherines.info. *Clubs*: Lansdowne, University Women's.

**PHILLIPS, Andrew Bassett**; Head, Legal Deposit Review, British Library, 1996–99; *b* 26 Sept. 1945; *s* of William Phillips and Doreen (*née* Harris); *m* 1976, Valerie Cuthbert; two *s* one *d*. *Educ*: Newport High Sch.; Reading Univ. (BA). MCLIP. British Nat. Bibliography Ltd, 1969–70; Research Officer, Nat. Libraries ADP Study, 1970–71; Admin. Officer, Nat. Council for Educnl Technol., 1971–73; British Library: various posts in Bibliographic Servs and Ref. (subseq. Humanities and Social Scis) Divs, 1973–86; Dir, Public Services and Planning and Admin, 1987–90; Dir, Humanities and Social Scis, 1990–96. Part-time Lectr, West London Coll., 1972–75. Director: Cedar Audio Ltd, 1992–94; Saga Continuation Ltd, 1993–99. Advr, British Univs Film and Video Council, 2000–06. Mem., Mgt Cttee, Hoxton Health, 2011–14. Member: Governing Body, City Lit. Inst., 1982–87; Archives Cttee, Barts Health (formerly Bart & The London) NHS Trust (formerly St Bartholomew's Hosp.), 2000–19; Works of Art Cttee, Homerton Univ. Hosp., 2008–12; Sec., Friends of the British Liby, 2004–06 (Mem. Council, 1990–2002); Trustee: Black Country Mus. Develt Trust, 2004–12; Guild of Royal Hosp. of St Bartholomew, 2010– (Chm., 2012–16); Age UK E London, 2012–. Hon. Fellow, Shakespeare's Birthplace, 2003– (Trustee, 1991–2003; Mem. Council, 2018–). *Publications*: (ed) The People's Heritage, 2000; (contrib.) Inventing the 20th Century, 2000; various reviews, articles. *Address*: 23 Meynell Road, E9 7AP. *T*: (020) 8985 7413. *Club*: London Press.

**PHILLIPS, Anne, (Mrs Basil Phillips)**; *see* Dickinson, V. A.

**PHILLIPS, Prof. Anne**, PhD; FBA 2003; FAcSS; Graham Wallas Professor of Political Science (formerly Professor of Gender Theory, then of Political and Gender Theory), London School of Economics, since 1999; *b* 2 June 1950; *d* of Frederick Phillips and Margaret Hill; *m* 1982, Ciaran Driver; two *s*. *Educ*: Univ. of Bristol (BSc Philos. and Pols 1971); Sch. of Oriental and African Studies, London (MSc W African Pols 1972); City Univ., London (PhD 1982). FAcSS (AcSS 2012). Lectr, 1975–88, Reader, 1988–90, in Politics, City of London Poly.; Prof. of Politics, London Guildhall Univ., 1990–99. Adjunct Prof., ANU, 2002–05. Hon. Dr phil Aalborg, 1999; Hon. LLD Bristol, 2013. *Publications*: Hidden Hands: women and economic policies, 1983; Divided Loyalties: dilemmas of sex and class, 1987; The Enigma of Colonialism, 1989; Engendering Democracy, 1991, 2nd edn 1997; Democracy and Difference, 1993; The Politics of Presence, 1995, 2nd edn 1998; Which Equalities Matter?, 1999; Multiculturalism without Culture, 2007; Gender and Culture, 2010; Our Bodies: whose property?, 2013; The Politics of the Human, 2015. *Recreations*: swimming, reading novels, gardening. *Address*: Government Department, London School of Economics, Houghton Street, WC2A 2AE. *T*: (020) 7955 6979, *Fax*: (020) 7955 6408. *E*: a.phillips@lse.ac.uk.

**PHILLIPS, Anne Fyfe**; *see* Pringle, Dame A. F.

**PHILLIPS, Rev. Canon Anthony Charles Julian**; Headmaster, King's School, Canterbury, 1986–96; *b* 2 June 1936; *s* of Arthur Reginald Phillips and Esmée Mary Phillips; *m* 1970, Victoria Ann, *d* of Vernon Bruce Stainton, OBE and Marion Elizabeth Stainton (*née* Reed); two *s* one *d*. *Educ*: Kelly Coll., Tavistock (schol.); King's Coll., London (BD, 1st cl.; AKC, 1st cl.; Archibald Robertson Prize, 1962; Jun. McCaul Hebrew Prize, 1963); Gonville and Caius Coll., Cambridge (PhD 1967); College of the Resurrection, Mirfield. Solicitor, 1958; ordained priest, 1967; Curate, Good Shepherd, Cambridge, 1966–69; Dean, Chaplain and Fellow, Trinity Hall, Cambridge, 1969–74; Chaplain and Fellow, 1975–86, Domestic Bursar, 1982–84, St John's Coll., Oxford; Lecturer in Theology: Jesus Coll., Oxford, 1975–86; Hertford Coll., Oxford, 1984–86; S. A. Cook Bye Fellow, Gonville and Caius Coll., 1984; Canon Theologian, Dio. of Truro, 1986–2002; Chapter Canon, Truro Cath., 2001–02, now Canon Emeritus. Hon. Chaplain to Bishop of Norwich, 1970–71; Examining Chaplain to: Bp of Oxford, 1979–86; Bp of Manchester, 1980–86; Bp of Wakefield, 1984–86; Hon. Canon, Canterbury Cathedral, 1987–96. Chaplain to High Sheriff, Oxon, 2016–17. Archbps of Canterbury and York Interfaith Cons. for Judaism, 1984–86. Rep., Art Fund Cornwall, 2014–15. Hon. Vice-Pres., Royal Cornwall Poly. Soc., 2011– (Dir, 2003–08; Chm., 2004–08; Pres., 2008–11). Governor: Sherborne Sch., 1997–2001; Sherborne Sch. for Girls, 1997–2001; Cornwall Coll., 1997–2001, 2004–05; SPCK, 1998–2006 (Chair of Publishing, 2000–05). SBStJ 2003. Freeman, City of London, 2004; Liveryman, Broderers' Co., 2005. *Publications*: Ancient Israel's Criminal Law, 1970; Deuteronomy (Cambridge Bible Commentary), 1973; God BC, 1977, rev. 2018; (ed) Israel's Prophetic Tradition, 1982; Lower Than the Angels, 1983, 2nd edn 1996; Preaching from the Psalter, 1987; The Passion of God, 1995; Essays on Biblical Law, 2002; Entering into the Mind of God, 2002; Standing up to God, 2005; David: a story of passion and tragedy, 2008; contrib. to: Words and Meanings (ed P. R. Ackroyd and B. Lindars), 1968; Witness to the Spirit (ed W. Harrington), 1979; The Ministry of the Word (ed G. Cuming), 1979; Heaven and Earth (ed A. Linzey and P. Wexler), 1986; Tradition and Unity (ed Dan Cohn-Sherbok), 1991; Glimpses of God (ed Dan Cohn-Sherbok), 1993; Splashes of God Light (ed T. Copley and others), 1997; Intelligent Faith (ed J. Quenby and J. MacDonald Smith), 2009; Reflecting on Retirement: content and discontent among Anglican clergy (ed T. Neal and L. J. Francis), 2019; articles in theol jls, The Times, Expository Times, etc. *Recreations*: gardening, beachcombing. *Address*: 47 Warwick Street, Oxford OX4 1SZ. *T*: (01865) 244871. *E*: a.phillips920@btinternet.com. *Club*: Sloane.

**PHILLIPS, Arlene**, CBE 2013 (OBE 2002); Choreographer, Creative Director and Producer, Arlene Phillips Hot Gossip Ltd, since 1978; *b* Manchester, 22 May 1943; *d* of Emanuel Phillips and Rita Phillips; two *d*. *Educ*: Manchester Central High Sch. for Girls; Muriel Tweedy's Sch. of Dance. Dance teacher: Muriel Tweedy's Sch. of Dance, 1962–66; Dance Centre, Floral St, 1968; Pineapple, 1979–84; creator and choreographer, Hot Gossip, dance gp, 1974; *choreographer*: films: Can't Stop The Music, 1980; Annie, 1982; Monty Python's The Meaning of Life, 1983; The Wind in the Willows, 1996; stage: Starlight Express, 1984, internat. tour, 2013; Grease, London, 1993, internat. tour, 1997, UK tour, 2017; (and dir) Saturday Night Fever, London, NY and internat. tour, 1998; We Will Rock You, London and world tour, 2002; (and dir) The Music of Andrew Lloyd Webber, US tour, 2005; The Sound of Music, London, 2006; The Wizard of Oz, London, 2011, Canada, 2012, US tour, 2013; Monty Python Live, 2014; (and dir) Brazouka, 2014; Whelan/Watson: Other Stories, London, 2015; (and staging) Utopia, Roundhouse, 2015; Jackie The Musical, UK tour, 2016; You and I Know, Candoco Dance Co., 2016; Allelujah!, Bridge Th., 2018; Grease the Musical, UK Tour, 2019; (and movement dir) A Midsummer Night's Dream, Bridge Th., 2019; *Creative Dir*, Judy – The Songbook of Judy Garland, New Victoria, 2015; *Director*: Strictly Come Dancing Live Tour, 2008, 2009; 27, Cockpit Th., 2016; Myth, The Other Palace, 2018; A Little Princess, RFH, 2018; Dir of Choreography, Manchester Commonwealth Games, 2002; Co-Producer, Midnight Tango (dance show), Aldwych and tours, 2011; Arlene!: the glitz, the glamour, the gossip, UK tour, 2017; *television*: choreographer: A Midsummer Night's Dream, BBC One, 2016; Candoco Dance Co. and Strictly Come Dancing professionals, Strictly Come Dancing, 2018; judge of television shows: Strictly Come Dancing, 2004–08; Strictly Dance Fever, 2005–06; So You Think You Can Dance?, 2010–11; Over the Rainbow, 2012; creator, television shows: (and appeared in) DanceX, 2007; Britannia High, 2008; Judge, West End Eurovision, 2018. Mem. Bd, 2009–11, Ambassador, 2011–, Sadler's Wells Th. Ambassador: Prince's Trust; Alzheimer's Soc.; Youth Dance England; Patron: Midlands Acad. of Dance and Drama; Laine Theatre Arts; Dance UK; Dance Umbrella; Urdan Acad.; Stella Mann Coll.; Liberatus Sch. of Dance and Drama; Candoco Dance Co.; Dance Proms 2014. Companion, Liverpool Inst. for Performing Arts, 2004. Hon. Mem., Internat. Dance Teachers' Assoc., 2006. Carl Alan Award for Stage/Theatre Outstanding Services to Dance, Internat. Dance Teachers' Assoc., 2007; Gold Badge Award, BASCA, 2011. *Publications*: Alana Dancing Star (children's book series), 2010; Dance to the Musicals, 2011. *Recreations*: theatre, dance, art, charity, family, cooking. *Address*: c/o Alex Segal, InterTalent Rights Group, InterTalent House, 46 Charlotte Street, W1T 2GS. *T*: (020) 7427 5681. *E*: roxie@hotgossipmail.com.

**PHILLIPS, Prof. Calbert Inglis**, FRCS, FRCSE; Professor of Ophthalmology, University of Edinburgh and Ophthalmic Surgeon, Royal Infirmary, Edinburgh, 1972–90, now Professor Emeritus; *b* 20 March 1925; *o s* of Rev. David Horner Phillips and Margaret Calbert Phillips; *m* 1962, Christina Anne Fulton, MB, FRCSE; one *s*. *Educ*: Glasgow High Sch.; Robert Gordon's Coll., Aberdeen; Aberdeen Univ. MB, ChB Aberdeen 1946; DPH Edinburgh 1950; FRCS 1955; MD Aberdeen 1957; PhD Bristol 1961; MSc Manchester 1969; FRCSE 1973. Lieut and Captain, RAMC, 1947–49. House Surgeon: Aberdeen Royal Infirmary, 1946–47 (House Phys., 1951); Aberdeen Maternity Hosp., 1949; Glasgow Eye Infirmary, 1950–51; Asst, Anatomy Dept, Glasgow Univ., 1951–52; Resident Registrar, Moorfields Eye Hosp., 1953–55; Sen. Registrar, St Thomas' Hosp. and Moorfields Eye Hosp., and Res. Asst, Inst. of Ophthalmology, 1955–58; Consultant Surg., Bristol Eye Hosp., 1958–63; Alexander Piggott Wernher Trav. Fellow, Dept of Ophthalmol., Harvard Univ., 1960–61; Consultant Ophthalmic Surg., St George's Hosp., 1963–65; Prof. of Ophthal., Manchester Univ., and Hon. Consultant Ophthalmic Surg. to United Manchester Hosps, 1965–72. Hon. FBOA 1975. *Publications*: (ed jtly) Clinical Practice and Economics, 1977; Basic Clinical Ophthalmology, 1984; Logic in Medicine, 1988, 2nd edn 1995; (jtly) Ophthalmology: a primer for medical students and practitioners, 1994; papers in Eur., Amer., and Japanese Jls of Ophthal., Nature, Brain, BMJ, etc, mainly on intra-ocular pressure and glaucoma, retinal detachments, ocular surgery and hereditary diseases. *Address*: 5 Braid Mount Crest, Edinburgh EH10 6JN.

**PHILLIPS, Caryl**, FRSL; writer; Professor of English, Yale University, since 2005; *b* 13 March 1958. *Educ*: Queen's Coll., Oxford (BA English 1979; Hon. Fellow, 2006). Writer in Residence: Literary Criterion Centre, Mysore, India, 1987; Univ. of Stockholm, Sweden, 1989; Nat. Inst. of Educn, Singapore, 1994; Amherst College, Massachusetts: Vis. Writer, 1990–92; Writer in Residence, 1992–94; Prof. of English and Writer in Residence, 1994–98; Barnard College, Columbia University: Prof. of English and Henry R. Luce Prof. of Migration and Social Order, 1998–2005; Dir, Initiatives in the Humanities, 2003–05. Visiting Professor: NY Univ., 1993; Univ. of WI, Barbados, 1999–2000; Dartmouth Univ., NH, 2008; Oxford Univ., 2009; Univ. of Virginia, 2016; Univ. of Liège, Belgium, 2017; UNESCO Vis. Prof., UEA, 2018. British Council Fiftieth Anniversary Fellow, 1984; Guggenheim Fellow, 1992; Rockefeller Foundn (Bellagio) Residency, 1993; Fellow, Centre for Scholars and Writers, NY Public Liby, 2002–03; Montgomery Fellow, Dartmouth Coll., NH, 2008. Ed., Faber Caribbean series, 1998–2001. FRSL 2000. Humanities Schol. of the Year, Univ. of WI, 1999. Hon. AM Amherst, 1995; DUniv: Leeds Metropolitan, 1997; York, 2003; Hon. LittD Leeds, 2003; Hon. MA Yale, 2006; Hon. DLitt: West Indies, 2010; Edinburgh, 2012; Hon. Dr Liège, 2015. Giles Cooper Award, BBC, 1984; Bursary in Drama, Arts Council of GB, 1984; Martin Luther King Meml Prize, 1987; James Tait Black Meml Prize, 1994; Lannan Foundn Literary Award, 1994. *Publications*: plays: Strange Fruit, 1981; Where There is Darkness, 1982; The Shelter, 1984; Rough Crossings, 1984; *novels*: The Final Passage, 1985; A State of Independence, 1986; Higher Ground, 1989; Cambridge, 1991; Crossing the River, 1993; The Nature of Blood, 1997; A Distant Shore, 2003 (Commonwealth Writers Prize, 2004); Dancing in the Dark, 2005 (PEN Open Book Award (jtly), 2006); In the Falling Snow, 2009; The Lost Child, 2015; A View of the Empire at Sunset, 2018; *screenplays*: Playing Away, 1987; The Mystic Masseur (Silver Ombu award for best screenplay, Mar del Plata Film Fest.), 2002; *non-fiction*: The European Tribe, 1987; The Atlantic Sound, 2000; A New World Order, 2001; Foreigners, 2007; Colour Me English, 2011; *anthology*: (ed) Extravagant Strangers, 1997; (ed) The Right Set: the Faber Book of Tennis, 1999. *Recreations*: running, golf. *Address*: c/o Georgia Garrett, Rogers Coleridge and White, 20 Powis Mews, W11 1JN.

**PHILLIPS, Sir David**; *see* Phillips, Sir J. D.

**PHILLIPS, Prof. David**, CBE 2012 (OBE 1999); FRS 2015; Professor of Physical Chemistry, 1989–2006, Hofmann Professor of Chemistry, 1999–2006, now Professor Emeritus, and Dean, Faculties of Life Sciences and Physical Sciences, 2002–06, Imperial College London; *b* 3 Dec. 1939; *s* of Stanley and Daphne Ivy Phillips; *m* 1970, Caroline Lucy Scoble; one *d*. *Educ*: South Shields Grammar-Technical Sch.; Univ. of Birmingham (BSc, PhD). Post doctoral Fellow, Univ. of Texas, 1964–66; Vis. Scientist, Inst. of Chemical Physics, Acad. of Scis of USSR, Moscow, 1966–67; Lectr 1967–73, Sen. Lectr 1973–76, Reader 1976–80, in Phys. Chem., Univ. of Southampton; Royal Institution of Great Britain: Wolfson Prof. of Natural Philosophy, 1980–89; Actg Dir, Jan.–Oct. 1986; Dep. Dir, 1986–89; Head, Dept of Chemistry, Imperial Coll., London, 1992–2002. Vice-Pres. and Gen. Officer, BAAS, 1988–89. Mem., Faraday Council, 1990–93, Pres., 2010–12, RSC. Nyholm Lectr, RSC, 1994. Chm., London Gifted and Talented, 2003–08. FRSC 1973; Fellow, Imperial Coll. London, 2008; Hon. FCGI 2004; Honorary Life Fellow: Royal Inst., 2005; BAAS, 2006. Hon. DSc: Birmingham, 2011; Southampton, 2012; Durham, 2013; Leicester, 2014; Westminster, 2014; Hon. LLD Bath, 2013. Michael Faraday Award, Royal Soc., 1997; Porter Medal, Eur. Photochemistry Assoc., Inter-American Photochem. Soc. and Oceanic Photochem. Assoc., 2010. *Publications*: (jtly) Time-Correlated Single-Photon Counting, 1984; Polymer Photophysics, 1985; (jtly) Jet Spectroscopy and Dynamics, 1995; over 598 res. papers and revs in sci. lit. on photochem., photophys. and lasers. *Recreations*: music, travel, tennis, theatre. *Address*: 195 Barnett Wood Lane, Ashtead, Surrey KT21 2LP. *T*: (01372) 274385. *Club*: Athenæum.

**PHILLIPS, His Honour (David) Alan**; a Circuit Judge, 1983–95; Chancellor, diocese of Bangor, 1988–95; *b* 21 July 1926; *s* of Stephen Thomas Phillips, MC and Elizabeth Mary Phillips; *m* 1960, Jean Louise (*née* Godsell); two *d*. *Educ*: Llanelli Grammar Sch.; University Coll., Oxford (MA). Left school, 1944. Served War, Army, 1944; commnd, 1946, RWF; Captain (GS), 1947; demobilised, 1948. Oxford, 1948–51. Lectr, 1952–59. Called to Bar, Gray's Inn, 1960. Stipendiary Magistrate for Mid-Glamorgan, 1975–83; a Recorder of the Crown Court, 1974–83. *Recreations*: music, chess, swimming.
*See also* Rt Hon. Sir S. E. Phillips.

**PHILLIPS, Prof. David George**, DPhil; FRHistS, FAcSS; Professor of Comparative Education, University of Oxford, 2000–12, now Emeritus; Fellow of St Edmund Hall, Oxford, 1984–2012, now Emeritus; b 15 Dec. 1944; s of late George and Doris Phillips; m 1968, Valerie Mary Bache; two d. Educ: Sir Walter St John's Sch., Battersea; BA London 1966; St Edmund Hall, Oxford (DipEd 1967; MA; DPhil 1984). Assistant teacher: Huntingdon Grammar Sch., 1967–69; Chipping Norton Sch., 1969–75; University of Oxford: Tutor, then Univ. Lectr, Dept of Educnl Studies, 1975–96; Reader in Comparative Educn, 1996–2000; Professorial Sen. Res. Fellow in Comparative Educn, 2012–13. Member: Teacher Educn Commn of Wissenschaftsrat, 1990–91; Council, 1992–94, Scientific Cttee, 1992–98, German Inst. for Internat. Educnl Res., Frankfurt-am-Main; Educnl Sci. Commn, Ministry of Sci., Res. and the Arts, Baden-Württemberg, 2003–04; Chm., British Assoc. for Internat. and Comparative Educn, 1998–2000; Emeritus Res. Fellow, Leverhulme Trust, 2012. FAcSS (AcSS 2002); FRHistS 2002. FRSA 1987. Editor, Oxford Review of Education, 1984–2003; Series Editor, Oxford Studies in Comparative Educn, 1991–; Ed., Res. in Comparative and Internat. Educn, 2006–16; Editor, Comparative Educn, 2015–19 (Chm. Editl Bd, 2009–15, 2019–). *Publications*: Zur Universitätsreform in der Britischen Besatzungszone 1945–48, 1983; (ed) German Universities After the Surrender, 1983; (with Veronica Stencel) The Second Foreign Language, 1983; (ed) Which Language?, 1989; (with Caroline Filmer-Sankey) Diversification in Modern Language Teaching, 1993; Pragmatismus und Idealismus: das Blaue Gutachten und die Britische Hochschulpolitik in Deutschland 1948, 1995; (ed) Education in Germany: tradition and reform in historical context, 1995; (ed jtly) Learning from Comparing, vol. 1, 1999, vol. 2, 2000; (ed) Education in Eastern Germany since Unification, 2000; Reflections on British Interest in Education in Germany in the Nineteenth Century, 2002; (jtly) Towards a Structural Typology of Cross-National Attraction in Education, 2002; (ed jtly) Can the Japanese Change Their Education System?, 2003; (ed jtly) Implementing European Union Education and Training Policy: a comparative study of issues in four member states, 2003; (ed jtly) Educational Policy Borrowing: historical perspectives, 2005; (jtly) Comparative and International Education: an introduction to theory, method and practice, 2006; The German Example: English interest in educational provision in Germany since 1800, 2011; Investigating Education in Germany: historical studies from a British perspective, 2015; Educating the Germans: people and policy in the British zone of Germany, 2018; (ed) British Scholars of Comparative Education: examining the work and influence of notable 19th and 20th century comparativists, 2020; *festschrift*: (ed Hubert Ertl) Cross-National Attraction in Education: accounts from England and Germany, 2006; numerous articles in jls. *Recreations*: art history, antiquarian books. *Address*: Department of Education, 15 Norham Gardens, Oxford OX2 6PY; St Edmund Hall, Oxford OX1 4AR.

**PHILLIPS, David John**; QC 1997; a Recorder, since 1998; a Deputy High Court Judge, since 2001; b 4 May 1953; s of Hon. Sir (John) Raymond Phillips MC, and of Hazel Bradbury Phillips; m 1981, Ann Nicola Beckett, d of late Ronald Beckett; one s one d. Educ: Rugby Sch.; Aix-en-Provence Univ.; Balliol Coll., Oxford (BA (Jurisprudence) 1977; MA 1996). Called to the Bar, Gray's Inn, 1976 (Arden, Atkin, Mould & Reid Prize, 1977), Bencher, 2004; admitted Bar of Gibraltar, 2004; Mem., Bar of Eastern Caribbean, 2005; Mem., Bar of Turks and Caicos Islands, 2016; admitted to Bar of Trinidad and Tobago, 2017; Mem., Wales and Chester Circuit, 1983; Asst Recorder, 1994–98; Hd of Chambers, 199 Strand, 2000–06; door tenant, 30 Park Place, 1986–; Consultant (Of Counsel): Karam and Missick, Providenciales, Turks and Caicos Is, 2013–19; Wessex Fairchild, Providenciales, Turks and Caicos Is, 2019–. Legal Chairman: FA Premier League Tribunal, 2003– (Lay Mem., FA Specialist Panel, 2003–); Sports Dispute Resolution Panel, 2003–; Judicial Chm., Nat. Greyhound Racing Club's Appeal Tribunal, 2006–. Dir, Disability Law Service, 1999–2014. Mem. Cttee, Barristers' Benevolent Assoc., 1993– (Jt Hon. Treas., 1999–). *Recreations*: hill walking, cinema. *Address*: Wilberforce Chambers, 8 New Square, Lincoln's Inn, WC2A 3QP. *T*: (020) 7306 0102. *E*: dphillips@wilberforce.co.uk.

**PHILLIPS, Diane Susan**, CB 2000; Director, Transport Strategy, Department for Transport (formerly the Environment, Transport and the Regions, then Department for Transport, Local Government and the Regions), 2000–02; b 29 Aug. 1942; d of Michael Keogh and Jessie (née Tite); m 1967, John Phillips; two d. Educ: Univ. of Wales. NEDO, 1967–72; Civil Service, 1972–2002: Principal, DoE, 1972–77, Cabinet Office, 1977–78; Asst Sec., Dept of Transport, 1978–80; Department of the Environment, then Department of the Environment, Transport and the Regions, 1981–2002: Grade 4, Local Govt Finance, 1988–90; Under Sec. (Grade 3) and Principal Finance Officer, Property Hldgs, 1990–94; Dir, Social Housing Policy and Resources, 1994–98; Dir, Roads and Traffic, 1998–2000; Dep. Hd, Integrated Transport Taskforce, 2000. Mem. Bd, London & Quadrant Housing Trust, 1998–2013 (Dep. Chm., 2010–13). Gov., St George's Coll., Weybridge, 1995–2004. *Address*: 60 Portmore Park Road, Weybridge, Surrey KT13 8EU.

**PHILLIPS, Rt Rev. Donald David**; Bishop of Rupert's Land, 2000–18; m Nancy. Educ: Univ. of Western Ontario (BSc 1976, MSc 1979); Huron Coll., Univ. of Western Ontario (MDiv 1981; Hon. DD 2002); Durham Univ. (PhD 2015). Ordained deacon, 1981, priest, 1981; incumbent, Lac La Biche, Alberta, 1981–84; Priest in charge, St Thomas Ch, Fort McMurray and St Paul's Ch, Fort Chipewyan, Alberta, 1984–87; incumbent, St Michael and All Angels, Moose Jaw, Sask, 1987–92; Ministries Develt Co-ordinator, 1992–96, Exec. Officer, 1997–2000, Dio. Qu'Appelle. Hon. Asst, Parish of St Matthew, Regina, Sask, 1992–2000.

**PHILLIPS, Sir (Gerald) Hayden**, GCB 2002 (KCB 1998; CB 1989); DL; Director, St Just Farms Ltd, since 1997; Chairman: IPSO Appointments Panel, since 2014; Reviewing Committee on the Export of Works of Art and Cultural Objects, since 2014; Independent Reviewer of Rulings of Advertising Standards Authority Council, since 2010; b 9 Feb. 1943; s of Gerald Phillips and Dorothy Phillips; m 1st, 1967, Dr Ann Watkins (marr. diss.); one s one d; 2nd, 1980, Hon. Laura Grenfell; one s two d. Educ: Cambridgeshire High Sch.; Clare Coll., Cambridge (MA); Yale Univ., USA (MA). Home Office: Asst Principal, 1967; Economic Adviser, 1970–72; Principal, 1972–74; Asst Sec., and Principal Private Sec. to Sec. of State for Home Dept, 1974–76; Dep. Chef de Cabinet to Pres., Commn of European Communities, 1977–79; Asst Sec., Home Office, 1979–81, Asst Under-Sec. of State, 1981–86; Dep. Sec., Cabinet Office (MPO, subseq. Office of the Minister for the Civil Service), 1986–88; Dep. Sec., HM Treasury, 1988–92; Permanent Secretary: DNH, later Dept for Culture, Media and Sport, 1992–98; LCD, 1998–2003; Dept for Constitutional Affairs, 2003–04; Clerk of the Crown in Chancery, 1998–2004. Reviewer: the Honours System, 2004; the Funding of Political Parties, 2006–07; Chm., Inter-Party Talks on Political Funding, 2007. Charities Consultant to HRH the Prince of Wales, 2004–09. Chm., NT, 2004–10. Chm., Digital Cinema Funding Partnership, 2010–14. Director: Global Solutions Ltd, 2005–08; Hanson Family Hldgs, 2007–13; Westhouse Hldgs, 2009–14; Chm., Hanson Westhouse Ltd, 2007–09. Adviser: Hanson Capital, 2004–06; Englefield Capital, 2004–11. Dir, Energy Saving Trust, 2011–18. Member: Council, KCL, 1993–99; Ct of Govs, Henley Mgt Coll., 1993–2002; Council, Marlborough Coll., 1997–2013 (Chm., 2006–13); Bd, Inst. of Advanced Legal Studies, 1998–2004; Fitzwilliam Mus. Trust, 1999–2005; Salisbury Cathedral Council, 2002–14; Chm., Salisbury Cathedral Fabric Adv. Cttee, 2006–. Lay Canon, Salisbury Cathedral, 2008–. Chm. Cttee, Wellington Collection, Apsley Hse, 2010–; Gov., Wilts Historic Buildings Trust, 2006– (Dep. Chm., 2007–17; Vice-Pres., 2017–). Patron, Southern Spinal Injuries Trust, 2007–. Hon. Bencher, Inner Temple, 1998. DL Wilts, 2007. Actor in film, Jane Eyre, 2011. *Publications*: Review of the Honours System, 2004; Strengthening Democracy: fair and sustainable funding of political parties, 2007. *Recreations*: theatre, other arts, shooting and fishing, India. *Address*: Homington Farm, Homington, Salisbury, Wilts SP5 4NG. *Clubs*: Brooks's, Pratt's.

**PHILLIPS, Dr Helen Mary**; Chair, Chesterfield Royal Hospital NHS Foundation Trust, since 2015; b Dublin, 29 May 1966; d of James Phillips and Anne Phillips (née Duggan); m 1st, 1991, Desmond Ryan (marr. diss. 2008); one s one d; 2nd, 2009, Adrian Belton, qv; one step s two step d. Educ: University Coll., Dublin (BSc Hons 1987; PhD 1993). Environment Agency: Regl Tech. Planning Manager, 1996–97, Regl Planning Manager, 1997–98, Midlands Reg.; Area Manager, Thames Reg., 1998–2001; Head of Strategic Develt, 2001; Dir, Wales, 2002–06; Chief Exec., Natural England, 2006–12; Dir of Customer Services and Networks, Yorkshire Water, 2012–14; Chm., Loop Customer Mgt Ltd, Kelda Gp, 2012–14. Lead Accounting Officer, Jt Nature Conservation Cttee, 2006–11. Mem., Legal Services Bd, 2015– (Interim Chm., 2017–18; Chm., 2018–). FRSB. *Recreations*: walking, shoes, handbags, chocolate. *Address*: Chesterfield Royal Hospital NHS Foundation Trust, Calow, Chesterfield, Derbys S44 5BL. *Club*: Farmers.

**PHILLIPS, Prof. Ian**, MD; FRCP, FRCPath, FFPH; Professor of Medical Microbiology, 1974–96 (at St Thomas' Hospital, 1974–82), and Clinical Dean, 1992–96, United Medical and Dental Schools of Guy's and St Thomas's Hospitals, now Emeritus Professor; b 10 April 1936; s of late Stanley Phillips and Emma (née Price). Educ: St John's Coll., Cambridge (MA, MD); St Thomas's Hosp. Med. Sch. (MB BChir). FRCPath 1981; FRCP 1983; FFPH (FFPHM 1996). House Officer, St Thomas' Hosp., 1961–62; Lecturer in Microbiology: St Thomas's Hosp. Med. Sch., 1962–66; Makerere UC, 1966–69; Sen. Lectr, 1969–72, Reader, 1972–74, St Thomas's Hosp. Med. Sch.; Chm., Dist Mgt Team, St Thomas' Hosp., 1978–79; Hon. Cons. Microbiologist, St Thomas' Hosp., subseq. Guy's and St Thomas's Hosp. NHS Trust, 1969–96, now Emeritus Consultant; Chm., Pathology, Guy's and St Thomas's Hosp. NHS Trust, 1990–96. Civil Consultant, RAF, 1979–2000. Mem., Veterinary Products Cttee, 1981–85. An editor, Clinical Microbiology and Infection, 1997–2005. Mem. Council, RCPath, 1974–76 and 1987–90; Chairman: Brit. Soc. for Antimicrobial Chemotherapy, 1979–82; Assoc. of Med. Microbiologists, 1989–93; Pres., European Soc. for Clinical Microbiol. and Infectious Diseases, 1995–96 (Fellow, 2018). Member: S London Botanical Inst.; BSBI. Hon. Mem., Croatian Acad. of Med. Sci., 1997. Freeman, City of London, 1975; Liveryman, Soc. of Apothecaries, 1975. *Publications*: (ed jtly) Laboratory Methods in Antimicrobial Chemotherapy, 1978; (jtly) Microbial Disease, 1979; contrib. chapters and papers. *Recreations*: botany, music, decorative domestic glass. *Clubs*: Athenæum, Royal Society of Medicine.

**PHILLIPS, (Ian) Peter**, OBE 2004; JP; Director, Kroll Buchler Phillips Ltd, 1999–2005; Chairman, Kroll (formerly Buchler Phillips) Lindquist Avey, 1997–2005; b 13 Oct. 1944; s of Bernard Phillips and Constance Mary Clayton; m 1970, Wendy Berne; one s one d. Educ: Highgate Sch.; Sorbonne, Paris. FCA, FIPA. Partner, Bernard Phillips & Co., 1968; UK Head of Corporate Recovery Services, Arthur Andersen & Co., 1982–88; Chm., Buchler Phillips Gp, 1988–99. Jt Administrator, British and Commonwealth Holdings, 1990; Court Receiver, Estate of Robert Maxwell, 1991. Dir, Jt Insolvency Monitoring Unit, 1997–98; Mem., Insolvency Tribunal, 1997–. Pres., Insolvency Practitioners Assoc., 1988–89. Member: Lord Chancellor's Adv. Cttee on JPs for Inner London, City and Westminster, 1999–2009; 2nd and 3rd Selection Panels, Gtr London Magistrates' Cts Authy, 2002–04. Mem., Global Adv. Bd, Centre for Internat. Business and Mgt, Judge Inst. of Mgt, Cambridge Univ., 1999–. Trustee: Israel-Palestine Centre for Res. and Inf., 1991–96; Papyrus (Prevention of Suicide) Co. Ltd, 2000–04; Restorative Justice Consortium, 2006–07. Treas., N Kensington Neighbourhood Law Centre, 1970–76. Chm., Hampstead Theatre, 1997–2001 (Dir, 1991–2004; Mem., Adv. Council, 2004–); Chair, Develt Gp (formerly Major Donors Cttee), Anna Freud Centre, 2012–17. Mem., British Acad. of Experts, 1991–. Accredited Relate Counsellor, 2006. JP Inner London, 1979 (Dep. Chm., Highbury Corner Bench, 2004–08). Mem., Magic Circle, 2003–. *Publications*: Life After Debt, 2010. *Recreations*: theatre, baroque and modern jazz music, horse riding, coastal path walking, close-up magic, singing. *Address*: The Fourth House, 5 Turner Drive, NW11 6TX. *T*: 07836 572277.

**PHILLIPS, Jeremy Gavin**; QC 2018; b London, 20 Jan. 1954; s of Peter and Josephine Phillips; m 1984, Mary Gould; three s two d. Educ: Harrow Sch.; Univ. of Southampton (BA Hons English Lit.). Admitted as solicitor, 1980; Partner, Cartwrights, Solicitors, 1982–84; Co-Founder and Partner, Holt Phillips, Solicitors, 1984–94; Equity Partner: Eversheds (Solicitors), 1994–2001; Osborne Clarke (Solicitors), 2001–04; called to the Bar, Inner Temple, 2004; in practice as barrister, 2004–; Accredited Mediator, 2007. Mem., Disciplinary Panel, LTA, 2019–. Trustee, Licensing Trade Charity, 2015–. Fellow, Inst. Licensing, 2017. Ed.-in-Chief, Paterson's Licensing Acts, 105th edn, 1997–. *Publications*: Phillips Licensing Law Guide, 1995, 3rd edn 2002; (jtly) Law of Regulatory Enforcement and Sanctions, 2001; (contrib.) Halsbury's Laws of England, vol. 26, 1999, vol. 67, 2008, vol. 13, 2009; (jtly) Smith and Monkcom: Law of Gambling, 4th edn 2017. *Recreations*: family, Medieval history, motorbike racing, squash, gardening, literature, travel. *Address*: Francis Taylor Building, Inner Temple, EC4Y 7BY. *T*: (020) 7353 8415. *E*: jeremy.phillips@ftbchambers.co.uk. *Clubs*: Reform; Jesters.
See also S. B. Phillips.

**PHILLIPS, Jeremy Patrick Manfred**; QC 1980; b 27 Feb. 1941; s of late Manfred Henry Phillips, CA, and late Irene Margaret (née Symondson); m 1962, Margaret Ann (née Adams) (marr. diss. 1968); m 1968, Virginia Gwendoline (née Dwyer) (marr. diss. 1974); one s (and one s decd); m 1976, Judith Gaskell (née Hetherington); two s two d. Educ: St Edmund's Sch., Hindhead, Surrey; Charterhouse. Apprentice Accountant, Thomson McLintock & Co., 1957–61. Called to Bar, Gray's Inn, 1964; in practice, accountancy and commercial law, 1964–2003 (won case in HK that resulted in first modern mobile tel. system); Head of Chambers: 2 Temple Gdns, 1990–98; New Ct Chambers, 2000–03; DTI Inspector, affairs of Queens Moat Houses plc, 1993. Owner and Dir of Ops, Kentwell Hall, Long Melford, Suffolk, 1971–; originator of domestic living history events in UK with Kentwell's Annual Historical Re-Creations of Tudor Domestic Life, 1978–, World War II domestic events, 1995–, Halloween event, Scaresville, 2007–. Founding Dir, CARE Britain. *Publications*: contrib. early edns of Cooper's Students' Manual of Auditing, Cooper's Manual of Auditing and various pamphlets, papers, guides, etc, on Kentwell Hall and Tudor period, on democracy and educn issues. *Recreations*: historic buildings, Tudor history, constitutional and educational issues, cricket, conversation. *Address*: Kentwell Hall, Long Melford, Suffolk CO10 9BA.

**PHILLIPS, Jessica Rose**; MP (Lab) Birmingham Yardley, since 2015; b Yardley, Birmingham, 9 Oct. 1981; m 2006, Tom Phillips; two s. Educ: Univ. of Leeds (BA Jt Hons Econ. and Social Hist. and Social Policy 2003); Univ. of Birmingham (Postgrad. Dip. Public Sector Mgt 2013). Project and Event Manager, Health Links, 2008–10; Business Develt

Manager, Sandwell Women's Aid, 2010–15. Mem. (Lab), Birmingham CC, 2012–16. Mem., Women and Equalities Select Cttee, 2015–. Victims' Champion, Birmingham, 2011. *Publications:* Everywoman: one woman's truth about speaking the truth, 2017; Truth to Power: seven ways to call time on B. S., 2019. *Address:* House of Commons, SW1A 0AA.

**PHILLIPS, His Honour John Andrew,** CBE 2006; a Circuit Judge, 1998–2016; Director of Training (Courts), Judicial College, 2012–16; *b* 26 May 1950; *s* of Jack and Mary Nolan Phillips; *m* 1993, Moira Margaret Kynnersley (*d* 2012); two *d*. *Educ:* Fitzwilliam Coll., Cambridge (MA). Mem., Fitzwilliam String Quartet, Quartet in Residence, York Univ., 1971–74; called to the Bar, Gray's Inn, 1976, Bencher, 2008; in practice at the Bar, 1977–98. Dir of Studies, Judicial Studies Bd of England and Wales, 2007–11. Hon. DLaws BPP Univ. Coll. of Professional Studies, 2012. *Recreation:* playing the violin.

**PHILLIPS, Sir (John) David,** Kt 2000; QPM 1994; lecturer and writer; *b* 22 April 1944; *s* of late Percy Phillips and Alfreda Phillips; *m* 1970, Nancy Wynn Rothwell; one *s*. *Educ:* Leigh Grammar Sch.; Manchester Univ. (BA 1st Cl. Hons Econs). Served: Lancs Constabulary, 1963–84; Gtr Manchester Constabulary, 1984–89; Dep. Chief Constable, Devon and Cornwall, 1989–93; Chief Constable of Kent, 1993–2003; Dir, Nat. Centre of Policing Excellence, 2003–05. Chm., Nat. Crime Faculty; Pres., ACPO, 2001–03. CCMI 2002. Hon. Fellow, Christchurch Coll., Canterbury, 1998. Hon. LLD Coventry, 2010. *Recreations:* history, golf.

**PHILLIPS, John Randall;** Member, 1995–99, Chairman, 1995–96, then Lord Mayor, 1996–97, Cardiff City and County Council; *b* 22 April 1940; *s* of James Phillips and Charlotte Phillips (*née* Phelps); *m* 1967, Margaret Ray Davies; one *s* one *d*. *Educ:* Cardiff High Sch.; University Coll., Cardiff (BA Econ. 1961). Dip. Soc. Studies 1967. Cardiff City Council, 1963–66; Glam CC, 1967–74; Mid Glam CC, 1974–96: Principal Trng Officer, 1974–82; Principal Asst (Child Abuse), 1982–89; Dist Social Services Officer, Cynon Valley, 1989–94; Principal Officer, 1994–96. Cardiff City Council: Member (Lab), 1972–96; Chm. of Personnel, 1974–76 and 1979–83; Dep. Leader, Labour Gp, 1986, Ldr, 1990–94; Vice Chm., 1987, Chm., 1990, Policy; Leader, 1990–94; Dep. Lord Mayor, 1994–95. Mem., Cardiff Bay Develt Corp., 1990–99. First Pres., UWIC, 1996–97. *Recreations:* politics, listening to music. *Address:* 15 Kyle Crescent, Whitchurch, Cardiff CF14 1ST. *T:* (029) 2062 4878.

**PHILLIPS, Sir Jonathan,** KCB 2009; Warden, Keble College, Oxford, since 2010; *b* 21 May 1952; *s* of Gilbert Reginald Phillips and Ruby May Phillips (*née* Hughes); *m* 1974, Amanda Rosemary Broomhead; two *s*. *Educ:* Queen Mary's Grammar Sch., Walsall; St John's Coll., Cambridge (BA 1973; PhD 1978); London Univ. Inst. of Educn (PGCE 1974). Department of Trade, later Department of Trade and Industry, 1977–93: seconded to CBI econs directorate, 1982–83; as Sec., Cttee of Inquiry into regulatory arrangements at Lloyd's, 1986–87; Asst Sec., 1987–93; Under-Sec., 1993; Dir, Exec. Agencies, Dept of Transport, 1993–96; Department of Trade and Industry: Dir, Investigations and Enforcement, 1996–98; Dir, Finance and Resource Mgt, 1998–2000; Dir Gen., Resources and Services, 2000–02; Operating Strategy Dir, Sea Systems, BAE Systems, 2002 (on secondment); Pol Dir, 2002–05, Perm. Sec., 2005–10, NI Office. Non-executive Director: Forward Trust Gp, 1995–96; Charlie Goldsmith Associates, 2011–. Mem. Bd, Cooperation Ireland, 2010–. Gov., St Saviour's and St Olave's Sch., Southwark, 1998–2005. Chm., Bd of Visitors, Pitt Rivers Mus., 2019–. Pres., Friends of the Oxford Bach Choir, 2012–; Trustee, Esmée Fairbairn Foundn, 2011– (Dep. Chair, 2019–); Chm. Trustees, Schola Cantorum, Oxford, 2013–. *Address:* Keble College, Oxford OX1 3PG. *Clubs:* Athenæum, Oxford and Cambridge.

**PHILLIPS, Prof. Judith Eleri,** OBE 2013; PhD; Professor of Gerontology, and Deputy Principal (Research), University of Stirling, since 2016; *b* Cardiff, 7 Feb. 1959; *d* of Thomas William Pugh Phillips and Bridget Phillips; *m* 1991, Peter. *Educ:* Pontypridd Girls' Grammar Sch.; University Coll. of Wales, Aberystwyth (BA Hons 1980); Stockholm Univ. (Dip. Social Sci. 1981); Jesus Coll., Oxford (MSc, CQSW 1983); Univ. of E Anglia (PhD 1989). Social worker, Wilts CC, 1983–85; Researcher, 1988–89, Lectr in Social Work, 1989–93, UEA; Keele University: Lectr in Social Work and Gerontol., 1993–98; Sen. Lectr, 1998–2001; Prof. of Social Gerontol., 2001–04; University of Wales, Swansea, later Swansea University: Prof. of Gerontol. and Social Work, 2004–16; Scientific Dir, Centre for Innovative Ageing, 2009–16; Dir, Res. Inst. for Applied Social Sci., 2009–16; Dep. Pro Vice Chancellor, 2011–16. Dir, Older People and Ageing R&D Network in Wales, 2006. Chair, Res. Cttee, Guide Dogs, 2015. Guest Professor: Umeå Univ., Sweden, 2011–13; Lund Univ., Sweden, 2012; Vis. Fellow, New Coll., Oxford, 2011; Vis. Sen. Res. Fellow, LSE, 2011–13. AcSS 2009; Fellow, British Soc. Gerontol., 2011; FLSW 2012. FRSA 2014. *Publications:* Social Work with Older People, 2006, 5th edn 2011; Care: key concepts, 2007; Ageing at the Intersection of Work and Home Life: blurring the boundaries, 2008; Critical Issues in Social Work with Older People, 2008; Key Concepts in Social Gerontology, 2010. *Recreations:* hill walking, history of tea shops, international public speaking. *Address:* Deputy Principal Office, University of Stirling, Stirling FK9 4LA.

**PHILLIPS, Leslie Samuel,** CBE 2008 (OBE 1998); actor, director, producer; *b* 20 April 1924; *s* of late Frederick and Cecelia Phillips; *m* 1st, 1948, Penelope Bartley (marr. diss. 1965; she *d* 1981); two *s* two *d*; 2nd, 1982, Angela Scoular (*d* 2011); one step *s*; 3rd, 2013, Zara Carr. *Educ:* Chingford Sch.; Italia Conti Stage Sch. Army, 1942–45 (Lieut, DLI; invalided out). *Theatre* includes: début, Peter Pan, London Palladium, 1937; Zeal of Thy House, Garrick, 1938; Otello, and Turandot, Covent Garden, 1939; Dear Octopus, Queen's, 1939–40; Nutmeg Tree, Lyric, 1941–42; The Doctor's Dilemma, Haymarket, 1942; Daddy Long-Legs, Comedy, 1947–48; Charley's Aunt, Saville, 1948; On Monday Next, Comedy, 1949; For Better, For Worse, Comedy, 1952–54; Diary of a Nobody, Arts, 1954; Lost Generation, Garrick, 1955; The Whole Truth, Aldwych, 1955–56; The Big Killing, Shaftesbury, 1961–62; Boeing-Boeing, Apollo, 1963–5; The Deadly Game (also dir), Savoy, 1967; The Man Most Likely To… (also dir), Vaudeville, 1968–69, tour, S Africa, 1970–71, Duke of York's, 1972, tour of Australia, 1974; Sextet, Criterion, 1977–78; Canaries Sometimes Sing, tour, 1980; Not Now Darling, Savoy, 1979, world tour, 1980; Pygmalion, tour, 1980; The Cherry Orchard, Haymarket, 1983; Chapter 17, tour, 1983; Passion Play, Wyndham's, 1984–85; Pride and Prejudice, tour, 1988; Taking Steps, world tour, 1989; Painting Churches, Playhouse, 1992; August, tour of Wales, 1994; Love for Love, Chichester, 1996; Merry Wives of Windsor, RSC, 1997; Camino Real, 1998; On The Whole It's Been Jolly Good, Edin. Fest., 1999, Hampstead, 2000; Naked Justice, W Yorks Playhouse, 2001, 2002; The Play What I Wrote, Wyndhams, 2003; more than 100 *films*, including: A Lassie from Lancashire, 1938; The Citadel, 1938; Four Feathers, 1938; Mikado, 1938; Climbing High, 1939; Proud Valley, 1939; Thief of Baghdad, 1939; Train of Events, 1949; Sound Barrier, 1949; Pool of London, 1950; Gamma People, 1955; The Smallest Show on Earth, 1956; Brothers in Law, 1956; High Flight, 1957; Les Girls, 1957; Carry on Nurse, 1958; I Was Monty's Double, 1958; Carry on Constable, 1959; This Other Eden, 1959; Ferdinando, 1959; Doctor in Love, 1960; Very Important Person, 1961; In the Doghouse, 1961; Raising the Wind, 1961; Crooks Anonymous, 1962; Fast Lady, 1962; The Longest Day, 1963; Doctor in Clover, 1965; You Must Be Joking, 1965; Maroc 7 (also prod.), 1966; Some Will Some Won't, 1969; Doctor in Trouble, 1970; Magnificent Seven Deadly Sins, 1971; Don't Just Lie There, 1973; Spanish Fly, 1975; Out of Africa, 1986; Empire of the Sun, 1987; Scandal, 1988; Mountains of the Moon, 1989; King Ralph, 1990; August, 1995; Day of the Jackal, 1997; Cinderella, 1999; Saving Grace, 2000; Lara Croft: Tomb Raider, 2001; Thunderpants, 2001; Harry Potter and the Philosopher's Stone, 2001; Collusion, 2002; Harry Potter and the Chamber of Secrets, 2002; Carry On Columbus, 2002; Churchill: the Hollywood years, 2002; Colour Me Kubrick, 2004; Walking With Shadows, 2004; Millions, 2005; Venus, 2007; Is Anybody There?, 2009; Harry Potter and the Deathly Hallows, Pt 2, 2011; *television* includes: Morning Departure (first TV from Alexandra Palace), 1948; My Wife Jacqueline, 1952; Our Man at St Mark's, 1963; Impasse, 1963; The Reluctant Debutante, 1965; The Gong Game, 1965; Foreign Affairs, 1966; Blandings Castle, 1967; Very Fine Line, 1968; The Suit, 1969; Casanova, 1973; Redundant and the Wife's Revenge, 1983; You'll Never See Me Again, 1983; Mr Palfrey of Westminster, 1985; Monte Carlo, 1986; Rumpole, 1988; Summer's Lease, 1989; Comic Strip, 1989, 1990, 1991; Chancer, 1989–90; Who Bombed Birmingham, 1990; Life After Life, 1990; Thacker, 1991; The Trials of Oz, 1991; Boon, 1992; Lovejoy, 1992; Bermuda Grace, 1993; The Changeling, 1993; Vanity Dies Hard, 1993; Love on a Branch Line, 1993; House of Windsor, 1994; Two Golden Balls, 1994; Honey for Tea, 1994; The Canterville Ghost, 1995; L for Liverpool, 1998; Dalziel & Pascoe, 1998; The Best of British, 2000; Sword of Honour, 2000; Take a Girl Like You, 2000; Into the Void, 2001; Legends, 2002; Monarch of the Glen, 2002; Holby City, 2002; Midsomer Murders, 2002; Unto the Wicked, 2002; Where The Heart Is, 2003; The Last Detective, 2007; Miss Marple, 2007; Harley Street, 2008; Edgar Wallace series: The Pale Horse, 1996; Tales from the Crypt, 1996; *radio* includes: The Navy Lark, 1959–76; Three Men in a Boat, 1962; Vera Lynn Story, 1973; Would the Last Businessman to Leave England Please Turn out the Light, 1977–78; Round the World in 80 Days, 1991–92; Red Riding Hood and the Wolf's Story, 1994; England Their England, 1994; Wind in the Willows, 1994; Truth in Dark Places, 1994–95; Falling Heads, 1995; Philip and Rowena, 1995; Envious Casca, 1996; Half a Sixpence, 1996; Me and Little Boots, 2000; Maclean the Memorex Years, 2000; Cousin Bette, 2000; Tales from the Backbench, 2001; Democracy and Language, 2001; Les Miserables, 2002; Hitchhiker's Guide to the Galaxy, 2003; Cads, 2004; Dr Who, 2004; presenter, Carry on Forever!, 2010. Vice Pres., Royal Theatrical Fund; Founder Mem., Theatre of Comedy; Vice Pres., Disabled Living Foundn, 2002–. Award for lifetime achievement in films, Evening Standard, 1997; Comic Icon Award, 2003, Greatest Living Englishman Award, 2006, Loaded mag.; Dilys Powell Award for Lifetime Achievement in Film, London Critics Circle, 2007; Best Supporting Actor, BIFA, 2007; Best Trouper Award, Oldie mag., 2007. *Publications:* Hello: the autobiography, 2006. *Recreations:* cats, restoration, racing, collecting, gardening, classical music, weaving, chess, all sport. *Address:* c/o Independent Talent Group Ltd, 40 Whitfield Street, W1T 2RH. *T:* (020) 7636 6565.

**PHILLIPS, Malcolm Edward,** MD; FRCP; Consultant Physician and Nephrologist, Imperial College Healthcare NHS Trust (formerly Charing Cross Hospital, then Hammersmith Hospitals NHS Trust), 1981–2005 (Director of Renal Services, 1994–2001); *b* 24 March 1940; *s* of Albert H. Phillips and Kathleen M. Phillips; *m* 1st, 1967, Rona Lendon (marr. diss. 2012); one *s* one *d*; 2nd, 2013, Shu-Ching Cheng; two *d*. *Educ:* Charing Cross Hosp. Med. Sch., London (MB BS 1964; MD 1979). MRCS 1964; FRCP 1986. Jun. hosp. med. posts, Fulham Hosp. and Charing Cross Hosp., 1964–81; Wellcome Trust Fellow, Univ. of Naples, 1970–72; Gen. Manager, 1989, Med. Dir, 1995–97, Charing Cross Hosp. Panellist, Fitness to Practise Panel, GMC, 2006–12; Chm., Fitness to Practise Panels, MPTS, 2012–14. Canterbury Trustbank Vis. Prof., Christchurch, NZ, 1997. Pres., W London Medico-Chirurgical Soc., 2005–06; Member: Internat. Assoc. for Hist. of Nephrol., 2015–; Mem., Eur. Assoc. of Professors Emeriti, 2016–. *Publications:* articles in jls. *Recreations:* cricket, philately.

**PHILLIPS, Margaret Corinna, (Mrs D. R. Hunt),** FRCO; Professor of Organ, Royal College of Music, since 1996; concert organist; *b* 16 Nov. 1950; *d* of John George Phillips and Cora Frances (*née* Hurford); *m* 1983, Dr David Richard Hunt, MA, ARCO. *Educ:* Sittingbourne Grammar Sch. for Girls; Maidstone Grammar Sch. for Girls; Royal Coll. of Music (ARCM). GRSM 1971; FRCO 1971. Director of Music, St Lawrence Jewry next Guildhall, London, 1976–85; Prof. of Organ and Harpsichord, London Coll. of Music, 1985–91; Tutor in Organ Studies, RNCM, 1993–97 (Vis. Tutor, 1997–2005). Co-founder with Dr D. R. Hunt, and Chm., English Organ Sch. and Museum, Milborne Port, Som, 1996–. Pres., IAO, 1997–99; Mem. Council, RCO, 1982–2003. Recitals throughout Europe, USA, Canada, Mexico and Australia; radio broadcasts, UK, Scandinavia, Netherlands, Australia, USA; numerous recordings incl. complete organ works of J. S. Bach. *Publications:* articles on style and performance of organ music. *Recreations:* reading, tennis, playing the violin. *Address:* The Manse, Chapel Lane, Milborne Port, Sherborne DT9 5DL. *T:* (01963) 250011. *W:* www.margaretphillips.org.uk.

**PHILLIPS, Captain Mark Anthony Peter,** CVO 1974; ADC(P); Chef d'Equipe and Coach, US Three Day Event Team, 1993–2012; Consultant, Gleneagles Mark Phillips Equestrian Centre, 1992–97 (Director, 1988–92); *b* 22 Sept. 1948; *s* of late P. W. G. Phillips, MC, and Anne Patricia (*née* Tiarks); *m* 1st, 1973, HRH The Princess Anne (marr. diss. 1992); one *s* one *d*; 2nd, 1997, Sandy Pflueger; one *d*. *Educ:* Marlborough Coll.; RMA Sandhurst. Joined 1st The Queen's Dragoon Guards, July 1969; Regimental duty, 1969–74; Company Instructor, RMA Sandhurst, 1974–77; Army Trng Directorate, MoD, 1977–78, retired. Personal ADC to HM the Queen, 1974–. Student, RAC Cirencester, 1978. Chm., British Olympic Equestrian Fund, subseq. British Equestrian Fedn Fund, 1989–2000. In Three Day Equestrian Event, GB winning teams: Team Championships: World, 1970; European, 1971; Olympic Gold Medallists (Team), Olympic Games, Munich, 1972; Olympic Silver Medallists (Team), Olympic Games, Seoul, 1988; Mem., Equestrian Team (Reserve), Olympic Games, Mexico, 1968 and Montreal, 1976. Winner, Badminton Three Day Event, 1971, 1972, 1974, 1981. Dir, Glos TEC, 1991–98. Hon. FBHS 2005. Liveryman: Farriers' Co.; Farmers' Co.; Carmen's Co.; Loriners' Co.; Freeman: City of London; Yeoman, Saddlers' Co. *Recreations:* riding, Rugby football, athletics. *Address:* Aston Farm, Cherington, Tetbury, Glos GL8 8SW. *Club:* (Hon. Mem.) Buck's.

*See also under Royal Family.*

**PHILLIPS, Mark Paul;** QC 1999; a Recorder, 2000–07; *b* 28 Dec. 1959; *s* of Norman John Phillips and Wendy Sharron Phillips; *m* 1984, Deborah Elizabeth Fisher (*d* 2010); one *s* two *d*; *m* 2011, Samantha Jayne Wilding; one *s* two step *d*. *Educ:* John Hampden Sch., High Wycombe; Univ. of Bristol (LLB 1982; LLM 1983). Called to the Bar, Inner Temple, 1984; in practice, 1986–; Asst Recorder, 1998–2000. Pres., Insolvency Lawyers' Assoc., 2002–03; Member: Council, Assoc. of Business Recovery Professionals, 2004–10 (Fellow, 2004); Internat. Insolvency Inst., 2007–. Founder and Mem. Bd, Debbie Fund, 2010–12. Gov., John Hampden Grammar Sch., 2014–. *Publications:* (ed jtly) Butterworths Insolvency Law Handbook, 1987, 13th edn 2011; contrib. chapter on Insolvency in: Byles on Bills of Exchange, 26th edn 1983; Paget's Law of Banking, 10th edn 1989 to 13th edn 2007; chap. on insolvency procedures in Insolvency of Banks: managing the risks, 1996. *Recreations:* dating my wife, family, watching football, motor sport. *Address:* 3–4 South Square, Gray's Inn, WC1R 5HP. *T:* (020) 7696 9900, *Fax:* (020) 7696 9911. *E:* markphillips@southsquare.com.

**PHILLIPS, (Mark) Trevor,** OBE 1999; broadcaster and journalist; Chairman, Green Park Executive Recruitment, since 2018; Co-founder and Director, Webber Phillips Data Analytics, since 2014; *b* 31 Dec. 1953; *s* of George Milton Phillips and Marjorie Eileen Phillips; *m* 1st, 1981, Asha Bhownagary (marr. diss. 2009); two *d*; 2nd, 2013, Helen Veale. *Educ:* Queen's Coll., Georgetown, Guyana; Imperial Coll., London (BSc; ARCS). Pres., NUS, 1978–80; London Weekend Television: researcher, 1980–81; producer, Black on Black, The Making of Britain, 1981–86; reporter, This Week, Thames TV, 1986–87; London Weekend Television: Editor, London Prog., 1987–92; Hd, Current Affairs, 1992–94; Presenter: London Prog., 1987–2000; Crosstalk, 1994–2000; The Material World, 1998–2000. Man. Dir, Pepper Prodns, 1994. Sen. Fellow, Policy Exchange, 2018–. Mem. (Lab), 2000–03, Chm., 2000–01 and 2002–03, Dep. Chm., 2001–02, London Assembly, GLA. Chairman: CRE, 2003–06; Index on Censorship, 2018–. Chairman: Runnymede Trust, 1993–98; Hampstead Theatre, 1993–97; London Arts Bd, 1997–2000; Mem. Bd, Barbican Arts Centre, 2013–19. Chair, Equality and Human Rights Commn, 2006–12; Mem., Social Integration Commn, 2014–16. Pres., John Lewis Partnership Council, 2015–18. Vice-Pres., RTS, 2000–. Fellow, Imperial Coll. London, 2007. FRSA 1995. Journalism Award, RTS, 1988 and 1993; Best Documentary Series (for Windrush), RTS, 1998. Chevalier, Légion d'Honneur (France), 2007. *Publications:* Windrush: the irresistible rise of multi-racial Britain, 1998; Britain's Slave Trade, 1999; Race and Faith: the deafening silence, 2016. *Recreations:* music, running, crosswords. *Clubs:* Athenæum, Groucho, Home House.

**PHILLIPS, Matthew James;** QC 2017; *b* Manchester, 26 Oct. 1969; *s* of Malcolm and Margaret Phillips; *m* 1999, Rachel Willmot; two *s*. *Educ:* Bolton Sch., Lancs; Trinity Coll., Oxford (MA Juris.); St Catharine's Coll., Cambridge (Dip. Internat. Law). Called to the Bar, Lincoln's Inn, 1993; in practice as barrister, specialising in personal injury, clinical negligence and sports law. *Recreations:* junior football management, cycling (road), the emotional rollercoaster that is BWFC! *Address:* Outer Temple Chambers, 222 Strand, WC2R 1BA. *T:* (020) 7353 6381.

**PHILLIPS, Max;** Assistant Under Secretary of State, Ministry of Defence, 1977–84; *b* 31 March 1924; *m* 1953, Patricia Moore; two *s* one *d* (and one *d* decd). *Educ:* Colston's Sch., Bristol; Christ's Hospital; Magdalene Coll., Cambridge (Schol.; 1st cl. Hist. Tripos, pts I and II; MA). Served War, RA, 1943–46. Appointed to Home Civil Service, 1949; Colonial Office, 1949–59; Sec., Nigeria Fiscal Commn, 1957–58; UKAEA, 1959–73; Procurement Exec., MoD, 1973–74; HM Treasury, 1974–77; retired 1984, re-employed as Asst Sec., MoD, 1984–87. Chm., Guildford Evening DFAS, 2003–06. Gov., Christ's Hospital, 1979– (Almoner, 1981–92). *Recreations:* modern myths, exploring the imagination and the countryside. *Address:* 2 Wilderness Farmhouse, Onslow Village, Guildford, Surrey GU2 7QP. *T:* (01483) 561308.

**PHILLIPS, Melanie;** columnist, The Times, since 2014; *b* 4 June 1951; *d* of late Alfred and Mabel Phillips; *m* 1974, Joshua Rufus Rozenberg, *qv*; one *s* one *d*. *Educ:* Putney High Sch. for Girls; St Anne's Coll., Oxford (BA 1973). Grad. trainee, Evening Echo, Hemel Hempstead, 1974–76; staff writer, New Society, 1976–77; Guardian: reporter, 1977; social services corresp., 1978–80; leader writer, 1980–84; news ed., 1984–87; Asst Ed. and columnist, 1987–93; columnist: Observer, 1993–98; Sunday Times, 1998–2001; Daily Mail, 2001–14. Panellist, The Moral Maze, BBC Radio 4. *Publications:* The Divided House, 1980; (with J. Dawson) Doctors' Dilemmas, 1984; All Must Have Prizes, 1996, 3rd edn 1998; The Sex-Change Society: feminised Britain and the neutered male, 1999; The Ascent of Woman, 2003, 2nd edn 2004; Londonistan, 2006; The World Turned Upside Down: the global battle over God, truth and power, 2010; Guardian Angel, 2013, 2nd edn 2018; The Legacy, 2018. *Recreations:* family, friends, theatre, cinema. *Address:* BCM Rozenberg, WC1N 3XX. *E:* melanie@melaniephillips.com. *W:* www.melaniephillips.com.

**PHILLIPS, Prof. Nelson William,** PhD; Abu Dhabi Chamber Professor of Innovation and Strategy (formerly Professor of Strategy and Organizational Behaviour), Imperial College Business School (formerly Tanaka Business School), Imperial College London, since 2005; *b* 7 Nov. 1962; *s* of Murray and Lucille Phillips. *Educ:* Univ. of Calgary (BSc, MBA); Univ. of Alberta (PhD 1995). Asst Prof., 1993–98, Associate Prof., 1998–2002, Faculty of Mgt, McGill Univ.; Beckwith Prof. of Mgt Studies and MBA Dir, Judge Inst. of Mgt, and Fellow, Hughes Hall, Cambridge Univ., 2002–05. *Publications:* (with C. Hardy) Discourse Analysis, 2002; contribs to Acad. of Mgt Jl, Organization Science, Organization Studies, Jl Mgt Studies. *Address:* Imperial College Business School, Imperial College London, S Kensington Campus, SW7 2AZ. *T:* (020) 7589 5111, *Fax:* (020) 7823 7685. *E:* n.phillips@imperial.ac.uk.

**PHILLIPS, Nigel James,** CBE 2013; Governor, Falkland Islands, and Commissioner for South Georgia and the South Sandwich Islands, since 2017; *b* UK, 1963; *s* of Brian and Jean Phillips; *m* 2005, Emma; one *d*. *Educ:* Durham Univ. Business Sch. (MBA 1997); King's Coll. London (MA 2001). CEng 2013; MIET. Joined RAF, 1984; jssc 2001; Sen. SO Plans, Defence Communications Services Agency, MoD, 2001–03; Defence Attaché, Stockholm, 2003–07; Dep. Comdt, Defence Coll. of Communications Information Systems, MoD, 2007–09; Defence Attaché, Warsaw, 2008–12; RCDS, 2013–14; Hd, Wider Europe Policy, MoD, 2015–16; Dep. Mil. Rep. to EU, 2016–17. *Recreations:* military history, walking black labradors. *Address:* The Coach House, 95 Victoria Road, Cirencester, Glos GL7 1ES.

**PHILLIPS, Prof. Paddy Andrew,** FRACP, FACP, FRCP; Chief Public Health Officer, Department of Health, Australia, since 2015; Chief Medical Officer, Department of Health, South Australia, since 2008; Professor of Medicine, Flinders University, Adelaide, since 1997; Consultant, Flinders Medical Centre and Repatriation Hospitals, Adelaide, since 1997 (Head of Medicine, 1997–2008); *b* 26 Oct. 1956; *s* of Walter Alfred Peter Phillips and Lilian Phillips (*née* Watt); one *s* one *d*. *Educ:* Univ. of Adelaide (MB, BS); Univ. of Oxford (DPhil 1983; MA 1997). Intern, Royal Adelaide Hosp., 1980; Hon. Sen. House Officer, John Radcliffe Hosp., Oxford, 1981–83; Resident MO and Registrar, Prince Henry's Hosp., Melbourne, 1984–86; Fellow in Clinical Pharmacology, 1987, Res. Fellow, 1988–90, Consultant, 1988–96, Austin Hosp., Melbourne; Sen. Lectr, 1990–94, Associate Prof., 1994–96, Dept of Medicine, Melbourne Univ.; May Reader in Medicine, Nuffield Dept of Clinical Medicine, Univ. of Oxford, and Professorial Fellow, New Coll., Oxford, 1996–97; Consultant, Oxford Radcliffe NHS Trust, 1996–97; Adjunct Prof., Duke Univ., 2002–; Affiliate Prof., Univ. of Adelaide, 2017–. Public Service Medal for Health Services, 2011. *Publications:* scientific papers in physiol., pharmacol., cardiovascular disease, health services research. *Recreations:* mountain and road cycling, wine, fly fishing, ski-ing, music. *Address:* South Australia Department of Health, Citicentre Building, Hindmarsh Square, Adelaide, SA 5000, Australia. *T:* (8) 82266000.

**PHILLIPS, Patricia Ruth;** HM Diplomatic Service, retired; Counsellor, Foreign and Commonwealth Office, 2010–14; *b* 11 March 1962; *d* of Alan and Diana Phillips. *Educ:* N London Collegiate Sch.; Newnham Coll., Cambridge (BA Hist. 1984); Open Univ. (MBA 2011); Univ. of Birmingham (MA Mil. Hist. 2018). MAFF, 1984–91; Fulbright Fellow, Univ. of Minnesota, 1991–92; First Secretary: Washington, 1992–97; FCO, 1997–2002; Counsellor (Econ.), The Hague, 2002–04; Dep. Hd of Mission, Amman, 2004–07; Ambassador to Angola and concurrently to São Tomé and Príncipe, 2007–09. *Recreations:* music, history.

**PHILLIPS, Dr Paul Lasseter,** CBE 2017 (OBE 2011); Principal and Chief Executive, Weston College Group, since 2001; *b* Newport, Gwent, 22 Oct. 1957; *s* of Kenneth and Hazel Phillips; partner, Julie Mears; two *s*. *Educ:* University Coll., Cardiff (Craddock Wells Schol.; BSc Special Hons Maths 1979; MEd Law/Econs 1987; PhD Cost Benefit Analysis of Post-16 Educn 1990). Research Officer: in Erythropoesis, University Hosp. of Wales, 1977; in Computer, Audit, Control and Security, Ferranti Computers, 1979; Prog. Advr, Univ. of Wales, Cardiff, 1979; Dep. Hd. of Maths, Rougemont Sch., Newport, 1980–82; Sen. Lectr, 1982–89, Hd of Dept, 1989–92, Pontypool Coll.; Dep. Principal, Ebbw Vale Coll., 1992–95; Gwent Tertiary College: Asst Dir, Usk Campus, 1995–97; Dir, Newport Campus, 1997–98; Vice Principal, 1998–2001. N Som Award for contribn to Weston-super-Mare, 2005. *Recreations:* Rugby, canal restoration, professional wrestling. *Address:* Weston College, Knightstone Road, Weston-super-Mare, Som BS23 2AL. *T:* (01934) 411447. *E:* principals.office@weston.ac.uk.

**PHILLIPS, Peter;** *see* Phillips, I. P.

**PHILLIPS, Peter Andrew Jestyn;** Chief Executive, Secretary of the Press Syndicate, and University Printer, Cambridge University Press, since 2012; Fellow, Wolfson College, Cambridge, since 2012; *b* Cardiff, 1 May 1962; *s* of late Dr Ernest Phillips and of Barbara Phillips; *m* 1988, Clare Higgins; two *s* one *d*. *Educ:* Culford Sch., Merton Coll., Oxford (BA 1st Cl. Maths); Harvard Business Sch. (AMP 2002); Univ. of Cambridge (MA). Associate Consultant, 1984–86, Consultant, 1986–89, Manager, 1989–91, Bain & Co.; Sen. Manager, Corporate Finance, S G Warburg, 1991–93; BBC: Hd, Corporate Planning, 1993–96; Finance Dir, 1997–2000, Chief Operating Officer, 2001–04, News; Dir, Business Develt, 2005–06; Bd Mem. and Partner, Strategy and Market Develts, Ofcom, 2006–10; Chief Operating Officer, CUP, 2010–12. Dir, Parly Broadcasting Ltd, 1998–2006. Advr, RCP, 2004–11. Chm., Sabre Trust, 1990–93; Trustee: John Schofield Trust, 1995–2011; Article 19, 2001–05; Crafts Council, 2004–11; Nuffield Trust, 2008–14; Cambridge Commonwealth, Eur. and Internat. Trust, 2016–. Pres., Publishers' Assoc., 2019– (Mem., Council, 2015–; Vice-Pres., 2018–19). *Recreations:* walking, small islands, chamber music, motorbikes, Arsenal FC, contemporary crafts. *Address:* Cambridge University Press, University Printing House, Shaftesbury Road, Cambridge CB2 8BS. *T:* (01223) 312393.

**PHILLIPS, Sir Peter (John),** Kt 1990; OBE 1983; Chairman, Principality Building Society, 1991–2000 (Deputy Chairman, 1988–91); *b* 18 June 1930; *s* of Walter Alfred Phillips and Victoria Mary Phillips; *m* 1956, Jean Gwendoline Williams; one *s* one *d*. *Educ:* Radley College; Pembroke College, Oxford (MA). Joined Aberthaw and Bristol Channel Portland Cement Co., 1956, Jt Man. Dir, 1964–83; Western Area Dir, Blue Circle Industries, 1983–84; Dep. Chm., 1985, Chm., 1987–93, A. B. Electronic Products Gp. Dep. Chm. Bd of Governors, Univ. of Glam., 1996–98; Chm. Council, Univ. of Wales, Cardiff, 1998–2004 (Vice-Chm., 1997–98). *Recreations:* walking, fishing, reading. *Address:* Fromheulog, Church Road, Llanbethian, Cowbridge CF71 7JF. *Club:* Cardiff and County.

**PHILLIPS, Peter Sayer;** Founder and Musical Director, The Tallis Scholars, since 1973; Music Critic, The Spectator, 1983–2016; Bodley Fellow, Merton College, Oxford, since 2010 (Director of Music, 2008–16); *b* 15 Oct. 1953; *s* of Nigel Sayer Phillips and Patricia Ann Witchell (*née* Wyatt); *m* 1st, 1987, Clio (marr. diss. 1993), *d* of late David Oliver Lloyd-Jacob, CBE; 2nd, 1997, Caroline Trevor; one *s*. *Educ:* Winchester Coll.; St John's Coll., Oxford (Organ Scholar). Teacher: Oxford Univ., 1976–81; Trinity Coll. of Music, 1980–84; RCM, 1981–88. Co-founder and Artistic Director: Gimell Records, 1980–; Tallis Scholars Summer Schs, Oakham, 2000–11 and Uppingham, 2012–14 (teacher, 2000–14), Seattle, 2005–13, Sydney, 2007–12. Has conducted Dutch Chamber Choir, Collegium Vocale Gent, BBC Singers, Intrada of Moscow, Musica Reservata Barcelona, El Leon de Oro, Chœur de Chambre de Namur, Latvian Radio Choir, London Internat. A Cappella Choral Competition, Estonian Philharmonic Chamber Choir. Mem., Early Music Cttee, Arts Council, 1987–88. Chm., Judges, London A Cappella Choir Competition, 2014–. cricket correspondent, Spectator, 1989; Prop. and Adv. Ed., Musical Times, 1995–. Many awards for recordings made by Tallis Scholars, incl. Gramophone Record of the Year, 1987, and Early Music Record of the Year, 1987, 1991, 1994 and 2005, Gramophone magazine, and Diapason d'Or de l'Année, 1989, 2012. Chevalier de l'Ordre des Arts et des Lettres (France), 2005. *Publications:* English Sacred Music 1549–1649, 1991; (contrib.) Companion to Medieval and Renaissance Music, 1992; What We Really Do, 2003, 2nd edn 2013; contrib. Spectator, Guardian, Times, Musical Times, New Republic, Listener, Early Music, Music and Letters, Royal Acad. magazine, Evening Standard, BBC Music Magazine, TLS, Sunday Telegraph. *Recreations:* black and white photography, cricket, cooking, Arabia. *Address:* 22 Gibson Square, N1 0RD. *T:* (020) 7226 8047; 48 rue des Francs Bourgeois, 75003 Paris, France. *T:* 42724461. *Clubs:* Chelsea Arts, MCC, Two Brydges.

**PHILLIPS, (Rachel) Sarah,** OBE 2005; DL; Chairman, Demelza Hospice Care for Children, 2012–18; *b* 8 Feb. 1943; *d* of late Air Cdre John Lawrance Kirby, CB, CBE, JP, DL and Rachel Kirby; *m* 1966, Peter, *s* of Maj.-Gen. Sir Farndale Phillips, KBE, CB, DSO, and Lady (Lovering Catherine) Phillips; one *s* one *d*. *Educ:* Benenden Sch.; Heidelberg. Qualified as: LTA coach, 1978; remedial tutor, Kingsbury Centre, Washington, 1983; diagnosed with MS, 1981. Trustee, 1992–2005, Chm., 1998–2005, Multiple Sclerosis Society of GB and NI; Chm., Colchester Br., MS Soc., 1989–98; Chm., Homes Cttee, MS Soc., 1993–98; Trustee, Internat. Fedn of MS Socs, now MS Internat. Fedn, 1997 (Pres. and Chm., 2004–11; Chm., Nominating Cttee, 2002–03, Hon. Sec., 2003–04). Chm., Disability Adv. Gp, NHS Appts Commn, 2003–07. Chm., Victim Support, 2005–11. Non-executive Director: Mid Essex Community and Mental Health Trust, 2000–01; N Essex Partnership NHS Foundn Trust (formerly N Essex Mental Health Partnership NHS Trust), 2001–13. Mem., Registration and Conduct Cttees, Gen. Social Care Council, 2003–12. Comr, Royal Hosp. Chelsea, 2007–12. Trustee, Leonard Cheshire, 1999–2002. DL Essex, 2005. *Recreations:* bridge, choral singing. *Address:* Wistaria House, Coggeshall, Essex CO6 1UF.

**PHILLIPS, Raymond Mark;** Policy Adviser to European Union, Department for International Development and World Bank and author of National Employment Plans for Central and East European Governments, since 1998; *b* 15 April 1944; *s* of Vernon Phillips and Claudia Phillips; *m* 1968, Janet Harris; four *s*. *Educ:* Cowbridge Grammar Sch.; UC Cardiff. Department of Employment: Operational Planning and Res., 1976–78; Pay Policy Advr, 1978–79; Asst Sec., Standing Commn on Pay Comparability, 1979–80; Regl Gen. Manager, Trng Services Agency, 1980–82; Exec. Dir, Employment Service, 1982–83; Regional Director: MSC, 1983–86; Employment and Enterprise Gp, 1986–87; Regl Dir, 1987–93, Dir of Inf. and Systems, 1993–95, Employment Service, Dept of Employment; Dir, Policy and Process Design, Employment Service, DfEE, 1995–97. *Recreations:* gardening, cosmology, tennis. *Address:* Stockport, Cheshire.

**PHILLIPS, Richard Charles Jonathan**; QC 1990; b 8 Aug. 1947; yr s of Air Commodore M. N. Phillips, MD, ChB, DMRD and Dorothy E. Phillips; m 1978, Alison Jane Francis (OBE 1991); one d. Educ: King's School, Ely; Sidney Sussex College, Cambridge (Exhibnr). Called to the Bar, Inner Temple, 1970. Asst Parly Boundary Comr, 1992–. Recreations: travel, natural history, photography, walking. Address: Francis Taylor Building, Temple, EC4Y 7BY. T: (020) 7353 8415.

**PHILLIPS, Dr Richard Peter**, CMG 2006; Director, Global Shared Services, British Council, 2009–10; b 2 May 1950; s of William Leslie Phillips and Dorothy May Phillips; m 1st, 1976, Alice Detoya (d 2003); one s one d; 2nd, 2006, Adele Sinclair (née McNaughton). Educ: Univ. of Bristol (BSc Hons Chem. 1971; PhD Inorganic Chem. 1975); Huddersfield Poly. (PGCE 1981); Open Univ. (MA Classical Studies 2015). Pt-time Tutor of Chem., Univ. of Bristol, 1971–74; Vis. Prof. of Chem., Mindanao State Univ., Philippines, 1974–76; Field Officer, Philippines, 1976–77, Field Dir, Indonesia, 1978–80, VSO; HM Diplomatic Service, 1981–82; joined British Council, 1982: Sci. Officer, Yugoslavia, 1983–85; Sen. Sci. Officer, London, 1985–89; Educn Officer/Dep. Dir, Indonesia, 1989–93; Hd, Mgt Services, London, 1993–95; Contract Ops Dir, Manchester, 1995–2000; Dir, Indonesia, 2000–03; Prog. Dir, Finance and Business Systems, 2003–06; Dir, Customer Services and Innovation, 2007–08; Dep. Dir, Resources, 2008–09. Publications: contrib. various papers to Chemical Communications and Jl Inorganic Chemistry. Recreations: tennis, sailing, reading, classical studies, ancient history, classical archaeology. Address: 107 Sussex Road, Petersfield, Hants GU31 4LB. E: rpphillips01@gmail.com.

**PHILLIPS, Rear Adm. Richard Thomas Ryder**, CB 1998; FNI; Vice Chairman, JMW Energy Ventures, Gibraltar, since 2015 (Vice Chairman, JMW Energy Ventures (Bahrain), 2013–15); Member, International Advisory Board, Mercantile Ports and Logistics Ltd; b 1 Feb. 1947; s of late Brig. Thomas Hall Phillips and Arabella Sadie Phillips; m 1st, 1969, Susan Elizabeth Groves (d 1996); one d; 2nd, 1999, Belinda Susan Kelway Round Turner; one step s one step d. Educ: Kingsland Grange, Shrewsbury; Wrekin Coll. BRNC Dartmouth, 1965; Commanding Officer: HMS Scimitar, 1974; HMS Hubberston, 1978; ndc Canberra, 1981; Directorate of Naval Plans, 1982; Commanding Officer: HMS Charybdis, 1985; HMS Scylla, 1986; Asst Dir, Defence Op. Requirements (Maritime), 1987; CO, HMS Cornwall, and Capt., 8 Frigate Sqn, 1988; Capt., RN Presentation Team, 1991; Cabinet Office Top Mgt Prog., 1992; COS, Flag Officer Surface Flotilla, 1992; CO, HMS Illustrious, 1993–96; ACDS Op. Requirements (Sea Systems), 1996–99. ADC to the Queen, 1993. Director: Marconi Naval Systems, 1999–2000; BAE SYSTEMS, 2000–04; East Africa Oil Co., 2013–14. Special Adviser: Internat. Energy Adv. Council, 2004–07; Oil and Gas Adv. Bd, Renaissance Capital, 2011–12; Mem., Exec. Adv. Bd, XSMG Defence, 2011–13. CEO/Clerk, Haberdashers' Co., 2005–13; Mem. Bd, Haberdashers' Aske's Fedn Trust Bd, 2014–18. Younger Brother, Trinity Hse, 1984. FNI 1999; Associate Fellow, RUSI, 2004. Recreations: shooting, gardening, sailing, ski-ing. Clubs: Royal Yacht Squadron, Brancaster Sailing.

**PHILLIPS, Sir Robin Francis**, 3rd Bt cr 1912; Owner and Principal, Ravenscourt Theatre School, London, 1989–2007; b 29 July 1940; s of Sir Lionel Francis Phillips, 2nd Bt, and Camilla Mary, er d of late Hugh Parker, 22 Chapel Street, Belgrave Square, SW1; S father, 1944. Educ: Aiglon Coll., Switzerland. Chief Air Traffic Control Officer, Biggin Hill, 1970–78; Hazel Malone Management, 1978–81; Devonair Radio, 1981–83; Radio Luxembourg, 1984; Hd of Casting, Corona Stage School, 1985–89. Heir: none.

**PHILLIPS, Prof. Robin Kenneth Stewart**, FRCS, FRCSE, FRCPSGlas; Consultant Surgeon, 1987–2017, and Clinical Director, Gastroenterology, Upper Gastrointestinal Surgery and Emergency Surgery, 2006–17, St Mark's Hospital, Harrow; medicolegal consultant, since 2017; b 18 Nov. 1952; s of John Fleetwood Stewart Phillips and Mary Gordon Phillips (née Shaw); m 1975, Janina Fairley Nowak; one s one d. Educ: Sherborne Sch. for Boys; Royal Free Hosp. Med. Sch. (MB BS 1975); MS London 1984. FRCS 1979; FRCSE 2002; FRCPSGlas ad eundem, 2004. Higher surgical trng with St Mary's Gp of Hosps, 1980–85; St Mark's Hospital: Resident Surgical Officer, 1986; Chm., Surgery, 1993–97; Dean, Acad. Inst., 1999–2002; Sen. Lectr in Surgery, St Bartholomew's Hosp., London, 1987–90; Consultant Surgeon, Homerton Hosp., London, 1990–93; Civilian Consultant in Colorectal Surgery to the RN, 2001–. Dir, CRUK (formerly ICRF) Polyposis Registry, 1993–2013. President: British Colostomy Assoc., 2001–05; Sect. of Coloproctology, RSocMed, 2006–07. Prof. of Colorectal Surgery, Imperial Coll., London, 2000–18, now Emeritus. Publications: edited: Familial adenomatous polyposis and other polyposis syndromes, 1994; Fistula-in-ano, 1996; A Companion to Specialist Surgical Practice: colorectal surgery, 1997, 5th edn 2014; Frontiers in Coloproctology, 2005; contrib. numerous peer-reviewed res. articles, mainly in familial adenomatous polyposis (an inherited form of bowel cancer), anal fistula and other painful conditions. Recreation: fly-fishing. Address: 7 Kewferry Drive, Northwood, Middx HA6 2NT. T: (01923) 827988, 07785 746987, Fax: (01923) 841330. E: robin.phillips@nhs.net, robin@rksphillips.go-plus.net. Club: Royal Society of Medicine.

**PHILLIPS, (Ronald) William**; Director: NB Selection Ltd, 1991–2002; Norman Broadbent International, 1998–2002; b 21 April 1949; s of late Ronald Phillips and Phoebe Nora Haynes; m 1979, Dorothy Parsons. Educ: Steyning Grammar Sch.; University College of Wales, Aberystwyth (BScEcon). Joined CS, 1971; served in Dept of Transport, PSA, DoE, Develt Commn (Private Sec. to Lord Northfield); Asst County Sec., Kent CC, 1979–80; UK Expert to EC Council of Ministers Wkg Party on Environmental Impact Assessment, 1980–83; Greater London Reg. Office, DoE (Local Govt Reorganisation), 1983–86; Head of Policy Unit, 1986–87, Man. Dir, 1987–91, Westminster CC. FRSA 1990; FCMI (FBIM 1990). JP Maidstone, 1992–96. Recreation: travel.

**PHILLIPS, Rory Andrew Livingstone**; QC 2002; b 30 May 1961. Educ: Eton; King's Coll., Cambridge (MA). Address: 3 Verulam Buildings, Gray's Inn, WC1R 5NT.

**PHILLIPS, Sarah**; see Phillips, R. S.

**PHILLIPS, Sharon Katherine, (Mrs Charles Cowling)**; Principal, King Edward VI College, Stourbridge, 2008–15; b Bristol, 17 Feb. 1957; d of Gordon and Gloria Damsell; m 1st, 1979, Paul Phillips (marr. diss. 1995); one s one d; 2nd, 2008, Charles Cowling. Educ: Churchill Coll., Cambridge (BA Hons English 1979; PGCE 1981; MA 1982); Open Univ. (BA Hons 1988); Reading Univ. (MA Lit. and Visual Arts 1995). Hd of English, Newbury Coll., 1990–95; North East Worcestershire College: Curriculum Manager, Humanities, 1995–97; Associate Dir, 1997–99; Dir of Quality, 1999–2001; Dep. Principal, Halesowen Coll., 2001–08. Publications: English Language and Literature A Level, 1994, 2nd edn 2000; English Literature Resource Bank, 1995; contrib. poetry to print and online jls and anthologies. Recreations: reading, visiting art galleries, looking, walking, spending time with husband, children and dogs.

**PHILLIPS, Dame Siân**, DBE 2016 (CBE 2000); actress; d of D. Phillips and Sally Phillips; m 1st, 1954, Dr D. H. Roy (marr. diss. 1960); 2nd, 1960, (Seamus) Peter O'Toole (marr. diss. 1979; he d 2013); two d; 3rd, 1979, Robin Sachs (marr. diss. 1992). Educ: Pontardawe Grammar Sch.; Univ. of Wales (Cardiff Coll.) (BA Hons English; Fellow, 1982); RADA (Maggie Albanesi Scholarship, 1956; Bancroft Gold Medal, 1958). BBC Radio Wales, mid 1940s–, and BBC TV Wales, early 1950s–; Newsreader and Announcer, and Mem. Rep. Co., BBC, 1953–55; toured for Welsh Arts Council with National Theatre Co., 1953–55; Arts Council Bursary to study drama outside Wales, 1955. Mem., Arts Council Drama Cttee, 1970–75. Governor: St David's Trust, 1970–73; Welsh Coll. of Music and Drama, 1992–. Theatre: London: Hedda Gabler, 1959; Ondine, and the Duchess of Malfi, 1960–61 (1st RSC season at Aldwych); The Lizard on the Rock, 1961; Gentle Jack, Maxibules, and The Night of the Iguana, 1964; Ride a Cock Horse, 1965; Man and Superman, and Man of Destiny, 1966; The Burglar, 1967; Epitaph for George Dillon, 1972; A Nightingale in Bloomsbury Square, 1973; The Gay Lord Quex, 1975; Spinechiller, 1978; You Never Can Tell, Lyric, Hammersmith, 1979; Pal Joey, Half Moon, 1980 and Albery, 1981; Dear Liar, Mermaid, 1982; Major Barbara, NT, 1982; Peg, Phoenix, 1984; Gigi, Lyric, Shaftesbury Ave., 1985; Thursday's Ladies, Apollo, 1987; Brel, Donmar, 1987; Paris Match, Garrick, 1989; Vanilla, Lyric, 1990; The Manchurian Candidate, Lyric, Hammersmith, and nat. tour, 1991; Painting Churches, Playhouse, 1992; The Glass Menagerie, Cambridge Theatre Co. nat. tour, 1989; Ghosts, Welsh Arts Council tour, and Sherman Theatre, Wales, 1993; The Lion in Winter, UK nat. tour, 1994; An Inspector Calls, NY, 1995; A Little Night Music, RNT, 1995; Marlene, nat. tour, 1996, Lyric, 1997, S Africa, Paris, 1998, NY, 1999; Lettice and Lovage, tour, 2001; My Old Lady, LA, 2001, NY, 2002; The Old Ladies, UK tour, 2003; The Dark, Donmar Th., 2004; The Play What I Wrote, UK tour, The Unexpected Man, UK tour, 2005; Great Expectations, RSC, 2005–06; Rockaby, Barbican and Gate, Dublin, 2006; Quartet, USA, 2006; Regrets Only, NY, 2007; Les Liaisons Dangereuses, NY, 2008; Calendar Girls, UK tour, 2008–09; Noel Coward Th., 2009; Juliet and Her Romeo, Th. Royal, Bristol, 2010; A Little Night Music, St Louis Opera, 2010; Siân Phillips Crossing Borders (solo show), Wiltons Music Hall, London, 2011, Pheasantry, London, 2012; Bittersweet (operetta), NY, 2011; Lovesong, tour for Frantic Assembly, 2011, then Lyric Hammersmith, 2012; Little Dogs, Nat. Th. of Wales, 2012; My Fair Lady, Royal Albert Hall, 2012; Cabaret, Savoy and tour, 2012 (Best Actress in a Vis. Prodn, Manchester Th. Awards, 2013); This is My Family, Crucible Studio, Sheffield, 2013 (Best Supporting Perf., UK Th. Awards, 2013); People, RNT UK tour, 2013; The Importance of Being Earnest, Shakespeare Th., Washington, 2013, Harold Pinter Th. and UK tour, 2014; Playing For Time, Crucible Th., Sheffield, 2015; Les Blancs, RNT, 2016; All the President's Men?, Vaudeville Th., 2017; Driving Miss Daisy, Bath Th. Royal and UK tour, 2017; concert tours, UK and US, 2000, UK 2001; Concert for Aberfan, Wales Millennium Centre, 2016; cabaret: NY, 2000, RNT and tour, 2001; Divas at the Donmar, Donmar Th., 2001; UK concert tour, 2003; Both Sides Now, touring UK and overseas, 2007–; solo cabaret in Welsh, S4C, 2013. TV drama series include: Shoulder to Shoulder, 1974; How Green was my Valley, 1975; I, Claudius, 1976; Boudicca, and Off to Philadelphia in the Morning, 1977; The Oresteia of Aeschylus, 1978; Crime and Punishment, 1979; Sean O'Casey (RTE), 1980; Winston Churchill, The Wilderness Years, 1981; Language and Landscape (6 bilingual films, Welsh and English), 1985; The Snow Spider, 1988; Shadow of the Noose, 1989; Emlyn's Moon, 1990; Perfect Scoundrels, 1990; Tonight at 8.30: Hands Across the Sea; The Astonished Heart; Ways and Means, 1991; The Borrowers, 1992, 1993; The Aristocrats, 1999; Nikita, The Magician's House, 2000; The Last Detective, 2002; Midsomer Murders, 2006; Canu Grwndi, 2006; TV films include: A Painful Case (RTE), 1985; While Reason Sleeps; Return to Endor, 1986 (USA); Siân (biographical), 1987, 2002; Heidi, 1993; Mind to Kill (also in Welsh), 1995; Summer Silence (musical, also in Welsh), 1995; The Green Hollow, 2016; TV documentary: To Provide All People, 2018. Films include: Becket, 1963; Goodbye Mr Chips, and Laughter in the Dark, 1968; Murphy's War, 1970; Under Milk Wood, 1971; The Clash of the Titans, 1979; Dune, 1984; Ewocks Again, and The Doctor and the Devils, 1985; Valmont, 1989; Age of Innocence, 1994; House of America, 1996; Alice Through the Looking Glass, 1999; Coming and Going, 2000; The Gigolos, 2007. Radio: Writing the Century, Radio 4, 2016; Hide the Moon, Radio 3, 2017; The Things We Never Said, Radio 4, 2017; The Aspern Papers, Radio 4, 2018; Hilda, Radio 4, 2018; The Macefield Plot, Radio 4, 2019. Has made recordings, incl. Peg, Gigi, I remember Mama, Pal Joey, Bewitched, Bothered and Bewildered, A Little Night Music, Marlene. RTS Annual Lecture (Eng. and Welsh transmissions), 1993. FRSA. FWNCMD, 1991; Fellow, Cardiff Coll., Univ. of Wales, 1983; Hon. Fellow: Polytechnic of Wales, 1988; Trinity Coll., Carms, 1998; Univ. of Wales Swansea, 1998. Hon. DLitt Wales, 1984. Critics Circle Award, New York Critics Award, and Famous 7 Critics Award, for Goodbye Mr Chips, 1969; BAFTA Award for How Green was my Valley and I, Claudius, 1978; Royal Television Soc. Award for I, Claudius (Best Performer), 1978; Lifetime Achievement Award, BAFTA Wales, 2000; St David Award for Culture, Welsh Govt, 2015; Audio Drama Lifetime Achievement Award, BBC, 2018. Mem., Gorsedd of Bards, 1960 (for services to drama in Wales). Publications: Siân Phillips' Needlepoint, 1987; autobiography: Private Faces, 1999; Public Places, 2001; gen. journalism (Vogue, Cosmopolitan, Daily Mail, 3 years for Radio Times, Country Living, Options). Recreations: walking, gardening, needlepoint, drawing. Address: c/o Dalzell Beresford, Paddock Suite, The Courtyard, 55 Charterhouse Street, EC1M 6HA.

**PHILLIPS, Simon Benjamin**; QC 2010; **His Honour Judge Simon Phillips**; a Circuit Judge, since 2015; b Watford, 24 Sept. 1961; s of late Peter John Phillips and Josephine Beryl Phillips (née Isaacs); m 1986, Hon. Sophia Rosalind Vane, d of 11th Baron Barnard, TD and of Lady Davina Barnard, e d of 6th Marquess of Exeter; two s one d. Educ: Harrow Sch.; Sussex Univ. (BA Law 1983); Trinity Hall, Cambridge (LLM 1984); Inns of Court Sch. of Law. Called to the Bar, Inner Temple, 1985 (Basil Nield Schol.), Bencher, 2018; in practice at the Bar, 1986–2015; a Recorder, 2002–15; Fee Paid Immigration Judge, 2006–15. Member: RFU Disciplinary Panel, 2012–; Bar Council, 2014; Lay Mem., Nat. Safeguarding Panel, 2012–15. Recreations: family, rural life, travel, squash, lawn tennis, padel tennis, golf, ski-ing. Address: Leeds Combined Court Centre, Court House, 1 Oxford Row, Leeds LS1 3BG. Clubs: Royal Automobile; Jesters; Alwoodley Golf.
See also J. G. Phillips.

**PHILLIPS, Prof. Simon Edward Victor**, PhD; FRSC; Director, Research Complex at Harwell, 2008–16; Visiting Professor of Molecular Biophysics, University of Oxford, since 2008; Adjunct Fellow, Linacre College, Oxford, since 2015; b Cirencester, 14 March 1950; s of Edward and Norah Mary Phillips; m 1974, Deborah Anne Cowell; two s. Educ: Cirencester Grammar Sch.; University Coll. London (BSc Chem. 1971; PhD Chem. 1974). FRSC 2002. Post-doctoral Fellow in Chem., Univ. of BC, Vancouver, 1974–76; scientist, MRC Lab. of Molecular Biol., Cambridge, 1976–82; Chargé de Recherche, Immunologie, Inst. Pasteur, Paris, 1982–85; University of Leeds: Lectr in Biophysics, 1985–89; Reader in Biophysics, 1989–92; SERC Sen. Fellow, 1989–94; Prof. of Molecular Biophysics, 1992–96; Astbury Prof. of Biophysics, 1996–2008; Dir, Astbury Centre for Structural Molecular Biol., 1999–2001; Dean for Res., Faculty of Biol Scis, 2001–04. Vis. Prof. of Biophysics, Univ. of Leeds, 2008–; Vis. Scientist, Brookhaven Nat. Lab., NY, 1980; EMBO Fellow, Inst. Pasteur, Paris, 1985; Internat. Res. Schol., Howard Hughes Med. Inst., USA, 1993–99. Pres., British Crystallographic Assoc., 2018–. Publications: contribs to scientific pubns. Recreations: music, gardening, theatre, wine, finding out how things work. Address: Research Complex at Harwell, Rutherford Appleton Laboratory, Harwell, Didcot OX11 0FA. T: (01235) 567700. E: simon.phillips@rc-harwell.ac.uk.

**PHILLIPS, Rt Hon. Sir Stephen (Edmund),** Kt 2013; PC 2019; **Rt Hon. Lord Justice Phillips;** a Lord Justice of Appeal, since 2019; *b* 10 Oct. 1961; *s* of His Honour (David) Alan Phillips, *qv*; *m* 1998, Sonia (*née* Tolaney). *Educ:* King's Sch., Chester; University Coll., Oxford (MA Oxon; Martin Wronker Prize, 1983). Called to the Bar, Gray's Inn, 1984 (Birkenhead Award, 1984; Reid Scholarship; David Karmel Prize, 1985; Bencher, 2006); an Asst Recorder, 1999–2000; a Recorder, 2000–13; QC 2002; a Dep. High Ct Judge, 2008–13; a Judge of the High Ct of Justice, QBD, 2013–19. *Recreations:* hill walking, football, tennis. *Address:* Royal Courts of Justice, Strand, WC2A 2LL.

**PHILLIPS, Stephen James;** freelance writer, producer and broadcaster; *b* 28 May 1947; *s* of James Ronald Phillips and Diana Betty Phillips (*née* Bradshaw); *m* 1988, Simone Lila Lopez; two *d*. *Educ:* Univ. of London (ext. BA Hons Ancient Hist.); St John's Coll., Cambridge (Dip. Classical Archaeol.). Reporter and critic, Yorks Evening Post, 1965–69; critic and feature writer, Daily Express, 1969–72; Manager, Holiday Village, Thasos, Greece, 1973; BBC Radio 4 reporter and presenter, 1973–76; Gen. Administrator, Prospect Theatre Co., Old Vic, 1976–78; presenter, Kaleidoscope and other BBC programmes, 1978–81; Arts Corresp., ITN and Channel Four, 1982–89; Series Ed., Signals, Channel 4, 1989–91; producer, The House of Bernarda Alba (film), 1991; exec. producer, Antelope Films, 1992–2000; Hd of Arts, 1991–95, Arts consultant, 1996–2000, Meridian Broadcasting; Culture/communications consultant: Arts Sponsorship Panel, J. Sainsbury plc, 1990–2003; RIBA, 2000–; Theatre Mgt Assoc., 2011–; Director and Executive Producer: Aarya Ltd, 2012–; Jazz Music Ltd, 2014–. Lectr, Dramatic Writing MA, 1997–2007, Vis. Res. Fellow, 1999–2007, Sussex Univ. Member: Arts Council of England, 1994–98 (Chm., Touring Adv. Panel, 1994–98); SE Arts Bd, 1999–2002; SE England Regl Assembly and Exec. Cttee, 2000–02; Vice Chm., SE Regl Cultural Consortium, 2000–03. Chairman: Isaac Newton Arts Trust, 2002–09; Anglo Chinese Creative Industries Assoc., 2010–12; British Architectural Trust, 2011–13. Board Member: Tricycle Theatre, Kilburn, 1982–2002 (Chm., 1984–94); English Nat. Ballet, 1996–2005; Chichester Fest. Theatre, 1999–2003; Chm., Arts for Everyone Lottery Panel, 1996–98. Chm., Friends of Herstmonceux Castle, 1995–2002; Trustee: Brighton's West Pier, 1997–2007; RIBA Cultural Trust, 2003–10 (Vice Chair, 2007–10); Patron, Brighton Dome Appeal. Hon. FRIBA 2003. *Recreations:* theatre, art, history, Mediterranean travel, family.

**PHILLIPS, Stephen James;** QC 2009; a Recorder, since 2009; *b* London, 9 March 1970; *s* of late Stewart Charles Phillips and of Janice Frances Phillips (*née* Woodall, now Pavey); *m* 1998, Fiona Jane Parkin (marr. diss 2013); one *s* two *d*. *Educ:* Canford Sch.; Oriel Coll., Oxford (BA Juris 1991; BCL 1992). Late 14/20 King's Hussars and Welsh Guards. Called to the Bar, Lincoln's Inn, 1993; in practice specialising in commercial litigation. MP (C) Sleaford and N Hykeham, 2010–Nov. 2016. Member: European Scrutiny Cttee, 2010–15; Public Accounts Cttee, 2014–16. Chm. of Govs, Frank Barnes Sch. for Deaf Children, 2006–10. *Recreation:* getting muddy with my kids. *Address:* 7 King's Bench Walk, Temple, EC4Y 7DS. *T:* (020) 7910 8300, *Fax:* (020) 7910 8400. *E:* clerks@7kbw.com. *Club:* Cavalry and Guards.

**PHILLIPS, Timothy Dewe,** CBE 2007; Chairman: All England Lawn Tennis and Croquet Club, 1999–2010; Committee of Management, Wimbledon Championships, 1999–2010; *b* 22 April 1942; *s* of late Warren Phillips and Marjorie Phillips (*née* Thornton); *m* 1969, Elizabeth Wheeldon; two *s* one *d*. *Educ:* Mill Hill Sch.; Merton Coll., Oxford (MA; Hon. Fellow 2008); Harvard Business Sch. (AMP). British Airways, 1966–2001: worked overseas in various mgt posts based in Hong Kong, Zambia, Brunei, Lebanon, The Gulf, Australia and Italy, 1969–83; Head Office, London, 1983–2001: General Manager: Africa, 1983–84; UK, 1984–86; Hd, Logistics and Dep. Ops Dir, 1986–88; Dep. Mktg Dir, 1989–91; Regl Gen. Manager, Europe, 1992–94; Hd, Regs, 1994–96; Hd, Community Relns, 1996–2001. Played in 3 of the 4 Grand Slam tennis events incl. Wimbledon; semi-finalist, Men's Doubles, US Nationals, 1964. Chm., Fields in Trust (NPFA), 2013–. Mem., Internat. Tennis Clubs of GB, France, US, Australia, Czech Republic and Hong Kong (Capt. Internat. Club of GB, 2012). Chm., Wimbledon Lawn Tennis Mus., 2011–17. *Recreations:* tennis, squash, hockey (Triple Blue at Oxford). *Clubs:* All England Lawn Tennis, Queen's, Roehampton; Vincent's (Oxford).

**PHILLIPS, Tom,** CBE 2002; RA 1989 (ARA 1984); RE 1987; RP 1999; painter, writer and composer; *b* 24 May 1937; *s* of David John Phillips and Margaret Agnes (*née* Arnold); *m* 1961, Jill Purdy (marr. diss. 1988); one *s* one *d*; *m* 1995, Fiona Maddocks, *qv*. *Educ:* St Catherine's College, Oxford (MA; Hon. Fellow, 1992); Camberwell School of Art. NDD. One man shows: AIA Galleries, 1965; Angela Flowers Gall., 1970–71; Marlborough Fine Art, 1973–75; Dante Works, Waddington Galleries, 1983; retrospective exhibitions: Gemeente Museum, The Hague, 1975; Kunsthalle, Basel, 1975; Serpentine, 1975; 50 years of Tom Phillips, Angela Flowers Gall., 1987; Mappin Art Gall., Sheffield, 1987; Nat. Gall., Jamaica, 1987; Bass Mus., Miami, 1988; Nat. Gall., Australia, 1988; City Art Inst., Sydney, 1988; Nat. Portrait Gall., 1989; N Carolina Mus., 1990; Royal Acad., 1992; V&A, 1992; Ulster Mus., 1993; Yale Center, USA, 1993; S London Art Gall., 1998; Dulwich Picture Gall., 1998; Modern Art Mus., Fort Worth, 2001; Flowers Gall., London, 2004, 2012, 2017; Flowers Gall., NY, 2005; Massachusetts Mus. of Contemp. Art, 2013; work in collections: British Museum, Tate Gall., V&A, Nat. Portrait Gall., Imperial War Mus., Ashmolean Mus., Oxford, Mus. Fine Arts, Budapest, MOMA NY, Philadelphia Museum, Bibliothèque Nationale, Paris, Gemeente Museum, Boymans Museum, Rotterdam, Nat. Museum, Stockholm, Nat. Gall. of Australia; designed: Armed Forces Conflict Meml, Westminster Abbey, 2008; tapestries for St Catherine's, Oxford; mosaics for Chapel of St George and English Martyrs, Westminster Cathedral, 2016; Shakespeare five ounce proof coins, silver and gold, Royal Mint, 2016; music: first perf. opera Irma, 1973, full version premiere, S London Gall., 2017; York, 1974; ICA, 1983; librettist, Heart of Darkness chamber opera, Linbury Th., Royal Opera Hse, 2011, Cadogan Hall, 2013; recordings incl. Irma, 1980 (new version, 1988); Intervalles/Music of Tom Phillips 1982; Six of Hearts, 1997; television: co-dir, Dante series, 1984–89 (1st prize Montreal Fest., 1990; Prix Italia, 1991); film scripts: Tom Phillips (Grierson Award, BFI, 1976; Golden Palm Award, Chicago, 1976); The Artist's Eye (TV film), 1988; Twenty Sites (TV film), 1989; designer, The Winter's Tale, Globe Theatre, 1997; designer and translator, Otello, ENO, 1998; designer, The Entertainer, Derby Playhouse, 2003, The Magic Flute, Opera Holland Park, 2008. Curator: Africa: the art of a continent, RA, 1995, Berlin and NY, 1996; We Are The People, NPG, 2004. Slade Prof. of Fine Art, Univ. of Oxford, 2005–06; Visitor, IAS, Princeton, 2005–11. Chairman: RA Library, 1987–95; RA Exhibns Cttee, 1995; Vice-Chm., British Copyright Council, 1984–88. Trustee: Ruskin House, 1996–2002; Nat. Portrait Gall., 1998–2006; BM, 1999–2007. Pres., Heatherley's Sch. of Art, 2003–11. Judge, Man Booker Prize for Fiction, 2017. Hon. Fellow, London Inst., 1999. Francis Williams Prize, V&A 1983; First Prize, Hunting Gp of Cos, 1988. *Publications:* Trailer, 1971; A Humument, 1980, 6th edn 2016; illustr. trans. Dante's Inferno, 1992; Works/Texts to 1974, 1975; Heart of a Humument, 1985; The Class of Forty-Seven, 1990; Works/Texts vol. II, 1992; Humument Supplement, 1992; Plato's Symposium, 1992; (with Salman Rushdie) Merely Connect, 1994; (ed) Africa: the art of a continent, 1995; Music in Art, 1997; Aspects of Art, 1997; (illustrator) Waiting for Godot, 2000; The Postcard Century, 2000; We Are The People, 2004; Merry Meetings, 2005; Goldweights: miniature sculptures from Ghana 1400–1900, 2010; Ashanti Weights, 2010; Vintage People on Photo Postcards: women and hats, 2010, Readers, 2010, Bicycles, 2011, Weddings, 2011; Menswear, 2012; Fantasy Transport, 2012; (illustrator) Cicero Orations, 2011; Humument Images to Accompany James Joyce's Ulysses, 2014; Irma an Opera: full score, 2014; The Sound in My Life, 2015; *Recreations:* ping pong, cricket, postcards. *Address:* 57 Talfourd Road, SE15 5NN. *T:* (020) 7701 3978, *Fax:* (020) 7703 2800. *E:* tom@tomphillips.co.uk. *Club:* Chelsea Arts.

**PHILLIPS, Sir Tom (Richard Vaughan),** KCMG 2010 (CMG 1998); HM Diplomatic Service, retired; Director, Centre for the Study of Modern Slavery, St Mary's University, Twickenham, since 2018; *b* 21 June 1950; *s* of late Comdr Tom Vaughan Gerald Phillips, DSC, OBE, RN and of Margaret Sproull (*née* Gameson); *m* 1986, Anne de la Motte; two *s*. *Educ:* Harlow Technical Coll.; Exeter Univ.; Jesus Coll., Oxford; Wolfson Coll., Oxford (MLitt). Journalist, West Herts and Watford Observer, 1969–72; DHSS, 1977–83; FCO, 1983–85; First Sec., Harare, 1985–88; FCO, 1988–90; Dep. Head of Mission and Consul-Gen., Tel Aviv, 1990–93; Counsellor, Washington, 1993–97; Hd, Eastern Adriatic Dept, FCO, 1997–99; High Comr to Uganda, 2000–02; UK Special Rep. for Afghanistan, 2002–06; Dir, S Asia and Afghanistan, FCO, 2003–06; Ambassador: to Israel, 2006–10; to Saudi Arabia, 2010–12. Comdt, RCDS, 2014–18. Internat. Advr, Internat. Sustainability Unit, Prince's Charities, 2013–14; Sen. Advr, GPW Ltd, 2013–14. Associate Fellow, Middle East Prog., RIIA, Chatham House, 2012–15. Member: Adv. Council, Wilton Park, 2012–15; Council of Advrs, RAND Europe, 2018–; Council, Lord Kitchener Nat. Meml Fund, 2018–. *Publications:* (as Tom Vaughan): No Second Prize, 1993; Sampler (poems), 2010; Envoy (poems), 2013.

**PHILLIPS, Trevor;** *see* Phillips, M. T.

**PHILLIPS, Trevor Thomas;** *see* Phillips, Tom.

**PHILLIPS, Vernon Francis,** CPFA; FCA; Chief Executive, Bedfordshire County Council, 1989–92; *b* 7 July 1930; *s* of Charles and May Phillips; *m* 1955, Valerie P. Jones; two *s* one *d*. *Educ:* Wilson Sch., Reading. CIPFA (Hons) 1954; ASAA 1958; FCA 1970. Berkshire CC, 1964–53; Swindon BC, 1953–55; Bristol City Council, 1955–58; Coventry City Council, 1958–61; Dep. Borough Treas., Luton CB, 1962–73; County Treas., Bedfordshire CC, 1973–89. Adviser to ACC, 1985–92. Member: Soc. of County Treas., 1973–; Assoc. of County Chief Execs, 1989–95; SOLACE, 1989–95. Chm., Bedford Citizens Housing Assoc., 1999–2004. Mem., Bedford Rotary Club. *Recreations:* reading, music (listening), dancing, walking, paperweights, stained glass windows, photography. *Address:* 55 Wentworth Drive, Bedford MK41 8QB. *T:* (01234) 345628.

**PHILLIPS, Victoria Mary;** Partner, since 2002, and Head, Employment Rights (Client Relations), since 2014, Thompsons Solicitors LLP; *b* Cheltenham, 15 May 1962; *d* of Ronald and Mary Phillips; *m* 1988, Paul Head (*d* 2014); two *s*. *Educ:* Pates' Grammar Sch. for Girls, Cheltenham; Univ. of East Anglia (LLB Hons 1983); Univ. of Westminster (Postgrad. Cert. Legal Practice 1994). Nat. Pres., NUS, 1986–88; Nat. Women's Officer, Labour Party, 1988–93. Admitted as solicitor, 1996; solicitor, 1996–2001, Hd, Employment Rights, 2003–14, Thompsons Solicitors. Mem., Internat. Justice Council, UN, 2012–16. Trustee: Tottenham GS Foundn, 2000–; Park Th., Finsbury Park, 2017–. Hon. LLD E Anglia, 2013. *Recreations:* politics, theatre, running. *Address:* Thompsons Solicitors, Congress House, Great Russell Street, WC1B 3LW. *T:* (020) 7290 0032. *E:* victoriaphillips@thompsons.law.co.uk.

**PHILLIPS, William;** *see* Phillips, R. W.

**PHILLIPS, Prof. William Daniel,** PhD; physicist; National Institute of Standards and Technology Fellow, since 1995; Distinguished University Professor, since 2001, and College Park Professor, since 2006, University of Maryland (Adjunct Professor, 1992–2001); Fellow, Joint Quantum Institute, Maryland, since 2006; *b* 5 Nov. 1948; *s* of William Cornelius Phillips and Mary Catherine Savine Phillips; *m* 1970, Jane Van Wynen; two *d*. *Educ:* Juniata Coll. (BS Physics 1970); Massachusetts Inst. of Technol. (PhD Physics 1976). Chaim Weizmann Fellow, MIT, 1976–78; physicist, Nat. Bureau of Standards, later Nat. Inst. of Standards and Technol., 1978–95. Eastman Vis. Prof., Oxford Univ., 2002–03. Fellow: Amer. Physical Soc., 1986; Optical Soc. of America, 1994 (Hon. Mem., 2004); Amer. Acad. of Arts and Scis, 1995. Member: NAS, 1997; Pontifical Acad. of Scis, 2004. Corresp. Mem., Mexican Acad. of Scis, 2016. FAAAS 2019. Gold Medal, Dept of Commerce, 1993; Michelson Medal, Franklin Inst., 1996; Nobel Prize in Physics, 1997; Schawlow Prize, Amer. Physical Soc., 1998; Richtmeyer Award, Amer. Assoc. Physics Teachers, 2000; Archie Mahan Prize, Optical Soc., 2002; Samuel J. Heyman Service to America Medal, Career Achievement Award, 2006; Moyal Medal, Macquarie Univ., 2010; Pioneer in Photonics Award, Duke Univ., 2013; Galileo Ferraris Prize, Istituto Nazionale Di Ricerca Metrologica, 2014. *Publications:* contrib. numerous articles in Physical Rev. Letters and other professional jls, and in proc. nat. and internat. confs. *Recreations:* photography, tennis, gospel music, Bible study. *Address:* 100 Bureau Drive, Stop 8424, National Institute of Standards and Technology, Gaithersburg, MD 20899–8424, USA.

**PHILLIPSON, Antony John;** HM Diplomatic Service; Consul General, New York, since 2017; HM Trade Commissioner for North America, since 2018; *b* Johannesburg, 13 Jan. 1971; *s* of Nicolas Guy Phillipson and Veronica Phillipson; *m* 2000, Julie Elizabeth Pilley; three *s*. *Educ:* Marlborough Coll.; Keble Coll., Oxford (BA Hons Mod. Hist. 1992). Department of Trade and Industry: Policy Officer, 1993–96; Private Sec., 1996–98, Prin. Private Sec., 1998–2000, to Sec. of State; First Sec., 2000–02, Counsellor, 2002–04, Washington; Private Sec. for Foreign Affairs to the Prime Minister, 2004–07; Hd, Iran Coordination Gp, FCO, 2007–10; High Comr to Singapore, 2011–15; Dir (EU Ext.), Eur. and Global Issues Secretariat, Cabinet Office, 2015–16; Dir, Trade and Partnerships, DExEU, 2016–17. *Recreations:* travel, current affairs, family. *Address:* c/o Foreign and Commonwealth Office, King Charles Street, SW1A 2AH. *Clubs:* British, Tanglin (Singapore); Singapore Cricket.

**PHILLIPSON, Bridget Maeve;** MP (Lab) Houghton and Sunderland South, since 2010; *b* Gateshead, 19 Dec. 1983; *d* of Clare Phillipson; *m* 2009, Lawrence Dimery; one *s* one *d*. *Educ:* St Robert of Newminster Catholic Sch., Washington; Hertford Coll., Oxford (BA Hons Modern Hist. 2005; MA). Sunderland CC, 2005–07; Manager, Wearside Women in Need refuge, 2007–10. An Opposition Whip, 2013–15. Member: Home Affairs Select Cttee, 2010–13; Speaker's Cttee on Electoral Commn, 2010–; Public Accounts Cttee, 2015–. Mem., Lab Party Nat. Policy Forum, 2002–04. Chm., Oxford Univ. Labour Club, 2003. *Recreations:* reading, music, running. *Address:* House of Commons, SW1A 0AA. *T:* (020) 7219 7087. *E:* bridget.phillipson.mp@parliament.uk.

**PHILLIPSON, Prof. David Walter,** LittD; FBA 2002; FSA; Director, Cambridge University Museum of Archaeology and Anthropology, 1981–2006 and Professor of African Archaeology, University of Cambridge, 2001–06; Fellow, Gonville and Caius College, Cambridge, 1988–2006, now Emeritus; *b* 17 Oct. 1942; *s* of late Herbert Phillipson and Mildred Phillipson (*née* Atkinson); *m* 1967, Laurel Lofgren; one *s* one *d*. *Educ:* Merchant Taylors' Sch., Northwood; Gonville and Caius Coll., Cambridge (BA 1964; MA 1968; PhD 1978; LittD 2003). Sec. and Inspector, Nat. Monuments Commn, N Rhodesia, then Zambia, 1964–73; Asst Dir, British Inst. in Eastern Africa, 1973–78; Keeper of

Archaeol., Ethnography and Hist., Glasgow Mus., 1979–81; Reader in African Prehistory, Univ. of Cambridge, 1991–2001. Ed., African Archaeol Rev., 1987–94. Reckitt Archaeol Lectr, British Acad., 2000; Dist. Lectr in African Archaeol., Univ. of Florida, 2006. Hon. Vis. Prof., Addis Ababa Univ., 2006. FSA 1979 (Frend Medal, 2005); Associate Fellow, Ethiopian Acad. of Scis, 2014. *Publications:* (ed) Mosi-oa-Tunya: a handbook to the Victoria Falls Region, 1975; Prehistory of Eastern Zambia, 1976; Later Prehistory of Eastern and Southern Africa, 1977; African Archaeology, 1985, 3rd edn 2005; The Monuments of Aksum, 1997; Ancient Ethiopia, 1998; Archaeology at Aksum, Ethiopia, 1993–97, 2000; Archaeology in Africa and in Museums, 2003; Ancient Churches of Ethiopia, 2009; Foundations of an African Civilisation, 2012; numerous contribs to ed vols and learned jls. *Recreation:* bibliomania. *Address:* 11 Brooklyn Terrace, Threshfield, Skipton, N Yorks BD23 5ER. *T:* (01756) 753965. *Club:* Oxford and Cambridge.

**PHILLPOT, Hereward Lindon,** QC 2015; *b* Hagworthingham, Lincs, 26 March 1973; *s* of Vernon and Meryl Phillpot; *m* 2001, Antonia Johnson; two *s* one *d. Educ:* Queen Elizabeth I Grammar Sch., Alford; Univ. of York (BA 1st Cl. Hons Hist.); City Univ. (Postgrad. DipLaw). Called to the Bar, Gray's Inn, 1997; in practice as barrister, specialising in planning and envmtl law, 1997–. Mem., Attorney Gen.'s A Panel of Jun. Counsel, 2010–. *Publications:* National Infrastructure Planning Handbook, 2015. *Recreations:* fishing, cycling, ski-ing. *Address:* Francis Taylor Building, Inner Temple, EC4Y 7BY.

**PHILP, Chris;** MP (C) Croydon South, since 2015; Parliamentary Under Secretary of State, Ministry of Justice, since 2019; *b* Bromley, 6 July 1976; *s* of Brian Philp and Edna Philp; *m* 2009, Elizabeth; one *s* one *d* (twins). *Educ:* St Olave's Grammar Sch., Orpington; University Coll., Oxford (MPhys 1st Cl.). Analyst, McKinsey & Co., 1998–2000; Co-Founder and Dir, Blueheath, 2000–04; Co-Founder and Chief Executive Officer: Pluto Capital, 2004–15; Pluto Finance. Contested (C) Hampstead and Kilburn, 2010. PPS, HM Treasury, 2017–18, MHCLG, 2018–19. Mem., Treasury Select Cttee, 2015–17. Vice-Chm. for Policy, Cons. Party, 2019–. *Publications:* (ed) Conservative Revival, 2006. *Recreations:* football, ski-ing, riding. *Address:* House of Commons, SW1A 0AA. *T:* (020) 7219 8026. *E:* chris.philp.mp@parliament.uk.

**PHILP, Prof. Ian,** CBE 2008; MD; FRCP; Professor of Global Ageing, University of Stirling, since 2017; Chief Executive Officer, Age Care Technologies Ltd, since 2018; Consultant to World Health Organisation, since 2019; *b* 14 Nov. 1958; *s* of Thomas Philp and Nancy Philp (*née* Yule); *m* 1984, Elizabeth Anne Boyd; one *s* two *d. Educ:* Univ. of Edinburgh (MB ChB, MD 1990). FRCP 1994. Trained in geriatric medicine, general medicine, rehabilitation and public health in UK and USA, 1981–90; Hon. Consultant and Sen. Lectr in Geriatric Medicine, Univ. of Southampton, 1990–94; Hon. Consultant and Marjorie Coote Prof. of Health Care for Older People, Univ. of Sheffield, 1994–2011; Med. Dir, NHS Warwickshire, 2009–11; Med. Dir and Consultant in Old Age Medicine, S Warwicks NHS Trust, 2011–13; Hon. Prof. of Health Care for Older People, Univ. of Warwick, 2011–16; CMO, Hull and E Yorks NHS Hosps Trust, 2013–15; Dep. Med. Dir for Older People, Heart of England NHS Foundn Trust, 2015–17. Nat. Dir for Older People (formerly Older People's Services and Neurol Conditions), Dept of Health, 2000–08. Founder, and Mem., Core Academic Gp, Sheffield Inst. for Studies on Ageing, 1999–2009. Developed EASY-Care and COPE Index, instruments for assessing needs of older people and family carers, used worldwide. Presenter, TV series, 100 Years Younger in 21 Days, 2018. Team Leader, UK Hosp. Doctor Team of the Year, 1999. Co-presenter, BBC TV series, How To Live Longer, 2006. Hon. FFPH 2008. Queen's Anniv. Prize for Higher Educn, 2000. *Publications:* (ed) Assessing Elderly People, 1994; (ed) Outcomes Assessment, 1998; (ed) Carers of Older People in Europe, 2001; numerous contribs to acad. and med. press on care of older people. *Recreations:* cinema, travelling with family.

**PHILPOT, His Honour Nicholas Anthony John;** a Circuit Judge, 1992–2010; a Deputy Circuit Judge, 2010–12; *b* 19 Dec. 1944; *s* of late Oliver Lawrence Spurling Philpot, MC, DFC, and Margaret Nathalie Forsyth (*née* Owen); *m* 2008, Bahia Naïdji; two *s* and one step *d. Educ:* Winchester Coll.; New Coll., Oxford (BA PPE 1966). VSO, Bolivia, 1966–67. Called to the Bar, Lincoln's Inn, 1970; Asst Recorder, 1987–90; Recorder, 1990–92.

**PHILPOT, Robert Terence Samuel;** freelance journalist and broadcaster, since 2014; Director, Progress, 2001–06, 2007–08 and 2010–14; *b* Chelmsford, Essex, 28 Dec. 1972; *s* of Terence Philpot and Mary Philpot; partner, Paul Lantsbury. *Educ:* Trinity Sch., Croydon; Univ. of Durham (BA 1st Cl. Hons Politics); Inst. of United States Studies, Univ. of London (MA (Dist.) Area Studies). Graduate Teaching Asst, Brunel Univ., 1996–99; Progress: Dep. Editor, 1998–99; Publications Editor, 2000–01; Special Adviser: to Sec. of State for NI, 2006–07; to Minister for the Olympics and for the Cabinet Office, 2009–10. *Publications:* (ed) The Purple Book, 2011; Margaret Thatcher: the honorary Jew, 2017. *Recreations:* travel, gym, reading, cinema.

**PHILPOTT, Hugh Stanley,** OBE 2018; HM Diplomatic Service; Ambassador to Turkmenistan, since 2019; *b* 24 Jan. 1961; *s* of Gordon Cecil Haig Philpott and Janet Philpott (*née* Guy, now Downer); *m* 1984, Janine Frederica Rule; one *d. Educ:* Brockenhurst Coll.; Open Univ. Barclays Bank Internat., 1979; FCO, 1980; Oslo, 1982–84; Third Secretary: Budapest, 1985–86; Arabic Lang. Trng, 1987–88; Baghdad, 1988–90; Second Secretary: FCO, 1990–93; Washington, 1993–97; First Secretary: DFID, 1997–99; FCO, 1999–2001; Counsellor and Dep. Hd of Mission, Muscat, 2001–04; Dep. Hd, Overseas Territories Dept, FCO, and Dep. Comr, British Indian Ocean Territory, 2005–07; Dep. Hd, Internat. Sci. and Innovation Gp, FCO, 2007–08; Hd, UK Sci. and Innovation Network, FCO and BIS, 2008–12; Russian Lang. Trng, 2012–13; Country Dir, UK Trade and Investment, 2013–14; Charge D'Affaires Astana, Kazakhstan, 2014; Tajiki Lang. Trng, 2014–15; Ambassador to Tajikistan, 2015–19. *Recreations:* computers, growing walnuts, opera, learning foreign languages. *Address:* c/o Foreign and Commonwealth Office, King Charles Street, SW1A 2AH; Crouttes, Orne, France.

**PHINBOW, Sandra Anne;** *b* Welwyn Garden City, 6 July 1973; *d* of Gerald Edward Head and Joan Sandra Charlotte Head; *m* 2015, Matthew John Phinbow; one *s*, and one *s* by a previous marriage. *Educ:* Thanet Coll. (Access to Sci. 2000); Univ. of Westminster (Cert. Higher Educn Biomed. Scis 2004); Univ. of Greenwich (BSc Hons Biomed. Sci. 2006); Univ. of Kent (MSc Sci., Communication and Society 2009). CBiol 2012–14, CSci 2012; FSB 2012–14. Jun. retained fire fighter, Kent Fire Service, 1989–91; served Army as soldier and HGV driver, NI, 1991–94 (Mil. Campaign Service Medal 1993). Biomed. scientist and specialist team leader, William Harvey Hosp., Ashford, Kent, 2002–07; Sales Account Manager, Leica Microsystems, 2008; Regl Manager, Schulke & Mayr, 2010–11; Biomed. Scientist, Cellular Pathology, John Radcliffe Hosp., 2011–15; Dermatology Product Specialist UK, Athrodax Healthcare Ltd, 2015–16; Area Sales Manager, Advanced Wound Care, Advancis Medical, 2016–17. Med. Advr Melanoma UK, 2015–. Founder, Witney Astro Telescopes Soc., 2010. Contributor, NHS Employers' Blog, 2013–. *Publications:* contrib. articles to Biomed. Scientist, Oxford Univ. Hosp. NHS Trust mag., STEMNET. *Recreations:* amateur astronomy, prog rock, general awesomeness. *E:* bms_nhs@yahoo.co.uk.

**PHIPPARD, Sonia Clare,** CBE 2015; Director-General, Environment, Rural and Marine (formerly Policy Delivery, then Environment and Rural), Department for Environment, Food and Rural Affairs, since 2015; *b* 8 Jan. 1960; *d* of Brig. Roy Phippard and Gillian Phippard (*née* Menzies); *m* 2001, Michael Hartley. *Educ:* Wadhurst Coll.; Somerville Coll., Oxford (BA Physics 1981). Joined Civil Service Department, later Cabinet Office (MPO), 1981: on secondment to DES, 1987–89; Private Sec. to Sec. of Cabinet, 1989–92; Asst Sec., Next Steps Project Dir, 1992–94; on secondment to Coopers and Lybrand, 1995–97; Dep. Dir, 1997–99, Head, 2000–01, Central Secretariat, Cabinet Office; Dir, Sustainable Agriculture and Livestock Products, 2001–06, Dir, Analysis and Common Agricl Policy Strategy, then Food and Farming (EU, Internat. and Evidence), 2006–10, Dir, Water and Flood Risk Mgt (formerly Water, Floods, Envmtl Risk and Regulation), 2010–15, DEFRA. *Recreations:* amateur dramatics, food, time with friends. *Address:* Department for Environment, Food and Rural Affairs, 2 Marsham Street, SW1P 4DF.

**PHIPPEN, (Conway) Paul;** Partner, Macfarlanes, Solicitors, 1989–2009; *b* 30 Jan. 1957; *s* of late Rev. Charles Dennis Phippen and of Margaret Helen Phippen; *m* 1981, Jennifer Caroline Nash; two *s* one *d. Educ:* Kingswood Sch., Bath; Exeter Univ. (LLB). Admitted solicitor, 1982; Man. Partner, Macfarlanes, 1999–2008.

**PHIPPS,** family name of **Marquess of Normanby**.

**PHIPPS, Belinda Clare;** Chair, Fawcett Society, 2013–18; Chief Executive Officer, Science Council, 2015–18; *b* 11 April 1958; *d* of Leonie May Kerslake; partner, Nigel John Simmons; three *d. Educ:* The Holt Grammar Sch., Wokingham; Bath Univ. (BSc Hons Microbiol. 1980); Ashridge Management Coll. (MBA 1992). Glaxo Pharmaceuticals, 1980–90; Man. Dir, NHS Blood Transfusion Service, 1991–94; co-ordinating Wells report on London Ambulance Service, 1995; CEO, East Berks Community Trust, 1996–99; Chief Exec., National Childbirth Trust (NCT), 1999–2014; Interim CEO, BMA, 2018–19. Non-exec. Dir, Dorset Healthcare Univ. NHS Foundn Trust, 2017–. Chm., Appt Bd, NMC, 2015–. Patron, Parent Infant Partnership, 2014–; Trustee, Pro Bono Economics, 2018–. Hon. LLD Bath, 2018. *Recreation:* ballroom dancing. *E:* belindaphipps@btinternet.com.

**PHIPPS, Constantine;** *see* Normanby, 5th Marquis of.

**PHIPPS, Maj. Gen. Jeremy Julian Joseph,** CB 1997; Director: Saladin Security Ltd, 2007–12; Bibury Club, Salisbury Racecourse, 2004–10; President, Scottish Borders Scouts Association, since 2017; *b* 30 June 1942; *s* of Lt Alan Phipps, RN (killed in action, 1943), 2nd *s* of Rt Hon. Sir Eric Phipps, GCB, GCMG, GCVO, and Hon. Veronica Phipps, 2nd *d* of 16th Lord Lovat, KT, GCVO, KCMG, CB, DSO; *m* 1974, Susan Louise, *d* of late Comdr Wilfrid and Patricia Crawford; one *s* one *d. Educ:* Ampleforth Coll.; RMA, Sandhurst. Commnd Queen's Own Hussars, 1962; served in Germany, Middle East, Far East; student, US Armed Forces Staff Coll., Norfolk, Va, 1980; commanded Queen's Own Hussars, 1981–83; COS, RMA, Sandhurst, 1983–85; Comdr 11th Armoured Bde, 1985–89; Dir Special Forces, 1989–93; Sen. British Loan Service Officer, Sultanate of Oman, 1993–96; retd 1997. Man. Dir, Network Internat., 1997–2000; Dir of Special Accounts, Control Risks Gp, 2000–02; Dir of Security, Jockey Club, 2002–03; Dir, Derby House Stabling, 2003–05; Dir of Global Risks, Group 4 Security, 2005–07. Order of Achievement (1st cl.), (Sultanate of Oman), 1995. *Recreations:* shooting, fishing. *Address:* Royal Bank of Scotland, 6 The Square, Kelso TD5 7HG. *Clubs:* White's; Houghton.
*See also* Sir C. E. Maclean of Dunconnel, Bt.

**PHIPPS, His Honour John Christopher;** a Circuit Judge, 1996–2012; *b* 29 Aug. 1946; *s* of Thomas Phipps and Jane Bridget Phipps; *m* 1969, Elizabeth Bower; one *s* three *d. Educ:* Liskeard GS, Cornwall; Univ. of Liverpool (LLB Hons 1967). Called to the Bar, Middle Temple, 1970; practised on Northern Circuit, 1971–96; Asst Recorder, 1989–93; Recorder, 1993–96. *Recreations:* theatre, opera, performing with amateur musical societies.

**PHIZACKERLEY, Ven. Gerald Robert;** Archdeacon of Chesterfield, 1978–96, now Emeritus; *b* 3 Oct. 1929; *s* of John Dawson and Lilian Mabel Ruthven Phizackerley; *m* 1959, Annette Catherine, *d* of Cecil Frank and Inez Florence Margaret Baker; one *s* one *d. Educ:* Queen Elizabeth Grammar School, Penrith; University Coll., Oxford (Open Exhibnr; MA); Wells Theological Coll. Curate of St Barnabas Church, Carlisle, 1954–57; Chaplain of Abingdon School, 1957–64; Rector of Gaywood, Bawsey and Mintlyn, Norfolk, 1964–78; Rural Dean of Lynn, 1968–78; Hon. Canon of Norwich Cathedral, 1975, of Derby Cathedral, 1978; Priest-in-charge, Ashford-in-the-Water with Sheldon, 1978–90. Fellow, Woodard Corporation, 1981. JP Norfolk, 1972. *Publications:* (ed) The Diaries of Maria Gyte of Sheldon, Derbyshire, 1913–1920, 1999. *Recreations:* books, theatre, Border collies. *Address:* Archway Cottage, Hall Road, Leamington Spa, Warwickshire CV32 5RA. *T:* (01926) 332740.

**PHOENIX, Prof. Ann,** FBA 2014; Professor of Psychosocial Studies (formerly Professor of Education), UCL Institute of Education, University College London (formerly Institute of Education, University of London), since 2007. Open University: Sen. Lectr in Psychol., then Reader, until 2003; Prof. of Social Sci. and Develtl Psychol., 2003–07; Co-Dir, Thomas Coram Res. Unit, Inst. of Educn, Univ. of London, 2007. Vis. Prof., Humanist Univ., Utrecht, 1997–98. Member, Editorial Board: Eur. Jl Women's Studies; Feminism and Psychol.; Race Ethnicity and Educn; Social Politics; Thymos; Jl Boyhood Studies; Young. FAcSS. Hon. PhD Umeå. *Publications:* Young Mothers?, 1991; (jtly) Crossfires: nationalism, racism and gender in Europe, 1995; (ed jtly) Standpoints and Differences, 1998; (jtly) Young Masculinities: understanding boys in contemporary societies, 2001; (with B. Tizard) Black, White or Mixed Race?, 2002; (with F. Husain) Parenting and Ethnicity, 2007; (jtly) Social Psychology Matters, 2007; (jtly) Environment in the Lives of Children and Families, 2017; contribs to learned jls. *Address:* Department of Social Science, UCL Institute of Education, University College London, 27–28 Woburn Square, WC1H 0AA.

**PHOENIX, Prof. David Andrew,** OBE 2010; PhD, DSc; FRCPE, FRSocMed; FRSB, FRSC, FIMA, FAcSS, PFHEA; DL; Vice Chancellor and Chief Executive, London South Bank University, since 2014; *b* Davyhulme, Gtr Manchester, 26 Feb. 1966; *s* of Derek Phoenix and Edna Marion Phoenix (*née* Tate); *m* 1994, Stephanie Jayne Bailey; one *s* two *d. Educ:* Univ. of Liverpool (BSc Biochem. 1987; PhD Biochem. 1991; DSc Biochem. 2009); Open Univ. (BA Maths 1993; MA Educn 1999; MBA Business 2005); London Business Sch. (Exec. Prog. 2008). CChem 1991; CBiol 1991; CMath 1999. Postdoctoral Res. Asst, Univ. of Liverpool, 1990; Postdoctoral Res. Fellow, Utrecht Univ., 1991–92; University of Central Lancashire: Lectr, 1992–94; Sen. Lectr, 1994–96; Reader, 1996–2000; Prof. of Biochem., 2000–13; Inaugural Hd, Forensic Sci., 2000–02; Dean, Sci. and Technol., 2002–08; Dep. Vice Chancellor and Vice Pres., 2008–13; Vis. Prof., 2013–18. Director: Environmental Ltd, 2002–04; UCLan Biomedical Technology (Shenzhen) Ltd, 2010–13 (Chm., 2010–13); UCLan Cyprus Ltd, 2011–13 (Chm., 2011–13); Consultant, SmithKline Beecham, 1993–95. Vis. Specialist in Clin. Biochem., Preston HA, 1993–96; Vis. Consultant in Clin. Biochem., Royal Preston Hosp., 1996–2014; Hon. Consultant in Clin. Biochem., Lancs Teaching Hosps NHS Trust, 2014–. Fellow, EMBO, 1990, 1991; Vis. Fellow, Univ. of Liverpool, 1996–99; Vis. Prof. in Bioinformatics, Moscow Inst. of Physical Engrg, 1996–2000; Dist. Vis. Prof., Univ. of

Ontario Inst. of Technol., 2004; Visiting Professor: Sichuan Univ., 2013–17; KCL, 2014–17. Trustee: Inst. of Biol., 1997–2000; Mus. of Sci. and Industry, Manchester, 2009–11 (Mem., Adv. Bd, 2015–); Darwin Community Acad., 2009–11; Sci. Mus. Gp, 2015–. Member: Preston and Chorley NHS Trusts Res. Directorate, 2001–03; Daresbury Lab. Facility Access Panel, 2006–10; Lord Chancellor's Adv. Sub-cttee for JPs, Lancs, 2005–08. Bioscis Discipline Consultant, Learning and Teaching Support Network, 2001–03; Nat. Teaching Fellowship Projs Bd, Higher Educn Acad., 2008–10; Ambassador, Diversity in Public Appts, Govt Equalities Office, 2009–10; Mem., Teaching, Quality and Student Experience Strategic Cttee, HEFCE, 2013–18. Director: Univs UK, 2015–; Nat. Centre for Univs and Business, 2016–; Chairman: MillionPlus, 2015–; S Bank Academies, 2016–. European Committee of Biology Associations: Comr for Biotechnol., 2000–02; UK Rep., 2003–07; Chm., Membership and Professional Recognition Panel, 2003–07. Internat. Advr, Sci. and HE, Univ. of Guyana, 2012–. FSS 1993–95; FRSB (FSB 2001); FRSC 2001; FHEA 2007, SFHEA 2008; FRSocMed 2007; FIMA 2008; FAcSS (AcSS 2012); FRCPE 2013; FRSA 2016. DL Greater London, 2015. DUniv Bolton, 2013. Individual Excellence Award, Vice-Premier Liu Yandong (China), 2014; Friendship Award (China), 2016. *Publications:* Introductory Mathematics for Life Scientists, 1997; (ed) Protein Targeting and Translocation, 1998; (ed) Transcription, 2001; (jtly) Antimicrobial Peptides, 2013; (jtly) Proliposomes: a manufacturing technology for pulmonary delivery via nebulization, 2014; (ed jtly) Novel Antimicrobial Agents and Strategies, 2014; 23 book chapters; approx. 125 conf. procs and 200 articles. *Recreations:* theatre, music, walking, travelling, science. *Address:* London South Bank University, 103 Borough Road, SE1 0AA. *T:* (020) 7815 6001, *Fax:* (020) 7815 6099. *E:* phoenixd@lsbu.ac.uk.

**PIACHAUD, Prof. David François James;** Professor of Social Policy (formerly Social Administration), London School of Economics, 1987–2016, now Emeritus; *b* 2 Oct. 1945; *s* of late Rev. Preb. François A. Piachaud and Mary R. Piachaud; *m* 1988, Louise K. Carpenter, *d* of late Rev. Dr E. F. Carpenter, KCVO; one *s* one *d*. *Educ:* Westminster Sch.; Christ Church, Oxford (MA); Univ. of Michigan (MPA). Economic Asst, DHSS, 1968–70; Lectr, 1970–83, Reader, 1983–87, LSE. Policy Advr, Prime Minister's Policy Unit, 1974–79. Associate: Centre for Analysis of Social Exclusion, 1997–; Asia Res. Centre, 2012–. Consultant: EU, 1976–79; OECD, 1982–84; World Bank, 1983–84, 2012; ILO, 1986; UNICEF, 2019. *Publications:* The Causes of Poverty (jtly), 1978; The Cost of a Child, 1979; (jtly) Child Support in the European Community, 1980; The Distribution and Redistribution of Incomes, 1982; (jtly) The Fields and Methods of Social Planning, 1984; (jtly) The Goals of Social Policy, 1989; (jtly) The Price of Food, 1997; (jtly) Understanding Social Exclusion, 2002; (jtly) Making Social Policy Work, 2007; (jtly) Colonialism and Welfare, 2011; (jtly) Social Protection, Economic Growth and Social Change, 2013; contribs to learned jls and periodicals. *Recreations:* walking with Tiger, metal sculpture, travelling. *Address:* c/o Department of Social Policy, London School of Economics, Houghton Street, WC2A 2AE.

**PIANO, Renzo;** architect; founder, Renzo Piano Building Workshop, 1992; *b* 14 Sept. 1937; *m* 1st, 1962, Magda Ardnino; two *s* one *d*; 2nd, 1992, Milly Rossato. *Educ:* Milan Poly. Sch. of Architecture. Founded with Peter Rice, Atelier Piano & Rice, 1977–92. Works include: Pompidou Centre, Paris (with Sir Richard Rogers), and IRCAM, 1977; Schlumberger research labs, Paris, 1984; Menil Collection Mus., Houston, 1986; S Nicola Football Stadium, Bari, Italy, 1990; Kansai Internat. Airport, Osaka, 1994; Concert Hall, hotel and shopping mall, Lingotto, Turin, 1994–96; Contemp. Art Mus. and Congress Centre, Lyon, 1996; Mus. of Sci. and Technol., Amsterdam, and Beyeler Foundn Mus., Basle, 1997; Daimler Benz projects for redevelopment of Potsdamer Platz, Berlin, 1997–98; KPN Telecom office tower, Rotterdam, 2000; Aurora Place high rise office block, Sydney, 2000; Central St Giles, London, 2010; Shard, London, 2012; Astrup Fearnley Mus. of Modern Art, Oslo, 2012; Whitney Mus. of American Art, New York, 2015; numerous exhibitions worldwide. Hon. FAIA, 1981; Hon. FRIBA, 1985; Hon. Fellow: Amer. Acad. of Arts and Scis, 1993; Amer. Acad. of Arts and Letters, 1994. RIBA Gold Medal, 1989; Kyoto Prize, Inamori Foundn, 1990; Erasmus Prize, Amsterdam, 1995; Pritzker Architect Prize, USA, 1998. Cavaliere di Gran Croce (Italy), 1989; Officier, Ordre Nat. du Mérite (France), 1994; Officier, Légion d'Honneur (France), 2000. *Publications:* (jtly) Antico è bello, il recupero della città, 1980; Chantier ouvert au public, 1985; Progetti e Architetture 1984–1986, 1986; Renzo Piano, 1987; (with R. Rogers) Du Plateau Beaubourg au Centre G. Pompidou, 1987; (jtly) Le Isole del tesoro, 1989; Renzo Piano Building Workshop 1964–1988, 1989; Renzo Piano Building and Projects 1971–1989, 1989; Renzo Piano Building Workshop 1964–1991: in search of a balance, 1992; The Making of Kansai International Airport Terminal, 1994; Giornale di Bordo, 1997; Fondation Beyeler: une maison de l'art, 1998. *Address:* Via Rubens 29, 16158 Genoa, Italy; 34 rue des Archives, 75004 Paris, France.

**PIATKUS, Judy;** strategic consultant, investor, coach, mentor and keynote speaker on entrepreneurship, future trends and conscious leadership, since 2008; Founder, ConsciousCafe, personal development network, since 2011; *b* 16 Oct. 1949; *d* of Ralph and Estelle Assersohn; *m* 1st, 1971, Brian Piatkus; one *s* two *d*; 2nd, 1990, Cyril Ashberg. *Educ:* S Hampstead High Sch. for Girls; Dip. Psychodynamic Psychotherapy 2001; Regent's Univ. London (MA Creative Leadership 2014). Founder, Man. Dir and Publisher, Piatkus Books, 1979–2007. *Publications:* (as Judy Ashberg): Little Book of Women's Wisdom, 2001; Lovers' Wisdom, 2004. *Recreation:* enjoying stimulating conversations with interesting people and constantly learning new things. *W:* www.judypiatkus.com.

**PIATT, Wendy Louisa,** DPhil; Senior Adviser, Higher Education, Wild Search, since 2018; *b* Heswall, Wirral, 17 Nov. 1970; *d* of Barrie Piatt and Ann Piatt. *Educ:* King's Coll. London (BA 1992); Lincoln Coll., Oxford (MPhil 1995; DPhil 1998). Hd of Academic Studies, Centre for Internat. Educn, Oxford, 1996–2000; Sen. Res. Fellow and Hd of Educn, IPPR, 2000–02; Sen. Policy Advr, DFES, 2002–04; Dep. Dir and Sen. Civil Servant, Prime Minister's Strategy Unit, 2004–07; Dir Gen., Russell Group, 2007–17. *Publications:* (with Tony Millns) Paying for Learning: the future of individual learning accounts, 2000; (with Peter Robinson) Opportunity for Whom?: options for the funding and structure of post-16 education, 2001; Diverse Missions: achieving excellence and equity in post-16 education, 2004; The UK Government's Approach to Public Service Reform, 2006. *Recreations:* reading, music, football, tennis.

**PICARDA, Hubert Alistair Paul;** QC 1992; *s* of late Pierre Adrien Picarda, Docteur en Droit (Paris), Avocat à la Cour d'Appel de Paris, Barrister, Middle Temple, and Winifred Laura (née Kemp); *m* 1976, Ann Hulse (marr. diss. 1995); one *s* one *d*; *m* 2000, Sarah Elizabeth, *d* of His Honour Judge William Alan Belcher Goss. *Educ:* Seaford Coll. Jun., Worthing; Westminster Sch.; Magdalen Coll., Oxford (Open Exhibnr in Classics; BA Jurisprudence 1961; MA; BCL 1963); University Coll. London (Bunnell Lewis Prize for Latin Verse, 1962). Called to the Bar, Inner Temple, 1962, *ad eundem* Lincoln's Inn and Gray's Inn, 1965; in practice at Chancery Bar, 1964–; Night Lawyer, Daily Express, 1964–72; Lectr, Holborn Coll. Law, Langs and Commerce, 1965–68. Visiting Lecturer: Malaysian Bar Council, 1994, 1995, 1996; Law Soc. of Singapore, 1994, 1996; Hong Kong, 1994; Sarawak, 1995; Singapore Legal Acad., 1999; Cayman Islands Law Sch., 2003; WA Lee Equity Lectr, Brisbane, 2001; Max Planck Inst., Heidelberg Univ., 2006; Insolvency Practitioners Assoc., Singapore, and Nat. Univ. of Singapore, 2007; Univ. of Melbourne, 2013; Univ. of Montréal, 2015. Mem., Senate and Bar Council, 1978–81. Pres., Charity Law Assoc., 1992–2005 (Mem., 2005–); Mem., Trust Law Cttee, 1995–. Pres., Inst. Conveyancers, 2000. Pres., Hardwicke Soc., 1968–72; Member: Classical Assoc.; Horatian Soc.; London Roman Law Gp. Managing Editor: Charity Law and Practice Rev., 1992–2004; Receivers, Administrators and Liquidators Qly, 1994–99 (Consulting Editor, 1999–); Member, Editorial Board: Butterworths Jl of Internat. Banking and Financial Law, 1995–; Trust Law Internat., 1992–. *Publications:* Study Guide to Law of Evidence, 1965; Law and Practice Relating to Charities, 1977, 4th edn 2010, suppl. 2014; Law Relating to Receivers, Managers and Administrators, 1984, 5th edn 2018; (ed) Receivers, in Halsbury's Laws of England, 4th edn, reissue, 1998; (ed) Charities, in Halsbury's Laws of England, 4th edn, reissue, 2001; (contrib.) Dictionary of British Classicists, 2004; contrib. legal periodicals and The Spectator. *Recreations:* Spain in World War II, Andalusian baroque churches, Latin, music, conversation. *Address:* Third Floor North, 9 Old Square, Lincoln's Inn, WC2A 3SR. *T:* (020) 7242 3566. *E:* hubert@hpicarda.com. *Clubs:* White's, Turf, Pratt's, Beefsteak.

**PICARDO, Hon. Fabian;** MP (Gibraltar Socialist Labour), since 2003; Chief Minister of Gibraltar, since 2011; *b* Gibraltar, 18 Feb. 1972; *m* 2011, Justine Olivero; two *s*. *Educ:* Bayside Comprehensive Sch., Gibraltar; Oriel Coll., Oxford (BA Juris. 1993); Inns of Court Sch. of Law. Called to the Bar, Middle Temple, 1994, Bencher, 2018; Associate, 1994–2000, Partner, 2000–, Hassans Internal Law Firm. Leader, Gibraltar Socialist Lab. Party, 2011– (Mem., 2002–). Hon. QC 2014. *Address:* Office of the Chief Minister, No 6 Convent Place, Gibraltar.

**PICHON, Liz;** author and illustrator, since 1990; *b* London, 16 Aug. 1963; *d* of Francis and Joan Pichon; *m* 1990, Mark Flannery; one *s* two *d*. *Educ:* Camberwell Sch. of Art (BA Hons Graphic Design). Art Dir, Jive Records, 1987–90. *Publications:* The Very Ugly Bug, 1988; Square Eyed Pat, 2003; My Big Brother Boris, 2004; Bored Bill, 2004; A Tale of Two Kitties, 2005; Beautiful Bananas, 2005; My Little Sister Doris, 2008; Penguins, 2008; Three Horrid Little Pigs, 2008; with R. Mortimer: Three Billy Goats Gruff, 2011; Red Riding Hood, 2013; Jack and the Jelly Bean Stalk, 2015; Tom Gates series: The Brilliant World of Tom Gates, 2011; Excellent Excuses, 2011; Everything's Amazing (sort of), 2012; Genius Ideas, 2012; Absolutely Fantastic, 2013; Extra Special Treats, 2013; The Best Book Day Ever, 2013; A Tiny Bit Lucky, 2014; Yes! No (Maybe…), 2015; Top of the Class, 2015; Super Good Skills, 2016; Dog Zombies Rule, 2016; Family, Friends and Furry Creatures, 2017; Epic Adventure, 2017; Biscuits, Bands and Very Big Plans, 2018; What Monster?, 2018; The Music Book, 2018; Mega Make and Do, 2019. *Recreations:* travel, swimming, family, art. *Address:* c/o David Higham Associates, 7–12 Noel Street, W1F 8GQ.

**PICK, Geoffrey Michael Boyd;** Director, London Metropolitan Archives, since 2013; *b* Wigan, Lancs, 15 May 1956; *s* of Rev. William Harry Pick and Audrey Joan Pick (née Boyd); *m* 1983, Jacqueline Andrews. *Educ:* Liverpool Coll., Liverpool; Bristol Univ. (BA Classics); Liverpool Univ. (Postgrad. Dip. Archive Admin). Archivist: Worcester Cathedral Liby, 1978–79; Lambeth Palace Liby, 1979–86; City of London: Dep. Record Keeper, Gtr London Record Office, 1986–95; Hd, Public Services, London Metropolitan Archives, 1995–2007; Hd, Learning and Access, London Metropolitan Archives, Keats Hse and Guildhall Art Gall., 2007–10; Hd, Guildhall Art Gall. and Keats Hse, 2010–13. Consultant in Ghana on govtl records mgt, Internat. Records Mgt Trust, 1996–97. Lectr, liby and archive postgrad. course, UCL, 2008–11. National Council on Archives: Chair: Nat. Surveys Wkg Party, 2001–; Public Services Quality Gp, 2004–14; Vice Chair, 2006–08; Chair, 2008–10. Museums, Libraries and Archives Council: Member: Inspiring Learning for All Think Tank, 2003–06; Comprehensive Performance Assessment Bd, 2005–07; Adult Learners Bd, 2009–10; Adv. Panel, NHMF, 2015–; Chair: London Archives Partnership, 2014–; Archive Service Accreditation Cttee, 2019–. Vice Chair, London Mus. Gp, 2005–12. Mem. Bd, 2010–14, Vice Chair, 2014–16, Chair, 2016–18, Archives and Records Assoc. of UK and Ireland. Co-founder and Mem. Cttee, 2003–12, LitHouses (Literary Homes and Mus of GB). Freeman, City of London, 2006. *Publications:* contrib. articles to professional archival jls. *Recreations:* ski-ing, ballroom dancing, allotment tending, guest lyricist/triangle player with the Saggy Bottom Boys. *Address:* London Metropolitan Archives, 40 Northampton Road, EC1R 0HB. *T:* (020) 7332 3833, 07950 157226. *E:* Geoff.Pick@cityoflondon.gov.uk.

**PICK, Hella Henrietta,** CBE 2000; writer and journalist; Director, Art and Culture Programme, Institute (formerly Weidenfeld Institute) for Strategic Dialogue, 2005–17, Senior Advisor, since 2017; Advisor, Editorial Intelligence, since 2017; *b* 24 April 1929; *d* of Ernst Pick and Johanna Marie Pick (née Spitz). *Educ:* Fairfield PNEU Sch., Ambleside; London Sch. of Econs (BSc Econ). Commercial Ed., West Africa mag., 1958–60; The Guardian: UN Corresp., 1960–67; Europe Corresp., 1967–72; Washington Corresp. 1972–75; East-West Affairs Corresp., 1975–82; Diplomatic Ed., 1983–94; Associate Foreign Affairs Ed., 1994–96. Consultant and Ameurus Conference Organiser, Club of Three, Weidenfeld Inst. for Strategic Dialogue, 1997–2005; Sen. Consultant, Inst. for Strategic Dialogue, 2005–. Mem., RIIA. Hon. Dr Sussex, 2018. Goldenes Ehrenzeichen (Austria), 1980; Grosses Verdienstkreuz (Germany), 2002. *Publications:* Simon Wiesenthal: a life in search of justice, 1996, 2nd edn 2000; Guilty Victim: Austria from the Holocaust to Haider, 2000. *Recreations:* walking, swimming, travel, opera. *Address:* Flat 11, 113/115 Haverstock Hill, NW3 4RY. *T:* (020) 7586 3072. *E:* hpick@aol.com. hp@isdglobal.org. *Clubs:* University Women's, PEN (also Austria).

**PICKARD, Prof. Christopher James,** PhD; FInstP; Sir Alan Cottrell Professor of Materials Science, University of Cambridge, since 2015; *b* Huntingdon, 1 July 1973; *s* of Robert and Daphne Claire Pickard; *m* 2007, Sylvie Marie Pauline Delacroix; one *s*. *Educ:* Oakham Sch.; Christ's Coll., Cambridge (BA 1994; PhD 1997). FInstP 2007. Postdoctoral Scholar, Nat. Center for High Perf. Computing, Taiwan, 1997–98; Res. Associate, Cavendish Lab., Univ. of Cambridge, 1998–99 and 2000–02; Hochschulassistent C1, Univ. of Kiel, 1999–2000; Res. Fellow, Darwin Coll., Cambridge, 2001–04; Fellow, Corpus Christi Coll., Cambridge, 2004–06; Reader in Physics, Univ. of St Andrews, 2006–08; Prof. of Physics, UCL, 2009–15. EPSRC Advanced Fellow, 2002–07; EPSRC Leadership Fellow, 2008–14. Rayleigh Medal and Prize, Inst. of Physics, 2015; Wolfson Res. Merit Award, Royal Soc., 2015. *Publications:* contribs to learned jls incl. Nature Physics, Nature Materials, Nature Chem., Jl Amer. Chem. Soc., Proc. NAS, Physical Rev. Letters. *Recreation:* fishing. *Address:* Department of Materials Science and Metallurgy, University of Cambridge, 27 Charles Babbage Road, Cambridge CB3 0FS.

**PICKARD, David Keith;** Director, BBC Proms, since 2015; *b* 8 April 1960; *s* of Roger Willows Pickard and June Mary Pickard; *m* 1991, Annette Elizabeth Finney; two *s*. *Educ:* King's Sch., Ely (Choir Sch.); St Albans Sch.; Corpus Christi Coll., Cambridge (Choral Schol.; MA Music). Co. Manager, Royal Opera, 1984–87; Administrator, New Shakespeare Co., 1987–89; Man. Dir, Kent Opera, 1989–90; Asst Dir, Japan Fest. 1991, 1990–92; Artistic Administrator, Eur. Arts Fest., 1992–93; Chief Exec., Orch. of Age of Enlightenment, 1993–2001; Gen. Dir, Glyndebourne, 2001–15. Trustee: Nat. Opera Studio, 2001–15; Shakespeare Globe Trust, 2005–14; Cambridge Univ. Music Soc., 2013–17; Charleston, 2016–. *Recreations:* playing piano duets, cooking.

**PICKARD, (James) Nigel**; Chief Executive, Spindrift Media, since 2014; Director: Dial Square 86, since 2014; Nevision Ltd, since 2015; *b* Worthing, 10 March 1952; *m* 1974, Hazel; two *s* one *d*. Film ed., floor manager, trainee dir, then Asst Dir, Southern TV, 1972–82; TVS: Sen. Dir, 1982–85, Exec. Prod., 1985–86, Children's Dept; Controller, Children's and Family Programming, 1986–92; Controller of Entertainment and Drama Features, Scottish TV, 1992–93; Dir of Progs, 1993–96, Gen. Manager, 1996–97, Family Channel; Vice-Pres. of Prodn, and Gen. Manager, Challenge TV, Flextech TV, 1997–98; Controller: Children's and Youth Progs, ITV Network Ltd, 1998–2000; Children's Progs, BBC, 2000–02; Dir of Progs, ITV, 2003–06; Dir of Family & Children's Programming, later Gp Dir, Family Entertainment and Drama, RDF Media Gp, 2006–10; Chief Exec., Zodiak MEAA/UK Family and Kids, 2010–14. Non-exec. Dir, Beano Studios, 2016–. Pres., TRX, 2016–. Chm., The Foundn, 2006–14. FRTS 2006. *Address:* Peasridge Farmhouse, Bubhurst Lane, Frittenden, Cranbrook TN17 2BD.

**PICKARD, John Anthony, (Tony);** professional tennis coach; *b* 13 Sept. 1934; *s* of John William Pickard and Harriet Haywood Pickard; *m* 1958, Janet Sisson; one *s* twin *d*. *Educ:* Ripley Sch.; Diocesan Sch., Derby; Derby Tech. Coll. Worked under Harry Hopman, Australia (LTA), 1953–54; Sherwood Foresters, 1954–56; Mem., British Davis Cup team, 1958–63; Dir, Chellaston Brick Co., Derby, 1965; Dir, 1967, Man. Dir, 1971, F. Sisson & Sons and subsidiaries, Langley Mill; Captain, under-21 tennis team, winning Galea Cup, 1972; non-playing Captain, British Davis Cup team, 1973–76, 1991–94. Professional tennis coach to Stefan Edberg, 1985–94, to Greg Rusedski, 1997–98. Pres., Notts LTA, 2002–17. GB Coach of the Year, 1988. *Recreations:* golf, walking, cars, spending time at home, football. *Clubs:* All England Lawn Tennis; International Tennis Clubs of GB, America, Germany, Sweden; Ripley Tennis; Lindrick Golf.

**PICKARD, Prof. John Douglas**, FRCS, FRCSE, FMedSci; Professor of Neurosurgery, University of Cambridge, 1991–2013, now Emeritus; Consultant Neurosurgeon, Addenbrooke's Hospital, Cambridge, 1991–2013; Chairman, Wolfson Brain Imaging Centre, 1995–2013; Professorial Fellow, St Catharine's College, Cambridge, 1991–2013, now Emeritus; *b* 21 March 1946; *s* of late Reginald James Pickard and Eileen Muriel Pickard (*née* Alexander); *m* 1971, Charlotte Mary, *d* of late Robert Stuart Townshend and Maureen Charlotte Townshend (*née* Moran); one *s* two *d* (and one *s* decd). *Educ:* King George V Grammar Sch., Southport; St Catharine's Coll., Cambridge (BA 1st Class 1967; MA); King's Coll. Hosp. Med. Sch., London (MB BChir 1970; MChir 1981 (distinction)). KCH, 1970–72; Inst. of Neurol Sci., Glasgow, 1972–73; Falkirk Hosp., 1973–74; Univ. of Pennsylvania Hosp., 1974–75; Registrar, Sen. Registrar, Lectr in Neurosurgery, Inst. of Neurol Sci., Glasgow, 1976–79; Consultant Neurosurgeon, Wessex Neurol Centre, Southampton, 1979–91; Sen. Lectr, 1979, Reader, 1984, Prof. of Clin. Neurol Scis, 1987–91, Univ. of Southampton. Dir, NIHR Brain Injury Healthcare Technol. Co-operative, 2012–17; Hon. Dir, NIHR Brain Injury MedTech Co-operative, 2018–. President: Soc. of British Neurological Surgeons, 2006–08; Soc. for Res. into Hydrocephalus and Spina Bifida, 2018–; Chm., Jt Neuroscis Council, 2007–10. Pres., Academia Eurasiana Neurochirurgica, 2011–13. Hon. Consultant Advr (Neurosurgery) to Army, 2009–. Founder Trustee, Brain and Spine Foundn, 1992; Trustee, Brain Res. Trust, 2012–. Founder FMedSci 1998. Dr *hc* Liege, 2008. Robert H. Pudenz Award for Excellence in Cerebro-Spinal Fluid Physiology Res., 2000; Guthrie Meml Prize, AMS, 2009; Medal for outstanding contribns to neurosurgery, Soc. British Neurol Surgeons, 2019. *Publications:* numerous articles in med. and sci. jls. *Recreations:* family life, golf. *Address:* Hermiston, Broadgait, Gullane EH31 2DH. *T:* (01620) 842557. *Clubs:* Athenæum; New (Edinburgh).

**PICKARD, Sir (John) Michael**, Kt 1997; FCA; Chairman: National House-Building Council, 1998–2002; London Docklands Development Corporation, 1992–98 (Deputy Chairman, 1991–92); Deputy Chairman, Epsom Downs Racecourses Ltd, 2003–06; *b* 29 July 1932; *s* of John Stanley Pickard and Winifred Joan Pickard; *m* 1959, Penelope Jane (*née* Catterall); three *s* one *d*. *Educ:* Oundle School. Finance Dir, British Printing Corp., 1965–68; Man. Dir, Trust Houses Ltd/Trusthouse Forte Ltd, 1968–71; Founder Chm., Happy Eater Ltd, 1972–86; Dep. Chief Exec., 1986–88, Chief Exec., 1988–92, Sears plc; Chairman: Grattan plc, 1978–84; Courage Ltd and Imperial Brewing & Leisure Ltd, 1981–86; Dep. Chief Exec., Imperial Gp plc, 1985–86; Chm., Freemans, 1988–92. Director: Brown Shipley Hldgs, 1986–93; Electra Investment Trust plc, 1989–2002; Nationwide Building Soc., 1991–94; Pinnacle Leisure Gp Ltd (formerly Wates Leisure), 1992–99; London First, 1992–2002 (Dep. Chm., 1998–2002); Bentalls plc, 1993–2001; Racecourse Leisure Corp., 1993–96; United Racecourses (Holdings) Ltd, 1995–2003; Chairman: Bullough plc, 1996–2002; Servus (formerly Opus) Hldgs, 1997–2001; London First Centre, 1998–2001; The Housing Forum, 1999–2002; Freeport, 2001–03. Dir, Surrey Cricket Bd Ltd, 2009–14; Dep. Pres., 2011–12, Pres., 2012–13, Surrey CCC. Chm. Council, Roedean Sch., 1980–91; Chm. of Govs, Oundle Sch., 2004–07 (Gov., 1988–2000). Member: Bd, BTA, 1968–71; Cttee, AA, 1994–99. Mem., Court of Assistants, Co. of Grocers, 1990– (Master, 1996). Hon. LLD E London, 1997. *Recreations:* cricket, golf, bridge, politics. *Clubs:* Boodle's, Pilgrims, MCC; Walton Heath Golf (Chm., 2003–08); Headley Cricket (Pres., 1986–); Surrey County Cricket; Dorking Rugby Football (Pres., 2007–12).

**PICKARD, Nigel**; *see* Pickard, J. N.

**PICKARD, Tony**; *see* Pickard, J. A.

**PICKEN, Ven. David Anthony**; Archdeacon of Newark, since 2012; *b* Hednesford, Staffs, 5 June 1963; *s* of Norman Anthony Picken and late Valerie Picken; *m* 1985, Catherine Ann Edwards. *Educ:* Kingsmead Comprehensive Sch.; Univ. of London (BA Hons 1984); Christ Church, Canterbury (PGCE 1985); Univ. of Nottingham (MA 1996). Teacher of Religious Studies: Seaford Head, 1985–86; Elizabethan High Sch., Retford, 1986–87; ordained deacon, 1990, priest, 1991; Asst Curate, Worth Team Ministry, 1990–93; Team Vicar and Hospital Chaplain, Wordsley Team Ministry, 1993–97; Team Rector: Wordsley, 1997–2004; High Wycombe, 2004–11; Area Dean, Wycombe, 2007–11. Hon. Canon: Christ Church, Oxford, 2011; Southwell, 2012. *Recreations:* theatre, sport, literature. *Address:* Jubilee House, Westgate, Southwell, Notts NG25 0JH. *E:* archdeacon-newark@southwell.anglican.org.

**PICKEN, Hon. Sir Simon**, Kt 2015; **Hon. Mr Justice Picken;** a Judge of the High Court, Queen's Bench Division, since 2015; a Presiding Judge, Wales Circuit, since 2018; *b* 23 April 1966; *s* of Keith and Ann Picken; *m* 1992, Sophie Victoria Seddon; one *s* three *d*. *Educ:* Cardiff High Sch.; University Coll., Cardiff (LLB Hons 1987); Magdalene Coll., Cambridge (LLM Starred 1st Cl. 1988). Called to the Bar, Middle Temple, 1989; in practice as a barrister, specialising in commercial law, 1989–2015; QC 2006; a Recorder, 2005–15; a Dep. High Court Judge, 2010–15; a Church Comr, 2013–15. *Publications:* Good Faith and Insurance Contracts, 3rd edn 2010, 4th edn 2018. *Recreations:* Rugby Union, Italy.

**PICKERING, Prof. Alan Durward**, PhD, DSc; CBiol, FRSB; Director, CEH Windermere (formerly Institute of Freshwater Ecology), 1995–2001 (acting Director, 1993–95); Independent Advisor, Department for Environment, Food and Rural Affairs, 2002–13; *b* 7 Sept. 1944; *s* of Frank Hadfield Pickering and Olive Pickering (*née* Page); *m* 1969, Christine Mary Pott; two *s* one *d*. *Educ:* Ecclesfield Grammar Sch.; Univ. of Nottingham (BSc 1st cl. Zoology 1966; PhD 1970; DSc 1986). CBiol, FRSB (FIBiol 1995). Res. Physiologist, Freshwater Biological Assoc., 1969–89; Head, Windermere Lab., 1989–93. Associate Prof., Dept of Biology and Biochemistry, Brunel Univ., 1991–2002. *Publications:* (ed) Stress and Fish, 1981; numerous articles in scientific jls. *Recreations:* gardening, woodwork, golf, sailing, travel.

**PICKERING, Alan Michael**, CBE 2004; Chairman, BESTrustees Ltd, since 2008; *b* 4 Dec. 1948; *s* of Frank and Betty Pickering; *m* 1982, Christine Tull. *Educ:* Exhall Grange Sch., Coventry; Univ. of Newcastle upon Tyne (BA Hons Politics and Social Admin). APMI 1981. With BR, 1967–69; Hd, Membership Services Dept, EETPU, 1972–92; Partner, then Sen. Consultant, Watson Wyatt, 1992–2008. Member: Occupational Pensions Bd, 1992–97; Bd, Pensions Regulator, 2005–13; Chairman: Nat. Assoc. of Pension Funds, 1999–2001; Plumbing Ind. Pension Scheme, 2001–; Eur. Fedn of Retirement Provision, 2001–04; Royal Mail Statutory Pension Scheme, 2012–. Mem., Rules Cttee, British Horseracing Authy, 2009–; Mem. Bd, Racehorse Owners Assoc., 2011– (Vice Pres., 2015–). Trustee: Life Academy (Pre-Retirement Assoc.), 2005–13 (Chm., 2006–13); Kosovan Pensions Savings Trust, 2012–15; Founder Trustee, Clara-Pensions, 2018–. Pres., Blackheath Harriers, 1992; Chm., Blackheath and Bromley Harriers Trust Co., 2017–. *Publications:* A Simpler Way to Better Pensions, 2002; Look Where You're Going, 2018. *Recreations:* running, gardening, horse racing, travel. *Club:* Blackheath and Bromley Harriers Athletic.

**PICKERING, Prof. Brian Thomas**; Deputy Vice-Chancellor, University of Bristol, 1992–2001, now Emeritus Professor (Hon. Fellow, 2002); *b* 24 May 1936; *s* of Thomas Pickering and Dorothy May Pickering; *m* 1965, Joan Perry (*d* 2005); two *d*. *Educ:* Haberdashers' Aske's Hatcham Boys' Sch.; Univ. of Bristol (BSc 1958; PhD 1961; DSc 1974). Research Biochemist, Hormone Res. Lab., Univ. of California, 1961–62; Scientific Staff, NIMR, MRC, 1963–65; University of Bristol: Lectr in Biochem. and Pharmacol., 1965–70 (Mem., MRC Gp for Res. in Neurosecretion); Lectr in Anatomy and Biochem., 1970–72; Reader in Anatomy and Biochem., 1972–78; Prof. of Anatomy and Head of Dept, 1978–92; Dean, Faculty of Medicine, 1985–87. Vis. Prof., Univ. of Geneva, 1977; Anatomical Soc. Review Lectr, 1984. Mem., Bristol & Weston HA, 1988–90; non-exec. Dir, United Bristol Healthcare NHS Trust, 1990–98. Mem., Animal Grants Bd, AFRC, 1988–94 (Chm., 1991–94). Associate Editor, Jl of Endocrinology, 1972–77. Sec. and Treasurer, 1971–77, Vice-Pres., 1986–90, Pres., 1990–94, European Soc. for Comparative Endocrinology; Sec., British Neuroendocrine Gp, 1986–92; mem., other learned bodies. Hon. Fellow, Romanian Acad. of Med. Sci., 1991. Hon. MD Carol Davila, Bucharest, 1994; Hon. LLD Bristol, 2001. Medal, Soc. for Endocrinology, 1977. *Publications:* contribs to professional jls. *Address:* 243 Canford Lane, Bristol BS9 3PD.

**PICKERING, Errol Neil**, PhD; Director General, International Hospital Federation, 1987–98; *b* 5 May 1938; *s* of Russell Gordon and Sylvia Mary Pickering. *Educ:* York Univ., Canada (BA Hons); Univ. of Toronto (DipHA); Univ. of New South Wales (PhD). Asst Administrator, St Michael's Hosp., Toronto, 1971–73; Executive Director: Aust. Council on Hosp. Standards, 1973–80; Aust. Hosp. Assoc., 1980–87. Dir, Health Care Risk Solutions Ltd, 1994–98. Pres., UNICEF Australia, 1984–86. Vice Pres., RSPCA, Gold Coast, 2006–. Chm., Internat. Assoc. Forum, 1990–92. Bd Mem., European Soc. of Assoc. Execs, 1995–98. *Publications:* many articles on hosp. and health policy issues. *Recreations:* classical music, bridge. *Address:* 13 Firestone Court, Robina Woods, Qld 4226, Australia.

**PICKERING, Janet Dolton**; Headmistress, Withington Girls' School, 2000–10; *b* 21 June 1949; *d* of George Browning and Marjorie Dolton Haywood; *m* 1971, William Ronald Pickering; two *s*. *Educ:* Bridlington High Sch.; Malton Grammar Sch.; Univ. of Sheffield (BSc 1st Cl. Biochem.). SRC res. student, Univ. of Sheffield, 1970–73; Scientific Officer, Hallamshire Hosp. Med. Sch., 1973–75; Teaching Fellow, Univ. of Leeds, 1975–79; freelance proof-reader, editor, indexer (sch. sci. texts and scientific jls), 1980–88; part-time teacher and tutor, Gordonstoun Sch., 1983–85; King's School, Canterbury, 1986–97: teacher, tutor, housemistress, 1990–94; Dep. Hd, 1994–97; Hd, St Bees Sch., Cumbria, 1998–2000. HMC/ISI Inspector, 1994–, Reporting Inspector, 2011–. Chm., Sen. Mistresses Gp, 1995–96, Mem., Inspections Cttee, 2004–10 (Chm., 2007–10), Mem. Council, 2007–10, GSA; Co-Chm., Sports Sub-Cttee, GSA/HMC, 2004–05; Bd Mem., ISI, 2007–10. Consultant, Ogden Trust, 2012–18. University of Manchester: Lay Mem., Assembly, 2007–18; Mem., Nominations Cttee, 2009–16. Governor: Copthorne Prep. Sch., 1995–97; Windlesham House Sch., 1996–98; Branwood Prep. Sch., 2001–08; Colfe's Sch., 2005–08; Chetham's Sch. of Music, 2005–15; Bury Grammar Schs, 2008–15. Hon. Fellow, Rank Foundn, 2010. *Publications:* (jtly) Nucleic Acid Biochemistry, 1982; (contrib.) Children's Britannica, 4th edn 1988; contrib. articles to Jl Gen. Micro., Inserm, Hum. Hered. *Recreations:* reading, theatre, cinema, natural history, travel, running. *Address:* 6 Castle Howard Drive, Malton, N Yorks YO17 7BA. *Club:* University Women's.

**PICKERING, His Honour Richard Edward Ingram**; a Circuit Judge, 1981–98; *b* 16 Aug. 1929; *s* of late Richard and Dorothy Pickering; *m* 1962, Jean Margaret Eley; two *s*. *Educ:* Birkenhead Sch.; Magdalene Coll., Cambridge (MA). Called to the Bar, Lincoln's Inn, 1953; has practised on Northern Circuit, 1955–81 (Junior, 1960–61); a Recorder of the Crown Court, 1977–81. Admitted as advocate in Manx Courts (Summerland Fire Inquiry), 1973–74. Councillor, Hoylake UDC, 1961–64; Legal Chm., Min. of Pensions and Nat. Insurance Tribunal, Liverpool, 1967–77; pt-time Chm., Liverpool Industrial Tribunal, 1977–79; Nominated Judge, NW Reg. (formerly Judicial Mem., Merseyside), Mental Health Rev. Tribunal, 1984–2001 (Legal Mem., 1967–79; Regional Chm., 1979–81); Northern Circuit Rep., Cttee, Council of Circuit Judges, 1984–89. Pres., League of Friends, Clatterbridge Hosp., 2001–11. *Recreations:* walking, bowls, gardening, study of military history. *Address:* Trelyon, Croft Drive, Caldy, Wirral CH48 2JN. *Clubs:* Athenæum (Liverpool) (Hon. Proprietor, 2012); Union (Cambridge).

**PICKERING, Robert Mark**; Chief Executive, JPMorgan Cazenove (formerly Cazenove Group plc), 2001–08; *b* 30 Nov. 1959; *s* of Richard Pickering and Lorna Pickering (*née* Browne); *m* 1st, 1983, Harriet Jump (marr. diss. 2005); two *s* one *d*; 2nd, 2006, Miho Umino; two *d*. *Educ:* Westminster Sch.; Lincoln Coll., Oxford (MA Law). Admitted solicitor, 1982; Solicitor: Allen & Overy, 1982–85; Cazenove & Co., 1985–2001 (Partner, 1993). Non-executive Director: Neptune Investment Mgt Ltd, 2009–16; Hikma Pharmaceuticals plc, 2011–; Itau BBA Internat. plc, 2012–; CLSA UK, 2014–17. *Recreations:* fishing, drinking wine, art, trying to stop rabbits eating my plants. *Clubs:* Garrick; Flyfishers'; Vincent's (Oxford).

**PICKERING, Thomas Reeve**; Vice Chairman, Hills & Company, since 2006; Board Member, International Crisis Group, since 2006; *b* Orange, NJ, 5 Nov. 1931; *s* of Hamilton R. Pickering and Sarah C. (*née* Chasteney); *m* 1955, Alice J. Stover (*d* 2011); one *s* one *d*. *Educ:* Bowdoin Coll. (AB); Fletcher Sch. of Law and Diplomacy (MA); Univ. of Melbourne (MA). Served to Lt-Comdr, USNR, 1956–59. Joined US For. Service, 1959; For. Affairs Officer, Arms Control and Disarmament Agency, 1961; Political Advr, US Delegn to 18 Nation Disarmament Conf., Geneva, 1962–64; Consul, Zanzibar, 1965–67; Counselor, Dep. Chief of Mission, Amer. Embassy, Dar-es-Salaam, 1967–69; Dep. Dir Bureau, Politico-Mil. Affairs, State Dept, 1969–73; Special Asst to Sec. of State and Exec. Sec., Dept of State, 1973–74; Amb. to Jordan, 1974–78; Asst Sec. for Bureau of Oceans, Internat. Environmental and Sci. Affairs, Washington, 1978–81; Ambassador: to Nigeria, 1981–83; to El Salvador, 1983–85; to Israel, 1986–88; Ambassador and US Perm. Rep. to UN, 1989–92; Ambassador: to India, 1992–93; to Russia, 1993–96; Under Sec. for Political Affairs, US Dept of State, 1997–2000. Sen. Vice Pres., Internat. Relations, Boeing Co., 2001–06. Member: Council, For. Relns, IISS, 1973–; Global Leadership Foundn, 2008–. Phi Beta Kappa. Hon. LLD: Bowdoin Coll., 1984; Atlantic Union Coll., 1990; Tufts Univ., 1990; Hebrew Union Coll., 1991; Willamette Univ., 1991; Drew Univ., 1991; Franklin Pierce Coll., 1991; Hofstra, 1992; Lafayette Coll., 1992. *Address:* Hills & Co., 1850 M Street NW, Suite 600, Washington, DC 20036, USA. *Club:* Cosmos (Washington).

**PICKETT, Prof. George Richard,** DPhil; FRS 1997; Professor of Low Temperature Physics, University of Lancaster, 1988, now Distinguished Professor. *Educ:* Magdalen Coll., Oxford (BA 1962; DPhil). Lectr, then Sen. Lectr, later Reader, Dept of Physics, Univ. of Lancaster. *Address:* Department of Physics, University of Lancaster LA1 4YB.

**PICKETT, Prof. John Anthony,** CBE 2004; PhD, DSc; FRS 1996; Professor of Biological Chemistry, Cardiff University, since 2017; *b* 21 April 1945; *s* of Samuel Victor Pickett and Lilian Frances Pickett (*née* Hoar); *m* 1970, Ulla Birgitta Skålen; one *s* one *d*. *Educ:* King Edward VII Grammar Sch., Coalville; Univ. of Surrey (BSc Hons Chem. 1967; PhD Organic Chem. 1971); DSc Nottingham 1993. CChem 1975, FRSC 1982; CSci 2004. Postdoctoral Fellow, UMIST, 1970–72; Chem. Dept, Brewing Res. Foundn (flavour active components of hops and malt), 1972–76; Dept of Insecticides and Fungicides, Rothamsted Exptl Stn (semiochem. aspects of insect chem. ecology), 1976–83; Hd, Dept of Insecticides and Fungicides, subseq. Biol and Ecol Chem. Dept, then Biol Chem. Dept, IACR-Rothamsted, then Rothamsted Res., 1984–2010; Scientific Dir, Rothamsted Centre for Sustainable Pest and Disease Mgt, 2007–10; Michael Elliott Distinguished Res. Fellow, 2010–17, Scientific Leader of Chem. Ecology, 2010–14, Rothamsted Research. Special Prof., later Vis. Prof., then Hon. Prof., Sch. of Biol., Univ. of Nottingham, 1991–. Lectures: Boyce Thompson Inst. for Plant Res., Cornell Univ., 1991; Alfred M. Boyce, Univ. of California, Riverside, 1993; Woolhouse, Soc. for Experimental Biology, York Univ., 1998; Barrington Meml, Univ. of Nottingham, 1999; Cameron-Gifford, Univ. of Newcastle, 2000; Andersonian Chem. Soc. Centenary, Univ. of Strathclyde, 2006; H. R. MacCarthy Pest Mgt, Univ. of BC, 2007; Croonian, Royal Soc., 2008; Cornell Univ. Ithaca, 2009; Wilson Baker, Univ. of Bristol, 2010. Mem. Council, Royal Soc., 2000–02. Pres., Royal Entomological Soc., 2014–16. Hon. FRES 2010. Hon. Mem., Chem. Soc. of Ethiopia, 2010. Foreign Associate, Nat. Acad. of Scis, USA, 2014. Hon. DSc Aberdeen, 2008. Rank Prize for Nutrition and Crop Husbandry, 1995; Silver Medal, Internat. Soc. of Chem. Ecology, 2002; Wolf Foundn Prize in Agriculture, 2008; Millennium Award, Associated Chambers of Commerce and Industry of India, 2011; Cert. of Distinction, Internat. Congress of Entomol., Daegu, Korea, 2012. *Publications:* over 530 papers and patents. *Recreation:* jazz trumpet playing. *Address:* School of Chemistry, Cardiff University, Main Building, Park Place, Cardiff CF10 3AT.

**PICKETT, Philip;** Director, New London Consort, since 1978. *Educ:* Guildhall Sch. of Music and Drama (Maisie Lewis Foundn Award; Wedgewood Award). Prof. of Recorder and Historical Performance Practice, GSMD, 1972–97. Began career as trumpet player; subseq. took up recorder, crumhorn, shawm, rackett, etc; as soloist, has performed with many leading ensembles, incl. Acad. of St Martin-in-the-Fields, London Chamber Orch., Polish Chamber Orch., English Chamber Orch., London Mozart Players; with New London Consort, performs a wide repertoire of medieval, Renaissance and Baroque music; resident early music ensemble, S Bank Centre; nat. and internat. concerts, operas and recitals, incl. BBC Proms, and regular performances at art fests. Dir of Early Music, Globe Theatre, 1993–; Artistic Director: Purcell Room Early Music Series, 1993–; Aldeburgh Early Music Fest., 1994–97 (also Founder); Early Music Fest., S Bank Centre, 1996–2003; Associate Artist, Bridgewater Hall, Manchester, 2010–. Appearances on radio and television; film soundtracks. Solo recordings incl. Handel recorder concertos and trio concertos, and Vivaldi and Telemann concertos. *Publications:* articles in books and jls.

**PICKETT-HEAPS, Prof. Jeremy David,** PhD; FRS 1995; FAA; Professor, 1988–2002, now Professorial Fellow, School of Botany, University of Melbourne; *b* 5 June 1940; *s* of Harold Arthur Pickett-Heaps and Edna Azura (*née* May); *m* 1st, 1965, Daphne Charmian Scott (*d* 1970); one *s* one *d*; 2nd, 1977, Julianne Francis Jack; two *s*. *Educ:* Clare Coll., Cambridge (BA; PhD 1965). Fellow, Research Sch. of Biol Sci., ANU, 1965–70; Prof., Dept of Molecular, Cellular and Developmental Biol., Univ. of Colorado, 1970–88. FAA 1992. *Publications:* Green Algae, 1972; numerous scientific res. papers. *Recreations:* various. *Address:* PO Box 247, Mallacoota, Vic 3892, Australia. *T:* (3) 51580123.

**PICKFORD, Meredith William;** QC 2015; *b* 13 April 1972; *s* of Nigel Pickford and Rosamund Pickford; two *s* one *d*. *Educ:* Chesterton Community Coll., Cambridge; Hills Road Sixth Form Coll., Cambridge; Clare Coll., Cambridge (BA Econs 1994); City Univ. (DipLaw 1998). Corporate Strategy Consultant, L/E/K Partnership, 1994–96; Econ. Consultant, Smithers & Co. Ltd, 1996–98; called to the Bar, Middle Temple, 1999; barrister specialising in competition law and economic regulation. *Address:* Monckton Chambers, 1–2 Raymond Buildings, Gray's Inn, WC1R 5NR. *T:* (020) 7405 7211, *Fax:* (020) 7405 2084.

**PICKFORD, Stephen John,** CB 2004; Associate Fellow, Royal Institute of International Affairs, Chatham House, since 2011; Managing Director, International and Finance Directorate, HM Treasury, 2007–09; *b* 26 Aug. 1950; *s* of Frank and May Pickford; *m* 1978, Carolyn M. Ruffle; two *s*. *Educ:* St John's Coll., Cambridge (BA Hons 1971; MA 1974); Univ. of British Columbia (MA 1984). Economist, Dept of Employment, 1971–79; HM Treasury: Economist, 1979–85; Dep. Press Sec., 1985–87; Sen. Economic Advr, 1987–89, 1993–98; Manager, Macroeconomics, New Zealand Treasury, 1989–93; UK Exec. Dir, IMF and World Bank, 1998–2001; Minister (Econ.), British Embassy, Washington, 1998–2001; Dir, Internat. Finance, 2001–06, Europe, 2006–07, HM Treasury. *Publications:* (contrib.) Government Economic Statistics, 1989; Chatham Hse pubns. *Recreations:* cycling, film.

**PICKING, Anne;** *see* Moffat, A.

**PICKLES,** Baron *cr* 2018 (Life Peer), of Brentwood and Ongar in the County of Essex; **Eric Jack Pickles,** Kt 2015; PC 2010; *b* 20 April 1952; *m* 1976, Irene. *Educ:* Greenhead Grammar Sch.; Leeds Polytechnic. Joined Conservative Party, 1968; Young Conservatives: Area Chm., 1976–78; Nat. Vice-Chm., 1978–80; Nat. Chm., 1980–81; Conservative Party: Member: Nat. Union Exec. Cttee, 1975–91; One Nation Forum, 1987–91; Nat. Local Govt Adv. Cttee, 1985– (Chm., 1992–93); Lectr, Cons. Agents Examination Courses, 1988–; Local Govt Editor, Newsline, 1990–92; a Vice-Chm., 1993–97; Dep. Chm., 2005–07. Bradford Council: Councillor, 1979–91; Chm., Social Services, 1982–84; Chm., Educn, 1984–86; Leader, Cons. Gp, 1987–91; Leader of Council, 1988–90. Dep. Leader, Cons. Gp, AMA, 1989–91. MP (C) Brentwood and Ongar, 1992–2017. PPS to Minister for Industry, 1993; Opposition frontbench spokesman on social security, 1998–2001; Shadow Transport Minister, 2001–02; Shadow Sec. of State for Local Govt and the Regions, 2002–07, for Communities and Local Govt, 2007–09; Sec. of State for Communities and Local Govt, 2010–15. Chm., All Party Film Gp, 1997–2004; Vice-Chm., Cons. Envmt, Transport and Regions Cttee, 1997–98. Chm., Conservative Party, 2009–10. UK Special Envoy on post-Holocaust Issues, 2015–; Hd, UK Delegn to Internat. Holocaust Remembrance Alliance, 2015–. Mem., Council of Europe, 1997–. Mem., Yorks Area RHA, 1982–90. Mem., Adv. Cttee on Business Appts, Jan. 2020–. Chm., Internat. Tracing Service, 2019–20. Co-Chair, UK Holocaust Meml Foundn, 2018–. *Recreations:* film buff, opera, serious walking.

**PICKSTOCK, Prof. Catherine Jane Crozier,** PhD; Norris-Hulse Professor of Divinity, University of Cambridge, since 2018; Fellow, Emmanuel College, Cambridge, since 1995; *b* New York City, 1970; *d* of Keith Pickstock and Janet Louise Pickstock (*née* Crozier); *m* 2002, Thomas Harrison; two *s* one *d*. *Educ:* Channing Sch., Highgate; St Catharine's Coll., Cambridge (BA 1991); Emmanuel Coll., Cambridge (PhD 1996). Faculty of Divinity, University of Cambridge: British Acad. Postdoctoral Fellow, 1998; Lectr in Philosophy of Religion, 2000–08; Reader in Philosophy and Theol., 2008–15; Prof. of Metaphysics and Poetics, 2015–18. *Publications:* After Writing: on the liturgical consummation of philosophy, 1998 (trans. French, 2013; Spanish, Serbo Croat); (ed jtly) Radical Orthodoxy: a new theology, 1998; (with J. Milbank) Truth in Aquinas, 2001; Thomas d'Aquin et la Quête Eucharistique, 2002; Povijest Osjetilnog Viška (The Surplus of Matter), 2011; Repetition and Identity, 2013; Truth and Event, 2018; contribs to Modern Theol. and Telos. *Recreations:* choral music, poetry, the music of Olivier Messiaen. *Address:* Emmanuel College, Cambridge CB2 3AP.

**PICKTHALL, Colin;** Chairman of Trustees, Ford Park Community Trust, 2007–16; *b* 13 Sept. 1944; *s* of Frank Pickthall and Edith (*née* Bonser), Dalton-in-Furness; *m* 1973, Judith Ann Tranter; two *d*. *Educ:* Univ. of Wales (BA); Univ. of Lancaster (MA). Teacher, Ruffwood Comprehensive Sch., Kirkby, 1967–70; Edge Hill College of Higher Education: Sen. Lectr in English Lit., 1970–83; Head, European Studies, 1983–92. County Councillor, Ormskirk, Lancs CC, 1989–93. Contested (Lab) Lancashire West, 1987; MP (Lab) Lancs W, 1992–2005; PPS to Sec. of State for Home Office, 1998–2001, for Foreign and Commonwealth Affairs, 2001–05. Mem., Ulverston Town Council, 2012– (Leader, 2016–). Chm., Keep Ulverston Special (anti-supermarket campaign), 2011–14. Founder, 2013, Chm., 2015–, Friends of Coronation Hall, Ulverston (Sec., 2013–15). *Recreations:* fell-walking, gardening, cricket, theatre. *Address:* 25 Fountain Street, Ulverston, Cumbria LA12 7EQ.

**PICKTHORN, Sir James (Francis Mann),** 3rd Bt *cr* 1959, of Orford, Suffolk; Partner, Pickthorn, estate agents and chartered surveyors, since 1994; *b* 18 Feb. 1955; *o s* of Sir Charles William Richards Pickthorn, 2nd Bt and of Helen Antonia, *o d* of Sir James Gow Mann, KCVO; *S* father, 1995; *m* 1998, Clare, *yr d* of Brian Craig-McFeely; two *s*. *Educ:* Eton; Reading Univ. (BSc Estate Management). With Healey & Baker, 1977–82; Debenham Tewson & Chinnocks, 1982–86; Kinney & Green, 1986–94 (Partner, 1991–94); founded Pickthorn, 1994. TA (HAC), 1978–98. *Recreation:* sailing. *Heir: s* William Edward Craig Pickthorn, *b* 2 Dec. 1998. *Address:* 45 Ringmer Avenue, SW6 5LP. *T:* (020) 7621 1380; (office) 8 Laurence Pountney Hill, EC4R 0BE.

**PICKUP, David Cunliffe;** Chief Executive, Sports Council Trust Company, 1993–94; Director General, Sports Council, 1988–93; *b* 17 Sept. 1936; *s* of Robert and Florence Pickup; *m* 1960, Patricia Moira Aileen (*née* Neill) (decd); two *s* (and one *s* decd). *Educ:* Bacup and Rawtenstall Grammar Sch. Min. of Education, 1955–63; MPBW, 1964–71 (incl. periods as Pvte Sec. to four Ministers); Department of the Environment: Prin. Pvte Sec. to Minister for Housing and Construction, 1971–72; Asst Sec., 1972; Housing, 1972–75; Personnel, 1975–77; Under Sec., 1977; Regl Dir, Northern Reg., 1977–80; Housing, 1980–84; Local Govt, 1984–85; Dep. Sec., Assoc. of Dist Councils, 1986–88. Dir, Bromley Mytime, 2004–16; Chairman: Proactive S London (formerly S London Sport and Physical Activity Partnership), 2013–15 (Vice Chm., 2010–13); ProActive Bromley, 2013–16. FRSA 1992. *Publications:* Not Another Messiah, 1996; Bracken Point, 2002; Legacy, 2005; Robbed of Air, 2008; Short Measures, 2012; Endgame, 2019. *Recreations:* reading, music, sport, walking. *Address:* 15 Sandford Road, Bromley, Kent BR2 9AL.

**PICKUP, David Francis William,** CB 2002; Attorney General of the Falkland Islands, 2007–11; *b* 28 May 1953; *s* of Joseph and Muriel Pickup; *m* 1975, Anne Elizabeth Round. *Educ:* Poole Grammar Sch.; Polytechnic of Central London (Univ. of London External LLB Hons). Called to the Bar, Lincoln's Inn, 1976, Gibraltar, 1988. Joined Treasury Solicitor's Dept as Legal Asst, 1978, Sen. Legal Asst, 1981; Grade 5 1987; Estabt Finance and Security Officer, 1988–90; Grade 3, Chancery Litigation Div., 1990; Legal Advr, MoD, 1991–95; Solicitor (Grade 2), HM Customs and Excise, subseq. HM Revenue and Customs, 1995–2005; Dir Gen., HMRC, 2006–07. *Recreations:* watching sport, listening to music, supporting and watching modern ballet, food and wine, travel, golf. *Address:* Post House, Marston, Pembridge, Leominster HR6 9JA. *T:* (01544) 388264. *E:* dfwp.aep@icloud.com. *Club:* Kington Golf.

**PICKUP, Ronald Alfred;** actor; *b* 7 June 1940; *s* of Eric and Daisy Pickup; *m* 1964, Lans Traverse, USA; one *s* one *d*. *Educ:* King's Sch., Chester; Leeds Univ. (BA); Royal Academy of Dramatic Art. Radio prodns, 1960s–1980s, incl. Hamlet in Hamlet; poetry readings, incl. adaptation of Jon Juan, by Byron, Prelude, by Wordsworth and selections of Wilfred Owen, Keats, Edward Thomas and Seamus Heaney. Repertory, Leicester, 1964; Royal Court, 1964 and 1965–66; National Theatre, 1965, 1966–73, 1977: appearances include: Rosalind, in all-male As You Like It, 1967; Richard II, 1972; Edmund, in Long Day's Journey into Night, 1971; Cassius, in Julius Caesar, 1977; Philip Madras, in The Madras House, 1977; Norman, in Norman Conquests, Globe, 1974; Play, Royal Court, 1976; Hobson's Choice, Lyric, Hammersmith, 1981; Astrov, in Uncle Vanya, Haymarket, 1982; Allmers in Little Eyolf, Lyric, Hammersmith, 1985; Gayev, in The Cherry Orchard, Aldwych, 1989; Amy's View, RNT, 1997, NY, 1999; Peer Gynt, Romeo and Juliet, RNT, 2000; Proof, Donmar Warehouse, 2002; Col Redfern in Look Back in Anger, Th. Royal, Bath, 2006; Uncle Vanya, Rose Th., Kingston, 2008; Waiting for Godot, tour then Th. Royal, Haymarket, 2010; Heartbreak House, Chichester, 2012; *films:* Three Sisters, 1969; Day of the Jackal, 1972; Joseph Andrews, 1976; 39 Steps, Zulu Dawn, 1978; Nijinsky, 1979; Never Say Never Again, John Paul II, 1983; Eleni, Camille (remake), 1984; The Mission, 1985; The Fourth Protocol, 1986; Bring Me the Head of Mavis Davis, 1996; Breathtaking, 1999; Evilenko, 2004; Greyfriars Bobby, 2006; Dark Floors, 2008; Prince of Persia, 2010; The Best Exotic Marigold Hotel, 2012; The Second Best Exotic Marigold Hotel, 2015; The Time of Their Lives, 2017; Darkest Hour, 2018; The Happy Prince, 2018; *television:* series and serials: Dragon's Opponent, 1973; Jennie, Fight Against Slavery, 1974; Tropic, 1979; Life of Giuseppe Verdi, 1982; Wagner, 1982; Life of Einstein, 1983; Moving, 1984; The Fortunes of War, 1987; Behaving Badly, 1988; A Time to Dance, 1992; My Friend Walter, 1992; The Riff Raff Element, 1993, 1994; Ivanhoe, 1996; Hornblower, 1998; Dalziel and Pascoe, 1999; The Worst Week of my Life, 2003–05; Feather Boy, 2004; Holby City, 2006–07; The Jury, 2011; Atlantis, Young Dracula, 2014; Downton Abbey, 2015; Vera, 2016; The Crown, 2016; Summer of Rockets, 2019; other: The Philanthropist, Ghost Trio, The Discretion of Dominic Ayres, 1977; Memories, Henry VIII, 1978; England's Green and Pleasant Land, Christ Hero, 1979; The Letter, Ivanhoe, 1981; Orwell on Jura, 1983; The Rivals, 1986; The Attic, Chekhov in Yalta, 1988; A Murder of Quality, 1990; Absolute

Hell, 1991; The War that Never Ends, 1991; The Golden Years, 1992; In the Cold Light of Day, 1994; Milner, 1994; A Case of Coincidence, 1994; A Very Open Prison, 1995; The Dying Day, Henry IV (title rôle), 1995; Cherished, 2003. Hon. DLitt Chester, 2012. *Recreations:* listening to music, walking, reading.

**PICKUP, Sarah Jane**, OBE 2014; Deputy Chief Executive, Local Government Association, since 2015; *b* Ramsgate, Kent, 29 Dec. 1962; *d* of Patrick and Anne Malone; *m* 1989, Michael Pickup; two *s* two *d*. *Educ:* Holy Trinity Convent, Bromley, Kent; Univ. of Sussex (BA Hons Econs 1984); W London Inst. of Higher Educn. CIPFA 1989. Trainee Acct, Richmond LBC, 1984–88; Hertfordshire County Council: Principal Tech. Asst, 1988–91; Principal Acct, 1991–93; Educn Finance Manager, 1993–95; Asst Dir, Adult Care Service, 1995–2003; Dir, Health and Community Services, 2003–13; Dep. Chief Exec., 2013–15. Pres., Assoc. of Dirs of Adult Social Services, 2012–13. FRSA. Freeman, City of London, 2019. *Recreations:* reading, family, theatre, yoga, swimming, ski-ing, music. *Address:* Local Government Association, Local Government House, Smith Square, SW1P 3HZ.

**PICTET, François-Charles;** Ambassador of Switzerland to Austria, 1990–94, and Ambassador on Special Mission to the Holy See, 1993–97; *b* Geneva, 21 July 1929; *e s* of Charles Pictet, Geneva, and Elisabeth (*née* Decazes), France; *m* 1st, 1954, Elisabeth Choisy (*d* 1980), Geneva; three *s*; 2nd, 1983, Countess Marie-Thérèse Althann, Austria. *Educ:* College Calvin, Geneva; Univ. of Geneva (Faculty of Law). Called to the Swiss Bar, 1954. Joined Swiss Federal Dept of Foreign Affairs, 1956; Attaché, Vienna, 1957; Sec., Moscow, 1958–60; 1st Sec., Ankara, 1961–66; Dep. Dir, Internat. Orgns, Dept of For. Affairs, Berne, 1966–75; Minister Plenipotentiary, 1975; Ambassador to Canada and (non-resident) to the Bahamas, 1975–79; Ambassador, Perm. Rep. to Internat. Orgns in Geneva, 1980–84; Ambassador to UK, 1984–89, to the Netherlands, 1989–90; Hd of Swiss Delegn to CSCE, Vienna, 1991–93. *Address:* 6 rue Robert-de-Traz, 1206 Geneva, Switzerland. *T:* (22) 7890086.

**PICTON, Julian Mark;** QC 2010; *b* Kingston-upon-Thames, 25 April 1964; *s* of Prof. Denis Charles Alec Picton and Jane Picton. *Educ:* Reigate Grammar Sch.; Oriel Coll., Oxford (BA Law). Called to the Bar, Middle Temple, 1988. Chair, Disability Gp, Bar Council, 2009–. Vice Chm., Essex Yeomanry Assoc., 2008–. *Publications:* (contrib.) McGregor on Damages, 17th edn 2003, 18th edn 2009. *Recreations:* buildings, English furniture, English porcelain. *Address:* The Manor House, Wisbech St Mary, Cambs PE13 4RY. *T:* (020) 7643 5000, *Fax:* (020) 7353 5778. *E:* julian.picton@hailshamchambers.com.

**PICTON, Martin Thomas; His Honour Judge Picton;** a Circuit Judge, since 2005; *b* 20 Jan. 1958; *s* of Gerald and Daphne Picton; *m* 1992, Dr Susan Wensley; three *s* one *d*. *Educ:* Haberdashers' Aske's Sch., New Cross; King's Coll. London (LLB). Called to the Bar, Middle Temple, 1981; tenant, Albion Chambers, Bristol, 1982–2005; a Recorder, 1998–2005. *Recreations:* running, ski-ing, bringing up four children. *Address:* Gloucester Crown Court, PO Box 9051 GL1 2XG. *T:* (01452) 420100, *Fax:* (01452) 833599.

**PIDCOCK, Laura Barbara;** MP (Lab) North West Durham, since 2017; *b* New Hartley, Northumberland. *Educ:* Manchester Metropolitan Univ. (BA Politics); Northumbria Univ. (MA Disaster Mgt and Sustainable Develt). VSO with HIV/Aids project in UK and Nigeria; mental health support worker, Manchester; Manager, Show Racism the Red Card. Mem. (Lab), Northumberland CC, 2013–17. Shadow Minister for Labour, 2018–. Mem., Justice Cttee, H of C, 2017–. *Address:* House of Commons, SW1A 0AA.

**PIDD, Prof. Michael,** PhD; Professor of Management Science, Lancaster University, 1992–2014, now Emeritus; *b* Sheffield, 1948; *s* of Ernest Pidd and Marion Pidd; *m* 1971, Sally Anne Nutt; two *d*. *Educ:* High Storrs Grammar Sch., Sheffield; Brunel Univ. (BTech 1970); Univ. of Birmingham (MSc 1971); Lancaster Univ. (PhD 2006). Operational Res. Analyst, Cadbury Schweppes, 1971–74; Lectr in Operational Res., Aston Univ., 1974–79; Lectr, 1979–89, Sen. Lectr, 1989–92, in Operational Res., Lancaster Univ. Pres., Operational Res. Soc., 2000–01. Chair, Business and Mgt Studies Panel, RAE 2008 and REF 2014. Member: Bd, Centre for Workforce Intelligence, 2012–14; Home Office Sci. Adv. Council, 2015–. Companion of Operational Res. 2011; FBAM 2009; FAcSS (AcSS 2012). *Publications:* Computer Simulation in Management Science, 1984, 5th edn 2004; (ed) Computer Modelling for Discrete Simulation, 1989; Tools for Thinking: modelling in management science, 1996, 3rd edn 2009; (ed) Systems Modelling: theory and practice, 2004; Measuring the Performance of Public Services: principles and practice, 2012; articles in jls relating to operational res. and computer simulation. *Recreations:* walking, family, church work, local charitable work. *Address:* Department of Management Science, Lancaster University, Lancaster LA1 4YX. *T:* (01524) 593870, *Fax:* (01524) 844885. *E:* m.pidd@lancaster.ac.uk.

**PIDDING, Baroness** *cr* 2015 (Life Peer), of Amersham in the County of Buckinghamshire; **Emma Samantha Pidding,** CBE 2014; Chairman, National Conservative Convention, 2012–15; partner, Tim Butcher. *Educ:* Brudenell Co. Secondary Sch.; Dr Challoner's High Sch. Work in retail, then private banking; Mktg and Events Manager, IT consultancy, Bucks; Consultant, ESP Consultancy, 2009–12. Conservative Party: joined 1986; Chm., Chesham and Amersham Young Conservatives, 1991–94; Dep. Chm., 1997–2000, Chm., 2000–03, Chesham and Amersham Cons. Assoc.; Area Dep. Chm., 2002–04, Area Chm., 2004–06, Oxon and Bucks; Vice Pres., 2006–08, Pres., 2009–10, Nat. Convention; Jt Performance Improvement Co-ordinator, 2010–12; Nat. Volunteer Parly By-election Co-ordinator, 2010–12. Pres., NI Conservatives, 2007–. Mem. (C), Chiltern DC, 1991–99. *Address:* House of Lords, SW1A 0PW.

**PIDDINGTON, Philip Michael,** CBE 1988; HM Diplomatic Service, retired; Counsellor, Foreign and Commonwealth Office, 1987–90; *b* 27 March 1931; *s* of Percy Howard Piddington and Florence Emma (*née* Pearson); *m* 1955, Sylvia Mary Price; one *s* one *d*. *Educ:* Waverley Grammar Sch., Birmingham. Served HM Forces, 1949–51. Entered Min. of Works, 1947; FO, 1952; Jedda, 1956; Tokyo, 1962–66; First Sec., Lagos, 1969–71; Consul: NY, 1971–73; Istanbul, 1973–77; First Sec., FCO, 1978–83; Counsellor and Consul-Gen., Brussels, 1983–87. *Recreations:* riding, walking, photography. *Address:* Hammond Lodge, Breakspear Road North, Harefield, Uxbridge UB9 6NA. *T:* (01895) 825004.

**PIDGEON, Caroline Valerie,** MBE 2013; Member (Lib Dem), London Assembly, Greater London Authority, since 2008; *b* Eastleigh, Hants, 29 Sept. 1972; *d* of Eric and Valerie Pidgeon; *m* 2006, Paul Miles; one *s*. *Educ:* Univ. of Wales, Aberystwyth (BSc Econ Hons). Political Researcher: Cllr Rose Colley, Southwark BC, 1994–96; Brent Council, 1996–99; Communications Manager: Croydon HA, 1999–2002; Guy's and St Thomas' NHS Foundn Trust, 2002–06. Mem. (Lib Dem), Southwark BC, 1998–2010 (Dep. Leader, 2002–04; Exec. Mem., for Educn, 2004–06, for Children's Services, 2006–08). Contested (Lib Dem) Vauxhall, 2010. *Recreations:* cinema, modern art. *Address:* Greater London Authority, City Hall, The Queen's Walk, SE1 2AA. *T:* (020) 7983 4362. *E:* caroline.pidgeon@london.gov.uk.

**PIEBALGS, Andris;** Chairman, Unity Party, Latvia, 2016–17; Senior Fellow, Florence School of Regulation, since 2015; *b* 17 Sept. 1957; *m* Anda; one *s* two *d*. *Educ:* Univ. of Latvia (degree in physics 1980). Teacher, then Headmaster, Secondary Sch. No 1, Valmiera, 1980–88; Desk Officer, then Hd of Dept, Min. of Educn, Latvia, 1988–90; Minister of Educn, 1990–93; MP, 1993–94; Minister of Finance, 1994–95; Ambassador to Estonia, 1995–97; Perm. Rep. of Latvia to EU, 1998–2003; Dep. Sec. of State, Min. of Foreign Affairs, 2003–04; Hd of Cabinet, Latvian Mem. of EC, 2004; Mem., EC, 2004–14.

**PIENAAR, Dame Erica (Christine),** DBE 2014; Director, Wey Education Schools Trust, since 2013; Executive Headteacher, Leathersellers' Federation of Schools, Lewisham, 2008–13; *b* Cape Town, S Africa, March 1952. *Educ:* Rockmouth Primary Sch., South Norwood; Coloma Convent Grammar Sch. for Girls; Goldsmiths' Coll., Univ. of London (BA); MBA. Teacher of Science, Bromley, 1973; Hd of Sci., Bullers Wood Sch., Chislehurst; Dep. Hd, Cator Park Sch., Bromley; Hd Teacher, Prendergast Sch., Lewisham, 1998–2008. Chm. Govs, John Ball Primary Sch., Blackheath. Hon. Freewoman, London Bor. of Lewisham, 2013. *Address:* Wey Education Schools Trust, 10 Orange Street, WC2H 7DQ.

**PIENAAR, John Adrian;** Presenter, Pienaar's Politics, BBC Radio Five-Live, since 2010; Deputy Political Editor, BBC News, since 2016; *b* 2 Nov. 1956; *s* of Eric and Johanna Pienaar; *m* 1st, 1980, Denise Walsh (marr. diss.); one *s* one *d*; 2nd, Penny Davies; two *d*. *Educ:* Ravenswood Sch., Bromley. Political staff, Press Assoc., 1980–86; Political Correspondent: Independent, 1986–92; BBC News, 1992–; Presenter, The Weekend News, 2006–10, Chief Political Correspondent, 2002–16, Radio Five-Live. *Recreations:* reading, history, novels, almost anything, watching films, near-obsessive fan of Crystal Palace FC. *Address:* BBC Westminster, 4 Millbank, SW1P 3JQ. *E:* john.pienaar@bbc.co.uk.

**PIEŃKOWSKI, Jan Michał;** author and illustrator, since 1958; *b* 8 Aug. 1936; *s* of late Jerzy Dominik Pieńkowski and Wanda Maria Pieńkowska. *Educ:* Cardinal Vaughan Sch., London; King's Coll., Cambridge (MA Classics and English). Art Dir, J. Walter Thompson, William Collins, and Time and Tide, London, 1958–61. Work includes graphics and murals, posters and greeting cards, children's TV, and book illustration. *Stage designs:* Meg and Mog Show, 1981–88; Beauty and the Beast, Royal Opera House, 1986; Théâtre de Complicité, 1988; Sleeping Beauty, Euro Disney, 1992; Beauty and the Beast, Kremlin Palace Th., 2013; Captain Blood's Revenge, Glyndebourne, 2013. Exhibn of original art works, Illustration Cupboard Gall., London, 2017. Kate Greenaway Medal, Library Assoc., 1972 and 1979; Lifetime Achievement Award, Book Trust, 2019. *Publications:* illustrator: A Necklace of Raindrops, by Joan Aiken, 1968, new edn 2009; The Kingdom under the Sea, 1971, new edn 2011; Tale of a One Way Street, 1978; Past Eight O'Clock, 1986; A Foot in the Grave, 1989 (new format edn with addnl artwork, 2013); M.O.L.E., 1993, etc; (co-author with Helen Nicoll and illustrator) Meg and Mog series, 1973–90 (televised, 2004); (co-author with David Walsher and illustrator) Meg and the Pirate, 2014; The Glass Mountain: tales from Poland, by David Walser, 2014; illustrator/author: Nursery series, 1973–91; Haunted House, 1979; Robot, 1981; Dinner Time, 1981 (new large-format edn 2007); Christmas, 1984; Little Monsters, 1986 (new large-format edn 2007); Small Talk, 1988; Easter, 1989; Fancy That, 1990; Phone Book, 1991; Christmas Kingdom, 1991; Door Bell, 1992; Road Hog, 1993; ABC Dinosaurs, 1993; Toilet Book, 1994; 1001 Words, 1994; Furrytails series, 1994; Nursery Cloth Books series, 1994; Botticelli's Bed and Breakfast, 1996; Nursery Pop-Up series, 1996–97; Tickle-me Books, 1997; Good Night, 1998; Bel and Bub series, 2000; The Monster Pet, 2000; Pizza!, 2001; The Cat with Nine Lives, 2001; The Animals went in Two by Two, 2001; Meg, Mog and Og, 2003; Meg's Mummy, 2004; The First Noël, 2004; The Fairy Tales, 2005; Mog's Missing, 2005; Haunted House, 25th anniversary edn, 2005; The First Christmas, 2006; Meg & Mog Touch and Feel Counting Book, 2006; The Thousand Nights and One Night, 2007; Meg and Mog, 35th anniversary edn, 2007, 40th birthday edn, 2012; Nut Cracker, 2008; In the Beginning, 2010; Meg Goes to Bed, 2010; A River of Stories: tales and poems from across the Commonwealth, 2011; Meg and the Dragon, 2015; Meg in the Jungle, 2016; Meg and the Romans, 2017; The Odyssey, retold by David Walser, 2019; Meg's Christmas, 2019. *Recreations:* keeping bantams, Latin, drawing from life on computer. *Address:* Oakgates, Barnes. *Club:* Polish Hearth.

**PIEPER, Philippa;** *see* Whitford, P.

**PIERCE, Rt Rev. Anthony Edward;** Bishop of Swansea and Brecon, 1999–2008; *b* 16 Jan. 1941; *s* of Gwynfor Pierce and Martha Jane Pierce (*née* Owen), *Educ:* Dynevor Sch., Swansea; University Coll., Swansea (BA Hons Hist. 1963); Linacre Coll., Oxford (BA Hons Theol 1965; MA 1971); Ripon Hall, Oxford. Deacon 1965, priest 1966; Curate: St Peter, Swansea, 1965–67; St Mary and Holy Trinity, Swansea, 1967–74; Vicar of Llwynderw, 1974–92; Priest-in-charge, St Barnabas, Swansea, 1992–96; Canon Res., Brecon Cathedral, 1993; Archdeacon of Gower, 1995–99; Vicar, St Mary, Swansea, 1996–99. Sec., Dio. Conf. and Dio. Patronage Bd, 1991–95; Dio. Dir of Educn, 1992–96. Mem., Prov. Selection Panel, 1984–97; Chm., Social Action Sect., 1985–90, Chm. Div. Social Responsibility, 1990–92, Prov. Bd of Mission. Chm., Ecumenical Aids Monitoring Gp (Wales), 1988–95. University College, Swansea: Bp's Chaplain to Anglican Students, 1971–74; Mem. Ct of Govs, 1981–2010 (Life Mem., 2010); Chaplain, 1984–88. Mem. Council, Univ. of Wales, Swansea, 1995–2010. Chaplain, Singleton Hosp., 1980–95; Co-ordinator, Hosp. Chaplains, 1982–95. Chair, Gwalia Housing Gp, 2009–15. Pres., Friends of Swansea Music Fest., 2002–. Hon. Fellow, Swansea Univ., 2011. Hon. Ed., Welsh Churchman, 1972–75. KStJ 2010 (Sub-Prelate, Order of St John, Priory of Wales, 2002–10). *Recreations:* reading, theatre, music. *Address:* 2 Coed Ceirios, Swansea Vale, Swansea SA7 0NU.

**PIERCE, Dame Karen (Elizabeth), (Dame Karen Roxburgh),** DCMG 2018 (CMG 2008); HM Diplomatic Service; UK Permanent Representative to the United Nations, New York (with rank of Ambassador), since 2018; *b* 23 Sept. 1959; *d* of late Derek Robert Pierce and Barbara Florence Pierce; *m* 1987, Charles Fergusson Roxburgh, *qv*; two *s*. *Educ:* Penwortham Girls' High Sch.; Girton Coll., Cambridge (BA Hons English 1981; MA 1991; Hon. Fellow, 2018); London Sch. of Econs and Pol Sci. (MSc Internat. Strategy and Diplomacy 2012). Joined FCO, 1981; Tokyo, 1984–87; Security Policy Dept, FCO, 1987–91; Washington, 1991–96; Eastern Dept, then Eastern Adriatic Dept, FCO, 1996–99: Head: Newsroom, FCO, 1999–2000; EU Dept (Bilateral), FCO, 2001–02; Eastern Adriatic Dept, FCO, 2002–06; Dep. Permanent Rep., UK Mission to UN, New York and Pres., UN Trusteeship Council, 2006–09; Dir, South Asia and Afghanistan, 2009–11; UK Perm. Rep. to UN and WTO, Geneva, 2012–15; Ambassador to Afghanistan, 2015–16; Chief Operating Officer, FCO, 2016–17; Dir Gen., Political, FCO, 2017–18. Mem., Bd of Trustees, NT, 2019–; Hon. Mem. Bd, Amer. Friends of NT, 2019–. *Recreations:* collecting ceramics, fridge magnets, theatre. *Address:* c/o Foreign and Commonwealth Office, King Charles Street, SW1A 2AH.

**PIERCY,** family name of **Baron Piercy.**

**PIERCY, 3rd Baron** *cr* 1945, *of Burford*; **James William Piercy**; *b* 19 Jan. 1946; *s* of 2nd Baron Piercy and Oonagh Lavinia (*d* 1990), *d* of late Major Edward John Lake Baylay, DSO; *S* father, 1981. *Educ*: Shrewsbury; Edinburgh Univ. (BSc 1968). AMIEE; FCCA. *Heir*: *b* Hon. Mark Edward Pelham Piercy [*b* 30 June 1953; *m* 1979, Vivien Angela, *d* of His Honour Evelyn Faithfull Monier-Williams; *one s three d*]. *Address*: 36 Richford Street, W6 7HP.

**PIERI, Frank**; Sheriff of South Strathclyde, Dumfries and Galloway at Airdrie, since 2009 (at Hamilton, 2005–09); *b* 10 Aug. 1954; *s* of Ralph Pieri and Teresa Pieri; *m* 1977, Dorothy Telfer; two *d*. *Educ*: St Aloysius Coll., Glasgow; Univ. of Glasgow (LLB 1974). Solicitor, 1976–93; called to the Scottish Bar, 1994; in practice as Advocate, 1994–2000; Immigration Adjudicator (full time), 2000–04. Member: Council, Scottish Law Agents Soc., 1991–93; Council of Immigration Judges, 2003. *Recreations*: ambling, crime fiction, opera, Partick Thistle FC. *Address*: Airdrie Sheriff Court, Graham Street, Airdrie ML6 6EE. *T*: (01236) 751121. *E*: sherifffpieri@scotcourts.gov.uk.

**PIERREHUMBERT, Prof. Raymond Thomas,** PhD; Halley Professor of Physics, University of Oxford, since 2015; Fellow, Jesus College, Oxford, since 2015; *b* USA. *Educ*: Harvard Coll. (AB Physics *magna cum laude* 1975); Massachusetts Inst. of Technol. (PhD 1980). Knox Fellow, Univ. of Cambridge, 1976–77; Asst Prof. of Meteorol., MIT, 1980–82; Res. Scientist, Geophysical Fluid Dynamics Lab., Nat. Oceanic and Atmospheric Admin, and concurrently Vis. Lectr, with rank of Associate Prof., Atmospheric and Oceanic Scis Prog. and Affiliated Faculty Mem., Applied and Computational Maths Prog., Princeton Univ., 1982–88; on sabbatical as Guest Investigator, Meteorologiska Inst., Stockholm Univ., 1987–88; Prof. of Geol. and Geophysics, Princeton Univ., 1988–89; Prof. of Geophysical Scis, 1989–2015, Louis Block Prof., 2005–15, Univ. of Chicago; John Simon Guggenheim Fellow, Lab. de Météorologie Dynamique, École Normale Supérieur, Paris, 1996–97. Kung Karl XVI Gustaf Vis. Prof., Stockholm, 2014–15; Vis. Dir de Recherche, École Polytéchnique, France, 2003–04. Ed., Jl Atmospheric Scis, 1988–91; Member: Editl Bd, Annual Revs of Earth and Planetary Sci., 2012–17; Sci. and Security Bd, Bull. Atomic Scientists, 2014–. Member: Nat. Res. Council Panel on Abrupt Climate Change and Societal Impacts, 2000–01; City of Chicago Mayor's Task Force on Climate Change, 2007–08; Nat. Res. Council Bd on Atmospheric Sci. and Climate, 2009–14. Fellow: Amer. Geophysical Union, 2006; Amer. Acad. Arts and Scis, 2015. Hon. PhD Stockholm, 2015. Chevalier, Ordre des Palmes Académiques (France). *Publications*: Principles of Planetary Climate, 2010; The Warming Papers, 2011; contrib. articles to scientific jls. *Address*: Atmospheric, Oceanic and Planetary Physics, University of Oxford, Parks Road, Oxford OX1 3PU.

**PIERS, Sir James (Desmond),** 11th Bt *cr* 1661, *of Tristernagh Abbey, Westmeath*; business lawyer, James Piers Law, since 2013; *b* 24 July 1947; *s* of Sir Charles Robert Fitzmaurice Piers, 10th Bt and Ann Blanche Scott (*d* 1975); *S* father, 1996; *m* 1975, Sandra Mae Dixon; *one s one d*. *Educ*: Univ. of Victoria (BA 1969); Univ. of British Columbia (LLB 1973). Called to the Bar, British Columbia, 1974; Partner, Russell & DuMoulin, subseq. Fasken Martineau DuMoulin, lawyers, 1983–2013. *Heir*: *s* Stephen James Piers, *b* 14 Sept. 1979.

**PIETRONI, Prof. Patrick Claude,** FRCP, FRCGP; Director, Centre for Psychological Therapies in Primary Care, University of Chester, since 2012; Public Health Associate Director, Mental Health Shropshire, since 2013; *b* 8 Nov. 1942; *s* of Michael and Jeannette Pietroni; *m* 1st, 1963, Theresa Wilkinson (marr. diss.); two *s* one *d*; 2nd, 1977, Marilyn Miller. *Educ*: Guy's Hosp. Med. Sch. (MB BS 1966). MRCP 1973, FRCP 2000; FRCGP 1985; MFPH (MFPHM 2000). MO, RAMC, 1967–69; Principal, Gen. Practice, 1971–; Associate Prof., Family Medicine, Univ. of Cincinnati, 1978–80; Sen. Lectr in Gen. Practice, St Mary's Hosp. Med. Sch., 1981–93; Prof. and Dir, Centre for Community Care and Primary Health, Univ. of Westminster, 1993–97; Dean, Postgrad. Gen. Practice, N Thames (West) Dept of Postgrad. Med. and Dental Educn, London Univ., 1996–2001; Dir, Educnl Support Unit, London Region, NHS Exec., 2001–04. Founder and Advr, Internat. Inst. for Study of Cuba, London Metropolitan Univ., 2008–. Dir, 4Ps Res. and Develt Unit, 2001–04. Hon. DSc Westminster, 2001. *Publications*: Holistic Living, 1986; The Greening of Medicine, 1990; Innovation in Community Care and Primary Health, 1995. *Recreations*: tennis, riding, bridge, opera.

**PIGEON, Michel,** PhD; Member (Québec Liberal) Charlesbourg, National Assembly of Québec, 2008–11; *b* 1945; *s* of Louis-Philippe Pigeon and Madeleine Gaudry; *m* 1968, Marie-José des Rivières; two *d*. *Educ*: Laval Univ. (BA 1963, BScA 1967); ICSTM (MPhil 1969); Univ. Pierre et Marie Curie, Paris (PhD 1984). Laval University: Department of Civil Engineering: Asst Prof., 1972–77; Associate Prof., 1977–87; Tenured Prof., 1987–2009; Dir, 1999–2001; Dir, Interuniv. Res. Centre on Concrete, 1992–98, 2000–01; Vice Dean, Res., Sci. and Engrg Faculty, 2001; Dean, Sci. and Engrg Faculty, 2002; Rector, 2002–07. *Publications*: (with R. Pleau) Durability of Concrete in Cold Climates, 1995; book chapters and articles in learned jls.

**PIGGOT, James Anderson, (Jay);** Headmaster, Epsom College, since 2012; *b* Belfast, 30 Dec. 1961; *s* of James and Joy Piggot; *m* 1994, Poppy Bromley-Challenor; two *s* one *d*. *Educ*: Campbell Coll., Belfast; University Coll., Cardiff (BA Hons English Lit. 1984); Univ. of Liverpool (MA English Renaissance Lit. 1986); Pembroke Coll., Cambridge (PGCE 1995). Teacher of English, Millfield Sch., Som, 1986–89; Asst Master, Eton Coll., 1989–2006 (House Master, Farrer Hse, 1999–2006); Headmaster, Campbell Coll., Belfast, 2006–12. Trustee, Swifts Sports Trust, –. Gov., Epsom Coll. of Malaysia, 2012–. Hon. Old Etonian. *Recreations*: reading, squash, golf, dog walking in North Cornwall. *Address*: Headmaster's House, Epsom College, College Road, Epsom, Surrey KT17 4JH. *T*: (01372) 821004. *E*: jaypiggot@icloud.com. *Clubs*: Royal Automobile; Trevose Golf and Country, St Enodoc Golf.

**PIGGOTT, Ven. Andrew John;** Archdeacon of Bath, 2005–17; *b* 27 Sept. 1951; *s* of late David Geoffrey John and Joyce Vera Piggott; *m* 1979, Ruth Elizabeth Morris; two *d*. *Educ*: Queen Mary Coll., London (BScEcon 1972); Leeds Univ. (PGCE 1973); Nottingham Univ. (DipTh 1984). Various teaching posts, 1973–83; ordained deacon, 1986, priest, 1987; Curate, St Philip with St James, Dorridge, 1986–89; Team Vicar, St Chad's, Kidderminster, 1989–94; Incumbent, St Lawrence, Biddulph, 1994–99; Church Pastoral Aid Society: Ministry and Vocations Advr, 1999–2001; Acting Gen. Dir, 2000–01; Patronage Sec., 2001–05. Mem., Gen. Synod, 2009–17.

**PIGGOTT, Lester Keith;** jockey, 1948–85 and 1990–95; trainer, 1985–87; *b* 5 Nov. 1935; *s* of late Keith Piggott and Iris Rickaby; *m* 1960, Susan Armstrong; two *d*. Selection of races won: the Derby (9 times): 1954 (on Never Say Die); 1957 (on Crepello); 1960 (on St Paddy); 1968 (on Sir Ivor); 1970 (on Nijinsky); 1972 (on Roberto); 1976 (on Empery); 1977 (on The Minstrel); 1983 (on Teenoso); St Leger (8 times); The Oaks (6 times); 2,000 guineas (5 times); 1,000 guineas (twice). In many seasons 1955–85 he rode well over 100 winners a year, in this country alone; rode 4,000th winner in Britain, 14 Aug. 1982; record 30th classic win, 1 May 1992; Champion Jockey 11 times, 1960, 1964–71, 1981, 1982; rode frequently in France; won Prix de l'Arc de Triomphe on Rheingold, 1973, on Alleged, 1977 and 1978; won Washington, DC, International on Sir Ivor, 1968 (first time since 1922 an English Derby winner raced in USA), on Karabas, 1969, on Argument, 1980. *Publications*: (with Sean Magee) Lester's Derbys, 2004; *relevant publication*: Lester, the Official Biography, by Dick Francis, 1986. *Recreations*: swimming, water ski-ing, golf.

**PIGNATELLI, Frank,** CBE 2005; pro bono adviser and mentor to individuals and charitable, voluntary and not-for-profit organisations, since 2006; Chief Executive, University for Industry, Scotland, 1999–2006; *b* 22 Dec. 1946; *s* of Frank and Elizabeth Pignatelli; *m* 1969, Rosetta Anne McFadyen; one *s* one *d*. *Educ*: Univ. of Glasgow (MA; DipEd, MEd); Jordanhill Coll. of Educn (Secondary Teachers Cert.). Teacher, St Mungo's Acad., Glasgow, 1970; Hd of Dept, St Gregory's Secondary Sch., Glasgow, 1974; Asst Headteacher, St Margaret Mary's Secondary Sch., Glasgow, 1977; Strathclyde Region: Educn Officer, Renfrew Div., 1978; Asst Dir of Educn, 1983; Depute Dir of Educn, 1985; Dir of Educn, 1988–96; Gp Dir, Human Resources, Associated Newspapers, London, 1996–97; Chm. and Man. Dir, Exec. Support and Develt Consultancy, 1997–2000; Chief Exec., ScotBIC, 1998–99. Hon. Lectr in Educn, 1988–90, Vis. Prof., 1990–, Univ. of Glasgow Sch. of Educn; Vis. Prof. of Mgt Educn, Univ. of Glasgow Business Sch., 1997–. Chairman: RIPA (West of Scotland), 1990–93; Scottish Mgt and Enterprise Council, 1999–; Scottish Skills and Employability Network, 1999–; Member: Adv. Scottish Council for Educn and Trng Targets, 1993–96; Bd, SCOTVEC, 1993–96 (Fellow, 1996); UK Nuffield Langs Inquiry, 1998–2000; Ministerial Trade Union Wkg Pty on Lifelong Learning, 2000–. Chairman: Technol. Review Gp, 1993–; Nat. Cttee for Review of Post 16 educn and trng, 1993–; Assoc. for Mgt Educn and Trng in Scotland, 1998–; Scottish Parlt Futures Forum Project Bd, 2007–08. Pres., Glasgow and West of Scotland Inst. of Mgt, 2001–; Hon. Pres., Scottish Assoc. for Language Teaching, 1998–2000. CCMI (CIMgt 2000; FBIM 1989; Pres., Renfrewshire, 1991–93). FRSA 1992; FSQA 1997; FICPD 1998; Fellow, Scotland's Colls, 2006. DUniv Paisley, 1993; Hon. DEd Abertay, 2003. *Publications*: Basic Knowledge 'O' French, 1974; Higher French Past Papers, 1975; Scottish Education Policy Review, 1994; contrib., World Year Book in Education, TES, Mgt of Educnl Policy - Scottish Perspectives. *Recreations*: swimming, genealogy, do-it-yourself, reading and all things French. *T*: 07867 862945. *E*: frank@pignatelli.co.uk.

**PIGOT, Sir George (Hugh),** 8th Bt *cr* 1764, *of Patshull, Staffs*; consultant, residential fire sprinkler system design and training; Proprietor, Padworth Hydroelectric, since 2011; *b* 28 Nov. 1946; *s* of Maj.-Gen. Sir Robert Pigot, 7th Bt, CB, OBE, DL, and Honor (*d* 1966), *d* of Captain Wilfred St Martin Gibbon; *S* father, 1986; *m* 1st, 1967, Judith Sandeman-Allen (marr. diss. 1973); one *d*; 2nd, 1980, Lucinda Jane (marr. diss. 1993), *d* of D. C. Spandler; two *s*; 3rd, 2006, Odette (marr. diss. 2008), *yr d* of Walter Stanley, Port Elizabeth, SA. *Educ*: Stowe. Man. Dir, Padworth Fisheries Ltd, 1981–95; Dir, Southern Trout Ltd, 1993–95 (Man. Dir, 1994–95); business consultant, Positive Response, 1995–; Sec.-Gen., 1998–2003, Administrator, 2007–, Residential Sprinkler Assoc.; Chief Exec., Fire Sprinkler Assoc., 2003–07; Dir, Integrated Fire Protection Ltd, 2008–12. Member: Council, British Trout Assoc., 1986–93 (Hon. Treas., 1990–92); Fish Farming Exec. Cttee, NFU, 1987–90 (Chm. Health and Technical Sub-Cttee, 1989–90). *Recreations*: classic cars, golf, hydroelectric generation. *Heir*: *s* George Douglas Hugh Pigot, *b* 17 Sept. 1982. *Address*: Mill House, Mill Lane, Padworth, near Reading, Berks RG7 4JX.

**PIGOTT, Prof. Christopher Donald,** PhD; Director, University Botanic Garden, Cambridge, 1984–95; *b* 7 April 1928; *s* of John Richards Pigott and Helen Constance Pigott (*née* Lee); *m* 1st, 1954, Margaret Elsie Beatson (*d* 1981); one *d*; 2nd, 1986, Sheila Lloyd (*née* Megaw). *Educ*: Mill Hill School; University of Cambridge. MA, PhD. Asst Lectr, and Lectr, Univ. of Sheffield, 1951–60; Univ. Lectr, Cambridge, 1960–64; Fellow of Emmanuel Coll., Cambridge, 1962–64; Prof. of Biology, Univ. of Lancaster, 1964–84, Prof. Emeritus, 1995–; Professorial Fellow, Emmanuel Coll., Cambridge, 1984–95, Emeritus Fellow, 2010. Member: Scientific Policy Cttee, Nature Conservancy Council, 1964–82; Scientific Adv. Cttee, Field Studies Council, 1964–68; Internat. Biol Prog., UK/Uganda Proj., Royal Soc. Cttee, 1965–74; Nature Conservancy, 1971–73; Council, 1980–92, Properties Cttee, 1990–2002, Nat. Trust; Home Grown Timber Adv. Cttee, 1987–94, Res. Users Adv. Gp, 1993–96, Forestry Commn. Vis. Prof., Botany and Microbiol., Univ. of Witwatersrand, 1975; Consultant, Nilsvlei Proj., CSRI Pretoria, 1975–81; Advr on univ. curricula for applied plant ecology, Min. of Sci. and Res., Algeria, 1980. Foreign Correspondent, Acad. d'Agriculture de France (Silviculture), 1982–. *Publications*: Lime-trees and Basswoods: a biological monograph of the genus Tilia, 2012; over 100 refereed contribs to sci. jls, books and symposia (ecology and physiology of plants). *Recreations*: walking, gardening, drawing. *Address*: Greenbank, Cartmel, Grange-over-Sands LA11 7ST.

**PIGOTT, Sir David John Berkeley,** 6th Bt *cr* 1808; *b* 16 Aug. 1955; *s* of Sir Berkeley Henry Sebastian Pigott, 5th Bt and of (Olive) Jean Pigott (*née* Balls); *S* father, 2017, but his name does not appear on the Official Roll of the Baronetage; *m* 1st, 1981, Alison Fletcher (marr. diss.); 2nd, 1986, Julie Wiffen (marr. diss.); one *d*. *Educ*: Moor Park, Ludlow; Hurn Court, Bournemouth. *Heir*: *b* Antony Charles Philip Pigott [*b* 1960; *m* 1st, 1985, Linda J. Watkins (*née* Read); two *d*; 2nd, 2013, Gina Knights; one *s*].

**PIGOTT, Ronald Wellesley,** FRCS, FRCSI; Consultant Plastic Surgeon, Frenchay Hospital, Bristol, 1969–93, Hon. Consultant, since 1993; *b* 16 Sept. 1932; *s* of Thomas Ian Wellesley Pigott and Kathleen Muriel (*née* Parsons); *m* 1958, Sheila King; four *s*. *Educ*: Oakham Sch., Rutland; Univ. of Dublin (BA, MB, BCh, BAO). FRCSE 1958; FRCSI 1960; FRCS 1962; FRCS (Plast). Short service commn, Parachute Field Ambulance, 1960–62. Sen. Registrar, Plastic Surgery, Stoke Mandeville Hosp., 1962–68; Robert Johnson Fellow, Univ. of Miami, 1967. Pioneered endoscopy of velopharyngeal isthmus in the condition of velopharyngeal incompetence; developed split screen recording of endoscopic and radiological examn of velopharyngeal isthmus with A. P. W. Makepeace; pioneered computer-based assessment of symmetry for application to cleft lip and nose deformity with B. Coghlan and D. Matthews. President: Eur. Assoc. of Plastic Surgeons, 1992–93; British Assoc. of Aesthetic Plastic Surgeons, 1993. James Halloran Bennet Medal in Surgery, 1956; James Berry Prize 1979, Jacksonian Prize 1979, RCS; Mowlem Award, Brit. Assoc. Plastic Surgeons, 1982. *Publications*: chapters regarding investigation and treatment of cleft lip and palate in: Advances in the Management of Cleft Lip and Palate, 1980; Clinics in Plastic Surgery, 1985; Scott Brown's Paediatric Otolaryngology, 5th edn 1987; Current Therapy in Plastic and Reconstructive Surgery, 1989; article on develt of endoscopy of palatopharyngeal isthmus, Proc. Royal Soc., 1977; articles in Lancet, Brit. Jl Plastic Surgery, Plastic Reconstructive Surgery, Annals Plastic Surgery, Scandinavian Jl Plastic Reconstructive Surgery. *Recreations*: formerly hockey (represented Ireland, University of Dublin and Army and Combined Services), tennis (represented Univ. of Dublin), painting, sculpture, gardening.

**PIGOTT-BROWN, Sir William Brian,** 3rd Bt *cr* 1902; *b* 20 Jan. 1941; *s* of Sir John Pigott-Brown, 2nd Bt (killed in action, 1942) and of Helen (who *m* 1948, Capt. Charles Raymond Radclyffe), *o d* of Major Gilbert Egerton Cotton, Priestland, Tarporley, Cheshire; *S* father, 1942. *Heir*: none.

**PIKE, Prof. (Edward) Roy,** PhD; FRS 1981; Clerk Maxwell Professor of Theoretical Physics, University of London at King's College, 1986–2010, now Professor Emeritus (Head of School of Physical Sciences and Engineering, 1991–94); *b* 4 Dec. 1929; *s of* Anthony Pike and Rosalind Irene Pike (*née* Davies); *m* 1955, Pamela Sawtell; one *s* two *d*. *Educ:* Southfield Grammar Sch., Oxford; University Coll., Cardiff (BSc, PhD; Fellow, 1981). CPhys, FInstP, CMath, FIMA, FRMS. Served Royal Corps of Signals, 1948–50. Fulbright Schol., Physics Dept, MIT, 1958–60; Royal Signals and Radar Estabt Physics Group, 1960: theoretical and experimental research condensed matter physics and optics; Individual Merit: SPSO 1967; DCSO 1973; CSO, 1984–90. Vis. Prof. of Maths, Imperial Coll., London, 1985–86. Chairman: Adam Hilger Ltd, 1981–85; Oval (114) Ltd, 1984–85; non-executive Director: Richard Clay plc, 1985–86; Stilo Technology Ltd, 1995–2004 (Chm., 1995–2002); Stilo Internat. plc, 2000–04 (Chm., 2000–02); Phonologica Ltd, 2004–06. Govt assessor, SRC Physics Cttee, 1973–76. Mem. Council: Inst. of Physics, 1976–85 (Vice-Pres. for Publications, 1981–85); European Physical Soc., 1981–83; Director: NATO Advanced Study Insts, 1973, 1976; NATO Advanced Res. Workshops, 1987–88, 1991 and 1996. Hon. Editor: Journal of Physics A, 1973–78; Optica Acta, 1978–83; Quantum Optics, 1989–94. Nat. Science Foundn Vis. Lectr, USA, 1959; Lectures: Univ. of Rome, 1976; Univ. of Bordeaux, 1977; Simon Fraser Univ., 1978; Univ. of Genoa, 1980. FKC 1993. Charles Parsons medal and lecture, Royal Society, 1975; MacRobert award (jtly) and lecture, Council of Engrg Instns, 1977; Worshipful Co. of Scientific Instrument Makers Annual Achievement award (jtly), 1978; Committee on Awards to Inventors award, 1980; Guthrie Medal and Prize, Inst. of Physics, 1996. Confrérie St-Etienne, 1980–. *Publications:* (jtly) The Quantum Theory of Radiation, 1995; (ed) High Power Gas Lasers, 1975; edited jointly: Photon Correlation and Light Beating Spectroscopy, 1974; Photon Correlation Spectroscopy and Velocimetry, 1977; Frontiers in Quantum Optics, 1986; Fractals, Noise and Chaos, 1987; Quantum Measurement and Chaos, 1987; Squeezed and Non-classical Light, 1988; Photons and Quantum Fluctuations, 1988; Inverse Problems in Scattering and Imaging, 1991; Photon Correlation and Light Scattering Spectroscopy, 1997; Scattering, 2002; (jtly) The Limits of Resolution, 2017; over 300 papers in scientific jls. *Recreations:* music, languages, woodwork. *Address:* 8 Bredon Grove, Malvern, Worcs WR14 3JR.

**PIKE, Rt Rev. Eric;** Bishop of Port Elizabeth, 1993–2001; *b* 11 Nov. 1936; *s of* Eric and Elizabeth Pike; *m* 1st, 1963, Wendy Anne Walker; one *s* one *d*; 2nd, 1977, Joyce Davidson; two step *s* three step *d*. *Educ:* Graaff Reinet Teachers' Training Coll. (Primary Teachers Cert. 1957); St Paul's Theol Coll., Grahamstown (DipTh 1968). Worked in Govt Service, Transkei, SA, 1955; taught at Queen's Coll. Boys' High Sch., 1958–65; ordained deacon, 1968, priest, 1969; Asst Priest, St John's, E London, 1969–71; Rector: St Paul's, Komga, 1971–72; St Mark's, E London, 1972–77; Archdeacon of E London and Operation Outreach, 1978–87; Rector, St Alban's, E London, 1987–89; Suffragan Bishop of Grahamstown, 1989–93. *Publications:* Who Do You Say I Am?, 2011; Waymarks for the Way, 2017. *Recreations:* walking, gardening. *Address:* 14 St John's Cottages, 77 Water Road, Walmer 6070, Port Elizabeth, South Africa.

**PIKE, Helen Laura;** Master, Magdalen College School, Oxford, since 2016; *b* Birkenhead, 28 March 1973; *d of* Barry and Margaret Pike; partner, Prof. George Garnett; two step *s* one step *d*. *Educ:* All Hallows RC High Sch., Penwortham; Cardinal Newman Coll., Preston; Christ Church, Oxford (MA Modern Hist.); Univ. of Michigan, Ann Arbor (MA Modern Hist.); Birkbeck, Univ. of London (MA Creative Writing); Open Univ. (PGCE). Teacher of Hist., Westminster Sch., 1998; teacher of Hist. and Politics, 1998–2003, Dep. Hd of Sixth Form, 2000–03, City of London Sch. for Boys; Teacher of Hist., 2003–05, Hd of Politics, 2005–09, St Paul's Sch.; Dir of Studies, Royal GS, Guildford, 2009–13; Headmistress, South Hampstead High Sch. GDST, 2013–16. Trustee: Activate Learning Educn Trust, 2017–; Mustard Seed Community Based Orgn, Uganda, 2018–. Ed., acad. hist. textbooks for Anthem Press, 2009–14. *Publications:* The Harlot's Press, 2011. *Recreations:* long-distance running, YMCA qualified instructor in Exercise to Music, writing fiction. *Address:* Magdalen College School, Oxford OX4 1DZ. *T:* (01865) 242191. *E:* master@mcsoxford.org. *Club:* Lansdowne.

**PIKE, Lt-Gen. Sir Hew (William Royston),** KCB 1997; DSO 1982; MBE 1977; General Officer Commanding and Director of Military Operations, Northern Ireland, 1998–2001; *b* 24 April 1943; *s of* Lt-Gen. Sir William Pike, KCB, CBE, DSO; *m* 1966, Jean, *d of* Col Donald Matheson, RAMC; one *s* two *d*. *Educ:* Winchester Coll.; RMA Sandhurst. Commissioned Parachute Regt, 1962; 3 Para, Middle East, British Guiana, UK, 1963–66; ADC, UK and Norway, 1966–67; 1 Para, Middle East, UK, 1967–70; Sch. of Infantry, 44 Para Bde (V), 1970–74; Staff College, 1975; Brigade Major, 16 Para Bde, 1976–77; Co. Comdr, 3 Para Germany and NI, 1978–79; CO, 3 Para, UK and Falkland Is Campaign, 1980–83 (despatches NI 1981); Comd 22 Armd Bde, Bergen-Hohne, 1987–90; RCDS 1990; GOC 3rd (UK) Div., 1992–94; Comdt, RMA, Sandhurst, 1994–95; Dep. C-in-C, and Inspector Gen. TA, HQ Land Comd, 1995–97; Dep. Comdr, SFOR, Bosnia, 1997–98. Lieut, HM Tower of London, 2004–07. Pres., Airborne Assault Normandy Trust, 2011–16. Dir, GAP Activity Projects, 2001–06. Chm. Govs, Treloar Sch., 2001–08, Trustee, Treloar Trust, 2001–08. Freeman, City of London, 1982. *Publications:* From the Front Line— Family Letters and Diaries: 1900 to the Falklands and Afghanistan, 2008. *Recreation:* country pursuits. *Address:* c/o Lloyds Bank, Castle Street, Farnham, Surrey.

**PIKE, Sir Michael (Edmund),** KCVO 1989; CMG 1984; HM Diplomatic Service, retired; *b* 4 Oct. 1931; *s of* Henry Pike and Eleanor Pike; *m* 1962, Catherine (*née* Lim); one *s* two *d*. *Educ:* Wimbledon Coll.; London Sch. of Econs and Pol Science; Brasenose Coll., Oxford (MA 1956). Service in HM Armed Forces, 1950–52. Editor, Cherwell, Oxford Univ., 1954; part-time News Reporter, Sunday Express, 1954–55; Feature Writer and Film Critic, Surrey Comet, 1955–56; joined HM Foreign (now Diplomatic) Service, 1956; Third Secretary: FO, 1956–57; Seoul, 1957–59; Second Secretary: Office of Comr Gen. for Singapore and SE Asia, 1960–62; Seoul, 1962–64; FO, 1964–68; First Sec., Warsaw, 1968–70; FCO, 1970–73; First Sec., Washington, 1973–75; Counsellor: Washington, 1975–78; Tel Aviv, 1978–82; RCDS, 1982; Ambassador to Vietnam, 1982–85; Minister and Dep. UK Perm. Rep. to NATO, Brussels, 1985–87; High Comr, Singapore, 1987–90. Political Affairs Advr, Sun Internat. Exploration and Production Co., 1991–93; Dir, AIB Govett Asian Smaller Cos Investment Trust, 1993–2001. Member: Bid Cttee, British Olympic Bid: Manchester 2000, 1991–93; Bid Cttee, English Commonwealth Games Bid, Manchester 2002, 1994–95; Sensitivity Review Unit, FCO, 1992–2001. Special Rep. of Sec. of State for Foreign and Commonwealth Affairs, 1992–99; HM Govt Co-ordinator, Conf., Britain in the World, 1995. Dir, Greenwich Millennium Trust, 1995–2000; Co-Chm., Greenwich Town Centre Management Agency, 1993–2001; Vice-Chm., Greenwich Develt Agency, 1998–2003 (Mem., 1997–2003); Member: Greenwich Tourism Partnership, 1998–2001; Cutty Sark Wkg Gp, Maritime Greenwich - World Heritage Site Partnership, 2002–04; Standards Cttee (formerly Probity and Conduct Panel), Greenwich London Bor., subseq. Royal Bor. Council, 2002– (Chm., 2009–12). Pres., Union of Catholic Students of GB, 1955–56; Director: Housing Justice (formerly Catholic Housing Aid Soc.), 1995–2004; Catholic Housing Aid Soc. (Central London), 2003–10; Nat. New Infant and Parent Network, 1995–99. Chm., Editorial Bd, Asian Affairs, 2002–14. *Recreations:* reading, running, contemplating London. *Address:* 5 Crooms Hill, SE10 8ER.

**PIKE, Peter Leslie;** *b* 26 June 1937; *s of* Leslie Henry Pike and Gladys (*née* Cunliffe); *m* 1962, Sheila Lillian Bull; two *d*. *Educ:* Hinchley Wood County Secondary Sch. (Commercial Dept); Kingston Technical Coll. Pt 1 Exam., Inst. of Bankers. National Service, RM, 1956–58. Midland Bank, 1954–62; Twinings Tea, 1962–63; Organiser/ Agent, Labour Party, 1963–73; Mullard (Simonstone) Ltd, 1973–83. Mem., GMBATU (Shop Steward, 1976–83). Member (Lab): Merton and Morden UDC, 1962–63; Burnley BC, 1976–84 (Leader, Labour Gp, 1980–83; Gp Sec., 1976–80). MP (Lab) Burnley, 1983–2005. Opposition front bench spokesperson: on Rural Affairs, 1990–92; on Housing, 1992–94. Member: Envmt Select Cttee, 1984–90; Procedural Select Cttee, 1995–97; Regulatory Reform Cttee (formerly Deregulation Select Cttee), 1995–2005 (Chm., 1997–2005); Modernisation Select Cttee, 1997–2005; Liaison Cttee, 1997–2005; Speakers Panel of Chairmen, 2001–05; Chm., Rights of Way Rev. Cttee, 1997–2005. All-Party Groups: Chairman: Romania Gp, 1994–2005; Southern Africa Gp; Mongolia Gp; Joint Chairman: Road Passenger Transport Gp, 1995–2005; Kidney Gp, 2001–05; Associate Parly Transport Forum, 1997–2001; Vice Chairman: Paper Industry Gp; Homelessness Gp; (Jt), Manufacturing Gp; Kashmir Gp, 2005; Secretary: Pakistan Gp, 1997–2005; Building Socs Gp, 1997–2005; Jt Sec., Overseas Develt Gp; Treas., Road Transport Study Gp, 1997–2000. Chm., PLP Envmt Cttee, 1987–90. Chairman: Clarets Trust, 2005–; E Lancs (formerly Burnley, Pendle and Rossendale) Learning Difficulties Partnership, 2005–12; Emmaus Burnley, 2005–14; Pennine (formerly Burnley Area) Community Credit Union, 2007–; Burnley Labour Party, 2008–17; Member Board: Burnley Youth Th., until 2012; Burnley Area Self Help Agency, 2005–15; Pendle CAB, 2005–11; SW Burnley Enterprise, 2005–12 (Chm., 2007–12); Burnley Homestart, 2006–08; Burnley Building Bridges, 2014–; Mem. Cttee, Burnley Civic Soc., 2005–; President: Burnley WEA, 2005–10; Friends of Freshfields, 2005–08; Hon. Pres., Burnley Municipal Choir and Orch., 2005–; Treas., Friends of St Peters, 2006–. Member: Nat. Trust, 1974–2011; CND; Anti-Apartheid. Hon. Fellow, Univ. of Central Lancs, 2011. *Recreation:* Burnley Football Club supporter. *Address:* 30 Deerpark Road, Burnley, Lancs BB10 4SD. *T:* (01282) 434719, 07976 891801. *E:* peterl.pike@btinternet.com.

**PIKE, Roy;** *see* Pike, E. R.

**PIKE, Roy Ernest;** Chief Executive, Torquay Boys' Grammar School Multi Academy Trust, since 2014; Headmaster, Torquay Boys' Grammar School, 1987–2013; *b* Taunton, 1 May 1948; *s of* Ernest and Nora Pike; *m* 1971, Philippa Gordon; two *s* four *d*. *Educ:* Ilminster Grammar Sch.; St Luke's Coll., Exeter (BEd 1970); University Coll. London (BA Hons 1977 ext.). Torquay Boys' Grammar School: History Teacher, 1970; Hd of Dept, 1975–83; Pastoral Hd, 1977–83; Dep. Headmaster, 1983–87. Mem. Cttee, Freedom and Autonomy for Schs - Nat. Assoc. (formerly Grant Maintained Schs Adv. Cttee, later Foundn and Voluntary Aided Schs Assoc., then Foundn and Aided Schs Nat. Assoc., subseq. Foundn, Aided Schs and Academies Nat. Assoc.), 1993–; Chm., Nat. Grammar Schs Assoc., 2011–13; Mem., Boys' Academic Selective Schs. Trustee, Torbay Coast and Countryside Trust, 2002– (Vice Chm.). FRSA. Hon. LLD Exeter, 2014. *Publications:* (contrib.) The Beacon School Experience: case studies in excellence, vol. 1, 2000, developing the curriculum, vol. 2, 2002. *Recreations:* family (12 grandchildren), tennis, country pursuits, conservation of natural and built environment.

**PIKE, Air Vice-Marshal Warwick John;** Director General, RAF Medical Services, 2002–04; *b* 31 Dec. 1944; *s of* late Captain Thomas Pike and Molly (*née* Buckley); *m* 1st, 1968, Susan Margaret Davies-Johns (*d* 2007); two *s* two *d*; 2nd, 2011, Shirley Jacqueline Cotterill. *Educ:* Sir John Port Sch.; Guy's Hosp., London (MB BS 1968); London Sch. of Hygiene and Tropical Medicine (MSc 1988). MRCS, LRCP 1968; DObstRCOG 1975; MRCGP 1975; DAvMed 1979; MFOM 1993. Joined RAF, 1970; served in UK, Singapore, Hong Kong and Germany; CO, Princess Mary's Hosp., Akrotiri, Cyprus, 1990–92; Dir, Med. Personnel, 1992–94; Asst Dir of Med. Co-ordination, Surgeon Gen.'s Dept, MoD, 1994–96; Dir, Primary Health Services, 1996–99; QHP 1997–2004; COS, later Chief Exec., Defence Secondary Care Agency, 1999–2002. *Recreations:* walking, theatre, history. *Address:* 7 Prebendal Green, Yarwell, Peterborough PE8 6PJ. *E:* wjpike@gmail.com. *Club:* Royal Air Force.

**PILA, Dr Jonathan Solomon,** FRS 2015; Reader in Mathematical Logic, University of Oxford, since 2010; Fellow, Wolfson College, Oxford, since 2010; *b* Melbourne, 28 July 1962; *s of* Joshua Pila and Mary Joan Pila (*née* Lloyd); *m* 1999, Justine FitzGerald; two *d*. *Educ:* Univ. of Melbourne (BSc Hons 1984); Stanford Univ. (PhD 1988). Asst Prof., Columbia Univ., 1989–92; Associate, 1993–94 and 1996–99, Sen. Fellow, 2000–04, Univ. of Melbourne; Asst Prof., McGill Univ., 2003–05; Lectr, 2005–07, Sen. Lectr, 2007–10, Univ. of Bristol. Mem., Inst. for Advanced Study, Princeton, 1988–89 and 2002–03. Dir and Manager, James Nelson Textile Gp, 1992–2002. MAE 2016. Clay Res. Award, 2011; Sen. Whitehead Prize, LMS, 2011; (jtly) Karp Prize, Assoc. for Symbolic Logic, 2013. *Publications:* articles in learned jls. *Address:* Mathematical Institute, University of Oxford, Andrew Wiles Building, Radcliffe Observatory Quarter, Woodstock Road, Oxford OX2 6GG.

**PILBROW, Fionn Peter Alexander;** QC 2019; *b* Hong Kong, 11 March 1976; *s of* David and Virginia Pilbrow; *m* 2003, Saritha Wilkinson; three *s*. *Educ:* Winchester Coll.; Balliol Coll., Oxford (BA 1998; MA 2005); St John's Coll., Cambridge (MPhil 1999); City Univ., London (DipLaw 2000); Inns of Court Sch. of Law (BVC 2001). Called to the Bar, Inner Temple, 2001; in practice as barrister, specialising in commercial law, 2002–. *Recreations:* family, travel, theatre, ski-ing, diving, sports. *Address:* Brick Court Chambers, 7–8 Essex Street, WC2R 3LD. *T:* (020) 7379 3550. *Clubs:* Queen's, 67 Pall Mall, Boodle's.

**PILBROW, Richard Hugh;** Founder and Chairman, Theatre Projects (formerly Theatre Projects Consultants), 1957–2006; *b* 28 April 1933; *s of* Arthur Gordon Pilbrow and Marjorie Pilbrow; *m* 1st, 1958, Viki Brinton; one *s* one *d*; 2nd, 1974, Molly Friedel; one *d*. *Educ:* Cranbrook Sch.; Central Sch. of Speech and Drama. Stage Manager, Teahouse of the August Moon, 1954; Lighting Designer for over 200 prodns in London, New York, Paris, Moscow and Sydney, incl.: Brand, 1959; Blitz, 1962; Zorba, 1968; Annie, 1978; The Little Foxes, Windy City, 1982; Singin' In the Rain, 1983; Heliotrope Bouquet, 1991; Four Baboons Adoring the Sun, 1992; The Magic Flute, LA, 1993; Showboat, 1993; The Life, 1997; Our Town, 2003; The Boy Friend, 2005; The Sleeping Beauty, Amer. Ballet Th., 2007; A Tale of Two Cities, 2008; Candida, 2010; Molly Sweeney, 2011; Dancing at Lughnasa, 2011; Transport, 2014; My Fair Lady, 2016; for Nat. Theatre Co., 1963–, incl. Hamlet, 1963, Love for Love, 1965, 1985, Rosencrantz and Guildenstern are Dead, 1966, Heartbreak House, 1975. Theatrical Producer in London of prodns incl.: A Funny Thing Happened on the Way to the Forum, 1963, 1986; Cabaret, 1968; Company, 1972; A Little Night Music, 1975; West Side Story, 1984; The Mysteries, Lyceum, 1985; I'm Not Rappaport, 1986. Film Prod., Swallows and Amazons, 1973; TV Productions: All You Need is Love—the story of popular music, 1975; Swallows and Amazons for Ever, 1984; Dir, Mister, 1971. Theatre Projects Consultants have been consultants on over 1500 theatres and arts centres, incl. Disney Concert Hall, LA, Kimmel Performing Arts Centre,

Philadelphia, New Amsterdam Theatre, NY, Nat. Theatre of GB, Barbican Theatre, and theatres and arts centres in Canada, Iran, Hong Kong, Saudi Arabia, Mexico, Iceland, Nigeria, Singapore, USA, etc. Co-founder, Soc. of British Theatre Designers, 1975; Fellow, Assoc. of British Theatre Technicians, 2003–; Pres., Assoc. of Lighting Designers, 2008– (Chm., 1982–85; Jt Pres., 2003–08); Member: Drama Panel, Arts Council of GB, 1968–70; Soc. of West End Theatre; Council, London Acad. of Music and Drama. Fellow, US Inst. of Theatre Tech., 2001. Hon. Fellow: Hong Kong Acad. for Performing Arts, 2010; Royal Central Sch. of Speech and Drama, 2012. FRSA. *Publications:* Stage Lighting, 1970, 3rd edn 1991; Stage Lighting Design, 1997; (with Patricia Mackay) The Walt Disney Concert Hall—The Backstage Story, 2003; A Theatre Project, 2011, 2nd edn 2015. *Recreations:* The Hebrides, cooking, dogs. *Address:* 78 Barrack Hill Road, Ridgefield, CT 06877, USA. *Club:* Garrick.

**PILDITCH, Sir John (Richard),** 5th Bt *cr* 1929, of Bartropps, Weybridge, Surrey; *b* London, 24 Sept. 1955; *o s* of Sir Richard Edward Pilditch, 4th Bt and of (Pauline) Elizabeth Pilditch (*née* Smith); *S* father, 2012. *Educ:* privately. *Recreation:* sailing.

**PILE, Sir Anthony (John Devereux),** 4th Bt *cr* 1900, of Kenilworth House, Rathgar, co. Dublin; MBE 2016; Chairman, Blue Skies Holdings, since 1997; *b* Bristol, 7 June 1947; *s* of Sir John Devereux Pile (*d* 1982), *yr s* of 2nd Bt and Katharine Mary (*d* 2010), *d* of late Austin George Shafe; *S* uncle, 2010; *m* 1977, Jenny Clare Youngman; two *s* one *d*. *Educ:* Durham Sch. Durham LI, then LI; Major, 1980. JP Northants, 1994–96. Hon. DSc Cranfield, 2011. *Recreations:* entrepreneurial activity in Africa and S America, reading, walking. *Heir: s* Thomas Charles Devereux Pile, *b* 6 April 1978. *Address:* The Manor House, Pitsford, Northants NN6 9AZ. *E:* anthony.pile@blueskies.com.

**PILGER, John Richard;** journalist, author and film-maker; *s* of Claude Pilger and Elsie (*née* Marheine); one *s* one *d*. *Educ:* Sydney High Sch. Cadet journalist, Sydney Daily Telegraph, Australia, qualified, 1961; freelance journalist, Italy, 1962; Reuter, London, 1962; feature writer, chief foreign correspondent, Daily Mirror, London, 1962–86 (reporter, Vietnam War, 1966–75, Cambodia, 1979–91, etc); columnist, New Statesman, 1991–2014; contributor: The Guardian (1970s–2014); The Independent, Sydney Morning Herald, The Age, Melbourne, Il Manifesto, Rome; contrib. websites incl. Counterpunch, Information Clearing House, Consortiumnews.com. Campaigns incl. Thalidomide 'X list' victims, and Australian Aboriginal land rights. Documentary film-maker, 1970–, films include: The Quiet Mutiny, 1970; A Faraway Country (Czechoslovakia), 1977; Year Zero: the silent death of Cambodia, 1979; Nicaragua, 1983; Japan Behind the Mask, 1986; The Last Dream, 1988; Death of a Nation: the Timor conspiracy, 1994; Vietnam: the last battle, 1995; Inside Burma: land of fear, 1996; Breaking the Mirror: the Murdoch Effect, 1997; Apartheid Did Not Die, 1998; Paying the Price: killing the children of Iraq, 2000; The New Rulers of the World, 2001; Palestine is Still the Issue, 2002; Breaking the Silence, 2003; Stealing a Nation, 2004; The War on Democracy, 2007; The War You Don't See, 2010; Utopia, 2013; The Coming War on China, 2016. Edward Wilson Fellow, Deakin Univ., Aust., 1995; Vis. Prof., Cornell Univ., USA, 2004–. Hon. DLitt: Staffordshire, 1994; Kingston, 1999; Rhodes Univ., SA, 2008; Lincoln, 2009; DPhil *hc* Dublin City, 1995; Hon. DArts Oxford Brookes, 1997; Hon. LLD St Andrews, 1999; DUniv Open, 2001. Order of Timor-Leste, 2017. Awards include: Descriptive Writer of the Year, 1966; Reporter of the Year, 1967; Journalist of the Year, 1967, 1979; Internat. Reporter of the Year, 1970; News Reporter of the Year, 1974; Campaigning Journalist of the Year, 1977; UN Media Peace Prize and Gold Medal, 1979–80; George Foster Peabody Award, USA, 1990; Reporters Sans Frontières Award, France, 1990; Richard Dimbleby Award, 1991; US TV Academy Award (Emmy), 1991; Premis Actual Award, Spain, 1996; Sophie Prize for Human Rights, 2003; RTS Award, 2005; Sydney Peace Prize, 2009; Grierson Trustees Award for Documentary Film-making, 2011; Internat. Journalism Prize, Mexico, 2017; Trinity Coll. Histl Soc. Medal, 2017. Order of Timor-Leste (East Timor), 2017. *Publications:* The Last Day, 1975; Aftermath: the struggle of Cambodia and Vietnam, 1981; The Outsiders, 1984; Heroes, 1986; A Secret Country, 1989; Distant Voices, 1992; Hidden Agendas, 1998; The New Rulers of the World, 2002; (ed) Tell Me No Lies: investigative journalism and its triumphs, 2004; Freedom Next Time, 2006. *Recreations:* swimming, sunning, mulling, reading. *Address:* 57 Hambalt Road, SW4 9EQ. *T:* (020) 8673 2848. *E:* jpilger2003@yahoo.co.uk. *W:* www.johnpilger.com, www.twitter.com/johnpilger.

**PILGRIM, Dr Mark Antony;** Chief Executive Officer, North of England Zoological Society (Chester Zoo), since 2010; *b* Portsmouth, 22 May 1964; *s* of Richard Pilgrim and Marjorie Pilgrim; *m* 2016, Kirstie Fraser; two *s* one *d*. *Educ:* Medina Primary Sch., Portsmouth; Springfield Comp. Sch., Portsmouth; North East London Poly. (BSc Hons); Liverpool John Moores Univ. (PhD 2010). North of England Zoological Society (Chester Zoo): bird keeper, 1988–90; Avicultural Deputy, 1990–98; Gen. Curator, Ops, 1998–2002; Hd, Animal and Plant Conservation Div., 2002–07; Conservation and Educn Dir, 2007–10. *Recreations:* travel, bird watching, horse riding. *Address:* Cedar House, Chester Zoo, Caughall Road, Upton, Chester, Cheshire CH2 1LH. *E:* m.pilgrim@chesterzoo.org.

**PILGRIM, Martin George;** non-executive director, since 2007; Chief Executive, Association of London Government, subseq. London Councils, 1997–2007; *b* 10 Feb. 1950; *s* of late George and Audrey Pilgrim; *m* 1974, Angela Muriel Staples; two *d*. *Educ:* Arden St Co. Primary Sch., Gillingham; Gillingham Grammar Sch.; Univ. of Kent at Canterbury (MA Mgt). CIPFA. Various posts, Kent CC, 1968–81; Association of Metropolitan Authorities: Under Sec. (Finance), 1981–96; Dep. Sec., 1996–97. Dir, Film London, 2005–11; Associate, Criticaleye, 2007–. Prince's Trust: Chm., London Regl Council, 2007–13; Chm., England Council, 2009–13; Trustee, 2009–10; Mem., Nat. Adv. Bd, 2010–13. Chair, London Sustainability Exchange, 2007–15. Trustee: Family and Childcare (formerly Daycare) Trust, 2007–18; Family Rights Gp, 2011– (Chm., 2016–); Young Women's Trust, 2013–; Swanswell, 2014–16; Diana Award, 2014–; Early Intervention Foundn, 2017–; Th. Royal Stratford E, 2017–. *Publications:* articles in acad. jls and local govt press. *Recreations:* keeping fit, hill-walking, moderate ski-ing, France and French. *Address:* Hoades Court, Hoath Road, Hoath, Canterbury, Kent CT3 4JL. *T:* (01227) 710625. *E:* mpilgrim@easynet.co.uk.

**PILKINGTON, Muriel Norma,** MA; educational consultant, since 1998; Headteacher, Wycombe High School, 1986–98; *b* 1 Jan. 1941; *d* of Norman Herbert Fosbury and Lilian Alice Fosbury; *m* 1st, 1962, Anthony Leonard Andrews; one *s*; 2nd, 1983, Derek Brogden Pilkington; one step *s* one step *d*. *Educ:* Woking County Grammar Sch.; Helene Lange Hochschule, Hamburg; Lady Margaret Hall, Oxford (BA 1962; MA 1970). Asst Teacher, Shephalbury Sch., Stevenage, 1962–64; 2nd in Dept, Hatfield Girls' Grammar Sch., 1964–66; Head of Dept/Faculty, Sir James Altham Sch., Watford, 1970–81; Dep. Head, Francis Bacon Sch., St Albans, 1981–86. Chm., Area 6 SHA, 1993–95. Consultant, Centre for Educnl Mgt, 1999–. Trustee: Whitmore Vale Housing Assoc., 1970–; London Arts Schs, 1994–2009 (Mem. Council, 2000–08). Governor: Bucks Chilterns UC (formerly Bucks Coll., Brunel Univ.), 1993–2006 (consultant/guest lectr, 1999; Vice Chm., Council, 2001–06); Dr Challoner's High Sch., 2003–13; Wimbledon High Sch., 2004–08. Contributor, Inst. for Sch. and Coll. Govs, 2003–07. Regular lectr, Oxfordshire Probus Clubs and U3As on local history. FRSA 1990. Hon. PhD Bucks Chilterns UC, 2006. *Publications:* A History of the Wycombe High School Guild 1910–2010, 2010; Past, Present and Future: a history of the Buckinghamshire New University, 2010; contribs to Educn Update pubns for Centre for Educn and Finance Mgt. *Recreations:* classical music, literature, languages. *Address:* 1 Bishops Farm Mill, Witan Way, Witney, Oxon OX28 4DG; (summer) 304A Residence Tinssimo Parc, Boulevard Simon Batlle, 66400 Ceret, France.

**PILKINGTON, Stephen Charles,** CBE 2005; QPM 1998; DL; PhD; Chief Constable, Avon and Somerset Constabulary, 1998–2005; *b* 4 June 1948; *s* of Charles Leonard Pilkington and Joan Pilkington; *m* 1974, Anne Bernadette Brett; three *s*. *Educ:* Queen Elizabeth Coll., Univ. of London (BSc 1st cl. Hons Biology, 1969; PhD Plant Physiology, 1973). Joined Metropolitan Police, 1972; Constable, Battersea; seconded to American Police Force, 1984; Dep. Asst Comr, Central London, 1996–97. DL Somerset, 2005. *Recreations:* walking, ornithology, Rugby (spectator), cycling, conservation volunteer (holidays).

**PILKINGTON, Sir Thomas Henry Milborne-Swinnerton-,** 14th Bt *cr* 1635; *b* 10 March 1934; *s* of Sir Arthur W. Milborne-Swinnerton-Pilkington, 13th Bt and Elizabeth Mary (she *m* 1950, A. Burke), *d* of late Major J. F. Harrison, King's Walden Bury, Hitchin; *S* father, 1952; *m* 1961, Susan, *e d* of N. S. R. Adamson, Durban, South Africa; one *s* two *d*. *Educ:* Eton College. Sen. Steward, Jockey Club, 1994–98. *Recreations:* golf, racing. *Heir: s* Richard Arthur Milborne-Swinnerton-Pilkington [*b* 4 Sept. 1964; *m* 1994, Katya (marr. diss. 2000), *d* of T. J. Clemence; one *d*; *m* 2001, Henrietta Kirk; two *d*]. *Address:* Parsonage Farm, King's Walden, Hitchin, Herts SG4 8LF. *Clubs:* White's, City of London.

**PILKINGTON, Victoria Lucy Annabel;** *see* Stapleton, V. L. A.

**PILL, Rt Hon Sir Malcolm (Thomas),** Kt 1988; PC 1995; a Lord Justice of Appeal, 1995–2013; *b* 11 March 1938; *s* of late Reginald Thomas Pill, MBE and Anne Pill (*née* Wright); *m* 1966, Roisin Pill (*née* Riordan), DL; two *s* one *d*. *Educ:* Whitchurch Grammar Sch.; Trinity Coll., Cambridge (MA, LLM); Dip. Hague Acad. of Internat. Law; Univ. of Buckingham (MA 2015). Served RA, 1956–58; Capt., Glamorgan Yeomanry (TA), 1958–67. Called to Bar, Gray's Inn, 1962, Bencher, 1987; Wales and Chester Circuit, 1963 (Treas., 1985–87; Presiding Judge, 1989–93); a Recorder, 1976–87; QC 1978; a Judge of the High Court, QBD, 1988–95; a Judge, Employment Appeal Tribunal, 1992–95. 3rd Sec., Foreign Office, 1963–64 (delegns to UN Gen. Assembly, ECOSOC, Human Rights Commn). Dep. Chm., Parly Boundary Commn for Wales, 1993–95. Chm., Assoc. of Judges of Wales, 2008–12. Chairman: UNA (Welsh Centre) Trust, 1969–77, 1980–87; Welsh Centre for Internat. Affairs, 1973–76; Eur. Parly Boundary Cttee for Wales, 1993. Chm., UK Cttee, Freedom from Hunger Campaign, 1978–87. Trustee, Dominic Barker Trust, 1997–2007. Hon. Fellow, Univ. of Wales Cardiff, 1998; Fellow, Aberystwyth Univ., 2011. Hon. LLD: Glamorgan, 1998; Wales, 2016. *Publications:* A Cardiff Family in the Forties, 1999; Choices and Chances 1948–1969, 2016; Montgomery: friends within, foes without, 2019; contribs to legal and military history jls. *Address:* 9 Westbourne Crescent, Whitchurch, Cardiff CF14 2BL. *Club:* Cardiff and County.

**PILLAY, Prof. Gerald John;** DL; DTheol, PhD; Vice-Chancellor and Rector, Liverpool Hope University, since 2005 (Rector and Chief Executive, Liverpool Hope University College, 2003–05); *b* 21 Dec. 1953; *s* of Jimmy and Theena Pillay; *m* 1983, Nirmala Pillay; two *s*. *Educ:* Univ. of Durban-Westville (BA 1975; BD 1978; DTheol 1985); Rhodes Univ. (PhD 1984). Lectr, then Sen. Lectr in Church Hist., Univ. of Durban-Westville, 1979–87; Prof. of Church Hist., Univ. of SA, 1988–97; Foundn Prof. of Theology and Dean of Liberal Arts, Otago Univ., NZ, 1997–2003. DL Merseyside, 2009. *Publications:* Voices of Liberation, vol. 1, Albert Lutuli, 1993; Religion at the Limits?: Pentecostalism among Indian South Africans, 1994; (ed) A History of Christianity in South Africa, vol. 1, 1994; contribs to numerous books and learned jls. *Recreations:* squash, gardening. *Address:* Liverpool Hope University, Hope Park, Liverpool L16 9JD. *T:* (0151) 291 3403, *Fax:* (0151) 291 3100. *E:* pillayg@hope.ac.uk.

**PILLING, Benjamin;** QC 2015; *b* Cambridge, Mass, 18 Dec. 1972; *s* of Sir Joseph (Grant) Pilling, *qv*; *m* 2000, Naomi Ruth Hillman; two *s* one *d*. *Educ:* Abingdon Sch.; Lincoln Coll., Oxford (BA Eng. Lit.); City Univ., London (DipLaw). Called to the Bar, Inner Temple, 1997; in practice as barrister in independent practice, 1998–. Trustee, Campden Charities, 2007–16. *Publications:* (contrib.) Halsbury's Laws, 2003. *Recreations:* cooking, wine, music, friends. *Address:* 4 Pump Court, Temple, EC4Y 7AN. *T:* (020) 7842 5555. *E:* bpilling@4pumpcourt.com. *Club:* Athenæum.

**PILLING, Sir Joseph (Grant),** KCB 2001 (CB 1995); Permanent Under-Secretary of State, Northern Ireland Office, 1997–2005; *b* 8 July 1945; *s* of late Fred and Eva Pilling; *m* 1968, (Patricia) Ann Cheetham; two *s*. *Educ:* Rochdale Grammar Sch.; King's Coll., London; Harvard. Asst Principal, 1966, Pvte Sec. to Minister of State, 1970, Home Office; Asst Pvte Sec. to Home Sec., 1970–71; NI Office, 1972; Harkness Fellow, Harvard Univ. and Univ. of Calif at Berkeley, 1972–74; Home Office, 1974–78; Pvte Sec. to Sec. of State for NI, 1978–79; Home Office, 1979–84; Under Sec., DHSS, 1984–87; Dir of Personnel and Finance, HM Prison Service, Home Office, 1987–90; Dep. Under Sec. of State, NI Office, 1990–91; Dir-Gen., HM Prison Service, Home Office, 1991–92; Prin. Estabt and Finance Officer, DoH, 1993–97. Strategic Reviewer of CAA, 2007–08; Mem., Rev. of 30 Year Rule, 2007–09; Reviewer, Govt's Official History Prog. 2009; Identity Comr, 2009–10; External Reviewer, IPSO, 2016; Chairman: Rev. Gp on Sen. Appts in C of E, 2005–07; Koestler Trust, 2006–13; Adv. Bd, Relationships Foundn, 2006–10; House of Bishops Wkg Gp on Human Sexuality, 2012–14; Ind. Commn on Referendums, 2017–18; Pres., 2006–, Chm., 2016–, New Bridge Foundn; Member: Adv. Council, Mgt Sch., Imperial Coll., London, 1989–97; Bd of Trustees, Macmillan Cancer Support, 2005–15; Council, Univ. of London, 2006–08; Dio. Bd of Finance, Oxford, 2006–09. *Club:* Athenæum.
*See also* B. *Pilling*.

**PILLING, Prof. Michael John,** CBE 2008; PhD; CChem, FRSC; Research Professor, University of Leeds, 2008–10, now Emeritus Professor; *b* 25 Sept. 1942; *s* of John and Joan Pilling; *m* 1966, Gwenda Madeline Harrison; one *s* one *d*. *Educ:* Bacup and Rawtenstall Grammar Sch.; Churchill Coll., Cambridge (MA, PhD). CChem, FRSC 1991. Cambridge University: SRC Fellow, 1967–68; Jun. Res. Fellow, Churchill Coll., 1967–70; ICI Fellow, 1969–70; Vis. Scientist, Nat. Bureau of Standards, USA, 1968–69; Lectr in Physical Chemistry, and Fellow and Tutor of Jesus Coll., Oxford Univ., 1970–89; Leeds University: Prof. of Physical Chem., 1989–2007; Pro-Vice-Chancellor, 1992–94; Hd of Sch. of Chem., 1995–98; Dean for Res., Faculty of Maths and Phys. Scis, 2000–02; Dir, NERC Distributed Inst. for Atmospheric Composition, 2007–10. Visiting Professor: Univ. of Oregon, 1975; Univ. of Maryland, 1980; Univ. of Rome, 1984; Stanford Univ., 1987. Pres., Faraday Div., RSC, 2003–06 (Vice Pres., 1991–98; Sec., 1992–98); Mem. Council, NERC, 1995–2000 (Chm., Atmospheric Science and Tech. Bd, 1995–2000); Chm., Air Quality Expert Gp, DEFRA, 2001–09. Hon. Dr rer. nat. 2007 and Hon. Prof., 2007, Eötvös Loránd Univ., Budapest. Lectures: John Jeyes, RSC, 2001; Dist. Guest, Envmtl Chm. Gp, RSC, 2006. Award in Reaction Kinetics, 1991, Michael Polanyi Medal, Gas Kinetics Gp, 1994, Award for Combustion and Hydrocarbon Oxidation Chem., 2001, RSC; Sugden Award, Combustion Inst., 1993; Haagen-Smit Prize, Atmospheric Envmt, 2010. *Publications:* Reaction Kinetics, 1975; (ed jtly) Modern Gas Kinetics, 1985; (jtly) Reaction Kinetics,

1995; (jtly) Unimolecular Reactions, 1996; (ed) Low Temperature Combustion and Autoignition, 1997; (jtly) The Mechanisms of Atmospheric Oxidation of the Oxygenates, 2011; res. papers in learned jls. *Recreations:* hill-walking, running, music. *Address:* School of Chemistry, University of Leeds, Leeds LS2 9JT. *T:* (0113) 343 6451. *E:* m.j.pilling@leeds.ac.uk.

**PILLING, Simon Richard**, QFSM 2014; Chief Fire Officer and Chief Executive, West Yorkshire Fire and Rescue Service, since 2018; *b* Leeds, 1965; *s* of Ian Pilling and Yvonne Pilling; *m* 1997, Kathryn Scott; one *s. Educ:* Ossett Comp. Sch.; Univ. of Central Lancashire (MSc Fire Comd and Mgt 2002); Coventry Univ. (MA Mgt Studies 2003). West Yorkshire Fire and Rescue Service: Dir, Fire Safety and Tech. Services, 2004–06; Dir, Ops, 2006–08; Dep. Chief Fire Officer, 2006–08. Queen's Golden Jubilee Medal, 2002; Fire Service Long Service and Good Conduct Medal, 2005; Queen's Diamond Jubilee Medal, 2012. *Recreation:* sporting activities.

**PILLMAN, (Annabel) Clare**, CB 2017; OBE 2000; Chief Executive, Natural Resources Wales, since 2018; *b* Liverpool, 20 Feb. 1965; *d* of late Joseph Robert Pillman and Joan Meirion Pillman (*née* Evans). *Educ:* Wycombe Abbey Sch.; St Andrews Univ. (MA); Courtauld Inst. of Art (MA). Joined Department for National Heritage, 1992: Private Sec., 1994–96; Head: Millennium Celebrations Team, 1996–2000; Architecture and Historic Envmt, 2001–03; Hd of Strategy, DCA, 2003–04; Area Dir, N Wales, 2004–07, Dir, Wales, 2007–11, HM Courts Service; Dir, DCMS, 2011–18. Trustee: Inst. of Cancer Res., 2003–13; Nat. Th. of Wales, 2013–. *Recreations:* medieval history, opera, walking the dog. *E:* clare.pillman@cyfoethnaturiolcymru.gov.uk. *Club:* Oriental.

**PILLOW, Nathan Charles**; QC 2015; *b* Ilkeston, Derbyshire, 9 Aug. 1974; *s* of Christopher Pillow and Susan Pillow; *m* 2002, Aleksandra; two *d. Educ:* Nottingham High Sch.; Magdalen Coll., Oxford (BA Hons Law and French Law 1996); Univ. of Paris II, Panthéon-Assas (Dip. French Law 1995). Called to the Bar, Gray's Inn, 1997; in practice as a barrister, specialising in commercial litigation and civil fraud, Essex Court Chambers, 1998–. Bar Professional Trng Course Chief Examnr for Civil Litigation, Bar Standards Bd, 2011–14. *Address:* Essex Court Chambers, 24 Lincoln's Inn Fields, WC2A 3EG. *T:* (020) 7813 8000, *Fax:* (020) 7813 8080. *E:* npillow@essexcourt.com.

**PINCH, Sarah Ann Boyd**; Managing Director, Pinch Point Communications, since 2013; *b* Plymouth, Devon, 11 Aug. 1972; *d* of John Ellis Pinch and Judith Leonora Pinch (*née* Stevens); *m* 2011, John Gleave; one *d. Educ:* Devonport High Sch. for Girls; Univ. of West of England (Postgrad. Cert. Mgt). Chartered Practitioner, CIPR, 2016. Asst Producer, BBC TV and Radio, 1990–2000; PR Manager, Christian Aid, 2000–02; Mktg and Communications Manager, Children's Hospice SW, 2002–04; Head: PR and Mktg, First South and Wales, 2004–06; Communications, First Capital Connect, 2006–08; Dir of Communications, Univ. Hosps Bristol NHS Foundn Trust, 2008–13. Ind. Advr, Nat. Assembly for Wales Commn, 2018–. Non-executive Director: HSE, 2015–; Filament PR, 2017–. Pres., CIPR, 2015. Chair, Taylor Bennett Foundn, 2017–. MInstD 2012. FCIPR 2013. *Publications:* The C Words: women in the boardroom, 2019. *Recreations:* mentoring future female leaders, supporting diversity in business and the arts, debate, discussion, running, cycling, cooking, fine wine. *T:* (0117) 962 4050. *E:* sarah@pinchpointcommunications.co.uk. *Clubs:* Civil Service, House of St Barnabas.

**PINCHAM, Roger James**, CBE 1982; Chairman, Venture Consultants Ltd, 1980–2014; Consultant: Gerrard, 2000–06; J. M. Finn & Co., 2006–10; *b* 19 Oct. 1935; *y s* of late Sam and Bessie Pincham; *m* 1965, Gisela von Ulardt (*d* 1974); one *s* two *d. Educ:* Wimbledon Park Primary Sch.; Kingston Grammar School. National Service, RAF, 1954–56. With Phillips & Drew, 1956–88, Partner, 1967–76, consultant, 1976–88. Mem., London Stock Exchange, 1963–91; MCSI (MSI 1992). Director: Market Access Internat., then Eur. Political Consultancy Gp, 1985–94; Gerrard Vivian Gray, subseq. Greig Middleton, 1988–2000; UKRD Ltd, 1991–2006; Cornwall Independent Radio Ltd, 1991–99; ICOR(LPG) Internat. Ltd, 1992–; County Sound Radio Network Ltd, 1998–2003. Contested (L) Leominster, 1970, Feb. and Oct. 1974, 1979, 1983. Liberal Party: Nat. Exec., 1974–75 and 1978–87; Assembly Cttee, 1974–87; Standing Cttee, 1975–83; Chm. of Liberal Party, 1979–82; Jt Negotiating Cttee with SDP, and signatory to A Fresh Start for Britain, 1981. Mem., Agenda Cttee, Congress for Democracy, 2001–. Pres., St John Ambulance, St Pancras Div., 1996–2000. Founder Chm., Gladstone Club, 1973–; First Chairman: Ind. Educnl Assoc., 1974–2007; St James and St Vedast Schools, 1974–2007; Mem. Council, City Appeal for Eng. Coll. in Prague, 1991–; Gov., Sidney Perry Foundn, 1993–; Founder Trustee, John Stuart Mill Inst., 1992–. Trustee: Princess Margarita of Romania Trust, 1994–2004; Nat. Benevolent Fund for the Aged, 2001–12. Pres., Lloyd George Soc., 1996–2012. Pres., Kington Eisteddfod, 1978. FRSA 1994. Fellow, Churchill Meml, Fulton, Mo, 1997–. Freeman, City of London. Liveryman: Barbers' Co. (Master, 1993–94); Founders' Co.; Freeman, Co. of Watermen and Lightermen. *Publications:* (jtly) New Deal for Rural Britain, 1977; (ed) New Deal for British Farmers, 1978; (contrib.) Dictionary of Liberal Biography, 1998; (contrib.) Standing for Justice, 2001; (contrib.) Sheila Rosenberg: a Renaissance lady, 2004. *Recreations:* gardening, cricket, visiting Aldeburgh and Kullu. *Address:* Babbacombe, Snape Bridge, Saxmundham, Suffolk IP17 1ST. *T:* (01728) 688010. *E:* rogerpincham@me.com. *Clubs:* Beefsteak, Reform, National Liberal, City of London, Royal Automobile; Woolhope Naturalists' Field.

**PINCHER, Rt Hon. Christopher (John)**; PC 2018; MP (C) Tamworth, since 2010; Minister of State, Foreign and Commonwealth Office, since 2019; *b* Walsall, 24 Sept. 1969; *s* of John and Sandra Pincher. *Educ:* Ounsdale Sch., Wombourne, Staffs; London Sch. of Econs and Pol Sci. (BSc (Econ) Govt and Hist. 1991). Exec., outsourcing practice, Accenture, 1993–2010. PPS to Foreign Sec., 2015–16; an Asst Govt Whip, 2016–17; Comptroller of HM Household (Govt Whip), 2017; Treasurer of HM Household (Dep. Chief Whip), 2018–19. Member: Energy and Climate Change Select Cttee, 2010–15; Regulatory Reform Cttee, 2015–17; Cttee of Selection, 2017–. *Recreations:* horse racing, motor sports, history. *Address:* House of Commons, SW1A 0AA. *T:* (020) 7219 7169. *E:* christopher.pincher.mp@parliament.uk. *Club:* Travellers.

**PINCHERA, Albert Anthony**; Principal, BP Con LLP, since 2009; *b* 2 Sept. 1947; *s* of Albert Storre Pinchera and Edith Pinchera (*née* DeLuca); *m* 1971, Linda Avril Garrad; one *d. Educ:* Upton House Sch.; University Coll. London (BSc Hons Geol.). Exploration Geologist, 1969–72; Boots Company plc: Buyer, 1972–74; Sen. Buyer, 1974–77; Asst Merchandise Controller, 1977–81; Mktg Controller, 1981–86; Business Gen. Manager, 1986–90; Man. Dir, Boots Opticians, 1990–95; Hd, Internat. Retail Develt, 1995–97; Chief Exec., Nat. Kidney Res. Fund, 1998–2003; Dir, Greater London Magistrates' Courts Authy, 2003–05; Dir, HM Courts Service, 2005–07; Chief Operating Officer, HMRC (Prosecutions), 2007–08. Non-exec. Dir, Queen's Univ. Hosp. Trust, 2001–06; Mem., NHS Postgrad. Medical Bd, 2007–11. Chair, League of Friends, Queen's Med. Centre, Nottingham, 2012–. *Recreations:* military history, art restoration. *Address:* The Old School House, Elston, Notts NG23 5NP.

**PINCHING, Prof. Anthony John**, DPhil; FRCP; Director: Pinner Music Festival, since 2016; Music in Pinner Series, since 2018; Chairman of Directors, Ludlow Song, since 2016; *b* 10 March 1947; *s* of John Pinching and Wilhelmina Hermina Pinching (*née* Jonkers); *m* 1971, Katherine Susan Sloper; two *s* two *d. Educ:* Sherborne Sch., Dorset; St John's Coll., Oxford (BA 1968); St Edmund Hall, Oxford; Oxford Univ. Med. Sch. (DPhil 1972; BM BCh, MA 1973). MRCP 1976; FRCP 1986. Royal Postgraduate Medical School, London: Registrar and Sen. Registrar, Medicine and Immunology, 1976–79; Res. Fellow (Immunology), 1979–82; St Mary's Hospital Medical School, London: Sen. Lectr in Clinical Immunology, 1982–89; Reader, 1989–92; Louis Freedman Prof. of Immunology, 1992–2003, and Hd, Div. of Molecular Pathology Infection and Immunity, 1998–2003, St Bartholomew's and the Royal London Sch. of Medicine and Dentistry, subseq. Bart's and The London Sch. of Medicine and Dentistry, QMW, London Univ.; Clinical Dir, Infection and Immunity, St Bartholomew's Hosp. and Royal Hosps NHS Trust, 1992–99; Associate Dean for Cornwall, Peninsula Medical Sch., 2003–11. Vis. Prof., Univ. of Malta, 1986. Dep. Chm., CMO's Wkg Gp on CFS/ME, 2000–02; Principal Med. Advr, Action for ME, 2002–11; Chm., CFS/ME Service Investment Steering Gp, DoH, 2003–06. Terrence Higgins Trust Award, 1986; Evian Health Award, 1990. *Publications:* (ed) AIDS and HIV Infection, 1986; (ed jtly) AIDS and HIV Infection: the wider perspective, 1988; (ed jtly) New Dictionary of Medical Ethics, 1997; res. papers on neuroanatomy, autoimmune disease, HIV and AIDS and other immuno-deficiency. *Recreations:* music, especially opera, playing clarinet, literature, especially 20th Century, writing poetry, walking, librettist for composer, Russell Pascoe, in choral works and song.

**PINDLING, Dame Marguerite (Matilda)**, GCMG 2014 (DCMG 2007); Governor General of the Bahamas, 2014–19 (Deputy to Governor General of the Bahamas, 2006–07 and 2012–14); *b* 26 June 1932; *d* of Ruebin and Viola McKenzie; *m* 1956, Rt Hon. Sir Lynden Oscar Pindling, KCMG, OM, PC (*d* 2000); two *s* two *d. Educ:* South Andros All Age Sch., Andros Is., Bahamas. Businesswoman. *Publications:* The Life and Times of Dame Marguerite Pindling, 2007. *Recreations:* charitable work, Bahamas Red Cross Society. *Address:* Lynmar, Skyline Drive, Nassau, NP, Bahamas.

**PINE, Courtney**, CBE 2009 (OBE 2000); jazz saxophonist; *b* 18 March 1964; *m* 1997, June Guishard; one *s* three *d.* Founder Mem., Jazz Warriors, 1985. Albums include: Journey to the Urge Within, 1987; Destiny's Song, 1988; The Vision's Tale, 1989; Closer to Home, 1990; Within the Realms of Our Dreams; To the Eyes of Creation; Modern Day Jazz Stories, 1995; Underground, 1997; Back in the Day, 2000; Devotion, 2003; Resistance, 2005; Transition in Tradition, 2009; Courtney Pine Band Live, 2010; Europa, 2011; House of Legends, 2012; Song (The Ballad Book), 2015; Black Notes from the Deep, 2017; has also produced and arranged albums; contrib. to albums by other artists, incl. Mick Jagger, and to Larry Adler tribute album; has toured internationally. Presenter, Jazz Crusade, Radio 2, 2001–08 (12 series). Jt producer, Jazzdaze (film), 2005. Hon. Prof., Thames Univ., 2005. Hon. DMus: Westminster, 2005; Southampton, 2010.

**PINE, Prof. Cynthia Margaret**, CBE 2006; PhD; Professor of Dental Public Health, since 2013, and Academic Lead and Head, Unit of Dental Public Health, since 2014, Institute of Dentistry, Barts and The London, Queen Mary University of London; Consultant in Dental Public Health, Salford Royal NHS Foundation Trust, since 2013; Managing Director, Kippax Design Ltd, since 2013; *b* 2 Oct. 1953; *d* of Frederick and Nora Freeman; *m* 1992, Geoffrey Pine; two *d*, and one step *s. Educ:* Swanshurst Grammar Sch., Birmingham; Univ. of Manchester (BDS 1976; PhD 1982); Univ. of Dundee (MBA Dist. 2001). FDSRCSE 1997; FDSRCS 2004. Lectr, in Child Dental Health, 1982–85, in Dental Public Health, 1985–92, Univ. of Manchester; Dental Epidemiologist, NW RHA, 1985–92; University of Dundee: Sen. Lectr, 1992–99, Reader, 1999–2001, in Dental Public Health; Prof. of Dental Public Health, 2001–02; Prof. of Dental Public Health and Primary Dental Care, 2002–08, Dean of Dental Studies, 2003–08, Univ. of Liverpool; Exec. Dean, Coll. (formerly Faculty) of Health and Social Care, 2008–12, Pro Vice-Chancellor Internat., 2010–12, Univ. of Salford. Hon. Consultant in Dental Public Health: Dundee Hosp., 1992–2001; Royal Liverpool Hosp., 2002–08; NHS Salford PCT, 2008–13. Dir, WHO Collaborating Centre in Res. in Oral Health of Deprived Communities, 2003–13. Non-exec. Dir, Aintree Univ. Hosp. NHS Foundn Trust, 2008–08; Mem., Health is Wealth Commn, 2007–08; Chm., NW Cttee of Res. for Patient Benefit, NIHR, 2011–. Chair, Fiveways Trust, 2007–09. Gov., Birkenhead Sixth Form Coll., 2005–08. FRSA 2007. Hon. FCGI 2014. *Publications:* Community Oral Health, 1997, 2nd edn 2007; over 100 articles in learned jls. *Recreations:* enjoying holidays with my family, reading, collecting porcelain, going to the Royal Ballet, being a grandmother. *Clubs:* Royal Society of Medicine, International Women's Forum.

**PINES, Prof. Jonathon Noë Joseph**, PhD; FRS 2016; FMedSci; Chris Marshall Professor of Cell Biology and Head, Division of Cancer Research, Institute of Cancer Research, since 2015; *b* London, 11 Oct. 1961; *s* of Malcolm Irvine Manoah Pines and Evelyn Iris Mary Pines; *m* 2015, Lola Rafieva. *Educ:* King's Coll. Sch., Wimbledon; Caius Coll., Cambridge (BA Hons Natural Scis (Biochem.) 1983; PhD 1988). Post-doctoral Fellow, Salk Inst., Calif, 1988–92; Gp Leader, Wellcome/CRC Inst., Cambridge, 1992–2001; Sen. Gp Leader, Gurdon Inst., Cambridge, 2001–15. FMedSci 2005. *Address:* Institute of Cancer Research, 237 Fulham Road, SW3 6JB. *T:* (020) 7153 5144. *E:* jon.pines@icr.ac.uk.

**PINI, John Peter Julian**; QC 2006; **His Honour Judge Pini**; a Circuit Judge, since 2014; Resident Judge, Lincoln Crown Court, since 2014; *b* 27 Nov. 1954; *s* of Pierino and Roberta Pini; *m* 1991, Yvonne Anne Coen, *qv*; one *s* one *d*, and one *d* from a previous marriage. *Educ:* Queen's Univ., Belfast (BA 1st Cl. Hons Philos. 1977); City Univ. (Dip. Law 1979). Called to the Bar, Gray's Inn, 1981 (Lord Justice Holker Exhibnr); criminal practitioner, SE Circuit, 1981–91, Midland Circuit, 1991–2014; Asst Recorder, 1999–2000; Recorder, 2000–14. Hon. Recorder of Lincoln, 2015–. *Recreations:* jazz guitar, cookery, family, golf (flog). *Address:* Lincoln Crown Court, The Castle, Castle Hill, Lincoln LN1 3GA.

**PINI, Yvonne Anne**; *see* Coen, Y. A.

**PINKER, Prof. Robert Arthur**, CBE 2005; independent reviewer, Press Complaints Commission, 2012–14 (international consultant, 2004–12); Professor of Social Administration, London School of Economics and Political Science, 1993–96, now Emeritus; *b* 27 May 1931; *s* of Dora Elizabeth and Joseph Pinker; *m* 1955, Jennifer Farrington Boulton (*d* 1994); two *d. Educ:* Holloway County Sch.; LSE (Cert. in Social Sci. and Admin 1959; BSc Sociology 1962; MSc Econ 1965). University of London: Head of Sociology Dept, Goldsmiths' Coll., 1964–72; Lewisham Prof. of Social Admin, Goldsmiths' Coll. and Bedford Coll., 1972–74; Prof. of Social Studies, Chelsea Coll., 1974–78; Prof. of Social Work Studies, LSE, 1978–93; Pro-Director, LSE, 1985–88; Pro-Vice-Chancellor for Social Scis, London Univ., 1989–90. Vis. Prof., Univ. of Ulster, 2012–. Press Complaints Commission: Mem., 1991–2004; Privacy Comr, 1994–2004; Acting Chm., 2002–03; Chm., Bosnia-Hercegovina Press Council, 2003–05. Chm., British Library Project on Family and Social Research, 1983–86; Mem., Council, Advertising Standards Authority, 1988–95. Chm., Deptford Challenge Trust, 2005–14. Chm. Governors, Centre for Policy on Ageing, 1988–94; Gov., BPMF, 1990–94; Mem. Council, Goldsmiths Coll., Univ. of London, 2001–07 (Hon. Fellow, 1999). Fellow, Soc. of Editors, 2004–. Chm., Editl Bd, Jl of Social Policy, 1981–86. Hon. LLD Ulster, 2016. *Publications:* English Hospital Statistics

1861–1938, 1964; Social Theory and Social Policy, 1971; The Idea of Welfare, 1979, re-issued 2019; Social Work in an Enterprise Society, 1990; (with R. Deacon and N. Lipton) Privacy and Personality Rights, 2010; Social Policy and Welfare Pluralism, 2017. *Recreations:* reading, writing, travel, unskilled gardening. *Address:* 76 Coleraine Road, Blackheath, SE3 7PE.

PINKER, Prof. Steven (Arthur), PhD; Johnstone Family Professor, Department of Psychology, Harvard University, since 2003; *b* Montreal, 18 Sept. 1954; *s of* Harry and Roslyn Pinker; US citizen; *m* 1st, 1980, Nancy Etcoff (marr. diss. 1992); 2nd, 1995, Ilavenil Subbiah (marr. diss.); 3rd, 2007, Rebecca Goldstein. *Educ:* McGill Univ. (BA Psychol. 1976); Harvard Univ. (PhD Exptl Psychol. 1979). Postdoctoral Fellow, Center for Cognitive Sci., MIT, 1979–80; Assistant Professor, Department of Psychology: Harvard Univ., 1980–81; Stanford Univ., 1981–82; Massachusetts Institute of Technology: Asst Prof., Dept of Psychol., 1982–85; Associate Prof., 1985–89, Prof., 1989–2003, Dept of Brain and Cognitive Scis; Co-Dir, Center for Cognitive Scis, 1985–94; Dir, McDonnell-Pew Center for Cognitive Neurosci., 1994–99; Margaret MacVicar Faculty Fellow, 2000; Peter de Florez Prof., 2000–03. Hon. DSc: McGill, 2005; Newcastle, 2005; Hon. PhD: Tel Aviv, 2003; Surrey, 2003; Tromso, 2008; Hon. DHL Albion Coll., 2007. Dist. Scientific Award, 1984, Boyd R. McCandless Young Scientist Award, 1986, Amer. Psychol Assoc.; Troland Res. Award, NAS, 1993; Golden Plate Award, Amer. Acad. Achievement, 1999; Henry Dale Prize, Royal Instn of GB, 2004; George Miller Prize, Cognitive Neurosci. Soc., 2010. *Publications:* Language Learnability and Language Development, 1984; (ed) Visual Cognition, 1985; (ed with J. Mehler) Connections and Symbols, 1988; Learnability and Cognition: the acquisition of argument structure, 1989; (ed with B. Levin) Lexical and Conceptual Semantics, 1992; The Language Instinct, 1994 (Wm James Bk Prize, Amer. Psychol Assoc., 1995; Public Interest Award, Linguistics Soc., of America, 1997); How the Mind Works, 1997 (LA Times Bk Prize, 1998; Wm James Bk Prize, Amer. Psychol Assoc. 1999); Words and Rules: the ingredients of language, 1999; The Blank Slate: the modern denial of human nature, 2002 (Eleanor Maccoby Book Prize, 2003, William James Book Prize, Amer. Psychol Assoc., 2003; Kistler Book Prize, Foundn for the Future, 2005); The Stuff of Thought: language as a window into human nature, 2007; The Better Angels of our Nature: the decline of violence in history and its causes, 2011; The Sense of Style: the thinking person's guide to writing in the 21st Century, 2014; Enlightenment Now: the case for reason, science, humanism and progress, 2018; contrib. articles to Science, Cognition, Cognitive Sci., Proc. Nat. Acad. of Scis and other jls. *Recreations:* bicycling, photography. *Address:* Department of Psychology, Harvard University, William James Hall, 33 Kirkland Street, Cambridge, MA 02138, USA. *E:* pinker@wjh.harvard.edu.

PINKERTON, Anthony James Moxon L.; *see* Lowther-Pinkerton.

PINKERTON, Prof. (Charles) Ross, MD; Professor of Oncology, University of Queensland, since 2003; Director, Oncology Unit, Children's Health Queensland (formerly Director of Paediatric Oncology, Royal Children's Hospital and Mater Children's Hospital), since 2007; *b* 6 Oct. 1950; *s* of late Prof. John Henry McKnight Pinkerton, CBE; *m* 1989, Janet Hardy; three *d*. *Educ:* Campbell Coll.; Queen's Univ., Belfast (MD 1981). Postgrad. trng in paediatrics, Dublin and London, 1976–80; trng in children's cancer, London and France, 1980–86. Consultant Paediatric Oncologist and Hd, Children's Unit, Royal Marsden Hosp., 1989–2003 (Sen. Res. Fellow, 1986–89); Prof. of Paediatric Oncology, Inst. of Cancer Res., London, 1995–2003; Dir of Cancer Services, Mater Hosps, Brisbane, 2003–07. Chm., UK Children's Cancer Study Gp, 2000–02. *Publications:* editor: Paediatric Oncology: clinical practice and controversies, 1991, 2nd edn 1997; Childhood Cancer Management, 1995; Clinical Challenges in Paediatric Oncology, 1998; over 200 papers on children's cancer management. *Recreation:* tennis. *Address:* 107 Ironbark Road, Chapel Hill, Qld 4069, Australia.

PINKERTON, Francis Trevor Woodman; a Judge of the Upper Tribunal (Immigration and Asylum Chamber), 2010–16; Resident Judge, Taylor House Hearing Centre, London, 2011–16; *b* Hitchin, Herts, 5 March 1946; *s of* Dr George Eustace Pinkerton, MC and Doreen Patricia Pinkerton (*née* Tooley); *m* 1st, 1974, Hilary Claire Youldon (marr. diss. 1994; she *m* 2003, Sir (Frederick Douglas) David Thomson, *qv*); one *s* one *d* (and one *d* decd); 2nd, 2015, Jacqueline Margaret Martin (*née* Carter). *Educ:* Gadebridge Park Sch., Hemel Hempstead; Tonbridge Sch., Kent; Coll. of Law, Lancaster Gate; Coll. of Law, Guildford. Admitted as solicitor, 1970; Legal Asst, Anglo American Corp., Johannesburg, 1971–72; Solicitor: Needham & Grant, Clements Inn, 1973–74; John Duncombe & Co., Cheltenham, 1974–75; Partner, Pinkerton Leeke & Co., 1976–99; Immigration Adjudicator (pt-time), 1996–99, salaried, 1999–2002; on secondment to S African Refugee Appeal Bd, 2002; Dep. Dist Judge (Civil), 2000–08; Resident Senior Immigration Judge: Central London, Asylum and Immigration Tribunal, 2002–10; First-tier Tribunal (Immigration and Asylum Chamber), Central London, 2010–16. *Recreations:* rowing, opera, ballet, singing, motorcycling, classic cars, ski-ing. *Clubs:* Remenham, London Rowing, Tideway Scullers School.

PINKERTON, Ross; *see* Pinkerton, C. R.

PINNER, Ruth Margaret, (Mrs M. J. Pinner); *see* Kempson, R. M.

PINNINGTON, Roger Adrian, TD 1967; consultant; *b* 27 Aug. 1932; *s of* William Austin Pinnington and Elsie Amy Pinnington; *m* 1st, 1961, Jean Heather Goodall (marr. diss. 1977); 2nd, 1978, Marjorie Ann Pearson; one *s* three *d*. *Educ:* Rydal Sch., Colwyn Bay; Lincoln Coll., Oxford (MA Law). Nat. Service, 1951–53. Marketing Dir, Jonas Woodhead & Sons, 1963–74; 1975–82: Vice Pres., TRW Europe Inc.; Man. Dir, CAM Gears Ltd; Pres., TRW Italia SpA; Dir Gen., Gemmer France; Pres., Torfinasa; Dep. Chm. and Chief Exec., UBM Gp, 1982–85; Dir, Norcros, 1985–86; Dir and Chief Exec., Royal Ordnance PLC, 1986–87; Dir and Gp Chief Exec., RHP, subseq. Pilgrim House Gp, 1987–89. Chairman: Telfos Hldgs, subseq. Jenbacher Hldgs (UK), 1991–95; Lynx Holdings PLC, 1992–98; Cortworth PLC, 1994–97; British World Aviation Ltd, later BWA Gp plc, 1994–2000; Huntingdon Internat. Hldgs plc, 1994–98 (Dep. Chm., 1998–99); Montanaro Hldgs Ltd, 1995–2001; Armour Gp plc, 1996–2001; SEA Gp, 2001–07. *Recreations:* gardening, arguing with Sally, collecting silver and porcelain sauce bottle labels, staying alive! *Address:* Whitelands Cottage, Pickhurst Road, Chiddingfold, Surrey GU8 4TS. *E:* pinnington@hotmail.com. *Club:* Vincent's (Oxford).

PINNOCK, family name of Baroness Pinnock.

PINNOCK, Baroness *cr* 2014 (Life Peer), of Cleckheaton in the County of West Yorkshire; Kathryn Mary Pinnock; *m* Andrew Pinnock, MA; three *c*. *Educ:* Univ. of Keele. History teacher. Mem. (Lib Dem) Kirklees Council, 1987– (Leader, 2000–06). Mem. Bd, Yorkshire Forward RDA, 2001–11. Non-exec. Dir, Yorkshire Water, 2008–17. Chm., 2008–12, Pres., 2012–18, Assoc. of Lib Dem Cllrs. Chm. Govs, Whitcliffe Mount Sch., 1998–2014; Mem. Governing Council, Univ. of Huddersfield, 2016–. Trustee, Huddersfield Contemporary Music Festival. Contested (Lib Dem) Batley and Spen, 1997, 2001. DUniv Huddersfield, 2015.

PINNOCK, Comdr Harry James, RN retd; Director, Cement Makers' Federation, 1979–87; *b* 6 April 1927; *s of* Frederick Walter Pinnock and Kate Ada (*née* Shepherd); *m* 1st, 1962, Fru Inger Connie Åhgren (*d* 1978); one *d*; 2nd, 2002, Deborah Olivares, USA. *Educ:* Sutton Valence Sch. Joined RN, 1945; Midshipman, HMS Nelson, 1945–47; Sub-Lieut/Lieut, HMS Belfast, Far East, 1948–50; RN Rhine Flotilla, 1951–52; Staff of First Sea Lord, 1952–55; Lt-Comdr, Mediterranean Minesweepers, 1955–57; HMS Ceylon, E of Suez, 1957–59; Staff of C-in-C Plymouth, 1960–61; HQ Allied Naval Forces, Northern Europe, Oslo, 1961–63; Comdr, MoD, 1964–67, retd. Cement Makers' Fedn, 1970–87. Chm., Gala Day Services, 2007–09. *Recreation:* travel. *Address:* Flat 7, Halyard Place, Trinity Way, Minehead TA24 6GL.

PINNOCK, Trevor, CBE 1992; ARCM; harpsichordist; conductor; Director, The English Concert, 1973–2003; *b* Canterbury, 16 Dec. 1946. *Educ:* Canterbury Cathedral Choir Sch.; Simon Langton Grammar Sch., Canterbury; Royal Coll. of Music, London (Foundn Scholar; Harpsichord and Organ Prizes). ARCM Hons (organ) 1965, FRCM 1996. London début with Galliard Harpsichord Trio (Jt Founder with Stephen Preston, flute and Anthony Pleeth, 'cello), 1966; solo début, Purcell Room, London, 1968. Formed The English Concert for purpose of performing music of baroque period on instruments in original condition or good modern copies, 1972, making its London début in English Bach Festival, Purcell Room, 1973. NY début at Metropolitan Opera, conducting Handel Giulio Cesare, 1988. Artistic Dir and Principal Conductor, 1991–96, Artistic Advr, 1996–98, Nat. Arts Centre Orch., Ottawa. Recordings of complete keyboard works of Rameau; Bach Toccatas, Partitas, Goldberg Variations, Concerti, Handel Messiah and Suites, Purcell Dido and Aeneas, orchestral and choral works of Bach, Handel, Vivaldi, complete symphonies of Mozart, etc. Hon. RAM 1988. Hon. DMus: Ottawa, 1993; Kent, 1995; Sheffield, 2005. Officier, Ordre des Arts et des Lettres (France), 1998. *Address:* c/o Ms Melanie Moult, Askonas Holt, 15 Fetter Lane, EC4A 1BW. *T:* (020) 7400 1700.

PINSENT, Sir Matthew (Clive), Kt 2005; CBE 2001 (MBE 1992); oarsman; International Rowing Umpire, since 2012; *b* 10 Oct. 1970; *s of* Rev. Ewen and Jean Pinsent; *m* 2002, Demetra Ekaterina Koutsoukos; twin *s* one *d*. *Educ:* Eton College; St Catherine's College, Oxford (BA Hons Geography 1993). Winner: coxless pairs: (with Tim Foster) Junior World Championship, 1988; (with Steven Redgrave): World Championship, 1991, 1993, 1994 and 1995; Olympic Gold Medal, 1992 and 1996; (with James Cracknell) coxed and coxless pairs, 2001, coxless pairs, 2002, World Championship; coxless fours: World Championship, 1997, 1998, 1999; Olympic Gold Medal, 2000 and 2004; Mem., Oxford Boat Race winning crew, 1990, 1991. Sports presenter, BBC, 2006–. Dir, JJB Sports plc, 2010–12. Mem., IOC, 2002–04. *Publications:* A Lifetime in a Race, 2004. *Recreations:* golf, flying. *Club:* Leander (Henley-on-Thames).

PINSENT, Sir Thomas Benjamin Roy, 4th Bt *cr* 1938, of Selly Hill, City of Birmingham; *b* 21 July 1967; *s of* Sir Christopher Roy Pinsent, 3rd Bt and of Susan Mary Pinsent (*née* Scorer); *S* father, 2015; *m* 2007, Angelika Waltraud Heinkel. *Heir: uncle* Michael Roy Pinsent [*b* 4 Feb. 1927; *m* 1952, Stella Marie Priestman (marr. diss.); one *s* two *d*].

PINSON, Barry; QC 1973; *b* 18 Dec. 1925; *s of* Thomas Alfred Pinson and Alice Cicily Pinsen; *m* 1950, Miriam Mary; one *s* one *d*; *m* 1977, Anne Kathleen Golby. *Educ:* King Edward's Sch., Birmingham; Univ. of Birmingham. LLB Hons 1945. Fellow Inst. Taxation. Mil. Service, 1944–47. Called to Bar, Gray's Inn, 1949, Bencher 1981. Trustee, RAF Museum, 1980–98; Chm., Addington Soc., 1987–90. *Publications:* Revenue Law, 17 edns. *Recreations:* music, theatre, photography. *T:* (020) 7798 8450.

PINTER, Rabbi Abraham, (Avraham); Principal, Yesodey Hatorah Schools, since 1994; Dean, Beer Miriam Seminary, since 2008; *b* London, 21 Jan. 1949; *s of* Rabbi Samuel Pinter and Gertrude Pinter; *m* 1971, Rachel, OBE (*d* 2014); two *s* five *d*. Mem. (Lab) Hackney BC, 1982–90. Chm., 1996–2015, Hon. Pres., 2015, Chizuk; Trustee, Union of Orthodox Hebrew Congregations, 1990– (Chm., External Affairs, 2015–); Chm., Ezer Lyoldos (Children and Families), 2016–. Founder Member: Jewish-Christian Forum of Stamford Hill; Muslim Jewish Forum; Chm., Orthodox Jewish Health Forum, Hackney. *Address:* 6 Northdene Gardens, N15 6LX. *T:* (020) 8826 5500, *Fax:* (020) 8826 5505. *E:* yeshatorah@aol.com.

PINTER, Lady Antonia; *see* Fraser, Antonia.

PINTER, Rabbi Avraham; *see* Pinter, Rabbi Abraham.

PINTO, Amanda Eve; QC 2006; a Recorder, since 2003; *b* 28 July 1960; *d of* John and Marigold Pinto; *m* 1987, Charles Spencer Porter; one *s* two *d*. *Educ:* St Paul's Girls' Sch., London; Gonville and Caius Coll., Cambridge (exhibnr; BA Law 1982; MA); Birkbeck Coll., London (Dip. Hist. of Art Distinction 1991). Called to the Bar, Middle Temple, 1983, Bencher, 2012; in practice as barrister, specialising in internat. corruption, fraud, money laundering, corporate and art crime. Dir, Internat. Affairs, Criminal Bar Assoc., 2007–13; Mem., Bar Council, 2015– (Vice Chair, 2019; Chair, 2020; Co-Chm., Internat. Rule of Law Panel, 2013–14; Chair, Internat. Cttee, 2015–); UK Rep., Internat. Criminal Bar Council, 2008–17. Trustee: Tate Members Council, 2013–16 (Dep. Chair, 2017–); Slynn Foundn, 2014–; Champion, First 100 Years, 2018–. *Publications:* (with M. Evans) Corporate Criminal Liability, 2003, 3rd edn 2013; (contrib. on corporate crime) Blackstone's Criminal Practice, 2011–; (contrib.) Smith, Owen and Bodnar on Asset Recovery, 2019. *Recreations:* art, theatre, walking my dog, ski-ing, travelling, baking cakes. *Address:* 33 Chancery Lane, WC2A 1EN. *T:* (020) 74409950. *E:* ap@33cllaw.com. *Club:* Hurlingham.

PIOT, Baron Prof. Peter, Hon. KCMG 2016 (Hon. CMG 2010); MD, PhD; FRCP, FMedSci; Professor of Global Health, and Director, London School of Hygiene and Tropical Medicine, since 2010; *b* Leuven, 17 Feb. 1949; *s of* René Piot and Joanna Pardon; *cr* Baron (Belgium) 1995; *m* 2012, Heidi Larson; two *s* one *d*. *Educ:* Koninklijk Atheneum Keerbergen; Univ. of Ghent (MD 1974); Univ. of Antwerp (PhD Microbiol. 1980). FRCP 2001. Asst Prof., Inst. of Tropical Medicine, Antwerp, 1974–92; Associate Prof., Univ. of Nairobi, 1986–87; Asst Dir, Global Prog. on AIDS, WHO, Geneva, 1992–94; Exec. Dir, UNAIDS and Under Sec. Gen., UN, Geneva, 1995–2008; Prof. of Global Health, Imperial Coll. London, 2009–10. Senior Fellow: Univ. of Washington, 1978–79; Gates Foundn, 2009. Chair, Strategic Coherence of ODA-funded Res. Bd, 2018–. FMedSci 2011. Hon. FFPH 2015. Mem., Royal Acad. of Medicine, Belgium, 1989; For. Mem., Nat. Acad. of Medicine (formerly Inst. of Medicine), NAS, 2000; Mem., German Nat. Acad. of Scis Leopoldina, 2018. Pres., King Baudouin Foundn, Brussels, 2007–11. Hideyo Noguchi Africa Prize for Med. Res., Japan, 2013; Prince Mahidol Award, 2014; Person of Year Award, Time, 2014; Canada Gairdner Global Health Award, 2015; Robert Koch Gold Medal, 2015; Prix Internat., Institut Nat. de la Santé et de la Recherche Médicale, 2015; Bloomberg Hopkins Centennial Award, 2016; Jimmy and Rosalynn Carter Humanitarian Award, 2017. Officer, Order of Leopard (Zaire), 1978; Commandeur: Ordre du Lion (Senegal), 2005; Nat. Order (Mali), 2008; Grand Official, Order of Henrique the Navigator (Portugal), 2007; Grand Cordon, Order of Rising Sun (Japan), 2018. *Publications:* Basic Laboratory Procedures in Clinical Bacteriology, 1991; Reproductive Tract Infections in Women, 1992; Aids in Africa: a handbook for physicians, 1992; L'Épidémie du Sida et la

Mondialisation des Risques, 2005; Sexually Transmitted Diseases, 2008; Over AIDS, 2009; Le Sida dans le Monde, 2011; No Time to Lose, 2012 (trans. Dutch, French, Japanese, Korean); AIDS: between science and politics, 2015 (trans. French, Japanese); over 580 scientific papers. *Address*: London School of Hygiene and Tropical Medicine, Keppel Street, WC1E 7HT. *E*: director@lshtm.ac.uk. *Club*: Athenæum.

**PIPE, Martin Charles**, CBE 2000; racehorse trainer, National Hunt and flat racing, 1977–2006; *b* 29 May 1945; *m* 1971, Mary Caroline; one *s*. First trainer's licence, 1977; first British trainer to saddle 200 winners in a season, 1989; trained more than 200 winners in a season 8 times, 1989–2006; fifteen times champion trainer, National Hunt, to 2005; holder of British record for jump winners trained with 3929 winners, 2014; trained 6 winners, Royal Ascot, 34 winners, Cheltenham Fest.; major wins include: Champion Hurdles, Granville Again, 1993, Make a Stand, 1997; Grand National, Miinnehoma, 1994; Welsh Grand National, five times; Hennessy Gold Cup, twice; Irish Hennessy Gold Cup; Mackeson Gold Cup, eight times. Hon. DSc Liverpool, 2007. *Publications*: (with Richard Pitman) Martin Pipe: the champion trainer's story, 1992. *Address*: Pond House, Nicholashayne, near Wellington, Somerset TA21 9QY.

**PIPER, Rev. Canon Clifford John**; Rector, St John the Evangelist, Forres, 2009–16 (Priest-in-charge, 2003–09); Dean of Moray, Ross and Caithness, 2009–14; *b* Tintagel, Cornwall, 8 April 1953; *s* of John Henry Piper and Lilian Mary Piper (*née* Knight); *m* 1974, Susan Ruth Greaves; one *s* one *d*. *Educ*: Aberdeen Univ. (Cert. Social Services); Theol Inst. of the Scottish Episcopal Church; Robert Gordon Univ. (Postgrad. Dip. Community Care). Principal Officer Social Work, then Area Social Work Manager Sutherland, Highland Council, 1983–98; ordained deacon, 1993, priest, 1994; Asst Curate, St Ninians, Invergordon, 1993–96; NSM, 1996–98, Priest-in-charge, 1998–2003, St Andrew's, Tain; Priest-in-charge, St Ninians, Invergordon, 2000–03; Canon, 2000–09, Hon. Canon, 2014–16, St Andrew's Cathedral, Inverness. Provincial Child Protection Officer, Scottish Episcopal Church, 1998–2000. *Recreations*: golf, walking, reading, information technology, horology, cooking, motorcycling. *Address*: 17 Craig Crescent, Tain, Ross-shire IV19 1JW. *T*: (01862) 892593. *E*: cliffpiper@hotmail.co.uk.

**PIPER, Rt Rev. Dr Reginald John**; Assistant Minister, St Michael's Anglican Cathedral, Wollongong, since 2010; Bishop of Wollongong, and an Assistant Bishop, Diocese of Sydney, 1993–2007; *b* 25 Feb. 1942; *s* of Leslie and Myra Elaine Piper; *m* 1967, Dorothy Patricia Lock; one *s* two *d* (and one *s* decd). *Educ*: Australian Nat. Univ. (BSc 1963); Moore Coll., Sydney (Theol. Schol. 1970); Melbourne Coll. of Divinity (BD 1975); Fuller Theol Seminary, LA (DMin 1992). Ordained deacon, 1966, priest, 1967; Curate: St Stephen's, Willoughby, 1966–69; St Clement's, Lalor Park, 1970–71; Rector: St Aidan's, Hurstville Grove, 1972–75; Christ Church, Kiama, 1975–79; Holy Trinity, Adelaide, 1980–93; St Paul's Anglican Ch, Gymea, 2007–10. *Publications*: The Ephesus Plan, 1998; Forty Days with the Risen Lord, 2005; The Ephesus Code, 2006; Ephesus and the New Humanity, 2010; From Rome with Love, 2013; The Life and Labours of Paul, 2016. *Address*: 111/201 Pioneer Road, Fairy Meadow, NSW 2519, Australia.

**PIPER, Thomas Stephen Towry**, MBE 2015; freelance theatre designer, since 1990; *b* London, 24 Nov. 1964; *s* of Sir David Towry Piper, CBE and of Anne Horatia Piper (*née* Richmond); *m* 1992, Caroline Rohais Millar; five *d*. *Educ*: Magdalen Coll. Sch., Oxford; Trinity Coll., Cambridge (Schol.; BA Art Hist.); Slade Sch. of Art (MA Th. Design). Associate Designer, RSC, 2004–14; designer: Histories Cycle, RSC, 2008 (jtly) Olivier Award for Best Costume Design); A Midsummer Night's Dream, RSC, 2016. Designer: (with A. Farlie) BM exhibn, Shakespeare, staging the world, 2012; (with P. Cummins) Blood Swept Lands and Seas of Red installation, Tower of London, 2014. Hon. Fellow, RWCMD, 2015. *Recreations*: cycling, theatre, photography, exhibitions, family. *Address*: 17 Lordship Park, N16 5UN. *T*: (020) 8802 2833. *E*: tom@tompiperdesign.co.uk.

**PIRANI, Rohan Carl**; Regional Employment Judge (South West), since 2018; *b* Bristol, 2 Oct. 1969; *s* of Mohamed and Roslyn Pirani; *m* 2007, Anna; two *s*. *Educ*: Birkenhead Sch.; Wadham Coll., Oxford (MA Juris 1991; BCL 1992); Univ. of Toronto (LLM 1993). Called to the Bar, Middle Temple, 1995; Mem., Old Square Chambers, 1996–2013. Fee-paid Employment Judge, 2005–13; Salaried Employment Judge, 2013–18; Dep. Chair, Central Arbitration Cttee, 2016. *Recreations*: mountain climbing, hill walking. *Address*: Bristol Civil and Family Justice Centre, 2 Redcliff Street, Bristol BS1 6GR.

**PIRIE, Madsen (Duncan)**, PhD; President, Adam Smith Institute, since 1977; *b* 24 Aug. 1940; *s* of Douglas Gordon Pirie and Eva (*née* Madsen). *Educ*: Univ. of Edinburgh (MA Hons 1970); Univ. of St Andrews (PhD 1974); MPhil Cantab 1997. Distinguished Vis. Prof. of Philosophy, Hillsdale Coll., Michigan, 1975–78; Sen. Vis. Fellow in Land Economy, Univ. of Cambridge, 2010–. Mem., Adv. Panel on Citizen's Charter, 1991–95. (Jtly) Nat. Free Enterprise Award, 2010. *Publications*: Trial and Error and the Idea of Progress, 1978, 2nd edn 2015; The Book of the Fallacy, 1985; Privatization, 1988; Micropolitics, 1988; (with Eamonn Butler) The Sherlock Holmes IQ Book, 1995; How to Win Every Argument, 2006; Children of the Night, 2007; Dark Visitor, 2007; The Waters of Andros, 2007; Freedom 101, 2008; Zero Base Policy, 2009; 101 Great Philosophers, 2009; The Emerald Warriors, 2011; Economics Made Simple, 2012; Think Tank: the story of the Adam Smith Institute, 2012; Tree Boy, 2012; Team Games, 2013; Why Liberty Works, 2014; Silver Dawn, 2014; Communications Command 1: Spelthorpe, 2016; Britain and the World in 2050, 2016. *Recreations*: calligraphy, cooking, motion pictures, science fiction. *Address*: Adam Smith Institute, 23 Great Smith Street, SW1P 3BL. *W*: www.madsen-pirie.com. *Clubs*: Oxford and Cambridge, East India, City University.

**PIRMOHAMED, Sir Munir**, Kt 2015; PhD; FRCP, FRCPE; FBPhS; FMedSci; FRSB; NHS Chair of Pharmacogenetics, since 2007, Director, Wolfson Centre for Personalised Medicine, since 2009, David Weatherall Professor of Medicine, since 2013, and Director, MRC Centre for Drug Safety Science, since 2014, University of Liverpool; Hon. Consultant Physician, Royal Liverpool University Hospital, since 1996; Executive Director, Liverpool Health Partners, 2015–18; *b* Ngora, Uganda, 29 Aug. 1962; *s* of Mohamedali and Malek Pirmohamed; *m* 1989, Jacqueline Anne Clark; two *s*. *Educ*: Univ. of Liverpool (MB ChB Hons 1985; PhD 1993). MRCP 1988, FRCP 2000; FRCPE 1999; FBPhS (FBPharmacolS 2004). University of Liverpool: MRC Trng Fellow, 1989–92; Sen. Clin. Res. Fellow, 1992–94; Lectr, 1994–95, Sen. Lectr, 1996–2000, Reader, 2000–01, Dept of Pharmacol.; Prof. of Clin. Pharmacol., 2001–13; Associate Exec. Pro Vice Chancellor (Clin. Res.), 2013–18. Sir Desmond Pond Fellow, Epilepsy Res. Foundn, 1992–95. Rand Lectr, British Pharmacol Soc., 2007; Dr Andrew Duncan Lect. and Medal, RCPE, 2016. Non-exec. Dir, NHS England, 2019–. Dir, Mersey Yellow Card Centre for Adverse Drug Reaction Monitoring, 1995–. Mem., Commn on Human Medicines, 2005–. Chair, Pharmacovigilance Expert Adv. Gp, 2006–. Mem., Cttee on Safety of Medicines, 2002–05 (Mem., Sub-cttee on Pharmacovigilance, 1996–2005). Pres., British Pharmacol Soc., Jan. 2020– (Chm., Clin. Section Cttee, 2012–18). Mem., UKRI-MRC, 2018–. MAE 2016. FMedSci 2013; FRSB 2018. Hon. FFPM 2017. British Assoc. of Pharmaceutical Physicians Prize, 1994, GSK Clin. Travelling Prize, 2002, British Pharmacol Soc.; Inaugural NIHR Sen. Investigator Award, 2008; William Withering Medal, RCP, 2010; IPIT Award for Public Service, Univ. of N Carolina, 2011; Stanley Davidson Lect. and Medal, RCPE, 2019. *Publications*: (ed) Textbook of Pharmacogenetics, 2006; contrib. articles on clin. pharmacol., drug safety and genetics to med. and scientific jls. *Recreations*: family, Arsenal Football Club, fast cars, movies. *Address*: Department of Molecular and Clinical Pharmacology, University of Liverpool, Liverpool L69 3GL. *T*: (0151) 794 5549. *E*: munirp@liverpool.ac.uk.

**PIRNIE, Graham John Campbell**; HM Diplomatic Service, retired; Counsellor and Deputy Head of Mission, Abu Dhabi, 1998–2001; *b* 9 Aug. 1941; *s* of late Ian Campbell Pirnie and of Emily Elizabeth Pirnie; *m* 1st, 1967, Kathleen Gunstone (marr. diss. 2001); two *s* one *d*; 2nd, 2001, Dora Ines Guerrero Velez. *Educ*: Surbiton Grammar Sch.; Birmingham Univ. (BSocSc). Graduate VSO, 1963–64; joined Foreign and Commonwealth Office, 1965: Information Res. Dept, 1965; FCO, 1966–68; Third Sec. and Vice Consul, Phnom Penh, 1968–70; Commercial Officer, Paris, 1970–74; Second Sec. (Commercial), The Hague, 1974–77; FCO, 1977–82; First Sec. and Consul, Geneva, 1982–86; JSDC 1986; FCO, 1986–89; Dep. Head of Mission and Consul, Quito, 1989–93; FCO, 1993–95; Ambassador to Paraguay, 1995–98. *Recreations*: town and country walking, natural history, antique/vintage clock restoration, reading, current affairs, ski-ing. *E*: graham.pirnie@btinternet.com.

**PIRNIE, Rear Adm. Ian Hugh**, CB 1992; DL; Chairman, Morecambe Bay Health Authority, 1994–2002; *b* 17 June 1935; *s* of late Hugh Pirnie, KPM and Linda Pirnie; *m* 1958, Sally Patricia (*née* Duckworth); three *d*. *Educ*: Christ's Hosp., Horsham; Pembroke Coll., Cambridge (MA). CEng 1986; FIEE 1986. Qualified in submarines, 1964; post-graduate educn, RMCS, Shrivenham, 1964–65, US Guided Missile Sch., Dam Neck, VA, 1966; sea service in aircraft carrier HMS Bulwark, destroyers HMS Finistere and HMS Antrim, and submarines HMS Resolution and HMS Repulse; Dir, Naval Officer Appts (Engrs), 1984–86; commanded RNEC, Manadon, Plymouth as ADC, 1986–88; Chief, Strategic Systems Exec., MoD (in overall charge of Trident procurement prog.), 1988–93, RN retd, 1993. Chairman: Furness Enterprise Ltd, 1993–2000; Ashworth High Security Hosp., 1999; non-executive Director: Cumbria Ambulance Service, 1992–94; Cumbria and Lancs Strategic Health Authy, 2002–06. Trustee, Francis C. Scott Charitable Trust, 1993–2011. DL Cumbria, 2000. *Recreations*: family, fell walking, opera, classical music, topiary.

**PIRRIE, David Blair**, FCIB; Director of International and Private Banking, Lloyds Bank Plc, 1992–97; *b* 15 Dec. 1938; *s* of John and Sylvia Pirrie; *m* 1966, Angela Sellos; three *s* one *d*. *Educ*: Strathallan Sch., Perthshire; Harvard Business Sch. (Management Develt). FCIB 1987. Lloyds Bank: Gen. Man., Brazil, 1975–81; Dir, Lloyds Bank International, 1981–83; Gen. Man., Gp HQ, 1983–85; Sen. Dir, Internat. Banking, 1985–87; Sen. Gen. Man., UK Retail Banking, 1987–89; Dir, UK Retail Banking, 1989–92. *Recreations*: golf, theatre, music.

**PISSARIDES, Sir Christopher (Antoniou)**, Kt 2013; PhD; FBA 2002; School Professor of Economics and Political Science, since 2012, and Regius Professor of Economics, since 2013, London School of Economics and Political Science (Professor of Economics, since 1986; Norman Sosnow Professor of Economics, 2006–12); *b* 20 Feb. 1948; *s* of Antonios and Evdokia Pissarides; *m* 1986, Francesca Michela Cassano (marr. diss. 2009); one *s* one *d*; *m* 2011, Liwa (Rachel) Ngai; one *s*. *Educ*: Essex Univ. (BA Econs 1970, MA Econs 1971); London Sch. of Econs and Pol Sci. (PhD 1974). Central Bank of Cyprus, 1974; Lectr, Univ. of Southampton, 1974–76; London School of Economics: Lectr, 1976–82; Reader, 1982–86; Prog. Dir, Centre for Econ. Performance, 1999–2007. Prof. of Eur. Studies, Univ. of Cyprus, 2013–; Helmut and Anna Pao Sohmen Prof. at Large, Inst. of Advanced Study, Univ. of Sci. and Technol., Hong Kong, 2013–; Pres., Growth Lab., St Petersburg State Univ., 2013–. Mem., Employment Taskforce, EC, 2003–04. Research Fellow: Centre for Economic Policy Res., London, 1994–; Inst. for Study of Labor (IZA), Bonn, 2001– (Prize in Labor Econs jtly), 2005). Associate Ed., Economica, 1996–2012 (Chm. Bd, 2007–12); Mem., Editl Bd, AEJ Macroeconomics, 2007–17. Specialist Advr, Treasury Cttee, H of C, 2001–05. Chm., Council of Nat. Economy, Cyprus, 2013–18; Mem., Monetary Policy Cttee, Central Bank of Cyprus, 2000–07. Member Council: REconS, 1996–2003; Econometric Soc., 2005–10; Eur. Econ. Assoc., 2005–12 (Pres., 2011). Mem., Interim Governing Bd, Univ. of Cyprus, 1989–95. Fellow: Econometric Soc., 1997; Soc. of Labor Economists, 2008; Academia Europaea; Acad. of Athens 2016. For. Hon. Mem., AEA, 2011. Hon. Dr: Cyprus, 2009; Athens Univ. of Econs, 2011; Essex, 2012; San Marcos Nat. Univ., Peru, 2014; San Antonio Abal del Cusco, Peru, 2015. Aristeion Award, Republic of Cyprus, 2008; (jtly) Nobel Prize in Economics, 2010; Gold Medal, Historical Soc. of TCD, 2012; Global Economy Prize, Kiel Inst. of World Economy, 2015. Grand Cross of Republic of Cyprus, 2011; Caballero, Congress of Republic of Peru, 2015. *Publications*: Labour Market Adjustment, 1976; Equilibrium Unemployment Theory, 1990, 2nd edn 2000; (jtly) After the Crisis: the way ahead, 2010; (with Dale T. Mortensen) Job Matching, Wage Dispersion and Unemployment, 2011; (jtly) Greece: beyond austerity, 2017; contribs to professional jls, conf. proc. and ed books. *Recreations*: cooking, gardening, walking. *Address*: London School of Economics and Political Science, Houghton Street, WC2A 2AE. *T*: (020) 7955 7513, *Fax*: (020) 7955 6092. *E*: c.pissarides@lse.ac.uk.

**PISTORIUS, Prof. Carl Wilhelm Irene, (Calie)**, CEng, FIET; Chief Executive, DeltaHedron Ltd, since 2017; *b* Pretoria, S Africa, 9 Aug. 1958; *s* of Carl Wilhelm Irene Pistorius and Iolanthé Pistorius (*née* Tancred); *m* 2005, Michèle Emily Olivier; two *d* by a previous marriage. *Educ*: High Sch., Menlo Park, Pretoria; Univ. of Pretoria (BSc(Eng) cum laude 1979; BEng Hons cum laude 1981); Ohio State Univ. (MS 1984; PhD 1986); Massachusetts Inst. of Technol. (SM 1994); Harvard Business Sch. (AMP 2003). CEng 2010; FIET 2010. University of Pretoria: Hd, Dept of Electrical and Electronic Engrg, 1989–94; Dir, Inst. for Technol Innovation, 1994–98; Dir, Inf. Technol., 1998–99; Dean, Faculty of Engrg, Built Envmt and Inf. Technol., 2000–01; Vice-Chancellor and Principal, 2001–09; Vice-Chancellor, Univ. of Hull, 2009–17. Fellow: S African Acad. of Engrg, 1999; S African Inst. of Electrical Engrs, 2002; FRSSAf 2002. *Publications*: (jtly) Introduction to the Uniform Geometrical Theory of Diffraction, 1990; articles in IEEE Trans on antennas and propagation research policy, technol forecasting, social change and innovation mgt. *Address*: DeltaHedron Ltd, 31–38 Queen Street, Hull HU1 1UU. *T*: 07540 671295. *E*: calie.pistorius@deltahedron.co.uk.

**PITA, Arthur**; choreographer; Artistic Director, Arthur Pita Productions, since 2003; *b* Johannesburg, SA, 21 Feb. 1972; *s* of Francisco Alberto Pita and Teresinha Delgado Pita; partner, Sir Matthew Christopher Bourne, qv. *Educ*: Johannesburg Art, Ballet, Drama and Music Sch. (matriculation); London Contemporary Dance Sch. (MA Dance and Choreography). Associate Artist: The Place, 2003–05; Jerwood DanceHouse DanceEast, 2013–15. *Choreographic works* include: Snow White in Black, Phoenix Dance Th., 2006; Mischief, in collaboration with Theatre Rites, 2007 (TMA Th. Award for Achievement in Dance, 2008); The Metamorphosis, Linbury Studio Th., Royal Opera House, 2011 (Critics' Circle Nat. Dance Award for Best Modern Choreography, 2012; South Bank Sky Arts Award, 2012); La Donna del Lago, ROH, 2013; (also Dir) Nobody's Baby - The World's Greatest Show, ROH, 2014; Carmen, ROH, 2015; The Little Match Girl, Lilian Baylis Studio, 2015; Rise and Fall of the City of Mahagonny, ROH, 2015; Run Mary Run (for Natalia Osipova), 2016; Cristaux, Ballet Black, Barbican Centre, 2016; The Wind, Royal Ballet, Covent Garden, 2017; The Little Match Girl, Dance City

Newcastle, 2017; Björk Ballet, War Meml Opera House, San Francisco, 2018; The Mother, Queen Elizabeth Hall, 2019. *Recreations:* travel, music, film, dog lover, nature. *Address:* Church Cottage, St Mary's Path, N1 2RR. *T:* 07940 548201. *E:* arthurpita@mac.com. *W:* www.arthurpita.com.

**PITCHER, Sir Desmond (Henry),** Kt 1992; CEng, FIET, FBCS; Chairman, United Utilities (formerly North West Water Group), 1993–98 (Director, 1990–98; Deputy Chairman, 1991–93); *b* 23 March 1935; *s* of George Charles and Alice Marion Pitcher; *m* 1st, 1961 (marr. diss.); twin *d*, 2nd, 1978 (marr. diss.); two *s*, 3rd, 1991, Norma Barbara Niven. *Educ:* Liverpool Coll. of Technology. MIEEE (USA). A. V. Roe & Co., Develt Engr, 1955; Automatic Telephone and Elec. Co. (now Plessey), Systems Engr, 1958; Univac Remington Rand (now Sperry Rand Ltd), Systems Engr, 1961; Sperry Univac: Dir, Systems, 1966; Managing Dir, 1971; Vice-Pres., 1974; Dir, Sperry Rand, 1971–76, Dep. Chm., 1974–76; Man. Dir, Leyland Truck and Bus Ltd, 1976–78; Dir, British Leyland, 1976–78; Man. Dir, Plessey Telecommunications and Office Systems, 1978–83; Dir, Plessey Co., 1979–83; Director: The Littlewoods Orgn, 1983–95 (Gp Chief Exec., 1983–93; Vice-Chm., 1993–95); National Westminster Bank, 1994–98 (Mem., Northern Adv. Bd, 1989–92). Chm. & Dir, Signbrick Ltd, 2001–12; Dir, Steeltower Ltd, 2001–05. Chairman: Mersey Barrage Co., 1986–96; Merseyside Develt Corp., 1991–98; Westminster Green Management Co. Ltd, 2010–. Pres., NW Chambers of Commerce, 1994–98. Vis. Prof. of Business Policy, Univ. of Manchester, 1993–98. Faraday Lectures, The Social Computer, IEE, 1974–75. Dir, CEI, 1979; Pres., TEMA, 1981–83. Dep. Chm., Everton Football Club, 1990–98 (Dir, 1987–98); Chm., Royal Liverpool Philharmonic Soc. Develt Trust, 1992–2005. Mem., Twickenham Regeneration Adv. Panel, Richmond upon Thames LBC, 2011–13. Chm. and Trustee, Rocking Horse Appeal, Royal Liverpool Children's NHS Trust, 1996–2005; Trustee, Outward Bound, 2005–07. DL Merseyside, 1992–99. Freeman, City of London, 1987; Liveryman, Co. of Information Technologists, 1992–. CCMI; FRIAS; FRSA 1987; Hon. FIDE; Hon. Fellow, Liverpool John Moores Univ., 1993. Knight, Order of St Hubert (Austria), 1991. *Publications:* Institution of Electrical Engineers Faraday Lectures, 1974–75; Water Under the Bridge: 30 years in industrial management (autobiog.), 2003; various lectures on social implications of computers and micro-electronics. *Recreations:* golf, music. *Address:* Pill Heath Place, Pill Heath, Andover, Hants SP11 0JG. *E:* desmondpitcher@aol.com. *Clubs:* Brooks's, Royal Automobile, Carlton; Royal Birkdale Golf; Royal Liverpool; Lancs CC.

**PITCHER, Rev. George Martell;** Chairman, Bridgit Group Ltd, since 2007; Editor-in-Chief, International Business Times UK, 2014–16; *b* Sherborne, Dorset, 30 May 1955; *s* of George Thomas Pitcher and Mary Pitcher (née Brownscombe); *m* 1985, Lynda Caire Silvana Mobbs; three *s* one *d*. *Educ:* Blundell's Sch., Devon; Birmingham Univ. (BA Hons Drama and Th. Arts); N Thames Ministerial Trng Course, Middx Univ. (BA Hons Theol.). Journalist, Haymarket Publishing Ltd, 1980–83; Man. Dir, BH Pubns Ltd, 1983–85; financial journalist, 1985–88, Industrial Ed., 1988–91, The Observer; Contributing Ed. and columnist, Mktg Week, 1988–2005; Luther Pendragon: Co-founder and Dir, 1992–95; Chief Exec., 1995–2000; Partner, 2000–05; Religion Ed. and columnist, Daily Telegraph, 2008–10; Sec. for Public Affairs to Archbp of Canterbury, 2010–11. Non-exec. Chm. and co-founder, Jericho Chambers, 2013–17. Contrib., Daily Mail, 2011–13; Associate Ed., Newsweek Europe, 2015 (Contrib. Ed., 2014–15); Hd, Editl Panel, IBT Media, 2014–15. Ordained deacon, 2005, priest, 2006; Curate, Dio. of London, 2005–08; Associate Priest, St Bride's, Fleet St, 2008–12; Chaplain, Guild of St Bride's, 2013–; non-stipendiary Priest-in-charge, Waldron, E Sussex, 2013–. Ext. Examiner, Univ. of Westminster, 2013–15. Vis. Fellow, LSE, 2018–. Governor: Battle Abbey Sch., 2011–19; Cross in Hand C of E Primary Sch., 2013–. Nat. Newspaper Industrial Journalist of Year, Industrial Soc., 1991. *Publications:* The Death of Spin, 2003; A Time to Live: the case against euthanasia and assisted suicide, 2010; A Dark Nativity (novel), 2017. *Recreations:* Sussex, pilgrimage, donkeys, woods, writing, theology. *Clubs:* Garrick, Lansdowne.

**PITCHERS, Hon. Sir Christopher (John),** Kt 2002; a Judge of the High Court, Queen's Bench Division, 2002–08; Commissioner, Royal Court of Jersey, 2008–17; *b* 2 Oct. 1942; *s* of late Thomas Pitchers and Melissa Pitchers; *m* 1965, Judith Stevenson, MBE (*d* 2006); two *s*. *Educ:* Uppingham Sch.; Worcester Coll., Oxford. MA. Called to the Bar, Inner Temple, 1965, Bencher, 1996; a Recorder, 1981–86; a Circuit Judge, 1986–2002. Dir of Studies, Judicial Studies Bd, 1996–97 (Mem., Criminal Cttee, 1991–95; Jt Dir, 1995–96). Hon. Sec., Council of HM Circuit Judges, 1992–95 (Pres., 1999). Vice-Pres., NACRO, 1994–2002. Hon. Vis. Prof., Nottingham Law Sch., 2008. Hon. LLD De Montfort, 2002.

**PITKEATHLEY,** family name of **Baroness Pitkeathley**.

**PITKEATHLEY,** Baroness *cr* 1997 (Life Peer), of Caversham in the Royal co. of Berkshire; **Jill Elizabeth Pitkeathley,** OBE 1993; Chair, Professional Standards Authority for Health and Social Care (formerly Council for Healthcare Regulatory Excellence), 2009–15; President, National Council for Voluntary Organisations; *b* 4 Jan. 1940; *d* of Roland Wilfred Bisson and Edith May Bisson (née Muston); *m* 1st, 1961, W. Pitkeathley (marr. diss. 1978); one *s* one *d*; 2nd, 2008, (John) David Emerson, *qv*. *Educ:* Ladies' Coll., Guernsey; Bristol Univ. (BA Econ). Social worker, 1961–64; Voluntary Service Co-ordinator, Manchester and Essex, 1970–83; Nat. Consumer Council, 1983–86; Dir, Nat. Council for Carers, 1986 until merger with Assoc. of Carers, 1988; Chief Exec., Carers Nat. Assoc., 1988–98; Chm., New Opportunities Fund, 1998–2004. Advr to Griffiths' Rev. of Community Care, 1986–88; Mem., Health Adv. Service, 1993–97; Chm. Adv. Gp, 1999–2000, Interim Chair, 2001–02, Gen. Social Care Council; Chair: Children and Families Court Adv. and Support Service, 2004–08; Adv. Panel on Futurebuilders, 2005–08; Adv. Body, Office of the Third Sector, Cabinet Office, 2008–11. Chair, Select Cttee on Charities, H of L, 2016–17. Dir, Big Society Trust, 2011– (Chm., 2015–18). President: Community Council for Berks, 1998–2013 (Vice-Pres., 1990–98); Volunteering England (formerly Nat. Centre for Volunteering), 2002; Vice Pres., Carers UK, 2003–; Pres., Eurocarers, 2007–11. Patron, Bracknell CVS. Mem. Bd of Governors, Nat. Inst. of Social Work, 1995–98. Trustee, Cumberland Lodge, 2011–. Hon. LLD: Bristol, 2002; London Metropolitan, 2002. *Publications:* When I Went Home, 1978; Mobilising Voluntary Resources, 1982; Volunteers in Hospitals, 1984; Supporting Volunteers, 1985; It's my duty, isn't it?, 1989; (with David Emerson) The Only Child, 1992; (with David Emerson) Age Gap Relationships, 1994; Cassandra and Jane: a personal journey through the lives of the Austen sisters, 2004; Dearest Cousin Jane: the story of Jane Austen's cousin, 2010. *Recreations:* gardening, grand-children, writing. *T:* (office) (020) 7219 0358.
*See also* C. M. Wilson.

**PITMAN, Rt Rev. Cyrus Clement James;** Bishop of Newfoundland, Eastern, and Labrador, 2004–13; *b* 24 March 1944; *s* of John and Ella Pitman; *m* 1968, Mary (née Lee); three *s* one *d*. *Educ:* Newfoundland Meml Univ. (BA); Queen's Coll., Newfoundland (LTh). Ordained deacon, 1967, priest, 1968; Curate, Channel, 1967–70; Incumbent, Flower's Cove, 1970–75; Rector, Meadows, 1975–80; Dir of Prog., Dio. W Newfoundland, 1980–82; Curate, St Mary the Virgin, St John's, 1982–87; Rector: Petty Harbour, 1987–90; St Paul, Goulds, Kilbride, 1990–93; All Saints, Conception Bay S, 1993–2000; St Mary the Virgin, St John's, 2000–03; Archdeacon, Avalon E and W, 2002–03; Exec. Archdeacon and Admin. Asst to Bishop of Eastern Newfoundland and Labrador, 2003–04. Regl Dean, Avalon W, 1990; Canon, Stall of St Columba, 1997. *Address:* c/o Synod Office, 19 King's Bridge Road, St John's, NL A1C 3K4, Canada. *T:* (709) 5766697, *Fax:* (709) 5767122. *E:* cpitman@anglicanenl.net.

**PITMAN, His Honour David Christian;** a Circuit Judge, 1986–2006; a Deputy Circuit Judge, 2006–08; *b* 1 Dec. 1936; 3rd *s* of Sir (Isaac) James Pitman, KBE, and Hon. Margaret Beaufort Pitman (née Lawson Johnston); *m* 1971, Christina Mary Malone-Lee; one *s* two *d*. *Educ:* Eton Coll.; Christ Church, Oxford (BA (PPE) 1961, MA 1964). Editorial role in publishing books in Initial Teaching Alphabet, 1960–63; called to Bar, Middle Temple, 1963; commenced practice, 1964; Asst Recorder, 1982; Recorder, 1986. National Service: 2nd Lieut, 60th Rifles, 1955–57; Territorial Army: Lieut Queen's Westminsters, KRRC, 1957–61; Captain, then Major, Queen's Royal Rifles (TA), 1961–67; Major, 5th (T) Bn RGJ, 1967–69. *Recreations:* music, the open air. *Address:* c/o The Crown Court, Snaresbrook, Hollybush Hill, E11 1QW.

**PITMAN, Jennifer Susan,** OBE 1998; professional racehorse trainer (National Hunt), 1975–99; *b* 11 June 1946; *d* of George and Mary Harvey; *m* 1st, 1965, Richard Pitman (marr. diss.); two *s*; 2nd, 1997, David Stait. *Educ:* Sarson Secondary Girls' School. Dir, Jenny Pitman Racing Ltd, 1975–99; Partner, DJS Racing, 1996. Training of major race winners includes: Midlands National, 1977 (Watafella), 1990 (Willsford); Massey Ferguson Gold Cup, Cheltenham, 1980 (Bueche Giorod); Welsh National, 1982 (Corbiere), 1983 (Burrough Hill Lad), 1986 (Stearsby); Grand National, 1983 (Corbiere), 1995 (Royal Athlete); Mildmay/Cazalet Gold Cup, 1983 (Burrough Hill Lad), 1986 (Stearsby), 1993 (Superior Finish); Cheltenham Gold Cup, 1984 (Burrough Hill Lad), 1991 (Garrison Savannah); King George VI Gold Cup, 1984 (Burrough Hill Lad); Hennessy Gold Cup, Newbury, 1984 (Burrough Hill Lad); Whitbread Trophy, 1985 (Smith's Man); Ritz Club Chase, Cheltenham, 1987 (Gainsay); Philip Cornes Saddle of Gold Final, Newbury, 1988 (Crumpet Delite); Welsh Champion Hurdle, 1991 (Wonderman), 1992 (Don Valentino); Scottish National, 1995 (Willsford). Piper Heidsieck Trainer of the Year, 1983/84, 1989/90. *Publications:* Glorious Uncertainty (autobiog.), 1984; Jenny Pitman: the autobiography, 1998; *novels:* On the Edge, 2002; Double Deal, 2002; The Dilemma, 2003; The Vendetta, 2004; The Inheritance, 2005. *Address:* Owl's Barn, Kintbury, Hungerford, Berks RG17 9SX. *Club:* International Sporting.

**PITMAN, Joanna Beaufort;** author and journalist; consultant on Japanese affairs; *b* London, 29 Sept. 1963; *d* of late Peter Pitman and Jenny Pitman; *m* 1st, 1996, Giles Worsley (*d* 2006); three *d*; 2nd, 2011, (Anthony) Patrick (Mycroft) Beeley. *Educ:* Westminster Sch.; St John's Coll., Cambridge (BA Japanese Studies 1986). Staff writer: Euromoney mag., 1987–88; Internat. Financing Review mag., 1988–89; The Times: Tokyo Bureau Chief, 1989–93; columnist and feature writer, London, 1993–2010; Exec., Hakluyt & Co., 2010–12. Trustee: Somerset House, 2009–16; Great Britain Sasakawa Foundn, 2010–17 (Vice Chair, 2018–); John Kobal Foundn, 2009–19; SAIDIA Kenya, 2016–; Dir, Baillie Gifford Japan Trust, 2018–. *Publications:* On Blondes, 2003; The Raphael Trail, 2006. *Recreations:* family, art, architecture, cooking. *Address:* c/o A. P. Watt, 12–26 Lexington Street, W1F 0LE.

**PITT, Brad;** *see* Pitt, W. B.

**PITT, Joanna;** *see* Read, J.

**PITT, Sir Michael (Edward),** Kt 2005; DL; CEng, FICE; Chairman, Pharmaceutical Services Negotiating Committee, since 2015; *b* 2 Feb. 1949; *s* of Albert and Doris Joan Pitt; *m* 1969, Anna Maria Di Claudio; two *d*. *Educ:* University College London (first class Hons BSc Engrg). CEng 1974; FICE 1989. Civil Servant, 1970–72; motorway design and construction, 1972–75; transportation planner in private sector and local govt, 1975–80; Asst County Surveyor, Northumberland, 1980–84; Dir of Property Services and Dir of Tech. Services, Humberside CC, 1984–90; Chief Executive: Cheshire CC, 1990–97; Kent CC, 1997–2005; Swindon BC, 2005–06; Chairman: South West Strategic HA, 2006–09; Infrastructure Planning Commn, 2009–12; Chair and Chief Exec., Planning Inspectorate, 2011–14; Chm., Legal Services Bd, 2014–18. DL Wilts, 2009. *Publications:* papers in technical jls. *Recreations:* family life, walking, bridge, choir, cycling, the voluntary sector.

**PITT, William Bradley, (Brad);** actor; *b* Shawnee, Oklahoma, 18 Dec. 1963; *s* of Bill Pitt and Jane Pitt (née Hillhouse); *m* 2000, Jennifer Aniston (marr. diss. 2005); *m* 2014, Angelina Jolie (marr. diss. 2019); one *s* two *d* (incl. twin *s* and *d*) and two adopted *s* one adopted *d*. *Educ:* Univ. of Missouri. *Films* include: as actor: Cutting Class, Happy Together, 1989; Across the Tracks, Thelma & Louise, Johnny Suede, 1991; Contact, Cool World, A River Runs Through It, 1992; Kalifornia, True Romance, 1993; The Favor, Interview with the Vampire, Legends of the Fall, 1994; Se7en, 1995; Twelve Monkeys, Sleepers, 1996; The Devil's Own, Seven Years in Tibet, The Dark Side of the Sun, 1997; Meet Joe Black, Fight Club, 1999; Snatch, 2000; The Mexican, Spy Game, 2001; Ocean's Eleven, 2002; Confessions of a Dangerous Mind, Full Frontal, 2003; Troy, 2004; Ocean's Twelve, Mr & Mrs Smith, 2005; Babel, 2006; Ocean's Thirteen, The Assassination of Jesse James by the Coward Robert Ford (also prod.) (Best Actor, Venice Film Fest.), 2007; Burn After Reading, 2008; The Curious Case of Benjamin Button, Inglourious Basterds, 2009; The Tree of Life, Moneyball, 2011 (also prod.); Killing Them Softly, 2012; World War Z (also prod.), 12 Years a Slave (also prod.), The Counsellor, 2013; Fury, 2014; By the Sea, 2015; The Big Short, Allied, 2016; War Machine, 2017; Ad Astra (also prod.), Once Upon a Time in Hollywood, 2019; as producer: God Grew Tired of Us, The Departed, Running with Scissors, 2006; Year of the Dog, The Tehuacan Project, A Mighty Heart, 2007; Pretty/Handsome, 2008; The Private Lives of Pippa Lee, 2009; television includes: as actor: Dallas, 1987–88; The Image, 1990; Glory Days (series), 1990; Freedom: a history of Us (series), 2003; Rx for Survival: a global health challenge (series), 2005. *Address:* c/o Creative Artists Agency, 2000 Avenue of the Stars, Los Angeles, CA 90067, USA.

**PITT, William F.;** *see* Fox-Pitt.

**PITT-BROOKE, John Stephen,** CB 2009; Chief Executive, Forces Pension Society, 2015–18; *b* 9 Sept. 1950; *s* of late Reginald Pitt-Brooke and Hilda (née Wright); *m* 1st, 1986, Rosalind (*d* 1996), *d* of late Prof. William Mulligan; two *s*; 2nd, 1999, Frances Way, *d* of B. T. McDade. *Educ:* Salford Grammar Sch.; Queens' Coll., Cambridge (MA). MoD, 1971–74; NI Office, 1974–77; Private Sec. to Minister of State for NI, 1975–77; MoD, 1978; NATO Defence Coll., 1980; Private Sec. to Permanent Under Sec., MoD, 1984–87; Cabinet Office, 1988–89; Ministry of Defence, 1989–2011: Head of Industrial Relns Div., 1989–92; Private Sec. to Sec. of State for Defence, 1992–94; Comd Sec., Land Comd, 1995–98; Fellow, Center for Internat. Affairs, Harvard Univ., 1998–99; Director General: Corporate Communications, 1999–2001; Civilian Personnel, 2001–04; Media and Communications, 2005–06; Secretariat, 2006–10; Hd, Civilian Review Team, 2010–11; Project Dir, Standard Life Charitable Trust, 2011–13. *Recreations:* family life, literature, Salisbury Cathedral, Manchester City Football Club. *Club:* MCC.

**PITT-RIVERS, Valerie**, CVO 2014; Lord-Lieutenant of Dorset, 2006–14 (Vice Lord-Lieutenant, 1999–2006); *b* 23 Jan. 1939; *d* of Derek and Eva Scott; *m* 1964, George Anthony Lane-Fox Pitt-Rivers, OBE, DL. *Educ*: Prior's Field, Godalming. Advertising and public relns, 1957–63; worked for NHS, charities and the arts in Dorset, 1970–. Non-exec. Dir and Vice Chm., W Dorset Gen. Hosps NHS Trust, 1991–98. Founder, 1987, Chm., 1987–98, Arts in Hospital Project for NHS, Dorchester. Pro Chancellor, Bournemouth Univ., 2014–19. DL Dorset, 1995. CStJ 2007. *Recreations*: gardens, opera. *Address*: Manor House, Hinton St Mary, Sturminster Newton, Dorset DT10 1NA.

**PITT-WATSON, David James**; Visiting Fellow, Judge Business School, Cambridge University, since 2019; *b* Aberdeen, 23 Sept. 1956; *s* of Ian Robertson Pitt-Watson and Helen Maud Pitt-Watson (*née* McCall); *m* 1989, Ursula Barnes; one *s* two *d*. *Educ*: Bearsden Acad.; Aberdeen Grammar Sch.; Queen's Coll., Oxford (BA PPE 1977); Stanford Univ. (MA 1980; MBA 1980). Investment Controller, 3i, 1977–78; Man. Dir, Braxton Associates, 1980–97; Asst Gen. Sec., Labour Party, 1997–99; Chief Exec., Hermes Focus Asset Mgt, 1999–2006; Sen. Advr, Hermes Fund Managers, 2008–09; Chair, Hermes Focus Asset Mgt, 2009–12. Dir, Oxford Analytica, 2006–15. Non-exec. Dir, KPMG, 2013–. Vis. Prof., Cranfield Univ., 1990–96; Exec. Fellow, London Business Sch., 2013–17. Pembroke Vis. Prof., Cambridge Univ., 2018. Chair, Finance Initiative, UNEP, 2013–16. Trustee: IPPR, 2004–; Oxfam (UK), 2011–17; NESTA, 2013–19. FRSA. *Publications*: The New Capitalists, 2006; Privatisation and Transition in Russia in the Early 1990s, 2013; What They Do With Your Money, 2016. *Recreations*: history, politics, singing, jogging. *Address*: 23 Dartmouth Park Road, NW5 1SU. *E*: david@pitt-watson.com.

**PITTAM, Jonathan Charles**; County Treasurer, Hampshire County Council, 1997–2010; *b* 9 June 1950; *s* of Brian and Sheila Pittam; *m* 1972, Mary Catherine Davey; two *s* one *d*. *Educ*: Tavistock Sch.; King's Coll., Univ. of London (BSc Hons). CPFA 1975. London Borough of Croydon: grad. trainee, 1971–73; Sen. Audit Asst, 1973; Accountant, 1973–75; Gp Accountant, 1975–76; Asst Prin. Accountant, 1976–78; Chief Accountant, 1979–80, Asst Dir, Finance and Admin, 1980–83, Cambs CC; Dep. Co. Treas., Hants CC, 1983–97; Treasurer: Hants Police Authy, 1997–2010; Hants Fire and Rescue Authy, 1997–2010. Expenditure Co-ordinator, LGA, 2005–10. Non-exec. Dir, Solent NHS Trust, 2011– (Chm., Finance Cttee, 2011–16; Chm., Audit Cttee, 2016–). Mem. Council, CIPFA, 2008–10 (Fellow, 2016); President: Soc. of County Treasurers, 2002–03; Assoc. of Local Authority Treasurers' Societies, 2004–10. *Address*: 25 Shepherds Down, Alresford, Hants SO24 9PP. *Club*: Rotary (Alresford) (Pres., 2015–16).

**PITTAWAY, David Michael**; QC 2000; a Recorder, since 2000; a Deputy High Court Judge (Queen's Bench Division), since 2008, and (Administration Court), since 2012; Head, Hailsham Chambers, since 2016; *b* 29 June 1955; *s* of late Michael Pittaway, JP, MRCVS, and of Heather Yvette Pittaway (*née* Scott); *m* 1983, Jill Suzanne Newsam, *d* of Dr Ian Douglas Newsam, MRCVS; two *s*. *Educ*: Uppingham Sch.; Sidney Sussex Coll., Cambridge (Exhibnr; MA). FCIArb 1994; Accredited Mediator 2000. Called to the Bar: Inner Temple, 1977 (Bencher, 1998; Treas., 2017); Gibraltar (Temp.), 2007; NI, 2011; Asst Recorder, 1998; Midland and Oxford Circuit. Bar Council: Mem., 1999–2005, 2008–11; Mem., Gen. Mgt Cttee, 2008–11; Chairman: Trng for Bar Cttee, 2008–11; Neuberger Monitoring Implementation Gp, 2010–11; Mem., Exec. Cttee, 1994–98 and 2004–09, 2012–, Chm., Educn Cttee, 2004–09, Inner Temple; Mem., 2008–11, Trustee, 2013–16, Council of Inns of Court. Actg Chancellor, Birmingham Dio., 2001–04; Chancellor, Peterborough Dio., 2006–. Legal Mem., Mental Health Review Tribunal, 2002–16; Legal Assessor: GMC, 2002–04; RCVS, 2004–17; Gen. Social Care Council, 2008–10. Course Dir, Clinical Negligence Seminars, 1998–2003, Chm., 2005–07, Professional Negligence Bar Assoc. Mem., Exec. Cttee, British Malaysian Soc., 2018–. Trustee, Nat. Educn Trust, 2011–14. Gov., Compton Verney Hse Trust, 2010–12 (Chm., Develt Bd, 2010–12). Mem. Council, Cheltenham Ladies Coll., 2012–. Freeman, City of London, 2016; Liveryman, Gardeners' Co., 2017. *Publications*: (contrib.) Atkin's Court Forms, vol. 8, Carriers, 1990, rev. edn 2010, vol. 29(2), Personal Injury, 1996, rev. edn 2014; Professional Negligence, 1996, rev. edn 2013, vol. 28, National Health Service, 2003, rev. edn 2014, vol. 27(2); (Gen. Ed.) Pittaway & Hammerton, Professional Negligence Cases, 1998; (contrib.) Advanced Civil Litigation: professional negligence in practice, 2000; (contrib.) Law and Ethics in Intensive Care, 2010. *Recreations*: gardening, travel, music. *Address*: Hailsham Chambers, 4 Paper Buildings, Temple, EC4Y 7EX. *T*: (020) 7643 5000. *Clubs*: Garrick, Royal Automobile.

**PITTS, His Honour Anthony Brian**; a Circuit Judge, 2002–16; *b* 18 May 1946; *s* of Sir Cyril Alfred Pitts and of Barbara Pitts; *m* 1980, Sally-Jane Spencer; one *s* one *d*. *Educ*: Pembroke Coll., Oxford (BA Law). Called to the Bar, Gray's Inn, 1975; a Recorder, 1997–2002. *Recreations*: motor sport, guitar, France.

**PITTS, Antony Philip David**; Composer and Founder-Director, Tonus Peregrinus, since 1990; Artistic Director, The Song Company, since 2016; *b* Farnborough, Kent, 24 March 1969; *s* of David and Rosemary Pitts; *m* 1989, Karen Jonckheere; three *s* two *d*. *Educ*: Tiffin Boys' Sch., Kingston-upon-Thames; New Coll., Oxford (MA 1st Cl. Hons Music). BBC, 1992–2005: Producer, 1994–98 (Facing the Radio, Radio Acad. BT Award, 1996); Sen. Producer, Radio 3, 1999–2005 (A Pebble in the Pond, Prix Italia, 2004); Sen. Lectr in Creative Technol., RAM, 2006–09. Founder: 1equalmusic, 2011; klangr Ltd, 2015–. Hon. FFCM, Central Sch. of Religion, Indiana, 2008. With Tonus Peregrinus: perf. at meml for Alexander Litvinenko, 2006; composer, oratorio, Jerusalem-Yerushalayim, 2008 (recorded 2017). Numerous recordings, incl. Passio, 2003 (Cannes Classical Award, 2004), Eton Choirbook, 2011, Missa Unitatis, 2016, In illo tempore, 2018. *Publications*: The Naxos Book of Carols, 2004; numerous music scores.

**PITTSBURGH, Assistant Bishop of**; *see* Scriven, Rt Rev. H. W.

**PIZARRO, Artur**; pianist; *b* Portugal. Performances with orchs incl. Philadelphia, LA Philharmonic, Baltimore Symphony, NHK Symphony (Tokyo), Montreal Symphony, Toronto Symphony, Hong Kong Philharmonic, Leipzig Chamber, Rotterdam Philharmonic, Vienna Symphony, Royal Philharmonic, BBC Symphony. Recitals worldwide. Numerous recordings. Winner, Leeds Internat. Piano Competition, 1990.

**PIZZEY, Erin Patria Margaret**; international founder of refuges for victims of domestic violence; *b* 19 Feb. 1939; *d* of late Cyril Edward Antony Carney, MBE and of Ruth Patricia Balfour-Last; *m* 1961, John Leo Pizzey (marr. diss. 1979); one *s* one *d*. *Educ*: St Antony's; Leweston Manor, Sherborne, Dorset. Somewhat chequered career as pioneering attracts frequent clashes with the law; appearances at such places as Acton Magistrates Court and the House of Lords could be considered milestones in the fulfilment of a career dedicated to defending women and children; Founder of first Shelter for Battered Wives (subseq. Women) and their children, 1971; helped fund and open Health Care Centre, Wandsworth Prison, 2001. Patron: Mankind Charity, 2004–; Derwentside Domestic Violence Forum, 2005–; Compassion in Care, 2005–; owner, www.Honest-Ribbon.org. Presenter, Domestic Violence is not a Gender Issue, Internat. Conf., Sacramento, 2008 (Lifetime Achievement Award); held lectures about domestic violence and child advocacy for Slovenia Ombudsman, 2008; contribs to: New Statesman, Sunday Times, Cosmopolitan. Member: Soc. of Authors; AFI; Smithsonian Instn; Royal Soc. of Literature. Patron, Care and Comfort Romania, 1998–. Attended Women of Achievement Lunch, Buckingham Palace, 2004. Diploma of Honour, Internat. order of volunteers for peace, 1981; Nancy Astor Award for Journalism, 1983; Distinguished Leadership Award, World Congress of Victimology, 1987; San Valentino d'Oro prize for lit., 1994. *Publications*: (as Erin Pizzey) Scream Quietly or the Neighbours Will Hear, 1974, 2nd edn 1978; Infernal Child (autobiog.), 1978; The Slut's Cookbook, 1981; Prone to Violence, 1982; Erin Pizzey Collects, 1983; Wild Child (autobiog.), 1996; (jtly) Grandmothers of the Revolution, 2000; (jtly) Women or Men - Who Are the Victims?, 2000; This Way to the Revolution (autobiog.), 2011; *novels*: The Watershed, 1983; In the Shadow of the Castle, 1984; The Pleasure Palace, 1986; First Lady, 1987; The Consul General's Daughter, 1988; The Snow Leopard of Shanghai, 1989; Other Lovers, 1991; Morning Star, 1991; Swimming with Dolphins, 1992; For the Love of a Stranger, 1993; Kisses, 1995; The Wicked World of Women, 1996; The Fame Game, 1999; This Way to the Revolution, 2011; poems and short stories. *Recreations*: reading, writing, cooking, antiques, violin, gardening, wine, travel. *Address*: Flat 5, 29 Lebanon Park, Twickenham TW1 3DH. *T*: (020) 8241 6541, 07967 136453. *E*: erin.pizzey@blueyonder.co.uk.

**PLACE, Joanna Ruth**; Chief Operating Officer, Bank of England, since 2017; *b* Derby, 21 June 1962; *d* of Frank Place and Stella Place; *m* 1999, Graeme Danton; one *s* two *d*. *Educ*: Fitzwilliam Coll., Cambridge (BSc Econ; PGCE Maths and PE). Teacher of Maths, Rainham Mark GS, 1984–86; Bank of England: Banking Supervisor, 1986–90; Internat. Div., 1990–92; Governor's Office, 1992–94; various managerial roles, 1994–2000; Hd, Monetary and Financial Statistics Div., 2000–04; Dir, Change, UK Border Agency, Home Office, 2004–07; Bank of England: Hd, Customer Banking, 2007–12; Dir, Regulatory Ops, 2012–14; Exec. Dir, Human Resources, 2014–17. Non-exec. Dir, CISI, 2016–. Gov., Woking High Sch., 2012–. *Recreations*: running, swimming, walking, family. *Address*: Bank of England, Threadneedle Street, EC2R 8AH. *T*: (020) 3461 4284. *E*: joanna.place@bankofengland.co.uk.

**PLAISTOWE, (William) Ian (David)**, FCA; Managing Practice Director of Audit and Business Advisory Practice for Europe, Middle East, Africa and India, Arthur Andersen, 1993–2002; *b* 18 Nov. 1942; *s* of late David William Plaistowe and Julia (*née* Ross Smith); *m* 1968, Carolyn Anne Noble Wilson; two *s* one *d*. *Educ*: Marlborough Coll.; Queens' Coll., Cambridge. Joined Arthur Andersen & Co., 1964; Partner, 1976; Head of Accounting and Audit practice, London, 1984–87; Dir of Acctg and Audit for UK and Ireland, 1987–93; Chm., Auditing Practices Bd of UK and Ireland, 1994–2002; Mem., Internat. Audit and Assurance Standards Bd, 2002–04. Institute of Chartered Accountants in England and Wales: Chairman: London Soc. of Chartered Accountants, 1981–82; Mem. Council, 1985–99; Vice-Pres., 1990–91; Dep. Pres., 1991–92; Pres., 1992–93. Chm., FPA, 2006–12; Dir, Abbeyfield Soc., 2009– (Chm., 2015–). Mem. Council, Univ. of Buckingham, 2003–. Chm., Beacon Sch., Amersham, 1999–2012. Master, Co. of Chartered Accountants in England and Wales, 2002–03. *Publications*: articles in learned jls. *Recreations*: golf, tennis, squash, ski-ing, gardening. *Address*: The Cross, 48 High Street, Watlington, Oxon OX49 5PY. *T*: (01491) 614068. *Clubs*: Carlton, Huntercombe Golf.

**PLANE, Robert Edward**, FRAM; solo and chamber clarinettist; Principal Clarinet, BBC National Orchestra of Wales, since 1999; *b* Great Yarmouth, 13 April 1969; *s* of Nathaniel and Kathleen Plane; *m* 1997, Lucy Gould; one *s* two *d*. *Educ*: Chetham's Sch. of Music; Univ. of Bristol (BA Hons); Royal Acad. of Music (MMus; Dip. RAM). LRAM 1991; ARAM; FRAM 2014. Principal Clarinet: Northern Sinfonia, 1992–99; City of Birmingham SO, 2010–11. Winner, Royal Over-Seas League Music Competition, 1992. *Recreation*: marathon running. *Address*: 16 Teilo Street, Cardiff CF11 9JN. *T*: 07966 206634. *E*: rob.e.plane@gmail.com. *W*: www.robertplane.com. *Club*: Royal Over-Seas League.

**PLANT**, family name of **Baron Plant of Highfield**.

**PLANT OF HIGHFIELD**, Baron *cr* 1992 (Life Peer), of Weelsby in the County of Humberside; **Raymond Plant**, PhD; DLitt; Professor of Jurisprudence and Legal Philosophy, King's College London, since 2001; *b* 19 March 1945; *s* of Stanley and Marjorie Plant; *m* 1967, Katherine Sylvia Dixon; three *s*. *Educ*: Havelock Sch., Grimsby; King's Coll. London (BA); Hull Univ. (PhD 1971). Lectr, then Sen. Lectr in Philosophy, Univ. of Manchester, 1967–79; Prof. of Politics, 1979–94, Pro-Chancellor, 1996–99, Res. Prof., 1999–2001, Univ. of Southampton; Master, St Catherine's Coll., Oxford, 1994–99. Vincent Wright Prof., Inst. d'Etudes Politiques de Paris, Sciences Po, 2008; Gresham Prof. of Divinity, 2012; Vis. Prof., Univ. of Winchester, 2007–. Lectures: Stevenson, Univ. of Glasgow, 1981; Agnes Cumming, UC Dublin, 1987; Stanton, 1989–90 and 1990–91, Boutwood, 2006, Univ. of Cambridge; Sarum, 1991, Bampton, 2007, Univ. of Oxford; Ferguson, Manchester Univ., 1994; Scott Holland, Manchester Cathedral, 1995; Charles Gore, Westminster Abbey, 1995; J. P. MacIntosh Meml, Edinburgh Univ., 1995; Eleanor Rathbone, Bristol Univ., 1997; G. Ganz, Southampton Univ., 2005; A. J. Milne, Durham, 2006; Zutshi-Smith, Bristol, 2010. Chair: Labour Party Commn on Electoral Systems, 1991–93; Fabian Soc. Commn on Taxation and Citizenship, 1999–2000. President: Acad. of Learned Socs in Social Scis, 2000–01; NCVO, 1997–2002. Times columnist, 1988–92. Chm., Centrepoint, 2002–04. Lay Canon, Winchester Cathedral, 2008–. FKC 2008. Hon. Fellow: Cardiff Univ., 2000; St Catherine's Coll., Oxford, 2000; Harris Manchester Coll., Oxford, 2001. Hon. DLitt: London Guildhall Univ., 1993; Hull, 1994; DUniv: York, 2007; Winchester, 2008; Tallinn, 2012; Hon. LLD Southampton, 2012. *Publications*: Hegel, 1974, 2nd edn 1984; Community and Ideology, 1974; Political Philosophy and Social Welfare, 1981; Philosophy, Politics and Citizenship, 1984; Conservative Capitalism in Britain and the United States: a critical appraisal, 1988; Modern Political Thought, 1991; Politics, Theology and History, 2001; The Neo-Liberal State, 2009. *Recreations*: music, opera, thinking about the garden, listening to my wife playing the piano, reading. *Address*: 6 Woodview Close, Bassett, Southampton SO16 3PZ. *T*: (023) 8076 9529. *Club*: Athenæum.

**PLANT, Dr Gordon Terence**, FRCP, FRCOphth; Consultant Neurologist, National Hospital for Neurology and Neurosurgery, Moorfields Eye Hospital and St Thomas' Hospital, since 1991; *b* 4 July 1952; *s* of Thomas Edmund Plant and Sheila May Plant (*née* Atkinson); *m* 1978, Marilyn Jane Dirkin; three *d*. *Educ*: Downing Coll., Cambridge (BA 1974, MA 1977; MB BChir 1978; MD 1987). FRCP 1993; FRCOphth 2005. Hse Physician, St Thomas' Hosp., 1977; Hse Surgeon, Kingston Gen. Hosp., 1978; SHO, Westminster Hosp., 1978; Nat. Hosp., Queen Sq., 1979; Registrar in Neurol., Addenbrooke's Hosp., 1980–82. Wellcome Trust Res. Associate, Physiol Lab., Cambridge, 1982–85; Registrar, Nat. Hosp., Queen Sq., 1985–91; MRC Travelling Fellow, Smith-Kettlewell Res. Inst., San Francisco, 1989. Visiting Professor: City Univ., 2005–; Wills Eye Inst., Philadelphia, 2011; Univ. Paris 5 René Descartes, 2018. Autumn Lectr, Assoc. British Neurologists, 2017; Bryan St L. Liddy Lectr, Canadian Ophthalmological Soc., 2018. Pres., Clin. Neurocsis Section, RSocMed, 2011–12. Founder, UK Neuro-Ophthalmol. Special Interest Gp, 2008– (Pres.). Member: British Is Neuro-ophthalmology Club, 1992– ; Ophthalmic Club, 1996– (Sec., 2012–). FEAN 2019. Hon. Fellow, Neurological Soc. of Thailand, 2014. Editor-in-Chief, Neuro-ophthalmology, 2008–18, Ed. Emeritus, 2019. Allvat Gulstrand Medal, Swedish Ophthalmol Soc., 2009; Claffey Medal, Sydney Eye

Hosp., 2009; Lang Medal, R.SocMed, 2010; Mooney Medal, Irish Ophthalmol Soc., 2013; Lettsomian Medal, Med. Soc. of London, 2016; Ida Mann Award, Univ. of Oxford, 2019. *Publications:* Optic Neuritis, 1986; contribs to med., neurol, ophthalmol and visual sci. jls. *Recreations:* music, painting, book collecting. *Address:* 246 Sheen Lane, SW14 8RL. *T:* (020) 3448 3388, *Fax:* (020) 3448 8994. *E:* gplant7@icloud.com.

**PLANT, Patrick Gerard;** Partner, Linklaters LLP, since 1994; *b* Manchester, 11 April 1962; *s* of Walter Patrick Plant and Margaret Mary Plant. *Educ:* Univ. of Manchester (LLB Hons Law 1983). Articled clerk, Wilsons, Salisbury, 1984–86; admitted as solicitor, 1986; Assistant Solicitor: Linklaters and Paines, London, 1986–89; Mallesons Stephen Jaques, Sydney, 1989–90; Linklaters LLP, London, 1990–: Asst Solicitor, 1990–94; Global Hd, Real Estate, 2003–11. Non-exec. Dir, Falcon Property Trust, 2012–14. Member: Bd, British Liby, 2012–; Council, RCA, 2016–. Hon. Lectr in Law, Faculty of Humanities, Univ. of Manchester, 2013–. Trustee, Royal Soc. for Blind Children (formerly Royal London Soc. for Blind People), 2014–. *Recreations:* 20th century British art, family. *Address:* Linklaters LLP, One Silk Street, EC2Y 8HQ. *T:* (020) 7456 4718, *Fax:* (020) 7456 2222. *E:* patrick.plant@linklaters.com.

**PLANT, Robert Anthony,** CBE 2009; singer and songwriter; solo singer, since 1980; *b* W Bromwich, Staffs, 20 Aug. 1948; *m* 1968, Maureen; one *s* one *d* (and one *s* decd). Lead singer, New Yardbirds, later Led Zeppelin, 1968–80; albums: Led Zeppelin, 1969; Led Zeppelin II, 1969; Led Zeppelin III, 1970; Untitled, 1971; Houses of the Holy, 1973; Physical Graffiti, 1975; Presence, 1976; In Through the Out Door, 1979; Coda, 1982; solo albums: Pictures at Eleven, 1982; The Principle of Moments, 1983; Shaken 'n' Stirred, 1985; Now and Zen, 1988; Manic Nirvana, 1989; Fate of Nations, 1993; Dreamland, 2002; Sixty Six to Timbuktu, 2003; with The Honeydrippers, The Honeydrippers Volume I, 1984; with Jimmy Page: No Quarter—Unledded, 1994; Walking into Clarksdale, 1998; with The Strange Sensation, Mighty ReArranger, 2005; with Alison Krauss, Raising Sand, 2007 (Grammy Award, 2009); with Band of Joy, Band of Joy, 2010; with Sensational Space Shifters, Lullaby and... The Ceaseless Roar, 2014; Carry Fire, 2017. *Address:* c/o Trinifold Management, 12 Oval Road, NW1 7DH.

**PLANTIN, Marcus;** healer and tutor, Ham Healing Centre, since 2005; *b* 23 Oct. 1945. Producer/director, BBC TV, 1970–84; London Weekend Television: Head of Light Entertainment, 1985–87; Controller of Entertainment, 1987–90; Dir of Progs, 1990–92; ITV Network Dir, 1992–97; Dir of Progs, LWT, 1997–2001; Dir of Entertainment, Granada, 2001–02; CEO, September Films, 2003–05. FRTS. *Address:* 4 Morgans House, Ham Common, Richmond TW10 7JU.

**PLASCHKES, Sarah Georgina;** QC 2011; **Her Honour Judge Plaschkes;** a Circuit Judge, since 2015; *b* Bournemouth; ; *Educ:* Bournemouth Sch. for Girls; Southampton Univ. (LLB). Called to the Bar, Inner Temple, 1988; barrister, specialising in professional discipline and criminal law, 1988–2015; a Recorder, 2004–15. *Address:* Kingston-upon-Thames Crown Court, 6–8 Penrhyn Road, Kingston-upon-Thames, Surrey KT1 2BB.

**PLASKITT, James Andrew;** Senior Counsel, Cicero Group, since 2014; *b* 23 June 1954; *s* of late Ronald Plaskitt and Phyllis Irene Plaskitt. *Educ:* Pilgrim Sch., Bedford; University Coll., Oxford (MPhil 1979; MA 1980). Lecturer in Politics: University Coll., Oxford, 1977–79; Christ Church, Oxford, 1984–86; Lectr in Govt, Brunel Univ., 1979–84; Oxford Analytica Ltd: Western European Editor, 1986–90; Dir of Consultancy, 1993–96. Mem. (Lab) Oxfordshire CC, 1985–97 (Leader, Labour Gp, 1990–96). Contested (Lab) Witney, 1992. MP (Lab) Warwick and Leamington, 1997–2010; contested (Lab) same seat, 2010. Parly Under-Sec. of State, DWP, 2005–08.

**PLASSNIK, Ursula,** DIur; Ambassador of Austria to Switzerland, since 2016; *b* 23 May 1956. *Educ:* elementary and grammar schs, Klagenfurt; High Sch., Funchal, P; Vienna Univ. (DIur 1978); Coll. of Europe, Bruges (Postgrad. Dip.). Federal Ministry for Foreign Affairs, 1981–2008: COS of Vice Chancellor, 1997–2000, Federal Chancellor, 2000–04, Dr Wolfgang Schüssel, Federal Chancellery; Ambassador to Switzerland, 2004; Minister: for Foreign Affairs, 2004–07; for European and Internat. Affairs, 2007–08; Ambassador to France, 2011–16. MP (People's Party) Austria, 2006–07, 2008–11. *Address:* Austrian Embassy, Kirchenfeldstrasse 77–79, 3005 Berne, Switzerland.

**PLATELL, Amanda Jane;** writer and broadcaster; columnist, Daily Mail, since 2007; *b* 12 Nov. 1957; *d* of Francis Ernest Platell and Norma June Platell. *Educ:* Univ. of Western Australia (BA Hons Philosophy and Politics). Dep. Ed., Today newspaper, 1987–92; Man. Ed., Mirror Gp, 1993; Mktg Dir, 1993–95, Man. Dir, 1995–96, The Independent; Acting Ed., Sunday Mirror, 1996–97; Ed., Sunday Express, 1998–99; Hd of Media, Cons. Party, 1999–2001. *Publications:* Scandal, 1999. *Recreations:* travelling, cooking, cars, writing.

**PLATT, Alison;** *see* Platt, E. A.

**PLATT, Anthony Michael Westlake,** CBE 1991; Chief Executive, London Chamber of Commerce and Industry, 1984–91; *b* 28 Sept. 1928; *s* of late James Westlake Platt, CBE and Veronica Norma Hope Platt (*née* Arnold); *m* 1st, 1952, Jennifer Susan Scott-Fox; three *s*; 2nd, 1984, Heather Mary Stubbs; one step *s* one step *d*; 3rd, 1987, Sarah Elizabeth Russell. *Educ:* Stowe School; Balliol College, Oxford (PPE 1951). Foreign Office, 1951, served Prague, 1953–54, NY, 1955–56; Shell Group of Cos: Switzerland, 1957; Guatemala, 1959; S Africa, 1961; Venezuela, 1963; London, 1969; The Hague, 1972; London, 1975–77 (Billiton UK); The Hague, 1977–78 (Billiton Internat.); Man. Dir, Consolidated Petroleum, London, 1979–84. Advr, Council of British Chambers in Europe, 1992–95. Freeman, City of London, 1991. *Publications:* (ed) Parallel 40 North to Eureka, 2000; Belovedest—A Marriage of Opposites, 2006. *Recreations:* walking, music, languages. *Address:* 17 Westgate Street, Bury St Edmunds, Suffolk IP33 1QG.

**PLATT, David Wallace;** QC 2011; *b* Northern Ireland, 1964; *s* of Christopher Platt and Susan Harriette La Nauze; *m* 2007, Jessica Perks; one *s* one *d*. *Educ:* Campbell Coll., Belfast; Trinity Hall, Cambridge (BA 1986; MA). Called to the Bar, Middle Temple, 1987; in practice as a barrister, specialising in personal injury, envmtl and insurance law. Presenter, BBC TV progs, The Stand and Dilemma, 1991–95. Contested (C) Cambridge, 1997. Governor: Churchill Gardens, 2003–11; Pimlico Sch., 2005–07. *Publications:* contrib. to various political and cultural jls. *Recreations:* walking, conservation, theatre, opera, J. R. R. Tolkien, Dorset. *Address:* Crown Office Chambers, Temple, EC4Y 7HJ. *T:* (020) 7797 8100. *E:* platt@crownofficechambers.com. *Club:* Brooks's.

**PLATT, Dame Denise,** DBE 2004 (CBE 1996); Chair: Local Innovation Award Scheme, 2009–10; Commission for Social Care Inspection, 2004–09; *b* 21 Feb. 1945; *d* of Victor Platt and May Platt (*née* Keeling). *Educ:* UCW, Cardiff (BSc Econ 1967); AIMSW 1968. Social Worker, then Sen. Social Worker, Middx Hosp., 1968–73; Sen. Social Worker, Guy's Hosp., 1973–76; Gp Leader, Southwark Social Services, 1976–78; Prin. Social Worker, Hammersmith Hosp., 1978–83; London Borough of Hammersmith and Fulham: Asst Dir, Social Services, 1983–86; Dir, 1986–95 (on leave of absence, 1994–95); Under Sec., Social Services, AMA, 1994–97; Hd of Social Services, LGA, 1997–98; Jt Hd, Social Care Gp, DoH, 1998–2001; Chief Inspector, Social Services Inspectorate, 1998–2004 and Dir of Children, Older People and Social Care Services, DoH, 2001–04. Pres., Assoc. Dirs of Social Services, 1993–94. Chm., Nat. AIDS Trust, 2006–16 (Trustee, 1987–98; Vice Chm., 1994–98); Trustee and Dir, FPA, 2005–10. Member: Central Council Educn and Trng in Social Work, 1994–98; Youth Justice Task Force, 1997–98; Disability Rights Task Force, 1997–98; Ind. Reference Gp on Mental Health, 1997–98; Review Team, Strategic Review of London's Health Services, 1997–98; Ind. Review Bd, Cheshire CC Fire and Rescue Service, 2007–16; Audit Commn, 2007–10; Cttee on Standards in Public Life, 2008–14; Commn on Assisted Dying, 2010–12; GMC, 2013–; Bd, SRA, 2010–. Mem., Adv. Bd, Sch. of Social Care Res., NIHR, LSE, 2008–. Trustee: NSPCC, 2007–17; Adventure Capital Fund, 2008–11; Lloyds (formerly Lloyds TSB) Foundn for England and Wales, 2011–16. Patron: Advocacy Plus, 2009–12; MHA, 2015–; Vice-Patron, Family Action, 2015–. Governor: Nat. Inst. for Social Work, 1995–98 (Chm., 1997–99); Univ. of Bedfordshire, 2006–12. Hon. Fellow, Univ. of Bedfordshire, 2014. Hon. DSocSc Brunel, 1998; Hon. LLD Brighton, 2008. *Publications:* various articles in social services press. *Recreations:* music, watercolours, walking, travel. *Club:* Reform.

**PLATT, Eleanor Frances;** QC 1982; a Recorder of the Crown Court, 1982–2004; a Deputy High Court Judge, Family Division, 1987–2004; *b* 6 May 1938; *er d* of late Dr Maurice Leon Platt and Sara Platt (*née* Stein), Hove, Sussex; *m* 1963; two *c*. *Educ:* Hove County School for Girls; University College London. LLB 1959. Called to the Bar, Gray's Inn, 1960; Jt Head of Specialist Family Law Chambers, 1990–2007. Mem., Matrimonial Causes Rule Cttee, 1986–90. Dep. Chm., NHS Tribunal, 1995–2001; Legal Assessor: Med. Practitioners Tribunal Service, GMC, 1995–2018; GDC, 2009–17; Investigation Cttee, GMC, 2017–; Mem., Gene Therapy Adv. Cttee, 1993–98. Treas., Family Law Bar Assoc., 1990–95 (Acting Chm., 1995); Pres., Jewish Family Mediation Register, 1998–. Chm., Law, Parly and Gen. Purposes Cttee, 1988–94, Dep. Chm. Defence Bd, 1997–2003, Vice Pres., 2003–06, Chm., Family Law Gp, , 2006–, Bd of Deputies of British Jews; Chm., New London Synagogue, 1994–99. Pres., Medico-Legal Soc., 2002–04 (Mem. Council, 1995–). Mem., Ethics and Jewish Genealogy Panel, Internat. Inst. for Jewish Genealogy, 2012–. *Recreations:* the arts, travel, grandchildren. *Address:* 10 Lincoln's Inn Fields, WC2A 3BP. *T:* (020) 7797 7900. *E:* Platt@1gc.com.

**PLATT, (Elizabeth) Alison, (Mrs William Ward),** CMG 2011; Group Chief Executive, Countrywide plc, 2014–18; *b* Oldham, 25 Feb. 1962; *d* of Gerard and Elizabeth Platt; *m* 2001, William Ward; one *s*. *Educ:* Adelphi House Grammar Sch., Salford. Mgt Prog., British Airways plc, 1980–93; Bupa Health and Wellbeing: Dir, Customer Service, 1993–95; Dir, Ops, 1995–98; Dep. Man. Dir, 1998–2004; Chief Operating Officer, Bupa Hosps, 2004–07; Bupa: Gp Develt Dir, 2007–09; Man. Dir, Europe, 2009–10; Divl Man. Dir, Europe and N America, 2010–12; Man. Dir, Internat. Develt Markets, 2012–14. Chair, Opportunity Now, 2009–13. Non-executive Director: FCO, 2005–10; Cable & Wireless Communications, 2012–16; Tesco plc, 2016–. *Recreations:* reading, running, football (watching).

**PLATT, Prof. Frances Mary,** PhD; FMedSci; Professor of Biochemistry and Pharmacology, University of Oxford, since 2008; Fellow, Merton College, Oxford, since 2007; *b* Shipley, W Yorks, 12 April 1961; *d* of David Judson and Helen Judson; *m* 1985, Nicholas Platt; one *s* one *d* (twins). *Educ:* Bradford Girls' Grammar Sch.; Imperial Coll. London (BSc Zool. 1982); Univ. of Bath (PhD Animal Physiol. 1986). Postdoctoral Res. Fellow, Washington Univ. Med. Sch., St Louis, 1986–87; Res. Scientist, Monsanto Co., St Louis, 1987–89; University of Oxford: Glycobiology Institute, Department of Biochemistry: Sen. Res. Scientist, Searle Res. Gp, 1989–93; Sen. Res. Fellow, 1993–96; Lister Institute Sen. Res. Fellow, 1996–2002; Reader in Glycobiol., 1999–2006; Reader, Dept of Pharmacol., 2006–08. MAE 2018. FMedSci 2011. *Recreations:* horse riding, gardening, keeping chickens. *Address:* Department of Pharmacology, University of Oxford, Mansfield Road, Oxford OX1 3QT. *E:* frances.platt@pharm.ox.ac.uk.

**PLATT, Howard Martin,** PhD; Member, Joint Nature Conservation Committee, since 2015; Deputy Chairman, Council for Nature Conservation and the Countryside, since 2015 (Director, Northern Ireland, since 2015); *b* London, 10 June 1947; *s* of Norman Platt and Edna Platt; *m* 1977, Ruth Jackson; two *s* one *d*. *Educ:* King's Sch., Macclesfield; Univ. of London ext. (BSc Hons 1st Cl. Zoology 1968); Queen's Univ., Belfast (PhD 1971). Zoologist, British Antarctic Survey, Cambridge, 1972–77; Hd, Nematode Section, Natural Hist. Mus., 1977–91; Man. Dir, KMM Marenco Ltd, Belfast, 1991–92; Hd, Conservation Sci., and Chief Scientist, NI Envmt Agency, 1992–2013. Hon. Prof., QUB, 2008. Dir, Ulster Wildlife Trust, 2014–. *Publications:* Free-living Marine Nematodes, Part I British Enoplids, 1983, Part II British Chromadorids, 1988, Part III British Monhysterida, 1998; 55 articles in scientific learned jls. *Recreations:* music, drumming, nature conservation, travel, family. *Address:* 76 Sicily Park, Belfast BT10 0AN. *T:* 07894 872122. *E:* howard.platt@sky.com.

**PLATT, Jane Christine,** CBE 2013; Chief Executive, National Savings and Investments, 2006–16; Chairman, LifeSight Pension Master Trust, since 2017; *b* 8 Jan. 1957; *d* of George Platt and Miriam Platt (*née* Knowles); *m* 1980, David Bill. *Educ:* St Catherine's Coll., Oxford (MA). Sen. Pension Fund Manager, Mercury Asset Mgt, 1982–88; Dir, Business Develt, 1988–94, Man. Dir, 1994–95, BZW Investment Management; Chief Operating Officer, Barclays Asset Mgt, 1995–96; CEO, Barclays Stockbrokers and Barclays Bank Trust Co., 1996–2001; Chief Operating Officer, (Business Divs) Reuters, 2001–04. Non-executive Director: Edinburgh UK Investment Trust Plc, 2004–06; Witan Plc, 2005–06; Royal London Gp, 2012–13; Financial Conduct Authy, 2013–19. Chartered Fellow, CISI, 2010. Mem., Cornhill Club. Hon. LLD Warwick, 2015; DUniv Huddersfield, 2016. *Recreation:* performing arts.

**PLATT, Joanne;** MP (Lab) Leigh, since 2017; two *c*. Advocacy worker, Willow, 2012–13. Mem. (Lab), Wigan MBC, 2012–17 (Cabinet Mem. for Children and Young People, 2014–17). Shadow Minister for the Cabinet Office, 2018–. *Address:* House of Commons, SW1A 0AA.

**PLATT, His Honour John Richard;** a Circuit Judge, 1992–2012; *b* 21 Nov. 1942; *s* of Arthur James Platt and Joan Platt; *m* 1986, Jayne Mary Webb; two *d*. *Educ:* Sherborne Sch.; Trinity Hall, Cambridge. Partner, Lee Davies & Co., Solicitors, 1969–82; Registrar and District Judge, Bow County Court, 1982–92. *Publications:* A Guide to Judicial Pensions for Circuit Judges, 1995; A Guide to Judicial Pensions for District Judges, 1996; A Guide to Judicial Pensions for Stipendiary Magistrates, 1996; A Guide to the Judicial Pensions and Retirement Act, 1997; contribs to Jordans Civil Court Service, New Law Jl, Liverpool Law Review, Family Law. *Recreations:* wine and food, music, travel.

**PLATT, Margaret;** *see* Wright, Margaret.

**PLATT, Sir Martin Philip,** 3rd Bt *cr* 1959, of Grindleford, co. Derby; *b* 9 March 1952; *o s* of Hon. Sir Peter Platt, 2nd Bt, AM and of Jean Halliday Platt (*née* Brentnall); *S* father, 2000; *m* 1971, Francis Corinne Moana, *d* of Trevor Samuel Conley; two *s* two *d*. *Heir: s* Philip Stephen Platt, *b* 17 Oct. 1972.

**PLATT, Michael Edward Horsfall;** Pensions Ombudsman, 1991–94; *b* 24 Aug. 1934; *s* of Fred Horsfall Platt and Alice Martha Taylor Platt (*née* Wilde). *Educ:* Taunton Sch.; The Queen's Coll., Oxford. Nat. Service, RAF, 1952–54. Min. of Labour, 1959; Min. of Pensions and Nat. Insurance, 1960; Min. of Social Security, 1966; Private Sec. to Minister of State, DHSS, 1968–70; Cabinet Office, 1970–71; DHSS, 1971–86; Chief Adjudication Officer, 1986–90. *Recreations:* theatre, music. *Address:* c/o Office of the Pensions Ombudsman, First Floor, 10 South Colonnade, Canary Wharf, E14 4PU. *T:* (020) 7630 2200.

**PLATT, Stephen, (Steve);** freelance editor and writer; *b* 29 Sept. 1954; *s* of Kenneth Norman Platt and Joyce (*née* Pritchard); one *d. Educ:* Longton High Sch., Stoke-on-Trent; Wade Deacon Sch., Widnes; LSE (BSc (Econ)). Teacher, Moss Brook Special Sch., Widnes, 1972–73; Dir, Self Help Housing Resource Library, Poly. of N London, 1977–80; Co-ordinator, Islington Community Housing, 1980–83; News Editor, subseq. Acting Editor, New Society, 1985–88; Editor: Roof, 1988; Midweek, 1988–89; columnist and writer, 1988–91; Editor, New Statesman and Society, 1991–96; freelance writer, 1996–. Editor, Enjoying the Countryside, 1988–93; Editl Consultant, Channel 4, 1996–2012; Website Editor: Time Team, 1999–2010; Dispatches, 1999–2005. Associate, HouseMark, 2010–. Hon. Chm., Medical Aid for Iraq, 1991–2010. *Publications:* various. *Recreations:* archaeology, amphibians, bears (real and fictional), countryside, football, growing things, mountains, music, poetry, running, long-distance walking. *Address:* 46 Tufnell Park Road, N7 0DT. *T:* (020) 7263 4185. *E:* steveplatt@gmail.com. *Club:* Port Vale.

**PLATT, Terence Charles,** CB 1996; Deputy Under-Secretary of State and Principal Establishment Officer, Home Office, 1992–96; *b* 22 Sept. 1936; *yr s* of Bertram Reginald Platt, QPM and Nina Platt; *m* 1959, Margaret Anne Cotmore; two *s. Educ:* St Olave's and St Saviour's Grammar School; Joint Services School for Linguists; Russian Interpreter. HM Immigration Officer, 1957; Asst Principal, Home Office, 1962; Principal, 1966; Cabinet Office, 1970; Principal Private Sec. to Sec. of State for NI (Rt Hon. William Whitelaw), 1972–73; Asst Sec., Home Office, 1973–81; Asst Under-Sec. of State and Princ. Estabt and Finance Officer, NI Office, 1981–82; Asst Under-Sec. of State and Dir of Regimes and Services, Prison Dept, Home Office, 1982–86; Asst Under-Sec. of State (Ops and Resources), Immigration and Nationality Dept, Home Office, 1986–92; Chief Inspector, Immigration Service, 1991–92. Mem., Civil Service Appeal Bd, 1997–2001. *Publications:* New Directions in Prison Design (Wkg Party Report), 1985. *Recreations:* photography, butterflies, water-colour painting.

**PLATT, Tracy Lynn;** *see* Brabin, T. L.

**PLATT, Prof. Trevor,** PhD; FRS 1998; FRSC 1990; Professorial Fellow, Plymouth Marine Laboratory, since 2014 (Executive Director, Partnership for Observation of the Global Oceans, 2008–14); *b* 12 Aug. 1942; *s* of John Platt and Lily Platt (*née* Hibbert); *m* 1988, Shuba Sathyendranath. *Educ:* Univ. of Nottingham (BSc); Univ. of Toronto (MA); Dalhousie Univ. (PhD 1970). Res. Scientist in Marine Ecology, 1965–72, Hd, Biol Oceanography, 1972–2002, Bedford Inst. of Oceanography, Nova Scotia. Chairman: Jt Global Ocean Flux Study, 1991–93; Internat. Ocean-colour Co-ordinating Gp, 1996–2005. Pres., Amer. Soc. Limnology and Oceanography, 1990–92. *Publications:* numerous res. papers in scholarly jls. *Recreations:* cycling, fly-fishing, languages, music. *Address:* Plymouth Marine Laboratory, Prospect Place, The Hoe, Plymouth, Devon PL1 3DH. *T:* (01752) 633100.

**PLATTEN, Rt Rev. Stephen George;** an Honorary Assistant Bishop: Diocese of London, since 2014; Diocese of Newcastle, since 2014; Diocese of Southwark, since 2015; *b* 17 May 1947; *s* of George Henry and Marjory Platten; *m* 1972, Rosslie Thompson; two *s. Educ:* Stationers' Company's Sch.; Univ. of London (BEd Hons 1972); Trinity Coll., Oxford (Dip. Theol. 1974; BD 2003); Cuddesdon Theol Coll. Shell Internat. Petroleum Co., 1966–68. Deacon 1975, Priest 1976; Asst Curate, St Andrew, Headington, Oxford, 1975–78; Chaplain and Tutor, Lincoln Theol Coll., 1978–82; Diocesan Dir of Ordinands and Canon Residentiary, Portsmouth Cathedral, 1983–89; Dir, post-ordination trng and continuing ministerial educn, Dio. Portsmouth, 1984–89; Archbishop of Canterbury's Sec. for Ecumenical Affairs, 1990–95; Dean of Norwich, 1995–2003; Bishop of Wakefield, 2003–14; Chaplain, Order of St John, S and W Yorks Priory, 2003–14; Rector, St Michael's, Cornhill, City of London, 2014–17; Chaplain, Guild Church of St Martin Ludgate, London, 2017–19. Hon. Canon: Canterbury Cathedral, 1990–95; St John's Cathedral, Musoma, Tanzania, 2008–. Anglican Sec., ARCIC (II), 1990–95; Chm., Liturgical Commn, 2005–14. Chairman: Soc. for Study of Christian Ethics, 1983–88; Govs, Anglican Centre in Rome, 2001–18; Council, Coll. of the Resurrection, 2004–14. Minister Provincial, European Province, Third Order, SSF, 1991–96. Dir, SCM Press, 1990–2003 (Chm., 2001–03); Member: Council, Hymns Ancient and Modern, 1997–2020 (Chm., 2014–20); Faith and Order Commn (formerly Adv. Gp), C of E, 2000–10, Faith and Order Commn, 2010–12; Cathedrals Fabric Commn for England, 2005–16. Mem., H of L, 2009–14. Member: Exec., Georgian Gp, 2014–16; Council, RSCM, 2014–16; Council, Guild of Church Musicians, 2014–16. Trustee: Hepworth Wakefield, 2007–14 (Emeritus Trustee, 2015); Media Standards Trust, 2008–15. Lectures: Cheney, Yale, 1998; Warburton, Lincoln's Inn, 2004. Guestmaster, Nikaean Club, 1990–95. Liveryman, Stationers' Co., 2004 (Mem., Ct of Assts, 2011–). Hon. FGCM 2012. Hon. DLitt East Anglia, 2003; DUniv Huddersfield, 2012. Lambeth Cross for Ecumenism, 2018. *Publications:* (series editor) Ethics and Our Choices, 1990–; (jtly) Spirit and Tradition: an essay on Change, 1996; Pilgrims, 1996; (ed jtly) New Soundings, 1997; Augustine's Legacy: authority and leadership in the Anglican Communion, 1997; (ed jtly) Flagships of the Spirit: cathedrals in society, 1998; Pilgrim Guide to Norwich, 1998; Cathedrals and Abbeys of England, 1999, 2nd edn 2011; Ink and Spirit, 2000; Rebuilding Jerusalem: the Church's hold on hearts and minds, 2007; Vocation: singing the Lord's song, 2007; Animating Liturgy: the dynamics of worship and the human community, 2017; Borderlands: exploring Northumberland and the Tweed, 2017; Border Country: tales from Northumberland and the Tweed Valley, 2019; contributor: Deacons in the Ministry of the Church, 1987; Spirituality and Psychology, 1990; Say One for Me, 1991; (and ed) Seeing Ourselves: who are the interpreters of contemporary society?, 1998; (and ed) The Retreat of the State, 1999; (and ed) Open Government, 2002; A New Dictionary of Liturgy and Worship, 2002; (and ed) Runcie: on reflection, 2002; (and ed) Anglicanism and the Western Tradition, 2003; Jesus in History, Thought and Culture, 2003, 2nd edn as Jesus: the complete guide, 2005; (and ed jtly) Dreaming Spires: cathedrals in a new age, 2006; In Search of Humanity and Deity: a celebration of John Macquarrie's theology, 2006; (and ed jtly) Reinhold Niebuhr and Contemporary Politics: God and power, 2010; Unity in Process: reflections on ecumenical activity, 2012; (and ed) Comfortable Words: polity, piety and the Book of Common Prayer, 2012; Liturgical Spirituality: Anglican reflections on the Church's prayer, 2013; (and ed) Oneness: the monastic tradition and the contemporary church, 2017; (and ed) Holy Ground: cathedrals in the 21st century, 2017; contribs to theol and educnl jls. *Recreations:* walking, music, literature, Land Rovers, Northumberland. *Address:* 22 Quay Walls, Berwick upon Tweed, Northumberland TD15 1HB. *E:* stephen.platten@icloud.com. *Clubs:* Athenæum (Mem., Gen. Cttee, 2017–19), City University.

**PLATTS, (Charles) Graham (Gregory); His Honour Judge Platts;** a Circuit Judge, since 2005; a Judge of the High Court, since 2008; Judge, Court of Protection, since 2018; *b* 25 Aug. 1956; *s* of Arthur Platts and Georgina Platts; *m* 1985, Hazel Carty; one *s* one *d. Educ:* Fitzwilliam Coll., Cambridge (BA 1977). Called to the Bar, Gray's Inn, 1978; in practice as barrister specialising in clinical negligence and personal injury, 1978–2005; Asst Recorder, 1999–2000; a Recorder, 2000–05. Pt-time Legal Mem., 2002–05, Mem., Restricted Patients' Panel, 2007–, Mental Health Rev. Tribunal. *Recreations:* piano, walking, ski-ing, Manchester City FC.

**PLATTS-MILLS, Mark Fortescue;** QC 1995; *b* 17 Jan. 1951; *s* of John Faithful Fortescue Platts-Mills, QC; *m* 1982, Dr Juliet Anne Britton; one *s. Educ:* Bryanston Sch.; Balliol Coll., Oxford (BA Eng. Sci. and Econ.). Called to the Bar, Inner Temple, 1974; Bencher, Lincoln's Inn, 2006. *Recreations:* gardening, hockey, cricket. *Address:* 8 New Square, Lincoln's Inn, WC2A 3QP.

**PLATTS-MILLS, Prof. Thomas Alexander,** FRS 2010; Professor of Medicine, Head of Division of Allergy and Clinical Immunology, and Head of Asthma and Allergic Diseases, University of Virginia, since 1982; *b* Colchester, 22 Nov. 1941; *s* of John Faithful Fortescue Platts-Mills, QC, and Janet Katherine Platts-Mills (*née* Cree); *m* 1970, Roberta Rosenstock; three *s* one *d. Educ:* University College Sch., Hampstead; Balliol Coll., Oxford (BA 1963; BM BCh 1967); St Thomas' Hospital, London. Fellow, Johns Hopkins Univ., 1971–74; Perm. Mem., Clinical Res. Centre, MRC, 1974–82. Pres., Amer. Acad. of Allergy, Asthma and Immunology, 2006–07. *Publications:* over 330 articles in scientific jls. *Recreations:* hiking, sailing. *Address:* University of Virginia School of Medicine, Box 801355, Charlottesville, VA 22908, USA. *T:* (434) 9245917. *E:* tap2z@virginia.edu.
*See also* M. F. Platts-Mills.

**PLAYER, Dr David Arnott,** FRCPE, FRCPsych, FFCM; District Medical Officer, South Birmingham Health Authority, 1987–91; *b* 2 April 1927; *s* of John Player and Agnes Gray; *m* 1955, Anne Darragh; two *s. Educ:* Calder Street Sch.; Bellahouston Acad., Glasgow; Glasgow Univ. (MB, ChB 1949; DPH 1960). DPM RCSI 1964; St Andrews Univ. (MA Hons 1995). House Surgeon, Dumfries and Galloway Royal Infirmary, 1950; Consultant in Dermatology and VD, RAMC (Far East), 1950–52; House Surgeon, Western Infirmary, Glasgow, 1952; House Physician, Bridge of Earn Hosp., 1952–53; House Surgeon (Obst., Gyn. and Paed.), Halifax Royal Infirmary, 1953–54; GP, W Cumberland and Dumfriesshire, 1954–59; Registrar (Infectious Diseases), Paisley Infectious Diseases Hosp., 1959–60; Asst MOH, Dumfriesshire, 1960–62; Registrar (Psychiatry), Crichton Royal Hosp., Dumfries, 1962–64; MOH, Dumfries Burgh, 1964–70; MO (Mental Health Div.), SHHD and Med. and Psych. Adviser to Sec. of State for Scotland on Scottish Prison and Borstal Service, 1970–73; Dir, Scottish Health Educn Group, 1973–82; Dir Gen., Health Educn Council, 1982–87. Hon. Vis. Prof., Dept of Clinical Epidemiology and Gen. Practice, Royal Free Hosp. Sch. of Medicine, 1983–. *Publications:* articles in Health Bulletin, Internat. Jl of Health Educn, Scottish Trade Union Review. *Recreations:* golf, cycling.

**PLAYER, Gary James;** professional golfer, since 1953; *b* Johannesburg, 1 Nov. 1935; *s* of Francis Harry Audley Player and late Muriel Marie Ferguson; *m* 1957, Vivienne, *d* of Jacob Wynand Verwey; two *s* four *d. Educ:* King Edward Sch., Johannesburg. Won first, Dunlop tournament, 1956; major championship wins include: British Open, 1959, 1968, 1974; US Masters, 1961, 1974, 1978; US PGA, 1962, 1972; US Open, 1965; S African Open, thirteen times, 1956–81; S African PGA, 1959, 1960, 1969, 1979, 1982; Australian Open, seven times, 1958–74; Johnnie Walker Trophy, Spain, 1984; World Match Play Tournament, 1965, 1966, 1968, 1971, 1973. *Publications:* Golf Begins at 50 (with Desmond Tolhurst), 1988; To Be the Best, 1991; The Meaning of Life, 2000.

**PLAYFAIR, Prudence Margaret;** *see* Leith, P. M.

**PLAYFORD, His Honour Jonathan Richard;** QC 1982; a Circuit Judge, 1998–2006; *b* 6 Aug. 1940; *s* of late Cecil R. B. Playford and Euphrasia J. Playford; *m* 1978, Jill Margaret Dunlop; one *s* one *d. Educ:* Eton Coll.; London Univ. (LLB). Called to the Bar, Inner Temple, 1962, Bencher, 1991; a Recorder, 1985–98. Mem., CICB, 1995–98. Freeman, Clockmakers' Co., 2004. *Recreations:* music, horology, golf. *Address:* c/o Reading Crown Court, Old Shire Hall, Forbury, Reading RG1 3EH. *Clubs:* Garrick; Huntercombe Golf (Henley); New Zealand Golf.

**PLAYLE, Colin;** Managing Director, Cicero, The Talking Company, 1995–2012; *b* 13 May 1933; *s* of James and Florence Playle; *m* 1st, 1957, Reena Mary Cuppleditch (marr. diss. 1975); two *d*; 2nd, 1976, Patricia Margaret Golds (*d* 1998); 3rd, 2007, Rosemary Margaret Henderson. *Educ:* University College London (BA Hons). CompIGasE. British Gas: Marketing and Customer Service, E Midlands Gas Bd, 1957–75; Regl Marketing Manager, E Midlands, 1975–78; Dir of Marketing, British Gas NE, 1978–86; Sen. Mem., British Gas Privatisation Team, 1986–91; HQ Dir, Industrial and Commercial Gas, London, 1988–91; Regl Chm., British Gas Scotland, 1991–94; Project Dir, Retail, 1994–95. Chm., Combined Heat and Power Assoc., 1991–93. Vis. Prof. in Business Studies, Liverpool Business Sch., 1997–2012. Co-ordinator, Azerbaijan, TAM programme, EBRD, 1999–2000. *Recreations:* ski-ing, ornithology, modern literature, theatrical productions. *Address:* Upton Barn, 83 Main Street, Upton, Newark, Notts NG23 5SY.

**PLEASENCE, Prof. Pascoe Thomas;** Professor of Empirical Legal Studies, University College London, since 2007; *b* London, 24 May 1965; *s* of Michael Cadman and Angela Pleasence; partner, Sophie Weeks; one *d. Educ:* Hampton Sch.; University Coll. London (BA Philosophy); St Edmund's Coll., Cambridge (MPhil Criminol. 1989); City Univ. (DipLaw); Inns of Court Sch. of Law. Called to the Bar, Middle Temple, 1991; Hd, Legal Services Res. Centre, London, 1995–2009; Sen. Res. Fellow, Law and Justice Foundn of NSW, Sydney, 2012–14; Man. Dir, Pascoe Pleasence Ltd, 2011–. *Publications:* Profiling Civil Litigation, 1996; Personal Injury Litigation in Practice, 1998; Local Legal Need, 2001; Causes of Action: civil law and social justice, 2004, 2nd edn 2006; Transforming Lives, 2007; Reaching Further, 2009; In Need of Advice?: findings of a small business legal needs benchmarking survey, 2013; Paths to Justice: a past, present and future road map, 2013; Reshaping Legal Services, 2014; How People Resolve Legal problems, 2014; contrib. articles to jls. *Recreations:* travel, music, swimming; formerly surf life saver, Queenscliff Beach, Sydney. *Address:* UCL Laws, Bentham House, Endsleigh Gardens, WC1H 0EG. *E:* p.pleasence@ucl.ac.uk.

**PLEDGER, Air Chief Marshal Sir Malcolm (David),** KCB 2001; OBE 1988; AFC 1981; *b* 24 July 1948; *m* 1969, Betty Barker Kershaw; two *s. Educ:* Newcastle Univ. (BSc 1st Cl. Chemistry 1970). Commnd RAF, 1970; served RAF Stations at Akrotiri, Shawbury, Sek Kong, Upavon, RAF Staff Coll., and MoD, 1972–85; OC 240 Operational Conversion Unit, RAF Odiham, 1985–88, incl. tour as OC 78 Sqdn, RAF Mount Pleasant, Falkland Is; Air Sec.'s Dept, 1988–90; Station Comdr, RAF Shawbury, 1990–92; rcds 1993; Air Officer Plans, HQ RAF Strike Command, 1993–97; COS, Dep. C-in-C and AOC, Directly Administered Units, HQ RAF Logistics Comd, 1997–99; Air Mem. for Logistics and AOC-in-C, RAF Logistics Comd, 1999; DCDS (Personnel), 1999–2002; Chief of Defence Logistics, MoD, 2002–04. *Recreation:* golf. *Club:* Royal Air Force.

**PLEMING, Nigel Peter**; QC 1992; a Judge of the Courts of Appeal of Jersey and Guernsey, 2007–18; *b* 13 March 1946; *s* of late Rev. Percy Francis Pleming and Cynthia Myra Pleming (later Mrs Leslie Tuxworth); *m* 1979, Evelyn Carol Joan Hoffmann; one *s* two *d*. *Educ*: King Edward VI Grammar Sch., Spilsby; Kingston Polytechnic (LLB); University Coll. London (LLM). Lectr, Kingston Poly., 1969–73; called to the Bar, Inner Temple, 1971, Bencher, 2001; in practice at the Bar, 1974–; Junior Counsel to the Crown (Common Law), 1987–92; Member: Belize Bar, 2010–; BVI Bar, 2013–; occasional Mem., Bars of Hong Kong, Cayman Is, and Trinidad and Tobago. Vice-Chm., Mental Health Act Commn, 1994–97; Mem., Govt working party on mental health reform, 1998–99. Mem., UK Res. Integrity Office, 2000–. Hon. LLD Kingston, 1999. *Recreations*: theatre, guitar, watching cricket. *Address*: 39 Essex Chambers, 81 Chancery Lane, WC2A 1DD. *T*: (020) 7832 1111. *Club*: Garrick.

**PLEMING, Richard Thomas Francis**; Teacher of English, Kensington Aldridge Academy, since 2017; *b* Cuckfield, Sussex, 20 May 1962; *s* of late Peter Pleming and Morag Pleming; *m* 1989, Rachel Crowther; one *s* four *d*. *Educ*: Pembroke Coll., Cambridge (BA 1st Cl. Hons Eng. 1984). Mktg Exec., Scottish Opera, 1984–85; Corporate Finance Exec., Schroders, 1985–88; Investment Controller, Investors in Industry, 1988–90; Teacher of English: St Paul's Sch., Barnes, 1990–91; Eton Coll., 1991–97; Hd of English, 1997–2007, Housemaster, 2006–11, St Edward's, Oxford; Headmaster, Wrekin Coll., 2011–13; Headmaster, Charterhouse, 2014–16. *Recreations*: hill walking, reading, opera, dogs, singing, church visiting, five-a-side football.

**PLENDER, John**; *see* Plender, W. J. T.

**PLENDER, Hon. Sir Richard (Owen)**, Kt 2008; a Judge of the High Court of Justice, Queen's Bench Division, 2008–10; Visiting Professor of Economic and Commercial Law, University of Groningen, Netherlands (Professor of Economic and Commercial Law, 2010–14); *b* 9 Oct. 1945; *s* of George Plender and Louise Mary (*née* Savage); *m* 1978, Patricia Clare (*née* Ward); two *d*. *Educ*: Dulwich Coll.; Queens' Coll., Cambridge (MA, LLB; LLD 1993); Univ. of Illinois (LLM; JSD 1972); Univ. of Sheffield (PhD 1973). Called to the Bar, Inner Temple, 1972, Bencher, 1996; in practice at the Bar, 1974–2008; QC 1989; Recorder, 1998–2008. Consultant, UN Law and Population Programme, 1972–74; Legal Adviser, UN High Comr for Refugees, 1974–78; Legal Sec., Court of Justice of European Communities, 1980–83; Dir of Studies, 1987, Dir of Res., 1988, and Lectr, 1998, Hague Acad. of Internat. Law; Dir, Centre of European Law, KCL, 1988–91; Special Legal Advr to States of Jersey, 1988–2008. Leverhulme Fellow, Yale Law Sch., 1980; British Acad. Fellow, Soviet Acad. of Sciences, 1985; Sen. Mem., Robinson Coll., Cambridge, 1983–; Associate Prof., Univ. de Paris II (Univ. de Droit, d'Economie et des Sciences Sociales), 1989–90; Hon. Vis. Prof., City Univ., 1991–. *Publications*: International Migration Law, 1972, 2nd edn 1988; (ed and contrib.) Fundamental Rights, 1973; Cases and Materials on the Law of the European Communities, 1980 (with J. Usher), 3rd edn 1993; A Practical Introduction to European Community Law, 1980; (with J. Peres Santos) Introducción al Derecho Comunitario Europeo, 1984; Basic Documents on International Migration Law, 1988, 3rd edn 2006; (ed and contrib.) Legal History and Comparative Law: essays in honour of Albert Kiralfy, 1990; The European Contracts Convention: the Rome Convention on the Choice of Law for Contracts, 1991, 3rd edn (with M. Wilderspin) as The European Private International Law of Obligations, 2009; (ed and contrib.) The European Courts Practice and Precedents, 1996, supplement 1997, as European Courts Procedure, 2000–; contribs in English, French, German and Spanish to jls and encyclopedias. *Recreations*: writing light verse, classical music (especially sacred choral).

**PLENDER, (William) John (Turner)**, FCA; writer and columnist, Financial Times, since 1981; *b* Cardiff, 9 May 1945; *s* of William Plender and late Averil Maud Plender (*née* Turnbull); *m* 1st, 1972, Sophia Mary, *e d* of late Alistair and Nancy Crombie (marr. diss. 1989); one *s* two *d*; 2nd, 1997, Stephanie Julia Michell, *d* of late David and Joan Harris; two *s*. *Educ*: Downside Sch.; Oriel Coll., Oxford (BA). FCA 1970. Chartered Accountant, Deloitte, Plender, Griffiths & Co., 1967–70; Staff writer: Investors Chronicle, 1970–71; The Times, 1972–74; Financial Ed., Economist, 1974–79; Mem., Planning Staff, FCO, 1980–81; freelance journalist, publisher, author and broadcaster, 1982–. Chm., Pensions and Investment Res. Consultants, 1992–2002. Non-executive Director: Quintain Estates and Development plc, 2002–10 (Chm., 2007–09); OMFIF, 2012– (Chm., 2014–18). Member: Co. Law Rev. Steering Gp, DTI, 1998–2001; Private Sector Adv. Gp on Corporate Governance, World Bank/OECD, 2002–. Mem., Quality of Mkts Adv. Cttee, London Stock Exchange, 1992–95; Chm., Adv. Council, Centre for Study of Financial Innovation, 1997–. Mem., Adv. Panel, Assoc. of Corporate Treasurers, 2002–19. Trustee, Pearson Pension Fund, 2010–. Sen. Wincott Award for Financial Journalism, 1994. *Publications*: That's The Way The Money Goes, 1981; (with P. Wallace) The Square Mile, 1985; A Stake in the Future, 1997; Going Off the Rails, 2003; (with A. Persaud) Ethics and Finance, 2007; Capitalism: money, morals and markets, 2015. *Recreations*: piano, art, literature, wine, walking. *Address*: c/o The Financial Times, Bracken House, 1 Friday Street, EC4M 9BT. *T*: (020) 7873 3000, *Fax*: (020) 7478 9438. *E*: john.plender@ft.com. *Club*: Travellers.

**PLENDERLEITH, Ian**, CBE 2002; Deputy Governor and Member, Monetary Policy Committee, South African Reserve Bank, 2003–05; Executive Director, 1994–2002, Member, Monetary Policy Committee, 1997–2002, Bank of England; Chairman, Sanlam UK Ltd, since 2016 (non-executive Director, since 2010); *b* 27 Sept. 1943; *s* of late Raymond William Plenderleith and Louise Helen Plenderleith (*née* Martin); *m* 1st, 1967, Kristina Mary Bentley (marr. diss. 2007); one *s* two *d*; 2nd, 2007, Elizabeth Ann Campbell Barrell. *Educ*: King Edward's Sch., Birmingham; Christ Church, Oxford (MA); Columbia Business Sch., NY (MBA; Beta Gamma Sigma Medal, 1971). Joined Bank of England, 1965; seconded to IMF, Washington DC, 1972–74; Private Sec. to Governor, 1976–79; Alternate Dir, EIB, 1980–86; Hd of Gilt-Edged Div., 1982–90; Asst Dir, 1986–90, Associate Dir, 1990–94. Dir, Bank of England Nominees Ltd, 1994–2002; Alternate Dir, BIS, 1994–2002; Sen. Broker to Comrs for Reduction of Nat. Debt, 1989–2002. Dir, London Stock Exchange (formerly Mem., Stock Exchange Council), 1989–2001 (Dep. Chm., 1996). Internat. Consultant, Invoice Clearing Bureau SA (Pty) Ltd, 2006–. Chairman: BH Macro Ltd, 2007–17; Morgan Stanley Internat. Ltd, 2014–18 (non-exec. Dir, 2011–18); non-executive Director: Sanlam Ltd, 2006–13; BMCE Bank Internat. (formerly Medicapital Bank plc), 2006–16; Bond Exchange of S Africa, 2007–09; Europe Arab Bank plc, 2009–12; Sanlam Private Investments (UK) Hldgs Ltd, 2013–16; Sanlam Life & Pensions Ltd, 2013–16. Sen. Advr, Anthem Corp. Finance, 2009–12. Chairman: Stock Borrowing and Lending Cttee, 1990–95; G-10 Gold and Foreign Exchange Cttee, 1995–2001; Sterling Money Mkts Liaison Gp, 1999–2002; Corporation for Public Deposits, 2003–05; SA Money Mkts Liaison Gp, 2004–05; Co-Chm., Govt Borrowers Forum, 1991–94; Mem., G-10 Cttee on Global Financial System, 1994–2002. Member: Editl Cttee, OECD Study on Debt Management, 1990–93; Legal Risk Rev. Cttee, 1991–92; Financial Law Panel, 1992–94; Global Borrowers and Investors Forum Adv. Bd, 2003–05; Sen. Adv. Council, Internat. Capital Mkts Assoc., 2006–12; Adv. Bd, Central Banking Pubns, 2006–. Member: Adv. Bd, Inst. of Archaeology Develt Trust, UCL, 1987–96; Bd of Overseers, Columbia Business Sch., 1991–2009 (Mem., Adv. Bd, London Alumni Club, 2002, 2006–); London Old Edwardians Assoc. Cttee, 1996–2004 (Vice-Pres., 2004–); Ext. Adv. Panel, Oxford Math. Inst., 2000–03; Oxford Business Alumni Adv. Bd, 2002–03; Adv. Bd, Witwatersrand Business Sch., 2007–12. Member: Fund-raising Planning Gp, St Bartholomew's Hosp., 1992–94; Fund-raising Planning Cttee, St Bartholomew's and The London Hosps, 1998–2003; Council, British Museum Soc., subseq. BM Friends, 1993–99, 2000–03 and 2005–12; BM Townley Steering Gp, 2002–03; Adv. Bd, Actors Centre, 2002–; Council (formerly Develt Council), Shakespeare's Globe, 2002–; Christ Church Develt Bd, 2008–15 (Mem. Bd, 2002–08, Mem., Finance Cttee, 1998–2003, Christ Church Campaign); Chm., Reed's Sch. Foundn Appeal, 2006–07; Jt Pres., Reed's Sch., 2016– (Gov., 2007–16; Chm., 2008–16). Dir, City Arts Trust, 1997–2003. FCSI (FSI 2006, MSI 1991); Mem., Assoc. of Black Securities and Investment Professionals, 2005–06; Mem., Internat. Bankers' Co., 2012–. Hon. Fellow, ACT, 1989 (Mem. Adv. Bd, 2007–). Liveryman, Innholders' Co., 1977 (Mem., Investment Cttee, 2007–). *Recreations*: archaeology, theatre, cricket, travel. *Address*: Goldneys, River, Petworth, W Sussex GU28 9AU. *Clubs*: Athenæum (Mem., 2007–, Chm., 2008–14, Investment Cttee), MCC; Tillington Cricket (Hon. Sec., 1983–2003).

**PLETNEV, Mikhail Vasilievich**; pianist, conductor and composer; *b* Archangel, Russia, 14 April 1957. *Educ*: Central Sch. of Music; Moscow State Conservatory (under Yakov Flier and Lev Vlasenko (piano), and Albert Leman (composition)). Founder and Principal Conductor, Russian Nat. Orch., 1990–99, now Conductor Laureate; Guest Conductor of orchs incl. Philharmonia, LSO, CBSO and Los Angeles Philharmonic. Piano recitals and tours with orchs worldwide; numerous recordings. Teacher, Moscow State Conservatory, 1981–. Works composed include: Classical Symphony; Triptych for Symphony Orch.; Fantasy on Kazakh Themes for Violin and Orch.; Capriccio for Piano and Orch.; Concerto for Viola and Orch. Gold Medal, Tchaikovsky Internat. Piano Competition, 1978; State Prize of Russia, 1995, 2002.

**PLEWMAN, Thomas**; QC 2016; *b* Johannesburg, S Africa, 7 July 1965; *s* of Christel Plewman and Ulla Tove Plewman; *m* 1992, Theresa Jane Fleming; one *s* one *d*. *Educ*: Univ. of Cape Town (BCom); Univ. of Witwatersrand (LLB); Magdalen Coll., Oxford (BCL). Admitted Advocate, SA, 1993; Advocate, High Court of SA, 1993–2008; Sen. Counsel, SA, 2008–; called to the Bar, Middle Temple, 2009; in practice as barrister specialising in commercial litigation, 2009–. *Recreations*: hiking, tennis, cycling. *Address*: Brick Court Chambers, 7–8 Essex Street, WC2R 3LD.

**PLEWS, Derek Alexander**; Policy Lead, Private Sector Employer Engagement, Ministry of Defence, since 2014; *b* 14 Dec. 1960; *s* of Albert Edward Plews and Doris Plews; *m* 1984, Sandra Elizabeth Joyce Ming; two *s*. *Educ*: Clondermott Sec. Sch., Londonderry; Open Univ. (BA Hons Hist. 2012); Univ. of Birmingham (MA 2014). Reporter, Belfast Telegraph, 1979–82; Actg Ed., Londonderry Sentinel, 1982–85; Press Officer, MoD, 1985–91; Chief Press Officer, Employment Dept, 1991–94; Dep. Hd of Inf., Dept of Transport, 1994–97; Hd of News, DETR, 1997–98; Press Sec. to Dep. Prime Minister, 1998–2001; Dir of Communications, Assoc. of Train Operating Cos, 2001; Dir of News, MoD, 2001–02; Dir of Communication, ODPM, then DCLG, 2002–06; Principal Consultant, Media Outcomes, 2006–07; Lt Col, Royal Irish Regt, attached to Defence Media Ops Centre, mobilized mil. service, SO1 Media Ops, HQ MND (SE), Basra, Iraq, 2007; full-time Reserve Service (Army), SO1 Jt Media Ops Team, Defence Media Ops Centre, RAF Uxbridge, then RAF Halton, 2008–11; Dir of Communications, Reading BC, 2011–14. *Recreations*: hill-walking, angling. *Address*: 6.D.28 Main Building, Ministry of Defence, Horseguards Avenue, SW1A 2HB.

**PLEYDELL-BOUVERIE**, family name of **Earl of Radnor**.

**PLEYDELL-BOUVERIE, Juliet**; *see* Bouverie, J. P.

**PLOMIN, Judith Frances**; *see* Dunn, J. F.

**PLOMIN, Prof. Robert**, PhD; FBA 2005; Research Professor in Behavioural Genetics, and Deputy Director, MRC Research Centre on Social, Genetic, and Developmental Psychiatry, Institute of Psychiatry, Psychology and Neuroscience (formerly Institute of Psychiatry), King's College, London, since 1994; *b* 20 Feb. 1948; *m* 1987, Judith Frances Dunn, *qv*. *Educ*: DePaul Univ., Chicago (BA Psychology 1970); Univ. of Texas, Austin (PhD Psychology 1974). University of Colorado: Faculty Fellow, Inst. for Behavioral Genetics, 1974–86; Asst Prof., 1974–78; Associate Prof., 1978–82; Prof., 1982–86; Dist. Prof. and Dir, Center for Develt and Health Genetics, Pennsylvania State Univ., 1986–94. Pres., Behavior Genetics Assoc., 1989–90. Ed., Sage Series on Individual Differences and Development, 1990–. *Publications*: (with A. H. Buss) Temperament: early developing personality traits, 1984; (with J. C. DeFries) Origins of Individual Differences in Infancy: the Colorado Adoption Project, 1985; Development, Genetics and Psychology, 1986; (ed with J. Dunn) The Study of Temperament: changes, continuities, and challenges, 1986; (jtly) Nature and Nurture in Infancy and Early Childhood, 1988; (with J. Dunn) Separate Lives: why siblings are so different, 1990; (jtly) Behavioral Genetics: a primer, 2nd edn 1990 to 6th edn 2014; (ed jtly) Nature and Nurture during Middle Childhood, 1994; (ed jtly) Separate Social Worlds of Siblings: impact of nonshared environment on development, 1994; Genetics and Experience: the interplay between nature and nurture, 1994; (jtly) The Relationship Code, 2000; Blueprint: how DNA makes us who we are, 2018; numerous articles in learned jls. *Address*: MRC Centre for Social, Genetic and Developmental Psychiatry, Institute of Psychiatry, Psychology and Neuroscience, King's College London, De Crespigny Park, Denmark Hill, SE5 8AF.

**PLOTKIN, Prof. Gordon David**, PhD; FRS 1992; FRSE; Professor of Computation Theory, Edinburgh University, since 1986; *b* 9 Sept. 1946; *s* of Manuel Plotkin and Mary (*née* Levin); *m* 1st, 1984, Lynda (*née* Stephenson) (marr. diss.); one *s*; 2nd, 1994, Hephzibah (*née* Kolban). *Educ*: Univ. of Glasgow (BSc 1967); Univ. of Edinburgh (PhD 1972). University of Edinburgh: Res. Associate and Res. Fellow, 1971–72; Lectr, 1975; Reader, 1982–86. BP Venture Res. Fellow, 1981–87; SERC Sen. Res. Fellow, 1992–97. MAE 1989. FRSE 1993. Royal Soc.–Wolfson Res. Merit Award, 2005–11. (Jtly) Test of Time Award, Logic in Computer Sci., 2007, 2017; Programming Langs Achievement Award, ACM Special Interest Gp on Programming Langs, 2010; Blaise Pascal Medal in Computational Scis and Information, Eur. Acad. of Scis, 2011; Milner Award, Royal Soc., 2012; Eur. Assoc. of Theoretical Computer Sci. Award, 2014; Lovelace Medal, BCS, 2019. *Publications*: (ed with G. Kahn) Semantics of Data Types, 1984; (ed with G. Huet) Logical Frameworks, 1991; (ed with J.-L. Lassez) Computational Logic: essays in honour of Alan Robinson, 1991; (ed jtly) Situation Theory and its Applications, 1991; (ed with G. Huet) Logical Environments, 1993; (ed with M. Dezani-Ciancaglini) Typed Lambda Calculi and Applications, 1995; (ed jtly) Proof, Language and Interaction: essays in honour of Robin Milner, 2000; contribs to jls of computer science and logic. *Recreations*: hill-walking, chess. *Address*: School of Informatics, University of Edinburgh, 10 Crichton Street, Edinburgh EH8 9AB.

**PLOTKIN, Prof. Henry Charles**, PhD; Professor of Psychobiology, University College London, 1993–2005, now Emeritus; *b* Johannesburg, 11 Dec. 1940; *s* of Bernard Solomon Plotkin and Edythe Plotkin (*née* Poplak); *m* 1st, 1965, Patricia Ruehl (marr. diss. 1970); 2nd, 1975, Victoria Mary Welch; one *s* one *d*. *Educ*: Univ. of Witwatersrand (BSc 1st cl. Hons

1964); University College London (PhD 1968). Res. Asst, Univ. of Witwatersrand, 1964; Res. Scientist, MRC Unit on Neural Mechanisms of Behaviour, 1965–72; MRC Travelling Fellowship, Stanford Univ., Calif, 1970–71; Department of Psychology, University College London: Lectr, 1972–88; Reader, 1988–93; Head of Dept, 1993–98. *Publications:* Darwin Machines and the Nature of Knowledge, 1994; Evolution in Mind, 1997; The Imagined World Made Real, 2002; Evolutionary Thought in Psychology, 2004; Necessary Knowledge, 2007; Evolutionary Worlds Without End, 2010; *edited:* (with D. A. Oakley) Brain, Behaviour and Evolution, 1979; Essays in Evolutionary Epistemology, 1982; The Role of Behaviour in Evolution, 1988; articles in learned jls. *Recreations:* family, Dorset cottage, books, music. *Address:* Department of Psychology, University College London, WC1E 6BT.

**PLOWDEN, Hon. Francis John**; Member, Judicial Appointments Commission, 2006–12; Chairman, Child Exploitation and On-line Protection Centre, 2010–13; Board Member, Serious Organised Crime Agency, 2009–13; *b* 25 June 1945; *s* of Lord Plowden, GBE, KCB, and Lady Plowden, DBE; *m* 1984, Geraldine Wickman; one *s*. *Educ:* Eton; Trinity Coll., Cambridge (BA 1966). FCA 1969. Cooper Brothers, then Coopers & Lybrand, subseq. PricewaterhouseCoopers: consulting and acctg experience, UK, Ghana, the Gambia and Zaire, 1966–76; Partner, Nigeria, 1976–79; on secondment to HM Treasury/Cabinet Office Financial Mgt Unit, 1982–85; Partner, 1985; Hd, Govt Consulting, 1987–95; Man. Partner Internat. Affairs, and Mem. Internat. Exec. Cttee, 1995–98; Global Govt Leader, 1998–2001. Chm., Nat. Council for Palliative Care, 2001–08. Director: ITNET plc, 2001–05; Hedra plc, 2007–08; Draxmont Ltd, 2010–. Member: Audit Cttee, BM, 2009–13; Bd, Children and Family Court Adv. and Support Services, 2012–; Asst Boundary Comr, Boundary Commn for England, 2011–13. Chm., Greenwich Foundn for Old Royal Naval Coll., 2003–11. Treas., Family Housing Assoc., 1979–84. Trustee: Royal Armouries, 1989–97; Royal Ballet Sch., 1989–2003; Anna Plowden Trust, 2000–; Edward James Foundn (W Dean Coll.), 2014–; CARE Internat. (UK), 2014–18. *Publications:* (with Sir Christopher Foster) The State Under Stress, 1996; Review of Court Fees in Child Care Proceedings, 2009. *Recreations:* walking, ballet, theatre, built and natural environment. *Address:* 4 Highbury Road, SW19 7PR. *T:* (020) 8879 9841. *E:* f.plowden@btopenworld.com. *Clubs:* Royal Automobile, MCC.

**PLOWDEN, Prof. Philip Edward Hartley Standish**; Vice-Chancellor and Chief Executive, Birmingham City University, since 2017; *b* London, 2 March 1961; *s* of Giles Plowden and Sarah Maconochie Plowden; *m* 2012, Dr Penelope Smith; one *s*. *Educ:* Ampleforth Coll.; Brasenose Coll., Oxford (BA Hons English 1982); Newcastle Univ. (LLM 1996). Admitted solicitor, 1993; called to the Bar, Middle Temple, 2001. Greater London CAB Service, 1984–89; Christian Fisher solicitors, 1991–93; School of Law, Northumbria University: Lectr, 1993–97; Principal Lectr, 1997–2002; Associate Dean, 2002–08; Chair in Law, 2005–11; Dean, 2008–11; Dep. Vice-Chancellor, Univ. of Derby, 2011–17. Mem. Bd, Office for Legal Complaints, 2014–17. Founder Trustee, Derby Mus and Art Galls Trust, 2012–17. Nat. Teaching Fellow, Higher Educn Acad., 2005. *Publications:* articles on advocacy, human rights and criminal litigation. *Recreations:* American football (viewing), science fiction, computer gaming.

**PLOWMAN, John Patrick**; consultant in transport safety, environmental policy and sustainability, since 2003; *b* 20 March 1944; *s* of late Robert and Ruth Plowman, Lane End, Bucks; *m* 1973, Daphne Margaret Brock Kennett; two *s* one *d*. *Educ:* St Edward's Sch., Oxford; Grenoble Univ.; University Coll., Univ. of Durham (BA). MoD, 1967–75: Private Office, Minister of State for Defence, 1969–71; Resident Observer, CSSB, 1975; Cabinet Office, 1976–78; MoD and UK Delegn to UN Law of Sea Conf., 1979–81; Asst Sec., DoE, 1982–86; Counsellor, UK Repn to EC, 1986–90; Head, Envmtl Protection (Europe), 1990–93; Regl Dir for NW, DoE and Dept of Transport, 1993–94; Dir, Wildlife and Countryside, DoE, then DETR, 1994–98; Dir, Road Safety and Envmt, DETR, 1998–2001; Chm., Driver and Vehicle Operator Gp, DETR, subseq. DTLR, then DfT, 2001–02; Gp Modernisation Dir, Driver and Vehicle Operator Gp, DfT, 2003. Served Royal Marines Reserve, 1968–71. Director and Trustee: Parly Adv. Council for Transport Safety, 2004–; Road Safety Foundn, 2009– (Chm., Older Drivers Task Force, 2015–); Dir, RoadSafe, 2006–. Chm., London Sustainable Develt Commn, 2009–14. Gov., Charlotte Sharman Sch., Southwark, 2002– (Chm., 2008–18). Freeman, City of London, 2010; Liveryman, Coachmakers' Co., 2010–. *Recreations:* music, fishing, gardening (English Gardening Sch., 2004), travel, book collecting. *Club:* Royal Over-Seas League.

**PLOWMAN, (Phillip) Jon**, OBE 2013; freelance executive TV producer, since 2006; *b* Hatfield, Herts, 4 July 1953; *s* of Charles Edward Plowman and Florence Joan Plowman (*née* Bentley); civil partnership 2007, Francis Matthews. *Educ:* Stanborough Sch., Welwyn Garden City; University Coll., Oxford (BA Hons). Asst Dir, Royal Court Th., 1971–75; Arts Council Drama Officer, 1978–79; Entertainment Producer, Granada TV, 1980–81; BBC TV: producer, 1981–94; Hd of Comedy Entertainment, 1994–2001; Hd of Comedy, 2001–06. Production credits include: Comic Relief, 1989 and 1991; French and Saunders, 1990–2004; Smith and Jones, 1990–92; Murder Most Horrid, 1991–94; Absolutely Fabulous, 1992–2014; The Vicar of Dibley, 1994–2007; Bottom, 1994; A Bit of Fry and Laurie, 1995; Executive Producer: Goodness Gracious Me, 1998–2001; Gimme, Gimme, Gimme, 1999–2001; The League of Gentlemen, 1999–2002; The Office, 2001–03; Little Britain, 2003–06; Beautiful People, 2008–09; Psychoville, 2009–11; Roger and Val Have Just Got In, 2011–12; Twenty Twelve, 2011–12; Inside No 9, 2014; W1A, 2014; producer, film, Absolutely Fabulous: the Movie, 2016. Mem., BAFTA. FRTS 2003; FRSA. Judges' Award for Outstanding Achievement in Broadcasting, RTS, 2006; Lifetime Achievement Award, Banff World TV Fest., 2007. *Publications:* How to Produce Comedy Bronze, 2018. *Recreations:* music, walking in the French Pyrenees, reading, Somerset. *Address:* c/o PBJ Management, 22 Rathbone Street, W1T 1LG. *T:* (020) 8743 8000. *E:* pjplowman@aol.com. *Club:* Soho House.

**PLOWRIGHT, Dame Joan (Ann), (The Lady Olivier)**, DBE 2004 (CBE 1970); leading actress with the National Theatre, 1963–74; Member of the RADA Council; Honorary President, English Stage Company, since 2009; *b* 28 Oct. 1929; *d* of late William Ernest Plowright and of Daisy Margaret (*née* Burton); *m* 1st, 1953, Roger Gage (marr. diss.); 2nd, 1961, (as Sir Laurence Olivier) Baron Olivier, OM (*d* 1989); one *s* two *d*. *Educ:* Scunthorpe Grammar School; Laban Art of Movement Studio; Old Vic Theatre School. First stage appearance in If Four Walls Told, Croydon Rep. Theatre, 1948; Bristol Old Vic and Mem. Old Vic Co., S Africa tour, 1952; first London appearance in The Duenna, Westminster, 1954; Moby Dick, Duke of York's, 1955; season of leading parts, Nottingham Playhouse, 1955–56; English Stage Co., Royal Court, 1956; The Crucible, Don Juan, The Death of Satan, Cards of Identity, The Good Woman of Setzuan, The Country Wife (transferred to Adelphi, 1957); The Chairs, The Making of Moo, Royal Court, 1957; The Entertainer, Palace, 1957; The Chairs, The Lesson, Phoenix, NY, 1958; The Entertainer, Royale, NY, 1958; The Chairs, The Lesson, Major Barbara, Royal Court, 1958; Hook, Line and Sinker, Piccadilly, 1958; Roots, Royal Court, Duke of York's, 1959; Rhinoceros, Royal Court, 1960; A Taste of Honey, Lyceum, NY, 1960 (Best Actress Tony Award); Rosmersholm, Greenwich, 1973; Saturday, Sunday, Monday, Queen's, 1974–75; The Sea Gull, Lyric, 1975; The Bed Before Yesterday, Lyric 1975 (Variety Club of GB Award, 1977); Filumena, Lyric, 1977 (Soc. of West End Theatre Award, 1978); Enjoy, Vaudeville, 1980; The Cherry Orchard, Haymarket, 1983; The House of Bernada Alba, Globe, 1986; Time and the Conways, Old Vic, 1990; If We are Women, Greenwich, 1995; Absolutely! (perhaps), Wyndham's, 2003; Chichester Festival: Uncle Vanya, The Chances, 1962; St Joan (Best Actress Evening Standard Award), Uncle Vanya, 1963; The Doctor's Dilemma, The Taming of the Shrew, 1972; Cavell, 1982; The Way of the World, 1984; National Theatre: St Joan, Uncle Vanya, Hobson's Choice, opening season, 1963; The Master Builder, 1964; Much Ado About Nothing, 1967, 1968; Three Sisters, 1967, 1968; Tartuffe, 1967, 1968; The Advertisement, 1968; Love's Labour's Lost, 1968; The Merchant of Venice, 1970; A Woman Killed With Kindness, 1971; The Rules of the Game, 1971; Eden End, 1974; Mrs Warren's Profession, 1985. Produced The Travails of Sancho Panza, 1969; directed: Rites, 1969; A Prayer for Wings, 1985; Married Love, 1988. *Films include:* The Entertainer, 1960; Three Sisters, 1970; Equus; Britannia Hospital, 1982; Wagner, Revolution, 1985; Drowning by Numbers, The Dressmaker, 1988; I Love You to Death, Avalon, 1989; Stalin, 1992 (Golden Globe Award, 1993); Enchanted April, 1993 (Golden Globe Award, 1993); Denis the Menace, A Place for Annie, A Pin for the Butterfly, Widow's Peak, Last Action Hero, 1993; On Promised Land, Hotel Sorrento, A Pyromaniac's Love Story, The Scarlett Letter, 1994; Mr Wrong, 1995; Jane Eyre, 101 Dalmatians, Surviving Picasso, 1996; The Assistant, 1996; Dance with Me, 1998; America Betrayed, 1998; Tea with Mussolini, 1999; Return to the Secret Garden, Frankie and Hazel, Global Heresy, 2000; Callas Forever, 2001; George and the Dragon, I Am David, 2002; Bringing Down the House, 2003; Mrs Palfrey at the Claremont, 2006; The Spiderwick Chronicles, 2007; Nothing Like a Dame, 2018; *films for TV:* The Merchant of Venice; Brimstone and Treacle, 1982; A Dedicated Man; Return of the Natives, 1994; Tom's Midnight Garden, 1998; This Could Be the Last Time, 1998; other *television* appearances include: Daphne Laureola, 1976; The Birthday Party, 1987; The Importance of Being Earnest, 1988; And a Nightingale Sang, 1989; House of Bernada Alba, 1991; Clothes in the Wardrobe, 1992. 18th annual Crystal Award, Women in Film, USA, 1994. Hon. DLitt Hull, 2001. *Publications:* And That's Not All (memoirs), 2001. *Recreations:* reading, music, entertaining. *Address:* c/o 7 Newham Lane, Steyning, W Sussex BN44 3LR.

**PLOWRIGHT, Jonathan Daniel**, FRAM; concert pianist, since 1985; Member of Keyboard Faculty, Royal Conservatoire of Scotland, since 2007; *b* Doncaster, 1959; *s* of Cyril James and Molly Plowright; *m* 1990, Diane Shaw. *Educ:* Stonyhurst Coll., Lancs; Royal Acad. of Music, London (Macfarren Gold Medal 1983); Peabody Conservatory of Music, Johns Hopkins Univ. FRAM 2013. Fulbright Schol., 1983. Débuts: Carnegie Recital Hall, NY, 1984; Southbank, London, 1985; winner, Eur. Piano Competition, 1989. World première perf. of Constant Lambert Piano Concerto, 1988; world première recordings of piano works by Sigismund Stojowski, 2003–04; has performed with leading orchestras and chamber ensembles and at major concert halls and music fests. *Publications:* contribs to magazines, incl. Musical Opinion, Klassisk Musikkmagasin (Norway), Internat. Piano Mag., Limelight (Australia). *Recreations:* watching cricket and Rugby, fishing, cooking. *E:* jonathan@jonathan.plowright.com. *W:* www.jonathanplowright.com. *Club:* Royal Over-Seas League (Hon. Mem.).

**PLOWRIGHT, Rosalind Anne, (Mrs J. A. Kaye)**, OBE 2007; mezzo-soprano; *b* 21 May 1949; *d* of Robert Arthur Plowright and Celia Adelaide Plowright; *m* 1984, J(ames) Anthony Kaye; one *s* one *d*. *Educ:* Notre Dame High Sch., Wigan; Royal Northern Coll. of Music, Manchester. LRAM. London Opera Centre, 1974–75; Glyndebourne Chorus and Touring Co., début as soprano, Agathe in Der Freischutz, 1975; WNO, ENO, Kent Opera, 1975–78; Miss Jessel in Turn of the Screw, ENO, 1979 (SWET award); début at Covent Garden as Ortlinde in Die Walküre, 1980; with Bern Opera, 1980–81, Frankfurt Opera and Munich Opera, 1981; débuts: in USA (Philadelphia and San Diego), Paris, Madrid and Hamburg, 1982; at La Scala, Milan, Edinburgh Fest., San Francisco and New York (Carnegie Hall), 1983; at Deutsche Oper, Berlin, 1984; in Houston, Pittsburgh, Verona, Montpellier and Venice, 1985; in Rome, Florence and Holland, 1986; in Tulsa, Buenos Aires, Santiago di Chile, Israel and Bonn, 1987; with NY Phil. and Paris Opera, 1987; in Lausanne, Geneva, Oviedo and Bilbao, 1988; in Zurich, Copenhagen, Lisbon and Torre del Lago, 1989; with Vienna State Opera, 1990; in Nice, 1991; in Wiesbaden, 1992; in Leeds, 1993; in Athens and Bregenz, 1994; BBC Prom. Concerts; with Berlin Deutsche Staatsoper, 1996; with Scottish Opera, 1999; with Opera New Zealand, 2000; with Opera Holland Park, 2002; with NY Metropolitan Opera; Paris Châtelet, 2003; with Florence Maggio Musicale, 2004; Tokyo, 2006; Seattle, 2008; Lisbon, 2009; Stuttgart and Madrid, 2011; Portland, Theater des Champs Elysées, Paris, 2013; Theater an der Wien, 2015; Státní Opera, Wexford Festival Opera 2016. Principal rôles as soprano include: Ariadne; Aida; Amelia in Un Ballo in Maschera; Leonora in Il Trovatore; Leonora in La Forza del Destino; Desdemona in Otello; Violetta in La Traviata; Medora in Il Corsaro; Elena in I Vespri Siciliani; Abigaille in Nabucco; Elisabetta in Don Carlos; Lady Macbeth; Manon Lescaut; Giorgetta in Il Tabarro; Suor Angelica; Norma; Alceste; Médée; Maddalena in Andrea Chénier; La Gioconda; Tatyana in Eugene Onegin; Tosca; principal rôles as mezzo-soprano include: Amneris in Aida; Kostelnicka in Jenufa; Fricka in Das Rheingold and Die Walküre; Ortrud in Lohengrin; Marfa in Khovanshchina; Gertrude in Hansel and Gretel; Klytämnestra in Elektra, Mme de Croissy in Dialogues des Carmelites; Herodias in Salome; Countess in Queen of Spades; Old Baroness in Vanessa; Mme de la Haltière in Cendrillon; Mamma Lucia in Cavalleria Rusticana. Has given recitals and concerts in UK, USA and Europe, made opera and concert recordings, and opera telecasts; acting début, House of Elliott, TV serial, 1993; The Man Who Made Husbands Jealous, TV, 1997; Two's a Crowd, UK th. tour, 2002. Teacher of singing; masterclasses at Royal Acad. of Music, Guildhall Sch. of Music, RNCM, Royal Conservatoire of Scotland, Trinity Coll., Portland, USA, Prague and Sweden. First prize, 7th Internat. Comp. for Opera Singers, Sofia, 1979; Prix Fondation Fanny Heldy, Acad. Nat. du Disque Lyrique, 1985. *Recreation:* fell walking. *Address:* c/o James Black Management, 9 Burnhams, Rye, E Sussex TN31 7LW. *W:* www.rosalindplowright.com, www.ros-sing.co.uk.

**PLUMB**, family name of **Baron Plumb**.

**PLUMB, Baron** *cr* 1987 (Life Peer), of Coleshill in the County of Warwickshire; **Charles Henry Plumb**, Kt 1973; DL; Member (C) The Cotswolds, European Parliament, 1979–99; *b* 27 March 1925; *s* of Charles and Louise Plumb; *m* 1947, Marjorie Dorothy Dunn (*d* 2019); one *s* two *d*. *Educ:* King Edward VI School, Nuneaton. National Farmers Union: Member Council, 1959; Vice-President, 1964, 1965; Deputy-President, 1966, 1967, 1968, 1969; President, 1970–79. European Parliament: Chm., Agricl Cttee, 1979–82; Leader, EDG, 1982–87; Pres., 1987–89; Co-Chm., EU/ACP Jt Assembly, 1994; Vice-Pres., EPP, 1994–97; Leader, British Conservatives, 1994–97. Mem., H of L, 1987–2017. Non-executive Director: Lloyds Bank, 1970–81; United Biscuits, 1970–80; Fisons, 1970–78. Chm., British Agricl Council, 1975–79. Chm., Agricultural Mortgage Corp., 1994–95. Mem., Duke of Northumberland's Cttee of Enquiry on Foot and Mouth Disease, 1967–68; Member Council: CBI; Animal Health Trust. Chm., Internat. Agricl Trng Programme, 1987–. Pres., Royal Agric. Soc. of England, 1977, Dep. Pres. 1978; President: Internat. Fedn of Agricl Producers, 1979–82; Comité des Organisations Professionnels Agricoles de la CEE (COPA), 1975–77. Pres., Nat. Fedn of Young Farmers' Clubs, 1976–; Patron, Warwicks Co. Fedn of YFC, 1974–; Hon. Pres., Ayrshire Cattle Soc. Pres., Nat. Sleep Assoc., 2000–. Founder and Trustee, Henry Plumb Foundn, 2013–. Chancellor,

Coventry Univ., 1995–; Gov., RAU (formerly RAC), Cirencester, 1995–. Liveryman, Farmers' Co. (Master, 2005–06). FRSA 1970; FRAgS 1974. DL Warwick 1977. Hon. Fellow, Wye Coll., London Univ., 1988. Hon. DSc: Cranfield, 1983; Silsoe Coll. of Technol., 1987; De Montfort, 1995; Hon. LLD Warwick, 1990; Hon. Dr: Cheltenham & Gloucester Coll. of HE, 1999; Public Service Ohio State, 2010. Gold Medal, RASE, 1983; Robert Schuman Gold Medal, France, 1989; Lifetime Achievement Awards: Farmers Weekly, 2013; Food and Farming Industry, 2014; Farmers Guardian, 2015. Ordén de Merito (Portugal), 1987; Order of Merit (Luxembourg), 1988; Grand Cross, Order of Civil Merit (Spain), 1989; Knight Comdr's Cross, Order of Merit (FRG), 1990 (Order of Merit, 1979); Grand Order of the Phoenix (Greece), 1997. *Recreations:* country pursuits, fishing. *Address:* The Dairy Farm, Maxstoke, Coleshill, Warwicks B46 2QJ. *T:* (01675) 463133, *Fax:* (01675) 464156. *Club:* Farmers.

PLUMB, Alan; *see* Plumb, R. A.

PLUMB, Caroline Bayantai, OBE 2016; Founder and Chief Executive Officer, Fluidly, since 2016; *b* Manchester, 23 Nov. 1978; *d* of Stephen Plumb and Eleanor Onon Plumb; *m* 2006, James Taylor; two *s* one *d*. *Educ:* Bolton Sch. Girls' Div.; St John's Coll., Oxford (MEng Engrg, Econs and Mgt 2000). Co-Founder and CEO, 2000–16, Chm., 2016–, FreshMinds. Prime Minister's Business Ambassador, UKTI, then DIT, 2010–18. *Recreations:* family, running, cards, eating chocolate. *Address:* Fluidly, 229–231 High Holborn, WC1V 7DA. *T:* (020) 7611 1000.

PLUMB, Paula Maria H.; *see* Hay-Plumb.

PLUMB, Prof. (Raymond) Alan, PhD; FRS 1998; Professor of Meteorology, 1988–2017, now Emeritus, and Director, Program in Atmospheres, Oceans and Climate, 2003–08, Massachusetts Institute of Technology; *b* 30 March 1948; *s* of Tom and Dorothy Plumb; *m* 1st, 1981, Janet Gormly (marr. diss. 2007); one *s* one *d*; 2nd, 2010, Donna Jane Bulpett. *Educ:* Manchester Univ. (BSc Physics 1969; PhD Astronomy 1972). SO, then SSO, Met. Office, Bracknell, 1972–76; Res. Scientist, then Principal Res. Scientist, CSIRO Div. of Atmospheric Res., Aspendale, Vic, 1976–88. Haurwitz Meml Lectr, Amer. Meteorol Soc., 2001. Fellow: Amer. Geophysical Union, 2000; Amer. Meteorol Soc., 2002. Jule G. Charney Award, Amer. Meteorol Soc., 2013. *Publications:* (ed with R. A. Vincent) Middle Atmosphere, 1989; (with J. C. Marshall) Atmosphere, Ocean, and Climate Dynamics, 2007; (with P. D. Clift) The Asian Monsoon, 2008; numerous papers in refereed scientific jls, incl. Jl Atmospheric Scis, Jl Geophysical Res. *Recreations:* angling, hiking. *Address:* 21 Regency Drive, Bedford, NH 03110, USA. *T:* (603) 4885057.

PLUMBLY, Sir Derek (John), KCMG 2001 (CMG 1991); HM Diplomatic Service, retired; Under Secretary General and Special Coordinator for Lebanon, United Nations, 2012–15; *b* 15 May 1948; *s* of late John C. Plumbly and Jean Elizabeth (*née* Baker); *m* 1979, Nadia Gohar; two *s* one *d*. *Educ:* Brockenhurst Grammar Sch.; Magdalen Coll., Oxford (BA PPE). VSO, Pakistan, 1970; Third Sec., FCO, 1972; MECAS, 1973; Second Sec., Jedda, 1975; First Sec., Cairo, 1977; FCO, 1980; First Sec., Washington, 1984; Dep. Head of Mission, Riyadh, 1988; Head of Chancery, UK Mission to UN, NY, 1992–96; Internat. Drugs Co-ordinator, and Dir, Drugs and Internat. Crime, FCO, 1996–97; Dir, Middle East and N Africa, FCO, 1997–2000; Ambassador: to Saudi Arabia, 2000–03; to Egypt, 2003–07. Chm., Assessment and Evaluation Commn, Comprehensive Peace Agreement, Sudan, 2008–11. Pres., Levantine Foundn, 2009–; Chairman: Arab British Centre, 2016–; Saudi British Soc., 2016–19. Trustee: British Univ. in Egypt, 2007–; New Giza Univ., 2017–. Vis. Prof., Middle East Studies, KCL, 2015–. DUniv Loughborough, 2008. *Club:* Travellers.

PLUMBLY-CLEGG, Richard, PhD; FREng; FRSC; Foundation Chief Executive, Lloyd's Register Foundation, since 2013; *b* Todmorden, Yorks, 9 Sept. 1957; *s* of John Clegg and Marilyn Clegg; three *s*; *m* 2018, Debbie Plumbly. *Educ:* Bingham Toothill Sch.; Brunel Univ. (BSc Applied Chem. 1980); Univ. of Salford (PhD Radiation Chem. 1984); Univ. of Lancaster (MBA 1989). FRSC 1996; FREng 2016. British Nuclear Fuels: graduate trainee; Health Physicist and Envmtl Modeller, 1985–95; Hd, Corporate Res. Lab., 1995–97; Gp Sci. Dir, 1997–2005; Univ. of Manchester: Founder Dir, Dalton Nuclear Inst., 2005–08; Associate Dean for Res., Fac. of Engrg and Physical Scis, 2007–08; Chief Scientific Advr, Atomic Weapons Establishment, 2008–09; Founder Dir, Nat. Nuclear Centre of Excellence, DECC, 2009–10; Global Nuclear Dir, Lloyd's Register, 2010–13. Trustee, Sci. Mus. Gp, 2016–. Visiting Professor: (Nuclear) Univ. of Manchester, 2011–; (Risk) Univ. of Liverpool, 2017–. Vis. Prof. (Public Understanding of Risk), 2017–. Advr to Dep. Pres. (Res. and Technol.), 2017–, NUS. Freeman, Shipwrights' Co., 2017. Hon. DSc Lancaster, 2017. *Recreations:* antique British clocks, clock watching, gardening, vintage Vespa scooters, Lebanese wine, the Winchester. *Address:* Lloyd's Register Foundation, 71 Fenchurch Street, EC3M 4BS. *T:* (020) 7423 1677. *E:* richard.clegg@lrfoundation.org.uk.

PLUMMER, (Arthur) Christopher (Orme), CC (Canada) 1968; actor; *b* Toronto, 13 Dec. 1929; *m* 1st, 1956, Tammy Lee Grimes; one *d*; 2nd, 1962, Patricia Audrey Lewis (marr. diss. 1966); 3rd, 1970, Elaine Regina Taylor. *Educ:* public and private schs, Montreal. French and English radio, Canada, 1949–52; Ottawa Rep. Theatre; Broadway: Starcross Story, 1951–52; Home is the Hero, 1953; The Dark is Light Enough, 1954 (Theatre World Award); The Lark, 1955; J. B., 1958 (Tony nomination); Royal Hunt of the Sun, 1965–66; Stratford, Conn, 1955: Mark Antony, Ferdinand; leading actor, Stratford Festival, Canada, 1956–67: Henry V, The Bastard, Hamlet, Leontes, Mercutio, Macbeth, Cyrano de Bergerac, Benedick, Aguecheek, Antony; Royal Shakespeare Co., Stratford-on-Avon, 1961–62: Benedick, Richard III; London debut as Henry II in Becket, Aldwych and Globe, 1961 (Evening Standard Best Actor Award, 1961); National Theatre, 1971–72: Amphitryon 38, Danton's Death; Broadway musical, Cyrano, 1973 (Outer Critics Circle Award and Tony Award for Best Actor in a Musical, NY Drama Desk Award); The Good Doctor, NY, 1974; Iago in Othello, NY, 1982 (Drama Desk Award); Macbeth, NY, 1988; No Man's Land, NY, 1994; Barrymore (one-man show), 1997 (Tony Award for Best Actor); King Lear, Stratford Fest., 2002, NY, 2004. Films: Stage-Struck, 1956; Across the Everglades, 1957; The Fall of the Roman Empire, 1963; The Sound of Music (Golden Badge of Honour, Austria), Daisy Clover, 1964; Triple Cross, 1966; Oedipus Rex, 1967; The Battle of Britain, 1968; Royal Hunt of the Sun, 1969; The Pyx, 1973; The Man Who Would Be King, 1975; Aces High, The Moneychangers (Emmy Award), 1976; International Velvet, The Silent Partner, 1978; Hanover Street, 1979; Murder by Decree, 1980 (Genie Award, Canada); The Disappearance, The Janitor, 1981; The Amateur, 1982; Dreamscape, 1984; Playing for Keeps, Lily in Love, 1985; Souvenir, 1989; Where The Heart Is, 1990; Twelve Monkeys, 1996; The Insider, 2000; Dracula 2001, Lucky Break, A Beautiful Mind, 2001; Ararat, Nicholas Nickleby, 2002; Blizzard, Gospel of John, 2003; National Treasure, 2004; Alexander, 2005; Inside Man, Syriana, 2006; Closing the Ring, 2007; Man in the Chair, 2008; The Imaginarium of Doctor Parnassus, 2009; The Last Station, 2010; Priest, The Girl with the Dragon Tattoo, Beginners, 2011 (Academy, Golden Globe and BAFTA Awards for Best Supporting Actor, 2012); Muhammad Ali's Greatest Fight (TV film), 2013; Danny Collins, Remember, 2015; The Man Who Invented Christmas, 2017; All the Money in the World, 2018 (Best Supporting Actor, Golden Globe Awards, 2018); Knives Out, 2019, and others. TV appearances, Britain, Denmark, and major N American networks, incl. Hamlet at Elsinore, BBC and Danish TV, 1964 (4 Emmy Award nominations). First entertainer to win Maple Leaf Award (Arts and Letters), 1982; Lifetime Achievement Award, Acad. of Canadian Cinema and Television, 2017. *Publications:* In Spite of Myself: a memoir, (USA), 2008. *Recreations:* tennis, ski-ing, piano. *Clubs:* Players, River (New York).

PLUMMER, Maj.-Gen. Brian Peter, CBE 2002; Clerk to Worshipful Company of Skinners, 2003–15; *b* 30 Aug. 1948. *Educ:* Univ. of Durham (BA). Commnd RWF, 1970; Regt and Staff Duty, 1974–85; jsdc, 1986; ASC, 1986–88; CO 1 RWF, 1989–91; HCSC, 1995; Comd, 1st Mechanised Bde, 1995–96; rcds, 1997; Comd, Combined Arms Trng Centre, 1998–99; Dir Gen. Trng Support, HQ Land Comd, 1999–2002. Col, RWF, 2001–05. *Address:* c/o RHQ RWF, Hightown Barracks, Wrexham, Clwyd LL13 8RD.

PLUMMER, Christopher; *see* Plummer, A. C. O.

PLUMPTON, Alan, CBE 1980; BSc; FREng, FIET; Chairman, Schlumberger plc, 1992–2001; Chairman, 1992–99, Director, 1999–2001, Beaufort Group PLC (formerly Beaufort Management Consultants); *b* 24 Nov. 1926; *s* of late John Plumpton and Doris Plumpton; *m* 1950, Audrey Smith; one *s* one *d*. *Educ:* Sunderland Technical Sch.; Durham Univ. (BSc Elec. Eng). FREng (FEng 1991). Pupil Engr, Sunderland Corp. Elec. Undertaking, 1942; various engrg and commercial appts, NEEB, 1948–61; Dist Manager, E Monmouthshire Dist, S Wales Electricity Bd, 1961–64. Admin. Staff Coll., Henley, 1963; Dep. Chief Commercial Engr, S Wales Elec. Bd, 1964–67; Chief Commercial Engr, S Wales Elec. Bd, 1967–72; Dep. Chm., London Elec. Bd, 1972–76, Chm., 1976–81; Dep. Chm., Electricity Council, 1981–86. Chairman: Ewbank Preece Group, 1986–92; Manx Electricity Authority, 1986–97; Schlumberger Measurement and Systems, 1988–92; Dir, Eleco Holdings, 1993–97. MInstD 1986; CCMI. Liveryman, Gardeners' Co. JP Mon, 1971–72. *Recreations:* golf, gardening. *Address:* Lockhill, Stubbs Wood, Amersham, Bucks HP6 6EX. *T:* (01494) 433791. *Club:* Harewood Downs Golf (Chm., 1996–98).

PLUMPTON, Denise Kathryn (Mrs P. J. Finney); Director of Information, Highways Agency, Department for Transport, 2005–10; *b* 31 Oct. 1954; *d* of late Dennis Plumpton and Mabel Jenny Plumpton; *m* 2015, Peter John Finney. *Educ:* Univ. of Sheffield (BSc 1st Cl. Hons Maths 1976). Cert. IoD 2010. Rover Gp, 1976–82; ISTEL, 1983–89; Powergen: Commercial Manager, 1989–96; IT Dir, 1996–99; Information Technology Director: TNT UK Ltd, 1999–2004; Sendo, 2004. Non-executive Director: Heart of Birmingham Teaching PCT, 2007–11; Centro, 2009–15; Reed Exhibns 360°IT - The Infrastructure Event, 2010; Sanctuary Gp, 2015–; Dir, Process Doctor, 2010–. Vice Chair, Birmingham S Central CCG, 2011–18. MInstD 1997–2015. *Recreation:* Judge for British Racing and Sports Car Club, MG Car Club and Classic Sports Car Club. *Address:* Solihull. *T:* 07713 780110. *E:* deniseplumpton@btinternet.com.

PLUMPTRE, family name of Baron FitzWalter.

PLUMPTRE, Hon. (Wyndham) George; Chief Executive, National Gardens Scheme, since 2011 (Deputy Chairman, 2009–10); *b* 24 April 1956; 3rd *s* of 21st Baron FitzWalter; *m* 1st, 1984, Alexandra Elizabeth Cantacuzene-Speransky (marr. diss. 2008); two *s* one *d*; 2nd, 2010, Annabel Louise Williams. *Educ:* Radley Coll.; Jesus Coll., Cambridge (BA Mod. Hist.). Author, journalist and lecturer, 1978–; contributor, Country Life, 1979–; Gardens Correspondent, 1993–95, columnist, 1995–97, The Times; Ed., Sotheby's Preview Mag., 1995–97; Dir, S Africa, Sotheby's, 1997–99; Founder and Editl Dir, greenfingers.com, 1999–2002; Publisher, Bonhams Mag., 2004–09. Trustee: Kent Gardens Trust, 1992–99; Nat. Gardens Scheme, 2005–10; Member: SE Regl Cttee, Nat. Trust, 1993–96; Arts and Library Sub Cttee, MCC, 2000–10. *Publications:* Royal Gardens, 1981; Collins Book of British Gardens, 1985; The Fast Set, 1985; The Latest Country Gardens, 1988; Homes of Cricket, 1988; Garden Ornament, 1989; Cricket Cartoons and Caricatures, 1989; Back Page Racing, 1989; The Golden Age of Cricket, 1990; The Water Garden, 1993; The Garden Makers, 1993; Great Gardens, Great Designers, 1994; Edward VII, 1995; The Country House Guide, 1996; Classic Planting, 1998; Royal Gardens of Europe, 2005; Heritage Gardens, 2007; (ed) The Gardens of England, 2013; The English Country House Garden, 2014, rev. edn 2018. *T:* (01483) 213906. *E:* gplumptre@ngs.org.uk.

PLUMSTEAD, Her Honour Isobel Mary, (Mrs N. J. Coleman); a Circuit Judge, 2001–14; authorised to sit as Judge of High Court, Family Division, 2002; Designated Family Judge: Cambridge, 2003–09; Peterborough and Cambridge, 2007–09; *b* 19 July 1947; *d* of John Archibald Plumstead, DFM, MA and Nancy Plumstead (*née* Drummond); *m* 1971, Nicholas John Coleman, *qv*; one *s* two *d*. *Educ:* Norwich High Sch. for Girls (GPDST); St Hugh's College, Oxford (BA 1969; MA 1985); Inns of Court Sch. of Law. Blackstone Entrance Scholar, 1967, Colombos Prize for Internat. Law, 1970, Harmsworth Scholar, 1970–73, Middle Temple. Called to the Bar, Middle Temple, 1970, Bencher 2006; Registrar, Principal Registry, Family Div. of High Court, 1990; District Judge, Principal Registry, Family Div. of the High Ct, 1990–2001; Asst Recorder, 1994–98; a Recorder, 1998–2001. Member: Independent Schs Tribunal, 1992–2000; Family Cttee (formerly Civil and Family Cttee), 1993–99, Main Bd, 1997–99, Judicial Studies Bd; Hon. Sec., Council of HM Circuit Judges, 2009–11 (Sen. Vice Pres., 2012; Pres., 2013). Trustee: New Parents' Infant Network (Newpin), 1989–96; Hackney and E London Family Mediation Service, 1993–96; Vice Pres., Family Mediators Assoc., 1999–. Gov., St Margaret's Sch., Hampstead, 1993–98. *Publications:* (contrib.) Emergency Remedies in the Family Courts, 1997; (contrib.) Rayden and Jackson on Divorce and Family Matters, 1997. *Recreation:* when time permits, spending the kids' inheritance. *Clubs:* Anmer Social; Hunstanton Golf.

PLUNKET, family name of Baron Plunket.

PLUNKET, 9th Baron *cr* 1827; Tyrone Shaun Terence Plunket; *b* 5 Feb. 1966; *s* of Hon. Shaun Albert Frederick Sheridan Plunket and of Judith Ann Plunket (*née* Power); *S* uncle, 2013; *m* 2000, Lucy Marguerite, *d* of late James Currie, MC; twin *s*. *Heir: s* Hon. Rory Peter Robin Plunket, *b* 11 March 2001.

PLUNKET GREENE, Dame Mary; *see* Quant, Dame M.

PLUNKETT, family name of Barons Dunsany and Louth.

PLUNKETT, (Andrew) Christopher; His Honour Judge Plunkett; a Circuit Judge, since 2005; *b* 31 March 1961; *s* of Anthony Penson Plunkett and Anne Malkin Plunkett; *m* 2001, Rachel Anne Stewart; two *s*. *Educ:* Warwick Univ. (LLB); Inns of Court Sch. of Law, London. Called to the Bar, Gray's Inn, 1983; a Recorder, 2002–05. *Recreation:* cycling, on and off road. *Address:* Worcester Combined Court, Shire Hall, Foregate Street, Worcester WR1 1EQ. *T:* (01905) 730800. *Clubs:* Cyclists' Touring, Rugged Meanderers'.

PLUTHERO, John; Chairman, MyAppConverter Ltd, 2014–19; *b* 10 Feb. 1964; *m*; three *c*. *Educ:* Colchester Royal Grammar Sch.; London Sch. of Econs (BSc 1st Cl. Hons Econs). ACA 1989. Dir, Chelsea Harbour, P&O Develts, 1990–94; Strategy and Planning, Bass plc, 1994–95; Business Review Dir, Dixons Gp, 1995–98; Man. Dir, Mastercare DSG, 1998–99; Founder, Freeserve plc, subseq. Freeserve.com plc, CEO, 1998–2002; Chief Exec., Energis plc, 2002–05; Cable & Wireless plc: Dir, UK Business, 2005–06; Gp Man. Dir and Exec. Chm., Worldwide, 2006–10; Exec. Chm., Internat., 2007–08; Exec. Chm., 2010–11; Chief Exec., 2010–11; Chm., Essensys, 2011. MInstD. *Recreation:* modern art.

**PLYMOUTH, 4th Earl of,** cr 1905; **Ivor Edward Other Windsor-Clive**; Viscount Windsor (UK 1905); 16th Baron Windsor (England, cr 1529); b 19 Nov. 1951; s of 3rd Earl of Plymouth and Caroline Helen Windsor-Clive; S father, 2018; m 1979, Caroline, d of late Frederick Nettlefold and Hon. Mrs Juliana Roberts; three s one d. Educ: Harrow; Royal Agricl Coll., Cirencester. Co-founder, and Dir, Centre for the Study of Modern Art, 1973. Chairman: Earl of Plymouth Estates Ltd, 1997–; Ludlow Food Centre Ltd, 2006–. Chm., Heart of England Reg., HHA, 1996–2001. FRSA. Recreation: cricket. Heir: s Viscount Windsor, qv. Address: Oakly Park, Ludlow, Shropshire SY8 2JW; 17 Farm Place, W8 7SX. Club: Brooks's.

**PLYMOUTH, Bishop Suffragan of,** since 2015; **Rt Rev. Nicholas Howard Paul McKinnel**; b Liverpool, 19 Aug. 1954; s of Hugh McKinnel and Hazel McKinnel; m 1981, Jacqueline Shipley; one s three d. Educ: Marlborough Coll.; Queens' Coll., Cambridge (BA 1975; MA 1979); Wycliffe Hall, Oxford (BA 1979; MA 1986). Ordained deacon, 1980, priest, 1981; Curate, St Mary's Church, W Kensington, 1980–83; Anglican Chaplain, Liverpool Univ., 1983–87; Rector: Hatherleigh, Meeth, Exbourne and Jacobstowe, 1987–94; Minster Church of St Andrew, Plymouth, 1994–2012; Bishop Suffragan of Crediton, 2012–15. Hon. DD Plymouth, 2013. Address: 108 Molesworth Road, Plymouth PL3 4AQ. T: (01752) 500059. E: bishop.of.plymouth@exeter.anglican.org.

**PLYMOUTH, Bishop of, (RC),** since 2014; **Rt Rev. Mark Anthony O'Toole**; b London, 22 June 1963; s of Marcus and Maura O'Toole. Educ: St Ignatius Primary Sch., Stamford Hill; St Thomas More Secondary Sch., Wood Green; Univ. of Leicester (BSc Geog. 1984); Allen Hall Seminary (BD 1989); Univ. of Oxford (MPhil 1992); Pontifical Univ., Leuven (STL 2000). Pastoral work, St Joan of Arc Parish, Highbury, 1989–90; ordained priest, 1990; Asst Priest, St Mary Magdalene Parish, Willesden Green, and part-time Lectr in Catechesis, 1992–97; Allen Hall Seminary: Lectr in Theology and Formation Advr to seminarians, 1997–2002; Dean of Studies, 1999–2002; Private Sec. to Cardinal Murphy-O'Connor, Archbishop of Westminster, 2002–08; Rector, Allen Hall Seminary, 2008–13; Ecumenical Canon: Truro Cathedral, 2014–; Exeter Cathedral, 2016–. Recreations: reading, swimming, film. Address: Bishop's House, 45 Cecil Street, Plymouth, Devon PL1 5RZ. T: (01752) 224414. E: bishopmark@prcdtr.org.uk.

**PLYMOUTH, Archdeacon of;** see Shutt, Ven. N. S.

**POCKLINGTON, Jeremy Mark;** Director General, Housing and Planning, Ministry of Housing, Communities and Local Government, since 2018; b Manchester, 13 Oct. 1973; s of David Pocklington and Valerie Pocklington; m 2005, Katy Jane Wigley. Educ: Manchester Grammar Sch.; Exeter Coll., Oxford (BA Mod. Hist. 1995; MPhil Econ. and Social Hist. (Distinction) 1997); INSEAD (MBA (Distinction) 2004). HM Treasury: joined, 1997; Head: Property Tax, 2004–06; Corporate and Private Finance, 2006–09; Cabinet Office: Director: Nat. Econ. Council Secretariat, 2009–10; Econ. and Domestic Affairs Secretariat, 2010–12; Enterprise and Growth Unit, HM Treasury, 2012–15; Dir Gen., Markets and Infrastructure, DECC, then BEIS; Dir Gen., Energy and Security, BEIS, 2016–18. Recreation: hillwalking. Address: Ministry of Housing, Communities and Local Government, 2 Marsham Street, SW1P 4DF.

**POCOCK, Sir Andrew (John),** KCMG 2015 (CMG 2008); PhD; HM Diplomatic Service, retired; High Commissioner to Nigeria, 2012–15; b 23 Aug. 1955; s of John Francis Pocock and Vida Erica Pocock (née Duruty); m 1995, Julie Mason. Educ: St Mary's Coll., Trinidad; Queen Mary Coll., London (BA, MA); Peterhouse, Cambridge (PhD 1987). Joined HM Diplomatic Service, 1981; Second, later First Sec., Lagos, 1983–86; First Secretary: Southern African Dept, FCO, 1986–87; Washington, 1988–92; Personnel Mgt Dept, FCO, 1992–94; Asst, S Asia Dept, FCO, 1994–95; Counsellor, on loan to RCDS, 1996; Dep. High Comr, Canberra, 1997–2001; Hd of African Dept (Southern), FCO, 2001–03; High Comr to Tanzania, 2003–06; Ambassador to Zimbabwe, 2006–09; Africa Dir, FCO, 2010; High Comr to Canada, 2011–12. Sec., Beit Trust, 2016–. Liveryman, Cutlers' Co., 1979–. Hubert Walter Award for Reconciliation, Lambeth Awards, 2016. Recreations: tennis, cricket, walking.

**POCOCK, Christopher James;** QC 2009; b Chatham, 3 Nov. 1960; s of Roy Allan Pocock and Shirley Ann Rose Pocock; m Karen Anne (marr. diss. 2013); two d. Educ: St Dunstan's Coll., Catford; Pembroke Coll., Oxford (BA Hons Juris.). Called to the Bar, Inner Temple, 1984; in practice as barrister specialising in family law. Recreations: fishing, scuba diving, amateur astronomy. Address: 1 King's Bench Walk, Temple, EC4Y 7DB. T: (020) 7936 1500, Fax: (020) 7936 1590. E: cpcockqc@1kbw.co.uk.

**POCOCK, Gordon James;** Director, Communications Educational Services Ltd, 1983–87; b 27 March 1933; s of late Leslie and Elizabeth Maud Pocock; m 1959, Audrey Singleton (d 1990). Educ: Royal Liberty Sch., Romford; Keble Coll., Oxford. Joined PO, 1954; Private Sec. to Dir Gen., 1958–59; Principal, 1960–68; Asst Sec., 1968–72; Dep. Dir, 1972–76; Dir, Ext. Telecommns, 1976–79; Dir, Telecommns Marketing, 1979, Sen. Dir, 1979–81; Chief Exec., Merlin Business Systems, BT, 1981–84. Fellow, Nolan Norton & Co., 1985–87. Publications: Corneille and Racine, 1973; Boileau and the Nature of Neo-Classicism, 1980; article on Nation, Community, Devolution and Sovereignty. Recreations: travel, theatre, local history. Address: 131 Lichfield Court, Sheen Road, Richmond, Surrey TW9 1AY. T: (020) 8940 7118.

**POCOCK, Margaret A.;** see Aderin-Pocock.

**PODGER, Geoffrey John Freeman,** CB 2003; Chief Executive, Health and Safety Executive, 2005–13; Acting Chief Executive, WorkSafe New Zealand, 2013–14; Chair, Management Board, Government Actuary's Department, since 2015; b 3 Aug. 1952; s of late Leonard and Beryl Podger. Educ: Worthing High Sch. for Boys; Pembroke Coll., Oxford (Open Scholar; BA Medieval and Modern Langs 1974; MA 1977). MoD, 1974–82; Internat. Staff, NATO HQ, Brussels, 1977–79; Department of Health and Social Security, subseq. Department of Health, 1982–96; loaned to Falkland Islands Govt as Sec. to Port Stanley Hosp. Fire Inquiry, 1985; Private Sec. to Chm. (subseq. Chief Exec.), NHS Management Bd and Sec. to Bd, 1985–87; Principal Private Sec. to Sec. of State for Social Services, 1987–88; Head, Internat. Relations Unit, 1992–93; Under Sec. for Health Promotion, 1993–96; Hd of Food Safety and Sci. Gp, MAFF, 1996–97; Hd, Jt Food Safety and Standards Gp, MAFF and DoH, 1997–2000; Chief Exec., Food Standards Agency, 2000–03; Exec. Dir, European Food Safety Authy, 2003–05. Vis. Sen. Res. Fellow, KCL Centre for Risk Mgt, 2014–. Mem. Council, Inst. for Employment Studies, 2006– (Mem. Bd, 2007–). Chairman: Occupational Safety and Health Consultants Register, 2011–; Nat. Compliance and Risk Qualifications, 2016–. Hon. Vice Pres., IOSH, 2007. Hon. Fellow, IIRSM, 2007; CCMI 2009. MInstD. Club: Athenæum.

**PODMORE, Dr Colin John;** Director, Forward in Faith, since 2013; b Redruth, 22 Feb. 1960; s of late Raymond Podmore and (Averil) Iris Podmore (née Collins). Educ: Bodmin Grammar Sch.; Bodmin Sch.; Keble Coll., Oxford (MA 1985; DPhil 1995); Selwyn Coll., Cambridge (PGCE 1983). Teacher, St Michael's C of E High Sch., Chorley, 1983–85; Asst Sec., Bd for Mission and Unity, Gen. Synod, 1988–91; Asst Sec., 1991–97, Dep. Sec., 1997–98, Council for Christian Unity; Secretary: Liturgical Publishing Gp, 1999–2002; CAC Rev. Gp, 1999–2001; House of Clergy of the Gen. Synod, 2002–11; Liturgical Commn, 2002–09; Dioceses Commn, 2002–11; Sen. Appts Rev. Gp, 2005–07; Clerk to the Gen. Synod, C of E, 2011–13. Parish Clerk, St Michael, Crooked Lane, London, 2004–. Mem. Council, Roehampton Univ., 2003–06. FRHistS 2002. Mem., Parish Clerks' Co., 2005– (Ct Asst, 2016–). Lanfranc Award for Educn and Scholarship, Archbp of Canterbury, 2017. Publications: The German Evangelical Churches: an introduction, 1992; (contrib.) Blackwell Dictionary of Evangelical Biography 1730–1860, 1995; (ed jtly) Leuenberg, Meissen and Porvoo, 1996; The Moravian Church in England 1728–1760, 1998; (ed and contrib.) Community-Unity-Communion: essays in honour of Mary Tanner, 1998; Prayers to Remember, 2001; (contrib.) New SCM Press Dictionary of Liturgy and Worship, 2002; (contrib.) Oxford Dictionary of National Biography, 2004; Aspects of Anglican Identity, 2005; (ed and contrib.) Maiden, Mother and Queen: Mary in the Anglican tradition, 2013; (ed and contrib.) Part of the One Church? The ordination of women and Anglican identity, 2014; (ed and contrib.) Fathers in God? Resources for reflection on women in the episcopate, 2015; (contrib.) Oxford History of Anglicanism, 2017; (contrib.) Oxford Handbook of the Oxford Movement, 2017; articles in various jls incl. Anglican and Episcopal History, Ecclesiastical Law Jl, Ecclesiology, Internat. Jl for Study of the Christian Church, Jl of Anglican Studies, Jl of Ecclesiastical History, Jl of Moravian History, Theology, Unitas Fratrum. Recreations: church history, travel, dining with friends, gardening. Club: Savile.

**POET, Bruno;** freelance lighting designer, since 1994; b Wimbledon, 1972; s of Robert Poet and Margarete Poet; m 2004, Annabel Ingram; one d. Educ: Oundle Sch.; Mansfield Coll., Oxford (BA Hons Geog.). Lighting designs include: theatre: Midnight's Children, 2003, Romeo and Juliet, 2008, RSC; Major Barbara, Volpone, Royal Exchange, Manchester, 2004; National Theatre: Aristocrats, 2005; The Enchantment, 2007; Every Good Boy Deserves Favour, 2009; Season's Greetings, 2010; Frankenstein, 2011 (Olivier Award for Lighting Design, 2012; Kt of Illumination Award, 2012; What's On Stage Award, 2012); London Road, 2012; Travelling Light, 2012; Timon of Athens, 2012; From Morning to Midnight, 2013; Treasure Island, 2014; Light Shining in Buckinghamshire, 2015; St George and the Dragon, 2017; Stories, 2018; A Midsummer Night's Dream, Dundee Rep., 2006 ((jtly) Best Design Award, Critics' Awards for Scotland, 2006–07); Phaedra, Donmar, 2006; Tobias and the Angel, 2006, A Prayer for My Daughter, 2008, The Human Comedy, 2010, The Convert, 2018, Young Vic; All About My Mother, 2007, Cause Célèbre, 2011, Old Vic; The Horse Marines, 2008, Grand Guignol, 2009, Chekhov in Hell, 2010, Th. Royal, Plymouth; Breakfast at Tiffany's, Th. Royal, Haymarket, 2009; Coram Boy, Bristol Old Vic, Colston Hall, 2011; Being Shakespeare, Trafalgar Studios, 2011; South Downs, The Browning Version, Minerva, Chichester, 2011; Fortune's Fool, Sweet Bird of Youth, Old Vic, 2013; From Here to Eternity, Shaftesbury Th., 2013; Miss Saigon, Prince Edward, 2014, transf. NY, 2017 and Japanese and UK tours, 2016; The Two Gentlemen of Verona, RSC, 2014; Faith Healer, Donomar, 2016; Oliver!, Leicester Curve, 2016; The Lion, the Witch and the Wardrobe, W Yorks Playhouse, 2017; Julius Caesar, Bridge, 2018; Tina: the musical, 2018; Amadeus, Royal Danish Opera, 2019; opera: Al Gran Sole Carico d'Amore, Staatsoper Berlin, Salzburg Fest.; L'Arbore di Diana, Barcelona, Madrid; Pelléas et Mélisande, Buenos Aires; Rusalka, Sydney Opera House (Australian Green Room Award); Rinaldo, Lyric Opera Chicago; Freischütz, Cavalleria Rusticana, I Pagliacci, Partenope, Il Trovatore, The Cunning Little Vixen, Royal Danish Opera; I Puritani, De Nederlandse, Grand Théâtre de Genève; The Enchanted Pig, Young Vic; Aida, The Marriage of Figaro, The Merry Widow, ENO; Il Trovatore, Den Jyske Opera, Turin, Bilbao; Carousel, Makropulos Case, Macbeth, NZ Opera; Don Giovanni, The Marriage of Figaro, Carmen, Den Norske Opera; From the House of the Dead, A Midsummer Night's Dream, Romeo et Juliette, Dido and Aeneas, Les Noces, Carousel, Opera North; A Midsummer Night's Dream, Linbury Studio; Das Portrait, Bregenzer Festspiele; Peter Grimes, Grand Théâtre de Genève; Una Cosa Rara, La Corte del Faraon, Valencia; Eine Florentinische Tragödie, Gianni Schicchi, Greek Nat. Opera; Varjak Paw, Opera Gp at Linbury Studio and UK tour; La Clemenza di Tito, Liceu, Barcelona, Oper Leipzig; Rigoletto, Aarhus; Macbeth, Scottish Opera-Go-Round; Macbeth, Il Trovatore, Opera Monte Carlo; Akhnaten, ENO and Metropolitan Opera, NY; Otello, The Rise and Fall of the City of Mahagonny, I Due Foscari, Don Giovanni, La Donna Del Lago, ROH; Carmen, ENO, Bregenz Festival, Austria; Don Giovanni, Shlomo Lahat Opera Hse; Marco Polo, Guangzhou Opera House; Oklahoma!, Grange Park Opera; ballet: Connectome, ROH, 2014; The Tempest, Birmingham Hippodrome, 2016; Other Stories, 2015, Les Enfants Terribles, 2017, The Unknown Soldier, 2018, Royal Ballet. Lighting designer: Garsington Opera, 1998–; for Sigur Ros, world tours, 2012–13 and 2017 (Kt of Illumination Award). Recreations: sailing, travel. Address: Dodbrook Cottage, Millbrook, Torpoint, Cornwall PL10 1AN. E: brunopoet@mac.com.

**POGGIO, Albert Andrew,** GMH 2014; OBE 2006 (MBE 1995); United Kingdom Representative of HM Government of Gibraltar, 1988–2016; b 18 Aug. 1946; s of late Joseph Ernest and Sally Poggio; m 1966, Sally Sofaer (marr. diss. 1987); one d; partner, Doreen Isobel Mellor. Educ: Christian Brothers Coll., Gibraltar; Robert Montefiore Sch., London; City of London Coll. Chairman: Westex Gp of Cos, 1980–88; Vital Health Gp, 1990–2003; Dir, 1996–, Sen. Vice Pres., 2003–09, Medcruise, Assoc. of Mediterranean Ports. Vice Pres., UK Overseas Territories Assoc., 1993–2000 (Chm., 2004 and 2014–15); Pres., Friends of British Overseas Territories Assoc., 2017. Chm., Calpe House Charitable Trust, 2017– (Vice Chm., 1989–2017; Chm., Calpe House Ltd, 2017–); Vice Chm., Friends of Gibraltar Heritage Trust, 2013–. Recreations: sports, military memorabilia, travelling. E: albert.poggio@gmail.com. Clubs: Royal Automobile, Casino Calpe (Gibraltar); Royal Gibraltar Yacht.

**POGSON, Abigail;** Managing Director, North Music Trust, Sage Gateshead, since 2015; b Halifax, 21 Sept. 1974; m 2015, John Fulljames; one s one d. Educ: Trinity Hall, Cambridge (BA Modern and Medieval Langs 1997); City Univ. (MA Cultural Mgt). Asst Co. Manager, ENO, 1998–2000; Gen. Manager, Music Th. Wales, 2000–03; Exec. Dir, Soc. for Promotion of New Music, 2003–08; Chief Exec., Spitalfields Music, 2008–15. Fellow, Clore Leadership Prog., 2007–08. Address: Sage Gateshead, St Mary's Square, Gateshead Quays, Gateshead NE8 2JR. T: (0191) 443 4601, Fax: (0191) 443 4551. E: abigail.pogson@sagegateshead.com.

**POGSON, Kevin Edward,** CBE 2006; Regional Director for London, HM Courts Service, 2006–10; b 5 Sept. 1950; s of Edward Pogson and Ivy (née Hubble); m (marr. diss.); two s. Educ: state schools in London. Joined Lord Chancellor's Department, 1967; various positions at HQ, 1967–79; Knightsbridge Crown Court, 1979–86; Personnel Dept, 1987–92; Dir of Finance, 1992–99, of Change, 1999–2001, Court Service; Circuit Adminr, SE Circuit, LCD, 2001–02; Dir of Field Services, Court Service, 2003–04; SE Circuit Adminr, Court Service, subseq. Regl Dir for SE, HM Courts Service, 2004–06. Recreations: chess, music, cooking. Club: UNATS Chess.

**POINTER, Martin John;** QC 1996; barrister; b 17 July 1953; s of late Michael Edward Pointer and Mary Isabel Pointer (née Simms); m 1st, 1985 (marr. diss. 1997); two s one d; 2nd, 2001, Janet Bridal. Educ: King's Sch., Grantham; Univ. of Leicester (LLB Hons). Called to the Bar, Gray's Inn, 1976 (Reid Schol., 1977). Fellow, Internat. Acad. of Family (formerly Matrimonial) Lawyers, 1994. Address: 1 Hare Court, Temple, EC4Y 7BE. T: (020) 7797 7070. Club: Travellers.

**POITIER, Sidney,** KBE (Hon.) 1974; actor, film and stage; director; *b* Miami, Florida, 20 Feb. 1927; *s* of Reginald Poitier and Evelyn (*née* Outten); *m* 1950, Juanita Hardy (marr. diss.); four *d*; *m* 1975, Joanna Shimkus; two *d*. *Educ:* private tutors; Western Senior High Sch., Nassau; Governor's High Sch., Nassau. Served War of 1941–45 with 1267th Medical Detachment, United States Army. Started acting with American Negro Theatre, 1946. *Plays include:* Anna Lucasta, Broadway, 1948; A Raisin in the Sun, Broadway, 1959; *films include:* Cry, the Beloved Country, 1952; Red Ball Express, 1952; Go, Man, Go, 1954; Blackboard Jungle, 1955; Goodbye, My Lady, 1956; Edge of the City, 1957; Band of Angels, 1957; Something of Value, 1957; The Mark of the Hawk, 1958; The Defiant Ones, 1958 (Silver Bear Award, Berlin Film Festival, and New York Critics Award, 1958); Porgy and Bess, 1959; A Raisin in the Sun, 1960; Paris Blues, 1960; Lilies of the Field, 1963 (award for Best Actor of 1963, Motion Picture Academy of Arts and Sciences); The Bedford Incident, 1965; The Slender Thread, 1966; A Patch of Blue, 1966; Duel at Diablo, 1966; To Sir With Love, 1967; In the Heat of the Night, 1967; Guess Who's Coming to Dinner, 1968; For Love of Ivy, 1968; They Call Me Mister Tibbs, 1971; The Organization, 1971; The Wilby Conspiracy, 1975; Deadly Pursuit, 1988; Sneakers, 1991; Separate But Equal, 1990; Children of the Dust, 1995; To Sir With Love II, 1996; Mandela and De Klerk, One Man, One Vote, 1997; The Jackal, 1998; David and Lisa, 1998; Free of Eden, 1999; The Simple Life of Noah Dearborn, 1999; director and actor: Buck and the Preacher, 1972; A Warm December, 1973; Uptown Saturday Night, 1974; Let's Do It Again, 1975; A Piece of the Action, 1977; *director:* Stir Crazy, 1981; Hanky Panky, 1982. Non-resident Ambassador of the Bahamas to Japan, 1997–2007, to UNESCO, 2003–. Hon. Acad. Award for Lifetime Achievement, 2002; Fellow, BAFTA, 2016. Presidential Medal of Freedom (USA), 2009. *Publications:* This Life (autobiography), 1980; The Measure of a Man: a spiritual autobiography, 2000; Life Beyond Measure: letters to my great-grandaughter, 2009. *Address:* c/o CAA, 2000 Avenue of the Stars, Los Angeles, CA 90067, USA.

**POKHILKO, Carol;** *see* Harrison, C.

**POLAK,** Baron *cr* 2015 (Life Peer), of Hertsmere in the County of Hertfordshire; **Stuart Polak,** CBE 2015; Chairman, TWC Associates; Senior Consultant, Jardine Lloyd Thompson. Youth and community worker, United Synagogue, Edgware; Officer, Bd of Deputies of British Jews, until 1989; Dir, Cons. Friends of Israel, 1989–2015 (Hon. Pres., 2015). *Address:* House of Lords, SW1A 0PW.

**POLANYI, Prof. Hon. John Charles;** PC (Can.) 1992; CC (Canada) 1979 (OC 1974); FRS 1971; FRSC 1966 (Hon. FRSC 1991); University Professor, since 1974, and Professor of Chemistry, since 1962, University of Toronto; *b* 23 Jan. 1929; *m* 1958, Anne Ferrar Davidson; one *s* one *d*; *m* 2004, Brenda Mary Bury. *Educ:* Manchester Grammar Sch.; Victoria Univ., Manchester (BSc, PhD, DSc). Research Fellow: Nat. Research Council, Ottawa, 1952–54; Princeton Univ., 1954–56; Univ. of Toronto: Lectr, 1956; Asst Prof., 1957–60; Assoc. Prof., 1960–62. Mem., Scientific Adv. Bd, Max Planck Inst. for Quantum Optics, Garching, Germany, 1982–92. Sloan Foundn Fellow, 1959–63; Guggenheim Meml Fellow, 1970–71, 1979–80; Sherman Fairchild Distinguished Scholar, CIT, 1982; Vis. Prof. of Chem., Texas A & M Univ., 1986; John W. Cowper Dist. Vis. Lectr, SUNY at Buffalo, 1986; Consolidated Bathurst Vis. Lectr, Concordia Univ., 1988; Beam Dist. Vis. Prof., Iowa Univ., 1992; Hitchcock Prof., Calif Univ., Berkeley, 1994; Lectures include: Centennial, Chem. Soc., 1965; Ohio State Univ., 1969 (and Mack Award); Reilly, Univ. of Notre Dame, 1970; Harkins Meml, Univ. of Chicago, 1971; Killam Meml Schol., 1974, 1975; F. J. Toole, Univ. of New Brunswick, 1974; Kistiakowsky, Harvard Univ., 1975; Camille and Henry Dreyfus, Kansas, 1975; Jacob Bronowski Meml, Toronto Univ., 1978; Hutchison, Rochester Univ., 1979; Priestley, Penn State Univ., 1980; Barré, Univ. of Montreal, 1982; Wiegand, Toronto Univ., 1984; Walker-Ames, Univ. of Washington, 1986; Morino, Japan, J. T. Wilson, Ont Sci. Centre, and Spiers Meml, Faraday Div., RSChem., 1987; Polanyi, IUPAC, W. B. Lewis, Atomic Energy of Canada Ltd, Killam, Univ. of Windsor, and Herzberg, Carleton Univ., 1988; C. R. Mueller, Purdue Univ., 1989; Phillips, Pittsburgh, 1991; Dove Meml, Toronto, 1992; Fritz London, Duke Univ., 1993; Linus Pauling, CIT, 1994; Hagey, Waterloo Univ., 1995. Hon. FRSE 1988; Hon. For. Mem., Amer. Acad. of Arts and Sciences, 1976; For. Associate, Nat. Acad. of Sciences, USA, 1978; Mem., Pontifical Acad. of Scis, 1986. Hon. DSc: Waterloo, 1970; Memorial, 1976; McMaster, 1977; Carleton, 1981; Harvard, 1982; Rensselaer, Brock, 1984; Lethbridge, Victoria, Ottawa, Sherbrooke, Laval, 1987; Manchester, York, 1988; Acadia, Univ. de Montréal, and Weizmann Inst. of Science, Israel, 1989; Univ. of Bari, Italy, Univ. of BC, and McGill Univ., 1990; Queen's, 1992; Free Univ., Berlin, 1993; Laurentian, Toronto, Liverpool, 1995; Hon. LLD: Trent, 1977; Dalhousie, 1983; St Francis Xavier, 1984; Concordia Univ., 1990; Calgary, 1994. Marlow Medal, Faraday Soc., 1963; Steacie Prize for Natural Scis, 1965; Chem. Inst. Canada Medal, 1976 (Noranda Award, 1967); Chem. Soc. Award, 1970; Henry Marshall Tory Medal, 1977, Michael Polanyi Medal, 1989, RSC; Remsen Award, Amer. Chem. Soc., 1978; (jtly) Wolf Prize in Chemistry, Wolf Foundn, Israel, 1982; (jtly) Nobel Prize for Chemistry, 1986; Killam Meml Prize, Canada Council, 1988; Royal Medal, 1989, Bakerian Prize, 1994, Royal Soc.; eponymous award, Canadian Soc. for Chem., 1992; Herzberg Canada Gold Medal, NSERC, 2008. KStJ 1987. *Film:* Concept in Reaction Dynamics, 1970. *Publications:* (with F. G. Griffiths) The Dangers of Nuclear War, 1979; papers in scientific jls, articles on science policy and on control of armaments. *Address:* Department of Chemistry, University of Toronto, 80 St George Street, Toronto, ON M5S 3H6, Canada; 1 Sullivan Street, Toronto, ON M5T 1B8, Canada.

**POLDEN, Martin Alan,** OBE 2006; Joint Founder, 1987, and Vice President, since 2011, Environmental Law Foundation (ELF) (Chairman, 1987–95); *b* 23 June 1928; *s* of Ralph Polden and Deborah Polden (*née* Tree); *m* 1956, Margaret Fry (*d* 1998); one *s* three *d*. *Educ:* Royal Grammar Sch., High Wycombe; LSE (LLB); Law Soc. Sch. of Law. Admitted solicitor, 1953; estabd Polden & Co., 1958, subseq. Polden Bishop & Gale, 1964; merged with Rubinstein Callingham, 1987, Sen. Partner, 1990–94; Consultant, Ross & Craig, 1994–2001. Member: All-Party Envmt Gp, 1993–; Planning and Envmtl Law Cttee, Law Soc., 1994–2002. Member: Green Alliance, 1990–; The Maccabaeans, 1993–; BAFTA, 1999–; Justice, 2000–. Founding Trustee, 1983–2003, Patron, 2003–, Gandhi Trust; Founding Trustee, Hugo Gryn Meml Trust, 1997–2011. Mem., Bd of Visitors, Wormwood Scrubs Prison, 1986–91. Fellow, Soc. for Advanced Legal Studies, 1998. FRSA 2000. *Publications:* The Law, the Environment and the Mosquito, 1990; The Environment and the Law: earth, air, fire and water, 1994; articles in legal and envmtl jls, and newspapers. *Recreations:* reading, writing, theatre, cinema, walking, grandchildering and philosophying with them. *Address:* London and Christchurch, Dorset. *Clubs:* MCC, City University.

**POLDEN, His Honour Richard;** a Circuit Judge, 2006–17; *b* 13 Nov. 1953; *s* of Stanley Richard Edward Polden and Gladys Mary Polden; *m* 1975, Susan James; one *s* one *d*. *Educ:* Knockhall Primary Sch.; Dartford Technical High Sch. for Boys; Coll. of Law, Guildford. Admitted Solicitor, 1978; joined Church Bruce Hawkes Brasington & Phillips Solicitors, Gravesend, 1978, Partner, 1980; a Dep. District Judge, 1993–95; District Judge, 1995; a Recorder, 2001–06; Designated Family Judge for Kent, 2008–14. *Recreations:* football, dog walking, foreign travel, trying to play golf. *Clubs:* Gravesend and Meopham Rotary; Gravesend 41; Mid Kent Golf.

**POLE;** *see* Carew Pole.

**POLE, Sir John (Chandos),** 6th Bt *cr* 1791, of Wolverton, Hampshire; company director; *b* 27 April 1952; *o s* of Sir Peter Van Notten Pole, 5th Bt and of Jean Emily, *d* of late Charles Douglas Stone, Borden, WA; *S* father, 2010; *m* 1973, Suzanne Norah, BAppSc(MT), *d* of late Harold Raymond Hughes, Nedlands, WA; two *s* one *d*. *Educ:* Hale Sch.; Curtin Univ., Perth. *Heir: s* Michael Van Notten Pole [*b* 12 May 1980; *m* 2007, Susan Lila, *d* of David William Kay; one *s* one *d*]. *Address:* 41 Webster Street, Nedlands, WA 6009, Australia.

**POLIAKOFF, Prof. Sir Martyn,** Kt 2015; CBE 2008; PhD; FRS 2002; FREng; Research Professor in Chemistry, University of Nottingham, since 1991; *b* 16 Dec. 1947; *s* of late Alexander Poliakoff, OBE and Ina Miriam Poliakoff (*née* Montagu); *m* 1969, Dr Janet Frances Keene; one *s* one *d*. *Educ:* Westminster Sch.; King's Coll., Cambridge (BA 1969, PhD 1973). CChem, FRSC 2002, Hon. FRSC 2015; CEng, FIChemE 2004; FREng 2017. Sen. Res. Officer, Dept of Inorganic Chem., Univ. of Newcastle upon Tyne, 1972–79; Lectr in Inorganic Chem., 1979–85, Reader, 1985–91, Univ. of Nottingham. Rutherford Lect., Royal Soc., 2012. Mem. Council, IChemE, 2009–13. Hon. Prof. of Chem., Moscow State Univ., 1999–. Foreign Sec. and Vice-Pres., Royal Soc., 2011–. MAE 2013. Hon. Member: Chem. Soc. of Ethiopia, 2008; Chinese Chem. Soc., 2015; Associate Member: Third World Acad. Sci., 2013; Ethiopian Acad. of Scis, 2014; Foreign Mem., Russian Acad. of Scis, 2012. FAAAS 2017. Hon. ScD E Anglia, 2008; Hon. DSc Heriot-Watt, 2011; Dr *hc* Tallinn Tech., 2016. Hansen Medal, IChemE, 2009; Leverhulme Medal, Royal Soc., 2010; Nyholm Prize for Education, 2011, Lord Lewis Prize, 2016, Longstaff Prize, 2019, RSC; James T. Grady - James T. Stack Award, ACS, 2019. *Publications:* contrib. scientific papers to chem. jls. *Recreations:* hill-walking, second-hand books, architecture. *Address:* School of Chemistry, University of Nottingham, Nottingham NG7 2RD. *T:* (0115) 951 3520, *Fax:* (0115) 951 3058. *E:* martyn.poliakoff@nottingham.ac.uk.
*See also* E. S. Coen, S. Poliakoff.

**POLIAKOFF, Stephen,** CBE 2007; playwright and film director; *b* 1 Dec. 1952; *s* of late Alexander Poliakoff, OBE and Ina Miriam Poliakoff (*née* Montagu); *m* 1983, Sandy Welch; one *s* one *d*. *Educ:* Westminster Sch.; King's Coll., Cambridge. *Plays:* writer: Clever Soldiers, 1974; The Carnation Gang, 1974; Hitting Town, 1975; City Sugar (Evening Standard Most Promising Playwright Award), 1976; Strawberry Fields, NT, Shout Across the River, RSC, 1978; The Summer Party, 1980; Favourite Nights, 1981; Breaking the Silence, RSC, 1984; Coming in to Land, NT, 1987; Playing With Trains, RSC, 1989; Sienna Red, nat. tour, 1992; Blinded by the Sun, RNT (Critics' Circle Best Play Award), 1996; Remember This, RNT, 1999; writer and director: Sweet Panic, Hampstead, 1996, Duke of York's, 2003; Talk of the City, RSC, 1998; My City, Almeida, 2011; *films:* writer: Bloody Kids, 1980; Runners, 1982; Soft Targets, 1982; writer and director: Hidden City, Close My Eyes (Evening Standard Best British Film Award), 1992; Century, 1995; The Tribe, 1998; Food of Love, 1998; Glorious 39, 2009; *TV plays include:* writer: Caught on a Train (BAFTA Award), 1980; She's Been Away (Venice Film Festival Prize); writer and director: Shooting the Past (serial) (Prix Italia), 1999; Perfect Strangers (serial), 2001 (Dennis Potter BAFTA Award, 2002); The Lost Prince (Emmy Award), 2003; Friends and Crocodiles, 2005; Gideon's Daughter, 2005; Joe's Palace, Capturing Mary, A Real Summer, 2007; Dancing on the Edge, 2013; Close to the Enemy (serial), 2016; Summer of Rockets (serial), 2019. *Publications:* all plays; Plays One, 1989; Plays Two, 1994; Plays Three, 1998. *Recreations:* watching cricket, going to the cinema. *Address:* 33 Devonia Road, N1 8JQ. *T:* (020) 7354 2695.
*See also* E. S. Coen, Sir M. Poliakoff.

**POLITO, Simon William;** Inquiry Chair, Competition and Markets Authority, 2014–18 (a Deputy Chairman and Board Member, Competition Commission, 2012–14); *b* Leics, 11 March 1949; *s* of John and Dodo Polito; *m* 1992, Helen Cormack; two *s*. *Educ:* Lancing Coll., Sussex; Liverpool Univ. (LLB Hons). Called to the Bar, Middle Temple, 1972; admitted as solicitor, 1976; Solicitor, 1976–82, Partner, 1982–2009, Consultant, 2009–11, Lovells. Mem., Jt Wkg Party on Competition Laws of UK and Irish Bars and Law Societies, 1991–2006 (Chm., 2006–11). Member: Panel, Competition Decisions Cttee, Financial Conduct Authy, 2019–; Competition Decisions Cttee and Enforcement Decisions Cttee, Payment Systems Regulator, 2019–. Mem. Court, Leathersellers' Co., 2007–19. Gov., Colfe's Sch., Lewisham, 1999–2016; Chm., Colfe's Charitable Trust, 2019–. *Recreations:* architecture and architectural history, gardening, horse-racing, travel, music, photography, all sports (now mainly as a spectator). *Address:* Old Vicarage, Taynton, Burford, Oxon OX18 4UH. *E:* simonpolito@aol.com. *Club:* Hurlingham.

**POLITZER, Prof. (Hugh) David,** PhD; Richard Chace Tolman Professor of Theoretical Astrophysics, California Institute of Technology, since 2004; *b* 31 Aug. 1949; *s* of Alan A. Politzer and Valerie T. Politzer (*née* Diamant). *Educ:* Michigan Univ. (BS 1969); Harvard Univ. (PhD 1974). Visiting Associate, 1975–76, Associate Prof., 1976–79, Prof. of Theoretical Physics, 1979–2004, Calif Inst. of Technol. (Jtly) Nobel Prize in Physics, 2004. *Address:* Particle Theory Group, California Institute of Technology, 1200 East California Boulevard, Pasadena, CA 91125, USA.

**POLIZZI, Hon. Olga, (Hon. Mrs William Shawcross),** CBE 1990; Director, Rocco Forte Hotels (formerly RF Hotels), since 1996; Director: Tresanton Hotel Ltd, since 1996; Hotel Endsleigh Ltd, since 2004; Millers Bespoke Bakery Ltd, since 1996; Forte plc, 1983–96 (Managing Director, Building and Design Department, 1980–96); *d* of Baron Forte; *m* 1st, 1966, Alessandro Polizzi di Sorrentino (*d* 1980); two *d*; 2nd, 1993, Hon. William Hartley Hume Shawcross, *qv*. *Educ:* St Mary's Sch., Ascot. Westminster City Councillor, 1989–94. Trustee: Italian Hosp. Fund, 1992–; Trusthouse Charitable Foundn, 1997– (Chm., 2008–); St Mary's Sch., Ascot, 1997– (Gov., 1988–97); Trustee and Gov., Landau Forte Acads. Pres., British Italian Soc. *Recreations:* walking, opera. *Address:* (office) 70 Jermyn Street, SW1Y 6NY.
*See also* Hon. Sir R. J. V. Forte, O. Peyton.

**POLKINGHORNE, Rev. Canon John Charlton,** KBE 1997; PhD; ScD; FRS 1974; Fellow, Queens' College, Cambridge, since 1996 (President, 1989–96; Hon. Fellow, 1996); *b* 16 Oct. 1930; *s* of George Baulkwill Polkinghorne and Dorothy Evelyn Polkinghorne (*née* Charlton); *m* 1955, Ruth Isobel Martin (*d* 2006); two *s* one *d*. *Educ:* Elmhurst Grammar Sch.; Perse Sch.; Trinity Coll., Cambridge (MA 1956; PhD 1955; ScD 1974; Hon. Fellow 2014); Westcott House, Cambridge, 1979–81. Commonwealth Fund Fellow, California Institute of Technology, 1955–56; Lecturer in Mathematical Physics, Univ. of Edinburgh, 1956–58; Cambridge University: Fellow, Trinity Coll., 1954–86; Lecturer in Applied Mathematics, 1958–65; Reader in Theoretical Physics, 1965–68; Prof. of Mathematical Physics, 1968–79; Fellow, Dean and Chaplain of Trinity Hall, Cambridge, 1986–89 (Hon. Fellow, 1989). Hon. Prof. of Theoretical Physics, Univ. of Kent at Canterbury, 1985. Ordained deacon 1981, priest 1982; Curate: St Andrew's, Chesterton, 1981–82; St Michael's, Bedminster, 1982–84; Vicar of St Cosmus and St Damian in the Blean, 1984–86; Canon Theologian, Liverpool Cathedral, 1994–2005; Six Preacher, Canterbury Cathedral, 1996–2006. Member: SRC, 1975–79; Human Genetics Adv. Commn, 1996–99; Human Genetics Commn, 2000–02; Chairman: Nuclear Phys Bd, 1978–79; Cttee to Review the Research Use of Fetuses and Fetal Material, 1988–89; Task Force to Review Services for Drugs Misusers, 1994–96; Adv. Cttee on Genetic Testing, 1996–99. Member: C of E

Doctrine Commn, 1989–95; Gen. Synod of C of E, 1990–2000. Chm. of Governors, Perse Sch., 1972–81; Governor, SPCK, 1984–2002. Licensed Reader, Diocese of Ely, 1975. Hon. DD: Kent, 1994; Durham, 1999; Gen. Theol. Seminary, NY, 2010; Wycliffe Coll., 2011; Hon. DSc: Exeter, 1994; Leicester, 1995; Marquette, 2003; Hon. DHum Hong Kong Baptist, 2006. Templeton Prize, 2002. *Publications:* (jtly) The Analytic S-Matrix, 1966; The Particle Play, 1979; Models of High Energy Processes, 1980; The Way the World Is, 1983; The Quantum World, 1984; One World, 1986; Science and Creation, 1988; Science and Providence, 1989; Rochester Roundabout, 1989; Reason and Reality, 1991; Science and Christian Belief, 1994; Quarks, Chaos and Christianity, 1994; Serious Talk, 1995; Scientists as Theologians, 1996; Beyond Science, 1996; Searching for Truth, 1996; Belief in God in an Age of Science, 1998; Science and Theology, 1998; Faith, Science and Understanding, 2000; (jtly) The End of the World and the Ends of Gods, 2000; (jtly) Faith in the Living God, 2001; (ed) The Work of Love, 2001; The God of Hope and the End of the World, 2002; Quantum Theory: a very short introduction, 2002; Living with Hope, 2003; Science and the Trinity, 2004; Exploring Reality, 2005; Quantum Physics and Theology, 2007; From Physicist to Priest: an autobiography, 2007; Theology in the Context of Science, 2008; (with N. Beale) Questions of Truth: fifty-one responses to questions about God, science, and belief, 2009; Encountering Scripture: a scientist explores the Bible, 2010; (ed) The Trinity and an Entangled World: relationality in physical science and theology, 2010; Science and Religion in Quest of Truth, 2011; many articles on elementary particle physics in learned journals. *Address:* Queens' College, Cambridge CB3 9ET.

**POLL, Prof. (David) Ian (Alistair),** OBE 2002; FREng, FRAeS, FCGI; Professor of Aerospace Engineering (formerly Professor of Aerodynamics), 1995–2012, now Professor Emeritus, Founder and Managing Director, Poll AeroSciences Ltd, since 2012; *b* 1 Oct. 1950; *s* of Ralph Angus Poll and Mary Poll (*née* Hall); *m* 1975, Elizabeth Mary Read; two *s* one *d*. *Educ:* Heckmondwike Grammar Sch.; Imperial Coll. London (BSc Hons); Cranfield Inst. of Technol. (PhD). FRAeS 1987; FREng (FEng 1996). Engineer, Future Projects, Hawker Siddeley Aviation, 1972–75; Res. Asst, 1975–78, Lectr, 1978–85, Sen. Lectr, 1985–87, Cranfield Inst. of Tech.; University of Manchester: Prof. of Aeronautical Engineering, and Dir of Goldstein Aeronaut. Engrg Lab., 1987–95; Man. Dir, Flow Science Ltd, 1990–95; Head, Dept of Engineering, 1991–94; Hd, Coll. of Aeronautics, subseq. Dir, Cranfield Coll. of Aeronautics, 1995–2004, Cranfield Univ. Cranfield Aerospace Ltd: Man. Dir, 1995–99; Tech. Dir, 1999–2004; Business Develt and Tech. Dir, 2004–12; non-exec. Dir, 2012–18. Mem., NERC, 2014–18. Royal Aeronautical Society: Mem. Council, 1996–2010; Vice Pres., 1998–2000; Pres., 2001; Chairman: Learned Soc. Bd, 1996–2000; Strategic Review Bd, 2000–01; Uninhabited Air Vehicle Cttee, 2005–; Cranfield Univ. Br., 1997–; von Karman Lectr, 2016. Member: Fluid Dynamics Panel, AGARD, 1990–97; Council, Air League, 1997–2012; Gen. Assembly, Internat. Council of the Aeronautical Scis, 1997–2012 (Chm., Programme Cttee, 2006–; Pres., 2008–10; Past Pres., 2011–12); Foresight Action Steering Cttee, SBAC, 1997–99; Aerospace Cttee, DTI, 1999–2004; Aerospace Technol. Steering Gp, DTI, 2004–; Council, Royal Acad. Engrg, 2004–07; Uninhabited Air Vehicle Steering Cttee, CAA, 2006–; Scientific Adv. Council, Home Office, 2012–14; Chm., Defence Sci. Adv. Council, MoD, 2011–14; Founder Mem., Greener-By-Design, 2000– (Mem., Steering Cttee, 2000–); Mem., Ind. Sci. and Technol. Advrs Register, MoD, 2014–. Vice-Pres., Confedn of European Aerospace Socs, 2001–04. FAIAA 2000, Hon. FAIAA 2012; ACGI 1972, FCGI 2004 (Vice Pres., City and Guilds Coll. Assoc., 2004–06). Hon. Fellow, Internat. Council Aeronautical Scis, 2012. Mem., RUSI, 2005. Liveryman, Co. of Coachmakers and Coach Harness Makers, 2001. Mem., British Model Flying Assoc. (A Cert. 2015). Wilbur and Orville Wright Lectr, 2002, Lanchester Lectr, 2008, RAeS; Dryden Lectr, AIAA, 2010. Hodgson Prize, 2001, Written Paper Prize, 2018, RAeS. *Publications:* more than 100 papers on aircraft envmtl impact, aircraft design and fluid mechanics in learned jls and for tech. conferences. *Recreations:* golf, aviation, wine and conversation. *Address:* Cranfield Aerospace Ltd, Cranfield, Beds MK43 0AL. *T:* (01234) 754743. *E:* d.i.a.poll@cranfield.ac.uk. *Clubs:* Athenæum, Royal Air Force.

**POLL, Ven. Martin George;** Canon of Windsor, Chaplain in the Great Park and Chaplain, Cumberland Lodge, since 2012; Canon Chaplain and Precentor, St George's Chapel, Windsor, since 2012; Domestic Chaplain to HM the Queen, Royal Chapel, Windsor Great Park, since 2014; *b* Enfield, Middx, 10 Dec. 1961; *s* of Maurice and Violet Poll; *m* 1984, Diana Hudson; one *s* one *d*. *Educ:* Edmonton Co. Sch.; Christchurch Coll., Canterbury (BA Hons); Ripon Coll., Cuddesdon (CTh). Ordained deacon 1987, priest 1988; Curate, John Keble Ch, Mill Hill, 1987–90; Chaplain: HMS Raleigh, 1990–92; Commando Helicopters, 1992–94; BRNC, Dartmouth, 1994–97; HMS Invincible, 1997–99; HM Naval Base, Faslane, 1999–2002; RNAS Yeovilton, 2002–04; Staff Chaplain, 2004–06; Fleet Staff Chaplain, 2006–07; Chaplain: HMS Illustrious, 2007; HM Naval Base, Portsmouth, 2007–10; Principal Anglican Chaplain, Archdeacon for RN and Dep. Chaplain of the Fleet (formerly Dir, Naval Chaplaincy Service), 2010–12. QHC 2010–12. Mem., Gen. Synod, C of E, 2010–. Governor: Royal Sch. Windsor Great Park, 2012–; St George's Sch., Windsor Castle, 2012–. Trustee: Assoc. of RN Officers, 2009–; Windsor Fest., 2012–. *Recreations:* amateur dramatics, choral singing, history, theatre. *Address:* Chaplain's Lodge, The Great Park, Windsor SL4 2HP.

**POLLACK, Anita Jean;** writer, since 2006; *b* NSW, Australia, 3 June 1946; *d* of late John and Kathleen Pollack; *m* 1986, Philip Bradbury; one *d*. *Educ:* City of London Polytechnic (BA 1979); Birkbeck Coll., Univ. of London (MSc Polit. Sociology 1981). Advertising copy writer, Australia, 1963–69; book editor, 1970–75; student, 1976–79; Research Asst to Rt Hon. Barbara Castle, MEP, 1981–89. MEP (Lab) London SW, 1989–99; Hd of Eur. Liaison, later Eur. Policy, English Heritage, 2000–06. Contested (Lab), EP elections: SE Region, 1999; London, 2004. *Publications:* Wreckers or Builders?: a history of Labour MEPs 1979–99, 2009; New Labour in Europe: leadership and lost opportunities, 2016. *Recreation:* family. *Address:* 139 Windsor Road, E7 0RA. *W:* www.anitapollack.eu.

**POLLARD, Prof. (Alan) Mark,** DPhil; Edward Hall Professor of Archaeological Science, since 2004 and Associate Head (Research), Social Sciences Division, since 2016, University of Oxford (Director, Research Laboratory for Archaeology and the History of Art, 2004–14); Fellow, Linacre College, Oxford, since 2004; *b* Takapuna, Auckland, NZ, 5 July 1954; *s* of Alan and Elizabeth Pollard; *m* 1993, Dr Rebecca Nicholson; two *d*. *Educ:* Univ. of York (BA Physics; DPhil Physics). Res. Fellow, Res. Lab. for Archaeol. and the Hist. of Art, Univ. of Oxford, 1978–84; New Blood Lectr in Chem. and Archaeol., UC Cardiff, 1984–90; University of Bradford: Prof. of Archaeol Scis, 1990–2004; Hd of Dept, 1990–99; Pro-Vice Chancellor, 1999–2004. Nat. Co-ordinator for Science-based Archaeol., 1997–2000. *Publications:* (jtly) Archaeological Chemistry, 1996, 3rd edn 2017; (jtly) Handbook of Archaeological Science, 2001; (jtly) Analytical Chemistry in Archaeology, 2007; numerous articles. *Recreations:* Morris dancing, fishing. *Address:* Research Laboratory for Archaeology and the History of Art, School of Archaeology, 1 South Parks Road, Oxford OX1 3TG. *T:* (01865) 285228. *E:* mark.pollard@rlaha.ox.ac.uk.

**POLLARD, Prof. Andrew John,** PhD; Professor of Education Policy and Practice, UCL Institute of Education, University College London (formerly Institute of Education, University of London), since 2006; Fellow of Wolfson College, Cambridge, since 2000; *b* 13 Nov. 1949; *s* of Michael and Anne Pollard; *m* 1971, Rosalind Croft; one *s* one *d*. *Educ:* Univ. of Leeds (BA 1971); Univ. of Lancaster (PGCE 1972); Univ. of Sheffield (MEd 1976; PhD 1981). Teaching in primary schools, 1972–81; Sen. Lectr, 1981–84, Principal Lectr, 1984–85, Oxford Poly.; Reader, 1985–90, Associate Dean, 1990–95, UWE; Prof. of Educn, Univ. of Bristol, 1996–2000; Prof. of Educn, Univ. of Cambridge, 2000–05; Dir, ESRC Teaching and Learning Res. Prog., 2002–09; Prof. of Educn, Graduate Sch. of Educn, Univ. of Bristol, 2011–15 (Vis. Prof., 2015–16). Chm., Educn Panel, REF 2014, HEFCE, 2011–14; Mem., Expert Panel on Review of National Curriculum, Dept for Educn, 2011. Chm., UK Strategic Forum for Res. in Educn, 2008–11; Dir, ESCalate, HEA, 2011. Chm., William Pollard & Co. Ltd, 1997–2014. Hon. DEd Edinburgh, 2010. *Publications:* The Social World of the Primary School, 1985; Reflective Teaching, 1987, 5th edn (as Reflective Teaching in Schools), 2019; (jtly) Changing English Primary Schools, 1994; The Social World of Children's Learning, 1996; (with A. Filer) The Social World of Pupil Career, 1999; (with P. Triggs) What Pupils Say: changing policy and practice in primary education, 2000; (with A. Filer) The Social World of Pupil Assessment, 2000; Professionalism and Pedagogy: a contemporary opportunity, 2010; (with M. James) Principles for Effective Pedagogy, 2011. *Recreations:* sailing, gardening, bird watching. *Address:* UCL Institute of Education, 20 Bedford Way, WC1H 0AL.

**POLLARD, Prof. Andrew John,** PhD; FRCPCH; FMedSci; Professor of Paediatric Infection and Immunity, University of Oxford, since 2008; Fellow, since 2006, and Vice Master, since 2017, St Cross College, Oxford; *b* 29 Aug. 1965; *s* of John and Helen Pollard; *m* 1993, Rachel Cowdrill; two *s* one *d*. *Educ:* St Peter's Sch., Southbourne, Bournemouth; Guy's Hosp. Med. Sch., Univ. of London (BSc 1986); St Bartholomew's Hosp. Med. Sch., Univ. of London (MB BS 1989); Imperial Coll. London (PhD 1999); DIC 1999; MA Oxon 2015. FRCPCH 1986; MRCP 1993. Trng in paediatrics, Birmingham Children's Hosp., BC Children's Hosp., Vancouver; Action Res. Trng Fellow, St Mary's Hosp., Paddington, 1995–98; Lectr in Infectious Disease, 2001–06, Reader in Paediatric Infectious Disease, 2006–08, Univ. of Oxford. Hon. Consultant Paediatrician, Children's Hosp., John Radcliffe, Oxford, 2001–. Mem., Strategic Adv. Gp of Experts, WHO, 2016–. Chair: Guidelines Develt Gp on meningitis in children, NICE, 2006–14; Topic Expert Gp on meningitis in children, NICE, 2011–13; Jt Cttee on Vaccination and Immunisation, DoH, subseq. DHSC, 2013–. Chair: Scientific Cttee, World Soc. for Paediatric Infectious Disease, 2009–13; Scientific Adv. Gp on Vaccines, EMEA, 2012–. Chair, Scientific Panel, Spencer Dayman Meningitis Labs Charity, 2002–05. Mem., Eur. Soc. for Paediatric Infectious Disease. Fellow: Univ. of BC, Vancouver, 2000; Paediatric Infectious Disease Soc. of America, 2009; FHEA 2002; FMedSci 2016. Sci. Honor and Truth Award, Clinical IPPA, La Paz, Bolivia, 2000; Bill Marshall Award, 2013, Educn and Communication Award, 2015, Eur. Soc. Paediatric Infectious Disease. *Publications:* over 500 contribs to scientific jls. *Recreations:* mountaineering (1st British ascent of Chamlang (7309m), Eastern Nepal, 1991; 1st British ascent of Jaonli (6632m), Gangotri reg. of Garhwal, Himalaya, India, 1988; dep. leader, British Everest Med. Expedn, 1994). *Address:* Department of Paediatrics, University of Oxford, Level 2, Children's Hospital, John Radcliffe, Oxford OX3 9DU. *T:* (01865) 231682. *E:* andrew.pollard@paediatrics.ox.ac.uk. *Club:* Alpine.

**POLLARD, Maj.-Gen. Anthony John Griffin,** CB 1992; CBE 1985; DL; General Officer Commanding, South West District, 1990–92, retired; *b* 8 April 1937; *s* of William Pollard and Anne Irene Griffin; *m* Marie-Luise; four *s*. *Educ:* Oakham Sch.; Jesus Coll., Cambridge. Commnd Royal Leics Regt, 1956; served Cyprus, Germany, Hong Kong, Borneo, Malta; Staff Coll., 1969; Staff 7 Armd Bde, 1970–72; Instr, Staff Coll., 1975–77; CO 1st Bn Royal Anglian Regt, 1977–79; (Norway, NI, Germany); QMG's Secretariat, 1980; Col, Tactical Doctrine, BAOR, 1981; Col, Ops and Tactical Doctrine, 1(BR) Corps, 1982; Comdr, British Forces, Belize, 1983–84; Comdt, Sch. of Infantry, 1984–87; Comdr, British Mil. Mission to Uganda, 1985–86; Dir Gen., Trng and Doctrine (Army), 1987–90. Dep. Col, Royal Anglian Regt, 1986–92; Colonel Commandant: Small Arms Sch. Corps, 1987–92; Queen's Div., 1990–92; Hon. Col Suffolk ACF, 1992–2000. Pres., Royal Tigers Assoc., 1996–2010. DL Suffolk, 1999. OStJ 2004 (Chm., St John Council, Suffolk, 2004–10). *Recreations:* family, fishing, gardening, archaeology, ancient buildings. *Club:* Victory Services (Vice Chm., 2003–08; Vice Pres., 2010–17).

**POLLARD, Sir Charles,** Kt 2001; QPM 1990; President, Restorative Solutions Community Interest Company, since 2018 (Chairman, 2006–18); *b* 4 Feb. 1945; *s* of Humphrey Charles Pollard and Margaret Isobel Pollard (*née* Philpott); *m* 1972, Erica Jane Allison Jack; two *s* one *d*. *Educ:* Oundle Sch.; Bristol Univ. (LLB). Metropolitan Police, 1964; Sussex Police, 1980; Asst Chief Constable, Thames Valley Police, 1985–88; Dep. Asst Comr, i/c No 5 (SW) Area of London, Metropolitan Police, 1988–91; Chief Constable, Thames Valley Police, 1991–2002. Chm., Quality of Service Cttee, ACPO, 1993–94; Vice-Chm., Thames Valley Partnership (working for safer communities), 1992–2002; Mem., Youth Justice Bd for England and Wales, 1998–2006 (actg Chm., 2003–04). Chairman: Winchester Restorative Justice Gp, 1999–2008; Justice Res. Consortium, 2002–05. Mem. Bd, Centre for Mgt and Policy Studies, 2000–02. Chm., Oxford Common Purpose, 1996–98; Vice Chm., Why Me?, Victims for Restorative Justice, 2009–16. Vis. Fellow, Nuffield Coll., Oxford, 1993–2001. Hon. LLD: Buckingham, 2001; Bristol, 2003. *Publications:* contribs to nat. media and learned jls on policing, criminal justice and restorative justice. *Recreations:* tennis, walking, family pursuits. *Address:* Restorative Solutions Community Interest Company, Unit 5, Albert House, The Pavilions, Ashton-on-Ribble, Preston PR2 2YD. *Club:* Royal Over-Seas League.

**POLLARD, Christopher Charles;** *b* 30 April 1957; *s* of Anthony Cecil and Margaret Noelle Pollard; *m* 1984, Margaret Ann Langlois; three *d*. *Educ:* Merchant Taylors' Sch., Northwood; Newland Park Coll. Gramophone, 1981–99: Editor, 1986–90; Man. Editor, 1990–93; Editl Dir, 1993–99. Director: Jethou, 1995–; Out of the Blue Productions, 2001–07; Songlines Publications, 2002–15; Kryotrans Internat., 2006–10; TOWER Cold Chain Solutions, 2009–; Themis Analytics, 2011–. *Recreations:* Rugby football, cricket, cars, music. *Address:* Beechcroft, Hotley Bottom, Great Missenden, Bucks HP16 9PL.

**POLLARD, Eve, (Lady Lloyd),** OBE 2008; *d* of late Ivor and Mimi Pollard; *m* 1st, 1968, Barry Winkleman (marr. diss. 1979); one *d*; 2nd, 1979, Sir Nicholas Lloyd, *qv*; one *s*. Fashion Editor: Honey, 1967–68; Daily Mirror Magazine, 1968–69; Women's Editor: Observer Magazine, 1970–71; Sunday Mirror, 1971–81; Asst Ed., Sunday People, 1981–83; Features Ed. and presenter, TV-am, 1983–85; Editor: Elle USA (launched magazine in NY), 1985–86; Sunday magazine, News of the World, 1986; You magazine, Mail on Sunday, 1986–87; Sunday Mirror and Sunday Mirror Magazine, 1987–91; Sunday Express and Sunday Express Magazine, 1991–94. Founder, Wedding Day magazine, 1999. Formerly contributor to Sunday Times. Member: English Tourism Council (formerly English Tourist Bd), 1993–2000; Competition Commn, 1999–2007; Mem., Newspaper Takeover Panel, Competition Commn, 1999–2007. Founder, Women in Journalism, 1995 (Hon. Life Pres.); Chair, Reporters Sans Frontières London, 2016–. Vice-Chm., Wellbeing of Women, 2003–. Vis. Fellow, Bournemouth Univ., 2001–. *Publications:* Jackie: biography of Mrs J. K. Onassis, 1971; (jtly) Splash, 1995; (jtly) Best of Enemies, 1996; (jtly) Double Trouble, 1997; Unfinished Business, 1998; Jack's Widow, 2006. *Address:* c/o Jackie Gill Management Ltd, 3 Warren Mews, W1T 6AN. *T:* (020) 7383 5550.
*See also* C. Winkleman.

**POLLARD, Fiona Ann;** Director, Heritage Events Ltd, since 2014; *b* Inverness, Scotland, 6 July 1965; *d* of George Alexander Milne Archibald and Margaret Archibald; *m* 1989, Brent Pollard; one *s* three *d*. *Educ*: Glenurquhart Secondary Sch.; Inverness Royal Acad.; Univ. of Aberdeen (MA Hons). Investment Banker: Barclays, 1988–91; Daiwa Europe Bank, 1991–93; NatWest Mkts, 1993–97; Goldman Sachs, 1997–98; Chair, Morrison Fashion Gp, 2007–09; Dep. Chair, Melton Mowbray Bldg Soc., 2014–. Board Member: SEEDA, 2004–07; Parkerville Children & Youth Care, 2010–13; VisitEngland, 2018–. Chair, Roman Baths Foundn, 2018–; Trustee, Friends of Victoria Art Gall., Bath, 2016–. Mem. Council, Christchurch Grammar Sch., WA, 2010–13. *Recreations:* food, art, family. *Address:* Heritage Events Ltd, 23 Queen Square, Bath BA1 2HX. *T:* (01225) 355373. *E:* fionapollard1@gmail.com.

**POLLARD, (George) Nicholas;** Chief Executive, Services Sound and Vision Corporation, 2009–15; *b* 15 Nov. 1950; *s* of Thomas Bewcastle Pollard and Helen Pollard; *m* 1981, Sally Jane Behenna; two *s*. *Educ*: Birkenhead Sch. Television journalist, BBC, 1977–80; ITN: television journalist, 1980–92; Exec. Producer, News at Ten, 1987–92; Producer, Election coverage, 1987, 1992; ind. producer, current affairs progs, 1992–94; Dir of Progs, Channel One TV, 1994–96; Hd of News, British Sky Broadcasting, 1996–2006. Mem., Adv. Panel, DCMS Free-to-Air Events Listing Review, 2009. Mem. Bd, Ofcom, 2016–18. Consultant and Advr, China Global Television Network, 2018–. *Recreations:* family, walking, reading.

**POLLARD, Prof. Jeffrey William,** PhD; FMedSci; FRSB; FRSE; FAAAS; Professor of Resilience Biology and Director, MRC Centre for Reproductive Health, University of Edinburgh, since 2012; *b* Rochford, Essex, 23 Jan. 1950; *s* of Clifford Pollard and Marjorie Althea Pollard; *m* 1981, Ooi-Thye Chong. *Educ:* Westcliff High Sch.; Univ. of Sheffield (BSc Special Hons 1971); Imperial Cancer Res. Fund/King's Coll. London (PhD 1974). Lectr, Queen Elizabeth Coll., subseq. King's Coll. London, 1980–88; Albert Einstein College of Medicine, New York: Associate Prof., 1988–93; Prof., 1993–; Louis Goldstein Swan Chair, 2008–17. Wellcome Sen. Investigator, 2013–. FAAAS 2011; FRSB (FSB 2013); FRSE 2015; FMedSci 2016. Medal of Honor, Amer. Cancer Soc., 2010. *Publications:* (ed) Evolutionary Theory: paths into the future, 1984; (ed) Methods in Molecular Biology: Animal Cell Culture, vol. 5 1990, 2nd edn (vol. 75) 1997, Plant Cell Culture, vol. 6 1990; over 250 articles in Nature, Sci., Cell, Immunity, Nature Reviews, etc. *Recreations:* Japanese art, music, wine and food, travel. *Address:* University of Edinburgh, Room C1.17, Queen's Medical Research Institute, 47 Little France Crescent, Edinburgh EH16 4TJ. *T:* (0131) 242 6231, *Fax:* (0131) 242 6441. *E:* jeff.pollard@ed.ac.uk.

**POLLARD, Joy Kerr;** *see* Larkcom, J. K.

**POLLARD, Kerry Patrick;** JP; *b* 27 April 1944; *s* of late Patrick Joseph Pollard and of Iris Betty Pollard; *m* 1966, Maralyn Murphy; five *s* two *d*. *Educ:* St Joseph's Primary Sch., Heywood, Lancs; Thornleigh Coll., Bolton. Engr, British Gas, 1960–92; Co-ordinator, Homes for Homeless People, 1992; Dir and Co. Sec., Cherry Tree Housing Assoc., 1992–97; Chair, NACRO Housing, 2011. Chair, Labour Housing Gp, 2010–. Member (Lab): St Albans DC, 1982–98; Herts CC, 1989–97. MP (Lab) St Albans, 1997–2005; contested (Lab) same seat, 1992, 2005, 2015. Hon. Fellow, Royal Coll. of Midwives, 2003. JP St Albans, 1984. *Recreations:* swimming, theatre, country walking.

**POLLARD, L. Edwin,** OBE 2003; High Commissioner for Barbados in the United Kingdom, 2003–08; *b* 21 May 1942; *m* 1968, Deanna Winifred Warner; one *s* one *d*. *Educ:* Combermere Sch., Barbados. CDipAF. Joined Barclays Bank plc, 1961: Staff and Industrial Relns Manager, Barclays, Caribbean; Asst Caribbean Dir (Mem., Barclays UK Exec. Cttee); Personal Sector and Offshore Dir; Product Develt and Mktg Dir, until 2000. Member Board: Barbados Inst. Banking and Finance; Securities Exchange of Barbados. FCIB. *Recreations:* golf, cricket, hockey, football. *Address:* c/o Barbados High Commission, 1 Great Russell Street, WC1B 3ND. *T:* (020) 7631 4975, *Fax:* (020) 7323 6872. *Club:* London Golf.

**POLLARD, Linda,** CBE 2013 (OBE 2004); DL; Chairman, Leeds Teaching Hospitals NHS Trust, since 2013; Founding Chairman, An Inspirational Journey, 2009–18; *b* Shipley, W Yorks, 13 Sept. 1945; *d* of William Edward Bannister and Ada Bannister; *m* 1973, David Ernest Pollard; one *s*, and one step *s* one step *d*. *Educ:* Bingley Grammar Sch. Regl Manager, Deal Marketing, London, 1967–70; Co-Founder and Man. Dir, Quorum Ltd, fashion retail, 1972–84; Founder and Man. Dir, Concept Marketing Ltd, 1985–95. Director: Andrews of Bradford (BMW) Ltd, 1980–96; Oak Lane Hldgs Ltd, 1991–2008; Mem. Bd, Real Radio Yorkshire, 2000–04; Regl Chm., Coutts Bank plc, 2005– (Nat. Women's Ambassador, 2008–10). Chairman: Bradford Property Forum, 2007–09; Two Percent Club, 2013– (Chm., Yorks, 2000–13). Non-exec. Dir, Bradford HA, 1994–96; Chairman: Bradford NHS Teaching Hosps Trust, 1996–2000; Bradford Dist Care Trust, 2002–04; West Yorks Strategic HA, 2004–06; Airedale, Bradford, Leeds NHS Cluster PCT, 2009–13; Adv. Bd, Leeds Inst. for Quality Healthcare; Member: NHS Improvement Chairs Adv. Gp, 2016–; NHS Improvement Gender Equality Gp, 2016–. Associate Mem., Fitness to Practise Cttee, GMC, 2001–05. Regl Chm., Learning and Skills Council, 2002–06; Mem., Strategy Cttee, HEFCE, 2007–09; non-exec. Mem. Bd, UCEA, 2010–12. Dep. Chm., Yorkshire Forward, 2004–12; Member, Board: Fair Cities Bradford, 2004–06; Northern Way, 2004–06; Welcome to Yorkshire, 2009–11. Chairman: Bradford Can Appeal, 2001–03; Born in Bradford Res. Appeal, 2005–07; Breast Cancer Haven Yorks, 2008–10; Leeds Innovation District Strategic Leadership Gp, 2017–; Trustee, Leeds Cares (formerly Leeds Teaching Hosps Foundn Charity), 2013–. Pro Chancellor and Chm. Council, Univ. of Leeds, 2007–13. JP Bradford, 1979; DL West Yorks, 2006. Hon. LLD Leeds, 2013. *Recreations:* keen gardener, travel, work. *T:* 07802 325532. *E:* linda@lindapollard.org. *Club:* Sloane.

**POLLARD, Luke;** MP (Lab Co-op) Plymouth Sutton and Devonport, since 2017; *b* Plymouth. *Educ:* Christleton High Sch.; Univ. of Exeter (BA 1st Cl. Politics 2001). Pres., Guild, Exeter Univ. Students' Union, 2001–02. Researcher to Rt Hon. George Foulkes, MP, 2003–05; Account Dir, Edelman, 2005–09; Hd, Public Affairs, 2009–13, Hd, Eur. Develt, 2013–14, ABTA; Dir, Field Consulting UK, 2015–17. Shadow Minister, DEFRA, 2018–. Mem., Transport Cttee, H of C, 2017–18. Contested (Lab Co-op): SW Devon, 2010; Plymouth Sutton and Devonport, 2015. *Address:* House of Commons, SW1A 0AA.

**POLLARD, Mark;** *see* Pollard, A. M.

**POLLARD, Nicholas;** *see* Pollard, G. N.

**POLLARD, His Honour Richard Frederick David;** a Circuit Judge, 1990–2006; Senior Circuit Judge, Nottingham Crown Court, 2002–06; *b* 26 April 1941; *s* of William Pollard and Anne Irene Pollard (*née* Griffin), CBE; *m* 1964, Angela Susan Hardy; one *s* two *d*. *Educ:* Oakham School; Trinity College Dublin (BA); Univ. of Cambridge (Dip. Crim.). Called to the Bar, Gray's Inn, 1967, Bencher, 2001. *Recreations:* walking, art nouveau, looking out of the window.

**POLLARD, Stephen Bernard;** Partner, WilmerHale, solicitors, since 2012; *b* London, 5 Sept. 1958; *s* of David Pollard and Pauline Pollard; *m* 1990, Margaret Ainscough; two *s* two *d*. *Educ:* Manchester Grammar Sch.; Pembroke Coll., Oxford (BA Hons Juris.). Admitted solicitor, 1985; Partner, Kingsley Napley, 1990–2011. *Recreations:* family, sport (especially swimming and cycling), walking, theatre, Fulham FC, film. *Address:* WilmerHale, 49 Park Lane, W1K 1PS. *T:* (020) 7872 1006. *E:* stephen.pollard@wilmerhale.com.

**POLLARD, Stephen Ian;** Editor, Jewish Chronicle, since 2008; *b* London, 18 Dec. 1964; *s* of Bernard Pollard, CB and of Regina Pollard; *m* 2007, Samantha Benjamin; one *s* one *d*. *Educ:* St Martin's Sch., Northwood; John Lyon Sch., Harrow; Mansfield Coll., Oxford (MA Modern Hist.). Res. asst to Rt Hon. Peter Shore, MP, 1989–92; Res. Dir, Fabian Soc., 1992–95; Hd of Res., Social Mkt Foundn, 1995–97; freelance writer, various newspapers, 1997–99; Chief Leader Writer and columnist, Daily Express, 1999–2001; Sen. Fellow, 2001–05, Pres., 2005–08, Centre for New Europe. Chm., Eur. Inst. for Study of Contemporary Antisemitism, 2007–08. Mem., Adv. Council, Reform, 2001. Fellow, Civitas, 2001–06. *Publications:* (with A. Adonis) A Class Act: the myth of Britain's classless society, 1997; David Blunkett, 2004; Ten Days that Changed the Nation: the making of modern Britain, 2009. *Recreations:* National Hunt racing, Tottenham Hotspur FC, classical music, opera, wine, good food, obscure public policy books. *Address:* Jewish Chronicle, 28 St Albans Lane, NW11 7QE. *T:* (020) 7415 1500. *E:* stephen@stephenpollard.net.

**POLLEN, Peregrine Michael Hungerford;** Executive Deputy Chairman, 1975–77, Deputy Chairman, 1977–82, Sotheby Parke Bernet and Co.; *b* 24 Jan. 1931; *s* of late Sir Walter Michael Hungerford Pollen, MC, JP, and Lady Pollen; *m* 1958, Patricia Helen Barry; one *s* two *d*. *Educ:* Eton Coll.; Christ Church, Oxford. National Service, KRRC, 1949–51. ADC to Sir Evelyn Baring, Governor of Kenya, 1955–57; Sotheby's, 1957–82: Dir, 1961; Pres., Sotheby Parke Bernet, New York, 1965–72. *Address:* The Farmhouse, Norton Hall, Mickleton, Glos GL55 6PU. *Clubs:* Brooks's, Beefsteak.

**POLLEN, Sir Richard (John Hungerford),** 8th Bt *cr* 1795, of Redenham, Hampshire; Independent Corporate Communications Consultant; *b* 3 Nov. 1946; *o s* of Sir John Michael Hungerford Pollen, 7th Bt and Angela Pollen (*née* Russi, later Henderson); S father, 2003; *m* 1971, Christianne Mary, *d* of Sir Godfrey Agnew, KCVO, CB; four *s* three *d* (and one *s* decd). *Educ:* Worth Sch. Capel-Cure Myers, 1964–68; Financial Times, 1970–71; Charles Barker, 1971–79; Valin Pollen, 1979–91; Richard Pollen & Co., 1990–94; Ludgate Pollen, 1994–96; Communication Consultant, Pollen Associates, 1996–2012. Mem., PRCA. FCIPR. *Publications:* (contrib.) The Management Audit, 1993; (contrib.) Maw on Corporate Governance, 1994. *Recreations:* running, riding, walking, golf, ski-ing. *Heir: s* William Richard Hungerford Pollen [*b* 28 June 1976; *m* 2007, Jennifer, *d* of Vance Kyte; one *s* two *d*]. *Clubs:* Royal Automobile; Rushmore Golf.

**POLLEY, Prof. Jacob Barnabas;** freelance writer, since 2001; Professor of Creative Writing, Newcastle University, since 2018; *b* Carlisle, 2 June 1975; *s* of Richard Andrew Polley and Susie Elizabeth Sinclair Brook; partner, 2009, Mai Lin Li; one *s*. *Educ:* Caldew Sch., Dalston; Lancaster Univ. (BA Hons English Lit. 1996; MA Creative Writing 1997). Lectr in Creative Writing, 2010–13, Sen. Lectr in Creative Writing, 2013–15, Univ. of St Andrews; Sen. Lectr in Creative Writing, Newcastle Univ., 2015–18. *Publications:* The Brink, 2003; Little Gods, 2006; Talk of the Town, 2009; The Havocs, 2012; Jackself, 2016. *Recreations:* not enough. *Address:* School of English Literature, Language and Linguistics, 3rd Floor, Percy Building, Newcastle University, Newcastle upon Tyne NE1 7RU. *T:* (0191) 208 7781. *E:* jake.polley@ncl.ac.uk.

**POLLI, Timothy James;** QC 2018; *b* Barnet, 25 Aug. 1973; *s* of Carlo Giuseppe Polli and Jennifer Mary Polli (*née* White); *m* 2003, Catherine Helen Aherne; one *s* one *d*. *Educ:* St Columba's Coll., St Albans; Hertford Coll., Oxford (MA Juris. 1994; BCL 1995). Res. Asst, Law Commn, 1996–97; called to the Bar, Middle Temple, 1997; pupil at 29 Bedford Row Chambers, 1997–98; in practice as barrister, specialising in property law, 1999–. *Recreations:* theatre, travel, tennis. *Address:* Tanfield Chambers, 2–5 Warwick Court, WC1R 5DJ. *T:* (020) 7421 5300, *Fax:* (020) 7421 5333.

**POLLINGTON, Viscount; John Andrew Bruce Savile;** *b* 30 Nov. 1959; *s* and heir of 8th Earl of Mexborough, *qv*; *m* 2019, Norma Isolde Findlay (*née* Phoenix).

**POLLINI, Maurizio;** pianist; *b* Milan, 5 Jan. 1942; *s* of Gino Pollini and Renata Melotti; *m* 1968, Maria Elisabetta Marzotto; one *s*. Has performed with all major orchestras, including: Chicago Symphony; Cleveland; Berlin Philharmonic; Boston Symphony; LPO; LSO; New York Philharmonic; Vienna Philharmonic; has played at Berlin, Prague, Salzburg and Vienna Fests. First Prize, Internat. Chopin Competition, Warsaw, 1960; Ernst von Siemens Music Prize, Munich, 1996. Has made numerous recordings. *Address:* c/o HarrisonParrott Ltd, The Ark, 201 Talgarth Road, W6 8BJ.

**POLLITT, Prof. Michael Gerald,** DPhil; Professor of Business Economics, Judge Business School, University of Cambridge, since 2014; Fellow, Sidney Sussex College, Cambridge, since 1994; *b* Belfast, 23 Oct. 1967; *s* of David Pollitt and Olive Pollitt; *m* 2000, Yvonne Mary Abbott; one *s* one *d*. *Educ:* Campbell Coll., Belfast; Sidney Sussex Coll., Cambridge (BA Econs 1989); Brasenose Coll., Oxford (MPhil Econs 1991; DPhil Econs 1994). University of Cambridge: Lectr in Applied Industrial Orgn, Faculty of Econs, 1994–99; Dir of Studies in Econs, 1995–, in Mgt, 1999–, Sidney Sussex Coll.; Judge Business School (formerly Judge Institute of Mgt Studies): Lectr in Business Econs, 1999–2001; Sen. Lectr, 2001–06; Reader, 2006–14; Asst Dir, Energy Policy Res. Gp, 2011–. Vis. Associate Prof., MIT, 2003. External Econ. Advr, Ofgem, 2007–11; Energy Advr, Consumers' Assoc., 2011–14; Member, Expert Advisory Panel: ORR, 2012–18; Ofwat, 2015–. Jt Academic Res. Dir, Centre on Regulation in Europe, 2018–. Convenor, Assoc. of Christian Economists UK, 2000–. Church Warden, Holy Trinity, Cambridge, 2004–07, 2013–14. Co-Editor, Economics of Energy and Envmtl Policy, 2011–16; Member, Editorial Board: Rev. of Industrial Orgn, 2004–; Competition and Regulation in Network Industries, 2013–; Utilities Policy, 2015–. *Publications:* Ownership and Performance in Electric Utilities, 1995; (ed with I. W. Jones) The Role of Business Ethics in Economic Performance, 1998; (jtly) MED2: competition and regulation in the European electricity industry, 1999; (ed with I. W. Jones) Understanding How Issues in Business Ethics Develop, 2002; (ed jtly) Private Initiatives in Infrastructure: priorities, incentives and performance, 2002; (ed jtly) Future Electricity Technologies and Systems, 2006; (jtly) Multinationals in their Communities: a social capital approach to corporate citizenship projects, 2007; (ed jtly) Delivering a Low Carbon Electricity System, 2008; (ed with T. Jamasb) The Future of Electricity Demand: customers, citizens and loads, 2011; (ed with S. Eyre) Competition and Regulation in Electricity Markets, 2016; over 80 papers in jls on energy economics, regulatory policy and business ethics. *Recreations:* family, cinema, philately, current affairs. *Address:* Judge Business School, University of Cambridge, Trumpington Street, Cambridge CB2 1AG. *T:* (01223) 339615. *E:* m.pollitt@jbs.cam.ac.uk.

**POLLITT, Nicola Kathryn;** HM Diplomatic Service; Ambassador to Nepal, since 2019; *b* London, 9 Feb. 1979; *d* of Adrian Pollitt and Catherine Pollitt; *m* 2018, Mark Perrin; one *s* one *d*. *Educ:* Clare Coll., Cambridge (BA Hons Law 2002); Univ. of Poitiers (Dip. French Law). Joined FCO, 2003; Hd, Child Abduction Unit, Consular Directorate, 2003–04; Desk Officer, EU Policy on Asia, EU Directorate, 2004–06; Second Sec. (Political), Oslo, 2006–09; Hd, Political Team, Kabul, 2010–11; Sen. Policy Advr for Afghanistan, Pakistan and India, Cabinet Office, 2011–13; Dep. Hd, Crisis Mgt Dept, FCO, 2013–14; Asst Private Sec. to the Prime Minister, 2014–15; Somalia Conf. Coordinator, 2016–17; Additional Dir, E Europe and Central Asia Directorate, 2017–18, FCO; full-time lang. trng, 2018–19. *Recreations:* cycling, walking, music. *Address:* c/o Foreign and Commonwealth Office, King Charles Street, SW1A 2AH. *E:* Nicola.Pollitt@fco.gov.uk.

**POLLOCK,** family name of **Viscount Hanworth.**

**POLLOCK, Alexander;** Sheriff of Grampian, Highland and Islands at Inverness, 2005–09 (at Inverness and Portree, 2001–05); *b* 21 July 1944; *s* of late Robert Faulds Pollock, OBE, and Margaret Findlay Pollock; *m* 1975, Verena Francesca Gertraud Alice Ursula Critchley; one *s* one *d*. *Educ:* Rutherglen Academy; Glasgow Academy; Brasenose Coll., Oxford (Domus Exhibnr; MA); Edinburgh Univ. (LLB); Univ. for Foreigners, Perugia. Solicitor, Bonar Mackenzie & Kermack, WS, 1970–73; passed advocate, 1973; Advocate Depute, 1990–91; Sheriff (floating) of Tayside, Central and Fife at Stirling, 1991–93; Sheriff of Grampian, Highland and Is at Aberdeen and Stonehaven, 1993–2001. Contested (C) Moray, 1987. MP (C): Moray and Nairn, 1979–83; Moray, 1983–87. PPS to Sec. of State for Scotland, 1982–86, to Sec. of State for Defence, 1986–87. Mem., Commons Select Cttee on Scottish Affairs, 1979–82, 1986–87. Sec., British-Austrian Parly Gp, 1979–87. Mem., Queen's Body Guard for Scotland, Royal Co. of Archers, 1984–. *Publications:* (contrib.) Stair Memorial Encyclopaedia of Scots Law. *Recreations:* music, cycling, dogs. *Address:* Drumdarrach, Forres, Moray, Scotland IV36 1DW. *Clubs:* New (Edinburgh); Highland (Inverness).

**POLLOCK, Prof. Allyson Mary;** Professor of Public Health and Director, Institute of Health and Society, Newcastle University, since 2017. *Educ:* Univ. of Dundee (BA Hons Physiol. 1979; MB ChB 1983); London Sch. of Hygiene and Tropical Medicine (MSc Community Medicine 1989). MFPH (MFPHM 1991), FFPH 1993; FRCGP 2012; FRCPE. Prof. of Health Policy and Health Services Res., Sch. of Public Policy, UCL, 1998–2005, Hon. Prof., 2005–; Dir, R&D, UCL Hosps NHS Trust, 1998–2005; Prof. of Internat. Public Health Policy, 2005–11, Dir, Centre for Internat. Public Health Policy, 2006–11, Univ. of Edinburgh; Prof. of Public Health Res. and Policy, and Co-Dir, Global Health, Policy and Innovation Unit, Centre for Primary Care and Public Health, QMUL, 2011–17, now Hon. Prof. *Publications:* NHS plc: the privatisation of our health care, 2004; The New NHS Explained, 2006; Tackling Rugby: what every parent should know about injuries, 2014; contrib. BMJ, British Jl of Gen. Practice, Lancet, Jl of PHM, Public Law, Public Money and Mgt. *Address:* Institute of Health and Society, Newcastle University, Baddiley-Clark Building, Richardson Road, Newcastle-upon-Tyne NE2 4AX. *T:* 07976 978304. *E:* allyson.pollock@ncl.ac.uk, allyson.pollock@gmail.com. *W:* www.allysonpollock.com.

**POLLOCK, Brian;** see Pollock, His Honour P. B.

**POLLOCK, Prof. Christopher John,** CBE 2002; PhD, DSc; Emeritus Professor, Institute of Biological, Environmental and Rural Sciences, Aberystwyth University (formerly University of Wales, Aberystwyth), 2009 (Hon. Professor of Rural Sciences, 1993–2009); Director, Institute of Grassland and Environmental Research, 1993–2007; *b* 28 March 1947; *s* of Neil Cunningham Pollock and Margaret Pollock (née Charlton); *m* 1970, Elizabeth Anne Bates; one *s* one *d*. *Educ:* Trinity Hall, Cambridge (BA 1968, MA 1972); Birmingham Univ. (PhD 1972; DSc 1993). Post-Doctoral Fellow, Botany Sch., Cambridge, 1971–74; joined Welsh Plant Breeding Station, later Inst. of Grassland and Envmtl Res., then Inst. of Biol, Envmtl and Rural Scis, 1974; Head, Res. Gp, 1985; Head, Envmtl Biology Dept, 1989. Fulbright Fellow, Univ. of California, Davis, 1978–79; NATO Sen. Res. Fellow, Purdue Univ., 1987–92; Hon. Professor: Univ. of Wales, Aberystwyth, 1993; Nottingham Univ., 1994–2006. Chairman: Scientific Steering Cttee for Farm-scale Trials of GM Crops, 1999–2005; Res. Priorities Gp for Sustainable Farming and Food, 2003–06; Adv. Cttee for Releases into the Envmt, 2003–13; Chief Scientific Advr to First Minister of Wales, 2007–08; Mem., BBSRC, 2008–14. FRSB (FIBiol 1997) FRAgS 2000; FLSW 2013. DUniv Birmingham, 2011. *Publications:* (jtly) Carbon Partitioning Within and Between Organisms, 1992; (with J. F. Farrar) The Biology of Fructans, 1993; approx. 100 reviews; papers in sci. jls. *Recreations:* golf, walking, woodwork. *Address:* Institute of Biological, Environmental and Rural Sciences, Aberystwyth University, Aberystwyth SY23 3AL. *T:* (01970) 624471. *Club:* St David's (Aberystwyth).

**POLLOCK, Sir David (Frederick),** 6th Bt *cr* 1866, of Hatton, Middlesex; *b* London, 13 April 1959; *o s* of Sir George Frederick Pollock, 5th Bt and Doreen Mumford Pollock (née Nash) (*d* 2012); *S* father, 2016; *m* 1985, Helena Ruth, *d* of L. J. Tompsett, OBE; one *d*. *Educ:* Eton Coll. Director: Amatis Films Ltd, 1983–; Hatton Farm Estates Ltd, 1997–. *Recreations:* ski-ing, golf. *Heir:* kinsman Julian Rivers Pollock [*b* 4 Dec. 1942; *m* 1969, Patricia Diana Downey; one *s* one *d*]. *Address:* 21 Meare Close, Tadworth, Surrey KT20 5RZ. *T:* (020) 3418 9742. *E:* david@amatis.co.uk. *Club:* Walton Heath Golf.

**POLLOCK, David John Frederick;** Trustee and Member of Board, Humanists UK; *b* 3 Feb. 1942; *s* of late Leslie William Pollock and Dorothy Emily (née Holt); *m* 1976, Lois Jaques (marr. diss. 1991; remarried 2017); one *s* one *d*. *Educ:* Beckenham and Penge Grammar Sch.; Keble Coll., Oxford (BA Lit. Hum. 1964; MA); London Business Sch. British Coal Corporation, 1964–90: Head of Central Secretariat, 1972–78; Head of Staff Planning and Orgn, 1980–90; Dir, ASH, 1991–94; Dir, Continence Foundn, 1996–2001. Mem., Hackney BC, 1974–78. Sec., Charity Law Reform Cttee, 1972–77. Trustee and Mem. Bd (formerly Mem., Exec. Cttee), Humanists UK (formerly British Humanist Assoc.), 1965–75 and 1997– (Chm., 1970–72); Mem. Bd, Rationalist Assoc. (formerly Rationalist Press Assoc.), 1979–2019 (Chm., 1989–91). Hd, Internat. Humanist and Ethical Union delegn to Council of Europe, 2013–17. Pres., Eur. Humanist Fedn, 2006–12. Treasurer, Hackney North Labour Party, 1989–92. *Publications:* Denial & Delay: the political history of smoking and health 1950–64, 1999; (contrib.) Representing Religion in the European Union, 2013; (contrib.) Belief, Law and Politics, 2014; (contrib.) Religious Freedom and the Law: emerging contexts for and from religion, 2018; articles in humanist, health and other jls. *Recreations:* theatre, gardening. *Address:* 13 Dunsmure Road, N16 5PU. *T:* (020) 8800 3542, 07866 806932, *Fax:* (020) 7502 0283. *E:* david.pollock@virgin.net. *W:* www.thinkingabouthumanism.org.

**POLLOCK, Sir Guy Maximilian Montagu-,** 6th Bt *cr* 1872; freelance photographer, Arcaid, since 2004; *b* 27 Aug. 1966; *s* of Sir Giles Hampden Montagu-Pollock, 5th Bt and Caroline Veronica Pollock (née Russell); *S* father, 2017, but his name does not appear on the Official Roll of the Baronetage. *Educ:* Eton Coll. Workshop Controller, BMW, 1984–96; Systems Controller, McLaren Cars Ltd, 1996–2004. *Heir: cousin* Jonathan David Montagu-Pollock [*b* 3 July 1947; *m* 1979, Deirdre Clare Binding; two *s*].

**POLLOCK, His Honour (Peter) Brian;** a Circuit Judge, 1987–2003; *b* 27 April 1936; *s* of late Brian Treherne Pollock and Helen Evelyn Pollock (née Holt-Wilson); *m* 1st, 1966, Joan Maryon Leggett (marr. diss. 1981); two *s* (and one *s* decd); 2nd, 1988, Jeannette Mary Nightingale; two step *s* one step *d*. *Educ:* St Lawrence College. Called to the Bar, Middle Temple, 1958. A Recorder of the Crown Court, 1986–87. *Recreations:* croquet, watching cricket, travel, walking, reading. *Address:* 18 Sanditon, Sidmouth, Devon EX10 8LL. *T:* (01395) 514425. *Clubs:* MCC; Sidmouth Cricket, Tennis and Croquet.

**POLLOCK-HULF, Isobel Anne,** OBE 2014; CEng, FIMechE; Visiting Professor in Engineering and Design, University of Leeds, since 2006; *b* Ballymoney, NI, 10 Nov. 1954; *d* of late Charles Wilson Pollock and Elisabeth Margaret Pollock (née Watson); *m* 1st, 1980, Graham Ramsden (*d* 1997); 2nd, 2015, Robin Hulf (*d* 2015). *Educ:* Dalriada, Ballymoney; Imperial Coll., London (BScEng 1976). CEng 1981; FIMechE 1991. ICI, 1976–87; DuPont, 1987–96; Beatson Clark, 1997–99; Dir, Benbane Engrg Consultants, 1999–. Engineering Council UK: Chm., Quality Assce Cttee, 2005–12; Mem., Trustee Bd, 2005–13; Associate, 2013–; Chairman: BIS (formerly DTI, then DIUS) Pathfinder Measurement Wkg Gp, subseq. Electromagnetics and Time Prog., then Quantum Electromagnetics and Time, 2006–15; BEIS (formerly BIS) Prog. Expert Gp for Electromagnetics and Time, subseq. Digital Prog. Expert Gp, 2015–; Steering Bd, Nat. Measurement Office, subseq. Nat. Measurement and Regulation Office, 2013–16; Mem. Bd, British Hallmarking Council, 2019–. Pres., IMechE, 2012–13 (Vice Pres., 2000–06; Dep. Pres., 2010–12). Mem., Sci. and Technol. Adv. Council, NPL, 2015–. Trustee: Audi Design Foundn, 1999–2010; HMS Warrior 1860, 2014–; Design and Technol. Assoc., 2014–17. Liveryman, Engineers' Co., 2003– (Master, 2016–17). FCGI. Hon. FIET 2016. Hon. DSc: Huddersfield, 2004; Leeds, 2016. *Recreations:* engineering heritage, history of measurement, family history research, bridge, golf. *Address:* School of Mechanical Engineering, University of Leeds, Woodhouse Lane, Leeds LS2 9JT. *Clubs:* Royal Automobile, Athenæum; Woodsome Hall Golf.

**POLONIUS, Sarah Amalia;** see Teichmann, S. A.

**POLTIMORE,** 7th Baron *cr* 1831; **Mark Coplestone Bampfylde;** Bt 1641; Chairman, Sotheby's Russia and Scandinavia, and Deputy Chairman, Sotheby's Europe, since 2007; *b* 8 June 1957; *s* of Captain the Hon. Anthony Gerard Hugh Bampfylde (*d* 1969) (*er s* of 6th Baron) and of Brita Yvonne (who *m* 2nd, 1975, Guy Elmes), *o d* of late Baron Rudolph Cederström; *S* grandfather, 1978; *m* 1982, Sally Anne, *d* of late Dr Norman Miles; two *s* one *d*. Christie's: Associate Dir, 1984–87; Dir, 1987–2000; Dep. Chm., 1998–2000; Man. Dir, Eauctionroom.com, 2000–02; Sen. Dir, Sotheby's, 2002–06; Chm., Sotheby's UK, 2006–07. *Publications:* (with Philip Hook) Popular Nineteenth Century Painting: a dictionary of European genre painters, 1986. *Heir: s* Hon. Henry Anthony Warwick Bampfylde, *b* 3 June 1985. *Address:* North Hidden Farm, Hungerford, Berks RG17 0PY. *Club:* White's.

**POLWARTH,** 11th Lord *cr* 1690 (Scot.); **Andrew Walter Hepburne Scott;** *b* 30 Nov. 1947; *s* of 10th Lord Polwarth, TD and Caroline Margaret (née Hay); *S* father, 2005; *m* 1971, Anna, *e d* of late Maj. J. F. H. Surtees, OBE, MC; two *s* two *d*. *Educ:* Eton; Trinity Hall, Cambridge. JP Roxburgh Div., Scottish Borders, 1997–2005. *Heir: s* Master of Polwarth, *qv*. *Club:* Knickerbocker (New York).

**POLWARTH; Master of;** Hon. **William Henry Hepburne Scott;** Head, London and South East, Brewin Dolphin Ltd; *b* 21 March 1973; *s* and *heir* of Lord Polwarth, *qv*; *m* 2008, Donna Louise, *d* of Maj. Gen. Anthony Neil Carlier, *qv*; two *s* one *d*. *Educ:* Charterhouse; Newcastle Univ. With Brewin Dolphin Ltd, 1996–. *Heir: s* Harry Walter Hepburne Scott, *b* 21 March 2010.

**POLYCHRONAKIS, John;** Chief Executive, Dudley Metropolitan Borough Council, 2008–15; *b* Liverpool, 22 Nov. 1952; *s* of George and Ann Polychronakis; *m* 1980, Jacqueline Greaves; one *s* one *d*. *Educ:* St Francis Xavier's Coll., Liverpool; Liverpool Univ. (LLB). Admitted as solicitor, 1977; Solicitor, Liverpool CC, 1977–83; Asst Dir, Sefton MBC, 1983–87; Sen. Asst Chief Legal Officer, 1987–92, Dir, Law and Property, 1992–2008, Dudley MBC. Company Secretary: Black Country Living Mus. Ltd, 1994–2015; Black Country Consortium Ltd, 2008–15. Pres., Assoc. of Council Secretaries and Solicitors, 2004. *Recreations:* running, cycling, walking.

**POLYNESIA, Bishop of,** since 2019; Most Rev. **Fereimi Cama;** Co-Archbishop, Anglican Church in Aotearoa, New Zealand and Polynesia, since 2019; *b* Fiji; *s* of late Alipate Vuli and Meraia Ranadi; *m* 1977, Mereadani Qio Cama (*d* 2017); one *s* two *d* and one adopted *s*. *Educ:* Onolevu District Sch., Fiji; Queen Victoria Sch., Fiji; Corpus Christi Teachers' Coll., Suva (Teaching Cert.); Univ. of Geneva (Cert. Ecumenical Studies); Univ. of Auckland (BTh). School teacher, 1977–94; ordained deacon, 1990; Dean, Holy Trinity Cathedral, Suva, 1999–2012; Vicar, St Peter's, Lautoka, Viti Levu, 2016–19. *Recreations:* working in my backyard garden, playing cricket. *Address:* PO Box 35, Suva, Fiji Islands. *T:* 9768766. *E:* cama.fereimi@gmail.com.

**POMEROY,** family name of **Viscount Harberton.**

**POMEROY, Sir Brian (Walter),** Kt 2012; CBE 2006; Chairman, Age UK, since 2018 (Trustee, since 2017); *b* 26 June 1944; *m* 1974, Hilary Susan Price; two *d*. *Educ:* King's Sch., Canterbury; Magdalene Coll., Cambridge (MA). FCA (ACA 1968). Partner, Touche Ross Mgt Consultants, subseq. Deloitte Consulting, 1975–99: on secondment as Under Sec., DTI, 1981–83; Man. Dir, 1987–95; Sen. Partner, 1995–99. Non-executive Director: Rover Gp plc, 1985–88; QBE Insurance Gp Ltd, 2014–. Member: Nat. Lottery Commn, 1999–2007 (Chm., 1999–2000, 2002–03); Audit Commn, 2003–09; Gambling Commn, 2007–11 (Chm., 2008–11). Mem., Cttee of Enquiry into Regulatory Arrangements at Lloyd's, 1986; Ind. Mem. Council, Lloyd's, 1996–2004; Dep. Chm., Lloyd's Regulatory Bd, 1996–2002. Chairman: Telecommunications Interconnection Cttee, 1988–91; Financial Inclusion Task Force, HM Treasury, 2005–11; Payments Council, 2007–09; Ind. Commn on Equitable Life Payments, 2010–11; Responsible Gambling Strategy Bd, 2012–13; Action Gp on Cross-Border Remittances, HM Treasury, 2014–; Pres., Financial Inclusion Commn, 2015–. Member: Disability Rights Task Force, 1997–99; Pensions Protection Investments Accreditation Bd, 2000–05; Bd, Social Market Foundn, 2000–18; Ind. Inquiry into Drug Testing at Work, Joseph Rowntree Foundn, 2003–04; Financial Reporting Rev. Panel, 2004–13. Non-executive Director: FSA, 2009–13; Financial Conduct Authy, 2013–16. Mem. Council, Mgt Consultants Assoc., 1996–99. Chairman: AIDS Awareness Trust, 1993–96; Centrepoint, 1993–2001; Eur. Public Health Foundn, 1997–2002; Homeless Link, 2001–05; Raleigh Internat., 2005–07; Kraszna Krausz Foundn, 2016–. Trustee: Money Advice Trust, 1999–2009 (Ambassador, 2010–); Children's Express, 2004–07; SPACE Studios, 2004–05; Lloyd's Charitable Trust, 2004–10; Photographers' Gall., 2006–13 (Chm. of Trustees, 2008–13); Photography Oxford, 2016–; Chm. of Trustees, The King's Consort, 2000–05. Mem., Awards Cttee, RPS, 2016–17. Master, Mgt Consultants' Co., 2000–01. FRSA 1994. *Recreations:* photography (ARPS 2004; MA 2006), listening to music, theatre, cycling. *Address:* 7 Ferncroft Avenue, NW3 7PG. *T:* 07785 304368. *E:* pomeroybw@aol.com.

**POMERY, (Susannah) Victoria (Louise),** OBE 2012; Director, Turner Contemporary, since 2002; *b* Wirksworth, Derbys, 30 Aug. 1964; *d* of Peter Pomery and Briar Pomery. *Educ:* Norton Hill Sch., Midsomer Norton; North Staffordshire Poly. (BA Hons Hist. of Design and Visual Arts); Birmingham Poly. (MA (Dist.) Hist. of Art and Design). Pt-time Lectr in Hist. of Art and Design, Stourbridge Coll. of Art and Design, 1989; Asst Curator, Mead Gall., Univ. of Warwick, Coventry, 1989–95; Exhibns Officer, Angel Row Gall., Nottingham, 1995–97; Sen. Curator, Tate Liverpool, 1997–2002. Hon. MA Univ. for the Creative Arts, 2013. *Publications:* (ed with Dr Christoph Grunenberg) Marc Quinn, 2002. *Recreations:* arts, walking, gardening. *Address:* Turner Contemporary, Rendezvous, Margate, Kent CT9 1HG. *T:* (01843) 233001. *E:* vpomery@turnercontemporary.org.

**POND, Christopher;** Chair, Lending Standards Board, since 2017; *b* 25 Sept. 1952; *s* of Charles Richard Pond and Doris Violet Pond; *m* 1990, Carole Tongue, *qv* (marr. diss. 1999); one *d*; *m* 2003, Lorraine Melvin; one *s* one *d*. *Educ:* Univ. of Sussex (BA Hons Econs). Research Asst in Econs, Birkbeck Coll., Univ. of London, 1974–75; Res. Officer, Low Pay Unit, 1975–78; Lectr in Econs, CS Coll., 1978–79; Dir, Low Pay Unit, 1980–97. Contested (Lab) Welwyn Hatfield, 1987; MP (Lab) Gravesham, 1997–2005; contested (Lab) same seat, 2005; Parly Under-Sec. of State, DWP, 2003–05. Chief Exec., Nat. Council for One Parent Families, subseq. One Parent Families|Gingerbread, 2005–08; Financial Services Authority: Dir, Financial Capability, 2007–10; Sen. Advr, 2010–11; Hd, Consumer Affairs, 2011–12; Vice Chm., Financial Inclusion Commn, 2014–. Partner and Hd, Public Affairs, Kreab Worldwide, 2013–16. Chm., Capacitybuilders UK Ltd, 2005–09; Director: Cape Claims Services Ltd, 2005–; Current Account Switch Service, 2016–. Chm., Standards Bd, Safe Home Income Plans, later Equity Release Council, 2012–. Chm., Wkg Gp on debt, Centre for Social Justice, 2012–14. Ind. Mem., Ethics and Responsibility Bd Sub-Cttee, HMRC, 2009–13; Mem., FinTech Delivery Panel, HM Treasury, 2017–. Vis. Lectr in Econs, Univ. of Kent, 1983–84; Hon. Vis. Prof. and Res. Fellow, Univ. of Surrey, 1984–86; Hon. Vis. Prof., Univ. of Middlesex, 1995–. Consultant, Open Univ., 1987–88 and 1991–92. Chairman: Credit Action, Money Charity, 2011–; Caxton Foundn, 2015–18. Vice Chm., End Child Poverty, 2007–09; Mem. Council, IFS, 2005–14; Trustee: Nat. Family and Parenting Inst., 2009–13; Family and Childcare Trust, 2013–18; Gamble Aware, 2017–; Zacchaeus 2000 Trust, 2017–; Money and Mental Health Policy Inst., 2018–. FRSA 1992. *Publications:* (jtly) To Him Who Hath, 1977; (jtly) Taxation and Social Policy, 1981; (contrib.) Old and New Poverty, 1995; Out of Poverty: towards prosperity, 1996; (contrib.) Working for Full Employment, 1997; (contrib.) Beyond 2002, 1999. *Recreations:* running, reading, family. *Address:* Lending Standards Board, Abbey House, 74–77 St John Street, EC1M 4DZ.

**PONDER, Sir Bruce (Anthony John),** Kt 2008; PhD; FRCP, FMedSci; FRS 2001; Li Ka Shing Professor of Oncology, University of Cambridge, 2006–11, now Emeritus; Director: Cancer Research UK Cambridge Institute, 2005–13, now Emeritus; Cambridge Cancer Centre, 2010–15; Fellow, Jesus College, Cambridge, 1993–2011, now Emeritus; *b* 25 April 1944; *s* of late Anthony West Ponder and Dorothy Mary Ponder (*née* Peachey); *m* 1969, Margaret Ann Hickinbotham; one *s* three *d*. *Educ:* Charterhouse Sch.; Jesus Coll., Cambridge (MA, MB BChir); St Thomas's Hosp. Med. Sch.; PhD London. FRCP 1987; FRCPath 2001–10. NHS hosp. appts, 1968–73; Clinical Research Fellow, ICRF, 1973–76; first Hamilton Fairley Fellow, CRC, at Harvard Med. Sch., 1977–78; Clinical Scientific Officer, ICRF, St Bartholomew's Hosp., 1978–80; Institute of Cancer Research: CRC Fellow and Sen. Lectr in Med., Royal Marsden Hosp., 1980–87; Reader in Human Cancer Genetics and Head, Section of Cancer Genetics, 1987–89; University of Cambridge: Dir, Cancer Res. UK (formerly CRC) Human Cancer Genetics Gp, 1989–2008; CRC Prof. of Human Cancer Genetics, 1992–96; CRUK (formerly CRC) Prof. of Oncology, 1996–2006. Mem., Bd of Dirs, Amer. Assoc. for Cancer Res., 2008–11 (Founding Mem. Academy, 2013); Pres., British Assoc. for Cancer Res., 2010–14. Hon. Consultant Physician: Royal Marsden Hosp., 1980–2003; Addenbrooke's Hosp., Cambridge, 1989–2014. Vis. Prof., Harvard Medical Sch., 2017–19. Croonian Lectr, RCP, 1998. Gibb Fellow, CRC, 1990, CRUK, 2013. Founder FMedSci 1998; Founding Fellow, European Acad. of Cancer Scis, 2011–. Trustee, CRUK, 2016–. Internat. Public Service Award, Nat. Neurofibromatosis Foundn, USA, 1992; Merck Prize, European Thyroid Assoc., 1996; Hamilton Fairley Award, European Soc. of Med. Oncology, 2004; Bertner Award, M. D. Anderson Hosp., 2007; Alfred Knudson Award for Cancer Genetics, Nat. Cancer Inst., USA, 2008; Ambuj Nath Bose Prize, RCP, 2008; Donald Ware Waddell Award for Cancer Res., Univ. of Arizona, 2010; Lifetime Achievement Award, CRUK, 2013. *Publications:* papers on genetics, cancer, developmental biology. *Recreations:* gardening, travel, golf, wine, photography. *Address:* Cancer Research UK Cambridge Institute, University of Cambridge, Li Ka Shing Centre, Robinson Way, Cambridge CB2 0RE. *T:* (01223) 761860; Sutton Fields, Bircham Road, Snettisham, Norfolk PE31 7NF. *Club:* Royal West Norfolk Golf (Brancaster).

**PONSOLLE, Patrick Henry Jean;** Chairman and Chief Executive Officer, Pajoma SA, since 1990; *b* 20 July 1944; *s* of Jean Ponsolle and Marie-Rose Ponsolle (*née* Courthaliac); *m* 2nd, 1983, Nathalie Elie-Lefebvre; two *d*, and two step *s* two step *d*. *Educ:* Lycée Janson-de-Sailly, Paris; Lycée Henri IV, Paris; Ecole Normale Supérieure; Institut d'Etudes Politiques, Paris; Ecole Nationale d'Administration. Adminr, Min. of Econ. and Finance, 1973–77; Financial Attaché, French Embassy, Washington, 1977–79; Ministry of Economy and Finance: Chargé de Mission to Dir of Forecasting, 1980; Dep. Chief of Staff of Laurent Fabius, Minister responsible for the budget, 1981–83; Gen. Sec., Nat. Accounts and Budget Commn, France, 1980–81; Compagnie de Suez: Asst Dir Gen., 1983–87; Dir Gen., 1988–93; Adminr, 1991–93; Jt Chm., 1994–96, Exec. Chm., 1996–2001, Eurotunnel Gp; Chm., Eurotunnel SA, 1994–2001; Man. Dir and Vice Chm., Morgan Stanley Internat. Ltd, and Pres., Morgan Stanley SA, 2001–09; Vice Chm., Rothschild Europe, 2009–14. Non-exec. Dir, Proparco, 2014–. Chm., GreenWish Africa REN, 2015–. *Address:* 3 rue Danton, 75006 Paris, France. *E:* p.ponsolle@sfr.fr.

**PONSONBY,** family name of **Earl of Bessborough,** and of **Barons de Mauley** and **Ponsonby of Shulbrede.**

**PONSONBY OF SHULBREDE,** 4th Baron *cr* 1930, of Shulbrede; **Frederick Matthew Thomas Ponsonby;** Baron Ponsonby of Roehampton (Life Peer), 2000; JP; *b* 27 Oct. 1958; *o s* of 3rd Baron and of Ursula Mary, *yr d* of Comdr Thomas Stanley Lane Fox-Pitt, OBE, RN; *S* father, 1990; *m* 1995, Sarah Catriona Pilkington Jackson; one *s* one *d*. *Educ:* Holland Park Comprehensive Sch.; University Coll., Cardiff; Imperial Coll., London. FIMMM (FIMM 1996); CEng 1997. Councillor (Lab), London Borough of Wandsworth, 1990–94. Opposition frontbench spokesman on educn, H of L, 1992–97. Member: Sub-cttee C, European Select Cttee, H of L, 1997–98; Select Cttee on Sci. and Technol., H of L, 1998–99; Select Cttee on Constitution, 2001–02. Delegate: Council of Europe and WEU, 1997–2001; OSCE, 2001–10. JP Westminster, 2006, Inner London Youth Panel, 2008, Gtr London Family Panel, 2012. *Heir: s* Hon. Cameron John Jackson Ponsonby, *b* 4 Aug. 1995. *Address:* House of Lords, SW1A 0PW.

**PONSONBY, Sir Charles (Ashley),** 3rd Bt *cr* 1956, of Wootton, co. Oxfordshire; DL; *b* 10 June 1951; *e s* of Sir Ashley Ponsonby, 2nd Bt, KCVO, MC and Lady Martha Butler, *yr d* of 6th Marquess of Ormonde, CVO, MC; *S* father, 2010; *m* 1983, Mary Priscilla Bromley Davenport; two *s* one *d*. *Educ:* Eton; Christ Church, Oxford (BA 1973; MA). FCA 1977. Worked in accountancy, corporate finance and financial public relations, 1973–2010. DL Oxon, 2014. *Heir: s* Arthur Ashley Ponsonby, *b* 15 Sept. 1984. *Address:* Woodleys, Woodstock, Oxon OX20 1HJ. *T:* (01993) 811717. *E:* cponsonby88@gmail.com. *Clubs:* Pratt's, White's.

**PONSONBY, Air Vice Marshal John Maurice Maynard,** OBE 1999; Senior Vice President, Customer Support and Training Worldwide, AgustaWestland, 2012–18 (Senior Vice President, Training, 2007–12); Managing Director, AgustaWestland Ltd, 2015–18; Chairman, Aviation Training International Ltd, 2011–18 (Director, 2007–18); Director, Rotorsim Srl, 2008–16; *b* 8 Aug. 1955; *s* of Myles and Anne Ponsonby; *m* 1980, Marie-José Van Huizen; one *s* two *d*. *Educ:* Ampleforth Coll. Commn Royal Green Jackets, 1975–83; commnd RAF, 1983; qualified helicopter instructor, Hong Kong, Germany and UK, 1983–88; Flight Comdr, Germany, NI and Falkland Is, 1988–91; Staff HQ RAF Germany, 1991; Staff Coll., 1992; Staff, HQ No 1 Gp, MoD, 1993–95; Comd 27 Sqdn RAF, 1995–98; PSO to CDS, MoD, 1998–2000; HCSC, 2000; Station Comdr, RAF Aldergrove and Comdr Jt Helicopter Force, NI, 2000–02; AO Plans HQ Strike Comd, 2002–04; AOC Trng Gp and Chief Exec., Trng Gp Defence Agency, 2005–07; COS Ops, HQ Air Comd, 2007. Founder Patron, Help for Heroes, 2011– (Trustee, 2007–11). QCVS 2002. *Recreations:* flying, golf, tennis, cricket, military history. *Address:* c/o Lloyds Bank, 38 Blue Boar Road, Salisbury, Wilts SP1 1DB. *E:* ponsonby.3@googlemail.com. *Clubs:* Royal Air Force, Royal Automobile.

**PONSONBY, Robert Noel,** CBE 1985; Controller of Music, BBC, 1972–85; *b* 19 Dec. 1926; *o s* of late Noel Ponsonby, BMus, Organist Christ Church Cathedral, Oxford, and Mary White-Thomson; *m* 1st, 1957, Una Mary (marr. diss.), *er d* of late W. J. Kenny; 2nd, 1977, Lesley Margaret Black (marr. diss.), *o d* of late G. T. Black. *Educ:* Eton; Trinity Coll., Oxford. MA Oxon, Eng. Litt. Commissioned Scots Guards, 1945–47. Organ Scholar, Trinity Coll., Oxford, 1948–50; staff of Glyndebourne Opera, 1951–55; Artistic Director of the Edinburgh International Festival, 1955–60; with Independent Television Authority, 1962–64; Gen. Administrator, Scottish Nat. Orchestra, 1964–72. Director: Commonwealth Arts Festival, Glasgow, 1965; Henry Wood Promenade Concerts, 1974–86; Artistic Dir, Canterbury Fest., 1987–88. Adminr, Friends of the Musicians Benevolent Fund, 1987–93. Artistic Adviser to Internat. Arts Guild of Bahamas, 1960–72. Chm., London Choral Soc., 1990–94; Programme Consultant, RPO, 1993–96. Mem., Music Adv. Panel, Arts Council of GB, 1986–89; Music Advr, Wingate Scholarships, 1988–2008. Trustee: Young Concert Artists Trust, 1984–89; Nash Concert Soc., 1988–2004; Michael Tippett Musical Foundn, 1989–2013. Governor, Purcell Sch., 1985–88. Originator, Choirbook for the Queen, 2012. Hon. RAM 1975; Hon. Mem., ISM, 1992. FRSA 1979. *Publications:* Short History of Oxford University Opera Club, 1950; Musical Heroes, 2009; In and Out of Tune, 2016. *Recreations:* bird-watching, English and Scottish painting, music. *Address:* 11 St Cuthbert's Road, NW2 3QJ.

**PONTEFRACT, Archdeacon of;** see Townley, Ven. P. K.

**PONTI, Signora Carlo;** see Loren, Sophia.

**PONTIN, John Graham,** OBE 2004; Chairman, JT Group Ltd, 1961; Founder Trustee, Converging World, since 2007; *b* 2 June 1937; *s* of Charles Cyril Pontin and Phyllis (*née* Frieze); *m* 1st, 1966, Gillian Margaret Harris (marr. diss. 1971); one *s* one *d*; 2nd, 1977, Sylviane Marie-Louise Aubel (*d* 1998). *Educ:* Bristol Tech. Sch. (Building). Founder, JT Group, 1961. Chm., Dartington Hall Trust, 1984–97 (Trustee, 1980–97); Trustee, Quartet Community Foundn (formerly Gtr Bristol Community Trust, then Gtr Bristol Foundn), 1987–98. FRSA. *Recreation:* passionate about acting on environmental global issues. *Club:* Reform.

**PONTIUS, His Honour Timothy Gordon;** a Circuit Judge, 1995–2016; a Specialist Circuit Judge, Central Criminal Court, 2008–16; *b* 5 Sept. 1948; *s* of Gordon Stuart Malzard Pontius and Elizabeth Mary (*née* Donaldson). *Educ:* Boroughmuir Sen. Secondary Sch., Edinburgh; London Univ. (external, LLB Hons). Called to the Bar, Middle Temple, 1972, Bencher, 2008; in practice at the Bar, 1972–88; Dep. Judge-Advocate, 1988–91; AJAG, 1991–95; a Recorder, 1993–95. *Recreations:* music, travel, swimming.

**POOBALAN, Very Rev. Dr Isaac Munuswamy;** Provost, St Andrew's Cathedral, Aberdeen, since 2015; *b* Vellore, S India, 14 July 1962; *s* of Subramani and Devasitham Poobalan; *m* 1995, Amudha Sujatha; one *s* one *d*. *Educ:* Don Bosco Higher, Vellore, India; Christian Medical Coll., Vellore, India (RGN 1984); Univ. of Edinburgh (BD 1994; MTh 1997); Pittsburgh Theol Seminary (DMin 2012). RGN, Christian Medical Coll., Vellore, 1984–87; RGN (Psych.), Directorate of Med. Services, Abu Dhabi, 1987–91; Commn on Graduates from Foreign Nursing Schs, Philadelphia; ordained deacon, 1994, priest, 1995; Curate, St Peter's, Edinburgh, 1994–97; Priest-in-charge, St Clement's, Aberdeen, 1997–2001; Rector, St John's, Aberdeen, 2001–15. Chm., Friends of Vellore, Scotland, 2008–. Mem., Grampian Theol Club, 2002–. Spiritual Dir, 2012–. *Publications:* Pain - a blessed suffering: reflections on Prof. Paul Brand, 2014. *Recreations:* music (fusion percussion), cricket (bowling), graphic design, liturgy. *Address:* 28 King Street, Aberdeen AB24 5AX. *T:* (01224) 640119. *E:* provost@aberdeen.Anglican.org.

**POOK, Jocelyn, (Mrs Dragan Aleksic);** musician and composer; *b* Birmingham, 14 Feb. 1960; *d* of Mary and Wilfred Pook; *m* 2003, Dragan Aleksic; one *d*. *Educ:* King Edward VI Upper Sch., Bury St Edmunds; Guildhall Sch. of Music and Drama (viola and piano 1983). AGSM 1982. Performer (viola) with The Communards, 1985–89; string arrangements and collaborations with artists incl. Peter Gabriel, Massive Attack, PJ Harvey, Mark Knopfler and Laurie Anderson. Composer of *film scores:* Eyes Wide Shut, 1999 (ASCAP Award, Chicago Film Award, 2000); L'Emploi du Temps, 2001; Gangs of New York, 2002; Wild Side, 2004; Merchant of Venice, 2005; Heidi, 2006; Caotica Ana, 2007; Brick Lane, 2008 (ASCAP Award); Room in Rome, 2010; Augustine, 2014; *opera:* Ingerland for Royal Opera Hse Linbury Studio, 2010; *theatre scores:* Speaking in Tunes, UK tour, incl. ICA and Tron Th., Glasgow, 2003–04 (British Composer Award (multi-media), BASCA, 2003); St Joan, NT, 2007 (Olivier Award for Best Music and Sound Design, 2008); King Charles III, Wyndhams and Music Box, NY, 2014–16 (BAFTA Award for Best Original Music, 2018); Macbeth, Shakespeare's Globe Th., 2016; Memorial, Barbican, 2018; *commissions include:* Mobile for BBC Proms/Kings Singers in collaboration with Andrew Motion, Royal Albert Hall, 2002; Hearing Voices for BBC Concert Orchestra, 2012; iTMOi for Sadlers Wells/ Akram Khan Co., 2013; Anxiety Fanfare for Mental Health Foundn, 2014 (New Music Biennial Composer, PRS Foundn, 2017); Drawing Life, Jewish Music Inst., 2014; *dance scores:* STRANGE FISH, DV8 Physical Th., 1992 (Prix Italia for Music & Arts, 1994); DESH, Akram Khan Co., worldwide tour incl. Sadlers Wells, 2011–14 (British Composer Award (stage works), BASCA, 2012); DUST, 2014 (Lest We Forget) and M-DAO, 2016 (She Said), for English Nat. Ballet. *Albums:* Deluge, 1998; Flood, 2000; Untold Things

**POOLE,** family name of **Baron Poole**.

**POOLE, 2nd Baron** *cr* 1958, *of Aldgate;* **David Charles Poole;** Director, RGA (UK) Ltd, 2002–15; *b* 6 Jan. 1945; *s* of 1st Baron Poole, PC, CBE, TD and Betty Margaret Gilkison (*d* 1988); *S* father, 1993; *m* 1967; one *s*; *m* 2004, Kate Watts. *Educ:* Dragon Sch., Oxford; Gordonstoun; Christ Church, Oxford (MA); INSEAD, Fontainebleau (MBA). Samuel Montagu & Co. Ltd, 1967–74; Bland Payne & Co. Ltd, 1974–78; Capel-Cure Myers, 1978–87; Bonomi Group, 1987–90; James Capel, 1990–92; Mem., Prime Minister's Policy Unit (on secondment), 1992–94; Gp Chief Exec., Sturge, subseq. Ockham, Hldgs plc, 1994–2002; Chm. Govs, West Hill Park Sch., Titchfield, 2009–14. *Recreations:* sailing, ballet. *Heir: s* Hon. Oliver John Poole [*b* 30 May 1972; two *d* by Kate White]. *E:* davidpoole300@hotmail.com. *Clubs:* Brooks's, City of London, Beefsteak; Island Sailing.

**POOLE, Anna Isabel;** QC (Scot.) 2012; Judge of Upper Tribunal (Administrative Appeals Chamber), since 2018; *b* Craigtoun, 11 Aug. 1970; *d* of David Poole and Julie Poole; *m* 2000; one *s* one *d*. *Educ:* Madras Coll., St Andrews; Somerville Coll., Oxford (BA Juris. 1991); Magdalen Coll., Oxford (MSt 1993). Admitted solicitor, England and Wales, 1996, Scotland, 1997; Advocate, 1998; First Standing Jun. Counsel to Scottish Govt, 2010–12; pt-time fee-paid Judge, First-tier Tribunal (Social Entitlement Chamber), 2014–18. Chancellor, Dio. of Argyll and the Isles, 2014–, Dio. of Edinburgh, 2019–. Arbitrator, Motor Insurers Bureau, 2017–. FCIArb 2018. Mem. Bd, Queen's Hall, Edinburgh, 2018–. *Publications:* (contrib.) Court of Session Practice, 2004–; articles in Juridical Rev., Scots Law Times, Scottish Law and Practice Qly, Judicial Rev., Internat. Insurance Law Rev., Jl of Law Soc. of Scotland. *Recreations:* music, walking, travel.
See also C. E. Poole.

**POOLE, Dame (Avril) Anne (Barker),** DBE 1992; Chief Nursing Officer, Department of Health (formerly of Health and Social Security), 1982–92; *b* 11 April 1934; *d* of Arthur George and Norah Heritage; *m* 1959, John Percy Poole. *Educ:* High Sch., Southampton. SRN 1955, SCM 1957, Health Visitors Cert., 1958. Asst Chief Nursing Officer, City of Westminster, 1967–69; Chief Nursing Officer, London Borough of Merton, 1969–73; Area Nursing Officer, Surrey AHA, 1974–81; Dep. Chief Nursing Officer, DHSS, 1981–82. Non-exec. Dir, SW Surrey HA, 1993–96; Mem., Criminal Injuries Compensation Panel, 1996–2006. Trustee, Marie Curie Cancer Care (formerly Marie Curie Meml Foundn), 1992–2001. FRSocMed 1993; CCMI (CBIM 1984).

**POOLE, Dr (Catherine) Eve;** Third Church Estates Commissioner, since 2018; *b* St Andrews, 5 Feb. 1972; *d* of David and Julie Poole; *m* 2007, Nathan Percival; twin *d*. *Educ:* Madras Coll., St Andrews; Westminster Coll., Connecticut; Durham Univ. (BA theol. 1993); Edinburgh Univ. (MBA 1998); Newnham Coll., Cambridge (PhD 2010). HEO, Church Commn, 1993–97; Dir, Scottish Redundant Churches Trust, 1997–98; Change Mgt Consultant, Deloitte, 1998–2002; Dep. Dir, Leadership Faculty, Ashridge Business Sch., 2002–18. Associate Research Fellow: William Temple Foundn, 2014–18; St Paul's Inst., 2016–18. Trustee: Christian Assoc. of Business Execs, 2005–11; Foundn for Ch Leadership, 2006–12; St Andrews Voices, 2016–18. Chm., Bd of Govs, Gordonstoun Sch., 2015–. *Publications:* (ed with Carla Millar) Ethical Leadership, 2010; The Church on Capitalism, 2010; Capitalism's Toxic Assumptions, 2015; Leadersmithing, 2017; Buying God, 2018. *Recreation:* sleeping. *Address:* Church Commissioners for England, Church House, Westminster, SW1P 3NZ. *T:* (020) 7898 1624. *E:* eve.poole@churchofengland.org. *Club:* Caledonian.
See also A. I. Poole.

**POOLE, David Arthur Ramsay;** Managing Director, Blue Circle Industries, 1987–89; *b* 30 Sept. 1935; *s* of late Arthur Poole and Viola Isbol (*née* Ramsay); *m* 1961, Jean Mary Male; three *d*. *Educ:* King's Sch., Canterbury; St Edmund Hall, Oxford (MA Jurisprudence). Nat. service, 2nd Lieut, RA, 1955–57. Baring Bros & Co., 1960–65; APCM Ltd (now BCI), 1965–70; Wm Brandts & Co., 1970–73; British Caledonian Gp, 1973–75; Blue Circle Industries, 1976–89. *Recreation:* travel. *Address:* Dalwood Cottage, Long Reach, Ockham, Surrey GU23 6PF. *T:* (01483) 284986. *Clubs:* East India, Royal Automobile.

**POOLE, David James,** PPRP (RP 1969); ARCA; artist; *b* 5 June 1931; *s* of Thomas Herbert Poole and Catherine Poole; *m* 1958, Iris Mary Toomer; three *s*. *Educ:* Stoneleigh Secondary Sch.; Wimbledon Sch. of Art; Royal Coll. of Art. National Service, RE, 1949–51. Sen. Lectr in Painting and Drawing, Wimbledon Sch. of Art, 1962–77. Pres., Royal Soc. of Portrait Painters, 1983–91. One-man exhibns, Zurich and London; exhibn of non-portrait work, Curwen and New Acad. Gall., London, 2008. Portraits include: the Queen, The Duke of Edinburgh, The Queen Mother, Prince Charles, Princess Anne, Princess Margaret, Earl Mountbatten of Burma and The Duke of Kent; Private Secretaries to the Queen: Sir Alan Lascelles, Sir Michael Adeane, Sir Martin Charteris, Sir Philip Moore, Sir William Heseltine, Sir Robert Fellowes, Sir Robin Janvrin; also distinguished members of govt, industry, commerce, medicine, the academic and legal professions. Work in private collections of the Queen and the Duke of Edinburgh, and in Australia, S Africa, Bermuda, France, W Germany, Switzerland, Saudi Arabia and USA. *Recreations:* French travel, food and drink. *Address:* Trinity Flint Barn, Weston Lane, Weston, Petersfield, Hants GU32 3NN. *T:* (01730) 265075.

**POOLE, Eve;** see Poole, C. E.

**POOLE, Isobel Anne,** OBE 2013; Sheriff of the Lothian and Borders, 1979–2007, at Edinburgh, 1986–2007; part-time Sheriff, all Scotland, 2007–11; *b* 9 Dec. 1941; *d* of late John Cecil Findlay Poole, DM Oxon, and Constance Mary (*née* Gilkes), SRN. *Educ:* Oxford High Sch. for Girls; Edinburgh Univ. (LLB). Admitted to Faculty of Advocates, 1964. Formerly Standing Jun. Counsel to Registrar Gen. for Scotland. Ext. Examr in Comparative Criminal Procedure, Edinburgh Univ., 2001, 2002. Member: Sheriffs' Council, 1980–85; Scottish Lawyers European Gp, 1977–; Franco-British Lawyers Assoc. Chm., Edinburgh Sir Walter Scott Club, 2004–07. *Publications:* contrib. to Oxford DNB. *Recreations:* country, arts, houses, gardens, friends. *Clubs:* New, Scottish Arts (Edinburgh).

**POOLE, Jennifer Nancy;** see Willott, J. N.

**POOLE, Nicholas James Harries;** Chief Executive, Chartered Institute of Library and Information Professionals, since 2015; *b* London, 6 June 1974; *s* of James and Jennifer Poole; *m* 2005, Emma Wright; two *d*. *Educ:* Sidney Sussex Coll., Cambridge (BA Hons Modern and Medieval Langs 1996). Policy Officer, MLA, 1998–2005; Chief Exec., Collections Trust, 2005–15. Chairman: Europeana Network, 2010–14; Internat. Council of Museums, UK, 2011–13. Trustee: CILIP, 2010–14 (Treas., 2012–13); Wikimedia UK, 2015–. *Recreations:* kayaking, running, art, family, building automata. *Address:* Chartered Institute of Library and Information Professionals, 7 Ridgemount Street, WC1E 7AE. *T:* (020) 7255 0500. *E:* nick.poole@cilip.org.uk.

**POOLE, Nigel David;** QC 2012; a Recorder, since 2009; a Deputy High Court Judge, since 2017; *b* Shipley, W Yorks, 10 Nov. 1965; *s* of Michael and Susan Poole; *m* 1999, Annmarie Danson; one *s* one *d*. *Educ:* Bradford Grammar Sch.; Queen's Coll., Oxford (BA Hons); City Univ., London (DipLaw); Inns of Court Sch. of Law. Called to the Bar, Middle Temple, 1989; in practice as barrister, specialising in clinical negligence and personal injury, 1989–; Head, Kings Chambers, 2017–. Legal Assessor, GMC, 2002–09. Panel Chair, Bar Tribunals and Adjudication Service, 2012–. *Recreations:* singing in a Gospel choir, open water swimming, fell walking. *Address:* Kings Chambers, 36 Young Street, Manchester M3 3FT. *T:* (0161) 832 9082. *E:* npoole@kingschambers.com.

**POOLE, Nigel Robert;** a Judge of the Upper Tribunal (Immigration and Asylum Chamber) (formerly a Senior Immigration Judge, Asylum and Immigration Tribunal), 2005–16; *b* Southampton, 22 March 1949; *s* of Alfred Poole and Phyllis Harley Poole (*née* Anstey); *m* 1971, Gloria Durkin (*d* 2007); one *s* one *d*. *Educ:* Regents Park Boys' Sch., Southampton; Cardiff Jt Law Sch. (LLB Hons); Coll. of Law, Guildford. Admitted solicitor, 1975; Partner, Blatch & Co., 1978–99. Chm. (fee paid), Appeals Service, 1984–2002; Immigration Adjudicator (fee paid), 1995–2000; Immigration Judge, 2000. Dep. District Chm., Social Entitlement Chamber, 2010–16. *Recreations:* enjoying time with my children and grandchildren, spending time with friends and family, growing tomatoes. *Address:* 12 The Greenways, Magor, Monmouthshire NP26 3LJ. *T:* 07776 166631. *E:* poole_nigel@hotmail.com.

**POOLES, Michael Philip Holmes;** QC 1999; a Recorder, 2000–12; *b* 14 Dec. 1955; *s* of late Dennis John Pooles and of Joan Ellen Pooles; *m* 1982, Fiona Grant Chalmers; two *s*. *Educ:* Perse Sch., Cambridge; Queen Mary Coll., Univ. of London (LLB). Called to the Bar, Inner Temple, 1978, Bencher, 2011; in practice at the Bar, 1980–; Asst Recorder, 2000. Hd, Hailsham Chambers, 2004–09. Mem., Bar Standards Bd, 2006–10. Gov., Perse Sch., 2001–18. *Publications:* (contrib.) Professional Negligence and Liability, 2001. *Recreations:* reading, gardening. *Address:* Hailsham Chambers, 4 Paper Buildings, Temple, EC4Y 7EX. *T:* (020) 7643 5000. *Club:* Royal Automobile.

**POOLEY, Dr Derek,** CBE 1995; Chief Executive, UK Atomic Energy Authority, 1996–97; *b* 28 Oct. 1937; *s* of Richard Pike Pooley and Evelyn Pooley; *m* 1961, Jennifer Mary Davey; two *s* one *d*. *Educ:* Sir James Smith's Sch., Camelford, Cornwall; Birmingham Univ. (BSc 1958; PhD 1961). FInstP 1979. A. A. Noyes Res. Fellow, Calif Inst. of Technol., Pasadena, 1961–62; UKAEA, Harwell: Res. Scientist, 1962–68; Leader of Defects Gp, later of Physics Applications Gp, 1968–76; Head of Materials Develt Div., 1976–81; Dir of Non-nuclear Energy Res., 1981–83; Chief Scientist, Dept of Energy, 1983–86; Dep. Dir, 1986–89, Dir, 1989–90, Atomic Energy Estabt, Winfrith, later AEA Technol.; Dir, AEA Thermal Reactor Services, 1990–91; Man. Dir, Nuclear Business Gp, AEA Technol., 1991–94; Chief Exec., UKAEA Govt Div., 1994–96. Consultant, Derek Pooley Associates, 1998–2011. Non-exec. Dir, UK Nirex Ltd, 1995–97; Dir, BNES Ltd, 1997–2000. Chm., Waste Management Technology Ltd, 2006–08. Pres., British Nuclear Energy Soc., 1992–94; Chm., Scientific and Technical Cttee, Euratom, 1994–99. Mem., EU Adv. Gp on Energy, 2002–08. *Publications:* Real Solids and Radiation, 1975; (contrib.) Radiation Damage Processes in Materials, 1975; (contrib.) Energy and Feedstocks in the Chemical Industry, 1983; A Radical Approach to Nuclear Decommissioning, 1995; (contrib.) Key Tasks for Future European Energy R&D, 2005. *Recreations:* history, astronomy, walking. *Address:* 11 Halls Close, Drayton, Abingdon, Oxon OX14 4LU. *T:* (01235) 559454.

**POOLEY, Peter,** CMG 1996; a Deputy Director General, European Commission, 1983–95, now an Hon. Director-General; *b* 19 June 1936; *er* (twin) *s* of late W. M. Pooley, OBE, and Grace Lidbury, Truro; *m* 1966, Janet Mary, *er d* of Jack Pearson, Banbury; one *s* one *d*. *Educ:* Brentwood Sch.; Clare Coll., Cambridge (BA). Joined MAFF as Asst Principal, 1959; seconded to: Diplomatic Service, 1961–63 and 1979–82 (Minister (Agric.), Office of UK Perm. Rep. to EEC, Brussels); CSD, 1977–79; Under-Sec., 1979, Fisheries Sec., 1982, MAFF; Dep. Dir Gen., for Agric., 1983–89, for Develt, 1989–95 (Actg DG, 1992–95), EC. Interim Sec.-Gen., COPA/COGECA, 1996. Chm., British African Business Assoc., 1996–2001; with Business Council Europe-Africa, 1996–2002 (Pres., 1998). Chm., UK Br., 2002–05, Vice Pres., 2005–09, AIACE. Lay Mem., Winchester Diocesan Synod, 2009–15. Chm., Alresford Soc., 2008–12. *Address:* 8 The Mulberries, Station Approach, Alresford, Hampshire SO24 9FL. *T:* (01962) 732779.
See also R. Pooley.

**POOLEY, Robin,** OBE 1997; Chairman, English Apples and Pears Ltd, 2000–07; *b* 19 June 1936; *yr* (twin) *s* of late W. Melville Pooley, OBE and Grace M. Pooley (*née* Lidbury); *m* 1972, Margaret Anne (*d* 2019), *yr d* of Jack Pearson, Banbury; one *d*. *Educ:* Brentwood School. Various posts, Towers & Co. Ltd, 1954–71; Gen. Manager, CWS Gp, 1971–76; Man. Dir, Buxted Poultry Ltd, 1976–81; Chief Exec., Potato Marketing Bd, 1981–88; Managing Director: Anglian Produce Ltd, 1988–97; Anglian Potato Services Ltd, 1988–97; Chairman: Pseedco Ltd, 1995–98; Abbey Gp Ltd, 1997–2002; United Pig Marketing Ltd, 1999–2003. Director: North Country Primestock Ltd, 1996–2003; Smith and Holbourne, then Garden Isle, Ltd, 1997–2006. Chm., NFU Corporate, 1998–2003; Mem. Council, NFU, 1996–2003. Chm., MAFF Enquiry into meat hygiene, 1999; Mem., Scientific and Economic Co-ordinating Cttee, Min. of Agriculture for Italy, 1998–2007. Special Lectr in Mgt, Univ. of Nottingham, 1996–2008. Pres., CUPGRA, 1999–2006, now Pres. Emeritus. Master, Co. of Butchers, 1987. *Recreations:* fly fishing, freemasonry, finally enjoying retirement! *Address:* Barn Hill House, Strumpshaw, Norfolk NR13 4NS. *T:* (01603) 715992. *Club:* Farmers.
See also P. Pooley.

**POON, Sir Dickson,** Kt 2015; CBE 2007; Founder and Group Executive Chairman, Dickson Group of Companies, since 1980; Chairman, Harvey Nichols Group, since 1991; philanthropist; *b* Hong Kong, 1956; *s* of late Poon Kam Kai; *m* 1st, Marjorie Yang (marr. diss.); one *d*; 2nd, 1988, Michelle Yeoh (marr. diss. 1991); 3rd, 2002, Pearl Yu. *Educ:* St Joseph's Coll., Hong Kong; Uppingham Sch.; Occidental Coll., Los Angeles. Apprentice, Chopard, watchmakers, Geneva; opened Dickson Watch and Jewellery, Hong Kong, 1980; bought S. T. Dupont, 1987, sold 2012; Dir, 1991–, Gp Exec. Chm., 1992–, Dickson Concepts (Internat.) Ltd; Chm., Tommy-Hilfiger Asia-Pacific Ltd. *Address:* Harvey Nichols Group Ltd, 365 Chiswick High Road, W4 4HS.

**POORE, Sir Roger Ricardo,** 7th Bt *cr* 1795, *of Rushall, Wiltshire; b* 21 Oct. 1930; *e s* of Nasionceno Poore, *b* of 5th Bt; *S* cousin, Sir Herbert Edward Poore, 6th Bt, but his name does not appear on the Official Roll of the Baronetage; *m* Norma Naso Poore (decd), *widow* of Roberto Poore. *Heir: nephew* Fernando Nasionceno Poore [*b* 1964; *m* Maria del Carmen; one *s*].

**POORTA, Amanda Felicity;** see Mackenzie, A. F.

**POOTS, Edwin;** Member (DemU) Lagan Valley, Northern Ireland Assembly, since 1998; *b* 1965; *m*; four *c. Educ*: Wallace High Sch., Lisburn; Greenmount Agricl Coll. Farmer, Lagan Valley. Mem., NI Forum, 1996–98. Mem. (DemU) Lisburn CC, 1997–2010 (Dep. Mayor, 2008–10). Minister for Culture, Arts and Leisure, 2007–08, for the Envmt, 2009–11, of Health, Social Services and Public Safety, 2011–14, NI. *Address*: Northern Ireland Assembly, Parliament Buildings, Belfast BT4 3XX; (office) Old Town Hall, 29 Castle Street, Lisburn, Co. Antrim BT27 4DH.

**POPAT,** family name of **Baron Popat.**

**POPAT,** Baron *cr* 2010 (Life Peer), of Harrow in the London Borough of Harrow; **Dolar Amarshi Popat;** *b* Uganda, 14 June 1953; *m* Sandhya; three *s*. ACMA 1977. Arrived in UK, 1971; worked as waiter to fund studies. Business and corporate finance specialist. Mem., Small and Medium Enterprises Exports Cttee, H of L, 2012–13. Cons. Party Whip, 2012–; a Lord in Waiting (Govt Whip), 2013–15. Prime Minister's Trade Envoy to Uganda and Rwanda, 2016–. Sec., Anglo-Asian Cons. Assoc.; Chm., One Nation Forum; Mem., Cons. Ethnic Diversity Council; Pres., Harrow E Cons. Assoc. Founding Chm., Cons. Friends of India. *Address*: House of Lords, SW1A 0PW. *T*: (020) 7219 0295.

**POPAT, Prashant;** QC 2008; barrister, since 1992; *b* Saroti, Uganda, 24 Sept. 1968; *s* of Shantilal and late Saroj Popat; *m* 1991, Pritti Lakhani; one *s* one *d*. *Educ*: Mansfield Coll., Oxford (MA Jurisprudence 1990). Called to the Bar, Gray's Inn, 1992, Bencher, 2015. Judicial Asst to Master of the Rolls, 1997. *Publications*: (jtly) Civil Advocacy: a practical guide, 1997, 2nd edn 2001; (contrib. ed.) Halsbury's Laws: practice and procedure, 2001; (ed jtly) International Product Law Manual, 2012. *Recreation*: as much as possible. *Address*: Henderson Chambers, 2 Harcourt Buildings, Temple, EC4Y 9DB. *T*: (020) 7583 9020, *Fax*: (020) 7583 2686. *E*: ppopat@hendersonchambers.co.uk.

**POPAT, Prof. Sita Helen,** PhD; Professor of Performance and Technology, University of Leeds, since 2011 (Head, School of Performance and Cultural Industries, 2010–15); *b* Lusaka, Zambia, 18 May 1967; *d* of Ratilal and Clare Chiba; *m* 1st, 1989, Kris Popat (marr. diss. 2010); two *s*; 2nd, 2011, Calvin Taylor (*d* 2019). *Educ*: Univ. of Leeds (BA Hons Dance 1998; PhD 2002). Sec., Royal Opera Hse, 1988–89; Lectr in Dance, Univ. of Leeds, 2002–11. Mem., Adv. Bd, AHRC, 2014–18. Trustee, DV8 Physical Th., 2010–16. *Publications*: Invisible Connections: dance, choreography and internet communities, 2006; (ed with J. Pitches) Performance Perspectives: a critical introduction, 2011; (ed with N. Salazar Sutil) Digital Movement: essays in motion technology and performance, 2015; contribs to scholarly jls on performance, the body and new media. *Recreations*: performance arts, family, walking, playing a gnome healer in World of Warcraft. *Address*: School of Performance and Cultural Industries, University of Leeds, Woodhouse Lane, Leeds LS2 9JT. *T*: (0113) 343 8716. *E*: s.popat@leeds.ac.uk.

**POPAT, (Surendra) Andrew,** CBE 1997; a Recorder, since 1998; *b* 31 Dec. 1943; *s* of late Dhirajlal Kurji Popat and Kashiben Popat (*née* Chitalia); *m* 1995, Suzanne Joy, *d* of late Edward James Wayman and Beatrice Joyce Wayman; one *s*. *Educ*: Univ. of London (LLB); Univ. of Calif, Berkeley (LLM). Called to the Bar, Lincoln's Inn, 1969; Mem., Inner Temple, 1985; Associate Attorney, Willkie Farr & Gallagher (NY), 1970–74; practising Barrister, specialising in criminal law, 1975–; Asst Recorder, 1992–98; Tribunal Judge, First-tier Chamber (Criminal Injuries Compensation Tribunal), 2009–. Legal Mem., Criminal Injuries Compensation Appeals Panel, 2000; Mem., Professional Performance Cttee, 2002, Chm., Fitness to Practise Panel, 2006–; GMC; Co-Chm., Professional Conduct Cttee, Gen. Osteopathic Council, 2003–07; Chm., Hearings of Appeals, Postgrad. Med. Educn and Trng Appeals Panel, 2004–; Mem., Fitness to Practise Panel, GDC, 2007–. Contested (C): Durham NE, 1983; Bradford S, 1992; London Reg., EP, 1999. Dir, John Patten's election campaign, 1987. Treas., Surbiton Cons. Assoc., 1985. Chm., Disraeli Club, 1993–. Trustee, Brooke Hosp. for Animals, 1998–2000. Freeman, City of London, 1987; Liveryman, Plaisterers' Co., 1987 (Mem. Ct of Assts, 2001, now Asst Emeritus). *Recreations*: travel, theatre, cricket, tennis. *Club*: MCC.

**POPE, His Holiness the;** *see* Francis, His Holiness.

**POPE EMERITUS, His Holiness Benedict XVI, (Joseph Alois Ratzinger);** *see* Benedict XVI, His Holiness.

**POPE, Cathryn Mary;** soprano; *b* 6 July 1957; *m* 1st, 1982, Stuart Petersen (marr. diss. 1998); 2nd, 2003, Martin Barrell. *Educ*: Royal College of Music (ARCM); National Opera Studio. Début, ENO: Sophie, in Werther, 1983; Anna, in Moses, 1986; Susanna, in Marriage of Figaro, 1987; Gretel, in Hansel and Gretel, 1987; Oksana, in Christmas Eve, 1988; Despina, in Così fan tutte, 1988; Pamina, in Die Zauberflöte, 1989; Micaëla, in Carmen, 1993; Tatyana, in Eugene Onegin, 1994; Amsterdam: début, Gretel, 1990; Mélisande, in Pelléas et Mélisande, 1991; Elvira, in Don Giovanni, and Susanna, 1991; Opera Europa: Nedda, in Pagliacci, 1995; Giorgetta, in Il Tabarro; Nantes: Le Prostitué, in La Ronde. Numerous recordings.

**POPE, Col Christopher Michael,** OBE 2003; Chief Operations Officer, HM Land Registry, since 2017; Director, Chabe Ltd, since 2014; *b* Wargrave, 31 Aug. 1960; *s* of Michael Pope and Marion Audrey Pope; *m* 1998, Deborah Jane Searle; two *s* two *d*. *Educ*: Maidenhead Grammar Sch.; Cranfield Univ. (BScEng Hons Civil Engrg 1985; MSc Defence Technol. 1992). Army officer, 1978–2005; retired in rank of Col. Gp Projects Dir, Tribal Gp plc, 2005–07; Hd, Operational Engrg Services, Laing O'Rourke, 2008–09; Dir of Transformation, London Bor. of Merton, 2009–11; Exec. Dir, Resources and Commercial Develt, London Bor. of Newham, 2011–14; Gp Chief Commercial Officer, 2015–17, Ops Dir, 2017, BIS, then BEIS. Dir, South Tees Site Co. Ltd, 2016–18. Non-exec. Dir, UK Shared Business Services Ltd, 2015–18. Mem. Bd, Local Space Ltd, 2011–14. *Recreations*: amateur dramatics, gardening, fishing. *Address*: 126 Victoria Road, Wargrave, Reading, Berks RG10 8AE.

**POPE, Geoffrey Robert;** Member (Lib Dem), London Assembly, Greater London Authority, 2005–08; *b* 9 April 1944; *s* of late George Pope and Stella Pope; *m* 1968, Margaret Victoria Thompson; one *s* one *d*. *Educ*: Kingsbury County Grammar Sch.; Hendon Coll. (HNC Applied Physics 1965). Mgt, SmithKline Beecham, 1969–98. Chm., Teddington Meml Hosp. and Community NHS Trust, 1998–2001; Dir, Kingston Hosp. NHS Trust, 2001–04. Chm., Addiction Care and Support Agency, 2000–. Mem. (Lib Dem) Richmond upon Thames LBC, 1982–98 (Mayor, 1989–90); Chm., Social Services, 1994–98). Chm., Transport Cttee, London Assembly, 2006–07. Treas., Citizens Advice Hounslow, 2017–. Chm., Twickenham and Richmond Lib Dems, 2009–12. *E*: geoff.pope1@gmail.com.

**POPE, George Maurice,** FRICS; independent surveyor, since 1999; *b* 12 Jan. 1943; *s* of Maj. John Pope; *m* 1968, Tessa Roselle Norman; one *s* two *d*. *Educ*: Eton. Capt., Coldstream Guards, 1962–69. With John D. Wood & Co., 1970–99. Chm., 1982–99. *Recreations*: racing, hunting, shooting, golf. *Address*: Grounds Farm House, Fernham Road, Uffington, near Faringdon, Oxon SN7 7RD. *T*: (01367) 820234, 07803 722121. *Clubs*: White's; Royal St George's Golf, Sunningdale Golf.

**POPE, Gregory James;** Assistant General Secretary, Catholic Bishops' Conference of England and Wales, since 2017 (Head of Parliamentary and Public Affairs (formerly Parliamentary Relations), 2013–17); *b* 29 Aug. 1960; *s* of Samuel J. Pope and Sheila M. (*née* Day); *m* 1985, Catherine M. Fallon; two *s* one *d*. *Educ*: St Mary's Coll., Blackburn; Univ. of Hull (BA Hons). Local govt officer, 1987–92. MP (Lab) Hyndburn, 1992–2010. An Asst Govt Whip, 1997–99; a Lord Comr of HM Treasury (Govt Whip), 1999–2001. Dep. Dir, Catholic Educn Service, 2010–13. *Recreations*: polite cyclist, realistic football follower. *Address*: Catholic Bishops' Conference of England and Wales, 39 Eccleston Square, SW1V 1BX.

**POPE, Jeffrey Charles;** Head, Factual Drama, ITV Studios (formerly Granada Productions, then ITV Productions), since 1998; *b* Cowley, Middx, 2 Oct. 1961; *s* of David Pope and Patricia Pope; *m* 1992, Tina Jane Phillips; three *s*. *Educ*: Hayes Co. Grammar Sch. NCTJ Qualified Journalist 1981 (Distinction). Journalist, Ealing Gazette, 1980–83; ITV: Researcher, Factual Progs, LWT, 1983–86; Producer, 1986–89; Editor, 1989–92 (progs incl. Friday Now, 1988–90, Crime Monthly, 1990–93); Exec. Producer, Factual Progs, 1992–98. *Television*: Executive Producer: See No Evil: the Moors Murders, 2006 (Drama Serial award (jtly), BAFTA, 2007); Appropriate Adult, 2011; The Moorside, 2017; writer: Mrs Biggs, 2013; Lucan, 2013; Little Boy Blue, 2017; co-writer and producer: The Widower, 2014; Hatton Garden, 2019; writer and producer: Cilla, 2014; A Confession, 2019; co-writer and co-producer, Cradle to Grave, 2015; *film*: co-writer, screenplay, Philomena, 2014 (Best Adapted Screenplay (jtly), BAFTA); writer, screenplay, Stan & Ollie, 2018. Mem., BAFTA, 1996–. Guild of British Newspaper Editors' Award, 1981; Alan Clarke Award, BAFTA, 2015. *Publications*: (with Simon Shaps) Michael Winner's True Crimes, 1992. *Recreations*: Laurel and Hardy films, travel/holidays, golf with my sons—they beat me but I enjoy their company. *Address*: c/o ITV Studios, 2 Waterhouse Square, 138–142 Holborn, EC1N 2AE.

**POPE, Jeremy James Richard,** OBE 1985; DL; Member of Board, English Farming and Food Partnership, 2008–10 (Chairman, 2003–08); *b* 15 July 1943; *s* of late Philip William Rolph Pope and Joyce Winifred Harcourt Pope (*née* Slade); *m* 1969, Hon. Jacqueline Best; three *s*. *Educ*: Charterhouse; Trinity Coll., Cambridge. Law tripos, MA. Solicitor. Eldridge, Pope & Co., 1969–99: Finance and Planning Dir, 1972–82; Jt Man. Dir, 1982–88; Man. Dir, 1988–99; Chairman: Eldridge, Pope Fine Wines Ltd, 1999–2000; Milk Link Ltd, 2000–05; Chilworth Science Park Ltd, 2001–04; Exeter Investment Gp plc, 2003–04 (non-exec. Dir, 1999–2003). Chm., Smaller Firms Council, CBI, 1981–83; Member: NEDC, 1981–85; Top Salaries Review Body, 1986–93; Exec. Cttee, Food and Drinks Fedn, 1986–89 (Dep. Pres., 1987–89). Member: Royal Commn on Environmental Pollution, 1984–92; Wessex Regl Rivers Adv. Cttee, NRA, 1994–95; Bd, Bournemouth, Dorset and Poole LSC, 2001–04; Sustainable Farming and Food Strategy Implementation Gp, DEFRA, 2002–05. Chairman: Winterbourne Hosp. plc, 1981–89; Trustees, Wessex Medical Trust, 1993–97 (Trustee, 1991–97); Dorset Private Sector Forum, 1997–2000; Bournemouth, Dorset & Poole Economic Partnership, 1997–99; SW Chamber of Rural Enterprise, 2001–04; Deputy Chairman: SW of England RDA, 1999–2004 (Bd Mem., 1998–2004); Dorset Olympic Bd, 2010–14. Mem., Wessex Regl Cttee, NT, 2008–10. Chm., Spirit of the Sea Ltd, 2010–13; Dir, Expia CIC Ltd, 2013–14. Dir, Weymouth and Portland Nat. Sailing Acad., 2004–13. Gov., Forres Sch., Swanage, 1984–92; Mem. Council, Southampton Univ., 1999–2004. Trustee: Devonshire and Dorset Regtl Charity, 1994–2000; Tank Mus., 2000–19; Jurassic Coast Trust (formerly World Heritage Coast Trust), 2004–; Chesil Trust, 2004–13; Springboard, 2009–12; Dorset Shrieval Charitable Trust, 2012–14; SafeWise, 2013–; Friends of Portland Prison, 2014–16; Dorset Natural History and Archaeol Soc., 2017–. Chm. Mgt Cttee, Mus. of Regts of Devon and Dorset, 1994–2000. DL 2008, High Sheriff, 2012–13, Dorset. Liveryman: Gunmakers' Co., 1988; Innholders' Co., 1991 (Master, 2008–09). FRAgS. Hon. DLitt Bournemouth, 1999. *Recreations*: shooting, fishing, gardening, beekeeping, cooking the resultant produce. *Address*: Field Cottage, West Compton, Dorchester, Dorset DT2 0EY. *T*: (01300) 320469.

**POPE, Prof. Stephen Bailey,** PhD, DSc (Eng); FRS 2007; FInstP; Sibley College Professor of Mechanical Engineering, Cornell University, 1998–2015, now Emeritus; *b* 26 Nov. 1949; *s* of Sir Joseph Albert Pope; *m* 1979, Linda Ann Syatt; one *s* one *d*. *Educ*: Rydal Sch., Colwyn Bay; Imperial Coll., London (BSc (Eng.); MSc; PhD 1976, DIC); DSc (Eng) London 1986. ACGI; FInstP 2004. Mech. Engrg, Imperial Coll., London, 1972–77; Res. Fellow, Applied Maths, CIT, 1977–78; Asst Prof., then Associate Prof., of Mech. Engrg, MIT, 1978–81; Associate Prof., then Prof. of Mech. and Aerospace Engrg, Cornell Univ., 1982–2015. Dir, TQ Gp Ltd, 1995–2011. Fellow: APS, 1991; Amer. Acad. Arts and Scis, 2007; Soc. for Industrial and Applied Maths, 2009; Amer. Soc. of Mech. Engrs, 2014; Mem., NAE, 2010. Zeldovich Gold Medal, Combustion Inst., 2008; Fluid Dynamics Prize, APS, 2009; Propellants and Combustion Award, AIAA, 2012. *Publications*: Turbulent Flows, 2000; scientific articles in combustion and fluid dynamics. *Address*: Sibley School of Mechanical and Aerospace Engineering, Upson Hall, Cornell University, Ithaca, NY 14853, USA. *T*: (607) 2554314. *E*: s.b.pope@cornell.edu.

**POPHAM, Stuart Godfrey,** CMG 2019; Chairman, Royal National Lifeboat Institution, since 2016 (Trustee, since 2013; Vice Chairman, 2015–16); *b* 20 July 1954; *s* of late George Godfrey Popham and Ena Majorie Popham; *m* 1978, Carolyn Dawe; one *s* two *d*. *Educ*: Southampton Univ. (LLB 1975). Admitted solicitor, 1978; joined Clifford-Turner, subseq. Clifford Chance, 1976: Partner, 1984; Hd of Finance, 2000–03; Sen. Partner, 2003–10; Vice-Chm. of Banking for EMEA, Citigroup, 2011–19. Non-exec. Dir, Legal & General Gp plc, 2011–16. Confederation of British Industry: Chm., 2008–10, Vice Chm., 2011, London Bd (Mem., 2005–11); Mem., Internat. Adv. Bd, 2005–10; Chm., TheCityUK, 2009–12. Member: Council, RIIA, 2005–18 (Chm., 2012–18); Adv. Forum, Saïd Business Sch., Oxford, 2005–13; Council, Birkbeck, Univ. of London, 2012–16 (Fellow, 2016); Bd of Advrs, Business Sch. Faculty, Univ. of Southampton, 2012–. Trustee, Chichester Harbour Trust, 2012–. Hon. QC 2011. DUniv: Middx, 2008; Southampton, 2013; Glamorgan, 2013. *Recreations*: sailing, theatre, ballet, water sports. *Address*: c/o Royal National Lifeboat Institution, West Quay, Poole, Dorset BH15 1HZ. *Club*: Royal Yacht Squadron.

**POPLE, Alison Ruth;** QC 2015; *b* Ulverston, 8 Nov. 1968; *d* of John Ravenhill Pople and Elizabeth Allan Pople; *m* 2001, Denis Fintan Barry; two *d*. *Educ*: Ulverston Victoria High Sch.; Huddersfield Poly. (LLB Hons Business Law). Called to the Bar, Middle Temple, 1993. *Address*: Cloth Fair Chambers, 39–40 Cloth Fair, EC1A 7NT. *T*: (020) 7710 6444. *E*: alisonpople@clothfairchambers.com.

**POPLI, Dame Nicola Anne;** *see* Cullum, Dame N. A.

**POPPLEWELL, Lady;** *see* Gloster, Rt Hon. Dame Elizabeth.

**POPPLEWELL, Rt Hon. Sir Andrew John**, Kt 2011; PC 2019; **Rt Hon. Lord Justice Popplewell**; a Lord Justice of Appeal, since 2019; *b* 14 Jan. 1959; *s* of Sir Oliver Popplewell, *qv* and late (Catharine) Margaret Popplewell; *m* 1984, Debra Ellen Lomas; one *s* two *d*. *Educ*: Radley Coll.; Downing Coll., Cambridge (MA 1st cl. Law). Called to the Bar, Inner Temple, 1981; QC 1997; Recorder, 2002–11; a Judge of the High Ct of Justice, QBD, 2011–19. *Address*: Royal Courts of Justice, Strand, WC2A 2LL. *Club*: Hawks (Cambridge).

**POPPLEWELL, Sir Oliver (Bury)**, Kt 1983; Judge of the High Court of Justice, Queen's Bench Division, 1983–99; *b* 15 Aug. 1927; *s* of late Frank and Nina Popplewell; *m* 1st, 1954, Catharine Margaret Storey (*d* 2001); four *s* (and one *s* decd); 2nd, 2008, Hon. Dame Elizabeth Gloster, *qv*. *Educ*: Charterhouse (Schol.); Queens' Coll., Cambridge (Class. exhibnr; BA 1950; LLB 1951); Harris Manchester Coll., Oxford (BA 2006; Hon. Fellow, 2006); London Sch. of Economics (MA 2008); Univ. of Buckingham (MA 2015). FCIArb 1996. CUCC, 1949–51. Called to the Bar, Inner Temple, 1951, Bencher, 1978; QC 1969; Chartered Arbitrator; Accredited Mediator, 2000. Recorder, Burton-on-Trent, 1970–71; Dep. Chm., Oxon QS, 1970–71; a Recorder of the Crown Court, 1972–82. Ind. Mem., Wages Councils, 1962–82, Chm. 1973–82; Mem., Home Office Adv. Bd on Restricted Patients, 1981–82; Vice-Chm., Parole Bd, 1986–87 (Mem., 1985–87); Mem., Parole Review Cttee, 1987–88; Pres., Employment Appeal Tribunal, 1986–88 (Mem., 1984–85); Mem., London Court of Internat. Arbitration, 2000–. Chairman: Inquiry into Crowd Safety and Control at sports grounds, 1985–86; Sports Dispute Panel, 2000–; English Rep., ICC Commn into Corruption, 1999; Mem., Ct of Arbitration for Sport, 2000–. MCC: Mem. Cttee, 1971–74, 1976–79, 1980–97; Trustee, 1983–94; Pres., 1994–96; Hon. Life Vice Pres., 2010. Gov., Sutton's Hosp. in Charterhouse, 1986–88. Trustee, Bletchley Park Trust, 1999–2008. Hon. LLD Buckingham, 2015. *Publications*: Benchmark: life, laughter and the law, 2003; Hallmark: a judge at Oxford, 2008; The Prime Minister and His Mistress, 2014; The Aphrodisiac of Power, 2016. *Recreations*: sailing, cricket, tennis, reading and writing. *Address*: Brick Court Chambers, 7 Essex Street, WC2R 3LD. *T*: (020) 7379 3550. *E*: oliver.popplewell@virgin.net. *Clubs*: Garrick, MCC; Hawks (Cambridge); Vincent's (Oxford); XL; Blakeney Sailing.
*See also Rt Hon. Sir A. J. Popplewell.*

**POPPY, Prof. Guy Matthew**, DPhil; FRSB; Professor of Ecology, University of Southampton, since 2004; Chief Scientific Adviser, Food Standards Agency, since 2014; *b* Kettering, Northants, 14 Sept. 1965; *s* of Victor and Pam Poppy; *m* 1990, Jenny Baverstock; one *s* one *d*. *Educ*: Tideway Sch.; Brighton, Hove and Sussex VIth Form Coll.; Imperial Coll. London (BSc ARCS 1987); Wolfson Coll., Oxford (DPhil 1990). FRSB (FSB 2002). Rothamsted Research: HSO, 1991–95; SSO, 1995–98; PSO, 1998–2001; University of Southampton: Sen. Lectr, 2001–03; Reader, 2003–04; Hd, Sch. of Biol Scis, 2009–11; Dir, Interdisciplinary Strategy, 2011–14. Visiting Professor: Oregon State Univ., 2008; Imperial Coll. London, 2009–. Trustee, Marwell Wildlife, 2004–14. *Publications*: (with M. J. Wilkinson) Geneflow from GM Plants, 2005; contrib. articles to jls incl. Nature. *Recreations*: cycling, fine wine, travelling, natural history. *Address*: Centre for Biological Sciences, Faculty of Environmental and Natural Sciences, Life Sciences Building 85, University of Southampton, Highfield Campus, Southampton SO17 1BJ. *T*: (023) 8059 3217. *E*: gmp@soton.ac.uk. *Club*: Farmers.

**PORCHESTER, Lord**; **George Kenneth Oliver Molyneux Herbert**; *b* 13 Oct. 1992; *s* and heir of Earl of Carnarvon, *qv*.

**PORRITT, Hon. Sir Jonathon (Espie)**, 2nd Bt *cr* 1963, of Hampstead, co. London; CBE 2000; freelance writer and broadcaster; Chairman, Sustainable Development Commission, 2000–09; *b* 6 July 1950; *s* of Baron Porritt, GCMG, GCVO, CBE and Kathleen Mary (*d* 1998), 2nd *d* of A. S. Peck; *S* to Btcy of father, 1994; *m* 1986, Sarah Elizabeth Staniforth, *qv*; two *d*. *Educ*: Eton; Magdalen Coll., Oxford (BA (First Cl.) Modern Languages). ILEA Teacher, 1975–84: Head of English and Drama, Burlington Danes School, W12, 1980–84; Director: Friends of The Earth, 1984–90; Forum for the Future, 1996–. Co-Founder, Prince of Wales's Business and Envmtl Prog., 1994–. Non-exec. Dir, Willmott-Dixon Hldgs, 2009–. Chancellor, Keele Univ., 2012–. Pres., Conservation Volunteers, 2014–. Presenter, Where on earth are we going?, BBC TV, 1990. Ecology Party: candidate: General Elections, 1979 and 1983; European Elections, 1979 and 1984; Local Elections, 1977, 1978, 1982; Party Council Member, 1978–80, 1982–84; Chairman, 1979–80, 1982–84. *Publications*: Seeing Green—the Politics of Ecology, 1984; Friends of the Earth Handbook, 1987; The Coming of the Greens, 1988; Where on Earth are We Going?, 1991; (ed) Save the Earth, 1991; Captain Eco (for children), 1991; Playing Safe: science and the environment, 2000; Capitalism as if the World Matters, 2005; The World We Made, 2013. *Recreation*: walking. *Heir*: *b* Hon. Jeremy Charles Porritt [*b* 19 Jan. 1953; *m* 1980, Penny, *d* of J. H. Moore; two *s*]. *Address*: 9 Lypiatt Terrace, Cheltenham, Glos GL50 2SX.

**PORRITT, Sarah Elizabeth, (Hon. Lady Porritt)**; see Staniforth, S. E.

**PORTAL, Jane Virginia**, FSA; Keeper, Department of Asia, British Museum, since 2014; *b* Malta, 25 Jan. 1955; *d* of late Arthur John Bowerman and of Joan Gwendoline Bowerman; *m* 1st, 1975, Matthew Portal (marr. diss. 2002); one *s* two *d*; 2nd, 2005, Robert Geoffrey William Anderson, *qv* (marr. diss. 2017). *Educ*: Girton Coll., Cambridge (BA Oriental Studies (Chinese) 1978); Beijing Univ. (Cert. Postgrad. Study in Chinese Archaeol. 1980); Korean Lang. Inst., Yonsei Univ., Seoul (Cert. 1995); Sch. of Oriental and African Studies, Univ. of London (BA Hons Korean Studies 1996); MA Cantab (Oriental Studies) 2001. Grad. intern, Fitzwilliam Mus., Cambridge, 1978–79; Asst Librarian, Cambridge Univ. Liby (Chinese Section). 1980–81; Chinese translator, BP Exploration Dept, London, 1981–83; Lectr in Chinese Art and Archaeol., Extra-Mural Dept, Univ. of London, 1981–87; British Museum: Curator: Dept of Oriental Antiquities, 1987–99; Dept of Asia, 1999–2006; Hd, Chinese and Korean Sections, Dept of Asia, 2006–08; Matsutaro Shoriki Chair of Art of Asia, Oceania and Africa, Mus. of Fine Arts, Boston, 2008–14. Affiliate, Leverett Hse, 2010, Res. Associate, Fairbank Center, 2011–, Harvard Univ. Member: Oriental Ceramic Soc., 1987–; Cttee, British Assoc. of Korean Studies, 1999–2008; Assoc. of Art Mus. Curators, USA, 2008–; Assoc. for Asian Studies, USA, 2008–. Hon. Mem., 48 Gp UK, 2007. FSA 2004. *Publications*: (contrib.) The British Museum Book of Chinese Art, 1993, new edn 2007; (contrib.) Pottery in the Making: ceramic traditions, 1997; Korea: art and archaeology, 2000; (ed) Chinese Love Poetry, 2004; Art Under Control in North Korea, 2005 (US and Korean edns 2005); (with C. Michaelson) Chinese Art in Detail, 2006; The Terracotta Warriors, 2007; Terra Cotta Warriors: guardians of China's First Emperor, 2008; (contrib.) Treasures from Shanghai - Ancient Chinese Bronzes and Jades, 2009; Arts of Korea: Museum of Fine Arts highlights, 2012; (with H. Kinoshita) Arts of China: Museum of Fine Arts highlights, 2012; contrib. articles and reviews to jls inc. Orientations, Arts of Asia, Apollo, Oriental Art, BM Mag., THES, Trans Oriental Ceramics Soc. *Recreations*: theatre, museums, travel, walking. *Address*: Department of Asia, British Museum, Great Russell Street, WC1B 3DG.

**PORTAL, Sir Jonathan (Francis)**, 6th Bt *cr* 1901; FCA; freelance accountant, since 1993; *b* 13 Jan. 1953; *s* of Sir Francis Spencer Portal, 5th Bt, and of Jane Mary, *d* of late Albert Henry Williams, OBE; *S* father, 1984; *m* 1982, Louisa Caroline, *er d* of Sir (Frederick) John (Charles Gordon) Hervey-Bathurst, 7th Bt; three *s*. *Educ*: Marlborough; Univ. of Edinburgh (BCom). FCA (ACA 1977). Gp Financial Controller, Henderson Admin, 1989–91; Finance Dir, Grosvenor Ventures Ltd, 1992–93. Friend, Friends of Winchester Cathedral (Trustee, 2010–14). Trustee, Step by Step Partnership Ltd, 2019. Mem. Court, Clothworkers' Co. (Master, 2019–20). *Heir*: *s* William Jonathan Francis Portal, *b* 1 Jan. 1987. *Address*: Burley Wood, Ashe, Basingstoke, Hants RG25 3AG.

**PORTARLINGTON**, 7th Earl of, *cr* 1785; **George Lionel Yuill Seymour Dawson-Damer**; Baron Dawson 1770; Viscount Carlow 1776; *b* 10 Aug. 1938; *er s* of Air Commodore Viscount Carlow (killed on active service, 1944) and Peggy (who *m* 2nd, 1945, Peter Nugent; she *d* 1963), *yr d* of late Charles Cambie; *S* grandfather, 1959; *m* 1961, Davina, *e d* of Sir Edward Windley, KCMG, KCVO; three *s* one *d*. *Educ*: Eton. Page of Honour to the Queen, 1953–55. Director: G. S. Yuill & Co. Ltd, Sydney, 1964–; Australian Stock Breeders Co. Ltd, Brisbane, 1966–94. *Recreations*: fishing, ski-ing, books. *Heir*: *s* Viscount Carlow, *qv*. *Address*: Gledswood, Melrose, Roxburghshire TD6 9DN. *T*: (01896) 822558; 118 Wolseley Road, Point Piper, NSW 2027, Australia. *T*: (2) 93639725. *Clubs*: Australian (Sydney); Royal Sydney Golf.

**PORTEN, Anthony Ralph**; QC 1988; *b* 1 March 1947; *s* of late Ralph Charles Porten and Joan Porten (*née* Edden); *m* 1970, Kathryn Mary (*née* Edwards); two *d*. *Educ*: Epsom Coll.; Emmanuel Coll., Cambridge (BA; Athletics Blue, 1967). Called to the Bar, Inner Temple, 1969, Bencher, 2002; joined Lincoln's Inn (*ad eund.*), 1973; Hd of Chambers, 2001–06; practising mainly in town and country planning and local government work. A Recorder, 1993–2001; Asst Boundary Comr, 2001–. Fellow, Soc. for Advanced Legal Studies, 1999. *Address*: Claremont Cottage, The Reeds Road, Frensham, Surrey GU10 3DQ. *T*: (01252) 793062. *Clubs*: Hawks (Cambridge); Probus Farnham (Chm., 2019); Claremont Park Golf; Farnham Golf.

**PORTEOUS, Prof. David John**, OBE 2013; PhD; FRCPE, FMedSci; FRSE; Professor of Human Molecular Genetics and Medicine, University of Edinburgh, since 1996; *b* 3 July 1954; *s* of John and Jean Porteous; *m* 1976, Rosemary Braid; three *d*. *Educ*: Aberdeen Grammar Sch.; Univ. of Edinburgh (BSc Biol Scis 1975; PhD Genetics 1978). FRCPE 2004. Res. Fellow, Univ. of Oxford, 1978–81; Jun. Res. Fellow, Wolfson Coll., Oxford, 1980–81; MRC Recombinant DNA Res. Fellow, MRC Mammalian Genome Unit, Edinburgh, 1981–84; MRC Human Genetics Unit, Edinburgh: Staff Scientist, 1984–86; scientific non-clinical career appt to MRC, Grade 1, 1986–93; Hd of Molecular Genetics, 1993–96. Scientific Advr, H of C Select Cttee on Sci. and Technol., 1994–96. Founder, Generation Scotland, 2001. Pioneered Cystic Fibrosis Gene Therapy, 1995; discovered DISC1, 2000. FMedSci 1999; FRSE 2001; Mem., EMBO, 2010. *Recreations*: walking, cycling, windsurfing, ski-ing, reading, cinema, travelling, family, France. *Address*: Medical Genetics Section, Centre for Genomic and Experimental Medicine, MRC IGMM, University of Edinburgh, Crewe Road South, Edinburgh EH4 2XU. *T*: (0131) 651 1040, *Fax*: (0131) 651 1059. *E*: david.porteous@ed.ac.uk.

**PORTER OF SPALDING**, Baron *cr* 2015 (Life Peer), of Spalding in the County of Lincolnshire; **Gary Andrew Porter**, CBE 2013; Chairman, Local Government Association, since 2015 (Vice Chairman, 2011–15); *m* Karen. *Educ*: De Montfort Univ. (BA Hons 2000); Canterbury Christ Church Univ. (Postgrad. Cert. 2011). Mem. (C), S Holland DC, 2001– (Leader, 2003–). Chm., Cons. Councillors' Association, 2013–. *Address*: House of Lords, SW1A 0PW.

**PORTER, Alan Fraser**; Group Company Secretary, since 2012, and Group General Counsel, since 2015, Prudential plc; *b* UK, 22 Sept. 1963; *s* of Air Vice-Marshal John Alan Porter, *qv*; *m* 1994, Manuela Lozano; one *s* one *d*. *Educ*: Warwick Sch.; City of London Poly. (LLB); London Sch. of Econs (LLM). Admitted solicitor, 1988; Attorney, State Bar of Calif, 1997; Solicitor, Simmons & Simmons, 1986–93; Asst Solicitor, BAT Industries plc, 1993–96; Co. Sec., Farmers Gp Inc., 1996–98; Business Develt Counsel, British American Tobacco plc, 1998–2000; Sen. Counsel, Brown & Williamson Tobacco Inc., 2000–02; Co. Sec., 2002–06, Hd of Mktg Legal, 2006–08, British American Tobacco plc; Gp Gen. Counsel, Tesco plc, 2008–12. Mem., Takeover Panel, 2006–. Vice-Chm., 2010–18, Chm., 2018–, GC100 Gp. Chm., Companies Cttee, CBI, 2006–15. Court Asst, Tobacco Pipe Makers' and Tobacco Blenders' Co., 2012–. FRSA. *Recreations*: music, football, theatre, art, literature. *Address*: Prudential plc, Laurence Pountney Hill, EC4R 0HH. *T*: (020) 7220 7588. *Club*: East India.

**PORTER, Alastair Robert Wilson**, CBE 1985; Secretary and Registrar, Royal College of Veterinary Surgeons, 1966–91, retired; barrister; *b* 28 Sept. 1928; *s* of late James and Olivia Porter (*née* Duncan); *m* 1954, Jennifer Mary Priaulx Forman; two *s* one *d*. *Educ*: Irvine Royal Academy; Glasgow Academy; Merton Coll., Oxford (MA). Called to Bar, Gray's Inn, 1952. Resident Magistrate, N Rhodesia, 1954; Registrar of High Court of N Rhodesia, 1961; Permanent Secretary: Min. of Justice, N Rhodesia, 1964; Min. of Justice, Govt of Republic of Zambia, Oct. 1964. Mem., Fedn (formerly Liaison Cttee) of Veterinarians of the EEC, 1966–86, Sec.-Gen., 1973–79; Chm., EEC's Adv. Cttee on Veterinary Trng, 1986–87 (Vice-Chm., 1981–86). Lectures: Wooldridge Meml, BVA Congress, 1976; MacKellar Meml, Western Counties Veterinary Assoc., Tavistock, 1978; Weipers, Glasgow Univ., 1985; Keith Entwhistle Meml, Cambridge Univ., 1987. Vice-Chm., Haywards Heath Police Community Forum, 2000–02; Chm., Univ. of the Third Age, Haywards Heath, 2007–08. Hon. Member: BVA, 1978; British Small Animals Vet. Assoc., 1991; Australian Vet. Assoc., 1991; Latvian Vet. Assoc., 1997; Fedn of Veterinarians of Europe, 2002; Hon. Associate, RCVS, 1979. Vice-Pres., Blue Cross, 2006–12 (Gov., 1991–2000; Chm., Bd of Govs, 1995–98; Pres., 2000–05). Hon. DVMS Glasgow, 1994. Centenary Prize, 1981, and Victory Medal, 1991, Central Vet. Soc.; Akademische Ehrenbürger, Hannover Veterinary Sch., 1988. *Publications*: (jtly) An Anatomy of Veterinary Europe, 1972. *Address*: 4 Savill Road, Lindfield, West Sussex RH16 2NX. *T*: (01444) 482001.
*See also Dr A. J. Porter.*

**PORTER, Amanda Eve**; see Pinto, A. E.

**PORTER, Sir Andrew Alexander Marshall H.**; see Horsbrugh-Porter.

**PORTER, Andrew James**; Partner, Brunswick Group, since 2014 (Director, 2012–14); *b* Welwyn Garden City, 28 Sept. 1972; *s* of Arthur George Porter and Eileen Porter (*née* Nickolls). *Educ*: Dame Alice Owen's Sch.; Warwick Univ. (BA Hons Hist. and Pols); Cardiff Univ. (Postgrad. Dip. Journalism). Reporter, 1997–98, London Ed., 1998–2000, Western Morning News; Political Ed., Sunday Business, 2000–03; Business Corresp., 2003–04, Dep. Political Ed., 2004–06, Sunday Times; Dep. Political Ed., The Sun, 2006–07; Political Ed., Daily Telegraph, 2007–11. *Recreations*: golf, football. *Clubs*: Royal Automobile; Old Fold Manor Golf.

**PORTER, Prof. Andrew Neil**, PhD; Rhodes Professor of Imperial History, King's College, London, 1993–2008, now Emeritus; *b* 12 Oct. 1945; *s* of Peter Tozer Porter and Muriel Betty Porter (*née* Luer); *m* 1972, Mary Faulkner; two *s*. *Educ*: Chester Cathedral Choir Sch.; Christ's Hosp., Horsham; St John's Coll., Cambridge (MA, PhD). LRAM. Lectr in History, Univ. of Manchester, 1970–71; King's College, London: Lectr in History, 1971–85; Reader, 1985–90; Head of History Dept, 1988–94 and 2000–01; Prof. of History,

1990–93; FKC 2005. Hon. Sec., RHistS, 1986–90 (FRHistS 1980); Convenor, History at Univs Defence Gp, 1992–96 (Mem., Steering Cttee, 1990–99); Chm., Adv. Council (formerly Bd of Mgt), Inst. of Commonwealth Studies, 1994–2001. Trustee, FCO Library, 2008–. Life Mem., Friends of the Inst. of Commonwealth Studies, 1980; Mem. Council, Friends of PRO, 1991–99. FRSA 1998. Editor, Jl of Imperial and Commonwealth History, 1979–90. *Publications:* The Origins of the South African War, 1980; Victorian Shipping, Business and Imperial Policy, 1986; (jtly) British Imperial Policy and Decolonization 1938–64, vol. 1, 1987, vol. 2, 1989; (ed jtly) Money, Finance and Empire 1790–1860, 1985; (ed jtly) Theory and Practice in the History of European Expansion Overseas, 1988; (ed) Atlas of British Overseas Expansion, 1991 (Japanese edn 1996); European Imperialism 1860–1914, 1994 (Korean edn 2001, Japanese edn 2006); (ed and contrib.) The Oxford History of the British Empire, Vol. III, The Nineteenth Century, 1999; (ed) Bibliography of Imperial, Colonial and Commonwealth History since 1600, 2002; (ed) The Imperial Horizons of British Protestant Missions, 1880–1914, 2003; Religion versus Empire? British Protestant Missionaries and Overseas Expansion 1700–1914 (Trevor Reese Meml Prize, Inst. of Commonwealth Studies), 2004. *Recreations:* playing chamber music, mountain walking, travel. *Address:* 5 Farm Close, High Street, Clun, Shropshire SY7 8LJ. *Club:* Clun Bowling.

**PORTER, Dr Angus James;** Co-Chairman, Direct Wines Ltd, since 2014 (non-executive Director, 2010–14); Chairman, McColl's Retail Group plc, since 2017 (non-executive Director, 2016–17); *b* Kitwe, Northern Rhodesia, 9 June 1957; *s* of Alastair Robert Wilson Porter, *qv*; *m* 1989, Kate Francis; two *s* one *d*. *Educ:* Jesus Coll., Cambridge (BA 1978; MA 1979; PhD 1982). Mars Confectionery: Product Manager, 1985–86; Sen. Product Manager, 1987–91; New Business Develt Manager, 1992–93; Impulse Sales Dir, 1994–95; Mktg Dir, 1995–98; Eur. Gen. Manager (Sugar Confectionery), 1998–99; Man. Dir, Consumer Div., BT, 1999–2003; Customer Dir, Abbey National, 2003–05; Chief Exec., Added Value, 2005–08; Gp Strategy Dir, Thomas Cook, 2008–09; Chief Exec., Professional Cricketers' Assoc., 2010–16. Non-executive Director: Tele Danmark Communications, 2011–; Punch Taverns plc, 2012–. *Recreations:* cricket, golf, cooking, photography. *Address:* 1 Beechwood Drive, Marlow, Bucks SL7 2DH. *T:* (01628) 471280. *E:* angus.porter@btinternet.com. *Club:* MCC.

**PORTER, Rt Rev. Anthony;** *see* Sherwood, Bishop Suffragan of.

**PORTER, Sister Bernadette Mary,** CBE 2005; PhD; Treasurer General, Society of the Sacred Heart, since 2010 (Provincial Treasurer, 2007–10); Vice-Chancellor, Roehampton University (formerly Rector and Chief Executive, Roehampton Institute, then University of Surrey Roehampton), 1999–2004 (Hon. Fellow, 2006); *b* 21 July 1952; *d* of Owen and Teresa Porter. *Educ:* Merrow Grange, Guildford; Digby Stuart Coll. (Cert Ed); King's Coll. London (BEd 1979; PhD 1989); Kingston Univ. (DMS). Mem., Soc. of the Sacred Heart, 1973–. Teacher: Woldingston Sch., 1973–75; Sacred Heart, Newcastle, 1975–78; Our Lady's Convent, 1980–82; Kalunga Girls' Sch., Masaka, Uganda, 1982–83; Roehampton Institute, London: Lectr, 1983–89; Coll. Principal, 1989–99; Sen. Pro-Rector, 1995–99. Member: Council of Church Colls, 1989–2004; Council, Univ. of Surrey, 1999–2004; UUK, 1999–2004; Southwark Cathedral Council, 2001–; Cumberlege Commn, 2006–07; Chm., Educn Cttee, RC dio. of Southwark, 2006–09. Mem., Internat. Women's Forum, 2000–07. Hon. Treas., Solidarity with S Sudan, 2010–12. Pres., English/French Speaking Treasurers Gen., 2011–12. Trustee: St Mary's Sch., Shaftesbury, 1999–2007; Higher Educn Foundn, 2002–05; Regent, Marymount Internat. Sch., 2002–05; Villiers Park Educnl Trust, 2004–07. Chm. Trustees, Regenerate.com, 2005–09; Mem., Neuro-disability Res. Trust, 2005–09. Patron, Coll., of Teachers, 2005–. Governor: Wimbledon Sch. of Art, 2003–07; Heythrop Coll., 2007–09. MInstD 1999. FRSA 1997. DUniv Middlesex, 2004; Hon. DLitt Leicester, 2012. *Publications:* contrib. various articles. *Recreations:* gardening, walking, travel, music. *Address:* 9 Bute Gardens, W6 7DR. *Club:* Reform.

**PORTER, David John;** Director, David Porter Communications with Human Touch, since 2010; Head of Drama, 1998–2002 and Co-ordinator of Performance Studies, 2002–10, Kirkley High School, Lowestoft; *b* 16 April 1948; *s* of late George Porter and of Margaret Porter; *m* 1978, Sarah Jane Shaw; two *s* two *d*. *Educ:* Lowestoft Grammar School; New College of Speech and Drama, London. Teacher, London, 1970–72; Dir and Co-Founder, Vivid Children's Theatre, 1972–78; Head of Drama, Benjamin Britten High School, Lowestoft, 1978–81; Conservative Party Agent: Eltham, 1982–83; Norwich North, 1983–84; Waveney, 1985–87. MP (C) Waveney, 1987–97; contested (C) same seat, 1997. Member, Select Committee: on Social Security, 1991–92; for Educn, 1992–96; for Educn and Employment, 1996–97. Dir, David Porter Freelance Communications, 1997–99. Examr in A-Level Perf. Studies and Drama, OCR, IGCSE Drama, Edexcel Drama, 1999–; Sen. Examr in Drama and Theatre A-Level, OCR, 2018–. *Publications:* Old Men's Dreams (novel), 2015; (jtly) Cambridge Technicals Performing Arts Level 3 Study Guide, 2016; (jtly) Edexcel AS and A Level Drama and Theatre Study Guide, 2016; (jtly) Edexcel GCSE Drama Study Guide, 2016; Wild Beasts and Plague (short stories), 2018; A Rebel's Journey (autobiog.), 2018; Scoffers Will Come (short stories), 2019. *Recreations:* family of 4 children and 8 grandchildren, Waveney area—past, present and future. *Address:* 11 Irex Road, Pakefield, Lowestoft, Suffolk NR33 7BU. *W:* www.davidporter.co.uk.

**PORTER, Prof. Dorothy Elizabeth, (Mrs B. P. Dolan),** PhD; FRHistS; Professor in History of the Health Sciences, since 2002 and Chair, 2004–09, Department of Anthropology, History and Social Medicine, University of California, San Francisco; *b* 8 June 1953; *d* of John Dudley Mayne Watkins and Eileen Catherine Watkins (*née* Justice); *m* 1st, 1987, Roy Sydney Porter, FBA (marr. diss. 1997; he *d* 2002); 2nd, 2000, Brian Patrick Dolan. *Educ:* Univ. of Sussex (BA Sociol. 1976; MA Urban and Regl Studies 1977); University Coll. London (PhD 1984). FRHistS 1991. Fellow, Wellcome Inst. for Hist. of Medicine, 1985–88; Res. Associate, UCLA, 1988–89; Res. Fellow, Univ. of Calif., San Francisco, 1989–90; Vis. Asst Prof., Harvard Univ., 1990–91; Birkbeck College, University of London: Lectr, 1991–94, Sen. Lectr, 1994–97; Wellcome Reader in Hist. of Medicine, 1997–98; Prof. in the Hist. of Sci. and Medicine, 1998–2002; Pro-Vice Master for Internat. and Res. Students, 2001–02. Mem., Soc. for Social Hist. of Medicine, 1981. Founding Mem., Internat. Network for Hist. of Public Health, 1991; Member: Amer. Assoc. for Hist. of Medicine, 1990; Eur. Assoc. for Hist. of Medicine and Health, 1994. *Publications:* (with R. Porter) In Sickness and In Health: the British experience 1650–1850, 1988; (with R. Porter) Patient's Progress: doctors and doctoring in Eighteenth Century England, 1989; (ed jtly) The Codification of Medical Ethics, vol. 1, The Eighteenth Century, 1992; (ed with R. Porter) Doctors, Politics and Society: historical essays, 1993; (Introd.) John Ryle, Changing Disciplines, 1994; (ed) The History of Health and the Modern State, 1994, 2nd edn 2006; (ed) Social Medicine and Medical Sociology in the Twentieth Century, 1997; Health, Civilisation and the State: a history of public health from ancient to modern times, 1999, 2nd edn 2005; Health Citizenship: essays on social medicine and bio-medical politics, 2012. *Address:* Department of Anthropology, History and Social Medicine, University of California, 3333 California Street, Suite 485, San Francisco, CA 94143–0850, USA. *T:* (415) 4768826, *Fax:* (415) 4769453. *E:* porterd@dahsm.ucsf.edu.

**PORTER, Henry Christopher Mansel;** writer and political campaigner; London Editor, Vanity Fair, since 1992; *b* 23 March 1953; *s* of Major H. R. M. Porter, MBE and Anne Victoria Porter (*née* Seymour); *m* 1990, Elizabeth Mary Elliot; two *d*. *Educ:* Wellington Coll.; Manchester Univ. (BA Hons). Columnist, Sunday Times, 1982–87; Editor: Illustrated London News, 1987–89; Correspondent Mag., 1989–90; Exec. Ed., Independent on Sunday, 1990–91; contributor, 1991–, to London Evening Standard, Guardian, Observer, Daily Telegraph, Independent on Sunday. Co-Dir, Convention on Modern Liberty, 2009–; Dir, The Convention. Chm., People's Vote Media Hub. *Publications:* Lies, Damned Lies, 1984; *novels:* Remembrance Day, 1999; A Spy's Life, 2001; Empire State, 2003; Brandenburg (CWA Ian Fleming Steel Dagger), 2005; The Master of the Fallen Chutes, 2008; The Dying Light, 2009; Firefly, 2018; White Hot Silence, 2019. *Recreations:* painting, walking, gardening, reading. *Address:* c/o Lloyds Private Banking, PO Box 1060 Heathside, 131 Pembroke Road, Clifton, Bristol BS99 1UX.

**PORTER, Janet S.;** *see* Street-Porter.

**PORTER, Air Vice-Marshal John Alan,** OBE 1973; CEng, FRAeS, FIET; Deputy Vice-Chancellor and Professor, University of Glamorgan, 1994–99, now Professor Emeritus, University of South Wales (formerly University of Glamorgan); *b* 29 Sept. 1934; *s* of late Alan and Etta Porter; *m* 1961, Sandra Rose (marr. diss.); two *s*; *m* 2002, Veronica Kennedy. *Educ:* Lawrence Sheriff School, Rugby; Bristol Univ. (BSc); Southampton Univ. (Dip Soton). Commissioned in Engineer Branch, RAF, 1953; appts in UK, USA and Cyprus, 1953–79; Royal College of Defence Studies, 1980; Dep. Gen. Manager, NATO MRCA Develt and Production Agency (NAMMA), Munich, 1981–84; Dir-Gen. Aircraft 2, MoD(PE), 1984–88; Dir-Gen., Communications, Inf. Systems and Orgn (RAF), 1988–89; RAF retd, 1989. Dir, Communications-Electronics Security Gp, 1989–91; Dir, Sci. and Technol., GCHQ, 1991–94. Public and Lead Gov., Guy's and St Thomas' Foundn Trust, 2013–. Vis. Fellow, Cranfield Univ., 1994–97. Chm. Council, University Coll. Plymouth St Mark and St John, 2008–12. Hon. DSc Glamorgan, 2005. *Recreations:* music, horology. *Address:* University of South Wales, Pontypridd, Mid Glam CF37 1DC. *Club:* Royal Air Force.
*See also* A. F. Porter.

**PORTER, (Jonathan) Mark,** FRCA; Consultant Anaesthetist, University Hospitals Coventry and Warwickshire NHS Trust, since 1998; *b* Newcastle-under-Lyme, 18 April 1962; *s* of John and Jean Porter; *m* 1989, Linda Barrow; one *s* one *d*. *Educ:* Univ. of Leicester (BSc Med. Sci. 1983; MB ChB 1989). FRCA 1994. Hse Officer, 1989–90; SHO (anaesthesia), Peterborough Dist Hosp., Leicester Royal Infirmary, Leicester Gen. Hosp. and Glenfield Gen. Hosp., Leicester, 1990–92; SHO (Intensive Care Unit and Emergency Dept), Derbys Royal Infirmary, Derby, 1992–93; Specialist Registrar (anaesthesia), Coventry, Nuneaton and Birmingham, 1993–98. Chm. Council, British Med. Assoc., 2012–17 (Mem. Council, 1992–98 and 2004–17; Chair: Jun. Doctors Cttee, 1997–98; Consultants Cttee, 2009–12). Hon. Col, 202 (Midlands) Field Hosp., 2014–19. *Recreations:* family, visiting Roman ruins. *Address:* University Hospital, Clifford Bridge Road, Coventry CV2 2DX. *E:* Mark.Porter@uhcw.nhs.uk.

**PORTER, Julie Louise Jo;** *see* Chappell, J. L. J.

**PORTER, Prof. Sir Keith (Macdonald),** Kt 2011; FRCS, FRCSE; Professor of Clinical Traumatology, University Hospitals Birmingham NHS Foundation Trust, University of Birmingham and Royal Centre for Defence Medicine, since 2005; *b* Swindon, 31 Dec. 1948; *s* of Albert Porter and Hilda Porter; *m* 2008, Shamim Donnelly; one *d*, and two *s* one *d* by a previous marriage. *Educ:* Marlborough Coll.; St Thomas's Hosp. Med. Sch., London (MB BS 1974). FRCS 1978; FRCSE 1998; FIMCRCSE 2001. Surgical Hse Officer, St Thomas's Hosp., London, 1974; Hse Physician, St Helier's Hosp., Carshalton, 1975; Surgical Hse Officer, Gen. and Thoracic Surgery, St Mary's Hosp., Portsmouth, 1975–76; gen. surgical rotation, Wolverhampton, 1977–79; higher surgical trng, Birmingham, 1979–86. Consultant Trauma Surgeon: Birmingham Accident Hosp., 1986–93; Selly Oak Hosp., 1986–2010; Birmingham Gen. Hosp., 1993–95; Queen Elizabeth Hosp., Birmingham, 2010–; Dir, NIHR Surgical Reconstruction and Microbiol. Centre, 2010–15; Clinical Lead for Military Trauma, Queen Elizabeth Hosp., Birmingham, 2003. OStJ 2012. Queen's Jubilee Medal, 2002; College Medal, RCSE, 2011. *Publications:* 15 books; 150 articles in learned jls. *Recreations:* my family, walking. *Address:* Longfield Cottage, Rowney Green, Alvechurch, Birmingham B48 7RB. *T:* 07989 408752. *E:* Keith.Porter@uhb.nhs.uk. *Club:* Royal Society of Medicine.

**PORTER, Leonard Keith;** Chairman, eAsset Management, 2014–17; *b* 17 March 1952; *s* of Leonard Oram Porter and Irene Anne Porter (*née* Whitfield); *m* 1983, Victoria Louise Wigham; one *s* two *d*. *Educ:* Grangefield Grammar Sch. for Boys, Stockton-on-Tees; Univ. of Leeds (BSc Hons Metallurgy). Commercial saturation diver, Subsea Offshore, 1977–81; Founder/Dir, MOM Gp, 1981–94; Dep. Chm. and Chief Exec., Marine Offshore Mgt, 1994–96; Dir, Global Transportation Business, Lloyds Register of Shipping, 1996–2003; Chief Exec., Rail Safety and Standards Bd, 2003–14. Non-executive Director: LPA Gp plc, 2014–; Jetwing Symphony Ltd (Sri Lanka), 2014–; Angel Trains Gp Ltd, 2015–. *Publications:* A Handbook for Underwater Inspectors, 1992. *Recreations:* golf, Rugby (now spectating), scuba diving, interest in Sri Lanka, sustainable development, Boxer dogs. *Address:* 13 Silver Lane, Purley, Surrey CR8 3HJ. *T:* (office) (020) 8660 1883. *E:* (home) dovecote13@aol.com, (office) len.porter13@gmail.com. *Club:* Woodcote Park Golf.

**PORTER, Margaret Jane;** *see* Dallman, M. J.

**PORTER, Marguerite Ann, (Mrs Nicky Henson),** MBE 2015; Guest Artist, Royal Ballet Co., since 1986 (Senior Principal Dancer, 1976–85); *b* 30 Nov. 1948; *d* of William Albert and Mary Porter; *m* (marr. diss.); *m* 1986, Nicky Henson, *qv*; one *s*. *Educ:* Doncaster. Joined Royal Ballet School, 1964; graduated to Royal Ballet Co., 1966; soloist, 1972; Principal, 1976; favourite roles include: Juliet in Romeo and Juliet, Manon, Natalia in A Month in the Country; The Queen in Matthew Bourne's Swan Lake, NY, 1999. *Film:* Comrade Lady. Dir, Yorkshire Ballet Seminars, 2005–; Gov., Royal Ballet, 2006–. Hon. Dr York, 2016. *Publications:* Ballerina: a dancer's life, 1989. *Recreations:* my family, friends.

**PORTER, Mark;** *see* Porter, J. M.

**PORTER, Mark Christopher Milsom,** MBE 2005; General Practitioner, Culverhay Surgery, Wotton-under-Edge, Gloucestershire, since 2006; Medical Correspondent, The Times, since 2009; Presenter, Inside Health, BBC Radio 4, since 2011; *b* Ross-on-Wye, Herefordshire, 12 Nov. 1962; *s* of Alan and Lesley Porter; *m* 1987, Ros Lovell; two *d*. *Educ:* Wycliffe Coll., Stonehouse, Glos; University Coll. London and Westminster Med. Sch. (MB BS 1986). DA 1989; DCH 1990; GP VTS 1990. Trng posts in medicine and surgery, A&E, anaesthetics, paediatrics, age care, psychiatry and obstetrics and gynaecol., 1986–91; Registrar, 1991, NHS GP Asst, 1992–2001, Locking Hill Surgery, Stroud; NHS GP Principal, Stroud, 2002–05. Presenter: BBC1, 1993–; BBC Radio 4, 2003–. Team Doctor, Ford World Rally Team, 1990–96. *Recreations:* fine wines, good food, trying to start classic cars. *E:* drmarkp@aol.com. *W:* drmarkporter.co.uk.

**PORTER, Mark Edward**; Design Consultant, Owner and Creative Director, Mark Porter Associates, since 2010; *b* 15 March 1960; *s* of Robert George Porter and Sybil Elizabeth Porter; *m* 2001, Elizabeth Hubbard; two *s*. *Educ*: Trinity Sch. of John Whitgift, Surrey; Trinity Coll., Oxford (BA Hons, MA 1985). Art Dir of several mags, 1986–93; freelance art dir and design consultant, 1993–95; The Guardian: Associate Art Dir, 1995–98; Art Dir, 1998–2000; Creative Ed., then Creative Dir, 2000–10. Mem., AGI, 2004. *Publications*: contrib. to many books and jls on mag. and newspaper design. *Recreations*: family, food and cooking, Hispanophilia. *Address*: 103 Sclater Street, E1 6HR.

**PORTER, Martin Hugh Ninnis**; QC 2006; *b* 3 Nov. 1962; *s* of late William Hugh Lancelot Porter and of Elizabeth Hilary Porter (*née* Oddie); *m* 1989, Dr Kelly Jean Stanhope; two *d*. *Educ*: St John's Coll., Cambridge (BA 1984; LLM 1985). Called to the Bar, Inner Temple, 1986. *Recreations*: cycling, ski-ing, flying and drinking at moderate speed. *Address*: 2 Temple Gardens, EC4Y 9AY. *T*: (020) 7822 1200, *Fax*: (020) 7822 1300. *E*: mporter@2tg.co.uk. *Club*: Thames Velo.

**PORTER, Richard Bruce**; Chairman, Fred Hollows Foundation (UK), 2009–18; *b* 20 Jan. 1942; *s* of Maynard Eustace Prettyman Porter and Irene Marjorie Porter; *m* 1965, Susan Mary Early; two *d*. *Educ*: St Joseph's Coll., Ipswich; City of London Coll. (BSc Econ). Account Supervisor, A. C. Nielsen Co., 1965–70; Divl Manager, Brooke Bond Oxo Ltd, 1970–74; Market Develt Manager, Mackenzie Hill Hldgs, 1974–75; Management Consultant, 1975–79, Sen. Manager and Partner, 1984–94, KPMG Management Consulting; Project Economist, Engineering Science Inc., 1979–84; Exec. Dir, Sight Savers Internat., 1994–2005; Dir of Ops, Internat. Agency for the Prevention of Blindness, 2005–08. *Publications*: (jtly) Science Parks and the Growth of High Technology, 1988. *Recreations*: tennis, hockey, reading, bridge, gardening. *Address*: 15 Park Road, Burgess Hill, W Sussex RH15 8EU. *T*: (01444) 232602. *Club*: Royal Over-Seas League.

**PORTER, Prof. Robert**, AC 2001; DM, DSc; FRACMA, FRACP, FAA; Director, Research Development, Faculty of Medicine, Health and Molecular Sciences, James Cook University, Queensland, 1999–2008 (Planning Dean (Medicine), 1998–99), now Honorary Adjunct Professor, Division of Tropical Health and Medicine; *b* 10 Sept. 1932; *s* of late William John Porter and Amy Porter (*née* Tottman); *m* 1961, Anne Dorothy Steell; two *s* two *d*. *Educ*: Univ. of Adelaide (BMedSc; DSc 1976); Univ. of Oxford (MA, BM BCh, DM). Rhodes Scholarship, South Australia, 1954; Radcliffe Travelling Fellowship in Med. Sci., University Coll., Oxford, 1962; Lectr, Univ. Lab. of Physiology, Oxford, 1960–67; Fellow, St Catherine's Coll., and Medical Tutor, Oxford, 1963–67; Prof. of Physiology and Chm., Dept of Physiology, Monash Univ., 1967–79; Howard Florey Prof. of Med. Res., and Dir, John Curtin Sch. of Med. Res., ANU, 1980–89; Dean, Faculty of Medicine, 1989–98, Dep. Vice Chancellor (Res.), 1992–93, Monash Univ. Vis. Scientist, Brain Res. Inst., UCLA Med. Center, 1963–64; Sen. Fulbright Travelling Fellow and Vis. Prof., Washington Univ. Sch. of Medicine, St Louis, Mo, 1973; Fogarty Scholar-in-Residence, NIH, 1986–87. Member: Bd of Dirs, Alfred Gp of Hosps and Monash Med. Centre, 1989–99; Bd of Govs, Menzies Sch. of Health Res., Darwin, 1985–92; Bd of Management, Baker Med. Res. Inst., 1980–99. Hon. DSc: Sydney, 2001; James Cook, 2009. Centenary Medal, Australia, 2003. *Publications*: (with C. G. Phillips) Corticospinal Neurones: their role in movement, 1977; (with R. N. Lemon) Corticospinal function and voluntary movement, 1993; articles on neurophysiology and control of movement by the brain. *Recreation*: reading. *Address*: 21 Tamarind Place, Twin Waters, Qld 4564, Australia. *T*: (7) 54570905.

**PORTER, Maj. Gen. Roderick John Murray**, MBE 1994; Chief Executive, Military Ministries International, since 2018; *b* Tamerton Foliot, Devon, 29 June 1960; *s* of John William Porter and Jane Elisabeth Porter (*née* Langdon); *m* 1987, Martina Marianne Heslam; three *s*. *Educ*: Lipsom Vale Primary Sch., Plymouth; Mount House Sch., Tavistock; Sherborne Sch.; RMA Sandhurst; Univ. of Newcastle upon Tyne (BA Hons Combined Studies (German and Hist.)); US Army War Coll. (Combined/Jt Force Land Component Commander's Course). Platoon Comd, 1981–82, Regtl Signals Officer, 1985–87, Adjt, 1987–89, 1 RWF; SO3 G3 (Ops), HQ 4th Armd Bde (Germany and Gulf), 1989–91; Army Staff Course Div. II, 1991–92 (psc†); COS, HQ 4th Armd Bde (Germany and Bosnia), 1992–94; Co. Comd, 1 RWF (UK and Bosnia), 1994–96; SO1 Policy ACDS Operational Requirements (Land), 1997–99; CO, 1 RWF (NI), 1999–2001; Dep. Dir, Equipt Capability (Direct Battlefield Engagement), MoD, 2001–03; HCSC, Shrivenham, 2003; Bde Comd, 3 Inf. Bde (NI), 2003–04, 8 Inf. Bde (NI), 2004–05; Dir, Equipt Plans, MoD, 2006–08; Dir, Force Strategic Engagement Cell, Multinat. Force HQ, Iraq, 2008–09; COS (Jt Warfare Develt), Permanent Joint HQ, Northwood, 2009–11. Dir-Gen., Royal Over-Seas League, 2011–17. Col, Royal Welsh, 2006–11; Col Comdt, Prince of Wales's Div., 2009–13. Pres., Armed Forces Christian Union, 2008–14. Army Rugby Union: Chm., 2005–11, Vice Pres., 2012–, Referees' Soc.; Life Vice Pres., 2012–; Chm., Combined Services Rugby Referees' Fedn, 2006–11. *Recreations*: most sports, especially cricket, golf, dinghy sailing and Rugby, hill walking, reading, military and ancient history, leading battlefield tours, music (especially classical, blues and rock; playing guitar, violin). *E*: roddyporter@googlemail.com.

**PORTER, Sally Curtis**; *see* Keeble, S. C.

**PORTER, Dame Shirley, (Lady Porter)**, DBE 1991; Councillor, Hyde Park Ward, 1974–93, Leader, 1983–91, Westminster City Council; Lord Mayor of Westminster, 1991–92; *b* 29 Nov. 1930; *d* of late Sir John (Edward) Cohen and Lady (Sarah) Cohen; *m* 1949, Sir Leslie Porter (*d* 2005); one *s* one *d*. *Educ*: Warren Sch., Worthing, Sussex; La Ramée, Lausanne, Switzerland. Founded Designers' Guild, 1970; Chairman: Neurotech Medical Systems, 1992–94; LBC, 1992–93; Dir, Capital Radio, 1982–88. Westminster City Council: Conservative Whip, 1974–77; Road Safety Cttee, 1974–82; Member: Co-ordinating Cttee, 1981–82; Chairman: Highways and Works Cttee, 1978–82 (Vice-Chm., 1977–78); Gen. Purposes Cttee, 1982–83; Policy Review Cttee, 1982–83; Policy and Resources Cttee, 1983–91. Chairman: (also Founder) WARS Campaign (Westminster Against Reckless Spending), 1981–84; Cleaner City Campaign, 1979–81; Pres., Eur. Conf. on Tourism and the Envmt, 1992; Vice-Pres., Cleaner London Campaign, 1979–81; Mem. Exec., Keep Britain Tidy Gp, 1977–81. Pres., British Inst. of Cleaning Science, 1991; Mem. Ct, Guild of Cleaners, 1976–2002. Former Dep. Chm., Bd, London Festival Ballet. Trustee: London Philharmonic Trust, 1991–93; London Inst. for Math. Scis. Patron, Wingate Community Med. Centers, Myanmar. Hon. Mem., London Community Cricket Assoc., 1989–. Governor, Tel Aviv Univ., 1982–; Internat. Fellow, Porter Sch. of Envmtl Studies, Tel Aviv Univ., 2001–. JP Inner London, 1972–84; DL Greater London, 1988–94. FRSA 1989. Hon. PhD Tel Aviv, 1991. *Recreations*: golf, tennis, ballet. *Club*: Dyrham Park Golf.

**PORTER, Stanley Leonard**, CB 2005; Director, Winterbourne Consultancy Ltd, since 2006; *b* 16 March 1945; *s* of Leonard James and Lilian Elizabeth Porter; *m* 1966, Mary Roche; two *s* one *d*. *Educ*: King Edward VI Grammar Sch., Chelmsford. MCIPS 1994; FRAeS 1996. Ministry of Defence, 1963–2006: Asst Private Sec. to Minister of State for Defence Procurement, 1971–73; Principal, Tornado Finance, 1979–81; Asst Dir, Commercial, 1981–87; Director: Commercial Policy, 1987–89; Finance and Secretariat, 1989–92; Principal Dir, Commercial, 1992–98; Dir Gen., Commercial, 1998–2006 and Exec. Dir, Defence Procurement Agency, 1999–2006. *Recreations*: my family, travel, gardening. *T*: 07767 375511. *E*: stanporter@tiscali.co.uk.

**PORTES, Hélène**; *see* Rey, H.

**PORTES, Prof. Jonathan**; Professor of Economics and Public Policy, King's College London, since 2017; *b* 18 April 1966; *s* of Prof. Richard David Portes, *qv*. *Educ*: Balliol Coll., Oxford (BA Hons 1987); Princeton Univ. (MPA 1994). HM Treasury: various posts, 1987–91; Private Sec. and Speechwriter to the Chancellor of the Exchequer, 1991–92; Project Leader, Debt Mgt Review, 1994–95; Sen. Consultant, Nat. Economic Research Associates, 1995–98; Special Consultant, IMF, 1998–99; Project Leader, Performance and Innovation Unit, Cabinet Office, 1999–2000; Partner, Develt Strategies, 2000–02; Dir, Work, Welfare and Poverty, 2002–06, Chief Economist (Work), 2002–08, Dir, Children and Poverty, 2006–08, DWP; Chief Economist, Cabinet Office, 2011, Dir, 2011–15, Principal Res. Fellow, 2015–16, NIESR. FAcSS. *Publications*: govt policy papers, econs jls and press articles; 50 Capitalism Ideas You Really Need to Know, 2016. *Recreations*: walking, cooking. *Address*: Department of Political Economy, King's College London, Bush House North-East, Aldwych, WC2B 4BG.

**PORTES, Prof. Richard David**, CBE 2003; DPhil; FBA 2004; Professor of Economics, London Business School, since 1995; President (formerly Director), Centre for Economic Policy Research, 1983–2016, now Hon. President; *b* 10 Dec. 1941; *s* of Herbert Portes and Abra Halperin Portes; *m* 1st, 1963, Bobbi Frank (marr. diss. 2005); one *s* one *d*; 2nd, 2006, Prof. Hélène Rey, *qv*; one *d*. *Educ*: Yale Univ. (BA 1962 *summa cum laude* maths and philosophy); Balliol and Nuffield Colls, Oxford (Rhodes Schol., Woodrow Wilson Fellow, Danforth Fellow; MA 1965; DPhil 1969; Hon. Fellow, Balliol Coll., 2014). Official Fellow and Tutor in Econs, Balliol Coll., Oxford, 1965–69; Asst Prof. of Econs and Internat. Affairs, Princeton Univ., 1969–72; Prof. of Econs, Birkbeck Coll., Univ. of London, 1972–94 (Head, Dept of Econs, 1975–77 and 1980–83). Dir d'Etudes, Ecole des Hautes Etudes en Sciences Sociales, Paris, 1978–2011. Guggenheim Fellow, 1977–78; British Acad. Overseas Vis. Fellow, 1977–78; Res. Associate, Nat. Bureau of Econ. Res., Cambridge, Mass, 1980–; Vis. Prof., Harvard Univ., 1977–78; Dist. Global Vis. Prof., Haas Business Sch., Univ. of Calif at Berkeley, 1999–2000; Joel Stern Vis. Prof. of Internat. Finance, Columbia Business Sch., 2003–04; Tommaso Padoa-Schioppa Prof. of Eur. Econ. and Monetary Integration, Eur. Univ. Inst., 2014–17. Vice-Chm., Econs Cttee, SSRC, 1981–84. Member: Bd of Dirs, Soc. for Econ. Analysis (Rev. of Econ. Studies), 1967–69, 1972–80 (Sec. 1974–77); Council on Foreign Relations, 1978–; Hon. Degrees Cttee, Univ. of London, 1984–89; Bellagio Gp on the Internat. Econ., 1990–; Franco-British Council, 1997–2002; Commn Economique de la Nation, France, 1999–2005; Conseil d'Admin, Fondation Banque de France, 1999–; ALSSS Commn on Social Scis, 2000–02; Gp of Econ. Policy Advrs, Presidency of EC, 2001–10; Euro-area Business Cycle Dating Cttee, CEPR, 2003–16; Bd of Dirs, CEPREMAP, 2006–; Comité d'Honneur, Centre des Professions Financières, France, 2008–; Adv. Scientific Cttee, 2014– (Chm., 2017), Gen. Bd, 2017–, European Systemic Risk Bd; Chm., Collegio di Probiviri, Società per il Mercato dei Titoli di Stato, 2001–. Fellow, Econometric Soc., 1983–; Sec.-Gen., Royal Econ. Soc., 1992–2008 (Mem. Council, 1986–92; Exec. Cttee, 1987–2008; Vice-Pres., 2009–); Council, European Econ. Assoc., 1992–96 (Fellow, 2004). Co-Chm., Bd of Governors, 1985–2016, and Sen. Editor, 1985–2014, Economic Policy. Pres., Richard and Margaret Merrell Foundn, 1996–. Hon. DSc Univ. Libre de Bruxelles, 2000; Hon. PhD: London Guildhall, 2000; Paris IX (Dauphine), 2013. *Publications*: (ed) Planning and Market Relations, 1971; The Polish Crisis, 1981; Deficits and Détente, 1983; (ed) Threats to International Financial Stability, 1987; (ed) Global Macroeconomics: policy conflict and cooperation, 1987; (ed) Blueprints for Exchange Rate Management, 1989; (ed) Macroeconomic Policies in an Interdependent World, 1989; (ed) Economic Transformation in Hungary and Poland, 1990; (ed) External Constraints on Macroeconomic Policy: the experience of Europe, 1991; (ed) The Path of Reform in Central and Eastern Europe, 1991; (ed) Economic Transformation in Central Europe, 1993; (ed) European Union Trade with Eastern Europe, 1995; Crisis? What Crisis? Orderly Workouts for Sovereign Debtors, 1995; Crises de la Dette, 2003; International Financial Stability, 2007; Macroeconomic Stability and Financial Regulation, 2009; (ed) the Social Value of the Financial Sector, 2013; contribs to many learned jls. *Recreation*: living beyond my means. *Address*: London Business School, Regent's Park, NW1 4SA. *T*: (020) 7000 8424. *E*: rportes@london.edu.

*See also* J. Portes.

**PORTILLO, Rt Hon. Michael (Denzil Xavier)**; PC 1992; broadcaster and journalist; *b* 26 May 1953; *s* of late Luis Gabriel Portillo and Cora Waldegrave Blyth; *m* 1982, Carolyn Claire Eadie. *Educ*: Harrow County Boys' School; Peterhouse, Cambridge (1st cl. Hons MA History). Ocean Transport & Trading Co., 1975–76; Conservative Res. Dept, 1976–79; Special Advr, Sec. of State for Energy, 1979–81; Kerr McGee Oil (UK) Ltd, 1981–83; Special Adviser: to Sec. of State for Trade and Industry, 1983; to Chancellor of the Exchequer, 1983–84. MP (C) Enfield, Southgate, Dec. 1984–1997; contested (C) same seat, 1997; MP (C) Kensington and Chelsea, Nov. 1999–2005. An Asst Govt Whip, 1986–87; Parly Under Sec. of State, DHSS, 1987–88; Minister of State, Dept of Transport, 1988–90; Minister of State for Local Govt, DoE, 1990–92; Chief Sec. to HM Treasury, 1992–94; Sec. of State for Employment, 1994–95, for Defence, 1995–97; Shadow Chancellor, 2000–01. Chm. Judges, Man Booker Prize, 2008. BBC TV: regular contributor to This Week, 2003–; writer and presenter: Great British Railway Journeys, 2009–; Great Continental Railway Journeys, 2012–; Railways of the Great War with Michael Portillo, 2014; Portillo's State Secrets, 2015; Great American Railroad Journeys, 2016–; Great Indian Railway Journeys, 2018; Portillo's Hidden History of Britain, 2018; Great Canadian Railroad Journeys, 2019. Columnist, The Sunday Times, 2004–10. *Publications*: Portillo's Hidden History of Britain, 2018. *W*: www.michaelportillo.co.uk. *Club*: Garrick.

**PORTLAND**, 12th Earl of, *cr* 1689; **Timothy Charles Robert Noel Bentinck**, MBE 2018; Viscount Woodstock, Baron Cirencester, 1689; Count of the Holy Roman Empire; actor (as Timothy Bentinck); *b* 1 June 1953; *s* of 11th Earl of Portland and Pauline (*d* 1967), *y d* of late Frederick William Mellowes; S father, 1997; *m* 1979, Judith Ann, *d* of John Robert Emerson; two *s*. *Educ*: Harrow; Univ. of East Anglia (BA Hons). Trained Bristol Old Vic Theatre Sch. Winner BBC Drama Schs Radio Competition, 1978. London theatre appearances include: Pirates of Penzance, Theatre Royal, Drury Lane, 1982; Reluctant Heroes, Theatre of Comedy, 1984; Hedda Gabler, King's Head, 1990; A Doll's House, Bridge Lane Theatre, London, 1992; Arcadia, Haymarket, 1994; Night Must Fall, Haymarket, 1996; Educating Rita, Watermill, 2010; Love Your Chocolates (one-man show), tour, 2013; Brexit, King's Head, and Pleasance, Edinburgh, 2018; *radio*: David Archer in The Archers, 1982–; over 75 plays; *films*: North Sea Hijack, 1979; Pirates of Penzance, 1981; Winter Flight, 1985; Year of the Comet, 1992; Twelfth Night, 1995; Enigma, 2000; Fast Girls, 2012; Us and Them, 2016; Fantastic Beasts and Where to Find Them, 2016; *television* includes: By the Sword Divided, 1983; Square Deal, 1989; Made in Heaven, 1990; Sharpe, 1993; Grange Hill, 1994; Strike Force, 1995; Prince Among Men,

1997; The Gathering Storm, 2002; Born and Bred, 2003; D-Day, Murder in Suburbia, 2004; Silent Witness, Frances Tuesday, The Thick of It, Broken News, Absolute Power, 2005; Heartbeat, 2006; Doctors, 2006, 2012; Kingdom, 2009; The Pride of Wade Ellison, 2011; The Royal Bodyguard, 2011–12; Twenty Twelve, 2012; Eastenders, 2013 and 2018; The Politician's Husband, Lucan, Gangsta Granny, 2013; The Game, 2015; War and Peace, Reg, Rillington Place, 2016; Doctor Who, The Last Post, Quacks, Crown Court, 2017; winner: University Challenge - The Professionals, 2004; Celebrity Mastermind 2011; Celebrity Eggheads, 2012; Pointless Celebrities, 2012; composer of theme music for Easy Money, BBC TV, 1984; voice artist, radio and TV commercials, narrations, audio books, computer games and dubbing on films and TV progs. Travel journalist, Mail on Sunday. Computer programmer. Inventor of The Hippo (child-carrying device). HGV licence. *Publications:* Colin the Camper Van (for children), 2015; Being David Archer: and other unusual ways of earning a living, 2017. *Recreations:* guitar, banjo, writing comedy songs, scuba diving, house renovation, website design, computer advice, Mongolian archery. *Heir:* s Viscount Woodstock, qv.

**PORTMAN,** family name of **Viscount Portman.**

**PORTMAN,** 10th Viscount cr 1873; **Christopher Edward Berkeley Portman;** Baron 1837; Chairman, Portman Settled Estates Ltd, since 1998; b 30 July 1958; s of 9th Viscount Portman and of Rosemary Joy Portman (née Farris); S father, 1999; m 1st, 1983, Caroline Steenson (marr. diss.); one s; 2nd, 1987, Patricia Martins Pim; two s. *Educ:* Marlborough Coll. Director: Agua Via Inc., Calif, 2004–; BioQ Pharma (formerly Bioquiddity Inc.), San Francisco, 2006–. Patron, Jurassica, 2016–. *Recreations:* molecular nanotechnology, computer science, reading. *Heir:* e s Hon. Luke Oliver Berkeley Portman, b 31 Aug. 1984. *Address:* Ground Floor, 40 Portman Square, W1H 6LT. *T:* (020) 7563 1400. *Clubs:* White's, Home House.

**PORTMAN, Rachel Mary Berkeley,** OBE 2010; composer; b Haslemere, 11 Dec. 1960; m; three d. *Educ:* Worcester Coll., Oxford (BA Music). *Compositions:* A Celebration, 2012; We Were There (carol), 2014; *for film and television include:* Experience Preferred… But Not Essential, 1982; The Storyteller (TV series), 1986–88, 1990; Life is Sweet, 1990; Oranges are Not the Only Fruit (TV series), 1990; Antonia & Jane, 1991; Where Angels Fear to Tread, 1991; Used People, 1992; The Joy Luck Club, 1993; Benny & Joon, 1993; Friends, 1993; Sirens, 1994; Only You, 1994; War of the Buttons, 1994; To Wong Foo, Thanks for Everything!, 1995; A Pyromaniac's Love Story, 1995; Smoke, 1995; The Adventures of Pinocchio, 1996; Marvin's Room, 1996; Emma, 1996 (Acad. Award for best orig. score, 1997); Addicted to Love, 1997; The Cider House Rules, 1999; Chocolat, 2000; The Emperor's New Clothes, 2001; Hart's War, 2002; The Truth About Charlie, 2002; Nicholas Nickleby, 2002; The Human Stain, 2003; Mona Lisa Smile, 2003; Lard, 2004; The Manchurian Candidate, 2004; Because of Winn-Dixie, 2005; Oliver Twist, 2006; The Lake House, 2006; Miss Potter, 2006; Infamous, 2006; The Duchess, 2008; Grey Gardens (TV), 2009; Never Let Me Go, 2010; The Snowflower of the Secret Fan, 2011; One Day, 2011; Endangered, 2011; His Way, 2011; The Vow, 2012; Bel Ami, 2012; Private Peaceful, 2012; Paradise, 2013; Girl Rising, 2013; The Right Kind of Wrong, 2013; Still Life, 2013; Belle, 2013; Dolphin Tale 2, 2014; Despite the Falling Snow, 2014; Bessie, 2015; Race, 2015; A Dog's Purpose, 2016; Their Finest, 2016; *for theatre:* The Little Prince (opera), 2003; Little House on the Prairie (musical), 2009; London Assurance, National Theatre Live, 2010; A Tale of Two Cities, Royal & Derngate, Northampton, 2014; The Water Diviner's Tale, BBC Proms, 2009. *W:* www.rachelportman.co.uk.

**PORTO, Sue;** Chief Executive, Brandon Trust, since 2018; b Weymouth, 8 Nov. 1969; d of Colin and Sylvia Iliffe; two s one d. *Educ:* Weymouth Grammar Sch.; Open Univ. Sen. Manager, HM Prison Service, incl. Hd, Nat. Trng and Clinical Support, Offending Behaviour Progs, 1992–2007; Dir, SW of England, Prince's Trust, 2007–10; Chief Exec., Beanstalk charity (formerly Volunteer Reading Help), 2010–15; CEO, St John's Hosp., Bath, 2015–18. *Recreations:* horses, running, mountain biking. *Address:* 290A Sandridge Common, Melksham SN12 7QS. *T:* 07590 069334.

**PORTSDOWN, Archdeacon of;** *no new appointment at time of going to press.*

**PORTSMOUTH,** 10th Earl of, cr 1743; **Quentin Gerard Carew Wallop;** DL; Viscount Lymington, Baron Wallop, 1720; Hereditary Bailiff of Burley, New Forest; b 25 July 1954; s of Oliver Kintzing Wallop (Viscount Lymington) (d 1984) and Ruth Violet (d 1978), yr d of Brig.-Gen. G. C. Sladen, CB, CMG, DSO, MC; S grandfather, 1984; m 1st, 1981, Candia (née McWilliam) (marr. diss. 1984); one s one d; 2nd, 1990, Annabel, d of Dr and Mrs Ian Fergusson; one d. *Educ:* Eton; Millfield. Non-exec. Dir, Grainger Trust plc, 1987–2002. Patron, Hants Br., BRCS, 1995–. Warden, St Andrew's Ch, Farleigh Wallop. Mem., Fishmongers' Co., 1997– (Mem., Court of Assts, 2006–). DL Hants, 2004. *Heir:* s Viscount Lymington, qv. *Address:* Farleigh House, Farleigh Wallop, Basingstoke, Hants RG25 2HT. *Clubs:* White's, Buck's, Pilgrims; International Association of Cape Horners; Hampshire Hunt.

**PORTSMOUTH, Bishop of,** since 2010; **Rt Rev. Christopher Richard James Foster;** b Wednesbury, Staffs, 7 Nov. 1953; s of Joseph James Frederick Foster and Elizabeth Foster (née Gibbs); m 1st, 1982, Julia Marie Jones (d 2001); one s one d; 2nd, 2006, Rev. Sally Elizabeth Davenport. *Educ:* University Coll., Univ. of Durham (BA 1975); Univ. of Manchester (MA (Econ.) 1977); Trinity Hall, Cambridge (BA 1979, MA 1983); Westcott House, Cambridge. Lectr in Economics, Univ. of Durham, 1976–77; ordained deacon, 1980, priest, 1981; Asst Curate, Tettenhall Regis, Wolverhampton, 1980–82; Chaplain, Wadham Coll., Oxford and Asst Priest, Univ. Church of St Mary, with St Cross and St Peter in the East, Oxford, 1982–86; Vicar, Christ Church, Southgate, London, 1986–94; CME Dir, Edmonton Episcopal Area, 1988–94; Sub Dean and Canon Residentiary, Cathedral and Abbey Church of St Alban, 1994–2001; Bishop Suffragan of Hertford, 2001–10. Took seat in H of L, 2014. Chair, Churches Funerals Gp, 2017–; Co-Chair, English and Welsh Anglican-Roman Catholic Cttee, 2018–; Member: Church Comrs Pastoral Cttee, 2013–14; Dioceses Commn, 2014–; Chm., Remuneration and Conditions of Service Cttee, 2017–, Mem., Ministry Council, 2017–, Archbishops' Council. Member, Council: Westcott House, Cambridge, 2004–12; Ripon Coll., Cuddesdon, 2014– (Chm., 2015–). Trustee, Churches Together in England, 2012–17 (Chair and Convenor, Enabling Gp, 2012–16). Governor: Univ. of Herts, 2002–10 (Chm., F and GP Cttee, 2007–10); Univ. of Portsmouth, 2014–. Hon. DLitt Herts, 2011. *Address:* Bishopsgrove, 26 Osborn Road, Fareham, Hants PO16 7DQ. *T:* (01329) 280247. *E:* bishop@portsmouth.anglican.org.

**PORTSMOUTH, Bishop of, (RC),** since 2012; **Rt Rev. Philip Egan;** b Altrincham, 14 Nov. 1955; s of Bill and Rosalie Egan. *Educ:* St Vincent's Primary Sch.; St Ambrose Coll.; King's Coll. London (BA); Allen Hall Seminary; Venerable English Coll., Rome (STL); Boston Coll. (MA); Univ. of Birmingham (PhD 2004). Ordained priest, 1984; Asst Priest, St Anthony's Woodhouse Park, 1985–88; Asst Chaplain, Fisher House, Chaplaincy to Univ. of Cambridge, 1988–91; Chaplain, Arrowe Park Hosp., Wirral, 1991–94; Dean of Studies and Prof. of Fundamental Theol., St Mary's Coll., Oscott, 1996–2007; Parish Priest, Our Lady and St Christopher's, Romiley, 2008–12. *Publications:* Philosophy and Catholic Theology: a primer, 2009. *Address:* Bishop's House, Bishop Crispian Way, Portsmouth PO1 3HG. *T:* (023) 9282 0894. *E:* bishop@portsmouthdiocese.org.uk.

**PORTSMOUTH, Dean of;** *see* Cane, Very Rev. A. W. N. S.

**PORTWOOD, Nigel David;** Secretary to the Delegates, and Chief Executive, Oxford University Press, since 2009; Fellow of Exeter College, Oxford, since 2009; b Plymouth, 6 Dec. 1965; s of Leslie and Ruth Portwood; m 1995, Hayley Frances Morse; one s two d. *Educ:* Queens' Coll., Cambridge (BA Engrg 1988; MA 1991); INSEAD (MBA 1994). Mgt Consultant, OC&C Strategy Consultants, 1990–95; Strategy and Develt Exec., 1995–96, Dir of Strategy, 1997–99, Pearson plc; CEO, Pearson Educn EMEA, 1999–2002; Chief Financial Officer, 2003–08, Exec. Vice-Pres., Global Ops, 2008–09, Penguin Gp. Mem., Governing Council, Nat. Coll. for Sch. Leadership, 2000–03. Mem. Council, Publishers Assoc., 2000–02 and 2009–15. Mem., Mgt Bd, Blavatnik Sch. of Govt, Oxford Univ., 2014–. *Address:* Oxford University Press, Great Clarendon Street, Oxford OX2 6DP.

**POSEN, Adam Simon,** Hon. CBE 2013; PhD; Senior Fellow, since 1997, and President, since 2013, Peterson Institute for International Economics (Deputy Director, 2007–09); b Boston, Mass, Dec. 1966; s of Harold Posen and Annette Posen; m 2000, Jennifer Sosin. *Educ:* Harvard Coll. (AB Govt 1988); Harvard Graduate Sch. of Arts and Scis (PhD Pol Econ. and Govt 1997). Nat. Sci. Foundn Graduate Fellow, Harvard Univ., 1988–92; Bosch Foundn Fellow, Germany, 1992–93; Okun Meml Fellow, Brookings Instn, 1993–94; Economist, Federal Reserve Bank of New York, 1994–97. Mem., Panel of Advrs, US Congressional Budget Office, 2007–11; External Mem., Monetary Policy Cttee, Bank of England, 2009–12. Mem., Bd of Dirs, Bruegel, 2007–. Co-Founder and Chm., Editl Bd, International Finance, 1997–; columnist: International Economy, 2007–09; Welt am Sonntag, 2007–; Eurointelligence syndicate, 2009–. *Publications:* Restoring Japan's Economic Growth, 1998 (trans. Japanese 1999); (jtly) Inflation Targeting: lessons from the international experience, 1999; (ed jtly and contrib.) Japan's Financial Crisis and its Parrallels to US Experience, 2000; (ed and contrib.) The Euro at Five: ready for a global role?, 2005; (ed jtly and contrib.) The Euro at Ten: the next global currency?, 2009; contrib. articles in jls incl. Brookings Papers on Econ. Activity, NBER Macroecons Annual, Oxford Econ. Papers and numerous Central Bank conf. vols. *Recreations:* cooking, urban walking, European travel. *Address:* Peterson Institute for International Economics, Washington, DC 20036–1903, USA.

**POSNANSKY, Jeremy Ross Leon;** QC 1994; a Deputy High Court Judge, since 1997; b 8 March 1951; s of late Anthony Posnansky and Evelyn Davis (formerly Posnansky), JP; m 1974, Julia Sadler, d of late Richard Sadler, MBE; two d. *Educ:* St Paul's Sch.; Coll. of Law. Called to the Bar, Gray's Inn, 1972 (Bencher, 2003), Antigua and Barbuda, 1995; in ind. practice at the Bar, 1972–2007; Asst Recorder, 1993–98; a Recorder, 1998–2002; admitted solicitor, 2007; Partner, 2007–16, Consultant, 2016–, Farrer & Co. LLP. Mem., Family Courts Business and Service Cttees, Inner London, 1991–94. Fellow, Internat. Acad. of Matrimonial Lawyers, 1996–2015. *Publications:* contrib. Internat. Family Law, Family Law. *Recreations:* travel, scuba diving, photography, gardening. *Address:* Farrer & Co., 66 Lincoln's Inn Fields, WC2A 3LH. *T:* (020) 3375 7000.

**POSNER, Lindsay Steven;** theatre director; b 6 June 1959; s of Dennis and Pauline Posner; m 2000, Megan Wheldon; one s two d. *Educ:* Exeter Univ. (BA Eng. Lit.); Royal Acad. Dramatic Art. Associate Dir, Royal Court Th., 1987–92; productions include: The Treatment; No One Sees the Video; Built on Sand; Blood; Downfall; Ambulance; Colquhoun and McBryde; Death and the Maiden, 1991 (Olivier Award for Best Play); Royal Shakespeare Co. productions include: Volpone, Taming of the Shrew, 1999; The Rivals, 2000; Twelfth Night, 2001; National Theatre: Tartuffe, 2002; Power, 2003; Almeida Theatre productions include: The Hypochondriac, Romance, Tom and Viv, Man and Boy, Dada, Love Counts, 2005–06; House of Games, 2010; The Turn of the Screw, 2013; other productions include: American Buffalo, Young Vic, 1997; After Darwin, Hampstead Th., 1998; Sexual Perversity in Chicago, Comedy, 2003; A Life in the Theatre, Apollo, 2004; Oleanna, Garrick, 2004; Fool for Love, Apollo, 2005; The Birthday Party, Duchess, 2005; Fiddler on the Roof, Crucible, Sheffield, 2006, transf. Savoy, 2007; 3 Sisters on Hope Street, Everyman, Liverpool, 2008; Carousel, Savoy, 2008; A View from the Bridge, Duke of York's, 2009; An Ideal Husband, Vaudeville, 2010; Butley, Duchess, 2011; Noises Off, Old Vic, 2011; Abigail's Party, Menier, 2012; Uncle Vanya, Vaudeville, 2012; The Winslow Boy, Old Vic, 2013; Relatively Speaking, Wyndham's, 2013; A Little Hotel on the Side, Th. Royal, Bath, 2013; Other Desert Cities, Old Vic, 2014; Hay Fever, Theatre Royal, Bath, 2014, transf. Duke of York's Th., 2015; Speed-the-Plow, Playhouse Th., 2014; Harvey, Birmingham Repertory Th., transf. Theatre Royal, 2015; Communicating Doors, Menier Chocolate Factory, 2015; She Stoops to Conquer, Theatre Royal, Bath, 2015; Dinner with Saddam, Menier Chocolate Factory, 2015; The End of Longing, Playhouse Th., 2016; The Truth, Menier Chocolate Factory, transf. Wyndham's, 2016; The Lie, Menier Chocolate Factory, 2017; Curtains, Rose Th., Kingston, 2018; *opera:* Giulio Cesare, Royal Opera Hse, 1997; Roberto Devereux, Holland Park, 2009; Tosca, The Grange, 2010; Rigoletto, Holland Park, 2011; television includes: The Maitlands, 1993; Two Oranges and a Mango, 1994. *Recreations:* Italian white wine, family, reading, a multiplicity of obsessions. *Address:* 58 Chaucer Road, W3 6DP. *T:* (020) 8993 5575. *E:* posner.lindsay50@googlemail.com.

**POSNETT, David Wilson,** OBE 2012; b Runcorn, 6 May 1942; s of Charles Christopher Posnett and Coralie Howard Posnett (née Wilson); m 2007, Sarah Anne Clare Addington; two s one d. *Educ:* Leys Sch., Cambridge; Trinity Coll., Cambridge (BA 1964; MA 1967). Chm. and Man. Dir, Leger Galls, fine art dealers, 1966–96. Trustee and Chm., Holburne Mus., 1999–2012. Chm., Soc. of London Art Dealers, 1991–93. Freeman, City of London, 1963; Liveryman, Leathersellers' Co., 1967.

**POST, Andrew John;** QC 2012; b London, 12 May 1962; s of Jack Post and Valerie Post; m 1995, Mary Aylmer. *Educ:* Radley Coll.; Trinity Coll., Cambridge (BA Hist. 1984); City Univ. (DipLaw). Called to the Bar, Middle Temple, 1988; in practice as a barrister, 1988–, specialising in medical law, incl. clinical negligence, healthcare and disciplinary cases, and in the law of costs; High Court legal assessor for costs appeals. Co-founder, Chadwell Award, 2010. *Recreations:* contemporary art, travel. *Address:* Hailsham Chambers, 4 Paper Buildings, Temple, EC4Y 7EX. *T:* (020) 7643 5000. *E:* clerks@hailshamchambers.com.

**POST, Martin Richard,** MA; Regional Schools Commissioner for North West London and South Central Region, Department for Education, 2014–19; b 3 Sept. 1958; s of Kenneth and Barbara Post; m 1999, Kate Watts; one s. *Educ:* Univ. of York (BA Eng. and Related Lit.); MA Educnl Mgt Open Univ. King's Sch., Rochester, 1982–84; Darwin Coll., Cambridge, 1984–85; Mill Hill Co. High Sch., 1985–89; Richard Hale Sch., 1989–95; Dep. Head (Pastoral and Finance), 1995–2000, Headmaster, 2000–14, Watford GS for Boys. Mem., School Teachers' Review Body, 2019–. FRSA 2004. *Recreations:* sports, reading, theatre.

**POSTE, Dr George (Henry)**, CBE 1999; FRCPath, FMedSci; FRS 1997; FRCVS; Chief Executive Officer, Health Technology Networks, since 2000; Chief Scientist, Complex Adaptive Systems Initiative, and Regents' Professor, Arizona State University, since 2009; *b* 30 April 1944; *s* of late John H. Poste and of Kathleen B. Poste; *m* 1992, Linda Suhler; one *s* two *d*. *Educ*: Bristol Univ. (BVSc 1st cl. hons 1966; DVM 1966; PhD Virology 1969). FRCVS 1987; FRCPath 1989; FRSB (FIBiol 1998). Lectr, RPMS, Univ. of London, 1969–72; Prof. of Experimental Pathology, SUNY, 1972–80; SmithKline Beckman, then SmithKline Beecham: Vice Pres., R&D, 1980–88; Pres., R&D Technologies, 1989–90; Vice Chm. and Exec. Vice Pres., R&D, 1990–91; Dir, 1992–99; Pres., R&D, 1992–97; Chief Sci. and Technol. Officer, 1997–99. Dir, Arizona Biodesign Institute, Arizona State Univ., 2003–09. Partner, Care Capital, Princeton, 2000–03; non-executive Chairman: diaDexus, 1997–2003; Structural Genomi X, 2000–01. Director: Illumina, 2000–; Monsanto, 2004–; Exelixis, 2005–; Caris Diagnostics, 2007–13; Caris Life Sciences, 2013–. Pitt Fellow, Pembroke Coll., Cambridge, 1995–2001; Fellow, Hoover Inst., Stanford Univ., 2000–06. Member: Human Genetics Adv. Cttee, 1996–99; US Defense Sci. Bd, 2000–09; Council for Foreign Relns, 2004–; US Nat. Acad. of Medicine, Forum on Microbial Threats, 2015–; Scientific Advisory Board: A. Alfred Taubman Inst., Univ. of Michigan, 2014–; Synthetic Genomics Inc.; Human Longevity Inc., 2016–; Vir Biotechnology, 2017–. Governor, Center for Molecular Medicine and Genetics, Stanford Univ., 1992–96. Founder FMedSci 1998. Hon. FRCP 1993; Hon. FRVC 2000. Hon. Fellow, UCL, 1999. Hon. DSc 1987, Hon. LLD 1995, Bristol; Hon. LLD Dundee, 1998; Hon. DSc Sussex, 1999. *Publications*: joint ed. of fifteen books; numerous reviews and papers in learned jls; column in FT. *Recreations*: automobile racing, military history, photography, helicopter piloting, exploring the deserts of American Southwest. *Address*: Health Technology Networks, 2338 Casmar Way, Gilbertsville, PA 19525, USA. *T*: (610) 7050828, *Fax*: (610) 7050810. *E*: gposte@healthtechnetwork.com; Complex Adaptive Systems Initiative, Arizona State University - SkySong, 1475 N Scottsdale Road, Suite 361, Scottsdale, AZ 85257-3538, USA. *T*: (480) 7278662, *Fax*: (480) 9652765. *E*: george.poste@asu.edu. *Club*: Athenæum.

**POSTGATE, Prof. (John) Nicholas**, FBA 1993; Professor of Assyriology, University of Cambridge, 1994–2013; Fellow, Trinity College, Cambridge, since 1982; *b* 5 Nov. 1945; *s* of Ormond Oliver Postgate and Patricia Mary Postgate (*née* Peet); *m* 1st, 1968, Carolyn June Prater (marr. diss. 1999); one *s* one *d*; 2nd, 1999, Sarah Helen Blakeney; one *s* two *d*. *Educ*: Winchester Coll.; Trinity Coll., Cambridge (BA Oriental Studies 1967; MA 1970). Lectr in Akkadian, SOAS, 1967–71; Fellow, Trinity Coll., Cambridge, 1970–74; Asst Dir, British Sch. of Archaeology, Iraq, 1971–75; Dir, British Archaeol. Expedn to Iraq, 1975–81; Lectr in Hist. and Archaeol. of Ancient Near East, 1981–85, Reader in Mesopotamian Studies, 1985–94, Univ. of Cambridge. Director of excavations: Abu Salabikh, S Iraq, 1975–89; Kilise Tepe, S Turkey, 1994–99, 2007–13. *Publications*: Neo-Assyrian Royal Grants and Decrees, 1969; The Governor's Palace Archive, 1973; Taxation and Conscription in the Assyrian Empire, 1974; Fifty Neo-Assyrian Legal Documents, 1976; The First Empires, 1977; (ed) Abu Salabikh Excavations, vols 1–4, 1983–93; (with S. M. Dalley) Tablets from Fort Shalmaneser, 1984; The archive of Urad-Šerua and his family, 1988; Early Mesopotamia: society and economy at the dawn of history, 1992; (with F. M. Fales) Imperial administrative records, pt I 1992, pt II 1995; (with B. K. Ismail) Texts from Nineveh, 1993; (ed jtly) Concise Dictionary of Akkadian, 1999; (ed jtly) Excavations at Kilise Tepe 1994–98, 2007; The Land of Assur and the Yoke of Assur, 2007; (ed) Languages of Iraq, Ancient and Modern, 2007; (with A. Y. Ahmad) Archives from the domestic wing of the North-West Palace at Kalhu/Nimrud, 2007; Bronze Age Bureaucracy: writing and the practice of government in Assyria, 2013; articles in Iraq and other learned jls. *Address*: Trinity College, Cambridge CB2 1TQ. *T*: (01223) 338443.

**POSTGATE, Matthew Leigh**, FIET; Chief Technology and Product Officer, BBC, since 2016; *b* Winchester, 10 Nov. 1974; *s* of Ian Postgate and Rosemary Lass; *m* 2014, Roni Katz; one *s*. *Educ*: Hills Road Sixth Form Coll., Cambridge; Univ. of Bristol (BSc Politics 1996); Univ. of Cape Town; Stanford Graduate Sch. of Business (Exec. Prog. 2011). FIET 2015. Dir, Diarymanager.com, 1999–2001; Consultant, Rufus Leonard, 2001–03; BBC: Exec. Producer, 2003–07; Controller Mobile, 2007–09; Controller R&D, 2008–14; Chief Technol. Officer, 2014–16. Dir, Youview Ltd, 2010–14. Mem., Raspberry Pi Foundn, 2015–. *Recreations*: information policy, automotive. *Address*: BBC, Broadcasting House, Portland Place, W1A 1AA. *E*: matthew.postgate@bbc.co.uk.

**POSTON, Prof. Graeme John**, FRCS, FRCSE; Professor of Surgery, University of Liverpool, 2011–18, now Emeritus; Consultant Surgeon, Aintree University Hospital, Liverpool, 2004–18; *b* Oldham, 6 Aug. 1955; *s* of Richard George Poston and Christine Poston; *m* 1981, June Henry. *Educ*: Hulme Grammar Sch., Oldham; St George's Hosp. Med. Sch., London (MB BS 1979; MS 1988). FRCS 1984; FRCSE 1984. Instructor in Surgery, Univ. of Texas, 1986–87; Lectr in Surgery, Univ. of London, 1988–91; Consultant Surgeon, Royal Liverpool University Hosp., 1991–2004. Chm., NHS Specialised Commng Internal Medicine Prog. of Care Bd, 2012–16. President: British Assoc. of Surgical Oncol., 2005–07; Assoc. of Upper Gastrointestinal Surgeons of GB and Ire., 2010–12; Eur. Soc. of Surgical Oncol., 2012–14; Mersey Medico-legal Soc., 2018–19; Liverpool and NW Surgical Soc., 2018. Hon. Prof. of Surgery, Chinese Coll. of Surgeons, 2017–. Hon. Fellow: American Surgical Assoc., 2017–; Assoc. of Surgeons of India, 2018–; Coll. of Surgeons of Sri Lanka, 2018–. Hon. DSc King George V Univ., Lucknow, 2015. *Publications*: Surgical Management of Hepatobiliary and Pancreatic Disorders, 2002, 2nd edn 2010; Textbook of Surgical Oncology, 2004, 2nd edn 2015; Liver Metastases, 2009; over 270 scientific papers. *Recreations*: trekking in high places (Kilimanjaro, Kalar Pattar, Annapurna Base Camp, Lakya La), exploration in Arctic and Antarctic, running Zero Gravity Float Spa in Altrincham. *Address*: Linkstone, 201 Serpentine North, Blundellsands, Liverpool L23 6TJ.

**POTA, Vikas;** Group Chief Executive Officer, Tmrw Digital Ltd, since 2018; *b* Nairobi, 3 Feb. 1974; *s* of Tansukhrai Pota and Hasmukh Pota (*née* Vacchrajani); *m* 2001, Tejal Shah; two *d*. *Educ*: Aston Univ. (BSc Combined Hons Business Mgt); London Business Sch. (Exec. Course on Corporate Finance, Accounting and Financial Analysis 2015); John F. Kennedy Sch. of Govt, Harvard Univ. (Exec. Course on Global Leadership and Public Policy for 21st Century 2015). Parly Dir, Labour Friends of India, 2001–03; Man. Dir, Saffron Chase, 2004–10; Gp Dir, Corporate Affairs, Gems Educn, 2010–15; CEO, 2010–18, Chm., 2018–, Varkey Foundn. Vis. Practitioner in Educn, Harvard Grad. Sch. of Educn, 2016–; Policy Leaders Fellow, Centre for Sci. and Policy, Univ. of Cambridge, 2017–; Hon. Lectr, Inst. of Educn, UCL, 2017–. Member, Board of Directors: ARC Skills, 2014–; Gems Learning Trust, 2015–. Mem., Expert Network, WRF, 2017–. Mem., RSA. Hon. DSc Aston, 2016. Young Global Leader, WEF, 2013. *Publications*: India Inc.: how India's top ten entrepreneurs are winning globally, 2010; The Global Teacher Status Index, 2013; (contrib.) Handbook of International Development and Education, 2015; Generation Z: what the world's young people think and feel, 2017. *Recreations*: music, travel, reading. *Address*: Tmrw Digital Ltd, 2nd Floor, St Albans House, 57–59 Haymarket, SW1Y 4QX. *T*: (020) 7593 4040. *E*: vikas.pota@varkeyfoundation.org. *Club*: Arts.

**POTOČNIK, Janez,** PhD; Co-Chairman, International Resource Panel, United Nations Environment Programme, since 2014; *b* 22 March 1958; *m*; two *s*. *Educ*: Univ. of Ljubljana (BEc, MEc; PhD 1993). Econ. Analyst, SDK (APP) Agency, Kranj, 1983–84; Asst Dir, Inst. of Macroecon. Analysis and Develt, Ljubljana, 1984–87; Sen. Researcher, Inst. for Econ. Res., Ljubljana, 1988–93; Dir, Inst. of Macroecon. Analysis and Develt, Ljubljana, 1993–2001; Minister Councillor, Office of the Prime Minister, Slovenia, 2001–02; Minister for European Affairs, 2002–04. Asst Prof., Faculty of Law, Univ. of Ljubljana, 1991–2004. Mem., Eur. Commn, 2004–14.

**POTTER, Christopher Frank Rendall**, OBE 2001; MA; Headmaster, Old Swinford Hospital, Stourbridge, 1978–2001; *b* 9 Sept. 1939; *s* of late Cedric Hardcastle Potter and Phyllis Potter (*née* Rendall); *m* 1971, Charlotte Ann Millis, San Francisco; two *s* three *d*. *Educ*: March Grammar Sch.; Trinity Coll., Cambridge (MA Classics). Ardingly College, Sussex: Asst Master, 1961–78; Head of Classics, 1964–78; Housemaster, 1966–78. Chief Examr in Archaeol., London Exam Bd, 1976–80. Chm., State Boarding Inf. Service, 1996–98. Schoolmaster Studentship, Christ Church, Oxford, 1989. Pres., Stourbridge Archaeol and Historical Soc., 1988; Chm., Ludlow Historical Res. Gp, 2005–07. Chm., Trustees, Knoll Sch., Kidderminster, 1989–2009; Gov., The Elms Sch., Colwall, 1984–2013 (Vice Chm., 1985–2004; Chm., 2004–12). Churchwarden, St Laurence's, Ludlow, 2003–07. *Publications*: (with T. W. Potter) Romano-British Village at Grandford, Cambridgeshire, 1980; (ed) Parish Register Transcripts: Romsley, Worcs, 1988; Stone, Worcs, 1989; (jtly) St Laurence's Church, Ludlow 1199–2009: the Parish Church and people, 2010. *Recreations*: Italian opera, genealogy, red wine, Horatian Society, Bean Club. *Address*: 21 Townsend Close, Ludlow SY8 1UN. *T*: (01584) 878770; Villa Keramika, Kokkino Chorio, Vamos 73008, Crete, Greece.

**POTTER, Ven. Christopher Nicholas Lynden;** Archdeacon of St Asaph, 2011–14; Rector of Caerwys and Bodfari, 2011–14; *b* 4 Oct. 1949; *s* of Sir (Joseph) Raymond (Lynden) Potter and (Daphne) Marguerite Potter; *m* 1973, Jenny Lees; three *s* one *d*. *Educ*: Haileybury Coll.; Univ. of Leeds (BA (Hons) English/Fine Art 1971); St Asaph Diocesan Ordination Trng Course. Lectr, Tutor and Librarian, Bradford Art Coll., 1971–73; self-employed furniture designer and cabinet maker, 1975–90; ordained deacon, 1993, priest, 1994; Curate, Flint, 1993–96; Vicar of grouped parishes of Llanfair DC, Llanelidan, Efenechtyd and Derwen, 1996–2001; Dean of St Asaph, 2001–11. *Recreations*: pilgrimage, hill walking, reading, mending things.

**POTTER, Damion Andrew;** HM Diplomatic Service; Ambassador to Panama, since 2017; *b* Chertsey, Surrey, 22 Sept. 1974; *s* of Brian Jack Potter and Beverley Ann Potter; *m* 2001, Susanna Karolina Malm; two *s* one *d*. *Educ*: Univ. of Warwick (BA Hons French and Hist. 1998; MA 20th Century Eur. Hist. 1999). Entered FCO, 2000; Desk Officer, EU Directorate, 2000, EU Press Officer, 2001, FCO; Hd, Media and PR, Stockholm, 2002–05; Hd, Russia Gp, FCO, 2006–07; Communications Dir for EMEA and Asia and Pacific, ESPN, 2007–09; Dir, Trade and Investment, Russia and former Soviet Union, Moscow, 2009–13; Dep. Rep., British Office, Taipei, 2013–17. *Address*: c/o Foreign and Commonwealth Office, King Charles Street, SW1A 2AH. *E*: damion.potter@gmail.com.

**POTTER, Dr David Edwin**, CBE 1997; FREng; Founder, and Chairman, Psion plc, 1980–2009 (Chief Executive, 1980–99); a Director, Bank of England, 2003–09; *b* 4 July 1943; *s* of Paul James Potter and Mary Agnes (*née* Snape); *m* 1969, Elaine Goldberg; three *s*. *Educ*: Trinity Coll., Cambridge (Exhibnr; MA); Imperial Coll., London (PhD 1970). Lectr, Blackett Lab., Imperial Coll., London, 1970–80. Commonwealth Schol., 1966–69; Asst Prof., UCLA, 1974. Director: Charterhouse Venture Fund Management Ltd, 1985–94; Press Assoc. Ltd, 1994–97 (Vice-Chm., 1995–97); London First Centre, 1994–2002; Finsbury Technology Trust, 1995–; Chairman: Symbian Ltd, 1998–2004; Knowledge=Power, 2000–02. Member: Nat. Cttee of Inquiry into Higher Educn (Dearing Cttee), 1996–97; HEFCE, 1997–2003; Council for Sci. and Technol., Cabinet Office, 1998–2004. Mem., London Regl Council, CBI, 1993–99. Vis. Fellow, Nuffield Coll., Oxford, 1998–2006. Gov., London Business Sch., 1998–2009. Founder and Trustee, Bureau of Investigative Journalism, 2009–. Lectures: Stockton, London Business Sch., 1998; Millennium, 10 Downing St, 1999; Tacitus, World Traders' Co., 2000. FRSA 1989; FREng 2001. Hon. Fellow: Imperial Coll., 1998; London Business Sch., 1998. Hon. DTech: Kingston, 1998; Oxford Brookes, 1999; Hon. DSc: Brunel, 1998; Westminster, 1998; Warwick, 1999; Sheffield, 1999; York, 2002; Edinburgh, 2002; Cape Town, 2012; Open, 2012. Mountbatten Medal for Outstanding Services to Electronics Industry, Nat. Electronics Council, 1994. *Publications*: Computational Physics, 1972; contribs to various physics jls. *Recreations*: tennis, golf, flute, bridge, reading, ideas. *Address*: (office) 5 Welbeck Street, W1G 9YQ. *Club*: Portland.

**POTTER, David Roger William;** Chairman: Gresham House Strategic (formerly New Media Spark, then Spark Ventures), since 2009 (non-executive Director, since 2002); Coeus Software, since 2018; Illustrated London News, since 2014 (non-executive Director, since 2013); *b* 27 July 1944; *s* of late William Edward Potter and Joan Louise (*née* Frost); *m* 1966, Joanna Trollope, *qv* (marr. diss. 1983); two *d*; *m* 1991, Teresa Jill Benson (*d* 2019); one *d*. *Educ*: Bryanston Sch.; University Coll., Oxford (MA). Nat. Discount Co., 1965–69; Managing Director: Credit Suisse First Boston and Credit Suisse White Weld, 1969–81; Samuel Montagu & Co. Ltd, 1981–89; Midland Montagu Corporate Banking, 1986–89; Gp Chief Exec., Guinness Mahon Holdings, 1990–98; Chm. and Chief Exec., Guinness Mahon & Co. Ltd, Merchant Bankers, 1990–98; Dep. Chm., Investec Bank (UK) Ltd, 1998–99. Chairman: EON Lifestyle, 2001–06; DictaScribe, 2003–03; Deltron Electronics, 2005–06; Camco Internat., 2006–10; Quercus Publishing, 2009–14 (Dir, 2006–14); Ortus VCT, 2011–13; non-executive Director: Maybox plc, 1987–90; Thomas Cook, 1989–91; Tyndal plc, 1989–91; Execution Noble (formerly Noble Gp), 2000–10; Rose Partnership, 2000; WMC Communications, 2001–03; Numerica Gp plc, 2003–05; Solar Integrated Technologies, 2004–09 (Chm., 2004–06); Ortus plc (formerly Guinness Flight VCT), 2006–; Vycon Inc., 2007–09; Vantis plc, 2009–10; Maven Income and Growth VCT 4, 2013–15; Fundsmith Emerging Equities Trust, 2014–; Mem., Adv. Bd, Alva Capital, 2016–18. Chm., London Film Commn, 1996–2000. Mem. Council, KCL, 1997–2007 (Treas., 1998–2007; FKC 2006); Mem. Adv. Council, Centre for the Study of Financial Innovation, 1990–. Chm., Nat. Film and Television Sch. Foundn, 2004– (Mem., 1997–2004); Mem., Develt Bd, 14–18 NOW, 2014–; Trustee: Step Together (formerly Youth for Britain, then Worldwide Volunteering for Young People, later Worldwide Volunteering), 1994–2018; Nelson Mandela Children Foundn, 1998–2015. Governor: Bryanston Sch., 1982–2007 (Fellow, 2016–); Godolphin and Latymer Sch., 2009–11. FRSA. *Recreations*: shooting, gardening, golf. *Address*: (office) Brook House, Donnington, Newbury, Berks RG14 2JT. *E*: david@davidpotter.org. *Clubs*: Garrick; Vincent's (Oxford); Swinley Forest Golf.

**POTTER, Jeremy Patrick L.;** *see* Lee-Potter.

**POTTER, Rt Hon. Sir Mark (Howard)**, Kt 1988; PC 1996; arbitrator, since 2010; President of the High Court Family Division and Head of Family Justice, 2005–10; President, Court of Protection, 2007–10; *b* 27 Aug. 1937; *s* of Prof. Harold Potter, LLD, PhD, and Beatrice Spencer Potter (*née* Crowder); *m* 1962, Undine Amanda Fay, *d* of Major James Miller, 5/6th Rajputana Rifles, and Bunty Miller, painter; two *s*. *Educ*: Perse Sch.,

Cambridge; Gonville and Caius Coll., Cambridge (Schol.; BA (Law Tripos) 1960; MA 1963; Hon. Fellow 1998). National Service, 15 Med. Regt RA, 1955–57 (commnd 1956); 289 Lt Parachute Regt RHA(TA), 1958–64. Asst Supervisor, Legal Studies, Girton, Gonville and Caius, Queens' and Sidney Sussex Colls, 1961–68; called to Bar, Gray's Inn, 1961, Bencher, 1987, Treasurer, 2004; in practice, 1962–88; QC 1980; a Recorder, 1986–88; a Judge of the High Court of Justice, QBD (Commercial Court), 1988–96; a Presiding Judge, Northern Circuit, 1991–94; a Lord Justice of Appeal, 1996–2005. Member: Supreme Ct Rule Cttee, 1980–84; Lord Chancellor's Civil Justice Review Cttee, 1985–88; Chm., Bar Public Affairs Cttee, 1987; Vice-Chm., Council of Legal Educn, 1989–91; Chairman: Lord Chancellor's Adv. Cttee on Legal Educn and Conduct, 1998–99; Legal Services Adv. Panel, subseq. Consultancy Panel, 2000–05; Co-Chm., Legal Educn and Trng Review Consultancy Panel, 2011–13. Mem. Council, Nottingham Univ., 1996–99. Trustee: Somerset House Trust, 1997–2016; Gt Ormond St Charity, 2010–14. Hon. FKC 2005. Hon. LLD London Guildhall, 2000. *Recreations*: family and sporting. *Address*: Fountain Court Chambers, Fountain Court, Temple, EC4Y 9DH. *Clubs*: Garrick, Saintsbury; St Enodoc Golf; Denham Golf.

**POTTER, Michael Nicholas**; co-founder and non-executive Chairman, Seven Publishing, 2008–10 (publishers of Sainsbury's Magazine) (Executive Chairman, 2003–08); *b* 17 Oct. 1949; *s* of Alan Edward and Evelyn Mabel Potter; *m* 1973, Janet Nyasa Griffiths; one *s* two *d*. *Educ*: Royal Grammar Sch., Guildford; London Univ. (BSc Econ. (ext.)). DipM, MCIM 1974. Joined Haymarket Publishing, 1971 (Publishing Dir, Campaign and Marketing, 1979–83); founded Redwood Publishing, 1983, Chm., 2001–03: launched over 50 mags, incl. BBC Top Gear, M & S Mag., Sky TV Guide. Dir, Prince's Trust Trading, 1999–2007; non-exec. Dir, 4 imprint plc, 2001–03. Mem. Council, Mktg Gp of GB, 1993–2011 (Chm., 1995–97); Dir, PPA, 1995–2003; Mem., Assoc. of Publishing Agencies, 1993 (Chm., 1994–95). Member, Development Board: Nat. Portrait Gall., 1999–2007; Royal Court Th., 1999–2007. Mem., Nat. Fundraising and Marketing Cttee, Cancer Research UK, 2009–11. FRSA 1998. Marcus Morris Award for contrib. to magazine ind., PPA, 1998. *Recreations*: cars, motor-racing, theatre, opera, cinema, cricket. *Address*: Garden Cottage, Crocker End, Nettlebed, Oxon RG9 5BJ.

**POTTER, Raymond**, CB 1990; Deputy Secretary, 1986–93 (Courts and Legal Services, 1986–91), Head of the Court Service and Deputy Clerk of the Crown in Chancery, 1989–93, Lord Chancellor's Department; *b* 26 March 1933; *s* of William Thomas Potter and Elsie May Potter; *m* 1959, Jennifer Mary Quicke; one *s*. *Educ*: Henry Thornton Grammar School. Called to the Bar, Inner Temple, 1971, Bencher, 1989. Central Office, Royal Courts of Justice, 1950; Western Circuit, 1963; Chief Clerk, Bristol Crown Court, 1972; Dep. Circuit Administrator, Western Circuit, 1976; Circuit Administrator, Northern Circuit, 1982–86. Vice-Pres., Southern Rent Assessment Panel, 2001–03 (Pres., SW Panel, 1995–2001); Standing Chm., Strategic Health Authy Review Panel, 2003–09. *Recreation*: painting. *Address*: 8 Robinson Way, Backwell, Bristol BS48 3BP. *Club*: Athenæum.

**POTTER, Rhona Lynn**; see Campbell, R. L.

**POTTER, Roderick John Conwy; His Honour Judge Potter**; a Circuit Judge, since 2010; Resident Judge, Manchester Crown Court, since 2014; *b* Shrewsbury, 8 June 1962; *s* of Robert Michael Conwy Potter and Christobel Ann Potter; *m* 1993, Ann Marie O'Brien; three *s*. *Educ*: Wandsworth Sch.; Trent Poly. (BA Hons Law). Admitted solicitor, 1987; Solicitor, Messrs Dunderdale Wignall, Manchester, 1987–92; Partner, Messrs Platt Halpern, 1992–2010; Higher Court Advocate, 1997; Recorder, 2004–10. Mem., Solicitors Disciplinary Tribunal, 1997–2010. *Recreations*: going on the match, Weller. *Address*: Manchester Crown Court, Minshull Street, Manchester M1 3FS.

**POTTER, Maj. Gen. Stephen John**, QVRM 2011; Director Reserves, Army, since 2018; *b* Carshalton, Surrey, 15 June 1959; *s* of Arthur Potter and Maureen Potter; *m* 1983, Sara Penelope Hornsey; one *s* one *d*. *Educ*: Cheltenham Grammar Sch.; Poly. of Wales (BSc Urban Estate Mgt). Chartered Surveyor, RICS. Director: Paragon Finance plc, 1990–2004; West Bromwich Building Soc., 2004–09. Army Reserve: Sqn Comd, Middle Yeomanry, 1990–93; 39 Signal Regt, 1993–95; 2nd in comd, 37 Signal Regt, 1995–98; CO, 35 Signal Regt, 1999–2001; Signal Operating Instructions Communications, 11 Signal Bde, then Comd, 12 Signal Gp (Col), 2001–03; Dep. Comd, 143 (W Mids) Bde, 2004–07; Col Trng, Sandhurst, 2008–11; rcds 2011–12; Assistant Commander: Support Comd, 2014–16; Home Comd, 2016–17. *Recreations*: sailing, ski-ing, walking, cycling. *Address*: Army Headquarters, Blenheim Building, Marlborough Lines, Andover SP11 8HJ. *Club*: Army and Navy (Dir, 2013–16).

**PÖTTERING, Hans-Gert**; Member, 1979–2014 and President, 2007–09, European Parliament; Chairman, Konrad Adenauer Foundation, 2010–17; *b* Bersenbrück, 15 Sept. 1945; two *s*. *Educ*: Univ. of Bonn; Univ. of Geneva; Institut des Hautes Études Internationales, Geneva. Res. Asst, 1976–79; Lectr, Univ. of Osnabrück, 1989; Hon. Prof., 1995. European Parliament: Subcttee on Security and Disarmament, 1984–94; Vice-Chm., EPP Gp, 1994–99; Chm., EPP–ED Gp, 1999–2007; Head, EPP's and EPP-ED Gp's Working Party: on 1996 Intergovtl Conf., 1994–96; on EU Enlargement, 1996–99. Land Chm., Europa-Union in Lower Saxony, 1981–91; Chm., Europa-Union Deutschland, 1997–99. Chairman: Osnabrück Dist, Junge Union, CDU, 1974–76; Bersenbrück Br., CDU, 1974–80; Osnabrück Dist, CDU, 1990–2010; Mem. Exec. Cttee, 1999–2009, and Federal Exec., 1999–2009, CDU; Mem., Bureau, EPP, 1999–2009. Hon. Dr: Babeș-Bolyai; Opole; Warmia and Mazury; Korea; Miguel de Cervantes; Bahçeşehir. Robert Schuman Medal, EPP, 1995; Walter Hallstein Prize, Frankfurt, 2007; René Cassin Medaille for Human Rights, Consultative Council Jewish Orgns, 2010; Polish-German Prize, 2011. Grand Cross of Merit (Germany), 2010; Grand Golden Medal of Merit (Austria), 2002; Mérite Européen en or (Luxembourg), 2002; Grand Cross, Order of St Gregory the Great, 2007; Great Cross of Merit of Queen Jelena with Sash and Star (Croatia), 2007; Grand Cross (Italy), 2008; Three-Star Medal (Latvia), 2009; Medal of Jaroslaw the Wise (Ukraine), 2009; Grand Cross of Civil Merit (Spain), 2011; Comdr, Legion of Honour (France), 2011; Cross of Terra Mariana 1st cl., 2013; Knight Comdr's Cross (Poland), 2013; Grand Cross (Hungary), 2013; Grand Cross, Order of Star (Romania), 2014; Grand Officer (Tunisia), 2016. *Publications*: Adenauers Sicherheitspolitik 1955–63, 1975; (with F. Wiehler) Die vergessenen Regionen, 1983; (with L. Kühnhardt) Europas vereinigte Staaten: Annäherungen an Werte und Ziele, 1993; (with L. Kühnhardt) Kontinent Europa: Kern, Übergänge, Grenzen, 1998; (with L. Kühnhardt) Weltpartner Europäische Union, 2001; Von der Vision zur Wirklichkeit: auf dem Weg zur Einigung Europas, 2004; Im Dienste Europas, 2009; Mein Europäischer Weg, 2014; Mein Europa, 2015.

**POTTERTON, Homan**; art historian and writer; Editor, 1993–2002, and publisher, 2000–02, Irish Arts Review; Director, National Gallery of Ireland, 1980–88; *b* 9 May 1946; sixth *s* of late Thomas Edward Potterton and Eileen Potterton (née Tong). *Educ*: Kilkenny Coll.; Trinity Coll., Dublin (BA 1968, MA 1973); Edinburgh Univ. (Dip. Hist. Art 1971). FSA 1981. Cataloguer, National Gall. of Ireland, 1971–73; Asst Keeper, National Gall., London, 1974–80. Mem. Bd, GPA Dublin Internat. Piano Competition, 1987–92. HRHA 1982. *Publications*: Irish Church Monuments 1570–1880, 1975; A Guide to the National Gallery, 1976, rev. edn 1980 (German, French, Italian and Japanese edns 1977); The National Gallery, London, 1977; Reynolds and Gainsborough: themes and painters in the National Gallery, 1976; Pageant and Panorama: the elegant world of Canaletto, 1978; (jtly) Irish Art and Architecture, 1978; Venetian Seventeenth Century Painting (National Gallery Exhibn Catalogue), 1979; introd. to National Gallery of Ireland Illustrated Summary Catalogue of Paintings, 1981; (jtly) National Gallery of Ireland, 50 Pictures, 1981; Dutch 17th and 18th Century Paintings in the National Gallery of Ireland: a complete catalogue, 1986; Rathcormick: a childhood recalled, 2001; Potterton People and Places: three centuries of an Irish family, 2006; Who do I think I am?: a memoir, 2017; Knockfane (novel), 2019; contrib. Burlington Mag., Apollo, Connoisseur, FT and Country Life. *Recreation*: genealogy. *Address*: 36 Abingdon Road, W8 6AS; Colombel Bas, 81140 Castelnau-de-Montmiral, France. *T*: and *Fax*: (5) 63405352. *E*: hpotterton@orange.fr. *W*: www.potterton.ie.

**POTTINGER, Frank Vernon Hunter**, RSA 1991; sculptor; *b* 1 Oct. 1932; *s* of William Pottinger and Veronica (née Irvine); *m* 1991, Evelyn Norah Smith (marr. diss. 2007); one step *s* two step *d*. *Educ*: Boroughmuir Secondary Sch.; Edinburgh Coll. of Art (DA 1963). Apprentice fitter engineer, 1948–53; nat. service, 1953–55; teacher: Portobello Secondary Sch., 1965–73; Aberdeen Coll. of Educn, 1973–85; vis. lectr, colls of art in Scotland, 1980–91; full-time artist, 1985–. *Address*: 30/5 Elbe Street, Edinburgh EH6 7HW. *T*: (0131) 553 5082.

**POTTINGER, Graham Robert**; Chief Executive, Scottish Mutual Assurance plc, 1997–2002 (Finance Director, 1992–96); Managing Director, Abbey National Financial Investment Services plc, 1997–2002; *b* 14 June 1949; *s* of Arthur and Mary Pottinger; *m* 1970, Dorothy McLean; one *s* one *d*. *Educ*: Jordanhill Coll. Sch., Glasgow; Glasgow Univ. (LLB). CA 1972; ACMA 1993. Peat Marwick Mitchell & Co., 1969–72; Partner, Deloitte Haskins & Sells, 1972–79; Controller, UK and Africa, Cargill Plc, 1980–92. Mem. Council, ICAS, 1995–2001.

**POTTINGER, Piers Julian Dominic**; Managing Director, Bonaly Consultancy Pte Ltd, since 2017; *b* 3 March 1954; *s* of late W. G. Pottinger; *m* 1979, Carolyn Ann Rhodes; one *s* three *d*. *Educ*: Edinburgh Acad.; Winchester Coll. Trainee, J. Henry Schroder Wagg, 1972–74; Res. Analyst, Laurence Prust and Co., 1974–78; Exec., Charles Barker, 1978–80; Dir, Media Relations Manufacturers, Hanover, NY, 1980–82; Man. Dir, Sterling Financial Public Relations, 1982–85; Man. Dir, then Chm., Bell Pottinger (formerly Lowe Bell) Financial, 1985–2009; Gp Man. Dir, then Dep. Chm., Chime Communications plc, 1993–2012; Chm., Pelham Bell Pottinger, subseq. Bell Pottinger Asia (Singapore), 2013–17; Dep. Chm., Bell Pottinger Private, 2012–17. Director: Newmarket Investments plc (formerly British Bloodstock Agency plc), 2001–06 (Chm., 2001–06); Northern Racing Ltd, 2002–05; Green Castle Consulting Ltd, 2019–; Chairman: Sportech plc, 2006–10; Mysquar plc (Singapore), 2014–18. Former Member: Bd, Scottish Ballet; Gen. Council, Poetry Soc. Trustee: Racing Welfare, 2009–12; Foundn for Liver Res. (formerly Liver Res. Trust), 2010–; Vice-Pres., Nat. Soc. for Epilepsy, 2004–. *Recreations*: horse racing, golf. *Address*: Flat 2, 29 Crockerton Road, SW17 7HE. *Clubs*: Garrick, Turf; New Zealand Golf.

**POTTS, Alexander James Kenneth**; QC 2018; Partner, Kennedys Law LLP, Hamilton, Bermuda, since 2017; *b* Nairobi, Kenya, 11 June 1976; *s* of James Richardson Potts, OBE and Maria Potts; *m* 2007, Priscillia Robineau; two *s* one *d*. *Educ*: Hazlegrove Hse; Winchester Coll. (Schol.; Hd of Sch.); Exeter Coll., Oxford (Schol.; BA Hons English Lang. and Lit. 1998); City Univ., London (Postgrad. DipLaw 1999); Inns of Court Sch. of Law (BVC 2000). Called to the Bar, Middle Temple, 2001; in practice as barrister: 4 Pump Court, Temple, 2000–07; Conyers Dill & Pearman, Bermuda, 2007–12; Judicial Asst, Court of Appeal, 2001. Pegasus Schol., 2004. *Recreations*: watersports, tennis, squash, writing, theatre, cinema, travel. *E*: alex.potts@kennedyslaw.com.

**POTTS, Archibold**; Director, Bewick Press, since 1989; *b* 27 Jan. 1932; *s* of late Ernest W. Potts and Ellen Potts; *m* 1957, Marguerite Elsie (née Elliott) (*d* 1983); one *s* one *d*. *Educ*: Monkwearmouth Central Sch., Sunderland; Ruskin and Oriel Colls, Oxford (Dip. Econ. and Pol Sci.), 1958; BA PPE 2nd cl. hons, 1960); ext. postgrad. student, London Univ. (Postgrad. CertEd 1964) and Durham Univ. (MEd 1969). Nat. Service, RAF, 1950–53. Railway Clerk, 1947–50 and 1953–56. Lecturer: N Oxfordshire Tech. Coll., 1961; York Tech. Coll., 1962–65; Rutherford Coll. of Technology and Newcastle upon Tyne Polytechnic, 1965–80; Head of Sch. of Business Admin, 1980–87, Associate Dean, Faculty of Business and Professional Studies, 1988, Newcastle upon Tyne Polytechnic. Moderator, history courses, Tyneside Open Coll. Network, 1992–2005. Tyne and Wear County Council: Councillor, 1979–86; Vice-Chm., Planning Cttee, 1981–86; Vice-Chm., Council, 1983–84; Chm., Council, 1984–85. Contested (Lab) Westmorland, 1979. Chm., NE Labour History Soc., 1990–96 (Vice Pres., 1997–2011; Pres., 2012–); Mem., Exec. Cttee, Soc. for Study of Labour History, 1987–96. *Publications*: Stand True, 1976; Bibliography of Northern Labour History, 1982–; (ed) Shipbuilders and Engineers, 1987; Jack Casey, the Sunderland Assassin, 1991; The Wearside Champions, 1993; Jack London, the forgotten champion, 1997; Zilliacus, a life for peace and socialism, 2002; Headlocks and Handbags, 2005; contributions to: Dictionary of Labour Biography, vol. 2 1974, vol. 4 1977, vol. 5 1979, vol. 9 1993, vol. 11 2003, vol. 12 2005, vol. 14 2018; Oxford DNB, 2004; articles on economics and history. *Recreations*: local history, watching old films. *Address*: 47 Graham Park Road, Gosforth, Newcastle upon Tyne NE3 4BJ. *T*: (0191) 284 5132. *Club*: Victory Service.

**POTTS, Prof. David Malcolm**, PhD, DSc; FREng, FICE; GCG Professor of Geotechnical Engineering, and Head, Department of Geotechnics, Imperial College London; *b* 26 April 1952; *s* of Leonard Francis Potts and Doris Florence Potts; *m* 1974, Deborah Margot Peel; two *d*. *Educ*: King's Coll., London (BSc Eng); Churchill Coll., Cambridge (PhD 1976); Imperial Coll., London (DSc 1996). FICE 1997; FREng 2001. Res. Engr, Shell, Netherlands, 1976–79; Imperial College of Science, Technology and Medicine, later Imperial College London: Lectr, 1979–89; Reader, 1989–94; Prof. of Analytical Soil Mechanics, 1994; Dep. Hd, Dept of Civil and Envmtl Engng, 2001. *Publications*: Finite Element Analysis in Geotechnical Engineering: theory, 1999; Finite Element Analysis in Geotechnical Engineering: application, 2001; numerous contribs to learned jls incl. Geotechnique, Internat. Jl Num. Anal. Meth. in Geomech., Internat. Jl Num. Meth. Engrg, Engrg Computations, Computers and Geotechnics, Canadian Geotechnical Jl, Computational Methods, Appl. Mech. Engrg, Geotechnical Engrg, Jl Geotechnical and Geoenvmtl Engrg. *Recreations*: fly fishing, swimming. *Address*: Geotechnics Section, Department of Civil and Environmental Engineering, Skempton Building, Imperial College London, South Kensington Campus, SW7 2AZ. *T*: (020) 7594 6084, *Fax*: (020) 7594 6150. *E*: d.potts@imperial.ac.uk.

**POTTS, Vice Adm. Duncan Laurence**, CB 2014; Director, Universal Defence and Security Solutions; *b* Malta, 10 March 1961; *s* of Major Gordon Potts and Jane Potts; *m* 1987, Pamela Sleigh; one *s* one *d*. *Educ*: Wellington Sch.; City Univ., London (BSc Hons Systems and Mgt 1983). Joined Royal Navy, 1979; commanded: HMS Brilliant, 1996; HMS Southampton, 1996–98; HMS Marlborough, 2000–02; Navy Plans and Asst to VCDS, MoD, 2002–06; rcds 2007; Comdr UK Task Gp, 2007–09, Coalition Maritime Comdr, N Gulf and Iraq, 2008; Hd of Planning, UK Jt Operational HQ, 2009–11; Commander: UK Maritime Forces, 2011–12; EU Counter Piracy Ops in Indian Ocean,

2011–12; Rear Adm. Surface Ships, 2011–12; Asst Chief of Naval Staff (Capability), 2013–14; Controller of the Navy, 2013–14; Dir Gen. Jt Force Develt and Defence Acad., 2014–18. Younger Brother, Trinity House, 2006–. *Recreations:* fly fishing, shooting, walking, keeping fit, reading, ski-ing.

**POTTS, James Rupert;** QC 2013; *b* London, 28 June 1970; *s* of Robin Potts and Rebeca Potts; *m* 2000, Diana; two *s* one *d*. *Educ*: Charterhouse Sch.; Magdalen Coll., Oxford (BA 1st Cl. Hons Mod. Hist.). Called to the Bar, Gray's Inn, 1994. *Publications*: contributions to: Practice and Procedure of the Companies Court, 1997; Company Directors: law and liability; Buckley on the Companies Acts. *Recreations:* history, walking, family. *E*: clerks@erskinechambers.com.

**POTTS, Paul John,** CBE 2009; Group Chief Executive, 2000–10, and a Director, 1995–2010, PA Group (Chairman, 2008–09); Editor-in-Chief, The Press Association, 1996–2006; *b* 21 Jan. 1950; *s* of late Michael Henry Potts and of Sylvia Brenda Potts; *m* 1st, 1976, Gabrielle Jane Fagan (marr. diss. 1994); one *s* two *d*; 2nd, 1994, Judith Anne Fielding. *Educ*: Worksop Coll. Gen. Reporter, Sheffield Star, 1968–74; Lobby Corresp., Yorkshire Post, 1974–78; General Reporter: Daily Telegraph, 1978–81; Mail on Sunday, 1981–82; Political Ed., News of the World, 1982–86; Political Ed., then Asst Ed., later Dep. Ed., Daily Express, 1986–95. Chm., CNW Gp (formerly Canada NewsWire), 2003–10 (Dir, 2000–09); Mem., Nomination Cttee, Reuters Founders Share Co. Ltd, 2002–07. Non-exec. Dir, Channel 4, 2012–18. Sen. Advr, SWNS Media Gp, 2014–. Mem., Code of Practice Cttee, 1996–2007. Vis. Prof. of Journalism, Univ. of Sheffield, 2010–. Trustee, IWM, 2016–18; Mem., First World War Centenary Adv. Gp., 2015–18. Patron, Sheffield Wednesday Supporters Trust, 2001. Gov., St Anselm's Sch., Bakewell, 2010–14. Hon. DLitt Sheffield, 2002. *Recreations:* history, horse racing, Sheffield Wednesday FC. *Club:* Garrick.

**POTTS, Timothy Faulkner,** DPhil; FSA; Director, J. Paul Getty Museum, Los Angeles, since 2012; *b* 17 June 1958; *s* of Ian Faulkner Potts and Judy Potts; one *s* one *d*. *Educ*: Univ. of Sydney (BA Hons 1980); DPhil Oxon 1987. Res. Lectr, 1985–87, British Acad. Postdoctoral Res. Fellow, 1987–90, Christ Church, Oxford; Associate and Dir, Lehman Bros, NY and London, 1990–94; Director: Nat. Gall. of Victoria, Melbourne, 1994–98; Kimbell Art Mus., Texas, 1998–2007; Fitzwilliam Mus., Cambridge, 2008–12; Fellow, Clare Coll., Cambridge, 2010–12. FSA 2010. *Publications*: Civilization: ancient treasures from the British Museum, 1990, 1997; Mesopotamia and the East: an archaeological and historical study of foreign relations *c* 3400–2000 BC, 1994; (ed jtly) Culture Through Objects: ancient Near Eastern studies in honour of P. R. S. Moorey, 2003; (ed) Kimbell Art Museum: handbook of the collection, 2003; (ed) The J. Paul Getty Museum: handbook of the collection, 2010; (ed) Golden Kingdoms: luxury arts in the ancient Americas, 2017; (ed) Beyond the Nile: Egypt and the classical world, 2018. *Address:* J. Paul Getty Museum, 1200 Getty Center Drive, Suite 1000, Los Angeles, CA 90049–1687, USA.

**POULSEN, Ole Lønsmann,** Hon. GCVO 2000; Kt Comdr, Order of Dannebrog, 2005 (Comdr 1999); Chairman of Board, Danish Medical Consultants Center, 2017–19; *b* 14 May 1945; *s* of Aage Lønsmann Poulsen, head teacher, and Tove Alice (*née* Gyldenstein); *m* 1973, Zareen Mehta; two *s*. *Educ:* Copenhagen Univ. (LLM 1971). Hd of Dept, Danchurchaid, 1969–73; joined Danish Diplomatic Service, 1973; Hd of Section, Min. of Foreign Affairs, Denmark, 1973–76; Advr, Asian Develt Bank, Manila, 1976–77; First Sec., New Delhi and Trade Comr, Bombay, 1977–80; Alternate Exec. Dir, World Bank, Washington, 1980–83; Dep. Head, 1983–85, Head, 1985–88, Dept of Internat. Develt Co-operation, then Under-Sec. for Multilateral Affairs (Ambassador), 1988–92, Min. of Foreign Affairs; Ambassador to Austria and Perm. Rep. to IAEA, UNIDO and UN, Vienna, also accredited to Slovenia and Bosnia Hercegovina, 1992–93; State Sec., Min. of Foreign Affairs, 1993–96; Ambassador: to UK, 1996–2001; to China, 2001–04; to Sweden, 2004–06; to India, 2006–10. Chm., Industrial Develt Bd, UNIDO, 1990–91. Alternate Gov., World Bank and Gov. for Asian, African and Interamerican Develt Banks, 1989–92 and 1993–96. Chairman: Scandinavian Seminar Coll., 1975–76; Nordic Develt Fund, 1990–91. Member: Bd, Rohde Nielsen Shippingline, 2010–18; Adv. Bd, Scandinavian Eye Centre, 2015–17. Grand Decoration of Honour with Sash (Austria), 1993; Grand Cross of Northern Star (Sweden), 2006. *Recreations:* music, literature, sport. *Address:* Sollerødlund 17, 2840 Holte, Denmark.

**POULTER, Brian Henry;** Secretary, Northern Ireland Audit Office, 1989–2000; *b* 1 Sept. 1941; *s* of William Henry Poulter, PhC, MPS, and Marjorie Elizabeth Everett McBride; *m* 1968, Margaret Ann Dodds; one *s* twin *d*. *Educ*: Regent House Grammar Sch., Newtownards. Qual. as certified accountant, 1966. Hill, Vellacott and Bailey, Chartered Accountants, 1959–62; entered NICS, 1962; Min. of Health and Local Govt, 1962–65; Min. of Health and Social Services, 1965–71; Deputy Principal: Local Enterprise Develt Unit, 1971–74; Dept of Commerce, 1974–75; Chief Auditor 1975–81, Dep. Dir 1981–82, Dir 1982–87, Exchequer and Audit Dept; Dir, NI Audit Office, 1987–88. *Recreations:* reading, walking, cricket. *Address:* 20 Manse Road, Newtownards, Co. Down BT23 4TP.

**POULTER, Dr Daniel Leonard James;** MP (C) Central Suffolk and North Ipswich, since 2010; *b* Beckenham, 30 Oct. 1978. *Educ*: Univ. of Bristol (LLB Hons); Univ. of London (MB BS); King's Coll., London (AKC). Medical doctor specialising in obstetrics and gynaecol. Mem. (C) Hastings BC, 2006–07; Dep. Leader, Reigate and Banstead BC, 2008–10. Parly Under-Sec. of State, DoH, 2012–15. Member: Health Select Cttee, 2011–12; House of Lords Reform Cttee, 2011–12; Energy and Climate Change Cttee, 2015–16; Scottish Affairs Cttee, 2015–17; Public Admin and Constitutional Affairs Cttee, 2016–17; Envmtl Audit Cttee, 2017–. *Publications*: articles in field of women's health. *Recreations:* Rugby, cricket, golf. *Address:* House of Commons, SW1A 0AA. *E:* daniel.poulter.mp@parliament.uk.

**POULTER, Jane Anne Marie;** *see* Bonvin, Her Honour J. A. M.

**POULTER, John William;** Chairman, RM plc, since 2013; *b* 22 Nov. 1942; *m* 1968, Margaret Winifred Thorn; one *s* one *d*. *Educ*: Berkhamsted Sch.; Queen's Coll., Oxford (MA Natural Sci.). Cambridge Instruments Gp, 1968, Marketing Dir, 1972–77; Dir and Gen. Manager, Robinsons Carton Packaging, 1977–81; Man. Dir, Vokes Ltd, and other BTR subsids, 1981–88; Spectris plc, 1988–2008: Gp Man. Dir, 1988–91; Chief Exec., 1991–2001. Chairman: Kymata Ltd, 1999–2001; Wyko Gp, 2001–04; Spectris plc, 2001–08; Snell & Wilcox Ltd, 2002–09; Filtronic plc, 2006–09; Zenergy Power plc, 2010–11; Hampson Gp plc, 2011–12; Exec. Chm., 4imprint plc, 2010–16; non-executive Director: Lloyds Smaller Cos Investment Trust plc, 1992–2002; Crest Packaging plc, 1993–96; BTP plc, 1997–2000; Kidde plc, 2000–05; RAC plc, 2002–05; Smaller Cos Value Trust plc, 2002–09; London Metal Exchange Ltd, 2003–05; MacQuarie European Infrastructure plc, 2003–05; Suffolk Life plc, 2006–09. Gov., Ipswich Sch., 2000–17. *Club:* Oxford and Cambridge.

**POULTON, Denise;** *see* Lewis, Denise.

**POULTON, Michael Graham;** playwright and adapter of classic and contemporary plays and novels; *b* 6 April 1947; *yr s* of late John William Lines Poulton and Ella Poulton (*née* Clayton). Asst Ed., Pergamon Press, Oxford, 1973–74; Ed., then Dep. Chief Ed., Religious Educn Press, A. Wheaton & Co., Exeter, 1974–77; Oxford University Press, Oxford: Sen. Ed., Educn Div. and Religious Educn, 1977–78; Man. Ed., Primary Educn and Children's Information Books, 1978–90; Creator, Oxford Reading Tree, 1979–90; Consultant, John Murray, Publisher, London, 1990–92; Advr, Northern Broadsides Th. Co., 1992–94. *Plays and adaptations*, 1994–: Chekhov's Uncle Vanya, Turgenev's Fortune's Fool, Chichester, 1996; Chekhov's Three Sisters, Birmingham Rep., 1998; Ibsen's Ghosts, Plymouth, 1999; Uncle Vanya, 1999, Strindberg's Dance of Death, 2001, Three Sisters, 2003, Euripides' Ion, 2004, Chekhov's The Seagull, 2005, Colchester; Uncle Vanya, NY, 2000; The York Mysteries, York Minster, 2000; Fortune's Fool, NY, 2002; Schiller's Don Carlos, Sheffield Crucible, transf. Gielgud, 2004; Ibsen's Hedda Gabler, W Yorks Playhouse and Liverpool Playhouse, 2006; Aeschylus' Myrmidons, Dublin, 2006; Chaucer's Canterbury Tales, Parts One and Two, RSC, Stratford, London, Washington and Spain, 2006; Strindberg's The Father, Chichester, 2006; Chekhov's The Cherry Orchard, Schiller's Mary Stuart, Clwyd Th. Cymru, 2007; Don Carlos, Dublin, 2007; Schiller's Don Carlos, Göteborgs Stadsteater, 2007–08, Copenhagen, 2008–09; Ibsen's Rosmersholm, Almeida, 2008; Ibsen's The Lady from The Sea, Birmingham Rep., 2008; The Cherry Orchard, 2008; Schiller's Wallenstein, 2009, Chichester; Malory's Morte d'Arthur, RSC, Stratford, 2010; Schiller's Luise Miller, Donmar Warehouse, 2011; Uncle Vanya, The Print Room, London, 2012; Anjin: The English Samurai, Horipro/RSC, Tokyo, Osaka, Yokohama, Sadler's Wells, 2013; Fortune's Fool, Old Vic, 2013; Wolf Hall and Bring Up the Bodies, RSC, Stratford, transf. Aldwych, 2014; A Tale of Two Cities, Northampton, 2014; Kenny Morgan, Arcola Th., 2016; Imperium Part I: Conspirator and Part II: Dictator, RSC, Stratford, 2017, transf. Gielgud, 2018. *Publications*: books for children; (contrib.) My First Play, 2013; *adaptations*: The York Mysteries, 2000; Uncle Vanya, 2001, rev. trans. 2012; Fortune's Fool, 2002, rev. trans. 2013; The Seagull, 2004; Don Carlos, 2005; The Canterbury Tales, 2005; The Father, 2006; The Cherry Orchard, 2008; Rosmersholm, 2008; Mary Stuart, 2009; Wallenstein, 2009; Morte d'Arthur, 2010; Bacchae, 2010; Luise Miller, 2011; Judgement Day, 2011; Anjin: the shogun and the English samurai, 2013; Wolf Hall and Bring Up the Bodies, 2013; A Tale of Two Cities, 2014; Ghosts, 2014. *Recreations:* Norfolk, dogs. *Address:* c/o Alan Brodie Representation Ltd, Paddock Suite, The Courtyard at 55 Charterhouse Street, EC1M 6HA. *Club:* Royal Over-Seas League.

**POULTON, Richard Christopher,** MA; Director of Development, Round Square International Association of Schools, 2003–05; *b* 21 June 1938; *e s* of Rev. Christopher Poulton and Aileen (*née* Sparrow); *m* 1965, Zara, *o d* of late Prof. P. Crossley-Holland and Mrs J. Crossley-Holland; two *s* one *d*. *Educ*: King's Coll., Taunton; Wesleyan Univ., Middletown, Conn, USA; Pembroke Coll., Cambridge (BA 1961, CertEd 1962, MA 1965). Asst Master: Bedford Sch., 1962–63; Beckenham and Penge Grammar Sch., 1963–66; Bryanston School: Asst Master, 1966–80; Head of History Dept, 1971–76; Housemaster, 1972–80; Headmaster, Wycliffe Coll., 1980–86; Head Master, Christ's Hospital, Horsham, 1987–96; Founder Head Master, Internat. Sch. of the Regents, Pattaya, Thailand, 1996–97; Develt Officer, Inner Cities Young People's Project, 1998–2000; Clerk, All Saints Educnl Trust, 2001–04. Chm. Govs, 2010–13, Chm. Trustees, 2011–13, Sir Robert Geffery's Acad. (formerly Sir Robert Geffery's Sch.), Cornwall; Governor: Oxford and Cambridge Examinations Bd, 1987–90; Aiglon Coll., Switzerland, 1998–2000; Royal Bridewell Hosp., 1999–2004 and 2006–08; Beausoleil Internat. Coll., Switzerland, 2003–12; Box Hill Sch., 2004–08; Presentation Gov., Christ's Hosp., 1999–. JP S Glos, 1985–86. Freeman, City of London, 1987; Liveryman, Ironmongers' Co., 1993– (Yeoman, 1990; Mem. Court, 1999–; Jun. Warden, 2006–07; Sen. Warden, 2007–08; Master, 2008–09). FRSA 1994. *Publications*: Victoria, Queen of a Changing Land, 1975; Kings and Commoners, 1977; A History of the Modern World, 1980. *Recreations:* writing, choral music. *Address:* 2 Hill Cottages, Hoyle Lane, Heyshott GU29 0DU.

**POUND, Sir John David,** 5th Bt *cr* 1905; *b* 1 Nov. 1946; *s* of Sir Derek Allen Pound, 4th Bt; *S* father, 1980; *m* 1st, 1968 (marr. diss.); one *s*; 2nd, 1978, Penelope Ann, *er d* of late Grahame Arthur Rayden, Bramhall, Cheshire; two *s*. *Heir: s* Robert John Pound [*b* 12 Feb. 1973; *m* 2005, Tessa, *o d* of Michael Froggatt]. *Address:* 15 Tripcony Court, Pelican Waters, Qld 4551, Australia.

**POUND, Rev. Canon Keith Salisbury;** a Chaplain to the Queen, 1988–2003; *b* 3 April 1933; *s* of Percy Salisbury Pound and Annie Florence Pound. *Educ*: Roan School, Blackheath; St Catharine's Coll., Cambridge (BA 1954, MA 1958); Cuddesdon Coll., Oxford. Curate, St Peter, St Helier, Dio. Southwark, 1957–61; Training Officer, Hollowford Training and Conference Centre, Sheffield, 1961–64; Warden 1964–67; Rector of Holy Trinity, Southwark, with St Matthew, Newington, 1968–78; RD, Southwark and Newington, 1973–78; Rector of Thamesmead, 1978–86; Sub-Dean of Woolwich, 1984–86; Dean of Greenwich, 1985–86; Chaplain-Gen. and Archdeacon to Prison Service, 1986–93; Chaplain to HM Prison, Grendon and Spring Hill, 1993–98. Hon. Canon of Southwark Cathedral, 1985–. *Publications*: Creeds and Controversies, 1976; Previous Convictions, 2012. *Recreations:* theatre, music, books, crosswords. *Address:* 1 Sinnock Square, High Street, Hastings, East Sussex TN34 3HQ. *T:* (01424) 428330. *Club:* Civil Service.

**POUND, Stephen Pelham;** MP (Lab) Ealing North, since 1997; *b* 3 July 1948; *s* of late Pelham Pound and Dominica James; *m* 1976, Marilyn Anne Griffiths; one *s* two *d*. *Educ*: London Sch. of Economics (BSc Econ., Dip. Indust. Relations). Seaman, 1967–69; Bus Conductor, 1969–70; Hosp. Porter, 1970–79; student, 1980–84; Housing Officer, Camden Council, 1984–88; Homeless Persons Officer, Hammersmith and Fulham Council, 1988–90; Housing Officer, Paddington Churches HA, 1990–97. Councillor, London Borough of Ealing, 1982–98; Mayor of Ealing, 1995–96. Opposition Whip, 2010; Shadow Minister of State for NI, 2011–. *Recreations:* Fulham FC, cricket, walking, collecting comics. *Address:* House of Commons, SW1A 0AA. *T:* (020) 7219 6238; 115 Milton Road, Hanwell, W7 1LG. *Clubs:* St Joseph's Catholic Social; Fulham Football Supporters'.

**POUNDER, Prof. Robert Edward, (Roy),** MD, DSc; FRCP; Professor of Medicine, Royal Free and University College Medical School, 1992–2005, now Professor Emeritus, University College London; Hon. Consultant Physician and Gastroenterologist, Royal Free Hospital, since 1986; *b* 31 May 1944; *s* of Edward Pounder and Annie Pounder (*née* Langdale); *m* 1972, Christine Lee; two *s*. *Educ*: Eltham Coll.; Peterhouse, Cambridge (BA 1st Cl. Hons Nat. Sci. 1966; BChir 1969; MB, MA 1970; MD 1977); Guy's Hosp. Med. Sch.; DSc (Med.) London 1992. MRCP 1971, FRCP 1984. Registrar, Central Middlesex Hosp., 1972–76; Sen. Registrar, St Thomas' Hosp., 1976–80; Royal Free Hospital School of Medicine: Sen. Lectr, 1980–85, Reader, 1985–92, in Medicine; Clin. Sub-Dean, 1986–88; Admissions Sub-Dean, 1992–95; Chm., Collegiate Cttee of Examrs, 1996–2003. Co-Founder and Chm., RotaGeek Ltd, 2010–. Non-exec. Dir, Camden and Islington HA, 1996–2002 (Vice-Chm., 2001–02). Royal College of Physicians: Mem. Council, 1987–89 and 1997–2000; Vice-Pres., 2002–04; Associate Internat. Dir, Australasia and FE, 2004–08. Member Council: British Digestive Foundn, 1987–98; British Soc. of Gastroenterology, 1996–2000 (Sec., 1982–86). Trustee, Alimentary Pharmacology and Therapeutics Trust, 1988–99. Chm., Friends of Peterhouse, 1999–2002 (Mem. Council, 1982–2002). Gov., St

Paul's Sch., London, 2001–10 (Dep. Chm., 2007–09). Founding Co-Editor, Alimentary Pharmacology and Therapeutics, 1987–2017; Ed.-in-Chief, GastroHep.com, 2000–18. Hon. FRACP 2007; Hon. FRCPI 2009. *Publications:* (ed) Long Cases in General Medicine, 1983, 2nd edn 1988; (ed) Doctor, There's Something Wrong with my Guts, 1985; (ed) Recent Advances in Gastroenterology, 6th edn 1986 to 10th edn 1994; (ed jtly) Diseases of the Gut and Pancreas, 1987, 2nd edn 1994 (trans. Italian and Greek); (ed jtly) Advanced Medicine, 1987; (ed jtly) A Colour Atlas of the Digestive System, 1989 (trans. Japanese); (ed) Landmark Papers: the histamine H$_2$-receptor antagonists, 1990; (ed jtly) Current Diagnosis and Treatment, 1996; (ed jtly) Inflammatory Bowel Disease, 1998; papers on pharmacological control of acid secretion, inflammatory bowel disease and med. workforce. *Recreations:* gardening, family life, travelling. *Address:* 19 Queensberry House, Friars Lane, Richmond-upon-Thames, Surrey TW9 1NT.

**POUNDS, Prof. Kenneth Alwyne,** CBE 1984; FRS 1981; Professor of Space Physics, 1973–2002, now Emeritus, and Leverhulme Fellow, 2003–05, University of Leicester; *b* 17 Nov. 1934; *s* of Harry and Dorothy Pounds; *m* 1st, 1961, Margaret Mary (*née* Connell); two *s* one *d*; 2nd, 1982, Joan Mary (*née* Millit); one *s* one *d*. *Educ:* Salt Sch., Shipley, Yorkshire; University Coll. London (BSc, PhD; Fellow, 1993). Department of Physics, University of Leicester: Asst Lectr, 1960; Lectr, 1961; Sen. Lectr, 1969; Prof., 1973; Hd, Dept of Physics and Astronomy, 1986–2002; Chief Exec., PPARC (on leave of absence from Univ. of Leicester), 1994–98. Member: SERC, 1980–84 (Chm., Astronomy, Space and Radio Bd); Management Bd, British Nat. Space Centre, 1986–88; Pres., RAS, 1990–92. Dist. Hon. Fellow, Univ. of Leicester, 2013. DUniv York, 1984; Hon. DSc: Loughborough, 1992; Sheffield Hallam, 1997; Warwick, 2001; Leicester, 2005. Gold Medal, RAS, 1989; Planetary Scientist of the Year, 2007; COSPAR Space Science Medal, 2008. *Publications:* many, in Monthly Notices, Nature, Astrophysical Jl, etc. *Recreations:* sport, music. *Address:* 12 Swale Close, Oadby, Leicester LE2 4GF. *T:* (0116) 271 9370.

**POUNTNEY, Sir David (Willoughby),** Kt 2019; CBE 1994; freelance director; Artistic Director, Welsh National Opera, 2011–19; *b* 10 Sept. 1947; *s* of late Dorothy and Willoughby Pountney; *m* 1st, 1980, Jane Henderson (marr. diss. 2001); one *s* one *d*; 2nd, 2007, Nicola Raab. *Educ:* St John's College Choir School, Cambridge; Radley College; St John's College, Cambridge (MA; Hon. Fellow, 2007). Joined Scottish Opera, 1970; 1st major production Katya Kabanova (Janácek), Wexford Fest., 1972; Dir of Productions, Scottish Opera, 1976–80; individual guest productions for all British Opera companies, also USA (Metropolitan Opera début, world première of The Voyage by Philip Glass, 1992), Aust., Italy, Germany, The Netherlands; Dir of Prodns, ENO, 1982–93; Intendant, Bregenzer Festspiele, 2003–14. Productions for ENO include: Rusalka (Dvorak); Osud (Janácek); Dr Faust (Busoni); Lady Macbeth of Mtsensk (Shostakovich); Wozzeck (Berg); Pelléas and Mélisande (Debussy); Don Carlos (Verdi); Falstaff (Verdi); The Adventures of Mr Broucek (Janácek); The Fairy Queen (Purcell); Nabucco (Verdi), 2000; for WNO: The Doctor of Myddfai (and libretto) (Peter Maxwell Davies), 1996; Khovanshchina, 2007, 2017; Lulu, 2013; The Cunning Little Vixen, 2013; Usher House/La chute de la maison Usher, 2014; Pelléas and Mélisande (Debussy), 2015; Figaro Gets a Divorce (and libretto), 2016; In Parenthesis, 2016; La forza del destino (Verdi), 2018; War and Peace (Prokofiev), 2018; Un ballo in maschera (Verdi), 2019; other major productions include: Julietta (Martinu), Opera North, 1997; Dalibor (Smetana), Scottish Opera, 1998; Guillaume Tell (Rossini), Vienna State Opera, 1998; Greek Passion, Bregenz, 1999, Royal Opera House, 2000; Faust (Gounod), Munich, 2000; Mr Emmet Takes a Walk (and libretto) (Peter Maxwell Davies), première, Orkney Fest., 2000; Jenufa, Vienna State Opera, 2002; Turandot, Salzburg Fest., 2002; Euryanthe, Netherlands Opera, 2003; La Juive, Zurich, 2007; Carmen, Bolshoi, Moscow, 2008; Die Soldaten, Lincoln Center Fest., NY, 2008; Paradise Moscow, Opera North, 2009; Chorus!, Houston Grand Opera, 2009; Die Frau Ohne Schatten, Zürich, 2009; The Passenger (Weinberg), world première, Bregenz Fest., 2010; Kommilitonen (Peter Maxwell Davies), world première, RAM, 2011, US première, Juilliard Sch., 2011; Portrait (Weinberg), Opera North and Nancy, 2011; Prince Igor, Zurich, 2012; (libretto) The Wasp Factory, world première, Bregenz Fest., 2013; Spuren der Verirrten (Philip Glass), world première, Linz, 2013; Die Zauberflöte (Mozart), Bregenz Fest. Seebühne, 2014; Elysium, Norske Opera, Oslo, 2016; Francesca da Rimini (Zandonai), 2018, Manon Lescaut, 2019, La Scala; Les Sept Péchés capitaux (Schönberg-Weill), Opéra National du Rhin, 2018; (libretto) Beauty and Sadness, world première, Lyric Th., Hong Kong Acad. for Performing Arts, 2019; Les Vêpres Siciliennes, Bonn, 2019. Martinu Medal, Prague, 2000. Hon. RAM 2012. Chevalier de l'Ordre des Arts et des Lettres (France), 1993; Cavalier, Order of Merit (Poland), 2013; Ehrenkreuz (Austria), 2014. *Publications:* (with Mark Elder and Peter Jonas) Power House, 1992; numerous trans. of opera, esp. Czech and Russian repertoire. *Recreations:* croquet, gardening, cooking. *Address:* Château d'Azu, 71230 St Romain sous Gourdon, France. *Club:* Garrick.

**POUYANNÉ, Patrick Jean;** Chevalier de la Légion d'Honneur, 2015; Chief Executive Officer, since 2014, and Chairman of Board, since 2015, Total SA; *b* Petit Quevilly, France, 24 June 1963; *s* of Bernard and Renée Pouyanné; *m* 1989, Anne Le Calvet; three *s* one *d*. *Educ:* École Polytechnique (Engr 1986); Corps des Mines (Chief Engr 1989). Tech. Advr to Prime Minister's office, 1993–95; COS, Telecommunication Minister, 1995–97; Chief Admin Officer, Total Angola, 1997–99; Man. Dir, Total Qatar, 1999–2002; Total SA: Senior Vice President: Finance, Exploration and Prodn, 2002–06; Strategy, Business Devel, R&D, Exploration and Prodn, 2006–11; Pres., Refining and Chemicals, 2011–14. *Recreations:* tennis, ski-ing, trips around the world. *Address:* Total SA, 2 place Jean Miller, 92078 Paris La Défense Cedex 6, France. *T:* 147443883. *E:* patrick.pouyanne@total.com.

**POVER, Alan John,** CMG 1990; HM Diplomatic Service, retired; High Commissioner to the Republic of Gambia, 1990–93; *b* 16 Dec. 1933; *s* of John Pover and Anne (*née* Hession); *m* 1964, Doreen Elizabeth Dawson; one *s* two *d*. *Educ:* Salesian College, Thornleigh, Bolton. Served HM Forces, 1953–55; Min. of Pensions and Nat. Insce, 1955–61; Commonwealth Relations Office, 1961; Second Secretary: Lagos, 1962–66; Tel Aviv, 1966–69; Second, later First, Sec., Karachi/Islamabad, 1969–73; First Sec., FCO, 1973–76; Consul, Cape Town, 1976–80; Counsellor, Diplomatic Service Inspector, 1983–86; Counsellor and Consul-Gen., Washington, 1986–90.

**POVEY, Sir Keith,** Kt 2001; QPM 1991; HM Chief Inspector of Constabulary, 2002–05; *b* 30 April 1943; *s* of late Trevor Roberts Povey and Dorothy (*née* Parsonnage); *m* 1964, Carol Ann Harvey; two *d*. *Educ:* Abbeydale Grammar Sch., Sheffield; Sheffield Univ. (BA Law). Joined Sheffield City Police, 1962; Chief Superintendent, S Yorks, seconded as Staff Officer to Sir Lawrence Byford, HMCIC, 1984–86; Asst Chief Constable, Humberside, 1986–90; Dep. Chief Constable, Northants, 1990–93; Chief Constable, Leics, 1993–97; HM Inspector of Constabulary, 1997–2001. Hon. Secretary: ACPO General Purposes Cttee, 1994–96 (Chm., 1996–97); ACPO Crime Prevention Sub-cttee, 1994–96 (Chm., 1996–97). Hon. LLD Sheffield, 2004; Hon. DCL Northumbria, 2005. *Recreations:* jogging, flying (private pilot's licence).

**POVOAS, Nigel John Spencer;** QC 2019; *b* Leicester, 23 July 1975; two *s* one *d*. *Educ:* Nottingham Trent Univ. (LLB 1st Cl. Hons 1996 (Prize for top 1st Cl.)). Called to the Bar, Lincoln's Inn, 1998; in practice as barrister, specialising in internat. law. *Recreations:* travel, art history, art, philosophy, psychology, tennis, golf, running. *Address:* 7 Bedford Row, Holborn, WC1R 4BX.

**POW, Rebecca Faye;** MP (C) Taunton Deane, since 2015; Parliamentary Under-Secretary of State, Department for Environment, Food and Rural Affairs, since 2019; *b* Somerset, 10 Oct. 1960; *m* Charles Clark; three *c*. *Educ:* Wye Coll., Univ. of London (BSc Hons Rural Envmt Studies 1982). Presenter, producer and dir, HTV, ITV West and Channel 4, 1989–2005, incl. Envmt Corresp., HTV; producer and presenter, Farming Today, BBC Radio 4; work for NFU; Dir, Pow Prodns, PR co., 1988–. PPS to Minister of State for Housing and Planning and Minister of State for London, 2016–17; PPS, DEFRA, 2017–19; Parly Under-Sec. of State, DCMS, 2019. Member: Envmtl Audit Cttee, 2015–16; Envmt Food and Rural Affairs Select Cttee, 2015–17; Digital, Cultural, Media and Sport Select Cttee, 2017–. Trustee, Somerset Wildlife Trust. *Address:* House of Commons, SW1A 0AA.

**POWELL;** *see* Baden-Powell.

**POWELL,** family name of **Baron Powell of Bayswater.**

**POWELL OF BAYSWATER, Baron** *cr* 2000 (Life Peer), of Canterbury in the County of Kent; **Charles David Powell,** KCMG 1990; Chairman, LVMH (UK), since 2000; *b* 6 July 1941; *s* of Air Vice-Marshal John Frederick Powell, OBE and Geraldine Ysolda Powell (*née* Moylan); *m* 1964, Carla Bonardi; two *s*. *Educ:* King's Sch., Canterbury; New Coll., Oxford (BA). Diplomatic Service, 1963–83: served Helsinki, Washington, Bonn, Brussels (UK Perm. Repn to EU); Counsellor, 1979; Special Counsellor for Rhodesia negotiations, 1979–80; Private Sec. and Advr on For. Affairs to the Prime Minister, 1983–91. Director: National Westminster Bank, 1991–2000; Jardine Matheson Hldgs, 1991–2000; Jardine Strategic Hldgs, 1991–2000 and 2018–; Matheson & Co., 1991–; Mandarin Oriental Hotel Gp, 1992–2018; Hong Kong Land Holdings, 1991–2000, 2008–; J. Rothschild Name Co., 1993–2003; Said Holdings, 1994–2000; LVMH Moët-Hennessy-Louis Vuitton, 1995–; British-Mediterranean Airways, 1998–2007 (Dep. Chm.); Caterpillar Inc., 2001–13; Textron Inc., 2001–16; Yell Gp, 2003–09; Schindler Holdings, 2003–13; Adv. Dir, Northern Trust Corp., 2015–; Chairman: Phillips, 1999–2001; Sagitta Asset Mgt Ltd, 2000–05; Safinvest, later Capital Generation Partners, 2006–13; Magna Hldgs Internat., 2007–13. Chairman: Internat. Adv. Bd, Rolls Royce, 2006–17 (Strategic Advr, 2017–); Adv. Bd, Bowmark, 2008–; Member: Eur. Adv. Bd, Hicks Muse Tate & Furst, 2001–05; Internat. Adv. Council, Textron Corp., 1995–2007; International Advisory Board: Barrick Gold, 2000–; Magna Corp., 2002–05; Alfa Capital Partners, 2004–10; Chubb (formerly ACE Insce), 2006–; Adv. Bd, Diligence, 2000–10; Adv. Bd, Thales UK, 2005–; Strategic Advr, BAe Systems, 2006–. Mem., Global Bd of Advrs, Council on Foreign Relns, NY, 2011–17. Vis. Prof., St Mary's Univ., Twickenham, 2019–. Chairman: Singapore British Business Council, 1994–2001; Atlantic Partnership, 2004–; Co-Chm., UK Govt Asia Task Force, 2006–14; Pres., China-Britain Business Council, 1998–2007. Mem., H of L Select Cttee on the Constitution, 2010–15, on Procedure, 2015–; Chm., All Party Parly Gp on Entrepreneurship, 2005–09; Mem., Jt Parly Cttee on Nat. Security Strategy, 2016–. Trustee: Aspen Inst., 1995–; British Mus., 2001–10; IISS, 2010–17; Chm., British Mus. Trust, 2011–; Chm., Trustees, Oxford Business Sch. Foundn, 1998–. Foundn Fellow, Somerville Coll., Oxford, 2016. Hon. Fellow, Ashmolean Mus., 2010; Hon. FKC 2017. Hon. DSc Shiv Nadar, India, 2019. Public Service Medal (Singapore), 1998. *Recreation:* walking. *Address:* House of Lords, SW1A 0PW.

*See also* Hon. H. E. Powell, Sir J. C. Powell, J. N. Powell.

**POWELL, Anthony,** RDI 1999; designer of sets and costumes for theatre and film, since 1958; *b* Manchester, 2 June 1935; *s* of Arthur Lawrence Powell and Alice Powell (*née* Woodhead). *Educ:* William Hulme's Grammar Sch., Manchester; St Andrews Coll., Dublin; Central Sch. of Arts and Crafts, London (Dip. with Dist.). Served RCS, British Army of occupation of the Rhine, 1953–55. Asst to Sir Cecil Beaton and Oliver Messel; Lectr in Th. Design, Central Sch. of Arts and Crafts, 1958–71; freelance design consultant, Sabre Sportswear and Jantzen Swimwear, 1966–69; building interior designs incl. refurbishment of Angel Hotel, Cardiff, 1950s–60s, and Sutton Place, 1981–83; art dir, photographic shoots with Earl of Snowdon for Issey Miyake, London, Tokyo, 1988–89; Agatha Christie and Archaeol. Exhibn, Essen, Vienna, Basle, Berlin and BM, London, 2001–02. Set and costume designs for: *theatre:* Women Beware Women, RSC, 1961; School for Scandal, Haymarket and NY, 1961 (Tony Award, 1963); Comedy of Errors, RSC and world tour, 1963; The Rivals, Haymarket, 1966; Fish Out of Water, Greenwich, 1971; Private Lives, Queen's, London, NY and US tour, 1972; The Confederacy and Tonight We Improvise, Chichester, 1974; Ring Round the Moon, Ahmanson Th., LA, 1975 (LA Drama Critics Circle Awards (sets and costumes)); Amadeus, Th. Marigny, Paris, 1981; Lettice and Lovage (costumes for Maggie Smith), NY, 1990; Hay Fever, Albery, and provincial tour, 1992; Trelawny of the Wells, RNT, 1992; Sunset Boulevard, Adelphi and LA, 1993, NY, 1994, Frankfurt and Toronto, 1995, Australian and US tour, 1996 (Dramalogue Critics Award, LA Drama Critics' Circle Award, 1993); Tom Sawyer (musical), NY, 2001; Anything Goes, RNT and Theatre Royal, 2002–03; Hedda Gabler, Th. Marigny, Paris, 2003; My Fair Lady, Th. du Châtelet, Paris, 2010, 2013–14, Mariinsky Th., St Petersburg, 2011–12, Chicago Opera, 2017; Singin' in the Rain, Th. du Châtelet, Paris, 2015–16, Grand Palais, Paris, 2017–18; *opera:* Rinaldo, Sadlers Wells, Komische Oper, Berlin, Dresden Opera, Halle Opera, 1960; La Belle Hélène, Il Seraglio, Sadler's Wells, 1962; Capriccio, Glyndebourne, 1963; Martins Lie (for US TV), 1965; Capriccio, Paris Opera, 2004; *films:* Royal Hunt of the Sun, 1968; Joe Egg, 1969; A Town Called Bastard, 1970; Nicholas and Alexandra, 1971; Travels with my Aunt, 1972 (Acad. Award, 1973); Papillon, 1973; That Lucky Touch, 1974; Buffalo Bill and the Indians, 1975; Sorcerer, 1976; Death on the Nile, 1977 (British Acad. Award and Acad. Award, 1979); Tess, 1979 (Acad. Award, 1981); Priest of Love, 1980; Evil Under the Sun, 1981; Indiana Jones and the Temple of Doom, 1983; Pirates, 1985 (César Award, France, 1987); Ishtar, 1986; Frantic, 1987; Indiana Jones and the Last Crusade, 1988; Hook, 1991; 101 Dalmatians (costumes for Glenn Close), 1996; The Avengers, 1997; The Ninth Gate, 1998; 102 Dalmatians, 1999; Miss Potter, 2006. RSA Scholar, 1958. Hon. FRCA 1997. Hon. Fellow, UAL, 2002. FRSA 2011. Hon. DDes Greenwich, 2003. Career Achievement Award, Costume Designers' Guild, Hollywood, 2000; Irene Sharaff Lifetime Achievement Award, Th. Develt Fund, NY, 2004; Tirelli Lifetime Achievement Award, Italy, 2007. *Recreations:* music, gardening, collecting, laughing. *Address:* c/o Michael McCoy, Independent Talent Group Ltd, 40 Whitfield Street, W1T 2RH. *T:* (020) 7636 6565; 07771 613696. *E:* michaelmccoy@independenttalent.com.

**POWELL, Sir Christopher;** *see* Powell, Sir J. C.

**POWELL, Gen. Colin Luther,** Hon. KCB 1993; Legion of Merit, Bronze Star, Air Medal, Purple Heart; Secretary of State, USA, 2001–05; Advisor, Kleiner Perkins (formerly Strategic Limited Partner, Kleiner, Perkins, Caufield & Byers), since 2005; *b* 5 April 1937; *s* of late Luther Powell and Maud Ariel Powell (*née* McKoy); *m* 1962, Alma V. Johnson; one *s* two *d*. *Educ:* City Coll. of New York (BS Geology); George Washington Univ. (MBA). Commissioned 2nd Lieut, US Army, 1958; White House Fellow, 1972–73; Comdr, 2nd

Brigade, 101st Airborne Div., 1976–77; exec. asst to Sec. of Energy, 1979; sen. mil. asst to Dep. Sec. of Defense, 1979–81; Asst Div. Comdr, 4th Inf. Div., Fort Carson, 1981–83; sen. mil. asst to Sec. of Defense, 1983–86; US V Corps, Europe, 1986–87; dep. asst to President 1987, asst 1987–89, for Nat. Security Affairs; General 1989; C-in-C, US Forces Command, Fort McPherson, April–Sept. 1989; Chm., Jt Chiefs of Staff, 1989–93. *Publications:* My American Journey (autobiog.), 1995 (UK title, A Soldier's Way); It Worked For Me: in life and leadership, 2012. *Recreations:* racquetball, restoring old Volvos. *Address:* (office) Suite 700, 909 North Washington Street, Alexandria, VA 22314, USA.

**POWELL, David Hebbert;** HM Diplomatic Service, retired; Ambassador to Norway, 2006–10; Policy Adviser, University of Kent, since 2014; *b* 29 April 1952; *s* of John Laycock Powell and Barbara Myrrha Powell (*née* Hebbert); *m* 1st, 1984, Gillian Mary Croft (marr. diss. 2010; she *d* 2010); one *d*; 2nd, 2010, Katerina Sternbergova; two *s* one *d*. *Educ:* Fitzwilliam Coll., Cambridge (BA 1974). MoD, 1974–85; FCO, 1985–88; First Sec., Tokyo, 1988–92; FCO, 1992–95; Counsellor: Cabinet Office, 1995–97; UK Delegn to NATO, 1997–2001; Asst Dir, Human Resources, FCO, 2002–06. Dir, KMTV, 2017–. Mem., London Library. *Recreations:* reading, chess, Victorian crime. *E:* david.h.powell@hotmail.com.

**POWELL, Debra Ann;** QC 2017; a Recorder, since 2018; *b* Brighton, 10 Nov. 1971; *d* of John and Barbara Powell; civil partnership 2007, Nicola Dale; one *d*. *Educ:* Brighton and Hove High Sch.; Nottingham Univ. (BA Law 1993); Inns of Court Sch. of Law (BVC 1995). Called to the Bar, Middle Temple, 1995. Jt Ed., Inquest Law Reports, 2001–11. *Publications:* (jtly) The Mental Health Act 1983 Explained, 2000, 2nd edn 2001; (contrib.) Medical Treatment: decisions and the law, 3rd edn. *Recreations:* singing, piano, ski-ing, family. *Address:* Serjeants' Inn Chambers, 85 Fleet Street, EC4Y 1AE. *T:* (020) 7427 5000. *E:* dpowellqc@serjeantsinn.com.

**POWELL, Earl Alexander, III,** PhD; Director, National Gallery of Art, Washington, 1992–2019; *b* 24 Oct. 1943; *s* of Earl Alexander Powell and Elizabeth Powell; *m* 1971, Nancy Landry; three *d*. *Educ:* A. B. Williams Coll.; Harvard Univ. (PhD 1974). A. M. Fogg Art Mus. Teaching Fellow in Fine Arts, Harvard Univ., 1970–74 (Travelling Fellowship, 1973–74); Curator, Michener Collection and Asst Prof. of Art History, Univ. of Texas at Austin, 1974–76; National Gallery of Art, Washington: Mus. Curator, Sen. Staff Asst to Asst Director and Chief Curator, 1976–78; Exec. Curator, 1979–80; Dir, LA County Mus. of Art, 1980–92. Chm., US Commn of Fine Arts, 2005–; Member: Amer. Acad. of Arts and Scis; Amer. Acad. Commn on the Humanities and Social Scis; Amer. Philos. Soc.; Cttee for Preservation of the White House; Fed. Council on Arts and Humanities; Friends of Art and Preservation in Embassies; Nat. Portrait Gall. Commn; President's Cttee on Arts and Humanities. Trustee: American Fedn of the Arts; Assoc. of Art Museum Dirs; John F. Kennedy Center for Performing Arts; Morris and Gwendolyn Cafritz Foundn; Nat. Trust for Historic Preservation; Norton Simon Mus.; White House Historical Assoc. Hon. DFA: Otis Parsons, 1987; Williams, 1993. Williams Bicentennial Medal, 1995; Centennial Medal, Harvard Grad. Sch. of Arts and Scis, 2008. King Olav Medal (Norway), 1978; Grand Official, Order of Infante D. Henrique (Portugal), 1995; Commendatore, Ordine al Merito (Italy), 1998; Chevalier, Légion d'Honneur (France), 2000; Officier, Ordre des Arts et des Lettres (France), 2004; Order of the Aztec Eagle (Mexico), 2007; Officer's Cross, Order of Merit (Hungary), 2009. *Publications:* Thomas Cole, 1990. *Clubs:* Metropolitan (Washington); Knickerbocker (New York).

**POWELL, Very Rev. Frances Elizabeth Fearn;** *see* Ward, Very Rev. F. E. F.

**POWELL, Rev. Gareth John;** Fellow, Farmington Institute, Harris Manchester College, Oxford, since 2019; *b* Neath, 10 Dec. 1970; *s* of Cyril Powell and Eirlys M. Powell; *m* 2002, Suzanne N. Thomas; two *d*. *Educ:* Westminster Coll., Oxford (BA 1992); Univ. of Birmingham (MA 1995); Queen's Coll., Birmingham. Minister, Coventry Circuit and Chaplain, Coventry Univ., 1997–99; Minister, Cardiff Circuit and Chaplain, Cardiff Univ., 1999–2009; Methodist Church of GB: President's Asst, 2009–10; Hd of Governance Support, 2010–12; Asst Sec., 2012–14, Sec., 2015–19, Methodist Conf. Ecumenical Canon, St Paul's Cathedral, 2016–. Mem. Council, Cardiff Univ., 2010–19 (Vice-Chair, 2016–19); Pro Chancellor, 2019–). Hon. Fellow: Wesley House, Cambridge, 2015–; Harris Manchester Coll., Oxford, 2019–. Trustee, Council for Christians and Jews, 2019–. *Publications:* Christian Community Now: ecclesiological investigations, 2008. *Recreations:* gardening, poetry, theatre, reading. *Address:* Methodist Church House, 25 Marylebone Road, NW1 5JR. *T:* (020) 7486 5502. *E:* gareth.powell@methodist.org.uk. *Club:* Athenæum.

**POWELL, (Geoffrey) Mark;** Chairman, Rathbone Brothers plc, 2003–11 (non-executive Chairman, 2008–11); *b* Streatham, London, 14 Jan. 1946; *s* of late Francis Turner Powell, MBE and Joan Audrey Powell (*née* Bartlett); *m* 1st, 1971, Veronica Joan Rowland (marr. diss. 2009); two *d*; 2nd, 2011, Margaret Elizabeth Victoria, (Alva), Patton (*née* Smyth). *Educ:* Tonbridge Sch.; Univ. of Durham (BA 1968). FCSI 1971. Powell Popham Dawes & Co., 1968–77, Partner, 1972–77; Laing & Cruickshank: Dir, 1977–89; Hd, Private Client Investment Mgt, 1980–86; CL-Alexanders Laing & Cruickshank Hldgs Ltd: Hd, Investment Mgt Div., 1986–87; Gp Chief Exec., 1987–89; Laurence Keen Ltd, later Rathbone Brothers plc: Chief Exec., 1989–97; Gp Man. Dir, 1995–2003; Dep. Chm., 1997–2003. Chm., SVM UK Active Fund plc, 2006–10; Dir, HgCapital Trust plc, 2010–18. Chm., Assoc. of Private Client Investment Managers and Stockbrokers, 2000–06. Mem., Takeover Panel, 2001–07 (Chm., Remuneration Cttee, 2004–07). Chm., Chichester Cathedral Restoration and Develt Trust, 2015–; Member: Investment Cttee, C of E Pensions Fund, 2007–15; Westminster Abbey Finance Adv. Cttee, 2012–. Mem. Council, REACH, 1996–2001. Trustee, Fight for Sight, 1999–2014. Chm. Govs, Haberdashers' Aske's Schs, Elstree, 2008–12 (Gov., 2001–13). Liveryman, Haberdashers' Co., 1968 (Master, 2008–09 and 2012–13). FRSA. *Recreations:* National Hunt racing, golf, theatre, opera, wine (Maître Emérite, La Commanderie de Vin de Bordeaux à Londres). *Address:* Rumbolds Farmhouse, Plaistow, W Sussex RH14 0PZ. *T:* (01403) 871514, 07774 842329. *E:* mark@gm-powell.com. *Clubs:* Boodle's, City of London, MCC; W Sussex Golf.

**POWELL, Greg;** Managing and Senior Partner, Powell Spencer & Partners Solicitors, since 1977; *b* London, 21 Jan. 1948; *s* of Victor Harold and Barbara Powell. *Educ:* London Sch. of Econs and Pol Sci. (LLB); Birkbeck Coll., Univ. of London (BSc). Admitted Solicitor, 1973. Pres., London Criminal Courts Solicitors' Assoc., 2007. Criminal Aid Lawyer of Year, 2004. *Publications:* (jtly) A Practical Guide to the Police and Criminal Evidence Act, 1984; In Love's Shawl (poetry), 2014. *Recreation:* gardening. *Address:* Powell Spencer & Partners Solicitors, 270 Kilburn High Road, NW6 2BY. *T:* (020) 7604 5600, *Fax:* (020) 7328 1221. *E:* gregpowell@psplaw.co.uk.

**POWELL, Hope Patricia,** CBE 2010 (OBE 2002); coach education instructor, since 2013; Consultant, FIFA, since 2013; UEFA Technical Observer, since 2013; Regional Coach Educator, Professional Football Association, since 2016; Manager, Brighton and Hove Albion Women's Football Club, since 2017; *b* London; *d* of Vernon Powell and Lynn Francis; partner, 1994, Michelle Pryce. *Educ:* Abbeywood Sch.; West London Inst. of Higher Educn. Football player: Millwall Lionesses, 1978–86, 1988–90; Friends of Fulham,

1986–88; Bromley, 1990–92; Croydon, 1992–98; 66 caps for England (35 goals; Vice Capt.). Football Develt Officer, Crystal Palace FC, 1993–96; Team Leader, Prince's Trust, 1996–98; Football Develt Officer, Lewisham LBC, 1998; Nat. Coach, England Women's Football, 1998–2013. Hon. LLD Roehampton, 2011; Hon. DA E London, 2012; DUniv Loughborough, 2009; Hon. MSc: Leeds Metropolitan, 2008; St Mark and St John, Plymouth, 2014; Hon. MA Nottingham, 2012. *Recreations:* family, friends, theatre, reading, walking, photography.

**POWELL, Hon. Hugh Eric,** CMG 2010; HM Diplomatic Service; Division Director, Geopolitical Risk, Macquarie Bank, 2015–19; *b* 16 Feb. 1967; *s* of Baron Powell of Bayswater, *qv*; *m* 1993, Catherine Young; three *s*. *Educ:* Eton; Balliol Coll., Oxford (BA Hons 1988); Kennedy Sch. of Govt, Harvard (MPA 1990). Audit Commn, 1990–91; joined FCO, 1991; Second Sec., Paris, 1993–97; FCO, 1997–2000; First Sec., Berlin, 2000–03; Dir, Policy on Internat. Orgns, MoD, 2004; Hd, Security Policy Gp, FCO, 2005–08; UK Senior Rep. in Southern Afghanistan, 2008–09; Dir, 2010–13, Dep. Nat. Security Advr, 2013–14, Nat. Security Secretariat, Cabinet Office. *Recreation:* Left Back. *Address:* 24855 Brown Latigo, Malibu, CA 90265, USA. *E:* cathandhughpowell@gmail.com.

**POWELL, Sir Ian (Clifford),** Kt 2017; Chairman: Capita plc, since 2017; Police Now, since 2016; *b* Coseley, W Midlands, 16 March 1956; *s* of Clifford Powell and Jean Powell; *m* 1977, June Morris; two *s* two *d*. *Educ:* High Arcal Grammar Sch., Sedgley; Wolverhampton Poly. (BA Hons Econ. 1977). FCA 1981. Price Waterhouse, later PricewaterhouseCoopers: Assurance, 1977–86; Business Recovery Services, 1986–2006; Partner, 1991; Member: UK Mgt Bd, 2006–08; Internat. Bd, 2008–16; Chm. and Sen. Partner, 2008–16. Member: World Business Council for Sustainable Develt, 2009; Adv. Council, City UK, 2010–16; Bd, London First, 2018–. Mem., Develt Cttee, Nat. Gall., 2013–; Mem., Bd of Trustees, Old Vic Th., 2016–; Trustee, Wellbeing of Women, 2016–. Hon. DBA Wolverhampton, 2010. Freedom, City of London, 2010; Mem., Co. of Chartered Accountants in England and Wales, 2010. *Recreations:* music, motor sport, football. *Address:* Capita plc, 30 Berners Street, W1T 3LR.

**POWELL, Prof. James Alfred,** OBE 1996; PhD, DSc; CEng; Eur Ing; FIOA, FCIOB, FASI; Professor of Academic Enterprise, Salford University, 2001–10, now Emeritus (Pro Vice Chancellor for Enterprise and Regional Affairs, 2001–10); Academic Director, PASCAL Universities for Modern Renaissance, since 2010; *b* Sutton, 30 Oct. 1945; *s* of James Herbert Powell and Eileen Powell (*née* Newell); *m* 1969, Jennifer Elizabeth Morton; one *s*. *Educ:* De Burgh Sch., Tadworth; UMIST (BSc, MSc; AUMIST); Salford Univ. (PhD 1984; DSc 2000). FIOA 1984; CEng 1996; FASI 1999. ICI Schol., Salford Univ., 1970–71; Lectr, then Sen. Res. Associate, Sch. of Architecture, Dundee Univ., 1971–74; School of Architecture, Portsmouth Polytechnic: Reader in Building Utilisation, 1975–84; Prof. of Design Studies, 1984–91; Hd of Dept, 1990–91; Dep. Dean of Technol., Hd of Dept of Engrg and Mfg Systems and Lucas Prof. of Design Systems, Brunel Univ., 1991–94; Lucas Prof. of Informing Design Technol., 1994–2001, Dir of Acad. Enterprise, 1999–2001, Salford Univ. Hon. Prof., Sch. of Educn, Glasgow Univ., 2011–. Science and Engineering Research Council: IT Applications Co-ordinator, 1988–93; Mem., Engrg Bd, 1988–93; Chm., Educn and Trng Cttee, 1988–93; IT Awareness in Engrg Co-ordinator, EPSRC, 1994. Mem., Learning Foresight Panel, OST, 1996–. Internat. Speaker, Nat. IT Council of Malaysia, 1998–. Sen. Advr, Aalto Camp for Societal Innovation, 2009–. UK Ambassador, Leonardo European Corporate Learning Awards, 2009–; UK Ambassador of Social Entrepreneurship in HE, 2010–. Designer, Menuhin Auditorium for Portsmouth String Quartet Fest., 1980. FRSA; FIMgt; MInstD. Mem., New Club, Paris, 2010–. DUniv Salford, 2016. Taylor Woodrow Prize, 1967; British Interactive Multi Media Award, 1978; European Multi Media Award, 1979; Artificial Intelligence in Learning Award, 1983; Award for Interactive Audio in Multi Media, European Multi Media Assoc., 1992; Queen's Award for Higher and Further Education, 1999; Shell LIVEWire North West Enterprise Award, 2001; North West Excellence Award for Innovative Excellence, 2002. *Publications:* Design: Science: Methods, 1981; Changing Design, 1982; Designing for Building Utilisation, 1984; Noise at Work Regulations, 1990, 2nd edn 1994; Intelligent Command and Control Acquisition and Review using Simulation, 1992; The Powell Report: review of SERC engineering education and training, 1993; Informing Technologies for Construction, Civil Engineering and Transport, 1993; Neural Computing, 1994; Engineering Decision Support, 1995; Virtual Reality and Rapid Prototyping, 1995; (jtly) Universities for a Modern Renaissance, 2009; Smart City Futures, 2009; (contrib.) Handbook of Engaged Scholarship: contemporary landscapes, future directions, vol. 1: institutional change, 2010; (contrib.) Building Prosperous Knowledge Cities: policies, plans and metrics, 2012; (contrib.) European Higher Education at a Crossroads, 2012. *Recreations:* meditation, Tai Chi, cycling, squash, yoga, boating, painting. *Address:* UPBEAT, 127 Hale Road, Hale, Lancs WA15 9HQ.

**POWELL, Sir James Richard Douglas,** 5th Bt *cr* 1897; *b* 17 Oct. 1962; *s* of Sir Nicholas Folliott Douglas Powell, 4th Bt and of Daphne Jean Powell (*née* Errington); S father, 2019; *m* 1st, 1991, Susanna (marr. diss. 2013); *e d* of David Murray Threipland; two *s* one *d*; 2nd, 2014, Elizabeth Anne Primrose, *e d* of Harrison Hartley Deacon. *Heir: s* Douglas James Folliott Powell, *b* 22 Oct. 1992.

**POWELL, Prof. Janet Tinka,** PhD, MD; FRCPath; Professor of Vascular Medicine, University of Warwick, 2000–04; Medical Director, University Hospitals of Coventry and Warwickshire NHS Trust, 2000–04; Professor (part time), running clinical trials in vascular surgery and medicine, Imperial College, London, since 2004; *b* 1 Aug. 1945; *d* of Reginald Y. Powell and Mina Powell; partner, Douglas W. Ribbons (*d* 2002); one *s* one *d*. *Educ:* Lady Margaret Hall, Oxford (BA); King's Coll. London (PhD 1972); Univ. of Miami (MD 1981). FRCPath 2001. Asst Prof. of Medicine (Pulmonary), Univ. of Miami Sch. of Medicine, 1978–79; Hse Surgeon, Ysbyty Glan Clwyd, 1982; Hse Physician, Bristol Royal Infirmary, 1982–83; SHO in Dermatol., Geriatrics and Medicine, St David's Hosp., Bangor, 1983; Charing Cross and Westminster Medical School: Lectr in Biochem. and Surgery, 1983–89; Sen. Lectr, 1989–91; Reader in Cardiovascular Biol., 1991–94; Prof. of Vascular Biol., 1994–97; Registrar in Chem. Pathol., Charing Cross Hosp., 1985–87; Imperial College School of Medicine: Chm., Vascular Scis and Diseases Gp, 1997–2000; Dean, 2000. Vis. Prof., ICSTM, subseq. Res. Prof., Imperial Coll. London, 2001–04. Member: BMA, 1982; British Matrix Biol. Soc., 1984; Biochem. Soc., 1985; Vascular Surgical Soc., 1990; Surgical Res. Soc., 1990; British Atherosclerosis Soc., 1999. Member: Amer. Soc. Biochem. & Molecular Biol., 1975; Eur. Soc. for Vascular Surgery, 1992. Ed., Eur. Jl of Vascular and Endovascular Surgery, 2004–; Associate Ed., Arteriosclerosis Thrombosis and Vascular Biol., 2012–. Lifetime Achievement Award, Vascular Soc. of GB and Ireland, 2012. *Publications:* numerous contribs to learned jls incl. New England Jl of Medicine, Lancet, BMJ and Nature. *Recreations:* hiking, cycling, theatre, film. *Address:* 8 The Square, Long Itchington, Warwickshire CV47 9PE. *E:* Jtp700@aol.com.

**POWELL, Sir (John) Christopher,** Kt 2009; Chairman, Advertising Standards Board of Finance, since 2010; *b* 4 Oct. 1943; *s* of Air Vice-Marshal John Frederick Powell, OBE and Geraldine Ysolda Powell (*née* Moylan); *m* 1973, Rosemary Jeanne Symmons; two *s* one *d*. *Educ:* St Peter's Sch., York; London Sch. of Econs (BSc Econ.). Worked in advertising agencies, in London, 1965–69; BMP, subseq. BMP DDB: Partner, 1969–82; Jt Man. Dir,

1975–85; Chief Exec., 1986–98; Chm., 1999–2003. Non-executive Director: Riverside Studios, 1989–2017 (Chm., 2010–17); United Business Media (formerly United News & Media) plc, 1995–2006; Dr Foster LLP, 2006–15 (Chm., 2009–15); Member: Adv. Bd (formerly Corporate Finance Adv. Panel), PricewaterhouseCoopers, 2005–16; Adv. Bd, Portland PR, 2009–; Chm., Parcel Genie, 2010–15. Dep. Chm., Riverside Community NHS Trust, 1994–2000; Chm., Ealing, Hammersmith & Hounslow HA, 2000–02. Chairman: British Council Creative Industries Adv. Panel, 2002–08; NESTA, 2003–09; Advertising Bd, Royal Mail, 2013–18; Dep. Chm., Public Diplomacy Bd, 2006–09; Mem. Bd, Britain in Europe, 2005–. Pres., Inst. Practitioners in Advertising, 1993–95. Trustee: IPPR, 1999– (Chm., 2001–08); Alzheimer's Soc., 2012–18. *Recreations:* tennis, gardening, theatre. *Address:* DDBLondon Ltd, 12 Bishop's Bridge Road, W2 6AA. *T:* (020) 7258 3979.

*See also Baron Powell of Bayswater, J. N. Powell.*

**POWELL, John Lewis;** QC 1990; a Recorder, 2000; a Deputy High Court Judge; *b* 14 Sept. 1950; *s* of Gwyn Powell and Lilian Mary Powell (*née* Griffiths); *m* 1973, Eva Zofia Lomnicka; one *s* two *d. Educ:* Christ Coll., Brecon; Amman Valley Grammar Sch.; Trinity Hall, Cambridge (MA, LLB). Called to the Bar, Middle Temple, 1974 (Harmsworth Schol.), Bencher 1998. Pres., Soc. of Construction Law, 1991–93; Member: Bar Council, 1997–2004 (Chm., Law Reform Cttee, 1997–98). Contested (Lab) Cardigan, 1979. *Publications:* (with R. Jackson, QC) Professional Negligence, 1982, 8th edn; (with Eva Lomnicka) Encyclopedia of Financial Services Law, 1987; Palmer's Company Law, 24th edn 1987, 25th edn 1992; Issues and Offers of Company Securities: the new regimes, 1988; various articles. *Recreation:* travel.

**POWELL, (John) Mark (Heywood);** QC 2006; a Recorder, since 1997; a Deputy High Court Judge, since 2008; a Judge of the First-tier Tribunal, and a President, Mental Health Review Tribunal for Wales, since 2012 (Deputy Chairman, since 2015); *b* 18 July 1952; *s* of John Harford Powell, OBE, MC, and Lucinda Joan Eve Powell; *m* 1998, Carole Mary Symons-Jones (marr. diss. 2016); two *s* one *d. Educ:* Rugby Sch.; University Coll. London (BA Hons Hist. 1974). Solicitor, then Partner, Hugh James, solicitors, 1977–; barrister and solicitor, High Court of NZ, 1990–; HM Coroner, Monmouthshire, 1983–. Chancellor: Dio. of Birmingham, 2012–; Dio. of Monmouth, 2015–. Chm., Assoc. of Lawyers for Children, 1999–2001. Mem. Gov. Body and Dep. Chm., Disciplinary Cttee, Ch of Wales, 2015–. Trustee: Triangle Trust, 2000–15; Tros Gynnal, 2005–14. *Recreations:* French history and French living, watching Ebbw Vale play Rugby. *E:* jmhp@hotmail.co.uk. *Clubs:* MCC; Dale Yacht; Ebbw Vale Rugby Football (Pres., 2002–); Club Athletic (Riberac).

**POWELL, Jonathan Charles Boyd;** JP; Bursar and Clerk to the Governors, St Augustine's Priory, Ealing, since 2017; *b* 21 Jan. 1960; *s* of late Jeremy Boyd Powell and of Evangeline Anne Powell (*née* Simons); *m* 1993, Sarah Rhiannon Morgan; one *s* one *d. Educ:* Wellington Coll.; Southampton Univ. (BA Hons French and German); Thames Valley Univ. (Grad. Dip. in Law). RN, 1983–89. RBL, 1990–2001 (Hd, Ops and Develt, 1997–2001); Chief Executive: IndependentAge, RUKBA, 2001–06; Vitalise, 2007–09; Queen Elizabeth's Foundn for Disabled People, 2010–16. Director: Crossways Trust Ltd, 2002–06; IndependentAge Enterprises Ltd, 2003–06; Careways Ltd, 2007–09; Vitalise Enterprises Ltd, 2007–09; Surrey Care Assoc., 2010–16 (Vice Chm., 2013–16). JP Ealing, 1995. *Address:* 22 Albany Road, W13 8PG. *E:* jpowell@sapriory.com.

**POWELL, Prof. Jonathan Leslie;** Professor of Media, Royal Holloway, University of London, since 2007; *b* 25 April 1947; *s* of James Dawson Powell and Phyllis Nora Sylvester (*née* Doubleday); *m* 1990, Sally Jane Brampton (marr. diss. 2007; she *d* 2016); one *d. Educ:* Sherborne; University of East Anglia. BA Hons (English and American Studies). Script editor and producer of drama, Granada TV, 1970–77; BBC TV: Producer, drama serials, 1977–83; Hd of Drama Series and Serials, 1983–87; Hd of Drama, 1987; Controller, BBC1, 1988–92; Dir of Drama and Co-prodn, Carlton TV, 1993–2007. *TV serials include:* Testament of Youth, 1979 (BAFTA award); Tinker Tailor Soldier Spy, 1979; Pride and Prejudice, 1980; Thérèse Raquin, 1980; The Bell, 1982; Smiley's People, 1982 (Peabody Medal, USA); The Old Men at the Zoo, 1983; Bleak House, 1985; Tender is the Night, 1985; A Perfect Spy, 1987. Royal Television Soc. Silver Award for outstanding achievement, 1979–80. *Address:* 1 First Avenue, W3 7JP.

**POWELL, Jonathan Nicholas;** Founder and Director, Inter Mediate, since 2011; *b* 14 Aug. 1956; *s* of Air Vice-Marshal John Frederick Powell, OBE and Geraldine Ysolda Powell (*née* Moylan); *m* 1st, 1980, Karen Elizabeth Drayne (marr. diss. 1997); two *s*; 2nd, 2007, Sarah Helm; two *d. Educ:* University Coll., Oxford (MA Hist.); Univ. of Pennsylvania (MA Hist.). With BBC, 1978; Granada TV, 1978–79; joined FCO, 1979; Lisbon, 1980–83; FCO, 1983–85; Member, British Delegation to: CDE, Stockholm, 1985; CSCE, Vienna, 1985–89; FCO, 1989–91; Washington, 1991–95; COS to Leader of the Opposition, 1995–97, to the Prime Minister, 1997–2007. Prime Minister's Envoy to Libya, 2014–16. Senior Adviser: Centre for Humanitarian Dialogue, Geneva, 2008–11; Save the Children, 2008–; Morgan Stanley, 2008–11; Electrum Gp (UK) LLP (formerly Tigris Financial), 2009–11. *Publications:* Great Hatred, Little Room, 2008; The New Machiavelli: how to wield power in the modern world, 2010; Talking to Terrorists: how to end armed conflicts, 2014. *Recreations:* sailing, tennis.

*See also Baron Powell of Bayswater, Sir J. C. Powell.*

**POWELL, Kenneth George;** architectural critic, consultant and journalist; Consultant Director, Twentieth Century Society, 1995–2002; *b* 17 March 1947; *s* of Alan Powell and Winifred Alice Powell (*née* Hill); *m* 1969, Susan Harris-Smith. *Educ:* Canton High Sch. for Boys, Cardiff; London Sch. of Econs (BA 1968); Univ. of Manchester (MA Arch 1979). Research Assistant: Inst. of Historical Res., London, 1971–74; History of Univ. of Oxford, 1974–77; Temp. Lectr in Hist., UCL, 1977–78; worked in museums and as freelance researcher, 1978–84; Sec., SAVE Britain's Heritage, 1984–87; Architectural Corresp., Daily Telegraph, 1987–94; freelance writer. Member: Art and Architecture Cttee, Westminster Cathedral, 1994–2003; London DAC, 1996–2007, 2011–; Historic Churches Cttee, Dio. of Leeds, 1996–2016; Fabric Cttee, Guildford Cathedral, 2006–12; Hon. Sec., Architectural Assoc., 2006–07 (Mem. Council, 2002–12). Hon. FRIBA 2000. *Publications:* Stansted: Norman Foster and the architecture of flight, 1991; Vauxhall Cross, 1992; (with R. Moore) Structures, Space and Skin, 1993; World Cities: London, 1993; Richard Rogers, 1994; Edward Cullinan Architects, 1995; Grand Central Terminal, 1996; Richard Rogers: complete works (I), 1999, (II), 2001, (III), 2006; Architecture Transformed, 1999; Jubilee Line Architecture, 2000; The City Transformed, 2000; (jtly) The National Portrait Gallery: an architectural history, 2000; New London Architecture, 2001, 2nd edn (with Cathy Strongman) as New London Architecture 2, 2007; The Modern House Today, 2001; Will Alsop: book 1, 2001, book 2, 2002; New Architecture in Britain, 2003; KPF: process and vision, 2003; Nottingham Transformed, 2006; 30 St Mary Axe: a tower for London, 2006; (with P. Barclay) Wembley Stadium: venue of legends, 2007; Powell and Moya: twentieth century architects, 2009; 21st Century London: the new architecture, 2011; (with N. Foster) Sainsbury Centre for the Visual Arts, 2011; (ed) Great Builders, 2011; Ahrends, Burton and Koralek: twentieth century architects, 2012; Wills Building: Foster + Partners, 2012; (ed) the Great Builders, 2012; London Buildings: David Walker Architects, 2014; (jtly) The Architecture of Jacques Ferrier, 2016; Arup Associates: twentieth century architects, 2018; Tower Bridge: a history, 2018; contrib. many articles in Country Life, Architects Jl, etc. *Recreations:* architecture, food, wine and places, preferably Mediterranean or Celtic, music, book collecting. *Address:* Flat 1, 78 Nightingale Lane, SW12 8NR. *T:* (020) 8673 3383.

**POWELL, Prof. Kenneth Leslie,** PhD; Chairman, ReViral Ltd, since 2012; Hon. Professor, University College London, since 2000; *b* 23 July 1949; *s* of Alec and Ada Powell; *m* 1st, 1968, Anne (marr. diss. 1974); 2nd, 1975, Dorothy J. M. Purifoy (*d* 2015); two *d*, and one step *s* one step *d. Educ:* Apsley Grammar Sch.; Univ. of Reading (BSc Microbiology 1970); Univ. of Birmingham (PhD 1973). Post-doctoral Fellow, 1973–75, Asst Prof., 1975–77, Baylor Coll. of Medicine, Houston; Lectr, 1978–85, Sen. Lectr, 1985–86, Univ. of Leeds; Wellcome Foundation: Head of: Biochemical Virology, 1986–88; Antiviral Res., 1988–90; Cell Biology, 1990–93; Biology, 1993–95; Dep. Dir, Cruciform Project, subseq. Wolfson Inst. for Biomed. Res., and Prof., UCL, 1995–2000. Vis. Prof., Univ. of Michigan, 1985. CEO, Inpharmatica Ltd, 1998–2000; Chief Exec., 1998–2007, Head, 2007–08, Arrow Therapeutics; Chairman: ITS Ltd, 2009–11; Pharmidex Ltd, 2009–11; Theolytics Ltd, 2018–; Exec. Chm., Q-Chip Ltd, later Midatech Plc, 2009–14. *Publications:* more than 50 articles in learned jls. *Address:* 12 Kepplestone Mews, Beckenham, Kent BR3 6AX.

**POWELL, Prof. Lawrie William,** AC 1990; MD, PhD; FRACP, FRCP; Professor of Medicine, University of Queensland, 1975, now Emeritus; Director of Research (formerly Research Co-ordinator), Royal Brisbane and Women's Hospital, since 2000; *s* of Victor Alexander Powell and Ellen Evelyn (*née* Davidson); *m* 1958, Margaret Emily Ingram; two *s* three *d. Educ:* Univ. of Queensland (MB BS 1958; MD 1965; PhD 1973); Univ. of London; Harvard Medical Sch. FRACP 1975; FRCP 1991. Dir, Qld Inst. of Med. Res., 1990–2000. Hon. Lectr, Royal Free Hosp. and Univ. of London, 1963–65; Vis. Prof., Harvard Medical Sch., 1972–73. Mem. Bd, Australian Stem Cell Centre, 2007–08. FTSE 1995–2008. Hon. FRCP Thailand, 1997. DUniv Griffith, 1996. *Publications:* Metals and the Liver, 1978; Fundamentals of Gastroenterology, 1975, 6th edn 1995; over 400 articles on liver disease and iron metabolism. *Recreations:* music, reading, chess, bushwalking. *Address:* Royal Brisbane and Women's Hospital, Brisbane, Qld 4029, Australia.

**POWELL, Lucy Maria;** MP (Lab Co-op) Manchester Central, since Nov. 2012; *b* Manchester, 10 Oct. 1974; *d* of John Lloyd Powell and Mary Powell; *m* 2009, James Williamson; one *s* one *d* and one step *s. Educ:* Parrs Wood High Sch.; Somerville Coll., Oxford; King's Coll. London (BSc Chem.). Parly asst to Glenda Jackson, MP, 1997–98, to Beverley Hughes, MP, 1998–99; PR rôle, later Hd, Regl Campaigning, then Campaign Dir, Britain in Europe, 1999–2005; Gov. relns, 2006–07, Leadership, Manchester Innovation Fund project, 2007–10, NESTA; Manager, Labour Party leadership campaign for Rt Hon. Edward Miliband, 2010; Actg COS, then Dep. COS to Leader of Opposition, 2010–12; Shadow Minister for Childcare and Children, 2013–14, for Cabinet Office, 2014–15; Shadow Sec. of State for Educn, 2015–16. Member: Transport Select Cttee, 2012–13; Educn Select Cttee, 2017–. *Address:* House of Commons, SW1A 0AA.

**POWELL, Mark;** *see* Powell, G. M.

**POWELL, Mark;** *see* Powell, J. M. H.

**POWELL, Nikolas Mark,** OBE 2018; Director, National Film and Television School, 2003–17; *b* 4 Nov. 1950; *s* of A. B. Powell and Jane Powell (*née* Weir); one *s* one *d. Educ:* Ampleforth Coll. Co-founder and Dir, Virgin Records, 1967–81; Co-Chm., Palace Gp of Cos Ltd, 1982–91; Chm., Scala Prodns Ltd, 1991–. Chm., 1995–2003, Vice Chm., 2004–16, European Film Acad. Board Director: Film Consortium, 1996–2003; Northern Irish Film and TV Commn, 2001–07. Mem., Bd of Trustees, 2007–, Chm., Film Cttee, BAFTA, 2009–15. *Clubs:* Soho House; European Producers (Mem. Bd, 2017–).

**POWELL, Peter James Barnard;** Vice-Chairman, James Grant Group, 2009–14 (Co-Founder and Executive Chairman, James Grant Management Ltd, 1984–2009); *b* Stourbridge, 24 March 1951; *s* of James and Margaret Powell. *Educ:* Uppingham. Radio disc jockey: launched first show on BBC Radio Birmingham, 1970; Radio 1, 1972; Radio Luxembourg, 1972–77; Radio 1, 1977–88; TV presenter: Top of the Pops, Montreux Rock Fest. (annually), Saturday Night Seaside Special, Oxford Roadshow, 1977–88. Dir, Formation Gp plc, 2008–09. Mem., RYA. *Recreations:* sailing, world travel, politics, music. *Clubs:* Royal Automobile; Royal Ocean Racing.

**POWELL, Richard Stephen;** HM Diplomatic Service, retired; Deputy High Commissioner, Lagos, 2007–10; *b* 19 Oct. 1959; *s* of late David Ronald and Audrey Grace Powell. *Educ:* Pwll Co. Primary Sch.; Llanelli Grammar Sch.; Emmanuel Coll., Cambridge (BA Natural Scis 1981); Imperial Coll., London (MBA 1997). Entered HM Diplomatic Service, 1981; FCO, 1981–82; Attaché, UK Mission to UN, NY, 1982; Third, later Second, Sec., Helsinki, 1983–88; FCO, 1988–92; First Secretary: Tokyo, 1992–96; FCO, 1997–2003; Dep. Hd of Mission, Helsinki, 2003–07; Dep. High Comr, Accra, 2007. *Publications:* (trans.) Against All Odds, by Jorma Ollila and Harri Saukkomaa, 2016. *Recreations:* pottering, pubs. *E:* Richard.Pwll@yahoo.co.uk.

**POWELL, Dame Sally (Ann Vickers),** DBE 2001; consultant private client solicitor, since 2008; *b* 2 Oct. 1955; *d* of Alan Vickers Powell and Ena Esther Powell (*née* Crewe); *m* 1996, Iain Coleman, *qv*; one *s. Educ:* Royal Ballet Sch.; Univ. of Southampton (LLB 1984); Coll. of Law (Law Soc. Finals). Sadler's Wells Royal Ballet, 1974–80; joined Lewis Silkin, Solicitors, 1985; with Glazer Delmar, Solicitors, until 1997. Mem. (Lab) Hammersmith and Fulham London BC, 1986–2014 (formerly Cabinet Mem. for Regeneration). Dep. Leader, Assoc. of London Govt; Chm., Gtr London Enterprise; Dep. Chm., Business Link for London; Mem. Bd, London Develt Agency, Dep. Leader, Labour Gp, LGA. Mem. Bd, W London Mental Health Trust, 2008–11. *Recreations:* theatre, opera, football.

**POWELL, Sandy,** OBE 2011; RDI 2013; costume designer for film and theatre; *b* London, 7 April 1960; *d* of Sydney and Maureen Powell. *Educ:* Sydenham High Sch. for Girls; St Martin's Sch. of Art; Central Sch. of Art. Costume design for films including: Caravaggio, 1986; The Last of England, Stormy Monday, For Queen and Country, 1988; Venus Peter, 1989; Shadow of China, Killing Dad or How to Love Your Mother, 1990; The Miracle, The Pope Must Die, Edward II, 1991; Orlando, The Crying Game, 1992; Wittgenstein, 1993; Being Human, Interview with the Vampire: The Vampire Chronicles, 1994; Rob Roy, 1995; Michael Collins, 1996; The Butcher Boy, The Wings of the Dove, 1997; Velvet Goldmine (BAFTA Award, 1998), Hilary and Jackie, Shakespeare in Love (Acad. Award, 1999), 1998; Felicia's Journey, Miss Julie, The End of the Affair, 1999; Far from Heaven, Gangs of New York, 2002; Sylvia, 2003; The Aviator, 2004 (Acad. Award, 2005); Mrs Henderson Presents, 2005; The Departed, 2006; The Other Boleyn Girl, 2008; The Young Victoria, 2009 (BAFTA Award, 2009, Acad. Award, 2010); Shutter Island, 2010; The Tempest, Hugo, 2011; The Wolf of Wall Street, 2014; Cinderella, Carol, 2015; Wonderstruck, How to Talk to Girls at Parties, 2017; Mary Poppins Returns, 2018; The Favourite, 2018 (BAFTA Award, 2019). *Address:* c/o Independent Talent Group, 40 Whitfield Street, W1T 2RH. *T:* (020) 7636 6565.

**POWELL, William Rhys;** barrister, arbitrator; *b* 3 Aug. 1948; *s* of late Rev. Canon Edward Powell and Anne Powell; *m* 1973, Elizabeth Vaudin; three *d. Educ:* Lancing College; Emmanuel College, Cambridge (BA 1970; MA 1973); DipArb Reading Univ. 2000. FCIArb 2001. Called to the Bar, Lincoln's Inn, 1971. MP (C) Corby, 1983–97; contested (C) same seat, 1997. PPS to Minister for Overseas Develt, 1985–86, to Sec. of State for the Envmt, 1990–92. Member, Select Committee: on Procedure, 1987–90; on Foreign Affairs, 1990–91; on Sci. and Technol., 1992–95; on Agriculture, 1995–97; Mem., Jt Parly Ecclesiastical Cttee, 1987–97; Joint Secretary: Cons. Back-bench For. Affairs Cttee, 1985 and 1987–90; Cons. Back-bench Defence Cttee, 1988–90; Chairman: All-Party Parly Gp for the Gulf, 1993–97; British-Italian Parly Gp, 1992–96; British-Taiwan Parly Gp, 1992–97; British-Mongolia Parly Gp, 1993–97; British-Tunisia Parly Gp, 1995–97. Jt Chm., CAABU, 1992–95; Mem. Council, British Atlantic Cttee, 1985–90. Fellow, Industry and Parlt Trust, 1991. As Private Mem. piloted Copyright (Computer Software) Amendment Act, 1985. Vis. Scholar, Academia Sinaca, Taiwan, 1999. *Address:* Regency Chambers, Archdeaconry House, 15 Gravel Walk, Minster Precincts, Peterborough PE1 1YU. *Clubs:* Dinosaurs; Corby Conservative.

**POWELL-SMITH, Christopher Brian,** TD 1985; Chairman, Black & Decker Group Inc., 1995–2012 (Director, 1980–2012); *b* 3 Oct. 1936; *s* of Edgar and Theodora Powell-Smith; *m* 1964, Jennifer Goslett; two *s* two *d. Educ:* City of London Sch. Asst Solicitor, McKenna & Co., 1959; Nat. Service, 4th Regt, RHA, 1959–61; McKenna & Co.: Partner, 1964–97; Finance Partner, 1975–84; Managing Partner, 1984–87; Head, Corporate Dept, 1987–92; Sen. Partner, 1992–97; Partner, Cameron McKenna, 1997–99. Non-exec. Chm., KBC Advanced Technology plc, 2004–08 (Dir, 1997–2008); non-exec. Dir, MPG Gp Ltd, 1998–2006. Chm., Richmond Parish Lands Charity, 2000–05. CO and Regimental Col, HAC, 1975–79. *Recreations:* golf, choral singing. *Address:* 23 Clarence Road, Kew, Richmond, Surrey TW9 3NL. *T:* (020) 8940 3949. *E:* chrispowellsmith@gmail.com. *Club:* Royal Mid-Surrey Golf.

**POWER, Sir Alastair John Cecil,** 4th Bt *cr* 1924, of Newlands Manor; *b* 15 Aug. 1958; *s* of Sir John Patrick McLannahan Power, 3rd Bt and of Melanie, *d* of Hon. Alastair Erskine; *S* father, 1984; *m* 1981, Virginia Newton; one *s* two *d. Heir: s* Mark Alastair John Power, *b* 15 Oct. 1989.

**POWER, Prof. Anne Elizabeth,** CBE 2000 (MBE 1983); PhD; Professor of Social Policy, since 1997, and Director, LSE Housing and Communities (formerly Postgraduate MSc/ Diploma in Housing), since 1987, London School of Economics. *Educ:* Univ. of Manchester (BA Mod. Langs); London Sch. of Econs (Dip. Social Admin 1964); Univ. of Wisconsin (MA Sociol. 1966); PhD London 1985. Teacher, Tanzania, 1963–64; with Martin Luther King's End Slums Campaign, Chicago, 1966; Warden, Africa Centre, London, 1966–67; Co-ordinator: Friends Neighbourhood House, Islington, 1967–72; N Islington Housing Rights Project, 1972–79; Nat. Consultant, Priority Estates Project, DoE, 1979–89; Advr, Welsh Office and Rhondda BC, 1989–93. Co-ordinator and Res. Dir, prog. with Brookings Instn on Weak Mkt Cities, funded by Joseph Rowntree Foundn and DCLG, 2005–10. Vis. Res. Associate, Dept of Social Policy, LSE, 1981–88. Founding Dir, Nat. Communities (formerly Tenants') Resource Centre, 1991– (Chm., 2010–); Dep. Dir, Centre for Analysis of Social Exclusion, 1997–2009. Adv. Mem., Panel of Experts to EC on urban problems; Member: Govt Sounding Bds, Housing, 1997, Urban, 2000; Urban Task Force, 1998; Sustainable Develt Commn, 2000–09; Expert Adv. Panel, Troubled Families Prog., 2012–. Hon. FRIBA 2002. *Publications:* Property Before People: the management of Twentieth Century council housing, 1987; Housing Management: a guide to quality and creativity, 1991; Hovels to High-rise, 1993; (with R. Tunstall) Swimming Against the Tide, 1995; (with R. Tunstall) Dangerous Disorder, 1997; Estates on the Edge, 1997; (with K. Mumford) The Slow Death of Great Cities?, 1999; (with R. Rogers) Cities for a Small Country, 2000; (with K. Mumford) East Enders: family and community in East London, 2003; (with K. Mumford) Boom or Abandonment, 2003; Census Briefs: (with R. Lupton) Minority Ethnic Groups in Britain, 2004; (with R. Lupton) The Growth and Decline of Cities and Regions, 2005; (with J. Houghton) Jigsaw City, 2007; City Survivors, 2007; (jtly) the Built Environment and Health Inequalities, 2009; (with Laura Lane) Soup Runs in Central London: the right help in the right place at the right time?, 2009; Phoenix Cities: the fall and rise of great industrial cities, 2010; (jtly) Family Futures: childhood and poverty in urban neighbourhoods, 2011; Cities for a Small Continent, 2016; numerous governmental reports; contrib. articles in press on social policy and housing issues. *Address:* CASE - LSE Housing and Communities, London School of Economics, Houghton Street, WC2A 2AE. *E:* anne.power@lse.ac.uk.

**POWER, Benjamin James;** Artistic Associate, Royal National Theatre, since 2019 (Associate Director, 2010–15; Deputy Artistic Director, 2015–19); *b* Macclesfield, Cheshire, 18 Aug. 1981; *s* of Jonathan and Carolyn Power; *m* 2007, Dione Miller; one *s. Educ:* Poynton Co. High Sch.; Clare Coll., Cambridge (BA 1st Cl. English 2002). Freelance writer, 2004–, including: for BBC, The Hollow Crown, series 1, 2013 and series 2, 2016; for NBC; for National Theatre: Emperor and Galilean, 2011; Medea, 2014; Husbands and Sons, 2015; The Lehman Trilogy, 2018; for Royal Shakespeare Co.: A Tender Thing, 2012; dramaturgy includes A Disappearing Number, Complicité, 2007; Associate Dir, Headlong Th., 2006–10; productions include: Faustus, 2006; Six Characters in Search of an Author, 2008. *Publications:* Paradise Lost, 2006; Faustus, 2007; Six Characters in Search of an Author, 2008; A Tender Thing, 2010; Emperor and Galilean, 2011; Medea, 2014; Husbands and Sons, 2016. *Recreations:* cooking, music, Shakespeare. *Address:* c/o Royal National Theatre, Upper Ground, SE1 9PX. *T:* (020) 7452 3000.

**POWER, Jonathan;** syndicated columnist, author, broadcaster and film maker, since 1966; *b* N Mimms, Herts, 4 June 1941; *s* of Patrick and Dorothy Power; four *d. Educ:* Liverpool Inst. High Sch.; Manchester Univ. (BA); Univ. of Wisconsin (MSc). Mem., Anti-Apartheid Soc., London Univ., 1962; Chm., Manchester Univ. Campaign for Nuclear Disarmament, 1963. Advr to peasant farmers in Tanzania, 1964; on staff of Martin Luther King in Chicago, 1966–67; maker of BBC Third Prog. radio documentaries, 1968–70; documentary films for BBC TV, incl. for World in Action and This Week for ITV, 1969–76; foreign affairs feature writer, Guardian, NY Times, The Times, Observer and Economist, 1970–75; foreign affairs columnist, 1975–90, foreign affairs commentator, 2003–06, Internat. Herald Tribune; regular contribs to Encounter and Prospect mags, 1972–2009; regular guest columnist, New York Times, Washington Post and Los Angeles Times; 65 full length interviews with world leaders for Internat. Herald Tribune, Washington Post, Times and Prospect mag.; weekly reviewer, NY Jl of Books, 2018–. Prod., BBC TV documentary, It's Ours Whatever They Say, 1972 (Silver Medal, Venice Film Fest.). Consultant, 1970s and 1980s: Internat. Red Cross; WCC; IFAD; UNICEF; Catholic Ch Commn for Justice and Peace in England and Wales. Editl Advr to Ind. Commn on Nuclear Disarmament and Common Security, 1981. Mem., Transnat. Foundn for Peace and Future Res., Sweden, 1995–. *Publications:* Economic Development, 1971; World of Hunger, 1976; Migrant Workers in Europe and the USA, 1979; Against Oblivion, 1981; Vision of Hope: fiftieth anniversary of the United Nations, 1995; Like Water on Stone: the story of Amnesty International, 2002; Conundrums of Humanity: the big foreign policy questions of our age, 2013; Ending War Crimes, Chasing the War Criminals, 2018. *Recreations:* walking, cycling, opera, ballet, history, jazz. *Address:* Adelgatan 6, Lund 22350, Sweden. *T:* 706510879. *E:* jonathanpower95@gmail.com.

**POWER, Lewis Niall;** QC 2011; *b* Belfast, 16 July 1965; *s* of Gerard and Rose Noel Power; *m* 1993, Anne McQuillan; one *s* two *d. Educ:* Our Lady and St Patrick's Coll., Knock, Belfast; Wolverhampton Univ. (LLB Hons). Called to the Bar, Gray's Inn, 1990; in practice as barrister specialising in criminal and internat. law. Lectr and Ext. Examr in Internat. Law, Birkbeck Coll., London, 1990–97. Member: Northern Irish Bar; Criminal Bar Assoc.; Internat. Bar Assoc.; Sussex Bar Mess. FA approved lawyer, 2011. *Recreations:* American law, laughter, golf, Irish sports, football, architecture, travel, international law, family.

**POWER, Mark;** photographer, since 1983; *b* Harpenden, Herts, 24 June 1959; *s* of Thomas Power and Doris Power (*née* Sillence); partner, 1989, Johanna Coles; one *s* one *d. Educ:* Brighton Poly. (BA 1st Cl. Hons Visual Communication/Fine Art 1981); Loughborough Coll. of Art (Foundn 1978). Mem., Network Photographers, 1988–2002; Magnum Photos: Nominee, 2002–05; Associate, 2005–07; Mem., 2007–; Sen. Lectr in Photography, 1992–2004; Prof. of Photography, 2004–17, Univ. of Brighton. Hon. FRPS 2017. *Publications: monographs:* The Shipping Forecast, 1996; Superstructure, 2000; The Treasury Project, 2002; 26 Different Endings, 2007; The Sound of Two Songs, 2010; Mass, 2012; Die Mauer ist Weg!, 2014; Destroying the Laboratory for the Sake of the Experiment, 2016; Good Morning, America, Vol 1, 2018, Vol 2, 2019. *Recreations:* walking, reading, collecting photobooks. *Address:* 171 Ditchling Road, Brighton BN1 6JB. *T:* 07850 358148. *E:* mark@markpower.co.uk.

**POWER, Prof. Michael Kevin,** PhD; FBA 2016; FCA; Professor of Accounting, London School of Economics and Political Science, since 1987; *b* Arbroath, Scotland, 16 July 1957; *s* of John Charles and Alice Flora Power; *m* 2002, Caroline Muller; three *s. Educ:* Devonport High Sch.; St Edmund Hall, Oxford (BA PPE 1979); Girton Coll., Cambridge (MPhil Hist. and Philosophy of Sci. 1980; PhD 1984); London Sch. of Econs and Political Sci. (MSc Accounting and Finance 1989). FCA 1987. With Deloitte Haskins & Sells, 1983–87. Dir, Centre for Analysis of Risk and Regulation, LSE, 2010–14. Non-executive Director: St James's Place plc, 2005–13; St James's Place Internat. plc, 2012– (Chm., 2012–); RIT Capital partners plc, 2014–. Hon. Fellow, Inst. for Risk Mgt, 2011–. Hon. DEc: St Gallen, 2009; Turku, 2016; Hon. DSocSc Uppsala, 2013. *Publications:* The Audit Society, 1997; Organized Uncertainty: designing a world of risk management, 2007; Riskwork: essays on the organizational life of risk management, 2016. *Recreations:* soccer, tennis, film, theatre, jazz. *Address:* Department of Accounting. London School of Economics and Political Science, Houghton Street, WC2A 2AE. *T:* (020) 7955 7228. *E:* m.k.power@lse.ac.uk.

**POWER, Nigel John;** QC 2010; barrister; *b* Oswestry, Shropshire, 30 Jan. 1968; *s* of John Power and Olive Power; *m* 1997, Kate Symms; one *s* one *d. Educ:* Our Lady and St Oswald's Catholic Prim. Sch., Oswestry; Fitzalan Comp. Sch., Oswestry; Oswestry Sch.; Univ. of Reading (LLB 1990). Called to the Bar, Inner Temple, 1992; in practice as barrister, specialising in crime. *Recreation:* playing and watching cricket and football. *Address:* 7 Harrington Street Chambers, 7 Harrington Street, Liverpool L2 9YH. *T:* (0151) 242 0707. *Club:* Liverpool Ramblers Association Football Club (Hon. Secretary).

**POWER, Prof. Philip Patrick,** PhD; FRS 2005; Professor of Chemistry, University of California, Davis. *Educ:* Trinity Coll., Dublin (BA 1974); PhD Sussex 1977. Joined Univ. of Calif, Davis, 1981. Alexander von Humboldt Award, 1992; Mond Medal, RSC, 2004. *Publications:* articles in learned jls. *Address:* Department of Chemistry, University of California, Davis, CA 95616, USA.

**POWER, Vince,** Hon. CBE 2006; Chief Executive, Music Festivals plc, 2011–12; *b* Co. Waterford, Ireland, 29 April 1947; *s* of late John Power and Brigid Power; *m* 1967 (marr. diss. 1979); three *c*; five *c* with former partners. *Educ:* Dungarvan Vocational Coll. Owner, chain of furniture shops, N London, 1964–82; Founder and Chm., Mean Fiddler Orgn, subseq. Mean Fiddler Music Gp plc, 1982–2005; founder, Vince Power Music Group, 2005–10; opened club, Mean Fiddler, Harlesden, 1982; founder of clubs and bars: Powerhaus, Islington, 1988, moved to Finsbury Park, 1996; Subterania, 1988; The Grand, 1991; Jazz Cafe, 1992; The Forum, 1993; The Garage, 1993; Upstairs at the Garage, 1994; Crossbar, 1995; Mean Fiddler, Dublin, 1995; The Palace, Luton, 1995; The Complex, 1996; The Cube, 1996; Power's Bar, 1996; Zd, 1996; Bartok, 1998; Ion Bar and Restaurant, 1998; Point 101, 1998; The Rex, 1999; One Seven Nine, 2001; G-A-Y, 2002; Union-Undeb, Cardiff, 2003; Berkeley Square Cafe, 2003; acquired nightclubs: London Astoria, 2000; LA2, renamed Mean Fiddler, 2000; Media, 2002; Tunnel, 2002; Universe, 2002; promoter of events: Reading Fest., 1989–2005; Fleadh, London, 1990–2005; Fleadh, Glasgow, 1992; Madstock, 1992, 1994, 1996, 1998; Fleadh Mor, Ireland, 1993; Neil Young, 1993; Phoenix Fest., 1993–97; Tribal Gathering, 1995–97; Paul Weller, 1996; The Sex Pistols, 1996; Big Love, 1996; Mount Universe, 1996; Jamiroquai, 1997; Fleadh New York, 1997–2005; Fleadh Chicago, 1998–2005; Fleadh San Francisco, 1998–2005; Creamfields, 1998; Pulp, 1998; Temptation, 1998; Fleadh Boston, 1999–2005; We Love…Homelands (formerly Homelands), 1999–2005; Homelands Scotland, 1999–2005; Homelands Ireland, 1999–2005; Leeds Fest., 1999–2005; Glasgow Green, 2000–05; Nat. Adventure Sports Weekender, 2001; Dr Music Fest., Spain, 2003; Benicassim Fest., 2006; Hop Farm Fest., 2008; Costa de Fuego Fest., 2012; operational manager, Glastonbury Fest., 2002–05; co-owner, Tramore racecourse.

**POWERS, Dr Alan Adrian Robelou,** FSA; art historian, critic, teacher and curator; *b* 5 Feb. 1955; *s* of Michael Powers and Frances Powers (*née* Wilson); *m* 1982, Susanna Curtis; one *s* one *d. Educ:* Bryanston Sch.; Clare Coll., Cambridge (BA 1977; PhD 1983). Dir, Judd Street Gall., 1985–91; Librarian and Tutor, Prince of Wales's Inst. of Architecture, 1992–2000; Sen. Lectr, 1999–2004, Reader, 2004–07, Prof. of Architecture and Cultural Hist., 2007–12, Univ. of Greenwich. Curator: Modern Britain 1929–39, Design Mus., 1999; Serge Chermayeff, Kettle's Yard, Cambridge, 2001; Eric Ravilious, Imagined Realities, Imperial War Mus., 2003; Mind into Matter, De La Warr Pavilion, Bexhill on Sea, 2009. Chairman: Twentieth Century Soc., 2007–12 (Vice-Chm., 1999–2007); Pollock's Toy Mus. Trust, 1999–. Mem., Art Workers' Guild. FSA 2009. Hon. FRIBA 2008. *Publications:* (jtly) The National Trust Book of the English House, 1985; Seaside Lithographs, 1986; The English Tivoli, 1988; Shop Fronts, 1989; Oliver Hill, 1989; Modern Block-Printed Textiles, 1992; Living with Books, 1999; Nature in Design, 1999; Francis Pollen, 1999; Living with Pictures, 2000; Serge Chermayeff, 2001; Front Cover, 2001; Children's Book Covers, 2003; The Twentieth Century House in Britain, 2004; Modern: the Modern movement in Britain, 2005; Modern Architectures in History: Britain, 2007; Art and Print: the Curwen story, 2008; Adlington, Craig and Collinge, 2009; Robin Hood Gardens Re-Visions, 2010; (jtly) British Murals and Decorative Painting 1920–1960, 2013; Eric Ravilious, 2013; 100 Years of Architecture, 2016; Edward Ardizzone: artist and illustrator, 2016; Enid Marx: the pleasures of pattern, 2018; Alan Powers: the art of an art historian, 2018; Bauhaus Goes West, 2019. *Recreations:* painting, printmaking. *Address:* 99 Judd Street, WC1H 9NE. *T:* (020) 7387 3154. *E:* alanpowers@icloud.com. *Club:* Double Crown.

**POWERS, Dr Michael John**; QC 1995; *b* 9 Feb. 1947; *o s* of late Reginald Frederick and of Kathleen Powers; *m* 1st, 1968, Meryl Hall (marr. diss. 2001); one *s* one *d*; 2nd, 2001, Pamela Barnes. *Educ:* Poole Grammar Sch.; Middlesex Hosp. Med. Sch., London Univ. (BSc, MB BS, DA). House Surgeon, Middlesex Hosp., 1972; House Physician, Royal S Hants Hosp., 1973; Sen. House Officer, Anaesthetics, Royal United Hosp., Bath, 1974; GP, Parson Drove, Cambs, 1975; Registrar in Anaesthetics, Northwick Park Hosp., Harrow, 1975–77; called to the Bar: Lincoln's Inn, 1979, Bencher, 1998; Trinidad and Tobago, 2012; HM Asst Dep. Coroner, Westminster, 1981–87. Pres., S of England Coroners' Soc., 1987–88. FFFLM 2007. Hon. LLD Plymouth, 2010. *Publications:* Thurston's Coronership: the law and practice on coroners, 1985; Medical Negligence, 1990, 5th edn (ed jtly), as Clinical Negligence, 2015; chapters in medical and legal texts on medico-legal subjects. *Recreations:* music, hill-walking, flying (former helicopter pilot). *Address:* Clerksroom, Equity House, Blackbrook Park Avenue, Taunton TA1 2PX. *T:* 0845 083 3000. *E:* powersqc@medneg.co.uk. *Clubs:* Garrick, Royal Society of Medicine.

**POWERS-FREELING, Laurel Claire**; senior banking advisor; Chairman, Sumitomo Mitsui Banking Corporation Europe, since 2015; *b* 16 May 1957; *d* of Lloyd M. Powers and Catharine Berry Powers; *m* 1989, Dr Anthony Nigel Stanley Freeling, *qv*; two *d*. *Educ:* Columbia Univ., NY (AB *cum laude*); Massachusetts Inst. of Technol. (Sloan Schol.); Univ. de Reims Champagne-Ardenne (Dip. Haute études du Goût). Sen. Consultant, Price Waterhouse, 1981–85; manager, McKinsey & Co., 1985–89; Corporate Finance, Morgan Stanley Internat., 1989–91; Dir, Corporate Strategy, Prudential Gp plc, 1991–94; Gp Finance Dir, Lloyds Abbey Life Gp plc, 1994–97; Lloyds TSB Group plc: Finance and Develt Dir, Retail, 1997–99; Man. Dir, Wealth Mgt, 1999–2001; Exec. Dir, Marks & Spencer Gp plc, 2001–04; CEO, Marks & Spencer Financial Services plc, 2001–04; Sen. Vice-Pres., UK Country Manager and Chm., American Express Insce Services Europe, 2005–07; Gp Chief Exec., Dubai First International, 2007–09. Non-exec. Dir, 2002–05, Sen. Advr, 2010–11, Bank of England; Sen. Gp Advr, Erste Bank Gp, 2008–10; non-executive Director: Bank of Ireland UK plc, 2010–; BBA-LIBOR Ltd, 2010–13; C. Hoare & Co., 2010–17; Findel plc, 2010–14; ACE Europe Gp, 2012–15; Premium Credit Ltd, 2012–15; Callcredit Information Gp, 2014–17; Chm., Uber UK, 2017–. Chairman: Nat. Joint Registry, 2011–; Cambridge Univ. Health Partners, 2018–. Chairman: Piccola Accademia di Montisi Music (formerly Montisi Harpsichord Performance Centre), Siena, 2005–12; Amer. Soc. for Royal Acad. of Music, 2011–16; Gov., RAM, 2007–16; Dir, English Concert, 2008–12. *Recreations:* needlework, cooking, gastronomy and wines. *Address:* Sumitomo Mitsui Banking Corporation Europe Ltd, 99 Queen Victoria Street, EC4V 4EH. *T:* 07789 273544. *E:* laurel@powers-freeling.com.

**POWERSCOURT**, 11th Viscount *cr* 1743 (Ire.); **Mervyn Anthony Wingfield**; Baron Wingfield 1743; Baron Powerscourt (UK) 1885; *b* 21 Aug. 1963; *s* of 10th Viscount Powerscourt and Wendy Ann Pauline Wingfield (*née* Slazenger), now Watson; *S* father, 2015; *m* 2010, Sarah Ann Hall. *Educ:* Postgrad. Dip Therapeutic Counselling. Reg. Mem., British Assoc. for Counselling and Psychotherapy; Founder and Counsellor, Wingfield Counselling, 2014–. *Heir:* none. *E:* awingfield@me.com. *T:* 07771 602464.

**POWIS**, 8th Earl of, *cr* 1804; **John George Herbert**; Baron Clive (Ire.), 1762; Baron Clive (GB), 1794; Viscount Clive, Baron Herbert of Chirbury, Baron Powis, 1804; *b* 19 May 1952; *s* of 7th Earl of Powis and of Hon. Katharine Odeyne de Grey, *d* of 8th Baron Walsingham, DSO, OBE; *S* father, 1993; *m* 1977, Marijke Sophia (marr. diss. 2016), *d* of Maarten Nanne Guther, Ancaster, Canada; two *s* two *d*; *m* 2018, Helen Frances, *d* of Anthony John Burgess, Tunbridge Wells. *Educ:* Wellington; McMaster Univ., Ontario, Canada (MA; PhD 1994). Formerly Lectr, McMaster Univ.; Asst Prof., Redeemer Coll., Ont, Canada, 1990–93. Hon. Fellow, Bangor Univ., 2011. *Heir:* s Viscount Clive, *qv*. *Address:* Powis Castle Estate Office, Welshpool, Powys SY21 8RG.

**POWLES, Prof. Raymond Leonard**, CBE 2003; MD; FRCP; FRCPath; Professor of Haemato-Oncology, University of London, at Institute of Cancer Research, 1997–2004, now Emeritus; Head, Leukaemia, Myeloma and Bone Marrow Transplant Units, Cancer Centre London, Wimbledon, since 2004; Director, London Haemato-oncology Ltd, since 2010; *b* 9 March 1938; *s* of late Leonard William David Powles and Florence Irene Powles (*née* Conolly); *m* 1980, Louise Jane Richmond; three *s* one *d*. *Educ:* Eltham Coll.; St Bartholomew's Hosp. Med. Coll. (BSc 1961; MB BS 1964; MD 1976). MRCP 1968, FRCP 1980; FRCPath 1993. House Physician and Surgeon, St Bartholomew's Hosp., 1965–66; RMO, Royal Marsden Hosp., 1967–68; Leukaemia Res. Fund Fellow, Ville Juif, Paris, 1968; Tata Meml Fund Fellow, Royal Marsden Hosp. and Inst. of Cancer Res., Sutton, 1969–72; SSO, ICRF, St Bartholomew's Hosp. and Royal Marsden Hosp., 1972–74; Physician in Charge, 1974–2003, and Gp Hd, Haemato-Oncology, 1993–2003, Leukaemia and Myeloma Units, Royal Marsden Hosp. Clin. Tutor, RCP, 1990; internat. lectures on leukaemia, myeloma and bone marrow transplantation. Member: MRC Wkg Party on Leukaemia, 1974–2003; Royal Marsden SHA, 1989–92; Standing Med. Adv. Sub-Cttee on Cancer, DoH, 1991–93; WHO Cttee on Internat. Programme Chernobyl Accident, 1990–92; Ind. Reconfiguration Panel, 2002–13; Healthcare Inspections Adv. Panel, Cabinet Office Public Sector Team, 2002–. Chm., Nuclear Accidents Sub-Cttee, European Gp for Blood and Marrow Transplantation, 2001–. Bd Mem., European Soc. Med. Oncology, 1985–90; Scientific Advr, Internat. Myeloma Foundn, 1995–; American Society of Hematology: Mem., Scientific Cttee on hemopoetic growth factors, 2004– (Chm., 2006–08); Chm., Ad-Hoc Scientific Cttee on plasma cell biol., 2008–10. Mem. Bd, BioPartners GmbH, 2000–07. Trustee, and Bd Mem., New Health Network, 2002–. Board Member: Bone Marrow Transplantation, 1986–; Experimental Haematology, 1992–. Founding Patron, New India Cancer Care Initiative, 2010–. Lifetime Mem., Eur. Blood and Marrow Soc., 2018. Lifetime Achievement Award, Cancer Patients Aid Assoc., India, 1999; Outstanding Contribn Award, Ind. Healthcare Awards, 2009; Pride of Britain Lifetime Achievement Award, 2013. *Publications:* more than 1200 sci. papers, articles, and chapters in books on leukaemia, myeloma and bone marrow transplantation. *Recreations:* sport, travel, cinema, theatre, photography (1st Prize, Photographic Section, RCP Art Exhibn, 2011). *Address:* Little Garratts, 19 Garratts Lane, Banstead, Surrey SM7 2EA. *T:* 07768 165882, *Fax:* (office) (020) 8605 9103. *E:* myeloma@clara.co.uk.
*See also* T. J. *Powles*.

**POWLES, His Honour Stephen Robert**; QC 1995; a Circuit Judge, 2005–14; *b* 7 June 1948; *s* of late Andrew Frederick Arthur Powles and Nora (*née* Bristol); *m* 1975, Geraldine Patricia Hilda Adamson; one *s* one *d*. *Educ:* Westminster Sch.; University Coll., Oxford (MA Engrg Sci.). Called to the Bar: Middle Temple, 1972 (Harmsworth Maj. Exhibnr, 1971; Astbury Law Schol., 1972); Lincoln's Inn (*ad eundem*), 1977; a Recorder, 1994–2005. CEDR registered mediator, 2001–. Member: Civil Mediation Council, 2002–; Tribunal Panel, Financial Reporting Council (formerly Accountancy Investigation and Discipline Bd, then Accountancy and Actuarial Discipline Bd), 2004–16; Parole Bd, 2006–16. Hon. CIMechE 2001. *Recreations:* hill-walking, sailing, theatre, my border terrier. *Club:* Garrick.

**POWLES, Prof. Trevor James**, CBE 2003; PhD; FRCP; Consultant Breast Oncologist: St Anthony's Hospital, 1978–2016; Lister Hospital, 2002–14; Cancer Centre London, Parkside Hospital, since 2013 (Medical Director, since 2010); Consultant Physician in Breast Cancer, 1978–2003, Head of Breast Cancer Unit, 1993–2003, and Medical Director, Common Tumours Division, 2000–03, Royal Marsden Hospital; Professor of Breast Oncology, Institute of Cancer Research, London University, 1998–2003, now Emeritus; *b* 8 March 1938; *s* of late Leonard William David Powles and Florence Irene Powles (*née* Conolly); *m* 1968, Penelope Margaret Meyers; two *s* one *d*. *Educ:* Eltham Coll.; St Bartholomew's Hosp. Med. Coll. (MB BS 1964); Inst. of Cancer Res. (PhD 1975). FRCP 1983. House Physician and Registrar, Hammersmith Hosp., 1967–68; Med. Registrar, St Bartholomew's Hosp., 1965–70; MRC Clin. Res. Fellow, Inst. of Cancer Res., 1971–73; Sen. Registrar and Sen. Lectr, Royal Marsden Hosp., 1974–78; Consultant Breast Oncologist, Parkside Oncology Clinic, 2003–10. Visiting Professor: M. D. Anderson Cancer Center, Houston, 1993; Dana Farber Cancer Center, Harvard, Boston, 1996; Tom Baker Cancer Centre, Calgary, 1998. Director: Oncotech Inc., Calif, 1996–2008; Intact Medical Inc. (formerly Neothermia Inc.), Ohio, 2000–16. Vice Pres., Internat. Soc. for Prevention of Cancer, 1996–2010. Chm., Cancer Centre London LLP, 2010–. Patron, Breast Cancer Care, 2003–. Trustee: Breast Cancer Now and Best Cancer Care (formerly Breakthrough Breast Cancer, then Breast Cancer Now), 2009– (Vice Chm., 2015–); Breast Cancer Res. Trust (Chm., 2015–). All Party Parly Gp Award for lifetime achievement in breast cancer, 2003; Brinker Award for Scientific Distinction, Komen Foundn, 2005; Ind. Healthcare Award, Laing & Buisson, 2009; Pride of Britain Lifetime Achievement Award, 2013. *Publications:* Breast Cancer Management, 1981; Prostaglandins and Cancer, 1982; Medical Management of Breast Cancer, 1991; scientific papers on diagnosis, prevention and treatment of breast cancer. *Recreations:* horse riding, ski-ing, reading, golf, fishing. *Address:* Green Hedges, Coulsdon Lane, Chipstead, Surrey CR5 3QL; Cancer Centre London, 49 Parkside, Wimbledon, SW19 5NB. *T:* (020) 8247 3384, *Fax:* (020) 8247 3385. *Club:* Royal Automobile.
*See also* R. L. *Powles*.

**POWLETT**; *see* Orde-Powlett.

**POWLEY, John Albert**; Enquiry Officer, Post Office, 1991–96; *b* 3 Aug. 1936; *s* of Albert and Evelyn Powley; *m* 1957, Jill (*née* Palmer); two *s* one *d*. *Educ:* Cambridge Grammar Sch.; Cambridgeshire Coll. of Arts and Technology. Apprenticeship, Pye Ltd, 1952–57; RAF, 1957–59; retail shop selling and servicing radio, television and electrical goods, 1960–84. Member (C): Cambs CC, 1967–77, 1997–2013 (Chm., Social Services Cttee, 1998–2005; Cabinet Mem. for finance and corp. services, 2005–07; Vice Chm., 2009–11; Chm., 2011–13); Cambridge City Council, 1967–79 (Leader, Cons. Group, 1973–79; Chm., Housing Cttee, 1972–74, 1976–79; Leader of Council, 1976–79). Contested (C): Harlow, 1979; Norwich S, 1987. MP (C) Norwich S, 1983–87. Chm., Soham Cons. Assoc., 1991–2001. Sec./Manager, Wensum Valley Golf Club, Taverham, Norfolk, 1989–90. Hon. Alderman for Cambs, 2014–. *Recreations:* golf, cricket, football. *Address:* 22 Juniper Drive, Ely, Cambs CB7 4TT. *T:* (01353) 661642.

**POWNALL, David**; novelist and playwright, since 1970; *b* 19 May 1938; *s* of John Charles Pownall and Elsie Pownall (*née* Russell); *m* 1962, Glenys Elsie Jones (marr. diss. 1973; she *d* 1995); one *s*; partner 1972–89, Mary Ellen Ray; one *s*; *m* 1993, Jean Alexander Sutton; one *s*. *Educ:* Greasby Primary Sch., Wirral; Lord Wandsworth Coll., Long Sutton; Keele Univ. (BA Hons 1960). Grad. Trainee, then Personnel Officer, Ford Motor Co., 1960–63; Personnel Manager, Anglo-American Corp., Zambian Copperbelt, 1963–69. FRSL 1976. Hon. DLitt Keele, 2000. John Whiting Award, 1981; Giles Cooper Award, 1981, 1985; Sony Silver Award, 1993, 1994, Sony Gold Award, 1995; Writers Guild Award, 2013. *Publications:* novels: The Raining Tree War, 1974; African Horse, 1975; God Perkins, 1977; Light on a Honeycomb, 1978; Beloved Latitudes, 1981; The White Cutter, 1987; The Gardener, 1988; Stagg and his Mother, 1990; The Sphinx and the Sybarites, 1993; The Catalogue of Men, 1999; The Ruling Passion, 2008; The Archivist, 2010; *plays:* The Dream of Chief Crazy Horse (for children), 1975; Music to Murder By, 1976; Motocar/Richard III Part Two, 1979; An Audience Called Edouard, 1979; Master Class, 1983; The Composer Plays, 1993; Elgar's Rondo, 1993; Death of a Faun, 1996; Radio Plays, 1998; Getting the Picture, 1998; Collected Plays, 2000; *short stories:* My Organic Uncle and other stories, 1976; The Bunch from Bananas (for children), 1980; *poetry:* Another Country, 1978; Poems, 2007; *non-fiction:* Between Ribble and Lune, 1980; Sound Theatre, 2011; Writing Master Class, 2014. *Recreations:* fishing, fell-walking, gardening, music, reading. *Address:* c/o Johnson & Alcock Ltd, Clerkenwell House, 45/47 Clerkenwell Green, EC1R 0HT. *T:* (020) 7251 0125.

**POWNALL, Brig. John Lionel**, OBE 1972; Deputy Chairman, Police Complaints Authority, 1986–93 (Member, 1985–86); *b* 10 May 1929; *yr s* of late John Cecil Glossop Pownall, CB and Margaret Nina Pownall (*née* Jesson); *m* 1962, Sylvia Joan Cameron Conn (*d* 2011), *d* of late J. Cameron Conn, WS and Florence Conn (*née* Lennox); two *s*. *Educ:* Rugby School; RMA Sandhurst. Commissioned 16th/5th Lancers, 1949; served Egypt, Cyrenaica, Tripolitania, BAOR, Hong Kong, Cyprus; psc, jssc; Comd 16th/5th The Queen's Royal Lancers, 1969–71; Adjutant-Gen.'s Secretariat, 1971–72; Officer i/c RAC Manning and Records, 1973–75; Col, GS Near East Land Forces/Land Forces Cyprus, 1975–78; Asst Dir, Defence Policy Staff, MoD, 1978–79; Brig. RAC, UKLF, 1979–82; Brig. GS, MoD, 1982–84; retired 1984. Col, 16th/5th The Queen's Royal Lancers, 1985–90. *Address:* 5 Park Way, Easebourne, Midhurst, W Sussex GU29 0AW. *Clubs:* Cavalry and Guards, Army and Navy.

**POWNALL, Sir Michael (Graham)**, KCB 2011; Clerk of the Parliaments, House of Lords, 2007–11; *b* 11 Oct. 1949; *s* of Raymond Pownall and Elisabeth Mary Pownall (*née* Robinson); *m* 1974, Deborah Ann (*d* 2013), *e d* of T. H. McQueen; two *d*. *Educ:* Repton Sch.; Exeter Univ. Joined Parliament Office, House of Lords, 1971: seconded to CSD as Private Sec. to Leader of House and Govt Chief Whip, 1980–83; Estabt Officer and Sec. to Chm. of Cttees, 1983–88; Principal Clerk of Private Bills, 1988–90; Principal Clerk, Overseas Office, 1988–95; Clerk of Cttees, 1991–95; Clerk of the Journals, 1995–96; Reading Clerk and Principal Finance Officer, 1997–2003; Clerk Asst, 2003–07. Trustee, History of Parliament Trust, 2007–11. Chm., Kensington and Chelsea br., Cruse, 2017–; Patron, Upper Room charity, 2014–. Lay Fellow, Sion Coll., 2016–. Pres., Old Reptonian Soc., 2018. Hon. LLD Exeter, 2012. *Recreations:* bird-watching, house in Italy. *T:* (020) 8994 0797. *Club:* Brooks's.

**POWNALL, (Stephen) Orlando (Fletcher)**; QC 2002; *b* 13 Nov. 1952; *s* of Alan Pownall and Carola Pownall (*née* Thielker); *m* 1978, Catherine Higgins; one *s* two *d*. *Educ:* Oundle Sch.; Faculté de Droit, Paris. Called to the Bar, Inner Temple, 1975, Bencher, 2007; Jun. Treasury Counsel, 1991–95; Sen. Treasury Counsel, CCC, 1995–2002; Hd of Chambers, 2 Hare Court, 2009–13. *Recreations:* Rugby, golf, painting, gardening, Liverpool FC. *Address:* 2 Hare Court, Temple, EC4Y 7BH. *T:* (020) 7353 5324.

**POWNEY, Christopher William Deacon**; Artistic Director, Royal Ballet School, since 2014; *b* Guildford, 2 June 1968; *s* of Robert David Powney and Jean Victoria Powney; *m* 2001, Didy Veldman; two *d*. *Educ:* Ballet Rambert (Dip. Dance 1987); Royal Ballet Sch. (PDTC 2004). Dancer: Northern Ballet Th., 1987–90; English Nat. Ballet, 1990–94; Rambert Dance Co., 1994–96, 1998–2000; Asst Artistic Dir, Ballet Central, 1996–98; Teacher: Royal Ballet Sch., 2000–05; Royal Conservatoire Den Haag, 2005–10; Dir, Dutch National Ballet Acad., 2010–14.

**POWRIE, Prof. Fiona Margaret,** DPhil; FRS 2011; Director, Kennedy Institute of Rheumatology and Professor, Nuffield Department of Orthopaedics, Rheumatology and Musculoskeletal Sciences, University of Oxford, since 2014; Fellow of Wadham College, Oxford, since 2014; *b* Luton, 1963. *Educ:* Univ. of Bath (BSc Biochem. 1985); Univ. of Oxford (DPhil). University of Oxford: Wellcome Trust Sen. Res. Fellow, 1996–2009; Prof. of Immunol., until 2009; Sidney Truelove Prof. of Gastroenterology, 2009–14; former Hd, Experimental Med. Div., Nuffield Dept of Clinical Med. Gov., Wellcome Trust, 2018–. Fellow, EMBO, 2013; FMedSci 2014. (Jtly) Louis-Jeantet Prize for Medicine, 2012. *Address:* Kennedy Institute of Rheumatology, University of Oxford, Roosevelt Drive, Headington, Oxford OX3 7FY.

**POWRIE, Prof. William,** PhD; CEng, FREng, FICE; Professor of Geotechnical Engineering, University of Southampton, since 1995 (Dean, Faculty of Engineering and the Environment, 2010–18); *b* 25 Sept. 1959; *s* of William Powrie and Jean (*née* Darby); *m* 1988, Dr Christine Lorraine Solomon; three *s* one *d*. *Educ:* St Catharine's Coll., Cambridge (BA Engrg 1982; MA 1986; PhD Soil Mechanics 1986); King's Coll., London (MSc Construction Law and Arbitration 1991). CEng 1991; FICE 1997; FREng 2009. Civil Engrg Trainee, British Rail (Eastern Reg.), 1978–82; Lectr in Civil Engrg, KCL, 1985–88; Queen Mary and Westfield College, London: Lectr in Civil Engrg, 1988–93; Reader in Civil Engrg, 1993–94; Hd, Sch. of Civil Engrg and the Envmt (formerly Dept of Civil and Envmtl Engrg), Univ. of Southampton, 1999–2008. Chm., Southampton Univ. Res. into Sustainability and Envmt, 1998–2007. Geotechnical Cons. to W. J. Groundwater Ltd, Bushey, 1987–; Director: WJ Associates Ltd (geotechnical consultants), 1992–2003; Envmtl Services Assoc. Res. Trust, 1998–2002. Sponsor, Scientists for Global Responsibility (formerly Architects and Engrs for Social Responsibility), 2000–; Trustee, Inst. for Sustainability, 2010–15. Chm., DEFRA Technologies Adv. Cttee for Biodegradable Municipal Waste, 2005–10. Hon. Editor and Chm. Editl Adv. Panel, ICE Procs (Geotech. Engrg), 1997–99, (Waste and Resource Mgt), 2005–09. *Publications:* Soil Mechanics: concepts and applications, 1997, 3rd edn 2014; *c* 125 papers in acad. and professional jls incl. Geotechnique, ICE Procs, Procs ASCE, Canadian Geotech. Jl, Jl of Petroleum Sci. and Engrg, Waste Mgt, Jl of Rail and Rapid Transit, Internat. Jl of Rock Mechanics and Mining Scis. *Recreations:* music (playing and listening, mainly classical and jazz, piano, church organ and alto saxophone), cycling, walking, DIY. *Address:* Faculty of Engineering and the Environment, University of Southampton, Highfield, Southampton SO17 1BJ. *T:* (023) 8059 3214, *Fax:* (023) 8067 7519. *E:* wp@soton.ac.uk.

**POWYS,** family name of **Baron Lilford**.

**POYNTER, Kieran Charles,** FCA; Chairman, BMO Global Asset Management (formerly F&C Asset Management) plc, since 2013 (non-executive Director, since 2009); *b* 20 Aug. 1950; *s* of Kenneth and Betty Poynter; *m* 1977, Marylyn Melvin; three *s* one *d*. *Educ:* Salesian Coll.; Imperial Coll., London (BSc, ARCS). FCA 1977. Price Waterhouse, 1971–98, PricewaterhouseCoopers, 1998–2008: articled clerk, 1971; Partner, 1982; Dir, Insce Services, 1982–95; Member: Supervisory Bd, 1993–95; Mgt Bd, 1995–2008; Man. Partner, 1996–2000; Chm. and Sen. Partner, 2000–08. Chm., Nomura European Hldgs plc, Nomura Internat. plc and Nomura Bank Internat. plc, 2009–15; non-executive Director: British American Tobacco plc, 2010–; Internat. Consolidated Airlines Gp SA, 2010–. Member: Insce Cttee, ICAEW, 1982–95; Life Accounting Cttee, ABI, 1992; Govt Task Force on Deregulation of Financial Services, 1993. Lloyd's Committees: Member: Accounting and Auditing Standards, 1988–90; Solvency and Reporting, 1994–95; Disputes Resolution Panel, 1996–97; Chm., Gooda Walker Loss Review, 1991–92. Member: Council for Industry and Higher Educn, 1997–2008; Council, NIESR, 2000–14; President's Cttee, CBI, 2001–08; Council, Prince of Wales' Internat. Business Leaders Forum, 2001–13 (Chm., Audit Cttee, 2007–11); Transatlantic Council, British American Business Inc., 2001–08; Steering Cttee, Heart of the City, 2003–11; Task Force on Ethnic Diversity, IPPR, 2005–06; President's Cttee, Employers Forum on Disability, 2006–11; Council, British Olympic Appeal, 2008–13. Trustee: Industry in London, 1999–2008; Royal Anniversary Trust, 2007–16 (Chm., 2010–16). Director: Royal Automobile Club Ltd, 2007–13; Digital Theatre Ltd (formerly Digital Theatre TV Ltd), 2009–12. KHS 1999. *Publications:* contrib. various insurance articles to professional jls. *Recreations:* golf, watching sport, shooting. *Address:* 15 Montpelier Mews, SW7 1HB. *T:* (020) 7581 5812, 07715 376784. *Clubs:* Royal Automobile, Brooks's; Quinta do Lago Golf.

**POYSER, Crispin John;** Clerk Adviser, Chamber and Committees, House of Commons, since 2018; *b* Nottingham, 9 Nov. 1957; *s* of Eric and Pamela Poyser; *m* 1994, Kristine Williams; one *s* one *d*. *Educ:* Ampleforth Coll.; Merton Coll., Oxford (BA 1978). House of Commons: Clerk: Cttee, Journal, Public Bill and Table Offices, 1978–2002; Treasury Select Cttee, 2002–05; Parly Advr, Cabinet Office, 2005–08; Principal Clerk, Cttee Office, 2008–11 and 2016–18; Clerk, Overseas Office, 2011–16. Jt Sec., Assoc. of Secretaries Gen. of Parlts, 1991–96. Sec., Soc. of Clerks-at-the-Table in Commonwealth Parlts, 2011–16. *Recreations:* classical ballet, history, reading, armchair sport. *Address:* Department of Chamber and Committee Services, House of Commons, SW1A 0AA. *T:* (020) 7219 3000.

**PRADA, Miuccia,** PhD; Head of Prada SpA, since 1978; *b* 1949; *d* of late Luisa Prada; *m* 1987, Patrizio Bertelli; two *s*. Mime artist, Teatro Piccolo, Milan. Joined Prada, 1970; launched: women's clothing collection, 1988; Miu Miu, 1992; men's collection, 1994. Internat. Award, Council of Fashion Designers of America, 2004. *Address:* Prada SpA, Via Andrea Maffei 2, 20135 Milan, Italy.

**PRAG, Prof. (Andrew) John (Nicholas Warburg),** MA, DPhil; FSA; Keeper of Archaeology, Manchester Museum, 1969–2004, now Hon. Professor; Professor of Archaeological Studies, University of Manchester, 2004–05, Professor Emeritus of Classics, since 2005; *b* 28 Aug. 1941; *s* of late Adolf Prag and Frede Charlotte (*née* Warburg); *m* 1969, Kay (*née* Wright); one *s* one *d*. *Educ:* Westminster Sch. (Queen's Scholar); Brasenose Coll., Oxford (Domus Exhibnr 1960; Hon. Scholar 1962; BA 1964; Dip. Classical Archaeol. 1966; Sen. Hulme Scholar, 1967; MA 1967; DPhil 1975). FSA 1977. Temp. Asst Keeper, Ashmolean Museum, Oxford, 1966–67; University of Manchester: Hon. Lectr, Dept of History, 1977–83, Dept of Archaeology, 1984–2005. Vis. Prof. of Classics, McMaster Univ., 1978; Vis. Fellow, British Sch. at Athens, 1994. Editor, Archaeological Reports, 1975–87. *Publications:* The Oresteia: iconographic and narrative tradition, 1985; (with Richard Neave) Making Faces Using the Forensic and Archaeological Evidence, 1997; (ed jtly) Periplous: papers on classical art and archaeology, 2000; (with J. Swaddling) Seianti Hanunia Tlesnasa: the story of an Etruscan noblewoman, 2002; (with Simon Timberlake) The Archaeology of Alderley Edge, 2005; The Story of Alderley: living with the Edge, 2016; articles on Greek art and archaeology in learned jls. *Recreations:* travel, cooking, music. *Address:* Manchester Museum, The University, Manchester M13 9PL. *T:* (0161) 275 2665. *E:* john.prag@manchester.ac.uk.
See also T. G. A. *Prag*.

**PRAG, Thomas Gregory Andrew;** Chairman, Media Support Partnership, since 2001; Director, iMedia Associates, since 2012; *b* 2 Jan. 1947; *s* of late Adolf Prag and Frede Charlotte Prag (*née* Warburg); *m* 1970, Angela Hughes; three *s*. *Educ:* Westminster Sch.; Brasenose Coll., Oxford (MA PPE). Producer/presenter, BBC Radio Oxford, 1970–78; Prog. Organiser, BBC Highland, 1978–81; Man. Dir, 1981–2000, Chm., 2000–01, Moray Firth Radio; Mem. for Scotland, Radio Authority, 2001–03; Mem., Scottish Adv. Cttee, Ofcom, 2004–12 (Chm., 2006–08). Pres., Inverness Chamber of Commerce, 1996–98; Member, Board: Inverness Harbour Trust, 2003–13 (Vice-Chm. 2009–13); Inverness Airport Business Park, 2012–17. Mem. Bd, Assoc. of Ind. Radio Contractors, subseq. Commercial Radio Cos Assoc., 1993–2000. Dir, 1993–2004, Chm., 2002–04, Highland Fest. Mem. Court (formerly Bd Governors), UHI (formerly UHI Millennium Inst.), 2002–13; Chm., UHI Millennium Inst. Develt Trust, 2004–07; Vice-Chairman: Highland Opportunity Ltd, 2012–17; Highlands and Islands Transport Partnership, 2014–15. Chairman: Inshes Community Assoc.; INBS Lib Dems. Mem. (Lib Dem), Highland Council, 2007–17 (Chm., Planning Envmt and Develt, later Planning, Develt and Infrastructure, 2012–15). Gov., Eden Court Theatre, 2007–17; Trustee, Highlanders Mus. FCMI (FBIM 1978); FRA 1998. Hon Fellow, UHI, 2014. *Recreations:* wife and family, acquiring old things - clocks, radios, etc - learning how to dispose of them, 1950 Convertible Daimler, casual gardener, sculler and cox, music, travel, Founder member of Truly Terrible Orchestra, 'cracking' tenor in Inverness Choral Society. *Address:* Windrush, Easter Muckovie, Inverness IV2 5BN. *E:* thomas@prags.co.uk. *Club:* Inverness Rotary (Pres., 2004–05).
See also A. J. N. W. *Prag*.

**PRAGER, Prof. Richard William,** PhD; CEng, FIET, FREng; Professor of Engineering, since 2008, and Head, Department of Engineering, since 2018, University of Cambridge; Fellow, Queens' College, Cambridge, since 1988; *b* London, 2 Feb. 1962; *s* of Paul Prager and Oonagh Margaret Bannister Prager (*née* Browne); *m* 1999, Dr Claire O'Brien; one *s* one *d*. *Educ:* Eton Coll.; Trinity Coll., Cambridge (BA 1984; MA 1988; PhD 1988). CEng, FIET 2008. University of Cambridge: Res. Fellow, 1988–91; Lectr, 1992–2000; Tutor to Res. Students, Queens' Coll., 1992–2004; Dir, Undergrad. Educn in Engrg, 1995–99; Sen. Lectr, 2000–02; Reader in Information Engrg, 2002–08; Dep. Hd, Engrg Dept (Teaching), 2006–12; Hd, Sch. of Technol., 2014–18. Mem., EPSRC Healthcare Strategic Adv. Team, 2008–16. Mem., Vis. Cttee, Mech. Engrg, Nat. Univ. of Singapore, 2013. Non-executive Director: Cambridge Centre for Advanced Res. and Educn in Singapore Ltd, 2014–18; Judge Business Sch. Exec. Educn Ltd, 2015–18; OCR Exams Ltd, 2016–; Cambridge Sustainability Ltd, 2016–18; Cambridge Inst. for Sustainability Leadership (Belgium) SPRL, 2017–18; Inst. for Manufacturing Educn and Consultancy Services Ltd, 2018–. Mem., Life Scis Jury, Blavatnik Awards for Young Scientists (UK), 2018–. FREng 2017. *Publications:* contribs to sci. and engrg jls on computer speech recognition and med. ultrasonic imaging. *Recreations:* opera, cycling, walking. *Address:* Engineering Department, University of Cambridge, Trumpington Street, Cambridge CB2 1PZ.

**PRAGNELL, Michael Patrick,** CBE 2017; Chairman and Trustee, Cancer Research UK, 2010–16; *b* Hindhead, Surrey, 19 Dec. 1946; *s* of George Pragnell and Margaret Pragnell (*née* Lowry); *m* 1983, Susan Williams; two *s*. *Educ:* Douai Sch.; St John's Coll., Oxford (MA); INSEAD (MBA). Courtaulds Ltd, 1968–72; Courtaulds N America Inc., 1972–74; First Nat. Bank of Chicago, 1974–75; Courtaulds plc, 1975–95: CEO, Coatings, 1986–92; Dir, 1990–95; Chief Financial Officer, 1992–94; CEO, Zeneca Agrochemicals, 1995–2000, Dir, 1997–2000, Zeneca, later AstraZeneca plc; Founder CEO and Dir, Syngenta AG, Switzerland, 2000–07. Mem., Supervisory Bd, Advanta BV, 1996–2000; non-executive Director: D. S. Smith plc, 1996–2000; VINCI SA, Paris, 2009–. Pres., CropLife Internat., 2002–05. Mem., Swiss-American Bd, Chamber of Commerce, 2005–07. Mem. Bd, 2009–18, Adv. Cttee, 2018–, INSEAD. *Recreations:* ski-ing, walking, shooting, theatre, opera, music, modern art, travel. *T:* 07789 986109. *E:* michael@pragnell.org.

**PRAITIES, Nigel Anthony;** Executive Editor, Pharmaceutical Journal, since 2018; *b* Harrogate, 1 April 1978; *s* of Robert Laurence and Marion Patricia Praties; partner, Kintaro Sawado. *Educ:* University Coll. London (BSc Hons Physiol.); Imperial Coll. London (MSc Sci. Communication). Freelance writer for Guardian; reporter, Research Fortnight mag., 2007; Pulse magazine: clin. reporter, 2007–12; Dep. Ed., 2012–14; Ed., 2014–18. Publication Ed. of Year, Med. Journalists Assoc. Awards, 2014; Ed. of Year, Business, British Soc. of Mag. Editors Awards, 2016. *Address:* Pharmaceutical Journal Publications, Royal Pharmaceutical Society, 66–68 East Smithfield, E1W 1AW.

**PRANCE, Sir Ghillean (Tolmie),** Kt 1995; DPhil; FRS 1993; FLS, FRSB; FRGS; VMH; Scientific Director, Eden Project, Cornwall, 1999–2013 (Trustee, 2009–18); *b* 13 July 1937; *s* of Basil Camden Prance, CIE, OBE and Margaret Hope Prance (*née* Tolmie); *m* 1961, Anne Elizabeth Hay; two *d*. *Educ:* Malvern Coll.; Keble Coll., Oxford (BA, MA, DPhil). FLS 1961; FRSB (FIBiol 1988). New York Botanical Garden: Res. Asst, 1963–66; Associate Curator, 1966–68; B. A. Krukoff Curator of Amazonian Botany, 1968–75; Dir of Research, 1975–81; Vice-Pres., 1977–81; Senior Vice-Pres., 1981–88; Dir, Royal Botanic Gdns, Kew, 1988–99. Adjunct Prof., City Univ. of NY, 1968–99; Vis. Prof. in Tropical Studies, Yale, 1983–89; Vis. Prof., Reading Univ., 1988–; McBryde Prof., 2000–02, McBryde Sen. Res. Fellow, 2006–, Nat. Tropical Botanical Gdn, Kalaheo, Hawaii; Dir of Graduate Studies, Instituto Nacional de Pesquisas da Amazônia, Manaus, Brazil, 1973–75; 29 botanical expedns to Amazonia. President: Assoc. of Tropical Biol., 1979–80 (Hon. Fellow, 2007); Amer. Assoc. of Plant Taxonomists, 1984–85; Systematics Assoc., 1989–91; Econ. Botany Soc., 1996–97; Linnean Soc., 1997–2000; Internat. Assoc. for Plant Taxonomy, 1999–2005; Inst. of Biology, 2000–02; Internat. Tree Foundn, 2005–; Chm., MEMO Project, 2006–. Mem. Council, RHS, 1990–2000. Chm., A Rocha Internat., 2008–12. FRGS 1989; Fellow: AAAS, 1990; Perak Acad., 2006; Corresponding Member: Brazilian Acad. of Scis, 1976; Botanical Soc. of America, 1994; Foreign Member: Royal Danish Acad. of Scis and Letters, 1988; Royal Swedish Acad. of Scis, 1989; Associate Mem., Third World Acad. of Scis, 1993; Hon. Mem., British Ecol Soc., 1996. Hon. Freeman, Gardeners' Co., 1997. Fil Dr *hc* Univ. Göteborgs, Sweden, 1983; Hon. DSc: Kent, Portsmouth, Kingston, 1994; St Andrews, 1995; Bergen Univ., Norway, 1996; Florida Internat. Univ., Herbert H. Lehman Coll., NY, and Sheffield Univ., 1997; Liverpool, 1998; Glasgow, Plymouth, 1999; Keele, Exeter, 2000; Gloucestershire, 2009. Henry Shaw Medal, Missouri Botanical Garden, St Louis, 1988; Linnean Medal, 1990; Internat. Cosmos Prize, Japan, 1993; Patron's Medal, RGS, 1994; Janaki Ammal Medal, Soc. of Ethnobotany, 1996; Internat. Award of Excellence, Botanical Res. Inst., Texas, 1998; Medalho do Mérito, Jardim Botânico, Rio de Janeiro, 1998; VMH 1999; Lifetime of Discovery Award, Discovery Channel and RGS, 1999; Fairchild Medal for Plant Exploration, Nat. Tropical Botanical Gdn, 2000; Dist. Econ. Botanist Award, Soc. of Econ. Botany, 2002; Graziela Maciel Barroso Prize, Botanical Soc. of Brazil, 2004; Allerton Award, Nat. Tropical Botanical Gdn, 2005; Gold Medal, New York Botanical Gdn, 2008. Ordem Nacional do Mérito Cientifico-Grã-Cruz (Brazil), 1995; Comendador da Ordem Nacional do Cruzeiro do Sul (Brazil), 2000; Order of the Rising Sun (Japan), 2012. *Publications:* Arvores de Manaus, 1975; Algumas Flores da Amazonia, 1976; Extinction is Forever, 1977; Biological Diversification in the Tropics, 1981; Amazonia: key environments, 1985; Leaves, 1986; Manual de Botânica Econômica do Maranhão, 1988; Flowers for all Seasons, 1989; Out of the Amazon, 1992; Bark, 1993; The Earth Under Threat: a Christian perspective, 1996; Rainforests: water, fire, earth and air, 1997; Chrysobalanaceae of the World, 2003;

Rainforest: light and spirit, 2008; Go to the Ant, 2013; That Glorious Forest, 2014. *Recreations:* flower stamp collecting, bird watching. *Address:* The Old Vicarage, Silver Street, Lyme Regis, Dorset DT7 3HS. *T:* (01297) 444991. *E:* siriain01@yahoo.co.uk. *Club:* Explorers (New York) (Fellow).

**PRANKERD, Thomas Arthur John,** FRCP; Professor of Clinical Haematology, 1965–79 and Dean, 1972–77, University College Hospital Medical School; Hon. Consultant Physician: University College Hospital; Whittington Hospital; *b* 11 Sept. 1924; *s* of late H. A. Prankerd, Barrister-at-Law, and J. D. Shorthose; *m* 1950, Margaret Vera Harrison Cripps (*d* 2015); two *s* (and one *s* one *d* decd). *Educ:* Charterhouse Sch.; St Bartholomew's Hospital Med. Sch. MD (London) Gold Medal 1949; FRCP 1962. Jr med. appts, St Bart's and University Coll. Hosp., 1947–60. Major, RAMC, 1948–50. Univ. Travelling Fellow, USA, 1953–54; Consultant Physician, University Coll. Hosp., 1960–65. Examr, RCP, and various univs. Goulstonian Lectr, RCP, 1963; Visiting Professor: Univ. of Perth, WA, 1972; Univ. of Cape Town, 1973. Mem., NE Thames RHA, 1976–79. Mem. Bd of Governors, UCH, 1972–74. Mem., Assoc. of Physicians, 1965. *Publications:* The Red Cell, 1961; Haematology in Medical Practice, 1968; articles in med. jls. *Recreations:* fishing, gardening, music. *Address:* 6 Stinsford House, Stinsford, Dorchester DT2 8PT. *T:* (01305) 751521.

**PRASAD, Dr Sunand,** RIBA; Senior Partner, Penoyre & Prasad Architects, since 1988; President, Royal Institute of British Architects, 2007–09; *b* 22 May 1950; *s* of Devi and Janaki Prasad; *m* 1st, 1982, Susan Francis (marr. diss. 2014); three *s*; 2nd, 2018, Gillian Horn; one *d*. *Educ:* Univ. of Cambridge Sch. of Architecture (MA); Architectural Assoc. (AA Dip.); PhD RCA 1988. RIBA 1987. Partner, Edward Cullinan Architects, 1978–84; Leverhulme Res. Fellow, RCA, 1985–88. Comr, Commn for Architecture and the Built Envmt, 1999–2006; Mem., Green Construction Bd, 2011–14. Member: Awards Gp, 1995–2000, Practice Cttee, 1999–2002, RIBA; Council, AA, 1997–2001; London Mayor's Design Adv. Gp, 2008–16; Built Envmt Expert, Design Council, 2013–; London Mayor's Design Advocate, 2017–; Advr, UK Govt Building Better Building Beautiful Commn, 2019–. Trustee: Article 25, 2008– (Chm., 2014–); Centre for Cities, 2010–14; Cape Farewell, 2011–14; UK Green Building Council, 2016–. Presenter, The Essay: Architecture, The Fourth R, BBC Radio 3, 2010. Chm., Editl Bd, Jl of Architecture, 2017– (Mem., 2014–). FRSA. Hon. Member: AIA 2008; RTPI 2009. Hon. FRIAS 2008; Hon. FRAIC 2010. Hon. DA UEL, 2009. *Publications:* contributor to: Le Corbusier: architect of the century, 1987; Paradigms of Indian Architecture, 1998; Macmillan Dictionary of Art, 1997; Design Quality, 2002; London: postcolonial city, 2002; Transformations: the architecture of Penoyre & Prasad, 2007; Changing Hospital Architecture, 2008; Retrofit for Purpose, 2014. *Recreations:* music, cycling. *Address:* Penoyre & Prasad Architects, 28–42 Banner Street, EC1Y 8QE. *T:* (020) 7250 3477. *E:* mail@penoyreprasad.com.

**PRASHAR, Baroness** *cr* 1999 (Life Peer), of Runnymede in the county of Surrey; **Usha Kumari Prashar,** CBE 1995; PC 2009; Chairman, Judicial Appointments Commission, 2006–10; Deputy Chairman, British Council, 2012–18; Member, Iraq Inquiry, 2009–16; *b* 29 June 1948; *d* of Nauhria Lal Prashar and Durga Devi Prashar; *m* 1973, Vijay Kumar Sharma. *Educ:* Duchess of Gloucester Sch., Nairobi; Wakefield Girls' High Sch. (Head Girl, 1966–67); Univ. of Leeds (BA Hons Pol Studies); Univ. of Glasgow (postgrad. Dip. Social Admin). Race Relations Bd, 1971–76; Asst Dir, Runnymede Trust, 1976–77, Dir, 1976–84; Res. Fellow, PSI, 1984–86; Dir, NCVO, 1986–91; Dep. Chm., 1992–2000, Chm., 2000–05, Nat. Literacy Trust. CS Comr (part-time), 1990–96; Chm., Parole Bd, 1997–2000; First CS Comr, 2000–05. Non-executive Director: Channel 4, 1992–99; Unite plc, 2001–04; ITV, 2005–10; Nationwide, 2017–. Vice-Chm., British Refugee Council, 1987–89. Member: Arts Council of GB, 1979–81, Arts Council of England, 1994–97; Study Commn on the Family, 1980–83; Social Security Adv. Cttee, 1980–83; Exec. Cttee, Child Poverty Action Gp, 1984–85; GLAA, 1984–86; London Food Commn, 1984–90; BBC Educnl Broadcasting Council, 1987–89; Adv. Council, Open College, 1987–89; Solicitors' Complaints Bureau, 1989–90; Royal Commn on Criminal Justice, 1991–93; Lord Chancellor's Adv. Cttee on Legal Educn and Conduct, 1991–97; Council, PSI, 1992–97; Bd, Energy Saving Trust, 1992–98; King's Fund, 1998–2002. President: UK Council for Internat. Student Affairs, 2006–; Community Foundn Network, 2007–; Hon. Vice-Pres., Council for Overseas Student Affairs, 1986–98. Trustee: Thames Help Trust, 1984–86; Charities Aid Foundn, 1986–91; Independent Broadcasting Telethon Trust, 1987–92; Acad. of Indian Dance, 1987–91; Camelot Foundn, 1996–2001; Ethnic Minority Foundn, 1997–2002; BBC World Service Trust, 2001–05; Miriam Rothschild and John Foster Trust, 2007–10; Cumberland Lodge, 2007– (Chm., 2019–); Chm., English Adv. Cttee, Nat. AIDS Trust, 1988–89; Gov., Ditchley Foundn, 2003–; Patron, Runnymede Trust, 2008–. Chancellor, De Montfort Univ., 2000–06 (Gov., 1996–2006). Trustee, 2001–11, Chm., 2001–08, Pres., 2008–11, Royal Commonwealth Soc. FRSA. Hon. Fellow, Goldsmiths' Coll., Univ. of London, 1992; Hon. Bencher, Inner Temple, 2012. Hon. LLD: De Montfort, 1994; South Bank Univ., 1994; Greenwich, 1999; Leeds Metropolitan, 1999; Ulster, 2000; Oxford Brookes, 2000; Hon. Dr: Leeds; Glasgow; Exeter; Aston; Kalinka Inst. of Social Sci., India, 2018. *Publications: contributed to:* Britain's Black Population, 1980; The System: a study of Lambeth Borough Council's race relations unit, 1981; Scarman and After, 1984; Sickle Cell Anaemia, Who Cares? a survey of screening, counselling, training and educational facilities in England, 1985; Routes or Road Blocks, a study of consultation arrangements between local authorities and local communities, 1985; Acheson and After: primary health care in the inner city, 1986. *Recreations:* reading, country walks, music, golf, international affairs. *Address:* House of Lords, SW1A 0PW.

**PRAT, Prof. Andrea,** PhD; FBA 2011; Richard Paul Richman Professor of Business, Columbia Business School, and Professor of Economics, Columbia University, New York, since 2012. *Educ:* Turin Univ. (Laurea in Economia e Commercio 1992); Stanford Univ. (PhD 1997). Fellow, Compagnia di San Paolo, Italy, 1992–94; Res. Asst, Stanford Univ., 1995–96; Marie Curie Fellow, EC, 1997–99; Asst Prof., Tilburg Univ., 1997–2000; Lectr, 2000–02, Reader, 2002–04, Prof. of Econs, 2004–13, Dept of Econs, LSE; Co-Dir, Prog. for Study of Econ. Orgn and Public Policy, Suntory and Toyota Internat. Centres for Econs and Related Disciplines, 2004–12. Man. Ed., 2005–09, Chair, 2010–13, Rev. of Econ. Studies; Associate Ed., Theoretical Econs, 2007–. Mem. Council, REconS. *Publications:* (contrib.) Oxford Handbook of Political Economy, 2006; (ed jtly) The Ruling Class: management and politics in modern Italy, 2010; contribs to Jl Finance, Rev. of Financial Studies, Jl Econ. Theory, Qly Jl Pol Sci., Econometrica, Jl Public Econs. *Address:* Graduate School of Business, Columbia University, 3022 Broadway, Uris 624, New York, NY 10027–6902, USA.

**PRATLEY, Alan Sawyer;** Deputy Financial Controller, Commission of the European Communities, 1990–98 (Director, Financial Control, 1986–90); *b* 25 Nov. 1933; *s* of Frederick Pratley and Hannah Pratley (*née* Sawyer); *m* 1st, 1960, Dorothea Rohland (marr. diss. 1979); two *d*; 2nd, 1979, Josette Kairis (marr. diss. 1994); one *d*; 3rd, 1996, Marie-Hélène Ledivelec. *Educ:* Latymer Upper School; Sidney Sussex Coll., Cambridge (BA Modern Languages (German, Russian)). Head, German Dept, Stratford Grammar Sch., West Ham, 1958–60; Asst Dir, Examinations, Civil Service Commn, 1960–68; Home Office, 1968–73; Commission of the European Communities: Head, Individual Rights Div., 1973–79; Dep. Chef de Cabinet to Christopher Tugendhat, 1979–80; Adviser to Michael O'Kennedy, 1980–81; Dir of Admin, 1981–86. *Recreations:* tennis, gardening. *Address:* 18 Avenue de l'Armée, 1040 Brussels, Belgium. *T:* and *Fax:* (2) 7352483. *E:* alan.pratley@skynet.be.

**PRATLEY, David Illingworth;** Principal, David Pratley Associates, 1996–2015; *b* 24 Dec. 1948; *s* of Arthur George Pratley and Olive Constance Illingworth; *m* 1st, 1996, Caryn Faure Walker (*née* Becker) (*d* 2004); 2nd, 2008, Diane Linda Fredericks (*née* Cane) (*d* 2017). *Educ:* Westminster Abbey Choir Sch.; Westminster Sch.; Univ. of Bristol (LLB). PRO, Thorndike Theatre, Leatherhead, 1970–71; Gen. Asst, Queen's Univ. Festival, Belfast, 1971–73; Dep. Dir, Merseyside Arts Assoc., 1973–76; Dir, Greater London Arts Assoc., 1976–81; Regl Dir, Arts Council of GB, 1981–86; Chief Exec., Royal Liverpool Philharmonic Soc., 1987–88; Man. Dir, Trinity Coll. of Music, 1988–91; Dir of Leisure, Tourism and Econ. Develt, Bath CC, 1992–96. Chm., Alliance Arts Panel, 1987–88; Council Mem., Nat. Campaign for the Arts, 1986–92 (Chm., 1988–92); Dir, Dance Umbrella Ltd, 1986– (Chm., 1990–92). Lottery Policy Advr, Arts Council England (formerly Arts Council of England), 1996–. Trustee, Sainsbury Internat. Arts Festival, 2009–15. Chairman: Poole Arts Trust, 2009–16; Wilts Music Centre, 2009–15. FRSA. *Recreations:* music, theatre and film, art, design and architecture, photography, gardens, sailing, walking, travel. *Address:* 5 Little Burn, Sway, Hampshire SO41 6DZ.

**PRATT,** family name of **Marquess Camden.**

**PRATT, James Simon H.;** *see* Healy-Pratt.

**PRATT, (Richard) Camden;** QC 1992; a Recorder, 1993–2013; a Deputy High Court Judge (Family Division), 1995–2013; *b* 14 Dec. 1947; *s* of late Richard Sheldon Pratt, MA Oxon, and Irene Gladys Pratt; *m* 1973, (Dorothy Jane) Marchia, *d* of late Capt. W. P. and Aphrodite Allsebrook. *Educ:* Boston Grammar Sch.; Westcliff High Sch.; Lincoln Coll., Oxford (Hanbury Law Scholar; MA Jurisp). Called to the Bar, Gray's Inn, 1970, Bencher, 2002. Chairman: Sussex Courts Liaison Cttee, 1993–2009; Sussex Sessions Bar Mess, 1994–2006; Mem., Area Criminal Justice Liaison Cttee, 1994–2002. *Recreations:* walking, sailing, Arsenal FC, travel, people. *E:* camdenprattqc@btinternet.com.

**PRATT, Richard Charles;** JP; regulatory consultant; *b* 3 Nov. 1949; *s* of Charles Pratt and Rosemary Pratt (*née* Robson); *m* 1974, Christine Whiteman; one *s*. *Educ:* Eltham Coll.; Bristol Univ. (BSc Politics and Econs 1972); Sch. of Oriental and African Studies, London Univ. (MA 1973). Joined Civil Service, 1973; Press Officer, Prime Minister's Office, 1975–76; Asst Private Sec., Lord Privy Seal's Office, 1976; Head of Pay Negotiations Br., CSD, 1977–80; Head of Special Employment Measures Br., Dept of Employment, 1980–82; HM Treasury: Head of NI Public Expenditure Br., 1982–84; Mem., Central Unit for UK Budget, 1984–86; Head of Gen. Expenditure Div., 1986–87; Economic Counsellor, Washington, 1987–90 (on secondment); Head, EC Div. (EMU and Trade Policy), 1990–93; Advr to Sec. of State for Social Services on Expenditure Review, DSS, 1993; Head of Securities and Mkts Div., HM Treasury, 1993–95; Dir of External Affairs, LIFFE, 1995–98; Dir Gen., Jersey Financial Services Commn, 1999–2003. Ombudsman for KPMG, 2004–; Special Advr, RSM Robson Rhodes, 2004–06; Director: UK Financial Services Compensation Scheme, 2004–09; Look Ahead Care and Support (formerly Look Ahead Housing), 2008–14. Chm., Friends of Urambo and Mwanhala, 2014–. JP E London, 2009. *Publications:* (ed) How to Combat Money Laundering and Terrorist Financing, 2005; (ed) Working Together: international cooperation between financial services regulators, 2007. *Recreations:* flying, travelling, guitar. *Address:* Redwoods, Ridgeway, Horsell, Surrey GU21 4QR.

**PRATT, Ven. Dr Richard David;** Archdeacon of West Cumberland, since 2009; *b* Cheltenham, 25 Dec. 1955; *s* of Kenneth Pratt and Margaret Pratt; *m* 1983, Diane Tomlinson; three *s*. *Educ:* Ranelagh Sch., Bracknell; Lincoln Coll., Oxford (Exhibnr; MA 1980); Lincoln Theol Coll. and Univ. of Nottingham (BCS 1984); Univ. of Birmingham (PhD 2001). Pt-time Porter, Broadmoor Hosp., 1972–74; VSO, Ghana Secondary Sch., Tamale, Ghana, 1977–79; Systems Analyst, Perkins Engines, Peterborough, 1979–81; ordained deacon, 1984, priest, 1985; Asst Curate, All Hallows, Wellingborough, 1984–87; Team Vicar, St Mark's, Kingsthorpe, 1987–92; Vicar, St Benedict's, Hunsbury, 1992–97; Priest-in-charge, St Cuthbert's, Carlisle, 1997–2008; Communications Officer, Dio. of Carlisle, 1997–2008. *Publications:* contribs to jls incl. Christian Community, Theology. *Recreations:* walking the Lakeland Fells, growing vegetables, the music of Bach. *Address:* 50 Stainburn Road, Workington, Cumbria CA14 1SN. *T:* (01900) 66190. *E:* richard.pratt@lincoln.oxon.org. *W:* www.prattr.org.

**PRATT, Richard James;** QC 2006; a Recorder, since 2000; *b* 22 June 1956; *s* of Gordon Francis Pratt and Audrey Pratt (*née* Upton-Prowse); *m* 1987, Kim Lorraine Emmerson; two *d*. *Educ:* St Mary's Coll., Crosby, Liverpool; Lanchester Poly., Coventry (BA Hons 1978). Called to the Bar, Gray's Inn, 1980, Bencher, 2010; in practice as barrister, 7 Harrington Street, Liverpool; Asst Recorder, 1997–2000; Leader, Northern Circuit, 2011–13. *Recreations:* watching Everton Football Club and old films, listening to music, practising ventriloquism. *Address:* 7 Harrington Street, Liverpool L2 9YH. *T:* (0151) 242 0707, *Fax:* (0151) 236 1120. *E:* Rickpratt2@aol.com. *Club:* John Mc's (Liverpool).

**PRATT, Prof. Robert John,** CBE 2003; FRCN; Professor of Nursing and Director, Richard Wells Research Centre, Thames Valley University, 1994–2010, now Emeritus Professor; *b* 27 June 1941; *s* of Loren Delbert Pratt and Mary Jane Stubbs, and step *s* of Leonard William Paulson. *Educ:* Univ. of London (DN 1974); New Coll. of Calif, San Francisco (BA (Humanities) 1981); Chelsea Coll., London (MSc (Health Educn) 1984). Served US Navy, Hospital Corpsman, Fleet Marine Force, 1959–63. Various nursing appts, USA and UK, 1964–71; Charge Nurse, Charing Cross Hosp., 1971–76; Hd, Dept of Professional and Vocational Studies, Charing Cross Hosp. Sch. of Nursing, 1978–86; Vice Principal, Riverside Coll. of Health Studies, London, 1986–94. Pres., Infection Control Nurses Assoc. of British Isles, 2000–06; Patron, UK Nat. HIV Nurses Assoc., 1999–. FRCN 1999; FHEA 2007; FRSA 2006. *Publications:* HIV & AIDS: a foundation for nursing and healthcare practice, 1986, 5th edn 2003; (jtly) Tuberculosis: a foundation for nursing and healthcare practice, 2005; frequent articles in a variety of nursing and med. peer-reviewed jls. *Recreations:* theatre, cinema, travel, reading. *Address:* Richard Wells Research Centre, University of West London, Paragon House, Boston Manor Road, Brentford, Middx TW8 9GA. *E:* robert.pratt5@btopenworld.com.

**PRATT, Roger Allan,** CBE 1996; Boundary Review Director, Conservative Party, since 2015; *b* 28 Dec. 1950; *s* of late Allan Pratt and Joyce Isobel Pratt (*née* Dodds); *m* 1st, 1975, Ann Heaton (marr. diss. 1993; she *d* 2010); one *s* one *d*; 2nd, 1993, Lynn Mary Tomlinson (marr. diss. 2011); one step *s* one step *d*; 3rd, 2014, Jane Thomas; two step *s* one step *d*. *Educ:* King Edward's Fiveways Sch., Birmingham. Organiser, E Midlands Area YC, 1971–72; NW Area Youth Develt Officer, 1972–74; Agent, Liverpool Wavertree Cons. Assoc., 1975–76; Nat. YC Organiser, 1976–79; Agent, Pendle, Burnley and Hyndburn Cons. Assocs, 1980–84; North West Area, then NW Region: Dep. Central Office Agent, 1984–89; Central Office Agent, 1989–93; Regl Dir, 1993; Dir, Cons. Pty in Scotland,

1993–97; Conservative Central Office: Dep. Dir, Campaigning Dept, 1997–98; Area Campaign Dir, London Western, and Regl Eur. Campaign Dir for London, 1998–2000; Dep. Dir of Ops, 2004; Boundary Rev. Project Dir, 2000–05, Dep. Dir of Campaigning, 2005–07, Cons. Campaign HQ; Acting Sec., Nat. Cons. Convention, 2005–07; Regl Dir, SW Conservatives, 2008–10; Boundary Rev. Manager, 2010–12; Dir, Welsh Cons. Party, 2012–15. *Recreation:* cricket. *Address:* Conservative Party, 4 Matthew Parker Street, Westminster, SW1H 9HQ.

**PRATT, Dr Rosemary Dorothea;** Director, Hostile State Activity and Cyber Unit, National Security Secretariat, Cabinet Office, since 2018; *b* Plymouth, 1 July 1967; *m* 1995, Dr Philip John Pratt; two *s* one *d*. *Educ:* Plymouth High Sch. for Girls; St Peter's Coll., Oxford (MA 1st Cl. German and Philosophy); University Coll. London (PhD 2000). Department for Education and Science, then Department for Education and subsequently Department for Education and Employment, 1990–2000: Pvte Sec. to Sec. of State, 1991–92; Hd, Literacy and Numeracy Strategy, 1992–99; Dep. Dir, Schs Plus, 2000–01; Deputy Director: Family Law and Mental Capacity, DCA, 2001–05; Policy and Performances, DCSF, 2007–09; Children and Young People Strategy, DCSF, subseq. DFE, 2009–11; Head: Preventing Extremism Unit, DFE, 2011–13; Prevent, Office of Security and Counter-Terrorism, Home Office, 2013–14; Director: Counter Extremism and Due Diligence, DFE, 2014–15; Europe, Data, Digital and Security Directorate, DCMS, 2016–17; EU and Trade Capability, DCMS, 2017. *Address:* Cabinet Office, 70 Whitehall, SW1A 2AS.

**PRATT, His Honour Simon;** a Circuit Judge, 1995–2012; *b* 23 June 1949; *s* of Harry James Roffey Pratt and Ann Loveday Pratt (*née* Peter); *m* 1974, Sheena Maynard; one *s* one *d*. Called to the Bar, Inner Temple, 1971; a Recorder, SE Circuit, 1989–95. Freeman, City of London, 1984. *Recreation:* dwindling. *Address:* 3 Temple Gardens, Temple, EC4Y 9AU. *T:* (020) 7353 3102.

**PREBBLE, Stuart Colin;** Director, StoryVault Ltd and Chairman, StoryVault Films, since 2010; *b* 15 April 1951; *s* of Dennis Stanley Prebble and Jean Margaret Prebble; *m* 1978, Marilyn Anne Charlton; one *d* (and one *d* decd). *Educ:* Univ. of Newcastle upon Tyne (BA Hons English Lang. and Lit.). Reporter, BBC TV News, 1975–80; Presenter, Granada TV, 1981; Producer, 1983–88, Editor, 1988–89, World in Action; Head of Regl Progs, Granada, 1989–90; Man. Dir, North East TV, 1990–91; Head of Factual Progs, Granada, 1992; Controller, ITV Network Factual Progs, 1993–96; Chief Exec., Granada Sky Broadcasting, 1996–98; Man. Dir, Channels and Interactive Media, Granada Media Gp, 1999; Chief Executive: ONdigital, subseq. ITV Digital, 1999–2002; ITV Network, 2001–02; Man. Dir, Liberty Bell Ltd, 2002–10 (Jt Man. Dir, 2002–05). *Publications:* A Power in the Land, 1988; The Lazarus File, 1989; The Official Grumpy Old Men Handbook, 2004; Grumpy Old Men: the secret diary, 2005; Grumpy Old Christmas, 2006; Grumpy Old Workers, 2007; Grumpy Old Drivers, 2008; Secrets of the Conqueror, 2011; The Insect Farm, 2015; The Bridge, 2017. *Recreations:* walking, cinema, music.

**PREBENSEN, Preben;** Chief Executive, Close Brothers Group plc, since 2009; *b* London, 19 Nov. 1956; *s* of Peter and Else Prebensen; *m* 1983, Annie Whitehead; three *s* one *d*. *Educ:* St Paul's Sch., London; Magdalene Coll., Cambridge (BA Hist. 1978). J. P. Morgan, later JP Morgan Chase: UK Corporate Finance, 1978–84; US Capital Mkts, 1984–91; Head, UK, Scandinavia and Holland, 1991–2001; Co-Head, Eur. Investment Banking, Chm., London Mgt Cttee and Mem., Global Investment Banking Cttee, 1996–2000; investment consultant, 2001–04; Chief Exec., Wellington Underwriting plc, 2004–06; Chief Investment Officer, Catlin Gp Ltd, 2006–09. Non-exec. Dir, British Land Co. plc, 2017–. *Recreations:* theatre, forestry, farming. *Address:* Close Brothers Group plc, 10 Crown Place, EC2A 4FT. *T:* (020) 7655 3100.

**PREECE, Prof. Michael Andrew,** MD; FRCP, FRCPCH; Professor of Child Health and Growth, Institute of Child Health, University College London, 1985–2007, now Emeritus; Medical Director, Great Ormond Street Hospital for Children, 2005–07; *b* 11 May 1944; *s* of Roy and Norah Preece; *m* 1977, Jan Baines; one *s*. *Educ:* Guy's Hosp. Med. Sch., Univ. of London (MB BS 1967; MD 1976; MSc 1977). FRCP 1982; FRCPCH 1997. Institute of Child Health, London University: Lectr In Growth and Develt, 1974–77; Sen. Lectr, 1977–83; Reader in Child Health and Growth, 1983–85. Visiting Professor: RPMS, later ICSM, 1994–2005; Hosp. for Sick Children, Univ. of Toronto, 2003; Lectures: Teale, RCP, 1990; Gaisford, Manchester Med. Soc., 1994. Mem., Selection Panel, Snowdon Trust, 2010–. Guthrie Medal, British Paediatric Assoc., 1980. *Publications:* (with J. M. Tanner) The Physiology of Human Growth, 1989; (jtly) The Cambridge Encyclopaedia of Human Growth and Development, 1998; (jtly) Neoplasia: growth and growth hormone treatment, 2004. *Recreations:* nature photography, theatre, sport (mostly watching nowadays). *E:* m.preece@ucl.ac.uk.

**PREECE, Ven. Roger Martin Howell;** Master, Royal Foundation of St Katharine, London, since 2019; *b* Grimsby, 25 Sept. 1964; *m* 1991, Catherine Hooper; three *d*. *Educ:* Imperial Coll. London (BSc Elec. Engrg); St Stephen's House, Oxford (MA Theol.). Exec., County Bank, Natwest, 1986–88; Manager, Accenture, 1998–92; Vice Pres., Bank of America, 1992–95; Man. Dir, Sumitomo Mitsui Banking Corp., 1995–98; Man. Dir, Capco, 1998–2003; ordained deacon 2006, priest, 2007; Curate, All Saints, Marple, Stockport, 2006–08; Vicar, St Mary's, Bowdon, Altrincham, 2008–15; Archdeacon of St Helens and Warrington, 2015–19. FRSA. *Recreations:* running, music. *Address:* Royal Foundation of St Katharine, 2 Butcher Row, Limehouse, E14 8DS.

**PREISS, Prof. David,** FRS 2004; Professor of Mathematics, University of Warwick, 2006–17, now Emeritus; *b* 21 Jan. 1947; *s* of Alfred and Marta Preiss; *m* 1977, Irena; one *d*. *Educ:* Charles Univ., Prague (RNDr (Dr of Natural Sci.) 1970; Candidate of Sci. 1979). Various posts, Charles Univ., Prague, 1970–89; Astor Prof. of Maths, UCL, 1990–2006. Vis. posts at univs in Jerusalem, Palermo, Santa Barbara and Vancouver. (Jtly) Ostrowski Prize, 2011. *Publications:* Fréchet Differentiability of Lipschitz Functions and Porous Sets in Banach Spaces (jtly), 2012; res. papers, chiefly in mathematical analysis, in scientific jls. *Address:* Mathematics Institute, University of Warwick, Coventry CV4 7AL. *E:* d.preiss@warwick.ac.uk.

**PRENDERGAST, Prof. Christopher Alan Joseph,** PhD; FBA 1996; Fellow, King's College, Cambridge, since 1970; Professor of Modern French Literature, Cambridge University, 1997–2003, now Professor Emeritus; *b* 27 Sept. 1942; *s* of James Prendergast and Celia (*née* Sevitt); *m* 1st, 1965, Shirley Busbridge (marr. diss. 1979); two *d*; 2nd, 1997, Inge Birgitte Siegumfeldt (marr. diss. 2008); one *d*; 3rd, 2016, Bridget Strevens Marzo. *Educ:* Keble Coll., Oxford (BA 1965; BPhil 1967); MA 1968, PhD 1989, Cantab. Lectr, Pembroke Coll., Oxford, 1967–68; Fellow, Downing Coll., Cambridge, 1968–70; Univ. Lectr, Cambridge Univ., 1968–89; Distinguished Prof. in French and Comparative Lit., Grad. Sch., CUNY, 1989–92; Reader in Modern French Lit., Cambridge Univ., 1992–97. Vis. Prof., 1998–2000, Hon. Prof., 2004, Univ. of Copenhagen, Denmark. MAE 2013; Mem., Amer. Acad. of Arts and Scis, 2015. Officier, Ordre des Palmes Académiques (France), 2019. *Publications:* Balzac: fiction and melodrama, 1978; The Order of Mimesis, 1986; (ed) Nineteenth-Century French Poetry, 1990; Paris and the Nineteenth Century, 1992; (ed jtly) Anthology of World Literature, 1994; (ed) Cultural Materialism, 1996; Napoleon and History Painting, 1997; The Triangle of Representation, 2000; (ed) Proust, In Search of Lost Time, 6 vols, 2002; (ed) Debating World Literature, 2004; The Classic: Sainte-Beuve and the nineteenth-century culture wars, 2007; The Fourteenth of July: and the taking of the Bastille, 2008; Mirages and Mad Beliefs: Proust the skeptic, 2013; (ed) A History of Modern French Literature, 2017; Counterfactuals: paths of the might have been, 2019. *Recreations:* gardening, cooking, opera. *Address:* 26 Bermuda Road, Cambridge CB4 3JX.

**PRENDERGAST, Sir (Walter) Kieran,** KCVO 1991; CMG 1990; HM Diplomatic Service, retired; Under-Secretary-General for Political Affairs, United Nations, New York, 1997–2005; *b* 2 July 1942; *s* of late Lt-Comdr J. H. Prendergast and Mai Hennessy; *m* 1967, Joan Reynolds; two *s* two *d*. *Educ:* St Patrick's College, Strathfield, Sydney, NSW; Salesian College, Chertsey; St Edmund Hall, Oxford. Turkish language student Istanbul, 1964; Ankara, 1965; FO (later FCO), 1967; 2nd Sec. Nicosia, 1969; 1st Sec. FCO, 1972; The Hague, 1973; Asst Private Sec. to Foreign and Commonwealth Sec. (Rt Hon. Anthony Crosland, Rt Hon. Dr David Owen), 1976; UK Mission to UN, NY, 1979 (detached for duty Jan.–March 1980 at Govt House, Salisbury, Rhodesia); Counsellor, Tel Aviv, 1982–86; Head of Southern African Dept, FCO, 1986–89; High Comr to Zimbabwe, 1989–92; High Comr to Kenya, 1992–95; Ambassador to Turkey, 1995–97. Sen. Advr, Centre for Humanitarian Dialogue, Geneva, 2006–. Mem., Internat. Adv. Bd, Independent Diplomat, 2007–; Counsellor, Dragoman Global, 2013–. Counsellor, ESU. Trustee, Beit Trust, 2009–. Pres., British Assoc. of Former UN Civil Servants, 2017–. Rhodesia Medal, 1980; Zimbabwe Independence Medal, 1980. *Recreations:* family, wine, walking, reading. *Address:* 5 Weston Court Barn, Pembridge HR6 9JE; 333 Milkwood Road, SE24 0HA; Bonneval, La Chapelle-aux-Saints, 19120, France. *T:* (555) 912960. *E:* prendergast@hdcentre.org. *Clubs:* Beefsteak, Garrick.

**PRENN, Helen Gillian;** see Robinson, H. G.

**PRENTER, Patrick Robert,** CBE 1995; Chairman, Mactaggart Scott Holdings, Loanhead, Midlothian, since 1991; Lord-Lieutenant for Midlothian, 2003–13; *b* 9 Sept. 1939; *s* of Robert Gibson Prenter, OBE and Katherine Emily Prenter (*née* Scott); *m* 1962, Susan, *d* of Francis Patrick, OBE and Isabel Patrick (*née* Spencer); two *s* two *d*. *Educ:* Loretto Sch., Musselburgh; Trinity Hall, Cambridge (BA Mech. Scis 1962). Man. Dir, 1967–99, Chm., 1991–2004, Mactaggart Scott & Co. Ltd. Tax Comr, 1985–2003. Dir, 1984–91, Vice Chm., 1990–91, Forth Ports Authy. Mem. Bd, Castle Rock Housing Assoc., 1975–2005 (Chm., 1995–2000). Pres., Scottish Engrg Employers' Assoc., 1985–86. Dir, Scottish Chamber Orch., 1995–2009. JP Midlothian, 1980–2003. Gov., Loretto Sch., 1982–89. *Recreations:* music, opera, reading, golf, tennis, ski-ing. *Address:* Carlyle House, 5/2 East Suffolk Park, Edinburgh EH16 5PL. *T:* (0131) 667 4635. *E:* patrick.prenter@mactag.com; 41 Ocean Quay, Harbour Island, Gordons Bay, Western Cape, 7150, South Africa. *Clubs:* New (Edinburgh); Hon. Company of Edinburgh Golfers; Free Foresters.

**PRENTICE, Dr Ann,** OBE 2006; Director, MRC Elsie Widdowson Laboratory (formerly MRC Resource, then MRC Collaborative Centre for Human Nutrition Research, later MRC Human Nutrition Research), since 1998; *b* 8 April 1952; *d* of Alexander Rubach and Beryl Ann Rubach; *m* 1976, Andrew Major Prentice (marr. diss. 2009); two *d*. *Educ:* Somerville Coll., Oxford (BA Hons Chemistry; MA 1977); Univ. of Surrey (MSc Med. Physics); Darwin Coll., Cambridge (PhD Natural Scis, 1978). Scientist, MRC Dunn Nutrition Gp, Keneba, Gambia, 1978–83; Scientist, 1984–91, Sen. Scientist, 1991–98, MRC Dunn Nutrition Unit, Cambridge. Hon. Prof., Shenyang Med. Coll., People's Republic of China, 1995–; Vis. Prof. KCL, 2003–09. Pres., Nutrition Soc., 2004–07. Chm., Sci. Adv. Cttee on Nutrition, 2010–. FRSB (FSB 2010); FMedSci 2012; FAfN 2011, Hon. FafN 2012; Hon. FRCPCH 2015. Hon. Dr Surrey, 2014. *Publications:* book chapters and reviews; numerous contribs to peer-reviewed scientific jls. *Recreations:* music, theatre, literature, foreign travel. *Address:* MRC Elsie Widdowson Laboratory, 120 Fulbourn Road, Cambridge CB1 9NL. *T:* (01223) 426356.

**PRENTICE, Aric John Andrew;** Director of Music, Organist and Master of the Choristers, Lincoln Cathedral, since 2003; *b* Nottingham, 9 April 1972; *s* of John Andrew Prentice and Elizabeth Mary, (Dizzy), Prentice (*née* Nicholls); *m* 2008, Clea, *d* of Prof. David Richard Tappin and Rosemary Jane Tappin (*née* Follows); one *s* one *d*. *Educ:* Chorister Sch., Durham; Trent Coll. (Music Scholar); Jesus Coll., Cambridge (Instrumental Exhibnr; BA 1993; MA); Middlesex Univ. (PGCE). LTCL 1990. Teacher of Music, Cheam High Sch., 1995–97; Hd, Music, 1997–2000, Hd, Expressive Arts, 2000–01, Eastwood Comp. Sch.; Dir, Music, Lincoln Minster Sch., 2001–16. *Recreations:* home improvement, watching cricket, failing to complete crosswords. *Address:* Lincoln Cathedral, 16 Minster Yard, Lincoln LN2 1PX. *T:* (01522) 504398. *E:* directorofmusic@lincolncathedral.com.

**PRENTICE, Bridget Theresa,** JP; Electoral Commissioner, 2014–18; *b* 28 Dec. 1952; *d* of James and Bridget Corr; *m* 1975, Gordon Prentice, *qv* (marr. diss. 2000). *Educ:* Glasgow Univ. (MA English Lit. and Mod. Hist.); London University: Avery Hill Coll. (PGCE); Southlands Coll. (Adv. Dip. in Careers Educn and Guidance); South Bank Univ. (LLB 1992). Teacher, ILEA, 1974–88. Councillor, Hammersmith and Fulham London BC, 1986–92. MP (Lab) Lewisham E, 1992–2010. An Asst Govt Whip, 1997–98 and 2003–05; Parly Under-Sec. of State, DCA, later MoJ, 2005–10. Dir, Bridget Prentice Associates, 2010–16; Ind. Consultant, The Pampered Chef, 2012–16. Chair, Blackheath Historic Bldgs Trust, 2011–14; Trustee: For Jimmy (formerly Jimmy Mizen Foundn), 2012–18; Age Exchange, 2012– (Chair, 2018–); Patron, Grove Park Community Gp, 2012–. Chm. Govs, Trinity Lewisham, 2013–18. Corporate Fellow, Woodard Foundn, 2014–. JP Inner London, 1985. Freewoman, London Bor. of Lewisham, 2016. *Recreations:* music, reading, crosswords, knitting, my three cats, football.

**PRENTICE, Christopher Norman Russell,** CMG 2009; HM Diplomatic Service, retired; Ambassador to Italy, 2011–16; *b* 5 Sept. 1954; *s* of Ronald Prentice and Sonia Prentice (*née* Bowring); *m* 1978, Marie-Josephine, (Nina), King; two *s* two *d*. *Educ:* Christ Church, Oxford (BA Lit.Hum., MA). Entered FCO, 1977; Arabic lang. student, MECAS, 1978; Third, later Second, Sec., Kuwait, 1980–83; First Secretary: on loan to Cabinet Office, 1983–85; Washington, 1985–89; FCO, 1989–94; Counsellor and Dep. Hd of Mission, Budapest, 1994–98; Counsellor, FCO, 1998–2002; Ambassador to Jordan, 2002–06; UK Special Rep., later FCO co-ordinator, Sudan Peace Process, 2006–07; Ambassador to Iraq, 2007–09; Special Envoy for Libya, March–May 2011. *Recreations:* music, sport, reading, mountains. *Clubs:* Athenæum, Beefsteak, MCC.

**PRENTICE, Prof. Daniel David;** Allen & Overy Professor of Corporate Law, Oxford University, 1991–2008, now Emeritus; Fellow of Pembroke College, Oxford, 1973–2008; *b* 7 Aug. 1941; *s* of Thomas James Prentice and Agnes Prentice (*née* Fox); *m* 1965, Judith Mary Keane; one *s* one *d*. *Educ:* St Malachy's Coll., Belfast; Queen's Univ., Belfast (LLB); Univ. of Chicago (JD); MA Oxford (by special resolution). Called to the Bar, Lincoln's Inn, 1982; Mem., Erskine Chambers. Associate Prof., Univ. of Ontario, 1966–68; Lectr, UCL,

1968–73; Lectr, 1973–90, Reader, 1991, Univ. of Oxford. Vis. Prof., various univs incl. UCL, 2008–. Asst Editor, Law Qly Rev., 1988–2008. *Publications*: (ed) Chitty, Law of Contracts, 25th edn 1983 to 29th edn 2004. *Address*: Erskine Chambers, 33 Chancery Lane, WC2A 1EN.

**PRENTICE, Gordon;** *b* 28 Jan. 1951; *s* of Esther and William Prentice; *m* 1975, Bridget Theresa Corr (*see* B. T. Prentice) (marr. diss. 2000); *m* 2011, Heather J. A. Halliday. *Educ*: Univ. of Glasgow (MA; Pres., Glasgow Univ. Union, 1972–73). Mercury House Publications, 1974–78; Local Govt Officer, 1978–81; Labour Party Policy Directorate, 1982–92. Mem. Council, London Borough of Hammersmith and Fulham, 1982–90 (Leader of Council, 1986–88). MP (Lab) Pendle, 1992–2010; contested (Lab) same seat, 2010. *Recreations*: cooking, hill walking, gardening.

**PRENTIS, David;** General Secretary, UNISON, since 2001 (Deputy General Secretary, 1993–2000); President, Trades Union Congress, 2007–08; *b* Leeds. *Educ*: QMC, Univ. of London (BA Hist.); Univ. of Warwick (MA Industrial Relns). Member: TUC Gen. Council (Mem. Exec. Cttee); Trade Union Labour Party Liaison Cttee; Econ. Commn and Jt Policy Cttee, Labour Party; Bd, ACAS, 2004–10. Comr, UK Commn for Employment and Skills. Director: IPPR; Catalyst. Pres., Unity Trust Bank plc; non-exec. Dir, Bank of England, 2012–19. Advr, Warwick Inst. of Governance and Public Mgt. Vis. Fellow, Nuffield Coll., Oxford. *Address*: UNISON Centre, 130 Euston Road, NW1 2AY.

**PRENTIS, Hon. Victoria Mary Boswell;** MP (C) Banbury, since 2015; *b* Banbury, 24 March 1971; *d* of Baron Boswell of Aynho, *qv*; *m* 1996, Sebastian Hugh Runton Prentis; two *d* (one *s* decd). *Educ*: Royal Holloway and Bedford New Coll., London (BA Hons English Lit.); Downing Coll., Cambridge (MA Law). Called to the Bar, Middle Temple, 1995; with Govt Legal Service, latterly Sen. CS, 1997–2014. PPS to Minister of State, Dft, 2016–17, to Lord Pres. of Council and Leader of H of C, 2017–. Mem., Justice Select Cttee, 2015–. Mem., Soc. of Cons. Lawyers. *Recreations*: the countryside, detective fiction, cider making, fundraising. *Address*: House of Commons, SW1A 0AA. *T*: (020) 7219 8756. *E*: victoria.prentis.mp@parliament.uk. *Clubs*: Carlton, Farmers.

**PRESCOTT,** family name of **Baron Prescott.**

**PRESCOTT,** Baron *cr* 2010 (Life Peer), of Kingston upon Hull in the County of East Yorkshire; **John Leslie Prescott;** *b* 31 May 1938; *s* of late John Herbert Prescott, JP and Phyllis Prescott; *m* 1961, Pauline Tilston; two *s*. *Educ*: Ellesmere Port Secondary Modern Sch.; WEA; correspondence courses; Ruskin Coll., Oxford (DipEcon/Pol Oxon); Hull Univ. (BSc Econ). Trainee Chef, 1953–55; Steward, Passenger Lines, Merchant Navy, 1955–63; Ruskin Coll., Oxford, 1963–65; Recruitment Officer, General and Municipal Workers Union (temp.), 1965; Hull Univ., 1965–68. Full-time Official, National Union of Seamen, 1968–70. Contested (Lab) Southport, 1966. MP (Lab) Kingston upon Hull (East), 1970–83, Hull East, 1983–97, Kingston upon Hull East, 1997–2010. PPS to Sec. of State for Trade, 1974–76; opposition spokesman on Transport, 1979–81; opposition front bench spokesman on Regional Affairs and Devolution, 1981–83, on Transport, 1983–84 and 1988–93, on Employment, 1984–87 and 1993–94, on Energy, 1987–89; Mem., Shadow Cabinet, 1983–97; PC 1994–2013; Sec. of State for the Envmt, Transport and the Regions, 1997–2001; Dep. Prime Minister, 1997–2007; First Sec. of State, 2001–07. Dep. Leader, Labour Party, 1994–2007. Member: Select Cttee Nationalized Industries, 1973–79; Council of Europe, 1972–75; European Parlt, 1975–79 (Leader, Labour Party Delegn, 1976–79); Leader, British Labour Delegn, Council of Europe and WEU, 2007–. Mem., NEC, Labour Party, 1989–. *Publications*: Not Wanted on Voyage, 1966; (jtly) Prezza: my story - pulling no punches, 2008. *Address*: House of Lords, SW1A 0PW.

**PRESCOTT, David Julian Brian;** Chief Executive, Blackwell's, since 2013; *b* Nottingham, 25 Oct. 1971; *s* of Brian and Christine Prescott; *m* 2003, Claire Sheehan; two *d*. *Educ*: Huddersfield Univ. (BA Histl and Pol Studies). Blackwell's: Goods-in Supervisor, Nottingham Trent, 1995–97; Manager, Univ. of Glamorgan, 1997–2000; Manager, Univ. of Cardiff, 2000–03; SW Regl Manager, 2001–03; Hd, Retail Ops, 2003–09; Hd of Sales, 2009–11, Man. Dir, 2011–13, Blackwell Ltd. Booksellers' Association: Chair, Acad. Professional and Specialist Booksellers' Gp, 2009–11; Vice Pres., 2011–. Mem., Book Soc. *Recreations*: guitar, sport, reading. *Address*: Blackwell's, 50 Broad Street, Oxford OX1 3BQ. *E*: david.prescott@blackwell.co.uk.

**PRESCOTT, Prof. Edward C.,** PhD; W. P. Carey Professor of Economics, since 2003, and Director, Center for Advanced Study in Economic Efficiency, since 2009, Arizona State University; Senior Monetary Adviser, Federal Reserve Bank of Minneapolis, since 2003 (Senior Adviser, Research Department, 1981–2003); *b* 26 Dec. 1940; *s* of William Clyde Prescott and Mathilde Helwig Prescott; *m* 1965, Janet Dale Simpson; two *s* one *d*. *Educ*: Swarthmore Coll., Penn (BA 1962); Case Inst. of Technol. (MS 1963); Carnegie Mellon Univ. (PhD 1967). Lectr, 1966–67, Asst Prof., 1967–71, Econs Dept, Univ. of Pennsylvania; Asst Prof., 1971–72, Associate Prof., 1972–75, Prof. of Econs, 1975–80, Carnegie-Mellon Univ.; Prof. of Econs, 1980–98, 1999–2003, Univ. of Minnesota; Prof. of Econs, Univ. of Chicago, 1998–99. Distinguished Adjunct Prof., ANU, 2013–. Irwin Plein Nemmers Prize, 2002; (jtly) Nobel Prize in Economics, 2004. *Publications*: (with S. L. Parente) Barriers to Riches, 2000; contrib. learned jls. *Address*: Department of Economics, W. P. Carey School of Business, Arizona State University, Tempe, AZ 85287–9801, USA; Research Department, Federal Reserve Bank of Minneapolis, 90 Hennepin Avenue, Minneapolis, MN 55401–1804, USA.

**PRESCOTT, John Barry,** AC 1996; Chairman, Aurizon Holdings Ltd (formerly Queensland Rail, then QR National Ltd), 2006–15; Member, Commonwealth Remuneration Tribunal, 2010–16; *b* 22 Oct. 1940; *s* of late John Norman Prescott and Margaret Ellen (*née* Brownie); *m* 1985, Jennifer Cahill; one *s* two *d* (and one *d* decd). *Educ*: N Sydney Boys' High Sch.; Univ. of NSW (BComm Industrial Relns). Joined The Broken Hill Pty Co. Ltd as Industrial Relns Trainee, 1958: various industrial relns positions, 1958–69; Superintendent, Industrial Relns, Shipping and Stevedoring, Newcastle and Sydney, 1969–74; Asst Fleet Manager, Ops, Newcastle, 1974–79; Exec. Asst to Gen. Manager, Transport, 1979–80; Manager Ops, Transport, 1980–82; Gen. Manager, Transport, 1982–87; Exec. Gen. Manager and Chief Exec. Officer, BHP Steel, 1987–91; Dir, 1988–98; Man. Dir and CEO, 1991–98. Chairman: Horizon Private Equity Pty Ltd, 1998–2005; ASC Pty Ltd (formerly Australian Submarine Corp.), 2000–09; Dir, Tubemakers of Aust. Ltd, 1988–92; non-executive Director: Normandy Mining Ltd, 1999–2002; Newmont Mining Corp., 2002–13; Member: Adv. Bd, Booz, Allen & Hamilton Inc., 1991–2003; Internat. Council, J. P. Morgan, 1994–2003; Asia Pacific Adv. Cttee, New York Stock Exchange Inc., 1995–2005. Chm., 2004–07, Patron, 2007–09, Sunshine Coast Business Council; Member Board: Business Council of Aust., 1995–97; Walter and Eliza Hall Inst. of Med. Res., 1994–98; Global Counsellor, Conference Bd, 2001–16 (Mem., Bd of Trustees, 1995–2001; Mem., Global Adv. Council, 2013–16). Mem. Internat. Council, 1991–2003, Mem., President's Circle, AustralAsiaCentre, 1999–2015, Asia Soc. Hon. LLD Monash, 1994; Hon. DSc NSW, 1995. *Publications*: (with Stephen Drotter) The Succession Pipeline: how to get the talent you need when you need it, 2018. *Recreations*: tennis, golf. *Address*: (office) Suite 1.02, Level 1, 11 Queens Road, Melbourne, Vic 3004, Australia. *Clubs*: Australian, Melbourne (Melbourne); Huntingdale Golf, National Golf (Vic), Twin Waters Golf, Noosa Springs Golf.

**PRESCOTT, Prof. John Herbert Dudley,** PhD; FRSB; FRAgS; Principal, Wye College, and Professor of Animal Production, University of London, 1988–2000, now Professor Emeritus; *b* 21 Feb. 1937; *s* of Herbert Prescott and Edith Vera Prescott; *m* 1960, Diana Margaret Mullock; two *s* two *d*. *Educ*: Haileybury; Univ. of Nottingham (BSc (Agric), PhD). FRSB (FIBiol 1983); FRAgS 1986. Lectr in Animal Prodn, Univ. of Newcastle upon Tyne, 1963–72; Animal Prodn Officer in Argentina, FAO, UN, 1972–74; Head of Animal Prodn Advisory and Develt, E of Scotland Coll. of Agric., 1974–78; Prof. of Animal Prodn, Univ. of Edinburgh, 1978–84, and Head of Animal Div., Edinburgh Sch. of Agric., 1978–84; Dir, Grassland, later Animal and Grassland, Res. Inst., 1984–86; Dir, Grassland and Animal Prodn Res., AFRC, 1986–88. Visiting Professor: Univ. of Reading, 1985–88; UCW, Aberystwyth, 1988. Non-exec. Dir, Natural Resources Internat. Ltd, 1997–2000 (Actg Chm., 1996). Chm., Tech. Cttee on Response to Nutrients, AFRC, 1988–94. British Council: Member: Cttee for Internat. Co-operation in Higher Educn, 1989–2000; Agric. and Vet. Adv. Cttee, 1988–96; Vice-Chm., Sci., Engrg and Envmt Adv. Cttee, 1997–2001. Member: Adv. Bd, Centre for Tropical Vet. Medicine, 1978–84; Board of Directors: Hill Farming Res. Orgn, 1980–84; Hannah Res. Inst., 1981–84; Scientific Adv. Cttee, 1990–92, Governing Body, 1992–97, Macaulay Land Use Res. Inst.; various cttees on cattle and beef, MLC, 1969–90. President: British Soc. of Animal Prodn, 1988; Agricl and Forestry Sect., BAAS, 1994–95; Mem. Council, British Grassland Soc., 1984–87. Chairman: Stapledon Meml Trust, 1992–2004; Natural Resources Internat. Foundn, 1997–2004; Trustee, E Malling Trust for Horticl Res., 1998–2010. Member: Gov. Body and Corp., Hadlow Coll., 1988–98; Council: RVC, 1988–98, 2001–04; Univ. of Kent, 1988–2000. Liveryman, Farmers' Co., 2000–. FRSA 2000. Hon. Fellow: Inst. for Grassland and Envmtl Res., 1989; Wye Coll., 2000; ICSTM, 2001. *Publications*: scientific papers in Animal Prodn and Agricultural Science; technical articles. *Recreations*: farming, walking, wildlife, the countryside.

**PRESCOTT, Lisa Ellen Buch;** *see* Christensen, L. E. B.

**PRESCOTT, Sir Mark,** 3rd Bt *cr* 1938, of Godmanchester; racehorse trainer, in Newmarket; *b* 3 March 1948; *s* of late Major W. R. Stanley Prescott (MP for Darwen Div., 1943–51; 2nd *s* of Colonel Sir William Prescott, 1st Bt) and Gwendolen (who *m* 2nd, 1952, Daniel Orme (*d* 1972); she *d* 1992), *oc* of late Leonard Aldridge, CBE; *S* uncle, Sir Richard Stanley Prescott, 2nd Bt, 1965. *Educ*: Harrow. *Address*: Heath House, Moulton Road, Newmarket, Suffolk CB8 8DU. *T*: (01638) 662117.

**PRESCOTT, Peter Richard Kyle;** QC 1990; *b* 23 Jan. 1943; *s* of Richard Stanley Prescott and Sarah Aitchison Shand; *m* 1st, 1967, Frances Rosemary Bland; two *s* one *d*; 2nd, 2014, Gillian Luciana Leddy. *Educ*: St Andrew's Scots' Sch., Argentina; St George's Coll., Argentina; Dulwich Coll.; University Coll. London (BSc); Queen Mary Coll., London (MSc Eng). Pres., Univ. of London Union. Called to the Bar, Lincoln's Inn, 1970, Bencher, 2001; in practice as a barrister, 1970–2012; a Dep. High Court Judge, 1997–2011. *Publications*: The Modern Law of Copyright (with Hugh Laddie, QC, and Mary Vitoria), 1980, 5th edn 2017; various articles. *Recreations*: music, reading, cooking, flying gliders. *Address*: Limehouse Marina, London.

**PRESCOTT-DECIE, Elizabeth Anne Scott,** MA; Head Mistress, Godolphin School, Salisbury, 1980–89; *b* 28 Dec. 1942; *d* of Thomas Scott Hannay and Doreen Hewitt Hannay; *m* 2000, John Prescott-Decie. *Educ*: Heathfield Sch., Ascot; St Hugh's Coll., Oxford (MA). Assistant Mistress: St Mary's Sch., Calne, 1966–70; Moreton Hall Sch., Shropshire, 1970–72; St Michael's, Burton Park, Petworth, 1973–75; Dep. Headmistress, St George's Sch., Ascot, 1975–80. Governor: Norman Ct Sch., W Tytherley, 1982–2012; Prior's Field Sch., Godalming, 1991–2013.

**PRESLAND, Frank George;** Chairman: Rocket Music Entertainment Group, 2010–12; William A. Bong Ltd, and other companies in Elton John Group, 2012–14 (Chief Executive, 1999–2012); *b* 27 Feb. 1944; *s* of Reginald Charles Presland and Elsie Presland; *m*; one *s* one *d*. *Educ*: London Sch. of Economics (BSc Econ); University Coll. of Rhodesia and Nyasaland (Fairbridge Schol.). Admitted solicitor, 1973; Partner, Frere Cholmeley, 1976–92; Chm., Frere Cholmeley Bischoff, 1992–98, when co. merged with Eversheds; Jt Chm., Eversheds, 1998–99. Chief Executive: Twentyfirst Artists Ltd, 2001–10; Sanctuary Gp plc, 2006–08. Dir, Edge VCT, 2005–16. Dir, Elstree UTC Ltd, 2012–15. Dir, Elton John AIDS Foundn, UK and USA, 1999–2014. Hon. FRAM 2010. *Recreation*: yachting. *E*: frank.presland@gmail.com. *Club*: Little Ship.

**PRESS, Dr Frank;** Principal, Washington Advisory Group, since 2011; Consultant, Huron Consulting Group, since 2011; *b* 4 Dec. 1924; *m* 1946, Billie Kallick (*d* 2009); one *s* one *d*. *Educ*: City Coll., NY (BS 1944); Columbia Univ. (MA 1946; PhD 1949). Columbia University: Res. Associate, 1946–49; Instr in Geology, 1949–51; Asst Prof. of Geology, 1951–52; Associate Prof., 1952–55; Prof. of Geophysics, 1955–65 and Dir, Seismol. Lab., 1957–65, CIT; Prof. of Geophysics and Chm., Dept of Earth and Planetary Scis, MIT, 1965–77; Sci. Advisor to Pres. and Dir, Office of Sci. and Tech. Policy, 1977–80; Prof., MIT, 1981; Pres., NAS, 1981–93; Cecil and Ida Green Sen. Fellow, Carnegie Instn of Washington, 1993–97. Member: President's Sci. Adv. Commn, 1961–64; Nat. Sci. Bd, 1970–; Lunar and Planetary Missions Bd, NASA; participant, bilateral scis agreement with People's Republic of China and USSR; US Deleg. to Nuclear Test Ban Negotiations, Geneva and Moscow. Mem., Acad. of Arts and Scis, and other US and internat. bodies. Life Mem., MIT Bd, 1985. Numerous awards, incl. Japan Prize, Sci. and Technol. Foundn of Japan, 1993, US Nat. Medal of Science, 1994, Lomonosov Gold Medal, Russian Acad. of Sci., 1998, and hon. degrees. Officer, Legion of Honour, 1989. *Publications*: (jtly) Propagation of Elastic Waves in Layered Media, 1957; (ed jtly) Physics and Chemistry of the Earth, 1957; (jtly) Earth, 1986; Understanding Earth, 1994, 4th edn 2005; numerous papers. *Address*: Building 5, Apt 306, Carolina Meadows, Chapel Hill, NC 27517, USA.

**PRESS, Prof. Malcolm Colin,** PhD; Vice-Chancellor and Chief Executive, Manchester Metropolitan University, since 2015; *b* 18 Sept. 1958; *s* of Kenneth and Sylvia Press. *Educ*: Kingsbury High Sch., London; Westfield Coll., Univ. of London (BSc (Envmtl Sci.) 1980); Univ. of Manchester (PhD (Botany) 1984). Res. Associate, UCL, 1985–89; Lectr, then Sen. Lectr, Univ. of Manchester, 1989–94; University of Sheffield: Reader, 1994–98; Prof. of Physiol Ecol., 1998–2008; Dir, Res. in the Envmt, 2001–08; Hd, Animal and Plant Scis, 2002–08; University of Birmingham: Prof. of Ecol. and Hd, Coll. of Life and Envmtl Scis, 2008–13; Pro-Vice-Chancellor, 2009–15; Dir, Inst. of Advanced Studies, 2012–15. Member: Sci. and Innovation Strategy Bd, NERC, 2007–10; Leadership, Governance and Mgt Strategic Adv. Cttee, HEFCE, 2016–18; Apprenticeship Delivery Bd, 2017–19; Bd, Inst. for Apprenticeships, then Inst. for Apprenticeships and Tech. Educn, 2018–; Dep. Chair, REF sub-panel for Biol Scis, 2011–14. Pres., British Ecol Soc., 2007–09 (Mem. Council, 1992–2001); Mem. Council, Soc. of Biol., 2009–10. Mem. Council, Nat. Trust, 2009–12; Trustee: Royal Botanic Gdns, Kew, 2012–18 (Mem., Kew Audit Cttee, 2013–15; Chm., Kew Sci. Cttee, 2014–18); WWF UK, 2014–. Ed., Jl Ecol., 2004–06.

*Publications:* scientific papers and contribs to books on ecol., agric. and forests. *Recreations:* Spanish language and culture, travel, walking the dog, gardening. *Address:* Manchester Metropolitan University, All Saints, Manchester M15 6BH. *T:* (0161) 247 1560. *E:* malcolm.press@mmu.ac.uk.

**PRESSDEE, Piers Charles William;** QC 2010; *b* London, 29 Dec. 1968; *s* of Comdr William Pressdee and Hilda Pressdee; *m* 1997, Sally Max; four *d. Educ:* St Paul's Sch., London; St John's Coll., Cambridge (BA Hons 1989); Inns of Court Sch. of Law. Called to the Bar, Middle Temple, 1991; in practice as barrister, specialising in children law, 1992–. Co-Chm., Assoc. of Lawyers for Children, 2008–10. *Publications:* Contact: the new deal, 2006; The Public Law Outline: the Court companion, 2008; (Contrib. Ed.) Halsbury's Laws of England, children vols, 2012. *Recreations:* my children, football (Chelsea season ticket holder), writing. *Address:* 29 Bedford Row, WC1R 4HE. *T:* (020) 7404 1044. *E:* ppressdee@29br.co.uk.

**PRESSLER, Christopher Carson;** University Librarian, and Director, John Rylands Library, University of Manchester, since 2019; *b* Belfast, 12 Aug. 1972; *s* of John Evans and Ruth Miller (*née* Pressler); partner, Brett Tryner. *Educ:* Grosvenor Grammar Sch., Belfast; Queen's Univ. Belfast (BA Hons); Nottingham Trent Univ. (MA); Univ. of Sheffield (MSc). IT Services Librarian, UCL, 1998–2000; JISC Prog. Manager, KCL, 2000–02; Hd of Arts Collections, Univ. of London, 2002–04; Dean, Information and Learning, Dartington Coll. of Arts, 2004–07; Director: Libraries and Archives, Univ. of Nottingham, 2007–10; Senate House Libraries, Univ. of London, 2010–13; Dir, Irish Modern Archives Res. Centre, 2013–19, Univ. Librarian, 2014–19, Dublin City Univ. FRSA 2004. *Publications:* Canning Circus, 2001; Director's Choice, Senate House Library, 2012; (ed) Senate House Library: historic collections, 2012; 94 Degrees in the Shade, 2016; The Leper Chapel, 2016; The White Whale, 2017. *Recreations:* writing novels, short stories and articles, listening to classical music and playing the violin, exploring England's most complicated county, Suffolk and Ireland's most exciting city, Dublin.

**PREST, (Adam) Charles;** QC 2016; a District Judge, since 2016; *b* Oxford, 29 March 1963; *s* of late John Michael Prest and of Susan Rippon Prest; *m* 2006, Fiona Clare Ford (*née* Pierce); one step *s* one step *d. Educ:* Abingdon Sch.; St John's Coll., Cambridge (BA 1985; MA); Cranmer Hall, Durham; Law Soc. (Dip. Local Govt Law and Practice). Admitted as solicitor, 1988; solicitor: Oates Hanson, Huddersfield, 1988–89 and 1990–91; E Sussex CC, 1991–94; Lee and Priestley, Leeds, 1994–2001; Dir, Legal Services, CAFCASS, 2001–05; Solicitor, Addleshaw Goddard, Leeds, 2005; called to the Bar, Inner Temple, 2005; in practice as barrister, Leeds, 2006–16. Consultant: Aire Centre, 2002–05; Joseph Rowntree Foundn, 2002–05; RCPCH, 2005–16; RSocMed, 2005–16. Editor: Butterworths Family Law Service, 1999–2019; Emergency Family Remedies, 2002–13; Family Law Precedents Service, 2004–15. *Publications:* Not Alone: a children's guide to care proceedings, 1995; Children Law: an interdisciplinary handbook, 2005; Family Law Case Library: Children, 2008, 3rd edn 2015, Family Law Case Library: Finance, 2008. *Recreations:* gardening, bee-keeping, walking, modern and some contemporary art. *Address:* Leeds Combined Court, 1 Oxford Row, Leeds LS1 3BG. *T:* (0113) 306 2800.

**PREST, Nicholas Martin,** CBE 2001; Chairman: Cohort plc, since 2006; Shephard Group Ltd, since 2007; *b* 3 April 1953; *s* of late Alan Richmond Prest and Pauline Chasey Prest (*née* Noble); *m* 1985, Anthea Joy Elisabeth Neal; one *s* two *d. Educ:* Manchester Grammar Sch.; Christ Church, Oxford (MA Hist. and Econs). Admin. trainee, 1974, Principal, 1980–82, MoD; joined United Scientific Hldgs Plc, later Alvis Plc, 1982; Gp Mktg Dir, 1985–89; Chief Exec., 1989–2004; Chm., 1996–2004. Chm., Aveva Gp plc, 2006–12. Chm., 2001–04, Mem. Council, 2006–09, Defence Manufrs Assoc.; Mem. Council, ADS, 2009–10; Mem., Nat. Defence Industries Council, 2001–04. *Recreations:* music, walking, shooting, watching cricket and Rugby. *Address:* Pilstone House, Llandogo, Monmouth NP25 4TH. *T:* (01594) 531007. *Clubs:* Cavalry and Guards, MCC.

**PRESTON,** family name of **Viscount Gormanston.**

**PRESTON;** see Campbell-Preston.

**PRESTON, Andrew;** Chief Executive Officer, Geometric Results International (formerly de Poel Group), since 2016; *b* Yorkshire, 1975; one *s* one *d.* Clin. Audit and Operational Mgt, Mid Yorks Hosps NHS Trust, 1995–2000; healthcare consultant, 1999–2000; Dir, Health, AXA Assistance, 1999–2001; Exec. Vice Pres., 2001–03, CEO, 2003–05, Clin. Solutions Gp; Managing Director: Clin. Services, Serco Health, 2005–07; Medacs Healthcare plc, 2007–12; Interim Chief Operating Officer, HB Healthcare, Hamilton Bradshaw Gp, 2013; Gp Man. Dir, de Poel Gp, 2013–16. *Publications:* (contrib.) Doing Business After Brexit: a practical guide to the legal changes, 2017; contribs to jls, Internat. Jl STD and AIDS, Rheumatology. *Address:* Geometric Results International, Booths Park 1, Chelford Road, Knutsford, Cheshire WA16 8GS. *T:* (01565) 682020. *E:* apreston@geometricresults.co.uk.

**PRESTON, Ben James;** Executive Editor, Sunday Times, since 2017; *b* Crosby, 24 Sept. 1963; *s* of late Peter John Preston and of Jean Mary Preston; *m* 1995, Janice Turner; two *s. Educ:* Alleyn's Sch., London; Bristol Univ. (BSSc Pols 1986); City Univ. (Dip. Journalism 1987). Reporter, Bristol Evening Post, 1987–89; Reporter, 1990–91, Educn Corresp., 1991–93, Press Assoc.; The Times: Educn Corresp., 1993–96; News Ed., 1997–99; Dep. Ed., 2000–08; Actg Ed., 2001; Exec. Ed., The Independent, 2008–09; Editor, Radio Times, 2009–17. *Recreations:* film, football, family. *Address:* Sunday Times, 1 London Bridge Street, SE1 9GF. *Club:* Millwall Football.

**PRESTON, David Michael;** mediator and law consultant; Partner, Hosack & Sutherland, Solicitors, Oban, 1978–2005; Chairman: Mental Health Tribunal for Scotland, since 2005; Private Rented Housing Panel, since 2011; Home Owners Housing Panel, since 2012; *b* 26 Aug. 1952; *s* of Robert Matthew Preston and Lily Stewart Preston; *m* 1975, Sheila Elizabeth McMeekin; two *s. Educ:* Hillhead High Sch., Glasgow; Univ. of Dundee (LLB 1974). Depute Procurator Fiscal (pt-time), 1976–79; Clerk to Gen. Comrs of Income Tax, 1976–. Legal Assessor, Gen. Teaching Council for Scotland, 2011–. Registrar, Episcopal Dio. Argyll and the Isles, 1977–2007. Mem. Council, 1990–2007, 2012–, Pres., 2002–03, Law Soc. of Scotland. Chm., Oban Youth and Community Assoc., 1980–2013. Sec., Atlantis Leisure, Oban, 1991–2000. *Recreations:* sailing, ski-ing, golf, reading, family. *Address:* Westbank, Duncraggan Road, Oban PA34 5DU. *Clubs:* Royal Highland Yacht, Oban Sailing (Cdre, 1992–93); Taynuilt and Hilton Park Golf.

**PRESTON, Hugh Geoffrey;** QC 2012; *b* Westow, N Yorks, 21 Oct. 1970; *s* of Brig. Roger Preston, CBE and Polly Preston; *m* 1998, the Noble Mary Louisa; two *s* two *d. Educ:* Eton Coll.; Durham Univ. (BA Hons Theol. 1992; DipLaw 1993). Called to the Bar, Middle Temple, 1994; in practice as a barrister, East Anglian Chambers, 1994–2000, 7 Bedford Row, 2000–. *Publications:* regular contrib. to legal jls. *Recreations:* shooting, gardening, cycling with my children, driving my Morris Traveller. *Address:* 7 Bedford Row, WC1R 4BS. *T:* (020) 7242 3555. *E:* hpreston@7br.co.uk.

**PRESTON, Jeffrey William,** CB 1989; Director General, Energy, Department of Trade and Industry, 1996–98; *b* 28 Jan. 1940; *s* of William and Sybil Grace Preston. *Educ:* Liverpool Collegiate Sch.; Hertford Coll., Oxford (MA Lit.Hum. 1966). Asst Principal, Min. of Aviation, 1963; Private Sec. to Permanent Sec., BoT, 1966; Principal: BoT, 1967; HM Treasury, 1970; DTI, 1973; Asst Sec., Dept of Trade, 1975–82; Under Sec. and Regional Dir, Yorks and Humberside Region, DTI, 1982–85; Dep. Sec., Industrial and Economic Affairs, Welsh Office, 1985–90; Dep. Dir Gen., OFT, 1990–96 (Acting Dir Gen., 1995). Mem. Bd, Oxford Inst. for Energy Studies, 1997–98. Vice-Pres., Hertford Soc., 2004– (Chm., 1987–95). FRSA. *Recreations:* travel, opera, wine. *T:* (020) 8940 7166. *Club:* Oxford and Cambridge (Chm., 1999–2001; Trustee, 2007–15).

**PRESTON, Kieran Thomas,** OBE 2006; FCIT, FCIPD; Director General, West Yorkshire Passenger Transport Executive, 1993–2014; *b* 30 Nov. 1950; *s* of Charles Edward Preston and Mary Kate Preston; *m* 1974, Denise Marie Gregory (*d* 2010); two *s. Educ:* Leeds Poly. (BA Hons Mgt and Admin). FCIT 1994. Local Govt Officer, various appts, 1972–89; Leeds City Council: Projects Dir, 1989–91; Actg Dir of Admin, 1991–92; Chief Services Officer, 1992–93. Chm., PTE Gp, 2001–05. FCIPD (FIPM 1992). *Recreations:* keeping fit, horse riding, football, cricket, judo, golf. *Address:* 15 Morritt Avenue, Leeds LS15 7EP.

**PRESTON, Mark Robin;** Group Chief Executive, Grosvenor, since 2008; Executive Trustee, Grosvenor Estate, since 2017; *b* Westow, 20 Jan. 1968; *s* of Roger St Clair Preston and Polly Mary Preston (*née* Marriot); *m* 1997, Kate Whittaker; one *s* two *d. Educ:* Eton Coll.; Reading Univ. (BSc Land Mgt). MRICS 1992. Joined Grosvenor, 1989; seconded to Hong Kong, 1995–97; Gp Fund Mgt Dir, 1997–2002; Pres., Grosvenor USA, San Francisco, 2002–06; Chief Exec., Grosvenor Britain and Ireland, 2006–08. Non-exec. Dir, London Bd, Royal & Sun Alliance, 2006–08. Non-exec. Dir, Sonae Sierra SGPS, 2008–. Mem. Bd, Assoc. of Foreign Investors in Real Estate, 2001– (Chm., 2007). Mem., North West Business Leadership Team, 2006–. *Recreation:* field sports. *Address:* Grosvenor, 70 Grosvenor Street, W1K 3JP. *T:* (020) 7408 0988. *Club:* Lansdowne.

**PRESTON, Sir Paul,** Kt 2018; CBE 2000; FRHistS; FBA 1994; Professor of International History, London School of Economics, since 1991; *b* 21 July 1946; *s* of Charles Ronald Preston and Alice Hoskisson; *m* 1983, Gabrielle Patricia Ashford-Hodges; two *s. Educ:* St Edward's Coll., Liverpool; Oriel Coll., Oxford (Hon. Fellow, 2017). Lectr in Modern History, Univ. of Reading, 1974–75; Queen Mary College, University of London: Lectr and Reader in Modern History, 1975–85; Prof. of History, 1985–91. Marcel Proust Chair, Academia Europea de Yuste, 2006. Mem., Institut d'Estudis Catalans, 2008. Hon. Dr: Tarragona, 2015; Liverpool, 2015; Extremadura, 2015; Valencia, 2015; Barcelona, 2016; Cantabria, 2019. Ramon Llull Internat. Prize, Catalonia, 2005; Pompeu Fabra Prize, Catalonia, 2012; Lluís Carulla Prize, Catalonia, 2013; Premi de projecció internacional, Barcelona, 2016. Comendador de la Orden de Mérito Civil (Spain), 1986; Gran Cruz, Orden de Isabel la Católica (Spain), 2007. *Publications:* (ed) Spain in Crisis, 1976; The Coming of the Spanish Civil War, 1978, 2nd edn 1994; (ed) Revolution and War in Spain 1931–1939, 1984; (with Denis Smyth) Spain, the EEC and NATO, 1984; The Triumph of Democracy in Spain, 1986; The Spanish Civil War 1936–1939, 1986; The Politics of Revenge, 1990; Franco, 1993 (Yorkshire Post Book of the Year, 1993); Las tres Españas del 36, 1998 (Así fue, 1998); Comrades! Portraits from the Spanish Civil War, 1999; Doves of War: four women of Spain, 2002; Juan Carlos: a people's king, 2004; We Saw Spain Die, 2008; The Spanish Holocaust, 2011; The Last Stalinist: the life of Santiago Carrillo, 2014; The Last Days of the Spanish Republic, 2016. *Recreations:* classical music, opera, modern fiction, wine, supporting Everton Football Club. *Address:* Department of International History, London School of Economics, Houghton Street, WC2A 2AE. *T:* (020) 7955 7107.

**PRESTON, Sir Philip (Charles Henry Hulton),** 8th Bt *cr* 1815, of Beeston St Lawrence, Norfolk; Partner, Bumphrey Preston Associates, architects, 1989–2011; *b* 30 Aug. 1946; *s* of Lt-Col Philip Henry Herbert Hulton Preston, OBE, MC and Katherine Janet Preston (*née* Broomhall); *S* cousin, 1999; *m* 1980, Kirsi Sylvi Annikki, *d* of Eino Yrjö Pullinen; one *s* two *d. Educ:* Nautical Coll., Pangbourne; Architectural Assoc. Sch. of Architecture. *Publications:* (ed jtly) The Battle of Crécy 1346, 2005. *Heir: s* Philip Thomas Henry Hulton Preston, *b* 15 Aug. 1990. *Address:* 32 rue Pierre Brossolette, 76680 Saint-Saëns, Normandie, France.

**PRESTON, Roberta Lynn;** see Gilchrist, R. L.

**PRESTON, Rosalind,** OBE 1993; Co-Chairman, Inter Faith Network for UK, 2000–10 (Co-Vice-Chairman, 1994–2000); Vice President, Board of Deputies of British Jews, 1991–94; *b* 29 March 1935; *d* of Benjamin and Marie Morris; *m* 1958, Ronald Preston; one *s* one *d. Educ:* Talbot Heath Sch., Bournemouth. Voluntary sector activity, 1960–; Nat. Pres., Nat. Council of Women, 1988–90; Hon. Vice Pres., British Section, Women's Internat. Zionist Orgn, 1999– (Vice Pres., 1993–99); Jt Hon. Sec., CCJ, 1996–2005. Dir (non-exec.), Harrow and Hillingdon Healthcare NHS Trust, 1994–96; Mental Health Manager, Central and NW London (formerly Brent, Kensington & Chelsea and Westminster) Mental Health NHS Trust, 2002–10. Chm., Nightingale Home, 2001–07. Trustee: Jewish Chronicle, 2000–11; Olive Tree Trust, 2004–08; Jewish Volunteering Network, 2008– (Pres., 2009–); WIZO UK, 2014–; Co-Chair, Jewish Human Rights Coalition UK, 2008–13. FRSA 1990. Paul Harris Fellow, Rotary Internat., 1992. *Recreations:* walking, volunteering, international/national news, family and friends. *Address:* 7 Woodside Close, Stanmore, Middx HA7 3AJ.

**PRESTON, Simon John,** CBE 2009 (OBE 2000); Organist and Master of the Choristers, Westminster Abbey, 1981–87; concert organist, since 1987; *b* 4 Aug. 1938; *m* Elizabeth Hays. *Educ:* Canford Sch.; King's Coll., Cambridge (Dr Mann Organ Student; BA 1961; MusB 1962; MA 1964). ARCM, FRAM. Sub Organist, Westminster Abbey, 1962–67; Acting Organist, St Albans Abbey, 1968–69; Organist and Tutor in Music, Christ Church, Oxford, 1970–81. Conductor, Oxford Bach Choir, 1971–74. Artistic Dir, Calgary Internat. Organ Comp., 1990–2002. Has performed with major orchestras incl. Berlin Philharmonic, LA Philharmonic and Boston SO, as well as British orchestras; soloist, Last Night of the Proms, 2005. Tours to USA and performance in Far East, Australia and major Eur. countries, incl. Russia. FRSA. Hon. FRCO 1975; Hon. FRCCO 1986; Hon. FRCM 1986. Hon. Student, Christ Church, Oxford, 2010. Edison Award, 1971; Grand Prix du Disque, 1979; Performer of the Year Award, NY Chapter, Amer. Guild of Organists, 1987. RCO Medal, 2014. *Recreations:* croquet, crosswords.

**PRESTON, Susanna;** see Gross, S.

**PRESTWICH, Prof. Michael Charles,** OBE 2010; FRHistS; FSA; Professor of History, University of Durham, 1986–2008, now Emeritus; *b* 30 Jan. 1943; *s* of late John Oswald Prestwich and Menna Prestwich; *m* 1973, Margaret Joan Daniel; two *s* one *d. Educ:* Charterhouse; Magdalen Coll., Oxford (MA); Christ Church, Oxford (DPhil). FSA 1980. Res. Lectr, Christ Church, Oxford, 1965–69; Lectr in Mediaeval History, Univ. of St Andrews, 1969–79; University of Durham: Reader in Medieval History, 1979–86; Pro-Vice-Chancellor, 1992–99; Sub-Warden, 1997–99. *Publications:* War, Politics and Finance under Edward I, 1972; The Three Edwards: war and state in England 1272–1377, 1980; Documents illustrating the Crisis of 1297–98 in England, 1980; Edward I, 1988; English

Politics in the Thirteenth Century, 1990; Armies and Warfare in the Middle Ages, 1996; Plantagenet England, 1225–1360, 2005; Knight, 2010; Medieval People, 2014; A Short History of the Hundred Years War, 2017; articles in learned jls. *Recreation:* ski-ing. *Address:* Langdale, Hillrise Lane, Longframlington, Morpeth, Northumberland NE65 8BN. *T:* (01665) 570684.

**PRETTEJOHN, Nicholas Edward Tucker;** Chairman: Scottish Widows Group, since 2014; Reach plc, since 2018; *b* 22 July 1960; *s of* Dr Edward Joseph Tucker Prettejohn and Diana Sally Prettejohn; *m* 1997, Claire Helen McKenna; two *d. Educ:* Balliol Coll., Oxford (BA 1st Cl. Hons PPE 1981; Pres., Oxford Union, 1980). Mgt Consultant, Bain & Co., 1982–91; Dir, Apax Partners, 1991–94; Dir of Corporate Strategy, NFC plc, 1994–95; Lloyd's of London: Head of Strategy, 1995–97; Man. Dir, Business Devlt Unit, 1997–99, and N America Business Unit, 1998–99; Chief Exec., 1999–2005; Chief Exec., Prudential UK and Europe, and Dir, Prudential plc, 2006–09. Non-executive Director: Legal and General plc, 2010–13; Lloyds Banking Gp, 2014–; Chm., Brit Insurance, 2011–13. Chm., Financial Services Practitioner Panel, 2007–09; Mem. Bd, Prudential Regulation Authy, Bank of England, 2013–14. Trustee, Royal Opera House, 2005–13; Mem., BBC Trust, 2014–17. Chairman: Britten-Pears Foundn, 2009–17; Bd of Govs, RNCM, 2012–. *Recreations:* opera, music, theatre, horse racing, golf.

**PRETTY, Prof. Jules Nicholas,** OBE 2006; Professor of Environment and Society, since 2000 and Director, Centre for Public Engagement, University of Essex; *b* Jos, Nigeria, 5 Oct. 1958; *s of* John and Susan Pretty; partner, Gill Boardman; one *s* one *d. Educ:* Denes High Sch., Lowestoft; Univ. of York (BA Hons Biol. 1979); Imperial Coll., London (MSc Envmtl Technol. 1981). Res. Officer, Imperial Coll., London, 1985–86; Res. Associate and Associate Dir, 1986–91, Dir, 1991–97, Sustainable Agric. Prog., Internat. Inst. for Envmt and Develt; University of Essex: Vis. Prof., 1997; Dir, Centre for Envmt and Society, 1997–99, 2000–04; Hd, Dept of Biol Scis, 2004–08; Pro-Vice-Chancellor, 2010; Dep. Vice-Chancellor, 2011–19. A. D. White Prof.-at-Large, Cornell Univ., 2001–07; Nat C. Robertson Vis. Prof., Emory Univ., Atlanta, 2007. Dep. Chm., UK Adv. Cttee on Releases to the Envmt, 1999–2009; Member: Strategy Bd, 2009–11, Food Security Strategy Adv. Panel, 2011–15, BBSRC; Lead Expert Gp, Foresight Food and Farming Futures Project, 2009–11; Expert Panel, UK Nat. Ecosystem Assessment, 2009–11; Expert Panel, Greening the Economies, Switzerland, 2014–; Wkg Gp, Health of the Public 2040, Acad. of Med. Scis, 2014–; Chair, Sustainable Intensification Innovation Lab., Kansas State Univ., 2014–. Member, Royal Society commn on Biological Approaches to Improving Crop Prodn, 2008–09, on People and the Planet, 2010–12. Chm., Essex Rural Commn, 2008–; Vice-President: Suffolk ACRE, 2009–; Rural Community Council of Essex, 2010–; Pres., Essex Wildlife Trust, 2019– (Trustee, 2005–09; Vice-Pres., 2010–19). Presenter: Ploughing Eden (also writer), BBC Radio 4, 1999; The Magic Bean (also co-writer), BBC TV, 2001; Silent Spring (also writer), BBC Radio 3 essay, 2012. Mem., Judges Panel, New Angle Prize for Literature, 2015. FRSB (FIBiol 2003); FRSA 2004; PFHEA 2017. Chief Ed., Internat. Jl of Agricl Sustainability, 2002–. Hon. Dr Ohio State, 2009. Presidential Medal (for agric. and food), British Sci. Fest., 2015. *Publications:* Unwelcome Harvest: agriculture and pollution (with G. R. Conway), 1991; Regenerating Agriculture: policies and practice for sustainability and self-reliance, 1995; (jtly) A Trainers' Guide to Participatory Learning and Action, 1995; The Living Land, 1998; (ed jtly) Fertile Ground: the impact of participatory watershed management, 1999; Agri-Culture: reconnecting people, land and nature, 2002; (ed) Guide to a Green Planet, 2002; (ed jtly) Waste Management, 2003; (ed) The Pesticide Detox: towards a more sustainable agriculture, 2005; (ed) The Earthscan Reader in Sustainable Agriculture, 2005; (ed) The Sage Major Work on the Environment, 2006; (jtly) Biological Approaches for Sustainable Soil Systems, 2006; (jtly) Guide to a Healthy Planet, 2006; (ed jtly) Sage Handbook on Environment and Society, 2007; The Earth Only Endures: on reconnecting with nature and our place in it, 2007; (ed) Sustainable Agriculture and Food, 4 vols, 2008; (jtly) Nature and Culture, 2010; This Luminous Coast (East Anglian nature book of the year, East Anglian Book Awards, 2011; New Angle Prize for Literature, 2013); (jtly) Eco-Cultures, 2014; The Edge of Extinction: travels with enduring people in vanishing lands, 2014; (ed jtly) Green Exercise: linking nature, health and well-being, 2016; The East Country: almanac tales of valley and shore, 2017 (Book of the Year, E Anglian Book Awards 2018); (with Z. Bharucha) The Sustainable Intensification of Agriculture, 2018; over 300 papers and articles. *Recreations:* tai chi, walking, cycling, gardening. *Address:* University of Essex, Wivenhoe Park, Colchester, Essex CO4 3SQ. *T:* (01206) 872436. *E:* jpretty@essex.ac.uk. *W:* www.julespretty.com, www.twitter.com/julespretty1.

**PRETTY, Dr Katharine Bridget,** CBE 2009; FSA, FSA (Scot.); Principal, Homerton College, Cambridge, 1991–2013 (Hon. Fellow, 2013); Deputy Vice-Chancellor, University of Cambridge, 2010–13 (Pro-Vice-Chancellor, 2004–10); *b* 18 Oct. 1945; *d of* M. W. and B. E. W. Hughes; *m* 1988, Prof. Tjeerd Hendrik van Andel (*d* 2010). *Educ:* King Edward VI High Sch. for Girls, Birmingham; New Hall, Cambridge (MA, PhD). New Hall, Cambridge: College Lectr and Fellow in Archaeology, 1972–91; Admissions Tutor, 1979–85; Sen. Tutor, 1985–91; Emeritus Fellow, 1995–; University of Cambridge: Member: Council of Senate, 1981–89; Financial Bd, 1986–96; Gen. Bd, 1997–2004; Chm. Council, Sch. of Humanities and Social Scis, 1997–2004; Sen. Fellow, McDonald Inst. for Archaeol Res., 2013–. Chairman: Rescue, 1978–83; OCR Examng Bd, 1998–2013. Pres., Council for British Archaeol., 2008–13 (Hon. Vice-Pres., 2015–). Trustee, Prince's Teaching Inst., 2007–15. Mem., Council, Durham Univ., 2014–. Vice-Pres., RSA, 1998–2004. FSA 2000 (Mem. Council, 2011–15); FSA (Scot.) 2013. Hon. Fellow, Harris Manchester Coll., Oxford, 2011. *Recreations:* archaeology, botany.

**PREVEZER, Susan Rachel;** QC 2000; a Recorder, since 2000; *b* 25 March 1959; *d of late* Prof. Sydney Prevezer and of Enid Margaret Prevezer (*née* Austin); *m* 1994, Benjamin Freedman; two *d. Educ:* St Paul's Girls' Sch.; Girton Coll., Cambridge (MA). Called to the Bar, Inner Temple, 1983. *Address:* Quinn Emanuel Urquhart & Sullivan LLP, 90 High Holborn, WC1V 6LJ.

**PREVITE, His Honour John Edward;** QC 1989; a Circuit Judge, 1992–2001; *b* 11 May 1934; *s of late* Lt Col K. E. Previte, OBE and Edith Frances (*née* Capper); *m* 1959, Hon. Phyllida Browne, *o d of* 6th Baron Kilmaine, CBE; two *s. Educ:* Wellington Coll.; Christ Church, Oxford (MA). Called to the Bar, Inner Temple, 1959, Bencher, 1986; a Recorder, Western Circuit, 1987–92. *Recreations:* sailing, skiffing, Real tennis, gardening.

**PREVOST, Sir Christopher (Gerald),** 6th Bt *cr* 1805; *b* 25 July 1935; *s of* Sir George James Augustine Prevost, 5th Bt and Muriel Emily (*d* 1939), *d of late* Lewis William Oram; *S father,* 1985; *m* 1964, Dolores Nelly, *o d of* Dezo Hoffmann; one *s* one *d. Educ:* Cranleigh School. Served Rifle Bde; Kenya Service Medal, 1955. IBM, 1955–61; Pitney-Bowes, 1963–76; founder of Mailtronic Ltd, manufacturers and suppliers of mailroom equipment, 1977, Chm. and Man. Dir, 1977–91; owner of water sports business, Algarve, Portugal, 1991–98. Mem., Huguenot Soc. *Heir: s* Nicholas Marc Prevost, *b* 13 March 1971.

**PRIAULX, Andrew Graham,** MBE 2008; racing driver; *b* 10 Aug. 1973; *s of* Graham Ernold Priaulx and Judith Anne Priaulx; *m* 1997, Joanne Le Tocq; one *s* one *d. Educ:* Elizabeth Coll., Guernsey. Winner, British Hillclimb Championship, 1995; competed Formula Renault and British Formula 3, 1996; winner, British Renault Spider Cup Championship, 1999–2002; competed British Formula 3, 2000–02; joined BMW UK team, 2003; winner: European Touring Car Championship, 2004; World Touring Car Championship, 2005, 2006, 2007. BMW Ambassador competing in DTM series, 2012, 2013, and in USCC with BMW Motorsport, USA, 2014; Awards include: Lifetime Ambassador, States of Guernsey, 2005; BBC SW Sports Personality of Year, 2005. Gold Medal, British Racing Drivers Club, 2007; Gold Medal, BARC, 2006, 2007. *Recreations:* running, boating, family. *Address:* Andy Priaulx Racing, 2/37 York Place, Harrogate HG1 5RH. *Clubs:* British Racing Drivers', Midland Automobile, British Automobile Racing.

**PRICE,** family name of **Baron Price**.

**PRICE, Baron** *cr* 2016 (Life Peer), of Sturminster Newton in the County of Dorset; **Mark Ian Price,** CVO 2014; *b* 2 March 1961; *s of* Graham and Marjorie Price; *m* 1991, Judith Caroline Bolt; two *d. Educ:* Lancaster Univ. (BA Archaeol). Managing Director: John Lewis, High Wycombe, 1992–95; John Lewis, Cheadle, 1995–98; Mktg Dir, 1998–2000, Dir of Selling and Mktg, 2000–05, Waitrose Ltd; Managing Director: Partnership Develt, John Lewis, 2005–07; Waitrose Ltd, 2007–16; Dir, John Lewis Partnership, 2005–16 (Dep. Chm., 2013–16). Chairman: Prince's Countryside Fund, 2010–16; Business in the Community, 2011–15; Bd of Trustees, Fairtrade Foundn, 2018–. Mem. Bd, Channel 4, 2010–16 (Dep. Chair, 2013–16). Minister of State: (Minister for Trade and Investment), BIS and FCO, 2016; DIT, 2016–17. Founder, Engaging Works, 2017–. *Publications:* The Great British Picnic Guide, 2008; Modern Manner, 2014; The Foolish King, 2016; Food Lover's Handbook, 2016; Fairness For All: unlocking the power of employee engagement, 2017; Six Steps to Workplace Happiness, 2017; Workplace Fables: 145 true life stories, 2017. *Recreations:* picnics, gardening, shooting, fishing, golf.

**PRICE, Adam;** Member (Plaid Cymru) Carmarthen East and Dinefwr, National Assembly for Wales, since 2016; Leader, Plaid Cymru, since 2018; *b* 23 Sept. 1968. *Educ:* Amman Valley Comprehensive Sch.; Saarland Univ.; Univ. of Wales Coll. of Cardiff (BA 1991). Res. Associate, Dept of City and Regl Planning, UWCC, 1991–93; Project Manager, 1993–95, Exec. Manager, 1995–96, Exec. Dir, 1996–98, Menter an Busnes; Man. Dir, Newidiem Econ. Develt Consultancy, 1998–2001; Public Innovation Lead, NESTA, 2012–16. Contested (Plaid Cymru) Gower, 1992. MP (Plaid Cymru) Carmarthen E and Dinefwr, 2001–10. *Publications:* The Collective Entrepreneur; (jtly) The Welsh Renaissance: innovation and inward investment in Wales, 1992; Rebuilding Our Communities: a new agenda for the valleys, 1993; Quiet Revolution? language, culture and economy in the nineties, 1994; The Diversity Dividend, 1996; (jtly) The Other Wales: the case for objective 1 funding post 1999, 1998. *Recreations:* contemporary culture, good friends, good food, travel. *Address:* National Assembly for Wales, Cardiff Bay, Cardiff CF99 1NA.

**PRICE, (Albert) John;** QC 2009; a Recorder, since 2007; *b* Bradford, Yorks, 29 April 1960; *s of* Albert and Eileen Price; *m* 1996, Ruth Caroline Sainsbury; four *d. Educ:* Jesus Coll., Oxford (BA Hons Juris.). Called to the Bar, Inner Temple, 1982. *Recreations:* golf, gardening. *Address:* 23 Essex Street, WC2R 3AA. *T:* (020) 7413 0353, *Fax:* (020) 7413 0374. *E:* JohnPrice@23es.com.

**PRICE, Bernard Albert,** CBE 1997; DL; County Clerk and Chief Executive, Staffordshire County Council, and Clerk to the Lieutenancy, 1983–2003; Clerk to the Staffordshire Police Authority, 1995–2003; *b* 6 Jan. 1944; *s of* Albert and Doris Price; *m* 1966, Christine Mary, *d of* Roy William Henry Combes; two *s* one *d. Educ:* Whitchurch Grammar Sch., Salop; King's Sch., Rochester, Kent; Merton Coll., Oxford (BA 1965, MA 1970). DMS, Wolverhampton Polytechnic, 1972. Articled, later Asst Solicitor, Worcs CC, 1966–70; Asst Solicitor, subseq. Dep. Dir of Admin, Staffs CC, 1970–80; Sen. Dep. Clerk, Staffs CC, 1980–83. Mem. Council, 2004–18, Hon. Sec., 2012–15, Staffs Wildlife Trust; Mem., W Midlands Regl Cttee, 2004–10, Dep. Chm., Midlands Adv. Bd, 2010–12, National Trust. Lay Mem., Chapter, 2004–09, Mem. Council, 2009–13, Lichfield Cathedral. Trustee, Abbots Bromley Hosp., 2011–19. DL Stafford, 2003. Hon. LLD Keele, 2002. *Recreations:* walking, Spain. *Address:* The Cottage, Yeatsall Lane, Abbots Bromley, Rugeley, Staffs WS15 3DY. *T:* (01283) 840269.

**PRICE, Christopher;** Head of Music, BBC Radio 1 and 1Xtra, since 2016; *b* Aylesbury, 17 July 1973; *s of* Brian Price and Carol Parker; *m* 2014, Courtney Connor. *Educ:* Univ. of Bristol (BA Mod. Langs). Producer, BBC Radio 1, 2000; Dir, Music Programming, MTV, 2006; Hd of Music, Last.fm, 2012. *Publications:* (jtly) Live Fast, Die Young: misadventures in rock 'n' roll America, 2010. *Recreations:* running, walking, writing, reading, guitar. *Address:* BBC, Broadcasting House, Portland Place, W1A 1AA.

**PRICE, Prof. Christopher Philip,** PhD; CSci; FRCPath; CChem, FRSC; FACB; Honorary Senior Fellow, University of Oxford, since 2016 (Visiting Professor in Clinical Biochemistry, 2002–16); Professor of Clinical Biochemistry, Queen Mary and Westfield College, University of London (formerly London Hospital Medical College), 1988–2001, Emeritus, 2002; *b* 28 Feb. 1945; *s of* Philip Bright Price and Frances Gwendoline Price; *m* 1968, Elizabeth Ann Dix; two *d. Educ:* Cirencester Grammar Sch.; Lanchester Poly. (BSc); Univ. of Birmingham (PhD 1973); MA Cantab 1983. CChem 1977; FRSC 1982; FRCPath 1989; FACB 2000; CSci 2005. Basic Grade Clin. Biochemist, Coventry and Warwickshire Hosp., 1967–72; Principal Grade Clin. Biochemist, E Birmingham Hosp., 1972–76; Consultant Clinical Biochemist: Southampton Gen. Hosp., 1976–80; Addenbrooke's Hosp., Cambridge, 1980–88; Dir of Pathol., The Royal Hosps, then Barts and the London, NHS Trust, 1995–2001; Vice-Pres., Outcomes Res., Diagnostics Div., Bayer HealthCare, Tarrytown, NY, 2002–05; Emeritus Prof. in Clinical Biochemistry, QMUL, 2006. Vis. Prof. in Med. Diagnostics, Cranfield Univ., 2005–08. Mem., Ind. Rev. of Pathology Services in England, 2006–08. Pres., Assoc. for Clinical Biochem., 2003–06. Hon. DSc: De Montfort, 1998; Coventry, 2011. *Publications:* Centrifugal Analysers in Clinical Chemistry, 1980; Recent Advances in Clinical Chemistry, Vol. 2, 1981, Vol. 3, 1985; Principles and Practice of Immunoassay, 1991, 2nd edn 1997; Point-of-Care Testing, 1999, 3rd edn 2010; Evidence-Based Laboratory Medicine, 2003, 2nd edn 2007; Point-of-Care Testing for Managers and Policymakers, 2006; Applying Evidence Based Laboratory Medicine: a step-by-step guide, 2008; Point-of-Care Testing: making innovation work for patient centred care, 2012. *Recreations:* walking, gardening.

**PRICE, Sir Curtis (Alexander),** KBE 2005; PhD; Warden, New College, Oxford, 2009–16; *b* 7 Sept. 1945; *s of* Dalias Price and Lillian Price (*née* Alexander); adopted British nationality, 2006; *m* 1981, Rhian Samuel; one step *s. Educ:* Southern Illinois Univ. (BA 1967); Harvard Univ. (AM 1970; PhD 1974). Washington University, St Louis: Asst Prof., 1974–79; Associate Prof., 1979–82; King's College London: Lectr, 1982–85; Reader in Historical Musicology, 1985–88; King Edward Prof. and Head of Dept of Music, 1988–95; FKC 1994; Principal, Royal Acad. of Music, 1995–2008. Guggenheim Fellow, 1982–83. Pres., Royal Musical Assoc., 1999–2002. Hon. RAM 1993; Hon. FRNCM 2001; Hon. FRCM 2002. Einstein Award, Amer. Musicol. Soc., 1979; Dent Medal, Royal Musical Assoc., 1985. *Publications:* Music in the Restoration Theatre, 1979; Henry Purcell and the London Stage, 1984; Dido and Aeneas: a critical score, 1986; The Impresario's Ten Commandments, 1992. *Address:* 16 Thackery Court, 75 Turnmill Street, EC1M 5SY. *E:* curtis.price@btinternet.com. *Club:* Garrick.

**PRICE, His Honour David**; a Circuit Judge, 2004–10; *b* 27 Sept. 1943; *s* of Bevan Glyn Price and Nora Price; *m* 1971, Jennifer Newton; two *s*. *Educ*: King Edward VI Sch., Stratford upon Avon; Univ. of Leeds (LLB). Called to the Bar, Inner Temple, 1968; in practice on Midland Circuit, 1968–93; a Recorder, 1992–2004. Asst Parly Boundary Comr, 1992; Chairman: Employment Tribunals, 1993–2004; Reinstatement Cttee, Reserve Forces, 1996–2004. *Recreations*: golf, music, theatre. *Club*: Luffenham Heath Golf.

**PRICE, David**; *see* Price, Geoffrey D.

**PRICE, David Jack**; QC 2011; Principal, David Price Solicitors & Advocates, since 1993; *b* London, 16 Oct. 1963; *s* of late Lionel and Judith Price; *m* 1992, Nicole Cohen; two *s* one *d*. *Educ*: Haberdashers' Aske's Sch., Elstree; Harvard High Sch., LA (ESU Schol.); Manchester Univ. (LLB 1986); Coll. of Law, Lancaster Gate. Admitted as solicitor, 1990; barrister, 1991; re-admitted as solicitor, 1992; Solicitor-Advocate, 1995. *Publications*: Defamation: law procedure and practice, 1995, 4th edn 2009. *Recreations*: balls (hitting, bowling and kicking), snow, sea and sand. *Address*: David Price Solicitors & Advocates, 21 Fleet Street, EC4Y 1AA. *T*: (020) 7353 9999, *Fax*: (020) 7353 9990. *E*: dprice@dpsa.uk. *Club*: MCC.

**PRICE, Dr David John**, CBE 2010; CEng, CSci; Chairman: Telesoft Technologies Ltd, since 2013; RTL Materials Ltd, since 2014; Symetrica Ltd, since 2015; Lontra Ltd, since 2016; *b* Hawkhurst, Kent, 27 March 1955; *s* of Ifan and Margaret Price; *m* 1979, Rosalynd Fiona Davidson; two *d*. *Educ*: Maidstone Grammar Sch.; University Coll. London (BSc 1977; PhD 1982). CEng 1984; CSci 2003. Thorn EMI: Prog. Manager, 1980–87, Chief Scientist, 1987–90, Defence Systems Div.; Systems Dir, 1990–93, Prog. Dir, 1993–95, Defence Gp; Chief Exec., Thomson-Thorn Missile Electronics, 1995–98; Managing Director: Thomson (UK) Hldgs Ltd, 1998–2000; Rolls-Royce Naval Marine, 2000–05; Chief Exec., Chemring Gp plc, 2005–12. Non-exec. Dir, AZ Electronic Materials plc, 2011–14; Chm., Optitune plc, 2014–18. Mem. Adv. Bd, DK Group BV, 2013–. Public Mem., Network Rail, 2013–15. Member: Defence Scientific Adv. Council, 1998–2005; Nat. Defence Industries Council, 2008–12. Member: Adv. Bd, Loughborough Univ. Business Sch., 2005–10; Council, Univ. of Southampton, 2010– (Hon. Treas., 2015–). Non-exec. Dir, Univ. Hosp. Southampton NHS Foundn Trust, 2014–18. Hon. DSc Cranfield, 2011. *Recreations*: opera, cinema, tennis, horse riding, reading, travel. *Address*: Ashe Hill, Ashe, Basingstoke, Hants RG25 3AE. *T*: (01256) 771228. *E*: dprice2703@aol.com.

**PRICE, David William James**; investment director and farmer; Chairman, F and C (formerly Foreign and Colonial) Management Ltd, 1999–2004; *b* 11 June 1947; *s* of Richard James Emlyn Price and Miriam Joan Dunsford; *m* 1971, Shervie Ann Lander Whitaker, *d* of Sir James Whitaker, 3rd Bt, OBE; one *s* one *d*. *Educ*: Ampleforth Coll.; Corpus Christi Coll., Oxford (MA). Director: Mercury Asset Management Gp, 1978–97 (Dep. Chm., 1985–97); S. G. Warburg and Co. Ltd, 1982–86; London Bd, Halifax Building Soc., 1993–96; Merrill Lynch European Investment (formerly Mercury Privatisation, then Mercury European Investment) Trust, 1994–2004; Scottish American Investment Co., 1997–; Booker plc, 1998–2000; Big Food Gp, 2000–04; Melchior Japan Investment Trust, 2006–11; Chairman: Aberdeen All Asia Investment (formerly Govett Asian Recovery, later Gartmore Asia Pacific) Trust, 1998–2009; Gartmore Absolute Growth & Income Trust, 2000–04; Iceland Group, 2001–04. Dir, Heritage Trust of Lincs, 1997–2012; Trustee, Orders of St John Care Trust, 2001–10. Councillor (C), London Borough of Lambeth, 1979–82. Mem. Council, KCL, 2001–08. OStJ; Kt, SMO Malta. *Recreations*: history, gardening. *Address*: Eastgate Manor, 137 Eastgate, Louth, Lincs LN11 9QG; Harrington Hall, Spilsby, Lincs PE23 4NH. *T*: (01790) 753764. *Clubs*: Brooks's; Lincolnshire.

**PRICE, Elizabeth**, PhD; artist; Lecturer in Fine Art, Ruskin School of Drawing and Fine Art, University of Oxford, 2012; Fellow, Lady Margaret Hall, Oxford, 2012; *b* Bradford, 1966. *Educ*: Ruskin Sch. of Art, Univ. of Oxford (BA Fine Art 1988); Royal Coll. of Art (MA Fine Art 1991); Univ. of Leeds (PhD Fine Art 1998). Principal Lectr, then Reader, Kingston Univ., until 2010; Arts Council England Helen Chadwick Fellow, Univ. of Oxford and British Sch. at Rome, 2010–11. Works include video installations: At the House of Mr X, 2007; Welcome (The Atrium), 2008; User Group Disco, 2009; The Tent, 2010; The Woolworths Choir of 1979, 2012; West Hinder, 2012; *solo exhibitions and screenings* include: Help, 2001, Denness, 2003, Mobile Home, London; Jerwood Artists Platform, Jerwood Space, London, 2004; Cry, 2006, O Fontana, 2008, The Woolworths Choir of 1979, 2012, MOT International; At the House of Mr X, Stanley Picker Gall., London, 2007, BFI, 2008; User Group Disco, Spike Island, Bristol, 2009, Whitechapel Gall., London, 2010, Contemp. Art Soc., London, 2013; Choir, New Mus., NY, Chisenhale Gall., London, 2011, Bielefelder Kunstverein, 2012; Here, Baltic, Gateshead, 2012; The Tent, Bloomberg SPACE, London, 2012; Sleep, MOT Internat., Brussels, 2014; Tate Britain, 2012; A Restoration, Ashmolean Mus., Oxford, 2016; Walker Gall., Minneapolis, 2018. Jarman Award, FLAMIN, 2011; Paul Hamlyn Award, 2012; Turner Prize, 2012; Contemporary Art Society Award, 2013.

**PRICE, Eric Hardiman Mockford**; Director, Robinson Brothers (Ryders Green) Ltd, 1985–2015; Proprietor, Batchworth Heath Farm (formerly Farm and Stud), since 2000; *b* 14 Nov. 1931; *s* of Frederick H. Price and Florence N. H. Price (*née* Mockford); *m* 1963, Diana M. S. Robinson; one *s* three *d*. *Educ*: St Marylebone Grammar Sch.; Christ's Coll., Cambridge. Econs Tripos, 1955; MA 1958. FREconS, 1956; FSS 1958; MInstPet 1992. Army service, 1950–52; HAC, 1952–57. Supply Dept, Esso Petroleum Co. Ltd, 1955–56; Economist: Central Electricity Authority, 1956–57; Electricity Council, 1957–58; British Iron & Steel Fedn, 1958–62; Chief Economist, Port of London Authority, 1962–67; Sen. Econ. Adviser, Min. of Transport, 1966–69; Chief Econ. Adviser, Min. of Transport, 1969–71; Dir of Econs, 1971–75, Under Sec., 1972–76, Dir of Econs and Stats, 1975–76, DoE; Under Sec., Econs and Stats Div., Depts of Industry, Trade and Consumer Protection, 1977–80; Head of Econs and Stats Div., Dept of Energy, 1980–92; Chief Econ. Advr, Dept of Energy, later DTI, 1980–93. Proprietor, Energy Economics Consultancy, 1995–99; Special Consultant, Nat. Econ. Res. Associates, 1993–98. Member: Soc. of Business Economists, 1961; Expert Adv. Gp on Entry into Freight Transport Market, EEC, 1973–75; Northern Regional Strategy Steering Gp, 1976–77; Expert Gp on Venture Capital for Industrial Innovation, EEC, 1978–79; Soc. of Strategic and Long-range Planning, 1980–; Council, Internat. Assoc. of Energy Economists, 1981–85; Energy Panel, SSRC, 1980–83; Council, British Inst. of Energy Economics, 1986–2006 (Mem., 1980–2005), Hon. Fellow, 2006; Vice-Chm., 1981–82 and 1988–89; Chm., 1982–85); Steering Cttee, Jt Energy Programme, RIIA, 1981–89, Steering Cttee, Energy and Envmtl Prog., 1989–; Adv. Council, Energy Econs Centre, Univ. of Surrey, 1989–93. UK rep., Econ. Res. Cttee, European Council of Ministers of Transport, 1968–76; UK rep. on Six Nations' Prog. on Govt Policies towards Technological Innovation in Industry, 1977–80; Mem., World Bank's Groupe des Sages on Econs of Global Warming, 1990–93. Member, Advisory Board: Transport Studies Unit, Oxford Univ., 1973–75; Centre for Res. in Industrial, Business and Admin Studies, Univ. of Warwick, 1977–80. FInstD 1990. Mem., U3A. *Publications*: various articles in learned jls on transport and industrial economics, energy and energy efficiency, investment, utilities, technological innovation in industry, regional planning, environmental abatement policies, and East European energy issues. *Recreations*: racehorse breeding, local history, horse racing. *Address*: Batchworth Heath Farm, London Road, Rickmansworth, Herts WD3 1QB. *Clubs*: Moor Park Golf (Hon. Mem.); Riverside Health and Leisure (Northwood, Middx).

**PRICE, Sir Francis (Caradoc Rose)**, 7th Bt *cr* 1815; QC (Can.) 1992; barrister and solicitor; Partner, Reynolds Mirth Richards and Farmer LLP, since 1979; *b* 9 Sept. 1950; *s* of Sir Rose Francis Price, 6th Bt and Kathleen June, *d* of late Norman W. Hutchinson, Melbourne; *S* father, 1979; *m* 1975, Marguerite Jean Trussler, retired Justice, Court of Queen's Bench, Alberta, *d* of late Roy S. Trussler, Victoria, BC; three *d*. *Educ*: Eton; Trinity College, Melbourne Univ. (Sen. Student 1971–72, LLB Hons 1973); Univ. of Alberta (LLM 1975); Canadian Petroleum Law Foundn Fellow, 1974–75. Admitted barrister and solicitor, Province of Alberta 1976, Northwest Territories 1978, Canada; Bencher, Law Soc. of Alberta, 1990–94. Lectr, 1979–89, and Course Head, 1983–89, Alberta Bar Admission Course. Chartered Arbitrator, Arbitration and Mediation Inst. of Canada, 1994. CLJ 2000. *Publications*: Pipelines in Western Canada, 1975; Mortgage Actions in Alberta, 1985; Conducting a Foreclosure Action, 1996; contribs to Alberta and Melbourne Univ. Law Revs, etc. *Recreations*: opera, cricket, theatre. *Heir*: *nephew* Benjamin William Rose Price, *b* 16 Sept. 1989. *Address*: 9626 95th Avenue, Edmonton, AB T6C 2A4, Canada. *Club*: Faculty (Edmonton).

**PRICE, Gareth**; broadcast management consultant, since 2005; *b* 30 Aug. 1939; *s* of Rowena and Morgan Price; *m* 1962, Mari Griffiths; two *s* one *d*. *Educ*: Aberaeron Grammar School and Ardwyn Grammar School, Aberystwyth; University College of Wales, Aberystwyth (BA Econ). Asst Lectr in Economics, Queen's Univ., Belfast, 1962–64; BBC Wales: Radio Producer, Current Affairs, 1964–66; Television Producer, Features and Documentaries, 1966–74; Dep. Head of Programmes, 1974–81; Head of Programmes, 1981–85; Controller, 1986–90; Thomson Foundation: Controller of Broadcasting, 1990–93; Dir, 1993–2005. Vice-Pres., Welsh Centre for Internat. Affairs, 2012– (Chm., 2003–12). Consultant, Asia-Pacific Broadcasting Union, 2010–. Vice-Chm., Communication and Inf. Cttee, UNESCO UK, 2006–10. Hon. Sec., Elizabeth R. Fund, 2006–15. Hon. Prof. of Communication, Univ. of Wales, Cardiff, 1994–99; Hon. Fellow, Univ. of Wales, Aberystwyth, 2000–. Elizabeth R Lifetime Achievement Award for Promoting Public Broadcasting, Commonwealth Broadcasting Assoc., 2006. *Publications*: David Lloyd George (with Emyr Price and Bryn Parry), 1981; Broadcast Management for Asians, 2006; The Broadcasters of BBC Wales, 1964–90, 2017. *Address*: 98 Pencisely Road, Cardiff CF5 1DQ. *E*: price.g@ntlworld.com.

**PRICE, Prof. (Geoffrey) David**, PhD; FGS; Professor of Mineral Physics, since 2006, and Vice Provost (Research), since 2007, University College London; *s* of Prof. Neville J. Price and Joan J. Price; *m* 1978, Sarah Lois Millar (*see* Prof. S. L. Price); one *s* one *d*. *Educ*: Latymer Upper Sch.; Clare Coll., Cambridge (MA; PhD 1980). Royal Soc. Res. Fellow, 1983–88; Reader in Mineral Physics, 1988–91, Prof. of Mineral Physics, 1991–2006, UCL and Birkbeck Coll., London Univ.; Hd, Dept of Earth Scis, 1992–2002 and 2004–05, Vice Dean (Res.), 2003–06, Exec. Dean, 2006–07, Math. and Physical Scis, UCL. Ed., Earth and Planetary Sci. Letters, 2005–07. Chairman: HEFCE REF 2014 sub-panel for Earth and Envmtl Scis, 2011–14; HEFCE REF 2021 Main Panel B (Maths, Physical Scis and Engrg); Policy Cttee, League of Eur. Res. Univs, 2014–; Mem., STFC, 2012–19. Pres., Mineralogical Soc. of GB, 2004–06 (Mem., 1977–; Schlumberger Medal, 1999); FGS 1992 (Murchison Medal, 2002); FMSA 1997; Fellow, Amer. Geophysical Union, 2005. MAE 2000. Non-exec. Dir, North Middlesex Univ. Hosp. NHS Trust, 2012–15. Chm. Govs, UCL Academy Sch., Camden, 2011–17. Mem., Editl Bd, The Conversation, 2014–17. Louis Néel Medal, Eur. Geoscis Union, 2006. *Publications*: over 270 papers in learned jls on mineralogy, geophysics and micropalaeontology. *Recreations*: philately, family history. *Address*: Office of Vice Provost (Research), University College London, 2 Taviton Street, WC1H 0BT. *T*: (020) 7679 8581. *E*: d.price@ucl.ac.uk. *Club*: Athenæum.

**PRICE, Geraint**; *see* Price, William G.

**PRICE, His Honour Gerald Alexander Lewin**; QC 1992; a Circuit Judge, 2000–10; *b* 13 Sept. 1948; *s* of Denis Lewin Price and Patricia Rosemary (*née* Metcalfe); *m* 1974, Theresa Elisabeth Iremonger-Watts; two *s*. *Educ*: Haileybury Coll.; College of Law; Inns of Court Law Sch. Called to the Bar, Middle Temple, 1969; in private practice, Cardiff, 1970–77; Bermuda: Resident Stipendiary Magistrate, 1977–81; Chief Stipendiary Magistrate and Sen. Coroner, 1981–84; in private practice, Cardiff, 1984–2000; a Recorder, 1990–2000. Chm., Liquor Licence Authority, Land Valuation Appeals Tribunal, Price Control Commn and Jury Revising Tribunal, 1981–84. Mem., Commonwealth Magistrates and Judges Assoc., 1984–. Mem., RYA. *Recreations*: travel, classical music, sunshine, motorboating in Menorca. *Club*: Menorca Cricket.

**PRICE, Prof. Huw**, PhD; FBA 2012; Bertrand Russell Professor of Philosophy, University of Cambridge, 2011–Sept. 2020; Fellow, Trinity College, Cambridge, since 2011; Academic Director, Leverhulme Centre for Future of Intelligence, since 2016; *b* 1953. *Educ*: Australian Nat. Univ. (BA 1976); Univ. of Oxford (MSc 1977); PhD Cantab 1981. Sydney Univ., 1989–2000, Prof. of Natural Metaphysics, 1997–2000; Prof. of Logic and Metaphysics, Univ. of Edinburgh, 2000–03; ARC Fedn Fellow, 2002–11, and Challis Prof. of Philosophy and Founding Dir, Centre for Time, 2002–12, Univ. of Sydney. Mem. Bd, Ada Lovelace Inst., Nuffield Foundn, 2018–. Consulting Ed., Stanford Encyclopedia of Philosophy, 1995–2006; Associate Ed., Australasian Jl Philosophy; Member, Editorial Advisory Board: Contemp. Pragmatism; Logic and Philosophy of Sci.; Eur. Jl for Philosophy of Sci. Past Pres., Australasian Assoc. Philosophy. FAHA 1994. *Publications*: Facts and the Function of Truth, 1988; Time's Arrow and Archimedes' Point, 1996; (ed with R. Corry) Naturalism Without Mirrors, 2011; Expressivism, Pragmatism and Representationalism, 2013; contribs to Jl Philosophy, Mind, British jl for Philosophy of Sci., Nature. *Address*: Faculty of Philosophy, University of Cambridge, Sidgwick Avenue, Cambridge CB3 9DA.

**PRICE, Isobel Clare M.**; *see* McKenzie-Price.

**PRICE, Jackie D.**; *see* Doyle-Price.

**PRICE, James Edward N.**; *see* Newton-Price.

**PRICE, Sir James Keith Peter Rugge-**, 10th Bt *cr* 1804, of Spring Grove, Richmond, Surrey; *b* 8 April 1967; *er s* of Sir Keith Rugge-Price, 9th Bt and of Jacqueline Mary Rugge-Price (*née* Loranger); *S* father, 2000, but his name does not appear on the Official Roll of the Baronetage. *Heir*: *b* Andrew Philip Richard Rugge-Price, *b* 6 Jan. 1970.

**PRICE, James Richard Kenrick**; QC 1995; *b* 14 Sept. 1948; *s* of Lt-Col Kenrick Jack Price, DSO, MC, 9th Lancers and Juliet Hermione, *d* of Marshal of the Royal Air Force Sir John Cotesworth Slessor, GCB, DSO, MC; *m* 1983, Hon. Virginia Yvonne, *d* of 5th Baron Mostyn, MC. *Educ*: Eton College; St Edmund Hall, Oxford. Called to the Bar, Inner Temple, 1974. Dir, Mostyn Estates Ltd, 1994–. *Recreations*: fine and decorative arts, gardening, mountains, ski-ing, Corfu. *Address*: 5 Gray's Inn Square, Gray's Inn, WC1R 5AH. *T*: (020) 7242 2902. *Clubs*: Brooks's, Beefsteak.

**PRICE, John**; *see* Price, A. J.

**PRICE, His Honour John Charles**; a Circuit Judge, 2003–15; *b* 8 March 1945; *s* of Hubert and Betty Price. *Educ*: Wrekin Coll., Wellington, Shropshire; The Hill Sch., Pottstown, Pa, USA; Univ. of Birmingham (LLB Hons). Called to the Bar, Gray's Inn, 1969, Bencher, 2009; in practice, 1969–2003; a Recorder of the Crown Court, 1990–2003. *Recreations*: tennis, sailing, ski-ing, maintaining friendships. *Club*: Garrick.

**PRICE, Prof. John Frederick**, MD; FRCP, FRCPCH; Consultant Paediatrician, King's College Hospital, 1978–2010; Professor of Paediatric Respiratory Medicine, University of London, since 1992; Clinical Director of Paediatrics, King's NHS Healthcare Trust, 1993–96 and 1999–2010; *b* 26 April 1944; *s* of Drs Cyril Frederick Price and Dora Elizabeth Price; *m* 1971, Dr Valerie Pickup; two *d*. *Educ*: Dulwich Coll.; St John's Coll., Cambridge (MB BCh; MA; MD 1986); Guy's Hosp., London. DCH 1973; FRCP 1985; FRCPCH 1997. MRC Trng Fellowship, Inst. of Child Health and Gt Ormond St Hosp., 1975–78; Hd, Acad. Dept of Child Health, 1995–98, and Chm., Div. of Child Health and Reproductive Medicine, 1995–98, GKT Med. and Dental Sch., KCL (formerly King's Coll. Sch. of Medicine and Dentistry), Univ. of London. Vis. Prof. and Ext. Examr, Hong Kong Univ. and Univ. of Malaya, 1997. Altounyan Address, Brit. Thoracic Soc., 1989; C. Elaine Field Lecture, Hong Kong Paediatric Soc., 1997, 2000. Sec., Paediatric Section, Royal Soc. Medicine, 1988–90; Chm., Brit. Paediatric Respiratory Soc., 1992–94; Council Member: Brit. Thoracic Soc., 1990–; European Respiratory Soc., 1990–95. Chm., Nat. Asthma Campaign, subseq. Asthma UK, 2003–09 (Trustee, 1990–2009; Vice Pres., 2010); Trustee: Brit. Lung Foundn, 1990–95; Demelza Hospice Care for Children, 2015–; Member: Med. Adv. Panel, Nat. Eczema Soc., 1987–91; Res. and Med. Adv. Cttee, Cystic Fibrosis Trust, 1993–98 (Trustee, 2010–17). Master, Fruiterers' Co., 2013. Associate Editor: Respiratory Medicine, 1987–93; European Respiratory Jl, 1990–93. *Publications*: (with J. Rees) ABC of Asthma, 1984, 3rd edn 1995; contrib. chapters in books; numerous articles in learned jls related to respiratory disease in childhood. *Recreations*: theatre, music, Austen, Trollope, conversations with family and friends. *Address*: Wychling Hall, Wichling, Kent ME9 0DJ. *Clubs*: Athenæum, Walbrook Ward; Hawks (Cambridge).

**PRICE, Leontyne**; Opera Prima Donna (Soprano), United States; *b* 10 Feb. 1927. *Educ*: Public Schools, Laurel, Mississippi; Central State College, Wilberforce, Ohio (BA); Juilliard Sch. of Music, NY. Four Saints, 1952; Porgy and Bess, 1952–54. Operatic Debut on TV, 1955, as Tosca; Concerts in America, England, Australia, Europe. Operatic debut as Madame Lidouine in Dialogues of Carmelites, San Francisco, 1957; Covent Garden, Verona Arena, Vienna Staatsoper, 1958; five roles, inc. Leonora in Il Trovatore, Madame Butterfly, Donna Anna in Don Giovanni, Metropolitan, 1960–61; Salzburg debut singing soprano lead in Missa Solemnis, 1959; Aida in Aida, Liu in Turandot, La Scala, 1960; opened season at Metropolitan in 1961 as Minnie in Fanciulla del West; opened new Metropolitan Opera House, 1966, as Cleopatra in world premiere of Samuel Barber's Antony and Cleopatra; debut Teatro Dell'Opera, Rome, in Aida, 1967; debut Paris Opera, in Aida, 1968; debut Teatro Colon, Buenos Aires, as Leonora in Il Trovatore, 1969; opened season at Metropolitan Opera, in Aida, 1969. Numerous recordings. Vice-Chm., Nat. Inst. for Music Theatre. Member: Metropolitan Opera Assoc.; Bd of Dirs, Dance Theatre of Harlem; Bd of Trustees, NY Univ. Life Mem., NAACP. Fellow, Amer. Acad. of Arts and Sciences. Hon. Dr of Music: Howard Univ., Washington, DC, 1962; Central State Coll., Wilberforce, Ohio, 1968; Hon. DHL, Dartmouth Univ., 1962; Hon. Dr of Humanities, Rust Coll., Holly Springs, Miss, 1968; Hon. Dr of Humane Letters, Fordham Univ., New York, 1969. Hon. Mem. Bd of Dirs, Campfire Girls, 1966. Presidential Medal of Freedom, 1965; Spingarn Medal, NAACP, 1965; Nat. Medal of Arts, 1985; 18 Grammy Awards, Nat. Acad. Recording Arts and Scis. Order of Merit (Italy), 1966; Commandeur, Ordre des Arts et des Lettres (France), 1986. *Recreations*: cooking, dancing, shopping for clothes, etc, antiques for homes in Rome and New York.

**PRICE, Nick**; golfer; founded Nick Price Golf Course Design, 2001; *b* Durban, 28 Jan. 1957; *m* Sue Price; one *s* two *d*. Wins include: US PGA, 1992, 1994; Open, Turnberry, 1994; Vardon Trophy, 1993; record for PGA Tournament lowest score (269), 1994. *Publications*: The Swing, 1997. *Address*: c/o Professional Golfers' Association Tour, 112 PGA Tour Boulevard, Ponte Vedra Beach, FL 32082, USA.

**PRICE, Nigel Stewart**; Master of the Senior Courts (formerly Supreme Court), Chancery Division, 1999–2019; *b* 18 May 1954; *s* of late Ernest Henry Price and Diana Price (*née* Lane). *Educ*: Billesley Infant and Jun. Schs; Moseley Grammar Sch., Birmingham; Christ's Coll., Cambridge (MA); Coll. of Law; City of Birmingham Poly.; Open Univ. (BA Hons Classics, French and Spanish 2010). Admitted solicitor, 1978; articled clerk and Asst Solicitor, Clifford-Turner, 1976–80; Asst Solicitor, Pinsent & Co., 1980–82; Lectr in Law, Univ. of Buckingham, 1983–86; Partner, Kimbell & Co., 1986–99; Dep. Master, Chancery Div., 1992–99; Immigration Adjudicator, 1996–98. Consulting Ed., Atkin's Court Forms, 2014–; Ed., Civil Procedure, 2015–. Alfred Syrett 2nd Prize, City of London Solicitors' Co., 1976. *Publications*: (ed and contrib.) Jowitt's Dictionary of English Law, 3rd edn 2010; contribs to legal jls. *Recreations*: languages, music, literature, ski-ing, dog walking. *Address*: c/o Chancery and Commercial Courts, Rolls Building, 110 Fetter Lane, EC4A 1NL.

**PRICE, Rt Rev. Peter Bryan**; Bishop of Bath and Wells, 2002–13; Assistant Bishop, Diocese of Southwark, since 2019; *b* 17 May 1944; *s* of Alec Henry Price and Phyllis Evelyn Mary Price; *m* 1967, Edith Margaret Burns (MBE 2010); four *s*. *Educ*: Redland Coll., Bristol (Cert Ed 1966); Oak Hill Theol Coll. (Dip. in Pastoral Studies, 1974); Heythrop Coll. (MPhil Studies 1993). Asst Master, Ashton Park Sch., Bristol, 1966–70; Tutor, Lindley Lodge, Nuneaton, 1970; Head of Religious Studies, Cordeaux Sch., Louth, 1970–72; ordained, 1974; Community Chaplain, Crookhorn, Portsmouth and Asst Curate, Christ Church, Portsdown, 1974–78; Chaplain, Scargill House, Kettlewell, 1978–80; Vicar, St Mary Magdalene, Addiscombe, Croydon, 1980–88; Canon Residentiary and Chancellor, Southwark Cathedral, 1988–91, Canon Emeritus, 1992–97; Gen. Sec., USPG, 1992–97; Area Bp, Kingston-upon-Thames, 1997–2002; an Hon. Asst Bp, Dio. of Salisbury, 2016–19. Chairman: Anglican Communion Pastoral Visitors, 2008–13; Conciliation Resources, 2013–19; Chair, Anglican Peace Initiative, 2020–. Mem., Inst. for Policy Develt, Univ. of Bath, 2014–16. Founding Trustee, Burns Price Foundn, 2015–. Vice Pres., Royal Bath and West Soc., 2014– (Pres. 2012–13). Visitor, Wadham Coll., Oxford, 2002–13. Entered House of Lords, 2008. Hon. LLD Bath, 2013. *Publications*: The Church as Kingdom, 1987; Seeds of the Word, 1996; Telling it as it is, 1998; Living Faith in the World through Word and Action, 1998; To Each their Place, 1999; Mark Today, 1999; Jesus Manifesto: reflections on St Luke's gospel, 2000; Undersong: listening to the soul, 2001; Playing the Blue Note, 2002; (with Jeanne Hinton) Changing Communities, 2003; (contrib.) The Value of Dialogue in Times of Hostility and Insecurity, 2016; Things that make for Peace: a Christian peacemaker in a world of war, 2018; A Shaking Reality: daily reflections for Advent, 2018. *Recreations*: painting, swimming, walking, conversation. *Address*: Flat 86, Whitgift House, 76 Brighton Road, South Croydon CR2 6AB.

**PRICE, Peter Nicholas**; European Strategy Counsel, since 1994; *b* 19 Feb. 1942; *s* of Rev. Dewi Emlyn Price and Kate Mary Price; *m* 1988, Joy Bhola; one *d*. *Educ*: Worcester Royal Grammar Sch.; Aberdare Boys' Grammar Sch.; Univ. of Southampton (BA (Law)); Coll. of Law, Guildford; KCL (Postgrad. Dip. in EC Law). Solicitor. Freelance broadcaster, 1962–67; Asst Solicitor, Glamorgan CC, 1967–68; solicitor in private practice, 1966–67 and 1968–85; part-time EC consultant: Payne Hicks Beach, 1990–93; Howard Kennedy, 1993–2001; pt-time Employment Judge (formerly Chm., Employment Tribunal), 2000–12. Contested (C) Gen. Elecns: Aberdare 1964, 1966; Caerphilly 1970; Nat. Vice-Chm., Young Conservatives, 1971–72; Mem., Nat. Union Exec. Cttee, 1969–72 and 1978–79; Vice-Chm., Cons. Pol Centre Nat. Cttee, 1978–79; Hon. Sec., For. Affairs Forum, 1977–79; Vice-Chm., Cons. Gp for Europe, 1979–81; Mem. Council, Eur. Movement, 1971–81. MEP (C): Lancashire W, 1979–84; London SE, 1984–94; Hon. MEP, 1994; European Parliament: Chm., Budgetary Control Cttee, 1989–92 (Vice-Chm., 1979–84, and its Rapporteur for series of 4 major reports on Community finances, 1985–86); spokesman for EDG, Legal Affairs Cttee, 1984–87, Budgets Cttee, 1986–89; Member: ACP/EEC Jt Assembly, 1981–94; Ext. Econ. Relns Cttee, 1992–94; delegns for relns with Japan, 1989–92, US Congress, 1992–94. Member: Lib Dem Federal Policy Cttee, 1998–; Alliance of Liberals and Democrats for Europe Party Council (formerly European Lib Dem and Reformist (Party) Council), 1999–; Lib Dem Federal Finance Cttee, 2001–06; Lib Dem Internat. Affairs Cttee, 2010–. Contested (Lib Dem) Wales, EP elecn, 1999. Standing Orders Comr, 1998–99, Mem., Commn on Powers of Nat. Assembly, 2002–04, Nat. Assembly for Wales. Non-executive Director: Bureau Veritas Quality Internat. Ltd, 1991–2001; Ravensbourne NHS Trust, 1998–99; Welsh Ambulance Services NHS Trust, 2005–13 (Vice Chm., 2010–12); Wales Audit Office, 2013–17; Chm., Bd of Governance, Jersey Audit Office, 2016–. Mem. Bd (formerly Exec. Cttee), Cymru Yfory/Tomorrow's Wales, 2004–16 (Chm., 2012–16). Mem., NEC, FPA, 1973–77 (Mem., then Chm., Long-term Planning Gp, 1973–76). Fellow, Industry and Parlt Trust, 1981–82; Vice-Pres., UK Cttee, Eur. Year of Small and Med.-sized Enterprises, 1983. Mem., RIIA. Vice-Pres., Llangollen Internat. Eisteddfod, 1981–. Gov., Thames Valley Univ., 1996–2005. *Publications*: misc. pol pamphlets and newspaper articles. *Recreations*: theatre, music, photography. *Address*: 37 Heol St Denys, Lisvane, Cardiff CF14 0RU. *T*: (029) 2076 1792; 60 Marlings Park Avenue, Chislehurst, Kent BR7 6RD. *T*: (01689) 820681. *E*: peterprice@btinternet.com.

**PRICE, Rev. Peter Owen**, CBE 1983; BA; FPhS; RN retired; Minister of Blantyre Old Parish Church, Glasgow, 1985–96; *b* Swansea, 18 April 1930; *e s* of late Idwal Price and Florence Price; *m* 1957, Margaret Trevan (*d* 1977); three *d*; *m* 1996, Mary Hamill Robertson (*d* 2008); *m* 2016, Christine Alexandra Cherry. *Educ*: Hutchesons' Grammar Sch., Glasgow; King Edward's Grammar Sch., Camp Hill, Birmingham; Wyggeston Sch., Leicester; Didsbury Theol Coll., Bristol. BA Open Univ. Ordained, 1960, Methodist Minister, Birmingham; commnd RN as Chaplain, 1960; served: HMS Collingwood, 1960; HQ 3 Cdo Bde, RM, 1962–64; Staff of C-in-C Med., 1964–68; RNAS Brawdy, 1968–69; HQ 3 Cdo Bde, 1969–70, HQ Cdo Forces, 1970–73, RM; HMS Raleigh, 1973; HMS Drake, 1974–78; BRNC Dartmouth, 1978–80; Principal Chaplain, Church of Scotland and Free Churches (Naval), MoD, 1981–84. Hon. Chaplain to the Queen, 1981. *Recreations*: freemasonry (Past Grand Chaplain, Grand Lodge of Scotland; Hon. Depute Provincial Grand Master, Lanarks Middle Ward; Member: Scottish Rite - 32nd Degree; Royal Order of Scotland), warm water sailing, music. *Address*: Duncraigan, 22 Old Bothwell Road, Bothwell, Glasgow G71 8AW.

**PRICE, His Honour Philip John**; QC 1989; a Circuit Judge, 1993–2008; Designated Family Judge, Cardiff, 1998–2006; *b* 16 May 1943; *s* of late Ernest and Eunice Price; *m* 1967, Mari Josephine Davies; one *s* two *d*. *Educ*: Cardiff High Sch.; Pembroke Coll., Oxford (MA). Lectr in Law, Univ. of Leeds, 1966–70; called to the Bar, Gray's Inn, 1969; in practice on Wales and Chester Circuit and Temple, 1971–93; a Recorder, 1985–93. Chancellor, Dio. Monmouth, 1992–2015; Pres., Disciplinary Tribunal, Church in Wales, 2001–05. Member: Mental Health Rev. Tribunal, 1995–2018; Cttee, Council of Circuit Judges, 1998–2007 (Sen. Vice Pres., 2007). Mem., 1993–2016, Chm., Standing Cttee, 2005–16, Governing Body, Church in Wales. Trustee, LATCH-Welsh Children's Cancer Charity, 1996–2015 (Chm., 2006–15; Pres., 2015–). *Recreations*: architecture, books, cricket. *Address*: HMCS Wales, Churchill House, Churchill Way, Cardiff CF10 2HH. *Club*: Cardiff and County.

**PRICE, Richard Alexander David**; Chief Economist, Department for International Trade, since 2016; *b* 18 Aug. 1967; *s* of Prof. Roger David Price and Heather Lynne Price; *m* 1999, Dr Luisa Affuso; one *s* one *d*. *Educ*: Hewett Sch., Norwich; Univ. of York (BA Econs 1987, MSc Econs 1989). Economist, HM Treasury, 1989–93; Nat. Econ. Res. Associates, 1993–97; Home and Legal Team, HM Treasury, 1997–99; Chief Economist, Home Office, 1999–2001; Performance and Innovation Unit, Cabinet Office, 2001; Strategy Advr to the Permanent Sec., Home Office, 2001–02; Hd of Enterprise Policy, HM Treasury, 2002–05; Chief Economist, 2005–11, and Dir of Corporate Performance, 2008–11, DEFRA; Chief Exec., Office of Rail Regulation, then Office of Rail and Road, 2011–16. Mem., Govt Economic Service Bd, 1999–2001, 2005–11; Founding Chair, 2013–15, Sen. Advr, 2015–16, UK Regulators' Network. Non-exec. Dir, ETC Venues Ltd, 2005–06; alternate non-exec. Dir, Capital for Enterprise Bd, 2005. Sec., Highbury Railway Allotments and Gardens Soc., 2009–. Chair, Freightliners City Farm, 2017–. FRSA. *Publications*: various policy and res. papers and articles on econ. regulation, infrastructure, entrepreneurship, migration, crime reduction, envmtl econs, globalisation and social impacts of policy. *Recreations*: modern and contemporary art, exploring Italy, travel and transport, food. *Address*: Department for International Trade, 3 Whitehall Place, SW1A 2AW. *E*: richard_price@larpnet.com.

**PRICE, Richard Mervyn**, OBE 1995; QC 1996; a Recorder, 2004–18; *b* 15 May 1948; *s* of late William James Price and Josephine May Price; *m* 1971, Caroline Sarah (marr. diss. 2007), *d* of Geoffrey and Mary Ball; one *s* two *d*. *Educ*: King Edward VII Sch., Sheffield; King's Coll., London (LLB Hons). Called to the Bar, Gray's Inn, 1969, Bencher, 2002; Accredited Mediator, 1997. Standing Counsel on Election Law to Conservative Central Office, 1986–. Mem., Bar Council, 1998–2002 (Vice-Chm., 2002–04, Chm., 2005, Professional Conduct and Complaints Cttee); Mem., Bar Standards Bd, 2006–07 (Chm., Conduct Cttee, 2006–07). Legal Assessor: to Disciplinary Cttee, RCVS, 2007–; to GMC, 2010–18. *Publications*: (ed) Parker's Law and Conduct of Elections, 2003–; (cons. ed.) Halsbury's Laws of England, Elections and Referendums, 5th edn 2014. *Recreations*: politics, theatre, films, music, walking, cycling. *Address*: 4–5 Gray's Inn Square, WC1R 5AH. *Clubs*: Garrick, Royal Automobile.

**PRICE, His Honour Richard Neville Meredith;** a Circuit Judge, 1996–2014; *b* 30 May 1945; *s* of Christopher Llewelyn Price and Valerie Ruby Price (*née* Greenham); *m* 1971, Avril Judith Lancaster; three *s. Educ:* Marsh Court, Stockbridge, Hants; Sutton Valence, Kent. Admitted solicitor, 1970; Asst Recorder, 1985–90; called to the Bar, Middle Temple, 1990; Recorder, 1990–96; Resident Judge, Portsmouth and Newport Crown Courts, 2004–11; Hon. Recorder, City of Portsmouth, 2006–11. *Recreations:* choral singing, sailing, reading, listening to music, appreciating Dr Who. *Clubs:* Bar Yacht; Seaview Yacht (IoW).

**PRICE, Richard Ralph,** FCA; Chairman, British Association for Performing Arts Medicine, since 2004; Director, Pearson Education Ltd, since 2014; *b* London, 1 Aug. 1944; *s* of Llewelyn Ralph Price and Vera Patricia Price; *m* 1967, Susan Jennifer Mary Smellie; one *s* one *d. Educ:* Glasgow Acad.; Watford Boys Grammar Sch.; Univ. Coll. of S Wales and Monmouthshire (BSc (Econ)). FCA 1969. Co-founder, BPP Hldgs plc, 1976, Chm., 1986–2002; Chm., EDI plc, 2004–12. Vice Pres., Action Med. Res., 2014– (Chm., 2008–14). Mem. Council, RCM, 2004–14 (Hon. FRCM 2015). Mem., Bach Choir (Chm., 2000–08). Hon. DLaws BPP, 2012. *Recreations:* golf, tennis, music, walking. *Clubs:* Brooks's; Denham Golf, Campden Hill Tennis; Royal Solent Yacht.

**PRICE, Sir Robert (John) G.;** *see* Green-Price.

**PRICE, Sally;** *see* Price, S. L.

**PRICE, Samantha Anna;** Headmistress, Benenden School, since 2014; *b* London, 13 Jan. 1974; *d* of Graham Rangeley Mitchell and Valerie Joy Mitchell, *qv*; *m* 2000, Rev. Iorwerth Price; one *s* one *d. Educ:* Malvern Girls' Coll.; Univ. of Edinburgh (MA Hons Hist. of Art 1997). Direct Mktg Officer, Tate Gall., 1997–99; Hd of History of Art and Hd of Year, Reading Blue Coat Sch., 1999–2003; teacher and housemistress, King's Sch., Canterbury, 2003–07; Dep. Head, Hereford Cathedral Sch., 2007–10; Head, Godolphin Sch., Salisbury, 2010–13. Governor: Brambletye Prep. Sch., 2014–; Tonbridge Sch., 2014–16; John Wallis C of E Acad., 2014–. Chair: Boarding Cttee, GSA; Wellbeing Cttee, HMC. *Recreations:* cycling, horseriding, opera appreciation. *Address:* Benenden School, Cranbrook Road, Benenden, Kent TN17 4AA. *T:* (01580) 240592. *E:* jmm@benenden.kent.sch.uk.

**PRICE, Sarah Helena;** HM Diplomatic Service; Head, Counter-Proliferation and Arms Control Centre, Foreign and Commonwealth Office, since 2018; *b* 4 June 1966; *d* of John Michael Anthony Price and Mary Price; *m* 2006, Simon McGrath; two *s. Educ:* Holy Child Sch., Edgbaston; Somerville Coll., Oxford (BA Hons Classics and Mod. Langs 1989). Joined FCO, 1990: Third Sec., FCO, 1990–92; Second Secretary: UK Delegn to CSCE, Helsinki, 1992; Prague, 1993–96; First Sec., FCO, 1996–99; on secondment to Finnish Foreign Ministry, 1999–2000; Dep. Hd of Mission, Belgrade, 2000–04; Dep. Hd, Counter-Proliferation Dept, 2004–07, Hd, Drugs and Internat. Crime Dept, 2008, Counsellor, Strategic Finance Directorate, 2009–10, Hd, Arabian Peninsula and Iraq Dept, 2011–13, FCO; Ambassador to Finland, 2014–17. *Address:* c/o Foreign and Commonwealth Office, King Charles Street, SW1A 2AH.

**PRICE, Prof. Sarah Lois, (Sally),** PhD; FRS 2017; Professor of Physical Chemistry, University College London, since 2000; *b* Watford, 24 Aug. 1956; *d* of David and Jane Millar; *m* 1978, (Geoffrey) David Price, *qv* (separated); one *s* one *d. Educ:* St Albans Grammar Sch. for Girls; Clare Coll., Cambridge (BA Natural Scis 1977; PhD Theoretical Chem. 1980). Postdoctoral Res. Associate, Univ. of Chicago, 1980–81; Postdoctoral Res. Asst, Univ. of Cambridge, 1981–85; Fellow, Fitzwilliam Coll., Cambridge, 1981–89; Royal Soc. Univ. Res. Fellow, Univ. of Cambridge, 1985–89, UCL, 1989–90; Lectr in Physical Chem., 1990–96, Reader, 1996–2000, UCL. *Publications:* contribs to learned jls incl. Chemistry, Jl Amer. Chem. Soc., Crystal Growth and Design, Jl Chem. Physics. *Recreations:* family, scientific conference travels, enjoying London, especially Camden, local Parochial Church Council. *Address:* Department of Chemistry, University College London, 20 Gordon Street, WC1H 0AJ.

**PRICE, Prof. Shirley Christine, (Mrs P. L. Lane),** PhD; FRSB, FBTS, FHEA, FRSC; Academic Director (Education), Student Progression and Learning Gain, since 2018, and Professor of Toxicology, since 2010, University of Surrey; *b* London, 3 March 1956; *d* of Cecil Price and Irene Price; *m* 1984, Peter Leslie Lane; one *s* one *d. Educ:* Honor Oak Grammar Sch., London; Chelsea Coll., Univ. of London (BSc (Hons) Biochem.); Univ. of Surrey (MSc Toxicol.; PhD Toxicopathology 1985). University of Surrey: Robens Institute of Industrial and Environmental Health and Safety: Res. Asst, 1980–83; Res. Fellow, 1983–85; Res. Fellow in Electron Microscopy, 1985–87; Manager of Histopathology, 1987–88; Manager, In Vivo Toxicol. Gp, 1988–98; School of Biomedical and Molecular Sciences: Tutor, 1998–2001; Sen. Tutor, 2001–04; Sen. Lectr and Dir of Postgrad. Studies, 2004–10; Associate Dean (Learning and Teaching), 2009–14; Hd, Academic Appeals and Academic Quality, 2014–18. Chm., UK Register of Toxicologists, 2007–12. Expert Toxicologist: Special Prog. of Res. Develt and Trng in Human Reproduction, WHO, 2000–04); Expert Adv. Gp on Veterinary Residues, 2005–; Expert Adv. Gp on Paediatric Medicines, 2009–; Mem., Commn on Human Medicines, 2014–. Mem., Kent, Surrey and Sussex Deanery Adv. Bd, 2011–. Gov., Royal Grammar Sch., Guildford, 2008–; Gov., 2015–, Trustee, 2018–, Godalming Coll. (Chair, Curriculum and Quality Cttee, 2018–) Eur. Registered Toxicologist, 2000. FHEA 2008; FBTS 2009 (Pres., April 2020–); FRSB (FSB 2012); FRSC 2015. Mem., Pharmacol Soc., 2015. *Publications:* Principles and Practice of Skin Toxicology, 2008; contrib. articles in jls incl. Eur. Jl of Pharmaceutical Scis, Jl of Further and Higher Educn, Jl of Applied Toxicol., Veterinary Record, Frontiers in Pharmacol. *Recreations:* theatre, singing in local choir, family, walking. *Address:* Office of the Vice Provost (Education), Senate House, University of Surrey, Guildford, Surrey GU2 7XH. *T:* (01483) 689215. *E:* s.price@surrey.ac.uk.

**PRICE, Prof. Susan Ann,** CBE 2016; JP; PhD; Vice Chancellor, Leeds Beckett (formerly Leeds Metropolitan) University, 2010–15; *b* South Shields, 11 Sept. 1956; *d* of Michael and Dorothea Price; *m* 1982, Dr Uwe Zemke. *Educ:* Salford Univ. (BSc 1st Cl. Hons Modern Langs); Salford Univ. and University Coll. London (PhD Linguistics 1982); Bradford Univ. (MBA). FCIL 2004. Lectr in Spanish, Bradford Univ., 1983–89; ESRC Fellow in Internat. Business, Manchester Univ., 1992–93; Dir of Academic Affairs, Dept of Modern Langs, Bradford Univ., 1993–97; Associate Dean, Faculty of Langs and Eur. Studies, UWE, 1998–2002; Pro Vice Chancellor (Academic), 2002–07, Dep. Vice Chancellor, 2007–08, Acting Vice Chancellor, 2008–09, Univ. of E London. Mem. Council, Univ. of Salford, 2015–. JP W Yorks, 2019. MCIM 1993; FCMI 2003; FHEA 2008; FRSA. Hon. DEd 2017. *Publications:* Comparative Constructions in Spanish and French Syntax, 1990, 2nd edn 2017. *Recreations:* travel, reading, food and wine.

**PRICE, Thomas;** QC 2010; *b* Burton on Trent, 23 March 1963; *s* of John Price and Josephine Maguire; *m* Claire Sugrue. *Educ:* Univ. of Southampton (LLB Hons). Called to the Bar, Inner Temple, 1985. *Recreations:* art, theatre, cooking, angling. *Address:* 25 Bedford Row, WC1R 4HD. *T:* (020) 7067 1500. *E:* tprice@25bedfordrow.com.

**PRICE, Tristan Robert Julian;** Chief Executive, M. P. Evans Group PLC, since 2016; *b* 24 Nov. 1966; *s* of Julian Price and Isolde (*née* Buchloh); *m* 1988, Judith Ann Torrance; three *s* one *d. Educ:* Tonbridge Sch.; Corpus Christi Coll., Cambridge (BA Hons Econs 1988; MA 1992); University Coll. London (MSc Econs 1993). FCA 2007 (ACA 1992).

Coopers & Lybrand, 1988–91; Treuhandanstalt, Berlin, 1992; joined FCO, 1993, Econ. Advr, 1993–98; Econs Dept, OECD, 1999–2002; rejoined FCO, 2003; Dep. Hd, Econ. Policy Dept, 2003; Hd, Financial Planning and Perf. Dept, 2003–06; M. P. Evans Gp PLC, 2006–, Gp Finance Dir, 2010–15. Mem. Council and Chair, Faculty of Finance and Mgt, later Business and Mgt Faculty, ICAEW, 2014–17. *Publications:* (jtly) OECD Economic Surveys: Baltic States, 1999, Brazil, 2000, Yugoslavia, 2002. *Recreations:* my children, skiing, cycling, eating good cheese. *Address:* M. P. Evans Group PLC, 3 Clanricarde Gardens, Tunbridge Wells, Kent TN1 1HQ.

**PRICE, Prof. (William) Geraint,** FRS 1988; FREng, FIMechE, FRINA; Professor of Ship Science, 1990–2009, now Emeritus, and Head of School of Engineering Sciences, 1998, University of Southampton; *b* 1 Aug. 1943; *s* of Thomas Price and Ursula Maude Price (*née* Roberts); *m* 1967, Jennifer Mary Whitten; two *d. Educ:* Merthyr Tydfil County Grammar Sch.; University Coll. Cardiff (Univ. of Wales) (G. H. Latham Open Sci. Scholar; BSc, PhD); Univ. of London (DSc(Eng)). FRINA 1980; FREng (FEng 1986); FIMechE 1989. Res. Asst, later Lectr, UCL, 1969–81; Reader in Applied Mechanics, Univ. of London, 1981–82; Prof. of Applied Mechanics, Brunel Univ., 1982–90. Fellow: Japan Soc. for Promotion of Science, 1987; Y. S. Hui Foundn, 2004. Pres., RINA, 2001–04. Foreign Mem., Chinese Acad. of Engrg, 2000. *Publications:* Probabilistic Theory of Ship Dynamics, 1974; Hydroelasticity of Ships, 1979. *Recreations:* walking, Rugby, golf, barbecuing. *Address:* Tŷ Gwyn, 45 Palmerston Way, Alverstoke, Gosport, Hants PO12 2LY. *T:* (023) 9235 1719.

**PRICE, William John R.;** *see* Rea Price.

**PRICE, Winford Hugh Protheroe,** OBE 1983; FCA; City Treasurer, Cardiff City Council, 1975–83; *b* 5 Feb. 1926; *s* of Martin Price and Doris Blanche Price. *Educ:* Cardiff High Sch. IPFA 1952; FCA 1954. Served War, RAFVR, 1944–48. City Treasurer's and Controller's Dept, Cardiff, 1942; Dep. City Treasurer, Cardiff, 1973–75. Public Works Loan Comr, 1979–83. Treasurer and Financial Adviser, Council for the Principality, 1975–83; Financial Adviser, Assoc. of Dist Councils Cttee for Wales, 1975–83; Treasurer: The Queen's Silver Jubilee Trust (S Glam), 1976–83; Royal National Eisteddfod of Wales (Cardiff), 1978. Occasional lectr on local govt topics. *Publications:* contrib. to jls. *Recreation:* chess.

**PRICE EVANS, David Alan;** *see* Evans, David A. P.

**PRICHARD, David Colville Mostyn,** MBE 2002; Headmaster, Wycliffe College, 1994–98; *b* 26 May 1934; *s* of Rev. George Mostyn Prichard and Joan Mary Mostyn Prichard; *m* 1992, Catherine Elizabeth Major (formerly Headmistress, Warwick Prep. Sch.). *Educ:* Radley Coll.; Pembroke Coll., Oxford (Captain of Boats; MA; Mem., Society Cttee, 1956–2005). FCollP. Asst Master, Monkton Combe Sch., 1955–68 (Dir, Centenary Appeal, 1962; Founder, GB 1st Vol. Police Cadets, 1964; CO, CCF, 1964–68); Headmaster, Port Regis, Motcombe Park, 1969–93. Founder, Nat. Conf. for Govs, Bursars and Heads, 1981–93; Chm., IAPS, 1989–90. Mem. Develt Cttee, SW Arts, 1998–2006. Trustee, Smallpeice Trust, 1980–2003; Chm., Smallpeice Enterprises, 1986–95; Co-Chm., Operation New World, 1992–99 (Trustee, 1992–); Vice President: Glos Pied Piper Appeal, 1995; Wycliffe Watermen, 1998–. Governor: Swanbourne House Sch., 1985–2000; Holmewood House Sch., 1987–98; Orwell Park Sch., 1995–98; St John's Sch., Chepstow, 1995–99; West Hill Park Sch., 1998–2002; Sherborne Prep. Sch., 1999–2006 (Chm., 2002–06); Mem., Govs' Adv. Body, Wycliffe Coll., 2006–11. Vice-Chm., Sherborne and District Soc., 2009–15. Trustee, Sherborne House Trust, 1998–2006. Mem. Cttee, Friends of Yeatman Hosp., 2000–03. Church Warden, Castleton Church, 1999–2005. Freeman, City of London, 1990; Liveryman, Loriners' Co., 1990–. FRSA. *Publications:* Training for Service, 1967. *Recreations:* education, travel, rowing (OUBC Isis VIII). *Address:* Thornhill Lodge, North Road, Sherborne, Dorset DT9 3JW. *T:* (01935) 816539. *Clubs:* National, Carlton; Leander.

**PRICHARD, Jonathan Layton,** CEng, FICE; Chief Executive, Institution of Chemical Engineers, since 2017; *b* Llanelli, 12 Feb. 1964; *s* of David Layton Prichard and Veronica Kay Prichard (*née* Evans); *m* 1989, Gillian Sarah Owen; two *s* one *d. Educ:* Shrewsbury Sch.; RMA Sandhurst; RMCS Shrivenham (BEng 1988). CEng 1998; CEnv 2004; FICE 2005. Served RE, 1983–2001. Dir, Membership, 2001–05, Dir, Engrg, 2005–07, ICE; Dir, Resources, High-Point Rendel, 2007–10; CEO, Engrg Council, 2010–17. Non-exec. Dir, Quality Assurance Agency for Higher Educn, 2012–17. Chair, Engineers Without Borders, 2017–. Served TA, 2003– (Col, 2007–); Actg Adjt, Engr and Logistic Staff Corps RE (V), 2004–. FInstRE 2009. Hon. FSE 2008. *Recreations:* sailing, ski-ing, DIY. *Address:* Institution of Chemical Engineers, Davis Building, Railway Terrace, Rugby CV21 3HQ. *E:* ceo@icheme.org. *Clubs:* Royal Air Force; Royal Engineer Yacht.

**PRICHARD, Mathew Caradoc Thomas,** CBE 1992; DL; Chairman, Agatha Christie Ltd, 1976–2016; *b* 21 Sept. 1943; *s* of late Major H. de B. Prichard and Rosalind Hicks; *m* 1st, 1967, Angela Caroline Maples (*d* 2004); one *s* two *d*; 2nd, 2007, Lucinda Mary Oliver. *Educ:* Eton College; New College, Oxford. BA (PPE). Penguin Books, 1965–69. Pres., Nat. Mus. of Wales, 1996–2002 (Mem. Court of Governors and Council, 1975–2007); Member: Welsh Arts Council, 1980–94 (Chm., 1988–94); Arts Council of GB, 1983–94. Chm., Artes Mundi, 2012–. High Sheriff, Glamorgan, 1972–73; DL S Glam, 1994. Prince of Wales Medal for Philanthropy, 2012. *Publications:* (ed) Agatha Christie's The Grand Tour: letters and photographs from the British Empire Expedition 1922, 2012. *Recreations:* golf, cricket, bridge. *Address:* Bettws Lodge, Bettws Newydd, Usk, Monmouthshire NP15 1JN. *T:* (01873) 881127. *Clubs:* Boodle's, MCC; Cardiff and County; Royal & Ancient Golf (St Andrews); Royal Porthcawl Golf.

**PRICHARD-JONES, Sir David John Walter,** 3rd Bt *cr* 1910, of Bron Menai, Anglesey; *b* 14 March 1943; *s* of Sir John Prichard-Jones, 2nd Bt and Heather, *er d* of Sir Walter Nugent, 4th Bt; *S* father, 2007. *Educ:* Ampleforth; Christ Church, Oxford (BA). *Heir:* cousin Richard Stephen Prichard-Jones [*b* 23 Nov. 1952; *m* 2000, Jane Emma Lewsley; one *s* two *d* (of whom one *s* one *d* are twins)]. *Address:* 17 Tresco House, 2 Sancroft Street, Kennington, SE11 5UQ.

**PRICKETT, Prof. (Alexander Thomas) Stephen,** PhD; FAHA; FEA; Honorary Professor of English, University of Kent at Canterbury, since 2008; *b* 4 June 1939; *s* of Rev. William Ewart Prickett and Barbara Browning (*née* Lyne); *m* 1st, 1967, Diana Joan Mabbutt; one *s* one *d*; 2nd, 1983, Maria Angelica Alvarez (marr. diss. 2001); 3rd, 2001, Patricia Erskine-Hill. *Educ:* Kent Coll., Canterbury; Trinity Hall, Cambridge (BA 1961; PhD 1968); University Coll., Oxford (DipEd). English teacher, Uzuakoli, E Nigeria, 1962–64; Asst Lectr, Lectr, and Reader, Univ. of Sussex, 1967–82; Prof. of English, ANU, Canberra, 1983–89; Regius Prof. of English Lang. and Lit., Univ. of Glasgow, 1990–2001; Margaret Root Brown Prof. of English and Dir, Armstrong Browning Liby, Baylor Univ., Texas, 2003–08. Vis. Lectr, Smith Coll., Mass, USA, 1970–71; Vis. Fulbright Prof., Univ. of Minnesota, 1979–80; Visiting Professor: of English, Duke Univ., USA, 2001–03; Univ. of Urbino, 2019. Trustee, Higher Educn Foundn, 1976–2004. President: Soc. for Study of Literature and Theology, 1991–2000; George MacDonald Soc., 1994–. FAHA 1986; Fellow, Soc. for Values in Higher Educn, USA, 1992; FRSA 1993; FEA 2004. Dr *hc:* Artois,

France, 2002; Bucharest, 2015. Lifetime Achievement Award, Conf. on Christianity and Literature, 2015. *Publications:* Do It Yourself Doom, 1962; Coleridge and Wordsworth: the poetry of growth, 1970, 2nd edn 1980; Romanticism and Religion, 1976; Victorian Fantasy, 1979, 3rd edn 2017; Words and the Word: language poetics and biblical interpretation, 1986, 2nd edn 1988; England and the French Revolution, 1988; Reading the Text: biblical criticism and literary theory, 1991; (jtly) The Bible, 1991; Origins of Narrative: the romantic appropriation of the Bible, 1996; (ed) World's Classics Bible, 1997; (jtly) The Bible and Literature: a reader, 1999; Narrative, Religion and Science, 2002; (ed) Education! Education! Education!: managerial ethics and the law of unintended consequences, 2002; Modernity and the Reinvention of Tradition, 2009; (ed) European Romanticism: a reader, 2010; (ed) The Edinburgh Companion to the Bible and the Arts, 2014; (Gen. Ed.) Bible and Literature: a history, 5 vols., 2020; Inner Space: culture, imagination and identity, 2020. *Recreations:* walking, ski-ing, drama, cruise lecturing.

**PRIDDIS, Rt Rev. Anthony Martin;** Bishop of Hereford, 2004–13; an Honorary Assistant Bishop: Diocese of Worcester, since 2013; Diocese of Gloucester, since 2014; *b* 15 March 1948; *s* of Ted and Joan Priddis; *m* 1973, Kathy Armstrong; two *s* one *d*. *Educ:* Corpus Christi Coll., Cambridge (BA 1969; MA 1973); New Coll., Oxford (DipTh 1971; MA 1975); Cuddesdon Coll., Oxford. Ordained deacon, 1972, priest, 1973; Asst Curate, New Addington, 1972–75; Chaplain, Christ Church, Oxford, 1975–80; Team Vicar, High Wycombe, 1980–86; Priest-in-charge, 1986–90, Rector, 1990–96, Amersham; RD of Amersham, 1992–96; Suffragan Bp of Warwick, 1996–2004. Chair and Mem., Central Safeguarding Liaison Gp, C of E, 2002–10; Chm., Rural Bishops' Panel, 2006–09; Mem., Rural Strategy Gp, 2009–. Entered H of L, 2009. Lay Mem. Bd, CEM (formerly FAEM), 2002–08; Mem., W Midlands Cultural Consortium, 2002–05. Co-Chm., Family Life and Marriage Educn Network, 2001–06. Hon. FRCEM (Hon. FFAEM 2005). *Publications:* (contrib.) Study of Spirituality, 1986; Forgiveness: a practical and pastoral companion, 2019; various articles for mags, local and nat. radio and television. *Recreations:* walking the dogs, music, golf, gardening, watching sport, fly-fishing. *Address:* Round Oak Cottage, Bridstow, Ross-on-Wye HR9 6QJ. *E:* anthony@priddis.me.

**PRIDDLE, Robert John,** CB 1994; energy consultant: Endless Energy, since 2002; Plexus Energy, since 2002; Editorial Consultant, World Energy Outlook, International Energy Agency, since 2003; *b* 9 Sept. 1938; *s* of late Albert Leslie Priddle and Alberta Edith Priddle; *m* 1962, Janice Elizabeth Gorham; two *s*. *Educ:* King's Coll. Sch., Wimbledon; Peterhouse, Cambridge (MA). Asst Principal, Min. of Aviation, 1960, Principal 1965; Private Sec. to Minister for Aerospace, 1971–73; Asst Sec., DTI, 1973, and Dept of Energy, 1974; Under Sec., Dept of Energy, 1977–85; Under Sec., DTI, 1985–89; Dep. Sec. and Dir Gen. of Energy Resources, Dept of Energy, subseq. DTI, 1989–92; Dep. Sec., Corporate and Consumer Affairs, DTI, 1992–94; Exec. Dir, Internat. Energy Agency, 1994–2002 (Chm., Governing Bd, 1991–92). Pres., Conf. of European Posts and Telecommunications Administrations, 1987–89. Mem., Financial Reporting Council, 1992–94. Chevalier de la Légion d'Honneur (France), 2001. *Publications:* Victoriana, 1959, 2nd edn 1963. *Address:* 1 Stable Court, Stodham Park, Liss, Hants GU33 7QX.

**PRIDEAUX, John Denys Charles Anstice,** CBE 1994; PhD; Chairman: Festiniog Railway Company, since 2006; Ffestiniog and Welsh Highland Railways Trust (formerly Festiniog Railway Trust), since 1998; Danube Eastern Railway Company, since 2013; *b* 8 Aug. 1944; *s* of Denys Robert Anstice-Prideaux and Frances Hester Dorothy Anstice-Prideaux (*née* Glaze); *m* 1972, Philippa Mary (*née* Morgan); one *s* one *d*. *Educ:* St Paul's; Univ. of Nottingham (BSc, PhD). British Railways: Operational Research, 1965; Area Manager, Newton Abbot, 1972; Strategic Planning Officer, 1974; Divl Manager, Birmingham, 1980; Dir, Policy Unit, 1983–86; Dir, 1986–91, Man. Dir, 1991, InterCity; Man. Dir, New Ventures, 1992–94; Chm., Union Railways, 1992–93; Director: Green Arrow, 1994–95; Docklands Light Railway, 1994–98; Chairman: Prideaux and Associates, 1994–99; Angel Train Contracts, 1996–98 (Dir, 1996–2008); Image Scan Hldgs Plc, 1998–2000; Altram (Manchester) Ltd, 1999–2003; Superlink Ltd, 2004–10. Member: Adv. Cttee on Trunk Road Assessment, 1977; Transport Cttee, SERC and ESRC, 1982; Planning and Envmt Cttee, ESRC, 1985; Special Advr on Railways, FIPRA Internat., 2005–. Mem., Council, Manchester Business School, 1987. *Publications:* railway histories, papers on management and transport. *Recreations:* rural affairs, farming, conservation, history, sailing, ski-ing, design. *Address:* Ffestiniog Railway Company, Harbour Station, Porthmadog, Gwynedd LL49 9NF.

**PRIDEAUX, Julian Humphrey,** OBE 1995; Deputy Director-General and Secretary, National Trust, 1997–2002; *b* 19 June 1942; 2nd *s* of Sir Humphrey Povah Treverbian Prideaux, OBE; *m* 1967, Jill, 3rd *d* of R. P. Roney-Dougal; two *s*. *Educ:* St Aubyn's, Rottingdean; Eton; Royal Agricultural Coll. (Dip. Estate Management). ARICS 1966, FRICS 1974. Land Agent with Burd & Evans, Shrewsbury, 1964–67; Agent to Col Hon. C. G. Cubitt and others, 1967–69; National Trust: Land Agent, Cornwall Region, 1969–77; Dir, Thames and Chilterns Region, 1978–86; Chief Agent, 1987–96. Mem. Council, 1987–2005, Trustee, 2003–05, Nat. Gardens Scheme; Trustee: Rural Housing Trust, 2001–14; Chelsea Physic Gdn, 2003–12; Goldsmiths Centre, 2007–12; Dorneywood Trust, 2010–. *Recreation:* walking. *Address:* Cromwell Lodge, 39 East Street, Coggeshall, Essex CO6 1SJ. *Club:* Farmers.

**PRIDHAM, Brian Robert;** HM Diplomatic Service, retired; Hon. Research Fellow, Centre for Arab Gulf Studies, University of Exeter, 1995–2000 (Research Fellow, 1983–95; Director, 1985–86, 1987–95); *b* 22 Feb. 1934; *s* of Reginald Buller Pridham and Emily Pridham (*née* Winser); *m* 1st, 1954, Fay Coles (marr. diss. 1996); three *s*; 2nd, Lorraine Patricia Waitt (*née* Moore). *Educ:* Hele's Sch., Exeter. MA Exon, 1984. RWAFF (Nigeria Regt), 1952–54; Foreign Office, 1954–57; MECAS, 1957–59; Bahrain, 1959; Vice-Consul, Muscat, 1959–62; Foreign Office, 1962–64; 2nd Sec., Algiers, 1964–66, 1st Sec., 1966–67; Foreign Office, 1967–70; Head of Chancery: La Paz, 1970–73; Abu Dhabi, 1973–75; Dir of MECAS, Shemlan, Lebanon, 1975–76; Counsellor, Khartoum, 1976–79; Head of Communications Ops Dept, FCO, 1979–81. University of Exeter: Lectr in Arabic, Dept of Arabic and Islamic Studies, 1984–87; Dep. Dir, Centre for Arab Gulf Studies, 1984–85. Dep. Hd, EU Observer Mission to Palestinian Elections, 1995–96; Hd, OSCE Observer Mission to Albanian Elections, 1997; Hd, EU Observer Mission to Tanzanian Elections, 2000. Jt Ed., New Arabian Studies series, 1994–2007. *Publications:* (ed) Contemporary Yemen: politics and historical background, 1984; (ed) Economy, Society and Culture in Contemporary Yemen, 1984; (ed) The Arab Gulf and the West, 1985; (ed) Oman: economic, social and strategic developments, 1986; The Arab Gulf and the Arab World, 1987; (trans.) Omani-French Relations 1715–1905, 1996; (trans.) A Permissible Narrative, 2010; (ed) My Early Life, 2010. *Recreations:* shrubs, photography.

**PRIDHAM, Brig. Robert,** OBE 1991; Clerk to the Grocers' Company, 2006–16; *b* 9 Dec. 1949; *s* of late Kenneth Reginald Pridham, Grenadier Guards, and Theresia Pridham (*née* Berkemeier); *m* 1979, Jane Elizabeth Stibbon; four *d*. *Educ:* Hele's Sch., Exeter; RMCS Shrivenham (BSc Applied Sci. 1975); Univ. of Westminster (MA Internat. Liaison and Commns 2007). CEng 1998; FICE 1998. Enlisted Grenadier Guards, 1968; RMA Sandhurst, 1969–70; commnd RE, 1970; Troop Comd, Berlin and Cyprus, 1971; RMCS Shrivenham; Aide/Speechwriter, US Congress, Washington, 1972–75; Troop Comd, BAOR and NI, 1975–77; 3 Field Sqn, NI and Oman, 1977–79; Instructor, RMA Sandhurst, 1980; Army Comd and Staff Coll., Shrivenham and Camberley, 1981–82; Defence Operational Analysis Estabt, UK and Berlin, 1983–85; OC 39 Field Sqn BAOR, Canada and Australia, 1985–87; SO2 Mil Sec., MoD, 1987–88; SO1 Defence (Budget) Prog., MoD, 1988–90; CO 39 Engr Regt, UK, RAF Germany and Gulf, 1990–91; CRE 3rd UK Div., UK and France, 1991–94; Comdt RSME, 1995–97; RCDS, London and E Asia, 1998; Dir Staff Ops SHAPE, Mons, 1999–2000; lang. trng, Germany, 2001–02; Defence Attaché, Berlin, 2002–06. Member: British-German Assoc.; British-German Officers Assoc. FCIL 2006; FCMI 2006; FInstRE 2009. *Recreations:* family, travel, France, Germany, opera, choral music, biographies, rowing, langlauf, watercolours. *Address:* Harnham Height, 148 Bouverie Avenue South, Salisbury, Wilts SP2 8EB. *T:* (01722) 333945.

**PRIEST, Christopher McKenzie;** author (novelist and dramatist), since 1968; *b* Cheadle, Cheshire, 14 July 1943; *s* of Walter Mackenzie Priest and Millicent Alice Priest; *m* 1988, Leigh Kennedy (marr. diss. 2011); one *s* one *d* (twins); partner, Nina Allan. *Educ:* Cheadle Hulme Sch. Jun. clerical posts, 1959–68. Mem., Mgt Cttee, Soc. of Authors, 1985–88. Vice Pres., H. G. Wells Soc., 2003–. Patron, Hastings and Rother CAB, 1999–2005. JP E Sussex, 1996–2013. Best Writer, European Award, 1983; Lifetime Achievement Award, Prix Utopia, 2001. *Publications:* Indoctrinaire, 1970; Fugue for a Darkening Island, 1972 (John W. Campbell Jr Meml Award, 1972); Inverted World, 1974 (BSFA Award, 1974); Real-Time World, 1974, rev. edn 2008; The Space Machine, 1976; A Dream of Wessex, 1977; (ed) Anticipations, 1978; An Infinite Summer, 1979; (ed with R. P. Holdstock) Stars of Albion, 1979; The Affirmation, 1981 (inspiration for exhibn of installation art, Chelsea Space, 2007); The Glamour, 1984; The Quiet Woman, 1990; The Book on the Edge of Forever, 1994; The Prestige, 1995 (James Tait Black Meml Prize, 1995; World Fantasy Award, 1996); The Extremes, 1999 (BSFA Award, 1999); The Dream Archipelago, 1999; The Separation, 2002 (Arthur C. Clarke Award, BSFA Award, 2002; Grand Prix de l'Imaginaire, 2005; SF ga Yomitai, best foreign novel pubd in Japan, 2008); Ersatz Wines, 2008; The Magic, 2008; 'It' Came from Outer Space, 2008; The Islanders, 2011 (John W. Campbell Jr Meml Award, BSFA Award, 2012; SF ga Yomitai, best foreign novel pubd in Japan, 2013); The Adjacent, 2013; L'Été de l'Infini, 2015; The Gradual, 2016; An American Story, 2018; Episodes, 2019; works translated into 23 languages. *Recreations:* reading, photography, cinema, aviation. *Address:* c/o United Agents, 12–26 Lexington Street, W1F 0LE. *T:* (020) 3214 0800. *E:* cp@christopher-priest.co.uk.

**PRIEST, Rear-Adm. Colin Herbert Dickinson C.;** *see* Cooke-Priest.

**PRIEST, Prof. Eric Ronald,** PhD; FRS 2002; FRSE; James Gregory Professor of Mathematics, 1997–2010 and Wardlaw Professor, 2002–10, University of St Andrews, now Professor Emeritus; *b* 7 Nov. 1943; *s* of Ronald Priest and Olive Vera Priest (*née* Dolan); *m* 1970, Clare Margaret Wilson; three *s* one *d*. *Educ:* Nottingham Univ. (BSc 1965); Leeds Univ. (MSc 1966; PhD 1969). FRSE 1985. St Andrews University: Lectr, 1968–77; Reader, 1977–83; Prof. of Theoretical Solar Physics, 1983–97. Lectures: Marlar, Rice Univ., 1991; Lindsay Meml, Washington, 1998; Birkeland, Norwegian Acad. of Scis and Letters, 2016. Mem., Norwegian Acad. Scis and Letters, 1994. Leverhulme Emeritus Fellow, 2011. Hon. DSc St Andrews, 2013. Hale Prize, AAS, 2002; Gold Medal, RAS, 2009; Payne-Gaposchkin Medal and Prize, Inst. of Physics, 2009; Hannes Alfvén Medal, Eur. Geophysical Union, 2017. *Publications:* Solar Magnetohydrodynamics, 1982 (trans. Russian 1985); (jtly) Plasma Astrophysics, 1994; (jtly) Magnetic Reconnection: MHD Theory and Applications, 2000; Magnetohydrodynamics of the Sun, 2014; *edited:* Solar Flare Magnetohydrodynamics, 1981; Solar System Magnetic Fields, 1985; Dynamics and Structure of Quiescent Solar Prominences, 1989; (jtly) Magnetic Flux Ropes, 1990; (jtly) Mechanisms of Chromospheric and Coronal Heating, 1991; (jtly) Advances in Solar System Magnetohydrodynamics, 1991 (trans. Russian 1995); (jtly) Reconnection in the Solar Corona and Magnetospheric Substorms, 1997; (jtly) A Crossroads for European Solar and Heliospheric Physics, 1998; (jtly) Reconnection of Magnetic Fields: MMD and collisionless theory and observations, 2007; Reason and Wonder: why science and faith need each other, 2016; over 460 res. papers and articles. *Recreations:* bridge, hill walking, aerobics, singing, having fun with my family. *Address:* Mathematical Institute, St Andrews University, St Andrews, Fife KY16 9SS. *T:* (01334) 463709.

**PRIESTLEY, Christopher;** writer, illustrator, painter; *b* Hull, 25 Aug. 1958; *s* of Thomas Victor and Rosina Priestley; *m* 1996, Sally May Coombes; one *s*. *Educ:* Manchester Poly. (BA Hons Graphic Design/Illustration 1980). Freelance illustrator and cartoonist, 1980–; cartoonist: Economist, 1990–96; Independent, 1996–98; strip cartoonist: Bestiary for Independent on Sunday, 1992–95; Babel for Observer, 1995–96; 7:30 for 8:00 for Independent, 1997–98; Payne's Grey for New Statesman, 2002–09; writer for children and teenagers, 2000–. *Exhibitions* include: Laing Art Prize, Mall Galls, London, 1987, 1991; Eastern Open, King's Lynn Arts Centre, Norfolk, 1992, 1993, 1999, 2010, 2013; Hunting/Observer Prize, Mall Galls, 1992, 1993; Sea Bones (one-man exhibn), Brazen Head Gall., Burnham Mkt, Norfolk, 1998; RA Summer Exhibn, 1992, 2012. *Publications:* Dog Magic!, 2000; Jail-Breaker Jack, 2001; My Story: Battle of Britain, 2002; Battle of Hastings, 2003; Witch Hunt, 2003; Death and the Arrow, 2004; The White Rider, 2004; Redwulf's Curse, 2005; New World, 2007; Uncle Montague's Tales of Terror, 2007; Tales of Terror from the Black Ship, 2008; Tales of Terror from the Tunnel's Mouth, 2009; The Dead of Winter, 2010; Blood Oath, 2011; Mister Creecher, 2011; The Teacher's Tales of Terror, 2011; Christmas Tales of Terror, 2012; Through Dead Eyes, 2013; The Dead Men Stood Together, 2013; The Last of the Spirits, 2014; The Wickford Doom, 2015; Anything That Isn't This, 2015; The Curse of the Werewolf Boy, 2017; Treasure of the Golden Skull, 2018; Attack of the Meteor Monsters, 2019. *Recreations:* hill-walking, nature, art, music, reading, cinema, talking, history, looking round old buildings and ancient sites, thinking. *Address:* c/o Philippa Milnes-Smith, Lucas Alexander Whitley, 2nd Floor, 16–17 Wardour Mews, W1F 8AT. *T:* (020) 7471 7900. *E:* admin@lawagency.co.uk.

**PRIESTLEY, Kathleen, (Kate), (Mrs Alan Humphreys);** *b* 25 Aug. 1949; *d* of late John Fletcher Taylor and Joan Taylor (*née* Hannon); *m* 1st, 1967 (marr. diss. 1983); one *s*; 2nd, 1985, Alan Humphreys. *Educ:* Notre Dame, Manchester; Manchester Univ. (CQSW); Edinburgh Univ. (MBA). Psychiatric social worker and Sen. Social Worker, Oldham, 1972–79; Manager, Mental Health Service, Salford, 1979–84; Chief Exec., Family Care, Edinburgh, 1984–89; Asst Dir, Social Services, Newcastle upon Tyne, 1989–92; Exec. Dir, Northern RHA, 1992–94; Department of Health: Dir, Purchase Performance Mgt, Northern and Yorkshire Reg., NHS Exec., 1994–97; Chief Exec., NHS Estates, 1998–2004; Chief Exec., Inventures, 2001–04; Chm., Leadership Centre for Local Govt, 2004–10. Non-exec. Dir, Scarborough Bldg Soc., 2001–09 (Vice-Chm., 2005–09); Chairman: Island Healthcare, 2003–10; Inspired Spaces, 2008–13; Shared Interest, 2010–15; Northumberland Tourism, 2012–14. Non-executive Director: Nat. Property Bd, Dept of Constitutional Affairs, 2003–07; Living Independently, EU, 2006–07; Govt Office NE, 2008–11. Chairman: Standing Cttee on Structural Safety, 2002–09; Mental Health NE, 2010–11; Scene CIC, 2010–12; Mem., Govt Skills Council, 2005. Trustee, BRE Trust (formerly Foundn for the Built Envmt), 2003–08. FRSA 1999. Mem., Council, Univ. of

Newcastle, 2005–13. Hon. Fellow: Univ. of Manchester, 1993; Univ. of York, 1995; Inst. Healthcare Engrg and Estate Mgt, 2000. CompICE 2003; MInstD. *Recreations:* graphology, cooking and entertaining, opera. *Address:* Kitty Frisk House, Corbridge Road, Hexham, Northumberland NE46 1UN. *T:* (01434) 601533.

**PRIESTLEY, Leslie William,** TD 1974; FCIB; FCIM; Chairman, Tenax Capital Ltd, 2005–13; *b* 22 Sept. 1933; *s* of Winifred and George Priestley; *m* 1960, Audrey Elizabeth (*née* Humber); one *s* one *d*. *Educ:* Shooters Hill Grammar School. Head of Marketing, Barclaycard, 1966–73; Asst Gen. Manager, Barclays Bank, 1974–77, Local Dir, 1978–79; Sec. Gen., Cttee of London Clearing Bankers, 1979–83; Dir, Bankers' Automated Clearing Services, 1979–83; Man. Dir, Barclays Insurance Services Co., 1983–84; Regional Gen. Manager, Barclays Bank, 1984–85; Dir and Chief Exec., TSB England & Wales plc (formerly TSB England and Wales and Central Trustee Savings Bank), 1985–89; Director: TSB Gp plc, 1986–89; Hill Samuel Bank, 1988–89; Pearce Signs Gp (formerly Pearce Gp Hldgs), 1989–2003. Chairman: CAA Pension Scheme Trustees, 1993–2003; Caviapen Investments Ltd, 1993–2003; Generali Pan Europe Ltd, 2006–14; Vice-Chm., Guernsey Financial Services Commn, 2003–05 (Mem., 1999–2005); Director: London Electricity plc (formerly London Electricity Board), 1984–97; Pinnacle Insurance, 1990–2003; Omnia/ICL, 1991–94; London Chamber of Commerce and Industry, 1993–96; Expatriate Management Ltd, 1994–99; Prudential Banking plc, 1996–2006; Egg plc, 2000–06; Currencies Direct Ltd, 2006–13. Banking Advr, Touche Ross & Co., 1990–96; Financial Services Advisor: ICL, 1991–97; Satyam Computer Services Ltd, 2005–08. Member: Monopolies and Mergers Commn, 1990–96; Bd, CAA, 1990–96. Member of Council: Chartered Inst. of Bankers, 1988–89; Assoc. for Payment Clearing Services, 1988–89. Vis. Fellow, UCNW, 1989–95. Consultant Editor, Bankers' Magazine, 1972–81. FCIB 1973; FCIM (FInstM 1987); CCMI; FRSA. *Publications:* (ed) Bank Lending with Management Accounts, 1981. *Recreations:* reading, gardening, swimming, golf. *Club:* Chislehurst Golf.

**PRIESTLEY, Philip John,** CBE 1996; HM Diplomatic Service, retired; High Commissioner to Belize, 2001–04; *b* 29 Aug. 1946; *s* of late Frederick Priestley and Caroline (*née* Rolfe); *m* 1972, Christine Rainforth; one *s* one *d*. *Educ:* Boston Grammar Sch.; Univ. of East Anglia (BA Hons). FCO 1969; served Sofia and Kinshasa; First Sec., FCO, 1976; Wellington, 1979–83; FCO, 1984–87; Commercial Counsellor and Dep. Head of Mission, Manila, 1987–90; Ambassador to Gabon, 1990–91; Fellow, Center for Internat. Affairs, Harvard Univ., 1991–92; Consul-Gen., Geneva, 1992–95; Hd, N America Dept, FCO, 1996–2000. Blue Diamond Ventures, 2006–08; Dir, BCB Hldgs Ltd, 2009–15. Mem., Adv. Bd, Friends of Belize, 2011–17. Trustee, West India Cttee, 2012–17. FRSA 1999. *Recreations:* walking, watching Rugby.

**PRIESTLEY, Dr Robert Henry;** owner, Ro-Po Publishing, since 2007; *b* 19 March 1946; *s* of late Henry Benjamin Priestley, MA, BSc and Margaret Alice (*née* Lambert); *m* 1970, Penelope Ann Fox, BSc; two *d*. *Educ:* Brunts Grammar Sch., Mansfield; Univ. of Southampton (BSc 1967); Univ. of Exeter (PhD 1972); CS Coll. (Dip. in Consultancy Practice, 1999). FRSB (FIBiol 1988). Plant Pathologist, Lord Rank Res. Centre, Rank Hovis McDougall, 1970–73; National Institute of Agricultural Botany: Cereal Pathologist, 1973–78; Head of Cereal Path. Section, 1978–82; Head of Plant Path. Dept, 1982–88; Gen. Sec., Inst. of Biol., 1989–97. Mgt consultant, HQ Strike Comd, RAF High Wycombe, 1998–2002; Principal Consultant and Lectr, Centre for Mgt and Policy Studies, Sunningdale Park, 2002–06. Sec., UK Cereal Pathogen Virulence Survey, 1974–82; Member: Council Fedn of British Plant Pathologists, 1980–81; Internat. Soc. for Plant Path., 1988–92; Treasurer, British Soc. for Plant Path., 1981–87; Member: British Nat. Cttee for Microbiology, 1982–89; Cttee of Management, Biol. Council, 1989–91; Bd, CSTI, 1989–97; Parly and Sci. Cttee, 1989–97; Chairman: European Communities Biol. Assoc., 1992–96; Eur. Biologist Registration Cttee, 1994–97. FCMI (FIMgt 1997). *Publications:* Football League Programmes of the late 1940s, 2007; consultancy reports; papers on diseases of crops; popular articles. *Recreations:* music, art, architecture, football.

**PRIESTLEY, Ven. Rosemary L.;** *see* Lain-Priestley.

**PRIESTLY, Paul Graham;** Permanent Secretary, Department for Regional Development, Northern Ireland, 2007–10; project finance and business development consultant, 2011–12; Strategic Adviser, Strategic Investment Board Ltd, since 2012; *b* Belfast, 30 March 1958; *s* of Samuel Robert and Clara Priestly; *m* 1984, Pamela Ann Hawkins; one *s* two *d*. *Educ:* Grosvenor Grammar Sch., Belfast; Queen's Univ., Belfast (BA Hons 1st Cl. Geog.). Joined NI Office, 1985; Hd, Policing Reforms Div., NI Office, 1998–2000; Principal Private Sec. to Sec. of State for NI, 2000–02; Hd, Criminal Justice Reform Div., 2002–03; Dir of Resources, 2003–07, NI Office; Dir of Policy and Strategy, Office of the First Minister and Dep. First Minister, NI, 2007. *Recreations:* hill-walking, reading natural and military history, sailing, playing guitar (badly).

**PRIESTMAN, Jane,** OBE 1991; FCSD; design management consultant; *b* 7 April 1930; *d* of late Reuben Stanley Herbert and Mary Elizabeth Herbert (*née* Ramply); *m* 1954, Arthur Martin Priestman (marr. diss. 1986); two *s*. *Educ:* Northwood College; Liverpool Coll. of Art (NDD, ATD). Design practice, 1954–75; Design Manager, Gen. Manager, Architecture and Design, BAA, 1975–86; Dir, Architecture and Design, BRB, 1986–91. Member: LRT Design Panel, 1985–89; Jaguar Styling Panel, 1988–91; Percentage for Art Steering Gp, Arts Council, 1989–91; Council, Design Council, 1996–99; Design Panel, SE England Region, 2000–; Design Review Panel, Home Office, 2003–. Vis. Prof. of Internat. Design, De Montfort Univ., 1997–2001. Enabler, CABE, 2001–11. Trustee, London Open House, 1995– (Chair of Trustees, 1998–2009). Governor: Commonwealth Inst., 1987–99; Kingston Univ. (formerly Kingston Polytechnic), 1988–96. Hon. FRIBA; FRSA. Hon. DDes: De Montfort, 1994; Sheffield Hallam, 1998. Ada Louise Huxtable Award, Architects Jl Women in Architecture Awards, 2015. *Recreations:* textiles, city architecture, opera, travel. *Address:* 30 Duncan Terrace, N1 8BS. *T:* (020) 7837 4525. *Club:* Architecture.
*See also* P. D. Priestman.

**PRIESTMAN, Paul Dominic;** designer; Chairman, PriestmanGoode, since 2016 (Director, since 1989); Global Creative Director, CRRC Sifang, since 2013; *b* UK, 8 June 1961; *s* of Arthur Martin Priestman and Jane Priestman, *qv*; *m* 1990, Hon. Tessa Mitford, *d* of 5th Baron Redesdale. *Educ:* St Christopher's Sch., Letchworth; Central St Martin's Coll. of Arts and Design (BA); Royal Coll. of Art (MA; MDes; Hon. Fellow, 2017). Member: Design Council, 2004–06 (Chair, Design Skills Adv. Panel, 2004–06); Exec., D&AD, 2005–07; Council, RCA, 2010–16. Pres., Design Business Assoc., 2001–03. Trustee, Design Council, 2016–17. Student Design Award, RSA; Melchett Meml Award, Design and Industries Assoc.; Award, 2nd Internat. Design Awards, Osaka; London Design Innovation Medal. *Address:* PriestmanGoode, 150 Great Portland Street, W1W 6QD. *T:* (020) 7580 3444. *E:* studio@priestmangoode.com.

**PRIMAROLO,** Baroness *cr* 2015 (Life Peer), of Windmill Hill in the City of Bristol; **Dawn Primarolo,** DBE 2014; PC 2002; *b* 2 May 1954; *m* 1972 (marr. diss.); one *s*; *m* 1990, Thomas Ian Ducat. *Educ:* Thomas Bennett Comprehensive Sch., Crawley; Bristol Poly.; Bristol Univ. Mem., Avon CC, 1985–87. MP (Lab) Bristol S, 1987–2015. Opposition front bench spokesman on health, 1992–94, on Treasury affairs, 1994–97; Financial Sec., HM Treasury, 1997–99; HM Paymaster Gen., 1999–2007; Minister of State: DoH, 2007–09; DCSF, 2009–10; Shadow Minister for Children, 2010; Second Dep. Chm. of Ways and Means and a Dep. Speaker, H of C, 2010–15. Mem., Select Cttee on Members' Interests, 1988–92. Chm., Remuneration Bd, Welsh Assembly, 2015–. Non-exec. Dir, Thompsons Solicitors, 2016–. Vis. Prof., UWE, 2016–. Hon. LLD Bristol, 2016.

**PRIMROSE,** family name of **Earl of Rosebery**.

**PRIMROSE, Prof. John Neil,** MD; Professor of Surgery, University of Southampton, since 1993; *s* of late William Murray Primrose and of Evelyn Primrose; partner, Ursula Ward; two *s* one *d*. *Educ:* Clydebank High Sch., Clydebank; Univ. of Glasgow (MB ChB Hons 1977; MD 1984). Lectr, then Sen. Lectr in Surgery, Univ. of Leeds, 1984–93; Hon. Consultant Surgeon, University Hosps Southampton NHS Foundn Trust (formerly Southampton Univ. Hosps NHS Trust), 1993–; Clin. Dir, NIHR Clin. Res. Network (Wessex), 2007–17. Pres., Assoc. of Surgeons of GB and Ireland, 2013–15. NIHR Sen. Investigator, 2016–. Visiting Professor: Emory Univ., Atlanta, 2018; Univ. of Glasgow, 2018. FMedSci 2016. *Publications:* contrib. papers and book chapters on surgery and cancer. *Recreations:* travel, ski-ing. *Address:* University Surgery (816), C Level, South Academic Block, Southampton General Hospital, Southampton, Hants SO16 6YD. *T:* (023) 8120 6143, *Fax:* (023) 8120 4020. *E:* j.n.primrose@soton.ac.uk.

**PRIMROSE, Sir John Ure,** 5th Bt *cr* 1903, of Redholme, Dumbreck, Govan; *b* 28 May 1960; *s* of Sir Alasdair Neil Primrose, 4th Bt and of Elaine Noreen, *d* of Edmund Cecil Lowndes, Buenos Aires; *S* father, 1986; *m* 1st, 1983, Marion Cecilia (marr. diss. 1987), *d* of Hans Otto Altgelt; two *d*; 2nd, Claudia Ines Schwarz. *Heir:* *b* Andrew Richard Primrose [*b* 19 Jan. 1966. *Educ:* St Peter's School and Military Acad. BA].

**PRIMUS, The;** *see* Strange, Most Rev. M. J., Bishop of Moray, Ross and Caithness.

**PRINCE, Conrad Stuart,** CB 2015; Distinguished Fellow, Royal United Services Institute, since 2018; *b* Bowdon, Cheshire, 1 Dec. 1966; *s* of late Kenneth Prince, MBE and Eileen Prince; *m* 1992, Helen Dennis. *Educ:* Manchester Grammar Sch.; Christ's Coll., Cambridge (BA Hons Hist. 1988; MPhil Internat. Relns 1989). Government Communications Headquarters, 1989–2015: Dir Gen., Ops, 2008–11; Dir Gen., Intelligence and Strategy, and Dep. Dir, 2011–15; HCSC, 2004; Cyber Security Ambassador, Defence and Security Orgn, UKTI, then DIT, 2015–18. Hon. Col, 7 Mil. Intelligence Bn, Intelligence Corps, 2015–. Mem., Adv. Bd, Albany Investment, 2018–; Sen. Advr, Boston Consultancy Gp, 2018–; Adviser: Nationwide Building Soc., 2016–; Pool Reinsurance, 2018–. *Recreations:* hill walking and other rural pursuits, historic motor sport. *Address:* Royal United Services Institute, 61 Whitehall, SW1A 2ET. *Clubs:* Oriental, Special Forces.

**PRINCE, David,** CBE 2009; Chief Executive, The Standards Board for England, 2004–08; *b* 31 May 1948; *s* of late Charles and Phyllis Grace Prince; *m* 1973, Davina Ann Pugh. *Educ:* Exeter Univ. (BA Hons English). CPFA. Hants CC Grad. Trainee, 1969–71; finance posts, Berks CC, 1971–76; Chief Accountant, Cambs CC, 1976–81, and Asst Co. Treasurer; Dep. Co. Treasurer, Herts CC, 1981–86; Dir, Finance and Admin, Cambs CC, 1986–91; Chief Exec., Leics CC, 1991–94; Audit Commission: Chief Exec., Dist Audit Service, then Dist Audit, 1994–2000; Dir of Ops, 2000–01; Dir of Strategy and Resources, 2001–03; Managing Dir, 2003–04. Mem., Cttee on Standards in Public Life, 2009–15; Lay Member: Gen. Social Care Council, 2007–12; Gen. Pharmaceutical Council, 2013–19; Independent Member: Leicestershire Police Authy, 2008–12; Governance, Risk and Audit Cttee, Bar Standards Bd, 2008–13; Audit and Corporate Governance Cttee (formerly Audit, Risk and Assurance Cttee, Care Quality Commn), 2012–15. Vis. Prof., Bath Spa Univ., 2015–. FRSA. *Recreations:* theatre, music, gardening.

**PRINCE, Jennifer Ann H.;** *see* Halpern Prince.

**PRINCE, Rose Amanda;** food writer and columnist, Daily Telegraph, since 2002; *b* 4 Dec. 1962; *d* of 2nd Baron Jeffreys and Sarah Clarke; *m* 1993, Dominic Prince; one *s* one *d*. *Educ:* Hatherop Castle Sch., Glos; St Mary's Wantage, Berks. Food columnist: Daily Express, 1998–2001; Evening Standard, 2007; cook, Spectator mag., 1998–2005; columnist: The Tablet, 2004–; Resurgence, 2006–08; Telegraph Mag., 2008–10; contributor, 1998–: Spectator, New Statesman, Saveur (USA), Daily Mail, Sunday Telegraph, The Times. Reporter, Food Prog., BBC Radio 4. Prod., TV series, In the Foot Steps of Elizabeth David, 1999. Mem., H of L Cttee of Inquiry into misregulation of meat industry, 2000. Founder, The Pocket Bakery, 2010; Dinner and Party, 2017. Glenfiddich Food Writer of the Year, 2001; Fortnum & Mason Food Writer of the Year, 2014. *Publications:* The New English Kitchen: changing the way you shop, cook and eat, 2005; The Savvy Shopper, 2006; The New English Table, 2008; The Good Produce Guide (annually), 2009–12; Kitchenella, 2010; The Pocket Bakery, 2013; Dinner and Party, 2017. *Recreations:* lunch, wine, sunbathing, reading, racing. *T:* 07968 359376. *E:* rose@roseprince.co.uk. *Club:* Bluebird.

**PRINCE, Susanne,** OBE 2004; DL; artist, since 1983; tourism provider, since 1985; organic farmer, since 1997; eco-tourism consultant, since 2001; *b* London, Aug. 1956; *d* of Brian and Breege Norrie; *m* 1976, Terence Prince; two *d*. *Educ:* Graham Balfour High Sch., Stafford. Artist in Swedish folk art, teaching in Sweden, 2005–. Food project Consultant, Univ. of Derby, 2001–08; Eco-tourism Consultant: for Belmont Mgt Consultants, in Transylvania, 2006–09; for Renewal of Peak Dist Envmtl Quality Mark, 2010–11. Member: Peak Dist Nat. Park Authy, 2000–09; Bd, Advantage W Midlands RDA, 2004–11; Rural Enterprise Panel (formerly Land Use and Access Panel), NT, 2005–14; Commn for Rural Communities, 2009–11; Bd, Staffs LEP, 2011. Chm., Sustainable Tourism Action Gp for Staffs, 2007–; Vice-Chm., Peak Dist Leader Action Gp, 2007–. Mem., Governing Council, Keele Univ., 2008–11. Trustee, Ilam Cross, 2005–. A West Midlands Greenleader, 2010. DL Staffs 2011. *Recreations:* avid reader, social media, walking, painting, cinema, friends and family, throwing balls for small dog and grandchildren. *Address:* Beechenhill Farm, Ilam, Ashbourne, Derbys DE6 2BD. *E:* info@beechenhill.co.uk.

**PRINDL, Dr Andreas Robert,** Hon. CBE 2001; Chairman, Nomura Bank International, 1990–97 (Managing Director, 1986–90); Deputy Chairman, Lloyd's, 2009–12 (Member of Council, since 2003); *b* 25 Nov. 1939; *s* of Frank Joseph Prindl and Vivian Prindl (*née* Mitchell); *m* 1st, 1963, Veronica Maria Koerber (marr. diss. 2004); one *s* one *d*; 2nd, 2009, Patricia Norland (*d* 2014). *Educ:* Princeton Univ. (BA); Univ. of Kentucky (MA, PhD). Morgan Guaranty Trust Company: NY and Frankfurt, 1964–70; Vice-Pres., IMM, London, 1970–76; Gen. Manager, Tokyo, 1976–80; CEO Saudi Internat. Bank, London, 1980–82; Vice-Pres., Mergers and Acquisitions, Morgan Guaranty, 1982–84; Man. Dir, Nomura Internat., 1984–86. Chm., Banking Industry Trng and Develt Council, 1994–96; Provost, Gresham Coll., 1996–99. President: Chartered Inst. of Bankers, 1994–95; Assoc. of Corporate Treasurers, 1996. Vis. Prof., People's Univ. of China, Beijing, 2000–. Chm., Good Vibrations, charity, 2009–14. Non-exec. Dir, ACE European Gp, 2012–16. Freeman, City of London, 1999; Liveryman: Musicians' Co., 1999– (Mem., Ct of Assts, 2001–; Master, 2006–07); World Traders' Co., 2000–11. Hon. Treas., C&G, 1998–2000. Hon. Fellow, Acad. of Moral Sci., Beijing, 1998. Hon. DSc City, 1996. *Publications:* (jtly) International Money Management, 1972 (trans. Italian as La Gestione Aziendale

Plurimonetaria, 1975); Foreign Exchange Risk, 1976 (trans. Japanese as Kawase Risuku, 1978; Spanish as El Riesgo de Cambio, 1980); Japanese Finance, 1981; Money in the Far East, 1986; (ed) Banking and Finance in Eastern Europe, 1992; (ed jtly) Ethical Conflicts in Finance, 1994; The First XV, 1995; A Companion to Lucca, 2000; A Companion to Angoulême, 2005 (trans. French as Du haut des remparts d'Angoulême, 2007); A Companion to Fauquier County, Virginia, 2008; A Companion to Rye and Winchelsea, 2015. *Recreations:* classical music, Asian art and history, travel (especially Japan and France). *Clubs:* Reform; Tokyo American (Tokyo).

**PRING, Prof. Richard Anthony;** Professor and Director of Department of Educational Studies, University of Oxford, 1989–2003; Fellow of Green College, Oxford, 1989–2003, now Emeritus; *b* 20 April 1938; *s* of Joseph Pring and Anne-Marie Pring; *m* 1970, Helen Faye Evans; three *d*. *Educ:* Gregorian Univ. and English College, Rome (PhL); University Coll. London (BA Hons Philosophy); Univ. of London Inst. of Education (PhD); College of St Mark and St John (PGCE). Asst Principal, Dept of Educn and Science, 1962–64; teacher in London comprehensive schools, 1965–67; Lectr in Education: Goldsmiths' Coll., 1967–70; Univ. of London Inst. of Educn, 1972–78; Prof. of Educn, Univ. of Exeter, 1978–89. Lead Dir, Nuffield Rev. of 14–19 Educn and Trng, 2003–09 (report, Education for All: the future of educn and trng for 14–19 year olds, 2009). Pres., Socialist Educn Assoc., 2008–16. Hon. DLitt: Kent, 1995; Inst. of Educn, Univ. of London, 2015. Editor, British Jl of Educational Studies, 1986–2001. Bene Merenti Medal (Pius XII), 1958. Annual Award of Distinction, Aga Khan Univ., Karachi, 2007. *Publications:* Knowledge and Schooling, 1976; Personal and Social Education, 1984; The New Curriculum, 1989; Closing the Gap: liberal education and vocational preparation, 1995; (ed with Geoffrey Walford) Affirming the Comprehensive Ideal, 1997; Philosophy of Educational Research, 2000, 3rd edn 2014; Philosophy of Education: aims, theory, common sense and research, 2004; (ed with G. Thomas) Evidence Based Practice in Education, 2004; John Dewey: a philosopher of education for our time?, 2007; (jtly) Education for All: the future of education and training for 14–19 year olds, 2009; The Life and Death of Secondary Education for All: dream or reality?, 2012; (ed with Martin Roberts) A Generation of Radical Educational Change: stories from the field, 2016; The Future of Publicly Funded Faith Schools: a critical perspective, 2018; Thinking Philosophically about Education, 2018. *Recreations:* cycling, writing, campaigning for comprehensive schools, swimming. *Address:* Green Templeton College, Woodstock Road, Oxford OX2 6HG.

**PRINGLE, Maj. Gen. Andrew Robert Douglas,** CB 2000; CBE 1992 (MBE 1980); President, Government Services (Global), Kellogg Brown and Root, 2015–17; *b* 9 Oct. 1946; *s* of late Douglas Alexander Pringle and Wendy Pringle (née Gordon); *m* 1975, Jane Carolyn Mitchison; one *s* two *d*. *Educ:* Wellington Coll.; RMA, Sandhurst; RMCS, Shrivenham (BSc Hons). Commnd RGJ, 1966: served in UK, Cyprus, NI, Germany, 1967–77; Staff Coll., Camberley, 1977–78; Staff and Regtl appts, NI, 1979–82; Directing Staff, Staff Coll., Camberley, 1983–85; CO, 3rd Bn, RGJ, 1985–88; MoD, 1988–91; Higher Comd and Staff Course, 1990; rcds, 1991; Cabinet Office, 1992–94; Commander: 20 Armoured Bde, 1994–96; UN Sector SW, Bosnia, 1995; Dir, Land Warfare, 1996–97; Comdr, Multi-Nat. Div. (SW), Bosnia, 1997–98; COS, Perm. Jt HQ, 1998–2001. Regtl (formerly Rep.) Col Comdt, Royal Green Jackets, 1999–2002; Col Comdt, 2nd Bn Royal Green Jackets, 1999–2001. Defence consultant, 2002–08; Dir, AP JOINTSOLUTIONS Ltd, 2003–08; Vice Pres., Govt and Defence, EMEA, 2008–09, Pres., Internat. Govt, Defence and Support Services (formerly Internat. Govt and Defence), 2010–14, Infrastructure Govt and Power (EMEA), 2014–15, Kellogg Brown and Root. Non-exec. Dir, Allocate (formerly Manpower) Software plc, 2004–15. Freeman, City of London, 2019; Liveryman, Fan Makers' Co., 2019. QCVS 1996 and 1998. *Recreations:* reading, skiing, Cresta Run, a little light farming, military history, antiques. *Clubs:* Army and Navy, Cavalry and Guards; St Moritz Tobogganing.

**PRINGLE, Dame Anne Fyfe,** DCMG 2010 (CMG 2004); HM Diplomatic Service, retired; UK Special Representative for Deportations with Assurance, 2012–15; *b* 13 Jan. 1955; *d* of late George Grant Pringle and Margaret Fyfe Pringle (née Cameron); *m* 1987, Bleddyn Glynne Leyshon Phillips. *Educ:* Glasgow High Sch. for Girls; St Andrews Univ. (MA Hons French and German). Joined FCO, 1977: Third Sec., Moscow, 1980–83; Vice Consul, San Francisco, 1983–85; Second Sec., UK Rep., Brussels, 1986–87; FCO, 1988–91; First Sec., Eur. Political Co-operation Secretariat, Brussels, 1991–93; Dep. Hd, Security Co-ordination Dept, then African Dept (Equatorial), FCO, 1994–96; Head, Common Foreign and Security Policy Dept, FCO, and European Correspondent, 1996–98; Head, Eastern Dept, FCO, 1998–2001; Ambassador to the Czech Republic, 2001–04; Dir, Strategy and Information, FCO, 2004–07; Ambassador to Russia, 2008–11. Public Appts Assessor, 2012–15. Non-exec. Dir, Ashmore plc, 2013–. Sen. Gov., St Andrews Univ., 2016–. Trustee, Shakespeare's Globe, 2016–. FRSA 2001. *Recreations:* sport, gardening, walking.

**PRINGLE, Caroline Jan;** *see* MacEwen, C. J.

**PRINGLE, Derek Raymond;** Cricket Correspondent, The Daily Telegraph, 2002–14; *b* Nairobi, 18 Sept. 1958; *s* of late Donald James Pringle and of Doris May Pringle (née Newton). *Educ:* St Mary's Sch., Nairobi; Felsted Sch., Essex; Fitzwilliam Coll., Cambridge (MA). Professional cricketer, Essex and England, 1978–93; Cricket Correspondent: Independent on Sunday, 1993–95; Independent, 1995–2002. *Publications:* England's Ashes, 2005; Pushing the Boundaries, 2018. *Recreations:* photography, music, conchology.

**PRINGLE, Hamish Patrick,** FIPA; Partner, Pringle and Pringle LLP, 2011–15; *b* Chiswick Mall, London, 1951; *s* of Robert Henry and Pamela Ann Pringle; *m* 1977, Vivienne Elizabeth Lloyd; three *s* one *d*. *Educ:* Trinity Coll., Glenalmond (Captain of Sch.), 1968–69); Trinity Coll., Oxford (BA PPE 1973). Account Exec., Ogilvy & Mather, 1973–75; Account Manager, McCormick Richards, 1975–76; Account Manager, 1976–77, Account Dir, 1978–79, Boase Massimi Pollitt; New Business Dir, McCormick Intermarco-Farner, 1980–82; Bd Dir, Abbott Mead Vickers SMS, 1982–86; Man. Dir, Madell Wilmot Pringle, 1986–90; Bd Dir, Leagas Delaney, 1990–92; CME KHHB: New Business Dir, 1992–94; Jt Man. Dir, 1994–95; Chm. and CEO, 1995–96; Chm. and CEO, K Advertising, 1996–97; Vice-Chm. and Dir of Mktg, Saatchi & Saatchi, 1997–99; Dir, Brand Beliefs, 1999–2001; Dir Gen., Inst. of Practitioners in Advertising, 2001–11. Strategic Advr, 23red, 2011–16. Member: Bd, Advertising Assoc., 2001–11; Advertising Standards Bd of Finance, 2001–11; Broadcasters' Audience Res. Bd, 2001–11; Bd, Eur. Assoc. of Communication Agencies, 2001–11; Broadcast Advertising Standards Bd of Finance, 2006–11; Council, ASA, 2011–17. Institute of Practitioners in Advertising: Society Chm., 1984–85; Mem. Council, 1985–86 and 1989–98; Member: Advertising Effectiveness Cttee, 1986–96 (Chm., 1993–96); President's Cttee, 1994–96. Mem., 1993–96, Chm., 1996–98, Gen. Mgt Cttee, Nat. Advertising Benevolent Soc.; Jt Chm., Fund-raising Cttee, Cinema and Television Benevolent Fund, 1994–95. FIPA 1992; Fellow, Mktg Soc., 2009. Mem., Mktg Gp of GB. Ron Miller Award, Nat. Advertising Benevolent Soc., 1998. *Publications:* (with M. Thompson) Brand Spirit: how cause related marketing builds brands, 1999; (with W. Gordon) Brand Manners: how to create the self-confident organisation to live the brand, 2001; Celebrity Sells, 2004; (with P. Field) Brand Immortality: how brands can live long and prosper, 2008; (with J. Marshall) Spending Advertising Money in the Digital Age: how to navigate the media flow, 2012. *Recreation:* art. *E:* hamish@pringleandpringle.co.uk. *T:* 07977 269778. *Club:* Soho House.

**PRINGLE, Ian Derek;** QC 2003; **His Honour Judge Pringle;** a Circuit Judge, since 2012; Resident Judge, Oxford Crown Court, since 2014; *b* 19 Jan. 1957; *s* of late Dr Derek Hair Pringle and of Anne Collier Pringle (née Caw); *m* 1980, Mary Seeney; one *s* one *d*. *Educ:* Edinburgh Acad.; St Catharine's Coll., Cambridge (MA). Called to the Bar, Gray's Inn, 1979, Bencher, 2009; in practice, specialising in criminal law; Mem., Guildhall Chambers, Bristol, 1981–2012; a Recorder, 1998–2012. Hon. Recorder, Oxford, 2014–. Mem. Council, Burden Neurol Inst., Bristol, 1996–2012. *Recreations:* history, sport, particularly football, Rugby, golf and athletics. *Address:* Oxford Crown Court, St Aldates, Oxford OX1 1TL. *Club:* Hibernian Football.

**PRINGLE, Jack Brown,** PPRIBA; Principal, since 2012, and Regional Director, Europe, Middle East and Africa, since 2017, Perkins+Will (formerly Pringle Brandon); President, Royal Institute of British Architects, 2005–07; Chairman, Construction Industry Council, 2012–14; *b* 13 March 1952; *s* of John and Grace Mason Pringle; *m* 2010 Holly Anne Porter; one *d*, and two *d* from a previous marriage. *Educ:* Bristol Univ. (BA Hons 1973; DipArch 1975). RIBA 1977. Architect: Powell and Moya, 1973–81; Jack Pringle Architects, 1981–86; Partner, Pringle Brandon, 1986–2012. Royal Institute of British Architects: Mem. Council, 1979–89 and 2003–; Vice-Pres. for Educn, 2003–; Chm., Professional Services Co., 2003–05. Chair: Article 25, 2007–14; Editl Bd, Jl of Architecture, 2012–16. FRSA. Hon. AIA 2006. Commandeur de l'Ordre des Arts et des Lettres (France), 2007. *Recreations:* flying (Private Pilot's Licence), racing offshore yachts, exhibitions, travelling with wife and daughters. *Address:* Perkins+Will, The White Chapel Building, 10 Whitechapel High Street, E1 8QQ. *T:* (020) 7466 1000, *Fax:* (020) 7466 1050.

**PRINGLE, Sir John (Kenneth),** Kt 1993; Justice of the High Court of Northern Ireland, 1993–99; *b* 23 June 1929; *s* of late Kenneth Pringle and Katie (née Batchen); *m* 1960, Ruth Henry; two *s* one *d*. *Educ:* Campbell Coll., Belfast; Queen's Univ., Belfast (BSc 1st Cl. Hons 1950; LLB 1st Cl. Hons 1953). Called to the Bar, NI, 1953, Bencher, 1973; QC (NI), 1970; Recorder of Belfast, 1984–93. Chm., Bar Council of NI, 1975–80. Member: Parades Commn for NI, 2000–05; Investigatory Powers Tribunal, 2001–06. *Recreations:* gardening, being outdoors.

**PRINGLE, Jonathan Helier W.;** *see* Watt-Pringle.

**PRINGLE, Margaret Ann;** Associate Director, Centre for the Study of Comprehensive Schools, 1995–2000; independent education consultant, 2000–10; *b* 28 Sept. 1946. *Educ:* Holton Park Girls' Grammar Sch.; Somerville College, Oxford (MA, BLitt English Lang. and Lit.). English Teacher, Selhurst High School, Croydon, 1972–76; Head of English, Thomas Calton School, Peckham, 1976–81; Dep. Head, George Green's School, Isle of Dogs, 1981–86; Head, Holland Park Sch., 1986–95. Mem., Ind. Monitoring Bd, HMP Wormwood Scrubs, 2004–. *Recreations:* all food, all music, choral singing, prison reform. *Address:* Flat 3, 64 Pembridge Villas, W11 3ET.

**PRINGLE, Prof. Michael Alexander Leary,** CBE 2001; FRCGP; Professor of General Practice, University of Nottingham, 1993–2010; President, Royal College of General Practitioners, 2012–15; *b* 14 May 1950; *s* of Alexander and Yvonne Pringle; *m* 1974, Nicola Mary Wood; three *d*. *Educ:* St Edward's Sch., Oxford; Guy's Hosp. Med. Sch. (MB BS 1973). FRCGP 1989. Vocational Trng Scheme for Gen. Practice, Reading, 1975–78. Principal in gen. practice, Collingham, Notts, 1979–2004; Lectr and Sen. Lectr, Dept of Gen. Practice, Univ. of Nottingham, 1983–93. GP Clinical Hd, NHS Connecting for Health, 2004–07. Chm. Council, RCGP, 1998–2001. Co-Chm., Expert Ref. Gp for Diabetes Nat. Service Framework, 1999–2002. Chm., change, grow, live (formerly Crime Reduction Initiatives), 2015– (Trustee, 2011–). FMedSci 1999. Hon. FRCP 2000. *Publications:* (jtly) Managing Change in Primary Care, 1991; (ed) Change and Teamwork in Primary Care, 1993; (ed) Fellowship by Assessment, 1995; (jtly) A Guide for New Principals, 1996; (ed) Primary Care: core values, 1998; contrib. numerous chapters in books, res. articles and editorials in jls. *Recreations:* chess, reading, Italy, walking. *E:* mikepringle@btinternet.com.

**PRINGLE, Michael Stanley Robert;** Member (Lib Dem) Edinburgh South, Scottish Parliament, 2003–11; *b* 25 Dec. 1945; *s* of Robert Stanley Valdemar Pringle and Pauline Olga Pringle (née Brian); *m* 1971, Margaret Isobel Gilfillan Birkett; two *s*. *Educ:* Edinburgh Acad. Bank teller, Inst. of Bankers of Scotland, Royal Bank of Scotland, 1965–71; Trainee Hotel Manager, North British Trust Hotels, 1971–74; Man. Dir, TMM Ltd, 1974–92. Member: Edinburgh DC, 1992–96; Lothian Regl Council, 1994–96; Edinburgh CC, 1995–2003. Contested (Lib Dem) Edinburgh S, Scottish Parlt, 2011. *Recreations:* fishing, wine tasting, sport, cooking.

**PRINGLE, Sir (Norman) Murray (Archibald MacGregor),** 10th Bt *cr* 1683 (NS) of Stichill, Roxburghshire; Director, Salama Ltd, since 2008; Director and Chief Finance Officer, Food Development Co. Ltd, since 2009; *b* Chunya, Tanzania, 3 Aug. 1941; *s* of Ronald Steuart Pringle (*d* 1968), *s* of 8th Bt, and Janet Patricia Pringle (née Pickford); a Privy Council Judgment given in 2016 concluded that he was entitled to succeed as the 10th Bt as his father, Ronald Steuart Pringle had retrospectively been proved to be the rightful heir to the 8th Bt; *m* 1st, 1966, Lysbet Watkins-Pitchford (marr. diss. 1991); one *s* one *d*; 2nd, 1992, Patricia Nadine Millem. *Educ:* Open Univ. (BA). FCIS, ChGP, FCMA, CMC, FIC, FCMI, CDipAF, DipCII, DipPFS. Mgt and Finance, Brooke Bond Liebig, 1961–73; Ops Exec., Commonwealth Develt Corp., 1973–81; Sen. Mgt Consultant, Deloitte Haskins and Sells, 1981–82; Mine Sec. and Commercial Manager, De Beers Botswana Mining Co., 1982–85; Jt Man. Dir, Rickards Pringle/Ernst and Young, 1985–87; Commn Sec. and Mem., Jt Perm. Tech. Commn, Lesotho Highlands Water Project (with Diplomatic status in Lesotho and S Africa), 1987–89; Chief Accountant, British Shops and Stores Assoc., 1990–91; Banking, Credit and Finance Expert, EC Internat. Consultant, 1991–2009. Trustee, Clan Pringle Assoc., 2013–. *Recreations:* walking and keep fit, reading, music, genealogy. *Heir: s* Alastair Steuart Ronald Pringle [*b* 23 May 1972; *m* 1999, Chanel Van Staden; four *d*]. *Address:* Cypress Cottage, Warrendene Road, Hughenden Valley, High Wycombe HP14 4LX. *T:* (01494) 562595. *E:* murraypringle@btinternet.com. *Clubs:* Nairobi (Nairobi); Ace (Cairo).

**PRIOR,** family name of **Baron Prior of Brampton.**

**PRIOR OF BRAMPTON,** Baron *cr* 2015 (Life Peer), of Swannington in the County of Norfolk; **David Gifford Leathes Prior;** chairman and director of various private companies; *b* 3 Dec. 1954; *s* of Baron Prior, PC; *m* 1987, Caroline Henrietta Holmes; twin *s* and *d*. *Educ:* Charterhouse; Pembroke Coll., Cambridge (Exhibnr; MA Law 1976). Called to the Bar, Gray's Inn, 1977; Commercial Dir, British Steel, 1980–87. MP (C) N Norfolk, 1997–2001; contested (C) same seat, 2001. Vice Chm., 1998–99, Dep. Chm. and Chief Exec., 1999–2001, Conservative Party. Chairman: Norfolk and Norwich University Hospital Trust, 2002–06 and 2007–13; Care Quality Commn, 2013–15; Univ. Coll.

London Hosps NHS Foundn Trust, 2017–18; NHS England, 2018–. Parly Under-Sec. of State, DoH, 2015–16, BEIS, 2016–17. *Recreations:* gardening, farming, most sports. *Address:* Swannington Manor, Swannington, Norwich NR9 5NR. *T:* (01603) 861560. *Club:* Royal Automobile.

**PRIOR, (Alice) Mary,** CVO 2017; MBE 1999; Lord-Lieutenant of the County of Bristol, 2007–17; Pro-Chancellor, University of Bristol, since 2014; *b* 22 April 1942; *d* of Harry Forty and Kathleen Louise Forty; *m* 1982, John Michael Prior; one *s* one *d*. *Educ:* Kingswood Grammar Sch. Bowater Paper Corp., 1959–65; Gen. Sales Manager, Sales Dir, then Sales and Mktg Dir, Alexandra plc, 1973–97. Trustee: St Monica Trust, 1999–2008; Quartet Community Foundn, 2004–10; Trustee and Dir, Viridor Credits Bd, 2015–. Patron, Bristol Cathedral Trust, 2005– (Trustee, 1988–2005). Patron or Pres., numerous charitable orgns in Bristol. Mem., Soc. of Merchant Venturers, 2008–. DL County of Bristol, 1996. DStJ 2011. *Recreations:* reading, gardening, music. *Address:* Youngwood Farm, Youngwood Lane, Nailsea, Bristol BS48 4NR. *T:* (01275) 852374. *E:* mary@youngwoodfarm.co.uk.

**PRIOR, Anthony Basil,** FRICS; Consultant Valuer to Institute of Revenues Rating & Valuation, 2001–16; Advisor to European Group of Valuers' Associations, 2005–15; *b* 23 March 1941; *s* of Rev. Christopher Prior and May Prior (née Theobald); *m* 1967, Susan Margaret Parry; two *s. Educ:* Commonweal Grammar Sch., Swindon. FRICS 1977; IRRV (Hons) 1988. Joined Valuation Office, 1967: Dist Valuer, Southampton, 1979–84; Superintending Valuer, Chief Valuer's Office, 1984–91; Regl Dir, Western Reg., later London Reg., 1991–98; Dir, Professional and Customer Services, and Mem., Mgt Bd, Valuation Office Agency, 1999–2001; Consultant Valuer to IOM Govt, 2001–07. Mem., Adv. Panel on Standards for the Planning Inspectorate, 2001–11. Member: Rating Valuers' Assoc., 1984; Council, IRRV, 1988–2001. Hon. Recognised European Valuer, 2009. *Publications:* (jtly) Encyclopedia on Contractors Basis of Valuation, 1990. *Recreations:* beekeeping, fly fishing, Greek and Roman history.

**PRIOR, (Christina) Claire;** *see* Doherty, C. C.

**PRIOR, Clifford James,** CBE 2002; Chief Executive Officer, Big Society Capital, since 2016; *b* 14 Feb. 1957; *s* of Colin Prior and Beatrice (née Maber). *Educ:* Alleyn's Sch., Dulwich; St Catherine's Coll., Oxford (BA Biochem. 1978). Counsellor: Andover Crisis Support Centre, 1978–80; Social Services, Tower Hamlets LBC, 1980–82; Housing Asst, 1982–84, Area Manager, 1984–85, Special Projects Co-ordinator, 1985–88, New Islington and Hackney Housing Assoc.; Housing Services Manager, 1988–90, Asst Dir of Policy and Inf., 1990–92, Dir of Policy and Planning, 1992–94, Stonham Housing Assoc.; Progs Dir, Mental Health Foundn, 1994–98; Chief Executive: Nat. Schizophrenia Fellowship, subseq. Rethink, 1998–2006; UnLtd, 2006–16. Vice Chairman: Homeless Network, 1996–99; Long Term Med. Conditions Alliance, 2000–06; Member: NHS Mental Health Task Force, 2000–06; NHS Modernisation Bd, 2000–04; Nat. Leadership Gp, 2005–06; Medicines Commn, 2004–05; Third Sector Commissioning Task Force, 2005–06; Healthcare Commn, 2007–09; Civil Society Adv. Body to Cabinet Office, 2008–11; Adv. Bd, Big Society Capital, 2011–16; Cabinet Office Skills Social Action Rev., 2012–13; UK Practitioner Council, 2016–18; UK Nat. Adv. Body for Impact Investment, 2018–; Adv. Bd, Nat. Lottery Community Fund, 2018–; Chm., Wkg Gp on Impact Investing Wholesalers, 2017–18. Chm., Health and Social Care Gp, ACEVO, 2005–06; Mem., Comic Relief UK Grants Cttee, 2007–15. Chm., FSE Trading Ltd, 2008–11; non-exec. Dir, UCL Partners, 2013–17. Trustee: Clore Social Leadership Prog., 2010–15; Empower Community Foundn, 2015–16; Internat. Venture Philanthropy Centre, 2018–; Founder Trustee, Local Trust, 2012–14; Chair, Mission Alignment Gp to G8 Social Impact Investment Taskforce, 2014–15. Founder Member and Treasurer: Stonewall Housing Assoc., 1983–87; Strutton Housing Assoc., 1987–90; Chm. Supported Housing, Circle 33 Housing Trust, 1992–98. *Recreations:* scuba diving, travel, film, music, friends. *Address:* Big Society Capital, New Fetter Place, 8–10 New Fetter Lane, EC4A 1AZ. *T:* (020) 7186 2507. *E:* cprior@bigsocietycapital.com. *W:* www.twitter.com/cliffprior.

**PRIOR, Joanna Melancy Lyndon;** Managing Director, Penguin General Books, Penguin Random House UK, since 2009; *b* Beckenham, Kent, 3 Feb. 1966; *d* of Hugh and Janet Prior; *m* 1995, Barry Blackmore; one *d. Educ:* James Allen's Girls' Sch., Dulwich; Pembroke Coll., Cambridge (BA 1987; MA). PA to Man. Dir, Macmillan Books Ltd, 1988–89; Publicist, William Heinemann, 1989–91; Publicity and Mktg Dir, Fourth Estate Publishing, 1991–98; Ed., Sunday Telegraph Mag., 1998; Publicity and Mktg Dir, Penguin Books Ltd, 1998–2009. Pres., Publishers' Assoc., 2015–16. Chm. Bd, Women's Prize for Fiction (formerly Bailey's Women's Prize for Fiction), 2015–. Trustee, Nat. Literacy Trust, 2015–. *Recreations:* theatre, cinema, art, walking, reading, painting, travel, friends and family, France. *Address:* Penguin General Books, 80 Strand, WC2R 0RL. *T:* (020) 7139 3250. *E:* jprior@penguinrandomhouse.co.uk.

**PRIOR, Mary;** *see* Prior, A. M.

**PRIOR, Mary;** QC 2017; a Recorder, since 2018; *b* Newbiggin by the Sea, 14 Oct. 1962; *d* of Raymond Bennett and Margaret Ellen Bennett; *m* 2006, Paul Stephen Prior; five *s. Educ:* Biddulph High Sch.; Chelmer Inst. (LLB Hons); Inns of Court Sch. of Law (BVC). Magistrates' Court Clerk, 1986–90; called to the Bar, Gray's Inn, 1990; in practice as barrister, specialising in criminal law, homicide and serious sexual offences; Sen. Crown Prosecutor, 1990–96; Ind. Bar, 1996–. Co-Chair, Midlands Br., Women in Criminal Law. *Recreations:* sing in Leicester Philharmonic Choir, avid supporter Leicester City FC and Darlington FC. *Address:* 36 Group, 4 Field Court, Gray's Inn, WC1R 5EF. *T:* (020) 7421 8000, *Fax:* (020) 7421 8035. *E:* mprior@36crime.co.uk.

**PRIOR-PALMER, Simon Erroll;** non-executive director, public, private and not-for-profit sectors, since 2005; Head, UK Investment Banking, Credit Suisse First Boston, 1987–98; *b* London, 5 Feb. 1951; *s* of Maj.-Gen. George Erroll Prior-Palmer, CB, DSO and Lady Doreen Hersey Winifred Prior-Palmer (née Hope); *m* 1984, Lady Julia Margaret Violet Lloyd George, *d* of 3rd Earl Lloyd George of Dwyfor; three *s* one *d. Educ:* Eton; Christ Church, Oxford (BA PPE 1973; MA). JP Morgan, London and NY, 1973–82; Credit Suisse First Boston, 1982–2005, Sen. Advr, 2003–05. Mem., Postal Services Commn, 2006–10; Sen. Advr, FSA, 2010–11. Non-executive Director: Inter Lotto (UK) Ltd, 2006–07; Gabriel Resources Ltd, 2006–12; Burani Designer Hldgs NV, 2007–09; DJI Hldgs plc, 2012–15 (Chm., 2013–15). Trustee, Macmillan Cancer Support, 2001–13. Co-sponsor, New Philanthropy Capital Charity Efficiency Report, 2018. FRSA 1989. *Recreations:* tennis, golf, ski-ing, unusual travel. *Club:* White's.
*See also* L. J. Green, Earl Lloyd George of Dwyfor.

**PRISK, (Michael) Mark;** MP (C) Hertford and Stortford, since 2001; Prime Minister's Trade and Investment Envoy to the Nordic and Baltic Nations, since 2014, and to Brazil, since 2016; *b* 12 June 1962; *s* of Michael Raymond Prisk and June Irene Prisk; *m* 1989, Lesley Jane Titcomb, *qv. Educ:* Truro Sch., Cornwall; Univ. of Reading (BSc (Hons) Land Mgt); Henley Business Sch. (Professional Cert Coaching, 2019). Knight Frank & Rutley, 1983–85; Chartered Surveyor, 1985–; Dir, Derrick, Wade & Waters, 1989–91; Principal: Mark Prisk Connection, 1991–97; mp2, 1997–2001. Shadow Financial Sec., 2002–03; Shadow Paymaster Gen., 2003–04; Opposition Whip, 2004–05; Shadow Minister, Small Business and Enterprise, 2005–08, Business, 2008–10; Minister of State, BIS, 2010–12; Minister of State (Minister for Housing), DCLG, 2012–13. Contested (C): Newham NW, 1992; Wansdyke, 1997. Non-exec. Dir, Edward Stanford Ltd, 2014–. Advisor, business coach and mentor. *Recreations:* piano, choral music, Rugby and cricket supporter, photography. *Address:* House of Commons, SW1A 0AA. *T:* (020) 7219 3000.

**PRITCHARD, Alison Alexis;** Chief Operating Officer, Government Digital Service, since 2017; *b* London, 29 June 1965; *d* of Terence Graham Pritchard and Sylvia Marion Pritchard; one *s* one *d. Educ:* Alleyn's Sch., Dulwich; Univ. of Bath (BSc Hons Econs and Politics 1987). Ministry of Defence: Desk Officer, Air Armaments (Finance and Secretariat), 1987–89, Secretariat Overseas (Commitments), 1989–91; Systems Analyst and Programmer, Army Staff Duties (IT), 1991–93; Project Manager, Dir Gen. IT Services, 1993–95; Implementation Officer, Service Personnel (Policy), 1995–96; Hd of Section, Naval Support Command (Secretariat), 1996; Hd of Finance, MoD Team Riyadh, 1996–2001; Dir, Chief Exec.'s Office, Office of Govt Commerce, HM Treasury, 2001–04; Cabinet Office: Dir, Ind. Air Travel Review, 2004–06; Hd of Business Strategy, Corporate Develt Gp, 2004–07; Dir of Progs, Lokahi Foundn (on secondment), 2006–07; Hd of Strategy, 2007–10, Hd of Delivery, 2010–12, Dir, 2014–16, Govt Equalities Office, Home Office; Hd of Gambling and Nat. Lottery, DCMS, 2012–14; Dir, Transformational Change, DEFRA, 2016–17. Dir and CEO, Kirrin Prodns Ltd, 2014–. Chair: Ind. Monitoring Bd, Harmondsworth Immigration Removal Centre, 2004–06; Nat. Forum for Immigration Removal Centres, 2006–07. *Recreation:* comedy writer and producer for radio. *Address:* Government Digital Service, White Chapel Building, 10 Whitechapel High Street, E1 8QS.

**PRITCHARD, David Alan,** CB 2006; Dean, Cardiff School of Management, Cardiff Metropolitan University (formerly University of Wales Institute, Cardiff), 2006–12, Consultant Adviser to Vice Chancellor, 2012–16; *b* 23 March 1946; *s* of John Merfyn Pritchard and Anne Louise Pritchard; *m* 1970, Kathryn Henton; two *s. Educ:* UCNW, Bangor (BA Hons Econs). Welsh Office: Head: Industry Policy Div., 1989; Health Strategy and Rev. Div., 1990–97; Local Govt Policy and Finance Div., 1997–99; Welsh Assembly Government: Corporate Planning Unit, 1999–2000; Gp Dir, Econ. Develt, then Econ. Develt and Transport, Dept, 2000–06. Non-exec. Dir, Carbon Trust, 2001–08. Volunteer, NHS, 2017–. Hon. Fellow, Cardiff Metropolitan Univ., 2012. Mem., Ordre des Chevaliers Bretvins, Bailliage du Pays de Galles, 2013. *Recreations:* walking, gardening, Liverpool FC, theatre, politics, wine, just being with my grandchildren. *Address:* Ty'r Ardd, Cardiff Road, Creigiau CF15 9NL. *T:* (029) 2089 0932.

**PRITCHARD, David Edward;** independent consultant (culture and environment), since 2008; *b* Jarrow, 7 Oct. 1958; *s* of David Lloyd Pritchard and Elizabeth Buchanan Young Pritchard (née Livingston). *Educ:* S Shields Grammar-Tech. Sch. for Boys; Durham Univ. (BSc Hons Zool. 1980); University Coll. London (MSc Conservation 1981). Royal Society for the Protection of Birds: res. ecologist/conservation planner, 1981–86; Casework Officer, 1986–90; Manager, Planning and Local Govt Unit, 1990–97; Hd, Site Protection and Wetlands Policy, 1997–99; Internat. Treaties Advr, 1999–2009. Non-executive Director: Wetlands Internat., 2001–07 (Chm., Prog. and Sci. Cttee, 2006–07; Associate Expert, 2014–); Jt Nature Conservation Cttee, 2006–12 (Chm., Audit and Risk Mgt Cttee, 2007–12). Assessor, Arts Council England, 2011–12. Ramsar Convention: Mem., Scientific and Tech. Rev. Panel, 1999–2012; Chm., Thematic Area 3, 2003–12; Jt Coordinator, Culture Network (formerly Co-Chm., Culture Wkg Gp), 2006–; Member: IUCN Specialist Gp on Cultural and Spiritual Values of Protected Areas, 2005–; Ind. Rev., Northumberland Nat. Park Authy, 2013–14; IUCN Connectivity Conservation Specialist Gp, 2017–; World Commn on Protected Areas, 2017–. Chm., UK Arts and Envrnt Network, 2008–; Member: Expert Network, UNESCO UK Commn, 2014–; Eur. Sci. Foundn Coll. of Expert Reviewers, 2017–; Reviewer: Marine and Freshwater Res., 2016–; Newton Prize, 2018–. Vis. Lectr, Durham Univ., 2013–; Adjunct Sen. Res. Fellow, Inst. for Land, Water and Soc., Charles Sturt Univ., 2018–. Trustee: Bedford Creative Arts, 2006–10 (Vice Chm., 2007–10); Centre for Contemp. Art and the Natural World, 2009–13; Queen's Hall Arts, 2015–. Hon. FCIWEM 2011. Wetland Conservation Award and Evian Special Prize, Ramsar, 2008. *Publications:* (ed jtly) Important Bird Areas in the UK, 1992; (ed) Strategic Environmental Assessment, 1992; (ed) Conservation Policy Directions, 1996; Dendros: horizons of change, 2006; (series ed.) Ramsar Handbooks for the Wise Use of Wetlands, 4th edn 2010; (with T. Papayannis) Culture and Wetlands in the Mediterranean: an evolving story, 2011; contrib. chapters in books; contrib. tech. papers. *Recreations:* hill-walking, tree art, photographing shadows, staring at the sea. *Address:* 20 Burswell Avenue, Hexham NE46 3JL.

**PRITCHARD, David Peter;** Acting Chairman, Euromoney Institutional Investor plc, 2018–19 (non-executive Director, 2008–09; Senior Independent Director, 2008–19); *b* 20 July 1944; *s* of Norman and Peggy Pritchard; *m* 1993, Elizabeth Cresswell; one *s* one *d. Educ:* Read Sch., Drax, Yorks; Southampton Univ. (BScEng 1966). Hawker Siddeley Aviation, 1966–71; Wm Brandt's Sons & Co., 1971–73; Edward Bates & Sons Ltd, 1973–78; Man. Dir, Citicorp Investment Bank, 1978–87; Vice Chm., Orion Royal Bank, 1987–88; Gen. Manager, Europe, Royal Bank of Canada, 1988–95; Treas., TSB Gp plc, 1995–96; on secondment to FSA, 1996–98; Gp Dir, Wholesale and Internat. Banking, 1998–2003, Dep. Chm., 2003–05, Lloyds TSB Gp plc. Chairman: Cheltenham & Gloucester, 2004–05; Songbird Estates plc, 2005–15; AIB Gp (UK) plc, 2007–16; non-executive Director: LCH.Clearnet Gp Ltd (formerly London Clearing House), 2001–07; Motability Tenth Anniv. Trust, 2003–; Scottish Widows plc, 2003–07; Allied Irish Banks plc, 2007–11; Advr, Highbrook Investors, 2016–. *Recreations:* cycling, photography. *Address:* 17 Thorney Crescent, SW11 3TT. *T:* (020) 7585 2253.

**PRITCHARD, Hon. Dame Frances Jean;** *see* Judd, Hon. Dame F. J.

**PRITCHARD, (Iorwerth) Gwynn;** broadcasting consultant and television producer; Secretary General, International Public Television (INPUT) (formerly International Public Television Screening Conference), 2001–06; *b* 1 Feb. 1946; *s* of late Rev. Islwyn Pritchard and Megan Mair Pritchard; *m* 1st, 1970, Marilyn Bartholomew (*d* 1994); two *s* one *d*; 2nd, 1998, Althea Sharp. *Educ:* Bolton Sch.; King's Coll., Cambridge (MA). Producer and Director: BBC Television, London, 1969–78; BBC Wales, 1979–82; HTV Wales, 1982–85; Commissioning Editor, 1985–88, Sen. Commissioning Editor for Educn, 1989–92, Channel 4; Hd of Welsh Progs, then of Welsh Broadcasting, BBC Cymru/Wales, 1992–2001. Pres., INPUT Internat. Bd, 1988–93. Trustee, Welsh Writers Trust, 1990–2017; Chm., Menter Iaith Bro Morgannwg/Vale of Glamorgan Lang. Initiative, 2011–13. Chm., Cardiff Unitarian Congregation, 2011–17; Mem., Exec. Cttee, Gen. Assembly of Unitarian and Free Christian Chs, 2015–17. Mem. Council, Coleg Harlech, 1992–2000; Gov., Ysgol Gynradd Pencae, 1992–2002. Winston Churchill Fellow, Winston Churchill Meml Trust, 1973; Huw Weldon Fellow, UCNW, Bangor, 1990–91. Chevalier de l'Ordre des Arts et des Lettres (France), 1990. *Recreations:* swimming, walking, cinema, reading. *Address:* 25 Westbourne Road, Penarth, Vale of Glamorgan CF64 3HA. *T:* (029) 2070 3608.

**PRITCHARD, Rt Rev. John Lawrence**; Bishop of Oxford, 2007–14; an Honorary Assistant Bishop: Diocese of Durham, since 2015; Diocese of Leeds, since 2015; *b* 22 April 1948; *s* of late Rev. Canon Neil Lawrence Pritchard and Winifred Mary Coverdale (*née* Savill); *m* 1972, Susan Wendy Claridge; two *d*. *Educ*: St Peter's Coll., Oxford (Dip. Theol., 1970; MA (Law) 1973; Hon. Fellow, 2007); St John's Coll., Durham (MLitt (Theol.) 1993). Ordained deacon, 1972, priest, 1973; Asst Curate, St Martin in the Bull Ring, Birmingham, 1972–76; Diocesan Youth Chaplain and Asst Dir of Educn, dio. of Bath and Wells, 1976–80; Vicar, St George's, Wilton, Taunton, 1980–88; Dir of Pastoral Studies, 1989–93, Warden, 1993–96, Cranmer Hall, St John's Coll., Durham; Archdeacon of Canterbury, 1996–2001; Bishop Suffragan of Jarrow, 2002–07. Took seat in H of L, 2011. Member: Gen. Synod of C of E, 1999–2001, 2007–; Bd, Church Army, 2003–11; Min. Council, 2008–11; Chm., C of E Bd of Educn, 2011–14. Bishops' Inspector, 1999–2004. Pres., St John's Coll., Durham, 2008–11. Pres., Guild of Health, 2003–14. *Publications*: Practical Theology in Action, 1996; The Intercessions Handbook, 1997; Beginning Again, 2000; Living the Gospel Stories Today, 2001; How to Pray, 2002; The Second Intercessions Handbook, 2004; Living Easter through the Year, 2005; Leading Intercessions, 2005; How to Explain your Faith, 2006; The Life and Work of a Priest, 2007; Going to Church: a user's guide, 2009; Pocket Prayers for Troubled Times, 2010; Living Jesus, 2010; God Lost and Found, 2011; Pocket Prayers for Pilgrims, 2011; Living Faithfully, 2013; Ten: why Christianity makes sense, 2014; The Journey: with Jesus to Jerusalem and the cross, 2014; Something More, 2016; The Intercession Resource Book, 2018; Five Events that Made Christianity, 2018. *Recreations*: photography, walking, travel, music, cricket, reading. *E*: johnlpritchard@btinternet.com.

**PRITCHARD, John Michael;** Founder and Chairman, Legalease Ltd, Publishers, since 1988; *b* 18 June 1949; *s* of Arthur Glyn Pritchard and Sybil Roderick Pritchard; *m* 1st, 1976, Mary Margaret Freeman (marr. diss. 1998); two *s* one *d*; 2nd, 1999, Hilary Baker. *Educ*: Penarth Grammar Sch.; Bristol Univ. Admitted solicitor, 1974; articled with Thompsons, solicitors, London; in practice with Powell Spencer, Kilburn, 1974–88. Editor: The Practical Lawyer, 1988–; Legal Business mag., 1990–; In House Lawyer mag., 1992–; Editor in Chief: Property Law Jl, 1997–; Employment Law Jl; Commercial Law Jl, Trusts and Estates Law Jl; Personal Injury Law Jl; Family Law Jl; Procurement and Outsourcing Law Jl; Gen. Counsel. *Publications*: (ed) Penguin Guide to the Law, 1982, 5th edn, as New Penguin Guide to the Law: your rights and the law explained, 2001; (ed) Legal 500, annually 1988–; Young Solicitors' Handbook, 1990, rev. edn 1991; (ed) Who's Who in the Law: eminent practising lawyers in the UK, 1991; (ed) European Legal 500, annually 1991–; Which Firm of Solicitors?, 1993; Legal Experts, annually 1994–; (ed) Commercial Client Directory: guide to legal service buyers at the UK's top 15,000 companies, 1996; (ed) Asia Pacific Legal 500, annually 1996–; Kanzleien in Deutschland, annually 1997–; (ed) Cabinets d'Avocats en France, annually, 1999–. *Recreations*: anything that does not involve lawyers. *Address*: Legalease Ltd, 188 Fleet Street, EC4A 2AG. *T*: (020) 7396 9292, *Fax*: (020) 7396 9300.

**PRITCHARD, Kenneth William,** OBE 1992; WS; part-time Sheriff, 2000–03 (Temporary Sheriff, 1995–99); Secretary of the Law Society of Scotland, 1976–97; *b* 14 Nov. 1933; *s* of Dr Kenneth Pritchard, MB, BS, DPH, and Isobel Pritchard, LDS (*née* Broom); *m* 1962, Gretta (*née* Murray), BL, MBA, WS; two *s* one *d*. *Educ*: Dundee High Sch.; Fettes Coll.; St Andrews Univ. (BL). National Service, Argyll and Sutherland Highlanders, 1955–57; commnd 2nd Lieut, 1956; TA 1957–62 (Captain). Joined J. & J. Scrimgeour, Solicitors, Dundee, 1957, Sen. Partner, 1970–76; WS 1984. Hon. Sheriff, Dundee, 1978. Member: Sheriff Court Rules Council, 1973–76; Lord Dunpark's Cttee Considering Reparation upon Criminal Conviction, 1973–77; Secretary, Scottish Council of Law Reporting, 1976–97. Governor, Moray House Coll. of Educn, 1982–84; Mem. Ct, Univ. of Dundee, 1990–93. Mem., National Trust for Scotland Jubilee Appeal Cttee, 1980–82. Pres., Dundee High Sch. Old Boys Club, 1975–76; Captain of the Former Pupil RFC, Dundee High Sch., 1959–62. Hon. Prof. of Law, Strathclyde Univ., 1986–94. *Recreation*: golf. *Address*: 22/4 Kinellan Road, Edinburgh EH12 6ES. *T*: (0131) 337 4294. *Clubs*: New, Bruntsfield Links Golfing Society (Edinburgh); Hon. Company of Edinburgh Golfers (Muirfield).

**PRITCHARD, Mark Andrew;** MP (C) The Wrekin, since 2005; *b* 22 Nov. 1966; *s* of late Francis Pritchard and of Romona Pritchard; *m* 1997, Sondra Janae Spaeth (marr. diss. 2013). *Educ*: London Guildhall Univ. (MA Mktg Mgt); CIM Postgrad. Dip. Mktg; Elim Coll. (Cert. Theol. and Pastoral Studies); Univ. of Buckingham (MA Internat. Diplomacy, 2013). Parly researcher, 1994–95; founder and owner: Pritchard Communications Ltd, 1999–2007; Next Steps Mkt Res. Ltd, 2002–06. Member: Harrow BC, 1993–94; Woking BC, 2000–03. Contested (C) Warley, 2001. Member: Envmtl Audit Select Cttee, 2005–07; DWP Select Cttee, 2006–08; Welsh Affairs Select Cttee, 2007–10; Transport Select Cttee, 2008–10; Jt Nat. Security Strategy Cttee, 2010–15; DFID Select Cttee, 2012–13; Speaker's Panel, 2015–; Human Rights Jt Cttee, 2015–17; Chm., All-Party Parly Gp on Abolition of Death Penalty (Jt Chm., 2012); Vice Chairman: All-Party Parly Gp on Social Care, 2005; ASEAN Parly Gp, 2010; Secretary: Cons. Party Defence Cttee, 2006; Cons. Parly Foreign Affairs Gp, 2006; 1922 Cttee, 2010–12; Vice Chm., Cons. Parly Foreign Affairs and Defence Cttee; Mem., Cons. Homeland Security Team, 2006–; Founding Mem. and Comr, Cons. Human Rights Commn, 2006–; Mem. Bd, Parliamentarians for Global Action, 2007–. Member: Parly Delegn to NATO, 2010–14; British Irish Parly Assembly, 2013–; UK Delegn to Council of Europe, 2015–. Dep. Chm., Internat. Office, Cons. Party, 2010–12. Member: Council, Bow Gp, 1993–94; Bd, Cons. Councillors Assoc., 2002–05. *Recreations*: writing comedy, trainee bird watcher, jazz, ski-ing, animal welfare. *Address*: c/o House of Commons, SW1A 0AA. *T*: (020) 7219 3000. *E*: pritchardm@parliament.uk.

**PRITCHARD, Dr Michael,** FRPS; Director, Education and Public Affairs, Royal Photographic Society, since 2018 (Chief Executive, 2011–18); *b* Watford, 21 Nov. 1964; *s* of Alan and Lesley Pritchard. *Educ*: Queen's Sch., Bushey; Univ. of Hull (BSc Hons Geog. 1986); De Montfort Univ. (PhD Hist. of Photography 2010). FRPS 1986. Photography specialist, Christie's London, 1986–2007; Res. Fellow, De Montfort Univ., 2009–10; Consultant, British Liby, 2011. *Publications*: Spy Camera, 1993; A Directory of London Photographers 1841–1908, 1994; Photographers, 2012; A History of Photography in 50 Cameras, 2014. *Recreations*: photography, museums, travel, cinema, hill-walking. *Address*: 61 Great Pulteney Street, Bath BA2 4DN. *T*: (01225) 424742. *E*: michael@mpritchard.com.

**PRITCHARD, Prof. Thomas Owen,** OBE 2005; JP; Chairman, Cynefin Environmental Ltd, consultants in sustainable development, 1991–2012; Deputy Chairman, National Heritage Memorial Fund, 1999–2005; Professorial Fellow, University of Wales; *b* 13 May 1932; *s* of late Owen and Mary Pritchard; *m* 1957, Enyd Ashton; one *s* one *d*. *Educ*: Botwnnog Grammar Sch.; Univ. of Wales (BSc Hons Botany and Agric. Botany); Univ. of Leeds (PhD Genetics). Midlands Regl Officer and Head of Educn, Nature Conservancy, 1957–67; Dep. Dir for Wales, Nature Conservancy—NERC, 1967–73; Dir for Wales, NCC, 1973–91. Consultant, Council of Europe, 1968. Vis. Prof., Dept of Forestry and Resource Management, Univ. of California, Berkeley, 1981–. Dir, CTF Training Ltd, 1982–91; Chairman: Coed Cymru Ltd, 1983–92; Slate Ecology Co. Ltd, 1995. Chairman: Bardsey Island Trust, 1987–93; Welsh Historic Gdns Trust, 1994–98 (Pres., 2001); Exec., POW Cttee, 1971–73; Country Cttee for Wales, Heritage Lottery Fund, 1999–2005; Envmt Protection Adv. Cttee for Wales, Envmt Agency, Wales, 2005; Vice Chm. (Educn), IUCN, 1966–73; former Chm. and Mem., conservation and envmtl bodies, nat. and internat. Member: Genetical Soc.; British Ecological Soc. Member: Ct of Govs and Council: Univ. of Wales, Bangor (formerly UC, Bangor), 1981–2002; Nat. Museum of Wales, 1981–91. Member: Gorsedd of Bards, Royal Nat. Eisteddfod; Hon. Soc. of Cymmrodorion. FRSA. JP Bangor, 1978. *Publications*: Cynefin y Cymro, 1989; numerous contribs to sci. and educn jls. *Recreation*: sailing. *Address*: Graig Lwyd, 134 Ffordd Penrhos, Bangor, Gwynedd LL57 2BX. *T*: (01248) 370401.

**PRITCHARD-JONES, Prof. Kathryn,** PhD; FRCPCH, FRCPE, FMedSci; Professor of Paediatric Oncology, University College London, since 2010; Honorary Consultant Oncologist, Great Ormond Street NHS Foundation Trust, since 2010; Chief Medical Officer, University College London Hospitals Cancer Collaborative (incorporating London Cancer), 2010–18; Cancer Programme Director, UCL Partners, 2010–19; *b* Coventry, 1958; *d* of John Pritchard-Jones and Marianne Pritchard-Jones; one *s* one *d*. *Educ*: John Port Comp. Sch., Etwall; St Hugh's Coll., Oxford (BA Physiol Sci. 1980; BM BCh 1983); MRC Human Genetics Unit, Univ. of Edinburgh (PhD 1992). FRCPCH 1997; FRCPE 1998. Jun. dr trng posts, paediatrics and paediatric oncology, Oxford, Newcastle and Adelaide, 1984–87; MRC Recombinant DNA trng fellowship, MRC Human Genetics Unit, Univ. of Edinburgh, 1987–92; Team Leader, 1993–2010, Prof. of Childhood Cancer Biol., 2004–10, Inst. of Cancer Res., Univ. of London; Consultant Paediatric Oncologist, Royal Marsden Hosp., 1994–2010. FMedSci 2012. *Publications*: over 250 articles in scientific jls on childhood cancer, particularly Wilms tumour and internat. childhood cancer survival benchmarking. *Recreations*: ski-ing, sailing, fine wines, mountain walking, foreign travel, Boris biking around London's sights. *Address*: UCLPartners, 170 Tottenham Court Road, W1T 7HA. *T*: (020) 7679 6393; UCL Institute of Child Health, 30 Guilford Street, WC1N 1EH. *T*: (020) 7905 2774. *E*: k.pritchard-jones@ucl.ac.uk.

**PRITCHETT, Matthew, (Matt),** MBE 2002; front page cartoonist for Daily Telegraph, since 1988; *b* 14 July 1964; *s* of Oliver Pritchett and Joan Pritchett (*née* Hill); *m* 1992, Pascale Charlotte Marie Smets; one *s* three *d*. *Educ*: Addey and Stanhope Sch.; St Martin's Sch. of Art. Freelance cartoonist for New Statesman, Punch and Spectator, 1986–88. Awards from: What the Papers Say, 1992, 2004, 2006; Cartoon Arts Trust, 1995, 1996, 1999, 2005, 2006, 2009, 2013; UK Press Gazette, 1996, 1998; British Press Awards, 2000, 2008, 2009, 2018; Sports Cartoonist of the Year, Sports Journalism Awards, 2013; Journalists' Charity Award, 2014. *Publications*: Best of Matt, annually, 1991–; 10 Years of Matt, 2001; 30 Years of Matt, 2018; Matt on Brexit, 2019. *Address*: c/o The Daily Telegraph, 111 Buckingham Palace Road, SW1W 0DT.

**PRITTIE,** family name of **Baron Dunalley**.

**PROBY, Sir William Henry,** 3rd Bt *cr* 1952, of Elton Hall, co. Huntingdon; CBE 2009; DL; farmer; *b* 13 June 1949; *s* of Sir Peter Proby, 2nd Bt and Blanche Harrison (*née* Cripps); *S* father, 2002; *m* 1974, Meredyth Anne, *d* of Timothy David Brentnall; four *d*. *Educ*: Eton; Lincoln Coll., Oxford (MA); Brooksby Coll. of Agric. FCA. Price Waterhouse & Co., 1971–76; Morgan Grenfell & Co., 1976–80; Chief Exec., MWP Ltd, 1980–82; Chm., Elton Estates Co. Ltd, 1982–. Chm., Retirement Advantage (formerly MGM Assce Ltd, then Marine and Gen. Mutual Life Assce Soc.), 2007– (non-exec. Dir, 2006–). Pres., Historic Houses Assoc., 1994–99; Chm., Nat. Trust, 2003–08. Mem. Adv. Council, Tate Britain, 1999–2010. Trustee, Nat. Portrait Gall., 2009–17 (Vice Chm., 2011–12; Chm., 2012–17). DL Cambs, 1995; High Sheriff, Cambs, 2001–02. *Address*: Elton Hall, Elton, Peterborough PE8 6SH. *T*: (01832) 280223, *Fax*: (01832) 280584. *E*: whp@eltonhall.com. *Clubs*: Brooks's, Boodle's, Dilettanti, Roxburghe.

**PROBYN, Calista Jane, (Mrs N. C. Dinnage); Her Honour Judge Probyn;** a Circuit Judge, since 2013; *b* Calgary, Canada, 23 July 1960; *d* of late Alfred John Probyn and Calista Helen Probyn; *m* 1995, Nicholas Charles Dinnage; one *s*. *Educ*: Llandrindod Wells High Sch.; Univ. of Westminster (LLB Hons). Inns of Court Sch. of Law. Called to the Bar, Middle Temple, 1988, Bencher, 2018; in practice as a barrister, specialising in family law, 1988–2013; a Recorder, 2003–13. *Recreations*: family life, walking, reading, theatre.

**PROCHASKA, Dr Alice Marjorie Sheila,** FRHistS; Principal, Somerville College, Oxford, 2010–17; Pro-Vice-Chancellor, University of Oxford, 2014–17; *b* 12 July 1947; *d* of John Harold Barwell and Hon. Sheila McNair; *m* 1971, Dr Franklyn Kimmel Prochaska; one *s* one *d*. *Educ*: Perse Sch. for Girls, Cambridge; Somerville Coll., Oxford (BA 1968; MA 1973; DPhil 1975; Hon. Fellow 2017). Assistant Keeper: London Museum, 1971–73; Public Record Office (Nat. Archives), 1975–84; Sec. and Librarian, Inst. of Historical Res., 1984–92; Dir of Special Collections, BL, 1992–2001; University Librarian, Yale Univ., 2001–10. Chm., Nat. Council on Archives, 1991–95; Mem., Royal Commn on Historical MSS, 1998–2001. Member: History Working Gp on Nat. Curriculum, DES, 1989–90; Council, RHistS, 1991–95 (Vice Pres., 1995–99); Heritage Educn Trust, 1992–2001; Hereford Mappa Mundi Trust, 1992–95; Adv. Council, Inst. of Historical Res., 1992–2001; Library Panel, Wellcome Inst., 1993–97; Adv. Panel, Qualidata, Univ. of Essex, 1995–98; Sir Winston Churchill Archive Trust, 1995–2001 (Chm., 2010–Dec. 2020); Steering Cttee, Digital Library Fedn, 2001–05 (Trustee, 2005–09); Adv. Council, Yale Center for British Art, 2002–10; Bd, Yale Univ. Press, 2005–10; Main Panel D, REF 2014, HEFCE, 2011–15; Steering Cttee, Conference of Colls, 2011–16, Supervisory Cttee, Recognised Ind. Centres, 2012–17 (Chm., 2012–17), Curators Bd of Univ. Libraries, 2014–17, Univ. of Oxford; Adv. Gp, Re-Imagine, India-UK Cultural Relns in the 21st Century, British Council, 2012–13; Bd of Advrs, Jindal Sch. of Liberal Arts and Humanities, O. P. Jindal Global Univ., Sonipat, India, 2015–; Gen. Fedn of Trades Unions Educn Trust, 2017–; Marshall Aid Commemoration Commn, 2017– (Chair, Educn Cttee, 2018–; Dep. Chair, 2019–). Chair: Section Panel, Rare Books and Manuscripts, IFLA, 1999–2003; Trustees of Lewis Walpole Library, 2001–10; Inst. of Histl Res. Trust, Univ. of London, 2017–; Mem., Historic Towns Trust, 2018–; Chm., Collections and Access Cttee, 2003–05, Mem., Res., Trng and Learning Cttee, 2005–06, Chair, Special Collections Wkg Gp, 2007–09, Assoc. of Res. Libraries; Bd Mem., Center for Res. Libraries, 2003–10 (Vice-Chair, 2005–07; Chair, 2007–09). Gov., London Guildhall Univ., 1995–2001. Hon. Fellow: Inst. of Histl Res., London Univ., 2001; RHUL, 2002. Hon. LLD Aberdeen, 2013. *Publications*: London in the Thirties, 1973; History of the General Federation of Trade Unions 1899–1980, 1982; Irish History from 1700: a guide to sources in the Public Record Office, 1986; (ed jtly with F. K. Prochaska) Margaretta Acworth's Georgian Cookery Book, 1987; contribs to books, learned jls and collections of conf. papers. *Recreations*: family life, walking, fine art and museums.

**PROCTER, Jane Hilary;** artist; media consultant, since 2002; *m* 1985, Thomas Charles Goldstaub; one *s* one *d*. *Educ*: Queen's Coll., Harley St. Fashion Asst, Vogue, 1974–75; Asst Fashion Editor, Good Housekeeping, 1975–77; Actg Fashion Editor, Woman's Jl, 1977–78; Fashion Writer, Country Life, 1978–80; Freelance Fashion Editor, The Times, Sunday Times and Daily Express, 1980–87; Editor: British W, 1987–88; Tatler, 1990–99; Editl Dir, PeopleNews Network, 1999–2002. *Publications*: Dress Your Best, 1983. *Recreations*: sailing, ski-ing. *E*: jane@janeprocter.net.

**PROCTER, John Michael;** Member (C) Yorkshire and the Humber, European Parliament, 2016–19; *b* Leeds, 7 Nov. 1966; *m* Rachael; two *c*. Dir, Strategic Facilities Mgt Ltd, 2014–. Mem. (C), Leeds CC, 1992–2018. Contested (C) Yorks and the Humber, EP, 2019. Mem. Bd, Northern Ballet; Dir, Leeds Grand Th. Enterprises Ltd, 2007–17.

**PROCTER, Robert John Dudley;** Chief Executive, Lincolnshire County Council, 1983–95; *b* 19 Oct. 1935; *s* of Luther Donald Procter and Edith Muriel Procter; *m* 1962, Adrienne Allen; one *s* one *d*. *Educ:* Cheltenham Grammar School. Admitted Solicitor, 1961. Articled Clerk, Glos CC, 1956–61; Assistant Solicitor: Bath City, 1961–63; Cumberland CC, 1963–65; Lindsey County Council: Sen. Asst Solicitor, 1965–69; Asst Clerk, 1969–71; Dep. Clerk, Kesteven CC, 1971–73; Dir of Personnel, 1973–77, Dir of Admin, 1977–83, Lincolnshire CC. Chm., Assoc. of County Chief Execs, 1994–95. Mem., Warner Cttee of Inquiry into recruitment and selection of staff in children's homes, 1992. Vice Chm., Linkage Community Trust, 2001–04; Treas., Lincoln Cathedral Community Assoc., 2001–06. Chm. Govs, Lincoln Christ's Hosp. Sch. and Foundn, 2001–05. Chm., Eastgate Lincoln Bowls Club, 2007–08. *Recreations:* horse racing, swimming, family history, bowls. *Address:* Flat 3, The Lodge, 38B Nettleham Road, Lincoln LN2 1RE. *T:* (01522) 532105.

**PROCTOR, His Honour Anthony James;** a Circuit Judge, 1988–2001; *b* 18 Sept. 1931; *s* of James Proctor and Savina Maud (*née* Horsfield); *m* 1964, Patricia Mary Bryan; one *d*. *Educ:* Mexborough Grammar Sch., Yorkshire; St Catharine's Coll., Cambridge (MA, LLM). Flying Officer, RAF, 1953–55. Articled to Sir Bernard Kenyon, County Hall, Wakefield, 1955–58; admitted Solicitor 1958. Sen. Prosecuting Solicitor, Sheffield Corp., 1959–64; Partner, Broomhead & Neals, Solicitors, Sheffield, 1964–74; Dist Registrar and County Court Registrar, Barrow in Furness, Lancaster, Preston, 1974–88; a Recorder, 1985–88; Hon. Recorder of Lancaster, 2000–05. Pres., Assoc. of Dist and Court Registrars, 1985–86. *Recreations:* photography, travel, genealogy.

**PROCTOR, Rev. John;** General Secretary, United Reformed Church, 2014–Aug. 2020; *b* Stirling, 22 Dec. 1952; *s* of Lawrence Proctor and Marion Proctor (*née* Davis); *m* 1977, Elaine Patricia Low; one *s* one *d*. *Educ:* Queen Mary's Grammar Sch., Walsall; St John's Coll., Cambridge (MA); Univ. of Glasgow (MSc; BD). Lectr in Statistics, Univ. of Glasgow, 1975–77; Church of Scotland Minister, Colston Milton, Glasgow, 1981–86; Dir of New Testament Studies, 1986–2014, Vice-Principal, 1997–2014, Westminster Coll., Cambridge. *Publications:* The People's Bible Commentary: Matthew, 2001; Westminster Bible Companion: first and second Corinthians, 2015. *Recreations:* following football and cricket, bird-watching. *Address:* United Reformed Church House, 86 Tavistock Place, WC1H 9RT. *T:* (020) 7916 2020.

**PROCTOR, (Keith) Harvey;** Private Secretary to the Duke and Duchess of Rutland, 2002–15; *b* 16 Jan. 1947; *s* of late Albert Proctor and Hilda Tegerdine. *Educ:* High School for Boys, Scarborough; Univ. of York (BA History Hons, 1969). Asst Director, Monday Club, 1969–71; Research Officer, Conservative 1970s Parliamentary Gp, 1971–72; Exec. Director, Parliamentary Digest Ltd, 1972–74; British Paper & Board Industry Federation: Asst Sec., 1974–78; Secretary, 1978–79; Consultant, 1979–87. Dir, Proctor's Shirts and Ties, 1992–2000. MP (C): Basildon, 1979–83; Billericay, 1983–87. Mem., Exec. Council, Monday Club, 1983–87. Chief Exec., Richmond Bor. Chamber of Commerce, 1996–98 (Vice-Pres., 1990–92; Pres., 1992–94). Trustee, SW London Community Foundn, 1993–94; Chairman: Richmond Town Centre Cttee, 1995–97; Parkview Court Residents' Assoc., 1996–97 (Sec., 1994–96); Co-Chm., Richmond Victorian Evening Cttee, 1999. Clerk, Earl of Rutland and Dr Fleming's Hosp. Trust, 2013–15. Editor, News and Views, 1991–98. *Publications:* Billericay in Old Picture Postcards, 1985; Credible and True (memoir), 2016. *Recreations:* collecting British contemporary art, walking boxer dogs, travelling.

**PROCTOR, Prof. Michael Richard Edward,** PhD, ScD; FRS 2006; FRAS, FIMA; Professor of Astrophysical Fluid Dynamics, University of Cambridge, 2000–17, now Emeritus; Provost of King's College, Cambridge, since 2013; *b* 19 Sept. 1950; *s* of Edward Francis Proctor and Stella Mary Major Proctor (*née* Jones); *m* 1st, 1973, Linda Irene Powell (marr. diss. 1998); two *s* one *d*; 2nd, 1999, Elizabeth Julia Colgate (*née* Nuttall); two step *s*. *Educ:* Stoke House Prep. Sch., Seaford; Shrewsbury Sch.; Trinity Coll., Cambridge (Entrance Scholar 1968; BA 1971, MA; PhD 1975; ScD 1994). FRAS 1977; FIMA 2007. University of Cambridge: Asst Lectr, 1977–81; Lectr, 1981–94; Reader, 1994–2000. Trinity College: Res. Fellow, 1974–77; Teaching Fellow, 1977–2013; Tutor, 1980–90, 1991–94; Dean, 1994–2006; Vice-Master, 2006–12. Instructor and Asst Prof., MIT, 1975–77. *Publications:* (with N. O. Weiss) Magnetoconvection, 2014; over 190 articles in learned jls. *Recreations:* gardening, rowing, foreign travel, theatre, concerts. *Address:* The Provost's Lodge, King's College, Cambridge CB2 1ST. *T:* (01223) 331253, *Fax:* (01223) 331195. *E:* provost@kings.cam.ac.uk. *Club:* Oxford and Cambridge.

**PROCTOR, Prof. Stephen John,** FRCP, FRCPath; Professor of Haematological Oncology, University of Newcastle upon Tyne, 1991, now Emeritus; *b* 21 Nov. 1945; *s* of Jack and Betty Proctor; *m* 1971, Susan; one *s* two *d*. *Educ:* Morley Grammar Sch.; Univ. of Newcastle upon Tyne (MB BS 1970). FRCP 1985; FRCPath 1989. Sen. Lectr in Medicine and Haematology, Univ. of Newcastle upon Tyne, 1982–91. *Publications:* over 200 peer reviewed articles in scientific jls and med. jls. *Recreations:* gardening, horticulture, enjoying Northumberland, motoring, travel. *Address:* Haematological Sciences, School of Clinical and Laboratory Sciences, Medical School, University of Newcastle upon Tyne, Framlington Place, Newcastle upon Tyne NE2 4HH. *T:* (0191) 208 7791. *E:* stephen.proctor@ncl.ac.uk.

**PROCTOR, William Angus;** Clerk of the Journals, House of Commons, 2003–04; *b* 1 May 1945; 3rd *s* of late George Longmate Proctor and Anne Ines Louie Proctor (*née* Angus); *m* 1969, Susan Irene Mottram; two *s* one *d*. *Educ:* Bristol Cathedral Sch. (chorister); Keele Univ. (BA Hons English and Political Instns; Pres., Students Union, 1965–66). A Clerk, H of C, 1968–70 and 1972–2004; Res. Associate, Manchester Univ., 1970–72; Delegn Sec., H of C Overseas Office, 1972–74; Clerk, Select Committees on: Sci. and Technol., 1974–77; Procedure, 1977–79; Transport, 1979–82; Foreign Affairs, 1982–87; Sec., H of C Commn, 1987–92; Principal Clerk: of Financial Cttees and Clerk, Treasury and CS Cttee, 1992–95; of Standing Cttees, 1995–97; of Bills, 1997–99; of Delegated Legislation, 1999–2003. Procedural Advr to Pres., Council of Europe Assembly, 1989–92. Occasional advr to overseas parliaments, 2004–. *Publications:* (jtly) The European Parliament, 1973; (ed) The Parliamentary Assembly of the Council of Europe: procedure and practice, 9th edn (with J. Sweetman) 1990; (Asst Ed. and contrib.) Erskine May's Parliamentary Practice, 22nd edn, 1997; contrib. articles and reviews to parly jls. *Recreations:* reading a lot of history, and writing my own. *E:* billproctor2012@hotmail.co.uk.

**PROCTOR-BEAUCHAMP, Sir Christopher Radstock;** *see* Beauchamp.

**PRODI, Romano;** Prime Minister of Italy, 1996–98 and 2006–08; Professor-at-Large, Watson Institute for International Studies, Brown University, 2009–13; Special Envoy for the Sahel, United Nations, 2012–14; *b* Scandiano, Italy, 9 Aug. 1939; *m* Flavia Franzoni; two *s*. *Educ:* Catholic Univ. of Milan (degree in law); LSE (post-grad. studies; Hon. Fellow). Asst in Political Econs, 1963–71, Prof. of Industrial Organisation and Industrial Policy, 1971–99, Univ. of Bologna; Researcher: Lombard Inst. of Economic and Social Studies, 1963–64; Stanford Res. Inst., 1968. Prof. of Econs and Indust. Politics, Free Univ. of Trento, 1973–74; Vis. Prof., Harvard Univ., 1974. Minister of Industry, 1978–79; Chm., Inst. for Industrial Reconstruction, 1982–89, 1993–94. Chm., Ulivo (centre-left coalition gp), 1995–2007; Pres., Democratic Party, 2007–08. MP (Ulivo), Italy, 1996–99; Pres., Eur. Commn, 1999–2004; MP (Union), Italy, 2006–08. Prof., China Europe Internat. Business Sch., Shanghai, 2010–15. Hon. Mem., Real Academia de Ciencias Morales y Políticas, Madrid. Hon. Dr: Madras; Sofia; Brown; Barcelona; Pisa; Ottawa; Seoul; Modena-Reggio; Hon. DCL Oxon, 2002. Premio Schumpeter, 1999.

**PROESCH, Gilbert,** RA 2017; artist; *b* Dolomites, Italy, 1943. *Educ:* Wolkenstein Sch. of Art; Hallein Sch. of Art; Munich Acad. of Art; St Martin's Sch. of Art. Collaboration with George Passmore, *qv*, as Gilbert and George. Gallery exhibitions include: Modern Fears, 1980, The Believing World, 1983, New Pictures, 1987, Worlds & Windows, 1990, New Democratic Pictures, 1992, Anthony d'Offay Gall.; The Rudimentary Pictures, Milton Keynes Gall., 2000; New Horny Pictures, White Cube$^2$, 2001; Perversive Pictures, NY, 2004; Jack Freak Pictures, White Cube, 2009, and European mus. tour, 2010; The Banners, White Cube, 2015; Gilbert and George: the beard pictures and their f\*\*\*osophy, White Cube, 2017; museum exhibitions include: The Paintings, 1971, Photo-Pieces 1971–80, 1981, Whitechapel Art Gall.; Pictures 1982 to 85, Hayward Gall., 1987; Enclosed and Enchanted, MOMA, Oxford, 2000; The Dirty Words Pictures (retrospective), Serpentine Gall., 2002; Gilbert & George: major exhibition (retrospective), Tate Modern, 2007, and US mus. tour, 2008; London Pictures, White Cube, 2012; living sculpture includes: The Red Sculpture; Underneath the Arches; The Singing Sculpture; Our New Sculpture. Work in permanent collections incl. Nat. Portrait Gall., Tate Modern and San Francisco Mus. of Modern Art. Represented GB, Venice Biennale, 2005. (Jtly) Turner Prize, 1986. *Publications:* (as Gilbert), with George Passmore: Lost Day; Oh, the Grand Old Duke of York; What Our Art Means. *Address:* c/o White Cube$^2$, 144–152 Bermondsey Street, SE1 3TQ.

**PROFFITT, Stuart Graham;** Publishing Director, Penguin Press, since 1998; *b* Bolton, 24 Aug. 1961; *s* of late Geoffrey Arnold Proffitt and of Sheila Patricia (*née* Whitehurst); *m* 2003, Anya Catherine Suschitzky; two *d*. *Educ:* Uppingham Sch., Rutland; Worcester Coll., Oxford (BA Modern Hist. 1982). Various posts, Collins, later HarperCollins, Publishers, 1983–92; Publisher, Trade Div., HarperCollins Publishers, 1992–98. Chair, Baillie Gifford Prize (formerly Samuel Johnson Prize) for Non-fiction, 1999–. London Library/Christie's Life in Literature Award, 2014. *Recreations:* reading, music, hill-walking. *Address:* c/o Penguin Books, 80 Strand, WC2R 0RL. *T:* (020) 7010 3000. *Club:* Brooks's.

**PROFIT, (George) Richard,** CBE 2003 (OBE 1980); AFC 1974; Board Member, and Group Director, Safety Regulation, Civil Aviation Authority, 1997–2003; *b* 31 Oct. 1940; *s* of Richard George Profit and Lillian Cotterill Profit; *m* 1965, Pamela Shepherd; one *d*. *Educ:* Oldershaw Grammar Sch.; Army Staff Coll., Camberley; RCDS. Commissioned Royal Air Force, 1961: operational pilot, UK, Singapore, Germany, 1963–77; Officer Commanding: No 3 (F) Sqdn, 1977–80; RAF Coltishall, 1982–85; Inspector of Flight Safety, 1987–90; retd in rank of Air Cdre, 1990; Dir, Safety, Security and Quality Assurance, NATS Ltd, 1990–97. Non-exec. Dir, Rail and Safety Standards Bd, 2003–10. *Publications:* Systematic Safety Management in the Air Traffic Services, 1995. *Recreations:* trout fishing, photography. *Club:* Royal Air Force.

**PROKHOROVA, Violetta;** *see* Elvin, V.

**PROOPS, Dr Anya Lucie Victoria;** QC 2016; *b* London. *Educ:* Godolphin and Latymer Sch.; Jesus Coll., Cambridge (BA 1992); London Sch. of Econs and Pol Sci. (PhD); City Univ. (DipLaw); Inns of Court Sch. of Law. Called to the Bar, Inner Temple, 1998. *Address:* 11KBW, 11 King's Bench Walk, Temple, EC4Y 7EQ. *T:* (020) 7632 8500.

**PROPHET, His Honour John;** a Circuit Judge, 1997–2006; a Judge of the Employment Appeal Tribunal, 2002–06; *b* 19 Nov. 1931; *s* of Benjamin and Elsie Prophet; *m* 1961, Pauline Newby; three *d*. *Educ:* Trinity Coll., Cambridge (MA). Called to the Bar, Lincoln's Inn, 1956; Shell International, 1956–60; private practice at the Bar, 1960–63; Sen. Lectr, Law Faculty, Leeds Univ., 1968–76; full-time Chm. of Industrial Tribunals, 1976–88; Regl Chm. of Industrial Tribunals, Yorkshire and Humberside, 1988–97; Pres., Industrial, subseq. Employment, Tribunals for England and Wales, 1997–2002. Consultant, Nat. Assoc. of Local Councils, 1968–89. *Publications:* The Structure of Government, 1968; The Parish Councillor's Guide, 1974, 17th edn 2000; Fair Rents, 1976; The Councillor, 1979, 11th edn 1997. *Recreations:* tennis, chess, gardening, eight grandchildren!

**PROPHIT, Penny Pauline;** Member, Board of Directors, Trustee and Chair, College Board of Trustees, Our Lady of the Lake Regional Medical Center, Baton Rouge, Louisiana, 2004; *b* 7 Feb. 1939; *d* of C. Alston Prophit and Hortense Callahan. *Educ:* Marillac Coll., St Louis Univ., USA (BSN); Catholic Univ. of America (MSN, DNSc, PhD). Asst Prof., Catholic Univ. of America, 1975; Associate Professor: Univ. of Southern Mississippi, 1975; Louisiana State Univ. Med. Center, 1975; Cons., WHO, Eur. Office, Copenhagen, 1977; Prof., Katholieke Univ., Leuven, Belgium, 1977; Prof. of Nursing Studies, 1983–92, Hd of Dept, 1983–88, Univ. of Edinburgh. Mental Welfare Comr for Scotland, 1985; Mem., UK Central Council for Nursing, Midwifery and Health Visiting, 1988. Delta Epsilon Sigma, Nat. Catholic Scholastic Honor Soc., 1966; Sigma Theta Tau, Internat. Nursing Scholastic Honor Soc., 1970; Sigma Epsilon Phi, Catholic Univ. of Amer. Honor Soc., 1975. *Publications:* (with Lynette Long) Understanding and Responding, 1982; res. articles on nursing care of the elderly, stress in nursing, interdisciplinary collaboration, etc. *Recreations:* jogging, reading and writing poetry and short stories, playing piano and listening to music of all kinds.

**PROPPER, Prof. Carol,** CBE 2010; DPhil; FBA 2014; Professor of Economics, Imperial College Business School, Imperial College London, since 2007. *Educ:* Univ. of Bristol (BSc Hons Econs and Econ. Hist. 1977); Oxford Univ. (MSc Social Res. and Social Policy 1981); Univ. of Toronto (Commonwealth Schol. 1982); Univ. of York (PhD Econs 1988). Community worker, Islington, 1977–79; Res. Officer, Nuffield Coll., Oxford, 1981–82; Res. Economist, NZ Inst. of Econ. Res., 1983–84; Res. Fellow, Centre for Health Econs, Univ. of York, 1986–87; Lectr in Econs, Brunel Univ., 1987–88; University of Bristol: Lectr, Sch. for Policy Studies and Dept of Econs, 1988–93; on secondment to DoH as Sen. Econ. Advr to NHS Exec. on Regulation of NHS Internal Mkt, 1993–94; Reader, 1993–94; Prof. of Econs of Public Policy, 1995–2015; Dir, Centre for Mkt and Public Orgn, 2002–04. Co-Dir, ESRC Centre for Analysis of Social Exclusion, LSE, 1997–2007. Res. Fellow, Centre for Econ. Policy Res., 1998; Vis. Prof., Inst. for Res. in Econs and Business Admin and Health Econs Bergen, Univ. of Bergen, 2004. Econ. Consultant, USAID/Govt of Jamaica, Tax Reform Project Jamaica, 1983. Mem., Health Steering Gp for Measuring NHS Productivity, DoH, 2003–05. Mem. Council, ESRC, 2005–09. Mem. Council, REconS, 2000–05. *Publications:* contribs to learned jls incl. Jl Political Econ., Econ. Jl, Jl Health Econs, Jl Population Econs, Jl Public Econs and Labour Econs. *Address:* Imperial College Business School, Imperial College London, Tanaka Building, South Kensington Campus, SW7 2AZ.

**PROSOR, Ron**; Abba Eban Professor of International Diplomacy, Lauder School of Government, Diplomacy and Strategy, Interdisciplinary Center, University of Herzliya, since 2016; Distinguished Fellow, Hudson Institute, since 2016; *m* Hadas; two *s* one *d*. *Educ*: Hebrew Univ. of Jerusalem (MA *cum laude* Pol Sci.). Joined Min. of Foreign Affairs of Israel, 1980; Spokesman, Israeli Embassy, Bonn, 1988–92; Dep. Dir, Eur. Div., 1992–93, Dir, Ops Centre, 1993–95, Min. of Foreign Affairs; Spokesman, Israeli Embassy, London, 1995–98; Minister-Counsellor, Pol Affairs, Washington, 1998–2002; Foreign Min. Spokesman, 2002–03; Dep. Dir Gen. for Strategic Affairs, Counter-Terrorism and Nuclear Disarmament, 2003; COS to Foreign Minister, 2003–04; Sen. Dep. Dir Gen., 2004, Dir Gen., 2004–07, Min. of Foreign Affairs; Ambassador of Israel to Court of St James's, 2007–11; Perm. Rep. of Israel to UN, 2011–15. Dist. Service Award, Min. of Foreign Affairs, Israel, 2002. *Address*: Interdisciplinary Center Herzliya, PO Box 167, Herzliya 4610101, Israel.

**PROSSER,** family name of **Baroness Prosser.**

**PROSSER,** Baroness *cr* 2004 (Life Peer), of Battersea in the London Borough of Wandsworth; **Margaret Theresa Prosser,** OBE 1997; *b* 22 Aug. 1937; *d* of Frederick James and Lillian (*née* Barry); *m* (marr. diss.); one *s* two *d*. *Educ*: St Philomena's Convent, Carshalton; North East London Polytechnic (Post Grad. Dip. in Advice and Inf. Studies, 1977). Associate Mem., Inst. of Legal Execs, 1982. Advice Centre Organiser, Southwark Community Develt Project, 1974–76; Advr, Southwark Law Project, 1976–83; Transport and General Workers' Union: official, 1983–2002; Nat. Sec., 1984–92; Nat. Organiser, 1992–99; Dep. Gen. Sec., 1999–2002. Pres., TUC, 1995–96. Non-exec. Dir, Royal Mail, 2004–10. Member: Equal Opportunities Commn, 1987–93; Employment Appeal Tribunal, 1995–2007; Central Arbitration Cttee, 2000–03; Low Pay Commn, 2000–05; Chair, Women's Nat. Commn, 2002–07; Dep. Chair, Commn for Equality and Human Rights, 2006–12. Treas., Labour Party, 1996–2001. *Recreations*: walking, gardening, reading.

**PROSSER, Benjamin Charles W.;** *see* Wegg-Prosser.

**PROSSER, Charles;** *see* Prosser, L. C.

**PROSSER, Sir David (John)**, Kt 2005; Chief Executive, Legal & General Group, 1991–2006; Joint Chairman, Investec plc, 2011–14 (Director, 2006–14); *b* 26 March 1944; *s* of Ronald and Dorothy Prosser; *m* 1971, Rosemary Margaret Snuggs; two *d*. *Educ*: Univ. of Wales (BSc). FIA. Sun Alliance Group, 1965–69; Hoare Govett, 1969–73; CIN Management, 1973–88; Legal & General, 1988–2006. Director: SWALEC, 1991–96; InterContinental Hotels Gp, 2003–08; Epsom Downs Racecourse, 2006–13. Chm., Financial Services Skills Council, 2004–06. Mem. of Bd, ABI, 1994–97, 1999–2006. *Recreation*: family life. *Club*: Royal Automobile (Chm., 2007–12).

**PROSSER, His Honour (Elvet) John;** QC 1978; a Circuit Judge, 1988–2001; a Deputy High Court Judge, 1984–2001; Resident Judge, Newport (Gwent) Crown Court, 1993–2001; *b* 10 July 1932; *s* of David and Hannah Prosser; *m* 1957, Mary Louise Cowdry; two *d*. *Educ*: Pontypridd Grammar Sch.; King's Coll., London Univ. LLB. Flt Lt, RAF, 1957–59. Called to the Bar, Gray's Inn, 1956, Bencher, 1986; Mem., Senate of Inns of Court and the Bar, 1980–87; a Recorder, 1972–88; Leader, Wales and Chester Circuit, 1984–87. Part-time Chm. of Industrial Tribunals, 1975–81. An Asst Boundary Comr for Wales, 1977–2001. *Recreations*: watching cricket and television. *Address*: 15 Redwood Court, Llanishen, Cardiff CF14 5RD. *Clubs*: East India, Devonshire, Sports and Public Schools; Cardiff and County (Cardiff).

**PROSSER, Gwynfor Mathews, (Gwyn);** *b* 27 April 1943; *s* of late Glyndwr Jenkin Prosser and of Edith Doreen Prosser; *m* 1972, Rodina Beaton MacLeod; one *s* two *d*. *Educ*: Dunvant Sch., Swansea; Swansea Secondary Tech. Sch. Nat. Dip. Mech. Engrg; First Cl. Cert. Steam and Motor Engrg; CEng, MIMarEST. Merchant Navy Engr Cadet, 1960–65; sea-going Marine Engr, 1965–72; shore-based Marine Engr, Greenock and Saudi Arabia, 1972–79; Chief Engr, Sealink, 1979–92; OPCS, 1992–96. MP (Lab) Dover, 1997–2010; contested (Lab) same seat, 2010. Mem., Select Cttee on Home Affairs, H of C, 2001–10. Chm., Associated Parly Ports and Merchant Navy Gp, 2002–10. Mem. (Lab), Kent CC, 1989–97 (Chm., Economic Develt Cttee, 1993–97). *Recreations*: hill walking, family outings, awaiting the revival of Welsh Rugby. *Club*: Marine Officers' (Dover).

**PROSSER, Sir Ian (Maurice Gray)**, Kt 1995; FCA; Chairman, InterContinental Hotels Group, 2003; Chairman and Chief Executive, 1987–2000, Executive Chairman, 2000–03, Bass PLC, later Six Continents PLC; *b* 5 July 1943; *s* of late Maurice and Freda Prosser; *m* 1st, 1964, Elizabeth Herman (marr. diss. 2003); two *d*; 2nd, 2003, Hilary Prewer. *Educ*: King Edward's School, Bath; Watford Grammar School; Birmingham Univ. (BComm). Coopers & Lybrand, 1964–69; Bass Charrington Ltd, later Bass PLC, subseq. Six Continents PLC, 1969–2003: Financial Dir, 1978–81, Vice Chm., 1982–87; Gp Man. Dir, 1984–87. Director: Boots Co., 1984–96; Lloyds TSB Gp (formerly Lloyds Bank), 1988–99; BP, 1997–2010 (Dep. Chm., 1999–2010); Glaxo SmithKline plc (formerly SmithKline Beecham PLC), 1999–2009; Hillshire Brands Co. (formerly Sara Lee Corp.), 2004–14; Chairman: NAAFI, 2008–; BP Pension Fund Trustees, 2010–; Aviva Staff Pension Fund, 2013–; GamCare, 2015–. Chm., Stock Exchange Listed Cos Adv. Cttee, 1992–98 (Mem., 1990–98). Chm., World Travel and Tourism Council, 2001–03. Chm., Brewers and Licensed Retailers Assoc. (formerly Brewers' Soc.), 1992–94 (Dir, 1983–2000). DUniv Birmingham, 2001. *Recreations*: theatre, music, bridge. *Clubs*: Home House; Leander; Phyllis Court.

**PROSSER, Prof. James Anthony William, (Tony),** FBA 2014; Professor of Public Law, University of Bristol, since 2002; *b* Ludlow, 3 May 1954; *s* of James Prosser and Flora Prosser; *m* 1998, Charlotte Villiers; one *s* one *d*. *Educ*: Ludlow Grammar Sch.; Univ. of Liverpool (LLB 1974). Res. Asst, Univ. of Southampton, 1974–76; Lectr in Law, Univ. of Hull, 1976–80; Lectr, 1980–89, Sen. Lectr, 1989–92, Univ. of Sheffield; John Millar Prof. of Law, Univ. of Glasgow, 1992–2002. Jean Monnet Fellow, European University Inst., Florence, 1987–88; Visiting Professor: Coll. of Europe, Bruges, 2009–; Univ. Paris-Dauphine, 2019. *Publications*: Nationalised Industries and Public Control, 1986; (with C. Graham) Privatizing Public Enterprises, 1991; Law and the Regulators, 1997; The Limits of Competition Law, 2005; The Regulatory Enterprise, 2010; The Economic Constitution, 2014. *Recreations*: hillwalking, cycling, travel, cinema, listening to modern jazz. *Address*: University of Bristol Law School, Wills Memorial Building, Queens Road, Bristol BS8 1RJ. *T*: (0117) 954 5302, *Fax*: (0117) 925 1870. *E*: t.prosser@bristol.ac.uk.

**PROSSER, Jeffrey;** Chairman, Queen Elizabeth Hospital King's Lynn (formerly King's Lynn and Wisbech Hospitals) NHS Trust, 2000–05; *b* 13 June 1942; *s* of Trevor and Beryl Prosser; *m* 1st, 1968, Margaret Sumpter (marr. diss. 1988); three *s*; 2nd, 1989, Sandra Walmsley. *Educ*: University Coll., Cardiff (Dip. Social Services); Leicester Univ. (Dip. Social Work); UEA (BA 2004; MA 2006). Social worker, Herts CC, 1968–72; Principal Social Worker, Northwick Park Hosp., 1972–74; Divl Manager, Cambs CC, 1974–79; Asst Dir, Haringey LBC, 1979–82; Area Dir, Devon CC, 1982–84; Dep. Dir of Social Services, Enfield LBC, 1984–86; Gen. Manager, Tower Hamlets HA, 1986–89; Dir of Community Care, Court Cavendish plc, 1989–92; Controller of Community Services, 1993–95, Dir of Community Services, 1995–99, Dir of Social Affairs, 1999, London Bor. of Barnet. Chm.,

Flagship Hsg Gp, 1999–2006; Vice Chm., Peddars Way Housing Assoc., 1998–99. Chm., Red2Green, 2004–07; Dir, impressionsprints ltd, 2007–10. Chm., Bd of Govs, Methvold High Sch., 2008–12. Mem., Weeting Parish Council, 2008– (Chm., 1999–2000). Trustee, AgeUK Norfolk, 2016– (Chm., 2018–). *Recreations*: gardening, cycling, photography, St Edmundsbury Male Voice Choir. *Address*: The Old Rectory, Rectory Lane, Weeting, Brandon, Suffolk IP27 0PX. *T*: (01842) 812672.

**PROSSER, His Honour John;** *see* Prosser, His Honour E. J.

**PROSSER, Kevin John;** QC 1996; tax barrister; a Recorder, 2000–15; a Deputy High Court Judge (Chancery Division), 2008–15; *b* 26 Aug. 1957; *s* of Sidney Ronald Prosser and Rita Lillian Prosser; *m* 1st, 1994, Mary Elizabeth Stokes (marr. diss. 2010); one *s* one *d*; 2nd, 2011, Rebecca Louise Murray. *Educ*: Broxbourne Sch.; UCL (LLB); St Edmund Hall, Oxford (BCL). Called to the Bar, Lincoln's Inn, 1982, Bencher, 2005; Asst Recorder, 2000; Hd of Chambers, 2015–. Chm., Revenue Bar Assoc., 2008–13. *Publications*: (with D. C. Potter) Tax Appeals, 1990. *Recreations*: opera, squash, reading. *Address*: 16 Bedford Row, WC1R 4EF. *T*: (020) 7414 8080. *Club*: Garrick.

**PROSSER, (Leslie) Charles,** DFA; Secretary, Royal Fine Art Commission for Scotland, 1976–2005; *b* 27 Oct. 1939; *s* of Dr Leslie John Prosser and Eleanor Alice May (*née* Chapman); *m* 1960, Coral Williams; one *s* two *d*. *Educ*: Sedbergh Sch.; Bath Acad. of Art, Corsham; Slade Sch. of Fine Art (DFA); Kungl. Akademien Konsthögskolan, Stockholm; Inst. of Educn, Leeds Univ. (DAEd). Asst Lectr in Fine Art, Blackpool Sch. of Art, 1962–64; Leverhulme European Arts Research Award, Stockholm, 1964–65; Lectr in Fine Art, Leeds Coll. of Art, later Jacob Kramer Coll. of Art, 1965–76; research in art educn, 1974–75. Ed., Royal Fine Art Commn for Scotland pubns, 1976–2005. Mem. UK Cttee, Hong Kong Architecture Exhibn, Edinburgh, 1996–97. Mem., Scotch Malt Whisky Soc., Leith, 1991–. FRSA 1997; Hon. FRIAS 1997; Hon. MRTPI 2002. *Publications*: contrib. to environmental design jls. *Recreations*: appreciating the art of planning our surroundings, unneeded walking, opining.

**PROSSER, Tony;** *see* Prosser, J. A. W.

**PROUD, Rt Rev. Andrew John;** Area Bishop of Reading, 2011–19; *b* 27 March 1954; *s* of late John Gascoigne Proud and of Joan Denise Proud; *m* 1977, Hon. (Fiona) Janice, PhD, *d* of 2nd Baron Brain; one *s* one *d*. *Educ*: King's Coll., London (BD 1979, AKC); Sch. of Oriental and African Studies, Univ. of London (MA 2001). Ordained deacon, 1980, priest, 1981; Asst Curate, Stansted Mountfitchet, 1980–83; Team Vicar, Borehamwood, 1983–90; Asst Priest, Bishop's Hatfield, 1990–92; Rector, E Barnet, 1992–2001; Chaplain, St Matthew's, Addis Ababa, 2002–07; Bishop's Asst for the Horn of Africa, 2004; Canon of Cairo, 2005; Area Bishop of Ethiopia and the Horn of Africa, 2007–11. *Recreations*: cooking, music, bird watching, reading, Ethiopia. *Address*: 21 Clarence Avenue, Northampton NN2 6NX.

**PROUDFOOT, Bruce;** *see* Proudfoot, V. B.

**PROUDFOOT, Prof. Nicholas Jarvis,** PhD; FRS 2005; Brownlee-Abraham Professor of Molecular Biology, University of Oxford, since 2003; Fellow of Brasenose College, Oxford, since 1982; *b* Chicago, 6 June 1951; *s* of Malcolm Jarvis Proudfoot and Mary Proudfoot (*née* MacDonald); *m* 1975, Anne Semple; two *s*. *Educ*: Bedford Coll., London (BSc Biochem. 1972); King's Coll., Cambridge (PhD Molecular Biol. 1975). MRC Laboratory of Molecular Biology, Cambridge: MRC Res. Student, 1972–75; Jun. Beit Meml Res. Fellow, 1975–78; MRC Scientific Staff, 1978–79; Jun. Res. Fellow, St John's Coll., Cambridge, 1976–79; Sen. Res. Fellow, CIT, 1979–80; Res. Associate, Harvard Univ., 1980–81; University of Oxford: Lectr in Chemical Pathology, Sir William Dunn Sch. of Pathology, 1981–96; Prof. of Experimental Pathology, 1996–2003; Tutor in Biochem., Brasenose Coll., 1982–2003. Mem. EMBO, 1982. Royal Soc./Wolfson Res. Merit Award, 2002–07. *Publications*: contrib. molecular biology/genetics jls. *Recreations*: amateur musician (horn player and baritone), walking, cycling. *E*: nicholas.proudfoot@path.ox.ac.uk.

**PROUDFOOT, Prof. (Vincent) Bruce,** OBE 1997; FSA 1963; FRSE 1979; FRGS; FRAI; Professor of Geography, University of St Andrews, 1974–93, Emeritus 1993; *b* 24 Sept. 1930; *s* of late Bruce Falconer Proudfoot; *m* 1961, Edwina Valmai Windram Field; two *s*. *Educ*: Royal Belfast Academical Instn; Queen's Univ., Belfast (BA, PhD). Research Officer, Nuffield Quaternary Research Unit, QUB, 1954–58; Lectr in Geography, QUB, 1958–59, Durham Univ., 1959–67; Tutor, 1960–63, Librarian, 1963–65, Hatfield Coll., Durham; Visiting Fellow, Univ. of Auckland, NZ, and Commonwealth Vis. Fellow, Australia, 1966; Associate Prof., 1967–70, Prof., 1970–74, Univ. of Alberta, Edmonton, Canada; Acting Chm., Dept of Geography, Univ. of Alberta, 1970–71; Co-ordinator, Socio-Economic Opportunity Studies, and Staff Consultant, Alberta Human Resources Research Council, 1971–72. Trustee, Nat. Mus. of Antiquities of Scotland, 1982–85. Chairman: Rural Geog. Study Gp, Inst. of British Geographers, 1980–84; Soc. for Landscape Studies, 1979–83. Royal Society of Edinburgh: Mem. Council, 1982–85 and 1990–91; Vice-Pres., 1985–88; Gen. Sec., 1991–96; Bicentenary Medal, 1997. Vice-Pres., Soc. of Antiquaries of Scotland, 1982–85; Pres., Section H (Anthrop. and Archaeol.), BAAS, 1985; Hon. Pres., Scottish Assoc. of Geography Teachers, 1982–84; Royal Scottish Geographical Society: Mem. Council, 1975–78, 1992–93; Chm. Council, 1993–99; Vice-Pres., 1993–; Hon. Editor, 1978–92; Fellow, 1991; Chm., Dundee Centre, 1993–99 (Mem., Cttee, 1976–93, 1999–2003); Treas., Scottish Church Heritage Research, 2010–. Lectures: Lister, BAAS, 1964; Annual, Soc. for Landscape Studies, 1983; Estyn Evans, QUB, 1985. FRSA. Hon. FRSGS 1991. *Publications*: The Downpatrick Gold Find, 1955; (with R. G. Ironside *et al*) Frontier Settlement Studies, 1974; (ed) Site, Environment and Economy, 1983; numerous papers in geographical, archaeological and soils jls. *Recreation*: gardening. *Address*: Westgate, Wardlaw Gardens, St Andrews, Scotland KY16 9DW. *T*: (01334) 473293. *Club*: Royal Scots (Edinburgh).

**PROUDMAN, (Antony) James;** Executive Director, UK Deposit Takers Supervision, Bank of England, since 2014; *b* Winchester, 13 Feb. 1967; *s* of Antony and Elizabeth Proudman; *m* 1992, Elizabeth Mills; one *s* one *d*. *Educ*: Winchester Coll.; Univ. of Bristol (BSc); London Sch. of Econs and Pol Sci. (MSc 1996). Bank of England: Internat. Div., 1988–91; Foreign Exchange Div., 1991–94; Monetary Analysis Directorate, 1996–2003; Private Sec. to Gov., 2003–06; Hd, Monetary Assessment and Strategy Div., 2006–11; Hd, MPC Secretariat, 2009–11; Hd, Sterling Mkts Div., 2011; on secondment with Lloyds Banking Gp, 2011–13; Hd, Strategic Plan Prog. Office, 2013–14. *Publications*: (ed with S. Redding) Openness and Growth, 1998; contrib. Philosophical Trans Royal Soc. *Recreations*: hiking, ski-ing, cricket, history. *Address*: Prudential Regulation Authority, Bank of England, 20 Moorgate, EC2R 6DA. *T*: (020) 3461 4167. *E*: James.Proudman@bankofengland.co.uk.

**PROUDMAN, Hon. Dame Sonia Rosemary Susan, (Hon. Dame Sonia Cartwright),** DBE 2008; a Judge of the High Court of Justice, Chancery Division, 2008–17; *b* 30 July 1949; *d* of late Kenneth Oliphant Proudman and Sati Proudman (*née* Hekimian); *m* 1987, Crispian Cartwright; one *d*. *Educ*: St Paul's Girls' Sch. (Foundn Schol.); Lady Margaret Hall, Oxford (Open Schol.; BA 1st Cl. Hons Jurisprudence 1971; MA 1973;

Hon. Fellow 2009). Called to the Bar, Lincoln's Inn, 1972 (Kennedy Schol., Buchanan Prize), Bencher, 1996; Oxford Univ. Eldon Law Schol., 1973; in practice at Chancery Bar, 1974–2008; QC 1994; Asst Recorder, 1996–2000; Recorder, 2000–08; Dep. High Court Judge, 2001–08. Mem., Panel of Chairmen, Competition Appeal Tribunal, 2008–17. Member: Oxford Law Faculty Adv. Bd, 2000; QC Selection Panel, 2005. *Recreation:* taking enormous notice of hats and backchat. *Clubs:* Hurlingham, CWIL.

**PROUT, David Michael,** CB 2018; PhD; Pro Vice-Chancellor (Planning and Resources), University of Oxford, since 2017; Fellow, Queen's College, Oxford, since 2018; *b* 14 March 1963; *s* of late Prof. Charles Keith Prout and of Lesley Craven Prout; *m* 1992, Penelope Sarah Gibbs; two *d. Educ:* Magdalen Coll. Sch., Oxford; Wadham Coll., Oxford (BA Hons (Mod. Hist.) 1985); Courtauld Inst. of Art, London (PhD 1991). Joined Civil Service, 1993; various posts, DoE, 1993–95; UK Perm. Repn to EU, 1995–98; Private Sec., 1999–2001, Principal Private Sec., 2001–04, to Dep. Prime Minister; Dir of Local Govt Policy, ODPM, subseq. DCLG, 2004–07; Exec. Dir, Planning and Bor. Develt, Royal Bor. of Kensington and Chelsea, 2007–09; Dir Gen., Localism (formerly Communities), DCLG, 2009–12; Dir Gen., High Speed Two, DfT, 2013–17. Non-exec. Dir, Radioactive Waste Mgt Ltd, 2018–. *Recreations:* cycling, tennis, cinema, family, travel. *Address:* University Offices, Wellington Square, Oxford OX1 2JD.

**PROVAN, James Lyal Clark;** politician, farmer, businessman; *b* 19 Dec. 1936; *s* of John Provan and Jean (*née* Clark); *m* 1960, Roweena Adele Lewis; twin *s* one *d. Educ:* Ardvreck Sch., Crieff; Oundle Sch., Northants; Royal Agricultural Coll., Cirencester. Member: Tayside Regional Council, 1978–82; Tay River Purification Bd, 1978–82. Chairman: McIntosh Donald Ltd, 1989–94; James McIntosh & Co., 1990–94. MEP (C): NE Scotland, 1979–89; S Downs W, 1994–99; SE Reg., England, 1999–2004; European Parliament: Quaestor, 1987–89; Cons. Chief Whip, 1994–96; Vice Pres. and Chief Whip, EPP, 1996–99; Vice Pres., 1999–2004; Member: Agriculture and Fisheries Cttee, 1979–89 (EDG spokesman on agricl and fisheries affairs, 1982–87); Environment, Consumer Affairs and Public Health Cttee, 1979–89; Chairman: Cross-Party Tourism Gp, 1996–2004; Conciliation Cttee to Council of Ministers, 1999–2004; Founder Chm., Internal Audit Cttee, 1992–94. Exec. Dir, Scottish Financial Enterprise, 1990–91; non-exec. Dir, CNH Global NV, 1999–2006 (Director: New Holland Holdings NV, 1995–99; New Holland NV, 1996–99). Mem. Bd, Rowett Res. Inst., 1990–2004 (Chm., 1992–98); Mem., AFRC, 1990–94. Area President, Scottish NFU, 1965 and 1971; Treasurer, Perth and E Perthshire Conservative Assoc., 1975–77; Member, Lord Lieutenant's Queen's Jubilee Appeal Cttee, 1977. FRAgS 2000. FRSA 1987. *Publications:* The European Community: an ever closer union?, 1989; Europe's Freedom to Farm, 1996, 1998; Europe's Fishing Blues, 1997. *Recreations:* country pursuits, sailing, flying, musical appreciation, travel. *Address:* Summerfield, Glenfarg, Perth PH2 9QD. *Clubs:* Farmers; Royal Perth Golfing Society.

**PROVAN, Marie;** *see* Staunton, M.

**PROVERA, Marco T.;** *see* Tronchetti Provera.

**PROWSE, Most Rev. Christopher Charles;** *see* Canberra and Goulburn, Archbishop of, (R.C).

**PROWSE, Philip (John);** theatre director and designer; Professor of Theatre Design, Slade School of Fine Art, University College London, 1999–2003 (Head of Theatre Design Department, 1995–2003), now Professor Emeritus; *b* 29 Dec. 1937; *s* of late Alan William Auger Prowse and Violet Beatrice (*née* Williamson). *Educ:* King's Sch., Worcester; Malvern Coll. of Art; Slade Sch. of Fine Art. Professional début: Diversions for Royal Ballet, Royal Opera House, 1961; subsequent prodns and designs for opera, ballet and drama including: Glasgow Citizens' Theatre; rep. theatres; West End theatres; Royal Nat. Theatre; RSC, Barbican; Old Vic Theatre; Royal Opera; Royal Ballet; ENO; Sadler's Wells Royal Ballet; Birmingham Royal Ballet; WNO; Scottish Opera; Opera North; English Nat. Ballet (Festival Ballet); Scottish Ballet; Chichester Fest. Theatre; prodns in Europe and US; festival appearances: Rome, Wiesbaden, Holland, Warsaw, Zurich, Belgrade, Edinburgh, Cologne, Hamburg, Venice, Parma, E Berlin, Halle, Caracas. Co-Dir, Glasgow Citizens' Theatre, 1970–2004. *Address:* c/o Cruickshank Cazenove, 97 Old South Lambeth Road, SW8 1XU.

**PRUCE, Daniel Robert;** HM Diplomatic Service; Ambassador to the Philippines, since 2017; *b* London, 24 July 1966; *s* of Stanley Pruce and Lilian Pruce; *m* 2015, Rachael Morgan. *Educ:* Univ. of Hull (BA French and Eng. 1989). Joined FCO, 1990; UK Perm. Repn to EU, 1993–97; FCO, 1997–99; UK Perm. Repn to EU, 2000–02; on secondment to Prime Minister's Press Office, 10 Downing Street, 2002–04; Dir, Organisation Proj., FCO, 2004–05; Hd, Economic and Central Europe Gp, FCO, 2006–08; Deputy Head of Mission: Bangkok, 2008–12; Madrid, 2012–16. *Address:* c/o Foreign and Commonwealth Office, King Charles Street, SW1A 2AH.

**PRUSINER, Prof. Stanley Ben,** MD; Professor of Neurology, since 1984, Professor of Biochemistry, since 1988 and Director, Institute for Neurodegenerative Diseases, since 1999, University of California, San Francisco; *b* 28 May 1942; *s* of Lawrence Albert Prusiner and Miriam Prusiner (*née* Spigel); two *d. Educ:* Univ. of Pennsylvania (AB 1964; MD 1968). University of California, San Francisco: Med. Intern, 1968–69; Resident in Neurology, 1972–74; Asst Prof. of Neurology, 1974–80; Associate Prof., 1980–84; Prof., 1984–; Prof. of Virology, Univ. of Calif, Berkeley, 1984–. FAAAS 1998. Foreign Mem., Royal Soc., 1997. Max Planck Res. Award, Alexander von Humboldt Foundn and Max Planck Soc., 1992; Gairdner Foundn Award, 1994; Wolf Prize for Medicine, 1996; Nobel Prize in Physiology or Medicine, 1997. *Publications:* (ed) The Enzymes of Glutamine Metabolism, 1973; Slow Transmissible Diseases of the Nervous System, 2 vols, 1979; Prions, 1987; Prion Diseases of Humans and Animals, 1992; Molecular and Genetic Basis of Neurologic Disease, 1993, 3rd edn 2003; Prions, Prions, Prions, 1996, 2nd edn as Prion Biology and Diseases, 2004; more than 300 articles in learned jls. *Address:* University of California, 675 Nelson Rising Lane, San Francisco, CA 94158, USA.

**PRYCE, (George) Terry,** CBE 1994; Chairman, G. T. Pryce (Farms) Ltd, since 1996; *b* 26 March 1934; *s* of Edwin Pryce and Hilda Florence (*née* Price); *m* 1957, Thurza Elizabeth Tatham, JP; two *s* one *d. Educ:* Welshpool Grammar Sch.; National Coll. of Food Technol. MFC, FIFST. Dir, various food cos in THF Gp, 1965–70; Asst Man. Dir, Dalgety (UK) Ltd, 1970–72; Man. Dir, Dalgety (UK) and Dir, DPLC, 1972–78; Man. Dir, 1978–81, Chief Exec., 1981–89, Dalgety PLC. Chairman: Solway Foods Ltd, 1990–94; York House Group Ltd, 1996–2003; Jas Bowman and Sons Ltd, 1999–2015 (Dir, 1991–); Dir, H. P. Bulmer Holdings PLC, 1984–94. Chm., British Soc. for Horticultural Res., later Horticulture Res. Internat., 1990–97; Council Member: AFRC, 1986–94; UK Food and Drink Fedn, 1987–89; Mem. Adv. Bd, Inst. of Food Res., 1988–94. Chm., UK Food Assoc., 1994–98. CCMI. *Recreation:* sport. *Address:* 89 Brookmans Avenue, Brookmans Park, Hatfield, Herts AL9 7QG. *T:* (01707) 642039. *Clubs:* Athenæum, MCC.
*See also* S. C. C. Pryce, T. J. R. Pryce.

**PRYCE, Jonathan,** CBE 2009; actor; *b* 1 June 1947; *m* 2014, Kate Fahy; two *s* one *d. Educ:* RADA. FRWCMD (FWCMD 1995). Patron: Friendship Works (formerly Friends United Network), 1992–; Facial Surgery Res. Foundn, Saving Faces, 2001–. *Theatre includes:* Comedians, Nottingham Playhouse, Old Vic, 1975, NY 1976 (Tony Award); title rôle, Hamlet, Royal Court, 1980 (Olivier Award); The Caretaker, Nat. Th., 1981; Accidental Death of an Anarchist, Broadway, 1984; The Seagull, Queen's, 1985; title rôle, Macbeth, RSC, 1986; Uncle Vanya, Vaudeville, 1988; Miss Saigon, Drury Lane, 1989 (Olivier Award and Variety Club Award), NY, 1991 (Tony Award for Best Actor in Musical, 1991); Oliver!, Palladium, 1994; My Fair Lady, RNT, transf. Theatre Royal, Drury Lane, 2001, Kennedy Centre, Washington, 2013; The Reckoning, Soho Th., 2003; The Goat, or Who is Sylvia, Almeida, 2004, transf. Apollo, 2004; Dirty Rotten Scoundrels, NY, 2006; Glengarry Glen Ross, Apollo, 2007; Dimetos, Donmar, The Caretaker, Liverpool Everyman, 2009, transf. Trafalgar Studios, 2010, world tour, 2012; King Lear, Almeida, 2012; The Merchant of Venice, Shakespeare's Globe, 2015, world tour, 2016; The Height of the Storm, West End and tour, 2018, transf. NY, 2019; *television includes:* Roger Doesn't Live Here Anymore (series), 1981; Timon of Athens, 1981; Martin Luther, 1983; Praying Mantis, 1983; Whose Line Is It Anyway?, 1988; The Man from the Pru, 1990; Selling Hitler, 1991; Mr Wroe's Virgins, 1993; Thicker Than Water, 1993; David, 1997; HR, 2007; The Baker Street Irregulars, 2007; My Zinc Bed, 2008; Clone, 2008; Cranford, 2009; Wolf Hall, 2015; Game of Thrones, 2015–16; To Walk Invisible: the Brontë sisters, 2016; Aberfan: The Green Hollow, 2016; Taboo, 2017; To Provide All People, 2018; *films include:* Something wicked this way comes, 1982; The Ploughman's Lunch, 1983; Brazil, 1985; The Doctor and the Devils, 1986; Haunted Honeymoon, 1986; Jumpin' Jack Flash, 1987; Consuming Passions, 1988; The Adventures of Baron Munchausen, 1988; The Rachel Papers, 1989; Glengarry Glen Ross, 1992; The Age of Innocence, 1992; Barbarians at the Gate, 1992; Great Moments in Aviation, 1993; A Business Affair, 1993; Shopping, 1994; Carrington, 1995 (Best Actor Award: Cannes, 1995; Evening Standard, 1996); Evita, 1996; Regeneration, 1997; Tomorrow Never Dies, 1997; Ronin, 1998; Stigmata, 1999; Very Annie Mary, 2001; Bride of the Wind, 2001; The Affair of the Necklace, 2002; Unconditional Love, 2002; Pirates of the Caribbean: The Curse of the Black Pearl, 2003; What a Girl Wants, 2003; De-Lovely, 2004; The Brothers Grimm, 2005; Pirates of the Caribbean: Dead Man's Chest, 2006; Pirates of the Caribbean: At World's End, 2007; Leatherheads, 2007; Bedtime Stories, 2008; GI Joe: The Rise of the Cobra, 2009; Hysteria, Borgriki, 2011; Dark Blood, 2012; GI Joe: Retaliation, 2013; Listen Up Philip, 2014; Under Milk Wood, 2014; The Salvation, 2014; Woman in Gold, 2015; Narcopolis, 2015; The White King, 2016; Dough, 2017; The Man Who Invented Christmas, 2017; The Wife, 2018; *recordings include:* Miss Saigon; Nine—the Concert; Under Milk Wood; Cabaret; Oliver!; Evita; Hey Mr Producer; My Fair Lady. Hon. Patron, Northern Lights Symphony Orchestra, 2010–. Hon. DLitt Liverpool, 2006. Special BAFTA Cymru, 2001; Cymru for the World Award, 2009. *Address:* c/o Julian Belfrage Associates, 3rd Floor, 9 Argyll Street, W1F 7TG.

**PRYCE, Rev. Canon Mark;** *see* Pryce, Rev. Canon R. M.

**PRYCE, Nancy Margaret;** *see* Edwards, N. M.

**PRYCE, Rev. Canon Dr (Robin) Mark;** Director of Ministry, Diocese of Birmingham, since 2017; a Chaplain to the Queen, since 2017; *b* Shrewsbury, 6 Sept. 1960; *s* of late George William Bryan Pryce and of Hazel Annie Pryce (*née* Richards). *Educ:* High Sch. for Boys, Oswestry; Univ. of Sussex (BA Hons 1982); Westcott House, Cambridge (CTh); Corpus Christi Coll., Cambridge (MA 1994); University of Birmingham (DPTh 2015). Ordained deacon, 1987, priest, 1988; Asst Curate, All Saints, West Bromwich, 1987–90; Fellow and Chaplain, 1990–2002, Tutor, 1992–2002, Dean of Chapel, 1996–2002, Corpus Christi Coll., Cambridge; Vicar, Old Church, Smethwick, 2002–06; Bishop's Advr for Clergy Continuing Ministerial Educn, Dio. of Birmingham, 2006–17. Part-time Chaplain, Sandwell District Gen. Hosp., 1990; County Chaplain, St John Ambulance, W Midlands, 2008–. Hon. Canon, Birmingham Cathedral, 2014–. Vis. Scholar, Sarum Coll., Salisbury, 2016–; Hon. Res. Fellow, Queen's Foundn Birmingham, 2017–. Chair of Trustees, Dorothy Parkes Healthy-Living Centre Ltd, 2002; Trustee, St Peter Saltley Trust, 2018–. FRSA. OStJ 2015. *Publications:* Finding a Voice: men, women and the community of the church, 1996; Literary Companion to the Lectionary, 2001; Literary Companion for Festivals, 2003; (jtly) Journeying with Mark, 2011, 2nd edn 2017; (jtly) Journeying with Luke, 2012; (jtly) Journeying with Matthew, 2013; (jtly) Journeying with John, 2014, 2nd edn 2016; (jtly) Making Nothing Happen: five poets explore faith and spirituality, 2014; Poetry, Practical Theology and Reflective Practice, 2019. *Recreations:* poetry, contemporary art, cooking, swimming, walking. *Address:* Church of England Birmingham, 1 Colmore Row, Birmingham B3 2BJ. *T:* (0121) 426 0430. *E:* markp@cofebirmingham.com.

**PRYCE, Prof. Roy;** Director, 1973–78, Senior Advisor for Direct Elections, 1978–79, Chief Advisor, 1979–81, Directorate General for Information, Commission of the European Communities; *b* 4 Oct. 1928; *s* of Thomas and Madeline Pryce; *m* 1954, Sheila Rose, *d* of Rt Hon. James Griffiths, CH; three *d. Educ:* Grammar Sch., Burton-on-Trent; Emmanuel Coll., Cambridge (MA, PhD). MA Oxon. Research Fellow: Emmanuel Coll., Cambridge, 1953–55; St Antony's Coll., Oxford, 1955–57; Head of London Information Office of High Authority of European Coal and Steel Community, 1957–60; Head of London Inf. Office, Jt Inf. Service of European Communities, 1960–64; Rockefeller Foundn Res. Fellow, 1964–65; Dir, Centre for Contemp. European Studies, Univ. of Sussex, 1965–73. Dir, 1983–90, Sen. Res. Fellow, 1990–99, Federal Trust for Educn and Res. Vis. Professorial Fellow, Centre for Contemporary European Studies, Univ. of Sussex, 1973–81; Visiting Professor: Coll. of Europe, Bruges, 1965–72; Eur. Univ. Inst., Florence, 1981–83; Eur. Inst. for Public Admin, Maastricht, 1983–88. *Publications:* The Italian Local Elections 1956, 1957; The Political Future of the European Community, 1962; (with John Pinder) Europe After de Gaulle, 1969, German and Ital. edns 1970; The Politics of the European Community, 1973; (ed) The Dynamics of European Union, 1987; (ed jtly) Maastricht and Beyond, 1994; Heathfield Park: a private estate and a Wealden town, 1996; Heathfield and Waldron: an illustrated history, 2000; Rotherfield Hall, 2002; Battle Abbey and the Websters, 2005; (jtly) Old Heathfield and Cade Street in the 19th Century, 2008. *Recreations:* gardening, local history.

**PRYCE, Simon Charles Conrad;** Chief Executive, Ultra Electronics, since 2018; *b* 8 Dec. 1961; *s* of (George) Terry Pryce, *qv* and Thurza Elizabeth Pryce (*née* Tatham); *m* 1997, Katharine Mary Childs; two *d. Educ:* Haberdashers' Aske's Sch., Elstree; Reading Univ. (BSc Food Scis). Chartered Accountant. Dir, Lazard, 1987–96; Sen. Vice Pres., JPMorgan, 1996–97; GKN plc: Dir, Corporate Finance, 1997–2001; Chief Financial Officer, Automotive, 2001–04; Chief Exec., Diversified Businesses Gp, 2004–07; Chief Exec., BBA Aviation plc, 2007–17. Non-exec. Dir, Electro Components plc, 2016–. Director: SMMT, 2005–07; General Aviation Manufacturers Assoc., 2010–. Mem. Council, Reading Univ., 2013– (Member: Investment Cttee, 2013–; Strategy and Finance Cttee, 2016–). MCSI (MSI 1997). FRAeS 2010. *Recreations:* sports, travel, performing arts, reading. *Clubs:* Athenaeum, Soho House, 5 Hertford Street, MCC.
*See also* T. J. R. Pryce.

**PRYCE, Terry;** *see* Pryce, G. T.

**PRYCE, Tim John Robert;** Managing Director, Terra Firma Capital Partners, 2016–19 (Chief Executive Officer, 2009–16); non-executive Director, Terra Firma Holdings Ltd, 2017–19; *b* Cleethorpes, 1 July 1965; *s* of (George) Terry Pryce, *qv*; civil partnership 2007, Jonathan Kemp. *Educ:* King's Coll. London and Pantheon Sorbonne, Paris (LLB English

Law 1988; Maîtrise French Law 1988; AKC 1988). Admitted as solicitor, 1991. Solicitor, Slaughter and May, 1989–96; General Counsel: GE Capital AFS Europe, 1996–98; Transamerica TDF Europe, 1998–2000; Team Hd, Nomura TMD-PFG, 2000–02; Gen. Counsel, Terra Firma Capital Partners, 2002–09. *Recreations:* theatre, ballet, opera, travel.
*See also S. C. C. Pryce.*

**PRYCE, Vicky;** Chief Economic Adviser, since 2014, and Member of Board, since 2016, Centre for Economics and Business Research; *b* Athens; *d* of late Nicolas Courmouzis and Voula Courmouzis; *m* 1st, 1972, G. Pryce (marr. diss. 1981); two *d*; 2nd, 1984, Christopher Murray Paul Huhne (*see* Rt Hon. C. M. P. Huhne) (marr. diss. 2011); two *s* one *d*. *Educ:* London Sch. of Econs and Pol Sci. (BSc Econs, MSc Monetary Econs). Economist, then Chief Economist, Williams & Glyn's Bank, 1973–83; Corporate Economist, Esso Europe, 1983–86; Chief Economist, then Partner, KPMG, 1986–2001; Chm., Good Corp., 2001–02; Partner, London Economics, 2001–02; Chief Economic Advr and Dir Gen., Econs, DTI, then BERR, later BIS, 2002–10; Dep. Hd, 2004–07, Jt Hd, 2007–10, Govt Economic Service; Sen. Man. Dir, FTI Consulting, 2010–13. Hon. Vis. Prof., Cass Business Sch., City Univ., 2002–06, 2008–11; Vis. Fellow, Nuffield Coll., Oxford, 2008–13; Adjunct Prof., Imperial Coll. Business Sch., Imperial Coll. London, 2010–13; Visiting Professor: Sch. of Econs and Finance, QMUL, 2011–13; Birmingham City Univ., 2014–; Aston Univ., 2015–; Hon. Prof., Guildhall Faculty of Business and Law, London Metropolitan Univ., 2014–17; Sen. Hon. Fellow and Mem. Court, Regent's Univ., 2018–. Mem. Internat. Adv. Bd, British Amer. Business Inc., 2003–13. Member: Standing Adv. Gp to Financial Reporting Rev. Panel, Financial Reporting Council, 2006–12; Exec. Cttee, 2010–12, Council, 2010–18, IFS; Panel on Monitoring the Economy, BIS, 2010–15; Adv. Bd, OMFIF, 2013–; Econ. Adv. Gp, British Chambers of Commerce, 2014–; non-exec. Mem. Cttee, NESTA, 2011–13. Fellow, Soc. of Professional Economists (formerly Soc. of Business Economists), 2005–. Mem. Court, Co. of Mgt Consultants, 2001–16 (Master, 2010–11); Companion, British Acad. of Mgt, 2018–. Member: Council, REconS, 2002–07; Council, Univ. of Kent, 2005–11; Adv. Bd, Centre for Internat. Business and Mgt, Brunel Univ., 2015– (Judge Inst., Cambridge, 1999–2013; Univ. of Bath Business Sch., 2013–15); Res. Adv. Bd, ABI, 2006–11; Council, AcSS, 2018–. Bd of Trustees: RSA, 2006–08; Centre for Economic Policy Res., 2010–13; Court, LSE, 2011–13; Sen. Common Room, St Anthony's Coll., Oxford, 2016–17. Member: Internat. Women's Forum, 2017–; London Chapter, Women Corporate Dirs Foundn, 2017–. Patron: Pro-Bono Economics, 2011–; Working Chance, 2014–. FAcSS (AcSS 2011). *Publications:* (ed jtly) Green Business, Green Values and Sustainability, 2011; Prisonomics: behind bars in Britain's failing prisons, 2013; Greekonomics: the Euro crisis and why politicians don't get it, 2013; (jtly) It's the Economy, Stupid, 2015; Why Women Need Quotas, 2015; (jtly) Redesigning Manufacturing, 2015. *Recreations:* theatre, cinema, Chelsea football supporter. *Clubs:* Reform, Groucho.

**PRYDE, Roderick Stokes,** OBE 1999; Director, Spain, British Council, 2009–15; Director, Roderick Pryde Consulting Ltd, since 2015; *b* 26 Jan. 1953; *s* of William Gerard Pryde and Patricia Mary Pryde; *m* 1989, Susanne Mona Graham Hamilton; one *s* three *d*. *Educ:* George Watson's Coll., Edinburgh; Univ. of Sussex (BA Hons); UCNW, Bangor (PGCE, TESL). Lectr, Univ. of Dijon, 1975–76; English Teaching Co-ordinator, Cie Française des Pneumatiques, Michelin, 1979–81; British Council, 1981–2015: Asst Regl Lang. Officer, London, 1981–83; Dir of Studies, Milan, 1983–87; Regional Director: Andalucia, 1987–88; Bilbao, 1988–89; Director: Kyoto and Western Japan, 1990–94; English Lang. Centre, Hong Kong, 1994–98; Portugal, 1998–2000; Dir, Educnl Enterprises, 2000–02; Asst Dir-Gen., 2002–05; Regl Dir, India and Sri Lanka, 2005–09. Mem. Bd, Wigtown Fest. Co., 2016–17. Prog. Advr, Edinburgh Internat. Culture Summit, 2016–. Mem., Friends Cttee, Ditchling Mus. of Art + Craft, 2018–. *Recreations:* walking, family, reading. *Address:* 1 Blackbrook Farm Cottages, Spatham Lane, Ditchling, E Sussex BN6 8XJ. *E:* rspryde@icloud.com.

**PRYKE, Sir Christopher Dudley,** 4th Bt *cr* 1926, of Wanstead, co. Essex; *b* 17 April 1946; *s* of William Dudley Pryke and Lucy Irene Pryke (*née* Madgett); *S* uncle, 1998; *m* 1st, 1973, Angela Gay Meek (marr. diss. 1986); one *s*; 2nd, 1999, Marilyn Wright, *d* of late Gerald William Henry Williamson. *Educ:* Hurstpierpoint. MRICS. *Heir: s* James Dudley Pryke [*b* 29 Dec. 1977; *m* 2013, Gemma Claire, *d* of Christopher Alan Mills; one *s* one *d*]. *Address:* 43 Bramble Rise, Cobham, Surrey KT11 2HP.

**PRYKE, Paula Shane, (Mrs P. Romaniuk),** OBE 2014; floral artist, interior and garden designer and author; *b* 29 April 1960; *d* of Ralph and Gladys Pryke; *m* 1987, Peter Romaniuk. *Educ:* Culford Sch.; Univ. of Leeds (BEd Hons Hist.). LRAM (Speech and Drama) 1985. Founder, Paula Pryke Flowers, London, 1998. Lectr and demonstrator on floral art around the world. Ambassador for Floral Industry Award, NFU, 2000. *Publications:* The New Floral Artist, 1993; Flower Innovations, 1995; Flower Celebrations, 1995; Simple Flowers, 1999; Candles, 1999; Wreaths and Garlands, 1999; Living Colour, 2001; Wedding Flowers, 2004; Classic Paula Pryke, 2004; The Flower School, 2006; Table Flowers, 2007; Seasonal Wreaths and Bouquets, 2008; Simply Pink, 2009; The Ultimate Floral Collection, 2010; Paula Pryke Wedding Flowers, 2015; Floristry, 2017. *Recreations:* gardening, cooking, the arts. *Address:* The Old Post Office, Dalham, Suffolk CB8 8TG. *T:* 07802 784166. *E:* paula@paulapryke.com.

**PRYKE, Roy Thomas;** Director of the Virtual Staff College, University of Exeter, 2000–06; *b* 30 Nov. 1940; *s* of Thomas George and Nellie Matilda Pryke; *m* 1962, Susan Pauline Andrew; one *s* three *d*. *Educ:* Univ. of Wales (BA Hons); Univ. of Manchester (PGCE). Teacher, Manchester, 1963–71; Education Officer, Devon, 1971–79; Deputy Chief Education Officer: Somerset, 1980–82; Devon, 1983–87; Dep. Chief Educn Officer and Head of Operations, Cambridgeshire, 1987–89; Dir, Educn Services, Kent CC, 1989–98. Adviser to: Council of Local Educn Authorities, 1992–98; ACC, 1994–97; LGA, 1997–98; Chm., Assoc. of Chief Educn Officers, 1996–97. Chm., DFEE Adv. Gp, Schs Improvement Internat., 1999–2002; Mem., President of Zimbabwe's Commn on Educn and Trng, 1998–99. Chm., Rolle Exmouth Ltd, 2010–14 (Vice Chm., 2014–17). Vis. Prof. of Educn, 1998–2000, Hon. Fellow, 2006, Univ. of Exeter. Chairman: Exmouth Community Assoc., 2007–18; Steering Gp, Exmouth Neighbourhood Plan, 2015–19. FRSA 1988; Hon. FCP 1991. Chevalier, Ordre des Palmes Académiques (France), 1994. *Publications:* contributor to: Open Plan Schools, 1978; The Head's Legal Guide, 1984; The Revolution in Education and Training, 1986; articles in Education Jl on curriculum and on education management. *Recreations:* foreign travel and languages, sailing, golf. *Address:* 1 West Checkstone, 2 Douglas Avenue, Exmouth, Devon EX8 2AU. *T:* (01395) 277173.

**PRYN, Maj.-Gen. William John,** OBE 1973; MB, BS; FRCS, FRCSEd; Director of Army Surgery, and Consulting Surgeon to the Army, 1985–88, retired; *b* 25 Jan. 1928; *s* of late Col Richard Harold Cotter Pryn, FRCS, late RAMC and Una St George Ormsby (*née* Roe); *m* 1st, 1952, Alison Lynette (marr. diss.), 2nd *d* of Captain Norman Arthur Cyril Hardy, RN; two *s* one *d*; 2nd, 1982, June de Medina (*d* 2017), *d* of Surg. Comdr Norman Bernard de Medina Greenstreet, RN; one step *s* one step *d*. *Educ:* Malvern Coll.; Guy's Hosp. Med. Sch., London Univ. (MB, BS 1951). MRCS, LRCP 1951; FRCS 1958; FRCSEd 1984. Trooper, 21st SAS Regt (Artists Rifles), TA, 1948–50. House appts, Gen. Hosp., Ramsgate and Royal Berks Hosp., Reading, 1951–52; commnd into RAMC, 1952; Regtl MO to No 9 Training Regt RE, 1952–53; surg. appts in mil. hosps in UK, Cyprus and N Africa, 1953–58; seconded as Surg. Registrar, Royal Postgrad. Med. Sch., Hammersmith Hosp., 1958–59; Officer i/c Surg. Div. and Consultant Surgeon to mil. hosps, Malaya, Singapore, N Borneo and UK, 1959–69; CO BMH Dhekelia, 1969–72; Sen. Consultant Surgeon in mil. hosps, UK and NI, 1972–77; Consulting Surgeon to BAOR, 1977–82; Consultant in Surgery to Royal Hosp., Chelsea, 1982–86; Hon. Consultant to S Dist, Kensington and Chelsea and Westminster AHA (T), 1981. Member: EUROMED Gp on Emergency Medicine, 1980–86; Specialty Bd in Surgery, and Reg. Trng Cttee in Gen. Surgery, Defence Medical Services, 1982–86; Med. Cttee, Defence Scientific Adv. Council, 1982–86; BMA, 1950–; Wessex Surgeons Club, 1976–. Member Council: RAMC, 1982–86; Mil. Surgical Soc., 1982–. Fellow, Assoc. of Surgeons of GB and Ireland, 1960 (Mem., Educn Adv. Cttee, 1982–86). QHS 1981–86. OStJ 1984. Mem., Editorial Bd, Injury, 1982–86. *Publications:* (contrib). Field Surgery Pocket Book, 1981; original articles in the Lancet and British Jl of Surgery. *Recreations:* fishing, shooting and other country pursuits, golf, tennis, sailing, gardening, joinery, house maintenance.

**PRYNNE, Andrew Geoffrey Lockyer;** QC 1995; *b* 28 May 1953; *s* of late Maj.-Gen. Michael Whitworth Prynne, CB, CBE and Jean Violet Prynne; *m* 1977, Catriona Mary Brougham; three *d*. *Educ:* Marlborough Coll.; Univ. of Southampton (LLB Hons). Called to the Bar, Middle Temple, 1975. Mem., Lord Chancellor's Multi-Party Actions Wkg Gp, 1997–2000. Asst Boundary Comr, 2000–05. CEDR Accredited Mediator, 2000. *Recreations:* sailing, shooting, theatre, music, ballet. *Address:* Temple Garden Chambers, 1 Harcourt Buildings, Temple, EC4Y 9DA. *T:* (020) 7583 1315. *Clubs:* Royal Yacht Squadron, Royal Solent Yacht, Royal Southampton Yacht; Bar Yacht.

**PRYOR, Arthur John,** CB 1997; PhD; competition consultant, since 1996; Head, Competition Policy Division, Department of Trade and Industry, 1993–96; *b* 7 March 1939; *s* of late Quinton Arthur Pryor, FRICS and Elsie Margaret (*née* Luscombe); *m* 1964, Marilyn Kay Petley; one *s* one *d*. *Educ:* Harrow County Grammar Sch.; Downing Coll., Cambridge (MA; PhD). Asst Lectr, then Lectr, in Spanish and Portuguese, UC Cardiff, 1963–66; Asst Principal, BoT and ECGD, 1966–69; Principal, DTI, 1970–73; First Sec., British Embassy, Washington, 1973–75; Principal, Dept of Trade, 1975–77; Assistant Secretary: Shipping Policy Div., Dept of Trade, 1977–80; Air Div., DoI, 1980–83; Department of Trade and Industry: Asst Sec., Internat. Trade Policy Div., 1984–85; Under Sec. and Regional Dir, W Midlands Region, 1985–88; Dir Gen., BNSC, 1988–93. Mem., Competition (formerly Monopolies and Mergers) Commn, 1998–2003; Competition Commn Appeal Panel, subseq. Competition Appeal Tribunal, 2000–11. *Publications:* contribs to modern lang., space and competition jls. *Recreations:* tennis, golf, book collecting. *Address:* c/o Competition Appeal Tribunal, Victoria House, Bloomsbury Place, WC1A 2EB. *T:* (020) 7979 7979.

**PRYOR, Dr Francis Manning Marlborough,** MBE 1999; archaeologist; Director of Archaeology, Flag Fen Bronze Age Centre, Peterborough, since 1987; *b* 13 Jan. 1945; *s* of late Robert Matthew Marlborough Pryor, MBE and Barbara Helen Pryor (*née* Robertson); *m* 1st, 1969, Sylvia Jean Page (marr. diss. 1977); one *d*; 2nd, 1988, Maisie Taylor. *Educ:* Eton; Trinity Coll., Cambridge (MA Archaeol. and Anthropol.; PhD 1985). Asst Curator, Royal Ontario Mus., Toronto, 1969–78; Welland Valley Field Officer, Cambs CC, 1978–82; Dir, Etton and Flag Fen Excavations, 1982–87. Vis. Prof. of Archaeol., Leicester Univ., 2007–. Pres., Council for British Archaeol., 1998–2005. Presenter, TV series: Britain BC, 2003; Britain AD, 2004. *Publications:* Excavations at Fengate, Peterborough, 4 vols, 1974–1984; Flag Fen, 1992; Prehistoric Farmers, 1998; Excavations at Etton, 1998; Sea Henge, 2001; The Flag Fen Basin, 2001; Britain BC, 2003; Britain AD, 2004; Britain in the Middle Ages, 2006; The Making of the British Landscape, 2010; The Birth of Modern Britain: a journey into Britain's archaeological past: 1550 to the present, 2011; The Lifers' Club (novel), 2014; Home: a time traveller's tales from Britain's prehistory, 2014; Stonehenge: the story of a sacred landscape, 2016; The Way, The Truth and The Dead (novel), 2017; Paths to the Past: encounters with Britain's hidden landscapes, 2018. *Recreations:* gardening, eating my own vegetables (it's about ingredients, not sauces). *Address:* Flag Fen Bronze Age Centre, The Droveway, Northey Road, Peterborough PE6 7QF. *T:* (01733) 313414, *Fax:* (01733) 349957.

**PRYOR, John Pembro,** MS; FRCS; consultant uroandrologist, retired; *b* 25 Aug. 1937; *s* of William Benjamin Pryor and Kathleen Pryor; *m* 1959, Marion Hopkins; four *s*. *Educ:* Reading Sch.; King's Coll. and King's Coll. Hosp. Med. Sch. (MB, BS). AKC 1961; FRCS 1967; MS London 1971. Training appointments: Doncaster Royal Infirm., 1965–66; Univ. of Calif, San Francisco, 1968–69; KCH and St Paul's Hosp., 1971–72; Consultant Urol Surgeon to KCH and St Peter's Hosp., 1975–94; Dean, Inst. of Urology, London Univ., 1978–85; Reader, Inst. of Urology, UCL and Hon. Cons. Urol Surgeon, St Peter's Hosp., 1994–99. Hunterian Prof., RCS, 1971 and 1995. Chairman: (first), British Andrology Soc., 1979–84; European Assoc. of Genital Microsurgeons, 1992–95; Impotence Assoc., 1999–2001; Eur. Sexual Alliance, 1999–2004; Trustees, Eur. Acad. for Sexual Medicine, 2004–07; Pres., Eur. Soc. for Impotence Research, 1999–2001. Treas., British Jl of Urology, 1991–99. St Peter's Medal, British Assoc. of Urol Surgeons, 1995. *Publications:* (ed jtly) Andrology, 1987; (ed) Urological prostheses, appliances and catheters, 1992; (jtly) Impotence: an integrated approach to clinical practice, 1992; articles on urology and andrology in scientific jls. *Address:* The Beacon, Channel Way, Fairlight, E Sussex TN35 4BP. *T:* (01424) 814949.

**PRYOR, His Honour Robert Charles;** QC 1983; a Circuit Judge, 1991–2004; *b* 10 Dec. 1938; *s* of Charles Selwyn Pryor and Olive Woodall Pryor; *m* 1969, Virginia Sykes; one *s* one *d*. *Educ:* Eton; Trinity Coll., Cambridge (BA). National Service, KRRC, 2nd Lieut 1958. Called to the Bar, Inner Temple, 1963; a Recorder, 1989–91. Director, Sun Life Corp. (formerly Sun Life Assurance) plc, 1977–91.
*See also Viscount Hampden.*

**PRYS-ROBERTS, Prof. Cedric,** DM; FRCA; Professor of Anaesthesia, University of Bristol, 1976–99, Emeritus since 2000; President, Royal College of Anaesthetists, 1994–97; *b* 8 Aug. 1935; *s* of late William Prys Roberts and Winifred Prys Roberts (*née* Osborne Jones); *m* 1961, Linda Joyce Bickerstaff; two *s* two *d*. *Educ:* Dulwich Coll.; St Bartholomew's Hosp. Med. Sch. (MB BS London); MA, DM Oxon; PhD Leeds. FANZCA; FRCA. Research Fellow, Univ. of Leeds, 1964–67; Clinical Reader in Anaesthetics, Oxford Univ., 1967–76; Fellow, Worcester Coll., Oxford, 1970–76; Hon. Cons. Anaesthetist, Radcliffe Infirmary, 1967–76; Prof. of Anaesthesia, Univ. of California, San Diego, 1974; Hon. Consultant Anaesthetist, Bristol Royal Infirmary and Bristol Royal Hosp. for Sick Children, 1976–99. Hunterian Prof., RCS, 1978. Hon. FCMSA 1996; Hon. FCAI (FFARCSI 1998). *Publications:* (ed) The Circulation in Anaesthesia, 1980; (ed) Pharmacokinetics of Anaesthesia, 1984; (ed) Monitoring in Anaesthesia and Intensive Care, 1994; (ed) International Practice of Anaesthesia, 2 vols, 1996; contribs to learned jls. *Recreations:* mountaineering, ski-ing, philately and postal history, music (playing trumpet), videography of birds. *Address:* Foxes Mead, Cleeve Hill Road, Cleeve, Bristol BS49 4PG.

**PRZYBORSKI, Prof. Stefan Alexander**, PhD; Professor of Cell Technology, Durham University, since 2000; *b* Norwich, 26 Oct. 1966; *s* of Stefan and Kathleen Przyborski; *m* 1996, Jane; two *d*. *Educ*: Univ. of Sheffield (BSc Anatomy and Cell Biol. 1989; PhD 1992); Durham Univ. (PGCE 2005). Wellcome Trust Postdoctoral Fellow, Univ. of Sheffield, 1992–95; MRC Postdoctoral Travelling Fellow, Jackson Lab., USA, 1995–97; Res. Scientist, Wyeth Neurosci., Princeton, NJ, 1997–98; J. G. Graves Sen. Med. Res. Fellow, Univ. of Sheffield, 1998–99. Director and Chief Scientific Officer: Reinnervate Ltd, 2002–14; Reprocell Europe Ltd, 2014–. Pres., Anatomical Soc., 2017–19. *Publications*: Technology Platforms for 3D Cell Culture, 2017; contribs to peer-reviewed pubns. *Recreations*: running, football, hiking, cycling, carpentry, DIY, music, cinema. *Address*: Department of Biosciences, Durham University, South Road, Durham DH1 3LE. *T*: (0191) 334 3988. *E*: stefan.przyborski@durham.ac.uk.

**PTASZYNSKI, André Jan**; theatre producer, trading as Pola Jones Ltd, since 1980; Head of Theatres, Really Useful Group, since 2011; *b* 7 May 1953; *s* of Wladyslaw Ptaszynski and Joan Ptaszynski (*née* Holmes); *m* 1985, Judith Terry; two *s* two *d*. *Educ*: Ipswich Sch.; Jesus Coll., Oxford (BA 1975, MA 1978). Associate Dir, Crucible Th., Sheffield, 1978–80; ind. theatre and television producer trading as Pola Jones Ltd, 1980–: produced over 50 West End and touring shows including: Return to the Forbidden Planet, West Side Story, Fosse, Chicago, Spend, Spend, Spend, Tommy, Show Boat, (with RSC, West End, N America and Australia) Matilda the Musical, Groundhog Day; produced sitcoms for BBC including Joking Apart (Bronze Rose, Montreux TV Fest., 1995); promoted live work of comedians including: Rowan Atkinson, Dave Allen, Victoria Wood, Eddie Izzard and League of Gentlemen; Chief Executive: Really Useful Th., 2000–05; Really Useful Gp, 2005–11. Member, Board: Oxford Stage Co., 1990–97; RNT, 2001–10; Mountview Acad. of Th. Arts, 2017–. Pres., Soc. of London Th., 1996–99. *Recreations*: fell-walking, cycling around London, reading, yoga, drinking wine on sunny terraces. *Address*: Hill Farm, Chiselhampton, Oxford OX44 7XH. *T*: (office) (01865) 400372. *E*: andre@polajones.com.

**PUAPUA, Rt Hon. Sir Tomasi**, GCMG 2002; KBE 1998; PC 1982; Governor General of Tuvalu, 1998–2003; *b* 10 Sept. 1938; *s* of Fitilau and Olive Puapua; *m* 1971, Riana Tabokai; two *s* two *d*. *Educ*: King George V Secondary Sch.; Fiji Sch. of Medicine; Otago Med. Sch., NZ (DPH). Gilbert and Ellice Islands Colony Government: gen. med. practitioner, 1964–70; MO, Public Health, 1971–76; Tuvalu: MP Vaitupu, 1977–98; Prime Minister, 1981–89; Speaker of Parliament, 1993–98. *Recreations*: cricket, fishing, gardening, reading. *Address*: c/o Government House, Funafuti, Tuvalu.

**PUBLICOVER, Ralph Martin**; HM Diplomatic Service, retired; *b* 2 May 1952; *s* of John Publicover and Nora (*née* Bates); *m* 1973, Rosemary Sheward; one *s* two *d*. *Educ*: Haberdashers' Aske's Sch., Elstree; Univ. of Manchester (BA Econ 1973); Sch. of Oriental and African Studies, London. Joined HM Diplomatic Service, 1976; Second, then First Sec., Dubai, 1979–81; First Sec. (Econ.), Ottawa, 1981–85; Assessments Staff, Cabinet Office, 1985–87; First Sec., Washington, 1989–92; Dep. Hd, Central Eur. Dept, FCO, 1992–94; Deputy Head of Mission: Bucharest, 1994–97; Lisbon, 1998–2003; Hd, Consular Crisis Gp, FCO, 2003–04; Ambassador to Angola, 2005–07; Clerk, Cttee Office, H of L, 2008–10. Sensitivity Reviewer, FCO, 2012–. *Recreations*: music, cricket, ancient monuments, ducks and geese. *Address*: 87 Great Brownings, College Road, SE21 7HR. *E*: ralphpublicover@ntlworld.com.

**PUDDEPHATT, Andrew Charles**, OBE 2003; Founder Director, Adapt, since 2017; Executive Chairman, Advisory Board, Global Partners Digital (formerly Global Partners and Associates), since 2016 (Managing Director, 2005–16); *b* 2 April 1950; *s* of Andrew Ross Puddephatt and Margaret McGuire; two *d*. *Educ*: Sidney Sussex College, Cambridge (BA 1971). Worked as teacher in 1970s; computer programmer, 1978–81. Councillor, Hackney Council, 1982–90 (Leader, 1986–89). Gen. Sec., NCCL, subseq. Liberty, 1989–95; Dir, Charter 88, 1995–99; Exec. Dir, Article 19, Internat. Centre Against Censorship, 1999–2005. Vis. Fellow, LSE, 2005–08. Chairman: Internat. Media Support (Denmark), 2011– (Dep. Chm., 2001–11); Internet Watch Foundn. Trustee, Sigfrid Rausing Trust, 2008–. *Recreations*: literature, music. *Address*: c/o Global Partners Digital, Second Home, 68–80 Hanbury Street, E1 5JL.

**PUDDEPHATT, Prof. Richard John**, OC 2007; PhD; FRS 1998; FRS (Can) 1991; Distinguished University Professor of Chemistry, University of Western Ontario, since 2005 (Professor of Chemistry, 1978–2005); *b* 12 Oct. 1943; *s* of late Harry and Ena Puddephatt; *m* 1979, Alice Ruth Poulton; one *s* one *d*. *Educ*: University Coll. London (BSc 1965; PhD 1968). Teaching Fellow, Univ. of Western Ont, 1968–70; Lectr, 1970–77, Sen. Lectr, 1977–78, Univ. of Liverpool. Canada Res. Chair, Univ. of Western Ont., 2001–. Sen. Editor, Canadian Jl Chem., 1998–. Royal Society of Chemistry: Noble Metals Award, 1991; Nyholm Award, 1997; Chemical Society of Canada: Alcan Award, 1985; Steacie Award, 1996; CIC Medal, 1998; Hellmuth Prize, 2000. *Publications*: The Periodic Table of the Elements, 1972, 2nd edn 1986; The Chemistry of Gold, 1978; contrib. numerous papers to learned jls, mostly on organometallic chemistry. *Recreations*: gardening, golf. *Address*: Department of Chemistry, University of Western Ontario, London, ON N6A 5B7, Canada. *T*: (519) 6792111.

**PUGH, Alun John**; writer and consultant specialising in public services and public consultations; *b* 9 June 1955; *s* of late Maurice Thomas Pugh, coal miner, and Violet Jane Pugh, nurse; *m* 1st, 1978, Janet Hughes (marr. diss. 2002); one *s* one *d*; 2nd, 2006, Mary Juliet Chaffé. *Educ*: Tonypandy Grammar Sch.; Poly. of Wales; UC, Cardiff. Lectr in Accounting, Bridgend Coll., 1983–87; Sen. Lectr, Newcastle Coll., 1987–92; Head of Sch., Llandrillo Coll., 1992–96; Asst Principal, W Cheshire Coll., 1996–99. Dir, Snowdonia Soc., 2008–10; Columnist, Daily Post, 2010–12. Mem. (Lab) Clwyd W, Nat. Assembly for Wales, 1999–2007; Dep. Health and Social Services Sec., 2000–01; Dep. Educn Minister, 2001–03; Minister for Culture, the Welsh Lang. and Sports, 2003–07. Contested (Lab): Clwyd West, Nat. Assembly for Wales, 2007; Arfon, 2010, 2015. Mem., British Mountaineering Council, 2009–. *Recreations*: mountaineering, cycling. *E*: alunpugh@hotmail.com.

**PUGH, Brett**, PhD; adviser on education strategic planning, since 2016; Director, School Standards and Workforce Group, Welsh Government, 2013–16; *b* Abertysswg, Caerphilly, 19 Feb. 1956; *s* of Gomer Pugh and Beatrice Rose Pugh; civil partnership 2006, Eric Serebro. *Educ*: Univ. of Warwick (BA Hons 1977; PGCE 1978; MEd 1983); Univ. of Glamorgan (MSc 1997); Univ. of Cardiff (PhD 2002). Secondary sch. teacher of English and Music, Warks, 1978–83, Caerphilly, 1983–89; primary sch. teacher, Redbridge, 1989, Tower Hamlets, 1989–91; Dep. Headteacher, St Mary's RC Primary Sch., Bridgend, 1991–94; Headteacher, Phillipstown Primary Sch., Caerphilly, 1995–98; Advr, Caerphilly CBC, 1998–2003; Chief Educn Officer, 2003–05, Dir of Educn, 2005–07, Blaenau Gwent BC; Chief Educn Officer, Newport, 2007–11; Hd, Sch. Standards Unit, Welsh Govt, 2011–13. Mem., Ind. Adv. Gp on Curriculum, 2016–, Chm., Delivery Gp for Educn Otherwise than at Sch., 2017–, Welsh Govt Chm., SE Wales Educn Consortium, 2007–11. Vice Chm., 2008–10, Chm., 2010–11, Assoc. of Dirs of Educn in Wales. Vis. Prof. of Educn, Univ. of South Wales, 2017– (Associate Advr, 2017). *Publications*: contribs to inspection reports, govt reports and plans. *Recreations*: church organist and music co-ordinator, theatre, ballet, opera, music, biblical studies, archaeology. *Address*: 165 Pontygwindy Road, Caerphilly, Gwent CF83 3HQ. *T*: 07971 848734. *E*: brett.pugh@talktalk.net.

**PUGH, David Samuel; His Honour Judge Pugh**; a Circuit Judge, since 2016; *b* 18 June 1954; *s* of Samuel Aubrey Pugh and Edith Lorraine Pugh; *m* 1987, Jacqueline Mary Pyle; one *s* one *d*. *Educ*: Hampton Grammar Sch.; Salford Univ. (BSc Civil Eng). Called to the Bar, Middle Temple, 1978; barrister, Francis Taylor Bldg, 1979–84; Legal Advr, Amec plc, 1984–87; barrister, East Anglian Chambers, 1987–2008, Hd of Chambers, 2005–08; a Dep. District Judge, 2002–08; a Recorder, 2008–16; a District Judge, 2008–16. Mem., Bar Conduct and Complaints Cttee, 1989–2001. *Recreations*: sailing, walking, tennis, ski-ing, saxophone. *Address*: Ipswich Crown Court, 1 Russell Road, Ipswich IP1 2AG. *T*: (01473) 228585. *Clubs*: Bar Yacht, Aldeburgh Yacht.

**PUGH, Dame Gillian (Mary)**, DBE 2005 (OBE 1998); Chief Executive, Coram Family (formerly Thomas Coram Foundation for Children), 1997–2005; Chair, National Children's Bureau, 2006–12; *b* 13 May 1944; *d* of late Robert Quested Drayson, DSC and Rachel Drayson; *m* 1975, Gareth Nigel Pugh (*d* 1981); one *d*; *m* 1989, Martin Waldron; one step *s* two step *d*. *Educ*: Ashford Sch. for Girls; Univ. of Exeter (BA Hons). Editor: Careers Res. and Adv. Centre, Cambridge, 1966–67; Humanities Curriculum Project, Schs Council/Nuffield Foundn, 1967–70; Asst Dir of Information, Schs Council for Curriculum and Examinations, 1970–74; National Children's Bureau: Sen. Information Officer, 1974–77; Sen. Develt Officer, 1980–86; Dir, Early Childhood Unit, 1986–97; Develt Officer, Voluntary Council for Handicapped Children, 1978–80. Jt Editor, Children & Society, 1992–2003. Vis. Prof., London Univ. Inst. of Educn, 2000–11. Member: Effective Preschool Educn Project Adv. Gp, DfEE, 1997–2006; Bd, Children's Workforce Develt Council, 2005–08; Bd, Trng and Develt Agency, 2006–11; Family Justice Rev. Panel, 2010–11; Chair, Cambridge Primary Rev. (formerly Primary Educn Rev.), 2006–09. President: Child Develt Soc., 1994–96; Nat. Childminding Assoc., 2009–12; Chm., Parenting Educn and Support Forum, 1999–2006; Vice President: Preschool Learning Alliance, 1998–2003; British Assoc. of Early Childhood Educn, 1998–2012; Chair of Governors: Thomas Coram Early Childhood Centre, 1998–2005; Christ Church Chorleywood C of E Sch., 2015–19 (Gov., 2013–19). Trustee: Nat. Family and Parenting Inst., 1999–2006; Friends Provident Charitable Foundn, 2005–09. Chair, Chiltern Choir, 2005–15. FRSA 1993. Hon. DEd: Manchester Metropolitan, 1994; West of England, 1998; DUniv Open, 1995; Hon. DLitt Sheffield, 2013. *Publications* include: (jtly) The Needs of Parents, 1984; Contemporary Issues in the Early Years, 1992, 6th edn 2013; Confident Parents, Confident Children, 1994; (jtly) Learning to Be a Parent, 1996; (jtly) Training to Work in the Early Years, 1998; London's Forgotten Children: Thomas Coram and the Foundling Hospital, 2007; (contrib.) Children, Their World, Their Education, 2009; (jtly) Exploring Chorleywood: a pictorial history, 2018. *Recreations*: gardening, choral singing, walking, golf. *Address*: Weathervane, Old Shire Lane, Chorleywood, Herts WD3 5PW. *T*: (01923) 285505.

**PUGH, Jeanette Mary**, CB 2008; PhD; Director, Gambling Commission, 2013–14; *b* Bognor Regis, 4 June 1959; *d* of William and Eileen Pugh. *Educ*: St Francis of Assisi Prim. Sch., Liverpool; La Sagesse High Sch., Liverpool; Univ. of Bradford (BA Hons 1st Cl. Mod. Langs); Univ. of Manchester Inst. of Sci. and Technol. (PhD Linguistics 1984). Res. Associate, then Proj. Officer, UMIST, 1985–91; Department for Education, then Department for Education and Employment, later Department for Education and Skills: various team leader posts, 1991–98; Divl Manager, Lifelong Learning and Technologies Div., 1998–2001; Divl Manager, Funding Directorate, 2001–02; Divl Manager, Strategy and Communications and Dep. Chief Exec., Connexions Service Nat. Unit, 2002–03; Transition Manager, Children and Families Directorate, 2003; Dir, Children's Workforce Unit, 2003–06; Dir, Safeguarding Gp, DfES, later DCSF, then DFE, 2006–13. *Recreations*: going to the theatre, reading.

**PUGH, Dr John David**; *b* 28 June 1948; *s* of James and Patricia Pugh; *m* 1971, Annette; one *s* three *d*. *Educ*: Maidstone Grammar Sch.; Durham Univ.; PhD Manchester; MPhil Nottingham; MA Liverpool. Head: Social Studies, Salesian High Sch., Bootle, 1972–83; Philosophy and Religious Studies, Merchant Taylors' Sch., Crosby, 1983–2001. Mem. (Lib Dem) Sefton MBC, 1987–2002 (Leader, Lib Dem Gp, 1992–2001; Leader of Council, 2000–01). MP (Lib Dem) Southport, 2001–17. *Publications*: The Christian Understanding of God, 1990. *Recreation*: cycling. *Address*: 27 The Walk, Birkdale, Southport, Lancs PR8 4BG. *T*: (01704) 569025. *Club*: National Liberal.

**PUGH, Paul William**; Director, KCBD Ltd, consultancy services, since 2015; *b* Liverpool, 5 Aug. 1960; *s* of James Pugh and Patricia Pugh; *m* 1982, Kathryn Burton; two *s* one *d*. *Educ*: Nottingham High Sch.; Jesus Coll., Cambridge (BA Hons Mod. Langs 1982). Home Office, 1984–2003: Pte Sec. to Home Sec., 1990–92; Hd, Operational Policing Policy Unit, 1996–99; Hd, Police Leadership and Powers Unit, 2000–03; Chief Exec., Central Police Trng and Develt Authy, 2003–04; Exec. Dir, NW London Strategic HA, 2005–07; Regl Dir, Govt Office for E of England, 2008–10; Exec. Dir of Ops, Identity and Passport Service, 2010–13; Chief Exec., then Registrar Gen., HM Passport Office, 2013–14. Non-exec. Dir, Inst. of Customer Service, 2015–. Trustee, Campus Educnl Trust, 2015–. Gov., Middlesex Univ., 2017–. *Recreations*: spending time with family and friends, shopping in John Lewis. *E*: pughpaul@hotmail.com.

**PUGSLEY, His Honour David Philip**; a Circuit Judge, 1992–2014; *b* 11 Dec. 1944; *s* of Rev. Clement Pugsley and Edith (*née* Schofield); *m* 1966, Judith Mary Mappin; two *d*. *Educ*: Shebbear College; St Catharine's College, Cambridge (MA); MPhil Birmingham, 1995. Called to the Bar, Middle Temple, 1968; practised Midland and Oxford Circuit until 1985; Chm. of Industrial Tribunals, Birmingham Reg., 1985–92; a Recorder, 1991–92. Pres., Council of Industrial Tribunal Chairmen, 1991–92; Mem., Parole Bd, 1999–2005, 2010–12. Mem., Editl Bd, Civil Court Procedure, 1999–. Freeman, City of London, 2006. *Publications*: (jtly) Industrial Tribunals Compensation for Loss of Pension Rights, 1990; (jtly) The Contract of Employment, 1997; (jtly) Butterworths Employment Compensation Calculator, 1999. *Recreations*: fly fishing, theatre. *Address*: Cruck Barn Cottage, The Green, Brailsford, Derbyshire DE6 3BX.

**PUIG de la BELLACASA, José Joaquín**, Hon. GCVO 1986; Knight of Calatrava; Counsellor of State, Spain, since 1997 (Chairman, Council for Foreign Affairs, 1995–97); *b* 5 June 1931; *s* of José Maria Puig de la Bellacasa and Consuelo de Urdampilleta; *m* 1960, Paz de Aznar Ybarra; four *s* two *d*. *Educ*: Areneros Jesuit Coll., Madrid; Madrid Univ. Barrister-at-law. Entered Diplomatic Service, 1959; Dirección General Política Exterior, 1961–62; Minister's Cabinet, 1962–69; Counsellor, Spanish Embassy, London, 1971–74; Private Sec. to Prince of Spain, 1974–75, to HM King Juan Carlos, 1975–76; Director-General: Co-op. Tecnica Internacional, 1976; Servicio Exterior, 1977–78; Under-Sec. of State for Foreign Affairs, 1978–80; Ambassador to Holy See, 1980–83; Ambassador to UK, 1983–90; Sec.-Gen., Spanish Royal Household, 1990–91; Ambassador to Portugal, 1991–95. Vice Chm., Paneuropean Union, Spain, 1999–. Hon. Fellow, QMC, 1987.

Grand Cross of Isabel la Católica; Grand Cross of Merito Naval; Encomienda de Numero de Carlos III; holds several foreign decorations. *Address:* Felipe IV 7, Madrid 28014, Spain. *Clubs:* Beefsteak, White's; Nuevo, Golf de Puerta de Hierro (Madrid); Real Club Maritimo del Abra (Bilbao).

**PULAY, Jessica Mary;** Co-Head of Policy and Markets and Member, Managing Board, United Kingdom Debt Management Office, since 2015; *b* London, 19 July 1966; *d* of late George Pulay and Katharine Frances Goddard Pulay (*née* Sachs, later Harman). *Educ:* Wycombe Abbey Sch.; Christ Church, Oxford (Open Schol.; BA Hons 1987; MA; Pres., Oxford Union, 1987). Coverage Officer, Credit Suisse First Boston Ltd, 1987–90; Staff Reporter, Economist, 1990; Exec. Dir, Goldman Sachs Internat. Ltd, 1991–97; Man. Dir, Deutsche Morgan Grenfell, 1997; Exec. Dir, Morgan Stanley Internat. Ltd, 1997–98; Manager, Funding, European Bank for Reconstruction and Develt, 1999–2004; Dep. Hd, Funding, EBRD, 2004–15. Mem., Council, Queen's Coll. London, 1998–2015 (Vice Chm., 2010–15; Chairman: Investment Cttee, 2000–06; Finance Cttee, 2006–08). Trustee: Nat. Centre for Languages, CILT, 2007–08; Wallace Collection, 2013– (Member: Audit Cttee, 2013– (Chm., 2016–); Investment Cttee, 2015–); Arts Foundn, 2014–16. MCIL 2004. *Address:* United Kingdom Debt Management Office, Eastcheap Court, 11 Philpot Lane, EC3M 8UD.

**PULFORD, Air Chief Marshal Sir Andrew (Douglas),** GCB 2016 (KCB 2013); CBE 2004; DL; Chief of the Air Staff, 2013–16; Air Aide-de-Camp to the Queen, 2013–16; *b* 22 March 1958; *s* of Douglas and Jean Pulford; *m* 1982, Nicola Jane Pearse; one *s* one *d*. *Educ:* Magnus Grammar Sch., Newark. Support helicopter pilot, 1978–92; Fleet Air Arm Exchange, 1980–82; RAAF Exchange, 1985–87; OC 18 Sqn, 1996–99; PSO to CAS, 1999–2000; HCSC, 2001; OC RAF Odiham and Chinook Wing, 2002–03; Dir Air Resources and Plans, MoD, 2004–06; AOC No 2 Gp, 2007–08; ACDS (Ops), 2008–10; Dep. C-in-C (Personnel) Air Comd, and Air Mem. for Personnel, 2010–13. DL Notts, 2019. *Recreations:* military history, motorcycling, old cars, sailing. *Club:* Royal Air Force.

**PULHAM, Mary Helen;** *see* Creagh, M. H.

**PULLAN, Prof. Brian Sebastian,** PhD; FBA 1985; Professor of Modern History, University of Manchester, 1973–98; *b* 10 Dec. 1935; *s* of late Horace William Virgo Pullan and Ella Lister Pullan; *m* 1962, Janet Elizabeth Maltby (*d* 2018); two *s*. *Educ:* Epsom Coll.; Trinity Coll., Cambridge (MA, PhD); MA Manchester. Nat. Service, RA, 1954–56. Cambridge University: Res. Fellow, Trinity Coll., 1961–63; Official Fellow, Queens' Coll., 1963–72; Univ. Asst Lectr in History, 1964–67; Lectr, 1967–72; Dean, Faculty of Arts, Manchester Univ., 1982–84. Feoffee of Chetham's Hosp. and Library, Manchester, 1981–2004. Corresp. Fellow, Ateneo Veneto, 1986. Serena Medal, British Academy, 1991. *Publications:* (ed) Sources for the History of Medieval Europe, 1966; (ed) Crisis and Change in the Venetian Economy in the Sixteenth and Seventeenth Centuries, 1968; Rich and Poor in Renaissance Venice, 1971; A History of Early Renaissance Italy, 1973; The Jews of Europe and the Inquisition of Venice, 1983; (ed with Susan Reynolds) Towns and Townspeople in Medieval and Renaissance Europe: essays in memory of Kenneth Hyde, 1990; (ed with David Chambers) Venice: a documentary history 1450–1630, 1992; Poverty and Charity: Europe, Italy, Venice, 1400–1700, 1994; (with Michele Abendstern) A History of the University of Manchester 1951–73, 2000; (ed with Maureen Mulholland and Anne Pullan) Judicial Tribunals in England and Europe 1200–1700, 2003; (with Michele Abendstern) A History of the University of Manchester 1973–90, 2004; (ed) A Portrait of the University of Manchester, 2007; Tolerance, Regulation and Rescue: dishonoured women and abandoned children in Italy, 1300–1800, 2016; articles and reviews in learned jls and collections. *Recreations:* dogs, theatre. *Address:* 33 Green Pastures, Heaton Mersey, Stockport SK4 3RB.

**PULLEN, Dr Roderick Allen;** HM Diplomatic Service, retired; Fellow, Trinity College, Cambridge, since 2006; *b* 11 April 1949; *s* of late Derrick and Celia Pullen; *m* 1971, Karen Lesley Sketchley; four *s* one *d*. *Educ:* Maidstone Grammar Sch.; Mansfield Coll., Oxford (MA); Sussex Univ. (DPhil). MoD, 1975–78; Second Sec., UK Delegn to NATO, 1978–80; MoD, 1980–81; First Sec., UK Delegn to CSCE, 1981–82; FCO, 1982–84; Dep. High Comr, Suva, 1984–88; FCO, 1988–90; Counsellor, Paris, 1990–94; Dep. High Comr, Nairobi, 1994–97; Dep. High Comr, Lagos, 1997–2000; High Comr, Ghana, 2000–04; Ambassador to Zimbabwe, 2004–06; UK Special Rep. to Sudan/Darfur Peace Process, 2006. Gov., Thomas Alleyne Acad. (formerly Thomas Alleyne Sch.), Stevenage, 2009–16. Trustee, Cambridge and Peterborough Probation Trust, 2010–14. Gov., Exmoor Fedn, 2018–. *Address:* Trinity College, Cambridge CB2 1TQ.

**PULLINGER, John James,** CB 2014; Chief Executive, UK Statistics Authority, National Statistician and Permanent Secretary, 2014–19; *b* 1 June 1959; *s* of Desmond and Kathleen Pullinger; *m* 1981, Alison Taylor; two *s* one *d*. *Educ:* Alleyn's Sch., Dulwich; Univ. of Exeter (BA 1st Cl. Hons Geog. and Stats 1980); Harvard Business Sch. (AMP 2003). Asst Statistician, then Sen. Asst Statistician, DTI, 1980–85; Section Hd, DoE, 1985–91; Hd of Pay Res., Office of Manpower Econs, 1991–92; Central Statistical Office, subseq. Office for National Statistics: Dir, Policy and Planning, 1992–96; Dir, Social and Regl Statistics, 1996–98; Exec. Dir, 1999–2004; Librarian, H of C, 2004–14. Pres., Royal Statistical Soc., 2013–14. *Recreations:* family, church, gardening, politics, current affairs.

**PULLMAN, Sir Philip (Nicholas Outram),** Kt 2019; CBE 2004; FRSL; author and playwright; *b* 19 Oct. 1946; *s* of late Alfred and Audrey Pullman (*née* Merrifield); *m* 1970, Judith Speller; two *s*. *Educ:* Ysgol Ardudwy, Harlech; Exeter Coll., Oxford (BA English Lang. and Lit. 1968; Hon. Fellow, 2004). Teacher, Oxford Middle Schools, 1973–86; Lectr (part-time), Westminster Coll., Oxford, 1986–96. Patron, Centre for the Children's Book, 2000. Pres., Soc. of Authors, 2013–. Mem., Guild of Rocking Horse Makers, 2007–. Hon. Freeman, City of Oxford, 2007. Hon. Prof., Bangor Univ., 2008. Hon. Fellow: Westminster Inst. of Educn, 1999; Univ. of Wales, Bangor, 2003. Hon. DLitt: Oxford Brookes, 2002; UEA, 2003; Oxford, 2009; Exeter, 2010; Bath, 2013; Anglia Ruskin, 2013; DUniv: UCE, 2003; Surrey, 2003; Open, 2008; Hon. LLD Dundee, 2007. Booksellers Assoc. Author of the Year, 2000, 2001; Author of the Year, Br. Bk Awards, 2002, 2018; Eleanor Farjeon Award, 2003; Astrid Lindgren Memorial Award, 2005. *Plays:* Sherlock Holmes and the Adventure of the Limehouse Horror, 1984; The Three Musketeers, 1985; Frankenstein, 1986; Puss in Boots, 1997. *Publications: novels and stories:* Galatea, 1978; Count Karlstein, 1982, illustrated edn 1991; The Ruby in the Smoke, 1985 (Children's Book Award, Internat. Reading Assoc., 1988; televised 2006); The Shadow in the North, 1987; How To Be Cool, 1987; Spring-Heeled Jack, 1989; The Broken Bridge, 1990; The Tiger in the Well, 1991; The White Mercedes, 1992, re-issued as The Butterfly Tattoo, 1998; The Wonderful Story of Aladdin and the Enchanted Lamp, 1993; The Tin Princess, 1994; Thunderbolt's Waxwork, 1994; The Gas-Fitters' Ball, 1995; The Firework-Maker's Daughter, 1995 (Smarties Gold Award, 1996); His Dark Materials: Book One: Northern Lights, 1995 (US title: The Golden Compass) (Guardian Children's Fiction Award, 1996; Carnegie Medal, 1996; British Book Award: Children's Book of the Year, 1996; filmed, 2007); Book Two: The Subtle Knife, 1997; Book Three: The Amber Spyglass, 2000 (British Book Award: Children's Book of the Year, 2001; Whitbread Book of the Year, 2002; trilogy adapted for stage by Nicholas Wright, NT, 2003; trilogy televised, 2019); Clockwork, or All Wound Up, 1996 (Smarties Silver Award, 1997); I Was a Rat!, 1999 (televised, 2001); Mossycoat, 1999; Puss in Boots, 2000; Lyra's Oxford, 2003; The Scarecrow and His Servant, 2004; Aladdin, 2004; Once Upon a Time in the North, 2008; The Good Man Jesus and the Scoundrel Christ, 2010; The Adventures of the New Cut Gang, 2011; Grimm Tales for Young and Old, 2012 (adapted for stage by Philip Wilson, Unicorn, 2018); The Adventures of John Blake, 2017; The Book of Dust, Vol. One: La Belle Sauvage, 2017 (Waterstones Book of the Year, 2017), Vol. Two: The Secret Commonwealth, 2019; *plays:* Sherlock Holmes and the Adventure of the Limehouse Horror, 1993; Frankenstein, 1992. *Recreations:* drawing, music. *Address:* c/o A. P. Watt Ltd, United Agents, 12–26 Lexington Street, W1F 0LE.

**PULLUM, Prof. Geoffrey Keith,** PhD; FBA 2009; Professor of General Linguistics, University of Edinburgh, since 2007; *b* Irvine, 8 March 1945; *s* of Keith Francis and Marjorie Joan Pullum; *m* 1st, 1967, Joan E. Rainford (marr. diss. 1993); one *s*; 2nd, 1994, Barbara Caroline Scholz (*d* 2011); 3rd, 2014, Patricia Catherine Shannon (*d* 2016). *Educ:* Eltham Coll.; Univ. of York (BA Hons Lang.); King's Coll., Cambridge; Univ. of London (PhD Gen. Linguistics 1976). Lectr, UCL, 1974–81; Prof. of Linguistics, 1981–2007, Dean of Grad. Studies and Res., 1987–93, Univ. of Calif, Santa Cruz; Fellow: Center for Advanced Study in Behavioral Scis, Stanford Univ., 1990–91; Radcliffe Inst. for Advanced Study, Harvard Univ., 2005–06. Gerard Vis. Prof. of Cognitive, Linguistic and Psychol Scis, Brown Univ., 2012–13. Fellow: Amer. Acad. of Arts and Scis, 2003; Linguistic Soc. of America, 2007. *Publications:* (ed with D. L. Goyvaerts) Essays on the Sound Pattern of English, 1975; (with G. Gazdar and E. H. Klein) A Bibliography of Contemporary Linguistic Research, 1978; Rule Interaction and the Organization of a Grammar, 1979; (ed with P. Jacobson) The Nature of Syntactic Representation, 1982; (ed with G. Gazdar and E. H. Klein) Order, Concord, and Constituency, 1983; (with G. Gazdar, E. H. Klein and I. A. Sag) Generalized Phrase Structure Grammar, 1985; (ed with D. C. Derbyshire) Handbook of Amazonian Languages, vol. 1, 1986, vol. 2, 1990, vol. 3, 1991, vol. 4, 1998; The Great Eskimo Vocabulary Hoax, 1991; (with W. A. Ladusaw) Phonetic Symbol Guide, 1986, 2nd edn 1996; (jtly) The Cambridge Grammar of the English Language, 2002; (with R. Huddleston) A Student's Introduction to English Grammar, 2005; (with M. Liberman) Far from the Madding Gerund and Other Dispatches from Language Log, 2006; Linguistics: why it matters, 2018; over 250 articles. *Recreations:* walking, swimming, playing guitar, writing, blogging. *Address:* 11 Gordon Terrace, Edinburgh EH16 5QW. *T:* (0131) 650 3603, *Fax:* (0131) 651 3190. *E:* pullum@gmail.com.

**PULLUM, Megan Michelle Elaine;** QC (Guernsey) 2012; HM Procureur (Attorney-General) and Receiver General, Guernsey, since 2016; *b* UK, 1971; *d* of Dr Geoffrey Pullum and Anne Pullum (*née* Steer); *m* 2009, Simon Guest; two *c*. *Educ:* Herts and Essex High Sch. for Girls; Univ. de Nantes, France (Dip. d'études universitaires générales 1, 1992); Univ. of Wales Coll. of Cardiff (LLB Jt Hons Law and French 1993); Coll. of Law, York 1994; Univ. of Glamorgan (LLM Eur. Law 2000); Univ. de Caen, France (Certificat d'études juridiques françaises et normandes 2005). Admitted as solicitor, 1996; called to the Guernsey Bar, 2006; Accredited Workplace and Employment Mediator, 2011; HM Comptroller and Dep. Receiver Gen., Guernsey, 2012–16. *Address:* c/o Law Offices of the Crown, St James Chambers, St Peter Port, Guernsey, Channel Islands GY1 2PA. *T:* (01481) 723355. *E:* law@gov.gg.

**PULMAN, Prof. Stephen Guy,** PhD; FBA 2001; Professor of Computational Linguistics, University of Oxford, 2006–17, now Emeritus; Fellow, Somerville College, Oxford, 2000–17, now Emeritus; Senior Natural Processing Research Scientist, Apple, since 2017; *b* 1 Oct. 1949; *s* of Raymond Pulman and Celia Margaret Pulman; *m* 1989, Nicola Jane Verney; one *s* two *d*. *Educ:* Bedford Coll., London (BA Hons English 1972); Univ. of Essex (MA Theoretical Linguistics 1974; PhD Linguistics 1977). Lecturer: Dept of Lang. and Linguistics, Univ. of Essex, 1977–78; Sch. of English and American Studies, UEA, 1978–84; University of Cambridge Computer Laboratory: Lectr, 1984–97; Reader in Computational Linguistics, 1997–2000; Dep. Hd, 1999–2000; Dir, 1988–97, Principal Scientist, 1998–2001, SRI Internat. (formerly Stanford Res. Inst.) Cambridge Computer Sci. Res. Centre; University of Oxford: Prof. of Gen. Linguistics, 2000–06; Dep. Hd, 2007–08, Hd, 2008–09, Computing Lab; Dep. Hd, Dept of Computer Sci., 2010–13. *Publications:* Word Meaning and Belief, 1983; (jtly) Computational Morphology: practical mechanisms for the English lexicon, 1992; contrib. papers to Computational Linguistics, Artificial Intelligence, Linguistics and Philosophy, Philosophical Trans of Royal Soc., etc. *Recreations:* gardening, bird-watching, walking, bell-ringing. *Address:* Somerville College, Oxford OX2 6HD.

**PULVERTAFT, Rear-Adm. David Martin,** CB 1990; Secretary, Defence, Press and Broadcasting Advisory Committee, 1992–99; *b* 26 March 1938; *s* of late Captain William Godfrey Pulvertaft, OBE, RN and Annie Joan Pulvertaft (*née* Martin); *m* 1961, Mary Rose Jeacock; one *s* two *d*. *Educ:* Canford Sch., Dorset; Britannia RN Coll., Dartmouth; RN Engineering Coll., Manadon. BSc (Eng) 1962. FIMechE 1989 (MIMechE 1974). HMS Ceylon, 1958–59; HMS Anchorite, Singapore, 1963–66; HMS Dreadnought, 1967–71; 10th Submarine Sqdn, 1971–72; HM Dockyard, Devonport, 1973–75; Nat. Defence Coll., Latimer, 1975–76; MoD 1976–78; HM Dockyard, Devonport, 1979–82; RCDS, 1983; MoD, 1984–87; Dir Gen. Aircraft (Navy), 1987–90; Dir Gen., Procurement and Support Orgn (Navy), 1990–92. Chm. of Trustees, Plymouth Naval Base Mus., 2001–05; Chm., SW Maritime Hist. Soc., 2000–03; Mem. Council, Soc. for Nautical Res., 2002–11, 2012–. Fellow, Soc. for Nautical Res., 2016. *Publications:* The Warship Figureheads of Portsmouth, 2009; Figureheads of the Royal Navy, 2011. *Recreations:* genealogy, printing, bookbinding, British warship figureheads. *Address:* Staffords, 3 Paternoster Row, Ottery St Mary, Devon EX11 1DP. *Club:* Army and Navy.

**PULZER, Prof. Peter George Julius,** PhD; FRHistS; Professorial Fellow, Institute for German Studies, University of Birmingham, 1996–99; Gladstone Professor of Government and Public Administration, University of Oxford, 1985–96, now Emeritus; Fellow of All Souls College, 1985–96, now Emeritus; *b* 20 May 1929; *s* of Felix and Margaret Pulzer; *m* 1962, Gillian Mary Marshall; two *s*. *Educ:* Surbiton County Grammar Sch.; King's Coll., Cambridge (1st Cl. Hons Historical Tripos 1950; PhD 1960); London Univ. (1st Cl. Hons BSc Econ 1954). FRHistS 1971. Lectr in Politics, Magdalen Coll. and Christ Church, Oxford, 1957–62; University Lectr in Politics, Oxford, 1960–84; Official Student and Tutor in Politics, Christ Church, 1962–84. Visiting Professor: Univ. of Wisconsin, 1965; Sch. of Advanced Internat. Studies, Johns Hopkins Univ., 1972; Univ. of Calif, LA, 1972; Eric Voegelin, Munich Univ., 1988; Potsdam Univ., 1993; Technical Univ., Dresden, 1997; Humboldt Univ., Berlin, 2000; Leipzig Univ., 2003; Max Kade, Lafayette Coll., Easton, Pennsylvania, 2004. Chairman: Academic Adv. Cttee, Centre for German-Jewish Studies, Univ. of Sussex, 1997–2009; Leo Baeck Inst., London, 1998–2013; Mem. Governing Body, Historisches Kolleg, Munich, 1993–97. Hon. Vice-Pres., Internat. Assoc. for the Study of Germany Politics, 1997–. Hon. Dr rer. soc. oec. Innsbruck, 2007; Hon. DPhil Vienna, 2012. Bundesverdienstkreuz (Germany), 2004; Grand Silver Medal of Honour for Meritorious Service to the Republic of Austria, 2008; Leo Baeck Medal of Recognition, Leo Baeck Inst., 2015. *Publications:* The Rise of Political Anti-Semitism in Germany and Austria, 1964, 2nd edn 1988 (German edn 1966); Political Representation and Elections in Britain, 1967, 3rd edn 1975; Jews and the German State, 1992, 2nd edn 2003; German Politics 1945–1995, 1995; Germany 1870–1945: politics, state formation and war, 1997; (ed with K. R. Luther) Austria 1945–1995: fifty years of the Second Republic, 1998; (ed with Wolfgang Benz) Jews in the Weimar Republic, 1998; (contrib.) German-Jewish History in Modern Times, 1998; contrib. to jls, year books and symposia. *Recreations:* opera, walking. *Address:* All Souls College, Oxford OX1 4AL.

PUNTER, Prof. David Godfrey, PhD; DLitt; FSAScot; FEA, FHEA; Professor of Poetry, University of Bristol, since 2016 (Professor of English, 2000–16); *b* 19 Nov. 1949; *s* of Douglas Herbert and Hilda Mary Punter; *m* 1988, Caroline Mary Case; one *s* two *d*. *Educ:* Fitzwilliam Coll., Cambridge (BA 1970; PhD 1984); DLitt Stirling, 1999. FSAScot; FEA. Lectr, 1973–84, Sen. Lectr, 1984–86, in English, UEA; Prof. of English and Hd of Dept, Chinese Univ. of Hong Kong, 1986–88; Prof. of English, 1988–2000, and Hd of Dept, 1988–94 and 1996, Univ. of Stirling; Dean, Grad. Studies, 2002–03, Res. Dean, 2003–09, Faculty of Arts, Univ. of Bristol. Vis. Prof. of Modern English, Fudan Univ., Shanghai, 1983. Dir, Develt of Univ. English Teaching Project, 1985–86. Chair, W Reg., RSA, 2012–14; Member, Board: Poetry Can, 2013–18; Literature Southwest, 2017–; Ledbury Poetry Fest., 2017–. Dir, Bristol Poetry Inst., 2014–18. Fellow, Inst. Contemp. Scotland; FRSA; FHEA. *Publications:* The Literature of Terror: a history of Gothic fictions from 1765 to the present day, 1980, 2nd edn 1996; (jtly) Romanticism and Ideology: studies in English writing 1765–1830, 1981; Blake, Hegel and Dialectic, 1982; The Hidden Script: writing and the unconscious, 1985; (ed) Introduction to Contemporary Cultural Studies, 1986; William Blake: selected poetry and prose, 1988; The Romantic Unconscious: a study in narcissism and patriarchy, 1989; Selected Poems of Philip Larkin: notes, 1991; (ed) William Blake: new casebook, 1996; Romanticism, 1997; William Blake's Songs of Innocence and of Experience: notes, 1998; Gothic Pathologies: the text, the body and the law, 1998; (ed with G. Byron) Spectral Readings: towards a Gothic geography, 1999; (ed) A Companion to the Gothic, 2000; Writing the Passions, 2000; Postcolonial Imaginings: fictions of a new world order, 2000; Philip Larkin's The Whitsun Weddings and Selected Poems: advanced notes, 2003; William Blake's Songs of Innocence and of Experience: advanced notes, 2003; (with G. Byron) The Gothic, 2004; The Influence of Postmodernism on Contemporary Writing, 2005; (ed) Francis Latham, The Midnight Bell, 2007; Metaphor, 2007; Modernity, 2007; Rapture: literature, addiction, secrecy, 2009; (ed) A New Companion to the Gothic, 2012; (ed jtly) The Encyclopaedia of the Gothic, 2013; The Literature of Pity, 2014; The Gothic Condition: terror, history and the psyche, 2016; *poetry:* China and Glass, 1985; Lost in the Supermarket, 1987; Asleep at the Wheel, 1996, Foreign Ministry, 2011; Selected Short Stories, 1999; Flashes in the Dark, 2015; Bristol: 21 poems, 2018; contrib. numerous articles and book chapters. *Recreations:* gardening, walking, collecting maps. *Address:* Department of English, University of Bristol, Bristol BS8 1TB. *T:* (0117) 928 8082, *Fax:* (0117) 928 8860. *E:* david.punter@bristol.ac.uk. *Clubs:* Oxford and Cambridge, Arts.

PURCELL, Brendan James; Director of Performance, British Rowing, since 2018; *b* Sydney, Australia, 29 April 1970; *s* of Dennis and Donna Purcell; *m* 1995, Sharleen Mills; three *s*. *Educ:* Villanova Coll., Coorparoo, Brisbane; Univ. of Queensland (BPhty 1991). Physiotherapist: Multiple Sclerosis Soc. (pt-time), 1993–94; Mater Public Hosp., 1995–97; private practice, 1998; Manager, Zillmere Stationery Solutions, 1999–2001; Talent Search Coach (pt-time), 2000, Junior Develt Coach, 2001, Queensland Acad. of Sport Kayak Squad; Hd Coach, Sprint Canoe, W Australian Inst. of Sport, 2001–03; Sen. Coach, Australian Canoeing, 2003–04; High Performance Manager, Diving Australia, 2005–06; Women's Hd Coach, 2007–08, Nat. Performance Coach, 2008–13, GB Canoeing-Sprint; Performance Dir, British Triathlon, 2013–18. *Recreations:* walking, BBQs, Rugby, family. *Address:* c/o British Rowing, 6 Lower Mall, Hammersmith, W6 9DJ. *T:* (020) 8237 6700. *E:* brendan.purcell@britishrowing.org.

PURCELL, Prof. Nicholas, FBA 2007; Camden Professor of Ancient History, University of Oxford, since 2011; Fellow, Brasenose College, Oxford, since 2011. *Educ:* Worcester Coll., Oxford (BA 1977). Prize Fellow, All Souls Coll., Oxford, 1977–79; Lectr in Ancient Hist., Univ. of Oxford and Fellow, St John's Coll., Oxford, 1979–2011. Vis. Sather Prof. of Classical Lit., Univ. of Calif, Berkeley, 2012. *Publications:* (with P. Horden) The Corrupting Sea: a study of Mediterranean history, 2000; (contrib.) The Cambridge Companion to the Age of Augustus, 2005; (contrib.) Mediterranean Urbanization 800–600 BC, 2005; (contrib.) Ancient Colonizations: analogies, similarity and differences, 2005; contribs to Amer. Jl Philol., Amer. Histl Rev. *Address:* Brasenose College, Oxford OX1 4AJ.

PURCELL, Philip James; President, Continental Investors LLC, since 2006; *b* 5 Sept. 1943; *m* 1964, Anne Marie McNamara; seven *s*. *Educ:* Univ. of Notre Dame (BBA 1964); LSE (MSc 1966); Univ. of Chicago (MBA 1967). Man. Dir, McKinsey & Co., 1967–78; Vice Pres. of Planning and Admin, Sears, Roebuck & Co., 1978–82; CEO, and Pres., subseq. Chm., Dean Witter Discover & Co., 1982–97; Chm. and CEO, Morgan Stanley Dean Witter & Co., subseq. Morgan Stanley, 1997–2005. Dir, NY Stock Exchange, 1991–96. Dir, AMR Corp., 2000–. *Address:* Continental Investors LLC, 227 West Monroe Street, Suite 5045, Chicago, IL 60606, USA.

PURCELL, Prof. Wendy Maria, PhD; Chief Executive, later Vice-Chancellor, President and Chief Executive, 2007–14, President, 2015, Emeritus Professor, 2016, University of Plymouth; *b* Kingsbury, 21 June 1961; *m* 1987, Geoff Hendron. *Educ:* Univ. of Plymouth (BSc Hons Biol Scis 1985); Hatfield Poly. and University Coll. London (PhD Immunopharmacology 1989). CBiol 1989, MRSB (MIBiol 1989). Lectr in Health Studies and Related Biosci. Progs, Roehampton Inst., 1990–92; University of Hertfordshire: Sen. Lectr in Physiol. and Pharmacol., 1992–93; Hd, Div. of Physiol., Pharmacol. and Toxicol., 1993–97; University of West of England: Associate Dean and Hd, Dept of Biol and Biomed. Scis, 1997–2000; Exec. Dean, Faculty of Applied Scis, 2000–05; Pro Vice-Chancellor (Res.), 2003–05; Dep. Vice-Chancellor, Univ. of Herts, 2005–07. Vis. Prof., T. H. Chan Sch. of Public Health, Harvard Univ., 2016–. Dir, United Planet, 2019–; non-exec. Dir, BIS, 2013–16. Fellow, Top Mgt Programme, 2001. Mem. Bd, Envmtl Assoc. for Univs and Colls, 2013–18; Trustee, Nat. Maritime Aquarium, 2008–18. FRSA. *Publications:* (jtly) Approaches to High Throughput Toxicity Screening, 1999; (contrib.) Going Global: identifying trends and drivers of international education, 2013; contribs to jls incl. Cellular Biochem., NeuroReport, Chem. Res. Toxicol., Pediatric Transplant, Neurotoxicol., Neurochem. Res., Perspectives: Policy and Practice in Higher Educn, PLoS One, Inside Higher Ed. *Recreations:* swimming, theatre, modern art. *E:* wendympurcell@gmail.com.

PURCHAS, Christopher Patrick Brooks; QC 1990; a Recorder, 1986–2018; *b* 20 June 1943; *s* of Rt Hon. Sir Francis Purchas, PC and Patricia Mona Kathleen Purchas; *m* 1st, 1974, Bronwen Mary Vaughan (marr. diss. 1995); two *d*; 2nd, 1998, Diana, widow of Dr Ian Hatrick. *Educ:* Summerfield Sch.; Marlborough Coll.; Trinity Coll., Cambridge (MA). Called to the Bar, Inner Temple, 1966, Bencher, 1995. *Recreations:* golf, tennis, shooting, ski-ing.

See also R. M. Purchas.

PURCHAS, Robin Michael; QC 1987; a Recorder, 1989–2019; Deputy High Court Judge, 1994–2019; *b* 12 June 1946; *s* of Rt Hon. Sir Francis Brooks Purchas, PC and Patricia Mona Kathleen Purchas; *m* 1970, Denise Anne Kerr Finlay; one *s* one *d*. *Educ:* Summerfields; Marlborough College; Trinity College, Cambridge (MA). Called to the Bar, Inner Temple, 1968, Bencher, 1996. Mem., Bar Council, 1999–2002 (Chm., Educn and Trng Cttee, 2000–02). *Recreations:* opera, music, fishing, tennis, ski-ing, sailing, shooting, golf. *Address:* (chambers) Francis Taylor Building, Temple, EC4Y 7BY. *T:* (020) 7353 8415. *Clubs:* Boodle's, Lansdowne, Queen's; Royal West Norfolk Golf; Royal Worlington and Newmarket Golf; Brancaster Staithe Sailing.

See also C. P. B. Purchas.

PURDEN, Roma Laurette, (Laurie), (Mrs J. K. Kotch), MBE 1973; journalist and writer; *b* 30 Sept. 1928; *d* of George Cecil Arnold Purden and Constance Mary Sheppard; *m* 1957, John Keith Kotch (*d* 1979); two *d*. *Educ:* Harecroft Sch., Tunbridge Wells. Fiction Editor, Home Notes, 1948–51; Asst Editor, Home Notes, 1951–52; Asst Editor, Woman's Own, 1952; Sen. Asst Editor, Girl, 1952–54; Editor of: Housewife, 1954–57; Home, 1957–62; House Beautiful, 1963–65; Good Housekeeping, 1965–73; Editor-in-Chief: Good Housekeeping, and Womancraft, 1973–77; Woman's Journal, 1978–88; Woman & Home, 1982–83. Dir, Brickfield Publications Ltd, 1978–80. Magazine Editor of the Year, 1979, British Soc. of Magazine Editors; Consumer Magazine of the Year awarded by Periodical Publishers Assoc. to Woman's Journal, 1985. *Address:* 30 Elizabeth Court, Milmans Street, SW10 0DA. *T:* (020) 7352 4166.

PURDEW, Stephen James; Director, and Co-owner, Champneys Health Resorts; *b* 25 May 1959; *s* of late Robert and of Dorothy Purdew; one *s*; *m* 2009, Isabelle Cave; one *s* one *d*. *Educ:* Midhurst Grammar Sch. Dir, Henlow Grange Health Farm, 1981– (Manager, 1981–90); acquisition of: Springs Health Hydro (Dir), 1990; Forest Mere Health Farm, 1997; Champneys, 2001, when all resorts rebranded under that name. *Address:* Champneys Health Resort, Henlow, Beds SG16 6DB. *T:* (01462) 811111, *Fax:* (01462) 815310.

PURDON, Col Timothy Corran Richard Brooke, LVO 2018; OBE 1995 (MBE 1980); Lieutenant, Her Majesty's Body Guard of the Honourable Corps of Gentleman at Arms, 2016–18; *b* Belfast, 17 Jan. 1949; *s* of Maj.-Gen. Corran William Brooke Purdon, CBE, MC, CPM; *m* 1979, Angela Mary Jean, *d* of Maj. R. N. Topham, Plas yn Grove, Ellesmere; one *s* two *d*. *Educ:* Glenalmond Coll.; RMA, Sandhurst. Commnd Irish Guards, 1969; served: Hong Kong, 1973; Belize, 1974; Germany, 1975; NI, 1976; Oman, Southern Oman Regt, 1976–78; Rhodesia/Zimbabwe (Ceasefire Monitoring Force Op. AGILA), 1979–80; Army Staff Coll., 1993; Co. Comdr, 1st Bn Irish Guards, 1984–86; SO2, Ops Orgn and Develt London Dist, 1987–89; SO1 Internal Security Advr to Saudi Nat. Guard, Saudi Arabia, 1989–91; DS, Army Staff Coll., 1991; CO, 1st Bn Welsh Guards, NI, 1992–94; SO1 Military Sec. 4, MoD, 1994–96; Dep. Comdr (Col), 3 Inf. Bde, NI, 1997–99. Hd of Membership, 1999–2003, Regl Manager, 2003–12, RBL. Regtl Adjt, Irish Guards, 2013–18. President: St John Ambulance, Devizes, 2002–18; St John Ambulance, Wilts, 2018–; Dir of Ceremonies (Internat.), Order of St John, 2011–13. KStJ 2011 (OstJ 1994; CStJ 2002). *Recreations:* military history, collecting lead soldiers, fishing, following Irish Rugby. *Address:* Coatefield House, Coate, Devizes, Wilts SN10 3LP. *E:* tpurdon@hotmail.co.uk. *Club:* Army and Navy.

PURDUE, Marie Theresa; see Conte-Helm, M. T.

PURDY, George; see Purdy, W. G.

PURDY, Quentin Alexander; a District Judge (Magistrates' Courts), 2003–18; *b* 23 Aug. 1960; *s* of late Gordon Purdy, OBE, FRCS and Margaret Purdy; *m* 1988, Elizabeth Audrey Hazelwood; two *d*. *Educ:* Gresham's Sch., Holt; Leicester Poly. (BA Hons 1982); Inns of Court Sch. of Law; University Coll. London (LLM 1985). Called to the Bar, Gray's Inn, 1983; barrister, Common Law Chambers, London, 1983–2003; Actg Metropolitan Stipendiary Magistrate, 1998–2000; Dep. Dist Judge (Magistrates' Courts), 2000–03. Deacon, Dormansland Baptist Church, 2001–08. Band Trust Award, 1983. *Publications:* (contrib. ed.) Archbold Magistrates' Courts Criminal Practice, 2012–17. *Recreations:* badminton, cycling, dog walking, foreign travel.

PURDY, (William) George, CBE 2002; Vice President, Scout Association, since 2007 (Chief Scout, 1996–2004); President, County Down Scouts, since 2008; Vice President, Northern Ireland Scouts, since 2012; *b* 16 April 1942; *s* of George Purdy and Amelia Jane Purdy (née McConnell); *m* 1969, Judith Sara Isabell Kerr; two *s*. *Educ:* Annadale Grammar Sch. NICS, 1960–91, 1993–96; Chief Exec., NI Software Industry Fedn, 1991–93. Scout Leader, 1962–94, Chief Comr, NI, 1994–96, Scout Assoc. *Recreations:* golf, Rugby, tennis, bowls, Probus, photography, music. *Address:* 16 Carshaulton Road, Donaghadee, Co. Down BT21 0QB.

PURKIS, Dr Andrew James, OBE 2002; Executive Director, Samworth Foundation, 2009–17; *b* 24 Jan. 1949; *s* of late Clifford Henry Purkis and Mildred Jeannie Purkis; *m* 1980, Jennifer Harwood Smith; one *s* one *d*. *Educ:* Highgate Sch.; Corpus Christi Coll., Oxford; St Antony's Coll., Oxford. 1st class Hons MA Mod. Hist. 1970; DPhil 1978. Home Civil Service, N Ireland Office, 1971; Private Sec. to Perm. Under-Sec. of State, NI Office, 1976–77; Head of Policy Unit, 1980, Asst Dir, 1986, NCVO; Dir, CPRE, 1987–91; Public Affairs Advr to the Archbishop of Canterbury, 1992–98; Chief Executive: Diana, Princess of Wales Meml Fund, 1998–2005; Tropical Health and Educn Trust, 2005–09. Member, Board: Contact a Family (charity), 1986–93; Green Alliance, 1992–2004; Charity Commn, 2007–10; Office of Ind. Adjudicator for Higher Educn, 2010–17 (Dep. Chair, 2014–17); Directory of Social Change, 2018–; Safe Passage, 2019; Ind. Mem., Parole Bd, 2010–14; Chair: Living Streets (formerly Pedestrians' Assoc.), 1999–2007; Empty Homes Agency, 2004–07; ActionAid UK, 2009–14; Mem., Internat. Bd, ActionAid, 2013–19 (Vice Chair, 2018–19). Blog on charity matters, www.andrewpurkis.wordpress.com. *Publications:* (with Paul Hodson) Housing and Community Care, 1982; (with Rosemary Allen) Health in the Round, 1983; Housing Associations in England and the Future of Voluntary Organisations, 2010; (contrib.) The Big Society Challenge, 2011. *Recreations:* walking, surf-riding, bird-watching, music, theatre. *Address:* 44 Bellamy Street, SW12 8BU. *T:* (020) 8675 2439.

PURKISS, Cathleen, (Kate); Her Honour Judge Purkiss; a Circuit Judge, since 2013; *b* Surrey, 7 Sept. 1962; *d* of Norman Charles Purkiss and Rena Purkiss (née Greensmythe); *m* 1992, Michael Alexander Curtis, *qv*; one *s* two *d*. *Educ:* University Coll. London (BA Hons Eng.); Poly. of Central London (DipLaw); Inns of Court Sch. of Law. Called to the Bar, Lincoln's Inn, 1988; a Recorder, 2009–13. *Recreations:* opera, theatre, cinema, watching football. *Club:* Arsenal Football.

PURKISS, Robert Ivan, MBE 2000; independent consultant on diversity and change management; *b* 11 Nov. 1945; *s* of Howard Flanagan and Betty Purkiss; *m* 1971, Monica Dell Richardson; two *d*. *Educ:* Toynbee Rd Boys' Sch.; Southampton Inst. of Higher Educn; Southampton Univ. (Dip. Industrial Relns). Chief Petty Officer, MN, 1961–72; Advr, Industrial Soc., 1972–74; Nat. Officer, Nat. Workers' Union of Jamaica, 1974–76; TGWU, 1976–2000 (Nat. Sec., 1989–2000); Chm., Eur. Monitoring Centre on Racism and Xenophobia, 2001–04. Member: CRE, 1993–2001; Central Arbitration Cttee, 2002–16. Ind. Assessor for Public Appts, DTI, 2001–; Ind. Mem., Hampshire Police Authy, 2003–12 (Chm., Personal and Professional Standards); Mem., Employment Tribunals, 2010–16 (Chair, 2013–15); Ind. Mem., Hampshire Police and Crime Panel, 2012– (Chair, Complaints Panel, 2012–); Chair: Black & Ethnic Minorities Network, 2004–10; Race and Diversity Policy, Assoc. of Police Authorities, 2005–08; Panel, Discrimination Discipline Cttee, FA, 2014–. Man. Dir, Different Realities Partnership, 2004–08. Lead Gov.,

Southampton Univ. Hosp. Trust, 2018–. *Publications:* contrib. numerous articles on anti-racism, industrial relns and diversity. *Recreations:* football referee (Mem., Southampton Referees Soc.; Race Relns and Equality Officer, 2002–, Develt Officer, 2012–, Wessex League (Chm., 2009–12)), athletics (Vice-Chm., Team Solent Athletics Club), AAA starter/marksman, grandchildren. *Address:* Penderyn, Norlands Drive, Otterbourne, Winchester SO21 2DT.

**PURNELL, Prof. Anthony John,** CEng, FREng; Head of Technology, British Cycling, since 2013; Fellow Commoner, Trinity Hall Cambridge, since 2013; *b* Carshalton, Surrey, 23 May 1958; *s of* John M. Purnell and Sylvia M. Purnell (*née* Vassierre); *m* 1994, Alison S. Nocton; one *s* one *d. Educ:* Univ. of Manchester Inst. of Sci. and Technol. (BSc); Massachusetts Inst. of Technol. (SM Mech. Engrg). CEng 2017; FREng 2017. Kennedy Schol., 1981–82. Founder and Chairman: Pi Res., 1986–92; Pi Technol., 1992–99; Pi Gp, 1999–2002; CEO, Premier Perf. Div., Ford Motor Co., 2002; Team Principal, Jaguar Racing F1, 2002–04; Tech. Advr, Fédn Internat. d'Automobile, 2005–10; Dir, Caesium Consultants LLP, 2005–. RAEng Vis. Prof., Univ. of Cambridge, 2007–. Dir, Milton Hall Estates, 2000–. *Recreations:* cycling, engineering. *Address:* Trinity Hall, Trinity Lane, Cambridge CB2 1TJ.

**PURNELL, Rt Hon. James;** PC 2007; Director, Radio and Education, BBC, since 2016 (Director: Strategy and Digital, 2013–16; Strategy and Education, 2016); *b* 2 March 1970; *s of* John and Janet Purnell; *m* 2015, Alexis Kirschbaum; one *d. Educ:* Balliol Coll., Oxford (BA PPE). Researcher for Tony Blair, MP, 1990–92; Strategy Consultant, Hydra Associates, 1992–94; Res. Fellow, Media and Communications, IPPR, 1994–95; Hd, Corporate Planning, BBC, 1995–97; Special Advr to Prime Minister on culture, media, sport and the knowledge econ., 1997–2001. Mem. (Lab) Islington BC, 1994–95 (Chairman: Early Years Cttee; Housing Cttee). MP (Lab) Stalybridge and Hyde, 2001–10. Asst Govt Whip, 2004–05; Parly Under-Sec. of State, DCMS, 2005–06; Minister of State, DWP, 2006–07; Sec. of State for Culture, Media and Sport, 2007–08, for Work and Pensions, 2008–09. Sen. Producer, Rare Day, 2010–13. Sen. Advr, Boston Consulting Gp, 2011–13. Member, Board: Nat. Theatre, 2010–15; RAJAR, 2019; Radioplayer, 2019 Gov., BFI, 2011–13. Chm., Trustees, IPPR, 2010–12; Trustee, Citizens UK, 2010–13. *Publications:* contrib. various publications for IPPR. *Recreations:* football, film, theatre, music.

**PURNELL, Nicholas Robert;** QC 1985; *b* 29 Jan. 1944; *s of* late Oliver Cuthbert Purnell and Pauline Purnell; *m* 1970, Melanie Stanway; four *s. Educ:* Oratory Sch.; Kely Coll. Cambridge (Open Exhibnr; MA). Called to the Bar, Middle Temple, 1968 (Astbury Schol.), Bencher 1990; Junior of Central Criminal Court Bar Mess, 1972–75; Prosecuting Counsel to Inland Revenue, 1977–79; Jun. Treasury Counsel, 1979–85; Recorder, 1986–2010; a Dep. High Court Judge, 1995–2014. Mem., Bar Council and Senate, 1973–77, 1982–85, 1989–91 (Chm., Legal Aid Fees Cttee, 1989–90); Member: Lord Chancellor's and Home Secretary's Working Party on the Training of the Judiciary, 1975–78; Crown Court Rules Cttee, 1982–88; Lord Chancellor's Adv. Cttee on Educn and Conduct, 1991–97; Criminal Cttee, Judicial Studies Bd, 1991–96. Chm., Criminal Bar Assoc., 1990–91. Governor, The Oratory Sch., 1994–2018. *Recreations:* living in France as much as possible, supporting Wimbledon AFC and En Avant de Guingamp. *Address:* Cloth Fair Chambers, 39–40 Cloth Fair, EC1A 7NT.
*See also* P. O. *Purnell.*

**PURNELL, Paul Oliver;** QC 1982; a Recorder, 1985–2011; *s of* late Oliver Cuthbert and Pauline Purnell; *m* 1966, Celia Consuelo Ocampo; one *s* two *d. Educ:* The Oratory Sch.; Jesus Coll., Oxford (MA). Served 4th/7th Royal Dragoon Guards, 1958–62. Called to the Bar, Inner Temple, 1962, Bencher, 1991; Head of Chambers, 2007–15. Jun. Treasury Counsel at Central Criminal Court, 1976–82. *Recreations:* motorcycling, publishing short stories and novellas. *Club:* Hurlingham.
*See also* N. R. *Purnell.*

**PURSE, Hugh Robert Leslie;** barrister; part-time Chairman of Employment (formerly Industrial) Tribunals, 1996–2003; *b* 22 Oct. 1943; *s of* Robert Purse and Elsie Purse (*née* Kemp). *Educ:* St Peter's School, York; King's College London (LLB). Called to the Bar, Gray's Inn, 1964 (Atkin Scholar). Legal Asst, Dept of Employment, 1969; Legal Adviser to Price Commission, 1978–79; Govt legal service, 1979–96: Legal Advr, Dept of Employment, and Principal Asst Treasury Solicitor, 1988–96.

**PURSEY, Nigel Thomas;** Chief Executive, Staffordshire County Council, 2003–07; *b* 4 Aug. 1949. *Educ:* Manchester Univ. (MusB). CPFA 1975. Trainee Accountant, Cheshire CC, 1971–75; Accountant, Mid Glamorgan CC, 1975–78; Wiltshire County Council: Group Accountant, 1978–81; Chief Admin. Assistant (Finance), 1981–83; Chief Accountant, 1983–86; Asst County Treasurer, 1986–92; Shropshire County Council: County Treas., 1992–97; Chief Exec., 1997–2003. Clerk to: Shropshire Lieutenancy, 1997–2003; Staffs Lieutenancy, 2003–07; Staffs Police Authy, 2003–07. Dep. Chm., Shropshire Learning and Skills Council, 2001–03; Mem. Bd and Chair of Audit Cttee, Children's Workforce Develt Council, 2008–12. Associate Master of the Music, Shrewsbury Abbey, 2001–. Treas., Pontesbury-Muheza Link Charity, 2008– (Trustee, 2012–); Trustee, Lingen Davies Appeal, 2010– (Chm., Trustees, 2012–16). Gov., Staffs Univ., 2003–07. *Recreations:* music, walking, bridge, family activities.

**PURSGLOVE, Thomas Christopher John;** MP (C) Corby, since 2015; an Assistant Government Whip, since 2019; *b* 5 Nov. 1988. *Educ:* Sir Christopher Hatton Sch., Wellingborough; Queen Mary Coll., Univ. of London (BA Politics). Pt-time work for Rt Hon. Douglas Hogg, MP, 2008–10; Parly Asst to Christopher Heaton-Harris, MP, 2010–15; Dir, Together Against Wind, 2014–17. PPS to Minister of State for Immigration, 2016–17, to Sec. of State for Internat. Trade 2017–19. Mem. (C), Wellingborough BC, 2007–15. *Recreations:* cricket, swimming, golf, running. *Address:* House of Commons, SW1A 0AA.

**PURSHOUSE, Michael,** PhD; CEng, FIET, FREng, FInstP, FIMA; independent technical and management consultant, since 2012; *b* Rotherham, 19 Sept. 1951; *s of* Edwin Purshouse and Rita Purshouse (*née* Bryars); *m* 1981, Sabine Gabriele Rohrssen; two *d. Educ:* St John's C of E Sch., Mexborough; Mexborough Grammar Sch.; Rolls-Royce Tech. Coll., Bristol; Sidney Sussex Coll., Cambridge (BAC Industrial Scholar; Coll. Scholar; BA 1973; Robert Angus Engrg Student; RAeS Geoffrey de Havilland Scholar; PhD 1978). CEng 1980; VDI 1983; FIET (FIEE 1996); FREng 2007; FInstP 2008; FIMA 2010. Undergrad. apprentice, BAC, Bristol, 1969–74; Acoustics Consultant, YARD Ltd, Glasgow, 1978–81; Res. Scientist, Fraunhofer-Gesellschaft, Stuttgart, Germany, 1981–83; Principal Consultant, YARD Ltd, 1984–92; Business Gp Manager, Naval Engrg, BAeSEMA Ltd, 1992–2000; Sen. Systems Engineer, Thales UK plc, 2000–12; Chief Engr, Thales Aircraft Carrier Team, 2000–03; Hd, Systems Engrg, Aircraft Carrier Alliance, 2003–06; Proj. Dir and Chief Engr, Thales-Boeing FRES System of Systems Integrator, 2007–10; Technical Dir, Thales UK Land Systems, 2010–12. Hon. Prof., Dept of Physics and Astronomy, Univ. of Glasgow, 1997–2010; Hon. Fellow, Sidney Sussex Coll., Cambridge, 2014– (Fellow Commoner, 2004–14); Lecturer: Warwick Univ., 2014–; UWE, 2014–. Pres., Cambridge Univ. Engrs' Assoc., 2012–17 (Mem. Exec. Cttee, 2007–12); Educn, Training and Careers Cttee, STFC, 2009–12. Chm., Glasgow Panel,

IMechE, 1992–95. Mem., Audit and Risk Cttee, 2014–17, Membership Panel 5, 2014–17, RAEng; Mem., Academic Accreditation Cttee, IET, 2016–. Vice-Pres., Stephenson Soc., Sidney Sussex Coll., 1996–2006; 1st Cl. Mem., Smeatonian Soc. of Civil Engrs, 2014–. Treas., Christ Ch PCC, Bradford-on-Avon, 2015–. Dir, Avonbrook Glade Ltd, 2012–. Freeman: Engineers' Co., 2011 (Liveryman, 2012–); City of London. *Recreations:* economics, European history and politics, visiting country estates, reading, music (play piano), dining out with friends and family, foreign travel. *Address:* c/o Sidney Sussex College, Cambridge CB2 3HU. *E:* mp458@cam.ac.uk. *Club:* Bath and County (Treas., 2015–19).

**PURSSELL, Anthony John Richard;** Vice-President, National Society for Epilepsy, since 2010 (Trustee, 1993–2008; Chairman, 1995–98); *b* 5 July 1926; *m* 1952, Ann Margaret Batchelor; two *s* one *d. Educ:* Oriel Coll., Oxford (MA Hons Chemistry). Managing Director: Arthur Guinness Son & Co. (Park Royal) Ltd, 1968; Arthur Guinness Son & Co. (Dublin) Ltd, 1973; Arthur Guinness & Sons plc, 1975–81; Jt Dep. Chm., 1981–83. Thames Valley and S Midlands Regl Bd, Lloyds Bank plc: Regl Dir, 1982–91; Chm., 1989–91. Member: IBA, 1976–81; Bd, CAA, 1984–90. Trustee and Hon. Treas., Oxfam, 1985–92. *Recreations:* travel, golf, books. *Address:* Allendale, 53 Bulstrode Way, Gerrards Cross, Bucks SL9 7QT. *Club:* Leander (Henley).

**PURVES, Elizabeth Mary, (Libby), (Mrs Paul Heiney),** OBE 1999; writer, broadcaster and theatre critic; *b* 2 Feb. 1950; *d of* late James Grant Purves, CMG; *m* 1980, Paul Heiney, *qv*; one *d* (one *s* decd). *Educ:* Convent of the Sacred Heart, Tunbridge Wells; St Anne's Coll., Oxford (1st Cl. Hons Eng. Lang. and Lit.). BBC Local Radio (Oxford), 1972–76; Radio 4: Reporter, 1976–79, Presenter, 1979–81, Today; Presenter, Midweek, 1983–2017. Editor, Tatler, March–Oct. 1983, resigned; columnist, 1990–, chief theatre critic, 2010–13, The Times. Pres., Council for Nat. Parks, 2000–01. Trustee, Nat. Maritime Mus., 1991–2001. Founder, Theatrecat.com, 2014. *Publications:* (ed) The Happy Unicorns, 1971; (ed) Adventures Under Sail, H. W. Tilman, 1982; Britain At Play, 1982; Sailing Weekend Book, 1985; How Not to be a Perfect Mother, 1986; Where Did You Leave the Admiral, 1987; (jtly) The English and their Horses, 1988; The Hurricane Tree, 1988; One Summer's Grace, 1989; How Not to Raise a Perfect Child, 1991; Getting the Story, 1993; Working Times, 1993; How Not to be a Perfect Family, 1994; (with Paul Heiney) Grumpers' Farm, 1996; Holy Smoke, 1998; Nature's Masterpiece: a family survival book, 2000; Radio - a True Love Story, 2002; That Was Midweek That Was, 2017; *novels:* Casting Off, 1995; A Long Walk in Wintertime, 1996; Home Leave, 1997; More Lives Than One, 1998; Regatta, 1999; Passing Go, 2000; A Free Woman, 2001; Mother Country, 2002; Continental Drift, 2003; Acting Up, 2004; Love Songs and Lies, 2007; Shadow Child, 2009. *Recreations:* sailing, walking, theatre, radio. *Address:* c/o The Times, 1 London Bridge Street, SE1 9GF. *Club:* Royal Cruising.

**PURVES, Sir William,** Kt 1993; CBE 1988; DSO 1951; Chairman, 1990–98, Chief Executive, 1990–92, HSBC Holdings plc; *b* 27 Dec. 1931; *s of* Andrew and Ida Purves; *m* 1st, 1958, Diana Troutbeck Richardson (marr. diss. 1988); two *s* two *d*; 2nd, 1989, Rebecca Jane Lewellen. *Educ:* Kelso High School. FIBScot; FCIB. National Service, with Commonwealth Div. in Korea (Subaltern; DSO). National Bank of Scotland, 1948–54; Hongkong and Shanghai Banking Corporation: Germany, Hong Kong, Malaysia, Singapore, Sri Lanka, Japan, 1954–70; Chief Accountant, Hong Kong, 1970; Manager, Tokyo, 1974; Sen. Manager Overseas Operations, 1976; Asst General Manager, Overseas Operations, 1978; General Manager, 1979–82; Executive Director, 1982–84; Dep. Chm., 1984–86; Chm. and Chief Exec., 1986–92; Chm., Midland Bank Plc, 1994–97 (Dir, 1987–90); Dir, Marine Midland Banks Inc., 1982–98. Chairman: British Bank of ME, 1979–98; Hakluyt & Co., Ltd, 2000–08; non-executive Director: Shell Transport and Trading, 1993–2002; Reuters Founders Share Co. Ltd, 1995–2009; Trident Safeguards Ltd, 1999–2003; BW Gp Ltd, 2003–12; Aquarius Platinum, 2004–12; Dep. Chm., Alstom, 1998–2003. Pres., Internat. Monetary Conf., 1992. Trustee and Dep. Chm., Imperial War Mus., 1996–2004. Hon. LLD: Sheffield, 1993; Hong Kong, 1994; Hon. DBA: Stirling, 1987; Hong Kong Poly., 1993; Napier, 1998; Hon. MBA Strathclyde, 1996; UMIST, 2001. GBM 1999. *Address:* Flat 1, Ebury House, 39 Elizabeth Street, SW1W 9RP. *Clubs:* Royal Automobile, Caledonian; Hong Kong Jockey, Hong Kong.

**PURVIS OF TWEED,** Baron *cr* 2013 (Life Peer), of East March in the Scottish Borders; **Jeremy Purvis;** Member (Lib Dem) Tweeddale, Ettrick and Lauderdale, Scottish Parliament, 2003–11; *b* 15 Jan. 1974; *s of* George Purvis and Eileen Purvis. *Educ:* Brunel Univ. (BSc Hons Politics and Mod. Hist.). Personal Asst to Sir David Steel, later Lord Steel of Aikwood, 1995–98. Director: GJW Scotland, 1998–2001; McEwan Purvis, 2001–03. Contested (Lib Dem) Midlothian S, Tweeddale and Lauderdale, 2011. Leader, Devo Plus Gp, 2012–13; Campaigns Dir, Keep Scotland Beautiful, 2013. *Recreations:* classic cars, painting, reading.

**PURVIS, Bryan John;** Head Master, William Hulme's Grammar School, Manchester, 1997–99; Founder, Hale Educational Consultancy, 2000; *b* 6 Aug. 1947; *s of* Robert Hunt Purvis and Eleanor Liddle Purvis; *m* 1969, Irene Anne Griffiths (*d* 2008); one *s* two *d. Educ:* Tynemouth High Sch.; Bedford Coll., London (BSc); Durham Univ. (MSc). Biology Master, St Joseph's Grammar Tech. Sch., Hebburn on Tyne, 1969–74; Dep. Headmaster and Head of Biology, King's Sch., Tynemouth, 1974–93; Head Master, Altrincham GS for Boys, 1993–97. Sen. Consultant, Nat. Coll. for Sch. Leadership, 2007–15. *Recreations:* gardening, hill-walking, watching football (Manchester City) and Rugby. *Address:* The Old Forge, 7A Church Brow, Bowdon, Altrincham, Cheshire WA14 2SF. *T:* (0161) 929 1053. *E:* BPrvs@aol.com. *Club:* St James' (Manchester).

**PURVIS, Dawn;** independent consultant, since 2015; Chief Executive, Victoria Housing Estates Ltd, since 2016; *b* 22 Oct. 1966; two *s. Educ:* Queen's Univ. Belfast (BA Hons 1st cl. Sociol. and Social Policy 2003). Researcher: Sch. of Envmtl Scis, Univ. of Ulster, Coleraine, 2004–06; Sch. of Sociology, Huddersfield Univ., 2006–07. Mem. for Belfast E, NI Assembly, Jan. 2007–2011 (PUP, 2007–10, Ind, 2010–11); contested (Ind) same seat, 2011. Leader, PUP, 2007–10. Mem., NI Policing Bd, 2006–07; Comr, Equality Commn for NI, 2019–. Prog. Dir, Marie Stopes NI, 2012–15. Chair, Healing Through Remembering, 2011–.

**PURVIS, Air Vice-Marshal Henry R.;** *see* Reed-Purvis.

**PURVIS, Iain Younie;** QC 2006; a Recorder, since 2010; a Deputy High Court Judge, since 2012; *b* 23 Aug. 1963; *s of* John Younie Purvis and Juliet Purvis (*née* Parker); *m* 1993, Beverley Jane Myers; two *s* one *d. Educ:* Royal Grammar Sch., High Wycombe; Clare Coll., Cambridge (BA Law 1984, MA); St Edmund Hall, Oxford (BCL). Called to the Bar, Gray's Inn, 1986. *Publications:* Working with Technology, 2001. *Recreations:* neolithic monuments, ski-ing, running. *Address:* 11 South Square, Gray's Inn, WC1R 5EY. *E:* ipurvis@11southsquare.com.

**PURVIS, John Robert,** CBE 1990; Partner, Purvis & Co., since 1986; *b* 6 July 1938; *s of* Lt-Col R. W. B. Purvis, MC, JP, and Mrs R. W. B. Purvis, JP; *m* 1962, Louise S. Durham; one *s* two *d. Educ:* Cargilfield, Barnton, Edinburgh; Trinity Coll., Glenalmond, Perthshire; St Salvator's Coll., Univ. of St Andrews (MA Hons). National Service, Lieut Scots Guards,

1956–58. First National City Bank, New York, 1962–69: London, 1962–63; New York, 1963–65; Milan, 1965–69; Treasurer, Noble Grossart Ltd, Edinburgh, 1969–73; Man. Dir, Gilmerton Management Services Ltd, 1973–92. MEP (C): Mid-Scotland and Fife, 1979–84, contested same seat, 1984; Scotland, 1999–2009. European Democratic Group, European Parliament: whip, 1980–82; spokesman on energy, research and technology, 1982–84; Vice-Pres., Economic and Monetary Affairs Cttee, EPP Gp, 2001–09. Vice Pres., Scottish Cons. and Unionist Assoc., 1987–89 (Chm., Industry Cttee, 1986–97); Mem., IBA, 1985–89 (Chm., Scottish Adv. Cttee, 1985–89); Mem., Scottish Adv. Cttee on Telecommunications, 1990–98. Chm., Financial Future, Brussels, 2009–. Director: James River Fine Papers Ltd, 1984–95; Edgar Astaire & Co. Ltd, 1993–94; Jamont NV, 1994–95; European Utilities Trust plc, 1994–2007; Curtis Fine Papers Ltd, 1995–2001; Crown Vantage Ltd, 1995–2001; Chairman: Kingdom FM Radio Ltd, 1998–2008 (Dir, 2008–13); Belgrave Capital Management Ltd, 1999–. *Publications*: (section 'Money') in Power and Manoeuvrability, 1978. *Address*: Brigton, St Andrews, Fife KY16 8NB. *T*: (01334) 475830. *E*: purvisco@jpurvis.co.uk. *Clubs*: Cavalry and Guards, Farmers; New (Edinburgh); Royal and Ancient (St Andrews).

**PURVIS, Sir Neville**, KCB 1992; Vice Admiral, retired; Chairman, Grays International of Cambridge, 2001–07; *b* 8 May 1936; *s* of Charles Geoffrey and Sylvia Rose Purvis; *m* 2nd, 1970, Alice Margaret (*née* Hill) (marr. diss. 1998); two *s*; 3rd, 2008, Susan Legh Bancroft. *Educ*: Charterhouse; Selwyn College, Cambridge (MA). BRNC Dartmouth, 1953; reading engineering at Cambridge, 1954–57; joined submarine service, 1959; served in HM Ships Turpin, 1960, Dreadnought, 1963, Repulse, 1967; Naval Staff, 1970; Sqdn Engineer Officer, 3rd Submarine Sqdn, 1973; Staff of Flag Officer, Submarines, 1975; RCDS 1980; in Command, HMS Collingwood, 1985–87; Dir Gen., Future Material Projects (Naval), 1987–88; Dir Gen., Naval Manpower and Trng, 1988–90; Mem., Admiralty Bd, and Chief of Fleet Support, 1991–94; Chief Exec., BSI, 1994–96; Dir Gen., British Safety Council, 1997–2001; Chm., Reliance Secure Task Mgt, 2001–05. Chm., Council, Friends of Nat. Maritime Mus., 2002–05; Chm. and Trustee, Marine Soc. and Sea Cadets, 2005–07 (Trustee, Sea Cadets Assoc., 2003–05). President: Westminster Br., Royal Soc. of St George, 2007–; London Br., Submariners Assoc., 2007–. FRSA 1992. *Recreation*: wining and dining. *Address*: 108 Homecross House, 21 Fishers Lane, Chiswick, W4 1YB.

**PURVIS, Prof. Stewart Peter**, CBE 2000; Professor of Television Journalism, City University, 2003–15; *b* 28 Oct. 1947; *s* of late Peter and Lydia Purvis; *m* 1st, 1972 (marr. diss. 1993); one *d*; 2nd, 2004, Jacqui Marson; two *s*. *Educ*: Dulwich Coll.; Univ. of Exeter (BA). Presenter, Harlech TV, 1968–69; BBC News trainee, 1969; ITN journalist, 1972; Programme Editor, News At Ten, 1980; Editor, Channel Four News, 1983; Independent Television News: Dep. Editor, 1986; Editor, 1989; Editor-in-Chief, 1991–95; Chief Exec., 1995–2003. Dir, ITN Ltd, 1989–2003; Pres., Euronews, 1998–2002. News Internat. Prof. of Broadcast Media, Univ. of Oxford, 2004–05. Partner, Content and Standards, Ofcom, 2007–10; Chairman: Digital Britain Media Literacy Wkg Gp, 2009; Consortium for Digital Participation, 2009–10. Mem., Adv. Cttee on BBC Charter Renewal, DCMS, 2016–17. Non-executive Director: Royal Marsden NHS Trust, 1999–2004; Channel Four, 2013–. Trustee, Services Sound and Vision Corp., 2013–17. FRTS 1991. Hon. LLD Exeter, 2005. BAFTA Award for Best News or Outside Broadcast, 1986, 1987; BPG Award for Best News or Current Affairs Prog., 1988; Gold Medal, RTS, 2009. *Publications*: (with J. Hulbert) When Reporters Cross the Line, 2013; Guy Burgess: the spy who knew everyone, 2016. *Address*: c/o Knight Ayton Management, 29 Gloucester Place, W1U 8HX. *E*: info@knightayton.co.uk.

**PUSEY, Prof. Charles Dickson**, DSc; FRCP, FRCPath, FMedSci, FRSB; Professor of Medicine, since 2003, and Head of Renal Section, Division of Medicine, since 1997, Imperial College, London (Head of Postgraduate Medicine, 2006–14); Hon. Consultant Physician, since 1984, and Lead Clinician, since 2001, Directorate of Renal Medicine and Transplantation, Imperial College Healthcare NHS Trust (formerly Hammersmith Hospitals NHS Trust). *Educ*: Corpus Christi Coll., Cambridge (BA 1969; MB BChir 1972; MA 1973); Guy's Hosp. Med. Sch., London Univ. (MSc 1983; DSc 2002). FRCP 1989; FRCPath 1997. House Officer and Jun. Med. Registrar, Guy's Hosp., 1972–74; Unit Med. Officer, Specialist then Sen. Specialist, in Medicine, RAF, 1974–79; Sen. Registrar, MRC Trng Fellow and Wellcome Trust Sen. Fellow in Clin. Sci., RPMS and Hammersmith Hosp., 1980–89; Sen. Lectr, Reader and then Prof. in Renal Medicine, RPMS and Imperial Coll., London, 1989–2002; Dir of Res. and Develt, 2005–08, Dir of Educn, 2008–11, Hammersmith Hosps NHS Trust, subseq. Imperial Coll. Healthcare NHS Trust. Acad. Registrar, RCP, 2001–05. Chm., Kidney Research UK, 2002–07. FMedSci 2002; Fellow, American Soc. of Nephrology, 2009; FRSB (FSB 2011). *Publications*: Fast Facts: Renal Disorders, 2006, 2nd edn 2013; over 450 articles, reviews, and book chapters in field of renal medicine. *Recreations*: tennis, walking, music. *Address*: Renal Section, Department of Medicine, Imperial College London, Hammersmith Campus, Du Cane Road, W12 0NN. *T*: (020) 8383 3152, *Fax*: (020) 8383 2062. *E*: c.pusey@imperial.ac.uk.

**PUSEY, Prof. Peter Nicholas**, PhD; FRS 1996; FRSE; FInstP; Professor of Physics, University of Edinburgh, 1991–2008, now Emeritus (Head, Department of Physics and Astronomy, 1994–97 and 2000–03); *b* 30 Dec. 1942; *s* of late Harold Kenneth Pusey and Edith Joan Pusey (*née* Sparks); *m* 1966, Elizabeth Ann Nind; two *d*. *Educ*: St Edward's Sch., Oxford; Clare Coll., Cambridge (MA); Univ. of Pittsburgh (PhD 1969). FInstP 1981; FRSE 1996. Postdoctoral Fellow, IBM T. J. Watson Res. Center, Yorktown Heights, NY, 1969–72; SPSO, later Grade 6, RSRE, Malvern, 1972–91. *Publications*: numerous contribs in scientific literature. *Address*: School of Physics and Astronomy, University of Edinburgh, Peter Guthrie Tait Road, Edinburgh EH9 3FD. *E*: p.n.pusey@ed.ac.uk.

**PUTIN, Vladimir Vladimirovich**; President of Russia, 2000–08 and since 2012; Leader, People's Front for Russia, since 2013; *b* Leningrad, 7 Oct. 1952; *s* of late Vladimir Putin and Maria Putin; *m* 1983, Lyudmila Shkrebneva (marr. diss. 2014); two *d*. *Educ*: Leningrad State Univ. (law degree 1975); St Petersburg Mining Univ. (PhD Econs 1997). With KGB, in USSR and Germany, 1975–90; Adviser: to Rector, Leningrad State Univ., 1990; to Mayor of Leningrad, 1990–91; Chm., Cttee on Foreign Relations, Office of the Mayor, St Petersburg, 1991–94; first Dep. Mayor, and Chm. Cttee on Foreign Relations, St Petersburg, 1994–96; first Dep. Hd, Gen. Mgt Dept of Presidential Admin, 1996–97; Hd of Control Dept, 1997–98, first Dep. Hd of Admin, 1998, Kremlin; Dir, Fed. Security Service, Russia, 1998–99; Sec., Security Council, Russia, 1999; Prime Minister of Russia, 1999, 2008–12; Chm., United Russia Party, 2008–12. Chm., Bd of Trustees, Russian Geographical Soc., 2009–. *Publications*: First Person (autobiog.), 2000; (with Arkady Rotenberg) The Art of Judo: from game to mastery, 2016. *Recreations*: mountain ski-ing, judo. *Address*: Office of the President, The Kremlin, Kremlevskaya Naberezhnaya, Moscow 103073, Russia.

**PUTNAM, Roger George**, CBE 2007; Visiting Professor of Automotive Business, City, University of London (formerly City University), since 2006; Chairman, Ford Motor Co. Ltd, 2002–05; *b* 17 Aug. 1945; *s* of George William Putnam and Peggy May Putnam (*née* Morgan); *m* 1969, Patricia Elizabeth Williams; one *s* one *d*. *Educ*: Haberdashers' Aske's Sch., Elstree. Public Relations Officer, 1966–68, Gen. Manager, Sales and Marketing, 1968–74, Lotus Cars Ltd; Director, Sales and Marketing: JCL Marine Ltd, 1974–76; Lotus Cars Ltd, 1976–82; Jaguar Cars Ltd, 1982–2002. Trustee, Jaguar Trust (formerly Jaguar Daimler Heritage Trust), 1985–2010; Chairman: Retail Motor Strategy Gp, BERR, later BIS, 2005–10; The Learning Grid, 2007–09. Non-exec. Director: Halcyon Days Ltd, 2002–11; ITM Power plc, 2006– (Chm., 2010–); Autologic Gp plc, 2007–08; Chm., Suila Ltd, 2008–17. Dir, SMMT, 2002–08 (Pres., 2005–06). Pres., CIM (Midland), 2002. FIMI 1984. *Recreations*: walking, photography, military history, theatre, reading. *Address*: Further Hill Grange, Ullenhall, Henley-in-Arden, Warwicks B95 5PN. *Club*: Royal Automobile.

**PUTTNAM**, family name of **Baron Puttnam**.

**PUTTNAM, Baron** *cr* 1997 (Life Peer), of Queensgate in the Royal Borough of Kensington and Chelsea; **David Terence Puttnam**, Kt 1995; CBE 1983; Chairman: Enigma Productions Ltd, since 1978; National Endowment for Science, Technology and the Arts, 1998–2003; Chairman, Atticus Education, since 2012; *b* 25 Feb. 1941; *s* of Leonard Arthur Puttnam and Marie Beatrice Puttnam; *m* 1961, Patricia Mary (*née* Jones); one *s* one *d*. *Educ*: Minchenden Grammar Sch., London; City and Guilds. Advertising, 1958–66; photography, 1966–68; film prodn, 1968–2000; public policy, 1988–. Producer of feature films including: Bugsy Malone, 1976 (four BAFTA awards); The Duellists, 1977 (Jury Prize, Cannes); Midnight Express, 1978 (two Acad. Awards, three BAFTA Awards); Chariots of Fire, 1981 (four Acad. Awards, three BAFTA Awards, incl. awards for best film); Local Hero, 1982 (two BAFTA Awards); The Killing Fields, 1985 (three Acad. Awards, eight BAFTA Awards incl. Best Film; David di Donatello award, Accademia del Cinema Italiano, 1985); The Mission, 1986 (Palme d'Or, Cannes, 1986, one Acad. Award, three BAFTA awards, David di Donatello award, Accademia del Cinema Italiano, 1987). Chm. and Chief Exec. Officer, Columbia Pictures, 1986–88. Dep. Chm., Channel Four, 2006–12. Visiting Professor: Drama Dept, Bristol Univ., 1986–98; Inst. of Educn, London Univ., 2008–13; Adjunct Professor: University Coll. Cork, 2012–; Sch. of Media and Communications, RMIT, 2018–. Digital Champion, Republic of Ireland, 2012–17. Chairman: Jt Scrutiny Cttee for Communications Bill, 2002; Jt Cttee on Draft Climate Change Bill, 2007; Hansard Soc.'s Commn on Communication of Parly Democracy, 2004–05; Digital Technol. and Democracy Cttee, H of L, 2019–; Prime Minister's Trade Envoy to Vietnam, Laos and Cambodia, 2012–16. Director: National Film Finance Corp., 1980–85; Anglia Television Gp, 1982–99; Survival Anglia TV Ltd, 1982–98; Claridge's Hotel, 1984–99; Village Roadshow Internat., 1988–98; Village Roadshow Corp., 1989–99; Chrysalis Group, 1993–96; Promethean World plc (formerly Chalkfree), 2006–15; Huntsworth plc, 2007–12; EMPGI (Ireland), 2012–; Chairman: Internat. Television Enterprises Ltd, 1988–99; Spectrum Strategy Consultants, 1999–2006; Futurelab, 2006–11; Dep. Chm., Profero, 2010–14 (Chm., 2007–10); Chm., Adv. Bd, Prime Hotels (UK) Ltd, 2011–14. Governor: National Film and Television Sch., 1974–96 (Chm., 1988–96; Life Pres., 2017); Central Sch. of Speech and Drama, 1993–96; LSE, 1997–2002 (Vis. Prof.); London Inst., 1998–2002; Member: Governing Council, Nat. Coll. for Sch. Leadership; Academic Adv. Bd, Inst. for Advanced Studies, Univ. of Bristol; Co-founder, European Media Business Sch., Madrid 1991. President: UNICEF UK, 2002–09 (Ambassador, 2010–); Film Distributors' Assoc., 2007–; Vice President: BAFTA, 1993–2004; CPRE, 1997–2007 (Pres., 1985–92). Member: British Screen Adv. Council, 1988–98; Adv. Cttee, Tate Gall. Liverpool, 1988–94; Arts Council Lottery Panel, 1995–98; Educn Standards Task Force, 1997–2002; Creative Industries Task Force, 1997–99; British Educnl Communications and Technol. Agency; Arts and Humanities Res. Bd; Senate, Engrg Council; Council, Hansard Soc., 2007–; Accenture Adv. Council, Ireland, 2013–; Nat. Forum for Enhancement of Teaching and Learning, Ireland, 2013–16; Bd, Commonwealth of Learning. Chairman: Arts Adv. Cttee, 1991–2003, Film, TV and Video Adv. Cttee, 1992–2001, Trustees, Science Mus., 1996–2003; British Council; Gen. Teaching Council, 1998–2001; Media and Culture Sector Adv. Gp, QCA, 2000–03; TSL Adv. Bd, 2010–18. Advr, DCSF, 1997–2005. Chair, Future for Public Services Television Inq., 2015–16. Chairman: Ateliers du cinéma européen 1991–94; Nat. Meml Arboretum, 1993–2003; Nat. Mus. of Photography, Film and Television, 1994–2003; Academic Bd, Pearson Coll., 2014–17; Nord Anglia Internat. Sch., Dublin, 2017–; Film London Exec. Task Force. Trustee: Tate Gall., 1986–93; Nat. Energy Foundn, 1990–98; IPPR, 1998–2011; Royal Acad. of Arts, 2000–03; Sunderland AFC Foundn, 2001–13; Thomson Foundn, 2003–; Forum for the Future, 1996–2004 (Chm., 1996–99); Eden Project, 2009–13; Transformation Trust, 2009–11; Baker Dearing Trust, 2010–13; Mohamed S. Farsi Foundn, 2011–19; Chm. Trustees, Nat. Teaching Awards, 1998–2008; Chm., North Music Trust, Sage Gateshead, 2007–13. Patron: Schools North East, 2008–; Dublin Bid for World Summit on Media for Children, 2020/2023, 2017–. Pres., Thirty Club, London, 2010–11. Hon. Mem., British Business Gp Vietnam, 2014–17. Internat. Ambassador, WWF. Hon. Chancellor: Univ. of Sunderland, 1998–2007; Open Univ., 2007–14. Lay Canon, Durham Cathedral, 2002–08. FRGS; FRSA; FRPS; Fellow: BFI, 1997; BAFTA, 2006; FCGI 1999; FRTS 2002; FRIA 2016. Founder Mem., Europ. Film Acad., 1988. Freedom: City of Sunderland, 2007; Metropolitan Bor. of Gateshead, 2014. Freeman, Educators' Guild. Charter Fellow, Coll. of Teachers, 2001. Fellow, Sam Spiegel Film Sch., Jerusalem, 2012. Hon. Fellow: Manchester Polytechnic, 1990; Inst. of Educn, London Univ., 2007; IPA, 2013; Nat. Film and Television Sch., 2014; Brit. Inst. of Professional Photographers. Hon. FCSD 1990; Hon. FLI 1994. Hon. Cork Person of the Yr, 2013. Hon. Life Mem., Royal Dublin Soc., 2018 (Hon. Mem., 2015). Hon. LLD Bristol, 1983; Hon. DLitt: Leicester, 1986; Sunderland, 1992; Bradford, 1993; Humberside, 1996; Westminster, 1997; Kent, 1998; London Guildhall, 1999; City, 2000; Nottingham, 2000; Heriot-Watt, 2001; Birmingham, 2002; Southampton, 2002; Keele, 2002; Abertay, 2003; Hon. LittD: Leeds, 1992; N London, 2001; Hon. DLit QUB, 2001; Hon. Dr of Drama RSAMD, 1998; Hon. DPhil Cheltenham and Gloucester Coll. of Higher Educn, 1998; Hon. DSc (Med.) Imperial Coll., London, 1999; Hon. DFA American Univ. in London, 2000; Hon. Dr: Navarra, Spain, 1999; Sheffield Hallam, 2000; King Alfred's Coll., Winchester, 2002; Herzen Univ., St Petersburg, 2003; Surrey, 2003; Thames Valley, 2004; Queen Margaret Univ. Coll., 2004; Brunel, 2004; Middx, 2004; Greenwich, 2004; Nottingham Trent, 2007; Open, 2007; Edinburgh, 2013; Griffiths, Brisbane, 2013; TCD, 2016; Bath Spa, 2017; Hon. DEd Sunderland, 2007. Michael Balcon Award for outstanding contribn to British Film Industry, 1982, Fellowship, 2006, BAFTA; Benjamin Franklin Medal, RSA, 1996; Crystal Award, World Economic Forum, 1997; President's Medal, RPS, 2003; Akiro Kurasawa Award, 2007; Bicentennial Medal, RSA, 2008; New Media Consortium Fellows Award (USA), 2012; T K Whitaker Award for Outstanding Contribn to Public Life, Inst. Banking, Ireland, 2019. Commandeur de l'Ordre des Arts et des Lettres (France), 2006 (Officier, 1992). *Publications*: (with Brian Wenham) The Third Age of Broadcasting, 1982; (jtly) Rural England, 1988; What Needs to Change?, 1996; Undeclared War, 1997; Movies and Money, 1998. *Recreations*: reading, watching movies. *Address*: House of Lords, SW1A 0PW. *Clubs*: Athenæum, Chelsea Arts, MCC.

**PUXLEY, James Henry Lavallin**; Lord-Lieutenant of Berkshire, since 2015 (Vice Lord-Lieutenant, 2011–15); *b* London, 23 Oct. 1948; *s* of John Philip Lavallin Puxley and Aline Carlos Puxley; *m* 1991, Deborah Ferguson; one *s* one *d*. *Educ*: Eton; Univ. of Bristol (BA); Royal Agricl Coll., Cirencester (Dip.). ARICS. Partner, Britton Poole and Burns, chartered surveyors, 1978–81; Dir, Welford Farms Ltd, 1981–; Partner: Elton Farm Partners,

1981–2011; Welford Estate Partners, 2012–. Chm., W Berks Anglo-American Community Relns Cttee, 1984–92. Hon. Comdr, RAF Welford, 2007–. DL Berks, 2005. CStJ 2018. *Recreations:* travel, theatre, walking. *Address:* Welford Park, Welford, Newbury, Berks RG20 8HU. *T:* (01488) 608691. *E:* jpuxley@welfordpark.co.uk. *Club:* Travellers.

**PWAISIHO, Rt Rev. William Alaha,** OBE 2004; Rector of Gawsworth, 1999–2019; an Hon. Assistant Bishop, Diocese of Chester, since 1997; *b* Solomon Is, 14 May 1948; *s of* Stephen Honiuhi and Esther Makatoro; *m* 1976, Sister Kate Kome Oikada; one *s* three *d* and one adopted *s*. *Educ:* C of E primary, sen. and secondary schs in Solomon Is; Bp Patterson Theol Coll., Kohimarama (Dip. in Theol. and Biblical Studies). Ordained deacon, 1974, priest, 1975; Chaplain to Archbp of Melanesia and to Central Police HQ, Honiara, 1976; Curate, Mission Bay, Auckland, NZ (first missionary priest from Melanesia), 1977–78; Chaplain and Tutor, Bp Patterson Theol Coll., 1979–80; Dean, St Barnabas Provincial Cathedral, Honiara, 1980–81; Diocesan Bishop, Malaita, 1981–89; Tutor, Melanesian Brotherhood HQ, Tabalia, 1989–90; (first) Gen. Sec., Melanesian Bd of Mission, Honiara, 1990–95; Parish Priest, E of Honiara, 1995–97; Curate, St Anne and St Francis, Sale, UK, 1997–99. Chaplain: to High Sheriff of Cheshire, 2002–03; to Mayor, Cheshire E Council, 2015–16. Hon. Chaplain, Crimebeat in England and Wales, 2004; Mem., Ethnic Minority Ind. Adv. Gp, Cheshire Constabulary. Member: Melanesian Mission UK; UK and NI Churches Together Pacific Forum. *Recreations:* football, Rugby, fishing, volleyball. *Address:* 1 Williams Way, Henbury, Macclesfield, Cheshire SK11 9NR. *Club:* Macclesfield Rotary (Pres., 2011–12).

**PYANT, Paul;** lighting designer, since 1980; *b* 22 July 1953; *s of* late Leonard Vincent Pyant and of Jean Phoebe Pyant (*née* Frampton); partner, Stephen Lawless. *Educ:* Royal Acad. of Dramatic Art (Hons Dip.). Lighting designs for: Glyndebourne Opera, 1974–, including: Death in Venice, Falstaff, 1990; Le Nozze di Figaro, 1991; Die Fledermaus, 2003; A Midsummer Night's Dream, 2006; English National Opera, 1985–, including: Xerxes, 1985; Lady Macbeth of Mtsensk, 1987; Street Scene (Scottish Opera/ENO), 1989; Royal National Theatre, 1988–, including: Wind in the Willows, 1990; The Madness of George III, 1991; Carousel, 1992 (NY, 1994, Japan, 1995); Candide, 1999; Streetcar Named Desire, 2003; Othello, 1997 (and Salzburg); 2000 Years, 2005; King Lear, 2014; Houston Grand Opera, 1989–, incl. New Year, 1989; Royal Opera House, 1991–; Royal Shakespeare Co., 1991–, including: Richard III, 1992; The Tempest, 1993; Northern Ballet Theatre, 1991–, including: Romeo and Juliet, 1991; Cinderella, 1993; Dracula, 1996; Donmar Warehouse, 1992–, including: Assassins, 1992; Cabaret, 1993; Company, 1995; English National Ballet, 1993–, incl. Cinderella, 1996; LA Opera, 1995–, incl. The Elixir of Love, 1996; *theatre* includes: Orpheus Descending, Th. Royal, Haymarket, 1988 (NY, 1989); Hamlet, Old Vic, 2004; The Woman in White, Palace Th., 2004 (NY, 2005); Lord of the Rings, Toronto, 2006, Th. Royal, Drury Lane, 2007; Aristo, Chichester, 2008; The Secret Garden, W Yorks Playhouse, 2009; Richard III, Old Vic, 2011; Charlie and the Chocolate Factory, Th. Royal, Drury Lane, 2013 (Olivier Award for Best Lighting Design, 2014); Oh What a Lovely War, Th. Royal, Stratford E, 2014; opera work includes: productions in USA: for Metropolitan Opera, Seattle Opera, San Francisco Opera and Chicago Opera; in Australia and NZ; in Europe, incl. La Scala, Milan; ballet productions for: Royal NZ Ballet, Norwegian Nat. Ballet, Boston Ballet, Atlanta Ballet, Colorado Ballet and Asami Maki Ballet, Tokyo. *Recreations:* steam locomotives, gardening. *Address:* The Old Coach House, Castle Ditch Lane, Lewes, E Sussex BN7 1YJ. *T:* (01273) 473960. *E:* PaulPyant@googlemail.com.

**PYATT, David John;** Principal Horn, Orchestra of the Royal Opera House, Covent Garden, since 2019; *b* 26 Sept. 1973; *s of* John Douglas Pyatt and Frances Margaret Pyatt; *m* 1997, Catherine Anne Whiteside; one *s* one *d*. *Educ:* Watford Boys' Grammar Sch.; Selwyn Coll., Cambridge. Guest Principal Horn, Scottish Opera, 1994–96; Co-Principal Horn, BBC Nat. Orch. of Wales, 1996–98; Principal Horn: LSO, 1998–2012; LPO, 2013–19. Professor of Horn, GSMD, 2012–. Young Musician of the Year, BBC, 1988; Gramophone Young Artist of the Year, 1996. *Recreations:* cooking, eating and drinking enough to keep up with the Wine Society brochures. *Address:* 16 Park Way, Rickmansworth, Herts WD3 7AT.

**PYCROFT, Stephen Gerard;** Executive Chairman, Mace, since 2013; *b* Bradford, 18 Oct. 1958; *s of* Arnold and Joyce Pycroft; *m* 1992, Joanne Camilleri (*d* 2006); one *s* one *d*. *Educ:* Nottingham Poly. (BSc Hons). ARICS 1982. With Bovis, 1985–93; Mace, 1993–: Bd Dir, 1995–; Chief Operating Officer, 2001–04; CEO, 2004–08; CEO and Chm., 2008–13. *Recreations:* cycling, golf. *Address:* Mace, 155 Moorgate, EC2M 6XB. *T:* (020) 3522 3055.

**PYE, Prof. (John) David,** FLS; Professor of Zoology, Queen Mary and Westfield College (formerly Queen Mary College), University of London, 1973–91, now Emeritus Professor, Queen Mary, University of London; *b* 14 May 1932; *s of* Wilfred Frank Pye and Gwenllian Pye (*née* Davies); *m* 1958, Dr Ade Pye (*née* Kuku), Sen. Lectr, UCL, retd. *Educ:* Queen Elizabeth's Grammar School for Boys, Mansfield; University Coll. of Wales, Aberystwyth (BSc 1954, 1st Cl. Hons 1955); Bedford Coll., London Univ. (PhD 1961). FZS 1956; FLS 1980; MInstP 2001, FInstP 2003. Research Asst, Inst. of Laryngology and Otology, London Univ., 1958–64; Lectr in Zoology, 1964–70, Reader, 1970–73, King's Coll. London; Head of Dept of Zoology and Comparative Physiology, Queen Mary Coll., 1977–82. A founder Dir, QMC Instruments Ltd, 1976–89. Linnean Society: Editor, Zoological Jl, 1981–85; Editl Sec. and Mem. Council, 1985–91; Vice-Pres., 1987–90; Mem., IEE Professional Gp Cttee E15, Radar, Sonar, Navigation and Avionics, 1983–86. Member Editorial Boards: Zool Soc., 1972–77, 1978–83, 1985–90; Jl of Exper. Biol., 1974–78; Jl of Comp. Physiol. A, 1978–96; Bioacoustics, 1987–. Royal Institution: Associate Mem., 1979–92; Mem., 1992–2002 (Hon. FRI 2002); delivered Friday discourses 1979, 1983, and televised Christmas Lects for Children, 1985–86; co-organizer, discussion evenings, 1994–2002; Mem. Council, 1999–2002; Vice Pres., 2001–02. Life Mem., Wildfowl and Wetlands Trust. Life Fellow RSPB. *Publications:* Bats, 1968; (with G. D. Sales) Ultrasonic Communication by Animals, 1974; (ed with R. J. Bench and A. Pye) Sound Reception in Mammals, 1975; Polarised Light in Science and Nature, 2001; articles and research papers. *Recreations:* bread baking and brewing, travel, arts. *Address:* Woodside, 24 St Mary's Avenue, Finchley, N3 1SN. *T:* (020) 8346 6869.

**PYE, Prof. Kenneth,** ScD, PhD; CGeol, FGS; Managing Director, Kenneth Pye Associates Ltd, since 2004 (Founder Director, since 2002); *b* 24 Aug. 1956; *s of* Leonard Pye and Joyce Pye; *m* 1st, 1979, Diane Cadman (marr. diss. 2007); one *s* one *d*; 2nd, 2014, Samantha Jayne Witton. *Educ:* Upholland Grammar Sch., Lancs; Hertford Coll., Oxford (Scholar; BA 1977; MA 1981); St John's Coll., Cambridge (PhD 1981; ScD 1992). CGeol 1995; FGS 1980. Cambridge University: NERC Postdoctoral Res. Fellow, 1980–82; Sarah Woodhead Res. Fellow, 1980–83, Non-stipendiary Fellow, 1983–89, Girton Coll.; Royal Society 1983 Univ. Res. Fellow, 1983–88; Reading University: Lectr in Quaternary Sedimentology, 1989–92; Reader in Sedimentology, 1992–94; Prof. of Envmtl Sedimentology, 1994–98; Royal Holloway, University of London: Prof. of Envmtl Geology, 1999–2004; Vis. Prof., 2004–07. Visiting Professor: Earth and Ocean Sci., Nat. Oceanography Centre, Southampton, 2011–; Sch. of Engrg and Envmt, Univ. of Southampton, 2013–. Founder Director: Cambridge Envmtl Research Consultants Ltd, 1986–95; K. Pye Associates, 1998–. Expert Witness, forensic geology (criminal and civil investigations). Leverhulme Trust Fellowship, 1991; Leverhulme Trust Sen. Res. Fellowship, 1996. Sedgwick Prize, Univ. of Cambridge, 1984; British Geomorphological Research Group: Wiley Award, 1989; Gordon Warwick Award, 1991. *Publications:* Chemical Sediments and Geomorphology, 1983; Aeolian Dust and Dust Deposits, 1987; Aeolian Sand and Sand Dunes, 1990, 2nd edn, 2009; Saltmarshes, 1992; The Dynamics and Environmental Context of Aeolian Sedimentary Systems, 1993; Aeolian Sediments Ancient and Modern, 1993; Sediment Transport and Depositional Processes, 1994; Environmental Change in Drylands, 1994; Backscattered Scanning Electron Microscopy and Image Analysis of Sediments and Sedimentary Rocks, 1998; Coastal and Estuarine Environments: sedimentology, geomorphology and geoarchaeology, 2000; Forensic Geoscience: principles, techniques and applications, 2004; Geological and Soil Evidence: forensic applications, 2007; The Measurement of Coastal Change, 2009; contribs to learned jls. *Recreations:* world travel, visiting historic sites and houses, collecting rocks and minerals, reading. *Address:* Kenneth Pye Associates Ltd, Thames Valley Science Park, Gateway Building, 1 Collegiate Square, Shinfield, Reading, Berks RG2 9LH. *T:* (0118) 304 1026.

**PYE, Dame Wendy (Edith),** DNZM 2013; MBE 1994; Owner and Director, Wendy Pye Publishing Ltd, since 1985; *b* Yarloop, WA; *d of* Thomas Jackson and Marie Louise Jackson; *m* 1965, Donald Norman Pye. *Educ:* Auckland Univ. of Technol. (mgt degree). With NZ Newspapers Ltd, from jun. journalist to manager of educative cos in publishing div. With Wendy Pye Publishing, publisher of early learning reading series (2700 titles), television series and online digital books and activities. NZ Rep., Apec Business Adv. Council, 2001–07. Co-Chairman: Capacity Building Wkg Gp, 2004; Technol. and Information Wkg Gp, 2007; Chm., Technol. Wkg Gp, 2005–06. Dir, NZ Trade and Enterprise, 2005–07. FInstD, NZ. *Address:* Private Bag 17.905, Greenlane, Auckland 1546, New Zealand. *T:* (9) 5253575. *E:* wendy@sunshine.co.nz. *Club:* Northern (Auckland).

**PYE, William Burns,** FRSS; sculptor; *b* 16 July 1938; *m* 1963, Susan Marsh; one *s* two *d*. *Educ:* Charterhouse; Wimbledon Sch. of Art; Royal Coll. of Art (ARCA). Vis. Prof., Calif. State Univ., 1975–76. Pres., Hampshire Sculpture Trust, 2002–. Directed film, Reflections, 1971. *Solo exhibitions:* Winchester Great Hall, 1979; Hong Kong (retrospective), 1987; RBS Gall., 2008; *public sculpture:* Zemran, South Bank, London, 1971 (grade II listed status, 2016); Curlicue, Greenland Dock, London, 1989; Cader Idris, Cardiff, 1998; *public water sculpture:* Slipstream and Jetstream, Gatwick Airport, 1988; Chalice, Fountain Sq., London, 1990; Water Wall and Portico, Expo '92, Seville, 1992; Orchid, the Peacocks, Woking, 1992; Cristos, St Christopher's Place, London, 1993; Confluence, Hertford, 1994; Downpour, British Embassy, Oman, 1995; Derby Cascade, Derby, 1995; Antony House, Cornwall, 1996; Archimedes Screw feature, West India Quay, London, 1997; Aquarena, Millennium Square, Bristol, 2000; Scaladaqua Tonda, Nat. Botanical Gardens, Wales, 2000; Tureen, St John's Coll., Cambridge, 2001; Monolith, Sunderland Winter Garden, 2001; Cornucopia, Millfield Sch., 2001; Scala Aquae Pembrochiana, Wilton House, 2001; Charybdis, Seaham Hall, Sunderland, 2001; Haberdashers' Co. new hall, 2002; Argosy, Lloyd's Register of Shipping, 2002; Divine Influx in Bath, Cross Bath, 2003; Jubilee Fountain, New Square, Lincoln's Inn, 2003; eight features for new gardens at Alnwick Castle, 2005; Sunken Garden, Aberglasney Gardens, Wales, 2005; font, Salisbury Cathedral, 2008; Hypanthium water piece, Univ. of BC Botanical Gdns, Vancouver, 2010; Water Pavilion, Drammen, Norway, 2011; Starburst, Sainsbury Lab., Cambridge, 2011; Cedra, Woolbeding House (Nat. Trust), Midhurst, 2012; Vortex CPFL, Campinas, Brazil, 2012; Vortex Bank Muscat, Brazil, 2012; Hydrodendron, Chateau La Trapperie, Belgium, 2013; Arroyo, Maggie's, Cheltenham, 2013; Thistle and Pergola fountains, Dumfries House, Scotland, 2014; Alchemilla, AELTC, 2016; Aquaverde, Grange Park, Toronto, 2017; *portrait bust of* Rt Hon. Douglas Hurd, Nat. Portrait Gall., 1996. FRSS (FRBS 1992). Hon. FRIBA 1993. Prix de Sculpture, Vth Internat. Sculpture Exhibn, Budapest; Peace Sculpture Prize, W Midlands CC, 1984; ABSA Awards for Best Sculpture in UK (Gatwick Airport), 1988, and in Scotland (Glasgow), 1989; UENO Royal Museum Award, Japan, 1989. *Recreation:* playing the flute. *Address:* 43 Hambalt Road, Clapham, SW4 9EQ. *T:* (home) (020) 8673 2318, (studio) (020) 8682 2727. *W:* www.williampye.com.

**PYE-JEARY, Anthony John;** Founder and Partner, Dewynters Ltd, 1975–2016 (Chief Executive Officer, 1998–2016); *b* London, 19 May 1949; *s of* Thomas Pye-Jeary and Peggy Pye-Jeary (*née* Banks); *m* 1985, Katharine Phillips; one *s*. *Educ:* Dulwich Coll. Advertising and promotions trainee, Rediffusion Television, 1966–68; ind. theatrical PR, 1969–75. *Recreations:* theatre, horse racing, Jumby Bay.

**PYKE, Elaine;** Executive Producer, New Pictures Ltd, since 2014; *b* Aberdare, Wales, 8 Feb. 1971; *d of* George Pyke and Margaret Pyke (*née* Hayter); partner, Richard George Dawson; two *d*. *Educ:* Howells Sch., Llandaff; Marlborough Coll.; Exeter Coll., Oxford; Rose Bruford Coll. of Drama. Actress, RSC, 1990–2000; Script Editor: Carlton TV, 2001–02; Thames Talkback, 2002; producer, Mediae Kenya, 2002–03; Sky One: Exec. Producer, 2003–04; Drama Comr, 2004–05; Controller of Drama, Sky TV, 2005–11; Controller, Sky Atlantic, 2011–14. Mem., BAFTA, 2009–. *T:* 07841 220871.

**PYLE, Dr Christopher John;** Head, Lancaster Royal Grammar School, since 2012; *b* Santiago, Chile, 14 June 1972; *s of* Leo and Dympna Pyle; *m* 1997, Sally Hoyle; three *s*. *Educ:* Henley Coll., Henley-on-Thames; Fitzwilliam Coll., Cambridge (BA Hons 1994; MA 1998; PhD 1998). NPQH 2011. Mgt trainee, Anglian Water, 1998–99; Teacher of Geog., 1999–2004, Hd of Geog., 2004–07, Dep. Hd, 2007–12, Perse Sch. *Recreations:* running, reading, fell walking, Devizes to Westminster canoe race. *Address:* Lancaster Royal Grammar School, East Road, Lancaster LA1 3EF. *T:* (01524) 580605.

**PYLE, Derek Colin Wilson;** Sheriff Principal of Grampian, Highland and Islands, since 2012; *b* 15 Oct. 1952; *s of* Colin Lawson Pyle and Mary Best Johnston Pyle; *m* 1980, Jean Blackwood Baillie May; six *s* one *d*. *Educ:* Royal High Sch., Edinburgh; Univ. of Edinburgh (LLB Hons). Law Apprentice, Lindsays, WS, Edinburgh, 1974–76; Partner, Dove Lockhart, WS, Solicitors, Edinburgh, 1977–80; Sole Partner, Wilson Pyle & Co., WS, Solicitors, Edinburgh, 1980–88; Partner, Henderson Boyd Jackson, WS, Solicitors, Edinburgh, 1989–99; Sheriff: of Tayside, Central and Fife, 2000–05; of Grampian, Highland and Islands at Inverness, 2005–08; of Tayside, Central and Fife at Dundee, 2008–12. *Recreations:* golf, hill-walking, writing unpublished best-sellers. *Address:* The Old Manor, Grange, Errol, Perthshire PH2 7SZ. *T:* (01821) 642198. *Club:* Craigielaw Golf.

**PYLE, Prof. John Adrian,** CBE 2017; DPhil, ScD; FRS 2004; FRSC; Director, Centre for Atmospheric Science, since 1992, and 1920 Professor of Physical Chemistry, 2007–18, University of Cambridge (Head, Department of Chemistry, 2015–18); Fellow, St Catharine's College, Cambridge, 1986–2018, now Emeritus; *b* 4 April 1951; *s of* Harold Pyle and Agnes Pyle (*née* Rimmer); *m* 1979, Elizabeth Caroline Lynnell Davies; one *s* two *d*. *Educ:* De La Salle Coll., Salford; Univ. of Durham (BSc Physics); Jesus Coll., Oxford (DPhil 1976). ScD Cantab 2012. FRSC 2015. Res. asst, Dept of Atmospheric Physics, Univ. of Oxford, 1976–82; Rutherford Appleton Lab., 1982–85; University of Cambridge: Lectr in Physical Chem., 1985–95; Reader in Atmospheric Chem., 1995–2000; Prof. of Atmospheric Sci., 2000–07; Head: Eur. Ozone Res. Co-ordinating Res. Unit, 1990–95; Atmospheric Chem. Modelling Support Unit, 1992–2005; Co-Dir, 2005–13, Chief Scientist, 2013–, NCAS. Member: Stratospheric Ozone Rev. Gp, DoE, later DEFRA, 1986– (Chm., 1988–); EC DG Res. Panel on Stratospheric Ozone, 1990–; Subcttee on

Envmtl. Sci., ACOST, 1990–92; NERC Sci. and Technol. Bd, then Sci. and Implementation Strategy Bd, 2000–02. Co-Chm., UNEP-WMO Ozone Scientific Adv. Panel, 2007–. Member, Council: Eur. Geophysical Soc., 1986–89; Royal Soc., 2009–11. MAE 1993. Sec. II, RMetS, 1979–84. John Jeyes Lect., RSC, 2009. Fellow, Amer. Geophysical Union, 2011. (Jtly) Eurotrac Award, Remote Sensing Soc., 1985; Interdisciplinary Award, RSC, 1991; (jtly) Körber Eur. Sci. Foundn Award, 1999; Adrian Gill Prize, RMetS, 2003; (jtly) NERC Internat. Impact Award and overall Impact Award, 2015; Davy Medal, Royal Soc., 2018. *Publications:* (ed jtly) Encyclopedia of Atmospheric Science, 2002, 2nd edn 2014; contrib. numerous papers to scientific jls. *Recreations:* hill walking, sport, supporting Bolton Wanderers. *Address:* Centre for Atmospheric Science, Department of Chemistry, Lensfield Road, Cambridge CB2 1EW. *T:* (01223) 336473. *E:* john.pyle@atm.ch.cam.ac.uk.

**PYLE, Leo Michael Peter;** a Recorder, since 2009; a District Judge (Magistrates' Courts), since 2011; *b* Beaconsfield, 30 Aug. 1961; *s* of Anthony Joseph and Mary Patricia Pyle; *m* 1987, Angela Claire Darke; one *s* two *d*. *Educ:* Slough Grammar Sch.; Liverpool Poly. (LLB Hons); Coll. of Law, Chester. Higher Courts (Criminal Proc.) Qualif. 2005. Admitted solicitor 1986; Partner: Page Nelson (formerly Page & Co.), Lincoln, 1992–2005; McKinnells, Lincoln, 2005–11. Dep. Dist Judge (Magistrates' Courts), 2000–11. *Recreation:* sport, watching and playing badly. *Address:* c/o Nottingham Justice Centre, Wilford Street, Nottingham NG2 1EE.

**PYLE, Nicholas John,** OBE 2010 (MBE 1999); HM Diplomatic Service; Deputy Governor, Gibraltar, since 2016; *b* 9 Dec. 1960; *m* 1993, Rosamund Day, MBE; two *s* one *d*. *Educ:* Bearwood Coll. Entered FCO, 1981; UKMIS, Geneva, 1984–86; Kabul, 1986–88; Jeddah, 1989–93; Second Sec. (Immigration) and Consul, Sri Lanka, 1996–99; Second Sec. (Pol), 2000–03, Dep. Hd of Mission, 2003–04, Barbados; Political Counsellor (Somalia), Nairobi, 2005–08; Special Advr to UN Sec.-Gen.'s Special Rep. to Somalia (on secondment), 2008–09; Deputy Head: E Africa and Gt Lakes Dept, FCO, 2010–12; Africa Dept Central and Southern, FCO, 2012–13; High Comr to Botswana, 2013–16; UK Rep. to Southern African Develt Community, 2013–15. *Address:* c/o Foreign and Commonwealth Office, King Charles Street, SW1A 2AH.

**PYLKKÄNEN, Juha, (Jussi);** Global President, Christie's, since 2015; *b* Helsinki, 27 May 1963; *m* 1986, Alison Green; one *s* one *d*. *Educ:* Lady Margaret Hall, Oxford (MA English Lit.). Christie's: Specialist, Old Master and Modern Prints, 1986–90; Associate Dir, Impressionist and Modern Art, 1990–95; Dir, Impressionist Dept, 1995–2000; Dep. Chm., Christie's, UK, 2000–06; Pres., Christie's Europe, Middle East and Russia (formerly Europe), 2005–14; Chm., Impressionist and Modern Art Dept, 2006–14. *Address:* Christie's, 8 King Street, St James's, SW1Y 6QT. *E:* jpylkkanen@christies.com.

**PYM, Richard Alan,** CBE 2015; FCA; Chairman: Bradford & Bingley plc, 2009–16 (Chief Executive, 2008; Executive Chairman, 2008–09); Northern Rock (Asset Management) plc, 2010–16; Allied Irish Banks, since 2014. *Educ:* Univ. of Warwick (BSc 1971). FCA 1974. Thomson McLintock & Co., 1971–75; British Gas plc, 1975–77; BAT Industries plc, 1978–82; The Burton Gp plc, 1983–92; Alliance & Leicester plc: Gp Finance Dir, 1993–2001; Man. Dir, Retail Banking, 2001–02; Gp Chief Exec., 2002–07; Chm., Co-operative Bank plc, 2013–14. Director: Selfridges plc, 1998–2003; Halfords plc, 2004–08 (Chm., 2006–08); Old Mutual, 2007–10; Chm., UK Asset Resolution Ltd, 2010–16. Vice-Pres., BBA, 2004–07.

**PYMAN, Avril;** *see* Sokolov, A.

**PYMONT, Christopher Howard;** QC 1996; a Recorder, since 2004; a Deputy High Court Judge, since 2008; *b* 16 March 1956; *s* of John and Joan Pymont; *m* 1996, Meriel Rosalind, *d* of Roger and late Ann Lester; two *s* one *d*. *Educ:* Marlborough Coll.; Christ Church, Oxford (BA Hons 1977, MA 1979). Called to the Bar, Gray's Inn, 1979; in practice at the Bar, 1980–; Hd of Chambers, 2012–. *Address:* Maitland Chambers, 7 Stone Buildings, Lincoln's Inn, WC2A 3SZ. *T:* (020) 7406 1200.

**PYNE, Kenneth John, (Ken);** cartoonist, since 1970; *b* London, 30 April 1951; *s* of John Ernest Pyne and Dorothy Maud Pyne; partner, Pamela Todd. *Educ:* Holloway Co. Sch., London. First cartoon published in Punch, 1967; contributed to: The Times, TES, Daily Mirror, Mail on Sunday, Private Eye, Punch, Independent, Evening Standard, Daily Telegraph, The People, Observer, Guardian, Manchester Evening News, Hampstead & Highgate Express, Sunday Times, The Oldie, Reader's Digest, Which, Stern (Germany), Today, Sunday Express, Marketing Week, Spectator, New Statesman, The Listener, Radio Times, Esquire, House Beautiful, Fedn of Small Businesses, MoneyMarketing, FM World, The Pavement, Cambridge Univ. Press, Literary Review, etc. *Exhibitions:* Cartoonist Gall., London, 1991 and 1996; Barbican Centre, 1992; Burgh House, Hampstead, 2001; *work in collections:* V&A Mus.; Cartoon Art Trust Mus.; Salon Internat. du Pressin et d'Humour, Switzerland. Member: British Cartoonist Assoc., 1979–; Professional Cartoonists' Orgn, 2008–; Burgh House (Hon. Friend, 2009). Professional Cartoonist Orgn. Cartoonist of Year, Cartoonist Club of GB, 1981; Strip Cartoonist of Year, 2001, Cartoonist of Year and Caricaturist of the Year, 2006, Cartoon Art Trust; Hampstead Cartoonist of The Year, Hampstead Village Voice, 2010, 2016. *Publications:* The Relationship, 1981; Martin Minton, 1982; Silly Mid-off, 1985; This Sporting Life, 1986; In the Bleak Mid-winter, 1987; (with Craig Brown) 1966 and All That, 2005; illustrated numerous book; work reproduced in numerous books. *Recreations:* walking, drawing, drinking, reading. *Address:* 15 Well Walk, Hampstead, NW3 1BY. *T:* (020) 7431 3480. *E:* pyne9@hotmail.com.

**PYOTT, David Edmund Ian,** CBE 2006; Chairman and Chief Executive Officer, Allergan Inc., California, 1998–2015; Chairman, Bioniz Therapeutics, since 2016; *b* London, 13 Oct. 1953; *s* of Robert Macgregor Pyott and Margaret Pyott (*née* Martin); *m* 1990, Julianna Racz; three *s* one *d*. *Educ:* Glasgow Acad.; Univ. of Edinburgh (MA); Univ. of Amsterdam (Dip. Eur. and Internat. Law); London Business Sch. (MBA). Sandoz AG, Basel: Hd, Strategic Planning, Nutrition Div., 1980–83; Marketing Manager, Nutrition Div., Malaysia, Singapore, 1984–86; Gen. Manager, Nutrition Div., Austria, 1986–89; Gen. Manager, Nutrition Div., Spain, 1990–92; Chief Exec., Nutrition Div., USA, 1993–95; Mem., Exec. Bd, 1995–; Mem., Exec. Bd, Novartis Internat. AG, Basel, 1995–97; Director: Avery Dennison Inc., Pasadena, Calif, 1999–; Edward Life Scis Corp., Irvine, Calif, 2000–. Director: California Healthcare Inst., 1998–; Biotechnol. Industry Orgn, 2005–. *Recreations:* ski-ing, mountaineering, cycling, travel, gardening, history.

**PYPER, Mark Christopher Spring-Rice,** OBE 2011; Principal (formerly Headmaster), Gordonstoun School, 1990–2011; *b* 13 Aug. 1947; *s* of late Arthur Spring-Rice Pyper and of Rosemary Isabel Pyper; *m* 1979, Jennifer Lindsay Gilderson; one *s* two *d*. *Educ:* Winchester College; Balliol College, Oxford; London Univ. (BA Mod. Hist. ext.). Asst Master, Stoke Brunswick Sch., East Grinstead, 1966–69; Asst Master, then Joint Headmaster, St Wilfrid's Sch., Seaford, 1969–79; Registrar, Housemaster, then Dep. Headmaster, Sevenoaks Sch., 1979–90. Dir, Sevenoaks Summer Festival, 1981–90. Member: SE Arts Cttee, 1984–90; HMC Community Service Cttee, 1995–2000; Council, Round Square Internat., 1995–2001 (Chm., Strategy Cttee, 1999–2001); Oxfordshire Deanery Synod, 2013–17. Chm. Bd, Oxford Teaching Schs Alliance Sch. Centred Initial Teacher Training, 2015–. Governor: Rosebrae Nursery Sch., Elgin, 1998–2002; Bellhaven Hill Sch., Dunbar, 2000–04; Ardvreck Sch., Crieff, 2004–07; Bedales Sch., Petersfield, 2012–17 (Chair, Educn Cttee, 2015–17); Westonbirt Sch., 2013–18; Governor and Chair Education Committee: Samworth Ch. Acad., 2011–13; Beaudesert Park Sch., 2011– (Chair, Bd, 2015–); Bloxham Sch., 2012–17. Educn Advr, Alexandria Trust, 2012–13. Fellow, Woodard Corp., 2012. Hon. Fellow, Rank Foundn, 2011. *E:* pyperm@hotmail.com. *Club:* MCC.

**PYPER, Susan Elizabeth;** Lord-Lieutenant of West Sussex, since 2008; *b* London, 12 Dec. 1951; *d* of Ronald Harrison and Joan Harrison; *m* 1987, Jonathan Pyper; one *s* one *d*. *Educ:* Prendergast Grammar Sch.; Univ. of Durham (BSc Hons); Chelsea Coll., London Univ. (Postgrad. Dip.). Forensic scientist, Metropolitan Police, 1973–76; Officer, RAF, 1976–87; Scientific Exec., Milupa (UK) Ltd, 1990–92; Chairman: Merton and Sutton Community NHS Trust, 1992–99; Sussex Weald and Downs NHS Trust, 1999–2002; Western Sussex NHS PCT, 2002–05; Royal W Sussex NHS Trust, 2005–09. Chm., Regl Envmt Protection Adv. Cttee, 2002–10; Mem., Regl Flood Defence Cttee, 2002–10. Lay Mem., Preliminary Investigation Cttee, RCVS, 1999–2006. Joint President: Sussex Community Foundn, 2008–; Action in Rural Sussex, 2009–; Sussex Historic Churches Trust, 2009–; Pres., South Downs Nat. Park Trust, 2018–; Vice President: SSAFA (formerly SSAFA Forces Help), Sussex; SE RFCA; Army Benevolent Fund, W Sussex; Weald and Downland Mus.; Patron: Chichester Harbour Trust; Pallant House Gall.; Chichester Cathedral Restoration Trust; Lodge Hill Trust; St Barnabas Hospice, Chichester, 2011; St Wilfrid's Hospice, Worthing, 2013; Vice Patron, Almshouse Assoc., 2015–. Jt Pres., Sussex Council, Order of St John. DStJ (CStJ 2009). *Recreations:* family, classical music, walking, ski-ing, outdoor pursuits, travel. *Address:* Fair Oaks, Monkmead Lane, W Chiltington, W Sussex RH20 2PF. *E:* jandspyper@btinternet.com.

**PYTCHES, Rt Rev. (George Edward) David;** Vicar of St Andrew's, Chorleywood, Rickmansworth, 1977–96; *b* 9 Jan. 1931; 9th *c* and 6th *s* of late Rev. Thomas Arthur Pytches and late Eirene Mildred Pytches (*née* Welldon); *m* 1958, Mary Trevisick; four *d*. *Educ:* Old Buckenham Hall, Norfolk; Framlingham Coll., Suffolk; Univ. of Bristol (BA); Trinity Coll., Bristol; MPhil Nottingham, 1984. Ordained deacon 1955, priest 1956; Asst Curate, St Ebbe's, Oxford, 1955–58; Asst Curate, Holy Trinity, Wallington, 1958–59; Missionary Priest in Chol Chol, Chile, 1959–62; in Valparaiso, Chile, 1962–68; Rural Dean, Valparaiso, 1966–70; Asst Bishop, 1970–72, Vicar General, 1971–72, Bishop, 1972–77, Dio. of Chile, Bolivia and Peru. Co-ordinator, Fellowship of Ind. Anglican Churches, 1992–; Founding Director, New Wine Family Conf., 1989–2000 (Trustee, 1999–); Founding Sponsor, and Trustee, Soul Survivor Youth Confs, 1993–2004; Co-ordinating Dir, Lakeside Family Conf., 1994–99. Dir, Kingdom Power Trust, 1987–2007. *Publications:* (contrib.) Bishop's Move, 1977; Come Holy Spirit, 1985; (contrib.) Riding the Third Wave, 1987; Does God Speak Today?, 1989; Some Said It Thundered, 1990; (jtly) New Wineskins, 1991; (contrib.) Planting New Churches, 1992; Prophecy in the Local Church, 1993; (contrib.) Recovering the Ground, 1995; (contrib.) Meeting John Wimber, 1996; (ed) John Wimber: his influence and legacy, 1998; Leadership for New Life, 1998; (ed) Burying the Bishop, 1999; (ed) Four Funerals and a Wedding, 1999; (ed) Out of the Mouths of Babes, 1999; Family Matters, 2002; Church Matters, 2002; Living at the Edge, 2002; (contrib.) Setting the Church of England Free, 2003; Can Anyone Be a Leader?, 2004; Upside Down Kingdom, 2007; If You Think My Preaching's Bad, Try My Jokes, 2008; What They Say About Prayer, 2011; The Way They Pray, 2015. *Recreations:* reading, travelling, enjoying twelve grandchildren. *Address:* 5 Churleswood Court, Shire Lane, Chorleywood, Rickmansworth, Herts WD3 5NH. *T:* (01923) 283763. *E:* pytches@btinternet.com.

# Q

**QADIR, Catherine Anne**; see Stephens, C. A.

**QASIM, Prof. Waseem**, PhD; National Institute of Health Research Professor of Cell and Gene Therapy, Great Ormond Street Institute of Child Health (formerly Institute of Child Health), University College London, since 2015; Consultant in Paediatric Immunology, Great Ormond Street Hospital NHS Trust, since 2007; *b* Bradford, 24 Feb. 1969; *s* of Mohammed and Rashida Qasim; *m* 2002, Sahar Hassan (marr. diss. 2010); two *d*. *Educ:* Bradford Grammar Sch.; Univ. of Newcastle upon Tyne (BMedSci 1st Cl. Hons 1991; MB BS 1993); University Coll. London (PhD 2002). MRCP 1996; MRCPCH 1997. Hse Physician and Hse Surgeon, Royal Victoria Infirmary, Newcastle upon Tyne, 1993–94; Senior House Officer: in Paediatrics, Nottingham City Hosp. and Queen's Med. Centre, Nottingham, 1994–96; in Immunol. and Infectious Diseases, Gt Ormond St Hosp., 1996; Specialist Registrar in Paediatrics, Northern Deanery, 1997–99; Vis. Registrar, Brisbane Children's Hosp., 1998–99; Institute of Child Health: Clin. Fellow, Molecular Immunol. Unit, 1999–2002; Clinician Scientist, 2003–07; Leukaemia Res. Sen. Lectr, 2007–12; Reader in Cell and Gene Therapy, UCL, 2012–15. *Publications:* contrib. articles, reviews and commentaries to jls incl. New England Jl Medicine, Sci., Translational Medicine, Nature Biotechnol., Jl Clin. Investigation, Blood, Molecular Therapy, Jl Allergy and Clin. Immunol., British Jl Haematol., Brain, Acta Neuropathologica. *Recreations:* gardening, cooking, Cerys on a Sunday morning. *Address:* Molecular and Cellular Immunology Unit, Wolfson Centre for Gene Therapy, Great Ormond Street Institute for Child Health, 30 Guilford Street, WC1N 1EH. *T:* (020) 7905 2794. *E:* w.qasim@ucl.ac.uk.

**QESKU, Pavli**; Ambassador of the Republic of Albania to the Court of St James's, 1993–97; writer of English-Albanian and Albanian-English dictionaries, since 1999; *b* 16 June 1943; *s* of Mihal and Vasilika Qesku; *m* 1973, Lidia Daka; one *s* one *d*. *Educ:* Tirana State Univ. (English Language). Translator at State publishing house, 1968; English teaching, 1975; translator and editor at publishing house, 1978; Ministry of Foreign Affairs, 1993. *Publications:* English Albanian Dictionary, 1999; English-Albanian and Albanian-English Dictionary, 2004; Comprehensive Albanian-English Dictionary, 2014. *Recreations:* reading, writing, music.

**QUADEN, Prof. Guy**, PhD; Governor, National Bank of Belgium, 1999–2011 (Director, 1988–99); Member, Governing Council and General Council, European Central Bank, 1999–2011; *b* 5 Aug. 1945; *m* Brigitte Tilman; two *s*. *Educ:* Univ. of Liège (grad. Econ 1967; PhD Econ 1973); La Sorbonne (grad. Econ and Soc. Scis 1972). University of Liège: First Asst, 1974–76; Lectr, 1977; Prof. in Economic Policy, 1978–88; Special Prof., 1988–. Mem. Bd Dirs, BIS, 1994–; Alternate Governor: IDA, 1994–2011; IBRD, 1999–2011; IFC, 1999–2011; Governor, IMF, 1999–2011. Member: Conseil supérieur des Finances; Institut des Comptes nationaux. Officier: Ordre de Léopold (Belgium), 1987; Légion d'Honneur (France), 2001. *Publications:* Le budget de l'Etat belge, 1980; La crise de finances publiques, 1984; L'économie belge dans la crise, 1987; Politique économique, 1985, 2nd edn 1991. *Recreations:* football, music, literature. *Address:* c/o National Bank of Belgium, Boulevard de Berlaimont 14, 1000 Brussels, Belgium.

**QUAH, Prof. Danny**; Li Ka Shing Professor of Economics, since 2016, and Dean, since 2018, Lee Kuan Yew School of Public Policy, National University of Singapore (Vice Dean (Academic Affairs), 2016–18); *b* Penang, Malaysia, 1958; *s* of Chong-eng Quah and Phaik-im Goh; *m* 2010, Aileen Lim; two *s*. *Educ:* Princeton Univ. (AB 1980); Harvard Univ. (PhD Econs 1986). Asst Prof., Econs Dept, MIT, 1986–91; London School of Economics and Political Science: Lectr, then Reader in Econs, 1991–95; Prof. of Econs, then Prof. of Econs and Internat. Develt, 1996–2016; Hd of Econs Dept, 2006–09; Co-Dir, Global Governance, 2009–11; Kuwait Prof., 2012–14; Dir, Kuwait Res. Prog., 2013–14; Dir, Swee Hock SE Asia Centre, 2014–16; Sen. Advr to Dir, 2015–16. Tan Chin Tuan Vis. Prof., Nat. Univ. of Singapore, 2010–16. *Publications:* (ed) Oxford Handbook of Information and Communication Technologies, 2007; articles in Amer. Econ. Rev., Econometrica, Jl of Pol Economy, Econ. Jl, European Econ. Rev., Jl of Econ. Growth, Scandinavian Jl of Econs, Jl of Monetary Econs, etc. *Recreations:* Taekwon-do, running, videogaming. *Address:* Lee Kuan Yew School of Public Policy, National University of Singapore, 469C Bukit Timah Road, Singapore 259772, Singapore. *T:* 66015506. *E:* D.Quah@nus.edu.sg.

**QUANT, Dame Mary, (Dame Mary Plunket Greene)**, DBE 2015 (OBE 1966); RDI 1969; Director, 1955–2000, Co-Chairman, 1991–2000, Mary Quant Group of companies; *b* 11 Feb. 1934; *d* of Jack and Mildred Quant; *m* 1957, Alexander Plunket Greene (*d* 1990); one *s*. *Educ:* Goldsmiths' College of Art (Hon. Fellow, 1993). Fashion designer. Founded Mary Quant Cosmetics, 1966. Mem., Design Council, 1971–74. Member: British/USA Bicentennial Liaison Cttee, 1973; Adv. Council, V&A Museum, 1976–78. Non-exec. Dir, House of Fraser, 1997–. Exhibitions: Mary Quant's London, London Museum, 1973–74; (retrospective) V&A, 2019. FCSD (FSIA 1967); Sen. FRCA 1991; FRSA 1996. Hon. Dr Wales; hon. degree, Winchester Sch. of Art, 2000. Maison Blanche Rex Award (US), 1964; Sunday Times Internat. Award, 1964; Piavola d'Oro Award (Italy), 1966; Annual Design Medal, Inst. of Industrial Artists and Designers, 1966; Hall of Fame Award, British Fashion Council, 1990. *Publications:* Quant by Quant, 1966; Colour by Quant, 1984; Quant on Make-up, 1986; Classic Make-up and Beauty Book, 1996; Mary Quant: my autobiography, 2012.

**QUANTRILL, William Ernest**; HM Diplomatic Service, retired; Ambassador to the Republic of Cameroon, and concurrently to the Central African Republic, Equatorial Guinea and the Republic of Chad, 1991–95; *b* 4 May 1939; *s* of late Ronald Frederick Quantrill and Norah Elsie Quantrill (*née* Matthews); *m* 1964, Rowena Mary Collins; three *s* one *d*. *Educ:* Colston's Sch., Bristol; Hatfield Coll., Univ. of Durham (BA Hons French). Entered FO, 1962; served Brussels, Havana, Manila, Lagos, 1964–80; Head of Training Dept, FCO, 1980–81; Dep. Head of Personnel Ops Dept, FCO, 1981–84; Counsellor and Hd of Chancery, Caracas, 1984–88; Dep. Gov., Gibraltar, 1988–90. *Recreations:* wild life, travel. *Address:* Tor House, 36 Newtown, Bradford-on-Avon, Wilts BA15 1NF. *T:* (01225) 866245.

**QUARMBY, David Anthony**, CBE 2003; MA, PhD; FCILT, FCIHT; consultant in transport, planning, tourism and economics, 2006–16; Chairman: RAC Foundation, 2009–13; Strategic Rail Authority, 2004–06 (Deputy Chairman, 2002–04; Member, 2001–06); *b* 22 July 1941; *s* of Frank Reginald and Dorothy Margaret Quarmby; *m* 1968, Hilmary Hunter; four *d*. *Educ:* Shrewsbury Sch.; King's Coll., Cambridge (MA); Leeds Univ. (PhD, Dip. Industrial Management). Asst Lectr, then Lectr, Dept of Management Studies, Leeds Univ., 1963; SSO, 1966–68, Economic Adviser, 1968–70, Economic Planning Directorate, Min. of Transport; London Transport Executive: Dir of Operational Research, 1970; Chief Commercial and Planning Officer, 1974; Mem., 1975–84; Man. Dir (Buses), 1978–84; Mem., London Regional Transport, 1984; Director: Homebase Ltd, 1987–89; Shaw's Supermarkets Inc., 1987–92; Jt Man. Dir, J. Sainsbury plc, 1988–96 (Dir, 1984–96). Chairman: English Tourist Bd, 1996–99; S London Business Leadership Ltd, 1996–99; British Tourist Authy, 1996–2003; Docklands Light Railway Ltd, 1999–2001 (Dir, 1998–2001); SeaBritain 2005 Steering Gp, Nat. Maritime Mus., 2003–05; English Tourism Intelligence Partnership, 2008–11; Winter Resilience Rev., DfT, 2010; Motorists' Forum, DfT, 2011–12; Freight Adv. Gp, Canal and River Trust, 2012–15; Transport Adv. Gp, Royal Bor. of Greenwich, 2013–15; Dep. Chm., S London Econ. Develt Alliance, 1999–2003; Director: New Millennium Experience Co. Ltd, 1997–2001 (Chm., May–Sept. 2000; Dep. Chm., 2000–01); London First, 1998–2002; BRB (Shadow Strategic Rail Authy), 1999–2001; Abellio Gp (formerly Ned Railways Ltd), 2007–11; Colin Buchanan & Partners Ltd, 2007–08; Member: RAC Public Policy Cttee, 1996–; Panel 2000, 1999–2002; London Sustainable Develt Commn, 2002–03; Ind. Transport Commn, 2007–10 (Chm., 2007–10); Greenwich Waterfront Regeneration Agency, 2008–11; Woolwich Regeneration Agency, 2011–14; Expert Adv. Panel, Airports Commn, 2013–15; Project Dir, Major Roads for the Future, Rees Jeffreys Road Fund, 2014–16. Chm., Retail Action Gp for Crime Prevention, Home Office, 1995–96; Mem., Crime Prevention Agency Bd, Home Office, 1995–97; non-exec. Dir, Dept of Transport Central Mgt Bd, 1996–97, DETR Bd, 1997–98; Mem. Bd, Transport for London, 2000–04 (Ministerial Advr, 1999–2000). Mem. Bd, Elderhostel Inc., 2006–09. Vice-President: Bus and Coach Council, 1981–84; CIT, 1987–91; Mem., Nat. Council, Freight Transport Assoc., 1985–88; Pres., Commercial Boat Operators Assoc., 2015–. Chm., Transport Res. Inst., Edinburgh Napier (formerly Napier) Univ., 2006–11. Member: London Educn Business Partnership, 1988–92; Sch. Curriculum and Assessment Authy, 1993–95; Southwark Diocesan Bd of Finance, 1982–85; London Adv. Bd, Salvation Army, 1982–87; Mem., Friends' Council, 2004–07, Trustee, 2005–13, Nat. Maritime Mus.; Trustee, St Paul's Cathedral Foundn, 2005–07; Mem., A12 Commn of Inquiry, 2008. Dir, and Chm. Develt Cttee, Blackheath Concert Halls, 1990–94. Gov., 1987–98 (Chm., 1995–98), Chm., Finance Cttee, 1991–95, James Allen's Girls' Sch., London; Mem. Ct, Greenwich Univ., 2000–08. Pres., Inst. of Logistics, 1996–99. CompOR; FTS 1997; FRSA 2006. Hon. DSc Huddersfield, 1999; Hon. DEng Napier, 2008. *Publications:* Factors Affecting Commuter Travel Behaviour (PhD Thesis, Leeds), 1967; contribs to Jl of Transport Economics and Policy, Regional Studies, Enterprise Management, Transport Times, and to other journals and books on transport, distribution, tourism, economics and operational research. *Recreations:* music, singing, walking, photography, family life. *Address:* 13 Shooters Hill Road, Blackheath, SE3 7AR.

**QUARME, Giles Thomas**, RIBA; Principal, Giles Quarme & Associates, since 1989; *b* Chelsea, London, 19 June 1951; *s* of Philip Anthony Thomas and Wendy Kathlene Quarme; *m* 1986, Margaret Henrietta Augusta Casely-Hayford, *qv*; one *d*. *Educ:* Marlborough Coll.; Univ. of East Anglia (BA Hons Art Hist. 1973); Univ. of Westminster (BA Hons Architecture 1976; DipArch 1979); Architectural Association (DipCons 1984). RIBA 1980. Sole practitioner in association with John Dickinson, RIBA, 1979–82; Co-Founder, Dickinson, Quarme & Associates, 1982–89. Surveyor of the Fabric, RNC, Greenwich, 1996–2009; Historic Bldg Advr to Foster & Partners on British Mus. Millennium proj., 1997. Projects include: restoration of Royal Victoria Patriotic Bldg Complex, Wandsworth, 1988 (Europa Nostra Award, 1988); restoration of High Comr of India's residence, London, 1995; restoration of 14 & 18 St Leonards Terrace, London, 1995; restoration of 49 Thames Street, Sunbury-on-Thames, 1996 (Spelthorne Design Award, 1996); Princess Diana Mus., Althorp Park, 1997; Queen Anne Court, RNC, Greenwich, 2000 (Civic Trust Award); Althorp House (RICS Award); Bentley Priory Battle of Britain Mus. Chm. Trustees, Ancient Monuments Soc., 2000– (Mem. Council, 1993–); Member: Adv. Cttee, 1991–92, Cttee, 1992, Save Britain's Heritage; British Acad. of Experts, 1993–; Exec. Council, ICOMOS UK, 1993–99; London Adv. Cttee, English Heritage, 1999–2014; Exec. Council, Georgian Gp, 1999–. FRSA 1986; Fellow, Royal Asiatic Soc., 1996. Freeman, Co. of Chartered Architects, 1994–. *Publications:* articles in ASCHB Transactions. *Recreations:* trying to understand historic events, analysing old buildings, walking on Exmoor. *Address:* 36 Smith Street, Chelsea, SW3 4EP. *T:* (020) 7582 0748; Giles Quarme & Associates, 7 Bishops Terrace, SE11 4UE. *E:* mail@quarme.com.

**QUARME, Margaret Henrietta Augusta**; see Casely-Hayford, M. H. A.

**QUARREN EVANS, His Honour (John) Kerry**; a Circuit Judge, on South Eastern circuit, 1980–95; *b* 4 July 1926; *s* of Hubert Royston Quarren Evans, MC and Violet Soule Quarren Evans (*née* George); *m* 1958, Janet Shaw Lawson; one *d* (one *s* decd). *Educ:* King Henry VIII Sch., Coventry; Cardiff High Sch.; Trinity Hall, Cambridge, 1948–51 (MA, LLM). 21st Glam. (Cardiff) Bn Home Guard, 1943–44; enlisted, Grenadier Gds, 1944; commnd Royal Welch Fusiliers, 1946, from OTS Bangalore; attd 2nd Bn The Welch Regt, Burma, 1946–47; Captain 1947. Admitted solicitor, 1953; Partner: Lyndon Moore & Co., Newport, 1954–71; T. S. Edwards & Son, Newport, 1971–80; Recorder, Wales and Chester Circuit, 1974–80. Clerk to Gen. Comrs of Income Tax, Dinas Powis Div., 1960–80; Chm., Newport Nat. Insurance Local Tribunal, 1968–71. *Recreations:* golf, Rugby football, oenology, staurologosophy, old things. *Address:* 17 Bulstrode Court, Gerrards Cross, Bucks SL9 7RR. *T:* (01753) 880819. *Clubs:* Arkaves (Cardiff); Woodpeckers, Denham Golf, Royal Porthcawl Golf, Crawshay's Welsh Rugby Football.

**QUARREY, David,** CMG 2015; HM Diplomatic Service; Ambassador to Israel, 2015–19; *b* 6 Jan. 1966; *m* Aldo Oliver Henriquez. Entered FCO, 1994; Second Sec. (Pol), Havana, 1995–2000; First Sec. (Pol), New Delhi, 2000–03; FCO, 2003–04; Private Sec. to Prime Minister, 2004–06; Dep. Dir, ME and N Africa, FCO, 2006–08; Counsellor and Hd, Pol Sect., Perm. Mission of UK to UN, 2008–12; Dir, Near East and N Africa, FCO, 2012–14. *Address:* c/o Foreign and Commonwealth Office, King Charles Street, SW1A 2AH.

**QUARTA, Roberto;** Partner, Clayton, Dubilier & Rice, since 2001; Chairman: Smith & Nephew plc, since 2014; WPP Group, since 2015; *b* 10 May 1949; *m;* one *s* one *d. Educ:* Italy and USA; Coll. of the Holy Cross, Mass, USA (BA 1971). Management Trainee, David Gessner, 1971–73; Worcester Controls Corp., 1973–78: Manager, Purchasing and Production Control; Vice-Pres., Internat. Procurement; BTR plc, 1979–85: Manufacturing Dir, Worcester Controls Corp.; Man. Dir, Worcester Controls UK; Group Man. Dir, Valves Group; Chief Exec., Hitchiner Manufacturing Corp., 1985–89; a Chief Divl Exec., BTR, 1989–93 (Dir, Main Bd, 1993); BBA Group plc: Dir, 1993–2007; Chief Exec., 1993–2000; Chm., 2000–07. Non-executive Director: PowerGen, 1996–2001; Equant NV, 2000–05; Azure Dynamics Corp., 2004–07; BAE Systems plc, 2005–11; Foster Wheeler AG, 2011; Spie SA, 2011; Smith & Nephew plc, 2013– (Chair, 2014–); Chm., IMI plc, 2011–15; Chm., Supervisory Bd, Rexel SA, 2007–. Former Trustee, Coll. of the Holy Cross. *Recreations:* aviation, music. *Address:* CD&R LLP, Cleveland House, 33 King Street, SW1Y 6RJ.

**QUARTANO, Ralph Nicholas,** CBE 1987; Chairman, PosTel Investment Management Ltd, 1987–91 (Chief Executive, 1983–87); *b* 3 Aug. 1927; *s* of late Charles and Vivienne Mary Quartano; *m* 1st, 1954, Cornelia Johanna de Gunst (*d* 1996); two *d;* 2nd, 2006, Kathryn Margaret Brown. *Educ:* Sherborne Sch.; Pembroke Coll., Cambridge (MA). Bataafsche Petroleum Mij., 1952–58; The Lummus Co., 1958–59; Temple Press, 1959–65; Man. Director: Heywood Temple Industrial Publications, 1965–68; Engineering Chemical and Marine Press, 1968–70. The Post Office, 1971–74: Sen. Dir, Central Finance, 1973–74; Chief Exec., Post Office Staff Superannuation Fund, 1974–83. Dir, 1985–93, Dep. Chm., 1987–93, SIB. Director: London American Energy NV, 1981–88; Britoil plc, 1982–88; 3i Group plc (formerly Investors in Industry), 1986–97; John Lewis Partnership Pensions Trust, 1986–89; Clerical Medical Investment Group, 1987–98; Booker plc, 1988–98; British Maritime Technology Ltd, 1988–97 (Chm., 1995–97); Heitman Financial LLC, 1991–2000; Laird Group, 1991–98; Enterprise Oil, 1991–97; Lyonnaise Pension Trustees Ltd, 1994–2005; Chm., Murray Emerging Economies Trust plc, 1994–98. Member: Engrg Council, 1981–83; City Capital Markets Cttee, 1985–93; Investment Cttee, Pensioen Fonds PGGM, Netherlands, 1986–98; Investment Cttee, KPN (formerly PTT) Pensioen, Netherlands, 1988–98; Financial Reporting Council, 1990–93. City Advr to Dir-Gen., CBI, 1985–93. Sloan Fellow of London Business School. Gov., BUPA, 1987–98. Mem. Council, 1993–99, and Treas., 1994–99, RSA. Trustee, Montevrdi Trust, 1986–93. *Address:* 20 Oakcroft Road, SE13 7ED. *T:* (020) 8852 1607. *Club:* Athenæum.

**QUAYLE, James Danforth, (Dan),** JD; Chairman, Cerberus Global Investments, LLC, New York, since 2000; Vice-President of the United States of America, 1989–93; *b* 4 Feb. 1947; *m* 1972, Marilyn Tucker; two *s* one *d. Educ:* DePauw Univ. (BS 1969); Indiana Univ. (JD 1974). Admitted to Indiana Bar, 1974. Journalist, 1965–69, Associate Publisher and Gen. Manager, 1974–76, Huntington Herald Press; Investigator, Consumer Protection Div., Office of the Attorney General, Indiana, 1970–71; Admin. Assistant to Gov. of Indiana, 1971–73; Dir, Inheritance Tax Div., Indiana, 1973–74; Professor of Business Law, Huntington Coll., 1975. Mem. of Congress, 1976–80; Mem. for Indiana, US Senate, 1981–88. Chm., Circle Investors, Inc., 1993–. Vis. Prof., Thunderbird Internat. Business Sch., 1997–99. *Publications:* Standing Firm, 1994; The American Family, 1996; Worth Fighting For, 1999. *Address:* 7001 North Scottsdale Road, Suite 2010, Scottsdale, AZ 85253, USA.

**QUAYLE, Quinton Mark;** HM Diplomatic Service, retired; Adviser to the President, Thai Beverage plc, since 2011; *b* 5 June 1955; *s* of late Eric Stanley Quayle and Elizabeth Jean (*née* Thorne); *m* 1979, Alison Marshall; two *s. Educ:* Humphry Davy GS; Bristol Univ. (BA). Entered HM Diplomatic Service, 1977; Third, later Second Sec., Bangkok, 1979–82; FCO, 1983–86; Ecole Nat. d'Admin, Paris, 1986–87; First Sec., Paris, 1987–91; FCO, 1991–93; on secondment to Price Waterhouse Management Consultants, 1993–94; Dir, Jt Export Promotion Directorate, FCO, 1994–96; Counsellor, Consul-Gen. and Dep. Hd of Mission, Jakarta, 1996–99; Internat. Gp Dir, Trade Partners UK, British Trade Internat., 1999–2002; Ambassador: to Romania, 2002–06; to Thailand, 2007–10. Senior Adviser: Asia, Sindicatum Sustainable Resources, 2011–; Prudential Assce, 2013–. Member: QC Appts Panel, 2013–17; HS2 Need to Sell Panel, 2017–. Non-exec. Dir, 2gether NHS Foundn Trust, 2016–18. Member, Board: Council for Licensed Conveyancers, 2016–; Cottsway Housing Assoc., 2018–. *Recreations:* book collecting, gardening. *Club:* Oriental.

**QUEENSBERRY,** 12th Marquess of, *cr* 1682; **David Harrington Angus Douglas;** Viscount Drumlanrig and Baron Douglas, 1628; Earl of Queensberry, 1633; Bt (Nova Scotia), 1668; late Royal Horse Guards; Professor of Ceramics, Royal College of Art, 1959–83; Partner, Queensberry Hunt design group; *b* 19 Dec. 1929; *s* of 11th Marquess of Queensberry and late Cathleen Mann; *S* father, 1954; *m* 1st, 1956, Mrs Ann Radford; two *d;* 2nd, 1969, Alexandra (marr. diss. 1986), *d* of Guy Wyndham Sich; two *s* one *d* (and one *s* decd); 3rd, 2000, Hsueh-Chun Liao; (one *d* decd). *Educ:* Eton. Dir, Highland Stoneware. Pres., Design and Industries Assoc., 1976–78. Trustee, Paolozzi Foundn. Sen. FRCA, 1990. Hon. DDes Staffordshire, 1993. *Heir: s* Viscount Drumlanrig, *qv.*

**QUEENSLAND, Metropolitan of;** *see* Brisbane, Archbishop of.

**QUEENSLAND, NORTH, Bishop of,** since 2019; **Rt Rev. Dr Keith Ronald Joseph;** *b* Hornsby, NSW, 8 Dec. 1960; *s* of Ron and Anne Joseph; one *s. Educ:* Ku-Ring-Gai High Sch., NSW; Macquarie Univ. (BA Hons; MA); Charles Sturt Univ. (DipTh); Univ. of Newcastle, NSW (PhD). Reserve and full-time service, RAAMC, 1980–2006, retired as Major. Lectr in Philosophy, Aust. Catholic Univ., 1993–98; Contract Manager, Aust. Federal Police, Solomon Islands, 2004–06; ordained deacon, 2005, priest, 2006; Lectr, Bishop Patteson Theol Coll., Kohimarama, Solomon Islands, 2006–10; Priest-in-charge, Parish of Mt Vincent and Weston, NSW, 2011–13; Dean, Christ Church Cathedral, Darwin, 2013–19; Adminr, Dio. of the NT, 2015–19. Chair, Aust. Hearing Human Res. Ethics Cttee, 2000–06; Member: Human Res. Ethics Cttee, Dept of Health, NT, 2014–19; Bd of Anglicare NT, 2013–19. Service Mem., Returned and Services League of Aust., 1999– (Vice-Pres., Darwin Sub-br., 2018–). Rugby Union Referee, 1975–2006. OStJ 2018. *Publications:* Professional Ethics, 1998; State, Society and Governance in Melanesia, 2008; contrib. articles in jls incl. New Doctor, Bioethics Outlook, Monash Bioethics Rev., Aust. Defence Force Jl, Anglican Ecocare Jl of Ecotheology. *Recreations:* reading, philately, golf, bush walking. *Address:* Anglican Diocese of North Queensland, PO Box 1244, Townsville, Qld 4810, Australia. *T:* (7) 47714175, *Fax:* (7) 47211756. *E:* bishopnq@anglicannq.org.

**QUELCH, Prof. John Anthony,** CBE 2011; DBA; Miller University Professor and Vice Provost, University of Miami, and Dean, Miami Business School, since 2017; *b* 8 Aug. 1951; *s* of late Norman Quelch and Laura Sally (*née* Jones); *m* 1978, Joyce Ann Huntley. *Educ:* Norwich Sch.; Exeter Coll., Oxford (BA 1972; Hon. Fellow, 2002); Wharton Sch., Univ. of Pennsylvania (MBA 1974); Harvard Univ. (DBA 1977; SM 1978). Asst Prof. of Business Admin, Univ. of Western Ontario, 1977–79; Harvard Business School: Asst Prof. of Business Admin, 1979–84, Associate Prof., 1984–88, Prof., 1988–93; Sebastian S. Kresge Prof. of Marketing, 1993–98; Dean and Prof. of Mktg, London Business Sch., 1998–2001; Sen. Associate Dean and Lincoln Filene Prof. of Business Admin, Harvard Business Sch., 2001–11; Dean, Vice Pres. and Distinguished Prof. of Internat. Mgt, China Europe Internat. Business Sch., Shanghai, 2011–13; Charles Edward Wilson Prof. of Business Admin, Harvard Business Sch., and Prof. of Health Policy and Mgt, Harvard Sch. of Public Health, 2013–17. La Caixa Vis. Prof. of Internat. Mgt and Chm., Academic Adv. Council, China Europe Internat. Business Sch., 2009. Chm., Massachusetts Port Authy, 2002–11. Non-executive Director: Reebok Internat. Ltd, 1985–97; European Communication Mgt Ltd, 1988–97; WPP Gp plc, 1988–2013; US Office Products Co., 1995–97; Pentland Gp plc, 1997–99; Blue Circle Industries plc, 2000–01; easyJet plc, 2000–03; Loyalty Management UK Ltd, 2003–06; Alere Inc., 2003–; Pepsi Bottling Gp, 2005–09; Gentiva Health Services, 2006–09; Epiphany Biosciences, 2007–09; BBC Worldwide Americas, 2007–10; Datalogix, 2014–15; Luvo, 2015–; Propel Media, 2015–16; Aramark, 2016. Mem. Adv. Bd, PricewaterhouseCoopers Corporate Finance, 2002–03. Director: Council of Better Business Bureaux, 1995–97; Graduate Mgt Admissions Council, 1999–2001; Accion Internat., 2003–06; Member: Council on Foreign Relns, 2009–; Trilateral Commn, 2012–. Mem., Internat. Adv. Bd, British Amer. Business Council (formerly British Amer. Business Inc.), 2001–; Mem., Adv. Bd, AT Kearney Global Policy Council, 2002–06; Dir, Americans For Oxford, 2006–11. Trustee, Univ. of Virgin Islands, 2018–. Hon. Chm., British Amer. Business Council of New England, 2008–11. Hon. Consul Gen. of Morocco in New England, 2004–17. CCMI (CIMgt 1998). FRSA 1998; FRGS 2009; Fellow, Amer. Acad. of Arts and Scis, 2017. Hon. Fellow, London Business Sch., 2008; Hon. PhD Vietnam National, 2011. *Publications:* (jtly) Advertising and Promotion Management, 1983; (jtly) Cases in Advertising and Promotion Management, 1983, 4th edn 1996; (jtly) Marketing Management, 1985, 2nd edn 1993; (jtly) Global Marketing Management, 1988, 5th edn 2005; How to Market to Consumers, 1989; Sales Promotion Management, 1989; (jtly) The Marketing Challenge of Europe 1992, 1990, 2nd edn 1991; (jtly) Ethics in Marketing, 1992; (jtly) Cases in Product Management, 1995; (jtly) Cases in Marketing Management and Strategy, 1996; (jtly) Cases in European Marketing Management, 1997; (jtly) Cases in Strategic Marketing Management: business strategies in Latin America, 2001; Business Strategies in Muslim Countries, 2001; (jtly) Marketing Management, 2004; (jtly) Problems and Cases in Health Care Marketing, 2004; (jtly) The Global Market, 2005; (jtly) The New Global Brands, 2006; (jtly) Business Solutions for the Global Poor, 2007; Readings in Modern Marketing, 2007; (jtly) Greater Good: how good marketing makes for better democracy, 2008; (jtly) All Business Is Local: why place matters more than ever in a global, virtual world, 2011; Consumers, Corporations and Public Health, 2016; Building a Culture of Health: a new imperative for business, 2016; (jtly) Choice Matters, 2018; (jtly) Compassionate Management of Mental Health, 2018; contribs to learned and professional jls. *Recreations:* squash, tennis. *Address:* Miami Business School, Jenkins Building 219, 5250 University Drive, Coral Gables, FL 33124–6520, USA. *T:* (305) 2849191. *Club:* Brooks's.

**QUENTIN, Caroline;** actress; *b* 11 July 1960; *d* of Frederick and Katie Emily Jones; adopted stage name of Quentin; *m* 1991, Paul James Martin, *qv* (marr. diss. 1999); *m* 2006, Sam Farmer; one *s* one *d. Educ:* Arts Educnl, Tring Park. *Theatre includes:* The Seagull, tour; Roots, RNT; Our Country's Good, Garrick; Low Level Panic, Sugar and Spice, Royal Court; Les Miserables, Barbican, transf. Palace; An Evening with Gary Lineker; A Game of Love and Chance, RNT; Les Enfants du Paradis, tour; Lysistrata; Mirandolina, Lyric, Hammersmith; The Live Bed Show, Garrick, 1994; The London Cuckolds, RNT, 1998; Life After Scandal, Hampstead, 2007; Pippin, Menier Chocolate Factory, 2012; Relative Values, Th. Royal, Bath, 2013, transf. Harold Pinter Th., 2014; Oh What a Lovely War, Th. Royal, Stratford E, 2014; The Life and Times of Fanny Hill, Bristol Old Vic, 2015; The Hypocrite, Hull Truck Th., transf. RSC, 2017; Me and My Girl, Chichester Fest. Th., 2018; The Provoked Wife, RSC, 2019; dir, Dead Funny, Palace, Watford, 1998. *Television includes: series:* Don't Tell Father, 1992; Men Behaving Badly, 1992–97; Jonathan Creek, 1997–2002; Kiss Me Kate, 1998–2002; The Innocent, 2001; Blue Murder, 2003–09; Life Begins, 2004–06; Von Trapped, 2004; Life of Riley, 2009; Dickensian, 2016; The World's Most Extraordinary Homes, 2017, 2018; *film:* An Evening with Gary Lineker, 1994. *Recreation:* bird-watching.

**QUEST, David Charles;** QC 2013; *b* Manchester, 1 June 1971; *s* of Barry Quest and Janet Quest; *m* 2004, Paula; two *s* one *d. Educ:* Manchester Grammar Sch.; Trinity Coll., Cambridge (BA 1991). Called to the Bar, Gray's Inn, 1993. *Address:* 3 Verulam Buildings, Gray's Inn, WC1R 5NT.

**QUICK, Dorothy, (Mrs Charles Denis Scanlan);** a District Judge (Magistrates' Courts) (formerly Metropolitan Stipendiary Magistrate), 1986–2010; *b* 10 Dec. 1944; *d* of Frederick and Doris Quick; *m* 1971, Charles Denis Scanlan; two *s. Educ:* Glanafan Grammar Sch., Port Talbot; University Coll. London (LLB). Called to the Bar, Inner Temple, 1969; barrister-at-law, 1969–86. Mem., British Acad. of Forensic Sciences, 1987–2010. *Recreations:* gardening, theatre, books. *Club:* Reform.

**QUICK, Robert Frederick,** QPM 2003; Chief Executive, BGS (formerly BlueLight Global Solutions) Ltd, since 2010; *b* London, 25 April 1959; *s* of Robert Edward Quick and Patricia Quick; *m* 2001, Judith Jane Clark; one *s* four *d. Educ:* Exeter Univ. (MBA with Dist.); Civil Service Coll. Top Managers Prog.; Police Staff Coll., Bramshill (Police Strategic Comd Course 2001); Univ. of Cambridge (Dip. Applied Criminol. 2001). Metropolitan Police Service: Constable, Lambeth, 1978–82; Detective Constable, Brixton, Lambeth, 1982–84; Sergeant, 1984–87; Detective Sergeant, 1987–90, Catford, Lewisham; Detective Inspector, Lambeth, 1990–92, Greenwich, 1994–95; Detective Chief Inspector, SE London Crime Squad, 1995–96, Croydon, 1996–97; SO to Asst Comr, 1997–98; Superintendent, Southwark, 1998–99; Detective Chief Superintendent, Anti-Corruption Comd, New Scotland Yard, 1999–2001; Comdr, New Scotland Yard, 2001–03; Dep. Chief Constable, 2003–04, Chief Constable, 2004–08, Surrey Police; Asst Comr, Specialist Ops, Metropolitan Police Service, 2008–09. Partner, RQC Solutions—Policing and Justice. MInstD 2001. *Recreations:* ski-ing, walking, motorcycling, collector of classic motorcycles and motorcars.

**QUICKE, Mary Eleanor,** MBE 2004; DL; Managing Director, Quicke's Traditional Ltd, since 1987; *b* Newton St Cyres, 1 May 1955; *d* of Sir John Godolphin Quicke, CBE and Prudence Tinné Quicke; *m* 1979, Tom Langdon-Davies; one *s* one *d. Educ:* Queen Elizabeth's Sch.; King's Coll. London (BA Hons English Lit. and Lang. 1977); Seale Hayne Coll. (Dip. Farm Mgt/BTEC 1984). FRAgS 2005. Columnist, Devon Life, 2015–. Member, Board: Dairy Sector, Agric. and Horticulture Develt Bd, 2012–97; Food Standards Agency, 2017–. Chairman: Maize Growers Assoc., 1990–91; Devon Co. Agricl Assoc., 2010–. Dir, Acad. of Cheese, 2016–; Mem., Guilde des Fromageurs, 2016–. Chair of Governors: Newton Cyres Primary Sch., 1999–2002; Queen Elizabeth Community Coll., 2005–08. Fellow, Inst. of Farm Mgt, 1998. DL Devon, 2018. Hon. Dr Plymouth, 2012. *Recreations:* gardening, walking, surfing. *Address:* Home Farm, Newton St Cyres, Exeter EX5 5AY. *T:* (01392) 851222. *E:* mary@quickes.co.uk.

**QUICKE, Rev. Michael John;** C. W. Koller Professor of Preaching and Communication, Northern Seminary (formerly Northern Baptist Theological Seminary), Chicago, 2000–14, now Emeritus Professor of Preaching; *b* 30 July 1945; *s* of George and Joan Quicke; *m* 1968, Carol Bentall; two *s*. *Educ:* Jesus Coll., Cambridge (MA); Regent's Park Coll., Oxford (MA). Nat. Sec. for Student Work, Baptist Union, 1967–69; Minister: Leamington Road Baptist Church, Blackburn, 1972–80; St Andrew's Street Baptist Church, Cambridge, 1980–93; Principal, Spurgeon's Coll., 1993–2000 (Dist. Vis. Scholar, 2016–). Interim Preacher, First Baptist Ch, Wheaton, Ill., 2000–02. Religious Advr, ITV, 1987–88. Mem. Council, Baptist Union of GB, 1976–2000; Vice Chm., Doctrine Commn, 1990–95, Mem., Worship Commn, 1995–2005, Mem., Church Leadership Commn, 2006–10, Baptist World Alliance. Member: Council of Mgt, Open Theol Coll., 1993–2000; Council, Evangelical Alliance, 1997–2000. Mem., Acad. of Homiletics, 1995–. Fellow, Coll. of Preachers, 1996 (Mem., Exec., 1996–2000); Consultant, US Lilly prog., Strengthening Quality of Preaching, 2014–17. Hon. DD William Jewell Coll., Liberty, USA, 1994. *Publications:* Christian Apologetics, 1976; Something to Declare, 1996; On the Way of Trust, 1997; Doing Theology in a Baptist Way, 2000; 360 Degree Preaching, 2003; 360 Degree Leadership, 2006; Preaching as Worship, 2011. *Recreations:* listening to sermons, music, travel, painting. *Address:* 14 Brierley Walk, Cambridge CB4 3NH.

**QUIGLEY, Anthony Leslie Coupland,** CEng, FIET; management consultant, since 2001; *b* 14 July 1946; *s* of late Leslie Quigley and Vera Barbara Rodaway (*née* Martin); *m* 1968, Monica Dean; one *s* two *d*. *Educ:* Apsley Grammar Sch.; Queen Mary Coll., Univ. of London (BSc Eng). Command Control and Computer Divs, ASWE, 1967–81 (Exchange Scientist, US Naval Surface Weapons Center, 1976–79); Supt, Command and Control Div., 1981–84, Hd, Command, Control and Assessment Gp, 1984–87, RARDE; Dep. Head, Science and Technology Assessment Office, Cabinet Office, 1987–90; Dir, SDI Participation Office, 1990–93, Asst Chief Scientific Advr (Nuclear), 1993–95, MoD; Under Sec., OST, 1995–99 (on secondment); Dir Gen., Scrutiny and Analysis, MoD, 1999–2001. Member: Council, Foundn for Sci. and Technol., 2001–18; Council, Univ. of Kent, 2006–17. Gov., Kent Community Health Foundn Trust, 2019–. MInstD. *Publications:* technical papers on radar tracking and command and control. *Address:* 21 Yew Tree Road, Tunbridge Wells, Kent TN4 0BD.

**QUIGLEY, Conor;** QC 2003; *b* 21 Feb. 1958; *s* of Edmond Gerard Quigley and Kathleen Theresa Quigley (*née* Murphy). *Educ:* King's Coll. London (LLB); MA Oxon. Called to the Bar, Gray's Inn, 1985; in practice as barrister specialising in EU law, 1985–. Fellow, LMH, Oxford Univ., 1991–96. Chm., Bar European Gp, 1992–94. *Publications:* European Community Contract Law, 1997; EC State Aid Law and Policy, 2002, 3rd edn 2015. *Recreations:* history, wine, Europe. *Address:* Serle Court, 6 New Square, Lincoln's Inn, WC2A 3QS. *T:* (020) 7242 6105, *Fax:* (020) 7400 4005. *E:* cquigley@serlecourt.co.uk.

**QUIGLEY, Air Vice-Marshal Michael,** CEng, FIExpE; Director, Safety and Environment, Quality and Technology (formerly Technical Director), Defence Equipment and Support, Ministry of Defence, 2015–18; *b* Retford, Notts, 12 Aug. 1965; *s* of late Geoffrey Michael Quigley and of Sandra May Quigley (*née* Cook, now Tredrea); *m* 1990, Belinda Jane Wheeler; one *s*. *Educ:* No 1 Sch. of Tech. Trng, RAF Halton (RAF Technician Apprenticeship, BTEC, HNC Aerospace Studies (Mech.) 1985); King's Coll. London (MA Defence Studies 2001); Cranfield Univ. (MSc Defence Acquisition Mgt 2008). CEng 2010; MIET 2010; FIExpE 2014. Aircraft Technician Apprentice, RAF Halton, 1982–85; Aircraft Technician (Tornado), RAF Honington, 1985–90; Initial Officer/Engr Officer Trng, RAF Cranwell, 1990–91; Jun. Engr Officer, 16 (Reserve) Sqdn, RAF Lossiemouth, 1991–92; OC Tornado Aircraft Servicing Flight, RAF Bruggen, 1993–95; SO, HQ Logistics Comd, RAF Brampton, 1996; Harrier Fleet Manager/Support Authy, RAF Wyton, 1996–98; Sen. Engr Officer, XI (Fighter) Sqdn, RAF Leeming, 1998–2000; acsc 2001; MA to Dir Gen., Equipt Support (Air), RAF Wyton, 2001–03; OC Engrg & Supply Wing, RAF Leuchars, 2003–05; Pegasus/Adour Engine Prog. Manager and Asst Dir Transformation, Harrier Integrated Project Team, RAF Wyton, 2005–08; Air Warfare Centre Chief Engr, MoD, Boscombe Down, 2008–11; Defence Equipment and Support, Abbey Wood: Short Range Air Defence Project Team Leader, 2011–12; Hd, Weapons Engrg and Hd, Defence Ordnance Safety Gp, 2012–15. *Recreations:* fell walking, gardening, photography, DIY, collecting books I never find time to read. *E:* info@rafclub.org.uk. *Club:* Royal Air Force.

**QUIGLEY, Rebecca;** theatre producer; Chief Executive Officer and Producer, Greene Light Stage plc, since 2017; *b* London, 1 July 1969; *d* of Gerry Quigley and Diane Quigley; *m* 2001, Elliott Rae; one *s*. *Educ:* Old Palace Sch., Croydon; Wimbledon Sch. of Art and Design, London; Guildhall Sch. of Music and Drama, London. Various positions, Pola Jones Assoc., 1995–2000; General Manager: Clear Channel, 2000–01; Tiger Aspect, 2001–03; Working Title Films, 2003–08; Exec. Producer, Stage Entertainment UK, 2008–11; CEO, Stage Entertainment UK, 2011–16. *Recreations:* safari holidays, wildlife adventures, walking.

**QUILTER, Sir Guy (Raymond Cuthbert),** 5th Bt *cr* 1897, of Bawdsey Manor, Suffolk; *b* 13 April 1967; *o s* of Sir Anthony Raymond Leopold Cuthbert Quilter, 4th Bt and Mary Elise (*d* 2013), *er d* of late Colonel Brian (Sherlock) Gooch, DSO, TD; *S* father, 2014; *m* 1992, Jenifer Redvers-Cox; three *s*. Rowed the Atlantic Ocean (E–W), 2003. *Heir: s* William Raymond Cuthbert Quilter, *b* 29 Nov. 1995.

**QUIN, Baroness** *cr* 2006 (Life Peer), of Gateshead in the County of Tyne and Wear; **Joyce Gwendolen Quin;** PC 1998; *b* 26 Nov. 1944; *d* of late Basil Godfrey Quin, MC and Ida (*née* Ritson); *m* 2010, Guy MacMullen. *Educ:* Univ. of Newcastle upon Tyne (BA French, 1st Cl. Hons); Univ. of London (MSc Internat. Relns). Research Asst, Internat. Dept, Labour Party Headquarters, Transport House, 1969–72; Lecturer in French, Univ. of Bath, 1972–76; Resident Tutor, St Mary's Coll., and Lectr in French and Politics, Univ. of Durham, 1977–79. Mem. (Lab) European Parliament, S Tyne and Wear, 1979–84, Tyne and Wear, 1984–89. MP (Lab) Gateshead E, 1987–97, Gateshead E and Washington W, 1997–2005. Opposition front bench spokesman on trade and industry, 1989–92, on employment, 1992–93, on European affairs, 1993–97; Minister of State: Home Office, 1997–98; (Minister for Europe), FCO, 1998–99, MAFF, 1999–2001; opposition spokesman on envmt, food and rural affairs, 2010–11. Member: Select Cttee on Treasury and Civil Service, 1987–89; EU Select Cttee, H of L, 2014–15 (Chm., EU Justice, Instns and Consumer Protection Sub-Cttee, 2014–15); Chairman: Franco-British Parly Relns Cttee, 2001–05; Regl Govt Gp, PLP, 2001–05; Mem., Franco-British Council, 2001–13 (Chm., 2007–13). Vice Chairman: NE Constit. Convention, 2001–05; Franco-British Soc., 2013–. Vis. Prof., Centre for Urban and Regl Develt Studies, Newcastle upon Tyne Univ., 2001–05; Vis. Parly Fellow, St Antony's Coll., Oxford, 2007–08. Mem. Court, Newcastle Univ., 2013–. President: Northumbrian Pipers Soc., 2009–; Northumberland Nat. Park Foundn, 2015–; Vice-Pres., Newcastle Assoc. of City Guides, 2017–; Chair, Strategic Bd, Tyne and Wear Archives and Museums, 2017–. Hon. Fellow: Sunderland Polytechnic, subseq. Univ. of Sunderland, 1986; St Mary's Coll., Durham Univ., 1994. Hon. Freeman, Bor. of Gateshead, 2006. Officier de la Légion d'Honneur (France), 2010. *Publications:* The British Constitution: continuity and change—an inside view, 2010; (with Moira Kilkenny) Angels of the North: notable women of the North-East, 2018; various articles in newspapers and journals. *Recreations:* North-East local history, music, theatre, walking, cycling. *Address:* House of Lords, SW1A 0PW.

**QUIN, Jeremy Mark;** MP (C) Horsham, since 2015; Comptroller of HM Household (Government Whip), since 2019; *b* Aylesbury, 24 Sept. 1968; *s* of Rev. David Quin and late Elizabeth Quin; *m* 2003, Joanna Healey. *Educ:* St Albans Sch.; Hertford Coll., Oxford (BA Hons Mod. Hist. 1990). Natwest Youth Mackenzie & Co. Ltd, 1990–99; BT Alex Brown, 1999–2000; a Man. Dir, Deutsche Bank, 2000–15; Sen. Corporate Finance Advr, HM Treasury, 2008–09 (on secondment). PPS to Minister of State, DExEU, 2016–17; Jt PPS to Sec. of State, DExEU, 2018; an Asst Govt Whip, 2018; a Lord Comr of HM Treasury (Govt Whip), 2018–19. Member: Work and Pensions Select Cttee, 2015–16; Regulatory Reform Cttee, 2015–18; Financial Inclusion Commn, 2017–18; Chm., All-Party Parly Gp on Credit Unions, 2017–18. Contested (C) Meirionnydd Nant Conwy, 1997. *Address:* House of Commons, SW1A 0AA. *E:* jeremy.quin.mp@parliament.uk.

**QUINAN, Lloyd;** Member (SNP) West Scotland, Scottish Parliament, 1999–2003; *b* 29 April 1957; *s* of Andrew and Ann Quinan. *Educ:* Queen Margaret Coll., Edinburgh. Actor, 1978–83; theatre dir, 1983–89; television presenter, producer and dir, 1989–99. Contested (SNP) Motherwell & Wishaw, Scottish Parlt, 2003. *Recreations:* reading, travel, music, football.

**QUINAULT, James Hjalmar René,** CBE 2011; Executive Director, Implementation Unit, Cabinet Office, since 2015; *b* London, 25 Oct. 1970; *s* of Francis Quinault and Wendy Horton; *m* 1993, Lucia Conybeare; two *s* one *d*. *Educ:* Madras Coll., St Andrews; Phillips Exeter Acad., NH, USA; Merton Coll., Oxford (BA Lit.Hum. 1992; MA 2013). Entered CS Fast Stream, 1993; Private Sec. to Cabinet Sec. and Hd of CS, 1996–97; Envmt, Rural and Housing Team, 1997–98, Hd, Gen. Expenditure Policy Team, 1998–2000, HM Treasury; Hd, Home Affairs Team, Economic and Domestic Secretariat, Cabinet Office, 2000–02; Hd of Strategy, Office of Criminal Justice Reform, Home Office, 2002–06; Dir, Managed Migration, Home Office, 2006; Hd, Defence, Diplomacy and Intelligence Spending, HM Treasury, 2006–11; Dir, Office of Cyber Security, Cabinet Office, 2011–15. *Recreations:* reading, walking, Irish traditional music. *Address:* Cabinet Office, 35 Great Smith Street, SW1P 3BQ. *T:* (020) 7271 8660.

**QUINCE, William James;** MP (C) Colchester, since 2015; Parliamentary Under Secretary of State, Department for Work and Pensions, since 2019; *b* Ascot; *s* of Nigel Anthony Quince and Jane Frances Quince; *m* 2009, Elinor Ann; two *d* (one *s* decd). *Educ:* Windsor Boys' Sch.; Univ. of Wales, Aberystwyth (LLB Hons Law); Univ. of West of England (DipLP 2012). Mkt Develt Exec., Concur Technologies Ltd, 2005–06; Customer Develt Manager, Britvic Soft Drinks plc, 2006–10; trainee solicitor, Asher Prior Bates, 2010–13; Solicitor, Thompson Smith and Puxon, 2013–15. Member (C): E Herts DC, 2007–08; Colchester BC, 2011–16. *Address:* (office) 37 Layer Road, Colchester, Essex CO2 7JW. *T:* 07944 098398. *E:* will.quince.mp@parliament.uk. *W:* www.willquince.com.

**QUINEY, Charles Benedictus Alexander, (Ben);** QC 2014; *b* London; *s* of Adrian Quiney and Indira Quiney; two *s*. *Educ:* Birkdale Sch., Sheffield; University Coll., Oxford (BA, BCL). Called to the Bar, Gray's Inn, 1998. *Address:* Crown Office Chambers, 2 Crown Office Row, Temple, EC4Y 7HJ.

**QUINLAN, Rt Rev. (Alan) Geoffrey;** a Bishop Suffragan, Diocese of Cape Town, 1988–98; now involved in spiritual direction, teaching, training and the conduct of retreats, quiet days, confirmations, preaching and leading weekly Bible study groups; *b* 20 Aug. 1933; *s* of late Robert Quinlan and Eileen Beatrice Quinlan; *m* 1963, Rosalind Arlen Sallie (*née* Reed) (*d* 2017); three *s* one *d*. *Educ:* Kelham Theological College. RAF, 1952–54. Ordained deacon 1958, priest 1959; Asst Curate, St Thomas's, Leigh, Lancs, 1958–61; Rector: St Margaret's, Bloemfontein, 1962–68; St Michael and All Angels, Sasolburg, OFS, 1968–72; Warden, Community of Resurrection of Our Lord, Grahamstown and Chaplain, Grahamstown Training Coll., 1972–76; Priest-in-Charge of Training in Ministries and Discipleship, Cape Town Diocese, 1976–80; Rector, All Saints, Plumstead, Cape Town, 1980–88. Canon, St George's Cathedral, Cape Town, 1980–88. *Publications:* A Manual for Worship Leaders; Discipleship and the Alternative Society; Church-wardens' Handbook; My Personal Prayer Book, 2006. *Recreations:* chess, reading, computers, music, painting. *Address:* 132 Woodley Road, Plumstead, Cape Town, 7800, South Africa.

**QUINLAN, Anthony James;** Chief Executive Officer, Laird Technologies (formerly Laird plc), since 2016; *b* London, 1965; *s* of Tony and Patricia Quinlan; *m* 1994, Stephanie Harrison; two *d*. *Educ:* Central Foundn Boys' Grammar Sch.; University Coll. of Wales, Aberystwyth (BSc Hons Chem. 1987). ACA 1991. Res. Chemist, Dow Corning, 1984–85; Audit Supervisor, Coopers & Lybrand, 1987–92; Marks and Spencer: Dir, Investor Relns, 2000–04; Dir, Finance, 2004–08; Gp Finance Dir, Drax Gp, 2008–15; Chief Financial Officer, Laird plc, 2015–16. Vice Chm., Port of London Authy, 2012–18. *Recreations:* gym, film, music, reading. *Address:* Laird Technologies, 100 Pall Mall, SW1Y 5NQ. *T:* (020) 7468 4040. *Clubs:* Royal Automobile, Home House.

**QUINLAN, Christopher John;** QC 2011; a Recorder, since 2009; *b* Bristol, 1 Oct. 1968; *s* of Margaret Rew (formerly Quinlan, *née* Broe); *m* 1996, Julia Donaldson; one *s* one *d*. *Educ:* Henbury Sch., Bristol; Manchester Poly. (LLB Hons). Called to the Bar, Inner Temple, 1992, Bencher, 2015. Judicial Panel Chm., World Rugby, 2017–; Mem., World Rugby Anti-Doping Adv. Cttee, 2015–; Legal Member: Nat. Anti-Doping Panel, 2008–; Nat. Safeguarding Panel, 2012–; Specialist Mem., FA Judicial Panel, 2008–; Legal Arbitrator, Sport Resolutions (UK) Panel of Arbitrators, 2006–; Dep. Chm., Table Tennis England Appeal Bd, 2016–. Author, Quinlan Review, 2016. *Recreations:* Eloise and Thomas, Bristol RFC, Liverpool FC, sailing. *Address:* Guildhall Chambers, 23 Broad Street, Bristol BS1 2HG. *T:* (0117) 930 9000, *Fax:* (0117) 930 3824. *E:* christopher.quinlan@guildhallchambers.co.uk; Farrar's Building, Temple, EC4Y 7BD. *Club:* Army and Navy.

**QUINLAN, Rt Rev. Geoffrey;** *see* Quinlan, Rt Rev. A. G.

**QUINN, Andrea Helen, (Mrs R. Champ);** conductor; Music Director and Chief Conductor, Symphony Orchestra of Norrlands Opera, Umeå, Sweden, 2005–09; *b* 22 Dec. 1964; *d* of Desmond Bone and Theresa Bone (*née* MacLaren) (who *m* 1971, John Quinn); *m* 1991, Dr Roderick Champ; one *s* two *d*. *Educ:* Nottingham Univ. (BA Hons); Royal Acad. of Music (Adv. Cert. in Conducting; ARAM 1999). Music Director: London Philharmonic Youth Orch., 1993–96; Royal Ballet, 1998–2001; NY City Ballet, 2001–06. Hon. FTCL 2000. *Recreations:* literature, endurance horse riding (member of Endurance GB and Arab Horse Soc.), animal husbandry, fine art. *Address:* Urishay Barn, Michaelchurch Escley, Herefordshire HR2 0LR. *T:* (01981) 510686. *E:* quinnchamp@gmail.com. *W:* www.andreaquinn.com.

**QUINN, Anthony;** writer; *b* Liverpool, 20 April 1964; *s* of Peter Quinn and late Margaret Quinn; *m* 2006, Rachel Cooke. *Educ:* St Francis Xavier's Coll., Liverpool; Pembroke Coll., Oxford (BA Classics). Freelance writer, 1986–88; Book Reviewer, Independent, 1988–95; Film Critic, Marie Claire, 1992–96; Arts Editor, Harper's & Queen, 1996–99; Film Critic, Independent, 1998–2013. Judge, Man Booker Prize, 2006. *Publications:* The Rescue Man,

2009; Half of the Human Race, 2011; The Streets, 2012; Curtain Call, 2015; Freya, 2016; Eureka, 2017; Our Friends in Berlin, 2018. *Recreations:* reading, wine drinking, party going, films, theatre, five-a-side football. *Address:* 30 St Paul's Place, N1 2QG. *T:* (020) 7704 0426. *E:* tonyquinn3@gmail.com. *Clubs:* Authors', Garrick.

**QUINN, Brian,** CBE 1996; Managing Director, Brian Quinn Consulting (formerly Brian Quinn Consultancy plc), 1996–2016; *b* 18 Nov. 1936; *s* of Thomas Quinn and Margaret (*née* Cairns); *m* 1961, Mary Bradley; two *s* one *d*. *Educ:* Glasgow Univ. (MA Hons); Manchester Univ. (MA Econs); Cornell Univ. (PhD). FCIBS 1995. Economist, African Dept, IMF, 1964–70, Rep., Sierra Leone, 1966–68; joined Bank of England, 1970: Economic Dir., 1970–74; Chief Cashier's Dept, 1974–77; Head of Information Div., 1977–82; Asst Dir, 1982–88; Head of Banking Supervision, 1986–88; Exec. Dir, 1988–96; Acting Dep. Gov., 1995. Chairman: Nomura Bank Internat., 1996–99; Celtic plc, 2000–07 (non-exec. Dir, 1996–2000); Bvalco Ltd, 2011–17. Non-executive Director: Bank Gesellschaft Berlin UK Ltd, 1996–2002; Britannic (formerly Britannia) Asset Mgt, 1998–2004; Sumitomo-Mitsui Banking Corp., 2000–02; Genworth Mortgage Inscе Europe, 2005–10; Qatar Finance Centre Regulatory Authy, 2006–11. Chm., Financial Markets Gp, LSE, 1996–2000. Advr, Singapore Govt, 1997–2002; Consultant: World Bank, 1997–2008; IMF, 1997–2003; McKinsey and Co., 1998–2008; Mem. Bd of Dirs, Toronto Centre, 2008–10 (Mem. Adv. Bd, 1998–2010); Chm., Banking Adv. Bd, 2008–10). Mem., City Disputes Panel, 2003–. Mem., Investigatory Chamber, UEFA Club Financial Control Body (formerly Vice Pres., UEFA Club Financial Control Panel), 2009–15. Glasgow University: Hon. Prof. of Econs and Finance, 2006–17; Mem., Strategic Adv. Bd, Business Sch., 2011–16. *Publications:* (contrib.) Surveys of African Economies, vol. 4, 1971; (contrib.) The New Inflation, 1976; articles in learned jls. *Recreations:* watching football, pilates. *Address:* 14 Homewood Road, St Albans, Herts AL1 4BH. *Club:* Reform.

**QUINN, Brian;** *see* Quinn, J. S. B.

**QUINN, Carolyn;** Presenter: PM programme, BBC Radio 4, since 2000; Westminster Hour, BBC Radio 4, since 2007; *b* 22 July 1961; *d* of late Edward James Quinn and of Maureen Quinn; *m* 2003, Nigel Paul Morris. *Educ:* St Joseph's RC Primary Sch., Crayford; Dartford Grammar Sch. for Girls; Kent Univ. (BA Hons French 1983); Inst. of Educn, Univ. of London (PGCE). Clerical worker, Charing Cross Hosp., London, 1984–85; Irish Post newspaper, London, 1985–86; trainee, BBC Radio, Local Radio Reporter Scheme, 1986–87; reporter/producer, BBC Radio Solent, 1987–89; BBC Westminster, covering Parlt and politics, 1989–; political corresp., BBC, 1994–2006; Presenter, Today prog., BBC Radio 4, 2004–08. *Recreations:* cycling, cinema, walking, jazz, playing bass guitar. *Address:* c/o BBC News Centre, Broadcasting House, Portland Place, W1A 1AA.

**QUINN, Geoffrey;** Chairman, T. M. Lewin, since 2018 (Director, since 1980; Chief Executive, 1993–2018); *b* Margate, 10 March 1959; *s* of Francis and Jennifer Quinn; *m* 1981, Janine Willis; one *s* two *d*. *Educ:* Hartsdown Comprehensive Sch., Westbrook, Kent. Salesman, Turnbull & Asser, 1976–80. *Recreations:* theatre, family, travel, Prince's Trust. *Address:* T. M. Lewin, 6–7 St Cross Street Courtyard, EC1N 8UA. *T:* (020) 7877 3500.

**QUINN, Gregory;** *see* Quinn, J. G.

**QUINN, (James) Gregory;** HM Diplomatic Service; High Commissioner to Guyana, and non-resident Ambassador to Suriname, since 2015; *b* Lurgan, NI, 16 June 1971; *s* of James Eric Quinn and Gwendoline Audrey Quinn; *m* 1995, Wendy Ann Dackombe. *Educ:* Univ. of Wales, Aberystwyth (BSc (Econ) Hons Internat. Politics and Internat. Hist. 1992); Open Univ. (MA Hist. 2008). Joined FCO, 1995; Res. Asst, then Asst Editor, Documents on British Policy Overseas, FCO Historians, 1995–98; Desk Officer for Estonia, Latvia and Lithuania, FCO, 1998–2000; Dep. Hd of Mission (temp. duty), Tallinn, 2000; Political, Press and Public Affairs Officer, Accra, 2000–03; Dep. Hd of Mission, Minsk, 2004–07; Iraq/Middle East Liaison Officer, Washington, seconded to State Dept, 2007–09; Hd, UN Political Team, FCO, 2009–12; Dep. Hd of Mission, Astana, 2012–14. Hon. LLD QUB, 2019. *Recreations:* golf, Rugby, cricket, walking, avid reader of non-fiction (especially on World War 2 and aviation). *Address:* Foreign and Commonwealth Office, King Charles Street, SW1A 2AH. *T:* (020) 7008 1500. *E:* greg.quinn@fco.gov.uk.

**QUINN, (James Steven) Brian;** Director General, International Institute of Communications, 2003–09; Honorary Irish Consul for the Bahamas, 2011–14; *b* 16 June 1936; *s* of James and Elizabeth Quinn; *m* 1st, 1962, Blanche Cecilia James (marr. diss. 1987); two *s* one *d*; 2nd, 2004, Catherine Mann. *Educ:* St Mary's Coll., Crosby; Waterpark Coll., Ireland; University Coll., Dublin (BCL, LLB). Barrister-at-law, Kings Inn, Dublin. Director: Johnson Radley, 1966–68; United Glass Containers, 1968–69; Head of Industrial Activities, Prices and Incomes Board, 1969–71; Dir, M. L. H. Consultants, 1971–79; Corporate Develt Advr, Midland Bank Internat., 1977–80; Chief Industrial Advr, Price Commn, 1977–78; Man. Dir, Visnews, 1980–86; Digital Computer Services: Dir, 1985–96; Chief Exec., 1989–92; Chm., 1992–96. Chairman: BrightStar Communications, 1983–85; BAJ Holdings, 1985–87; Harmer Holbrook, 1987–88; Signet Online, 1996–99; Loan Line Ltd, 1997–2000; Central Equipment Hldgs Ltd, 2003–04; Director: Telematique Services, 1985–90; QM Security Ltd; IP Solutions Internat., Bahamas, 2009–13 (Dep. Chm., 2010–13). Telecom res. into cross border transmissions, TCD, 1995–97. Institute of Management (formerly British Institute of Management): CCMI (CBIM 1985; FBIM 1978); Mem. Council, 1981–87, 1990–98; Mem. Finance Cttee, 1981–84; Chm., City of London Branch, 1981–83; Vice Pres., 1983–90; Chm., Gtr London Regl Council, 1990–94. International Institute of Communications: Trustee, 1982–88, 1992–97; Chm., Exec. Cttee, 1984–88; Pres., 1988–91; Life Trustee, 2009. Mem., Exec. Cttee, Inst. of European Trade and Technology, 1983–96. Trustee: Internat. Center of Communications, San Diego State Univ., 1990–2006. Chm., Finance Cttee, Great Japan Exhibn, 1979–82. Chm., Editl Bd, Professional Manager, 1993–98. *Recreations:* golf, reading, veteran vehicles. *Address:* Hicks Grove House, Halls Green, Weston, Herts SG4 7DX. *Clubs:* Athenæum, Lansdowne; Royal Nassau Sailing.

**QUINN, Jane Elisabeth,** OBE 2014; Founding Partner, Public Relations Consultant and Director, Bolton & Quinn Ltd, since 1981; *b* 2 March 1949; *d* of Dr Francis Prime and Barbara Prime; *m* 1st, 1971, Stephen Quinn (marr. diss. 1998); three *s*; 2nd, 2000, Martin Duignan. *Educ:* Convent of the Sacred Heart, Tunbridge Wells; Queen's Coll., London. Media buyer, Ogilvy & Mather, 1969–70; PR Exec., Prime Associates, 1970–72; Publicity Exec., Riverside Studios, 1978–81. Dir, Michael Clark Co., 2005–15. Director: Art Baby, 2003–; Inst. of Imagination (formerly London Children's Mus.), 2010–18; Coronet Th., 2016–; Fluxus Art Projects, 2018–. *Address:* Bolton & Quinn Ltd, 6 Addison Avenue, W11 4QR.

**QUINN, John Louie Marie;** QC 2017; Attorney General for Isle of Man, since 2017 (Acting Attorney General, 2013–17); Member, Legislative Council, Isle of Man, since 2013; *b* Douglas, IOM, 9 May 1954; *s* of James and Josephine Quinn; *m* 1986, Heather Callow; six *s* one *d*. *Educ:* St Joseph's Coll., Upholland, Lancs; Chester Coll. of Law. Admitted as Advocate, 1978; with Quinn Kneale Advocates, 1978–2009; Gp Legal Counsel, Sefton Gp plc, 2009–13. Chm., Bank of Ireland (IOM) Ltd, 2003–13. Pres., IOM Law Soc.,

1998–2001. Chm., Hospice Care IOM, 2001–10. *Recreations:* hobby farming, theatre, family. *Address:* Attorney General's Chambers, 2nd Floor, Belgravia House, Circular Road, Douglas, Isle of Man IM1 1AE. *T:* (01624) 685452. *E:* john.quinn@attgen.gov.im.

**QUINN, Lawrence William;** Programme and Projects Director, SNC-Lavalin-Atkins, since 2016; *b* 25 Dec. 1956; *s* of late Jimmy Quinn and Sheila Quinn; *m* 1982, Ann Eames. *Educ:* Pennine Way Schs, Carlisle; Harraby Sch., Carlisle; Hatfield Poly. (BSc). CEng; FICE. Formerly Planning Develt Engr, London NE, Railtrack; Rail Projects Delivery Manager, Bechtel, 2005–15. MP (Lab) Scarborough and Whitby, 1997–2005; contested (Lab) same seat, 2005. PPS to Minister of State, DTI, 2001–02, Cabinet Office, 2002–05. Chm., All Party Railways (formerly Rail Freight) Gp, 1997–2005; Secretary: Labour backbench Agriculture Cttee, 1997–2001; All Party Brazil Gp, 2000–05; Chairman: All Party Saudi Arabia Gp, 1998–2005; All Party Underground Space Gp, 2003–05. Sec., PLP Yorks and Humber Gp, 2001–05; PLP Rep., Nat. Policy Forum, 2001–05; Labour Party Policy Comr, 2001–. Sec., 2008–12, Chm., 2012–17, Railway Civil Engineers' Assoc.; Chairman: Railway Engrg Forum, 2013–15; ICE London, 2015– (Mem., Regl Bd, 2013–); Founder Mem., High Speed Rail Leaders Gp, 2013–. *Address:* 23 Academy Drive, Dringhouses, York YO24 1UJ.

**QUINN, Leo;** Group Chief Executive, Balfour Beatty plc, since 2015; *b* 13 Dec. 1956; *s* of Kevin and Mary Quinn; *m* 1993, Elaine Fitzpatrick; two *s*. *Educ:* Portsmouth Poly. (BSc Hons Civil Engrg 1979); Imperial Coll., London (DIC Mgt Sci. 1982). Civil Engr, Balfour Beatty Construction, 1979–81; Planning Manager, Texas Instruments, UK and Portugal, 1982–84; Honeywell, 1984–2000: various posts in UK, Europe and USA; Pres., Honeywell H&BC Enterprise Solutions Worldwide, 2000; Pres. Europe, ME and Africa, Tridium Inc., 2000–01; Chief Operating Officer, Prodn Mgt Div., Invensys plc (USA), 2001–04; CEO, De La Rue, 2004–09; Chief Exec., QinetiQ Gp plc, 2009–14. Non-executive Director: Tomkins PLC, 2007–09; Betfair, 2011–14. *Recreations:* ski-ing, theatre, water sports, shooting, horse racing. *Address:* Balfour Beatty plc, The Curve, Axis Business Park, Hurricane Way, Langley SL3 8AG. *E:* leo.quinn@balfourbeatty.com.

**QUINN, Lisa Dawn;** Director, Link Asset Services, since 2017; *b* Salford, 3 Oct. 1967; *d* of Joseph Watson Quinn and Betty Joyce Quinn. *Educ:* Salford Coll. of Technol.; Liverpool John Moores Univ. MAAT 1990; CPFA 1996. Macclesfield Borough Council: Clerical Asst, 1986–90; Accountancy Technician, 1990–94; Sen. Accountant, 1994–2002; Gp Accountant, 2002–03; Financial Gp Manager, 2003–06; Service Manager, Financial Services, 2006; Corporate Manager, Finance and Asset Mgt, 2006–09; Interim Chief Finance Officer, Cheshire East Shadow Authy, 2008–09; Cheshire East Council: Borough Treas. and Hd of Assets, 2009–11; Dir of Finance and Business Services, 2011–13; Dir of Local Authy Treasury and Capital Finance, Sector Gp, 2013; Dir, Capita Asset Services, Treasury Solutions, 2013–17. *Recreations:* travel, walking, reading, archaeology, ancient history, Arthurian legends, oh yes, and work. *Address:* Link Asset Services, 65 Gresham Street, EC2V 7NQ.

**QUINN, Matthew John;** Distinguished Visiting Fellow, Sustainable Places Research Institute, Cardiff University, since 2017; *b* Leicester, 21 July 1963; *s* of John and June Quinn. *Educ:* Gateway Sch., Leicester; Hertford Coll., Oxford (BA Lit.Hum. 1986; MA). Admin. trainee, DoE and Dept of Transport, 1986–89; Private Sec. to Perm. Sec., Dept of Transport, 1989–90; Hd of Branch, Envmt White Paper Div., DoE, 1990–92; Nuffield and Leverhulme Travelling Fellow, 1992–93; Hd of Br., Planning Policy Div., DoE, 1993–95; Dir, Envmt and Transport, Govt Office for SW, 1995–98; Dir, Policy Unit, Nat. Assembly for Wales, 1998–2003; Hd, of Strategy, 2003–06, of Envmt Protection and Quality, 2006–07, Dir, Envmt, Sustainability and Housing, then Envmt and Sustainable Develt, 2007–17, Welsh Assembly Govt, later Welsh Govt. Non-exec. Dir, Carbon Trust, 2008–11. Dir and Trustee, Gregynog Festival, 2008–. *Publications:* (contrib.) British Planning Policy in Transition, 1996; (contrib.) Introduction to Planning Practice, 2000. *Recreations:* classical music, gadgets. *Address:* Sustainable Places Research Institute, 33 Park Place, Cardiff CF10 3BA.

**QUINN, Richard;** *see* Quinn, T. R.

**QUINN, Ruairi;** TD (Lab) Dublin South-East, 1977–81 and 1982–2016; *b* 2 April 1946; *s* of Malachi Quinn and Julia Quinn; *m* 1st, 1969, Nicola Underwood; one *s* one *d*; 2nd, 1990, Liz Allman; one *s*. *Educ:* University Coll., Dublin (BArch, Higher Dip. in Ekistics). Dublin City Council: Mem., 1974–77; Leader, Lab Gp and Civic Alliance, 1991–93. Mem., Seanad Eireann, 1976–77 and 1981–82; Minister of State, Envmt, 1982–83; Minister: for Labour, 1984–87, and for Public Service, 1986–87; for Enterprise and Employment, 1993–94; for Finance, 1995–97; for Educn and Skills, 2011–14. Leader, Irish Labour Party, 1997–2002. Chair, Inst. of Internat. and European Affairs, 2017–. Adjunct Prof., Trinity Business Sch., TCD, 2016–. *Publications:* Straight Left: a journey in politics, 2006; contrib. to Architects Jl, Irish Architect, Ekistics, Tilt. *Recreations:* reading, cooking, walking, music, gardening, cycling.

**QUINN, Stephen,** CB 2008; Permanent Secretary, Department of Enterprise, Trade and Investment, Northern Ireland, 2006–09; *b* 22 Aug. 1950; *s* of Thomas Charles Quinn and Jane Quinn (*née* Kirkpatrick); *m* 1983, Deirdre Mary Brady. *Educ:* Portora Royal Sch., Enniskillen; Trinity Coll., Dublin (BA Hons Hist. and Pol Sci.). Northern Ireland Civil Service: Dept of Finance, 1974–86 (Sec., Kincora Inquiry, 1984–85); Assistant Secretary: Dept of Health and Social Services, 1986–87; Dept of Finance and Personnel, 1987–90; Dept of Educn, 1990–92; Central Secretariat, 1992–94; Under Secretary: Dept of Finance and Personnel, 1994–98; DoE, 1998–99; Permanent Secretary: DoE, 1999–2002; Dept for Regl Develt, 2002–06.

**QUINN, Terence James;** Editor-in-Chief, APN Regional Newspapers, Australia and New Zealand, 2004–10; *b* 17 Nov. 1951; *s* of Thomas Quinn and Shirley (*née* Anderson); *m* 1973, Patricia Anna-Maria Gillespie; one *s* one *d* (and one *s* decd). *Educ:* St Aloysius Coll., Glasgow. Editor: Telegraph & Argus, Bradford, 1984–89; Evening News, Edinburgh, 1989–92; Dep. Editl Dir, 1992–94, Editl Dir, 1994, Thomson Regl Newspapers; Editor, Daily Record, 1994–98; Sen. Vice Pres., Readership, Thomson Newspapers (US), 1998–2000; Pres., Reader Inc. (US), 2000–02; Publisher, Fairfax Sundays, NZ, 2002–04. *Publications:* The Scoop (novel), 2018. *Recreations:* tennis, sailing, golf.

**QUINN, Dr Terence John,** CBE 2004; FRS 2002; Emeritus Director, Bureau International des Poids et Mesures, Sèvres, France, since 2004 (Deputy Director, 1977–88; Director, 1988–2003); *b* 19 March 1938; *s* of John Henry and Olive Hilda Quinn; *m* 1962, Renée Marie Goujard; two *s*. *Educ:* Univ. of Southampton (BSc 1959); Univ. of Oxford (DPhil 1963). National Physical Laboratory, Teddington: Jun. Res. Fellow, 1962–64; Staff Mem., 1964–77. Vis. Scientist, Nat. Bureau of Standards, Washington, DC, 1967–68; Royal Soc. Vis. Fellow, Cavendish Lab., and Dist. Vis. Fellow, Christ's Coll., Cambridge, 1984–85. Corresp. Mem., Bureau des Longitudes, Paris, 2011. Chm., Paris Decorative and Fine Arts Soc., 2014–. Pres., British Luncheon 1916, Paris, 2016. Fellow: IOP 1975; Fellow, APS, 1995; FAAAS 2001. Hon. Prof., Birmingham Univ., 2000. Hon. Dr Conservatoire Nat. des Arts et Métiers, Paris, 2000. Editor, Notes & Records of the Royal Soc., 2004–07. *Publications:* Temperature, 1983, 2nd edn 1990; From Artefacts to Atoms: the BIPM and the search for ultimate measurement standards, 2011; papers in sci. press on thermometry, radiometry, mass standards, lab. gravitational experiments, fundamental phys. constants and history of metrology and the Metre Convention. *Recreations:* photography, bee keeping, violin playing. *Address:* 92 rue Brancas, 92310 Sèvres, France. *T:* (1) 46230656. *E:* tjqfrs@gmail.com. *Club:* Athenæum.

**QUINN, (Thomas) Richard;** flat jockey, 1978–2006 and since 2007; *b* 2 Dec. 1961; *s* of late Thomas Quinn and of Helen Quinn (*née* McDonald); *m* 1990, Fiona Christine Johnson (marr. diss. 1993); one *s* one *d*; *m* 2007, Alex. *Educ:* Bannockburn High Sch. First winner, Kempton, 1981; Champion Apprentice, Europe, 1983, GB, 1984; 2nd in Jockey's Championship, 1996, 1999. Winning races include: Irish Oaks, 1986, 1990; French 1,000 Guineas, 1986; St Leger, 1990, 2001; Irish St Leger, 1990, 1995; Dewhurst Stakes, 1990; Prix Royal Oak, 1992; Italian Derby, 1994; Juddmonte Lockinge Stakes, 1996; Prix Vermeille, 1998; Oaks, 2000; has ridden winners in 25 countries worldwide. Vice-Pres., Jockeys Assoc., 1992. *Address:* c/o Jockey Club, 42 Portman Square, W1H 0EN.

**QUINNEY, Prof. Robert James Henry,** FRCO; Associate Professor, Faculty of Music, University of Oxford, since 2014; Organist and Tutor in Music, New College, Oxford, since 2014; *b* Nottingham, 16 March 1976; *s* of David and Lynne Quinney; *m* 2000, Cecilia Osmond (marr. diss. 2019); one *s* two *d*. *Educ:* King's Coll., Cambridge (BA Music 1998; MPhil Musicology 1999). FRCO 1996. Asst Master of Music, Westminster Cathedral, 2000–04; Sub-organist, Westminster Abbey, 2004–13; Dir of Music, Peterborough Cathedral, 2013–14. *Recreations:* running, ironing, laughter, silence. *Address:* New College, Oxford OX1 3BN. *T:* (01865) 279500. *E:* robert.quinney@new.ox.ac.uk.

**QUIRK, Barry John,** CBE 2001; PhD; Chief Executive, Royal Borough of Kensington and Chelsea, since 2017; *b* 20 Nov. 1953; *s* of John Quirk and Iris (*née* Cope; now Aldridge); *m* 2009, Katherine Kerswell; three *s* one *d* by former marriage. *Educ:* London Univ. (ext. BSc Hons 1975); Portsmouth Poly. (PhD 1984). Head of Corporate Policy, London Borough of Newham, 1987; Asst Chief Exec., 1987–94, Chief Exec., 1994–2017, London Borough of Lewisham. Non-exec. Dir, HM Customs and Excise, subseq. Revenue and Customs, 2002–06. Pres., 2005–06, Chm., 2006–08, SOLACE. Vis. Fellow of Social Policy and Politics, Goldsmiths Coll., Univ. of London, 1998–2006. Associate, Inst. for Govt, 2010–15. *Publications:* Re-imagining Government: public leadership and management in challenging times, 2011.

**QUIRKE, Pauline;** actress; *b* 8 July 1959; *m* Steve; one *s* one *d*. *Educ:* Anna Scher Theatre Sch., London. Appeared in Dixon of Dock Green, BBC TV, 1968; *television series include:* Angels, 1976; Shine on Harvey Moon, 1982; Rockliffe's Babies, 1987; Birds of a Feather (12 series), 1989–98, 2014–16; Jobs for the Girls, 1993; First Sign of Madness, 1996; Double Nougat, 1996; Real Women, 1997–99; Maisie Raine, 1998–99; Down to Earth, 2000–03; Office Gossip, 2001; Being April, 2002; North and South, 2004; Missing, 2009; Emmerdale, 2010–12; Broadchurch, 2013, 2015; You, Me and the Apocalypse, 2015; *television drama includes:* The Sculptress, 1996; Our Boy, 1997; Deadly Summer, 1997; David Copperfield, 1999; The Flint Street Nativity, 1999; Carrie's War, 2003. *Films include:* Little Dorrit, 1986; Getting it Right, 1988; The Return of the Soldiers, 1988; Still Lives—Distant Voices, 1989; The Canterville Ghost, 1997; Check-out Girl, 1998; Arthur's Dyke, 2000; Redemption Road, 2001. *Theatre includes:* A Tale of Two Cities, Royal Court Theatre, 1979; Birds of a Feather, New Victoria, Woking, 2012, tour, 2012–13. Opened The Pauline Quirke Academy of Performing Arts, 2007.

**QUIRKE, Prof. Philip,** PhD; FRCPath, FMedSci; Professor of Pathology, Head, Pathology and Data Analytics (formerly Pathology and Tumour Biology), since 1997, and Sub Dean, Academic Training, since 2007, University of Leeds; Honorary Consultant, Leeds Teaching Hospitals NHS Trust, since 1990; *b* Romford, Essex, 14 Dec. 1955; *s* of Daniel Quirke and Barbara Quirke; *m* 1984, Judith Wyatt; one *s* one *d*. *Educ:* Coopers Company Grammar Sch., Mile End, subseq. Coopers' Company and Coborn Comp. Sch., Upminster; Univ. of Southampton (BM 1980); Univ. of Leeds (PhD 1987). MRCPath 1983, FRCPath 1997. University of Leeds: Lectr, 1982–90; Sen. Lectr, 1990–95; Reader, 1995–97. Hd, Histopathol. and Molecular Pathol., Leeds Teaching Hosps NHS Trust, 1991–2004. Lead Pathology NHS England Bowel Cancer Screening Prog., 2007–. NIHR Sen. Investigator, 2015. Pres., Pathol Soc. of GB and Ire., 2015–18. FMedSci 2014; FRCSE *ad hominem* 2017. Hon. FFPath, RCPI, 2019. *Publications:* (ed jtly) PCR: a practical approach, 1991; (with M. F. Dixon) Aids to Pathology, 3rd edn 1993. *Recreations:* travel, films, photography, dining. *Address:* Pathology and Data Analytics, Wellcome Trust Brenner Building, Saint James's University Hospital, Beckett Street, Leeds, W Yorks LS9 7TF.

**QURESHI, Bashir Ahmad,** FRCGP, FRCPCH; medical journalist, since 1964; expert witness, since 1992; general practitioner, Hounslow, 1969–2016; *b* 25 Sept. 1935; four *d* (one *s* decd). *Educ:* Nishtar Medical Coll., Multan, Pakistan (MB BS); DHMSA 1974; DCH 1976; DPMSA 1980. AFOM 1978; MRCGP 1976, FRCGP 1984; MICGP 1984; MFFP 1993; MRCPCH 1998, FRCPCH 2006; FFSRH (FFFP 2006), Hon. FFSRH 2016. MO Paediatrics, Nishtar Hosp., Multan, Pakistan, 1961–64; med. doctor, UK hosps, 1964–69; MO (pt-time), British Army and HM Prisons, 1998–; Expert Witness in cultural, religious and ethnic issues in litigation, UK, 1992–; Expert Witness in GP clinical negligence, 1992–. Mem. Council, RCGP, 1990–; Chm. Council, 1997–98, Emeritus Vice Pres., 2005–, RSPH (formerly RSH); Dep. Chm. and Sec., Nat. Assoc. of Sessional GPs, 2007–11 (Mem., BMA Subcttee, 1998–2017); Chm., NHS Trusts Assoc., 2006–10. Dep. Chm., Local Med. Cttee, Hounslow, 2003–12; Med. Advr, London Area, British Red Cross, 2006–. Lectr in transcultural litigation and transcultural medicine, 1989–2003; lectr, Army Med. Coll., Westminster, later Portsmouth, 1990–2003. Life Mem., BMA, 2014; BMA Ambassador, 2018–. Vice Pres., Hounslow Conservative Assoc., 2005–. Mem. Council, Conservative Med. Soc., 1988–; Vice Pres., Conservative Health, 2009–. Member: Ct of Govs, LSHTM, 2004–; Trustees Bd, English PEN, 2008–12; Life Mem., Coll. of St George, Windsor Castle, 1986. Member: Med. Music Soc. of London; London Music Soc.; NHS Retirement Fellowship. Assessor: for annual Med. Book Competition, BMA Liby, 1995–; for Queen's Anniversary Prizes for Higher and Further Educn, 1997–. Hon. FRSPH (Hon. FRSH 1998); Hon. Member: APHA, 1998; GP Sect., RSM, 1998 (Pres., 2000–01). Badge of Honour, British Red Cross, 1999; Plaque of Recognition, H of L, 2001. *Publications:* Transcultural Medicine: dealing with patients from different cultures, religions and ethnicities, 1989, 2nd edn 1994; contrib. 12 chapters in med. books; 321 articles in med. jls; handouts and 385 lects to med. meetings, mainly UK, USA, India and Tanzania. *Recreations:* cinema, writing short stories, music, dancing, travel, reading, theatre, dining out, holidays, public speaking, guest broadcasting on British TV and radio, social media comments; Twitter, Facebook and LinkedIn. *T:* 07710 402276, *T:* and *Fax:* (020) 8570 4008. *E:* drbashirqureshi@hotmail.com. *W:* www.drbashirqureshi.com. *Clubs:* Royal Society of Medicine; Society of Authors; English PEN.

**QURESHI, Murad;** Member (Lab) London Assembly, Greater London Authority, 2004–16; *b* 27 May 1965. *Educ:* Univ. of E Anglia (BA 1987); University Coll. London (MSc 1993). Mem. (Lab) Westminster CC, 1998–2006. Member: Metropolitan Police Authy, 2004–06; London Fire and Emergency Planning Authy, 2004–12. Contested (Lab) London Assembly, GLA, 2016. *Recreations:* football and cricket (playing and watching).

**QURESHI, Yasmin;** MP (Lab) Bolton South East, since 2010; *b* Pakistan, 5 July 1963; *d* of Mohammad Qureshi and Sakina Beg; *m* 2008, Nadeem Ashraf Butt. *Educ:* Westfield Sch.; South Bank Poly. (BA Law 1984); Council of Legal Educn; University Coll. London (LLM 1987). Called to the Bar, Lincoln's Inn, 1985; in practice as barrister, 1987–; Crown Prosecutor, CPS, 1987–2000; Hd, Criminal Legal Section, UN Mission, Kosovo, 2000–01; Dir, Dept of Judicial Admin, Kosovo, 2001–02; Policy Adviser, CPS, 2002–04; Human Rights Advr to Mayor of London, 2004–08; barrister: 2 King's Bench Walk Chambers, 2004–08; Kenworthy's Chambers, Manchester, 2008–10. Contested (Lab) Brent E, 2005. Shadow Minister for Justice, 2016–. Member: Justice Select Cttee, 2010–15; Foreign Affairs Select Cttee, 2015–16; Political and Constitutional Reform Cttee, 2011; Privacy and Injunctions Jt Cttee, 2011–12; Home Affairs Cttee, 2013–15; High Speed Rail (London-W Midlands) Bill Select Cttee, 2014–15. *Address:* House of Commons, SW1A 0AA.

**QUYSNER, David William,** CBE 2008; Chairman, Abingworth Management Ltd, 2002–14; *b* Westhoughton, Lancs, 26 Dec. 1946; *s* of late Charles William Quysner and Marjorie Alice Quysner; *m* 1971, Lindsay Jean Parris (*née* Biggs); one *s* two *d*. *Educ:* Bolton Sch.; Selwyn Coll., Cambridge (BA 1969; MA); London Business Sch. (London Exec. Prog. 27). Investment Exec., 1968–76, Local Dir, 1976–82, Industrial and Commercial Finance Corp. Ltd; Dir, 1982–94, Man. Dir, 1994–2002, Abingworth Mgt Ltd. Chairman: RCM Technology Trust plc, subseq. Allianz Technology Trust plc, 2004–14; Capital for Enterprise Ltd, 2008–12; Director: ANGLE plc, 2004–14; Foresight 2 VCT plc, 2004–15; MRC Technology Ltd, 2004–14; Private Equity Investor plc, 2004–14. Dir, British Venture Capital Assoc., 1992–98 (Chm., 1996–97). *Recreations:* travel, opera, cricket. *Address:* The Old Vicarage, Selmeston, Polegate, E Sussex BN26 6TY. *T:* (01323) 811515. *E:* quysner@abingworth.com. *Club:* MCC.

# R

**RA JONG-YIL, Dr;** University Distinguished Professor, Gachon University, Republic of Korea, since 2016; Chair Professor, National Defense University, Republic of Korea, since 2018; *b* 5 Dec. 1940; *s* of Ra Iong-Gwyn and Ra Gwi-Nye; *m* 1968, Ra Jae-Ja; one *s* three *d*. *Educ:* Seoul Nat. Univ. (BA Pol Sci., MA Pol Sci.); Trinity Coll., Cambridge (PhD Internat. Relns, 1972). Kyung Hee University, Korea: Prof. of Pol Sci., 1972–; Dean: Coll. of Econs and Pol Sci., 1980–81; Grad. Sch., 1988–92. Fellow Commoner, Churchill Coll., Cambridge, 1981; Fulbright Sen. Fellow, Univ. of Southern Calif, 1985. Vice-Chm., Forum of Democratic Leaders in Asia-Pacific, 1994; Mem., Exec. Cttee and Special Asst to Pres., Nat. Congress for New Politics, 1996–97; Hd, Admin. Office, Presidential Transition Cttee, 1997; 2nd and 1st Dir, Nat. Security Planning Bd, 1998; 1st Dir, Nat. Intelligence Service, 1998–99; Director-General: Res. Inst. of Peace Studies, 1999–2000; Circle Millennium Korea, 1999–2000; Special Assistant: to Pres., Foreign and Security Affairs, Millennium Democratic Party, 1999–2000; to Dir-Gen., Foreign Affairs, Nat. Intelligence Service, 2000–01; Ambassador of Republic of Korea to UK, 2001–03; Nat. Security Advr to Pres., 2003–04; Ambassador to Japan, 2004–07. Chm., Cttee on Ideological Conflict, Presidential Commn on Social Cohesion, 2008–; Mem., Presidential Cttee of Preparation for Unification, 2014–. National Commission for Human Rights: Member: Policy Adv. Cttee, 2012–14; Special Cttee on Internat. Human Rights, 2013–15; Internat. Human Rights Cttee, 2015–17; Chm., Special Cttee on Human Rights in N Korea, 2013–15. Mem., Special Adv. Cttee to Pres., Korean Red Cross, 2015–. Pres., Woosuk Univ., Korea, 2007–11; Univ. Dist. Prof., Hangyang Univ., Korea, 2011–16. *Publications:* Co-operation and Conflict, 1986; Points of Departure, 1992; Human Beings and Politics, 1995; Preparing for the New Millennium, 1998; Fairy Stories of Ra, Jong-Yil, 2006; Bibimbap Story, 2008; The Discovery of the World, 2008 (Korean edn 2009); The Wizard of River Nakdong, 2010; (trans.) Fiction and Politics in the Modern World, 2012; (trans.) Aristotle's Politics, 2012; The Forgotten Terrorist, 2013; (contrib.) Alternative Political Systems in Asia; A Most Trivial Salvation, 2015; The Son-in-Law of Theocracy, 2016; Asia in 2015, 2016; Shyukusei no Ouchiyou, 2017; Inside North Korean Theocracy, 2019. *Recreations:* tennis, golf, Kendo, Aikido. *Address:* Gachon University, 1342 Seongnam-Daero, Sujeong-Gu, Seongnam-Si, Gyeonggi-Do 13120, Republic of Korea; Songpa-gu, Joongdae-ro 24, Olympic Family Apts #211–204, Republic of Korea. *Club:* Seoul.

**RAAB, Rt Hon. Dominic (Rennie);** PC 2018; MP (C) Esher and Walton, since 2010; Secretary of State for Foreign and Commonwealth Affairs, since 2019; *b* Bucks, 25 Feb. 1974; *m* 2005, Erika Rey; two *s*. *Educ:* Dr Challoner's Grammar Sch., Amersham; Lady Margaret Hall, Oxford (BA Law); Jesus Coll., Cambridge (LLM). Internat. lawyer; Linklaters, incl. secondments to Liberty and in Brussels advising on EU and WTO law, 1998–2000; entered FCO, 2000; advr on legal issues, 2000–03; First Sec. (Legal), The Hague, 2003–06; COS to Shadow Home Sec., 2006–08, to Shadow Justice Sec., 2008–10. Parly Under-Sec. of State, 2015–16, Minister of State, 2017–18, MoJ; Minister of State (Minister for Housing), MHCLG, 2018; Sec. of State for Exiting the EU, 2018. Member: Jt Cttee on Human Rights, 2010–13; Educn Select Cttee, 2013–15; Cttee on Exiting the EU, 2016–17. *Publications:* The Assault on Liberty: what went wrong with rights, 2009. *Recreations:* sport (karate black belt 3rd dan, boxing), theatre, travel. *Address:* House of Commons, SW1A 0AA.

**RABAN, Antony John;** Conseiller, Relations Internationales, Association Bernard Gregory, 2003–07 (Committee Member, 1996–2002; Membre d'Honneur, since 2005); *s* of Rev. Harry Priaulx Raban and Freda Mary Raban (*née* Probert); *m* 1965, Sandra Gilham Brown. *Educ:* St John's Sch., Leatherhead; Corpus Christi Coll., Cambridge (MA Hist.). Asst Master, Doncaster GS, 1964–67; Careers Officer, 1967–69, Professional Asst, 1969–71, Cambs & Isle of Ely CC; Asst Sec. (Careers Advr), Oxford Univ. Careers Service, 1971–74; Careers Advr, 1974–92, Dir, 1992–2002, Cambridge Univ. Careers Service. Chm., Assoc. of Grad. Careers Adv. Services, 1979–81; Pres., Eur. Forum on Student Guidance, 1988–92; Mem. Council, CRAC, 1998–2002. *Publications:* Working in the European Union: a guide for graduate recruiters and job-seekers, 1985, 4th edn 1995; The Entry of New Graduates into the European Labour Market, 1991; From PhD to Employment, 2000, 2nd edn 2003; numerous reports and contribs to professional jls. *Recreations:* art history, France.

**RABAN, Jonathan,** FRSL; essayist, travel writer, novelist; *b* 14 June 1942; *s* of late Rev. Canon J. Peter C. P. Raban and Monica Raban (*née* Sandison); *m* 1992, Jean Lenihan (marr. diss.); one *d*. *Educ:* Univ. of Hull (BA Hons English). Lecturer in English and American Literature: UCW, Aberystwyth, 1965–67; Univ. of E Anglia, 1967–69; professional writer, 1969–. FRSL 1975. Hon. DLitt Hull, 2005. *Publications:* The Technique of Modern Fiction, 1969; Mark Twain: Huckleberry Finn, 1969; The Society of the Poem, 1971; Soft City, 1973; Arabia Through the Looking Glass, 1979; Old Glory, 1981 (Heinemann Award, RSL, 1982; Thomas Cook Award, 1982); Foreign Land, 1985; Coasting, 1986; For Love and Money, 1987; God, Man & Mrs Thatcher, 1989; Hunting Mister Heartbreak, 1990 (Thomas Cook Award, 1991); (ed) The Oxford Book of the Sea, 1992; Bad Land, 1996 (National Book Critics Circle Award, 1997; PEN Award for creative non-fiction, 1997); Passage to Juneau, 1999; Waxwings, 2003; My Holy War, 2005; Surveillance, 2006; Driving Home: an American scrapbook, 2010. *Recreation:* sailing. *Address:* c/o Aitken Alexander Associates Ltd, 291 Gray's Inn Road, WC1X 8EB. *Clubs:* Groucho; Rainier (Seattle).

**RABBATTS, Dame Heather (Victoria),** DBE 2016 (CBE 2000); Managing Director, Cove Pictures (formerly Smuggler Entertainment LLP), since 2013; *b* 6 Dec. 1955; *d* of Thomas Rabbatts and Hyacinth Rabbatts; one *s* by Edmund Gerard O'Sullivan; *m* 2001, Michael Lee, OBE (*d* 2018); one step *s*. *Educ:* London Sch. of Econs (BA Hons Hist.; MSc). Called to the Bar, Lincoln's Inn, 1981. Equalities Officer, then Parly Liaison Officer, Local Govt Inf. Unit, 1983–86; London Borough of Hammersmith and Fulham: Hd, Women's Dept, 1987–89; Dir of Personnel, 1989–91; Dep. Chief Exec. and Dir, Strategic Services, 1991–93; Chief Executive: Merton LBC, 1993–95; Lambeth LBC, 1995–2000; Man. Dir, 4Learning, Channel 4, 2002–06; Chief Exec., 2006–09, non-exec. Dir, 2009–10, Millwall Hldgs; Exec. Dep. Chm., Millwall FC, 2006–09; Chm., Shed Media plc, 2009–10. A Gov., BBC, 1999–2002. Non-executive Director: Bank of England, 2003–07; Crossrail, 2008–14; Grosvenor (Britain and Ireland), 2009–; Malaria No More, 2010–14; FA, 2011–17; Supervisory Bd, FCO, 2012–15. Member: Bd, Qualifications and Curriculum Authority, 1997–99; Bd, British Council, 1998–2004; ESRC, 1998–2000; Bd, UK Film Council, 2003–11; Bd, Royal Opera House, 2009–17; Chm., Soho Th., 2018–. Gov., LSE, 1997–2004. Hon. DSc Aston. *Recreations:* opera, literature, champagne, theatre. *Address:* Cove Pictures (registered office), 16 Carlisle Street, W1D 3BT.

**RABBI, The Chief;** *see* Mirvis, E.

**RABBITT, Prof. Patrick Michael Anthony,** PhD; Research Professor in Gerontology and Cognitive Psychology, and Director, Age and Cognitive Research Centre, University of Manchester, 1983–2004, now Emeritus Professor; *b* 23 Sept. 1934; *s* of Joseph Bernard Rabbitt and Edna Maude Smith; *m* 1st, 1955, Adriana Habers (marr. diss. 1976); one *s* two *d*; 2nd, 1976, Dorothy Vera Bishop, *qv*. *Educ:* Queens' Coll., Cambridge (MA, PhD); MA Oxon; Manchester Univ. (MSc). Scientific Staff, MRC Applied Psychology Unit, Cambridge, 1962–68; Univ. Lectr in Psychology, and Official Fellow, Queen's Coll., Univ. of Oxford, 1968–82; Prof. of Psychology, Univ. of Durham, 1982–83. University of Western Australia: Adjunct Prof. of Psychology, 1991–2003; Hon. Res. Fellow, then Sen. Res. Fellow, 2003–15; Sen. Res. Fellow (formerly Hon. Res. Fellow), and Associate Mem., Dept of Exptl Psychol., Univ. of Oxford, 2004–. FRSA 1997; Founding Fellow, British Gerontological Soc., 2009. Mem., Eur. Acad., 2013. Hon. Mem., Experimental Psychol. Soc., 1999; Hon. FBPsS 1995. Hon. DSc Western Australia, 2001. *Publications:* (ed) Cognitive Gerontology, 1990; Methodology of Frontal and Executive Function, 1997; Inside Psychology, 2009; Cognitive Gerontology, 2009; The Aging Mind: an owner's manual, 2015; Cognitive Development and the Ageing Process, 2019; 380 papers in learned jls. *Recreations:* gin, nostalgia. *Address:* Department of Experimental Psychology, University of Oxford, Anna Watts Building, Radcliffe Observatory Quarter, Woodstock Road, Oxford OX2 6GG; 10 North Parade Avenue, Oxford OX2 6LX.

**RABBITTS, Prof. Terence Howard,** PhD; FRS 1987; FMedSci; Professor of Molecular Biology, University of Oxford, 2012–Feb. 2020; Professor of Molecular Immunology, Institute of Cancer Research, from March 2020; *b* 17 June 1946; *s* of Joan and Frederick Rabbitts; *m* 1984, Pamela Gage; one *d*, and one step *s* one step *d*. *Educ:* John Ruskin Grammar School; Univ. of East Anglia (BSc); Nat. Inst. for Medical Research (PhD). Research Fellow, Dept of Genetics, Univ. of Edinburgh, 1971–73; Mem., Scientific Staff, 1973–2006, Jt Hd of Protein and Nucleic Acid Div., 1988–2002, MRC Lab. of Molecular Biology, Cambridge; Dir, Leeds Inst. of Molecular Medicine, Univ. of Leeds, 2006–11. Non-executive Director: Aptuscan, 2010–11; Aberterno, 2014–15. Chair, Scientific Advisory Board: Cambridge Antibody Tech., 1990–97; Quadrant Healthcare, 1992–2000; Kymab, 2010–15; Orbit Discovery, 2016– (Founder, 2015; Mem., non-exec. Bd, 2016–); Founder, Quadrucept Ltd, 2016; Member: Sci. Adv. Bd, Domantis, 2001–08; Oakes Lyman Consolidated Hldgs Ltd, 2002–07; Med. Adv. Bd, OLK Investments, 2007–10; Oryzon Genomics, 2009–16; DiThera, 2009–12; Biosceptre, 2010–; Avacta, 2012–. Mem., Hooke Cttee, Royal Soc., 2012–15. Mem., EMBO, 1981–. FMedSci 1998 (Mem. Council, 2009–11); FRSocMed 2005. Associate Mem., Amer. Assoc. for Cancer Res., 1991. Colworth Medal, 1981, Ciba Medal and Prize, 1993, Biochemical Soc.; Clotten Foundn Prize, 2015. *Publications:* papers in scientific jls. *Address:* (until Feb. 2020) Weatherall Institute of Molecular Medicine, MRC Molecular Haematology Unit, University of Oxford, John Radcliffe Hospital, Headington, Oxford OX3 9DS; (from March 2020) Institute of Cancer Research, 15 Cotswold Road, Sutton SM2 5NG.

**RABENIRINA, Rt Rev. Remi Joseph;** Archbishop of the Indian Ocean, 1995–2005, Archbishop Emeritus, 2013; Bishop of Antananarivo, 1984–2008; *b* 6 March 1938; *s* of Joseph Razafindrabe and Josephine Ramanantenasoa; *m* 1971, Elisabeth Razaizanany; two *s* four *d*. *Educ:* Protestant Church schs; St Paul's Theol Coll., Ambatoharanana, Madagascar; Univ. of Madagascar; St Chad's Theol Coll., Lichfield; Ecumenical Inst. of Bossey, Switzerland. School teacher, 1958–61; Parish Priest: St James', Toamasina, 1967–68; St Matthew's, Antsiranana, 1968–73; St John's, Ambohimangakely (Antananarivo), 1973–84; Diocesan Chancellor, Antananarivo, 1982–84. Chevalier, Officier, Commandeur, Grand Officier et Grand Croix de deuxième classe de l'Ordre National (Malagasy). *Publications:* (in Malagasy) An Open Door: a short history of the beginning of the Anglican Church in Northern Madagascar, 1969; (trans.) J. C. Fenton, Preaching the Cross, 1990; Some of the Saints (biogs of Saints remembered in the Anglican Church Calendar, Madagascar), 1998. *Recreations:* reading, writing. *Address:* Fonenana Nirina I, Andranomahery, Anosiala, 105 Ambohidratrimo, Madagascar. T: (34) 2020827.

**RABINOWITZ, Laurence Anton;** QC 2002; *b* 3 May 1960; *s* of Joseph and Mary Rabinowitz; *m* 1989, Suzanne Benster; two *s* one *d*. *Educ:* Univ. of Witwatersrand (BA, LLB); Merton Coll., Oxford (BA, BCL). Called to the Bar, Middle Temple, 1987, Bencher, 2008; in practice specialising in commercial law; Jun. Counsel to Crown, Chancery, 1995–2002; a Dep. High Court Judge, 2016–. Gov., N London Collegiate Sch., 2008–. *Publications:* (ed) Weinberg and Blank on Take-overs and Mergers, 5th edn, 1989. *Recreations:* sport, music, reading. *Address:* (chambers) One Essex Court, Temple, EC4Y 9AR. T: (020) 7583 2000, Fax: (020) 7583 0118. E: lrabinowitz@oeclaw.co.uk.

**RACE, (Denys Alan) Reg;** management and policy consultant; Founder and Director, Quality Health management consultants, 1993–2015; *b* 23 June 1947; *s* of Denys and Elsie Race; *m* 1983, Mandy Moore. *Educ:* Sale Grammar School; Univ. of Kent (BA (Politics and Sociology), PhD (Politics)). Senior Research Officer, National Union of Public Employees, 1972. MP (Lab) Haringey, Wood Green, 1979–83. Contested (Lab) Chesterfield, 2001. Head of Programme Office, GLC, 1983–86; Special Res. Officer, ACTT, 1986; County Dir, Derbys County Council, 1988. Parly Advr, Local Govt Inf. Unit and Local Authy Assocs, 1986–88; Advr, Health Policy Adv. Unit, 1989–93. Chair, St Mildred's Area Community Assoc., Canterbury, 2016–.

**RACE, John William B.;** *see* Burton-Race.

**RACE, Reg;** *see* Race, D. A. R.

**RACEY, Prof. Paul Adrian**, FRSE; FRSB; Regius Professor of Natural History, University of Aberdeen, 1993–2009, now Emeritus; Visiting Professor, University of Exeter, Cornwall Campus, since 2007; *b* 7 May 1944; *s* of Albert and Esme Racey; *m* 1968, Anna Priscilla Notcutt; three *s*. *Educ*: Ratcliffe Coll.; Downing Coll., Cambridge (MA); London Univ. (PhD); Univ. of Aberdeen (DSc). FRSB (FIBiol 1987); FRSE 1992. Rothamsted Experimental Station, 1965–66; Zoological Soc. of London, 1966–71; Res. Fellow, Univ. of Liverpool, 1971–73; University of Aberdeen: Lectr and Sen. Lectr in Zoology, 1973–85; Prof. of Zoology, 1985–93. Chairman: Bat (formerly Chiroptera) Specialist Gp, IUCN Species Survival Commn, 1986–2014; Bat Conservation Trust, 1990–96 (Hon. Sci. and Conservation Advr, 1996–); Member: Scottish Exam. Bd, 1985–90; Management Cttee, Scottish Univs Res. and Reactor Centre, 1991–95 (Mem. Sci. Adv. Bd, 1986–90); Council, Fauna & Flora International (formerly Fauna & Flora Preservation Soc.), 1990–2012 (Chm., Conservation Cttee, 1993–2012; Vice-Pres., 2006–12); Bd of Govs, Macaulay Land Use Res. Inst., 1990–2001; NCC for Scotland, 1991–92; Terrestrial and Freshwater Sci. Cttee, NERC, 1991–94; Exec. Cttee, Mammal Soc., 1991–98; Res. Bd, 1992–94, Scientific Adv. Cttee, 1994–2001 (Chm., 1996–2001), SE Regl Bd, 1996–97, Scottish Natural Heritage; Council, Zool Soc. of London, 1999–2003 (Vice Pres., 2001–03); Member: Adv. Cttee for Sci. and Conservation, 1996–2000 (Chm., 1999–2000); Awards Cttee, 2003–07); Council for Scotland, WWF, 1997–2000; Bat Expert Panel, Natural England, 2018–. *Publications*: numerous res. papers in professional jls. *Recreations*: riding, sailing, walking. *Address*: Chapel Cottage, Prazegooth Lane, Cadgwith, Ruan Minor, Helston, Cornwall TR12 7LA. *T*: (01326) 291255.

**RADAELLI, Prof. Paolo Giuseppe**, PhD; FInstP; Dr Lee's Professor of Experimental Philosophy, since 2008, and Associate Head, Oxford Physics and Head, Oxford Condensed Matter Physics, since 2011, University of Oxford; Fellow of Wadham College, Oxford, since 2008; *b* Milan, 11 Oct. 1961; *s* of Bruno Radaelli and Annamaria Trovato Radaelli; *m* 1988, Anna Raimondi; one *s* one *d*. *Educ*: Liceo G. Garducci, Milan (Maturità Classica 1980); Università degli Studi, Milan (Laurea Physics 1986); Illinois Inst. of Technol. (PhD Physics 1992). FInstP 2012. Res. Associate, Inst. for Technol. of Non-conventional Metals, CNR, Milan, 1988–89; Res. Associate and Lectr, Illinois Inst. of Technol., 1989–90; Grad. Res. Asst, 1990–92, Post-doctoral Res. Asst, 1992–93, Materials Sci. Div., Argonne Nat. Lab.; Post-doctoral Res. Asst, Lab. de Cristallographie-CNRS, Grenoble, 1993–94; Scientist, Institut Laue-Langevin, Grenoble, 1994–98; Scientist, 1998–2003, STFC Fellow, 2003–08, ISIS, STFC. Vis. Prof., UCL, 2002–. Knight, Order of the Star of Italy, 2017. *Publications*: Symmetry in Crystallography, 2011; articles in Nature, Science, Physical Rev. Letters, Physical Rev. *Recreations*: piano, sailing. *Address*: Clarendon Laboratory, Department of Physics, University of Oxford, Parks Road, Oxford OX1 3PU.

**RADAKIN, Adm. Antony David**, CB 2018; First Sea Lord and Chief of the Naval Staff, since 2019; First and Principal Naval Aide-de-Camp to the Queen, since 2019; *b* Oldham, 10 Nov. 1965; *s* of Brian John Radakin and Dorothy Radakin (*née* Sanderson); *m* 1995, Louise Sarah Carron; four *s*. *Educ*: St Brendan's Coll.; Southampton Univ. (LLB Hons 1989); King's Coll. London (MA Internat. Defence Relns 2000). Commnd 1990; watchkeeping, HMS Leeds Castle, 1990–91; Navigating Officer, HMS Charybdis and HMS Andromeda, 1991–92; CO, HMS Blazer, 1993–95; called to the Bar, Middle Temple, 1996; PWO, HMS Beaver, 1996–98; Mem. Staff, BRNC, 1998–99; acsc 1999–2000; MA to Under Sec. of State for Defence, 2000–02; CO, HMS Norfolk, 2002–04; Captain i/c Operation Telic, Iraq, 2006–07; PJHQ Plans, 2007–08; MA to VCDS, 2008–09; hcsc 2010; Cdre i/c Operation Telic, Iraq, 2010–11; Comdr, Portsmouth Naval Base, 2011–12; Hd of Strategy Mgt, MoD, 2012–14; Rear Adm. Surface Ships, and Comdr, UK Maritime Forces, 2014–16; COS, Jt Forces Comd, 2016–18; Second Sea Lord and Dep. Chief of the Naval Staff, 2018–19. Chm., Surface Warfare Officer Assoc., 2014–16. Pres., RN Squash Assoc., 2014–. *Recreations*: follows most sports and active participant in squash, sailing, ski-ing and mountain biking. *Club*: Royal Navy of 1765 and 1785 (Vice Chm., 2017–19).

**RADCLIFFE, Andrew Allen**; QC 2000; *b* 21 Jan. 1952; *s* of Reginald Allen Radcliffe and Sheila Radcliffe (*née* McNeil); *m* 1977 (marr. diss. 1990); two *s* one *d*. *Educ*: Birkenhead Sch.; St Edmund Hall, Oxford (BA Hons 1974). Called to the Bar, Middle Temple, 1975; Asst Recorder, 1998–2000; Recorder, 2000–11. Mem. Cttee, Criminal Bar Assoc., 1998–2001. *Address*: 2 Hare Court, Temple, EC4Y 7BH. *T*: (020) 7353 5324. *Club*: Radlett Cricket.

**RADCLIFFE, Daniel Jacob**; actor; *b* London, 23 July 1989; *s* of Alan Radcliffe and Marcia Gresham. *Educ*: Sussex House Sch.; City of London Sch. *Television*: David Copperfield, 1999; My Boy Jack, 2007; A Young Doctor's Notebook, 2012–13; The Gamechangers, 2015; *films*: The Tailor of Panama, Harry Potter and the Philosopher's Stone, 2001; Harry Potter and the Chamber of Secrets, 2002; Harry Potter and the Prisoner of Azkaban, 2004; Harry Potter and the Goblet of Fire, 2005; Harry Potter and the Order of the Phoenix, December Boys, 2007; Harry Potter and the Half-Blood Prince, 2009; Harry Potter and the Deathly Hallows: Part 1, 2010; Harry Potter and the Deathly Hallows: Part 2, 2011; The Woman in Black, 2012; Kill Your Darlings, Horns, What If, 2013; Trainwreck, Victor Frankenstein, 2015; Now You See Me 2, Imperium, Swiss Army Man, 2016; Jungle, 2017; *theatre*: Equus, Gielgud, 2007, NY, 2008; How to Succeed in Business Without Really Trying, NY, 2011; The Cripple of Inishmaan, Noël Coward, 2013, NY, 2014; Privacy, NY, 2016; Rosencrantz and Guildenstern are Dead, Old Vic, 2017; The Lifespan of a Fact, NY, 2018. *Address*: c/o ARG Talent Agency, 4A Exmoor Street, W10 6BD. *T*: (020) 7436 6400. *E*: argall@argtalent.com.

**RADCLIFFE, Francis Charles Joseph**; *b* 23 Oct. 1939; *s* of Charles Joseph Basil Nicholas Radcliffe and Norah Radcliffe (*née* Percy); *m* 1968, Nicolette, *d* of Eugene Randag; one *s* two *d*. *Educ*: Ampleforth Coll.; Gonville and Caius Coll., Cambridge (MA). Called to the Bar, Gray's Inn, 1962; a Recorder of the Crown Court, 1979, until submitted 'Lawful marriage is good, just and indissoluble' (1540 Henry VIII c. 38). Contested (Christian: stop abortion candidate) York, 1979; founded York Christian Party, 1981. Chm., Life, York. *Recreations*: shooting, beagling, gardening, etc.

**RADCLIFFE, Nora**; Member (Lib Dem) Gordon, Scottish Parliament, 1999–2007; *b* 4 March 1946; *d* of late James Stuart MacPherson and Doreen MacPherson (*née* McRobb); *m* 1972, Michael Anthony Radcliffe; one *s* one *d*. *Educ*: Bowmore Primary Sch.; Peterculter Primary Sch.; High Sch. for Girls, Aberdeen; Aberdeen Univ. Hotel mgt, 1968–72; Grampian Health Board: Community Liaison Team, 1993–96; Primary Care Develt Team, 1996–99. Mem. (Lib Dem), Gordon DC, 1988–92. Contested (Lib Dem) Gordon, Scottish Parlt, 2007. *Recreations*: reading, walking, good food. *Address*: 3 King Street, Inverurie, Aberdeenshire AB51 4SY. *T*: (01467) 622575.

**RADCLIFFE, Paula Jane**, MBE 2002; professional athlete; BBC commentator and athletics pundit, since 2013; *b* 17 Dec. 1973; *d* of Peter Radcliffe and Patricia Radcliffe; *m* 2000, Gary Lough; one *s* one *d*. *Educ*: Loughborough Univ. (1st cl. Hons Mod. European Studies 1996). World Junior Champion, cross-country, 1992; European Champion: cross-country, 1998, 2003; 10,000m, 2002; Silver Medal for 10,000m, World Championships, 1999; World Champion: half marathon, 2000, 2001, 2003; cross-country, 2001, 2002; marathon, 2005; Commonwealth Champion, 5000m, 2002; winner of London Marathon, 2002, 2003 (World Record, 2 hours 15 mins 25 secs), 2005; winner of Chicago Marathon, 2002; winner of New York Marathon, 2004, 2007, 2008; European Record Holder: 10,000m (30 mins 1.09 secs, 2002), half marathon (1 hour 6 mins 47 secs, 2001); marathon; GB Record Holder: 3000m (8 mins 22.20 secs, 2002), 5000m (14 mins 29.11 secs, 2004), 10,000m (30 mins 1.10 secs, 2002), half marathon, marathon. GB Women's Team Captain, 1998, 2005. Mem., IAAF Athletes' Commn, 2003– (Vice Chair, 2015–). UN Envmt Ambassador for Clean Air, 2018–. DUniv: De Montfort, 2001; Loughborough, 2002. London Marathon Lifetime Achievement Award, 2015. *Publications*: Paula: my story so far, 2004; How to Run, 2011. *Recreations*: athletics!, travel, reading. *Club*: Bedford and County Athletic.

**RADCLIFFE, Sir Sebastian Everard**, 7th Bt *cr* 1813; *b* 8 June 1972; *s* of Sir Joseph Benedict Everard Henry Radcliffe, 6th Bt, MC and of Marcia Anne Helen (who *m* 1988, H. M. S. Tanner), *y d* of Major David Turville Constable Maxwell, Bosworth Hall, Husbands Bosworth, Rugby; *S* father, 1975; *m* 2005, Jacinta (*née* Lynch); one *s* two *d*. *Heir*: *s* Hugh Everard Benedict Radcliffe, *b* 8 Jan. 2013. *Address*: Le Château de Cheseaux, 1033 Cheseaux, Vaud, Switzerland.

**RADCLIFFE, Fr Timothy Peter Joseph**, OP; Master of the Order of Preachers (Dominicans), 1992–2001; Sarum Canon of Salisbury Cathedral, since 2007; Councillor, Pontifical Council for Justice and Peace, since 2013; *b* 22 Aug. 1945; 3rd *s* of late Hugh John Reginald Joseph Radcliffe, MBE, and Marie-Therese, *d* of Maj.-Gen. Sir Cecil Pereira, KCB, CMG; *g s* of Sir Everard Radcliffe, 5th Bt. *Educ*: Downside; St John's College, Oxford (MA; Hon. Fellow, 1993). Entered Dominican Order, 1965; Chaplain to Imperial Coll., 1976–78; taught theology at Blackfriars, Oxford, 1978–88; Prior of Blackfriars, 1982–88; Faculty of Theology, Oxford Univ., 1985–88; Provincial of the English Province, OP, 1988–92. John Toohey Schol. in Residence, Sydney Univ., 1984. Grand Chancellor: Pontifical Univ. of St Thomas (Angelicum), Rome, 1992–2001; Univ. of Santo Tomas, Manila, 1992–2001; Theol. Faculty, Fribourg, 1992–2001; Ecole Biblique, Jerusalem, 1992–2001. Mem. Bd, Las Casas Inst., Blackfriars, Oxford, 2009– (Dir, 2014–17). Trustee (formerly Mem. Bd), 2002–16, and Mem. Develt Bd, 2010–16, CAFOD; Trustee, Fellowship and Aid to Christians of the East, 2018–. Pres., Conf. of Major Religious Superiors, 1991–92. Mem. Bd, New Blackfriars, 2003 (Chm., Editl Bd, 1983–88). Mem., Theol Commn, Caritas Internationalis, 2008–. Patron: Margaret Beaufort Inst., Cambridge, 1992–; Eckhart Soc., 1999–; Embrace the Middle East, 2015–. Freedom, City of London, 2013. Hon. STD Providence Coll., RI, 1993; Hon. LLD: Barry Univ., Florida, 1996; Molloy Coll., NY, 2005; Hon. DHumLit: Ohio Dominican Coll., 1996; Dominican Univ., Chicago, 2002; Aquinas Inst., St Louis Univ., 2007; Siena Heights Univ., 2007; Felician Coll., New Jersey, 2010; Hon. DD: Oxford, 2003; Fribourg, 2016; Hon. Dr Univ. Catholique de l'Ouest, 2006. Prix de littérature religieuse, Le syndicat des libraires de littérature religieuse de France, 2001; Spiritualités d'aujourd'hui, Le Centre Méditerranéen de Littérature, 2001. Hon. Citizen: Augusta (Italy); Sepahua (Peru). *Publications*: El Manantial de la Esperanza Salamanca, 1998; Sing a New Song: the Christian vocation, 2000; I Call You Friends, 2001; Seven Last Words, 2004; What is the Point of Being a Christian?, 2005 (trans. French; Prix des Lecteurs de la Procure, 2006; Michael Ramsey Prize, 2007); (ed) Just One Year, 2006; Why Go to Church?: the drama of the Eucharist, 2008; Essere Cristiani nel XXI Secolo: una spiritualità per il nostro tempo, 2011; Take the Plunge: living baptism and confirmation, 2012; (jtly) Le livre noir de la condition des chrétiens dans le monde, 2014; Parole di Oggi, 2014; Stations of the Cross, 2015; Il bordo del mistero, 2016; Alive in God: a Christian imagination, 2019; articles in books and periodicals. *Recreations*: walking, talking with friends, reading novels and poetry. *Address*: Blackfriars, St Giles, Oxford OX1 3LY. *T*: (01865) 278422. *E*: timothy.radcliffe@english.op.org.

**RADCLYFFE, Sarah**; Managing Director, Sarah Radclyffe Productions Ltd, since 1993; *b* 14 Nov. 1950; *d* of late Charles Raymond Radclyffe, LVO and Helen Egerton Radclyffe; one *s* by Graham Bradstreet; *m* 1996, William Godfrey; one *s*. *Educ*: Heathfield Sch., Ascot. Jt Founder, 1984, Jt Man. Dir, 1984–93, Working Title; *films* produced include: My Beautiful Laundrette, 1984; Caravaggio, 1985; Wish You Were Here, 1985; Paperhouse, 1987; Sammy and Rosie Get Laid, 1988; A World Apart, 1988; Fools of Fortune, 1989; Robin Hood, 1990; Edward II, 1991; Sirens, 1993; Second Best, 1993; Bent, 1997; Cousin Bette, 1997; Les Misérables, 1997; The War Zone, 1998; There's Only One Jimmy Grimble, 1999; Love's Brother, 2003; Tara Road, 2004; Free Jimmy, 2006; How About You, 2007; Cirque du Freak: The Vampire's Assistant, 2009; The Edge of Love, 2008; Good Morning Karachi, 2011; Close, 2018. Non-exec. Dir, Channel Four TV, 1995–99; Gov., BFI, 1996–99; Dir, Film Council, 2000–04. Simon Olswang Business Woman of the Year Award, 1993. *Recreations*: travel, ski-ing. *Address*: Sarah Radclyffe Productions Ltd, Lew House, Lew, near Bampton, Oxon OX18 2AZ. *E*: sarah@srpltd.co.uk.

**RADDA, Prof. Sir George (Karoly)**, Kt 2000; CBE 1993; MA, DPhil; FRS 1980; Professor and Head, Department of Physiology, Anatomy and Genetics, University of Oxford, 2005–08, now Emeritus Professor of Molecular Cardiology; *b* 9 June 1936; *s* of Dr Gyula Radda and Dr Anna Bernolak; *m* 1st, 1961, Mary O'Brien (marr. diss. 1995); two *s* one *d*. 2nd, 1995, Sue Bailey. *Educ*: Pannonhalma, Hungary; Eötvös Univ., Budapest, Hungary; Merton Coll., Oxford (BA Cl. 1, Chem., 1960; DPhil 1962). Res. Associate, Univ. of California, 1962–63; University of Oxford: Lectr in Organic Chemistry, St John's Coll., 1963–64; Fellow and Tutor in Organic Chem., Merton Coll., 1964–84; Lectr in Biochem., 1966–84, Hd of Dept of Biochem., 1991–96; British Heart Foundn Prof. of Molecular Cardiol., 1984–2003 (on leave of absence, 1996–2003); Chief Exec., MRC, 1996–2003; Professorial Fellow, Merton Coll., Oxford, 1984–2003 and 2005–08, now Emeritus Fellow; Chairman: Singapore Bioimaging Consortium, 2005–10; Biomedical Res. Council, Agency for Sci., Technol. and Res., Singapore, 2009–16. Vis. Prof., Cleveland Clinic, 1987. Medical Research Council: Mem. Council, 1988–92; Chm., Cell Biology and Disorders Bd, 1988–92; Chm., Human Genome Directed Programme Cttee, 1992–96; Hon. Dir, Unit of Biochemical and Clin. Magnetic Resonance, 1988–96. Member of Council: Royal Soc., 1990–92; ICRF, 1991–96 (Chm., Scientific Adv. Cttee, 1994–96). Res. Dir, Lab. of Metabolic Medicine, Singapore, 2005–; Sen. Advr, Dean's Office, Nat. Univ. Health System, Singapore, 2009–. Non-exec. Dir, BTG plc, 1999–2005. Mem., various Editorial Bds of scientific jls including: Editor, Biochemical and Biophysical Research Communications, 1977–85; Man. Editor, Biochimica et Biophysica Acta, 1977–94 (Chm. Editl Bd, 1989–94); Mem. Editorial Bd, Interface, 2004–09. Founder Mem., Oxford Enzyme Gp, 1970–86; Pres., Soc. for Magnetic Resonance in Medicine, 1985–86. Mem., Fachbeirat, Max Planck Inst. für Systemphysiologie, Dortmund, 1987–93; Internat. Adv. Council Mem., Biomed. Res. Council, Singapore, 2003–06 (Bd Mem., 2005–). Trustee, Cancer Res. UK, 2003–06 (Dep. Chm., 2005–06). Mem., EMBO, 1997; MAE 1999; Fellow: Soc. of Magnetic Resonance, 1994; Internat. Acad. Cardiovascular Scis, 2001; ISMAR, 2008; Founding Fellow, Internat. Soc. Heart Res., 2000. Founder FMedSci 1998. Hon. Member: Eur. Soc. of Magnetic Resonance and Biol., 2007; Hungarian Acad. of Scis, 2010; Hungarian Soc. of Cardiol., 2013. Hon. FRCR 1985; Hon. MRCP 1987, Hon. FRCP 1997; Hon. Fellow, Amer. Heart Assoc., 1988. Hon. DM Bern, 1985; Hon. DSc (Med) London, 1991; Hon. DSc: Stirling, 1998; Sheffield, 1999; Debrecen, Hungary, 2001; Birmingham, 2003; Univ. de la Méditerranée, 2003; Aberdeen,

2004; Düsseldorf, 2004; Semmelweis Univ., Budapest, 2004; Hull, 2005; Leicester, 2006. Colworth Medal, Biochem. Soc., 1969; Feldberg Prize, Feldberg Foundn, 1982; British Heart Foundn Prize and Gold Medal for cardiovascular research, 1982; CIBA Medal and Prize, Biochem. Soc., 1983; Gold Medal, Soc. for Magnetic Resonance in Medicine, 1984; Buchanan Medal, Royal Soc., 1987; Internat. Lectr and Citation, Amer. Heart Assoc., 1987; Skinner Lecture and Medal, RCR, 1989; Rank Prize in Nutrition, 1991; Medal of Merit, Internat. Acad. of Cardiovascular Res., 2006; Public Service Medal, Friends of Singapore, 2008; Semmelweis Budapest Award, 2011; Biospectrum Asia Pacific Lifetime Award, 2013. Hon. Citizen of Republic of Singapore, 2015. Commander's Cross, Order of Merit (Hungary), 2016; Corvin-Ianc Award (Hungary), 2018 (Mem., Corvin-Ianc Testulet). *Publications:* articles in books and in jls of biochemistry and medicine. *Recreations:* opera, swimming, jazz. *Address:* Merton College, Oxford OX1 4JD.

**RADER, Gen. Paul Alexander;** General of the Salvation Army, 1994–99; *b* 14 March 1934; *s* of Lt-Col Lyell Rader and Gladys (*née* Damon); *m* 1956, (Frances) Kay Fuller; one *s* two *d*. *Educ:* Asbury Coll. and Seminary, USA (BA, BD); Southern Baptist Seminary (MTh); Fuller Theol Seminary (DMiss). Salvation Army: trng work in Korea, 1962–73; Trng Principal, 1973; Educn Sec., 1974–76; Asst Chief Sec., 1976, Chief Sec., 1977–84, Korea; Trng Principal, USA Eastern Territory, 1984–87; Divl Comdr, 1987–89; Chief Sec., 1989; Territorial Comdr, USA Western, 1989–94. Pres., Asbury Coll., Wilmore, Ky, 2000–06. Hon. LLD Asbury Coll., USA, 1984; Hon. DD: Asbury Theol Seminary, USA, 1995; Roberts Wesleyan Coll., USA, 1998; Hon. LHD Greenville Coll., USA, 1997. *Publications:* (with Kay Rader) To Seize this Day of Salvation, 2015. *Recreations:* jogging, reading, music. *Address:* 3953 Rock Ledge Lane, Lexington, KY 40513, USA.

**RADFORD, Dr David;** Chairman, NHS Devon, Plymouth and Torbay, 2011–13 (Chairman, Devon Primary Care Trust, later NHS Devon, 2006–11); *b* 22 April 1949; *s* of Ken and Dorothy Radford; *m* 1st, 1970, Josephine Mogridge; one *d*; 2nd, 1976, Madeleine Margaret Simms; two *d*. *Educ:* RN Sch., Malta; St John's Sch., Singapore; Manchester Univ. (BSc Hons Chem., MSc Organisation of Technology, PhD). Consumer Services Manager, CWS, 1974–75; Res. Dir, Welsh Consumer Council, 1975–77; Head of Res., Inst. of Housing, 1977–81; Asst Dir of Housing, Wolverhampton MBC, 1981–86; Asst Chief Exec., Wolverhampton MBC, 1986–90; Asst Chief Exec., Northants CC, 1990–97; Chief Exec., Somerset CC, 1997–2002; Lead Govt Official, Plymouth CC, 2003–06. Chm., SW Constitutional Convention, 2003–06. *Recreations:* hill and coast walking, concert-going, sailing.

**RADFORD, His Honour David Wyn;** Circuit Judge, 1996–2017; Senior Circuit Judge, 2002–17; a Deputy Circuit Judge, since 2017; *b* 3 Jan. 1947; *s* of late Robert Edwin Radford, CB and Eleanor Margaret Radford (*née* Jones); *m* 1972, Nadine Radford, *qv*; two *s* two *d*. *Educ:* Cranleigh Sch.; Selwyn Coll., Cambridge (MA, LLM). Called to the Bar, Gray's Inn, 1969, Bencher, 2008; Asst Recorder, 1988; Recorder, 1993. Hon. Recorder of Redbridge, 2009–17. *Recreations:* supporting Manchester City FC and Brentford FC, chairing Chaos Theory charitable trust, cruise ship speaker, reading widely, travel, spending time with family. *E:* judgeradford@gmail.com.

**RADFORD, Rev. Georgina Margaret, (Gina),** FRCP, FFPH; Deputy Chief Medical Officer, 2015–19; *b* 25 April 1955; *d* of Edward Arthur Radford and Elsie (*née* Burdon). *Educ:* Guildford Co. Grammar Sch. for Girls; Royal Free Hosp. Sch. of Medicine (MB BS 1979). DCH 1982; DRCOG 1983; MFPHM 1989, FFPH (FFPHM 1997); FRCP 2002. Consultant in Public Health Medicine, S and W Surrey DHA, 1988–94; Dir of Public Health, S and W Devon HA, 1994–97; Hd, Public Health Develt Unit, NHS Exec., DoH, 1997–99; Regl Dir of Public Health, E of England, DoH, 2000–06; Dir of Public Health, NHS Fife, 2006–08; former Consultant in Public Health, Cambridgeshire PCT; Public Health Adviser: Anglia Cancer Network, 2009–13; Anglia Heart and Stroke Network, 2009–13; Centre Dir, Norfolk, Suffolk, Cambridge and Essex, PHE, 2013–14. Vis. Prof., UEA, 2017. Ordained deacon, 2016, priest, 2017; non-Stipendiary Minister, Ely, 2016–19; Team Vicar, Exeter, 2019–. Hon. FRCGP. *Recreations:* riding, singing/music, reading, travel, village duck warden.

**RADFORD, Nadine Poggioli;** QC 1995; *m* 1972, His Honour David Wyn Radford, *qv*; two *s* two *d*. Called to the Bar, Lincoln's Inn, 1974, Bencher, 1999. *Address:* 3 Temple Gardens, EC4Y 9AU.

**RADFORD, Prof. Peter Frank,** PhD; Professor, Department of Sport Sciences, Brunel University, 1997–2005 (Hon. Professor Associate, School of Sport and Education, 2007; Visiting Professor, 2012–14); *b* 20 Sept. 1939; *s* of Frank Radford and Lillian E. Radford (*née* Marks); *m* 1961, Margaret M. (*née* Beard); one *d*. *Educ:* Tettenhall Coll.; Cardiff Coll. of Educn (Dip. of Physical Educn); Purdue Univ., USA (MSc); Univ. of Glasgow (PhD 1978). Mem., GB Athletics Teams, 1958–64: held British 100m record, 1958–78; World Records: Jun. 100m and Jun. 200m, 1958; Indoor 50m, 1959; 200m and 220 yards, 1960; 4 × 110 yards Relay, 1963; Bronze Medals, 100m and 4 × 100m Relay, Olympic Games, Rome, 1960. Lectr and Asst Prof., Sch. of Physical Educn and Athletics, McMaster Univ., 1967–75; University of Glasgow: Professor and Head of Departments of: Physical Educn and Recreation, 1976–87; Physical Educn and Sports Sci., 1987–94 (Titular Prof., 1997–2004); Head of Dept, 1997–2000, Dir of Res., 2000–05, Dept of Sport Scis, Brunel Univ. Non-exec. Dir, Performance Brunel Ltd, 2004–. Vice-Chm., 1992–93, Chm., 1993–94, Exec. Chm., 1994–97, British Athletic Fedn. Scottish Sports Council: Mem., 1983–90; Mem., 1988–91, Chm., 1991–96, Drug Adv. Gp; Chm., Rev. of Coaching in Sport, 1991–93. Mem., Internat. Wkg Gp on Anti-Doping in Sport, 1991–93; Vice-Chm., 1992–94, Chm., 1994–98, Internat. Doping Convention, Council of Europe; Member: Saudi/British Memorandum of Understanding for Sport and Youth Welfare, 1990–2007; Compliance with Commitments Project, Council of Europe, 1998–99. Pres., Nat. Union of Track Statisticians, 2009–. Chm., Burford and Dist. Soc., 2016–18. Pres., Old Tettenhallian Club, 2016–17. Fellow, Folger Shakespeare Liby, Washington DC, 2018. Hon. DSc Wolverhampton, 2006. *Publications:* The Celebrated Captain Barclay, 2001; 1866 and All That…: the story of the world's first National Athletics Championships, 2016; contrib. to various jls, conf. proc. and books on topics of sport, sports history and women's history. *Recreations:* sports history 1650–1850, 18th and 19th century sporting art, gardening. *Address:* Bank House, 8 Sheep Street, Burford, Oxon OX18 4LT. *T:* (01993) 824836.

**RADFORD, Prof. Sheena Elizabeth,** PhD; FRS 2014; FMedSci; Astbury Professor of Biophysics, since 2014, Professor of Structural Molecular Biology, since 2000, and Director, Astbury Centre for Structural Molecular Biology, since 2012, University of Leeds; *m* Prof. Alan Berry. *Educ:* Univ. of Birmingham (BSc 1984); St John's Coll., Cambridge (PhD 1987). Royal Soc. Univ. Res. Fellow, Oxford Centre for Molecular Scis, Univ. of Oxford, 1991–95; Lectr, 1995–98, Reader in Structural Molecular Biol., 1998–2000, Univ. of Leeds. Fellow, EMBO, 2007. FMedSci 2010. Colworth Medal, Biochem. Soc., 1996; Astra Zeneca Prize, Royal Soc., 2005; Carl Branden Award, Protein Soc., 2013. *Publications:* contribs to learned jls incl. Nature Chem. Biol., Molecular Cell, Jl Amer. Chem. Soc., Jl Biol Chem. *Address:* Astbury Centre for Structural Molecular Biology, School of Molecular and Cellular Biology, University of Leeds, Leeds LS2 9JT.

**RADFORD, Lt Gen. Timothy Buchan,** CB 2016; DSO 2010; OBE 2006 (MBE 1994); Deputy Supreme Allied Commander Europe (in rank of Gen.), from April 2020; *b* Dalton, Lancs, 23 Feb. 1963; *s* of Colin and Inge Radford; *m* 2001, Tracey Mary Titterington; two *s* one *d*. *Educ:* Methodist Coll. Belfast; Rugby Sch.; Durham Univ. (BA Hons Politics); King's Coll. London (MA War Studies). Joined Army, 1984; regtl duty and command, NI, Sierra Leone, Balkans, Iraq, 1984–2006; i/c 19 Lt Bde (Comd Task Force Helmand, Afghanistan), 2009; Hd, Overseas Ops, MoD, 2010–11; COS HQ ISAF Jt Comd, Kabul, Afghanistan, 2012; GOC Force Troops Comd, 2013–15; COS Land Forces, Army HQ, 2015; Dep. Comdr Resolute Support, 2015–16; Comdr ARRC, 2016–19. Pres., Army Lawn Tennis Assoc., 2012–. QCVS 2013. Officer, Legion of Merit (USA), 2018. *Recreations:* family, tennis, gardening, art history. *Address:* c/o Military Secretary, Army Personnel Centre, Kentigern House, 65 Brown Street, Glasgow G2 8EX.

**RADFORD, Timothy Robin;** Science Editor, The Guardian, 1992–2005; *b* NZ, 9 Oct. 1940; *s* of Keith Ballantyne Radford and Agnes Radford; *m* 1964, Maureen Grace Coveney; one *s* one *d*. *Educ:* Sacred Heart Coll., Auckland. Reporter, NZ Herald, 1957–60; sub-ed., Fishing News, London, 1961–62; reporter, Hull Daily Mail, 1963–65; sub-ed., Dover Express, 1965–68; COI, 1968–73; joined The Guardian, 1973: Letters Ed., 1975–77; Arts Ed., 1977–80; Dep. Features Ed., 1980–88; Literary Ed., 1989–91. FRGS 1990. *Publications:* The Crisis of Life on Earth, 1990; (ed) Frontiers 01: science and technology 2001–02, 2002; (ed) Frontiers 03: new writing on cutting edge science by leading scientists, 2003; The Address Book: our place in the scheme of things, 2011; The Consolations of Physics, 2018. *Recreations:* reading, walking, travel. *Address:* 41 Downside Close, Eastbourne, E Sussex BN20 8EL.

**RADICE, Baron** *cr* 2001 (Life Peer), of Chester-le-Street in the County of Durham; **Giles Heneage Radice;** PC 1999; *b* 4 Oct. 1936. *Educ:* Winchester; Magdalen Coll., Oxford. Head of Research Dept, General and Municipal Workers' Union (GMWU), 1966–73. MP (Lab) Chester-le-Street, March 1973–1983, Durham North, 1983–2001. Opposition front bench spokesman on foreign affairs, 1981, on employment, 1981–83, on education, 1983–87; Mem., Treasury and Civil Service Select Cttee, 1987–96; Chairman: Public Service Select Cttee, 1996–97; Treasury Select Cttee, 1997–2001. Chm., EU Economic and Financial Affairs Sub-cttee, H of L, 2002–06; Mem., EU External Affairs Sub-cttee, H of L, 2011–15. Mem., Council, Policy Studies Inst., 1978–83. Chairman: European Movt, 1995–2001; British Assoc. for Central and Eastern Europe, 1997–2008 (Vice Chm., 1991–97); Franco British Council, 2002–07; Policy Network, 2007–09. Parly Fellow, St Antony's Coll., Oxford, 1994–95. Order of Merit (Germany), 1996; Légion d'Honneur (France), 2004. *Publications:* Democratic Socialism, 1965; (ed jointly) More Power to People, 1968; (co-author) Will Thorne, 1974; The Industrial Democrats, 1978; (co-author) Socialists in Recession, 1986; Labour's Path to Power: the new revisionism, 1989; Offshore: Britain and the European idea, 1992; The New Germans, 1995; (ed) What Needs to Change, 1996; Friends & Rivals, 2002; Diaries 1980–2001: the political diaries of Giles Radice, 2004; The Tortoise and the Hares, 2008; Trio, 2010; Odd Couples: the great political pairings of modern Britain, 2015. *Recreations:* reading, travel. *Address:* The Longhouse, 3 Gelston, near Grantham, Lincs NG32 2AE.

**RADICE, Elizabeth Joy;** Headmistress, Haberdashers' Aske's School for Girls, Elstree, 2005–11; *b* 5 Feb. 1951; *d* of Donald and Joy Stephenson; *m* 1973, William Radice; two *d*. *Educ:* Wycombe Abbey Sch., High Wycombe; Somerville Coll., Oxford (BA Hons 1972). Hd of English, Sch. of St Helen and St Katharine, Abingdon, 1985–92; Dir of Studies, Royal Grammar Sch., Newcastle-upon-Tyne, 1996–98; Headmistress, Channing Sch., Highgate, London, 1999–2005. *Recreations:* books, theatre, film, cooking.

**RADICE, Vittorio;** Chief Executive, La Rinascente, since 2005; *b* Como, Italy, 2 April 1957; *m* Gemma; two *s*. *Educ:* Univ. of Milan. Head of Worldwide Sourcing, Home Furnishings Dept, Associated Merchandising Corp.; Buying Dir, Habitat Internat., 1990–92; Man. Dir, Habitat UK, 1992–96; Man. Dir, 1996–98, Chief Exec., 1998–2003, Selfridges plc; Exec. Dir, Home, Marks and Spencer plc, 2003–04. Non-executive Director: Abbey (formerly Abbey National) plc, 2001–04; Shoppers Stop India, 2001–06; McArthurGlen, 2005–; Ishaan Real Estate plc, 2006–; Conran Hldgs, 2011–.

**RADNOR, 9th Earl of,** *cr* 1765; **William Pleydell-Bouverie;** Bt 1714; Viscount Folkestone, Baron Longford, 1747; Baron Pleydell-Bouverie, 1765; *b* 5 Jan. 1955; *s* of 8th Earl of Radnor and of Anne (who later *m* Vice-Adm. Sir John Cox, KCB), *d* of Donald Seth-Smith, MC; *S* father, 2008; *m* 1996, Melissa, *d* of late James Keith Edward Stanford, OBE; four *s* two *d*. *Educ:* Harrow; Royal Agricultural Coll., Cirencester. Landowner and farmer, 1980s; with Christie's, 2008–. Gov., French Hosp., 'La Providence', Rochester, 2008–15. Trustee, Creative Foundn, Folkestone. Patron of two livings. FRSA. *Recreations:* photography, looking at art, ski-ing. *Heir: s* Viscount Folkestone, *qv*. *Address:* Estate Office, Longford Castle, Salisbury, Wilts SP5 4ED.

**RADOMSKY, Rabbi David;** educational consultant, since 2006; *b* 4 Sept. 1956; *s* of Benjamin and Rachel Radomsky; *m* 1981, Naomi; three *s* one *d*. *Educ:* BA Hons, MA (Dist.); Teaching Dip. NPQH. Ordained rabbi; rabbi/teacher, Mid Rashiat Noam Yeshiva High Sch., Israel, 1982–85; Communal Rabbi, Dublin, 1985–88; Rabbi, Wembley Synagogue, 1988–93; pt-time Lectr, Jews' Coll., 1991–93; Dep. Headteacher, Immanuel Coll., 1993–2000; Headteacher, Hasmonean High Sch., 2000–06. *E:* david@radomsky.co.uk.

**RADWAY, Jonathan Mark;** a District Judge (Magistrates' Courts), since 2011; *b* London, 6 Feb. 1955; *s* of John and Patricia Radway; *m* 1st, 1981, Margaret Rimmer (marr. diss. 2011); one *s* one *d*; 2nd, 2015, Cheryl Wright. *Educ:* Ardingly Coll.; Mid-Essex Tech. Coll. (LLB Hons London ext.); Inns of Court Sch. of Law. CEDR Accredited Mediator 2007. Called to the Bar, Middle Temple, 1977; Justices' Clerk, Huntingdon, Peterborough and Fenland Divs and Clerk to Cambs Magistrates' Courts Cttee, 1987–96; Justices' Chief Exec., Herts, 1996–2004; Actg Metropolitan Stipendiary Magistrate, subseq. Dep. Dist Judge (Magistrates' Courts), 1999–2011; Performance Dir, Courts Service, 2004–05. Internat. Consultancy with Agencia Consulting and British Embassies in Zagreb, Kyiv and Belgrade, undertaking Judicial Reform progs in Croatia, Ukraine and Serbia, 2006–11. Dir, Confugium Film Ltd, 2006–11; non-exec. Dir, Peterborough and Stamford Hosps NHS Foundn Trust, 2005–11 (Dep. Chm., 2006–11). Lay Mem., Chapter of Peterborough Cathedral, 2002–05. *Recreations:* travel, heritage railways, horology, playing the piano. *Address:* Stratford Magistrates' Court, 389–397 High Street, E15 4SB.

**RAE, Hon. Lady; Rita Emilia Anna Rae;** a Senator of the College of Justice in Scotland, since 2014; *d* of Alexander Smith Cowie Rae and Bianca Bruno. *Educ:* Univ. of Edinburgh (LLB Hons). Apprentice, 1972–74, Asst Solicitor, 1974–76, Biggart Baillie & Gifford, Glasgow; Asst Solicitor and Partner, Ross Harper & Murphy, Glasgow, 1976–81; admitted Advocate, 1982; Temporary Sheriff, 1988–97; QC (Scot.) 1992; Sheriff of Glasgow and Strathkelvin, 1997–2014; Temporary Judge of High Ct, 2004–14; Upper Tribunal Judge (Immigration and Asylum), 2017–18. Tutor in Advocacy and Pleading, Strathclyde Univ., 1979–82; Member: Scottish Council on Human Bioethics, 1996–98; Legal 40, Univ. of Glasgow, 2010–. Vice-Chm., Parole Bd for Scotland, 2005–07 (Mem., 2001–07); Member: Sentencing Commn for Scotland, 2003–06; SACRO, 1998–; Nat. Strategic Adv. Gp on

Violence Reduction, 2011–. Sec., Glasgow Bar Assoc., 1981–82. Chm., Glasgow Br., Scottish Assoc. for Study of Offending (formerly Scottish Assoc. for Study of Delinquency), 2003–14 (Life Mem.; Hon. Pres., 2014). Mem. Bd, Conforti Inst., Coatbridge, 2011–17. Ambassador for 'Young Citizens', London, 2018–. *Recreations:* classical music, opera, theatre, walking, gardening, learning piano. *Address:* Supreme Courts, Parliament House, 11 Parliament Square, Edinburgh EH1 1RQ. *T:* (0131) 225 2595.

**RAE, Barbara Davis,** CBE 1999; RA 1996; RSA 1992; RGI; FRCA; FRSE; painter and master printmaker; *d* of James Rae and Mary (*née* Young); *m*; one *s*. *Educ:* Morrison's Acad., Crieff; Edinburgh Coll. of Art (Dip.; Postgrad. Travelling Schol.); Moray House Coll. of Education. Art Teacher: Ainsley Park Comprehensive, Edinburgh, 1968–69; Portobello Secondary Sch., Edinburgh, 1969–72; Lectr in Drawing, Painting and Printmaking, Aberdeen Coll. of Educn, 1972–75; Lectr in Drawing and Painting, Glasgow Sch. of Art, 1975–96. Mem., Royal Fine Art Commn for Scotland, 1995–2005. Solo exhibitions include: New '57 Gall., Edinburgh, 1967, 1971; Univ. of York, 1969; Univ. of Aberdeen and Aberdeen Art Gall., 1974; Peterloo Gall., Manchester, 1975; Stirling Gall. and Greenock Arts Guild, 1976; Univ. of Edinburgh, 1978, 1979; Gilbert Parr Gall., London, 1977; Scottish Gall., Edinburgh, 1979, 1983, 1987, 1988, 1990, 1995, 1998, 2000, 2002, 2003, 2005, 2006; annual solo exhibns from 1995 of paintings and of prints in major galls of Edinburgh, Edinburgh Internat. Fest. of Arts, Royal Scottish Acad., St Andrews Univ., Aberdeen Univ., Portland Gall. and other London and Richmond galls, plus Royal Acad. of Arts, Bath, Chichester, Belfast, Dublin, Oslo, Santa Fe, NY, Chicago, Gibraltar and Mexico City; art works in private and commercial collections worldwide, and museums in Scotland, England, Ire. and Washington, USA; commissions include: tapestry for Festival Theatre, Edinburgh, 1994; rug for Royal Mus. of Scotland, 1999; portraits. RSW 1975, now Hon. Fellow; Hon. FRCA 2005 (FRCA 2003); Hon. RE 2009; Hon. FRIAS 2018. Hon. DArts Napier, 1999; Hon. DLitt: Aberdeen, 2003; St Andrews, 2008. Awards: Arts Council, 1968; Major Arts Council, 1975–81; Guthrie Medal, RSA, 1977; May Marshall Brown, RSW Centenary Exhibn, 1979; RSA Sir Wm Gillies Travel, 1983; Calouste Gulbenkian Printmaking, 1983; Alexander Graham Munro, RSW, 1989; Hunting Gp Prizewinner, 1990; Scottish PO Bd, RSA, 1990; Scottish Amicable, RGI, 1990; W. J. Burness, Royal Scottish Acad., 1990. *Relevant publications:* Barbara Rae, by B. Hare *et al*, 2008; Barbara Rae Prints, by A. Lambirth *et al*, 2010; Barbara Rae: sketchbooks, by Gareth Wardell *et al*, 2011; Barbara Rae: the Northwest Passage, by Tagak Curley *et al*, 2018; Barbara Rae: Arctic sketchbooks. *Recreation:* travelling.

**RAE, Fiona Elizabeth,** RA 2002; artist; Professor of Painting, Royal Academy Schools, 2011–15; *b* 10 Oct. 1963; *d* of Alexander Edward Ian Rae and Pamela Christine Rae; *m* 2002, Daniel Jonathan Perfect. *Educ:* Croydon Coll. of Art (Foundn Course Fine Art 1984); Goldsmiths Coll., London Univ. (BA 1st Cl. Hons Fine Art 1987; Hon. Fellow 2015). Artist Trustee, Tate, 2005–09. Selected *solo exhibitions:* Kunsthalle Basel, 1992; ICA, London, 1993–94; Galerie Nathalie Obadia, Paris, 1994, 2000, 2004, 2009, 2013; Buchmann Galerie, Cologne, 2000, 2005; Carré d'Art - Musée d'art contemporain de Nîmes, 2002–03; Tate Modern Restaurant commn, 2002–05; Timothy Taylor Gall., London, 2003, 2008, 2013, 2015; commn for Art Site, BBC Broadcasting House Public Art Prog., London, 2003; PaceWildenstein, NY, 2006, The Pace Gall., 2010; Buchmann Galerie, Berlin, 2011, 2014, 2016, 2018; Leeds Art Gall., 2012; New Art Gall., Walsall, 2012; Towner, Eastbourne, 2013; Nottingham Castle Mus. and Art Gall., 2014; Southampton City Art Gall., 2014; Buchmann Galerie, Lugano, 2017; Hakgojae Cheongdam, Seoul, 2018; selected *group exhibitions:* Freeze, Surrey Docks, London, 1988; Aperto, La Biennale di Venezia XLIV, 1990; Turner Prize Exhibn, Tate Gall., London, 1991; Unbound: Possibilities in Painting, Hayward Gall., London, 1994; Sensation: Young British Artists from the Saatchi Collection, RA, London, Hamburger Bahnhof - Mus. für Gegenwart, Berlin and Brooklyn Mus. of Art, NY, 1997–2000; Painting Pictures: Painting and Media in the Digital Age, Kunstmus. Wolfsburg, 2003; Pictograms: the Loneliness of Signs, Kunstmus. Stuttgart, 2006–07; Reset: Werke aus der Sammlung Marx, Hamburger Bahnhof - Mus. für Gegenwart, Berlin, 2007–08; Classified: Contemporary British Art from Tate Collection, Tate Britain, 2009; Babel, FRAC Auvergne, 2020; New Art Now, Birmingham Mus. and Art Gall., 2010; Encounter, ICA Singapore, 2012; Globetrotter, Essl Mus., 2014; Non Figuratif, Centre d'Art Contemporain Meymac, 2016; Darkness into Light, Millennium Gall., Sheffield, 2018. *Relevant publication:* Fiona Rae, by S. Wallis and J.-P. Criqui, 2002. *Address:* Galerie Nathalie Obadia, 3 rue du Cloître Saint-Merri, 75004 Paris, France. *E:* info@nathalieobadia.com.

**RAE, Gordon Hamilton;** Director General, Royal Horticultural Society, 1993–99; *b* 12 Sept. 1938; *s* of Peter and Gwendoline Elizabeth Rae; *m* 1965, Judith Elizabeth Pickup; one *s* two *d*. *Educ:* Bablake Sch., Coventry; Wye Coll., Univ. of London (BSc Agric. Hons); Clare Coll., Cambridge (Dip. Agric.); Imperial Coll. of Tropical Agric., Trinidad (DTA). Agricl and Dist Agricl Officer, HM Colonial Service, Kenya, 1962–65; ICI, 1965–93: Gen. Manager, Agricl Chemicals Div., ICI do Brasil, São Paulo, 1980–84; Gen. Manager, ICI Garden and Professional Products, 1989–92. Non-exec. Dir, D. J. Squire & Co. Ltd, 1999–2007. LRPS 2012; CPAGB 2016. Jt Patron, Garden Media Guild, 2007–; Patron, Grayshott Gardeners, 2015–. FCIHort (FIHort 1996). VMH 1999. *Recreations:* gardening, family, travel, photography. *Address:* New House, Church Lane, Grayshott, Hindhead, Surrey GU26 6LY. *T:* (01428) 606025. *Club:* Farmers.

**RAE, Dr John;** Vice-Chairman, AWE plc, 2001–02 (Chief Executive, 2000–01); *b* 29 Sept. 1942; *s* of late John Rae and Marion Rae (*née* Dow); *m* 1968, Irene (*née* Cassells); one *s* one *d*. *Educ:* Rutherglen Academy; University of Glasgow (BSc 1964, PhD 1967). FInstE 1987; FInstP 1996. Lecturing and research in physics: Univ. of Glasgow, 1967–68; Univ. of Texas, 1968–70; Univ. Libre, Brussels, 1970–72; Queen Mary College London, 1972–74; Theoretical Physics Div., Harwell: Industrial Fellow, 1974–76; Leader, Theory of Fluids Group, 1976–85; Acting Div. Head, 1985; Chief Scientist, Dept of Energy, 1986–89; Chief Exec., AEA Envmt & Energy, 1990–93; Business Develt Dir, 1993–95; Dir, Nat. Envmtl Technology Centre, 1994–95, AEA Technology; Man. Dir, NPL Mgt Ltd, 1995–2000. Member: SERC, 1986–89; NERC, 1986–89. Pres., NPL Sports Club, 1996–2000. Freeman, City of London, 1997; Liveryman, Scientific Instrument Makers' Co., 1997–. *Publications:* scientific papers in professional jls. *Recreations:* music, especially singing; gardening, astronomy.

**RAE, Rita Emilia Ann;** *see* Rae, Hon. Lady.

**RAE, Hon. Robert Keith;** PC (Can.) 1998; CC 2015 (OC 2000); OOnt 2004; QC (Can.) 1984; Senior Counsel, Olthius Kleer Townshend LLP, Toronto, since 2019 (Senior Partner, 2014–18); MP (Liberal) Toronto Centre, Canada, 2008–June 2013; interim Leader, Liberal Party, 2011–13; *b* 2 Aug. 1948; *s* of Saul Rae and Lois (*née* George); *m* 1980, Arlene Perly; three *d*. *Educ:* Ecole Internationale, Geneva; Univ. of Toronto (BA Hons 1969; LLB 1977); Balliol Coll., Oxford (BPhil 1971). MP for Broadview-Greenwood, Ontario, 1978–82; Finance Critic, New Democratic Party, 1979–82; MPP (NDP) York South, Ontario, 1982–95; Leader, Ontario New Democrats, 1982–96; Leader, Official Opposition, Ontario legislature, 1987–90; Premier of Ontario, 1990–95. Partner, Goodmans LLP (formerly Goodmans Phillips & Vineberg), 1996–2007. Director: Tembec Ltd, 1997–2006; Trojan Technologies, 2001–06. Sen. Fellow, Massey Coll., 1997–; University of Toronto: Adjunct Prof., 1997–99; Sen. Dist. Fellow, Sch. of Public Policy and Governance, 2013–; Prof. of Public Policy, 2018–. Dir, Canadian Ditchley Foundn, 1997–2006. Chairman: Forum of Fedns, 1999–2006; Royal Conservatory of Music, 2000; Toronto SO, 2002; Canadian Unity Council, 2002–06. Trustee, University Health Network, 1999–2006. Gov., Univ. of Toronto, 1999–2006; Nat. spokesperson, Leukemia Res. Fund of Canada, 1996–. Hon. LLD: Law Soc. of Upper Canada, 1998; Toronto, 1999; many other instns in Canada and elsewhere. *Publications:* From Protest to Power, 1996; The Three Questions, 1998; Canada in the Balance, 2006; Exporting Democracy: the risks and rewards of pursuing a good idea, 2010; What's Happening to Politics, 2015. *Recreations:* tennis, golf, ski-ing, fishing, reading. *Address:* Olthius Kleer Townshend LLP, 8th Floor, 250 University Avenue, Toronto, ON M5H 3E5, Canada.

**RAE, Air Vice-Marshal William McCulloch,** CB 1993; Director, United Services Trustees (formerly United Services Trustee), 1996–2015; *b* 22 June 1940; *s* of William Brewster Rae and Margaret Rae; *m* 1964, Helen, *d* of Thomas and Eileen Reading; two *d*. *Educ:* Aberdeen Grammar School; psc, ndc, rcds. RAF 1958; Nos 213, 10, 55 Sqns, 1960–64; CFS (helicopter element), 1965–67; Radar Res. Flying Unit, Pershore, 1968–70; Sqn Comdr, 6 FTS, 1970–72; Inspectorate of Recruiting, 1973; RAF Staff Coll., 1974; Air Sec's Dept, 1975–77; NDC, 1978; OC 360 Sqn, 1979–81; CDS Staff, 1981–82; Central Policy Staff, MoD, 1982–85; Station Comdr, RAF Finningley, 1985–87; RCDS, 1988; Branch Chief, Policy, SHAPE, 1989–91; Sen. DS (Air), RCDS, 1992–95; Sen. Assessor, Charter Mark, Cabinet Office, 1996–97. Dealer in early English barometers, 1997–2007. *Recreations:* antiques, fly-fishing, wine, golf. *Club:* Royal Air Force.

**RAEBURN, David Antony;** Grammatikos (tutor in Ancient Greek Language), Faculty of Literae Humaniores, 1991–96, Grocyn Lecturer, 1992–96, University of Oxford; *b* 22 May 1927; *e s* of late Walter Augustus Leopold Raeburn, QC; *m* 1961, Mary Faith, *d* of Arthur Hubbard, Salisbury, Rhodesia (*d* 2013); two adopted *s* one adopted *d*. *Educ:* Charterhouse; Christ Church, Oxford (Schol., MA). 1st cl. hons Hon. Mods, 2nd in Greats. Nat. Service, 1949–51: Temp. Captain, RAEC. Asst Master: Bristol Grammar Sch., 1951–54; Bradfield Coll., 1955–58 (prod. Greek Play, 1955 and 1958); Senior Classics Master, Alleyn's Sch., Dulwich, 1958–62; Headmaster: Beckenham and Penge Grammar Sch., 1963–70 (school's name changed to Langley Park School for Boys, Beckenham in 1969); Whitgift Sch., Croydon, 1970–91. Schoolteacher Fellow-Commoner, Jesus Coll., Cambridge, 1980. New College, Oxford: Vis. Fellow, 1997; Coll. Lectr, 2000–16, Rodewald Lector in Classical Langs, 2003–15. Chm. Classics Cttee, Schs Council, 1974–80; Pres., Jt Assoc. of Classical Teachers, 1983–85 (Dir, Greek Summer Sch., 1968–85); Treas., HMC, 1984–89. FRSA 1969. *Publications:* trans. Ovid, Metamorphoses, 2004; trans. Sophocles, Electra and Other Plays, 2008; (jtly) The Agamemnon of Aeschylus: a commentary for students, 2011; Greek Tragedies as Plays for Performance, 2016; essays on education; articles on Greek tragedy and Greek play production. *Recreation:* play production (produced Cambridge Greek Play, 1980, 1983; Oxford Greek Play, 1996; ten prodns of Greek tragedies, New Coll., 2007–19; numerous prodns of Shakespeare, etc. with sch. and univ. students). *Address:* 41 Ritchie Court, 380 Banbury Road, Oxford OX2 7PW. *T:* (01865) 553075.

**RAEBURN, Michael Edward Norman;** (4th Bt, *cr* 1923, but does not use the title); *b* 12 Nov. 1954; *s* of Sir Edward Alfred Raeburn, 3rd Bt, and Joan, *d* of Frederick Hill; *S* father, 1977; *m* 1979, Penelope Henrietta Theodora (marr. diss. 1997), *d* of Alfred Louis Penn; two *s* three *d*; *m* 2005, Yvette Graham. *Heir:* *s* Christopher Edward Alfred Raeburn, *b* 4 Dec. 1981.

**RAEBURN, Susan Adiel Ogilvie;** QC (Scot.) 1991; Sheriff of Grampian, Highlands and Islands at Elgin, 2011–15; *b* 23 April 1954; *d* of George Ferguson Raeburn and Rose Anne Bainbridge (*née* Morison). *Educ:* St Margaret's Sch. for Girls, Aberdeen; Edinburgh Univ. (LLB). Admitted to Faculty of Advocates, 1977; temp. Sheriff, 1988–93; Sheriff of Glasgow and Strathkelvin, 1993–2011. Part-time Chairman: Social Security Appeal Tribunals, 1986–92; Med. Appeal Tribunals, 1992–93. *Recreations:* travel, the arts.

**RAESIDE, Alison Louise; Her Honour Judge Raeside;** a Circuit Judge, since 2011; Designated Family Judge, Surrey, since 2019; *b* London, 3 Dec. 1958; *d* of Major John Powell and Gertrude Powell; *m* 1985, Mark Andrew Raeside, *qv*; three *s* one *d*. *Educ:* Godolphin and Latymer Sch., Hammersmith; Univ. of Manchester. Called to the Bar, Inner Temple, 1982; a District Judge, 2000–11. *Address:* Guildford County Court, Mary Road, Guildford GU1 4PS.

**RAESIDE, Mark Andrew;** QC 2002; **His Honour Judge Mark Raeside;** a Specialist Senior Circuit Judge, since 2013; *b* 27 Nov. 1955; *s* of Dr John Robertson Raeside and Annelie Raeside; *m* 1985, Alison Louise (*see* A. L. Raeside); three *s* one *d*. *Educ:* Univ. of Kent; Wolfson Coll., Cambridge (BA, MPhil). Called to the Bar, Middle Temple, 1982, Bencher, 2011. FCIArb 2001. Accredited Mediator, 2003. Military Cross (2nd class) (Estonia), 2004. *Recreations:* country and community life at West Sussex and Wester Ross estates, family life. *Address:* Leeds Combined Court Centre, The Courthouse, 1 Oxford Row, Leeds LS1 3BG. *Club:* Garrick.

**RAFF, Prof. Jordan,** PhD; César Milstein Professor of Cancer Cell Biology, University of Oxford, since 2009; Fellow, Lincoln College, Oxford, since 2009; *b* Montreal, 2 Nov. 1964; *s* of Prof. Martin Charles Raff, *qv* and Edith Dorsey Raff; *m* 1990, Rachel Crook; two *s* one *d*. *Educ:* Bristol Univ. (BSc); Imperial Coll. London (PhD 1989). Post-doctoral Fellow, Univ. of Calif, San Francisco, 1990–94; Gp Leader, 1994–2004, Sen. Gp Leader, 2004–08, Wellcome Trust/CRC, then CRUK Inst., later Gurdon Inst., Univ. of Cambridge. Member: British Soc. of Cell Biol., 1988– (Pres., 2011–18); Amer. Soc. of Cell Biol., 1988–. Mem., EMBO, 2011. FMedSci 2018. Editor-in-Chief, Biology Open, 2011–18. *Publications:* Why Don't People Like Me?, 1999; contrib. Cell. *Recreation:* have you met my family? *Address:* Sir William Dunn School of Pathology, University of Oxford, South Parks Road, Oxford OX1 3RE. *E:* jordan.raff@path.ox.ac.uk.

**RAFF, Prof. Martin Charles,** CBE 2009; FRS 1985; Professor of Biology, 1979–2002, now Emeritus, and Hon. Fellow, since 2004, University College London; Affiliated Member, MRC Laboratory for Molecular Cell Biology, since 1995; *b* 15 Jan. 1938; *s* of David and Reba Raff; *m* 1979, Carol Winter; two *s* one *d* by a previous marriage. *Educ:* McGill Univ. (BSc; MD; CM). House Officer, Royal Victoria Hosp., Montreal, 1963–65; Resident in Neurology, Massachusetts General Hosp., 1965–68; Postdoctoral Fellow, Nat. Inst. for Med. Res., 1968–71; Sen. Res. Fellow, UCL, 1971–79; Dir, MRC Develt Neurobiology Programme, 1971–2002. Chm., UK Life Scis Cttee, 1997–2001. Pres., British Soc. of Cell Biology, 1991–95. Founder FMedSci 1998. Foreign Hon. Mem., American Acad. of Arts and Scis, 1999; For. Associate Mem., NAS, US, 2003. Hon. DSc McGill, 2005; Vrije Univ. Brussel, 2007. *Publications:* (jtly) T and B Lymphocytes, 1973; (jtly) Molecular Biology of the Cell, 1983, 6th edn 2015; (jtly) Essential Cell Biology, 1997, 5th edn 2019.
*See also J. Raff.*

**RAFFAELLI, Surgeon Vice Adm. Philip Iain**, CB 2012; FFOM, FRCP; Surgeon General, Ministry of Defence, 2009–12; *b* Kirkcaldy, Fife, 24 Nov. 1955; *s* of Nello and Margaret Raffaelli; *m* 2006, Fiona Ivy Buchanan; one *s* two *d. Educ*: St Andrew's High Sch., Kirkcaldy; Edinburgh Univ. (BSc Med. Sci. 1976; MB ChB 1979); London Sch. of Hygiene and Tropical Medicine (MSc 1987). MRCGP 1984; AFOM 1987, FFOM 1997; FRCP 1989. MO, HMS Renown, 1981–82; GP Trng, RN Hosp. Haslar and RM Deal, 1982–85; Dep. Sqn MO, Faslane, 1985–87; Sen. MO (Submarine Medicine), Inst. of Naval Medicine, 1988–89; Principal MO, HMS Neptune, 1990–92; Naval MO Health (Portsmouth), 1992–94; Submarine Flotilla MO, 1994–95; jsdc 1995; Med Op 2 (NATO) 1996–97. Prof. of Naval Occupational Medicine, 1997–99; Dir, Health (Navy), 1999–2002; MO i/c, Inst. of Naval Medicine, 2003–04; Chief Exec., Defence Med. Educn and Trng Agency, 2004–06; Dir, Med. Ops Capability, 2006–08; Dir Gen., Strategic Change and Inspector Gen., 2008–09. QHP, 2006–. Mem., Mgt Bd, 1999–2002, Chief Examr, 2002–05, Faculty of Occupational Medicine. Mem., Ct of Govs, LSHTM, 2007–; Gov., Univ. Hosp. of Birmingham Foundn Trust, 2009–12. Mem., Adv. Bd, Tickets for Troops, 2012–. Assoc. Officer, Gosport Conservatives, 2014–. Mem. (C), Gosport BC, 2016–. Hon. Fellow, Assoc. Surgeons of GB and Ireland, 2011. CStJ 2012. Order of Mil. Med. Merit (USA), 2011. *Recreations*: music, reading, gardening, travel, family. *Address*: Chadwick House, 14 St Mark's Road, Alverstoke, Gosport, Hants PO12 2DA. *T*: (023) 9236 2415. *E*: philip.raffaelli@gmail.com.

**RAFFAN, Keith William Twort**; Member (Lib Dem) Scotland Mid and Fife, Scottish Parliament, 1999–Jan. 2005; *b* 21 June 1949; *s* of A. W. Raffan, TD, MB, ChB, FFARCS and late Jean Crampton Raffan (*née* Twort), MB, ChB. *Educ*: Robert Gordon's Coll., Aberdeen; Trinity Coll., Glenalmond; Corpus Christi Coll., Cambridge (BA 1971; MA 1977). Parly Correspondent and sketch writer, Daily Express, 1981–83; internat. public relns consultant, NY, 1992–94; presenter, Welsh Agenda, HTV, 1994–98. Contested (C) Dulwich, Feb. 1974, and East Aberdeenshire, Oct. 1974; MP (C) Delyn, 1983–92. Mem., Select Cttee on Welsh Affairs, 1983–92. Introduced: Controlled Drugs (Penalties) Act (Private Member's Bill, 1985); Tourism (Overseas Promotion) (Wales) Act, 1991. Chief spokesman on home affairs, Scottish Lib Dem Party, 1998. Nat. Chm., PEST, 1970–74. *Clubs*: Chelsea Arts, Royal Automobile.

**RAFFARIN, Jean-Pierre**; Grand Officier de la Légion d'Honneur; Grand Croix, Ordre National du Mérite; Member for Vienne (UMP), French Senate, 2005–17 (Vice President, 2011–14); Prime Minister of France, 2002–05; *b* 3 Aug. 1948; *s* of Jean Raffarin and Renée (*née* Michaud); *m* 1980, Anne-Marie Perrier; one *d. Educ*: Lycée Henri IV, Poitiers; Faculté de Droit, Paris-Assas; Ecole Supérieure de Commerce, Paris. Mktg Dept, Cafés Jacques Vabre, 1973–76; Advr, Office of Minister of Labour, 1976–81; Lectr, Inst. d'Etudes Politiques, Paris, 1979–88; Dir-Gen., Bernard Krief Communications, 1981–88; Gen. delegate, Inst. Euro-92, 1988–89. MEP (RPR–UDF), Poitou-Charentes, 1989–95; elected Mem. of Senate, for Vienne, 1995, 1997, 2004; Minister of Small and Medium Sized Businesses, Trade and Small Scale Industry, 1995–97. City Councillor, Poitiers, 1977–95; Regl Councillor, 1986–88, Chm., Regl Council, 1988–2002, Poitou-Charentes; Dep. Mayor, Chasseneuil-du-Poitou, 1995–2001. Nat. Delegate, Dep. Sec.-Gen. and Mem., Pol Bureau, 1977, Nat. Sec., 1989–95, PR; Dep. Sec.-Gen. and Spokesman, 1993–95, Sec.-Gen., 1995–97, UDF; Vice-Chm., Démocratie Libérale, 1997–2002. Pres., Assoc. of the Regions of France, 1998–2002; Pres., Leaders for Peace, 2018–. *Publications*: La vie en jaune, 1977; La publicité, nerf de la communication, 1983; L'avenir a ses racines, 1986; Nous sommes tous les régionaux, 1988; Pour une morale de l'action, 1992; Le livre de l'Atlantique, 1994; Pour une nouvelle gouvernance, 2002. *Recreations*: contemporary painting, regional literature.

**RAFFERTY, Angela Margaret Mary**; QC 2015; Her Honour Judge Rafferty; a Circuit Judge, since 2019; *b* Coleraine, NI, 19 March 1970; *d* of Michael Rafferty and Patricia Rafferty; *m* 2004, Gregory Lloyd Perrins, *qv*; two *d. Educ*: Trinity Coll., Cambridge (BA 1992; Whitaker Scholar in Law). Called to the Bar, Lincoln's Inn, 1995. Recorder, 2009–19. Chair, Criminal Bar Assoc., 2017–18. *Address*: Central Criminal Court, Old Bailey, EC4M 7EH.

**RAFFERTY, Rt Hon. Dame Anne (Judith), (Dame Anne Barker)**, DBE 2000; PC 2011; Rt Hon. Lady Justice Rafferty; a Lord Justice of Appeal, since 2011; *m* 1977, Brian John Barker, *qv*; three *d* (and one *d* decd). *Educ*: Univ. of Sheffield (LLB; Hon. LLD 2005). Called to the Bar, Gray's Inn, 1973, Inner Temple *ad eundem*, 1996; Bencher, Gray's Inn, 1998; QC 1990; a Recorder, 1991–2000; Head of Chambers, 1994–2000; a Dep. High Court Judge, 1996–2000; a Judge of the High Court of Justice, Queen's Bench Div., 2000–11; Presiding Judge, SE Circuit, 2003–06. Criminal Bar Association: Mem. Cttee, 1986–89; Sec., 1989–91; Vice-Chm., 1993–95; Chm., 1995–97; Chm., Bar Conf., 1992. Chm., Judicial Coll., 2014–; Vice Chm., Criminal Procedure Rule Cttee, 2012–17. Mem., Royal Commn on Criminal Justice, 1991–93; Comr, Judicial Appts Commn, 2017– (Vice Chm., 2017–). Member: SE Circuit Cttee, 1987–90; Pigot Cttee, 1988–89; Circuit Cttee, SE Circuit, 1991–94; Criminal Cttee, Judicial Studies Bd, 1998–2000; Sentencing Council, 2010–12. Gov., Expert Witness Inst., 1997–99. Chancellor, Univ. of Sheffield, 2015–. Mem., Appeal Ct, Oxford Univ., 2003–. Mem. Council, Eastbourne Coll., 1993–2006. *Recreations*: Apostrophe Chambers, sea swimming. *Address*: Royal Courts of Justice, Strand, WC2A 2LL.
*See also* P. A. Darling.

**RAFFERTY, Kevin Robert**; Editor in Chief, PlainWords Media, London, Hong Kong and Osaka, since 2003; Columnist, South China Morning Post, Hong Kong, since 2006; *b* 5 Nov. 1944; *s* of Leo and Thérèse Rafferty; *m* 2009, Prof. Mikako Hayashi. *Educ*: Marist Coll., Kingston upon Hull; Queen's Coll., Oxford (MA). Journalistic training, The Guardian, Sun, 1966–69; Financial Times, 1970–76, Asia Editor, 1973–76; Founder Editor, Business Times Malaysia, 1976–77; Consultant Editor, Indian Express Gp, 1978–79; Foreign Correspondent, Financial Times, 1980; Asia Pacific Editor, Institutional Investor, 1981–87; Ed., The Universe, 1987–88. Founder Editor, then Associate Editor, Asia and Pacific Review, Saffron Walden, 1980–93; Managing Editor: Internat. Media Partners, NY, 1989–96; World Bank, Washington, 1997–99; Business Editor, then Actg Editor, Hong Kong Standard, 1999–2001; Editor in Chief, Business Day, Thailand, 2001–05; Editor/Publisher, HandaiGlobal, 2014–16. Columnist, The Japan Times, Tokyo, 2006–17; Opinion writer, Indian Express, 2019–. Prof., Inst. for Academic Initiatives, Osaka Univ., 2013–16. *Publications*: City on the Rocks: Hong Kong's uncertain future, 1989; Inside Japan's Power Houses, 1995; India: briefing book, 2007; Faces of the Bank's World (calendars), 1998, 1999. *Recreations*: travelling, meeting ordinary people, reading, taking photographs. *E*: plainwordseditor@gmail.com. *Clubs*: Oxford and Cambridge; Foreign Correspondents (Hong Kong).

**RAFFERTY, Stuart**; QC 2009; His Honour Judge Rafferty; a Circuit Judge, since 2012; *b* Mexborough, Yorks, 22 Sept. 1952; *s* of Ronald Stuart and Nellie Rafferty; *m* 1983, Ann Saxby; two *s. Educ*: Long Eaton Grammar Sch.; Lanchester Poly., Coventry (BA Hons Business Law); Inns of Court Sch. of Law. Called to the Bar, Gray's Inn, 1975; in practice as barrister specialising in crime; a Recorder (Crime), 2001–12, (Civil), 2004–12. *Recreations*: family life, gardening, music, the theatre, walking, convivial company. *Address*: Nottingham Crown Court, 60 Canal Street, Nottingham NG1 7EL. *Club*: Reform.

**RAFTERY, Prof. John James**, PhD; Vice-Chancellor, London Metropolitan University, 2014–18; *b* Ireland, Sept. 1956. *Educ*: University Coll., Cork; Liverpool Poly. (PhD 1984). Prof., Univ. of Greenwich; Prof. of Real Estate and Construction Econs, Hong Kong Poly. Univ., 1994–2000; Oxford Brookes University: Hd, Sch. of Architecture, 2000; Dean of Architecture and Built Envmt, 2000–09; Pro-Vice-Chancellor (Internat.), then Pro-Vice-Chancellor (Student Experience), 2005–14. Mem., UN Global Humanitarian Forum, 2008–10. *Publications*: Principles of Building Economics, 1991; Models for Construction Cost and Price Forecasting, 1991; (ed jtly) The Construction Sector in the Asian Economies, 2004; (jtly) Risk Management in Projects, 2nd edn 2005; contrib. scientific papers on econs and risk mgt in construction sector, econ. develt in Asia and on psychol characteristics of entrepreneurs.

**RAGGATT, Timothy Walter Harold**; QC 1993; a Recorder, since 1994; *b* 13 April 1950; *s* of late Walter George and Norah Margaret Raggatt; *m* 2017, Vanessa Sarah Bradford. *Educ*: Redditch County High Sch.; King's Coll. London (LLB 1971). Called to the Bar, Inner Temple, 1972, Bencher, 1999; Tutor, Inns of Court Sch. of Law, 1972–73; in practice on Midland and Oxford Circuit, 1974–; an Asst Recorder, 1991–94; Hd of Chambers, 4 King's Bench Walk, 2003–. Mem., Professional Assoc. of Diving Instructors, 1992–. *Recreations*: golf, scuba diving, bridge. *Address*: 4 King's Bench Walk, Temple, EC4Y 7DL; St Philips Chambers, 55 Temple Row, Birmingham B2 5LS. *Clubs*: Royal Automobile; Blackwell Golf (Birmingham), Royal Cinque Ports Golf.

**RAGHUNATHAN, Prof. Madabusi Santanam**, Padma Bhushan, 2012 (Padma Shri, 2001); PhD; FRS 2000; FIASc, FNA; Distinguished Visiting Professor, DAE-UM Centre for Excellence in Basic Sciences, Mumbai, since 2017; *b* 11 Aug. 1941; *s* of Madabusi Sudarsanam Iyengar Santanam and Ambuja Santanam; *m* 1968, Ramaa Rangarajan; one *s. Educ*: Vivekananda Coll., Univ. of Madras (BA Hons 1960); Bombay Univ. (PhD 1966). Tata Institute of Fundamental Research: Associate Prof., 1966–70; Prof., 1970–80; Sen. Prof., 1980–90; Distinguished Prof., 1990–97; Prof. of Eminence, 1997–2006; Homi Bhabha Prof., 2006–11. Dist. Guest Prof., IIT Bombay, 2011–17. FIASc 1974; FNA 1975; Fellow, Third World Acad. of Scis, 1994. Bhatnagar Award, Council of Scientific and Industrial Res., India, 1977; Third World Acad. Award, Trieste, 1991. *Publications*: Discrete Subgroups of Lie Groups, 1972; contrib. papers to Annals of Maths, Inventiones Mathematicae, etc. *Address*: Department of Mathematics, DAE-UM Centre for Excellence in Basic Sciences, University of Mumbai, Vidyanagari Campus, Kalina, Santacruz (East), Mumbai 400098, India. *T*: (home) (22) 25504766.

**RAGLAN**, 6th Baron *cr* 1852; **Geoffrey Somerset**; *b* Usk, Monmouthshire, 29 Aug. 1932; *yr s* of 4th Baron Raglan and Hon. Julia Hamilton, CStJ (*d* 1971), *d* of 11th Baron Belhaven and Stenton, CIE; *S* brother, 2010; *m* 1956, Caroline Rachel (*d* 2014), *d* of late Col E. R. Hill, DSO; two *d* (one *s* decd). *Educ*: Dragon Sch.; Westminster; Royal Agricultural Coll., Cirencester. Nat. Service, Grenadier Guards, 1952–54. Sales Promoter, Standard Motor Co., 1957–60; Gp Mktg Manager, Lambourn Engrg Gp, 1960–71; wine shipper, 1971–94. Member: Berks CC, 1966–75; Newbury DC, 1978–83; Oxon CC, 1988–93. Mem., Thames Valley Valuation Tribunals, 1987–2004 (a Chm., 1996–2004). Chm., Vale of White Horse Dist, CPRE, 2000–04. *Recreations*: shooting, conservation. Heir: *g s* Inigo Arthur Fitzroy Somerset, *b* 6 July 2004. *Address*: Manor Farm Cottage, Stanford-in-the-Vale, Faringdon, Oxon SN7 8NN. *T*: (01367) 710558. *E*: geoffrey.somerset@btinternet.com.

**RAHMAN, Prof. Atta-ur-**, Nishan-i-Imtiaz, 2002; PhD, ScD; FRS 2006; Director, H. E. J. Research Institute of Chemistry, 1990–2008, Patron in Chief, International Center for Chemical and Biological Sciences, since 2008, and Professor Emeritus, 2010, University of Karachi; Coordinator General, Organization of Islamic Conference Standing Committee on Scientific and Technological Cooperation, 1996–2012; President: Pakistan Academy of Sciences, 2003–06 and 2011–14 (Vice President, 1997–2001); Network of Academies of Science of Islamic Countries, since 2004; *b* Delhi, 22 Sept. 1942; *s* of Jameel-Ur-Rahman and Amtul Subhan Begum; *m* Nargis Jamal; four *s. Educ*: Karachi Univ. (BSc 1963; MSc 1964); King's Coll., Cambridge (PhD 1968; ScD 1987; Hon. Life Fellow, 2007). Karachi University: Lectr, 1964–69; Asst Prof., 1969–74; Associate Prof., 1974–76; Prof. 1981–90; Co-Director, H. E. J. Research Inst. of Chem., 1977–80 and 1981–90. D. A. A. D. Fellow, Univ. of Tübingen, 1979; Einstein Prof., Chinese Acad. of Scis, 2013. Government of Pakistan: Minister: for Sci. and Technol., 2000–02; Min. of Educn, 2002; Min. of Sci. and Technol., 2003–04; Chm., Higher Educn Commn, 2002–08; Advr to Prime Minister for Sci. and Technol., 2005–07. Higher Educn Commn Dist. Nat. Prof., 2011. Pres., Chem. Soc. of Pakistan, 1992; Vice-Pres. (Central and S Asia), Acad. of Scis for the Developing World, 2007–. Editor: Studies in Natural Products Chemistry series, vols 1–35, 1986–; Current Medicinal Chem., Organic Synthesis, Organic Chem., Pharmaceutical Analysis, Nanosci., Analytical Chem., Bioactive Compounds, Chemical Biol.; Medicinal Chem.; Nanosci. and Nanotechnol.—Asia; Natural Products Jl. FRSC 1981; Fellow: Pakistan Acad. of Scis, 1982; Islamic Acad. of Scis, 1988; Third World Acad. of Scis; Korean Acad. of Sci. and Technol., 2004; Inst. of Chemistry, Colombo, 2014; Einstein Prof. 2013, Foreign Mem., 2015, Chinese Acad. of Scis. Foreign Fellow: Korean Acad. of Scis; Chinese Chem. Soc. Consultant, Educn Forum Asia, 2015–. Hon. DEd Coventry, 2007; Hon. DSc: Sir Syed Engrg Univ., Karachi, 2003; Gomal Univ., 2004; Univ. of Karachi, 2005; Bradford, 2010; Hon. PhD: Asian Inst. of Technol., Thailand, 2010; Univ. of Technol., Mara, Malaysia, 2011. Islamic Gold Medal, 1977, Open Gold Medal, 1984, Pakistan Acad. Scis; Fedn of Pakistan Chambers of Commerce and Industry Prize for Technol Innovation, 1985; Scientist of the Yr Award, Pakistan, 1987; Islamic Orgn Prize, Kuwait Foundn for Advancement of Scis, 1988; Babai Urdu Award, 1994; Pakistan Acad. Scis-Infaq Foundn Prize, Gold Medal, 1996; UNESCO Sci. Prize, 1999; Award for Chem. Scis, 1999, Prize for Instn Bldg (Italy), 2009, Third World Acad. Scis; Econ. Cooperation Orgn Prize, 2000; Chem. Award, Islamic Educnl, Scientific and Cultural Orgn, 2001; Engro Excellence Award, 2010; Internat. Scientific Corpn Award, Chinese Acad. of Scis, 2014. Nishan-i-Imtiaz (Pakistan), 2002 (Tamgha-i-Imtiaz, 1983; Sitara-i-Imtiaz, 1991; Hilal-i-Imtiaz, 1998); Gold Medal (Kuwait), 1980; Order of Golden Sash (Austria), 2007; Friendship Award (China), 2014. *Publications*: Biosynthesis of Indole Alkaloids (with A. Basha), 1983; Nuclear Magnetic Resonance, 1986; One and Two Dimensional Nuclear Magnetic Resonance Spectroscopy, 1989; (with Zahir Shah) Stereoselective Synthesis in Organic Chemistry, 1993; (with M. I. Choudhary) Solving Problems with Nuclear Magnetic Resonance Spectroscopy, 1996, 2nd edn 2016; contrib. over 253 books and jls; over 900 res. articles; 37 patents. *Address*: H. E. J. Research Institute of Chemistry, International Centre for Chemical and Biological Sciences, University of Karachi, Karachi 75270, Pakistan.

**RAHMAN, (Sadeqa) Shaheen;** QC 2017; *b* Bristol, 3 July 1973; *d* of Mohammad Azizar Rahman and Razia Sultana Rahman; *m* 2006, Christopher Payne; two *d. Educ:* Redland High Sch. for Girls; Birmingham Univ. (BA English); Coll. of Law (CPE); Inns of Court Sch. of Law (BVC). Called to the Bar, Gray's Inn, 1996; in practice as barrister, specialising in public and healthcare law, 1996–. *Recreations:* cinema, cooking, travel, family. *Address:* 1 Crown Office Row, Temple, EC4Y 7HH. *T:* (020) 7797 7550. *E:* shaheen.rahman@1cor.com.

**RAILTON, David;** QC 1996; a Recorder, since 2000; a Deputy High Court Judge, since 2013; *b* 5 June 1957; *s* of late Andrew Scott Railton, MC and of Margaret Elizabeth Railton (*née* Armit); *m* 1996, Sinéad Major; one *s* one *d. Educ:* Balliol Coll., Oxford (BA). Called to the Bar, Gray's Inn, 1979, Bencher, 2005. *Recreations:* cricket, golf. *Address:* Fountain Court, Temple, EC4Y 9DH.

**RAILTON, Elizabeth Jane,** CBE 2006; Director for Children's Services Self-Improvement, Children's Improvement Board, Local Government Association, 2011–12; *b* 21 Nov. 1952; *d* of John and Jill Nisbet; *m* 1974, James Lancelot Railton (*d* 2012); two *s. Educ:* Somerville Coll., Oxford (MA, MSc). CQSW 1978. Social worker, 1974–86; Hertfordshire County Council: Social Services Manager, 1986–91; Asst Dir of Social Services, 1991–95; Dep. Dir, Social Services, 1995–96; Dir, Social Services, Cambs CC, 1998–2002; Essex County Council: Dep. Chief Exec., Learning and Social Care, 2003–05; Dir, Children's Services, 2005–06; Nat. Programmes Dir, Serco Ltd, 2007–11 (Together for Children, 2007–08; Together for Children and Together for Disabled Children, 2008–11; Together for Children and Learners, 2009–11). Hon. Sec., Assoc. of Dirs of Social Services, 2002–06. Trustee: British Assoc. Adoption and Fostering, 2001–06; Nat. Children's Bureau, 2015–; non-exec. Dir, Slough Children's Services Trust, 2015–19. *Recreations:* shopping, travel, theatre, opera.

**RAINBIRD, Sharon;** *see* Horgan, S.

**RAINBOW, Prof. Philip Stephen,** DSc, PhD; CBiol, FRSB, FLS, FMBA; Keeper of Zoology, 1997–2013 and Head, Department of Life Sciences, 2012–13, Natural History Museum (Director of Science, 2011); *b* 21 Oct. 1950; *s* of Frank Evelyn Rainbow, OBE and Joyce May Victoria Rainbow (*née* Turner); *m* 1973, Mary Meaken; two *s. Educ:* Bedford Sch., Bedford; Clare Coll., Cambridge (MA); UCNW, Bangor (PhD 1975; DSc 1994). CBiol 1998, FRSB (FIBiol 1998). Queen Mary College, later Queen Mary and Westfield College, University of London: Lectr, 1975–89; Reader in Marine Biology, 1989–94; Prof. of Marine Biology, 1994–97; Head, Sch. of Biol Scis, 1995–97; Vis. Prof., 1997–2013. Mem., Darwin Initiative Adv. Cttee, DEFRA, 2003–09. Gov. and Mem. Council, Marine Biol Assoc. UK, 2008–; Mem., Bd of Trustees, Nat. Biodiversity Network, 2008–13. FLS 1985; FMBA 2014. *Publications:* (ed jtly) Aspects of Decapod Crustacean Biology, 1988; (ed jtly) Heavy Metals in the Marine Environment, 1990; (ed jtly) Ecotoxicology of Metals in Invertebrates, 1993; (jtly) Biomonitoring of Trace Aquatic Contaminants, 1993, 2nd edn 1994; (ed jtly) Forecasting the Environmental Fate and Effects of Chemicals, 2001; (jtly) Metal Contamination in Aquatic Environments: science and lateral management, 2008; (ed jtly) Environmental Assessment of Estuarine Ecosystems, 2009; (ed jtly) Tolerance to Environmental Contaminants, 2011; (ed jtly) Ecological Biomarkers: indicators of ecotoxicological effects, 2012; Trace Metals in the Environment and Living Organisms: the British Isles as a case study, 2018; numerous papers in scientific jls. *Recreations:* natural history, watching cricket and Rugby. *E:* philipstephenrainbow@gmail.com. *Club:* Tetrapods.

**RAINE, Craig Anthony;** poet; Fellow of New College, Oxford, 1991–2010, now Emeritus; Editor, Areté, since 1999; *b* 3 Dec. 1944; *s* of Norman Edward Raine and Olive Marie Raine; *m* 1972, Ann Pasternak Slater; one *d* three *s. Educ:* Barnard Castle Sch.; Exeter Coll., Oxford (BA Hons in English; BPhil). College Lecturer, Oxford University: Exeter Coll., 1971–72; Lincoln Coll., 1974–75; Exeter Coll., 1975–76; Christ Church, 1976–79. Books Editor, New Review, 1977–78; Editor, Quarto, 1979–80; Poetry Editor: New Statesman, 1981; Faber & Faber, 1981–91. Cholmondeley Poetry Award, 1983; Sunday Times Writer of the Year, 1998. *Publications:* The Onion, Memory, 1978, 5th edn 1986; A Martian Sends a Postcard Home, 1979, 8th edn 1990; A Free Translation, 1981, 2nd edn 1981; Rich, 1984, 3rd edn 1985; The Electrification of the Soviet Union, 1986; (ed) A Choice of Kipling's Prose, 1987; The Prophetic Book, 1988; '1953', 1990; Haydn and the Valve Trumpet (essays), 1990; (ed) Rudyard Kipling: selected poetry, 1992; History: the home movie, 1994; Clay. Whereabouts Unknown, 1996; (ed jtly) New Writing 7, 1998; A la recherche du temps perdu, 2000; In Defence of T. S. Eliot (essays), 2000; Collected Poems 1978–1999, 2000; (ed) Rudyard Kipling: The Wish House and other stories, 2002; T. S. Eliot, 2006; Heartbreak (novel), 2010; How Snow Falls (poetry), 2010; The Divine Comedy (novel), 2012; More Dynamite (essays), 2013; My Grandmother's Glass Eye: a look at poetry, 2016. *Recreations:* music, ski-ing. *Address:* c/o New College, Oxford OX1 3BN.

**RAINE, John Stephen;** County Director, then Chief Executive, Derbyshire County Council, 1989–97; *b* 13 April 1941; *s* of Alan and Ruby Raine; *m* 1961, Josephine Elizabeth Marlow; two *s. Educ:* Sir Joseph Williamson's Mathematical School, Rochester. MCIPR. Journalist; Kent Messenger, Sheffield Morning Telegraph, Sheffield Star, Raymond's News Agency, 1957–70; Press Officer, East Midlands Gas, 1970–73; Derbyshire County Council: County Public Relations Officer, 1973–79; Asst to Clerk and Chief Exec., 1979–81; Asst Chief Exec., 1981–88; Dep. County Dir, 1988–89. Chairman: Derbys Probation Bd, 2001–07; Nat. Assoc. of Probation Bds for England and Wales, 2004–07. Chairman: Hearing Aid Council, 1997–2003; Derbys Assoc. for the Blind, 1997–2007. Non-exec. Dir, Chesterfield and N Derbys Royal Hosp. NHS Trust, 1998–2006; Chairman: Derbys County NHS PCT, 2006–09; Scottish Borders NHS Bd, 2011–19; Ind. Chm., Child Protection Cttee, Scottish Borders, 2010–12. *Recreations:* motor cars, travel, learning piano. *Address:* Woodstock Bank, Chiefswood Road, Melrose, Scottish Borders TD6 9QH. *T:* (01896) 822008.

**RAINE, June Munro,** CBE 2009; FRCP, FRCPE; interim Chief Executive, Medicines and Healthcare products Regulatory Agency, since 2019; *b* 20 June 1952; *d* of David Harris and Isobel Harris (*née* Munro); *m* 1975, Prof. Anthony Evan Gerald Raine (*d* 1995); one *s* one *d. Educ:* Herts & Essex High Sch.; Somerville Coll., Oxford (BA Hons 1st Cl. 1974; MSc 1976; BM BCh 1978). MRCP 1980, FRCP 2003; MRCGP 1982; FRCPE 1995. Department of Health: SMO, Medicines Div., 1985–89; Gp Manager, Medicines Control Agency, 1989–98; Principal Assessor to Medicines Commn, 1992–2005; Dir, Post-Licensing Div., Medicines Control Agency, 1998–2003; Dir, Post-Licensing Div., then Vigilance and Risk Mgt of Medicines Div., Medicines and Healthcare products Regulatory Agency, 2003–19. Mem., wkg gps on aspects of pharmaceutical regulation, EC; Chm., Pharmacovigilance Risk Assessment Cttee, Eur. Medicines Agency, 2012–18. FRSocMed 2000. Hon. FBPhS (Hon. FBPharmacolS 2015). *Publications:* papers on pharmacology, adverse drug effects and regulation of medicines. *Recreations:* music, opera, travel. *Address:* Medicines and Healthcare products Regulatory Agency, 10 South Colonnade, Canary Wharf, E14 4PU.

**RAINE, Sandra Margaret;** private consultant on company secretarial matters, 2007–14; *b* 7 March 1958; *d* of Charles Kitchener Lovell and Mary Rosaline Lovell (*née* O'Hare); *m* 1980, Ian Henry Raine. *Educ:* Univ. of Newcastle upon Tyne (BA Hons Sociol. and Social Admin). ACIS 1986. Pensions Asst, Dunlop Ltd, 1980; Admin. Officer, NE Council on Alcoholism, 1980–82; Sen. Admin. Asst, Newcastle upon Tyne Poly., 1982–85; Asst Co-ordinator, Urban Programmes, Gateshead MBC, 1985–86; Asst Divl Dir, Berks Social Services, 1986–90; Asst Co. Sec., AA, 1990–91; Ben Fund Sec., Chartered Inst. Building, 1992–94; Sec. and Chief Exec., IGasE, 1994–99; Co. Sec., Paddington Churches Housing Assoc., subseq. Gp Co. Sec., Genesis Housing Gp Ltd, 1999–2003; Exec. Dir, Internat. Headache Soc., 2003–05. Trustee, subseq. Chm., Inst. of Plumbing and Heating Engrg, 2005–11. Liveryman, Plumbers' Co., 2007 (Ct Asst, 2016–). *Recreations:* keep fit, reading, genealogy. *Club:* Nirvana (Berkshire).

**RAINEY, Mary Teresa,** OBE 2015; Deputy Chair, Channel 4, since 2016 (non-executive Director, since 2012); *d* of Peter and Margaret Rainey. *Educ:* Glasgow Univ. (MA Hons); Aston Univ. Corporate Hd of Planning, Chiat/Day, US, 1983–89; CEO, Chiat/Day, London, 1989–93; Founding Partner, Rainey Kelly Campbell Roalfe, 1993–99; Jt CEO, 1999–2003, Chm., 2003–05, Rainey Kelly Campbell Roalfe/Y&R. Founder and Dir, horsesmouth.co.uk, 2005–. Chm., Think Ltd, 2008–15; non-executive Director: WH Smith, 2003–08; SMG, 2005–07; Pinewood Gp, 2015–; Hays plc, 2015–; Charlotte Street Partners Ltd, 2015–. Mem., Nat. Skills Forum, 2007–12; Vice Chm., Creative Skillset, 2009–. Chm., Marketing Gp of GB, 2005–06. Mem., Women's Advertising Club of London, 1991–; Pres., Thirty Club, 2012–13. *Publications:* numerous contribs to jls of advertising and mkt res. industries. *Recreations:* reading, music, hill-walking. *E:* mt@mtrainey.com.

**RAINEY, Philip Carslake;** QC 2010; *b* Tyneside, 25 Oct. 1968; *s* of George Rainey and Mavis Storey; *m* 1995, Helen Staples; two *s* one *d. Educ:* King's Sch., Tynemouth; Univ. of Leicester (LLB 1989). Called to the Bar, Middle Temple, 1990; in practice as barrister, 1991–; Hd of Chambers, 2013–. Mem., Civil Procedure Rule Cttee, 2001–08. Member: Property Bar Assoc., 2000–; Chancery Bar Assoc., 2007–. MCIArb 1999. *Publications:* (jtly) Service Charges and Management, 2006, 3rd edn 2013; (jtly) Rent Review, 2008; (contrib.) Smith and Monkcom: The Law of Gambling, 3rd edn 2009, 4th edn 2017; (jtly) Megarry's Manual of the Law of Real Property, 9th edn 2014. *Recreations:* family, sailing (fairweather), history. *Address:* Tanfield Chambers, 2–5 Warwick Court, WC1R 5DJ. *T:* (020) 7421 5300, *Fax:* (020) 7421 5333. *E:* clerks@tanfieldchambers.co.uk.

**RAINEY, Simon Piers Nicholas,** FCIArb; QC 2000; a Recorder, since 2001; a Deputy High Court Judge, since 2008; *b* 14 Feb. 1958; *s* of Peter Michael Rainey and Theresa Cora Rainey (*née* Heffernan); *m* 1st, 1986, Pia Witlox (marr. diss. 1999); twin *s* one *d*; 2nd, 2000, Charlotte Rice. *Educ:* Cranbrook Sch.; Corpus Christi Coll., Cambridge (BA 1st Cl. Hons Law 1980; MA 1984); Univ. Libre de Bruxelles (Licence en Droit Européen (Dist) 1981). FCIArb 2013. Called to the Bar, Lincoln's Inn, 1982; Western Circuit. Vis. Fellow, Inst. of Internat. Trade and Shipping Law, 2010, Hon. Prof., Coll. of Business, Economics and Law, 2013, Univ. of Swansea. *Publications:* Maritime Laws of West Africa, 1985; Ship Sale and Purchase, 1993; Law of Tug and Tow, 1996, 4th edn 2018; Law and Practice of Voyage Charterparties, 2009; Cargo Claims: from The Hague to the Rotterdam Rules, 2010; Pollution at Sea: law and liability, 2012; Carriage of Goods by Land, Sea and Air, 2014; Shipbuilding, Sale and Finance, 2015; Offshore Contracts and Liability, 2016; International Trade and Carriage of Goods, 2017. *Recreations:* classical music, print-collecting, ski-ing. *Address:* Quadrant Chambers, 10 Fleet Street, EC4Y 1AU. *T:* (020) 7583 4444. *E:* simon.rainey@quadrantchambers.com.

**RAINFORD, Rev. Canon (Robert) Graham;** Head of Religious Studies (Theology, Philosophy, Religion), Sussex House School, Cadogan Square, since 2011; *b* 23 April 1955; *s* of late Robert Rainford and Mary Madeline Victory Rainford (*née* Saunders); *m* 1979 (marr. diss. 2006); two *s* one *d*; *m* 2006, Anne Barrett. *Educ:* Bootle Grammar Sch. for Boys; St Martin's Coll. of Educn, Lancaster (Cert Ed; BEd); St Stephen's House, Oxford (Cert. Theol. 1983). Schoolmaster, Seedfield Sch., Bury, 1977–81. Ordained deacon, 1983, priest, 1984; Curate, St Catherine with St Alban and St Paul, Burnley, 1983–86; Priest-in-charge, 1986–89, Vicar, 1989–2003, St Christopher, Hawes Side, Blackpool; Priest-in-charge, St Nicholas, Marton Moss, Blackpool, 2001–03; Area Dean of Blackpool, 2000–03; Sen. Chaplain to the Bishop of Dover and Canterbury Chaplain to the Archbishop of Canterbury, 2003–05; Priest Administrator, 2005–08, Asst Priest, 2008–12, Associate Priest, 2012–15, Holy Trinity Church, Sloane Street. Permission to officiate, Dio. of London, 2015–. Industrial Chaplain, Blackpool Pleasure Beach, 1987–2003; Chaplain, 1988–2012, Mem. Council, 2011–12, Actors' Church Union; Asst Theatre Chaplain, Marlowe Th., Canterbury, 2004–05; Theatre Chaplain, Garrick Th., London, 2011–12; Chaplain, Peter Jones, Sloane Sq., 2012–15. Chm., House of Clergy, Blackburn Diocesan Synod, 2000–03; Hon. Canon, Blackburn Cathedral, 2001–03. Hon. Chaplain, Garden House Sch., Chelsea; Hon. Asst Chaplain, Lister Hosp., Chelsea, 2008–12. Member: London Diocesan Synod, 2012–15; Bishop of London's Council, 2012–15. Chairman of Governors: Marton Primary Sch., 1991–2003; Holy Trinity C of E Primary Sch., Chelsea, 2006–15; Vice Chm. Govs, Hawes Side Primary Sch., Blackpool; Gov., St George's C of E High Sch., Blackpool, 2002–03. Non-magisterial Mem., Lord-Lieut of Lancs Adv. Cttee. *Recreations:* travel (pilgrimage), theatre, opera, music, art, architecture, reading, cooking, gardening, photography, walking, sailing, allotmenteering. *Address:* Sussex House School, 68 Cadogan Square, SW1X 0EA. *E:* gr@sussexhouseschool.co.uk.

**RAINGER, Peter,** CBE 1978; FRS 1982; FREng; Deputy Director of Engineering, British Broadcasting Corporation, 1978–84, retired; *b* 17 May 1924; *s* of Cyril and Ethel Rainger; *m* 1st, 1953, Josephine Campbell (decd); two *s*; 2nd, 1972, Barbara Gibson. *Educ:* Northampton Engrg Coll.; London Univ. (BSc(Eng)). CEng, FIET; FREng (FEng 1979). British Broadcasting Corporation: Head of Designs Dept, 1968–71; Head of Research Dept, 1971–76; Asst Dir of Engrg, 1976–78. Chairman: Professional Gp E14, IEE, 1973–76; various working parties, EBU, 1971–84. Fellow, Royal Television Soc., 1969. Geoffrey Parr Award, Royal TV Soc., 1964; J. J. Thompson Premium, IEE, 1966; TV Acad. Award, Nat. Acad. of Arts and Scis, 1968; David Sarnoff Gold Medal, SMPTE, 1972. *Publications:* Satellite Broadcasting, 1985; technical papers in IEE, Royal TV Soc. and SMPTE jls. *Recreations:* painting, model engineering. *Address:* 22 Mill Meadow, Milford on Sea, Hants SO41 0UG.

**RAINHAM, Tina Jeanette;** *see* Landale, T. J.

**RAINSFORD, (David) Mark;** QC 2006; *b* 3 May 1962; *s* of David and June Rainsford; *m* 1991, Fiona Caroline Munro; one *s* four *d. Educ:* London Sch. of Econs (LLB Hons). Called to the Bar, Lincoln's Inn, 1985; in practice as a barrister, 33 Chancery Lane, specialising in corporate wrongdoing. *Recreation:* tennis. *Address:* The Old House, 27 Leyton Road, Harpenden, Herts AL5 2JB. *E:* mr@33cllaw.com.

**RAISER, Rev. Dr Konrad;** General Secretary, World Council of Churches, 1993–2003; *b* Magdeburg, 25 Jan. 1938; *m* 1967, Elisabeth von Weizsäcker; four *s. Educ:* Univ. of Tübingen (DTheol 1970). Ordained into German Evangelical Ch, 1964; Asst Pastor, Württemberg, 1963–65; Lectr, Protestant Theol. Faculty, Tübingen, 1967–69; World

Council of Churches: Study Sec., Commn on Faith and Order, 1969–73; Dep. Gen. Sec., 1973–83; Prof. of Systematic Theol. and Ecumenics, and Dir, Ecumenical Inst., Protestant Theol. Faculty, Univ. of Ruhr, 1983–93. *Publications*: Identität und Sozialität, 1971; Ökumene im Übergang, 1989 (Ecumenism in Transition, 1991); (contrib.) Dictionary of the Ecumenical Movement, 1991; Wir stehen noch am Anfang, 1994; To Be the Church, 1997; For a Culture of Life, 2002; Hoffen auf Gerechtigkeit und Versöhnung, 2002; Schritte auf dem Weg der Ökumene, 2005; Religion–Macht–Politik, 2010 (Religion, Power, Politics, 2013); Ökumene zwischen Kirche und Welt, 2013; 500 Jahre Reformation: weltweit, 2016; The Challenge of Transformation, 2018; many essays and articles. *Address*: Zikadenweg 14, 14055 Berlin, Germany.

**RAISMAN, John Michael,** CBE 1983; Chairman, Shell UK Ltd, 1979–85; *b* 12 Feb. 1929; *er s* of Sir Jeremy Raisman, GCMG, GCIE, KCSI, and late Renee Mary Raisman; *m* 1953, Evelyn Anne (*d* 2019), *d* of Brig. J. I. Muirhead, CIE, MC; one *s* two *d* (and one *d* decd). *Educ*: Dragon Sch., Oxford; Rugby Sch.; The Queen's Coll., Oxford (Jodrell Schol., MA Lit Hum). Joined Royal Dutch/Shell Group, 1953; served in Brazil, 1954–60; General Manager, Shell Panama, 1961–62; Asst to Exploration and Production Co-ordinator, The Hague, 1963–65; Gen. Man., Shell Co. of Turkey, 1966–69; President, Shell Sekiyu K. K. Japan, 1970–73; Head, European Supply and Marketing, 1974–77; Man. Dir, Shell UK Oil, 1977–78; Regional Co-ordinator, UK and Eire, Shell Internat. Pet. Co. Ltd, 1978–85; Shell UK Ltd: Dep. Chm., 1978–79; Chief Exec., 1978–85; Govt Dir, 1984–87, Dep. Chm., 1987–91, British Telecom. Chm., British Biotech plc, 1995–98 (Dir, 1993–98); Director: Vickers PLC, 1981–90; Glaxo Hldgs PLC, 1982–90; Lloyds Bank Plc, 1985–95; Lloyds Merchant Bank Hldgs Ltd, 1985–87; Candover Investments PLC, 1990–98; Tandem Computers Ltd, 1991–97; Lloyds TSB plc, 1996–98. Chairman: Adv. Council, London Enterprise Agency, 1979–85; UK Oil Industry Emergency Cttee, 1980–85; Council of Industry for Management Educn, 1981–85; Investment Bd, Electra-Candover Partners, 1985–95. Member: Council, CBI, 1979–90 (Chm., CBI Europe Cttee, 1980–88; Mem., President's Cttee, 1980–88); Council, Inst. of Petroleum, 1979–81; Council, Inst. for Fiscal Studies, 1982–2016; Governing Council, Business in the Community, 1982–85; Council, UK Centre for Econ. and Environmental Develt, 1985–89; Royal Commn on Environmental Pollution, 1986–87; Chm., Electronics Industry EDC, 1986–87. Chairman: Langs Lead Body, 1990–95; Council for Industry and Higher Educn, 1991–98 (Mem., 1988–98); Dep. Chm., Nat. Commn on Educn, 1991–2000; Pres., Council for Educn in World Citizenship, 1992–2003. Mem., Council for Charitable Support, 1986–91; Chairman: RA Trust, 1987–96 (Emeritus Trustee, RA, 1996–); Trustees, British Empire and Commonwealth Mus., 2003–06. Governor, NIESR, 1983–2016; Pro-Chancellor, Aston Univ., 1987–93. CCMI (CBIM 1980). DUniv Stirling, 1983; Hon. LLD: Aberdeen, 1985; Manchester, 1986; UWE, 1998; Hon. DSc Aston, 1992. *Recreations*: reading, music, theatre. *Address*: Netheravon House, Netheravon Road South, W4 2PY. *Club*: Brooks's.

**RAJAH, Eason Thurai;** QC 2011; a Recorder, since 2016; *b* Ipoh, Malaysia, 18 Jan. 1967; *s* of N. T. Rajah and Gnanambigai Rajah; *m* 1993, Ann Collier; one *s* one *d*. *Educ*: Epsom Coll.; Univ. of Nottingham (LLB Hons). Called to the Bar, Gray's Inn, 1989; in practice as a barrister specialising in Chancery law; Advocate and Solicitor, High Court of Malaya, 1991. An Editor, Court of Protection Law Reports, 2012–. *Publications*: (ed) Mellows Taxation for Executors and Trustees (looseleaf), 2006–. *Address*: 10 Old Square, Lincoln's Inn, WC2A 3SU. *T*: (020) 7405 0758. *E*: clerks@tenoldsquare.com.

**RAJAN, Amol;** BBC Media Editor, since 2016; Presenter, The Media Show, BBC Radio 4, since 2017; *b* Calcutta, 4 July 1983; *s* of P. Varadarajan and Sunanda Joshi Rajan; *m* 2013, Charlotte Rosemary Faircloth; one *s*. *Educ*: Graveney Sch.; Downing Coll., Cambridge (BA Hons English Lit. 2005). Asst Desk Officer, Eastern Adriatic Dept, FCO, 2001–02; on-screen audience researcher, The Wright Stuff, Channel 5, 2005–07; news reporter, sports news corresp., 2007–09, Dep. Comment Ed., 2009–10, The Independent; Media Advr to Evgeny Lebedev, owner of The Independent and London Evening Standard, 2010–13; Ed., The Independent, 2013–16. *Publications*: Twirlymen: the unlikely history of cricket's greatest spin bowlers, 2011. *Recreations*: cricket, reggae, avoiding lifts.

**RAJOY BREY, Mariano;** Prime Minister of Spain, 2011–18; *b* Santiago de Compostela, 27 March 1955; *m* 1996, Elvira Fernández Balboa; two *s*. *Educ*: Univ. of Santiago de Compostela (LLB). Registrar of Deeds, Pres., Local and Provincial Press, Pontevedra. Mem. (People's Alliance), Galician Regl Parlt, 1981; Gen. Dir, Instnl Relns, Xunta de Galicia; Pres., Provincial de Pontevedra, 1983–86; Vice Pres., Xunta de Galicia, 1986–87; Minister: of Public Admin, 1996–99; of Educn and Culture, 1999–2000; First Dep. Prime Minister and Minister of Interior, 2001–02; First Dep. Prime Minister and Speaker, and Minister of the Presidency, 2002–03. Popular Party: Mem., Nat. Exec. Cttee, 1989–2018; Dep. Sec. Gen., 1999–2003; Gen. Sec., 2003–04; Pres., 2004–18. *Publications*: In Confidence (autobiog.), 2011.

**RAKE, Sir Michael Derek Vaughan,** Kt 2007; FCA; Chairman: Majid Al Futtam Holdings; New Day, since 2018; William Pitt Fellow, Pembroke College, Cambridge, since 2010; *b* 17 Jan. 1948; *s* of Derek Shannon Vaughan Rake and Rosamund Rake (*née* Barrett); *m* 1st, 1970, Julia (*née* Cook); three *s*; 2nd, 1986, Caroline (*née* Thomas); one *s*. *Educ*: Wellington Coll. FCA 1970. Turquands Barton Mayhew, London and Brussels, 1968–74; KPMG: Brussels, 1974; Partner, 1979–; Partner i/c of Audit, Belgium and Luxembourg, 1983–86; Sen. Resident Partner, ME, 1986–89; Partner, London office, 1989–; Mem., UK Bd, 1991– (Chm., 1998–); Regl Man. Partner, SE Reg., 1992–94; Chief Exec., London and SE Reg., 1994–96; Chief Operating Officer, UK, 1996–98; Sen. Partner, KPMG UK, 1998–2006; Chairman: KPMG Europe, 1999–2002; KPMG Internat., 2002–07; British Telecommunications plc, 2007–17; easyJet plc, 2010–13 (Dep. Chm., 2009–10); Worldpay, 2015–18. Director: Barclays Gp plc, 2008–15 (Dep. Chm., 2012–15); FRC, 2008–11; S&P Global (formerly McGraw Hill Inc.), 2008–. Mem., Task Force on US/UK Regulation, DTI, 2006; Chm., UK Commn for Employment and Skills, 2007–10; BVCA Guidelines Monitoring Gp, 2008–13. Chm., BITC, 2004–07; Pres., CBI, 2013–15; Chm., ICC, 2015–; Member: Bd, Prince of Wales Internat. Business Leaders Forum, 1999–2007; Bd, Transatlantic Business Dialogue, 2004–; Bd, Business for New Europe, 2006–; Internat. Business Council, World Econ. Forum, 2006–12; Global Adv. Bd, Oxford Univ. Centre for Corporate Reputation, 2008–; Sen. Advr, Chatham House, 2008–. Chm., Great Ormond St Hosp., 2017–. Trustee, Prince of Wales Charitable Foundn, 2011–16. Gov., Wellington Coll., 2007–16 (Chm. and Vice Pres., 2010–16). Vice Pres., RNIB, 2003–; FCGI 2012. *Recreations*: tennis, ski-ing. *Club*: Guards Polo Club (Mem. Bd, 2005–).

**RALEIGH, Dr Jean Margaret Macdonald C.;** *see* Curtis-Raleigh.

**RALLI, Sir David (Charles),** 4th Bt *cr* 1912, of Park Street, City of Westminster; farmer; *b* London, 5 April 1946; *o s* of Sir Godfrey Victor Ralli, 3rd Bt, TD and Nora Margaret Forman (*d* 1990); *S* father, 2010; *m* 1975, Jacqueline Cecilia, *d* of late David Smith; one *s* one *d*. *Educ*: Eton; Harper Adams Agricultural Coll. Chm., Dereham Farm Services, 1985–87; Dir, Mid Norfolk Farmers, 1985–93; Chm., Norfolk Gp, Game Conservancy, 1993–97. Founder, Guineafowl Trust Safaris, 1996. Mem. (C), Breckland DC, 1987–95 (Chm., Envmtl Health Cttee, 1990–95). Chm. of Govs, St Andrews First Sch., N Pickenham, 1992–94. Area Pres., St John Ambulance, SW Norfolk, 2005–; Pres., Mid Norfolk Cons. Assoc., 2014–. Liveryman, Farmers' Co., 1985. OStJ 2014. *Recreations*: golf, fishing, shooting. *Heir*: *s* Philip Neil David Ralli [*b* 31 March 1983; *m* 2017, Shannon Tham, Singapore; one *s* one *d* (twins)]. *Address*: Panworth Hall, Ashill, Thetford, Norfolk IP25 7BB. *T*: (01760) 440852. *E*: davidralli62@gmail.com. *Clubs*: White's, Farmers.
*See also* Sir A. R. Milburn, Bt.

**RALLING, (Antony) Christopher,** OBE 1992; FRGS; freelance writer/director; *b* 12 April 1929; *s* of Harold St George Ralling and Dorothy Blanche Ralling; *m* 1963, Angela Norma (*née* Gardner); one *d*. *Educ*: Charterhouse; Wadham Coll., Oxford (BA 2nd Cl. Hons English). Joined BBC External Services, Scriptwriter, 1955; British Meml Foundn Fellowship to Australia, 1959; Dep. Editor, Panorama, BBC TV, 1964; joined BBC TV Documentaries, 1966; directed The Search for the Nile, 1972 (Amer. Acad. Award, 1972; Peabody Award, 1972); Mem., British Everest Expedn, 1975; produced The Voyage of Charles Darwin, 1978 (British Acad. Award, 1978; Desmond Davies British Acad. Award, 1978; RTS Silver Medal, 1979); Hd of Documentaries, BBC TV, 1980; left BBC to start Dolphin Productions, 1982; directed: The History of Africa, 1984; Chasing a Rainbow (Josephine Baker), 1986 (Amer. Acad. Award, 1986); Prince Charles at Forty, LWT, 1988; The Kon-Tiki Man, BBC, 1989; The Buried Mirror, BBC, 1992; A Diplomat in Japan, BBC, 1992; Return to Everest, Channel 4, 1993. FRGS 1978. *Publications*: Muggeridge Through the Microphone, 1967; The Voyage of Charles Darwin, 1978; Shackleton, 1983; The Kon-Tiki Man, 1990; Scrapbook for Jessica (personal memoir), 2017. *Recreations*: tennis, ski-ing. *Address*: Tankerville Cottage, Kingston Hill, Surrey KT2 7JH. *Club*: Alpine.

**RALLS, His Honour Peter John Henry;** QC 1997; a Circuit Judge, 2008–16; *b* 18 July 1947; *s* of Ivan Jack Douglas Ralls and Sybil Gladys Child; *m* 1st, 1979, Anne Elizabeth Marriott (marr. diss. 1986); 2nd, 1997, Tonia Anne Clark; two *s* one *d*. *Educ*: Royal Russell Sch., Surrey; UCL (LLB Hons). Called to the Bar, Middle Temple, 1972; admitted Solicitor, 1981; returned to the Bar, 1982; an Asst Recorder, 1998–2000; a Recorder, 2000–08. Chm., Cowes Combined Clubs, 2001–. *Recreations*: yacht racing, cricket. *Clubs*: Brooks's, MCC; Royal London Yacht; Royal Yacht Squadron.

**RALPH, Richard Peter,** CMG 1997; CVO 1991; HM Diplomatic Service, retired; *b* 27 April 1946; *s* of Peter and Marion Ralph; *m* 1st, 1970 (marr. diss. 2001); one *s* one *d*; 2nd, 2002, Jemma Victoria Elizabeth Marlor; one *d*. *Educ*: King's Sch., Canterbury; Edinburgh Univ. (MSc). Third Sec., FCO, 1969–70; Third, later Second, Sec., Vientiane, Laos, 1970–73; Second, later First, Sec., Lisbon, 1974–77; FCO, 1977–81; Head of Chancery, Harare, Zimbabwe, 1981–85; Counsellor, FCO, 1985–89; Head of Chancery and Congressional Counsellor, Washington, 1989–93; Ambassador to Latvia, 1993–95; Gov., Falkland Is, and Comr for S Georgia and S Sandwich Is, 1996–99; Ambassador: to Romania and to Moldova, 1999–2002; to Peru, 2003–06. Chairman: Anglo-Peruvian Soc., 2006–09; S Georgia Soc., 2006–09. *Recreations*: reading, travel, philanthropy, tennis. *Address*: 51 High Street, Sandwich, Kent CT13 9EG.

**RALSTON, Gen. Joseph W.,** DFC 1967; DSM 1990; Vice Chairman, The Cohen Group, since 2003; *b* 4 Nov. 1943; *m* 1989, Diana Dougherty; one *s* one *d*, and one step *s* one step *d*. *Educ*: Miami Univ. (BA Chemistry 1965); Central Michigan Univ. (MA Personnel Mgt 1976); John F. Kennedy Sch. of Govt, Harvard Univ. Commissioned USAF, Reserve Officer Trng Corps Program, 1965; F-105 Pilot, Laos and N Vietnam; US Army Comd and Gen. Staff Coll., 1976; Nat. War Coll., Washington, 1984; Asst Dep. COS (Ops), and Dep. COS (Requirements), HQ Tactical Air Comd, 1987–90; Dir, Tactical Progs, 1990–91, Opnl Requirements, 1991–92, HQ USAF; Comdr, Alaskan Comd, 11 Air Force, Alaskan N Amer. Aerospace Defense Comd Reg., and Jt Task Force Alaska, 1992–94; Dep. COS (Plans and Ops), HQ USAF, 1994–95; Comdr, Air Combat Comd, 1995–96; Vice Chm., Jt Chiefs of Staff, 1996–2000; SACEUR, NATO, and C-in-C, US European Comd, 2000–03. US Legion of Merit, DDSM, MSM, Air Medal, Air Force Commendation Medal. Highest degree, Mil. Order of Merit (Morocco), 1996; Officer, Legion of Honour (France), 1997; Kt Comdr's Cross, Order of Merit (Germany), 1999; Grand Cross, Royal Norwegian Order of Merit (Norway), 2000. *Recreations*: hunting, fishing, gardening. *Address*: The Cohen Group, 500 8th Street NW, Suite 200, Washington, DC 20004, USA.

**RALTON, Alexander Julius; His Honour Judge Ralton;** a Circuit Judge, since 2018; *b* London, 6 Nov. 1967; *s* of late Cyril Ralton and of Helen Penelope Ralton; *m* 1995, Kim Savage; one *s* one *d*. *Educ*: Harrow Sch.; Univ. of East Anglia (LLB Hons). Called to the Bar, Lincoln's Inn, 1990; Dep. Dist Judge, 2005–09; Dist Judge, 2009; Recorder, 2017–18. *Publications*: contribs to jls incl. Family Law Jl, Elder Law Jl. *Recreations*: competitive running (up to and beyond marathon distance), triathlon (Ironman 2016 and 2017), tennis, horse riding, hiking, films and gadgets especially sporting ones. *Address*: Chippenham, Wilts.

**RAMADAN, Prof. Tariq,** PhD; His Highness Sheikh Hamad Bin Khalifa Al-Thani Professor of Contemporary Islamic Studies, University of Oxford, since 2009; Fellow, St Antony's College, since 2009 (Visiting Fellow, 2005–06; Research Fellow, 2006–09); Executive Director, Centre for Islamic Legislation and Ethics, Qatar Faculty of Islamic Studies, since 2012; *b* Geneva, 26 Aug. 1962. *Educ*: Univ. of Geneva (MA Phil. and French Lit.; PhD Phil. and Islamic Studies). Dean, Collège de Saussure, Geneva, 1988–92; Prof. of Islamology, Fribourg Univ., 1997–2003; Prof. of Islamic Studies, Notre Dame Univ., 2004; Senior Research Fellow: Lokahi Foundn, 2005–; Doshisha Univ., Kyoto, 2007–18; Vis. Prof., Erasmus Univ., Rotterdam, 2007–09. European of the Year, European Voice/The Economist, 2006. *Publications*: To Be a European Muslim, 1999; Muslims in France: the way towards coexistence, 1999; Western Muslims and the Future of Islam, 2003; Islam, the West, and Challenges of Modernity, 2003; The Messenger: the meanings of the life of Muhammad, 2007; In the Footsteps of the Prophet: lessons from the life of Muhammad, 2007; Radical Reform: Islamic ethics and liberation, 2009; What I believe, 2009; The Quest for Meaning, 2010; The Arab Awakening: Islam and the new Middle East, 2012; Islam: the essentials, 2017. *Address*: St Antony's College, 62 Woodstock Road OX2 6JF. *T*: (01865) 284780.

**RAMADHANI, Rt Rev. John Acland;** Bishop of Zanzibar and Tanga, 1980–2000, Bishop of Zanzibar, 2000–02; *b* 1 Aug. 1932. *Educ*: Univ. of Birmingham (DipTh 1975); Univ. of Dar-es-Salaam (BA 1967); Queen's Coll., Birmingham. Deacon 1975, Birmingham; priest 1976, Dar-es-Salaam; Asst Chaplain, Queen's Coll., Birmingham, 1975–76; Warden, St Mark's Theol Coll., Dar-es-Salaam, 1976–80; Archbishop of Tanzania, 1984–98. *Address*: PO Box 5, Mkunazini, Zanzibar, Tanzania.

**RAMAGE, Dr James Cumming,** CPhys, FInstP; CEng, FREng; Chairman: Tesla Engineering Ltd, since 1995; Storrington Industries Ltd, since 2005; *b* Kilmarnock, 28 March 1951; *s* of James T. Ramage and Eva B. Ramage; *m* 1975, Jane C. Freer; two *d*. *Educ*: Univ. of Glasgow (BSc Maths and Natural Philosophy 1973); Balliol Coll., Oxford (DPhil Semiconductor Physics 1976). CPhys 1994; FInstP 1994; CEng 2010; FREng 2014. Lecturer in Physics: Balliol Coll., Oxford, 1976–77; Open Univ., 1977–80; Man. Dir, VG Gas Analysis Ltd, 1981–85; Chief Exec., VG Instruments Inc., 1985–88; Man. Dir, VG Scientific Ltd, 1988–90; Exec. Dir, VG Instruments plc, 1986–90; Divl Man. Dir (Inorganic Instrumentation), Fisons Instruments, 1990–94. Non-exec. Dir, Microsaic Systems plc, 2010–17. (Jtly) Katharine Burr Blodgett Gold Medal and Prize, Inst. of Physics, 2018. *Recreations*: family, gardening, dinghy sailing. *Address*: Tesla Engineering Ltd, Water Lane, Storrington, W Sussex RH20 3EA. *E*: ramage@tesla.co.uk.

**RAMAGE, Prof. Robert,** DSc; FRS 1992; CChem, FRSC; FRSE; Forbes Professor of Organic Chemistry, University of Edinburgh, 1984–2001; *b* 4 Oct. 1935; *s* of Robert Bain Ramage and Jessie Boag Ramage; *m* 1961, Joan Fraser Paterson; three *d*. *Educ*: Whitehill Sen. Secondary Sch., Glasgow; Univ. of Glasgow (BSc Hons 1958; PhD 1961; DSc 1982). Fulbright Fellow and Fellow of Harvard Coll., 1961–63; Research at Woodward Res. Inst., 1963–64; Lectr then Sen. Lectr, Univ. of Liverpool, 1964–77; Prof., 1977–84, Head of Dept, 1979–84, UMIST; Head, Dept of Chem., Univ. of Edinburgh, 1987–90, 1997–2000; Dir, Edinburgh Centre for Protein Technology, 1996–2000; Scientific Dir, 2002–07 and Vice Pres., 2004–07, Almac Scis (Scotland) Ltd (formerly Albachem Ltd, then CSS Albachem). FRSE 1986. Dr (*hc*) Lille. *Recreations:* sport, gardening, current affairs.

**RAMAKRISHNAN, Prof. Tiruppattur Venkatachalamurti,** FRS 2000; DST Year of Science Professor; DAE Homi Bhabha Professor, Department of Physics, Banaras Hindu University, 2003–08, now Emeritus; Distinguished Associate, Centre for Condensed Matter Theory, Department of Physics, Indian Institute of Science, Bangalore, since 2003; *b* 14 Aug. 1941; *s* of Tiruppattur Ramaseshayyar Venkatachala-Murti and Jayalakshmi Murti; *m* 1970, Meera Rao; one *s* one *d*. *Educ*: Banaras Hindu Univ., Varanasi (BSc 1959; MSc 1961); Columbia Univ., NY (PhD 1966). Lectr, 1966, Asst Prof., 1967, Indian Inst. of Technol., Kanpur; Asst Res. Physicist, UCSD, 1968–70; Asst Prof., 1970–77, Prof. of Physics, 1977–80, Indian Inst. of Technol., Kanpur; Prof. of Physics, 1981–84 and 1986–2003, INSA Srinivasa Ramanujan Res. Prof., 1997–2002, Indian Inst. of Sci., Bangalore; Prof. of Physics, Banaras Hindu Univ., 1984–86. Vis. Res. Physicist, 1978–81, Vis. Prof., 1990–91, Princeton Univ. Consultant, Bell Labs, 1979–81. Pres., Indian Acad. of Scis, 2004–06. Fellow: INSA, 1984; APS, 1984; Third World Acad. of Scis, 1990. Padma Sri, 2001. *Publications:* (jtly) Physics, 1988, 2nd edn 1994; (with C. N. R. Rao) Superconductivity Today, 1990, 2nd edn 1997; about 120 research papers and 6 review articles. *Recreation:* trekking. *Address:* Centre for Condensed Matter Theory, Department of Physics, Indian Institute of Science, Bangalore 560012, India. *T:* (80) 23600591, (94) 48363379.

**RAMAKRISHNAN, Sir Venkatraman,** Kt 2012; PhD; FRS 2003; Senior Scientist and Group Leader, Structural Studies Division, MRC Laboratory of Molecular Biology, Cambridge, since 1999; President, Royal Society, since 2015. *Educ:* Baroda Univ., India (BSc 1971); Ohio Univ. (PhD 1976); Univ. of Calif, San Diego. Postdoctoral Fellow, Dept of Chem., Yale Univ., 1978–82; Res. Staff, Oak Ridge Nat. Lab., 1982–83; Brookhaven National Laboratory: Asst Biophysicist, 1983–85; Associate Biophysicist, 1985–88; Biophysicist, 1988–94; Sen. Biophysicist, 1994–95; Prof., Biochem. Dept, Univ. of Utah, 1995–99. (Jtly) Nobel Prize in Chemistry, 2009. *Address:* Structural Studies Division, MRC Laboratory of Molecular Biology, Francis Crick Avenue, Cambridge CB2 0QH.

**RAMAPHOSA, (Matamela) Cyril;** President, African National Congress, since 2017 (Deputy President, 2012–17); President, Republic of South Africa, since 2018 (Deputy President, 2014–18); *b* 17 Nov. 1952; *s* of late Samuel Ramaphosa and of Erdmuth Ramaphosa; *m* 1996, Tshepo Motsepe; two *s* two *d*. *Educ:* Sekano-Ntoane High Sch., Soweto; Univ. of North, Turfloop (BProc 1981). Detained under Terrorism Act for 11 months, 1974, and 6 months, 1976; active in Black People's Convention, 1975; articled clerk, Attorney Henry Dolovitz, 1977; Legal Advr, Council of Unions of SA, 1981–82; First Gen. Sec., NUM, SA, 1982–91; arrested and detained under Riotous Assemblies Act, 1984; organised first legal one day strike by black mineworkers, 1984; African National Congress: Mem., Nat. Exec. Cttee, 1991–; Sec.-Gen., 1991–96; Leader, ANC Delegn to Multi-Party Negotiations, 1992–94; Chm., Constitutional Assembly, Govt of Nat. Unity, 1994–96. Exec. Dep. Chm., New Africa Investments Ltd, 1996–99; Chm. and Chief Exec., Molope Gp, 1999–2000; Chairman: Rebhold Services (Pty), 2000–03; Shanduka Gp, 2000–13; non-executive Chairman: MCI Gp, 2003; MTN Gp; Bidvest Gp Ltd; Standard Bank Ltd; former joint non-executive Chairman: Mondi plc; Mondi Ltd. Mem., Adv. Council, SAB Miller plc. Former Dep. Chm., Commonwealth Business Council. Vis. Prof. of Law, Stanford Univ., USA, 1991. Hon. Dr: Massachusetts, 1992; Univ. of the North, 2002; Hon. PhD Port Elizabeth, 1995; Hon. LLD: Natal, 1997; Cape Town, 1997; Lesotho, 2002. *Recreation:* fly-fishing. *Address:* (office) Union Buildings, Private Bag X1000, Pretoria, 0001, South Africa. *Club:* River (Johannesburg).

**RAMASAMY, Selvaraju;** QC 2018; a Recorder, since 2009; *b* Kendal, Cumbria, 22 Jan. 1970; *s* of Govindasamy Ramasamy and Jeanne Ramasamy; *m* 2019, Catherine Collins; one *s* one *d*. *Educ:* Sedbergh Sch.; Queen Mary and Westfield Coll., Univ. of London (LLB 1991); University Coll. London (LLM 1993). Called to the Bar, Inner Temple, 1992; in practice as a barrister, 1994–. Member: Bar Council, 1997–2000 (Mem., Race Relns Cttee, 1997–2000); Cttee, Criminal Bar Assoc., 1997–2000 and 2008–09; Prosecuting Panel for Disciplinary Hearings, Bar Standards Bd, 2009. *Recreations:* tennis, guitar. *Address:* QEB Hollis Whiteman, 1–2 Laurence Pountney Hill, EC4R 0EU. *T:* (020) 7933 8855, *Fax:* (020) 7929 3732. *E:* barristers@qebholliswhiteman.co.uk. *Club:* Queen's.

**RAMBAHADUR LIMBU, Captain,** VC 1966; MVO 1984; HM the Queen's Gurkha Orderly Officer, 1983–84; employed in Sultanate of Negara Brunei Darussalam, 1985–92; *b* Nov. 1939; *s* of late Tekbir Limbu; *m* 1st, 1960, Tikamaya Limbuni (*d* 1966); two *s*; 2nd, 1967, Punimaya Limbuni; three *s*. Army Cert. of Educn 1st cl. Enlisted 10th Princess Mary's Own Gurkha Rifles, 1957; served on ops in Borneo (VC); promoted Sergeant, 1971; WO II, 1976; commissioned, 1977. Hon. Captain (Gurkha Commnd Officer), 1985. *Publications:* My Life Story, 1978. *Recreations:* football, volleyball, badminton, basketball. *Address:* Ward No 13 Damak, Nagar Palika, PO Box Damak, District Jhapa, Mechi Zone, East Nepal. *Clubs:* VC and GC Association, Royal Society of St George (England).

**RAMCHANDANI, Prof. Paul Gulab,** DPhil; LEGO® Professor of Play in Education Development and Learning, University of Cambridge, since 2018; *b* Maidstone, 12 Jan. 1968; *s* of Gulab and Bridget Ramchandani. *Educ:* Marlwood Sch.; Univ. of Southampton (BM 1991); Univ. of Leeds (MMedSci 2001); London Sch. of Hygiene and Tropical Medicine, Univ. of London (MSc 2002); Univ. of Oxford (DPhil 2006). NHS doctor, 1991–; Res. Fellow, 2001–06, Sen. Res. Fellow, 2006–12, Univ. of Oxford; Reader, 2012–16, Prof. of Child and Adolescent Mental Health, 2016–17, Imperial College London; Consultant Child and Adolescent Psychiatrist, Central and NW London NHS Trust, 2012–17. *Recreations:* music, football, interpretive dance. *Address:* Faculty of Education, University of Cambridge, 184 Hills Road, Cambridge CB2 8PQ.

**RAMGOOLAM, Dr the Hon. Navinchandra,** GCSK 2008; FRCP; Member, National Assembly, Mauritius, 1991–2014; Prime Minister of Republic of Mauritius, 1995–2000 and 2005–14; *b* 14 July 1947; *s* of Rt Hon. Sir Seewoosagur Ramgoolam, GCMG, PC (First Prime Minister of Mauritius) and Lady Sushil Ramgoolam; *m* 1979, Veena Brizmohun. *Educ:* Royal Coll. of Surgeons, Dublin; London Sch. of Econs (LLB Hons 1990; Hon. Fellow, 1998); Inns of Court Sch. of Law. LRCP, LRCSI 1975; FRCP 2009. Called to the Bar, Inner Temple, 1993, Overseas Bencher, 2011. Mauritius Labour Party: Leader, 1991–; Pres., 1991–92. Leader of the Opposition, 1991–95 and 2000–05. Hon. Freeman, Rodrigues, 2007. *Dr hc:* Mauritius, 1998; Aligarh Muslim, India, 1998; Jawaharlal Nehru, India, 2005; Hon. DSc Padmashree Dr D. Y. Patil Univ., India, 2009; Hon. Dr Staffordshire, 2010; Hon. DLaws, Kurukshetra Univ., Haryana, India, 2012. Wilberforce Medal, Wilberforce Lect. Trust, 2007; Rajiv Gandhi Award, India, 2007; Pravasi Bharatiya Samman Award, India, 2008; Prix Louise Michel, CEPS, Paris, 2008; Order of Rule of Law, World Jurist Assoc., USA, 2011. Grand Officier, Légion d'Honneur (France), 2006. *Recreation:* reading.

**RAMIN, Ileana, (Mme Manfred Ramin);** see Cotrubas, I.

**RAMMELL, William Ernest;** Vice-Chancellor and Chief Executive, University of Bedfordshire, since 2012; *b* 10 Oct. 1959; *s* of William Ernest Rammell and Joan Elizabeth Rammell; *m* 1983, Beryl Jarhall; one *s* one *d*. *Educ:* University Coll., Cardiff (BA French). Pres., Cardiff Students' Union, 1982–83; mgt trainee, BR, 1983–84; NUS Regl Official, 1984–87; Hd of Youth Services, Basildon Council, 1987–89; General Manager: Students' Union, KCL, 1989–94; Univ. of London Union, 1994–97. MP (Lab) Harlow, 1997–2010; contested (Lab) same seat, 2010. PPS to Sec. of State for Culture, Media and Sport, 2001–02; Parly Under-Sec. of State, FCO, 2002–05; Minister of State: (Minister for Univs), DfES, 2005–07; DIUS, 2007–08; FCO, 2008–09; (Minister for Armed Forces), MoD, 2009–10. Dep. Vice-Chancellor, Univ. of Plymouth, 2011–12. Chm., Lab Movt for Europe. *Recreations:* football, cricket, socialising. *Address:* 9 Orchard Croft, Harlow, Essex CM20 3BA. *T:* (01279) 439706.

**RAMOS, Gen. Fidel Valdez;** Founder and Chairman, Ramos Peace and Development Foundation; President of the Philippines, 1992–98; *b* 18 March 1928; *s* of Narciso Ramos and Angela (*née* Valdez); *m* Amelita Martinez; five *d*. *Educ:* Nat. Univ. of Manila; USMA W Point; Univ. of Illinois. Active service in Korea and Vietnam; Dep. Chief of Staff, 1981, Chief of Staff, 1986, Philippines Armed Forces; Sec. of Nat. Defence, 1988. Leader, People's Power Party. Chm. Council of Advrs, Boao Forum for Asia, 2010–. Légion d'Honneur (France), 1987. *Address:* Ramos Peace and Development Foundation, 26th Floor, Export Bank Plaza, Corner Senator Gil Puyat and Chino Roces Avenues, 1200 Makati City, Philippines; 120 Maria Cristina Street, Ayala Alabang Village, Muntinlupa City, Philippines.

**RAMOS-HORTA, José;** President of Timor-Leste, 2007–12; *b* Dili, E Timor, 26 Dec. 1949; *s* of late Francisco Horta and of Natalina Ramos Filipe Horta; *m* 1978, Ana Pessoa (marr. diss.); one *s*. *Educ:* Hague Acad. of Internat. Law; Internat. Inst. of Human Rights, Strasbourg; Columbia Univ., NY; Antioch Univ. (MA 1984). Journalist, radio and TV correspondent, 1969–74; Minister for Ext. Affairs and Inf., E Timor, Dec. 1975; Perm. Rep. for Fretilin to UN, NY, 1976–89; Public Affairs and Media Dir, Embassy of Mozambique, Washington, 1987–88; Special Rep. of Nat. Council of Maubere Resistance, 1991; Foreign Minister, 2002–06, Prime Minister, 2006–07, E Timor; Special Rep. and Hd, UN Integrated Peacebuilding Office in Guinea-Bissau, 2013–14; Chm., UN High-Level Ind. Panel on Peace Operations, 2014–15. Founder Dir and Lectr, Diplomacy Trng Prog., 1990, and Vis. Prof., 1996, Law Faculty, Univ. of NSW. Member: Peace Action Council, Unrepresented Nations and Peoples Orgn, The Hague (UNPO Award, 1996); Exec. Council, Internat. Service for Human Rights, Geneva; Bd, E Timor Human Rights Centre, Melbourne. Sen. Associate Mem., St Antony's Coll., Oxford, 1987. Nobel Peace Prize (jtly), 1996. Order of Freedom (Portugal), 1996. *Publications:* Funu: the unfinished saga of East Timor, 1987; contrib. to newspapers and periodicals in Portugal, France, USA and Australia. *Recreation:* tennis.

**RAMOTAR, Donald;** President, Republic of Guyana, 2011–15; General Secretary, People's Progressive Party, Guyana, 1997–2013; *b* Caria-Caria, Essequibo River, 22 Oct. 1950; *s* of Sam Ramotar and Olive Constantine; *m* 1974, Deolatchmee; two *s* one *d*. *Educ:* Univ. of Guyana (Econs degree); Technical Inst. (electronics). Worked as a journalist. People's Progressive Party: joined, 1967; party representative in Czechoslovakia, 1983–88; represented the party and Progressive Youth Orgn at many internat. fora. *Publications:* contrib. to People's Progressive Party Mirror newspaper and Thunder mag. *Recreations:* reading, long walks. *E:* donald.ramotar@gmail.com.

**RAMPEN, Prof. William Hugh Salvin, (Win),** PhD; FREng; CEng; FIMechE; FRSE; Professor of Energy Storage, University of Edinburgh, since 2014; Founder, 1994, and Founder Director, Artemis Intelligent Power Ltd, since 2014 (Managing Director, 1994–2013); *b* Oakville, Ont, 1956; *s* of Leonardus Rampen and Sybil Rampen (*née* Calverley); *m* 1988, Dr Rosemary Dixon; one *s* two *d*. *Educ:* Ryerson Univ., Toronto (BTech 1977); Univ. of New Brunswick (MScE 1986); Univ. of Edinburgh (PhD 1993). CEng 2011; FIMechE 2011; FREng 2012. Res. Associate, Univ. of Edinburgh, 1978–81; Lectr, Ryerson Univ., 1981–86; Res. Fellow, Univ. of Edinburgh, 1987–93. FRSA; FRSE 2017. *Publications:* many papers and patents in subject area of Digital Displacement® Hydraulics. *Recreations:* hill running, old machinery, farming. *Address:* Artemis Intelligent Power Ltd, Unit 3, Edgefield Industrial Estate, Loanhead, Midlothian EH20 9TB. *T:* (0131) 440 6262. *E:* w.rampen@artemisip.com.

**RAMPHAL, Sir Shridath Surendranath,** OE 1983; GCMG 1990 (CMG 1966); OM (Jamaica) 1990; OCC 1991; Kt 1970; QC (Guyana) 1965, SC 1966; Secretary-General of the Commonwealth, 1975–90; *b* 3 Oct. 1928; *s* of James and Grace Ramphal; *m* 1951, Lois Winifred King; two *s* two *d*. *Educ:* King's Coll., London (LLM 1952; FKC 1975). Called to the Bar, Gray's Inn, 1951 (Hon. Bencher 1981). Colonial Legal Probationer, 1951; Arden and Atkin Prize, 1952; John Simon Guggenheim Fellow, Harvard Law Sch., 1962. Crown Counsel, British Guiana, 1953–54; Asst to Attorney-Gen., 1954–56; Legal Draftsman, 1956–58; First Legal Draftsman, West Indies, 1958–59; Solicitor-Gen., British Guiana, 1959–61; Asst Attorney-Gen., West Indies, 1961–62, Attorney-Gen., Guyana, 1965–73; Minister of State for External Affairs, Guyana, 1967–72; Foreign Minister and Attorney General, Guyana, 1972–73; Minister, Foreign Affairs and Justice, 1973–75; Mem., Nat. Assembly, Guyana, 1965–75. Member: Ind. (Brandt) Commn on Internat. Devlot Issues, 1977–83; Ind. (Palme) Commn on Disarmament and Security Issues, 1980–89; Ind. Commn on Internat. Humanitarian Issues, 1983–88; World (Brundtland) Commn on Environment and Devlot, 1984–87; South Commn, 1987–90; Carnegie Commn on Preventing Deadly Conflict, 1994–98; Chm., W Indian Commn, 1990–92; Co-Chm., Commn on Global Governance, 1992–2000. Special Advr, Sec. Gen., UN Conf. on Envmt and Devlot, 1992; Chm., UN Cttee on Devlot Planning, 1984–87; Chief Negotiator on Ext. Economic Relations in Caribbean Reg., 1997–2001; Facilitator, Belize-Guatemala Dispute, 2002–02; Counsel, Guyana-Suriname UN Convention on the Law of the Sea Arbitration, 2004–07. Chairman: Internat. Adv. Cttee, Future Generations Alliance Foundn, Kyoto, 1994–97; Bd, Internat. Inst. for Democracy and Electoral Assistance, Stockholm, 1995–2001; Pres., Internat. Steering Cttee, Leadership in Envmt and Devlot, 1991–98; Member: Bd, Internat. Devlot Res. Centre, Ottawa, 1994–98; Council, Internat. Negotiating Network, Carter Centre, Atlanta, 1991–97. Mem., Internat. Commn of Jurists, 1970–. Chancellor: Univ. of Guyana, 1988–92; Univ. of Warwick, 1989–2002; Univ. of WI, 1989–2003. Visiting Professor: Exeter Univ., 1988; Faculty of Laws, KCL, 1988. Toronto Univ., 1995; Osgoode Hall Law Sch., Univ. of York, Toronto, 1995. FRSA 1981; CCMI (CBIM 1986). Fellow, LSE, 1979; Hon. Fellow, Magdalen Coll., Oxford, 1982; Companion, Leicester Poly., 1991. Hon. LLD: Panjab, 1975; Southampton, 1976; St Francis Xavier, NS, 1978; Univ. of WI, 1978; Aberdeen, 1979; Cape Coast, Ghana, 1980; London, 1981; Benin, Nigeria, 1982; Hull, 1983; Yale, 1985; Cambridge, 1985; Warwick, 1988; York, Ont, 1988; Malta, 1989; Otago, 1990; DUniv: Surrey, 1979; Essex, 1980;

Hon. DHL: Simmons Coll., Boston, 1982; Duke Univ., 1985; Hon. DCL: Oxon, 1982; E Anglia, 1983; Durham, 1985; Hon. DLitt: Bradford, 1985; Indira Gandhi Nat. Open Univ., New Delhi, 1989; Hon. DSc Cranfield Inst. of Technology, 1987. Albert Medal, RSA, 1988; Internat. Educn Award, Richmond Coll., 1988; Rene Dubos Human Envmt Award, 1993. AC 1982; ONZ 1990; Comdr, Order of Golden Ark (Netherlands), 1994. *Publications:* One World to Share: selected speeches of the Commonwealth Secretary-General 1975–79, 1979; Nkrumah and the Eighties: Kwame Nkrumah Memorial Lectures, 1980; Sovereignty and Solidarity: Callander Memorial Lectures, 1981; Some in Light and Some in Darkness: the long shadow of slavery (Wilberforce Lecture), 1983; The Message not the Messenger (STC Communication Lecture), 1985; The Trampling of the Grass (Economic Commn for Africa Silver Jubilee Lecture), 1985; Inseparable Humanity: an anthology of reflections of Shridath Ramphal (ed Ron Sanders), 1988; An End to Otherness (eight speeches by the Commonwealth Secretary-General), 1990; Our Country, The Planet, 1992; Glimpses of a Global Life (memoirs), 2014; contrib. various political, legal and other jls incl. International and Comparative Law Qly, Caribbean Qly, Public Law, Guyana Jl, Round Table, Foreign Policy, Third World Qly, RSA Jl Internat. Affairs. *Address:* The Garden House, Pleasant Hall Drive, Dayrells Road, Christchurch BB14030, Barbados, West Indies. *T:* 435 7531. *Clubs:* Athenæum, Royal Automobile, Travellers.

**RAMPHUL, Sir Indurduth,** Kt 1991; Governor, Bank of Mauritius, 1982–96; *b* 10 Oct. 1931; *m* 1962, Taramatee Seedoyal; one *s* one *d*. *Educ:* Univ. of Exeter (Dip. Public Admin). Asst Sec., Min. of Finance, 1966–67; Bank of Mauritius: Manager, 1967; Chief Manager, 1970; Man. Dir, 1973. Alternate Governor, IMF for Mauritius, 1982–96. *Recreations:* reading, swimming. *Address:* 9 Buswell Avenue, Quatre Bornes, Mauritius. *T:* 4541643, *Fax:* 4540559. *E:* sir.indur@intnet.mu. *Clubs:* Mauritius Turf; Cadets.

**RAMPLING, Christopher Maxwell,** MBE 2005; HM Diplomatic Service; Ambassador to Lebanon, since 2018; *b* London, 8 Oct. 1973; *s* of Michael Rampling and Deirdre Rampling; *m* 2008, Lies Lauwers; one *s* one *d*. *Educ:* Durham Univ. (BA Hons). Joined FCO, 1999; Political and Press Officer, Tripoli, 2002–05; Team Leader, Turkey Team, 2005–07, Dep. Hd, Counter Proliferation Dept, 2007–09, FCO; Dep. Hd of Mission, Amman, 2009–13; Hd, Corporate Services Prog., FCO, 2013–14; UK Dep. Ambassador to EU's Political and Security Cttee, 2014–18. *Recreations:* football (Brentford FC), cricket, hiking, running, music, family. *Address:* c/o Foreign and Commonwealth Office, King Charles Street, SW1A 2AH. *E:* chris.rampling@fco.gov.uk. *Club:* MCC.

**RAMROOP, Andrew Madan,** OBE 2009; Director, Maurice Sedwell Ltd, since 1988; *b* Tunapuna, Trinidad, 10 Nov. 1952; *s* of John Shunnin Ramroop and Baby Ramroop; *m* 2018, Daniela Fierro; one *s* one *d*. *Educ:* London Coll. of Fashion. Apprentice tailor, 1966–70; Huntsman, Savile Row, 1970–72; Maurice Sedwell Ltd, 1974–. Principal, Savile Row Acad., 2007–. Mem., Nat. Adv. Bd, W. E. B. Du Bois Inst., Harvard Univ., 2002–. Hon. Prof., Distinction in Field of Tailoring, London Inst., 2001; Vis. Prof., Univ. of the Arts, London. Chaconia Gold Medal (Trinidad and Tobago), 2005. *Recreations:* cricket, badminton. *Address:* Maurice Sedwell Ltd, 19 Savile Row, W1S 3PP. *T:* (020) 7734 0824. *E:* andrew@mauricesedwell.com.

**RAMSAY,** family name of **Earl of Dalhousie**.

**RAMSAY, Lord; Simon David Ramsay;** Captain, 1st Battalion, Scots Guards; *b* 18 April 1981; *s* and *heir* of Earl of Dalhousie, *qv*; *m* 2016, Kaitlin Marie, *d* of John J. Kubinsky, Sr, of Charlotte, NC; one *s*. *Educ:* Harrow. *Recreations:* history of art, sculpture, country sports. *Heir: s* Hon. William Fox Ramsay, *b* 25 Aug. 2017. *Address:* Brechin Castle, Brechin, Angus DD9 6SG.

**RAMSAY OF CARTVALE,** Baroness *cr* 1996 (Life Peer), of Langside in the City of Glasgow; **Meta Ramsay;** international affairs consultant; a Deputy Speaker, House of Lords, 2002–06; *b* 12 July 1936; *d* of Alexander Ramsay and Sheila Ramsay (*née* Jackson). *Educ:* Hutchesons' Girls' Grammar Sch.; Univ. of Glasgow (MA, MEd); Graduate Inst. of Internat. Studies, Geneva. President: Students' Rep. Council, Univ. of Glasgow, 1958–59; Scottish Union of Students, 1959–60; Associate Sec. for Europe, Co-ordinating Secretariat, Nat. Unions of Students, Leiden, Netherlands, 1960–63; Manager, Fund for Internat. Student Co-operation, 1963–67; HM Diplomatic Service, 1969–91: Stockholm, 1970–73; Helsinki, 1981–85; Counsellor, FCO, 1987–91. Foreign Policy Advr to Leader of Opposition, 1992–94; Special Advr to Shadow Sec. of State for Trade and Industry, 1994–95; a Baroness in Waiting (Govt Whip), 1997–2001. Member: Intelligence and Security Cttee, 1997, 2005–07; Jt Cttee on Nat. Security Strategy, 2010–14. Mem., Labour Finance and Industry Gp, 1997–. Mem., UK Parly delegn to NATO Parly Assembly, 2003–. Chm., Atlantic Council of the UK, 2001–10. Co-Chair, Scottish Constitutional Convention, 1997–99; Chm., Scotland in Europe, 2004–. Hon. Vis. Res. Fellow in Peace Studies, Univ. of Bradford, 1996. Mem., Lewisham CHC, 1992–94. Chm., Bd of Governors, Fairlawn Primary Sch., Lewisham, 1991–97. Member: RIIA; Inst. of Jewish Policy Res.; Fabian Soc.; Labour Movement in Europe; Co-operative Party. FRSA 1995. Hon. DLitt Bradford, 1997; DUniv: Glasgow, 2004; Stirling, 2009. *Recreations:* theatre, opera, ballet. *Address:* House of Lords, SW1A 0PW. *T:* (020) 7219 5353. *Clubs:* Reform, University Women's.

**RAMSAY, Sir Alexander William Burnett,** 7th Bt *cr* 1806, of Balmain (also *heir-pres*. to Btcy of Burnett, *cr* 1626 (Nova Scotia), of Leys, Kincardineshire, which became dormant, 1959, on death of Sir Alexander Edwin Burnett of Leys, and was not claimed by Sir Alexander Burnett Ramsay, 6th Bt, of Balmain); *b* 4 Aug. 1938; *s* of Sir Alexander Burnett Ramsay, 6th Bt and Isabel Ellice, *e d* of late William Whitney, Woodstock, New South Wales; *S* father, 1965; *m* 1963, Neryl Eileen, *d* of J. C. Smith Thornton, Trangie, NSW; three *s*. *Heir: s* Alexander David Ramsay [*b* 20 Aug. 1966; *m* 1990, Annette Yvonne, *d* of H. M. Plummer; three *d*]. *Address:* Bulbah, Warren, NSW 2824, Australia.

**RAMSAY, Sir Allan (John Heppel Ramsay),** KBE 1992; CMG 1989; HM Diplomatic Service, retired; Ambassador to the Kingdom of Morocco, 1992–96; *b* 19 Oct. 1937; *s* of Norman Ramsay Ramsay and Evelyn Faith Sorel-Cameron; *m* 1966, Pauline Thérèse Lescher; two *s* one *d*. *Educ:* Bedford Sch.; RMA Sandhurst; Durham Univ. Served Army, 1957–70: Somerset Light Infantry, 1957–64; Trucial Oman Scouts, 1964–66; DLI, 1966–68. MECAS, 1968–69; entered FCO, 1970; First Sec. (Commercial), Cairo, 1973–76; First Sec. and Hd of Chancery, Kabul, 1976–78; Counsellor and Head of Chancery: Baghdad, 1980–83; Mexico City, 1983–85; Ambassador: to Lebanon, 1988–90; to Sudan, 1990–91. *Address:* Le Genest, 53190 Landivy, France.

**RAMSAY, Andrew Charles Bruce,** CB 2007; Director General, Partnerships and Programmes, Department for Culture, Media and Sport, 2008–11; *b* 30 May 1951; *s* of Norman Bruce Ramsay and Marysha Octavia Ramsay; *m* 1983, Katharine Celia Marsh; two *d*. *Educ:* Winchester Coll.; Bedford Coll., London Univ. (BA). Joined DoE, 1974; Private Sec. to Parly Sec., Dept of Transport, 1978–80; Principal, DoE and Dept of Transport, 1980–85; Asst Sec., DoE, 1986–93; Under Sec. and Head of Arts, Sport and Lottery Gp, DNH, 1993–96; Under Sec. and Hd of Finance, Personnel and Lottery, then Corporate Services, Gp, DNH then DCMS, 1996–2000; Dir Gen., Creative Industries, Broadcasting, Gambling and Lottery Gp, 2000–04, Econ. Impact, 2004–06, Culture, Creativity and Economy, 2006–08, DCMS. *Recreations:* gardening, opera, birds, moths. *Address:* West Hall, Sedgeford, Hunstanton, Norfolk PE36 5NX.

**RAMSAY, Andrew Vernon,** CEng, FIET; FCIS; Chief Executive Officer (formerly Executive Director), Engineering Council, 2002–10 (Acting Director, 2001–02); *b* 7 July 1948; *s* of Douglas Charles Ramsay and Dorothy Isobel Ramsay (*née* Shankland); *m* 1971, Ruth Irene Mullen; one *s* one *d*. *Educ:* Churchill Coll., Cambridge (MA). CEng 1979; FIET (FIEE 2000). Student apprentice, AEI, 1966–70; Project Engr, GEC, 1970–72; various posts, CEGB, 1973–79; Dep. Sec., 1979–84, Sec. and CEO, 1985–97, CIBSE; Dir for Engrs Regulation, Engrg Council, 1997–2001; Construction Industry Council: Sec., 1988–90; Mem., 1990–97. Member, Board: QAA, 2006–10; Mathematics in Educn and Industry, 2011–; Chm., Adv. Cttee on Degree Awarding Powers, 2015–. Gov., Univ. for the Creative Arts, 2011–. FCIS 1982. *Recreations:* cycling, S London Swimming Club.

**RAMSAY, Douglas John;** Parliamentary Counsel, 2004–11; *b* 29 Nov. 1959; *s* of Douglas Ramsay and Susan McFadyen Ramsay; *m* 1999, Gillian Platt; one *s* one *d*. *Educ:* Northgate Grammar Sch., Ipswich; Univ. of Leeds (LLB 1981); Chester Coll. of Law. Articled clerk, then solicitor, Tittmuss, Sainer & Webb, 1982–87; Office of the Parliamentary Counsel: Asst Parly Counsel, 1987–91; Sen. Asst Parly Counsel, 1991–94; Principal Asst Parly Counsel, 1994–98; Dep. Parly Counsel, 1998–2004, seconded: to Law Commn, 1999–2002; to Tax Law Rewrite, 2006–09. *Recreations:* Rugby, football, my family. *Address:* c/o Office of the Parliamentary Counsel, 1 Horse Guards Road, SW1A 2HQ.

**RAMSAY, Gordon James,** OBE 2006; chef, restaurateur and television personality; *b* 8 Nov. 1966; *s* of late Gordon Scott Ramsay and Helen Ramsay (*née* Mitchell); *m* 1996, Cayetana Elizabeth Hutcheson; two *s* three *d* (of whom one *s* one *d* are twins). *Educ:* Stratford-upon-Avon High Sch.; North Oxon Tech. Coll., Banbury (HND Hotel Mgt 1987). Professional footballer, Glasgow Rangers FC, 1982–85; worked: with Marco Pierre White at Harvey's, 1989–91; with Albert Roux at La Gavroche, 1992–93; in Paris kitchens of Guy Savoy and Joël Robuchon, 1993–94; chef/proprietor: Aubergine restaurant, 1994–98 (Michelin Star, 1995, 1997); Gordon Ramsay Restaurant, Royal Hospital Road, Chelsea, 1998– (Michelin Star, 2001); Pétrus, Mayfair, 1999–2003, at The Berkeley, 2003–08 (Michelin Star, 2000); Amaryllis, Glasgow, 2001–04 (Michelin Star, 2002); Gordon Ramsay at Claridge's, 2001–13 (Michelin Star, 2003); Gordon Ramsay at The Connaught, 2002–07 (Michelin Star, 2003); The Savoy Grill, 2003–07 (Michelin Star, 2004), 2010–; Boxwood at The Berkeley, 2003–10; Maze, Grosvenor Square, 2005–; Gordon Ramsay at The London, NY, 2006–09; Gordon Ramsay at The Trianon Palace Hotel, Versailles, 2008– (2 Michelin Stars, 2009); York & Albany, 2008–; Foxtrot Oscar, 2008–; Maze Grill, 2008–; Bread Street Kitchen, One New Change, 2011–; GR Steak, Las Vegas, 2012–; Opal by Gordon Ramsay, Doha, 2012–; Gordon Ramsay Doha, 2012–; Fat Cow, LA, 2012–; Gordon Ramsay Pub & Grill, Las Vegas, 2012–; Gordon Ramsay BurGR, Las Vegas, 2012–; Union Street Café, 2013–; Bread Street Kitchen & Bar, Hong Kong, 2014–; Heddon Street Kitchen, 2014–; Pressoir d'Argent, Bordeaux, 2015– (2 Michelin Stars, 2017); Gordon Ramsay Fish & Chips, Las Vegas, 2015–; Lucky Cat, London, 2019–. Television series include: Hell's Kitchen, 2004; Ramsay's Kitchen Nightmares, 2004– (BAFTA Award, 2005); The F Word, 2005–; Ramsay's Kitchen Nightmares USA, 2007–; Cookalong Live, 2008; Gordon's Great Escape, 2010–; Ramsay's Best Restaurant, 2010; Christmas with Gordon, 2010; Gordon's Christmas Cookalong Live, 2011, 2012; Hotel Hell, USA, 2012, 2014; Gordon Behind Bars, 2012; Gordon Ramsay's Ultimate Cookery Course, 2012; Ramsay's Hotel Hell, 2013, 2016; Ramsay's Costa del Nightmares, 2014; Gordon Ramsay on Cocaine, 2017; Gordon, Gino and Fred's Road Trip, 2018; Gordon Ramsay: Uncharted, 2019. *Publications:* Passion for Flavour, 1996; Passion for Seafood, 1999; A Chef for All Seasons, 2000; Just Desserts, 2001; Gordon Ramsay's Secrets, 2003; Gordon Ramsay's Kitchen Heaven, 2004; Gordon Ramsay Makes it Easy, 2005; Gordon Ramsay's Sunday Dinners, 2006; The F Word, 2006; Humble Pie (autobiog.), 2006; Gordon Ramsay's Fast Food, 2007; Cooking for Friends, 2008; Gordon Ramsay's Healthy Appetite, 2008; Gordon Ramsay's Great British Pub Food, 2009; Gordon Ramsay's World Kitchen: recipes from The F Word, 2009; Gordon Ramsay's Great Escape: 100 of my favourite Indian recipes, 2010; Ramsay's Best Menus, 2010; Christmas with Gordon, 2010; Gordon's Great Escape: Southeast Asia, 2011; Gordon Ramsay's Ultimate Cookery Course, 2012; Bread Street Kitchen, 2016. *Recreations:* salmon fishing, scuba diving, long distance running. *Address:* Gordon Ramsay Group, 539–547 Wandsworth Road, SW8 3JD. *T:* (020) 7592 1370.

**RAMSAY, Prof. John Graham,** CBE 1992; FRS 1973; Professor of Geology, Eidgenössische Technische Hochschule and University of Zürich, 1977–92, now Professor Emeritus; *b* 17 June 1931; *s* of Robert William Ramsay and Kathleen May Ramsay; *m* 1st, 1952, Sylvia Hiorns (marr. diss. 1957); 2nd, 1960, Christine Marden (marr. diss. 1987); three *d* (and one *d* decd); 3rd, 1990, Dorothee Dietrich. *Educ:* Edmonton County Grammar Sch.; Imperial Coll., London. DSc, PhD, DIC, BSc, ARCS, FGS. Musician, Corps of Royal Engineers, 1955–57; academic staff Imperial Coll., London, 1957–73: Prof. of Geology, 1966–73; Prof. of Earth Sciences, Leeds Univ., 1973–76. Mem., NERC, 1989–92. Vice-Pres., Société Géologique de France, 1973. Hon. Prof. of Earth Sci., Univ. of Cardiff, 2002; Hon. Prof. of Geology, Ben-Gurion Univ., 2008. For. Associate, US Nat. Acad. of Scis, 1985. Dr hc Rennes, 1978. *Publications:* Folding and Fracturing of Rocks, 1967; The Techniques of Modern Structural Geology, vol. 1, 1983, vol. 2, 1987, vol. 3, 2000. *Recreations:* music composition, chamber music, ski-ing, writing poetry. *Address:* Cratoule, Issirac, 30760 St Julien de Peyrolas, France.

**RAMSAY, Jonathan William Alexander,** FRCS; Consultant Urologist, Charing Cross Hospital, since 1988; West Middlesex Hospital, since 1988; *b* 27 Oct. 1953; *s* of late Raymond Ramsay, MBE, FRCS and Lillian Jane Ramsay, MBE (*née* Bateman); *m* 1983, Priscilla Jaqueline Russell Webster; two *s* one *d*. *Educ:* Bradfield Coll.; St Bartholomew's Hosp. Med. Coll. (MB BS, MS). FRCS 1981. Qualified, St Bartholomew's Hosp. (Brackenbury Schol.), 1977; Chief Asst (Urology), St Bartholomew's, 1985–88; Hon. Consultant Urologist, St Luke's Hosp. for Clergy, 1989–. Examr, Intercollegiate Speciality Bd in Urology, 2008–. Mem., Clinical Senate, NHS London, 2012–. Royal College of Surgeons: Regl Specialty Advr, 1995–2000; Mem., Court of Examrs, 1997–2005; Regl Advr, 1999–2006; Dir, Professional Affairs, 2010–. Sec., Sect. Urology, RSocMed, 2006. President: W London Medico-Chirurgical Soc., 1999; Eur. Intrarenal Surgery Soc., 1999–. Fellow, Eur. Bd of Urology, 1991. *Publications:* contribs on treatment of stones by minimally invasive means and investigations of male fertility. *Recreations:* fishing, sailing. *Address:* Dovoswood, Maidensgrove, Henley-on-Thames, Oxon RG9 6HN; 18 Devonshire Street, W1G 7AF. *Club:* Flyfishers'.

**RAMSAY, Nicholas Harvey;** Member (C) Monmouth, National Assembly for Wales, since 2007; *b* 10 June 1975; *s* of Graham George Ramsay and Carole Ann Mann, and step *s* of Andrew John Mann. *Educ:* Univ. of Durham (BA Jt Hons English and Philosophy); Cardiff Univ. (Postgrad. Dip. Applied Linguistics). Driving instructor, 2000–01; press officer/researcher, Nat. Assembly for Wales, 2001–07. Mem. (C) Monmouthshire CC, 2004–08. Mem., Lions Club Internat. *Recreations:* tennis, reading, keen pub quizzer. *Address:* National Assembly for Wales, Cardiff Bay, Cardiff CF99 1NA. *T:* 0300 200 7211. *E:* Nicholas.Ramsay@assembly.wales.

**RAMSAY, Patrick George Alexander;** Controller, BBC Scotland, 1979–83; retired; *b* 14 April 1926; *yr s* of late Rt Rev. Ronald Erskine Ramsay, sometime Bishop of Malmesbury, and Winifred Constance Ramsay (*née* Partridge); *m* 1948, Hope Seymour Dorothy, *y d* of late Rt Rev. Algernon Markham, sometime Bishop of Grantham, and Winifred Edith Markham (*née* Barne) (*d* 2013); two *s. Educ:* Marlborough Coll.; Jesus Coll., Cambridge (MA). Served War, Royal Navy (Fleet Air Arm), 1944–46. Joined BBC as Report Writer, Eastern European Desk, Monitoring Service, 1949; Liaison Officer, US Foreign Broadcasts Information Service, Cyprus, 1951–52; Asst, Appts Dept, 1953–56; Sen. Admin. Asst, External Broadcasting, 1956–58; Admin. Officer News and Head of News Administration, 1958–64; Planning Manager, Television Programme Planning, 1964–66; Asst Controller: Programme Services, 1966–69; Programme Planning, 1969–72; Controller, Programme Services, 1972–79. General Managerial Advr, Oman Broadcasting Service, 1984–85. A Dir, Windsor Festival Soc., 1973–76. Councillor and Alderman, Royal Borough of New Windsor, 1962–67; Chm., Windsor and Eton Soc., 1971–76. Chm., Windsor Liberal Assoc., 1961–66. *Recreations:* fellwalking, gardening, foreign travel, history, looking in junk shops, thwarting bureaucrats. *Address:* Hafod House, Broad Street, Presteigne, Powys LD8 2AD.

**RAMSAY, Richard Alexander McGregor;** Director, The Shareholder Executive, 2007–11; *b* 27 Dec. 1949; *s* of Alexander John McGregor Ramsay and Beatrice Kent La Nauze; *m* 1975, Elizabeth Catherine Margaret Blackwood; one *s* one *d. Educ:* Dalhousie Sch.; Trinity Coll., Glenalmond; Aberdeen Univ. (MA Hons in Politics and Sociology). ACA 1975; FCA. Price Waterhouse & Co., 1972–75; Grindlay Brandts, 1976–78; Hill Samuel & Co. Ltd, 1979–87 (Dir, 1984–87); on secondment as Dir, Industrial Develt Unit, DTI, 1984–86; Dir, 1988–91, Man. Dir, Corporate Finance Div., 1991–93, Barclays De Zoete Wedd; Director: Ivory & Sime, 1993–94; Ivory & Sime Investment Mgt, 1994–96; Finance Dir, Aberdeen FC, 1997–2000; Man. Dir for Regulation and Financial Affairs, Ofgem, 2001–03; Dir, Intelli Corporate Finance Ltd, 2003–09 (Vice Chm., 2003–05). Non-executive Director: Artemis AiM VCT plc, 2001–09 (Chm., 2001–03); Xploite plc, 2007–09; Castleton Tech. (formerly Redstone) plc, 2010–14 (Chm., 2011–13); Castle Trust plc, 2011– (Chm., 2015–17); Seneca Global Income and Growth (formerly Midas Income and Growth) Trust, 2013– (Chm., 2014–); John Laing Envmtl Assets Gp Ltd, 2014–; URICA Ltd, 2012– (Chm., 2012–15); Chairman: Wolsey Group Ltd, 2008–; Northcourt Ltd, 2011–; Redcentric plc, 2013–14. Consultant, Armstrong Bonham Carter, 2007–17. *Recreations:* hill walking, ski-ing, classic cars, gardening. *Address:* The Little Priory, Sandy Lane, South Nutfield, Surrey RH1 4EJ. *T:* (01737) 822329.

**RAMSAY, Robert,** CMG 2000; DPhil; Director General for Research, European Parliament, 1989–99; *b* 11 Sept. 1940; *s* of Robert and Mabel Hamilton Ramsay; *m* 1963, Patricia Buckley (*d* 2009); four *s* (and one *s* decd). *Educ:* Royal Belfast Academical Instn; Queen's Univ., Belfast (BA Hons); Univ. of Ulster (DPhil 1979). Commonwealth Fellow, Victoria Univ. of Wellington, 1963–65; entered NICS, 1965; Principal Private Sec. to Prime Minister, 1971–72; European Dir, Inward Investment, Brussels, 1972–74; Sec. to Economic Council, 1974–76; Principal Private Sec. to Sec. of State for NI, 1976–78; Under Sec., DoE, 1978–83; Sec. Gen., EDG, EP, 1983–87; Dir, President's Office, EP, 1987–89. Sen. Policy Advr on EU affairs, PRM European Lobbyists, Brussels, 1999–. Leverhulme Fellow, 1978. *Publications:* The Corsican Time Bomb, 1983; Ringside Seats, 2009; Calling the Shots, 2015. *Recreations:* sailing, European literature. *E:* rr@clanramsay.eu. *Club:* Carlton.

**RAMSAY-FAIRFAX-LUCY,** Sir Edmund John William Hugh Cameron; *see* Fairfax-Lucy.

**RAMSBOTHAM,** family name of **Baron Ramsbotham.**

**RAMSBOTHAM,** Baron *cr* 2005 (Life Peer), of Kensington, in the Royal Borough of Kensington and Chelsea; **Gen. David John Ramsbotham,** GCB 1993 (KCB 1987); CBE 1980 (OBE 1974); HM Chief Inspector of Prisons for England and Wales, 1995–2001; *b* 6 Nov. 1934; *s* of Rt Rev. J. A. Ramsbotham; *m* 1958, Susan Caroline (*née* Dickinson); two *s. Educ:* Haileybury Coll.; Corpus Christi Coll., Cambridge (BA 1957, MA 1973; Hon. Fellow, 2001). Nat. Service, 1952–54; Rifle Bde, UK and BAOR, 1958–62; seconded to KAR, 1962–63; Staff Coll., 1964; Rifle Bde, Far East, 1965; Staff, 7 Armoured Bde, 1966–68; 3 and 2 Green Jackets (BAOR), 1968–71; MA to CGS (Lt-Col), 1971–73; CO, 2 RGJ, 1974–76; Staff, 4 Armd Div., BAOR, 1976–78; Comd, 39 Infantry Bde, 1978–80; RCDS, 1981; Dir of Public Relns (Army), 1982–84; Comdr, 3 Armd Div., 1984–87; Comdr, UK Field Army and Inspector Gen., TA, 1987–90; Adjt Gen., 1990–93; ADC Gen. to the Queen, 1990–93. Dir of Internat. Affairs, DSL Ltd, 1994–99. Chm., Hillingdon Hosp. NHS Trust, 1995. Mem. Council, IISS, 1996–2002. Col Comdt, 2nd Battalion, The Royal Green Jackets, 1987–92; Hon. Col, Cambridge Univ. OTC, 1987–93; Hon. Bencher, Gray's Inn, 2002. FRSA 1999; FCGI 2000. Hon. FRCSLT 2012. Hon. DCL: Huddersfield, 1999; E London, 2002; Nottingham Trent, 2002; Birmingham, 2002; Keele, 2004; Portsmouth, 2004; Kent, 2004. *Publications:* Prisongate (memoirs), 2003. *Recreations:* sailing, gardening, art and art history. *Club:* Beefsteak.

*See also* Hon. J. D. A. *Ramsbotham.*

**RAMSBOTHAM, Hon. James David Alexander,** CBE 2019; DL; Chief Executive, North East England Chamber of Commerce, since 2006; *b* Iserlohn, Germany (BAOR), 30 Aug. 1959; *s* of Baron Ramsbotham, *qv; m* 1984, Carolyn Sarah Jane Fenwick; one *s* one *d. Educ:* Harrow Sch.; Durham Univ. (BA Geog.). ACIB 1992. Commnd RGJ, 1978; served with RGJ and PPCLI, Canada; resigned commn, 1989. Corporate Banking Dir and Marketing Dir, Barclays Bank, 1989–2003; Exec. Vice Chm., ESH Gp, 2003–06. Chm., NE, LSC, 2005–10. Chm., Darlington Building Soc., 2006–18. Hon. Col, The Rifles, Co. Durham, 2009–. Chm. Trustees, DLI, 2012–; Pres., NE Br., RGJ Regtl Assoc., 2015–. FAIA 2016. Hon. DBA Sunderland, 2017. *Recreations:* sailing, ski-ing, country pursuits. *Address:* North East England Chamber of Commerce, Aykley Heads, Durham DH1 5TS. *Clubs:* Pitt; Rifles Officers'; Northern Counties; Royal Yachting Association.

**RAMSBOTHAM, Prof. Oliver Peter,** PhD; Emeritus Professor of Conflict Resolution, University of Bradford, 2002 (Professor of Peace Studies and Head, Department of Peace Studies, 1999–2002); President, Conflict Research Society, since 2002; *b* 27 Oct. 1943; *er s* of Hon. Sir Peter Ramsbotham, GCMG, GCVO, (3rd Viscount Soulbury, but did not use the title) and Frances Marie Massie (*née* Blomfield); *S* father, 2010 as 4th Viscount Soulbury, but does not use the title; *m* 1965, Meredith Anne, *o d* of Brian Jones; three *s. Educ:* Eton; University Coll., Oxford (BA 1965); Univ. of Bradford (PhD). Chm. Bd, Oxford Res. Gp, 2007–13 (Mem. Bd, 2002–13); Dept of Peace Studies, Univ. of Bradford, 1991–2002. Co-Ed., Routledge Studies in Peace and Conflict Resolution. *Publications:* (jtly) Humanitarian Intervention in Contemporary Conflict, 1996; (jtly) The Crescent and the Cross: Muslim and Christian approaches to war and peace, 1997; Islam, Christianity and Humanitarian Intervention, 1997; (jtly) Contemporary Conflict Resolution: the prevention, management and resolution of deadly conflict, 1999, 4th edn 2016; (ed jtly) Peacekeeping and Conflict Resolution, 2000; Transforming Violent Conflict: radical disagreement, dialogue and survival, 2010; (jtly) Contemporary Conflict Resolution Reader, 2015; When Conflict Resolution Fails, 2017; over 100 refereed jl articles. *Heir:* (to Viscountcy) *s* Hon. Edward Herwald Ramsbotham, *b* 8 July 1966. *Address:* Flat 7 Museum Chambers, Bury Place, WC1A 2LD.

**RAMSBOTTOM, Paul Benjamin;** Chief Executive (formerly Executive Secretary), Wolfson Foundation, since 2007; Chief Executive (formerly Secretary), Wolfson Family Charitable Trust, since 2007; *b* 27 May 1976; *s* of Benjamin Ashworth Ramsbottom and Jean Margaret Ramsbottom (*née* Kelsall); *m* 2002, Karen Rachel Taylor; four *d. Educ:* St Albans Sch.; Corpus Christi Coll., Oxford (BA 1st Cl. Hons Modern Hist. 1997; MSt 1998). With Wolfson Foundation, 1998–: Grants Adminr, 1998–2000; Asst Exec. Sec., 2000–01; Dep. Exec. Sec., 2001–06. CCB Fellow, Univ. of Oxford, 2009–. Chm., Savannah Educn Trust, 2004–; Chair, Foundns Forum, 2013–. Mem. Ct, LSHTM, 2009–14. FRSocMed 2007. Trustee, Mercy Ships UK, 2015–. Hon. DLitt Bedfordshire, 2013. *Recreations:* exotic travel and food, theology, various sports. *Address:* The Wolfson Foundation, 8 Queen Anne Street, W1G 9LD. *T:* (020) 7323 5730, *Fax:* (020) 7323 3241.

**RAMSBURY, Bishop Suffragan of,** since 2019; **Rt Rev. Dr Andrew Paul Rumsey;** *b* Hitchin, Herts, 11 Feb. 1968; *s* of Rev. Canon Philip Rumsey and Elizabeth Rumsey; *m* 1998, Rebecca Louise Rigby; one *s* two *d. Educ:* Univ. of Reading (BA Hons Hist. 1989); Ridley Hall, Cambridge (MA Pastoral Theol. 1998); King's Coll. London (DThMin 2016). Ordained deacon, 1997, priest, 1998; Vicar, Christ Church, Gipsy Hill, 2001–11; Rector, St Mary's, Oxted and Tandridge, 2011–19. *Publications:* Strangely Warmed, 2009; Parish: an Anglican theology of place, 2017. *Recreations:* songwriting, classic cars, cats. *Address:* Ramsbury Office, Church House, Salisbury, Wilts SP1 2QB. *T:* (01722) 438662. *E:* bishop.ramsbury@salisbury.anglican.org.

**RAMSDEN, Sir David Edward John,** Kt 2015; CBE 2004; Deputy Governor for Markets and Banking, Member of Monetary Policy Committee, Financial Policy Committee and Prudential Regulation Committee, Bank of England, since 2017; *b* 9 Feb. 1964; *s* of late William Ramsden, OBE and of Elizabeth Ramsden (now Thompson); *m* 1993, Niccola Shearman; one *s* one *d. Educ:* Brasenose Coll., Oxford; London Sch. of Econs. Economist posts in DHSS and HM Treasury, 1986–98; HM Treasury: Head: EMU Policy Team, 1999–2003; O'Donnell Rev. Team, 2003; Dir, Tax and Budget, 2004–05; Dir, Macroeconomics and Fiscal Policy Gp, 2006–07; Man. Dir, later Dir Gen., 2007–17; Chief Economic Advr, 2008–17; Jt Hd, 2007–10, Hd, 2010–17, Govt Economic Service. Pres., Soc. of Professional (formerly Business) Economists, 2012–. Trustee, Pro Bono Economics, 2010–. *Recreations:* cycling, climbing, walking, reading. *Address:* Bank of England, Threadneedle Street, EC2R 8AH.

**RAMSDEN, Rt Hon. James Edward;** PC 1963; *b* 1 Nov. 1923; *s* of late Capt. Edward Ramsden, MC, and Geraldine Ramsden, OBE; *m* 1949, Juliet Barbara Anna, *y d* of late Col Sir Charles Ponsonby, 1st Bt, TD, and Hon. Lady Ponsonby, *d* of 1st Baron Hunsdon; three *s* two *d. Educ:* Eton; Trinity College, Oxford (MA). Commnd KRRC, 1942; served North-West Europe with Rifle Brigade, 1944–45. MP (C) Harrogate, WR Yorks, March 1954–Feb. 1974; PPS to Home Secretary, Nov. 1959–Oct. 1960; Under-Sec. and Financial Sec., War Office, Oct. 1960–Oct. 1963; Sec. of State for War, 1963–64; Minister of Defence for the Army, April–Oct. 1964. Director: UK Board, Colonial Mutual Life Assurance Society, 1966–72; Standard Telephones and Cables, 1971–81; Prudential Assurance Co. Ltd, 1972–91 (Dep. Chm., 1976–82); Prudential Corp. Ltd, 1979–91 (Dep. Chm., 1979–82). Dir, London Clinic, 1973–96 (Chm., 1984–96). Chm., The Hackfall Trust, 1988–. Mem., Historic Buildings Council for England, 1971–72. Pres., Northern Horticultural Soc., 1996–2001. *Address:* 14 High Agnesgate, Ripon, North Yorks HG4 1QR. *Club:* Pratt's.

**RAMSDEN, James Michael Scott;** QC 2016; *b* Sheffield, 25 June 1964; *s* of John Ramsden, CBE and Cynthia Ramsden; *m* 1990, Ruth Isobel; two *s* one *d. Educ:* Lady Manners Sch., Bakewell; Univ. of Leicester (LLB). Called to the Bar, Middle Temple, 1987; Attorney Gen.'s panel for asset tracing, 2008. Member: Lord's Taverners; NFU; South Devon Cattle Breeders Club. *Publications:* (contrib. ed.) Butterworths Commercial Law Digest. *Recreations:* beef genetics, Cornish League cricket, sea fishing, hedge laying, sleep. *Address:* 39 Essex Chambers, 81 Chancery Lane, WC2A 1DD. *T:* (020) 7832 1111. *E:* james.ramsdenqc@39essex.com. *Clubs:* MCC; Tideford Cricket.

**RAMSDEN, Sir John (Charles Josslyn),** 9th Bt *cr* 1689, of Byram, Yorks; HM Diplomatic Service, retired; Ambassador to Croatia, 2004–08; *b* 19 Aug. 1950; *s* of Sir Caryl Oliver Imbert Ramsden, 8th Bt, CMG, CVO, and Anne, *d* of Sir Charles Wickham, KCMG, KBE, DSO; *S* father, 1987; *m* 1985, (Jennifer) Jane Bevan; two *d. Educ:* Eton; Trinity Coll., Cambridge (MA). With merchant bank, Dawnay, Day & Co. Ltd, 1972–74. Entered FCO, 1975; 2nd Sec., Dakar, 1976; 1st Sec., MBFR, Vienna, 1978; 1st Sec., Head of Chancery and Consul, Hanoi, 1980; FCO, 1982–90; Counsellor, E Berlin, 1990; Counsellor and Dep. Hd of Mission, Berlin, 1991–93; Hd, Information Dept, FCO, 1993–96; UK Dep. Perm. Rep. to UN, Geneva, 1996–99; Hd, Central and NW Europe Dept, FCO, 1999–2003. Accredited Mediator, 2009; Partner, Ambassador Partnership (formerly ADRg Ambassadors) LLP, 2009–15. Mem., Lord Chancellor's Adv. Council on Nat. Records and Archives, 2014–18. Trustee, Mus. of E Asian Art, Bath, 2010–15. Patron, British Croatian Soc., 2010–. *Publications:* Send Golden Syrup, 2017; Hanoi After the War, 2018; The Box in the Attic, 2019.

**RAMSDEN, Prof. Richard Thomas,** MBE 2015; FRCS; Consultant Otolaryngologist, Manchester Royal Infirmary, 1977–2009; Professor of Otolaryngology, University of Manchester, 1994–2009; *b* 30 Dec. 1944; *s* of late Thomas William Ramsden and Elaine Napier Ramsden (*née* Meikle); *m* 1st, 1968, Wendy Margaret Johnson (marr. diss. 1984); one *s* two *d;* 2nd, 1987, Eileen Gillian Richardson (*née* Whitehurst); two step *s. Educ:* Madras Coll., St Andrews; St Andrews Univ. (MB ChB 1968). FRCS 1977. Registrar in Otolaryngol., 1972–74, Sen. Registrar, 1974–75, RNTNEH; Sen. Registrar, Otolaryngol., London Hosp., 1975–77. TWJ Travelling Fellow to N America, 1978. Lectures: Subramaniam, Indian Soc. of Otolaryngol., McBride, Univ. of Edinburgh, 1987; Dalby, Otology Section, RSocMed, 1992; Younis, Pakistan Soc. of Otolaryngol., 1993; Wilde, Irish Otolaryngol Soc., Graham Fraser, Otology Section, RSocMed, 1994; Goldman, Groote Schuur Hosp., Univ. of Cape Town, 1998; Yearsley, RCS, 2001; Gordon Smyth, BAO-HNS, 2004; Susan Bellman, British Assoc. of Audiol Physicians, 2004; William F. House, American Neurol. Soc., 2005; Philip Stell, N of Eng. Otolaryngol. Soc., 2006; Block Jacobson, Univ. of Dundee, 2008; Hunterian Oration, Hunterian Soc., 2008; Thomas Simm Littler, British Soc. of Audiology, 2009; Stirk Adams, Midland Inst. of Otology, 2012; Brinkmann, Univ. of Nijmegen, 2013; Toynbee, RCS, 2013. Pres., British Assoc. of Otolaryngologists-Head and Neck Surgeons, 2006–09. Trustee: Dowager Countess Eleanor Peel Trust, 2009–; William Alwyn Foundn, 2014–; Hearing Dogs for Deaf People; Patron, Nat. Assoc. for Deafened People. FRCSE (ad hominem) 2000. Hon. Member: German ENT Soc.; Irish ENT Soc.; Danish ENT Soc.; Amer. Otological Soc. (Corresp. Mem., 2006); Slovak Soc. of Otolaryngol. and Head and Neck Surgery; German Skull Base Soc. Dalby Prize, W. J. Harrison Prize, RSocMed; Jobson Horne Prize, BMA.

*Publications:* chapters on aspects of otology and neuro-otology; contrib. learned jls of otology and neuro-otology. *Recreations:* playing the bassoon, trying to resuscitate the golf, observing the maturation of the grandchildren, history of medicine. *Address:* Church House, 28 High Street, Thame, Oxon OX9 2AA. *T:* (01844) 212421. *Clubs:* Royal Society of Medicine; St Andrews New Golf; Middlesex County Cricket.

**RAMSEY, Dr Frances Madeleine Ross;** Head, Godolphin and Latymer School, since 2017; *b* Dunfermline, 4 Dec. 1964; *d* of John Moullin Davies and Elizabeth Nesta Davies (*née* Ross); *m* 1988, Christopher Bronk Ramsey; one *s* one *d*. *Educ:* Dragon Sch., Oxford; Oakham Sch.; Merton Coll., Oxford (BA Modern Hist. 1986; DPhil Medieval Hist. 1991). Westminster School: Teacher of Hist., 1992–2009; Hd of Hist., 1996–98; Dir of Studies, 1998–2002; Master of Queen's Scholars, 2003–09; Principal, Queen's Coll., London, 2009–17. *Publications:* (ed) English Episcopal Acta, Vol X (Bath and Wells, 1061–1205), 1995. *Recreations:* riding, ski-ing. *Address:* Godolphin and Latymer School, Iffley Road, Hammersmith, W6 0PG. *T:* (020) 8741 1935.

**RAMSEY, Brig. Gael Kathleen,** CBE 1992 (MBE 1976); Chief Executive, British Executive Service Overseas, 1997–2004; *b* 8 June 1942; *d* of Lt Col William Hammond, MBE and Kathleen Hammond; *m* 1977 (marr. diss. 1996). *Educ:* Convent of Good Shepherd, Singapore; High Sch. for Girls, Worcester, Gloucester and Dover. Commissioned, WRAC, 1968; Dir, WRAC, 1989–92; ADC to the Queen, 1989–92; Dir Women (Army), 1992; Comdr, Aldershot Bde Area, 1992–95, retd. Dep. Col Comdt, AGC, 1998–2002. Dir, Arnhem Wharf Residential Mgt Co. Ltd, 2003– (Chm., 2011–17). Freeman, City of London, 1991; Member: Guild of Freemen of City of London, 1992–; WRAC Assoc., 1989– (Life Mem.). FInstD 1995. *Recreations:* golf, tennis, reading, needlework, travel, messing about with plants. *Club:* Royal Cinque Ports Yacht.

**RAMSEY, Hon. Sir Vivian (Arthur),** Kt 2005; FREng; a Judge of the High Court, Queen's Bench Division, 2005–14; Judge in charge, Technology and Construction Court, 2007–10; International Judge, Singapore International Commercial Court, since 2015; *b* 24 May 1950; *s* of Rt Rev. Ian Thomas Ramsey and late Margretta Ramsey (*née* McKay); *m* 1974, Barbara Walker; two *s* two *d*. *Educ:* Harley Sch., Rochester, NY; Abingdon Sch., Oxon; Oriel Coll., Oxford (MA); City Univ. (Dip. Law). CEng, MICE 1977, FICE 2011; FREng 2013. Civil and Structural Engineer, Ove Arup & Partners, 1972–77, 1979–80; called to the Bar, Middle Temple, 1979, Bencher, 2002. Barrister and Arbitrator, 1981–2005; QC 1992; Head of Keating Chambers, 2002–05; Asst Recorder, 1998–2000; a Recorder, 2000–05. Special Prof., Dept of Civil Engineering, Nottingham Univ., 1990–2010; Vis. Prof., Centre of Construction Law, KCL, 2007–. Chm., Swanley Action Gp, 1989–2005. Fellow: American Coll. of Construction Lawyers, 2005– (Co-Chm., Internat. Cttee, 2008–11); Internat. Acad. of Construction Law (Pres., 2013–15); Liveryman, Constructors' Co., 2009 (Freeman, 1995; Master, 2019–20); Hon. Freeman, Paviors' Co., 2011. President's Medal, 2010, Internat. Medal, 2018, Soc. of Construction Law; Clare Edwards Award, Technol. and Construction Solicitors' Assoc., 2010. Editor, 1984–2005, Consultant Ed., 2005–, Construction Law Jl. *Publications:* (ed) Keating on Building Contracts, 7th edn, 2000, 10th edn, 2016. *Recreations:* building renovation, vineyards.

**RAMZAN GOLANT, Farah,** CBE 2011; Chief Executive, Europe and Middle East, kyu Collective, since 2018; *b* Kenya, 11 May 1964; *d* of Fateh and Gulshan Ramzan; *m* 1990, Dr Benjamin Golant; one *s* one *d*. *Educ:* Emmanuel Coll., Cambridge (BA Hons Mod. and Medieval Langs 1987). Abbott Mead Vickers BBDO (formerly Abbott Mead Vickers), 1990–2012: Man. Dir, 2003–05; CEO, 2005–10; Exec. Chm., 2010–12; Mem., Worldwide Bd, BBDO, 2007–12; Chief Executive: All3Media, 2012–14; Girl Effect, 2015–18. Member: Bd, National Theatre, 2008–16; Cambridge Judge Business Sch., 2012–18; Prime Minister's Business Adv. Gp, 2013–15 Business Ambassador for Creative Industries of Britain, 2013–15); Bd, Save the Children, 2015–17; Bd, Aldo Gp, 2015–; Bd, Sadler's Wells, 2017–; Trustee, Prince's Trust Internat., 2018–. *Recreations:* tennis, dance, arts, cinema. *Address:* kyu EMEA, 6th Floor, Herbal House, 8 Back Hill, EC1R 5EN. *Club:* Thirty.

**RANA, Baron** *cr* 2004 (Life Peer), of Malone in the County of Antrim; **Diljit Singh Rana,** MBE 1996; JP; Founder and Managing Director, Andras House Ltd, since 1981; *b* 20 Sept. 1938; *s* of Paras Ram Rana; *m* 1966, Uma Passi; two *s*. *Educ:* Punjab Univ. (BA (Econs) 1958). Founder and Chm., Indian Business Forum, 1985. Founder, Rana Charitable Trust, 1996; Chm., Thanksgiving Square, Belfast, 2002–. Vice Pres., UNICEF, 2004–08. Chm., Sanghol Educn Complex, India, 2004–. Pres., Global Orgn of People of Indian Origin, 2009–. Hon. Indian Consul in NI, 2004–. President: S Belfast Safer Towns Assoc., 1991–93; Belfast Chamber of Trade, 1991–92; NI Chamber of Commerce and Industry, 2004–05; NI Hon. Consular Assoc., 2008–. Gov., Lagan Coll., 1990–94. Hon. Dr: Ulster, 1999; QUB, 2003; Bengal Engrg and Sci. Univ., 2008. JP Belfast, 1986. Pravasi Bharatiya Samman Award (India), 2007. *Address:* 13 Malone Park, Belfast BT9 6NH. *Clubs:* Ulster Reform, Dunmurry Golf (Belfast).

**RANA, Kamlesh Kaur;** a District Judge (Magistrates' Courts), since 2016; *b* Dar-es-Salaam, Tanzania, 16 Feb. 1964; *d* of Hari Singh Sewak and Gurdev Kaur Sewak; *m* 1987, Narinderpal Singh Rana; two *s*. *Educ:* St Bernard's Catholic Grammar Sch.; Kingston Poly. (LLB Hons); Guildford Law Coll. (Solicitor's Finals). Admitted as Solicitor, 1994; Legal Advr, 1989–2016; a Dep. District Judge (Magistrates' Courts), 2009–16; a Fee-paid Judge, First-tier Tribunal, Social Entitlement Chamber, 2011–16. *Recreations:* travel, books, films.

**RANA, Manveen;** reporter, Today Programme, BBC Radio 4, since 2018; *b* London, 25 July 1980; *d* of Amrik S. Rana and Surinder Rana (*née* Sangha). *Educ:* Durham Univ. (BA Hons Econs). Journalist, Daily Telegraph and Sunday Telegraph, 2001–03; researcher, BBC Radio 4 News progs, 2003–05; journalist, World at One, PM, Broadcasting House, iPM, World This Weekend, BBC Radio 4, 2005–18. Peabody Award, Grady Coll. of Journalism, 2015; ARIAS, Radio Acad. Silver Award for News Coverage, 2016; Award for Radio, One World Media, 2016; Foreign Press Assoc. Award, 2016; Award for Humanitarian Journalist of Year, AidEx, 2016; Award for Outstanding Internat. News Coverage, UN Dept of Public Information, 2016; Gold Award for Best Documentary, 2016, Grand Jury Prize, 2016, NY Internat. Radio Fest.; Sue Lloyd Roberts Media Award, Women on the Move Awards, 2018. *Recreations:* travel, reading, theatre, drinking spectacularly good cocktails and making spectacularly bad ones. *Address:* c/o Today Programme, BBC Radio 4, New Broadcasting House, Portland Place, W1A 1AA. *E:* Manveen.Rana@bbc.co.uk. *Club:* 12 Hay Hill.

**RANASINGHE, (Kulatilaka Arthanayake) Parinda;** Chief Justice of Sri Lanka, 1988–91; *b* 20 Aug. 1926; *s* of Solomon Ranasinghe and Somawathie Ranasinghe; *m* 1956, Chitra (*née* Mapaguneratne); one *s* three *d*. *Educ:* Royal Coll., Colombo. Advocate of the Supreme Court; appointed Magistrate, 1958; District Judge, 1966–74; High Court Judge, 1974–78; Judge, Court of Appeal, 1978–82, Pres. 1982; Judge, Supreme Court, 1982–88. *Recreation:* walking. *Address:* 18/48 Muhandiram E. D. Dabare Mawatha, Colombo 5, Sri Lanka. *T:* (1) 508310.

**RAND, Ian;** Chief Executive Officer, Business Banking, Barclays UK, since 2016; *b* Kent, 1969. *Educ:* RMA, Sandhurst; Royal Mil. Coll. of Sci. (BSc Design and Inf. Systems 1993). Served Army, 1988–2000. Chief Operating Officer: for Global Res., JP Morgan Chase, 2000–08; for Coverage, 2008–14, for Corporate Banking, 2014–16, Barclays Bank. QCVS 1997. *Recreations:* cycling, dinghy sailing, learning blues piano. *Address:* c/o Barclays Bank, 1 Churchill Place, E14 5HP. *E:* ian.rand@barclays.com.

**RANDALL,** family name of **Baron Randall of Uxbridge.**

**RANDALL OF UXBRIDGE,** Baron *cr* 2018 (Life Peer), of Uxbridge in the London Borough of Hillingdon; **Alexander John Randall,** Kt 2013; PC 2010; *b* 5 Aug. 1955; *s* of late Alec Albert Randall and Joyce Margaret (*née* Gore); *m* 1986, Katherine Frances Gray; two *s* one *d*. *Educ:* Rutland House Sch., Hillingdon; Merchant Taylors' Sch., Herts; SSEES, Univ. of London (BA Hons Serbo-Croat Lang. and Lit. 1979). Dir, Randalls of Uxbridge Ltd, 1981– (Man. Dir, 1986–97). MP (C) Uxbridge, Aug. 1997–2010, Uxbridge and S Ruislip, 2010–15. An Opposition Whip, 2000–March 2003, July 2003–05; Opposition Asst Chief Whip, 2005–10; Treasurer of HM Household (Dep. Chief Whip), 2010–13; Special Advr to Prime Minister, 2017–19. Dir, Colne Valley CIC, 2015–17. Mem. Council, RSPB, 2015–17; Vice-Chm., Bd of Trustees, Human Trafficking Foundn, 2014–; Trustee: Hillingdon Partnership Trust, 2015–17; Saracens Sports Foundn, 2016–. *Recreations:* wildlife especially ornithology, theatre, opera, travel, sport. *Clubs:* Oriental; Saracens Rugby Football, Middlesex County Cricket.

*See also* P. A. Gore-Randall.

**RANDALL, Jeff William;** Editor-at-Large, The Daily Telegraph, 2005–13; Presenter, Jeff Randall Live, Sky Television, 2007–14; *b* 3 Oct. 1954; *s* of late Jeffrey Charles Randall and Grace Annie (*née* Hawkridge); *m* 1986, Susan Diane Fidler; one *d*. *Educ:* Royal Liberty Grammar Sch., Romford; Univ. of Nottingham (BA Hons Econs); Univ. of Florida. Hawkins Publishers, 1982–85; Asst Editor, Financial Weekly, 1985–86; City Corresp., Sunday Telegraph, 1986–88; The Sunday Times: Dep. City Editor, 1988–89; City Editor, 1989–94; City and Business Editor, 1994–95; Asst Editor and Sports Editor, 1996–97; Editor, Sunday Business, 1997–2001; Business Ed., BBC, 2001–05. Dir, Times Newspapers, 1994–95; Dep. Chm., Financial Dynamics Ltd, 1995–96. Columnist, Sunday Telegraph, 2002–04. Non-executive Director: Babcock Internat. plc, 2014–; Sandown Park Racecourse, 2014–; BDO, 2017–. Vis. Fellow, Univ. of Oxford Business Sch., 2008. Hon. Prof., Nottingham Univ. Business Sch., 2011. Mem. Council, Nottingham Univ., 2013–16. Hon. DLit: Anglia Poly. Univ., 2001; Univ. of Nottingham, 2006; Hon. DBA BPP Univ. Coll., 2011. Financial Journalist of the Year, FT-Analysis, 1991; Business Journalist of the Year, London Press Club, 2001; Sony Gold Award for best radio sports prog., The Bankrupt Game, BBC 5 Live, 2002; Broadcast Journalist of the Year and Decade of Excellence Award, Business Journalist of the Year Awards, 2003; Harold Wincott Award for Best Business Broadcaster, 2004; Communicator of the Year Award, PR Week, 2004; Best Broadcast Feature, Where's My Pension Gone?, Business Journalist of the Year Awards, 2007. *Publications:* (contrib.) The Day that Shook the World, 2001. *Recreations:* golf, horseracing. *Address:* c/o Babcock International, 33 Wigmore Street, W1U 1QX. *Clubs:* Brooks's; Thorndon Park Golf.

**RANDALL, John Norman;** Registrar General for Scotland, 1999–2003; *b* 1 Aug. 1945; *s* of Frederick William Randall and Daphne Constance Randall (*née* Gawn); *m* 1st, 1967, Sandra Philpott (marr. diss. 1991); one *s* one *d*; 2nd, 1997, Eileen Wilson (marr. diss. 2014); 3rd, 2016, Angela Clare. *Educ:* Bromley Grammar Sch.; Bristol Univ. (BA Hons Geography); Glasgow Univ. (MPhil Town and Regl Planning 1968; MPhil Econs 1979). Economist: Dept of Economic Affairs, 1968–70; Scottish Office, 1970–85; Dep. Registrar Gen. for Scotland, 1985–89; Asst Sec., Scottish Office, 1989–99. Trustee, Islands Book Trust, 2002–15; Mem. Council, Butterfly Conservation, 2002–06. Chm., Co-Chomunn na Pairc, 2007–13; Dir, Pairc Trust, 2008–16. *Recreations:* hill walking, natural history, island history, Gaelic. *Address:* 31 Lemreway, South Lochs, Isle of Lewis HS2 9RD.

**RANDALL, John Paul,** CBE 2015; international consultant on higher education and professional training, since 2001; *b* 23 Nov. 1947; *s* of late E. T. (Ted) Randall and Mollie Randall (*née* Macrae); *m* (marr. diss.); one *s* one *d*; 2nd, 1993, Marie Catherine Hague. *Educ:* Wallington County Grammar Sch. for Boys; Univ. of York (BA Hons Biol and Educn 1971). National Union of Students: Dep. Pres., 1971–73; Pres., 1973–75; Civil Service Union: Asst Sec., 1975–77; Asst Gen. Sec., 1977–81; Dep. Gen. Sec., 1981–87; Dir, Professional Standards and Develt, Law Soc., 1987–97; Chief Exec., QAA, 1997–2001. Chm., Skills for Justice (Justice Sector Skills Council), 2003–10. Mem. Council, NCVQ, 1992–97 (Chm., Accreditation Cttee, 1993–96; Chm., NVQ Policy Cttee, 1996–97; Mem. Jt Cttee, NCVQ and Schools Curriculum and Assessment Authy, 1996–97); Mem. Bd, Internat. Network of QAAs, 1999–2001. Member: Information Tribunal, 2003–10; Legal Services Consultative Panel, 2004–09; Gen. Regulatory Chamber (Information Rights and Estate Agents' jurisdictions), Tribunals Service, 2010– (Consumer Credit, 2010–14). Independent Chair: Police Adv. Bd for Eng. and Wales, 2004–14; Police Negotiating Bd, 2004–15; Chairman: Police Adv. Bd for NI, 2007–14; Scottish Police Consultative Forum, 2013–15; Consultative Gp, Coll. of Policing, 2014–15. Lay Assessor: Nat. Clin. Assessment Service (formerly Authy), 2003–11; PMETB, 2006–10; Lay Trng Partner, GMC, 2010–13. Quality Assurance Dir, Internat. Compliance Assoc., 2002–13. Vis. Academic Advr, Univ. of HK, 2002; Tech. Sec., UGC (Hong Kong), 2003–04, 2010–11, 2014–15; Specialist Consultant, Asia Develt Bank Tech. Assistance Project, Commn on Higher Educn, Philippines, 2004; Consultant, Hong Kong Council on Academic Accreditation, 2005–08. Sen. Res. Fellow, Legal Services Inst. (formerly Legal Services Policy Inst.), Univ. (formerly Coll.) of Law, 2008–13. Mem. Council, C&G, 1999–2015 (Mem., Trustee Bd (formerly Exec. Cttee), 2004–13). Mem. Bd of Mgt, Focus Housing Assoc., 1996–99. FRSA 1998. FCGI 2007. Hon. LLD Nottingham Trent, 1998. Special Award, Univ. Council Jamaica, 2017. *Publications:* (contrib.) Higher Education Re-formed, 2000; Collective Bargaining for a Modernised Workforce, 2006; articles in educnl and legal jls. *Recreations:* walking, music, opera, wine, travel, jogging. *Address:* Orchard Cottage, The Rampings, Longdon, Worcs GL20 6AL. *E:* john.randall23@btopenworld.com. *Clubs:* South London Harriers, Orion Harriers.

**RANDALL, John Yeoman;** QC 1995; *b* 26 April 1956; *s* of late Richard Randall and of Jean Randall; *m* 1982, Christine Robinson (marr. diss. 2018); one *s* one *d*. *Educ:* Rugby Sch.; Loomis Inst., USA; Jesus Coll., Cambridge (MA). Called to the Bar: Lincoln's Inn, 1978, Bencher, 2003; NSW, 1979; WA, 2001; in practice at English Bar, 1980–; an Asst Recorder, 1995–99; a Recorder, 1999–2016; a Dep. High Court Judge, 2000–16. Hd of Chambers, 2001–04. Mem., Legal Services Consultative Panel, 2000–09. Vis. Fellow, 2004–13, Adjunct Prof., 2013–, Univ. of NSW; Sen. Fellow, Melbourne Law Sch., 2014–17. *Publications:* (with Sarah Green) The Tort of Conversion, 2009. *Recreations:* travel, sports, music. *Address:* St Philip's Chambers, 55 Temple Row, Birmingham B2 5LS. *T:* (0121) 246 7000, *Fax:* (0121) 246 7001. *E:* commercial@st-philips.com.

**RANDALL, Philip Allan G.;** *see* Gore-Randall.

**RANDALL-PAGE, Peter,** RA 2015; sculptor; *b* Rochford, Essex, 1954; *m* Charlotte Eve; one *s* one *d*. *Educ*: Bath Acad. of Arts (BA Hons 1977). *Solo exhibitions* include: Sculpture and Drawings, Leeds City Art Galls, 1992; Stones, Sunlight and Shadows, New Art Centre, Roche Court, 2008–09; Yorkshire Sculpture Park, 2009–10; New Sculpture and Works on Paper, Peninsula Arts and Plymouth City Mus. and Art Gall., Plymouth, 2014; Arte Sella and Villa Panza, Italy, 2015; *group exhibitions* include Gwangju Biennale, South Korea, 2004; work in collections incl. Tate Gall., BM; commissions include: Univ. of Iowa, 2011; Univ. of Music, Karlsruhe, 2013; Univ. of Birmingham, 2014; Fitzroy Place, London, 2015. Hon. DArts Plymouth, 1999; Hon. DLitt: York St John, 2009; Exeter, 2010; Bath Spa, 2013. *W*: www.peterrandall-page.com.

**RANDELL, Charles David,** CBE 2016; Chairman: Financial Conduct Authority, since 2018; Payment Systems Regulator, since 2018; *b* Rheindahlen, 6 June 1958; *s* of Keith and Annette Randell; *m* 1983, Celia Van Oss; three *s*. *Educ*: Streete Court Prep. Sch.; Bradfield Coll.; Trinity Coll., Oxford (BA Juris. 1979); College of Law, Guildford. Slaughter and May: Articled Clerk, 1980–82; Solicitor, 1982–89; Partner, Corporate Dept, 1989–2013; Ext. Mem., Prudential Regulation Authy, Bank of England, 2013–18. Non-executive Director: DECC, 2014–16 (Chair, Audit and Risk Cttee, 2015–16); BEIS, 2016–18. Vis. Fellow, Centre for Commercial Law Studies, QMUL, 2011–. Member, Editorial Board: PLC Corporate Law, 1990–2013; Law and Financial Markets Review, 2012–14. *Publications*: (jtly) Public Company Takeovers in Germany, 2002; various articles relating to financial regulation, corporate law and corporate governance. *Recreations*: sailing, theatre, travel.

**RANDENIYA, Vijith,** OBE 2007; Chief Fire Officer, West Midlands Fire Service, 2009–13; *b* Croydon, 21 July 1960; *s* of Sarath Randeniya and Kamala Randeniya; *m* 2005, Shindo Barquer. *Educ*: Selhurst High Sch.; Univ. of Wales, Bangor (BA Hons Mod. Hist. 1981); Coventry Univ. (MA Mgt 2002). Firefighter, latterly Gp Comdr, London Fire Bde, 1983–98; Hd, Ops, Nottinghamshire Fire and Rescue Service, 1998–2000; West Midlands Fire Service: Asst Chief Fire Officer, 2000–03; Dep. Chief Fire Officer, 2003–09. Chm., Bd of Trustees, Birmingham St Mary's Hospice, 2014–17. FRSA. Mem., Lunar Soc. Hon. DSc Aston, 2010. *Recreations*: Victorian house refurbishments, military history, JFK memorabilia, cooking, shopping. *Club*: Royal Air Force.

**RANDEREE, Shabir Ahmed,** CBE 2013; Executive Chairman, DCD London and Mutual plc, since 1990; *b* Durban, 12 March 1962; *s* of Ahmed Randeree and Fareda Randeree; *m* 1989, Ruwaida; three *s*. *Educ*: Kingston Poly. (BA Hons Accounting and Finance 1984); Schiller Internat. Univ., London (MBA 1986). Various posts within DCD Gp Divisions, 1986–90; Dep. Chm., Al Baraka Bank Ltd, South Africa, 2002–; Chm., European Islamic Investment Bank plc, 2005–12; Director: Islamic Bank of Britain plc, 2003–08; BankIslami Ltd, 2005–16. Chancellor, UEL, 2016–. Member: Young Presidents' Orgn, 2003–; Council, Prince's Trust, 2016–. *Address*: DCD London and Mutual plc, 90 Long Acre, WC2E 9RA. *T*: (020) 7324 2000. *E*: sr@dcdgroup.com.

**RANDERSON,** family name of **Baroness Randerson**.

**RANDERSON, Baroness** *cr* 2011 (Life Peer), of Roath Park in the City of Cardiff; **Jennifer Elizabeth Randerson;** JP; *b* 26 May 1948; *m* 1970, Dr Peter Frederick Randerson; one *s* one *d*. *Educ*: Bedford Coll., London Univ. (BA Hons History); Inst. of Educn, London Univ. (PGCE 1970). Teacher: Sydenham High Sch., 1970–72; Spalding High Sch., 1972–74; Llanishen High Sch., 1974–76; Lectr, Coleg Glan Hafren, Cardiff, 1976–99. Member (L, then Lib Dem): Cardiff City Council, 1983–96; Cardiff County Council, 1995–2000 (Leader of Opposition, 1995–99). Mem. (Lib Dem) Cardiff Central, Nat. Assembly for Wales, 1999–2011. National Assembly for Wales: Sec., then Minister, for Culture, Sports and the Welsh Lang., 2000–03; Lib Dem spokesperson on economic develt and finance, 2003–05, on health, finance and equal opportunities, 2005–07, on health, social services, local govt and finance, 2007–09, on educn, economy and transport, 2009–11, on transport, 2015–. Parly Under-Sec. of State, Wales Office, 2012–15; spokesperson on NI, H of L, 2012–15. Chair of Exec., Welsh Lib Dems, 1988–90. Contested: (L) Cardiff S and Penarth, 1987; (Lib Dem) Cardiff Central, 1992, 1997. Pro Chancellor, 2017–19, Chancellor, 2019–, Cardiff Univ. JP Cardiff 1982. *Recreations*: travel, theatre and concert going, gardening. *Address*: House of Lords, SW1A 0PW.

**RANDLE, James Neville,** FREng, RDI 1994; engineering consultant, since 1992, and Chairman, since 1994, Randle Engineering and Design; Chief Executive Officer, Lea Francis Ltd, 2000–10 (Director, 1997–2010); *b* Birmingham, 24 April 1938; *s* of James Randle and Florence (*née* Wilkins); *m* 1963, Jean Violet Allen (*d* 2006); one *s* one *d*. *Educ*: Waverley Grammar Sch., Birmingham. MIMechE 1969, FIMechE 1980; FREng (FEng 1988). Rover Car Company: apprentice, 1954–59; design and develt engr, 1959–63; Project Manager, 1963–65; Jaguar: R&D Engr, 1965–72; Chief Res. Engr, 1972–78; Vehicle Engrg Dir, 1978–80; Product Engrg Dir, 1980–91. Hon. Prof., 1992–2006, Dir, Automotive Engrg Centre, 1993–2006, Univ. of Birmingham. Non-exec. Dir, Volvo Aero Turbines, 1992–98. Institution of Mechanical Engineers: Mem. Bd, 1979–88, Chm., 1986–87, Automobile Div.; Mem. Council, 1986–93. Member: Prince Philip Design Prize Cttee, 1992–95 and 1997–2002; Misha Black Awards Cttee for Design Educn, 1992–. Pres., Engrg Div., BAAS, 1995–96. Chm., 2007–11, Pres., 2016–, Coventry Aeroplane Club. FInstD 1986. FRSA 1989. Hon. FCSD 2000. James Clayton Prize, 1986, Crompton Lanchester Medal, 1986, IMechE. *Publications*: technical papers and presentations on automobile engrg and Jaguar and Lea Francis histories. *Recreations*: flying powered aircraft (private pilot's licence and owner), sailing (yacht master's certificate), ski-ing, hill walking, designing automobiles. *Address*: Pear Tree House, High Street, Welford on Avon, Warwickshire CV37 8EF.

**RANDLE, Prof. Valerie,** PhD, DSc; Professor of Materials Engineering, Swansea University (formerly University of Wales Swansea), 1999–2013, now Emeritus (Head of Materials Research Centre, 2007–09); *b* 8 May 1953; *d* of Bertram and Edith Brushfield; *m* 1st, 1971, Michael Randle (decd); one *s* one *d*; 2nd, 2006, Victor Pinheiro (decd); 3rd, 2017, Prof. Christopher Norris. *Educ*: Univ. of Wales, Cardiff (BSc 1983; PhD 1986; DSc 1996). FIMMM 1993; CEng 1998. Royal Soc. Univ. Res. Fellow, Bristol Univ., 1987–92, UC of Swansea, 1992–95; Sen. Lectr, 1995–97, Reader, 1997–99, UC of Swansea, then Univ. of Wales Swansea. Volunteer, Cruse Bereavement Care. Welsh Woman of the Year, 1998. *Publications*: Microtexture Determination and its Applications, 1992, 2nd edn 2003; Grain Boundary Geometry in Polycrystals, 1993; (jtly) An Atlas of Backscatter Kikuchi Diffraction Patterns, 1994; The Role of the Coincidence Site Lattice in Grain Boundary Engineering, 1996; (with Olaf Engler) Introduction to Texture Analysis: macrotexture, microtexture and orientation mapping, 2000, 2nd edn 2009; In the Long Run (novel), 2018; 350 scientific papers in learned jls. *Recreations*: walking, swimming, yoga, meditation, singing, writing fiction. *T*: 07732 357348. *E*: valeriepinheiro@gmail.com.

**RANDOLPH, Fergus Mark Harry;** QC 2009; *b* London, 6 Oct. 1961; *s* of late Peter and Rippy Randolph; *m* 1991, Griet Descheemaeker; three *s*. *Educ*: Harrow Sch.; Buckingham Univ. (LLB); Univ. of Aix-en-Provence (Licence en Droit). Called to the Bar, Middle Temple, 1985, Bencher, 2011; called to the Bar, Brussels, 2018; in practice as barrister specialising in EU and competition law, Brick Court Chambers, 1991–. Liveryman, Cutlers' Co., 1992–. *Publications*: Commercial Agency and Distribution Agreements, 1987; Shipping and EC Competition Law, 1991; Banking Secrecy, 1993; (jtly) Guide to the Commercial Agents Regulations, 1994, 3rd edn 2010. *Recreations*: running, fishing, stalking, opera. *Address*: Brick Court Chambers, 7–8 Essex Street, WC2R 3LD. *T*: (020) 7379 3550, *Fax*: (020) 7379 3558. *E*: fergus.randolph@brickcourt.co.uk.

**RANDOLPH, Prof. Mark Felton,** PhD; FRS 2011; FREng; FAA; Professor of Civil Engineering, Centre for Offshore Foundation Systems, University of Western Australia, since 1990; Director, Advanced Geomechanics, since 1994; *b* 3 July 1951; *s* of late Lt-Col John Hervey Randolph and Dorothy Elizabeth Randolph (*née* Eyre). *Educ*: Sherborne Sch.; Queen's Coll., Oxford (BA 1973; MA 1978); St John's Coll., Cambridge (PhD 1978). CPEng 1987; FIEAust 1994; FREng 2002. Scientific Officer, 1973–75, Higher Scientific Officer, 1975–77, BRE; Fellow, St John's Coll., Cambridge, 1977–86; Asst Lectr, 1978–83, Lectr, 1983–86, Engrg Dept, Univ. of Cambridge; University of Western Australia: Sen. Lectr, 1986–89; Associate Prof., 1989–90; Dir, Centre for Offshore Foundn Systems, 1997–2005. Fedn Fellow, Australian Res. Council, 2005–10. FTSE 1993; FAA 2000. *Publications*: (jtly) Piling Engineering, 1985, 3rd edn 2009; (jtly) Offshore Geotechnical Engineering, 2011; contrib. articles to geotech. engrg jls. *Recreations*: hiking, tennis, theatre, bridge. *Address*: Centre for Offshore Foundation Systems (MO53), University of Western Australia, 35 Stirling Highway, Crawley, WA 6009, Australia. *T*: (61) 864883075, *Fax*: (61) 864881044. *E*: mark.randolph@uwa.edu.au.

**RANDS, Dr Michael Russell Wheldon;** Executive Director, Cambridge Conservation Initiative, since 2009; *b* 2 Aug. 1956; *s* of late Russell Fuller Rands and Freda Millicent Rands; *m* 1984, Dr Gillian Frances Porter Goff; one *s* one *d*. *Educ*: Univ. of E Anglia (BSc Hons Envmtl Sci. 1978); Wolfson Coll., Oxford (DPhil 1982). Res. Biologist, Game Conservancy, 1982–86; Programme Dir, ICBP, 1986–94; Dir, Strategic Planning and Policy, 1994–96, Dir and Chief Exec., 1996–2009, BirdLife Internat. *Publications*: (with P. J. Hudson) Ecology and Management of Gamebirds, 1988; contrib. numerous papers to learned jls. *Recreations*: bird-watching, travelling with family, music. *Address*: David Attenborough Building, University of Cambridge, Trumpington Street, Cambridge CB2 3QZ.

**RANELAGH, John O'B.;** *see* O'Beirne Ranelagh.

**RANFURLY,** 8th Earl of, *cr* 1831 (Ire.); **Edward John Knox;** Baron Welles 1781; Viscount Northland 1791; Baron Ranfurly (UK) 1826; *b* Chichester, 21 May 1957; *s* of 7th Earl of Ranfurly and Rosemary (*née* Vesey Holt); *S* father, 2018; *m* 1994, Johannah Humphrey Walton; one *s* one *d*. *Educ*: Leys Sch., Cambridge; Loughborough Univ. (BSc). *Heir*: *s* Viscount Northland, *qv*. *Address*: 9 Parkgate, SE3 9XF.

**RANG, Prof. Humphrey Peter,** DPhil; FRS 1980; Director, Sandoz, later Novartis, 1983–97, Institute for Medical Research, and Professor of Pharmacology, 1979–83 and 1995–2001, now Emeritus, University College London; *b* 13 June 1936; *s* of Charles Rang and Sybil Rang; *m* 1992, Isobel Heyman. *Educ*: University Coll. Sch.; University Coll. London (MSc 1960); UCH Med. Sch. (MB, BS 1961); Balliol Coll., Oxford (DPhil 1965). J. H. Burn Res. Fellow, Dept of Pharmacol., Oxford, 1961–65; Vis. Res. Associate, Albert Einstein Coll. of Medicine, NY, 1966–67; Univ. Lectr in Pharmacol., Oxford, 1966–72; Fellow and Tutor in Physiol., Lincoln Coll., Oxford, 1967–72; Prof. of Pharmacology: Univ. of Southampton, 1972–74; St George's Hosp. Med. Sch., London, 1974–79; Fellow, 1983, and Vis. Prof., 1983–95, UCL. Pres., British Pharmacol Soc., 2014–16. Founder FMedSci 1998. *Publications*: Drug Receptors, 1973; Pharmacology, 1987; Drug Discovery and Development, 2006. *Recreations*: sailing, music, painting. *Address*: 1 Willow Road, NW3 1TH.

**RANGARAJAN, (Francis) Vijay (Narasimhan),** CMG 2015; PhD; HM Diplomatic Service; Ambassador to Brazil, since 2017; *b* New Delhi, 22 Sept. 1969; *s* of Lakshmi Narasimhan Rangarajan and Joyce Rangarajan; *m* 2000, Rosemary, (Rosie), Frances Cox; two *s*. *Educ*: Cranbrook Sch.; Selwyn Coll., Cambridge (BA Hons 1990, Pt III Maths; PhD Astrophysics 1995). Joined FCO, 1995; Second, later First Sec., UK Perm. Repn, Brussels, 1997–99; Pte Sec. to Perm. Under-Sec., FCO, 1999–2001; Hd of Eur. Defence, FCO, 2001–03; Dep. Hd of Mission, Mexico, 2003–06; Hd of Justice and Home Affairs, UK Repn, Brussels, 2006–09; Constitution Dir, MoJ and Cabinet Office, 2009–11; Multilateral Policy Dir, 2011–13, Europe Dir, 2013–16, FCO. *Publications*: papers in Monthly Notices of RAS and Astrophysical Jl. *Recreations*: singing (former Chair, City Chamber Choir, Holst Singers), cycling, kites, technology, family. *Address*: Foreign and Commonwealth Office, King Charles Street, SW1A 2AH. *E*: vijay.rangarajan@fco.gov.uk.

**RANGER, Raminder Singh,** CBE 2016 (MBE 2005); Founder and Chairman: Sun Mark Ltd, since 1995; Sea, Air and Land Forwarding Ltd, since 1987; *b* Gujranwala, 1947; *s* of late Shaheed Nanak Singh and Harbaus Kaur; *m* Renu; three *d*. *Educ*: Government Coll., Chandigarh (BA). Migrated to UK, 1971; worked for KFC, later district manager; ran sub post office/newsagent's shop; store manager, Dixons. Chm., British-Sikh Assoc. Trustee, Gandhi Meml Trust. Fellow, Prince's Trust. Hon. DLitt West London, 2016. *Publications*: From Nothing to Everything (autobiog.), 2014. *Address*: Sun Mark Ltd, Sun House, 428 Long Drive, Greenford, Middx UB6 8UH.

*[Created a Baron (Life Peer), 2019 but title not gazetted at time of going to press.]*

**RANK-BROADLEY, Ian,** FRSS; sculptor, since 1976; *b* 4 Sept. 1952; *s* of late John Kenneth Broadley and Barbara Anne Broadley (*née* Barker); *m* 1980, Hazel G. Rank; one *s* one *d*. *Educ*: Epsom Sch. of Art; Slade Sch. of Fine Art; University Coll. London (Boise Travelling Schol., Italy). FRSS (FRBS 1994). Effigy of: HM Queen Elizabeth II, for use on UK and Commonwealth coinage, 1998, and Golden Jubilee hallmark, 2002; HM Queen Elizabeth the Queen Mother, for Centenary Crown, 2000; the Queen for Golden Jubilee Crown and Medal, 2002; HRH Prince of Wales for 60th Birthday Crown, 2008; the Queen for Diamond Jubilee Crown and Kilo Coin, 2012; King George VI and Queen Elizabeth Diamond Stakes Trophy, 2005; Armed Forces Meml, Nat. Meml Arboretum, 2007; Portrait of HM Queen Elizabeth II, for Supreme Court, 2009; St Matthew, for St Matthew's Church, Northampton, 2009; Colet Meml, St Paul's Cathedral, 2010; Royal Anglian Regt Meml, Imperial War Mus., Duxford, 2010; Lord Lovat, Sword Beach, Ouistreham, Normandy, 2014; commissioned by Duke of Cambridge and Prince Harry to create sculpture of Princess Diana for grounds of Kensington Palace, 2018. *Works in public collections*: British Mus.; Nat. Portrait Gall.; Imperial War Mus.; Royal Mus. of Scotland; Fitzwilliam Mus.; Goldsmiths' Hall; London Library; Staatliche Mus., Berlin; Rijksmus., Leiden; Nat. Collection of Finland; Royal Swedish Coin Cabinet; All England Lawn Tennis & Croquet Club. Trustee, Prince's Sch. of Traditional Arts, 2010–14. Brother, Art Workers' Guild, 1995 (Mem. Cttee, 1999–2002; Trustee, 2002–05); Freeman, City of London, 1996; Liveryman, Goldsmiths' Co., 2009 (Mem., Modern Collection Cttee, 2004–10). Prizewinner, XI Biennale Dantesca, Ravenna, Italy, 1996; first prize, Goldsmiths' Craft and Design Council Awards, 2000, 2002; Olin-Stones Prize, Soc. of Portrait Sculptors, 2002, 2010; Marsh Award for Public Sculpture, Public Monument and Sculpture Assoc., 2008; Lifetime Achievement Award, Vicenza Numismatica, 2012. *Recreations*: yoga, gardening, swimming. *Address*: Green Farm, Nastend, Stonehouse, Glos GL10 3RS. *T*: (01453) 791424. *E*: irb@ianrank-broadley.co.uk.

**RANKEILLOUR**, 5th Baron *cr* 1932, of Buxted, co. Sussex; **Michael Richard Hope;** *b* 21 Oct. 1940; *s* of Hon. Richard Frederick Hope, OBE, *y s* of 1st Baron and Helen Hope (*née* Lambart); *S* cousin, 2005; *m* 1964, Elizabeth Rosemary (*d* 2019), *e d* of Col F. H. Fuller; one *s* two *d*. *Educ:* Downside Sch.; Loughborough Coll. (Engrg Dip.). Prodn engr then mgt trainee, Pye Gp, Cambridge, 1961; IBM UK: tech. sales, 1965; Original Equipment Manufr Gp, 1969; marketing mgt, 1974; new business mgt, computer sales, 1979; retired 1997. Trustee: Norwich Open Christmas, 1993–; All Saints Centre, 2003–; Songbird Survival, 2004–; St John's Catholic Cathedral, 2012–. *Recreations:* fishing, wildlife. *Heir: s* Hon. James Francis Richard Hope [*b* 5 Aug. 1968; *m* 2000, Felicity Gallimore; one *s*]. *Address:* St Margarets, Priory Road, Beccles, Suffolk NR34 9NJ. *T:* (01502) 470032. *E:* mandrhope@btinternet.com.

**RANKIN, Ian James,** OBE 2002; DL; novelist; *b* 28 April 1960; *s* of James Hill Rankin and Isobel Rankin (*née* Vickers); *m* 1986, Anna Miranda Harvey; two *s*. *Educ:* Beath Sen. High Sch.; Univ. of Edinburgh (MA Hons). Tax Collector, then punk musician, then alcohol researcher, then swineherd, then music journalist, 1986–90. Fulbright/Chandler Fellow, USA, 1991–92. Vis. Prof. of Creative Writing, UEA, 2016–17. Chm., Crime Writers Assoc., 1999–2000 (Short Story Dagger, 1994, 1996); Mem., Detection Club, 1998–. Co-writer, stage play: Dark Road, Royal Lyceum, Edinburgh, 2013; Rebus: Long Shadows, Birmingham Repertory Th., 2018. Book and culture reviewer, radio and newspapers. FRSE 2015; FRSL 2016. DL City of Edinburgh, 2007. Hon. DLitt: Abertay Dundee, 1999; St Andrews, 2000; Edinburgh, 2003; Open, 2005; Hull, 2006. Cartier Diamond Dagger Award for Lifetime Achievement, 2005. *Publications:* The Flood, 1986; Watchman, 1988; Westwind, 1989; Beggars Banquet, 2002; Doors Open, 2008 (adapted for TV, 2012); The Complaints, 2009; Dark Entries (graphic novel), 2009; The Impossible Dead, 2011; *Inspector Rebus series:* Knots and Crosses, 1987; Hide and Seek, 1990; Tooth and Nail, 1992; A Good Hanging and other stories, 1992; Strip Jack, 1992; The Black Book, 1993; Mortal Causes, 1994; Let it Bleed, 1995; Black and Blue (CWA Gold Dagger award), 1997; The Hanging Garden (Grand Prix du Roman Noir), 1998; Death is not the End (novella), 1998; Dead Souls, 1999; Set in Darkness, 2000; The Falls, 2001; Resurrection Men (MWA Edgar award), 2001; Question of Blood, 2003; Fleshmarket Close, 2004 (Best Crime Novel, British Book Awards, 2005); The Naming of the Dead, 2006 (Best Crime Novel, British Book Awards, 2007); Exit Music, 2007; Standing in Another Man's Grave, 2012; Saints of the Shadow Bible, 2013; The Beat Goes On (short stories), 2014; Even Dogs in the Wild, 2015; Rather Be the Devil, 2016; In a House of Lies, 2018; *as Jack Harvey:* Witch Hunt, 1993; Bleeding Hearts, 1994; Blood Hunt, 1995. *Recreations:* couch potato, regular visitor to Edinburgh pubs, '70s rock music. *Address:* c/o Rogers, Coleridge & White, 20 Powis Mews, W11 1JN. *Club:* Oyster (Edinburgh).

**RANKIN, Sir Ian (Niall),** 4th Bt *cr* 1898, of Bryngwyn, Much Dewchurch, Co. Hereford; Chairman, I. N. Rankin Oil Ltd, since 1981; *b* 19 Dec. 1932; *s* of Lt-Col Arthur Niall Rankin (*d* 1965) (*yr s* of 2nd Bt) and Lady Jean Rankin, DCVO; *S* uncle, 1988; *m* 1st, 1959, Alexandra (marr. diss.), *d* of Adm. Sir Laurence Durlacher, KCB, OBE, DSC; one *s* one *d*; 2nd, 1980, Mrs June Norman (marr. diss. 1998), *d* of late Captain Thomas Marsham-Townshend; one *s*; 3rd, 2013, Mrs Prudence Lane Fox (*née* Sporborg). *Educ:* Eton College; Christ Church, Oxford (MA). Lieut, Scots Guards. Chm., Slumberfleece Ltd, 1979–; Director: Lindsay and Williams Ltd, 1973; Bayfine Ltd and subsidiaries, 1974–85 (Jt Chm., 1974–81); Highgate Optical and Industrial Co. Ltd and subsidiary, 1976–84 (Jt Chm., 1976–81); New Arcadia Explorations Ltd, 1987–; Bristol Scotts, 1993–2001. Patron, Samaritans, 1991–; Mem. Council, Alexandra Rose Day, 1970–. Gov., Moorfields Eye Hosp., 2005–. *Publications:* Doomsday Just Ahead, 2004. *Recreations:* shooting, ski-ing, chess. *Heir: s* Gavin Niall Rankin, *b* 19 May 1962. *Address:* 97 Elgin Avenue, W9 2DA. *T:* (office) (020) 7286 0251, (home) (020) 7286 5117. *Clubs:* White's, Beefsteak, Pratt's; Royal Yacht Squadron.

**RANKIN, James Deans,** FREng, FIChemE; Senior Science and Technology Associate, ICI, 1995–2000; Technology Transfer Director, Molecular Materials Centre, University of Manchester, 2002–08; *b* 17 Feb. 1943; *s* of Dr James Deans Rankin and Florence Elizabeth (*née* Wight); *m* 1973, Susan Margaret Adams; one *s* one *d*. *Educ:* Merchiston Castle Sch., Edinburgh; Gonville and Caius Coll., Cambridge (MA). FREng (FEng 1987); FIChemE 1987. Joined ICI, 1965: Agricl Div., 1965–83; Process Technology Gp Manager, New Sci. Gp, 1983–88; Melinex R&D Manager, 1988–93; Technology, 1993–2000. Royal Acad. of Engrg Vis. Prof. of Engrg Design, Univ. of Oxford, 1997–2000; Vis. Prof., Univ. of Manchester (formerly UMIST), 2000–14. *Recreations:* steam boats, motoring.

**RANKIN, John James,** CMG 2016; HM Diplomatic Service; Governor and Commander-in-Chief of Bermuda, since 2016; *b* 12 March 1957; *s* of late James Rankin, CBE, and Agnes Rankin (*née* Stobie); *m* 1987, Lesley Marshall (marr. diss. 2019); one *s* two *d*. *Educ:* Hutchesons' Boys' Grammar Sch.; Univ. of Glasgow (LLB 1st Cl. Hons); McGill Univ., Montreal (LLM with distinction). Solicitor and Mem., Law Soc. of Scotland. Lectr in Public Law, Univ. of Aberdeen, 1984–88; Asst, then Sen. Asst Legal Advr, FCO, 1988–90; Legal Advr, UKMIS and UKDIS, Geneva, 1991–94; Legal Counsellor, FCO, 1995; Dep. Head, OSCE Dept, 1996–98; Counsellor and Dep. Head of Mission, Dublin, 1999–2003; Consul Gen., Boston, 2003–07; Dir, Americas, FCO, 2008–10; High Comr to Sri Lanka and (non-res.) to the Maldives, 2011–15; Chargé d'Affaires, Nepal, 2015. *Publications:* articles on Scots law and international law. *Recreations:* tennis, golf, gardening, food, Scottish literature. *Address:* c/o Foreign and Commonwealth Office, King Charles Street, SW1A 2AH.

**RANKIN, Maggie Mary;** *see* Gee, M. M.

**RANKIN, Rear-Adm. Neil Erskine,** CB 1995; CBE 1988; Chairman, Scottish Environment LINK, 2000–03; *b* 24 Dec. 1940; *s* of late James Hall Rankin and of Jean Laura Rankin (*née* Honeyman); *m* 1969, Jillian Mary Cobb; one *s* one *d*. *Educ:* HMS Conway; BRNC Dartmouth. Joined RN 1958; pilot's wings, 1963; CO HMS Achilles, 1977; CO HMS Bacchante, 1978; Comdr (Air), RNAS Yeovilton, 1979, HMS Invincible, 1981; Naval Air Warfare, MoD, 1982; COS, Flag Officer Third Flotilla, 1984; CO, Captain F8, HMS Andromeda, 1985; Sen. Naval Officer, Middle East, 1985; Dep. Dir, Naval Warfare, MoD, 1987; CO HMS Ark Royal, 1990; Comdr, British Forces Falkland Is, 1992–93; FO, Portsmouth, 1993–96. Chm., Caledonian MacBrayne Ltd, 1996–99. Director: Portsmouth Naval Base Property Trust, 1997–; Royal Yacht Britannia Trust, 1999– (Chm., 2002–). Chm., Scottish Seabird Centre, 1997–2012; Mem., Central Council, King George's Fund for Sailors, 1997. Trustee, RZSScot, 2000. Mem., RNSA, 1995–. Comr, Queen Victoria Sch., Dunblane, 1999–. Liveryman, Shipwrights' Co., 1992; Younger Brother, Trinity House, 1993–; Mem., Incorporation of Hammermen, Glasgow, 1998–. *Recreations:* Rugby (former Pres., Combined Services RFU and RNRU, Pres., United Services Portsmouth RFC, 1994–96), sailing, golf. *Clubs:* Royal Navy of 1765 and 1785, Naval; Royal Naval Golfing; North Berwick Golf; Gullane Golf; Royal Yacht Squadron; Royal Naval and Royal Albert Yacht; East Lothian Yacht.

**RANKIN, Robert Craig McPherson,** CompICE; Chairman, BKR Financial Ltd, 1988–2004; Director, British Shipbuilders, 1985–91; *b* 15 Aug. 1937; *s* of Robert Craig Rankin and Julia Rankin (*née* Duff); *m* 1963, Alison Barbara Black Douglas; one *s* one *d*. *Educ:* The Academy, Ayr; Royal College of Science and Technology, Glasgow. CompICE 1987. Dir, Balfour Beatty Construction (Scotland) Ltd, 1973–74; Dir 1974–83, Exec. Dir 1983–85, Balfour Beatty Construction Ltd; Balfour Beatty Ltd: Dir, 1983–88; Dep. Man. Dir, 1985–86; Man. Dir, 1986–87; Chief Exec., 1986–88; Dir, BICC PLC, 1987–88; Non-executive Director: London & Edinburgh Trust PLC, 1988–91; LDDC, 1989–93. CCMI (CBIM 1987). *Recreations:* opera, music.

**RANKIN, Shaun;** Executive Chef, Ormer Mayfair, since 2016; Shaun Rankin, Grantley Hall, since 2019; *b* Yorks, 7 March 1972; *s* of John Rankin and Judith Rankin; *m* 2007, Cheryl; two *s*. *Educ:* Ferryhill Comp. Sch.; Thames Valley Univ., Slough. Longueville Manor, 1994; Hd Chef, Bohemia (Michelin Star, 2005), 2002–13; Partner, Don Street Deli, 2013–; Chef Dir, Ormer Jersey (Michelin Star), 2013–17. Consultant, 12 Hay Hill Members Club, 2014–17. Ambassador, Jersey Royal Co., 2011–; British Celebrity Ambassador, Teenage Cancer Trust, 2013–. Patron, Caring Cooks Charity, 2016–. *Publications:* Shaun Rankin's Seasoned Islands, 2010; contributor: Yes Chef!, 2009; Nigel Haworth's Obsession, 2010; The Good Food Guide Recipes, 2011. *Recreations:* fishing, ski-ing, foraging. *Address:* Ormer Mayfair, 7–12 Half Moon Street, W1J 7BH.

**RANKIN, Prof. Susan Kathleen,** PhD; FBA 2009; FSA; Professor of Medieval Music, University of Cambridge, since 2006; Fellow of Emmanuel College, Cambridge, since 1984; *b* Belfast; *d* of (James) Frederick Rankin and Dr Kathleen Rankin; *m* 1999, Prof. David Michael Ganz. *Educ:* Victoria Coll., Belfast; Newnham Coll., Cambridge (BA 1975; PhD 1982); King's Coll., London (MMus 1976). Res. Fellow, Emmanuel Coll., Cambridge, 1981–84; Asst Lectr, 1990–93, Lectr, 1993–99, Reader in Medieval Music, 1999–2006, Univ. of Cambridge. Vis. Helen Waddell Prof., QUB, 2000–05. Member: Council, Plainsong and Mediæval Music Soc., 1984–; Council, Henry Bradshaw Soc., 1993– (Chm., 2013–); Cttee, Early English Church Music, 2005–. Gov., Forest Sch., London, 2000–12. FSA 2006; MAE 2007. Corresp. Mem., American Musicological Soc., 2015; Corresp. Fellow, Medieval Acad. of America, 2016. Dent Medal, Royal Musical Assoc., 1995. *Publications:* The Music of the Medieval Liturgical Drama in France and England, 2 vols, 1989; (ed with D. Hiley) Music in the Medieval English Liturgy: Plainsong and Mediæval Music Society centennial essays, 1993; (ed with W. Arlt) Stiftsbibliothek St Gallen Codices 484 & 381, 3 vols, 1996; The Winchester Troper, Introduction and Facsimile, 2007; Writing Sounds in Carolingian Europe: the invention of musical notation, 2018; numerous book chapters and articles in jls incl. Early Music, Early Music History, Jl of Amer. Musicological Soc., Anglo-Saxon England and Revue bénédictine. *Recreations:* music, European art, Irish sea. *Address:* Emmanuel College, Cambridge CB2 3AP. *T:* (01223) 334206. *E:* skr1000@cam.ac.uk.

**RANKINE, Fiona Grace;** *see* McLeod, F. G.

**RANKINE, Jean Morag, (Mrs N. A. Hall);** Deputy Director of the British Museum, 1983–97; *b* 5 Sept. 1941; *d* of late Alan Rankine and Margaret Mary Sloan Rankine (*née* Reid); *m* 1992, Norman Anthony Hall. *Educ:* Central Newcastle High Sch.; University College London (BA, MPhil; Fellow, 1990); Univ. of Copenhagen. Grad. Assistant, Durham Univ. Library, 1966–67; British Museum: Res. Assistant, Dept of Printed Books, 1967–73; Asst Keeper, Director's Office, 1973–78; Head of Public Services, 1978–83. *Recreations:* sculling, ski-ing, fell-walking, opera, motorcycling. *Address:* 49 Hartington Road, W4 3TS. *Clubs:* Thames Rowing; Mortlake, Anglian and Alpha Rowing; Clydesdale Amateur Rowing (Glasgow).

**RANN, Hon. Michael David,** CNZM 2009; AC 2016; Chief Executive Officer, Rann Strategy Group, since 2016; *b* Sidcup, Kent, 5 Jan. 1953; *s* of Frederick George and Winifred Hetty Rann; *m* 1st, 1982, Jennifer Russell (marr. diss.); one *s* one *d*; 2nd, 2006, Sasha Carruozzo. *Educ:* Northcote Coll., NZ; Auckland Univ. (MA). Political Journalist, Radio NZ, 1976–77; Press Secretary: to Premier of SA, 1977–79, 1982–85; to Leader of the Opposition, 1979–82. MHA (ALP) Briggs, 1985–93, Ramsay, 1993–2012, SA. South Australia Government: Minister: for Employment and Further Educn, of Youth Affairs, of Aboriginal Affairs, and Assisting Minister of Ethnic Affairs, 1989–92; for Business and Regl Develt, of Tourism and of State Services, 1992–93; Dep. Leader of the Opposition, and Shadow Minister for Regl Develt, Employment, Training and Further Educn, 1993–94; Leader of the Opposition, 1994–2002; Shadow Minister: for Industry, Manufacturing and Small Business, 1994–95; for Economic Develt, 1994–2002; for Jobs, 1998 and 2000–02; for Industry, 1999–2000; Premier of SA, 2002–11; Minister: for Volunteers, 2002–06; for the Arts and for Econ. Develt, 2002–11; for Social Inclusion, 2004–11; for Sustainability and Climate Change, 2006–11. Mem., Parly Public Works Standing Cttee, 1986–89. Nat. Pres., 2008, Nat. Vice Pres., 2009, ALP. High Comr for Australia in the UK, 2012–14; Ambassador of Australia to Italy, Libya, Albania and San Marino, 2014–16. Member: Australian Aboriginal Affairs Council, 1989–92; Australian Educn Council, 1990–92; SA Manuf. Council (Dep. Chm., 1992–93); Dep. Chm., Automotive Industry Task Force; Chair, Internat. States and Regions Network, 2008–11, Mem., Internat. Leadership Council, 2011–12, Climate Gp. Chm., Low Carbon Australia Ltd, 2012. Mem. Bd, Techsearch, 1986–89; Member Council: SA Inst. of Technol., 1986–89; Univ. of SA, 1994–97. Member: Commonwealth War Graves Commn, 2012–14; King's Commn for London, 2016–; Trustee, Imperial War Mus., 2012–14. Professorial Fellow, Flinders Univ., 2012–; Adjunct Prof., Carnegie Mellon Univ., 2012–; Vis. Sen. Res. Fellow, Univ. of Auckland, 2012–; Vis. Prof., Policy Inst., KCL, 2016–. Sen. Fellow, Center for National Policy, Washington, DC, 2012–. Philip of Macedonia Award, Fed. Pan Macedonian Assoc., Australia, 1996; Nikki (Victory) Award, Aust. Hellenic Council, 1997. *Recreations:* reading, films, travel, soccer, arts, writing. *E:* mike@rannstrategygroup.com. *Clubs:* Reform; Northern (NZ); South Adelaide Football, Port Adelaide Football.

**RANNARD, Prof. Steven Paul,** DPhil; FRSC; Professor of Chemistry, University of Liverpool, since 2007; *b* Orpington; *s* of Alfred James Rannard and Patricia Mary Bruce Rannard (*née* Ta'Bois); *m* 1992, Amanda Jane Bates; one *s* one *d*. *Educ:* Holyhead Secondary Sch.; Univ. of Sussex (BSc Hons 1988; DPhil 1992). FRSC 2007. Res. Associate, Cookson Technol. Centre, 1992–93; Principal Scientist: Courtaulds Strategic and Corporate Res., 1993–96; Courtaulds Coatings and Sealants, 1996–98; Unilever Research and Development - Port Sunlight Laboratory: Molecular Sci. Unit Leader, 1998–2001; Functional Ingredients Sci. Area Leader, 2001–05; Molecular and Nano Technols Discovery Platform Dir, 2005–07. Vis. Prof., Univ. of Liverpool, 2003–07; Vis. Lectr, Univ. of Sussex, 1999–2001; RSC Industrial Lecturer: Strathclyde Univ., 2001; Univ. of Sussex, 2002; Royal Soc. Industry Fellow, 2005–09. Co-Founder and CSO, IOTA NanoSolutions Ltd, 2005–13 (IOTA NanoSolutions Industrial Sen. Res. Fellow, 2007–10); Co-Founder and non-exec. Dir, Hydra Polymers Ltd, 2007–12; Co-Founder, 2014, Dir, 2019–, Tandem Nano Ltd. Mem., Welsh Govt Sêr Cymru (Rising Stars) Delivery Bd, 2012–18. Member: Applied Polymer Sci. Cttee, Inst. of Materials, 1997–2000; UK Cttee, RSC/SCI Macro Gp, 1998–2002; Innovate UK Emerging Technologies and Industries Steering Gp, 2015–18; Co-Founder and Mem. Cttee, Recent Appointees in Polymer Sci. Gp, 1999–2004. Mem., Mgt Team, Manchester Organic Materials Innovation Centre, 2002–06. Vice-Chair and Co-Founder, British Soc. for Nanomedicine, 2012–. Trustee, High Polymer Res. Gp, 2001–06. Co-Founder and Co-Ed. in Chief, Jl Interdisciplinary Nanomedicine, 2015–. *Publications:* contrib.

chapters to scientific text books; contribs to peer-reviewed scientific jls; co-inventor for 59 patent families. *Recreations:* theatre, cinema, reading, music, walking, photography, travel. *Address:* Department of Chemistry, University of Liverpool, Crown Street, Liverpool L69 7ZD. *T:* (0151) 794 3501. *E:* srannard@liv.ac.uk.

**RANSFORD, John Anthony,** CBE 1997; Chief Executive, Local Government Association, 2009–11 (Deputy Chief Executive, 2005–08); *b* 19 Sept. 1948; *s* of Sydney George Ransford and Ethel Alice Ransford (*née* Peters); *m* 1971, Liz Hainsworth; one *s* one *d*. *Educ:* Letchworth Grammar Sch.; Univ. of Sussex (BA Hons Sociol.; MSocWork). CQSW 1972. Probation Officer, SE London Probation and After-Care Service, 1972–74; Kirklees Metropolitan Council: Trng Officer, Social Services Dept, 1974–77; Health Liaison Officer, 1977–79; Asst Dir, Social Services, 1979–82, Dir, 1982–87; Actg Chief Exec., 1987; Dir, Social Services, 1988–94, Chief Exec., 1994–99, N Yorks CC; Hd, Social Affairs, Health and Housing, subseq. Dir, Educn and Social Policy, LGA, 1999–2005. Chm., Spurriergate Trading Co., York, 2013–18; non-exec. Dir, Care Mgt Gp, 2013–18; Bd Dir, HC-One Ltd, 2014–. Trustee, Dunhill Medical Trust, 2013–. Hon. Sec., Assoc. of Dirs of Social Services, 1993–96. *Recreations:* theatre, foreign travel, current affairs. *E:* jaransford@gmail.com.

**RANSON, Lee;** Chief Executive Officer, Eversheds Sutherland, since 2017; *b* Skegness, 16 Dec. 1964; *s* of Brian William Ranson and Lynnora Ranson; *m* 1990, Alexis Fionna; one *s* two *d*. *Educ:* Wilmslow Boys' Grammar Sch.; Hull Univ. (LLB). Solicitor, Eversheds, then Eversheds Sutherland, 1990–: Hd, Real Estate, 2005–08; Man. Partner, 2009–17. *Recreations:* golf, walking, boxing. *Address:* 4 Ogden Road, Bramhall, Stockport, Cheshire SK7 1HJ. *T:* 07771 891772. *E:* leeranson@eversheds-sutherland.com.

**RANTZEN, Dame Esther (Louise), (Dame Esther Wilcox),** DBE 2015 (CBE 2006; OBE 1991); television producer/presenter, since 1968; journalist; charity campaigner; *b* 22 June 1940; *d* of late Harry Rantzen and Katherine Rantzen; *m* 1977, Desmond John Wilcox (*d* 2000); one *s* two *d*. *Educ:* North London Collegiate Sch.; Somerville Coll., Oxford (MA; Hon. Fellow 2011). Studio manager making dramatic sound effects, BBC Radio, 1963; BBC TV: Researcher, 1965; Dir, 1967; Reporter, Braden's Week, 1968–72; Producer/Presenter, That's Life, 1973–94, scriptwriter, 1976–94; Producer, documentary series, The Big Time, 1976; Presenter: Esther Interviews …, 1988; Hearts of Gold, 1988; Esther, 1994–2002; That's Esther, 1999–; The Baby Boomer's Guide to Growing Old, 2017; House Trap, 2018; Producer/Presenter, Drugwatch, Childwatch, The Lost Babies, How to Have a Good Death and other progs on social issues; reporter/producer, various documentaries, religious and current affairs TV progs. Member: Nat. Consumer Council, 1981–90; Health Educn Authority, 1989–95; Task Force to review services for drug misusers, DoH, 1994. President: ChildLine, 2006– (Chair, 1986–2006); Action for ME (formerly Assoc. of Young People with ME), 1996–; Founder and Trustee, 2012, Pres., 2014–, Silver Line (Chm., 2012–14); a Vice-President: Nat. Deaf Children's Soc.; Rennie Grove Hospice Care (formerly Iain Rennie Hospice at Home); Action on Hearing Loss; Vice-Patron, Rose Road Appeal (people with disabilities in S Hants); Patron: DEMAND (furniture for the disabled); SIMR (Seriously Ill for Medical Research); Livability (formerly John Grooms Assoc.); Hillingdon Manor Sch. for Autistic Children, 1999–; The New Sch. at West Heath (The Princess Diana Sch.), 2000–; Campaign for Courtesy; North London Hospice; Nat. Assoc. for People Abused in Childhood; Families in Care; Bristol Grandparents' Support Gp; Siblings Together; Red Balloon; Compassion in Dying; Operation Encompass, 2016–; Ambassador, BHF. Champion, Community Legal Service, 2000. Chair, 4Children Commn into the Family, 2009–. Trustee, NSPCC, 2006–18 (Hon. Mem., 1989). Contested (Ind Rantzen) Luton South, 2010. FRTS 1995. Hon. DLitt: Southampton Inst. for FE, 1994; South Bank, 2000; Portsmouth, 2003; Wolverhampton, 2009; Staffordshire, 2009; Hon. Fellow, Liverpool John Moore's Univ., 2008. Personality of 1974, RTS award; BBC TV Personality of 1975, Variety Club of GB; European Soc. for Organ Transplant Award, 1985; Special Judges' Award for Journalism, RTS, 1986; Richard Dimbleby Award, BAFTA, 1988; Snowdon Award for Services to Disabled People, 1996; RTS Hall of Fame Award, 1998; Lifetime Achievement Award, Women in Film and TV, 2005. SSstJ 1992. *Publications:* (with Desmond Wilcox): Kill the Chocolate Biscuit, 1981; Baby Love, 1985; (with Shaun Woodward) Ben: the story of Ben Hardwick, 1985; Esther (autobiog.), 2001; A Secret Life (novel), 2003; If Not Now, When?: living the baby boomer adventure, 2008; Running Out of Tears, 2011. *Recreations:* family life, gardening. *Address:* c/o Billy Marsh Associates/Avalon, 4a Exmoor Street, W10 6BD.

**RAO, Prof. Calyampudi Radhakrishna,** Padma Vibhushan, 2001; FRS 1967; Eberly Professor of Statistics, Pennsylvania State University, 1988–2001, now Emeritus (Director, Center for Multivariate Analysis, 2001–10); Research Professor, University at Buffalo, since 2010; *b* 10 Sept. 1920; *s* of C. D. Naidu and A. Laksmikantamma; *m* 1948, C. Bhargavi Rao; one *s* one *d*. *Educ:* Andhra Univ. (MA, 1st Class Maths 1940); Calcutta Univ. (MA, 1st Class Statistics 1943; Gold Medal); PhD 1948, ScD, Cambridge (Hon. Fellow, King's Coll., Cambridge, 1975). Indian Statistical Institute: Superintending Statistician, 1943–49; Professor and Head of Division of Theoretical Research and Training, 1949–64; Dir, Res. and Training Sch., 1964–76 (Sec., 1972–76); Jawaharlal Nehru Professor, 1976–84. Univ. Prof., Univ. of Pittsburgh, 1979–88. Nat. Prof., India, 1987–92. Co-editor, Sankhya, Indian Jl of Statistics, 1964–72, Editor, 1972–96. Member, Internat. Statistical Inst., 1951 (Mem. Statistical Educn Cttee, 1958–; Treasurer, 1962–65; Pres.-elect, 1975–77, Pres., 1977–79, Hon. Mem. 1982); Chm., Indian Nat. Cttee for Statistics, 1962–70; President: Biometric Soc., 1973–75 (Hon. Life Mem., 1986); Indian Econometric Soc., 1971–76; Forum for Interdisciplinary Mathematics, 1982–84. Fellow: Indian Nat. Sci. Acad., 1953 (Vice-Pres., 1973, 1974); Inst. of Math. Statistics, USA, 1958 (Pres., 1976–77); Amer. Statistical Assoc., 1972; Econometric Soc., 1972; Indian Acad. of Scis, 1974; Founder Fellow: Third World Sci. Acad., 1983; Nat. Acad. of Scis, India, 1988; Nat. Acad. of Scis, USA, 1995; Foreign Mem., Lithuanian Acad. of Scis, 1997. Hon. Fellow: Royal Stat. Soc., 1969; Amer. Acad. of Arts and Scis, 1975; Calcutta Stat. Assoc., 1985; Biometric Soc., 1986; Finnish Statistical Soc., 1990; Inst. of Combinatorics and its Applications, 1995; Portuguese Statistical Soc., 2002; Eur. Acad. of Scis, 2009. Shanti Swarup Bhatnagar Memorial Award, 1963; Guy Medal in Silver, 1965, Guy Medal in Gold, 2011, Royal Stat. Soc.; Padma Bhushan, 1968; Meghnad Saha Medal, 1969; J. C. Bose Gold Medal, 1979; S. S. Wilke's Meml Medal, 1989; Mahalanobis Birth Centenary Gold Medal, 1996; Dist. Achievement Medal, Sect. on Stats and Envmt, Amer. Stat. Assoc., 1997; Carol and Emanuel Parzen Prize for statistical innovation, Texas A&M Univ., 2000; US Nat. Medal of Sci., 2001; Army Wilkes Medal, 2002; Srinivasa Ramanujan Medal, 2003; Mahalanobis Award, ISI, 2003; India Sci. Award, 2010; Neyman Medal, Polish Statistical Soc., 2014; Sirdar Patel Lifetime Achievement Award, 2015. Hon. DSc: Andhra; Leningrad; Athens; Osmania; Ohio State; Philippines; Tampere; Neuchatel; Poznan; Indian Statistical Inst.; Colorado State; Hyderabad; Barcelona; Slovak Acad. of Scis; Guelph; Munich; Venkateswara; Waterloo; Brasilia; Athens; Kent; Cyprus; Wollongong; Oakland; Calcutta; Pretoria; Nova de Lisboa; Madras; Visva-Bharati; Univ. of San Marcos; Lima; Univ. of Rhode Island; Jawaharlal Tech. Univ.; Univ. of Colombo; Karnataka; Univ. at Buffalo; Rashtria Vidyapeth; Tirupati; Indian Inst. of Technol., Kharagpur; Hon. DLit Delhi. Hon. Prof., Univ. of San Marcos, Lima. *Publications:* (with Mahalanobis and Majumdar) Anthropometric Survey of the United Provinces, 1941, a statistical study, 1949; Advanced Statistical Methods in Biometric Research, 1952; (with Mukherjee and Trevor) The Ancient Inhabitants of Jebal Moya, 1955; (with Majumdar) Bengal Anthropometric Survey, 1945, a statistical study, 1959; Linear Statistical Inference and its Applications, 1965; (with A. Matthai and S. K. Mitra) Formulae and Tables for Statistical Work, 1966; Computers and the Future of Human Society, 1968; (with S. K. Mitra) The Generalised Inverse of Matrices and its Applications, 1971; (with A. M. Kagan and Yu. V. Linnik) Characterization Problems of Mathematical Statistics, 1973; (with J. Kleffe) Estimation of Variance Components and its Applications, 1988; Statistics and Truth, 1989; (with H. Toutenburg) Linear Models, 1995; (with D. N. Shanbhag) Choquet-Deny Type Functional Equations with Applications to Stochastic Models, 1994; (with M. B. Rao) Matrix Algebra and its Applications to Statistics and Econometrics, 1998. *Address:* CR Rao Advanced Institute of Mathematics, Statistics and Computer Science, University of Hyderabad Campus, Prof. C. R. Rao Road, Hyderabad 500046, India.

**RAO, Prof. Chintamani Nagesa Ramachandra,** Padma Shri, 1974; Padma Vibhushan, 1985; Bharat Ratna, 2014; FRS 1982; CChem, FRSC; Hon. President and Linus Pauling Research Professor, Jawaharlal Nehru Centre for Advanced Scientific Research, Bangalore, India, since 2000 (President, 1989–99); Albert Einstein Research Professor, 1995–99; Distinguished Research Fellow, Department of Materials Science, University of Cambridge, since 2007; *b* 30 June 1934; *s* of H. Nagesa Rao; *m* 1960, Indumati; one *s* one *d*. *Educ:* Banaras Univ. (MSc); Univ. of Mysore (DSc); Univ. of Purdue, USA (PhD). Research Chemist, Univ. of California, Berkeley, 1958–59; Lectr, Indian Inst. of Science, 1959–63; Prof., Indian Inst. of Technology, Kanpur, 1963–76, Head of Chemistry Dept, 1964–68, Dean of Research, 1969–72; Jawaharlal Nehru Fellow, 1973–75; Indian Institute of Science, Bangalore: Founder Chm., Solid State and Structural Chemistry Unit and Materials Res. Laboratory, 1977–84; Dir, 1984–94; Hon. Prof., 1994–. Commonwealth Vis. Prof., Univ. of Oxford, and Fellow, St Catherine's Coll., 1974–75; Jawaharlal Nehru Vis. Prof., Univ. of Cambridge, and Professorial Fellow, King's Coll., Cambridge, 1983–84; Linnett Vis. Prof., Univ. of Cambridge, 1998; Gauss Prof., Acad. of Scis, Göttingen, 2003; Albert Einstein Prof., Chinese Acad. of Scis, 2012 (Foreign Fellow). Blackett Lectr, Royal Soc., 1991. US Nat. Acad. of Sci. Lect., 1993. Visiting Professor: Purdue Univ., USA, 1967–68, 1982 (Adjunct Prof., 2004–); Univ. Joseph Fourier, Grenoble, 1990; Univ. of Southampton, 2007–10; Distinguished Visiting Professor: La Trobe Univ., Melbourne; UCLA, Berkeley, 2008–11; Dist. Vis. Prof. of Materials, UCLA, Santa Barbara, 1995–; Dist. Adjunct Prof., Temple Univ., PA, 2016. Hon. Prof., Univ. of Wales, Cardiff, 1993–97. President: INSA, 1985–86; IUPAC, 1985–87; Indian Sci. Congress, 1987–88; Indian Acad. of Scis, 1989–91; Materials Res. Soc. of India, 1989–91. Member: First Nat. Cttee of Science and Technology, Govt of India, 1971–74; Science Adv. Cttee to Union Cabinet of India, 1981–86 (Chm., 1997–98); Atomic Energy Commn of India, 1986–2014; Chm., Science Adv. Council to Prime Minister, 1985–89, 2004–14. Member: Gen. Council, ICSU; Internat. Sci. Adv. Bd, UNESCO, 1996–99. Wigner Meml Lect., Oakridge, 2015. Foreign Member: Slovenian Acad. of Scis, 1983; Serbian Acad. of Scis, 1986; Amer. Acad. of Arts and Scis, 1986; USSR Acad. of Scis, 1988; Czechoslovak Acad. of Scis, 1988; Polish Acad. of Scis, 1988; US Nat. Acad. of Scis, 1990; Pontifical Acad. of Scis, 1990; Academia Europaea, 1997; Brazilian Acad. of Scis, 1997; European Acad. of Arts, Scis and Humanities, 1997; Japan Acad., 1998; Royal Spanish Acad. of Scis, 1999; French Acad. of Scis, 2000; Centennial Foreign Fellowship, Amer. Chemical Soc., 1976; Founder Mem., Third World Acad. of Scis, 1983– (Pres., 2000–); Internat. Mem. (formerly Foreign Mem.), Amer. Philosophical Soc., 1995; Foreign Fellow, Royal Soc. of Canada. Hon. Fellow: UWCC, 1997; St Catherine's Coll., Oxford, 2007; Hon. FRSC 1989; Hon. FInstP 2006. Hon. doctorates from 79 universities include: Hon. DSc: Purdue, 1982; Bordeaux, 1983; Sri Venkateswara, 1984; Roorkee, 1985; Banaras, Osmania, Mangalore and Manipur, 1987; Anna, Mysore, Burdwan, 1988; Wroclaw, 1989; Andhra, Karnataka, 1990; Bangalore, Hyderabad, Indian Inst. of Technology, Kharagpur, 1991; Oxford, 2007; Temple 2017. Many awards and medals, incl.: Marlow Medal of Faraday Soc. (London), 1967; Bhatnagar Prize, 1968; Royal Soc. of Chemistry (London) Medal, 1981; Centennial For. Fellowship of Amer. Chemical Soc., 1976; Hevrovsky Gold Medal, Czech. Acad. of Scis, 1989; Golden Jubilee Prize, CSIR, 1991; P. C. Ray Meml Award, 1994; Sahabdeen Award for Sci., Sri Lanka, 1994; Medal for Chemistry, Third World Acad. of Scis, 1995; Albert Einstein Gold Medal, UNESCO, 1996; Shatabdi Puraskar prize, Indian Sci. Congress Assoc., 1999; Centenary Medal, RSC, 2000; Hughes Medal, Royal Soc., 2000; Millennium Plaque of Honour, Indian Sci. Cong., 2001; Somiya Award, Internat. Union of Materials Res., 2004; India Sci. Prize, 2005; (jtly) Dan David Internat. Prize for Materials Sci., 2005; Chemical Pioneer, Amer. Inst. of Chemists, 2005; Nikkei Asia Prize for Sci. and Technol. and Innovation, 2008; Royal Medal, Royal Soc., 2009; August-Wilhelm-von-Hoffmann Medal, German Chem. Soc., 2010; Ernesto Illy Trieste Sci. Prize, 2011; Von Hippel Award, Materials Res. Soc., USA, 2017; first Sheikh Saud Internat. Prize for Materials Res., UAE, 2019. Comdr, Order of Rio Branco (Brazil), 2002; Chevalier, Légion d'Honneur (France), 2005; Order of Friendship (Russia), 2009; Order of Rising Sun, Gold and Silver Star (Japan), 2015. *Publications:* 52 books including: Ultraviolet and Visible Spectroscopy, 1960, 3rd edn 1975; Chemical Applications of Infrared Spectroscopy, 1963; Spectroscopy in Inorganic Chemistry, 1970; Modern Aspects of Solid State Chemistry, 1970; University General Chemistry, 1973; Solid State Chemistry, 1974; Phase Transitions in Solids, 1978; Preparation and Characterization of Materials, 1981; The Metallic and the Non-metallic States of Matter, 1985; New Directions in Solid State Chemistry, 1986; Chemistry of Oxide Superconductors, 1988; Chemical and Structural Aspects of High Temperature Oxide Superconductors, 1988; Bismuth and Thallium Superconductors, 1989; Advances in Catalyst Design, 1991; Chemistry of High Temperature Superconductors, 1991; Chemistry of Advanced Materials, 1992; Chemical Approaches to the Synthesis of Inorganic Materials, 1994; Transition Metal Oxides, 1995; Metal-Insulator Transition Revisited, 1995; Understanding Chemistry, 1999; Superconductivity Today, 1999; 1730 research papers. *Recreations:* gourmet cooking, gardening. *Address:* Jawaharlal Nehru Centre for Advanced Scientific Research, Jakkur Post, Bangalore 560064, India. *T:* (office) (80) 23653075, *T:* (home) (80) 23601410.

**RAPER, Maj.-Gen. Anthony John,** CB 2006; CBE 1996 (MBE 1987); Quartermaster General, Ministry of Defence, 2002–06; *b* 14 April 1950. *Educ:* RMA Sandhurst; Selwyn Coll., Cambridge (BA 1974, MA 1976). Commnd Royal Signals, 1970; posts in UK, Germany, Cyprus, Bosnia and NATO; Commander: 4th Armoured Div. and Signal Regt, 1988–91; 1st Signal Bde, Allied Comd Europe, 1994–95; Defence Intelligence Staff; Directorate of Land Warfare; directing staff, RMA Sandhurst and Staff Coll.; Dir, Operational Requirements for Inf. and Communication Services; Chief Exec., Defence Communications Services Agency, 1998–2002; Dir Gen. Strategy and Logistics Develt, 2002–04; Defence Logistics Transformation Prog. Team Leader, 2004–06. Sen. Defence (formerly Defence and Security) Advr, PwC, 2011–.

**RAPHAEL, Adam Eliot Geoffrey;** Editor, Good Hotel Guide, since 2004; *b* 22 April 1938; *s* of Geoffrey George Raphael and Nancy Raphael (*née* Rose); *m* 1970, Caroline Rayner Ellis; one *s* one *d*. *Educ:* Arnold House; Charterhouse; Oriel Coll., Oxford (BA Hons History). 2nd Lieut Royal Artillery, 1956–58. Copy Boy, Washington Post, USA, 1961; Swindon Evening Advertiser, 1962–63; Film Critic, Bath Evening Chronicle, 1963–64; The Guardian: Reporter, 1965; Motoring Correspondent, 1967–68; Foreign

Correspondent, Washington and S Africa, 1969–73; Consumer Affairs Columnist, 1974–76; Political Correspondent, The Observer, 1976–81, Political Editor, 1981–86; Presenter, Newsnight, BBC TV, 1987–88; an Asst Editor, 1988, Exec. Editor, 1988–93, The Observer; writer on Home Affairs, 1994, political correspondent, 1994–2004, The Economist. Awards include: Granada Investigative Journalist of the Year, 1973; British Press Awards, Journalist of the Year, 1973. *Publications*: My Learned Friends, 1989; Ultimate Risk: the inside story of the Lloyd's catastrophe, 1994. *Recreations*: tennis, golf, ski-ing. *Address*: 50 Addison Avenue, W11 4QP. *T*: (020) 7603 9133. *Clubs*: Garrick, Hurlingham.

**RAPHAEL, Caroline Sarah;** Director and Producer, Dora Productions, since 2015; *b* 15 Jan. 1958; *d* of Arnold Raphael and Lily Suzanne (*née* Shaffer); *m* 1st, 1982, Michael Eaves (marr. diss. 2001); one *s*; 2nd, 2011, Paul Keers. *Educ*: Putney High Sch.; Manchester Univ. (BA Hons Drama). Theatre director: Nuffield Theatre, 1980–81; Bristol Old Vic, 1981–83; Gate Theatre, London, 1983; Literary Agent and Publisher, Chappel's Music, 1983; joined BBC Radio, 1984: Script Reader, Producer, Editor Drama, 1984–90; Editor Drama, Features, Youth Programmes, Radio 5, 1990–94; Hd of Drama, BBC Radio, 1994–97; Commng Editor, Comedy, Drama, Fiction, Arts Features, BBC Radio 4, 1997–2015; Editl Strategy for BBC Radio 4 Extra, 2012–15; Editl Dir, Penguin Random House Audio, 2015–16. Teacher of audio drama writing and production, Central St Martins, Creative Skillset and AudioTrain (formerly RIGTrain), 2015–; Associate Lectr, Central St Martins, UAL, 2018–. Mem. Bd, Paines Plough Theatre Co., 1996–2000; Council Mem., NYT, 2005–07. Vice-Chair, AudioUK (formerly Radio Independents Gp), 2017–. FRSA. Producer, The Red, BBC Radio 4, 2017 (Best Single Drama, BBC Audio Drama Awards, 2018). *Recreations*: listening to radio, reading, cooking, comedy, going to theatre, cinema and art exhibitions. *E*: mail@doraproductions.co.uk.

**RAPHAEL, Frederic Michael;** author; *b* 14 Aug. 1931; *s* of late Cedric Michael Raphael and Irene Rose Raphael (*née* Mauser); *m* 1955, Sylvia Betty Glatt; two *s* (one *d* decd). *Educ*: Charterhouse; St John's Coll., Cambridge (Maj. Schol. in Classics; MA (Hons)). FRSL 1964. Jackson Knight Meml Lectr, Exeter Univ., 2011. *Publications*: *novels*: Obbligato, 1956; The Earlsdon Way, 1958; The Limits of Love, 1960; A Wild Surmise, 1961; The Graduate Wife, 1962; The Trouble with England, 1962; Lindmann, 1963; Darling, 1965; Orchestra and Beginners, 1967; Like Men Betrayed, 1970; Who Were You With Last Night?, 1971; April, June and November, 1972; Richard's Things, 1973; California Time, 1975; The Glittering Prizes, 1976; Heaven and Earth, 1985; After the War, 1988 (adapted for television, 1989); The Hidden I, 1990; A Double Life, 1993; Old Scores, 1995; Coast to Coast, 1998; Fame and Fortune, 2007; Final Demands, 2010; Private Views, 2015; *short stories*: Sleeps Six, 1979; Oxbridge Blues, 1980 (also pubd as scripts of TV plays, 1984); Think of England, 1986; The Latin Lover, 1994; All His Sons, 1999; *biography*: Somerset Maugham and his World, 1977; Byron, 1982; *memoir*: Eyes Wide Open: a memoir of Stanley Kubrick and Eyes Wide Shut, 1999; A Spoilt Boy (autobiog.), 2003; Going Up (autobiog.), 2015; Personal Terms series: Personal Terms (notebooks 1951–1969), 2001; Rough Copy (notebooks 1970–1973), 2004; Cuts and Bruises (notebooks 1974–1978), 2006; Ticks and Crosses (notebooks 1978–1981), 2008; Ifs and Buts (notebooks 1978–79), 2011; There and Then (notebooks 1980–83), 2013; On the Contrary (notebooks 1983–88), 2017; *essays*: Bookmarks (ed), 1975; Cracks in the Ice, 1979; Of Gods and Men, 1992; France, the Four Seasons, 1994; The Necessity of Anti-Semitism, 1997; Karl Popper, 1998; (ed jtly and contrib.) The Great Philosophers from Socrates to Turing, 2000; The Benefits of Doubts, 2003; Some Talk of Alexander, 2006; A Jew Among the Romans: Flavius Josephus and his legacy, 2013; J. Robert Oppenheimer, For Example, 2013; Anti-Semitism, 2015; Antiquity Matters, 2017; *screenplays*: Nothing but the Best, 1964; Darling, 1965 (Academy Award); Two For The Road, 1967; Far From the Madding Crowd, 1967; A Severed Head, 1972; Daisy Miller, 1974; The Glittering Prizes, 1976 (sequence of TV plays) (Writer of the Year 1976, Royal TV Soc.); Rogue Male, 1976; (and directed) Something's Wrong (TV), 1978; School Play (TV), 1979; The Best of Friends (TV), 1979; Richard's Things, 1981; After the War (TV series), 1989; (and directed) The Man In The Brooks Brothers Shirt, 1991 (ACE Award); Eyes Wide Shut, 1999; For God's Sake (TV documentary series), 1998; Coast to Coast, 2004; *plays*: From The Greek, Arts, Cambridge, 1979; The Daedalus Dimension (radio), 1982; The Thought of Lydia (radio), 1988; The Empty Jew (radio), 1993; A Thousand Kisses (radio), 2011; Jake Liebowitz (radio), 2013; *translations*: Petronius: Satyrica, 2003; (with Kenneth McLeish): Poems of Catullus, 1976; The Oresteia, 1978 (televised as The Serpent Son, BBC, 1979); The Complete Plays of Aeschylus, 1991; Medea, 1994; Hippolytus, 1997; Aias, 1998; Bacchae, 1999; *correspondence*: (with Joseph Epstein) Distant Intimacy, 2013; (with Joseph Epstein) Where Were We?: a deepening friendship, 2017. *Recreations*: tennis, bridge, having gardened. *Address*: c/o Louise Greenberg Books Ltd, End House, Church Crescent, N3 1BG.

**RAPHAEL, Philip Montague, (Monty);** Special Counsel, Peters & Peters Solicitors LLP, 2005–18; *b* 8 Feb. 1937; *s* of Solomon and Sarah Raphael; *m* 1963, Leona Hartley; one *s* three *d* and one *s* decd). *Educ*: Davenant Sch.; University Coll. London (LLB Hons). Admitted solicitor, 1962; Partner, Peters & Peters, 1965–2005. Vis. Prof., Kingston Univ., 2004–. Mem. Bd, Fraud Adv. Panel. Hon. Solicitor, Howard League for Penal Reform. Hon. QC 2011. *Publications*: The Proceeds of Crime Act: how it will work in practice, 2003; Blackstone's Guide to the Bribery Act, 2010; Bribery Law and Practice, 2016. *Recreations*: obsessing about London, arts, travel, thinking very vigorously about exercise.

**RAPIER, Gillian Barbara;** *see* Westerman, G. B.

**RAPINET, Michael William;** a Vice-President, 1997–2002, and Acting Vice-President, 2003–05, Immigration Appeal Tribunal; *b* 13 April 1935; *s* of Charles Herbert Rapinet and Eleanor Adelaide Rapinet (*née* Hunt); *m* 1962, Christina Mary (*d* 2015), *d* of Captain William Eric Brockman, CBE, RN; one *s* one *d*. *Educ*: St Edward's Coll., Malta; St Joseph's Coll., London. Admitted Solicitor, 1957; Sen. Partner, Kidd Rapinet, 1958–85. Pt-time Chm., Industrial Tribunals, 1987–91; pt-time Chm., 1989–92, Chm., 1992–97, Immigration Tribunal. Pres., Council of Immigration Judges, 2000–01. Member (C): Wandsworth LBC, 1958–62; Berks CC, 1968–75 (Chm., Schs Cttee; Member: Finance Cttee; Personnel and Mgt Cttee). Freeman, Tallow Chandlers' Co. (Liveryman, 1983–2016). Founder: Order of Malta Homes Trust, 1975; Orders of St John Care Trust (formerly Orders of St John Trust), 1975. CStJ 1988; Kt of Magistral Grace, 1973, Kt Grand Cross, 1996, SMO (Malta). *Publications*: Our Lords the Sick: a history of the Orders of St John Care Trust, 2012. *Recreations*: fishing, gardening, walking, reading, theatre, music. *Address*: Greenlands, Townsend Road, Streatley-on-Thames, Berks RG8 9LH. *T*: (01491) 871740. *Club*: Carlton.

**RAPLEY, Prof. Christopher Graham,** CBE 2003; PhD; Professor of Climate Science, University College London, since 2009; *b* 8 April 1947; *s* of Ronald Rapley and Barbara Helen Rapley (*née* Stubbs); *m* 1970, Norma Khan; twin *d*. *Educ*: Jesus Coll., Oxford (BA Hons Physics 1969; MA 1974; four shooting half blues); Manchester Univ. (MSc Radio Astronomy 1970); UCL (PhD X-ray Astronomy 1976). Prof. of Remote Sensing Sci., UCL, 1991–97; Director: British Antarctic Survey, 1998–2007; Science Museum, 2007–10. Fellow: St Edmund's Coll., Cambridge, 1999–; UCL, 2008–. Exec. Dir, Internat. Geosphere-Biosphere Prog., Royal Swedish Acad. of Scis, 1994–97; Chm., ICSU Planning Gp, 2003–04, Mem., Jt Cttee, 2005–, for Internat. Polar Year 2007–08; Sen. Vis. Scientist, NASA Jet Propulsion Lab., 2006–; Chairman: UCL Communicating Climate Sci. Policy Commn, 2012–14; London Climate Change Partnership, 2013–19; UCL Communicating Climate Sci. Policy Commn II, 2017–. Pres., Internat. Scientific Cttee on Antarctic Res., 2006–08 (Vice Pres., 2000–04); Member: Earth Sci. Adv. Council, ESA, 2000–01; UK Deleg., Governing Council, ESF, 2000–03; Global Envmtl Res. Cttee, Royal Soc., 2007–12; ESA Dir Gen's High Level Sci. Policy Adv. Cttee, 2013–16 (Chm., 2014–16); Sci. Adv. Bd, Sci. Mus. Gp, 2019–. Vis. Prof., Imperial Coll. London, 2009–. Hon. Professor: UCL, 1998; UEA, 1999–. Mem., Adv. Council, Winston Churchill Meml Trust, 2008–10, 2013–. Science Consultant: Climate Change - The Facts (documentary), 2019; One Strange Rock (series), 2019. Patron, Surrey Climate Change Commn, 2019–. Co-writer and performer, 2071 - The World We'll Leave our Grandchildren, Royal Court, 2014. MAE 2010. Hon. DSc: Bristol, 2008; UEA, 2010–. Edinburgh Science Medal, Edinburgh Internat. Sci. Fest., 2008. *Publications*: more than 250 res. papers on space astronomy, Earth remote sensing, climate change, earth system sci., sci. communication. *Recreation*: digital photography. *Address*: Department of Earth Sciences, University College London, Room 301c, Kathleen Lonsdale Building, Gower Street, WC1E 6BT. *E*: chris.g.rapley@ucl.ac.uk.

**RAPSON, Sarah Oonagh;** Director, Authorisations, Financial Conduct Authority, since 2016; *b* London, 20 June 1967; *d* of Neil Rapson and Anne Rapson; *m* 2005, Rob McIvor; one *s*. *Educ*: Lancaster Univ. (BSc Maths 1988); London Business Sch. (MBA 2003). ACIB 1996. Manager, Branch Develt, Woolwich, later Barclays, 1991–2001; Strategy and Implementation Manager, American Express, 2003–05; Identity and Passport Service: Ops Dir, 2005–07; Exec. Dir, Service Planning and Delivery, 2007–10; Chief Exec., Identity and Passport Service, 2010–13; Registrar Gen. for England and Wales, 2010–14; interim Dir Gen., 2013–14, Dir Gen., 2014–16, UK Visas and Immigration, Home Office. Non-exec. Dir, N Middx Univ. Hosp. Trust, 2017–. *Address*: Financial Conduct Authority, 12 Endeavour Square, E20 1JN.

**RAPSON, Sydney Norman John,** BEM 1984; *b* 17 April 1942; *s* of late Sidney Rapson and of Doris Rapson (*née* Fisher); *m* 1967, Phyllis Edna, *d* of Frank and Beatrice Williams; one *s* one *d*. *Educ*: Southsea and Paulsgrove Secondary Modern Sch.; Portsmouth Dockyard Coll. Apprentice aircraft fitter, 1958–63, Aircraft Engr, 1963–97, MoD. Member (Lab): Portsmouth CC, 1971–97 (Lord Mayor, 1990–91; Hon. Alderman, 1999); Hants CC, 1973–76. Non-exec. Dir, Portsmouth Healthcare NHS Trust, 1993–97 (Gov., Portsmouth Hosp. Trust, 2007–). MP (Lab) Portsmouth N, 1997–2005; Team PPS, MoD, 2003–05. Dir, Paulsgrove Learning and Leisure Community, 2006–09. Freeman: City of London, 1990; City of Portsmouth, 2016. Imperial Service Medal, 1998. *Address*: 79 Washbrook Road, Paulsgrove, Portsmouth, Hants PO6 3SB.

**RASCH, Sir Simon (Anthony Carne),** 4th Bt *cr* 1903, of Woodhill, Danbury, Essex; *b* 26 Feb. 1948; *s* of Sir Richard Guy Carne Rasch, 3rd Bt and Anne Mary (*d* 1989), *e d* of Maj. John Henry Dent-Brocklehurst, OBE; *S* father, 1996; *m* 1987, Julia, *er d* of Maj. Michael Godwin Plantagenet Stourton; one *s* one *d*. *Educ*: Eton; RAC Cirencester. MRICS (ARICS 1973). A Page of Honour to HM The Queen, 1962–64. *Heir*: *s* Toby Richard Carne Rasch, *b* 28 Sept. 1994. *Address*: Priors Farm, Semley, Shaftesbury, Dorset SP7 9BP.

**RASHID, Faisal;** MP (Lab) Warrington South, since 2017; *m* Aleeza. *Educ*: Nat. Coll. of Business Admin and Econ., Lahore (MBA). Team Manager, HBOS, 1999–2005; business manager, NatWest Bank, Warrington, 2006–17. Mem. (Lab), Warrington BC, 2011–17 (Mayor, 2016–17). Mem., Internat. Trade Cttee, H of C, 2017–. Non-exec. Dir, Network Warrington. Trustee, St Rocco's Hospice. Mem., Warrington Parish Council, 2012–17. *Address*: House of Commons, SW1A 0AA.

**RASHLEIGH, Sir Richard (Harry),** 6th Bt *cr* 1831; management accountant; self-employed, since 1990; *b* 8 July 1958; *s* of Sir Harry Evelyn Battie Rashleigh, 5th Bt and Honora Elizabeth (*d* 1987), *d* of George Stuart Sneyd; *S* father, 1984; *m* 1996, Emma (*d* 2013), *o d* of John McGougan and Jennifer (*née* Dyke; she *m* 1987, Sir Antony Acland, *qv*); one *s* one *d*. *Educ*: Allhallows School, Dorset. Management Accountant with Arthur Guinness Son & Co., 1980–82; Dexion-Comino International Ltd, 1982–84; United Biscuits, 1985–88; Wessex Housing, 1988–90. *Recreations*: sailing, tennis, shooting. *Heir*: *s* David William Augustine Rashleigh, *b* 1 April 1997. *Address*: Menabilly, Par, Cornwall PL24 2TN. *T*: (01726) 815432. *Club*: Royal Fowey Yacht.

**RASMUSSEN, Anders Fogh,** Hon. KCMG 2015; Secretary-General, NATO, 2009–14; Founder and Chairman, Rasmussen Global, since 2014; *b* 26 Jan. 1953; *s* of Knud Rasmussen and Martha (*née* Fogh Andersen); *m* 1978, Anne-Mette; one *s* two *d*. *Educ*: Univ. of Aarhus (MSc Econs 1978). Consultant, Danish Fedn of Crafts and Small Industries, 1978–87. MP (L) Greve, Denmark, 1978–2009; Minister: for Taxation, 1987–92; for Econ. Affairs, 1990–92; spokesman for Liberal Party, 1992–98; Prime Minister of Denmark, 2001–09; Vice-Chairman: Housing Cttee, 1981–86; Econ. and Pol Affairs Cttee, 1993–98; Foreign Policy Bd, 1998–2001. Liberal Party: Mem., Mgt Cttee, 1984–87 and 1992–2009, Chm., 1998–2001, Parly Party; Vice-Chm., 1985–98, Chm., 1998–2009, nat. orgn. Nat. Chm., Liberal Youth of Denmark, 1974–76. Dr *hc*: George Washington, 2002; Corvinus, Budapest, 2008; Bucharest, 2013; Kaunas, 2014; Hon. LLD Hampden-Sydney Coll., Va, 2003; Hon. DPhil Haifa, 2008. Awards: Adam Smith Award, 1993; Politician of the Year, Danish Mktg Assoc., 1998; Liberal of the Year, Jongeren Organisatie Vrijheid en Democratie, Holland, 2002; European Leader, Polish Leaders Forum, 2003; European of the Year, Danish Eur. Movt, 2003; Robert Schuman Medal, EP, 2003; Best Leader in Denmark, 2005; Årets Erhvervspolitiker, Dansk Erhvervssammenslutning, 2005; Dist. Leadership Award, US Atlantic Council, 2013; Hillary Rodham Clinton Award, Georgetown Univ., 2014; Global Leadership Award, Chicago Council on Global Affairs, 2014. Medal of Merit in Gold (Denmark), 2002; Commander 1st Cl., Order of the Dannebrog (Denmark), 2002. Foreign decorations include: Grand Cross: Order of Merit (Portugal), 1992; Order of Merit (Germany), 2002; Order of Merit (Poland), 2003; Order of the Oak Crown (Luxembourg), 2003; Order of Nicaragua, 2003; Order of Star (Romania), 2004; Order of Polar Star (Sweden); Great Cross, Order Pedro Joaquín Chamorro (Nicaragua), 2003; Grand Duke Gediminas (Lithuania), 2004; Three Star Order (Latvia), 2005; Order of Stara Planina First Class (Bulgaria), 2006. *Publications*: Opgør med skattesystemet, 1979; Kampen om boligen, 1982; Fra socialstat til minimalstat, 1993; The Will to Lead: America's indispensable role in the global fight for freedom, 2016.

**RASMUSSEN, Lars Løkke;** MP (L) Frederiksborg, Denmark, since 1994; Prime Minister of Denmark, 2009–11 and 2015–19; *b* Vejle, Denmark, 15 May 1964; *m* 1998, Sólrun Jákupsdóttir; two *s* one *d*. *Educ*: Univ. of Copenhagen (LLM 1992). Mem., Græsted-Gilleleje Municipal Council, 1986–97; County Mayor, Frederiksborg County, 1998–2001. Minister for the Interior and Health, 2001–07, for Finance, 2007–09. Vice Chm., 1998–2009, Chm., 2009–19, Liberal Party. Nat. Chm., Young Liberals, 1986–89. Comdr 1st Cl., Order of the Dannebrog (Denmark), 2009; Grand Cross, Order of the Phoenix (Greece), 2009. *Publications*: Foreningshåndbogen, 1994; Hvis jeg bli'r gammel (If I Get Old), 1997; Løkkeland: Lars Løkke Rasmussens Danmark, 2006. *Address*: Folketinget, Christiansborg, 1240 Copenhagen K, Denmark.

**RASMUSSEN, Poul Nyrup;** Member (Social Democrats) for Denmark, European Parliament, 2004–09; *b* 15 June 1943; *s* of Oluf Nyrup Rasmussen and Vera Nyrup Rasmussen; *m* 1st (marr. diss.); (one *d* decd); 2nd (marr. diss.); 3rd, 1994, Lone Dybkjær. *Educ:* Esbjerg Statsskole; Univ. of Copenhagen (MA Econs). With Danish Trade Union Council, 1980–86: in Brussels, 1980–81; Chief Economist, 1981–86; Man. Dir, Employees' Capital Pension Fund, 1986–88. Chm., SDP, 1992–2002 (Dep. Chm., 1987–92); MP (SDP) Herning-Kredsen, Denmark, 1988–2004; Prime Minister of Denmark, 1993–2001. Pres., PES, 2004–11. Former Chm. Bd, Lindoe Offshore Renewables Center.

**RASSOOL, Bertrand Louis Maurice;** sustainable development consultant; Executive Director, Ecowatt Co. Ltd, Seychelles, since 2014; *b* 10 April 1957; *m* 1978, Estelle Gontier; one *s* two *d*. *Educ:* London Sch. of Econs (BSc Econs (Mathematical Econs and Econometrics)). Central Bank of Seychelles: economist, 1980; Asst Dir of Res., 1981–86; Dir of Res., 1986–88; Dir Gen., Planning and Econ. Co-operation Div., Min. of Planning and Ext. Relns, 1988–93; Principal Secretary: Min. of Foreign Affairs, Planning and Envmt, 1993–94; Min. of Industry, 1994–98; Min. of Tourism and Civil Aviation, 1998–99; High Comr of Seychelles to UK, 1999–2003. Gp Dep. CEO, British American Investment Gp (Mauritius), 2006–11 (Dir, 2005–11; Executive Chairman: Tourism and Leisure Div., 2008–09; Energy and Envmt Div., 2009–11). Non-executive Director: Trading Emissions plc (UK), 2007– (Advr, 2005–); Central Bank of Seychelles, 2012–. *Recreations:* fishing, chess, horse-racing. *Address:* Ecowatt Co. Ltd, PO Box 116, Victoria, Mahé, Seychelles.

**RASUL, Prof. Imran,** PhD; FBA 2019; Professor of Economics, University College London, since 2005; *b* London, 29 July 1974; *s* of Ghulam and Kaniz Rasul; *m* 2005, Prof. Oriana Bandiera, *qv*; one *s* one *d*. *Educ:* London Sch. of Econs and Pol Sci. (BSc Econs; PhD Econs 2003); University Coll., Oxford (MPhil Econs). Asst Prof. of Econs, Grad. Sch. of Business, Univ. of Chicago, 2002–05. *Recreations:* cricket, travel, yoga, gym. *Address:* Department of Economics, University College London, Room 205, Drayton House, 30 Gordon Square, WC1H 0AX. *E:* i.rasul@ucl.ac.uk.

**RATCLIFF, Antony Robin Napier;** Deputy Chairman and Chief Executive, Eagle Star Insurance, 1985–87; Visiting Professor, Sir John Cass Business School, City of London (formerly City University Business School), 1987–2005; *b* 26 Sept. 1925; *m* 1956, Helga Belohlawek (*d* 2014), Vienna; one *s*. FIA 1953; Aktuar, DAV, 1994; ASA. Nat. Correspondent for England, Internat. Actuarial Assoc., 1965–70; Mem. Council, Assoc. of British Insurers (formerly British Insurance Assoc.), 1969–87. Pres., Inst. of Actuaries, 1980–82; Vice-President: London Insce Inst., 1964–; Chartered Insce Inst., 1983–84. Hon. Mem., Assoc. internat. pour l'Etude de l'Economie de l'Assurance, 1991–2009 (Vice-Pres., 1986–90). Trustee, Soc. for the Protection of Life from Fire, 1989–2012 (Chm., 1998–2000). Mem., Evangelische Forschungs-akad., Berlin. Corresponding Member: Deutsche Gesellschaft für Versicherungsmathematik; Verein zur Förderung der Versicherungswirtschaft. Trustee, St Paul's German Evangelical Reformed Ch Trust; Extraordinary Mem. of Synod, German-speaking Protestant Congregations in GB, 2003–12. Messenger and Brown Prize-Winner, Inst. of Actuaries, 1963. Hon. DLitt City, 1986. Officer's Cross, Order of Merit (Germany), 2007. *Publications:* (jtly) Lessons from Central Forecasting, 1965; (jtly) Strategic Planning for Financial Institutions, 1974; (jtly) A House in Town, 1984; The Annals of the German Evangelical Reformed St Paul's Church, 2019; contribs to Jl of Inst. of Actuaries, Trans of Internat. Congress of Actuaries, Jl London Insce Inst., Jl Chartered Insce Inst., Blätter der Deutschen Gesellschaft für Versicherungsmathematik. *Address:* 8 Evelyn Terrace, Richmond, Surrey TW9 2TQ. *Clubs:* Actuaries, Anglo-Austrian Society.

**RATCLIFFE, Frederick William,** CBE 1994; MA, PhD; JP; University Librarian, University of Cambridge, 1980–94, now Emeritus; Life Fellow, since 1994 (Fellow, 1980–94), and Parker Librarian, 1995–2000, Corpus Christi College, Cambridge; *b* 28 May 1927; *y s* of late Sydney and Dora Ratcliffe, Leek, Staffs; *m* 1952, Joyce Brierley; two *s* one *d*. *Educ:* Leek High Sch., Staffs; Manchester Univ. (MA, PhD); MA Cantab. Served in N Staffs Regt, 1945–48. Manchester University: Graduate Res. Scholarship, 1951; Res. Studentship in Arts, 1952; Asst Cataloguer and Cataloguer, 1954–62; Sub-Librarian, Glasgow Univ., 1962–63; Dep. Librarian, Univ. of Newcastle upon Tyne, 1963–65; University Librarian, 1965–80, Dir, John Rylands University Library, 1972–80, Manchester University. Trustee, St Deiniol's Library, Hawarden, 1975–98 (Hon. Fellow, 2000). Hon. Lectr in Historical Bibliography, Manchester Univ., 1970–80; External Prof., Dept of Library and Inf. Studies, Loughborough Univ., 1981–86; Hon. Res. Fellow, Dept of Library, Archive and Inf. Studies, UCL, 1987; Sandars Reader in Bibliography, Cambridge Univ., 1988–89. Founder, later Pres., Consortium of Univ. Res. Libraries, 1984–94; Chm., Library Panel, The Wellcome Trust, 1988–94. Fellow, Chapter of Woodard Schools (Eastern Div.), 1981–97, now Emeritus (Vice-Provost, 1994–97). Chm., Adv. Cttee, Nat. Preservation Office, 1984–94. Trustee: Cambridge Foundn, 1989–94; Malaysian Commonwealth Studies Centre, 1994–98. Hon. FCLIP (Hon. FLA 1986). JP Stockport, 1972–80, Cambridge, 1981–97. Encomienda de la Orden del Merito Civil (Spain), 1988. *Publications:* Die Psalmenübersetzung Heinrichs von Mügeln, 1965; Preservation Policies and Conservation in British Libraries, 1984; many articles in learned journals. *Recreations:* book collecting, hand printing, cricket. *Address:* Ridge House, The Street, Rickinghall Superior, Diss, Norfolk IP22 1DY. *T:* (01379) 898232, (01379) 897199.

**RATCLIFFE, Sir James A.,** Kt 2018; Chairman and Founder, INEOS plc, since 1998; *b* 18 Oct. 1952; *s* of Alan and Marie Ratcliffe; two *s* one *d*. *Educ:* Univ. of Birmingham (BSc); London Business Sch. (MBA). ACMA. CEO, Inspec, 1992–98 (Founder, 1992). *Recreations:* ski-ing, running, mountains, wine.

**RATCLIFFE, (John) Michael;** writer and editor; *b* 15 June 1935; *s* of Donald Ratcliffe and Joyce Lilian Dilks; civil partnership 2006, *m* 2015, Howard Lichterman. *Educ:* Cheadle Hulme Sch.; Christ's Coll., Cambridge (MA). Trainee journalist, Sheffield Telegraph, 1959–61; Asst Literary and Arts Editor, Sunday Times, 1962–67; Literary Editor, 1967–72, chief book reviewer, 1972–82, The Times; freelance writer, 1982–83; theatre critic, 1984–89, Literary Ed., 1990–95, Contributing Ed., 1995–96, Observer; freelance writer, 1996–. Commended Critic of the Year, British Press Awards, 1989. Officer, Order of Merit (FRG), 2003. *Publications:* The Novel Today, 1968; The Bodley Head 1887–1987 (completed for J. W. Lambert), 1987. *Recreations:* music, travel, art, architecture, walking, reading, film, cooking. *Address:* Flat 6, The Design Works, 93–99 Goswell Road, EC1V 7EY. *T:* (020) 7490 8372. *E:* ratcliffe296@gmail.com.

**RATCLIFFE, Sir Peter (John),** Kt 2014; MD; FRCP, FMedSci; FRS 2002; Professor of Clinical Medicine, since 2016 (Nuffield Professor of Clinical Medicine, 2004–16), Director, Target Discovery Institute, since 2016, Director of Clinical Research, Francis Crick Institute, since 2016, and Member, Ludwig Institute for Cancer Research, since 2013, University of Oxford; Fellow, Magdalen College, Oxford, since 2004; Honorary Consultant in Acute General Medicine, John Radcliffe Hospital, Oxford University Hospitals NHS Trust, since 1990; *b* 14 May 1954; *s* of William and Alice Margaret Ratcliffe; *m* 1983, Fiona Mary MacDougall; two *s* two *d*. *Educ:* Lancaster Royal Grammar Sch.; Gonville and Caius Coll., Cambridge (MD 1987; Hon. Fellow, 2014); St Bartholomew's Hosp., London (MB ChB). FRCP 1995. University of Oxford: Wellcome Sen. Fellow, 1990–92; Fellow, Jesus Coll., 1992–2004; Prof. of Renal Medicine, 1996–2004. FMedSci 2002; Member: EMBO, 2006; Amer. Acad. of Arts and Scis, 2007. Dr *hc* Zurich, 2017. Louis-Jeantet Prize for Medicine, Fondation Louis-Jeantet, 2009; Canada Gairdner Award, Gairdner Foundn, 2010; Robert J. and Claire Pasarow Foundn Award, 2011; Baly Medal, RCP, 2011; Scientific Grand Prix of Instn Lefoulon-Delalande, Inst. of France, 2012; Jakob-Herz-Preis, Friedrich-Alexander-Universität, Erlangen-Nürnberg, 2012; Wiley Prize for Biomedical Res., 2014; Albert Lasker Basic Med. Res. Award, 2016; Buchanan Medal, Royal Soc., 2017; Massry Prize, 2018. *Publications:* contribs on aspects of renal and cell biology, particularly processes involved in cellular oxygen sensing. *Recreations:* fell-walking, gardening (when pressed). *Address:* Manor Farmhouse, 17 Church Street, Kidlington, Oxon OX5 2BA.

**RATFORD, Sir David (John Edward),** KCMG 1994 (CMG 1984); CVO 1979; HM Diplomatic Service, retired; translator and language consultant, University of Lund, Sweden, since 1997; *b* 22 April 1934; *s* of George Ratford and Lilian (*née* Jones); *m* 1960, Ulla Monica (*d* 2013), *d* of Oskar and Gurli Jerneck, Stockholm; two *d*. *Educ:* Whitgift Middle Sch.; Selwyn Coll., Cambridge (1st Cl. Hons Mod. and Med. Langs). National Service (Intell. Corps), 1953–55. Exchequer and Audit Dept, 1952; FO, 1955; 3rd Sec., Prague, 1959–61; 2nd Sec., Mogadishu, 1961–63; 2nd, later 1st Sec., FO, 1963–68; 1st Sec. (Commercial), Moscow, 1968–71; FCO, 1971–74; Counsellor (Agric. and Econ.), Paris, 1974–78; Counsellor, Copenhagen, 1978–82; Minister, Moscow, 1983–85; Asst Under-Sec., of State (Europe), 1986–90, and Dep. Political Dir, 1987–90, FCO; UK Rep., Permanent Council of WEU, 1986–90; Ambassador to Norway, 1990–94. Chm., Tushinskaya Trust, 1996–2011. Comdr, Order of the Dannebrog, Denmark, 1979. *Publications:* translations from Swedish: Zetterquist, A Europe of the Member States or of the Citizens?, 2002; Pihl Atmer, Stockholm Town Hall and its Architect, Ragnar Östberg, 2011; Jönsson, Jerneck and Arvidson, Politics and Development in a Globalised World, 2012; Per Gedin, Manilla, 2012. *Recreations:* music, travel. *Address:* Apt 4, 20 Cabanel Place, Kennington, SE11 6BD; Käringön, Bohuslän, Sweden. *Club:* Travellers.

**RATHBAND, Very Rev. Kenneth William;** Dean of St Andrews, Dunkeld and Dunblane, since 2007; Rector, Holy Trinity, Dunfermline, and of St Margaret's, Lunan Head, since 2018; *b* 1960. *Educ:* Edinburgh Theol Coll.; Edinburgh Univ. (BD 1986). Ordained deacon, 1986, priest, 1987; Asst Curate, St Paul's Cathedral, Dundee, 1986–88; Team Vicar, St Martin's, Dundee, 1988–89; Asst Curate, St Philips and St James', Edinburgh, 1990–91; Rector, St Ninian's, Alyth, with St Catherine's, Blairgowrie, and St Anne's, Coupar Angus, 1991–2018. *E:* krathband@btinternet.com.

**RATHBONE, Prof. Dominic William,** PhD; Professor of Ancient History, King's College London, since 2003; *b* 8 Feb. 1957; *s* of late Norman and Christine Rathbone; *m* 1993, Yvette Erete. *Educ:* Christ's Hosp., Horsham; Jesus Coll., Cambridge (BA Classics; PhD 1986). Lectr in Classics, Univ. of Aberdeen, 1981–84; Lectr, 1985–93, Reader, 1993–2003, in Ancient Hist., KCL. *Publications:* Economic Rationalism and Rural Society in Third-Century AD Egypt, 1991; (ed jtly) Cambridge Ancient History, vol. xi, 2001; (ed jtly) Egypt from Alexander to the Copts: an archaeological and historical guide, 2004. *Recreations:* travel, DIY. *Address:* Department of Classics, King's College London, Strand, WC2R 2LS. *T:* (020) 7848 2343. *E:* dominic.rathbone@kcl.ac.uk.

**RATHBONE, Jenny;** Member (Lab) Cardiff Central, National Assembly for Wales, since 2011; *b* Liverpool, 12 Feb. 1950; *d* of late Bertram Lyle Rathbone and Elizabeth Eleanor Rathbone; partner, John Uden; one *s* one *d*. *Educ:* Univ. of Essex (BA Govt (Latin America) 1972); London Metropolitan Univ. (Nat. Professional Qual. in Integrated Centre Leadership 2006). Researcher and reporter, World in Action, Granada TV, 1979–87; Producer, The Money Programme, BBC, 1989–96. Mem. (Lab) Islington LBC, 1998–2002. Contested (Lab) Cardiff Central, 2010. Chm., Ind. Rev. Panels, NHS London, 1995–2003; Prog. Manager, Sure Start Hillmarton, Islington, 2002–07. Chm., All Wales Prog. Monitoring Cttee, 2013–15. Trustee: Eleanor Rathbone Charitable Trust, 1984–; Good Food Llanedeyrn, 2017–. *Recreations:* outdoor swimming, bicycling, films, family. *Address:* National Assembly for Wales, Cardiff Bay, Cardiff CF99 1NA. *T:* 0300 200 7112. *E:* Jenny.Rathbone@assembly.wales.

**RATHBONE, William,** OBE 2012; Director and Chief Executive, Royal United Kingdom Beneficent Association and Universal Beneficent Association, 1988–2001; *b* 5 June 1936; *s* of William Rathbone and Margaret Hester (*née* Lubbock); *m* 1st, 1960, Sarah Kynaston Mainwaring (*d* 2006); one *s* one *d*, 2nd, 2010, Carolyn Wendy Dorothy, *widow* of David O. Lloyd-Jacob, CBE. *Educ:* Radley Coll.; Christ Church, Oxford (MA 2nd Cl. Hons PPE 1959); IMEDE, Lausanne (Dip. Business Studies 1972). Nat. Service, RA, 1954–56. Ocean Group PLC, 1959–88: Elder Dempster Lines, 1959–69; tanker and bulk carrier div., 1969–71; Dir, Wm Cory & Sons Ltd, 1973–74; Gen. Manager, Ocean Inchcape Ltd, 1974–79; Exec. Dir, Gastransco Ltd, 1979–88. Dir, Rathbone Bros plc, 1994–2003. Trustee, Queen's Nursing Inst., 1974– (Vice-Chm., 1974–99); Pres., Community and Dist Nursing Assoc., 1984–99; Vice Pres., Christ Church (Oxford) United Clubs, 1991–. Trustee: Eleanor Rathbone Charitable Trust, 1958–; New England Co., 1974–; St Peter's Convent, Woking, 1992–2007; Hadfield Trust, 1997–; Southwark Cathedral Millennium Trust, 1998–2012; British Mus. Friends, 2003–12 (Vice-Chm., 2005–11). Mem., Develt Bd, Christ Church, 2002–. Gov., Centre for Policy on Ageing, 2000–02. Liveryman, Skinners' Co., 1969–. Trustee, Skinners' Almshouse Charity, 2009–12. *Recreations:* fishing, the arts, friends. *Address:* 7 Brynmaer Road, SW11 4EN. *T:* (020) 7978 1935. *Clubs:* Brooks's; Leander (Henley-on-Thames).

**RATHCAVAN, 3rd Baron** *cr* 1953, of The Braid, Co. Antrim; **Hugh Detmar Torrens O'Neill;** Bt 1929; *b* 14 June 1939; *s* of 2nd Baron Rathcavan, PC (NI) and his 1st wife, Clare Désirée (*d* 1956), *d* of late Detmar Blow; *S* father, 1994; *m* 1983, Sylvie Marie-Thérèse Wichard du Perron; one *s*. *Educ:* Eton. Captain, Irish Guards. Financial journalism, Observer, Irish Times, FT; Dep. Chm., IPEC Europe, 1978–82; Chairman: Northern Ireland Airports, 1986–92; NI Tourist Board, 1988–96; Cleggan Estate Co. Ltd, 1996–; Brasserie St Quentin 2002 Ltd, 2002–08; non-executive Director: St Quentin, 1980–94; The Spectator, 1982–84; Old Bushmills Distillery Co., 1989–99; Savoy Management, 1989–94; Northern Bank Ltd, 1990–97; Berkeley Hotel Co. Ltd, 1995–97; Brompton Bar and Grill Ltd, 2008–14. Mem., BTA, 1988–96. Member: H of L European Select Cttee D, 1995–99; British-Irish Interparly Body, 1995–99. Trustee, Newman Foundn, 1998–. *Recreations:* food, travel. *Heir:* *s* Hon. François Hugh Nial O'Neill, *b* 26 June 1984. *Address:* Cleggan Lodge, Ballymena, Co. Antrim BT43 7JW. *T:* (028) 2568 4209, *Fax:* (028) 2568 4552; 14 Thurloe Place, SW7 2RZ. *T:* (020) 7584 5293, *Fax:* (020) 7823 8846. *E:* lordrathcavan@btopenworld.com. *Club:* Beefsteak.

**RATHCREEDAN, 3rd Baron** *cr* 1916; **Christopher John Norton;** Director, Norton & Brooksbank Ltd, Pedigree Livestock Auctioneers, since 2003; *b* 3 June 1949; *er s* of 2nd Baron Rathcreedan, TD and Ann Pauline (*d* 2007), *d* of late Capt. William Bastian, RN; *S* father, 1990; *m* 1978, Lavinia Anne Ross, *d* of late A. G. R. Ormiston; two *d*. *Educ:* Wellington Coll.; RAC Cirencester. Partner, Hobsons, Pedigree Livestock Auctioneers; founded Norton & Brooksbank, 1983, Partner, 1983–2003. *Recreations:* horse racing, gardening. *Heir:* *b* Hon. Adam Gregory Norton [*b* 2 April 1952; *m* 1980, Hilary Shelton, *d* of Edmond Ryan; two *d*]. *Address:* Stoke Common House, Purton Stoke, Swindon, Wilts SN5 4LL. *T:* (01793) 772492. *Club:* Turf.

**RATHDONNELL**, 5th Baron cr 1868; **Thomas Benjamin McClintock Bunbury**; b 17 Sept. 1938; o s of William, 4th Baron Rathdonnell and Pamela (d 1989), e d of late John Malcolm Drew; S father, 1959; m 1965, Jessica Harriet, d of George Gilbert Butler, Scatorish, Bennettsbridge, Co. Kilkenny; three s one d. Educ: Charterhouse; Royal Naval College, Dartmouth. Lieutenant RN. Heir: s Hon. William Leopold McClintock Bunbury [b 6 July 1966; m 2002, Emily Henrietta Dacres Dixon]. Address: Lisnavagh, Rathvilly, County Carlow, Ireland. T: (59) 9161104.

**RATLEDGE, Prof. Colin**, PhD; CChem, FRSC; CBiol, FRSB; Professor of Microbial Biochemistry, University of Hull, 1983–2004, now Emeritus; b 9 Oct. 1936; s of Fred Ratledge and Freda Smith Ratledge (née Proudlock); m 1961, Janet Vivien Bottomley; one s two d. Educ: Bury High Sch.; Manchester Univ. (BSc Tech, PhD). AMCST; CChem, FRSC 1970; CBiol, FRSB (FIBiol 1982). Res. Fellowship, MRC Ireland, 1960–64; Res. Scientist, Unilever plc, 1964–67; Hull University, 1967–: Lectr, 1967–73; Sen. Lectr, 1973–77; Reader, 1977–83; Head of Dept of Biochemistry, 1986–88. Visiting Lecturer: Australian Soc. of Microbiol., 1986; NZ Soc. of Microbiol., 1986; Kathleen Barton Wright Meml Lectr (Inst. of Biol./Soc. Gen. Microbiol.), 1995; Visiting Professor: Univ. of Malaya, 1993; Hong Kong Poly., 1994, 2001–02; Univ. of OFS, Bloemfontein, 1994; Ben-Gurion Univ. of the Negev, Israel, 2008; Univ. of Malaysia, 2008; Jiangnan Univ., China, 2010–13; Hon. Dir, Colin Ratledge Center for Microbial Pipids, Shandong Univ. of Technology, China, 2015–. Mem., AFRC Food Res. Cttee, 1989–92; Chairman: AFRC Food Res. Grants Bd, 1989–92; AFRC Food-borne Pathogens Co-ord. Prog., 1992–95; Brit. Co-ordinating Cttee for Biotechnology, 1989–91; Inst. of Biol. Industrial Biol. Cttee, 1992–2001; Vice-Pres., SCI, 1993–96 (Chm. Biotechnol. Gp, 1990–91; Mem. Council, 1991–93); Sec., Internat. Cttee of Envmtl and Applied Microbiology, 1991–94; Mem., Biotechnology Cttee, Internat. Union of Biochemistry, 1984–97. Fellow, Internat. Inst. of Biotechnology, 1993. Editor: World Jl of Microbiol. and Biotechnol., 1987–2004; Biotechnology Techniques, 1988–99; Biotechnology Letters, 1996–2017. Hon. PhD Ben Gurion, Israel, 2018. Stephen S. Chang Award, Amer. Oil Chemists' Soc., 2011. Publications: The Mycobacteria, 1977; Co-Editor: Microbial Technology: current state, future prospects, 1979; The Biology of the Mycobacteria, vol. 1 1982, vol. 2 1983, vol. 3 1989; Biotechnology for the Oils and Fats Industry, 1984; Microbial Technology in the Developing World, 1987; Microbial Lipids, vol. 1 1988, vol. 2 1989; Microbial Physiology and Manufacturing Industry, 1988; Biotechnology: Social and Economic Impact, 1992; Industrial Application of Single Cell Oils, 1992; Biochemistry of Microbial Degradation, 1993; Mycobacteria: molecular biology and virulence, 1999; Basic Biotechnology, 3rd edn 2006; Single Cell Oils, 2005, 2nd edn 2010; numerous scientific papers in biol science jls. Recreations: enjoying my grandchildren, hill walking, bonsai gardening, bridge. Address: Department of Biological Sciences, University of Hull, Hull HU6 7RX. E: c.ratledge@hull.ac.uk; (home) 49 Church Drive, Leven, Beverley, E Yorks HU17 5LH. T: (01964) 542690.

**RATNER, Gerald Irving**; Chief Executive, geraldonline, since 2003; after-dinner/ conference speaker; b 1 Nov. 1949; s of Leslie and Rachelle Ratner; m 1st (marr. diss. 1989); two d; 2nd, 1989, Moira Day; one s one d. Educ: Hendon Co. Grammar Sch. Chm. and Chief Exec., Ratners Gp, 1986–92. Director: Norweb, 1989–91; Workshop Health & Fitness Club, Henley, 1997–2003. Publications: The Rise and Fall... and Rise Again (autobiog.), 2007. Recreation: road cycling.

**RATTEE, Sir Donald (Keith)**, Kt 1989; a Judge of the High Court of Justice, Chancery Division, 1993–2000 (Family Division, 1989–93); b 9 March 1937; s of Charles Ronald and Dorothy Rattee; m 1964, Diana Mary, d of John Leslie and Florence Elizabeth Howl; four d. Educ: Clacton County High School; Trinity Hall, Cambridge (Schol.; 1st cl. Pts I and II Law Tripos; MA, LLB). Called to Bar, Lincoln's Inn, 1962, Bencher, 1985, Treas., 2006; Second Junior Counsel to the Inland Revenue (Chancery), 1972–77; QC 1977; Attorney Gen. of the Duchy of Lancaster, 1986–89; a Recorder, 1989. Liaison Judge, Family Div. (NE Circuit), 1990–93; Mem., Gen. Council of the Bar, 1970–74. Chm., Inns of Court and Bar Educnl Trust, 1997–2004. Recreations: reading, music, theatre. Address: 29 Shirley Avenue, Cheam, Surrey SM2 7QS. Clubs: Royal Automobile; Banstead Downs Golf (Banstead); Thurlestone Golf (Thurlestone, Devon).

**RATTLE, Sir Simon**, OM 2014; Kt 1994; CBE 1987; Chief Conductor and Artistic Director, Berlin Philharmonic Orchestra, 2002–18; Principal Guest Conductor, Orchestra of the Age of Enlightenment, since 1992; Principal Conductor and Music Director, London Symphony Orchestra, since 2017; b Liverpool, 19 Jan. 1955; m 1st, 1980, Elise Ross (marr. diss. 1995), American soprano; two s; 2nd, 1996, Candace Allen (marr. diss. 2008); 3rd, 2008, Magdalena Kozena; two s one d. Won Bournemouth John Player Internat. Conducting Comp., when aged 19. Has conducted: Bournemouth Sinfonietta; Philharmonia; Northern Sinfonia; London Philharmonic; London Sinfonietta; Berliner Philharmoniker; Boston Symphony; Chicago Symphony; Cleveland; Concertgebouw; Stockholm Philharmonic; Toronto Symphony, etc. Débuts: Festival Hall, 1976; Glyndebourne, 1977; ENO, 1985; Royal Opera, 1990; Vienna Philharmonic, 1993; Philadelphia, 1993; Royal Albert Hall (Proms etc), 1976–; Asst Conductor, BBC Scottish Symphony Orch., 1977–80; Principal Conductor and Artistic Advr, 1980–90, Music Dir, 1990–98, CBSO. Associate Conductor, Royal Liverpool Philharmonic Soc., 1977–80; Principal Conductor, London Choral Soc., 1979–84; Artistic Dir, South Bank Summer Music, 1981–83; Principal Guest Conductor: Rotterdam Philharmonic, 1981–84; Los Angeles Philharmonic, 1981–92. Exclusive contract with EMI Records. Hon. Fellow, St Anne's Coll., Oxford, 1991. Hon. DMus: Birmingham, 1985; Birmingham Poly., 1985; Oxford, 1999. Shakespeare Prize, Toepfer Foundn, Hamburg, 1996; Albert Medal, RSA, 1997; Comenius Award, 2004; Hon. Schiller Award, 2005; Urania Medal, 2006; Goldena Kamera Award, 2006. Chevalier des Arts et des Lettres (France), 1995. Address: c/o Askonas Holt Ltd, 15 Fetter Lane, EC4A 1BW. T: (020) 7400 1700.

**RATTRAY, Sandy Campbell**; Chief Investment Officer, Man Group, since 2016; b Saigon, Vietnam, 21 Aug. 1969; s of Robin and Ulla Rattray; m 2001, Fiona Ross; two s one d. Educ: Jesus Coll., Cambridge (BA Econs and Natural Scis 1991). Goldman Sachs: Associate, 1992–97; Exec. Dir, 1997–2002; Man. Dir, 2002–07; Asset Manager, Man GLG, 2007–10; Chief Investment Officer, Man Systematic Strategies, 2010–13; CEO, Man AHL, 2013–17. Recreations: sailing, ski-ing, modern architecture, walking, cycling, piano playing. Address: Man Group, 2 Swan Lane, EC4R 3AD. T: (020) 7144 1292. E: sandy.rattray@man.com. Clubs: Lansdowne; Royal Solent Yacht.

**RATZINGER, Joseph Alois**; see Benedict XVI, His Holiness.

**RAU, Prof. Raghavendra**, PhD; Sir Evelyn de Rothschild Professor of Finance, University of Cambridge, since 2011. Educ: Delhi Univ. (BSc Hons 1987); Indian Inst. of Mgt, Bangalore (MBA 1989); INSEAD (MSc 1993; PhD 1997). Associate Prof., Purdue Univ., 1997–2008; Principal, Barclays Global Investors, 2008–09. Vis. Associate Prof., UCLA, 2005–06; Vis. Prof., Univ. of Calif at Berkeley, 2009–11, 2017–19. Publications: articles in Jl of Finance, Jl of Financial Econs, Rev. of Financial Studies, Mgt Sci., Jl of Accounting Res., Accounting Rev. Recreations: aikido, iaido. Address: Cambridge Judge Business School, University of Cambridge, Trumpington Street, Cambridge CB2 1AG.

**RAUF, Mariya A.**; see Afzal Rauf.

**RAUSING, Dr (Anna) Lisbet (Kristina), (Mrs Peter Baldwin)**, FLS; Founder, 2001, and Member, Donor Board, since 2006, Arcadia; Director, Ingleby Farms and Forests, since 2005; b Lund, Sweden, 9 June 1960; d of late Hans A. Rausing, Hon. KBE and of Märit Rausing (née Norrby); m 1st, 1988, Prof. Joseph Leo Koerner (marr. diss. 2002); one s one d; 2nd, 2002, Prof. Peter Baldwin. Educ: Univ. of Calif, Berkeley (BA summa cum laude 1984); Harvard Univ. (MA Hist. 1987; PhD Hist. 1993). Lectr in Hist. of Sci., 1993–94, Asst Prof., 1994–96, Dept of Hist. of Sci., Harvard Univ.; Sen. Res. Investigator, 2000–02, Sen. Res. Fellow, 2002–11, Centre for Hist. of Sci., Technol. and Medicine, Imperial Coll. London. Dir, Tetra Laval Gp of Industries, 1984–95; Mem., Supervisory Bd, Ecolean, 2001–. Member: Bd of Overseers, Stockholm Sch. of Econs, 1993–2007; Founding Council, Inst. for Philanthropy, 2000–07; Bd, Courtauld Inst., 2004–08 (Mem., Investment Adv. Cttee, 2004–07); Bd of Overseers, Harvard Univ., 2005–11 (Mem., Cttee to Visit Harvard Liby, 1998–2011); Internat. Adv. Bd, Israel Nat. Liby, 2011–14; Univ. Council Sub-Cttee, West Campus, Yale Univ., 2012–14; Co-Chm., Planning Cttee, Harvard Campaign, Harvard Univ., 2012–; Rothschild Archive Academic Adv. Cttee, 2016–. Vis. Sen. Res. Fellow, Dept of Hist., KCL, 2013–; Associate, Dept of Hist. of Sci., Harvard Univ., 2018–. Vice President: Fauna and Flora Internat., 2000– (Mem. Council, 2004–07); Kent Wildlife Trust, 2011–; Sussex Wildlife Trust, 2011–. Trustee, Yad Hanadiv, 2001–11; Member, Advisory Board: Sutton Trust, 2004–08; Smithsonian Nat. Mus. of Natural History, 2011–14; Cambridge Conservation Initiative, 2012–; Mem., Agricultural Forum, 2015–. FLS 2001. Fellow, Royal Swedish Acad. of Agric. and Forestry, 2015. Hon. FBA 2006; Hon. FRSB (Hon. FSB 2014). Hon. Dr: SOAS, 2004; Imperial Coll. London, 2007; Uppsala, 2007. Publications: Linnaeus: nature and nation, 1999; contrib. articles, newspaper commentary and book reviews. Address: Nyland, Sixth Floor, 5 Young Street, W8 5EH. T: (020) 7361 4911, Fax: (020) 7361 4949. E: celia.hamer@nyland.org.uk. Clubs: Athenæum, Reform, Farmers, National Liberal, Harvard (UK); Harvard (New York).
See also S. M. E. Rausing.

**RAUSING, Kirsten**; DL; Owner and General Manager, Lanwades Stud, since 1980; Director, British Bloodstock Agency Ltd, since 2010; b Lund, Sweden, 6 June 1952; d of Dr Gad Rausing and Dr Birgit Rausing (née Mayne). Educ: in Sweden, France and Ireland. Work at Airlie Stud, Ireland, 1977–80. Non-executive Director: Tetra Pak, 1983–; Tetra Laval Gp, 1983–. Director: British Bloodstock Agency plc, 2004–10; Jockey Club Estates Co. Ltd; National Stud. Chm., Veterinary Commn, 1994–2004, Hon. Pres., 2012–, Eur. Fedn of Thoroughbred Breeders' Assocs (Paris); Chairman: Equine Industry Liaison Cttee, Animal Health Trust, 2002–12; Fedn Européenne des Eleveurs de Pur Sang, Paris, 2002–05; Thoroughbred Breeders' Assoc., GB, 2008–12; Internat. Thoroughbred Breeders' Fedn, 2017–. Mem., Cttee of Enquiry into Veterinary Res., RCVS. Member: Scientific Adv. Gp, Equine Fertility Unit, Univ. of Cambridge/Thoroughbred Breeders' Assoc.; Ext. Adv. Cttee, Liverpool Univ. Veterinary Coll.; Cataloguing Standards Cttee, Soc. of Internat. Thoroughbred Auctioneers. Founder and Chm., Alborada Trust, 2001–; Mem., Animal Health Trust. Patron, Asha Centre. Hon. Fellow, Wolfson Coll., Cambridge, 2009. Hon. Associate, RCVS, 2013. DL Suffolk, 2016. DUniv E Anglia, 2008. Address: c/o Tetra Laval International, SA, 70 Avenue Général-Guisan, PO Box 430, 1009 Pully, Switzerland. Club: Jockey.

**RAUSING, Lisbet**; see Rausing, A. L. K.

**RAUSING, Sigrid Maria Elisabet**; Publisher: Portobello Books, since 2005; Granta Publications, since 2005; Editor, Granta magazine, since 2014; b 29 Jan. 1962; d of late Hans A. Rausing, Hon. KBE and of Märit Rausing (née Norrby); m 1st, 1996 (marr. diss. 2002); one s; 2nd, 2003, Eric Antony Abraham, qv. Educ: York Univ. (BA Hist.); University Coll. London (PhD Anthropol. 1997). Chm., Sigrid Rausing Trust, 1996–. Hon. Fellow, Dept of Anthropol., UCL, 1997–98. Emeritus Mem. Bd, Human Rights Watch Internat., 1997–; Mem., Adv. Bd, Coalition for Internat. Criminal Court, 2010–15; Emeritus Mem. Bd, Order of Teaspoon. Trustee, Charleston Trust, 2008–13. Judge: Amnesty Media Awards, 2009, 2010; Index on Censorship Media Awards, 2012; Per Anger Prize. Mem. Council, RCA, 2018–. Hon. Fellow: LSE, 2010; St Anthony's Coll., Oxford, 2014; Morrell Fellow, Univ. of York, 2012. DUniv: York, 2014; Open, 2016; Hon. DLitt Kent, 2016. Human Rights Award, Internat. Service, 2004; Special Award for Philanthropy, Beacon Fellowship, 2005; Changing Face of Philanthropy Award, Women's Funding Network, 2006. Publications: History, Memory and Identity in Post-Soviet Estonia, 2004; Everything Is Wonderful, 2014; Mayhem, 2017. Recreations: walking, reading, conservation. Address: 12–14 Addison Avenue, W11 4QR.
See also A. L. K. Rausing.

**RAVEN, Amanda**; see Game, A.

**RAVEN, Prof. James Russell**, PhD, LittD; FBA 2019; FSA, FRHistS, FLS; Professor of Modern History, University of Essex, since 2004; Senior Research Fellow, Magdalene College, Cambridge, since 2012; b Colchester, 13 April 1959; s of Leonard Raven and Eileen Raven; m 2000, Karen Jane Walden-Smith, qv; two s. Educ: Gilberd Sch., Colchester; Clare Coll., Cambridge (BA 1981; MA 1985; PhD 1985); MA Oxon 1997; LittD Cantab 2012. FRHistS 2000; FSA 2007; FLS 2016. University of Cambridge: Drapers' Res. Fellow, 1985–89, Fellow, 1989–90, Pembroke Coll.; Munby Fellow, 1989–90; Dir, Studies in Hist., and Fellow and Lectr, Magdalene Coll., 1990–96; Newton Trust Lectr, Hist. Faculty, 1994–96; University of Oxford: Lectr, Mod. Hist. Faculty, 1996–2000; Reader in Social and Cultural Hist., 2000–04; Fellow, Mansfield Coll., 1996–2004. Dir, Cambridge Proj. for Book Trust, 1990–. Visiting Fellow: Newberry Liby, Chicago, 1986; Amer. Antiquarian Soc., 1986 and 1995 (Mem., 1997); Lewis Walpole Liby, Yale Univ., 1994–95; Magdalene Coll., Cambridge, 2003–04; Marsh's Liby, Dublin, 2015; McLean Fellow, Liby Co. of Philadelphia, 1996; Vis. Scholar, Pembroke Coll., Cambridge, 2005–07; British Acad. Res. Reader, 2005–07. Lectures: Karmiole, LA, 2008; Panizzi, BL, 2010; Jackson, Toronto, 2016. Dep. Chm., ESU, 2014– (Gov., 2000–06 and 2012–; Chm., Educn Cttee, 2018–); Chm., Lindemann Trust, 2014–. Gov., Wisbech Grammar Sch., 2014–. Member: Mid-Atlantic Gp, 1997–; Pilgrims Soc. of GB, 2006–. Vice-Pres., Bibliographical Soc., 2012–. Trustee, Marks Hall Estate, Essex, 2007–. Contested (Lib Dem): Colchester N, 1992; N Essex, 2005, 2010. Seeley Medal, 1986, Thirlwall Prize, 1986, Univ. of Cambridge. Publications: Judging New Wealth: popular publishing and responses to commerce in England, 1750–1800, 1992; (ed jtly) The Practice and Representation of Reading in England, 1996; (ed) Free Print and Non-Commercial Publishing since 1700, 2000; (jtly) The English Novel 1770–1829, 2 vols, 2000; London Booksellers and American Customers: Transatlantic literary community and the Charleston Library Society, 1748–1811, 2002; (ed) Lost Libraries: the destruction of book collections since antiquity, 2004; The Business of Books: booksellers and the English book trade 1450–1850, 2007 (DeLong Book Hist. Prize, Soc. for Hist. of Authorship, Reading and Publishing, 2008); (ed) Books Between Europe and the Americas, 2011; Bookscape: geographies of printing and publishing in London before 1800, 2014; Publishing Business in Eighteenth-Century England, 2014; Lost Mansions: essays on the destruction of the country house, 2015; What is the History of the Book?, 2018; (ed) The Oxford Illustrated History of the Book, 2020; over 90 articles in learned jls and chapters in books, 1985–. *Recreations:* family, painting, theatre, writing, tennis. *Address:* Magdalene College, Cambridge CB3 0AG. *T:* (01223) 332100. *E:* jr42@cam.ac.uk.

**RAVEN, Prof. John Albert,** FRS 1990; FRSE; CBiol, FRSB; Boyd Baxter Professor of Biology, University of Dundee, 1995–2008, now Emeritus; *b* 25 June 1941; *s* of John Harold Edward Raven and Evelyn Raven; *m* 1985, Linda Lea Handley. *Educ:* Wimbish County Primary Sch.; Friends' Sch., Saffron Walden; St John's College, Cambridge (MA, PhD). FRSE 1981; CBiol, FRSB (FIBiol 1998). University of Cambridge: Research Fellow, and Official Fellow, St John's Coll., 1966–71; Univ. Demonstrator in Botany, 1968–71; Lectr, and Reader, 1971–80, Prof. (personal chair), 1980–95, Dept of Biol Scis, Univ. of Dundee. FMBA. Hon. FLS. Hon. PhD Umeå, Sweden, 1995. *Publications:* Energetics and Transport in Aquatic Plants, 1984; (with Paul Falkowski) Aquatic Photosynthesis, 1997, 2nd edn 2007; numerous papers in learned jls and chapters in multi-author vols. *Recreations:* aviation, walking, literature. *Address:* Spital Beag, Waterside, Invergowrie, Dundee DD2 5DQ.

**RAVEN, Karen Jane;** *see* Walden-Smith, K. J.

**RAVEN, Martin Clark;** HM Diplomatic Service, retired; Consul-General, São Paulo, and Director, Trade and Investment, Brazil, 2006–10; *b* 10 March 1954; *s* of Basil Raven and Betty Raven (*née* Gilbert); *m* 1978, Philippa Michale Morrice Ruddick; two *s*. *Educ:* Bury Grammar Sch., Lancs; Univ. of Sussex (BA Intellectual Hist.). Joined HM Diplomatic Service, 1976: Korea/Mongolia Desk, then Yugoslavia/Albania Desk, FCO, 1976–78; Third Sec., Lagos, 1978; Hindi lang. trng, SOAS, 1979; Third, later Second Sec., Delhi, 1979–83; First Secretary: N America, then Non-Proliferation Depts, FCO, 1983–88; Human Rights and Social Issues, UK Mission to UN, NY and Alternate Rep. to Commn on Human Rights, 1988–92; Dep. Hd, S Atlantic and Antarctic Dept, FCO and Dep. Comr, British Antarctic Territory, 1993–96; Hd, Drugs and Internat. Crime Dept, FCO, 1996–98; Counsellor, Dep. Hd of Mission and Consul Gen., Stockholm, 1998–2001; on secondment as Dir, Services, Aid and Export Finance, Business Gp, Trade Partners UK, later UK Trade & Investment, 2001–06. Dir, BESO, 2001–05. Non-exec. Chm., VG Partner, 2012–15. Chairman: Anglo Latin American Foundn, 2010–15; Nominations Cttee, EnglishUK, 2012–; Vice-Chm., Brazil Wkg Gp, TheCityUK, 2011–14. *Recreations:* cycling, cinema, food, theatre, reading novels, listening to music, watching football and cricket, eating olives. *E:* martin.raven@hotmail.com.

**RAVENSCROFT, Ven. Raymond Lockwood;** Archdeacon of Cornwall and Canon Librarian of Truro Cathedral, 1988–96; *b* 15 Sept. 1931; *s* of Cecil and Amy Ravenscroft; *m* 1957, Ann (*née* Stockwell) (*d* 2008); one *s* one *d*. *Educ:* Sea Point Boys' High School, Cape Town, SA; Leeds Univ. (BA Gen. 1953); College of the Resurrection, Mirfield. Assistant Curate: St Alban's, Goodwood, Cape, SA, 1955–58; St John's Pro-Cathedral, Bulawayo, S Rhodesia, 1958–59; Rector of Francistown, Bechuanaland, 1959–62; Asst Curate, St Ives, Cornwall, 1962–64; Vicar: All Saints, Falmouth, 1964–68; St Stephen by Launceston with St Thomas, 1968–74; Team Rector of Probus Team Ministry, 1974–88; RD of Powder, 1977–81; Hon. Canon of Truro Cathedral, 1982–88. *Recreations:* walking, reading, local history. *Address:* 14 Treviglas Rise, Probus, Truro, Cornwall TR2 4LJ. *T:* (01726) 382630.

**RAVENSDALE, 4th Baron** *cr* 1911; **Daniel Nicholas Mosley;** Project Director, Atkins, since 2015; *b* Nottingham, 10 Oct. 1982; *s* of late Shaun Nicholas Mosley and Teresa Frances Mosley; *S* grandfather, 2017; *m* 2010, Rachael Carter; three *s*. *Educ:* Univ. of Sheffield (MEng 1st Aerospace Engrg 2006). CEng, MIMechE 2010. Systems Engr, 2006–11, Project Manager, 2011–15, Atkins. Elected Mem., H of L, 2019–. *Recreations:* family, cycling, reading, politics, philosophy, economics, science. *Heir:* *s* Hon. Alexander Lucas Mosley, *b* 12 April 2012. *Address:* Atkins, Derwent House, RTC Business Park, London Road, Derby DE24 8UP. *E:* mosled83@hotmail.com.

**RAVENSWORTH, 9th Baron** *cr* 1821; **Thomas Arthur Hamish Liddell;** Bt 1642; *b* 27 Oct. 1954; *s* of 8th Baron Ravensworth and Wendy, *d* of J. S. Bell; *S* father, 2004; *m* 1983, Linda, *d* of H. Thompson; one *s* one *d*. *Educ:* Gordonstoun; RAC Cirencester. *Heir:* *s* Hon. Henry Arthur Thomas Liddell, *b* 27 Nov. 1987.

**RAVIV, Moshe;** Ambassador of Israel to the Court of St James's, 1993–97; *b* Romania, 23 April 1935; *s* of David and Elka Raviv; *m* 1955, Hanna Kaspi; two *s* one *d*. *Educ:* Hebrew Univ., Jerusalem; Univ. of London (grad. Internat. Relations). Israel Ministry of Foreign Affairs: 2nd Sec., London, 1961–63; Office of Foreign Minister, Mrs Golda Meir, 1964–65; Political Sec. to Foreign Minister, Abba Eban, 1966–68; Counsellor, Washington, 1968–74; Dir, E European Div., 1974–76; Dir, N American Div., 1976–78; Ambassador to the Philippines, 1978–81; Dir, Economic Div., 1981–83; Minister, London, 1983–88; Dep. Dir Gen., i/c Information, 1988–93. *Publications:* Israel At Fifty: five decades of struggle for peace, 1998. *Recreations:* reading, chess, jogging.

**RAW, Geoffrey David;** Chief Executive, Brighton and Hove City Council, since 2015; *b* Newcastle upon Tyne, 1962; *s* of David and Detta Raw; *m* Dr Susan Chuichi Baxter; one *d*. *Educ:* St Cuthbert's Grammar Sch., Newcastle upon Tyne; Univ. of E Anglia (BA Hons); Oxford Brookes Univ. (Dip. and MSc Town Planning). Wembley Project Co-ordinator, 1998–2001, Dir, Envmtl Policy and Performance, 2001–02, London Bor. of Brent; Hd, Strategic Options, HM Treasury, 2002–03; Nat. Prog. Manager, 2003–05, Asst Dir, London Investment, 2005–08, Housing Corp.; Dir, Design Develt and Strategy, London Develt Agency, 2008–10; Strategic Dir Place, Brighton and Hove CC, 2010–15. *Recreations:* travel, gym, cooking, gardening, art. *Address:* Brighton and Hove City Council, Hove Town Hall, Norton Road, Hove BN3 3BQ. *T:* (01273) 291132. *E:* geoff.raw@brighton-hove.gov.uk.

**RAWBONE, Rear-Adm. Alfred Raymond,** CB 1976; AFC 1951; *b* 19 April 1923; *s* of A. Rawbone and Mrs E. D. Rawbone (*née* Wall); *m* 1943, Iris Alicia (*née* Willshaw); one *s* one *d*. *Educ:* Saltley Grammar Sch., Birmingham. Joined RN, 1942; 809 Sqdn War Service, 1943; CO 736 Sqdn, 1953; CO 897 Sqdn, 1955; CO Loch Killisport, 1959–60; Comdr (Air) Lossiemouth and HMS Ark Royal, 1961–63; Chief Staff Officer to Flag Officer Naval Air Comd, 1965–67; CO HMS Dido, 1968–69; CO RNAS Yeovilton, 1970–72; CO HMS Kent, 1972–73; Dep. ACOS (Operations), SHAPE, 1974–76. Comdr 1958; Captain 1964; Rear-Adm. 1974. Director: Vincents of Yeovil, 1983–86; Vindata, 1984–86; Vincents (Bridgewater) Ltd, 1984–86. *Address:* Wisteria House, 12 Wessex Court, Church Street, Henstridge, Templecombe, Som BA8 0AU.

**RAWCLIFFE, Prof. Carole,** PhD; FSA, FRHistS; Professor of Medieval History, University of East Anglia, 2002–16, now Emerita; *b* 18 Sept. 1946; *d* of Lewis and Betty Rawcliffe. *Educ:* Univ. of Sheffield (BA; PhD 1975). FRHistS 1978; FSA 2004. Asst Keeper, Commn on Historical MSS, 1972–74; Co-ed., medieval vols of The History of Parliament, 1974–92; University of East Anglia: Sen. Res. Fellow, Sch. of Hist., 1992–95; Sen. Lectr, 1995–98; Dir, Centre of E Anglian Studies, 1997–98 and 2005–08; Reader in Medical Hist., 1998–2002. Vis. Fellow, Huntington Liby, Calif, 1984. Mem. Council, Norfolk Record Soc., 2008– (Chair, 2012–). Trustee, Hungate Medieval Art Mus., Norwich, 2008–. Hon. Fellow, Norfolk Medico-Chirurgical Soc., 2003. *Publications:* The Staffords, Earls of Stafford and Dukes of Buckingham, 1978; (ed jtly) The History of Parliament: the House of Commons 1386–1421, 1993; Medicine and Society in Later Medieval England, 1995; Sources for the History of Medicine in Later Medieval England, 1995; The Hospitals of Medieval Norwich, 1995; Medicine for the Soul, 1999; (with R. G. Wilson) The History of Norwich, 2004; Leprosy in Medieval England, 2006; Urban Bodies: communal health in late medieval English towns and cities, 2013; The Norwich Chamberlains' Accounts 1539–1545, 2019; (ed jtly) Policing the Urban Environment in Premodern Europe, 2019; contribs to numerous collections of essays and learned jls on medieval medical, social and religious history. *Recreations:* art, music, dog-walking. *Address:* School of History, University of East Anglia, Norwich NR4 7TJ. *T:* (01603) 592872, *Fax:* (01603) 593519. *E:* c.rawcliffe@uea.ac.uk.

**RAWKINS, His Honour Jeremy John Bruce;** a Circuit Judge, 2008–16; Designated Family Judge for Lancashire, 2011–16; *b* Preston; *s* of Robert Arthur Rawkins and Sally Joan Rawkins; *m* 1978, Jane Blake; two *s* two *d*. Admitted solicitor, 1974; Dep. District Judge, 1988–94; District judge, 1994–2008; Recorder, 2001–08. *Address:* c/o Designated Family Centre, Sessions House, Lancaster Road, Preston PR1 2PD.

**RAWLINGS, Baroness** *cr* 1994 (Life Peer), of Burnham Westgate in the County of Norfolk; **Patricia Elizabeth Rawlings;** a Baroness in Waiting (Government Whip), 2010–12; an Extra Baroness in Waiting, since 2012; *b* 27 Jan. 1939; *d* of late Louis Rawlings and Mary (*née* Boas de Winter); *m* 1962, David Wolfson (*see* Baron Wolfson of Sunningdale) (marr. diss. 1967). *Educ:* Oak Hall, Haslemere, Surrey; Le Manoir, Lausanne; Florence Univ.; University Coll. London (BA Hons; Fellow 2005); London School of Economics (post grad. diploma course, Internat. Relns). Children's Care Cttee, LCC, 1959–61; WNHR Nursing, Westminster Hosp., until 1968. Contested (C): Sheffield Central, 1983; Doncaster Central, 1987. MEP (C) Essex SW, 1989–94; contested (C) Essex West and Hertfordshire East, Eur. parly elecns, 1994. European Parliament, 1989–94: EPP British Section Rep. on Conservative Nat. Union; Vice Pres., Albanian, Bulgarian and Romanian Delegn; EDG spokesman on Culture Cttee, substitute on Foreign Affairs Cttee; Dep. Whip, 1989–92. Opposition Whip, H of L, 1997–98; Shadow Minister for Internat. Develt and Foreign Affairs, H of L, 1998–2010; govt spokesman for DCMS and Scotland, 2010–12. British Red Cross Society: Mem., 1964–; Chm., Appeals, London Br., until 1988; Nat. Badge of Honour, 1981, Hon. Vice Pres., 1988; Patron, London Br., 1997–. Member Council: British Bd of Video Classification, 1986–89; Peace through NATO; British Assoc. for Central and Eastern Europe, 1994–2008; Mem. Adv. Council, PYBT, 1998–; Special Advr to Ministry on Inner Cities, DoE, 1987–88. President: British Internat. Freight Assoc., 1991–92; NCVO, 2002–07; British Antique Dealers Assoc., 2005–12; Hon. Pres., Friends of BADA Trust, 2013–. Chm. Council, KCL, 1998–2007. Chm. of Govs, English Coll. Foundn, Prague, 2008–16. Dir, English Chamber Orch. and Music Soc., 1980–2001. Trustee, Chevening Estate, 2002–. FKC 2003. Hon. LittD Buckingham, 1998. Hon. Plaquette, Nat. Assembly of Republic of Bulgaria, 2007. Order of the Rose, Silver Class (Bulgaria), 1991; Grand Official, Order of the Southern Cross (Brazil), 1997. *Recreations:* music, art, golf, ski-ing, travel. *Address:* House of Lords, SW1A 0PW. *Clubs:* Grillions, Pilgrims; Royal West Norfolk Golf.

**RAWLINGS, Brian Kenneth; His Honour Judge Rawlings;** a Circuit Judge, since 2015; *b* Birmingham, 14 June 1962; *s* of Alan Ivor Rawlings and Olive Gwendoline Rawlings; *m* 2005, Cheryl Elaine Bernadette Jones; one *d*. *Educ:* Moseley Sch., Birmingham; University Coll., Cardiff (LLB Hons Law). Admitted as solicitor, 1986; solicitor, Eversheds LLP, specialising in corporate restructuring, banking and corporate law; Higher Rights of Audience, 2000; Licensed Insolvency Practitioner, 2001; a Recorder, 2008–15. *Address:* Stoke-on-Trent Combined Courts Centre, Bethesda Street, Hanley, Stoke-on-Trent ST1 3BP.

**RAWLINGS, Christopher;** Regional Director, Middle East and North Africa, British Council, since 2017; *b* Aylesbury, Bucks, 20 April 1968; *s* of Frederick Ernest Rawlings and Mary Louise Rawlings (*née* Vallange); *m* 2003, Priyanka Rakheja; one *s* one *d*. *Educ:* Malvern Coll.; Durham Univ. (BSc Hons). With British Council, 1992–: Contract Manager, 1992–95, Contract Dir, 1995–98, HQ Manchester; Hd, Develt Services, India, 1998–2000; Sen. Exec. Asst to Dir-Gen., HQ London, 2000–03; Director: Bosnia and Herzegovina, 2003–07; Mexico, 2007–12; Colombia, 2012–16; Hong Kong, and Cluster Lead, NE Asia, 2016–17. *Recreations:* exercise and horse riding, reading and holding books, pen and ink, jazz, rock, Latin and classical music as listener and occasional performer. *Address:* British Council, Tariq Bin Zaid Street (near Rashid Hospital), PO Box 1636, Dubai, United Arab Emirates. *T:* 043135592, *Fax:* 043370703; Foreign and Commonwealth Office, BFPO 5416, West End Road, Ruislip, Middx HA4 6EP. *E:* chris.rawlings@britishcouncil.org.

**RAWLINGS, Gillian Felicity;** *see* Douglas, G. F.

**RAWLINGS, Hugh Fenton,** CB 2011; PhD; FLSW; Director, Constitutional Affairs and Inter-Governmental Relations, Welsh Government (formerly Welsh Assembly Government), since 2011; *b* 24 Nov. 1950; *s* of William Rawlings and late Marion Rawlings (*née* Hughes), OBE; *m* 1981, (Felicity) Gillian Douglas, *qv*; one *s* one *d*. *Educ:* Worcester Coll., Oxford (BA Juris. 1973); London Sch. of Econs (PhD 1977). Lectr in Law, Univ. of Bristol, 1976–88; Welsh Office: Principal, Local Govt Finance Div., 1988–94; Hd, Culture and Recreation Div., 1994–97; Dep. Hd, Devolution Unit, 1997–99; National Assembly for Wales: Hd, European Affairs Div., 1999–2002; Sec., Commn on Local Govt Electoral Arrangements in Wales, 2002–03; Hd, Open Govt and Constitutional Affairs Div., 2003–04; Dir, Local Govt, Public Service and Culture, subseq. Local Govt and Culture, 2004–07; Dir, Strategic Policy, Legislation and Communications, later Constitutional Affairs, Equality and Communications, 2007–09, Dir, Dept of First Minister and Cabinet, 2009–11, Welsh Assembly Govt. Hon. Vis. Prof., Wales Governance Centre, Cardiff Univ., 2011–. FLSW 2019. *Publications:* Law and the Electoral Process, 1988; articles in acad. legal jls. *Recreations:* reading, music, theatre, worrying about Welsh Rugby. *Address:* 62 Adventurers Quay, Pierhead Road, Cardiff Bay, Cardiff CF10 4NQ; Welsh Government, Crown Buildings, Cathays Park, Cardiff CF10 3NQ. *T:* 03000 256532. *E:* hugh.rawlings@gov.wales.

**RAWLINGS, Flt Lieut Jerry John;** President, Republic of Ghana, 1992–2001; African Union High Representative for Somalia, 2010; *b* 22 June 1947; *s* of John Rawlings and Victoria Agbotui; *m* 1977, Nana Konadu Agyeman; one *s* three *d*. *Educ:* Achimota Sch., Accra; Ghana Military Acad. Enlisted in Ghana Air Force, 1967; commnd Pilot Officer, 1969; tried for mutiny, May 1979; forcibly released from cell, June 1979, by popular uprising; became Chm., Armed Forces Revolutionary Council; handed over to democratically elected Govt, Sept. 1979; overthrew Govt, Dec. 1981; Chm., Provisional Nat. Defence Council, 1982–92. *Recreations:* flying, swimming, riding, reading.

**RAWLINGS, Ven. John Edmund Frank;** Archdeacon of Totnes, 2005–14, now Archdeacon Emeritus; *b* 15 April 1947; *s* of Edward and Ivy Rawlings; *m* 1969, Janette Mary Rawlings (*née* Alexander); one *s* one *d*. *Educ:* Godalming Grammar Sch.; King's Coll., London (AKC 1969); St Augustine's Coll., Canterbury. Ordained deacon, 1970, priest

1971; Curate: St Margaret's, Rainham, 1970–73; Tattenham Corner and Burgh Heath, 1973–76; Chaplain, RN, 1976–92; Vicar, Tavistock and Gulworthy, 1992–2005; RD Tavistock, 1997–2002; Preb., Exeter Cathedral, 1999–2005. *Recreations:* gardening, cooking, music (organ playing). *Address:* 9 Rosemount Lane, Honiton, Devon EX14 1RJ. *T:* (01404) 43404. *E:* rawlings1@btinternet.com.

**RAWLINGS, Menna Frances,** CMG 2014; HM Diplomatic Service; Director General, Economic and Global Issues, Foreign and Commonwealth Office, since 2019; *b* Hillingdon, 16 Sept. 1967; *d* of Christopher and Ann Hornung; *m* 2001, Mark Rawlings; one *s* two *d*. *Educ:* Northwood Comprehensive Sch.; London Sch. of Econs and Pol Sci. (BSc (Econs) Internat. Relns 1989); Open Univ. (MBA 2011). FCIPD 2012. Entered FCO, 1989; Third, later Second Sec., UK Repn, Brussels, 1991–93; Second Sec. (Econ./Envmt), Nairobi, 1993–96; FCO, 1997; First Sec., Tel Aviv, 1998–2002; Private Sec. to Perm. Sec., FCO, 2002–04; Dep. Hd of Mission, Accra, 2005–08; Counsellor, Corporate Services and Consul.-Gen., Washington, 2008–11; Dir, Human Resources, FCO, 2011–14; High Comr to Australia, 2015–19. *Recreations:* family, sport (running, ski-ing, cycling), Chelsea FC, music. *Address:* c/o Foreign and Commonwealth Office, King Charles Street, SW1A 2AH.

**RAWLINGS, Prof. Rees David,** PhD, DSc; CEng; Professor of Materials Science, 1993–2007, now Emeritus and Visiting Professor, and Pro Rector (Educational Quality), 2000–08, Imperial College, London; *b* 30 Sept. 1942; *s* of Aubrey Rhys Islwyn Rawlings and Daphne Irene Rawlings (*née* Sangster); *m* 1964, Ann Margaret Halliday; two *d*. *Educ:* Sir Thomas Rich High Sch., Gloucester; Imperial Coll. (BSc Engrg 1st cl. Hons 1964; PhD Metallurgy 1967; Fellow 2009); ARSM 1964; DIC 1967; DSc London 1989. CEng 1980; FIMMM (FIM 1985); FHEA (ILTM 2000). Imperial College: Lectr, 1966–81; Reader, 1981–93; acting Hd, Earth Resources Engrg, 1996–98; Dean, Royal Sch. of Mines, 1995–98; Mem. Governing Body, 1995–98; Mem. Court, 1998–2008; Partner, Matcon (Materials Consultants), 1974–90. Vis. Prof., RCA, 2008–12. Subject Specialist Assessor: HEFCE, 1996–98; HEFCW, 1997–98. Mem., Dist. Adv. Bd, Jl Materials Science, 2015– (Dep. Ed., 1993–2002; Co-Ed.-in-Chief, 2002–08; Reviews Ed., 2008–15); Ed., Jl Materials Science Letters, 2002– (Dep. Ed., 1993–2002); Mem. Adv. Bd, Metal and Materials Internat., 2003–. Trustee, Montessori St Nicholas Charity, 2000–. Mem., Isle of Purbeck Arts Club. Hon. FRCA, 2001. FCGI 2002. L. B. Pfeil Medal and Prize, Inst. of Materials, 1990. *Publications:* (jtly) Materials Science, 1974, 5th edn 2003; (jtly) Composite Materials: engineering and science, 1994; articles in learned jls, conf. proceedings and books on materials science. *Recreations:* sport (Pres., Imperial Coll. Rugby Football Club, 2008–), gardening, art, theatre. *Address:* The Elms, 13 Wolverton Avenue, Kingston upon Thames, Surrey KT2 7QF. *Club:* Kingston Athletic and Polytechnic Harriers.

**RAWLINS, Brig. Gordon John,** OBE 1986; business development consultant, specialising in the Third Sector; *b* 22 April 1944; *s* of Arthur and Joyce Rawlins; *m* 1st, 1965, Ann Beard (*d* 1986); one *s*; 2nd, 1986, Margaret Anne Ravenscroft; one step *s* one step *d*. *Educ:* Peter Symond's, Winchester; Welbeck College; RMA Sandhurst; RMCS Shrivenham (BSc Eng). psc. Commissioned REME, 1964; served Aden, Oman, Jordan, Hong Kong, BAOR, UK, 1964–77; Staff Coll., 1978; MoD 1978–80; 2 i/c 5 Armd Wksp, REME, BAOR, 1981–82; CO 7 Armd Wksp, REME, BAOR, 1982–84; MoD, 1984–87 (Sec. to COS Cttee, 1987); Comd Maint., 1 (BR) Corps, BAOR, 1988. Sec., Instn of Production, subseq. Manufacturing, Engrs, 1988–91; Dep. Sec., 1991–2000, Dir, Members Services, 2000–02, IEE. Trustee, FirstLight Trust, 2016–17. Liveryman, Turners' Co., 1991. *Recreations:* travel, walking the dogs, watching Rugby and cricket. *Address:* Hall Barn Farm, Ingleby Arncliffe, Northallerton DL6 3PE.

**RAWLINS, Hon. Sir Hugh (Anthony),** Kt 2012; Chief Justice, Eastern Caribbean Supreme Court, 2008–12; Judge, International Administrative Tribunal, International Labour Organization, Geneva, since 2012; Course Director, LLM Legislative Drafting, Faculty of Law, University of the West Indies, 2012–14; *b* Gingerland, St Kitts and Nevis; *s* of William Joseph Rawlins and Veronica Rawlins; *m* Claudette Norville; two *d*. *Educ:* Univ. of West Indies (BA Hons 1974; LLB Hons 1983; LLM 1993); Norman Manley Law Sch., Jamaica (Legal Educn Cert. 1985); Inst. Advanced Legal Studies, Univ. of London. Undergrad. teacher, 1969–71, grad. teacher, 1974–76, high schs; Government of St Kitts and Nevis: Hd, Dept of Labour (Ag.), 1977–79; Asst Sec., Min. of Agric., Lands, Housing and Labour, 1976–85; Crown Counsel, 1985–88, Registrar of the High Court and Addnl Magistrate, 1988–89, Solicitor Gen. and Perm. Sec., Legal Dept, 1989–95, St Kitts and Nevis; Temp. Lectr in Law, 1994, Lectr in Law, 1995–2000, UWI; Master, Eastern Caribbean Supreme Court, 2000–02; High Court Judge, Antigua and Barbuda, Dominica and BVI, 2002–05; Mem., Judicial and Legal Services Commn, BVI, 2004–05; Justice of Appeal, Eastern Caribbean Supreme Court, 2005–08; Chm., Judicial and Legal Services Commns, BVI, Anguilla and Eastern Caribbean Supreme Court, 2008–12; Mem., Regl Judicial and Legal Services Commn of Caribbean Court of Justice, 2009–12. Eastern Caribbean Supreme Court: Chm., Judicial Ethics Cttee, 2004–06; Chm., Judicial Educn Inst., 2004–07. Mem. Adv. Cttee, Commonwealth Judicial Educn Inst., Dalhousie Univ. Sch. of Law, Halifax, NS, 2006– (Fellow, 2004). UNITAR Fellow, Acad. Internat. Law, The Hague, 1986. Associate Fellow, Soc. of Advanced Legal Studies, Univ. of London, 1995–. Seventieth Anniv. Award for Excellence and Leadership, Univ. of WI, 2018. *Publications:* contrib. articles on law subjects to Caribbean Law Rev., Caribbean Law Bulletin, Jl Transnat. Law and Policy. *Recreations:* athletics, soccer, cricket, tennis, swimming. *Address:* PO Box 720, Bridgetown, Barbados BB11000, West Indies. *T:* 2554798.

**RAWLINS, Prof. (John) Nicholas (Pepys),** DPhil; FMedSci; FBPsS; Master, Morningside College, Chinese University of Hong Kong, since 2018; *b* 31 May 1949; *s* of Surg. Vice-Adm. Sir John Stuart Pepys Rawlins, KBE; *m* 1986, Prof. Susan Lynn Hurley (*d* 2007); two *s*. *Educ:* Winchester Coll.; University Coll., Oxford (BA 1971, MA 1976; DPhil 1977). University of Oxford: Department of Experimental Psychology: MRC Res. Asst, 1975–81; Royal Soc. Henry Head Fellow in Neurol., 1981–83; Univ. Lectr in Psychol., 1983–98; Prof. of Behavioural Neurosci., 1998–2005; Watts Prof. of Psychol., 2005–10; Associate Head, Med. Scis Div., 2008–10; Pro-Vice-Chancellor, Develt and Ext. Affairs, 2010–17; Prof. of Behavioural Neurosci., 2010–17, now Emeritus; University College, Oxford: Weir Jun. Res. Fellow, 1978–81; Sen. Res. Fellow, 1981–87; Sir Jules Thorne Fellow and Praelector in Psychol., 1987–2005; Professorial Fellow, 2005–07; Emeritus Fellow, 2008–; Professorial Fellow, Wolfson Coll., Oxford, 2008–17, now Emeritus; Vice Pres., Internat. Affairs and Develt, Toulouse Sch. of Econs, 2017–18. Special Vis. Prof., Univ. of Nottingham, 2009–; Fogarty Foundn Res. Fellow, Johns Hopkins Univ., 1979–80. Neurosci. Grants Cttee, MRC, 1986–90; Wellcome Trust: Neurosci. Grants Cttee, 1995–2000; Mem., 2000–02, Chm., 2002–04, Basic Sci. Interest Gp; Co-Chm., Neurosci. Panel, 2004–07; Chm., Neurosci. Panel Cognitive and Higher Systems, 2004–07; Mem., Neurosci. Strategy Cttee, 2004–07. Nuffield Council Panel on Bioethics, 2001–03. Trustee, Schizophrenia Res. Trust, 1995–. FMedSci 2006; FBPsS 2011. *Publications:* (jtly) Brain Power: working out the human mind, 1999; over 200 articles in learned jls. *Recreations:* wine, cooking, gardens, walking, landscape, architecture, ski-ing, snorkelling. *Address:* Master's Lodge, Morningside College, Chinese University of Hong Kong, Shatin, New Territories, Hong Kong SAR. *E:* nickrawlins@cuhk.edu.hk.

**RAWLINS, Sir Michael (David),** GBE 2017; Kt 1999; MD; FRCP, FRCPE, FFPM, FMedSci; Ruth and Lionel Jacobson Professor of Clinical Pharmacology, University of Newcastle upon Tyne, 1973–2006, now Emeritus; Chairman, National Institute for Health and Clinical Excellence (formerly for Clinical Excellence), 1999–2013; President, Royal Society of Medicine, 2012–14; Chairman, Medicines and Healthcare Products Regulatory Agency, since 2014; *b* 28 March 1941; *s* of Rev. Jack and Evelyn Daphne Rawlins; *m* 1963, Elizabeth Cadbury Hambly (marr. diss. 2005); three *d*. *Educ:* St Thomas's Hosp. Med. Sch., London (BSc 1962; MB BS 1965); MD London 1973. FRCP 1977; FRCPE 1987; FFPM 1989 (Hon. FFPM 2015). Lectr in Medicine, St Thomas's Hosp., London, 1967–71; Sen. Registrar, Hammersmith Hosp., London, 1971–72; Consultant Clinical Pharmacologist, Newcastle upon Tyne NHS Trust, 1973–2006. Chm., Eastern Academic Health Sci. Network, 2013–14. Vis. Res. Fellow, Karolinska Inst., Stockholm, Sweden, 1972–73; Public Orator, Univ. of Newcastle upon Tyne, 1990–93; Ruiting van Swieten Vis. Prof., Academic Med. Centre, Amsterdam, 1998; Hon. Prof., LSHTM, 2000–; Guest Prof., Univ. of Remnin, Beijing, 2012–15. Pres., NE Council on Addictions, 1991–2000; Chairman: Adv. Council on Misuse of Drugs, 1998–2008; UK Biobank, 2012–19; Vice-Chm., Northern RHA, 1990–94; Member: Nat. Cttee on Pharmacology, 1977–83; Cttee on the Safety of Medicines, 1980–98 (Chm., 1993–98); Cttee on Toxicity, 1989–92; Standing Gp on Health Technology Assessment, 1993–95. Chm., Newcastle SDP, 1981–84. Bradshaw Lectr, RCP, 1986; Welcome Lectr, Soc. of Apothecaries, 1996; Samuel Gee Lectr, 2005, Harveian Orator, 2008, RCP; Stevens Lectr, RSocMed, 2010; Crookshank Lectr, RCR, 2010; Stanley Davidson Lectr, RCPE, 2010; Fear Meml Lectr, Univ. of Dalhousie, 2011; Jephcott Lectr, RSocMed, 2015. DL Tyne and Wear, 1999–2008. FRSocMed 1972; Founder FMedSci 1998; FKC 2013. Hon. FRCA 2000; Hon. FBPhS (Hon. FBPharmacolS 2005); Hon. Fellow, Royal Statistical Soc. 2009; Hon. FRCS 2012; Hon. FRCGP 2013; Hon. FRCR 2013; Hon. FFPH 2017; Hon. FRSocMed 2017. DUniv York, 2007; Hon. DCL Newcastle, 2008; Hon. DSc: Univ. of Scis, Philadelphia, 2010; Cambridge, 2015; Hon. MD Sheffield, 2011. Univ. Medal, Helsinki, 1978; William Withering Medal, RCP, 1994; Dixon Medal, Ulster Med. Soc., 1995; Lilly Medal, British Pharmacol Soc., 1997; Paracelsus Medal, Univ. of Amsterdam, 1998; Bradlaw Oration and Medal, FDS RCS, 2002; Hutchinson Medal, RSocMed, 2003; Galen Medal, Soc. of Apothecaries, 2011; Donebedian Lifetime Achievement Award, Internat. Soc. of Pharmacoeconomics and Outcomes Res., 2011; Prince Mahidol Award for Medicine, 2012; Lifetime Achievement Award, European Assoc. of Clinical Therapeutics, 2013. *Publications:* Variability in Human Drug Response, 1973; (ed) Textbook of Pharmaceutical Medicine, 1994; (ed) Patients, the Public and Priorities in Healthcare, 2009; Evidence for Decision-Making in Therapeutics, 2011; articles on clinical pharmacology in med. and scientific jls. *Recreation:* music. *Address:* 16 Friend Street, EC1V 7NS.

**RAWLINS, Nicholas;** *see* Rawlins, J. N. P.

**RAWLINS, Brig. Peregrine Peter,** MBE 1983; Clerk to the Grocers' Company, 1998–2006; *b* 3 March 1946; *s* of Lt-Col John Walter Rawlins, Northamptonshire Regt, and Elizabeth Joan Rawlins (*née* Delmé-Radcliffe); *m* 1976, Marlis Müller; one *s* one *d*. *Educ:* Malvern Coll.; RMA, Sandhurst; Lincoln Coll., Oxford (BA Hons Geography 1970). Royal Anglian Regiment: commnd 2nd Bn, 1966; Comd, 2nd Bn, 1985–87; Dep. Col, 1996–98. Staff Coll., 1978; Directing Staff, RMCS, 1988–90; COS, Directorate of Infantry, 1990–92; NATO Defence Coll., Rome, 1992; Defence Attaché, Bonn, 1992–96; Dep. Comdt, RMCS, 1996–98, retd. Gov., Dauntsey's Sch., 2007–. *Recreations:* bird/butterfly conservation, golf, gardening, fishing. *Address:* The Grey House, Low Road, Little Cheverell, Devizes, Wilts SN10 4JS.

**RAWLINS, Peter Jonathan,** FCA; business strategy consultant and executive coach, Rawlins Strategy Consulting, since 1994; *b* 30 April 1951; *e s* of late Kenneth Raymond Ivan Rawlins and Constance Amande Rawlins (*née* Malzy); *m* 1st, 1973, Louise Langton (marr. diss. 1999); one *s* one *d*; 2nd, 2000, Christina Conway; three *s* one *d*. *Educ:* Arnold House Sch.; St Edward's Sch., Oxford; Keble Coll., Oxford (Hons English Lang. and Lit.; MA). Arthur Andersen & Co., 1972–85: Manager, 1977; Partner, 1983; UK Practice Develt Partner, 1984; full-time secondment to Lloyd's of London as PA to Chief Exec. and Dep. Chm., 1983–84; Dir, Sturge Holdings, and Man. Dir, R. W. Sturge & Co., 1985–89; Chief Exec., Internat., subseq. London, Stock Exchange, 1989–93; Director: Sturge Lloyd's Agencies, 1986–89; Wise Speke Holdings, 1987–89; non-exec. Dir, Lloyd-Roberts & Gilkes, 1989–94; Man. Dir (Europe, ME and Africa), Siegel & Gale Ltd, 1996–97; Director: Scala Business Solutions, NV, 1998–2000; Logistics Resources Ltd, 1999–2002; Oyster Partners Ltd, 2001–02; Cognito Ltd, 2007–09; Chm., Higham Gp plc, 2004–05. Mem., Cttee, Lloyd's Underwriting Agents Assoc., 1986–89 (Treasurer, 1986–87; Dep. Chm., 1988); Mem., standing cttees, Council of Lloyd's, 1985–89. Non-exec. Dir, Royal Bournemouth and Christchurch Hosps NHS Foundn Trust, 2005–07. Director: London Sinfonietta Trust, 1985–88; Half Moon Theatre, 1986–88; Mem. Council and Dir, ABSA, 1982–96; Dir and Trustee, London City Ballet Trust, 1986–93; Mem., Develt Council, RNT, 1991–95; Vice-Chm., 2000, Chm., 2000–02, Spitalfields Fest. Chairman: London First Neighbourhood Approach, 1993–95; Assoc. for Res. into Stammering in Children, 1993–. FRSA 1990. *Recreations:* performing arts, tennis, Rugby, travelling. *Address:* The White House, Hadlow Road, Tonbridge, Kent TN11 0AE. *T:* (01732) 852248. *E:* peter@pjrawlins.co.uk. *Clubs:* City of London, MCC.

**RAWLINSON, Sir Anthony Henry John,** 5th Bt *cr* 1891; photographer and inventor; *b* 1 May 1936; *s* of Sir Alfred Frederick Rawlinson, 4th Bt and Bessie Ford Taylor (*d* 1996), *d* of Frank Raymond Emmatt, Harrogate; *S* father, 1969; *m* 1st, 1960, Penelope Byng Noel (marr. diss. 1967), 2nd *d* of Rear-Adm. G. J. B. Noel, RN; one *s* one *d*; 2nd, 1967, Pauline Strickland (marr. diss. 1976), *d* of J. H. Hardy, Sydney; one *s*; 3rd, 1977, Helen Leone (marr. diss. 1997), *d* of T. M. Kennedy, Scotland; one *s*; 4th, 2013, Rosalind Snaith, *d* of Robert Everett. *Educ:* Millfield School. Coldstream Guards, 1954–56. *Recreations:* tennis, sailing. *Heir: s* Alexander Noel Rawlinson, *b* 15 July 1964.

**RAWLINSON, Charles Frederick Melville,** MBE 2012; Deputy Chairman, Britten Sinfonia, 1997–2013 (Director, 1988–2013); Member, Advisory Council, since 2013); *b* 18 March 1934; *s* of Rowland Henry Rawlinson and Olivia Melville Rawlinson; *m* 1962, Jill Rosalind Wesley; three *d*. *Educ:* Canford Sch.; Jesus Coll., Cambridge (MA). FCA, FCT. With A. E. Limehouse & Co., Chartered Accts, 1955–58; Peat Marwick Mitchell & Co., 1958–62; Morgan Grenfell & Co. Ltd, Bankers, 1962–94: Dir, 1970–87; Jt Chm., 1985–87; Morgan Grenfell Group PLC: Dir, 1985–88; Vice-Chm., 1987–88; Sen. Advr, 1988–94; Chm., Morgan Grenfell (Asia), Singapore, 1976–88, Hon. Pres., 1988–93; seconded as Man. Dir, Investment Bank of Ireland Ltd, Dublin, 1966–68; Director: Jefferson Smurfit Gp, 1969–83; Associated Paper Industries plc, 1972–91 (Chm., 1979–91); Yule Catto plc, 1975–85; Willis Faber plc, 1981–89; Hedley Wright & Co. Ltd, 1994–99; Chm., Boxford Suffolk Gp, 1992–2000. Sen. Advr, West Merchant Bank, 1994–97. Chairman: The Hundred Gp of Finance Dirs, 1984–86; Industrial Mems Adv. Cttee on Ethics, ICAEW, 1991–99; Member: Chartered Accountants' Jt Ethics Cttee, 1994–2001; Council, ICAEW, 1995–97; Exec. Cttee, Jt Disciplinary Scheme, 1995–2010. Mem., Council, Order of St Etheldreda, Ely Cathedral, 1999–2017; Trustee, Ely Cathedral Trust, 2007–. Chm., Peache Trustees, 1980–2002; Hon. Vice Pres., Ambition (formerly NABC—Clubs for Young People), 1995–2017 (Jt Hon. Treas., 1983–91; Dep. Chm., 1989–92; Chm., 1992–94).

Member: Soc. of St Radegund, Jesus Coll., Cambridge, 1994–; Vice Chancellor's Circle, Univ. of Cambridge, 2011–. FRSA. *Recreations:* music, sailing, travel. *Address:* The Old Forge, Arkesden, Saffron Walden, Essex CB11 4EX. *E:* post@oldforge.org. *Club:* Brooks's.
*See also under Royal Family.*

**RAWLINSON, David Ian, (Iain);** Principal, Rawlinson Partners Ltd, since 2005; Consulting Partner, Vico Partners Ltd, since 2017; *b* Liverpool, 18 Sept. 1958; *s* of (James) Keith McClure Rawlinson and Griselda Maxwell Rawlinson (*née* Carlisle); *m* 1st, 1991 (marr. diss. 1995); 2nd, 1997 (marr. diss. 2013); one *s* one *d*. *Educ:* Birkenhead Sch.; Jesus Coll., Cambridge (BA 1980). Called to the Bar, Lincoln's Inn, 1981; corporate finance roles, Lazard Brothers & Co. Ltd, 1986–94; Robert Fleming London, 1994–95; Robert Fleming Johannesburg, 1995–2000; Hd, Corporate Finance, Robert Fleming South Africa, subseq. Fleming Martin, 1997–2000; Dir, SA Hldg Bd, RF Hldgs SA Ltd, 2000; Chief Operating Officer, Fleming Family & Partners Ltd, 2000–02; Chief Exec., FF&P Advisory Ltd, 2000–04; Sen. Advr, Fleming Family & Partners Ltd, 2004–05; Chief Exec., Highland Star Gp, 2004–05; Dir, Strategy, Good Governance Gp, 2004–08; Chairman: Monarch Airlines Ltd, 2009–11; Monarch Gp, 2009–14. Non-executive Director: Dana Petroleum plc, 2004–10; Sindicatum Carbon Capital Ltd, 2007–10; Edgo Energy Ltd, 2007–09; Lithic Metals and Energy Ltd, 2007–09; Parkmead Gp plc, 2010–. Chairman: Tusk Trust, 2005–13 (Vice Pres., 2014–); (and Founder) Online Radio Broadcasting (formerly StudyVox) Foundn Ltd, 2009–; Rainmaker Foundn, 2013–14; Dep. Chm., Global Philanthropic Ltd, 2007–13. Non-exec. Dir, Royal Bournemouth and Christchurch Hosps NHS Foundn Trust, 2017–. Chm., Govs, Walhampton Sch., Lymington, 2018–. Fellow, Centre for Social Innovation, Cambridge Judge Business Sch., 2016–. *Recreations:* writing, broadcasting, sailing, music, Scotland, Africa. *T:* 07799 882382. *E:* iain@rawlinsonpartners.com. *Clubs:* Beaulieu River Sailing, Royal Southampton Yacht, Royal Lymington Yacht.

**RAWLINSON, Ivor Jon,** OBE 1988; HM Diplomatic Service, retired; *b* 24 Jan. 1942; *s* of Vivian Hugh Rawlinson and Hermione (*née* Curry); *m* 1976, Catherine Paule Caudal; one *s* two *d*. *Educ:* Christ Church, Oxford (MA). Joined FO, 1964; Polish lang. student, 1965–66; Warsaw, 1966–69; Bridgetown, 1969–71 (course at Univ. of W Indies); Second Sec., News Dept, FCO, 1971–73; Asst Private Sec. to Minister of State, FCO, 1973–74; Second Sec. (Econ.), Paris, 1974–78; First Secretary: FCO, 1978–80; (Commercial), Mexico City, 1980–84; Consul, Florence and Consul-Gen., San Marino, 1984–88; First Sec., later Counsellor (Inspectorate), FCO, 1988–93; RCDS, 1993; Consul-Gen., Montreal, 1993–98; Ambassador to Tunisia, 1999–2002; Hd, FCO Outplacement, 2002–07. Dir, Northcote Books Ltd, 2013–15. Gov., Ryde Sch., IoW, 2005–12 (Vice-Chm., 2006–11). Chm., Pimpernel Trust, 2013–18 (Trustee, 2006–13). *Publications:* Tunisian Dreams: a novel, 2012. *Recreations:* painting, writing, restoring farmhouse in France. *Address:* 29 Broxash Road, SW11 6AD. *T:* (020) 7228 5261.

**RAWLINSON, Mark Stobart;** Chairman, UK Investment Banking, Morgan Stanley, since 2016; *b* Eccles, Manchester, 3 May 1957; *s* of Thomas Stobart Rawlinson and Barbara Rawlinson; *m* 1984, Julia Shepherd; three *s*. *Educ:* Haberdashers' Aske's Sch., Elstree; Sidney Sussex Coll., Cambridge (BA Hons 1979; MA Hons Law 1980); Guildford Law Sch. (Professional Exams Pt II). Freshfields Bruckhaus Deringer LLP (formerly Freshfields): articled clerk, 1982–84; Associate, 1984–90; Mergers and Acquisitions Partner, 1990–2016; Hd, Trainee Recruitment, 2008–09; Hd, Corporate Dept, 2008–11; Hd, London office, 2011–14. Lead non-exec. Dir, MoJ, 2018–. *Recreations:* sport (4 Peaks Challenge, 1997, Engadin cross country ski marathon, 2005), Rugby, cricket, golf. *Address:* Morgan Stanley Investment Banking, 25 Cabot Square, Canary Wharf, E14 4QA. *Club:* Hawks (Cambridge).

**RAWLINSON, Richard Anthony;** Managing Director, Axion Leadership Ltd, since 2015; *b* 11 Feb. 1957; *s* of Sir Anthony Rawlinson, KCB and Lady (Mary) Rawlinson; *m* 1991, Sharon Sofer; two *s*. *Educ:* Eton Coll. (King's Schol.); Christ Church, Oxford (BA Politics and Econs 1978; MA); Harvard Business Sch. (Baker Schol.; MBA 1983). J. Henry Schroder Wagg & Co. Ltd, 1978–81; Associates Fellow, Harvard Business Sch., 1983–84; Monitor Company: Cambridge, Mass, 1984–85; London, 1985–89; Tokyo, 1989–93; Hong Kong, 1994–96; London, 1996–2001; Partner (formerly Dir), Monitor Co. Gp LP, 1993–2001. Chm. and Man. Dir, W. P. Stewart & Co. Ltd, 2001–02; Dep. Man. Dir, W. P. Stewart & Co Ltd, Bermuda, 2001–02; Vice Pres., Booz Allen Hamilton Inc., later Booz & Co., then Strategy&, 2004–15 (Dir, 2010–13). Mem., Competition (formerly Monopolies and Mergers) Commn, 1998–2005. FRGS 2002. *Publications:* (contrib.) Competition in Global Industries, 1986; articles in Harvard Business Review, Strategy & Business. *Recreation:* mountain walking. *Address:* 3 Britannia Studios, 49A Britannia Road, SW6 2HJ. *Clubs:* Oxford and Cambridge, Hurlingham.

**RAWNSLEY, Andrew Nicholas James;** author, broadcaster and journalist; Chief Political Commentator and Associate Editor, The Observer, since 1993; *b* 5 Jan. 1962; *s* of Eric Rawnsley and Barbara Rawnsley (*née* Butler); *m* 1990, Jane Leslie Hall; three *d*. *Educ:* Lawrence Sheriff Grammar Sch., Rugby; Rugby Sch.; Sidney Sussex Coll., Cambridge (schol.; 1st Cl. Hons Hist.; MA; Hon. Fellow 2018). BBC, 1983–85; The Guardian: reporter, 1985–87; sketchwriter, 1987–93. Ed.-in-Chief, PoliticsHome.com, 2008–09. TV presenter: A Week in Politics, 1989–97; series: The Agenda, 1996; Bye Bye Blues, 1997; Blair's Year, 1998; What the Papers Say, incl. Rev. of the Year, 2002–07; The Sunday Edition, 2006–08; The Rise and Fall of Tony Blair, 2007; Gordon Brown: where did it all go wrong?, 2008; Crash Gordon: the inside story of the financial crisis, 2009; Cameron Uncovered, 2010; Roses and Thorns: the inside story of the coalition, 2011. Radio presenter: The Westminster Hour, 1998–2006; The Unauthorised Biography of the United Kingdom, 1999; Leader Conference, 2011–; Beyond Westminster, 2008–11. Trustee, Speakers Trust, 2019–. FRSA 2001. Student Journalist of Year, Guardian/NUS Student Media Awards, 1982; Young Journalist of Year, British Press Awards, 1987; Columnist of Year, What the Papers Say Awards, 2000; Journalist of the Year, Channel Four Pol Awards, 2003; Political Journalist of the Year, Public Affairs Awards, 2006; Commentator of Year, House Mag. Awards, 2008; Chair's Choice, Editorial Intelligence Comment Awards, 2015. *Publications:* Servants of the People: the inside story of New Labour, 2000, revd edn 2001 (Channel 4/Politico Book of the Year, 2001); Crash Gordon: the inside story of the financial crisis, 2009; The End of the Party: the rise and fall of New Labour, 2010. *Recreations:* books, movies, mah-jong, sailing, ski-ing. *Address:* The Observer, Kings Place, 90 York Way, N1 9GU. *T:* (020) 3353 4255. *E:* Andrew.Rawnsley@Observer.co.uk; Press Gallery, House of Commons, SW1A 1AA.

**RAWORTH, Sophie;** Presenter, BBC News; *b* Redhill, Surrey, 15 May 1968; *d* of Richard and Jenny Raworth; *m* 2003, Richard Winter; one *s* two *d*. *Educ:* Bute House Prep. Sch., Hammersmith; Putney High Sch.; St Paul's Girls' Sch.; Univ. of Manchester (BA Jt Hons French and German 1991); City Univ., London (Postgrad. Dip. Broadcast Journalism 1992). Joined BBC as trainee, 1992; reporter, BBC GMR Manchester, 1992–93; producer, Brussels office, 1993–95; Presenter: (and reporter) BBC Look North Leeds, 1995–97; BBC Breakfast, 1997–2002; (and reporter) Tomorrow's World, 1999–2002; BBC Six O'Clock News, 2003–06; BBC One O'Clock News, 2006–. TV presenter: Dream Lives, 2001; Judgemental, 2002; The Trouble with Working Women, 2009; Crimewatch Roadshow, 2009; Panorama: Swine Flu, 2009, Too Much Too Young?, 2011; The Big Personality Test, 2010; Moneywatch, 2010; Parents Under Pressure, 2010; Britain's Royal Weddings, 2011; The Royal Wedding, 2011; Watchdog Daily, 2013; The Watchdog Test House, 2014; Chelsea Flower Show, 2014–; The Queen's Longest Reign, 2015; Watchdog, 2015–; The People Remember, 2015. Judge, Baileys Women's Prize for Fiction, 2014. Hon. DArts City, 2013. *Recreations:* running, cycling, books, theatre. *Address:* BBC News Centre, Broadcasting House, Portland Place, W1A 1AA.

**RAWSON, Prof. Dame Jessica (Mary),** DBE 2002 (CBE 1994); LittD; FBA 1990; Warden, Merton College, Oxford, 1994–2010, now Honorary Fellow; Professor of Chinese Art and Archaeology, University of Oxford, since 2000; Slade Professor of Fine Art, University of Cambridge, 2013–14; Fellow, St John's College, Cambridge, 2013–14; *b* 20 Jan. 1943; *d* of Roger Nathaniel Quirk and Paula Quirk; *m* 1968, John Rawson; one *d*. *Educ:* New Hall, Cambridge (BA Hons History; LittD 1991; Hon. Fellow, 1997); London Univ. (BA Hons Chinese Lang. and Lit.). Asst Principal, Min. of Health, 1965–67; Department of Oriental Antiquities, British Museum: Asst Keeper II, 1967–71; Asst Keeper I, 1971–76; Dep. Keeper, 1976–87; Keeper, 1987–94; Pro-Vice-Chancellor, Univ. of Oxford, 2005–10. Visiting Professor: Kunsthistorisches Inst., Heidelberg, 1989, 2011; Dept of Art, Univ. of Chicago, 1994; Peking Univ., 2017; Hon. Professor: Xi'an Jiaotong Univ., 2007–; Univ. of Sci. and Technol., Beijing, 2008–. Lectures: Barlow, Sussex Univ., 1979; Leventritt Meml, Harvard, 1989; A. J. Pope, Smithsonian Instn, 1991; Harvey Buchanan, Cleveland Mus. of Art, 1993; Pratt Inst., 1998; Beatrice Blackwood, Oxford, 1999; Millennium, Oxford, 2000; Creighton, Univ. of London, 2000; K. S. Lo, Hong Kong, 2009; Heinz-Goetze, Heidelberg, 2011; Frederick Mote, Princeton, 2011; Mok, Chinese Univ. of Hong Kong, 2011; William Cohn, Univ. of Oxford, 2014; Leon Levy, New York Univ., 2015; Sir Percival David, London, 2016. Member: Nuffield Langs Inquiry, 1998–99; British Library Bd, 1999–2003; Scholars' Council, Library of Congress, Washington, 2005–11. Academic Advr to Centre for Ancient Civilization, Inst. of Archaeol., Chinese Acad. of Social Scis, 2000–; Consultant to Res. Dept, Palace Mus., Beijing, 2014–; Ambassador, Inst. of Archaeol., Shaanxi Province, 2014–. Chm., Oriental Ceramic Soc., 1993–96; Vice-Chm., Exec. Cttee, GB-China Centre, 1985–87. Governor: SOAS, Univ. of London, 1998–2003; Latymer and Godolphin Sch., 2004–08; St Paul's Girls' Sch., 2009–14. Hon. DSc St Andrews, 1997; Hon. DLitt: London, 1998; Sussex, 1998; Newcastle, 1999; Hon. Dr: Xi'an Jiaotong, 2007; Univ. of Sci. and Technol., Beijing, 2008. Freer Medal, Freer Gall., Smithsonian Instn, Washington DC, 2017. *Publications:* Chinese Jade Throughout the Ages (with John Ayers), 1975; Animals in Art, 1977; Ancient China, Art and Archaeology, 1980; Chinese Ornament: the lotus and the dragon, 1984; Chinese Bronzes: art and ritual, 1987; The Bella and P. P. Chiu Collection of Ancient Chinese Bronzes, 1988; Western Zhou Ritual Bronzes from the Arthur M. Sackler Collections, 1990; (with Emma Bunker) Ancient Chinese and Ordos Bronzes, 1990; (ed) The British Museum Book of Chinese Art, 1992; Chinese Jade from the Neolithic to the Qing, 1995; Mysteries of Ancient China, 1996; (with Evelyn Rawski) China, The Three Emperors 1662–1795, 2005; Treasures from Shanghai, Ancient Chinese Bronzes and Jades, 2009; (ed with Kristian Göransson) China's Terracotta Army, 2010; Ancestors and Eternity: essays on Chinese archaeology and art, 2011; Lotus and Dragon: studies of Chinese ornament, 2019; contrib. Proc. of British Acad. and learned jls. *Address:* Merton College, Merton Street, Oxford OX1 4JD. *T:* (01865) 276310.

**RAWSON, Prof. Kenneth John,** MSc; FREng; RCNC; consultant; Professor and Head of Department of Design and Technology, 1983–89, Dean of Education and Design, 1983–89, Brunel University; *b* 27 Oct. 1926; *s* of late Arthur William Rawson and Beatrice Anne Rawson; *m* 1950, Rhona Florence Gill; two *s* one *d*. *Educ:* Northern Grammar Sch., Portsmouth; HM Dockyard Technical Coll., Portsmouth; RN Colls, Keyham and Greenwich. RCNC; FREng (FEng 1984); FRINA. WhSch. At sea, 1950–51; Naval Construction Res. Estabt, Dunfermline, 1951–53; Ship Design, Admiralty, 1953–57; Lloyd's Register of Shipping, 1957–59; Ship and Weapons Design, MoD, Bath, 1959–69; Naval Staff, London, 1969–72; Prof. of Naval Architecture, University Coll., Univ. of London, 1972–77; Ministry of Defence, Bath: Head of Forward Design, Ship Dept, 1977–79; Dep. Dir, Ship Design and Chief Naval Architect (Under Sec.), 1979–83. Hon. DEng Portsmouth, 1995. *Publications:* Photoelasticity and the Engineer, 1953; (with E. C. Tupper) Basic Ship Theory, 1968, 5th edn 2001; Ever the Apprentice, 2006; contrib. numerous technical publications. *Recreations:* cabinet making, gardening, walking. *Address:* Moorlands, The Street, Chilcompton, Radstock BA3 4HB. *T:* (01761) 232793.

**RAWSON, Air Vice-Marshal Paul David,** CB 2007; Regional Director (Riyadh), Rolls-Royce International, 2007–17; Managing Director and Chief Executive Officer, Rolls-Royce Saudi Arabia Ltd, 2009–17; *b* 13 March 1953; *s* of Geoffrey and Joyce Rawson; *m* 1975, Janet Elizabeth Fewster; one *s*. *Educ:* RAF Cranwell (HND Mech. Engrg); Open Univ. (BA). Joined RAF, 1972; completed Engr Officer trng, 1975; appts at Brize Norton, Waddington, Farnborough and Binbrook, 1975–83; Tech. Staff Officer, Ordnance Bd, then RAF Marham, subseq. Sen. Engr Officer, RAF Unit, Goose Bay, Canada, 1983–90; RAF St Athan, 1991–93; leader, VC10 Support Authy, Wyton, 1993–95; Sen. Engr Officer, St Athan, 1996–98; Logistics Support Services Agency, Wyton, 1998–2000; RCDS, 2000; ACOS Logistics, HQ Strike Comd, 2002–04; Team Comdr, MoD Saudi Arabian Armed Forces Project, 2004–06; Chief of Staff Support, HQ Strike Comd, 2006–07. *Recreations:* DIY, travel, hill walking, ski-ing, gardening. *Address:* 29 Spaldwick Road, Stow Longa PE28 0TL. *T:* 07772 224820. *E:* rawsonpd@hotmail.com.

**RAWSTHORN, Alice,** OBE 2014; design critic and historian; *b* 15 Nov. 1958; *née* Judith Alison Rawsthorn; *d* of Peter Rawsthorn and Joan Rawsthorn (*née* Schofield). *Educ:* Clare Coll., Cambridge (MA). Grad. trainee journalist, Thomson Org., 1980–83; Journalist: Campaign Mag., 1983–85; Financial Times, 1985–2001; Dir, Design Mus., 2001–06; Columnist, NY Times, 2006–17. Chm., Design Adv. Gp, British Council, 2003–07; Mem., Arts Council England, 2007–13 (Lead Advr on Visual Arts, 2004–07; Chm., Turning Point Review of Contemporary Visual Arts, 2003–06; Member: Visual Arts Bd, 2008–09; Arts Policy Cttee, 2010–13); Mem., Honours Cttee for Arts and Media, 2019–. Chm., Trustees, Chisenhale Gall., 2013–; Trustee: Whitechapel Gall., 1998–2018 (Chm., 2014–15); Michael Clark Co., 2013–18 (Chm., 2015–18); Hepworth Wakefield, 2018– (Chm., 2018–). Member: Global Agenda Council on Design, WEF, 2008–15; Writers at Liberty, 2014–. Hon. Sen. FRCA. Hon. Dr UAL, 2014. *Publications:* Yves Saint Laurent: a biography, 1996; Marc Newson, 2000; Hello World: where design meets life, 2013; Design as an Attitude, 2018; *contributor:* Frieze Projects 2003–2005, 2006; Fashion Theory: a reader, 2007; Marti Guixe: don't buy it if you don't need it, 2007; Women of Design, 2008; Rises in the East: a gallery in Whitechapel, 2009; AC|DC: contemporary art, contemporary design, 2009; Articulado, 2010; 220° Virus Monobloc, 2010; Hella Jongerius: misfit, 2011; Ronan and Erwan Bouroullec: bivouac, 2012; Formafantasma, 2014; Martino Gamper: design is a state of mind, 2014; Richard Hamilton, 2014; How Social Design Changes our World, 2014; Design and Violence, 2015; Designing Everyday Life, 2015; Michael Craig-Martin: transience, 2015; Aldo Bakker, 2016; Hella Jongerius: I don't have a favourite colour, 2016; The Frieze A to Z of Contemporary Art, 2016; My Top Tens, 2017; As Seen:

exhibitions that made design history, 2017; Be the Future—Back to the Future, 2017; Crafts: today's anthology for tomorrow's crafts, 2018. *Recreations:* art, architecture, film, literature, fashion, cycling, hiking, Manchester United. *Address:* c/o Toby Mundy Associates, 38 Berkeley Square, W1J 5AE. *W:* www.alicerawsthorn.com.

**RAWSTHORNE, Anthony Robert;** a Senior Clerk, House of Lords, 2001–05; *b* 25 Jan. 1943; *s* of Frederic Leslie and Nora Rawsthorne; *m* 1967, Beverley Jean Osborne; one *s* two *d*. *Educ:* Ampleforth College; Wadham College, Oxford. Home Office, 1966–97: Asst Sec., 1977; Crime Policy Planning Unit, 1977–79; Establishment Dept, 1979–82; Sec., Falkland Islands Review Cttee, 1982; Principal Private Sec., 1983; Immigration and Nationality Dept, 1983–86; Assistant Under-Secretary: Establishment Dept, 1986–91; Equal Opportunities and Gen. Dept, 1991; Asst Under-Sec., then Dep. Dir-Gen., Policy, Immigration and Nationality Directorate, 1991–97; Dir, Customs Policy, and a Comr, HM Customs and Excise, 1997–2000. Mem., Fitness to Practise Panel (formerly Professional Conduct Cttee), GMC, 2001–12. *Recreations:* bridge, squash, holidays in France and Italy.

**RAWSTHORNE, Rt Rev. John;** Bishop of Hallam, (RC), 1997–2014, now Bishop Emeritus; *b* Crosby, Merseyside, 12 Nov. 1936. Priest, 1962; Titular Bishop of Rotdon and an Auxiliary Bishop of Liverpool, 1981–97. Pres., St Joseph's Coll., 1982–90.

**RAY, Christopher,** PhD; Reporting Inspector, Independent Schools Inspectorate, since 2014; *b* 10 Dec. 1951; *m* 1976, Carol Elizabeth Morrison. *Educ:* Rochdale Grammar Sch.; UCL (BA; Pres. Students' Union, 1974–75); Churchill Coll., Cambridge (PhD 1982); Balliol Coll., Oxford. Admin and Overseas Depts, Bank of England, 1976–78; Asst Master Physics, Marlborough Coll., 1982–83; Sci. Educn Ed., OUP, 1984–88; Fellow, Nat. Univ. of Singapore, 1988–89; Asst Prof., Portland State Univ., Oregon, 1989–91; Teacher and Director of Studies: Framlingham Coll., 1991–96; King's Coll. Sch., Wimbledon, 1996–2001; Headmaster, John Lyon Sch., Harrow, 2001–04; High Master, Manchester Grammar Sch., 2004–13. Vis. Lectr in Philos. of Space and Time, Univ. of Oxford, 1987–88. Principal Sci. Scrutineer, QCA, 2000–02. Chm., HMC, 2012–13; Mem., UK Internat. Educn Council, BIS, 2013–16. Gov., King's Sch., Chester, 2011–13. *Publications:* The Evolution of Relativity, 1987; Time, Space and Philosophy, 1991; (contrib.) A Companion to the Philosophy of Science, 2000; (contrib.) The Head Speaks Out, 2008. *Recreations:* fell-walking, opera and ballet, crime fiction. *Club:* East India.

**RAY, Edward Ernest,** CBE 1988; Director, 1986–2013, and Chairman, 1995–2013, C. T. Baker Ltd; Senior Partner, Spicer and Pegler, Chartered Accountants, 1984–88 (Partner, 1957); *b* 6 Nov. 1924; *s* of Walter James Ray and Cecilia May Ray; *m* 1949, Margaret Elizabeth, *d* of George Bull; two *s*. *Educ:* Holloway Co. Sch.; London Univ. (External) (BCom). Served RN, 1943–46. Inst. of Chartered Accountants: Mem., 1950; FCA 1955; Council Mem., 1973; Vice Pres., 1980; Dep. Pres., 1981; Pres., 1982, 1983. Chm., London Chartered Accountants, 1972–73. Dir, SIB, 1985–90; Chm., Investors' Compensation Scheme Ltd, 1988–91; Member: City Capital Markets Cttee, 1984–88; Marketing of Investments Bd Organising Cttee, 1984–88. *Publications:* Partnership Taxation, 1972, 3rd edn 1987; (jtly) VAT for Accountants and Businessmen, 1972; contrib. accountancy magazines. *Recreations:* walking, birdwatching, golf.

**RAY, Jane Rosemary;** illustrator of children's books; *b* 11 June 1960; *d* of Donald Edwin Ray and Barbara May Ray (*née* Rowley); *m* 1988, David Temple; one *s* two *d*. *Educ:* Middlesex Univ. (BA Hons 3-D Design (Ceramics)). Artist-in-Residence, Islington Centre for Refugees and Migrants, 2015–. *Publications:* author and illustrator: Noah's Ark, 1991; The Story of Creation, 1992; The Story of Christmas, 1992; Twelve Dancing Princesses, 1996; Hansel and Gretel, 1997; Can you catch a Mermaid, 2002; Adam and Eve and the Garden of Eden, 2004; The Apple Pip Princess, 2007; The Dolls House Fairy, 2009; Snow White, 2009; Ahmed and the Feathergirl, 2010; The Twelve Days of Christmas, 2011; Cinderella, 2012; The Emperor's Nightingale and other Feathery Tales, 2013; The Elephant's Garden, 2017; illustrator: A Balloon for Grandad, by Nigel Gray, 1989; The Happy Prince, by Oscar Wilde, 1994; Song of the Earth, by Mary Hoffman, 1995; Sun, Moon and Stars, by Mary Hoffman, 1998; Fairy Tales, by Berlie Doherty, 2000; Orchard Book of Love and Friendship, by Geraldine McCaughrean, 2000; The Bold Boy, by Malachy Doyle, 2001; The King of Capri, by Jeanette Winterson, 2003; Romeo and Juliet, re-written by Michael Rosen, 2004; Jinnie Ghost, by Berlie Doherty, 2005; Moonbird, by Joyce Dunbar, 2006; The Lost Happy Endings, by Carol Ann Duffy, 2006; Stories of Sun, Stone and Sea, by Sally Pomme Clayton, 2012; Zeraffa Giraffa, by Dianne Hofmeyr, 2014; Heartsong, by Kevin Crossley-Holland, 2015; The Glassmaker's Daughter, by Dianne Hofmeyr, 2017; Corey's Rock, by Sita Brahmachari, 2018; The Unicorn Prince, by Saviour Pirotta, 2018; Hummingbird, by Nicola Davies, 2019; various books illus. for Folio Soc., including: Myths and Legends of the Near and Middle East, 2003; Celtic Myths and Legends, 2006. *Recreations:* reading, gardening, listening to music, singing, general domesticity. *Address:* c/o Hilary Delamere, The Agency, 24 Pottery Lane, Holland Park, W11 4LZ. *T:* (home) (020) 8442 1748. *E:* janeray41@gmail.com. *W:* www.janeray.com.

**RAY, Prof. John David,** FBA 2004; FSA; Herbert Thompson Professor of Egyptology, University of Cambridge, 2005–13, now Emeritus (Reader, 1977–2005); Fellow, Selwyn College, Cambridge, since 1979; *b* 22 Dec. 1945; *s* of late Albert Ray and Edith Ray (*née* Millward); *m* 1997, Sonia Ofelia Falaschi. *Educ:* Latymer Upper Sch.; Trinity Hall, Cambridge (BA 1968, MA 1971; Thomas Young Medal). Res. Asst, Dept of Egyptian Antiquities, BM, 1970; Lectr in Egyptology, Univ. of Birmingham, 1970–77. Visiting Professor: Univ. of Chicago, 1984; Yale Univ., 1988. Reviewer: TLS, 1981–; The Times, 2001–. FSA 2000. *Publications:* The Archive of Hor, 1976; Reflections of Osiris: lives from Ancient Egypt, 2001; Demotic Papyri and Ostraca from Qasr Ibrim, 2005; The Rosetta Stone, 2007; Demotic, Hieroglyphic and Greek Inscriptions from the Sacred Animal Necropolis, North Saqqâra, 2011; Demotic Ostraca from the Sacred Animal Necropolis, North Saqqâra, 2013; (with J. Malek) Graffiti from the Memphite Serapeum, 2017; articles in Jl of Egyptian Archaeology, Lingua Aegyptia, Kadmos, etc. *Recreations:* listening to Beethoven, reading Patrick O'Brian, being walked by a golden retriever. *Address:* Selwyn College, Cambridge CB3 9DQ. *E:* jdr1000@cam.ac.uk.

**RAY, Kenneth Richard,** OBE 1996; FDSRCS, FRCS; Dean, Faculty of Dental Surgery, Royal College of Surgeons of England, 1992–95; Chairman, Joint Committee for Specialist Training in Dentistry, 1996–98; *b* 25 Jan. 1930; *s* of late John Thomas Ray and Edith Rose (*née* Hobbs); *m* 1958, Pamela Ann Thomas; one *s* two *d*. *Educ:* City of Oxford High Sch.; Univ. of Birmingham (LDS, BDS). FDSRCS 1959; FRCS 1995; FRACDS 1995. Hse Surgeon, Gen. Hosp., Birmingham, 1955; Sen. Hse Officer, Midlands Regl Plastic and Jaw Surgery Centre, 1956; Registrar, then Sen. Registrar, Royal Dental Hosp. of London and St George's Hosp., 1957–60; Sen. Lectr and Hon. Cons. in Oral Surgery, Univ. of London at Royal Dental Hosp. Sch. of Dental Surgery, 1960–73; Cons. in Oral Surgery, Royal Berks Hosp., Reading and Oxford RHA, 1963–92. Mem., GDC, 1993–95. Chm., Central Cttee for Hosp. Dental Services, 1979–86; Mem., Jt Consultants Cttee, 1979–86 and 1992–95. Royal College of Surgeons: Mem. Bd, Fac. of Dental Surgery, 1981–95; Vice-Dean, 1989; Colyer Gold Medal, 1999; British Dental Association: Mem. Council, 1979–87; Pres., Berks, Bucks and Oxon Br., 1978; Pres., Hosp. Gp, 1979; Pres., BAOMS, 1985. UK Rep., EC Dental Liaison Cttee, 1981–89; UK Rep., EC Adv. Cttee on Trng of Dental Practitioners, 1981–92. Hon. Fellow, BDA, 1990; Hon. FDSRCSE 1997; Hon. FDSRCPSGlas 1998. *Publications:* articles in learned jls and contrib. to textbooks on oral and maxillofacial surgery, local analgesia and health service planning. *Recreations:* fell-walking, natural history, English inns. *Club:* Royal Society of Medicine.

**RAY, Piali;** see Ray Mahasay, P.

**RAY, Hon. Robert (Francis);** Chairman, Australian Political Exchange Council, 2009–13; Senator for Victoria, 1981–2008; *b* Melbourne, 8 April 1947; *m* (Victoria) Jane Petheram. *Educ:* Monash Univ.; Rusden State Coll. Former technical sch. teacher. Australian Labor Party: Mem., 1966–; Deleg., Vic. State Conf., 1970–96; Mem., Nat. Exec., 1983–98; Minister for Home Affairs and Dep. Manager of Govt Business in the Senate, 1987; Minister assisting the Minister for Transport and Communications, 1988; Minister for Immigration, Local Govt and Ethnic Affairs, 1988–90; Manager of Govt Business in the Senate, 1988–91; Minister for Defence, 1990–96; Dep. Leader of Govt in Senate, 1993–96. Chm., Victorian Managed Insurance Authy, 2010–11. Mem. Council, Australian Strategic Policy Inst., 2010.

**RAY, Vincent Edward;** journalist, since 1987; writer, trainer and broadcaster; *b* London, 2 June 1957; *s* of Victor and Peggy Ray; partner, Sara Lee; two *s* one *d*. *Educ:* Wallington Co. Grammar Sch.; Bristol Coll. of Art (BA Hons Ceramics 1978); City of London Poly. (MA Politics 1987). Dir, Lincoln Hannah Ltd, 1981–87; BBC: Ceefax, 1987–88; producer, Nine O'Clock News, 1988–90; Foreign Field producer, 1990–93; Foreign Ed., 1993–96; World News Ed., 1996–99; Exec. Ed., News, 1999–2002; Dep. Hd, Newsgathering, 2002–05; Dir, BBC Coll. of Journalism, 2005–10. Visiting Professor: New York Univ., 2003–06; Bournemouth Univ., 2010–. Trustee, Rory Peck Trust, 1997–2004; Chm., Trustees, Ockenden Internat. Mem., Flying Gazebo Walking Soc. Distinguished Media Leadership Award, Dart Centre, 2004. *Publications:* The Reporter's Friend, 2002; The Television News Handbook, 2003. *Recreations:* walking in Greenwich Park, reading, art, storytelling, gadgets. *E:* vinray@me.com. *Club:* Frontline.

**RAY, Rt Rev. William James;** Bishop of North Queensland, 2007–18; *b* Yarram, Vic, 19 Oct. 1950; *s* of Vernon Henry Ray and Violet June Colbert; *m* 1978, Robin Adele, *d* of Rees William Llewellyn and Beryll Allison Koeteveld; one *s* one *d*. *Educ:* Yarram High Sch.; Frankston Teachers' Coll. (Teaching Dip.); Western Australian Coll. of Educn (BEd); Australian Coll. of Theology (ThL); Duke Univ., USA (MRE). Teacher, Stradbroke Primary Sch., 1973–75; Headteacher, Seaspray Primary Sch., 1976–77; Youth Officer, Dio. of Brisbane, 1978–81; Youth and Children's Officer, St Luke's, Toowoomba, 1981–83, 1986–87; Educn Officer, Dio. of Gippsland, 1987–91; Ministry Trng Officer, Dio. of Rockhampton, 1991–96; ordained priest, 1992; Rector, St Luke's, Wandal, 1996–99; Dir Gen., Bd of Religious Educn, 2000–01 (Mem., 1974–97); Vicar: St George's, E Ivanhoe, 2001–03; St John the Divine, Croydon, 2003–07; Archdeacon of Maroondah, Melbourne, 2004–07. Chair, Diocesan Catechumenate Working Gp, 2002–18; Mem., Archbishop in CI Exec., 2004–18. CI Crescent Lagoon Sch., 1980–2018; MACE; Founding Mem., Academic Bd, Inst. of Theol. Educn, 1993–97; Trainer, Australian Educn for Ministry, 2005–07. Chaplain, Scouting Assoc., 1977–99. KCSJ. *Recreations:* walking, bushwalking, reading biographies and newspapers, cycling, movies, cooking.

**RAY MAHASAY, Piali,** OBE 2002; Founder Director and Chief Executive Officer, Sampad Asian Arts and Heritage, since 1990; *b* Calcutta, India, 9 Oct. 1956; *d* of Binoy Krishna Ghosh and Bani Ghosh; *m* 1978, Dr Sugat Raymahasay. *Educ:* Queen of Missions Convent, Calcutta; Loreto Coll., Calcutta (BA (Dist.) 1975; MA 1st Cl. Hist. and Indology 1980; BEd 1st Cl. 1982); Cranfield Coll. of Mgt (Mgt and Strategic Leadership course 1998). Artist, dancer and choreographer, UK, 1982–98. Mem., Music and Dance Panels, 1988–89, Cultural Diversity Cttee, 2000–02, Arts Council England. Founder Mem., Aditi (nat. orgn for S Asian dance), 1991; Founder and Mem., S Asian Dance Alliance UK, 2002–. Board Member: Birmingham Royal Ballet, 1988–; Rambert Dance Co., 2004–07; Chitraleka Dance Acad., 2005–; One Dance UK, 2017–. Mem. Cttee, Birmingham Royal Inst. for Blind, 1996–98. Trustee, UK Asian Women's Conf., 1999–. Producer, Moving Earth (outdoor dance prodns with 220 dancers) and Mandala (multimedia finale), London 2012 Fest.; Dir, Utsav 2017: Birmingham's Year of S Asian Culture; Artistic Dir, Birmingham Weekender, 2017; Jt Artistic Dir, Athletes' Homecoming and launch of Commonwealth Games, Birmingham, 2018. DUniv Central England, 2006. Outstanding Business Person of Year, Birmingham Chamber of Commerce, 2009; British Indian Arts and Culture Award, 2015. *Recreations:* travelling, reading. *Address:* 24 Selly Wick Drive, Selly Park, Birmingham B29 7JH. *T:* (0121) 472 3934. *E:* piali@sampad.org.uk.

**RAYFIELD, Rt Rev. Lee Stephen;** see Swindon, Bishop Suffragan of.

**RAYLEIGH, 6th Baron** *cr* 1821; **John Gerald Strutt;** Company Chairman, since 1988; *b* 4 June 1960; *s* of Hon. Charles Richard Strutt (*d* 1981) (2nd *s* of 4th Baron) and of Hon. Jean Elizabeth, *d* of 1st Viscount Davidson, GCVO, CH, CB, PC; *S* uncle, 1988; *m* 1991, Annabel Kate, *d* of late W. G. Patterson; four *s*. *Educ:* Eton College; Royal Agricultural College, Cirencester. Welsh Guards, 1980–84. Chm., Lord Rayleigh's Farms Ltd, 1988–. *Recreations:* cricket, gardening, shooting, silviculture. *Heir: s* Hon. John Frederick Strutt, *b* 29 March 1993. *Clubs:* Brooks's, White's, MCC.
*See also* Baroness Jenkin of Kennington, Hon. Sir B. C. Jenkin.

**RAYMOND, Meurig David,** CBE 2019 (MBE 2005); DL; FRAgS; farmer, since 1968; President, National Farmers' Union of England and Wales, 2014–18; *b* Haverfordwest, Pembs, 28 Nov. 1952; *s* of Thomas Andrew Raymond and Dinah Mary Raymond; *m* 1972, Hilary Charmaine Williams; two *s* one *d*. *Educ:* Mandrowen Primary Sch.; Fishguard Secondary Sch.; Pembrokeshire Coll. (C&G Dip. Agric.); Wye Coll., Univ. of London (Advanced Farm Mgt Course 1985). National Farmers' Union: Co. Chm., Pembrokeshire, 1989; Welsh Treas., 1992–2004; Pembrokeshire Council delegate, 1995–2004; Vice-Pres., 2004–06; Dep. Pres., 2006–14. Member: Food from Britain Council, 1997–2003; Home Grown Cereals Authy, 1997–2004; Agricl Wages Bd, 1998–2004. FRAgS 2000. DL Dyfed, 2019. Hon. DSc Harper Adams, 2014. *Recreations:* politics, sport. *Address:* Trenewydd Fawr, Croesgoch, Haverfordwest, Pembs SA62 5JY. *E:* meurigraymond@btinternet.com. *Club:* Farmers.

**RAYMOND, Robert Jacques;** director of banks and funds, retired 2014; *b* 30 June 1933; *s* of Henri Raymond and Andrée (*née* Aubrière); *m* 1970, Monique Brémond, MD. *Educ:* Sorbonne (Masters Econs 1955). With Bank of France, 1951–94: Audit Dept, 1958–66; Rep. in NY, 1966–67; Hd, Balance of Payments Div., 1969–73; Director: Internat. Affairs, 1973–75; Monetary Stats and Analysis, 1975–76; Dep. Sec. Gen., Conseil Nat. du Crédit, 1975–81; Dep. Hd, 1976–82, Dir Gen., 1982–90, Res. Dept; Dir Gen., Credit Dept, 1990–94; Dir Gen., European Monetary Inst., 1994–98; Perm. Rep. of European Central Bank to IMF, Washington, 1999; Chm. and CEO, Banque CPR-Paris, 1999–2001. Mem. Bd, various public financial instns in Paris, 1981–94. Chm., monetary experts, Cttee of Govs of EEC, 1981–91. Officier de la Légion d'Honneur (France), 1996 (Chevalier, 1984); Officier, Ordre national du Mérite (France), 1988. *Publications:* La Monnaie, 1976; (jtly) Les relations économiques et monétaires internationales, 1982, 3rd edn 1986; Les institutions monétaires en France, 1991, 2nd edn 1996; L'unification monétaire en Europe, 1993, 2nd edn 1996; L'Euro et l'unité de l'Europe, 2001. *Address:* 5 rue de Beaujolais, 75001 Paris, France.

**RAYNE, Hon. Robert (Anthony);** Chairman, Derwent London plc, 2007–19; *b* 30 Jan. 1949; *s* of Baron Rayne and late Margaret Marco; *m* 1974, Jane Blackburn (separated); one *s* one *d. Educ:* Malvern Coll.; New York Inst. of Finance. Dir, 1983–2001, CEO, 2001–07, London Merchant Securities plc; CEO, 2007–10, Chm., 2010–11, LMS (formerly Leo Capital plc (Dir, 2006–); Director: First Leisure Corp. plc, 1983–2000; Westpool Investment Trust plc, 1984–; Weatherford Internat. Inc. (US), 1987–2016; First Call Gp plc, 1996–98; Crown Sports plc, 2001–03; Chairman: Golden Rose Communications plc, 1991–99; London Jazz Radio, 1991–99. Trustee: Rayne Foundn and Rayne Trust, 1977– (Chm., 2004–); The Place To Be, 1993–2018; Imperial Coll. Fund, 2007–18. MInstD. *Recreations:* art, theatre, music. *E:* rrayne@lmscapital.com, rrayne@sqpltd.com.

**RAYNER, Angela;** MP (Lab) Ashton-under-Lyne, since 2015; *b* Stockport, 28 March 1980; *d* of Martyn and Lynne Bowen; one *s*; *m* 2010, Mark Rayner; two *s. Educ:* Bridgehall Primary Sch.; Avondale High Sch.; Stockport Coll. (British Sign Lang., Care, Counselling). Home help, private sector and local govt, 1998–2005. Trade union lay activist, 2002–15. Samaritan, 1997–2000. Shadow Sec. of State for Educn, 2016–. *Address:* House of Commons, SW1A 0AA. *T:* (020) 7219 8782. *E:* angela.rayner.mp@parliament.uk.

**RAYNER, David Edward,** CBE 1992; Director, South East Trains Ltd, 2003–06; *b* 26 Jan. 1940; *s* of Marjory and Gilbert Rayner; *m* 1966, Enid Cutty; two *d. Educ:* St Peter's School, York; Durham University (BSc Hons). Joined British Railways, 1963; Passenger Marketing Manager, BR Board, 1982; Dep. Gen. Manager, BR, London Midland Region, 1984–86; Gen. Manager, BR, Eastern Region, 1986–87; British Railways Board: Mem., 1987–94; Jt Man. Dir, 1987–89; Man. Dir, Engrg and Operations, 1989–92; Man. Dir, Safety and Operations, 1992–94; Bd Mem., Railtrack Gp, 1994–97; Dir Safety and Standards, Railtrack, 1994–97. Non-executive Chairman: Rail Investments Ltd, 1998–99; Oakburn Properties plc, 1998–2004; non-executive Director: Coll. of Railway Technol., subseq. Catalis Rail Trng, Ltd, 1998–2003 (Chm., 1998–2002); Connex Transport UK (formerly Connex Rail) Ltd, 1998–2003. Chm., Rail Industry Training Council, 1992–95. Vis. Prof., UCL, 1998–2008. Trustee: Science Mus., 1997–2006; York and N Yorks Community Foundn, 2000–07; York Museums (formerly York Museums and Gall.) Trust, 2002–07; York Glaziers Trust, 2004–; St Peter's Foundn, 2005–10. Gov., York Co. of Merchant Adventurers, 2012–13. Hon. Col, Railway Sqn, RLC (TA), 1992–99. *Recreation:* collector.

**RAYNER, Jay;** freelance writer, journalist, broadcaster and musician; *b* 14 Sept. 1966; *s* of late Desmond Rayner and Claire Berenice Rayner, OBE; *m* 1992, Pat Gordon Smith; two *s. Educ:* Leeds Univ. (BA Hons Pol Studies 1987). Editor, Leeds Student newspaper, 1987–88; freelance journalist, The Observer, The Guardian, Independent on Sunday, Cosmopolitan and others, 1988–92; Feature Writer: The Guardian, 1992–93; Mail on Sunday, 1993–96; The Observer, 1996–, Restaurant Critic, 1999–. Presenter, BBC Radio: Stop Press, 1995–97; Papertalk, 1997–99 (Magazine Prog. of the Year, Sony Radio Awards, 1999); The Food Quiz, 2003–06; The Kitchen Cabinet, 2012–; contributor: MasterChef, 2006–, The One Show, 2009–16, BBC TV; Top Chef Masters, US TV, 2009. Leader, Jay Rayner Quartet (live recording, A Night of Food and Agony, 2017). Podcast, Out to Lunch with Jay Rayner, 2019–. Young Journalist of the Year, 1991, Critic of the Year, 2006, British Press Awards; Restaurant Critic of the Year, Glenfiddich Food and Drink Awards, 2001; Derek Cooper Award for Campaigning and Investigative Food Writing, Guild of Food Writers, 2013; Restaurant Writer of the Year, Fortnum & Mason Food and Drink Awards, 2018. *Publications:* Star Dust Falling, 2002; The Man Who Ate the World, 2008; A Greedy Man in a Hungry World, 2013; My Dining Hell: twenty ways to have a lousy night out, 2015; The Ten (Food) Commandments, 2016; Wasted Calories and Ruined Nights, 2018; My Last Supper, 2019; *novels:* The Marble Kiss, 1994; Day of Atonement, 1998; The Apologist, 2004; The Oyster House Siege, 2007; contrib. to Arena, Esquire, Gourmet, Food and Wine. *Recreations:* jazz piano, cooking, my kids. *Address:* c/o Curtis Brown Group Ltd, Haymarket House, 28–29 Haymarket, SW1Y 4SP. *T:* (020) 7393 4400, *Fax:* (020) 7393 4401. *E:* jay.rayner@observer.co.uk.

**RAYNER, Rt Rev. Keith,** AO 1987; Archbishop of Melbourne and Metropolitan of the Province of Victoria, 1990–99; Primate of Australia, 1991–99 (Acting Primate, 1989–91); *b* 22 Nov. 1929; *s* of Sidney and Gladys Rayner, Brisbane; *m* 1963, Audrey Fletcher (*d* 2011); one *s* two *d. Educ:* C of E Grammar Sch., Brisbane; Univ. of Queensland (BA 1951; PhD 1964). Deacon, 1953; Priest, 1953. Chaplain, St Francis' Theol Coll., Brisbane, 1954; Mem., Brotherhood of St John, Dalby, 1955–58; Vice-Warden, St John's Coll., Brisbane, 1958; Rotary Foundn Fellow, Harvard Univ., 1958–59; Vicar, St Barnabas', Sunnybank, 1959–63; Rector, St Peter's, Wynnum, 1963–69; Bishop of Wangaratta, 1969–75; Archbishop of Adelaide and Metropolitan of South Australia, 1975–90. Pres., Christian Conference of Asia, 1977–81; Chm., International Anglican Theological and Doctrinal Commission, 1980–88. Hon. ThD Aust. Coll. of Theology, 1987; DUniv Griffith, 2001. *Address:* 36 Highfield Avenue, St Georges, SA 5064, Australia.

**RAYNER, Miranda;** *see* Hughes, Miranda.

**RAYNER, Prof. Peter John Wynn,** PhD; Professor of Signal Processing, University of Cambridge, 1998–2002, now Emeritus; Fellow, Christ's College, Cambridge, 1969–2002, now Emeritus; *b* 22 July 1941; *s* of John Austin Rayner and Amelia Victoria Rayner; *m* 1960, Patricia Ann Gray; two *d. Educ:* Univ. of Aston (PhD 1968); MA Cantab 1969. Student apprentice, Pye TVT Ltd, 1957–62; Sen. Engr, Cambridge Consultants, 1962–65; Res. Student, Univ. of Aston, 1965–68; Cambridge University: Lectr, Dept of Engrg, 1968–90; Dir, Studies in Engrg, Christ's Coll., 1971–99; Reader in Inf. Engrg, 1990–98. Dir, Cedar Audio Ltd, 1989–; Advr to Bd, Autonomy Corp., 2000–12. *Publications:* (with S. J. Godsill) Digital Audio Restoration, 1998; book chapters; numerous contribs to learned jls. *Recreations:* scuba-diving, flamenco and blues guitar, gardening, cycling. *Address:* 69 High Street, Oakington, Cambs CB24 3AG. *T:* (01223) 234203.

**RAYNER, Samuel Alan Miles,** DL; Managing Director, 1974–2016, Chairman, since 2016, Lakeland Ltd (formerly Lakeland Plastics Ltd); *b* 31 May 1953; *s* of Alan and Dorothy Rayner; *m* 1978, Judy McIlvenny; two *s* one *d*. High Sheriff, 2015–16, DL 2016, Cumbria. *Address:* Lakeland Ltd, Alexandra Buildings, Windermere LA23 1BQ.

**RAYNER, Prof. Steve,** PhD; James Martin Professor of Science and Civilization, University of Oxford, since 2003 (Director, Institute for Science, Innovation and Society (formerly James Martin Institute for Science and Civilization), 2003–18); Fellow, Keble College, Oxford, since 2003; *b* 22 May 1953; *s* of Harry Rayner and Esmé Rayner; *m* 1994, Heather Katz; one *d. Educ:* Univ. of Kent (BA Philos. and Theol. 1974); University Coll. London (PhD Anthropol. 1979). Res. Associate, Russell Sage Foundn, 1980–81; Vis. Schol., Boston Univ. Sch. of Public Health, 1982; Sen. Res. Staff, Oak Ridge Nat. Lab., 1983–91; Chief Scientist, Pacific Northwest Nat. Lab., 1991–99; Prof. of Envmt and Public Affairs, Columbia Univ., 1999–2003. Adjunct Asst Prof., Univ. of Tennessee, 1986; Vis. Associate Prof., Cornell Univ., 1990; Adjunct Associate Prof., Virginia Polytech., 1997–98; Hon. Prof. of Climate Change and Society, Univ. of Copenhagen, 2008–13; ANZSOG Goyder Vis. Prof. in Public Sector Policy and Mgt, Flinders Univ., 2013–14. Dir, ESRC Sci. in Society Prog., 2002–08. Member: Intergovtl Panel on Climate Change, 1999–2007; Royal Commn on Envmtl Pollution, 2003–09; Adv. Bd, UK Climate Impacts Prog., 2004–11; Wkg Gp on Geoengrg the Climate, Royal Soc., 2009. Mem., Lead Expert Gp, UK Foresight Prog. on Future of Cities, 2013–16. Mem., Bd of Dirs, Foundn for Law, Justice and Soc., 2006–12. Mem., Council, RAI, 2018–. Sen. Fellow, Breakthrough Inst., 2010–. *Publications:* (with Jonathan Gross) Measuring Culture, 1985; (with James Flanagan) Rules, Decisions and Inequality, 1988; (with Robin Cantor and Stuart Henry) Making Markets, 1992; (with Elizabeth Malone) Human Choice and Climate Change, 4 vols, 1998; (with Peter Healey) Unnatural Selection, 2009; (with Mark Caine) The Hartwell Approach to Climate Policy, 2015; (with Theresa Scavenius) Institutional Capacity for Climate Change Response, 2018; articles in Climatic Change, Global Envmtl Change, Ecol Econs, Energy Policy, Sci. and Public Policy, Science, Nature, Govt and Opposition, Social Studies of Sci., Risk Analysis, Evaluation Review, Econ. and Political Wkly, Industry and Higher Educn. *Recreations:* gardening, narrowboating. *Address:* Institute for Science, Innovation and Society, University of Oxford, 64 Banbury Road, Oxford OX2 6PN. *T:* (01865) 288938. *E:* steve.rayner@insis.ox.ac.uk.

**RAYNER JAMES, Jonathan Elwyn;** *see* James, Jonathan E. R.

**RAYNES, Prof. (Edward) Peter,** FRS 1987; Professor of Optoelectronic Engineering, University of Oxford, 1998–2010, now Emeritus; Fellow of St Cross College, Oxford, 1998–2010, now Emeritus; Honorary Visiting Professor, Department of Chemistry, University of York, since 2011 (Leverhulme Emeritus Fellow, 2010–12); *b* 4 July 1945; *s* of Edward Gordon and Ethel Mary Raynes; *m* 1970, Madeline Ord; two *s. Educ:* St Peter's School, York; Gonville and Caius College, Cambridge (MA, PhD). Hon. FInstP. Royal Signals and Radar Establishment, 1971–92: SPSO, 1981; DCSO, 1988–92; Chief Scientist, 1992–95, Dir of Res., 1995–98, Sharp Labs of Europe Ltd, Oxford. Hon. DSc Hull, 2012. Rank Prize for Opto-electronics, 1980; Paterson Medal, Inst. of Physics, 1986; Special Recognition Award, 1987, Jan Rajchman Prize, 2009, Soc. for Information Display. *Publications:* (ed jtly) Liquid Crystals: their physics, chemistry and applications, 1983; (ed jtly) Handbook of Visual Display Technology, 2012; (ed jtly) Handbook of Liquid Crystals, 2014; numerous scientific papers and patents. *Recreations:* choral singing, hill walking. *Address:* Department of Chemistry, University of York, York YO10 5DD. *T:* (01904) 322527.

**RAYNHAM, Viscount; Thomas Charles Townshend;** *b* 2 Nov. 1977; *s* and *heir* of Marquess Townshend, *qv*; *m* 2011, Octavia Legge; one *s* one *d. Educ:* Oundle; RAC Cirencester (BSc Estate Mgt 2000). Chartered Surveyor. Land Agent, Bidwells, Cambridge, 2002–06; Hd of Agricultural Investment, Knight Frank, 2006–16; Chief Exec., Raynham Estate, 2016–. Chm., HHA Next Generation Gp, 2013–16.

**RAYNOR, Andrew Paul;** entrepreneur; Chief Executive, Shakespeare Martineau (formerly Shakespeares Legal) LLP, 2015–19; *b* 24 May 1957; *s* of Laurence Edwin Raynor and Pamela Sylvia Raynor (*née* Skelton); *m* 1980, Karen Jane Robertson; three *d. Educ:* Leicester Polytech. (BA Hons Business Studies). FCA 1981. Partner, Stoy Hayward East Midlands, 1986; BDO Stoy Hayward East Midlands: Hd, Corporate Finance, 1994–97; Hd, Business Develt, 1997–2000; Managing Partner, 2000–01; Finance Dir, Tenon Group plc, 2002–03; Chief Exec., Tenon Gp, later RSM Tenon Gp plc, 2003–12; Chief Client Officer, Shakespeares Legal LLP, 2013–15. *Publications:* various articles in financial related jls. *Recreations:* running, travel, old and new motorcycles, competing with classic racing cars. *E:* andypraynor@gmail.com.

**RAYNOR, Keith Hugh; His Honour Judge Keith Raynor;** a Circuit Judge, since 2015; Diversity and Community Relations Judge, since 2015; *b* Nairobi, Kenya, 3 May 1964; *s* of Regtl Sgt Major Granville Vincent Raynor, Royal Norfolk Regt and Audrey Kathleen Raynor (*née* Ward); *m* 1994, Joanna Carolyn Truman; two *s. Educ:* Duke of York's Royal Mil. Sch.; Trent Poly. (LLB Hons). Admitted Solicitor, 1990; Asst Solicitor, Lovell White Durrant, 1990–91; Army Officer, Army Legal Services, 1991–94; called to the Bar, Lincoln's Inn, 1995; Sen. Associate, Clayton Utz, Perth, WA, 1995–96; in practice as solicitor advocate, 1996–2004, as barrister, 2004–15; a Recorder, 2005–15; UN Prosecutor: Extraordinary Chambers in Courts of Cambodia (Khmer Rouge Tribunal), 2012–14; Iraq Historic Allegations Prosecutions Team, 2014–15; Deployable Civilian Expert, Stabilisation Unit, 2012–18; Vice Pres., Kosovo Specialist Chambers, The Hague, 2017–. *Recreations:* travel, hill-walking, cycling, open-water swimming, watching Rugby. *Address:* Woolwich Crown Court, 2 Belmarsh Road, Thamesmead, SE28 0EY. *Clubs:* Victory Services; Derby Rugby Football.

**RAYNOR, His Honour Philip Ronald;** QC 1994; a Circuit Judge, 2001–17; Specialist Circuit Judge, Technology and Construction Court, Manchester, 2006–17; *b* 20 Jan. 1950; *s* of Wilfred and Sheila Raynor; *m* 1974, Judith Braunsberg; one *s* one *d. Educ:* Roundhay Sch., Leeds; Christ's Coll., Cambridge (Schol., MA). Lectr in Law, Univ. of Manchester, 1971–74; called to the Bar, Inner Temple, 1973; in practice, 1973–2001; a Recorder, 1993–2001; Head of Chambers, 40 King Street, Manchester, 1996–2001. *Recreations:* travel, opera, dining out. *Address:* c/o Manchester Civil Justice Centre, 1 Bridge Street West, Manchester M60 9DJ.

**RAYNSFORD, Alison Jane;** *b* 20 Jan. 1954; *d* of late Michael John Ward and Lilian Ward (*née* Lomas); *m* 1975 (marr. diss. 2007); two *d*; *m* 2012, Rt Hon. Wyvill Richard Nicolls Raynsford, (Rt Hon. Nick), *qv. Educ:* North East London Polytechnic. Parly Asst to Rt Hon. Roy Hattersley, MP, 1987–92; Advr to Rt Hon. Nick Raynsford, MP, 1992–2005. MP (Lab) Plymouth Devonport, 2005–10, Plymouth, Moor View, 2010–15; contested (Lab) same seat, 2015. PPS to Minister of State for Europe, 2006–07; an Asst Govt Whip, 2007–08; PPS to Sec. of State for Transport, 2008–09; Shadow Minister for Housing, 2010–11; Shadow Defence Minister, 2010–15. Member: Select Cttee for Communities and Local Govt, 2005–06; Regulatory Reform Select Cttee, 2005–07; Chairman: Select Cttee for SW, 2009–10; All Party Gp for Local Govt, 2006–08. Trustee, Horizons Plymouth, 2016–. Patron, Devon and Cornwall Lupus Gp, 2012–. *Recreations:* reading, walking, swimming, gardening.

**RAYNSFORD, Rt Hon. Wyvill Richard Nicolls, (Rt Hon. Nick);** PC 2001; *b* 28 Jan. 1945; *s* of Wyvill Raynsford and Patricia Raynsford (*née* Dunn); *m* 1st, 1968, Anne Raynsford (*née* Jelley) (marr. diss. 2011); three *d*; 2nd, 2012, Alison Jane Seabeck (*see* A. J. Raynsford). *Educ:* Repton Sch.; Sidney Sussex Coll., Cambridge (MA); Chelsea Sch. of Art (DipAD). Market research, A. C. Nielsen Co. Ltd, 1966–68; Gen. Sec., Soc. for Co-operative Dwellings, 1972–73; SHAC: Emergency Officer, 1973–74; Research Officer, 1974–76; Dir, 1976–86; Partner, 1987–90, Dir, 1990–92, Raynsford and Morris, housing consultants; Dir, Raynsford Dallison Associates, housing consultants, 1992–93; Consultant, HACAS, 1993–97. Councillor (Lab) London Borough of Hammersmith & Fulham, 1971–75 (Chm., Leisure and Recreation Cttee, 1972–74). MP (Lab) Fulham, April 1986–1987; contested (Lab) same seat, 1987; MP (Lab) Greenwich, 1992–97, Greenwich and Woolwich, 1997–2015. Opposition front bench spokesman on London, 1993–97, on housing, 1994–97; Parly Under-Sec. of State, DoE and Dept of Transport, subseq. DETR,

1997–99; Minister of State: DETR, 1999–2001; DTLR, 2001–02; ODPM, 2002–05. Mem., Envmt Select Cttee, 1992–93. Chairman: NHBC Foundn, 2006–; Triathlon Homes, 2010–17; Construction Industry Council Approved Inspectors Register Ltd, 2015–; Tideway Reporting Bd, 2016–; Heylo Housing Registered Provider, 2017–; Hon. Vice Chm., Construction Industry Council, 2010– (Chm., 2006–08); Dep. Chm., Crossrail Ltd, 2019–. Chair, Raynsford Rev. of Planning, TCPA (Report as Planning 2020, 2018). President: Constructionarium, 2008–17; Town and Country Planning Assoc., 2015–. Hon. FICE 2005; Hon. FRTPI 2006; Hon. FRIBA 2007; Hon. MRICS 2008; Hon. MCIH 2009. *Publications*: A Guide to Housing Benefit, 1982, 7th edn 1986; Substance not Spin, 2016. *Recreation*: photography.

**RAZ, Prof. Joseph,** FBA 1987; Professor of the Philosophy of Law, 1985–2006, Research Professor in the Philosophy of Law, 2006–09, University of Oxford; Fellow of Balliol College, Oxford, 1985–2006, now Emeritus; Professor, Columbia Law School, New York, since 2002; Research Professor (part-time), King's College London, since 2011; *b* 21 March 1939. *Educ*: Hebrew University, Jerusalem (MJur 1963); University Coll., Oxford (DPhil 1967). Lectr, Hebrew Univ., Jerusalem, 1967–70; Research Fellow, Nuffield Coll., Oxford, 1970–72; Tutorial Fellow, Balliol Coll., Oxford, 1972–85. Vis. Prof., Columbia Law Sch., NY, 1995–2002. For. Hon. Mem., Amer. Acad. of Arts and Scis, 1992. Hon. Dr: Catholic Univ., Brussels, 1993; Hebrew Univ., Jerusalem, 2014; Hon. PhD, KCL, 2008. Tang Prize in Rule of Law, 2018. *Publications*: The Concept of a Legal System, 1970, 2nd edn 1980; Practical Reason and Norms, 1975, 2nd edn 1990; The Authority of Law, 1979; The Morality of Freedom, 1986; Ethics in the Public Domain, 1994, rev. edn 1995; Engaging Reason, 2000; Value, Respect and Attachment, 2001; The Practice of Value, 2003; Between Authority and Interpretation, 2009; From Normativity to Responsibility, 2011. *Address*: Columbia Law School, 435 W 110 Street, New York, NY 10027, USA.

**RAZZALL,** family name of **Baron Razzall**.

**RAZZALL, Baron** *cr* 1997 (Life Peer), of Mortlake in the London Borough of Richmond; **Edward Timothy Razzall,** CBE 1993; Partner, RT Associates, since 2012; *b* 12 June 1943; *s* of late Leonard Humphrey and Muriel Razzall; *m* 1st, 1965, Elizabeth Christina Wilkinson (marr. diss. 1974); *one s one d*; 2nd, 1982, Deirdre Bourke Martineau (née Taylor Smith) (marr. diss. 2003). *Educ*: St Paul's Sch.; Worcester Coll., Oxford (Open Schol.; BA). Teaching Associate, Northwestern Univ., Chicago, 1965–66; with Frere Cholmeley Bischoff, solicitors, 1966–96 (Partner, 1973–96); Partner, Argonaut Associates, 1996–2012. Councillor (L), Mortlake Ward, London Borough of Richmond, 1974–98; Dep. Leader, Richmond Council, 1983–97. Treasurer: Liberal Party, 1986–87; Liberal Democrats, 1987–2000; Chm., Lib Dem Campaign Cttee, 2000–06; Lib Dem spokesman, H of L, on trade and industry, 1998–2014, Treasury, 2014–15, Cabinet Office, 2015–16, manufacturing industry, 2016–. Chm., Boxhill Technologies plc, 2009–; Dep. Chm., Just Loans plc, 2015–19. Pres., Assoc. of Lib Dem Councillors, 1990–95. European Lawyer of Year, Inst. of Lawyers in Europe, 1992. *Publications*: Chance Encounters: tales from a varied life, 2014. *Recreation*: all sports. *Address*: Spring Cottage, Swallowcliffe, Salisbury, Wilts SP3 5PA. *Clubs*: National Liberal, Soho House, MCC.

**REA,** family name of **Baron Rea**.

**REA, 3rd Baron** *cr* 1937, of Eskdale; **John Nicolas Rea,** MD; Bt 1935; General Medical Practitioner, Kentish Town, NW5, 1957–62 and 1968–93; *b* 6 June 1928; *s* of Hon. James Russell Rea (*d* 1954) (2nd *s* of 1st Baron) and Betty Marion (*d* 1965), *d* of Arthur Bevan, MD; *S* uncle, 1981; *m* 1st, 1951, Elizabeth Anne (marr. diss. 1991), *d* of late William Hensman Robinson; four *s* two *d*; 2nd, 1991, Judith Mary, *d* of late Norman Powell. *Educ*: Dartington Hall School; Belmont Hill School, Mass, USA; Dauntsey's School; Christ's Coll., Cambridge Univ.; UCH Medical Sch. MA, MD (Cantab); FRCGP; DPH, DCH, DObstRCOG. Research Fellow in Paediatrics, Lagos, Nigeria, 1962–65; Lecturer in Social Medicine, St Thomas's Hosp. Medical School, 1966–68. Trustee, 1985–2015, Pres., 2015–, UK Health Forum (formerly Nat. Forum for Prevention of Coronary Heart Disease, then Nat. Heart Forum); Chm., Parly Food & Health Forum, 1997–2014. Opposition spokesman on health, develt and co-operation, H of L, 1992–97; elected Mem., H of L, 1999. FRSocMed (Pres., Section of Gen. Practice, 1985–86). *Publications*: Interactions of Infection and Nutrition (MD Thesis, Cambridge Univ.), 1969; (jtly) Learning Teaching— an evaluation of a course for GP Teachers, 1980; articles on epidemiology and medical education in various journals. *Recreations*: music (bassoon), gardening. *Heir*: *s* Hon. Matthew James Rea, *b* 28 March 1956. *Address*: 1–2 Littledene Cottages, Glynde, E Sussex BN8 6LA. *T*: (weekdays) (020) 7607 0546.

**REA, Christopher William Wallace;** Broadcast Controller (formerly Head of Communications), World Rugby (formerly International Rugby Board, 2000–15; *b* 22 Oct. 1943; *s* of Col William Wallace Rea and Helen Rea; *m* 1974, Daphne Theresa Manning; one *d*. *Educ*: High Sch. of Dundee; Univ. of St Andrews (MA). With BBC Radio Sports Dept, 1972–81; Rugby and Golf Corresp., Scotsman, 1981–84; Publisher and Ed., Rugby News Mag., 1984–88; Presenter, BBC TV Rugby Special, 1988–94; Asst Sec., then Head, Marketing and Public Affairs, MCC, 1995–2000. Rugby Corresp., Independent on Sunday, 1990–2000. Played Rugby Union for Scotland, 1968–71 (13 Caps); Mem., British Lions tour to NZ, 1971; played for Barbarians, 1971. *Publications*: Illustrated History of Rugby Union, 1977; Injured Pride, 1980; Scotland's Grand Slam, 1984. *Recreations*: golf, hill walking. *Clubs*: Royal and Ancient (St Andrews), Royal Worlington Golf.

**REA, Prof. Sir Desmond,** Kt 2005; OBE 1996; PhD; non-executive Chairman, NIJobs.com, 2010–14; non-executive Director, Security Industry Authority, 2013–18; *b* 4 March 1937; *s* of Samuel and Annie Rea; *m* 1969, Irene Maeve Williamson, Prof. Emeritus; four *d*. *Educ*: Queen's Univ., Belfast (BSc Econs, MSc Econs; PhD); Univ. of Calif, Berkeley (MBA). Queen's University, Belfast: Lectr, then Sen. Lectr, in Business Admin, 1969–75; Asst Dean, Faculty of Econs and Social Scis, 1973–75; Hd of Dept and Prof. of Human Resource Mgt, Ulster Polytech., subseq. Univ. of Ulster, 1975–95, now Prof. Emeritus. Chairman (part-time): NI Schs Exams Council, 1987–90; NI Schs Exams and Assessment Council, 1990–94; NI Council for Curriculum, Exams and Assessment, 1994–98; NI Local Govt Staff Commn, 1989–96; NI Lab. Relns Agency, 1996–2002; Chm., 2001–09, Ind. Mem., 2001–11, NI Policing Bd. Chm., Jt Ind. Gp for Study and Action, 2016– (Mem., 1980–). Mem. Bd, Anglo-Irish Encounter, 1983–2004. Chm., Ulster Orchestra Soc. Ltd, 2008–12. Chm., Bd of Govs, Methodist Coll., Belfast, 2000–04; non-exec. Chm., Stranmillis Univ. Coll., QUB, 2013–. Ed., Quarterly Economic Outlook and Business Review, First Trust Bank, 1984–2010. Hon. LLD Ulster, 2010. *Publications*: (ed) Political Co-operation in Divided Societies: a series of papers relevant to the conflict in Northern Ireland, 1981; (with Robin Mansfield) Policing in Northern Ireland: delivering the new beginning?, 2014; (with Hugh Orde) Bear in Mind These Dead: the Omagh bombing and policing, 2016. *Recreations*: reading, classical music, Rugby. *Address*: c/o Stranmillis University College, Queen's University Belfast, Stranmillis Road, Belfast BT9 5DY.

**REA, Rev. Ernest;** freelance broadcaster and writer; Head of Religious Broadcasting, BBC, 1989–2001; *b* 6 Sept. 1945; *s* of Ernest Rea and Mary Wylie (née Blue); *m* 1st, 1973, Kay (née Kilpatrick) (marr. diss 1994); two *s*; 2nd, 1995, Gaynor (née Vaughan Jones). *Educ*: Methodist Coll., Belfast; Queen's Univ., Belfast; Union Theological Coll., Belfast. Asst Minister, Woodvale Park Presb. Ch, Belfast, 1971–74; Minister, Bannside Presb. Ch, Banbridge, Co. Down, 1974–79; Religious Broadcasting Producer, BBC Belfast, 1979–84; Sen. Religious Broadcasting Producer, BBC S and W, 1984–88; Editor, Network Radio, BBC S and W, 1988–89; Hd of Religious Progs, BBC Radio, 1989–93. Presenter, Beyond Belief, BBC Radio 4, 2001–. *Recreations*: reading, watching cricket, playing golf, theatre, music. *Address*: The Coach House, Beechfield Road, Alderley Edge, Cheshire SK9 7AU.

**REA, James Alexander;** Director of Broadcasting, Global, since 2019 (Group Head of News, 2011–19); *b* Middlesbrough, 18 April 1980; *s* of Julie Ann Rea; *m* 2009, Jennifer Cunliffe; one *s* one *d*. *Educ*: St David's RC Secondary Sch., Middlesbrough. Journalist, Century Radio, 1996–2000; presenter, Border TV, 1998–99; News Ed., Real Radio, 2000–07; Sen. Broadcast Journalist, Newsbeat, BBC Radio 1, 2006–07; Gp Hd of News, 2007–10, Editl Dir, 2010–11, GMG Radio; Managing Editor: LBC, 2011–19; Heart, 2017–19. Non-exec. Dir, Ind. Radio News, 2011–. Dir, Broadcast Journalism Trng Council, 2019–. *Address*: Global Radio, 30 Leicester Square, WC2H 7LA.

**REA, Dr John Rowland,** FBA 1981; Lecturer in Documentary Papyrology, University of Oxford, 1965–96; Senior Research Fellow, Balliol College, Oxford, 1969–96, now Emeritus Fellow; *b* 28 Oct. 1933; *s* of Thomas Arthur Rea and Elsie Rea (née Ward); *m* 1959, Mary Ogden. *Educ*: Methodist Coll., Belfast; Queen's Univ., Belfast (BA); University Coll. London (PhD). Asst Keeper, Public Record Office, 1957–61; Res. Lectr, Christ Church, Oxford, 1961–65. *Publications*: The Oxyrhynchus Papyri, Vol. XL, 1972, Vol. XLVI, 1978, Vol. LI, 1984, Vol LV, 1988, Vol. LVIII, 1991, LXIII, 1996, also contribs to Vols XXVII, XXXI, XXXIII, XXXIV, XXXVI, XLI, XLIII, XLIX, L, LXII, LXIV; (with P. J. Sijpesteijn) Corpus Papyrorum Raineri V, 1976; articles in classical jls. *Address*: Aurolaine, 1 Shirley Drive, St Leonards-on-Sea, East Sussex TN37 7JW.

**REA, Rupert Lascelles P.;** *see* Pennant-Rea.

**REA, Stephen James;** actor and director; *b* Belfast, 31 Oct. 1949; *s* of James Rea and Jane Rea (née Logue); *m* 1983, Dolours Price (marr. diss.; she *d* 2013); two *s*. *Educ*: Queen's Univ., Belfast. Trained at Abbey Theatre Sch., Dublin. Jt Founder, Field Day Theatre Co., 1980. *Theatre includes*: The Shadow of a Gunman; The Cherry Orchard; Miss Julie; High Society; Endgame; The Freedom of the City; Translations; The Communication Cord; Saint Oscar; Boesman and Lena; Hightime and Riot Act; Double Cross; Pentecost; Making History; Someone Who'll Watch Over Me; Uncle Vanya; Ashes to Ashes; Playboy of the Western World; Comedians; The Shaughraun; Cyrano de Bergerac, 2004; Kicking a Dead Horse, 2008; Ballyturk, 2014; Cyprus Avenue, 2016, 2019; *director*: Three Sisters; The Cure at Troy; Northern Star. *Films include*: Angel, Loose Connections, 1983; Company of Wolves, 1984; The Doctor and the Devils, 1986; Life is Sweet, 1991; The Crying Game, 1992; Bad Behaviour, 1993; Princess Caraboo, Angie, Interview with the Vampire, 1994; Prêt-à-Porter, Between the Devil and the Deep Blue Sea, 1995; All Men are Mortal, Michael Collins, 1996; Trojan Eddie, A Further Gesture, 1997; The Butcher Boy, Still Crazy, 1998; In Dreams, The Life Before This, Guinevere, 1999; The End of the Affair, I Could Read the Sky, 2000; Evelyn, 2003; Bloom, Breakfast at Pluto, V for Vendetta, 2006; River Queen, 2008; Stuck, Nothing Personal, 2009; Ondine, The Heavy, 2010; Blackthorn, Stella Days, Underworld: Awakening, 2012; Black '47, 2018. *Television includes*: Four Days in July, 1984; The Kidnapper in Shergar, 1986; Hedda Gabler, 1993; The Shadow of a Gunman, 1995; Citizen X, 1995; Crime of the Century, 1996; Father & Son, 2010; The Shadow Line, 2011; Utopia, 2013; The Honourable Woman, 2014 (BAFTA Award for Best Supporting Actor, 2015); Dickensian, 2015; War and Peace, 2016; Cyprus Avenue, 2019. *Address*: c/o Independent Talent Group Ltd, 40 Whitfield Street, W1T 2RH.

**REA PRICE, (William) John,** OBE 1991; Director, National Children's Bureau, 1991–98; *b* 15 March 1937; *s* of late John Caxton Rea Price and of Mary Hilda Rea Price. *Educ*: University College Sch.; Corpus Christi Coll., Cambridge (MA); LSE (DSA; Cert. Applied Social Studies). London Probation Service, 1962–65; London Borough of Islington Children's Dept, 1965–68; Nat. Inst. for Social Work, 1968–69; Home Office, Community Develt Project, 1969–72; Dir of Social Services, London Borough of Islington, 1972–90. Lead Inspector, Children and Young People, HM Inspectorate of Prisons, 1999–2005. Pres., Assoc. of Dirs of Social Services, 1989–90. *Recreations*: cycling, archaeology, history of landscape. *E*: John.Reaprice@btinternet.com.

**READ, Albert Nathaniel;** Managing Director, Condé Nast Britain, since 2017; *b* London, 5 Jan. 1970; *s* of Piers Paul Read, *qv*; *m* 2003, Catherine Emma Ostler, *qv*; one *s* two *d*. *Educ*: New Coll., Oxford (BA Classics 1992); INSEAD, France (MBA 2000). Comment and Literary Ed., 1995–97, Hd of Features, 1997–99, Daily Express; Asia Pacific Business Dir, 2001–06, Dep. Planning Dir, 2003–06, Condé Nast Internat.; Gen. Manager, 2006–12, Dep. Man. Dir, 2012–17, Condé Nast Britain. *Recreations*: walking, cooking, reading. *Address*: Condé Nast Publications Ltd, Vogue House, 1 Hanover Square, W1S 1JU. *T*: (020) 7152 3362. *E*: albert.read@condenast.co.uk. *Club*: Soho House.

**READ, Catherine Emma;** *see* Ostler, C. E.

**READ, Sir David (John),** Kt 2007; PhD; FRS 1990; Professor of Plant Sciences, Sheffield University, 1990–2004, now Emeritus; *b* 20 Jan. 1939; *s* of O. Read; *m* (marr. diss.); one *s*. *Educ*: Sexey's Sch., Bruton, Som; Hull Univ. (BSc 1960; PhD 1963). Sheffield University: Jun. Res. Fellow, 1963–66; Asst Lectr, 1966–69; Lectr, 1969–79; Sen. Lectr, 1979–81; Reader in Plant Sci., 1981–90. Chairman: Bd of Dirs, Rothamsted Research, 2003–09; Res. Adv. Bd, Forestry Commn, 2004. Vice-Pres. and Biol Sec., Royal Soc., 2003–08. Mem. Bd Govs, Macaulay Land Res. Inst., 2003. *Publications*: editor of numerous books and author of papers in learned jls mostly on subject of symbiosis, specifically the mycorrhizal symbiosis between plant roots and fungi. *Recreations*: walking, botany. *Address*: Minestone Cottage, Youlgrave, Bakewell, Derbys DE45 1WD. *T*: (01629) 636360.

**READ, Emma Rosemary;** Founder and Managing Director, Emporium Productions, since 2015; *b* London, 1962; *d* of Anthony Read and Rosemary Elizabeth Read; *m* 2001, Robert Blagden; two *s*. *Educ*: Girton Coll., Cambridge (BA Natural Scis 1983). TV producer, BBC TV and freelance, 1983–98, series incl. Video Diaries; Hd, UK Documentaries, Mosaic Films, 1998–2000; Commissioning Editor: UK and EMEA, Discovery Communications, 2000–05; Factual and Features, BSkyB, 2005–10; Creative Dir, 2010, Hd, 2010–15, Factual and Features, ITN Prodns. Dir, Bd, Internat. Documentary Fest., Sheffield, 2004–13; Mem., Adv. Cttee, Guardian Edinburgh Internat. Television Fest., 2015. Member: Faraday and Kohn Awards Cttee, Royal Soc., 2008–14; Winton Book Prize Jury, Royal Soc., 2015. Mem., BAFTA. *Recreations*: cinema, theatre, reading, writing, walking, restoring derelict French houses. *Address*: Emporium Productions, 33 Oval Road, NW1 7EA. *T*: (020) 7184 7777. *E*: emmar@emporiumproductions.co.uk.

**READ, Prof. Frank Henry,** FRS 1984; consultant engineer in charged particle optics, since 2002; Founder Director, CPO Ltd, since 2000; Professor Emeritus, University of Manchester (formerly Victoria University of Manchester), since 2002; *b* 6 Oct. 1934; *s* of late Frank Charles Read and Florence Louise (*née* Wright); *m* 1961, Anne Stuart (*née* Wallace); two *s* two *d*. *Educ*: Haberdashers' Aske's Hampstead Sch. (Foundn Scholar, 1946); Royal Coll. of Science, Univ. of London (Royal Scholar, 1952; ARCS 1955; BSc 1955). PhD 1959, DSc 1975, Victoria Univ. of Manchester. FInstP 1968; FIET (FIEE 1998); CEng; CPhys. University of Manchester: Lectr, 1959; Sen. Lectr, 1969; Reader, 1974; Prof. of Physics, 1975–98; Langworthy Prof. of Physics, 1998–2001; Res. Dean, Faculty of Sci., 1993–95; Res. Prof., 2001–02. Vis. Scientist: Univ. of Paris, 1974; Univ. of Colorado, 1974–75; Inst. for Atomic and Molecular Physics, Amsterdam, 1979–80. Consultant to industry, 1976–. Vice Pres., Inst. of Physics, 1985–89 (Chm., IOP Publishing Ltd, 1985–89); Member: Science Bd, SERC, 1987–90; Council, Royal Soc., 1987–89. Holweck Medal and Prize, Inst. of Physics and Soc. Française de Physique, 2000. Hon. Editor, Jl of Physics B, Atomic and Molecular Physics, 1980–84. *Publications*: (with E. Harting) Electrostatic Lenses, 1976; Electromagnetic Radiation, 1980; over 200 papers in physics and instrumentation jls. *Recreations*: stone-masonry, landscaping, bridge. *Address*: Deakins Cottage, Orleton, Ludlow SY8 4HN. *T*: (01568) 780955.

**READ, Graham Stephen;** QC 2003; *b* 17 Sept. 1957; *s* of late Peter Denis Read and Dorothy Ruby Read; *m* 1983, Frances Margaret Catherine Daley; two *d*. *Educ*: Queen Mary's, Basingstoke; Trinity Hall, Cambridge (MA). Called to the Bar, Gray's Inn, 1981 (Arden Schol. 1980; Holker Schol. 1981). *Publications*: contrib. to various legal pubns. *Recreations*: walking, Roman and 20th century European history, concerts. *Address*: Devereux Chambers, Queen Elizabeth Building, Temple, EC4Y 9BS. *T*: (020) 7353 7534, *Fax*: (020) 7353 1724.
See also M. P. Read.

**READ, Harry;** British Commissioner, Salvation Army, 1987–90; Editor, Words of Life, 1990–2000; *b* 17 May 1924; *s* of Robert and Florence Read; *m* 1950, Winifred Humphries (*d* 2007); one *s* one *d*. *Educ*: Sir William Worsley Sch., Grange Town, Middlesbrough. Served RCS, 1942–47 (6th Airborne Div., 1943–45). Commnd Salvation Army Officer, 1948; pastoral work, 1948–54; Lectr, Internat. Training Coll., 1954–62; pastoral work, 1962–64; Divl Youth Sec., 1964–66; Lectr, Internat. Training Coll., 1966–72; Dir, Information Services, 1972–75; Divl Comdr, 1975–78; Principal, Internat. Training Coll., 1978–81; Chief Sec., Canada Territory, 1981–84; Territorial Comdr, Australia Eastern Territory, 1984–87. Chevalier, Légion d'Honneur (France), 2016. *Publications*: No Heart More Tender, 2010; Heart-Talk, 2013. *Recreations*: writing, hymns, poetry. *Address*: Flat 1 Dean Park Grange, 15A Cavendish Road, Bournemouth, Dorset BH1 1QX. *T*: (01202) 381758.

**READ, Imelda Mary, (Mel);** Member (Lab) East Midlands Region, European Parliament, 1999–2004 (Leicester, 1989–94; Nottingham and Leicestershire North West, 1994–99); *b* Hillingdon, 8 Jan. 1939; *d* of Robert Alan Hocking and Teresa Mary Hocking; *m*; one *s* one *d*, and one step *s*. *Educ*: Bishopshalt Sch., Hillingdon, Middx; Nottingham Univ. (BA Hons 1977). Laboratory technician, Plessey, 1963–74; researcher, Trent Polytechnic, 1977–80; Lectr, Trent Polytechnic and other instns, 1980–84; Employment Officer, Nottingham Community Relations Council, 1984–89. European Parliament: Chair, British Labour Gp, 1990–92; Quaestor, 1992–94. Contested (Lab): Melton, 1979; Leicestershire NW, 1983. Member: Nat. Exec. Council, ASTMS, 1975; NEC, MSF; TUC Women's Adv. Cttee; Chair, Regl TUC Women's Cttee. Hon. Pres., European Cervical Cancer Assoc., 2003–09. *Publications*: (jtly) Against a Rising Tide, 1992. *Recreations*: beekeeping, gardening.

**READ, Joanna;** Director and Chief Executive, Yvonne Arnaud Theatre, since 2019; *b* Stroud, 8 March 1968; *d* of Michael Read and April Read; *m* 1997, Nicolas Pitt; two *d*. *Educ*: Bristol Univ. (BA Hons Drama). Asst Dir, Young Vic, 1991–92; Educn Dir, Birmingham Repertory Th., 1993–97; Associate Dir, Bolton Octagon Th., 1997–99; Artistic Dir and Jt Chief Exec., Salisbury Playhouse, 1999–2007; freelance dir and writer, 2007–10; Principal, LAMDA, 2010–19. Pres., Guildford Shakespeare Co., 2015– (Chm., 2011–14). Trustee, Regl Th. Young Dirs Scheme, 2013–. *Recreations*: writing pantomimes, running. *Address*: Yvonne Arnaud Theatre, Millbrook, Guildford GU1 3UX. *T*: (01483) 443903. *E*: jread@yvonne-arnaud.co.uk.

**READ, Keith Frank,** CBE 1997; CEng; FIET; FCGI; consultant; Chief Executive (formerly Director General), Institute of Marine Engineering, Science and Technology (formerly Institute of Marine Engineers), 1999–2009; *b* 25 April 1944; *s* of Alan George Read, OBE and Dorothy Maud Read (*née* Richardson); *m* 1966, Sheila Roberts; one *s* two *d*. *Educ*: King's Sch., Bruton; Britannia Royal Naval Coll., Dartmouth; Royal Naval Engrg Coll., Manadon. CEng 1972; FIET (FIEE 1988); FIMarEST (FIMarE 1998), Hon. FIMarEST 2009. Joined Royal Navy, 1962: trng appts, 1963–67; HM Submarine Ocelot, 1968–69; Nuclear Reactor Course, RNC, Greenwich, 1969; HM Submarine Sovereign, 1970–73; Sen. Engr, HM Submarine Repulse, 1974–76; Staff of Capt. Submarine Sea Trng, 1976–79; Comdr 1980; Sch. Comdr, HMS Collingwood, 1980; Ops (E), MoD, 1981–84; jsdc 1984; Exec. Officer, Clyde Submarine Base, 1984–88; Capt. 1988; Dep. Dir, Naval Logistic Plans, 1989; rcds 1990; Capt. Surface Ship Acceptance, 1991–92; Naval Attaché, Rome and Albania, 1992–96; retd RN, 1996; Manager, Southern Europe, Ganley Gp, 1997–98. Dir, Engrg and Technol. Bd, 2001–02, 2008–09; Mem. Bd, Science Council, 2003–12 (Vice Chair, 2009–12). Director: Marine South East, 2008–12; Meadowside Freehold Ltd, 2018–. Chm., Cttee of Chief Execs of Engrg Instns, 2004–09. Member: Adv. Bd, Greenwich Maritime Inst., 1999–2010; Tech. Cttee, 2002–14, Council, 2010–14, RNLI (Vice Pres., 2014–). Trustee: RSA, 2012–18; IMarEST Pension Fund, 2013–. Chair, W Hatch Parish Council, 2016–. FRSA 2000; FCGI 2009. *Recreations*: family, Italy, music, theatre, sailing.

**READ, Leonard Ernest, (Nipper),** QPM 1976; National Security Adviser to the Museums and Galleries Commission, 1978–86; *b* 31 March 1925; *m* 1st, 1951, Marion Alexandra Millar (marr. diss. 1979); one *d*; 2nd, 1980, Patricia Margaret Allen. *Educ*: elementary schools. Worked at Players Tobacco factory, Nottingham, 1939–43; Petty Officer, RN, 1943–46; joined Metropolitan Police, 1947; served in all ranks of CID; Det. Chief Supt on Murder Squad, 1967; Asst Chief Constable, Notts Combined Constabulary, 1970; National Co-ordinator of Regional Crime Squads for England and Wales, 1972–76. British Boxing Board of Control: Mem. Council, 1976–82; Admin. Steward, 1982–88; Vice Chm., 1988–96, Chm., 1996–2000; Vice Pres. 1991–97, Pres., 1997–2005; Vice Pres., 1989–, Sen. Vice Pres. 1997–2001, World Boxing Council; Vice-Pres., World Boxing Assoc., 1989–2001. Freeman, City of London, 1983. *Publications*: with James Morton: Nipper (autobiog.), 1991; Nipper Read: the man who nicked the Krays (autobiog.), 2001. *Recreations*: home computing, playing the keyboard. *Address*: 23 North Barn, Broxbourne, Herts EN10 6RR.

**READ, Malcolm James;** District Judge (Magistrates' Courts) (formerly Metropolitan Stipendiary Magistrate), 1993–2013; *b* 4 May 1948; *s* of Frank James Cruickshank Read and Anne Elizabeth (*née* Oldershaw); *m*; one *s* by previous marriage. *Educ*: Wallington Independent Grammar Sch.; Council of Legal Educn. Called to the Bar, Gray's Inn, 1979; Clerk to Justices, Lewes Magistrates' Court, 1980–81; Clerk to: Hastings, Bexhill, Battle and Rye Justices, 1981–91; E Sussex Magistrates' Courts Cttee, 1981–91; in private practice, Brighton, 1991–93. *Recreations*: motor-cycling, golf (occasionally).

**READ, Mark;** Chief Executive Officer, WPP plc, since 2018; *b* London, 19 Nov. 1966; *s* of Ian and Linda Read. *Educ*: Trinity Coll., Cambridge (MA Econs 1988); Harvard Univ. (Henry Fellow 1999); INSEAD (MBA 2003). Corporate Develt, WPP, 1989–95; Principal, Booz Allen & Hamilton, 1995–99; CEO, Webrewards, 1999–2001; WPP plc: Dir of Strategy, 2002–12; Exec. Dir, 2006–15; CEO, WPP Digital, 2006–15; Global CEO, Wunderman, 2015–18; Chief Operating Officer, WPP plc, 2018. *Recreations*: ski-ing, sailing, wine, food. *Address*: WPP plc, Sea Containers, 18 Upper Ground, SE1 9GL.

**READ, Dr Martin Peter,** CBE 2011; Chairman: Wincanton plc, since 2018; Senior Salaries Review Body, since 2015; *b* 16 Feb. 1950; *s* of late Peter Denis Read and Dorothy Ruby Read; *m* 1974, Marian Eleanor Gilbart; one *s* one *d*. *Educ*: Queen Mary's Grammar Sch., Basingstoke; Peterhouse, Cambridge (BA Nat. Scis 1971); Merton Coll., Oxford (DPhil Physics 1974; Hon. Fellow, 2006). CDipAF 1976; FIET (FIEE 2005). Posts in sales and marketing, finance, ops, and systems develt, UK and overseas, Overseas Containers Ltd, 1974–81; Corp. Commercial Dir, Marine Coatings, 1981–84, Gen. Manager, Europe, 1984–85, International Paint, part of Courtaulds; joined GEC Marconi, 1985; Gen. Manager, Marconi Secure Radio, 1986–87; Dir, Marconi Defence Systems Ltd, 1987–89; Man. Dir, Marconi Command and Control Systems Ltd, 1989–91; Gp Man. Dir, Marconi Radar and Control Systems Gp, 1991–93; Gp Chief Exec., Logica, later LogicaCMG plc, 1993–2007. Chairman: Laird plc, 2014–18; Low Carbon Contracts Co., 2014–18; Electricity Settlements Co., 2014–18; non-executive Director: ASDA Gp plc, 1996–99; Southampton Innovations Ltd, 1999–2003; Boots Gp plc, 1999–2006; British Airways plc, 2000–09; Siemens Hldgs plc, 2008–09; Aegis Gp plc, 2009–13; Invensys plc, 2009–14; Lloyd's, 2009–18. Senior Adviser: Candover Partners, 2008–09; HCL, 2008–12; Actis, 2011–13; Zensar Technologies, 2013–17. Mem., President's Cttee, 2004–07, Internat. Adv. Bd, 2007–10, CBI; Dir, Strategy Bd, DTI, 2005–06; led govt review on improving efficiency of back office systems and IT across the public sector, 2008–09; led govt review on mgt information, 2012; non-exec. Dir, UK Govt Efficiency and Reform Bd, 2010–15. Chm., Remuneration Consultants Gp, 2010–19. Director: Portsmouth Housing Assoc., 1993–2007; Shelter, 2004–10 (Mem. Finance Cttee, 2000–04); Trustee: Hampshire Technology Centre, 1990–; Southern Focus (formerly Portsmouth Housing Trust, 1992–2000. Mem., Nat. Centre for Univs and Business (formerly Council for Industry and Higher Educn), 2000–07 (Trustee, 2007–14). Gov., Highbury Coll., Portsmouth, 1989–99; Member: Council, Southampton Univ., 1999–2015 (Vice Chm., 2008–15); Cambridge Univ. Library Adv. (formerly Vis.) Cttee, 2007–19 (Chm., 2015–19); Council, Shakespeare's Globe, 2010–. Hon. DTech Loughborough, 2000. Gold Medal, Chartered Mgt Inst., 2007. *Publications*: article in Jl of Applied Physics. *Recreations*: French and German novels, drama, military history, travel, gardening. *Address*: c/o Company Secretary, Wincanton plc, Methuen Park, Chippenham, Wilts SN14 0WT.
See also G. S. Read.

**READ, Mel;** see Read, I. M.

**READ, Paul John Z.;** see Zollinger-Read.

**READ, Piers Paul;** author; *b* 7 March 1941; 3rd *s* of Sir Herbert Read, DSO, MC and late Margaret Read, Stonegrave, York; *m* 1967, Emily Albertine, *o d* of Evelyn Basil Boothby, CMG and Susan Boothby; two *s* two *d*. *Educ*: Ampleforth Coll.; St John's Coll., Cambridge (MA). Artist-in-residence, Ford Foundn, Berlin, 1963–64; Sub-Editor, Times Literary Supplement, 1965; Harkness Fellow, Commonwealth Fund, NY, 1967–68. Member: Council, Inst. of Contemporary Arts, 1971–75; Cttee of Management, Soc. of Authors, 1973–76; Literature Panel, Arts Council, 1975–77; Council, RSL, 2001–07. Adjunct Prof. of Writing, Columbia Univ., NY, 1980. Bd Mem., Aid to the Church in Need, 1988–2012. Trustee, Catholic Nat. Liby, 1998–2010. Governor: Cardinal Manning Boys' Sch., 1985–91; More House Sch., 1996–2000. Chm., Catholic Writers' Guild (the Keys), 1992–97 (Vice-Pres., 1997–). Screenplay: Verbrechen mit Vorbedacht, 1967; TV plays: Coincidence, 1968; The House on Highbury Hill, 1972; The Childhood Friend, 1974; Margaret Clitheroe, 1977; radio play: The Family Firm, 1970. *Publications*: novels: Game in Heaven with Tussy Marx, 1966; The Junkers, 1968 (Sir Geoffrey Faber Meml Prize); Monk Dawson, 1969 (Hawthornden Prize and Somerset Maugham Award; filmed 1997); The Professor's Daughter, 1971; The Upstart, 1973; Polonaise, 1976; A Married Man, 1979 (televised 1983); The Villa Golitsyn, 1981; The Free Frenchman, 1986 (televised 1989); A Season in the West, 1988 (James Tait Black Meml Prize); On the Third Day, 1990; A Patriot in Berlin, 1995; Knights of the Cross, 1997; Alice in Exile, 2001; The Death of a Pope, 2009; The Misogynist, 2010; Scarpia, 2015; *non-fiction*: Alive, 1974 (filmed 1992); The Train Robbers, 1978; Quo Vadis?: the subversion of the Catholic Church, 1991; Ablaze: the story of Chernobyl, 1993; The Templars, 1999; Alec Guinness, The Authorised Biography, 2003; Hell and Other Destinations, 2006; The Dreyfus Affair: the story of the most infamous miscarriage of justice in French history, 2012. *Address*: 23 Ashchurch Park Villas, W12 9SP.
See also A. N. Read.

**READ, Prof. Randy John,** PhD; FRS 2014; Professor of Protein Crystallography, University of Cambridge, since 1998; *b* 9 June 1957; *s* of John and Anne Read; *m* 1995, Penelope Effie Stein; one *s* one *d*. *Educ*: McCoy High Sch., Medicine Hat; Univ. of Alberta, Edmonton (BSc 1979; PhD 1986). Asst Prof., 1988–93, Associate Prof., 1993–98, Univ. of Alberta. Max Perutz Prize, Eur. Crystallographic Assoc., 2013; Rosario Prize, Instituto de Física de São Carlos, 2014. *Publications*: contrib. papers on methods in protein crystallography and applications to medically relevant proteins. *Address*: Cambridge Institute for Medical Research, The Keith Peters Building, Hills Road, Cambridge CB2 0XY. *T*: (01223) 336500, *Fax*: (01223) 336827. *E*: rjr27@cam.ac.uk.

**READE, Brian Anthony;** HM Diplomatic Service, retired; *b* 5 Feb. 1940; *s* of Stanley Robert Reade and Emily Doris (*née* Lee); *m* 1964, Averille van Eugen; one *s* one *d*. *Educ*: King Henry VIII Sch., Coventry; Univ. of Leeds (BA Hons 1963). Interlang Ltd, 1963–64; Lectr, City of Westminster Coll., 1964–65; 2nd Sec., FCO, 1965–69; 2nd Sec., Bangkok, 1970–71; 1st Sec., 1971–74; FCO, 1974–77; Consul (Econ.), Consulate-General, Düsseldorf, 1977–81; FCO, 1981–82; 1st Sec., Bangkok, 1982–84; Counsellor (ESCAP), Bangkok, 1984–86; Counsellor, FCO, 1986–93. *Recreations*: watching sport, conversation, reading. *Clubs*: Coventry Rugby Football; Royal Bangkok Sports (Thailand).

**READE, David Jarrett;** QC 2006; *b* 20 April 1961; *s* of John and Margaret Reade; *m* 1989, Linda Jane Whitfield; two *d*. *Educ*: Prince Henry's High Sch., Evesham; Univ. of Birmingham (LLB 1982). Called to the Bar, Middle Temple, 1983, Bencher, 2009. Mem., Tufty Club, RoSPA, 1967–. Trustee, London Library, 2012. *Publications*: (jtly) The Law of Industrial Action and Trade Union Recognition, 2004, 3rd edn 2018; (contrib.) Transfer of Undertakings, 2007; (jtly) A guide to the Equality Act, 2010; (jtly) Blackstone's Employment Law Manual, 2013, 2019. *Recreations:* tennis, football (W Bromwich Albion), Rugby, music. *Address:* Littleton Chambers, 3 King's Bench Walk North, Temple, EC4Y 7HR. *T:* (020) 7797 8600. *E:* dr@djreade.com.

**READE, Sir Kenneth Roy,** 13th Bt *cr* 1661, of Barton, Berkshire; *b* 23 March 1926; *s* of Leverne Elton Reade (*d* 1943; 5th *s* of Sir George Compton Reade, 9th Bt), and Norma B. Ward; *S* cousin, 1982; *m* 1944, Doreen D. Vinsant (*d* 2006); three *d*. *Heir:* none.

**READE, Rt Rev. Nicholas Stewart;** Bishop of Blackburn, 2004–12; an Honorary Assistant Bishop: Diocese of Europe, since 2013; Diocese of Chichester, since 2014; *b* 9 Dec. 1946; *s* of late Sqdn Ldr Charles Sturrock Reade and Eileen Vandermere (*née* Fleming); *m* 1971, Christine Jasper, *d* of late Very Rev. R. C. D. Jasper, CBE, DD and Ethel Jasper; one *d*. *Educ:* Elizabeth Coll., Guernsey; Univ. of Leeds (BA, DipTh); Coll. of the Resurrection, Mirfield. Ordained deacon, 1973, priest, 1974; Assistant Curate: St Chad's, Coseley, 1973–75; St Nicholas, Codsall, and Priest-in-charge of Holy Cross, Bilbrook, 1975–78; Vicar, St Peter's, Upper Gornal and Chaplain, Burton Road Hosp., Dudley, 1978–82; Vicar: St Dunstan's, Mayfield, 1982–88; St Mary's, Eastbourne, 1988–97; Archdeacon of Lewes and Hastings, 1997–2004. Rural Dean: Dallington, 1982–88; Eastbourne, 1988–97; Canon of Chichester Cathedral, 1990–2004 (Prebendary, 1990–97); Hon. Asst Priest, All Saints, Sidley, 2013–; Actg Priest in Charge, St Barnabas', Bexhill, 2014–16. Member: Gen. Synod of C of E, 1995–2000, 2002–12; Dioceses Commn. 2001–05; Sen. Appts Gp (Episcopal), 2007–12; Urban Bishops' Panel, 2010–12; Chairman: Chichester Dio. Liturgical Cttee, 1989–97; Ministry Div., Cttee for Ministry of and among Deaf and Disabled People, 2008–12. Entered H of L, 2009. President: Eastbourne and Dist Police Court Mission, 1994–2017; Crowhurst Christian Healing Centre, 2001–13; Vice Pres., Blackburn Diocesan Prayer Book Soc., 2010–. Trustee: St Wilfrid's Hospice, Eastbourne, 1995–98; UC, Chichester, 2000–03; House of Bishops Healing Group, 2005–11; Christ Church St Leonards Old Buildings Trust, 2013–. Patron: Rosemere Cancer Foundn, 2005–12; Derian House Children's Hospice, Chorley, 2006–12; Skipton-East Lancs Rail Action Partnership, 2006–; Stonyhurst Christian Heritage Centre, 2011–; Caring and Sharing E Sussex, 2012–. Warden, Guild of St Raphael, 2009–13. FRSA 2010. Companion, Order of Star of Ethiopia, 2012. *Recreations:* cycling, steam trains, modern ecclesiastical and political biographies. *Address:* 5 Warnham Gardens, Cooden, Bexhill-on-Sea, E Sussex TN39 3SP. *T:* (01424) 842673. *E:* nicholas.reade@btinternet.com.

**READER, David George;** HM Diplomatic Service, retired; *b* 1 Oct. 1947; *s* of late Stanley Reader and of Annie Reader; *m* 1969, Elaine McKnight; one *s* one *d*. *Educ:* Barrow Grammar Sch. Entered FO, later FCO, 1964; Warsaw, 1969–72; Paris, 1972–74; Bucharest, 1974–76; FCO, 1976–79; Kinshasa, 1979–82; Kathmandu, 1982–84; FCO, 1984–87; Consul, Brisbane, 1987–92; First Sec. and Consul, Belgrade, 1992–96; FCO, 1996–98; Dir, Trade & Investment, Cairo, 1998–2001; High Comr, Kingdom of Swaziland, 2001–05; Ambassador to Cambodia, 2005–08; Special Rep. for Sec. of State for Foreign and Commonwealth Affairs, 2009–18. *Address:* c/o Foreign and Commonwealth Office, King Charles Street, SW1A 2AH.

**READER, Martin Sheldon;** Headmaster, Cranleigh School, since 2014; *b* 28 May 1967; *s* of Phillip John Reader and Juliet Elaine Reader; *m* 1994, Amanda Elizabeth Dyton; one *s* one *d*. *Educ:* St Olave's Grammar Sch.; University Coll., Oxford (Exhibitioner; BA Hons Eng. Lang. and Lit. 1989; MPhil Eng. Studies 1991; MA 1993); Homerton Coll., Cambridge (QTS 2002); Univ. of Hull (MBA 2004). Assistant Master: St Edward's Sch., Oxford, 1991–97; Oundle Sch., 1997–2002; Dep. Head, Laxton Sch. (subseq. merged with Oundle), 2000–02; Dep. Head, 2002–04, Sen. Dep. Head, 2004–06, Reigate Grammar Sch.; Headmaster, Wellington Sch., Somerset, 2006–14. Mem. Bd, Nat. Exec., Boarding Schs' Assoc., 2016– (Vice Chm., 2017–18; Chm., 2018–). Trustee, Hawk and Owl Trust, 2014–. *Recreations:* birdwatching, ski-ing, gym, reading, spending time with family, local church involvement. *Address:* Cranleigh School, Horseshoe Lane, Cranleigh, Surrey GU6 8QQ. *T:* (01483) 273677, *Fax:* (01483) 273696. *E:* mrp@cranleigh.org.

**READER, Nigel Frederick,** CBE 2004; Member of Board, Animal and Plant Health Agency, since 2017; non-executive Board Member, Environment Bank; Independent Member, Audit and Risk Assurance Committee: Joint Nature Conservation Committee; Rural Payments Agency; *b* Tunbridge Wells, 11 Feb. 1948; *s* of Frederick George Reader and Nora Reader (*née* Weeden); *m* 1991, Margaret Caroline Knight; three *d*. *Educ:* Skinners' Grammar Sch., Tunbridge Wells; Sidney Sussex Coll., Cambridge (MA). Sen. finance manager posts, Wessex Water, 1975–88; Regl Gen. Manager (Wessex), 1989–91, Finance Dir, 1992–96, NRA; Finance Dir, Envmt Agency, 1996–2009; Member, Board: Marine Mgt Orgn, 2010; Natural England, 2011–18; Natural Resources Wales, 2012. Mem., CIMA, 1973. Trustee and Chm., Audit Cttee, Wateraid, 1999–2011; Trustee and Treas., Excellent Develt, 2015–. *Recreations:* singer/entertainer at care homes, running, travel. *Address:* Little Croft, New Road, Trull, Taunton, Som TA3 7NJ. *T:* (01823) 323184, 07885 259581. *E:* nigelreader@aol.com.

**READER, Ven. Trevor Alan John,** PhD; Archdeacon of Portsdown, 2006–13; *b* 3 Aug. 1946; *s* of Clement and Lucy Reader; *m* 1st, 1968, Lesley Suzanne Taubman (*d* 2005); six *d*; 2nd, 2008, Linda Margaret Parks. *Educ:* Portsmouth Poly. (BSc 1968, MSc 1970, Zoology (London Univ. external); PhD 1972); Southern Dios, MTS, Salisbury and Wells Theol Coll. Research Asst, 1968–72, Lectr/Sen. Lectr, 1972–86, Portsmouth Poly. Ordained deacon, 1986, priest, 1987; Asst Curate, St Mary, Alverstoke, 1986–89; Priest i/c, St Mary, Hook-with-Warsash, 1989–98; Priest i/c, Holy Trinity, Blendworth, with St Michael and all Angels, Chalton, with St Hubert, Idsworth, and Diocesan Dir of Non-Stipendiary Ministry, dio. Portsmouth, 1998–2003; Archdeacon of IoW, 2003–06. Bp of Portsmouth's Liaison Officer for Prisons, 2003–06; Bp of Portsmouth's Advr to Hospital Chaplaincy, 2006–13. Dir, Portsmouth Educn Business Partnership, 2004–10. *Publications:* (jtly) Teaching Christianity at Key Stage 2, 2001; (jtly) Reflective Learning, 2009; 16 articles relating to work in parasitology in scientific jls. *Recreations:* walking, surfing, reading, vegetable gardening, relaxing with family. *Address:* 54 David Newberry Drive, Lee on the Solent, Hants PO13 8FE.

**READHEAD, Simon John Howard;** QC 2006; a Recorder of the Crown and County Court, since 2000; *b* 3 Feb. 1956; *s* of Frederick John Readhead and Kathleen Mary Readhead; *m* 1987, Siobhan Elizabeth Mary O'Mahony; two *s*. *Educ:* Tonbridge Sch.; Lincoln Coll., Oxford (MA, BCL). Called to the Bar, Middle Temple, 1979, Bencher, 2012; Jun., Midland and Oxford Circuit, 1989–90. Asst Recorder, 1995–2000. Lectr in Law, Hammersmith and W London Coll., 1979–81. Mem., Costs Panel, Gen. Council of the Bar, 1995–2009. Member, Management Committee: Permanent Exhibn of Judicial and Legal Costume, Royal Courts of Justice, 1979– (Trustee, 2009–); Rolls Building Art and Educnl Trust, 2011– (Trustee, 2011–). Mem., Medico-Legal Soc., 2014– (Mem. Council, 2017–). Chm. Govs, King's House Sch., Richmond, 2007–13. *Address:* 1 Chancery Lane, WC2A 1LF. *T:* (020) 7092 2900, *Fax:* (020) 7404 9876. *E:* sreadhead@1chancerylane.com.

**READING, 4th Marquess of,** *cr* 1926; **Simon Charles Henry Rufus Isaacs;** Baron 1914; Viscount 1916; Earl 1917; Viscount Erleigh 1917; *b* 18 May 1942; *e s* of 3rd Marquess of Reading, MBE, MC, and Margot Irene, *yr d* of late Percy Duke, OBE; *S* father, 1980; *m* 1979, Melinda Victoria, *yr d* of late Richard Dewar, Cecily Hill, Cirencester, Glos; one *s* two *d*. *Educ:* Eton. Served 1st Queen's Dragoon Guards, 1961–64. Member of Stock Exchange, 1970–74. Chm., Visionscape Gp, 2017–; Director: Cure Internat., 2004–18; Mertens House (St Petersburg), 2008–; Raven Resources, 2015–; Unibin Resources, 2016–; Remit Radar, 2016–. Mem., Adv. Bd, Orthus Capital, 2018–. Chm., Crosswinds, 2001–; Trustee, Garden Tomb, Jerusalem, 2002–08. Patron: Nelson Trust, 1985–; Barnabas Fund, 1998– (Chair, 2016–); Jewish Nat. Fund, 2016–. *Heir: s* Viscount Erleigh, *qv*. *Address:* 7 Cecily Hill, Cirencester, Glos GL7 2EF. *Clubs:* Cavalry and Guards, MCC, All England Lawn Tennis and Croquet; Stoke Park (Pres., 2005–07).

**READING, Area Bishop of,** since 2019; **Rt Rev. Olivia Josephine Graham;** *b* Dartford, 21 June 1956; *d* of Michael William Graham and Rachel Mildred Graham; *m* 1989, Keith Malcolm Glenny; two *s* one *d*. *Educ:* Cobham Hall, Kent; Stake Farm Coll., Kent; Univ. of E Anglia (BA Hons 1st Cl. 1984); St Albans and Oxford Ministry Course (CTh 1997). Teaching, Africa, 1974–81; Co-ord., UN Refugee Educn Prog., World Univ. Service, Djibouti, 1984–86; Dep. Country Dir, Oxfam Somalia, 1986–88; Co-ord., Arid Lands Information Network, Oxfam, 1988–93; ordained deacon, 1997, priest, 1998; non-stipendiary Curate, St Mary's, Garsington, 1997–98; Curate, St Mary's, Princes Risborough, 1998–2001; Vicar, St Peter's, Burnham, 2001–07; Parish Develt Advr, Oxford Archdeaconry, 2007–13; Archdeacon of Berkshire, 2013–19. Hon. Canon, Christ Church Cath., Oxford, 2012–. *Recreations:* walking, swimming, reading, inventive cooking, playing with paint, good comedy, music. *Address:* Bishop's House, Tidmarsh Lane, Tidmarsh, Reading RG8 8HA. *T:* (0118) 984 1216. *E:* bishopreading@oxford.anglican.org.

**READING, David Michael Ronald,** OBE 2005; Director, Food Allergy Support, 2009–18; *b* 17 Aug. 1947; *s* of Ronald George Frederick and Winifred Mabel Reading; *m* 1987, Sylvia Anne Cruickshank; two *d* (and one *d* decd). *Educ:* Godalming County Grammar Sch. Reporter, Surrey Advertiser, 1965–69; Sub-editor: Aldershot News, 1970–72, 1975–80, 1982–88, 1993–98; Reading Evening Post, 1972–73; Bedfordshire Times, 1973–74; Oxford Mail, 1974–75; Licensee Mag., 1980–82; Dep. Ed., Wokingham Times, 1988–93. Dir, Anaphylaxis Campaign, 1996–2009. *Recreations:* writing novels, guitar playing, films, ornithology, tai chi, photography. *Address:* 8 Wey Close, Ash, Aldershot, Hants GU12 6LY.

**READING, (Ian) Malcolm,** RIBA; Founder, 1996, Malcolm Reading & Associates (now Malcolm Reading Consultants); specialist adviser on architecture and the built environment; *b* 11 June 1957; *s* of Harold William Reading and Margaret (*née* Fletcher); *m* 1988, Catherine Jane Ormell; one *s*. *Educ:* George Heriot's Sch., Edinburgh; Univ. of Bristol (BA Arch. 1979; DipArch 1983). RIBA 1986. Bernard Hartley, architects, 1983–86; Andrews Downie and Partners, architects, 1986–89; Moxley Frankl Architects, 1989–90; Dir, Architecture and Design, British Council, 1990–96. Chm., Consultative Cttee, Tower of London World Heritage Site, UNESCO, 2008–. Member: Public Art Panel for Supreme Court of UK, 2007–09; Royal Household Audit Cttee for the Sovereign Grant, 2015–. Trustee: Historic Royal Palaces, London, 2005–14; Edinburgh World Heritage, 2012–15; English Heritage, 2015–18; Mem., Historic Estate Conservation Cttee, 2015–18. FRSA 1993. Hon. FRGS 2005. *Publications:* Lubetkin and Tecton: architecture and social commitment, 1981; Lubetkin and Tecton, 1992. *Recreations:* cycling, walking, photography. *Address:* (office) 8 Lincoln's Inn Fields, WC2A 3BP. *E:* malcolm@malcolmreading.com.

**READING, Dr Peter Richard;** Director, Peter Reading Strategic Consulting Ltd, since 2007; Chief Executive, Northern Lincolnshire and Goole Hospitals NHS Foundation Trust, since 2017; *b* 1 May 1956; *s* of Dr Harold Garnar Reading and late Barbara Mary Reading (*née* Hancock); *m* 2001, Dr Catherine Austin (*née* Fountain); one *s* two *d*, and two step *d*. *Educ:* St Edward's Sch., Oxford; Gonville and Caius Coll., Cambridge (MA; Exhibnr, Sen. Exhibnr); Birmingham Univ. (PhD); Moscow State Univ. (British Council Res. Schol.); London Sch. of Econs and Pol Sci. (Public Sector Mgt Prog.). Health service mgt posts in London, 1984–94; Chief Executive: Lewisham and Guy's Mental Health NHS Trust, 1994–98; UCL Hosps NHS Trust, 1998–2000; Univ. Hosps of Leicester NHS Trust, 2000–07; mgt consultant, freelance and PwC, 2007–17; Interim Chief Executive: Doncaster and Bassetlaw NHS Foundn Trust, 2010–11; Peterborough and Stamford Hosps NHS Foundn Trust, 2012–14; Associate Dir, PwC, 2014–17. CCMI 2006. *Recreations:* history, pig keeping, Oxford United, 1960s and 1970s popular music. *T:* 07813 438932. *E:* info@peterreading.co.uk.

**REAMSBOTTOM, Barry Arthur;** a Senior Secretary to the Speaker of the House of Commons, 2002–09; *b* 4 April 1949; *s* of Agnes Reamsbottom. *Educ:* St Peter's RC Secondary Sch., Aberdeen; Aberdeen Academy. Scientific Asst, Isaac Spencer & Co., Aberdeen, 1966–69; Social Security Officer, DHSS, Aberdeen, 1969–76; Area Officer, NUPE, Edinburgh, 1976–79; Civil and Public Services Association: Head of Educn Dept, 1979–87; Editor, Press Officer, 1987–92; Gen. Sec., 1992–98; Gen. Sec., PCS, 1998–2002. Mem., NUJ, 1987–. Bereavement counsellor, Trinity Hospice, London, 2007–14. *Recreations:* reading, golf, art appreciation, politics, music, taking photographs, laughter and the love of friends. *Address:* 156 Bedford Hill, SW12 9HW.

**REANEY, Trevor Eccles,** CBE 2016; Clerk and Chief Executive (formerly Clerk and Director General), Northern Ireland Assembly, 2008–16; *b* Lisburn, Co. Antrim, 3 July 1959; *s* of John James and Norah Violet Reaney; *m* 1978, Elizabeth Ann Dunlop; three *s* one *d*. *Educ:* Ballymena Acad.; Open Univ. (MBA 1995). Gen. Manager, Stormont Estate Refreshment Club, 1983–87; Sen. Operations Manager, Compass Services (UK), 1987–90; Dir, Commercial Services, Southern Educn and Liby Bd, 1990–96; Chief Executive: Craigavon BC, 1996–2003; NI Policing Bd, 2004–08. *Recreations:* walking, sport, local church.

**REARDON, Rev. John Patrick,** OBE 1999; General Secretary, Council of Churches for Britain and Ireland, 1990–99; Moderator, General Assembly of the United Reformed Church, 1995–96; *b* 15 June 1933; *s* of John Samuel Reardon and Ivy Hilda Reardon; *m* 1957, Molly Pamela Young; four *s* one *d*. *Educ:* Gravesend Grammar Sch. for Boys; University College London (BA Hons English); King's College London (postgraduate Cert. in Educn). Teacher, London and Gravesend, 1958–61; Minister, Horsham Congregational Church, 1961–68 (Chm., Sussex Congregational Union, 1967); Minister, Trinity Congregational Church, St Albans, 1968–72 (Chm., Herts Congregational Union, 1971–72); Sec., Church and Society Dept, 1972–90, and Dep. Gen. Sec., 1983–90, URC. *Publications:* More Everyday Prayers (contrib.), 1982; (ed) Leaves from the Tree of Peace, 1986; (ed) Threads of Creation, 1989; Together Met, Together Bound, 2007. *Recreations:* literature (modern fiction and poetry), travel. *Address:* 1 Newbolt Close, Newport Pagnell, Bucks MK16 8ND. *T:* (01908) 217559.

**REARDON, Katherine Genevieve;** Editor-in-Chief, Times Luxx, since 2018; *b* New York, 20 Nov. 1968; *d* of Patrick Reardon and Polly Reardon (*née* Peverley, later Wood); one *s* one *d* (twins). *Educ:* Cheltenham Ladies' Coll.; Stowe Sch. Fashion Asst, US Vogue, 1988–90; Fashion Dir, Tatler, 1990–97; Contrib. Editor, Vanity Fair, 1999–2011; Founder, Toptips.com, 2007–11; Editor, Tatler, 2011–17. Columnist, fashion, 1999–2001, jewellery, 2003–06, The Times. Mem., CRUK, 2007–. *Publications:* Top Tips for Girls, 2008; Top Tips for Life, 2010. *Recreations:* riding, tidying.

**REARDON SMITH, Sir (William) Antony (John),** 4th Bt *cr* 1920, of Appledore, Devon; Chairman, GEM Containers Ltd, 2013–16; *b* 20 June 1937; *e s* of Sir William Reardon Reardon-Smith, 3rd Bt and his 1st wife, Nesta Florence Phillips (*d* 1959); *S* father, 1995; *m* 1962, Susan Wight, *d* of Henry Wight Gibson; three *s* one *d*. *Educ:* Wycliffe Coll. Nat. Service, RN, Suez, 1956. Sir William Reardon Smith & Sons Ltd and Reardon Smith Line plc, 1957–85 (Dir, 1959–85); Director: London World Trade Centre, 1986–87; Milford Haven Port Authority, 1988–99; Marine and Port Services Ltd, Milford Docks, 1990–99. Chm., N Eastern Rubber Co. Ltd, 1980–2004. Member: Baltic Exchange, 1959–87 (Dir, 1982–87; Assoc. Mem., 1990–92); Chamber of Shipping Documentary Cttee, 1963–72 (Chm., 1968–72); Documentary Council, Baltic and Internat. Conf., 1964–82. Dir, UK Protection and Indemnity Club and Freight, Demurrage and Defence Assoc., 1968–80. Trustee: Royal Merchant Navy Sch. Foundn, 1966–2003 (Vice-Pres., 1992–); Bearwood Coll., 1966–2003; Trustee and Chm., Joseph Strong Frazer Trust, 1980–; Member: Council, King George's Fund for Sailors, 1981–95; City of London Cttee, RNLI, 1976–2006. Clerk, Fuellers' Co., 2002–14 (Hon. Liveryman, 2014); Liveryman: World Traders' Co., 1986–; Poulters' Co., 1991–; Shipwrights' Co., 1994–. GCLJ 2002 (KLJ 1997; Bailiff, 2002–08, now Bailiff Emeritus). *Recreations:* golf, shooting. *Heir: s* William Nicolas Henry Reardon Smith [*b* 10 June 1963; *m* 2001, Julia, *er d* of D. Martin Slade]. *Address:* 26 Merrick Square, SE1 4JB. *T:* (020) 7403 5723.

**REASON, Prof. James Tootle,** CBE 2003; FBA 1999; FRAeS; FBPsS; Professor of Psychology, University of Manchester, 1977–2001, now Emeritus; *b* 1 May 1938; *s* of late George Stanley Tootle and Hilda Alice Reason; *m* 1964, Rea Jaari; two *d*. *Educ:* Royal Masonic Sch.; Univ. of Manchester (BSc 1962); Univ. of Leicester (PhD 1967). FBPsS 1988; FRAeS 1998. RAF Inst. of Aviation Medicine, 1962–64; Lectr and Reader, Dept of Psychology, Univ. of Leicester, 1964–76. Hon. DSc Aberdeen, 2002. Dist. Foreign Colleague Award, US Human Factors and Ergonomics Soc., 1995. Hon. FRCGP 2006; Hon. Fellow, Safety and Reliability Soc., 2011. Dist. Service Award, RoSPA, 2006. *Publications:* Man in Motion, 1974; Motion Sickness, 1975; Human Error, 1990; Beyond Aviation Human Factors, 1995; Managing the Risks of Organizational Accidents, 1997; Managing Maintenance Error, 2003; The Human Contribution: unsafe acts, accidents and heroic recoveries, 2008; A Life in Error, 2013. *Recreations:* reading, writing, viewing. *Address:* 96 Cliveden Gages, Taplow, Bucks SL6 0GB. *T:* (01268) 666485. *E:* jim@jamesreason.com.

**REAY, 15th Lord** *cr* 1628, of Reay, Caithness; **Aeneas Simon Mackay;** Bt (NS) 1627; Baron Mackay van Ophemert and Zennewijnen, Netherlands, 1822; Chief of Clan Mackay; Director, Montrose Advisers LLP, since 2011; Principal and Co-founder, Montrose Partners LLP, 2003–11; *b* 20 March 1965; *s* of 14th Lord Reay and of Hon. Annabel Thérèse Fraser (*see* A. T. Keswick); *S* father, 2013; *m* 2010, Mia, *er d* of Markus Ruulio, Helsinki; two *s* one *d*. *Educ:* Westminster School; Brown Univ., USA. Associate, Salomon Brothers, 1987–91; Robert Fleming, later JP Morgan, 1992–2003. Elected Mem., H of L, 2019. *Recreations:* most sports, especially football, cricket and shooting. *Heir: s* Master of Reay, *qv*.

**REAY, Master of; Hon. Alexander Shimi Markus Mackay;** *b* 21 April 2010; *s* and heir of Lord Reay, *qv*.

**REAY, David William;** Chairman, Northumberland Mental Health NHS Trust, 1992–2001; *b* 28 May 1940; *s* of late Stanley Reay and Madge Reay (*née* Hall); *m* 1964, Constance Susan Gibney; two *d*. *Educ:* Monkwearmouth Grammar School, Sunderland; Newcastle upon Tyne Polytechnic. Independent Television Authority, 1960–62; Alpha Television (ATV and ABC) Services Ltd, 1962–64; Tyne Tees Television Ltd, 1964–72; HTV Ltd: Engineering Manager, 1972–75; Chief Engineer, 1975–79; Dir of Engineering, 1979–84; Man. Dir, 1984–91, Chief Exec., 1991, Tyne Tees Television Hldgs. Chairman: Hadrian Television Ltd, 1988–91; Legend Television Ltd, 1989–91; Man. Dir, Tyne Tees Television Ltd, 1984–91; Director: Tyne Tees Music, 1984–91; Tyne Tees Enterprises, 1984–91; ITCA, now ITVA, 1984–91; Independent Television Publications, 1984–89; Tube Productions, 1986–91; ITN, 1990–91; Tyne and Wear Develt Corp., 1986–88; The Wearside Opportunity Ltd, 1989–94. Mem. Council, Univ. of Newcastle upon Tyne, 1989–94. CCMI (CBIM 1987); FRTS 1984; FRSA 1992. *Recreations:* walking, reading, music, watching soccer (particularly Sunderland AFC). *Address:* 11 The Links, Ascot, Berks SL5 7TN.

**REAY, Prof. Diane,** PhD; Professor of Education, University of Cambridge, 2005–16, now Emerita; *b* 21 July 1949; *d* of Arthur James Sutton and Lilian Mary Sutton (*née* Smart); *m* 1971, Keith Reay (marr. diss. 1995); one *s* one *d*. *Educ:* Ashby Girls' Grammar Sch., Ashby-de-la-Zouch; Univ. of Newcastle upon Tyne (BA Hons Pols and Econs 1970; PGCE 1971); Inst. of Educn, London (MA 1987); South Bank Univ. (PhD 1995). Teacher, ILEA, 1971–90; Advr, Islington LEA, 1990–92; Res. Scholar, South Bank Univ., 1992–95; Res. Fellow, 1995–2001, Sen. Lectr, 2001–03, KCL; Prof., London Metropolitan Univ., 2003–05. Vis. Prof. of Sociol., LSE, 2017–. Member: 2008 RAE Educn Panel; 2014 REF Educn Panel; ESRC Res. Grants Bd, 2006–. FAcSS (AcSS 2007). *Publications:* Class Work: mothers' involvement in their children's schooling, 1998; (ed jtly) Activating Participation: parents and teachers working towards partnership, 2004; (jtly) Degrees of Choice: social class, race and gender in higher education, 2005; (jtly) White Middle Class Identities and Urban Schooling, 2011; Miseducation: inequality, education and the working classes, 2017. *Address:* Faculty of Education, University of Cambridge, Hills Road, Cambridge CB2 8PQ. *T:* (01223) 767600, *Fax:* (01223) 767602.

**REAY-SMITH, Richard Philip Morley;** DL; Chairman, Painshill Park Trust, since 2018 (first Chairman, 1980–85; Vice-Chairman, 1985–2018); *b* 24 Nov. 1941; *m* 1972, Susan Margaret Hill; two *s*. *Educ:* Stowe Sch.; Durham Univ. (LLB); Harvard Business Sch. (AMP). Barclays Bank, 1963–98: Local Dir, Shrewsbury, 1984–87; Dep. Chief Exec., Central Retail Services Div., 1987–91; Chief Exec., Barclaycard, 1991–94; Man. Dir, Personal Banking, 1995–98; Chm., Barclays Life Assurance Co. Ltd, 1996–98; Chief Exec., UK Retail Banking, 1998. Director: Visa Internat. Services Assoc., 1991–98; Legal & General Bank Ltd, 2001–03. Chm., Surrey Compact, 2008–13. DL Surrey, 2004. FRSA. *Recreations:* sailing, music, travel, classic and vintage motorsport.

**REBSTOCK, Dame Paula (Rae),** DNZM 2016 (CNZM 2009); independent economic consultant, since 2009; Chair, Board of Directors, Accident Compensation Corporation, New Zealand, since 2012; *b* Great Falls, Montana, USA, 9 Aug. 1957; *d* of Roy and Wilma Rebstock; partner, Ulf Schoefisch; two *d*. *Educ:* Univ. of Oregon (BSc Econs 1986); London Sch. of Econs and Pol Sci. (DipEcon 1987; MSc Econs 1988). Econ. Advr, Dept of Prime Minister and Cabinet, NZ, 1990–92; Gen. Manager, Labour Mkt Policy, Dept of Labour, NZ, 1992–97; New Zealand Commerce Commission: Mem., 1998–2003; Chair, 2003–09; Chair, Expert Panel for Oversight of Change Prog., Probation Service, Dept of Corrections, NZ, 2009–11; Ministry of Social Development, NZ: Chair: Welfare Wkg Gp, 2010–11; Work and Income Bd, 2012–15; Expert Panel on Modernising Child, Youth and Family, 2015–16. Chair: Insce and Savings Ombudsman Commn, NZ, 2009–17; Vulnerable Children's Bd, Govt of NZ, 2016–18; Dep. Chair, NZ Railways Corp., 2009–18. Chair: Kiwi Gp Hldgs Ltd, 2018–; Ngati Whatua Orakei Wai Maia, 2018–; Director: Auckland Transport, 2014–; Vector Ltd, 2019–. Mem., Adv. Bd, Univ. of Auckland Business Sch., 2006–17. Member: NZ Inst. Dirs, 2005; Global Women NZ, 2009. *Publications:* (ed with M. Prebble) Incentives and Labour Supply: modelling taxes and benefits, 1992. *Recreations:* boating, cinema, family.

**REBUCK,** Baroness *cr* 2014 (Life Peer), of Bloomsbury in the London Borough of Camden; **Gail Ruth Rebuck,** DBE 2009 (CBE 2000); Chairman, Penguin Random House UK, and Director, Penguin Random House, since 2013; *b* 10 Feb. 1952; *d* of Gordon and Mavis Rebuck; *m* 1985, Philip Gould (later Baron Gould of Brookwood; *d* 2011); two *d*. *Educ:* Lycée Français de Londres; Univ. of Sussex (BA). Production Asst, Grisewood & Dempsey, 1975–76; Editor, then Publisher, Robert Nicholson Publications, 1976–78; Publisher, Hamlyn Paperbacks, 1978–82; Publishing Dir, Century Publishing, 1982–85; Publisher, Century Hutchinson, 1985–89; Chm., Random House Div., Random Century, 1989–91; Chm. and Chief Exec., Random House UK, then Random House Gp Ltd, 1991–2013. Non-executive Director: BSkyB, 2002–12; Koovs plc, 2014–; Belmond Ltd, 2015–; Guardian Media Gp, 2016–. Mem., Creative Industries Taskforce, 1997–2000. Non-exec. Dir, Work Foundn, 2001–08. Trustee: IPPR, 1993–2003; Nat. Literacy Trust, 2007–14; Cheltenham Festivals, 2013–16 (Chm. Literature Fest., 2013–16). Member: Court, Univ. of Sussex, 1997–; Council, RCA, 1999– (Chair, 2015–). FRSA 1989. *Recreations:* reading, travel. *Address:* Penguin Random House UK, 20 Vauxhall Bridge Road, SW1V 2SA. *T:* (020) 7840 8886.

**RECKLESS, Mark John;** Member for South Wales East, National Assembly for Wales, since 2016 (UK Ind, 2016–17; C, since 2017); *b* 6 Dec. 1970; *m* 2011, Catriona; two *s* one *d*. *Educ:* Marlborough Coll.; Christ Church, Oxford (BA PPE); Columbia Business Sch., NY (MBA); Coll. of Law (LLB). UK Economist, Warburgs, 1993–97; Booz Allen Hamilton, 1999–2001; Cons. Party Policy Unit, 2002–04. Called to the Bar, Lincoln's Inn, 2007; Herbert Smith LLP, 2007–10. Mem. (C) Medway Council, 2007–11. Mem., Kent Police Authy, 2007–11. Contested (C) Medway, 2001, 2005. MP (C) Rochester and Strood, 2010–Sept. 2014, (UK Ind) Rochester and Strood, Nov. 2014–2015; contested (UK Ind) same seat, 2015. Mem., Home Affairs Select Cttee, 2010–14. *Publications:* Euromoney Guide to the London Financial Markets, 1996; The Euro: bad for business, 1998; Conveyor Belt to Crime, 2003; (jtly) The Drivers of Regulations, 2004; (jtly) Direct Democracy, 2005. *Address:* National Assembly for Wales, Cardiff Bay, Cardiff CF99 1NA.

**RECORD, Neil Peter;** Chairman: Record plc (formerly N. P. Record Ltd), since 1983 (Chief Executive Officer, 1983–2010); Institute of Economic Affairs, since 2015 (Trustee, since 2008); Global Warming Policy Forum Ltd, since 2019; *b* Oxford, 26 June 1953; *s* of Peter Douglas Record and Cherry Kathleen Record; *m* 1980, Carol Steven (marr. diss. 2000); two *s* one *d*; partner, 2000, Julie Catherine Wealthall (*née* Adams); one step *s* one step *d*. *Educ:* Magdalen Coll. Sch., Oxford; Balliol Coll., Oxford (MA Psychol. and Philosophy 1975); Essex Univ. (Dip. Econs (Dist.) 1976); University Coll. London (MSc Econs (Dist.) 1977). FCT 1993. Economist, Bank of England, 1977–78; Commodity Economist, 1978–80, Commodity Buyer, 1980–83, Mars Ltd. Vis. Fellow, Nuffield Coll., Oxford, 2008–16 (Mem., Investment Cttee, 2004–17; Chm., Remuneration Cttee, 2018–). Chm., Family Heart Assoc., 1991–92. Gov., Magdalen Coll. Sch., Oxford, 2008– (Vice Chm., 2014–). FRSA. *Publications:* Currency Overlay, 2003. *Recreations:* tennis, skiing, opera, architecture and art, travel. *Address:* Record plc, Morgan House, Madeira Walk, Windsor, Berks SL4 1EP. *T:* (01753) 605849. *E:* fkalra@recordcm.com.

**REDDAWAY, Sir David (Norman),** KCMG 2013 (CMG 1993); MBE 1980; HM Diplomatic Service, retired; Chief Executive and Clerk, Goldsmiths' Company, since 2016; *b* 26 April 1953; *s* of late George Frank Norman Reddaway, CBE and Jean Reddaway, OBE (*née* Brett); *m* 1981, Roshan Taliyeh Firouz (marr. diss. 2019); two *s* one *d*. *Educ:* Oundle Sch. (Schol.); Fitzwilliam Coll., Cambridge (Exhibnr; MA Hist.). Volunteer teacher, Ethiopia, 1972. Joined FCO, 1975; language student, SOAS, 1976 and Iran, 1977; Tehran: Third Sec. later Second Sec. (Commercial), 1977–78; Second Sec. later First Sec. (Chancery), 1978–80; First Secretary: (Chancery), Madrid, 1980–84; FCO, 1985–86; Private Sec. to Minister of State, 1986–88; (Chancery) New Delhi, 1988–90; Chargé d'Affaires, Tehran, 1990–93 (Counsellor, 1991); Minister, Buenos Aires, 1993–97; Hd, Southern European Dept, FCO, 1997–99; Dir, Public Services, FCO, 1999–2001; UK Special Rep. for Afghanistan, 2002; Vis. Fellow, Harvard Univ., 2002–03; High Comr, Canada, 2003–06; Ambassador: to Ireland, 2006–09; to Turkey, 2009–14. Advr to Bd, 2014–15, non-exec. Dir, 2015–, Beko plc. Member: Adv. Bd, Sch. of Mgt, Univ. of Bath, 2014–18; Council, Goldsmiths, Univ. of London, 2016–. Mem., Council of Experts, Democratic Progress Inst., 2015–. *Recreations:* rowing, kayaking, Persian carpets and art. *Club:* Hawks (Cambridge).

**REDDICLIFFE, Paul,** OBE 1998; HM Diplomatic Service, retired; Research Analyst for Cambodia, Laos, Thailand, and Vietnam, Foreign and Commonwealth Office, 1997–2008; *b* March 1945; *m* 1974, Wee Siok Boi; two *s*. *Educ:* Bedford Mod. Sch.; Jesus Coll., Oxford (MA Lit. Hum. 1967); Sch. of Oriental and African Studies, Univ. of London (MA SE Asian Studies 1973); Univ. of Kent. VSO, Vientiane, Laos, 1968–70 and 1971–72; joined HM Diplomatic Service, 1977; Indochina Analyst, Res. Dept, FCO, 1977–85; First Sec., Canberra, 1985–89; Indochina Analyst, 1989–92, Hd, S and SE Asia Section, 1992–94, Res. later Res. and Analysis, Dept, FCO; Ambassador to Kingdom of Cambodia, 1994–97. *Recreations:* bird-watching, books, P. G. Wodehouse, history. *Address:* c/o Foreign and Commonwealth Office, King Charles Street, SW1A 2AH.

**REDDIHOUGH, His Honour John Hargreaves;** a Circuit Judge, 2000–17; a Deputy Circuit Judge, since 2018; *b* 6 Dec. 1947; *s* of Frank Hargreaves Reddihough and Mabel Grace Reddihough (*née* Warner); *m* 1981, Sally Margaret Fryer; one *s* one *d*. *Educ:* Manchester Grammar Sch.; Univ. of Birmingham (LLB Hons). Called to the Bar, Gray's Inn, 1969; barrister, 1971–2000; Asst Recorder, 1991–94; Recorder, 1994–2000; Resident Judge, Grimsby Combined Court, 2001–09. *Recreations:* ski-ing, gardening, music, travel, reading, sport, walking, bowls. *Address:* c/o Reading Crown Court, Old Shire Hall, The Forbury, Reading RG1 3EH. *T:* (0118) 967 4400.

**REDDINGTON, (Clifford) Michael;** Chief Executive, Liverpool City Council, 1986–88; *b* 14 Sept. 1932; *s* of Thomas Reddington and Gertrude (*née* Kenny); *m* 1968 Ursula Moor. *Educ:* St Michael's Coll., Leeds; St Edward's Coll., Liverpool; Liverpool Univ. (BCom 1953); Open Univ. (Dip. Maths 2013). CPFA (IPFA 1958). Served RAF, 1958–60. City Treasury, Liverpool, 1953–58 and 1960–86; Dep. City Treasurer, 1974, City Treasurer, 1982–86. Mem., Ind. Inquiry into Capital Market Activities of London Borough of Hammersmith and Fulham, 1990. Investigating Accountant, Disciplinary Scheme, CIPFA, 1991–98. Member: Regulatory Cttee, CIPFA, 2011–19; Conduct Cttee, Inst. of Financial Accountants, 2013–. Chairman: Liverpool Welsh Choral Union, 1990–93;

Convocation, Univ. of Liverpool, 1993–96; Trust Fund Manager, Hillsborough Disaster Appeal Fund, 1989–98; Chm., James Bulger Meml Trust, 1993–98. Mem. Governing Body, and Chm. Finance Cttee, Nugent Care Soc., 1992–2005. Member: World Bank mission to govts of Macedonia, Latvia, Armenia and Yugoslavia, 1999–2010; IMF missions to govt of Bosnia-Herzegovina, 2003. Sec. Treas., NW and N Wales Br., RHS Rhododendron Camellia and Magnolia Gp, 1990–2017. *Recreations:* cycling, fell walking, gardening. *Address:* Entwood, 18 Westwood Road, Noctorum, Prenton CH43 9RQ. *T:* (0151) 652 6081. *Club:* Athenæum (Liverpool).

**REDDROP, Gemma;** *see* Bodinetz, G.

**REDESDALE,** 6th Baron *cr* 1902; **Rupert Bertram Mitford;** Baron Mitford (Life Peer), 2000; *b* 18 July 1967; *s* of 5th Baron and of Sarah Georgina Cranstoun, *d* of Brig. Alston Cranstoun Todd, OBE; *S* father, 1991; *m* 1998, Helen, *e d* of David Shipsey; two *s* two *d*. *Educ:* Highgate Sch.; Newcastle Univ. (BA Hons Archaeology). Outdoor instructor, Fernwood Adventure Centre, South Africa, 1990–91. Lib Dem spokesman on overseas development, H of L, 1993–99, on defence, 2000–05, on energy, 2005–09, on agriculture, 2006–09; Member: H of L Select Cttee on Sci. and Technology, 1994–97; EU (D) Agric. Select Cttee, 1998–2000. Mem. Council, IAM, 1995–; Pres., Natural Gas Vehicle Assoc., 1997–2004; Chairman: Anaerobic and Biogas Assoc., 2009–12; Low Energy Co. (UK), 2013–; Chief Executive Officer: Carbon Management Assoc., 2013–; Energy Managers Assoc., 2013–. Chair, Red Squirrel Protection Partnership, 2006–. Hon. Vice Pres., Raleigh Internat., 2000–. *Recreations:* caving, climbing, ski-ing. *Heir: s* Hon. Bertram David Mitford, *b* 29 May 2000. *Address:* House of Lords, SW1A 0PW. *Club:* Newcastle University Caving.

**REDFERN,** family name of **Baroness Redfern.**

**REDFERN,** Baroness *cr* 2015 (Life Peer), of the Isle of Axholme in the County of Lincolnshire; **Elizabeth Marie Redfern;** Member (C), North Lincolnshire Council, since 1996 (Leader, 2006–07 and 2011–17); *b* Winterton, 25 Sept. 1947; *m* 1974, Gordon Redfern (*d* 2009); two *d*. *Educ:* Winterton Comprehensive Sch.; North Lindsey Coll., Scunthorpe. Former Marketing Dir of chemical and agricl machinery co.; co-owner, seed merchanting business. Director: Humber LEP, 2011–; Greater Lincs LEP, 2011–; Humberside Airport, 2011–; Humber Bridge Bd, 2012–14 (Chm.); Humber Local Transport Bd; North Lincs Homes; Humber UTC Bd; Rail North Ltd, 2013–. Director: North Lincs PCT; North Lincs Acute Trust. North Lincolnshire Council: Dep. Leader, Cons. Gp, 1995–2003; Dep. Leader, 2003–06; Leader, Cons. Gp, 2007–10. Member (C): Belton Parish Council, 1987–; Epworth Town Parish Council. Chancellor, N Lincs Children's Univ., 2016–. *Recreations:* walking in and around the Isle of Axholme with three dogs, charity work, active role with five grandchildren, gardening, theatre, sport. *Address:* Chancel House, 5 Queen Street, Epworth, N Lincs DN9 1HG. *E:* eredfern008@btinternet.com.

**REDFERN, Rt Rev. Dr Alastair Llewellyn John;** Bishop of Derby, 2005–18; *b* 1 Sept. 1948; *s* of Victor Redfern and Audrey Joan Redfern; *m* 1st, 1974, Jane Valerie Straw (*d* 2004); two *d*; 2nd, 2006, Caroline Elizabeth Boddington, *qv*. *Educ:* Christ Church, Oxford (MA Modern Hist.); Trinity Coll., Cambridge (MA Theol.); Westcott House, Cambridge; PhD Theol. Bristol. Curate, Tettenhall Regis, dio. Lichfield, 1976–79; Lectr in Church History, 1979–87, Vice Principal, 1985–87, Ripon Coll., Cuddesdon; Dir, Oxford Inst. for Church and Society, 1979–83; Curate, All Saints, Cuddesdon, 1983–87; Canon Theologian, Bristol Cathedral, 1987–97; Bishop Suffragan of Grantham, 1997–2005. Dean of Stamford, 1997–2005; Canon and Preb., Lincoln Cathedral, 2000–05. Mem., H of L, 2010. *Publications:* Ministry and Priesthood, 1999; Being Anglican, 2000; Growing the Kingdom, 2009; Public Space and Private Faith: a challenge to the churches, 2009; Thomas Hobbes and the Limits of Democracy, 2009; Community and Conflict, 2011; Out of the Depths, 2012; Leadership of the People of God, 2013; Discipleship: a call and commission, 2013; Mission in Action, 2014; Living in Love: mysticism in a material world, 2014; Sacrifice Remembered, 2014; The Word on the Street, 2015; Peace That Passes Understanding, 2016; The Challenge of Our Christian Calling, 2016; The Church: a workshop of salvation, 2016; Shaping the Spiritual Life, 2017; The Clewer Initiative: T. T. Carter and the fight against modern slavery, 2017; Truth: an unanswered question, 2018. *Recreations:* reading, walking. *E:* bishopalastair.redfern@gmail.com.

**REDFERN, Michael Howard;** QC 1993; a Recorder, since 1999; *b* 30 Nov. 1943; *s* of Lionel William Redfern and Kathleen Roylance Redfern (*née* Brownston); *m* 1st, 1966, Sylvia Newlands (marr. diss. 1989); one *d*; 2nd, 1991, Diana Barbara Eaglestone, *qv*; one *d*, and two step *d*. *Educ:* Stretford Grammar Sch. for Boys; Leeds Univ. (LLB Hons). Teacher, 1967–68; Lectr in Law, 1968–69; called to the Bar, Inner Temple, 1970, Bencher, 2002. Lifetime Achievement Award, Manchester Legal Awards, 2015. *Recreations:* music, sport (preferably participating), travel, history. *Address:* St Johns Buildings, 24a–28 St John Street, Manchester M3 4DJ.

**REDFORD, (Charles) Robert;** American actor and director; Founder, 1981, and President, Sundance Institute; *b* 18 Aug. 1937; *s* of Charles Redford and Martha (*née* Hart); *m* 1958, Lola Jean Van Wagenen (marr. diss. 1985); one *s* two *d*; *m* 2009, Sibylle Szaggars. *Educ:* Van Nuys High Sch.; Univ. of Colorado; Pratt Inst., Brooklyn; Amer. Acad. of Dramatic Arts. *Theatre:* appearances include: Tall Story, Broadway, 1959; Sunday in New York, Broadway, 1961–62; Barefoot in the Park, Biltmore, NY, 1963–64; *television:* appearances include, The Iceman Cometh, 1960; *films* include: as actor: War Hunt, 1962; Inside Daisy Clover, 1965; Barefoot in the Park, 1967; Butch Cassidy and the Sundance Kid, 1969; The Candidate, 1972; The Way We Were, 1973; The Sting, 1973; The Great Gatsby, 1974; All the President's Men, 1976; The Electric Horseman, 1979; The Natural, 1984; Out of Africa, 1985; Legal Eagles, 1986; Havana, 1990; Sneakers, 1992; Up Close and Personal, 1996; Spy Game, 2001; The Last Castle, 2002; The Clearing, 2004; An Unfinished Life, 2006; All is Lost, 2013; Captain America: The Winter Soldier, 2014; Truth, A Walk in the Woods, 2015; Pete's Dragon, 2016; The Old Man and the Gun, 2018; Avengers: Endgame, 2019; as director: Ordinary People, 1980 (Acad. Award for Best Dir, 1981); Milagro Beanfield War (also prod.), 1988; A River Runs Through It, 1992; Indecent Proposal (also actor), 1993; The River Wild, 1995; The Horse Whisperer (also actor), 1998; The Legend of Bagger Vance, 2001; Lions for Lambs (also actor), 2007; The Conspirator, 2011; The Company You Keep (also actor), 2012; exec. prod., The Mustang, 2019. Hon. Academy Award, 2002; Chaplin Award, Film Soc. of Lincoln Center, 2015; Presidential Medal of Freedom (USA), 2016. *Publications:* The Outlaw Trail, 1978. *Address: c/o* Sundance Institute, PO Box 684429, Park City, UT 84068, USA.

**REDGRAVE, Adrian Robert Frank;** QC 1992; a Recorder of the Crown Court, since 1985; *b* 1 Sept. 1944; *s* of Cecil Frank Redgrave and Doris Edith Redgrave; *m* 1967, Ann Cooper; two *s* one *d*. *Educ:* Abingdon Sch.; Univ. of Exeter (LLB 1966). Called to the Bar, Inner Temple, 1968. *Recreations:* tennis, wine, garden, France, Bangalore Phall. *Address:* Cornwall Street Chambers, 85–87 Cornwall Street, Birmingham B3 3BY. *T:* (01865) 311066.

**REDGRAVE, Diane Catherine; Her Honour Judge Redgrave;** a Circuit Judge, since 2008; *b* 28 May 1953; *d* of Norman Redgrave and Kathleen Redgrave; *m* 1981, Nicholas Harvey; one *s* one *d*. *Educ:* Notre Dame Collegiate Sch. for Girls, Leeds; Bristol Polytech. (BA Hons (Law) 1974). Lectr in Law, Leeds Polytech., 1974–78; Vis. Lectr in Law, Dept of Econs, Bradford Univ., 1976–77. Called to the Bar, Middle Temple, 1977, Bencher, 2012; District Judge, Principal Registry, Family Div., 1998–2008; Recorder, 2002–08. *Recreations:* my family, walking, ski-ing, reading, gardening. *Address:* Bromley County Court, Court House, College Road, Bromley BR1 3PX.

**REDGRAVE, Sir Steven (Geoffrey),** Kt 2001; CBE 1997 (MBE 1987); DL; oarsman; sports consultant; *b* 23 March 1962; *m* 1988, Elizabeth Ann Callaway; one *s* two *d*. *Educ:* Great Marlow Sch. Represented: Marlow Rowing Club, 1976–2000; Leander, 1987–2000. Rowed coxless pairs with Andrew Holmes, until 1989, then with Matthew Pinsent; subseq. rowed coxless fours with Matthew Pinsent, James Cracknell and Tim Foster; winner: Commonwealth Games, 1986 (single sculls, coxed fours, coxless pairs); World Championships, coxed pairs, 1986, coxless pairs, 1987, 1991, 1993, 1994 and 1995; Gold Medal, Olympic Games, 1984 (coxed fours), 1988, 1992 and 1996 (coxless pairs), 2000 (coxless fours); Gold Medal, World Championships, coxless fours, 1997, 1998 and 1999. High Perf. Dir, Chinese nat. rowing team, 2018–. Founded Sir Steve Redgrave Charitable Trust, 2001; Pres., British Assoc. of Snowsport Instructors, 2012–; Chm., Henley Royal Regatta, 2014–; Vice President: Diabetes UK; British Olympic Assoc. Hon. DCL. DL Bucks, 2001. *Publications:* Steven Redgrave's Complete Book of Rowing, 1992; (with Nick Townsend): A Golden Age (autobiog.), 2000; You Can Win at Life!, 2005; Inspired, 2009; Enduring Success, 2010; Great Olympic Moments, 2011. *Address:* PO Box 3400, Marlow, Bucks SL7 3QE. *T:* (01628) 483021. *Club:* Leander (Henley-on-Thames).

**REDGRAVE, Vanessa,** CBE 1967; actress, since 1957; *b* 30 Jan. 1937; *d* of late Sir Michael Redgrave, CBE, and Rachel Kempson; *m* 1962, Tony Richardson (marr. diss. 1967; he *d* 1991); one *d* (and one *d* decd); one *s* by Franco Nero. *Educ:* Queensgate School; Central School of Speech and Drama. Frinton Summer Repertory, 1957; Touch of the Sun, Saville, 1958; Midsummer Night's Dream, Stratford, 1959; Look on Tempests, 1960; The Tiger and the Horse, 1960; Lady from the Sea, 1960; Royal Shakespeare Theatre Company: As You Like It, 1961, Taming of the Shrew, 1961, Cymbeline, 1962; The Seagull, 1964; The Prime of Miss Jean Brodie, Wyndham's, 1966; Daniel Deronda, 1969; Cato Street, 1971; The Threepenny Opera, Prince of Wales, 1972; Twelfth Night, Shaw Theatre, 1972; Antony and Cleopatra, Bankside Globe, 1973; Design for Living, Phoenix, 1973; Macbeth, LA, 1974; Lady from the Sea, NY, 1976, Roundhouse, 1979; The Aspern Papers, Haymarket, 1984; The Seagull, Queen's, 1985; Chekhov's Women, Lyric, 1985; The Taming of the Shrew and Antony and Cleopatra, Haymarket, 1986; Ghosts, Young Vic, transf. Wyndham's, 1986; Touch of the Poet, Young Vic, transf. Comedy, 1988; Orpheus Descending, Haymarket, 1988, NY, 1989; A Madhouse in Goa, Lyric, Hammersmith, 1989; Three Sisters, Queen's, 1990; When She Danced, Globe, 1991; Heartbreak House, Haymarket, 1992; The Liberation of Skopje, Antony and Cleopatra, Riverside, 1995; John Gabriel Borkman, NT, 1996; The Tempest, Globe, 2000; The Cherry Orchard, RNT, 2000; Lady Windermere's Fan, Haymarket, 2002; Long Day's Journey into Night, NY (Best Actress, Tony Award), 2003; Hecuba, Albery, 2005; The Year of Magical Thinking, NT, 2008; Driving Miss Daisy, Wyndham's, 2011; The Revisionist, Cherry Lane Th., NY, 2013; Much Ado About Nothing, Old Vic, 2013; Richard III, Almeida, 2016; The Inheritance, Young Vic, transf. Noël Coward, 2018. *Films:* Morgan—A Suitable Case for Treatment, 1966 (Cannes Fest. Award, Best Actress 1966); The Sailor from Gibraltar, 1967; Blow-Up, 1967; Camelot, 1967; Red White and Zero, 1967; Charge of the Light Brigade, 1968; Isadora, 1968; A Quiet Place in the Country, 1968; The Seagull, 1969; Drop-Out, 1970; La Vacanza, 1970; The Trojan Women, 1971; The Devils, 1971; Mary, Queen of Scots, 1972; Murder on the Orient Express, 1974; Out of Season, 1975; Seven Per Cent Solution, 1975; Julia, 1976 (Academy Award, 1977; Golden Globe Award); Agatha, 1978; Yanks, 1978; Bear Island, 1978; Playing for Time, 1980; My Body, My Child, 1981; Wagner, 1983; The Bostonians, 1984; Wetherby, 1985; Steaming, 1985; Comrades, 1987; Prick Up Your Ears, 1987; Consuming Passions, 1988; A Man For All Seasons, 1988; Orpheus Descending, 1990; Young Catherine, 1990; Whatever Happened to Baby Jane, 1990; The Ballad of the Sad Café, 1991; Howards End, 1992; The House of the Spirits, 1994; Mother's Boys, 1994; Little Odessa, 1995; A Month by the Lake, 1996; Mission: Impossible, 1996; Looking for Richard, 1997; Wilde, 1997; Smilla's Feeling for Snow, 1997; Mrs Dalloway, 1998; Deep Impact, 1998; Cradle Will Rock, 2000; Venus, 2007; Evening, 2007; Letters to Juliet, 2010; Anonymous, 2011; Song for Marion, 2013; The Butler, 2013; The Secret Scripture, 2017; Mrs Lowry and Son, 2019. Television incl. The Gathering Storm, 2002 (Best Actress, BPG awards, 2003); The Day of the Triffids, 2009; The Thirteenth Tale, 2013. Fellow, BAFTA, 2010. *Publications:* Pussies and Tigers (anthology of writings of school children), 1963; Vanessa Redgrave: an autobiography, 1991. *Address: c/o* Gavin Barker Associates, 2d Wimpole Street, W1G 0EB.
*See also* Joely Richardson.

**REDHEAD, Prof. Michael Logan Gonne,** FBA 1991; Professor of History and Philosophy of Science, Cambridge University, 1987–97; Fellow, Wolfson College, Cambridge, 1988–97, now Emeritus Fellow (Vice-President, 1992–96; Acting President, 1992–93); *b* 30 Dec. 1929; *s* of Robert Arthur Redhead and Christabel Lucy Gonne Browning; *m* 1964, Jennifer Anne Hill (*d* 2010); three *s*. *Educ:* Westminster Sch.; University College London (BSc 1st Cl. Hons Physics 1950; PhD Mathematical Phys. 1970). FInstP 1982. Dir, Redhead Properties Ltd, 1962; Partner, Galveston Estates, 1970; Lectr, Sen. Lectr in Philosophy of Science, 1981–84, Prof., Philosophy of Physics, 1984–85, Chelsea Coll., Univ. of London; Prof. of Philosophy of Physics, King's College London, 1985–87; Hd, 1987–93, Chm., 1993–95, Dept of Hist. and Philosophy of Sci., Cambridge Univ.; Dir of Studies, Christ's Coll., Trinity Hall and St Catharine's Coll., Cambridge, 1989–97; London School of Economics: Actg Dir, 1998–2001, Co-Dir, 2001–, Centre for Philosophy of Natural and Social Sci.; Centennial Prof. of Philosophy, 1999–2002. Tarner Lectr, Trinity Coll., Cambridge, 1991–94; Visiting Fellow: Pittsburgh Univ., 1985; Princeton Univ., 1991; LSE, 1994; All Souls Coll., Oxford, 1995; Vis. Prof., Essex Univ., 2004–07. Leverhulme Emeritus Fellow, 2008. Pres., British Soc. for Philos. of Sci., 1989–91; Trustee, Archive Trust for Res. in Math. Scis and Philosophy, 2008–12. Mem., Acad. Internat. de Philosophie des Sciences, 1995. FKC 2000. Lakatos Award in Philosophy of Science, 1988. Editor, Studies in History and Philosophy of Modern Physics, 1993–2001. *Publications:* Incompleteness, Nonlocality and Realism, 1987; From Physics to Metaphysics, 1995; (with T. Debs) Objectivity, Invariance and Convention, 2007; (with S. Groom) God, Belief and Explanation, 2011; papers in learned jls. *Recreations:* tennis, poetry, books, music. *Address:* 119 Rivermead Court, Hurlingham, SW6 3SD. *T:* (020) 7736 6767. *Clubs:* Athenæum, Hurlingham.

**REDHOUSE, Naomi**; a District Judge (Magistrates' Courts), since 2010; b London, 1 Dec. 1955; d of late Alexander Redhouse and Diana Redhouse (née Behr); one s one d. Educ: Hendon Co. Grammar Sch.; King's Coll., Cambridge (BA 1977); Coll. of Law. Admitted solicitor, 1984; a Dep. District Judge (Magistrates' Courts), 2003–10. Publications: with Mark Ashford: Defending Young People in the Criminal Justice System, 3rd edn 2006; Blackstone's Youth Court Handbook 2014–15, 2013. Recreations: walking, eating, cooking, friends.

**REDING, Dr Viviane**; Member (Christian Democrats) for Luxembourg, European Parliament, 2014–18; b 27 April 1951; m; three s. Educ: Sorbonne, Paris (PhD). Journalist, Luxemburger Wort, 1978–99; Pres., Luxembourg Union of Journalists, 1986–98. MP (PCS) Luxembourg, 1979–89; MEP (EPP) Luxembourg, 1989–99; Mem., 1999–2014, a Vice-Pres., 2010–14, EC. Nat. Pres., Christian-Social Women, 1988–93; Vice Pres., Parti Chrétien-Social, Luxembourg, 1995–99.

**REDMAN, Rev. Anthony James**, FRICS; Partner, 1985–2017, Practice Consultant, since 2017, Whitworth Co. Partnership LLP, Architects and Surveyors (Managing Partner, 1985–2002); b 1 May 1951; s of late Alan Redman and Diana Redman (née Cooke); m 1974, Caroline Blackwood Ford; two d. Educ: Walton-on-Thames Secondary Modern Sch.; Surbiton Grammar Sch.; Univ. of Reading (BSc Hons Estate Mgt); East Anglian MTS; Anglia Ruskin Univ. (MA Pastoral Theol. 2005). FRICS 1998; IHBC 1998. Surveyor: Lister Drew and Associates, 1972–74; Suffolk CC, 1974–79; Asst Surveyor, Whitworth & Hall, 1979–85. Surveyor of Fabric, St Edmundsbury Cathedral, 1991–2016. Chm., RICS Bldg Conservation Gp, 1997–2000; Mem., RICS Conservation Bd, 2000–03. Ordained deacon, 2003, priest, 2004; NSM, N Bury Team, 2003–05; Associate priest SSM (formerly Asst priest NSM), Blackbourne Team, 2006–; Asst Rural Dean, Ixworth Deanery, 2017–; Asst Diocesan Dir of Ordinands, 2017–. Member: Gen. Synod of C of E, (laity) 1989–2003 and (clergy) 2010–15 (Mem., Church Buildings Council, 2010–15); Council for Care of Churches, 1990–2001 (Jt Vice Chm., 1996–2001); Westminster Abbey Fabric Adv. Commn, 1998–; St Albans DAC, 1998–2004; Cathedrals Fabric Commn for England, 1999–2003; Cathedrals Measure Revision Cttee, 2001–02; Peterborough DAC, 2010–; Archbishop of Canterbury's Anglican/Romanian Orthodox Consultative Cttee, 2013–. Bishop's Advr for SSM Ministry, 2016–. Mem., Baptist Union Listed Bldg Adv. Panel, 1997–2010. Mem., Romanian Hospice of Hope Appeal Cttee, 2003–09; Trustee: Hospices of Hope, 2016– (Vice Chm., 2018–); Suffolk Historic Churches Trust, 2017–; Suffolk Preservation Soc., 2017–. Liveryman, Masons' Co., 2009–. Freeman, City of London, 2009. Mem., Order of St Edmund, 2017. Publications: (ed jtly) A Guide to Church Inspection and Repair, 1996; (ed with M. Carnell) A Taste of Transylvania, 2006. Recreations: gardening, painting, Romania, architectural history, avoiding household maintenance. Address: (office) 18 Hatter Street, Bury St Edmunds, Suffolk IP33 1NE. T: (01284) 760421. E: tredman@whitworth.co.uk

**REDMAN, Prof. Christopher Willard George**, FRCP, FRCOG; Consultant and Clinical Professor of Obstetric Medicine, Nuffield Department of Obstetrics and Gynaecology, Oxford University, 1992–2009, now Emeritus; Fellow of Lady Margaret Hall, Oxford, 1988–2009, now Honorary Research Fellow; b 30 Nov. 1941; s of late Roderick Oliver Redman and Annie Kathleen Redman (née Bancroft); m 1964, Corinna Susan Page; four s one d. Educ: St John's Coll., Cambridge (MA; MB, BChir). FRCP 1981; FRCOG (ad eund) 1993. Oxford University: Clinical Lectr, Dept of Regius Prof. of Medicine, 1970–76; Univ. Lectr and Consultant, Nuffield Dept of Obstetrics and Gynaecol., 1976–89; Clinical Reader and Cons., 1989–92. Pres., Internat. Soc. for Study of Hypertension in Pregnancy, 2006–08. Publications: scientific articles about pre-eclampsia in med. jls. Recreation: hill-walking. Address: Nuffield Department of Obstetrics and Gynaecology, John Radcliffe Maternity Hospital, Headington, Oxford OX3 9DU. T: (01865) 221009.

**REDMAYNE, Charles George Mariner**; Chief Executive Officer, HarperCollins UK, since 2013; b London, 30 Aug. 1966; s of Richard Redmayne and late Maxine Redmayne (née Brodrick, later Gray); m 1993, Annabel Jane Grayburn; one s one d. Educ: Eton Coll.; RMA, Sandhurst. Work in advertising and mktg; Founder: RCL Communications, 1993; Blink TV, 1996; Mykindaplace Ltd, 2000–06; Hd, Commercial Partnerships, Sky Online Business Unit, BSkyB, 2006–08; HarperCollins: Gp Digital Dir, HarperCollins UK, 2008–09; Exec. Vice Pres. and Chief Digital Officer, NY, 2009–11; CEO, Pottermore, 2011–13. Pres., Publishers Assoc., 2018–19. Recreations: cricket, tennis, ski-ing, golf, shooting, wine, reading, Scrabble, friends. Address: HarperCollins UK, The News Building, 1 London Bridge Street, SE1 9GF. T: (020) 8307 4399. E: Charlie.Redmayne@HarperCollins.co.uk. Club: Hurlingham.

**REDMAYNE, Clive**; retired aeronautical engineer; b 27 July 1927; s of late Procter Hubert Redmayne and Emma (née Torkington); m 1952, Vera Muriel, d of late Wilfred Toplis and Elsie Maud Toplis; one s one d. Educ: Stockport Sch. BSc (Hons Maths) London External. CEng, MIMechE. Fairey Aviation Co.: apprentice, 1944–48; Stress Office, 1948–50; English Electric Co., Warton: Stress Office, 1950–51; A. V. Roe & Co., Chadderton: Stress Office, 1951–55; A. V. Roe & Co., Weapons Research Div., Woodford: Head of Structural Analysis, 1955–62; Structures Dept, RAE, 1962–67; Asst Director, Project Time and Cost Analysis, Min. of Technology, 1967–70; Sen. Officers' War Course, RNC, Greenwich, 1970; Asst Dir, MRCA, MoD(PE), 1970–74; Division Leader, Systems Engrg, NATO MRCA Management Agency (NAMMA), Munich, 1974–76; Chief Supt, A&AEE, Boscombe Down, 1976–78; Dir, Harrier Projects, MoD(PE), 1978–80; Director General, Future Projects, MoD(PE), 1980–81; Dir Gen. Aircraft 3, Procurement Exec., MoD, 1981–84. Recreations: reading, chess, bridge. Address: 6 Hanna Court, 195–199 Wilmslow Road, Handforth, Cheshire SK9 3JX. T: (01625) 526315.

**REDMAYNE, Sir Giles (Martin)**, 3rd Bt cr 1964, of Rushcliffe, co. Nottingham; Managing Director, Purpose Design, since 2004; b Chelmsford, 1 Dec. 1968; s of Hon. Sir Nicholas John Redmayne, 2nd Bt, and Ann Redmayne (née Saunders) (d 1985); S father, 2008; m 1994, Claire Ann O'Halloran; three s. Educ: Radley Coll. Man. Dir, Reef Design, 1996–2010. Recreations: shooting, ski-ing. Heir: s George Martin John Redmayne, b 13 April 2001. Address: Walcote Lodge, Walcote, Lutterworth, Leics LE17 4JR. E: redmayne@atlas.co.uk.

**REDMOND, Sir Anthony (Gerard)**, Kt 2011; CPFA; Chairman and Chief Executive, Commission for Local Administration, and Local Government Ombudsman, 2001–10; b 18 May 1945; s of Alfonso and Florence Redmond; m 1973, Christine Mary Pinnington; two s two d. Educ: St Mary's Coll., Crosby. CPFA 1968. IRRV 2011. Liverpool City Council: various accountancy and audit posts, 1962–75; Chief Accountant, 1975–78; Dep. Treas., Wigan MBC, 1978–82; Treasurer: and Dep. Chief Exec., Knowsley MBC, 1982–87; Merseyside Police Authy, 1985–87; W London Waste Authy, 1987–2001; Chief Exec., London Borough of Harrow, 1987–2001. Mem., Local Govt Boundary Commn for England, 2011–18; Chm., Consumer Council for Water (London and SE), 2013–. Treas., UNICEF UK, 2011–. Course Dir, Public Admin Internat., 2012–. FRSA 1994; Fellow, CPA Australia, 2012. Friend: Royal Opera Hse; Royal Acad., until 2017; Nat. Trust; Patron, Allied Dancing Assoc., 2012–. Recreations: sport, theatre, ballet, good food and fine wines. Clubs: MCC; Wasps Rugby, Waterloo Rugby (Blundellsands), Lancashire Rugby.

**REDMOND, Ian Michael**, OBE 2006; CBiol, FZS, FLS; independent wildlife biologist, since 1979; Consultant: Born Free Foundation, since 1987; UN Food and Agriculture Organisation, since 2009; Ambassador, UNEP Convention on Migratory Species, since 2010; Ambassador and Consultant, Virtual Ecotourism, since 2012; b 11 April 1954; s of Maj. Peter Redmond, RAMC (retd) and Margaret Redmond; m 1982, Caroline Ireland; two s. Educ: Beverley Grammar Sch., E Yorks; Kelvin Hall High Sch.; Univ. of Keele (BSc Hons Biol. with Geol. 1976). FZS 1979; MRSB (MIBiol 1985), CBiol 1986. Res. Asst to Dr Dian Fossey, Karisoke Res. Centre, Rwanda, 1976–78; zoologist, Operation Drake, PNG, 1979; field conservationist, Fauna Preservation Soc., Mt Gorilla Project, Rwanda, 1980; zoologist/botanist, Operation Drake, Kenya, 1980; estabd Mt Elgon Elephant Caves Res. Project, Kenya, 1981–. Hon. Res. Associate, Dept of Psychol., Univ. of Hull, 1981–. Mem., Primate Specialist Gp, IUCN Species Survival Commn, 2000–. Scientific Advr for, and sometimes featured in, over 100 natural history documentaries, e.g. by BBC, Nat. Geographic, US, German and French TV, 1977–; documentaries include: Pembe ya Ndovu (we want ivory and we want more now) (Exec. Producer), 2014; When Giants Fall (Prod./biol consultant), 2014; The Gorilla Family and Me, 2015; The Elephant Family and Me, 2016; Close Calls on Camera, 2017; Wild Daze, 2018; Der Verbündete der Höhlenelefanten, 2018; freelance lecturer: UK and Africa, 1978–; N America, 1986–; public speaker: Foyles Lecture Agency, 1980–2000; Gordon Poole Agency, 2006–; Vis. Lectr, Oxford Brookes Univ., 2011–. Freelance natural history photo-journalist, 1982–; reporter, BBC Wildlife Mag., 1983–84; Leader, Wildlife Special Interest Tours, 1983–. Consultant, 1986–, various conservation and animal welfare orgns, including: Dian Fossey Gorilla Fund (formerly Digit Fund); Internat. Fund for Animal Welfare; Internat. Primate Protection League; WSPA, etc. Accredited observer: Convention on Internat. Trade in Endangered Species of Wild Fauna and Flora, Lausanne, 1989, Kyoto, 1992, Fort Lauderdale, 1994, Harare, 1997, Nairobi, 2000, Santiago, Chile, 2002, Bangkok, 2004 and 2013, The Hague, 2007, Doha, 2010, Bangkok, 2013; Johannesburg, 2016; Convention on Biological Diversity, Kuala Lumpur, 2004, Curitiba, 2006, Bonn, 2008, Nagoya, 2010; UN Framework Convention on Climate Change, Bali, 2007, Poznan, 2008, Copenhagen, 2009, Paris, 2015; UNEP Convention on Migratory Species, Rome, 2008, Bergen, 2011. Founder: and Co-ordinator, African Ele-Fund, 1987– (Co-founder, Elefriends, subseq. part of Born Free Foundn, 1989); and Chm., UK Rhino Gp, 1993–2003; and Chm., Ape Alliance, 1996–; Hd, Tech. Support Team, 2001–05, Chief Consultant, 2005–09, Envoy, 2009–12, Consultant, 2012–, UNEP/UNESCO Great Ape Survival Partnership (formerly Project, and under contract to Born Free Foundn and UNEP, 2001–11); Consultant, The Last of the Great Apes (3D film), 2012. Mem., British Herpetological Soc., 1981–. Member: Yorks Wildlife Trust, 1970–; Jersey Wildlife Preservation Trust, 1973–; Fauna and Flora Internat., 1978–; E African Wildlife Soc., 1980–; Elephant Res. Foundn (formerly Elephant Interest Gp), 1982–; Primate Soc. of GB, 1982– (Mem. Conservation Wkg Party, 1988–; Mem. Council, 1996–99, 2012–16; Ed., Primate Eye, 2016–); Wildlife Conservation Soc. of Tanzania, 1992–; Elephant, Primates and Rhino/Tiger Wkg Gps, Species Survival Network, 1995–; Mem. Bd, Internat. Primate Protection League, 2018–. Trustee: Orangutan Foundn-UK, 1993–; The Gorilla Organization (formerly Dian Fossey Gorilla Fund Europe), 2004– (Chm., Bd of Trustees, 2012–); Great Ape Film Initiative, 2006–; Thin Green Line Foundn (UK), 2014–. TEDx talk on Gardeners of the Forest (apes and elephants), Southampton, 2014. Co-founder, www.Ecostreamz.com, 2017. Ambassador, UN Year of the Gorilla, 2009. FLS 2008. DUniv Oxford Brookes, 2011; Hon. DSc: Roehampton, 2014; Keele, 2018. Conservation Award, Internat. Fund for Animal Welfare, 2013; Animal Heroes Award, RSPCA/Mirror, 2017. Publications: The Elephant in the Bush, 1990; (with V. Harrison) The World of Elephants, 1990; Monkeys and Apes, 1990; Wildlife at Risk: Gorillas, 1990; Wildlife at Risk: Elephants, 1990; The Elephant Book, 1990, 2nd edn 2001 (Friends of the Earth Earthworm Award, 1991); (jtly) Elephants - the Deciding Decade (Canada), 1991, 2nd edn 1997, UK edn as Elephants, Saving the Gentle Giants, 1993; Eyewitness Elephant, 1993; Eyewitness Gorilla and other primates, 1995; The Primate Family Tree: primates of the world, 2008; (jtly) Last Stand of the Gorilla: environmental crime and conflict in the Congo Basin, 2010; (jtly) Stolen Apes, 2013; (contrib.) Gorilla Pathology and Health: with a catalogue of preserved materials, 2017; (ed and contrib.) Remembering Great Apes, 2018; contrib. numerous scientific reports and papers, news reports and feature articles to wildlife mags worldwide, and newspapers incl. Guardian, Sunday Times, Kuwait Times, Arab Post, Hong Kong Standard, Jakarta Post, Daily Mirror, Geographical Mag., Wanderlust, Travel Africa, Nat. Geographic, BBC Wildlife Mag. Recreations: natural history, travel, outdoor activities, collecting antiquarian books and 78rpm records, minimum-intervention gardening and home maintenance. Address: Ape Alliance, c/o RSPCA Building, Lansdown, Stroud, Glos GL5 1BG. T: and Fax: (01453) 765228. E: ele@globalnet.co.uk. W: www.twitter.com/4apes.

**REDMOND, Imelda**, CBE 2010; National Director, Healthwatch England, since 2017; b 7 June 1959; d of Andy and Alice Redmond; m Jo Clare; one step s. Educ: Froebel Inst. (BA Hons (Social Admin) Univ. of London). Dir, Markfield Project, 1989–98; Dep. CEO, 1998–2003, Chief Exec., 2003–11, Carers UK; Dir, Policy and Public Affairs, Marie Curie Cancer Care, 2011–14; Chief Exec., 4Children, 2015–16.

**REDMOND, Phil**, CBE 2004; writer and television producer; Founder, The Mersey Television Co. Ltd (Chairman, 1981–2005); Chairman, Merseyfilm, since 2003; m Alexis Jane Redmond. Educ: Univ. of Liverpool (BA Hons). Writer, Grange Hill, 1978–81; Executive Producer: Brookside, 1982–2003; Hollyoaks, 1996–2005; Grange Hill, 2002–08. Creative Chair, 2008 Eur. Capital of Culture, Liverpool, 2007–09. Chm. of Trustees, National Museums and Galleries of Liverpool, 2008–17. Hon. Prof. of Media, 1989, Fellow, 1989, Ambassador Fellow, 2010, Liverpool John Moores Univ. FRSA 1996. Hon. DLitt: Chester, 2010; Liverpool, 2010. Hon. Freedom, City of Liverpool, 2018. Recreations: photography, boating, digital media. Address: (office) Merseyfilm, Tirley Garth, Willington, Tarporley, Cheshire CW6 0RQ.

**REDSHAW, Peter Robert Gransden**; HM Diplomatic Service, retired; Group Security Adviser, Gallaher Ltd, 1996–2004; b 16 April 1942; s of late Robert Henry Gransden Redshaw and Audrey Nita Redshaw (née Ward); m 1970, Margaret Shaun (née Mizon) (d 2013); one s two d. Educ: Boxgrove School; Charterhouse; Trinity College, Cambridge (MA). ACA. Price Waterhouse, 1964–67; FCO, 1968; Kampala, 1970–73; 1st Sec., 1971; FCO, 1973; Lagos, 1982–85; Counsellor, 1985; FCO, 1985–88; Kuala Lumpur, 1988–91; FCO, 1992–96. Recreations: books, history, sailing, travel. Clubs: Kampala; Woking Tennis & Croquet.

**REDSHAW, Tina Susan**; HM Diplomatic Service; Ambassador to Cambodia, since 2018; b 25 Jan. 1961; d of Trevor Redshaw and Doreen Cooper; m 2001, Phong Phun Khogapun; one d. Educ: York Univ. (BA Hons Lang./Linguistics); Open Univ. (MSc Develt Mgt). Voluntary Service Overseas: Prog. Dir, China, 1990–94; Regl Prog. Manager, SE Asia, 1994–99; entered FCO, 1999; China Hong Kong Dept, 1999–2000; First Sec., Beijing, 2000–03; Ambassador, E Timor, 2003–06; Hd of Environment, Energy and Infrastructure, UK Trade and Investment, Beijing, 2007–11; Dep. Hd, Climate Change, FCO, 2011–13; Consul-Gen., Chongqing, China, 2013–16. Recreations: photography, theatre, dance, jazz music, swimming, creative writing. E: tina.redshaw@fco.gov.uk.

**REDWOOD, Rt Hon. Sir John (Alan),** Kt 2019; PC 1993; DPhil; MP (C) Wokingham, since 1987; b 15 June 1951; s of William Charles Redwood and Amy Emma Redwood (née Champion); m 1974, Gail Felicity Chippington (marr. diss. 2004); one s one d. Educ: Kent Coll., Canterbury; Magdalen and St Antony's Colls, Oxford; MA, DPhil Oxon. MCSI. Fellow, All Souls Coll., Oxford, 1972–87, 2003–05, 2007–. Investment Adviser, Robert Fleming & Co., 1973–77; Investment Manager and Dir, N. M. Rothschild & Sons, 1977–87; Norcros plc: Dir, 1985–89; Jt Dep. Chm., 1986–87; non-exec. Chm., 1987–89. Non-executive Chairman: Hare Hatch Hldgs Ltd (formerly Mabey Securities), 1999–2008; Concentric plc, 2003–08; Pan Asset Capital Mgt, 2007–09; non-exec. Dir, BNB, 2001–07. Investment Advr, CS (formerly Evercore) Pan Asset, 2007–. Adviser, Treasury and Civil Service Select Cttee, 1981; Head of PM's Policy Unit, 1983–85. Councillor, Oxfordshire CC, 1973–77. Contested (C) Peckham, 1982. Parly Under Sec. of State, DTI, 1989–90; Minister of State: DTI, 1990–92; DoE, 1992–93; Sec. of State for Wales, 1993–95; Opposition front bench spokesman on trade and industry, 1997–99, on the envmt, 1999–2000; Shadow Sec. of State for De-regulation, 2004–05. Head, Cons. Parly Campaigns Unit, 2000–01; Chairman: Cons. Party Policy Review on Econ. Competitiveness, 2005–10; Cons. Economic Affairs Cttee, 2010–15; Cons. Treasury Cttee, 2015–. Vis. Prof., Middx Business Sch., 2000–. Governor of various schools, 1974–83. Qualified Ind. Financial Advr, CISI, 2012; Chartered Fellow, CISI. Publications: Reason, Ridicule and Religion, 1976; Public Enterprise in Crisis, 1980; (with John Hatch) Value for Money Audits, 1981; (with John Hatch) Controlling Public Industries, 1982; Going for Broke, 1984; Equity for Everyman, 1986; Popular Capitalism, 1988; The Global Marketplace, 1994; The Single Currency, 1995; Action Not Words, 1996; Our Currency, Our Country, 1997; The Death of Britain?, 1999; Stars and Strife, 2001; Just Say No, 2001; Singing the Blues, 2004; Superpower Struggles, 2005; I Want to Make a Difference, 2006; After the Credit Crunch, 2009; The Future of the Euro, 2012; We Don't Believe You, 2019; pamphlets on Cons. matters. Recreations: water sports, village cricket, daily blog (www.johnredwood.com). Address: House of Commons, SW1A 0AA. T: (office) (020) 7219 4205, (home) (020) 7976 6603. W: www.johnredwoodsdiary.com.

**REDWOOD, Sir Peter (Boverton),** 3rd Bt cr 1911; Colonel, late King's Own Scottish Borderers, retired 1987; b 1 Dec. 1937; o s of Sir Thomas Boverton Redwood, 2nd Bt, TD, and Ruth Mary Redwood (née Creighton, then Blair); S father, 1974; m 1964, Gilian, o d of John Lee Waddington Wood, Limuru, Kenya; three d. Educ: Gordonstoun. National Service, 1956–58, 2nd Lieut, Seaforth Highlanders; regular commn, KOSB, 1959; served in UK (despatches 1972), BAOR, Netherlands, ME, Africa and Far East; Staff Coll., Camberley, 1970; Nat. Defence Coll., Latimer, 1978–79. Dir, SERCO-IAL Ltd, 1992–95. Vice-Pres., Royal Bath and West of England Soc., 2013–. Mem., Queen's Body Guard for Scotland (Royal Co. of Archers). Liveryman, Goldsmiths' Co. Recreations: shooting, silver and silversmithing, archery. Heir: half-b Robert Boverton Redwood [b 24 June 1953; m 1978, Mary Elizabeth Wright; one s one d]. Address: c/o Svenska Handelsbanken AB, London Road Office Park, London Road, Salisbury, Wilts SP1 3HP.

**REECE, Damian John;** Managing Partner, Instinctif Partners (formerly Managing Partner and Deputy Chief Executive, College Hill Capital Markets), since 2013; b Yalding, Kent, 15 Oct. 1966; s of Malcolm Reece and Sheila Reece; m 1995, Page Shepherd; one s one d. Educ: St Joseph's RC Sch., Horwich; Thornleigh Salesian Coll., Bolton; Univ. of Manchester (BA Econs). Staff writer, Investors Chronicle, 1993–94; Dep. Personal Finance Ed., The Sunday Telegraph, 1994–98; Consumer Industries Corresp., Sunday Business, 1998–99; Asst City Ed., The Sunday Telegraph, 1999–2003; City Ed., The Independent, 2003–05; Dep. City Ed., 2005–06, City Ed., 2006–07, The Daily Telegraph; Hd of Business, Telegraph Media Gp, 2007–13. Personal Finance Journalist of Year, 1996; Consumer Industries Journalist of Year, 2000. Publications: The Sunday Telegraph A–Z Guide to Family Finance, 1996. Recreations: family, the great outdoors, music and the arts, sport, clocks. Address: 116 Wilberforce Road, N4 2SU. T: 07931 598593, (020) 7457 2020. E: damian.reece@instinctif.com.

**REECE, Dr Henry Michael;** Secretary to Delegates, and Chief Executive, Oxford University Press, 1998–2009; Fellow of Jesus College, Oxford, 1998–2009, now Emeritus; b 10 Aug. 1953; s of David Reece and Persis Rebecca Reece; m (marr. diss. 2005); m 2009, Susan Norine Froud. Educ: Univ. of Bristol (BA 1st Cl. Hons); St John's Coll., Oxford (DPhil Modern Hist. 1981; Hon. Fellow 2010). Tutor in Hist., Univ. of Exeter, 1977–78; Prentice Hall International: Field Sales Editor, 1979–82; Academic Sales Manager, 1982–84; UK Sales Manager, 1984–85; Asst Vice-Pres., Simon & Schuster Internat., 1985–88; Exec. Ed., Allyn & Bacon (US), 1988–91; Man. Dir, Pitman Publishing, 1991–94; Executive Director: Longman Gp Ltd, 1994–95; Pearson Professional, 1995–97. Mem. Council, Publishers Assoc., 1999–2006 (Pres., 2004–05). Hon. DLitt Oxford, 2010. Publications: The Army in Cromwellian England, 1649–1660, 2013. Recreations: reading crime novels, watching Wales win at Rugby, cycling, kayaking, walking the dog. Address: Jesus College, Turl Street, Oxford OX1 3DW.

**REECE, Jason; His Honour Judge Reece;** a Circuit Judge, since 2018; b Wolverhampton, 28 Dec. 1968; s of Terence and Barbara Reece; m 1993, Ila Patel; one d. Educ: Pool Hayes Community Sch.; Nottingham Univ. (BA Hons Hist. 1990; MPhil Hist. 1992); Hughes Hall, Cambridge (PGCE 1992); Nottingham Trent Univ. (Postgrad. DipLaw 1999; BVC 2000). Teacher, King's Sch., Peterborough, 1992–98; called to the Bar, Inner Temple, 2000; in practice as barrister, St Mary's Chambers, Nottingham, 2000–16 (Jt Hd of Chambers, 2013–16); a Dep. Dist Judge, 2010–16; Dist Judge, 2016–18. Vis. Fellow, Nottingham Law Sch., 2013–. Contested (Lab) Huntingdon, 1997; Newark, 2005. Jt Ed., Notts Annual Bird Report, 2008–. Publications: The Status of Birds in Nottinghamshire, 2009. Recreations: birding, gardening, natural history, books, cricket, political history. Address: Lincoln County Court and Family Court, 360 High Street, Lincoln LN5 7PS. T: (01522) 551500. E: enquiries@lincoln.countycourt.gsi.gov.uk.

**REECE, Richard Marsden,** DPhil; FSA; Reader in Late Roman Archaeology and Numismatics, Institute of Archaeology, University College London, 1994–99; b 25 March 1939; o s of Richard Marsden Reece and Alice Reece (née Wedel). Educ: Cirencester Grammar Sch.; UCL (BSc Biochem. 1961); Wadham Coll., Oxford (DipEd 1962; DPhil 1972). FSA 1968. Asst Master, St John's Sch., Leatherhead, 1962–65; Head of Chem. Dept, St George's Sch., Harpenden, 1966–68; London Institute of Archaeology, subseq. Institute of Archaeology, University College London: Lectr, 1970–81; Sen. Lectr, 1981–93; Tutor to Arts students, 1988–91. Linecar Lectr, British Numismatic Soc., 2011. Chairman: John Jones Trust, 2014–; Powell's Educnl Foundn, 2015–18. Hon. Pres., Scientific Cttee, Jl Archaeol Numismatics, 2011–. Membre d'Honneur, Romanian Numismatic Soc.; Hon. FRNS 2003 (RNS Medal 2009). Derek Allen Award, British Acad., 2014. Publications: Roman Coins, 1970; Excavations on Iona 1964–74, 1981; Coinage in Roman Britain, 1987, revd edn as Coinage of Roman Britain, 2002; My Roman Britain, 1988; Later Roman Empire, 1999; Roman Coins and Archaeology: collected papers, 2003; Cotswold Studies V, 2015; articles in learned jls. Recreations: reading novels, music. Address: The Apple Loft, The Waterloo, Cirencester, Glos GL7 2PZ.

**REED, Rt Hon. Lord; Robert John Reed;** PC 2008; a Justice, since 2012, and President, from Jan. 2020, Supreme Court of the United Kingdom (Deputy President, 2018–Jan. 2020); b 7 Sept. 1956; s of George and Elizabeth Reed; m 1988, Jane Mylne; two d. Educ: George Watson's Coll.; Univ. of Edinburgh (LLB 1st Cl. Hons; Vans Dunlop Schol.); Balliol Coll., Oxford (DPhil). Admitted to Faculty of Advocates, 1983; called to the Bar, Inner Temple, 1991, Bencher, 2012; Standing Junior Counsel: Scottish Educn Dept, 1988–89; Scottish Office Home and Health Dept, 1989–95; QC (Scot.) 1995; Advocate Depute, 1996–98; a Senator of the Coll. of Justice in Scotland, 1998–2012; a Judge of the Outer House of the Court of Session, 1998–2008; Principal Commercial Judge, 2006–08; Mem., Inner House, 2008–12; ad hoc Judge, European Court of Human Rights, 1999–; a non-perm. Judge, Hong Kong Court of Final Appeal, 2017–. Expert advr, EU/Council of Europe Jt Initiative with Turkey, 2002–04. Chm., Franco-British Judicial Co-operation Cttee, 2005–12; Pres., EU Forum of Judges for the Envmt, 2006–08; Mem. Adv. Bd, 2001–06, Trustee, 2015–, British Inst. Internat. and Comparative Law; Mem. Adv. Bd, UN Task Force on Access to Justice, 2006–09. Convener, Children in Scotland, 2006–12. Chm., Centre for Commercial Law, Univ. of Edinburgh, 2008–12; Visitor: Balliol Coll., Oxford, 2011–; Linacre Coll., Oxford, 2018–; St Cross Coll., Oxford, 2018–; Wolfson Coll., Oxford, 2018– (Hon. Fellow, 2018). Hon. Prof., Univ. of Glasgow, 2006–. High Steward, Univ. of Oxford, 2018–. Scottish Ed., European Law Reports, 1997–2011. FRSE 2015. Hon. LLD Glasgow, 2013. Publications: (with J. M. Murdoch) Human Rights Law in Scotland, 2001, 4th edn 2017; contribs to various books and jls on public law. Recreation: music. Address: Supreme Court of the United Kingdom, Parliament Square, SW1P 3BD.
[To be created a Baron (Life Peer), but title not gazetted at time of going to press.]

**REED, Sir Alec (Edward),** Kt 2011; CBE 1994; Founder, Reed Executive PLC, 1960; b 16 Feb. 1934; s of Leonard Reed and Annie Underwood; m 1961, Adrianne Mary Eyre; two s one d. Educ: Grammar School. FCMA. Founded: Medicare PLC; ICC PLC; Reed Business Sch.; Womankind Worldwide; Ethiopiaid UK, Australia, Ireland, Canada; Women @ Risk; Acad. of Enterprise; Alec Reed Acad.; The Big Give. President: Inst. of Employment Consultants, 1974–78; Internat. Confedn of Private Employment Agency Assocs, 1978–81. Hon. Prof., Enterprise and Innovation, Royal Holloway, Univ. of London, 1993–2003 (Hon. Fellow, RHBNC, 1988); Vis. Prof., London Metropolitan (formerly London Guildhall) Univ., 1999–2004; Hon. Prof., Warwick Univ., 2001–14. Mem. Council, RHC, 1979–85. Fellow, Beacon Fellowship Charitable Trust, 2010 (Beacon Prize, 2010). Hon. PhD London Guildhall, 1999; DUniv Open, 2012. Publications: Innovation in Human Resource Management, 2002; Capitalism is Dead, Peoplism Rules, 2003; I Love Mondays (autobiog.), 2012. Recreations: family, ballet, cinema, tennis, riding, portrait painting, bridge. Address: Reed Foundation, The Peak, 5 Wilton Road, SW1V 1AN.
See also J. A. Reed.

**REED, Andrew John,** OBE 2012; Director, Saje Impact, since 2010; b 17 Sept. 1964; s of James Donald Reed and Margaret Anne Reed; m 1992, Sarah Elizabeth Chester. Educ: Riverside Jun. Sch.; Stonehill High Sch.; Longslade Community Coll.; Leicester Poly. (BA Hons Public Admin 1987). Parly Asst to Keith Vaz, MP, 1987–88; Urban Regeneration Officer, Leicester CC, 1988–90; Sen. Economic Develt Officer, 1990–94, European Officer, 1994–97, Leics CC. MP (Lab and Co-op) Loughborough, 1997–2010; contested (Lab and Co-op) same seat, 2010. Parliamentary Private Secretary: to Minister for Sport, 2000–01; to Sec. of State for Envmt, Food and Rural Affairs, 2001–03; to Paymaster General, 2005–07. Director: Special Olympics Bd, 2010–; Amateur Swimming Assoc., 2010–13; Sports Think Tank, 2011–; Sport and Recreation Alliance, 2011– (Chm., 2011–15); Chairman: Leics and Rutland Sport, 2005–18; Volleyball England Foundn, 2011–13; Mem. Bd, British Basketball League Foundn, 2011–. Sen. Partner, Green and Gold Partnership, 2013–17; non-exec. Dir, EP Partners, 2015–; Mem. Bd and Vice Chair, Leicester and Leics Enterprise Partnership. Mem., Evangelical Alliance Council, 2009–14. Trustee: Richard Engelhardt Trust, 2010–; Sports Chaplaincy UK, 2013–18; World Vision UK, 2013–19. Vis. Prof. of Sports Policy and Develt, Liverpool John Moores Univ., 2014–. Recreations: Rugby, fitness, tennis, running, Member, Openheaven Church, Loughborough. Address: 17 Nursery Lane, Quorn, Loughborough, Leics LE12 8BH. Clubs: Birstall Rugby Football, Leicester Rugby Football.

**REED, Anna Jane;** see Boase, A. J.

**REED, Air Cdre April Anne,** RRC 1981; Director of RAF Nursing Services, 1984–85, retired; b 25 Jan. 1930; d of Captain Basil Duck Reed, RN, and Nancy Mignon Ethel Reed. Educ: Channing Sch., Highgate. SRN, SCM. SRN training, Middlesex Hosp., 1948–52; midwifery training, Royal Maternity Hosp., Belfast, 1953; joined Royal Air Force, 1954; Dep. Matron, 1970; Sen. Matron, 1976; Principal Matron, 1981; Matron in Chief (Director), 1984. Recreations: sailing, ornithology, antiques, gardening, interest in oriental carpets. Address: 1 Garners Row, Walsingham Road, Burnham Thorpe, King's Lynn, Norfolk PE31 8HN. Club: Royal Air Force.

**REED, Barry St George Austin,** CBE 1988; MC 1951; Chairman, Austin Reed Group PLC, 1973–96; b 5 May 1931; s of late Douglas Austin Reed and Mary Ellen (née Philpott); m 1st 1956, Patricia (née Bristow) (d 2002); one s one d; 2nd, 2005, Mary Rose (née Lee Warner), widow of N. S. Farquharson. Educ: Rugby Sch. Commnd Middlesex Regt (DCO), 1950; served Korea, 1950–51; TA, 1951–60. Joined Austin Reed Group, 1953; Dir, 1958–99; Man. Dir, 1966–85. National Westminster Bank: Dir, City and West End Regions, 1980–87; Dir, 1987–90; Chm., Eastern Regl Adv. Bd, 1987–92; Dir, UK Adv. Bd, 1990–92. Pres., Menswear Assoc. of Britain, 1966–67; Chairman: Retail Alliance, 1967–70; British Knitting and Clothing Export Council, 1985–89; Dir, British Apparel and Textile Confedn, 1992–99; Member: Bd, Retail Trading-Standards Assoc., 1964–78; Consumer Protection Adv. Cttee, 1973–79; European Trade Cttee, 1975–84; Cttee, Fleming American Exempt Fund, 1979–94; Council, Royal Warrant Holders Assoc., 1980–2012 (Pres., 1990). Dir, Independent Broadcasting Telethon Trust Ltd, 1991–94. Pres., Vale of York Cons. Assoc., 1995–2000. Dir, Hambleton and Richmondshire Partnership Against Crime, 1997–99. Chm., Queen Elizabeth Scholarship Trust, 1990–95; Trustee, Third Age Challenge Trust, 1994–96. Member: Ripon and Leeds Dio. Synod, 1997–2006; Ripon and Leeds Dio. Bd of Finance, 1997–2009; Vice-Chm., 1997–2000, Chm., 2000–03, Ripon and Leeds Dio. Parsonages Bd; Chm., Ripon and Leeds Dio. Property and Estates Cttee, 2003–09. Freeman, City of London, 1963; Liveryman, Glovers' Co., 1963– (Master, 1980–81). DL Greater London, 1977–99; Rep. DL, London Borough of Hackney, 1980–86. FRSA. Publications: papers in clothing, textile and banking jls. Recreations: travel, gardens, reading. Address: The Old School, East Witton, Leyburn, N Yorks DL8 4SN. T: (01969) 625817. Clubs: Army and Navy, Pilgrims, MCC.
See also L. D. Reed.

**REED, David;** Regional Employment Judge (formerly Regional Chairman of Employment Tribunals), Newcastle upon Tyne, 1998–2017; b 11 Oct. 1946; s of Thomas and Olive Reed; m 1976, Sylvia Mary Thompson. Educ: London Univ. (LLB ext.). Admitted Solicitor (William Hutton Prize), 1972, in practice, 1972–91; full-time Chm., Industrial Tribunals, 1991–2017; Fee-paid Employment Judge, 2017–19.

**REED, Gavin Barras;** *b* 13 Nov. 1934; *s* of late Lt-Col Edward Reed and Greta Milburn (*née* Pybus); *m* 1957, Muriel Joyce, *d* of late Humphrey Vaughan Rowlands; one *s* three *d*. *Educ*: Eton; Trinity Coll., Cambridge (BA). National Service, Fleet Air Arm Pilot, 1953–55. Joined Newcastle Breweries Ltd, 1958; Dir, Scottish & Newcastle Breweries Ltd, 1970–94; Gp Man. Dir, 1988–91, Gp Vice-Chm., 1991–94, Scottish & Newcastle plc; Chairman: Wainhomes plc, 1994–98; Harmeny Educn Trust Ltd, 1995–2005; John Menzies plc, 1997–2002 (Dir, 1992–2002); Hamilton & Inches Ltd, 1998–2011; Maclay Gp plc, 2001–12; Dir, Burtonwood Brewery plc, 1996–2005. Chm., N Region, CBI, 1987–88. Liveryman, Brewers' Co., 1992–. *Recreation:* travelling. *Address:* West Farnley Grange, Corbridge, Northumberland NE45 5RP. *Club:* New (Edinburgh).

**REED, James Andrew;** Chairman: Reed Executive Ltd, since 2004; Reed Global Ltd, since 2008; *b* Woking, 12 April 1963; *s* of Sir Alec Edward Reed, *qv*; *m* 1991, Nicola Arkell; three *s* three *d*. *Educ*: St Paul's Sch., London; Christ Church, Oxford (MA Hons PPE); Harvard Business Sch. (MBA). Exec. Asst, Body Shop plc, 1984–85; Media Planner and Buyer, Saatchi & Saatchi plc, 1986; Project Adminr, Afghanaid, 1987–88; Producer, BBC Television, 1990–94; Reed Executive plc: non-exec. Dir, 1991–94; Ops Dir, 1994–96; Chief Operating Officer, 1996–97; Chief Exec., 1997–2004; Chairman: Reed Learning Ltd, 2004–; Reed in Partnership, 2004–; Reed Online Ltd, 2004–. Founder, Keep Britain Working Campaign, 2009. FCIPD 2003. *Publications:* (jtly) Put Your Mindset to Work, 2011; Why You?: 101 interview questions you'll never fear again, 2014. *Recreations:* cinema, horse riding, mountaineering, running, scuba diving, tennis. *Address:* Reed Executive Ltd, Dragon Court, 27–29 Macklin Street, WC2B 5LX. *T:* (020) 7616 2301. *E:* james.reed@reedglobal.com. *Club:* Brooks's.

**REED, Jamieson Ronald, (Jamie);** Head of Development and Community Relations, Sellafield Ltd, since 2017; *b* 4 Aug. 1973; *s* of Ronald and Gloria Reed; *m*; three *s* one *d*. *Educ*: Whitehaven Sch.; Manchester Univ. (BA English 1994); Univ. of Leicester (MA Mass Communications 2000). Researcher: EP, 1995–97; and Advr, Labour Gp, Cumbria CC, 1997–2000; Manager, TU and Community Sellafield Campaign, 2000–01; Public Affairs, BNFL, 2001–05. MP (Lab) Copeland, 2005–Jan. 2017. *Recreations:* spending time with my family, American literature, modern history, music, football, fell walking, Rugby League. *Address:* Sellafield Ltd, Seascale, Cumbria CA20 1PG.

**REED, Jane Barbara,** CBE 2000; Director, Times Newspaper Holdings Ltd, since 2002; Director of Corporate Affairs, News International plc, 1989–2000; 2nd *d* of late William and Gwendoline Reed, Letchworth, Herts. *Educ*: Royal Masonic Sch.; sundry further educational establishments. Journalist on numerous magazines; returned to Woman's Own, 1965; Editor, 1970–79; Publisher, IPC Women's Monthly Group, 1979–81; Editor-in-Chief, Woman magazine, 1981–82; IPC Magazines: Asst Man. Dir, Specialist Educn and Leisure Gp, 1983; Man. Dir, Holborn Publishing Gp, 1983–85; Man. Editor (Features), Today, News (UK) Ltd, 1985–86; Man. Editor, Today, 1986–89. Mem., Editl Bd, British Journalism Rev., 2004–12. Pres., Media Soc., 1995. Trustee (formerly Mem. Council), Nat. Literacy Trust, 1992–2016; Trustee, Media Trust, 1994–2014. Member: Royal Soc. COPUS, 1986–96; Nuffield Council for Bio-ethics, 1991–94; Council, Nat. Acad. of Writing, 2001–09. Trustee, St Katharine and Shadwell Trust, 1992–2009. Gov., Lady Margaret Sch., Fulham, 2011–. *Publications:* Girl About Town, 1964; (jtly) Kitchen Sink—or Swim?, 1982. *Address:* Fulham.

**REED, Ven. John Peter Cyril;** Archdeacon of Taunton, 1999–2016; *b* 21 May 1951; *s* of C. Gordon Reed and M. Joan Reed (*née* Stenning); *m* 1979, Gillian Mary Coles; one *s* one *d*. *Educ*: Monkton Combe Sch., Bath; King's Coll. London (BD, AKC 1978); Ripon Coll., Cuddesdon. With Imperial Group, 1969–73; Research and Marketing, Wales & the West Ltd, Cardiff, 1973–75. Deacon 1979, priest 1980; Curate, Croydon Parish Church, 1979–82; Precentor, St Albans Abbey, 1982–86; Rector, Timsbury and Priston and Chaplain for Rural Affairs, Archdeaconry of Bath, 1986–93; Team Rector, Ilminster and Dist Team Ministry, 1993–99. *Recreations:* family, cricket, tennis, fishing, countryside. *Address:* 11 Morwellham Cottages, Tavistock, Devon PL19 8JL. *T:* (01822) 834105. *E:* john.morwellham@hotmail.com.

**REED, (John William) Rupert;** QC 2014; *b* Dunfermline, 27 Nov. 1969; *s* of late Comdr Robert Reed, RN and of Joan Reed; *m* 2004, Anna Jane Boase, *qv*; one *s* two *d*. *Educ*: Sandroyd Sch.; Sherborne Sch.; Lincoln Coll., Oxford (BA Mod. Hist. and French 1992); Downing Coll., Cambridge (BA Law 1994); Harvard Law Sch. (LLM Law 1995). Called to the Bar, Lincoln's Inn, 1996, Cayman Is (ad hoc), 1999; in practice as a barrister, Wilberforce Chambers, 1997–2017, Serle Court Chambers, 2017–; Attorney Gen.'s C Panel of Treasury Counsel, 2000–05; Registered Advocate, DIFC Courts, 2009–. *Publications:* (jtly) Rules of the DIFC Courts, 2016; articles in Company, Banking and Commercial Law. *Recreations:* family, working from home, lunching with newspaper, cycling, classical and world music, French cinema, Arab news media. *Address:* Serle Court Chambers, 6 New Square, Lincoln's Inn, WC2A 3QS. *E:* rreed@serlecourt.co.uk.

**REED, Dame Julie Thérèse;** *see* Mellor, Dame J. T.

**REED, Laurance Douglas;** *b* 4 Dec. 1937; *s* of late Douglas Austin Reed and Mary Ellen Reed (*née* Philpott). *Educ*: Gresham's Sch., Holt; University Coll., Oxford (MA). Nat. Service, RN, 1956–58; worked and studied on Continent (Brussels, Bruges, Leyden, Luxembourg, Strasbourg, Paris, Rome, Bologna, Geneva), 1963–66; Public Sector Research Unit, 1967–69. MP (C) Bolton East, 1970–Feb. 1974; PPS to Chancellor of Duchy of Lancaster, 1973–74. Jt Sec., Parly and Scientific Cttee, 1971–74; Mem., Select Cttee on Science and Technology, 1971–74. *Publications:* Europe in a Shrinking World, 1967; An Ocean of Waste, 1972; Political Consequences of North Sea Oil, 1973; The Soay of Our Forefathers, 1986; Philpott of Fordingbridge, 1994; A Marginal Seat, 2012; Mary's Letters, 2013; A Midshipman on the Warrior, 2014. *Recreations:* gardening, historical research. *Address:* 14 Calumet, Reynolds Road, Beaconsfield, Bucks HP9 2LZ. *T:* (01494) 673153. *Clubs:* Carlton; Coningsby.
 See also B. St G. A. Reed.

**REED, Leslie Edwin,** PhD; Chief Industrial Air Pollution Inspector, Health and Safety Executive, 1981–85; *b* 6 Feb. 1925; *s* of Edwin George and Maud Gladys Reed; *m* 1947, Ruby; two *s*. *Educ*: Sir George Monoux Grammar Sch., Walthamstow; University Coll. London (BScEng, MScEng, PhD). Engineering Officer, RNVR, 1945–47; Fuel Research Station, 1950–58; Warren Spring Laboratory, 1958–70; Central Unit on Environmental Pollution, DoE, 1970–79; Head, Air and Noise Div., DoE, 1979–81. *Address:* 5 Devey Close, Knebworth, Herts SG3 6EN. *T:* (01438) 813272.

**REED, Dr Malcolm Christopher,** CBE 2004; FCILT, FCIHT, FIES; Chief Executive, Transport Scotland, 2005–09; *b* 24 Nov. 1944; *s* of James and Lilian Reed; marr. diss.; two *d*. *Educ*: Blue Coat Sch., Durham; Royal Grammar Sch., Newcastle upon Tyne; St Catherine's Coll., Oxford (MA); Nuffield Coll., Oxford; DPhil Oxon 1971. Asst Grade 1, Bodleian Liby, Oxford, 1968–69; Lectr, Dept of Econ. Hist., Univ. of Glasgow, 1969–74; Researcher, then Associate Dir, Planning Exchange, Glasgow, 1974–75; Planner, then Chief Public Transport Co-ordinator, Gtr Glasgow PTE, 1975–79; Strathclyde Regional Council: Chief Policy Planner, 1979–80; Sen. Exec. Officer, 1980–90; Asst Chief Exec., 1990–96; Dir Gen., Strathclyde PTE, 1997–2005. Adviser: Virgin Trains, 2009–14; Abellio UK, 2013–14. Interim Clerk, E Ayrshire Council, 1995. Chair, Contract Assurance Cttee, Nexus (Tyne and Wear Passenger Transport Exec.), 2009 (Mem., Metro Transition Asscn Cttee, 2016–17). Railway Heritage Committee: Mem., 1994–99; Dep. Chm., 1996–99; Member: Adv. Cttee, Rail Safety & Standards Bd, 2003–05; Adv. Panel, Railway Heritage Trust, 2007–; Adv. Panel, Centre for Transport Res., Univ. of Aberdeen, 2008–15; Council, Instn of Engrs and Shipbuilders in Scotland, 2008–11. Trustee, City of Durham Trust, 2011–. FCILT (FCIT 1993); FCIHT (FIHT 2006); CIES 2007, FIES 2014. Hon. Fellow, Instn of Railway Operators, 2014. FRSA. *Publications:* (ed) Railways in the Victorian Economy, 1969; Investment in Railways in Britain, 1975; A History of James Capel & Co., 1975; The London & North Western Railway: a history, 1996; contribs to Econ. Hist. Rev., Transport Hist., Scottish Jl Political Econ. *Recreations:* hill-walking, gardening, listening to music. *E:* malcolm.reed@live.co.uk. *Club:* Western (Glasgow).

**REED, Matthew Graham;** Chief Executive, Marie Curie, since 2019; *b* Reading, 29 Aug. 1968; *s* of Graham and Patricia Reed; *m* 1995, Dr Jennifer Candy; one *s* one *d*. *Educ*: Ranelagh Sch.; Univ. of Nottingham (BEng 1989); Ripon Coll. Cuddesdon (BA Oxon 1992, MA 1993); Univ. of Surrey (MSc 2003). Ordained deacon, 1993, priest, 1994; Parish priest: Oxton, Merseyside, 1993–97; Marlow, Bucks, 1997–2002; Christian Aid: Mktg Manager, 2002–04; Community Dir, 2004–08; Mktg Dir, 2008–10; Chief Exec., Cystic Fibrosis Trust, 2010–12; Chief Exec., Children's Soc., 2012–19 (Trustee, 2010–12). Trustee, Children England, 2013–19. FRSA 2013. *Address:* Marie Curie, 89 Albert Embankment, SE1 7TP. *T:* (020) 7599 7130. *E:* matthew.reed@mariecurie.org.uk.

**REED, Paul Stuart Malcolm;** QC 2010; *b* London, 16 June 1959; *s* of Alfred Reed and Betty Patricia Reed (*née* Bryant); *m* 1990, Helen Garthwaite; one *s* one *d*. *Educ*: Skinners' Sch., Tunbridge Wells; King's Coll. London (LLB 1987; MSc 1990). Called to the Bar, Inner Temple, 1988; in practice as a barrister, specialising in commercial, insurance and construction; Head of Chambers, 2011–. *Publications:* Accessory Liability and Remedies, 2010; Cases That Changed The World, 2011; Construction All Risks Insurance, 2014, 2nd edn 2016; Construction Professional Indemnity Insurance, 2018. *Recreation:* sailing. *Address:* Hardwicke Building, New Square, Lincoln's Inn, WC2A 3SB. *T:* (020) 7242 2523. *E:* paul.reed@hardwicke.co.uk. *Club:* Bar Yacht.

**REED, Penelope Jane;** QC 2009; a Recorder, since 2010; a Deputy High Court Judge, since 2013; mediator, since 2009; *b* Epping, Essex, 13 June 1961; *d* of Robert Arthur Reed and Jean Audrey Reed; *m* 1986, Mark Simon Wilce; one *s* one *d*. *Educ*: Loughton Co. High Sch.; King's Coll., London (LLB); Inns of Court Sch. of Law. Called to the Bar, Inner Temple, 1983, Bencher, 2017; in practice as barrister specialising in Chancery law; Hd of Chambers, 2018–. Mem., QC Appts Panel, 2018–. Chair, Chancery Bar Assoc., 2014–16 (Vice Chair, 2013–14). *Publications:* A Practical Guide to the Trustee Act 2000, 2001; With the Best Will in the World, 2002; Trusts and Estates Law Handbook, 2002, 3rd edn 2008; Inheritance Act Claims, 2007, 2nd edn 2017; Risk and Negligence in Wills, Trusts and Estates, 2009, 2nd edn 2014. *Recreations:* walking, reading, theatre. *Address:* 5 Stone Buildings, Lincoln's Inn, WC2A 3XT. *T:* (020) 7242 6201, *Fax:* (020) 7831 8102. *E:* preed@5sblaw.com.

**REED, Philip Howard,** OBE 2008; Director, Churchill War Rooms (formerly Cabinet War Rooms, then Churchill Museum and Cabinet War Rooms), 1993–2016, HMS Belfast, 2010–16, and Executive Director, American Air Museum in Britain, 2014–16, Imperial War Museum; Director, Phil Reed Museum Consulting, since 2016; *b* 2 Nov. 1950; *s* of late William Reed and Mary Reed (*née* Fearon); *m* 1982, Sally Blaxland. *Educ*: Univ. of Leicester (BA Hons German 1973); Univ. of Bristol (MA 1974). Lexicographer, Harrap's Ltd, 1973–74; Dep. Keeper, Dept of Documents, Imperial War Mus., 1974–93. Exec. Vice Pres. (Exec. Dir), Churchill Centre, 2008–10. *Publications:* various academic articles, papers and forewords. *Recreations:* opera, fine wines and haute cuisine.

**REED, Robert John;** *see* Reed, Rt Hon. Lord.

**REED, Prof. Roger Charles,** PhD; FREng; Professor of Engineering Science and Materials, University of Oxford, since 2013; Fellow, St Anne's College, Oxford, since 2012; Founder and Director, OxMet Technologies Ltd, since 2017; *b* London, 23 Nov. 1965; *s* of Frank and Celia Reed; *m* 1996, Joanna Copeman; one *s*. *Educ*: Dulwich Coll.; Corpus Christi Coll., Cambridge (BA 1987; MA 1990; PhD 1990). Lectr, Imperial Coll. London, 1990–94; Asst Dir of Res., Univ. of Cambridge, 1994–2001; Prof. and Canada Res. Prof., Univ. of BC, 2001–04; Prof. and Dir of Res., Univ. of Birmingham, 2005–12. FREng 2017. *Publications:* The Superalloys: fundamentals and applications, 2006; contrib. papers to learned jls incl. Acta Materialia, Materials Sci. & Engrg, Materials Sci. Technol. *Recreations:* sports, particularly football and running, wine, food and cooking, parties and fun, travelling and international relations. *Address:* University of Oxford, Begbroke Science Park, Begbroke Hill, Woodstock Road, Begbroke, Oxford OX5 1PF. *T:* (01865) 613069, 613450. *E:* roger.reed@eng.ox.ac.uk.

**REED, Roger William Hampson;** FCIS; Chairman, South East Arts Board, 1995–2001; Member, Arts Council of England, 1996–98; Chairman, Pallant House Gallery Trust, 2002–07; *b* 23 Oct. 1938; *s* of late Thomas Henry Walter Reed and Lily Reed (*née* Hampson); *m* 1961, Jane Noelle Madeline Bowring Gabriel; one *s* one *d*. *Educ*: Trinity Sch. of John Whitgift; City of London Coll. FCIS 1968; FIET (FIEE 1990). Mgt trainee, Albright and Wilson Gp, 1957–61; Asst Co. Sec., Powell Duffryn Gp, 1961–62; Jt Chief Accountant, John Mowlem Gp, 1962–68; Ewbank Preece Group: Dir and Co. Sec., 1968–91; Chm., 1991–93; Chm., Old Ship Hotel (Brighton) Ltd, 1979–93; Dir, Regency Bldg Soc., 1984–88. Partner, Gratwicke Farm, 1982–2018. Founder Dir, Sussex Enterprise (formerly Sussex TEC), 1991–95. Chm., Sussex Br., Inst. Dirs, 1986–89. Trustee, Brighton Fest. Trust and Dir, Brighton Fest. Soc., 1980–95. Chm., Royal Alexandra Hosp. for Sick Children Centenary Fund and Rockinghorse Appeal, 1991–2004. Gov., Hurstpierpoint Coll., 1989–2001. Fellow, Woodard Foundn, 1993–2001. High Sheriff, 2004–05, DL 2005, W Sussex. FCIM 1982. *Recreations:* the arts, cooking and entertaining, sport. *Address:* 37 St Luke's Street, Chelsea, SW3 3RP. *Clubs:* Savile, MCC; Sussex; W Sussex Golf (Pulborough).

**REED, Rupert;** *see* Reed, J. W. R.

**REED, Ruth Madeline,** RIBA; Director, Green Planning Studio Ltd (formerly Green Planning Solutions LLP), since 2013 (Partner (part-time), 2007–13); President, Royal Institute of British Architects, 2009–11; *b* Winchester, 28 Sept. 1956; *d* of Roger and Pamela Green; *m* Donald Reed (marr. diss. 2010); two *d*. *Educ*: Harlescott Grange Prim. Sch., Shrewsbury; Wakeman Sch., Shrewsbury; Sheffield Univ. (BA 1978; DipArch 1981; MA 1982). RIBA 1983. Architectural Asst, Welmar (Yorkshire) Ltd, 1981–83; Architect, Hadfield Cawkwell Davidson and Partners, 1983–87; Sen. Architect, S Yorks Housing Assoc., 1988–90; Sole Practitioner, 1992–2002, Partner, 2002–06, Reed Architects. Course Dir, 2005–12, Prof. of Archit Practice and Dir of Archit Studies, 2012–13, Birmingham Sch. of Architecture, UCE, later Birmingham City Univ. Pres., Royal Soc. of Architects in

Wales, 2003–05; Vice Pres. Membership, RIBA, 2005–07. *Recreations:* gardening and collecting plants, walking, photography, reading maps. *Address:* Green Planning Studio Ltd, Unit D - Lunesdale, Upton Magna Business Park, Upton Magna, Shrewsbury SY4 4TT. *E:* ruth.reed@gpsltd.co.uk.

**REED, Steven Mark Ward,** OBE 2013; MP (Lab Co-op) Croydon North, since Nov. 2012; *b* St Albans, 12 Nov. 1963; *s* of Royston and Thelma Reed. *Educ:* Sheffield Univ. (BA English). Thomson, 1990–97; Law Soc., 1997–2001; Home Office, 1997–98; Pannell Kerr Forster, Accountants, 1998–99; Thomson, 2001–02; Wolters Kluwer, 2002–08. Mem. (Lab) Lambeth LBC, 1998–12 (Leader, 2006–12). Member: Exec. Bd, for Housing, 2009–10, for Children and Young People's Services, 2010–12, London Councils; Bd, London Enterprise Partnership, 2010–12; Chm., London Young People's Educn and Skills Bd, 2010–12; Co-Chair, Nine Elms Strategy Bd, 2010–12; Dep. Chm., LGA, 2010–12; Chm., Central London Forward; Chair, Cooperative Councils Innovation Network, 2010–12 (Patron, 2012–). Shadow Minister for: Home Affairs, 2013–15; Communities and Local Govt, 2015–16; Culture, Media and Sport, subseq. Digital, Culture, Media and Sport, 2016–. *Address:* House of Commons, SW1A 0AA; (office) 908 London Road, Thornton Heath CR7 7PE.

**REED, Prof. Terence James, (Jim),** FBA 1987; Taylor Professor of the German Language and Literature, University of Oxford, 1989–2004, now Emeritus; Fellow, Queen's College, Oxford, 1989–2004, Hon. Fellow, 2007; *b* 16 April 1937; *s* of William Reed and Ellen (*née* Silcox); *m* 1960, Ann Macpherson; one *s* one *d*. *Educ:* Shooters Hill Grammar Sch., Woolwich; Brasenose Coll., Oxford (MA). Sen. Scholar, Christ Church, Oxford, 1960–61; Jun. Res. Fellow, Brasenose Coll., Oxford, 1961–63; Fellow and Tutor in Mod. Langs, St John's Coll., Oxford, 1963–88 (Hon. Fellow, 1997). Schiller Prof., Univ. of Jena, 1999. Vis. Res. Scholar, Univ. of Göttingen, 2004–05. Pres., English Goethe Soc., 1995–; Mem., Council, Goethe Soc., Weimar, 2003–11. Corresponding Member: Collegium Europaeum, Jena, 1991; Göttingen Acad. of Scis, 1997. Hon. DPhil Freiburg, 2010. Gold Medal, Goethe Soc., Weimar, 1999; Res. Prize, Humboldt Foundn, 2002. Co-founder and Editor, Oxford German Studies, 1965–; Editor, Oxford Magazine, 1985–2004. *Publications:* (ed) Death in Venice, 1972 (German edn 1983); Thomas Mann, The Uses of Tradition, 1974, 2nd edn 1997; The Classical Centre: Goethe and Weimar 1775–1832, 1980 (German edn 1982); Goethe, 1984 (German edn 1999; also Hebrew, Japanese, Korean, Persian and Spanish edns); (trans.) Heinrich Heine: Deutschland, a not so sentimental journey, 1986; Schiller, 1991; Death in Venice: making and unmaking a master, 1994; (trans. with D. Cram) Heinrich Heine, Poems, 1997; (trans.) Goethe: The Flight to Italy: diaries and letters 1786, 1999; (ed) Goethe: poems, 1999; (ed and trans. jtly) Goethe: poems, 2000; Humanpraxis Literatur (essays), 2001; (ed jtly) Thomas Mann: Erzählungen 1893–1912, 2 vols (text and commentary), 2004; Mehr Licht in Deutschland: kleine Geschichte der Aufklärung, 2009; Light in Germany: scenes from an unknown Enlightenment, 2015; Genesis: the making of literary works from Homer to Celan, 2020. *Recreations:* hill walking, talking to people. *Address:* 91 Eynsham Road, Oxford OX2 9BY. *T:* (01865) 862946.

**REED-PURVIS, Air Vice-Marshal Henry,** CB 1982; OBE 1972; Sales Director, British Aerospace Dynamics Group, 1983–89; *b* 1 July 1928; *s* of late Henry Reed and of Nancy Reed-Purvis; *m* 1951, Isabel Price; three *d*. *Educ:* King James I School, Durham; Durham Univ. BSc Hons 1950. Entered RAF, 1950; various Op. Sqdns, 1951–58; Instr, Jt Nuclear Biological and Chemical Sch., 1958–60; RMCS Shrivenham (Nuclear Sci. and Tech.), 1961; MoD Staff, 1962–64; OC No 63 Sqdn, RAF Regt, Malaya, 1964–66; Exchange Duties, USAF, 1966–69; USAF War Coll., 1969–70; OC No 5 Wing RAF Regt, 1970–72; Gp Capt. Regt, HQ Strike Comd, 1972–74, HQ RAF Germany, 1974–76; ADC to the Queen, 1974–76; Dir, RAF Regt, 1976–79; Comdt Gen. RAF Regt and Dir Gen. of Security (RAF) 1979–83. Dir, Forces Help Soc. and Lord Roberts Workshops, 1986–97; Council Mem., Trustee and Dir, SSAFA/Forces Help, 1997–99. Vice Pres., Council for Cadet Rifle Shooting, 1985–. Pres., 2120 Sqdn ATC Welfare Cttee, 1995–2000. *Recreations:* golf, bridge and music. *Address:* 9 Turville Barns, Eastleach, near Cirencester, Glos GL7 3QB.

**REEDER, John;** QC 1989; *b* 18 Jan. 1949; *s* of Frederick and Barbara Reeder; *m* 1st, 1971, Barbara Kotlarz (marr. diss. 1994); 2nd, 1995, Pauline Madden. *Educ:* Catholic Coll., Preston; University Coll. London (LLM); PhD Birmingham 1976. Called to the Bar, Gray's Inn, 1971, NSW 1986. Lectr in Law, Univ. of Birmingham, 1971–76; commenced practice, 1976; Junior Counsel to the Treasury (Admiralty), 1981–89; a Recorder, 1991–97; Lloyd's salvage arbitrator, 1991–2005, 2006–09; CEDR Mediator, 2003–. Lawyer, PNG, 1984. Mem., Ferrari Owners' Club, 2003–. *Recreations:* motorsport, travel. *Address:* 72 Bracondale Road, Norwich NR1 2BE.

**REEDIE, Sir Craig (Collins),** GBE 2018 (CBE 1999); Kt 2006; President, World Anti-Doping Agency, since 2014 (Board Member, since 2000); Vice-President, International Olympic Committee, 2012–16 (Member, since 1994; Member, Executive Board, 2009–16); *b* 6 May 1941; *s* of late Robert Lindsay Reedie and Anne Reedie; *m* 1967, Rosemary Jane Biggart; one *s* one *d*. *Educ:* High Sch., Stirling; Univ. of Glasgow (MA, LLB). Sec. and Pres., Scottish Badminton Union, 1966–81; Council Mem., Chm. and Pres. of Internat. Badminton Fedn, 1970–84; Mem. Council and Treas., Gen. Assoc. of Internat. Sports Fedns, 1984–92; Chm., British Olympic Assoc., 1992–2005. Board Member: Manchester 2002 Ltd, 2000–02; London 2012, 2003–05; London Organising Cttee for the Olympic Games, 2005–13; Olympic Lottery Distributor, 2005–13. Mem., NHS Resource Allocation Steering Gp, 1998–99. FRSA 1995. DUniv: Glasgow, 2001; Stirling, 2014; Hon. LLD St Andrews, 2005; Hon. LLD: Brunel, 2007; W of Scotland, 2011; Hon. DBA Lincoln, 2009; Hon. DSc Glasgow Caledonian, 2013. *Recreations:* reading, golf, sport, sport and more sport. *Address:* Senara, Hazelwood Road, Bridge of Weir PA11 3DB. *T:* (01505) 613434. *Clubs:* East India; Royal & Ancient Golf (St Andrews), Western Gailes Golf, Ranfurly Castle Golf.

**REEDIJK, Alexander;** General Director, Scottish Opera, since 2006; *b* Lower Hutt, Wellington, NZ, 31 Dec. 1960; *s* of Leendert and Jacoba Reedijk; *m* 2002, Anne Goldrick; one *s* one *d*. *Educ:* Wainuiomata Coll., NZ; Victoria Univ., Wellington, NZ. Freelance roles incl. stage manager, dresser, lighting designer for shows and events in NZ, Ireland, England and Scotland, 1982–88; Production Manager: Opera Ireland, 1985–89; Assembly Th., Edinburgh Fest., 1988–94; Wexford Opera Fest., 1989–91; Tech. Dir, May Fest., Glasgow, 1989–91; New Zealand Festival: Tech. Dir, 1991–2008; Dep. Exec. Dir, 1998–2000 (incl. Producer, Edinburgh Mil. Tattoo in NZ); Exec. Dir, 2000–02; Studio Manager, Riverside Studios, 1994–96; Gen. Dir, Nat. Business Rev., NZ Opera, 2002–06. Convener, NZ Entry to Prague Quadrennial, 1999; Assessor, Creative NZ, 2002–04. Chair, Beacon Arts Centre, Greenock; Vice Chair, Citizens Th., Glasgow, 2017–; Trustee: Downstage Th., Wellington, 1999–2002; Christchurch Arts Fest., 2001–05; NZ Opera Trng Sch., 2002–; Auckland Fest., 2003–06; Nat. Opera Studio, London, 2006–. Fellow, Royal Conservatoire of Scotland, 2011. *Recreations:* opera, sailing, family, theatre. *Address:* Scottish Opera, 39 Elmbank Crescent, Glasgow G2 4PT. *T:* (0141) 248 4567. *E:* alex.reedijk@scottishopera.org.uk.

**REEDS, Graham Joseph;** QC 2009; **His Honour Judge Reeds;** a Circuit Judge, since 2018; *b* Glossop, Derbys; *s* of Ernest Reeds and Glenys Reeds; *m* 1988, Madeleine Carne; one *s* one *d*. *Educ:* Hulme Grammar Sch., Oldham; Univ. of Sheffield (LLB Hons). Called to the Bar, Middle Temple, 1984; barrister, 11 King's Bench Walk, 1986–2006; a Recorder, 2002–18; Sen. Counsel, Serious Organised Crime Agency, 2006–09; a Principal Advocate for CPS, 2008–18, Principal Counsel, 2010–18. CD-ROMs: (jtly) Family Finance Toolkit, 1996–2003; (jtly) Personal Injury Toolkit, 1997, 7th edn 2011. *Recreations:* football, high altitude mountaineering (climbed to 7,000m on Everest, 2002). *Address:* Sheffield Crown Court, The Law Courts, West Bar, Sheffield S3 8PH.

**REEDY, Norris John, (Jack);** media consultant and lecturer, since 1994; *b* 1934; *s* of John Reedy; *m* 1964, Sheila Campbell McGregor; one *d*. *Educ:* Chorlton High Sch., Manchester; Univ. of Sheffield. Newspaper journalist, 1956–82, incl. Sunday Times and Guardian; Birmingham Post, 1964–82 (Editor, 1974–82); Regl Officer, Midlands, IBA, 1983–88; Sen. Nat. and Regl Officer, ITC, 1988–94; PRO, Inst. of Dirs (Midland Br.), 1994–99. Tutor in media skills and public speaking, RCN, 1995–2008. Mem., Coventry and Warwickshire Selection Panel, The Prince's Trust, 1998–2010; Chm., Warwickshire Badger Gp, 2005–; Vice Chm., Badger Trust, 2006–10. Pres., Guild of British Newspaper Editors, 1981 (former Chm. W Midlands Region, and Nat. Vice-Pres.); Sec., Midlands Centre, Royal Television Soc. Chm., House Cttee, Birmingham Press Club. Churchwarden, St Laurence, Rowington, 2005–. *Recreations:* astronomy, riding, natural history, painting, photography. *Address:* The Old Manor, Rowington, near Warwick CV35 7DJ. *T:* (01564) 783129.

**REEKIE, Jonathan Alistair James,** CBE 2013; Director, Somerset House Trust, since 2014; *b* 2 Sept. 1964; *s* of Dr Andrew Reekie and Virginia Reekie; two *d*. *Educ:* Bristol Poly. (BA Business Studies). Co. Co-ordinator, Glyndebourne Fest., 1987–91; Gen. Manager, Almeida Th., 1991–97; Dir, Almeida Opera, 1991–2003; Chief Exec., Aldeburgh Music, 1997–2014 (Trustee, 2009–12). Mem., Bd of Dirs, Musica Nel Chiostro, Batignano, Italy, 1989–2005. Advr, Arts Prog. Cttee, Paul Hamlyn Foundn, 2007–. Trustee, Arts Foundn, 2000–. Hon. FRAM 2010; Hon. DMus UEA, 2010. *Address:* Somerset House Trust, Somerset House, Strand, WC2R 1LA.

**REEKS, David Robin,** MBE 2015; TD 1974; Vice Lord-Lieutenant of Lanarkshire, 2002–10; *b* 15 June 1935; *s* of Harry and Dorothy Reeks; *m* 1958, Kathleen Stephens; one *s* one *d*. *Educ:* Canford Sch.; London Univ. (BSc Eng ext.). Rig Design Engr, UKAEA, Dounreay, 1962–67; Reactor Thermal Engr, SSEB, 1967–89; Reactor Performance and Safety Engr, Scottish Nuclear, 1989–94. Mem. Cttee, and Volunteer Convoy Leader, Edinburgh Direct Aid to Bosnia and Kosovo, 1994–. TA, RE and RCT, 1962–90. DL Lanarks, 1989. *Recreations:* hill-walking, Scottish country dancing, part-time tour manager Great Rail Journeys. *Address:* 3 Cedar Place, Strathaven, Lanarks ML10 6DW. *T:* and *Fax:* (01357) 521695. *E:* d.reeks@talktalk.net.

**REES OF LUDLOW,** Baron *cr* 2005 (Life Peer), of Ludlow in the county of Shropshire; **Martin John Rees,** OM 2007; Kt 1992; FRS 1979; Fellow, Trinity College, Cambridge, since 2012 (Master, 2004–12); Astronomer Royal, since 1995; *b* 23 June 1942; *s* of late Reginald J. and Joan Rees; *m* 1986, Caroline Humphrey (*see* Dame C. Humphrey). *Educ:* Shrewsbury Sch.; Trinity Coll., Cambridge; MA, PhD (Cantab). Fellow, Jesus Coll., Cambridge, 1967–69 (Hon. Fellow, 1996); Research Associate, California Inst. of Technology, 1967–68 and 1971; Mem., Inst. for Advanced Study, Princeton, 1969–70; Prof., Univ. of Sussex, 1972–73; Cambridge University: Plumian Prof. of Astronomy and Experimental Philosophy, 1973–91; Dir, Inst. of Astronomy, 1977–82 and 1987–91; Royal Soc. Res. Prof., 1992–2003; Prof. of Cosmology and Astrophysics, 2002–09; Fellow of King's Coll., Cambridge, 1969–72 and 1973–2003. Visiting Professor: Harvard Univ., 1972, 1986–88; Inst. for Advanced Studies, Princeton, 1982, 1995; Imperial Coll., London, 2001–; Hitchcock Vis. Prof., UC Berkeley, 1994; Regents Fellow of Smithsonian Instn, Washington, 1984–88; Oort Prof., Leiden, 1999. Lectures: H. P. Robertson Meml, US Nat. Acad. Sci., 1975; Bakerian, Royal Soc., 1982; Danz, Univ. of Washington, 1984; Pauli, Zurich, 1999; Leverhulme, 1999; Scribner, Princeton, 2000; Russell, Amer. Astron. Soc., 2004; Messenger, Cornell Univ., 2005; Gifford, Scottish Univs, 2007; Reith, BBC, 2010; Romanes, Oxford, 2011. Trustee: BM, 1996–2002; NESTA, 1998–2001; Inst. for Adv. Study, Princeton, 1998–; Kennedy Meml Trust, 1999–2004; IPPR, 2001–09; Nat. Mus. of Sci. and Industry, 2003–11; Gates Cambridge Trust, 2007–14. President: RAS, 1992–94; BAAS, 1994–95; Royal Soc., 2005–10; Chm., Science Adv. Cttee, ESA, 1976–78; Member: Council, Royal Soc., 1983–85 and 1993–95; PPARC, 1994–97. Member: Academia Europaea, 1989; Pontifical Acad. of Sci., 1990; For. Hon. Mem., Amer. Acad. of Arts and Sciences, 1975; Foreign Associate, Nat. Acad. of Sciences, USA, 1982; Foreign Member: Amer. Phil. Soc., 1993; Royal Swedish Acad. Sci., 1993; Russian Acad. of Sci., 1994; Norwegian Acad. of Arts and Letters, 1996; Accademia Lincei, Rome, 1996; Royal Netherlands Acad. of Arts and Sciences, 1998; Finnish Acad. of Sci. and Letters, 2004; Japan Acad., 2015; Associate Mem., TWAS: the Acad. of Scis for the Developing World, 2008. Hon. FInstP 2001; Hon. FREng 2007; Hon. FMedSci 2011; Hon. FBA 2012; Hon. FLSW 2016. Hon. Fellow: Cardiff Univ., 1998; Darwin Coll., Cambridge, 2004; John Moores Univ., 2008; King's Coll., Cambridge, 2007; Clare Hall, Cambridge, 2016; Robinson Coll., Cambridge, 2019. Hon. DSc: Sussex, 1990; Leicester, 1993; Copenhagen, 1994; Keele, Newcastle and Uppsala, 1995; Toronto, 1997; Durham, 1999; Oxford, 2000; Ohio and Exeter, 2006; Hull, 2007; Liverpool, 2008; Yale, 2008; McMaster, 2009; E Anglia, 2009; Melbourne, 2010; Portsmouth, 2011; Sydney, 2012; ETH Zurich, 2012; Cambridge, 2014; Greenwich, 2014; Harvard, 2016; Leeds 2017; DUniv Open, 2008; Hon. DLitt London, 2011; Bath, 2015. Heinemann Prize, Amer. Inst. Physics, 1984; Gold Medal, RAS, 1987; Guthrie Medal and Prize, Inst. of Physics, 1989; Balzan Prize, Balzan Foundn, 1989; Schwarzschild Medal, Astron. ges., 1989; Bruce Gold Medal, Astron. Soc. of Pacific, 1993; Bower Award for Science, Franklin Inst., 1998; Rossi Prize, American Astron. Soc., 2000; Cosmology Prize, Gruber Foundn, 2001; Einstein Award, World Cultural Council, 2003; Michael Faraday Award, Royal Soc., 2004; (jtly) Crafoord Prize, Royal Swedish Acad., 2005; Niels Bohr Medal, UNESCO, 2005; Templeton Prize, John Templeton Foundn, 2011; Newton Prize, Inst. of Physics, 2012; Chancellor's Medal, Univ. of Calif, Santa Cruz, 2012; Dirac Prize, ICTP Trieste, 2013; Nierenberg Prize, Scripps Inst., 2015. Officier, Ordre des Arts et des Lettres (France), 1991; Gold and Silver Star, Order of Rising Sun (Japan), 2015. *Publications:* Perspectives in Astrophysical Cosmology, 1995; (with M. Begelman) Gravity's Fatal Attraction: black holes in the universe, 1996, 3rd edn 2020; Before the Beginning, 1997; Just Six Numbers, 1999; Our Cosmic Habitat, 2001; Our Final Century?, 2003; From Here to Infinity: scientific horizons, 2011; (ed) Universe, 2012; On the Future: prospects for humanity, 2018; mainly scientific papers; numerous general articles. *Address:* c/o Trinity College, Cambridge CB2 1TQ. *T:* (01223) 338412, (office) (01223) 337548.

**REES, Allen Brynmor;** Regional Chairman, Employment (formerly Industrial) Tribunals, Birmingham, 1995–2004; *b* 11 May 1936; *s* of late Allen Brynmor Rees and Elsie Louise Rees (*née* Hitchcock); *m* 1961, Nerys Eleanor Evans; two *d*. *Educ:* Monmouth Sch.; UCW, Aberystwyth (LLB Hons 1958). Admitted Solicitor (with Hons), 1961. Partner, Francis Ryan and Co., 1961–62; Solicitor, SW Div., NCB, 1962; Rexall Drug and Chemical Co., 1962–65; Rees Page (incorp. Page Son and Elias, Skidmore Hares and Co., and Darbey-Scott-Rees), 1965–93, Sen. Partner, 1974–93; Chm., Employment (formerly Industrial)

Tribunals, 1993–2004. Prin. Solicitor, Birmingham Midshires Building Soc., 1976–93. Chairman: W Midlands Rent Assessment Panel, 1968–93; Social Security Tribunals, 1980–93; Employment (formerly Industrial) Tribunals, Birmingham, 1993–95; Reserve Forces Appeal Tribunal, 2003–; Mem. Cttee, Legal Aid Bd, 1975–93. Columnist (Solicitors' Notebook), Solicitors' Jl, 1968–92; Ed., Employment Tribunals Chairman's Handbook, 1999–2006. *Recreations:* canoeing, ski-ing, gardening, walking, watching Rugby. *Address:* Rossleigh, Shaw Lane, Albrighton, Wolverhampton WV7 3DS. *Club:* Old Monmothians (Monmouth).

**REES, Prof. Andrew Jackson;** Professorial Fellow, Medical University of Vienna, 2010–15, now Professor Emeritus (Marie Curie Professor, 2007–10); *b* 11 June 1946; *s* of late Gordon Jackson Rees and of Elisabeth Rees; *m* 1st, 1972, Ann Duncan (marr. diss. 1974); 2nd, 1979, Daphne Elizabeth Wood (marr. diss. 1985); two *d*; 3rd, 1999, Renate Kain; two *c*. *Educ:* King William's Coll., Isle of Man; Liverpool Univ. (MB ChB 1969); London Univ. (MSc). Trained in gen. medicine and nephrology, at Liverpool, Guy's, and Hammersmith Hosps, 1969–79; Consultant Physician, Hammersmith Hosp., 1979–90; Prof. of Nephrology, RPMS, 1990–94; Regius Prof. of Medicine, Univ. of Aberdeen, 1994–2007. Vis. Prof., Nat. Jewish Hosp., Denver, 1983–84; Goulstonian Lectr, RCP, 1984. Chair: UK Renal Genetics Gp, 2005–07; European Kidney Health Alliance, 2007–11. Pres., Nephrology Section, RSocMed, 1994–95. Vice-Pres., Kidney Res. UK (formerly Nat. Kidney Res. Fund), 2000– (Chm., 1995–2000); Pres., Renal Assoc. of GB and Ireland, 2001–04; Mem. Council, Internat. Soc. of Nephrology, 1998–2003. FMedSci 2000; FRSB (FSB 2009). *Publications:* (ed with C. D. Pusey) Rapidly Progressive Glomerulonephritis, 1998; papers on pathogenesis and treatment of glomerulonephritis. *Recreations:* contemporary theatre and music, ski-ing. *Address:* Mauerbachstrasse 10, 1140 Vienna, Austria.

**REES, (Anthony) John (David);** educational consultant, since 2003; *b* 20 July 1943; *s* of Richard Frederick and Betty Rees; one *s* one *d* (and one *d* decd). *Educ:* Newcastle Royal Grammar Sch.; Clare Coll., Cambridge (Exhibnr; BA 2nd Cl. Hons Geog.); PGCE 1966. Head of Economics, Harrow Sch., 1966–80; Head Master, Blundell's Sch., Tiverton, Devon, 1980–92; Rector, Edinburgh Acad., 1992–95; Director: Harrow Sch. Develt Trust, 1995–97; The Bradfield Foundn, 1998–2000; school master, Cheltenham Coll., 2000–03. Established Notting Dale Urban Study Centre, 1972; Vis. Tutor, London Inst. of Education, 1973–2007. Member Executive Committee: Queen's Silver Jubilee Appeal, 1976–82; and Admin. Council, Royal Jubilee Trusts, 1978–82; Chairman: Prince's Trust for Devon, 1981–83; Youth Clubs UK, 1987–89; Founder Dir, Mid Devon Enterprise Agency, 1984–91; Chm., Crested, 1996–97. Member: CoSIRA Cttee for Devon, 1981–83; Council, Drake Fellowship, 1981–; Admiralty Interview Bd, 1981–2005; Cttee, HMC, 1986–91; Prince of Wales Community Venture, 1985–; Council, Prince's Trust for Wales, 2009–; Board: Devon and Cornwall Prince's Youth Business Trust, 1987–92; Fairbridge in Scotland, 1992–95; Trustee: SFIA Educnl Trust, 1996–2014; Talley Community Woodland, 2007– (Chm., 2009–). *Publications:* articles on economics and community service in many jls incl. Economics, Youth in Society, etc. *Recreations:* hill walking, family and friends.

**REES, Barbara;** *see* Wilding, B.

**REES, Caroline, (Lady Rees of Ludlow);** *see* Humphrey, Dame Caroline.

**REES, Caroline Elizabeth;** QC 2018; a Recorder, since 2014; *b* Llanelli, 20 April 1972; *d* of Harold Royston Rees and Elizabeth Mary Rees; *m* 1998, Eugene Egan; one *s* one *d*. *Educ:* Ysgol Gyfun Y Strade, Llanelli; Univ. of Birmingham (LLB Hons 1993); Inns of Court Sch. of Law. Called to the Bar, Gray's Inn, 1994; barrister in ind. practice, Cardiff, 1994–; Mem., Wales and Chester Circuit, 1995–. *Recreations:* running (including London Marathon, 2016 and New York Marathon, 2017), wine, supporting my children from hockey/Rugby touchlines. *Address:* 30 Park Place, Cardiff CF10 3BS. *T:* (029) 2039 8421. *E:* cr@30parkplace.co.uk.

**REES, Celia,** FEA; writer; *b* Solihull, 17 June 1949; *d* of Wilfred Taylor and Lilla Taylor (*née* Goodway); *m* 1972, Terence Rees; one *d*. *Educ:* Tudor Grange Grammar Sch. for Girls, Solihull; Univ. of Warwick (BA Hons Hist. and Politics); Birmingham Univ. (PGCE, MEd). Teacher of English: Binley Park Comp. Sch., Coventry, 1972–81; Stoke Park Sch. and Community Coll., Coventry, 1981–82; Whitley Abbey Sch., Coventry, 1983–89; further educn lectr (pt-time), Henley Coll. of Further Educn, Coventry, 1990–97; Tutor in Open Studies (pt-time), Univ. of Warwick, 1997–2001. Chair, Children's Writers and Illustrators Gp, 2007–09; Mem., Mgt Cttee, 2016–, Soc. of Authors'. FEA 2011. *Publications:* Every Step You Take, 1993; The Bailey Game, 1994; Colour her Dead, 1994; Blood Sinister, 1996; Midnight Hour, 1997; Ghost Chamber, 1997; The Vanished, 1997; Soul Taker, 1998; Truth or Dare, 2000 (Stockport Book Award, 2001); The Cunning Man, 2000; Witch Child, 2000 (Cassa di Risparmio di Cento di Letteratura per Ragazzi, 2001; Prix Sorcières, 2003); Trap in Time, 2001; City of Shadows, 2002; The Host Rides Out, 2002; Sorceress, 2002; Pirates!, 2003 (Thumbs Up!, Michigan Libraries Award, 2004); The Wish House, 2005; The Stone Testament, 2007; Sovay, 2008; The Fool's Girl, 2010; This Is Not Forgiveness, 2012; Glass Town Wars, 2018. *Recreations:* reading, film, walking, swimming, yoga and meditation, travel, seeing friends. *Address:* 195 Rugby Road, Milverton, Leamington Spa, Warwickshire CV32 6DX.

**REES, Christina Elizabeth;** MP (Lab) Neath, since 2015; *b* 21 Feb. 1954; *m* 1981, Rt Hon. Ronald Davies, *qv* (marr. diss. 2000); one *d*. *Educ:* Cynffig Comprehensive Sch.; Ystrad Mynach Coll.; Univ. of Wales Coll. of Cardiff (LLB Hons 1995). Auditor, S Glamorgan CC, 1979–84; Constituency Sec., H of C, 1984–96; called to the Bar, 1996; in practice as barrister, Cardiff, 1997–98; Develt Officer and Nat. Coach, Wales Squash and Racketball, 2003–15; Squash Professional, Vale Hotel, 2004–14. Mem. (Lab): Mid-Glamorgan CC, 1988–95; Porthcawl Town Council, 2012–15; Bridgend CBC, 2012–15. Shadow Sec. of State for Wales, 2017–. Member: Welsh Affairs Select Cttee, 2015–16; Justice Select Cttee, 2015. Contested (Lab): Arfon, Nat. Assembly for Wales, 2011; Wales, EP, 2014. JP 1990. Female Coach of Year, Sport Wales, 2008. *Address:* House of Commons, SW1A 0AA.

**REES, Christina Henking Muller,** CBE 2015; communications, media and public relations consultant, since 1985; writer, since 1986; broadcaster, since 1990; campaigner, since 1990; executive coach, since 2003; Dean of Little Gidding, Cambridgeshire, 2016; *b* 6 July 1953; *d* of John Muller, Jr and Carol Benton Muller; *m* 1978, Christopher Rees, *s* of late Richard Rees and Margaret (*née* Head); two *d*. *Educ:* Pomona Coll., Calif (BA English 1975); King's Coll., London (MA Theology 1998). Asst PR Officer, Children's Soc., 1985–87. Sen. Partner, Media Maxima, 1990–. Member: Gen. Synod of C of E, 1990–2015; Archbishops' Council, 1999–2000, 2006–15; Chair: Women and the Church, 1996–2010; Women on the Move, 1999–; spokesperson, Movt for Ordination of Women, 1992–94. Mem., Central Religious Adv. Cttee, 2003–08. Trustee: Li Tim-Oi Foundn, 1997– (Vice Chm.); Christian Assoc. of Business Executives, 2007–18; Bible Soc., 2013–; Horstead Youth Centre, 2018–; Church Urban Fund, 2019–; Dir, The Churchfield Trust, 2000–12. Consultant: IBA, 1979; BBC Children in Need Appeal, 1997–2000; Ernst & Young, 2011–13. Gov., Ripon Coll. Cuddesdon, 2000–15 (Hon. Fellow, 2014); Chaplain (pt-time), Beeston Hall Sch., 2018–. Contribs to radio and TV progs, 1990–, incl. Thought for the Day, Radio 4, 1991–2006, Pause for Thought, Radio 2, 2008–10. FRSA 2005. *Publications:* Sea Urchin, 1990; The Divine Embrace, 2000; (ed) Voices of This Calling, 2002; Feast + Fast: food for Lent and Easter, 2011; Feast + Fast: food for Advent and Christmas, 2012; contrib. to The Times, Guardian, Independent, Christian publications, etc. *Recreations:* beachcombing, improving Anglo-American relations, cross country walking. *Address:* Semaphore Lodge, 30 Weybourne Road, Sheringham, Norfolk NR26 8HF. *E:* christina@mediamaxima.com.

**REES, Sir David Allan, (Sir Dai Rees),** Kt 1993; BSc, PhD, DSc; FRCPE, FMedSci; FRS 1981; FRSC, FRSB, FLSW; Medical Research Council scientist, 1996–2001; *b* 28 April 1936; *s* of James Allan Rees and Elsie Bolam; *m* 1959, Myfanwy Margaret Parry Owen; two *s* one *d*. *Educ:* Hawarden Grammar Sch., Clwyd; University Coll. of N Wales, Bangor, Gwynedd (BSc 1956; PhD 1959; Hon. Fellow, 1988); DSc Edinburgh, 1970. FRCPE 1999. DSIR Res. Fellow, University Coll., Bangor, 1959, and Univ. of Edinburgh, 1960; Asst Lectr in Chem., 1961, Lectr, 1962–70, Univ. of Edinburgh; Section Manager, 1970–72, Principal Scientist, 1972–82, and Sci. Policy Exec., 1978–82, Unilever Res., Colworth Lab.; Chm., Science Policy Gp for Unilever Res., 1979–82. Associate Dir (pt-time), MRC Unit for Cell Biophysics, KCL, 1980–82; Dir, Nat. Inst. for Med. Res., Mill Hill, 1982–87; Sec., subseq. Chief Exec., MRC, 1987–96. Vis. Professorial Fellow, University Coll., Cardiff, 1972–77. Philips Lecture, Royal Soc., 1984. Member: MRC, 1984–96; Council, Royal Soc., 1985–87. Pres., ESF, 1994–99. FKC 1989. Founder FMedSci 1998; FLSW 2010. Hon. FRCP 1986. Hon. DSc: Edinburgh, 1989; Wales, 1991; Stirling, 1995; Leicester, 1997; DUniv York, 2007. Colworth Medal, Biochemical Soc., 1970; Carbohydrate Award, Chemical Soc., 1970. *Publications:* various, on carbohydrate chem. and biochem. and cell biology. *Recreations:* river boats, reading, listening to music. *Address:* Ford Cottage, 1 High Street, Denford, Kettering, Northants NN14 4EQ. *T:* (01832) 733502. *E:* dairees1@btinternet.com.

**REES, David Benjamin;** QC 2017; a Recorder, since 2012; a Deputy High Court Judge, since 2018; *b* Sevenoaks, 6 Sept. 1971; *s* of Benjamin Barrie Rees and Susan Rees; *m* 2006, Alison Louise Barnett. *Educ:* Sherborne Sch.; St Anne's Coll., Oxford (BA Hons Juris.); Inns of Court Sch. of Law. Called to the Bar, Lincoln's Inn, 1994; in ind. practice as barrister, specialising in wills, trusts, and court of protection work, 1995–. Dep. Chancellor, Dio. Leicester, 2014–. Gen. Ed., Heywood and Massey: Court of Protection Practice, 2006–. *Address:* 5 Stone Buildings, Lincoln's Inn, WC2A 3XT. *T:* (020) 7242 6201. *E:* clerks@5sblaw.com.

**REES, His Honour (David) Wyn;** a Circuit Judge, 2005–13; Deputy Designated Family Judge for South Wales, 2006–13; authorised to sit as a Judge of the High Court, Family Division, 2011–13; a Deputy Circuit Judge, 2013–16; *b* 6 Jan. 1948; *s* of late David Daniel Rees and Mariann Rees; *m* 1972, Gillian Anne Davies; two *d*. *Educ:* Ysgol Gynradd Gymraeg Aberdâr; Mountain Ash Grammar Sch.; University Coll. of Wales, Aberystwyth (BSc Hons 1969). Mem., Aberdare UDC, 1970–74. Admitted solicitor, 1973; Partner, Spicketts, Solicitors, Pontypridd, 1974–88; Dep. Registrar and Dist Registrar, 1984–88; Registrar and Dist Registrar, subseq. Dist Judge, 1988–2005; Asst Recorder, 1994–98; Recorder, 1998–2005; Diversity and Community Relations Judge (formerly Ethnic Minority Liaison Judge) for SE Wales (formerly S Wales), 2005–11. Judicial Studies Board: Dir, Seminars for Dist Judges, 1996–2001; Mem., Civil and Family Cttees, 1996–2001; Mem., Main Bd, 1999–2001; Mem., Equal Treatment Adv. Cttee, 2007–11. Member: Lord Chancellor's Standing Cttee for Welsh Lang., 1999–2005; Law and Admin of Justice Terminology Subject Gp, Welsh Lang. Bd, 2007–12; Chm., Mgt Cttee, Pontypridd Children's Contact Centre, 2006–12; Mem., Expert Wkg Gp on Future Direction for Child Contact Centres, 2011–13. Mem., 2011–16, Chm., 2012–13, Legislative Sub-Cttee, Assoc. of Judges of Wales. Pres., Pontypridd and Rhondda Law Soc., 1985–86. Hon. Mem., Gorsedd of Bards, 2003–. *Recreations:* walking Wales, foreign travel, golf, the company of family and friends.

**REES, Edward Parry;** QC 1998; *b* 18 June 1949; *s* of Edward Howell Rees and Margaret Rees Parry; *m* 1983, Kathleen Wiltshire; one *s* one *d*. *Educ:* University Coll. of Wales, Aberystwyth (LLB Hons); Open Univ. (MA History). Called to the Bar, Gray's Inn, 1973. Hon. Fellow in Criminal Process, Univ. of Kent, 1992. Chm. Trustees, Huddleston Centre, E London, 2017–. *Publications:* Blackstone's Guide to the Proceeds of Crime Act 2002, 2003, 5th edn 2013; The Law of Public Order and Protest, 2010. *Recreations:* family, garden.

**REES, Eleri Mair; Her Honour Judge Rees;** a Circuit Judge, and Liaison Judge for the Welsh Language, since 2002; a Senior Circuit Judge, Resident Judge, Cardiff Crown Court, and Recorder of Cardiff, since 2012; *b* 7 July 1953; *d* of late Ieuan Morgan and Sarah Alice Morgan (*née* James); *m* 1975, Alan Rees. *Educ:* Ardwyn Grammar Sch., Aberystwyth; Univ. of Liverpool (LLB Hons). Called to the Bar, Gray's Inn, 1975, Bencher, 2013. Clerk to Justices, Bexley Magistrates' Court, 1983–94; Metropolitan Stipendiary Magistrate, subseq. Dist Judge (Magistrates' Courts), 1994–2002; a Recorder, 1997–2002. Editor, Family Court Reporter, 1992–94. Mem., Magisterial Cttee, Judicial Studies Bd, 1989–94. *Publications:* contrib. various jls on subject of family law. *Recreations:* travel, cookery, ski-ing. *Address:* c/o Cardiff Crown Court, The Law Courts, Cathays Park, Cardiff CF10 3PG.

**REES, Gareth David;** QC 2003; Partner, King & Spalding International LLP, since 2017; *b* 2 July 1956; *s* of Baron Merlyn-Rees, PC and Colleen (*née* Cleveley); *m* 2000, Lucia Boddington; two *d*, and one *s* two *d* from former marriage. *Educ:* Harrow Co. Sch. for Boys; Reading Univ. (BA Hons). Called to the Bar, Gray's Inn, 1981; in practice as barrister, 1981–2012; Exec. Counsel, Accountancy and Actuarial Discipline Bd, later Dir of Enforcement and Gen. Counsel, Enforcement Div., Financial Reporting Council, 2012–17. *Recreations:* sport, music, family, cinema. *Address:* King & Spalding International LLP, 125 Old Broad Street. *E:* gr@garethreesqc.com. *Club:* MCC.

**REES, Prof. Geraint Ellis;** PhD; FMedSci; Professor of Cognitive Neurology, Wellcome Centre for Human Neuroimaging (formerly Wellcome Trust Centre for Neuroimaging), Institute of Neurology, since 2003, and Dean, Faculty of Life Sciences, since 2014, University College London; *b* 27 Nov. 1967; *s* of Olav Anelyf Rees and Rosemary Ann Rees (*née* Dawson); *m* 2000, Rebecca Ruth Roylance; one *s* one *d*. *Educ:* Gonville and Caius Coll., Cambridge (BA Med. Sci. Tripos 1988); New Coll., Oxford (BM BCh 1991); University Coll. London (PhD 1999). MRCP 1994; FRCP 2008. Pre-registration surgery, Glasgow Royal Infirmary, and medicine, John Radcliffe Hosp., Oxford, 1991–92; post-registration SHO posts at Hammersmith Hosp., Royal Brompton Hosp., St Thomas' Hosp. and National Hosp., 1991–94; Registrar, Queen Mary's Hosp., Roehampton, 1994–95; University College London: Clin. Res. Fellow, Inst. of Neurol., 1995–99; Dir, Inst. of Cognitive Neurosci., 2009–14; Dep. Hd, Faculty of Brain Scis, 2011–14; non-exec. Mem., Bd of Dirs, UCL Business plc, 2015–; Wellcome Advanced Fellow: CIT, 1999–2001; Inst. of Cognitive Neurosci., UCL, 2001–02. Hon. Consultant, National Hosp. for Neurol. and Neurosurgery, 2004–. FMedSci 2010. *Publications:* (ed jtly) Neurobiology of Attention, 2005; contrib. numerous articles to acad. jls and acad. monographs. *Recreation:* attempting to achieve a better work/life balance. *Address:* Wellcome Centre for Human Neuroimaging, 12 Queen Square, WC1N 3BG. *T:* (020) 7679 5496, *Fax:* (020) 7813 1420. *E:* g.rees@ucl.ac.uk.

**REES, Hefin Ednyfed**; QC 2013; a Recorder, since 2008; *b* Liverpool, 1969; *s* of Rev. Dr D. Ben Rees and Meinwen Rees; *m* 1995, Dr Bethan; two *s*. *Educ*: King David High Sch., Liverpool; Durham Univ. (BA (Hons) Law); Inns of Court Sch. of Law. FCIArb 2011. Called to the Bar: Inner Temple, 1992; St Vincent and the Grenadines, E Caribbean Circuit, 2010; Ireland, 2012; Grand Cayman Is, 2015; BVI, 2017. Founder and Chm., Assoc. of London Welsh Lawyers, 2011–. *Publications*: (contrib.) Construction Contracts, 2013; contrib. Suffolk Transnational Law Rev., 2000. *Recreations*: charity work in Africa, travelling. *Address*: 3 Verulam Buildings, Gray's Inn, WC1R 5NT. *E*: hrees@3vb.com. *Club*: Travellers.

**REES, Helen**; *see* Young, H.

**REES, Hugh Francis E.**; *see* Ellis-Rees.

**REES, Huw**; *see* Rees, O. H.

**REES, John**; *see* Rees, A. J. D., and Rees, P. J.

**REES, Rev. Canon John**; *see* Rees, Rev. Canon V. J. H.

**REES, John Charles**; QC 1991; *b* 22 May 1949; *s* of Ronald Leslie Rees and Martha Therese Rees; *m* 1970, Dianne Elizabeth Kirby; three *s* one *d*. *Educ*: St Illtyd's College, Cardiff; Jesus College, Cambridge (double first class Hons; BA (Law), LLB (Internat. Law), MA, LLM; repr. Univ. in boxing and Association Football; boxing Blue). Called to the Bar, Lincoln's Inn, 1972. Trustee and Gov., St John's College, Cardiff, 1987–2010, 2016–. Chm., British Boxing Board of Control, 2014–18. *Recreations*: all sport, esp. boxing and Association Football; theatre. *Address*: Marleigh Lodge, Druidstone Road, Old St Mellons, Cardiff CF3 6XD. *T*: (029) 2079 4918; 28 Cathedral Road, Cardiff CF11 9LJ. *Club*: Hawks (Cambridge).

*See also J. E. Rees.*

**REES, John Samuel**; Editor, Western Mail, 1981–87; *b* 23 Oct. 1931; *s* of John Richard Rees and Mary Jane Rees; *m* 1957, Ruth Jewell; one *s* one *d*. *Educ*: Cyfarthfa Castle Grammar Sch., Merthyr Tydfil. Nat. Service, Welch Regt and RAEC, 1950–52. Reporter, 1948–50, Sports Editor, 1952–54, Merthyr Express; The Star, Sheffield: Reporter, 1954–56; Sub Editor, 1956–58; Dep. Chief Sub Editor, 1958–59; Dep. Sports Editor, 1959–61; Asst Editor, 1961–66; Dep. Editor, Evening Echo, Hemel Hempstead, 1966–69; Editor: Evening Mail, Slough and Hounslow, 1969–72; The Journal, Newcastle upon Tyne, 1972–76; Evening Post-Echo, Hemel Hempstead, 1976–79, Asst Man. Dir, Evening Post-Echo Ltd, 1979–81. Lectr, Centre for Journalism Studies, Univ. of Wales Coll. of Cardiff, 1988–92. *Recreations*: marquetry, watching cricket and rugby, walking, gardening.

**REES, Jonathan David**; QC 2010; *b* Cardiff, 18 Oct. 1961; *s* of John Geraint Rees and Caroline Fay Rees; *m* 1988, Clare Marian Gray; one *s* one *d*. *Educ*: Cardiff High Sch.; Stowe Sch.; Jesus Coll., Oxford (BA Hons 1984). Called to the Bar, Gray's Inn, 1987; Jun. Treasury Counsel, 2002–08; Sen. Treasury Counsel, 2008–15. *Recreations*: Welsh Rugby, Spurs, everything London has to offer. *Address*: 2 Hare Court, Temple, EC4Y 7BH. *T*: (020) 7353 5324. *E*: JonathanRees@2harecourt.com. *Club*: Cardiff and County.

**REES, Jonathan Elystan**; QC 2019; *b* Cardiff, 27 Feb. 1977; *s* of John Charles Rees, *qv*; *m* 2006, Claire Louise Jacklin; one *s* one *d*. *Educ*: St John's Coll., Cardiff; St David's Catholic VI Form Coll., Cardiff; Jesus Coll., Cambridge (BA 1st Cl. Hons Law 1999). Called to the Bar, Inner Temple, 2000; in practice as barrister, 2000–. Mem. Bd, Legal Wales Foundn, 2014–. Jun. Sec., Wales and Chester Circuit, 2017–19. *Recreations*: supporting Cardiff City FC and Welsh national football and Rugby teams, hill walking, running, lead guitar, watching son play sport and daughter perform ballet. *Address*: Apex Chambers, 20 Cathedral Road, Cardiff CF11 9LJ. *T*: (029) 2023 2032. *E*: jonathan.reesQC@apexchambers.net; 5 Paper Buildings, Temple, EC4Y 7HB. *T*: (020) 7583 6117. *E*: jr@5pb.co.uk. *Club*: Hawks' (Cambridge).

**REES, Prof. Jonathan Laurence**, FRCP, FRCPE, FMedSci; Grant Professor of Dermatology, University of Edinburgh, since 2000; *b* 10 Oct. 1957; *s* of William Rees and Maura (*née* West); *m* 1983, Anne Bradbury (marr. diss. 2006); two *d*; *m* 2007, Lisa Naysmith. *Educ*: Newcastle Univ. (BMedSci 1st Cl. Hons 1981; MB BS Hons 1982). MRCP 1985, FRCP 1993; FRCPE 2001. Vis. Fellow, 1st Hautklinik, Allgemeines Krankenhaus der Stadt Wien, Vienna, 1986; MRC Trng Fellow, Univ. of Newcastle upon Tyne, 1987–89; MRC Clinician Scientist, CNRS/INSERM Lab. de Génétique Moléculaire des Eucaryotes, Strasbourg, 1989–91; Prof. of Dermatology, Univ. of Newcastle upon Tyne, 1992–99. FMedSci 1998. *Publications*: papers on genetics of skin disease, particularly pigment genetics ("red hair gene") and skin cancer; more recently, papers on semi-automated skin cancer diagnostic systems and learning in dermatology. *Recreations*: Rugby, avoiding formal occasions and wondering when the machines will take over. *Address*: Department of Dermatology, University of Edinburgh, Level 1, The Lauriston Building, Lauriston Place, Edinburgh EH3 9HA. *T*: (0131) 536 2041, *Fax*: (0131) 229 8769. *E*: reestheskin@me.com.

**REES, Jonathan Nigel**; Director General and Accounting Officer, Government Equalities Office, 2008–13; *b* 29 Sept. 1955; *s* of late Arthur Ernest Rees and Thelma Maureen Rees; *m* 1996, Kathryn Jayne Taylor; one *s* one *d*. *Educ*: Jesus Coll., Oxford (MA Hons Modern History). Joined DTI, 1977; Private Sec. to Minister for Trade, 1981–84; EC, 1984–86 (on secondment); DTI, 1986–89; Industry Counsellor, UK Rep. to EU, 1989–94; Prime Minister's Policy Unit, 1994–97; Dir, Citizen's Charter Unit, then Modernising Public Services Gp, Cabinet Office, 1997–2000; Dir, Consumer and Competition Policy, DTI, 2000–04; Dep. Dir Gen., later Dep. Chief Exec. (Policy), HSE, 2004–08. Independent Director: Lending Standards Bd, 2014–; Office of Ind. Adjudicator for Higher Educn, 2018–. Non-exec. Dir, Ombudsman Services, 2013–18. Trustee: Citizens Advice, 2011–17; NACAB Pension Fund, 2012–17; Employers Network on Equality and Inclusion, 2013–. Ind. Dir, Personal Finance Soc., 2015–. *Recreations*: sport, travel, theatre. *Club*: MCC.

**REES, Dame Judith (Anne)**, DBE 2013 (CBE 2005); PhD; Professor of Environmental and Resources Management, 1995–2016, Vice-Chair, Grantham Research Institute on Climate Change and the Environment, since 2014 (Director, 2008–12; Co-Director, 2012–14), and Professorial Research Fellow, since 2016, London School of Economics and Political Science (Hon. Fellow, 2016); *b* 26 Aug. 1944; *d* of late Douglas S. Hart and Eva M. Hart (*née* Haynes); *m* 1st, 1968, Prof. Raymond Rees, *qv* (marr. diss. 1972); 2nd, 1981, Prof. David Keith Crozier Jones. *Educ*: Bilborough Grammar Sch., Nottingham; London Sch. of Economics (BSc Econ 1965; MPhil 1967; PhD 1978). Lectr, Agricl Econs, Wye Coll., London Univ., 1967–69; Lectr, 1969–85, Sen. Lectr, 1985–89, in Geography, LSE; University of Hull: Prof. of Geography, 1989–95; Dean of Sch. of Geography and Earth Resources, 1991–93; Pro-Vice Chancellor, 1993–95; London School of Economics and Political Science: Pro-Dir, then Dep. Dir, 1998–2004; Dir, 2011–12; Dir, ESRC Centre for Climate Change Econs and Policy, 2008–13. Nat. Water and Sewerage Policy Advr, Australian Dept of Urban and Regl Develt, 1974–75. Economic and Social Research Council: Member: Trng Bd, 1994–98; Global Envmtl Change Cttee, 1995–98; Council, 2004–10; Dutch Nat. Climate Res. Progs, Internat. Scientific Adv. Council, 2011–14; Member: Exec. Panel on Pollution Res., SSRC, 1977–80; Adv. Cttee, Centre for Regulated Industries, 1990–2007; Technical Adv. Cttee, Global Water Partnership, 1996–2010; Competition (formerly Monopolies and Mergers) Commn, 1996–2002; Link/Teaching Co. Scheme Bd, OST, 1997–2002; UN Sec. Gen's Adv. Bd on Water and Sanitation, 2004–16; UN Water Task Force on Water and Climate Change, 2010–14; Scientific Adv. Cttee, Energy Climate House, Centre for Eur. Policy Studies; Chm., Ofwat Southern Customer Service Cttee, 1990–96. Royal Geographical Society: Mem. Council, 1979–82 and 2012–18; Vice Pres., 1995–97; Press., 2012–15; Mem. Council, Inst. of British Geographers, 1981–83. Hon. DSc Hull, 2012. *Publications*: Industrial Demands for Water, 1969; Natural Resources Allocation, Economics and Policy, 1985, 2nd edn 1990, repr. 2018; (jtly) The International Oil Industry: an interdisciplinary perspective, 1987; (jtly) Troubled Water, 1987; Water for Life, 1993; articles on water resources and envmtl mgt in books and learned jls. *Address*: Grantham Research Institute, Pethick-Lawrence House, London School of Economics and Political Science, Houghton Street, WC2A 2AE. *T*: (020) 7955 6228.

**REES, Laurence Mark**; Chairman, LR History Ltd (formerly History Media TV Ltd, then LR History TV Ltd), since 2011; *b* 19 Jan. 1957; *s* of late Alan Rees and Margaret Julia Rees (*née* Mark); *m* 1987, Helena Brewer; two *s* one *d*. *Educ*: Solihull Sch.; Worcester Coll., Oxford (BA). Joined BBC TV, 1978: prodn trainee, 1978–79; writer/producer/dir, 1982–; Ed., Timewatch, BBC2, 1992–2002; Hd, History Progs Unit, BBC TV, 1999–2000; Creative Dir, BBC TV History Progs, 2000–08. Founder, writer and producer, WW2History.com, 2009– (Best in Class in Educn and Ref., Interactive Media Awards, 2011). Sen. Vis. Fellow, Internat. Hist. Dept, LSE, 2009–16. *Productions* include: Crisis (drama documentary), 1987; A British Betrayal, 1991; We Have Ways of Making You Think (History of Propaganda series), 1992; Nazis: a warning from history (series; awards include: BAFTA, IDA, Peabody, BPG), 1997; War of the Century (series), 1999; Horror in the East (series), 2000; Auschwitz: the Nazis and the 'Final Solution' (series; Grierson Award, History Today Prize), 2005; World War Two: behind closed doors, 2008; The Dark Charisma of Adolf Hitler (series), 2012; Touched by Auschwitz, 2015; as Executive Producer, awards include: Emmy Awards, 1994 (2) and 1996; Amnesty Press Award, 1994; Internat. Documentary Assoc. Award, 1997; Western Heritage Award, 2000. Hon. DLitt Sheffield, 2005; DUniv Open, 2011. Lifetime Achievement Award, History Makers, 2009. *Publications*: Electric Beach (novel), 1990; Selling Politics, 1992; Nazis: a warning from history, 1997; War of the Century, 1999; Horror in the East, 2001; Auschwitz: the Nazis and the 'Final Solution', 2005 (History Book of the Year, British Book Awards, 2006); Their Darkest Hour: people tested to the extreme in World War Two, 2007; World War Two: behind closed doors, 2008; The Dark Charisma of Adolf Hitler: leading millions into the abyss, 2012; The Holocaust, 2017. *Recreation*: my three children. *Address*: c/o Andrew Nurnberg Associates, 20–23 Greville Street, EC1N 8SS. *T*: (020) 7327 0400.

**REES, Prof. Dame Lesley Howard**, DBE 2001; MD, DSc; FRCP; FRCPath; FMedSci; Professor of Chemical Endocrinology, Bart's and The London School of Medicine and Dentistry, Queen Mary (formerly St Bartholomew's Hospital Medical College), University of London, 1978–2006, now Emeritus; *b* 17 Nov. 1942; *d* of Howard Leslie Davis and Charlotte Patricia Siegrid Young; *m* 1969, Gareth Mervyn Rees, FRCS, FRCP. *Educ*: Pate's Grammar Sch. for Girls, Cheltenham; Malvern Girls' Coll.; London Univ. (MB BS 1965; MD 1972; MSc 1974; DSc 1989). MRCP 1967, FRCP 1979; MRCPath 1976, FRCPath 1988. Editor, Clinical Endocrinology, 1979–84; Sub-dean, 1983–88, Dean, 1989–95, St Bartholomew's Hosp. Med. Coll.; Public Orator, London Univ., 1984–86. Chm., Soc. for Endocrinology, 1984–87; Sec.-Gen., Internat. Soc. of Endocrinology, 1984–2005. Mem., Press Complaints Commn, 1991–94. Royal College of Physicians: Dir, Internat. Office, 1997–99; Dir, Educn Dept, 1997–2001. Founder FMedSci 1998. Hon. Fellow, QMUL, 2006. *Recreations*: music, poetry, reading, administrative gardening. *Address*: 23 Church Row, Hampstead, NW3 6UP. *T*: (020) 7794 4936; 2 Impasse du Petit St Martin, La Flotte en Ré, 17630 Ile de Ré, France. *Club*: Royal Air Force.

**REES, Madeleine Selina**, OBE 2014; Secretary General, Women's International League for Peace and Freedom, since 2010; *b* Cardiff, 26 March 1957; *d* of David and Margaret Rees; civil partnership 2006, Yulia Krieger; one *d*. *Educ*: Sutton Coldfield Grammar Sch. for Girls; University Coll. of Wales, Aberystwyth (BA Hons Hist.; PGCE); Univ. of Central England (Law). Teacher, 1980–88; admitted as solicitor, 1990; Solicitor, 1990–96, Partner, 1994–96, Tyndallwoods; Office of the Ombudsman, Bosnia, 1996–97; Head, Bosnia, 1997–2006, Gender Unit, Geneva, 2006–10, Office of UN High Comr for Human Rights. Vis. Prof. in Practice, LSE, 2016–. Hon. DSocSc Edinburgh, 2015. *Recreations*: family, biking, walking dogs, reading (watching Game of Thrones). *Address*: Women's International League for Peace and Freedom, 41 Rue de Varembé, 1211 Geneva 20, Switzerland. *T*: (22) 9197080. *E*: mrees@wilpf.ch.

**REES, Mary**; *see* Rees, S. M.

**REES, Sir Meuric**; *see* Rees, Sir R. E. M.

**REES, Prof. Michael Ralph**, FRCP, FRCR; Professor of Cardiovascular Studies, since 2005 and University Director of Medical Development, since 2012, Bangor University (formerly University of Wales, Bangor); *b* Hammersmith, 19 April 1950; *s* of William Morris Rees and Herta Klara Rees (*née* Teichmann); *m* 1992, Ann Patricia Clements; two *d*. *Educ*: Shene Grammar Sch., East Sheen; Univ. of East Anglia (BSc 1971); Univ. of Sheffield (MB ChB 1976). DMRD 1982; Eur. Bd of Cardiac Radiol. 2011; Cert Ed 2011; Postgrad. Cert. Clin. Leadership 2016. FRCR 1983; FRCP 1999. Consultant Cardioradiologist, Leeds, 1984–93; Consulting Prof., Stanford Univ., Calif, 1992–93; Prof. of Radiol Scis, Keele Univ., 1993–95; Prof. of Clinical Radiol., Univ. of Bristol, 1995–2005. Hon. Clinical Sen. Lectr, Univ. of Leeds, 1998–2002. Vis. Prof., Glyndŵr and Chester Univs, 2018–. Mem. Council, BMA, 2008– (Chm., 2003–07, Co-Chm., 2007–, Academic Staff Cttee). Pres., Eur. Soc. of Cardiac Radiol., 2008–11. Member: UK Healthcare Educn Adv. Cttee, 2009–12; Health Educn Nat. Strategic Exchange, 2009–. Betsi Cadwalladr University Health Board: Associate Mem., 2015–; Chm., Health Professions Forum, 2015–; Med. Dir, Workforce and Professionalism, 2015–. FHEA 2005; FAcadMed 2015. Hon. PhD Ionnina, 2006. Medal, BMA, 2008. *Publications*: book chapters and over 100 papers in scientific jls. *Recreation*: medical politics. *Address*: 3 Kings Oak, Colwyn Bay, Conwy LL29 0AJ. *T*: (01492) 531242. *E*: michael.rees@bangor.ac.uk.

**REES, Natasha Rachel**; Partner and Senior Equity Partner, since 2008, and Head of Property Litigation, since 2012, Forsters LLP; *b* Northwood, 24 Jan. 1966; *d* of Brian Frederick Rees and Julia Rees; *m* 2009, Michael Gaskel Griffiths; one *s* one *d*. *Educ*: Tormead Sch., Surrey; Rugby Sch.; Univ. of Edinburgh (BSc Hons Biol. and Psychol. 1989); Coll. of Law (Solicitors Finals, CPE 1993). Admitted solicitor, 1995; joined Lewis Silkin, 1993, solicitor, 1995–98; solicitor: Pinsent Masons, 1998–2001; Forsters LLP, 2001–. Member: Law Soc.; Property Litigation Assoc. *Recreation*: cycling between European cities. *Address*: 116 Milton Grove, N16 8QY. *T*: (020) 7863 8385. *E*: natasha.rees@forsters.co.uk. *Club*: Reform.

**REES, Owen**, CB 1991; Deputy Chairman, Qualifications, Curriculum and Assessment Authority for Wales, 1997–2006; *b* 26 Dec. 1934; *s* of late John Trevor and Esther Rees, Trimsaran, Carmarthenshire; *m* 1958, Elizabeth Gosby (*d* 1991); one *s* two *d*. *Educ*: Llanelli Grammar Sch.; Univ. of Manchester. BA(Econ). Bank of London and South America, 1957; regional development work in Cardiff, Birmingham and London, BoT, 1959–69; Cabinet Office, 1969–71; Welsh Office, 1971–94: Asst Sec. (European Div.), 1972; Under Sec., 1977–94; Sec. for Welsh Educn, 1977–78; Head, Educn Dept, 1978–80; Dir, Industry Dept, 1980–85; Head, Economic and Regl Policy Gp, 1985–90; Head, Agriculture Dept, 1990–94. *Address*: 4 Llandennis Green, Cyncoed, Cardiff CF23 6JX. *T*: (029) 2075 9712.

**REES, (Owen) Huw; His Honour Judge Huw Rees;** a Circuit Judge, since 2016; *b* Llanelli, Carmarthenshire, 6 Oct. 1960; *s* of Henry John Rees and Pamela Maureen Rees; partner, David Geraint Phillips. *Educ*: Llanelli Grammar Sch. for Boys; University Coll. of Wales, Aberystwyth (LLB); Inns of Court Sch. of Law. Called to the Bar, Gray's Inn, 1983; in practice at the Bar, 1983–2016; a Recorder, 2008–16. Pres., Mental Health Rev. Tribunal for Wales, 2012–; Chm., Police Misconduct Tribunals, 2014–. *Recreations*: watching most sports, especially Llanelli Scarlets, piano, biographies, journalism, Welsh culture, Colonia de Sant Jordi. *Address*: c/o Caernarfon Criminal Justice Centre, Llanberis Road, Caernarfon LL55 2DF. *T*: (01286) 669700. *Club*: Royal Welsh Yacht.

**REES, Prof. (Peter) John,** FRCP, FRCPE; Professor of Medical Education, King's College London School of Medicine, 2006–15, now Emeritus; *b* 2 March 1949; *s* of Joseph Thomas Rees and Doris Mary Williams; *m* 1973, Helen Mary Heath; one *s* one *d*. *Educ*: Whitchurch Grammar Sch., Cardiff; Christ's Coll., Cambridge (MB BChir; MA; MD); Guy's Hosp., London. FRCP 1988; FRCPE 2002. Guy's Hospital, later UMDS of Guy's and St Thomas' Hospitals, then Guy's, King's and St Thomas' Hospitals Medical and Dental School of King's College London, subseq. King's College London School of Medicine: Lectr, 1979–83; Sen. Lectr in Medicine, 1983–2006; Consultant Physician, 1983–2010; Asst Clin. Dean, 1993–2000; Gp Clin. Dir for Acute Med. Services, 1995–2000; Dep. Chm., Academic Bd, 1996–98; Site Dean, Guy's Hosp., 2000–05; Dean, Undergrad. Educn, 2005–10; Mem. Bd, Global Health Centre, 2010–. Non-exec. Mem., Lewisham and N Southwark HA, 1990–92; non-executive Director: Mildmay Mission Hosp., 1992–2005; Lewisham Hosp. Trust Bd, 1995–2006; Mem. Exec. Cttee, British Lung Foundn, 1988–95. FKC 2010. *Publications*: (jtly) ABC of Asthma, 1984, 6th edn 2009; (jtly) Practical Management of Asthma, 1985, 2nd edn 1996; A Medical Catechism, 1986; (jtly) A New Short Textbook of Medicine, 1988; Diagnostic Tests in Respiratory Medicine, 1988; Asthma: family doctor guide, 1988; (jtly) A Colour Atlas of Asthma, 1989; (jtly) Aids to Clinical Pharmacology and Therapeutics, 1993; (jtly) Principles of Clinical Medicine, 1995; (jtly) Asthma: current perspectives, 1996; (jtly) 100 Cases in Clinical Medicine, 2000, 3rd edn 2014; (jtly) Essential Clinical Medicine, 2009. *Recreations*: theatre, opera, squash, running. *Address*: Global Health Centre, Weston Education Centre, King's College London, 10 Cutcombe Road, SE5 9RJ.

**REES, Peter John;** QC 2009; FCIArb; Counsel and Arbitrator, Thirty Nine Essex Chambers, since 2014; *b* Wendover, 21 April 1957; *s* of Leslie Marchant Rees and Betty Rees; *m* 1st; one *d*; 2nd, 1999, Nicola Jane Mumford. *Educ*: Downing Coll., Cambridge (BA 1978); Nottingham Trent Univ. (MBA 1999). FCIArb 1997. Admitted solicitor, 1981; Partner, Norton Rose, 1987–2006; Partner, Debevoise & Plimpton LLP, 2006–10; Legal Dir and Exec. Cttee Mem., Royal Dutch Shell plc, 2011–14. Co-Chm., Internat. Construction Projs Cttee, IBA, 1999–2001; Chairman: Technol. and Construction Solicitors Assoc., 2000–04; Bd of Mgt, CIArb, 2008–09. Member: Council, ICC UK, 2006–17; Court, London Court of Internat. Arbitration, 2012– (Vice Pres., 2017–); Bd, Internat. Inst. for Conflict Prevention and Resolution, 2012–17; Governing Body, Internat. Court of Arbitration, ICC, 2012–14. *Publications*: (with A. Briggs) Civil Jurisdiction and Judgments, 1993, 5th edn 2009. *Recreations*: Association Football, golf, scuba diving, gardening. *Address*: 39 Essex Chambers, 81 Chancery Lane, WC2A 1DD. *E*: peter.rees@39essex.com. *Clubs*: Hawks; Richmond Golf.

**REES, Prof. Peter Wynne,** CBE 2015; FRTPI; Professor of Places and City Planning, The Bartlett, UCL Faculty of the Built Environment, since 2014; *b* 26 Sept. 1948; *s* of Gwynne Rees, MM, CEng, MIMechE, FMES, and late Elizabeth Rodda Rees (*née* Hynam). *Educ*: Pontardawe Grammar Sch.; Whitchurch Grammar Sch., Cardiff; Bartlett Sch. of Architecture, UCL (BSc Hons); Welsh Sch. of Architecture, Univ. of Wales (BArch); Polytechnic of the South Bank (BTP). Architectural Asst, Historic Bldgs Div., GLC, 1971–72; Asst to Gordon Cullen, CBE, RDI, FSIA, 1973–75; Architect, Historic Areas Conservation, DoE, 1975–79; UK Rep., Council of Europe Wkg Parties studying New Uses for Historic Buildings and The Economics of Building Conservation, 1977–78; Asst Chief Planning Officer, London Bor. of Lambeth, 1979–85; Controller of Planning, 1985–87, The City Planning Officer, 1987–2014, Corp. of London, later City of London Corp. Trustee: Building Conservation Trust, 1985–91; Architecture Foundn, 2014–17. Founder Mem. and Dir, British Council for Offices, 1989–. London Rep., EC (formerly European) Working Party on Technological Impact on Future Urban Change, 1989–92; Member: Steering Gp, London World City Study, 1990–91; Officers' Gp, London Pride Partnership, 1994–98; London Office Review Panel, 1996–2014. Hon. Mem., AA, 2014. FRSA 1988. Hon. FRIBA 2011. Hon. DSc London South Bank, 2014. President's Award, British Council for Offices, 2003; Barbara Miller Award, Faculty of Building, 2004; Outstanding Contribution, Offices Awards, 2010; Award for Outstanding Contribn to Property, Estates Gazette, 2013; Property Award, Coll. of Estate Mgt, 2014. *Publications*: City of London Local Plan, 1989; City of London Unitary Development Plans, 1994 and 2002; contribs to professional studies and jls. *Recreations*: tidying, playing the viola, watching paint dry. *Address*: The Bartlett, UCL Faculty of the Built Environment, Central House, 14 Upper Woburn Place, WC1H 0NN. *E*: peter.rees@ucl.ac.uk.

**REES, Philip;** a Recorder of the Crown Court, 1983–2008; *b* 1 Dec. 1941; *s* of John Trevor Rees and Olwen Muriel Rees; *m* 1969, Catherine Good; one *s* one *d*. *Educ*: Monmouth Sch.; Bristol Univ. (LLB Hons). Called to the Bar, Middle Temple, 1965. Asst Boundary Comr, 1996–2008. *Recreations*: music, sport. *Address*: 35 South Rise, Llanishen, Cardiff CF14 0RF. *T*: (029) 2075 4364. *Club*: Cardiff and County (Cardiff).

**REES, Prof. Philip Howell,** CBE 2004; PhD; FBA 1998; FAcSS, FRGS; Professor of Population Geography, University of Leeds, 1990–2009, now Emeritus; *b* 17 Sept. 1944; *s* of Foster and Mona Rees; *m* 1968, Laura Campbell; one *s* one *d*. *Educ*: King Edward's Sch., Birmingham; St Catharine's Coll., Cambridge (BA Geog. 1966; MA 1970); Univ. of Chicago (MA Geog. 1968; PhD 1973). FRGS 1971. University of Leeds: Lectr, 1970–80; Reader, 1980–90. Hofstee Vis. Fellow, Netherlands Interdisciplinary Demographic Inst., The Hague, 1995; Dist. Vis. Fellow, Univ. of Adelaide, 1996. Mem., Adv. Cttee on Resource Allocation, NHS England, 2006–16. Series Ed., Internat. Population Studies, 2009–17. FAcSS (AcSS 2013). Gill Meml Award, 1996, Victoria Medal, 2009, RGS. *Publications*: Spatial Population Analysis, 1977; Residential Patterns in American Cities, 1979; (ed jtly) Population Structures and Models, 1985; (ed jtly) Migration Processes and Patterns, Vol. 2, 1992; (ed jtly) Population Migration in the European Union, 1996; (jtly) The Determinants of Migration Flows in England, 1998; (ed jtly) The Census Data System, 2002; (jtly) The Development of a Migration Model, 2002; e-Learning for Geographers, 2009. *Recreation*: walking. *Address*: School of Geography, University of Leeds, Leeds LS2 9JT. *T*: 07584 098247; (home) 3 Mavis Lane, Cookridge, Leeds LS16 7LL. *T*: (0113) 267 6968.

**REES, Prof. Ray;** Professor of Economics, University of Munich, 1993–2008, now Emeritus (Dean of Economics Faculty, 1999–2000); *b* 19 Sept. 1943; *s* of Gwyn Rees and Violet May (*née* Powell); *m* 1976, Denise Sylvia (*née* Stinson); two *s*. *Educ*: Dyffryn Grammar Sch., Port Talbot; London School of Economics and Political Science (MScEcon). Lectr 1966–76, Reader 1976–78, Queen Mary Coll., Univ. of London; Economic Advr, HM Treasury (on secondment), 1968–72; Prof. of Econs, UC, Cardiff, 1978–87; Prof. of Econs, Univ. of Guelph, Ont, 1987–93. Member (part-time), Monopolies and Mergers Commn, 1985–87. *Publications*: A Dictionary of Economics, 1968, 3rd edn 1984; Public Enterprise Economics, 1975, 3rd edn 1992; Microeconomics, 1981, 3rd edn 2004; Economics: a mathematical introduction, 1991; Introduction to Game Theory, 1992; The Theory of Principal and Agent, 1992; Mathematics for Economics, 1996, 3rd edn 2011; The Economics of Public Utilities, 2006; The Microeconomics of Insurance, 2008; Public Economics and the Household, 2009; articles in Economic Jl, Amer. Econ. Rev., Jl of Political Econ., Jl of Public Econs, Economica, and others. *Recreations*: playing the guitar, walking in the Alps and the Snowdonia National Park. *Address*: Bwlchcoediog Uchaf, Cwm Cewydd, Machynlleth, Powys SY20 9EE. *T*: (01650) 531652.

**REES, Sir (Richard Ellis) Meuric,** Kt 2007; CBE 1982; JP; FRAgS; Lord-Lieutenant for Gwynedd, 1990–99; Vice Chairman, Hill Farming Advisory Committee (Chairman, Committee for Wales); *b* Pantydwr, Radnorshire, 1924; *m*; three *d*. President: YFC in Wales, 1961; Merioneth Agricl Soc., 1972; Royal Welsh Agricl Show, 1978; former Chm., Welsh Council of NFU; Mem., CLA. Member: Agricl Trng Bd, 1974 (Chm., Cttee for Wales); Countryside Commn, 1981 (Chm., Cttee for Wales). Governor: Welsh Agricl Coll., Aberystwyth; Coleg Meirionnydd, Dolgellau; Inst. of Grassland and Animal Production, 1987; Inst. of Grassland and Environmental Res., 1990. Mem., Tywyn UDC, 1967–73. Chm., N Wales Police Authority, 1982–84. JP Tywyn, 1957 (Chm. of Bench, 1974–94); High Sheriff of Gwynedd, 1982–83; DL Gwynedd, 1988. FRAgS 1973. Hon. MSc Wales, 1999. KStJ 1997. *Address*: Esguan Hall, Tywyn, Gwynedd LL36 9HR.

**REES, Susan Barbara;** *see* Lambert, S. B.

**REES, Prof. (Susan) Mary,** PhD; FRS 2002; Professor of Mathematics, University of Liverpool, 2002–18, now Emeritus; *b* 31 July 1953; *d* of Prof. David Rees, FRS and Joan Rees. *Educ*: St Hugh's Coll., Oxford (BA 1974, MSc 1975); Univ. of Warwick (PhD Maths 1978). Asst, then Associate Prof. of Maths, Univ. of Minnesota, 1982–84; Lectr, 1984–90, Sen. Lectr, 1990–2002, Univ. of Liverpool. *Publications*: contribs to Acta Mathematicae, Annales de l'Ecole Normale Supérieure, Jls of London Mathematical Soc., Inventiones Mathematicae, Ergodic Theory and Dynamical Systems, Asterisque, etc. *Recreations*: late start runner, at nearly 60, then cross-country at 61 and first marathon at 62, walking, choir-singing, listening to music, reading, gardening. *Address*: Department of Mathematical Sciences, Mathematics and Oceanography Building, University of Liverpool, Peach Street, Liverpool L69 7ZL. *E*: maryrees@liverpool.ac.uk.

**REES, Prof. Dame Teresa Lesley,** DBE 2015 (CBE 2003); PhD; FAcSS; FLSW; Professor of Social Sciences, Cardiff University, 2000–15, now Emerita (Pro Vice Chancellor, 2004–10); Director for Wales (formerly Associate Director), Leadership Foundation for Higher Education, 2010–13; *b* 11 June 1949; *d* of Gordon Leslie Baggs and Vera Geddes-Ruffle; *m* 1974, Gareth Meredydd Rees (marr. diss. 2004); two *s*. *Educ*: Univ. of Exeter (BA Hons Sociology and Politics); PhD Wales 1993. Res. Officer, Univ. of Exeter, 1970–73; Res. Fellow, UWIST, 1973–76; Sen. Res. Asst, Mid Glamorgan CC, 1977–78; University College, Cardiff: Res. Fellow, 1976–77, 1978–88; Dir, Social Res. Unit, and Lectr in Sociology, 1988–92; Bristol University: Sen. Res. Fellow, 1993–94; Reader, 1994–95; Prof. of Labour Mkt Studies, 1995–2000. Fellow, Sunningdale Inst., Nat. Sch. of Govt, 2007–12. Member: EOC, 1996–2002; BBC Audience Council Wales, 2007–12. Hon. Pres., S Wales Br., WEA, 1996–2014. FAcSS (AcSS 2001); FLSW 2012. FRSA. Hon. Fellow, Univ. of Lampeter, 2006. Hon. DSocSci QUB, 2012; Hon. LLD: Bath, 2012; Exeter, 2014; Bristol, 2016; Aberdeen, 2016; S Wales, 2017. *Publications*: (ed jtly) Youth Unemployment and State Intervention, 1982; (ed jtly) Our Sisters' Land: the changing identities of women in Wales, 1994; Women and the Labour Market, 1992; Mainstreaming Equality in the European Union, 1998; Women and Work, 1999; (jtly) Adult Guidance and the Learning Society, 2000. *Recreation*: campaigning for gender equality. *Address*: School of Social Sciences, Cardiff University, Glamorgan Building, King Edward VII Avenue, Cardiff CF10 3WT.

**REES, Victoria Kirstyn;** *see* Williams, V. K.

**REES, Rev. Canon (Vivian) John (Howard);** Principal Registrar, Province of Canterbury, since 2000; Chaplain to the Queen, since 2014; *b* 21 April 1951; *s* of Herbert John Rees and Beryl Rees; *m* 1980, Dianne Elizabeth Hamilton; two *d*. *Educ*: Skinners' Sch., Tunbridge Wells; Southampton Univ. (LLB 1972); Wycliffe Hall, Oxford (MA); MPhil Leeds 1984. Admitted Solicitor, 1975; Ecclesiastical Notary; Asst Solicitor, Cooke Matheson & Co., 1975–76; Hosp. Administrator, Multan, Pakistan, 1976; ordained deacon 1979, priest 1980; Asst Curate, Moor Allerton Team Ministry, Leeds, 1979–82; Chaplain and Tutor, Sierra Leone Theol Hall, Freetown, 1982–85; with Winckworth Sherwood, 1986– (Partner, 1988–; Sen. Partner, 2013–). Proctor in Convocation for Oxford, 1995–2000; Legal Advr, ACC, 1994–; Diocesan Registrar, Dio. Oxford, 1998–; Registrar: Court of Arches and Court of Ecclesiastical Causes Reserved, 2000–; Clergy Discipline Tribunals, 2006–. Provincial Canon, Canterbury Cathedral, 2001–; Hon. Canon, Christ Church, Oxford, 2017–. Mem., Legal Adv. Commn, General Synod, 2000– (Vice-Chm., 2001–). Treas., 1995–2015, Chm., 2015–, Ecclesiastical Law Soc. *Recreations*: photography, walking, cycling, second-hand bookshops. *Address*: (office) 2 Chawley Park, Oxford OX2 9GG. *T*: (01865) 297200, *Fax*: (020) 7593 0309. *E*: jrees@wslaw.co.uk; (home) 36 Cumnor Hill, Oxford OX2 9HB. *T*: and *Fax*: (01865) 865875. *E*: vjhrees@btinternet.com. *Clubs*: Athenæum, Nobody's Friends.

**REES, His Honour Wyn;** *see* Rees, His Honour D. W.

**REES LEAHY, Prof. Helen Blodwen,** PhD; Director, Centre for Museology, 2002–17, and Professor of Museology, 2013–17, now Professor Emerita, School of Arts, Languages and Cultures (formerly School of Art History and Archaeology, then School of Arts, Histories and Cultures), University of Manchester; *b* 23 Aug. 1960; *d* of late Edward Elgar Rees and of Dorothy Rees (*née* Banham); *m* 1997, Dr Michael Gordon Leahy. *Educ*: Gaisford High Sch. for Girls, Worthing; New Hall, Cambridge (MA); City Univ.; Univ. of Manchester (PhD 1999). Information Officer, Conran Foundn, 1984–86; Curator, 1986–89, Dir, 1989–92, Design Mus.; Communications Dir, Eureka!, The Mus. for Children, 1992; Asst Dir and Head of Public Affairs, NACF, 1992–95; University of Manchester: Lectr in Art Gall. and Mus. Studies, 2000–07, Sen. Lectr, 2007–13, Sch. of Arts, Histories and Cultures (formerly Sch. of Art History and Archaeol); Dir, External

Relns, 2010–13. Curatorial Consultant, Elizabeth Gaskell's House, Manchester, 2013–. Member: Adv. Panel, Arts Council of England, 1992–95; Design Adv. Cttee, RSA, 1990–94; Visual Arts Advr, NW Arts Bd, 1996–. Gov., Dean Clough Foundn (formerly Design Dimension Educnl Trust), 1990–. Trustee: Cardiff Old Library Trust, 1995–2000; Cornerhouse, Manchester, 1996–2003; Yorkshire Sculpture Park, 2002–. Editor (and contrib.) Design Museum Publications, 1989–92. *Publications*: 14:24 British Youth Culture, 1986; (contrib.) The Authority of the Consumer, ed Nigel Whiteley, 1993; (contrib.) The Culture of Craft, ed Peter Dormer, 1997; (contrib.) Art History and its Institutions, ed Elizabeth Mansfield, 2002; (contrib.) Museum Materialities, 2009; (ed) Art City Spectacle: the 1857 Manchester Art Treasures Exhibition revisited, 2009; (contrib.) Performance, Learning, Heritage, 2010; (contrib.) The Thing About Museums, 2011; (contrib.) Sculpture and Archaeology, 2011; Museum Bodies: the politics and practices of visiting and viewing, 2012; (contrib.) Museums and Biographies, 2012; articles in jls. *Recreations*: hand weaving, Bach, listening and playing. *Address*: 17 River Street, Manchester M1 5BG. *T*: (0161) 236 2717; Centre for Museology, School of Arts, Languages and Cultures, University of Manchester, Oxford Road, Manchester M13 9PL. *E*: helen.rees@manchester.ac.uk.

**REES-MOGG, Rt Hon. Jacob (William);** PC 2019; MP (C) North East Somerset, since 2010; Leader of the House of Commons and Lord President of the Council, since 2019; *b* 24 May 1969; *s* of Baron Rees-Mogg and of Gillian Shakespeare Rees-Mogg (*née* Morris); *m* 2007, Helena de Chair; five *s* one *d*. *Educ*: Eton Coll.; Trinity Coll., Oxford (BA Hist. 1991). Investment Analyst, J. Rothschild Investment Mgt, 1991–93; Dir, Lloyd George Mgt, Hong Kong, 1992–96, London, 1996–2007; Sen. Partner and Founder, Somerset Capital Mgt, 2007–. Contested (C): Central Fife, 1997; The Wrekin, 2001. Member, Select Committee: on Procedure, 2010–15; on Eur. Scrutiny, 2010–17; Treasury, 2015–17; on Exiting the EU, 2017–. *Publications*: The Victorians, 2019. *Address*: House of Commons, SW1A 0AA; Gournay Court, West Harptree, Somerset BS40 6EB. *T*: (01761) 221027.

**REES-WILLIAMS,** family name of **Baron Ogmore**.

**REES-WILLIAMS, Jonathan,** FRCO; Organist and Master of the Choristers, St George's Chapel, Windsor Castle, 1991–2002; *b* 10 Feb. 1949; *s* of Ivor and Barbara Rees-Williams; *m* 1985, Helen Patricia Harling; one *s* two *d*. *Educ*: Kilburn Grammar Sch.; Royal Academy of Music; New Coll., Oxford (Organ Scholar; MA 1972). LRAM, DipRAM 1969; ARAM 1984; FRCO 1968. Organist: St Edmund, Yeading, 1967; Church of the Ascension, Wembley, 1968; Actg Organist, New Coll., Oxford, 1972; Assistant Organist: Hampstead Parish Church and St Clement Danes, 1972–74; Salisbury Cathedral, 1974–78; Dir of Music, Salisbury Cathedral Sch., 1974–78; Organist and Master of Choristers, Lichfield Cathedral, 1978–91; Conductor, Lichfield Cathedral Special Choir, 1978–91. Chorusmaster, Portsmouth Festival Choir, 1974–78; Accompanist and Asst Dir, Salisbury Musical Soc., 1974–78. *Recreations*: cycling, wine, railways, vintage model railways.

**REESE, Prof. Colin Bernard,** PhD, ScD; FRS 1981; FRSC; Daniell Professor of Chemistry, King's College, University of London, 1973–98, now Emeritus; *b* 29 July 1930; *s* of Joseph and Emily Reese; *m* 1968, Susanne Bird; one *s* one *d*. *Educ*: Dartington Hall Sch.; Clare Coll., Cambridge (BA 1953, PhD 1956, MA 1957, ScD 1972). 1851 Sen. Student, 1956–58; Research Fellow: Clare Coll., Cambridge, 1956–59; Harvard Univ., 1957–58; Official Fellow and Dir of Studies in Chem., Clare Coll., 1959–73; Cambridge University: Univ. Demonstrator in Chem., 1959–63; Asst Dir of Res., 1963–64; Univ. Lectr in Chem., 1964–73. FKC 1989. *Publications*: scientific papers, mainly in chemical jls. *Address*: 21 Rozel Road, SW4 0EY. *T*: (020) 7498 0230.

**REESE, Colin Edward;** QC 1987; a Recorder, 1994–2015; Deputy Judge, Technology and Construction Court (formerly Deputy Official Referee), High Court, 1994–2015; *b* 28 March 1950; *s* of late Robert Edward Reese and Katharine Reese (*née* Moore); *m* 1978, Diana Janet Anderson; two *s* one *d*. *Educ*: Hawarden Grammar School; King Edward VI School, Southampton; Fitzwilliam College, Cambridge (BA 1972; MA 1976). Called to the Bar, Gray's Inn, 1973 (Mould Schol., 1974; Bencher, 1998); admitted, *ad eund*, Lincoln's Inn, 1976; in practice, 1975–2014. An Asst Parly Boundary Comr, 1992–2006. Legal Mem., Restricted Patients' Panel, First-tier Tribunal (Mental Health) (formerly Mental Health Review Tribunals), 2000–15. Vice-Chm., Qualifications Cttee, 2006–11, Mem., Complaints Cttee, 2004–09, Bar Standards Bd. Vice Chm., 1997–2000, Chm., 2000–03, Technol. and Construction (formerly Official Referees) Bar Assoc. Dir, Bar Mutual Indemnity Fund Ltd, 2001–13. Pres., Cambridge Univ. Law Soc., 1971–72. Liveryman, Bakers' Co., 1991– (Mem., Ct of Assts, 2010; Master, 2015–16). *Address*: c/o 1 Atkin Building, Gray's Inn, WC1R 5AT. *T*: (020) 7404 0102.

**REEVE, Anne Elizabeth;** *see* Longfield, A. E.

**REEVE, Derek Charles;** financial consultant; Director of Finance and Information Systems, Deputy Town Clerk and Deputy Chief Executive, Royal Borough of Kensington and Chelsea, 1991–2002; *b* 7 Dec. 1946; *s* of Charles Reeve and Sylvia Reeve (*née* Prynne); *m* 1968, Janice Rosina Williamson; one *s* one *d*. *Educ*: Dame Alice Owen's Grammar Sch. for Boys, Islington; Tottenham and E Ham Tech. Colls. Various posts, Islington LBC, 1965–74; Asst Borough Treas., Greenwich LBC, 1974–79; Dep. Dir of Finance, RBK&C, 1979–91. Actg Clerk, Western Riverside Waste Authy, 2005–06. Pres., Soc. of London Treasurers, 2000–01. Vice-Chairman of Governors: Sweyne Co. Primary Sch., Swanscombe, Kent, 2002– (Chm., Finance Cttee, 2002–); Manor Sch., Swanscombe, Dartford, 2009– (Chm., Interim Governing Body, 2008–09). *Recreations*: golf, painting (watercolours), reading, gardening, music, following Arsenal FC, genealogy, fly-fishing, running art clubs for primary schoolchildren. *Address*: 5 Red Lodge Crescent, Bexley, Kent DA5 2JR. *Clubs*: The Warren; Birchwood Park Golf (Wilmington).

**REEVE, John;** non-executive Chairman, Temple Bar Investment Trust PLC, 2003–18 (Director, 1992–2018); Director, Premium Credit Ltd, since 2012; *b* 13 July 1944; *s* of Clifford Alfred Reeve and Irene Mary Turnidge Reeve; *m* 1974, Sally Diane Welton; one *d*. *Educ*: Westcliff High School (Grammar). FCA. Selbey Smith & Earle, 1962–67; Peat Marwick McLintock, 1967–68; Vickers, Roneo Vickers Group, 1968–76; Wilkinson Match, 1976–77; Amalgamated Metal Corp., 1977–80; Group Finance Director: British Aluminium Co., 1980–83; Mercantile House Holdings, 1983–87; Dep. Man. Dir, 1988, Man. Dir, 1989, Sun Life Assurance Society plc; Gp Man. Dir, 1990–95, non-exec. Dir, 1995–96, Sun Life Corp. plc; Exec. Chm., Willis Corroon, subseq. Willis, Gp Ltd, 1995–2000. Non-executive Chairman: Alea Gp Hldgs (Bermuda) Ltd, 2003–07; Coverzones Ltd, 2007–10. Director: The English Concert, 1987– (Chm., 1993–2006); HMC Group plc, 1988–94; London First, 1998–2002. Pres., Inst. of Business Ethics, 1997–2000 (Mem. Adv. Council, 1986–91; Dep. Pres., 1991–96). Chm., E London Business Alliance, 2000–02; Member: E London Partnership Bd, 1991–2000 (Chm., 1996–2000); Council, BITC, 1995–2000; Life Insce Council, 1991–94, Bd, 1993–95, ABI; Bd, 1993–2001, Exec. Cttee, 1996–2001, Internat. Insurance Soc. Inc. Governor: Res. into Ageing, 1991–96; NIESR, 1995–2000. CCMI. FRSA 1999. *Recreations*: yachting, music, theatre. *Address*: Cliff Dene, 24 Cliff Parade, Leigh-on-Sea, Essex SS9 1BB. *T*: (01702) 477563. *E*: reevej@compuserve.com. *Clubs*: Athenæum, Royal Ocean Racing; Essex Yacht.

**REEVE, Rear Adm. Jonathon,** CB 2003; CEng; Deputy Chief Executive, Warship Support Agency, and Navy Board Member for Logistics, 2001–04; *b* 1 Oct. 1949; *e s* of late Lawrence Alick Reeve and of Joan Reeve; *m* 1980, Jennifer Anne, *d* of late Guy and of Betty Wickman; one *s* one *d*. *Educ*: Marlborough Coll.; St Catharine's Coll., Cambridge (MA 1972). CEng, MIEE 1978, FIET (FIEE 2000). Joined Royal Navy, 1967: qualified submarines, 1974; HMS Renown, 1974–76; HMS Dreadnought, 1979–82; RNSC, 1982; Naval Sec.'s Dept, MoD, 1982–84; Strategic Systems Exec., 1985–88; Naval Manpower Trng, 1989–91; Capt. 1991; Asst Dir, MoD Defence Systems, 1991–93; Head of Integrated Logistics Support (Navy), Ship Support Agency, MoD, 1994–96; rcds 1997; Cdre 1998; Naval Base Comdr, Devonport, 1998–2000; COS (Corporate Develt) to C-in-C Fleet, 2000. Dir, OMG, 2006–. *Recreations*: golf, tennis, gardening, dancing. *Address*: c/o Naval Secretary, Fleet Headquarters, Whale Island, Portsmouth, Hants PO1 3LS.

**REEVE, Prof. Michael David,** FBA 1984; Fellow, Pembroke College, Cambridge, since 1984; *b* 11 Jan. 1943; *s* of Arthur Reeve and Edith Mary Barrett; *m* 1970, Elizabeth Klingaman (marr. diss. 1999); two *s* one *d*. *Educ*: King Edward's Sch., Birmingham; Balliol Coll., Oxford (MA). Harmsworth Senior Scholar, Merton Coll., Oxford, 1964–65; Woodhouse Research Fellow, St John's Coll., Oxford, 1965–66; Tutorial Fellow, Exeter Coll., Oxford, 1966–84, now Emeritus Fellow; Kennedy Prof. of Latin, 1984–2006, Dir of Res., Faculty of Classics, 2006–07, Sandars Reader in Bibliography, 2012, Cambridge Univ. Visiting Professor: Univ. of Hamburg, 1976; McMaster Univ., 1979; Univ. of Toronto, 1982–83. Chm., Adv. Council, Warburg Inst., 2008–13. Fellow, Società Internazionale per lo Studio del Medioevo Latino, 1996; Corresp. Mem., Akademie der Wissenschaften, Göttingen, 1990; Foreign Member: Istituto Lombardo, Milan, 1993; Accademia Nazionale dei Lincei, Rome, 2017; Accademico della Classe di Studi Greci e Latini, Biblioteca Ambrosiana, Milan, 2014. Editor, Classical Quarterly, 1981–86. *Publications*: Longus, Daphnis and Chloe, 1982; contribs to Texts and Transmission, ed L. D. Reynolds, 1983; Cicero, Pro Quinctio, 1992; Vegetius, Epitoma rei militaris, 2004; Geoffrey of Monmouth, De gestis Britonum, 2007; Manuscripts and Methods, 2011; articles in European and transatlantic jls. *Recreations*: chess, music, gardening, mountain walking. *Address*: Pembroke College, Cambridge CB2 1RF.

**REEVE, Philip John;** author and illustrator; *b* Brighton, 28 Feb. 1966; *s* of Michael and Jean Reeve; *m* 1998, Sarah Hedley; one *s*. *Educ*: Stanley Deason High Sch., Brighton; Cambs Coll. of Arts and Technol. (HND BTEC (Illustration)). Freelance illustrator, 1990–; author, 2001–. *Publications*: Mortal Engines, 2001 (Guardian Children's Fiction Prize, Nestlé Book Prize, Blue Peter Book of Year; filmed, 2018); Predator's Gold, 2003; Infernal Devices, 2005; A Darkling Plain, 2006; Larklight, 2006; Here Lies Arthur, 2007 (Carnegie Medal, CILIP, 2008); Starcross, 2007; Mothstorm, 2008; Fever Crumb, 2009; No Such Thing as Dragons, 2009; A Web of Air, 2010; Scrivener's Moon, 2011; Goblins, 2012; Goblin Quest, 2014; Railhead, 2015; Black Light Express, 2016; Station Zero, 2018; Night Flights, 2018; with Sarah McIntyre: Oliver and the Seawigs, 2013; Cakes in Space, 2014; Pugs of the Frozen North, 2015; Jinks and O'Hare Funfair Repair, 2016; Pug-a-Doodle-Do, 2017; The Legend of Kevin, 2018. *Recreation*: walking on Dartmoor, horseback and bicycle. *Address*: c/o Lucas Alexander Whitley, 14 Vernon Street, W14 0RJ. *T*: (020) 7471 7900.

**REEVE, Robin Martin,** MA; Head Master, King's College School, Wimbledon, 1980–97; *b* 22 Nov. 1934; *s* of Percy Martin Reeve and Cicely Nora Parker; *m* 1959, Brianne Ruth Hall; one *s* two *d*. *Educ*: Hampton Sch.; Gonville and Caius Coll., Cambridge (Foundation Schol.; BA 1957; MA). Asst Master, King's Coll. Sch., Wimbledon, 1958–62; Head of History Dept, 1962–80, and Dir of Studies, 1975–80, Lancing Coll. Member: CATE, 1993–94; ISC (formerly ISJC), 1991–99; Council, Brighton Coll., 1997–99; Council, Lancing Coll., 1997–2009 (Chm., 1999–2008). *Publications*: The Industrial Revolution 1750–1850, 1971. *Recreations*: English history and architecture, gardening. *Address*: The Old Rectory, Coombes, Lancing, W Sussex BN15 0RS. *Club*: Athenæum.

**REEVE, Roy Stephen,** CMG 1998; HM Diplomatic Service, retired; Consultant, Conciliation Resources, since 2010; *b* 20 Aug. 1941; *s* of Ernest Arthur Reeve and Joan Elizabeth (*née* Thomas); *m* 1964, Gill Lee; two *d*. *Educ*: Dulwich Coll.; LSE (BSc Econs 1965; MSc 1966). Joined FCO, 1966; Moscow, 1968–71; First Secretary: FCO, 1973–78; (Commercial) Moscow, 1978–80; Counsellor on loan to Home Civil Service, 1983–85; Dep. Consul-General, Johannesburg, 1985–88; Hd, Commercial Management and Export Dept, FCO, 1988–91; Consul-Gen., Sydney, 1991–95; Ambassador to Ukraine, 1995–99; OSCE Ambassador: to Armenia, 1999–2003; to Georgia, 2003–07; Hd, EU Planning Team, and Dep. Hd, EU Rule of Law Mission, Kosovo, 2008–10. Hon. Sen. Res. Fellow, Centre for Russian and E European Studies, Univ. of Birmingham, 1999–. Chair, British Georgian Soc., 2014–18. *Recreations*: Rugby Union, scuba diving.

**REEVE, Simon Alan;** author, since 1996, and television presenter, since 2002; *b* London, July 1972; *s* of Alan Edward Reeve and Cynthia Mary Reeve; *m* 2007, Anya Courts; one *s*. *Educ*: Twyford High Sch., Acton. Charity shop volunteer, 1989–91; post boy, then staff writer and Dep. Night News Ed., Sunday Times, 1991–96; Man. Ed., Vision Investigations, 1996–97. Presenter of television programmes: Meet the Stans, 2003; House of Saud, 2004; Places That Don't Exist, 2005; Equator, 2006; Tropic of Capricorn, 2008; Tropic of Cancer, 2010; Indian Ocean, 2012; Australia, 2013; Sacred Rivers, 2014; Caribbean, 2015; Greece, 2016; The Big Life Fix, 2017; Turkey with Simon Reeve, 2017; Russia with Simon Reeve, 2017; Burma with Simon Reeve, 2018; Mediterranean with Simon Reeve, 2018. Ness Award, RGS, 2012; Outstanding Contribn Award, One World Broadcasting Trust; Special Contribn Award, Travel Media Awards, 2015; John Tompkins Natural History Award, Internat. Moving Image Soc., 2019. *Publications*: The New Jackals: Ramzi Yousef, Osama bin Laden and the future of terrorism, 1998; One Day in September: the full story of the 1972 Munich Olympics massacre, 2000, repr. 2006 (adapted as Oscar-winning documentary film, 2000); Tropic of Capricorn: circling the world on a southern adventure, 2008; Step by Step (autobiog.), 2018; contribs to periodicals incl. Time, Esquire, Observer, Sunday Times. *Recreations*: chopping wood, sunny beaches, long walks, cold beer, beautiful views, memorable adventures. *Address*: c/o United Agents. 12–26 Lexington Street, W1F 0LE.

**REEVE, Timothy Iain;** Deputy Director and Chief Operating Officer, Victoria & Albert Museum, since 2013; *b* Kings Lynn, 13 March 1973; *s* of Terry Reeve and Elizabeth Taylor (*née* Blelska); two *s*. *Educ*: Christ's Hosp. Sch., Horsham; Royal Holloway, Univ. of London (BA Ancient Hist. 1994); INSEAD (Internat. Exec. Prog. 2011). English Heritage: Archivist, 1996–97; Exhibitions Manager, 1997–2002; Hd of Property Develt, 2002–04; Dir, Historic Properties, 2004–13. Dir, Design Dundee Ltd, 2018–. Mem., Strategic Adv. Bd, Hunterian Mus., 2018–. Trustee: Assoc. of Leading Visitor Attractions, 2011–13; Nat. Meml Arboretum, 2014–18; Canal and River Trust, 2016–; Painting in Hosps, 2018–. Life Mem., English Heritage; Mem., NT. *Recreations*: iron age hill forts, heritage, cricket, football, books, museums, running. *Address*: Victoria & Albert Museum, South Kensington, SW7 2RL. *T*: (020) 7942 2161. *E*: t.reeve@vam.ac.uk.

**REEVELL, Simon Justin;** *b* Doncaster, 2 March 1966; *s* of Stephen and Jean Reevell; *m* 2001, Louise Cooke. *Educ*: Boston Spa Comprehensive Sch. (MoD (Army) VI Form Scholarship); Manchester Poly. (BA Hons Econs; MoD (Army) Univ. Cadetship); Poly. of Central London (DipLaw); Inns of Court Sch. of Law (Denning Scholar, Hardwicke

Scholar, Thomas More Bursar). PWO Regt of Yorks, 1985–89. Called to the Bar, Lincoln's Inn, 1990; in practice as a barrister, specialising in military and criminal law, NE Circuit and London, 1990–. MP (C) Dewsbury, 2010–15; contested (C) same seat, 2015. Court Martial Ed., Westlaw UK Insight, 2013–. *Club:* Farmers.

**REEVES, Antony Robert;** Chief Executive, Liverpool City Council, since 2018; *b* 10 Feb. 1965; *s* of Bob and Jackie Reeves; *m* 2002, Kathryn; one *s*. *Educ:* Bristol Poly. (BA Hons); Huddersfield Univ. (MBA 1996). Housing Officer, 1989, Sen. Housing Officer, 1989–90, Stockport MBC; Estate Action Team Leader, 1990, District Housing Manager, 1990–92, Calderdale MBC; Barnsley Metropolitan Borough Council: Prin. Housing Officer, 1992–93; Hd of Housing Ops, 1993–95; Hd of Housing, 1995–99; Actg Prog. Dir of Health, Home Care Services, 1999–2000; Exec. Dir of Housing and Property Services, 2000–03; Dep. Chief Exec., Wakefield MDC, 2003–06; Chief Exec., City of Bradford MDC, 2006–14; Partner, Local Govt Advisory, Deloitte, 2015–18. *Recreations:* scuba diving, walking, golf, Rugby, reading, travel. *Address:* Liverpool City Council, Municipal Buildings, Dale Street, Liverpool L2 2DH.

**REEVES, Dr Colin Leslie,** CBE 1999; self-employed healthcare consultant, since 2003; *b* 4 April 1949; *s* of Leslie and Isabelle Reeves. *m* 1978, Christine Lloyd; two *d*. *Educ:* Birkenhead Sch.; Clare Coll., Cambridge (BA 1970; MA); UCNW, Bangor (MSc 1971; PhD 1973); DBA Cornell Univ. 1990. CPFA (IPFA 1976). Lectr, UCNW, Bangor, 1971–73; Accountancy and Audit Assistant, Warrington County Borough, 1973–75; Asst Treas., Ellesmere Port and Neston BC, 1975–80; Deputy Director of Finance: Stratford-on-Avon DC, 1980–84; NW Thames RHA, 1984–85; Director of Finance: Paddington and N Kensington DHA, 1985–86; NW Thames RHA, 1986–94; Dir of Finance and Performance, NHS Exec., 1994–2001; Dir, Accountancy Foundn Rev. Bd, 2001–03. Vice Chm. and Chm., Audit Cttee, Oxford Radcliffe Hosps NHS Trust, 2005–09. Member: Adv. Cttee on Mentally Disordered Offenders, 1993–94; Culyer Cttee on R&D, 1993–94; NHS Steering Gps on Capitation and on Capital, 1993–94; Chancellor of Exchequer's Pvte Finance Panel, 1994–95; Butler Cttee on review of Audit Commn, 1995; CMO's Nat. Screening Cttee, 1996–2001; Review of ONS, reporting to HM Treasury, 1999; Bd, Accountancy NTO, 1999–2001; Co-ordinating Gp on Audit and Accounting Issues, DTI/HM Treasury, 2002; Consultative Cttee on Review of the Listing Regime, FSA, 2002. Mem., Finance and Audit Cttee, Oxfam Internat., 2009–10. Hon. Treasurer: Headway (brain injury charity), 2002–; Florence Nightingale Foundn, 2011–; Goring and Streatley Fest., 2014–. Member: NT; RSPB; Woodland Trust. *Publications:* The Applicability of the Monetary Base Hypothesis to the UK, the USA, France and West Germany, 1974; contrib. professional jls. *Recreations:* sport, especially cricket and golf, history of Test Match cricket, hockey (former regl internat. and county player). *Address:* Battle Hill, Elvendon Road, Goring-on-Thames, Oxon RG8 0DT. *T:* (01491) 872166; La Loma, Las Lomas, 29500 Alora, Malaga, Spain. *Clubs:* Royal Automobile, MCC; Goring and Streatley Golf; Flying Ferrets Golf Soc.; Henley Hawks Rugby Football.

**REEVES, Dr David Alan;** Managing Director, DRC Consulting Ltd, since 2009; Director and Co-Founder, E:Fundamentals, London, since 2014; *b* London, UK, 8 March 1947; *s* of Edward Arthur and Madge Dora Reeves; *m* 1st, 1968, Margaret Micklethwaite (marr. diss.); two *d*; 2nd, 1998, Eiko Yamanouchi; one *d*. *Educ:* Univ. of East Anglia (BSc); Univ. of Cambridge and Univ. of East Anglia (PhD 1971). Regl Manager, S Africa, RJR Nabisco, 1984–87; Mktg Dir, RJR Switzerland and Austria, 1987–89; Global Brand Manager, RJR Camel, 1989–91; Vice Pres., Mktg, RJR Mitsubishi TV, Tokyo, 1991–95; Sony Computer Entertainment (Europe): Man. Dir, Germany, Austria and Switzerland, 1995–99; Vice Pres., Mktg and Sales, London, 1999–2003; Pres. and Chief Operating Officer, 2003–09; CEO, 2005–09; Chief Operating Officer, Capcom EMEA, 2010–13; Consultant, Quantic Gp, 2012–17. Chm., Near East Digital Ventures, Dubai, 2009–17; Dir, RED Entertainment Dubai, 2010–; Sen. Ind. Dir, Keywords Internat. plc, Dublin, 2013–. Trustee: Rabin Ezra Scholarship Trust, 2007–; Sense (UK), 2009–; Autistica, UK, 2013–; Sense UK, 2014–; Nat. Autistic Soc., 2015–; St John Ambulance, 2015–. *Recreations:* National Ski Patrol (Instructor), tennis, PADI scuba. *Address:* 2 Midgarth Close, Oxshott, Surrey KT22 0JY. *T:* (01372) 841527. *E:* David.Reeves26@yahoo.co.uk.

**REEVES, Rev. Donald St John,** MBE 2008; Rector, St James's Church, Piccadilly, 1980–98; *b* 18 May 1934; *s* of Henry and Barbara Reeves. *Educ:* Sherborne; Queens' Coll., Cambridge (BA Hons 1957); Cuddesdon Theol Coll. 2nd Lieut, Royal Sussex Regt, 1952–54. Lectr, British Council, Beirut, 1957–60; Tutor, Brasted Theol Coll., 1960–61; Cuddesdon Theol Coll., 1961–63; deacon, 1963, priest, 1964; Curate, All Saints, Maidstone, 1963–65; Chaplain to Bishop of Southwark, 1965–68; Vicar of St Peter's, Morden, 1969–80. Mem., Gen. Synod of C of E, 1990–94. Dir, The Soul of Europe, 1999–. MLitt Lambeth, 2003. *Publications:* (ed) Church and State, 1984; For God's Sake, 1988; Making Sense of Religion, 1989; Down to Earth: a new vision, 1995; The Memoirs of "A Very Dangerous Man", 2009. *Recreations:* playing the organ, watching TV soaps. *Address:* The Coach House, Church Street, Crediton EX17 2AQ. *T:* (01363) 775100, *Fax:* (01363) 773911. *Club:* Athenæum.

**REEVES, Ellie;** MP (Lab) Lewisham West and Penge, since 2017; *d* of Graham Reeves and Sally Reeves; *m* 2012, John Robert Cryer, *qv*; one *s*. *Educ:* Cator Park Secondary Sch.; Univ. of Oxford. Called to the Bar; in practice as barrister specialising in employment rights law incl. maternity rights; trade union lawyer. Mem., Justice Cttee, H of C, 2017–. *Address:* House of Commons, SW1A 0AA.

**REEVES, Dame Helen May,** DBE 1999 (OBE 1986); Chief Executive (formerly Director), Victim Support (formerly National Association of Victim Support Schemes), 1980–2005; *b* 22 Aug. 1945; *d* of Leslie Percival William Reeves and Helen Edith Reeves (*née* Brown). *Educ:* Dartford Grammar School for Girls; Nottingham University (BA Hons Social Admin. 1966). Probation Officer, Inner London Probation Service, 1967–79 (Senior Probation Officer, 1975–79). Member: Nat. Bd for Crime Prevention, 1993–95; Govt Working Gp on Vulnerable and Intimidated Witnesses, 1998–99; Home Office Steering Gp on Review of Sexual Offences, 1999; EU Cttee of Experts on Victims of Crime, 1998–99; Ind. Review of Criminal Stats, 2006; Chm., Council of Europe Expert Cttee on Victims of Crime and Terrorism, 2005–06. Vice Pres., World Soc. of Victimology, 1994–2006; Chm., Eur. Forum for Victim Services, 2001–05. Member: Howard League Commn on Future of English Prisons, 2005–09; RSA Risk Commn, 2006–09; Adv. Bd, Tim Parry Johnathan Ball Foundn for Peace, 2005–11 (Trustee, 2011–15). Chair: Blackheath Decorative and Fine Arts Soc., 2011–14; Blackheath Soc., 2014–18 (Vice Chair, 2018–); Arts Soc. Blackheath, 2017–18. Hon. MA Nottingham, 1998; Hon. LLD: Warwick, 2001; Southampton Solent, 2004; Nottingham, 2014. *Recreations:* social and local history and architecture, food, gardens, fine and decorative arts.

**REEVES, Marc Barnaby;** Editor in Chief, Midlands, Reach plc (formerly Trinity Mirror), since 2014; Editor, Birmingham Mail, since 2014; *b* 25 Nov. 1965; *s* of late Frederick Reeves and Mai Reeves (then Barnes); *m* 1st, 1988 (marr. diss.); two *d*; 2nd, 2014, Claire Procter. *Educ:* St Teresa's Primary Sch., Birmingham; Handsworth Grammar Sch., Birmingham; Birmingham Poly.; Oxford Brookes Univ. (CMS 2002; DMS 2003). Dep. Ed., Walsall Advertiser, 1988–89; Sub-ed., Focus Newspapers, Birmingham, 1989–91; Revise Ed., Computer Newspaper Services, Howden, 1991–92; Prodn Ed., Northampton Chronicle & Echo, 1992–94; Dep. Ed., Cumberland News, 1994–97; Ed., Reading Chronicle, 1997–2000; Editl Dir, Trinity Mirror Southern, 2000–06; Editor: Birmingham Post, 2006–09; TheBusinessDesk.com W Midlands, 2010–12; Partner, RJF Public Affairs Ltd, 2011–13; Publishing Dir, Trinity Mirror Midlands, 2013–14. Mem., Lunar Soc. *Recreations:* collecting music, wine and bourbon, military and political history, lazing in the garden.

**REEVES, Martin Robert,** PhD; Chief Executive, Coventry City Council, since 2009; *b* Chatham, Kent, 30 May 1970; *s* of David Reeves and Margaret Reeves; *m* 2006, Lucy Ann Parker; two *d*. *Educ:* Sheffield City Poly. (BA Hons Mgt 1991); Loughborough Univ. (MSc (dist.) Rec. Mgt 1993); Cheltenham and Gloucester Coll. of HE (PGCFHE 1998); Loughborough Univ. (PhD 2000). Nat. Press and PR Officer, Disability Sport England, 1991–92; Lectr and Researcher, Cheltenham and Gloucester Coll. of HE, 1997–2000; Policy and Res. Manager, Reigate and Banstead BC, 2000–01; Hd of Policy, Performance and Business Support, Waltham Forest LBC, 2001–03; Hd, Performance Improvement, Westminster CC, 2003–06; Asst Chief Exec., 2006–08, Chief Exec., 2008–09, Beds CC; Interim Chief Exec., W Midlands Combined Authy, 2016–17. *Recreations:* all sport, travel, photography. *Address:* Coventry City Council, Council House, Earl Street, Coventry CV1 5RR. *T:* (024) 7683 1100, *Fax:* (024) 7683 3680. *E:* martin.reeves@coventry.gov.uk.

**REEVES, Rachel Jane;** MP (Lab) Leeds West, since 2010; *b* 13 Feb. 1979; *d* of Graham Reeves and Sally Reeves. *Educ:* New Coll., Oxford (BA Hons PPE); London Sch. of Econs and Pol Sci. (MSc Econs). Economist: Bank of England, 2000–02, 2003–09; British Embassy, Washington, 2002–03; Business Planner, Halifax Bank of Scotland, 2006–09. Shadow Chief Sec. to the Treasury, 2011–13; Shadow Sec. of State for Work and Pensions, 2013–15. Mem., Treasury Select Cttee, 2015–17; Chm., Select Cttee on Business, Energy and Industrial Strategy, 2017–. Contested (Lab) Bromley and Chislehurst, 2005, June 2006. *Publications:* Why Vote Labour?, 2010; Women of Westminster: the MPs who changed politics, 2019; contrib. Jl of Pol Econ. *Recreations:* swimming, walking, tennis, theatre. *Address:* House of Commons, SW1A 0AA; (office) Unit 8A, Bramley Shopping Centre, Bramley, Leeds LS13 2ET. *T:* (0113) 255 2311. *E:* rreevesmp@gmail.com.

**REEVES, William Desmond,** CB 1993; Secretary, UK Management Board, PricewaterhouseCoopers, 1998–2004; *b* 26 May 1937; *s* of late Thomas Norman and Anne Reeves; *m* 1967, Aase Birte Christensen; two *d*. *Educ:* Darwen Grammar Sch.; King's Coll., Cambridge (BA Hist.). National service, RAEC, 1959–61. Joined Admiralty as Asst Principal, 1961; MoD, 1964; Asst Sec., 1973; seconded to Pay Board, 1973–74; Asst Under Sec. of State, Air, MoD (PE), 1982–84; Resources and Progs, MoD, 1984; Systems, Office of Management and Budget, MoD, 1985–88; Under Sec., Cabinet Office, 1989–92; Asst Under Sec. of State (Commitments), MoD, 1992–94. Partnership Sec., Coopers & Lybrand, 1994–98. *Recreation:* supporting Blackburn Rovers. *Address:* 2 Downs Bridge Road, Beckenham, Kent BR3 5HX.

**REFFELL, Adm. Sir Derek (Roy),** KCB 1984; Governor and Commander-in-Chief, Gibraltar, 1989–93; *b* 6 Oct. 1928; *s* of late Edward (Roy) and Murielle Reffell; *m* 1956, Janne Gronow Davis (*d* 2013); one *s* one *d*. *Educ:* Culford Sch., Suffolk; Royal Naval Coll., Dartmouth. Various ships at Home, Mediterranean, West Indies and Far East, 1946–63; qualified Navigating Officer, 1954; Comdr 1963; Comd HMS Sirius, 1966–67; Comdr BRNC Dartmouth, 1968–69; Captain 1970; Naval Staff, 1971–74; Comd HMS Hermes, 1974–76; Director Naval Warfare, 1976–78; Commodore Amphibious Warfare, 1978–79; Asst Chief of Naval Staff (Policy), 1979–82; Flag Officer Third Flotilla and Comdr Anti-Submarine Group Two, 1982–83; Flag Officer, Naval Air Comd, 1983–84; Controller of the Navy, 1984–89, retd. Governor, Royal Sch., Hindhead, 1995–98. Trustee, Special Olympics UK, 1998–2002. Chm., Friends of Gibraltar Heritage Soc., 1994–2004. Master, Coachmakers' Company, 1998–99. KStJ 1989. *Recreations:* golf, birdwatching.

**REFFO, Geraldine Mary Nicole,** CMG 2009; Founder and Managing Director, Gerry Reffo Coaching and Consulting Ltd, since 2009; *b* London, 17 Jan. 1959; *d* of Gerald Francis Reffo and Josephine Mary Reffo. *Educ:* Open Univ. (MBA 1995). Clerical Officer, 1975–82, Auditor, 1982–89, Dept of Employment; Foreign and Commonwealth Office: Sen. Auditor, 1989–93; Dep. Hd, Internal Audit, 1993–96; Hd, Personnel Mgt Unit, 1998–2001; Asst Dir, Human Resources, 2001–03; Hd, Learning and Develt, 2003–09. Mem., Inst. of Internal Auditors, 1985. *Publications:* (with V. Wark) Leadership PQ, 2014. *Recreations:* walking (dog), reading, horse racing, house in France. *E:* greffo2000@yahoo.co.uk. *T:* 07788 428340.

**REFSON, Dame Benita (Margaret),** DBE 2016 (OBE 2007); President, Place2Be, since 2014; *b* London, 9 Sept. 1947; *d* of late Gerald and Anne Ronson; one *s* two *d*. *Educ:* Sarum Hall; Roedean Sch.; Paris; Regent's Coll. and Westminster Pastoral Foundn (Qualified Counsellor). Trainee psychiatric social worker; fashion ed., Vogue; Founding Trustee and Dir, 1994–2002, CEO, 2002–13, Place2Be. Advr, Educn and Learning Cttee, Paul Hamlyn Foundn. Trustee: Children and Success Schs Trust, 2013–; RAPt, 2013–. Hon. LLD E London, 2009; Hon. DLit (Educn) Inst. of Educn, 2014. *Recreations:* walking, piano lessons, dog walking, fashion, spending time with children and grandchildren, film and theatre. *Address:* Place2B, 175 St John Street, Clerkenwell, EC1V 4LW. *T:* (020) 7923 5500. *Club:* Reform.

**REGAN, Rt Rev. Edwin;** Bishop of Wrexham, (RC), 1994–2012, now Bishop Emeritus; *b* 31 Dec. 1935; *s* of James Regan and Elizabeth Ellen Regan (*née* Hoskins). *Educ:* St Joseph's RC Primary Sch., Aberavon; Port Talbot County Grammar Sch.; St John's Coll., Waterford, Eire; Corpus Christi Coll., London. Priest, 1959; Curate, Neath, 1959–66; Adviser in RE, Archdio. Cardiff, 1967–87; Chaplain, St Clare's Convent, Porthcawl, 1967–71; Administrator, St David's Cathedral, Cardiff, 1971–84; Parish Priest: St Helen's, Barry, 1984–89; St Mary's, Bridgend, 1989–94; Blaenau Ffestiniog, 2012–. Apostolic Administrator, Archdio. of Cardiff, 2000–01. *Recreations:* reading, gentle walking and exercises. *Address:* 5 Plas Avenue, Prestatyn LL19 9NH.

**REGAN, Prof. Lesley, (Mrs John Summerfield),** MD; FRCOG; Professor and Head of Department of Obstetrics and Gynaecology, Imperial College at St Mary's Hospital, London, since 1996; Deputy Head, Division of Surgery, Oncology, Reproductive Biology and Anaesthetics, Imperial College London, since 2005; President, Royal College of Obstetricians and Gynaecologists, 2016–19; *b* 8 March 1956; *d* of Jack Regan and Dorothy Hull (*née* Thorne); *m* 1990, Prof. John Summerfield; twin *d*, and two step *s* two step *d*. *Educ:* Royal Free Hosp. Sch. of Medicine (MB BS 1980; MD 1989). MRCOG 1985, FRCOG 1998. Sen. Registrar in Obstetrics and Gynaecology, Addenbrooke's Hosp., Cambridge, 1986–90; Teaching Fellow (Medicine), 1986–90, Dir of Medical Studies, 1987–90, Girton Coll., Cambridge; Sen. Res. Associate, MRC Embryo and Gamete Res. Gp, Univ. of Cambridge, 1987–89; Sen. Lectr, ICSM, and Hon. Consultant in Obstetrics and Gynaecology, St Mary's Hosp., London, 1990–96; Director: Miscarriage Service, St Mary's Hosp., 1990–; Subspecialty Trng Prog. in Reproductive Medicine for ICSM at St Mary's and Hammersmith Hosps, 1995–; Clinical Dir, Maternity, 2000–03, Gynaecology, 2002–05, St Mary's Hosp. Rosenfelder Vis. Fellow, Boston, USA, 1999; Vis. Prof., Harvard Centre of Excellence for Women's Health, 2000–02; RCOG Vis. Lectr to S Africa, 2004; Lectures: Alexander Gordon, Aberdeen Univ., 2003; Lettsomian, Med. Soc. of London,

2004; Green-Armytage, RCOG, 2006. Non-exec. Dir, W Middx Univ. Hosp. NHS Trust, 2006–08. Mem., HFEA, 2008–. Professional Advisor: Miscarriage Assoc., 1992–; CHANA, 1994–; Industrial Relns Soc., 1994–; Twins and Multiple Births Assoc., 1996–. Mem., Expert Adv. Panels in Reproductive Medicine and Contraception, 1997, Women's Sexual and Reproduction Rights Cttee, 2008–, FIGO; Member: Wellcome Trust Adv. Bd (Clinical Interest Gp), 2002–04; Gynaecol Vis. Soc.; Soc. for Gynaecol Investigation, USA; Council, 2006–, Academic Cttee, 2006–, Finance and Exec., 2008–, RCOG. Sec., Assoc. of Professors and Gynaecologists, 2001–07; Pres., Assoc. of Early Pregnancy Units in the UK, 2005–. Trustee: Inst. of Obstetrics and Gynaecology, 1996–; Save the Baby, 1998–; Wellbeing of Women, 2009–. Woman of Achievement Award, 2005, for services to reproductive medicine. *Publications*: Miscarriage: what every woman needs to know, 1997, 2nd edn 2001; Your Pregnancy Week by Week, 2005; numerous chapters in reproductive medicine textbooks; scientific articles on sporadic and recurrent pregnancy loss and uterine fibroids in BMJ, Lancet, Human Reproduction, British Jl of Obstetrics and Gynaecol., Amer. Jls of Obstetrics and Gynaecol. *Recreations*: mother to my twin girls, opera, creating a garden in the South of France. *Address*: Department of Obstetrics and Gynaecology, Imperial College at St Mary's Hospital London, South Wharf Road, Paddington, W2 1NY. *T*: (020) 7886 1798. *E*: l.regan@imperial.ac.uk.

**REGAN, Maj.-Gen. Michael Dalrymple,** CB 1996; OBE 1985; Controller, The Army Benevolent Fund, 1997–2003; *b* 6 Jan. 1942; *s* of late M. L. R. Regan and G. I. Regan (*née* Dalrymple); *m* 1974, Victoria, *o d* of late Comdr V. C. Grenfell, DSO; two *d*. *Educ*: St Boniface's Coll.; RMA, Sandhurst. Commnd 1st KSLI, 1962; served Germany, Malaysia, Cyprus and NI; Instructor, Sch. of Infantry, 1968–70; Adjutant, 3rd LI, 1971–73; Staff Coll., Camberley, 1973–74; BM, 12th Mech. Bde, 1975–76; Company Comdr, 1st LI, 1977–78; MA to C-in-C, UKLF, 1979–82; CO, 3rd LI, 1982–84 (mentioned in Despatches); Col MS 2, MoD, 1985; Comdr, 20th Armd Bde, 1986–87; RCDS, 1988; DCOS, HQ UKLF, 1989–91; GOC Wales and Western Dist, 1991–94; Dir Gen., AGC, 1994–95; COS, HQ Adjt Gen., 1995–96. Col, LI, 1992–96; Asst Col Comdt, AGC, 1995–96. Chm. Trustees, Shropshire Regimental Mus., 1998–2003; Trustee: Army Dependants Assurance Trust, 2003–12; Royal Commonwealth Ex-Services League, 2006–12 (Council Mem., 2003–12). *Recreations*: golf, ski-ing, sailing. *Clubs*: MCC, Army and Navy.

**REGAN, Michael John;** HM Diplomatic Service, retired; Senior Adviser, G3 Good Governance Group Ltd, (Managing Partner (formerly Executive Director), 2010); *b* 17 Aug. 1955; *s* of late Brig. John Joseph Regan, OBE and Edith Nancy Cunliffe; *m* 1986, Carolyn Gaye Black; two *s*. *Educ*: St George's Coll., Weybridge; Nottingham Univ. (BA Jt Hons Econs and Agricl Econs). SSC, 3rd RTR, 1977–82. Insurance Broker, Fenchurch Gp, 1982–83; joined Diplomatic Service, 1983; FCO, 1983–86; Kabul, 1986–88; FCO, 1988–89; First Sec. (Chancery/Economic), Dubai, 1989–91, FCO, 1991–95; Counsellor (ESCAP), Bangkok, 1995–98; FCO, 1998–2004; Counsellor, Harare, 2004–07; Baghdad, 2007–08; Counsellor, FCO, 2008–10. *Recreations*: hockey, tennis, golf, sailing, walking. *Clubs*: Frontline; Hankley Common Golf; Frensham Fly Fishers.

**REGAN-DENHAM, Ashten;** Member (SNP) Edinburgh Eastern, Scottish Parliament, since 2016; Minister for Community Safety, since 2018; *b* Lanark, 8 March 1974; *d* of Michael Regan and Marianne Regan (*née* McLellan); *m* 2000, Robert Denham (marr. diss. 2018); twin *s*. *Educ*: Keele Univ. (BA Hons Internat. Relns 1995); Open Univ. (MSc Develt Mgt 2012). PR and Mktg Officer, ScottClem, 1998–2001; Sen. Account Exec., Spreckley Partners, 2001–02; Events Exec., Zinc Mgt, 2002; Account Manager, Rocket PR, 2002–03; Digital Mktg, Tearfund, 2012–13; Hd, Campaigns, Common Weal, Scotland, 2013–15. *Recreation*: chip connoisseur. *Address*: Scottish Parliament, Edinburgh EH99 1SP. *T*: (0131) 348 5922. *E*: ash.denham.msp@parliament.scot.

**REGO, Dame (Maria) Paula (Figueiroa),** DBE 2010; RA 2016; artist; *b* 26 Jan. 1935; *d* of José Fernandes Figueiroa Rego and Maria de S José Paiva Figueiroa Rego; *m* 1959, Victor Willing (*d* 1988); one *s* two *d*. *Educ*: St Julian's Sch., Carcavelos, Portugal; Slade School of Fine Art, UCL. First Associate Artist, Nat. Gall., Jan.–Dec. 1990. Selected solo exhibitions: (1st at) Soc. Nat. de Belas Artes, Lisbon, 1965; Gal. S Mamede, Lisbon, 1971; Gal. Modulo, Porto, 1977; Gal. III, Lisbon, 1978; Air Gall., London, 1981; Edward Totah Gall., 1982, 1985, 1987; Arnolfini, 1983; Art Palace, NY, 1985; Gulbenkian Foundn, 1988, 1999, 2012; Serpentine Gall. (retrospective), 1988; Marlborough Graphics (nursery rhymes), 1989; Nat. Gall., 1991–92; Marlborough Gall., 1992, 1994; Tate Gall., Liverpool (retrospective), 1997; Dulwich Picture Gall., 1998; Gulbenkian Foundn, Lisbon, 1999; Abbot Hall, Kendal, 2001; Yale Centre for British Art, 2002; Marlborough Fine Art, 2003, 2006, 2008, 2010; Tate Britain, 2004; Serralves Museum, Oporto, 2004–05; prints (retrospective), Talbot Rice Gall., Edinburgh, then Brighton Mus. and tour, 2005–07; Mus. Nacional Centro de Arte Reina Sofia, Madrid (retrospective), 2007, then Nat. Mus. of Women in the Arts, Washington, DC; Marlborough, NY, 2008; print retrospective, École des Beaux Arts, Nîmes, 2008; Marco Monterrey, 2010, then Pinacoteca do Estado, São Paulo, 2011; Marlborough Fine Art, 2013, 2014, 2017; Musée de l'Orangerie, Paris, 2018; Milton Keynes Gall. (retrospective), 2019. Many collective shows include: ICA, 1965; S Paulo Biennale, 1969, 1985; British Art Show, 1985, 2000; Hayward Gall., 1994 and 1996; Saatchi Gall., 1994–95; Encounters, Nat. Gall., 2000; also in Japan, Australia, all over Europe. Large painting, Crivelli's Garden, in restaurant of Sainsbury Wing, Nat. Gall., 1992. Sen. Fellow, RCA, 1989. Hon. Fellow, Murray Edwards Coll., Cambridge, 2013. Hon. DLitt: St Andrews, 1999; E Anglia, 1999; Oxford, 2005; Hon. DFA Rhode Island Sch. of Design, 2000; Hon. Dr: London Inst., 2002; UCL, 2004; DUniv Roehampton, 2005; Hon. LittD Cambridge, 2015. Premio Penagos, Fundación MAPFRE, 2010. *Relevant Publications*: Paula Rego, by John McEwen, 1992, 3rd edn 2006; Paula Rego, by Fiona Bradley, 2002; Paula Rego: the complete graphic work, by T. G. Rosenthal, 2003, 2nd edn 2012; Paula Rego's Map of Memory, by Dr Maria Lisboa, 2003; Behind the Scenes, by John McEwen, 2008. *Recreations*: going to the movies, plays. *Address*: c/o Marlborough Fine Art, 6 Albemarle Street, W1S 4BY. *T*: (020) 7629 5161.

**REHÁK, Dr Lubomír;** Ambassador of Slovakia to the Court of St James's, since 2015; *b* Topolcany, 24 Feb. 1970; *m* 1998, Dana; two *d*. *Educ*: Moscow State Inst. of Internat. Relns (MA 1992; PhD 1997). Entered Diplomatic Service of Slovakia, 1993; Third Sec., Moscow, 1993–98; Dep. Hd of Mission, Lisbon, 1999–2003; Eur. Correspondent, Min. of Foreign Affairs, 2003–06; Hd of Mission, Minsk, 2006–08; Ambassador: to EU Political and Security Cttee, Brussels, 2008–10; to Kazakhstan, 2011–12; Political Dir, Ministry of Foreign Affairs, 2010–11 and 2012–15. Knight Comdr of Merit (with Star), Sacred Military Constantinian Order of St George, 2017. *Recreations*: music, history. *Address*: Embassy of Slovakia, 25 Kensington Palace Gardens, W8 4QY. *T*: (020) 7313 6470, *Fax*: (020) 7313 6481. *E*: emb.london@mzv.sk.

**REHN, Olli Ilmari,** DPhil; Governor and Chairman, Bank of Finland, since 2018 (Member of Board, 2017–18); *b* Mikkeli, Finland, 31 March 1962; *s* of Tauno and Vuokko Rehn; *m* 1995, Merja Maria Hakkarainen; one *d*. *Educ*: Macalester Coll., St Paul, Minn; Univ. of Helsinki (Master Soc. Sci. Political Sci. 1989); St Antony's Coll., Oxford (DPhil Internat. Political Econ. 1996). Mem., City Council, Helsinki, 1988–94; MP (Centre Party), 1991–95; Special Advr to Prime Minister, 1992–93; MEP, 1995–96; Hd of Cabinet, EC, 1998–2002; Prof. and Dir of Res., Dept of Political Sci. and Centre for European Studies, Univ. of Helsinki, 2002–03; Econ. Policy Advr to Prime Minister, 2003–04; Mem., EC, 2004–14; MEP (Alliance of Liberals and Democrats for Europe), 2014–15; MP (Centre Party) Helsinki Dist, 2015–17; Minister of Econ. Affairs, 2015–16. Chm., Financial Supervisory Authy, Finland, 2017–18. Chm., Centre Youth, Finland, 1987–89; Dep. Chm., Centre Party, 1988–94. Chm., Finnish Delegn to Council of Europe, 1991–95; Vice-Pres., European Movement of Finland, 1996–98. Chm., Football League of Finland, 1996–97. Player, association football, 1968–: FC Mikkelin Palloilijat (youth teams, 1968–78; 1st team, 1979–82); FC Finnish Parliament, 1991–; Finland Utd of Brussels, 1995–2015; CS Eurocommission II, 1998–2002. Columnist in several newspapers and mags, 1985–. *Publications*: Pieni valtio Euroopan Unionissa (A Small State in the European Union), 1996; European Challenges of the Finnish EU Presidency, 2nd edn 1998; (contrib.) Liberalism in the European Union: the way forward, 2004; Europe's Next Frontiers, 2006; Suomen eurooppalainen valinta ei ole suhdannepolitikkaa, 2006; Myrskyn silmässä, 2012. *Recreations*: political economy, rock and jazz, reading.

**REICH, Sir Erich (Arieh),** Kt 2010; Founder and Managing Director, Classic Tours, 1989–2014; *b* Vienna, 1935; *s* of late Sigmund Reich and Mina Reich; *m* 2003, Linda Esther Haase; three *s* two *d*. Manager, Client Services, 1970–76, Ops Dir, 1976–80, Thomson Holidays; Gen. Manager, 1980–84, Man. Dir of Tour Ops, 1984–89, Thomas Cook. Chm., Kindertransport Gp, Assoc. of Jewish Refugees, 2007–. *Recreations*: classical music, swimming.

**REICH, Steve;** composer; *b* 3 Oct. 1936; *s* of Leonard Reich and June Carroll (*née* Sillman); *m* 1976, Beryl Korot; one *s*, and one *s* from previous *m*. *Educ*: Cornell Univ. (BA Hons Philos. 1957); Juilliard Sch. of Music; Mills Coll. (MA Music 1963); Inst. for African Studies, Univ. of Ghana. Guggenheim Fellow, 1978; Montgomery Fellow, Dartmouth Coll., 2000. Mem., AAAL, 1994. Founded ensemble, Steve Reich and Musicians, 1966, toured the world, 1971–. Music performed by major orchestras, including: NY Philharmonic; San Francisco Symphony; St Louis Symphony; Brooklyn Philharmonic; LA Philharmonic; BBC Symphony; London Symphony Orch.; commissions received include: Fest. d'Automne, Paris for 200th Anniv. of French Revolution, 1989; BBC Proms in honour of centennial, 1995. Member: Amer. Acad. of Arts and Letters, 1994; Bavarian Acad. of Fine Arts, 1995. Hon. DMus: Calif Inst. of the Arts, 2002; SUNY, Buffalo, 2008; New England Conservatory of Music, 2009; Juilliard Sch. of Music, 2010. Schuman Prize, Columbia Univ., 2000; Premium Imperial in Music, 2006; Polar Prize, 2007; Pulitzer Prize in Music, 2009. Commandeur, Ordre des Arts et des Lettres (France), 1999. *Compositions include*: Drumming, 1971; Music for 18 Musicians, 1976 (Grammy Award for Best Small Ensemble recording, 1996); Eight Lines, 1979–83; Tehillim, 1981; The Desert Music, 1984; Sextet, 1985; Different Trains, 1988 (Grammy Award for Best Contemporary Composition, 1990); The Cave, 1993; Nagoyd Marimba, 1994; City Life, 1995; Proverb, 1995; Triple Quartet, 1999; Three Tales, 2002; Cello Counterpoint, 2003; You Are (variations), 2004; Daniel Variations, 2006, 2x5, 2007; Double Sextet, 2008 (Pulitzer Prize, 2009); Mallet Quartet, 2009; WTC 9/11, 2010; Radio Rewrite, 2013; Quartet, 2014; Pulse: music for winds, strings, piano and electric bass, 2015; Runner, 2016; Music for Ensemble and Orchestra, 2018; Reich/Richter, 2019. *Publications*: Writings About Music, 1974; Writings on Music 1965–2000, 2002. *Address*: c/o Andrew Rosner, Rayfield Allied, Studio 26 China Works, 100 Black Prince Road, SE1 7SJ.

**REICHLIN, Prof. Lucrezia,** PhD; FBA 2013; Professor of Economics, London Business School, since 2008 (Chair, Economic Department, 2011–14); *b* Rome; *d* of Alfredo Reichlin and Luciana Castellina. *Educ*: Univ. of Modena (Laurea in Econs 1980); New York Univ. (PhD 1986). Adjunct Prof., Barnard Coll., Columbia Univ., NY, 1985–86; Jean Monnet Fellow, 1986–87, and Res. Fellow, 1987–88, European Univ. Inst., Florence; Dep. Dir, Res. Dept, Observatoire Français des Conjunctures Economiques, Fondation Nat. des Scis Politiques, Paris, 1988–93; Vis. Associate Prof., Grad. Sch. of Business, Columbia Univ., 1993–94; Prof. Ordinaire of Econs, Univ. Libre de Bruxelles, Belgium, 1994–2004; Dir Gen. Res., Eur. Central Bank, 2005–08. Prog. Co-Dir, Internat. Macroecons, 1999–2004, Scientific Dir, 2011–13, Centre for Econ. Policy Res. Visiting Professor: Res. Dept, Bank of Italy, 2000–01; Econ. Dept, NY Univ., 2001–02; Houblon-Norman Sen. Fellow, Bank of England, 2004. Co-Founder and Dir, Now-Casting Econs Ltd. Co-Ed., Jl Applied Econometrics, 2009–12; Ed., Internat. Jl of Central Banking, 2016–. Columnist, Corriere della Sera, 2011–. Non-executive Director: Unicredit Banking Gp, 2009–; Messaggerie Italiane Gp, 2012–; Ageas Insce Gp, 2014–; Eurobank Ergasias SA, 2016–. Chair, Scientific Council, Breugel, Brussels, 2013–16. Mem., Adv. Bd, Centre for Internat. Macroecons and Finance, Univ. of Cambridge. Co-author, Geneva Report, 2014. *Publications*: contrib. papers to jls incl. Amer. Econ. Rev., Rev. of Econ. Studies, Rev. of Econs and Stats, Jl Econometrics, Jl Monetary Econs, Jl Amer. Statistical Assoc., Jl Eur. Econ. Assoc. *Address*: London Business School, Regent's Park, NW1 4SA.

**REID,** family name of **Baron Reid of Cardowan**.

**REID OF CARDOWAN,** Baron *cr* 2010 (Life Peer), of Stepps in Lanarkshire; **John Reid;** PC 1998; PhD; Chairman, Celtic plc, 2007–11; a Senior Advisor, Chertoff Group, since 2010; *b* 8 May 1947; *s* of late Thomas Reid and Mary Reid; *m* 1st, 1969, Catherine (*née* McGowan) (*d* 1998); two *s*; 2nd, 2002, Carine Adler. *Educ*: St Patrick's Senior Secondary Sch., Coatbridge; Stirling Univ. (BA History, PhD Economic History). Scottish Research Officer, Labour Party, 1979–83; Political Adviser to Rt Hon. Neil Kinnock, 1983–86; Scottish Organiser, Trades Unionists for Labour, 1986–87. MP (Lab) Motherwell N, 1987–97, Hamilton N and Bellshill, 1997–2005, Airdrie and Shotts, 2005–10. Opposition spokesman on children, 1989–90, on defence, 1990–97; Minister of State, MoD, 1997–98; Minister of Transport, 1998–99; Secretary of State: for Scotland, 1999–2001; for Northern Ireland, 2001–02; Minister without Portfolio and Chair, Labour Party, 2002–03; Leader of the H of C and Pres. of the Council, 2003; Secretary of State: for Health, 2003–05; for Defence, 2005–06; for the Home Dept, 2006–07. Member: Public Accounts Cttee, 1988–89; Armed Forces Cttee and Reserved Forces Cttee, 1996–97; Internat. Relns Cttee, H of L, 2016–. Hon. Prof. and Chair, Inst. for Strategy, Resilience and Security (formerly Inst. for Security and Resilience Studies), UCL, 2008–. Fellow, Armed Forces Parly Scheme, 1990–. *Publications*: (jtly) Cyber Doctrine: toward a framework for learning resilience, 2011. *Recreations*: football, reading history, crossword puzzles. *Address*: House of Lords, SW1A 0PW.

**REID, Sir Alan;** see Reid, Sir P. A.

**REID, Alan;** *b* 7 Aug. 1954; *s* of James Smith Reid and Catherine Graham Reid (*née* Steele). *Educ*: Prestwick Acad.; Ayr Acad.; Strathclyde Univ. (BSc Hons Pure & Applied Maths). Strathclyde Regional Council: Maths Teacher, 1976–77; Computer Programmer, 1977–85; Computer Project Manager, Glasgow Univ., 1985–2001. MP (Lib Dem) Argyll and Bute, 2001–15; contested (Lib Dem) same seat, 2015, 2017; contested (Lib Dem) Argyll and Bute, Scottish Parlt, 2016. Mem. (Lib Dem), Argyll and Bute Council, 2017–. *Recreations*: playing chess, walking, reading, watching TV.

**REID, Air Vice-Marshal Alastair Norman Crawford;** Defence Medical Director, since 2018; *b* Dorchester, 23 June 1961; *s* of Robin Reid and Audrey Reid; *m* 1994, Sylvia Challis; one *s* one *d*. *Educ:* Kelvinside Acad.; Univ. of Glasgow (MB ChB 1983); Univ. of Aberdeen (MSc 2003). DRCOG 1986; DAvMed 1998; FFOM 2014. Gen. Practice Principal, NHS, 1983–89; Med. Officer, Royal Flying Doctor Service, WA, 1990–91; Civilian Med. Practitioner, MoD, 1992–93; joined RAF, 1993; Air Officer Med. Ops and Comdt, RAF Centre of Aviation Medicine, 2014–16; Hd of Med. Policy and Inf. Systems, HQ Surg. Gen., 2016–18. QHP 2014. *Recreations:* sailing, photography, cycling, vintage tractor restoration. *Address:* Headquarters Joint Medical Group, Defence Medical Services Whittington, Lichfield WS14 9PY. *T:* (01543) 434249. *E:* alastair.reid519@mod.gov.uk. *Club:* Royal Air Force.

**REID, Dr Alexander Arthur Luttrell;** Director-General, Royal Institute of British Architects, 1994–2000; *b* 11 Jan. 1941; *s* of late Capt. Philip Reid, RN and of Louisa (*née* Luttrell); *m* 1st, 1964, Sara Louise Coleridge (marr. diss. 1987); two *d*; 2nd, 1988, Sian Tudor Roberts; one *s* one *d*. *Educ:* Winchester Coll. (Schol.); Trinity Coll., Cambridge (MA); University Coll., London (MSc; PhD 1974). Served RN, Lieut (helicopter pilot), 1962–67. Post Office Telecommunications: Hd, Long Range Studies, 1972–77; Director: Prestel, 1977–80; Business Systems, 1980–83; Acorn Computer Gp PLC, 1984–85; Octagon Investment Mgt Ltd, 1984–2010; MJP Architects Ltd, 2007–18; Chief Exec., DEGW Ltd, 1991–94. Mem. (Lib Dem), Cambs CC, 2003–09. Royal College of Art: Council Mem., 1988–90; Chm., 1990–93. *Recreations:* carpentry, sailing. *Address:* 79 Grantchester Meadows, Cambridge CB3 9JL. *T:* 07748 654008.

**REID, Andrew Scott;** HM Coroner, Inner North London District of Greater London, 2002–12; *b* 2 March 1965; *m* 2007, Suzanne Ellen Greenaway; twin *s* two *d* from a previous marriage. *Educ:* Univ. of Nottingham Med. Sch. (BMedSci 1986; BM BS 1988); Nottingham Trent Univ. Sch. of Law (Postgrad. Dip. Law 1992; Solicitors Final Exam 1993). Pre-registration, sen. house officer and registrar posts in gen. medicine, surgery and histopathol., 1988–92; temp. Lectr in Human Morphol., Univ. of Nottingham, 1989–90; admitted solicitor, specialising in med. law and clin. negligence, 1995; In-house Solicitor and/or Clinical Risk Manager: NHS Litigation Authy, 1998–99; NHS Exec. Regl Medicolegal Service, 1999–2001; NW London Hosps NHS Trust, 2001–02. Asst Dep. Coroner, Notts, 1995–98; Dep. Coroner, N London, 1998–2002. Hon. Sen. Lectr in Pathology, Inst. of Cell and Molecular Sci., Queen Mary's Sch. of Medicine and Dentistry, London Univ., 2005–08. Legal Mem., Mental Health Rev. Tribunal, 2002. Mem., Human Tissue Authy, 2005–12. Member: BMA, 1987; Coroners' Soc. of England and Wales, 1995. FRSocMed 1997; FFFLM 2006 (Vice Pres., 2010–12). *Publications:* (contrib.) The Pathology of Trauma, ed Prof. J. K. Mason, 2nd edn 1993; contrib. papers on epithelial cell kinetics, breast cancer and industrial disease to med. jls. *Recreation:* trying to enjoy life between moderation and excess as appropriate.

**REID, Andrew Stephen;** Senior Partner, RMPI (formerly Reid Minty) LLP, Solicitors, since 1980; Deputy High Court Costs Judge (formerly Deputy Supreme Court Taxing Master), since 1991; Deputy District Judge: Principal Registry of the Family Division, since 2001; South Eastern Circuit, since 2002; Deputy Adjudicator, HM Land Registry, since 2007; *b* 2 March 1954; *s* of Leon Ralph Reid and Fay Marion Reid; partner, Corrina Bithell; one *d*. *Educ:* University College Sch.; University Coll. London (LLB Hons). ACIArb 1979, MCIArb. Admitted solicitor, 1979; founded Reid Minty, Solicitors, 1980. Mem., Radio Authy, 1994–99. Farmer, 1981–, established Belmont Children's Farm, Mill Hill, 2009–. Racehorse trainer/breeder, London, until 2016 (trained winner of Eider Chase, 1992, bred and trained winner of all weather Derby, plus 200 other winners). Dir, Belmont Farm Nursery Sch., 2018–. Non-exec. Dep. Treas., 2013–14, non-exec. Nat. Treas., 2014–15, UKIP; Mem., Cons. Party, 2015–. Trustee, RAF Mus., 2011–. Liveryman, Coachmakers' and Coach Harness Makers' Co., 2008. Jt Master, S Devon Fox Hounds, 2015–17. *Recreations:* polo, hunting, gardening, horse breeding, shooting, carriage driving, sailing, flying, classic car collector. *Address:* (office) Moss House, 15–16 Brooks Mews, W1K 4DS. *Clubs:* MCC, Alfred's; Belmont Polo; Guards' Polo; Oakley Hunt; Leander (Henley-on-Thames); Royal Dart Yacht; Stoke Gabriel Boating Assoc.

**REID, Caroline Jean Vernon;** Hon. Director General, European Investment Bank, since 2004; *b* 6 April 1948; *d* of late Colin Beever and of Dorothy Beever; *m* 1970, Michael Francis Reid; two *s*. *Educ:* Lycée Châteaubriand, Rome; Bedford High Sch. for Girls; Univ. of Bristol (BSc Hons Econs and Stats). Asst economist, British Gas Council, 1969–71; with NIESR, 1972–74; joined European Investment Bank, 1974: Energy Economist, 1974–85; loan officer, Energy/Envmt Div., Dept for Lending, Rome, 1985–88, Hd of Div., 1988–94; Dir, Italy Dept, 1994–99; Dir Gen., Projects Directorate, 1999–2001; Hd of Infrastructure and Project Finance, Banca OPI SpA, SanPaolo Imi Banking Gp, 2001–07. *Address:* Via Palestro 11, 00185 Rome, Italy. *E:* cjvreid@gmail.com.

**REID, Caroline Oldcorn,** PhD; a District Judge, Principal Registry, Family Division, 2006–15 (Deputy District Judge, 2003–06); *b* 6 April 1948; *d* of late John Patterson Reid and Olwen Reid; *m* 1983, Dr Frank Patrick Burton, *qv*; two *s* one *d*. *Educ:* Holt Grammar Sch., Wokingham; Univ. of Sheffield (BA Hons Hist. 1969; PhD 1976); City Univ. (Dip Law 1981). Tutor Organiser, WEA, Sheffield, 1974–80; called to the Bar, Middle Temple, 1982; in practice as a barrister, 1984–2006, 14 Gray's Inn Square, 1994–2006. *Publications:* (contrib.) Evidence in Family Proceedings, 1999; (contrib.) Child Abuse, 3rd edn 2003; (contrib.) The Family Court Practice, 2007–. *Recreations:* relaxing with my family, Suffolk, reading, cooking, old things, garden design.

**REID, Sir Charles Edward James,** 4th Bt *cr* 1897; *b* 24 June 1956; *s* of Sir Alexander James Reid, 3rd Bt and of Michaela Ann Reid (*née* Kier); *S* father, 2019, but his name does not appear on the Official Roll of the Baronetage; *m* 1991, Nancy Annie Macnicol (marr. diss.); one *s*. *Heir: s* Marcus James Reid, *b* 1994.

**REID, Sir David (Edward),** Kt 2012; Chairman, Intertek Group plc, since 2012; *b* Ndola, Zambia, 5 Feb. 1947; *s* of late Robert Barron Reid and Mary Reid (*née* Johnston); *m* 1973, Prunella Alexandra Hiatt; two *d*. *Educ:* Fettes Coll., Edinburgh. CA 1970. Supervisor, then Sen. Auditor, Peat Marwick Mitchell, Paris, 1970–73; Chief Accountant, Philips Electronics (UK) Ltd, 1973–79; Finance Dir, Internat. Stores Ltd, British American Tobacco plc, 1979–85; Director: Tesco plc, 1985– (Chm., 2004–11); Westbury plc, 1989–96; De Vere Gp (formerly Greenalls Gp plc), 1994–2002; Legal and General Gp plc, 1995–97; non-exec. Dir, Reed Elsevier plc, 2003–13; Chm., Kwik-Fit Gp Ltd, 2006–11. Mem., Global Sen. Adv. Bd, Jefferies Internat., 2012–19. Business Ambassador, UK Trade & Investment, 2010–13. Chm., Whizz-Kidz Ltd, 2008–. Hon. DBA Robert Gordon, 2005; Hon. LLD Aberdeen, 2006. *Recreation:* Rugby (former Chm., London Scottish Rugby Club). *Address:* Intertek Group plc, 33 Cavendish Square, W1G 0PS. *T:* (020) 7396 3400. *E:* david.reid@intertek.com. *Club:* Caledonian.

**REID, Dominic;** *see* Reid, J. D.

**REID, Elizabeth Margaret;** Chief Executive, Specialist Schools and Academies Trust (formerly Technology Colleges, then Specialist Schools, Trust), 2001–11; PhD student in History of Chinese Art, School of Oriental and African Studies, University of London, since 2016; *b* 16 April 1947; *d* of late John A. McConachie, MB ChB, FRCPE and J. Margaret McConachie, MB ChB; *m* 1st, 1970, Robin Reid, MA (marr. diss. 1975); 2nd, 1982, Martin J. Monk, BA Hons Oxon (marr. diss. 2000). *Educ:* Aberdeen Univ. (MA Hons 1969); London Univ. (MA Educnl Admin 1980); Courtauld Inst. of Art (Grad. Dip. 2014); Sch. of Oriental and African Studies, Univ. of London (MA Hist. of Art and Archaeol. of E Asia 2015). Asst Principal, CS, 1969–70; Inner London Education Authority: schoolteacher, 1970–78; Advr for 16–19 educn, 1978–79; Professional Asst, London Borough of Ealing, 1979–80; Asst Educn Officer, London Borough of Haringey, 1980–83; Sen. Principal Officer (Educn), AMA, 1983–85; Inner London Education Authority: Admin. Head, Further and Higher Educn Br., 1985–88; Dep. Dir of Educn (Further and Higher Educn), 1988–89; Dep. Provost, London Guildhall Univ. (formerly City of London Poly.), 1989–93; Director of Education: Lothian Regional Council, 1993–96; City of Edinburgh Council, 1996–98; London Borough of Hackney, 1998–2000. Vice Chm., Scottish Qualifications Authy, 1996–98; Mem. Bd, QCDA (formerly QCA), 2009–11. Mem. Bd, Enterprise Educn Trust (formerly Understanding Industry), 2000–16. Member: Ct of Govs, Univ. of the Arts, London (formerly London Inst.), 2001–13 (Chair, Finance Cttee, 2009–13); Fashion Retail Acad., 2006–15; Bd, City and Islington Coll., 2007–14. Dir, Muban Educnl Trust, 2009–; Trustee, Royal Female Sch. of Art Foundn, 2015–18. Fellow, Inst. of Educn, 2008. FRSA 1989; FSQA 1998; Fellow and Icebreaker of the Year, 48 Gp Club, 2007. *Publications:* (contrib.) Central and Local Control of Education After the Education Reform Act 1988, ed R. Morris, 1990; (contrib.) The Future of Higher Education, ed T. Schuller, 1991; (with R. Morris and J. Fowler) Education Act 93: a critical guide, 1993. *Recreations:* theatre, opera, reading, history of art (East and West). *E:* elizabethreid@sky.com.

**REID, Prof. Gavin Clydesdale,** PhD, DLitt; Professor of Economics, University of St Andrews, 1991–2013, now Honorary Professor in Economics and Finance; Member, Competition Appeal Tribunal, 2011–18; Senior Research Associate, Centre for Business Research, Judge Business School, University of Cambridge, since 2019; *b* Glasgow, 25 Aug. 1946; *s* of late Lt Col Alexander Macfarlane Reid, BSc and Sheila Macgregor Reid (*née* Jackson); *m* 1st, 1967, Margaret Morrice McGregor, MA, JP, DL (marr. diss. 1983); one *s* and one step *s*; 2nd, 1986, Maureen Johnson Bagnall, MB, ChB, BSc (marr. diss. 2007); one *s* two *d* and one step *s*; 3rd, 2008, Julia Anne Smith, BCom, PhD, FCMA; two *d*. *Educ:* Lyndhurst Prep. Sch.; Frimley and Camberley Grammar Sch.; Univ. of Aberdeen (MA 1st Cl. Hons Econ. Sci. 1969; Stephen Schol.); Univ. of Southampton (MSc Econ. Theory and Econometrics 1971; SSRC Schol.); Univ. of Edinburgh (PhD Industrial Orgn 1975); Univ. of Aberdeen (DLitt Small Business Enterprise 2012). Lectr, 1971–84, Sen. Lectr, 1984–90, Reader in Econs, 1990–91, Actg Hd, Econs, 1991, Univ. of Edinburgh; Founder and Dir, Centre for Res. into Industry, Enterprise, Finance and the Firm, Univ. of St Andrews, 1991–2013; Prof. of Enterprise and Innovation, Business Sch., UWS, 2013–14; Prof. of Business Mgt and Strategy, and Hd, Dundee Business Sch., Abertay Univ., 2014–18. Visiting Professor: Queen's Univ., Ont, 1981–82; Univ. of Denver, 1984; Univ. of Nice, 1998; Vis. Schol., Darwin Coll., Cambridge, 1987–88; Vis. Prof. in Accounting and Finance, Univ. of Strathclyde, 2007–15. Research Fellow: Leverhulme Trust, 1989–90; Nuffield Foundn, 1997–98. Advisor: Centre for Business Res., Univ. of Cambridge, 2009–; Keynes Centre, UC Cork, 2015–. External Examiner: Univ. of Aberdeen, 1979, 2014–15; Univ. of WI, 1986–88; UC Cork, 1994–2008; Univ. of Malawi, 1998–2001; Univ. of Durham, 1999–2006; Univ. of Cambridge, 2001–09; Univ. of Glasgow, 2015–17. President: Scottish Econ. Soc., 1999–2002; Nat. Conf. of Univ. Profs, 2003–06; Inst. of Contemporary Scotland, 2005–06. Chairman: ESRC Network of Industrial Economists, 1997–2001; Scottish Inst. for Enterprise Res. Forum, 2002–03; ESRC Seminars in Accounting, Finance and Econs, 2006–08. FFCS 2000; FRSA 2000. Hon. DBA Abertay Dundee, 2010; DLitt Aberdeen, 2012. Medal of Honour, Scottish Econ. Soc., 2017. *Publications:* The Kinked Demand Curve Analysis of Oligopoly, 1981; Theories of Industrial Organization, 1987; (jtly) The Small Entrepreneurial Firm, 1988; Classical Economic Growth, 1989; Small Business Enterprise, 1993; (jtly) Profiles in Small Business, 1993; Venture Capital Investment, 1998; (jtly) Information System Development in the Small Firm, 2000; The Foundations of Small Business Enterprise, 2007; (jtly) Risk Appraisal and Venture Capital in High Technology New Ventures, 2008; contrib. papers to learned jls in economics, accounting and finance incl. Economic Jl, Economica, Oxford Econ. Papers, Rev. of Industrial Orgn, Internat. Jl of Industrial Orgn, Jl of Industrial Econs, Small Business Econs, Managerial and Decision Econs, Eur. Jl Finance, Entrepreneurship Theory and Practice, Mgt Accounting Res., Critical Perspectives on Accounting, Accounting and Business Res. *Recreations:* reading, poetry, music, running, badminton. *Address:* School of Economics and Finance, University of St Andrews, Castlecliffe, The Scores, St Andrews KY16 9AR. *E:* gcr@st-andrews.ac.uk, gr432@cam.ac.uk. *Clubs:* Reform, Royal Over-Seas League; St Andrews Golf.

**REID, Rt Rev. Gavin Hunter,** OBE 2000; Bishop Suffragan of Maidstone, 1992–2000; an Honorary Assistant Bishop, Diocese of St Edmundsbury and Ipswich, since 2008; *b* 24 May 1934; *s* of Arthur William Reid and Jean Smith Reid (*née* Guthrie); *m* 1959, Mary Eleanor Smith; two *s* one *d*. *Educ:* Roan Sch., Greenwich; Queen Mary Coll. and King's Coll., London Univ. (BA 1956); Oak Hill Theol Coll. Ordained, Chelmsford Cathedral: deacon, 1960; priest, 1961; Assistant Curate: St Paul's, East Ham, 1960–63; Rainham Parish Church, 1963–66; Publications Sec., CPAS, 1966–71; Editorial Sec., United Soc. for Christian Lit., 1971–74; Sec. for Evangelism, 1974–90, Consultant Missioner, 1990–92, CPAS; Advr, Gen. Synod Bd of Mission, 1990–92. Seconded: Nat. Dir, Mission England, 1982–85; Project Dir, Mission 89, 1988–89. Chairman: Archbishops' Adv. Gp for the Millennium, 1995–2000; CPAS Council of Reference, 2005–08. Pres., British Youth for Christ, 2001–04. *Publications:* The Gagging of God, 1969; The Elaborate Funeral, 1972; A New Happiness, 1974; To Be Confirmed, 1977; Good News to Share, 1979; Starting Out Together, 1981; To Reach a Nation, 1987; Beyond Aids, 1987; Lights that Shine, 1991; Brushing up on Believing, 1991; Our Place in his Story, 1994; To Canterbury with Love, 2002; various symposia. *Recreations:* golf, sailing, walking, birdwatching. *Address:* 17 Richard Crampton Road, Beccles, Suffolk NR34 9HN.

**REID, Rt Hon. Sir George (Newlands),** Kt 2012; PC 2004; Member, UK Electoral Commission, 2010–13; Chairman, Remuneration Board, National Assembly for Wales, 2010–13; Lord-Lieutenant of Clackmannanshire, 2011–14; Professorial Fellow, University of Stirling, since 2014; *b* 4 June 1939; *s* of late George Reid, company director, and of Margaret Forsyth; *m* 1968, Daphne Ann MacColl; one *d*, and one *d* from previous marriage. *Educ:* Tullibody Sch.; Dollar Academy; Univ. of St Andrews (MA Hons). Pres., Students' Representative Council. Features Writer, Scottish Daily Express, 1962; Reporter, Scottish Television, 1964; Producer, Granada Television, 1965; Head of News and Current Affairs (Scottish Television), 1968; presenter, BBC, 1979. Head of Inf., 1984–86, Dir of Public Affairs, 1986–90, Dir of Internat. Campaign for Victims of War, 1990–92, League of Red Cross and Red Crescent Socs, Geneva. MP (SNP) Stirlingshire E and Clackmannan, Feb. 1974–1979; Mem., British Parly Delegn to Council of Europe and WEU, 1977–79. Scottish Parliament: Mem. Mid Scotland & Fife, 1999–2003, Ochil, 2003–07 (SNP,

1999–2003, when elected Presiding Officer); Dep. Presiding Officer, 1999–2003; Presiding Officer, 2003–07; Convener: Scottish Parly Bureau, 2003–07; Scottish Parly Corporate Body, 2003–07. Mem., Standing Council on Europe, Scottish Govt, 2016–. Chair, Strategic Rev. of Governance, NI Assembly, 2007–08. Dir, Strategic Rev., NT for Scotland, 2009–10. Vice-Convener, SNP, 1997–99. Contested (SNP) Ochil, 1997. Ind. Advr, Scottish Ministerial Code, 2008–11. Lord High Comr, Gen. Assembly, Ch of Scotland, 2008 and 2009. Dir, Scottish Council Res. Inst., 1974–77. Visiting Professor: Glasgow Univ., 2006–10; Stirling Univ., 2008–14; Professorial Fellow, London Acad. of Diplomacy, 2014–17. Vice Chm., Carnegie Commn on Civil Soc., 2006–09; Mem., Caucasus-Caspian Commn, 2007–08. Chair, Scottish Press Awards, 2008–11. Trustee: Glasgow Culture and Sport, 2007–13; Royal Edinburgh (formerly Edinburgh) Military Tattoo, 2007–13 (Vice-Patron, 2013–). Chief Red Cross deleg. to Armenia, Dec. 1988–Jan. 1989. FRSE 2015. Hon LLD: St Andrews, 2005; Glasgow, 2009; DUniv: Queen Margaret UC, 2006; Edinburgh, 2007; Stirling, 2008. *Address*: Coneyhill House, Bridge of Allan, Stirling FK9 4DU.

**REID, Rev. Canon Gordon;** *see* Reid, Very Rev. Canon W. G.

**REID, Gordon John,** MBE 2017; professional wheelchair tennis player; *b* Helensburgh, 2 Oct. 1991; *s* of Graham and Alison Reid. Started playing wheelchair tennis, 2005; GB Nat. Champion, 2007; rankings: World No 1 Junior, 2009; World No 1, Doubles, 2015; World No 1, Singles, 2016; competed at Paralympic Games: Singles: Beijing, 2008; London, 2012; Rio de Janeiro, 2016 (Gold Medal); Doubles: Beijing, 2008; London, 2012; Rio de Janeiro, 2016 (Silver Medal); Singles: winner: Australian Open, Wimbledon, 2016; Doubles: winner: US Open, 2015, 2017; French Open, 2015, 2016; Wimbledon, 2016, 2017, 2018; Australian Open, 2017; winner, Masters Doubles, 2013, 2015, 2017. *Recreation*: wheelchair basketball. *E*: Paul@Paulregan.org. *T*: 07957 959675. *W*: www.gordonreidtennis.com.

**REID, Prof. Graeme Thomas,** PhD; CEng; FInstP, FIET; FRSE; Professor of Science and Research Policy, University College London, since 2014; *b* Thorne, Yorks, 4 July 1955; *s* of Tom and Jean Reid; *m* 1978, Victoria Jane Raban-Williams; one *d*. *Educ*: Musselburgh Grammar Sch.; Robert Gordon's Inst. of Technol. (BSc Physical Scis 1979); Strathclyde Univ. (PhD Mech. Engrg 1988). CEng 1989; FInstP 1998; FIET 2001. NEL, 1979–88; DTI, Cabinet Office, HM Treasury, UKTI and BIS, 1988–2014. Strategic Advr, Nat. Centre for Univs and Business, 2014–; Specialist Advr, Sci. and Technol. Cttee, H of L, 2015–18; Mem., high level gp on EU exit, univs, res. and innovation, UK Govt, 2017–; Leader of Reviews: of innovation centres, SFC, 2016; of govt-funded res. and innovation for Welsh Govt, 2017–18. Vis. Prof., Sch. of Govt and Public Policy, Univ. of Strathclyde, 2018–. Mem. Council, Research England, 2018–. Chm., Campaign for Sci. and Engrg, 2014–. Trustee, Assoc. of Med. Res. Charities, 2014–. FRSE 2019. *Recreations*: cycling, gardening, being in Rutland. *Address*: Office of the Vice Provost (Research), University College London, 2 Taviton Street, WC1H 0BT. *T*: 07740 613069. *E*: graeme.reid@ucl.ac.uk.

**REID, Graham Livingstone,** CB 1991; Director General of Strategy, International and Analytical Services, Department for Education and Employment, 1995–97; *b* 30 June 1937; *s* of late William L. Reid and of Louise M. Reid; *m* 1st, 1973, Eileen M. Loudfoot (marr. diss. 1983); 2nd, 1985, Sheila Rothwell (*d* 1997); 3rd, 2008, Mavis Waller. *Educ*: Univ. of St Andrews (MA); Queen's Univ., Kingston, Canada (MA). Dept of Social and Economic Res., Univ. of Glasgow: Asst Lectr in Applied Economics, 1960, Lectr 1963, Sen. Lectr 1968, Reader 1971; Sen. Econ. Adviser and Head of Econs and Statistics Unit, Scottish Office, 1973–75; Dir, Manpower Intelligence and Planning Div., MSC, 1975–84; Department of Employment: Chief Economic Adviser and Hd, Economic and Social Div., 1984–88 and Dir, Enterprise and Deregulation Unit, 1987; Dep. Sec., Manpower Policy, 1988–90, Resources and Strategy, 1991, Indust. Relns and Internat. Directorate, 1991–95. Vis. Associate Prof., Mich State Univ., 1967; Vis. Res. Fellow, Queen's Univ., Canada, 1969. FRSA 1996. *Publications*: Fringe Benefits, Labour Costs and Social Security (ed with D. J. Robertson), 1965; (with K. J. Allen) Nationalised Industries, 1970, 3rd edn 1975; (with L. C. Hunter and D. Boddy) Labour Problems of Technological Change, 1970; (with K. J. Allen and D. J. Harris) The Nationalised Fuel Industries, 1973; contrib. to Econ. Jl, Brit. Jl of Indust. Relations, Scot. Jl of Polit. Econ., Indust & Lab. Relns Rev. *Recreations*: theatre, reading, music. *Address*: 24 Barley Way, Marlow SL7 2UG. *T*: (01628) 483720. *Club*: Phyllis Court (Henley-on-Thames).

**REID, Henry William, (Harry);** writer; *b* 23 Sept. 1947; *s* of late William Reid and Catherine Robertson Craighead Reid (*née* Maclean); *m* 1980, Julie Wilson Davidson; one *d*. *Educ*: Aberdeen Grammar Sch.; Fettes Coll.; Worcester Coll., Oxford (BA). The Scotsman: reporter, sports writer, leader writer, 1970–73; educn correspondent, 1973–77; Features Ed., 1977–81; Sport and Leisure Ed., Sunday Standard, 1981–82; Exec. Ed., 1982–83, Dep. Ed., 1983–97, Ed., 1997–2000, columnist, 2004–, The Herald, Glasgow. Vis. Fellow, Faculty of Divinity, Univ. of Edinburgh, 2001–02. Mem., Church and Soc. Council, Ch of Scotland, 2005–06. Gov., Fettes Coll., 2002–12. DUniv Glasgow, 2001; Dr *hc* Edinburgh, 2001. Oliver Brown Award, Scots Independent, 2008. *Publications*: Dear Country: a quest for England, 1992; Outside Verdict: an old kirk in a new Scotland, 2002; Deadline: the story of the Scottish press, 2006; Reformation: the dangerous birth of the modern world, 2009. *Recreations*: exploring Scotland and European cities, hill walking, supporting Aberdeen FC, reading novels, listening to Bob Dylan. *Address*: 12 Comely Bank, Edinburgh EH4 1AN. *T*: (0131) 332 6690.

**REID, Iain;** arts consultant, retired; *b* 27 March 1942; *s* of Jean Reid (*née* Money) and George Aitken Reid; *m* 1st, 1968, Judith Coke; 2nd, 1982, Kay Barlow; one *s* one *d*. *Educ*: Uppingham; RADA; Lancaster Univ. (MA). Actor, 1963–73; theatre administrator, 1973–77; Drama Officer, Greater London Arts, 1977–82; Dir of Arts, Calouste Gulbenkian Foundn (UK), 1982–89; Dir, Arts Co-ordination, later Arts Develt, Arts Council of GB, 1989–94; Dir of Combined Arts, Arts Council of England, 1994–98; Dean, Arts Educnl Sch., London, 1998–2006. Examnr, Trinity Coll., London, 2008–17. *E*: Kay.in@btinternet.com.

**REID, His Honour James Robert;** QC 1980; a Circuit Judge, 1999–2013; *b* 23 Jan. 1943; *s* of late Judge J. A. Reid, MC and Jean Ethel Reid; *m* 1st, 1974, Anne Prudence Wakefield, *qv* (marr. diss. 2002); two *s* one *d*; 2nd, 2012, Rosalba Effenberg (*née* de Lisi). *Educ*: Marlborough Coll.; New Coll., Oxford (MA). FCIArb 1992. Called to the Bar, Lincoln's Inn, 1965, Bencher, 1988 (Treas., 2011); Recorder, 1985–99; Dep. High Court Judge, 1985–2013; Additional Judge of Employment Appeal Tribunal, 2000–11; Designated Civil Judge, Surrey Courts, 2004–12; Legal Mem., Lands Tribunal, subseq. Judge of the Upper Chamber (Lands), 2006–11. Mem., Senate of Inns of Court and the Bar, 1977–80; Mem., Gen. Council of the Bar, 1990–96 (Chm., Professional Conduct Cttee, 1995–96). Chm., Barristers Benevolent Assoc., 1995–99 (Hon. Jt Treas., 1986–91; Dep. Chm., 1991–95). Dir, Bar Mutual Indemnity Fund Ltd, 1996–99. Mem., Court of Arbitration for Sport, 1999–; Chairman: Football League Appeal Cttee, 2000–; Professional Football Compensation Cttee, 2008–.

**REID, Prof. Janice Clare,** AC 2015 (AM 1998); FASSA; Vice-Chancellor and President, University of Western Sydney, 1998–2013, now Emeritus Professor; *b* 19 Sept. 1947; *d* of Keith M. Reid and Joan C. Reid; one *d*. *Educ*: Presbyterian Girls' Coll., Adelaide; Univ. of Adelaide (BSc); Univ. of Hawaii (MA); Stanford Univ., USA (MA, PhD). FASSA 1991. High sch. teacher, PNG, 1968–69; Res. Officer/Asst, Dept of Community Medicine, Univ. of NSW, 1974–75; Sen. Lectr, then Associate Prof., Sch. of Public Health and Tropical Medicine, 1979–90, and Dir, Centre for Crosscultural Studies in Health and Medicine, 1988–92, Univ. of Sydney; Foundn Hd, Sch. of Community Health, Cumberland Coll. of Health Scis, 1987–91; Prof. of Community Health, Univ. of Sydney, 1990–91; Pro Vice-Chancellor (Acad.), Qld Univ. of Technol., 1991–98. Chm. or mem., various Nat. Health and MRC standing cttees, 1992–96; Member: Higher Educn Council, 1996–98; Gtr Western Sydney Econ. Develt Bd, 1998–2000; Council, Assoc. of Commonwealth Univs, 1999; Integral Energy Bd, 2000–06; Fed. Council on Australian/Latin American Relns, 2001–06 (Chm., Educn Action Gp, 2003–06); Higher Educn Cttee, Ministerial Ref. Gp, Nat. Higher Educn Rev., 2002; Governing Bd, OECD Instnl Mgt in Higher Educn Prog., 2005–08 (Vice-Chm., 2007–08); Steering Cttee, Internat. Talloires Univ. Network, 2005–14 (Vice-Chm., 2011–14); Bd, NSW Health Clinical Excellence Commn, 2007–14; Bd, Agency for Clinical Innovation, 2007–14; Expert Ref. Gp, Commonwealth Tertiary Educn Quality Standards, 2009–10; Innovation and Productivity Council, NSW, 2011–12; Convenor, NSW Vice-Chancellors' Cttee, 2012. Mem., Regl Adv. Council, St Vincent's Hosp., NSW, 2014– (Mem., Clin. Governance and Safety Cttee, 2017–). Mem. Bd, UniSuper Ltd, 2006–12. Mem., Australian Inst. Aboriginal and Torres Is Studies, 1981–; Dep. Chm., Qld Inst. Med. Res., 1994–97. Chm., Founder and Convener, Australian Soc. of Med. Anthropol., 1981–82. Member: Qld Mus. Bd, 1992–97; Nat. Cultural Heritage Cttee, 2011–13; Council, Nat. Liby of Australia, 2012–15; Council, Univ. of S Pacific, 2014–18. Mem. Council, Blue Mts GS, 1998–2002; Gov., Westmead Millennium Inst., 2001–05. Mem. Adv. Bd, Western Sydney Salvation Army, 2001–10. Trustee, Kedumba Drawing Award, 2001–02, 2004–10; Mem. Trust, NSW Art Gall., 2004–12. Chair, Pacific Friends of the Global Fund, 2015–18. Hon. DLitt Western Sydney, 2013; Hon. DMedSci Sydney, 2017. Wellcome Medal, RAI, 1984. Centenary Medal, Australia, 2003. *Publications*: (ed) Body Land and Spirit, 1982; Sorcerers and Healing Spirits, 1983; edited with P. Trompf: The Health of Immigrant Australia, 1990; The Health of Aboriginal Australia, 1991; contrib. numerous chapters, papers and reports to various jls, incl. Social Sci. and Medicine, particularly on Aborigines, migrants and refugees and health. *Address*: NSW, Australia. *E*: janice.reid1@gmail.com.

**REID, John Boyd,** AO 1980; LLB; FAIM, FAICD; CPEng, FIEAust; Chairman Emeritus, Australian Graduate School of Management, since 2000 (Board Member, 1991–2002); Chairman, James Hardie Industries Ltd, 1973–96 (Director, 1964–96); *b* 27 Dec. 1929; *s* of Sir John Thyne Reid, CMG. *Educ*: Scotch College; Melbourne Univ. Chm., Comsteel Vickers Ltd, 1983–86; Vice-Chm., Qantas Airways, 1981–86 (Dir, 1977–86); Director: Broken Hill Pty Co., 1972–97; Barclays Internat. Australia, 1982–85; Bell Resources Ltd, 1987–88; Peregrine Capital Australia Ltd, 1991–95; Focus Publishing, 1991–2003. Chm., Australian Bicentennial Authy, 1979–85; Dir, World Expo 88, 1986–89; Member: Admin. Review Cttee, 1975–76; Ind. Inquiry into Commonwealth Serum Labs, 1978; Patron, Australia Indonesia Business Co-operation Cttee, 1979–88 (Pres., 1973–79); Dir, Thailand-Australia Foundn Ltd, 1993–96; Mem., Internat. Adv. Bd, Swiss Banking Corp., 1986–97; Chm., Review of Commonwealth Admin, 1981–82. Trustee and Internat. Counsellor, Conference Bd USA; Internat. Council, Stanford Res. Inst., USA. Chairman: NSW Educn and Trng Foundn, 1989–93; Cttee, Aust. Scout Educn and Trng Foundn, 1991; Museum of Contemp. Art, 1994–98. Chm. Council, Pymble Ladies Coll., 1975–82 (Mem., 1965–75); Governor, Ian Clunies Ross Meml Foundn, 1975–2000; Chm., Sydney Adv. Cttee, 1995–97, and Red Shield Appeal, 1993–94, Salvation Army. Mem., Inst. of Company Dirs. Life Governor, AIM (Sydney Div.). Hon. Fellow, Univ. of Sydney, 2004. Hon. DBus Charles Sturt Univ., NSW; Hon. PhD Queensland; DUniv Qld Univ. of Technol., 2002. Melbourne Univ. Graduate Sch. of Business Admin Award, 1983; John Storey Medal, AIM, 1985. *Club*: Queensland.

**REID, (John) Dominic,** OBE 2003; Pageantmaster, Lord Mayor's Show, since 1992; Principal, Reid and Reid, since 1992; Partner, John and Sylvia Reid, since 2011; Chief Executive Officer, Invictus Games Foundation, since 2015; Mentor, Mentore Consulting LLP, since 2016; Founding Partner, Sequitur, since 2017; *b* 24 Sept. 1961; *s* of late John Reid, OBE, DL and of Sylvia Reid; *m* 1991, Suzanne Jessup (*née* Schultz); one *d*. *Educ*: Oundle Sch. (Music Scholar); Downing Coll., Cambridge; University College London. RIBA 1991. 2nd Lt, 49 Field Regt, Royal Artillery, 1981. Architect: Doshi-Raje, Ahmedabad, India, 1984–85; Austin-Smith:Lord, 1986–89; Richard Horden Associates Ltd, 1989–90; John and Sylvia Reid, 1990–92; Dir, Designer's Collaborative, 1996–2000; Chief Exec., London Film Commission, 1999–2000; Exec. Dir, Oxford and Cambridge Boat Race, 2000–04; Pageantmaster, The Queen's Golden Jubilee, 2002; Dir, 2010 Anniversary Prog., Royal Soc., 2007–10. Director: Chatsworth Country Fair, 2013; Holkham Country Fair, 2013; of Events, Invictus Games, 2014. Gov., Mus. of London, 2013–17. Hon. Col, City of London and NE Sector ACF, 2015–. Sergeant-at-Mace, Royal Soc., 2010–. HM Lieut for City of London, 2009–. Liveryman, Grocers' Co., 1999–. OStJ 1999. *Publications*: (ed jtly) Lord Mayor's Show: 800 years 1215–2015, 2015. *Recreations*: telemarking, sailing, cycling, shooting, sartorial correctness. *E*: dominic@reidandreid.com. *Clubs*: HAC; Leander.

**REID, Prof. John Low,** OBE 2001; DM; Regius Professor of Medicine and Therapeutics, University of Glasgow, 1989–2009, now Emeritus Professor and Hon. Senior Research Fellow; Medical Director, Scottish Advisory Committee on Distinction Awards, Scottish Government (formerly Executive) Health Department, 2005–09; *b* 1 Oct. 1943; *s* of Dr James Reid and Irene M. Dale; *m* 1964, Randa Pharaon (*d* 2014); one *s* one *d*. *Educ*: Fettes Coll., Edinburgh; Magdalen Coll., Oxford. MA; DM. FRCP 1986; FRCPGlas 1979; FRCPI 1997; FRSE 1995; FBPhS (FBPharmacolS 2009). House Officer, Radcliffe Infirmary, Oxford, and Brompton Hosp., 1967–70; Res. Fellow, RPMS, 1970–73; Vis. Fellow, Nat. Inst. of Mental Health, USA, 1973–74; Royal Postgraduate Medical School: Sen. Lectr in Clin. Pharmacol., and Consultant Physician, 1975–77; Reader in Clin. Pharmacol., 1977–78; Regius Prof. of Materia Medica, Univ. of Glasgow, 1978–89; Clinical Dir, Acute Medicine, 1993–2000, Chm., Div. of Medicine, 2000–06, N Glasgow Univ. Hosps NHS Trust. Founder FMedSci 1998. *Publications*: Central Action of Drugs in Regulation of Blood Pressure, 1975; Lecture Notes in Clinical Pharmacology, 1982; Handbook of Hypertension, 1983; papers on cardiovascular and neurological diseases in clinical and pharmacological journals. *Recreations*: books, gardening, the outdoors. *Address*: Maryland, Black Bull Lane, Fencott, Oxon OX5 2RD. *T*: (01865) 331023.

**REID, Dr Julia;** Member for South West Region and Gibraltar, European Parliament, 2014–19 (UK Ind, 2014–18; Ind, 2018–19); *b* Brockley, SE London, 16 July 1952; *d* of John and Joan Rudman; *m* 1st, 1970 (marr. diss. 1986); one *s*; 2nd, 1987, Kenneth Reid. *Educ*: Honor Oak Grammar Sch.; Sudbury Girls' High Sch.; John Bentley Sch., Calne; Univ. of

Bath (BSc Hons Biochem. 1990; PhD Pharmacol. 1998). Hd of Academic Res. and Lab. Manager, Diabetes and Lipid Res. Lab., Royal United Hosp., Bath, 1999–2009. Parly Asst to Trevor Colman, MEP, 2011. Mem. (UK Ind) Calne Town Council, 2013. Contested (UK Ind): SW Reg., EP, 2009; Chippenham, 2010, 2015.

**REID, Prof. Kenneth Bannerman Milne,** PhD; FRS 1997; Professor of Immunochemistry, University of Oxford, 1993–2008; Fellow, Green College, Oxford, 1986–2008, now Emeritus; Director, MRC Immunochemistry Unit, Oxford University, 1985–2008; *b* 22 Sept. 1943; *s* of John McBean Reid and Maria Anderson (*née* Smith); *m* 1969, Margery Robertson Gilmour; one *s* two *d*. *Educ*: Univ. of Aberdeen (BSc 1965; PhD 1968). SO, Fisheries Res. Unit, Aberdeen Univ., 1968–69; ICI Res. Fellowship, Dept Biochem., Univ. of Oxford, 1969–70; Mem., Scientific Staff, 1970–84, Dep. Dir, 1984–85, MRC Immunochemistry Unit, Dept of Biochemistry, Univ. of Oxford. Fellow, EMBO, 1991; Founder FMedSci 1998. Second Wellcome Trust Lecture Award, 1981; Eur. Complement Network Medal for lifetime achievement in complement res., 2013. *Publications*: Complement, 1988, 2nd edn 1995; author or co-author of numerous papers in jls such as Nature, Biochem. Jl, Jl Immunology. *Recreations*: hill-walking, racket sports (squash, tennis). *Address*: 4 Peacock Road, Headington, Oxford OX3 0DQ; Green Templeton College, at the Radcliffe Observatory, Woodstock Road, Oxford OX2 6HG.

**REID, Prof. Kenneth Gilbert Cameron,** CBE 2005; WS; FRSE; FBA 2008; Professor of Scots Law, University of Edinburgh, since 2008; *b* 25 March 1954; *s* of Gilbert Beith Reid and Mary Henry Reid (*née* Sinclair); *m* 1981, Elspeth Christie; two *s* one *d*. *Educ*: Loretto; St John's Coll., Cambridge (MA); Univ. of Edinburgh (LLB). Admitted solicitor, 1980; WS 1999. University of Edinburgh: Lectr in Law, 1980–91; Sen. Lectr, 1991–94; Prof. of Property Law, 1994–2008; Mem., Scottish Law Commn, 1995–2005. Visiting Professor: Tulane Law Sch., New Orleans, 2003; Loyola Univ., New Orleans, 2013. Fellow: Business and Law Res. Centre, Radboud Univ., Nijmegen, 2005–09; Stellenbosch Inst. for Advanced Study, 2015. Ed., Edinburgh Law Review, 2006–10. FRSE 2000. Hon. LLD Cape Town, 2015. *Publications*: (jtly) The Laws of Scotland: Stair Memorial Encyclopaedia, Vol. 18, 1993, rev. edn as The Law of Property in Scotland, 1996; (with G. L. Gretton) Conveyancing, 1993, 5th edn 2018; (ed jtly) A History of Private Law in Scotland, 2000; Abolition of Feudal Tenure in Scotland, 2003; (ed jtly) Mixed Legal Systems in Comparative Perspective: property and obligations in Scotland and South Africa, 2004; (ed jtly) Exploring the Law of Succession: studies national, historical and comparative, 2007; (ed jtly) Towards an EU Directive on Protected Funds, 2009; (ed jtly) Testamentary Formalities, 2011; (ed jtly) Intestate Succession, 2015; (with G. L. Gretton) Land Registration, 2017; numerous papers in learned jls. *Recreations*: classical music, both listening and doing. *Address*: School of Law, University of Edinburgh, Old College, South Bridge, Edinburgh EH8 9YL. *T*: (0131) 650 2015.

**REID, Lesley Munro;** *see* Shand, L. M.

**REID, Leslie,** CBE 1978; HM Diplomatic Service, retired; Director General, The Association of British Mining Equipment Companies, 1980–83; *b* 24 May 1919; *s* of late Frederick Sharples and Mary Reid; *m* 1942, Norah Moorcroft (*d* 2011); three *d*. *Educ*: King George V Sch., Southport, Lancs. Served War of 1939–45, W Europe and SEAC, Major, XX The Lancashire Fusiliers. Board of Trade, 1947–49; Asst Trade Commissioner: Salisbury, Rhodesia, 1949–55; Edmonton, Alberta, 1955–56; Trade Comr, Vancouver, 1956–60; Principal, BoT, 1960–62; Trade Comr and Economic Advisor, British High Commn, Cyprus, 1962–64; BoT, 1964–66; 1st Sec., FCO, 1966–68; Sen. Commercial Sec., British High Commn, Jamaica, and 1st Sec., British Embassy, Port-au-Prince, Haiti, 1968–70; Commercial and Economic Counsellor, Ghana, 1970–73; Consul Gen., Cleveland, Ohio, 1973–79. *Recreations*: golf, reading. *Address*: Kingsdowne, Albert Terrace, Norwich NR2 2JD.

**REID, Lynne Elizabeth;** *see* Frostick, L. E.

**REID, Malcolm Herbert Marcus;** Chief Executive, Life Assurance and Unit Trust Regulatory Organisation, 1986–89; *b* 2 March 1927; *s* of late Marcus Reid and Winifred Stephens; *m* 1st, 1956, Eleanor (*d* 1974), *d* of late H. G. Evans, MC; four *s*; 2nd, 1975, Daphne (*d* 2000), *e d* of Sir John Griffin, QC; 3rd, 2004, Carol Stephens, *d* of late E. Deason. *Educ*: Merchant Taylors' Sch.; St John's Coll., Oxford. Served in Navy, 1945–48 and in RNVR, 1949–53. Entered Board of Trade, 1951; Private Secretary to Permanent Secretary, 1954–57; Trade Comr in Ottawa, 1957–60; Board of Trade, 1960–63; Private Secretary to successive Prime Ministers, 1963–66; Commercial Counsellor, Madrid, 1967–71; Asst Sec., DTI, 1972–74; Under Sec., Dept of Industry, 1974–78, of Trade, 1978–83, DTI, 1983–84; Registrar, Registry of Life Assurance Commn, 1984–86. Dir, Mercury Life Assurance Co. Ltd, 1989–97. Mem., Appeal Cttee, ICA, 1990–96. *Recreations*: National Hunt racing, inland waterways. *Address*: 3 Church Street, St Ives, Cambs PE27 6DG. *T*: (01480) 468367. *Club*: Oxford and Cambridge.

**REID, Melanie Frances,** MBE 2016; columnist, since 2007, and writer, Spinal Column, since 2010, The Times; *b* Barnet, Herts, 13 April 1957; *d* of Ronald Ogilvy Reid and Edith Elizabeth Reid (*née* Oakman); *m* 1st, 1982, Clifford Martin (marr. diss. 1992); one *s*; 2nd, 1996, David McNeil. *Educ*: Ormskirk Grammar Sch.; Univ. of Edinburgh (MA Hons 1980). Graduate trainee, 1980–82, Woman's Editor, 1983–87, The Scotsman; Associate Ed., Sunday Mail, 1987–2000; Sen. Writer, The Express, 2000–01; Sen. Asst Ed., The Herald, 2001–07. Mem., Carnegie Commn for Rural Community Devel, 2004–07. Co-writer (with Sally Beamish), Spinal Chords for Orch. of Age of Enlightenment, 2011. Journalist of the Year, Scottish Press Awards, 2010; Columnist of the Year - Broadsheet, Press Awards, 2011; Columnist of the Year, BSME Awards, 2017. DUniv Stirling, 2014. *Publications*: (with G. Fisher) The Boy from Nowhere, 2015; The World I Fell Out Of, 2019. *Recreations*: amateur bird-watching, painful physiotherapy. *Address*: The Times, 1 London Bridge Street, SE1 9GF. *E*: melanie.reid@thetimes.co.uk.

**REID, Prof. Miles Anthony,** PhD; FRS 2002; Professor, Mathematics Institute, University of Warwick, since 1992; *b* 30 Jan. 1948; *s* of John Rollo Reid and Edna Mary Reid (*née* Frost); *m* 1978, Nayo Hagino; three *d*. *Educ*: Petit Lycée Condorcet, Paris; Bournemouth Sch. for Boys; Trinity Coll., Cambridge (BA 1969, PhD 1972, MA 1973). Res. Fellow, Christ's Coll., Cambridge, 1973–78; Lectr, 1978–89, Reader, 1989–92, Maths Inst., Univ. of Warwick. Visiting Professor: Univ. of Tokyo, 1990; Nagoya Univ., 1996–97; British Hispanic Foundn Queen Victoria Eugenia Prof. of Doctoral Studies, Complutense Univ., Madrid, 2002–03. *Address*: Mathematics Institute, University of Warwick, Coventry CV4 7AL. *T*: (024) 7652 3523, *Fax*: (024) 7652 4182. *E*: miles@maths.warwick.ac.uk.

**REID, Prof. Nancy Margaret,** OC 2014; PhD; FRS 2018; FRSE; FRSC; Professor, since 1988, University Professor of Statistical Sciences, since 2003, and Canada Research Chair, since 2007, University of Toronto; *b* St Catharines, Ont, 17 Sept. 1952; *d* of Robert Edwin Reid and Ruth Reid (*née* Canning); *m* 2001, Donald A. S. Fraser; two *d*. *Educ*: A. N. Myer Secondary Sch., Niagara Falls, Canada; Univ. of Waterloo (BMath 1974); Univ. of British Columbia (MSc 1976); Stanford Univ. (PhD 1979). Postdoctoral Fellow, Imperial Coll., London, 1979–80; Asst Prof., 1980–85, Associate Prof., 1985–86, UBC; Associate Prof., Univ. of Toronto, 1986–88. Dir, Canadian Statistical Scis Inst., 2015–. FRSC 2001; FRSE 2015. *Publications*: (with D. R. Cox) The Theory of Design of Experiments, 2000; (jtly) Applied Asymptotics: case studies in higher order asymptotics, 2007; contribs to scholarly jls. *Recreations*: cycling, hiking, reading. *Address*: 98 Dinnick Crescent, Toronto, ON M4N 1L8, Canada. *T*: (416) 4822911. *E*: reid@utstat.utoronto.ca.

**REID, Paul Campbell;** QC 2001; a Recorder of the Crown Court, since 1993; *b* 27 March 1949; *s* of Stuart Wemyss Reid and Elsie Reid; *m* 1978, Pauline Brown; two *s*. *Educ*: Merchant Taylors' Sch., Crosby; Christ's Coll., Cambridge (MA). Called to the Bar, Gray's Inn, 1973; an Assistant Recorder, 1989–93. *Recreations*: tennis, amateur dramatics, acoustic guitar. *Address*: Lincoln House Chambers, Tower 12, The Avenue North, Spinningfields, 18–22 Bridge Street, Manchester M3 3BZ. *T*: (0161) 832 5701.

**REID, Maj.-Gen. Peter Daer,** CB 1981; *b* 5 Aug. 1925; *s* of Col S. D. Reid and Dorothy Hungerford (*née* Jackson); *m* 1958, Catherine Fleetwood (*née* Boodle); two *s* two *d*. *Educ*: Cheltenham College; Wadham Coll., Oxford. Commissioned into Coldstream Guards, 1945; transferred Royal Dragoons, 1947; served: Germany, Egypt, Malaya, Gibraltar, Morocco; Staff Coll., 1959; Comdg Officer, The Royal Dragoons, 1965–68; student, Royal College of Defence Studies, 1973; Commander RAC, 3rd Div., 1974–76; Dir, RAC, 1976–78; Chief Exec., Main Battle Tank 80 Proj., 1979–80; Dir, Armoured Warfare Studies, 1981; Defence Advr, GKN, 1983–88; Mil. Advr, Howden Airdynamics, 1982–88; Associate Mem., Burdeshaw Associates Ltd (USA), 1982–94; Defence Consultant, Vickers Defence Systems Ltd, 1989–94. *Publications*: A Brief History of Medieval Warfare, 2008. *Recreations*: sailing, ski-ing, fishing, bird watching. *Clubs*: Army and Navy; Royal Western Yacht; Kandahar Ski.

**REID, Philip;** *see* under Ingrams, R. R.

**REID, Sir (Philip) Alan,** GCVO 2012 (KCVO 2007); Keeper of the Privy Purse, Treasurer to the Queen, and Receiver-General of the Duchy of Lancaster, 2002–17; an Extra Equerry to the Queen, since 2017; Chairman, Duchy of Lancaster, since 2018; *b* 18 Jan. 1947; *s* of Philip Reid and Margaret Reid (*née* McKerracher); *m* 1971, Maureen Petrie; one *s* one *d*. *Educ*: Fettes Coll.; St Andrews Univ. (LLB Hons). Internat. Chm., KMG Tax Advisors, 1982–87; Nat. Dir of Taxation, KMG Thomson McLintock, 1983–87; KPMG Management Consultancy: Eur. Exec. Chm., 1994–98; UK Head, 1994–98; Global Chm., 1996–98; KPMG: UK Chief Financial Officer, 1998–2001; Eur. Chief Financial Officer, 1999–2001; Global Chief Financial Officer, 1999–2001; UK Chief Operating Officer, 2001–02. Pres., Mgt Consultancies' Assoc., 1997. Mem. Council, King's Fund, 2002–12. Trustee: Royal Collection Trust, 2002–17; Historic Royal Palaces, 2002–15 (Dep. Chm., 2007–15); Chm., Queen's Trust (formerly Queen's Silver Jubilee Trust), 2007–19. Pres., King George Fund for Actors and Actresses, 2011–. Vice Pres., RNLI, 2014– (Trustee, 2009–14; Treas., 2011–14). Gov., King Edward VII's Hosp. Sister Agnes, 2004–13. Mem., ICAS, 1973; Fellow, Inst. Taxation, 1979. *Recreations*: family, Arsenal, cinema, theatre, golf, ski-ing. *Club*: MCC.

**REID, Sir Robert Paul, (Sir Bob),** Kt 1990; Chairman: ICE Clear Europe, 2007–16; ICE Futures Europe (formerly International Petroleum Exchange), 1999–2015; Deputy Governor, Bank of Scotland, 1997–2004 (Director, 1997–2004); non-executive Director, HBOS, 2001–04; *b* 1 May 1934; *m* 1958, Joan Mary (*d* 2017); three *s*. *Educ*: St Andrews Univ. (MA Pol Econ. and Mod. Hist.). Joined Shell, 1956; Sarawak Oilfields and Brunei, 1956–59; Nigeria 1959–67 (Head of Personnel); Africa and S Asia Regional Orgn, 1967–68; PA and Planning Adviser to Chairman, Shell & BP Services, Kenya, 1968–70; Man. Dir, Nigeria, 1970–74; Man. Dir, Thailand, 1974–78; Vice-Pres., Internat. Aviation and Products Trading, 1978–80; Exec. Dir, Downstream Oil, Shell Co. of Australia, 1980–83; Co-Ordinator for Supply and Marketing, London, 1983; Dir, Shell International Petroleum Co., 1984–90; Chm. and Chief Exec., Shell UK, 1985–90; Chairman: BRB, 1990–95; London Electricity plc, 1994–97; Sears plc, 1995–99; British-Borneo Oil & Gas plc, 1995–2000; Sondex Ltd, 1999–2002. Director: British Borneo Petroleum, 1993–2000; AVIS Europe, 1997–2004 (Chm., 2002–04); Sun Life Assurance Co. of Canada, subseq. Sun Life Financial, 1997–2004; Siemens plc, 1998–2006; Diligenta Ltd, 2005–; Jubilant Energy NV, 2007–15; EEA Helicopter Operations, 2008–17. Chairman: Foundn for Management Educn, 1986–2003; BIM, 1988–90; Council, Industrial Soc., 1993–98; Foundn for Young Musicians, 1994–; Learning Through Landscapes, 2000–; Conservatoire for Dance and Drama, 2001–11. Dir, Merchants Trust, 1995–2008. Chancellor, Robert Gordon Univ., 1993–2004. CCMI. Hon. LLD: St Andrews, 1987; Aberdeen, 1988; Sheffield Hallam, 1995; South Bank, 1995; Hon. DSc Salford, 1990. *Recreations*: golf, opera. *Address*: 24 Ashley Gardens, Ambrosden Avenue, SW1P 1QD. *Clubs*: MCC; Royal and Ancient Golf; Royal Melbourne (Melbourne); Royal Mid-Surrey Golf, Frilford Heath Golf.

**REID, Dame Seona (Elizabeth),** DBE 2014 (CBE 2008); FRSE; Director, Glasgow School of Art, 1999–2013; *b* 21 Jan. 1950; *d* of George Robert Hall and Isobel Margaret Reid. *Educ*: Park Sch., Glasgow; Strathclyde Univ. (BA Hons Sociology); Liverpool Univ. (DBA). Business Manager, Lincoln Theatre Royal, 1972–73; Press and Publicity Officer, Northern Dance Theatre, 1973–76; Press and PRO, Ballet Rambert, 1976–79; freelance Arts consultant, 1979–80; Dir, Shape, 1980–87; Asst Dir, Strategy and Regl Develt, Greater London Arts, 1987–90; Dir, Scottish Arts Council, 1990–99. Bd Mem., Cove Park, 2004–19 (Chm., 2013–19). Hon. Prof., Univ. of Glasgow, 1999. Dep. Chm., NHMF and HLF, and Chm., Scottish Cttee, Heritage Lottery Fund (formerly Trustee for Scotland, NHMF), 2011–19; Scottish Comr to UK-US Fulbright Commn, 2011–18. Chairman: Nat. Theatre of Scotland, 2013–; Scotland Adv. Cttee, British Council, 2019–; Panel Mem., Children's Hearings Scotland, 2019–. Trustee: Tate Gall., 2013–; Edinburgh Internat. Cultural Summit, 2015–. FRSA 1991; FRSE 2015. Hon. DArts Robert Gordon Univ., Aberdeen, 1995; Hon. DLitt: Glasgow, 2001; Strathclyde, 2009; Hon. DLit Glasgow Caledonian, 2004. *Recreations*: walking, birdwatching, travel, arts.

**REID, Simon H. C.;** Head Master, Christ's Hospital, Horsham, since 2017; *b* Johannesburg, 19 Oct. 1961; *s* of Derric Reid and Pamela Reid (*née* Gray); *m* 1985, Michèle C. La Hausse de Lalouvière; one *s* one *d*. *Educ*: Hilton Coll., Natal; Univ. of the Witwatersrand (BA; Higher Dip. Educn). Teacher of English: Brentwood School, 1986–88; Stowe Sch., 1988–93; Dep. Hd of English, 1993–98, Housemaster, 1998–2004, Christ's Hospital Sch.; Dep. Hd, Worksop Coll., Notts, 2004–11; Principal, Gordonstoun Sch., 2011–17. Gov., Itchingfield Primary Sch., W Sussex, 2000–04. *Recreations*: reading, photography, ski-ing. *Address*: Christ's Hospital, Horsham, W Sussex RH13 0LJ.

**REID, Stephen Ashton;** Deputy Vice Chancellor (Chief Operating Officer) (formerly Deputy Rector), University of the Arts, London, since 2011; *b* 13 May 1949; *s* of Tom and Enid Reid. *Educ*: Brighton, Hove & Sussex Grammar Sch.; City of Westminster Coll.; UMIST; Pembroke Coll., Oxford; Harvard Business Sch. Personnel Mgt, BBC, 1975–79; Industrial Relns and Design Mgt, Granada TV, 1980–87; General Manager: Granada TV News Ops, 1987–90; BBC Wales, 1991–93; Controller: Resources Regs BBC, 1993–95; Services, BBC, 1995–97; Projects Dir, BBC Resources, 1998–99; Chief Exec., energywatch, 2000–03; Dir of Ops, Tanaka Business Sch., 2004–08, Project Prog. Dir, 2009–10, Imperial Coll. London. *Recreations*: piano playing, sport, modern fiction. *Address*: 272 High Holborn, WC1V 7EY.

**REID, Very Rev. Canon William Gordon**; Dean, Southwark Deanery, Diocese of Pennsylvania, since 2017; *b* 28 Jan. 1943; *s* of William Albert Reid and Elizabeth Jean Inglis. *Educ*: Galashiels Academy; Edinburgh Univ. (MA); Keble Coll., Oxford (MA); Cuddesdon College. Deacon 1967, priest 1968; Curate, St Salvador's, Edinburgh, 1967–69; Chaplain and Tutor, Salisbury Theological Coll., 1969–72; Rector, St Michael and All Saints, Edinburgh, 1972–84; Provost of St Andrew's Cathedral, Inverness, 1984–88; Chaplain of St Nicolas, Ankara, 1988–89, of St Peter and St Sigfrid's Church, Stockholm, 1989–92; Canon, Gibraltar Cathedral, 1992–98; Vicar-Gen., Dio. of Gibraltar in Europe, 1992–2003; Archdeacon in Europe, 1996–98; Priest-in-Charge, St Michael, Cornhill with St Peter le Poer, 1997–98; Dean of Gibraltar, 1998–2000; Archdeacon of Italy and Malta, and Chaplain of All Saints, Milan, 2000–03; Rector, St Clement's, Philadelphia, USA, 2004–15, now Rector Emeritus. Canon Emeritus, Gibraltar Cathedral, 2004. Councillor, Lothian Regional Council, 1974–84; Chm., Lothian and Borders Police Bd, 1982–84. *Publications*: (ed) The Wind from the Stars, 1992; Every Comfort at Golgotha, 1999. *Recreations*: travel and languages, Church and politics. *Address*: 1203 Pine Street, Philadelphia, PA 19107, USA. *Club*: New (Edinburgh).

**REID, Sir William (Kennedy)**, KCB 1996 (CB 1981); Chairman: Advisory Committee on Distinction Awards, 1997–2000; Mental Welfare Commission for Scotland, 1997–2000; Parliamentary Commissioner for Administration, and Health Service Commissioner for England, Scotland and Wales, 1990–96; *b* 15 Feb. 1931; 3rd *s* of late James and Elspet Reid; *m* 1959, Ann, *d* of Rev. Donald Campbell; two *s* one *d*. *Educ*: Robert Gordon's Coll.; George Watson's Coll.; Univ. of Edinburgh; Trinity Coll., Cambridge. MA 1st cl. Classics Edinburgh and Cantab. Ferguson scholar 1952; Craven scholar 1956. Nat. service, 1952–54. Min. of Educn, 1956; Cabinet Office, 1964; Private Sec. to Sec. of Cabinet, 1965–67; Sec., Council for Scientific Policy, 1967–72; Under Sec., 1974–78, Accountant-General, 1976–78, DES; Dep. Sec. (Central Services), Scottish Office, 1978–84; Sec., SHHD, 1984–90. Chm. of Govs, Scottish Police Coll., 1984–90. Member: Council on Tribunals, 1990–96; Commns for Local Administration in England and in Wales, 1990–96. A Dir, Internat. Ombudsman Inst., 1992–96. Chm. Council, St George's Sch. for Girls, 1997–2003. Lectures: Crookshank, RCR, 1994; Sydenham, Soc. of Apothecaries, 1994; Hunt, RCGP, 1996. Chm., Edinburgh Fest. of Music, Speech and Drama, 2006–10. Chm., Scottish Churches Architectural Heritage Trust, 2011–12. Queen Mother Fellow, Nuffield Trust, 1998. FRCPE 1997; FRSE 1999; Hon. FRCSE 2002. Hon. LLD: Aberdeen, 1996; Reading, 1998; Hon. DLitt Napier, 1998. *Recreation*: versification. *Address*: Darroch House, 9/1 East Suffolk Park, Edinburgh EH16 5PL. *Club*: New (Edinburgh).

**REID, William Macpherson**; Sheriff of Tayside, Central and Fife, 1983–2004; *b* 6 April 1938; *s* of William Andrew Reid and Mabel McLeod; *m* 1971, Vivien Anne Eddy; three *d*. *Educ*: Elgin Academy; Aberdeen Univ.; Edinburgh Univ. MA; LLB. Admitted Advocate, 1963; Sheriff of: Lothian and Borders, 1978; Glasgow and Strathkelvin, 1978–83. *Address*: Middlehall, Muckhart, Dollar, Clackmannanshire FK14 7JJ.

**REID BANKS, Lynne**; *see* Banks.

**REIDHAVEN, Viscount, (Master of Seafield); James Andrew Ogilvie-Grant**; *b* 30 Nov. 1963; *s* and *heir* of Earl of Seafield, *qv*. *Educ*: Harrow.

**REIDY, Andrea Jane**, OBE 2005; HM Diplomatic Service, retired; international political risk and governance consultant, 2010–12; *b* 24 Nov. 1958; one *d*; *m* Stan Hauff. *Educ*: South Bank Univ. (BA Hons Modern Langs and Internat. Business). Teaching, Caracas, Venezuela and British Embassy, Caracas, 1977–89; Internat. Policy, DoE, 1994–95; entered FCO, 1995; Desk Officer, Venezuela, Ecuador and Peru, Latin America Dept, FCO, 1995–97; Second Sec., Bratislava, 1997–2000; Dep. High Comr, Freetown, 2000–02; Hd, Global Opportunity Fund, FCO, 2003; Hd, UK Office, Coalition Provisional Authy, 2003–04, First Sec. (Political), 2004–05, Baghdad; Communications Team Leader, Prism Prog., FCO, 2005–06; Consul Gen. for Northern Iraq, Ebril, 2006–07; Ambassador to Eritrea, 2008–10. *Recreations*: hiking, the outdoors, bridge, travelling.

**REIF, Prof. Stefan Clive**, PhD, LittD; Professor of Medieval Hebrew Studies, Faculty of Oriental Studies, University of Cambridge, 1998–2006, now Emeritus; Fellow of St John's College, Cambridge, since 1998; Founder Director, Genizah Research Unit, 1973–2006, and Head, Oriental Division, 1983–2006, Cambridge University Library; *b* 21 Jan. 1944; *s* of late Peter (Pinhas) and Annie Reif (*née* Rapstoff); *m* 1967, Shulamit (*d* 2010), *d* of late Edmund and Ella Stekel; one *s* one *d*. *Educ*: Jews' Coll., Univ. of London (BA 1964); PhD London 1969; MA Cantab 1976; LittD Cantab 2002. Lectr in Hebrew and Semitic Langs, Univ. of Glasgow, 1968–72; Asst Prof. of Hebrew Lang. and Lit., Dropsie Coll., Philadelphia, 1972–73. Visiting Professor: Hebrew Univ. of Jerusalem, 1989, 1996–97; Univ. of Pennsylvania, 2001. President: Jewish Historical Soc. of England, 1991–92; British Assoc. for Jewish Studies, 1992; Cambridge Theological Soc., 2002–04. Hon. PhD Haifa, 2014. *Publications*: Shabbethai Sofer and his Prayer-Book, 1979; (ed) Interpreting the Hebrew Bible, 1982; Published Material from the Cambridge Genizah Collections, 1988; (ed) Genizah Research After Ninety Years, 1992; Judaism and Hebrew Prayer, 1993; Hebrew Manuscripts at Cambridge University Library, 1997; A Jewish Archive from Old Cairo, 2000; Why Medieval Hebrew Studies?, 2001; (ed) The Cambridge Genizah Collections: their contents and significance, 2002; Problems with Prayers, 2006; Charles Taylor and the Genizah Collection, 2009; Ha-Tefillah Ha-Yehudit, 2010; (ed) Death in Jewish Life: burial and mourning customs among the Jews of Europe and nearby communities, 2014; (ed) Religious Identity Markers, 2015; (ed) Ancient Jewish Prayers and Emotions, 2015; Jewish Prayer Texts from the Cairo Genizah, 2016; Jews, Bible and Prayer, 2017; (ed) Discovering, Deciphering and Dissenting: Ben Sira's manuscripts after 120 years, 2018; about 420 articles. *Recreations*: football, cooking matza-brei for his grandchildren, opera. *Address*: St John's College, Cambridge CB2 1TP. *T*: (01223) 338786.

**REIGATE, Archdeacon of**; *see* Astin, Ven. M. A. E.

**REIHER, Sir Frederick (Bernard Carl)**, KCMG 2010 (CMG 1982); KBE 1992; Investment and finance consultant, 1992; Chairman, Air Niugini, since 2014 (Director, since 2005; Deputy Chairman, 2013–14); *b* 7 Feb. 1945; *s* of William and Ruth Reiher; *m* 1974, Helen Perpetua; two *s* two *d*. *Educ*: Chanel Coll., Rabaul; Holy Spirit National Seminary, Port Moresby; Univ. of Papua New Guinea (BD). Private Sec. to Minister for Finance, PNG 1973–76. Joined Diplomatic Service, 1976; established Diplomatic Mission for PNG in London, 1977; High Comr for PNG in London, 1978–80, concurrently accredited Ambassador to FRG, Belgium, EEC and Israel; Sec. of Dept of Prime Minister, PNG, 1980–82; formerly High Comr for PNG in Canberra; COS to Prime Minister of PNG, 2001. Chairman: Harcos Trading (PNG) Ltd, 1982–91; PNG Agriculture Bank, 1986–91; PNG Nat. Airline Commn, 1992; Dir, Harrisons & Crosfield (PNG) Ltd, 1982–91. Chm., Nat. Honours and Awards Council, 2005–11. *Address*: PO Box 7500, Boroko, Papua New Guinea. *Clubs*: Aviat Social & Sporting, South Pacific Motor Sports, Royal Yacht, PNG Pistol.

**REIK, Prof. Wolf**, MD; FRS 2010; FMedSci; Principal Investigator, since 1989, and Head, Laboratory of Developmental Genetics and Imprinting, since 1992, Babraham Institute, Cambridge; Associate Faculty, Wellcome (formerly Wellcome Trust) Sanger Institute, since 2012 (Co-Founder and Member, Sanger-EBI Single-Cell Genomics Centre, since 2013); *b* Aachen, Germany, 22 Aug. 1957; *s* of Prof. Dr Helmut Reik and Rosemarie Reik; *m* 1989, Dr Cristina Rada; one *s* one *d*. *Educ*: Univ. of Hamburg (MD 1985). EMBO Postdoctoral Fellow, Univ. of Cambridge, 1985–87; Fellow, Lister Inst. of Preventive Medicine, Cambridge, 1987–93; Babraham Institute, Cambridge: Hd, Prog. of Develtl Genetics, 1997–2004; Associate Dir of Res., 2004–; Hd, Epigenetics (formerly Epigenetics and Chromatin) Prog., 2008–. Mem., EMBO 2003; MAE 2011. Hon. Prof. of Epigenetics, Dept of Physiol., Develt and Neurosci., Univ. of Cambridge, 2008–. FMedSci 2013. Wellcome Prize in Physiol., 1994. *Publications*: over 200 res. articles; contrib. articles on epigenetics to res. jls. *Recreations*: music, reading, cooking, skiing, bicycling. *Address*: Babraham Institute, Cambridge CB22 3AT. *T*: (01223) 496336. *E*: wolf.reik@babraham.ac.uk.

**REILLY, David**, FRCP; Lead Consultant Physician, NHS Centre for Integrative Care, 1990–2016 (Director, Adhom Academic Departments, 1985–2016); National Lead Clinician for Integrative Care, Scottish Government Health Department, 2008–11 (part-time secondment); Co-Founder and Co-Director, TheWEL: Wellness Enhancement Learning Programme (formerly AdHominem charity), since 1998; Hon. Senior Lecturer in Medicine, Glasgow University, since 1991; *b* 4 May 1955. *Educ*: Glasgow Univ. (MB ChB with commendation). MRCP 1981, FRCP 1993; MRCGP 1982; MFHom 1983, FFHom 1989. Various trng posts in conventional medicine and mind body medicine and holism; RCCM/MRC Res. Fellow, Univ. Dept of Medicine, 1987–91, Hon. Sen. Registrar in Gen. Medicine, 1994–, Glasgow Royal Infirmary. Visiting Faculty Member: Harvard Med. Sch., 1994–2004; Weill Cornell Univ., Doha, Qatar, 2015–; Vis. Prof., Univ. of Maryland Sch. of Med., 1999–. Co-founding Ed., Interprofessional Care, 1992–96; Internat. Ed., Alternative Therapies in Health and Medicine, 1995–96. Hon. DSc Westminster, 2013. RAMC Meml Prize, 1978; Merit Award, Gtr Glasgow Health Council, 1998; NHS Merit Award, 2001; Person of the Year, Dynamic Place Awards, 2004. *Publications*: contrib. to numerous scientific pubns and book chapters exploring human healing and integrative processes. *Recreations*: family, nature, musician, writer. *W*: www.davidreilly.net.

**REILLY, David Nicholas, (Nick)**, CBE 2000; Chairman, Asia-Pacific, MSX International Inc., 2012–15; Independent Director, WABCO Holdings Inc., since 2014; *b* 17 Dec. 1949; *s* of late John Reilly and of Mona Reilly; *m* 1976, Susan Haig; one *s* two *d*. *Educ*: Harrow Sch.; St Catharine's Coll., Cambridge (MA). Investment Analyst, 1971–74; joined Gen. Motors, 1974; Finance Dir, Moto Diesel Mexicana, 1980–83; Supply Dir, Vauxhall Motors, 1984–87; Vice Pres., IBC, 1987–90; Manufg Dir, Vauxhall Ellesmere Port, 1990–94; Vice Pres., Quality, Gen. Motors Europe, 1994–96; Man. Dir, 1996–2001, Chm., 1996–2001, Vauxhall Motors Ltd; Chm., IBC Vehicles, 1996–2001; Vice Pres., 1997–2006, Gp Vice-Pres., 2006–09, Gen. Motors Corp.; Vice-Pres. of Sales, Mktg and Aftersales, Gen. Motors Europe, 2001–02; Pres. and CEO, 2002–06, Chm., 2006–09, GM Daewoo Auto and Technol.; Pres., Gen. Motors Asia Pacific Ops, 2006–09; Pres., Gen. Motors Internat. Ops, 2009; Exec. Vice-Pres., Gen. Motors Corp., 2009–12; Pres., Gen. Motors Europe, 2009–11; Chief Exec., 2009–11, Chm., 2011–12, Supervisory Bd, Opel/Vauxhall. Mem. Bd, Saab GB, 1996–2000. Chairman: Chester, Ellesmere, Wirral TEC, 1990–94; Trng Standards Council, 1997–2001; Adult Learning Inspectorate, 2001. Mem., Commn for Integrated Transport, 1999–2001. Pres., SMMT, 2001–02 (Vice Pres., 1996–2001). Chm., Econ. Affairs Cttee, CBI, 1999–2001. Chm., Oundle Sch. Foundn, 1997–2001. FIMI 1990 (Vice Pres., 1995). Trustee, Trinity Sailing Foundn, 2016–.

**REILLY, Mary Margaret**, FCA; Partner, Deloitte (formerly Deloitte & Touche) LLP, 1987–2013; *b* 22 May 1953; *d* of John Reilly and Helena Reilly; *m* 1979, Mark Corby; one *s* one *d*. *Educ*: Notre Dame Collegiate Sch., Leeds; University Coll. London (BA Hist.); London Business Sch. ACA 1978, FCA 1988. Chm., London Develt Agency, 2004–08. Chm. London Reg., Council, CBI, 2004–06. Non-executive Director: Crown Agents Ltd, 2013–17; DfT, 2013–18; Travelzoo Inc., 2013–; Woodford Investment Mgt LLP, 2014–16; Ferrexpo plc, 2015–19; Cape plc, 2016–17; Essentra plc, 2017–; MITIE plc, 2017–. Fellow, UCL, 2010. *Recreations*: travel, theatre, music, cooking. *Club*: Reform.

**REILLY, Michael David**, PhD; HM Diplomatic Service, retired; Chief Representative, China, BAE Systems, 2011–14; *b* 1 March 1955; *s* of late Hugh Aidan Reilly and Mary Sheila Reilly; *m* 1981, Won-Kyong Kang; one *s* one *d*. *Educ*: Ulverston Grammar Sch.; Barnard Castle Sch.; Univ. of Liverpool (BA 1975; PhD 1986); Yonsei Univ., Seoul. Joined HM Diplomatic Service, 1978; Seoul, 1979–84; First Secretary: FCO, 1984–88; UK Delegn to OECD, Paris, 1988–91; Seoul, 1991–93; FCO, 1994–96; Dep. Hd of Mission, Manila, 1997–2000; Head: Cultural Relns, subseq. Culture, Scholarships and Sport, Dept, FCO, 2000–02; SE Asia Dept, FCO, 2003–05; Dir, British Trade and Cultural Office, Taipei, 2005–09; on secondment to BAE Systems as Dir, Far East, 2009–10. Dir, Visiting Arts, 2000–03. Chairman: Coral Cay Conservation Trust, 2013–16; Coral Restoration Foundn Europe, 2014–18. Sen. Fellow, Taiwan Studies Prog., Nottingham Univ., 2015–; Vis. Fellow, Academia Sinica, Taiwan, 2016, 2019. Co. Sec., Welshpool and Llanfair Light Rlwy Preservation Co., 2016–. Taiwan Friendship Medal. *Publications*: Towards an EU-Taiwan Investment Agreement, 2017; Narrow Gauge Railways of Taiwan, 2018; (with D. Huang) The Implications of Brexit for East Asia, 2018; articles in academic jls and railway press. *Recreations*: hiking, running, steam engines. *Address*: 6 Reed Place, West Byfleet, Surrey KT14 6AX. *Club*: Pyrford Puffers.

**REILLY, Nick**; *see* Reilly, D. N.

**REILLY, Thomas Saul Anthony**; HM Diplomatic Service; Ambassador to Morocco, since 2017 (also to Mauritania, 2017–18); *b* Canterbury, Kent, 17 Nov. 1970; *s* of John Reilly and Penelope Reilly (*née* Bary); *m* 2005, Alix Leah Catherine Fearn; two *d*. *Educ*: Simon Langton Boys' Grammar Sch., Canterbury; London Sch. of Econs and Pol Sci. (LLB 1994). Associate Solicitor: Taylor Joynson Garrett, London and Brussels, 1995–98; Van Bael & Bellis, Brussels, 1998–99; entered FCO, 2000; Political Officer, Buenos Aires, 2001–03; Arabic lang. trng, 2004; Political Officer, Sana'a and Kuwait, 2004–05; Deputy Head: Counter Terrorism Dept, FCO, 2006–08; Climate Change Dept, FCO, 2008–10; Dep. Ambassador, Egypt, 2010–12; Hd, Govt Relns, Shell UK Ltd, 2012–15; Sen. Advr, Internat. Govt Relns and Regulatory Affairs, Shell, 2015–17. *Recreations*: sailing, running, climbing, swimming, polo, snow-boarding, trekking, surfing, reading, carpentry, bread-making, learning languages. *Address*: British Embassy, Rabat, Morocco. *T*: 537633354. *E*: Thomas.Reilly@fco.gov.uk.

**REIMAN, Dr Donald Henry**; Editor, Shelley and his Circle, Carl H. Pforzheimer Collection, New York Public Library, since 1986; Adjunct Professor of English, University of Delaware, 1992; *b* 17 May 1934; *s* of Mildred A. (Pearce) Reiman and Henry Ward Reiman; *m* 1st, 1958, Mary A. Warner (marr. diss. 1974); one *d*; 2nd, 1975, Hélène Dworzan (*d* 2017). *Educ*: Coll. of Wooster, Ohio (BA 1956); Hon. LittD 1981); Univ. of Illinois (MA 1957; PhD 1960). Instructor, 1960–62, Asst Prof. 1962–64, Duke Univ.; Associate Prof., Univ. of Wisconsin, Milwaukee, 1964–65; Editor, Shelley and his Circle, Carl H. Pforzheimer Liby, 1965–86. James P. R. Lyell Reader in Bibliography, Oxford

Univ., 1988–89. Gen. Editor, Manuscripts of the Younger Romantics, 1984–98 (29 vols); Editor-in-Chief, Bodleian Shelley MSS, 1984–2000 (23 vols). *Publications*: Shelley's The Triumph of Life, 1965; Percy Bysshe Shelley, 1969, 2nd edn 1990; (ed) The Romantics Reviewed, 9 Vols, 1972; (ed) Shelley and his Circle, vols V–VI, 1973, Vols VII–VIII, 1986, (ed with D. D. Fischer) Vols IX–X, 2002; (ed with D. D. Fischer) Byron on the Continent, 1974; (ed with S. B. Powers) Shelley's Poetry and Prose, 1977, 2nd edn (with N. Fraistat), 2001; (ed) The Romantic Context: Poetry, 128 vols, 1976–79; (ed jtly) The Evidence of the Imagination, 1978; English Romantic Poetry 1800–1835, 1979; Romantic Texts and Contexts, 1987; Intervals of Inspiration, 1988; The Study of Modern Manuscripts, 1993; (ed with N. Fraistat) The Complete Poetry of Percy Bysshe Shelley, vol. I, 2000, vol. II, 2004; contribs to scholarly books, reviews and learned jls. *E*: dhreiman@udel.edu.

**REIMANN, Fiona Mary;** *see* Gribble, F. M.

**REINFELDT, Fredrik;** Chair, Extractive Industries Transparency Initiative, since 2016; *b* 4 Aug. 1965; *s* of Bruno and Birgitta Reinfeldt; *m* 1992, Filippa; two *s* one *d*. *Educ*: Stockholm Univ. (BSc Business Admin and Econs 1990). Dep. Chm., Swedish Conscripts Council, Swedish Defence Staff, 1986; Skandinaviska Enskilda Banken, Täby, 1986, 1987. Young Moderates: Dep. Chm., 1988–90, Chm., 1990–92, Regl Section, Stockholm; Mem., 1990–92, Chm., 1992–95, Exec. Cttee. Dep. Sec., 1990–91, Sec., 1991, to Stockholm City Comr. Mem., Riksdag, 1991–2014; Alternate, Riksdag Cttee, on Taxation, 1991–94, on EU Affairs, 2001–02; Mem., 1994–2001, Dep. Chm., 2002–03, Riksdag Cttee on Finance, 1994–2001; Chm., Riksdag Cttee on Justice, 2001–02; Alternate, 2002–03, Mem., 2003–06, Riksdag Adv. Council on For. Affairs. Moderate Party: Mem. Regl Section, Stockholm, 1992–2003; Mem., 1999–2003, Leader and First Dep. Chm., 2002–03, Chm., 2003–15, Exec. Cttee, Moderate Party Gp, Riksdag; Chm., Moderate Party of Sweden, 2003–15; Prime Minister of Sweden, 2006–14. Sen. Advr, EMEA, Bank of America Merrill Lynch, subseq. Bank of America, 2016–. *Publications*: Det sovande folket, 1993; Projekt Europa: sex unga européer on Europasamarbetet, 1993; Nostalgitrippen, 1995; Stenen i handen på den starke, 1995; Väljarkryss: personvalshandbok, 2001; Halvvägs, 2015.

**REINHARDT, Prof. Tobias,** DPhil; Corpus Christi Professor of the Latin Language and Literature, University of Oxford, since 2008; Fellow, Corpus Christi College, Oxford, since 2008; *b* Gross-Gerau, Germany, 31 Aug. 1971; *s* of Mathias and Sabine Reinhardt; *m* 1997, Eva Maria Martin; one *s* one *d*. *Educ*: Kronberg-Gymnasium, Aschaffenburg, Germany; Univ. of Frankfurt (Staatsexamen); Corpus Christi Coll., Oxford (DPhil 2000). Jun. Res. Fellow in Ancient Philosophy, Merton Coll., Oxford, 2001–02; Lectr in Classical Langs and Lit., Univ. of Oxford, 2002–08; Fellow and Tutor in Latin and Greek, Somerville Coll., Oxford, 2002–08. *Publications*: Das Buch E der Aristotelischen Topik, 2000; Cicero's Topica, 2003; (with M. Winterbottom) Quintilian Book 2, 2006; contrib. learned jls. *Address*: Corpus Christi College, Oxford OX1 4JF.

**REINTON, Sigurd Evang,** Hon. CBE 2007; Chairman, Aubin Holdings Ltd, since 2017; *b* 9 Nov. 1941; *s* of Dr Lars Reinton and Ingrid Evang Reinton (*née* Evang); *m* 1966, Arlette Jeanne Gisele Dufresne; two *d*. *Educ*: Lund Univ. (MBA 1964). Sales Dir, Audio-Nike AB, 1964–66; Account Supervisor, Young & Rubicam, 1966–68; Associate, 1968–76, Principal, 1976–81, Dir, 1981–88, McKinsey & Co., Inc.; Chm., Express Aviation Services, 1988–91; Dir, Aubin Hldgs Ltd, 1988–98; Chairman: Mayday Healthcare NHS Trust, 1997–99; London Ambulance Service NHS Trust, 1999–2009. Director: NATS Hldgs Ltd, 2007–13; Monitor, 2012–16; NHS Improvement, 2016–18. Dir, Freewheel Film Finance Ltd, 2000–03. Mem., Nat. Council, NHS Confedn, 1998–2007; Dir, Ambulance Services Network (formerly Ambulance Services Assoc.), 2005–09 (Mem. Nat. Council, 2001–05); Mem., Adv. Bd, The Foundation, 2005–10. *Publications*: contrib. McKinsey Qly and Financial Times on corporate leadership. *Recreations*: flying (private pilot's licence/instrument rating), sailing, theatre. *Address*: 8 Wickham Way, Beckenham, Kent BR3 3AA. *Clubs*: Royal Automobile; Yacht Club de Carolles (Normandy).

**REIS e SOUSA, Prof. Caetano,** DPhil; FMedSci; FRS 2019; Professor of Immunology, Department of Medicine, Imperial College London, since 2013; Assistant Research Director, Senior Group Leader, and Head, Immunobiology Laboratory, Francis Crick Institute, since 2015 (Head, Immunobiology Laboratory, Cancer Research UK, London Research Institute (formerly Imperial Cancer Research Fund), 1998–2015); *b* 24 Feb. 1968; *s* of Artur and Margarida Reis e Sousa. *Educ*: United World Coll. of the Atlantic; Imperial Coll. of Sci., Technol. and Medicine, London (BSc Hons Biol. 1989); Hertford Coll., Oxford (DPhil Immunology 1992). Vis. Fellow, 1993–97, Vis. Associate, 1998, Nat. Inst. of Allergy and Infectious Diseases, NIH, Bethesda; Res. Scientist, 1998–2003, Sen. Scientist, 2003–05, Sen. Gp Leader, 2003–15, CRUK, London Res. Inst. (formerly ICRF). Hon. Sen. Res. Fellow, 1998–2003, Hon. Reader, 2003–05, Hon. Prof., 2005–, Dept of Immunology and Molecular Pathology, UCL; Hon. Reader, 2004–05, Hon. Prof., 2005–09, Centre for Molecular Oncology, Inst. of Cancer, QMUL; Hon. Prof., KCL, 2014–. FMedSci 2006. Mem., EMBO, 2016. BD Bioscis Award, Eur. Macrophage and Dendritic Cell Soc., 2003; Liliane Bettencourt Award for Life Scis, Fondation Bettencourt-Schueller, 2008; Eur. Soc. for Clinical Investigation Award for Excellence in Basic/Translational Res., 2011; Louis-Jeantet Prize for Medicine, Fondation Louis-Jeantet, 2017. Officer, Order of Sant'iago da Espada (Portugal), 2009. *Publications*: numerous articles in scientific jls. *Recreations*: reading, music, diving. *Address*: Francis Crick Institute, 1 Midland Road, NW1 1AT. *E*: caetano@crick.ac.uk.

**REISS, Charles Alexander;** Political Editor, Evening Standard, 1985–2004; *b* 23 March 1942; *s* of Dr Joseph Charles Reiss and Jenny Francisca Reiss; *m* 1978, Sue Rosemary Newson-Smith; three *d*. *Educ*: Bryanston Sch., Dorset. Reporter: Hampstead & Highgate Express, 1964–66; London office, Glasgow Citizen, and Scottish Daily Express, 1966–68; Press Officer, Labour Party, 1968–71; Lobby Correspondent: E Anglia Daily Times, etc, 1971–73; Birmingham Post, 1973–75; Political Correspondent: and leader writer, Evening News, 1975–80; and chief leader writer, Evening Standard, 1980–85. Chm., Parly Lobby Journalists, 1995–96. Mem., Govt Communications Review Gp, 2003. Trustee, Kennet and Avon Canal Trust, 2009. *Recreations*: opera, theatre, reading, travel, ranting. *Club*: Royal Automobile.

**REISS, David Anthony;** Chairman, Reiss (Holdings) Ltd, since 1992 (Managing Director, 1992–2017); *b* London, 15 May 1943; *s* of late Joshua Reiss and Rita Reiss; *m* 1966, Rosemary June; one *s* one *d* (and one *d* decd). *Educ*: Carmel Coll.; Kingsway Day Coll., Oxon. Manufacturers' agent, 1964–66; co-founder, Oliver Shirts, shirt manufg co., 1966–71; opened Reiss store, Bishopsgate, London, 1971; opened flagship store, King's Road, Chelsea, 1980; own label brand, 1992; launched Women's Wear Div., 2000; opened flagship store, NY, 2003. *Recreations*: sport, soccer (Mem., Diamond Club), Arsenal, plays tennis and golf, running. *Address*: Reiss Building, 12 Picton Place, W1U 1BW. *T*: (020) 3075 2000, *Fax*: (020) 3075 2001. *E*: david.reiss@reiss.com.

**REISS, Rev. Prof. Michael Jonathan,** PhD; FRSB, FAcSS; Professor of Science Education, UCL Institute of Education, University College London (formerly Institute of Education, University of London), since 2001 (Head, School of Science, Mathematics and Technology, 2001–07; Associate Director, then Pro-Director, Research and Development, 2009–14); *b* 11 Jan. 1958; *s* of Herbert and Ann Reiss (*née* Scott); *m* 1982, Jenny L. Chapman. *Educ*: Westminster Sch., London; Trinity Coll., Cambridge (BA 1st Cl. Hons Natural Scis 1978; MA 1982; PhD 1982; PGCE 1983); E Anglian Ministerial Trng Course; Cambs Consultancy in Counselling (Grad. Counsellor 1993); Open Univ. (MBA 2002). FRSB (FIBiol 1990); FAcSS (AcSS 2010). Teacher, Hills Rd VIth Form Coll., Cambridge, 1983–88 (Hd, Social Biol., 1987); University of Cambridge: Lectr and Tutor, Dept of Educn, 1988–94; Sen. Lectr, 1994–98; Reader in Educn and Bioethics, 1998–2000; Tutor, Homerton Coll., 1994–2000. Inaugural Ed., Sex Education, 1999–2011. Dir of Educn, Royal Soc., 2006–08. Chief Exec., Sci. Learning Centre, London, 2003–13. Ordained deacon, 1990, priest, 1991; Priest-in-charge, Boxworth, Elsworth and Knapwell, 1996–99, Toft, 2003–05, Dio. Ely. Specialist Adviser: to H of L Select Cttee on Animals in Scientific Procedures, 2001–02; to H of C Educn Cttee on Personal, Social, Health and Econ. Educn, 2014–15. Chm., Biosci. for Society Strategy Panel, BBSRC, 2004–07. Member: Adv. Cttee on Novel Foods and Processes, 1998–2001; Cttee, Farm Animal Welfare Council, 2004–12; Nuffield Council on Bioethics, 2019–. Vice-President: Inst. Biol., 1994–97; British Sci. Assoc., 2009–15. Hon. Visiting Professor: Univ. of York, 2000–; Univ. of Birmingham, 2009–12; Univ. of Leeds, 2013–17; Univ. of Kiel, 2016–; Visiting Professor: Kristianstad Univ., Sweden, 2002; Univ. of WA, 2017; Docent, Univ. of Helsinki, 2004–; Hon. Prof., RVC, 2012. Hon. Fellow, British Sci. Assoc., 2010. FRSA 2006. Freeman, Salters' Co., 2004 (Liveryman, 2010; Mem. Court, 2014; Master, 2017). *Publications*: The Allometry of Growth and Reproduction, 1989; Science Education for a Pluralist Society, 1993; (with R. Straughan) Improving Nature?: the science and ethics of genetic engineering, 1996 (trans. Chinese, Croatian, Japanese, Polish and Portuguese); (with J. L. Chapman) Ecology: principles and applications, 1992, 2nd edn 1999 (trans. Chinese and Italian); Understanding Science Lessons: five years of science teaching, 2000; (with J. M. Halstead) Values in Sex Education: from principles to practice, 2003; (with J. White) An Aims-Based Curriculum, 2013; contrib. numerous acad. papers, chapters, curriculum materials, reports and other books. *Recreations*: visiting art galleries and museums, trying to keep fit. *Address*: UCL Institute of Education, University College London, WC1H 0AL. *T*: (020) 7612 6800. *E*: m.reiss@ucl.ac.uk. *Club*: Athenæum.

**REISS, Rev. Canon Robert Paul;** Canon Treasurer, 2005–13, and Sub-Dean, 2011–13, Westminster Abbey, now Canon Emeritus; *b* 20 Jan. 1943; *s* of Paul Michael Reiss and Beryl Aileen Reiss (*née* Bryant); *m* 1985, Dixie Nichols; one *d*. *Educ*: Haberdashers' Aske's Sch., Hampstead; Trinity Coll., Cambridge (MA); Westcott House, Cambridge; Theol Inst., Bucharest, Rumania; PhD Lambeth 2012. Ordained deacon, 1969, priest, 1970; Asst Curate, St John's Wood Parish Church, London, 1969–73; Asst Missioner, Rajshahi, dio. of Dacca, Bangladesh, 1973; Chaplain, Trinity Coll., Cambridge, 1973–78; Selection Sec., ACCM, 1978–85 (Sen. Selection Sec., 1983–85); Team Rector of Grantham, dio. of Lincoln, 1986–96; Archdeacon of Surrey, 1996–2005. Mem., General Synod of C of E, 1990–2005. Trustee, Churches Conservation Trust, 2002–08. *Publications*: (contrib.) Say One for Me, 1992; The Testing of Vocation: 100 years of ministry selection in the Church of England, 2013; Sceptical Christianity, 2016. *Recreations*: cricket, golf. *Address*: 35 Addington Square, SE5 7LB. *Clubs*: Garrick, MCC; Worplesdon Golf.

**REITH,** family name of **Baron Reith**.

**REITH,** 3rd Baron *cr* 1940, of Stonehaven; **James Harry John Reith;** Founder and Director, Reith Partners (Woodfuel) Ltd, 2006–18; *b* Perth, 2 June 1971; *s* of Christopher John Reith (2nd Baron but did not use the title) and (Penelope Margaret) Ann Reith (*née* Morris); *S* father, 2017; *m* 2002, Fiona Ann Knox; one *s* one *d*. *Educ*: Merchiston Castle Sch., Edinburgh; Univ. of Edinburgh (BSc Hons Agric., Forestry and Rural Econs). Forest/Estate Manager, 1993–99; running family farm and (pt-time) timber mktg, 1999–2000; forest mgt and farming (pt-time), 2000–. Mem. Bd, Woodheat Assoc. (subsid. of Renewable Energy Assoc.), 2017–. Mem., Central Scotland Forestry Forum, 2017–. *Recreations*: Cub Leader, animals, walking, fishing, curling. *Heir*: *s* Hon. Harry Joseph John Reith, *b* 19 Sept. 2006. *Address*: Whitebank Farm, Methven, Perth PH1 3QU. *Club*: Royal Caledonian Curling.

**REITH, Fiona Lennox;** QC (Scot.) 1996; Sheriff of Lothian and Borders at Edinburgh, since 2007; *b* 17 July 1955; *d* of late Patrick Donald Metcalfe Munro and Francesca Diana Munro (*née* Fendall, later Sutherland); *m* 1979, David Stewart Reith, WS (marr. diss. 1990). *Educ*: Perth Acad.; Aberdeen Univ. (LLB). Solicitor, Edinburgh, 1979–82; admitted WS 1981; admitted to Faculty of Advocates, 1983; Standing Jun. Counsel in Scotland to Home Office, 1989–92; Advocate-Depute, 1992–95; Standing Jun. Counsel to Scottish Office Envmt Dept, 1995–96; Sheriff: of Tayside Central and Fife at Perth, 1999–2000; of Glasgow and Strathkelvin, 2000–07. Specialist Sheriff, all-Scotland Sheriff Personal Injury Court, 2015–. Member: Sheriff Courts Rules Council, 1989–93; Council, Sheriffs' Assoc., 2003–06, 2009–12; Criminal Courts Rules Council, 2004–11; Parole Bd for Scotland, 2004–07 (Vice-Chm., 2008–09); Civil Justice Adv. Gp, 2004–05; Information and Communications Technol. Cttee, Judicial Council for Scotland, 2011–12. External Examr in Professional Conduct, Faculty of Advocates, 2000–06. FSAScot. *Recreations*: walking, theatre, good food and wine, travel, pilates, enthusiastic supporter of Edinburgh International Book Festival and Edinburgh International Festival. *Address*: Sheriffs' Chambers, Sheriff Court House, 27 Chambers Street, Edinburgh EH1 1LB. *T*: (0131) 225 2525. *Club*: New (Edinburgh).

**REITH, Gen. Sir John (George),** KCB 2003 (CB 2000); CBE 1991 (OBE 1989); Lead Senior Mentor, NATO, 2008–14; Deputy Supreme Allied Commander Europe, 2004–07; *b* 17 Nov. 1948; *s* of John and Jean Reith; *m* 1st, 1971, Cherry Parker; one *s* one *d*; 2nd, 1987, June Nightingale; two *s*. *Educ*: Elliots Green; RMA Sandhurst. Commnd, 1969; CO 1st Bn Parachute Regt, 1986–88 (despatches 1986); COS 1 Armd Div., 1988–91; Comd, 4 Armd Bde, 1992–94; Comd, UN Sector SW Bosnia, 1994; Dir, Internat. Orgns, 1994, Dir, Mil. Ops, 1995–97, MoD; Comdr, ACE Mobile Force (Land), 1997–99; Comdr, Albania Force, 1999; ACDS (Policy), MoD, 2000–01; Chief of Jt Ops, Permt Jt HQ, 2001–04. Chm. of Govs, Millfield Sch., 2010–17. Freeman, City of London, 2000. QCVS 1994. *Recreations*: hill walking, gardening, good food. *Club*: Army and Navy.

**REITH, Lesley-Anne;** *see* Alexander, L.-A.

**REITH, Martin;** HM Diplomatic Service, retired; *b* 6 Dec. 1935; *s* of late James Reith and Christian (*née* Innes); *m* 1964, Ann Purves; four *s*. *Educ*: Royal High Sch. of Edinburgh. Served: India (Calcutta), 1957–59; Uganda, 1962–66; Scottish Office, Edinburgh, 1966–68; Australia (Canberra), 1969–72; Asst Head of Central and Southern Africa Dept, FCO, 1974–77; Commercial Sec., Beirut, 1977–78; Dep. Hd, UN Dept, FCO, 1979; Counsellor, NATO Def. Coll., Rome, 1980; Dep. High Comr, Malta, 1980–83; High Comr, Swaziland, 1983–87; Ambassador, Republic of Cameroon, 1987–91. *Recreations*: bridge, bowling, family history, bird-watching, travel. *Address*: Ardnagaul House, Strathtay, by Pitlochry, Perthshire PH9 0PG.

**REITH, Hon. Peter Keaston,** AM 2019; writer and political commentator; *b* 15 July 1950; *s* of Dr A. C. Reith and E. V. Sambell; *m* (marr. diss.); four *s*; *m* Kerrie. *Educ*: Brighton Grammar Sch., Vic; Monash Univ. (BEc, LLB). Solicitor, 1974–82. MP (L) Flinders, Victoria, 1984–2001; Shadow Attorney-Gen., 1987–88; Shadow Industrial Relns,

1988–89; Shadow Minister of Educn, 1989–90; Shadow Treas., 1990–93; Dep. Leader of Opposition, 1990–93; Shadow Special Minister of State, 1993; Shadow Minister for Defence, 1994; responsibility for Native Title legislation, 1994; Shadow Minister: for Foreign Affairs, 1994–95; of Industrial Relns and Manager, Opposition Business in the House, 1995–96; Leader, House of Representatives, 1996–2001; Minister assisting Prime Minister for Public Service, 1996–97; Minister: for Industrial Relns, 1996–97; for Employment, Workplace Relns and Small Business, 1998–2000; for Defence, 2000–01. Dir, EBRD, 2003–09. Chm., Gas Market Rev. for Govt of Victoria, 2013. Pres., Shire, Phillip Is. Council, 1980–81. Sec., Newhaven Coll., Phillip Is., 1977–82. *Recreations:* farming, reading. *E:* peter@reith.com.au.

**REKER,** Birke; *see* Häcker, B.

**REMEDIOS, Prof. John Joseph,** DPhil; Professor of Earth Observation Science, since 2010, and Director, National Centre for Earth Observation, since 2014, University of Leicester; *b* Addis Ababa, 20 July 1964; *s* of Lucas and Anne Remedios; *m* 2001, Gabrielle Loftus; one *s* one *d. Educ:* Salesian Coll., Battersea; University Coll., Oxford (BA; MA; DPhil 1991). Res. Associate in Atmospheric Oceanic and Planetary Physics, Univ. of Oxford, 1988–2000; Res. Fellow, St Peter's Coll., Oxford, 1991–2001; Leicester University: Lectr, 2000–06; Sen. Lectr, 2006–10; Hd, Earth Observation Sci., 2002–14. *Publications:* contrib. articles to Jl Geophysical Res., Atmospheric Chemistry and Physics, Remote Sensing of Envmt. *Recreations:* sport, parish and lay community life, music. *Address:* National Centre for Earth Observation, Michael Atiyah Building, University of Leicester, University Road, Leicester LE1 7RH.

**REMFRY, Prof. David,** MBE 2001; RA 2006; RWS 1987; artist; *b* Worthing, 1942. *Educ:* Hull Coll. of Art. *Solo exhibitions* include: Ferens Art Gall., Hull, 1975, 2005; Middlesbrough Art Gall., 1981; NPG, 1992; Boca Raton Mus. of Art, Florida, 1999, 2002; MoMA PSI Contemp. Art Center, NY, 2001; V&A Mus., 2003; DeLand Mus. of Art, Florida, 2017; has exhibited in USA, Holland and Germany in solo and gp exhibns. Eranda Prof. of Drawing, Royal Acad. Schs, 2016–18. Hon. DA Lincoln, 2007. Hugh Casson Drawing Prize, Royal Acad. Arts, 2010. *Publications:* David Remfry Dancers, 2001; We Think the World of You, 2015. *Address:* c/o Royal Academy of Arts, Piccadilly, W1J 0BD. *E:* studio@davidremfry.com. *Clubs:* Groucho, Soho House, Chelsea Arts, Arts, Academicians Room.

**REMNANT,** family name of **Baron Remnant.**

**REMNANT,** 3rd Baron *cr* 1928, of Wenhaston; **James Wogan Remnant,** CVO 1979; FCA; Bt 1917; Director, Bank of Scotland, 1989–96 (Director 1973–96, and Chairman, 1979–92, London Board); Chairman, National Provident Institution, 1990–95 (Director, 1963–95); *b* 23 Oct. 1930; *s* of 2nd Baron Remnant, MBE and Dowager Lady Remnant (*d* 1990); *S* father, 1967; *m* 1953, Serena Jane Loehnis, *o d* of Sir Clive Loehnis, KCMG; three *s* one *d. Educ:* Eton. FCA 1955. Nat. Service, Coldstream Guards, 1948–50 (Lt). Partner, Touche Ross & Co., 1958–70; Man. Dir, 1970–80, Chm., 1981–89, Touche, Remnant & Co.; Chairman: TR City of London Trust, 1978–90 (Dir, 1973–90); TR Pacific Investment Trust, 1987–94. Dep. Chm., Ultramar, 1981–91 (Dir, 1970–91); Director: Australia and New Zealand Banking Group, 1968–81 (Mem., Internat. Bd of Advice, 1987–91); Union Discount Co. of London, 1968–92 (Dep. Chm., 1970–86); London Merchant Securities, 1994–2002; London Authorities Mutual, 2007–09, and other cos. Chm., Assoc. of Investment Trust Cos, 1977–79. A Church Comr, 1976–84. Chm., Institutional Shareholders Cttee 1977–78. Trustee, Royal Jubilee Trusts, 1990–2000 (Hon. Treasurer, 1972–80; Chm., 1980–89); President: Wokingham Constituency Cons. Assoc., 1981–96; Nat. Council of YMCAs, 1983–96; Florence Nightingale Foundn, 1987–2004; Chairman: Learning Through Landscapes Trust, 1989–2000; Friends of Anglican Communion Fund, 2009–14; Patron, Orders of St John Care Trust, 2002–14. Master, Salters' Co., 1995–96. GCStJ (Bailiff of Egle, 1993–99). *Heir:* s Hon. Philip John Remnant, *qv. Address:* 53a Northfield End, Henley-on-Thames RG9 2JJ.

**REMNANT, Hon. Philip John,** CBE 2011; Senior Adviser, Credit Suisse, 2006–13; Chairman, Shareholder Executive, 2007–12; *b* 20 Dec. 1954; *s* and *heir* of Baron Remnant, *qv; m* 1977, Caroline Elizabeth Clare Cavendish; one *s* two *d. Educ:* Eton Coll.; New Coll., Oxford (MA Law). ACA 1979. Peat, Marwick, Mitchell & Co., 1976–82; Kleinwort Benson Ltd, 1982–90 (Dir, 1988–90); Barclays de Zoete Wedd, 1990–97: Man. Dir, 1992–97; Hd, UK Corporate Finance, 1993–94; Dep. Hd, Global Corporate Finance, 1995–96; Co-Hd, Global M&A, 1997; Man. Dir and Dep. Hd, UK Investment Banking, Credit Suisse First Boston, 1997–2001; Dir Gen., 2001–03 (on secondment) and 2010, Dep. Chm., 2012–; Takeover Panel; Hd, UK Investment Banking, Credit Suisse First Boston, 2003–04; Vice-Chm., Credit Suisse First Boston Europe, 2003–06. Member Board: Northern Rock plc, 2008–09; UK Financial Investments Ltd, 2009–18 (Sen. Ind. Dir, 2014–18); Northern Rock (Asset Mgt) plc, 2009–10; Chairman: City of London Investment Trust plc, 2011–; M&G Gp Ltd, 2016–18; Sen. Ind. Dir, Prudential plc, 2013–; non-exec. Dir, Severn Trent plc, 2014–. JP Central London, 2009–16. Hon. Bencher, Inner Temple, 2015. Master, Salters' Co., 2018–19. *Address:* Ham Farm House, Baughurst, Basingstoke, Hants RG26 5SD.

**REMNICK, David Jay;** Editor, The New Yorker, since 1998; *b* 29 Oct. 1958; *m* 1987, Esther B. Fein; two *s* one *d. Educ:* Princeton Univ. (BA). Washington Post: staff writer, 1982–88; Moscow corresp., 1988–92; staff writer, The New Yorker, 1992–98. Vis. Fellow, Council on Foreign Relns. *Publications:* Lenin's Tomb, 1993 (Pulitzer Prize, George Polk Award, 1994); Resurrection, 1997; The Devil Problem (and Other True Stories), 1997; King of the World, 1998; Reporting: writings from The New Yorker, 2007; The Bridge: the life and rise of Barack Obama, 2010. *Address:* The New Yorker, 1 World Trade Center, New York, NY 10007, USA.

**RENALS, Sir Stanley,** 4th Bt *cr* 1895; formerly in the Merchant Navy; *b* 20 May 1923; 2nd *s* of Sir James Herbert Renals, 2nd Bt; *S* brother, Sir Herbert Renals, 3rd Bt, 1961; *m* 1957, Maria Dolores Rodriguez Pinto, *d* of late José Rodriguez Ruiz; one *s. Educ:* City of London Freemen's School. *Heir:* s Stanley Michael Renals, BSc, CEng, MIMechE, MIProdE [*b* 14 Jan. 1958; *m* 1982, Jacqueline Riley; one *s* one *d*]. *Address:* St Helens, Nep Town Road, Henfield, West Sussex BN5 9DU.

**RENDLESHAM,** 9th Baron *cr* 1806 (Ire.); **Charles William Brooke Thellusson;** *b* 10 Jan. 1954; *o s* of 8th Baron Rendlesham and his 2nd wife, Clare, *d* of Lt-Col D. H. G. McCririck; *S* father, 1999; *m* 1988, Lucille Clare, *d* of Rev. Henry Ian Gordon Cumming; one *d. Educ:* Eton. *Heir: cousin* James Hugh Thellusson [*b* 7 Jan. 1961; *m* 1995, Jennifer Louise Owers; one *s* one *d*].

**RENFREW,** family name of **Baron Renfrew of Kaimsthorn.**

**RENFREW OF KAIMSTHORN,** Baron *cr* 1991 (Life Peer), of Hurlet in the District of Renfrew; **Andrew Colin Renfrew,** FBA 1980; Disney Professor of Archaeology, University of Cambridge, 1981–2004; Director, 1991–2004, Senior Fellow, since 2004, McDonald Institute for Archaeological Research, Cambridge; *b* 25 July 1937; *s* of late Archibald Renfrew and Helena Douglas Renfrew (*née* Savage); *m* 1965, Jane Margaret, *d* of Ven. Walter Frederick Ewbank; two *s* one *d. Educ:* St Albans Sch.; St John's Coll., Cambridge (Exhibnr; Hon. Fellow, 2004); British Sch. of Archaeology, Athens. Pt I Nat. Scis Tripos 1960; BA 1st cl. hons Archaeol. and Anthrop. Tripos 1962; MA 1964; PhD 1965; ScD 1976. Pres., Cambridge Union Soc., 1961; Sir Joseph Larmor Award 1961. Nat. Service, Flying Officer (Signals), RAF, 1956–58. Res. Fellow, St John's Coll., Cambridge, 1968; Bulgarian Govt Schol., 1966; University of Sheffield: Lectr in Prehistory and Archaeol., 1965–70; Sen. Lectr, 1970–72; Reader, 1972; Prof. of Archaeology, Southampton Univ., 1972–81; Professorial Fellow, St John's Coll., Cambridge, 1981–86; Jesus College, Cambridge: Master, 1986–97; Professorial Fellow, 1997–2004; Emeritus Fellow and Hon. Fellow, 2004–. Vis. Lectr, Univ. of Calif at Los Angeles, 1967 and 2005. Contested (C) Sheffield Brightside, 1968; Chm., Sheffield Brightside Conserv. Assoc., 1968–72. Member: Ancient Monuments Bd for England, 1974–84; Royal Commn on Historical Monuments (England), 1977–87; Historic Buildings and Monuments Commn for England, 1984–86; Ancient Monuments Adv. Cttee, 1984–2001; UK Nat. Commn for UNESCO, 1984–86 (Mem. Culture Adv. Cttee, 1984–86); Exec. Cttee, NACF, 2001–10; Trustee: Antiquity Trust, 1974–2014; British Mus., 1991–2001; Chm., Hants Archaeol Cttee, 1974–81; a Vice-Pres., RAI, 1982–85. Chm., Governors, The Leys, 1984–92; Chm. Council, British Sch. at Athens, 2004–10. Chairman: All Party Parly Archaeol Cttee, 2002–; Treasure Valuation Cttee, 2011–. Lectures: Dalrymple in Archaeol., Univ. of Glasgow, 1975 and 2000; George Grant MacCurdy, Harvard, 1977; Patten, Indiana Univ., 1982; Harvey, New Mexico Univ., 1982; Hill, Univ. of Minnesota, 1987; Tanner, Stanford Univ., 1993; Neubergh, Univ. of Göteborg, 1997; Hitchcock, Univ. of Calif, Berkeley, 1997; Kroon, Amsterdam, 1999; McDonald, Cambridge Univ., 1999; Rhind, Edinburgh, 2001; Sackler, Nat. Acad. of Scis, Washington, DC, 2005. Excavations: Saliagos near Antiparos, 1964–65; Sitagroi, Macedonia, 1968–70; Phylakopi in Melos, 1974–76; Quanterness, Orkney, 1972–74; Maes Howe, 1973–74; Ring of Brodgar, 1974; Liddle Farm, 1973–74; Markiani, Amorgos, 1987; Keros, 2006–08. FSA 1968 (Vice-Pres., 1987–92); FSAScot 1970 (Hon. FSAScot 2001); Hon. FRSE 2001; Hon. Fellow, Archaeol. Soc. of Athens, 1990. For. Associate, Nat. Acad. of Scis, USA, 1997; Corresponding Member: Österreichische Akad. der Wissenschaften, 2000; Deutsches Archaeologisches Institut, 2004; Russian Acad. of Scis, 2006; Amer. Philosophical Soc., 2006. Freeman, City of London, 1987. Hon. LittD: Sheffield, 1987; Southampton, 1991; Liverpool, 2005; Dr *hc*: Athens, 1991; Pontificia Univ. Católica del Peru, 2009; Hon. DLitt: Edinburgh, 2005; St Andrews, 2006; Kent, 2007; London, 2008. Rivers Meml Medal, 1979, Huxley Meml Medal, 1991, RAI; Fyssen Prize, Fyssen Foundn, Paris, 1996; Lucy Wharton Drexel Medal, Univ. of Pennsylvania Mus., 2003; Latsis Prize, Eur. Sci. Foundn, 2003; Balzan Foundn Prize, 2004. *Publications:* (with J. D. Evans) Excavations at Saliagos near Antiparos, 1968; The Emergence of Civilisation, 1972; (ed) The Explanation of Culture Change, 1973; Before Civilisation, 1973; (ed) British Prehistory, a New Outline, 1974; Investigations in Orkney, 1979; (ed) Transformations: Mathematical Approaches to Culture Change, 1979; Problems in European Prehistory, 1979; (with J. M. Wagstaff) An Island Polity, 1982; (ed) Theory and Explanation in Archaeology, 1982; Approaches to Social Archaeology, 1984; The Prehistory of Orkney, 1985; The Archaeology of Cult, 1985; Archaeology and Language, 1987; (with G. Daniel) The Idea of Prehistory, 1988; The Cycladic Spirit, 1991; (with P. Bahn) Archaeology, 1991; (ed) America Past, America Present, 2000; Loot, Legitimacy and Ownership, 2000; (ed) Archaeogenetics, 2000; Figuring It Out, 2003; (with P. Bahn) Archaeology, the Key Concepts, 2005; (ed with P. Forster) Phylogenetic Methods and the Prehistory of Languages, 2006; (ed jtly) Markiani, Amorgos: an early bronze age fortified settlement, 2006; Prehistory, the Making of the Human Mind, 2007; (ed) Excavations at Phylakopi in Melos 1974–77, 2007; (with I. Morley) The Archaeology of Measurement, 2010; (ed jtly) The Settlement at Dhaskalio, 2013; articles in archaeol jls. *Recreations:* modern art, travel. *Address:* McDonald Institute for Archaeological Research, Downing Street, Cambridge CB2 3ER. *T:* (01223) 333521. *Clubs:* Athenæum, Oxford and Cambridge.

See also Hon. M. A. Renfrew.

**RENFREW, Hon. Magnus Archibald;** Founder and Managing Director, ART HQ Group, since 2016; *b* Winchester, 5 Nov. 1975; *s* of Baron Renfrew of Kaimsthorn, *qv*; *m* 2004, Emma Louise Williamson; three *s. Educ:* St Faith's, Cambridge; Leys Sch., Cambridge; Univ. of St Andrews (MA 1st Cl. Hons Art Hist. 1999; OE Saunders Prize for Art Hist. 1999). Specialist in Scottish Art, Bonhams, Edinburgh, 1999–2002; Bonhams, London: Specialist: in 20th Century British Art, 2002–04; in Modern and Contemporary Art, 2004–06; in Contemporary Asian Art, 2004–06; Manager and Hd of Exhibns, Contrasts Gall., Shanghai, 2006–07; Fair Dir, ART HK, Hong Kong Internat. Art Fair, Hong Kong, 2007–12; Dir, Asia, and Mem., Exec. Cttee, Art Basel, 2012–14; Dep. Chm., Asia, and Dir, Fine Arts, Asia, Bonhams, 2014–16. Mem., Hong Kong Arts Develt Council, 2014–16; Chm., Adv. Council, Para Site, Hong Kong, 2015–. Associate Gov., Foreign Correspondents Club, Hong Kong, 2018–19. FSAScot 2001. Young Global Leader, WEF, 2013. *Recreations:* family, art. *Address:* 1D Tower 1, Hillsborough Court, 18 Old Peak Road, Hong Kong. *E:* info@magnusrenfrew.com. *Club:* Brooks's.

**RENNARD,** Baron *cr* 1999 (Life Peer), of Wavertree in the county of Merseyside; **Christopher John Rennard,** MBE 1989; Chief Executive, Liberal Democrats, 2003–09 (Director of Campaigns and Elections, 1989–2003); Director of Communications, British Healthcare Trades Association, since 2011; *b* 8 July 1960; *s* of late Cecil Langton Rennard and Jean Winifred Rennard (*née* Watson); *m* 1989, Ann McTegart. *Educ:* Mosspits Lane County Primary Sch.; Liverpool Blue Coat Sch.; Univ. of Liverpool (BA Hons Politics and Economics). Liberal Party: Agent, Liverpool Mossley Hill constituency, 1982–84; Area Agent, East Midlands region, 1984–88; Election Co-ordinator, Social & Liberal Democrats, 1988–89. *Publications:* Winning Here: my campaigning life: memoirs volume 1, 2018. *Recreations:* cooking, wine, France. *Address:* 19 Stockwell Park Road, SW9 0AP.

**RENNELL,** 4th Baron *cr* 1933, of Rodd, co. Hereford; **James Roderick David Tremayne Rodd;** Founder, SocialHabitats.co, since 2017; *b* 9 March 1978; *o s* of 3rd Baron Rennell and Phyllis (*née* Neill); *S* father, 2006. *Educ:* Wellesley House; Bryanston; Latymer; De Montfort Univ. Event Mktg Manager, Vision Nine (formerly Sports Vision), 2009–13; Mktg Manager, Park Hyatt Maldives, 2013–14; Mktg and Content Manager, Four Seasons Hotels and Resorts, 2014–17. *Recreations:* wide range of sports, esp. surfing, golf, cricket. *Heir:* none. *E:* jamesrodd9@me.com.

**RENNET, Roderick James,** CBE 2000; CEng; FICE; Chief Executive, East of Scotland Water, 1996–2000; *b* 25 March 1942; *s* of James Mowat Rennet and Rachel Rennet; *m* 1965, Lesley Margaret Irving Love; one *s* one *d. Educ:* Dundee Inst. of Technol. (BSc Hons). CEng 1969; FICE 1986; FCIWEM (FIWEM 1987); FIWO 1992. Civil engg apprentice, Dundee Harbour Trust, 1960–62; asst engr, Chester CBC, 1966–68; asst engr, then sen. engr, Durham CC, 1969–70; sen. engr, then principal engr, Dundee Corp., 1970–75; Tayside Regional Council: Depute Dir of Water Services, 1975–87; Dir of Water Services, 1988–95. *Recreations:* hill-walking, photography, cycling. *Address:* 1A Polwarth Terrace, Edinburgh EH11 1NF.

**RENNIE, David James;** His Honour Judge Rennie; a Circuit Judge, since 2001; b 8 March 1953; s of Michael Rennie and Margaret Rennie (née McGrath); partner, Catherine O'Shea; two s. Educ: Cranleigh Sch.; Kingston Poly. (BA Hons Law). Called to the Bar, Inner Temple, 1976; in practice, specialising in criminal law; a Recorder, 1998–2001. Recreations: spending time in France, cooking, cinema, painting. Address: Lewes Combined Court Centre, The Law Courts, High Street, Lewes, E Sussex BN7 1YB.

**RENNIE, William Cowan;** Member (Lib Dem) Fife North East, Scottish Parliament, since 2016 (Scotland Mid and Fife, 2011–16); Leader, Scottish Lib Dems, since 2011; b 27 Sept. 1967; s of Alexander and Peta Rennie; m 1992, Janet Macfarlane; two s. Educ: Paisley Coll. of Technol. (BSc 1989). Agent for Paul Tyler, MP, 1990–94; Campaign Officer, Liberal Democrats, 1994–97; Chief Exec., Scottish Liberal Democrats, 1997–2001; self-employed consultant, 2001–03; Account Dir, McEwan Purvis, 2003–06; self-employed communications consultant, 2010–11. MP (Lib Dem) Dunfermline and W Fife, Feb. 2006–2010; contested (Lib Dem) same seat, 2010. Recreation: running. Address: Scottish Parliament, Edinburgh EH99 1SP. Club: Carnegie Harriers.

**RENNISON, Air Vice-Marshal David Ralph Grey,** CB 2005; Vice President, Saudi Arabia Typhoon Aircraft Programme, BAE Systems Saudi Arabia, 2009–14; consultant in defence sector, 2014–16; b 28 June 1951; s of Brian and Elizabeth Rennison; m 1975, Anne Scarth; one s one d. Educ: Royal Sch., Armagh; UMIST (BSc Electrical Engrg and Electronics); Univ. of Cranfield (MSc Corporate Mgt); RAF Coll., Cranwell. Joined RAF, 1970; various jun. officer appts, 1975–82; 3 Sqn Ldr appts, 1982–89; student, RAF Staff Coll., 1989; OC Engrg Wing, RAF Wildenrath, 1990–92; Wing Comdr Appointer, RAF Personnel Agency, 1992–94; Gp Capt., RAF Signals Engrg Estabt, 1994–97; Station Comdr, RAF Sealand, 1997–98; ACOS Communications and Inf. Systems, HQ Strike Comd, 1999–2002; Dir, Defence Inf. Infrastructure Prog., MoD, 2002–03; COS (Support), HQ Strike Comd, 2003–05; Air Mem. for Logistics, and Dir Gen. Logistics (Strike Envmt), Defence Logistics Orgn, MoD, 2006–07; Dir, Internat. Maintenance and Logistics Ops, later Future Capability and Internat. Support, Military Air Solutions, BAE Systems, 2007–09. Recreations: social golf, walking, jogging. Address: Pear Tree Cottage, Mill Lane, Calcot, Reading, Berks RG31 7RF.

**RENSHAW, Sir (John) David,** 4th Bt cr 1903, of Coldharbour, Wivelsfield, Sussex; b 9 Oct. 1945; s of Sir Maurice Renshaw, 3rd Bt and his 1st wife, Isabel Bassett (née Popkin); S father, 2002; m 1970, Jennifer Murray (marr. diss. 1988); one s two d. Educ: Ashmole Sch., Southgate. Army, 1960–69; NAAFI, 1970–74; Meat and Livestock Commn, 1974–88; self-employed furniture maker, 1990–2002. Recreations: ski-ing, travel, cycling, family history. Heir: s Thomas Charles Bine Renshaw, b 3 March 1976. Address: 3 Hunts Field Drive, Gretton, Northants NN17 3GD.

**RENTON,** family name of **Baron Renton of Mount Harry.**

**RENTON OF MOUNT HARRY,** Baron cr 1997 (Life Peer), of Offham in the co. of Sussex; **Ronald Timothy Renton;** PC 1989; DL; b 28 May 1932; yr s of R. K. D. Renton, CBE, and Mrs Renton, MBE; m 1960, Alice Fergusson of Kilkerran, Ayrshire; two s two d (and one d decd). Educ: Eton Coll. (King's Schol.); Magdalen Coll., Oxford (Roberts Gawen Schol.). First cl. degree in History, MA Oxon. Joined C. Tennant Sons & Co. Ltd, London, 1954; with Tennants' subsidiaries in Canada, 1957–62; Dir, C. Tennant Sons & Co. Ltd and Managing Dir of Tennant Trading Ltd, 1964–73; Director: Silvermines Ltd, 1967–84; Australia & New Zealand Banking Group, 1967–76; Fleming Continental European Investment Trust, 1992–2003 (Chm., 1999–2003), and other cos. Mem., BBC Gen. Adv. Council, 1982–84; Vice Chm., British Council, 1992–97; Mem., British Council Bd, 1997–99. Contested (C) Sheffield Park Div., 1970. MP (C) Mid-Sussex, Feb. 1974–1997. PPS to Rt Hon. John Biffen, MP, 1979–81, to Rt Hon. Geoffrey Howe, MP, 1983–84; Parly Under Sec. of State, FCO, 1985–87; Minister of State: FCO, 1985–87; Home Office, 1987–89; Parly Sec. to HM Treasury and Govt Chief Whip, 1989–90; Minister of State, Privy Council Office (Minister for the Arts), 1990–92. Mem., H of L, 1997–2016. Member: Select Cttee on Nationalised Industries, 1974–79; Select Cttee on Nat. Heritage, 1995–97; Vice-Chm., Cons. Parly Trade Cttee, 1974–79; Chairman: Parly British-Hong Kong All-Party Gp, 1992–97; Cons. Foreign and Commonwealth Council, 1982–84; Member: Sub-Cttee A, 1997–2001, Sub-Cttee D, 2002–16 (Chm., 2003–06), EC Cttee, H of L; Chm., Information Cttee, H of L, 2006–16; Vice-Pres., 1978–80, Pres., 1980–84, Cons. Trade Unionists; Fellow, Industry and Parlt Trust, 1977–79. Member: Adv. Bd, Know-How Fund for Central and Eastern Europe, 1992–2000; Develt Council, Parham Trust, 1992–2000; Criterion Theatre Trust, 1992–97; APEX. DL East Sussex, 2004. Pres. Council, Roedean Sch., 1998–2005 (Mem., 1982–97). Trustee: Mental Health Foundn, 1985–89; Brighton West Pier Trust, 1997–2005. Founding Pres. (with Mick Jagger), Nat. Music Day, 1992–97; Chairman: Outsider Art Archive, 1995–2001; Sussex Downs Conservation Bd, 1997–2005; South Downs Jt Cttee, 2005–09; Pres., Fedn of Sussex Amenity Socs, 2009–14. Mem. Council, Univ. of Sussex, 2000–07; Pres. Council, Brighton Coll., 2007–11. Publications: The Dangerous Edge (novel), 1994; Hostage to Fortune (novel), 1997; Chief Whip: the role, history and black arts of parliamentary whipping, 2004. Recreations: writing, messing about in boats, listening to opera, cultivating a Sussex vineyard.

**RENTON, Andrew David;** Keeper of Art, Amgueddfa Cymru - National Museum of Wales, since 2015; b Castleford, 2 Oct. 1961; s of David and Jean Renton; m 1987, Linnea Altshuler. Educ: Queen's Coll., Oxford (BA Lit.Hum. 1984); Univ. of Nottingham (PGCE 1988); Univ. of Manchester (Postgrad. Dip. Art Gall. and Mus. Studies 1993). Teacher: of English, Fudan Univ., Shanghai, 1985–86; of English, Hangzhou Univ., China, 1986–87; of Classics, Newcastle-under-Lyme Sch., 1988–92; National Museums and Galleries on Merseyside: Asst Curator, 1993–96; Curator, Lady Lever Art Gall., 1997–99; National Museum of Wales: Curator, Applied Art, 1999–2005; Hd, Applied Art, 2005–15. Trustee, Crafts Study Centre, Farnham, 2008–. Recreations: travel, languages, walking, cricket, crosswords, museums. Address: Amgueddfa Cymru - National Museum of Wales, Cathays Park, Cardiff CF10 3NP. T: (029) 2057 3275. E: andrew.renton@museumwales.ac.uk.

**RENTON, Ian;** see Renton, R. I.

**RENTON, Nicholas William;** Resident Judge (formerly Regional Adjudicator), 2004–15, and Upper Tribunal Judge, 2008–18, Birmingham; b Crewe, 25 July 1948; s of William John Renton and Mary Renton (née Holland); m 1975, Mary Joyce Garrett; one s one d. Educ: Warwick Sch.; Univ. of Kent, Canterbury (BA Hons 1970). Admitted solicitor, 1974; in private practice, Coventry, 1974–92. Part-time Chairman: Social Security Appeal Tribunal, 1985–2000; Disability Appeal Tribunal, 1985–2000; Child Support Appeal Tribunal, 1985–2000; pt-time Immigration Adjudicator, 1990–2000; salaried Immigration Adjudicator, 2000–04. Recreations: Coventry City FC, reading, history.

**RENTON, (Robert) Ian;** Regional Director, South West, Jockey Club, since 2012; b London, 1 Nov. 1958; s of Alec Renton and Susan Renton; m 2007, Jean Keane; one s one d. Educ: Shrewsbury Sch.; Magdalen Coll., Cambridge (BA 1981). Manager, Davy's of London, 1982–84; Asst Manager, Cheltenham Racecourse, 1985–87; Manager, Salisbury and Wincanton Racecourse, 1988–2001; Clerk of the Course, Aintree Racecourse, 1993–2001; Man. Dir, Arena Leisure, 2001–12. Director: Racecourse Assoc., 2000–07; British Horseracing Authy, 2007–09. Recreations: tennis, ski-ing, wine. Address: Cheltenham Racecourse, Cheltenham, Glos GL50 4SH. T: (01242) 513014. E: ian.renton@thejockeyclub.co.uk.

**RENTOUL, John Tindal;** journalist; Chief Political Commentator, The Independent, since 2016; b Kalimpong, India, 25 Sept. 1958; s of Robert Wylie Rentoul and Mary Claire Rentoul (née Tindal); m 2003; one s two d. Educ: Bristol Grammar Sch.; Wolverhampton Grammar Sch.; King's Coll., Cambridge (BA Eng. Lit. 1980). Reporter, Accountancy Age, 1981–83; reporter, 1983–87, Dep. Editor, 1987–88, New Statesman; reporter, On The Record, BBC1, 1988–95; Political Corresp., 1995–97, Chief Leader Writer, 1997–2004, The Independent; Chief Political Commentator, Independent on Sunday, 2004–16. Vis. Fellow, 2008–12, Vis. Prof., 2012–15, contemp. hist., QMUL; Vis. Prof., KCL, 2014–. Publications: The Rich Get Richer: the growth of inequality in Britain in the 1980s, 1987; Me and Mine: the triumph of the new individualism?, 1989; Tony Blair, 1995, 2nd edn 1996; Tony Blair: Prime Minister, 2001, 3rd edn 2013; The Banned List: a manifesto against jargon and cliché, 2011; Questions to Which the Answer is No, 2012; Listellany: a miscellany of very British top tens from politics to pop, 2014; (with Jon Davis) Heroes or Villains? The Blair Government Reconsidered, 2019. Recreations: Spotify, quizzes. Address: The Independent, Northcliffe House, 2 Derry Street, W8 5HF. E: j.rentoul@independent.co.uk.

**RENTZENBRINK, Catherine Marion;** writer and journalist; b Truro, Cornwall, 8 Jan. 1973; d of (Matthew) Kevin Mintern and Margaret Mintern; m 2009, Erwyn Rentzenbrink; one s. Educ: Univ. of Leeds (BA Hons 1996). Bell and Crown pub and travel, 1996–2002; Waterstone's: bookseller, Harrods, 2002–04; Events Manager, Oxford St, 2004–06; Asst Manager, Hatchards, 2006–08; Manager, Teddington, 2008–09, Richmond, 2009–10; Publisher Relationship Manager, 2010–11; Publisher Liaison Manager, 2011–12; New Fiction Reviewer, 2012–13, Associate Editor, 2013–15, Contributing Editor, 2015–17, The Bookseller; Proj. Dir, Quick Reads, 2012–16. Publications: The Last Act of Love (memoir), 2015; A Manual for Heartache (memoir), 2017. Recreations: reading excessively, day dreaming. E: cathyrentzenbrink@hotmail.com.

**RENUCCI, Ronaldo Alfredo;** QC (Scot.) 2018; b Glasgow, 23 Sept. 1962; s of Alfredo Renucci and Moira Renucci (née MacGregor); m 1987, Lindsay Dargie; one s two d. Educ: St Aloysius' Coll., Glasgow; Univ. of Dundee (LLB; DipLP). Admitted as solicitor, 1996; Partner, Galletly & Co. Solicitors, 1988–2001; admitted to Faculty of Advocates, 2001; Advocate, 2001–18. Pres., Scottish Criminal Bar Assoc., 2018–. Recreations: family, antiques, cycling, classic cars, reading, collecting. Address: Woodside House, Woodside, Blairgowrie, Perthshire PH13 9WQ. T: (01828) 670342, 07977 092180. E: ronnie.renucci@blackchambers.co.uk.

**RENWICK,** family name of **Barons Renwick** and **Renwick of Clifton.**

**RENWICK,** 2nd Baron cr 1964, of Coombe; **Harry Andrew Renwick;** Bt 1927; b 10 Oct. 1935; s of 1st Baron Renwick, KBE, and Mrs John Ormiston, Miserden House, Stroud, er d of late Major Harold Parkes, Alveston, Stratford-on-Avon; S father, 1973; m 1st, 1965, Susan Jane (marr. diss. 1988), d of late Captain Kenneth S. B. Lucking and Mrs Moir P. Stormonth-Darling, Lednathie, Glen Prosen, Angus; two s; 2nd, 1989, Mrs Homayoun Mazandi, d of late Col Mahmoud Yazdanparst Pakzad. Educ: Eton. Grenadier Guards (National Service), 1955–56. Partner, W. Greenwell & Co., 1964–80; Dir, General Technology Systems Ltd, 1975–93; Chm., European Information Society Group, 1994–2000 (Pres., 2000–). Mem., H of L Select Cttee on the European Communities, 1988–92, on Science and Technology, 1992–95; Hon. Sec., Parly Information Technology Cttee, 1991–2000 (Vice-Pres., 2006–). Vice-Pres., British Dyslexia Assoc., 1982– (Chm., 1977–82); Chm., Dyslexia Educnl Trust, 1986–2002. Heir: s Hon. Robert James Renwick, b 19 Aug. 1966. Club: Turf.

**RENWICK OF CLIFTON,** Baron cr 1997 (Life Peer), of Chelsea in the Royal Borough of Kensington and Chelsea; **Robin William Renwick,** KCMG 1989 (CMG 1980); Vice-Chairman: Investment Banking, JP Morgan Europe, 2001–14; JP Morgan Cazenove, 2005–14; Director, Stonehage Fleming Family and Partners, since 2014 (Deputy Chairman, Fleming Family and Partners, 2000–14); b 13 Dec. 1937; s of late Richard Renwick, Edinburgh, and Clarice (née Henderson); m Annie; one s one d. Educ: St Paul's Sch.; Jesus Coll., Cambridge (Hon. Fellow, 1992); Univ. of Paris (Sorbonne). Army, 1956–58. Entered Foreign Service, 1963; Dakar, 1963–64; FO, 1964–66; New Delhi, 1966–69; Private Sec. to Minister of State, FCO, 1970–72; First Sec., Paris, 1972–76; Counsellor, Cabinet Office, 1976–78; Rhodesia Dept, FCO, 1978–80; Political Adviser to Governor of Rhodesia, 1980; Vis. Fellow, Center for Internat. Affairs, Harvard, 1980–81; Head of Chancery, Washington, 1981–84; Asst Under Sec. of State, FCO, 1984–87; Ambassador to S Africa, 1987–91; Ambassador to Washington, 1991–95. Mem., H of L, 1997–2018. Dir, 1996–2000, Dep. Chm., 1999–2000, Robert Fleming Hldgs Ltd. Chairman: Save & Prosper Gp, 1996–98; Fluor Ltd, 1996–2011; Kropz plc, 2018–; Director: Compagnie Financière Richemont AG, 1995–2017 (Sen. Ind. Dir; Sen. Advr, 2017–); British Airways plc, 1996–2005; Liberty Internat., 1996–2000; Canal Plus, 1997–2000; BHP Billiton plc, 1997–2005; Fluor Corp., 1997–2008; SABMiller plc (formerly South African Breweries), 1999–2008; Harmony Gold, 1999–2004; KAZ Minerals (formerly Kazakhmys) plc, 2005–15; Gem Diamonds Ltd, 2007–08; Excelsior Mining Co., 2014–; Mem. Sen. Adv. Bd, Appian Capital, 2018–. Trustee, The Economist, 1996–2009. Dir, Open Europe, 2012–17. FRSA. Hon. LLD: Wits Univ., 1990; Amer. Univ. in London, 1993; Hon. DLitt: Coll. of William and Mary, 1993; Oglethorpe Univ., 1995. Publications: Economic Sanctions, 1981; Fighting with Allies, 1996, rev. edn 2017; Unconventional Diplomacy, 1997; A Journey with Margaret Thatcher: foreign policy under the Iron Lady, 2013; Helen Suzman, 2014; Ready for Hillary?, 2014; The End of Apartheid: a diary of a revolution, 2015; How to Steal a Country, 2018; Not Quite a Diplomat: a memoir, 2019. Recreations: tennis, fly fishing. Address: 9 South Street, W1K 2XA. T: (020) 7907 2618. Clubs: Brooks's, Hurlingham, Queen's.

**RENWICK, David Peter;** scriptwriter and author, since 1974; b 4 Sept. 1951; s of James George Renwick and Winifred May Renwick (née Smith); m 1994, Eleanor Florence (née Hogarth). Educ: Luton Grammar Sch.; Luton Sixth Form Coll.; Harlow Tech. Coll. (Nat. Proficiency Cert. in Journalism). Reporter/Sub-Editor, Luton News, 1970–74. (With Andrew Marshall) creator and writer: The Burkiss Way, BBC Radio 4; television: End of Part One, 1979–80; Whoops Apocalypse, 1982; The Steam Video Company, 1984; Hot Metal, 1986–88; Alexei Sayle's Stuff, 1989–91; If You See God, Tell Him, 1993; solo creator and writer: One Foot in the Grave, 1989–2000; Jonathan Creek, 1997–2016 (also dir, 2009–13); Love Soup, 2005–08; stage play, Angry Old Men, 1994; radio, Desolation Jests, BBC Radio 4, 2016. Publications: One Foot in the Grave, 1993. Address: c/o Wilson Wright LLP, Thavies Inn House, 3/4 Holborn Circus, EC1N 2HA. T: (020) 7832 0444.

**RENWICK, Sir Richard Eustace**, 4th Bt *cr* 1921; *b* 13 Jan. 1938; *er s* of Sir Eustace Deuchar Renwick, 3rd Bt, and Diana Mary, *e d* of Colonel Bernard Cruddas, DSO; *S* father, 1973; *m* 1966, Caroline Anne, *er d* of Major Rupert Milburn; three *s*. *Educ*: Eton. *Heir*: *s* Charles Richard Renwick [*b* 10 April 1967; *m* 1993, Jane Ann Lyles (*née* Bush) (marr. diss. 2003); two *s*; *m* 2018, Nicola Helen Erskine (*née* Read)]. *Address*: Whalton House, Whalton, Morpeth, Northumberland NE61 3UZ. *T*: (01670) 775383. *Club*: Northern Counties (Newcastle).

**REPP, Richard Cooper**, DPhil; Master, St Cross College, Oxford, 1987–2003; *b* 1 April 1936; *s* of Robert Mathias Repp, Jun., and Martha Repp (*née* Cooper); *m* 1972, Catherine Ross MacLennan; one *s* one *d*. *Educ*: Shady Side Acad., Pittsburgh; Williams Coll., Mass (BA); Worcester Coll., Oxford (1st Cl. Hons Oriental Studies, MA, DPhil; Hon. Fellow 1989). Instr in Humanities, Robert Coll., Istanbul, 1959–62; Oxford University: Univ. Lectr in Turkish History, 1963–2003; Sen. Proctor, 1979–80; Vice-Chm., Staff Cttee, 1982–84; Member: Gen. Bd of the Faculties, 1982–84, 1985–89; Hebdomadal Council, 1991–2000; Pro-Vice-Chancellor, 1994–2003; Linacre College: Fellow, 1964–87, Hon. Fellow, 1987; Sen. Tutor, 1985–87. Boskey Distinguished Vis. Prof. of History, Williams Coll., Mass., 2008. Chm., Visitors of the Ashmolean Mus., 1995–2002. Hon. Fellow, St Cross Coll., Oxford, 2003. Bicentennial Medal, Williams Coll., Mass, 2004. *Publications*: The Müfti of Istanbul, 1986; various articles on Ottoman history. *Recreations*: gardening, music. *Address*: St Cross College, Oxford OX1 3LZ. *T*: (01865) 278490.

**REPTON, Bishop Suffragan of**, since 2016; **Rt Rev. Janet Elizabeth McFarlane**; *b* Stoke-on-Trent, 25 Nov. 1964; *d* of David James McFarlane and Anne McFarlane; *m* 2004, Andrew Alexander George Ridoutt. *Educ*: Univ. of Sheffield (BMedSci 1987); St John's Coll., Univ. of Durham (BA 1992); Cranmer Hall, Univ. of Durham (DipMin 1993). Speech Therapist, N Staffs HA, 1987–90; ordained deacon, 1993, priest, 1994; Curate, Stafford Team Ministry, 1993–96; Chaplain: Ely Cathedral, 1996–99; to Bishop of Norwich, 2000–09; Dir of Commns, Dio. of Norwich, 1999–2016; Archdeacon of Norwich, 2009–16; Warden of Readers, Dio. of Norwich, 2015–16. *Publications*: (compiled) Pocket Prayers for Advent and Christmas, 2009; Pocket Prayers of Blessing, 2012; regular contribs to Reflections for Daily Prayer, 2010–. *Address*: Repton House, 39 Hickton Road, Swanwick, Alfreton, Derbys DE55 1AF. *E*: bishopofrepton@derby.anglican.org.

**RESTIEAUX, Mary Catherine**, RDI 2011; freelance weaver and textile designer, since 1974; *b* Norwich, 31 Aug. 1945; *d* of late Stephen Restieaux and Catherine Restieaux (*née* Freeman); *m* 2003, Robin White; one *d*. *Educ*: Cambridge Coll. of Art and Technol. (BA 1967); Hammersmith Coll. of Art, London (Cert. Textiles 1972); Royal Coll. of Art (MA Textiles 1974). Established studio, 1974; Textile Res. Fellow, RCA, 1974–80; Index of Selected Makers, Crafts Council, 1979; Mem., First Eleven Studio, textile design, 1991–. Vis. Lectr, Chelsea Coll. of Art and Design, Goldsmiths' Coll., Central St Martins Coll. of Art and Design, Surrey (formerly West Surrey) Coll. of Art and Design, Camberwell Coll. of Art, 1976–98; study days in own studio for students from RCA, Chelsea Coll. of Art and Design, Central St Martins Coll. of Art and Design, and Middlesex Univ. (formerly Middlesex Poly.), 1988–. Work in public collections including: V&A; British Acad.; Govt Art Collection; Craft Study Centre, Farnham; Crafts Council; Nat. Mus. of Mod. Art, Kyoto. Hon. FRCA 2005. Gold Medal, Gestaltendes Handwerk, Munich, 1993; Traditional Technique Prize, 4th Internat. Textile Competition, Kyoto, 1994; Silver Medal, Weavers' Co., 2009. *Address*: 19 Rollscourt Avenue, SE24 0EA. *T*: (020) 7733 3637.

**RESTREPO-LONDOÑO, Andrés**; Order of Boyacá, Colombia; private financial consultant, since 1993; President, Empresa Colombiana de Petróleos-ECOPETROL, 1988–92; *b* 20 Jan. 1942; *m* 1968, Ghislaine Ibiza; one *s* three *d*. *Educ*: Universidad de Antioquia; Université de Paris (postgraduate courses, 1966). Professor and Head of Economic Dept, Univ. de Antioquia, 1967–68; Gen. Man., La Primavera chain of stores, 1969–76; Finance Man., Empresas Públicas de Medellín, 1976–79; Gen. Man., Carbones de Colombia (Colombian Coal Bd), 1979–80; Minister for Economic Develt, 1980–81; Ambassador to UK, 1981–82. Chm., Proban SA (Banana Exporting Co.), 1983–84; Pres., Industrias e Inversiones Samper SA (Cement Co.), 1985–88. Dir, Colombia Móvil SAESP, 2006–. Order Sol of Perú; Order Cruzeiro do Sul, Brazil. *Publications*: Carbones Térmicos en Colombia, Bases para una Política Contractual, 1981; several articles in El Colombiano, daily newspaper of Medellín, Colombia. *Recreations*: fishing, tennis. *Address*: Calle 136A No. 73–17, Bogotá, Colombia; (office) Calle 93B No. 12–30 Of. 305, Bogotá, Colombia. *T*: (1) 6217905, 6217954. *Club*: Lagartos (Bogotá).

**REUBEN, David**; Joint Chief Executive Officer, Reuben Brothers SA, since 1988; Trustee, Reuben Brothers Foundation, since 2002; *b* 14 Sept. 1938; *s* of David Sassoon Reuben and Nancy Reuben; *m* 1976, Debra; two *s* one *d*. *Educ*: Sir Jacob Sassoon High Sch.; Sir John Cass Coll., London (non-degree course Metallurgy). Mountstar Metals, 1958–74, Dir, until 1972; Dir, Metal Traders Gp, 1974–77; Chm., Trans World Metals Gp, 1977–2000. *Recreations*: painting, writing, golf, other sports. *Clubs*: Hurlingham; Wentworth, Coombe Hill Golf.

**REUBEN, Simon David**; Principal, Reuben Brothers, since 2000; *s* of David Sassoon Reuben and Nancy Reuben; *m* 1973, Joyce Nounou; one *d*. *Educ*: Sir Jacob Sassoon High Sch.; Sir John Cass Coll., London (degree not completed). Principal and Managing Director: J. Holdsworth & Co. Ltd, 1966–77; Devereux Gp of Cos, 1970–77; Dir and Jt Principal, Trans World Metals Gp, 1977–2000; Director: Reuben Brothers Ltd, 1988; Global Switch Hldgs, 2011. Trustee, Reuben Foundn, 2002–. *Recreations*: film, art, history, politics. *E*: sreuben@libello.com. *Clubs*: Hurlingham; Yacht Club de Monaco; Monte-Carlo Tennis; Automobile Club de Monaco.
See also D. Reuben.

**REUPKE, Michael**; journalist, 1962–89; *b* Potsdam, Germany, 20 Nov. 1936; *s* of Dr Willm Reupke and Dr Frances G. Reupke (*née* Kinnear); *m* 1963, (Helen) Elizabeth Restrick; one *s* two *d*. *Educ*: Latymer Uppr Sch., London; Jesus Coll., Cambridge (MA Mod. Langs); Collège d'Europe, Bruges. Pilot Officer, RAF, 1957–58. Joined Reuters, 1962; reporter, France, Switzerland, Guinea and West Germany, 1962–69; Asst European Manager, Gen. News Div., 1970–72; Chief Rep., West Germany, 1973–74; Manager, Latin America and the Caribbean, 1975–77; Editor-in-Chief, 1978–89; Gen. Manager, 1989. Director: Visnews, 1985–89; Compex (formerly Company Information Exchange), 1992–2009. Mem. Bd, Radio Authy, 1994–99. Member: IPI, 1978–97; Internat. Inst. of Communications, 1987–2003. Trustee, Reuter Foundn, 1982–89. Founder Chm., Michael Reupke Foundn, 2015–. Volunteer in post-stroke rehabilitation res., Oxford Univ., 2009–; Founder Mem., Stroke Survivors' Club, Chinnor, 2009–. FRSA 2017. *Recreations*: travel, cooking, wine (dégustateur officiel, concours des grands vins de France, 1997–2013). *Address*: 27A Upper High Street, Thame, Oxon OX9 3EX. *Clubs*: Royal Air Force; Leander (Henley-on-Thames).

**REUTER, Edzard**; Chairman, Board of Management, Daimler-Benz, 1987–95. *Educ*: Univs of Berlin and Göttingen (maths and physics); Free Univ. of Berlin (law). Research Asst, Free Univ. of Berlin Law Faculty, 1954–56; Universum Film, 1957–62; Manager, TV prod. section, Bertelsmann Group, Munich, 1962–64; Daimler-Benz: exec., finance dept, 1964; responsible for management planning and organization, 1971; Dep. Mem., Bd, 1973; Full Mem., Exec. Bd, 1976. Mem., Bd of Trustees, Ernst Reuter Foundn, Berlin, 1988–; Chm., Bd of Trustees, Helga and Edzard Foundn, Stuttgart, 1998–. Hon. Citizen, Berlin, 1998. *Publications*: Vom Geist der Wirtschaft, 1986; Horizonte der Wirtschaft, 1993; Schein und Wirklichkeit, 1998; Der schmale Grat des Lebens, 2007; Die Stunde der Heuchler, 2010; Egorepublik Deutschland, 2013; Eingemischt, 2016. *Address*: Taldorfer Strasse 14A, 70599 Stuttgart, Germany.

**REVELSTOKE, 7th Baron** *cr* 1885, of Membland, Devon; **Alexander Rupert Baring**; *b* 9 April 1970; *er s* of 6th Baron Revelstoke and Aneta (*née* Fisher); *S* father, 2012. *Heir*: *b* Hon. Thomas James Baring, *b* 4 Dec. 1971. *Address*: Lambay, Rush, Co. Dublin, Eire.

**REW, Paul Francis**, FCA; Partner, PricewaterhouseCoopers (formerly Price Waterhouse), 1987–2010; non-executive Director, Northumbrian Water Group plc, since 2010; *b* 1953; *s* of late Lt Col Peter Rew and of Diana Edith Rew; *m* 1982, Mary Ellen Pleasant; two *d*. *Educ*: Churcher's Coll., Petersfield; Exeter Univ. (BSc Engrg Sci.). ACA 1977; FCA 1983. Price Waterhouse: articled, London, 1974; Johannesburg office, 1982–84; Partner, 1987; UK Energy and Utilities leader, 2001–07; on secondment to DTI as Under Sec. and Dir, Industrial Develt Unit, 1992–94. Non-executive Director: Met Office, 2010–16; Sustainable Develt Commn, 2010–11; DEFRA, 2011–18; Care Quality Commn, 2014–. Mem., Steering Bd, Insolvency Service, 1992–94. Member: Bd of Mgt, St Bartholomew's and Queen Alexandra's Coll. of Nursing and Midwifery, 1990–95; Adv. Bd, Univ. of Exeter Business Sch., 2010–.

**REY, Prof. Hélène**, Hon. OBE 2016; PhD; FBA 2011; Professor of Economics, since 2007, and Lord Raj Bagri Professor of Economics, since 2016, London Business School; *b* Brioude, France, 13 March 1970; *d* of Denis and Andrée Rey; *m* 2006, Prof. Richard David Portes, *qv*; one *d*. *Educ*: Ecole Nationale de la Statistique et de l'Administration Economique; Stanford Univ. (MSc 1994); Ecole des Hautes Etudes en Sciences Sociales (PhD 1998); London Sch. of Econs and Pol Sci. (PhD 1998). London School of Economics and Political Science: Lectr, 1997–2000; Asst Prof., 2000–06; Prof. of Econs and Internat. Affairs, Econs Dept, Woodrow Wilson Sch., Princeton Univ., 2006–07. Alfred P. Sloan Fellow, 2005–07. Member: Bd, Autorité de Contrôle Prudentiel, France, 2010– (Founding Chair, Scientific Cttee); Conseil d'Analyse Economique, France, 2010–. Bernácer Prize, 2006. *Publications*: Reforming the International Monetary System, 2011; contribs to Political Econ., Amer. Econ. Rev., Qly Jl Econs, Rev. of Econ. Studies. *Address*: London Business School, Regent's Park, NW1 4SA. *T*: 07966 908412, *Fax*: (020) 7000 7001. *E*: hrey@london.edu.

**REYNOLD, Frederic**; QC 1982; *b* 7 Jan. 1936; *s* of late Henry and Regina Reynold. *Educ*: Battersea Grammar School; Magdalen College, Oxford. BA Hons Jurisprudence. Called to the Bar, Gray's Inn, 1960, Bencher, 1991; commenced practice, 1963. *Publications*: The Judge as Lawmaker, 1967; Disagreement and Dissent in Judicial Decision-Making, 2013; Chance, Cheek and Some Heroics, 2018. *Recreations*: too numerous to specify. *Address*: 5 Hillcrest, 51 Ladbroke Grove, W11 3AX. *T*: (020) 7229 3848.

**REYNOLDS, Christopher Douglas**; Chief Executive Officer, Games Marketing Ltd, since 2004; *b* 24 March 1957; *s* of Geoffrey Butler and Margaret Williams (*née* Reynolds); *m* 1993, Deborah Pegden; one *s* one *d*. *Educ*: Ellesmere Coll.; St John's Coll., Durham Univ. (BA 1978). Mktg trainee, Grants of St James's, 1978–80; Product Manager, Eden Vale, 1980–82; various roles, incl. Mktg and Sales Dir, Europe, Dunlop Slazenger Internat. Ltd, 1982–90; Vice-Pres., Apparel, Internat. Div., Reebok Internat. Ltd, 1990–93; Brand Dir, Pringle of Scotland, 1994–95; Vice-Pres., Mktg, Sara Lee Champion Europe, Florence, 1995–97; Founder Partner, Pegden Reynolds Consultancy, 1997–2000; Man. Dir, British Horseracing Bd, 2000–02. Non-executive Chairman: iKnowledge Ltd, 2002–06; Sound Decisions Ltd, 2007–12 (non-exec. Dir, 2002–07). MInstD 2000. *Recreations*: golf, tennis, family, wines - passionate collector/imbiber. *T*: (01483) 417679. *Clubs*: MCC; Hankley Common Golf (Tilford, Surrey); Guildford and Godalming Rugby.

**REYNOLDS, Prof. David**, CBE 2002; Deputy Pro Vice-Chancellor, Professor of Education, and Head, School of Education, Swansea University, since 2016; *b* 3 May 1949; *s* of Colin Reynolds and Joyce Reynolds (*née* Jones); *m* 1994, Meriel Jones; two step *s*. *Educ*: Norwich Sch.; Univ. of Essex. Mem., Scientific Staff, MRC, 1971–75; Lectr in Social Admin, UC Cardiff, 1976–82; Lectr, then Sen. Lectr in Educn, UC Cardiff, subseq. UWCC, 1983–93; Professor: of Educn, Univ. of Newcastle upon Tyne, 1993–99; of Sch. Effectiveness and Sch. Improvement, Loughborough Univ., 1999–2000; of Leadership and Sch. Effectiveness, Univ. of Exeter, 2000–05; of Educn, Univ. of Plymouth, 2005–11; of Educational Effectiveness, Univ. of Southampton, 2011–16. Guest Prof., Univ. of Shenyang, China, 2005–; Visiting Professor: Univ. of Southampton, 2007–10; Univ. of Balearic Isles, 2008–. Mem., Literacy Task Force, 1996–97; Chm., Numeracy Task Force, 1997–98; Department for Education and Employment, subseq. Department for Education and Skills: Member: Literacy and Numeracy Strategy Gp, 1998–2001; Value Added Adv. Gp, 2003–05; Adviser: Teachers' Gp, 1999–2000; Standards and Effectiveness Unit, 2001–01; City Acad. Support Service, 2002–03; Innovation Unit, 2003–06; Sen. Educnl Policy Advr, Dept for Educn and Skills, Welsh Govt, 2011–13. Member Board: British Educnl Communications and Technol. Agency, 1999–2003; TDA (formerly TTA), 2000–06; Educnl Broadcasting Council for Wales, 2005–07. Consultant, Tribal Educn, 2003–10. Non-exec. Dir, Goal plc, 2000–02. Trustee/Dir, E-ACT Academies, 2009–13. Gov., Clifton Coll., 2003–; Chm., The Innovation Trust (Monkseaton Community High Sch.), 2007–13. FRSA 1996. Co-Ed., School Effectiveness and Improvement: an internat. jl of res., policy and practice, 1991–2005. *Publications*: jointly: (ed) Studying School Effectiveness, 1985; The Comprehensive Experiment, 1987; Education Policies: controversies and critiques, 1989; (ed) School Effectiveness and School Improvement, 1989; International School Effects Research, 1992; (ed) School Effectiveness, 1992; Advances in School Effectiveness Research, 1994; (ed) Merging Traditions, 1996; Making Good Schools, 1996; (ed) Dilemmas of Decentralisation, 1996; Worlds Apart?, 1996; Improving Schools: performance and potential, 1999; The International Handbook of School Effectiveness Research, 2000; World Class Schools, 2002; Effective Teaching, 2001, 4th edn as Effective Teaching: evidence practice, 2017; Failure Free Education? The Past, Present and Future of School Effectiveness and Improvement, 2010; School Effectiveness and Improvement: research, policy and practice, 2012; The Routledge International Handbook of Educational Effectiveness and Improvement, 2016; contrib. articles to acad. jls, professional jls and popular media. *Recreations*: walking, wine, travelling, opera. *Address*: Tondrugwaer Farm, Cross Inn, Llantrisant CF72 8NZ. *T*: (01443) 223417. *E*: david@davidreynoldsconsulting.com.

**REYNOLDS, Prof. David James**, PhD; FBA 2005; Professor of International History, University of Cambridge, since 2002; Fellow of Christ's College, Cambridge, since 1983; *b* 17 Feb. 1952; *s* of late Leslie Reynolds and Marian Reynolds (*née* Kay); *m* 1977, Margaret Philpott Ray; one *s*. *Educ*: Dulwich Coll.; Gonville and Caius Coll., Cambridge (BA, MA,

PhD 1980). Choate Fellow, 1973–74, Warren Fellow, 1980–81, Harvard Univ.; Res. Fellow, Gonville and Caius Coll., Cambridge, 1978–80, 1981–83; University of Cambridge: Asst Lectr in History, 1984–88; Lectr, 1988–97; Reader in Internat. History, 1997–2002; Chm., History Faculty, 2013–15. Writer and presenter, BBC TV: Churchill's Forgotten Years, 2005; The Improbable Mr Attlee, 2005; Summits (3-part series), 2008; Armistice, 2008; Nixon in the Den, 2010; World War Two: 1941 and the Man of Steel, 2011; World War Two: 1942 and Hitler's soft underbelly, 2012; Long Shadow (3-part series), 2014; World War Two: 1945 and the Wheelchair President, 2015; America, Empire of Liberty (90-part series), BBC Radio 4, 2008–09 (Voice of the Listener and Viewer Award for Best New Radio Prog., 2008). *Publications*: The Creation of the Anglo-American Alliance, 1937–41, 1981 (Bernath Prize, Soc. for Historians of Amer. For. Relns, 1982); (jtly) An Ocean Apart: the relationship between Britain and America in the 20th century, 1988; Britannia Overruled: British policy and world power in the 20th century, 1991; (ed jtly) Allies at War: the Soviet, American, and British experience 1939–45, 1994; (ed) The Origins of the Cold War in Europe, 1994; Rich Relations: the American occupation of Britain 1942–45, 1995 (Soc. for Mil. Hist. Distinguished Book Award, 1996); One World Divisible: a global history since 1945, 2000; From Munich to Pearl Harbor: Roosevelt's America and the origins of the Second World War, 2001; In Command of History: Churchill fighting and writing the Second World War, 2004 (Wolfson Hist. Prize, 2005); From World War to Cold War: Churchill, Roosevelt and the international history of the 1940s, 2006; Summits: six meetings that shaped the twentieth century, 2007; (ed jtly) FDR's World: war, peace and legacies, 2008; America, Empire of Liberty: a new history, 2009; The Long Shadow: the Great War and the twentieth century, 2013 (Hessell-Tiltman Prize, English PEN, 2014); (ed jtly) Transcending the Cold War: summits, statecraft, and the dissolution of bipolarity in Europe, 2016; (jtly) The Kremlin Letters: Stalin's wartime correspondence with Churchill and Roosevelt, 2018. *Address*: Christ's College, Cambridge CB2 3BU. *T*: (01223) 334900.

**REYNOLDS, Deborah,** CB 2008; PhD; Chief Veterinary Officer and Director General, Animal Health and Welfare, Department for Environment, Food and Rural Affairs, 2004–07; Visiting Professor, Royal Veterinary College, since 2008; *b* 29 May 1952; *m*; one *s*. *Educ*: Univ. of Bristol (BVSc 1975); Univ. of Reading (PhD 1983). MRCVS. Vet. Res. Officer, Inst. of Animal Health; Vet. Investigation Service, State Vet. Service, MAFF, 1984–91; MAFF, 1991–94; Hd, Bacteriol. Dept, Vet. Labs Agency, 1994–97; Hd of Endemic Animal Diseases and Zoonoses, MAFF, 1997–2001; Veterinary Dir, Food Standards Agency, 2001–04. Member, Board: HPA, 2008–13; Berkshire West NHS PCT, 2008–11; Partner Gov., Royal Berks Hosp. Foundn Trust, 2009–11. Chm., Natural Envmt (formerly Nature Conservation) Panel, NT, 2009–15. Affiliate Prof., Colorado State Univ., 2008–. Mem. Council, British Trust for Ornithol., 2016–. Chm. Govs, Abbey Sch., Reading, 2014–17. *Address*: Brimstone Cottage, Upper Bucklebury, near Reading, Berks RG7 6QX. *T*: (01635) 860254, 07976 297190.

**REYNOLDS, Emma;** MP (Lab) Wolverhampton North East, since 2010; *b* Wolverhampton, 2 Nov. 1977; *m* 2016, Richard Stevens. *Educ*: Wadham Coll., Oxford (BA PPE). Policy Researcher, Small Business Europe, Brussels, 2001–03; Pol Advr to Pres., Party of Eur. Socialists, 2004–06; Special Advr to Minister of State for Europe, FCO, 2006–07, to Parly Sec. to HM Treasury (Govt Chief Whip), 2007–08; Sen. Consultant, Cogitamus Ltd, 2009–10. Shadow Minister for Europe, 2011–13, for Housing, 2013–15; Shadow Sec. of State for Communities and Local Govt, 2015. Member: Health Select Cttee, 2015–16; Cttee on Exiting the EU, 2016–. *Recreations*: running, swimming, cinema. *Address*: (office) 492A Stafford Road, Wolverhampton WV10 6AN. *E*: emma.reynolds.mp@parliament.uk.

**REYNOLDS, Dame Fiona Claire, (Mrs R. W. T. Merrill),** DBE 2008 (CBE 1998); Master, Emmanuel College, Cambridge, since 2013; *b* 29 March 1958; *d* of Jeffrey Alan Reynolds and Margaret Mary (*née* Watson); *m* 1981, Robert William Tinsley Merrill; three *d*. *Educ*: Rugby High Sch. for Girls; Newnham Coll., Cambridge (MA, MPhil 1980). Sec., Council for Nat. Parks, 1980–87; Asst Dir, 1987–91, Dir, 1992–98, CPRE; Dir, Women's Unit, Cabinet Office, 1998–2000; Dir-Gen., Nat. Trust, 2001–12. Non-exec. Dir, Wessex Water Services, 2012–; Sen. non-exec. Dir, BBC, 2012–17. Chair: Green Alliance, 2014–; Cathedrals Fabric Commn for England, 2015–; Internat. Nat. Trusts Orgn, 2015–. Hon. FBA 2012. Trustee, Grosvenor Estate, 2018–. Global 500 Award, UN Envmt Programme, 1990. *Recreations*: hillwalking, classical music and opera, reading. *Address*: Master's Lodge, Emmanuel College, Cambridge CB2 3AP.

**REYNOLDS, Prof. Francis Martin Baillie,** DCL; FBA 1988; Professor of Law, University of Oxford, 1992–2000, now Emeritus; Fellow of Worcester College, Oxford, 1960–2000, now Emeritus; *b* 11 Nov. 1932; *s* of Eustace Baillie Reynolds and Emma Margaret Hanby Reynolds (*née* Holmes); *m* 1965, Susan Claire Shillito; two *s* one *d*. *Educ*: Winchester Coll.; Worcester Coll., Oxford (BA 1956; BCL 1957; MA 1960; DCL 1986). Bigelow Teaching Fellow, Univ. of Chicago, 1957–58. Called to the Bar, Inner Temple, 1961, Hon. Bencher 1979. Reader in Law, Oxford Univ., 1977–92. Visiting Professor, Nat. Univ. of Singapore, UCL, Univ. of Melbourne, Monash Univ., Otago Univ., Univ. of Sydney, Univ. of Auckland, Univ. of Hong Kong, Singapore Mgt Univ.; Hon. Prof. of Internat. Maritime Law, Internat. Maritime Law Inst., Malta. Hon. QC 1993. Gen. Editor, Lloyd's Maritime and Commercial Law Qly, 1983–87; Editor, Law Qly Review, 1987–2014. *Publications*: (ed jtly) Chitty on Contracts, 24th edn 1977 to 32nd edn 2015; (ed jtly) Benjamin's Sale of Goods, 1st edn 1974, to 9th edn 2014; Bowstead on Agency, (ed jtly) 13th edn 1968 to 18th edn as Bowstead and Reynolds on Agency 2006, (contrib.) 19th edn 2010 to 20th edn 2014; (ed jtly) English Private Law, 2000, 2nd edn 2008; (with Sir Guenter Treitel) Carver on Bills of Lading, 2001, 4th edn 2017; published lectures and contribs to legal jls. *Recreations*: music, walking. *Address*: 61 Charlbury Road, Oxford OX2 6UX. *T*: (01865) 559323.

**REYNOLDS, Gillian,** MBE 1999; Radio Critic, Sunday Times, since 2018; *b* 15 Nov. 1935; *d* of Charles Morton and Ada (*née* Kelly); *m* 1958, Stanley Reynolds (marr. diss. 1982; he *d* 2016); three *s*. *Educ*: St Anne's Coll., Oxford (MA; Hon. Fellow, 1996); Mount Holyoke Coll., South Hadley, Mass, USA. TV journalist, 1964–; Radio Critic: The Guardian, 1967–74; Daily Telegraph, 1975–2018; Programme Controller, Radio City, Liverpool, 1974–75. Vis. Fellow, Bournemouth Univ. Media Sch., 2002. Trustee: Nat. Museums Liverpool (formerly Nat. Museums and Galls on Merseyside), 2001–08; Nat. Media Mus., 2009–. Chm., Charles Parker Archive Trust, 1986–2009. Fellow (first to be apptd), Radio Acad., 1990; FRTS 1996. Hon. Fellow, Liverpool John Moores Univ., 2004. Hon. DLitt Lancaster, 2012. Media Soc. Award for distinguished contrib. to journalism, 1999; Special Award for contribn to public service broadcast, Voice of Listener and Viewer, 2015. *Recreations*: listening to the radio, the company of friends. *Address*: Flat 3, 1 Linden Gardens, W2 4HA. *T*: (020) 7229 1893.

**REYNOLDS, James Edward;** BBC News Correspondent, since 1998; *b* 20 May 1974; *s* of Paul and Louise Reynolds. *Educ*: Westminster Sch.; Christ's Coll., Cambridge (BA Hons Modern Langs 1996). Joined BBC, 1997; S America corresp., 1998–2001; Middle East corresp., 2001–06; China corresp., 2006–09; Iranian affairs corresp., 2010–12; Istanbul corresp., 2012–14; Rome corresp., 2014–. Nieman Fellow, Harvard Univ., 2009–10. *Recreations*: studying the effects of galactic trash, floating in the Dead Sea. *Address*: c/o BBC Broadcasting House, Portland Place, W1A 1AA. *T*: (020) 7743 8000. *E*: james.reynolds@bbc.co.uk.

**REYNOLDS, Sir James Francis,** 4th Bt *cr* 1923, of Woolton, co. Lancaster; music producer and mix engineer; *b* 10 July 1971; *s* of Sir David James Reynolds, 3rd Bt and of Charlotte Reynolds (*née* Baumgartner); *S* father, 2015; *m* 2004, Camilla Anne Stewart; one *s* one *d*. *Educ*: Worth Abbey. *Recreation*: sport. *Heir*: *s* Frederik James Reynolds, *b* 9 Sept. 2005.

**REYNOLDS, (James) Kirk;** QC 1993; *b* 24 March 1951; *s* of late James Reynolds, sometime Judge of the High Ct, Eastern Reg. of Nigeria, and of Alexandra Mary (*née* Strain); civil partnership 2007, Holger Andreas Baehr. *Educ*: Campbell Coll., Belfast; Peterhouse, Cambridge (MA). Called to the Bar, Middle Temple, 1974; Bencher, 2000. FCIArb 2014. Hon. Mem., RICS, 1997. Hon. LLD Bedfordshire, 2009. *Publications*: The Handbook of Rent Review, 1981 (Australian edn 2009); The Renewal of Business Tenancies, 1985, 4th edn 2012; Dilapidations: the modern law and practice, 1995, 5th edn 2013; Essentials of Rent Review, 1995. *Address*: Falcon Chambers, Falcon Court, EC4Y 1AA. *T*: (020) 7353 2484.

**REYNOLDS, John;** Director and Fellow, SAMI Consulting, St Andrews Management Institute, since 2006; *b* 14 Nov. 1950; *s* of Albert Victor Reynolds and Nina Eileen Reynolds (*née* Wolfenden); *m* 1973, Brenda O'Doherty; one *s* one *d*. *Educ*: HMS Worcester; UWIST (BSc Maritime Studies 1975). Navigating Officer, P&OSNCo., 1966–75; Res Scientist, Nat. Maritime Inst., 1975–84; Department of Trade and Industry, 1984–89: Shipbuilding Policy Div., 1984–87; Eur. Mgt of Technol. Prog., 1985–86; Tech. Asst to Chief Engr and Scientist, 1987–89; Head of Mobile Radio Licensing, Radiocommunications Agency, 1989–90; Dir of Resources, Lab. of Govt Chemist, 1991–96; Director: Radiocommunications Agency, 1996–98; Future and Innovation Unit, DTI, 1998–2001; Gp Dir, Strategy and Communications Gp, British Trade Internat., subseq. UK Trade and Investment, 2001–04; Dir, Capabilities Programme, DTI, 2005–06. *Recreations*: tennis, cycling, gardening. *Address*: SAMI Consulting, The Rectory, 1 Toomers' Wharf, Canal Walk, Newbury RG14 1DY.

**REYNOLDS, John;** Depute Provost, City of Aberdeen, 2012–17 (Lord Provost and Lord-Lieutenant, 2003–07; a Baillie, since 2007); *b* 5 April 1949; *s* of William and Anne Reynolds; *m* 1970, Helen Will; one *s* two *d*. *Educ*: Blackpool Grammar Sch. Posts in: entertainment ind. throughout UK, 1966–70; electrical retail trade, with Electric Rentals Gp/Granada, and John Reynolds news agency, 1970–96; self employed in travel business, Scottish Choice Itineraries, and news agency, 1996–2017. Member (Lib Dem): Aberdeen DC, 1986–96; Grampian Regl Council, 1994–96; Mem., Aberdeen CC, 1995– (Lib Dem, 1995–2012, Ind, 2012–) (Mem., 1996–, Convenor, 2017–, Licensing Cttee; Member: Audit and Risk Cttee, 2003–; Staff Governance Cttee, 2018–; Lead Cllr for Internat. Trade and Econ. Develt, 2006–). Vice Chm., Transport Gp, North Sea Commn, 2018–. Vice Chairman: E of Scotland Eur. Consortium, 2018–; E of Scotland Pension Fund, 2018–. Member: Grampian Jt Fire Bd; Aberdeen Licensing Bd. Comr, Northern Lighthouse Bd, 2003–07. Director: Aberdeen YMCA, 2007–; Aberdeen Seafarers Centre, 2011–; Aberdeen Exhibn and Conf. Centre, 2012–19; Elevator; Transition Extreme. President: Voluntary Service Aberdeen, 2003–07; Aberdeen Br., RNLI, 2003–07; Vice-Pres., Shipwrecked Fishermen and Mariners' Royal Benevolent Soc., 2003–07; Mem., Local Adv. Cttee, Royal Nat. Mission to Deep Sea Fishermen. Trustee, Nat. Liby of Scotland, 2003–07. Patron: Mental Health Aberdeen, 2003–07; Aberdeen Internat. Youth Fest., 2003–. Hon. Pres., Aberdeen Scout Council. Hon. Prof., Marat Ospanov Medical Univ. (formerly Acad.), 2006–. Burgess of Guild, City of Aberdeen, 1990. JP Aberdeen, 2003–07 (Chm., JPs Adv. Cttee). OStJ 2005. *Recreations*: music, theatre, DIY, socialising. *Address*: Aberdeen City Council, Town House, Aberdeen AB10 1LP. *T*: (01224) 522637, *Fax*: (01224) 523747. *E*: jreynolds@aberdeencity.gov.uk.

**REYNOLDS, Jonathan Neil;** MP (Lab Co-op) Stalybridge and Hyde, since 2010; *b* 28 Aug. 1980; *s* of Keith and Judith Reynolds; *m* 2008, Claire Johnston; one *s* one *d*. *Educ*: Houghton Kepier Comprehensive Sch.; Sunderland City Coll.; Manchester Univ. (BA Politics and Modern Hist.); BPP Law Sch., Manchester. Political asst to James Purnell, MP; trainee solicitor, Addleshaw Goddard LLP, Manchester until 2010. Mem. (Lab Co-op) Tameside MBC, 2007–11. An Opposition Asst Whip, 2010–11; Shadow Minister for Energy and Climate Change, 2013–15, for Transport, 2015–16; Shadow Econ. Sec., 2016–. Mem., Select Cttee on Sci. and Technol., 2010–12; Sec., All Party Parly Gp on the Armed Forces, 2010. *Address*: House of Commons, SW1A 0AA.

**REYNOLDS, Joyce Maire,** FBA 1982; Fellow of Newnham College, 1951–84, now Hon. Fellow, and Reader in Roman Historical Epigraphy, 1983–84, University of Cambridge; *b* 18 Dec. 1918; *d* of late William Howe Reynolds and Nellie Farmer Reynolds. *Educ*: Walthamstow County High Sch. for Girls; St Paul's Girls' Sch., Hammersmith; Somerville Coll., Oxford (Hon. Fellow, 1988). Temp. Civil Servant, BoT, 1941–46; Rome Scholar, British Sch. at Rome, 1946–48; Lectr in Ancient History, King's Coll., Newcastle upon Tyne, 1948–51; Cambridge University: Asst Lectr in Classics, 1952–57; Univ. Lectr 1957–83; Dir of Studies in Classics, 1951–79 and Lectr in Classics, 1951–84, Newnham Coll. Woolley Travelling Fellow, Somerville Coll., Oxford, 1961; Mem., Inst. for Advanced Study, Princeton, USA, 1984–85; Vis. Prof., Univ. of Calif at Berkeley, 1987. President: Soc. for Libyan Studies, 1981–86; Soc. for the Promotion of Roman Studies, 1986–89. Corresponding Member: German Archaeol Inst., 1971–; Austrian Archaeol Inst., 1991–. Hon. DLitt Newcastle upon Tyne, 1984; Hon. LittD Cantab, 2018. Gold Medal, Soc. of Antiquaries of London, 2004; Sir Frederic Kenyon Medal, British Acad., 2017. *Publications*: (with J. B. Ward Perkins) The Inscriptions of Roman Tripolitania, 1952; Aphrodisias and Rome, 1982; (with R. Tannenbaum) Jews and Godfearers at Aphrodisias, 1987; (ed) Christian Monuments of Cyrenaica, 2003; articles on Roman history and epigraphy in jls, 1951–. *Recreation*: walking. *Address*: Newnham College, Cambridge CB3 9DF.

**REYNOLDS, Kirk;** *see* Reynolds, J. K.

**REYNOLDS, His Honour Martin Paul;** a Circuit Judge, 1995–2006; a Deputy Circuit Judge, 2006–11; *b* 25 Dec. 1936; *s* of Cedric Hinton Fleetwood Reynolds and Doris Margaret (*née* Bryan); *m* 1961, Gaynor Margaret Phillips; three *s*. *Educ*: University College Sch., Hampstead; St Edmund Hall, Oxford (MA). ACIArb 1982. Called to the Bar, Inner Temple, 1962. Mem., Parole Bd, 2006–16; Pres., later Tribunal Judge, Mental Health Rev. Tribunal (Restricted Cases), 1997–2011. Councillor, London Borough of Islington, 1968–71 and 1972–82. Contested (Lab) Harrow West, Oct. 1994. *Recreations*: navigating waterways in a Dutch barge, foreign travel, gastronomy, music, supporting Arsenal, grandchildren. *Clubs*: Savage; Bar Yacht.

**REYNOLDS, Dr Martin Richard Finch**; Associate Director of Health Policy and Public Health, East Riding Health Authority, 1993–99; *b* 26 July 1943; 2nd *s* of Gerald Finch Reynolds and Frances Bertha (*née* Locke); *m* 1965, Shelagh (*née* Gray) (*d* 2010); two *d*. *Educ*: Newton Abbot Grammar Sch.; Univ. of Bristol. MB ChB, DPH; FFPHM; FRCP. House posts in medicine, surgery, infectious diseases and paediatrics, 1966–67; Dep. Med. Officer, Glos CC, 1967–70; Sen. Dep. Med. Officer, Bristol City and Asst Sen. Med. Officer, SW Regional Hosp. Bd, 1970–74; Dist Community Physician, Southmead Dist of Avon AHA (Teaching) and Med. Officer for Environmental Health, Northavon Dist Council, 1974–79; Area Med. Officer, Wilts AHA, 1979–80; Regional MO/Chief Med. Advr, South Western RHA, 1980–86; Specialist in Community Medicine, 1986–89, Consultant in Public Health Medicine, 1989–93, Hull HA. Registrar, FPHM, 1995–97. Voluntary work with Mission Assist (formerly Wycliffe Associates) for Bible trans., 1999–. *Publications*: contrib. various articles in professional jls on subjects in community medicine.

**REYNOLDS, Dr Roy Gregory**, CMG 2000; Chief Executive, Commonwealth Development Corporation, 1994–99; *b* 4 May 1939; *s* of Henry Herbert Reynolds and Alice Emily Reynolds; *m* 1963, Monica Cecelia; one *s* one *d*. *Educ*: George Dixon Grammar Sch., Birmingham; Birmingham Univ. (BSc Chem. Eng 1960); Imperial Coll., London (PhD 1964). Shell Internat. Petroleum Co., 1964–92, Man. Dir, Shell UK Oil, 1988–92. Dir, 1999–2009, Chm., 2003–09, J P Morgan Emerging Markets Investment Trust (formerly Fleming Emerging Markets Trust). Non-exec. Dir, LASMO plc, 1997–2001. *Recreations*: keeping fit, golf. *Club*: Royal Automobile.

**REYNOLDS, Susan Mary Grace**, FRHistS; FBA 1993; historian; Honorary Research Fellow, Institute of Historical Research, since 1993; *b* 27 Jan. 1929; *d* of Hugh Reynolds and Maisie Reynolds (*née* Morten). *Educ*: The Study, Montreal; Howell's Sch., Denbigh; Lady Margaret Hall, Oxford (History Cl. II, MA); Dip. Archive Admin, UCL. FRHistS 1968. Archive Asst, 1951–52; Victoria County Histories, 1952–59; school teacher, 1959–64; Fellow and Tutor in Modern History, LMH, Oxford, 1964–86, Emeritus Fellow, 1986; Lectr in Modern History, Oxford Univ., 1965–86. Visiting Professor: Dartmouth Coll., USA, 1986–87; Central European Univ., Budapest, 1994. *Publications*: (ed) Register of Roger Martival, Bishop of Salisbury, vol. 3, 1965; Introduction to the History of English Medieval Towns, 1977; Kingdoms and Communities in Western Europe 900–1300, 1984, 2nd edn 1997; Fiefs and Vassals, 1994; Ideas and Solidarities of the Medieval Laity, 1995; Before Eminent Domain: toward a history of expropriation for the common good, 2010; The Middle Ages without Feudalism, 2012; articles in historical jls. *Address*: 19 Ridgmount Gardens, WC1E 7AR. *T*: (020) 7636 9043.

**REYNOLDS, Prof. Vernon**, PhD; Professor of Biological Anthropology, University of Oxford, 1996–2001, now Professor Emeritus; Fellow, Magdalen College, Oxford, 1987–2001, now Fellow Emeritus; Emeritus Fellow, School of Anthropology, University of Oxford, since 2008; *b* 14 Dec. 1935; *s* of Heinz Emil Max Rheinhold and Eva Marianne Rheinhold (*née* Rudenberg); name changed to Reynolds, 1949; *m* 1960, Frances Glover; one *s* one *d*. *Educ*: Collyer's Sch.; University Coll. London (BA Hons; PhD 1962). Univ. of London Travelling Schol. to study wild chimpanzees in Uganda, 1962; Lecturer: in Anthropol., Bristol Univ., 1966–72; in Biol Anthropol., Oxford Univ., 1972–96. Hon. Sen. Res. Fellow, Univ. of Sussex, 2002–. Founder and Hd, Budongo Forest Project, Uganda, 1990–. President's Award, Amer. Soc. Primatologists, 2000; Chm.'s Award, Cttee for Res. and Exploration, Nat. Geographic Soc., 2000. *Publications*: Budongo: a forest and its chimpanzees, 1965; The Apes, 1967; The Biology of Human Action, 1976, 2nd edn 1980; (jtly) Primate Social Behaviour, 1993; (jtly) The Biology of Religion, 1983, 2nd edn 1994; The Chimpanzees of the Budongo Forest, 2005; edited jointly: Human Behaviour and Adaptation, 1978; The Meaning of Primate Signals, 1984; The Sociobiology of Ethnocentrism, 1987; Fertility and Resources, 1990; Mating and Marriage, 1991; The Aquatic Ape: fact or fiction?, 1991; Human Populations: diversity and adaptation, 1995; Survival and Religion, 1995; contributed chapters; contrib. scientific jls. *Recreations*: dinghy sailing, bee-keeping. *Address*: Orchard House, West Street, Alfriston, E Sussex BN26 5UX. *T*: (01323) 871136. *E*: vreynolds@btopenworld.com.

**REYNTIENS, Nicholas Patrick**, OBE 1976; Head of Fine Art, Central School of Art and Design, London, 1976–86; *b* 11 Dec. 1925; *s* of Nicholas Serge Reyntiens, OBE, and Janet MacRae; *m* 1953, Anne Bruce (*d* 2006); two *s* two *d*. *Educ*: Ampleforth; Edinburgh Coll. of Art (DA). Served Scots Guards, 1943–47. St Marylebone Sch. of Art, 1947–50; Edinburgh Coll. of Art, 1950–51. Founder (with wife, Anne Bruce, the painter), Reyntiens Trust, which ran art sch., Burleighfield, where pupils from UK, Ireland, France, Germany, Japan, Canada, Australia, New Zealand, US and Iceland learned art of stained glass, and which had facilities for tapestry design and teaching, a printing house for editioning in lithography, etching and silkscreen, as well as workshops for stained glass, ceramics, drawing and painting. Has lectured in USA, Spain, Mexico, France and Switzerland; British Council lectr, India, 1995–96; occasional Vis. Prof., Pilchuck Sch. of Glass, Washington State, USA. Many commissions, including glass for Liverpool RC Metropolitan Cathedral; for 35 years interpreted painters' designs into stained glass, as well as own commissions for stained glass, 1953–, including baptistery window, Coventry Cathedral, Eton Coll. Chapel, Churchill Coll., Cambridge, Robinson Coll., Cambridge, St Margaret's Westminster (all with John Piper), Derby Cathedral and Liverpool Metropolitan Cathedral Blessed Sacrament Chapel (with Ceri Richards), All Saints Basingstoke (with Cecil Collins); completed glazing of Christ Church Hall, Oxford, 1980–84; designed and painted Great West Window, Southwell Minster, Notts, 1995; commnd with son, John, to design and paint Lady Chapel, and entire south transept, Ampleforth Abbey, 2002; collaboration with G. Jones, designed and painted eight windows, Church of St Martin, Cochem, Germany, 2009. Retrospective exhibn of autonomous panels, Ontario, 1990. Member: Court, RCA; Adv. Cttee in Decoration, Brompton Oratory; Adv. Cttee in Decoration, Westminster Cathedral; Adv. Cttee, Westminster Abbey, 1981–95. Art Critic, Catholic Herald; art correspondent, The Oldie. Hon. Dr Edinburgh. *Publications*: Technique of Stained Glass, 1967, 2nd edn 1977; The Beauty of Stained Glass, 1990; has written for architectural, art, literary and political magazines and on cooking for Harpers & Queen. *Address*: Winterbourne Lodge, Ilford Bridges Farm, close Stocklinch, Ilminster, Som TA19 9HZ. *T*: (01460) 52241.

**RHIND, Prof. David William**, CBE 2001; FRS 2002; Director General and Chief Executive, Ordnance Survey, 1992–98; Vice-Chancellor and Principal, City University, 1998–2007; Member of Court, Bank of England, 2006–09; *b* 29 Nov. 1943; *s* of late William Rhind and Christina Rhind; *m* 1966, Christine Young; one *s* two *d*. *Educ*: Berwick Grammar School; Bristol Univ. (BSc); Edinburgh Univ. (PhD); London Univ. (DSc). FRGS; FRICS 1991; FSS 2004. Research Fellow, Royal College of Art, 1969–73; Lectr then Reader, Univ. of Durham, 1973–81; Birkbeck College, London University: Prof. of Geography, 1982–91; Dean, Faculty of Economics, 1984–86; Governor, 1986–90; Hon. Fellow, 2000. Visiting Fellow: Internat. Trng Centre, Netherlands, 1975; ANU, 1979. Vice-Pres., Internat. Cartographic Assoc., 1984–91; Mem., Govt Cttee on Enquiry into handling of geographic inf., 1985–87; Advisor, H of L Select Cttee on Sci. and Tech., 1983–84; Mem., ESRC, 1996–2000. Chm., Portsmouth Hosps NHS Trust, 2009–12. Chairman: Bloomsbury Computing Consortium Mgt Cttee, 1988–91; Royal Soc. Ordnance Survey Scientific Cttee, 1989–91; Commn on Social Scis, Acad. of Learned Socs for Social Scis, 2000–03; Statistics Commn, 2003–08 (Mem., 2000–03); Higher Educn Staff Develt Agency, 2001–04; Islington Improvement Bd, 2003–04; Socio-Econ. Cttee, Nuclear Decommng Authy, 2006–08; Adv. Panel on Public Sector Inf., 2008–15; Governing Bd, Cohort and Longitudinal Studies Enhancement Resources, ESRC, 2013–; Member: UK Statistics Authy, 2008–15 (Dep. Chm., 2012–15); Royal Soc. Section 10 Cttee, 2010–12; Public Sector Transparency Bd, 2013–15; State Honours Cttee, 2018–. President: Remote Sensing and Photogrammetric Soc., 2003–09; British Exploring (formerly British Schs Exploring) Soc., 2010–18 (Vice-Pres., 2007–10). Trustee, Nuffield Foundn, 2008–18 (Chm., 2010–18); Chm., Bank of England Pension Trustees, 2009–12. Governor: City of London Girls' Sch., 1999–2001; Ashridge Mgt Coll., 2000–04; NIESR, 2004–. Mem. Council, 2003–04, Mem. F and GP Cttee, 2003–08, Royal Soc.; Hon. Sec., RGS, 1988–91. CCMI (CIMgt 1998). Hon. FBA 2002; Hon. FCII 2004. Hon. Fellow, QMUL, 2007. Hon. DSc: Bristol, 1993; Loughborough, 1996; Southampton, 1998; Kingston, 1999; Durham, 2001; London Metropolitan, 2003; Royal Holloway, London, 2004; St Petersburg State Poly., 2007; Edinburgh, 2009; City Univ. London, 2011; Aberdeen, 2015. Centenary Medal, RSGS, 1992; Patron's Medal, RGS, 1997; Decade Award for Achievement, Assoc. for Geographic Inf., 1997. *Publications*: (jtly) Land Use, 1980; The Census User's Handbook, 1983; (jtly) Atlas of EEC Affairs, 1984; (jtly) Geographical Information Systems, 1991, revised 1999; (jtly) Postcodes: the new geography, 1992; Framework for the World, 1997; (jtly) Geographical Information Systems and Science, 2001, 4th edn 2015; numerous papers on map-making, geographical information systems and information policy. *Recreations*: travelling, mowing the lawn, coping with seven grandchildren. *Address*: 1 Cold Harbour Close, Wickham, Hants PO17 5PT.

**RHODES, Andrew Jon**; Registrar and Chief Operating Officer, Swansea University, since 2018; *b* Neath, 10 Oct. 1977; *m* 2005, Sarah Nichols; one *s* one *d*. *Educ*: Cefn Saeson Comprehensive Sch.; Neath Coll.; Univ. of Wales, Swansea (BA Hons; MPhil Hist.). Shop asst and sen. trolleyboy, Safeway Stores, 1995–99; Contact Centre Team Leader, NTL, 1999–2001; Technol. Solutions Consultant, PricewaterhouseCoopers, 2001–02; Prin. Officer, Bridgend County BC, 2002–05; Dir, Customer Services, 2007–09, Products and Services, 2009–10, DVLA; Chief Operating Officer, Food Standards Agency, 2010–15; Benefit Services Dir, 2015–16, Dir Gen., Ops, 2016–18, DWP. Mem., Ind. Air Audit Cttee, RAF Air Comd, 2013–. *Recreations*: bad trumpet playing, collecting old bank notes, being pedantic. *Address*: Swansea University, Singleton Park, Swansea SA2 8PP. *Club*: Royal Air Force.

**RHODES, Prof. Daniela**, PhD; FRS 2007; Professor, School of Biological Sciences, since 2011, Professor, Lee Kong Chian School of Medicine, since 2012, and Director, Institute of Structural Biology, since 2014, Nanyang Technological University, Singapore. *Educ*: Tekniska Hogskolan, Orebro (Dip. Chem. Engrg 1969); Univ. of Cambridge (PhD 1982). MRC Laboratory of Molecular Biology: Gp Leader, 1983–94; Sen. Scientist, 1994–2011; Dir of Studies, 2003–06; Fellow, Clare Hall, Cambridge, 1992–2013, now Emeritus Fellow. Former Visiting Professor: La Sapienza, Rome; Rockefeller Univ., NY. Mem., EMBO, 1996 (Mem., 2007–12, Chm., 2009–12, Council). MAE 2011. *Publications*: contribs to jls incl. Molecular Cell, Molecular Biol., Proc. NAS. *Address*: School of Biological Sciences, Nanyang Technological University, 50 Nanyang Avenue, Singapore 639798.

**RHODES, Gary**, OBE 2006; chef and restaurateur; *b* 22 April 1960; *s* of Jean Rhodes (*née* Ferris) and step *s* of John Smellie; *m* 1989, (Yolanda) Jennifer Adkins; two *s*. *Educ*: Thanet Technical Coll., Broadstairs (C&G qualifs; Student of the Year, Chef of the Year, 1979). Commis, then Chef de Partie, Amsterdam Hilton, 1979–81; Sous Chef: Reform Club, 1982–83; Capital Hotel, Knightsbridge, 1983–85; Head Chef: Whitehall, Broxted, 1985–86; Castle Hotel, Taunton, 1986–90 (Michelin Star, annually, 1986–90); The Greenhouse, London, 1990–96 (Michelin Star, 1996); Chef and Co-Proprietor: city rhodes, 1997–2003 (Michelin Star, annually 1997–2003); Rhodes in the Square, 1998–2003 (Michelin Star, 1998–2003); Rhodes & Co., Manchester, and Edinburgh, 1999–2002 (Bib Gourmand Award, 2001); Rhodes at the Calabash Hotel, Grenada, 2003–; Rhodes Twenty Four, 2003– (Michelin Star, 2004–); Arcadian Rhodes, P&O liner, 2005–11; Oriana Rhodes, P&O liner, 2006–11; Rhodes D7, Dublin, 2006–09; Rhodes W1 Restaurant, London, 2007– (Michelin Star, 2008–); Rhodes W1 (formerly Mezzanine), Dubai, 2007–; Kings Rhodes, 2008–09; Rhodes South, 2008–10; Rhodes Twenty 10, Dubai; Rhodes The Dome, Plymouth. Jt owner, Rhokett Patisserie, 2002–. Hon. Prof., Thames Valley Univ., 2003. FCGI 2005. *Television series*: Hot Chefs, 1988; Rhodes Around Britain, 1994; More Rhodes Around Britain, 1995; Open Rhodes Around Britain, 1996; Gary Rhodes, 1997; Gary's Perfect Christmas, 1998; Gary Rhodes' New British Classics, 1999; Masterchef, 2001; At the Table, 2001; Spring into Summer, 2002; Autumn into Winter, 2002; Hell's Kitchen, 2005; Rhodes Across India, 2007; Rhodes Across China, 2008; Rhodes Across the Caribbean, 2009; Rhodes Across Italy, 2010; columnist, BBC Good Food magazine, 1996–. *Publications*: Rhodes Around Britain, 1994; More Rhodes Around Britain, 1995; Open Rhodes Around Britain, 1996; Short-cut Rhodes, 1997; Fabulous Food, 1997; Sweet Dreams, 1998; New British Classics, 1999; At the Table, 2000; Spring into Summer, 2002; Autumn into Winter, 2002; The Complete Cookery Year, 2003; Keeping it Simple, 2005; Time to Eat, 2007; Rhodes 365, 2008. *Recreations*: driving, art, fashion. *Clubs*: Les Ambassadeurs, St James's.

**RHODES, John Andrew**; independent public transport consultant, 1999–2014; *b* 22 May 1949; *s* of George and Elsie Rhodes; *m* 1985, Marie Catherine Carleton. *Educ*: Queen Elizabeth Sch., Barnet; Wadham Coll., Oxford (MA Mod. History). Civil Service: various posts in DoE, Cabinet Office, Dept of Transport, 1971–87; Dir Gen., W Yorks PTE, 1988–92; Strategy and Planning Advr, BRB, 1992–93; Dir, Passenger Services Gp, Office of Rail Regulator, 1993–99. Chm., railway industry Delay Attribution Bd, 2004–14. Non-exec. Dir, E and N Herts NHS Trust, 2000–02. Chm., Bishop's Stortford Civic Soc., 2000–07; Pres., Bishop's Stortford Civic Fedn, 2014– (Vice-Chm., 2007–12). Hon. Sen. Res. Fellow, Constitution Unit, UCL, 2001–12. *Recreations*: music, history, gardening. *Address*: 26 Warwick Road, Bishop's Stortford, Herts CM23 5NW. *T*: (01279) 656482.
*See also* P. J. Rhodes.

**RHODES, Sir John (Christopher Douglas)**, 4th Bt *cr* 1919; *b* 24 May 1946; *s* of Sir Christopher Rhodes, 3rd Bt, and Mary Florence, *d* of late Dr Douglas Wardleworth; *S* father, 1964. *Heir*: *b* Michael Philip James Rhodes [*b* 3 April 1948; *m* 1973, Susan, *d* of Patrick Roney-Dougal; one *d*].

**RHODES, Prof. John David**, CBE 2000 (OBE 1992); PhD, DSc; FRS 1993; FREng; Chairman, 1994, Group Chief Executive, 2006, Filtronic plc (formerly Filtronic Comtek plc); Industrial Professor, Leeds University, since 1981, now Emeritus; *b* 9 Oct. 1943; *s* of Jack and Florence Rhodes; *m* 1965, Barbara Margaret Pearce; one *s* one *d*. *Educ*: Univ. of Leeds (BSc, PhD, DSc). FIEEE 1980; FIET (FIEE 1984); FREng (FEng 1987). Leeds University: Res. Asst, 1964–66; Res. Fellow, 1966–67; Sen. Res. Engr, Microwave Develt Labs, USA, 1967–69; Leeds University: Lectr, 1969–72; Reader, 1972–75; Prof., 1975–81.

Chm., and CEO Filtronic Ltd, 1977–2004. Hon. DEng: Bradford, 1988; Leeds, 2004; Hon. DSc Napier, 1995. Prince Philip Medal, Royal Acad. of Engrg, 2003. *Publications:* Theory of Electrical Filters, 1976. *Recreation:* golf. *Address:* Dabarda, West Winds, Moor Lane, Menston, Ilkley LS29 6QD.

**RHODES, John David McKinnon;** Advice Volunteer, Southwark Day Centre for Asylum Seekers, since 2016 (Trustee, since 2017); *b* 20 Aug. 1950; *s* of late John Ivor McKinnon Rhodes, CMG and Eden Annetta Rhodes; *m* 1984, Sarah Elizabeth Rickard; two *s* one *d*. *Educ:* Dulwich Coll.; Sussex Univ. (BA Hons); London Business Sch. (Sloan Fellow 1983). With Lithotype Inc., 1971–72; joined Department of Trade and Industry, 1972: Principal Private Sec. to Sec. of State for Trade, 1981–83; Asst Sec., Internat. Projects, 1984–86; Director: British Trade and Investment Office (USA), NY, 1987–90; EC Single Market Policy, 1991–94; Electricity and Nuclear Fuels, 1994–96; Nuclear Sponsorship, 1996–97; Sec., Low Pay Commn, 1997–98; Director: Infrastructure and Energy Projects, 1998–2000; BNFL Partnership Team, 2000–02; Dir, Innovation Gp, 2002–04; voluntary and public sector consultancy, 2005; Hd of Financial Capability, Citizens Advice, 2006–11. Advice Volunteer, Southwark CAB, 2012–16; Trustee: St Andrew's Westminster Youth Club, 2015–; Southwark Law Centre, 2015– (Chair, 2018–). *Recreations:* family, friends, cooking, walking. *Address:* 31 Holly Grove, SE15 5DF. *E:* jdmrhodes@btinternet.com.

**RHODES, Prof. Jonathan Michael,** MD; FRCP, FMedSci; Professor of Medicine, University of Liverpool, 1995–2014, now Emeritus; Consultant Gastroenterologist, Royal Liverpool University Hospital, 1991–2015; *b* 21 April 1949; *s* of late Wilfred Harry Rhodes and Ellen Linda Rhodes (*née* Wreford); *m* 1st, 1978, Elizabeth Geraldine Helen Morris (*d* 2007); three *d*; 2nd, 2009, Collette Marie Clifford. *Educ:* Kingston Grammar Sch.; St John's Coll., Cambridge (MA); St Thomas's Hosp. Med. Sch. (MD 1982). FRCP 1989. House surgeon, St Thomas' Hosp., 1973; house physician and SHO, Kingston Hosp., 1974–75; SHO, Hammersmith Hosp., 1976; Registrar and Res. Fellow, Royal Free Hosp., 1976–81; Sen. Registrar, Queen Elizabeth and Selly Oak Hosps, Birmingham, 1981–85; Sen. Lectr, 1985–91, Reader, 1991–95, Univ. of Liverpool. Pres.-elect, 2002–03, Pres., 2003–04, Liverpool Medical Inst. Pres., British Soc. Gastroenterology, 2010–12; Chm., Gastroenterology Speciality Cttee, RCP, 1997–2001; Member: Exec. Cttee, Assoc. Physicians, 1999–2001; Council, RCP, 2003–06. FMedSci 1999. Avery Jones Res. Medal, British Soc. Gastroenterology, 1989; Bengt Ihre Medal, Swedish Med. Assoc., 2005. *Publications:* (ed jtly) Inflammatory Bowel Disease, 3rd edn 1997; contrib. papers on inflammatory bowel disease, colon cancer, lectins and glycobiology. *Recreations:* fell-walking, classical guitar, rowing coaching. *Address:* Department of Cellular and Molecular Physiology, Institute of Translational Medicine, University of Liverpool, Henry Wellcome Laboratory, Nuffield Building, Crown Street, Liverpool L69 3GE. *T:* (0151) 794 6822. *Clubs:* Hawks (Cambridge); Leander (Henley); Bristol Owners.

**RHODES, Nicholas Piers;** QC 2008; a Recorder, since 2002; *b* 26 April 1958; *s* of Colin and Charlotte Rhodes; *m* 1999, Sally Ann Matthews; two *s*. *Educ:* Dover Coll. Jun. Sch.; Dover Coll.; Univ. of E Anglia (LLB Hons); Inns of Court Sch. of Law. Called to the Bar, Lincoln's Inn, 1981. *Recreation:* military history. *Address:* Charter Chambers, 33 John Street, WC1N 2AT. *T:* (020) 7618 4400, *Fax:* (020) 7618 4401. *E:* Nick.Rhodes@charterchambers.com.

**RHODES, Prof. Peter John,** FBA 1987; Professor of Ancient History, University of Durham, 1983–2005, Hon. Professor, since 2005; *b* 10 Aug. 1940; *s* of George Thomas Rhodes and Elsie Leonora Rhodes (*née* Pugh); *m* 1971, Jan Teresa Adamson (marr. diss. 2001, she *d* 2014). *Educ:* Queen Elizabeth's Boys' Grammar Sch., Barnet; Wadham Coll., Oxford (minor schol.; BA 1st cl. Mods, 1st cl. Greats); Merton Coll., Oxford (MA; DPhil). Harmsworth Schol., Merton Coll., Oxford, 1963–65; Craven Fellow, Oxford Univ., 1963–65; Lectr in Classics and Ancient History, 1965, Sen. Lectr, 1977, Durham Univ. Jun. Fellow, Center for Hellenic Studies, Washington, DC, 1978–79; Visiting Fellow: Wolfson Coll., Oxford, 1984; Univ. of New England, Aust., 1988; Corpus Christi Coll., Oxford, 1993; All Souls Coll., Oxford, 1998; Leverhulme Res. Fellow, 1994–95; Langford Family Eminent Scholar, Florida State Univ., 2002; Mem., Inst. for Advanced Study, Princeton, USA, 1988–89; Invitation Fellow, Japan Soc. for the Promotion of Sci., 2005; Fellow, Fondazione Lorenzo Valla, 2010. Sackler Lectr, Tel Aviv Univ., 2013. Pres., Classical Assoc., 2014–15. Foreign Mem., Royal Danish Acad., 2005. Chancellor's Medal, Durham Univ., 2015. *Publications:* The Athenian Boule, 1972; Greek Historical Inscriptions 359–323 BC, 1972; Commentary on the Aristotelian Athenaion Politeia, 1981; (trans.) Aristotle: the Athenian Constitution, 1984; The Athenian Empire, 1985; The Greek City States: a source book, 1986, 2nd edn 2007; (ed) Thucydides Book II, 1988; (ed) Thucydides Book III, 1994; (with D. M. Lewis) The Decrees of the Greek States, 1997; (ed with L. G. Mitchell) The Development of the Polis in Archaic Greece, 1997; (ed) Thucydides Book IV.1–Book V.24, 1999; Ancient Democracy and Modern Ideology, 2003; (with R. Osborne) Greek Historical Inscriptions 404–323 BC, 2003; (ed) Athenian Democracy, 2004; A History of the Classical Greek World 478–323 BC, 2005, 2nd edn 2010; (ed with E. E. Bridges and E. M. Hall) Cultural Responses to the Persian Wars, 2007; (ed with J. L. Marr) The 'Old Oligarch', 2008; (trans. and commentary with M. Hammond) Thucydides: the Peloponnesian War, 2009; Alcibiades, 2011; A Short History of Ancient Greece, 2014; (ed) Thucydides Book I, 2014; Atthis, 2014; (ed, trans. and commentary with D. F. Leão) The Laws of Solon, 2015; Thucydides, 2015; Ktema Es Aiei (A Possession for All Time), 2015; (ed with V. Gouschin) Deformations and Crises of Ancient Civil Communities, 2015; Aristotele, Costituzione degli Ateniesi, 2016; The Athenian Constitution Written in the School of Aristotle, 2017; (with R. Osborne) Greek Historical Inscriptions 478–404 BC, 2017; Periclean Athens, 2018; articles and reviews in jls. *Recreations:* music, typography, travel. *Address:* Department of Classics, University of Durham, 38 North Bailey, Durham DH1 3EU. *T:* (0191) 334 1670.
See also J. A. Rhodes.

**RHODES, Richard David Walton;** JP; Police and Crime Commissioner (C) for Cumbria, 2012–16; *b* 20 April 1942; *er s* of Harry Walton Rhodes and Dorothy Rhodes (*née* Fairhurst); *m* 1966, Stephanie Heyes, 2nd *d* of Frederic William Heyes and Catherine Heyes; two *d*. *Educ:* Rossall Sch.; St John's Coll., Durham (BA 1963); Hertford Coll., Oxford (DipEd 1964). Asst Master, St John's Sch., Leatherhead, 1964–75 (Founder Housemaster, Montgomery House, 1973–75); Deputy Headmaster, Arnold Sch., Blackpool, 1975–79; Headmaster, 1979–87; Headmaster, then Principal, Rossall Sch., 1987–2001. Member: Lancs CC Social Services Adv. Cttee, 1992–2001; Lancs Magistrates' Courts Cttee, 1993–96. Chairman: NW Div., HMC, 1987; Northern ISIS, 1993–95. Lay Member: Family Health Services Appeal Authy, 2002–10; First-tier Tribunal Service, 2010–12. Member: Independent Remuneration Panel, South Lakeland DC, 2003–08; Cumbria Probation Bd, 2004–08; Chair: Cumbria Bd, Nat. Probation Service, 2008–10; Cumbria Probation Trust, 2011–12; non-exec. Dir, Probation Assoc., 2011–12. JP Member: Cumbria Courts Bd, 2004–07; Cumbrian Lancs Courts Bd, 2007–11. Chairman: Cumbria Cons. Assoc., 2017–; Staveley in Cartmel Parish Council, 2019–. Member Council: Univ. of Salford, 1987–93; Lawrence House Sch., Lytham St Annes, 1988–93; Trustee, Lawrence House Trust, 1994–97 (Chm., 2000–08); Gov., Terra Nova Sch., Jodrell Bank, 1989–2005 (Chm. Govs, 2000–05). JP Fylde, 1978, Wyre, 1999, Furness, 2002. *Recreations:* photography, sports, motoring, gardening in the Lake District. *Address:* Fairview, Staveley in Cartmel, Newby Bridge, Ulverston, Cumbria LA12 8NS. *T:* (01539) 531634.

**RHODES, Robert Elliott;** QC 1989; a Recorder, 1987–2018; *b* 2 Aug. 1945; *s* of late Gilbert R. Rhodes, FCA and Elly, who *m* 2nd, Leopold Brook (he *d* 2007); *m* 1971, Georgina Caroline (marr. diss. 1996), *d* of late Jack Gerald Clarfelt; two *s* one *d*. *Educ:* St Paul's School; Pembroke Coll., Oxford (MA). Called to the Bar, Inner Temple, 1968, Bencher, 2007. Accredited Mediator, 2007; qualified Arbitrator, 2013. Second Prosecuting Counsel to Inland Revenue at Central Criminal Court and Inner London Crown Courts, 1979, First Prosecuting Counsel, 1981–89. Hd of Chambers, 1998–2003. Senior International Mediation Expert: Mainland-Hong Kong Mediation Center, 2017–; Internat. Dispute Resolution and Risk Mgt Inst., 2018–. Deputy Chairman: IMRO Membership Tribunal Panel, 1992–2001; ICAEW Appeal Cttee, 1998–2004; a Financial Reporting Council (formerly AIDB, then AADB) Chm. of Disciplinary Tribunals, 2004–14. Advr, Arbitration and ADR Center, Central Univ. of Finance and Econs, Beijing, 2012–; Member: Panel of Mediators, China Council for Promotion of Internat. Trade, 2013–16; Panel of Mediators and Arbitrators, Lang Fang Arbitration Commn, People's Republic of China, 2013; Mediator Panel, Japan Internat. Mediation Center, Kyoto, 2018–; Panel of Mediators, Internat. Ct of Arbitration for Sport, Switzerland, 2018–; Panel of Arbitrators: Thai Arbitration Inst., 2013–; Chinese Arbitration Inst., 2013–; Arbitration and Mediation Ct of the Caribbean; arbitrator, Global Panel of Dist. Neutrals, Internat. Inst. for Conflict Prevention and Resolution, 2014–. *Recreations:* opera, ballet, theatre, reading, art, cricket, real tennis, former international fencer. *Address:* Outer Temple, 222–225 Strand, WC2R 1BA. *T:* (020) 7353 6381. *Clubs:* Garrick, MCC; Epee.

**RHODES, Dame Zandra (Lindsey),** DBE 2014 (CBE 1997); RDI 1976; DesRCA, FCSD; Managing Director, Zandra Rhodes Enterprises; Chancellor, University for the Creative Arts, 2010–18; *b* 19 Sept. 1940; *d* of Albert James Rhodes and Beatrice Ellen (*née* Twigg). *Educ:* Medway Technical Sch. for Girls, Chatham; Medway Coll. of Art; Royal Coll. of Art (DesRCA 1964). FSIAD 1982. With Alexander MacIntyre, set up print factory and studio, 1965; sold designs (and converted them on to cloth) to Foale and Tuffin and Roger Nelson; formed partnership with Sylvia Ayton and began producing dresses using her own prints, 1966; opened Fulham Road Clothes Shop, designing dresses as well as prints, first in partnership, 1967–68, then (Fulham Road shop closed) alone, producing first clothes range in which she revolutionised use of prints in clothes by cutting round patterns to make shapes never before used; took collection to USA, 1969; sold to Fortnum and Mason, London, 1969, Piero de Monzi, 1971; began building up name and business in USA (known for her annual spectacular Fantasy Shows); also started designing in jersey and revolutionised its treatment with lettuce edges and seams on the outside; with Knight and Stirling founded Zandra Rhodes (UK) Ltd and Zandra Rhodes (Shops) Ltd, 1975–86; opened first shop in London, 1975; others opened in Bloomingdale's NY, Marshall Field, Chicago, Seibu, Tokyo and Harrods, London, 1976; new factory premises opened in Hammersmith, London, 1984; closed Mayfair shop, 1991, to show on a more personal and individual scale in her Hammersmith showroom. Since 1976 Zandra Rhodes has tried to reach a wider public through licensing her name in UK, USA, Australia and Japan, making full use of the Zandra Rhodes textile design talent for: wallpapers and furnishing fabrics, bathmats, men's ties, sheets and bed linen, printed shawls and scarves, hosiery, teatowels, kitchen accessories and jewellery. Notable licences include: Eve Stillman Lingerie (USA), 1977, Wamsutta sheets and pillowcases (USA), 1976, CVP Designs interior fabrics and settings (UK), 1977, Philip Hockley Decorative Furs (UK), 1986 and Zandra Rhodes Saris (India), 1987 (which she launched with 'West meets East' shows of Saris and Shalwar Chamises in Bombay and Delhi—the first Western designer to do so), Littlewoods Catalogues (UK), 1988 for printed T-shirts and Intasia sweaters; Hilmet silk scarves and men's ties (UK); 1989; Bonnay perfume, Coats Patons needlepoint (UK), 1993; Pologeorgis Furs (USA), Zandra Rhodes II handpainted ready-to-wear collection (HK, China), 1995; Grattons Catalogue sheets and duvets (UK), 1996; range of printed tops for Topshop (UK), 2002; Jewellery Licence, 2002; China licence for Royal Doulton, 2004. Designed stand with furniture and carpet for Hanover Expo, 2000. Designed: costumes for Magic Flute, San Diego Opera, 2001; costumes and sets for: Pearl Fishers, San Diego and Michigan, 2004, San Francisco and NY, 2005; Aida, ENO, 2007. Solo exhibitions: Oriel, Cardiff (Welsh Arts Council), 1978; Texas Gall., Houston, 1981; Otis Parsons, Los Angeles, 1981; La Jolla Museum of Contemporary Art, San Diego, 1982; ADITI Creative Power, Barbican Centre, 1982; Sch. of Art Inst., Chicago, 1982; Parsons Sch. of Design, NY, 1982; Art Museum of Santa Cruz Co., Calif, 1983; retrospective exhibition of 'Works of Art' with textiles, Museum of Art, El Paso, Texas, 1984; retrospective of Garments & Textiles (also Lead Speaker for Art to Wear exhibn), Columbus, Ohio, 1987; retrospectives for Seibu Seed Hall, Seibu, Tokyo, 1987 and 1991; Mint Mus., N Carolina, 1992; Athenæum Liby, La Jolla, 1996; water colour exhibition: Dyansen Galls, NY, LA and New Orleans, 1989; major group exhibitions: Nat. Gall. of Australia, 1993; V&A, 1994; RCA 1996. Work represented in major costume collections: UK: V&A; City Mus. and Art Gall., Stoke-on-Trent; Bath Mus.; Royal Pavilion Brighton Mus.; Platt Fields Costume Mus., Manchester; City Art Gall., Leeds; overseas: Metropolitan Mus., NY; Chicago Historical Soc.; Smithsonian Instn; Royal Ontario Mus.; Mus. of Applied Arts and Scis, Sydney; Nat. Mus. of Victoria, Melbourne; La Jolla Mus. of Contemp. Art; LA County Mus. of Art. Opening speaker, Famous Women of Fashion, Smithsonian Instn, Washington, 1978. Founded Fashion & Textile Mus., Bermondsey, 1996, opened to public, 2003. Hon. DFA Internat. Fine Arts Coll., Miami, Florida, 1986; Hon. Dr RCA, 1986; Hon. DD CNAA, 1987; Hon. DLitt Westminster, 2000; Hon. Dr London Inst., 2000; Hon. DHL Acad. of Art Coll., San Francisco, 2001. Designer of the Year, English Fashion Trade UK, 1972; Emmy Award for Best Costume Designs in Romeo and Juliet on Ice, CBS TV, 1984; Woman of Distinction award, Northwood Inst., Dallas, 1986; Top UK Textile Designer, Observer, 1990; Hall of Fame Award, British Fashion Council, 1995; citations and commendations from USA estabs. *Publications:* The Art of Zandra Rhodes, 1984, US edn 1985; The Zandra Rhodes Collection by Brother, 1988. *Recreations:* travelling, drawing, gardening, cooking. *Address:* (office) 79–85 Bermondsey Street, SE1 3XF. *T:* (020) 7403 5333, *Fax:* (020) 7403 0555. *E:* zrhodesent@newham.ac.uk.

**RHYMES, Rupert John,** OBE 2002; Trustee and Chairman, The Theatres Trust, 2002–09; Director, 2002–07 and Chairman, 2003–07, Bristol Old Vic; Vice President, Frank Matcham Society, since 2016 (Chairman, 2011–16); *b* 24 June 1940; *s* of Elson John Rhymes and Phyllis Rhymes (*née* Rawlings); *m* 1970, Susan Mary Chennells; one *s* one *d*. *Educ:* King Edward's Sch., Bath; Magdalen Coll., Oxford (BA Mod. Hist. 1962; MA). Box Office Clerk, RSC, Aldwych Theatre, 1962; Asst Manager, Sadler's Wells Theatre, 1963; Theatre Manager, Nat. Theatre, Old Vic, 1963–69; Sadler's Wells Opera, then English National Opera, 1969–87: Asst to Admin. Dir, then Head of Press and Publicity, then Gen. Manager, 1969–72, Co. Sec., and Admin. Dir, 1972–87; Chief Executive: SOLT, 1987–2001; Theatrical Mgt Assoc., 1987–2001. Chm., Oxford Stage Co., 1987–97. Director: West End Theatre Managers, 1978–87 (Pres., 1979–82; Vice Pres., 1982–83); Theatre Investment Fund, 1982–2010; Nat. Campaign for the Arts, 1988–2001 (Vice Chm., 1999–2001); Nat. Council for Drama Trng, 1997–2001. Director: JFMG Ltd,

1997–2009; Wheelshare, 2007–12; Peter Saunders Gp Ltd, 2007–19; Perspectiv, 2017–. Founding Mem., later Mem. Exec. Council, Performing Arts Employers Assocs League, Europe, 1991–2001 (Chm., 2000–01). Trustee: Raymond Mander and Joe Mitchenson Theatre Collection, 1977–2001 (Chm., 1986–2001); Motley Design Course, 1985–; Chichester Fest. Theatre, 1998–2000; Stephen Arlen Meml Fund, 1993–; Olivier Foundn, 2007–09; Peggy Ramsay Foundn, 2009–15. Gov., Central Sch. of Speech and Drama, 1990–2002 (Vice Chm., 1991–92). *Recreations:* finding time for theatre, protesting against further destruction in the city of Bath. *Address:* Honeysuckle Farm, Perrymead, Bath BA2 5AU. *T:* (01225) 834188.

**RHYS,** family name of **Baron Dynevor**.

**RHYS, Judith Stella, (Judi);** Chief Executive Officer, Tenovus Cancer Care, since 2019; *b* Neath, Wales, 28 March 1960; *d* of Mervyn Landeg and late Margaret Landeg; *m* 1st, 1981, Dr Stephen Bowsher (marr. diss. 2005); two *s*; 2nd, 2007, Dr Martin Rhys; one step *s* one step *d. Educ:* St Clare's Convent Grammar Sch., Porthcawl; Porthcawl Comprehensive Sch.; Open Univ. (BA Hons 1991; PGCE 2002); Univ. of Wales Coll. of Medicine (MSc 1995). Health promotion specialist, Mid-Glamorgan, 1990–99; Associate Lectr (pt-time), 1992–2003, Staff Tutor, 1999–2003, Open Univ.; Trng and Develt Manager, Cardiff Univ., 2003–05; Health Improvement Team Leader, Caerphilly CBC, 2005–06; Director: Diabetes UK, 2006–08; MS Soc., 2008–13; Chief Executive Officer: Arthritis Care, 2013–17; British Liver Trust, 2017–19. Springboard consultancy trainer, 2008–. Ind. Mem., Public Health Wales NHS Trust, 2017–. Non-exec. Dir, Sport Wales, 2018–. Mem. Bd, Samaritans Cymru, 2014–19. Trustee, Nat. Voices, 2015–18. *Recreations:* running, travel, the arts, walking. *Address:* Public Health Wales, 2 Capital Quarter, Tyndall Street, Cardiff CF10 4BZ. *T:* 07506 856534. *E:* judirhys@gmail.com.

**RHYS-JAMES, Shani,** MBE 2006; artist; *b* 2 May 1953; *d* of Harold Marcus Rhys-James and Jean (*née* Barker); *m* 1977, Stephen Alexander West; two *s. Educ:* Parliament Hill Girls' Sch.; Loughborough Coll. of Art; St Martin's Sch. of Art (BA Hons). Major touring exhibitions: Blood Ties, Wrexham Arts Centre, 1993; Facing the Self, Oriel Mostyn, Llandudno, 1997; The Black Cot, Aberystwyth Arts Centre, 2003; one person shows: Beaux Arts Gall., Bath, 1992; Martin Tinney Gall., Cardiff, 1993, 1995, 1998, 2003, 2005, 2008, 2010; The Inner Room, Stephen Lacey Gall., London, 2000; Connaught Brown Gall., London, 2009, 2012, 2015; Hillsboro Fine Art, Dublin, 2010; Aberystwyth Arts Centre, and tour, 2013; The Rivalry of Flowers, Kings Place Gall., London, and tour, 2013; Oriel Tegfryn, 2014; Distillation, Nat. Liby of Wales, 2015; Ceredigion Mus., 2015. Artist Advr, Purchasing Panel, Derek Williams Trust, Nat. Mus. Wales, 2006–11. Residency, Columbia Univ., NY, 2015. Hon. Fellow: UWIC, 2007; Hereford Coll. of Art, 2008. Mem., RCA, 1994. Gold Medal, Nat. Eisteddfod, 1992; Hunting/Observer Prize 1993; Welsh BBC Artist of the Year Award, 1994; Jerwood Painting Prize, 2003; Creative Wales Award, Welsh Arts Council, 2006. *Publications:* Facing the Self, 1997; The Inner Room, 2000; (with Eve Ropek) The Black Cot, 2003; Imaging the Imagination, 2005; 'Cassandra's Rant' artists book, 2006; The Rivalry of Flowers, 2013; The Spider, the Plants and the Black Black Cot, 2015; exhibition catalogues. *Recreations:* writing, vegetable gardening, restoring, music. *Address:* Dolpebyll, Llangadfan, Powys SY21 0PU. *T:* (01938) 820469. *E:* shanirhysjames@btinternet.com.

**RHYS JONES, Griffith,** OBE 2019; actor, writer, director and producer; *b* 16 Nov. 1953; *s* of Elwyn Rhys Jones and Gwynneth Margaret Jones; *m* 1981, Joanna Frances Harris; one *s* one *d. Educ:* Brentwood Sch.; Emmanuel Coll., Cambridge (Hon. Fellow 2007). BBC Radio Producer, 1976–79; *television:* Not the Nine O'Clock News (also co-writer), 1979–81; Alas Smith and Jones (also co-writer), 1982–87; Porterhouse Blue (serial), 1987; The World according to Smith and Jones, 1987; Small Doses (series of short plays) (writer, Boat People), 1989; A View of Harry Clark, 1989; Smith and Jones (also co-writer), 1992, 1995, 1997, 1998; Demob (drama series), 1993; Bookworm (presenter), 1994–2000; Restoration (presenter), 2003, 2004; Mine All Mine (drama serial), 2004; The Secret Life of Arthur Ransome, 2005; Betjeman and Me, 2006; Kipling: a remembrance tale, 2006; Restoration Village (presenter), 2006; Building Britain, 2007; A Pembrokeshire Farm, 2006, 2009; Three Men in a Boat, 2006, 2008–11; Mountain (writer and presenter), 2007; Charles Dickens and the Invention of Christmas, 2007; Greatest Cities of the World with Griff Rhys Jones, 2008, 2010; The Heart of Thomas Hardy, 2008; It'll be Alright on the Night, 2008; Losing It, 2008; Why Poetry Matters, 2009; Rivers with Griff Rhys Jones, 2009; The Prince's Welsh Village, 2010; Hidden Treasures of… (presenter), 2011; Three Men Go to Venice, 2011; A Short History of Everything Else, 2012; Britain's Lost Routes with Griff Rhys Jones, 2012; The Wind in the Willows, 2012; Burma, My Father and the Forgotten Army, 2013; A Great Welsh Adventure with Griff Rhys Jones, 2014; A Poet in New York (exec. prod.), 2014; National Treasures of Wales, 2014; The Quizeum, 2015; Slow Train Through Africa, 2015; Griff's Great Britain, 2016; Murder on the Blackpool Express, 2017; *theatre:* Charley's Aunt, 1983; Trumpets and Raspberries, 1985; The Alchemist, 1985; Arturo Ui, 1987; Smith & Jones (also co-writer), 1989–98; Thark, 1989; The Wind in the Willows, RNT, 1990; dir, Twelfth Night, RSC, 1991; The Revengers' Comedies, Strand, 1991; An Absolute Turkey, Globe, 1994; Plunder, Savoy, 1996; The Front Page, Donmar, 1997; Horse and Carriage, W Yorks Playhouse, 2001; Oliver, Drury Lane, 2009–10; (solo stand-up) Jones & Smith, UK tour, 2016; The Miser, Garrick, 2017; *films:* Morons from Outer Space, 1985; Wilt, 1989; As You Like It, 1992; Staggered, 1994; Up and Under, 1998; Taliesin Jones, 2000; Puckoon, 2003; *opera:* Die Fledermaus, Royal Opera Covent Garden, 1989; *radio* series: (also writer) Do Go On, 1997–; (also writer) Griff Rhys Jones show, 2000–03. President: Civic Trust, 2008–09; Civic Voice, 2009–; Vice Pres., Victorian Soc. Director: TalkBack, Advertising and Production; Playback, 1987–; Smith Jones Campbell (formerly Smith Jones Brown & Cassie), 1988–99; Modern Television, 2005–. Chm., Hackney Empire Appeal Cttee, 1998–2004. FRWCMD (FWCMD 1997); FRSA 2002. *Publications:* (jtly) The Smith and Jones World Atlas, 1983; The Lavishly Tooled Smith and Jones, 1986; (jtly) Janet lives with Mel and Griff, 1988; (jtly) Smith & Jones Head to Head, 1992; To the Baltic with Bob, 2003; Semi-Detached, 2006; Mountain: exploring Britain's high places, 2007; Rivers: a voyage into the heart of Britain, 2009; Insufficiently Welsh, 2014. *Address:* c/o Troika, 180 Great Portland Street, W1W 5QZ.

**RHYS JONES, Sandra Yvonne, (Sandi),** OBE 1998; FCIOB; management consultant, change agent and advocate for women in construction; Founding Partner, RhysJones Consultants, since 1976; *b* 26 May 1946; *d* of Ralph and Stella Wyndham; *m* 1968, Roderick Rhys Jones; three *s. Educ:* King's Coll., London (MSc Construction Law and Arbitration 1994). Accredited Mediator, Centre for Dispute Resolution, 1995. Work in advertising, tech. journalism and PR, 1964–76. Non-executive Director: DLR, 1998–2000; Simons Gp Ltd, 2002–09; Engrg UK, 2008–14; Envirobuild Ltd; Kennington Place Mgt. Chair and mem., govt and construction industry wkg gps, 1994–2004. Chair of Trustees, Women's Educn in Building, 1997–2002; Dep. Chair of Trustees, Royal Marines Mus., 2002–12; Mem., SeaMore Project Bd, Nat. Mus. of RN, 2015–. Mem., Develt Gp, London Mozart Players. ACIArb 1993; MCIM 1998; CCMI 2012; FCIOB 2003; FWES 2015. Hon. Dr Sheffield Hallam, 2005. *Publications:* Tomorrow's Team: women and men in construction, 1996; (contrib.) Managing Diversity and Equality in Construction, 2006; Never Waste a Good Crisis, 2009. *Recreations:* building projects, slow food, fast conversation with family and friends, music, trying to write better haiku in less time. *E:* sandi@rhysjones.com.

**RHYS WILLIAMS, Sir (Arthur) Gareth (Ludovic Emrys),** 3rd Bt *cr* 1918, of Miskin, Parish of Llantrisant, Co. Glamorgan; CEng, FIET, FIMechE; Government Chief Commercial Officer, Cabinet Office, since 2016; *b* 9 Nov. 1961; *s* of Sir Brandon Rhys Williams, 2nd Bt, MP and Caroline Susan, *e d* of L. A. Foster; *S* father, 1988; *m* 1996, Harriet, *d* of Maj. Tom Codner; two *s* one *d. Educ:* Eton; Durham Univ. (BSc Hons Eng); Insead (MBA). Materials Manager, Lucas CAV, 1987–88; Managing Director: NFI Electronics, 1990–93; Rexam Custom Europe, 1992–96; Reg. Man. Dir, Central Europe, BPB plc, 1996–2000; Chief Executive Officer: Vitec Gp plc, 2001–08; Capital Safety Ltd, 2008–10; Charter Internat. plc, 2011–12; PHS Gp plc, 2012–15. Mem. Council, FFI, 2012–. CCMI. *Recreations:* sailing, conjuring, shooting, travel. *Heir: s* Ludo Dhaulagiri Rhys Williams, *b* 12 Oct. 2001. *Address:* 9 Matheson Road, W14 8SN. *Club:* Garrick.

**RIBBANS, Prof. Geoffrey Wilfrid,** MA; Kenan University Professor of Hispanic Studies, Brown University, USA, 1978–99, now Emeritus; *b* 15 April 1927; *o s* of late Wilfrid Henry Ribbans and Rose Matilda Burton; *m* 1956, Magdalena Cumming (*née* Willmann) (*d* 2004), Cologne; one *s* two *d. Educ:* Sir George Monoux Grammar Sch., Walthamstow; King's Coll., Univ. of London. BA Hons Spanish 1st cl., 1948; MA 1953. Asst Lectr, Queen's Univ., Belfast, 1951–52; Asst, St Salvator's Coll., Univ. of St Andrews, 1952–53; Univ. of Sheffield: Asst Lectr, 1953–55; Lectr, 1955–61; Sen. Lectr, 1961–63; Gilmour Prof. of Spanish, Univ. of Liverpool, 1963–78; First Director, Centre for Latin-American Studies, 1966–70; Dean, Faculty of Arts, 1977–78; Chm., Dept of Hispanic and Italian Studies, Brown Univ., USA, 1981–84. Andrew Mellon Vis. Prof., Univ. of Pittsburgh, 1970–71; Leverhulme Res. Fellow, 1975; NEH Univ. Fellowship, 1991; Hon. Prof., Univ. of Sheffield, 1994–; Vis. Prof., Univ. of Salamanca, 1995. Lectures: Fundación Juan March, Madrid, 1984; E. Allison Peers, Univ. of Liverpool, 1985, 1994; Norman Maccoll, Univ. of Cambridge, 1985; Fordham Cervantes, NY, 1988; Raimundo Lida Meml, Harvard, 1998; Joan Gili Meml, Anglo-Catalan Soc., Edinburgh, 2009. Vice-Pres., Internat. Assoc. of Hispanists, 1974–80 (Pres., Local Organising Cttee, 8th Congress, Brown Univ., 1983); Pres., Anglo-Catalan Soc., 1976–78. Dir, Liverpool Playhouse, 1974–78. Editor, Bulletin of Hispanic Studies, 1963–78. Hon. Fellow, Inst. of Linguists, 1972. Corresp. Member: Real Academia de Buenas Letras, Barcelona, 1978; Hispanic Soc. of Amer., 1981. Hon. Mem., N American Catalan Soc., 2001. MA *ad eund* Brown Univ., 1979. Special Prize for excellence in Galdós Studies, Las Palmas, 1997. Encomienda de la Orden de Isabel la Católica (Spain), 1997; J. M. Batista i Roca Prize for contributions to Catalan studies, Barcelona, 2000. *Publications:* Catalunya i València vistes pels viatgers anglesos del segle XVIIIè, 1955, 2nd edn 1993; Niebla y Soledad: aspectos de Unamuno y Machado, 1971; ed, Soledades, Galerías, otros poemas, by Antonio Machado, 1975, 17th rev. edn 2008; Antonio Machado (1875–1939): poetry and integrity, 1975; B. Pérez Galdós: Fortunata y Jacinta, a critical guide, 1977 (trans. Spanish 1989); (ed) Campos de Castilla, by Antonio Machado, 1989, 14th rev. edn 2003; History and Fiction in Galdós's Narratives, 1993; Conflicts and Conciliations: the evolution of Galdós's Fortunata y Jacinta, 1997; numerous articles on Spanish and Catalan literature in specialised publications; *festschrift:* Hispanic Studies in Honour of Geoffrey Ribbans, 1992. *Recreations:* travel, fine art. *Address:* 310 Elmgrove Avenue, Providence, RI 02906–4252, USA.

**RIBEIRO,** family name of **Baron Ribeiro**.

**RIBEIRO, Baron** *cr* 2010 (Life Peer), of Achimota in the Republic of Ghana and of Ovington in the County of Hampshire; **Bernard Francisco Ribeiro,** Kt 2009; CBE 2004; FRCS; FRCP; Consultant General Surgeon, Basildon University Hospital, 1979–2008; President, Royal College of Surgeons of England, 2005–08; *b* 20 Jan. 1944; *s* of Miguel Augustus Ribeiro and Matilda Ribeiro; *m* 1968, Elisabeth Jean Orr; one *s* three *d* (incl. twin *d). Educ:* Dean Close Sch., Cheltenham; Middlesex Hosp. Med. Sch., London (MB BS 1967). LRCP 1967; MRCS 1967, FRCS 1972; FRCSEd (*ad hominem*) 2002; FRCP 2006; FRCA 2008; FRCPSGlas (*qua surgeon ad eundem*) 2008. Registrar, then Sen. Registrar, Middlesex Hosp., 1972–78; Lectr in Urology, Ghana Med. Sch., Accra, 1974. Mem. Bd of Visitors, HM Prison Chelmsford, 1982–92; Surgical Advr to Expert Adv. Gp on Aids (EAGA) and UK Adv. Panel for health care workers infected with blood-borne viruses (UKAP), DoH, 1994–2003; Vis. Prof., Dept of Surgery, Univ. of N Carolina, 2006–07. Hon. Sec., 1991–96, Pres., 1999–2000, Assoc. of Surgeons of GB and Ire; Mem. Council, RCS, 1998–2008 (Mem., Ct of Examrs, 1998–2004; Chm., Quality Assurance and Inspection, 2002–05; Sen. Vice-Pres., 2004–05); Med. Vice Chm. E England, Adv. Cttee on Clinical Excellence Awards, 2002–05; Consultant, Adv. Bd, Amer. Coll. of Surgeons/Health Policy Res. Inst., 2009–14; Chairman: Res. Panel, Pelican Cancer Foundn, 2009–17; Ind. Reconfiguration Panel, 2012–; Confidential Reporting System in Surgery, 2012–. Member: H of L EU Home Affairs Sub-Cttee, 2015–; H of L Refreshment Cttee, 2015–17; Select Cttee on Long Term Sustainability of the NHS, 2016–17. Charles Saint Lect., S Africa, 2007; Arthur Li Oration, Hong Kong, 2007; Vicary Lect., RCS, 2008; Joseph H. Ogura Lect., Triological Soc., Chicago, 2011. Patron: Achimota Trust, 2011–; Operation Hernia, 2011–; RCS, 2011; Lifebox, 2012–; Phi, 2013–. Mem., Exec. Cttee, Assoc. of Cons. Peers, 2012–15. Mem., Test and Itchen Assoc., 1989–. Liveryman, Co. of Barbers, 1997– (Mem., Ct of Assts, 2006–; Master, 2013–14). Mem., Editl Internat. Adv. Bd, Archives of Surgery, 2000–09. Mem. Council, Dean Close Sch., Cheltenham, 2006– (Trustee, 2010–12; Pres., 2016–); Pres., Old Decanians Soc., 2014–. Fellow, Acad. of Medicine, Malaysia, 2006; Hon. Fellow: Ghana Coll. of Physicians and Surgeons, 2006; Caribbean Coll. of Surgeons, 2007; Hon. FDSRCS 2006; Hon. FRCSI 2008; Hon. FACS 2008; Hon. FFGDP(UK) 2009; Hon. Mem., Acad. Nationale de Chirurgie, 2008. Hon. DSc Anglia Ruskin, 2008; Hon. DEng Bath, 2012. Hon. Liveryman, Cutlers' Co., 2008. Officer, Order of the Volta (Ghana), 2008. *Publications:* (contrib.) Concise Surgery, 1998; (contrib.) Emergency Surgery: principles and practice, 2006; contrib. Archives of Surgery, Bull. of RCS. *Recreations:* fishing, riparian activities, shooting, interest in the history of war. *Address:* House of Lords, SW1A 0PW. *T:* (020) 7219 5353. *E:* ribeirob@parliament.uk. *Clubs:* Flyfishers'; Surgical Sixty Travelling.

**RIBEIRO, Roberto Alexandre Vieira;** Hon. Mr Justice Ribeiro; Permanent Judge, Hong Kong Court of Final Appeal, since 2000; *b* 20 March 1949; *s* of late Gilberto and Eleanora Vieira Ribeiro; *m* 1974, Susan Elizabeth Swan (marr. diss. 2017); *m* 2017, Katherine Yip Ching. *Educ:* La Salle Coll., Hong Kong; London Sch. of Econs (LLB 1971, LLM 1972; Hon. Fellow, 2007). Called to the Bar, Inner Temple (Hon. Bencher, 2003) and Hong Kong, 1978; Lectr, Faculty of Law, Univ. of Hong Kong, 1972–79; in practice at Hong Kong Bar, 1979–99; QC (Hong Kong) 1990; Judge, Court of First Instance, 1999, Justice of Appeal, 2000, Hong Kong. Mem., Judicial Officers Recommendation Commn, 2008–14. Pres., Alliance Française, Hong Kong, 2000–16. Board Member: Hong Kong Internat. Film Fest., 2004–; Hong Kong Arts Fest. Soc., 2008–. Hon. Fellow, St Hugh's Coll., Oxford, 2016. Hon. LLD Hong Kong, 2019. Chevalier, l'Ordre des Arts et des Lettres (France), 2002; Comdr, Ordre des Palmes Académiques (France), 2007; Officier de la Légion d'Honneur (France), 2015 (Chevalier, 2002). *Recreations:* wine, books, travel, music. *Address:* Court of Final Appeal, 8 Jackson Road, Central, Hong Kong. *T:* 21230012, *Fax:* 21210303. *E:* rribeiro@netvigator.com. *Clubs:* Hong Kong, Lusitano, American (Hong Kong).

**RICARD, Alexandre**; Chairman and Chief Executive Officer, Pernod Ricard, since 2015. *Educ:* Ecole Supérieure de Commerce, Paris; Univ. of Pennsylvania (MA Internat. Global Studies 2001); Wharton Sch., Univ. of Pennsylvania (MBA 2001). Strategy consultant, Accenture; Mergers and Acquisitions Consultant, Morgan Stanley; joined Audit and Develt Dept, Pernod Ricard, 2003; Chief Financial Officer, Irish Distillers Pernod Ricard, Dublin, 2004–06; Chm. and CEO, Pernod Ricard Asia Duty Free, Hong Kong, 2006–08; CEO, Irish Distillers Pernod Ricard, 2008–11; Pernod Ricard: Man. Dir, Distribn Network, Paris, 2011–12; Mem., Exec. Bd, 2011–; Dep. CEO and Chief Operating Officer, 2012–15. *Address:* Pernod Ricard, 12 place des Etats-Unis, 75116 Paris, France.

**RICE**; see Spring Rice, family name of Baron Monteagle of Brandon.

**RICE**; see Talbot Rice.

**RICE, Sir (Charles) Duncan**, Kt 2009; FRSE; Principal and Vice-Chancellor, University of Aberdeen, 1996–2010; *b* 20 Oct. 1942; *s* of James Inglis Rice and Jane Meauras Findlay (*née* Scroggie); *m* 1967, Susan Ilene Wunsch (see Dame S. I. Rice); two *s* one *d*. *Educ:* Univ. of Aberdeen (MA 1st Cl. Hons Hist. 1964); Univ. of Edinburgh (PhD 1969). FRHistS 1996; FRSE 1998. Lectr, Univ. of Aberdeen, 1966–69; Yale University: Asst Prof. of Hist., 1970–75; Associate Prof., 1975–79; Prof. of History, Hamilton Coll., Clinton, NY, 1979–85; New York University: Prof. of History, 1985–96; Dean, Faculty of Arts and Sci., 1985–94; Vice-Chancellor, 1994–96. Dir, BT Scotland, 1998–2002; Vice Chm., Grampian Enterprise Ltd, 1999–2006. Board Member: Univs and Colls Employers' Assoc., 1997–2007; Rowett Res. Inst., 1998–2012; Scottish Opera, 1998–2004; Scottish Ballet, 1998–2003; Glasgow Life, 2011–14; Member: Council, Nat. Trust for Scotland, 1998–2004; Heritage Lottery Fund Cttee for Scotland, 2005–10. Chm., Global Philanthropic, Europe, 2011–17. Trustee, CASE Europe, 2005–10 (Chm. Bd, 2007–10). Chm., UK Socrates-Erasmus Council, 1999–2008. FRSA 1996. Hon. DHL New York, 2004; Hon. DEd Robert Gordon, 2005; Hon. DHC Edinburgh, 2010; Hon. LLD Aberdeen, 2011. *Publications:* The Rise and Fall of Black Slavery, 1975; The Scots Abolitionists 1831–1961, 1982. *Recreations:* contemporary Scottish literature, opera, studio ceramics, salmon fishing.

**RICE, Condoleezza**, PhD; Professor of Political Science, and Senior Fellow, Hoover Institution, since 2009, and Professor of Political Economy, Graduate School of Business, Stanford University; *b* Birmingham, Ala, 14 Nov. 1954. *Educ:* Univ. of Denver (BA Internat. Relns 1974; PhD 1981); Univ. of Notre Dame, Indiana. Prof., Stanford Univ., Calif, 1981–88; Dir, Soviet and E Eur. Affairs, Nat. Security Council, Special Asst to Pres. for nat. security affairs and Sen. Dir for Soviet Affairs, 1988–91; Stanford University, California: Prof., 1991–93; Provost, 1993–99; on leave of absence as foreign policy advr to George W. Bush, 2000–01; Nat. Security Advr, and Asst to the Pres. for Nat. Security Affairs, 2001–05; Secretary of State, USA, 2005–09. Dir, KiOR, 2011–. Hon. Dr Notre Dame, 1995. *Publications:* Uncertain Allegiance: the Soviet Union and the Czechoslovak Army, 1984; (with A. Dallin) The Gorbachev Era, 1986; (with P. Zelikow) Germany Unified and Europe Transformed, 1995; Extraordinary, Ordinary People: a memoir of family, 2010; No Higher Honour: a memoir of my years in Washington, 2011; Democracy: stories from the long road to freedom, 2017; (with Amy B. Zegart) Political Risk, 2018; contrib. numerous articles on Soviet and E European foreign and defense policy. *Address:* Hoover Institution, Stanford University, Stanford, CA 94305–6010, USA.

**RICE, Maj.-Gen. Sir Desmond (Hind Garrett)**, KCVO 1989 (CVO 1985); CBE 1976 (OBE 1970); Vice Adjutant General, 1978–79; *b* 1 Dec. 1924; *s* of Arthur Garrett Rice and Alice Constance (*née* Henman); *m* 1954, Denise Ann (*née* Ravenscroft); one *d*. *Educ:* Marlborough College. Commissioned into The Queen's Bays, 1944; psc 1954; 1st The Queen's Dragoon Guards, 1958; jssc 1963; First Comdg Officer, The Royal Yeomanry, 1967–69; Col GS 4 Div., 1970–73; BGS (MO) MoD, 1973–75; rcds 1976; Director of Manning (Army), 1977–78. Col, 1st The Queen's Dragoon Guards, 1980–86. Sec., Central Chancery of Orders of Knighthood, 1980–89. An Extra Gentleman Usher to HM the Queen, 1989–. *Recreations:* field sports, gardening. *Address:* Castle Grove, Castle Street, Bampton, Tiverton, Devon EX16 9NS. *T:* (01398) 332718. *Club:* Cavalry and Guards.

**RICE, Sir Duncan**; see Rice, Sir C. D.

**RICE, Maureen**; see Rice-Knight, M.

**RICE, Maurice**; see Rice, T. M.

**RICE, Dr Patricia**; Senior Research Fellow and Associate Head (Research), Department of Economics, University of Oxford, since 2007; *b* Plymouth, 17 Nov. 1951; *d* of George Alfred Rice and Marion Annette Rice (*née* Gale); *m* 1983, Prof. Anthony James Venables, *qv*; one *s* one *d*. *Educ:* Plymouth High Sch. for Girls; Univ. of Warwick (BSc 1st Cl. Hons 1973; MA 1974); Harvard Univ. (Frank Knox Schol.); Nuffield Coll., Oxford (DPhil 1981). Lectr in Econs, Univ. of Sussex, 1977–89; University of Southampton: Lectr in Econs, 1989–99; Sen. Lectr, 1999–2007; Hd of Econs, 2003–06. Vis. Prof. of Econs, Univ. of BC, 1982–83. Res. Consultant, World Bank, 1999. Academic Assessor for Fast Stream Economist Recruitment Service, HM Govt, 1994–97; Member: Adv. Panel, DCLG, 2007–10; Sch. Teacher Rev. Bd, 2011– (Chair, 2014–). Mem. Council, REconS, 2006–11. *Publications:* contribs to acad. jls on labour econs and regl econs. *Address:* Department of Economics, University of Oxford, Manor Road Building, Manor Road, Oxford OX1 3UQ.

**RICE, Rowena C.**; see Collins Rice.

**RICE, Dame Susan (Ilene), (Lady Rice)**, DBE 2018 (CBE 2005); FCIBS; FRSE; Chairman: Scottish Water, since 2015; Business Stream, since 2015; Scottish Fiscal Commission, since 2014; *b* 7 March 1946; *m* 1967, C(harles) Duncan Rice (see Sir C. D. Rice); two *s* one *d*. *Educ:* Wellesley Coll., Mass (BA); Univ. of Aberdeen (MLitt). Chartered Banker; FCIBS 2000; FRSE 2001. Dean, Saybrook Coll., Yale Univ., 1973–79; Staff Aide to Pres., Hamilton Coll., 1980–81; Dean of Students, Colgate Univ., 1981–86; Sen. Vice Pres. and Div. Hd, Nat West Bancorp, 1986–96; Dir, Business Projects, Hd, Branch Banking, then Man. Dir, Personal Banking, Bank of Scotland, 1997–2000; Chm. and Chief Exec., Lloyds TSB Scotland, 2000–09; Man. Dir, Lloyds Banking Gp Scotland, 2009–14. Non-executive Director: SSE plc (formerly Scottish & Southern Energy plc), 2003–14; Bank of England, 2007–14; Big Society Capital, 2011–18; J Sainsbury plc, 2013–; Nat. Centre for Univs and Business, 2013–14; Banking Standards Bd, 2015–; North American Income Trust, 2015–; C. Hoare & Co., 2018–. Pres., Scottish Council of Develt and Industry, 2012–. Regent, RCSE, 2011. CCMI 2003; FRSA 2004. Hon. DBA: Robert Gordon Univ., 2001; Queen Margaret, 2008; Dr *hc* Edinburgh, 2003; Hon. DLitt Heriot-Watt, 2004; DUniv: Paisley, 2005; Glasgow, 2007; Hon. LLD Aberdeen, 2008; Hon. DLaws Glasgow Caledonian, 2017. *Recreations:* modern art, fly fishing, opera, walking. *Address:* Scottish Water, Castle House, 6 Castle Drive, Carnegie Campus, Dunfermline KY11 8GG.

**RICE, Prof. (Thomas) Maurice**, PhD; FRS 2002; Professor of Physics, Eidgenössische Technische Hochschule Hönggerberg, Zürich, 1981–2004, now Emeritus; *b* 26 Jan. 1939; *s* of James P. Rice and Maureen K. Rice (*née* Quinn); *m* 1966, Helen D. Spreiter; one *s* two *d*. *Educ:* University Coll., Dublin (BSc 1959, MSc 1960); Churchill Coll., Cambridge (PhD 1964). Asst Lectr, Birmingham Univ., 1963–64; Res. Associate, Univ. of Calif., San Diego, 1964–66; Mem., tech. staff, Bell Labs, Murray Hill, NJ, 1966–81. *Address:* Theoretische Physik, ETH Hönggerberg, 8093 Zürich, Switzerland. *T:* (1) 6332581, *Fax:* (1) 6331115. *E:* rice@itp.phys.ethz.ch.

**RICE, Sir Timothy (Miles Bindon)**, Kt 1994; writer and broadcaster; *b* 10 Nov. 1944; *s* of late Hugh Gordon Rice and Joan Odette Rice; *m* 1974, Jane Artereta McIntosh; one *s* one *d*; partner, Nell Sully; one *d*. *Educ:* Lancing Coll. EMI Records, 1966–68; Norrie Paramor Org., 1968–69. Lyrics for stage musicals (with music by Andrew Lloyd Webber): The Likes of Us, 1965; Joseph and the Amazing Technicolor Dreamcoat, 1968; Jesus Christ Superstar, 1970 (Emmy Award, 2018); Evita, 1976; Cricket, 1986; The Wizard of Oz, 2011 (some songs only); (with music by Stephen Oliver) Blondel, 1983; (with music by Benny Andersson and Björn Ulvaeus) Chess, 1984; (with music by Michel Berger and book by Luc Plamondon) Tycoon, 1992; (with music by Alan Menken) Beauty and the Beast, 1994 (some songs only); (with music by John Farrar) Heathcliff, 1996; (with music by Alan Menken) King David, 1997; (with music by Elton John) Aida, 1998; (with music by Stuart Brayson) From Here to Eternity, 2013; Aladdin, 2016 (some songs only); lyrics for film musicals: (with music by Alan Menken) Aladdin, 1992; Beauty and the Beast, 2017; (with music by Elton John) The Lion King, 1994, expanded for theatre, 1997; (with music by Elton John) The Road to El Dorado, 2000; (with music by Tchaikovsky) Nutcracker - The True Story, 2009; (with various composers) Jock of the Bushfeld, 2010. Producer, Anything Goes, Prince Edward Theatre, 1989. Lyrics for songs, 1975–, with other composers, incl. Marvin Hamlisch, Rick Wakeman, Vangelis, Paul McCartney, Mike Batt, Francis Lai, John Barry, Freddie Mercury, Richard Kerr, Burt Bacharach, Graham Gouldman, Michael Kamen, Malcolm Arnold, Lalo Schifrin, Pete Hobbs and Ennio Morricone. Awards include: Oscar and Golden Globe for Best Original Film Song, A Whole New World (music by Alan Menken), 1992, for Can You Feel the Love Tonight (music by Elton John), 1994 and for You Must Love Me (music by Andrew Lloyd Webber), 1996; 13 Ivor Novello Awards, 3 Tony Awards and 6 Grammy Awards (incl. Song of the Year for A Whole New World, 1993); Star, Hollywood Walk of Fame, 2008; Olivier Special Award, 2012. Researcher, writer and presenter, Tim Rice's American Pie (52-part series), BBC Radio 2, 2010–11. Film début as actor in insultingly small rôle, The Survivor, 1980; even smaller rôle in About A Boy, 2002. Cameron Mackintosh Vis. Prof. of Contemporary Theatre, Univ. of Oxford, 2003. Chairman: Foundn for Sport and the Arts, 1991–2013; Lancing Coll. Develt, 2006–; Trustee, Chance to Shine, 2005–; Pres., London Liby, 2017–. Former Pres., Lord's Taverners. Fellow, BASCA, 2010. *Publications:* Heartaches Cricketers' Almanack, yearly, 1975–; (ed) Lord's Taverners Sticky Wicket Book, 1979; Treasures of Lord's, 1989; Oh, What a Circus (autobiog.), 1999; (with Andrew Lloyd Webber): Evita, 1978; Joseph and the Amazing Technicolor Dreamcoat, 1982; (jtly) Guinness Books of British Hit Singles and Albums and associated pubns, 1977–96, 31 books in all; (jtly) The Complete Eurovision Song Contest Companion, 1998. *Recreations:* cricket, history of popular music, chickens. *Clubs:* Garrick, MCC (Pres., 2002–03; Trustee, 2006–11), Groucho, Dramatists', Saints and Sinners (Chm., 1990), Soho House; Cricket Writers.

**RICE, Tony**; see Rice, W. A.

**RICE, Victor Albert**; Chief Executive, LucasVarity plc, 1996–99; President, Ravelin LLC, 1999; *b* 7 March 1941; *o s* of late Albert Edward Rice and of Rosina Emmeline (*née* Pallant); *m* 1984, Corinne Sutcliffe. Left sch. at 16 to join Finance Dept, Ford UK, 1957; various finance posts with Ford, Cummins and Chrysler, 1957–70; Comptroller, Northern European Ops, Perkins Engines Gp, 1970–75; Corporate Comptroller, Massey Ferguson (Perkins' parent co.), 1975–78; Varity Corporation: Pres. and Chief Operating Officer, 1978–80; Chm. and CEO, 1980–96. Liveryman, Glaziers' Co., 1978–. Mem. Council, Univ. of Buffalo, 1999. *Recreations:* golf, gardening, opera, ballet, theatre.

**RICE, William Anthony, (Tony)**; Chairman: Dechra Pharmaceuticals plc, since 2016; Ultra Electronics plc, since 2019; *b* London, 9 March 1952; *s* of William Norman and Eileen Mary Rice; *m* 1985, Jan Sherlaw Grandison; two *s*. *Educ:* Kingswood Primary Sch., Norwood; King Edward VI Grammar Sch., Chelmsford; City of London Coll. (BA Hons Business Studies 1974); Cranfield Univ. (MBA 1990). CIMA 1977. Finance rôles, British Telecommunications, 1974–78; finance and treasury rôles, British Gas, 1978–86; Finance Manager, 1986–88, Asst Treas., 1988–91, Treas., 1991–96, Man. Dir, Commercial Aircraft, 1997–99, BAE Systems; Chief Executive Officer: Tunstall plc, 2002–05; Cable & Wireless, 2005–08; Cable & Wireless Communications, 2008–13. Chm., Alexander Mann plc, 2009–13; Senior Independent Director: Spirit plc, 2006–15; Halma plc, 2014–. Non-exec. Dir, Whittington Health NHS Trust, 2014– (Chm., Finance, 2014–). FCT 1986. Trustee: Help the Aged, 2005–09; Shelter, 2013–17 (Chm., Audit Cttee, 2013–17). *Recreations:* family, walking, ski-ing, golf, supporting Crystal Palace, art, theatre, intellectual curiosity. *Address:* c/o Dechra Pharmaceuticals, 24 Cheshire Avenue, Cheshire Business Park, Lostock Gralam, Northwich, Cheshire CW9 7UA. *T:* (01606) 814730.

**RICE-KNIGHT, Maureen, (Maureen Rice)**; Editorial Director, Cedar Publishing, since 2010; *b* 13 Dec. 1958; *d* of Patrick Rice and Anastasia Rice (*née* McGuire); *m* 1986, David Peter Knight; one *s* one *d*. *Educ:* Gumley House Convent Grammar Sch., Isleworth; Polytechnic of Central London (BA Hons Media Studies; BA Hons Journalism). Magazines: Features Editor, Mizz, 1985; Dep. Editor, No 1, 1985; Editor, Mizz, 1986; Editor, 19, 1988; Editor, Options, 1991–98; Editor, Psychologies, 2005–09. Mem. Cttee, Women in Journalism (Co-Chm., 2010–11). FRSA. Editor of Year Awards: (Consumer Mags), PPA, 2008; (Lifestyle Mags), BSME, 2008. *Recreations:* reading, cinema, food, walking, arts.

**RICH, Harry Paul**; board member, regulator, executive coach and business advisor, since 2017; Founder, More Potential Limited, 2017; Registrar of Consultant Lobbyists, since 2018; Chief Executive, Royal Institute of British Architects, 2009–16; *b* Birmingham, 15 Jan. 1958; *s* of late Walter Rich and of Doreen Rich (*née* Seager, now Coleman); civil partnership 2006, *m* 2015, Richard Scandrett. *Educ:* King Edward VI Camp Hill Sch., Birmingham; Birmingham Univ. (LLB Hons); Coll. of Law, London. Admitted as solicitor, 1983; Solicitor, Warner Cranston, 1981–83; Managing Director: Rich & Pattison Ltd, 1984–94; Tandem (UK) Ltd, 1995–98; Dir, 1999–2003, Dep. Chief Exec., 2003–07, Design Council; Chief Exec., Enterprise Insight, 2007–09. Chm., New Moon Pubns plc, 1990–93. Member: Council, ASA, 1997–2003; Charter Compliance Panel, Press Complaints Commn, 2007–09; Bd, Press Recognition Panel, 2014–; BIS/DCMS Creative Industries Council, 2013–16. Chm., Student and Academic Campaign for Soviet Jews, 1983–88; Mem., Exec. Cttee, Bd of Deputies of British Jews, 1985–94. Mem., Internat. Adv. Council, Design Mgt Inst., USA, 2004–11. Chm., JAT (Jewish sexual health charity),

1998–2007. Mem., Law Soc., 1983–; Affiliate Mem., RIBA, 2010. Trustee: Harbour Foundn, 2017–; Open Coll. of Arts, 2018–. Governor: Univ. for Creative Arts, 2009–18; Glasgow Sch. of Art, 2018–. MInstD 2000; CCMI 2012. FRSA. JP London 1998–2001. *Recreations:* theatre and music, enquiring and understanding. *Club:* Groucho.

**RICH, Marcus;** Chief Executive, TI Media (formerly IPC Media Ltd, then Time Inc. (UK) Ltd), since 2014; *b* Wisbech, 21 June 1959; *s* of Eric Rich and Pamela Rich (*née* White); *m* 2004, Liza Hill; three *s* one *d*. *Educ:* King's Lynn Grammar Sch.; Norfolk Coll. of Arts and Technol. (HND 1980); Coll. for Distributive Trades (CAM Dip. 1982). Mgt Trainee, Foster Refrigeration UK, 1978–82; Res. Manager, Emap Nationals, 1982–83; Mktg Manager, Emap Business, 1983–85; Gp Account Dir, McCann Erickson, 1985–92; Mktg Dir, Emap Images, 1992–94; Publishing Dir, Emap Metro, 1994–97; Man. Dir, Emap Australia, 1997–99; Pres., Emap Metro LLC USA, 1999–2002; Managing Director: FHM Worldwide, 2002–04; Emap Performance, 2004–05; Emap Advertising, 2005–06; Gp Man. Dir, Bauer Advertising and Bauer Consumer Media Lifestyle Mags, 2006–08; Man. Dir, Mail on Sunday Dail Mail and Gen. Trust, 2008–14. *Recreations:* horse riding, ski-ing, music. *Address:* TI Media Ltd, 161 Marsh Wall, E14 9AP. *T:* (020) 3148 5102. *E:* marcus.rich@ti-media.com.

**RICH, His Honour Michael Samuel;** QC 1980; a Circuit Judge, 1991–2005; *b* 18 Aug. 1933; *s* of late Sidney Frank Rich, OBE and of Erna Babette; *m* 1963, Janice Sarita Benedictus (*d* 2011); three *s* one *d*. *Educ:* Dulwich Coll.; Wadham Coll., Oxford (MA, 1st Class Hons PPE). Called to the Bar, Middle Temple, 1958 (Bencher, 1985; Reader, 2006); a Recorder, 1986–91; Deputy High Court Judge: Chancery Div., 1992–2005; QBD, 1993–2005. Mem., Lands Tribunal, 1993–2006. Hon. Pres., Dulwich Soc., 2001–11. Medal of Merit, Boy Scouts Assoc., 1970. *Publications:* (jtly) Hill's Law of Town and Country Planning, 5th edn, 1968. *Address:* 5 John Adam House, 17–19 John Adam Street, WC2N 6JG. *Clubs:* Garrick, Dulwich; Maccabæans.

**RICH, Nigel Mervyn Sutherland,** CBE 1995; Chairman, Urban Logistics, since 2017; *b* 30 Oct. 1945; *s* of Charles Albert Rich and Mina Mackintosh Rich; *m* 1970, Cynthia Elizabeth (*née* Davies); two *s* two *d*. *Educ:* Sedbergh Sch.; New Coll., Oxford (MA). FCA. Deloittes, London and New York, 1967–73; Jardine Matheson, Hong Kong, Johannesburg, Manila, 1974–94; Man. Dir, Jardine Matheson Holdings, 1989–94; Chief Exec., Trafalgar House, 1994–96. Chairman: Hamptons Gp, 1997–2005; Exel plc (formerly Ocean Gp), 1997–2005; CP Ships, 2001–05; SEGRO (formerly Slough Estates) plc, 2006–16; Xchanging plc, 2008–11 (Dep. Chm., 2006–08); Pacific Industrial and Logistics, 2017–; Director: Matheson & Co., 1994–; British Empire Securities, 2012–. Hon. Steward, HK Jockey Club, 1994–. Freeman, City of London, 1970; Master, Tobacco Pipemakers' and Tobacco Blenders' Co., 2008–09. *Recreations:* golf, horseracing. *Clubs:* Boodle's, Hurlingham, Turf, MCC; Royal and Ancient Golf (Mem., Gen. Cttee, 2012–15); Royal St George's Golf; Royal County Down Golf; New Zealand Golf; Leopard Creek Golf (S Africa).

**RICHARD, Dame Alison (Fettes),** DBE 2010; PhD; Vice-Chancellor, Cambridge University, 2003–10; Fellow of Newnham College, Cambridge, 2003–10, now Hon. Fellow; *b* 1 March 1948; *d* of Gavin and Joyce Richard; *m* 1976, Robert E. Dewar (*d* 2013); two *d* (one *s* decd). *Educ:* Queenswood; Newnham Coll., Cambridge (BA 1969, MA); Queen Elizabeth Coll., London (PhD 1973). Yale University: Asst Prof., 1972–80; Associate Prof., 1980–86; Prof. of Anthropol., 1986–2003; Provost, 1994–2002; Franklin Muzzy Crosby Prof. of the Human Envmt, 1998–2003, Emerita, 2003–; Sen. Res. Scientist, 2011–; Dir, Yale Peabody Mus. of Natural Hist., 1991–94; Co-dir, Prog. of Conservation and Develt in Southern Madagascar, 1977–. Consultant, Species Survival Commn, IUCN, 1982–90. Chair, Advisory Board: Cambridge Conservation Initiative, 2011–; Perrett Laver, 2012–; Member, Editorial Board: Folia Primatologica, 1982–95; Amer. Jl of Primatology, 1988–97. Member: Sci. Adv. Council, L. S. B. Leakey Foundn, 1986–96; Physical Anthropol. Rev. Panel, NSF, 1988–91; Sci. Adv. Council, Wenner-Gren Foundn for Anthropol Res., 1991–94; Nat. Council, 1992–95, Bd, 1995–2004, WWF-US; Bd, Liz Claiborne/Art Ortenberg Foundn, 1998–2014; Adv. Bd, Luc Hoffmann Inst., 2017– (Chair, 2011–16). Trustee: WWF Internat., 2007–16; Howard Hughes Med. Inst., 2008–; Liz Claiborne/Art Ortenberg Foundn, 2014–. DL Cambs, 2004–10. Hon. Dr: Peking, 2004; Antananarivo, Madagascar, 2005; York, Canada, 2006; Edinburgh, 2006; QUB, 2008; Anglia Ruskin, 2008; Yale, 2009; Chinese Univ. of HK, 2009; EWHA Women's Univ., Korea, 2009; Exeter, 2010; Cambridge, 2011; Hong Kong Poly. Univ., 2015. Officier, Ordre National (Madagascar), 2005. *Publications:* Behavioral Variation: case study of a Malagasy lemur, 1978; Primates in Nature, 1985; contrib. numerous scientific articles on primate evolution, ecology and social behaviour to acad. jls. *Recreations:* opera, gardening, cooking. *Club:* Athenæum.

**RICHARD, Sir Cliff,** Kt 1995; OBE 1980; singer, actor; *b* 14 Oct. 1940; *s* of late Rodger Webb and Dorothy Webb; *né* Harry Rodger Webb; changed name to Cliff Richard, 1958. *Educ:* Riversmead Sch., Cheshunt. Awarded 14 Gold Discs for records: Living Doll, 1959; The Young Ones, 1962; Bachelor Boy, 1962; Lucky Lips, 1963; Congratulations, 1968; Power to all Our Friends, 1973; Devil Woman, 1976; We Don't Talk Anymore, 1979; Wired for Sound, 1981; Daddy's Home, 1981; Living Doll (with The Young Ones), 1986; All I Ask of You (with Sarah Brightman), 1986; Mistletoe and Wine, 1988; The Millennium Prayer, 1999; also 37 Silver Discs and 3 Platinum Discs (Daddy's Home, 1981; All I Ask of You, 1986; The Millennium Prayer, 1999). Films: Serious Charge, 1959; Expresso Bongo, 1960; The Young Ones, 1962; Summer Holiday, 1963; Wonderful Life, 1964; Finders Keepers, 1966; Two a Penny, 1968; His Land, 1970; Take Me High, 1973. Own TV series, ATV and BBC. Stage: rep. and variety seasons; Time, Dominion, 1986–87; Heathcliff, Apollo, 1997. Top Box Office Star of GB, 1962–63 and 1963–64; UK's best-selling singles artist of all time, 2004. 50th anniversary in music business, 2008–09; 50th anniversary internat. reunion tour with The Shadows, 2009–10; Bold as Brass tour, 2010; Soulicious UK tour, 2011; Still Reelin' and A Rockin' tour, 2013; 75th Birthday tour, 2015; 60th Anniv. Tour, 2018; Diamond Encore Tour, 2019. *Publications:* Questions, 1970; The Way I See It, 1972; The Way I See It Now, 1975; Which One's Cliff, 1977; Happy Christmas from Cliff, 1980; You, Me and Jesus, 1983; Mine to Share, 1984; Jesus, Me and You, 1985; Single-minded, 1988; Mine Forever, 1989; Jesus Here and Now, 1996; My Story: a celebration of 40 years in show business, 1998; (with Penny Junor) My Life, My Way, 2008. *Recreation:* tennis. *Address:* c/o PO Box 423, Leatherhead, Surrey KT22 2HJ. *T:* (01372) 467752. *Club:* All England Lawn Tennis and Croquet.

**RICHARDS,** family name of **Barons Milverton** and **Richards of Herstmonceux**.

**RICHARDS OF HERSTMONCEUX,** Baron *cr* 2014 (Life Peer), of Emsworth in the County of Hampshire; **Gen. David Julian Richards,** GCB 2011 (KCB 2007); CBE 2000; DSO 2001; DL; Chairman: Palliser Associates Ltd, since 2013; Equilibrium Global Ltd, since 2013; Chief of the Defence Staff, 2010–13; Aide-de-Camp General to the Queen, 2008–13; *b* 4 March 1952; *s* of John Downie Richards and Pamela Mary Richards (*née* Reeves); *m* 1978, Caroline Reyne (*née* Bond); two *d*. *Educ:* Eastbourne Coll. (Hd Boy, Capt. of Rugger); UWCC (BA Politics and Econs 1974). CO 3rd Regt RHA, 1991–94; Col Army Plans, 1994–96; Comdr 4th Armoured Bde, 1996–98; Comdr Jt Force HQ, 1998–2001; Commander British Joint Task Force: East Timor, 1999; Sierra Leone, 2000; COS ACE RRC, 2001–02; ACGS, 2002–04; Commander: ARRC, 2005–07; NATO Internat. Security and Assistance Force, Afghanistan, 2006–07; C-in-C, Land Forces, 2008–09; Chief of Gen. Staff, 2009–10. Member: RUSI, 1992– (Mem. Council, 1995–96); European Leadership Network, 2014–. Colonel Commandant: RA, 2005–12; Bde of Gurkhas, 2007–12; Media Ops Gp TA, 2008–12. Sen. Advr, IISS, 2013–18. Dep. Grand Pres., Royal Commonwealth Ex-Services League, 2013–. President: Combined Services Polo Assoc., 2010–17; Combined Ops Pilotage Parties, 2011–; Mil. Historical Soc., 2012–; League of Remembrance, 2014–; Adv. Panel, Homes for Heroes, 2016–; Vice Pres., Forces Pension Soc., 2014–. Patron: Afghan Appeal Fund, 2007–; Armed Forces Moslem Assoc., 2008–; Wilts Search and Rescue, 2009–11; Dougie Dalzell MC Trust, 2010–; Row to Recovery, 2010–; The Garrison, 2013–; UK Assoc. for the Blind Schs of Sierra Leone, 2014–; L'Orchestre du Monde, 2014–; James Myatt Sailing Trust for Young People, 2014–; Manor Trust, Bedhampton, 2016–; Emsworth Meml Gdn, 2016–; Nat. Sikh War Meml Trust, 2016–; Vice Patron, Blind Veterans UK, 2012–; Contributor, Speakers for Schs, 2011–. Admiral, Army Sailing Assoc., 2008–10. DL Hants, 2014. *Publications:* (ed jtly) Victory Among People—Lessons from Countering Insurgency and Stabilising Fragile States, 2011; (contrib.) Oxford Handbook of War, 2012; (contrib.) Blair's Generals, 2013; (autobiog.) Taking Command, 2014; articles in RUSI Jl, SA Inst. of Internat. Affairs Jl, The Times, British Army Rev., RA Jl and other mil. pubns. *Recreations:* offshore sailing, military history, riding, gardening, opera. *Address:* c/o Regimental Headquarters Royal Artillery, Royal Artillery Barracks, Larkhill, Salisbury, Wilts SP4 8QT. *T:* (01980) 845788. *Clubs:* Army and Navy, Cavalry and Guards, Pitt; Royal Artillery Yacht (Adm., 2012–), Royal Cruising, Kiel Yacht, Royal Yacht Squadron.

**RICHARDS, Prof. (Adrian) John,** PhD; Professor of Botany, University of Newcastle upon Tyne, 2002–04, now Professor Emeritus; *b* 26 Jan. 1943; *s* of Dr Taliesin Richards and Roonie Eileen Richards; *m* 1966, Sheila Mackie; one *s* two *d*. *Educ:* Leighton Park Sch., Reading; University Coll., Durham (BSc 1964; PhD 1968). Demonstrator, Botany Sch., Univ. of Oxford, 1967–70; University of Newcastle upon Tyne: Lectr, 1970–85; Sen. Lectr, 1985–96; Reader in Botany, 1996–2002. Mem., Jt Rock Gdn Cttee, RHS, 1995– (Vice-Chair, 2010–). Vice-President: Botanical Soc. of British Isles, 2002–; Alpine Gdn Soc., 2013– (Pres., 2003–06). *Publications:* Plant Breeding Systems, 1986, 2nd edn 1997; Primula, 1993, 2nd edn 2003; (with A. A. Dudman) Dandelions of the British Isles, 1997; Mountain Flower Walks: the Greek mainland, 2008; numerous botanical papers, esp. in New Phytologist and Heredity. *Recreations:* Alpine gardening, plant exploration, mountain walking (especially in Greece), birding, photographing butterflies. *Address:* School of Biology, Ridley Building, University of Newcastle upon Tyne NE1 7RU. *T:* (0191) 222 8839, *Fax:* (0191) 222 5229.

**RICHARDS, Anne Helen,** CVO 2014; CBE 2015; FRSE; Chief Executive Officer, Fidelity International, since 2018; *b* 7 Aug. 1964; *d* of Michael and Helen Finnigan; *m* 1991, Matthew John Richards; two *s*. *Educ:* Univ. of Edinburgh (BSc Hons Electronics and Elec. Engrg 1985); INSEAD (MBA 1992); CDipAF 1991. CEng 1992; MIET 1992; Chartered FCSI 2010 (FSI 2007). Res. Fellow, European Lab. for Particle Physics, CERN, 1985–88; Consultant, Cambridge Consultants Ltd, 1989–91; Analyst, Alliance Capital Ltd, 1992–94; Portfolio Manager, J P Morgan Investment Mgt, 1994–98; Man. Dir, Merrill Lynch Investment Managers, 1999–2002; Jt Man. Dir, Edinburgh Fund Managers plc, 2002–03; Chief Investment Officer, 2003–16, Exec. Dir, 2011–16, Aberdeen Asset Mgt plc; CEO, M&G Gp Ltd, 2016–18. Dir, Prudential plc, 2016–. Non-exec. Dir, esure Gp plc, 2012–16. Mem. Council, Duchy of Lancaster, 2005–14; Director: Scottish Financial Enterprise, 2006–12; Nuclear Liabilities Fund, 2008–11. Hd, Practitioner Panel, Financial Conducts Authy, 2017–. Chm., CERN & Soc. Foundn Bd, 2014–; Dir and Trustee, EveryChild, 2005–13; Dir, Scottish Chamber Orch., 2008–14. Gov., Caledonian Res. Foundn, 2007–09. Mem., 2007–14, Vice Convener, 2014–, Ct, Univ. of Edinburgh. FRSE 2016. Hon. DLitt Heriot-Watt, 2013. *Recreations:* music, mountains, family, gardening. *Address:* Fidelity International, 4 Cannon Street, EC4M 5AB.

**RICHARDS, (Anthony) Charles,** CVO 2012 (LVO 2006; MVO 1997); Deputy Master of HM Household and Equerry to the Queen, since 1999; *b* 20 Feb. 1953; *s* of Dudley Raymond Richards and Eleonora Caroline Richards (*née* Otter); *m* 1978, Serena Anne Spencer; two *s* (and one *s* decd). *Educ:* Marlborough Coll.; RMA Sandhurst. Commissioned Welsh Guards, 1973; served with 1st Bn Welsh Guards, UK and BAOR, 1973–82; seconded 1st Bn 2nd Gurkha Rifles, Hong Kong, 1982–84; Staff Coll., 1985; BAOR, 1986–90; 2 i/c 1st Bn Welsh Guards, UK, 1990–92; Staff Officer, HQ London Dist, 1992–94; Equerry to the Duke of Edinburgh, 1994–97; Div. Lt Col, Foot Guards, 1997–99, retired 1999. Long and Faithful Service Medal, Royal Household, 2015. *Recreations:* shooting, fishing, travel. *Address:* Rotherby Grange, Melton Mowbray, Leics LE14 2LP. *T:* (01664) 434206.

**RICHARDS, Brian Henry,** CEng, FIET; *b* 19 July 1938; *s* of Alfred Edward Richards and Lilian Maud Richards (*née* Bennett); *m* 1961, Jane Wilkins; one *s* one *d*. *Educ:* Buckhurst Hill County Grammar Sch.; St John's College, Cambridge (Mech. Sci. Tripos, 1st Class Hons 1959, BA 1960; MA 1965). GEC Electronics, later Marconi Defence Systems, 1960–87: Guided Weapons Division: various develt, systems, project and gen. management appts, 1960–84; Dir, Guided Weapons, 1985; RCDS, 1986; Asst Man. Dir, 1987; Technical Dir, Hunting Engineering, 1988–90; Chief Exec., Atomic Weapons Estabt, 1990–94; Weapon Systems Dir, 1995–2001, Special Projects Dir, 2001–02, Dynamics Div., GEC-Marconi Dynamics, later Missile Systems Div., Alenia-Marconi Systems; Projects Advr, MBDA UK, 2002–03. Consultant, Defence Res. Progs, Soc. of British Aerospace Cos, subseq. ADS, 2002–10. *Recreations:* golf, listening to music, reading, travel, gardening, dabbling in the stock market, being a grandparent to four grandsons and one granddaughter!

**RICHARDS, Sir Brian (Mansel),** Kt 1997; CBE 1990; PhD; Chairman: Alizyme plc, 1996–2009; Xenetic plc (formerly Lipoxen plc), 2005–14; *b* 19 Sept. 1932; *s* of Cyril Mansel Richards and Gwendolyn Hyde Richards; *m* 1st, 1952, Joan Lambert Breese (marr. diss. 2003); one *s* one *d*; 2nd, 2003, June Clark-Richards. *Educ:* Lewis Sch., Pengam, Glam; University Coll. of Wales, Aberystwyth (BSc); King's College London (PhD). British Empire Cancer Fellowship, 1955–57; Nuffield Fellowship, 1957; MRC Biophysics Research Unit, 1957–64; Reader in Biology, Univ. of London, 1964–66; Research Div., G. D. Searle & Co., 1966–86; Vice-Pres., UK Preclinical R&D, 1980–86; Chairman: British Bio-technology Ltd, 1986–89; British Bio-technology Gp, 1989–94; Oxford BioMedica plc, 1996–98; CeNes Ltd, 1996–98; LGC (Holdings) Ltd, 1996–2001; Peptide Therapeutics Group plc, 1997 (Exec. Chm., 1995–97; Dir, 1998–2003); Cozart Biosciences Ltd, 2001–07; MAN Alternative Investments Ltd, 2001–07. Director: Prelude Trust plc, 1997–2003; Innogenetics SA, 1997–2005; Drug Royalty Corp., 1998–2002; Summit (formerly Vastox) plc, 2005–08; Aitua Ltd, 2006–. Hon. Prof. in Life Scis, UCW, Aberystwyth, 1991–. Chm., Biotechnology Working Party, CBI, 1988; Mem., Res. and Manufg Cttee, CBI, 1988; Mem., Sci. Bd, SERC, 1987; Chairman: Biotechnology Jt Adv. Bd, SERC/DTI, 1989; Science-based Cos Cttee, London Stock Exchange, 1994; Member: Adv. Cttee for Genetic Modification (previously Manipulation), HSE, 1984–96; Gene

Therapy Adv. Cttee, DoH, 1994–98; BBSRC, 1994–97; Consultant on Biotechnology, OECD, 1987; Specialist Advr, H of L Select Cttee II on Biotechnol. Regulation, 1993. Chm., Roslin Inst., 1995–99. Hon. DSc Abertay Dundee, 1997. *Publications:* papers in sci. jls. *Recreation:* travel.

**RICHARDS, Carol Anne Seymour-;** *see* Seymour, C. A.

**RICHARDS, Charles;** *see* Richards, Anthony C.

**RICHARDS, Clare Mary Joan;** *see* Spottiswoode, C. M. J.

**RICHARDS, Rt Hon. Sir David (Anthony Stewart),** Kt 2003; PC 2015; **Rt Hon. Lord Justice David Richards;** a Lord Justice of Appeal, since 2015; Vice Chancellor, County Palatine of Lancaster, 2008–11; *b* 9 June 1951; *s* of late Kenneth Richards, MBE and Winifred Richards; *m* 1979, Gillian, *er d* of Lt-Col W. A. Taylor; one *s* twin *d*. *Educ:* Oundle; Trinity Coll., Cambridge (BA 1973; MA 1980). Called to the Bar, Inner Temple, 1974; Bencher, Lincoln's Inn, 2000; a Judge of the High Court, Chancery Div., 2003–15. Junior Counsel (Chancery), DTI, 1989–92; QC 1992. Contrib., 2000–, Jt Gen. Ed., 2009, Buckley on the Companies Acts. *Address:* Royal Courts of Justice, Strand, WC2A 2LL. *Club:* Garrick.

**RICHARDS, Sir David (Gerald),** Kt 2006; *b* 3 Oct. 1943; *m* Janet; one *s* one *d*. *Educ:* Comprehensive sch. Mech. engr with own business, 1970–2000; Chairman: Sheffield Wednesday FC, 1990–2000; Premier League (formerly FA Premier League), 1999–2013; Football Foundn, 2003–08.

**RICHARDS, David Pender,** CBE 2005; Chairman: Prodrive, since 1983; Aston Martin Lagonda Ltd, 2007–13; *b* 3 June 1952; *s* of Geoffrey and Eileen Richards; *m* 1976, Karen Danahur; two *s* one *d*. *Educ:* Brynhyfryd Sch., Ruthin. Chartered accountancy articles, Cooke & Co., Liverpool, 1970–75; professional rally driver, 1976–81; World Rally Champion, 1981; Team Principal, BAR F1, 2002–04. Chm., Motor Sports Assoc., 2018–. *Recreations:* flying, tennis, classic sports cars, sailing, time with the family. *Address:* Prodrive, Banbury, Oxon OX16 4XD. *Clubs:* Royal Automobile; British Racing Drivers' (Silverstone).

**RICHARDS, David Thomas;** Director of Governance, Welsh Government (formerly Welsh Assembly Government), since 2010; *b* 30 Nov. 1954; *s* of Ralph Henry Richards and Brenda Mary Elizabeth Richards; *m* 1979, Veryan Cumming Black; one *s* two *d*. *Educ:* Whitchurch High Sch., Cardiff; New Univ. of Ulster, Coleraine (BA Philosophy). Exec. Officer, DTI, 1978–79; Welsh Office: fast stream trainee, 1979–83; Principal: Housing Div., 1983–86; Local Govt Finance Div., 1986–90; Assistant Secretary: Econ. Policy Div., 1990–92; Industrial Policy Div., 1992–94; Finance Programmes Div., 1994–97; Principal Finance Officer, 1997–99; Welsh Assembly Government: Finance Dir, 1999–2006; Dir, Governance in Health Project, later Governance in Wales Prog., 2006–08; Dir of Public Private Partnerships, 2008–10; Dir of Strategic Investment, 2010; Principal Accounting Officer, Welsh Govt, 2012. Chm., Steering Bd, UK Intellectual Property Office (formerly Patent Office), 2001–11. *Recreations:* playing the harp, cooking. *Address:* Welsh Government, Cathays Park, Cardiff CF10 3NQ. *T:* (029) 2082 5006.

**RICHARDS, His Honour (David) Wyn;** a Circuit Judge, 1998–2008; *b* 22 Sept. 1943; *s* of late Evan Gwylfa Richards and Florence Margretta Richards (*née* Evans); *m* 1972, Thelma Frances Hall; five *s*. *Educ:* Gwendraeth GS; Llanelli GS; Trinity Hall, Cambridge. Called to the Bar, 1968; a Recorder, 1985–98. Asst Comr, Boundary Commn for Wales, 1982–86, 1992–96. *Address:* c/o Swansea Civil Justice Centre, Caravella House, Quay West, Quay Parade, Swansea SA1 1SP.

**RICHARDS, Prof. Duncan Brett,** FRCP, FBPhS; Climax Professor of Clinical Therapeutics and Head, Centre for Clinical Therapeutics, Botnar Research Centre, University of Oxford, since 2019; Fellow, St Hilda's College, Oxford, since 2019; *b* Crawley, Sussex, 14 May 1970; *s* of Dr David Richards and Averil Richards; *m* 2000, Dr Fiona Cooke; one *s* three *d*. *Educ:* Perse Sch., Cambridge; Merton Coll., Oxford (BA; BM BCh 1995). FRCP 2015; FBPhS 2012; FFPM 2015. Clin. Lectr, Clin. Pharmacol., Univ. of Oxford, 1998–2003; GlaxoSmithKline: Dir, Clinical Develt, 2003–11; Vice Pres. and Clinical Hd, 2011–13, Hd, 2013–16, GSK Academic Discovery Perf. Unit; Medicine Develt Leader, 2016–17; Hd of Translational Medicine, Future Pipeline Discovery, 2017–18; Dir, GSK Clin. Unit, Cambridge, 2017–19; Hd of Clin. Pharmacol. and Experimental Medicine, 2018–19. *Publications:* Oxford Handbook of Practical Drug Therapy, 2008, 2nd edn 2011. *Address:* St Hilda's College, Cowley Place, Oxford OX4 1DY.

**RICHARDS, Edward Charles,** CBE 2015; Managing Partner, Flint Global, since 2015; *b* 29 Aug. 1965; *s* of Donald and Pat Richards; partner, Delyth Evans, *qv*; one *s* one *d*. *Educ:* London Sch. of Econs (BSc 1987; MSc 1989); London Business Sch. (Corp. Finance 1996); Harvard Business Sch. (AMP 2005). Researcher, Diverse Prodns, 1988–89; Policy Advr, Nat. Communications Union, 1989–90; Advr to Gordon Brown, MP, 1990–92; Sen. Consultant, London Econs, 1992–95; Controller, Corporate Strategy, BBC, 1995–99; Sen. Advr, Prime Minister's Office, 1999–2003; Sen. Partner, 2003–05, Chief Operating Officer, 2005–06, Chief Exec., 2006–14, Ofcom; Chair, Financial Services Trade Assoc. Review, 2015–16. *Recreations:* music, fiction, film/theatre, sport.

**RICHARDS, Sir Francis Neville,** KCMG 2002 (CMG 1994); CVO 1991; DL; Director, Government Communications Headquarters, 1998–2003; Governor and Commander-in-Chief, Gibraltar, 2003–06; *b* 18 Nov. 1945; *s* of Sir (Francis) Brooks Richards, KCMG, DSC and Hazel Myfanwy, *d* of Lt-Col Stanley Price Williams, CIE; *m* 1971, Gillian Bruce Nevill, *d* of late I. S. Nevill, MC and of Dr L. M. B. Dawson; one *s* one *d*. *Educ:* Eton; King's Coll., Cambridge (MA). Royal Green Jackets, 1967 (invalided, 1969). FCO, 1969; Moscow, 1971; UK Delegn to MBFR negotiations, Vienna, 1973; FCO, 1976–85 (Asst Private Sec. to Sec. of State, 1981–82); Economic and Commercial Counsellor, New Delhi, 1985–88; FCO, 1988–90 (Head, S Asian Dept); High Comr, Windhoek, 1990–92; Minister, Moscow, 1992–95; Dir (Europe), FCO, 1995–97; Dep. Under-Sec. of State, FCO, 1997–98. Chm., Nat. Security Inspectorate, 2007–13; Dir, Centre for Studies in Security and Diplomacy, 2007–10, Hon. Sen. Fellow, 2010–, Univ. of Birmingham. Chm., Internat. Adv. Bd, Altimo, 2008–13. Co. Pres., SSAFA Glos, 2007–. Chm., Bletchley Park Trust, 2007–12; Trustee, Imperial War Mus., 2007–16 (Dep. Chm., 2009–11; Chm., 2011–16). Mem., 2013–18, Chm., 2018–, Adv. Bd, Sch. of Mgt, Univ. of Bath. Chm. Govs, Rendcomb Coll., 2016–. Hon. Col 167 Catering Support Regt, RLC, 2012–15. DL Glos, 2007. DUniv Birmingham, 2012; Hon. LLD Bath, 2017. KStJ 2003. *Recreations:* walking, travelling, riding. *Clubs:* Special Forces, Brooks's.

**RICHARDS, Graham;** *see* Richards, William G.

**RICHARDS, Ian;** HM Diplomatic Service; Ambassador to Eritrea, 2016–19; *b* Dorking, 7 Oct. 1962; *s* of late Arthur W. W. Richards and of Inez R. J. Richards (*née* Johns). *Educ:* Dorking Grammar Sch.; Emmanuel Coll., Cambridge (BA Modern and Medieval Langs 1984; MA). Entered FCO, 1993; Desk Officer, UN Disarmament, FCO, 1993–94; lang. trng. (Mandarin), 1994–96; Consul, Commercial/Econ., Shanghai, 1996–99; First Sec., Beijing, 2000–01; Head: Political and Mil. Team, Afghanistan Unit, FCO, 2002; Econ. Crime Team, Econ. Policy Dept, FCO, 2002–04; Theme Manager, Commn for Africa, 2004–05; Special Advr to Dep. Dir-Gen., OPCW (on secondment), 2005–11; Hd, Overseas Resources, UKTI, 2011–13; Chargé d'Affaires, Ashgabat, 2013; Dep. Hd of Mission, Caracas and Chargé d'Affaires, Conakry and Bamako, 2014; Chargé d'Affaires, Conakry and Migration Advr, UKMIS Geneva, 2015. Ebola Medal, 2015. *Recreations:* music, travel, theatre. *Address:* c/o Foreign and Commonwealth Office, King Charles Street, SW1A 2AH. *E:* ian.richards@fco.gov.uk.

**RICHARDS, Sir (Isaac) Vivian (Alexander),** KGN 1999; OBE 1994; cricketer; Chairman, West Indies Selection Committee, 2002–04; *b* St Johns, Antigua, 7 March 1952; *s* of Malcolm Richards; *m* Miriam Lewis; one *s* one *d*. *Educ:* Antigua Grammar School. First class débuts, Leeward Islands, 1971, India (for WI), 1974; played for: Somerset, 1974–86; Queensland, 1976–77; Rishton, Lancs League, 1987; Glamorgan, 1990–93; Capt., WI Cricket Team, 1985–91; played in 100th Test Match, 1988; scored 100th first class century, 1988; 100th Test Match catch, 1988; highest Test score, 291, *v* England, Oval, 1976; highest first class score, 322, *v* Warwicks, Taunton, 1985; fastest Test century *v* England, Antigua, 1986; highest number of Test runs by a West Indian batsman, 1991. WI team coach, tour of NZ, 1999. An ICC Ambassador. Hon. DLitt Exeter, 1986. *Publications:* (with David Foot) Viv Richards (autobiog.), 1982; (with Patrick Murphy) Cricket Masterclass, 1988; (with Michael Middles) Hitting across the Line (autobiog.), 1991; (with Bob Harris) Sir Vivian (autobiog.), 2000. *Recreations:* golf, tennis, music, football. *Address:* 36 Novello Street, SW6 4JB. *T:* (020) 7736 7420.

**RICHARDS, Jeremy Simon; His Honour Judge Jeremy Richards;** a Circuit Judge, since 2004; *b* 18 Sept. 1959; *s* of Richard Elwyn Richards and Rosemary Isobel Richards; *m* 1990, Lesley Isobel Seaton (*née* Buist); one *s* one *d*. *Educ:* Tywyn Sch.; UCW, Aberystwyth (LLB Hons). Called to the Bar, Gray's Inn, 1981; in practice as barrister, 1981–2004, specialising in children and family work for Official Solicitor, guardians and local authorities. Chm. (pt-time), Employment Tribunals, 1996–2004; Asst Recorder, 1998–2000, Recorder, 2000–04; Designated Family Judge for Norfolk, 2007–19. *Recreations:* sailing, cooking. *Address:* Norwich County Court, The Law Courts, Bishopgate, Norwich NR3 1UR. *T:* (01603) 728200. *Clubs:* Norfolk (Norwich); Norfolk Punt.

**RICHARDS, John;** *see* Richards, Adrian J. and Richards, Robert J. G.

**RICHARDS, Dr John Arthur,** OBE 1997; Leader, Climate Change Programme, British Council, 2007–08; Secretary, Putney Bridge Canoe Club, since 2009; *b* 28 Nov. 1946; *s* of Clifford Alban Richards and Helen Mary Richards (*née* Shaw); *m* 1980, Asha Kasbekar; two *s*. *Educ:* Faringdon Sch.; The Coll., Swindon; Univ. of Surrey (BSc Hons (Chem.) 1969); Univ. of Nottingham (PhD (Organometallic Chem.) 1975). Plessey Co. Ltd: res., Allen Clarke Res. Centre, 1967–68; Manager, Components Gp, 1969–72; res., Centre de la recherche scientifique, Bordeaux, 1975–76; British Council: London, 1976–77; Bombay, 1977–80; Sci. Officer and Dep. Dir, Japan, 1981–87; on secondment to Cabinet Office, 1987–89; Dir, Sci. and Technol. Dept, London, 1989–92; Hd, Educn and Sci. Dept, 1992–94; Director: Thailand, 1995–2000; Hungary, 2000–03; Nigeria, 2003–06. *Recreations:* reading, canoeing and other water sports, travelling. *Address:* c/o Putney Bridge Canoe Club, 28 Cristowe Road, SW6 3QE. *Club:* Canoe England.

**RICHARDS, Julian Charles,** FSA; independent archaeologist, broadcaster, writer and educator, since 2004; *b* Nottingham, 22 Nov. 1951; *s* of Albert Charles Richards and Helen Mary Richards; *m* 1987, Susan Jean Lobb; one *s*. *Educ:* Nottingham Boys High Sch.; Reading Univ. (BA Hons Archaeol.). FSA 1992. Field archaeologist and project manager, Berks Archaeol Unit and Wessex Archaeol., 1975–91; Partner, AC Archaeol., 1991–94; fieldworker, English Heritage, 1994–97; presenter and writer: Meet the Ancestors, 1998–2004, Blood of the Vikings, 2002, BBC TV; Mapping the Town, BBC Radio 4, 1999–2005. Arts Soc. lectr, 2016–. Hon. PhD Archaeol. Bishop Grosseteste Lincoln, 2016. *Publications:* Stonehenge, 1991; Meet the Ancestors, 1999; Blood of the Vikings, 2001, rev. edn 2002; Stonehenge: a history in photographs, 2004; Stonehenge: the story so far, 2007, rev. edn 2017. *Recreations:* classic cars and historic motorsport, Stonehenge trivia, lecturing, ceramic history. *Address:* Foyle Hill House, Foyle Hill, Shaftesbury, Dorset SP7 0PT. *T:* (01747) 851531. *E:* julian@archaemedia.co.uk.

**RICHARDS, Prof. Keith Sheldon,** PhD; Professor of Geography, University of Cambridge, 1995–2014, now Emeritus; Fellow of Emmanuel College, Cambridge, since 1984 (Professorial Fellow, since 1995); *b* 25 May 1949; *s* of Maurice and Jean Richards; *m* 1973, Susan Mary Brooks. *Educ:* Falmouth Grammar Sch.; Jesus Coll., Cambridge (MA 1974; PhD 1975). Lectr, then Sen. Lectr, Lanchester Poly., 1973–78; Lectr, then Sen. Lectr, Univ. of Hull, 1978–84; University of Cambridge: Lectr, 1984–95; Reader in Physical Geog., 1995; Head of Geography Dept, 1994–99; Dir, Scott Polar Res. Inst., 1997–2002. Chm., Brit. Geomorph. Res. Gp, 1994–95; Member: various NERC Cttees, 1990–93, 1995–97, Peer Review Coll., 2004–07; ESRC Peer Rev. Coll., 2010–12. Vice-Pres. (Research), RGS, 2004–07; Pres., BAAS Geography Section, 2005–06. Mem./Chm., 2001 and 2008 RAE Panels, and 2014 REF Panels. FRSA 2005; Fellow, British Soc. for Geomorph., 2014. Cuthbert Peek Award, 1983, Founders Medal, 2013, RGS; Linton Award, British Soc. for Geomorph., 2015. *Publications:* Stochastic Processes in One-dimensional Series: an introduction, 1979; (ed jtly) Geomorphological Techniques, 1982; Rivers: form and process in alluvial channels, 1982; (ed jtly) Geomorphology and Soils, 1985; (ed) River Channels: environment and process, 1987; (ed jtly) Slope Stability: geotechnical engineering and geomorphology, 1987; (ed jtly) Landform Monitoring, Modelling and Analysis, 1998; (ed jtly) Glacier Hydrology and Hydrochemistry, 1998; (jtly) Arsenic Pollution: a global synthesis, 2009; over 200 papers and chapters on geomorphol., hydrology, river and slope processes, etc. in various jls and edited books. *Recreations:* travel, walking, opera, theatre, cinema. *Address:* Department of Geography, University of Cambridge, Cambridge CB2 3EN. *T:* (01223) 333393.

**RICHARDS, Louise;** Trade Union and Communications Co-ordinator, Nicaragua Solidarity Campaign, since 2013; *b* 11 July 1951; *d* of William and Evelyn Greene; *m* 1977, Anthony Richards. *Educ:* Univ. of Leicester (BA Hons). Head of International Department: NALGO, 1983–93; UNISON, 1993–2003; Chief Executive: War on Want, 2003–07; Computer Aid Internat., 2007–09; Dir of Policy and Campaigns, Inst. of Fundraising, 2009–12. Bd Mem., Community HEART, 2003–. *Recreations:* music, theatre, film.

**RICHARDS, Prof. Martin Paul Meredith;** Professor of Family Research, 1997–2005, now Emeritus, and Director of the Centre for Family Research, 1969–2005, Cambridge University; *b* 26 Jan. 1940; *s* of Paul Westmacott Richards and Sarah Anne Richards (*née* Hotham); *m* 1st, 1961, Evelyn Cowdy (marr. diss. 1966); 2nd, 1999, Sarah Smalley. *Educ:* Westminster Sch.; Trinity Coll., Cambridge (BA 1962; MA 1965; PhD 1965; ScD 1999). SRC Post-Doctoral Fellow, 1965–67; University of Cambridge: Res. Fellow, Trinity Coll., 1965–69; Mental Health Res. Fund Fellowship, 1970; Lectr in Social Psychology, 1970–89; Reader in Human Develt, 1989–97; Chm., Faculty of Soc. and Pol Scis, 1997, Head of Dept, 1996–99. Member: Biomedical Ethics (formerly Medicine and Society) Panel, Wellcome Trust, 1998–2006; Human Genetics Commn, 2000–05; Ethics and Governance

Council, UK Biobank, 2006–14 (Vice Chm., 2008–14); Nuffield Council on Bioethics, 2012–15. Vis. Fellow, Princeton Univ., 1966–67; Visitor, Centre for Cognitive Studies, Harvard Univ., 1967 and 1968; Winegard Vis. Prof., Univ. of Guelph, 1987; Hon. Vis. Prof., City Univ., 1992–94; de Lissa Fellow, Univ. of SA, 1993; William Evans Vis. Fellow, Univ. of Otago, 1997. Chm., Bardsey Is Trust, 1993–2000. *Publications*: (ed jtly) Race, Culture and Intelligence, 1972; (ed) The Integration of a Child into a Social World, 1974; (ed jtly) Benefits and Hazards of the New Obstetrics, 1977; (ed jtly) Separation and Special Care Baby Units, 1978; Infancy: the world of the newborn, 1980; (ed jtly) Parent-Baby Attachment in Premature Infants, 1983; Children in Social Worlds, 1986; (with J. Burgoyne and R. Ormrod) Divorce Matters, 1987; (ed jtly) The Politics of Maternity Care, 1990; (ed jtly) Obstetrics in the 1990s, 1992; (with J. Reibstein) Sexual Arrangements, 1992; (ed jtly) The Troubled Helix, 1996; (ed jtly) What is a Parent?, 1999; (ed jtly) Body Lore and Laws, 2002; (ed jtly) The Blackwell Companion to the Sociology of Families, 2003; (ed jtly) Children and their Families: contact, rights and welfare, 2003; (jtly) Supporting Children Through Family Change, 2003; (ed jtly) Kinship Matters, 2006; (ed jtly) Death Rites and Rights, 2007; (ed jtly) The Limits of Consent, 2009; (ed jtly) Regulating Autonomy, 2009; (ed jtly) Birth Rites and Rights, 2011; (ed jtly) Reproductive Donation, 2012; (ed jtly) Relatedness in Assisted Reproduction, 2014; (ed jtly) The Wiley Blackwell Companion to the Sociology of Families, 2014; (ed jtly) Regulating Reproductive Donation, 2015. *Recreations*: bird-watching, listening to blue grass music, alpine gardening, grandchildren. *Address*: c/o Centre for Family Research, University of Cambridge, Free School Lane, Cambridge CB2 3RQ.

**RICHARDS, Menna,** OBE 2010; Director (formerly Controller), BBC Wales, 2000–11; *b* 27 Feb. 1953; *d* of late Penri T. Richards and Dilys M. Richards; *m* 1985, Patrick Hannan (MBE 1994), journalist and broadcaster (*d* 2009). *Educ*: Maesteg Grammar Sch.; UCW, Aberystwyth (BA). Journalist, BBC Wales, 1975–83; HTV Wales: journalist, 1983–91; Controller, Factual and Gen. Programmes, 1991–93; Dir of Programmes, 1993–97; Man. Dir, 1997–99. Non-executive Director: Welsh Water, 2010–; WNO, 2010–18; Principality Building Soc., 2012–15. Vice-Pres., RWCMD, 2007–. Chair, ALOUD Charity, 2016–. Hon. Mem., Royal Soc. of Architects, Wales, 2017; Hon. Fellow: Univ. of Wales, Aberystwyth, 1999; NE Wales Inst., 2004; Cardiff Univ., 2007; Univ. of Wales, Lampeter, 2008; Cardiff Metropolitan Univ., 2012. FRTS 2001. DUniv Glamorgan, 2008; Hon. Dr Swansea, 2013. BBC NOW Hoddinott Medal, 2014; BAFTA Outstanding Contribn to Television, 2015. *Recreations*: music, family, friends. *Clubs*: Royal Over-Seas League; Newport Boat.

**RICHARDS, Prof. Sir Michael (Adrian),** Kt 2010; CBE 2001; MD; FRCP; Sainsbury Professor of Palliative Medicine, King's College London School of Medicine (formerly Guy's, King's and St Thomas' School of Medicine, King's College London), 1995–99; Chairman, National Cancer Research Institute, 2006–08; Chief Inspector of Hospitals, Care Quality Commission, 2013–17; *b* 14 July 1951; *s* of Donald Hibbert Richards and Peronelle Imogen (*née* Armitage-Smith). *Educ*: Dragon Sch., Oxford; Radley Coll.; Trinity Coll., Cambridge (MA); St Bartholomew's Hosp., London (MB BChir, MD 1988). FRCP 1993. ICRF Res. Fellow, St Bartholomew's Hosp., 1982–86; ICRF Sen. Lectr, 1986–91, Reader in Med. Oncology, 1991–95, Guy's Hosp., London; Clinical Dir of Cancer Services, Guy's and St Thomas' Hosps, 1993–99; Nat. Cancer Dir, DoH, 1999–2013; Dir for Reducing Premature Mortality (Domain 1), NHS England, 2012–13. Non-exec. Dir, DoH, subseq. DHSC, 2017–. Trustee, CRUK, 2017–. *Publications*: papers on breast cancer, cancer service delivery, palliative care, quality of life. *Recreations*: hill-walking, classical music. *Address*: 42 Liberia Road, N5 1JR.

**RICHARDS, Maj.-Gen. Nigel William Fairbairn,** CB 1998; OBE 1987; Chairman, Confederation of British Service and Ex-Service Organisations, 1999–2002; *b* 15 Aug. 1945; *s* of late Lt-Col William Fairbairn Richards RA and of Marjorie May Richards; *m* 1968, Christine Anne Helen Woods; two *s* one *d*. *Educ*: Eastbourne Coll.; RMA Sandhurst; Peterhouse, Cambridge (MA). Commissioned, RA, 1965; regtl duty, 1966–76, UK, Germany, NI, Cyprus, Malaya; RN Staff Coll., 1976–77; MoD, 1978–80; Comd J Anti-Tank Battery, RHA, 1980–81; Directing Staff, RMCS, 1982–83; CO 7 Para Regt, RHA, 1983–86; MoD, 1986–88; Higher Comd and Staff Course, 1988; Comdr 5 Airborne Brigade, 1989–90; RCDS 1991; Dir Army Staff Duties, MoD, 1991–93; Chief of Combat Support, HQ Allied Command Europe Rapid Reaction Corps, 1994–96; GOC 4th Div., 1996–98. President: British Forces South Western Europe, 1994–96; Army Boxing and Hockey, 1996–98. Hon. Col, 7 Para Regt RHA, 1999–2005; Col Comdt, RA, 2001–06. Chm., Peterhouse Soc., 2001–04. *Recreations*: cricket, fishing, ski-ing, golf. *Address*: 6 Park Road, Winchester, Hants SO22 6AA. *Club*: Army and Navy.

**RICHARDS, Peter Graham Gordon;** a District Judge (Magistrates' Courts) (formerly Stipendiary Magistrate), Staffordshire, 1991–2008; *b* 16 July 1939; *s* of David Gordon and Irene Florence Richards; *m* 1965, Jeanette Uncles (*d* 1997); two *d*. *Educ*: Univ. of London (LLM 1966). Schoolmaster, 1962–65; Lectr, 1965–68; called to the Bar, Middle Temple, 1968; Midland and Oxford Circuit, 1968–91. *Recreations*: sports broadcasting, travel, theatre, astronomy. *Address*: c/o Law Courts, Baker Street, Fenton, Stoke on Trent ST4 3BX.

**RICHARDS, His Honour Philip Brian;** a Circuit Judge, 2001–16; *b* 3 Aug. 1946; *s* of late Glyn Bevan Richards and Nancy Gwenhwyfar Richards (*née* Evans); *m* 1st, 1971, Dorothy Louise George (marr. diss.); two *d*; 2nd, 1994, Julia Jones; one *d*, and one step *s*. *Educ*: Univ. of Bristol (LLB Hons). Called to the Bar, Inner Temple, 1969; Asst Recorder, 1995–2000; Recorder, 2000–01. *Publications*: (jtly) Government of Wales Bill, 1996; Report on Judicial training in the Welsh language, 2003. *Recreations*: music, sport, theatre, literature, the history, culture, languages and constitution of Wales. *Clubs*: Cardiff and County; Mountain Ash Rugby Football.

**RICHARDS, (Robert) John (Godwin);** Senior Advisor, Värde Partners Europe Ltd, since 2011; *b* 11 Jan. 1956; *m* 1987, Amanda Joseph; two *s*. *Educ*: Poly. of Wales (BSc). FRICS. Joined Hammerson plc, 1981; Dir, 1990–2009; UK Develt Dir, 1990–93; UK Man. Dir, 1993–97; Internat. Man. Dir, 1997–99; Chief Exec., 1999–2009. President: British Council of Shopping Centres, 2003–04; British Property Fedn, 2010–11.

**RICHARDS, Sandra Anne;** see Phinbow, S. A.

**RICHARDS, Stephen;** Chief Political Commentator, Independent, since 2000; *b* London, 6 June 1960; *s* of Keith and Val Richards; *m* 2010, Barbara Schofield; one *s* one *d*. *Educ*: Christ's Coll., Finchley; Univ. of York (BA Hons Hist.). BBC: Community Affairs Corresp., 1987–90; Political Corresp., 1990–96; Political Ed., New Statesman, 1996–2000. *Publications*: Preparing for Power, 1997; Whatever it Takes: a history of New Labour, 2010; The Rise of the Outsiders: how mainstream politics lost its way, 2017. *Recreations*: running, watching football, performing one-man show.

**RICHARDS, Rt Hon. Sir Stephen (Price),** Kt 1997; PC 2005; a Lord Justice of Appeal, 2005–16; *b* 8 Dec. 1950; *s* of late (Richard) Alun Richards; *m* 1976, Lucy Elizabeth Stubbings, MA; two *s* one *d*. *Educ*: King's Coll. Sch., Wimbledon; St John's Coll., Oxford (open schol.; BA Lit.Hum. 1972; BA Jurisprudence 1974; MA 1977; Hon. Fellow, 2008). Called to the Bar, Gray's Inn, 1975 (Arden Schol. and Bacon Schol.; Bencher, 1992); Second Jun. Counsel, 1987–89, Standing Counsel, 1989–91, to Dir Gen. of Fair Trading; a Jun. Counsel to the Crown, 1990–91, First Jun. Treasury Counsel, Common Law, 1992–97; an Asst Recorder, 1992–96; a Recorder, 1996–97; a Judge of High Court of Justice, QBD, 1997–2005; a Presiding Judge, Wales and Chester Circuit, 2000–03; Dep. Hd of Civil Justice, 2013–16. Dep. Chm., Boundary Commn for Wales, 2001–05. Governor, King's Coll. Sch., Wimbledon, 1998–2007 (Chm., 2004–07). Hon. LLD Glamorgan, 2004. *Publications*: (ed jtly) Chitty on Contracts, 25th edn 1983, 26th edn 1989. *Recreations*: walking, relaxing in the Welsh hills.

**RICHARDS, Sir Vivian;** see Richards, Sir I. V. A.

**RICHARDS, Prof. (William) Graham,** CBE 2001; DPhil, DSc; FRS 2018; Professor of Chemistry, 1996–2007, now Emeritus, and Chairman of Chemistry, 1997–2006, Oxford University; Fellow of Brasenose College, Oxford, since 1966; *b* 1 Oct. 1939; *o s* of Percy Richards and Julia Richards (*née* Evans); *m* 1st, 1970, Jessamy Kershaw (*d* 1988); two *s*; 2nd, 1996, Mary Elizabeth Phillips. *Educ*: Birkenhead Sch.; Brasenose Coll., Oxford (MA; DPhil 1964; DSc 1985). ICI Res. Fellow, Balliol Coll., Oxford, 1964 (Hon. Fellow, 2006); Res. Fellow, CNRS, Paris, 1965; Lectr, 1966–94, Reader in Computational Chemistry, 1994–96, Dept of Physical Chemistry, Oxford Univ. Director: Oxford Molecular Gp plc, 1989–99 (Founding Scientist, 1989, Chm., 1990–93); Isis Innovation Ltd, 1994–2007; Catalyst Biomedica Ltd, 1998–2003; IP Gp Plc (formerly IP2IPO Gp), 2000–13 (Chm., 2004–06; Venture Partner, 2013–); Oxeco Plc, 2006–10; TdeltaS, 2007–12; Crysalin Ltd, 2008–10; Chm. and Founding Scientist, Oxford Drug Design Ltd (formerly Inhibox Ltd), 2002–. Res. Schol., Stanford Univ., 1975–76; Visiting Professor: Univ. of Calif at Berkeley, 1975–76; Stanford Univ., 1978–82. Mem., Bd of Dirs, Assoc. for Internat. Cancer Res., 1995–99. Member: Council, RSC, 2005–12; African Inst. of Mathematical Scis, 2005–; Council, Royal Inst., 2006–08. Editor, Jl of Molecular Graphics, 1984–96. Hon. FRSC 2018. Marlow Medal, 1972, Award for Theoretical Chem., 1989, RSC; Lloyd of Kilgerran Prize, Foundn for Sci. and Technol., 1996; Mullard Award, Royal Soc., 1998; Italgas Prize, 2001; Award for Computers in Chemical and Pharmaceutical Res., American Chemical Soc., 2004; Richard J. Bolte Award, Sci. History Inst., 2018. *Publications*: Ab Initio Molecular Orbital Calculations for Chemists, 1970, 2nd edn 1983; Bibliography of Ab Initio Wave Functions, 1971, supplements, 1974, 1978, 1981; Entropy and Energy Levels, 1974; Structure and Spectra of Atoms, 1976; Quantum Pharmacology, 1977, 2nd edn 1983; Spin-Orbit Coupling in Molecules, 1981; Structure and Spectra of Molecules, 1985; The Problems of Chemistry, 1986; Computer-Aided Molecular Design, 1989; Energy Levels of Atoms and Molecules, 1994; Computational Chemistry, 1995; An Introduction to Statistical Thermodynamics, 1995; Spin-outs: creating business from university intellectual property, 2009; 50 Years at Oxford, 2011; University Intellectual Property: a source of finance and impact, 2012; Entrepreneurship: a case study from two view points, 2016. *Recreations*: sport, running, swimming. *Address*: Brasenose College, Oxford OX1 4AJ. *T*: (01865) 277830. *Club*: Vincent's (Oxford).

**RICHARDS, Wyn;** see Richards, His Honour D. W.

**RICHARDSON,** family name of **Baroness Richardson of Calow**.

**RICHARDSON OF CALOW, Baroness** *cr* 1998 (Life Peer), of Calow in the co. of Derbyshire; **Rev. Kathleen Margaret Richardson,** OBE 1996; Moderator, Churches' Commission for Inter-Faith Relations, 1999–2006; *b* 24 Feb. 1938; *d* of Francis and Margaret Fountain; *m* 1964, Ian David Godfrey Richardson; three *d*. *Educ*: St Helena Sch., Chesterfield; Stockwell Coll. (Cert Ed); Deaconess Coll., Ilkley; Wesley House, Cambridge. School teacher, 1958–61. Wesley Deaconess, Champness Hall, Rochdale, 1961–64; Lay Worker, Team Ministry, Stevenage, 1973–77; Methodist Minister 1976–; Minister, Denby Dale and Clayton West Circuit, 1979–87; ordained presbyter, 1980; Chm., West Yorks Dist, 1987–95. Pres., Methodist Conf., 1992–93; Moderator, Free Church Federal Council, subseq. Free Churches' Council, 1995–99; a President, Churches Together in England, 1995–99; Chm., Commn on Urban Life and Faith, 2004–06. Mem., H of L, 1998–2018. Hon. DLitt Bradford, 1994; Hon. LLD Liverpool, 1999; Hon. DD Birmingham, 2000. *Recreations*: reading, needlework.

**RICHARDSON, Sir Anthony (Lewis),** 3rd Bt *cr* 1924; *b* 5 Aug. 1950; *s* of Sir Leslie Lewis Richardson, 2nd Bt, and of Joy Patricia, Lady Richardson, *d* of P. J. Rillstone, Johannesburg; *S* father, 1985; *m* 1985, Honor Gillian Dauney; one *s* one *d*. *Educ*: Diocesan College, Cape Town, S Africa. Stockbroker with L. Messel & Co., London, 1973–75; Insurance Broker with C. T. Bowring, London and Johannesburg, 1975–76; Stockbroker with Fergusson Bros, Hall, Stewart & Co., Johannesburg and Cape Town, 1976–78; Stockbroker with W. Greenwell & Co., London, 1979–81; with Rowe & Pitman, subseq. S. G. Warburg Securities, then SBC Warburg, London, 1981–99 (Dir, 1986–99), seconded to Potter Partners, Melbourne and Sydney, 1986–89, seconded to SBC Warburg, Johannesburg, 1996–99; Dir, Barclays Private Bank, London, 1999–. *Recreations*: various sports, photography. *Heir*: *s* William Lewis Richardson, *b* 15 Oct. 1992. *Clubs*: Boodle's, Hurlingham.

**RICHARDSON, Prof. Brian Frederick,** FBA 2003; Professor of Italian Language, University of Leeds, 1996–2012, now Emeritus; *b* 6 Dec. 1946; *s* of late Ronald Frederick Richardson, CBE and Anne Elizabeth Richardson (*née* McArdle); *m* 1973, Catherine Normand; three *d*. *Educ*: Lincoln Coll., Oxford (MA); Bedford Coll., London (MPhil). Lecturer in Italian: Univ. of Strathclyde, 1970–72; Univ. of Aberdeen, 1972–76; Lectr, 1977–89, Sen. Lectr, 1989–96, Univ. of Leeds. Gen. Editor, Modern Language Review, 2004–13. *Publications*: (ed) N. Machiavelli, Il principe, 1979; (ed) Trattati sull'ortografia del volgare, 1984; Print Culture in Renaissance Italy, 1994; Printing, Writers and Readers in Renaissance Italy, 1999; (ed) G. F. Fortunio, Regole grammaticali della volgar lingua, 2001; Manuscript Culture in Renaissance Italy, 2009. *Recreations*: music, walking, gardening. *Address*: School of Languages, Cultures and Societies, University of Leeds, Leeds LS2 9JT.

**RICHARDSON, Prof. David J.,** PhD; Professor of Microbial Biochemistry, since 2001, and Vice-Chancellor, since 2014, University of East Anglia; *m* Andrea Blanchflower; two *c*. *Educ*: Univ. of Keele (BSc); Univ. of Birmingham (PhD 1988). Postdoctoral Res. Associate, Dept of Biochem., Univ. of Oxford, 1988–91; University of East Anglia: Lectr, 1991–98, Reader, 1998–2001, Sch. of Biol Scis; Associate Dean, 2004–07, Exec. Dean, 2008–11, Faculty of Sci.; Pro-Vice Chancellor, Enterprise and Engagement, 2011–12; Dep. Vice-Chancellor, 2012–14. Wolfson Merit Fellow, Royal Soc., 2008–13. Mem. Bd, 2012–, Chm., 2016–, Norwich Res. Park. Mem., BBSRC, 2012–16. Non-exec. Dir, Norfolk and Norwich Univ. Hosps NHS Foundn Trust, 2014–. Pres., Royal Norfolk Agricl Assoc., 2016–17. Fleming Medal, Soc. for Gen. Microbiol., 1999. *Publications*: articles in jls. *Address*: University of East Anglia, Norwich, Norfolk NR4 7TJ.

**RICHARDSON, His Honour Rev. David John;** a Circuit Judge, 2000–18; an Additional Judge of the Employment Appeal Tribunal, 2003; *b* 23 June 1950; *s* of Abraham Eric Richardson and Gwendoline Richardson (*née* Ballard); *m* 1980, Jennifer Margaret Richardson (*née* Cooke); one *s* one *d*. *Educ*: John Ruskin Grammar Sch., Croydon; Trinity Hall, Cambridge (BA 1971, MA; LLB 1972); Southwark Ordination Trng Course. Called to the Bar, Middle Temple, 1973; in practice, 1973–2000; an Asst Recorder, 1992–97; a Recorder, 1997–2000. Judicial Mem., Parole Bd, 2018–. Ordained deacon, 1985, priest, 1986; Hon. Curate, Emmanuel Church, S Croydon, 1985–2006. *Recreations:* walking, reading, supporter of Crystal Palace FC.

**RICHARDSON, David John;** Chief Executive, International Cricket Council, 2012–19; *b* Johannesburg, 16 Sept. 1959; *s* of John Henry Richardson and Margaret Ann Richardson; *m* 1985, Jennifer Elizabeth Grüttner; three *s*. *Educ:* Marist Brothers Coll., Port Elizabeth; Univ. of Port Elizabeth (BComm; LLB 1982); London Business Sch. (Sen. Exec. Prog. 2008). Played 1st class cricket for Eastern Province and South Africa, 1978–98 (Captain, Eastern Province, 1987–88); represented South Africa (wicket keeper/batsman) in 42 Tests and 122 One Day Internats. Dir, Pagdens Inc., attorneys, 1985–98; Business Dir, ESPM Legends (Pty) Ltd, subseq. Octagon SA (Pty) Ltd, sports mktg and events, 1998–2002; Gen. Manager, Cricket, ICC, 2002–12. Cricket Commentator, M-Net Supersport, 2000–02. Member: World Cricket Cttee, MCC, 2009–; Internat. Adv. Bd, World Acad. of Sport, 2013. Alumni Achievers Award, Nelson Mandela Metropolitan Univ., 2010. *Recreations:* golf, reading, family. *Club:* MCC (Hon. Life Mem., 2002).

**RICHARDSON, Prof. David John,** PhD; FRS 2018; FREng; Professor of Optoelectronics, since 1999, and Deputy Director, Optoelectronics Research Centre, since 2000, University of Southampton; *b* Southampton, 9 Jan. 1964; *s* of John and Anne Richardson; *m* 1994, Julia Hill; four *d*. *Educ:* St George's RC Sch., Southampton; Taunton's Coll., Southampton; Univ. of Sussex (BSc Hons; PhD Physics 1989). Res. student, Inst. Laue-Langevin, Grenoble, 1985–89; Res. Fellow, 1989–92, Royal Soc. Univ. Res. Fellow, 1992–2002, Univ. of Southampton. Consultant, SPI Lasers Ltd, 2000–16; CSO/Dir, Lumenisity Ltd, 2017–. FREng 2009. *Publications:* (jtly) Ultra-cold Neutrons, 1991; contribs to tech. jls. *Recreations:* golf, walking, family. *Address:* Optoelectronics Research Centre, University of Southampton, Highfield, Southampton SO17 1BJ. *T:* (023) 8059 4524. *E:* djr1@soton.ac.uk.

**RICHARDSON, Very Rev. Canon David John Leyburn,** AO 2016; OBE 2013; Archbishop of Canterbury's Representative to the Holy See, and Director, Anglican Centre in Rome, 2008–13; *b* Townsville, Qld, 14 March 1946; *s* of David James Leyburn Richardson and Alice May Richardson (*née* Tansey); *m* 1972, Margaret Rosalind Lewis; one *s* one *d*. *Educ:* Univ. of Queensland (BA 1969); St Barnabas' Coll., Adelaide (ThL 1970); Melbourne Coll. of Divinity (BD 1975); Univ. of Birmingham (Dip. in Pastoral Theol. 1976). Ordained deacon, 1970, priest, 1971; Assistant: St Paul's, Maryborough, 1972–73; Ipswich, 1974–75; St Francis, Birmingham, 1975–76; Chaplain, Girton Coll., Cambridge and Asst Curate, Great St Mary's Church, 1976–79; Sub-Warden, St Barnabas' Coll., Adelaide, 1979–82; Rector, Christ Church, St Lucia, Brisbane, 1982–88; Rector, 1988–89, Dean, 1989–99, St Peter's Cathedral, Adelaide; Dean, St Paul's Cathedral, Melbourne, 1999–2008, now Emeritus. Member: Gen. Synod, and Standing Cttee of Gen. Synod, Anglican Ch of Australia, 1988–2007; Bd of Election of Primate of Anglican Ch of Australia, 2007–08. Hon. Canon, Canterbury Cathedral, 2010–13, now Emeritus. Exec. Sec., Nat. Liturgical Commn, 1985–99; Nat. Rep., Anglican Consultative Council, 1992–2002. Mem., Ethics Cttee, Wakefield St Hosp., Adelaide, 1991–99. Gov., St Peter's Collegiate Girls Sch., Adelaide, 1989–98; Dep. Chm., Council, St Peter's Coll., Adelaide, 1998–99; Mem. Council, Melbourne Girls Grammar, 1999–2008. ChStJ 1996. *Recreations:* music, literature. *Clubs:* Adelaide, Melbourne.

**RICHARDSON, Prof. Genevra Mercy,** CBE 2007; FBA 2007; Professor of Law, King's College London, since 2005; *b* 1 Sept. 1948; *d* of John Lawrence Richardson and Josephine Juliet Richardson; *m* 1977, Oliver Thorold (*see* Sir A. O. Thorold); one *s* one *d*. *Educ:* King's Coll., London (LLB, LLM). Res. Officer, Centre for Socio-Legal Studies, Oxford, 1974–78; Lectr, UEA, 1979–87; Lectr, 1987–89, Reader, 1989–94, Prof. of Public Law, 1994–2005, Dean, Faculty of Law, 1996–99, QMW, subseq. Queen Mary, Univ. of London. Chm., Expert Cttee Advising Ministers on Reform of Mental Health Legislation, 1998–99. Mem., Administrative Justice & Tribunals Council (formerly Council on Tribunals), 2001–10. Member: Mental Health Act Commn, 1987–92; Animal Procedures Cttee, 1998–2006; Chairman: Prisoner's Advice Service, 1994–2002; Appointing Authy for Phase 1 Ethics Cttees, 2009–12. Mem. Council, MRC, 2001–08. Vice Pres., Public Policy, British Acad., 2016–. Trustee: Nuffield Foundn, 2002–14; Med. Res. Foundn, 2006–14. Hon. FRCPsych 2004. *Recreations:* walking, travel. *Address:* School of Law, King's College, Strand, WC2R 2LS. *E:* genevra.richardson@kcl.ac.uk.

**RICHARDSON, Prof. Guy Peel,** PhD; FRS 2009; Professorial Fellow, Hearing Research Centre, School of Life Sciences, University of Sussex, since 2004. *Educ:* Univ. of Sussex (BSc Neurosci. 1975; PhD 1980). Univ. of Sussex, 1984–. Member, Research Advisory Panel: Deafness Research UK; RNID. FMedSci 2013. *Publications:* articles in jls. *Address:* School of Life Sciences, University of Sussex, Falmer, Brighton BN1 9QG.

**RICHARDSON, Hugh;** Head, Delegation of European Commission to Tokyo, 2006–09; Ambassador of European Union to Japan, 2009–10; *b* 12 May 1947; *s* of Robert Richardson and Pauline (*née* Broadhurst); *m* (marr. diss.); two *s* three *d*; *m* 2000, Lisbeth Van Impe. *Educ:* Pembroke Coll., Oxford (BA 1969; BCL 1970; MA 2002). Commission of the European Communities: with Secretariat Gen., 1974–79; Directorate-Gen. for External Relns, 1979–84; Counsellor and Dep. Head, Tokyo Delegn, 1984–88; Asst to DG for External Relns, 1988–91; Dir, Rights and Obligations, Directorate-Gen. for Personnel and Admin, 1991–96; Deputy Director General: Jt Res. Centre, 1996–2002; DG Res., 2002–04; DG EuropeAid Co-operation Office, 2004–06. *Publications:* EC-Japan Relations: after adolescence, 1989. *Recreations:* sailing, ski-ing, running.

**RICHARDSON, James Colin,** CB 2019; PhD; Chief Economist, National Infrastructure Commission, since 2016; *b* Windsor, 5 Oct. 1965; *s* of Colin Richardson and Anne Richardson; *m* 2001, Rebecca Stanley; one *d*. *Educ:* Balliol Coll., Oxford (BA Hons PPE 1988); London Sch. of Econs and Pol Sci. (PhD Econs 1999). Chief Microeconomist, 2007–12, Dir, Public Spending, 2008–12, Dir, Fiscal, and Dep. Chief Economic Advr, 2012–16, HM Treasury. Dir, HM Treasury UK Sovereign Sukuk, 2014–16. Mem., ESRC, 2013–17. *Recreations:* photography, running, family, reading, theatre. *E:* James.Richardson@nic.gov.uk.

**RICHARDSON, Rev. Canon James John,** OBE 2007; Hon. Canon Pastor, 2009–14, Hon. Assistant Priest, since 2014, Sherborne Abbey; *b* 28 March 1941; *s* of late James John Richardson and Gladys May (*née* Evans); *m* 1966, Janet Rosemary Welstand; two *s* one *d*. *Educ:* Catford Central Sch.; Hull Univ. (BA); Sheffield Univ. (DipEd); Cuddesdon Coll., Oxford; Leicester Univ. Assistant Master, Westfield Comp. Sch., Sheffield, 1964–66; Curate, St Peter's Collegiate Church, Wolverhampton, 1969–72; Priest i/c, All Saints, Hanley, Stoke-on-Trent, 1972–75; Rector of Nantwich, 1975–82; Vicar of Leeds, 1982–88; Exec. Dir, CCJ, 1988–92; Priest-in-Charge: Gt Brington, Whilton and Norton (Northampton), dio. of Peterborough, 1993–96; E Haddon and Holdenby, Church and Chapel Brampton and Harlestone, 1994–96; St Augustine, Bournemouth, 2001–08; Team Rector, Bournemouth Town Centre Parish, 1996–2008. Hon. Canon, 1982–88, Canon Emeritus, 1988–, Ripon Cathedral. Chaplain: to Earl Spencer, 1993–96; to High Sheriff of Northants, 1995–96; to Mayor of Bournemouth, 2002–03 and 2006–07; to High Sheriff of Dorset, 2007–08. Chm., Racial Harassment Commn, Leeds, 1986–87; N of England Vice-Pres., UN Year of Peace, 1986–87. Chairman: Bournemouth Town Centre Detached Youth Project, 1997–2008; Churches Together in Bournemouth, 1998–2002; Director: Bournemouth Millennium Co., 1998–99; Hope FM Radio, 1998–2001. Member: Council, Centre for the Study of Judaism and Jewish/Christian Relations, Selly Oak Coll., 1989–94; Internat. Council of Christians and Jews Adv. Cttee, 1992–96; Council, Order of St John, Dorset, 2010–13. Member: Partnership Steering Cttee, Bournemouth BC, 2001–03; Bournemouth BC Standards Bd, 2003– (Vice-Chm., 2003–07; Chm., 2007–08); Bournemouth BC Schs Orgn Cttee, 2003–06; Bournemouth Town Centre Mgt Bd, 2003–08. Mem. Court, Leeds Univ., 1986–88; Chairman of Governors: Abbey Grange High Sch., Leeds, 1982–88; Leeds Grammar Sch., 1983–88; Governor: Leeds Girls' High Sch., 1982–88; Leeds Music Fest., 1982–88; Chm. Steering Gp, New Church Secondary Sch. for Bournemouth, 2001–03. FRSA 1991. Hon. Freeman, Bor. of Bournemouth, 2008. *Publications:* (contrib.) Four Score Years, 1989; contrib. Yorkshire Post, 1982–90. *Recreations:* leading pilgrimages to Israel, biography—especially life and times of Rupert Brooke, deciphering Tudor churchwardens' accounts. *Address:* 23 Mount Pleasant, Clerk Bank, Leek, Staffs ST13 5HB. *T:* (01538) 398748. *E:* Canonrichardson@btinternet.com.

**RICHARDSON, Jennifer;** *see* Brown, J.

**RICHARDSON, Prof. Jeremy John,** PhD; Fellow, 1998–2003, and Senior Tutor, 2001–03, Nuffield College, Oxford, now Emeritus Fellow; Professor, National Centre for Research on Europe, University of Canterbury, New Zealand, since 2008; *b* 15 June 1942; *s* of Samuel Radcliffe Richardson and Sarah Doris Richardson; *m* 1966, Anne Philippsen (marr. diss. 1993); one *s* one *d*; *m* 1994, Sonia Pauline Mazey; two *d*. *Educ:* Univ. of Keele (BA Hons Politics and Econs); Univ. of Manchester (MA Econ; PhD 1970). Asst Lectr, Lectr, then Reader, Univ. of Keele, 1966–82; Professor: Dept of Politics, Univ. of Strathclyde, 1982–92; Univ. of Warwick, 1992–95; Univ. of Essex, 1995–98; Nuffield Prof. of Comparative European Politics and Dir, Centre for European Politics, Economics and Society, Oxford Univ., 1998–2001. Ed., Jl of European Public Policy, 1993–. Hon. Dr Pol Sci., Umeå, 1995. *Publications:* The Policy-Making Process, 1969; (ed with R. Kimber) Campaigning for the Environment, 1974; (ed with R. Kimber) Pressure Groups in Britain: a reader, 1974; (with A. Grant Jordan) Governing Under Pressure: the policy process in a post-parliamentary democracy, 1979; (ed with R. Henning) Policy Responses to Unemployment in Western Democracies, 1984; (with J. Moon) Unemployment in the UK: politics and policies, 1985; (with A Grant Jordan) Government & Pressure Groups in Britain, 1987; (ed jtly) The Politics of Economic Crisis: lessons from Western Europe, 1989; (jtly) Local Partnership and the Unemployment Crisis in Britain, 1989; (with G. Dudley) Politics and Steel in Britain 1967–1988, 1990; (ed) Privatisation and Deregulation in Canada and Britain, 1990; (with S. Mazey) Lobbying in the European Community, 1993; (ed) Pressure Groups, 1993; (jtly) True Blues: the politics of Conservative Party membership, 1994; (jtly) Networks for Water Policy: a comparative perspective, 1994; (with W. Maloney) Managing Policy Change in Britain: the politics of water policy, 1995; (ed) European Union: power and policy-making, 1996, 4th edn (ed with S. Mazey) 2015; (with G. Dudley) Why Does Policy Change?: lessons from British transport policy 1945–1999, 2000; (with D. Coen) Lobbying in the European Union: institutions, actors and issues, 2009; Constructing a Policy-Making State?: policy dynamics in the European Union, 2012; (with S. Mazey) European Union: power and policy-making, 2015; British Policy-Making and the Need for a Post-Brexit Policy Style, 2018. *Recreations:* gardening, DIY, walking. *Address:* 30 Queen's Avenue, Fendalton, Christchurch 8014, New Zealand. *T:* (3) 3559161.

**RICHARDSON, Jeremy William;** QC 2000; **His Honour Judge Jeremy Richardson;** a Circuit Judge, since 2009; a Senior Circuit Judge, since 2018; Resident Judge, Sheffield Combined Court Centre, since 2018; *b* 3 April 1958; *s* of late Thomas William Sydney Raymond Richardson and of Jean Mary Richardson (*née* Revill); *m* 2006, David Carruthers. *Educ:* Forest Sch.; Queen Mary Coll., Univ. of London (LLB Hons 1979). Called to the Bar, Inner Temple, 1980, Bencher, 2007; in practice at the Bar, NE Circuit, 1982–2009; Asst Recorder, 1998–2000; Recorder, 2000–09; Dep. High Court Judge, Family Div., 2004–09; Designated Civil Judge for Humberside, 2009–15; Recorder: of Hull and E Riding, 2015–18; of Sheffield, 2018; Resident Judge of the Humber Courts (Hull and Grimsby), 2015–18. Mem., Gen. Council of the Bar, 1992–94. Sec., NE Circuit, 1991–96. *Address:* Sheffield Combined Court Centre, The Law Courts, 50 West Bar, Sheffield S3 8PH.

**RICHARDSON, Joely;** actress; *b* 9 Jan. 1965; *d* of late Tony Richardson and of Vanessa Redgrave, *qv*; *m* 1992, Tim Bevan, *qv* (marr. diss. 2001); one *d*. *Educ:* Lycée Français de Londres; St Paul's Girls' Sch.; Pinellas Park High Sch., Florida; Thacher Sch., Calif; RADA. West End début, Steel Magnolias, Lyric, 1989; Lady Windermere's Fan, Haymarket, 2002; The Lady from the Sea, Rose Th., Kingston, 2012; Ivanov, Classic Stage Co., NY, 2012; The Wars of the Roses, Rose Th., Kingston, 2015. *Films include:* Wetherby, 1985; Drowning by Numbers, 1988; Shining Through, Rebecca's Daughters, 1992; Sister, My Sister, 1995; Loch Ness, Believe Me, 101 Dalmatians, Hollow Reed, 1996; Event Horizon, 1997; Wrestling with Alligators, Under Heaven, 1998; Maybe Baby, Return to Me, The Patriot, 2000; The Affair of the Necklace, 2002; Anonymous, The Girl with the Dragon Tattoo, 2011; Red Lights, 2012; Thanks for Sharing, 2013; Vampire Academy, Endless Love, 2014; Maggie, The Messenger, 2015; Snowden, The Hatton Garden Job, 2016; Red Sparrow, In Darkness, Surviving Christmas with the Relatives, 2018; *television includes:* Body Contact, 1987; Behaving Badly, 1989; Heading Home, 1991; The Storyteller, Lady Chatterley's Lover, 1993; The Tribe, Echo, 1998; Nip/Tuck, 2004–10; Wallis and Edward, 2005; Fatal Contact, 2007; Day of the Triffids, 2009; Emerald City, 2016.

**RICHARDSON, John Charles;** Managing Director, Historical Publications Ltd, since 1971; *b* 7 June 1935; *s* of Joseph and Vera Richardson; *m* 1st, 1957, Laura Caroline Bourne Webb (marr. diss. 1962); two *s*; 2nd, 1966, Elizabeth Noel Ballard (marr. diss. 1981); two *s*; 3rd, 1981, Helen Warnock English. *Educ:* Barking Abbey GS. J. Walter Thompson, 1965–72; KMP, 1974–84. Member: St Pancras BC, 1959–66; Camden BC, 1966–71. Joint Founder: GLAA, 1966; Camden Arts Centre, 1966; Chm., Bubble Theatre Co., 1968–74. Chm., Camden Hist. Soc., 1970–. *Publications:* The Local Historian's Encyclopedia, 1974; Covent Garden, 1979; Highgate: its history since the fifteenth century, 1983; Hampstead One Thousand, 1985; Islington Past, 1988; Highgate Past, 1989; Camden Town and Primrose Hill Past, 1991; London and its People, 1995; Covent Garden Past, 1995; Kentish Town Past, 1997; A History of Camden, 1999; The Annals of London, 2000; The Camden Town Book, 2007. *Recreations:* visiting the London Library, architecture. *Address:* 14 Saddleton Road, Whitstable, Kent CT5 4JD. *T:* (01227) 272605.

**RICHARDSON, Rt Rev. John Henry;** Suffragan Bishop of Bedford, 1994–2002; an Hon. Assistant Bishop, Dioceses of Carlisle and Newcastle, since 2003; *b* 11 July 1937; *s* of John Farquhar Richardson and Elizabeth Mary Richardson; *m* 1963, Felicity-Anne Lowes; three *d*. *Educ:* Winchester; Trinity Hall, Cambridge (BA 1961; MA 1965); Cuddesdon Coll., Oxford. Nat. Service, 1956–58 (despatches, Malaya, 1958). Ordained deacon, 1963, priest, 1964; Asst Curate, St George's, Stevenage, 1963–66; Curate, St Mary's, Eastbourne, 1966–68; Vicar: St Paul's, Chipperfield, 1968–75; St Mary's, Rickmansworth, 1975–86; RD, Rickmansworth, 1977–86; Vicar, St Michael's, Bishop's Stortford, 1986–93; Hon.

Canon, St Albans Cathedral, 1986–2002. Hon. Fellow, Luton Univ., 2003. *Recreations:* walking, bird-watching, fishing, energetic gardening. *Address:* The Old Rectory, Bewcastle, Carlisle, Cumbria CA6 6PS. *T:* (016977) 48389. *E:* bishop.bewcastle@aol.co.uk. *Clubs:* Royal Automobile; Leander.

**RICHARDSON, Very Rev. John Stephen;** Assistant Priest, Romney Marsh Benefice, since 2016; Chairman, Aquila, Diocese of Canterbury Multi-Academy Trust, since 2014; *b* 2 April 1950; *s* of James Geoffrey and Myra Richardson; *m* 1972, Elizabeth Susan Wiltshire; one *s* two *d* (and one *s* decd). *Educ:* Haslingden Grammar Sch.; Univ. of Southampton (BA Hons Theology); St John's Theological Coll., Nottingham. Deacon 1974, priest 1975; Asst Curate, St Michael's, Bramcote, 1974–77; Priest-in-Charge, Emmanuel Church, Radipole and Melcombe Regis, 1977–80; Asst Diocesan Missioner and Lay Trainer Adviser, dio. of Salisbury and Priest-in-Charge of Stinsford, Winterborne Monkton and Winterborne Came with Witcombe, 1980–83; Vicar of Christ Church, Nailsea, 1983–90; Adviser in Evangelism, dio. of Bath and Wells, 1985–90; Provost, subseq. Dean, of Bradford, 1990–2001; Vicar of Wye and Brook with Hastingleigh, and Chaplain, Imperial Coll. London (Wye Agricultural Coll., later Wye Coll.), 2001–09; Area Dean of West Bridge, 2003–09; Priest-in-charge: Boughton Aluph and Eastwell, 2004–09, and of Hinxhill, 2007–09; Holy Trinity, Margate, 2009–16; Asst Area Dean of Thanet, 2009–15; Advr to Bishop of Dover on Deliverance Ministry, 2010–. Dir, Spring Harvest, 1998–2003 and 2007–11; Chm., Spring Harvest Charitable Trust, 1998–2012. Chaplain, W Yorks Police, 1995–2001. Bishop's Selector, ABM, 1993–97. Mem., General Synod, 1993–2001. Member: Exec. Bd, Common Purpose, 1992–2000; BBC North Adv. Panel, 1990–94; Bradford Breakthrough, 1992–2001; Council, Evangelical Alliance Management Gp, 1994–2000; Council, Scripture Union, 2000–07; Archbishop's Council, Dio. of Canterbury, 2013–15; Canterbury Diocesan Bd of Educn, 2013–. Mem. Council, Bradford Chamber of Commerce, 1992–2001. Director: Mildmay Hosp., 2004– (Chm., 2007–); Kent Community Housing Trust, 2005–08. Trustee: Acorn Healing Trust, 1990–2007; Spennithorne Hall, 1990–98; Northumbria Community, 2006–09. Council Mem., St John's Theological Coll., Nottingham, 1988–94; Governor: Bradford Grammar Sch., 1990–2001; Giggleswick Sch., 1993–2001; Bradford Cathedral Community Coll. (formerly Fairfax Sch., then Bowling Community Coll.), 1994–2001. Chaplain to: High Sheriff, W Yorks, 1994–95, 2000–01; High Sheriff, Kent, 2004–05. Dir, Monnaie Chapel, Guernsey, 2013–. MInstD 1994. *Publications:* Ten Rural Churches, 1988. *Recreations:* football, cricket, North Western Municipal Bus Operators, walking, writing, broadcasting. *Address:* The Rectory, 135 High Street, Dymchurch, Kent TN29 0LD. *T:* (01303) 980027. *E:* vicarjsr@icloud.com.

**RICHARDSON, John Stephen;** Director, St Andrew's School, Turi, Kenya, 2015–17; education consultant, since 2010; *b* 2 Dec. 1953; *s* of Rev. James H. Richardson and Rachel Richardson (*née* Varley); *m* 1989, Ruth W. Vardy; two *s* one *d*. *Educ:* Rossall Sch.; Selwyn Coll., Cambridge (BA 1976; PGCE 1977; MA 1978). Dean Close School, Cheltenham, 1977–84: Teacher of Maths, Housemaster and Curriculum Dir; OC CCF/RAF Section; Eton College, 1984–92: Teacher of Maths, House List, Chapel Steward; Master i/c U16 Rowing; OC CCF/RAF Section; Treas., Eton Action; Headmaster: Culford Sch., Bury St Edmunds, 1992–2004; Cheltenham Coll., 2004–10. ISI Inspector, 1993–2004; Chm., East Div., HMC, 2000–02; Mem., NAHT, 1992–2010. Vice Chm., Curriculum Evaluation and Mgt Centre, Durham Univ., 2000–04. Mem. Council of Reference, Cheltenham Youth for Christ, 2007–08. Trustee, Ind. Schs Christian Alliance, 1994–2002. Chm. Govs, Kingham Hill Sch., 2012–18; Trustee, Kingham Hill Trust, 2012–18; Vice Chm. Govs, Elstree Sch., 2012–15; Gov., Wrekin Old Hall Schs, 2015–16. FRSA 2007. Foundn Fellow, Univ. of Gloucester, 2006–10. *Recreations:* reading, sailing, mountaineering. *Address:* White Gables, Moorend Road, Charlton Kings, Cheltenham, Glos GL53 9BN. *T:* (01242) 250754. *E:* jsr1253@gmail.com.

**RICHARDSON, Kenneth Augustus,** CVO 1994; CBE 1989; JP; Secretary to the Cabinet, Bermuda, 1984–93; *b* 13 Feb. 1939; *s* of Augustus J. Richardson; *m* 1966, Brenda Joyce (*née* Smith); one *s* one *d*. *Educ:* Howard Univ., Washington (BSc); Manchester Polytechnic (Dip. Personnel Admin and Labour Relations). Teacher, Sandys Secondary School, Bermuda, 1964; Admin. Cadet, Colonial Sec.'s Office, 1967; Training and Recruitment Officer, Bermuda Govt, 1969; Perm. Sec., Labour and Home Affairs, 1974. Chm., Employment Tribunal, 1990–. Fellow, Bermuda Coll., 1994. Hon. Life Vice Pres., Bermuda Football Assoc., 1994. MIPM 1973; MInstD 1988. JP 1984. *Recreation:* sport (soccer, tennis). *Address:* Mahogany, 19 Trimingham Hill, Paget PG 05, Bermuda; PO Box HM 1703, Hamilton HM GX, Bermuda. *T:* 236 1788.

**RICHARDSON, Prof. Louise Mary,** PhD; FRSE; Vice-Chancellor, University of Oxford, since 2016; *b* Dublin, 8 June; *d* of Arthur and Julie Richardson; *m* 1988, Thomas Jevon; one *s* two *d*. *Educ:* Trinity Coll., Dublin (BA Hist., 1980; MA Hist. 1982); Univ. of California, Los Angeles (MA Pol Sci. 1981); Harvard Univ. (MA Govt 1984; PhD Govt 1989). FRSE 2010. Asst Prof. of Govt, 1989–94, Associate Prof., 1994–2001, Harvard Univ.; Lectr on Law, Harvard Law Sch., 2001–08; Exec. Dean, Radcliffe Inst. for Advanced Study, 2001–08; Principal and Vice-Chancellor, 2009–15, Prof. of Internat. Relns, 2010–15, Univ. of St Andrews. Mem., Council of Econ. Advrs, Scottish Govt, 2011–15. Member, Board: Carnegie Corp., 2013–; Booker Prize Foundn, 2014–. Member: Amer. Acad. of Arts and Scis, 2016; Acad. of Social Scis, 2016. Hon. MRIA 2015. Hon. Dr: Moscow State Inst. of Internat. Relns, 2013; Hon. DSSc QUB, 2015; Hon. LLD: Aberdeen, 2015; UWI, 2016; Notre Dame, 2018; Hon. DLitt St Andrews, 2016; Hon. DSc TCD, 2016; Hon. DPhil Edinburgh, 2017. *Publications:* When Allies Differ, 1996; What Terrorists Want, 2006; (ed) The Roots of Terrorism, 2006; (ed jtly) Democracy and Counterterrorism: lessons from the past, 2007. *Address:* University of Oxford, Wellington Square, Oxford OX1 2JD. *T:* (01865) 280458. *E:* vcweb@admin.ox.ac.uk.

**RICHARDSON, Malcolm,** OBE 2018; JP; Chief Executive, Acuta Ltd, since 1994; Vice President, Magistrates' Association, since 2017 (Deputy Chairman, 2010–15; National Chairman, 2015–17); *b* Derby, 30 Aug. 1948; *s* of Alfred and Mary Lloyd Richardson; *m* 1970, Judith Mary Barker; one *s*. *Educ:* Bemrose Sch., Derby; Sir John Cass Coll. (BSc Maths 1969). Systems Engr, IBM UK Ltd, 1969–75; Software Developer, IBM Corp., 1975–78; IBM UK Ltd: Systems Manager, 1978–83; Consultancy Services Manager, 1983–90; Business Sch. Manager, 1990–94. Mem., Family Justice Council, 2004–08. JP Avon, 1989; Chm., N Avon Magistrates, 2004–06. Columnist, Family Law jl, 2015–. FRSA 2016. *Publications:* (contrib.) The Magistracy at the Crossroads, 2012. *Recreations:* travel, food, wine, art, theatre, opera, fine weather gardening, collecting ties, pocket handkerchiefs and Starbuck's city mugs. *Address:* Dean House, Oldbury on Severn BS35 1PL. *T:* (01454) 411560. *E:* malcolm.richardson@acuta.co.uk. *Club:* Army and Navy.

**RICHARDSON, Margaret Ann,** OBE 2005; FSA; Curator, Sir John Soane's Museum, 1995–2005 (Assistant Curator, 1985–95); *b* 11 Sept. 1937; *d* of late James Ballard and Edna (*née* Johnstone); *m* 1963, Anthony George Richardson; two *d*. *Educ:* Harrogate Coll.; University Coll. London (BA Hons; Fellow, 2001); Courtauld Inst. of Art (Acad. Dip.). FSA 1996. Asst Curator, 1963–68, Jt Dep. Curator, 1972–85, Drawings Collection, British Architectural Liby. Pres., Twentieth Century Soc., 1995–2003 (Mem. Cttee, 1984–2003); Trustee: Save Britain's Heritage, 1975–2015; Lutyens Trust, 1984– (Chm., 1994–2001); Greenwich Foundn for RNC, 1997–2004; Member, Council: Nat. Trust, 2002–11; Soc. of Antiquaries, 2010–14. Hon. Curator of Architecture, RA, 2005–15. Hon. FRIBA 1994. *Publications:* (ed) RIBA Catalogue series, vols A, B, C–F, and S, 1969–76; Edwin Lutyens, 1973; Lutyens and the Sea Captain, 1981; (jtly) Great Drawings from the RIBA, 1983; Architects of the Arts and Crafts Movement, 1983; 66 Portland Place: the London headquarters of the RIBA, 1984; (jtly) The Art of the Architect, 1984; Sketches by Lutyens, 1994; (ed jtly) John Soane Architect: master of space and light, 1999. *Address:* 64 Albert Street, NW1 7NR. *T:* (020) 7387 7940.

*See also V. Richardson.*

**RICHARDSON, Martin Hugo;** QC (Scot.) 2017; *b* St Andrews, 26 Aug. 1974; *s* of John Stuart Richardson and Patricia Helen Richardson (*née* Robotham); *m* 2000; two *s*. *Educ:* Madras Coll., St Andrews; Edinburgh Acad.; Univ. of Edinburgh (LLB Hons 1996; DipLP 1998); Rijks Universiteit, Leiden (LLM 1997). Admitted: solicitor, 2000; Advocate, 2004. *Recreations:* walking, reading. *Address:* Advocates Library, Faculty of Advocates, Edinburgh EH1 1RF.

**RICHARDSON, Dame Mary,** DBE 2001; Chief Executive, HSBC Global Education Trust, 1999–2008; *b* 26 Feb. 1936; *d* of Lt George Arthur Habgood, RN, and Anna Jane Habgood; *m* 1960, Dr Donald Arthur Richardson; one *s* one *d*. *Educ:* Notre Dame High Sch., Wigan; Liverpool Univ. (BA 1957; DipEd 1958). Officer, WRAC, 1954–60. Pt-time teacher, St Adrian's Jun. Sch., 1963–72; Hd of Sixth Form, then Hd of English, Marlborough Sch., St Albans, 1977–85; Dep. Hd, Convent of Jesus and Mary, Willesden, 1985–86; Principal, Convent of Jesus and Mary Lang. Coll., Harlesden, 1986–99. Chm., Steering Gp, London Challenge Cadet Partnership Pilot Project, DFE/MoD, 2007–11. Chm., Adv. Cttee on educn to HRH Prince Seeiso, 2008–11. Mem., Nat. Coll. Sch. Leadership, 2008–11; Founding Ambassador, Teach First, 2008–. President: London Youth Trust, 2003–05; SOS Children's Villages, UK, 2008–; Vice President: Internat. Friendship League, 2012–; Marine Soc. and Sea Cadets, 2014– (Mem. Bd, 2007–14). Member, Advisory Board: Send a Cow, Africa, 2014–; Finito Educn, 2016–. Governor: Thornton Coll., Bucks, 1994–2017 (Vice Chm., 1995–2017); City of London Schs (Boys), 2000–18; ESU, 2005–14 (Dep. Chm., 2008–11; Chm., 2011–14); Royal Alexandra and Albert Sch., Reigate, 2006–; Richmond Internat. Univ., London, 2010– (Dep. Chair, Bd of Trustees, 2017–); Mem., Develt Cttee, Ripon Theol Coll., Cuddesdon, 2008–11; Hon. Vice-Pres., Commonwealth Youth Orch. and Choir, 2012–. Honorary Trustee: Dulverton Trust, 2003–; Vitol Foundn, 2008–17; Shakespeare's Globe, 2008–15 (Mem. Council, 2015–); Internat. Centre for Circulatory Health, Imperial Coll. London, 2011–18; Member, Board: Oxford Literary Fest., 2006–; Cadet Bursary Fund, 2015–; Cadet Forces Health Check Gp, 2015–; John Paul II Foundn for Sport, 2015–; Airey Neave Trust, 2016–; Chm., Four Pillars (of Good Governance), 2009–14. FRSA 1996. CCMI 2011. Freeman, City of London, 2000; Guild of Educators; Basketmakers' Co. Hon. Dr Brunel, 2005; Hon. DHumLit Richmond, 2007; Hon. DSc City, 2008. *Publications:* Free to Play, Free to Pretend, Free to Imagine, drama textbooks for use in primary schs, 1972; contrib. professional periodicals. *Address:* 1A Abbey Avenue, St Albans, Herts AL3 4BJ. *T:* (01727) 859039. *E:* damemary@btinternet.com. *Clubs:* Army and Navy, Victory Services.

**RICHARDSON, Michael Elliot;** Director of Continuing Education and Lifelong Learning and Director, Institute of Continuing Education (formerly Director of Continuing Education and Secretary, Board of Continuing Education), University of Cambridge, 1990–2003; Fellow of Wolfson College, Cambridge, 1990–2003, now Emeritus; *b* 29 Sept. 1938; *s* of late Rev. Emery Lonsdale Richardson and Margaret Ann Richardson (née Elliot); *m* 1968, Gillian Miles Jones (*d* 2016); two *d*. *Educ:* Pocklington Sch., York; St John's Coll., Cambridge (MA 1967); Lincoln Theol Coll.; Univ. of Nottingham (DipAE 1970). FCIPD. Schoolmaster, Middlesbrough Boys' High Sch., 1964–65; Adult Educn Tutor, Ibstock Community Coll., 1965–67; Principal, Alfreton Hall Adult Educn Centre, 1967–69; Open University, 1969–90: Dep. Regl Dir, Northern, 1969–76; Regl Dir, NW, 1976–79; Dir, Educnl Services for Contg Educn, 1979–81; Pro-Dir, 1981–84, Dir, 1984–86, Centre for Contg Educn; Pro-Vice Chancellor, Contg Educn, 1985–90. Chm., Council for Educn and Training of Youth and Community Workers, 1985–90; Sec., UACE, 1998–2002 (Mem. Council, 1990–2003, now Life Mem.); Mem. Council, CRAC, 1990–98; Mem., numerous cttees and boards, 1980–. Trustee, Nat. Extension Coll., 1988–2003. Pres., Rotary Club of Tynedale, 2009–10. DUniv Open 1994. FRSA. *Publications:* Preparing to Study, 1979; Continuing Education for the Post Industrial Society, 1982; contribs to educn jls. *Recreations:* gardening, angling, walking. *Address:* 8 St Wilfred's Road, Corbridge, Northumberland NE45 5DE.

**RICHARDSON, Michael John,** CB 2005; Chairman, Teachers' Pension Scheme Pensions Board, 2014–18; *b* 17 March 1946; *s* of Philip George Richardson, MBE and Susan Rowena (*née* Pearce); *m* 1967, Celia, *d* of Rev. Canon Peter and Daphne Bradshaw; one *s* one *d*. *Educ:* Eton Coll.; St Edmund Hall, Oxford (BA Lit.Hum. 1968). Joined HM Diplomatic Service, 1968; Hong Kong, 1969–71; 3rd, later 2nd Sec., Peking, 1972–74; 1st Secretary: FCO, 1974–75; EEC, 1976; Western European Dept, FCO, 1977–78; Private Secretary to: Minister of State, 1978–79; Lord Privy Seal, 1979–80; 1st Sec., Rome, 1980–85; Asst Head, EC Dept, 1985; Head, EC Presidency Unit, FCO, 1986–87; Department for Education, later DFEE, 1987–2001: Under Sec., 1992; Dir for Qualifications, 1995–98; Dir for Employment Policy, 1998–2001; Department for Work and Pensions: Director: for Work, Welfare and Fraud, 2001–02; for Work and Welfare Strategy, 2002–03; for Work, Welfare and Poverty, 2003–06. Dep. Chm., London & Quadrant Housing Assoc., 1998–2010. Chairman: Lewisham PCT, subseq. NHS Lewisham, 2007–11; Jt Cttee of SE London NHS PCTs, 2009–11. Trustee, Transformation Trust, 2011–16. *Recreations:* family, reading, gardening, theatre-going, adventurous travel, visiting parish churches.

**RICHARDSON, Miranda;** actress; *b* 3 March 1958; *d* of William Alan Richardson and Marian Georgina Townsend. *Educ:* St Wyburn, Southport, Merseyside; Southport High Sch. for Girls; Bristol Old Vic Theatre Sch. Repertory: Manchester Library Theatre, 1979–80; Derby Playhouse, Duke's Playhouse, Lancaster, Bristol Old Vic and Leicester Haymarket, 1982–83; West End début, Moving, Queen's, 1980–81; Royal Court: Edmund, 1985; A Lie of the Mind, 1987; Etta Jenks, 1990; Grasses of a Thousand Colours, 2009; National Theatre: The Changeling, and Mountain Language, 1988; The Designated Mourner, 1996; Orlando, Edinburgh Fest., 1996; Aunt Dan and Lemon, Almeida, 1999. *Television:* series include: Agony; Sorrell and Son; Blackadder II and III; Die Kinder, 1990; The True Adventures of Christopher Columbus, 1992; A Dance to the Music of Time, 1998; The Life and Times of Vivienne Vyle, 2007; Parade's End, 2012; World Without End, 2013; Girlfriends, 2018; Curfew, Good Omens, 2019; plays include: The Master Builder; The Demon Lover; After Pilkington; Sweet as You Are (RTS Award, 1987–88); Ball-trap on the Côte Sauvage, 1989; Old Times, 1991; Merlin, 1998; Alice in Wonderland, 2000; The Lost Prince, 2003; Gideon's Daughter, 2006; Mapp and Lucia, 2014; An Inspector Calls, 2015; And Then There Were None, 2015; *films:* Dance with a Stranger (role, Ruth Ellis) (City Limits Best Film Actress, 1985; Evening Standard Best Actress, 1985; Variety Club Most Promising Artiste, 1985); Underworld; Death of the Heart; Empire of the Sun; The Mad Monkey; Eat the Rich; Redemption, 1991; Enchanted April, 1992 (Golden Globe Award, Best Comedy Actress, 1993); Mr Wakefield's Crusade, The

Bachelor, 1992; Damage (BAFTA Award, Best Supporting Actress, 1993; NY Critics Circle Award; Film Critics Circle, Best Actress 1994; Royal Variety Club of GB, Best Film Actress of 1994); The Crying Game, 1992; Century, 1993; Tom and Viv (Best Actress, Nat. Bd of Review of Motion Pictures), La Nuit et Le Moment, 1994; Kansas City, Evening Star, 1996; Swann, 1997; Designated Mourner, Apostle, All For Love, Jacob Two Two and the Hooded Fang, The Big Brass Ring, 1998; Sleepy Hollow, Chicken Run (voice), Snow White, 2000; The Hours, Spider, 2001; The Actors, 2002; Rage on Placid Lake, Falling Angels, The Prince and Me, Phantom of the Opera, 2003; Harry Potter and the Goblet of Fire, 2005; Wah Wah, Spinning into Butter, Puffball, Southland Tales, 2006; Fred Claus, Provoked: a True Story, 2007; The Young Victoria, 2009; Harry Potter and the Deathly Hallows, Pt 1, Made in Dagenham, 2010; Belle, 2014; Testament of Youth, And Then There Were None, 2015; iBoy, Churchill, Stronger, 2017. Chm. Judges, Women's Prize for Fiction, 2013. *Recreations:* reading, walking, softball, gardening, music, junkshops, occasional art, animals. *Address:* c/o Independent Talent Group Ltd, 40 Whitfield Street, W1T 2RH.

**RICHARDSON, Rev. Neil Graham,** PhD; President, Methodist Conference, 2003–04; *b* 2 Dec. 1943; *s* of John and Ethel Richardson; *m* 1972, Rhiannon Bradshaw; three *s*. *Educ:* Queen's Coll., Oxford (BA Classics, Modern Hist.; MA 1970); Wesley House, Cambridge (BA Theol. 1971); Bristol Univ. (MLitt 1977, PhD 1992). Asst Tutor, Wesley Coll., Bristol, 1971–73; Minister, Oxford Circuit, 1973–77; Ecumenical Lectr, Bishop's Hostel, Lincoln, 1977–81; Minister, Manchester Mission Circuit, and Chaplain to Manchester Univ., 1981–84; Wesley College, Bristol: Tutor in New Testament Studies, 1984–95; Principal, 1995–2001; Superintendent Minister, Leeds NE Circuit, 2001–07. Res. Fellow, Queen's Coll., Birmingham, 2007–08. *Publications:* Was Jesus Divine?, 1979; The Panorama of Luke, 1982; Preaching from Scripture, 1983; Paul's Language About God, 1994; God in the New Testament, 1999; Paul for Today: new perspectives on a controversial apostle, 2009; John for Today, 2010; (with G. Lovell) Sustaining Preachers and Preaching, 2011; Who on Earth is God?, 2014. *Recreation:* marathon running (London Marathon, 1995, 1999, 2000, 2004–07, 2010; first UK national Church leader to run the London Marathon whilst in office). *Address:* 14 Mortimer Drive, Orleton SY8 4JW.

**RICHARDSON, Dr Nigel Peter Vincent;** education consultant, appraiser and author; Headmaster, The Perse School, Cambridge, 1994–2008; *b* 29 June 1948; *s* of Vincent Boys Richardson and Jean Frances (*née* Wrangles); *m* 1979, (Averon) Joy James; two *s*. *Educ:* Highgate Sch.; Trinity Hall, Cambridge (MA Hist.); Bristol Univ. (PGCE); University Coll. London (PhD 2007). Uppingham School: Hist. Dept, 1971–89; Sixth Form Tutor, 1977–83; Second Master, 1983–89; Headmaster, Dragon Sch., Oxford, 1989–92; Dep. Headmaster and Dir of Studies, King's Sch., Macclesfield, 1992–94. Course Dir, Bell Sch., Cambridge, 1976–82. Chm., HMC, 2007 (Vice-Chm., 2007–08). Syndic, Cambridge Univ. Press, 2009–14. Question compiler, Top of the Form, BBC Radio 4, 1982–87. Governor: Greycotes Sch., Oxford, 1989–92; King's Coll. Sch., Cambridge, 1998–2004; King's Sch., Ely, 2008–13 (Chm., Educn Cttee, 2010–13); Norwich Sch., 2008–13; Magdalen Coll. Sch., Oxford, 2008–19; Mem., Educn Cttee, 2008– (Chm., 2014–), Mem., Council, 2013–, Haileybury Coll.; Mem. Bd, Assoc. of Governing Bodies of Ind. Schs, 2014–20. Walter Hines Page Scholar, ESU, 2003. Ed., Conference and Common Room, 1999–2002; Series Ed. and Contrib., Leading Schools book series, HMC, 2006–12. *Publications:* The Effective Use of Time, 1984, 2nd edn 1989; First Steps in Leadership, 1987; Typhoid in Uppingham: analysis of a Victorian town and school in crisis 1875–77, 2008 (British Assoc. for Local Hist. Award, 2008); Thring of Uppingham: Victorian educator, 2014; various histories and biographies for school use; contrib. TES, The Times, Daily Telegraph, Daily Mail, etc. *Recreations:* history, music, writing, sport, gardening, travel. *Address:* 6 High Meadow, Harston, Cambridge CB22 7TR. *T:* (01223) 872469. *E:* NPVRichardson@btinternet.com.

**RICHARDSON, Rev. Paul;** Assistant Bishop of Newcastle, 1998–2009; *b* 16 Jan. 1947; *s* of late William and Ilene Richardson. *Educ:* Keswick Sch.; The Queen's Coll., Oxford (BA (Mod. History) 1968, (Theol.) 1970; MA 1975); Harvard Divinity Sch.; Cuddesdon Theol Coll. Ordained deacon, 1972, priest, 1973; Asst Curate, St John's, Earlsfield, 1972–75; Asst Chaplain, Oslo, Norway, 1975–77; Mission Priest, Nambaiyufa, PNG, 1977–79; Lectr, 1979–81, Principal, 1981–85, Newton Theol Coll.; Dean, St John's Cathedral, Port Moresby, 1985–86; Bishop of Aipo Rongo, PNG, 1987–95; Bishop of Wangaratta, 1995–97. Re-ordained in RC Church, 2011. *Recreations:* reading, walking, travel. *Address:* 86 Fitzalan Street, Lambeth, SE11 6QU. *T:* (020) 7091 4299. *Club:* Oxford and Cambridge.

**RICHARDSON, Paul Brayshaw;** a District Judge (Magistrates' Courts), 2002–14; *b* 21 June 1948; *s* of Ronald and Enid Richardson; *m* 1973, Valerie Madeleine Hine; one *s* one *d*. *Educ:* Berkhamsted Sch.; Trinity Coll., Oxford (MA). Called to the Bar, Middle Temple, 1972; in practice as barrister, Northern Circuit, with chambers in Manchester, 1973–2002; Actg Stipendiary Magistrate, 1995–2002. *Recreations:* fly fishing, cricket, jugband music.

**RICHARDSON, Prof. Peter Damian,** FRS 1986; Professor of Engineering and Physiology, Brown University, USA, 1984–2015, now Emeritus; *b* West Wickham, Kent, 22 Aug. 1935; *s* of late Reginald William Merrells Richardson and Marie Stuart Naomi (*née* Ouseley). *Educ:* Imperial College, Univ. of London (BSc (Eng) 1955; PhD 1958; DSc (Eng) 1974; ACGI 1955; DIC 1958; DSc 1983); MA Brown Univ. 1965. Demonstrator, Imperial Coll., 1955–58; Brown University: Vis. Lectr, 1958–59; Research Associate, 1959–60; Asst Prof. of Engrg, 1960–65; Associate Prof. of Engrg, 1965–68; Prof. of Engrg, 1968–84; Chair, University Faculty, 1987– (Vice-Chair, 1986–87; Parliamentarian, 1989–). Sen. Vis. Fellow, Univ. of London, 1967; Prof. d'échange, Univ. of Paris, 1968; leave at: Orta Doğu Teknik Univ., Ankara, 1969; Abteilung Physiologie, Medizinische Fakultat, RWTH Aachen, 1976; Univ. of Pisa, 1983; Lab. de Recherche sur les macromolecules, Univ. de Paris XIII, 1991. FASME 1983; Founding Fellow, AIMBE, 1991; FCGI 2003; Inaugural Fellow, Biomedical Engrg Soc., 2005. Hon. FRCP 2010. Humboldt-Preis, A. von Humboldt Sen. Scientist Award, 1976; Laureate in Medicine, Ernst Jung Foundn, 1987; President's Award for Excellence in Faculty Governance, Brown Univ., 2010. *Publications:* (with M. Steiner) Principles of Cell Adhesion, 1995; numerous articles in learned jls. *Recreations:* photography, travel, country life. *Address:* Box D, Brown University, 184 Hope Street, Providence, Rhode Island 02912–9104, USA.

**RICHARDSON, Hon. Ruth Margaret;** consultant and company director; Ruth Richardson (NZ) Ltd, strategic and economic policy advice, since 1994; *b* 13 Dec. 1950; *d* of Ross Pearce Richardson and Rita Joan Richardson; *m* 1975, Andrew Evan Wright; one *s* one *d*. *Educ:* Canterbury Univ., NZ (LLB Hons 1971). Admitted to the Bar, 1973; Legal Adviser: Law Reform Div., Dept of Justice, 1972–75; Federated Farmers of NZ, 1975–80. MP (Nat. Party) Selwyn, NZ, 1981–94; Opposition spokesman: on Education and on Youth Issues, 1984–87; on Finance, 1987–90; Minister of Finance, 1990–93. Dir, Reserve Bank of NZ, 1999–2004. Chairman: Jade Software Corp. Ltd, 1998–2016; NZ Merino Co. Ltd; Adv. Cttee, Kula Fund II; Syft Technologies Ltd; Kiwi Innovation Network; Director: Synlait Milk Ltd; Bank of China (NZ). *Recreations:* running, swimming, gardening. *Address:* 713 Newtons Road, RD5, Christchurch 7675, New Zealand. *T:* (3) 3479146.

**RICHARDSON, Sarah Jane; Her Honour Judge Sarah Richardson;** a Circuit Judge, since 2015; a Designated Civil Judge for Hull and Grimsby, since 2017. *Educ:* Nottingham Univ. (BA 1st Cl. Hons Law 1992). Called to the Bar, Inner Temple, 1993; a Dep. Dist Judge, 2005–08; a Dist Judge, 2008–15. *Address:* Hull Combined Court Centre, Lowgate, Hull HU1 2EZ.

**RICHARDSON, Sir Simon Alaisdair S.;** *see* Stewart-Richardson.

**RICHARDSON, Prof. Stephen Michael,** CBE 2015; PhD; FREng; FIChemE; Professor of Chemical Engineering, 1994–2016, now Emeritus, and Associate Provost, 2013–16, Imperial College London; *b* London, 8 Dec. 1951; *s* of late David Richardson and of Frances Joan Richardson; *m* 1976, Hilary Joy Burgess; one *s* two *d*. *Educ:* Imperial Coll., London (BSc (Eng) 1972; PhD 1976). FIChemE 1990; FREng 1996. Rolls-Royce Res. Asst, 1975, 1851 Res. Fellow, 1976–78, Univ. of Cambridge; Imperial College, London: Lectr, Dept of Chem. Engrg, 1978–87; Sen. Lectr, 1987–92; Reader, 1992–94; Hd of Dept, 2001–08; Principal, Faculty of Engrg, 2008–10; Dep. Rector, 2009–13. FCGI 1999; FHEA 2007. *Publications:* Fluid Mechanics, 1989. *Recreations:* gardening, walking, classical music. *Address:* Department of Chemical Engineering, Imperial College London, S Kensington, SW7 2AZ. *E:* s.m.richardson@imperial.ac.uk.

**RICHARDSON, Sir Thomas (Legh),** KCMG 2000 (CMG 1991); HM Diplomatic Service; Ambassador to Italy and (non-resident) to San Marino, 1996–2000; *b* 6 Feb. 1941; *s* of Arthur Legh Turnour Richardson and Penelope Margaret Richardson; *m* 1979, Alexandra Frazier Wasiqullah (*née* Ratcliff). *Educ:* Westminster Sch.; Christ Church, Oxford. MA (Hist.). Joined Foreign Office, 1962; seconded to Univ. of Ghana, 1962–63; FO, 1963–65; Third Sec., Dar-es-Salaam, 1965–66; Vice-Consul (Commercial), Milan, 1967–70; seconded to N. M. Rothschild & Sons, 1970; FCO, 1971–74; First Sec., UK Mission to UN, 1974–78; FCO, 1978–80; seconded to Central Policy Review Staff, Cabinet Office, 1980–81; Head of Chancery, Rome, 1982–86; Head of Economic Relns Dept, FCO, 1986–89; UK Dep. Perm. Rep. to UN, with personal rank of Ambassador, 1989–94; Dep. Pol Dir and Asst Under-Sec. of State (Western and Southern Europe), FCO, 1994–96. Governor: British Inst. of Florence, 2001–08 (Chm., 2003–08); Monte San Martino Trust, 2003–15; Mem. Council, British Sch. at Rome, 2002–06. Hon. Pres., British-Italian Soc., 2007–18. *Recreations:* reading, walking, travel, music.

**RICHARDSON, Victoria;** architecture and design writer, editor and curator; *b* London, 16 Oct. 1968; *d* of Anthony Richardson and Margaret Ann Richardson, *qv*. *Educ:* Central St Martins (Foundn in Art 1988); Univ. of Westminster (BA Hons Arch. 1992); Napier Univ. (NCTJ Newspaper Writing 1995); King's Coll. London (MA Early Modern Hist., 2016). Asst Ed., Public Sector Bldg, 1995–96; Ed., Public Service & Local Govt, 1996–97; Sen. Reporter, 1997–2000, Dep. Ed., 2000–02, RIBA Jl; Ed., Blueprint, 2004–10; Dir, Architecture, Design and Fashion, British Council, 2010–16; Associate Dir, London Sch. of Architecture, 2017–18. Co-Dir, London Fest. of Architecture, 2010–14. Chair, Architecture Centre Network, 2007–09; Member: London Cultural Strategy Gp, 2008–16; Adv. Cttee, V&A Dundee, 2014–. Mem. Council, AA, 2015–17 (Hon. Treas., 2016–17). Trustee, Campaign for Drawing, 2004–11. Hon. FRIBA 2015. *Publications:* In Defence of the Dome, 1999; New Vernacular Architecture, 2001; The Dungeness Box, 2003. *T:* 07496 727178. *E:* vicky@vickyrichardson.com.

**RICHARDSON, Prof. William Boys,** DPhil; General Secretary, Headmasters' and Headmistresses' Conference, 2011–18; *b* Barnet, 13 July 1956; *s* of late Vincent Richardson and of Jean Richardson (*née* Wrangles); partner, Susan Shallcross; one *s*; *m* 1991, Ellen Renner; one *s*. *Educ:* Highgate Sch.; Univ. of Bristol (BA); New Coll., Oxford (DPhil 1993). Gen. mgt trainee, industrial relns manager, Unilever plc, 1982–85; British Petroleum Fellow, Univ. of Warwick, 1986–95; Lectr, then Sen. Lectr, Univ. of Sheffield, 1995–2000; Prof. of Educn, and Dir, Res. Centre for the Learning Society, 2000–11, Public Orator, 2003–05, Univ. of Exeter. Hon. Prof., Univ. of Exeter, 2011–. Mem. Editl Bd, 1998–, Reviews Ed., 1998–2010, Hist. of Educn. Dir, Educn Policy MA prog., DfEE, 1998–2007. Chief Examr, Inst. of Educn, Univ. of London, 2002–05. Dir, ISC, 2011–. Mem., Governing Council, Univ. of Exeter, 2004–07. Chm., Archives and Records Assoc., 2018–. Sec., Queen St Gp, 2018–. Trustee: Coombeshead Coll. Trust, 2007–11 (Chm., 2010–11); Creative Educn Trust, 2010– (Vice Chm., 2013–). *Publications:* (jtly) Teachers into Business and Industry, 1989; (jtly) The Reform of Post-16 Education and Training in England and Wales, 1993; (jtly) Something Borrowed, Something Learned?: the transatlantic market in education and training reform, 1993; (with G. Stanton) Qualifications for the Future: a study of tripartite and other divisions in post-16 education and training, 1997; (with G. McCulloch) Educational Research in Historical Settings, 2000; (jtly) Social Change in the History of British Education, 2008; (contrib.) Oxford Dictionary of National Biography (1532–1677), 2004; res. reports, evaluation studies and teaching pubns. *Recreations:* histories, landscapes, lost causes. *Address:* Headmasters' and Headmistresses' Conference, 12 The Point, Rockingham Road, Market Harborough, Leics LE16 7QU. *E:* gensec@hmc.org.uk. *Club:* Athenæum.

**RICHARDSON, Prof. William David,** PhD; FRS 2013; FMedSci; FLS; Professor of Biology, since 1993, and Director, 2012–16, Wolfson Institute for Biomedical Research, University College London; *b* Belfast, 18 Aug. 1951; *s* of Walter Richardson and Olive Richardson (*née* Woods); *m* 1977, Susan Anne Powell (*née* Wray); one *s* one *d*. *Educ:* Royal Belfast Academical Instn; Univ. of Manchester (BSc 1st Cl. Phys 1973); King's Coll. London (PhD Biophys 1978). Internat. Fellow, NIH, Bethesda, Md, 1978–82; Staff Scientist, NIMR, Mill Hill, London, 1982–85; University College London: Lectr in Molecular Genetics, 1985–90; Reader in Biology, 1990–93; Hd of Dept, 2000–06; Wolfson Inst. for Biological Res., 1999–. FLS 2008; FMedSci 2010. *Publications:* over 130 articles in scientific jls and books, mainly on develtl neurosci. (specialty oligodendrocytes, the myelin-forming cells of central nervous system). *Recreations:* fencing in earlier years, more recently squash, beekeeping, lifelong motorcyclist. *Address:* Wolfson Institute for Biomedical Research, University College London, Gower Street, WC1E 6BT. *T:* (020) 7679 6729. *E:* w.richardson@ucl.ac.uk.

**RICHARDSON-BUNBURY, Sir Thomas William;** *see* Bunbury.

**RICHARDSON-WALSH, Kate Louise,** OBE 2017 (MBE 2015); hockey coach and consultant, since 2017; *b* Withington, Manchester, 9 May 1980; *d* of John Walsh and Barbara Walsh; *m* 2013, Helen Richardson (Helen Richardson-Walsh, MBE). *Educ:* Priestnall High Sch., Stockport; Aquinas Coll., Stockport; Brunel Univ. (BSc Hons 2003). Hockey player, England and GB hockey teams, 1999–2016, Captain, England and GB hockey teams, 2003–16. Silver Medal, 2002, 2014, Bronze Medal, 2006, 2010, Commonwealth Games; Bronze Medal, World Cup, 2010; Bronze Medal, London Olympic Games, 2012, Gold Medal, Rio de Janeiro Olympic Games, 2016; Gold Medal, European Championships, 2015. Hon. Fellow: Brunel Univ., 2011; Liverpool John Moores Univ., 2014. Hon. Dr Brunel, 2017. *Recreations:* sport, reading, cooking, fashion, travel.

**RICHBOROUGH, Bishop Suffragan of,** since 2011; **Rt Rev. Norman Banks;** Provincial Episcopal Visitor, Province of Canterbury, since 2011; an Honorary Assistant Bishop: Diocese of St Edmundsbury and Ipswich, since 2011; Diocese of Norwich, since 2012; Diocese of Ely, since 2012; Diocese of Guildford, since 2012; Diocese of Chelmsford, since 2012; Diocese of St Albans, since 2013; Diocese of Lincoln, since 2015; Diocese of Gibraltar in Europe, since 2015; Diocese of Rochester, since 2016; *b* Wallsend, Tyne and Wear, 4 April 1954; *s* of Francis John Banks and Elizabeth Jane Banks. *Educ:* Oriel Coll., Oxford (MA 1980); St Stephen's House, Oxford (CTh 1982). Ordained deacon, 1982, priest, 1983; Curate, 1982–87, Priest-in-charge, 1987–90, Christchurch with St Ann, Newcastle; Vicar, St Paul's, Whitley Bay, 1990–2000; Vicar, Walsingham, Houghton and the Barshams, Norfolk, 2000–11; Rural Dean, Burnham and Walsingham, 2008–11; Chaplain to the Queen, 2008–11; Chaplain to the High Sheriff of Norfolk, 2011. *Address:* Parkside House, Abbey Mill Lane, St Albans, Herts AL3 4HE. *T:* (01727) 836358. *E:* bishop@richborough.org.uk, secretary@richborough.org.uk.

**RICHENS, Prof. Paul Nicholas,** RIBA; Professor of Architectural Computing, University of Bath, 2005–15; *b* Cambridge, 24 July 1946; *s* of Richard Hook Richens and Ruth Hamilton Richens (*née* Scott); partner, Clare Gilmour; two *s* two *d*; *m* 2004, Megan Yakeley (marr. diss. 2013); one *d*; *m* 2014, Prof. Heather van der Lely (*d* 2014); *m* 2019, Prof. Mary Hepworth. *Educ:* Cambridgeshire High Sch. for Boys; King's Coll., Cambridge (BA 1968; DipArch). RIBA 1989. Software developer, 1969–84, Dir, 1984–86, Applied Research of Cambridge; Technical Dir, McDonnell Douglas AEC Systems Co., 1986–89; University of Cambridge: Asst Dir of Res., 1989–2000; Dir, Martin Centre for Architectural and Urban Studies, 1992–2002; Reader in Architectural Computing, 2000–05; Vice Master, Churchill Coll., Cambridge, 2000–05; Dir, Centre for Advanced Studies in Arch., Univ. of Bath, 2007–09. *Recreations:* feeding friends, trespassing. *Address:* Ivy House, Cavendish Road, Bath BA1 2UE.

**RICHER,** family name of **Baroness Altmann.**

**RICHER, Julian,** LVO 2007; Founder and Managing Director, Richer Sounds plc, since 1978; *b* 9 March 1959; *s* of Percy Isaac Richer and Ursula Marion (*née* Haller); *m* 1982, Rosemary Louise Hamlet. *Educ:* Clifton Coll., Bristol. Salesman, Hi-Fi Markets Ltd, 1977; Founder and Chairman: JR Properties, 1989–; Audio Partnership plc, 1994–2010; Richer Consulting Ltd, 1996–2002; The Richer Partnership, 1997–2009; JR Publishing, 1998–; Lomo Ltd, 1998–2007; Definitely Mktg Ltd, 2000–05; Richer Unsigned, 2014–; Chairman: Home Ltd, 1999–2003; Grey Frog plc, 2000–04. Non-executive Director: Duchy Originals Ltd, 1998–2006; Urban Spaces Ltd, 1999–2003; Knutsford plc, 1999–2002; Poptones plc, 2000–05; WILink.com plc, 2000–03; Tax Watch Ltd, 2018. Chm., Business Develt Gp, Henry Doubleday Res. Assoc., 1998–2002. Founder and Trustee: Persula Foundn, 1994–; Acts 435, 2009–; ASB Help, 2013–; Mem., Leadership Gp, Amnesty Internat., 2004–07; Patron; Big Issue, 1999; Youth Clubs UK 90th Anniv., 2000; Ambassador: Centrepoint, 2000–01; Amnesty Internat., 2017–; Vice-Pres., RSPCA, 2002–; Dep. Chm. and Mem., New Horizons Develt Bd, 1997–2002, Mem., Adv. Bd, 2002–04, RNIB. Dir, Whizz-Kids 10th Birthday Bd, 1999–2007. Hon. DBA: Kingston, 2001; Bournemouth, 2002. Richer Sounds plc awarded Royal Warrant, 2011. *Publications:* The Richer Way, 1995, 6th edn 2017; Richer on Leadership, 1999; A Richer Life (private pubn), 2010; The Ethical Capitalist, 2018. *Recreations:* drumming in and managing the band Ten Millennia, reading, travelling. *Address:* c/o Richer Sounds plc, Richer House, Hankey Place, SE1 4BB. *T:* (020) 7403 1310.

**RICHES, Anne Clare, (Mrs T. C. Coltman),** OBE 1999; DL; FSA; free-lance architectural historian, since 1989; *b* 12 April 1943; *d* of late Rt Rev. Kenneth Riches and of Kathleen Mary Riches (*née* Dixon); *m* 1989, Timothy Charles Coltman. *Educ:* Headington Sch., Oxford; Edinburgh Univ. (MA 1965; Dip. Hist. of Art 1966). FSA 1985. Historian, Historic Bldgs Div., GLC, 1966–78; Inspector, then Principal Inspector, Historic Bldgs and Monuments Directorate, Scottish Develt Dept, 1978–89. Society of Architectural Historians of Great Britain: Sec., 1978–83; Conf. Sec., 1978–85; Chm., 1985–88. Member: Adv. Panel, Railway Heritage Trust, 1985–2006; Nat. Cttee, Assoc. of Preservation Trusts, 1989–95; RCHME, 1991–99; Royal Commn on Ancient and Historical Monuments of Scotland, 1995–2004; Church Bldgs Council (formerly Council for Care of Churches), 2001–13. Trustee: Scottish Historic Bldgs Trust, 1989–2009; Theatres Trust, 1996–2005; Doddington Hall Conservation Charity, 2006–19; Heritage Trust for Lincolnshire: Dir, 1990–; Chm., 2002–12; Chm., Archaeol. Adv. Cttee, 1991–94; Chm., Bldgs Adv. Cttee, 1992–. Mem., Lincoln Cathedral Fabric Council, 1998–. DL Lincs, 2006. Chancellor's Medal, Univ. of Lincoln, 2013. *Publications:* (with R. Barber) A Dictionary of Fabulous Beasts, 1972; Victorian Church Building and Restoration in Suffolk, 1982; (jtly) Building of Scotland: Glasgow, 1990; (with R. Close) Buildings of Scotland: Ayrshire and Arran, 2012; contrib. Architectl Hist. *Recreations:* gardening, hill-farming, visiting buildings. *Address:* Skellingthorpe Hall, Lincoln LN6 5UU. *T:* (01522) 694609.

**RICHES, Lucinda Jane,** CBE 2017; non-executive Director: ICG Enterprise Trust (formerly Graphite Enterprise Trust plc), since 2011; British Standards Institution, since 2012 (Adviser, 2011–12); CRH plc, since 2015; Ashtead Group plc, since 2016; Greencoat UK Wind plc, since 2019; *b* Dorking, Surrey, 26 July 1961; *d* of late Kenneth Riches and Margaret Riches; three *d*. *Educ:* St Teresa's Convent, Effingham; Rosebery Grammar Sch., Epsom; Brasenose Coll., Oxford (BA PPE 1983; Exhibnr); Univ. of Pennsylvania (MA Pol Sci. 1984, Thouron Scholar). Grad. trng course, Chase Manhattan Bank, 1984–85; S. G. Warburg, and subseq. firms, then UBS, 1986–2007: Hd, US Equity Capital Mkts, NY, 1992–94; Hd, Eur. Equity Capital Mkts, 1995–99; Global Hd, Equity Capital Mkts, 1999–2007; Mem. Bd, UBS Investment Bank, 2001–07; non-executive Director: UK Financial Investments Ltd, 2009–18; Diverse Income Trust plc, 2011–18; non-exec. Mem., Partnership Bd, King & Wood Mallesons LLP (formerly S J Berwin LLP), 2012–16. Pres., Brasenose Soc., 2011–12. Trustee, Sue Ryder (formerly Sue Ryder Care), 2008–17. *Recreations:* family, walking, theatre, music. *E:* lucinda.riches@hotmail.co.uk.

**RICHMOND,** 11th Duke of, *cr* 1675, **LENNOX,** 11th Duke of, *cr* 1675 (Scot.), **AND GORDON,** 6th Duke of, *cr* 1876; **Charles Henry Gordon Lennox;** Baron Settrington, Earl of March, 1675; Lord of Torboulton, Earl of Darnley (Scot.), 1675; Earl of Kinrara, 1876; Duc d'Aubigny (France), 1684; Hereditary Constable of Inverness Castle; DL; *b* 8 Jan. 1955; *s* of 10th Duke of Richmond, Lennox and Gordon, and Susan Monica, *d* of late Col C. E. Grenville-Grey, CBE; *S* father, 2017; *m* 1st, 1976, Sally (marr. diss. 1989), *d* of late Maurice Clayton and of Mrs Denis Irwin; one *d*; 2nd, 1991, Hon. Janet Elizabeth, *d* of 3rd Viscount Astor and of Bronwen, *d* of His Honour Sir (John) Alan Pugh; three *s* one *d* (of whom one *s* one *d* are twins). *Educ:* Eton. Chm., Goodwood Gp of Cos, 1991–. Pres., BARC; Life Vice-Pres., RAC. Patron, TT Riders Assoc. Honorary Member: British Racing Drivers' Club; 500 Owners Club; Guild of Motoring Writers. DL W Sussex, 2006. *Heir: s* Earl of March and Kinrara, *qv*. *Address:* Goodwood House, Chichester, West Sussex PO18 0PY.

**RICHMOND, Bernard Grant;** QC 2006; a Recorder, since 2002; an Assistant Coroner (formerly Assistant Deputy Coroner), since 2012; *b* 25 May 1965; *s* of James Richmond and Carol Richmond (*née* Linstead); *m* 1995, Christa Elfriede, *d* of Rudolf and Ruth Veile. *Educ:* Stratford Comp. Sch.; City of London Poly. (LLB Hons 1986). Called to the Bar, Middle Temple, 1988, Bencher, 2005; in practice as a barrister, 1988–; apptd to Faculty, Middle Temple Advocacy, 1995, Dir of Studies, 2006–09 and 2011–. Chair, Mgt Cttee, 2007–, Dep. Vice Pres., 2012–, British Judo Council. *Recreations:* judo, Real tennis, battling with German grammar, conversing with my cats, alto saxophone. *Address:* Lamb Building, Temple, EC4Y 7AS. *T:* (020) 7797 7788. *E:* bernardrichmond@lambbuilding.co.uk. *Clubs:* Dantai Seishin Judokwai; Hyde Real Tennis.

**RICHMOND, Sir David (Frank),** KBE 2008; CMG 2004; HM Diplomatic Service, retired; Director General, Defence and Intelligence, Foreign and Commonwealth Office, 2004–07; Adviser, Bell Pottinger, 2007–15; *b* 9 July 1954; *s* of Frank George Richmond and Constance Lillian Richmond (*née* Hilling); *m* 1990, Caroline Matagne; one *s* one *d*. *Educ:* Merchant Taylors' Sch.; Trinity Hall, Cambridge (BA). FCO, 1976; MECAS, 1977–78; Baghdad, 1979–82; Second, later First Sec., FCO, 1982–87; UK Rep., Brussels, 1987–91; Dep. Head, Near East and N Africa Dept, FCO, 1991–94; Head, Economic Relations Dept, FCO, 1994–96; Head of Chancery, UK Mission to UN, NY, 1996–2000; UK Rep. to Pol and Security Cttee, EU and UK Perm. Rep. to WEU, Brussels, with rank of Ambassador, 2000–03; UK Special Rep. for Iraq, 2004. Gov., Ditchley Foundn, 2004–12. Chm., British Lebanese Assoc., 2012–; CEO, Brazzaville Foundn for Peace and Conservation, 2015–. *Address:* 12 Carlisle Mansions, Carlisle Place, SW1P 1HX.

**RICHMOND, Sir Mark (Henry),** Kt 1986; PhD, ScD; FRS 1980; Member, School of Public Policy, University College London, 1996–2005; *b* 1 Feb. 1931; *s* of Harold Sylvester Richmond and Dorothy Plaistowe Richmond; *m* 1st, 1958, Shirley Jean Townrow (marr. diss. 1999); one *s* one *d* (and one *d* decd); 2nd, 2000, Sheila Travers. *Educ:* Epsom Coll.; Clare Coll., Cambridge (BA, PhD, ScD). Scientific Staff, MRC, 1958–65; Reader in Molecular Biology, Univ. of Edinburgh, 1965–68; Prof. of Bacteriology, Univ. of Bristol, 1968–81; Vice-Chancellor, and Prof. of Molecular Microbiol., Victoria Univ. of Manchester, 1981–90; Chm., SERC, 1990–94 (Mem., 1981–85); Gp Hd of Res., Glaxo Hldgs, 1993–95. Director: Whittington Hosp. NHS Trust, 1996–98; Core Gp plc, 1997–99; Ark Therapeutics plc, 1997–2010; Genentech Inc., 1999–2005; OSI Pharmaceuticals Inc., 1999–2006; Cytos AG, 1999–2011. Member: Bd, PHLS, 1976–85; Fulbright Cttee, 1980–84; Chairman: British Nat. Cttee for Microbiol., 1980–85; CVCP, 1987–89; Cttee on Microbiological Food Safety, 1989–91; Member: Genetic Manipulation Adv. Gp, 1976–84; Adv. Cttee on Genetic Manipulation, 1984–85; Internat. Scientific Adv. Bd, UNESCO, 1996–2001; Council, Cancer Res. UK (formerly CRC), 1997–2002 (Chm., CRC Technology, 1997–2002; Chm., Cancer Res. Ventures, 1999–2002). Pres., Epsom Coll., 1992–2001. Member: IBM Academic Adv. Bd, 1984–90; Knox Fellowship Cttee, 1984–87; CIBA-Geigy Fellowship Trust, 1984–91; Jarrett Cttee for University Efficiency, 1985; Governing Body, Lister Inst., 1987–90; Council, ACU, 1988–90; Council, Royal Northern Coll. of Music, 1990–92; Educn Cttee, Royal Anniversary Trust, 1994–97; Trustee: Nat. Gall., 1994–2000; Tate Gall., 1995–99; Dyson Perrins Mus., Worcester, 1993–2001. Hon. Fellow, Pembroke Coll., Cambridge, 2011. *Publications:* several in microbiology and biochemistry jls. *Recreation:* increasing idleness. *Address:* Flat 16, St Andrew's Mansions, Dorset Street, W1U 4EQ. *Club:* Athenæum.

**RICHMOND, Prof. Peter,** PhD, DSc; FInstP; Visiting Professor, Department of Physics, Trinity College Dublin, 1998–2008 (European Union Marie Curie Fellow, 1998); *b* 4 March 1943; *s* of John Eric Richmond and Nellie (*née* Scholey); *m* 1st, 1967, Christine M. Jackson (*d* 1995); one *s* one *d*; 2nd, 2005, Mairin Breathnach. *Educ:* Whitcliffe Mount Grammar Sch., Cleckheaton; Queen Mary Coll., London (BSc, PhD); London Univ. (DSc). ICI Res. Fellow, Univ. of Kent, 1967–69; Univ. of NSW, 1969–71; Queen Elizabeth II Res. Fellow, Inst. of Advanced Studies, ANU, 1971–73; Unilever Res., 1973–82; Hd, Process Physics, AFRC Food Res. Inst., Norwich, 1982–86; Prof., Univ. of Loughborough, 1985–88; Dir, AFRC Inst. of Food Res., Norwich Lab., 1986–92; Gen. Manager, CWS, 1992–96; Dir, EPM Associates Ltd, 1998–2008. Hon. Prof., UEA, 1986–99; Sen. Vis. Fellow, Univ. Coll. Dublin, 2008–14; Vis. Prof., Open Univ., 2010–13. Mem., MAFF/DoH Adv. Cttee on novel foods and processes, 1988–94; Chairman, P10, Physics of Risk, 2004–07, Physics of Competition and Conflict, 2008–12, Eur. Co-operation in Scientific and Tech. Res. Mem., Exam. Cttee, Radio Soc. GB (formerly Radio Communications Foundn), 2013– (Chm., 2017–); Public Mem., NHS Res. for Patient Benefit Panel, 2016–; Lay Mem., Res. Cttee, Norfolk and Suffolk NHS Trust, 2018–. *Publications:* (with R. D. Bee and J. Mingins) Food Colloids, 1989; (with P. J. Frazier and A. Donald) Starch Structure and Functionality, 1997; (with J. Mimkes and S. Hutzler) Econophysics and Physical Economics: an introduction, 2013; contribs to learned jls on econophysics, complex systems, statistical physics, colloid and polymer physics and food physics. *Recreations:* music, walking, talking and eating with friends. *Club:* Athenæum.

**RICHMOND, Timothy Stewart,** OBE 2016 (MBE (mil.) 1985); TD 1982; FCA; Vice Lord-Lieutenant of Nottinghamshire, since 2008; chartered accountant, consultant and adviser in business direction; *b* Edingley, 17 Nov. 1947; *s* of Stewart Richmond Sylvester Richmond and Nancie Richmond (*née* Barber); *m* 1974, Susan Carol Spencer; two *s* two *d*. *Educ:* Birkdale Sch., Sheffield; Nottingham High Sch. ACA 1970; FCA 1979. Pannell Kerr Forster (PKF), Chartered Accountants: articles, 1966–70; qualified Asst, Manager, 1970–74; Partner, 1974–98; Man. Partner, Nottingham firm, 1980–85; Nat. Man. Partner, UK firm, 1985–94; Chm., internat. firm, 1994–98; Partner: Richmond Waine, later GTN, 1998–2008; Mazars, 2002–03; Arc Mediators LLP, 2009–11; Arc Partnership Consultants LLP, 2011–13. Chairman: Huthwaite Internat. Ltd, 1998–; Clegg Gp Ltd, 2008–10 (non-exec. Dir, 2000–); Dir, Legal Practice Consortium Ltd, 2006–11. Mem., Monopolies and Mergers Commn, subseq. Competition Commn, 1997–2003. Dir, Nottingham HA, 1989–91. Chm., Nottingham and Notts Futures (formerly Connexions Notts) Ltd, 2001–. Dir, Notts Community Foundn, 2003–05. Chm., English Churches Housing Gp, 1994–98. Pres., Nottingham, Derby and Lincoln Dist Soc. of Chartered Accountants, 2006–07 (Vice and Dep. Pres., 2004–06); Mem., Members Services Bd, ICAEW, 2007–12. Mem. Council, Chartered Mgt Inst., 1998–2002 (CCMI). Dep. Chm., Nottingham Trent Univ. (formerly Nottingham Poly.), 1989–97 (Gov., 1984–98); Gov., New Coll., Nottingham, 2008–10; Chm., Portland Coll., 2014– (Gov., 2013). Member: Southwell Cath. Council, 2000–07, 2012–; Council of Friends of Southwell Cath., 2006–; Southwell Cathedral Chapter, 2017–. Trustee, Notts Community Safety Trust, 2002–09; Patron, Notts Hospice, 2011–. Chm. Bd, Nat. Council, Reserve Forces and Cadets Assoc., 2011–14 (Vice Chm. (Army), 2003–11; Chm., E Midlands Assoc., 2003–12); Mem., Ext. Scrutiny Gp into Future Reserves 2020, 2012–18. Commnd Royal Regt of Artillery TA, 1971 (2nd Lieut); OC (Maj.) 307 (S Notts Hussars Yeo. RHA) Observation Post Battery (V), 1982–85 (Sen. Officer, 1995–2002; Hon. Col, 2002–14); CO (Lt Col), E Midlands Univs OTC, 1988–91 (Hon. Col, 2005–13); Dep. Bde Comdr (Col), 49 and 54 Bdes and TA Col for E Midlands, 1991–95; ADC (TA) to the Queen, 1992–95; Comdt, Notts ACF, 1997–2001. Hon. Col, S Notts Hussars, 2014–. DL 1990, High Sheriff, 2002–03, Notts. Hon. DBA Nottingham Trent, 1998. *Recreations:* sailing, gardening. *Address:* Newark, Notts. *Clubs:* Army and Navy; Nottingham.

**RICHMOND, Zoé;** *see* Whitley, Z.

**RICHMOND-WATSON, Julian Howard;** Chairman, Thoroughbred Breeders Association, since 2015; *b* 6 Dec. 1947; *s* of late Sonny and Jean Richmond-Watson; *m* 1972, Sarah Gee; four *s*. *Educ:* Hawtreys Sch.; Radley Coll. Man. Dir and Chm. of private cos in the property, quarrying and packing fields. Mem., various racecourse boards. Senior Steward, Jockey Club, 2003–09; Chm., Newmarket Racecourse, 2010–17. *Recreations:* horse-racing, shooting. *Address:* Wakefield Lodge, Pottersbury, Northants NN12 7QX. *E:* Julianrw@wakefieldestate.co.uk. *Clubs:* Boodle's, Jockey.

**RICHMOND AND CRAVEN, Archdeacon of;** *see* Gough, Ven. J. R. B.

**RICHTER, Max;** composer; *b* Hamelin, Germany, 22 March 1966; *s* of Lutz Richter and Ursula Meyer; *m* 1991, Yulia Mahr; one *s* two *d*. *Educ:* Bedford Modern Sch.; Univ. of Edinburgh; Royal Acad. of Music (BMus Hons; ARAM 2013). Co-founder, Piano Circus, classical ensemble, 1989–99. Solo albums: Memoryhouse, 2002; The Blue Notebooks, 2004; Songs From Before, 2006; 24 Postcards in Full Colour, 2008; Infra, 2010; Recomposed: Vivaldi's Four Seasons, 2012 (ECHO Klassik Award, 2013); SLEEP, 2015; film, ballet and theatre collaborations, 2004–; film soundtracks include: Waltz with Bashir, 2008 (Best Composer, Eur. Film Prize); Shutter Island, 2010; Sarah's Key, 2010; Perfect Sense, 2011; Lore, 2012 (Best Film Music, Bavarian Film Awards, 2013); Disconnect, 2012; Testament of Youth, 2014; Mary Queen of Scots, 2019; television soundtracks incl. The Leftovers, 2014; theatre includes: Black Watch, NT of Scotland, 2011; Macbeth, NY, 2012; chamber opera, Sum, 2012; work with Royal Ballet in collaboration with choreographer, Wayne McGregor incl. Infra, 2008, Woolf Works, 2015; Kairos for Ballet Zurich, 2015; works used by Joffrey Ballet, Nederlands Dans Teatre, NYC Ballet, Amer. Ballet Th., Dutch Nat. Ballet, Dresden Semper Oper, Ballet du Rhin, Northern Ballet, New English Ballet Th.; art collaborations: at White Cube; Future Self, Lunds Konsthall, Sweden, 2011; Rain Room, Barbican and MOMA, 2012. *Publications:* Memoryhouse, 2002; The Blue Notebooks, 2004; Songs From Before, 2006; 24 Postcards in Full Colour, 2008; Infra, 2010; SUM, 2012; The Four Seasons Recomposed, 2013; Woolf Works, 2015; SLEEP, 2015. *Recreations:* butterflies, astronomy, analogue synthesis, poetry. *E:* directors@studiorichtermahr.com.

**RICKARD, Rear Adm. Hugh Wilson,** CBE 1996; business consultant, since 2013; Director, Hugh Rickard Associates Ltd, since 2013; South Division Strategic Business Partner, BrightHouse, 2012–13; *b* 1 Sept. 1948; *s* of Charles Thomas Rickard and Isobel Rickard; *m* 1982, Patricia Ann Seager; two *s* one *d*. *Educ:* Surbiton Co. Grammar Sch.; Northern Poly. (BSc London Hons). MCIL (MIL 1994). Joined RN, 1972; qualified as Meteorological and Oceanographic Officer, 1974; Naval Staff Course, 1982; UK Defence and Naval Attaché, The Hague, 1992–95; CO, HMS Raleigh, 1995–98; Sen. Naval DS, RCDS, 1998–2000. Chief Exec., Lib Dems, 2000–03. Chief Exec., Royal Anniversary Trust, 2004–06; Bursar, Claremont Fan Court Sch., 2006–09; BrightHouse: Learning and Develt Manager, 2009–10; Nat. Customer Service Manager, 2010–11; Regl Manager, 2011–12. *Recreations:* sailing, hill-walking. *Address:* Mulberry Place, 29 Aldwick Avenue, Aldwick, W Sussex PO21 3AQ. *T:* (01243) 840954.

**RICKARD, Josanne Penelope Jeanne;** Partner, Shearman & Sterling (London) LLP, 2006–19; *b* Redruth, 1 Oct. 1949; *d* of John and Jeanne Rickard; *m* 1981, John Sawrey King; two *d*. *Educ:* Malvern Girls' Coll.; King's Coll. London (LLB). Articled Clerk, Kenneth Brown Baker Baker, 1971–73; admitted as solicitor, 1973; Associate, Cameron Kemm, 1973–75; Freshfields Bruckhaus Deringer: Associate, 1975–81; Partner, 1981–2006; on secondment to Lloyd's of London as Dir, Legal Services, 1994–96; Hd, London Dispute Resolution, 1996–2000; Jt Hd, Global Dispute Resolution, 2000–05. Chm., Mkt Supervision and Rev. Cttee, Lloyd's of London, 2013–. Dep. Chm., St Paul's Sch., 2010–14. *Recreations:* family, golf, tennis, travel. *E:* jo.rickard@btconnect.com. *Club:* Roehampton.

**RICKARDS, Joanne Elisabeth;** Partner, Mishcon de Reya LLP, since 2017; *b* Harbury, Warwickshire, 7 Oct. 1963; *d* of Stan Rickards and Maureen Rickards; *m* (marr. diss.); one *s* one *d*. *Educ:* Leamington Coll. for Girls; University Coll. London (LLB Hons). Admitted as solicitor, 1989; articled, 1986, Partner, 1992–2009, Peters & Peters; Partner: DLA Piper (UK) LLP, 2010–14; Kingsley Napley, 2014–17. *Recreations:* dancing, reading, collecting twentieth century ceramics, gardening, theatre and ballet, flea markets. *Address:* Mishcon de Reya LLP, Africa House, 70 Kingsway, WC2B 6AH. *T:* (020) 3321 6697. *E:* jo.rickards@mishcon.com.

**RICKERD, Martin John Kilburn,** OBE 2004; MVO 1985; HM Diplomatic Service, retired; freelance copy-editor and proofreader; *b* 17 Aug. 1954; *s* of John Rickerd and Anne Rickerd (*née* Kilburn, later Greener); *m* 1976, Charmain Gwendoline Napier; two *s*. *Educ:* Lord Weymouth Sch. HM Diplomatic Service, 1972–2010: FCO, 1972–75; UK Delegn to NATO, Brussels, 1975–77; Wellington, 1977–80; Asst Private Sec. to Parly Under Sec. of State, FCO, 1980–82; Third Sec., Bridgetown, 1982–86; Consul, Milan, 1986–91; First Sec., FCO, 1991–95; Hd of Chancery, Singapore, 1995–98; on secondment to Standard Chartered Bank, London, 1998–2000; Dep. Hd of Mission, Abidjan, 2000–03; Hd, N America Team, FCO, 2003–05; Consul Gen., Atlanta, USA, 2005–09. Professional Mem., Soc. for Editors and Proofreaders (E of England Coordinator, 2015–18). Mem., Queen's English Soc. Vice-Chm., Friends of Tiddenfoot Waterside Park, 2011–14; Mem. Cttee, Holbeach Br., RBL, 2015–18; Sec., Cambs Centre, Morgan Sports Car Club, 2016–18. *Publications:* The Patriotic Art: random recollections from a (mostly) diplomatic career, 2012. *E:* martin.rickerd@gmail.com.

**RICKETS, Brig. Reginald Anthony Scott, (Tony);** Chairman, Relate Glasgow, 2008–11; *b* 13 Dec. 1929; *s* of Captain R. H. Rickets and Mrs V. C. Rickets (*née* Morgan); *m* 1952, Elizabeth Ann Serjeant; one *s* one *d*. *Educ:* St George's Coll., Weybridge; RMA Sandhurst. 2nd Lieut, RE, 1949; served with airborne, armoured and field engrs in UK, Cyrenaica, Egypt, Malaya, Borneo, Hong Kong and BAOR; special employment military forces Malaya, 1955–59; Staff Coll., Camberley, 1962; BM Engr Gp, BAOR, 1963–66; OC 67 Gurkha Ind. Field Sqn, 1966–68; DS Staff Coll., 1968–70; Comdt Gurkha Engrs/CRE Hong Kong, 1970–73; COS British Sector, Berlin, 1973–77; Col GS RSME, 1977–78; Chief Engr UKLF, 1978–81. Man. Dir, Irvine Develt Corp., 1981–95. Director: Enterprise Ayrshire, 1990–97; Kelvin Travel, 1995–98; Nobel Exhibn Trust, (The Big Idea), 1997–2002; Chm., Irvine Housing Assoc., 2002–07. President: Ayrshire Chamber of Industries, 1983–86; Ayrshire Chamber of Commerce and Industry, 1989–91; German-British Chamber of Industry and Commerce in Scotland, 1998–; Mem. Exec. Bd, Scottish Council (Develt and Industry), 1990–92. Chm., ASSET Enterprise Trust, 1996–97. Mem. Exec. Bd, Scottish Maritime Mus., 1986–. *Recreation:* sailing. *Address:* Burnbrae Cottage, Montgreenan, Ayrshire KA13 7QZ. *Club:* Royal Engineer Yacht (Commodore, 1979–81).

**RICKETT, William Francis Sebastian,** CB 2010; Director General, Energy Markets and Infrastructure (formerly Energy), Department of Energy and Climate Change (formerly Department of Trade and Industry, then Department for Business, Enterprise and Regulatory Reform), 2006–09; *b* 23 Feb. 1953; *s* of Sir Denis Rickett, KCMG, CB and of Dr Ruth Pauline Rickett (*née* Armstrong); *m* 1979, Lucy Caroline Clark; one *s* one *d*. *Educ:* Trinity Coll., Cambridge (BA 1974). Joined Department of Energy, 1975; Private Sec. to Perm. Under Sec. of State, 1977; Principal, 1978; Private Sec. to Prime Minister, 1981–83; seconded to Kleinwort Benson Ltd, 1983–85; Asst Sec., Oil Div., Dept of Energy, 1985; Asst Sec., Electricity Privatisation, 1987; Grade 4, Electricity Div., 1989; Under Sec., 1990; Dir Gen., Energy Efficiency Office, Dept of Energy, 1990–92, DoE, 1992–93; Dir of Finance (Central) and Principal Finance Officer, DoE, 1993–97; Dir of Town and Country Planning, DoE, then DETR, 1997–98; Dep. Sec. and Hd, Economic and Domestic Secretariat, Cabinet Office, 1998–2000; Hd, Integrated Transport Taskforce, subseq. Dir-Gen., Transport Strategy and Planning, DETR, 2000–01; Dir-Gen., Transport Strategy, Roads, Local and Maritime Transport, then Transport Strategy, Roads and Local Transport, then Strategy, Finance and Delivery, DTLR, subseq. DfT, 2001–04; on secondment to Ernst & Young from DfT, 2004–06. Chm., Governing Bd, Internat. Energy Agency, 2007–09. Director: Oxford Inst. for Energy Studies, 2007–09; Cambridge Econ. Policy Associates Ltd, 2009– (Chm., 2013–); Nat. Renewable Energy Centre Ltd, 2010–13; Eggborough Power Ltd, 2010–15; Impax Envmtl Markets plc, 2011–; Helius Energy plc, 2011–15; Greencoat UK Wind plc, 2013–; Smart DCC Ltd, 2013–. Ind. energy expert, Which?, 2011–12; Sen. Advr, Cleveland Associates Ltd, 2011–. Mem. Adv. Bd, Energy Policy Res. Gp, Cambridge Univ., 2009–17 (Dep. Chair, 2018–). Hon. FEI 2010. *Recreations:* family, sports, dog.

**RICKETTS,** family name of **Baron Ricketts**.

**RICKETTS, Baron** *cr* 2016 (Life Peer), of Shortlands in the County of Kent; **Peter Forbes Ricketts,** GCMG 2011 (KCMG 2003; CMG 1999); GCVO 2014; HM Diplomatic Service, retired; Ambassador to France, 2012–16; *b* 30 Sept. 1952; *s* of Maurice and Dilys Ricketts; *m* 1980, Suzanne Julia Horlington; one *s* one *d*. *Educ:* Bishop Vesey's Grammar Sch.; Pembroke Coll., Oxford (MA; Hon. Fellow, 2007). Joined FCO, 1974; Singapore, 1975–78; UK Delegn to NATO, 1978–81; FCO, 1981–86, Private Sec. to Sec. of State for Foreign and Commonwealth Affairs, 1983–86; Washington, 1986–89; FCO, 1989–94, Head, Hong Kong Dept, 1991–94; Economic and Financial Counsellor, Paris, 1994–97; Dep. Pol Dir, FCO, 1997–99; Dir, Internat. Security, FCO, 1999–2000; Chm., Jt Intelligence Cttee, Cabinet Office (on secondment), 2000–01; Pol Dir, FCO, 2001–03; UK Perm. Rep., UK Delegn to NATO, 2003–06; Permanent Under-Sec. of State, and Hd of Diplomatic Service, 2006–10; Nat. Security Advr, 2010–11. Non-exec. Dir, Groupe Engie, 2016–; Strategic Advr, Lockheed Martin UK, 2016–. Chm., Normandy Meml Trust, 2017–; Sec. for Foreign Correspondence, RA, 2019–. Trustee, Royal Acad. Develt Trust, 2017–. *Recreation:* Victorian art and literature. *Address:* House of Lords, SW1A 0PW.

**RICKETTS, Prof. Martin John,** DPhil; Professor of Economic Organisation, University of Buckingham, 1987–2019, now Emeritus; *b* 10 May 1948; *s* of Leonard Alfred Ricketts and Gertrude Dorothy (*née* Elgar); *m* 1975, Diana Barbara Greenwood; one *s* one *d*. *Educ:* City of Bath Boys' Sch.; Univ. of Newcastle upon Tyne (BA Hons Econ.); Univ. of York (DPhil). Econ. Asst, Industrial Policy Gp, 1970–72; Res. Fellow, Inst. Econ. and Social Res., Univ. of York, 1975–77; University College at Buckingham, later University of Buckingham: Lectr in Econs, 1977–82; Sen. Lectr, 1982–85; Reader, 1985–87; Dean, Sch. of Business (formerly Sch. of Accountancy, Business and Econs), 1993–97; Pro-Vice-Chancellor, 1993; Dean of Humanities, 2002–15. Economic Dir, NEDO, 1991–92. Vis. Prof., Virginia Poly. Inst. and State Univ., 1984. Hon. Prof., Heriot-Watt Univ., 1996. Trustee: Inst. of Econ. Affairs, 1992–; Inst. of Internat. Monetary Res., 2016–. Chm., Buckingham Summer Fest., 2004–. *Publications:* (with M. G. Webb) The Economics of Energy, 1980; The Economics of Business Enterprise: new approaches to the firm, 1987, 4th edn as The Economics of Business Enterprise: an introduction to economic organisation and the theory of the firm, 2019; The Many Ways of Governance: perspectives on the control of the firm, 1999; papers on public finance, public choice, housing econs and econ. orgn. *Recreations:* music, student of piano and oboe. *Address:* Church Gate, Water Stratford MK18 5DX; Department of Economics and International Studies, University of Buckingham, Hunter Street, Buckingham MK18 1EG.

**RICKETTS, Simon;** Partner, Town Legal LLP, since 2016; *b* Lyndhurst, Hants, 25 June 1963; *s* of Brian Edward Ricketts and Joy Margaret Ricketts; *m* 1994, Sarah Louise Mastin; one *s* one *d*. *Educ:* King Edward VI Sch., Southampton; Queen Mary and Westfield Coll., Univ. of London (LLB Hons). Called to the Bar, Inner Temple, 1985; admitted as solicitor, 1991; Herbert Oppenheimer Nathan & Vandyk, 1987–88; Lovell White Durrant, 1988–97; S J Berwin, 1997–2013, Partner, 1999–2013; Partner, King & Wood Mallesons, 2013–16. Trustee, Theatres Trust, 2017–. FRSA. *Publications:* (jtly) Localism and Planning, 2012. *Recreations:* family, creative arts, blog-writing. *Address:* Town Legal LLP, 1 Wood Wall Buildings, EC2M 5PG. *E:* simon.ricketts@townlegal.com.

**RICKETTS, Simon Anthony;** Chief Information Officer, Rolls Royce plc, 2009–16; *b* Shoreham by Sea, Sussex, 17 Dec. 1954; *s* of late Herbert Arthur Ricketts and Pamela Anne Ricketts (*née* Forteware); *m* 1st, 1978, Monica Anne Ball (marr. diss. 2004); one *d*; 2nd, 2004, Jo Mary Fearn. *Educ:* Hastings Secondary Sch. for Boys; Univ. of East Anglia (BSc Hons Maths 1976); Univ. of Sussex (MSc Statistics 1980). British Steel Corporation: Operational Res. Gp, 1980–84; BSC Cumbria, 1984–86; Central Mgt Services, 1986–90; Cadbury Schweppes plc: Man. Dir, ITNet Ltd, 1990–94 (non-exec. Dir, ITNet Ltd, subseq. ITNet plc, 1994–2004); Ops Dir, Trebor Bassett Ltd, 1994–98; Gp IT Dir, 1998–2000; Chief Information Officer, 2000–03; Gp Information Systems Dir, Scottish & Newcastle plc, 2003–07; Global Transformation Dir, Logica plc, 2008–09. Director: Bar Box Ltd, 2004–08; UKCeB, 2010–. Non-executive Director: Strategic Thought plc, 2005–09 (Mem., Audit Cttee, 2005–09; Chm., Remuneration Cttee, 2005–09); National Savings and Investments, 2007–14 (Mem., Audit Cttee, 2007–14); HMRC, 2014–; Payment Systems Regulator, 2017–. Mem., Growth Bd, Tricentis, 2017–. Sen. Advr to Perm. Sec., Home Office, 2017–. Associate Fellow, 2014–16, Hon Prof., 2016–, Warwick Univ. Business Sch. *Recreations:* historic motor vehicles, running, cycling, political and economic history, music, house restoration. *T:* 07733 308766. *E:* simon@simonricketts.co.uk. *Clubs:* Royal Automobile; Warwickshire Golf and Country.

**RICKETTS, Simon Henry Martin,** CB 2000; Ministry of Defence, 1975–2011; *b* 23 July 1941; *s* of late Ralph Robert Ricketts and Margaret Adeliza Mary (*née* Royds); *m* 1973, Annabel Ophelia Clare Lea (*d* 2003); one *s* one *d*. *Educ:* Ampleforth; Magdalen Coll., Oxford (BA Hons History). Senior Systems Analyst, George Wimpey & Co., 1963–71; Lectr in Liberal Studies, Hammersmith Coll. of Art and Building, 1967–68; Kulu Trekking Agency, 1971; Teacher, British Inst. of Florence, 1971–73; Royalties Clerk, Cape & Chatto Services, 1973–75. Mem., Friends of Georgian Soc. of Jamaica, 2001– (Trustee, 2004–07). *Publications:* (ed) The English Country House Chapel: building a Protestant tradition, by Annabel Ricketts, 2007. *Address:* c/o Lloyds, 8 Fore Street, Budleigh Salterton, Devon EX9 6NQ. *Club:* Athenæum.

**RICKETTS, Sir Stephen Tristram,** 9th Bt *cr* 1828, of The Elms, Gloucestershire, and Beaumont Leys, Leicestershire; *b* 24 Dec. 1974; *s* of Sir (Robert) Tristram Ricketts, 8th Bt and of Ann Ricketts (*née* Lewis); *S* father, 2007; *m* 2009, Amy, *d* of Richard Robinson-Horley; two *s*. *Educ:* Winchester; Exeter Univ. *Heir: s* Freddy Tristram Ricketts, *b* 2 Aug. 2010.

**RICKFORD, Jonathan Braithwaite Keevil,** CBE 2001; solicitor, 1985–2010; regulatory consultant, 1996–2010; Professorial Fellow, British Institute of International and Comparative Law, 2006–08 (Director, Company Law Centre, 2003–06); *b* 7 Dec. 1944; *s* of R. B. K. Rickford, MD, FRCS, FRCOG and of Dorothy Rickford (*née* Lathan); *m* 1968, Dora R. Sargant; one *s* two *d. Educ:* Sherborne School; Magdalen College, Oxford (MA (Jurisp.); BCL). Barrister, 1970–85. Teaching Associate, Univ. of California Sch. of Law, 1968–69; Lectr in Law, LSE, 1969–72; Legal Asst, Dept of Trade, 1972–73; Senior Legal Assistant: Dept of Prices and Consumer Protection, 1974–76; Law Officers' Dept, Attorney General's Chambers, 1976–79; Dept of Trade and Industry (formerly Dept of Trade): Asst Solicitor (Company Law), 1979–82; Under Sec. (Legal), 1982–85; Solicitor, 1985–87; British Telecom: Solicitor and Chief Legal Advr, 1987–89; Dir of Govt Relns, 1989–93; Dir of Corporate Strategy, 1993–96; Project Dir, DTI's Review of Company Law, 1998–2001; Unilever Prof. in Eur. Corporate Law, Univ. of Leiden, Netherlands, 2002. Vis. Prof. of Law, LSE, 2003–09. Mem., Competition (formerly Monopolies and Mergers) Commn, 1997–2004. Member: Europe Cttee, CBI, 1993–98; Council, European Policy Forum, 1993–2014. FRSA 1992. *Publications:* (ed) The European Company, 2002; articles in learned jls. *Recreation:* sailing.

**RICKINSON, Prof. Alan Bernard,** PhD; FRS 1997; Professor of Cancer Studies, University of Birmingham, since 1983; *b* 12 Nov. 1943; *s* of Lawrence and Annie Rickinson; *m* 1968, Barbara; one *s* two *d. Educ:* Corpus Christi Coll., Cambridge (MA, PhD 1969). Hon. FRCP 1996. *Recreations:* walking, poetry. *Address:* Institute of Cancer and Genomic Sciences, College of Medical and Dental Sciences, University of Birmingham, Edgbaston, Birmingham B15 2TT. *T:* (0121) 414 4492.

**RICKLETON, James David John;** Owner Director, Mills Jakeby Ltd, since 2017; *b* 26 Aug. 1959; *s* of Jack and Jenifer Mary Rickleton; *m* 1998, Carol Anne Lyons (marr. diss. 2013); one *s* one *d. Educ:* Newcastle upon Tyne Poly. (BA Hons (Econs) 1980); City of London Poly. IPFA 1985. National Audit Office, 1981–2014: Audit trainee, 1981–86; Sen. Auditor, Financial Audit Tech. Support Team, 1986–88; Audit Manager, DES, 1988–92; Private Sec. to Comptroller and Auditor Gen., 1992–95; Dir of Audit, 1995–2003; Asst Auditor Gen., 2003–09; Dir Gen., Finance and Commerce, 2009–14; Finance Dir, Market Operator Services Ltd, 2015–16; Finance Dir and Consultant, Indepen Ltd, 2016–17. *Recreations:* golf, reading, Newcastle United FC.

**RICKS, Dr Catherine Louise;** Chief Master, King Edward's School, Birmingham, since 2019; *b* 16 March 1961; *d* of Paul George Koralek, *qv*; *m* 1983, David Bruce Ricks. *Educ:* Camden Sch. for Girls, London; Balliol Coll., Oxford (MA Eng. Lit. 1982; DPhil Eng. Lit. 2014). Assistant Teacher: St Paul's Girls' Sch., 1985–87; King Edward's Sch., Birmingham, 1987–90; Latymer Upper Sch., 1990–92; Hd of Eng., St Edward's Sch., Oxford, 1992–97; Dep. Hd (Academic), Highgate Sch., 1997–2002; Head, Sevenoaks Sch., 2002–19. *Address:* King Edward's School, Edgbaston Park Road, Birmingham B15 2UA. *T:* (0121) 472 1672.

**RICKS, Sir Christopher Bruce,** Kt 2009; FBA 1975; Warren Professor of the Humanities, Boston University, since 1998 (Professor of English, 1986–97); Professor of Poetry, University of Oxford, 2004–09; *b* 18 Sept. 1933; *s* of James Bruce Ricks and Gabrielle Roszak; *m* 1st, 1956, Kirsten Jensen (marr. diss.); two *s* two *d*; 2nd, 1977, Judith Aronson; one *s* two *d. Educ:* King Alfred's Sch., Wantage; Balliol Coll., Oxford (BA 1956; BLitt 1958; MA 1960). Hon. Fellow, 1989). 2nd Lieut, Green Howards, 1952. Andrew Bradley Jun. Res. Fellow, Balliol Coll., Oxford, 1957; Fellow of Worcester Coll., Oxford, 1958–68 (Hon. Fellow, 1990); Prof. of English, Bristol Univ., 1968–75; University of Cambridge: Prof. of English, 1975–82; King Edward VII Prof. of English Lit., 1982–86; Fellow, Christ's Coll., 1975–86 (Hon. Fellow, 1993). Visiting Professor: Berkeley and Stanford, 1965; Smith Coll., 1967; Harvard, 1971; Wesleyan, 1974; Brandeis, 1977, 1981, 1984. Lectures: Lord Northcliffe, UCL, 1972; Alexander, Univ. of Toronto, 1987; T. S. Eliot, Univ. of Kent, 1988; Clarendon, Univ. of Oxford, 1990; Clark, Trinity Coll., Cambridge, 1991. Pres., Assoc. of Literary Scholars and Critics, 2007–08. A Vice-Pres., Tennyson Soc.; Pres., Housman Soc. Chm. Judges, Man Booker Internat. Prize, 2013. Co-editor, Essays in Criticism. Fellow, American Acad. of Arts and Scis, 1991. Hon. DLitt: Oxon, 1998; Bristol, 2003; Western, Ont, 2016. George Orwell Meml Prize, 1979; Beefeater Club Prize for Literature, 1980; Andrew W. Mellon Dist. Achievement Award, 2004. *Publications:* Milton's Grand Style, 1963; (ed) The Poems of Tennyson, 1969, new edn 1987; Tennyson, 1972, rev. edn 1989; Keats and Embarrassment, 1974; (ed with Leonard Michaels) The State of the Language, 1980, new edn 1990; The Force of Poetry, 1984; (ed) The New Oxford Book of Victorian Verse, 1987; (ed) A. E. Housman: Collected Poems and Selected Prose, 1988; T. S. Eliot and Prejudice, 1988; (ed with William Vance) The Faber Book of America, 1992; Beckett's Dying Words, 1993; Essays in Appreciation, 1996; (ed) Inventions of the March Hare: poems 1909–1917 by T. S. Eliot, 1996; (ed) The Oxford Book of English Verse, 1999; (ed) Selected Poems of James Henry, 2002; Reviewery, 2002; Allusion to the Poets, 2002; Dylan's Visions of Sin, 2003; Decisions and Revisions in T. S. Eliot, 2003; (ed) New and Selected Poems of Samuel Menashe, 2005; Tennyson: selected poems, 2007; True Friendship: Geoffrey Hill, Anthony Hecht, and Robert Lowell under the sign of Eliot and Pound, 2010; (ed) What Maisie Knew, 2010; (ed) Joining Music with Reason: 34 poets, British and American, Oxford 2004–2009, 2010; (ed) Samuel Rogers: table-talk and recollections, 2011; (ed with Lisa Nemrow and Julie Nemrow) The Lyrics: since 1962, by Bob Dylan, 2014; (ed with Jim McCue) The Poems of T. S. Eliot, vol. I, Collected and Uncollected Poems, 2015, vol. II, Practical Cats & Further Verses, 2015. *Address:* 39 Martin Street, Cambridge, MA 02138, USA. *T:* (617) 3547887; Lasborough Cottage, Lasborough Park, near Tetbury, Glos GL8 8UF. *T:* (01666) 890252.

**RICKS, Robert Neville;** Deputy Legal Adviser, Treasury Advisory Division, Treasury Solicitor's Department, 1998–2002; *b* 29 June 1942; *s* of Sir John Plowman Ricks. *Educ:* Highgate Sch.; Worcester Coll., Oxford (MA). Admitted Solicitor, 1967. Entered Treasury Solicitor's Dept as Legal Asst, 1969; Sen. Legal Asst, 1973; Asst Solicitor, 1981; Prin. Asst Solicitor, 1986; Legal Advr, DES, then DfEE, 1990–97; Special Projects Dir, Treasury Solicitor's Dept, 1997–98. *Recreations:* collecting original cartoons, wine. *Address:* 2 Eaton Terrace, Aberavon Road, E3 5AJ. *T:* (020) 8981 3722.

**RICKSON, Ian;** freelance director; *b* 8 Nov. 1963; *s* of Richard and Eileen Rickson; one *s* by Kate Gould; *m* 2006, Polly Teale; one *d. Educ:* Essex Univ. (BA Eng and Eur. Lit. Hons); Goldsmiths' Coll., London Univ. (PGTC; Hon. Fellow, 2005). Freelance Dir, King's Head, The Gate, Chichester Fest. Theatre; Special Projects Dir, Young People's Th., 1991–92, Associate Dir, 1993–98, Royal Court Theatre; Artistic Dir, Royal Court Th., 1998–2006. Plays directed include: Me and My Friend, Chichester, 1992; The House of Yes, Gate Th., 1993; La Serva Padrona (opera), Broomhill, 1993; The Day I Stood Still, RNT, 1997; The Hothouse, NT, 2007; Parlour Song, Almeida, 2009; Hedda Gabler, NY, 2009; The Children's Hour, Betrayal, Comedy, 2011; Hamlet, Young Vic, 2011; Old Times, Harold Pinter Th., 2013; Electra, Old Vic, 2014; The Red Lion, RNT, 2015; The Nest, Young Vic, 2016; The Goat, or Who is Sylvia?, Th. Royal Haymarket, 2017; Against, Almeida, 2017; The Birthday Party, Harold Pinter Th., 2018; Translations, NT, 2018, 2019; Rosmersholm, Duke of York's, 2019; *Royal Court Theatre:* Wildfire, Sab, Killers, 1992; Some Voices, Ashes and Sand, 1994; Mojo, transf. Chicago, Pale Horse, 1995, Harold Pinter Th., 2013; Chicago, The Lights, 1996; The Weir, 1997, transf. Duke of York's, then NY, 1998; Dublin Carol, 2000; Mouth to Mouth, transf. Albery, 2001; The Night Heron, 2002; Fallout, 2003; The Sweetest Swing in Baseball, 2004; Alice Trilogy, 2005; The Winterling, Krapp's Last Tape, 2006; The Seagull, 2007, transf. NY, 2008; Jerusalem, 2009, transf. Apollo, 2010, NY 2011; The River, 2012. Films directed: Krapp's Last Tape (BBC), 2007; Fallout (C4), 2008; The Clear Road Ahead, 2010.

**RIDDELL, Alan Gordon;** Associate Director, IRIS Consulting, since 2007; *b* 8 Sept. 1948; *s* of George Riddell and Elizabeth (*née* Mellin); *m* 1976, Barbara Kelly; two *d. Educ:* Greenock Acad.; Glasgow Univ. (MA Hons Mod. Hist. and Pol Econ.). History teacher, Greenock Acad., 1971–74; Hd of History, Eyemouth High Sch., 1974–75; Department of the Environment, 1975–97: Asst Private Sec. to Minister of Housing, 1981–83; Inner Cities Div., 1983–86; Private Rented Sector Div., 1986–87; Private Sec. to Minister for Local Govt, 1987–90; Hd, Private Rented Sector Div., 1990–92; Principal Private Sec. to Sec. of State, 1992–94; Sec., Cttee on Standards in Public Life (Nolan Cttee), 1994–97; Hd, Regeneration Policy Div., DETR, 1997–98; Regl Dir, Govt Office for E of England, 1998–2002; Dir of Ops, Neighbourhood Renewal Unit, subseq. Dir of Local Develt and Renewal, ODPM, then DCLG, 2002–07. Chm., Standards Cttee, Sevenoaks DC, 2001. *Recreations:* walking, boats.

**RIDDELL, Alexander Hill, (Sandy);** public sector management consultant, since 2017; Chair, Mental Welfare Commission for Scotland, since 2019 (Member, 2017–19); Chair, Audit, Information Governance and Risk Management Committee, since 2018); *b* Inverness, 30 July 1956; *s* of Malcolm and Esther Riddell; *m* 1978, Sheila Fraser; two *d. Educ:* Moray Hse Coll., Edinburgh (DipSW 1978); Open Univ. (BA Hons Social Sci. 1994); Univ. of Stirling (MSc Social Work Mgt 1997). Highland Regional Council: Social Worker, 1978–85; Area Team Leader, 1985–89; Principal Officer, Community Care, 1989–94; Asst Dir, Elderly Services, 1994–96; Hd, Client Services, 1996–2002, Hd of Ops, 2002–05, Highland Council; Dir, Community Services, 2005–11, Corporate Dir, Educn and Social Care, 2011–14, Moray Council; Dir, Health and Social Care Partnership, Fife, 2014–16. Mem. Bd, NHS Grampian, 2018–. Pres., Assoc. of Dirs of Social Work, 2013–14; Founder, Social Work Scotland, 2013–14. *Recreations:* family, travel, music, gardening. *T:* 07936 057653. *E:* sandy.riddell@outlook.com.

**RIDDELL, Christopher Barry,** OBE 2019; political cartoonist and illustrator; Political Cartoonist, The Observer, since 1995; Children's Laureate, 2015–17; *b* 13 April 1962; *s* of Morris and Pamela Riddell; *m* 1987, Joanna Burroughes; two *s* one *d. Educ:* Archbishop Tenison's Grammar Sch., London; Epsom Sch. of Art and Design (Foundn); Brighton Polytech. Art Sch. (BA 1st cl. Hons (Illustration)). Cartoonist: The Economist, 1988–96; The New Statesman, 1998–2006; Political Cartoonist, Independent and Independent on Sunday, 1990–95; Cover Artist, Literary Review, 1996–. *Publications:* Ben and the Bear, 1986; Humphrey Goes to the Ball, 1986; Humphrey of the Rovers, 1986; Humphrey the Hippo, 1986; Humphrey's New Trousers, 1986; Mr Underbed, 1986, 2nd edn 1997; Bird's New Shoes, 1987; The Fibbs, 1987; The Trouble with Elephants, 1988; When the Walrus Comes, 1989; The Wish Factory, 1990; The Bear Dance, 1990; The Emperor of Absurdia, 2006; The Da Vinci Cod: and other illustrations to unwritten books, 2006; Ottoline and the Yellow Cat, 2007; Ottoline Goes to School, 2007; Ottoline at Sea, 2007; Alienography, 2010; Goth Girl and the Ghost of a Mouse (Costa Children's Book Award), 2013; with Richard Platt: The Castle Diary: the journal of Tobias Burgess, 1999; The Pirate Diary: the journal of Jake Carpenter, 2001 (Kate Greenaway Medal, 2002); Platypus, 2001; Platypus and the Lucky Day, 2002; with Martin Jenkins: Jonathan Swift's Gulliver (Kate Greenaway Medal), 2004; Don Quixote, 2009; with Paul Stewart: The Edge Chronicles series, 1998–; The Rabbit and Hedgehog series, 1998–2001; The Blobheads series, 2000; The Muddle Earth series, 2003; Fergus Crane (Smarties Book Prize), 2004; Corby Flood (Nestlé Book Prize), 2005; Hugo Pepper (Nestlé Book Prize), 2006; Barnaby Grimes: curse of the nightwolf, 2007; Wyrmeweald, 2010; with Neil Gaiman: The Graveyard Book, 2008 (Carnegie Prize, 2010); Coraline, 2012; Fortunately, the Milk, 2013; The Sleeper and the Spindle, 2014 (Kate Greenaway Medal, 2016); My Little Book of Big Freedoms: the human rights act in pictures, 2017; illus. for many other authors. *Recreations:* writing, drawing, talking. *Address:* The Observer, Kings Place, 90 York Way, N1 9GU. *Club:* Academy.

**RIDDELL, His Honour Nicholas Peter;** a Circuit Judge, 1995–2008; *b* 24 April 1941; *s* of late Peter John Archibald Riddell and Cynthia Mary Riddell (later Douglas); *m* 1976, Barbara Helen Glucksmann; three *d. Educ:* Harrow; Magdalene Coll., Cambridge (BA Cantab). Called to the Bar, Inner Temple, 1964; practised at the Bar, 1964–95. Mem. Bd, Circle 33 Housing Trust Ltd, 1998. *Address:* 18 Myddelton Square, EC1R 1YE. *T:* (020) 7837 4034.

**RIDDELL, Norman Malcolm Marshall;** Vice Chairman, OneFamily (formerly Family Investments), 2006–14 and 2015–16 (Chairman, 2014–15); *b* 30 June 1947; *s* of Malcolm Riddell and Euphemia Richardson Riddell (*née* Wight); *m* 1969, Leila Jean White; three *s. Educ:* George Heriot's Sch., Edinburgh. MCIBS; AIIMR. National Commercial Bank and Royal Bank of Scotland, 1965–78; Man. Dir, Britannia Investment Services, 1978–86; Chief Executive: Capital House Investment Management, 1986–93; INVESCO plc, 1993–96; Chairman: United Overseas Gp plc, 1997–99; Savoy Asset Mgt plc, 1997–2000; Norman Riddell and Associates Ltd, subseq. Novitas Partners LLP, 1997–2009. Director: Charterhouse Gp, 1986–89; Life Assce Hldg Corp., 1995–2004; Asset Management Investment Co., 1997–2002; Clubhaus, 1999–2004; Improvement Pathway, 1999–2002; Pathway One VCT plc, 2001–07; Invesco UK Ltd, 2011–16. *Recreations:* gardening, most sports, travel, music, fine wine.

**RIDDELL, Rt Hon. Peter (John Robert),** CBE 2012; PC 2010; Commissioner for Public Appointments, since 2016; Director, Institute for Government, 2012–16 (Senior Fellow, 2008–11); *b* 14 Oct. 1948; *s* of late Kenneth Robert Riddell and Freda Riddell (*née* Young); *m* 1994, Avril Walker; one *d. Educ:* Dulwich Coll.; Sidney Sussex Coll., Cambridge (BA Hist. and Econs 1970, MA; Hon. Fellow, 2005). Joined Financial Times, 1970: Property Corresp., 1972–74; Lex Column, 1975–76; Economics Corresp., 1976–81; Political Editor, 1981–88; US Editor and Washington Bureau Chief, 1989–91; joined The Times, 1991: Political Columnist, 1991–2010; Political Editor, 1992–93; Asst Editor (Politics), subseq. Chief Political Commentator, 1993–2010. Member: Privy Council Review of Treatment of UK Detainees, 2010–11; Parly and Political Service Honours Cttee, 2012–16. Regular broadcaster, Week in Westminster, Talking Politics, Radio 4, and on TV. Vis. Prof. of Political History, QMW, 2000–03. Chairman: Parly Press Gall., 1997; Hansard Soc., 2007–12 (Mem., 1995– ). Gov., Dulwich Coll., 2009– (Chm., 2015– ). FRHistS 1998; FAcSS (AcSS 2012). Hon. Fellow, Pol Studies Assoc., 2007. Freeman, City of London, 2012. Hon. DLitt: Greenwich, 2001; Edinburgh, 2007. Wincott Award for Economic and Financial Journalism, 1981; House Magazine Political Journalist of the Year, 1986; Political Columnist of the Year, Political Studies Assoc., 2004; Pres.'s Medal, British Acad., 2010. *Publications:* The Thatcher Government, 1983, rev. edn 1985; The Thatcher Decade, 1989, rev. edn as The Thatcher Era, 1991; Honest Opportunism, the rise of the career politician, 1993, rev. edn 1996; Parliament under Pressure, 1998, rev. edn as Parliament under Blair, 2000; Hug Them Close, 2003 (Pol Book of Year, Channel 4 Pol Awards, 2004); The Unfulfilled Prime Minister, 2005; In Defence of Politicians - In Spite of Themselves, 2011; 15 Minutes of Power: the uncertain life of British ministers, 2019;

contrib. chaps in books, including: A Conservative Revolution?, 1994; The Major Effect, 1994; The Blair Effect, 2001; British Politics since 1945, 2001; Reinventing Britain: Constitutional change under New Labour, 2007; So You Want to be a Political Journalist, 2011; The Coalition Effect, 2010–2015, 2015; contrib. to Spectator, New Statesman, Political Qly, British Journalism Rev., TLS, Jl of Legislative Studies. *Recreations:* watching cricket, opera, theatre. *Address:* Public Appointments Commission, 1 Horse Guards Road, SW1A 2HQ. *Clubs:* Garrick, MCC.

**RIDDELL, Richard Rodford,** PhD; education academic, freelance writer and researcher; Senior Lecturer, Bath Spa University, since 2009; *b* 28 Jan. 1953; *m* 1975, Millie Mitchell; one *s* one *d*. *Educ:* Manchester Grammar Sch.; Magdalen Coll., Oxford (MA); Madeley Coll. of Educn (PGCE); Bulmershe Coll. of Higher Educn (MPhil); Bath Spa Univ. (PhD 2012). Teacher: John Mason Sch., Abingdon, 1975–77; Waingel's Copse Sch., Reading, 1977–81; Asst Educn Officer, Wilts CC, 1981–86; Educn Officer, Notts CC, 1986–90; Asst Dir of Educn, Avon CC, 1990–95; Dir of Educn, Bristol CC, 1995–2002; Jt Hd of Educn, Amnesty Internat. UK, 2005–08. Vis. Fellow, UWE, 2002–. FRSA 1999; FHEA 2017. *Publications:* Schools For Our Cities, 2003; Aspiration, Identity and Self-Belief, 2010; Equity, Trust and the Self-improving Schools System, 2016. *E:* richardxvriddell@gmail.com.

**RIDDELL, Sandy;** see Riddell, A. H.

**RIDDELL, Sir Walter (John Buchanan),** 14th Bt *cr* 1628 (NS), of Riddell, Roxburghshire; *b* 10 June 1974; *e s* of Sir John Riddell, 13th Bt, KCVO and of Hon. Sarah, LVO, *o d* of Baron Richardson of Duntisbourne, KG, MBE, TD, PC; *S* father, 2010; *m* 2003, Lucy, *d* of Selwyn J. Awdry; one *s* three *d* (of whom one *s* one *d* are twins). *Heir:* s Finlay John Buchanan Riddell, *b* 2 June 2004.

**RIDDICK, Graham Edward Galloway;** Director: Norman Broadbent, 2007–09; Ashurst Executives, since 2010; *b* 26 Aug. 1955; *s* of late John Julian Riddick and Cecilia Margaret Riddick (née Ruggles-Brise); *m* 1988, Sarah Northcroft; one *s* two *d*. *Educ:* Stowe Sch., Buckingham; Univ. of Warwick (Chm., Warwick Univ. Cons. Assoc.). Sales management with Procter & Gamble, 1977–82; Coca-Cola, 1982–87. Gp Mktg Dir, subseq. Gp Mktg and Communications Dir, Onyx Environmental Gp plc, 1997–2000; Business Develt Dir, DeHavilland Information Services plc, 2000–05; Commercial Dir, Adfero Ltd, 2005–07. MP (C) Colne Valley, 1987–97 (first Cons. MP in Colne Valley for 102 years); contested (C) same seat, 1997. PPS to Financial Sec. to HM Treasury, 1990–92, to Sec. of State for Transport, 1992–94. Mem., Educn Select Cttee, 1994–96; Vice Chm., Cons. Trade and Industry Cttee, 1990; Secretary: Cons. Employment Cttee, 1988–90; All Party Textiles Gp, 1988–97. Pres., Yorks CPC, 1993–97. *Recreations:* fishing, shooting, sports, photography, bridge.

**RIDDING, John Joseph;** Chief Executive, Financial Times Group, since 2006; *b* Birmingham, 25 June 1965; *s* of Mike and Moira Ridding; *m* 2003, Lizzie Allen; two *s* two *d*. *Educ:* Bedales Sch.; University Coll., Oxford (BA 1st Cl. PPE). Hd, Econs and Asia Pacific desks, Oxford Analytica, 1987; joined Financial Times, 1988: Korea corresp., 1990–92; Paris corresp., 1993–95; Companies Reporter, 1995–98; Man. Ed., 1998–2001; Dep. Ed., 2001–03; Publisher, FT Asia; Chm., Pearson Asia, 2003–06; Pres., Pearson Professional, 2013–15. *Recreations:* music, running, surfing, scuba diving. *Address:* Financial Times, Bracken House, 1 Friday Street, EC4M 9BT. *E:* john.ridding@ft.com.

**RIDDLE, Howard Charles Fraser,** CBE 2018; Senior District Judge (Chief Magistrate), 2010–16; a District Judge (Magistrates' Courts) (formerly Metropolitan Stipendiary Magistrate), 1995–2016; *b* 13 Aug. 1947; *s* of Cecil Riddle and Eithne Riddle (née McKenna); *m* 1974, Susan Hilary Hurst; two *d*. *Educ:* Judd Sch., Tonbridge; London School of Economics (LLB); Coll. of Law. Admitted Solicitor, 1978. Sub-Editor, Penguin Books, 1969–70; Editor, McGill-Queens University Press, 1970–71; Publications Officer, Humanities and Social Science Res. Council, Canada, 1971–76; Solicitor, Edward Fail, Bradshaw and Waterson, 1976–95 (Sen. Partner, 1985–95). Vice-Chm., London Area Cttee, Legal Aid Bd, 1993–95; Mem., Sentencing Adv. Panel, 2004–10 (Vice-Chm., 2007–10); Chm., Legal Cttee, Council of Dist Judges (Magistrates' Courts), 2008–11; Hon. Bencher, Gray's Inn, 2012. Member, Editorial Board: Blackstone's Criminal Practice, 2012–17; Criminal Law Review, 2012–17, now Hon. Mem. *Publications:* (Contrib. Ed.) Wilkinson's Road Traffic Offences, 2008–12; (contrib.) Blackstone's Criminal Practice, 2011–12. *Recreations:* village activities, Rugby football, tennis, visiting France. *Club:* Tonbridge Juddians Rugby Football.

**RIDDLE, Kathryn Elizabeth,** OBE 2013; JP; DL; Senior Independent Director, Christie Hospital NHS Foundation Trust, Manchester, since 2016; *b* Halifax, 4 Aug. 1945; *d* of Maj. George Foster, MBE and Doris Foster; *m* 1967, Anthony Riddle; three *s*. *Educ:* High Sch., Retford, Notts; Univ. of Sheffield (BA Hons Econs 1967; LLB 1986). Tutor in Law, Univ. of Sheffield, 1986–98. Chairman: Sheffield FHSA, 1994–96; Sheffield HA, 1996–2001; S Yorks HA, 2001–06; Yorks and the Humber Strategic HA, then NHS N of England, 2006–13; Health Educn Yorks and the Humber, 2013–16. Pro Chancellor and Chm. Council, Univ. of Sheffield, 2003–13 (Mem., Alumni Bd, 2013–). Hon. Col, Univ. of Sheffield OTC, 2009–14. JP Sheffield, 1975; High Sheriff, 1998–99, DL, 1999, S Yorks. Hon. DLitt Sheffield, 2013. *Recreations:* family, friends, cooking, Rugby Union, travelling in Spain.

**RIDDLE, Dr Philip Keitch,** OBE 2008; consultant, researcher and tutor; Researcher and Tutor, University of Edinburgh Business School, 2015–18; *b* 6 May 1952; *s* of Clifford Stanley Frederick Riddle and Anne Munro Riddle (née Black); *m* 1977, Catherine Mary Riddle (née Adams); three *s*. *Educ:* Dunfermline High Sch.; Trinity Hall, Cambridge (BA 1973, MA 1977); Univ. of Edinburgh (MBA 1977; PhD 2018). Shell Group: various posts, marketing and trading, 1977–82; Hd, Oil and Gas Trading, Brunei Shell, 1982–85; Business Develt Manager, Shell Internat. Gas, 1985–88; Area Co-ordination, S America, Shell Internat., 1988–91; Man. Dir, Shell Namibia, 1991–94; Regl Develt Dir, Shell S Africa, 1994–95; Vice-Pres., Shell LPG Europe, 1995–99; Chm., Maximedia, 2000–01; CEO, VisitScotland, 2001–10. Hon. Consul (Namibia), Govt of the Netherlands, 1991–94. Counsellor, Prince's Scotland Youth Business Trust, 2000–10. Tourism Development Adviser: Tajikistan, 2013–15; Kyrgyzstan, 2018. Hon. Prof., Queen Margaret Univ., Edinburgh, 2011–16. *Recreations:* ski-ing, walking, reading, travel, making sense of Scotland. *E:* philriddle@blueyonder.co.uk.

**RIDER, Prof. Barry Alexander Kenneth,** OBE 2014; PhD; Director, Institute of Advanced Legal Studies, University of London, 1995–2004, Hon. Senior Research Fellow, since 2004; Fellow Commoner, Jesus College, Cambridge, since 2001; Professorial Fellow, Centre of Development Studies (formerly Development Studies Committee), University of Cambridge, since 2008; Professor of Comparative Law, Renmin University, China, since 2011; *b* 30 May 1952; *s* of Kenneth Leopold Rider and Alexina Elsie Rider (née Bremner); *m* 1976, Normalita Antonina Furto Rosales; one *d*. *Educ:* Bexleyheath Boys' Secondary Modern Sch.; Poly. of N London (Intermediate Ext. LLB 1970); Queen Mary Coll., London (LLB Hons 1973; PhD 1976); Jesus Coll., Cambridge (MA 1976; PhD 1978). Called to the Bar, Inner Temple, 1977, Bencher, 2010. Univ. teaching officer, Univ. of Cambridge, 1980–95; Fellow, 1976–2001, Dean, 1989–96, Jesus Coll., Cambridge. Master of Witan Hall, incorp. Gyosei Internat. Coll., 2002–03. Vis. Sen. Fellow, Centre for Commercial Law Studies, QMC, 1979–90; University of London: Chm., Acad. Policy and Standards Cttee, Sch. of Advanced Study, 1997–2004; Mem., Bd of Mgt, Inst. of US Studies, 1997–2004. Prof. of Law, and Dir, LLM Progs, Law Sch., BPP Univ. (formerly BPP University Coll.), 2008–; Prof. of Public Law, Centre for the Rule of Law and Wenlan Scholar Prof., Zhongnan Univ. of Economics and Law, China, 2017–. Various visiting academic appts, inc. Florida Univ., 1990–; Paul Hastings Prof. of Commercial Law, Univ. of Hong Kong, 2003. Honorary Professor: Dept of Mercantile Law, Univ. of the Free State (formerly Univ. of OFS), RSA, 1998–; Beijing Normal Univ., 2006–; Supreme People's Procuratorate Univ., PRC, 2006–; Renmin Univ., 2006– (Special Counsellor, Develt, Renmin Law Sch., 2015–); of Comparative Law, Univ. of Palermo, 2019–. General Editor: Company Lawyer, 1980–; European Business Law Rev., 1996–2005; Jl Financial Crime, 1994–; Jl Money Laundering Control, 1996–; Amicus Curiae, 1997–; Internat. and Comparative Corporate Law Jl, 1998–; Internat. Jl of Disclosure and Governance, 2003–08; Editor: CUP series on Corporate Law, 1996–; Kluwer series on Company and Financial Law, 1997–2006; Butterworth's series on Compliance, 2002–06. Hd, Commonwealth Commercial Crime Unit, 1981–89; Exec. Dir, Centre for Internat. Documentation on Organised and Econ. Crime, 1989–. Special Advr to H of C Select Cttee on Trade and Industry, 1989–93. Internat. Gen. Counsel, Internat. Compliance Assoc., 2007–09. Chairman: Exec. Cttee, Soc. for Advanced Legal Studies, 1997–2004 (Mem., 2006–); Hamlyn Trust for Legal Educn, 2001–05. Former Consultant to various govtl agencies and to internat. bodies, incl. UNDP, IMF, Commonwealth Fund for Tech. Co-operation, Asian Develt Bank, and Commonwealth Secretariat. Consultant: Beachcroft LLP (formerly Beachcroft Wansbroughs), 2004–06; Islamic Financial Services Bd, 2005–16; of Counsel, Bryan Cave LLP, 2008–12. Member: Bd of Advrs, Internat. Council for Capital Formation, 2003–07; Adv. Bd, Centre for Financial Crime and Security Studies, RUSI, 2015–17; Adv. Cttee, China Overseas-educated Scholars Foundn, YICAI Foundn, 2015–; Chair, Adv. Council, UK Sichuan Business Assoc., 2017–. International Advisor: New England Sch. of Law, 2002–; Faculty of Law, Univ. of Cyprus, 2003–; Centre for Criminology, Univ. of Hong Kong, 2004–; Inst. of Criminal Justice, Beijing, 2006–. Mem. Court, City Univ., 2001–17. Freeman, City of London, 1984; Mem., Court of Assts, 1998–, Master, 2007–08, Co. of Pattenmakers; Freeman, Guild of Educators, 2008–. Fellow, Inst. of Professional Investigators, 1980; FRSA 1997. Hon. Fellow: Soc. for Advanced Legal Studies, 2004; Inst. of Nat. Security Studies, Min. of Defence, Sri Lanka, 2018–. Hon. LLD: Dickinson Law Sch., USA, 1996; Free State, RSA, 2001. *Publications:* (jtly) The Regulation of Insider Trading, 1979; Insider Trading, 1983; (jtly) Guide to the Financial Services Act, 1987, 2nd edn 1989; (jtly) Insider Crime, 1993; (jtly) Guide to Financial Services Regulation, 1997; (jtly) Anti-Money Laundering Guide, 1999; (jtly) Market Abuse and Insider Dealing, 2002, 3rd edn 2016; *edited:* The Regulation of the British Securities Industry, 1979, CCH Financial Services Reporter, 3 vols, 1987; The Fiduciary, the Insider and the Conflict, 1995; Money Laundering Control, 1996; Corruption: the enemy within, 1997; Developments in European Company Law, vol. I 1997, vol. II 1998; International Tracing of Assets, 2 vols, 1997; Commercial Law in a Global Context, 1998; The Corporate Dimension, 1998; The Realm of Company Law, 1998; (jtly) The Prevention and Control of International Financial Crime, 2010; (jtly) Strategies for the Development of Islamic Capital Markets, 2011; International Financial Crime, 2015; contrib. to numerous books and legal periodicals on company law, financial law and control of economic crime. *Recreations:* riding, historic houses. *Address:* Institute of Advanced Legal Studies, Charles Clore House, 17 Russell Square, WC1B 5DR. *T:* (020) 7862 5800; Jesus College, Cambridge CB5 8BL. *T:* (01223) 339339. *E:* b.rider@jesus.cam.ac.uk. *Clubs:* Athenæum, Oxford and Cambridge, Civil Service.

**RIDER, Gill,** CB 2011; non-executive Director: Charles Taylor plc, since 2012; Pennon plc, since 2012; Invertek plc, since 2015; President, Chartered Institute of Personnel and Development, 2010–15; *b* London, 24 Oct. 1954; *d* of William and Ethel Rider; *m* 1986, David Paul Burke. *Educ:* Univ. of Southampton (BSc Hons Biol.; PhD Botany). FCIPD 2008, CCIPD 2015. Accenture, 1979–2006: Man. Partner, Utilities Practice, Europe and S Africa, 1998–99; Mem., Global Exec. Cttee, 1999–2006; Man. Partner, Resources Operating Unit, EMEA, India and S America, 1999–2002; Chief Leadership Officer, 2002–06; Dir-Gen., CS Capability Gp, Cabinet Office, 2006–11. Non-exec. Dir, De La Rue plc, 2006–15. Chm. Council, Univ. of Southampton, 2012–18. *Recreations:* entertaining, gardening, motor-racing, travel. *E:* gill.rider@mac.com.

**RIDER, Stephen Henry;** Presenter: Legends series, Sky Sports F1, since 2012; British Touring Car Championship, ITV; *b* 28 April 1950; *s* of Alfred Charles Rider and Shirley Jeanette (née Walls); *m* 1985, Jane Eydmann; one *s* one *d*. *Educ:* Roan Grammar Sch., Blackheath. Local sports journalist, S London and sports presenter for London Broadcasting, 1969–76; Sports Presenter: Anglia TV, 1976–80; ITV Network, incl., World of Sport, 1980 Olympics, Midweek Sports Special, Network Golf, 1980–85; Network Presenter for BBC Sport: Main Presenter, Sportsnight, 1985–92; network golf coverage; Olympic Games, Seoul, 1988, Barcelona, 1992, Atlanta, 1996, Sydney, 2000, Athens, 2004; Commonwealth Games, 1986, 1990, 1994, 1998 and 2002; main network golf presenter, 1991–2005; motor sport specialist; Presenter: Grandstand, 1985–2005 (Main Presenter, 1992–2005); BBC Sports Personality of the Year, 1986–2005; F1 Grand Prix, ITV, 2006–08; ITV Football (incl. Champions League and World Cup, 2006), 2006–10; Rugby World Cup, ITV, 2011. Sports Presenter of Year, TRIC, 1994, RTS, 1995. *Publications:* 50 Years of Sports Personality of the Year, 2003; Europe at the Masters, 2006; My Chequered Career: thirty-five years of televising motorsport, 2012. *Recreations:* golf, family. *Address:* c/o Blackburn Management, Argyll House, All Saints Passage, SW18 1EP.

**RIDGE, Keith William,** CBE 2014; PhD; Chief Pharmaceutical Officer, NHS Improvement (formerly NHS England), Department of Health and Social Care (formerly Department of Health) and Health Education England (formerly Chief Pharmaceutical Officer, Department of Health), since 2006; *b* Romford, Essex, 15 Feb. 1962; *s* of Cyril Ridge and Gwen Ridge; *m* 1989, Susan Caroline Sands; one *s* one *d*. *Educ:* University College London (BPharm 1st Cl. Hons 1987; MSc (Dist.) 1991); Univ. of Manchester (PhD 1998). Registered Pharmacist 1988. Res. Pharmacist, Roche Pharmaceuticals, 1988–90; various hosp. pharmacist posts, Whittington Hosp. NHS Trust, 1990–96; Principal Pharmacist, DoH, 1996–2000; Chief Pharmacist: North Glasgow Univ. NHS Trust, 2000–05; Univ. Hosps Birmingham, 2005–06. Vis. Prof., Dept of Medicine, Imperial Coll. London, 2013–. *Publications:* articles in learned jls. *Recreations:* family, angling, theatre, cooking. *Address:* NHS England, Skipton House, 80 London Road, SE1 6LH. *T:* (020) 7972 2833, *Fax:* (020) 7972 1186. *E:* Keith.Ridge@dhsc.gov.uk, Keith.Ridge@nhs.net.

**RIDGWAY, Lt-Gen. Sir Andrew Peter,** KBE 2011 (CBE 1995); CB 2001; DL; Lieutenant-Governor and Commander-in-Chief, Jersey, 2006–11; Executive Chairman, Confederation of Service Charities, 2014–16; *b* 20 March 1950; *s* of late Robert Hamilton Ridgway and Betty Patricia Ridgway (née Crane); *m* 1974, Valerie Elizabeth Shawe; three *s* one *d*. *Educ:* Hele's Sch., Exeter; RMA, Sandhurst; St John's Coll., Cambridge (MPhil). Commnd RTR, 1970: served Germany, NI, Belize, Bosnia, Kuwait, Macedonia, Kosovo and UK; CO, 3 RTR, 1991–92; Col, Army Prog., MoD, 1992–93; Comdr, 7 Armd Bde,

1993–95 (Comdr, UN Sector SW Bosnia Herzegovina, Feb.–Nov. 1994); Dir, Operational Capability, MoD, 1995–97; Chief, Jt Rapid Deployment Force, 1997–98; COS, ACE RRC, 1998–2001 (COS, Kosovo Force, 1999); Hd, Defence Trng Review Implementation Team, 2001–02; Dir Gen. Trng and Educn, MoD, 2002; Chief of Defence Intelligence, MoD, 2003–06. Col Comdt, RTR, 1999–2006; Hon. Colonel: Cambridge Univ. OTC, 2003–13; Westminster Dragoons, 2008–14; Jersey Field Sqdn RE, 2010–14. Dir, Army Ice Sports, 1999–2006; Chm., British Bobsleigh, 2010–14. Mem., Judicial Appts Commn, 2012–17; Chm., Adv. Cttee, War Pension Tribunals, 2014–16. Strategic Advr, Cyber Security, JT Global, 2014–. Mem., Adv. Bd, King's Centre for Mil. Health Res., KCL, 2014–16. Pres., SSAFA Devon, 2017–. Trustee, Bishopsteignton Heritage, 2017–; Chm., Tank Mus., 2018–. DL Devon, 2018. KStJ 2009 (CStJ 2007). *Recreations:* golf, fishing, walking, bobsleigh, beekeeping. *Club:* Army and Navy.

**RIDGWAY, David Frederick Charles,** CMG 2000; OBE 1988; HM Diplomatic Service, retired; Assessor, Foreign and Commonwealth Office, 2001–07; Partner, CONSULAT Business Consultancy, 2002–14; *b* 9 June 1941; *m* 1966, Dora Beatriz Siles; one *s* one *d.* Entered FO, 1960; served La Paz, Colombo and Durban, 1963–77; First Sec. (Commercial), Buenos Aires, 1980–82; FCO, 1982–84; Chargé d'Affaires ai, San Salvador, 1984–87; FCO, 1988–91; Dir of Trade Promotion, Madrid, 1991–95; Ambassador to: Bolivia, 1995–98; Cuba, 1998–2001. Chairman: Anglo-Central American Soc., 2005–07; Cuba Studies Trust, 2007–13. *Address:* 178 Rivermead Court, Ranelagh Gardens, SW6 3SF.

**RIDGWELL, Angela;** Chief Executive and Director of Resources, Lancashire County Council, since 2018; *b* Cambridge, 24 July 1964; *d* of Ronald Stenning and Jean Stenning; *m* 1985, Howard Ridgwell; one *d.* CIPFA 1991. Dir, Resources, Bridgnorth DC, 2000–02; Dir, Finance and ICT, Coventry CC, 2002–06; Chief Exec., Thurrock BC, 2007–08; Man. Dir, Angie Ridgwell Associates Ltd, 2009–; Strategic Dir, Business Change, Bristol CC, 2013; Dir Gen., Corp. Services, DECC, 2013–16; Dir Gen., Finance and Corporate Services, BEIS, 2016–17. Freedom, City of London, 2016. *Recreations:* triathlon, walking, family, theatre, ballet. *Address:* Lancashire County Council, PO Box 78, County Hall, Fishergate, Preston, Lancs PR1 8XJ. *T:* (01772) 536260. *E:* angie.ridgwell@lancashire.gov.uk.

**RIDLEY,** family name of **Viscount Ridley.**

**RIDLEY,** 5th Viscount *cr* 1900; **Matthew White Ridley,** DL; DPhil; FRSL; FMedSci; Baron Wensleydale 1900; Bt 1756; *b* 7 Feb. 1958; *o s* of 4th Viscount Ridley, KG, GCVO, TD and Lady Anne Lumley (*d* 2006), 3rd *d* of 11th Earl of Scarborough, KG, GCSI, GCIE, GCVO, PC; *S* father, 2012; *m* 1989, Prof. Anya Hurlbert, *d* of Dr Robert Hurlbert, Houston, Texas; one *s* one *d. Educ:* Eton Coll.; Magdalen Coll., Oxford (BA Zoology 1979; DPhil Zoology 1983). Science Editor, 1983–87, Washington corresp., 1987–90, American Editor, 1990–92, The Economist; columnist: Sunday and Daily Telegraph, 1993–2000; The Times, 2013–. Chairman: Northern 2 VCT, 1999–2008; Northern Rock plc, 2004–07 (Dir, 1994–2007); Director: Northern Investors, 1994–2007; PA Holdings Ltd, 1999–2008. Chm., Internat. Centre for Life, 1996–2003. Elected Mem., H of L, 2013. DL Northumberland, 2007. FRSL 1999; FMedSci 2004. *Publications:* Warts and All, 1989; The Red Queen, 1993; The Origins of Virtue, 1996; Genome, 1999; Nature Via Nurture, 2003; Francis Crick, 2006; The Rational Optimist: how prosperity evolves, 2010; The Evolution of Everything, 2015. *Recreations:* fly fishing, natural history. *Heir: s* Hon. Matthew White Ridley, *b* 27 Sept. 1993. *Address:* Blagdon Hall, Seaton Burn, Newcastle upon Tyne NE13 6DD.

**RIDLEY, Sir Adam (Nicholas),** Kt 1985; Director General, London Investment Banking Association, 2000–05, Senior Adviser, 2005–06; non-executive Director, Equitas Group of Companies, since 2014; *b* 14 May 1942; *s* of late Jasper Maurice Alexander Ridley and Helen Cressida Ridley (*née* Bonham Carter); *m* 1981, Margaret Anne Passmore; three *s* (inc. twin *s*). *Educ:* Eton Coll.; Balliol Coll., Oxford (1st cl. hons PPE 1965); Univ. of California, Berkeley. Foreign Office, 1965, seconded to DEA, 1965–68; Harkness Fellow, Univ. of California, Berkeley, 1968–69; HM Treasury, 1970–71, seconded to CPRS, 1971–74; Economic Advr to shadow cabinet and Asst Dir, 1974–79, Dir, 1979, Cons. Res. Dept; Special Advr to Chancellor of the Exchequer, 1979–84, to Chancellor of the Duchy of Lancaster, 1985. Director: Hambros Bank, 1985–97; Hambros PLC, 1985–97; Sunday Newspaper Publishing PLC, 1988–90 (Chm., 1990); non-executive Director: Assoc. of Lloyds Members, 1987– (Vice Chm., 1994–); Leopold Joseph Holdings, 1997–2004; Morgan Stanley Bank Internat., 2006–13; Hampden Agencies Ltd, 2007–12; Equitas Ltd, 2009–; Equitas Reinsce Ltd, 2009–; Equitas Hldgs Ltd, 2009–; Equitas Insce Ltd, 2009–. Chm., Names Adv. Cttee, 1995–96, Mem. Council, 1997–99, Mem., Regulatory Bd, 1997–99, Lloyds of London. Mem., National Lottery Charities Bd, 1994–2000 (Dep. Chm., 1995–2000). Mem. Council, British Sch. at Athens, 2003– (Vice Chm., 2010–17). *Publications:* articles on regional policy, public spending, international and Eastern European economics, financial regulation, charities, and music. *Recreations:* music, pictures, travel. *Club:* Political Economy.

**RIDLEY, Prof. Anne Jacqueline,** PhD; FRS 2017; FRSB; FMedSci; Professor of Cell Biology and Head, School of Cellular and Molecular Medicine, University of Bristol, since 2018; *b* Oxford, 3 April 1963; *d* of Kenneth Ridley and Jane Ridley; *m* 1990, Edward Kay; two *d. Educ:* Clare Coll., Cambridge (BA Hons Natural Scis 1985); Imperial Cancer Res. Fund, Univ. of London (PhD 1989). Post-doctoral Fellow: MIT, Cambridge, 1989–90; Inst. of Cancer Res., London, 1990–93; University College London: Mem., Ludwig Inst. for Cancer Res., 1993–2007; Lectr, 1995–2001; Reader, 2001–03; Prof., 2003–07; Prof. of Cell Biol., KCL, 2007–17. Mem. Council, Amer. Soc. for Cell Biol., 2006–08. Mem., EMBO, 2003. FRSB (FSB 2009); FMedSci 2012. Hon. FRMS, 2014. *Publications:* over 200 articles in biochem., cell biol. and med. jls. *Recreation:* music (play viola and piano). *Address:* School of Cellular and Molecular Medicine, Biomedical Sciences Building, University of Bristol, University Walk, Bristol BS8 1TD. *E:* anne.ridley@bristol.ac.uk.

**RIDLEY, Prof. Brian Kidd,** FRS 1994; Research Professor of Physics, University of Essex, 1991–2008, now Professor Emeritus; *b* 2 March 1931; *s* of Oliver Archbold Ridley and Lillian Beatrice Ridley; *m* 1959, Sylvia Jean Nicholls; one *s* one *d. Educ:* Univ. of Durham (BSc 1st Cl. Hons Physics, PhD). CPhys, FInstP. Research Physicist, Mullard Research Lab., Redhill, 1956–64; Essex University: Lectr in Physics, 1964–67; Sen. Lectr, 1967–71; Reader, 1971–84; Prof., 1984–91. Dist. Vis. Prof., Cornell Univ., 1967; Vis. Prof. at univs in USA, Denmark, Sweden and Holland. Paul Dirac Medal and Prize, Inst. of Physics, 2001. *Publications:* Time, Space and Things, 1976, 3rd edn 1995; The Physical Environment, 1979; Quantum Processors in Semiconductors, 1982, 5th edn 2013; Electrons and Phonons in Semiconductor Multilayers, 1997, 2nd edn 2009; On Science, 2001; Reforming Science: beyond belief, 2010; Hybrid Phonons in Nanostructures, 2017. *Recreations:* tennis, piano.

**RIDLEY, Prof. Frederick Fernand,** OBE 1978; PhD; Professor of Political Theory and Institutions, University of Liverpool, 1965–95, now Emeritus, and Senior Fellow, School of Management (formerly Institute of Public Administration and Management), 1995–2005; *b* 11 Aug. 1928; *s* of late J. and G. A. Ridley; *m* 1967, Paula Frances Cooper Ridley, *qv*; two *s* one *d. Educ:* The Hall, Hampstead; Highgate Sch.; LSE (BScEcon, PhD); Univs of Paris and Berlin. Lectr, Univ. of Liverpool, 1958–65. Vis. Professor: Graduate Sch. of Public Affairs, Univ. of Pittsburgh, 1968; Coll. of Europe, Bruges, 1975–83. Manpower Services Commission, Merseyside: Chm., Job Creation Prog., 1975–77; Vice-Chm., 1978–87, Chm., 1987–88, Area Manpower Bd. Member: Jt Univ. Council for Social and Public Admin, 1964–95 (Chm., 1972–74); Exec., Pol Studies Assoc., 1967–75 (Hon. Vice-Pres., 1995–); Council, Hansard Soc., 1970–94; Pol Science Cttee, SSRC, 1972–76; Cttee, European Gp on Public Admin, 1973–92; Public and Social Admin Bd, CNAA, 1975–82; Social Studies Res. Cttee, CNAA, 1980–83 (Chm.); Academic Cttee, Assoc. Internat. de la Fonction Publique, 1988–93; Vice-Pres., Rencontres Européennes des Fonctions Publiques/Entretiens Universitaires pour l'Admin en Europe, 1990–2001. Member: Exec., Merseyside Arts (RAA), 1979–84; Adv. Council, Granada Foundn, 1984–98; Council, Hochschule für Verwaltungswissenschaft, Speyer, 1993–2005; Trustee, Friends of Merseyside Museums and Galleries, 1977–85. Pres., Politics Assoc., 1976–81 (Hon. Fellow, 1995). Editor: Political Studies, 1969–75; Parliamentary Affairs, 1975–2004. *Publications:* Public Administration in France, 1964; Revolutionary Syndicalism in France, 1970; The Study of Government, 1975; numerous articles and edited vols on political sci. and public admin. *Address:* Riversdale House, Grassendale Park, Liverpool L19 0LR. *T:* (0151) 427 1630.

**RIDLEY, Michael;** *see* Ridley, R. M.

**RIDLEY, Sir Michael (Kershaw),** KCVO 2000 (CVO 1992); Clerk of the Council, Duchy of Lancaster, 1981–2000; *b* 7 Dec. 1937; *s* of late George K. and Mary Ridley; *m* 1968, Diana Loraine McLernon; two *s. Educ:* Stowe; Magdalene College, Cambridge. MA. FRICS. Grosvenor Estate, Canada and USA, 1965–69, London, 1969–72; Property Manager, British & Commonwealth Shipping Co., 1972–81. A Gen. Comr of Income Tax, 1984–98. Chm., Standards Cttee, RBK&C, 2001–06. Mem., Adv. Panel, Greenwich Hosp., 1978–2002. Mem. Court, Lancaster Univ., 1981–2000. Trustee: St Martin-in-the-Fields Almshouse Assoc., 1991–2005; Anne Duchess of Westminster Charity, 2004–18. Pres., Assoc. of Lancastrians in London, 2000. *Recreation:* golf. *Address:* 27 Musgrave Crescent, SW6 4QE. *Clubs:* Garrick; Royal Mid-Surrey Golf.

**RIDLEY, Paula Frances Cooper,** CBE 2008 (OBE 1996); JP; DL; MA; Chairman, Board of Trustees, Victoria and Albert Museum, 1998–2007; Director: Gulbenkian Foundation (UK), 1999–2007; English National Ballet, 2011–13; *b* 27 Sept. 1944; *d* of Ondrej Clyne and Ellen (*née* Cooper); *m* 1967, Frederick Fernand Ridley, *qv*; two *s* one *d. Educ:* Kendal High Sch., Westmorland; Univ. of Liverpool (BA, MA). Lectr in Politics and Public Admin, Liverpool Polytechnic, 1966–71; Proj. Co-ordinator, Regeneration Projects Ltd, 1981–84; Dir, Community Initiatives Res. Trust, 1983–90; Consultant, BAT Industries Small Businesses Ltd, 1983–95; Bd Mem., Brunswick Small Business Centre Ltd, 1984–95; Associate, CEI Consultants, 1984–88. Chairman: Liverpool Housing Action Trust, 1992–2005; Public Interest Gen. Council, Office for Public Mgt, 2003–07; Dir, Merseyside Develt Corp., 1991–98. Mem., Royal Commn on Long Term Care for the Elderly, 1997–99. Presenter and Assoc. Editor, Granada Action, 1989–92; Mem., IBA, 1982–88. Chm., Stocktonwood County Primary Sch., 1976–79; Member: Liverpool Heritage Bureau, 1971–88; Management Cttee, Liverpool Victoria Settlement, 1971–86 (Vice-Chm., 1977–86); Granada Telethon Trust, 1988–94. Trustee: Tate Gall., 1988–98; Nat. Gall., 1995–98; Chm., Tate Gall., Liverpool, 1988–98. Liverpool University: Lady Pres., Guild of Undergraduates, Clerk of Convocation, 1972–74; Member: Court, 1972–; Council, 1998–2007; Life Governor, Liverpool and Huyton Colls, 1979–94. Merseyside Civic Society: Hon. Sec., 1971–82; Vice-Chm., 1982–86; Chm., 1986–91. Chm., Liverpool Biennial of Contemporary Art, 2008–16; Chair: Nat. Student Drama Fest., 2009–12; Civic Voice, 2010–13. JP Liverpool, 1977. DL Merseyside, 1989. Hon. FRIBA 2005. Hon. Fellow, Liverpool John Moores Univ., 2002. Hon. LLD Liverpool, 2003. *Address:* 69 Thomas More House, Barbican, EC2Y 8BT. *T:* (020) 7628 8573.

**RIDLEY, (Robert) Michael;** Principal, Royal Belfast Academical Institution, 1990–2006; *b* 8 Jan. 1947; *s* of Maurice Roy Ridley and Jean Evelyn Lawther (*née* Carlisle); *m* 1985, Jennifer Mary Pearson; two *d. Educ:* Clifton Coll.; St Edmund Hall, Oxford (MA, Cert Ed). Wellington Coll., Berks, 1970–82 (Housemaster, 1975–82); Hd of English, Merchiston Castle Sch., Edinburgh, 1982–86; Headmaster, Denstone Coll., 1986–90. Mem., Rotary Club, Belfast, 1990–. *Recreations:* cricket (Oxford Blue, 1968–70; Ireland 1968), golf, reading, travel. *Clubs:* Ulster Reform (Belfast); Vincent's (Oxford); Royal County Down Golf (Newcastle, Co. Down); Boat of Garten Golf (Inverness-shire).

**RIDLEY, Prof. Tony Melville,** CBE 1986; FREng, FICE, FCILT; Professor of Transport Engineering (formerly Rees Jeffreys Professor), 1991–99, and Head of Department of Civil and Environmental Engineering (formerly Department of Civil Engineering), 1997–99, Imperial College of Science, Technology and Medicine, University of London, now Professor Emeritus, Imperial College London; *b* 10 Nov. 1933; *s* of late John Edward and Olive Ridley; *m* 1959, Jane (*née* Dickinson); two *s* one *d. Educ:* Durham Sch.; King's Coll. Newcastle, Univ. of Durham (BSc); Northwestern Univ., Ill (MS); Univ. of California, Berkeley (PhD); Stanford Univ., Calif (Sen. Exec. Prog.). Nuclear Power Group, 1957–62; Univ. of California, 1962–65; Chief Research Officer, Highways and Transportation, GLC, 1965–69; Director General, Tyne and Wear Passenger Transport Exec., 1969–75; Man. Dir, Hong Kong Mass Transit Rly Corp., 1975–80; Bd Mem., 1980–88, Man. Dir (Rlys), 1980–85, LTE, then LRT; Chm., 1985–88, Man. Dir, 1985–88, Chief Exec., 1988, London Underground Ltd; Man. Dir-Project, Eurotunnel, 1989–90 (Dir, 1987–90). Chm., Docklands Light Railway Ltd, 1987–88; Dir, London Transport Internat., 1982–88. Sen. Transport Advr, London 2012 Olympic Bid, 2004–05; Mem., Ind. Dispute Avoidance Panel for London 2012, 2008–. Chm., Building Schs for the Future Investments LLP, 2007–10. Dir, Major Projects Assoc., 1995–2009. President: Light Rail Transit Assoc., 1974–92; Assoc. for Project Mgt, 1999–2003; Commonwealth Engineers Council, 2000–09; Internat. Pres., CILT (formerly CIT), 1999–2001 (Vice-Pres., 1987–90); Member: Council, ICE, 1990–97 (Chm., Transport Bd, 1990–93; Vice Pres., 1992–95; Pres., 1995–96); Senate, Engrg Council, 1997–2000 (Chm., Bd for the Engrg Profession, 1997–99); Exec. Council, WFEO, 2000–09; Task Force 10 (Sci., Technol. and Innovation), UN Millennium Project, 2002–05; Minister of Transport's Internat. Adv. Panel, Singapore, 2007–10; Chm., Steering Gp, Global Transport Knowledge Partnership, 2008–10. Trustee, RAC Foundn for Motoring, 1999–2009 (Mem., Public Policy Cttee, 1997–2010). Freeman, City of London, 1982; Hon. Fellow, Paviors' Co., 2006. FREng (FEng 1992); FHKIE, FITE, FCIHT (FIHT 1992) (Highways Award, 1988). FCGI 1996. Hon. FAPM 1996; Hon. FIA 1999. Hon. DTech Napier, 1996; Hon. DEng Newcastle upon Tyne, 1997. Herbert Crow Award (1st recipient), Carmen's Co., 2001; President's Award, Engrg Council, 2002. *Publications:* Engineering in Perspective: lessons for a successful career, 2017; articles in transport, engrg and other jls. *Recreations:* walking, theatre, music, international affairs. *Address:* Orchard Lodge, Stichens Green, Streatley, Berks RG8 9SU. *T:* (01491) 871075. *Clubs:* Royal Automobile; Hong Kong, Jockey (Hong Kong).

**RIDLEY-THOMAS, Roger;** Managing Director, Thomson Regional Newspapers Ltd, 1989–94; *b* 14 July 1939; *s* of late John Montague Ridley-Thomas, MB, ChB, FRCSE, Norwich, and Christina Anne (*née* Seex); *m* 1962, Sandra Grace McBeth Young; two *s* two *d. Educ:* Gresham's Sch. Served Royal Norfolk Regt, 1958–60. Newspaper Publisher:

Eastern Counties Newspapers, 1960–65; Thomson Regional Newspapers, 1965–94 (Dir, 1985–94); Managing Director: Aberdeen Journals, 1980–84; Scotsman Publications, 1984–89; Director: Caledonian Offset, 1979–94; Radio Forth, 1978–81; TRN Viewdata, 1978–89; Thomson Scottish Organisation, 1984–89; Northfield Newspapers, 1984–89; The Scotsman Communications, 1984–94; The Scotsman Publications, 1984–94; Central Publications, 1984–94; Aberdeen Journals, 1980–84, 1990–94; Belfast Telegraph Newspapers, 1990–94; Chester Chronicle, 1990–94; Newcastle Chronicle & Journal, 1990–94; Western Mail & Echo, 1990–94; Cardrona Ltd, 1995–2015; Milex Ltd, 1996–2005; Adscene Gp plc, 1996–99; Roys (Wroxham) Ltd, 1997–2014 (Chm., 2004–14); Norfolk Christmas Trees Ltd, 2000–08; Chairman: Anglia FM, 1996–98; NorCor Hldgs plc, 1996–2000. Director: Aberdeen Chamber of Commerce, 1981–84; Scottish Business in the Community, 1984–89; Scottish Business Achievement Award Trust, 1985–2003; Edinburgh Ch. of Commerce and Manufrs, 1985–88. Pres., Scottish Daily Newspaper Soc., 1983–85; Mem. Council, CBI, 1983–86; Mem., Scottish Wildlife Appeal Cttee, 1985–88. *Recreations:* shooting, golf, tennis, travel.

**RIDOUT, Amanda Jane;** Founder and Chief Executive Officer, Boldwood Books, since 2019; *b* Norfolk, Va, 7 April 1960; *d* of Archibald Thomas Ridout and Elizabeth Ann Ridout; *m* 1995, Clive Cohen; one *s*. *Educ:* Godolphin Sch., Salisbury; Univ. of Bristol (BA). Sales Exec., Cassell Publishers, 1982–85; Sales Director: Thorsons Publishing Gp, 1985–90; Reed Publishers, 1990–93; Sales and Mktg Dir, Hodder and Stoughton, 1993–96; Managing Director: Headline Publishing, 1996–2001; Harper Collins Publishers, 2001–09; Phaidon Press, 2010–13; CEO, Head of Zeus, 2013–17 (non-exec. Dir, 2017–18). Bd Dir, Ind. Publishers Guild, 2015–. Mem., Book Soc., 2001– (Chair, 2014–15). FRSA. Mem., Stationers' Co., 1991–. *Recreations:* film, theatre, opera. *Address:* 23 Bowerdean Street, SW6 3TN. *Club:* Groucho.

**RIDPATH, Ian William;** author, broadcaster and lecturer on astronomy and space; *b* 1 May 1947; *s* of late Alfred William Joseph Ridpath and Irene Florence Ridpath (*née* Walton). *Educ:* Beal Grammar Sch., Woodford. FRAS 1988 (Council Mem., 2004–07). Mem., IAU, 2015. Member: Soc. of Authors; Assoc. of British Sci. Writers. Editor: Popular Astronomy (qly mag.), 1986–89; Oxford Dictionary of Astronomy, 1997–; The Antiquarian Astronomer, 2015–. Klumpke-Roberts Award, Astronomical Soc. of the Pacific, 2012. *Publications:* Worlds Beyond, 1975; (ed) Encyclopedia of Astronomy and Space, 1976; Messages from the Stars, 1978; The Young Astronomer's Handbook, 1981; Hamlyn Encyclopedia of Space, 1981; Life off Earth, 1983; Collins Pocket Guide to Stars and Planets, 1984, 5th edn as Collins Stars and Planets Guide, 2017; The Night Sky, 1985; (jtly) A Comet Called Halley, 1985; Concise Handbook of Astronomy, 1986; Dictionary of Astronomy and Astronautics, 1987; The Monthly Sky Guide, 1987, 10th edn 2019; Go Skywatching, 1987; Star Tales, 1988, 2nd edn 2018; (ed) Norton's Star Atlas, 18th edn 1989, 20th edn 2003; Giant Book of Space, 1989; Pocket Guide to Astronomy, 1990; Space, 1991; Book of the Universe, 1991; Philip's Atlas of Stars and Planets, 1992, 4th edn 2004; (ed) Oxford Dictionary of Astronomy, 1997, 3rd edn 2018; Handbook of Stars and Planets, 1998, 3rd edn 2010; Gem Stars, 1999; (ed) Collins Encyclopedia of the Universe, 2001; The Times Space, 2002; The Times Universe, 2004; Eyewitness Companion to Astronomy, 2006; Philip's Astronomy Starter Pack, 2011, 3rd edn 2018; Exploring Stars and Planets, 2011, 2nd edn 2016; Astronomy: a visual guide, 2018; Philip's Star Chart, 2018; *for children:* Discovering Space, 1972; (ed) Man and Materials (series): Oil, Coal, Gas, Stone, Plastics, Minerals, 1975; Signs of Life, 1977; Space, 1979; Secrets of Space, 1980; Spacecraft, 1981; Stars and Planets, 1981; Secrets of the Sky, 1985; The Sun, 1987; The Stars, 1987; Outer Space, 1987; *contributions to:* Reader's Digest Library of Modern Knowledge, 1978; Hutchinson 20th Century Encyclopedia, 1987; Microsoft Encarta Encyclopedia, 1997–2008; Dorling Kindersley Universe, 2005–; Dorling Kindersley Stars, 2016. *Recreations:* collecting antique star atlases and astronomically related stamps, distance running (Race Dir, Polytechnic Marathon, 1993–95), horse racing, cruise ship lecturing. *Address:* 48 Otho Court, Brentford, Middlesex TW8 8PY. *T:* (020) 8568 6100. *E:* ian@ianridpath.com. *W:* www.ianridpath.com. *Club:* Royal Southern Yacht.

**RIESEBERG, Prof. Loren Henry,** PhD; FRS 2010; FRSC; FRSB; Professor of Botany, University of British Columbia, since 2006. *Educ:* Southern Coll., Chattanooga (BA Biol. 1981); Univ. of Tennessee (MS Botany 1984); Washington State Univ. (PhD Botany 1987). Asst Prof. of Botany, Claremont Graduate Sch., 1987–93; Department of Biology, Indiana University: Associate Prof., 1993–97; Prof., 1997–2004; Distinguished Prof., 2004–; Dir, Plant Scis Prog., 1996–2000; Associate Chair for Res. and Facilities, 2000–04. Pres., Amer. Genetics Assoc., 2006. FAAAS 2003; Fellow, Amer. Acad. of Arts and Scis, 2004; FRSB (FSB 2010); FRSC 2010. *Address:* Rieseberg Laboratory, Department of Botany, University of British Columbia, 6270 University Boulevard, Vancouver, BC V6T 1Z4, Canada.

**RIESS, Prof. Adam Guy,** PhD; Distinguished Astronomer, Space Telescope Science Institute, since 1999; Thomas J. Barber Professor of Physics and Astronomy, Johns Hopkins University, since 2006; *b* Washington, DC, 16 Dec. 1969; *s* of late Michael and Doris Riess; *m* 1998, Nancy Joy Schondorf. *Educ:* Massachusetts Inst. of Technol. (AB Physics 1992); Harvard Univ. (AM Astrophysics 1994; PhD Astrophysics 1996). Miller Fellow, Univ. of Calif, Berkeley, 1996–99. Kavli Frontier of Sci. Fellow, 2007; MacArthur Fellow, 2008. Fellow, Amer. Physical Soc., 2011. Mem., NAS, 2009. Hon. Mem., Amer. Acad. Arts and Scis, 2008. Trumpler Award, Astronomical Soc. of Pacific, 1999; Sci. Award, Assoc. of Univs for Res. in Astronomy, 2000; Bok Prize, Harvard Univ., 2001; Helen B. Warner Prize, Amer. Astronomical Soc., 2003; Raymond and Beverley Sackler Prize, Tel-Aviv Univ., 2004; Shaw Prize, Shaw Foundn, 2006; Gruber Prize in Cosmol., Gruber Foundn, 2007; Einstein Medal, Albert Einstein Soc., 2011; Exceptional Scientific Achievement Award, NASA, 2011; (jtly) Nobel Prize in Physics, 2011. *Publications:* contribs to jls incl. Astrophysical Jl, Astronomical Jl. *Address:* Department of Physics and Astronomy, Bloomberg 207, Johns Hopkins University, 3400 N Charles Street, Baltimore, MD 21218–2686, USA.

**RIFKIN, Joshua;** Founder, and Director, The Bach Ensemble, since 1978; *b* 22 April 1944; *s* of Harry H. Rifkin and Dorothy (*née* Helsh); *m* 1st, 1970, Louise Litterick (marr. diss. 1984); 2nd, 1995, Helen Palmer; one *d*. *Educ:* Juilliard Sch. of Music (BS 1964); Princeton Univ. (MFA 1969). Musical Consultant, later Musical Dir, Nonesuch Records, NY, 1963–75; Brandeis University: Instructor, 1970–71; Asst Prof., 1971–77; Associate Prof., 1977–82. Visiting Professor, 1973–2002: NY Univ.; Harvard Univ.; Yale Univ.; Rutgers Univ.; Bard Coll.; Princeton Univ.; Stanford Univ.; King's Coll. London; Basel Univ.; Ohio State Univ.; Dortmund Univ. (Gambrinus Prof.); Munich Univ.; Univ. of N Carolina at Chapel Hill. Numerous concerts with Bach Ensemble in UK, Europe, US and Canada; Guest Conductor: English Chamber Orch., 1983, 1984; Scottish Chamber Orch., 1984, 1994; St Louis SO, 1985; Schola Cantorum Basiliensis, 1986, 1990, 1993, 1997, 2000; Victoria State SO, 1989; San Francisco SO, 1989; St Paul Chamber Orch., 1989; LA Chamber Orch., 1990; City of Glasgow SO, 1992; Cappella Coloniensis, Germany, 1993, 1994; Orch. Haydn/Bolzano, 1995; Solistas de México, BBC Concert Orch., and City of London Sinfonia, 1996; Jerusalem SO, Prague Chamber Orch., 1997; Nat. Arts Centre Orch., Houston SO, Camerata de las Américas, 1999; Bayerische Staatsoper, Munich, 2001; Israel Camerata, Jerusalem, 2002. Numerous recordings. Fellow, Wissenschaftskolleg, Berlin, 1984–86. Hon. PhD Dortmund, 1999. *Publications:* contrib. New Grove Dictionary of Music and Musicians, 1980; numerous articles in scholarly jls. *Recreations:* food, wine, cinema, theatre, computers, fiction. *E:* jrifkin@compuserve.com.

**RIFKIND, Charles Gabriel;** Principal, Rifkind Associates, since 2015; *b* Wolverhampton, 24 Jan. 1958; *s* of late Dr Joseph Rifkind and Renee Rifkind; *m* 1986, Simone Frances Sandelson; two *s*, and two step *s*. *Educ:* Clifton Coll. (Hd of Sch., 1976). BA Law. Called to the Bar, Gray's Inn, 1981. Dir, Rifkind and Levy Partnership, property develt, 1981–2015. Partner, MCC, Vision for Lord's, 2003–13. Facilitated Global Cities Exhibn, 2007, Mem., Corp. Adv. Gp, 2011–17, Tate Mus.; Mem., Develt Cttee, 2011–18, Trustee, 2012–19, Design Mus. Fellow, Duke of Edinburgh's Internat. Awards, 2008, Chm., Business Adv. Gp, Duke of Edinburgh's Internat. Award Foundn, 2010–11. Chm., Develt Gp, Juvenile Diabetes Res. Foundn, 2010–15; Member, Board: Wellington Hosp. Appeal, 2010–16; Internat. Med. and Scis Fundraising Cttee, British Red Cross, 2011–15. Gov., Arnold House Sch., 2002–17 (Life Pres., 2017). Trustee, Visitors' Art Foundation, 2017–. *Recreations:* golf, playing and watching tennis, cycling. *Address:* Rifkind Associates, 17 Hall Road, St John's Wood, NW8 9RF. *T:* (020) 7289 4444, *Fax:* (020) 7289 2028. *E:* charles@rifkindassociates.com. *Clubs:* Queen's; Frilford Heath Golf, Queenwood Golf.

**RIFKIND, Rt Hon. Sir Malcolm (Leslie),** KCMG 1997; PC 1986; QC (Scot.) 1985; *b* 21 June 1946; *yr s* of late E. Rifkind, Edinburgh; *m* 1970, Edith Amalia Rifkind (*née* Steinberg); one *s* one *d*. *Educ:* George Watson's Coll.; Edinburgh Univ. LLB, MSc. Lectured at Univ. of Rhodesia, 1967–68. Visiting Professor: Inst. for Advanced Studies in the Humanities, Edinburgh Univ., 1998; Dept of War Studies, KCL, 2015–. Called to Scottish Bar, 1970. Contested (C) Edinburgh, Central, 1970; MP (C) Edinburgh, Pentlands, Feb. 1974–1997; contested (C) same seat, 1997, 2001; MP (C) Kensington and Chelsea, 2005–10, Kensington, 2010–15. Opposition front bench spokesman on Scottish Affairs, 1975–76; Parly Under Sec. of State, Scottish Office, 1979–82, FCO, 1982–83; Minister of State, FCO, 1983–86; Secretary of State: for Scotland, 1986–90; for Transport, 1990–92; for Defence, 1992–95; for Foreign and Commonwealth Affairs, 1995–97; Opposition front bench spokesman on work and pensions, 2005. Jt Sec., Cons. Foreign and Commonwealth Affairs Cttee, 1978; Member: Select Cttee on Eur. Secondary Legislation, 1975–76; Select Cttee on Overseas Develt, 1978–79; Chm., Intelligence and Security Cttee, 2010–15. Non-exec. Dir, Unilever plc, 2010–15. Member: Bd, Nuclear Threat Initiative, 2014–; Panel of Eminent Persons on Eur. Security, OSCE, 2015–16; Sen. Associate Fellow, RUSI, 2015–. Hon. Pres., Scottish Young Conservatives, 1975–76; Pres., Scottish Cons.-Unionist Party, 1998–2002. Mem., Royal Co. of Archers, Queen's Body Guard for Scotland, 1992; Hon. Col, 162 Movt Control Regt (V), RLC, 1997–2005; Hon. Col, City of Edinburgh Univs OTC, 2004–14 (Hon. Dep. Col, 1999–2004). Pres., Edinburgh Univ. Develt Trust, 2004–14. Hon. LLD Napier, 1998; Dr *hc* Edinburgh, 2003. Commander: Order of Merit (Poland), 1998; Order of Grand Duke Gediminas (Lithuania), 2002. *Publications:* Power and Pragmatism: the memoirs of Malcolm Rifkind, 2016. *Recreations:* walking, reading, field sports. *E:* rifkind@malcolmrifkind.co.uk. *Clubs:* Pratt's, White's; New (Edinburgh).

**RIGBY, Sir Anthony (John),** 3rd Bt *cr* 1929, of Long Durford, Rogate. co. Sussex; *b* 3 Oct. 1946; *e s* of Lt-Col Sir (Hugh) John (Macbeth) Rigby, 2nd Bt and Mary Patricia Erskine Rigby (*née* Leacock); *S* father, 1999; *m* 1978, Mary Oliver; three *s* one *d*. *Educ:* Rugby. Heir: *e s* Oliver Hugh Rigby, *b* 20 Aug. 1979.

**RIGBY, Brian,** CBE 2003; Chairman, Walnut Tree Enterprises Ltd, since 2003; *b* 30 Aug. 1944; *s* of Donald Rigby and Margaret Rigby (*née* Dorrity); *m* 1986, Ann Passmore; one *s*. *Educ:* Birkenhead Sch.; Hertford Coll., Oxford (MA 1970); LSE (MSc 1972). Principal, DoE, 1971–77; British Telecommunications: joined, 1977; Dir, London, 1988–88; Dep. Man. Dir, Enterprises, 1988–92; Dir, Supply Mgt, 1992–97; Dir, Procurement Gp, HM Treasury, 1997–2000; Dep. Chief Exec., Office of Govt Commerce, 2000–03. Vis. Fellow, Warwick Business Sch., 2003–. Director: Oxford Radcliffe Hosp. NHS Trust, 2004–10; Partnership for Schools, 2005–12; Educn Funding Agency, 2012–. *Recreations:* people, places.

**RIGBY, Bryan;** Chairman, Anglo German Foundation, 1998–2009 (Trustee, since 1992); *b* 9 Jan. 1933; *s* of William George Rigby and Lily Rigby; *m* 1978, Marian Rosamund; one *s* one *d* of a former marriage, and one step *s* one step *d*. *Educ:* Wigan Grammar Sch.; King's Coll., London (BSc Special Chemistry, Dip. Chem. Engrg). UKAEA Industrial Gp, Capenhurst, 1955–60; Beecham Gp, London and Amsterdam, 1960–64; Laporte Industries (Holdings) Ltd, 1964–78; Dep. Dir-Gen., CBI, 1978–83; Man. Dir, UK Ops, 1984–87, UK, Ireland and Scandinavia, 1987–93; BASF Group; Chairman: Streamline Hldgs, 1994–98; Elliott Ross Associates, 1998–2003. Dir, MEDEVA plc, 1993–99. Mem., Social Security Adv. Cttee, 1994–99; Chm., Nurses' Pay Review Body, 1995–98. Vice-Pres., BAAS, 1992–96; Gov., Henley Management Coll., 1993–2002. Chm., Scannappeal, 1999–2011. *Recreations:* music, golf, gardening. *Address:* Cluny, 61 Penn Road, Beaconsfield, Bucks HP9 2LW. *T:* (01494) 673206. *Club:* Reform.

**RIGBY, Elizabeth Frances;** Political Editor, Sky News, since 2019; *b* Colchester, 19 Feb. 1976; *d* of Michael Rigby and Edith Rigby; partner, Angelo Acanfora; one *s* one *d*. *Educ:* Beaconsfield High Sch.; Fitzwilliam Coll., Cambridge (BA Hons Social and Political Sci. 1997); Centre of Latin American Studies, Univ. of London (MA Latin Amer. Studies). Financial Times: graduate trainee, 1998–2001; Hedge Fund Corresp., 2001–04; Retail Corresp., 2004–08; Consumer Industries Editor, 2008–10; Chief Political Corresp., 2010–12; Dep. Political Editor, 2012–15; Media Editor, The Times, 2015–16; Sky News: Sen. Political Corresp., 2016–18; Dep. Political Editor, 2018–19. *Recreations:* running, Northern Soul, cooking, tennis. *Address:* Sky News, 4 Millbank, SW1P 3JA. *E:* beth.rigby@sky.uk.

**RIGBY, Jean Prescott, (Mrs Jamie Hayes);** mezzo-soprano; Principal, English National Opera, 1982–90; *d* of late Thomas Boulton Rigby and Margaret Annie Rigby; *m* 1987, Jamie Hayes; three *s*. *Educ:* Birmingham Sch. of Music (ABSM 1976); Royal Acad. of Music (Dip. RAM; Hon. ARAM 1984; Hon. FRAM 1989). ARCM 1979; ABC 1996. Début: Royal Opera House, Covent Garden, 1983; Glyndebourne Festival Opera, 1984; rôles, 1990–, include: Nicklaus, in The Tales of Hoffmann, Olga in Eugene Onegin, Royal Opera; Isabella, in The Italian Girl in Algiers, Buxton; title rôle, La Cenerentola, and Idamante in Idomeneo, Garsington; Charlotte, in Werther, San Diego and Seattle; Irene, in Theodora, Geneviève, in Pelléas and Mélisande, Eduige, in Rodelinda, Hippolyta, in A Midsummer Night's Dream, and Emilia, in Otello, Glyndebourne; *English National Opera:* Penelope, in The Return of Ulysses; title rôle, in The Rape of Lucretia; Amastris, in Xerxes; Rosina, in The Barber of Seville; Helen, in King Priam; Maddalena, in Rigoletto; Ruth, in The Pirates of Penzance; Suzuki, in Madam Butterfly; Mrs Ford, in Sir John in Love. Several TV performances, videos and over fifty recordings. Hon. Fellow, Birmingham Conservatoire, 2007. Santley Award, Musicians' Co., 2016. *Recreations:* British heritage, sport, cooking.

**RIGBY, Sir Peter,** Kt 2002; Founder, Chairman and Chief Executive, Rigby Group Plc (formerly Specialist Computer Holdings Plc), since 1975; *b* 29 Sept. 1943; *s* of late John and Phyllis Rigby; two *s*. President, SCC Plc and subsidiaries, UK, France, Holland, Spain, Romania, Vietnam, 1982–; Chairman: Eden Hotel Collection (formerly Mallory Court Hotel), 1995–; Patriot Aerospace Gp, 2002–, incorporating British Internat. Helicopters Ltd, Veritair Aviation Ltd, Patriot Aviation Ltd, London Helicopter Centres Ltd; Coventry and Warwicks Develt Partnership LLP, 2011–; Coventry and Warwickshire LEP, 2012–14 (Mem. Bd, 2011–14); Regl and City Airports Mgt, 2013–. Chm., Millennium Point Trust, Birmingham, 1996–2003; Founder and Trustee, Rigby Foundn, 1995–; Trustee, Shakespeare Hospice, 2017–. Patron, Acorns Children's Hospice, 1993–2007. DL W Midlands, 2000–18. Liveryman, Hon. Co. of Air Pilots (formerly GAPAN), 2009–. HGC, 601 (Co. of London) Sqdn, RAuxAF, 2017–. FRAeS 2014. DUniv Central England, 1998; Hon. DSc Aston, 2003. *Recreations:* flying, classical music. *Address:* Rigby Group Plc, Bridgeway House, Stratford-upon-Avon CV37 6YX. *T:* (01789) 610000. *E:* peter@rigbygroupplc.com.

**RIGBY, Prof. Peter William Jack,** PhD; FRS 2010; FMedSci; Professor of Developmental Biology, Institute of Cancer Research, University of London, 2001–12, now Emeritus; Member, Board of Governors, Wellcome Trust, 2008–16 (Deputy Chairman, 2010–13); *b* 7 July 1947; *s* of late Jack Rigby and Lorna Rigby; *m* 1st, 1971, Paula Webb (marr. diss. 1983); 2nd, 1985, Julia Maidment; one *s*. *Educ:* Lower Sch. of John Lyon, Harrow; Jesus Coll., Cambridge (BA, PhD). MRC Lab. of Molecular Biol., Cambridge, 1971–73; Helen Hay Whitney Foundn Fellow, Stanford Univ. Med. Sch., 1973–76; Imperial College London: Lectr, then Sen. Lectr in Biochem., 1976–83; Reader in Tumour Virology, 1983–86; Vis. Prof., 1986–94 and 2000–08; Head, Div. of Eukaryotic Molecular Genetics, NIMR, MRC, 1986–2000 (Head, Genes and Cellular Controls Gp, 1986–96); Chief Exec., Inst. of Cancer Res., 1999–2011. Chm., MRC Gene Therapy Co-ordinating Cttee, 1992–96; Member: MRC Cell Bd, 1988–92; EMBO, 1979; Science Council, Celltech, 1982–2003; Scientific Cttee, Cancer Res. Campaign, 1983–88, 1996–99; Strategy Bd, BBSRC, 2004–06; Bd, Genome Res. Ltd, The Wellcome Trust Sanger Inst., 2006–14; Council, Marie Curie (formerly Marie Curie Cancer Care), 2008–18 (Chm., Cancer Res. Cttee, 2008–10); Bd, Co. of Biologists, 2016–; Bd, Natural Resources Wales, 2018–. Chairman, Scientific Advisory Board: Topotarget (formerly Prolifix Ltd), 1996–2008; Hexagen Technology Ltd, 1996–98; Oxford Gene Technology, 2012–16; Member, Scientific Advisory Board: Somatix Therapy Corp., 1989–97; deVGen NV, 1998–2000; KuDOS Pharmaceuticals, 1999–2006; Australian Regenerative Medicine Inst., 2011–18. Non-executive Director: Royal Marsden NHS Foundn Trust, 2001–11; Proacta Therapeutics, 2001–03. Member: Council, Acad. of Med. Scis, 2002–04; Bd of Govs, Beatson Inst. for Cancer Res., Glasgow, 2003–06 (Dep. Chm., 2006–07); Council, St George's, Univ. of London (formerly St George's Hosp. Med. Sch.), 2003–10; Bd of Trustees, Univ. of London, 2008–11; Bd of Govs, Royal Brompton and Harefield NHS Foundn Trust, 2009–13; Chair, Bd of Trustee Dirs, Babraham Inst., 2014–. Chm. Medical Res. Cttee, and Mem. Nat. Council, Muscular Dystrophy Campaign, 2003–07; Mem., Wellcome Trust Principal Res. Fellowship Interview Cttee, 2004–07. FMedSci 1999. European Editor, Cell, 1984–97. *Publications:* papers on molecular biology in sci. jls. *Recreations:* narrow boats, listening to music, sport. *Address:* Chester Beatty Laboratories: Institute of Cancer Research, 237 Fulham Road, SW3 6JB. *T:* (020) 7153 5125. *Clubs:* Athenæum, Middlesex CC.

**RIGBY, Prof. Susan;** Vice-Chancellor, Bath Spa University, since 2018; *b* Oldham, Lancs, 5 Aug. 1965; *d* of Brian and Marjorie Rigby; *m* 1993, Rev. Canon Dr Michael Jeremy Fuller, *qv*; two *s*. *Educ:* Samuel King's Sch., Alston; Exeter Coll., Oxford (MA); Emmanuel Coll., Cambridge (PhD 1990). SO, Geol Mus., London, 1986–87; Jun. Res. Fellow, Emmanuel Coll., Cambridge, 1990–92; Biostratigrapher for British Geol Survey, 1992–95; Lectr in Palaeontol. and Stratigraphy, Univ. of Leicester, 1992–95; University of Edinburgh: Lectr, then Sen. Lectr, 1995–2008; Hd, Grant Inst. Earth Scis, 2005–08; Asst Principal, 2009–12; Vice Principal, Learning and Teaching, 2012–15; Dep. Vice-Chancellor, Univ. of Lincoln, 2015–18. Hon. Prof., Univ. of Edinburgh, 2016–19. PFHEA 2012. *Publications:* (with C. V. Milsom) Fossils at a Glance, 2003, 2nd edn 2019; contribs to scientific papers on palaeontol. *Recreations:* opera, lieder recitals, walking in the Hebrides, football. *Address:* Bath Spa University, Newton Park, Newton St Loe, Bath BA2 9BN. *T:* (01225) 875510. *E:* Vice-Chancellor@bathspa.ac.uk.

**RIGG, Dame Diana,** DBE 1994 (CBE 1988); actress; *b* Doncaster, Yorks, 20 July 1938; *d* of Louis Rigg and Beryl Helliwell; *m* 1982, Archibald Stirling; one *d*. *Educ:* Fulneck Girls' Sch., Pudsey. Trained for the stage at Royal Academy of Dramatic Art. First appearance on stage in RADA prod. in York Festival, at Theatre Royal, York, summer, 1957 (Natella Abashwili in The Caucasian Chalk Circle); after appearing in repertory in Chesterfield and in York she joined the Royal Shakespeare Company, Stratford-upon-Avon, 1959; first appearance in London, Aldwych Theatre, 1961 (2nd Ondine, Violanta and Princess Berthe in Ondine); at same theatre, in repertory (The Devils, Becket, The Taming of the Shrew), 1961; (Madame de Tourvel, The Art of Seduction), 1962; Royal Shakespeare, Stratford-upon-Avon, April 1962 (Helena in A Midsummer Night's Dream, Bianca in The Taming of the Shrew, Lady Macduff in Macbeth, Adriana in The Comedy of Errors, Cordelia in King Lear); subseq. appeared in the last production at the Aldwych, Dec. 1962, followed by Adriana in The Comedy of Errors and Monica Stettler in The Physicists, 1963. Toured the provinces, spring, 1963, in A Midsummer Night's Dream; subseq. appeared at the Royal Shakespeare, Stratford, and at the Aldwych, in Comedy of Errors, Dec. 1963; again played Cordelia in King Lear, 1964, prior to touring with both plays for the British Council, in Europe, the USSR, and the US; during this tour she first appeared in New York (State Theatre), 1964, in same plays; Viola in Twelfth Night, Stratford, June 1966; Heloise in Abelard and Heloise, Wyndham's, 1970, also at the Atkinson, New York, 1971; joined The National Theatre, 1972: in Jumpers, 'Tis Pity She's a Whore and Lady Macbeth in Macbeth, 1972; The Misanthrope, 1973, Washington and NY, 1975; Phaedra Britannica, 1975 (Plays and Players Award for Best Actress); The Guardsman, 1978; Pygmalion, Albery, 1974; Night and Day, Phoenix, 1978 (Plays and Players award, 1979); Colette, USA, 1982; Heartbreak House, Haymarket, 1983; Little Eyolf, Lyric, Hammersmith, 1985; Antony and Cleopatra, Chichester, 1985; Wildfire, Phoenix, 1986; Follies, Shaftesbury, 1987; Love Letters, San Francisco, 1990; All for Love, Almeida, 1991; Berlin Bertie, Royal Court, 1992; Medea, Almeida, 1992, transf. Wyndhams, 1993–94 (Evening Standard Drama Award), then NY, 1994 (Tony Award); Mother Courage, RNT, 1995; Who's Afraid of Virginia Woolf?, Almeida, 1996; Phèdre, and Britannicus, Albery, 1998; Humble Boy, RNT, 2001; Suddenly Last Summer, Albery, 2004; Honour, Wyndham's, 2006; All About my Mother, Old Vic, 2007; The Cherry Orchard, Chichester, 2008; Hay Fever, Chichester, 2009; Pygmalion, Garrick, 2011; *films include:* A Midsummer Night's Dream, Assassination Bureau, On Her Majesty's Secret Service, Julius Caesar, The Hospital, Theatre of Blood, A Little Night Music, The Great Muppet Caper, Evil Under the Sun (Film Actress of the Year Award, Variety Club, 1983), A Good Man in Africa, Heidi, The Painted Veil, Breathe; *television appearances include:* Sentimental Agent, The Comedy of Errors, The Avengers (Special Award, BAFTA, 2000), Married Alive, Diana (US series), In This House of Brede (US), Three Piece Suite, The Serpent Son, Hedda Gabler, The Marquise, Little Eyolf, King Lear, Witness of the Prosecution, Bleak House, Mother Love (BAFTA award), Unexplained Laughter, Moll Flanders (serial), Rebecca (Emmy Award for Best Supporting Actress, 1997), The Mrs Bradley Mysteries, Victoria and Albert, Charles II: The Power and the Passion, Game of Thrones, Professor Branestawm 2, Victoria, Detectorists, and others. Chair, MacRoberts Arts Centre; Mem., BM Develt Fund. A Vice-Pres., Baby Life Support Systems (BLISS), 1984–. Cameron Mackintosh Vis. Prof. of Contemporary Theatre, Oxford Univ., 1999; Emeritus Fellow, St Catherine's Coll., Oxford. Chancellor, Stirling Univ., 1997–2008. Foreign Hon. Mem., American Acad. of Arts and Scis. *Publications:* No Turn Unstoned, 1982; So to the Land, 1994. *Recreations:* reading, trying to get organized. *Address:* c/o Dalzell and Beresford, Paddock Suite, The Courtyard, 55 Charterhouse Street, EC1M 6HA.

**RIGG, (Ian) Malcolm;** Director, Policy Studies Institute, 2004–13, now Visiting Research Fellow; *b* 31 Jan. 1947; *s* of Donald Appleby Rigg and Marjorie Isobel Connell Rigg (*née* Smiley); *m* 1982, Lesley Saunders, DPhil; one *s*, and one step *s* one step *d*. *Educ:* Magdalen College Sch., Oxford; Enfield Coll. of Technol. (BA Business Studies). Director: IFF Res., 1978–82; Sample Surveys, 1982–83; Sen. Res. Fellow, PSI, 1984–90; Head of Inf., Consumers' Assoc., 1990–94; Dir of Res., COI Communications, 1994–97; Managing Director: BMRB Social Res., 1997–2000; BMRB Internat., 2001–04. Mem., Ofgem Panel for Electricity Stakeholder Engagement Scheme, 2012–. Market Research Society: Mem. Council, 1995–97; Vice-Chm., 1996–97; Chairman: Professional Standards Cttee, 1995–97; Professional Develt Adv. Bd, 1997–2004. Mem. Cttee, Assoc. of Res. Centres in Soc. Scis, 2005–. Mem., Bd of Trustees, Involve, 2010–. Chm., Slough CAB, 2013–; Exec. Dir, Slough Healthwatch, 2013–. FAcSS. Mem., PSI Team, HEFCE Strategic Rev. of Sustainable Develt in Higher Educn in England, 2008. *Publications:* Training in Britain: individuals' perspectives, 1989; Continuing Training in Firms and Trainer Development in Britain, 1991; (jtly) Electronic Government: the view from the queue, 1999; (jtly) Food Labels and Food Choice: what do people actually understand and use?, 2012. *Recreations:* tandem triathlon, cycling up hills, social justice, music festivals, avant-garde jazz, poetry, Tottenham Hotspur season ticket holder (an annual entitlement to hope with minimal chance of fulfilment). *Address:* 15 Herschel Street, Slough SL1 1PB. *T:* (01753) 576432. *E:* malcolm.rigg@btinternet.com.

**RIGGE, Marianne, (Mrs Trevor Goodchild),** OBE 2000; Director, College of Health, 1983–2003; *b* 10 May 1948; *d* of late Dr Patrick Noel O'Mahony and Elizabeth Nora O'Mahony (*née* Daly); *m* 1st, 1968, John Simon Rigge; two *d* (one *s* decd); 2nd, 1990, Trevor Goodchild. *Educ:* St Angela's Ursuline Convent, London; University College London (BA Hons French). PA, Consumers' Assoc., 1971–76; Res. Asst to Chm., Nat. Consumer Council, 1976–77; founder Dir, Mutual Aid Centre, 1977–83. Member: Clinical Outcomes Gp, 1993–97; Clinical Systems Gp, 1997–2000; NICE Partners Council, 1999–2002; Nat. Access Taskforce, 2000–02. Non-exec. Dir, Whipps Cross Univ. Hosp. NHS Trust, 2001–08. Editor, Self Health, 1985–87; columnist, Health Service Jl, 1999–2003. *Publications:* (with Michael Young) Mutual Aid in a Selfish Society, 1979; Building Societies and the Consumer, 1981; Hello, Can I Help You, 1981; Prospects for Worker Co-operatives in Europe, 1981; (with Michael Young) Revolution from Within, 1983; Annual Guide to Hospital Waiting Lists, 1984–92. *Recreations:* gardening, cooking, music. *Address:* 157 Whipps Cross Road, E11 1NP. *T:* (020) 8530 4420.

**RIGGS, David George;** Corporate Finance Executive, Australian Government Solicitor, 2014–16 (Chief Financial Officer, 1998–2014); *b* 6 May 1942. *Educ:* Bury GS; Manchester Univ. (BA Econ.). CPFA (IPFA 1963). With Bury CBC, 1958–68; Greater London Council, 1968–82: Finance Officer, 1968–74; Hd of Public Services Finance, 1974–76; Asst Comptroller of Finance, 1976–82; Dir of Finance, ILEA, 1982–90; Dir of Finance, Benefits Agency, 1991–98. *Address:* 48 Jacka Crescent, Campbell, ACT 2612, Australia.

**RIGNEY, Andrew James;** QC 2010; *b* Oldham, 26 Aug. 1967; *s* of Arthur George Rigney and Mary Rigney; *m* 1998, Jane Allison; one *s* two *d*. *Educ:* Hulme Grammar Sch., Oldham; Christ's Coll., Cambridge (BA 1989; MA 1993); City Univ. (DipLaw 1991). Called to the Bar, Gray's Inn, 1992; in practice as barrister, specialising in construction, energy, internat. arbitration, insurance and professional indemnity. *Recreations:* family, reading, music, travel. *Address:* Crown Office Chambers, 2 Crown Office Row, Temple, EC4Y 7HJ. *T:* (020) 7797 8100, *Fax:* (020) 7797 8101.

**RIIS-JØRGENSEN, Birger;** Ambassador of Denmark to Italy and also accredited to Malta and San Marino, 2011–16; *b* 13 Jan. 1949; *s* of Jens and Thyra Jørgensen; *m* 1978, Karin Rasmussen; two *s*. *Educ:* Univ. of Copenhagen (MA Hist. 1974); studies in Sweden and USA. Res. Librarian, Royal Liby, Copenhagen, 1975; joined Danish Foreign Service, 1976; First Sec., Danish Delegn to NATO, Brussels, 1979–83; Hd of Section, Min. of For. Affairs, and Sec. to For. Affairs Cttee of Parlt, 1983–86; Counsellor, Secretariat for Eur. Political Co-operation, Brussels, 1987–88; Hd of Section and Dep. Hd of Dept, Danish Internat. Develt Agency, 1989–91; Ministry of Foreign Affairs: Hd, Africa Dept, 1991–94; Hd, Middle East and Latin America Dept, 1994–96; Under-Sec. for Bilateral Affairs, 1996–2000; State Sec. and Hd of Trade Council of Denmark, 2000–06; Ambassador to the Court of St James's, 2006–11. Sen. Advr to Danish authorities, Rasmussen Global and other companies, 2017–; columnist and lectr, 2017–. Member Board of Directors: Industrialisation Fund for Developing Countries, 1996–2000; Fund for Industrialisation of Eastern Europe, 1996–2000; Care Denmark, 2018–; Danish Co-Chm., US/Denmark/Greenland Cttee for Econ., Technical, Scientific and Cultural Co-operation, 2004–06. Comdr of First Class, Order of the Dannebrog (Denmark), 2009. *Recreations:* tennis, bicycling, sea-kayaking, swimming, modern history, classical music. *Address:* Lille Strandstraede 12, 1254 Copenhagen K, Denmark. *T:* 61427232. *E:* b.riis@riisint.dk. *Club:* Athenæum.

**RILEY, Bridget Louise,** CH 1999; CBE 1972; artist; *b* 24 April 1931; *d* of late John Riley and Louise (*née* Gladstone). *Educ:* Cheltenham Ladies' College; Goldsmiths' School of Art; Royal College of Art. ARCA 1955. Mem., RSA. Solo exhibitions include: Gall. One, London, 1962–63; Richard Feigen Gall., NY, 1965, 1967, 1968; Robert Fraser Gall., London, 1965, 1967; (with Philip King) XXXIV Biennale Venice, 1968; Rowan Gall., London, 1969, 1976, 1977, 1981; (retrospective) Arts Council of GB touring exhibn, Hanover, Berne, Dusseldorf, Turin, Prague, 1970–72, Hayward Gall., London, 1971; Paintings and Drawings, 1961–73, Arts Council of GB touring exhibn, 1973–74; Sidney Janis Gall., NY, 1975, 1978; (retrospective) touring exhibn, US, Aust., Japan, 1978–80; Working with Colour, Arts Council of GB touring exhibn, 1984–85; SW Galls Assoc. Scotland touring exhibn, 1986–87; Paintings 82–92, touring exhibn, Germany and Hayward Gall., London, 1992–93; Recent Paintings and Gouaches, 1980–1995, touring exhibn, Cambridge, Exeter, Waddington Galls, Leeds, Dublin, 1995–97; Karsten Schubert, London, 1996, 2004, 2008, 2009, 2011, 2012; Paintings from the 60s and 70s, Serpentine Gall., London, 1999; Paintings 1982–2000 and Early Works on Paper, PaceWildenstein, NY, 2000; Reconnaissance, DIA Center for Arts, NY, 2001; (retrospective) Tate Britain, 2003; Paintings and Drawings, 1961–2004, British Council touring exhibn, Mus. of Contemp. Art, Sydney, Aust., City Gall., Wellington, 2004–05; Recent Paintings and Gouaches, PaceWildenstein, NY, 2007; (retrospective) Musée d'Art, Paris, 2008; Flashback, Walker Gall., 2009–10; From Life, NPG, 2010; (retrospective) Colour, Stripes, Planes and Curves, Kettle's Yard, Cambridge, 2011; (retrospective) Works 1960–1966, Hazlitt Holland-Hibbert, London, 2012; (retrospective) The Stripe Paintings, David

Zwirner Gall., 2014; The Curve Paintings 1961–2014, De La Warr Pavilion, Bexhill on Sea, 2015; (retrospective) Learning from Seurat, Courtauld Gall., 2015; Paintings, 1963–2015, Scottish Nat. Gall. of Modern Art, 2016; Recent Paintings 2014–2017, David Zwirner Gall., 2018; Painting Now, Sprüth Magers Gall., 2018; (retrospective) Scottish Nat. Gall., 2019; (retrospective) Hayward Gall., 2019. Public collections include: Tate Gallery; Victoria and Albert Museum; Arts Council; British Council; Museum of Modern Art, New York; Australian Nat. Gallery, Canberra; Museum of Modern Art, Pasadena; Ferens Art Gallery, Hull; Allbright Knox, Buffalo, USA; Museum of Contemporary Art, Chicago; Ulster Museum, Ireland; Stedelijk Museum, Amsterdam; Berne Kunsthalle; Mus. of Modern Art, Tokyo. Designed Colour Moves, for Ballet Rambert, 1983. Trustee, Nat. Gallery, 1981–88. Hon. DLitt: Manchester, 1976; Ulster, 1986; Oxford, 1993; Cambridge, 1995; De Montfort, 1996; Exeter, 1997; London, 2005. AICA critics Prize, 1963; Stuyvesant Bursary, 1964; Ohara Mus. Prize, Tokyo, 1972; Gold Medal, Grafik Biennale, Norway, 1980; Praemium Imperiale for Painting, 2003.

**RILEY, Christopher John;** economic consultant; Associate, Oxera Consulting Ltd, since 2005; *b* 20 Jan. 1947; *s* of Bernard Francis Riley and Phyllis (*née* Wigley); *m* 1982, Helen Marion Mynett; two *s*. *Educ:* Ratcliffe Coll., Leicester; Wadham Coll., Oxford (MA Maths); Univ. of East Anglia (MA Econs). Economist, HM Treasury, 1969–77; Res. Fellow, Nuffield Coll., Oxford, 1977–78; Sen. Economic Advr, 1978–88, Under Sec., 1988–95, HM Treasury; Chief Economist, DoE, subseq. DETR, then DTLR, later DfT, 1995–2005. *Publications:* various articles in books and learned jls. *Recreation:* music - especially choral singing. *Address:* 10 Briarwood Road, SW4 9PX. *T:* (020) 7720 6263. *E:* chris@h-riley.gotadsl.co.uk.

**RILEY, Prof. Eleanor Mary,** PhD; FMedSci; FRSB; Professor of Immunology and Director, Roslin Institute, University of Edinburgh, since 2017; *b* Wrexham, N Wales, 30 June 1956; *d* of Robert Malcolm Riley and Yvonne Mary Riley (*née* Hall). *Educ:* Banbury Grammar Sch.; Univ. of Bristol (BSc Cellular Pathol. 1978; BVSc 1980); Univ. of Liverpool (PhD 1985). Intern in Veterinary Pathol., Cornell Univ., 1980–81; Sen. Scientist, MRC Labs, The Gambia, 1985–90; Wellcome Trust Sen. Res. Fellow, Univ. of Edinburgh, 1990–98; Prof. of Infectious Disease Immunology, LSHTM, Univ. of London, 1998–2017. Consultant, USAID Malaria Vaccine Develt Prog., 2013–. Chair, Biosci. for Health Strategy Adv. Panel, BBSRC, 2014–; Dep. Chair, Infections and Immunity Bd, MRC, 2015–18; Mem., UKRI-MRC, 2018–. FMedSci 2014; FRSB (FSB 2015). Ed., Parasite Immunol., 2002–. *Recreations:* walking, local politics, yoga, theatre, tidying the garden, coffee. *Address:* Roslin Institute, University of Edinburgh, Easter Bush, Midlothian EH25 9RD. *T:* (0131) 651 9100. *E:* director@roslin.ed.ac.uk.

**RILEY, Jamie Spencer;** QC 2019; *b* High Wycombe, Bucks, 2 Aug. 1971; *s* of Keith Riley and Janet Riley (now Wetherman); *m* 2000, Samantha Chippindall; one *s* one *d*. *Educ:* Royal Grammar Sch., High Wycombe; Downing Coll., Cambridge (BA 1993). Called to the Bar, Lincoln's Inn, 1995. *Recreations:* opera, wine, theatre, cinema, walking, ski-ing, travel, rowing, cycling. *Address:* Littleton Chambers, 3 Kings Bench Walk North, Temple, EC4Y 7HR. *T:* (020) 7797 8600. *E:* jr@littletonchambers.co.uk. *Club:* Leander (Henley-on-Thames).

**RILEY, Lt-Gen. Jonathon Peter,** CB 2008; DSO 1996; Director, Generalship Ltd, since 2012; *b* 16 Jan. 1955; *s* of John St John Riley and Joyce Riley (*née* Outen); *m* 1st, 1980, Kathryn Mary Beard (marr. diss. 2000); one *s* one *d*; 2nd, 2009, Sara Elinor Edwards, *qv* (marr. diss. 2017); one *d*. *Educ:* St Mary's, Beverley; Kingston Grammar Sch.; UCL (BA Geog. 1979); Leeds Univ. (MA Hist. 1989); Cranfield Univ. (PhD 2006). Commnd Queen's Royal Regt, 1974; Staff Coll., 1987; Bde Major, 6th Armd Bde, 1989; transferred to RWF, 1990; mil. observer, Balkan war, 1992–93; DS, Staff Coll., 1993–94; CO, 1 RWF, 1994–96; COS, 1st Armd Div., 1996–98; Dep. Comdt, Multinat. Div. (SW), Bosnia, 1998–99; Commander: 1 Mechanized Bde, Sierra Leone, 1999–2001; Jt Task Force Comd, and Mil. Advr to Govt of Sierra Leone, 2000–01; Dep. Comdt, Staff Coll., 2001–03; Dep. Comdg Gen., New Iraqi Army, 2003; rcds 2004; GOC British Troops, Iraq, and Comdg Gen., Multinat. Div. (SE), Iraq, 2004–05; Sen. British Mil. Advr, US Central Comd, 2005–07; Dep. Comdr, NATO Internat. Security Assistance Force, Afghanistan, 2007–08; Dir-Gen. and Master of the Royal Armouries, 2009–12. Col, Royal Welch Fusiliers, 2005–06. Vis. Prof. in War Studies, KCL, 2010, 2013–; Fellow in Internat. Politics, Univ. of Aberystwyth, 2011–12; ext. examiner in defence mgt and technol., Cranfield Univ., 2009–14; Vis. Sen. Mentor, Baltic Defence Coll., 2016–. Mem., Welsh Govt World War I Commemoration Prog. Bd, 2013–. Expert Witness, Internat. Criminal Court, 2012–. Chm., Royal Welch Fusiliers Mus. Trust, 2005–; Trustee: CDISS, 2006–08; Strata Florida Project, 2016–17; Mem., Catholic Records Soc., 2005–17. Pres., Harlech Internat. Associates, 2013–; Patron: LINKS, 2013–; Military Preparation Coll. Trust, 2014–. Liveryman, Armourers' and Brasiers' Co., 2011. Officer, Legion of Merit (US), 2005; NATO MSM, 2009. *Publications:* History of the Queen's, 1988; From Pole to Pole, 1989, 2nd edn 2001; Soldiers of the Queen, 1992; White Dragon, 1995; Napoleon and the World War 1813, 2000; The Royal Welch Fusiliers 1945–2000, 2001; The Life and Campaigns of General Hughie Stockwell, 2006; Napoleon as a General, 2007; (ed) That Astonishing Infantry, 2007, repr. 2017; Decisive Battles, 2010; (ed) Up to Mametz and Beyond, 2010, 2nd rev. edn 2018; A Matter of Honour, 2011; 1813: empire at bay, 2013; (contrib.) British Generals in Blair's Wars, 2013; The Last Ironsides, 2014, 2nd rev. edn 2016; The First Colonial Soldiers, vol. 1, 2014, vol. 2, 2015; Oft in Danger: the life and campaigns of General Sir Anthony Farrar-Hockley, 2015; (contrib.) British Army Battlefield Guide to the Great War, vol. 2, 2017; (jtly) The Royal Welch Fusiliers, Part One, Nov. 1918–May 1940 and Part Two, June 1940–Dec. 1945, 2019; Ghosts of Old Companions, 2019. *Recreations:* field sports, white water rafting, rowing, historical research, poetry and English literature. *Clubs:* Naval and Military, Victory Services.

**RILEY, Very Rev. Kenneth Joseph,** OBE 2003; Dean of Manchester, 1993–2005, now Emeritus; *b* 25 June 1940; *s* of Arthur and Mary Josephine Riley; *m* 1968, Margaret; two *d*. *Educ:* Holywell GS; UCW, Aberystwyth (BA 1961); Linacre Coll., Oxford (BA 1964; MA); Wycliffe Hall, Oxford. Ordained deacon, 1964, priest, 1965; Asst Curate, Emmanuel Ch, Fazakerley, Liverpool, 1964–66; Chaplain: Brasted Place Coll., 1966–69; Oundle Sch., 1969–74; Liverpool Univ., 1974–83; Vicar, Mossley Hill, Liverpool, 1975–83; RD, Childwall, 1982–83; Canon Treas., 1983–87, Canon Precentor, 1987–93, Liverpool Cathedral. *Publications:* Liverpool Cathedral, 1987. *Recreations:* music, drama, films. *Address:* 4 Lindisfarne Road, Alnwick, Northumberland NE66 1AU. *T:* (01665) 799174.

**RILEY, Philip Stephen;** Chairman: Orion Media Ltd, 2015–16 (Chief Executive, 2009–15); Koala Television, since 2015; *b* 4 June 1959; *s* of James and Marie Riley; *m* 1992, Jean Fiveash; one *s* two *d*. *Educ:* Loughborough Univ. (BSc Hons 1980); Columbia Business Sch. (MBA Beta Gamma Sigma 1988). Prog. Dir, BRMB Radio, 1989–90; Managing Director: Radio Aire, 1990–94; 100.7 Heart FM, 1994–96; Man. Dir, 1996–99, Chief Exec., 1999–2007, Chrysalis Radio. Member, Board: Commercial Radio Companies' Assoc., 1994–2007; Radio Advertising Bureau, 1996–2007; RAJAR, 2004–07. Trustee, Acorns Children's Hospice Trust, 2014–. Chair of Judges, UK Aria Awards, 2016–.

**RILEY, Stephen Michael,** FSA; Director, Maritime Heritage, National Maritime Museum, Greenwich, 2002–07; *b* 4 April 1950; *s* of Jack and Constance Riley; partner, Jane Avard Weeks; one *s* one *d*. *Educ:* Liverpool Univ. (BA Hons 1972); Univ. of Leicester (Post-grad. Cert. in Mus. Studies 1974). FSA 2007. Curatorial trainee, Maritime Hist., Merseyside Co. Mus, Liverpool, 1972–76; National Maritime Museum, Greenwich: Dep. Hd, Dept of Ships and Antiquities, 1986–92; Director: Property and Tech. Services, 1993–95; Display Div., 1995–98; Neptune Court Re-develt Project, 1998–99; Nat. Maritime Mus. Galls, 1999–2001. *Recreations:* classic boats and classic cars, photography, travel, reading, music, gardening.

**RILEY-SMITH, Tobias Augustine William;** QC 2016; a Recorder, since 2019; *b* Hammersmith, 19 Oct. 1969; *s* of late Prof. Jonathan Simon Christopher Riley-Smith and of Marie-Louise Jeannetta Riley-Smith (*née* Field); *m* 2003, Tamara Jane Trefusis; one *s* two *d*. *Educ:* Eton Coll.; Trinity Coll., Cambridge (BA 1991; MA 1995); City Univ. (DipLaw); Inns of Court Sch. of Law. PR Officer, John Groom's Assoc. for Disabled People, 1991–93; called to the Bar, Middle Temple, 1995; in practice as barrister, 1995–; Mem., Attorney Gen.'s London A Panel of Jun. Counsel, 2012–16. Freeman, Merchant Taylors' Co. Hon. Fellow, Chartered Inst. of Credit Mgt, 2015. EsqStJ 1995. Kt of Grace and Devotion, SMO, Malta, 2002. *Publications:* (contrib.) Product Liability, Law and Insurance, 2000; (jtly) Blackstone's Guide to the Consumer Credit Act 2006, 2006; (jtly) Butterworth's Commercial and Consumer Law Handbook, 2015. *Recreation:* family. *Address:* Henderson Chambers, 2 Harcourt Buildings, Temple, EC4Y 9DB. *T:* (020) 7583 9020, *Fax:* (020) 7583 2686. *E:* triley-smith@hendersonchambers.co.uk. *Club:* Beefsteak.

**RIMER, Rt Hon. Sir Colin (Percy Farquharson),** Kt 1994; PC 2007; a Lord Justice of Appeal, 2007–14; *b* 30 Jan. 1944; *s* of late Kenneth Rowland Rimer and Maria Eugenia Rimer (*née* Farquharson); *m* 1970, Penelope Ann Gibbs; two *s* one *d*. *Educ:* Dulwich Coll.; Trinity Hall, Cambridge (MA, LLB; Hon. Fellow, 2009). Legal Assistant, Inst. of Comparative Law, Paris, 1967–68; called to the Bar, Lincoln's Inn, 1968, Bencher, 1994; QC 1988; in practice, 1969–94; a Judge of the High Court of Justice, Chancery Div., 1994–2007. *Recreations:* music, novels, walking.

**RIMER, Jennifer;** Head Teacher, St Mary's Music School, Edinburgh, 1996–2013; *b* Kirkcaldy; *d* of James and Margaret Whitelaw; *m* 1971, David Rimer; three *d*. *Educ:* Buckhaven High Sch., Fife; Univ. of Edinburgh (BMus Hons 1969; DipEd 1970). LRAM 1968; Hon. ARAM 2009. Teacher, Church High Sch., Newcastle, 1970–72; Principal Teacher, Music, St David's High Sch., Dalkeith, 1972–77; Music and Piano Teacher, 1982–93, Hd, Acad. Music, Careers and Guidance, 1993–96, St Mary's Music Sch., Edinburgh. Music and Piano Teacher, George Heriot's Sch., Edinburgh, 2013–. Examiner, setter and marker, SQA, 1978–. Founder Fellow, Inst. of Contemp. Scotland, 2000; Member: Eur. Piano Teachers' Assoc., 1975–; Sch. Leaders Scotland (formerly Headteachers' Assoc. of Scotland), 2001–13. Gov., George Heriot's Sch., 1990–2000; Director: Edinburgh Youth Orch., 1990–93; Nat. Youth Orch. of Scotland, 2009–17. *Publications:* contrib. Jl of Scottish Educn. *Recreations:* family, theatre, opera, concerts, art galleries, piano, viola, books, youth orchestras, walking, yoga. *E:* jennifer_rimer@hotmail.com.

**RIMINGTON, John David,** CB 1987; Director-General, Health and Safety Executive, 1984–95; *b* 27 June 1935; *s* of late John William Rimington, MBE, and of Mabel Dorrington; *m* 1963, Dame Stella Rimington, *qv*; two *d*. *Educ:* Nottingham High Sch.; Jesus Coll., Cambridge (Cl. I Hons History, MA). Nat. Service Commn, RA, 1954–56. Joined BoT, 1959; seconded HM Treasury (work on decimal currency), 1961; Principal, Tariff Div., BoT, 1963; 1st Sec. (Economic), New Delhi, 1965; Mergers Div., DTI, 1969; Dept of Employment, 1970; Asst Sec. 1972 (Employment Policy and Manpower); Counsellor, Social and Regional Policy, UK perm. representation to EEC, Brussels, 1974; MSC, 1977–81; Under Sec. 1978; Dir, Safety Policy Div., HSE, 1981–83; Dep. Sec., 1984; Permanent Sec., 1992. Non-executive Director: Magnox Electric, 1998; BNFL, 1998–2000; Angel Trains Gp (formerly Angel Train Contracts) Ltd, 1999–2006. Mem. Nat. Council, 1995–2008, Vice Pres., 2001–07, Hon. Vice-Pres., 2008–, Consumers' Assoc. Visiting Professor: Univ. of Strathclyde, 1997–99; Salford Univ., 1999–. CCMI (CIMgt 1993). Hon. DSc Sheffield, 1995. *Publications:* From Erewash to Radegund (memoir), 2017; articles on risk; contrib. to RIPA Jl, New Asia Review, Trans IChemE, Pol Quarterly, etc. *Recreations:* playing the piano, gardening, watching cricket. *Address:* 9 Highbury Hill, N5 1SU. *Club:* Athenæum.

**RIMINGTON, Dame Stella,** DCB 1996; Director General, Security Service, 1992–96; *b* 1935; *m* 1963, John David Rimington, *qv*; two *d*. *Educ:* Nottingham High Sch. for Girls; Edinburgh Univ. (MA). Security Service, 1969. Non-executive Director: Marks & Spencer plc, 1997–2004; Whitehead Mann GKR (formerly GKR), 1997–2001; BG plc, 1997–2000; BG Gp, 2000–05; Royal Marsden NHS Trust, 1998–2001. Chm., Inst. of Cancer Res., 1997–2001. Chm. of Judges, Man Booker Prize, 2011. Trustee: RAF Mus., 1998–2001; Refuge, 2007–. Hon. Air Cdre, No 7006 (VR) Intelligence Sqn, RAuxAF, 1997–2001. Hon. LLD: Nottingham, 1995; Exeter, 1996; London Metropolitan, 2004; Liverpool, 2005; Hon. DSocSc Nottingham Trent, 2009. *Publications:* Open Secret (autobiog.), 2001; novels: At Risk, 2004; Secret Asset, 2006; Illegal Action, 2007; Dead Line, 2008; Present Danger, 2009; Rip Tide, 2011; The Geneva Trap, 2012; Close Call, 2014; Breaking Cover, 2016; The Moscow Sleepers, 2018. *Address:* PO Box 1604, SW1P 1XB.

**RIMMER, Marie Elizabeth,** CBE 2005; MP (Lab) St Helens South and Whiston, since 2015; *b* St Helens, 27 April 1947. With Pilkington Glass, 1962–99, incl. Stats and Accounts Dept, buyer of engrg equipt for glass prodn lines, and Health and Safety Advr, Float Glass Manufg. Mem. (Lab), St Helens MBC, 1978– (Leader, 1985–93, 1999–2006, 2010–13). Shadow Minister for Disabled People, 2017–. Trustee, St Helens Hope Centre. *Address:* House of Commons, SW1A 0AA.

**RIMMER, Nicholas Patrick Edward;** a District Judge, Magistrates' Courts, since 2016; *b* Reading, 25 July 1979; *s* of Dr Maurus Euan Rimmer and late Ciaran Catherine Rimmer (*née* Molan). *Educ:* Oratory Prep. Sch.; Oratory Sch., Woodcote, Oxon; Trinity Coll. Dublin (BA English Studies 2001; MA 2004); Coll. of Law (Postgrad. DipLaw 2003); Inns of Court Sch. of Law (BVC 2004). Paralegal, Kingsley Napley Solicitors, 2001–03; called to the Bar, Lincoln's Inn, 2004; in practice as barrister, 2004–16; a Dep. Dist Judge (Magistrates' Courts), 2012–16. Ind. Costs Adjudicator, Legal Aid Agency, 2013–16. Equality and Diversity Officer, UK Assoc. of Part-Time Judges, 2014–16. Mem., Commonwealth Magistrates' and Judges' Assoc., 2016–. Volunteer, Lawyers Without Borders, 2014–. *Publications:* As They Say..., 2000. *Recreations:* theatre, concerts, music, cars, gymnasium, restaurants, travelling, reading, church (Roman Catholic). *Address:* 61 Walton Street, Knightsbridge, SW3 2JU. *E:* nicholasrimmer@hotmail.com. *Club:* Victory Services.

**RIMMER, Paul Derek James;** Director, Ministry of Defence, since 2014; *b* Birmingham, 17 April 1960; *s* of James Derek Rimmer and Sylvia Rimmer (*née* Baker-Sherman); *m* 1990, Jill Mary Venables Turner; two *s*. *Educ:* Bishop Vesey's Grammar Sch., Sutton Coldfield; Univ. of Keele (BA (Hons) Internat. Relns). Ministry of Defence: Defence Intelligence Staff, 1983; jsdc, 1993–94; Procurement Exec., 1994; Overseas Secretariat, 2000; Principal

Private Sec. to Sec. of State for Defence, 2008–09; Chief of the Assessments Staff, Cabinet Office, 2009 (on secondment); COS (Policy and Finance), Perm. Jt HQ, 2012–14. Hon. Col, 3MI Bn Intelligence Corps, 2011–; Hon. Air Cdre 7010 (VR) Sqdn, Royal Aux. Air Force, 2018–. *Recreations:* my family, hill walking, military history. *Address:* c/o Ministry of Defence, Main Building, Whitehall, SW1A 2HB.

**RIMMER, Air Vice-Marshal Thomas William,** CB 2001; OBE 1987; FRAeS, FRGS; Commander, British Forces Cyprus, 2000–03; *b* 16 Dec. 1948; *s* of William Thompson Rimmer and Elizabeth Comrie Rimmer (*née* Baird); *m* 1976, Sarah Caroline Hale; one *s* one *d*. *Educ:* Morrison's Academy, Crieff; Montpellier Univ., France; Edinburgh Univ. (MA Hons 1970). FRAeS 1997. Graduated RAF Cranwell, 1972; served Central Flying Sch., RAF Linton-on-Ouse, RAF Bruggen, RAF Coltishall, to 1983; French Air Force Staff Coll., 1983–84; Chief Instructor, RAF Cottesmore, 1984–87; HQ RAF Germany, 1987–89; Head, RAF Presentation Team, 1989–90; Station Comdr, RAF Cottesmore, 1990–92; Senior UK Mil. Officer, WEU, 1992–94; rcds 1995; MoD, 1996–98; AOC and Comdt, RAF Coll., Cranwell, 1999–2000. Chm., Govs, Framlingham Coll., 2017–. FRGS 2010. Liveryman, Tallow Chandlers' Co., 1992– (Warden, 2011–14). QCVSA 1983. *Recreations:* offshore sailing, golf, gardening (mechanical), vintage tractors. *Clubs:* Royal Air Force; RAF Yacht, RAF Sailing Assoc., Royal Cruising.

**RIMMINGTON, Rosemary Jean Neil;** *see* Conley, R. J. N.

**RINGEN, Mary Christina;** *see* Chamberlain, M. C.

**RINGEN, Prof. Stein;** Professor of Sociology and Social Policy, University of Oxford, 1990–2012, now Emeritus; Fellow of Green Templeton College (formerly Green College), Oxford, 1990–2012, now Emeritus; Visiting Professor of Political Economy, King's College London, since 2017; *b* 5 July 1945; *s* of John Ringen and Anna Ringen (*née* Simengard); *m* 2002, Prof. Mary Christina Chamberlain, *qv*. *Educ:* Univ. of Oslo (MA, dr. philos.). Broadcasting reporter, Norwegian Broadcasting Corp., 1970–71; Fellow, Internat. Peace Res. Inst., Oslo, 1971–72; Head of Secretariat, Norwegian Level of Living Study, 1972–76; Fellow, Inst. for Social Res., Oslo, 1976–78; Head of Res., Min. of Consumer Affairs and Govt Admin, Oslo, 1978–83; Prof. of Welfare Studies, Univ. of Stockholm, 1983–86; Sen. Res. Scientist, Central Bureau of Statistics, Oslo, 1986–88; Asst Dir Gen., Min. of Justice, Oslo, 1988–90. Mem., Royal Commn on Human Values, Norway, 1998–2001. Adjunct Prof., Lillehammer University Coll., 2009–15; Hon. Professor: Central China Normal Univ., 2012–; Sun Yat-sen Univ., 2014–; Vis. Prof., Richmond, the American Internat. Univ., London, 2012–. Fellow: European Acad. of Sociol., 2009; Norwegian Acad. of Lit. and Freedom of Expression, 2017. FRSA. Hon. Dr Masaryk Univ., Czech Republic, 2008. *Publications:* The Possibility of Politics, 1987, 3rd edn 2006; Citizens, Families and Reform, 1997, 2nd edn 2005; Reformdemokratie, 1997; The Family in Question, 1998; Veien til det gode liv, 2000; What Democracy Is For, 2007; The Liberal Vision and Other Essays on Democracy and Progress, 2007; The Economic Consequences of Mr Brown: how a strong government was defeated by a weak system of governance, 2009; The Korean State and Social Policy: how South Korea lifted itself from poverty and dictatorship to affluence and democracy, 2011; Nation of Devils: democracy and the problem of obedience, 2013; The Perfect Dictatorship: China in the 21st century, 2016. *Address:* Department of Political Economy, King's College London, Strand Campus, Bush House (North East Wing), 30 Aldwych, WC2B 4BG. *E:* stein.ringen@kcl.ac.uk.

**RINGROSE, Adrian Michael;** Chairman: Taziker Industrial Ltd, since 2017; Syrinix Ltd, since 2017; Churches Fire Security Ltd, since 2017; Warwick Estates Property Management Ltd, since 2017; *b* 9 April 1967; *s* of Prof. John Robert Ringrose, *qv*; *m* 1995, Frances Jacombs; one *s* two *d*. *Educ:* Univ. of Liverpool (BA Hons Pol Theory and Instns 1988). MCIM 1991. London Electricity plc: Business Analyst, 1990–92; Commercial Manager, 1992–97; Hd, Business Develt, Building & Property Gp, 1997–2001; Man. Dir, Interserve FM Ltd, 2001–03; Chief Exec., Interserve plc, 2003–17. Chm., Public Services Strategy Bd, CBI, 2009–13. Pres., Business Services Assoc., 2007–10. *Recreations:* family, sport, music, film, travel.

**RINGROSE, Ven. Hedley Sidney;** Archdeacon of Cheltenham, 1998–2009, now Emeritus; *b* 29 June 1942; *s* of Sidney and Clara Ringrose; *m* 1969, Rosemary Anne Palmer; one *s* two *d*. *Educ:* West Oxfordshire Coll.; Salisbury Theol Coll.; BA Open Univ. 1979. Deacon 1968, priest 1969; Curate: Bishopston, Bristol, 1968–71; Easthampstead, Berks, 1971–75; Vicar, St George, Gloucester with Whaddon, 1975–88; RD Gloucester City, 1983–88; Vicar of Cirencester, 1988–98; RD Cirencester, 1989–97; Hon. Canon, 1986–98, Reserved Canonry, 1998–2009, Gloucester Cathedral; Actg Archdeacon of Malmesbury, dio. Bristol, 2010–11; Interim Archdeacon of Oxford, 2011–13. Chairman: Dio. Bd of Patronage, 1990–98; Dio. House of Clergy, 1994–98; Dio. Bd of Education, 1998–2009. Mem., Gen. Synod of C of E, 1990–2005. Governor: Rendcomb Coll., 2000–; St Mary's and St Margaret's Schs, Calne, 2011–; Dir, Oxford Diocesan Schs Trust, 2012–14. Trustee: Glenfall House, 1998–2009; Foundn of St Matthias, 1998–2009 (Chm., 2005–10); Sylvanus Lysons Trust, 2000–09. Mem., Conservation Bd, Cotswold AONB, 2015–19 (Mem., Grants Cttee, 2016–18). *Recreations:* travel, family and friends, grandchildren, cycling, driving, DIY, gardening, reading. *Address:* 131 North Street, Calne, Wilts SN11 0HL. *T:* (01249) 821215. *E:* hedleyringrose@gmail.com.

**RINGROSE, Prof. John Robert,** FRS 1977; FRSE; Professor of Pure Mathematics, 1964–93, now Emeritus, and a Pro-Vice-Chancellor, 1983–88, University of Newcastle upon Tyne; *b* 21 Dec. 1932; *s* of Albert Frederick Ringrose and Elsie Lilian Ringrose (*née* Roberts); *m* 1956, Jean Margaret Bates; three *s*. *Educ:* Buckhurst Hill County High School, Chigwell, Essex; St John's Coll., Cambridge (MA, PhD). Lecturer in Mathematics: King's Coll., Newcastle upon Tyne, 1957–61; Univ. of Cambridge (also Fellow of St John's Coll.), 1961–63; Sen. Lectr in Mathematics, Univ. of Newcastle upon Tyne, 1963–64. Pres., London Mathematical Soc., 1992–94. *Publications:* Compact Non-self-adjoint Operators, 1971; (with R. V. Kadison) Fundamentals of the Theory of Operator Algebras, 1983; mathematical papers in various research jls. *Address:* 15 Longmeadows, Ponteland, Newcastle upon Tyne NE20 9DX.
*See also* A. M. Ringrose.

**RINGROSE, Peter Stuart,** PhD; Chairman, Biotechnology and Biological Sciences Research Council, 2003–09; *b* 9 Oct. 1945; *s* of Arthur Ringrose and Roma Margaret Ringrose (*née* Roberts); *m* 1966, Nancy Elaine Palmer; two *s* one *d*. *Educ:* Alderman Newton's Grammar Sch., Leicester; Corpus Christi Coll., Cambridge (BA 1967; PhD 1971). Hd Biochemistry, Hoffmann La Roche, UK, 1970–79; Div. Hd, Sandoz Forschungs-Institut, Vienna, 1979–82; Sen. Vice Pres., Global Drug Discovery, Pfizer Inc., UK, 1982–96; CSO, Bristol-Myers Squibb Co., NY, and Pres., Pharmaceutical Res. Inst., Princeton, 1997–2002. Chm. Pharmaceutical R&D Heads, Hever Gp, 1999–2002; non-exec. Director: Cambridge Antibody Technology, 2003–06 (Chm., Scientific Adv. Bd, 2003–06); Astex Therapeutics, 2005–11; Rigel Pharmaceuticals, 2005–19 (Chm., Sci. and Clinical Trials Adv. Cttee, 2015–19); Biotica Technology Ltd, 2007–12; Technol. Strategy Bd, 2007–09; Theravance Inc., 2010–14; Theravance Biopharma, 2014– (Chm., Sci. and Technol. Adv. Cttee, 2014–); Member Scientific Advisory Board: Accenture Life Sciences,

2003–07; Merlin Biosciences, 2003–05; Cempra Pharmaceuticals, 2006–12; Schering-Plough Inc., 2007–09. Council Mem., Foundn for Sci. and Technol., UK, 2003–. Member: Policy Adv. Bd, Centre for Medicines Res. Internat., 1994–2001; Sci. and Regulatory Exec., Pharmaceutical Res. and Manufacturers of America, 1997–2002; US Council on Competitiveness, 1998–2002. Member: Chancellor's Ct of Benefactors, Oxford Univ., 1998–2003; Chemistry Adv. Bd, Cambridge Univ., 2001–13; Bd of Governors, NY Acad. of Sciences, 2001–05. William Pitt Fellow, Pembroke Coll., Cambridge, 1998–2006 (Life Hon. Fellow, 2006). Mem., Speldhurst Parish Council, 2011–12. *Recreations:* grandchildren, sketching, historical fiction, swimming, travelling, archaeology. *Club:* Athenæum.

**RINK, John Stuart;** Managing Partner, Allen & Overy, 1994–2003; *b* 25 Oct. 1946; *s* of Paul Lothar Max Rink and Mary Ida McCall Rink (*née* Moore); *m* 1971, Elizabeth Mary Pitkethly; one *s* one *d*. *Educ:* Sedbergh Sch.; London Univ. (LLB ext.). Allen & Overy: Trainee Solicitor, 1970–72; Asst Solicitor, 1972–77; Partner, 1977–2003; Man. Partner, Litigation Dept, 1989–94; Legal Dir, British Aerospace, 1994–95 (on secondment). Director: Brixton plc, 2003–06; Eversheds, 2004–09; RSM Robson Rhodes, 2004–06. Dep. Chm., Teach First, 2008–16 (Trustee, 2006–16). Gov., Sedbergh Sch., 2008–16. *Recreations:* golf, Rugby, walking, opera. *Address:* 2 Camp View, Wimbledon, SW19 4UL. *T:* (020) 8947 4800. *Clubs:* MCC; City Law; Royal Wimbledon Golf; Royal West Norfolk Golf; Windermere Golf; Silloth Golf; Windermere Motor Boat Racing.

**RINTOUL, Dr Gordon Charles,** CBE 2012; FRSE; Director, National Museums Scotland, since 2002; *b* 29 May 1955; *s* of Henry Rintoul and Janet Rintoul (*née* Brown); *m* 1997, Stephanie Jane Budden; one *s*. *Educ:* Allan Glen's Sch., Glasgow; Univ. of Edinburgh (BSc Hons Physics); Univ. of Manchester (MSc Sci., Technol. and Society; PhD Hist. of Sci. and Technol. 1982). Dip. Museums Assoc. Res. Supervisor, Chem. Mus. Develt Project, 1982–84; Consultant and Tutor, Open Univ., Milton Keynes, 1984; Curator, Colour Mus., Bradford, 1984–87; Dir, Catalyst: Mus. of the Chem. Industry, 1987–98; Chief Exec., Sheffield Galls and Museums Trust, 1998–2002. Member: Registration Cttee, Resource: Council for Museums, Archives and Libraries, 1995–2002; Bd, Scottish Cultural Resources Access Network (SCRAN), 2002–06; Leadership Gp, Scottish Tourism Forum, 2010–12; Bd, Destination Edinburgh Ltd, 2010–11; Bd of Dirs, Marketing Edinburgh Ltd, 2011–. Member Council: Assoc. of Ind. Museums, 1989–2002 (Treas., 1991–97); Museums Assoc., 1998–2004 (Mem., Collections Strategy Gp, 2009–12). FRSE 2018. Dr *hc* Edinburgh, 2013; DUniv Edinburgh Napier, 2013. *Recreations:* travel, reading, cooking. *Address:* National Museums Scotland, Chambers Street, Edinburgh EH1 1JF. *T:* (0131) 247 4260. *E:* g.rintoul@nms.ac.uk.

**RIORDAN, Prof. Colin Bryan,** PhD; President and Vice-Chancellor, Cardiff University, since 2012; *b* Paderborn, 27 July 1959; *s* of late Bryan Victor Riordan and Elisabeth Riordan; *m* 1991, Karin Alderson (marr. diss. 2013); two *d*. *Educ:* Liverpool Collegiate Sch.; Univ. of Manchester (BA 1st Cl. Hons German 1981; PhD 1986). Lektor, Julius-Maximilians Univ., Würzburg, 1982–84; University of Wales, Swansea: Lectr in German, 1986–94; Sen. Lectr in German, 1994–98; Hd, Dept of German, 1998–2003; University of Newcastle upon Tyne: Prof. of German, 1998–2007; Hd, Sch. of Modern Langs, 2001–04; Dean, Postgrad. Studies, Faculty of Humanities and Social Scis, 2004–05; Provost and Pro-Vice-Chancellor, 2005–07; Vice-Chancellor, Univ. of Essex, 2007–12. *Publications:* The Ethics of Narration, 1989; (with G. Butzphal) Studium Wirtschaftsdeutsch, 1990; (ed) Peter Schneider, 1993; (ed) Peter Schneider, 1995; (ed jtly) German Writers and the Cold War, 1945–61, 1992; (ed) Green Thought in German Culture, 1997; (ed) Jurek Becker, 1998; (ed jtly) Aesthetics and Politics in Modern German Culture: festschrift in honour of Rhys W. Williams, 2010; contribs to jls incl. Jl Eur. Studies, Modern Lang. Rev., Johnson-Jahrbuch. *Address:* Vice-Chancellor's Office, Cardiff University, Main Building, Park Place, Cardiff CF10 3AT.

**RIORDAN, Linda;** *b* 31 May 1953; *d* of John Foulds Haigh and Mary Alice Haigh (*née* Helliwell); *m* 1979, Alan Riordan (*d* 2007). *Educ:* Univ. of Bradford (BSc Hons). Formerly in banking. Pvte Sec. to Alice Mahon, MP, 2001–05. Mem. (Lab), Calderdale MBC, 1995–2006. MP (Lab and Co-op) Halifax, 2005–15.

**RIORDAN, Stephen Vaughan;** QC 1992; a Recorder, since 1990; *b* 18 Feb. 1950; *s* of Charles Maurice Riordan and Betty Moryfdd Riordan; *m* 1983, Jane Elizabeth Thomas; two *d*. *Educ:* Wimbledon Coll.; Univ. of Liverpool (LLB Hons). Called to the Bar, Inner Temple, 1972; Asst Recorder, 1986–90. *Recreation:* singing.

**RIORDAN, Thomas Messenger;** Chief Executive, Leeds City Council, since 2010; *b* 9 April 1968; *s* of late Michael Riordan and of Juliet Riordan; *m* Louise; one *s* one *d*. *Educ:* Trinity Coll., Oxford (BA Hons Mod. Hist. 1989); Imperial Coll., London (MBA 1st Cl. 1997). Joined Civil Service, 1990, fast stream incl. rep. UK on internat. envmtl policy negotiations (climate change and biodiversity), 1990–96; Operational Hd, RDA Proj. Team, Govt Office for Yorkshire and Humber, 1997–99; Yorkshire Forward: Hd, Strategy, 1999–2000; Exec. Dir, Strategy and Policy, 2000–05; Dep. Chief Exec., 2005–06; Chief Exec., 2006–10. Trustee, Centre for Cities, 2012–. Patron, St Gemma's Hospice, Leeds, 2015–. Hon. DLitt Bradford, 2008. *Publications:* articles on regl develt for Smith Inst. and New Local Govt Network. *Recreations:* football, Middlesbrough Football Club, horse racing, competitive dominoes, music. *Address:* Leeds City Council, Civic Hall, Calverley Street, Leeds LS1 1UR. *T:* (0113) 247 4554, *Fax:* (0113) 247 4870. *E:* tom.riordan@leeds.gov.uk. *W:* www.twitter.com/tomriordan. *Club:* Northallerton Working Men's.

**RIPERT, David Clément;** Founder and Chief Executive Officer, Poplar, since 2018; *b* Ottawa, 20 Sept. 1978; *s* of Jean-Maurice Ripert and Claudine Ripert-Landler. *Educ:* École des Hautes Etudes Commerciales du Nord, France (MA Mgt); Loyola Marymount Univ., LA (MBA). Mgt consultant, Capgemini Ernst & Young, 2001–02; Dir, Prodn and Distribution, IM Global Films, 2002–06; Manager, Original Content, Netflix, 2006–08; Vice Pres., Content, Dailymotion, 2008–12; Hd, YouTube Spaces, EMEA, Google, 2012–18; Investor and Advr, Tétu, 2018. Associate Judge, Webby Awards. Member: Founder's Forum; Virtual Reality and Augmented Reality Assoc.; French Tech. London; Google Campus. Trustee, Board of Directors: Sadler's Wells Trust, 2016–; Save the Children UK, 2017–.

**RIPLEY, Prof. Brian David,** PhD; FRSE; Professor of Applied Statistics, University of Oxford, 1990–2014, now Emeritus; Fellow, St Peter's College, Oxford, 1990–2014, now Emeritus; *b* 29 April 1952; *s* of Eric Lewis Ripley and Sylvia May Ripley (*née* Gould); *m* 1973, Ruth Mary Appleton. *Educ:* Farnborough Grammar Sch.; Churchill Coll., Cambridge (MA, PhD). FIMS 1987; FRSE 1990. Lectr in Statistics, Imperial Coll., London, 1976–80; Reader, Univ. of London, 1980–83; Prof. of Statistics, Univ. of Strathclyde, 1983–90. Mem., Internat. Statistical Inst., 1982. Adams Prize, Univ. of Cambridge, 1987. *Publications:* Spatial Statistics, 1981; Stochastic Simulation, 1987; Statistical Inference for Spatial Processes, 1988; Modern Applied Statistics with S-Plus, 1994, 3rd edn 1999; Pattern Recognition and Neural Networks, 1996; S Programming, 2000; numerous papers on statistics and applications in astronomy, biology, chemistry and earth sciences. *Recreation:* natural history. *Address:* Department of Statistics, University of Oxford, 24–29 St Giles', Oxford OX1 3LB. *T:* (01865) 272861.

**RIPLEY, John Kenneth,** ACMA, CGMA; Chair: CABI (formerly CAB International), 2011–15 (Director, since 2009); Church Mission Society, 2010–15; *b* Farnborough, 29 April 1952; *s* of Eric Ripley and Sylvia May Ripley (*née* Gould); *m* 1978, Anne Waring; two *d* (and one *d* decd). *Educ:* Farnborough Grammar Sch.; Trinity Coll., Cambridge (BA 1973). ACMA, CGMA 1980. Unilever: specialist, 1973–76; Mgt Accountant, van den Berghs, 1976–80, Internat. Specialities Div., Netherlands, 1980–82, Lever Bros, 1982–85; Commercial Dir, Loders Croklaan, Netherlands, 1985–89, Agribusiness, 1989–92; Finance Dir, Central Asia and Latin America, 1992–96; Hd, Strategy, 1996–2000; Chief Financial Officer, HPC Div., 2001–05; Dep. Chief Financial Officer, 2005–08; Hd, Corporate Develt, 2008. Governor: Howard of Effingham Sch., Leatherhead, 2002–13; Kingston Univ., 2010–16; Eastwick Schs, 2011–16. Non-executive Director: Great Ormond Street Hosp., 2012–15; Howard Partnership Trust, 2013–16. *Recreations:* travel, photography. *T:* (01372) 450227.
See also B. D. Ripley.

**RIPLEY, Sir William (Huw),** 5th Bt *cr* 1880; *b* 13 April 1950; *s* of Major Sir Hugh Ripley, 4th Bt and Dorothy Mary Dunlop Ripley; *S* father, 2003. *Educ:* Eton; McGill Univ., Montreal. Smallholder and local journalist. *Heir:* none.

**RIPLEY-DUGGAN, Gregory Alan;** Executive Producer, Hampstead Theatre, London, since 2010; *b* Leatherhead, 20 July 1958; *s* of Eric Ripley-Duggan and Olive Adelaide Ripley-Duggan; partner, Pascale Giudicelli; one *d*. *Educ:* St Peter's and Merrow Grange Comp. Sch.; Downing Coll., Cambridge (BA Eng. Lit. 1980). Independent West End producer, 1990–; Exec. Producer, Shakespeare's Globe, 1996–2006; Interim Exec. Producer, Headlong, 2008–09; Associate Producer, Kingston Rose, 2010–. Chm., League of Independent Producers, 2011–; Mem., SOLT, 2001–. *Recreations:* classical music, literature, following cricket, carpentry. *Address:* Hampstead Theatre, Eton Avenue, NW3 3EU. *T:* (020) 7449 4200. *E:* grd@ripleyduggan.com. *Club:* Groucho.

**RIPON, Area Bishop of,** since 2018; **Rt Rev. Dr Helen-Ann Macleod Hartley;** *b* Edinburgh, 28 May 1973; *d* of James Francis and Patricia Francis; *m* 2003, Myles Hartley. *Educ:* St Anthony's RC Girls Sch.; Univ. of St Andrews (MTheol Hons 1995); Princeton Theol Seminary (ThM 1996); Worcester Coll., Oxford (MPhil 2000; DPhil 2005; Hon. Fellow, 2015). Ordained deacon, 2005, priest, 2006; Curate, Wheatley Team, Oxford, 2005–09; Dir of Biblical Studies, Ripon Coll., Cuddesdon, 2009–12 (Hon. Fellow 2014); Dean for the New Zealand Dioceses, Coll. of St John the Evangelist, Auckland, 2012–14; Bishop of Waikato, 2014–18. Hon. Fellow, Harris Manchester Coll., Oxford, 2017. Hon. PhD Educn Sunderland, 2019. *Publications:* Making Sense of the Bible, 2011. *Recreations:* walking, water-colour painting, astronomy. *Address:* Redwood, New Road, Sharow, Ripon, N Yorks HG4 5BS. *T:* (01765) 601094. *E:* bishop.helenann@leeds.anglican.org.

**RIPON, Dean of;** *see* Dobson, Very Rev. J. R.

**RIPPENGAL, Derek,** CB 1982; QC 1980; Counsel to Chairman of Committees, House of Lords, 1977–99; *b* 8 Sept. 1928; *s* of William Thomas Rippengal and Margaret Mary Rippengal (*née* Parry); *m* 1963, Elizabeth Melrose (*d* 1973); one *d* (one *s* decd). *Educ:* Hampton Grammar Sch.; St Catharine's Coll., Cambridge (Scholar; MA). Called to Bar, Middle Temple, 1953 (Harmsworth schol.). Entered Treasury Solicitor's Office, 1958, after Chancery Bar and univ. posts; Sen. Legal Asst, 1961; Asst Treasury Solicitor, 1967; Principal Asst Treasury Solicitor, 1971; Solicitor to DTI, 1972–73; Dep. Parly Counsel, 1973–74, Parly Counsel, 1974–76, Law Commn. *Publications:* (contrib.) Halsbury's Laws of England, vol. 34 (Parliament), 4th edn, 1997. *Recreations:* music, fishing. *Address:* 62 Gwydir Street, Cambridge CB1 2LL. *Club:* Athenæum.

**RIPPON, Amanda Jayne; Her Honour Judge Rippon;** a Circuit Judge, since 2016; *b* Leeds, 16 Dec. 1967; *d* of Victor and Jacqueline Field; *m* 1996, Matthew James Rippon; two *s*. *Educ:* Lancaster Univ. (BA Hons Politics); City Univ. London (DipLaw); Inns of Court Sch. of Law. Called to the Bar, Gray's Inn, 1993; in practice as barrister, specialising in crime, 1993–2016; Hd of Chambers, New Park Court, Newcastle, 2015–16; a Recorder, 2008–16. *Recreations:* travel, theatre, cinema, reading. *Address:* The Law Courts, Quayside, Newcastle upon Tyne NE1 3LA. *T:* (0191) 201 2000. *E:* HHJ.Amanda.Rippon@ejudiciary.net.

**RIPPON, Angela May,** CBE 2017 (OBE 2004); broadcaster; presenter, Rip Off Britain, BBC TV, since 2010; *b* 12 Oct. 1944; *d* of late John Rippon and Edna Rippon; *m* 1967, Christopher Dare (marr. diss.). *Educ:* Plymouth Public Grammar Sch. Journalist, The Independent, Plymouth; presenter and reporter, BBC TV, Plymouth, 1966–69; editor, producer and presenter, Westward TV, 1967–73; reporter, nat. news, 1973–75, newsreader, 1975–81, BBC TV; co-founder, and presenter, TV-am, 1983; arts and entertainment correspondent, WNEV-TV, Boston, USA, 1984–85; presenter, LBC, 1990–94. *Television series include:* presenter: Angela Rippon Reporting, 1980–81; Antiques Roadshow, 1980–83; In the Country, 1980–83; Top Gear, 1980–83; Masterteam, 1985–87; Come Dancing, 1988–91; What's My Line, 1988–90; Live with Angela Rippon, 2002–04; Sun, Sea and Bargain Spotting, 2004–09; Cash in the Attic, 2006–; Holiday Hit Squad, 2012–; Amazing Greys, 2014; The Truth about Dementia, 2016; How to Stay Young, 2016–17; Health Truth or Scare, 2017; compère, Eurovision Song Contest, 1976; also presenter, radio progs. Vis. Prof., Consumer Journalism, Lincoln Univ., 2010–. Chm., English Nat. Ballet, 2000–04. Vice-Pres., British Red Cross, 1999–; Ambassador: Alzheimer's Soc., 2009–; Silver Swans, RAD, 2017–; Patron, Kidney Res. UK, 2009–11; Co-Chm., Prime Minister's Dementia Friendly Communities Cttee, 2011–. Pres., Lady Taverners, 2011–16. TRIC Newsreader of the Year, 1975, 1976, 1977. Hon. DHum Amer. Coll. in London, 1994; Hon. DArts Plymouth, 2012; Hon. DCL Newcastle, 2014. European Woman of Achievement, Women's EU, 2002; Lifetime Achievement Award, Women in Film and TV Awards, 2013. *Publications:* Riding, 1980; In the Country, 1980; Victoria Plum (children's stories), 1981; Mark Phillips: the man and his horses, 1982; Angela Rippon's West Country, 1983; Badminton: a celebration, 1987; Fabulous at 50 and Beyond, 2003. *Address:* c/o Knight Ayton Management, 29 Gloucester Place, W1U 8HX.

**RISBY,** Baron *cr* 2010 (Life Peer), of Haverhill in the County of Suffolk; **Richard John Grenville Spring;** *b* 24 Sept. 1946; *s* of late H. J. A. Spring and Marjorie (*née* Watson-Morris); *m* 1979, Hon. Jane (marr. diss. 1993), *o d* of 8th Baron Henniker, KCMG, CVO, MC; one *s* one *d*. *Educ:* Rondebosch, Cape; Univ. of Cape Town); Magdalene Coll., Cambridge (MA Econs). Vice-Pres., Merrill Lynch Ltd, 1976–86; Dep. Man. Dir, E. F. Hutton Internat. Associates, 1986–88; Exec. Dir, Shearson Lehman Hutton, 1988–89; Man. Director, Xerox Furman Selz, 1989–92. Contested (C) Ashton-under-Lyne, 1983. MP (C) Bury St Edmunds, 1992–97, W Suffolk, 1997–2010. PPS to Min. of State, DTI, 1996, to Ministers for the armed forces and for defence procurement, 1996–97; Opposition front bench spokesman on culture, media and sport, 1997–2000, on foreign and Commonwealth affairs, 2000–04; Shadow Financial Services Minister, 2004–05; Shadow Paymaster Gen., 2005. Member: Employment Select Cttee, 1992–94; NI Select Cttee, 1994–97; Health Select Cttee, 1995–97; Vice Chairman: All Party Racing and Bloodstock Cttee, 1997–98; All Party Mobile Telephone Gp, 2004; Chm., All Party Mauritius Gp, 2008–10. A Vice Chm., Cons. Party, and Co-Chm., Cons. City Circle, 2006–10. Pres., Arts and Heritage Cttee, Bow Gp, 1992–97. Prime Ministerial Trade Envoy to Algeria, 2012–. Mem., Horserace Betting Levy Bd, 2016–. European Elections Campaign Co-ordinator, 1989; Chm., Westminster CPC, 1990; Dep.-Chm., Small Business Bureau, 1997– (Chm., Parly Adv. Gp, 1992–2010). Chm., British-Ukranian Soc., 2007–. Gov., Westminster Foundn for Democracy, 2001–10. Pres., Assoc. for Decentralised Energy, 2013–. Mem., Adv. Bd, Newsmax, 2013–. Patron: Cons. City Future, 2010–; London Mag., 2013–; Open Reach, 2013–. *Recreations:* country pursuits, English watercolours. *Address:* House of Lords, SW1A 0PW. *Club:* Boodle's.

**RISIUS, Maj. Gen. His Honour Gordon,** CB 2000; a Circuit Judge, 2003–14; *b* 10 July 1945; *s* of late Rudolf Risius and Irene Risius (*née* Spier); *m* 1980, Lucinda Mary, *d* of Marshal of the Royal Air Force Sir Michael James Beetham, GCB, CBE, DFC, AFC; one *s* two *d*. *Educ:* University College Sch.; Coll. of Law. Admitted Solicitor, 1972; commnd as Capt., Army Legal Services, 1973; served HQ Land Forces Hong Kong, HQ BAOR, HQ NI, MoD, HQ 4th Armd Div., HQ Land Forces Cyprus; Col, Army Legal Services 2, MoD, 1992–94; Brig. Legal, HQ BAOR/UKSC (Germany), 1994–95; Brig. Legal, HQ Land Command, 1995–96; Brig. Prosecutions, 1997; Dir, Army Legal Services and Army Prosecuting Authy, 1997–2003. Asst Recorder, 1991–95; a Recorder, 1995–2003; a Vice-Pres., Immigration Appeal Tribunal, 2003–05; a Sen. Judge, Sovereign Base Areas Court, Cyprus, 2007–14; Resident Judge, Oxford Crown Court, 2010–14. Dep. Col Comdt, AGC, 2004–09. Vice-Pres., 1997–2003, Hon. Pres., 2003–, Internat. Soc. for Military Law and the Law of War; Mem., Internat. Inst. of Humanitarian Law, 1994–2003. Hon. Recorder of Oxford, 2011–14. *Publications:* articles on the law of war. *Recreations:* music, reading, computers, travel.

**RIST, Prof. John Michael,** FRSC; Professore Incaricato, Istituto Patristico Augustinianum, Rome, 1998–2016; *b* 6 July 1936; *s* of Robert Ward Rist and Phoebe May (*née* Mansfield); *m* 1960, Anna Thérèse (*née* Vogler); two *s* two *d*. *Educ:* Trinity Coll., Cambridge (BA 1959, MA 1963). FRSC 1976. Univ. of Toronto: firstly Lectr, finally Prof. of Classics, 1959–80; Chm., Grad. Dept of Classics, 1971–75; Regius Prof. of Classics, Aberdeen Univ., 1980–83; Prof. of Classics and Philosophy, Univ. of Toronto, 1983–96, Emeritus Prof., 1997. Kurt Pritzl O. P. Prof. of Philosophy, Catholic Univ. of America, 2012–16. Hon. PhilDr Santa Croce, Rome, 2002. Aquinas Medal, Amer. Catholic Philosophical Assoc., 2014. Hon. Chief and Father of Tiv tribe, Benue State, Nigeria, 2017. *Publications:* Eros and Psyche, Canada 1964; Plotinus: the road to reality, 1967; Stoic Philosophy, 1969; Epicurus: an introduction, 1972; (ed) The Stoics, USA 1978; On the Independence of Matthew and Mark, 1978; Human Value, 1982; Platonism and its Christian Heritage, 1985; The Mind of Aristotle, 1989; Augustine, 1994; Man, Soul and Body, 1996; On Inoculating Moral Philosophy Against God, 2000; Real Ethics, 2001; What is Truth?, 2008; Plato: the discovery of the foundations of ethics, 2012; Augustine Deformed, 2014; Reading Augustine: ethics, politics and psychology in the twenty-first century, 2017; contrib. classical and phil jls. *Recreations:* travel, swimming, hill-walking. *Address:* 14 St Luke's Street, Cambridge CB4 3DA.

**RITBLAT, Jamie William Jeremy;** Founder and Chief Executive, since 1995 and Chairman, since 2001, Delancey; *b* London, 18 Feb. 1967; *s* of Sir John Henry Ritblat, *qv*; *m* 1995, Joanna Henrietta Jackson; one *s* three *d*. *Educ:* Hall Sch.; Eton Coll.; Univ. of Bristol. Morgan Grenfell, 1986–90, Associate Dir, 1989–90; British Land Company plc, 1990–95, Dir, 1992–95 (Consultant, 1995–97); Founder, Freehold Portfolios Estates, 1995. Non-exec. Chm., Mitheredge Capital, 2017–. Trustee: Gordon Russell Trust, 2002–12 (Patron, 2012–14); Bathurst Estate, 2012–; Dir, Main Bd, 2005–14, Nat. Campaign Bd, 2007–11, Maggie's Cancer Caring Centres. Mem. Council, KCL, 2006–15 (Vice Chm., 2014–15; Chm., Estates Bd, 2007–15; Mem., Chm.'s Cttee, 2008–15); FKC 2012. Dep. Chm., Real Estates Adv. Bd, Tate Britain, 2008–15; Gov., 2009–16, Chm. Estates Cttee, 2010–16, Southbank Centre. Member: Bd, Heritage of London Trust, 2016–; Internat. Cttee, V&A, 2017–. Freeman, City of London, 1996. FRSA. *Recreations:* ski-ing, Real tennis, farming, shooting, bees, art. *Address:* Delancey, Lansdowne House, Berkeley Square, W1J 6ER. *E:* jamie.ritblat@delancey.com. *Clubs:* MCC (Mem., Estates Cttee, 2011); Boodle's, Queen's, Royal Automobile.

**RITBLAT, Jillian Rosemary, (Lady Ritblat),** OBE 2017; Member of Council, Royal College of Art, since 2010 (Chair, Fashion Gala, 2012–14); Trustee: Design Museum, 2010–19 (Member, Curatorial Committee, since 2018); Garden Museum, since 2010; *b* Newcastle upon Tyne, 14 Dec. 1942; *d* of Max Leonard Slotover and Peggy Cherna (*née* Cohen); *m* 1st, 1966, Elie Zilkha (marr. diss. 1981); one *s* one *d*; 2nd, 1986, Sir John Henry Ritblat, *qv*. *Educ:* Newcastle-upon-Tyne Ch High Sch.; Roedean; Westfield Coll., Univ. of London (BA Hons Hist. of Art). Called to the Bar, Gray's Inn, 1964; pupillage to Robin Simpson, QC, 1964–65; Alt. Deleg. for Internat. Council of Jewish Women, UN, Geneva, 1977–79; Patrons of New Art Tate Gallery: founding mem., 1982–; events organiser, 1984–87; Chm., 1987–90; Mem., Acquisitions Sub-Cttee, 1992–93 and 2000–01; Mem., Internat. Council, Tate Gall., 1995– (Vice-Chm., 1996–2001). Member: Cttee, British Friends of Art Museums of Israel, 1980–; Modern Art Oxford (formerly MOMA, Oxford), 1986– (Mem. Council, 1993–2010); Internat. Council, Jerusalem Mus., 1987–; Adv. Council, Friends of Tate Gall., 1990–2002; Special Events Cttee, NACF, 1991–92; William Townsend Mems Lecture Cttee, 1991–; Bd, Jerusalem Music Centre, 1991–; Bd, New Contemporaries, 1991–2016 (Vice Chair, 1992–2016); Arts Council Appraisal for W Midlands Arts, 1994; Develt Cttee, RAM, 2002–10 (Cttee of Honour, 2010–); Bd, British Archtl Trust Bd (formerly RIBA Trust), 2006–12; Internat. Council, Wallace Collection, 2008–; RIBA Gold Medal Cttee, 2017. Design Trustee, Public Art Comrs Agency, 1996–99; Trustee: Tate Foundn, 2006–13 (Hon. Mem., 2013–); Patron, Nat. Alliance for Art, Architecture and Design, 1994–97; Founding Patron, South Downs Soc., 2014–. Co-Curator: The Curator's Egg, Anthony Reynolds Gall., 1994; One Woman's Wardrobe, V&A, 1998–99 (Catalogue Design and Art Direction Silver Award for Graphic Design, D&AD, 1999); Exec. Producer, Normal Conservative Rebels: Gilbert & George in China, Edinburgh Film Fest., 1998 (Gold Medal, Chicago Film Fest.). Jury Member: Painting in the Eighties, 1987; Turner Prize, 1988; BA New Artist Award, 1990; Swiss Bank Corp. Euro Art Competition, 1994 and 1995; NatWest 90s Prize for Art, 1994 and 1995; FT Arts and Business Awards, 2000 and 2001; RIBA Regl Award, Building Commn, 2001; Royal Instn Nature Niche Prize, 2007; Manser Prize, RIBA, 2012. Hon. FRAM 2011; Hon. FRIBA 2013. *Recreations:* art, opera, travel, food, people. *Address:* Lansdowne House, Berkeley Square, W1J 6ER.

**RITBLAT, Sir John (Henry),** Kt 2006; FRICS; Chairman, The British Land Company PLC, 1970–2006 (Managing Director, 1970–2004; Hon. President, 2007); *b* 3 Oct. 1935; *m* 1st, 1960, Isabel Paja (*d* 1979); two *s* one *d*; 2nd, 1986, Jillian Rosemary Zilkha (see J. R. Ritblat). *Educ:* Dulwich Coll.; London Univ. College of Estate Management. FRICS 2000. Articles with West End firm of Surveyors and Valuers, 1952–58. Founder Partner, Conrad Ritblat & Co., Consultant Surveyors and Valuers, 1958; Chairman: Conrad Ritblat Gp plc, 1993–97; Colliers Conrad Ritblat Erdman, 2000–; Colliers Internat. (UK) Ltd, 2010–12. Comr, Crown Estate Paving Commn, 1969–2012, now Comr Emeritus. Hon. Surveyor, Seafarers UK (formerly King George's Fund for Sailors), 1979– (Vice Pres., 2010). Member: Council, Business in the Community, 1987–; Prince of Wales' Royal Parks Tree Appeal Cttee, 1987–; British Olympic Assoc., 1979; Olympic Appeal Cttee, 1984, 1988, 1996 and 2000. Chairman: Trustees, Wallace Collection, 2005–14; Wallace Collection Foundn (formerly Hertford House Trust), 2014–; Trustee, Tate Foundn, 2006–15 (Hon. Mem., 2015–); Member: Patrons of British Art, Tate Gall.; English Heritage; Royal Horticultural Soc.; Architecture Club; SPAB; NACF; British Heritage Bd, 1995–2003 and 2015–; Council, Royal Instn, 2002 (Life Fellow, 2001; Vice-Pres., 2008); Life Member: Nat. Trust; Zool Soc. of London; Georgian Gp; RGS; Trollope Soc. Patron, Investment Property Forum, 1999–. Pres., London Festival of Architecture, 2010. Trustee, Zool Soc. of London Develt Trust, 1986–89. Trustee, Internat. Students' Trust; Mem., Bd of Govs, Internat. Students' House, 2003–14 (Vice-Chm., 2007–14; Vice-Pres., 2014–). Patron, London Fedn of Boys' Clubs Centenary Appeal; Founder Sponsor, Young Explorers Trust; Sponsor: RGS, 1982–85; (sole), British Nat. Ski Championships, 1978–; Pres., British Ski and Snowboard (formerly British Ski Fedn, then British Ski and Snowboard Fedn), 1994– (Vice-Pres., 1984–89). Member, Board of Governors: London Business Sch., 1990–2014 (Hon. Fellow, 2000; Chm. Govs, 2006–14; Chm., 2013–14, Mem., 2014–, Estates Cttee); The Weizmann Inst., 1991–2012; Dir and Gov., RAM, 1998–2012 (Dep. Chm., 1999–2012; Hon. Fellow, 2000; Hon. Trustee, 2014–); Gov., 2003–12, Consultant, 2012–, Dulwich Coll. FRGS 1982; CCMI; Life FRSA. Freeman, City of London, 1996. Hon. FRIBA 2006. Hon. DLitt: London Metropolitan, 2005; Buckingham, 2013; Hon. DSc London Business Sch., 2014. *Recreations:* antiquarian books and libraries, bees, Real tennis, golf, ski-ing, opera, ballet. *Address:* Lansdowne House, 57 Berkeley Square, W1J 6ER. *Clubs:* Carlton, Royal Automobile, MCC, The Pilgrims, Queen's; Cresta (St Moritz).

*See also J. W. J. Ritblat.*

**RITCHEY, Ian**, PhD; CEng, FIMechE, FREng; Group Chief Engineer, Rolls-Royce plc, since 2017; *b* Durham, 10 Sept. 1964; *s* of Alan and Elisabeth Ritchey; *m* 1992, Alison Charlewood; one *s* one *d. Educ:* Royal Grammar Sch., Newcastle upon Tyne; Trinity Coll., Cambridge (MA; PhD 1992); Stanford Univ. (MS). CEng 1995; FIMechE 2014; FREng 2017. Rolls-Royce plc, 1992–98; Prof. of Engrg Design, Newcastle Univ., 1998–2000; Rolls-Royce plc: Hd of Res. and Technol. (Marine), 2000–02; Exec. Vice Pres., Engrg and Technol. (Commercial Marine), 2002–04; Chief Engr, Res. and Technol. (Civil), 2004–09; Hd of Aerospace Res. and Technol. 2009–10; Dir, Engrg and Technol. Defence UK, 2010–15; Engrg Dir, Defence Aerospace, 2015–17. *Address:* Rolls-Royce plc, PO Box 31, Derby DE24 8BJ. *T:* (01332) 247110. *E:* ian.ritchey@rolls-royce.com.

**RITCHIE**, family name of **Baron Ritchie of Dundee**.

**RITCHIE OF DUNDEE**, 6th Baron *cr* 1905; **Charles Rupert Rendall Ritchie**; drama and Alexander Technique teacher; *b* 15 March 1958; *s* of 5th Baron Ritchie of Dundee and Anne (*née* Johnstone); *S* father, 2008; one *s, b* 1994, by Irene Pels Leusden; *m* 2003, Celina Lucie Traill (marr. diss. 2005); one *s* one *d* (twins); *m* 2010, Mrs Harriet J. Draper (*née* Hague). *Educ:* Brickwall Sch., Northiam. LAMDA examiner. *Heir: s* Hon. Sebastian Ritchie, *b* 31 July 2004.

**RITCHIE, Andrew George**; QC 2009; *b* 4 April 1960; *s* of H. D. Ritchie and J. P. Ritchie; *m* 1st, 1988, Victoria Wilberforce (marr. diss. 2011); one *s* one *d;* 2nd, 2012, Charlotte Chaliha, MRCOG. *Educ:* Magdalene Coll., Cambridge (BA 1981). Admitted solicitor, 1984; called to the Bar, Inner Temple, 1985. Mem., Funding Appeal Cttee, LSC, 1998–2001. Member, Executive Committee: Assoc. of Personal Injury Lawyers, 1996–99; Chm., Personal Injury Bar Assoc., 2014–16. Man. Dir, Personal Injury Claims Arbitration Service, 2014–. Gen. Ed., Kemp & Kemp: Law Practice and Procedure, 2005–; Mem., Editl Bd, Kemp & Kemp on Quantum, 2004–18. *Publications:* Medical Evidence in Whiplash Cases, 1998; MIB Claims, 2001, 3rd edn 2008; Asbestos Claims, 2007; Manual Handling Claims, 2008; (ed) Guide to RTA Liability, 2009, 2nd edn 2012. *Recreations:* ski-ing, sailing. *Address:* 9 Gough Square, EC4A 3DG. *T:* (020) 7832 0500, *Fax:* (020) 7353 1344.

**RITCHIE, Maj.-Gen. Andrew Stephenson**, CBE 1999; Director, Goodenough College, 2006–18; *b* 30 July 1953; *er s* of Rev. Canon David Caldwell Ritchie and Dilys (*née* Stephenson); *m* 1981, Camilla Trollope; one *s* two *d. Educ:* Harrow County Boys' Sch.; RMA Sandhurst; Durham Univ. (BA Hons). Commnd RA 1973; regtl service, UK, Belize, Rhodesia, Germany, 1974–84; sc 1985; SO 2 Dir of Mil. Ops, MoD, 1986–87; 3 RHA, Germany, Cyprus, UK, 1988–90; SO 1 Dir of Army Plans, MoD, 1990–92; CO 1 RHA, UK, 1992–95; COS 3 (UK) Div./Multinational Div. SW, Bosnia, 1995–96; hcsc, 1997; Comdr RA 3 (UK) Div., 1997–98; Dir Personal Services (Army), 1998–2000; rcds, 2001; Dir Corporate Communications (Army), MoD, 2001–02; GOC 4th Div., 2002–03; Comdt, RMA Sandhurst, 2003–06. Chairman: Larkhill Equestrian Ltd, 2018–; Carthusia Ltd, 2019–. Trustee, Larkhill Racecourse, 2008–. Dir, Regular Forces Employment Assoc., 2010–. Chm. Govs, The Charterhouse, 2018–. Mem. Council, Marlborough Coll., 2006–15; Gov., Princess Helena Coll., 2006–14. *Recreations:* opera, racing, gardening. *Address:* The Old Farmhouse, Mill Lane, Poulshot, Devizes, Wilts SN10 1SA. *E:* andrew.ritchie3007@gmail.com. *Club:* Boodle's.

**RITCHIE, Anna**, OBE 1997; PhD; FSA; consultant archaeologist; *b* 28 Sept. 1943; *d* of George and Margaret Bachelier; *m* 1968, Graham Ritchie; one *s* one *d. Educ:* UC, Cardiff (BA Hons); Univ. of Edinburgh (PhD 1970; Hon. Fellow, 2000). FSA 1977. Member, Ancient Monuments Bd for Scotland, 1990–99. Trustee: Nat. Museums of Scotland, 1993–2003; BM, 1999–2004. Vice-Pres., Soc. of Antiquaries of London, 1988–92; Pres., Soc. of Antiquaries of Scotland, 1990–93. Hon. FSAScot 2007. *Publications:* Orkney and Shetland, 1985; Picts, 1989; Viking Scotland, 1993; Perceptions of the Picts from Eumenius to John Buchan, 1994; Prehistoric Orkney, 1995; Orkney, 1996; Shetland, 1997; Iona, 1997; Govan and its Carved Stones, 1999; Hogbacks at Govan and Beyond, 2004; Killellan Farm, Ardnave, Islay, 2005; On the Fringe of Neolithic Europe: excavation of a chambered cairn, Holm of Papa Westray, Orkney, 2009; A Shetland Antiquarian: James Thomas Irvine of Yell, 2011; with G. Ritchie: Scotland: archaeology and early history, 1981; Scotland: an Oxford archaeological guide, 1998; with I. Scott: People of Early Scotland from Contemporary Images, 2006; Pictish and Viking-Age Carvings from Shetland, 2009. *Address:* 11 Powderhall Rigg, Edinburgh EH7 4GG. *T:* (0131) 556 1128.

**RITCHIE, Cameron**; President, Law Society of Scotland, 2011–12 (Vice President, 2010–11); *b* Paisley, 25 Sept. 1952; *s* of Alexander McPherson Ritchie and Jane Cameron Ritchie (*née* Brown); *m* 1981, Hazel Fraser; two *s. Educ:* John Neilson Instn, Paisley; Univ. of Glasgow (LLB). Admitted as solicitor Advocate in criminal law, 1995; Procurator Fiscal, Stirling and Alloa, 1996–2002; Area Procurator Fiscal, Fife, 2002–10. *Recreations:* golf, walking. *Address:* 9 Coxburn Brae, Bridge of Allan FK9 4PS. *T:* (01786) 834200. *E:* cameron3@btinternet.com.

**RITCHIE, Prof. David Alastair**, DPhil; FInstP; Professor of Experimental Physics, Cavendish Laboratory, University of Cambridge, since 2002; Fellow, Robinson College, Cambridge, since 1991; Professor of Semiconductor Science and Technology, Swansea University, since 2018; *b* Watford, 11 March 1959; *s* of Charles and Patricia, (Betty), Ritchie; *m* 1989, Linda Elizabeth Miller (marr. diss. 2013); two *d. Educ:* Watford Grammar Sch. for Boys; Hertford Coll., Oxford (BA Physics 1980); Univ. of Sussex (DPhil Physics 1986). FInstP 2005. Res. Asst, Univ. of Sussex, 1984–85; University of Cambridge: Res. Associate, 1985–91; Asst Dir of Res., 1991–99; Reader of Exptl Physics, 1999–2002; Dep. Hd, Cavendish Lab., 2009–13. Gov., Watford GS for Boys, 2005–. Tabor Medal and Prize, Inst. of Physics, 2008. *Publications:* contrib. jl papers on physics and technol. of III–V semiconductors. *Recreations:* reading, running, cycling, exploring the Gower peninsula and northern Portugal, playing the guitar (badly). *Address:* Cavendish Laboratory, J. J. Thomson Avenue, Cambridge CB3 0HE. *T:* (01223) 337331, *Fax:* (01223) 337271. *E:* dar11@cam.ac.uk.

**RITCHIE, David Robert**, CB 2001; Regional Director, Government Office for West Midlands, 1994–2001; *b* 10 March 1948; *s* of late James Ritchie and Edith Ritchie (*née* Watts); *m* 1989, Joan Gibbons. *Educ:* Manchester Grammar School; St John's College, Cambridge (BA, MA). Min. of Transport, 1970; DoE, 1970; Regl Dir, W Midlands Regl Office, Depts of the Envmt and Transport, 1989–94. Mem., First-tier Tribunal, Gen. Regulatory Chamber (formerly Adjudication Panel for England), 2002–18; Chm., Nat. Urban Forestry Unit, 2003–06. Mem., Bishop's Council, Dio. Birmingham, 1992–2004. Dir, Univ. Hosp. Birmingham NHS Foundn Trust, 2006–13. Gov., The Queen's Foundn, 2013–16 (Vice-Pres., 2002–07; Pres., 2007–13). *Recreations:* fell-walking, cooking. *Address:* 14 Ashfield Road, Birmingham B14 7AS.

**RITCHIE, Prof. Donald Andrew**, CBE 2005; DL; FRSE; Professor of Genetics, University of Liverpool, 1978–2003, now Emeritus; Deputy Chairman, Environment Agency, 2001–05; *b* 9 July 1938; *s* of Andrew Ritchie and Winifred Laura (*née* Parkinson); *m* 1962, Margaret Jeanne (*née* Collister); one *s* one *d. Educ:* Latymer Sch., London; Univ. of Leicester (BSc 1959); RPMS, London (PhD 1964). FRSB (FIBiol 1978), CBiol 1985; FRSE 1979. MRC Microbial Genetics Res. Unit, London, 1959–64; Res. Associate, Biophysics Dept, Johns Hopkins Univ., 1964–66; Lectr, 1966–72, Sen. Lectr, 1972–78, Virology Dept, Univ. of Glasgow; Pro-Vice-Chancellor, Liverpool Univ., 1992–95. Royal Soc. Leverhulme Trust Sen. Res. Fellow, 1991–92; Royal Acad. of Engrg Vis. Prof., Univ. of Liverpool, 2004–06. Member: Science Bd, SERC, 1989–92; Biotechnol. Jt Adv. Bd, DTI, 1990–95; NERC, 1990–95; Bd, Envmt Agency, 1998–2005. Mem. Council, Marine Biol Assoc., 1991–94; Professional Affairs Officer, Soc. for Gen. Microbiol., 1998–2001; Mem., Environment Cttee, 1996–99 and Finance Cttee, 1996–2002, Inst. of Biol. Chairman: Mil. Educn Cttee, Liverpool Univ., 1995–2006; Council of Mil. Educn Cttees of UK Univs, 2004–12; Mem., Mil. Educn Cttee, City of Edinburgh Univs, 2012–18. Member: Council, Liverpool Sch. of Tropical Medicine, 1993–99; RFCA (formerly TAVRA), NW England & IOM, 1995–2011; Bd of Mgt, Shrewsbury House Youth Club, Everton, 2007–. Chairman: Merseyside Reg., NACF, 1996–2000; Liverpool Scottish Mus. Trust, 1999–. Trustee, RSE Scotland Foundn, 2009–19 (Chm., 2013–19; Hon. Sec., 2019–). Governor: IOM Internat. Business Sch., 2000–11; Shrewsbury Sch., 2003–12 (Dep. Chm., 2007–12). One-man show of paintings, Shrewsbury Sch., 2012. Mem., SE Scotland Cttee, St John Priory of Scotland, 2012–; MStJ 2016. Hon. Col Liverpool Univ. OTC, 2001–07. DL Merseyside, 2002. *Publications:* (with T. H. Pennington) Molecular Virology, 1971; (with K. M. Smith) Introduction to Virology, 1980; pubns on microbial molecular genetics and environmental microbiology in learned jls. *Recreations:* painting, gardening, walking, photography. *Address:* Allanbank, Gavinton, Duns, Berwickshire TD11 3QT. *T:* (01361) 882547. *E:* donald.ritchie167@btinternet.com. *Club:* Athenæum (Liverpool).

**RITCHIE, Sister Frances Dorothy Lyon, (Sister Frances Dominica)**, OBE 2006; DL; FRCN; Sister of All Saints Community, since 1966; Founder: Helen House Children's Hospice, 1982; Douglas House, Respice for Young People, 2003; *b* 21 Dec. 1942; *d* of Thomas Norman Ritchie and Margaret Armstrong Ritchie (*née* Paterson). *Educ:* Cheltenham Ladies' Coll.; Hosp. for Sick Children, Gt Ormond St (RSCN); Middlesex Hosp. (RGN). FRCN 1983. Entered Soc. of All Saints, Sisters of the Poor, 1966; professed, 1969; Mother Superior, 1977–89. Trustee: Helen & Douglas House, 2002–15; The Porch, 2016–; Founder and Trustee, REACT, 2017–; Pres., FACT (Falsely Accused Carers, Teachers and other professionals), 2016–. Patron, Internat. Children's Palliative Care Network. Hon. FRCPCH 1998. MUniv Open, 2003; Hon. Dr: Oxford Brookes, 2003; London Metropolitan, 2004; Northampton, 2012. DL Oxon, 2001. *Publications:* Just My Reflection: helping families to do things their way when their child dies, 1997, 2nd edn 2007. *Recreations:* dog walking at dawn, being alone in a country cottage with no television, telephone or alarm clock for a week at a time, friends. *Address:* All Saints, 15A Magdalen Road, Oxford OX4 1RW. *T:* 07762 019357.

**RITCHIE, Hamish Martin Johnston**; Chairman, Marsh & McLennan Companies UK Ltd, 2000–04; *b* 22 Feb. 1942; *s* of late James Martin Ritchie and Noreen Mary Louise Ritchie; *m* 1967, Judith Carol Young; one *s* one *d. Educ:* Loretto Sch.; Christ Church, Oxford (MA). Man. Dir, Hogg Robinson UK Ltd, 1980–81 (Dir, 1974–80); Chairman: Bowring London Ltd, 1981–93; Marsh Mercer Holdings Ltd (formerly Bowring Gp), 1983–; and Chief Exec., Bowring Marsh & McLennan Ltd, 1985–96; Marsh Europe SA, 1992–2001; Dir, Marsh Ltd, 1997–2005. Director: RAC, 1990–99; Halma plc, 1997–2002. Chm., BIBA, 2002–04 (Dep. Chm., 1987–91); Pres., Insurance Inst. of London, 1995–96. CCMI (CIMgt 1985). Trustee: Princess Royal Trust for Carers, 2000–05; Tower Hill Improvement Trust, 2005–11; Chm., Oldhurst Trust, 2003–. Member: Barbican Centre Cttee, 2005–06; Develt Council, Historic Royal Palaces, 2005–06. Gov., English Nat. Ballet, 2001–05. *Recreations:* music, golf. *Address:* Oldhurst, 35 Bulstrode Way, Gerrards Cross, Bucks SL9 7QT. *T:* (01753) 883262. *Clubs:* MCC, Royal Automobile; Royal & Ancient Golf (St Andrews) (Capt. 2008–09), Denham Golf, Rye Golf.

*See also S. M. Ritchie.*

**RITCHIE, Ian Carl**, CBE 2000; RA 1998; RIBA; RIAI; Principal, Ian Ritchie Architects, since 1981; *b* 24 June 1947; *s* of Christopher Charles Ritchie and Mabel Berenice (*née* Long); *m* 1972, Jocelyne van den Bossche; one *s. Educ:* Varndean, Brighton; Liverpool Sch. of Architecture; Polytechnic of Central London Sch. of Architecture (Dip. Arch. distinction). ARB 1979. With Foster Associates, 1972–76; in private practice in France, 1976–78; Partner, Chrysalis Architects, 1979–81; Co-founder and Dir, 1981–87, Consultant, 1987–90, RFR (Rice Francis Ritchie); Reg. German architect, 1993–99, 2019–. Major works include: Ecology Gall., Nat. Hist. Mus.; B8, Stockley Park, London; Roy Square housing, Limehouse, London; Eagle Rock House, E Sussex; Culture Centre, Albert, France; roofs, Louvre Sculpture Courts, and Louvre Pyramids, Paris; roof and glass facades, Mus. Nat. de Science, Techniques et de l'Industrie, La Villette, Paris; pharmacy, Boves, France; Fluy House, Picardy, France; Terrasson Cultural Greenhouse, France; HV Pylons for EDF, France (Millennium Product award, Design Council, 1999); glass towers, Centro de Arte Reina Sofia, Madrid; Leipzig Glashalle; Bermondsey Underground Stn, Crystal Palace Concert Platform (Millennium Product award, Design Council, 1999), and Wood Lane Underground Stn, London (Stn Excellence, HSBC Rail Bus. Awards, Rail Stn of Year Award, Nat. Transport Awards, 2009); Scotland's Home of the Future, Glasgow (Regeneration of Scotland Supreme Award, 2000); White City, London; Spire Monument, Dublin; Internat. Rowing Centre, Royal Albert Dock, London; Light Monument, Milan; Plymouth Th. Royal Production Centre; RSC Courtyard Th.; King Solomon Acad., Westminster; Sainsbury Wellcome Centre, UCL (Design Through Innovation Award, 2017); Dylon Housing, London; RSC The Other Place; Mercers' Walk, Covent Gdn (Bldg of Year, Constructing Excellence awards, 2017); RAM Th. and Recital Hall (RICS Projects of Year Award, 2017; RIBA London Bldg of Year, RIBA Nat. Award, RIBA London Award, FX Internat. Interior Design Award, UK Wood Award, UK Property Award, British Construction Industry Award, New London Architecture Award, 2018;

Architecture Award, Retrofit Award, Architects' Jl, 2018; Civic Trust Award, Peter Lord Award, Inst. Acoustics, Specification Award, Architects' Jl, World Architecture Community Award, 2019); Farsons Business Park, Malta; LSHTM; works in public collections: RA; Centro de Arte Reina Sofia, Madrid; Lodz Gall., Poland; Hugh Lane Gall., Dublin. Mem., Royal Fine Art Commn, now CABE, 1995–2001, now Emeritus Comr; Mem., Design and Built Envmt Cttees, Royal Commn for the Exhibn of 1851, 1999–2011. Architectural Adviser: Natural Hist. Mus., 1991–95; to the Lord Chancellor, 1999–2004; BM, 2004–06; Adviser: Ove Arup Foundn, 2002–; to Pres., Columbia Univ., NY, 2008–; to Centre for Urban Sci. and Progress, New York Univ., 2013–15; Backstage Trust, 2013–. External examiner, RIBA, 1986–. Vis. Prof., Vienna Technical Univ., 1994–95; Special Prof., Sch. of Civil Engrg, Leeds Univ., 2001–04; Prof. of Architecture, RA, 2005–12; Hon. Vis. Prof., Liverpool Univ., 2009–. Mem., Technology Foresight Construction Panel, 1996–98. Chm., Europan UK, 1997–2003. Mem. Council, 1999, 2005–07, 2014–16, Chm., Collections and Library Cttee, 2000–09, RA. Council Mem., Steel Construction Inst., 1994–97; Architects' Council of Europe rep. on European Construction Technology Platform, 2005–07. Gov., RSC, 2000–16 (Mem., Internat. Council, 2005–11). Chairman: RIBA Stirling Awards, 2006; RIAS Andrew Doolan Award, 2009. FRSA; Fellow, Soc. of Facade Engrg, 2012; Mem., Akademie der Künste, Berlin, 2013. Hon. FRIAS 2009; Hon. FAIA 2010; Hon. FRAM 2018. Hon. DLitt Westminster, 2000; Hon. Dr Milan Poly., 2019. Tableau de l'Ordre des Architectes Français, 1982; Architectural Design Silver Medal, 1982; IRITECNA (Italian state construction industry) European Prize, 1992; Eric Lyons Meml Award, for European housing, 1992; Robert Matthew Award, Commonwealth Assoc. of Architects, 1994; Du Pont Benedictus Award, 1997; AIA Awards, 1997, 2003, 2008; Civic Trust Awards, 1993, 1998, 2003 (two); Arts Bldg of the Year Award, Royal Fine Art Commn, 1998; Stephen Lawrence Prize, 1998; RIBA Awards, 1998 (two), 2000, 2003, 2004, 2007, 2018; Concrete Soc. Award, 2000; Acad. d'Architecture Grand Médaille d'Argent, 2000; Sports Bldg of the Year Award, Royal Fine Art Commn, 2000; Internat. Outstanding Structure Award, IABSE, 2000; Special Award, 2000, Civil Engrg Award, 2002, Major Bldg Project of the Year, 2016, British Construction Industry; Historic Structures Award, 2002, Structural Achievement Award, 2002, ICE; Bldg of the Year Award, Royal Fine Art Commn, 2003; Innovation in Copper Award, Copper Develt Assoc. (UK), 2000, 2003; HSBC Rail Business Award, 2009; UK Nat. Winner, 3R Awards, 2011; RAIA Award, 2011; BCO Award, 2011; Nat. Winner, BCI Awards, 2016; Overall Winner, 2016, Best Façade Design and Engrg, 2016, Leading Eur. Architecture Forum; Midland Counties Regl Awards Arts Winner, IStructE, 2016; AR Future Projects Commendation, 2017; German Design Award - Architecture, 2018. *Publications:* (Well) Connected Architecture, 1994; The Biggest Glass Palace in the World, 1997; Ian Ritchie Technoecology, 1999; Plymouth Theatre Royal TR2, 2003; The Spire, 2004; The RSC Courtyard Theatre, 2006; The Leipzig Glass Hall, 2007; Lines: poems and etchings, 2010; (with Roger Connah) Being: an architect, 2014. *Recreations:* art, swimming, reading, writing, theatre, supporting the Reds. *Address:* (office) 110 Three Colt Street, E14 8AZ. *T:* (020) 7338 1100. *E:* iritchie@ianritchiearchitects.co.uk.

**RITCHIE, Ian Charles Stewart;** festival director, artistic curator and music specialist; Artistic Director, Setúbal Music Festival, since 2010; *b* 19 June 1953; *s* of Kenneth John Stewart Ritchie and Wanda Margaret Angela Ritchie; *m* 1st, 1977, Angela Mary (marr. diss. 1993); two *d*; 2nd, 1997, Kathryn Alexandra McDowell, *qv. Educ:* Stowe Sch.; Royal Coll. of Music; Trinity Coll., Cambridge (MA); Guildhall Sch. of Music and Drama. General Manager, City of London Sinfonia, 1979–84; Artistic Dir, City of London Fest., 1983–84; Man. Dir, Scottish Chamber Orchestra, 1984–93; Gen. Dir, Opera North, 1993–94; arts mgt consultant, 1994–2005; Dir, City of London Fest., 2005–13. Artistic Co-Dir, 1988–93, Dir, 2004–05, St Magnus Fest., Orkney; Artistic Dir, The Musical Brain, 2010–. Director/Trustee: Tenebrae Choir; City Music Foundn; Music Action Internat. Vis. Prof., London Metropolitan Univ., 2012–. *Recreations:* wine, walking and song. *Address:* 167 Liverpool Road, N1 0RF. *T:* (020) 7837 6665. *E:* ian@ianritchie.org. *Clubs:* MCC; New (Edinburgh).

**RITCHIE, Ian Cleland,** CBE 2003; FRSE; CEng, FREng, FBCS; Chairman: Computer Application Services Ltd, since 2005; Krotos Ltd, since 2013; Tern plc, since 2017; Wyld Networks, since 2019; *b* 29 June 1950; *s* of late Alexander Ritchie and Jean Russell Ritchie (*née* Fowler); *m* 1974, Barbara Allan Cowie (*d* 2001); one *s* one *d. Educ:* Heriot-Watt Univ. (BSc Hons Computer Sci. 1973). CEng 1991; FBCS 1992. Develt Engr/ Manager, ICL, 1974–83; CEO and Man. Dir, Office Workstations Ltd (OWL), Edinburgh and Seattle, 1984–92 (OWL pioneered develt of hypertext (web-browsing) technol.; sold to Panasonic, 1989); special project, Heriot-Watt Univ., 1992–94. Chairman: Voxar Ltd, 1994–2002 (non-exec. Dir, 1994–2004); Orbital Software Gp Ltd, 1995–2001; Active Navigation (formerly Multicosm) Ltd, 1997–2004; Digital Bridges Ltd, 2000–03 (Dir, 2003–05); Sonaptic Ltd, 2003–06; Interactive University Ltd, 2003–08; Scapa Ltd, 2006–10; Caspian Learning Ltd, 2007–11; Interactive Design Inst. Ltd, 2007–15; Iomart plc, 2008–18; Blipfoto Ltd, 2012–15; Cogbooks Ltd, 2013–16; Red Fox Media, 2012–16; Dep. Chm., Vis Entertainment (formerly Vis Interactive) plc, 1995–2004. Director: Northern Venture Trust PLC, 1996–2001; Scran, 1996–2004; Indigo Active Vision Systems Ltd, 1997–2000; Epic Gp PLC, 1998–2004; Scottish Enterprise, 1999–2005; Channel 4 TV, 2000–06; Bletchley Park Trust, 2000–09; Scottish Science Trust, 2001–03; Mindwarp Pavilion Ltd, 2001–02; Dynamic Earth, 2004–18 (Chm., 2010–18); GO Gp, 2008–12; ShotScope Ltd, 2017–. Chairman: Generation Science, 2005–09; Connect Scotland, 2006–08. Director: Edinburgh Internat. Film Fest., 2002–10; Nat. Museums Scotland (formerly Nat. Museums of Scotland), 2003–10; Edinburgh Internat. Sci. Fest., 2005–19. Member: PPARC, 1999–2002; SHEFC, 2002–05; SFC, 2005–07; Scottish Council for Develt and Industry, 2018–. Dir, Scottish Inst. for Enterprise, 2001–06. Trustee: Nominet Trust, 2008–14; Saltire Foundn, 2009–17; Dave Hume Trust, 2008–18. Pres., BCS, 1998–99; Vice Pres., Business, RSE, 2012–16; Hon. Treas., RAEng, 2012–16. Hon. Prof., Heriot-Watt Univ., 1993–. FREng 2001; FRSE 2003. DUniv Heriot-Watt, 2000; Hon. DSc Robert Gordon, 2001; Hon. DBA Abertay Dundee, 2002; Dr *hc* Edinburgh, 2003. *Publications:* New Media Publishing: opportunities from the digital revolution, 1996; contrib. various technol. papers and articles. *Recreations:* travel, theatre and arts, web-browsing. *Address:* Coppertop, Green Lane, Lasswade EH18 1HE. *T:* (0131) 663 9486, 07973 214024. *W:* www.coppertop.co.uk.

**RITCHIE, Ian Kristensen,** FRCSE, FRCSE(Orth), FRCPE; Consultant Orthopaedic Surgeon, Forth Valley, 1992–2012; President, Royal College of Surgeons of Edinburgh, 2012–15 (Vice-President, 2009–12); *b* Syria, 2 Jan. 1953; *s* of James Ritchie and Mette Ritchie (*née* Kristensen); *m* 1986, Alyson M. Dow; three *d. Educ:* Lochaber High Sch.; Gordon Schs, Huntly; Univ. of Aberdeen (MB ChB 1977). FRCSE 1984; FRCSE(Orth) 1990. Surgeon Lieut, RN, 1978–83; Surgical Trng, Aberdeen, 1983–92. Convener, Trainer Trng, 1996–2009, Dir, Surgical Trng, 2005–09, RCSE. Non-exec. Dir, NHS Greater Glasgow and Clyde Health Bd. Hon. FRACS; Hon. FCSHK. *Recreations:* music, family, walking. *Address:* 13 Abercromby Place, Stirling FK8 2QP.

**RITCHIE, Ian Russell,** OBE 2018; Chief Executive, Rugby Football Union, 2012–17; Chairman, Premiership Rugby, since 2018; *b* 27 Nov. 1953; *s* of Hugh Russell Ritchie and Sheelah Ritchie; *m* 1982, Jill Evelyn Middleton-Walker; two *s. Educ:* Leeds Grammar Sch.; Trinity Coll., Oxford (MA Jurisprudence). Called to the Bar, Middle Temple, 1976. Practised at the Bar, 1976–78; Industrial Relations Advr, EEF, 1978–80; Granada TV, 1980–88 (Head of Prodn Services, 1987–88); Dir of Resources, 1988–91, Man. Dir, 1991–93, Tyne Tees TV; Gp Dep. Chief Exec., Yorkshire Tyne Tees TV, 1992–93; Managing Director: Nottingham Studios, Central Television, 1993–94; London News Network, 1994–96; Chief Exec., 1996, Chief Operating Officer, 1996–97, Channel 5 Broadcasting; Partner and Man. Dir, Russell Reynolds Associates, 1997–98; CEO, Middle East Broadcasting, 1998–2000; CEO, Associated Press Television News, 2000–03; Vice-Pres., Global Business, and Man. Dir, Associated Press Internat., 2003–05; Chief Exec., AELTC, 2005–12. Consultant, Onside Law, 2018–. Director: West Ham United plc, 1999–2002; Wembley Nat. Stadium Ltd, 2008–11; Ind. Dir, Football League Ltd, 2004–12. Member Council: LTA, 2006–09; FA, 2008–12; World Rugby Council, 2016–17; Ryder Cup Cttee, 2019–. Chm., Vincent's Appeal Trust Co., 2018–. FRSA. *Recreations:* golf, tennis, theatre, music. *Address:* Virginia Water, Surrey. *Club:* Vincent's (Oxford).

**RITCHIE, Jean Harris, (Mrs G. T. K. Boney);** QC 1992; *b* 6 April 1947; *d* of late Walter Weir Ritchie and Lily (*née* Goodwin); *m* 1976, Guy Thomas Knowles Boney, *qv*; two *s. Educ:* King's Coll., London (LLB); McGill Univ., Montreal (LLM); Open Univ. (BA 2014). Called to the Bar, Gray's Inn, 1970 (Churchill Schol., 1968; Bencher, 2000); on Western Circuit; a Recorder, 1993–2009; Head of Chambers, 2000–04. Chairman: Clunis Inquiry (care in the community for patients suffering from schizophrenia), 1993–94; Inquiry into Clinical Governance (arising from actions of Rodney Ledward), 1999–2000. Member: Supreme Ct Rule Cttee, 1993–97; Judicial Studies Bd, 1998–2001 (Mem., Civil Cttee, 1997–2001); QC Selection Panel, 2006–12. Chm. Council, Winchester Cathedral, 2011–. Member: Med. Ethics Cttee, King Edward VII Hosp., 2003–16; City Panel, Treloar Trust, 2005–08. Trustee, Bromley Trust, 2007–18. Fellow, Winchester Coll., 2008–18. Chm. Govs, Norman Court Prep. Sch., W Tytherley, 1996–2000. *Publications:* (contrib.) Safe Practice in Obstetrics and Gynaecology, ed R. V. Clements, 1994. *Recreations:* family, grandchildren, dog walking. *Address:* King's Head House, Stockbridge, Hants SO20 6EU.

**RITCHIE, Dr John Hindle,** MBE 1985; architect; development management consultant; *b* 4 June 1937; *s* of Charles A. Ritchie; *m* 1963, Anne B. M. Leyland; two *d. Educ:* Royal Grammar School, Newcastle upon Tyne; Univ. of Liverpool (BArch Hons); Univ. of Sheffield (PhD Building Science). RIBA 1965. Served RN, 1956–58. Science Research Council, 1963–66; Town Planner, Liverpool City Council, 1966–69; Rowntree Housing Trust, Univ. of Liverpool, 1969–72; R&D Architect, Cheshire County Council, 1972–74; Asst County Planner (Envmt), Merseyside CC, 1974–80; Merseyside Development Corporation: Dir of Develt, 1980–85; Chief Exec. and Mem., 1985–91. Chm., Merseyside Educn Training Enterprise Ltd, 1986–91; Member: Merseyside Tourism Bd, 1986–88; Internat. Organising Cttee, Grand Regatta Columbus '92, 1986–92; Board: Gardners Row Business Centre, 1987–90; Merseyside Enterprise Trust, 1988–91; Instant Muscle Ltd, 1993–95; Merseyside Sculptors Guild, 1993–97; Wirral Community Healthcare Trust, 1993–95; Landscape Trust, 1996–2001. Mem., Lord Chancellor's Panel of Ind. Inspectors, 1994–2003; consultant inspector, Planning Inspectorate, 2003–05. Gov., Liverpool Community Coll., 1995–2011. Major projects include: natural resource management, pollution control, land reclamation and urban conservation progs and projects, Merseyside Strategic Plan; Liverpool South Docks and Riverside reclamation and develt, Liverpool Internat. Garden Fest., 1984 (Civic Trust Award); Landscape Inst. 75th Anniv. Award, 2004); Albert Dock Conservation (European Gold Medal, 1986; Civic Trust Jubilee Award, 1987). CCMI; CBIM; FRSA. *Publications:* scientific and planning papers on urban environment obsolescence and regeneration. *Address:* Cartref, 46 The Mount, Heswall, Wirral CH60 4RD. *E:* johnritchie37@talktalk.net.

**RITCHIE, Kathryn Alexandra;** see McDowell, K. A.

**RITCHIE, Dr Kenneth George Hutchison;** Chief Executive, Electoral Reform Society, 1997–2010 (Member, Board, since 2012); *b* 8 Dec. 1946; *s* of late William Ritchie and Margaret Morton Ritchie (*née* Hutchison); *m* 1985, Elizabeth Anne Black; one *s* one *d. Educ:* George Heriot's Sch., Edinburgh; Edinburgh Univ. (BSc); Aston Univ. (PhD 1981). Maths teacher, VSO, Tanzania, 1968–69; systems analyst, ICI, 1970–73; Hd, Internat. Service, UNA, 1976–83; Exec. Dir, Appropriate Health Resources and Technologies Action Gp, 1983–88; Dep. Dir, British Refugee Council, 1988–94; UK Dir, Intermediate Technol., 1994–96. Co-ordinator, All-Party Parly Human Rights Gp, 2011. Hon. Treas., War on Want, 1980–85; Treas., Western Sahara Campaign, 1984–. Mem., Council for Advancement of Arab-British Understanding, 1989–94. Dir, Make Votes Count, 1998–2010; Bd Mem., FairVote/Center for Voting and Democracy, Washington, 2004–10. Member: Exec. Cttee, Labour Campaign for Electoral Reform, 2010–; Republic, 2011–; Reform Foundn, 2011– (Chm., 2011–). Mem. (Lab), Daventry DC, 2016–. Contested (Lab): Beckenham, 1987 and 1992; Daventry, 1997. *Publications:* (with L. Baston) Don't Take No for an Answer: the 2011 referendum and the future of electoral reform, 2011; (contrib.) Electoral Systems, 2012; Fixing our Broken Democracy: the case for total representation, 2012; The Saharawi Struggle for Self-Determination: a history of the campaign in Britain, 2014; Total Representation: an electoral system to resolve Italy's democratic crisis, 2014; The Elephant in the House, 2015; The Reform Debates: an agenda for a better democracy, 2016. *Recreations:* golf, music, walking the dog. *Address:* 37 Kilsby Road, Barby, Rugby CV23 8TU. *T:* (01788) 890942.

**RITCHIE, Prof. Sir Lewis (Duthie),** Kt 2011; OBE 2001; FRSE; James Mackenzie Professor of General Practice, University of Aberdeen, since 1992; associate general practitioner, since 2012; *b* Fraserburgh, 26 June 1952; *s* of Lewis Duthie Ritchie and Sheila Gladys Ritchie; *m* 1978, Heather Skelton. *Educ:* Fraserburgh Acad.; Univ. of Aberdeen (BSc Chem. 1978; MB ChB (Commendation) 1978; MD 1993); Univ. of Edinburgh (MSc Community Medicine 1982). DRCOG 1980; FFPH (FFPHM 1993); FRCGP 1994; FRCPEd 1995; FBCS 2004; CEng 1993; CITP 2004. Principal GP, Peterhead Health Centre and Community Hosp., 1984–2012; Lectr in Gen. Practice, 1984–92, Hd, Dept of Gen. Practice and Primary Care, 1992–2007, Univ. of Aberdeen; Consultant in Public Health Medicine, Grampian Health Bd, 1987–92; Hon. Consultant in Public Health Medicine, 1993–2012 and 2014–, Dir of Public Health, 2012–14, NHS Grampian. Hon. Prof. of Primary Care and Public Health, Univ. of Highlands and Is, 2014–; Hon. Prof. of Gen. Practice, Univ. of Edinburgh, 2015–. Lectures: Richard Scott, Univ. of Edinburgh, 2007; James Mackenzie, RCGP, 2010; Stock Meml, Assoc. of Port Health Authorities, 2012; Fulton, RCGP W Scotland, 2012; DARE, FPH, 2014. Mem., Harveian Soc. FRSE 2016. Hon. FRCPGlas 2015; Hon. FRCSE 2017. John Perry Prize, BCS, 1991; Stokoe Award, RCGP, 1992; Blackwell Prize, Univ. of Aberdeen, 1995; Eric Elder Medal, Royal NZ Coll. of GPs, 2007; Provost Medal, RCGP NE Scotland, 2010. *Publications:* Computers in Primary Care, 1984, 2nd edn 1986 (trans. Spanish 1991); contrib. chapters, reports and papers on computers, telemedicine, cardiovascular prevention and mgt, cancer, community hosps and intermediate care, immunisation, community pharmacy, professionalism and excellence in medicine; nat. revs of health services and healthcare provision in Scotland.

*Recreations:* Church, classical music, art appreciation, reading (particularly military and naval history), dog walking, civilian gallantry, RNLI. *Address:* Cramond, 79 Strichen Road, Fraserburgh, Aberdeenshire AB43 9QJ. *T:* (01346) 510191, *Fax:* (01346) 515598. *E:* l.d.ritchie@abdn.ac.uk. *Clubs:* New, Aesculapian (Edinburgh).

**RITCHIE, Margaret;** *b* 25 March 1958; *d* of late John Ritchie and Rose Ritchie (*née* Drumm). *Educ:* Queen's Univ., Belfast (BA). Mem. (SDLP) Down DC, 1985–2009. Mem., NI Forum, 1996. Parly Asst to Edward McGrady, MP, 1987–2003. Mem. (SDLP) S Down, NI Assembly, 2003–12; Minister for Social Develt, NI, 2007–10. MP (SDLP) S Down, 2010–17; contested (SDLP) same seat, 2017. Mem., Envmt, Food and Rural Affairs Select Cttee, 2012–17. Leader, SDLP, 2010–11. Member: Ark Housing Assoc., NI, 2017–; Cttee for Health and Wellbeing, 2017–.

*[Created a Baroness (Life Peer), 2019 but title not gazetted at time of going to press.]*

**RITCHIE, Margaret Claire;** Headmistress of Queen Mary School, Lytham, 1981–98; *b* 18 Sept. 1937; *d* of Roderick M. Ritchie, Edinburgh. *Educ:* Leeds Girls' High Sch.; Univ. of Leeds (BSc); London Univ. (PGCE). Asst Mistress, St Leonards Sch., St Andrews, 1960–64; Head of Science Dept, Wycombe Abbey Sch., High Wycombe, 1964–71; Headmistress, Queenswood Sch., 1972–81. JP Fylde, 1991–99, Preston PSD, 1999–2007. *Address:* 29 Walmer Road, Lytham St Annes, Lancs FY8 3HL.

**RITCHIE, Peter,** FCCA; Head of Finance, Fife Council, 1995–2001; *b* 16 March 1951. *Educ:* Kirkland High Sch.; Buckhaven High Sch.; Dundee Coll. of Commerce. FCCA 1975. Fife CC, 1969–75; Fife Regional Council, 1975–2001: Chief Accountant, 1980–84; Sen. Asst Dir of Finance, 1984–88; Dep. Dir of Finance, 1988–95. *Recreations:* travelling, hill-walking, gardening, theatre, cinema, photography.

**RITCHIE, Shirley Anne;** *see* Anwyl, Her Honour S. A.

**RITCHIE, Stuart Martin;** QC 2012; a Recorder, since 2018; *b* Beaconsfield, 27 July 1970; *s* of Hamish Martin Johnston Ritchie, *qv*; *m* 2001, Victoria Maclean; one *s* one *d*. *Educ:* Radley Coll., Abingdon; Christ Church, Oxford (BA Mod Langs 1993); Coll. of Law (CPE 1994). Called to the Bar, Middle Temple, 1995, Bencher, 2014; in practice as a barrister, Littleton Chambers, 1996–2016, Fountain Court Chambers, 2016–. Mediator. *Publications:* Fiduciary Duties: directors and employees, 2008, 2nd edn 2015. *Recreations:* classical music, piano and organ, golf, trustee of Gerald Finzi charitable trust and other private charities. *Address:* Fountain Court Chambers, Fountain Court, Temple, EC4Y 9DH. *T:* (020) 7583 3335. *E:* smr@fountaincourt.co.uk. *Clubs:* Hurlingham; Denham Golf, Rye Golf, Royal and Ancient Golf.

**RITCHIE, Susan Rosemary;** *see* Foister, S. R.

**RITCHIE, Prof. William,** OBE 1994; PhD; FRSGS; FRICS; FRSE; Director, Aberdeen Institute of Coastal Science and Management, King's College, University of Aberdeen, 2002–11; *b* 22 March 1940; *s* of Alexander Ritchie and Rebecca Smith Ritchie; *m* 1965, Elizabeth A. Bell; two *s* one *d*. *Educ:* Glasgow Univ. (BSc, PhD 1966). FRSGS 1980; FRSE 1982; FRICS 1989. Research Asst, Glasgow Univ., 1963; Aberdeen University: Lectr, 1964–72; Sen. Lectr, 1972–79; Prof., 1979–95; Dean, 1988–89; Vice Principal, 1989–95; Vice-Chancellor, Lancaster Univ., 1995–2002; Interim Dir, Macaulay Inst., Aberdeen, 2006. Post-doctoral Vis. Prof. and Hon. Prof. appts in geog. and coastal geog., Louisiana State Univ., USA, at various times, 1971–95; Adjunct Prof., World Maritime Univ., Malmo, 2003–. Chm., Scottish Aquaculture Res. Forum, 2003–. DUniv Stirling, 2003; Hon. DSc Lancaster, 2003. *Publications:* Mapping for Field Scientists, 1977; Surveying and Mapping for Field Scientists, 1988, 4th edn 1996; The Environmental Impact of the Wreck of the Braer, 1994; numerous papers mainly in jls of physical and coastal geog. and envmtl mgt.

**RITTER, Prof. Mary Alice,** OBE 2014; DPhil; FRCPath, FRSB, FCGI; Professor of Immunology, Imperial College London, 1991–2011, now Emeritus; International Ambassador, EIT Climate-KIC, since 2015 (Chief Executive Officer, 2010–14); *b* 19 Dec. 1943; *d* of Douglas and Iris Buchanan Smith; *m* 1st, 1967, James Ritter (marr. diss. 1973); 2nd, 1976, Roger Morris; three *s*. *Educ:* Berkhamsted Sch. for Girls; St Hilda's Coll., Oxford (BA Hons Zool. 1966; Dip. Physical Anthropol. 1967; MA 1971); Wolfson Coll., Oxford (DPhil 1971). FRCPath 2006. FCGI 2006. Res. Associate, Univ. of Conn, 1976–78; Res. Fellow, ICRF, 1978–84; Royal Postgraduate Medical School, London, later Imperial College, London: Lectr in Immunol., 1982–86; Sen. Lectr, 1986–88; Reader, 1988–91; Vice Dean (Educn), 1992–97; Asst Vice Principal (Postgrad. Medicine), 1998–2000; Dir, Grad. Sch. of Life Scis and Medicine, 1999–2006; Hd, Dept of Immunol., 2004–06; Pro-Rector: for Postgrad. Affairs, 2004–07; for Internat. Affairs, 2005–11. Mem. Council, and Chm. Scientific Adv. Panel, Action Res., 1997–2000; Member: Non-Clin. Trng and Career Develt Panel, MRC, 2005–09; Non-Clin. Careers Cttee, Acad. of Med. Scis, 2006–11; Prime Minister's Initiative for Higher Educn, 2006–11. Chm., Evaluation Panel, UK-India Educn and Res. Initiative, 2006–08; Vice Chm., Council for Doctoral Educn, European Univs Assoc., 2007–12; Chm., External Adv. Bd, Res. Councils UK Vitae Prog., 2008–10 (Chm., Annual Conf., UKGRAD Prog., subseq. Vitae Prog., 2005–10). Member: AgroParisTech Council, 2007–12; Internat. Adv. Panel, A*Star Grad. Acad., Singapore, 2007–12; Internat. Panel of Advrs, Inst. of Advanced Studies, Singapore, 2008–; Mgt Bd, GlobalTech, 2008–11; Pro Tem Gov. Bd, Lee Kong Chian Sch. of Medicine, 2010–12; Rectors' Bd, League of Eur. Res. Univs, 2010–11; Strategic Cttee, Univ. Pierre et Marie Curie, Paris VI, 2011–15; Res., Innovation and Sci. Policy Experts Adv. Panel, Directorate Gen. for Res. and Innovation, Eur. Commn, 2015–; Fellowship Evaluation Panel, Nat. Res. Foundn, Singapore, 2015–; Adv. Bd, Bernal Inst., Univ. of Limerick, 2018–. FRSA 2004. *Publications:* (with I. N. Crispe) The Thymus, 1992 (trans. Japanese 1993); contrib. numerous articles to peer-reviewed scientific learned jls. *Recreations:* travelling, gardening, cycling, biography, baroque music, ballet, opera. *Address:* EIT Climate-KIC, 34–37 Liverpool Street, EC2M 7PP. *E:* m.ritter@imperial.ac.uk, mary.ritter@climate-kic.org.

**RITTERMAN, Dame Janet (Elizabeth),** DBE 2002; PhD; Vice-President, Royal College of Music, since 2005 (Director, 1993–2005); *b* 1 Dec. 1941; *d* of Charles Eric Palmer and Laurie Helen Palmer; *m* 1970, Gerrard Peter Ritterman (*d* 2015). *Educ:* North Sydney Girls' High Sch.; NSW State Conservatorium of Music; Univ. of Durham (BMus 1971); King's Coll. London (MMus 1977); Goldsmiths' Coll., Univ. of London (PhD 1985). Pianist, accompanist, chamber music player; Senior Lecturer in Music: Middlesex Poly., 1975–79; Goldsmiths' Coll., Univ. of London, 1980–87; Dartington College of Arts: Head of Music, 1987–90; Dean, Academic Affairs, 1988–90; Acting Principal, 1990–91; Principal, 1991–93; Hon. Vis. Prof. of Music Educn, Univ. of Plymouth, 1993–2005. Chm., Assoc. Bd of Royal Schs of Music (Publishing) Ltd, 1993–2005. Former Mem., music educn and arts orgns; Member: Arts Council, 2000–02 (Mem., Music Panel, 1992–98); DfES Adv. Cttee, Music and Dance Scheme, 2001–05; Chm., Postgrad. Cttee, AHRB, 2002–04 (Mem. Postgrad. Panel, 1999–2002); Mem., Nominating Cttee, AHRC, 2005–08. Member: Council, Royal Musical Assoc., 1994–2004 (Vice-Pres., 1998–2004); Bd, ENO, 1996–2004; Bd, NYO, 1999–2008; Bd of Dirs, The Voices Foundn, 2005–12; Adv. Council, Inst. of Germanic and Romance Studies, 2005–11, Inst. of Musical Res., 2006–14, Univ. of London; Adv. Bd, Inst. for Advanced Studies in the Humanities, Univ. of Edinburgh, 2005–13; Bd, Sch. of Advanced Study, Univ. of London, 2008–14; Vice-Pres., Nat. Assoc. of Youth Orchestras, 1993–2005. Chairman: Adv. Council, Arts Res. Ltd, 1997–2005; Fedn of British Conservatoires, 1998–2003; Arts Res. Bd, Fonds zur Förderung der wissenschaftlichen Forschung, Austria, 2009–17; Member: Wissenschaftsrat, Bundesministerium für Wissenschaft und Forschung, Austria, 2003–12; Bd of Dirs, Anglo-Austrian Soc., 2005–11 (Chm., 2019–); Conseil de fondation, Haute École de Musique Genève, Switzerland, 2009–; Aufsichtsrat, Fonds zur Förderung der wissenschaftlichen Forschung, Austria, 2015–. Strategic Develt Advr, Orpheus Inst., Ghent, Belgium, 2009–. Chancellor, Middlesex Univ., 2013– (Mem., Governing Body, 2006–13); Member: Governing Body: Heythrop Coll., 1996–2006; Dartington Coll. of Arts, 2005–08; Falmouth Univ. (formerly UC Falmouth), 2008–16 (Dep. Chm., 2013–16); RWCMD, 2010–16; Council, Goldsmiths Coll., later Goldsmiths, Univ. of London, 2002–07; Governor: Assoc. Bd, Royal Schs of Music, 1993–2005; Purcell Sch., 1996–2000; Plymouth Coll. of Art, 2016–. Mem., Nuffield Foundn Educn Adv. Cttee, 2007–10. Trustee: Countess of Munster Musical Trust, 1993–; Plymouth Chamber Music Trust, 2006–10; EU Chamber Orch., 2012–; Belcea Quartet Trust, 2012–. Mem. Ct, Musicians' Co., 2005–11. FRNCM 1996; Fellow: Nene Coll., 1997; Dartington Coll. of Arts, 1997; High Educn Acad., 2007; Heythrop Coll., Univ. of London, 2008; Goldsmiths, Univ. of London, 2009. Hon. RAM 1995; Hon. GSMD 2000; Hon. Sen. Fellow, RCA 2004. DUniv: Central England, 1996; Middx, 2005; Hon. DLitt Ulster, 2004; Hon. DMus: Sydney, 2010; Royal Coll. of Music, 2017. Ehrenkreuz für Wissenschaft und Kunst (1st cl.) (Austria), 2017. *Publications:* articles in learned jls, France and UK. *Recreations:* reading, theatre-going, country walking. *E:* jritterman@blueyonder.co.uk. *Club:* Athenæum.

**RITTNER, Luke Philip Hardwick,** CBE 2017; Chief Executive, Royal Academy of Dance (formerly of Dancing), since 1999; *b* 24 May 1947; *s* of late George Stephen Hardwick Rittner and Joane (*née* Thunder); *m* 1974, Corinna Frances Edholm; one *d*. *Educ:* Blackfriars School, Laxton; City of Bath Technical Coll.; Dartington Coll. of Arts; London Acad. of Music and Dramatic Art. Asst Administrator, Bath Festival, 1968–71, Jt Administrator, 1971–74, Administrative Director, 1974–76; Founder, and Dir, Assoc. for Business Sponsorship of the Arts, 1976–83; Sec. Gen., Arts Council of GB, 1983–90; Dir, Marketing and Communications, then Corporate Affairs, Sotheby's Europe, 1992–99. Chm., English Shakespeare Co., 1990–94. UK Cultural Dir, Expo '92, Seville; Corporate Advr on cultural sponsorship to: Eurotunnel; J. Sainsbury plc. Non-exec. Bd Mem., Carlton Television, 1991–93. Member: Adv. Council, V&A Museum, 1980–83; Music Panel, British Council, 1979–83; Drama Panel, 1992–94, 2007–09, 2012–13, Dance Panel, 2003–04, Olivier Awards; Council, and Chm., Exec. Bd, LAMDA, 1994–2017; Jury, Walpole Awards for Cultural Excellence, 2006–16; Arts and Media Honours Adv. Cttee, 2012–17; Judging Panel, Legacy 10 Awards, 2013–18; Founder Mem., Adv. Develt Bd, Cambridge Summer Music Fest., 2010–18. Chm., London Choral Soc., subseq. London Chorus, 1994–2005. Trustee: Bath Preservation Trust, 1968–73; Theatre Royal, Bath, 1979–82; City Ballet of London, 1997–2000; Foundn Trustee, Holburne Museum, Bath, 1981–83; Gov., Conservatoire for Dance and Drama, 2004–13. Patron, Dartington Coll. of Arts, 2002–18. Hon. DA Bath, 2004; Hon. DCL Durham, 2005. *Recreations:* the arts, people, travel. *Address:* Royal Academy of Dance, 36 Battersea Square, SW11 3RA. *Club:* Garrick.

**RIVA, Hilary,** OBE 2009; Chairman, Development Committee, British Fashion Council, 2009–10 (Chief Executive, 2005–09); *b* Mansfield, 3 April 1957; three *s*. *Educ:* Poly. of Central London (BA Hons Soc. Sci. 1984). Arcadia Group: Buying and Merchandising Controller, Topshop, 1980–90; Buying and Merchandising Dir, Burton Gp, 1990–96; Man. Dir, Evans, 1996–98; Man. Dir, Dorothy Perkins, Topshop, Evans, Principles, 1998–2000; Man. Dir, Evans, Wallis, Warehouse, Principles, 2000–01; Man. Dir, Rubicon Retail Ltd, 2001–05. Non-executive Director: Shaftesbury plc, 2010–19; London & Partners Ltd, 2011–17; Asos plc, 2014–; Shepherd Neame Ltd, 2016–. *Address:* Abbey House, Abbey Road, Faversham ME13 7BE. *T:* (01795) 834744.

**RIVERDALE,** 3rd Baron *cr* 1935, of Sheffield, co. York; **Anthony Robert Balfour;** Bt 1929; *b* 23 Feb. 1960; *s* of Hon. Mark Robin Balfour (*d* 1995) and Susan Ann Phillips (*d* 1996); *S* grandfather, 1998. *Educ:* Wellington. *Heir:* cousin Arthur Michael Balfour [*b* 24 Nov. 1938; *m* 1962, Rita Ann Farce; two *s* one *d*].

**RIVERS, Deborah Ann;** *see* Cadman, D. A.

**RIVERS, Kenneth John,** CEng, FIChemE, FEI; Chief Executive, Refining NZ, New Zealand, 2007–12; President, Institution of Chemical Engineers, 2018–19; *b* Harrogate, 14 Jan. 1952; *s* of John Francis Rivers and Hilda Anne Rivers; *m* 1982, Carole Ann Huggins; two *d*. *Educ:* Harrogate High Sch.; Trinity Hall, Cambridge (BA 1974; MA 1978). CEng 1980; FIChemE 2000. Gen. Manager/Refinery Manager, Shell UK Oil Ltd, 2000–07. Chair: Buncefield Standard Task Gp, 2006–07; Midstream Oil Sector Govt and Industry Task Force, 2014–16; Control of Major Accident Hazards Strategic Forum, 2014–. Pres., Council, UK Petroleum Industry Assoc., 2001–07. Hon. Treas., IChemE, 2014–18. FEI 2018. Hon. Fellow, Northtec: Tai Tokerau Wananga, NZ, 2012. *Recreations:* music, theatre, supporting Leeds United and All Blacks. *Address:* Cherry Cottage, Little Heath, Christelton, Chester CH3 7AN. *T:* (01244) 637587. *E:* ken.j.rivers@gmail.com.

**RIVERS, Valerie Lane-Fox P.;** *see* Pitt-Rivers.

**RIVETT, Dr Geoffrey Christopher;** Senior Principal Medical Officer, Department of Health (formerly of Health and Social Security), 1985–92; *b* 11 Aug. 1932; *s* of Frank Andrew James Rivett and Catherine Mary Rivett; *m* 1976, Elizabeth Barbara Hartman; two *s* by previous marriage. *Educ:* Manchester Grammar Sch.; Brasenose Coll., Oxford (MA 1st Cl. Hons Animal Physiol.); Univ. Coll. Hosp. (BM, BCh); FRCGP, DObst RCOG. House Officer, Radcliffe Inf., Oxford, 1957; House Phys., London Chest Hosp., 1958; RAMC, 1958–60; GP, Milton Keynes, 1960–72; DHSS, subseq. DoH, 1972–92. Vice Chm., Council of Govs, Homerton NHS Foundn Trust, 2007–13. Liveryman: Soc. of Apothecaries, 1981–; Co. of Barbers, 1993–. ARPS 1971. *Publications:* The Development of the London Hospital System 1823–1982, 1986, 2nd edn as The Development of the London Hospital System 1823–2015, 2015; From Cradle to Grave: fifty years of the NHS, 1998, 2nd edn 2015. *Recreations:* photography, contemporary NHS history, web authoring. *Address:* 173 Shakespeare Tower, Barbican, EC2Y 8DR. *T:* (020) 7786 9617. *E:* geoffrey@rivett.net. *W:* www.nhshistory.net. *Club:* Royal Society of Medicine.

**RIVETT, James Peter;** QC 2019; *b* Norwich, 8 Sept. 1979; *s* of Dr James Frederick Rivett and Jane Margaret Rivett (*née* Walsh); *m* 2015, Olivia Charlotte Rose Cole; one *s*. *Educ:* Norwich Sch.; Royal Acad. of Music (Jun. Exhibnr); Clare Coll., Cambridge (MA); Corpus Christi Coll., Cambridge (MPhil). Called to the Bar, Lincoln's Inn, 2004; in practice as a barrister, 2004–. Attorney-Gen.'s Panel of Counsel, 2009–19. Consultant Lectr, Sotheby's Inst. of Art, 2013–. *Recreations:* classical music, farming, poets, British art. *Address:* Pump Court Tax Chambers, 16 Bedford Row, WC1R 4EF. *T:* (020) 7414 8080. *E:* clerks@pumptax.com.

**RIVETT-CARNAC, Sir Jonathan James,** 10th Bt *cr* 1836, of Derby; Chairman, Finch & Partners, since 2012; *b* 14 June 1962; *er s* of Sir Miles James Rivett-Carnac, 9th Bt and of April Sally (*née* Villar); *S* father, 2009; *m* 2013, Reiko, *d* of Setsuko Kiuchi, Tokyo, Japan; one *d. Educ:* Harrow. Dir, Lulu Guinness Ltd, 2011. *Heir: b* Simon Miles Rivett-Carnac [*b* 10 Feb. 1966; *m* 1994, Sarah Jane Petrie; two *s*]. *Clubs:* White's, Brooks's.

**RIVIERE, Rev. Canon Jonathan Byam Valentine,** LVO 2015; Rector, Sandringham Group of Parishes, and Domestic Chaplain to the Queen, since 2003; Chaplain to the Queen, since 2007; Rural Dean of Heacham and Rising, 2013–17; *b* 4 Feb. 1954; *s* of late Anthony and of Ann Riviere; *m* 1987, Clare Hudson; two *s* one *d. Educ:* Westminster; RAC Cirencester; Cuddesdon Coll. Ordained deacon, 1983, priest, 1984; Curate, Wymondham, 1983–88; Team Vicar, Quidenham, 1988–94; Priest i/c, 1994, Rector, 1995–2003, Somerleyton Gp of Parishes. Hon. Canon, Norwich Cathedral, 2014–. *Recreation:* sailing. *Address:* The Rectory, Sandringham, Norfolk PE35 6EH. *T:* (01485) 540587.

**RIVLIN, His Honour Geoffrey;** QC 1979; Adviser to Director, Serious Fraud Office, 2012–15; *b* 28 Nov. 1940; *s* of late M. Allenby Rivlin and late May Rivlin; *m* 1974, Maureen Smith, Hon. ARAM, Prof. of Violin, RAM; two *d. Educ:* Bootham Sch.; Leeds Univ. (LLB). Called to the Bar, Middle Temple, 1963 (Colombos Prize, Internat. Law); Bencher, 1987; Reader, 2007. NE Circuit Junior 1967; a Recorder, 1978–89; a Circuit Judge, 1989–2004; a Sen. Circuit Judge and Resident Judge, Southwark Crown Ct, 2004–11. Mem., Senate of Inns of Court and the Bar, 1976–79. Chm. Adv. Bd, Computer Crime Centre, QMW, 1996–2002. Mem., Investigatory Powers Tribunal, 2012–16. Mem. (Ind), Westminster CC, 2012–16. Hon. Recorder, City of Westminster, 2008–11. Chm., Bar Council review into future of criminal bar, 2014–15. Consultant: Commonwealth Secretariat, 2016–18; EU Council, 2017–18; Gov. of Mauritius, 2017–; RSLegal, 2017–. Mem. Ethics Cttee, Assoc. of Child Psychotherapists, 2017–. Trustee, Fine Cell Work charity, 2012–16 (Chm., 2012–14). Governor: St Christopher's Sch., Hampstead, 1990–99; NLCS, Edgware, 1993–2003. *Publications:* First Steps in the Law, 1999, 7th edn 2015; Judges and Schools, 2002; Criminal Justice, Advocacy and the Bar, 2015. *T:* (020) 3655 7801.

**RIX, Rear Adm. Anthony John,** CB 2009; defence and security consultant, since 2010; Founder, Ocean Matrix Ltd, since 2010; Director, Sirius Insight AI Ltd, since 2017; *b* 12 Aug. 1956; *s* of Sir John Rix, MBE, and Sylvia Gene Rix (*née* Howe). *Educ:* Sherborne Sch.; Britannia RNC. Joined RN, 1975; Commanding Officer: HMS Glasgow, 1995–96; HMS Marlborough, 1999–2000; Flag Officer Sea Trng, 2006–07; COS to Comdr Allied Naval Forces Southern Europe, 2007–09. Dir, MAST Ltd, 2016–17. QCVS 2006. *Recreations:* walking, fishing, sailing. *Address:* West Sussex GU31 5NE. *E:* Anthony.Rix@btinternet.com. *Clubs:* Royal Yacht Squadron; Trinity House.

**RIX, Rt Hon. Sir Bernard (Anthony),** Kt 1993; PC 2000; a Lord Justice of Appeal, 2000–13; a Justice of Appeal, Court of Appeal, Cayman Islands, since 2013; a Judge of Singapore International Commercial Court, since 2015; Professor of International Commercial Law, Queen Mary University of London, since 2013; international arbitrator and mediator; *b* 8 Dec. 1944; *s* of late Otto Rix and Sadie Silverberg; *m* 1983, Hon. Karen Debra, *er d* of Baron Young of Graffham, *qv*; three *s* two *d* (incl. twin *s*). *Educ:* St Paul's School, London; New College, Oxford (BA: Lit.Hum. 1966, Jur. 1968; MA; Hon. Fellow 2007); Harvard Law School (Kennedy Scholar 1968; LLM 1969). FCIArb 1999. Called to Bar, Inner Temple, 1970 (Bencher, 1990; Reader, 2004, Treasurer, 2005); QC 1981; a Recorder, 1990–93; a Judge of the High Court, QBD, 1993–2000; Judge in charge of Commercial List, 1998–99. Member: Senate, Inns of Court and Bar, 1981–83; Bar Council, 1981–83. Chm., Commercial Bar Assoc., 1992–93. President: Harvard Law Sch. Assoc. of UK, 2002–15; British Insurance Law Assoc., 2007 (Vice-Pres., 2006). Dir, London Philharmonic Orchestra, 1986–2014 (Mem., Adv. Council, 2014–). Vice-Chm., Central Council for Jewish Community Services, 1994–96 (author, report on youth services and orgns, 1994). Dir, Spiro Inst., 1995–99. Chm., British Friends of Bar-Ilan Univ., 1987–99 (Hon. Vice-Pres., 1999–); Mem. Bd of Trustees, Bar-Ilan Univ., 1988–99; Chm., 2003–15, Mem., 2015–, Adv. Council, Centre of Commercial Law Studies, QMUL; Trustee and Dir, British Inst. of Internat. and Comparative Law, 2003–12. Vis. Prof., Singapore Mgt Univ., 2015. Patron, Wiener Library, 2006–; Chairman: Coexist House, 2015–; Razumovsky Trust, 2019– Hon. Fellow, QMUL, 2008. *Recreations:* music, opera, Italy, formerly fencing. *Address:* 20 Essex Street, WC2R 3AL. *T:* (020) 7842 1200.

**RIX, Dr (Edward) Martyn;** freelance writer and botanist, since 1978; Editor, Curtis's Botanical Magazine, since 2003; *b* 15 Aug. 1943; *s* of Edward Lionel Reussner Rix and Elizabeth Joyce Rix; *m* 1983, Alison Jane Goatcher; two *d. Educ:* Sherborne Sch., Dorset; Trinity Coll., Dublin (MA); Corpus Christi Coll., Cambridge (PhD). Res. Fellow, Univ. of Zürich, 1971–73; botanist, RHS, Wisley, 1974–78. FLS 2006. Gold Veitch Meml Medal, RHS, 1999; Tercentenary Bronze Medal, Linnean Soc. of London, 2008. *Publications:* The Art of the Botanist, 1981; Growing Bulbs, 1983; The Redouté Album, 1990; Subtropical and Dry Climate Plants, 2006; with R. Phillips: Bulbs, 1981; Freshwater Fish, 1985; Roses, 1988; Shrubs, 1989; Perennials, 2 vols, 1991; Vegetables, 1993; The Quest for the Rose, 1993; Conservatory and Indoor Plants, 1997; Annuals, 1999; The Botanical Garden, 2002; (with S. Sherwood) Treasures of Botanical Art, 2008. *Recreations:* fishing, sailing, travel. *Address:* c/o Macmillan Publishers Ltd, 20 New Wharf Road, N1 9RR.

**RIX, Michael David;** National Officer, GMB, since 2005; *b* 11 April 1963; *s* of Roy Rix; *m* 1984; one *s* one *d. Educ:* Primrose Hill High Sch., Leeds; Bradford and Ilkley TUC Coll.; various TUC/ASLEF educn projects. Left sch. at 16 with no formal qualifications; work experience, Yorks copper works, 1979; trainee driver, BR, Leeds, 1979–86; qualified BR driver, 1986. Leeds ASLEF: Mem., Br. Cttee, 1980–84; Asst Br. Sec., 1984–98; Br. Sec., 1988–98; Negotiating Chair, 1992; Dist Council Chm., 1995; Dist Sec., No 3 Reg., 1998; Gen. Sec., ASLEF, 1998–2003. Mem., TUC General Council, 2001–03. Mem., Labour Party, 1980–97, 2000–. Mem., Co-op Soc., Wortley Hall, PPPS. *Recreations:* football, especially Leeds United, watching Rugby league, watching Yorkshire CCC, swimming, reading, very little time though to pursue. *Address:* c/o GMB National Office, Mary Turner House, 22 Stephenson Way, Euston, NW1 2HD.

**RIZA, Alper Ali;** QC 1991; a Recorder of the Crown Court, since 2000; *b* 16 March 1948; *s* of Ali Riza and Elli Liasides; *m* 1981, Vanessa Frances Hall-Smith, *qv* (marr. diss. 2009); two *d. Educ:* American Academy, Larnaca, Cyprus; English Sch., Nicosia. Called to the Bar, Gray's Inn, 1973. Pupillage, 1974–75; Turnpike Lane Law and Advice, 1975–77; Appeals Lawyer, Jt Council for Welfare of Immigrants, 1977–82; private practice, 1982–. Founder Mem., Assoc. of Greek, Turkish and Cypriot Affairs, 1990–. Fellow, Inst. of Advanced Legal Studies; Mem., RIIA. *Recreations:* music, philosophy, drinking and smoking, sport, walking around London W2 and W11 esp. Hyde Park, Kensington Gardens and Holland Park. *Address:* Goldsmith Chambers, Goldsmith Building, Temple, EC4Y 7BL.

**RIZZARDO, Dr Ezio,** AC 2018; FRS 2010; CSIRO Fellow, since 2000, Project Leader, Engineered Polymers, since 1978, and Leader, Polymer Production Program, Cooperative Research Centre, since 1994, CSIRO; *b* Onigo, Italy, 26 Dec. 1943; *s* of Gino Rizzardo and Ottorina Bresolin; *m* 1968, Jeannette Angela Dodds; one *s* one *d. Educ:* Univ. of NSW (BSc 1st Cl. Hons 1966); Univ. of Sydney (PhD 1969). Postdoctoral Fellow: Rice Univ., Houston, 1969–71; Research Inst. for Medicine and Chem., Cambridge, Mass, 1971–73; Res. Fellow, ANU, 1973–76; CSIRO: Sen. Res. Scientist, 1976–2000; Manager, Polymers Prog., 1980–98; Proj. Leader, Polymeric Biomaterials, 1988–92; Chief Res. Scientist, 1992–2000. Inventor/co-inventor on 37 worldwide patent families. FRACI 1981; FTSE 1994; FAA 2002. Aust. Polymer Medal, 1992, Applied Res. Medal, 1996, H. G. Smith Meml Medal, 2003, RACI; Most Prolific Inventor Award, 2001, Chairman's Gold Medal, CSIRO; Centenary Medal, Australia, 2003; Prime Minister's Prize for Sci., Australia, 2011; Luminary of Aust. Chemistry, RACI, 2011; ATSE Clunies Ross Award, 2014; RCS Macro Gp UK Medal for Outstanding Achievement, 2014; Thomson Reuters Highly Cited Researcher, 2015. *Publications:* articles and book chapters on organic chemistry and polymer sci. *Address:* CSIRO, Locked Bag 10, Clayton South, Vic 3169, Australia.

**RIZZI, Carlo;** conductor; Musical Director, Welsh National Opera, 1992–2001 and 2004–08, now Conductor Laureate; *b* 19 July 1960. *Educ:* Milan Conservatoire; Accademia Musicale Chigiana, Siena. Débuts: Australian Opera Co., 1989; Netherlands Opera, 1989; Royal Opera, 1990; WNO, 1991; Deutsche Oper, Berlin, 1992; Cologne Opera, 1992; La Scala, 1992; Israel Philharmonic, 1993; Metropolitan Opera, NY, 1993; Pesaro, 1994; Edinburgh Fest., 1996; Chicago Lyric Opera, 1996; has made numerous recordings.

**ROACHE, Timothy John;** General Secretary, GMB, since 2016; *b* Reading, 6 April 1962; *s* of Peter and Audrey Roache; *m* 2006, Mandy Chamberlain; one *s* two *d. Educ:* Hendon Sch., N London; Middlesex Poly. GMB Union (formerly General and Municipal Workers' Union): post room clerk, 1979–84; Legal Officer, 1984–89; Regl Organiser, 1989–99; Sen. Organiser, 1999–2007; Regl Sec., Yorks and N Derbys, 2007–16. *Recreations:* pursuing fairness and equality for all, coaching kids football, cinema, following Arsenal FC, battling the expanding waistline! *Address:* GMB, 22 Stephenson Way, Euston, NW1 2HD. *T:* (020) 7391 6700. *E:* tim.roache@gmb.org.uk.

**ROADS, Dr Christopher Herbert;** consultant in museums and audio-visual archives; Acting Chairman and (Founding) Managing Director, Historic Arms Exhibitions and Forts LLC, Oman, since 2001; Director, Bait ar Rudaydah Centre of Excellence of Historic Arms, Birkat al Mauz, Oman, since 2019; *b* 3 Jan. 1934; *s* of late Herbert Clifford Roads and Vera Iris Roads; *m* 1976, Charlotte Alicia Dorothy Mary Lothian (marr. diss.); one *d. Educ:* Cambridge and County Sch.; Trinity Hall, Cambridge (Double 1st Cl. Hist.; PhD 1961). Nat. Service, 2nd Lieut, RA, Egypt, 1952–54. Adviser to WO on Disposal of Amnesty Arms, 1961–62; Imperial War Museum: Keeper of Dept of Records, 1962–70; Dep. Dir-Gen. at Main Building, Southwark, 1964–79, at Duxford, Cambridge, 1976–79 (Founder), HMS Belfast, Pool of London, 1978–79 (Founder); Dir, Museums & Archives Develt Associates Ltd, 1977–85; Dir, Nat. Sound Archive, 1983–92; Associate Dir (Consultancy), R&D Dept, BL, 1992–94. UNESCO consultant designing major audio visual archives or museums in Philippines, Panama, Bolivia, Kuwait, Jordan, Saudi Arabia, etc, 1976–. Founder and Dir, Cambridge Coral/Starfish Res. Gp, 1968–; Founding Chairman: Sudanese British Develt Co., 1972–79; Photoair Services Ltd, 1972–80; Director: Nat. Discography Ltd, 1986–92; Historic Cable Ship John W. Mackay, 1986–; AVT Communications Ltd, 1988–92; Cedar Audio Ltd, 1989–92; Green Metals Ltd, 2011–; Founding Consultant and Dir, Green Alloys LLC, 2013–; Director: Green Pyramid LLC (formerly Nizbridge Metals LLC), 2015–; Nizbridge LLC, 2017–. Founder, 2013, Sen. Res. Fellow and Acting Vice Chair (Admin and Finance), 2016–, Dept of Materials Sci. and Metallurgy, Univ. of Nizwa in association with Dept of Materials Sci. and Metallurgy, Univ. of Cambridge, Consultant to Chancellor, Univ. of Nizwa, 2013–. Chm., Coral Conservation Trust, 1972–; President: Historical Breechloading Small Arms Assoc., 1973–, Pres. for Life, 2003; Internat. Film and TV Council (UNESCO Category A), 1990–92 (Pres., Archives Commn, 1970–); Hon. Pres., World Expeditionary Assoc. (Vice Pres., 1971); Vice President: Duxford Aviation Soc., 1974–; English Eight Club, 1980–; Cambridge Univ. Rifle Assoc., 1987– (Mem. Council, 1955–87; Double Half Blue in Rifle Shooting); Mem. Council, Scientific Exploration Soc., 1971–82; Sec., Nat. Archives Cttee, Internat. Assoc. of Sound Archives, 1988–92; Hon. Sec., Cambridge Univ. Long Range Rifle Club, 1979–2008 (Pres., 2008–); Mem., Home Office Reference Panel for Historic Firearms, 1997–2003; Chm., Heritage Arms Rescue, 1996–. Trustee: HMS Belfast Trust, 1970–78; Nat. Life Stories Collection, 1986–92; NSA Wild Life Sound Trust, 1986–92. Adjt, English VIII, 1964–88. Churchill Fellowship, 1970; Vis. Fellow, Centre of Internat. Studies, Univ. of Cambridge, 1983–84. FRGS. Liveryman, Gunmakers' Co., 1996; Freeman, City of London, 1996. Silver Jubilee Medal, 1977. Order of Independence, 2nd cl. (Jordan), 1977. *Publications:* The British Soldier's Firearm, 1850–1864, 1964; (jtly) New Studies on the Crown of Thorns Starfish, 1970; The Story of the Gun, 1978. *Recreations:* rifle shooting, marine and submarine exploration, wind surfing, motorcycling, videography. *Address:* The White House, 90 High Street, Melbourn, near Royston, Herts SG8 6AL. *T:* (01763) 260866, *Fax:* (01763) 262521; DX 12 Urbanización Bahia Dorada, 29693 Estepona, Málaga, Spain. *T:* and *Fax:* (95) 2796407; Historic Arms Exhibitions and Forts LLC, PO Box 3726, P. Code 112, Ruwi, Muscat, Sultanate of Oman. *T:* (residence) 99797326, *T:* and *Fax:* (office) 24501218. *Clubs:* Oxford and Cambridge; Hawks (Cambridge).

**ROADS, Elizabeth Ann,** LVO 2012 (MVO 1990); Secretary, Order of the Thistle, since 2014; *b* Iserlohn, Germany, 5 July 1951; *d* of Lt Col James Bruce, MC and Mary Hope Bruce (*née* Sinclair); *m* 1983, Maj. Christopher George William Roads, TD; two *s* one *d. Educ:* Lansdowne House Sch., Edinburgh; Edinburgh Napier Univ. (LLB 2012). Christie, Manson & Woods, London, 1970–74; Court of the Lord Lyon, 1975–2018: Lyon Clerk and Keeper of the Records, 1986–2018; Linlithgow Pursuivant Extraordinary, 1987; Carrick Pursuivant of Arms, 1992–2010; Asst Sec., Order of the Thistle, 2008–14; Lord Lyon *ad interim,* 2017–18. Hon. Treas., Scottish Record Soc., 1997–2011; Chm., Scottish Records Assoc., 2010–15 (Councillor, 2018–); Trustee, Scottish Council on Archives, 2015– (Vice Chair, 2016–). President: Old Edinburgh Club, 2013–16 (Hon. Sec., 2012–13); Bureau Permanent des Congrès Internationaux des Sciences Généalogique et Héraldique, 2017–; Vice Pres., Heraldry Soc. of Scotland, 2016–. Councillor, Dean's Council, Merchant Guildry of Stirling, 2014–. Lay Rep., St Mary's Ch, Aberfoyle, 2018–. FSAScot 1986; FSA 2013; Fellow: Heraldry Soc. of Scotland, 1996; Royal Heraldry Soc. of Canada, 2004; Heraldry Soc. of New Zealand, 2018; FHS 2018; Academician, Academie Internationale d'Héraldique, 2008. Silver Jubilee Medal, 1977; Golden Jubilee Medal, 2002; Diamond Jubilee Medal, 2012. OStJ 1999 (Chapter Mem., Priory of Scotland, OStJ, 2018–). *Publications:* The Chapel of the Order of the Thistle, 2009; articles in heraldic and genealogical jls. *Recreations:* history, reading, genealogical research, the countryside. *Address:* Duchray House, Aberfoyle, Stirling FK8 3XL.

**ROBARDS, Prof. Anthony William,** OBE 2002; PhD, DSc; FRSB; HSBC Professor of Innovation, University of York, 2001–09, now Emeritus Professor; Consultant, AWR1 Associates, since 2009; *b* 9 April 1940; *s* of Albert Charles Robards, Lamberhurst, Kent, and Kathleen Emily Robards; *m* 1st, 1962, Ruth Bulpett (marr. diss. 1985); one *s* one *d;* 2nd,

1987, Eva Christina, d of Bo Knutson-Ek, Lidingo, Sweden. *Educ:* Skinners' Sch.; UCL (BSc 1962; PhD 1966; DSc 1977); Inst. of Educn, Univ. of London (PGCE 1963); Dip RMS 1976. FRSB (FIBiol 1978). Department of Biology, University of York: Lectr, 1966–70; Sen. Lectr, 1970–79; Reader, 1979–88; Prof. of Biol., 1988–2003; Pro-Vice-Chancellor for Ext. Relns, 1996–2004; Director: Inst. for Applied Biol., 1986–95; Industrial Develt, 1988–96. Visiting Research Fellow: ANU, 1975; Univ. of Stockholm, 1986. Dir, York Science Park (Innovation Centre) Ltd, 1994– (Chm., 1995–2006); Chm., York Science Park Ltd, 1995–2012; Exec. Chm., York Sci. and Innovation Grand Tour Ltd, 2011–; non-exec. Chm., YorkTest Gp Ltd, 1999–2009. Trustee, Yorks Cancer Res., 2006–16 (Dep. Chm., 2009–10; Chm., 2010–16); Chair, York Archaeological Trust, 2017–. Mem., Co. of Merchant Adventurers, City of York, 1991– (Gov., 2008–09). *Publications:* (with U. B. Sleytr) Low Temperature Methods in Biological Electron Microscopy, 1985; 130 scientific articles. *Recreations:* horology, sailing, opera, photography. *Address:* Shrubbery Cottage, Nun Monkton, Yorks YO26 8EW. *T:* 07912 717458. *E:* Anthony.Robards@york.ac.uk, AnthonyRobards@aol.com.

**ROBARTS, (Anthony) Julian;** Director and Chief Executive, Iveagh Trustees Ltd, 1993–98; Managing Director, Coutts & Co., 1986–91; *b* 6 May 1937; *s* of late Lt-Col Anthony V. C. Robarts, DL and Grizel Mary Robarts (Grant); *m* 1961, Edwina Beryl Hobson; two *s* one *d*. *Educ:* Eton College. National Service, 11th Hussars (PAO), 1955–57; joined Coutts & Co., 1958, Dir, 1963, Dep. Man. Dir, 1976–86; Director: Coutts Finance Co., 1967–91; F. Bolton Group, 1970–2008; International Fund for Institutions Inc., USA, 1983–93; Chm., Hill Martin, 1993–2004; Regional Dir, Nat. Westminster Bank, 1971–92. Hon. Treasurer, 1969–2001, Vice-Pres., 2001–09, Union Jack Club. Trustee: Beit Med. Meml Fellowships, 1993–2001; Sargent Cancer Care for Children, 1997–2000. *Recreations:* gardening, opera. *Address:* Beacon Field House, The Causeway, Therfield, Royston, Herts SG8 9PP. *Clubs:* Brooks's, MCC.

**ROBATHAN,** family name of **Baron Robathan**.

**ROBATHAN, Baron** *cr* 2015 (Life Peer), of Poultney in the County of Leicestershire; **Andrew Robert George Robathan;** PC 2010; farmer; *b* 17 July 1951; *s* of late Robert Douglas Brice Robathan and Sheena Mary Martin Robathan (*née* Gimson); *m* 1991, Rachael Maunder; one *s* one *d*. *Educ:* Merchant Taylors' Sch., Northwood; Oriel Coll., Oxford (MA). Served Coldstream Guards, 1974–89 (Officer, SAS, 1981–83, HQ, 1984–87), resigned as Major; rejoined Army for Gulf War, Jan.–April 1991 (COS, POW Guard Force). Councillor, London Borough of Hammersmith and Fulham, 1990–92. MP (C) Blaby, 1992–2010, S Leicestershire, 2010–15. PPS to Minister of State for Nat. Heritage, 1995–97; opposition spokesman on: trade and industry, 2002–03; internat. develt, 2003; defence, 2004–05; Dep. Opposition Chief Whip, 2005–10; Parly Under-Sec. of State, 2010–12, Minister of State, 2012–13, MoD; Minister of State, NI Office, 2013–14. Mem., Internat. Develt Select Cttee, 1997–2002, 2003–04; Chm., 1994–97, Vice-Chm., 1997–2010, All-Party Cycling Gp; Vice Chairman: Parly Renewable and Sustainable Energy Gp, 1992–94, 1997–2010; Cons. back bench Defence Cttee, 1993–94, 1997–2001 (Chm., 1994–95); Cons. NI Cttee, 1994–95, 1997–2001; Cons. Defence and Internat. Affairs Policy Gp, 2001–02. Captain, Tug of War Team, 1995–2000, Clay Pigeon Team, 1997–2007, H of C. Mem. Bd, Indict, 1998–2001; Trustee, Halo Trust, 2000–06 (Chm., 2003–06). *Recreations:* hill-walking, ski-ing, shooting, architecture, history, conservation. *Address:* House of Lords, SW1A 0PW.

**ROBB, Andrew Mackenzie,** FCMA, FCT; Chairman, Tata Steel Europe Ltd, 2009–19 (Independent Director, 2003–19); Independent Director, Jaguar Land Rover plc, since 2009; *b* Birmingham, Sept. 1942; *s* of William and Kathleen Robb; *m*; two *d*. *Educ:* Rugby Sch. FCMA 1968; JDipMA 1973; FCT 1980. Accountant: T. Wall & Sons Ltd, 1964–69; Hoskyns Gp Ltd, 1969–71; Financial Controller, 1971–83, Gp Finance Dir, 1983–89, P & O Steam Navigation Co.; Exec. Dir, Pilkington plc, 1989–2003 (Gp Finance Dir, 1989–2001). Independent Director, Kesa Electricals plc, 2003–12; Paypoint plc, 2004–14; Laird plc, 2004–12; Tata Steel Ltd (India), 2007–17. Mem., Urgent Issues Taskforce, Accounting Standards Bd, 1992–97. Chm. Trustees, Pilkington Superannuation Scheme, 2000–14. Freeman, City of London, 1998. *Recreations:* golf, opera, travel. *E:* robbandrew62@gmail.com. *Clubs:* Royal Automobile; Guards Polo; Goodwood Golf.

**ROBB, (David) Campbell;** Chief Executive, Joseph Rowntree Foundation, since 2017; *b* Glasgow, 14 May 1969; two *d*; partner, Kim Davies. *Educ:* Univ. of Edinburgh (MA Hons Pols and Mod. Hist.). Researcher for David Blunkett, MP, 1993–94; Press Officer for Chris Smith, MP, 1996–97; Hd of Campaigns, 1998–2001, Dir, Public Policy, 2001–05, NCVO; Advr to HM Treasury, 2005; Dir Gen., Office of the Third Sector, 2006–09 and Social Exclusion Task Force, 2009, Cabinet Office; Chief Exec., Shelter, 2010–16. Hon. LLD York St Johns, 2018. *Recreations:* music, cooking, travelling. *Address:* Joseph Rowntree Foundation, The Homestead, 40 Water End, York YO30 6WP.

**ROBB, Dr Graham Macdonald,** FRSL; writer; *b* Manchester, 2 June 1958; *s* of Gordon James Robb and Joyce Robb (*née* Gall); *m* 1986, Margaret Gay Hambrick. *Educ:* Worcester Royal Grammar Sch.; Exeter Coll., Oxford (BA, MA); Goldsmiths' Coll., London (PGCE); Vanderbilt Univ. (MA; PhD 1986). British Acad. Post-doctoral Fellow, Exeter Coll., Oxford, 1987–90. FRSL 1999. Grande Médaille de la Ville de Paris, 2012. Chevalier, Ordre des Arts et des Lettres (France), 2009. *Publications:* Le Corsaire-Satan en Silhouette, 1985; Baudelaire lecteur de Balzac, 1988; (ed) Scènes de la vie de bohème, 1988; (adapted trans.) Baudelaire, 1989; La Poésie de Baudelaire et la poésie française, 1993; Balzac, 1994; Unlocking Mallarmé, 1996 (MLA Prize for Ind. Scholars, 1997); Victor Hugo, 1997 (Whitbread Biog. Prize; Heinemann Award, RSL); Rimbaud, 2000; Strangers: homosexual love in the nineteenth century, 2003; The Discovery of France, 2007 (Duff Cooper Prize, 2008; Ondaatje Prize, RSL, 2008); Parisians: an adventure history of Paris, 2010; The Ancient Paths: discovering the lost map of Celtic Europe, 2013; Cols and Passes of the British Isles, 2016; The Debatable Land: the lost world between Scotland and England, 2018; contribs to TLS, London Rev. of Books, NY Rev. of Books, Spectator. *Recreations:* road cycling, sylviculture. *Address:* c/o Rogers, Coleridge & White Ltd, 20 Powis Mews, W11 1JN. *E:* info@rcwlitagency.com.

**ROBB, Sir John (Weddell),** Kt 1999; Chairman, British Energy, 1995–2001; *b* 27 April 1936; *s* of John and Isabella Robb; *m* 1965, Janet Teanby; two *s* one *d*. *Educ:* Daniel Stewart's College, Edinburgh. Beecham Group: Marketing Exec., Toiletry Div., Beecham Products, 1966; Man. Dir, Beecham (Far East), Kuala Lumpur, 1971; Vice-Pres., W. Hemisphere Div., Beecham Products, USA, 1974; Man. Dir, Food and Drink Div., Beecham Products, 1976; Group Board, 1980; Chm., Food and Drink Div., 1980; Chm., Beecham Products, 1984–85; Gp Man. Dir, 1985–88; Wellcome Plc: Dep. Chief Exec., 1989–90; Chief Exec., 1990–95; Chm., 1994–95. Non-exec. Dir, Uniq plc (formerly Unigate), 1996–2002. Dep. Chm., Horserace Betting Levy Bd, 1993–2006; Trustee, Royal Botanic Gdn, Edinburgh, 1997–2002. *Recreations:* golf, gardening, racing. *Clubs:* Turf; Sunningdale.

**ROBB, Kenneth Richard;** Sheriff of South Strathclyde, Dumfries and Galloway at Stranraer, since 2008 and at Dumfries, since 2013 (at Kirkcudbright, 2008–13); *b* Larbert, 3 Sept. 1954; *s* of Richard Robb and Mary Robb; *m* 1977, Susan Ringrose; one *d*. *Educ:* Falkirk High Sch.; Edinburgh Univ. (LLB Hons). Admitted solicitor, 1978; private legal practice, 1976–2000; pt-time Immigration Judge, 2002–08; pt-time Employment Judge, 2005–08; pt-time Sheriff, 2006–08. Mem., Scottish Solicitors' Discipline Tribunal, 1998–2008. Mem. Council, Law Soc. of Scotland, 1987–97. Member, disciplinary panels: GMC, 2000–05; ACCA, 2002–08; Soc. of Actuaries, 2003–07. Mem. Council, Sheriffs' Assoc., 2012–15. *Publications:* (contrib. ed) Scottish Family Law Service, 1995. *Recreations:* hill-walking, history, holidays. *Address:* Sheriff Courthouse, Lewis Street, Stranraer DG9 7AA.

**ROBB, Prof. Michael Alfred,** PhD, DSc; FRS 2000; Professor of Chemistry, Imperial College, London, since 2004; *b* 19 Feb. 1944; *s* of Robert Fredrick Robb and Dorothy Estelle Robb; *m* 1st, 1967, Brenda Elizabeth Donald (*d* 2000); one *s*; 2nd, 2001, Elaine Murphy (*see* Baroness Murphy). *Educ:* Toronto Univ. (PhD 1970); DSc London 1987. King's College, London: Lectr, 1971–88; Reader, 1988–92; Prof. of Chemistry, 1992–2003; Hd, Dept of Chemistry, 2000–03. *Publications:* Theoretical Chemistry for Electronic Excited States, 2018; 375 articles in chemistry jls. *Address:* Department of Chemistry, Imperial College London, SW7 2AZ. *T:* (020) 7594 5757.

**ROBBIE, David Andrew;** Finance Director, Rexam plc, 2005–16; *b* Greenmount, Lancs; *s* of Frank Robbie and Dorothy Robbie (*née* Holt). *Educ:* St Andrews Univ. (MA). ACA 1990. Finance Director: CMG plc, 2000–03; Royal P&O Nedlloyd NV, 2004–05. Non-executive Director: BBC, 2007–10; Almeida Theatre, 2007–10; First Group plc, 2017–. Trustee, Aldeburgh Music, 2010–. *Recreations:* theatre, opera, travelling.

**ROBBINS, Barbara Jacquelyn;** *see* Sahakian, B. J.

**ROBBINS, Christopher William;** academic; HM Diplomatic Service, retired; *b* 16 June 1946. *Educ:* Skinners' Sch., Tunbridge Wells; Univ. of Sussex (BA); Warburg Inst., Univ. of London (MPhil); Univ. of York (PhD). Lectr in Philosophy, Univ. of York, 1969–75; Principal, Welsh Office, 1975–77; Adminr, Directorate of Economic and Social Affairs, Council of Europe, 1977–84; joined HM Diplomatic Service, 1984; EC Dept, FCO, 1984–87; First Sec., New Delhi, 1987–90; Asst Head, Central and Southern Africa Dept, 1990–91; Head, Projects and Export Policy Branch I, DTI (on secondment), 1991–94; Commercial Counsellor, The Hague, 1994–98, and Consul-Gen., Amsterdam, 1996–98; Ambassador to Lithuania, 1998–2001; Minister-Counsellor (formerly Consul Gen.) and Dep. Hd of Mission, Seoul, 2001–05. Leader of Philosophy Gp, Mallorca, 2006–12. Tutor in Philosophy, Univ. of York, 2013–15; Vis. Prof., Faculty of Philosophy, Vilnius Univ., 2017. *Publications:* (contrib.) La Santé Rationnée?, 1981; (contrib.) The End of an Illusion, 1984; articles on Sartre, Blaise Pascal and practical ethics in philosophical and social policy jls. *Recreation:* the enjoyment of beauty.

**ROBBINS, James;** Diplomatic Correspondent, BBC, since 1998; *b* 19 Jan. 1954; *s* of late (Richard) Michael Robbins, CBE and (Rose Margaret) Elspeth Robbins (*née* Bannatyne); *m* 1981, Gillian Gee; one *d*. *Educ:* Westminster Sch.; Christ Church, Oxford (BA Hons PPE). BBC: News Trainee, 1977; Reporter: Belfast, 1979–83; BBC News, 1983–87; Southern Africa Corresp., 1987–91; Europe Corresp., 1992–97. *Recreations:* opera, music, tennis, cooking, walking, looking out of train windows. *Address:* 3rd Floor Bridge, BBC New Broadcasting House, Portland Place, W1A 1AA. *E:* james.robbins@bbc.co.uk.

**ROBBINS, Lydia Akrigg;** *see* Brown, L. A.

**ROBBINS, Sir Oliver,** KCMG 2019; CB 2015; Prime Minister's Europe Adviser, Cabinet Office, 2017–19; *b* 20 April 1975; *s* of Derek and Diana Robbins; *m* 2005, Sherry Birkbeck; three *s*. *Educ:* Hertford Coll., Oxford (BA Hons PPE 1996). HM Treasury, 1996–2006: Hd, Corporate and Private Finance, 2003–06; Hd, Defence, Diplomacy and Intelligence, 2006; Principal Private Sec. to the Prime Minister, 2006–07; Dir, Prime Minister's Private Office, 2007; Cabinet Office: Dir, Intelligence and Security, 2007–10; Dep. Nat. Security Advr and Dir Gen., 2010–12; Dir Gen., Civil Service, Cabinet Office, 2014–15; Second Perm. Sec., Home Office, 2015–16; Perm. Sec., DExEU, 2016–17. Vis. Fellow, Heywood Foundn and Univ. of Oxford, 2019–. *Recreations:* walking, cooking. *Club:* National Liberal.

**ROBBINS, Ven. Stephen,** CB 2011; Archdeacon for the Army, 2004–11; Chaplain General, Ministry of Defence Chaplains (Army), 2008–11; Honorary Canon, Salisbury Cathedral, 2007–11, now Canon Emeritus; *b* 11 Aug. 1953; *s* of Joseph and Jane Robbins; *m* 1976, Susan Florence McCann (*d* 2009); one *s* one *d*; *m* 2011, Dr Lydia Akrigg Brown, *qv*. *Educ:* Jarrow Grammar Sch.; King's Coll., London (BD, AKC 1974). Ordained deacon, 1976, priest, 1977; Curate, Tudhoe Grange, Spennymoor, 1976–80; Priest-in-charge, then Vicar, Harlow Green, Gateshead, 1980–87; joined RAChD, 1987; Regtl Chaplain in Germany, 1987–94; Chaplain, Army Trng Regt, Bassingbourn, 1994–97; Sen. Chaplain, 8 Infantry Bde, Londonderry, 1997–99; Armed Forces Chaplaincy Centre, 1999–2001; Chaplain, RMA Sandhurst, 2001–02; Assistant Chaplain General: Germany, 2002–03; HQ Land Comd, 2003–06; Dir of Training, 2006–07, Dep. Chaplain Gen., 2007–08, MoD Chaplains (Army). QHC 2005–11. Permission to Officiate, Salisbury, Newcastle and Europe, 2011; Chaplain to Bishop of Salisbury, 2012–15; Bishop of Salisbury's Advr on Deliverance, 2016–. Hon. Chaplain, Royal Regt of Artillery, 2017. Pres., SSAFA Wilts, 2012–. Liveryman, Farriers' Co., 2017; Freeman, City of London, 2017. *Recreations:* exploring Neolithic and Bronze Age earthworks, Newcastle United, trying to find a beer I don't like. *Address:* Mill Leat, West Gomeldon, Salisbury, Wilts SP4 6JY. *E:* venstephen@gmail.com.

**ROBBINS, His Honour Stephen Dennis;** a Circuit Judge, 1994–2018; *b* 11 Jan. 1948; *s* of late Lt-Col Dennis Robbins, OBE, TD and Joan Robbins (*née* Mason); *m* 1974, Amanda Smith, JP; three *d*. *Educ:* Orwell Park; Marlborough; Coll. d'Europe, Bruges (Churchill Award). Infantry, HAC, 1966–69. Called to the Bar, Gray's Inn, 1969; practised SE Circuit, 1972–94; Asst Recorder, 1983–87; Recorder, 1987–94. Former Mem., Overseas Cttee, Bar Council; Hon. Sec., London Common Law Bar Cttee; Hon. Legal Advr, Katharine Lowe Centre, Battersea, 1974–79. Pres., Mental Health Rev. Tribunals, 1994. Mem., Parole Bd, 2001–07. *Recreations:* collecting ephemera, shooting, swimming, walking, music. *Address:* Hillcrest Farm, Sevington, near Ashford, Kent TN24 0LJ. *T:* (01233) 502732; 1/2 The Studios, 17/19 Edge Street, Kensington Church Street, W8 7PN. *T:* (020) 7727 7216.

**ROBBINS, Prof. Trevor William,** CBE 2012; PhD; FBPsS, FMedSci, FBPhS; FRS 2005; Professor of Experimental Psychology and Head of Department of Psychology (formerly Department of Experimental Psychology), 2002–17, now Emeritus Professor, and Director, Centre for Behavioural and Clinical Neuroscience Institute, since 2005, University of Cambridge (Professor of Cognitive Neuroscience, 1997–2002); Fellow, 1990–2017, and Angharad Dodds John Fellow in Mental Health and Neuropsychiatry, 2012–17, Downing College, Cambridge; *b* 26 Nov. 1949; *s* of William Walter Robbins and Eileen Hilda Robbins; *m* 1979, Prof. Barbara Jacquelyn Sahakian, *qv*; two *d*. *Educ:* Battersea GS; Jesus Coll., Cambridge (Schol.; BA 1st cl. Hons; MA; PhD). FBPsS 1990. Univ. Demonstrator, 1973–78, Univ. Lectr, 1978–92, Reader in Cognitive Neuroscience, 1992–97, Dept of Exptl Psychology, Univ. of Cambridge. Chm. and

Council Mem., Neuroscience Bd, MRC, 1995–99 (Mem., 1989–93); Council Mem., European Neuroscience Assoc., 1996–98; President: European Behavioural Pharmacology Soc., 1992–94; British Assoc. for Psychopharmacology, 1996–98; British Neurosci. Assoc., 2009–11. Ed., Psychopharmacology, 1980–. Fred Kavli Dist. Internat. Scientist Lectr, Soc. for Neurosci., 2005. Foreign Mem., Amer. Coll. of Neuropsychopharmacology, 1994–. FMedSci 1999; Fellow, Amer. Acad. of Psychol Sci., 2010; FBPhS 2017. Hon. Prof., Fudan Univ., Shanghai, 2018. Spearman Medal, BPsS, 1982; D. G. Marquis Award, Amer. Psychol Assoc., 1997; Dist. Scientist Award, European Behavioural Pharmacol. Soc., 2001; Medal, Coll. de France, 2004; Prize for Neuronal Plasticity, Fondn Ipsen, 2005; (jtly) Distinguished Scientific Contribn Award, American Psychol Assoc., 2011; (jtly) Brain Prize, Grete Lundbeck Foundn, 2014; Life Achievement Award, British Assoc. for Psychopharmacology, 2015; Robert Sommer Award, 2016; Gold Medal, Soc. for Biol Psychiatry, 2017; Patricia Goldman-Rakic Award for outstanding res. in cognitive neuroscis, Brain and Behavior Foundn/Yale Univ., 2017; Lifetime Achievement Award for Dist. Contribs to Psychol Knowledge, BPsS, 2019. *Publications*: (ed jtly) Psychology for Medicine, 1988; (ed jtly) The Prefrontal Cortex, 1998; Disorders of Brain and Mind 2, 2003; (ed jtly) Drugs and the Future, 2007; (ed jtly) Neurobiology of Addiction: new vistas, 2010; (ed jtly) Decision-making, Affect and Learning, 2011; (ed jtly) Cognitive Search: evolution, algorithms and the brain, 2012; (ed jtly) Translational Neuropsychopharmacology, 2016; more than 850 articles in learned books and jls. *Recreations*: chess, cricket, cinema, theatre, modern literature, visual arts, opera. *Address*: Department of Psychology, University of Cambridge, Downing Street, Cambridge CB2 3EB. *T*: (01223) 333551, *Fax*: (01223) 333564. *E*: twr2@cam.ac.uk.

**ROBBS, John Edward;** Director, Marine and Fisheries, Department for Environment, Food and Rural Affairs, 2011–15; *b* 26 June 1955; *s* of Eric and Christine Robbs; *m* 1989, Jacqueline Tozer; two *s*. *Educ*: King Edward VII Sch., King's Lynn; Queens' Coll., Cambridge (MA); London Sch. of Econs (MSc Econ). Joined Ministry of Agriculture, Fisheries and Food, 1977: Private Sec. to Perm. Sec., 1981–82; Private Sec. to Minister, 1982–83; on secondment to UK Perm. Repn to EU, Brussels, 1985–89; Head: of Envmt Task Force Div., 1991–94; of Conservation Policy Div., 1994–95; of Fisheries (Common Fisheries Policy) Div., 1995–99; of EU Internat. Div., 1999–2000; of Food Industry, Competitiveness and Flood Defence Gp, 2000–01; Dir, Food Industry and Crops, 2001–06, Wildlife and Countryside, 2006–11, DEFRA. *Recreations*: family, friends, gardening.

**ROBERG, Rabbi Meir;** Inspector of schools, UK, since 1997; Senior Advisor, Lauder Yeshurun Foundation, Berlin, since 2007; Rabbi, Kehal Adass Yisroel congregation, Berlin, since 2012; *b* 25 June 1937; *s* of late Julius and Hannchen Roberg; *m* 1961, Mirjam Nager; three *s* two *d*. *Educ*: Manchester Grammar Sch. (Gratrix Scholar); Talmudical Coll., Israel (Rabbinical Diploma); Univ. of London (BA 1st Cl. Hons 1960; DipEd 1970; MPhil 1972). Asst Teacher, 1960–62, Dep. Head, 1962–65, Yavneh Grammar Sch., London; Hasmonean High School: Asst Teacher and Head of Classics, 1965–71; Dep. Head, 1971–80; Headmaster, 1980–93; Principal of Jewish Day Sch and Dean of Talmudical Coll., Kiev, 1993–95; Hon. Consultant for Jewish schs and colls estabd in Ukraine following independence, 1995–2005. Lectr, Colls of Further Educn, 1962–93; Headmaster, Middx Regl Centre, 1965–73. Delegate, Internat. Religious Conf., Jerusalem, 1963 and 1980. Member: Keren Hatorah; Hendon Adass; Massoret Inst. (Chm., 1980–95); Assoc. of Headteachers of Jewish Day Schs (Pres., 1991–93; Life Pres., 1993–). *Publications*: (contrib.) Responsa Literature, 1996, 1998, 2000; reviews for Comparative Education, Jewish Tribune, and Parent-Teacher Monthly (NY). *Recreations*: Talmudic research, hiking. *Address*: 19 Sorotzkin Street, Jerusalem, Israel.

**ROBERTS,** family name of **Barons Clwyd** and **Roberts of Llandudno**.

**ROBERTS OF LLANDUDNO,** Baron *cr* 2004 (Life Peer), of Llandudno in the County of Gwynedd; **Rev. John Roger Roberts;** Superintendent Methodist Minister: Llangollen, 1965–70, Llandudno, 1983–2002; *b* 23 Oct. 1935; s of Thomas Charles and Alice Ellen Roberts; *m* 1962, Eirlys Ann (*d* 1995); one *s* two *d*. *Educ*: John Bright Grammar Sch., Llandudno; Univ. of Wales, Bangor (BA Hons); Handsworth Methodist Coll., Birmingham. Methodist Minister, 1958–. President: Welsh Liberal Party, 1981–84; Welsh Lib Dems, 1990–96. Contested Conwy: (L) 1979; (L/Alliance) 1983, 1987; (Lib Dem) 1992, 1997. *Recreations*: travel, walking, music. *Address*: 22 Garth Court, Abbey Road, Llandudno, Conwy LL30 2HF. *T*: (01492) 876690; House of Lords, SW1A 0PW. *E*: jrogerroberts@aol.com.

**ROBERTS, Sir Adam;** *see* Roberts, Sir E. A.

**ROBERTS, Prof. Alan Clive,** OBE 2001 (MBE 1982); TD 1969; JP; DL; PhD; Professor of Biomaterials in Surgery, University of Hull, since 1994; Consultant: Nuffield Hospital, Leeds, 2002–10; Bradford Institute for Health Research, since 2012; *b* 28 April 1934; *s* of Major William Roberts, MBE and Kathleen Roberts; *m* 1956, Margaret Mary Shaw; two *s*. *Educ*: Gregg Sch., Newcastle upon Tyne; MPhil CNAA 1975; PhD Bradford Univ. 1988. CBiol 1971; FRSB (FIBiol 1987); CIMechE 1995; FRSC 2019. Nat. Service, 1950–54. Scientific Officer, Royal Victoria Infirmary, Newcastle, 1954–56; Sen. Scientific Officer, Leeds Hosps, 1956–60; Prin. Clin. Scientist, Dept of Plastic Surgery, 1960–67, Consultant Clin. Scientist, 1990–, St Luke's Hosp., Bradford; Vis. Sen. Res. Fellow, Biomedical Scis, 1961–, Dir, Biomaterials Res. Unit, 1990–, Jt Dir, Inst. of Health Res., 1993–2003, Hon. Prof., 2000, Univ. of Bradford; Dir of R&D, Bradford Hosps NHS Trust, 1992–2003. Council of Europe Res. Fellow, Sweden, 1968. ADC to the Queen, 1980–83. Royal Society of Medicine: Mem. Council, 2000–09; Hon. Sub Dean, N Yorks, 2001–04; Treas., 2004–07; Vice Pres., 2007–09; Stuart Lectr, Edinburgh, 2009; Pres., Technol. in Medicine Sect., 2010–; Chm., Academic Bd, 2016–17; Stevens Lect., 2015; Ambassador, 2018–. President: British Inst. of Surgical Tech., 1998– (Pres., 1996–99); Bradford Medico-Chirurgical Soc., 1995; Mem., Leeds Medico-Chirurgical Soc., 2017–; Chm., Bradford Res. Ethics Cttee, 2003–12; Partner, Health Professions Council, 2004–06; Clin. Dir, Prosthetic Solutions, Univ. of Bradford, 2005–. Ambassador, Overseas Plastic Surgery Appeal, 2018–. Mem., NY Acad. of Scis, 1987. Chm., COMEC, 1990–96; University of Leeds: Crown Rep., 1985–86; Chm., Court and Council, 1986–; Pro-Chancellor, 1986–2000; Dir, Westwood Hall, 1987–; Chm., Mil. Educn Cttee, 1996–2005; Dir, Univ. of Leeds Foundn, 1986–2000; Examiner: Sch. of Clin. Dentistry, Univ. of Sheffield, 1995–96; Dental Sch., Univ. of Malta, 2004–; Chm., Adv. Bd, Inst. of Cancer Therapeutics, Univ. of Bradford, 2009–. Visiting Professor: Inst. of Bioenrgrg, Brunel Univ., 2009–; Huddersfield Univ., 2019–. Trustee: Edward Boyle Trust, 1986–97; Yorks Sculpture Park, 1995–2017; Isherwood Trust, 2004–08. Mem. Council, BRCS, 1995 (Pres., W Yorks, 1983–2004; Badge of Honour, 1992); Vice Chm., Mil., Yorks and Humber, RFCA, 1997–2001. President: W Yorks SSAFA, 2000–17 (Chm., 1985–99); Leeds NSPCC, 2002–; S and W Yorks, RBL, 2019– (Chm., Leeds RBL, 1983–2019); Chm., W Riding Artillery Trust, 1983–; Trustee: ARNI Trust, 2007–; Maritime Heritage Foundn (formerly British Maritime Heritage Foundn), 2011–. Founder and Pres., Univ. of Leeds Defence Studies Dining Club, 1973–. Lt-Col Comdg, 1972–79, Hon. Col, 1980–90, Regtl Col, 2000–, Leeds Univ. OTC; Col and Dep. Comdr, NE Dist TA, 1980–83; Hon. Col, 269 Batt., RA, 1990–; Col Comdt, RA, 1996–; Mem., HAC, 2000–. Patron, Age Concern, 1994–. Governor: Pocklington Sch., 1990–2001; Gateways Sch., Leeds, 2000–06. Hon. Freeman and Liveryman, Clothworkers' Co., 2000–. JP Leeds, 1977; DL W Yorks, 1982. CGIA, 1969, 1976, FCGI 1990 (Pres., City and Guilds Assoc., 1998–2003); FRSocMed 1993, Hon. FRSocMed, 2010; FLS 1998; Fellow, Med. Soc. of London, 2008–18. Hon. LLD Leeds, 2000; Hon. DSc: London, 2005; Bradford, 2007; Hon. DTech Brunel, 2007. Prince Philip Medal for Science, C&G, 1970; Convocation Medal, Univ. of Leeds, 2008; RSocMed Medal, 2018. Lead researcher and inventor of: Silskin prosthetic skin, 1980; Indermil Tissue Adhesive, 1993; Zeflosil Prosthetic Adhesive, 2007. KStJ 2010 (CStJ 2002; Chm. Council, S & W Yorks, 2004–); Kt Comdr of Merit, Mil. Constantinian Order of St George, 2011. Companion, Order of the League of Mercy, 2002. Gentleman Usher, Imperial Soc. of Kts Bachelor, 2009–. Kt Grand Officer, Royal Order of Eagle of Georgia, 2015; Medal of Merit, Royal House of Georgia, 2017. *Publications*: Obturators and Prosthesis for Cleft Palate, 1968; Facial Restoration by Prosthetic Means, 1975; Maxillo-Facial Prosthetics: a multi-disciplinary practice, 1975; numerous articles in med. and dental jls. *Recreations*: sculpture, silversmithing, avoiding holidays. *Address*: The Grange, Rein Road, Morley, Leeds, W Yorks LS27 0HZ. *T*: (0113) 253 4632. *E*: roberts@132acr.com. *Club*: Army and Navy.

**ROBERTS, Prof. Alan Madoc,** PhD; FRS 2015; Professor of Zoology, University of Bristol, 1991–2013, now Emeritus; *b* Rugby, Warwickshire, 24 Aug. 1941; *s* of Vernon and Mary Roberts; *m* 1st, 1963, Naomi Collet (marr. diss. 1973); one *s* one *d*; 2nd, 1973, Pamela Reynolds (marr. diss. 1985); one *d*; 3rd, 1991, Joanna Wright. *Educ*: Rugby Sch.; Trinity Coll., Cambridge (BA Natural Scis 1963); Univ. of Calif, Los Angeles (PhD Zool. 1967). University of Bristol: SRC Fellow, 1967–70; Lectr in Zool., 1970–82; Reader in Zool., 1982–91. *Publications*: contrib. papers to scientific jls. *Recreations*: gardening, making things, early music, collecting porcelain. *Address*: School of Biological Sciences, University of Bristol, Life Science Building, 24 Tyndall Avenue, Bristol BS8 1TQ. *T*: (0117) 394 1328. *E*: a.roberts@bristol.ac.uk.

**ROBERTS, Alfred,** PhD; Chief Executive, Institution of Engineering and Technology (formerly Institution of Electrical Engineers), 1999–2007; *b* 24 June 1945; *s* of Oswald and Ellen Roberts; *m* 1978, Elizabeth Ann King; one *s* one *d*. *Educ*: University Coll. London (BSc 1st cl. Hons 1967); Univ. of Manchester (PhD 1970). Central Electricity Generating Board: Res. Officer, 1971–73; Section Manager, Applied Physics, 1973–75; Div. Head, Engrg Sci., 1975–81; Regl Financial Controller, 1981–85; Gp Financial Controller, 1985–88; Dir, Engrg Services, 1988–89; Commercial Dir, PowerGen plc, 1989–98. *Publications*: articles in Nuclear Physics; conf. proceedings on nucleon transfer reactions; conf. papers on privatisation and deregulation of the electricity industry. *Recreations*: science, technology, history, music, literature, football.

**ROBERTS, Allan Deverell,** CB 2013; Counsel to the Chairman of Committees, House of Lords, 2002–13; *b* 14 July 1950; *s* of Irfon Roberts and Patricia Mary (*née* Allan); *m* 1991, Irene Anne Graham Reilly; two *s* (and one *s* decd). *Educ*: Eton Coll. (King's Schol.); Magdalen Coll., Oxford (MA). Solicitor in private practice, 1974–76; Solicitor's Office, DHSS, 1976–96, Under-Sec. (Legal), 1989–96; Dir, Legal (Envmt, Planning and Countryside), DoE, 1996–97; Dir, Legal (Envmt, Housing and Local Govt), DETR, 1997–99; Dir, Legal (Legislation Unit), DETR, subseq. DTLR, 1999–2002. *Recreations*: tegestology, football, gardening, decorative arts.

**ROBERTS, Alwyn;** Pro Vice Chancellor, University of Wales, Bangor, 1994–97; *b* 26 Aug. 1933; *s* of late Rev. Howell Roberts and Buddug Roberts; *m* 1960, Mair Rowlands Williams; one *s*. *Educ*: Penygroes Grammar Sch.; Univ. of Wales, Aberystwyth and Bangor (BA, LLB); Univ. of Cambridge (MA). Tutor, Westminster Coll., Cambridge, 1959; Principal, Pachhunga Meml Govt Coll., Aijal, Assam, India, 1960–67; Lectr in Social Admin, University Coll., Swansea, 1967–70; University College of North Wales, later University of Wales, Bangor: Lectr, subseq. Sen. Lectr, Dept of Social Theory and Instns, 1970–79; Dir of Extra Mural Studies, 1979–95; Vice Principal, 1985–94. BBC National Governor for Wales, 1979–86; Chm., Broadcasting Council for Wales, 1979–86 (Mem., 1974–78); Member: Welsh Fourth TV Channel Authy, 1981–86; Gwynedd CC, 1973–81 (Chm., Social Services Cttee, 1977–81); Gwynedd AHA, 1973–80; Royal Commn on Legal Services, 1976–79; Parole Bd, 1987–90. Pres., Royal National Eisteddfod of Wales, 1994–96 (Vice-Pres., 1987–89; Chm., 1989–92; Mem. Council, 1979–); Chm., Acen (Cyf.), 1989–2010; Vice Chm., Arts Council of Wales, 1994–2000; Mem. Bd, Cwmni Theatr Cymru, 1982–86. Pro Chancellor, Bangor Univ., 2013– (Mem., Council, 2005–12). Fellow, Nat. Eisteddfod of Wales, 2005. Hon. Fellow, Univ. of Wales, Aberystwyth, 1999. Hon. LLD Wales, 2000. *Address*: Brithdir, 43 Talycae, Tregarth, Bangor, Gwynedd LL57 4AE. *T*: (01248) 600007.

**ROBERTS, Andrew,** PhD; FRSL, FRHistS; writer; *b* 13 Jan. 1963; *s* of Simon and Katie Roberts; *m* 1st, 1995, Camilla Henderson (marr. diss. 2001); one *s* one *d*; 2nd, 2007, Susan Gilchrist, *qv*. *Educ*: Cranleigh Sch.; Gonville and Caius Coll., Cambridge (exhibnr, Hon. Sen. Schol.; BA 1st Cl. Hons Hist.; MA; Chm., 1984, Pres., 2016–, CU Cons. Assoc.; Mem., Ct of Benefactors, 2002–06); PhD Cantab 2011. Corporate broker, Robert Fleming Securities Ltd, 1985–88; freelance journalist, broadcaster and book reviewer, 1988–; USA corresp., Standpoint mag., 2011–. Guest Curator, Morgan Liby, NYC, 2001–12, incl. 'Churchill and the Power of Words', 2011–12. Merrill Family Vis. Prof., Cornell Univ., 2013; Vis. Prof., Dept of War Studies, KCL, 2016–. Trustee: Roberts Foundn, 1989–; Margaret Thatcher Archive Trust, 2005–; NPG, 2013–; Dir, Frank Harry Guggenheim Foundn, 2009; Member: Exec. Cttee, Friends of Lambeth Palace Library, 2003–11; Bd, Internat. Friends of London Liby, 2011–; Acad. Adv. Cttee, Nat. Churchill Liby and Center, George Washington Univ., 2013–. Member, Council: Bruges Gp, 2003–; Freedom Assoc., 2003–; British Weights and Measures Assoc., 2003–; Centre for Policy Studies, 2003–; Centre for Social Cohesion, 2007–; Global Vision, 2008–; European Foundn, 2008–; Hougoumont Project, 2008–; Mem., Adv. Council, UK Nat. Defence Assoc., 2009–; Mem., Internat. Bd, Canadian Inst. for Jewish Res., 2010–; Contributing Mem. Bd, Wkg Gp on Mil. Hist. and Contemporary Conflict, Hoover Instn, 2013–; Mem., Academic Bd, Historians for Britain, 2014–; Chm., Adv. Bd, CANZUK Union Institutes, 2016–. Founder Mem., Friends of Israel Initiative, 2010–. Chm., Cons. Party Adv. Panel on Sch. History Teaching, 2005. Mem. Academic Council, Henry Jackson Soc., 2011. Founder-Pres., Cliveden Literary Fest., 2017–. Judge, Elizabeth Longford Historical Biography Prize, 2003, 2005–; Chairman: Judges Panel, Hessell-Tiltman History Prize, 2009; Judges, Guggenheim-Lehrman Prize for Mil. Hist., 2012–; Mem., Rev. Cttee, Dan David Prize, 2012. Hon. Co-Chair, Chm.'s Council, 2011–, Lewis Lehrman Dist. Fellow, 2014–, NY Histl Soc.; Hon. Member: Guild of Battlefield Guides, 2006; Internat. Churchill Soc. (UK), 2007 (Mem. Bd, 2016–); Vice-Pres., Internat. Guild of Battlefield Guides, 2010–. FRSL 2001; FRHistS 2016. Hon. DHL Westminster Coll., Fulton, Mo, 2000. Lion of Judah Award, Canadian Inst. for Jewish Res., 2010; William Penn Award, Penn Club, 2012; Pride of Century Award, British Schs and Univs Club, USA, 2012; Bradley Prize, Lynde and Harry Bradley Foundn, 2016; Edmund Burke Award, 2019. *Publications*: The Holy Fox: a life of Lord Halifax, 1991; Eminent Churchillians, 1994; The Aachen Memorandum, 1995; Salisbury: Victorian Titan, 1999 (James Stern Silver Pen Award, Wolfson Award for Hist., 2000); The House of Windsor, 2000; Napoleon and Wellington, 2001; Hitler and Churchill: secrets of leadership, 2003; (ed) What Might Have Been, 2004; Waterloo:

Napoleon's Last Gamble, 2005; (ed) The Correspondence Between Mr Disraeli and Mrs Brydges Willyams, 2006; A History of the English-Speaking Peoples since 1900, 2006 (Intercollegiate Studies Inst. Book Award, 2007); (ed) The Art of War, vol. 1 2008, vol. 2 2009; Masters and Commanders, 2008 (Emery Reves Prize, Churchill Centre, 2009); The Storm of War: a new history of the Second World War, 2009 (British Army Mil. Book of Year, 2010); (ed) Letters to Vicky: the correspondence between Queen Victoria and her daughter Vicky, Empress of Germany, 1858–1901, 2011; (ed) Love, Tommy, 2012; Napoleon the Great, 2014 (Prix du Jury des Grands Prix de la Fondation Napoléon, 2014; LA Times Biography Prize, 2015); Elegy: the first day on the Somme, 2015; Churchill: walking with destiny, 2018. *Recreation:* Corinthian Bagatelle. *Address:* 22 South Eaton Place, SW1W 9JA. *T:* (020) 7730 3091. *E:* andrew@andrew-roberts.net. *Clubs:* Pratt's, Brooks's, Garrick, Beefsteak, Saintsbury, Miller's Academy (Hon. Mem.), Fox, 5 Hertford Street (Hon. Mem.); Brook (New York); Spectacle (Milwaukee) (Hon. Mem.); Other (Wisconsin) (Hon. Mem.).

**ROBERTS, Air Vice-Marshal Andrew Lyle,** CB 1992; CBE 1983; AFC 1969; FRAeS; General Manager for Jennifer Bate, international concert organist, since 2001; *b* 19 May 1938; *s* of Ronald and Norah Roberts; *m* 1962; three *d*. *Educ:* Cranbrook Sch.; RAF Coll., Cranwell. Commnd RAF, 1958; ADC to AOC No 18 Gp, 1965–66; Flight Comdr, 201 Sqdn, 1967–68 (AFC); RNSC, 1969; Personal Air Sec. to Parly Under-Sec. of State (RAF), MoD, 1970–71; i/c 236 Operational Conversion Unit, 1972–74; US Armed Forces Staff Coll., 1974; staff, SACLANT, 1975–77; i/c RAF Kinloss, 1977–79; Gp Capt. Ops, HQ Strike Command, 1980–82 (CBE); RCDS, 1983; Dir, Air Plans, MoD, 1984–86; C of S, HQ No 18 Gp, 1987–89; ACDS (Concepts), 1987–92; Hd of RAF Manpower Structure Study Team, 1992–94. Chm. of Public Inquiries, Lord Chancellor's Panel of Ind. Inspectors, 1994–2010. Vice-Pres., Coastal Comd and Maritime Air Assoc., 2002– (founding Chm., 1995–2002); President: Brockenhurst Br., RBL, 2006–; Shackleton Assoc., 2018–. Trustee, Gwennili Trust (sailing for the disabled), 1995–2011. Organist, St Paul's Cathedral, Valletta, 1961. *Recreations:* cross-country and hill walking, natural history, classical music, church organ, choral singing, off-shore sailing. *Address:* 28 Oakenbrow, Sway, Lymington, Hants SO41 6DY. *Club:* Royal Air Force.

**ROBERTS, Ann;** *see* Clwyd, Rt Hon. Ann.

**ROBERTS, (Anthony) John,** CBE 1991; Board Member, 1985–2002, and Chief Executive, 1995–2002, Royal Mail Group (formerly The Post Office, then Consignia plc); Chairman, Post Office Ltd (formerly Post Office Counters Ltd), 1993–2002; *b* 26 Aug. 1944; *s* of Douglas and Margaret Roberts; *m* 1970, Diana June (*née* Lamdin); two *s*. *Educ:* Hampton Sch.; Exeter Univ. (BA Hons). Open Entrant, Administrative Class Civil Service, The Post Office, 1967; PA to Dep. Chairman and Chief Executive, 1969–71; Principal, Long Range Planning, 1971–74; Controller Personnel and Finance, North Western Postal Board, 1974–76; Principal Private Sec. to Chairman, 1976–77; Director, Chairman's Office, 1977–80; Secretary Designate, 1980–81, Sec., 1981–82; Dir, 1981–85, Man. Dir, 1985–93, Counter Services, subseq. Post Office Counters Ltd; Man. Dir, Gp Services, 1993–95; Chm., Subscription Services, 1993–95. Advr, Deloitte Consulting, 2003–05. Chm., South Thames TEC, 1989–92; Dir, Internat. Posts Corp., 1996–2003; Bd Mem., 2004–11, Dep. Chm., 2005–11, British Educnl Communications and Technol. Agency; Member: Govt New Deal Task Force, 1997–2003; CBI Educn and Trng Affairs Cttee, 1998–2003; Home Office Strategic Delivery Bd, 2003–05; Royal Mail Stamp Adv. Cttee, 2003–; Bd, Ofsted, 2007–10. Mem. Council, Inst. of Employment Studies, 1995–2003 (Pres., 1998–2003); Governor: Henley Mgt Coll., 1996–2006 (Hon. Fellow, 2008); Eur. Foundn for Quality Management, 1996–2001 (Pres., 1998–2001); Chm., Bd of Pension Trustees, Inst. of Cancer Res. Pension Fund, 2013– (Mem., 2012–13; Mem. Inst. of Cancer Res., 2012). FRSA 1992. Freeman, City of London, 1983. *Recreations:* golf, gardening, music. *Clubs:* MCC; Betchworth Park Golf; Harlequins Rugby Football.

**ROBERTS, Barbara Haig;** *see* MacGibbon, B. H.

**ROBERTS, Benjamin Andrew;** Deputy Chief Executive, British Film Institute, since 2018 (Director, Lottery Film Fund, 2012); *b* Coventry, 1 April 1975; *s* of James and Jennifer Roberts; civil partnership 2012, Chris Morriss. *Educ:* Bablake Sch., Coventry; Coventry Univ. (Dip. Fine Art 1994); Leeds Univ. (BA Hons English 1997). Hd of Distribn, Metrodome, 1998–2003; Vice Pres., Worldwide Acquisitions, Universal Pictures, 2003–07; CEO, Protagonist Pictures, 2007–12. Member: BAFTA; Eur. Film Acad. *Address:* British Film Institute, 21 Stephen Street, W1T 1LN. *T:* (020) 7173 3222. *E:* ben.roberts@bfi.org.uk. *Club:* Soho House.

**ROBERTS, Brian Stanley;** HM Diplomatic Service, retired; *b* 1 Feb. 1936; *s* of Stanley Victor Roberts and Flora May (*née* McInnes); *m* 1st, 1961, Phyllis Hazel Barber (marr. diss. 1976); two *s*; 2nd, 1985, Jane Catharine Chisholm; one *d*. *Educ:* Christ's Coll., Cambridge (MA); Courtauld Institute, London (MA). Served Royal Navy, 1955–57. Staff, Edinburgh Univ., 1960–62; Lecturer in Art History, Goldsmiths' Coll., London, 1962–69; entered FCO, 1970: First Secretary, Cape Town/Pretoria, 1972; FCO, 1974; attached to Hong Kong Govt, 1977; FCO, 1980; Counsellor, Stockholm, 1983–87; Cabinet Office, 1987. Teacher, Art Hist., Cheltenham Ladies' Coll., 1988–89; Head of Art Hist., Putney High Sch., 1989–97. *Recreations:* walking, looking at pictures. *Club:* Lansdowne.

**ROBERTS, Dr Brynley Francis,** CBE 1993; Librarian, National Library of Wales, 1985–94; Moderator, General Assembly of the Presbyterian Church of Wales, 2001–02; *b* 3 Feb. 1931; *s* of Robert F. Roberts and Laura Jane Roberts (*née* Williams); *m* 1957, Rhiannon Campbell; twin *s*. *Educ:* Grammar School, Aberdare; University College of Wales, Aberystwyth (BA Hons Welsh, MA, PhD). Fellow, Univ. of Wales, 1956–57; Lectr, Sen. Lectr, Reader, Dept of Welsh, University Coll. of Wales, Aberystwyth, 1957–78; Prof. of Welsh Language and Literature, University Coll. Swansea, 1978–85. Sir John Rhys Fellow, Jesus Coll., Oxford, 1973–74; Leverhulme Emeritus Fellow, 1997; Res. Associate, Dublin Inst. for Advanced Studies, 2000–11. Chairman: United Theological Coll., Aberystwyth, 1977–98; Gwasg Pantycelyn, Caernarfon, 1977–98. Pres., Welsh Library Assoc., 1985–94; Chm., Welsh Books Council, 1989–94 (Vice-Chm., 1986–89; Mem., 1994–2012); Mem., HEFCW, 1993–2000. Editor: Dictionary of Welsh Biography, 1987–2014); Y Traethodydd, 1999–2015. Hon. Fellow: Univ. of Wales, Swansea, 1996; Univ. of Wales, Aberystwyth, 2000; Coleg Cymraeg Cenedlaethol, 2017; Hon. Prof., Cardiff, 2001; Hon. Sen. Res. Fellow, Centre for Advanced Welsh and Celtic Studies, Univ. of Wales, 2009. FLSW 2011. Hon. FCLIP (Hon. FLA 1994). Hon. DLitt Wales, 1996. Sir Ellis Griffith Prize, 1962, Vernam Hull Prize, 2005, Univ. of Wales; Medal, Hon. Soc. of Cymmrodorion, 2007. *Publications:* Gwassanaeth Meir, 1961; Brut y Brenhinedd, 1971, 2nd edn 1984; Cyfranc Lludd a Llefelys, 1975; Brut Tysilio, 1980; Edward Lhuyd: the making of a scientist, 1980; Gerald of Wales, 1982; Itinerary through Wales, 1989; Studies on Middle Welsh Literature, 1992; (ed) Y Bywgraffiadur Cymreig 1951–1970, 1997; (ed) Dictionary of Welsh Biography 1941–1970, 2001; Breudwyt Maxen Wledic, 2005; (with Dewi W. Evans) Edward Lhwyd, Archaeologia Britannica: texts and translations, 2009; Anwir Anwedhys Y Mae Yn I Ysgrivennv Ymma: rhai o ymylnodau Edward Lhwyd, 2009; Ar drywydd Edward Lhwyd, 2013; articles in learned jls. *Recreations:* reminiscing, gardening, music. *Address:* Hengwrt, Llanbadarn Road, Aberystwyth SY23 1HB. *T:* (01970) 623577.

**ROBERTS, Prof. Callum Michael,** PhD; Professor of Marine Conservation, University of York, since 2002; *b* Pitlochry, 14 April 1962; *s* of Peter Alva Roberts and Margaret Jean Roberts; *m* 1987, Julie Patricia Hawkins; two *d*. *Educ:* York Univ. (BSc Hons Biol. 1983; PhD Biol. 1986). Research Associate: Univ. of York, 1987; Univ. of Liverpool and Suez Canal Univ., 1987–90; Sen. Res. Associate, Univ. of Newcastle upon Tyne, 1990–92; Res. Asst Prof., Univ. of Virgin Is, 1992–95. Hrdy Vis. Prof., Harvard Univ., 2001. Grand Prix des Scis de la Mer Albert I Monaco, 2017. *Publications:* Marine Ecology of the Arabian Region, 1992; Reef Fisheries, 1996; Fully Protected Marine Reserves: a guide, 1999; The Unnatural History of the Sea, 2007; Ocean of Life: how our seas are changing, 2012; Secrets of the Seas, 2016; Reel Life: an underwater memoir, 2019. *Recreations:* scuba-diving, hiking, collecting and reading old books, writing, fish watching. *Address:* Department of Environment and Geography, University of York, Heslington, York YO10 5DD. *T:* (01904) 324066, *Fax:* (01904) 324998. *E:* callum.roberts@york.ac.uk.

**ROBERTS, Sir Carl Bertrand Westerby,** KCN 2015; CMG 2012; High Commissioner of Antigua and Barbuda to the Court of St James's, and concurrently Ambassador to France, Germany, Spain and Italy, 2004–14; *b* St John's, Antigua and Barbuda, 13 Oct. 1948; *s* of late Arthur E. S. Roberts and of Audrey E. Roberts; *m* 1974, Pauline Margaret A.; two *s* one *d*. *Educ:* Antigua Grammar Sch.; Northeastern Univ., Boston (BSEE Hons *magna cum laude* 1982); Univ. of WI, Barbados (MBA 1995); Univ. of Bradford (DBA 2004). Joined Cable & Wireless (WI) Ltd, 1967; Gen. Manager, Montserrat, 1995–97; Chief Executive: Cable & Wireless Dominica, 1997–2002; Cable & Wireless St Kitts & Nevis, 2002–04. Perm. Rep., UNESCO, Paris, 2004; Dep. Perm. Rep., WTO, Geneva, 2004. *Recreations:* cricket, tennis, golf, reading, singing. *Address:* c/o High Commission for Antigua and Barbuda, 2nd Floor, 45 Crawford Place, W1H 4LP. *Club:* Rotary (London).

**ROBERTS, Caroline Mary;** *see* Shea, C. M.

**ROBERTS, Cedric P.;** *see* Prys-Roberts.

**ROBERTS, Ceridwen Mary, (Mrs S. G. Panke),** OBE 2013; FAcSS; FLSW; Senior Research Fellow, Department of Social Policy and Intervention, University of Oxford, since 2001; *b* Kingston-upon-Hull, 24 Dec. 1947; *d* of Thomas John Roberts and Kathleen Roberts (*née* Cowley); *m* 1988, Stephen Gerald Panke. *Educ:* Lady Eleanor Holles Sch.; Univ. of Sussex (BA Hons Hist. 1970); Univ. of Bristol (Postgrad. DipSocSc (Sociol.)); Imperial Coll. London. Lectr in Industrial Sociol., Trent Poly., 1975–78; Sen. Res. Officer, then Principal Research Officer, Dept of Employment, 1978–92; Dir, Family Policy Studies Centre, 1992–2001. Former Member: Strategic Res. Cttee, ESRC; Adv. Cttee, Nat. Centre for Res. Methods; Member: Governing Body, Wales Centre for Public Policy (formerly Public Policy Inst. for Wales); Adv. Cttee, Welsh Inst. of Social and Econ. Res., Data and Methods. Chairman: Social Res. Assoc., 2002–06 (Patron, 2015–); Strategic Society Centre, 2010–. Mem. Bd, Acad. of Social Sci., 2012–17. Mem. Bd, Honourable Soc. of Cymmrodorion, 2004– (Chm., 2016–). Trustee, Highgate Cemetery, 2011–17. FAcSS 2012; FLSW 2012. *Publications:* (with J. Martin) Women and Employment: a lifetime perspective, 1984; book chapters, articles, monographs and policy res. briefings. *Recreations:* politics, campaigning for social science, dogs, gardening, entertaining friends, travel, going to music festivals. *Address:* 96 North Road, Highgate, N6 4AA. *T:* (020) 8347 9957. *E:* Ceridwen.roberts@btopenworld.com.

**ROBERTS, Prof. Charlotte Ann, (Mrs S. J. Gardner),** PhD; FBA 2014; Professor of Archaeology, Durham University, since 2004; *b* Harrogate, 25 May 1957; *d* of Neville Harpin Roberts and Elizabeth Ann Roberts; *m* 2003, Stewart James Gardner. *Educ:* St James' Hosp., Leeds (SRN 1978); Leicester Univ. (BA Hons Archaeol Studies 1982); Sheffield Univ. (MA Envmtl Archaeol. 1983); Bradford Univ. (PhD Human Bioarchaeol. 1988). Staff Nurse, Burns Unit, St Lawrence Hosp., Chepstow, 1979; University of Bradford: Res. Asst, 1983–88; Lectr in Palaeopathol., 1989–94; Sen. Lectr in Biol Anthropol., 1994–99; Reader in Archaeol., Durham Univ., 2000–04. Leverhulme Trust Sen. Res. Fellow, 2006–08; Nuffield Foundn Res. Fellow, 2006–07. Panel Mem. (Archaeol.), REF 2014 and 2021. President: Paleopathol. Assoc., 2011–13; British Assoc. for Biol Anthropol. and Osteoarchaeol., 2015–18. Excellence in Teaching Award, Univ. of Bradford, 1999; Excellence in Doctoral Supervision Award, Durham Univ., 2009; Eve Cockburn Service Award, Paleopathol. Assoc., 2017. *Publications:* (ed jtly) Burial Archaeology: current research, methods and developments, 1989; (ed jtly) Studies in Crime: an introduction to forensic archaeology, 1995; (with K. Manchester) The Archaeology of Disease, 1995, 3rd edn 2005; (ed jtly) Proceedings of the International Congress on the Evolution and Palaeoepidemiology of the Infectious Diseases, 2002; (with M. Cox) Health and Disease in Britain: from prehistory to the present day, 2003; (with J. E. Buikstra) The Bioarchaeology of Tuberculosis: a global perspective on a re-emerging disease, 2003; Human Remains in Archaeology: a handbook, 2009, 2nd edn 2018; (ed jtly) The Global History of Paleopathology: pioneers and prospects, 2012; (ed jtly) The Backbone of Europe: health, diet, work and violence over two millennia, 2019; contrib. papers to jls, incl. Amer. Jl Physical Anthropol. and chapters in books. *Recreations:* fell running, cycling, hiking, gardening, border collies, flower arranging, bell ringing, WI, flute playing, Scotland exploring, travel to developing countries, folk music, cross country ski-ing, yoga, choir member, birdwatcher, natural history. *Address:* Department of Archaeology, Durham University, South Road, Durham DH1 3LE. *T:* (0191) 334 1154, *Fax:* (0191) 334 1101.

**ROBERTS, Christine Elizabeth;** a Judge of the Upper Tribunal (Immigration and Asylum Chamber), 2010–16; *b* Newcastle upon Tyne, 31 May 1950; *d* of William Crawford and Edna Crawford (*née* Osborne); *m* 1972, Adrian Roberts; one *s*. *Educ:* Whitley Bay Grammar Sch.; Univ. of Manchester (LLB Hons). Admitted solicitor, 1975; in practice as a solicitor, 1975–95; Immigration Adjudicator (full-time), 1995–2002; Regl Adjudicator, Bradford, 2002–05; Resident Judge, Bradford, 2005–16; Upper Tribunal Dep. Judge (Immigration and Asylum Chamber), 2016–. *Recreations:* reading, world cinema, theatre, cricket, walking.

**ROBERTS, Christopher William,** CB 1986; Deputy Secretary, 1983–97, and Director-General of Trade Policy, 1987–97, Department of Trade and Industry; Senior Trade Adviser, Covington and Burling, 1998–2011; *b* 4 Nov. 1937; *s* of Frank Roberts and Evelyn Dorothy Roberts. *Educ:* Rugby Sch.; Magdalen Coll., Oxford (MA). Lectr in Classics, Pembroke Coll., Oxford, 1959–60; Asst Principal, BoT, 1960; Second Sec. (Commercial), British High Commn, New Delhi, 1962–64; Asst Private Sec. to Pres. of BoT, 1964–65; Principal, 1965; Cabinet Office, 1966–68; Private Sec. to Prime Minister, 1970–73; Asst Sec., 1972; Dept of Trade, 1973–77; Under Secretary: Dept of Prices and Consumer Protection, 1977–79; Dept of Trade, 1979–82; Chief Exec., BOTB, 1983–87. Non-exec. Dir, NHBC, 1998–2004. Chairman: Wine Standards Bd, 1999–2006; Liberalisation of Trade in Services Cttee, Internat. Financial Services London, 2000–05; Policy Cttee, European Services Forum, 2002–08. Master, Turners Co., 2009–10. *Recreations:* travel, cricket, opera. *Address:* Tall Timbers, High Drive, Woldingham, Surrey CR3 7ED. *Clubs:* Oxford and Cambridge, MCC.

**ROBERTS, Colin,** CVO 2006; HM Diplomatic Service; Senior Adviser (EU Exit), UK Governance Group, Cabinet Office, since 2017; *b* 31 July 1959; *s* of John Jeffrey Roberts and Avril Joyce Roberts (*née* Dowding); *m* 2000, Camilla Frances Mary Blair; two *s*. *Educ:* Winchester Coll.; King's Coll., Cambridge (BA Eng. Lit., MA); Courtauld Inst. of Art

(MPhil 1982). Lectr, Ritsumeikan Univ., Kyoto, 1983–84; called to the Bar, Inner Temple, 1986; in private legal practice, 1986–89; entered HM Diplomatic Service, 1989; Second Sec. (Econ.), later First Sec. (Pol), Tokyo, 1990–94; First Secretary: EU Dept (Internal), FCO, 1995–96; (Pol/Mil.), Paris, 1997–98; Hd, Common Foreign and Security Policy Dept, FCO, 1998–2000; Pol Counsellor, Tokyo, 2001–04; Ambassador to Lithuania, 2004–08; Dir, Overseas Territories, FCO, 2008–12; Comr, British Indian Ocean Territory and British Antarctic Territory, 2008–12; Dir, Eastern Europe and Central Asia, FCO, 2012–13; Gov., Falkland Is and Comr, S Georgia and S Sandwich Is, 2014–17. FRGS 2017. *Recreations:* mountain sports, natural history, tennis, reading. *Address:* c/o Foreign and Commonwealth Office, King Charles Street, SW1A 2AH. *Club:* Travellers.

**ROBERTS, David Francis,** CMG 2003; consultant on agricultural trade issues; Deputy Director General responsible for external trade policy in agriculture, European Commission, 1996–2002; *m* 1974, Astrid Suhr Henriksen; two *s* one *d*. *Educ:* Priory Grammar School, Shrewsbury; Worcester College, Oxford (MA). Joined MAFF, 1964; seconded to FCO as First Sec. (Agric.), Copenhagen, 1971–74; Principal Private Sec. to Minister of Agriculture, 1975–76; seconded to HM Treasury as Head of Agric. Div., 1979–80; Under Sec., 1985, seconded to FCO as Minister (Agric.), UK Repn to the European Communities, Brussels, 1985–90; Dep. Dir Gen., resp. for agricl support, DG VI, EC, 1990–96. *Recreations:* sailing, squash, rowing, racketball.

**ROBERTS, David George;** HM Diplomatic Service, retired; Founder Director, Dagero Ltd, international business advice, 2010–16; *b* 11 April 1955; *s* of David Ceredig Roberts, Dolgellau, and Margaret Roberts (*née* Burns); *m* 1985, Rosmarie Rita Kunz, Winterthur, Switzerland; one *s* one *d*. *Educ:* Bishop Vesey's Grammar Sch., Sutton Coldfield; Pembroke Coll., Oxford (BA Hons Mod. Hist. 1976; MA 1983). Joined FCO, 1976: Desk Officer, E Germany and WEU, 1976–77; Third, later Second, Sec. (Chancery), Jakarta, 1977–81; Second Sec. (Chancery), Havana, 1981–83; Desk Officer for nuclear deterrence, strategic defence and test ban matters, Defence and Arms Control and Disarmament Depts, FCO, 1983–86; Section Head for N Africa, Near East and N Africa Dept, FCO, 1986–88; First Secretary: (Eur. and Econ. Affairs), Madrid, 1988–90; (EU and Financial Affairs), Paris, 1990–94; Deputy Head: Hong Kong Dept, FCO, 1994–96; of Mission, and Consul Gen., Santiago, 1996–2000; of Mission, Dir of Trade and Investment and Consul Gen., Switzerland and Liechtenstein, 2000–05; Hd, Global Business, subseq. Sustainable Develt and Business, Gp, FCO, 2005–08. Internat. Advr, 3i Gp plc, 2008–09; Sen. Advr to Gov., Turks and Caicos Is, 2009. *Recreations:* enjoying languages (Spanish, French, German, Indonesian), rowing, keeping fit, reading, gardening, classical music, eating and drinking.

**ROBERTS, (David) Gwilym (Morris),** CBE 1987; FREng; Chairman, Acer Group Ltd, 1987–92; *b* 24 July 1925; *er s* of late Edward and Edith Roberts of Crosby; *m* 1st, 1960, Rosemary Elizabeth Emily (*d* 1973), *d* of late J. E. Giles of Tavistock; one *s* one *d*; 2nd, 1978, Wendy Ann, *d* of late Dr J. K. Moore of Beckenham and Alfriston. *Educ:* Merchant Taylors' School, Crosby; Sidney Sussex College, Cambridge (Minor Scholar, MA; Hon. Fellow, 1993). FICE, FIMechE; FREng (FEng 1986). Engineering Officer, RNVR, 1945–47; Lieut Comdr RNR, retired 1961. Asst Engineer, 1947–55, Partner, 1956–90 (Sen. Partner, 1981–90), John Taylor & Sons; principally development of water and wastewater projects, UK towns and regions, and Abu Dhabi, Bahrain, Egypt, Iraq, Kuwait, Mauritius, Qatar, Saudi Arabia and Thailand. Director: Acer Gp Ltd, 1987–92; various transportation projects in UK and abroad. Vis. Prof., Loughborough Univ., 1991–95. Chairman: BGS Programme Bd, 1989–93; Football Stadia Adv. Design Council, 1990–93; 2nd Severn Crossing Technical Adjudication Panel, 1991–97; Member: UK Cttee, IAWPRC, 1967–83; Bd of Control, AMBRIC (American British Consultants), 1978–92; (Construction Industry) Group of Eight, 1983–85, 1987–88; President: IPHE, 1968–69 (IPHE Silver Medal 1974; Gold Medal 1987); ICE, 1986–87 (Vice-Pres., 1983–86; Overseas Premium, 1978; Halcrow Premium, 1985; George Stephenson Medal, 1986); Smeatonian Soc. of Civil Engrs, 2009. Council Member: Brighton Polytechnic, 1983–86; NERC, 1987–93; CIRIA, 1988–92. Member: Exec. Cttee, British Egyptian Soc., 1991–93; Nat. Cttee, British-Arab Univ. Assoc., 1991–93; Council, Newcomen Soc., 2010–12. Governor: Chailey Sch., 1988–92; Roedean Sch., 1989–93. Freeman, City of London, 1977; Liveryman: Engineers' Co., 1985; Constructors' Co., 1990; Water Conservators' Co., 2000. Hon. FCIWEM. *Publications:* (co-author) Civil Engineering Procedure, 3rd edn 1979; Built By Oil, 1995; From Kendal's Coffee House to Great George Street, 1995; Chelsea to Cairo, 2006; Engineering Hitler's Downfall: the brains that enabled victory, 2018; papers to Royal Soc., Arab League, ICE, IPHE, Newcomen Soc. *Recreations:* golf, engineering history, family history. *Address:* 33 High Hurst Close, Newick, E Sussex BN8 4NJ. *T:* (01825) 722603. *Clubs:* Oxford and Cambridge; Piltdown Golf.

**ROBERTS, David Ian;** Co-Founder and Chief Executive, Edinburgh House Estates (Holdings) Ltd, since 2001; Co-Founder, Estama GmbH, 2007; *b* Greenock, 29 Sept. 1956; *s* of Romley Lewis Roberts and Anne Roberts; *m* 1993, Philippa Thornton (marr. diss. 2011); three *s* three *d*. *Educ:* Paisley Univ. (BA Land Econs). Chief Exec., Bourne End Properties plc, 1997–2001. Founder, David Roberts Art Foundn, 2007. *Recreations:* art collecting, ski-ing, fishing, golf. *Address:* Edinburgh House Estates (Holdings) Ltd, 17 Hanover Square, W1S 1BN. *T:* (020) 7383 8300. *E:* dir@ehel.co.uk. *Clubs:* Annabel's, Harry's Bar, Morton's, Arts.

**ROBERTS, (David) Paul,** OBE 2008; Managing Director, Improvement and Development Agency, 2009–10; Chairman, Board of Directors, Innovation Unit, since 2014 (Director, since 2011); *b* 6 Sept. 1947; *s* of Percival and Nancy Roberts; *m* 1969, Helen Margaret Shone; two *d*. *Educ:* Univ. of Bristol (BSc Hons 1969; CertEd 1970); Cambridge Inst. Educn (AdvDip 1982). Maths Teacher, then Dir of Studies, Ipswich Sch., 1970–74; Dep. Hd Teacher, Harlington Upper Sch., Beds, 1974–83; Chief Inspector, then Dep. Dir of Educn, Notts CC, 1983–97; Dir of Educn, Nottingham CC, 1997–2001. Dir, Guideline Careers Co. Ltd, 1997–2001; Dir, Capita Strategic Educn Services, and Dir of Educn, Haringey Council, 2001–04; Improvement and Development Agency: Strategic Advr, Children and Children's Services, 2004–05; Dir, Strategy and Develt, 2005–09. Advr to DCMS and DFE (formerly DfES, then DCSF) Ministers on Creativity in Schs, 2005–10; Chairman: Creative and Cultural Educn Bd, DCSF and DCMS, 2007–08; of Trustees, Creativity, Culture and Educn, 2008–17; Member: Cultural Educn Bd, DfE and DCMS, 2013–16; Music Educn Hub Adv. Bd, DfE, 2014–17. National Endowment for Science, Technology and the Arts: Member: Fellowship Prog. Cttee, 2004–06; Innovation Cttee, 2006–10; Public Services Innovation Lab. Bd, 2009–12; Creative Councils Steering Gp, 2012–13; Nat. Council, Arts Council England, 2017–; Durham Commn on Creativity and Educn, 2017–; Associated Bd of Royal Schs of Music Commn on Music Educn, 2017–. Mem., Warwick Commn on Future of Cultural Value, 2014–15. Chm., Nottingham Music Educn Hub, 2013–17; Member, Board of Directors: Mountview Acad. of Theatre Arts, 2010– (Dep. Chm., 2013–); Nottingham Contemp., 2010– (Dep. Chm., 2012–); Greenwood Acads Trust, 2010–14. FRSA 1999. *Publications:* Nurturing Creativity in Young People, 2006; (jtly) Organisational Innovation in Public Services, 2013; (jtly) The Virtuous Circle: why creativity and cultural education matter, 2014; articles in educnl and maths jls. *Recreations:* arts, hill-walking. *Address:* 55 Dunster Road, West Bridgford, Nottingham NG2 6JE. *T:* 07799 408229. *E:* paulroberts9994@gmail.com.

**ROBERTS, Dennis Laurie Harold;** Director of Methodology, Office for National Statistics, 2011–12; *b* 24 Jan. 1949; *s* of William Roberts and Vera Roberts; *m* 1980, Anne Mary Hillhouse; one *s*. *Educ:* Sheffield Univ. (BA, MSc). CSO, 1971–76; DoE, 1976–83; MoD, 1983–85; Department of the Environment: Head: Local Govt Finance Div., 1985–89; Water Envmt Div., 1989–92; Finance Div., 1992–94; OPCS, 1994–96; Dir, Socio-Economic Stats and Analysis Gp, 1996–98, Dir, Corp. Services Gp, 1998–99, ONS; Dir, Roads and Traffic Directorate, DETR, 2000–01; Dir, Road Transport Directorate, DTLR, then DfT, 2001–03; Dir, Registration Services and Dep. Registrar General for England and Wales, 2004–08; Dir, Surveys and Admin. Sources, 2008–11, ONS. *Recreations:* walking, reading, watching football.

**ROBERTS, Derek Franklyn,** FCII, FCIB; Chairman, Yorkshire Building Society, 1997–2001; *b* 16 Oct. 1942; *s* of Frank Roberts, MBE, and May Evelyn Roberts; *m* 1969, Jacqueline (*née* Velho); two *s* one *d*. *Educ:* Park High Grammar Sch., Birkenhead; Liverpool Coll. of Commerce; Harvard Business Sch. (AMP (Grad.)). Royal Insurance Co. Ltd, 1961–72; Huddersfield Building Society: Insce Services Man., 1972; apptd to Executive, as Business Develt Man., 1975; Develt Man., 1979; on formation of Yorkshire Building Soc., 1982, apptd Asst Gen. Man. (Marketing); Dir and Chief Exec., 1987–96. Director: BWD Securities plc, 1988–92; Yorkshire Water Services (formerly Yorkshire Water), 1996–2005; Kelda Gp plc, 1999–2005. Dir, Bradford City Challenge Ltd, 1993–97; Mem., W Yorks Rural Develt Cttee, 1992–96. CCMI. *Address:* The Ark, 20 Arkenley Lane, Almondbury, Huddersfield HD4 6SQ. *T:* (01484) 426414. *Clubs:* Huddersfield Golf, Woodsome Hall Golf; Huddersfield Rugby Union FC.

**ROBERTS, Sir Derek (Harry),** Kt 1995; CBE 1983; FRS 1980; FREng, FInstP; Provost of University College London, 1989–99 and 2002–03; *b* 28 March 1932; *s* of Harry and Alice Roberts; *m* 1958, Winifred (*née* Short); one *s* one *d*. *Educ:* Manchester Central High Sch.; Manchester Univ. (BSc). Joined Plessey Co.'s Caswell Res. Lab., 1953; Gen. Man., Plessey Semiconductors, 1967; Dir, Allen Clark Res. Centre, 1969; Man. Dir, Plessey Microelectronics Div., 1973; Technical Dir, 1983–85, Jt Dep. Man. Dir (Technical), 1985–88, GEC. Pres., BAAS, 1996–97. Hon. DSc: Bath, 1982; Loughborough, 1984; City, 1985; Lancaster, 1986; Manchester, 1987; Salford, Essex, London, 1988; DUniv Open, 1984. *Publications:* about 20 pubns in scientific and technical jls. *Recreations:* reading, gardening. *Address:* University College London, Gower Street, WC1E 6BT. *T:* (020) 7679 7234.

**ROBERTS, Sir (Edward) Adam,** KCMG 2002; FBA 1990; Montague Burton Professor of International Relations, 1986–2007, Senior Research Fellow, Department of Politics and International Relations, since 2008, Oxford University; Fellow of Balliol College, Oxford, 1986–2007, now Emeritus; President, British Academy, 2009–13; *b* 29 Aug. 1940; *s* of late Michael Roberts, poet and Janet Roberts, OBE, writer (as Janet Adam Smith); *m* 1966, Frances P. Dunn; one *s* one *d*. *Educ:* Westminster School; Magdalen College, Oxford (Open Schol.; Stanhope Hist. Essay Prize, 1961; BA 1962, MA 1981). Asst Editor, Peace News Ltd, 1962–65; Noel Buxton Student in Internat. Relations, LSE, 1965–68; Lectr in Internat. Relations, LSE, 1968–81; Alastair Buchan Reader in Internat. Relations, Oxford Univ., and Professorial Fellow, St Antony's Coll., Oxford, 1981–86; Leverhulme Res. Fellow, 2000–03. Mem., Council for Sci. and Technol., 2010–13. Member, Council: RIIA, 1985–91; IISS, 2002–08; Member: Adv. Bd, UK Defence Acad., 2003–15; Bd of Advrs, Lieber Inst. for Law and Land Warfare, US Military Acad., West Point, 2016–. Gov., Ditchley Foundn, 2001–11. Hon. Fellow: LSE, 1997; St Antony's Coll., Oxford, 2006; Cumbria Univ., 2014. For. Mem., Amer. Acad. of Arts and Scis, 2011; Mem., Amer. Philosophical Soc., 2013; MAE 2013. Hon. DSocSc KCL, 2010; Hon. LLD Aberdeen, 2012; Hon. Dr Internat. Politics Aoyama Gakuin, Tokyo, 2012; Hon. DLitt Bath, 2014. *Publications:* (ed) The Strategy of Civilian Defence, 1967; (jtly) Czechoslovakia 1968, 1969; Nations in Arms, 1976, 2nd edn 1986; (ed jtly) Documents on the Laws of War, 1982, 3rd edn 2000; (ed jtly) United Nations, Divided World, 1988, 2nd edn 1993; (ed jtly) Hugo Grotius and International Relations, 1990; Humanitarian Action in War, 1996; (ed jtly) The United Nations Security Council and War, 2008; (ed jtly) Civil Resistance and Power Politics, 2009; (ed) Democracy, Sovereignty and Terror, 2012; (ed jtly) Civil Resistance in the Arab Spring: triumphs and disasters, 2016. *Recreations:* mountaineering, cycling. *Address:* Balliol College, Oxford OX1 3BJ. *Club:* Alpine (Trustee, 2013–).

**ROBERTS, (Edward) Matthew (Giles);** Chief Executive Officer, Intu Properties plc, since 2019; *b* London, 8 Aug. 1963; *s* of David Gwilym Morris Roberts and Rosemary Elizabeth Roberts (*née* Giles); *m* 1993, Vanessa Anne Wright; one *s* two *d*. *Educ:* Sherborne Sch.; Durham Univ. (BA Econs). FCA 1999. Coopers and Lybrand, 1985–89; Burton Gp, 1989–95; Finance Director: Topshop and Topman, 1995–96; Debenhams plc, 1996–2003; Chief Financial Officer, Gala, subseq. Gala Coral Gp, 2004–08; Chief Financial Officer, Intu Properties plc, 2010–19. Non-exec. Dir, Marstons plc, 2017–. *Recreations:* golf, tennis, running, National Hunt racing, watching Brighton and Hove Albion. *Address:* Intu Properties plc, 40 Broadway, SW1H 0BT. *T:* (020) 7960 1353. *E:* matthew.roberts@intu.co.uk. *Clubs:* MCC, Turf; Rye Golf, Royal St George's Golf.

**ROBERTS, Eifion;** *see* Roberts, His Honour H. E. P.

**ROBERTS, Rt Hon. Elizabeth S.;** *see* Saville Roberts, Rt Hon. E.

**ROBERTS, Emyr Gordon,** PhD; Chief Executive, Natural Resources Wales, 2012–17; *b* 6 Sept. 1958; *s* of Gordon and Awena Wyn Roberts; *m* 1999, Karen Turner; one *s* one *d*. *Educ:* Univ. of Reading (BA Hons 1979); Univ. of Wales, Aberystwyth (PhD 1988). NFU, 1982–91; Welsh Office: Principal, 1991–97; Hd, Financial Planning Div., 1997–2000; Hd, Econ. Planning Div., Nat. Assembly for Wales, 2001–03; Chief Exec., Welsh European Funding Office, 2003–05; Welsh Assembly Government, subseq. Welsh Government: Dir, Dept for Social Justice and Regeneration, later Social Justice and Local Govt, 2005–09; Dir Gen., Public Services and Local Govt Delivery, 2009–10; Dir Gen., Children, Educn, Lifelong Learning and Skills, subseq. Dept for Educn and Skills, 2010–12. Mem., Ind. Welsh Pay Rev. Body, 2019–. Trustee, Alzheimer's Soc., 2014–. Mem. Council, Aberystwyth Univ., 2015– (Chair, 2018–; Fellow, 2013). Hon. Prof., Swansea Univ., 2017–. Hon. FSE 2018. *E:* emr27@aber.ac.uk.

**ROBERTS, Prof. Gareth Owen,** PhD; FRS 2013; Professor of Statistics and Director, Centre for Research in Statistical Methodology, University of Warwick, since 2007; *b* Liverpool, 1964; *s* of Alun Roberts and Ceri Roberts; *m* 1998, Deborah Tait; one *s* one *d*. *Educ:* Blue Coat Sch., Liverpool; Jesus Coll., Oxford (BA 1st Cl. Hons Maths 1985); Univ. of Warwick (PhD Statistics 1988). Lecturer in Statistics: Dept of Maths, Univ. of Nottingham, 1988–91; Dept of Pure Maths and Mathematical Statistics, Univ. of Cambridge, 1992–98; Prof. of Statistics, Dept of Maths and Statistics, Lancaster Univ., 1998–2007. FSS 1998. Medallion Lect., 2009, Blackwell Lect., 2014, Inst. for Mathematical Statistics. Guy Medal, Bronze, 1997, Silver, 2008, Royal Statistical Soc.; Rollo Davidson Prize, 1999. *Publications:* over 140 articles in acad. jls. *Recreations:* bridge, music, cycling, walking. *Address:* Department of Statistics, University of Warwick, Coventry CV4 7AL. *T:* (024) 7657 4812, *Fax:* (024) 7652 4532. *E:* gareth.o.roberts@warwick.ac.uk.

**ROBERTS, George Arnott**; Head of Administration Department, House of Commons, 1988–91; *b* 16 April 1930; *s* of David Roberts and Doris (*née* Sykes); *m* 1956, Georgina (*née* Gower); two *s* one *d*. *Educ*: Rastrick Grammar Sch.; London Univ. (extra-mural). Min. of Labour, then Dept of Employment, 1947–74; Advisory, Conciliation and Arbitration Service, 1974–85: Sec., Central Arbitration Cttee, 1978–80; Dir of Administration, 1980–83; Dir, London Region, 1983–85; House of Commons, 1985–91: Hd of Establishment Office, 1985–88. *Recreation*: gardening.

**ROBERTS, Sir Gilbert (Howland Rookehurst)**, 7th Bt *cr* 1809; *b* 31 May 1934; *s* of Sir Thomas Langdon Howland Roberts, 6th Bt, CBE, and of Evelyn Margaret, *o d* of late H. Fielding-Hall; *S* father, 1979; *m* 1958, Ines, *o d* of late A. Labunski; one *s* one *d*. *Educ*: Rugby; Gonville and Caius Coll., Cambridge (BA 1957). CEng, MIMechE. *Heir*: *s* Howland Langdon Roberts, *b* 19 Aug. 1961. *Address*: 3340 Cliff Drive, Santa Barbara, CA 93109–1079, USA.

**ROBERTS, Prof. Gordon Carl Kenmure**, PhD; Professor of Biochemistry, University of Leicester, 1986–2008, Emeritus Professor, 2011 (Honorary Professor, 2008–11); *b* 28 May 1943; *s* of Rev. Douglas M. A. K. Roberts and Hilda (*née* Engelmann); *m* 1963, Hilary Margaret Lepper; two *s* one *d*. *Educ*: University Coll., London (BSc Hons Biochem. 1964); PhD Biochem. London 1967. Res. Chemist, Merck Sharp & Dohme Res. Labs, Rahway, NJ, 1967–69; Member scientific staff: MRC Molecular Pharmacol. Res. Unit, Dept of Pharmacol., Univ. of Cambridge, 1969–72; NIMR, 1972–86; University of Leicester: Director: Henry Wellcome Labs for Structural Biol. (formerly Leicester Biol NMR Centre), 1986–2008; Centre for Mechanisms of Human Toxicity, 1991–2000; Head: Dept of Biochemistry, 2000–04; Sch. of Biol Scis, 2004–08. Pres., IUPAB, 2011–14. Ed.-in-Chief, Encyclopaedia of Biophysics, 5 vols, 2012. *Publications*: NMR in Molecular Biology (with O. Jardetzky), 1981; (ed) NMR of Biological Macromolecules, 1993; (ed with L.-Y. Lian) Protein NMR: practical techniques and applications, 2011; numerous papers in scientific jls. *Recreations*: gardening, genealogy. *Address*: Leicester Institute of Structural Biology, Department of Molecular and Cell Biology, Henry Wellcome Building, University of Leicester, Lancaster Road, Leicester LE1 7RH.

**ROBERTS, Gwilym**; *see* Roberts, D. G. M.

**ROBERTS, Howard Edward**, OBE 2008; QC (Guernsey) 2000; Lieutenant Bailiff of Guernsey, since 2017; *b* Suffolkbrowse, 19 April 1956; *s* of Basil Roberts and Lorna Roberts (*née* Heyworth); *m* 1977, Janice Dronsfield; two *s*. *Educ*: Cheadle Mosely Grammar Sch., Cheshire; Gonville and Caius Coll., Cambridge (MA); Univ. of Caen, France. Called to the Bar, Middle Temple, 1978, Guernsey, 1988; Legal Asst, MAFF, 1980–83; Legislative Draftsman, Guernsey, 1983–90; Crown Advocate, Guernsey, 1990–99; HM Comptroller (Solicitor-Gen.), Guernsey, 1999–2009; HM Procureur (Attorney-Gen.) and Receiver Gen., Guernsey, 2009–16. Mem., Guernsey Choral and Orchestral Soc. *Recreations*: choral music, gardening. *Address*: Royal Court House, St Peter Port, Guernsey GY1 2PB.

**ROBERTS, Sir Hugh (Ashley)**, GCVO 2010 (KCVO 2001; CVO 1998; LVO 1995); FSA; Director of the Royal Collection and Surveyor of the Queen's Works of Art, 1996–2010, now Surveyor Emeritus; *b* 20 April 1948; *s* of late Rt Rev. Edward James Keymer Roberts, sometime Bishop of Ely, and Dorothy Frances, *d* of Rev. Canon Edwin David Bowser; *m* 1975, Hon. Priscilla Jane Stephanie Low (*see* Hon. P. J. S. Roberts); two *d*. *Educ*: Winchester Coll.; Corpus Christi Coll., Cambridge (MA; Hon. Fellow 2011). FSA 1994. With Christie Manson and Woods, 1970–87 (Dir, 1978–87); Dep. Surveyor of the Queen's Works of Art, 1988–96. Mem., Sec. of State's Adv. Gp, Historic Royal Palaces Agency, 1990–98. Mem., Fabric Adv. Cttee, St George's Chapel, Windsor, 1998–. Member: Exec. Cttee, NACF, 1988–2000; Arts Panel, NT, 1988–2014 (Chm., 1997–2010); Council, Attingham Trust, 1988–2010 (Patron, 2010–); Conservation Cttee, Devonshire Collection, 2008– (Chm., 2008–); Mgt Cttee, Wellington Collection (Apsley House), 2015–. Trustee: Harewood House Trust, 1986–; Cobbe Collection Trust, 1997–; Historic Royal Palaces Trust, 1998–2010; Great Steward of Scotland's Dumfries House Trust, 2007–14; Wallace Collection, 2013–17; Trustee and Gov., Royal Pavilion and Museums Foundn (formerly Friends of Royal Pavilion Art Gall. and Brighton Mus.), 2008–16. Mem., Internat. Council, Preservation Soc. of Newport Co., RI, 2011–. Mem., Soc. of Dilettanti, 1991–. *Publications*: For the King's Pleasure: the furnishing and decoration of George IV's apartments at Windsor Castle, 2001; The Queen's Diamonds, 2012; contrib. to Furniture History, Burlington Mag., Apollo, etc. *Recreations*: cooking, gardening. *Address*: 33 East Lockinge, near Wantage, Oxon OX12 8QG. *T*: (01235) 835708. *Clubs*: Brooks's, Grillions; Nobody's Friends.

**ROBERTS, His Honour (Hugh) Eifion (Pritchard)**; QC 1971; DL; a Circuit Judge, 1977–98; *b* 22 Nov. 1927; *er s* of late Rev. and Mrs E. P. Roberts, Anglesey; *m* 1958, Buddug Williams; one *s* two *d*. *Educ*: Beaumaris Grammar Sch.; University Coll. of Wales, Aberystwyth (LLB); Exeter Coll., Oxford (BCL). Called to Bar, Gray's Inn, 1953; practised on Wales and Chester Circuit, Sept. 1953–July 1977. Dep. Chairman: Anglesey QS, 1966–71; Denbighshire QS, 1970–71; a Recorder of the Crown Court, 1972–77. Formerly Asst Parly Boundary Comr for Wales; Mem. for Wales of the Crawford Cttee on Broadcasting Coverage. Hon. Fellow, Bangor Univ., 2009. Hon. LLD Wales, 2014. *Recreation*: gardening. *Address*: Maes-y-Rhedyn, Gresford Road, Llay, Wrexham LL12 0NN. *T*: (01978) 852292.

**ROBERTS, Prof. Ian Gareth**, PhD, LittD; FBA 2007; Professor of Linguistics, since 2000, and Head, Section of Theoretical and Applied Linguistics, since 2019, University of Cambridge; Fellow, Downing College, Cambridge, since 2000; *b* 23 Oct. 1957; *s* of Idris Michael Roberts and Dorothy Sybil Roberts (*née* Moody); *m* 1993, Lucia Cavalli; one *s* one *d*. *Educ*: Stamford Sch.; Eirias High Sch., Colwyn Bay; UCNW (Bangor) (BA Hons Linguistics 1979); Univ. of Southern Calif (PhD 1985); LittD Cantab 2016. Translator, Motor Ind. Res. Assoc., Nuneaton, 1980–81; University of Geneva: Asst de linguistique anglaise, 1985–86; Maître-asst de linguistique générale, 1986–91; Professor: of Linguistics, UCNW (Bangor), then Univ. of Wales, Bangor, 1991–96; of English Linguistics, Univ. of Stuttgart, 1996–2000; Hd, Dept of Linguistics, 2001–05, Chair, Faculty of Modern and Medieval Langs, 2011–15, Univ. of Cambridge. Ed., Jl Linguistics, 1994–2000. MAE 2008. Pres., Soc. Linguistica Europaea, 2012–13. Hon. Dr Bucharest, 2013. *Publications*: The Representation of Implicit and Dethematised Subjects, 1987; Verbs and Diachronic Syntax, 1993; Comparative Syntax, 1996; Syntactic Change, 2003; Principles and Parameters in a VSO Language, 2005; Diachronic Syntax, 2007; Agreement and Head Movement, 2010; The Wonders of Language, 2017; The Final Over Final Condition: a syntactic universal, 2017; Parameter Hierarchies and Universal Grammar, 2019; contrib. numerous articles to learned jls. *Recreations*: reading, walking, music. *Address*: Downing College, Cambridge CB2 1DQ. *T*: (01223) 334834.

**ROBERTS, Ian White**; HM Diplomatic Service, retired; Hon. Visiting Fellow, 1985–99, Official Historian, since 1999, School of Slavonic and East European Studies, University College London; *b* 29 March 1927; *s* of George Dodd Roberts and Jessie Dickson Roberts (*née* White); *m* 1956, Pamela Johnston; one *d*. *Educ*: Royal Masonic Sch., Bushey, Herts; Gonville and Caius Coll., Cambridge (MA 1st Cl. Hons Mod. Langs). Served Royal Air Force (Pilot Officer), 1948–50; postgrad. student, Cambridge (Scarbrough Award), 1950. Joined Foreign Office, 1951; Klagenfurt, 1952; Munich, 1954; Berlin, 1955; FCO, 1957–61; Second (later First) Secretary, Budapest, 1961–63; FCO, 1963; Bujumbura, 1965; FCO, 1965–66; Buenos Aires, 1966; FCO, 1969–74; Oslo, 1974–76; FCO, 1976–84; Counsellor, 1976. Special Advr, Finnish Inst., London, 2009. *Publications*: Nicholas I and the Russian Intervention in Hungary, 1991; History of School of Slavonic and East European Studies, University College London, 1991, 2nd edn 2009; articles in philatelic and other jls incl. East-West Rev. and publications of FCO Historical Dept. *Recreations*: music, reading. *Address*: c/o Lloyds, 1 Butler Place, SW1H 0PR. *Club*: Travellers (Hon. Mem., 2014).

**ROBERTS, Sir Ivor (Anthony)**, KCMG 2000 (CMG 1995); FCIL; President, Trinity College, Oxford, 2006–17 (Hon. Fellow, 2017); HM Diplomatic Service, retired; *b* 24 Sept. 1946; *s* of late Leonard Moore Roberts and Rosa Maria Roberts (*née* Fusco); *m* 1974, Elizabeth Bray Bernard Smith; two *s* one *d*. *Educ*: St Mary's Coll., Crosby; Keble Coll., Oxford (Gomm schol.; MA; Hon. Fellow 2001); FCIL (FIL 1991). Entered HM Diplomatic Service, 1968; MECAS, 1969; Third, later Second Sec., Paris, 1970–73; Second, later First Sec., FCO, 1973–78; First Sec., Canberra, 1978–82; First Sec., later Counsellor, FCO, 1982–88; Minister and Dep. Head of Mission, Madrid, 1989–93; Chargé d'Affaires, Belgrade, 1994–96; Ambassador to Yugoslavia, 1996–97; Sen. Associate Mem., St Antony's Coll., Oxford, 1997–98; Ambassador: to Ireland, 1999–2003; to Italy and to San Marino, 2003–06. Chm. Council, British Sch. of Archaeol. and Fine Arts, Rome, 2008–12. Chm., Keats-Shelley Meml Assoc., 2018–. Patron, Venice in Peril Fund, 2006–. Pres., Oxford Univ. RFC, 2013–. Freeman, City of London, 2009. *Publications*: (ed) Satow's Diplomatic Practice, 6th edn 2009, 7th edn 2016; Razgovori s Miloševićem, 2012; (contrib.) The Past is Never Dead: Balkan legacies of the Great War, 2015; Conversations with Milošević, 2016. *Recreations*: opera, ski-ing, golf, photography. *Clubs*: Oxford and Cambridge, Beefsteak; Downhill Only (Wengen).

**ROBERTS, Sir James Elton Denby Buchanan**, 4th Bt *cr* 1909, of Milner Field, Bingley, W Riding of Yorks; *b* 12 July 1966; *o s* of David Gordon Denby Roberts (*d* 1971), 3rd *s* of 2nd Bt, and of Diana Frances Roberts (*née* Wilson-Jones, now Buchanan); adopted by his step-father and assumed surname of Roberts-Buchanan, later reverted to Roberts and assumed Buchanan as a forename; *S* uncle, 2012, but his name does not appear on the Official Roll of the Baronetage; *m* 1994, Lisa Jane, *d* of Ian Ross Stirling; one *s* three *d*. *Educ*: George Watson's Coll., Edinburgh; Harper Adams Agric. Coll. *Heir*: *s* John David Denby Roberts, *b* 29 Dec. 1999. *Address*: Lawhill House, Trinity Gask, by Auchterarder, Perthshire PH3 1LJ.

**ROBERTS, Hon. Jane**; *see* Roberts, Hon. P. J. S.

**ROBERTS, Dame Jane (Elisabeth)**, DBE 2004; FRCPsych; Consultant Child and Adolescent Psychiatrist, Whittington Health (formerly Islington Primary Care Trust), 1993–2016 (Medical Director, 2002–06; Director, Quality and Performance, 2006–10); Research Fellow in Public Leadership, Open University Business School, since 2016; *b* 23 Aug. 1955; *d* of Rev. Dr Fred Roberts and Nia Lora Roberts; *m* 2005, Prof. David Brian Dunger, *qv*; one *s* and one step *d*. *Educ*: Bristol Univ. (MB ChB 1980); Brunel Univ. (MSc 1991). MRCP 1983; MRCPsych 1986, FRCPsych 2004. Jun. posts in paediatrics, 1980–84; Registrar, Psychiatry, Maudsley Hosp., 1984–87; Sen. Registrar, Child and Adolescent Psychiatry, Tavistock Clinic, 1987–92; Locum Consultant, Child and Adolescent Psychiatry, Camden and Islington Community Health Services, NHS Trust, 1992–93. London Borough of Camden Council: Mem., 1996–2006; Dep. Leader, 1994–98, Leader, 2000–05; Chair, Educn Cttee, 1998–2000. Chair, Councillors' Commn, 2007–09. Interim Clin. Dir, Commissioning Support for London, 2010. Mem. Bd, OFSTED, 2007–11. Trustee: IPPR, 2005–16; Parenting UK, 2006–12 (Chair, 2006–12); Dir, New Local Govt Network, 2006– (Chair, 2012–); Member: Central Council, Socialist Health Assoc., 2006–17; Dr Foster Ethics Cttee, 2008–15; Ethics Cttee, Assoc. of Child Psychotherapists, 2012–; Gov. Body, Public Policy Inst. for Wales, 2013–; Remuneration Bd, Nat. Assembly for Wales, 2015–. Chm., Adv. Council, Compass Educn Inquiry, 2013–14. Lay Rep., Ethics Cttee, Zool Soc. of London, 2007–. Trustee, Freedom from Torture (formerly Med. Foundn for the Care of Victims of Torture), 2010–14. Sen. Associate Fellow, Warwick Business Sch., 2006–15; Vis. Fellow, Open Univ., 2015–16. Governor: Eleanor Palmer Primary Sch., Camden, 2010–14; Regent High Sch., Camden, 2012–; Kings Cross Acad., 2015–; Mem., Camden Partnership for Educnl Excellence, 2012–16. Hon. Fellow, UCL, 2005. Hon. DLaws Bristol, 2007. *Publications*: (ed with Dr S. Kraemer) The Politics of Attachment, 1996; Losing Political Office, 2017; academic articles in paediatrics and psychiatry. *Address*: 4 Tapestry Apartments, 1 Canal Reach, N1C 4AZ.

**ROBERTS, Hon. Dame Jennifer (Mary)**, DBE 2014; **Hon. Mrs Justice Roberts**; a Judge of the High Court, Family Division, since 2014; Family Division Liaison Judge, Western Circuit, since 2018. *Educ*: LLB 1st Cl. Hons. Called to the Bar, Inner Temple, 1988; Recorder, 2000–14; QC 2009; Dep. High Ct Judge, 2011–14. MCIArb 2013. Fellow, Internat. Acad. of Family (formerly Matrimonial) Lawyers, 2011. Hon. DLitt Southampton, 2017. *Address*: Royal Courts of Justice, Strand, WC2A 2LL.

**ROBERTS, His Honour Jeremy Michael Graham**; QC 1982; Member, Parole Board, since 2010; *b* 26 April 1941; *s* of late Lt-Col J. M. H. Roberts and E. D. Roberts; *m* 1964, Sally Priscilla Johnson, *d* of late Col F. P. Johnson, OBE. *Educ*: Winchester; Brasenose Coll., Oxford (BA). Called to the Bar, Inner Temple, 1965, Bencher, 1992. Recorder, 1981–2000; Perm. Judge, Central Criminal Court, 2000–11. Head of Chambers, 1997–2000. Mem., Press Complaints Commn, 2011–14. *Recreations*: racing, reading, theatre, opera, canals. *Address*: 21 The Butts, Brentford, Middx TW8 8BJ.

**ROBERTS, John**; *see* Roberts, A. J.

**ROBERTS, John Charles Quentin**; Hon. Chairman, International Advisory Board of All-Russia State Library for Foreign Literature, Moscow, 2004–16 (Member, 1991–93; Co-Chairman, 1994–2004); Director, Britain-Russia Centre (formerly Great Britain–USSR Association), 1974–93; *b* 4 April 1933; *s* of Hubert and Emilie Roberts; *m* 1959, Dinah Webster-Williams (marr. diss.); one *s* one *d*. *Educ*: Quainton Hall; King's Coll., Taunton (open scholar); Merton Coll., Oxford (MA). Royal Air Force CSC Interpreter, 1953; Russian Language Tutor, SSEES, Univ. of London, 1953; Shell International Petroleum Co. Ltd, 1956; Shell Co. of E Africa Ltd: Representative, Zanzibar and S Tanganyika, 1957, Kenya Highlands, 1958; PA to Man. Dir, Shell Austria AG Vienna, 1960; Pressed Steel Co. Ltd, Oxford, 1961; Asst Master, Marlborough Coll., 1963–74. Chairman: Organising Cttee for British Week in Siberia, 1978; Steering Cttee, British Month in USSR (Kiev), 1990. Mem. Council, Amer. Friends of the Russian Country Estate Inc., Washington, 1998–2003. Member Council: SSEES, Univ. of London, 1981–93; Academia Rossica, 2000–06; Vice Pres., Assoc. of Teachers of Russian, 1984–89. Governor, Cobham Hall, 1984–88. Trustee: Serge Rachmaninoff Foundn, 2002–06; Keston Inst., Oxford, 2003–07; Friends of Chelsea & Westminster Hosp., 2005–11. Hon. Life Mem., GB-Russia Soc., 2002. Mem., Editl Adv. Bd, Herald of Europe, Moscow, 2001–16. Tyutchev Gold Medal, Internat. Pushkin Foundn, 2004; Internat. Nikolai Karamzin Medal, Herald of Europe and Egor Gaidar Foundn, 2012. *Publications*: Speak Clearly into the Chandelier: cultural politics between Britain and Russia 1973–2000, 2000 (Russian lang. edn 2001, Znamya Award); The Colour of Poppies (trans. from French), 2005; If Only I Could Fly: children's poems from Russia, 2012; contribs to specialist jls. *Recreations:* family, friends old and new, the arts. *Address:* 147 Beaufort Street, SW3 6BS. *T:* (020) 7376 3452. *Club:* Athenæum.

**ROBERTS, John Edward**, CBE 2004; FREng, FIET, FCCA; Chairman: Halite Energy Group, since 2010; Electricity North West, since 2014; *b* 2 March 1946; *s* of Arthur and Dora Roberts; *m* 1970, Pamela Baxter; one *s* one *d*. *Educ:* Liverpool Univ. (BEng). FCCA 1983; CEng, FIET (FIEE 1988); FREng 2002; DMS. Merseyside and North Wales Electricity Board, subseq. Manweb: Chief Accountant, 1984–90; Finance Dir, 1990–91; Man. Dir, 1991–92; Chief Exec., 1992–95; Chief Executive: S Wales Electricity, then Hyder Utilities, 1996–99; United Utilities, 1999–2006. Dir, Hyder Gp, 1996–99. Chairman: Black Rock New Energy Investment Trust, 2011–14; RBC Europe Ltd, 2009–17; First Utility, 2013–16. Mem., Royal Commn on Envmtl Pollution, 1998–2002. CCMI. Hon. Fellow, Liverpool John Moores Univ., 2004. DL Merseyside, 2006. Hon. DEng Liverpool, 2004. *Recreations:* scuba diving, walking, gardening.

**ROBERTS, Dr John Esmond**; independent consultant on international treaties on chemicals and waste management, 2015; Deputy Director (part time), Common Agricultural Policy Direct Payments, Department for Environment, Food and Rural Affairs, 2011–15; *b* Bristol, 29 June 1951; *s* of Bill and Marian Roberts; *m* 1989, Lucy-Anne Collier; one *s* one *d*. *Educ:* Bishop Wordsworth Sch., Salisbury; Keble Coll., Oxford (MA, DPhil Chem. 1975). DoE, later DEFRA, 1975–2015; on secondment to Cabinet Secretariat, 1985–87; Divisional Manager: Local Govt Finance – Grants, 1987–91; Housing Gp Secretariat, 1991–92; Housing, Private Rented Sector, 1992–96; on secondment to LGA, 1996–97; Divisional Manager: Urban Policy, 1997–2001; Marine Envmt, 2001–06; Hd, Chemicals and Nanotechnologies, 2006–09, Hd, Noise and Local Envmtl Quality, 2008–09; Sec., Royal Commn on Envmtl Pollution, 2009–11. Mem., Mgt Bd, Eur. Chemicals Agency, 2007–09. Vice Pres., Stockholm Convention on Persistent Organic Pollutants, 2007–09; an expert gp Co-Chair, Minamata Convention on Mercury Pollution, 2007–16. *Recreations:* St Luke's Church, Wimbledon Park, Fulham Football Club.

**ROBERTS, His Honour John Houghton**; DL; a Circuit Judge, 1993–2012; *b* 14 Dec. 1947; *s* of John Noel Roberts and Ida Roberts, Irby, Wirral; *m* 1st, 1972, Anna Elizabeth (marr. diss. 1990), *e d* of Peter and Elizabeth Sheppard; three *s*; 2nd, 1991, Mary, *er d* of Frederic and Patricia Wilkinson, Blundellsands. *Educ:* Calday Grange Grammar Sch., West Kirby; Trinity Hall, Cambridge (Schol.; BA 1st Cl. Hons Law Tripos; MA). Lectr in Law, Liverpool Univ., 1969–71; called to the Bar, Middle Temple, 1970 (Harmsworth Major Entrance Exhibn 1968; Astbury Law Schol. 1970). Practised Northern Circuit, 1970–93. Asst Recorder, 1983; Recorder, 1988–93; Resident Judge, Bolton Crown Court, 1997–2001. President: Wirral Hospice St John's, 2014–; Cheshire Union of Golf Clubs, 2015. Mem., Bd of Regents, Liverpool Hope Univ., 2013–. Church Warden, 2013–15. DL Merseyside, 2016. *Recreations:* Rugby football, golf, cricket, music, reading. *Clubs:* Athenæum, Artists (Liverpool); Heswall Golf; Oxton Cricket.

**ROBERTS, Dr John Laing**; independent consultant in health and economic and sustainable development policy, since 1997; Adviser: to the Indian Ocean Commission, since 2004; to the Commonwealth Secretariat, 2004–16; *b* 26 Dec. 1939; *s* of Charles F. Roberts and May Roberts; *m* 1st, 1963, Meriel F. Dawes (marr. diss. 1980); three *d*; 2nd, 1981, Judith Mary Hare (marr. diss. 2002); 3rd, 2002, Bibi Bilkis Sheik Janny. *Educ:* Latymer Upper School; Univ. of Birmingham. PhD, MSc, BSocSc. FHA. NHS Nat. Administrative Trainee, 1962–63; Senior Administrative Asst, United Birmingham Hosps, 1964–66; Sen. Res. Associate, Dept of Social Medicine, Univ. of Birmingham, 1966–69; Dep. Dir, Res. Div., Health Education Council, 1969–74; Operational Services Gen. Administrator, S Glamorgan AHA (T), 1974–77; Regional Gen. Administrator, W Midlands RHA, 1977–82; Regional Administrator, 1983–85, Regl Prevention Manager, 1985–89, N Western RHA; Regl Advr in Health Services, WHO Office for Europe, Copenhagen, 1990–92; Consultant, WHO Office for Europe, 1992–94; Health Economist/Planner, Min. of Econ. Planning and Develt, Mauritius, 1994–98. Adviser to Government: of Malawi, 1999–2001; of Mauritius, 2000–04; consultant to UNEP on Africa envmt outlook, 2001–02; advr to UNEP, 2002–08; consulting Ed. to Bank of Mauritius, 2013–15. Columnist, Weekly mag., Mauritius, 2013–. Associate Prof., Dept of Econs and Statistics, Univ. of Mauritius, 2006–08. Dir, Adhealth, 1989–96. Hon. Sen. Res. Fellow, Manchester Univ., 1990–2000. Vice Pres., Mauritian Writers' Assoc., 2014–16. Mem. Editl Bd, Internat. Jl of Health Promotion, 1996–2015. *Publications:* If Only: death and injury from accidents, 1977; The Big Kill: death, disease and cost of smoking in England and Wales, 1985; (ed jtly) Saving Small and Island States, 2010; (ed jtly) Tools for Mainstreaming Sustainable Development in Small States, 2011; The Big Divide: progress with MDGs in small states, 2012; The Divided Region: progressing Rio + 20 outcomes, 2014; Exile: views from a distant land, 2018; papers on health education, health service administration, health and economics, the environment and sustainable development; PhD thesis, Studies of Information Systems for Health Service Resource Planning and Control. *Recreations:* swimming, beach walking, tennis, travel writing, poetry. *Address:* 5 Ranmore Court, 101 Worple Road, SW19 8HB; Habasha, Morcellement Mont Choisy, Mont Choisy, Mauritius. *T:* 2655187. *E:* john.laing@hotmail.com.

**ROBERTS, His Honour John Mervyn**; a Circuit Judge, 1999–2011; *b* 19 Feb. 1941; *s* of late Mervyn and Catherine Roberts; *m* 1972, Phillippa Ann Critien; one *d*. *Educ:* Hereford Cathedral Sch.; King's Coll., London (LLB Hons 1962). Called to the Bar, Inner Temple, 1963, Bencher, 2007; in practice at the Bar, 1963–99; a Recorder, 1994–99. Member: Criminal Injuries Compensation Bd, 1998–99; Parole Bd, 2002–14. *Recreations:* music, travel. *Address:* c/o 5 Essex Court, Temple, EC4Y 9AH.

**ROBERTS, Rear-Adm. John Oliver**, CB 1976; MNI; Managing Director, Demak Ltd, International Consultants, 1983–98; *b* 4 April 1924; *er s* of J. V. and M. C. Roberts; *m* 1st, 1950, Lady Hermione Mary Morton Stuart (marr. diss. 1960; she *d* 1969); one *d*; 2nd, 1963, Honor Marigold Gordon Gray (marr. diss. 1987); one *s* one *d*; 3rd, 1987, Sheila Violet Mary Traub (*née* Barker) (*d* 2012); 4th, 2014, Gillian Ffrench Reckitt (*née* Nobbs). *Educ:* RN Coll., Dartmouth. Served War: Midshipman, HM Ships Renown and Tartar, 1941–43; Sub-Lt, HMS Serapis, 1943–44; Lieut, 1945; Pilot Trng, 1944–46. HMS Triumph, 1947–49; RNAS, Lossiemouth, 1949–51; Flag-Lt to FOGT, 1952; Lt-Comdr, 1953; HMAS Vengeance and Sydney, 1953–54; RNVR, Southern Air Div., 1954–56; CO, No 803 Sqdn, HMS Eagle, 1957–58; Comdr, 1958; RNAS, Brawdy, 1958–60; CO, HMS St Bride's Bay, 1960–61; Naval Staff, 1962–64; Captain, 1964; CSO, Flag Officer Aircraft Carriers, 1964–66; CO, HMS Galatea, 1966–68; Naval Staff, 1968–70; CO, HMS Ark Royal, 1971–72; Rear-Adm., 1972; Flag Officer Sea Training, 1972–74; COS to C-in-C Fleet, 1974–76; Flag Officer, Naval Air Command, 1976–78. Non-exec. Dir, Aeronautical & General Instruments Ltd, 1981–82 (Head of Marketing and Sales, Defence Systems Div., 1980–81); Dir Gen., British Printing Industries Fedn, 1981–82. FRSA. *Recreations:* Rugby football, cricket, athletics, sailing, ski-ing. *Address:* 22 St Anne's Road, Whitstable, Kent CT5 2DW. *Club:* East India, Devonshire, Sports and Public Schools.

**ROBERTS, Julia Fiona**; actress; *b* Smyrna, Georgia, 28 Oct. 1967; *d* of late Walter Roberts and of Betty Roberts; *m* 1st, 1993, Lyle Lovett (marr. diss. 1995); 2nd, 2002, Danny Moder; two *s* one *d* (of whom one *s* one *d* are twins). *Educ:* Campbell High Sch., Georgia. *Stage:* Three Days of Rain, NY, 2006; *films include:* Satisfaction, Mystic Pizza, 1988; Steel Magnolias, 1989 (Best Supporting Actress, Golden Globe Awards, 1990); Blood Red, Pretty Woman (Best Actress, Golden Globe Awards, 1991), Flatliners, 1990; Sleeping with the Enemy, Hook, Dying Young, 1991; The Pelican Brief, I Love Trouble, Prêt-à-Porter, 1994; Something to Talk About, 1995; Mary Reilly, Everybody Says I Love You, Michael Collins, 1996; My Best Friend's Wedding, Conspiracy Theory, 1997; Stepmom, 1998; Notting Hill, Runaway Bride, 1999; Erin Brockovich, 2000 (Academy Award for Best Actress, 2000; Best Actress, BAFTA Awards, Golden Globe Awards, Screen Actors' Guild Awards, 2001); The Mexican, America's Sweethearts, 2001; Ocean's Eleven, 2002; Confessions of a Dangerous Mind, Full Frontal, 2003; Mona Lisa Smile, 2004; Closer, Ocean's Twelve, 2005; Ocean's Thirteen, Charlie Wilson's War, 2007; Duplicity, Fireflies in the Garden, 2009; Valentine's Day, Eat Pray Love, 2010; Larry Crowne, 2011; Mirror, Mirror, 2012; August: Osage County, 2014 (also prod.); Secret in their Eyes, Money Monster, Mother's Day, 2016; Wonder, 2017; Ben is Back, 2019; *television includes:* Crime Story, 1988; Baja Oklahoma, 1988; In the Wild, 1988; Homecoming, 2018.

**ROBERTS, Ven. Kevin Thomas**; Director, ReSource for Anglican Renewal Ministries, Telford (formerly Somerset), since 2016; Public Preacher, Diocese of Lichfield, since 2018; *b* Saltburn by the Sea, 11 Oct. 1955; *s* of Abel and Margaret Roberts; *m* 1982, Rev. Anne Waine; two *s* one *d*. *Educ:* Queens' Coll., Cambridge (BA Hons 1978; MA 1982); Nottingham Univ. (BA Hons 1982). Ordained deacon, 1983, priest, 1984; Assistant Curate: Beverley Minster, 1983–86; St John the Evangelist, Woodley, Oxfordshire, 1986–91; Vicar, Holy Trinity, Meole Brace, 1991–2009; Rural Dean, Shrewsbury, 1998–2008. Preb., Lichfield Cathedral, 2002–08; Rural Dean, Brampton, 2015–16; Archdeacon of Carlisle, and Canon Residentiary, Carlisle Cathedral, 2009–16; Acting Archdeacon of Wells, 2016–17. Chm., Carlisle Diocesan Bd of Educn, 2009–16. *Recreations:* reading, photography, Middlesbrough FC. *Address:* (home) 9 Bickerton Grove, Lawley, Telford, Shropshire TF3 5JL. *T:* 07880 762868. *E:* revsroberts55@gmail.com; (office) Meeting Point House, Southwater Square, Telford, Shropshire TF3 4HS. *E:* kevinroberts@resource-arm.net. *T:* (01952) 371300.

**ROBERTS, Prof. Kevin William Stuart**, DPhil; FBA 2007; Sir John Hicks Professor of Economics, University of Oxford, since 1999; Fellow, Nuffield College, Oxford, since 1999; *b* 29 Feb. 1952; *s* of Basil Roberts and Dorothy Roberts (*née* Heaven); *m* 1st, 1981, Julia Clarke (marr. diss. 1996); two *d*; 2nd, 2014, Sophie Petersen. *Educ:* Cheltenham Grammar Sch.; Univ. of Essex (BA Math. Econ. 1973); Nuffield Coll., Oxford (BPhil Econ. 1975; DPhil Econ. 1977). Jun. Res. Fellow, St John's Coll., Oxford, 1975–77; Asst Prof., MIT, 1977–78; Univ. Lectr and Official Fellow, St Catherine's Coll., Oxford, 1978–82; Professor of Econ. Theory, Univ. of Warwick, 1982–87; of Economics, LSE, 1987–99. Fellow, Econometric Soc., 1984. *Publications:* articles in internat. learned jls incl. Econometrica and Rev. Econ. Studies. *Address:* Nuffield College, Oxford OX1 1NF. *T:* (01865) 278601.

**ROBERTS, Lisa**; QC 2015; *b* Manchester, 2 Feb. 1969; *d* of Dr Geraint Roberts and Shirley Roberts; *m* 1994, Jonathan Bourne; one *s* one *d*. *Educ:* Salendine Nook Comprehensive Sch., Huddersfield; Huddersfield New Coll.; St Catherine's Coll., Oxford (BA Hons); Huddersfield Univ. (CPE); Inns of Court Sch. of Law (BVC). Called to the Bar, Lincoln's Inn, 1993; in practice as barrister, specialising in criminal and regulatory law, 1993–; Attorney Gen., Northern Circuit. Member: Criminal Bar Assoc.; Health and Safety Lawyers Assoc. *Recreations:* tennis, eating out, concerts, theatre, holidaying with family. *Address:* Lincoln House Chambers, Tower 12, Bridge Street, Manchester M3 3BZ. *T:* (0161) 832 5701, (0870) 458 0592. *E:* lisa.robertsqc@lincolnhousechambers.com.

**ROBERTS, Lynn Deborah**; a Circuit Judge, since 2012; **Her Honour Judge Lynn Roberts**; *b* 25 Oct. 1956; *d* of Henry and Eva Roberts; *m* 1994, John Watson (*d* 2007); one *s* one *d*, and one step *s* one step *d*. *Educ:* South Hampstead High Sch.; Brasenose Coll., Oxford (BA Hons (Mod. Hist.) 1979); Coll. of Law. Solicitor, 1986–88, Partner, 1988–2001, Hodge Jones and Allen; Dep. District Judge, County Courts, 1999–2001; Dep. District Judge, 1999–2001, District Judge, 2001–12, Principal Registry, Family Div.; Designated Family Judge for Essex and Suffolk, 2014–. Chair of Trustees, Melos Sinfonia, 2014–. *Publications:* (contrib.) Raydon and Jackson, Divorce and Family Matters, 18th edn 2004. *Recreations:* music, crosswords, country walks. *Address:* Chelmsford County Court, Priory Place, New London Road, Chelmsford, Essex CM2 0PP.

**ROBERTS, Martin Geoffrey**; Senior Consultant, Beachcroft Regulatory (formerly Beachcroft Wansborough) Consulting, 2003–09; *b* 3 July 1946; *s* of Arthur and Mary Roberts; *m* 1969, Christine Muriel George (*d* 2008); two *s*. *Educ:* Priory Grammar Sch., Shrewsbury; Worcester Coll., Oxford (MA). Min. of Technology, 1970; Private Sec. to Minister without Portfolio, 1973–74; seconded: to FCO, 1979–82; to DoE as Controller, Yorks and Humberside Regl Office, 1984–85; Sec., BOTB, 1985–89; Hd of Investigations Div., 1992–96, Dir, Finance and Resource Mgt, 1996–98, DTI; Dir, Insurance, HM Treasury, 1998; Dir, Inscne and Friendly Socs, 1999–2002, Sen. Inscne Advr, 2002–03, FSA. Dir, PensionsRisk LLP, 2007–09. Chm., Friendly Socs Commn, 1998–2002; Member: Exports Guarantee Adv. Council, 2003–12; St Helena Financial Services Regulatory Authy, 2011–17. Non-executive Director: Ealing PCT, 2009–13; Hillingdon PCT, 2011–13 (Interim Chm., 2010–11); NHS Outer NW London, 2011–12; NHS NW London, 2012–13. Mem., Exec. Cttee, 1998–2003, Chm., Tech. Cttee, 2000–03, Internat. Assoc. of Inscne Supervisors. *Recreation:* sailing.

**ROBERTS, Matthew**; *see* Roberts, E. M. G.

**ROBERTS, Michael**; *see* Roberts, Thomas M.

**ROBERTS, Michael Andrew**; Chief Executive, Water UK, since 2016; *b* Santiago de Chile, 14 May 1966; *s* of Michael Francis Roberts and Georgina Sara Olmos Adriazola; *m* 1st, 2004, Michelle Cora Farrell (*d* 2008); 2nd, 2012, Emma Kate Wild; one *s* one *d*. *Educ:* Prior Park Coll., Bath; St Benet's Hall, Oxford (BA Hons Mod. Hist. 1987). Account Manager, Decision Makers, 1989–91; CBI, 1991–2008, Dir, Business Envmt, 2000–08; Chief Exec., Assoc. of Train Operating Cos, 2008–15; Dir-Gen., Rail Delivery Gp, 2013–15. Member: Standing Adv. Cttee on Trunk Road Assessment, 1996–99; Dep. Prime Minister's Panel on Transport White Paper, 1997–98; Commn for Integrated Transport, 2000–08. Non-exec. Dir, Carbon Trust, 2001–08. *Recreations:* football, running, ski-ing, rowing. *Address:* Water UK, 3rd Floor, 36 Broadway, SW1H 0BH. *T:* (020) 7344 1800. *E:* mroberts@water.org.uk. *Club:* Molesey Boat.

**ROBERTS, Surgeon Rear Adm. Michael Atholl F.**; *see* Farquharson-Roberts.

**ROBERTS, Rev. Canon Michael Graham Vernon**; Principal, Westcott House, Cambridge, 1993–2006; *b* 4 Aug. 1943; *s* of Walter Graham Southall Roberts and Pamela Middleton Roberts (*née* Abel, now Murray); *m* 1970, Susan Elizabeth (*née* Merry); one *s* two *d*. *Educ:* Eton Coll.; Keble Coll., Oxford (BA 1965; MA); Cuddesdon Coll.; Church Divinity Sch. of Pacific, Berkeley, Calif. (MDiv 1967). Curate, Exmouth, 1967–70;

Chaplain, Clare Coll., Cambridge, 1970–74; Vicar, St Mark, Bromley, 1974–79; Tutor, Queen's Coll., Birmingham, 1979–85; Team Rector, High Wycombe, 1985–90; Vice-Principal, Westcott House, Cambridge, 1990–93. Hon. Canon, Ely Cathedral, 2004–. *Recreations:* gardening, walking, theological education, reading. *Address:* Hurleys, Sand Street, Milverton, Somerset TA4 1JN. *T:* (01823) 401071.

**ROBERTS, Michael John Wyn,** CVO 2008; HM Diplomatic Service, retired; Ambassador to Slovakia, 2007–10; consultant on governance and international affairs, since 2011; *b* 4 July 1960; *s* of late Denys Murray Wyn Roberts and of Diana Roberts (*née* Marshall); *m* 1985, Margaret Anne Ozanne; one *s* two *d*. *Educ:* Bryanston Sch.; Brasenose Coll., Oxford (MA). Joined HM Diplomatic Service, 1984; Second, then First Sec., Athens, 1987–91; FCO, 1991–95; First Sec., UK Perm. Repn to EU, Brussels, 1995–99; Hd of Div., European Secretariat, Cabinet Office, 1999–2003; Dep. Hd of Mission, Ankara, 2004–07. Chm., British Czech and Slovak Assoc., 2014–17. Trustee: EU Baroque Orch., 2012–17; Depaul Slovensko, 2012–; Fieri Consort, 2018–. *Recreations:* Central and Eastern Europe, music, walking.

**ROBERTS, Prof. Michael Symmons,** FRSL; poet; Professor of Poetry, Manchester Metropolitan University, since 2009; *b* Preston, Lancs, 13 Oct. 1963; *s* of David Symmons Roberts and Iris Roberts; *m* 1991, Ruth Humphreys; three *s*. *Educ:* St Bartholomew's Comprehensive Sch., Newbury; Regent's Park Coll., Oxford (BA Hons Philosophy and Theol. 1986). Radio producer, 1989–95; TV producer (documentaries), 1995–99, BBC; Hd of Develt, BBC Religion and Ethics, 1999–2001; freelance writer, 2001–05; Sen. Lectr in English, Manchester Metropolitan Univ., 2005–09. FEA 2012; FRSL 2014. *Publications: poetry:* Soft Keys, 1993; Raising Sparks, 1996; Burning Babylon, 2001; Corpus, 2004 (Whitbread Poetry Award, 2004); The Half Healed, 2008; Drysalter, 2013 (Costa Poetry Award, 2013; Forward Poetry Prize, 2013); Selected Poems, 2016; Mancunia, 2017; *fiction:* Patrick's Alphabet, 2006; Breath, 2008; *non-fiction:* (with Paul Farley) Edgelands, 2011; (with Paul Farley) Deaths of the Poets, 2017; *libretti:* (with composer James MacMillan): Raising Sparks, 1997; Quickening, 1998; Parthenogenesis, 2000; The Birds of Rhiannon, 2002; Chosen, 2003; Sun Dogs, 2006; The Sacrifice, 2007; Clemency, 2011; New-Made for a King, 2014; (with composer Emily Howard) The Anvil, 2019; *translation:* Schubert's Winterreise, 2009. *Recreations:* music, film, theatre, sport, season ticket holder at Old Trafford. *Address:* c/o Anna Webber, United Agents, 12–26 Lexington Street, W1F 0LE. *T:* (020) 3214 0876. *E:* awebber@unitedagents.co.uk. *W:* www.symmonsroberts.com.

**ROBERTS, Michèle Brigitte;** novelist and poet; Professor of Creative Writing, University of East Anglia, 2002–07, now Emeritus; *b* 20 May 1949; *d* of Reginald George Roberts and Monique Pauline Joseph (*née* Caulle); *m* 1st, 1983, Howard Burns (marr. diss. 1987); 2nd, 1991, Laurence James Latter (marr. diss. 2005). *Educ:* Somerville Coll., Oxford (MA); University Coll. London. MCLIP (ALA 1972); FRSL 1995. British Council Librarian, Bangkok, 1973–74; writer, 1974–; Poetry Editor: Spare Rib, 1974; City Limits, 1981–83. Vis. Fellow in Creative Writing, UEA, 1992; Research Fellow in Writing, 1995–96, Vis. Prof., 1996–2001, Nottingham Trent Univ.; Writer-in-Residence, York Univ., 2008. Tutor, Autobiog. Unit, MA in Life-Writing, UEA, 2009–11. Chm., Lit. Cttee, British Council, 1998–2001. Member: Soc. of Authors; PEN Translation Cttee, 2008–11. Chevalier, Ordre des Arts et des Lettres (France), 2001. *Publications: novels:* A Piece of the Night, 1978; The Visitation, 1983; The Wild Girl, 1984; The Book of Mrs Noah, 1987; In the Red Kitchen, 1990; Daughters of the House, 1992 (W. H. Smith Literary Award, 1993); Flesh and Blood, 1994; Impossible Saints, 1997; Fair Exchange, 1999; The Looking-Glass, 2000; The Mistressclass, 2003; Reader, I Married Him, 2005; Ignorance, 2012; The Walworth Beauty, 2017; *stories:* During Mother's Absence, 1993; Playing Sardines, 2001; Mud: stories of sex and love, 2010; *memoir:* Paper Houses, 2007; (jtly) The Lille Diaries, 2016; *poetry:* The Mirror of the Mother, 1986; Psyche and the Hurricane, 1991; All the Selves I Was, 1995; The Heretic's Feast, 2012; The Hunter's House, 2013; *plays:* The Journeywoman, 1988; Child-Lover, 1995; *film:* The Heavenly Twins, 1993; *essays:* Food, Sex and God: on inspiration and writing, 1998; Silly Lady Novelists?, 2016; *artist's books* (jointly): Poems, 2001; Fifteen Beads, 2003; Dark City Light City, 2007; The Secret Staircase, 2008; The Dark and Marvellous Room, 2013; *anthology:* (ed jtly) Mind Readings, 1996. *Recreations:* cooking, gardening, drawing, painting. *Address:* c/o Charles Walker, United Agents, 12–26 Lexington Street, W1F 0LE.

**ROBERTS, Patrick John;** Owner, Cognis Public Relations, 2006–17; *b* 21 Oct. 1942; *s* of Frank and Hilda Mary Roberts; *m* 1978, Alison Mary Taylor; one *s* one *d*. *Educ:* Rotherham Grammar Sch.; Lincoln Coll., Oxford (BA Hons Modern Langs). Foreign Office, 1965; Bangkok, 1966; FCO, 1970; First Sec., Lagos, 1971; FCO, 1974; UK Repn to EEC, Brussels, 1977; FCO, 1980; Counsellor (Inf.), Paris, 1984. Edelman Public Relations Worldwide: Dir of Eur. Affairs, 1989–90; Dir of Public, then Business and Corporate, Affairs, 1991–95; Dep. Man. Dir, 1995–99. Consultant, Abel Hadden and Co. Ltd, 1999–2002; Principal Consultant, Kaizo, 2002–06. *Recreations:* cooking, photography. *Address:* 81 Fawnbrake Avenue, SE24 0BG. *T:* (020) 7274 3530. *Club:* Oxford and Cambridge.

**ROBERTS, Paul;** *see* Roberts, D. P.

**ROBERTS, Prof. Paul Harry,** PhD, ScD; FRS 1979; FRAS; Professor of Mathematics, 1986–2010, now Emeritus, and Professor of Geophysical Sciences, Institute of Geophysics and Planetary Physics, now Distinguished Research Professor of Mathematics, University of California at Los Angeles; *b* 13 Sept. 1929; *s* of Percy Harry Roberts and Ethel Frances (*née* Mann); *m* 1989, Mary Frances (*née* Tabrett). *Educ:* Ardwyn Grammar Sch., Aberystwyth; University Coll. of Wales, Aberystwyth; Gonville and Caius Coll., Cambridge (George Green Student; BA, MA, PhD, ScD). FRAS 1955. Res. Associate, Univ. of Chicago, 1954–55; Scientific Officer, AWRE, 1955–56; ICI Fellow in Physics, 1956–59, Lectr in Phys, 1959–61, Univ. of Durham; Associate Prof. of Astronomy, Univ. of Chicago, 1961–63; Prof. of Applied Maths, Univ. of Newcastle upon Tyne, 1963–85. Fellow: Amer. Geophysical Union; Amer. Acad. of Arts and Scis, 2001. Editor, 1976–91, Mem. Editl Bd, 1991–, Geophysical and Astrophysical Fluid Dynamics. John Adam Fleming Medal, Amer. Geophysical Union, 1999. *Publications:* An Introduction to Magnetohydrodynamics, 1967; contrib. to Geophys. and Astrophys. Fluid Dyn., Jl Low Temp. Phys., Astrophys. Jl, Jl Fluid Mech., Jl Phys. Soc., Nature, Science, and Proc. and Trans Royal Soc. *Recreations:* playing bassoon, chess. *Address:* Department of Mathematics, University of California at Los Angeles, Los Angeles, CA 90095-1555, USA.

**ROBERTS, Peter John Martin;** Headmaster, The King's School, Canterbury, since 2011; *b* 31 May 1963; *s* of Alfred John Victor and Pamela Roberts; *m* 1990, Marie Toudic; three *d*. *Educ:* Tiffin Boys' Sch., Kingston upon Thames; Merton Coll., Oxford (MA 1st cl. Hons (Mod. Hist.) 1985); Inst. of Educn, London (PGCE 1986). Winchester College: Asst Master, 1986–90; Hd of History, 1990–97; Master in Coll. (Housemaster to the Scholars), 1991–2003; Headmaster, Bradfield Coll., 2003–11. Hon. Canon, Canterbury Cathedral, 2012. *Recreations:* sailing, book binding, calligraphy. *Address:* The King's School, 25 The Precincts, Canterbury, Kent CT1 2ES.

**ROBERTS, Phil;** Chief Executive, City and County of Swansea Council, since 2016; *b* Blackpool, 20 April 1961; *s* of Alwyn Pennant Roberts and Mavis Roberts; *m* 1986, Deborah; three *s*. *Educ:* Bath Univ. (BSc Hons Econs 1984); London Sch. of Econs and Pol Sci. (Postgrad. DH (Dist.) 1986). District and City of Swansea Council, later City and County of Swansea Council, 1986–: Hd of Housing, 2003–04; Interim Dir of Social Services and Housing, 2004–05; Dir of Regeneration, then Corporate Dir of Place, 2006–16. Hon. Lectr, Univ. of Cardiff, 1990–93. *Recreations:* musician, walking, ornithology (Mem., RSPB), Swansea City FC (Premier Club Mem.). *Address:* City and County of Swansea Council, The Guildhall, Swansea SA1 4PE. *T:* (01792) 637525. *E:* phil.roberts@swansea.gov.uk.

**ROBERTS, Philip Duncan;** QC 2018; *b* Berks, 28 Dec. 1973; *s* of Keith and Christine Roberts; *m* 1995, Penny Craven, MBE; two *d*. Called to the Bar, Inner Temple, 1996; in practice as barrister, specialising in intellectual property.

**ROBERTS, Hon. (Priscilla) Jane (Stephanie), (Hon. Lady Roberts),** DCVO 2013 (CVO 2004; LVO 1995; MVO 1985); Curator of the Print Room, 1975–2013 and Librarian, 2002–13, Royal Library, Windsor Castle; *b* 4 Sept. 1949; *d* of 1st Baron Aldington, KCMG, CBE, DSO, TD, PC; *m* 1975, Hugh Ashley Roberts (*see* Sir H. A. Roberts); two *d*. *Educ:* Cranborne Chase School; Westfield College, Univ. of London (BA Hons); Courtauld Inst., Univ. of London (MA). Gov., British Inst. of Florence, 2002–; Trustee, Royal Drawing Sch., 2014–. Visitor, Ashmolean Mus., 2015–. *Publications:* Holbein, 1979; Leonardo: Codex Hammer, 1981; Master Drawings in the Royal Collection, 1985; Royal Artists, 1987; A Dictionary of Michelangelo's Watermarks, 1988; (jtly) Leonardo da Vinci, 1989; A Souvenir Album of Sandby Views of Windsor, 1990; A King's Purchase: King George III and the Collection of Consul Smith, 1993; Holbein and the Court of Henry VIII, 1993; Views of Windsor: watercolours by Thomas and Paul Sandby, 1995; Royal Landscape: the gardens and parks of Windsor, 1997; Ten Religious Masterpieces: a Millennium Celebration, 2000; (ed and contrib.) Royal Treasures: a Golden Jubilee celebration, 2002; (ed and contrib.) George III and Queen Charlotte: patronage, collecting and Court taste, 2004; (jtly) Unfolding Pictures: fans in the Royal Collection, 2005; Queen Elizabeth II: a birthday souvenir album, 2006; Five Gold Rings: a royal wedding souvenir album, 2007; Charles, Prince of Wales: a birthday souvenir album, 2008; Queen Elizabeth II: a Diamond Jubilee souvenir album, 2011; (jtly) Long to Reign Over Us, 2015; (contrib.) Windsor Castle: a thousand years of a royal palace, 2018; articles in Burlington Magazine, Apollo, Report of Soc. of Friends of St George's. *Recreations:* singing, sewing, playing the piano. *Address:* 33 East Lockinge, Wantage, Oxon OX12 8QG. *Clubs:* Athenæum, Roxburghe, Grillions.

**ROBERTS, Ven. Raymond Harcourt,** CB 1984; Chairman, Customer Service Committee for Wales, Office of Water Services, 1990–2001; licensed to officiate, diocese of Llandaff, since 1995; *b* 14 April 1931; *s* of Thomas Roberts and Carrie Maud Roberts. *Educ:* Pontywaun Grammar Sch., Risca, Mon; St Edmund Hall, Oxford (MA English); St Michael's Theol Coll., Llandaff. Nat. Service, RN, 1949–51. Deacon 1956, priest 1957, dio. of Monmouth (Curate of Bassaleg); Chaplain RNVR, 1958, RN, 1959; Destroyers and Frigates, Far East, 1959; HMS Pembroke, 1962; Dartmouth Trng Sqdn, 1963; RM Commando Course, 1965; 45 Commando, S. Arabia, 1965; RN Engrg Coll., 1967; HMS Bulwark, 1968; BRNC Dartmouth, 1970; HMS Ark Royal, 1974; Commando Trng Centre, RM, 1975; HMS Drake and HM Naval Base, Plymouth, 1979; Chaplain of the Fleet and Archdeacon for RN, 1980–84, Archdeacon Emeritus, 1985–; QHC, 1980–84; Hon. Canon, Cathedral of Holy Trinity, Gibraltar, 1980–84; Gen. Sec., Jerusalem and ME Church Assoc., 1985–89; licensed, dio. of Guildford, 1986–91; Hon. Chaplain, Llandaff Cathedral, 1991–95. Mem., Nat. Customer Council, Ofwat, 1993–2001. Liveryman, Livery Co. of Wales (formerly Welsh Livery Guild), 1993– (Chaplain, 1993–2007); Chaplain: to the High Sheriff of S Glam, 1993–94; Drapers' Co., 1996–97; Submariners Assoc., 2000–06. Governor, Rougemont Sch., Gwent, 1993–2004. *Recreations:* cooking and listening to Mozart, not necessarily simultaneously. *Address:* 13 Cwm Lane, Rogerstone, Newport, S Wales NP10 9AF. *T:* (01633) 895721.

**ROBERTS, Richard (David Hallam);** occasional academic and writer (seldom published), yachtmaster (unqualified), bookbinder's mate, semi-competent househusband, gardener, woodman, antiquarian cyclist; *b* 27 July 1931; *s* of Arthur Hallam Roberts, Barrister-at-law, sometime Attorney-General, Zanzibar, and Ruvé Constance Jessie Roberts; *m* 1960, Wendy Ewen Mount; three *s*. *Educ:* King's Sch., Canterbury; Jesus Coll., Cambridge. Commissioned into RA 6th Field Regt, 1952. Asst Master, King's Sch., Canterbury, 1956; Housemaster, 1957; Head of Modern Language Dept, 1961; Senior Housemaster, 1965; Headmaster: Wycliffe Coll., Stonehouse, 1967–80; King Edward's Sch., Witley, 1980–85. Chairman: Alde and Ore Assoc., 1991–94; Orford Town Trust, 1995–99. *Publications:* Ten Footers and All That, 2017. *Club:* Orford Sailing.

**ROBERTS, Richard James Lloyd; His Honour Judge Richard Roberts;** a Circuit Judge, since 2018; *b* Coalville, Leics, 19 Aug. 1961; *s* of Rev. Richard Lloyd Roberts and Mary Roberts; *m* 2000, Catriona Mackenzie Smith; one *s* one *d*. *Educ:* St Martin's Sch., Brentwood; Anglia Ruskin Univ. (BA Hons). Called to the Bar, Middle Temple, 1983; in practice as a barrister, Temple Garden Chambers, specialising in personal injury and clinical negligence, 1984–2009; an Immigration Judge, 2007–09; a Master of the Senior (formerly Supreme) Ct, QBD, 2009–18. Mem., CICAP, 2008–09. Member: Injury Cttee, Civil Justice Council, 2009–10; Civil Procedure Rule Cttee, 2014–18. Sec., Assoc. of High Court Masters, 2010–13. Tutor, Judicial Coll., 2015–. *Publications:* (ed jtly) Civil Procedure (The White Book), 2010. *Recreations:* playing the piano, listening to classical and popular music, literature, travel. *Address:* Central London County Court, Royal Courts of Justice, Thomas More Building, Strand, WC2A 2LL.

**ROBERTS, Sir Richard (John),** Kt 2008; PhD; FRS 1995; Chief Scientific Officer, New England Biolabs, since 2005 (Director of Research, 1992–2005); *b* Derby, 6 Sept. 1943; *s* of John Walter Roberts and Edna Wilhelmina Roberts; *m* 1st, 1965, Elizabeth Dyson; one *s* one *d*; 2nd, 1986, Jean (*née* Tagliabue); one *s* one *d*. *Educ:* City of Bath Boys' Sch.; Sheffield Univ. (BSc Chem. 1965; PhD 1968). Harvard University: Res. Fellow, 1969–70; Res. Associate in Biochem., 1971–72; Cold Spring Harbor Laboratory: Sen. Staff Investigator, 1972–86; Asst Dir for Research, 1986–92. Miller Prof., UC Berkeley, 1991. Dist. Scientist and Res. Schol., Boston Univ., 2003–. Chm., Scientific Adv. Bd, Celera, 1998–2002; Advr to Dir, NASA Astrobiol. Prog., 2000–. Dir, InVivo Therapeutics, 2009–. Pres., Bd of Trustees, Ocean Genome Legacy, 2004–. Exec. Editor, Nucleic Acids Res., 1987–2009 (Mem. Editl Bd, 1977–87); Panel Mem., NLM Study Section, Comp. Biol., 1993–95. Fellow, Science Mus., London, 2009. Hon. MD: Uppsala, 1992; Bath, 1994; Hon. DSc Sheffield, 1994. (Jtly) Nobel Prize in Physiology or Medicine, 1993. *Publications:* numerous papers on restriction endonucleases, DNA methylases, computational molecular biology. *Recreations:* collecting games, croquet. *Address:* New England Biolabs, 240 County Road, Ipswich, MA 01938-2723, USA. *T:* (978) 3807405.

**ROBERTS, Prof. Ronald John,** PhD; FRCPath, FRSB, FRCVS; FRSE; Commander, Most Noble Order of the Crown (Thailand), 1992; Professor of Aquatic Pathobiology and Director, Institute of Aquaculture, University of Stirling, 1971–96, now Professor Emeritus; *b* 28 March 1941; *s* of Ronald George Roberts and Marjorie Kneale; *m* 1964, Helen, *d* of

Gordon Gregor Macgregor; two s. Educ: Campbeltown Grammar Sch., Argyll; Univ. of Glasgow Vet. Sch. (PhD, BVMS). FRSB (FIBiol 1984); FRCPath 1988; FRCVS 1992; FRSE 1978. Univ. of Glasgow: Asst in Microbiology, 1964–66; Lectr in Vet. Pathology, 1966–71. Hagerman Dist. Vis. Prof., Univ. of Idaho, 1997–2017; Vis. Prof., Univ. of Malaysia Terengganu, 2009–10; Adjunct Prof., Washington State Univ., 2010–17. Consultant in Fish Diseases: Dept Agric. and Fisheries for Scotland, 1968–71; ODA, subseq. DFID, 1974–2001; FAO, Rome, 1978–83; World Bank, 1989. Dir, Machrihanish Marine Envmtl Res. Lab., 1991–96. Member: Cabinet Office Science Panel, 1993–94; Res. Grants Panel, SFHEFC (formerly SHEFC), 2001–10; Vice-Chm., 2003–06, Mem., 2006–09, Animal Health and Welfare Panel, European Food Safety Authy. Editor: Jl Fish Diseases, 1978–2015; Aquaculture Research (formerly Aquaculture and Fisheries Management), 1988–2000. Chairman: Stirling Aquaculture, 1987–95; Heronpisces Ltd, 2003–; Bradan Ltd, 2003–; Director: Stirling Salmon, 1987–94; Tarbert Fyne Foods, 1987–90; Stirling Aquatic Technology, 1987–90; Campbeltown and Kintyre Enterprise, 1992–2005 (Chm., 1996–2005); Landcatch Ltd, 1996–2011. Scientific Advr, Lithgow Gp, 1996–2011. Chm., Argyll and Bute Countryside Trust, 1994–2004; Sec., Lady Linda McCartney Meml Trust, 2000–. Foundn Fellow, World Aquatic Veterinary Medical Assoc., 2013. Buckland Prof. and Medallist, 1985–86; C-Vet Award, BVA, 1989; Dalrymple-Champneys Cup and Medal, BVA, 1990. Publications: (with C. J. Shepherd) Handbook of Salmon and Trout Diseases, 1974, 3rd edn 1996; Fish Pathology, 1978, 4th edn 2012; various scientific publications on histopathology of fishes. Recreations: arboriculture, rhododendron culture, admiring and conserving the Scottish natural environment. Address: 9 Alexander Drive, Bridge of Allan, Stirling FK9 4QB. T: (01786) 833078; Carrick Point Farm, Ardnacross Shorelands, by Campbeltown, Argyll PA28 5QR. T: (01586) 554417.

**ROBERTS, Sir Samuel,** 4th Bt cr 1919, of Ecclesall and Queen's Tower, City of Sheffield; barrister; b 16 April 1948; s of Sir Peter Geoffrey Roberts, 3rd Bt, and Judith Randell (d 1998), d of late Randell G. Hempson; S father, 1985; m 1977, Georgina Ann (DL Norfolk, 2013), yr d of David Cory; one s three d. Educ: Harrow School; Sheffield Univ. (LLB); Manchester Business School. Called to the Bar, Inner Temple, 1972. Chm., Cleyfield Properties Ltd, 1984–. Publications: Follow the Master: the Roberts book 5th edn, 2013. Heir: s Samuel Roberts, b 12 Aug. 1989. Address: Cockley Cley Hall, Swaffham, Norfolk PE37 8AG.

**ROBERTS, Maj. Gen. Sir Sebastian (John Lechmere),** KCVO 2007; OBE 1993; Chairman, The Military Mutual, since 2014; General Officer Commanding London District and Officer Commanding Household Division, 2003–07; b 7 Jan. 1954; s of Brig. John Mark Herbert Roberts, OBE and Nicola Helen Lechmere Roberts (née Macaskie); m 1979, Elizabeth Anne Muir; two s two d. Educ: Ampleforth; Balliol Coll., Oxford (BA, MA); RMA, Sandhurst; Army Staff Coll., Camberley. Commnd Irish Guards, 1977; Captain, Rendezvous Point Comdr, Op AGILA, Southern Rhodesia, 1979–80; Major, COS, 4th Armd Bde, Münster, 1987–89; Co. Comdr, Irish Guards, Belize and Berlin, 1989–91; Lt Col, MA to CGS, MoD, 1991–93; CO, 1st Bn, Irish Guards, London and E Tyrone, 1993–96; Col, Land Warfare 2 (Doctrine), Upavon, 1996–99; Brig., Dir Public Relns (Army), MoD, 1999–2002; rcds 2003. COS, RCDS, 2007–09. Regtl Lt Col, 1999–2008, Col, 2008–11, Irish Guards; Col Comdt, Media Ops Gp (Volunteers), 2006–09. Hon. Col, 256 (City of London) Field Hosp. (Volunteers), 2007–13; Hon. Col, London Irish Rifles, 2012–19. Chm., Soc. for Army Historical Res., 2009–13. Pres., Army Art Soc., 2014–17. Gov., St Mary's Sch., Shaftesbury, 2009–17 (Chm. Govs, 2010–17). Queen's Rep., Trustees of Royal Armouries, 2011–. Patron, Equata, 2015–. Liveryman, Girdlers' Co., 2005. Publications: The Bullingdon War Mag, 1976; Bertie Meets the Queen, 1978; Soldiering: the military covenant, 1998; RCDS Strategy Handbook, 2009. Recreations: painting and drawing, conversation, rebus letters, public speaking, prayer, eating, drinking, travelling, reading, writing, 9 brothers and sisters, 7 grandchildren, shooting. Clubs: Beefsteak, Pitt, Aspinalls, Buck's, Cavalry and Guards.

**ROBERTS, Stephen Cheveley;** Principal, Stamford Endowed Schools, 2008–16; b 23 Aug. 1956; s of David Roberts and Elizabeth Roberts (née Thornborough); m 1985, Joanna Meryl Cunnison; two s. Educ: Mill Hill Sch.; University Coll., Oxford (BA 1978; PGCE 1979; MA 1982). Credit Analyst, Orion Bank, 1979–80; Asst Master, Christ's Hosp., Horsham, 1980–86; Oundle School: Hd of Physics, 1986–90; Housemaster, 1990–93; Headmaster, Felsted Sch., 1993–2008. Sen. Advr, RSAcademics Ltd, 2017–. Governor: Royal Hosp. Sch., Holbeach, 2009–12; Perse Sch., Cambridge, 2016–; Haileybury Coll., Hertford, 2016–. Recreations: golf, hockey, music, reading. Club: Vincent's (Oxford).

**ROBERTS, Stephen Pritchard;** baritone; professional singer, since 1972; b 8 Feb. 1949; s of Edward Henry Roberts and Violet Pritchard. Educ: Royal College of Music (schol.). ARCM 1969; GRSM 1971. Professional Lay-Cleric, Westminster Cathedral Choir, 1972–76; sang regularly in London, UK and Europe, with all major orchs and choral socs; also sang in USA, Canada, Israel, Hong Kong, Singapore and S America. Mem., Vocal Faculty, RCM, 1993–; Ext. Examnr, UK music colls incl. RAM and Trinity Coll. of Music; mem. judging panel, various UK singing competitions and prizes. Opera rôles include: Count, in Marriage of Figaro; Falke, in Die Fledermaus; Ubalde, in Armide; Ramiro, in Ravel's L'Heure Espagnole; Aeneas, in Dido and Aeneas; Don Quixote, in Master Peter's Puppet Show; Mittenhofer, in Elegy for Young Lovers; television appearances include: Britten's War Requiem; Weill's Seven Deadly Sins; Delius' Sea Drift; Handel's Jeptha; Handel's Judas Maccabaeus; Penderecki's St Luke Passion, 1983 Proms; Walton's Belshazzar's Feast, 1984 Proms; recordings include: Tippett's King Priam; Birtwistle's Punch and Judy; Gluck's Armide; Orff's Carmina Burana; Vaughan Williams' Five Mystical Songs, Epithalamion, Sea Symphony, Fantasia on Christmas Carols, Hodie, and Serenade; Elgar's Apostles, and Caractacus; Penderecki's St Luke Passion; Fauré's Requiem; Dyson's Canterbury Pilgrims; Stravinsky songs; English song recordings incl. Gurney, Finzi, Somervell, Bennett and Howells; works by J. S. Bach, C. P. E. Bach and Duruflé. Address: 144 Gleneagle Road, SW16 6BA. T: (020) 8516 8830.

**ROBERTS, Stewart Brian,** MA; Headmaster, Dauntsey's School, 1997–2012; b 21 March 1952; s of late Evan John and Joyce Roberts; m 1985, Anna Susan Norman (d 2011); one s one d. Educ: Birkenhead Sch.; St Peter's Coll., Oxford (BA 1974; PGCE 1975; MA 1978). Asst Master, Birkenhead Sch., 1975–78; Asst Master, 1978–93, (Housemaster, 1984–93), Shrewsbury Sch.; Headmaster-des., Chand Bagh Sch., Lahore, 1994; Second Master, Dauntsey's Sch., 1995–97. Mem., P&O Scholarship Bd, 2001–05. Governor: St Francis Sch., Pewsey, 1997–2002; Shiplake Coll., 2003–11; Thomas Telford Sch., 2012–; Moreton Hall, 2012–18 (Chm., 2018); Madeley Acad., 2014– (Chm., 2017–); Walsall Acad., 2015–. Freeman, City of London, 2000. Address: Upper Stanway, Rushbury, Shropshire SY6 7EF.

**ROBERTS, Susan;** see Gilchrist, S.

**ROBERTS, Susan Holt,** CBE 2009; FRCP; National Clinical Director for Diabetes, Department of Health, 2003–08; b 28 Aug. 1945; d of David Holt Roberts and Joyce Eastoe Roberts (née How); m 1971, Christopher Kenneth Drinkwater; two d. Educ: Middlesex Hospital Medical Sch., London (BSc 1966; MB BS 1969); Univ. of Newcastle upon Tyne (MSc Clin. Biochem. 1975). FRCP 1986. Lectr in Medicine, Meml Univ. of Newfoundland, 1974–76; Consultant Physician, Northumbria Healthcare Trust, 1978–2008 (Chair, Year of Care Partnerships, 2010–). Hon. FRCGP 2012. Publications: articles and book chapters on med. topics incl. women in medicine, diabetes, healthcare delivery and patient educn. Recreations: walking, gardening, knitting, cats. Address: 30 Battle Hill, Hexham, Northumberland NE46 2EB. T: (01434) 600352. E: sue.roberts@gofo.co.uk.

**ROBERTS, Dr (Thomas) Michael,** CBE 2009; CBiol, FRSB; Chief Executive, Central Science Laboratory, Department for Environment, Food and Rural Affairs, 2001–08, now Consultant; b 12 May 1948; e s of late Robert Stanley Roberts and Mary Roberts (née Cliffe); m 1968, Ann Vaughan-Williams; one s two d. Educ: St Asaph Grammar Sch.; Univ. of Wales, Swansea (BSc 1969; PhD 1972). CBiol 1991; FRSB (FIBiol 1991); MCIEEM (MIEEM 1995). Asst Prof., Dept of Botany, Univ. of Toronto, 1972–74; Lectr, Dept of Botany, Univ. of Liverpool, 1974–78; Section Head, Terrestrial Ecology, Biology Section, CEGB, 1978–89; Dir, Inst. of Terrestrial Ecology, 1989–99, Dir, Centre for Ecology and Hydrology, 1999–2001, NERC. Ext. Examiner, York Univ., 1993–2008. Member: DoE Adv. Cttee on Hazardous Substances, 1992–2000; HSE Adv. Cttee on Genetic Modification, 1994–99; MAFF Adv. Cttee on Pesticides, 1996–2001; Adv. Bd, Jt Inst. for Food and Nutrition, Food and Drug Admin/Univ. of Maryland, USA, 2002–08; Veterinary Residues Cttee, DEFRA, 2005–16; Royal Commn on Envmtl Pollution, 2009–11; non-exec. Bd Mem., Nat. Non-Food Crops Centre, 2008–13 (Chm., 2013–); Chm., UK Man and Biosphere Cttee, 1993–2001; Trustee, Nat. Biodiversity Network, 2000–01. Mem. Bd, Yorks and Humber Sci. and Innovation Council, 2006–08. Mem., Yorks Philosophical Soc., 2003–. Vice-Pres., Reigate Priory CC and Little Shelford CC, 2000–. Ed., Jl of Applied Ecology, 1981–86. Publications: Planning and Ecology, 1984; Ecological Aspects of Radionuclide Releases, 1985; numerous articles on applied ecology in learned jls. Recreations: club cricket, golf, gardening. Club: Easingwold Golf (Chm., 2011–16).

**ROBERTS, Timothy David;** QC 2003; a Recorder, since 1993; b 4 Oct. 1955; s of Norman and Heather Roberts; m 1986, Angela Shakespeare; two d. Educ: Guisborough Grammar Sch.; Southampton Univ. (LLB Hons). Called to the Bar, Gray's Inn, 1978, Bencher, 2007; Public Solicitor, Solomon Islands, 1979–81; joined Fountain Chambers, 1982, Hd of Chambers, 2000–10; in practice, specialising in criminal law. Recreations: music, sailing. Address: Fountain Chambers, Cleveland Business Centre, 1 Watson Street, Middlesbrough, Cleveland TS1 2RQ. T: (01642) 804040, Fax: (01642) 804060. Club: Runswick Bay Sailing.

**ROBERTS CAIRNS, Patricia Rose Marie, (Mrs D. A. O. Cairns),** OBE 2000; freelance editorial consultant; Consultant, National Magazine Co., since 1999; b 27 Nov. 1947; d of late Maj. William Roberts, MBE, RA and Catherine (née Slawson); m 1993, Dr David A. O. Cairns (d 2014). Educ: St Barnabas Sch., Woodford Green; Open Univ. (BA 2007). Reporter, Independent Newspapers, Essex, 1965–68; features writer, IPC mags, 1968–72; Founder Editor, Girl About Town (London's first free mag.), 1972–80; feature writer, Femail, Daily Mail, 1980–82; Associate Editor, Family Circle, 1982–84; Editor, Over 21, 1984–89; Founder Editor, House Beautiful, 1989–95; Editor-in-Chief, Good Housekeeping, 1995–99. Member: Editl Cttee, Periodical Trng Council, 1992–; Women of Year Cttee, 1993–; BSME Cttee, 1993–99; Editl Public Affairs Cttee, PPA, 1993–99; Press Complaints Commn, 1998–99. FRSA. Launch Editor of Year, BSME, 1990; Editor of Year, PPA, 1992. Publications: Living Images: styling yourself to success, 1990; House Beautiful Home Handbook, 1992. Address: Cliff Cottage, 49 Meads Street, Eastbourne BN20 7RN.

**ROBERTS-WEST, Lt-Col George Arthur Alston-;** see West.

**ROBERTSHAW, His Honour Patrick Edward;** a Circuit Judge, 1994–2010; b 7 July 1945; s of late George Edward Robertshaw and May (née Tallis); m 1st, 1972, Sally Christine Greenburgh (née Searle) (d 2016); two s two d; 2nd, 2018, Judith Elizabeth Bousfield (née Whitehead). Educ: Hipperholme Grammar Sch.; Southampton Univ. (LLB). Called to the Bar, Inner Temple, 1968; a Recorder, 1989–94. Mem., Parole Bd, 2010–. Publications: The Inglorious Twelfth: the study of a 1950s murder trial, 2005; No Smoking Gun: exposure of a 1950s miscarriage of justice, 2012; contrib. to legal periodicals. Recreations: reading, listening to music, travel, photography.

**ROBERTSON,** family name of **Barons Robertson of Oakridge, Robertson of Port Ellen** and **Wharton**.

**ROBERTSON OF OAKRIDGE,** 3rd Baron cr 1961; **William Brian Elworthy Robertson;** Bt 1919; Investment Agent, Strutt and Parker LLP, since 2006; b Roehampton, 15 Nov. 1975; o s of 2nd Baron Robertson of Oakridge and of Celia Jane, d of William R. Elworthy; S father, 2009. Educ: BA Hons English Lit. MRICS. Admitted Solicitor of the Supreme Court; Solicitor: Ashurst, 2001–05; Reed Smith, 2005; Schulte Roth & Zabel, 2006. Mem., Salters' Co. Heir: none. T: 07970 822274. E: willahr@hotmail.com.

**ROBERTSON OF PORT ELLEN,** Baron cr 1999 (Life Peer), of Islay in Argyll and Bute; **George Islay MacNeill Robertson,** KT 2004; GCMG 2004; PC 1997; Special Adviser to BP plc, since 2013; Chairman, BP Russian Investments, since 2015; Chancellor of the Order of St Michael and St George, since 2011; b 12 April 1946; s of George Philip Robertson and Marion I. Robertson; m 1970, Sandra Wallace; two s one d. Educ: Dunoon Grammar Sch.; Univ. of Dundee (MA Hons 1968). Res. Asst, Tayside Study, 1968–69; Scottish Organiser, G&MWU, 1970–78. MP (Lab) Hamilton, 1978–97, Hamilton South, 1997–99. PPS to Sec. of State for Social Services, 1979; opposition spokesman on Scottish Affairs, 1979–80, on Defence, 1980–81, on Foreign and Commonwealth Affairs, 1981–93; principal spokesman on European Affairs, 1984–93; principal opposition front bench spokesman on Scotland, 1993–97; Sec. of State for Defence, 1997–99. Sec.-Gen., NATO, 1999–2003. Chm., Scottish Labour Party, 1977–78; Mem., Scottish Exec. of Lab. Party, 1973–79, 1993–97. Dep. Chm., 2004–06, Sen. Internat. Advr, 2007–10, Cable & Wireless plc; Chm., Cable & Wireless Internat., 2006–10; Sen. Internat. Advr, Cable and Wireless Communications plc, 2010–15; Dep. Chm., TNK-BP, 2006–13; non-executive Director: Smiths Gp plc, 2004–06; Weir Gp plc, 2004–14; Edinburgh Military Tattoo, 2015– (Vice Chm., 2018–). Sen. Counsellor, Cohen Gp, USA, 2004–; Adviser: Engelfield Capital, 2004–11; Royal Bank of Canada, 2004–06. Vice Chm. Bd, British Council, 1985–94; Member: Council, RIIA, 1984–91 (Jt Pres., 2001–11); Adv. Council, European Council on Foreign Relations, 2008–; Council, IISS, 2013–; Adv. Bd, Centre for European Reform, 2014–. Vis. Prof., KCL, 2018–. Chm., Commn on Global Road Safety (Make Roads Safe), 2004–15. Chm., John Smith Meml Trust, 2004–08; Trustee: British Forces Foundn, 2006–; Queen Elizabeth Diamond Jubilee Trust, 2012–; FIA Foundn, 2015– (Chm., 2015–); Patron: Scottish Burned Children Trust, 2001–; Islay Book Fest., 2009–; Dunblane Centre, 2009–; Disability Trust, 2010–; Paratroop Regt Afghanistan Trust, 2012–; Mus. of Islay Trust, 2013–. Chm., Council, Ditchley Foundn, 2009–17 (Gov., 1989–; Dep. Chm., 2008). Mem. Adv. Bd, Commemoration of World War One, 2012–. Hon. Regtl Col, London Scottish (Volunteers), 2000–16. Mem. Court and Elder Brother, Trinity Hse, 2001–. Pres., Hamilton Burns Club, 2002. Hon. Guild Brother, Guildry of Stirling, 2004. FRSA 1999. Hon. FRSE 2003; Hon. Sen. Fellow, Foreign Policy Assoc., USA, 2000; Hon. Prof. of Politics, Stirling Univ., 2009–. Hon. LLD: Dundee, Bradford,

2000; Baku State Univ., Azerbaijan, 2001; Romanian Nat. Sch. of Pol and Admin. Studies, 2003; French Univ., Yerevan, Armenia, 2003; Azerbaijan Acad. of Scis, 2003; St Andrews, 2003; Glasgow Caledonian, 2004; Hon. DSc RMCS Cranfield, 2000; DUniv: Paisley, 2006; Stirling, 2008; Lincoln, 2008. Knight Grand Cross: Order of Merit (Italy), 2003; Order of Oranje-Nassau (Netherlands), 2003; Comdr Grand Cross, Order of Three Stars (Latvia), 2004; Grand Cross: Order of the Star (Romania), 2000; Order of Merit (Germany), 2003; Order of Merit (Poland), 2003; Order of Merit (Hungary), 2003; Order of Merit (Luxembourg), 2003; Order of Isabel the Catholic (Spain), 2003; Order of Jesus (Portugal), 2003; Order of Grand Duke Gedeminos (Lithuania), 2003; Order of Stara Planina (Bulgaria), 2003; Order of King Petar Kresimir IV (Croatia), 2003; Order of Yaroslav the Wise (Ukraine), 2005; Grand Cordon, Order of Leopold (Belgium), 2003; Presidential Medal of Freedom (USA), 2003; First Class: Order of the Tarra Mariana (Estonia), 2004; Order of the White Two-Arm Cross (Slovakia), 2004; Order for Exceptional Services (Slovenia), 2006; Golden Medal of Freedom (Kosovo), 2016; Order of George Skanderbeg (Albania), 2019. *Publications*: Islay and Jura: photographs, 2006; (jtly) Dunblane: its people in a century of change, 2012. *Recreations*: reading, family, photography, golf. *Address*: House of Lords, SW1A 0PW. *E*: robertsong@parliament.uk. *Clubs*: Army and Navy; Islay Golf; Dunblane New Golf.

**ROBERTSON, Aidan Malcolm David;** QC 2009; *b* Newcastle upon Tyne, 19 Dec. 1961; *s* of William David Duncan and Veronica Gloria Robertson; *m* 2005, Beverley Anne Blakeney; one *s* two *d* (of whom one *s* one *d* are twins). *Educ*: Jesus Coll., Cambridge (BA 1984; LLM 1985). Solicitor, 1988–95; called to the Bar, Middle Temple, 1995. Lectr in Law, Univ. of Oxford, 1990–96, Vis. Prof. in Law, 2015– (Vis. Lectr, 2002–15); Fellow and Tutor in Law, Wadham Coll., Oxford, 1990–99. *Publications*: (with N. Green) Commercial Agreements and Competition Law, 2nd edn 1997; (with D. Vaughan) Law of the European Union (looseleaf encyclopedia), 2003. *Recreations*: swimming, Newcastle United. *Address*: Brick Court Chambers, 7–8 Essex Street, WC2R 3LD. *T*: (020) 7379 3550, *Fax*: (020) 7379 7558. *E*: aidan.robertson@brickcourt.co.uk. *Club*: Royal Automobile.

**ROBERTSON, Alastair,** PhD; consultant on research strategy and agribusiness; Group Executive, Food, Health and Life Science Industries, CSIRO, 2009–13; *b* 18 July 1949; *s* of Robert Russell Robertson and Brenda Scott Robertson; *m* 1975, Wendy Kathleen Purchase; one *s* one *d*. *Educ*: Univ. of Bath (BSc Hons Applied Biology 1973; PhD Plant Biochemistry 1976). FRSC 1983; FIFST 1983. Postdoctoral Fellow, Univ. of Cambridge, 1976–79; Process Biochemist, Sigma Chemical Co., 1979–81; Head of Chemistry and Biochemistry, 1981–86, Dir of Food Science, 1986–92, Campden and Chorley Wood Food Res. Assoc.; Head of Res. and Develt, 1992–95, Technical Dir, 1995–2000, Safeway Stores plc; Dir, Inst. of Food Res., BBSRC, 2000–03; Chief Exec., Food Sci. Australia, 2003–05; Gp Exec., CSIRO Agribusiness, 2005–07; Dep. Chief Exec., CSIRO Sci. Strategy and Investment, 2007–09. Hon. Prof., UEA, 2000–03; Res. Prof., Univ. of Tasmania, 2004–13. *Publications*: 50 articles in jls on biochemistry and food sci. areas. *Recreations*: gardening, music, angling, sports. *E*: aw1.robertson@gmail.com.

**ROBERTSON, Andrew Ogilvie,** CBE 2018 (OBE 1994); Senior Partner, T. C. Young, 1994–2006; *b* 30 June 1943; *s* of Alexander McArthur Ogilvie Robertson and Charlotte Rachel Robertson (*née* Cuthbert); *m* 1974, Sheila Sturton; two *s*. *Educ*: Sedbergh Sch.; Edinburgh Univ. (LLB 1964). Apprentice Solicitor, Maclay Murray & Spens, 1964–67; Asst Solicitor, 1967–68, Partner, 1968–2006, T. C. Young. Secretary: Erskine Hosp., 1976–2002 (Vice-Pres., 2006; Chm., 2011–16); Fedn of Community Clydeside-based Housing Assocs, 1978–93 (also Treas.); Briggait Co. Ltd, 1983–88; Princess Royal Trust for Carers, 1990–2006 (Legal Advr, 1990–2006; Trustee, 2006–12); Chairman: Post Office Users' Council for Scotland, 1988–99; Gtr Glasgow Community and Mental Health Services NHS Trust, 1994–97; Glasgow Royal Infirmary Univ. NHS Trust, 1997–99; Gtr Glasgow Primary Care NHS Trust, 1998–2004; Member: POUNC, 1988–99; Gtr Glasgow Health Bd, 1999–2015 (Vice-Chm., 2004–07; Chm., 2007–15). Carers Champion for Glasgow, 2015–17. Chairman: Lintel Trust (formerly Scottish Housing Assocs Charitable Trust), 1990–2007; LAR Housing Trust, 2016–; Trustee: Housing Assocs Charitable Trust (UK), 1990–97; Music in Hosps, 2006–13; Vice Pres., Carers Trust, 2012–. Non-exec. Dir, Scottish Building Soc., 1994–2008 (Chm., 2003–06). Dir, Scotcash, 2007–11. Gov., Sedbergh Sch., 2000–08. Hon. DSc Glasgow, 2015. *Recreations*: climbing, sailing, swimming, reading, fishing. *Address*: Burnside Cottage, Main Street, Drymen G63 0BQ. *Clubs*: East India; Western (Glasgow).

**ROBERTSON, Rt Hon. Angus Struan Carolus;** PC 2015; *b* 28 Sept. 1969. *Educ*: Broughton High Sch., Edinburgh; Univ. of Aberdeen (MA 1991). News Editor, Austrian Broadcasting Corp., 1991; reporter, BBC, Austria, etc, 1991–99; communications consultant and journalist, 1999–. MP (SNP) Moray, 2017–17; contested (SNP) same seat, 2017. SNP spokesman on foreign affairs, 2001–15, on defence, 2003; SNP Leader, H of C, 2007–17. SNP Campaign Director: Scottish Parlt elections 2007 and 2011, Scottish independence referendum, 2014. Mem., Intelligence and Security Cttee, 2015–17. Contested (SNP) Midlothian, Scottish Parlt, 1999.

**ROBERTSON, Hon. Sir Bruce;** see Robertson, Hon. Sir J. B.

**ROBERTSON, Rev. Charles,** LVO 2005; Parish Minister, Canongate (The Kirk of Holyroodhouse), 1978–2005, now Minister Emeritus; Chaplain to the Queen in Scotland, 1991–2010, Extra Chaplain to the Queen in Scotland, since 2010; *b* 22 Oct. 1940; *s* of late Thomas Robertson and Elizabeth Halley; *m* 1965, Alison Margaret Malloch; one *s* two *d*. *Educ*: Camphill School, Paisley; Edinburgh Univ. (MA); New College, Edinburgh. Asst Minister, North Morningside, Edinburgh, 1964–65; Parish Minister, Kiltearn, Ross-shire, 1965–78. Chaplain to Lord High Comr, 1990, 1991, 1996 (the Princess Royal). Convener, Gen. Assembly's Panel on Worship, 1995–99 (Sec., 1982–95); C of S rep. on Joint Liturgical Group, 1984–99 (Chm., 1994–99). Mem., Broadcasting Standards Council, 1988–91, 1992–93. Chaplain: Clan Donnachaidh Soc., 1981–96; New Club, Edinburgh, 1986–2015; Moray House Coll. of Educn, then Edinburgh Univ. at Moray House, 1986–2002; No 2 (City of Edinburgh) Maritime HQ Unit, 1987–99, No 603 (City of Edinburgh) Sqn, 1999–2015, RAAF; to the High Constables and Guard of Honour of Holyroodhouse, 1993–2009 (Chaplain Emeritus, 2009); Incorp. of Goldsmiths of City of Edinburgh, 2000–; Edinburgh Merchants' Co., 2002–; Convenery of Trades of Edinburgh, 2005–16; Incorporation of Bonnetmakers and Dyers of Edinburgh, 2008–16. Lectr, St Colm's Coll., 1980–94. Mem., Historic Buildings Council for Scotland, 1990–99. Chairman: Bd of Queensberry House Hosp., 1989–96 (Mem., 1978–96); Queensberry Trust, 1996–; Gov., St Columba's Hospice, 1986–2005; Trustee: Edinburgh Old Town Trust, 1987–94; Edinburgh Old Town Charitable Trust, 1994–; Edinburgh World Heritage Trust, 1999–2000; Church Hymnary Trust, 1987–; Carnegie Trust for the Univs of Scotland, 2005–15; Soc. for the Benefit of Sons and Daughters of the Clergy of the Church of Scotland, 2003– (Chm., 2009–); Pres., Church Service Soc., 1988–91. Hon. Life Mem. No 603 (City of Edinburgh) Squadron Assoc., 2013. JP Edinburgh, 1980–2006. Sec. of cttees which compiled Hymns for a Day, 1983, Songs of God's People, 1988, Worshipping Together, 1991, Clann ag Urnaigh, 1991, Common Order, 1994, Common Ground, 1998; Sec., Cttee to Revise Church Hymnary, 1995–2004. *Publications*: (ed)
Singing the Faith, 1990; (ed) St Margaret Queen of Scotland and her Chapel, 1994; (jtly) By Lamplight, 2000. *Recreations*: Scottish and Edinburgh history and literature, hymnody, collecting Canongate miscellanea. *Address*: 3 Ross Gardens, Edinburgh EH9 3BS. *T*: (0131) 662 9025. *Clubs*: Puffin's, New (Hon. Mem.), Royal Scots (Hon. Mem.) (Edinburgh).

**ROBERTSON, Christine Joyce;** see Howe, C. J.

**ROBERTSON, Corin Jean Stella;** HM Diplomatic Service; Ambassador to Mexico, since 2018; *b* Sheffield, 15 Jan. 1972; *d* of Prof. William John Leatherbarrow, *qv*; *m* 1996, James Francis Robertson; one *s* one *d*. *Educ*: King Edward VII Sch., Sheffield; Queens' Coll., Cambridge (BA Hons Modern Langs 1994). Entered FCO, 1994; Desk Officer, Greece/Cyprus, Southern Eur. Dept, FCO, 1994–95; Japanese lang. trng, 1995–97; Second Sec., Global Issues, Tokyo, 1997–2000; Hd, EU-Gibraltar Section, Eur. Directorate, FCO, 2000–02; Hd, EP Section, 2002–04, First Sec. (Antici), 2004–06, UK Perm. Repn to EU, Brussels; Business Engagement Advr, FCO, 2007–08; Jt Hd, Counter-Terrorism Dept, FCO, 2008–11; Dep. High Comr, Ottawa, 2011–14; Dir, Estates and Security, FCO, 2014–17. *Recreations*: reading, spending time with family, playing netball, Netflix box-sets. *Address*: c/o Foreign and Commonwealth Office, King Charles Street, SW1A 2AH.

**ROBERTSON, Daphne Jean Black;** Sheriff of Lothian and Borders at Edinburgh, 1996–2000; *b* 31 March 1937; *d* of Rev. Robert Black Kincaid and Ann Parker Collins; *m* 1965, Donald Buchanan Robertson, QC (*d* 2012). *Educ*: Hillhead High Sch.; Greenock Acad.; Edinburgh Univ. (MA); Glasgow Univ. (LLB). Admitted solicitor, 1961; WS 1977; Sheriff of Glasgow and Strathkelvin, 1979–96; pt-time Sheriff, 2000–07.

**ROBERTSON, Douglas;** see Robertson, J. D. M.

**ROBERTSON, Fiona Mary Cecile;** Vice Lord-Lieutenant of Fife, since 2015; *b* Greenock, 25 Aug. 1954; *d* of David and Pamela Collen; *m* 1993, William Brian Robertson; two *s*. *Educ*: St Leonards Sch., St Andrews; Aberdeen Sch. of Physiotherapy (MCSP 1976); Univ. of Southampton (MSc Rehabilitation Studies 1993). Physiotherapist, 1977–2016; Res. Physiotherapist, Univ. of Oxford, 1988–90; Physiotherapy Lectr, Queen Margaret Univ., Edinburgh, 1994–2004. Trustee: Carnegie Dunfermline and Hero Fund Trusts, 2005–; Carnegie UK Trust, 2016–. DL Fife, 2007. *Recreations*: family, keeping fit, family history research, arts. *E*: fionarobertson13@gmail.com.

**ROBERTSON, Geoffrey Ronald,** AO 2018; QC 1988; barrister; author; *b* 30 Sept. 1946; *s* of Francis Albert Robertson and Bernice Joy (*née* Beattie); *m* 1990, Kathryn Marie Lette, *qv* (marr. diss. 2018); one *s* one *d*. *Educ*: Epping Boys' High Sch.; Univ. of Sydney (BA 1966; LLB Hons 1970); University Coll., Oxford (BCL 1972; Rhodes Schol.). Called to the Bar, Middle Temple, 1973, Bencher, 1997; Supreme Court of NSW, 1977, of Antigua, 1990, of Trinidad, 1992, of Malaysia, 1998, of Hong Kong, 2001, of Fiji, 2002, of Anguilla, 2007. An Asst Recorder, 1993–99; a Recorder, 1999–2012. Founder and Head, Doughty Street Chambers, 1990–. Visiting Professor: Univ. of NSW, 1977; Birkbeck Coll., and Queen Mary, London Univ., 1997–; New Coll. of the Humanities, 2012–; Vis. Fellow, Warwick Univ., 1980–81. Consultant on Human Rights to Attorney Gen. of Australia, 1983; Consultant (Commonwealth Secretariat) to Constitutional Convention, Seychelles, 1993. Chm., Inquiry into Press Council, 1982–83; Counsel: Royal Commn on Arms Trafficking, Antigua, 1990–91; Commn on Admin of Justice, Trinidad, 2000. Appeal Judge, UN Special Ct for Sierra Leone, 2002–07 (and Pres., 2002–04). Chm., Commn on UN Internal Justice Reform, 2006–07; Mem., UN Internal Justice Council, 2008–12. Member: BFI Wkg Party on New Technologies, 1984; Exec. Council, ICA, 1987–97; Freedom of Inf. Campaign, 1987–; Charter 88, 1988–96; Justice, 1991–. Chm., BMA Cttee on Medical Inf. and Patient Privacy, 1994. Chm., Common Sense, 1998–. *Television*: Moderator, Hypotheticals, 1981–; writer and presenter, Tree of Liberty, 1982; Chm., The World This Week, 1987; writer and narrator, 44 Days (documentary), 1992. Editor, legal column, The Guardian, 1980–85. Hon. LLD: Sydney, 2008; Brunel, 2010; Romanian Nat. Sch. of Pol Scis, 2011. Freedom of Information Award, 1993; Award for dist. in internat. law, NY Bar Assoc., 2011. *Publications*: The Trials of Oz (play), 1973 (televised 1991); Whose Conspiracy?, 1974; Reluctant Judas, 1976; Obscenity, 1979; People Against the Press, 1983; (with A. Nicol) Media Law, 1984, 5th edn 2007; Hypotheticals, 1986; Does Dracula have Aids?, 1987; Freedom, the Individual and the Law, 6th edn 1989, 7th edn 1993; Geoffrey Robertson's Hypotheticals, 1991; The Justice Game, 1998; Crimes Against Humanity, 1999, 4th edn 2012; The Tyrannicide Brief, 2005; The Levellers: the Putney debates, 2007; Statute of Liberty, 2009; Was there an Armenian Genocide?, 2009; The Case of the Pope: Vatican accountability for human rights abuses, 2010; The 1988 Iranian Prison Massacres, 2010; Human Rights Fact-Finding: some legal and ethical dilemmas, 2010; Who Wants Diego Garcia? Decolonisation, Torture and Indigenous Rights, 2012; Mullahs Without Mercy: human rights and nuclear weapons, 2012; Dreaming Too Loud: reflections on a race apart, 2013; Stephen Ward Was Innocent, OK, 2013; An Inconvenient Genocide: who now remembers the Armenians?, 2014; Rather His Own Man: in court with tyrants, tarts and troublemakers (memoir), 2018; contribs to anthologies and learned jls. *Recreations*: tennis, opera, fishing. *Address*: Doughty Street Chambers, 54 Doughty Street, WC1N 2LS. *T*: (020) 7404 1313, *Fax*: (020) 7404 2283. *E*: g.robertson@doughtystreet.co.uk.

**ROBERTSON, Air Marshal Graeme Alan,** CBE 1988 (OBE 1985); Managing Director, Blackbourne Wells Ltd, since 2003; *b* 22 Feb. 1945; *s* of Ronald James Harold Robertson, DFC and Constance Rosemary (*née* Freeman); *m* 1972, Barbara Ellen (*née* Mardon); one *d*. *Educ*: Bancroft's Sch.; RAF Coll., Cranwell; BA Open Univ. Pilot: 8 Sqn, 1968–69; 6 Sqn, 1970–72; 228 OCU, 1972–73; Asst Ops Officer, 550 TFTS, USAF, 1973–76; Flight Comdr, 56 Sqn, 1976–77; RAF Staff Coll., 1977–78; OR/Air Plans Staff, MoD, 1978–82; Commanding Officer: 92 Sqn, 1982–84; 23 Sqn, 1984–85; RAF Wattisham, 1985–87; Hon. ADC to the Queen, 1985–87; Dir of Air Staff Briefing and Co-ordination, MoD, 1987–88; RCDS, 1989; Dir of Defence Programmes, MoD, 1990–91; Dep. C-in-C, RAF Germany, 1991–93; AOC No 2 Gp, 1993–94; ACDS (Programmes), MoD, 1994–96; C of S and Dep. C-in-C, Strike Comd, 1996–98; Hon. Col, 77 Engr Regt (Vols), 1996–99. Defence and Air Advr, BAe, subseq. Sen. Mil. Advr, BAE Systems, 1999–2003. Co-ordinator, British-American Community Relns, MoD, 2004–10. Trustee, David Vasey Prize, 2018–. FRSA 1995; FRAeS 1997. Freeman, City of London, 1997; Clerk, Hon. Co. of Glos, 2013–18. QCVSA 1973. *Recreations*: field sports, sailing, winter sports, the arts. *Address*: c/o National Westminster Bank, Sleaford, Lincs NG34 7BF. *Clubs*: Royal Air Force, MCC.

**ROBERTSON, Rt Hon. Sir Hugh (Michael),** KCMG 2014; PC 2012; DL; FRGS; Chairman: British Olympic Association, since 2016 (Vice Chairman, 2015–16); Racing Authority, since 2019 (Shadow Racing Authority, 2018–19); *b* 9 Oct. 1962; *s* of George and June Robertson; *m* 2002, Anna Copson; one *s*. *Educ*: King's Sch., Canterbury; RMA Sandhurst; Reading Univ. (BSc Hons Land Mgt (Property Investment); Dist. Fellow, 2014). Served Life Guards, 1985–95 (Armourers' and Brasiers' Prize, 1986): active service: NI, 1988; UN Cyprus, 1988; Gulf War, 1991; Bosnia, 1994; i/c Household Cavalry on Queen's Birthday Parade and State Opening of Parlt as Field Officer of the Escort, 1993; Silver Stick Adjutant, 1994–95; retd in rank of Major; Schroder Investment Mgt, 1995–2001 (Asst Dir, 1999–2001). MP (C) Faversham and Mid Kent, 2001–15. An Opposition Whip, 2002–04; Shadow Sports Minister, 2004–05; Shadow Minister for Sport and the Olympics, 2005–10; Parly Under-Sec. of State (Minister for Sport and the Olympics), 2010–12, Minister of State (Minister for Sport and Tourism), 2012–13, DCMS; Minister of State, FCO, 2013–14. Sec., Parly Fruit Gp, 2001–10; Chm., All Party UN Gp, 2005–08. Gov., Westminster Foundn for Democracy, 2005–08. Vice Chm., Internat. Relns, Falcon and Associates, 2016–17 (Dir, 2015–17). Chm., Canterbury Cathedral Appeal, 2016–. Trustee, Chelsea FC Foundn, 2016–. DL Kent, 2015. FRGS 1995. Sultan of Brunei's Personal Order of Merit, 1993; Internat. Paralympic Cttee Merit Award, 2012; Sport and Recreation Alliance Emeritus Award, 2014. *Recreations*: cricket, hockey. *Address*: British Olympic Association, 101 Cavendish Street, W1W 6XH. *Clubs*: Cavalry and Guards, Pratt's, MCC (Playing Mem.).

**ROBERTSON, Iain Samuel,** CBE 2002; CA; Chairman, Corporate Banking and Financial Markets, Royal Bank of Scotland, 2001–05 (Chief Executive, 2000–01); *b* 27 Dec. 1945; *s* of Alfred and Kathleen Robertson; *m* 1972, Morag; two *s* two *d*. *Educ*: Jordanhill College Sch.; Glasgow Univ. (LLB). Industry and professional practice, 1966–72; Civil Servant, 1972–83; Dir, Locate in Scotland, 1983–86; Chief Exec., SDA, 1987–90; Gp Finance Dir, County Natwest, 1990–92; Royal Bank of Scotland: Man. Dir, Corporate and Instnl Banking Div., 1992–98; Chief Exec., UK Bank, 1998–2000. Non-executive Director: Scottish Development Finance, 1983–90; Selective Assets Trust plc, 1989–96; British Empire Securities & Gen. Trust plc, 1995–2007; BT (Scotland), 2004–08; Cairn Capital Ltd, 2004–08; John Menzies plc, 2004–09. *Recreations*: golf, reading.

**ROBERTSON, Ian,** CA; President, Institute of Chartered Accountants of Scotland, 2004–05; *b* 10 Aug. 1947; *s* of James Love Robertson and Mary Hughes Robertson (née Reid); *m* 1st, 1968, Susan Moira Scott (marr. diss.); two *s* one *d*; 2nd, 2001, Fiona Ann Hervey. *Educ*: Queen's Park Sch., Glasgow. CA 1969. Chief Accountant, Whitbread Scotland Ltd, 1973–76; Dir, J. & A. Ferguson Ltd, 1976–82; Chief Accountant, United Biscuits, Glasgow, 1982–84; Financial Controller, Terry's of York, 1984–87; Finance Dir, Dairy Div., 1987–90, Gp Finance Controller, 1991–94, Northern Foods plc; Finance Dir, 1994–2003, Gp Chief Exec., 2003–07, Wilson Bowden plc. Non-executive Director: Homes & Communities Agency, 2008–16 (Chm., Audit Cttee, 2008–16); Leeds Building Soc., 2008–15 (Chm., Audit Cttee, 2010–15). Member: Financial Reporting Council, 2004–07; Audit Adv. Bd, Scottish Parlt Corporate Body, 2007–14, 2017–18 (Chm., 2009–14); Ind. Mem., Audit Cttee, DCLG, 2012–16. Ext. Expert, Audit Cttee, UN Jt Staff Pension Fund, 2010–14 (Dep. Chm., 2012–14). Institute of Chartered Accountants, Scotland: Mem. Council, 1996–2003; Sen. Vice-Pres., 2003–04; Convener, Investigations Cttee, 2010–17, 2019–. Ind. Mem., Finance Cttee, Royal Coll. of Surgeons of England, 2016–18. Mem. (C), 1973–84, Chm., 1980–84, Eastwood DC. Mem., Collingham with Linton Parish Council, 2015–18. Chm., Elmet & Rothwell Cons. Assoc., 2017– (Dep. Chm., 2016–17). CCMI 2004 (FCMI 1976). *Recreations*: reading, music, travel, walking, politics. *E*: ianrobertsonca@gmail.com.

**ROBERTSON, Prof. Ian Hamilton,** PhD; Professor of Psychology, Trinity College Dublin, 1999–2016, now Emeritus; Co-Director, Global Brain Health Institute, since 2015; *b* Lennoxtown, Scotland, 26 April 1951; *s* of John M. Robertson and Anne D. Robertson; *m* 1984, Dr Fiona O'Doherty; two *s* one *d*. *Educ*: Allan Glen's Sch., Glasgow; Univ. of Glasgow (BSc Psychol. 1973); Inst. of Psychiatry, Univ. of London (MPhil 1978); Univ. of London (PhD 1988). FBPsS 1987. Clin. Psychologist, Tayside Health Bd, 1978–82; Sen. Clin. Psychologist, Royal Edinburgh Hosp., 1982–84; Hd Neuropsychologist, Astley Ainslie Hosp., Edinburgh, 1984–91; Sen. Scientist, MRC Cognition and Brain Scis Unit, Cambridge, 1991–99. Fellow, Hughes Hall, Cambridge, 1994–99. MRC Travelling Fellow, Univ. La Sapienza, Rome, 1989; Visiting Professor: UCL, 1996–; Bangor Univ., 1996–; Staff Scientist, Rotman Res. Inst., Univ. of Toronto, 1995–; T. Boone Pickens Dist. Scientist, Center for Brain Health, Univ. of Texas, Dallas, 2016–. MRIA 2007; MAE 2018; Fellow, Amer. Assoc. for Psychological Sci., 2013. FRSA 2011. *Publications*: Problem Drinking, 1981, 3rd edn 1997; Controlled Drinking, 1981; Unilateral Neglect, 1993; Spatial Neglect, 1999; Mind Sculpture, 1999; Cognitive Neurorehabilitation, 2002, 2nd edn 2008; The Mind's Eye, 2002; Handbook of Neuropsychology, vol. 9, 2003; Stay Sharp, 2006; The Winner Effect, 2012; The Stress Test, 2016. *Recreations*: boating, fishing, choral singing, tennis. *Address*: Institute of Neuroscience, Trinity College Dublin, Lloyd Building, Dublin 2, Ireland. *T*: (87) 2850478, (1) 8962684. *E*: iroberts@tcd.ie.

**ROBERTSON, Ian Stuart,** CMG 2012; Member, Board of Management, BMW AG, 2008–18, and Head of Sales and Marketing, BMW, 2008–17; *b* Shropshire, 5 June 1958. *Educ*: University Coll. Cardiff (BSc Maritime Studies 1979). Joined Rover Gp, 1979: Plant Director: Drews Lane, 1988–90; Powertrain, 1990–91; Purchasing Dir, 1991–94; Man. Dir, Land Rover Vehicles, 1994–99; Man. Dir, BMW SA, 1999–2005; Chm. and Chief Exec., Rolls-Royce Motor Cars Ltd, 2005–12. Non-exec. Dir, Dyson, 2013–15, 2018–. Hon. DSc Aston, 2011.

**ROBERTSON, James Andrew Stainton,** PhD; Director, Health, Value for Money Studies, 1995–2005, Private Finance Value for Money Studies, 2005–10 and Chief Economist, 2006–10, National Audit Office; *b* 23 April 1949; *s* of James Robertson and Margaret Elodie Robertson; *m* 1979, Ann Leatherbarrow; one *s* one *d*. *Educ*: Highgate Sch.; Univ. of Essex (BA Econs); LSE (MSc Econs, PhD). Sen. Econ. Asst and Econ. Advr, Dept of Employment, 1975–82; Econ. Advr, Dept of Energy, 1982–86; Senior Economic Adviser: DTI, 1986–89; Dept of Transport, 1989–90; Hd of Industrial and Regl Econs, DTI, 1990–93; Chief Econ. Advr, Dept of Employment, subseq. DFEE, 1993–95. *Publications*: contrib. various learned jls. *Recreations*: family, do-it-yourself, gardening.

**ROBERTSON, Hon. Sir (James) Bruce,** KNZM 2010; Judge, Qatar International Court (formerly Qatar Financial Centre Civil and Commercial Court), since 2011; Presiding Judge, Court of Appeal of Vanuatu, since 1996; President, Court of Appeal of Pitcairn, 2011–19; *b* Dunedin, NZ, 15 Feb. 1944; *s* of Finlay and Olive Mary Robertson; *m* 1969, Lyn Radford; two *s* one *d*. *Educ*: Otago Boys' High Sch.; Univ. of Otago (BA, LLB); Univ. of Virginia (LLM). Lectr (pt-time), Univ. of Otago, 1968–85; Partner, Ross Dowling Marquet & Griffin, Dunedin, 1969–87; Judge, High Court of NZ, 1987–2005; Judge of Ct of Appeal, NZ, 2005–10. Chief Comr of Intelligence Warrants (formerly Comr of Security Warrants, 2013–; Judge, High Court, Turks and Caicos Is, 2014–. Mem., PNG Leadership Tribunal, 2011; Chair: NZ Financial Advrs Disciplinary Cttee, 2011–; NZ Sports Tribunal, 2012–; Commonwealth Secretariat Sen. Internat. Judicial Advr to Commn of Nat. Inquiry, Maldives, 2012. Pres., NZ Law Commn, 2001–05. Mem. Council, Univ. of Otago, 1969–88 (Pro-Chancellor, 1982–88); Dep. Chm., Auckland Inst. of Technol., 1991–95. Council, Duke of Edinburgh Award Scheme, 1980–86; Council of Legal Educn, 1982–86. President: Otago Dist Law Soc., 1982; Legal Res. Foundn, 1990–99. Chairman: Rugby World Cup Authy, 2010–12; Online Media Standards Authy, 2012–17. Chm., Bd, Presbyterian Support Central, 2010–13. Visitor, Univ. of S Pacific, 2012–. Ed. in Chief, Introduction to Advocacy, 2009–. Hon. LLD Otago, 1990. GSM (Vanuatu), 2012. *Publications*: (consulting ed.) Adams on Criminal Law, 1992–2015; (consulting ed.) Essays on Criminal Law, 2004; (contrib.) The Promise of Law Reform, 2005. *Recreations*: reading, walking, bridge. *Address*: 22A Orchard Street, Wadestown, Wellington 6012, New Zealand. *T*: 44721935, (mobile) 21657726. *E*: jbruce.robertson@gmail.com. *Clubs*: Dunedin, Wellington.

**ROBERTSON, (James) Douglas (Moir),** CBE 1992; DL; Chairman, Surrey Primary Care Trust, 2006–10; *b* Stalybridge, 15 Nov. 1938; *s* of late George Robertson and Jessie Barrie (née Brough); *m* 1963, Caroline Blanche; two *s* one *d*. *Educ*: Dunfermline High Sch.; Trinity Acad., Edinburgh; Heriot-Watt Coll. Chartered Quantity Surveyor; ARICS 1961, FRICS 1969. Founder and Principal, Surveyors Collaborative, 1969–95. Director: Building Cost Information Service Ltd, RICS, 1962–95; Bobbett and Robertson, 1994–96; Research Park Developments Ltd, 1995–; Surrey Social and Market Research Ltd, 1999–2011; Chairman: Airports Policy Consortium, 1984–93; Building Data Banks Ltd, 1985–95. Chm., 1987–90, Leader, 1990–93, Surrey CC. Chm., Envmt Cttee, Assoc. of CCs, 1990–92. Pro-Chancellor, Univ. of Surrey, 1998–2007, now Emeritus (Chm. Council, 1995–98); Chm. Council, Federal Univ. of Surrey, 2000–04. Chairman: Bournewood Community and Mental Health NHS Trust, 1997–2002; N Surrey PCT, 2002–06. Chm., Nat. Crimebeat, 1998–2005. Trustee, Surrey Hist. Trust, 1998–. FCMI 1971; FRSA 1989. DL 1988, High Sheriff 1997, Surrey. Hon. Dr Laws Roehampton, 2006; DUniv Surrey, 2007. *Publications*: Property Occupancy Analysis, 1970; Maintenance Price Book, 1980; Guide to House Rebuilding Costs, 1988; papers on economics of construction industry, cost indices and trends, and regl govts. *Recreations*: golf, music, travel. *Address*: 16 Homewaters Avenue, Sunbury-on-Thames, Middx TW16 6NS. *T*: (01932) 786624, *Fax*: (01932) 786190. *E*: jdmrobertson@aol.com.

**ROBERTSON, Jane Elizabeth Louise;** *see* Cooper, J. E. L.

**ROBERTSON, John;** *b* 17 April 1952; *s* of Charles Robertson and Agnes Millen Robertson (née Webster); *m* 1973, Eleanor Munro; three *d*. *Educ*: Shawlands Acad.; Langside Coll.; Stow Coll. (HNC Electrical Engrg). GPO, subseq. PO, then British Telecom, 1969–2000 (Customer Service Field Manager, BT, 1991–2000). MP (Lab) Glasgow Anniesland, Nov. 2000–2005, Glasgow NW, 2005–15; contested (Lab) same seat, 2015. Parliamentary Private Secretary: to Minister of State for ME, FCO, 2005–08; to Chief Sec. to the Treasury, 2008–09; to Sec. of State, DWP, 2009–10; to Shadow Sec. of State, Home Office, 2010–15. Mem., Select Cttee on Energy and Climate Change, 2009–15; Chairman, All Party Parliamentary Groups: on telecommunications, subseq. communications, 2002–15; on music, 2005–15 (Sec., 2003–05); on nuclear energy, 2005–15; on Nigeria, 2005; on Angola, 2007. *Recreations*: football, cricket, reading, music. *Clubs*: Garrowhill Cricket, Cambus Athletic Football, Old Kilpatrick Bowling (Glasgow).

**ROBERTSON, Prof. John,** PhD; FRS 2015; FIEEE; Professor of Electronics, since 2002 and Director of Research, Engineering Department, since 2017, University of Cambridge (Head, Electrical Engineering Division, 2014–16); *b* Manchester, 1950; *s* of John Alexander and Jeannette Robertson; *m* 1983, Christine Ann Girling; one *s* one *d*. *Educ*: Sandbach Sch.; Churchill Coll., Cambridge (BA Natural Scis 1971; PhD Physics 1975). FIEEE 2012. Research Officer: Central Electricity Res. Labs, Leatherhead, CEGB, 1975–90; Nat. Power, 1990–94; University of Cambridge: Res. Associate, 1994–96; Lectr, 1996–99, Reader, 1999–2002, Engrg Dept. Vis. Associate Prof., Univ. of Illinois, Urbana Champagne, 1981–82; Vis. Prof., Waseda Univ., Tokyo, 2007–09. Fellow: Materials Res. Soc., 2010; Amer. Physical Soc., 2011. *Publications*: contrib. papers to scientific jls. *Recreations*: squash, tennis, walking. *Address*: Department of Engineering, University of Cambridge, Trumpington Street, Cambridge CB2 1PZ. *T*: (01223) 748331. *E*: jr@cam.ac.uk.

**ROBERTSON, Prof. John Charles,** DPhil; Professor of the History of Political Thought, University of Cambridge, 2010–18, now Emeritus; Fellow, Clare College, Cambridge, 2010–19; *b* Dundee, 28 Sept. 1951; *s* of Sir Lewis Findlay Robertson, CBE and Elspeth Robertson (née Badenoch); *m* 1977, Prof. Maxine Louise Berg, *qv*; three *d*. *Educ*: Trinity Coll., Glenalmond; Wadham Coll., Oxford (BA Mod. Hist. 1972; DPhil Mod. Hist. 1980). Res. Lectr, Christ Church, Oxford, 1975–80; Lectr in Mod. Hist., Univ. of Oxford, 1980–2010; Fellow and Tutor in Mod. Hist., St Hugh's Coll., Oxford, 1980–2010 (Hon. Fellow, 2011). Vis. appointments: Inst. for Advanced Studies in the Humanities, Univ. of Edinburgh, 1986; Folger Shakespeare Liby, Washington, DC, 1991; École des Hautes Études en Sciences Sociales, Paris, 2013. Carlyle Lectr, Univ. of Oxford, 2016; Benedict Lectr, Univ. of Boston, 2016. Foreign Mem., Accademia di Scienze Morali e Politiche, Società Nazionale di Scienze, Lettere e Arte, Naples, 2013. *Publications*: The Scottish Enlightenment and the Militia Issue, 1985; (ed) A Union for Empire: political thought and the British Union of 1707, 1995; The Case for the Enlightenment: Scotland and Naples 1680–1760, 2005; (ed with S. Mortimer) The Intellectual Consequences of Religious Heterodoxy 1600–1750, 2012; The Enlightenment: a very short introduction, 2015; articles in histl jls and collected vols on enlightenment, historiography and political thought 1600–1800. *Recreations*: cricket, walking, Italy (esp. Naples and the South). *Address*: Clare College, Cambridge CB2 1TL. *T*: 07984 658189. *E*: jcr57@cam.ac.uk; 99 Glisson Road, Cambridge CB1 2HQ. *T*: (01223) 353228.

**ROBERTSON, John David H.;** *see* Home Robertson.

**ROBERTSON, Rear Adm. John Keith,** CB 1983; FIET; *b* 16 July 1926; *s* of G. M. and J. L. Robertson; *m* 1951, Kathleen (née Bayntun); one *s* three *d*. *Educ*: RNC Dartmouth; Clare Coll., Cambridge (BA 1949). FIET (FIEE 1981). RNC Dartmouth, 1940–43; served, 1943–83 (Clare Coll., Cambridge, 1946–49): HM Ships Queen Elizabeth, Zest, Gabbard, Aisne and Decoy; Staff, RNC Dartmouth; Grad. Recruiting; Weapon Engr Officer, HMS Centaur; Comdr, RNEC Manadon; RCDS; Captain Technical Intell. (Navy), 1974–76; Captain Fleet Maintenance, Portsmouth, 1976–78; Dir, Naval Recruiting, 1978–79; Dir, Management and Support of Intelligence, MoD, 1980–82; ACDS (Intelligence), 1982–83. *Recreations*: hockey, tennis, golf, wood carving. *Address*: Alpina, Kingsdown, Corsham, Wilts SN13 8BJ. *Clubs*: Corkscrew (Bath); Kingsdown Golf.

**ROBERTSON, John Shaw;** educational consultant, since 2010; Rector, Dollar Academy, 1994–2010; *b* Glasgow, 7 April 1950; *s* of David and Margaret Robertson; *m* 1973, Mary Roy; one *s* one *d*. *Educ*: Univ. of Glasgow (MA English Lang. and Lit.; DipEd). English master, Housemaster, then Asst Headmaster, Daniel Stewart's & Melville Coll., 1973–87; Dep. Rector, Dollar Acad., 1987–93. Principal Examr, English (H), Scottish Exam. Bd, 1990–94. Headmasters' and Headmistresses' Conference: Member: Academic Policy Cttee, 1997–2003; Membership Cttee, 2003– (Chm., 2007–10); Chm., Scottish Div., 2000. Governor: Longridge Towers Sch., 2007–18; St Mary's, Melrose, 2008–; High Sch. of Dundee, 2010–; various educnl consultancies. Hon. Life Mem., Dollar Burns Club. *Publications*: Stewart's Melville: the first ten years, 1984; contrib. articles on educn, curriculum, assessment and on Robertson Davies, Canadian novelist. *Recreations*: cricket (Scottish), music (English), literature (international). *Address*: Sheardale, 11 Riverside Drive, Kelso TD5 7RH. *E*: johnandmaryrobertson@gmail.com. *Clubs*: East India, Lansdowne; Scottish Cricket Union (Life Member).

**ROBERTSON, John William;** Director, John Robertson Architects, since 2005; *b* 27 Aug. 1956; *s* of Ian Middleton Strachan Robertson and Agnes Ramsey Seaton Robertson; *m* 1984, Judy Peacock; one *s* two *d*. *Educ*: Univ. of Dundee (BSc 1976); Univ. of Liverpool (BArch Hons 1979). RIBA 1981. Partner, Fitzroy Robinson Partnership, 1986–93; Dir, Hurley Robertson and Associates, 1993–2005. Projects include: One Great St Helens, London (British Council for Offices Award, 2000); restoration and refurbishment of Daily

Express Bldg, Fleet Street (Royal Fine Art Commn Award, 2001; City Heritage Award, 2002); 10 Queen St Place, EC4 (British Council for Offices Award, 2007); Park House, Finsbury Circus, 2008; 107 Cheapside, EC2, 199 Bishopsgate, EC2, Bush House, Aldwych, 2013; refurbishment of Great Arthur House, EC1; Crossrail over-station developments at Moorgate and Farringdon stations. Mem., City Architectural Forum, 1994–. *Publications*: contrib. Architecture Today, RIBA Jl. *Recreations*: bagpiping, golf, ski-ing, Norfolk terriers, cycling, mountain walking. *Address*: John Robertson Architects, 111 Southwark Street, SE1 0JF. *T*: (020) 7633 5100, *Fax*: (020) 7620 0091. *E*: john.robertson@jra.co.uk. *Clubs*: Royal Automobile; Berkshire Golf.

**ROBERTSON, Kathryn Marie**; *see* Lette, K. M.

**ROBERTSON, Rt Rev. Larry**; *see* Yukon, Bishop of.

**ROBERTSON, Laurence Anthony**; MP (C) Tewkesbury, since 1997; *b* 29 March 1958; *s* of James Robertson and Jean (*née* Larkin); *m* 1st, 1989, Susan (*née* Lees) (marr. diss. 2014); two step *d*; 2nd, 2015, Anne Marie (*née* Adams). *Educ*: St James C of E Sch., Farnworth; Farnworth Grammar Sch.; Bolton Inst. Higher Educn. Work study engr, 1976–82; industrial consultant, 1982–92; charity fundraising, 1992–97 (raised about £2 million for various charities). Contested (C): Makerfield, 1987; Ashfield, 1992. An Opposition Whip, 2001–03; Opposition front bench spokesman on economic affairs, 2003–05; Shadow Minister for NI, 2005–10. Chm., NI Affairs Select Cttee, 2010–17; Member: Envmt Audit Select Cttee, 1997–99; Social Security Select Cttee, 1999–2001; European Scrutiny Select Cttee, 1999–2002; Educn and Skills Select Cttee, 2001; Panel of Chairs, 2017–; Jt Cttee on Consolidation of Bills, 1997–2001; Chm., All Party Parly Gp on Ethiopia and Djibouti, 2009–, on Engrg, 2017–; Jt Chm., All Party Parly Gp on Racing and Bloodstock, 2010–; Co-Chm., British Irish Parly Assembly, 2011–17. Secretary: Cons. Back Bench Constitutional Cttee, 1997–2001; 92 Gp, 2001–02. *Recreations*: sport (ran 6 marathons), particularly horseracing and golf, reading, writing, history. *Address*: House of Commons, SW1A 0AA. *T*: (020) 7219 4196; 22 High Street, Tewkesbury GL20 6DL. *T*: (01684) 291640.

**ROBERTSON, Nelson**; *see* Robertson, W. N.

**ROBERTSON, Nicholas John**, OBE 2011; Chief Executive Officer, ASOS.com, 1999–2015 (non-executive Director, since 2015); *b* Woking, Nov. 1967; *s* of John Spencer Robertson and Cynthia Mary Robertson; *m* 2004, Janine Coulson; two *d*. *Educ*: Canford Sch., Wimborne. Young and Rubicam, 1987–92; Carat UK, 1992–96; Entertainment Marketing UK Ltd, 1996–99. Chm. and Trustee, Asos Foundn. *Recreations*: ski-ing, Chelsea FC, cycling. *Address*: ASOS.com, Greater London House, Hampstead Road, NW1 7FB. *T*: (020) 7756 1000, *Fax*: (020) 7756 1001.

**ROBERTSON, Prof. Norman Robert Ean**, CBE 1991; FDSRCPSGlas; Professor of Orthodontics, 1970–92, Dean of the Dental School, 1985–92, University of Wales College of Medicine; Hon. Consulting Orthodontist, South Glamorgan Health Authority, since 1992 (Hon. Consultant in Orthodontics, 1970–92); *b* 13 March 1931; *s* of late Robert Robertson and Jean Robertson (*née* Dunbar); *m* 1954, Morag Wyllie (d 2014), *d* of George McNicol, MA; three *s* two *d*. *Educ*: Hamilton Acad.; Glasgow Univ. (BDS); Manchester Univ. (MDS 1962; DDS 1969). FDSRCPSGlas 1967. Registrar, then Sen. Registrar in Orthodontics, Glasgow Dental Hosp., 1957–59; Lectr in Orthodontics, 1960–62, Sen. Lectr in Orthodontics, 1962–70, Manchester Univ. Member: GDC, 1985–94; Standing Dental Adv. Cttee, 1989–92; S Glamorgan HA, 1976–92. *Publications*: Oral Orthopaedics and Orthodontics for Cleft Lip and Palate, 1983; articles in dental and med. jls. *Recreation*: painting. *Address*: 26 Heol Tyn y Cae, Rhiwbina, Cardiff CF14 6DJ. *T*: (029) 2061 3439.

**ROBERTSON, Patricia**; QC 2006; *b* 1 Aug. 1964; *d* of George and Sheila Robertson; *m* 1991, Tom Henry; two *s* one *d*. *Educ*: St George's Sch., Edinburgh; Balliol Coll., Oxford (BA Mod. Hist.); City Univ. (Dip. Law). Called to the Bar, Inner Temple, 1988, Bencher, 2011; in practice as a barrister, 1989–, specialising in commercial law, banking and financial services, professional negligence and regulatory law; a Dep. High Court Judge, 2016–. CEDR accredited mediator, 2004–. Mem., Bar Standards Bd, 2010–15 (Vice Chm., 2013–15). Mem., Mediterranean Gardening Soc. *Publications*: (contrib.) Law of Bank Payment, ed by Brindle and Cox, 1996, 2004; (contrib.) Professional Negligence and Liability, ed by M. Simpson, 2006. *Recreations*: gardening on a grand scale, faking Renaissance masterpieces (for pleasure, not profit). *Address*: Fountain Court, Temple, EC4Y 9DH. *T*: (020) 7583 3335, *Fax*: (020) 7353 0329. *E*: pr@fountaincourt.co.uk.

**ROBERTSON, Raymond Scott**; Director of Public Affairs (formerly Development Director), Halogen Communications, since 2002; *b* 11 Dec. 1959; *s* of late James Robertson and Marion Robertson. *Educ*: Glasgow Univ. (MA Hist. and Politics); Jordanhill Coll. Teacher, Hist. and Mod. Studies, Smithycroft Secondary Sch., Glasgow, 1982–83, Dumbarton Acad., 1983–89; NE Political Dir, 1989–92, Vice-Chm., 1993–95, Chm., 1997–2001, Scottish Cons. Party. MP (C) Aberdeen South, 1992–97; contested (C): same seat, 1997; Eastwood, 2001. PPS to Min. of State, NI Office, 1994–95; Parly Under-Sec. of State, Scottish Office, 1995–97.

**ROBERTSON, Prof. Ritchie Neil Ninian**, DPhil; FBA 2004; Taylor Professor of German Language and Literature, University of Oxford, since 2010; Fellow of Queen's College, Oxford, since 2010; *b* 25 Dec. 1952; *s* of Alexander Ritchie Robertson and Elizabeth Robertson (*née* Ninian); *m* 1999, Katharine Mary Nicholas; one step *s* one step *d*. *Educ*: Nairn Acad.; Univ. of Edinburgh (MA 1st class Honours: English 1974; German 1976); Lincoln Coll., Oxford (DPhil 1981). Montgomery Tutorial Fellow, Lincoln Coll., Oxford, 1979–84; Fellow and Dir of Studies in Modern Langs, Downing Coll., Cambridge, 1984–89; Lectr in German, 1989–99, Prof. of German, 1999–2010, Univ. of Oxford; Official Fellow, St John's Coll., Oxford, 1989–2010. Ed., Austrian Studies, 1990–99; Germanic Ed., MLR, 2000–10. *Publications*: Kafka: Judaism, politics and literature, 1985 (trans. German 1988); Heine, 1988 (trans. German 1997); The 'Jewish Question' in German Literature 1749–1939, 1999; (ed) The Cambridge Companion to Thomas Mann, 2002; Kafka: a very short introduction, 2004 (trans. Japanese 2007, Chinese 2008, German 2009); (ed with Katrin Kohl) A History of Austrian Literature 1918–2000, 2006; Mock-Epic Poetry from Pope to Heine, 2009; (ed) Lessing and the German Enlightenment, 2013; Goethe: a very short introduction, 2016; Enlightenment and Religion in German and Austrian Literature, 2017; A New History of the Enlightenment, 2020. *Address*: 31 Frenchay Road, Oxford OX2 6TG; Faculty of Modern Languages, 47 Wellington Square, Oxford OX1 2JF. *E*: ritchie.robertson@mod-langs.ox.ac.uk.

**ROBERTSON, Robert Henry**; Australian diplomat, retired; *b* 23 Dec. 1929; *s* of James Rowland Robertson and Hester Mary (*née* Kay); *m* 2nd, 1958, Jill Bryant Uther (marr. diss. 1982); two *s* one *d*; 3rd, 1986, Isabelle Costa de Beauregard, *d* of Comte and Comtesse René Costa de Beauregard. *Educ*: Geelong Church of England Grammar Sch.; Trinity Coll., Univ. of Melbourne (LLB). Third Secretary, Australian High Commn, Karachi, 1954–56; Second Sec., Mission to UN, New York, 1958–61; First Sec., later Counsellor, Washington, 1964–67; Ambassador to Jugoslavia, Romania and Bulgaria, 1971–73; Asst Sec., Personnel Br., Dept of Foreign Affairs, Canberra, 1974–75; First Asst Sec., Western Div., 1975–76, Management and Foreign Service Div., 1976–77; Ambassador to Italy, 1977–81; Dep. High Comr in London, 1981–84; Perm. Rep. to UN in Geneva, 1984–88; Ambassador to Argentina, Uruguay and Paraguay, 1989–92. Chm., Exec. Cttee, UN High Comr for Refugees, 1987–88. *Address*: 53 Williams Road, Mount Eliza, Vic 3930, Australia. *T*: and *Fax*: (3) 97752078. *Club*: Melbourne.

**ROBERTSON, Shirley Ann, (Mrs J. Boag)**, OBE 2005 (MBE 2001); DL; sailor and television presenter; *b* 15 July 1968; *d* of Iain Robertson and Elizabeth Ann Robertson (*née* Burnett); *m* 2001, Jamie Boag; one *s* one *d* (twins). *Educ*: Moray House, Edinburgh (BA Hons Recreation Mgt). Competitive Laser Cl. sailing, 1983–88, Europe Cl., 1988–2000; Extreme 40 Catamaran Sailing Series, 2007–. Member GB sailing team, Olympic Games: Barcelona, 1992; Atlanta, 1996; Gold Medal: Women's Singlehanded Europe Cl., Olympic Games, Sydney, 2000; three-person Women's Yngling Keelboat Cl., Olympic Games, Athens, 2004. World Sailor of the Year, ISAF, 2000. DL Isle of Wight, 2014. *Address*: c/o Into the Blue, One The Parade, Cowes PO31 7QJ. *Club*: Royal Corinthian Yacht.

**ROBERTSON, Sir Simon (Manwaring)**, Kt 2010; Partner, Simon Robertson Associates LLP (formerly Managing Partner, Simon Robertson Associates, then Partner, Robertson Robey Associates), since 2005; *b* 4 March 1941; *s* of David Lars Manwaring Robertson, CVO; *m* 1965, Virginia Stewart Norman; one *s* two *d*. *Educ*: Eton. Joined Kleinwort Benson, 1963; Dir, 1977–97; Dep. Chm., 1992–96; Chm., 1996–97; Man. Dir, Goldman Sachs Internat. and Pres., Goldman Sachs Europe Ltd, 1997–2005. Chm., Rolls-Royce plc, 2005–13 (Dir, 2004–13); non-executive Director: Inchcape, 1996–2005; London Stock Exchange, 1998–2001; Berry Bros & Rudd, 1998–2018; Invensys, 1999–2005; Royal Opera House Covent Garden Ltd, 2002–12; Economist Newspaper Ltd, 2005–17; HSBC Hldgs PLC, 2006–16 (Sen. Ind. Dir, 2007–15; Dep. Chm., 2010–16); Troy Asset Mgt Ltd, 2012–; Evercore Partners Inc., 2017–; Mem., Internat. Adv. Bd, Brown Advisory, 2015–. Vis. Prof., Dept of Political Economy, KCL, 2016–. Trustee: Eden Project, 2000–15; St Paul's Foundn, 2000–05; Royal Opera House Endowment Fund 2000, 2001–; Royal Acad. Trust, 2001–07 (Chm.); Ambassador, Winston Churchill Meml Trust, 2017–. Pres., UK Chapter, Légion d'Honneur, 2017–. Officier: Ordre des Arts et des Lettres (France), 2011; Légion d'Honneur (France), 2014. *Recreations*: ski-ing, walking in the Alps. *Clubs*: Boodle's, White's; Racquet (New York).

**ROBERTSON, Stanley Stewart John**, CBE 1998; safety engineering consultant, retired; Managing Director, Robertson Safety Engineering Services Ltd, 1998–2010; Director, Metro Solutions Ltd, 2005–12; *b* 14 July 1938; *s* of Jock Stanley Robertson and Florence Kathleen Robertson (*née* Carpenter); *m* 1961, Valerie Housley; two *s* two *d*. *Educ*: Liverpool Poly. (Dip. EE 1961). CEng 1973; FIET (FIEE 1987); FCILT (FCIT 1998). Student engrg apprentice, UKAEA, 1956–62; Asst Electrical Engr, CEGB, 1961–67; Elec. Engrg Manager, Shell Chemicals UK, 1967–74; Health and Safety Executive: Sen. Electrical Inspector, 1974–77; Dep. Superintending Inspector, 1977–80; Superintending Inspector, 1980–91; Dep. Chief Inspector and Regl Dir, 1991–93; HM Chief Inspector of Railways, 1993–98. Chairman: HSE Tech. Cttee investigating radio frequency ignition hazards, St Fergus, Scotland, 1979; Rly Industry Adv. Cttee, HSC, 1993–98; HSE Cttee investigating safety of Forth Rail Bridge, 1995–96; Mem., HSE Tech. Cttee investigating collapse of railway tunnels at Heathrow Airport and New Austrian Tunnelling Method, 1994. Health and Safety Advr, Taiwan High Speed Rail Corp., 1999–2006; Railway Safety Advr, Roads & Transport Authy, Dubai, 2008–09. Chm., Nat. Inspection Council for Elec. Installation Contracting, 1993–95. Non-exec. Dir, NQA Ltd, 1993–95. *Publications*: several tech. papers on electrical and railway safety matters. *Recreations*: music, gardening. *E*: ssjrcbe@hotmail.com.

**ROBERTSON, Stephen James**; Chief Executive Officer, Thames Water Utilities Ltd, 2016–19; *b* Edinburgh, 2 April 1958; *s* of late James Robertson and of Patricia Robertson; *m* 1986, Heather Baxter. *Educ*: Univ. of Edinburgh (MA Hist. and Politics 1980); London Sch. of Econs and Pol Sci. (MSc 1984). BT Group plc: manager roles, 1981–94; Sen. Vice Pres., Network and Customer Service, then Sen. Vice Pres., Network, Systems and Ops, Concert BT/MCI JV, Reston, Va, 1994–98; Dir, Data and IP Products, 1998–99; Man. Dir, Eur. Network Services, Colt Telecoms, 1999–2002; Man. Dir, Network Ops, British Telecommunications – BT Wholesale, 2002–05; CEO, Openreach, 2005–11; CEO, Truphone Ltd, 2011–16. *Recreations*: opera, running, music, rallying, football.

**ROBERTSON, Stephen Peter**; Chairman, Retail Economics, since 2016; *b* Essex, 1954; *m* Susan; three *s* two *d*. *Educ*: Univ. of Nottingham (BSc Hons Chem.). Eur. Mktg Manager, Mars Inc., 1986–92; Marketing Director: Mattel Toys, 1992–93; B&Q plc, 1993–2000; Chm., Screwfix Direct, 2000–02; Dir, Gp Communications, Kingfisher plc, 2002–04 (incl. Man. Dir, Ellen MacArthur sponsorship); Marketing Director: (interim) WH Smith plc, 2004; Woolworths Gp plc, 2004–07; Dir Gen., British Retail Consortium, 2008–12. Chairman: Business West, 2013–16; Bristol Energy & Technol. Services, 2019–. Non-executive Director: Fresca Gp Ltd, 2005–08; Nat. Portrait Gall. Co., 2008–11; Timpson Gp, 2010–; Hargreaves Lansdown plc, 2011–; Clipper Logistics plc, 2014–; Footasylum plc, 2017–19. Mem., Expert Adv. Panel on High Streets, DCLG, 2018–19. Fellow and former Chm., Marketing Soc. CCMI 2013. FRSA 2013. Hon. DBA UWE, 2017.

**ROBERTSON, Stuart Douglas**; Regional Employment Judge, North East Region, Employment Tribunals (England and Wales), since 2017 (North West Region, 2015–17); *b* Bradford, 1 May 1957; *s* of Ian and Joan Robertson; *m* 2017, Jane Ellis; one *s* one *d*. *Educ*: Bradford Grammar Sch.; Trinity Hall, Cambridge (BA Law 1979; MA 1983); Coll. of Law, Chester. Solicitor in private practice, 1982–2004; Fee-paid Employment Judge, 1994; Salaried Employment Judge, 2004; Registrar, Dio. Bradford, 2002–04. *Recreations*: long-distance walking, hill-walking, Rugby League. *Address*: Regional Office of the Employment Tribunals, City Exchange, 11 Albion Street, Leeds LS1 5ES. *T*: (0113) 245 9741.

**ROBERTSON, Tina**; *see* Tietjen, T.

**ROBERTSON, (William) Nelson**, CBE 1996; FCII; Director, Alliance Trust, 1996–2002; *b* 14 Dec. 1933; *s* of James Bogue and Eleanor Robertson; *m* 1964, Sheila Catherine Spence (d 2013); two *d*. *Educ*: Berwick Grammar Sch.; Edinburgh Univ. (MA). FCII 1963. Served RA, 1955–57. General Accident Fire & Life Assurance Corporation Ltd, later General Accident plc, 1958–95: Asst Gen. Man. (Overseas), 1972; Gen. Man., 1980; Dir, 1984; Dep. Chief Gen. Man., 1989; Gp Chief Exec., 1990–95. Director: Morrison Construction Gp, 1995–2001; Second Alliance Trust, 1996–2002; Edinburgh New Tiger Trust, 1996–2001; Scottish Community (formerly Caledonian) Foundn, 1996–99; Supervisory Bd, Scottish Amicable, 1997–2004; Edinburgh Leveraged Income Trust plc, 2001–02; Edinburgh Zeros 2008 plc, 2001–02. Bd Mem., ABI, 1991–95. Mem. Court, Univ. of Abertay, Dundee, 1996–99. *Recreations*: hill-walking, gardening. *Club*: Caledonian.

**ROBERTSON-MACLEOD, (Roderick) James (Andrew)**; Consultant, G4S (formerly Group 4 Securicor), 2006–16; *b* 5 March 1951; *s* of Col Roderick Robertson-Macleod and Daphne Robertson-Macleod; *m* 1992, Karen Barclay; one *s* two *d*. *Educ*: Milton Abbey. Commnd Royal Green Jackets, 1970–80; Private Sec. to HSH Princess Grace of Monaco,

1980–82; Dir, Markham Sports Sponsorship, 1982–91; Chief Exec., Raleigh International, 1991–2003; Dir, Project Support, AEGIS Defence Services, 2004–06. *Recreations:* tennis, Real tennis, ski-ing, walking. *Address:* Hill House, Coneyhurst, W Sussex RH14 9DL. *T:* (01403) 786877. *E:* jrobmac@btinternet.com.

**ROBINS, David Anthony;** Chairman: Asian Total Return Investment Company plc (formerly Henderson TR Pacific Investment Trust plc, then Henderson Asian Growth Trust), 2004–15 (Director, 2002–15); Fidelity Japanese Values plc, since 2012 (Director, since 2011); Hackney Empire Ltd, 2003–13 (Director, 2001–13); Oriel Securities Ltd, 2007–14; *b* 2 Sept. 1949; *s* of John Anthony Robins and Ruth Wenefrede Robins (*née* Thomas); *m* 1981, Joanna Christina Botting; two *s* one *d*. *Educ:* University Coll. London (BSc Econ). Economic Analyst, Investment and Res. Dept, Commonwealth Bank, Sydney, Australia, 1973–74; Economist, Overseas Dept, Bank of England, 1976–78; Exec., Japanese Dept, James Capel, 1978–80; Chief Internat. Economist, Phillips & Drew, 1980–86; Hd of Res., UBS Phillips & Drew Ltd, Tokyo, 1986–88; Hd, Internat. Securities Dept, UBS Securities Inc., NY, 1988–90; Functional Advr, Securities and Res., Union Bank of Switzerland, Zurich, 1990–93; Chief Exec. Officer, UBS UK Ltd, 1994–98; Exec. Vice Pres. and Hd, Region Europe, Union Bank of Switzerland, 1997–98; Chm. and Chief Exec. Officer, ING Barings, 1998–2000; Mem., Exec. Bd, ING Gp, 2000. Chm., New Philanthropy Capital, 2001–09; Non-executive Director: MPC Investors Ltd, 2001–07; Bending Light Ltd, 2001–17; LCH Clearnet Ltd, 2001–07 (Chm., 2003–07); Meggitt plc, 2002–14; EMG Gp Ltd, 2004–10; Serralux (formerly Serrasolar) Inc., 2011–; Pemberton Capital Advrs LLP, 2013–17; NHBS Ltd, 2014–; Sen. Ind. Dir, SVG Capital plc, 2013–17; Advr, Millennium Associates AG, 2015–17. Dep. Chm., E London Business Alliance, 2000–06. Mem., Investment Adv. Cttee, Univs Superannuation Scheme, 2004–08. Mem., RIIA, 1982; MCSI 1997; FInstD 2011 (MInstD 2002); FRSA 2003. Gov., Eltham Coll., 2001–13 (Chm., 2004–13). *Recreations:* travel, walking, gardening, wine.

**ROBINS, John Vernon Harry;** Chairman, Xchanging plc, 2000–08; *b* 21 Feb. 1939; *s* of Col William Vernon Harry Robins, DSO and Charlotte Mary (*née* Grier); *m* 1962, Elizabeth Mary Banister; two *s* one *d*. *Educ:* Winchester Coll. Mil. Service, 2nd Lieut 2/10 Princess Mary's Own Gurkha Rifles, 1959–61. Man. Dir, SNS Communications Ltd, 1966–74; Chief Exec., Bally Gp (UK) Ltd, 1974–79; Group Financial Director: Fitch Lovell plc, 1979–84; Willis Faber, subseq. Willis Corroon Gp plc, 1984–94; Chief Exec., Guardian Royal Exchange plc, 1994–99; Chairman: Hyder plc, 1998–2000; Lane, Clark and Peacock (Actuaries), 2000–03; Austin Reed Gp plc, 2000–06. Director: Wellington Underwriting plc, 1999–2001; Axa Asia Pacific Hldgs Ltd, Melbourne, 1999–2002; Alexander Forbes Ltd (SA), 2002– (Dep. Chm., 2004–07); Xchanging Insure Hldgs Ltd, 2008–12. Chm., Policyholders Protection Bd, 1998–2000. Mem., Barbican Centre Bd, 2003–08. *Recreations:* clocks, Baroque music, grand-children. *Club:* Brooks's (Chm., 2015–17).

**ROBINS, Group Captain Leonard Edward,** CBE (mil.) 1979; AE 1958 (and 2 clasps); Inspector, Royal Auxiliary Air Force, 1973–83; *b* 2 Nov. 1921; *yr s* of late Joseph Robins, Bandmaster RM, and late Louisa Josephine (*née* Kent); *m* 1949, Jean Ethelwynne (Headteacher) (*d* 1985), *d* of late Roy and Bessie Searle, Ryde, IoW. *Educ:* Singlegate, Mitcham, Surrey; City Day Continuation School, EC. Central Civil Service, GPO, 1936; War service, Radar Br., RAF, UK, SEAC, Ceylon, India, 1941–46; resumed with GPO, 1946; Min. of Health, 1948; Min. of Housing and Local Govt, 1962; DoE, 1970–80, retired. Airman, No 3700 (Co. of London) Radar Reporting Unit RAuxAF, 1950; Commissioned 1953, radar branch; transf. to No 1 (Co. of Hertford) Maritime HQ Unit RAuxAF, intelligence duties, 1960; OC No 1 Maritime Headquarters Unit, RAuxAF, 1969–73; Gp Capt., Inspector RAuxAF, 1973–83. ADC to the Queen, 1974–83. Selected Air Force Mem., Greater London TAVRA, 1973–83 and City of London TAVRA, 1980–84; Mem., HAC, 1997–. Patron, World War II Air Forces Radar Reunion, 2001, presided at Reunions, annually, 2003–10. Lord Mayor of London's personal staff, as researcher and speech writer, 1977–78, 1980–81, 1982–83 and 1986–94. Pres., Wandsworth Victim Support Scheme, 1980–87. Trustee, Royal Foundn of Greycoat Hosp., 1983–88. Life Vice Pres., City of London Sqdn, RAuxAF, 2015. Freeman, City of London, 1976. Coronation Medal, 1953; Silver Jubilee Medal, 1977. Officer of Merit with Swords, SMO Malta, 1986. DL Greater London, 1978–97, Rep. DL, Bor. of Wandsworth, 1979–97. FCMI. EsqStJ 1986. *Recreations:* naval, military and aviation history, book hunting, kipping, speech writing. *Address:* 5 Varley Terrace, Dean Street, Liskeard, Cornwall PL14 4AN. *T:* (01579) 348740.

**ROBINS, Sir Ralph (Harry),** Kt 1988; DL; FREng; FRAeS; Chairman, Rolls-Royce plc, 1992–2003; *b* 16 June 1932; *s* of Leonard Haddon and Maud Lillian Robins; *m* 1962, Patricia Maureen Grimes; two *d*. *Educ:* Imperial Coll., Univ. of London (BSc; ACGI; FIC 1993). MIMechE; FREng (FEng 1988); FRAeS 1990. Development Engr, Rolls-Royce, Derby, 1955–66; Exec. Vice-Pres., Rolls-Royce Inc., 1971; Man. Dir, RR Industrial & Marine Div., 1973; Commercial Dir, RR Ltd, 1978; Chm., International Aero Engines AG, 1983–84; Rolls-Royce plc: Man. Dir, 1984–89; Dep. Chm., 1989–92; Chief Exec., 1990–92. Chairman: Adv. Bd, Hakluyt, 2005–15; Freastream Aircraft Ltd, 2005–; GAMA Aviation plc, 2015–. Non-executive Director: Standard Chartered plc, 1988–2004; Schroders plc, 1990–2002; Marks & Spencer plc, 1992–2001; Cable and Wireless plc, 1994–2003 (non-exec. Chm., 1998–2003); Marshall of Cambridge Hldgs (formerly Marshall Hldgs) Ltd, 2004–16. Chm., Defence Industries Council, 1986–2003; Pres., SBAC, 1986–87. Mem., Council for Sci. and Technology, 1993–98. DL Derbys, 2000. FCGI 1990. Hon. FRAeS; Hon. FIMechE 1996. Hon. DSc: Cranfield, 1990; Nottingham, 2002; Cambridge, 2008; DUniv Derby, 1992; Hon. DBA Strathclyde, 1996; Hon. DEng Sheffield, 2001. Commander's Cross, Order of Merit (Germany), 1996. *Recreations:* golf, music, classic cars. *Clubs:* Athenæum, Royal Air Force.

**ROBINS, Maj.-Gen. William John Pherrick,** CB 1998; OBE 1984 (MBE 1979); CEng, FIET; FBCS; Director, Bill Robins Ltd, since 2003; *b* 28 July 1941; *s* of John Robins and Helen Hamilton (*née* Urry); *m* 1st, 1967, Anne Marie Cornu (marr. diss. 1985); one *s* one *d*; 2nd, 1993, Kathy Nash. *Educ:* Henry Mellish Grammar Sch., Nottingham; Welbeck Coll.; RMA Sandhurst; RMCS Shrivenham (BSc (Eng) London, 1966); Staff Coll. Camberley; Cranfield Inst. of Technology (MPhil (Information Systems) 1993). CEng 1991, FIET (FIEE 1992), FBCS 1995. 16 Parachute Bde, 1966–70; Special Communications, 1970–72; Germany and UK, 1972–79; CO 14 Signal Regt (Electronic Warfare), 1979–82; Mil. Asst to MGO, 1982–84; Army ADP Co-ordinator, 1984–87; Project Dir, 1987–89; Dir, CIS (Army), 1989–92; ACDS (Command, Control, Communications and Information Systems), 1992–94; Dir Gen., Information and Communication Services, MoD, 1995–98. Director: Marconi Radar and Defence Systems, 1998–99; Alenia Marconi Systems, 1999–2000; BAE SYSTEMS: Future Systems Dir, 2000–01; Dir, C4ISTAR Develt Avionics Gp, 2001–02; Dir, Advanced Concepts C4ISR Gp, 2002–03. Vis. Prof., Cranfield Univ., 2003–. Freeman, Information Technologists' Co., 2004. Hon. Fellow, Sch. of Defence Management, Cranfield Univ., 1994; Associate FRUSI 2002. *Recreations:* cartoons, looking at pictures, making high quality compost, running, hill walking. *Address:* c/o RHQ Royal Signals, Blandford Camp, Dorset DT11 8RH. *Clubs:* Special Forces, Army and Navy.

**ROBINSON,** family name of **Baron Martonmere.**

**ROBINSON, Alastair;** *see* Robinson, F. A. L.

**ROBINSON, Alice; Her Honour Judge Alice Robinson;** a Circuit Judge, since 2007; a Deputy High Court Judge of the Administrative Court, since 2010; Resident Judge, Croydon Crown Court, since 2017; Hon. Recorder of Croydon, since 2017; *b* Brentwood, Essex, 13 June 1959; *d* of Anthony Robinson and Anne Mary Robinson; *m* 1988, Antony John Cronk; one *s* one *d*. *Educ:* Haverstock Comp. Sch., London; University Coll., Cardiff (LLB 1st Cl. Hons 1982). Called to the Bar, Gray's Inn, 1983; in practice as barrister specialising in planning, property and public law; Supplementary Panel of Jun. Counsel to the Crown, Common Law, 1992–99; Recorder, 2003–07. Sen. Judge of Sovereign Base Areas of Akrotiri and Dhekelia, Cyprus, 2012–. Legal Mem., 2007–16, Mem., Restricted Patients Panel, 2007–16, Mental Health Rev. Tribunal; Mem., Lands Tribunal, 2009–. Asst Ed., Encyclopaedia of Planning Law and Practice, 2004–07. *Publications:* various articles in Jl of Planning Law and Judicial Rev. on Planning and Public Law. *Recreations:* hill walking, choral singing, films, cooking. *Address:* Croydon Crown Court, The Law Courts, Altyre Road, Croydon CB9 5AB.

**ROBINSON, Alwyn Arnold;** Managing Director, Daily Mail, 1975–89; *b* 15 Nov. 1929. Mem., Press Council, 1977–87 (Jt Vice-Chm., 1982–83).

**ROBINSON, Ann;** *see* Robinson, M. A.

**ROBINSON, Dr Ann;** Director General, National Association of Pension Funds Ltd, 1995–2000; *b* 28 Jan. 1937; *d* of Edwin Samuel James and Dora (*née* Thorne); *m* 1961, Michael Finlay Robinson; two *s*. *Educ:* St Anne's Coll., Oxford (MA); McGill Univ. (MA, PhD). Financial journalist, Beaverbrook Newspapers, 1959–61; University Lecturer: Durham, 1962–65; Bristol, 1970–72; Bath, 1972–75; Cardiff, 1972–89 (Sen. Lectr, 1987–89); Head of Policy Unit, Inst. of Dirs, 1989–95. Director: Great Western Hldgs, 1996–98; Almeida Capital, 2001–09. ICSA Vis. Prof. of Corporate Governance, Bournemouth Univ., 2000–03. Member: Equal Opportunities Commn, 1980–85; Econ. and Social Cttee, EEC, 1986–93 (Chm., Industry Section, 1990–92); Welsh Arts Council, 1991–93; HEFCW, 1993–97; Competition (formerly Monopolies and Mergers) Commn, 1993–99; Bd, Harwich Haven Authy, 1999–2006; Pensions Protection and Investments Accreditation Bd, 2001–06; London Pensions Fund Authy, 2001–05. Dir, WNO, 1992–94. Member: Council, RIIA, 1991–97; Bd of Academic Govs, Richmond Coll., London, 1992–2014; Bd of Govs, Commonwealth Inst., 1992–97; Council, Clifton Coll. (Vice-Chm. Council, 1998–2003); Council, City Univ., 1998–2002. Trustee: Foundn for Business Responsibilities, 1997–2003; Dixons Retirement and Employee Security Scheme, 2000–06; Wye Valley Chamber Music Festival, 2009–. Contested (C) S E Wales, EP election, 1979. *Publications:* Parliament and Public Spending, 1978; (jtly) Tax Policy Making in the United Kingdom, 1984; In or Out?: an impartial guide to the EU, 2016; articles in acad. jls and chapters on public expenditure control by Parliament. *Recreation:* gardening. *Address:* Northridge House, Usk Road, Shirenewton, Monmouthshire NP16 6RZ. *Club:* Reform.

**ROBINSON, Dame (Ann) Louise,** DBE 2018; MD; FRCGP; Professor of Primary Care and Ageing, since 2008, and Regius Professor of Ageing, since 2017, Newcastle University; *b* Durham, 27 Oct. 1961; *d* of George and Elizabeth Robinson; two *s*. *Educ:* Newcastle Univ. (MB BS 1985; MD 1999). FRCGP 2014. GP, St Bede's Med. Practice, Sunderland, 1990–93; Newcastle University: Lectr in Primary Care, 1993–99; Sen. Lectr in Primary Care, 1999–2008; Dir, Inst. for Ageing, 2014–19. *Recreations:* cinema, theatre, art, travelling, family. *Address:* Biomedical Research Building (2nd Floor), Campus for Ageing and Vitality, Newcastle University, Newcastle upon Tyne NE4 5PL. *T:* (0191) 208 7013, *Fax:* (0191) 208 1101. *E:* a.l.robinson@newcastle.ac.uk.

**ROBINSON, Anne Josephine;** journalist; *b* 26 Sept. 1944; *d* of late Bernard James Robinson and Anne Josephine Robinson (*née* Wilson); *m* 1st, 1968, Charles Martin Wilson, *qv* (marr. diss. 1973); one *d*; 2nd, 1980, John Penrose (marr. diss. 2008). *Educ:* Farnborough Hill Convent; Les Ambassadrices, Paris. Reporter: Daily Mail, 1967–68; Sunday Times, 1968–77; Daily Mirror: Women's Editor, 1979–80; Asst Editor and columnist, 1980–93; columnist: Today, 1993–95; The Times, 1993–95; The Sun, 1995–97; Daily Telegraph, 1995–2005; The Express, 1997–98; The Times, 1998–2001. Presenter: Anne Robinson Show, Radio 2, 1988–93; Watchdog, 1993–2001 and 2009; for BBC Television: Points of View, 1987–96 (also writer); Watchdog, 1993–2001, 2009–15; The Weakest Link, 2000–12 (also USA, 2001–02); Test the Nation, annually, 2002–07; Travels with My Unfit Mother, 2004; What's the Problem?, 2005; My Life in Books, 2011–12; Anne Robinson's Britain, 2016. Hon. Fellow, Liverpool John Moores Univ., 1996. *Publications:* Memoirs of an Unfit Mother, 2001. *Recreations:* dogs, houses, gossip, decently cooked food, having opinions. *E:* office@victoriagrove.co.uk. *Club:* Bibury Tennis (Pres.).

**ROBINSON, Sir Anthony, (Sir Tony),** Kt 2013; actor and writer; Vice-President, British Actors' Equity, 1996–2000; Member, Labour Party National Executive, 2001–04; Ambassador, Alzheimer's Society, since 2009; *b* 15 Aug. 1946; *s* of Leslie Kenneth Robinson and Phyllis Joan Robinson; one *s* one *d*; *m* 2011, Louise Hobbs. *Educ:* Wanstead Co. High Sch.; Central Sch. of Speech and Drama. Numerous appearances as child actor, incl. original stage version of Oliver!; theatre dir, 1968–78; work with Chichester Festival Th., RSC and NT; nationwide tour of 40 Years On, 1997; Tony Robinson's Cunning Night Out (on tour), 2005–07; The Wind in the Willows, Duchess Th., 2013; *television* includes: Joey (documentary); Baldrick in Blackadder (4 series), 1983–89; Sheriff of Nottingham in Maid Marian and Her Merry Men (4 series) (also writer); My Wonderful Life (3 series), 1997–99; presenter of TV programmes, incl. Blood and Honey (OT series) (also writer); Time Team (20 series); The Good Book Guide; The Worst Jobs in History (2 series); The Real Da Vinci Code, 2005; Me & My Mum, 2006; Tony Robinson's Crime and Punishment, 2008; Blitz Street, 2010; Birth of Britain, 2010; Tony Robinson's Gods and Monsters, 2011; Tony Robinson's Walking Through History, 2012; Tony Robinson's World War One, 2014; Time Crashers, 2015; Tony Robinson's Wild West, 2015; Hidden Britain by Drone, 2016, 2018; Tony Robinson's Coast to Coast, 2017; Britain's Great Cathedrals, 2018; Egyptian Tomb Hunting, 2018; Around the World by Train, 2019; The Thames: Britain's Great River with Tony Robinson, 2019; documentaries in Africa for Comic Relief; writer for TV: Fat Tulip's Garden; Odysseus: the greatest hero of them all (13 episodes); *film:* The Never Ending Story III. Hon. MA: Bristol, 1999; East London, 2003; Hon. PhD: Open, 2005; Exeter, 2005; Oxford Brookes, 2006; Chester, 2011. RTS and BAFTA awards; Internat. Prix Jeunesse. *Publications:* for children: Boodicaa and the Romans, 1989; Robert the Incredible Chicken, 1989; Keeping Mum/Driving Ambition, 1992; Hit Plays, 1992; Blood and Honey: story of Saul and David, 1993; Tony Robinson's Kings and Queens, 2000; Maid Marian and Her Merry Men series: How the Band Got Together, 1989; Beast of Bolsover, 1990; Whitish Knight, 1990; Rabies in Love, 1991; Worksop Egg Fairy, 1991; It Came From Outer Space, 1992; with Richard Curtis: Odysseus Goes Through Hell, 1996; Odysseus, Superhero!, 1996; Theseus, Monster-killer!, 1996; The Worst Children's Jobs in History, 2005 (Blue Peter Factual Book of the Yr, 2005); Bad Kids, 2009; (series) Tony Robinson's Weird World of Wonders, 2012–14 (Blue Peter Factual Book of the Yr, 2013, for World War II); for adults: (with Mick Aston)

Archaeology is Rubbish: a beginners guide to excavation, 2002; In Search of British Heroes, 2003; The Worst Jobs in History, 2004; Tony Robinson's History of Australia, 2011; No Cunning Plan (autobiog.), 2016. *Recreations:* politics, Bristol City Football Club. *Address:* c/o Jeremy Hicks Associates, 15 Arlington Road, NW1 7ER.

**ROBINSON, Anthony John de G.**; *see* de Garr Robinson.

**ROBINSON, Rt Rev. Anthony William;** *see* Wakefield, Area Bishop of.

**ROBINSON, Ariadne Elizabeth S.;** *see* Singares Robinson.

**ROBINSON, Bill;** *see* Robinson, Patrick W.

**ROBINSON, Boz;** *see* Robinson, Air Vice-Marshal B. L.

**ROBINSON, Brian Gordon,** CBE 1996; QFSM 1992; FIFireE; Commissioner for Fire and Emergency Planning (formerly Chief Officer, then Chief Fire Officer and Chief Executive), London Fire Brigade, 1991–2003; *b* 21 April 1947; *s* of Gordon and Theodora Robinson, Colchester, Essex; *m* 1996, Charmian Lesley Houslander-Green. FIFireE 1992. Joined London Fire Brigade, 1968; Accelerated Promotion Course, 1974; Sen. Course Dir, 1982, Fire Service Coll.; Divl Comdr, London, 1983; Asst Chief Officer, 1985; Dep. Chief Officer, 1990. President: Assoc. for Specialist Fire Protection, until 2017; Fire Sector Fedn. OStJ 1992. *Recreation:* golf.

**ROBINSON, Air Vice-Marshal Brian Lewis, (Boz);** Managing Director, Boz! Ltd, 2002–07; Joint Managing Director, Boz Asia Co. Ltd, 2007–19; *b* 2 July 1936; *s* of Frederick Lewis Robinson and Ida (*née* Croft); *m* 1962, Ann Faithfull; one *s* one *d. Educ:* Bradford Grammar Sch. (Queen's Scout). Served, 1954–76: 74 Sqn; Oxford Univ. Air Sqn; 73 Sqn; Canberra Trials Unit; Directorate of Flight Safety, MoD; 60 Course RAF Staff Coll., 1970; RAF Valley; 2 ATAF Germany; Canadian Forces Comd and Staff Coll., and 411 Air Reserve Sqn, Toronto; Chief Instr, 4 Flying Trng Sch., 1976–78, OC, RAF Valley, 1978–80; Internat. Mil. Staff HQ, NATO, Brussels, 1980–82; Defence and Air Attaché, Moscow, 1983–86; Dir of Orgn and Quartering, RAF, MoD, 1986–88; RAF Long-term Deployment Study, 1988; AOC Directly Administered Units, and AO Admin, HQ Strike Command, 1989–91. Sen. Partner, Belmont Consultants, then Sole Exec., Belmont Aviation, 1991–2001. Display pilot: (Gnat), Kennet Aviation, 1997–2001; (Hunter): Classic Jets, 2001–02; Thunder City, Cape Town, 2001–02; Hunter Flying Club, 2002; (Gnat and Hunter), Delta Jets, 2002; Flying Instr, Bristol Flying Centre, 1997–2001; Mem., British Precision Flying Team, Krakow, 1998. Editor, Flight Safety section, Air Clues, 1967–69. RAF Rally Champion, 1962; Mem., RAF and British Bobsleigh teams, 1967–74. President: 74 Tiger Sqdn Assoc., 1992–2008; British Aviation Archaeol. Council, 2000–16. Brexit Party, 2019–. Gov., Edgehill Coll., Bideford, 1997–2001. Humanities Teacher, Utaloy Internat. Sch., Guangzhou, China, 2006–07. FRAeS 2000–08. King Hussein Meml Sword, Royal Internat. Air Tattoo Cottesmore, 2001. *Recreation:* writing. *Address:* Glebe House, Barrington, Ilminster, Somerset TA19 0JB. *E:* bozbozrob@gmail.com.
*See also* (Sir) N. J. Wakeley (Bt).

**ROBINSON, Dame Carol Vivien,** DBE 2013; FRS 2004; FMedSci; Dr Lee's Professor of Chemistry, University of Oxford, since 2009; Fellow, Exeter College, Oxford, since 2009; President, Royal Society of Chemistry, 2018–July 2020; *b* 10 April 1956; two *s* one *d. Educ:* Canterbury Coll. of Technol. (ONC; HNC); Medway and Maidstone Coll. of Technol. (Grad. RSC); Univ. of Wales (MSc); Churchill Coll., Cambridge (PhD 1982). Technician, Pfizer, 1972–79; MRC Trng Fellow, Univ. of Bristol, 1982–83; Postdoctoral Res. Fellow, 1991–95, Royal Soc. Univ. Res. Fellow, 1995–2001, Univ. of Oxford; Prof. of Mass Spectrometry, Univ. of Cambridge, 2001–09; Royal Soc. Res. Prof., Univ. of Cambridge, 2006–09, Univ. of Oxford, 2009–16. Foreign Associate, US NAS, 2017–. FMedSci 2009. Hon. FRSC 2016. Biemann Medal, Amer. Soc. for Mass Spectrometry, 2003; Rosalind Franklin Award, Royal Soc., 2004; Davy Medal, Royal Soc., 2010; Royal Medal, Royal Soc., 2019. *Publications:* 465 pubns inc. book chapters.

**ROBINSON, Christopher John,** CVO 1992 (LVO 1986); CBE 2004; Fellow, since 1991, and Organist and Director of Music, 1991–2003, St John's College, Cambridge; *b* 20 April 1936; *s* of late Prebendary John Robinson, Malvern, Worcs; *m* 1962, Shirley Ann, *d* of H. F. Churchman, Sawston, Cambs; one *s* one *d. Educ:* St Michael's Coll., Tenbury; Rugby; Christ Church, Oxford (BMus); MA (Oxon and Cantab). FRCO; Hon. RAM. Assistant Organist of Christ Church, Oxford, 1955–58; Assistant Organist of New College, Oxford, 1957–58; Music Master at Oundle School, 1959–62; Assistant Organist of Worcester Cathedral, 1962–63; Organist and Master of Choristers: Worcester Cathedral, 1963–74; St George's Chapel, Windsor Castle, 1975–91; Acting Dir of Music, Clare Coll., Cambridge, 2005–06. Conductor: City of Birmingham Choir, 1963–2002; Oxford Bach Choir, 1977–97; Leith Hill Musical Festival, 1977–80. President: RCO, 1982–84; Friends of Cathedral Music, 2004–16; Vice-Pres., Herbert Howells Soc., 2012–. Chm., Ouseley Trust, 2002–07. Hon. Fellow, Birmingham City Univ. (formerly Birmingham Poly., later Univ. of Central England), 1990. Hon. FGCM 2002. Hon. MMus Birmingham, 1987; MusD Lambeth, 2002. *Recreations:* watching cricket, travel. *Address:* St John's College, Cambridge CB2 1TP.

**ROBINSON, Sir Christopher Philipse,** 8th Bt *cr* 1854, of Toronto; *b* 10 Nov. 1938; *s* of Christopher Robinson, QC (*d* 1974) (*g s* of 1st Bt) and Neville Taylor (*d* 1991), *d* of Rear-Adm. Walter Rockwell Gherardi, USN; *S* kinsman, Sir John Beverley Robinson, 7th Bt, 1988, but his name does not appear on the Official Roll of the Baronetage; *m* 1962, Barbara Judith, *d* of late Richard Duncan (marr. diss.); two *s* (and one *s* decd). *Heir: s* Peter Duncan Robinson [*b* 31 July 1967; *m* Jennifer Ann Martin; two *s* one *d*].

**ROBINSON, Prof. Colin,** FSS, FEI; Professor of Economics, University of Surrey, 1968–2000, now Emeritus; Editorial Director, Institute of Economic Affairs, 1992–2002; *b* 7 Sept. 1932; *s* of late James Robinson and Elsie (*née* Brownhill); *m* 1st, 1957, Olga West; two *s*; 2nd, 1983, Eileen Marshall; two *s* two *d. Educ:* Univ. of Manchester (BA Econ). FSS 1970; FEI (FInstPet 1985). Economist, Procter and Gamble, 1957–60; Economist, subseq. Head of Economics Dept, Esso Petroleum Co., 1960–66; Econ. Advr, Natural Gas, Esso Europe, 1966–68. Mem., Monopolies and Mergers Commn, 1992–98. Fellow, Soc. of Business Economists, 2000. Outstanding Contribution to the Profession Award, Internat. Assoc. for Energy Economics, 1998. *Publications:* Business Forecasting, 1970; (with Jon Morgan) North Sea Oil in the Future, 1978; (with Eileen Marshall) Can Coal Be Saved?, 1985; Energy Policy, 1993; Arthur Seldon: a life for liberty, 2009; papers on energy economics and regulation in learned jls. *Recreations:* walking, music, home improvements.

**ROBINSON, Cynthia Ann,** OBE 2019; consultant in nutrition and exercise, since 1982; Chief Executive, Extend Exercise, 2013–18; *b* 28 June 1951; *d* of Andrew Ian Robinson and Alys Congreve Sandys Robinson. *Educ:* Univ. of Nottingham (BSc Hons Biochem. 1972). RNutr 1991; CDipAF 1993. Res. Biochemist, Roche Products, 1972–75; Res. Nutritionist, Slimming Magazine, 1975–80; Mkt Res. Exec., AGB Ltd, 1980–82; Hd of Communications, Cow & Gate, 1991–93; Dir of Communications, Marie Curie Cancer Care, 1993–98; Chief Exec., Fitness Industry Assoc., 1998–99; Chief Exec., Queen Elizabeth's Foundn for Disabled People, 2001–10; Personal Trainer, 2012, Exercise Referral, 2013, SkillsActive. Dir, RYA, 1999–2002, 2004–07. Mem. Council, Royal Inst. of Navigation, 2004–11 (Chm., Small Craft Gp, 2007–14). Freeman, Hon. Co. of Air Pilots (formerly GAPAN), 2005. Cdre, City Livery Yacht Club, 2016–18 (Rear Cdre, 2013; Vice Cdre, 2014). FRIN 2004. J. E. D. Williams Medal for Outstanding Service, Royal Inst. of Navigation, 2014. *Publications:* (contrib.) Good Health Fact Book, 1995. *Recreations:* sailing (RYA Yachtmaster Offshore instructor, 1983–, examiner, 1994–), gliding (British Gliding Assoc. instructor, 1984–90), flying. *Address:* c/o Royal Institute of Navigation, 1 Kensington Gore, SW7 2AT.

**ROBINSON, Daniel Michael;** QC 2019; *b* Preston, Lancs; *s* of Michael Robinson and Anne Eileen Bleasdale; *m* 2006, Vicki Haydock; one *s* three *d. Educ:* Queen Elizabeth's Grammar Sch., Blackburn; Univ. of Wales Inst. of Sci. and Technol. (BSc (Tech) Hons Applied Psychol.). Called to the Bar, Lincoln's Inn, 1993. *Recreations:* listening to music, reading, watching sport, birdwatching. *Address:* 5KBW, 5 King's Bench Walk, Temple, EC4Y 7DN. *T:* (020) 7353 5638. *E:* Danny.robinson@5kbw.co.uk.

**ROBINSON, Prof. David Antony,** PhD; Director, International Corporate Coaching Pty Ltd, 2003–11; Vice Chancellor and President, Monash University, 1997–2002; *b* 24 July 1941; *s* of Harry Robinson and Marjorie Newcombe Robinson (*née* Patchett); *m* 1st, 1965, Marjorie Rose Collins (marr. diss. 1970); 2nd, 1976, Yvonne Ann Salter (marr. diss. 2003); 3rd, 2006, Gael Edith Hayes. *Educ:* Royal Masonic Schs; University Coll., Swansea (BA, PhD 1967). University College, Swansea: Res. Asst, Dept of Sociol., 1964–67; Res. Fellow, DHSS Med. Sociol. Res. Centre, 1967–71; Lectr, then Sen. Lectr, DHSS-MRC Addiction Res. Unit, Inst. of Psychiatry, Univ. of London, 1974–80; University of Hull: Sen. Lectr and Actg Dir, 1980–82, Dir, 1982–91, Inst. for Health Studies; Prof. of Health Studies, 1984–91; Hd of Dept, Social Policy and Professional Studies, 1985–86; Dean, Sch. of Social and Pol Scis, 1986–89; Pro Vice-Chancellor, 1989–91; Co-Dir, ESRC Addiction Res. Centre, Univs of Hull and York, 1983–88; Dir, WHO Collaborating Centre for Res. and Trng in Psycho-social and Econ. Aspects of Health, 1986–91; Vice-Chancellor and Pres., Univ. of S Australia, 1992–96, Prof. Emeritus, 1999. Member: Editl Bd, Brit. Jl of Addiction, 1978–89; Editl Adv. Bd, Sociol. of Health and Illness, 1987–90. Member: Exec. Council of Soc. for Study of Addictions, 1979–82; Exec. Cttee, Nat. Council on Alcoholism, 1979–82; Exec. Cttee, Nat. Council on Gambling, 1980–87; Health Services Res. Cttee, MRC, 1981–84; Social Affairs Cttee, ESRC, 1982–85. Member: Australian Vice Chancellors Cttee, 1992–2002, Dir, 1995–96; Business/Higher Educn Round Table, 1992–97 (Dir, 1995–98); Australian Higher Educn Industrial Assoc., 1992–97 (Mem., Exec. Cttee, 1993–97; Vice Pres., 1995–97); Univ. Grants Cttee, HK, 2002; Aust. Govt Rep., Univ. Grants Cttee, Univ. of S Pacific, 2001–02. Chm., VERNet Pty Ltd, 2005–07. Director: Open Learning Agency of Australia Pty Ltd, 1994–2002; Foundn for Family and Private Business, 1997–2000; Monash Univ. Sunway Campus Malaysia Sdn Bhd, 1998–2002; Monash Univ. S Africa Ltd, 2000–02; Monash Southern Africa (Pty) Ltd, 2000–02; Vice-Chm., Olympic Games Knowledge Services Inc., 2002. Chm. Council, Victorian Inst. of Forensic Mental Health, 1998–2000. FAIM 1993; FAICD 2005. FRSA 1990. *Publications:* (jtly) Hospitals, Children and their Families, 1970; The Process of Becoming Ill, 1971; Patients, Practitioners and Medical Care: aspects of medical sociology, 1973, 2nd edn 1978; From Drinking to Alcoholism: a sociological commentary, 1976; (ed jtly) Studies in Everyday Medical Life, 1976; (with S. Henry) Self-help and Health: mutual aid for modern problems, 1977; Talking Out of Alcoholism: the self-help process of Alcoholics Anonymous, 1979; (with Y. Robinson) From Self-help to Health: a guide to self-help groups, 1979; (ed) Alcohol Problems: reviews, research and recommendations, 1979; (with P. Tether) Preventing Alcohol Problems: a guide to local action, 1986; (ed jtly) Local Action on Alcohol Problems, 1989; (ed jtly) Controlling Legal Addictions, 1989; (ed jtly) Manipulating Consumption: information, law and voluntary controls, 1990; (with A. Maynard et al) Social Care and HIV-AIDS, 1993; contrib. numerous pamphlets, book chapters and papers in learned and professional jls. *Recreations:* walking, bridge, painting, cinema. *Address:* 55/1 Sandilands Street, South Melbourne, Vic 3205, Australia. *E:* robinsonda2@bigpond.com. *Club:* Melbourne.

**ROBINSON, (David) Duncan,** CBE 2008; Director and Marlay Curator, Fitzwilliam Museum, Cambridge, 1995–2007; Master, Magdalene College, Cambridge, 2002–12 (Hon. Fellow, 2012); Deputy Vice-Chancellor, University of Cambridge, 2005–12; *b* 27 June 1943; *s* of Tom and Ann Robinson; *m* 1967, Elizabeth Anne Sutton; one *s* two *d. Educ:* King Edward VI Sch., Macclesfield; Clare Coll., Cambridge (MA); Yale Univ. (Mellon Fellow, 1965–67; MA). Asst Keeper of Paintings and Drawings, 1970–76, Keeper, 1976–81, Fitzwilliam Museum, Cambridge; Fellow and Coll. Lectr, Clare Coll., Cambridge, 1975–81; Dir, Yale Center for British Art, New Haven, Conn, and Chief Exec., Paul Mellon Centre for Studies in British Art, London, 1981–95; Adjunct Prof. of History of Art, and Fellow of Berkeley Coll., Yale Univ., 1981–95; Professorial Fellow, Clare Coll., Cambridge, 1995–2002, Fellow Emeritus, 2002. Mem. Cttee of Management, Kettle's Yard, Cambridge Univ., 1970–81, 1995–2007 (Chm., Exhibns Cttee, 1970–81). Member: Art Panel, Eastern Arts Assoc., 1973–81 (Chm., 1979–81); Arts Council of GB, 1981 (Mem., 1978–81, Vice-Chm., 1981, Art Panel); Museums and Collections Cttee, English Heritage, 1996–2002; Assoc. of Art Mus. Dirs (USA), 1982–88; Bd of Managers, Lewis Walpole Library, Farmington Ct, USA, 1982–95; Council of Management, The William Blake Trust, 1983–2012; Vis. Cttee, Dept of Paintings Conservation, Metropolitan Museum of Art, NY, 1984–94; Walpole Soc., 1983–2005 (Mem. Council, 1985–87, 1995–2000); Connecticut Acad. of Arts and Scis, 1991–95; Univ. Museums Gp, 1995–2002 (Sec., 1997–99); Adv. Council, Paul Mellon Centre for Studies in British Art, 1997–2002; Arts and Humanities Res. Bd, 1998–2003; Adv. Cttee, Foster Art and Wilderness Foundn, Palo Alto, Calif, 2016–; Chairman: Art and Artifacts Indemnity Adv. Panel (USA), 1992–94 (Mem., 1991); Jardine Foundn Scholarship Cttee, Hong Kong, 2006–12; City of Cambridge Public Art Panel, 2009–15. Member, Board of Directors: New Haven Colony Historical Soc., 1991–94; Amer. Friends of Georgian Gp, 1992–95; E of England Museums, Libraries and Archives Council (formerly Mus Service East of England), 2001–03; The Burlington Magazine Publications Ltd, 2003–11. Gov., Yale Univ. Press, 1987–95. Trustee: Yale Univ. Press, London, 1990–2014; Charleston Trust (USA), 1990–92; Fitzwilliam Mus. Trust, 1995–2007; Wingfield Arts Trust, 2001–03; Burlington Magazine Foundn, 2003–; Crafts Study Centre, Surrey Inst. of Art and Design, 2004–08; Henry Moore Foundn, 2006–14 (Chm., 2008–14); Royal Collection, 2006–12; The Chantrey Bequest, 2010–15; Chairman of Trustees: Prince's Drawing Sch., 2007–13; Cambridge and County Folk Museum, 2011–13; Hon. Treas., NW Essex Collection Trust, 2003–07 (Chm., 2002–03). Governor: SE Museums Service, 1997–99; Gainsborough's House Soc., 1998–2002. Pres., Friends of Stanley Spencer Gall., Cookham, 1998–2015; Vice-Pres., NADFAS, 2000–06. FRSA 1990; FSA 2006. DL Cambs, 2004–15. Organised Arts Council exhibitions: Stanley Spencer, 1975; William Nicholson, 1980. *Publications:* Companion Volume to the Kelmscott Chaucer, 1975, re-issued as Morris, Burne-Jones and the Kelmscott Chaucer, 1982; Stanley Spencer, 1979, rev. edn 1990; (with Stephen Wildman) Morris & Company in Cambridge, 1980; Town, Country, Shore & Sea: English Watercolours from van Dyck to Paul Nash, 1982; Man and Measure: the paintings of Tom Wood, 1996; The Yale Center for British Art: a tribute to the genius of Louis I. Kahn, 1997; The Fitzwilliam Museum

1848–1998: one hundred and fifty years of collecting, 1998; An Introduction to the Work of John Golding, 1929–2012, 2017; catalogues; articles and reviews in Apollo, Burlington Magazine, etc. *Address:* 796 Crossfield Circle, Naples, FL 34104, USA. *Clubs:* Oxford and Cambridge; Elizabethan (Yale).

**ROBINSON, David Julien;** film critic and historian and festival director; *b* 6 Aug. 1930; *s* of Edward Robinson and Dorothy Evelyn (*née* Overton). *Educ:* Lincoln Sch.; King's Coll., Cambridge (BA Hons). Associate Editor, Sight and Sound, and Editor, Monthly Film Bulletin, 1956–58; Programme Dir, NFT, 1959; Film Critic: Financial Times, 1959–74; The Times, 1974–92; Editor, Contrast, 1962–63. Director: Garrett Robinson Co., 1987–88; The Davids Film Co., 1988–2013. Dir, Edinburgh Film Fest., 1989–91; Director: Channel 4 Young Film Maker of the Year Comp., Edinburgh Film Fest., 1992–95; Pordenone Silent Film Fest., Italy, 1997–2015 (Dir Emeritus, 2016). Has curated exhibns, incl. Musique et Cinéma muet, Musée d'Orsay, Paris, 1995. Films produced and directed: Hetty King—Performer, 1969; (Co-dir) Keeping Love Alive, 1987; (Co-dir) Sophisticated Lady, 1989. *Publications:* Hollywood in the Twenties, 1969; Buster Keaton, 1969; The Great Funnies, 1972; World Cinema, 1973, 2nd edn 1980 (US edn The History of World Cinema, 1974, 1980); Chaplin: the mirror of opinion, 1983; Chaplin: his life and art, 1985, 2001; (ed and trans.) Luis Buñuel (J. F. Aranda); (ed and trans.) Cinema in Revolution (anthology); (ed jtly) The Illustrated History of the Cinema, 1986; Music of the Shadows, 1990; Masterpieces of Animation 1833–1908, 1991; Richard Attenborough, 1992; Georges Méliès, 1993; Lantern Images: iconography of the magic lantern 1440–1880, 1993; Sight and Sound Chronology of the Cinema, 1994–95; Musique et cinéma muet, 1995; Charlot—entre rires et larmes, 1995; Peepshow to Palace, 1995; (jtly) Light and Image: incunabula of the motion picture, 1996; Alexander Shiryaev, Master of Movement, 2009; The World of Limelight, 2014; The Freak Chaplin's Final Legacy, 2019. *Recreations:* collecting optical toys, model theatres. *Address:* 2 Chandos House, 27–28 Westgate Buildings, Bath BA1 1EF. *T:* (01225) 465838.

**ROBINSON, Derek Anthony,** DPhil; Keeper, Science Museum, London, 1978–99; *b* 21 April 1942; *e s* of late Charles Frederick Robinson and Mary Margaret Robinson; *m* 1965, Susan Gibson (*d* 1991); two *s*. *Educ:* Hymers Coll., Hull; The Queen's Coll., Oxford (Hastings Scholar; BA 1963; MA, DPhil 1967). MRSC 2001. Post-doctoral Res. Fellow, Dept of Chemistry, Univ. of Reading, 1967–69; Mem. scientific staff, Molecular Pharmacology Unit of MRC, Cambridge, 1969–72; Sen. Asst in Res., Dept of Haematol Medicine, Cambridge Univ. Med. Sch., 1972–74; Science Museum: Asst Keeper I, Dept of Chem., 1974–77; Dep. Keeper (formerly Asst Keeper I), Wellcome Mus. of History of Medicine, and Sec. of Adv. Council, 1977–78; Keeper, Dept of Museum Services, 1978–87; Keeper, Dept of Physical Scis, later Head of Sci. Gp, then Head of Phys. Scis and Engrg Gp, 1987–98; Asst Dir (actg) and Hd of Collections, 1998–99. Mem., British Nat. Cttee for History of Sci., Medicine and Technology, 1987–88; Mem., CGLI, 1984–; Dir, Bd, Mus. Documentation Assoc., 1989–92. Trustee, Nat. Gas Mus., 1999–. Hon. Sec., Artefacts annual internat. confs, 2000–09. *Publications:* contributions to: 2nd edn Acridines, ed R. M. Acheson, 1973; Vol. VI, The History of Technology, ed T. I. Williams, 1978; Cambridge General Encyclopaedia, ed D. Crystal, 1990; Making of the Modern World: milestones of science and technology, ed N. Cossons, 1992; Instruments of Science: an historical encyclopaedia, ed R. F. Bud and D. J. Warner, 1998; Musei, saperi e culture, Atti del Convegno, ed M. Gregorio, 2002; (ed jtly and contrib.) Chymica Acta: an autobiographical memoir, by Frank Greenaway, 2007; papers on heterocyclic chemistry, molecular pharmacol., and leukaemia chemotherapy, in Jl Chem. Soc., Brit. Jl Pharmacol., and Biochem. Soc. Trans. *Recreations:* living and gardening in France, travel. *Address:* 3 Broadwater Avenue, Letchworth Garden City, Herts SG6 3HE. *T:* (01462) 686961. *E:* derekanthonyrobinson@gmail.com. *Club:* Athenæum.

**ROBINSON, Dickon Hugh Wheelwright,** CBE 2003; cider maker; *s* of Hugh and Nancy Robinson; *m* 1969, Charlotte; three *s* one *d*. *Educ:* St George's Sch., Hong Kong; King's Sch., Bruton; Portsmouth Coll. of Art (Dip Arch). RIBA 1971. Dept of Architecture, GLC, 1966–67; Scientific Control Systems (SCICON), 1969–74; Sir John Burnet Tait Architects (hosp. design partnership), 1972–74; Westwood, Piet Poole and Smart, Architects, 1974–75; Housing Dept, Camden LBC, 1976–88; Dir, Develt and Tech. Services, Peabody Trust, 1988–2004; Man. Dir, Peabody Enterprises, 2004–05. Vis. Prof., Mackintosh Sch. of Architecture, 2004–09. Mem., Urban Regeneration Panel, Bath & NE Som DC, 2004–13. Chairman: Cabespace, 2003–07; Building Futures, RIBA, 2005–14; Living Architecture, 2007–17. Member: Urban Panel, English Heritage, 2000–15; Commn for Architecture and Built Envmt, 2000–07; Cathedrals Fabric Commn for England, 2009–; London and SE Regl Adv. Bd, Nat. Trust, 2018–. Founder Member: Save Piccadilly Campaign, 1972–74; and First Chm., Soho Housing Assoc., 1973–80. Mem., Policy Cttee, British Property Fedn, 2000–03. Member: Mgt Cttee, Vision for London, 1994–98; Mgt Cttee, Centrepoint, 1995–99; Council, Urban Villages Forum, 1996–99; Mgt Cttee, St Mungo's, 1999–2000. Mem., Foyer Fedn for Youth, 1992 (Chm., 1994–2001). FRSA 1995. *Recreations:* twentieth century fine and applied art, architecture and books, apples, cider-making, orchards and trees, challenging received wisdom. *Address:* 4 Morgan House, 127 Long Acre, Covent Garden, WC2E 9AA. *E:* dickon@dickonrobinson.co.uk. *Club:* Architecture.

**ROBINSON, Sir Dominick Christopher L.;** *see* Lynch-Robinson.

**ROBINSON, Duncan;** *see* Robinson, David D.

**ROBINSON, Emma-Jane,** PhD; heritage consultant and researcher; University Librarian, University of London Library, 1994–2003; *b* 19 Aug. 1953; *d* of late Harold Frederick Wensley Cory and Yvonne Margaret Cory (*née* Hales); *m* 1974, Dr David John Robinson. *Educ:* Westonbirt Sch.; University Coll. of Wales, Aberystwyth (BSc); Inst. of Educn, London Univ. (PhD 2008). MCLIP (ALA 1981). Asst Librarian, then Sub-Librarian, Univ. of London Liby, 1989–94. Member: Consortium of Univ. Res. Libraries, 1994–2003; Consortium of European Res. Libraries, 1994–2003; Res. Libraries Gp, 1994–2003; BL Arts, Humanities and Social Scis Adv. Bd, 1997–2003. Chair and Co. Dir, Frome Heritage Mus., 2014–. FRSA 1995. *Publications:* articles on cultural landscapes in academic and professional jls. *Recreations:* walking, botanising, archaeologising. *Address:* 101 Colindeep Lane, Colindale, NW9 6DD.

**ROBINSON, Eric;** Chief Executive Officer, Disclosure and Barring Service, since 2019; *b* 28 May 1960; *s* of Eric Robinson and Margaret Robinson; partner, Jacqueline Pratt; one *s* two *d*. *Educ:* University Coll. Cardiff (BSc; DMS). Qualified as social worker, 1982; Assistant Director of Social Services: Knowsley MBC, 1995–97; Lincs CC, 1997–2001; Director of Social Services: Enfield LBC, 2001–03; Cambridgeshire CC, 2003–05; Corporate Dir, Social Care and Health, 2005–10, Dep. Chief Exec. and Dir for People, 2010–15, Staffordshire CC; Chief Exec., Wirral Council, 2015–19. *Recreations:* being a father, family life, Liverpool Football Club.

**ROBINSON, (Francis) Alastair (Lavie);** Group Vice-Chairman, Barclays Bank, 1992–96; *b* 19 Sept. 1937; *s* of late Stephen and Patricia Robinson; *m* 1961, Lavinia Elizabeth Napier; two *d*. *Educ:* Eton. Nat Service, 4th/7th Royal Dragoon Guards, 1956–58 (2nd Lieut). Mercantile Credit: management trainee, 1959; Gen. Manager, 1971; Mem.

Board, 1978; Chief Exec. Officer and Pres., Barclays American, USA, 1981; Regional Gen. Manager, Asia-Barclays International, 1984; Barclays Bank: Dir Personnel, 1987; Exec. Dir, UK Ops, 1990–92; Vice Chm., iOS Gp and Exec. Dir, Banking Div., 1992–96. Non-executive Director: RMC Gp plc, 1996–2005; Marshall of Cambridge (Hldgs) Ltd, 1996–2006; Portman Bldg Soc., 1998–2004. Chm., St Nicholas Hospice, Bury St Edmunds, 2008–12. *Recreations:* music, country pursuits, gardening.

**ROBINSON, Prof. Francis Christopher Rowland,** CBE 2006; DL; PhD; Professor of History of South Asia, University of London, since 1990; *b* Southgate, 23 Nov. 1944; *s* of late Leonard Robinson and Joyce Robinson (*née* King); *m* 1971, Patricia Courtenay Hughes; one *s* one *d*. *Educ:* County Grammar Sch. for Boys, Bexhill-on-Sea; Trinity Coll., Cambridge (MA, PhD). Prize Fellow, Trinity Coll., Cambridge, 1969–73; Royal Holloway College, then Royal Holloway and Bedford New College, subseq. Royal Holloway, University of London: Lectr in History, 1973–85; Reader, 1985–90; Hd of Dept, 1990–96; Mem., Council, 1991–2004; Vice-Principal (Res. and Enterprise), 1997–2003; Sen. Vice-Principal, 2003–04; Mem., Academic Cttee, 1994–, Council, 1995–98, London Univ. Vis. Prof., S Asia Program, 1982 and 1986, Near East Program, 1985, Jackson Sch. of Internat. Studies, Univ. of Washington; Directeur d'Etudes Associé, Ecole des Hautes Etudes en Sciences Sociales, Paris, 1985; Vis. Fellow, 2005–08, Sultan of Oman Fellow, 2008–11, Sen. Res. Associate, 2011–, Oxford Centre for Islamic Studies; Vis. Prof., Faculty of History, Oxford Univ., 2008–11; Sen. Golding Fellow, Brasenose Coll., Oxford, 2009–13; Mellon Vis. Prof. of Islamic Studies, Univ. of Chicago, 2015–16. Member, Board of Management: Inst. of Histl Research, 1994–99; Inst. of Commonwealth Studies, 1994–99. Mem., SE England - India Adv. Bd, 2007–09. Pres., RAS, 1997–2000, 2003–06 (Vice-Pres., 2000–03, 2014–17); Mem. Council, Soc. for S Asian Studies, 1998–2002. Trustee: Charles Wallace (Pakistan) Trust, 1999–2006 (Chm. of Trustees, 2001–06); Surrey History Trust, 2001–; Sir Ernest Cassel Educnl Trust, 2005– (Chm., 2008–). Governor: King Edward's Sch., Witley, 2002–12; Jubilee High Sch., Addlestone, 2002–04 (Chm., Jubilee Internat. High Sch. Trust, 2012–13). Vice-Pres., Surrey Youth Clubs, 2017–. Ed.-in-Chief, Past in the Present Books, 2006–11. FRSA 1997. DL Surrey, 2011. Iqbal Centenary Medal (Pakistan), 1978; Sheikh Zaki Yamani Medal, Iqbal Acad. UK, 2008. *Publications:* Separatism among Indian Muslims: the politics of the United Provinces' Muslims 1860–1923, 1974, 2nd edn 1993; (with F. Harcourt) Twentieth Century World History: a select bibliography, 1979; Atlas of the Islamic World since 1500, 1982; (with P. R. Brass) Indian National Congress and Indian Society 1885–1985, 1987; Varieties of South Asian Islam, 1988; (ed) Cambridge Encyclopedia of India, Pakistan, Bangladesh, Sri Lanka, 1989; (ed) Cambridge Illustrated History of the Islamic World, 1996; Islam and Muslim History in South Asia, 2000; The 'Ulama of Farangi Mahall and Islamic Culture in South Asia, 2001; Islam, South Asia and the West, 2007; The Mughal Emperors and the Islamic Dynasties of India, Iran and Central Asia 1206–1925, 2007; (ed) New Cambridge History of Islam, vol. 5: Islam in the Age of Western Dominance, 2010; Jamal Mian: the life of Maulana Jamaluddin Abdul Wahab of Farangi Mahall 1919–2012, 2017; The Muslim World in Modern South Asia: power, authority, education, 2019; contrib. Modern Asian Studies, Asian Affairs, S Asia, Jl of Islamic Studies, Encyclopedia of Islam, Indian Sociology, etc. *Recreations:* ball games, gardening, people, books, travel, food and wine. *Address:* Department of History, Royal Holloway, University of London, Egham, Surrey TW20 0EX. *T:* (01784) 443300. *Clubs:* Athenæum; Hawks.

**ROBINSON, Gavin James;** MP (DemU) Belfast East, since 2015; *b* Belfast, 22 Nov. 1984; *s* of John Calvert Robinson and Claire Allison Robinson (*née* Nesbitt); *m* 2011, Lindsay Witherow; one *s*. *Educ:* Grosvenor Grammar Sch.; Univ. of Ulster (LLB Hons Law); Queen's Univ., Belfast (MA Irish Politics; CPLS). Called to the Bar, NI, 2008; Special Advr to First Minister of NI, 2011–12, 2013–15. Mem., Defence Select Cttee, 2016–. Mem. (DemU), Belfast CC, 2010–15 (Alderman, 2012–15; Gp Leader, DUP, 2014–15); Lord Mayor of Belfast, 2012–13. *Recreations:* Rugby, reading, cooking, travel. *Address:* (office) 96 Belmont Avenue, Belfast BT4 3DE. *E:* gavin.robinson.mp@parliament.uk. *Club:* Ulster Reform.

**ROBINSON, Gemma Mary;** *see* Taylor, G. M.

**ROBINSON, Geoffrey;** MP (Lab) Coventry North West, since March 1976; *b* 25 May 1938; *s* of Robert Norman Robinson and Dorothy Jane Robinson (*née* Skelly); *m* 1967, Marie Elena Giorgio; one *s* one *d*. *Educ:* Emanuel School; Cambridge and Yale Univs. Labour Party Research Assistant, 1965–68; Senior Executive, Industrial Reorganisation Corporation, 1968–70; Financial Controller, British Leyland, 1971–72; Managing Director, Leyland Innocenti, Milan, 1972–73; Chief Exec., Jaguar Cars, Coventry, 1973–75; Chief Exec. (unpaid), Meriden Motor Cycle Workers' Co-op., 1978–80 (Dir, 1980–82). Chm., TransTec PLC, 1986–97. Dir, W Midlands Enterprise Bd, 1980–84. Opposition spokesman on science, 1982–83, on regional affairs and industry, 1983–86; HM Paymaster General, 1997–98. *Publications:* The Unconventional Minister: my life inside New Labour, 2000. *Recreations:* reading, architecture, gardens, football. *Address:* House of Commons, SW1A 0AA. *T:* (020) 7219 3000.

**ROBINSON, Dr Geoffrey Walter,** CBE 1998; FREng, FIET, FBCS; Director General and Chief Executive, Ordnance Survey, 1998–99; *b* 9 Nov. 1945; *s* of late George Robinson and Edith Margaret (*née* Wilson); *m* 1967, Edwina Jones; one *s* one *d*. *Educ:* Aireborough Grammar Sch.; Nottingham Univ. (BSc 1st Cl. Maths; PhD). IBM UK: Lab. posts, 1969–82; Manager of Scientific Centre, 1982–84; Technical Progs Advr, 1984–85; Technical Dir, 1986–88; Dir, Laboratories, 1988–92, 1994–96; Vice Pres., Networking Software Div., 1994–96; Dir of Technol., 1996–97; Chm., Transarc Corp., 1994–96; Dir, Pirelli UK, 2002–05. Chief Advr on Sci. and Technol., DTI, 1992–94. Dep. Chm., Foundn for Sci. and Technol., 1998–2000. Member: SERC, 1992–94; NERC, 1992–94; PPARC, 1994–98; CCLRC, 1995–98; Bd, QAA, 1997–2000; Bd, British Geol Survey, 2001– (Chm., 2002–04). Liveryman, Co. of Inf. Technologists, 1992. Gov., King Alfred's Coll., Winchester, 1993–99 (Hon. DTech 1992). FBCS 1994 (Pres., 1995–96); FIET (FIEE 1994) (Vice Pres., IEE, 1998–2000); FREng (FEng 1994). DUniv Leeds Metropolitan, 1997. *Publications:* articles on science, technol. and society. *Recreation:* music. *Address:* Fardale, Hookwood Lane, Ampfield, Romsey, Hants SO51 9BZ. *T:* (023) 8026 1837. *E:* gwr@fardale.org.

**ROBINSON, George,** MBE 2015; Member (DemU) East Londonderry, Northern Ireland Assembly, since 2003; *b* Limavady, 30 May 1941; *m*; one *s* one *d*. *Educ:* Limavady Tech. Coll. Civil servant, retired. Mem. (DemU), Limavady BC, 1985–2015 (Mayor, 2002). Mem., Regl Develt Cttee, NI Assembly. *Address:* (office) 6–8 Catherine Street, Limavady, Co. Londonderry BT49 9DB.

**ROBINSON, Sir Gerrard Jude, (Sir Gerry),** Kt 2004; Chairman: Nurse Plus Ltd, since 2015; Partnerships in Children's Services Ltd, since 2013; *b* 23 Oct. 1948; *s* of Anthony and Elizabeth Ann Robinson; *m* 1st, 1970, Maria Ann Borg (marr. diss. 1990); one *s* one *d*; 2nd, 1990, Heather Peta Leaman; one *s* one *d*. *Educ:* St Mary's Coll., Castlehead. FCMA 1991. Works Accountant, Lesney Products, 1970–74; Financial Controller, Lex Industrial Distribution and Hire, 1974–80; Coca Cola: Finance Dir, 1980–81; Sales and Mkting Dir, 1981–83; Man. Dir, 1983–84; Man. Dir, Grand Metropolitan Contract Services, 1984–87; Chief Exec., Compass Gp plc, 1987–91; Granada Group plc: Chief Exec., 1991–96; Chm.,

1996–2000; Dir, 2001–03; Chairman: LWT, 1994–96; ITN, 1995–97; BSkyB, 1995–98; Granada Compass plc, 2000–01; Allied Domecq, 2002–05; Moto Hospitality Ltd, 2006–15. Presenter television documentaries: I'll Show Them Who's Boss, 2003; Can Gerry Robinson Fix the NHS? (series), 2007; Can Gerry Robinson Fix Dementia Care Homes?, 2009; Gerry's Big Decision, 2009; Can't Take It with You, 2011. Chm., Arts Council of England, later Arts Council England, 1998–2004. *Publications:* I'll Show Them Who's Boss: the six secrets of successful management, 2004. *Recreations:* golf, opera, chess, ski-ing, reading, music. *Club:* Wisley Golf.

**ROBINSON, Rear Adm. Guy Antony,** OBE 2013; Deputy Commander, Naval Striking and Support Forces NATO, since 2017; *b* Dunfermline, 9 April 1967; *s* of Brian and Judy Robinson; *m* 1998, Melanie Suzanne Rees; one *s* one *d*. *Educ:* Bembridge Sch., IoW; King's Coll. London (MA Defence Studies 2001). Joined RN, 1986; warfare officer, 1986; Commanding Officer: HMS Guernsey, 1998–2000; HMS Edinburgh, 2001–03; Programmer, MoD, 2004–06; Comdr, Sea Trng, FOST, 2007; Asst Hd, Develt, Concepts and Doctrine Centre, 2008–10; CO, HMS Daring, 2010–12; ACOS (Warfare), Navy Comd, 2013–15; Dep. Comdr, UK Maritime Forces, 2015–16; rcds, 2016–17. *Address:* STRIKFORNATO, Lisbon, BFPO 6.

**ROBINSON, Helen Gillian, (Mrs Oliver Prenn),** OBE 1992; Chief Executive, The New West End Co., 2000–05; *b* 4 Jan. 1940; *d* of Dr John Christopher Wharton and Gertrude Margaret (*née* Dingwall); *m* 1st, 1959, Philip Henry Robinson (marr. diss. 1979; he *d* 2018); one *d* (one *s* decd); 2nd, 1980, Desmond Preston (*d* 1995); 3rd, 2009, Oliver Prenn. *Educ:* Roedean. Fashion Ed., UK and USA, Vogue Mag., 1960–70; Exec. Ed., Vogue Mag., 1970–75; Dir, Debenhams plc, 1975–86; Gp Mktg Dir, Condé Nast Pubns, 1986–88; Gp Man. Dir, Thomas Goode & Co. Ltd, 1988–93; general marketing and design mgt consultancies, 1993–96; Dir of Mktg, Asprey Gp, 1996–98; Mgt Consultant, MIA Pty Australia, 1999. Non-executive Director: BAA, 1978–95; LRT, 1984–95; London Electricity Plc, 1989–94; Churchill China Plc, 1996–98. Royal College of Art: Mem. Council, 1982–2000 (Vice Chm., 1992–2000); Chm., Staff Cttee, 1985–2000; Sen. Fellow, 2001. Gov. and Trustee (formerly Gov. and Mem., Exec. Cttee), Commonwealth Inst., 1994–2007; Trustee, Commonwealth Educn Trust, 2007–16. Mem., Design Mgt Adv. Gp, London Business Sch., 1985–95. World Wide Fund for Nature: Trustee and Chm., WWF (UK) Ltd, 1989–95; Mem., Council of Ambassadors, 1999–2006 (Fellow, 2006–). Mem. Council, Cottage Homes (Retail Trade Charity), 1995–96. FRSA 1990; Hon. FCSD 1994. *Recreations:* performing and visual arts, cooking, nature, family. *Address:* 47 Hyde Park Gate, SW7 5DU. *T:* (020) 7584 8870, *Fax:* (020) 7584 8910.

**ROBINSON, Sir Ian,** Kt 2000; FREng, FIChemE; Chief Executive, Scottish Power plc, 1995–2001; *b* 3 May 1942; *s* of Thomas Mottram Robinson and Eva Iris Robinson (*née* Bird); *m* 1967, Kathleen Crawford Leay; one *s* one *d*. *Educ:* Leeds Univ. (BSc); Harvard Univ. FIChemE 1982; FREng (FEng 1994). With Kellogg International Co. Ltd, 1964–72; Managing Director: Ralph M. Parsons Co. Ltd, 1972–86; John Brown Engrs & Constructors, 1986–92; Dir and Chm., Engrg Div., Trafalgar House plc, 1992–95. Chairman: Amey plc, 2001–03; Ladbrokes plc (formerly Hilton Gp plc), 2001–09. Non-executive Director: Siemens plc, 2002–13; Scottish & Newcastle plc, 2004–08; Compass Gp plc, 2006–15 (Sen. Ind. Dir). Member: Takeover Panel, 2003–17; Adv. Bd, CVC Capital Partners, 2004–06. Chm., Scottish Enterprise, 2001–03. *Recreations:* golf, gardening. *Club:* Royal Automobile.

**ROBINSON, Iris;** *b* 6 Sept. 1949; *d* of Joseph and Mary Collins; *m* 1970, Peter David Robinson, *qv*; two *s* one *d*. *Educ:* Knockbreda Intermediate Sch.; Cregagh Tech. Coll. Mem. (DemU) Castlereagh BC, 1989–2010 (Mayor 1992, 1995, 2000). Mem. (DemU) Strangford, NI Assembly, 1999–2010. MP (DemU) Strangford, 2001–10. *Recreation:* interior design.

**ROBINSON, Jancis Mary, (Mrs N. L. Lander),** OBE 2003; MW; wine writer and online publisher; *b* 22 April 1950; *d* of late Thomas Edward Robinson and Ann Sheelagh Margaret Robinson (née Conacher); *m* 1981, Nicholas Laurence Lander, *qv*; one *s* two *d*. *Educ:* Carlisle and County High Sch. for Girls; St Anne's Coll., Oxford (MA). Editor, Wine & Spirit, 1976–80; Founder and Editor, Drinker's Digest (subseq. Which? Wine Monthly), 1977–82; Editor, Which? Wine Guide, 1980–82; Sunday Times Wine Corresp., 1980–86; Evening Standard Wine Corresp., 1987–88; Financial Times Wine Corresp., 1989–; freelance journalism, particularly on wine, food and people, 1980–; freelance television and radio broadcasting, on various subjects, 1983–; Writer/Presenter: The Wine Programme, 1983 (Glenfiddich Trophy), 1985, 1987; Jancis Robinson Meets…, 1987; Matters of Taste, 1989, 1991; Vintners' Tales, 1992, 1998; Jancis Robinson's Wine Course, 1995 (Glenfiddich Trophy); The Food Chain, 1996; Taste, 1999; wine judging and lecturing, 1983–; Wine Consultant, British Airways, 1995–2010. Director: Eden Productions Ltd, 1989–2003 and 2010–; JancisRobinson.com, 2003–. Proprietor and principal contrib., jancisrobinson.com, 2000–. Mem., Wine Cttee, Royal Household, 2005–. Hon. Pres., Wine and Spirit Educn Trust, 2012–15. Freeman, City of London, 2013; Hon. Freeman, Vintners' Co., 2013. DUniv Open, 1997. VDP Golden Pin of Honour, Prädikat Wine Estates, Germany, 2016. Officier, Ordre du Mérite Agricole (France), 2016 (Chevalier, 2010); Comendador da Ordem do Mérito Empresarial (Portugal). *Publications:* The Wine Book, 1979, rev. edn 1983; The Great Wine Book, 1982 (Glenfiddich Award); Masterglass, 1983, rev. edn 1987; How to Choose and Enjoy Wine, 1984; Vines, Grapes and Wines, 1986 (André Simon Meml Prize, Wine Guild Award, Clicquot Book of the Year); Jancis Robinson's Adventures with Food and Wine, 1987; Jancis Robinson on the Demon Drink, 1988; Vintage Timecharts, 1989; (ed) The Oxford Companion to Wine, 1994 (6 internat. awards), 4th edn 2015; Jancis Robinson's Wine Course, 1995, revd edn 2003; Jancis Robinson's Guide to Wine Grapes, 1996; Confessions of a Wine Lover (autobiog.), 1997; Jancis Robinson's Wine Tasting Workbook, 2000; Jancis Robinson's Concise Wine Companion, 2001; (with Hugh Johnson) The World Atlas of Wine, 5th edn 2001 to 8th edn 2019; How to Taste (Wine), 2008; (with Hugh Johnson) Concise World Atlas of Wine, 2009; (with J. Harding and J. Vouillamoz) Wine Grapes, 2012; (with Linda Murphy) American Wine, 2013; The 24-Hour Wine Expert, 2016. *Recreations:* wine, food and words. *E:* jancis@jancisrobinson.com. *W:* www.JancisRobinson.com.

**ROBINSON, Jane;** *see* Morrice, J.

**ROBINSON, Joanna Lesley;** *see* Simons, J. L.

**ROBINSON, John Harris,** CBE 2014; FREng, FIChemE; Chairman: MHA (Methodist Homes), since 2017; Abbeyfield Society, 2009–15 (non-executive Director, 2007–15); Operating Partner, Duke Street Capital, 2001–10; *b* 22 Dec. 1940; *s* of Thomas and Florence Robinson; *m* 1963, Doreen Alice Gardner; one *s* one *d*. *Educ:* Woodhouse Grove Sch.; Birmingham Univ. (BSc). CEng 1968, FREng (FEng 1998); FIChemE 1983. ICI plc, 1962–65; Fisons plc, 1965–70; PA Consulting Gp, 1970–75; Woodhouse and Rixson, 1975–79; Smith & Nephew plc: Man. Dir, Healthcare Div., 1979–82; Dir, 1982–89; Dep. Chief Exec., 1989–90; Chief Exec., 1990–97; Chm., 1997–2000; Chairman: Low & Bonar PLC, 1997–2001; UK Coal (formerly RJB Mining) plc, 1997–2003; George Wimpey plc, 1999–2007; Railtrack, 2001–02; Paragon Healthcare Gp, 2002–06; Bespak, later Consort Medical plc, 2004–09; Affinity Healthcare Ltd, 2005–10; Oasis Healthcare Ltd, 2007–10; Rheon Ltd, 2017–; non-executive Director: Delta plc, 1993–2001; Esporta Gp Ltd, 2006–07. Chm., Healthcare Sector Gp, DTI, 1996–2001; Mem., Industrial Develt Adv. Bd, DTI, 1998–2001. Mem., President's Cttee, CBI, 2001–07 (Chm., Technol. and Innovation Cttee, 1998–2001). Chm., MacRobert Award, RAEng, 2010–14. Governor: Hymers Coll., Hull, 1983–2012; Woodhouse Grove Sch., 2003–13; Chm. Council and Pro-Chancellor, Hull Univ., 1998–2006; Mem., Cttee of Univ. Chairmen, 1998–2006. Trustee: Methodist Ind. Schools Trust, 2012–17; Livability, 2014–; RCS, 2014–; Chm., Engineers Trust, 2012–. President: IChemE, 1999; Inst. of Mgt, 2002. Liveryman, Engineers' Co. (Master, 2010–11). CCMI (CIMgt 1991); FRSA 1992. Hon. DEng Birmingham, 2000; DUniv Bradford, 2000; Hon. DBA' Lincoln, 2002; Hon. DSc Hull, 2006. *Recreations:* golf, cricket, theatre, long distance walking. *Address:* 146 Artillery Mansions, Victoria Street, SW1H 0HX. *T:* (020) 7222 7303. *Clubs:* Athenæum; Brough Golf (E Yorks).

**ROBINSON, Sir John (James Michael Laud),** 11th Bt *cr* 1660; Vice Lord-Lieutenant of Northamptonshire, 2008–14; *b* 19 Jan. 1943; *s* of Michael Frederick Laud Robinson (*d* 1971) and Elizabeth (*née* Bridge); *S* grandfather, 1975; *m* 1968, Gayle Elizabeth (*née* Keyes) (High Sheriff, Northants, 2001–02); two *s* one *d*. *Educ:* Eton; Trinity Coll., Dublin (MA, Economics and Political Science). Chartered Financial Analyst. Chairman: St Andrews Hosp., Northampton, 1984–94; Northampton Gen. Hosp. NHS Trust, 1994–99. Pres., British Red Cross, Northants Br., 1982–90. DL Northants, 1984. *Heir: s* Mark Christopher Michael Villiers Robinson [*b* 23 April 1972; *m* 1st, 2002, Paula (marr. diss.), *d* of late Donald Hendrick; one *d*; 2nd, 2009, Emma, *d* of Douglas Ainscough; two *d*]. *Address:* Cranford Hall, Cranford, Kettering, Northants NN14 4AL.

**ROBINSON, Very Rev. (John) Kenneth;** Dean of Gibraltar, 2000–03, now Emeritus; *b* 17 Dec. 1936; *s* of John Robinson and Elizabeth Ellen Robinson (*née* Blackburn); *m* 1965, Merrylyn Kay (*née* Young); one *s* one *d*. *Educ:* Balshaw's Grammar Sch., Leyland, Lancs; KCL (BD 1961). Ordained deacon, 1962, priest 1963; Assistant Curate: St Chad, Poulton-le-Fylde, 1962–65; Lancaster Priory, 1965–66; Chaplain, St John's Army Children's Sch., Singapore, 1966–68; Vicar, Holy Trinity, Colne, Lancs, 1968–70; Dir of Educn, dio. Windward Is, WI, 1971–74; Vicar, St Luke, Skerton, Lancaster, 1974–81; Area Sec., USPG, 1981–91; Minor Canon, St Edmundsbury Cathedral, 1982–91; Chaplain, Greater Lisbon, Portugal, 1991–2000; Archdeacon of Gibraltar, 1994–2002. *Recreations:* swimming, crossword puzzles, cooking. *Address:* 9 Poplar Drive, Coppull, Chorley, Lancs PR7 4LS.

**ROBINSON, John Martin Cotton,** DPhil, DLitt; FSA; antiquary and writer; *b* 10 Sept. 1948; *s* of John Cotton Robinson and Ellen Anne Cecilia Robinson, *e d* of George Adams, Cape Town, S Africa. *Educ:* Fort Augustus Abbey; St Andrews Univ. (MA 1st Cl. Hons 1970; DLitt 2002); Oriel Coll., Oxford (DPhil 1974). FSA 1979. Historic Buildings Div., GLC, 1974–86; Inspector, English Heritage, 1986–88; Partner, Historic Buildings Consultants, 1989–2013. Librarian to Duke of Norfolk, 1978–. Fitzalan Pursuivant Extraordinary, 1982–88; Maltravers Herald Extraordinary, 1988–. Heraldic Advr, NT, 1996–. Vice-Chm., Georgian Gp, 1990–2014 (Mem., Campaigns Cttee, 2017–); Chm., Art and Architecture Cttee, Westminster Cathedral, 1996–; Member: Prince of Wales Restoration Cttee, Windsor Castle, 1993–94; NW Cttee, NT, 1994–2005; Trustee: Abbot Hall Art Gall., 1990–2015; Rectory Soc., 2015–; Cumbria Historic Churches Trust, 2018–. KM 1980 (Hon. Archivist, 2017–). Architectural Writer, Country Life, 1973–; Architectural Editor, Survey of London, 1978–80. *Publications:* The Wyatts, 1979; Georgian Model Farms, 1980; Dukes of Norfolk, 1982; Latest Country Houses, 1983; Cardinal Consalvi, 1987; (with Thomas Woodcock) Oxford Guide to Heraldry, 1988; Temples of Delight, 1990; Guide to Country Houses of the North West, 1991; Treasures of English Churches, 1995; (with David Neave) Francis Johnson, Architect, 2001; The Staffords, 2002; The Regency Country House, 2005; Grass Seed in June, 2006; Arundel Castle, 2011; Felling the Ancient Oaks, How England Lost its Great Estates, 2012; James Wyatt, Architect to George III, 2012; Requisitioned: the British country house in the Second World War, 2014; The Travellers Club: a bicentennial history, 2018. *Address:* Beckside House, Barbon, Carnforth, Lancs LA6 2LT. *T:* (office) (020) 7831 4398, 07810 188000. *E:* Johnmentmore@gmail.com. *Clubs:* Travellers, Beefsteak, Pratt's, Pitt, XV, Roxburghe (Sec., 1990–).

**ROBINSON, Dr Keith;** Chief Executive, Wiltshire Council, 2009–10 (Chief Executive, Wiltshire County Council, 1996–2009); *b* 12 July 1951; *s* of Wes and Eileen Robinson; *m* 1976, Anne Elizabeth Wilkinson; one *s* one *d*. *Educ:* Sidney Sussex Coll., Cambridge (MA); Durham Univ. (MA); Manchester Univ. (PhD). Dept of Educn and Science, 1975–85; Leics CC, 1985–88; Bucks CC, 1988–93; Wilts CC, 1993–2009. *Recreations:* jazz, marathon running. *E:* robinson9thelays@btinternet.com.

**ROBINSON, Very Rev. Kenneth;** *see* Robinson, Very Rev. J. K.

**ROBINSON, Sir Kenneth,** Kt 2003; PhD; author, educator and educational consultant; *b* 4 March 1950; *s* of James Robinson and Ethel Robinson; *m* 1982, Marie Therese Watts; one *s* one *d*. *Educ:* Univ. of Leeds (BEd 1972); Inst. of Educn, Univ. of London (PhD 1982). Dir, Nat. Curriculum Council for Arts in Schs, 1985–89; Prof. of Educn, Univ. of Warwick, 1989–2001, now Emeritus; Sen. Advr, J. Paul Getty Trust, Los Angeles, 2001–06. Dir of Culture, Creativity and the Young, Council of Europe, 1996–98; Chm., Nat. Adv. Cttee on Creative and Cultural Educn, 1998–99. FRSA 1988. Athena Award, Rhode Island Sch. of Design, 2004; Peabody Medal, Peabody Inst., 2007; Benjamin Franklin Medal, RSA, 2008; LEGO Prize for Internat. Achievement in Educn, 2011; Sir Arthur C. Clarke Imagination Award, 2012. *Publications:* Learning Through Drama, 1977; Exploring Theatre and Education, 1980; (jtly) The Arts in Schools, 1982; The Arts and Higher Education, 1983; The Arts 5–16, 1990; Arts Education in Europe, 1997; All Our Futures: creativity, culture and education, 1999; Out of Our Minds: learning to be creative, 2001, rev. edn 2011; The Element: how finding your passion changes everything, 2009; Finding Your Element: how to discover your talents and passions and transform your life, 2014; (jtly) Creative Schools: revolutionizing education from the ground up, 2015; (jtly) You, Your Child and School, 2018. *Recreations:* theatre, music, cinema.

**ROBINSON, Kenneth William;** Member (UU) Antrim East, Northern Ireland Assembly, 1998–2011; *b* Belfast, 2 June 1942; *s* of Joseph Robinson and Anne Elizabeth (*née* Semple); *m* 1964, Louisa Morrison; three *s*. *Educ:* Whitehouse Primary Sch.; Ballyclare High Sch.; Stranmillis Coll. (Teacher's Cert. 1963); Queen's Univ., Belfast (BEd 1979). Principal Teacher: Lisfearty Primary Sch., 1975–77; Argyle Primary Sch., 1977–80; Cavehill Primary Sch., 1980–96. Mem., and Vice-Chm. Educn Cttee, N Eastern Educn and Liby Bd, 1985–93. Mem. (UU), Newtownabbey BC, 1985–2015 (Mayor, 1991–92; Vice Chm., Econ. Develt Cttee, 1995–96, 2011–12); Mem., Newtownabbey Dist Partnership Bd, 1996–97. Chm., S Antrim Unionist Assoc., 1985–87. Governor: E Antrim Inst. Higher and Further Educn, 1985–93; Whiteabbey Primary Sch., 1985–2015; Hollybank Primary Sch., 1985–2016. Vice-Chm., Newtownabbey-Dorsten Twinning Assoc., 2001–03. *Recreations:* foreign travel, caravanning, historical research, Association Football, swimming. *Address:* 5 Sycamore Close, Jordanstown, Newtownabbey, Co. Antrim BT37 0PL. *T:* (028) 9086 6056.

**ROBINSON, Dame Louise;** *see* Robinson, Dame A. L.

**ROBINSON, Louise Anne**; Headmistress, Merchant Taylors' Girls' School, Crosby, 2006–18; *b* Rochdale, 15 Dec. 1960; *m* 1986, Edward Philip Robinson; one *s*. *Educ*: Univ. of York (BA Hons Computer Sci. and Maths 1982); Univ. of Liverpool (PGCE 1983; MEd 2002). NPQH 1999. Teacher of Maths and Computer Sci., then Hd, Dept of Computing, later Sen. Teacher of Admin, Bolton Sch. Girls' Div., 1983–95; Dep. Hd, Manchester High Sch. for Girls, 1995–2001; Principal, Howell's Sch., Denbigh, 2001–06. Pres., GSA, 2012. *Recreations*: ski-ing, reading, sci-fi.

**ROBINSON, Prof. Margaret Scott**, PhD; FRS 2012; FMedSci; Professor of Molecular Cell Biology, University of Cambridge, since 2003; *b* Schenectady, NY, 29 Dec. 1951; *d* of Arthur W. Robinson, Jr and Cynthia Button Robinson; *m* 1985, John Vincent Kilmartin, *qv*; one *d*. *Educ*: Baldwin Sch., Bryn Mawr, USA; Smith Coll. (BA); Harvard Univ. (PhD 1982). Postdoctoral Fellow, MRC Lab. of Molecular Biology, 1982–89; University of Cambridge: Wellcome Sen. Res. Fellow, 1989–99; Wellcome Principal Fellow, 1999–. FMedSci 2001. Mem., EMBO, 2001. *Publications*: papers in sci. jls on cell biology. *Recreations*: reading, opera, theatre, swimming, knitting, cooking. *Address*: Cambridge Institute for Medical Research, University of Cambridge, Cambridge Biomedical Campus, Wellcome-MRC Building, Hills Road, Cambridge CB2 0XY. *T*: (01223) 330163. *E*: msr12@cam.ac.uk.

**ROBINSON, Mark**; *see* Robinson, S. M. P.

**ROBINSON, Mark Noel Foster**; Executive Director, Commonwealth Press Union, 1997–2002; *b* 26 Dec. 1946; *s* of late John Foster Robinson, CBE, TD and Margaret Eve Hannah Paterson; *m* 1982, Vivien Radclyffe (*née* Pilkington) (*d* 2004); one *s* one *d*. *Educ*: Harrow School; Christ Church, Oxford. MA Hons Modern History. Called to the Bar, Middle Temple, 1975. Research Assistant to Patrick Cormack, MP, 1970–71; Special Asst to US Congressman Hon. F. Bradford Morse, 1971–72; Special Asst to Chief of UN Emergency Operation in Bangladesh, 1972–73; Second Officer, Exec. Office, UN Secretary-General, 1974–77; Asst Dir, Commonwealth Secretariat, 1977–83. Consultant, 1987, Dir, 1988–91, non-exec. Dir, 1991–94, Leopold Joseph & Sons Ltd; non-exec. Dir, Leopold Joseph Hldgs, 1994–95. MP (C): Newport West, 1983–87; Somerton and Frome, 1992–97; contested (C): Newport West, 1987; Somerton and Frome, 1997. PPS to Sec. of State for Wales, 1984–85; Parly Under Sec. of State, Welsh Office, 1985–87; PPS to Minister for Overseas Develt and to Parly Under-Sec. of State, FCO, 1992–94, to Sec. of State for Foreign and Commonwealth Affairs, 1994–95, to Chief Sec. to Treasury, 1995–97. Member: Foreign Affairs Select Cttee, 1983–84; Welsh Affairs Cttee, 1992–97. Chm., UN Parly Gp, 1992–98 (Hon. Sec., 1983–85; Vice Chm., 1996–97); Mem. Cttee, British American Parly Gp, 1996–97. Mem., Commonwealth Develt Corp., 1988–92; Chm., Council for Educn in the Commonwealth, 1999–2005; Dir, Friends of the Commonwealth Foundn, 2008–. Mem. Council, Winston Churchill Meml Trust, 1993–. Fellow, Industry and Parlt Trust, 1985. Member: RUSI, 1984; RIIA, 1984. FCMI (FBIM 1983); FRSA 1990. *Recreations*: include the countryside and fishing. *Clubs*: Brooks's, Pratt's, Travellers.

**ROBINSON, Mary**; President, and Chairman, Board of Trustees, Mary Robinson Foundation - Climate Justice, since 2010; *b* 21 May 1944; *d* of Aubrey and Tessa Bourke; *m* 1970, Nicholas Robinson; two *s* one *d*. *Educ*: Trinity Coll. Dublin (MA, LLB 1967; Hon. Fellow 1991); Harvard Law Sch. (LLM 1968). Called to the Bar, King's Inns, Dublin, 1967 (Hon. Bencher, 1991), Middle Temple, 1973 (Hon. Bencher, 1991); SC 1980. Reid Prof. of Constitutional and Criminal Law, 1969–75, Lectr in EC Law, 1975–90, TCD. Mem., Irish Senate, 1969–89; Pres. of Ireland, 1990–97; UN High Comr for Human Rights, 1997–2002; UN Special Envoy to Gt Lakes, 2013–14, for Climate Change, 2014–15. Member: Adv. Bd, Common Market Law Review, 1976–90; Internat. Commn of Jurists, 1987–90 and 2004– (Pres., 2008–11); Adv. Cttee, Inter-Rights, 1984–90; Vaccine Fund Bd, 2001–; Global Commn on Internat. Migration, 2003–; Adv. Bd, Sustainable Energy for All, 2011–; Lead Gp of Scaling Up Nutrition, UN, 2012–. Pres., Realizing Rights, Ethical Globalization Initiative, 2002–10. Chair, Council of Women World Leaders, 2003–. Hon. Pres., Oxfam Ltd, 2002–12. Chancellor, Dublin Univ., 1998–. Extraordinary Prof., Univ. of Pretoria, 2003–; Prof. of Practice, Columbia Univ., 2004–. Chair, Irish Chamber Orch., 2003–. Mem., Haut Conseil de la Francophonie, 2003–. Member: The Elders, 2007–; Club of Madrid, 2002– (Vice Pres., 2004–). Patron, Inst. of Human Rights and Business, 2012– (Founding Chair, 2009–12). MRIA 1992; Mem., Amer. Phil Soc., 1998. Hon. Fellow: Hertford Coll., Oxford, 1999; LSE, 1999. Hon. FRCOG 1995; Hon. FRCPsych; Hon. FRCPI; Hon. FRCSI; Hon. FIEI; Hon. FRSE 2015. DCL Oxford (by diploma), 1993; hon. doctorates: Austin; Basle; Brown; Buenos Aires; Caledonian; Cambridge; Columbia; Costa Rica; Coventry; Dublin; Dublin City; Dublin Inst. of Technol.; Duke; Edinburgh; Emory; Essex; Florence; Fordham; Harvard; Leuven; Liverpool; London; McGill; Melbourne; Mongolia; Montpellier; Northeastern; Nottingham; Nova, Lisbon; NUI; Open; Poznan; QUB; Rennes; St Andrews; St Mary's, Halifax; Schweitzer Internat.; Geneva; Seoul; S Africa; Toronto; Uppsala; Victoria; Wales; Wheaton; Winnipeg; Yale. Presidential Medal of Freedom (USA), 2009. Grand Cross: Order of Merit, Chile, 2002; Order of the Southern Cross (Brazil), 2002; Military Order of Christ (Portugal), 2003; Grand Officier, Légion d'Honneur (France), 2003; Condecoración, Aquila Azteca (Mexico), 2002. *Publications*: Everybody Matters (memoir), 2012. *Address*: Mary Robinson Foundation - Climate Justice, Trinity College, 6 Leinster Street South, Dublin 2, Ireland; Massbrook House, Ballina, Co. Mayo, Ireland.

**ROBINSON, Mary Josephine**; MP (C) Cheadle, since 2015; *b* 23 Aug. 1955; *m* Stephen Robinson; four *c*. Co-founder, Robinson Rose, Accountants, until 2008; proprietor, Mary Felicity Design, 2008. Mem. (C), S Ribble BC, 2007–13. Mem., Communities and Local Govt Select Cttee, 2015–. *Address*: House of Commons, SW1A 0AA.

**ROBINSON, (Maurice) Richard**; President, since 1974, Chief Executive Officer, since 1975 and Chairman, since 1982, Scholastic Corporation; *b* 15 May 1937; *s* of Maurice Richard Robinson and Florence Liddell; *m* 1986, Helen Benham (marr. diss.); two *s*. *Educ*: Harvard Univ. (BA magna cum laude); Teachers Coll., Columbia Univ.; St Catharine's Coll., Cambridge. Teacher, Evanston High Sch., Ill, 1960–62; Scholastic: Asst Editor, 1962–64; Editorial Dir, 1964–70; Publisher, 1971–74. Trustee, American Mus. of Natural History, NY. *Recreations*: tennis, swimming, jogging, books. *Address*: c/o Scholastic Corporation, 557 Broadway, New York, NY 10012, USA. *T*: (212) 3436700, *Fax*: (212) 3436701. *E*: drobinson@scholastic.com. *Clubs*: University, Century (New York).

**ROBINSON, Michael John**, CMG 1993; HM Diplomatic Service, retired; *b* 19 Dec. 1946; *s* of George Robinson and Beryl Florence Naldrett Robinson; *m* 1971, Anne Jamieson Scott; two *s* two *d*. *Educ*: Cheadle Hulme Sch.; Worcester Coll., Oxford (BA Hons Mod. Langs). Third Sec., FCO, 1969; Russian lang. student, 1969; Third, subseq. Second, Sec., Moscow, 1970; Second, subseq. First, Sec., Madrid, 1972; FCO, 1977; UK Delegn to CSCE, Madrid, 1980; First Sec. and Head of Chancery, Madrid, 1981; Chef de Cabinet to Sec. Gen., OECD, Paris (on secondment), 1982; Dep. Head, UK Delegn to UNESCO, Paris, 1985; First Sec., subseq. Counsellor, FCO, 1986; Dep. Head of Mission and Consul-Gen., subseq. Chargé d'Affaires, Belgrade, 1990; Dep. Gov., Gibraltar, 1995–98; on secondment as: Pol Advr, OSCE Presence in Albania, Tirana, 1999–2001; Sen. Pol Advr, OSCE Mission to Belgrade, Yugoslavia, 2001–02; Head of OSCE Office, Podgorica, Montenegro, 2002–03; Anti-trafficking Adviser to Govt of Albania, Tirana, 2003–07 (on secondment to Internat. Criminal Investigative Trng Assistance Prog., US Dept of Justice). Vis. Fellow, RIIA, 1994. *Publications*: Managing Milosevic's Serbia, 1995. *Recreations*: reading, music, travel. *E*: mrobinson102@hotmail.com. *Club*: Royal Gibraltar Yacht.

**ROBINSON, Michael R.**; *see* Rowan-Robinson, G. M.

**ROBINSON, Michael Stuart**; Chief Executive, British Safety Council, since 2015; *b* 17 May 1964; *s* of Albert Edward Robinson and Mary Robinson; *m* 1994, Lucie Kate Bailey; one *s* one *d*. *Educ*: Portsmouth Poly. (BSc Hons Computer Sci.). ACA 1989. Audit Manager, Price Waterhouse, 1986–92; Chief Internal Auditor, Black Horse Financial Services, 1992–97; Chief Executive: Clerical Med. Internat., 1997–2005; HBOS Europe Financial Services, 2005–06; UK Hydrographic Office, 2006–11; Co-Founder and CEO, Global Navigation Solutions Ltd, 2012–14. *Recreations*: music, tennis, ski-ing, sailing. *Address*: British Safety Council, 70 Chancellor's Road, W6 9RS.

**ROBINSON, (Moureen) Ann**; independent energy expert, since 2016; independent consultant, since 2018; Partner, Rush Communication Strategic Consultancy, 2003–18; Director of Consumer Policy, uSwitch, 2005–16; Director of Public Awareness, Health Information Standard, 2008–14; *d* of William and Winifred Flatley; *m* Peter Crawford Robinson. DHSS, 1969–74; Central Policy Review Staff, 1974–77; nurses and midwives pay, educn and professional matters, 1981–85; liaison with Health Authorities, NHS planning and review, 1985–86; social security operations, 1986–93; Dir of Policy and Planning, Benefits Agency, DSS, 1990–93; Chief Exec., The Spastics Soc., then Scope, 1993–95; Head, Govt Consultancy Computer Sciences Corp., 1995–96; Dir-Gen., British Retail Consortium, 1997–99; Chairman: Gas Consumers Council, 2000; London Electricity Consumer Cttee, 2000; energywatch (formerly Gas and Electricity Consumers Council), 2000–03; Ascertiva Ltd, 2012–15; non-exec. Dir, Gas and Electricity Markets Authy, 2018–. Member: GMC, 2003–12; Prison Service Pay Review Body, 2004–08; Adv. Panel, Ofwat, 2017–. Chm., Victim Support London, 1999–2001; Trustee, Foundn for Credit Counselling, 2000–08. *Recreations*: walking, fine wine, bridge. *E*: annrob@ntlworld.com.

**ROBINSON, Canon Prof. Muriel Anita**, OBE 2013; PhD; DL; Vice Chancellor, Bishop Grosseteste University (formerly Principal, Bishop Grosseteste College, then Bishop Grosseteste University College), Lincoln, 2003–13, now Emeritus Professor; *b* 21 Feb. 1954; *d* of Albert and Anita Robinson; *m* 1981, Richard Mosiewicz. *Educ*: Furzedown Coll., London (BEd English and Educn Studies 1976); Univ. of London Inst. of Educn (MA Lang. and Lit. 1985; PhD 1995). Teaching in primary schs, ILEA, 1976–85; Brighton Polytechnic, subseq. University of Brighton School of Education: Lectr, 1985, Sen. Lectr, 1987, English in Educn; Course Leader, 1990–97; Principal Lectr, 1993; Co-ordinator, Professional Develt Award Scheme, 1994–98; Dep. Hd of Sch., 1998–2000; Vice Principal, Newman Coll. of Higher Educn, Birmingham, 2000–03. Chair, Lincoln Diocesan Bd of Educn, 2012–15; Lay Mem. for Dio. Lincoln, Gen. Synod of C of E, 2015–; Mem., Council, 2016–, Lay Canon, 2018–, Lincoln Cath. Mem. Bd, Open Coll. of Arts, 2013–16. Trustee: Mukherjee Trust, 2012–16; Mere Charity, 2016–. Fellow, Higher Educn Acad. DL Lincs, 2013. *Publications*: Children Reading Print and Television, 1997; extensive range of chapters in learned books and articles in jls, mainly in field of children and media educn. *Recreations*: music, reading, film, cycling, walking, travel. *Address*: Bishop Grosseteste University, Lincoln LN1 3DY. *E*: m.robinson@bishopg.ac.uk.

**ROBINSON, Neil**; Director: Global Marketing and Communications, ABP (China) Holdings, since 2013; Sino-European Trade and Investment Services Ltd, since 2016; *b* 25 April 1958; *s* of Arthur and Margery Robinson; *m* 1988, Susie Elizabeth Campbell; one *s*. *Educ*: Anfield Comprehensive Sch. Journalist: S Yorks Times, 1977–79; Evening Chronicle, Newcastle, 1979–86; freelance journalist various nat. newspapers, 1982; Border Television: News Ed., 1986–87; Producer (various programmes), 1987–88; Head of News and Current Affairs, 1988–90; Controller of Programmes, 1990–2000; Dir of Programmes, 2000–04; Interim Dir of Communications, Liverpool Culture Co., European Capital of Culture, 2005–06; Communications Consultant, London 2012 Olympic Games, 2006–09; Dir of Business Develt, Ten Alps Digital, 2007–09; Hd of Central Marketing, HM Treasury, 2009; Hd of Digital, British Army, MoD, 2010; Creative Dir, Global Cities Ltd, 2011–13. Dir, Cumbria Inward Investment Agency Ltd, 1997–. European Bd Mem., Co-op. Internat. de la Recherche et d'Actions en Matière de Communication, 1998–. Dir, NW Media Charitable Trust Ltd, 1998–99. Member: Northern Production Fund Panel, Northern Arts, 1993–2000; Cttee, BAFTA Scotland, 1998–2003. Mem., RTS, 1988; FRSA 1995. *Address*: Fayrefield, High Bank Hill, Kirkoswald, Cumbria CA10 1EZ. *Club*: Groucho.

**ROBINSON, Nicholas Anthony**; Presenter, Today Programme, since 2015, and Political Thinking podcast, BBC Radio Four; *b* 5 Oct. 1963; *s* of E. D. (Robbie) Robinson and Evelyn Robinson; *m* 1991, Pippa Markus; two *s* one *d*. *Educ*: University Coll., Oxford (BA Hons PPE). BBC, 1986–2002: Producer, then Dep. Ed., On The Record, 1988–92; Ed., The Vote Race, 1992; Dep. Ed., Panorama, 1992–95; Political Corresp., BBC News, 1995–97; Presenter, Radio Five Live, 1997–98; Chief Political Corresp., News 24, 1999–2002; Presenter, Westminster Live, 2001–02; Political Editor: ITV News, 2003–05; BBC, 2005–15. Columnist, The Times, 2003–05. *Publications*: Live From Downing Street: the inside story of politics, power and the media, 2012; Election Notebook: the inside story of the battle over Britain's future and my personal battle to report it, 2015. *Recreations*: Alice, Will and Harry, sailing, theatre, opera, Orford. *Address*: c/o BBC News Centre, New Broadcasting House, Portland Place, W1A 1AA. *E*: NickRobinsondesk@gmail.com.

**ROBINSON, Dr Patrick William, (Bill)**; Senior Adviser, KPMG, since 2016; *b* 6 Jan. 1943; *s* of Harold Desmond Robinson and Joyce Grover; *m* 1st, 1966, Heather Jackson (*d* 1995); two *s* one *d*; 2nd, 1997, Priscilla Stille; two step *s*. *Educ*: Bryanston Sch.; St Edmund Hall, Oxford; DPhil Sussex 1969; MSc LSE 1971. Economic Asst, 10 Downing Street, 1969–70; Cabinet Office, 1970–71; Economic Adviser, HM Treasury, 1971–74; Head of Div., European Commn, 1974–78; Sen. Res. Fellow, London Business Sch., 1979–86; Adviser, Treasury and Civil Service Cttee, 1981–86; Dir, Inst. for Fiscal Studies, 1986–91; econ. columnist, The Independent, 1989–91; Special Advr to Chancellor of Exchequer, 1991–93; Dir, London Economics, 1993–99; Hd UK Business Economist, Corporate Finance and Recovery (formerly Financial Adv. Services), PricewaterhouseCoopers, 1999–2007; Hd of Econs, 2007–12, Chm., Econs and Regulation, 2012–15, KPMG Forensic; Chief Economist, KPMG, 2015–16. Mem. Council, IFS, 2013–. Trustee, Tavistock Centre for Medical Psychology, 2006–11. Mem., Retail Prices Index Adv. Cttee, 1988–91. Gov., Trinity Laban Conservatoire of Music and Dance, 2016–. Editor: Exchange Rate Outlook, LBS, 1979–86; Economic Outlook, LBS, 1980–86; IFS Green Budget, 1987–91. *Publications*: Medium Term Exchange Rate Guidelines for Business Planning, 1983; Britain's Borrowing Problem, 1993; numerous articles. *Recreations*: bassoon playing, opera, bridge, ski-ing, windsurfing, writing musicals. *Address*: KPMG, 15 Canada Square, E14 5GL. *T*: 07715 704743. *Club*: Reform.

**ROBINSON, Paul Anthony**; Chief Executive and Chairman, Paul Robinson Associates, leadership coaching, since 2014; *b* Birmingham, 9 Sept. 1953; *s* of Frank and Marie Robinson; *m* 1986, Alison Margaret Cheadle; one *s* one *d*. *Educ*: Leeds Univ. (BA Hons Hist. 1975); Christ's Coll., Liverpool (PGCE 1977). Auditor, Price Waterhouse, 1975–76; teacher, Doncaster GS, 1977–83; Professional Asst, Leics CC, 1983–85; Asst Educn Officer, Cambs CC, 1986–89; Asst Co. Educn Officer, Essex CC, 1989–92; Dep. Dir of Educn, 1992–94, Dir of Educn, 1994–2007, Dir of Children's Services, 2007–14, Wandsworth BC. Chm., London Aggregation Body, 2002–. Chm., Assoc. of London Chief Educn Officers, 1997–2004. Chm., London Grid for Learning Trust Co., 1995–. Mem., S London Local Educn and Trng Bd, 2012–14. Gov., S Thames Further Educn Coll., 2001–15. Chevalier, Ordre des Palmes Académiques (France), 2003. *Publications*: (contrib.) School Development Planning, 1989. *Recreations*: golf, gym, Rugby coaching, tennis, scuba-diving (divemaster, Aquanaut Club, Kingston), theatre, cinema, eating and food, anything to do with castles. *Address*: Hinchley Drive, Esher, Surrey KT10 0BZ. *T*: (020) 8398 3988. *E*: paul.robinson93@ntlworld.com. *Clubs*: Richmond Golf; Sandown Sports.

**ROBINSON, Air Vice-Marshal Paul Anthony**, OBE 1994; FRAeS; defence and security consultant; *b* 8 Aug. 1949; *s* of Anthony and Eira Robinson; *m* 1971, Sarah Wood; one *s* one *d*. *Educ*: Peter Symonds' Sch., Winchester; RAF Coll., Cranwell; RAF Staff Coll., Bracknell. FRAeS 2001. Joined RAF, 1967; Harrier pilot, 1972–77, 1983–85 and 1989–91; qualified flying instructor, 1978; instructed on Gnat, Hawk, Harrier, Jetstream, Tutor and Vigilant aircraft; MoD (OR), 1987–89; OC 233 Operational Conversion Unit (Harrier), 1989–91; HQ 1 Gp, 1991–93; HQ 2 Gp, 1994–96; Stn Comdr, RAF Coll., Cranwell, 1996–98; COS, British Forces, Cyprus, 1998–2000; Comdt, CFS, 2000–01; Dep. Chief of Jt Ops, 2001–04. RAFR flying instructor, 2004–14. Officer, RAFVR, 2014–. Mem., Mgt Bd, Lincs Bomber Command Meml Trust, 2013–. Member: Chapter and Lay Canon, Lincoln Cath., 2012–; Bishop's Council and Synod, Dio. Lincoln, 2012–18. Trustee: Historic Lincoln Trust, 2014–; Assoc. of English Cathedrals, 2015–. Liveryman, Hon. Co. of Air Pilots (formerly GAPAN), 2007. *Recreations*: sailing, fishing, shooting, golf, charity and other voluntary work. *Club*: Royal Air Force.

**ROBINSON, Paul Nicholas**; Chief Executive Officer, Creative Media Partners, since 2013; Managing Director, Aser Kids, Aser Media, since 2016; *b* 31 Dec. 1957; *s* of Harold George Robert Robinson and Sonja Diana Robinson; *m* 1983, Gill; two *s*. *Educ*: Camberley Grammar Sch.; Manchester Univ. (BSc Hons Metallurgy 1978); Univ. of Bradford Sch. of Mgt (MBA Dist. 1996). Prog. Dir, Chiltern Radio Network, 1987–90; Head: of Programmes, BBC Radio 1, 1990–94; of Strategy and Develt, BBC, 1994–96; Man. Dir, Talk Radio UK, 1996–98; Vice-Pres., Walt Disney TV Internat., 1998–2000; Sen. Vice Pres., and Hd, Worldwide Prog. Strategy, Disney/ABC Cable Networks, 2000–03; Principal, PR Media Consulting, 2004–09; Man. Dir, KidsCo Ltd, 2007–11; Pres. Internat., A Squared Entertainment LLC, 2012–13; CEO, Radio Academy, 2013–14; Exec. Vice Pres., Your Family Entertainment AG, 2014–16. Chm., East London Radio, 2015–. Judge: BAFTA Awards; Sony Radio Awards. Member: Radio Acad., 1985; RTS 1998. *Recreations*: music, the gym, travel, freelance broadcasting.

**ROBINSON, Dr Peter**; writer; *b* Castleford, Yorks, 17 March 1950; *s* of Clifford and Miriam Robinson; *m* 1993, Sheila K. Halladay; one *s*. *Educ*: Univ. of Leeds (BA English Lit. 1974); Univ. of Windsor, Ont (MA English and Creative Writing 1975); York Univ., Toronto (PhD English Lit. 1982). Lecturer: in English, Humber Coll., Toronto, 1983–86; in English, Seneca Coll., Toronto, 1987–97; in Creative Writing (pt-time), Univ. of Toronto, 1997–2013. *Publications*: Caedmon's Song (US edn as The First Cut), 1990; No Cure for Love, 1995, re-issued 2015; Before the Poison, 2011; Seven Years (novella), 2017; *Inspector Banks mystery series*: Gallows View, 1987; A Dedicated Man, 1988; A Necessary End, 1989; The Hanging Valley, 1989; Past Reason Hated, 1991; Wednesday's Child, 1992; Dry Bones that Dream (US edn as Final Account), 1994; Innocent Graves, 1996; Dead Right (US edn as Blood at the Root), 1997; Not Safe After Dark and Other Stories, 1998, expanded edn 2002; In a Dry Season, 1999; Cold is the Grave, 2000; Aftermath, 2001; The Summer That Never Was (US edn as Close to Home), 2003; Playing with Fire, 2004; Strange Affair, 2005; Piece of My Heart, 2006; Friend of the Devil, 2007; All the Colours of Darkness, 2008; The Price of Love (short stories), 2009; Bad Boy, 2010; Watching the Dark, 2012; Children of the Revolution, 2013; Abattoir Blues, 2014; When the Music's Over, 2016; Sleeping in the Ground, 2017; Careless Love, 2018; Many Rivers to Cross, 2019. *Recreations*: music, travel, reading, walking, cinema. *E*: peterrobinson388@btinternet.com. *Club*: Detection.

**ROBINSON, Rt Hon. Peter (David)**; PC 2007; Member (DemU) Belfast East, Northern Ireland Assembly, 1998–2016; First Minister, Northern Ireland, 2008–16; *b* 29 Dec. 1948; *s* of David McCrea Robinson and Sheliah Robinson; *m* 1970, Iris Collins (*see* I. Robinson); two *s* one *d*. *Educ*: Annadale Grammar School; Castlereagh Further Education College. Gen. Secretary, Ulster Democratic Unionist Party, 1975–79, Dep. Leader, 1980–87, Leader, 2008–15. MP (DemU) Belfast E, 1979–2010 (resigned seat Dec. 1985 in protest against Anglo-Irish Agreement; re-elected Jan. 1986); contested (DemU) same seat, 2010. Member: (DemU) Belfast E, NI Assembly, 1982–86; NI Forum, 1996–98. Minister for Regl Develt, 1999–2000 and 2001–02, of Finance and Personnel, 2007–08, NI. Member, Castlereagh Borough Council, 1977–2007; Deputy Mayor, 1978; Mayor of Castlereagh, 1986. Member: Select Cttee on NI, 1994–2005; All-Party Cttee on Shipbuilding, 1992. Mem., NI Sports Council, 1986. *Publications*: (jtly) Ulster— the facts, 1982; booklets include: The North Answers Back, 1970; Capital Punishment for Capital Crime, 1978; Ulster in Peril, 1981; Their Cry Was "No Surrender", 1989; The Union Under Fire, 1995. *Recreations*: golf, bowling. *Address*: 51 Gransha Road, Dundonald, Northern Ireland BT16 2HB. *E*: probin1690@aol.com.

**ROBINSON, Sir Peter Frank**, 4th Bt *cr* 1908 of Hawthornden, Cape Province and Dudley House, City of Westminster; *b* Cape Town, SA, 23 June 1949; *o s* of Sir Wilfred Henry Frederick Robinson, 3rd Bt and Margaret Alison Kathleen Mellish; *S* father, 2012; *m* 1988, Alison Jane Bradley; three *d*. *Educ*: Diocesan Coll. Sch., Rondebosch; Univ. of Cape Town (BA); St John's Coll., Cambridge (MA). Chm., Berwin Leighton Paisner, 1994–2012. *Heir*: none. *Address*: 14 Wellgarth Road, NW11 7HS. *Clubs*: Royal Wimbledon Golf, Hampstead Golf.

**ROBINSON, Peter James**, FCIS, FCIB; Chairman, Cobra Holdings plc, 2006–12; Group Chief Executive, Forester Holdings (Europe) Ltd (formerly Forester UK, then Foresters UK Group), 1998–2006 (non-executive Director, 2006–13); *b* 28 April 1941; *s* of Percival Albert Robinson and Lillian Caroline (*née* Pantling); *m* 1st, 1963 (marr. diss.); twin *s* one *d*; 2nd, 1984, Janice Helen Jones; two *d*. *Educ*: Erith Co. Grammar Sch.; City of London Poly. FCIS 1967; FCIB 1967. Woolwich Building Society: mgt trainee, 1963–68; PA to Jt CEOs, 1968–70; Ops and Mkting Manager, 1970–72; Co. Sec., 1972–75; Asst Gen. Manager (Develt), 1975–81; Gen. Manager (Ops), 1981–86; Dep. Chief Exec. and Dir, 1986–91; Man. Dir, 1991–95; Gp Chief Exec., Woolwich Building Soc., 1995; management consultant, 1997–98. Chm., Metropolitan Assoc. of Building Socs, 1992. Freeman, City of London, 1982. MInstD 1988; CCMI (CIMgt 1991). *Publications*: contrib. articles to Finance Gazette, Economist, Mgt Today, various newspapers. *Recreations*: cricket, golf, gardening, dogs. *Address*: The White House, Rushmore Hill, Knockholt, Kent TN14 7NS. *Clubs*: Royal Automobile, MCC.

**ROBINSON, Ven. Peter John Alan**; Archdeacon of Lindisfarne, since 2008; *b* Carshalton, Surrey, 8 Dec. 1961; *s* of Alan and Sylvia Robinson; *m* 1986, Sarah Frances Walker; two *s*. *Educ*: Tiffin Boys Grammar Sch., Kingston-upon-Thames; St John's Coll., Cambridge (BA Hons 1983); St John's Coll., Univ. of Durham (BA Hons 1992; PhD 1997). Exec., Burmah Castrol, 1983–90; ordained deacon, 1995, priest, 1996; Asst Curate, North Shields, 1995–99; Priest-in-charge: St Martin's, Byker, 1999–2008; St Michael's, Byker, 2001–08. Dir, Urban Ministry and Theology Project, Newcastle E Deanery, 1999–2008. Chair: Lindisfarne Regl Trng Partnership, 2009–17; Newcastle Diocesan Educn Bd, 2014–. Chm., William Temple Foundn, 2009–. Trustee: Woodhorn Charitable Trust, 2009–; Lord Crewe's Charity, 2019–. Hon. Canon, Newcastle Cathedral, 2007–08. *Recreations*: fell-walking (especially in Northumberland), cricket, music (especially opera), reading (contemporary novels), travel (especially in Europe), family occasions, teaching theology. *Address*: 4 Acomb Close, Morpeth, Northumberland NE61 2YH. *T*: (01670) 503810, 07786 642124. *E*: p.robinson@newcastle.anglican.org.

**ROBINSON, Prof. Peter Michael**, FBA 2000; Tooke Professor of Economic Science and Statistics, London School of Economics and Political Science, 1995–2018, now Emeritus (Professor of Econometrics, 1984–95); Leverhulme Trust Personal Research Professor, 1998–2003; *b* 20 April 1947; *s* of Maurice Allan Robinson and Brenda Margaret (*née* Ponsford); *m* 1981, Wendy Rhea Brandmark; one *d*. *Educ*: Brockenhurst Grammar Sch.; University Coll. London (BSc); London School of Economics (MSc); Australian National Univ. (PhD). Lectr, LSE, 1969–70; Asst Prof. 1973–77, Associate Prof. 1977–79, Harvard Univ.; Associate Prof., Univ. of British Columbia, 1979–80; Prof., Univ. of Surrey, 1980–84. Fellow: Econometric Soc., 1989; Centre for Microdata Methods and Practice, 2003–; Spatial Econometrics Assoc., 2006–; Modelling and Simulation Soc. of Australia and NZ, 2007– (Biennial Medallist, 2007); Granger Centre for Time Series Econometrics, 2007–; FIMS 2000; FRSA 1999. Cátedra de Excelencia, Universidad Carlos III, Madrid, 2010, 2013. Mem., ISI, 2005–. Dr *hc* Universidad Carlos III, Madrid, 2000. Best Paper Award, Japan Statistical Soc., 2009. Co-Editor: Econometric Theory, 1989–91 (Mem., Adv. Bd, 2005–); Econometrica, 1991–96; Jl of Econometrics, 1997–2013 (Mem., Exec. Council, 2014–); Jl of Time Series Analysis, 2013–17 (Adv. Ed., 2018–). *Publications*: (ed with M. Rosenblatt) Time Series Analysis, 1996; (ed) Time Series with Long Memory, 2003; articles in books, and in learned jls, incl. Econometrica, Annals of Statistics. *Recreation*: walking. *Address*: Department of Economics, London School of Economics and Political Science, Houghton Street, WC2A 2AE. *T*: (020) 7955 7516.

**ROBINSON, Philip**; Chief Executive, City of Bradford Metropolitan District Council, 2003–05; *b* 2 March 1949; *s* of late Clifford and Vera Robinson; *m* 1974, Irene Langdale. *Educ*: Grange Grammar Sch., Bradford. IPFA, IRRV. City of Bradford Metropolitan District Council: Principal Accountant, 1982–85; Asst Dir of Finance, 1985–87; Dir of Finance, 1987–95; Strategic Dir (Corporate Services), 1995–2000; Asst Chief Exec. (Policy and Corporate Support), 2000–03. *Recreations*: walking, music, theatre.

**ROBINSON, Philip Edward Donald**; Vice Chancellor, University of Chichester (formerly Principal, University College Chichester), 1996–2007; *b* 13 April 1943; *s* of late James Edward Robinson and Phyllis Robinson (*née* Colclough); *m* 1st, 1967, Pamela Joan Bolton (*d* 1972); one *d*; 2nd, 1975, Linda Jane Whitelaw (*d* 2009); one *s* two *d*. *Educ*: Haslingden Grammar Sch.; St Paul's Coll., Cheltenham (CertEd 1964); Goldsmiths' Coll., London (BScSoc 1969); Inst. of Educn, London (MSc Econ. 1971); Univ. of Oxford (Advanced Dip. in Local History, 2009; MSc English Local History, 2011). Lectr, then Sen. Lectr, Univ. of Keele, 1974–83; Hd of Educn, Westminster Coll., Oxford, 1983–87; Dean of Educn, then Sen. Pro Rector and Principal of Froebel Coll., Roehampton Inst., London, 1987–96. Inter-Univ. Council Vis. Fellow, Univ. Sains Malaysia, 1977–78. Chm., Council of Ch Univs and Colls, 2001–03; Vice Chm., GuildHE (formerly Standing Conf. of Principals), 2003–06; Bd Mem., QAA, 2000–04. Mem. Bd, Chichester Fest. Th., 2005–17. Vice Chm., Bd of Govs, Central Sch. of Speech and Drama, 2003–10; Gov., Chichester High Sch. for Girls, 1997–2003; Mem., Bd of Govs, South Downs Coll., 2005–09. Trustee, Univ. of Chichester Acad. Trust, 2013–17. Chm., Chichester Local Hist. Soc., 2018–. DUniv Chichester, 2015. *Publications*: Education and Poverty, 1976, 2nd edn 2014; Perspectives on the Sociology of Education, 1981 (trans. Korean 1991), 2nd edn 2017; (with F. J. Coffield and J. Sarsby) A Cycle of Deprivation?, 1981; articles relating to educnl policy. *Recreations*: theatre, 18th century maritime history, local history, Rugby Union football, 18th and 19th century music.

**ROBINSON, Richard**; *see* Robinson, Maurice R.

**ROBINSON, Richard John; His Honour Judge Richard Robinson**; a Circuit Judge, since 2018; *b* 4 Aug. 1952; *s* of Peter Norton and Patricia Helen Robinson; *m* 1987, Joanna Lesley Simons, *qv* (marr. diss. 2010). *Educ*: Trinity Hall, Cambridge (BA 1974); SOAS, London (LLM 1976). Called to the Bar, Middle Temple, 1977, also Gray's Inn *ad eundem*; in practice as barrister, 1977–2002; District Judge, Principal Registry, Family Div., later Central Family Court, 2002–18. *Publications*: (jtly) A Practical Guide to Family Proceedings, 6th edn, 2017. *Recreations*: nature conservation (London Wildlife Trust, Galapagos Conservation Trust), birdwatching (partic. in hot climates), parkrun. *Address*: Medway County Court, 47–67 High Street, Chatham, Kent ME4 4DW. *Clubs*: Norwich City Football; Charlton Athletic Football.

**ROBINSON, Sian Christina**; *see* MacLeod, S. C.

**ROBINSON, (Simon) Mark (Peter)**; Member (DemU) South Belfast, Northern Ireland Assembly, 1998–2007; *b* 12 May 1959; *s* of Desmond and Evelyne Robinson. *Educ*: Knockbreda High Sch.; Castlereagh Coll. of Further Educn (HNC); Belfast Coll. of Technol. Mechanical engr, 1977–89; Gen. Manager, 1989–95; Man. Dir, DCR Engrg, 1995–99. Mem. (DemU) Castlereagh BC, 1997–2005. Former Governor: Knockbreda High Sch.; Belvoir Park Primary Sch. *Recreations*: musical theatre, golf.

**ROBINSON, Stephen Joseph**, OBE 1971; FRS 1976; FREng, FIET, FInstP; Director, Royal Signals and Radar Establishment, 1990–91 (Deputy Director, 1985–89); *b* 6 Aug. 1931; *s* of Joseph Allan Robinson and Ethel (*née* Bunting); *m* 1957, Monica Mabs Scott (marr. diss. 1987); one *s* one *d*. *Educ*: Sebright Sch., Wolverley; Jesus Coll., Cambridge (MA Natural Sciences). RAF, 1950–51. Mullard Res. Labs, 1954–72; MEL Div., Philips Industries (formerly MEL Equipment Co. Ltd), 1972–79; Product Dir, 1973–79; Man. Dir, Pye TVT Ltd, 1980–84. Man. Dir, Cambridge Angle Mgt Co., 1992–2016. Vis. Prof., Birmingham Univ., 1990–91. Mem. Council, Royal Soc., 1982–. Mem., Exec. Cttee, Campaign for Sci. and Engrg, 1995–2010.

**ROBINSON, Steve John**; Chief Executive, Cheshire West and Chester Council, 2009–16; *b* Evesham, Worcs, 2 March 1956; *s* of John and Lorna Robinson; *m* 1989, Nicola Dixon; one *s*. *Educ*: Abbey High Sch., Redditch; Univ. of Aston (BSc Envmtl Health 1979); Wolverhampton Poly. (Postgrad. Dip. Mgt Studies 1985). Trainee Envmtl Health Officer,

Coventry CC, 1975–79; Envmtl Health Officer, 1979–81, Housing Agency Co-ordinator, 1981–86, Sandwell BC; Prin. Housing Officer, 1986–91, Chief Housing Renewal Officer, 1991–96, Wolverhampton BC; Hd, Urban Renewal Service, Liverpool CC, 1996–98; Chief Exec., S Liverpool Housing, 1998–99; Asst Dir, Regeneration, Liverpool CC, 1999–2001; Dir, Riverside Housing Assoc., Liverpool, 2001–02; Chief Exec., Walsall Housing Gp, 2002–03; Stoke-on-Trent City Council: Dir, Housing and Consumer Protection, 2003–05; Dir, Community and Adult Services, 2005–06; Chief Exec., 2006–08. Clerk to Lord Mayor of Chester, 2009–16. Comr, Local Govt Boundary Commn for England, 2017–. Mem., Birmingham Ind. Improvement Panel, 2015–19. *Recreations:* walking, gardening, cycling, golf. *Club:* Chester Business.

**ROBINSON, Timothy James;** tenor; *b* 10 May 1964; *s* of John Robinson and Sheila Robinson; *m* 1990, Elizabeth Marcus; two *s*. *Educ:* Uppingham Sch.; New Coll., Oxford (BA 1985); Guildhall Sch. of Music and Drama. Operatic début, Kudrjas in Katya Kabanova, Glyndebourne Touring Opera, 1992; other Glyndebourne Fest. rôles incl. Jacquino in Fidelio, Grimoaldo in Rodelinda, Lysander in Midsummer Night's Dream; rôles with ENO incl. Fenton in Falstaff, Male Chorus in Rape of Lucretia, Captain Vere in Billy Budd, Peter Quint in Turn of the Screw; Principal, Royal Opera House, Covent Garden, 1995–2001, rôles incl. Ferrando in Cosi fan tutte, Froh in Das Rheingold, Jupiter in Semele, Vasek in The Bartered Bride; has also sung with Aix Opera, Opéra National de Paris, Salzburg Opera, Hamburg Opera, Lyon Opera, Welsh Nat. Opera, Bavarian State Opera, Bilbao Opera. Has appeared in concert with leading orchestras incl. Royal Philharmonic, Berlin Philharmonic, Leipzig Gewandhaus and Vienna Philharmonic. Numerous recordings. *Recreations:* good food and wine, anything to do with sport, family holidays. *Address:* c/o Askonas Holt, 15 Fetter Lane, EC4A 1BW.

**ROBINSON, Timothy Michael;** Chief Executive, LGC Group Ltd, since 2013; *b* Eaglescliffe, 9 Aug. 1963; *s* of Michael Robinson and Sheila Robinson; *m* 1992, Victoria Davies; one *s* one *d*. *Educ:* Pocklington Sch.; Univ. of Leeds (BSc Hons Physiology). Engr, mktg, Gen. Manager, IBM, 1984–94; Man. Dir, UK, Silicon Graphics, 1994–97; Chief Exec., DCS Gp plc, 1997–2001; Sen. Vice Pres., Thales, 2001–05; Chief Executive: Xafinity, 2005–10; Talaris, 2010–13. Non-exec. Dir, Camelot, 2002–10. Non-executive Member Board: UKTI, 2006–12; DFID, 2013–; non-exec. Chair, Open GI, 2016–. Non-exec. Mem., Audit Cttee, Oxfam, 2006–12. FInstD 2009; FRSA. Freeman, Information Technologists' Co., 2000. *Recreations:* Real tennis, triathlon, vintage Alvis, trekking, making lists. *Address:* LGC Group Ltd, Queens Road, Teddington, Middx TW11 0LY. *T:* (020) 8943 7400. *E:* tim.robinson@lgcgroup.com. *Clubs:* Royal Automobile; Radley College Real Tennis.

**ROBINSON, Maj. Gen. Timothy Patrick,** CBE 2015 (OBE 2007); Partner, Schillings, since 2016; *b* Wegberg, W Germany, 25 Nov. 1967; *s* of Alan and Yvonne Robinson; *m* 1996, Kate Woodrow (marr. diss. 2017); two *d*. *Educ:* Rendcomb Coll.; Exeter Univ. (BA Law 1990); Cranfield Univ. (MBA 2000); King's Coll. London (MA Defence Studies 2001). Mil. Asst to CGS, 2000–02; SO1, Middle East Plans, PJHQ, 2005–07; CO, 9th/12th Royal Lancers, 2007–09; Comdr, 1 Mechanised Bde, 2010–12; ACOS (Ops), 2012–14; Mem., RCDS, 2015; COS, Field Army, 2015. *Publications:* ADP Operations, 2010. *Recreations:* theatre, art and music, conservation. *T:* (020) 7034 9000. *Clubs:* Cavalry and Guards, Conduit.

**ROBINSON, Sir Tony;** *see* Robinson, Sir A.

**ROBINSON, Vivian;** QC 1986; Partner, McGuireWoods London LLP, 2011–19; *b* 29 July 1944; *s* of late William and Ann Robinson; *m* 1975, Louise Marriner; one *s* two *d*. *Educ:* Queen Elizabeth Grammar School, Wakefield; The Leys School, Cambridge; Sidney Sussex College, Cambridge (BA). Called to the Bar, Inner Temple, 1967 (Bencher, 1991; Treas., 2009); a Recorder, 1986–2016. Gen. Counsel, SFO, 2009–11. Liveryman, Gardeners' Co., 1976– (Mem., Court of Assistants, 1989–; Master, 2000–01). *Clubs:* Garrick, MCC, Pilgrims.

**ROBINSON, William Good;** Deputy Secretary, Department of the Civil Service, Northern Ireland, 1978–80, retired; *b* 20 May 1919; *s* of William Robinson and Elizabeth Ann (*née* Good); *m* 1947, Wilhelmina Vaughan; two *d*. *Educ:* Clones High Sch.; Queen's Univ. of Belfast (BScEcon, BA). Served War, RAF, 1941–46 (Flt Lieut, Navigator). Entered NI Civil Service, 1938; Min. of Labour and National Insurance, NI, 1946–63; Principal, Min. of Home Affairs, NI, 1963; Asst Sec., 1967; Sen. Asst Sec., NI Office, 1973. *Recreations:* do-it-yourself, reading history. *Address:* Stormochree, 47 Castlehill Road, Belfast BT4 3GN. *T:* (028) 9020 7386.

**ROBINSON, Yasmin;** *see* Sewell, Y.

**ROBISON, Maj. Gen. Garry Stuart,** CB 2010; Chief of Staff (Capability) to Commander-in-Chief Fleet, 2008–11; Head of Global Security, Bechtel, since 2014 (Risk Manager, 2011–12; In Country Operations Manager (BP West Nile Delta, Egypt), 2012–14); *b* 10 June 1958; *s* of late George Desmond Robison and of Carole Margaret Robison (*née* Pugh); *m* 1982, Bridget Anne Clark; one *s* two *d*. *Educ:* Bemrose Grammar Sch., Derby; Christ's Coll., Cambridge (MPhil Internat. Relns 1999). Royal Marines: Officer trng, 1976–77; Company Comdr, 40 Commando, 1988–89; CO, 45 Commando, 1999–2000; Dep. Comdr, Iraq Survey Gp, 2003; Comdt, Commando Trng Centre, 2004–06; Comdr UK Amphibious Forces, 2006–08; Comdt Gen. RM, 2006–09, and Captain of Deal Castle, 2009; Dep. Comdr (Stability), HQ Internat. Security and Assistance Force, Afghanistan, 2007. Vice Pres., RN and RM Children's Fund, 2006–19. Hon. Vice President: RN Cricket, 2011– (Pres., 2007–11); RN Football, 2011– (Vice Pres., 2009–11). Freeman, City of London, 2010; Liveryman, Plaisterers' Co., 2010. DUniv Derby, 2011. *Recreations:* golf, cricket, football, music. *Club:* Free Foresters Cricket.

**ROBISON, Shona;** Member (SNP) Dundee City East, Scottish Parliament, since 2011 (North East Scotland, 1999–2003; Dundee East, 2003–11); *b* 26 May 1966; *d* of Robin and Dorothy Robison; *m* 1997, Stewart Hosie, *qv*; one *d*. *Educ:* Alva Acad.; Glasgow Univ.; Jordanhill Coll. Sen. Community Worker, City of Glasgow Council, 1993–99. Scottish Parliament: Shadow Minister, Health (formerly Health and Community Care) Cttee, 2003–07; Minister for Public Health, 2007–11, for Sport, 2009–14, for Commonwealth Games, 2011–14; Cabinet Sec. for Health, Wellbeing and Sport, then Health and Sport, 2014–18. Contested (SNP) Dundee E, 1997. *Address:* Scottish Parliament, Edinburgh EH99 1SP.

**ROBLES, Marisa,** FRCM; harpist; Professor of Harp, Royal College of Music, 1971, now Visiting Professor; *b* 4 May 1937; *d* of Cristobal Robles and Maria Bonilla; *m* 1985, David Bean; two *s* one *d* by previous marriage. *Educ:* Madrid National Sch.; Royal Madrid Conservatoire. Prof. of Harp, Royal Madrid Conservatoire, 1958–60. Recitals and solo appearances with major orchestras in UK, Europe, Africa, Canada, USA, South America, Japan, China and Australia. Mem., UK Harp Assoc. Recordings include concerti by Handel, Dittersdorf, Boildieu, Debussy, Rodrigo, Moreno-Buendia, solo repertoire by Beethoven, Mozart, Fauré, Hasselmans, Tournier, Guridi and others, and chamber music by Alwyn, Roussel, Britten, Ravel, Debussy and others. Hon. Royal Madrid Conservatoire 1958; Hon. RCM 1973; FRCM 1983. *Recreations:* theatre, gardening, indoor plants, family life in general. *Address:* 38 Luttrell Avenue, Putney, SW15 6PE. *T:* (020) 8785 2204. *Club:* Royal Over-Seas League.

**ROBLIN, David,** FRCP, FMedSci; Chief Operating Officer and President of Research and Development, Summit Therapeutics, Oxford, UK and Cambridge, USA, since 2017; *b* Neath, W Glamorgan, 25 Sept. 1966; *s* of John and Margaret Diana Roblin; *m* 1992, Sallyanne Kite; two *s* one *d*. *Educ:* Ysgol Gyfyn Cwmtawe, Swansea; St George's Hosp. Med. Sch., Univ. of London (BSc 1st Cl. Hons Biochem. 1987; MB BS Hons 1991). FRCP 2004; FFPM 2014; FMedSci 2017. NHS Clin. Practice, St George's and St Bartholomew's Hosp., 1991–95; Clinician, Pfizer, 1995–97; Hd, Therapy Area for Anti-Infectives, Bayer Pharma, 1997–99; Sen. Clinician, Pfizer, 1999–2003; Hd, Clin. R&D Europe and Worldwide Endocrinol. Develt, Pfizer VP, 2003–07; Hd of Res., Site Hd, CMO, Europe R&D, Pfizer SVP, 2008–11; Chief Operating Officer and Dir, Scientific Translation, 2014–17, Chm., Scientific Translation, 2017–, Francis Crick Inst. Hon. Professor: of Medicine, Sch. of Medicine, Swansea Univ., 2013–; of Translational Medicine, St George's Hosp. Med. Sch., 2015–. Dir, Innovative Medicines Initiative, 2010–11; non-exec. Dir, Sosei-Heptares, 2018–. *Recreations:* walking, running, travel. *Address:* Summit Therapeutics, 136A Eastern Avenue, Milton Park, Abingdon, Oxon OX14 4SB. *E:* david.roblin@summitplc.com.

**ROBOROUGH,** 4th Baron *cr* 1938, of Maristow, co. Devon; **Massey John Henry Lopes;** Bt 1805; *b* 22 Dec. 1969; *s* of 3rd Baron Roborough and Robyn Zenda Carol Lopes (*née* Bromwich); *S* father, 2015; *m* 1996, Jean Campbell Sorell Underwood; two *s* one *d*. *Heir: s* Hon. Henry Massey Peter Lopes, *b* 30 July 1997.

**ROBOTTOM, Dame Marlene (Anne),** DBE 2000; Headteacher, Mulberry School for Girls, Tower Hamlets, London, 1991–2006; education consultant, 2006–15; *b* 10 July 1950; *d* of Alan Joseph Robottom and Patricia Annie Robottom (*née* Gilkes). *Educ:* Coll. of All Saints, London (CertEd 1971); NE London Poly. (BEd 1981); Poly. of E London (MSc 1989). Tower Hamlets, subseq. Mulberry School: Teacher, 1971–72; Dep. Head of Dept, 1972–77; Hd of Dept, 1977–78; Hd of House, 1979–80; Hd of House and Second Dep. Headteacher, 1980–87; First Dep. Headteacher (Curriculum), 1987–90. *Recreations:* theatre, music, the arts, antiques and restoration.

**ROBSON, Agnes;** Head of Corporate Services, Scottish Executive, 2000–04; *b* 6 Oct. 1946; *d* of John Wight and Agnes Margaret Wight (*née* Stark); *m* 1969, Godfrey Robson (marr. diss.); one *s*. *Educ:* Holy Cross Acad., Edinburgh; Edinburgh Univ. (MA Hons Politics and Mod. Hist.). Civil Servant, Dept of Employment, 1968–79; joined Scottish Office, 1985: Industry Department: Head: Energy Div., 1988–89; Nuclear Energy Div., 1989–90; Urban Policy Div., 1990–92; Dir, Primary Care, NHS Mgt Exec., Health Dept, 1992–2000. Mem., Scottish Health Council, 2005–11. Non-executive Director: Royal Scottish Nat. Orch., 2006–13; Citizens Advice Edinburgh, 2008–14; Citizens Advice Scotland, 2010–17. Gov., Royal Conservatoire of Scotland, 2013–. *Recreations:* opera, contemporary Scottish painting.

**ROBSON, Alan;** General Secretary, Confederation of Shipbuilding and Engineering Unions, 1993–2005; *b* 24 Dec. 1941; *s* of John William Robson and Bridgit Robson; *m* 1964, Joyce Lydia (*d* 2006). *Educ:* Ellison C of E Sch. Fitter-turner, 1958–90; Asst Gen. Sec., AEU, 1990–93. *Recreations:* reading, supporting the arts, football. *Address:* 20 York Avenue, Jarrow, Tyne and Wear NE32 5LT. *Clubs:* Labour, Elmfield, Ex-Service Men's (Jarrow).

**ROBSON, Prof. Alan David,** AO 2013 (AM 2003); PhD; FTSE, FAIAST; FACE; Hackett Professor of Agriculture, University of Western Australia, 1996–2012, now Emeritus Professor; *b* 1 Feb. 1945; *s* of Thomas Robson and Anne Robson (*née* Cummings); *m* 1966, Gwenda Clarice Ferris; one *s* two *d*. *Educ:* Univ. of Melbourne (BAgrSc); Univ. of Western Australia (PhD 1970). FACE 2004. Res. agronomist, 1972–73; University of Western Australia: Lectr, 1974–80; Sen. Lectr, 1980–82; Associate Prof., 1982–83; Prof., 1984–2012; Dir, Centre for Legumes in Mediterranean Agric., 1992–93; Dep. Vice Chancellor, 1993–2004; Vice Chancellor, 2004–12. Chairman: Gp of Eight Univs, 2007–10; Worldwide Univs Network, 2010–11; HE Standards Panel, Australian Govt, 2012–; WA Biosecurity Council, 2012–15. Chm. of Trustees, WA Mus., 2012–. FTSE 1989; FAIAST (FAIAS 1989). Hon. DLitt Western Australia, 2015. Leading CEO for Advancement of Women Award, Equal Opportunity for Women in Workplace Agency, Australia, 2011. *Publications:* (ed) Copper in Soils and Plants, 1981; (ed) Soil Acidity and Plant Growth, 1989; (ed) Zinc in Soil and Plants, 1993; (ed) Management of Mycorrhizas in Agriculture, Horticulture and Forestry, 1994; numerous scientific contribs on mineral nutrition of plants. *Recreations:* sport, reading. *Address:* School of Agriculture and Environment, University of Western Australia, 35 Stirling Highway, Crawley, WA 6009, Australia. *E:* Alan.Robson@uwa.edu.au.

**ROBSON, Bryan,** OBE 1990; Manager, Sheffield United Football Club, 2007–08; Head Coach, Thailand National Football Team, 2009–11; *b* 11 Jan. 1957; *s* of Brian and Maureen Robson; *m* 1978, Denise Brindley; one *s* two *d*. *Educ:* Lord Lawson Comprehensive Sch., Birtley. Player: West Bromwich Albion FC, 1974–81; Manchester United FC, 1981–94 (captain, winning team: FA Cup, 1983, 1985, 1990; European Cup Winners' Cup, 1991; Premier League, 1993, 1994); Manager: Middlesbrough FC, 1994–2001 (player-manager, 1994–97); Bradford City FC, 2003–04; W Bromwich Albion FC, 2004–06. Global Ambassador for Manchester United FC, 2008–17. Player, England Football Team, 1980–91 (90 appearances, 65 as captain, 26 goals). Hon. BA: Manchester, 1992; Salford, 1992. *Publications:* United I Stand (autobiog.), 1983. *Recreations:* horse racing, golf. *Clubs:* West Bromwich Albion Football, Manchester United, Middlesbrough.

**ROBSON, Carol;** *see* Robson, E. C.

**ROBSON, Elizabeth;** *see* Howlett, E.

**ROBSON, (Elizabeth) Carol;** HM Diplomatic Service, retired; Head, United Nations and Commonwealth Department, Department for International Development, 2004–05 (on secondment); *b* 14 Jan. 1955; *d* of James Henry Robson and Laura Robson (*née* Jacobson). *Educ:* Carlisle and County High Sch.; York Univ. (BA Physics 1977). Entered Diplomatic Service, 1977; Latin America floater, 1980–81; Russian lang. trng, 1981–82; Ulaanbaatar, 1983; Moscow, 1983–84; FCO, 1984; UKMIS, Geneva, 1987–92; Asst Head, SE Asia Dept, 1992–95; Head, Transcaucasus and Central Asia Unit, 1995–96; Counsellor, Consul-Gen. and Dep. Head of Mission, Stockholm, 1996–98; Dep. Dir, Ditchley Foundn, 1998–2001 (on special leave); Counsellor and Dep. Hd of Mission, Copenhagen, 2002–04. *Recreations:* diverse, including cooking, antiques, art, gardening, travel, visiting historic sites and houses, reading.

**ROBSON, Eric,** DL; freelance writer and broadcaster, since 1979; farmer, 1987–2009; *b* 31 Dec. 1946; *s* of James Walter Robson and Agnes Gourlay Robson; *m* 1st, 1976, Mary Armstrong (marr. diss. 1984); one *s* one *d*; 2nd, 1988, Annette Steinhilber; one *s* two *d*. *Educ:* Carlisle Grammar Sch. Border TV, 1966–; BBC TV and Radio, 1976–; BBC outside broadcast commentator, Trooping the Colour, the Cenotaph, handover of Hong Kong; Chm., Gardeners' Question Time, BBC Radio, 1995–2019; documentary producer and presenter. Chairman: Striding Edge Ltd, 1994–; Cumbria Tourist Bd, 2002–; Wainwright Soc., 2002–. Trustee, Tullie House Mus. and Art Gall. Trust, 2012–. DL Cumbria, 2004. *Publications*: Great Railway Journeys of the World, 1981; Northumbria, 1998; Out of Town, 2002; After Wainwright, 2004; The Border Line, 2006; Outside Broadcaster, 2007; The Zoo, 2007; Wainwright's TV Walks, 2008; Abroad, 2014. *Recreations*: painting, fell walking, cooking, avoiding housework. *Address*: Crag House Farm, Wasdale, Cumbria CA19 1UT. *T*: (01946) 726301. *Club*: Farmers.

**ROBSON, Euan Macfarlane;** Associate, Caledonia Public Affairs Ltd (formerly Caledonia Consulting), since 2008; *b* 17 Feb. 1954; *m* 1984, Valerie Young; two *d*. *Educ*: Univ. of Newcastle upon Tyne (BA Hons History 1976); Univ. of Strathclyde (MSc Political Sci. 1984). Teacher, King Edward VI Sch., Morpeth, 1977–79; Dep. Sec., Gas Consumers' Northern Council, Newcastle upon Tyne, 1981–86; Scottish Manager, Gas Consumers' Council, 1986–99. Mem. (L/All), Northumberland CC, 1981–89 (Chm., Highways Cttee, 1988–89; Hon. Alderman, 1989); L/All Gp Sec., 1981–87; Mem. (Lib Dem), Scottish Borders Council, 2017–. Contested (L/All) Hexham, 1983, 1987. Scottish Parliament: Mem. (Lib Dem) Roxburgh and Berwickshire, 1999–2007; Lib Dem Rural Affairs spokesman, 1998–99, Justice and Home Affairs spokesman, 1999–2001, Health and Communities spokesman, 2005–07; Dep. Minister for Parlt, subseq. for Parly Business, 2001–03, for Educn and Young People, 2003–05; Convener, Lib Dem Parly party, 2005–07. Contested (Lib Dem): Roxburgh and Berwicks, 2007, Ettrick, Roxburgh and Berwicks, 2011, Scottish Parlt; Scotland, Eur. Parlt, 2009. River Tweed Comr, 1994–2001. Founding Mem., Consumer Safety Internat.; Life Mem., Nat. Trust for Scotland. Chair, Borders Consortium of CAB, 2013–17. *Publications*: The Consumers' View of the 1990 EU Gas Appliances' Directive, 1991; George Houston: nature's limner, 1997; (contrib.) Kirkcudbright: 100 years of an artists' colony, 2000; Scotland, Poland and the European Union, 2002; Charles Oppenheimer: from craftsman to artist, 2012. *Recreation*: angling. *Address*: Elmbank, Tweedsyde Park, Kelso, Roxburghshire TD5 7RF. *T*: (01573) 225279.

**ROBSON, Frank Elms,** OBE 1991; Partner, Winckworth Sherwood (formerly Winckworth & Pemberton), Solicitors, Oxford and Westminster, 1962–98 (Senior Partner, 1990–94); *b* 14 Dec. 1931; *s* of Joseph A. Robson and Barbara Robson; *m* 1958, Helen (*née* Jackson) (*d* 2004); four *s* one *d*. *Educ*: King Edward VI Grammar Sch., Morpeth; Selwyn Coll., Cambridge (MA). Admitted solicitor, 1954. Registrar, Dio. Oxford, 1970–2000; Joint Registrar, Province of Canterbury, 1982–2000. Chm., Ecclesiastical Law Soc., 1996–2002; Vice-Chm., Legal Adv. Commn, Gen. Synod of C of E, 1990–2002. DCL Lambeth, 1991. *Recreation*: Northumberland. *Address*: 2 Simms Close, Middle Road, Stanton St John, Oxford OX33 1HB. *T*: (01865) 351393.

**ROBSON, Godfrey,** CB 2002; Chairman, Frontline Consultants, 2003–13 (Director, 2003–13); *b* 5 Nov. 1946; *s* of late William James Robson and Mary Finn; *m* (marr. diss.); one *s*. *Educ*: St Joseph's Coll., Dumfries; Edinburgh Univ. (MA). Joined Scottish Office, 1970; Pvte Sec. to Parly Under-Sec. of State, 1973–74, to Minister of State, 1974; Prin. Pvte Sec. to Sec. of State for Scotland, 1979–81; Assistant Secretary: Roads and Transport, 1981–86; Local Govt Finance, 1986–89; Under Sec., 1989; Scottish Fisheries Sec., 1989–93; Scottish Executive (formerly Scottish Office): Under Sec., Industrial Expansion, subseq. Economic and Industrial Affairs, 1993–2000; Dir of Health Policy, 2000–02. Sen. Policy Advr, ICAP, Washington DC, 2004–16. Non-executive Director: Lloyds TSB Scotland, 2001–13; TSB Bank plc, 2013–15. Founding Chm., Nat. Jubilee Hosp., Clydebank, 2002–03; Dir and Trustee, Caledonia Youth, 2003–12. Sec., Episcopal Dio. of Edinburgh, 2017–. *Recreations*: walking, travel by other means, reading history. *Address*: 50 East Trinity Road, Edinburgh EH5 3EN. *T*: (0131) 552 9519; Chemin Sous Baye, 84110 Vaison la Romaine, France. *T*: (4) 90371832.

**ROBSON, John Gair,** PhD, ScD; FRS 2003; Senior Research Professor in Vision Science, University of Houston, 1997; Fellow of Gonville and Caius College, Cambridge, since 1965 (Life Fellow, 1995); *b* 27 June 1936; *s* of Thomas Robson and Kathleen (*née* Elwell); *m* 1958, Jane Macdonald; two *s* two *d*. *Educ*: Shrewsbury Sch.; St John's Coll., Cambridge (BA; PhD 1962; ScD 2004). Vis. Scientist, Bell Labs, Murray Hill, 1964; Vis. Prof. Northwestern Univ., 1964; Demonstrator in Physiol., 1962–65, Lectr in Physiol., 1966–83, Reader in Neurophysiol., 1983–96, Univ. of Cambridge. Champness Lectr, Spectacle Makers' Co., 1990. (Jtly) Friedenwald Award, Assoc. for Res. in Vision and Ophthalmol., 1983; Edgar J. Tillyer Award, Optical Soc. of America, 1996. *Publications*: numerous contribs on vision and visual neurophysiology to learned jls. *Address*: Herring's House, Wilbraham Road, Fulbourn, Cambridge CB21 5EU. *T*: (01223) 880277.

**ROBSON, Rev. John Phillips,** LVO 1999; Chaplain to the Queen, 1993–2002; an Extra Chaplain to the Queen, since 2002; Chaplain of the Queen's Chapel of the Savoy and Chaplain of the Royal Victorian Order, 1989–2002; *b* 22 July 1932; *s* of Thomas Herbert and Nellie Julia Robson. *Educ*: Hele's School, Exeter; Brentwood School; St Edmund Hall, Oxford (Liddon Exhibnr 1954); King's College London (AKC 1958). Deacon 1959, priest 1960; Curate, Huddersfield Parish Church, 1959–62; Asst Chaplain 1962–65, Senior Chaplain 1965–80, Christ's Hospital, Horsham; Senior Chaplain of Wellington College, Berks, 1980–89. *Recreations*: cinema, theatre, technology, watching sport, Orthodox iconography. *Address*: Charterhouse, Charterhouse Square, EC1M 6AN. *T*: (020) 7101 9263. *Club*: Garrick.

**ROBSON, Mark Hunter,** FIMA, FCMA; CMath, CSci, CGMA; Senior Adviser, Bank of England, 2015; *b* Southend-on-Sea, 10 Aug. 1958; *s* of Peter William Robson and Shirley Marion Robson; *m* 1st, 1989, Amanda Louise Knox (marr. diss. 2000); two *d*; 2nd, 2006, Lara Jane Hays (marr. diss. 2017); two *s*. *Educ*: Westcliff High Sch. for Boys; St John's Coll., Oxford (BA Maths and Philosophy 1979, MA 1982; MPhil Econs 1985). FIMA 1990; CMath 1992; FCMA 2004; CSci 2005; CGMA 2012. HM Inspector of Taxes, 1980–83, Econ. Advr, 1985–90, Bd of Inland Revenue; Res. Fellow, Financial Mkts Gp, LSE, 1987–89; Sen. Manager, Tax Consultancy, KPMG Peat Marwick, 1990–93; Principal Administrator, Fiscal Affairs, OECD, 1993–95; Advr/Manager, Financial Stability, Bank of England, 1995–98; Tax Policy Advr, Thailand, IMF, 1998–99; Sen. Manager, Finance, Bank of England, 1999–2003; Treas. and Official Fellow, Lady Margaret Hall, Oxford, 2003–07, Hon. Res. Fellow, 2008–; Bank of England: Sen. Manager, Banking Services, 2008–09; Hd of Monetary and Financial Statistics, 2009–12; Hd of Statistics and Regulatory Data, 2012–15. Mem., Audit Cttee, London Bor. of Islington, 2008–12. Member: Grants Assessment Panel, 2010–14, Bd, 2015–17, ESRC; Social Scis Main Panel, HEFCE REF 2014, 2011–14; Bd, HEFCE, 2012–18; Commonwealth Scholarship Commn, 2014–17. Mem. Council, IMA, 1997–2000; Mem. Council and Exec. Cttee, Inst. for Fiscal Studies, 1997–; Mem., Governing Council, Centre for the Study of Financial Innovation, 2004–. Treasurer: Royal Statistical Soc., 2003–07; REconS, 2008–16 (Vice Pres., 2016–); Science Council, 2013–15. Mem. Council, City Univ., 2002–11; Vice Chm., London Metropolitan Univ., 2010–14. Gov., City of London Acad., Islington, 2008–11. Liveryman, Internat. Bankers' Co., 2006–. *Recreations*: family, reading, music, theatre, Roman Catholicism, charity governance, collegiate rowing.

**ROBSON, Mark William;** Director, English and Examinations, British Council, since 2010; *b* Newcastle upon Tyne, 2 Nov. 1960; *s* of William and Doris Robson; *m* 1995, Patricia Voets; two *d*. *Educ*: Latymer Upper Sch.; Univ. of Southampton (BSc Econs and Stats 1982). Mkt Res. Exec., MORI, 1982–84; Mkt Res. Exec., 1984–86, Sen. Brand Manager, 1986–88, Mkt Res. Manager, 1988–91, Colgate-Palmolive; Market Research Manager: Jamont, 1991–93; Eridania Beghin-Say, 1993–95; Dir, Mktg and Export, Carapelli Firenze, 1995–98; Vice-Pres., Sales and Mktg, Georgia-Pacific EMEA, 1998–2007; Dir, Ops, British Council, 2007–10. *Recreations*: football, football coaching, running, music, family. *Address*: British Council, 10 Spring Gardens, SW1A 2BN.

**ROBSON, Air Vice-Marshal Robert Michael,** OBE 1971; freelance journalist; sheep farmer, 1987–96; *b* 22 April 1935; *s* of Dr John Alexander and Edith Robson; *m* 1959, Brenda Margaret (*née* Croysdill); one *s* two *d*. *Educ*: Sherborne; RMA Sandhurst. Commissioned 1955; RAF Regt, 1958; Navigator Training, 1959; Strike Squadrons, 1965; Sqdn Comdr, RAF Coll., 1968; Defence Adviser to British High Comr, Sri Lanka, 1972; Nat. Defence Coll., 1973; CO 27 Sqdn, 1974–75; MoD staff duties, 1978; CO RAF Gatow, 1978–80; ADC to the Queen, 1979–80; RCDS 1981; Dir of Initial Officer Training, RAF Coll., 1982–84; Dir of Public Relations, RAF, 1984–87; Hd, RAF Study of Officers' Terms of Service, 1987; retired. Chairman: Turbo (UK) Ltd, 1995–98; Fuel Mechanics Ltd, 1995–97; Dir, Advanced Technology Industries Ltd, 1993–97; Chm., Prince's Trust, Lincs, 1993–96; Dir and Chm., Witham Hall Trust, 1995–2003; Gov., Witham Hall Sch., 1988–2006 (Chm. Govs, 1995–2003; Vice-Pres., 2003–06). Pres., SSAFA Forces Help, Lincs, 2010 (Vice-Pres., 2001–10). FCMI (FBIM 1980). *Recreations*: fly fishing, gardening. *Club*: Royal Air Force.

**ROBSON, Rt Rev. Stephen;** *see* Dunkeld, Bishop of, (R.C.).

**ROBSON, Sir Stephen Arthur, (Sir Steve),** Kt 2000; CB 1997; PhD; Second Permanent Secretary, Finance, Regulation and Industry, HM Treasury, 1997–2001; *b* 30 Sept. 1943; *s* of Arthur Cyril Robson and Lilian Marianne (*née* Peabody); *m* 1974, Meredith Hilary Lancashire; two *s*. *Educ*: Pocklington Sch.; St John's Coll., Cambridge (MA, PhD); Stanford Univ., USA (MA). Joined Civil Service (HM Treasury), 1969; Private Sec. to Chancellor of the Exchequer, 1974–76; seconded to Investors in Industry plc, 1976–78; Under Sec., Defence Policy and Material Gp, 1987–89, Public Enterprises and Privatisation Gp, 1990–93; Dep. Sec., Industry and Financial Instns, later Finance, Regulation and Industry, 1993–97. Non-executive Director: Royal Bank of Scotland, 2001–09; J P Morgan Cazenove (formerly Cazenove), 2001–10; Partnerships UK, 2001–08; Xstrata, 2002–13; Financial Reporting Council, 2007–13; KPMG, 2010–15; Kuwait Energy, 2014–17. *Recreation*: sailing. *Club*: Bosham Sailing.

**ROCH, Rt Hon. Sir John (Ormond),** Kt 1985; PC 1993; a Lord Justice of Appeal, 1993–2000; *b* 19 April 1934; *s* of Frederick Ormond Roch and Vera Elizabeth (*née* Chamberlain); *m* 1st, 1967, Anne Elizabeth Greany (*d* 1994); three *d*; 2nd, 1996, Mrs Susan Angela Parry. *Educ*: Wrekin Coll.; Clare Coll., Cambridge (BA, LLB). Called to Bar, Gray's Inn, 1961, Bencher, 1985; QC 1976; a Recorder, 1975–85; a Judge of the High Court of Justice, QBD, 1985–93; Presiding Judge, Wales and Chester Circuit, 1986–90. Vice-Pres., RNLI, 2006– (Gov. and Mem. Mgt Cttee, 1996–2006). President: Haverfordwest Civic Soc., 2006–; Old Wrekinian Assoc., 2007–13; Atlantic Challenge, Pembrokeshire Gig Assoc., 2010–14. *Recreations*: sailing, music. *Club*: Dale Yacht.

**ROCHA, John,** CBE 2002; fashion designer, since 1980; *b* Hong Kong, 23 Aug. 1953; *s* of Henry and Cecilia Rocha; *m* 1990, Odette Gleeson; one *s* two *d*. *Educ*: Croydon Coll. of Art and Design (Dip. Fashion). Estabd career, Dublin, late 1970s; worked in Milan, 1988–90, subseq. estabd John Rocha; launched: John Rocha at Waterford Crystal, 1997; John Rocha at Debenhams, 2000; John Rocha Jewellery, 2002; opened shop, 15A Dover St, London, 2007. Hon. DLitt Ulster, 1994; Hon. MA, Univ. of the Creative Arts, 2008. British Designer of the Year, British Fashion Awards, 1994. *Publications*: Texture, Form, Purity, Detail, 2002. *Recreation*: fly fishing. *Address*: 10 Ely Place, Dublin 2, Ireland. *T*: (1) 6629225, *Fax*: (1) 6629226. *E*: info@johnrocha.ie. *W*: www.johnrocha.ie. *Clubs*: h, Groucho.

**ROCHAT, Dr Philippe Henri Pierre;** Secretary General, International Civil Aviation Organization, 1991–97; former Executive Director, Air Transport Action Group, Geneva; *b* 19 Oct. 1942; *m* 1967, Catherine Dupuy; two *s* one *d*. *Educ*: Gymnase de Lausanne; Lausanne Univ. (LLB 1966; LLD 1974). Journalist and reporter, Swiss Radio-TV, 1967–74; Asst to Dep. Dir, Federal Office for Civil Aviation, Bern, 1975–77; Admin. and Commercial Dir, Geneva Airport, 1977–85; International Civil Aviation Organisation Council: Alternate Rep. of Belgium, 1985–86; Rep. of Switzerland, 1986–89; Dir, Mkting and Envmt, Geneva Airport, 1989–91. Air Law Professor: Geneva Univ.; Lausanne Univ. *Publications*: articles, reports and lectures on civil aviation and envmt, airports' structure and mgt, challenges in civil aviation, etc. *Recreations*: ski-ing, tennis, hiking, various cultural activities.

**ROCHDALE,** 3rd Viscount *cr* 1960; **Jonathan Hugo Durival Kemp;** human intelligence entrepreneur, creator of SmartWisdom, information athlete (platinum); Managing Director, SmartWisdom, since 1999; Baron 1913; *b* Edinburgh, 10 June 1961; *s* of 2nd Viscount Rochdale and of Serena Jane Kemp (*née* Clark-Hall, now Hanson); *S* father, 2015; one *d*. *Educ*: Stowe Sch.; Westminster Univ. (Postgrad. Dip. Mgt); Cass Business Sch. (MSc Shipping, Trade and Finance). Metropolitan Police, 1982–93. MInstD. *Publications*: (jtly) two sci. papers on knowledge mgt. *Recreation*: photography. *Heir*: *nephew* George Thomas Kemp, *b* 2001. *T*: 07786 526529. *E*: jkemp@smartwisdom.com, Jonathan@viscountrochdale.com. *Clubs*: Royal Automobile, h.

**ROCHDALE, Archdeacon of;** *see* Vann, Ven. C. E.

**ROCHE,** family name of **Baron Fermoy.**

**ROCHE, Most Rev. Arthur;** Archbishop Secretary of the Congregation of Divine Worship and Discipline of the Sacraments, Vatican City, since 2012; *b* 6 March 1950; *s* of Arthur Francis Roche and Frances Roche (*née* Day). *Educ*: Christleton Hall, Chester; English Coll., Valladolid; Pontifical Gregorian Univ., Rome (STL). Ordained priest, 1975; Asst Priest, Holy Rood, Barnsley, 1975–77; Sec. to Rt Rev. Gordon Wheeler, Bishop of Leeds, 1977–82; Vice-Chancellor, 1979–89, Financial Administrator, 1986–90, Dio. of Leeds; Asst Priest, Leeds Cathedral, 1982–89; Parish Priest, St Wilfrids's, Leeds, 1989–91; Spiritual Dir, Venerable English Coll., Rome, 1992–96; Gen. Sec. to Catholic Bps' Conf. of England and Wales, 1996–2001; Auxiliary Bishop of Westminster, 2001–02; Coadjutor Bishop of Leeds, 2002–04; Bishop of Leeds, (RC), 2004–12. Hon. Ecumenical Canon: Wakefield Cath., 2006–; Bradford Cath., 2008–. Titular Bishop of Rusticiana, 2001–02. Chm., Dept of Christian Life and Worship, Catholic Bps' Conf. of England and Wales, 2004–12. Chm., Internat. Commn for English in the Liturgy, 2002–12. Co-ordinator of the Papal Visit to York, 1982. Prelate of Honour to Pope John Paul II. KC★HS 2010; Conventual Chaplain Grand Cross *ad honorem* of Knight of Malta, 2018. *Recreations*: walking, reading, music, travel. *Address*: Piazza Pio XII, 10, 00120 Città del Vaticano, Italy. *T*: (6) 69884005, *Fax*: (6) 69882866.

**ROCHE, Barbara Maureen;** Chairman: Migration Matters Trust, since 2012; Praxis, since 2013; *b* 13 April 1954; *d* of late Barnett Margolis and Hannah (*née* Lopes Dias); *m* 1977, Patrick Roche; one *d*. *Educ:* JFS Comprehensive Sch., Camden; Lady Margaret Hall, Oxford (BA). Called to the Bar, Middle Temple, 1977. MP (Lab) Hornsey and Wood Green, 1992–2005; contested (Lab) same seat, 2005. Parly Under-Sec. of State, DTI, 1997–98; Financial Sec., HM Treasury, 1999; Minister of State: Home Office, 1999–2001; Cabinet Office, 2001–02; ODPM, 2002–03. Chm., Metropolitan Housing Partnership, 2009–13 (Bd Mem., 2006–13; Dep. Chm., 2008–09). Chm., Metropolitan Support Trust, 2007–09; Trustee, Oxford Literary and Debating Union Trust, 2012–. Former Vis. Fellow, Univ. of Teesside; Vis. Prof., Univ. of Sunderland, 2008–11. Associate Fellow, IPPR, 2009–10. Chm., Migration Mus. Project, 2006–. *Recreations:* theatre, detective fiction.

**ROCHE, David Lawrence Redmond;** owner, David Roche Enterprises Ltd, since 2011; *b* 8 May 1961; *s* of Lawrence and Jocelyn Roche; *m* 1987, Johanna Kari; three *s*. *Educ:* Worth Sch.; Durham Univ. (BA Hons Psychol. 1983). Prodn Planner, Burlington Klopman, 1984–86; Stock Control Manager, Hornes Ltd, 1986–89; Ops Manager, HMV UK Ltd, 1989–95; Product Director: HMV Europe Ltd, 1995–2002; Waterstone's Ltd, 2002–05; Chief Executive, Borders UK and Ireland Ltd, 2006–08; Gp Sales and Trade Mktg Dir, HarperCollins Publishing, 2008–11. Pres., Booksellers Assoc. UK & Ire, 2005–07. Non-executive Chair: London Book Fair, 2012–; BookBrunch Ltd, 2018– (Exec. Chm., 2016–18); Chair, New Writing North, 2015–; Trustee, Booktrust, 2008–15. Hon. Fellow, Univ. of Central Lancs, 2017. *Recreations:* travel, Rugby, golf, squash, ski-ing, scuba diving, cooking, wine, reading and, now, sleeping. *Address:* 25 Kingston Hill Place, Kingston upon Thames, Surrey KT2 7QY. *T:* (020) 8546 1023. *Clubs:* Soho House, MCC; Royal Wimbledon Golf.

**ROCHE, Sir David (O'Grady),** 5th Bt *cr* 1838 of Carass, Limerick; FCA; *b* 21 Sept. 1947; *s* of Sir Standish O'Grady Roche, 4th Bt, DSO, and of Evelyn Laura, *d* of Major William Andon; *S* father, 1977; *m* 1971, Hon. (Helen) Alexandra Briscoe Frewen (MBE 2017), *d* of 3rd Viscount Selby; one *s* one *d* (and one *s* decd). *Educ:* Wellington Coll., Berks; Trinity Coll., Dublin. Qualified as Chartered Accountant with Peat Marwick Mitchell, 1974; Sen. Manager, UK Banking, Samuel Montagu & Co. Ltd, 1976–78; Chm. and Finance Dir, Carlton Real Estate plc, 1978–82; Chairman: Echo Hotel plc, 1983–93; Plaza Hldgs Ltd, 2003–. Led consortium that won competition to redevelop Battersea Power Station and subseq. sold site, 1986. Mem., Prime Minister of Estonia's Tax Reform Commn, 1992–93. Dir of private cos in sectors of energy, leisure, shipping and Eastern European property, 1994–2002. Served with HAC, 1973–77. Mem. (C), Hammersmith and Fulham LBC, 1978–82. Dep. Chm., Standing Council of the Baronetage, 2012–. Mem., RYA. *Heir: s* David Alexander O'Grady Roche, *b* 28 Jan. 1976. *Address:* Bridge House, Starbotton, Skipton, N Yorks BD23 5HY. *T:* (01756) 760863; 20 Lancaster Mews, W2 3QE. *E:* davidroche20@yahoo.co.uk. *Clubs:* Buck's; Royal Yacht Squadron; Kildare Street (Dublin).

**ROCHE, Sir Henry John, (Sir Harry),** Kt 1999; Chairman, Press Association, 1995–2008 (non-executive Director, 1988–2008); *b* 13 Jan. 1934; *s* of Henry Joseph Roche and Mary Ann Roche; *m* 1st, 1956, Shirley May Foreman (marr. diss. 1986); three *s*; 2nd, 1986, Heather Worthington. *Educ:* George Mitchell Sch., Leyton; Watford Coll. of Technol. (HND Printing Technol.). Apprentice engraver, until 1959; worked on shopfloor of Daily Mirror, 1959–69; Dep. Prodn Controller, Daily Mirror, 1969–70; Northern Prodn Controller, Mirror Gp Newspapers, Manchester, 1970–73; Prodn Dir, 1973–77, Man. Dir, 1977–85, Manchester Evening News; Man. Dir, The Guardian, 1985–88; Chm. and Chief Exec., Guardian Media Gp Plc, 1988–96; Chm., GMTV, 1989–92. Director: Johnston Press plc, 1993–2004 (Dep. Chm., 1995–2004); Jazz FM (formerly Golden Rose Communications) plc, 1995–2002 (Chm., 1999–2002). Chairman: Press Standards Bd of Finance Ltd, 1991–2003; Orgn for Promoting Understanding in Society, 1998–2002; Dep. Chm., Printers Charitable Corp., 1996–2000 (Dir, 1985–2000; Pres., 1993). Mem. Council, CPU, 1988–. FIP3 (FIOP 1993 (Pres., 1996–98)). Freeman, City of London, 1993. *Recreations:* golf, ski-ing, music (particularly jazz). *Clubs:* Royal Automobile; Dunham Forest Golf and Country (Cheshire).

**ROCHE, Nicola,** CBE 2013; Director of Strategy, Sporting Assets, since 2017; *b* 27 Dec. 1956; *d* of Ronald and Shirley Roche. *Educ:* Harrogate Grammar Sch.; Univ. of York (BA Hons Hist. 1979). Birkbeck Coll., London (MA Hist. 1986). EDG, 1979–82; Prime Minister's Office, 1982–86; EDG, 1987–91; City and Inner London N TEC, 1991–93; Labour Attaché, Brussels, The Hague and Luxembourg, 1993–98; Private Office, DfEE, 1998–2001; Hd, Strategic Policy Team, then Dir for Identity Cards, Children and Coroners, Home Office, 2001–04; Dir of Sport, 2004–07, Dir of Strategy, then of Staging, later of Ops, Govt Olympic Exec., 2007–13, DCMS; Chief Exec., TdFHub2014 Ltd, 2013–14; self-employed business consultant, 2015–16. Non-exec. Dir, British Showjumping, 2013–16. Mem. Bd, UK Sport, 2014–. Trustee: Rees Care Leavers Foundn (formerly Care Leavers Foundn), 2013–18; Dame Kelly Holmes Trust, 2017–. *Recreations:* athletics, walking, history, art, riding.

**ROCHE, Patrick John;** Member (NIU), Lagan Valley, Northern Ireland Assembly, 1999–2003 (UKU, 1998–99); *b* 4 March 1940; *m*. *Educ:* Trinity Coll., Dublin (BA Hons Econs and Politics); Durham Univ. (MA Politics). Posts in banking, 1957–66; Lecturer: in Economics, Ulster Univ., 1974–95; in Philosophy of Religion, Irish Baptist Coll., 1978–. *Publications:* (ed jtly) The Northern Ireland Question: myth and reality, 1991, perspectives and policies, 1994, Unionism, nationalism and partition, 1999; (jtly) An Economics Lesson for Irish Nationalists, 1996; The Appeasement of Terrorism and the Belfast Agreement, 2000; The Northern Ireland Question: the peace process and the Belfast Agreement, 2009. *Recreation:* cycling.

**ROCHESTER, 3rd Baron,** of the 4th creation, *cr* 1931, of Rochester in the County of Kent; **David Charles Lamb;** *s* of 2nd Baron Rochester; *S* father, 2017, but does not use the title. *Heir: s* Hon. Daniel Lamb, *b* 12 June 1971.

**ROCHESTER, Bishop of,** since 2010; **Rt Rev. James Henry Langstaff;** Bishop to HM Prisons, since 2013; *b* 27 June 1956; *s* of Henry, (Harry), Langstaff and Jillian Langstaff (*née* Brooks, now Harper); *m* 1977, Bridget Streatfeild; one *s* one *d*. *Educ:* St Catherine's Coll., Oxford (BA (PPE) 1977, MA 1981); Univ. of Nottingham (BA (Theol.) 1980); St John's Coll., Nottingham (Dip. Pastoral Studies). Ordained deacon, 1981, priest, 1982; Asst Curate, St Peter, Farnborough, 1981–86; Vicar, St Matthew, Duddeston and St Clement, Nechells, 1986–96; RD, Birmingham City, 1995–96; Chaplain to Bp of Birmingham, 1996–2000; Rector, Holy Trinity, Sutton Coldfield, 2000–04; Area Dean, Sutton Coldfield, 2002–04; Bishop Suffragan of Lynn, 2004–10. Took seat in H of L, 2014. Tutor, Aston Trng Scheme, 1987–97. Mem., E of England Regl Assembly, 2006–10, Regl Strategy Bd, 2010. Non-exec. Dir, Good Hope Hosp. NHS Trust, 2003–06. Mem. Bd, FCH Housing and Care, 1998–2002; Chairman: Flagship Housing Gp, 2006–10; Housing Justice, 2008–. *Recreations:* ski-ing, walking, music, theatre, travel, current affairs. *Address:* Bishopscourt, 24 St Margaret's Street, Rochester, Kent ME1 1TS.

**ROCHESTER, Dean of;** *see* Hesketh, Very Rev. P. J.

**ROCHESTER, Archdeacon of;** *see* Wooding Jones, Ven. A. D.

**ROCHESTER, Terence Anthony,** CB 1997; *b* 30 May 1937; *s* of Arthur Alfred Rochester and Winifred Mabel Rochester (*née* Smith); *m* 1966, Margaret Alexandra Fleming; one *s* one *d*. *Educ:* Southwest Essex Sch. British Rail, 1953–59, 1961–65; Nat. Service, 2nd Lieut, RE, 1959–61; joined Dept of Transport, 1965; various posts, 1965–87; Director: Transport Eastern Region, 1987–89; Transport W Midlands Region, 1989–90; Construction Programme, W Midlands, 1990–91; Chief Highway Engineer, 1991–97; Civil Engrg and Envmtl Policy Dir, 1994–96, Quality Services Dir, 1996–97, Highways Agency. Chairman: Tech. Cttee B/525 Bldg and Civil Engrg Structures, BSI, 1997–2000; Construction Clients' Forum, 1997–2000; Mem., Govt Cttee on Thaumasite, 1998–99. Res. Fellow, Transport Res. Foundn. Pres., CIRIA, 1998–2001; Hon. Mem., British World Road Assoc. *Recreations:* music, walking, DIY.

**ROCHFORD, Thomas Nicholas Beverley; His Honour Judge Rochford;** a Circuit Judge, since 2019; *b* London, 1961; *s* of James Rochford and Elizabeth Rochford; *m* 1995, Deirdre Shields; two *d*. *Educ:* Ampleforth Coll.; Gonville and Caius Coll., Cambridge (MA). Called to the Bar, Inner Temple, 1984; a Recorder, 2005–19. *Address:* Aylesbury Crown Court, Walton Street, Aylesbury HP21 7FT.

**ROCK,** family name of **Baroness Rock.**

**ROCK, Baroness** *cr* 2015 (Life Peer), of Stratton in the County of Dorset; **Kate Harriet Alexandra Rock;** Senior Advisor: Boden, since 2014; Instinctif Partners, since 2017; *b* London, 9 Oct. 1968; *d* of Thomas Pope and Anna Pope; *m* 1999, Caspar Rock; one *s* one *d*. *Educ:* Hanford Sch.; Sherborne Sch. for Girls; Oxford Poly. (BA Hons). Work in corporate communications and business relations; Partner, Retail and Luxury Brands team, College Hill PR, 1996–2008; Conservative Party: Hd, Business Develt, 2008–10; Dir, Business Engagement, 2010–15; Vice Chm. with special responsibility for business, 2015–16. Member, Select Cttee on Artificial Intelligence, 2017–18, on Rural Economy, 2018–19. Member: Mgt Bd, Red Tape Initiative Ltd, 2017–19; Adv. Bd, Onward, 2018–; Bd, Centre for Data Ethics and Innovation, 2018–. Non-executive Director: Imagination Technologies, 2014–17 (Chm., Remuneration Cttee, 2016–17); First News, 2014–17; Wrackleford Farms Ltd, 2017–; Real World Technologies Ltd, 2017–; Keller Gp, 2018–. Gov., Burlington Danes Acad., 2012–. Vis. Parly Fellow, St Antony's Coll., Oxford, 2017. Speaker, Speakers for Schs, 2015–; Founding Ambassador, Women supporting Women, Princes Trust, 2018–. *Recreations:* reading, running, ski-ing, tennis, Dorset countryside. *Clubs:* Queen's; Marden's (Klosters).

**ROCK, David Annison,** PPRIBA; FCSD; President, Royal Institute of British Architects, 1997–99; Partner, Camp 5, since 1992; *b* 27 May 1929; *s* of Thomas Henry Rock and Muriel Rock (*née* Barton); *m* 1st, 1954, Daphne Elizabeth Richards (marr. diss. 1986); three *s* two *d*; 2nd, 1989, Lesley Patricia Murray. *Educ:* Bede Grammar Sch., Sunderland; King's Coll., Durham (BArch Hons 1952; CertTP 1953). ARIBA 1953, FRIBA 1967; MSIAD 1963, FCSD 1978. 2nd Lieut, RE, 1953–55. With Basil Spence and Partners, 1952–53 and 1955–59; David Rock Architect, 1958–59; Associate Partner, 1959–64, Equity Partner, 1964–71, Grenfell Baines & Hargreaves, later Building Design Partnership; Chm. and Man. Dir, Rock Townsend, 1971–92. Inventor, Workspace concept (sharing by several firms of central support services in a building), 1971; first RIBA/ARCUK approved Archt Developer, 1973. Major projects include: Bumpus Bookshop, W1, 1958; Univ. of Surrey Develt Plan, 1965; UN HQ and Austrian Nat. Conf. Centre, Vienna, 1970; Middlesex Poly., Bounds Green, 1975–88; (with Ralph Erskine) The London Ark, Hammersmith, 1993. Graham Willis Vis. Prof., Univ. of Sheffield, 1990–92. Founder Chairman and Director: 5 Dryden Street Collective, 1971–82; Barley Mow Workspace Ltd, 1973–92; Joint Founder: Construction Industry Council, 1986; Urban Design Alliance, 1997. Royal Institute of British Architects: Mem./Chm., Architecture Award Bds for 14 UK Regs, 1960–77; Mem., Vis. Bds, 20 univs and polys, 1973–81; Mem. Council, 1970–76, 1986–88, 1995–2001; Vice-Pres., 1987–88, 1995–97. Member: Architecture Bd, CNAA, 1975–81; Housing the Arts Cttee, Arts Council of GB, 1981–84; Lottery Awards Panel, Sports Council, 1995–97; Specialist Assessor, HEFCE, 1994–95; Hd, Lottery Architecture Unit, Arts Council of England, 1995–99. Finance Dir, HCL Ltd, 2003–05 and 2006–13. Chm., Soc. of Architect Artists, 1986–92; Pres., Architects Benevolent Soc., 2003–07 (Vice Pres., 2000–03, 2007–); Patron, Twentieth Century Soc., 2012–. Trustee: Montgomery Sculpture Trust, 2000–05; S Norfolk Buildings Preservation Trust, 2003–05. Hon. Treas., Harleston and Waveney Art Trail Collective, 2008–12. *Solo painting exhibitions:* Durham, and Covent Garden, 1977; Ditchling, 1994; Harleston, 2007; Spitalfields, London, 2010; Norwich, 2011. Hon. FAIA 2002 (Hon. AIA 1998). Glover Medal, Northern Architectl Assoc., 1949; Henry Bell Saint Bequest, Univ. of Durham, 1950; Crown Prize, Walpamur Co., 1951; Soane Medallion, 1954, Owen Jones Studentship prize, 1960, RIBA; President's Medal, AIA, 1998. *Publications:* Vivat Ware!: strategies to enhance a historic town, 1974; The Grassroot Developers: a handbook for town development trusts, 1979; *illustrated:* B. Allsopp, Decoration and Furniture, 1950; D. Senior, Your Architect, 1964; articles and reviews in prof. and technical pubns, 1961–. *Recreations:* work, painting, watching TV sport. *Address:* Camp 5, The Beeches, 13 London Road, Harleston, Norfolk IP20 9BH. *T:* and *Fax:* (01379) 854897. *E:* david.rock1@keme.co.uk.

**ROCK, Prof. Paul Elliot,** FBA 2000; Professor of Social Institutions, London School of Economics and Political Science, 1995–2008, now Emeritus; *b* 4 Aug. 1943; *s* of Ashley Rock and Charlotte (*née* Dickson); *m* 1965, Barbara Ravid (*d* 1998); two *s*. *Educ:* London School of Economics (BScSoc); Nuffield Coll., Oxford (DPhil). London School of Economics: Asst Lectr, 1967; Lectr, 1970; Sen. Lectr, 1976; Reader in Sociology, 1980; Reader in Social Institutions, 1981; Prof. of Sociology, 1986–95; Dir, Mannheim Centre for Study of Criminology and Criminal Justice, 1992–95. Visiting Professor: Princeton Univ., 1974–75; ANU, 2005–; Univ. of Macau, 2016–19; Univ. of Cambridge, 2017–18; Vis. Schol., Ministry of Solicitor Gen. of Canada, 1981–82; Fellow, Center for Advanced Study of Behavioral Scis, Stanford, Calif, 1996; Resident, Rockefeller Foundn Study Center, Bellagio, 2003; Vis. Prof. of Criminology, Univ. of Pennsylvania, 2006–10. Apptd by Cabinet Office to work on official history of criminal justice, 2009–14. FRSA 1997. DUniv Middx, 2000. *Publications:* Making People Pay, 1973; Deviant Behaviour, 1973; The Making of Symbolic Interactionism, 1979; (with D. Downes) Understanding Deviance, 1982, 7th edn 2016; A View from the Shadows, 1986; Helping Victims of Crime, 1990; The Social World of an English Crown Court, 1993; Reconstructing a Women's Prison, 1996; After Homicide, 1998; Constructing Victims' Rights, 2004; Victims, Policy-Making and Criminology Theory: selected essays, 2010. *Address:* London School of Economics and Political Science, Houghton Street, Aldwych, WC2A 2AE. *T:* (020) 7955 7296.

**ROCKEY, Patricia Mary, (Mrs D. C. Rockey);** *see* Broadfoot, P. M.

**ROCKLEY, 4th Baron** *cr* 1934, of Lytchett Heath, Dorset; **Anthony Robert Cecil;** *b* 29 July 1961; *o s* of 3rd Baron Rockley and Lady Sarah Cadogan (*d* 2017), *d* of 7th Earl Cadogan, MC; *S* father, 2011; *m* 1988, Katherine Jane, *d* of G. A. Whalley; one *s* two *d*. *Educ:* Eton; Gonville and Caius Coll., Cambridge (BA 1983; MA 1987). *Heir: s* Hon. William Evelyn Cecil, *b* 7 July 1996. *Address:* Lytchett Heath, Poole, Dorset BH16 6AE.

**ROCKLIN, David Samuel;** Chairman, Norton Opax, 1973–89; *b* 15 Aug. 1931; *s* of Alfred Rocklin and Ada Rebecca Rocklin; *m* 1955, Dorothy Ann (*d* 2011); two *s* two *d*. *Educ*: Hele's School, Exeter. Managing Director, Norton Opax, 1969–73. *Recreations*: books, travel, music, painting, good food and conversation.

**ROCKSAVAGE, Earl of; Alexander Hugh George Cholmondeley;** *b* 12 Oct. 2009; *er* twin *s* and *heir* of Marquess of Cholmondeley, *qv*.

**RODAN, Hon. Stephen Charles;** President of Tynwald, Isle of Man, since 2016 (Speaker, House of Keys, 2006–16); *b* 1954; *s* of Robert Rodan and Betty Rodan; *m* 1977, Ana Maria Valentina Ballesteros Torres, Mexico City; two *d*. *Educ*: High Sch., Glasgow; Univ. of Edinburgh; Heriot-Watt Univ. (BSc Hons Pharmacy 1977). MRPharmS 1978. Pharmacist, Elgin, Inverness, 1978–80; Pharmacy Manager, Bermuda, 1980–87; Pharmacy Proprietor, I of M, 1987–. Mem., Laxey Village Commn, 1991–95 (Chm., 1993–95). MHK, Garff, 1995–2016. Isle of Man Government: Chm., Planning Cttee, 1997–99; Minister: for Educn, 1999–2004; for Health and Soc. Security, 2004–06. Chairman: Liberal Club, Univ. of Edinburgh, 1974–76; Scottish Young Liberals, 1974–76; Mem. Nat. Exec., Scottish Liberal Party, 1975–77. Contested (Scots L) Moray and Nairn, 1979. Pres., Caledonian Soc. of Bermuda, 1983–85. Pipe Major, Cair Vie Manx Pipe Band, 1992–95. Chm., Laxey and Lonan Heritage Trust, 1995–2014. Pres., Laxey and Lonan Br., 1998–, Isle of Man Co., 2012–, RBL. *Recreations*: travel, Burns' suppers, pipes, friends and family. *Address*: Orry's Mount, Ballaragh Road, Laxey, Isle of Man IM4 7PE. *T*: and *Fax*: (01624) 861514. *E*: steve.rodan@gov.im.

**RODD,** family name of **Baron Rennell**.

**RODDA, James, (Jim),** FCA; Financial Director, National Film and Television School, 1996–2005; *s* of George Rodda and Ruby (*née* Thompson); *m* 1st, 1967, Angela Hopkinson (*d* 2014); one *s* two *d*; 2nd, 2015, Elizabeth Hardy. *Educ*: Maldon Grammar Sch.; Reading Univ. (BA Hons); Leicester Univ. (PGCE). FCA 1971 (prizewinner final Pt 2). Spicer and Pegler, 1967–71; Coopers and Lybrand, 1971–77; Thomas Cook Group, 1977–84; Lonconex Group, 1984–85; Mercantile Credit, 1985–86; London Commodity Exchange, 1986–91; Dir of Finance and Admin, House of Commons, 1991–96. Vol. Chm. then Treas., Berks, Bucks and Oxon Gp, 1994–97, Vol. Nat. Treas., 2006–10, Nat. Council for Conservation of Plants and Gardens, later Plant Heritage. *Recreations*: railway rambling, Chiltern Soc. (No HS2 across the Chilterns Campaign).

**RODDA, Dr John Carrol,** FRMetS; FRGS; President, International Association of Hydrological Sciences, 1995–2001; *b* 15 Aug. 1934; *s* of late J. Allen Rodda and Eleanor M. Rodda; *m* 1961, Annabel Brailsford Edwards; two *s*. *Educ*: UCW, Aberystwyth (BSc 1956; DipEd 1957; PhD 1960; DSc 1979). FRMetS 1961; MCIWEM 1976. DSIR Res. Fellow, 1960–62, Hydrologist, 1962–65, Hydraulics Res. Station, Wallingford; Hd, Catchment Res., Inst. Hydrology, Wallingford, 1965–69 and 1970–72; Consultant, WMO, Geneva, 1969–70 (on secondment); Head: Envmtl Pollution and Resources Unit, Directorate Gen. of Res., DoE, 1972–74; Data Acquisition Br., Water Data Unit, Reading, DoE, 1974–82; Asst Dir, Inst. Hydrology, Wallingford, 1982–88; Dir, Hydrology and Water Resources Dept, WMO, Geneva, 1988–95. Visiting Professor: Dept of Geog., Univ. of Strathclyde, 1976–79; Internat. Inst. for Infrastructure, Hydraulics & Envmt, Delft, 1976–97; Univ. of Perugia, 1983; Hon. Prof., Inst. Geog. and Earth Scis, Univ. of Aberystwyth (formerly Univ. of Wales, Aberystwyth), 1995–. Ed., 1972–79, Sec.-Gen., 1979–87, Internat. Assoc. Hydrological Sci.; Sec./Treas., ICSU/Union Internat. des Assocs et Organismes Techniques Cttee on Water Res., 1982–87; Mem., Scientific Cttee on Water Res., ICSU, 1991–95; Mem. Exec. Cttee, IUGG, 1995–2001. UN International Decade for Natural Disaster Reduction: Member: Prep. Cttee, 1988–90; Scientific and Tech. Cttee, 1990–95; Chm., UN Admin. Co-ordinating Cttee, Sub-cttee on Water Resources, 1990–92; Chairman: Prog. Rev. Gp IV, Centre for Ecol. and Hydrol., NERC, 1996–2000; Commn on Water, World Humanities Action Trust, 1998–2000; Member: Bd of Govs, World Water Council, 1999–2001; Regl Envmt Protection Adv. Cttee, Envmt Agency, 2007–11. Associate. Dir, Hydro-GIS Ltd, 2006–. Mem., Amer. Geophysical Union, 1960; Hon. Member: British Hydrological Soc., 1983; Amer. Water Resources Assoc., 1992; Hungarian Hydrological Soc., 1992. Chm., Oxon Agenda 21 Planning Gp, 1997–2001; Vice-Chm., Trust for Oxon's Envmt, 2001–03 (Mem. Bd, 1998–2000). Fellow, NERC Centre for Ecol. and Hydrol., 2004. FRGS 2003. Hon. Fellow, IUGG, 2015. Hugh Robert Mill Prize, RMetS, 1980; Internat. Hydrology Prize, Internat. Assoc. of Hydrol Scis/UNESCO/WMO, 2004. *Publications*: (jtly) Systematic Hydrology, 1976; (ed) Facets of Hydrology, 1976, Facets of Hydrology II, 1985 (trans. Russian); (jtly) Global Water Resource Issues, 1994; (ed jtly) Land Surface Processes in Hydrology: trials and tribulations of modeling and measurement, 1997; (ed jtly) World Water Resources at the Beginning of the Twenty-First Century, 2003; (ed jtly) The Basis of Civilisation - Water Science?, 2004; (ed jtly) The Role of Hydrology in Water Resources Management, 2009; (ed jtly) Progress in Modern Hydrology: past, present and future, 2015. *Recreations*: music, painting, environment. *Address*: Ynyslas, Brightwell cum Sotwell, Wallingford, Oxon OX10 0RG. *E*: jandarodda@waitrose.com.

**RODDA, Mathew Richard Allen;** MP (Lab) Reading East, since 2017; *b* 15 Dec. 1966; *m* Sarah; two *c*. *Educ*: Univ. of Sussex. Former journalist, Coventry Telegraph and Independent; civil servant, DFE; voluntary sector project manager. Mem. (Lab), Reading BC, 2011–. Shadow Minister for Buses, 2018–. Contested (Lab): E Surrey, 2010; Reading E, 2015. *Address*: House of Commons, SW1A 0AA.

**RODDAM;** *see* Holderness-Roddam.

**RODDEN, Prof. Thomas Anthony,** PhD; FREng; Professor of Computer Science, Nottingham University, since 2001; Chief Scientific Adviser, Department for Digital, Culture, Media and Sport, since 2019; *b* Glasgow, 18 Dec. 1962; *s* of Patrick and Bridget Rodden; *m* 2007, Boriana Koleva; two *d*. *Educ*: Univ. of Strathclyde (BSc Computer Sci. 1985); Univ. of Lancaster (PhD Computer Sci. 1990). Lectr, 1990–96, Prof. of Computer Sci., 1996–2001, Lancaster Univ.; on secondment from Univ. of Nottingham as Dep. Chief Exec., 2016–18, Dep. Exec. Chair, 2018–19, EPSRC. FREng 2018. *Address*: School of Computer Science, Jubilee Campus, Nottingham University, Nottingham NG8 2BB.

**RODDICK, (George) Winston,** CB 2004; QC 1986; Police and Crime Commissioner (Ind) for North Wales, 2012–16; Chairman, Association of Police and Crime Commissioners, 2015–16; *b* Caernarfon, 2 Oct. 1940; *s* of William and Aelwen Roddick; *m* 1966, Cennin Parry; one *s* one *d*. *Educ*: Sir Huw Owen GS, Caernarfon; Tal Handaq, Malta; University Coll. London (LLB, LLM). Called to the Bar, Gray's Inn, 1968, Bencher, 1997; a Recorder, 1987–2012; Counsel Gen. to Nat. Assembly for Wales, 1998–2003; Leader, Wales and Chester Circuit, 2007–10. Member: Gen. Council of the Bar, 1992–95 and 2007–12; Professional Conduct Cttee of the Bar, 1994–96; Employed Barristers Cttee, Bar Council, 2000–03; Chm., Bristol and Cardiff Chancery Bar Assoc., 1996–98. Hon. Recorder, Caernarfon, 2001–12. Member: ITC, 1998; S4C Authy, 2005–12. Member: Welsh Language Bd, 1988–93; Lord Chancellor's Adv. Cttee on Statute Law, 1999–2003; Standing Cttee on use of Welsh lang. in legal proceedings, 1999–2003. Vice Pres., Aberystwyth Univ. (formerly Univ. of Wales, Aberystwyth), 2000–11 (Hon. Fellow, 1999). Vice Pres., Caernarfon Male Voice Choir, 1994–. Patron, Caernarfon RFC, 1994–. Mem., Gorsedd of Bards, 2004–. *Recreation*: fishing. *Address*: 9 Park Place Chambers, Cardiff CF10 3DP. *T*: (029) 2038 2731; Ely Place Chambers, 13 Ely Place, EC1N 6RY. *Clubs*: Caernarfon Sailing, Caernarfon Bowls, Caernarfon Rugby.

**RODECK, Prof. Charles Henry,** DSc; FRCOG, FRCPath, FMedSci; Professor of Obstetrics and Gynaecology, University College London, 1990–2007, now Emeritus; *b* 23 Aug. 1944; *s* of Heinz and Charlotte Rodeck; *m* 1971, Elisabeth (*née* Rampton); one *s* one *d*. *Educ*: University College London (BSc Anatomy 1966; Fellow 2003); UCH Med. Sch. (MB BS 1969); DSc (Med) London 1991. MRCOG 1975; FRCOG 1987; FRCPath 1994. House appts to 1975; King's College Hospital Medical School: Registrar, 1975; Lectr, 1976; Sen. Lectr/Consultant, 1978; Dir, Harris Birthright Res. Centre for Fetal Medicine, 1983–86; Prof., Inst. of Obstetrics and Gynaecol., RPMS, Queen Charlotte's and Chelsea Hosp., 1986–90. Member, Council: Obst. and Gyn. Sect., RSocMed; British Assoc. of Perinatal Med.; RCOG, 1991–92, 1996–2001 (Chm., Subspeciality Bd, 1989–92); Mem., Working Party on Antenatal Diagnosis, RCP, 1986–89; Chm., Steering Gp for Fetal Tissue Bank, MRC, 1989–92; Mem., EEC Working Party on Chorion Villus Sampling, 1983–85; Mem., Antenatal Screening Subgroup, DoH, 2001–05. Examr, RCOG and Univs of Aberdeen, Brussels, Dublin, Leiden, London, Nottingham, Oxford, Reading, Singapore, Stockholm; Visiting Professor: USA Univs; Hong Kong Univ. Pres., Internat. Fetal Medicine and Surgery Soc., 1986; Chm., Assoc. of Profs of Obst. and Gyn., 1995–2000; Chm., Fedn of Assocs of Clinical Profs, 2000–07; Pres., Internat. Soc. for Prenatal Diagnosis, 2002–06. J. Y. Simpson Oration, 2000, William Meredith Fletcher Shaw Oration, 2002, Founder's Lect., 2010, RCOG. Founder FMedSci 1998. Hon. Member: Italian Soc. of Perinatol., 1982; Indian Soc. for Prenatal Diagnosis and Therapy, 1984; S African Soc. of Obstetrics and Gynaecol., 1985; British Assoc. of Perinatal Medicine, 1992; Soc. of Obstetrics and Gynaecol. of Nigeria, 1999; Soc. of Perinatol., Bogota, 2002. Hon. Fellow: Amer. Inst. of Ultrasound in Medicine, 1990; Soc. of Maternal Fetal Medicine of USA, 2008; Nat. Acad. of Medicine of Argentina, 2008. Mem., edit bds of professional jls, UK and overseas; Ed. for Europe, 1985–2005, Ed.-in-Chief, 2005–07, Prenatal Diagnosis. James Blundell Medal, British Blood Transfusion Soc., 2002; Eardley Holland Medal, RCOG, 2010; Ian Donald Gold Medal, Internat. Soc. of Ultrasound in Obst. and Gyn., 2014; Inaugural Pioneer Award, Internat. Soc. for Prenatal Diagnosis, 2018. *Publications*: (ed) Prenatal Diagnosis, 1984; (ed) Fetal Diagnosis of Genetic Defects, 1987; (ed) Fetal Medicine, 1989; (co-ed) Prenatal Diagnosis and Screening, 1992; (co-ed) Fetus and Neonate, 1993; (co-ed) Fetal Medicine: basic science and clinical practice, 1999, 2nd edn 2009; over 500 articles on prenatal diagnosis and fetal medicine. *Recreations*: stroking the cats, looking out of aeroplanes, the Wigmore Hall, Tottenham Hotspur. *Club*: Athenæum.

**RODEN, 10th Earl of,** *cr* 1771 (Ire.); **Robert Jocelyn;** Baron Newport 1743; Viscount Jocelyn 1755; Bt 1665; *b* 25 Aug. 1938; *s* of 9th Earl of Roden and Clodagh Rose (*d* 1989), *d* of Edward Robert Kennedy; *S* father, 1993; *m* 1st, 1970, Sara Cecilia (marr. diss. 1982), *d* of Brig. Andrew Dunlop; one *d*; 2nd, 1986, Ann Margareta Maria, *d* of Dr Gunnar Henning; one *s*. *Educ*: Stowe. *Heir*: *s* Viscount Jocelyn, *qv*.

**RODEN, Michael;** Principal, University of Birmingham School, 2014–18; *b* Rotherham, S Yorks, 15 Oct. 1959; *s* of Stanley and Kathleen Freda Roden; *m* 1982, Alison Mary Tonks; two *s* one *d*. *Educ*: Swinton Comprehensive Sch., Rotherham; Manchester Univ. (BSc Geog., PGCE). NPQH 2003. Asst Master, King Edward's Sch., Birmingham, 1982–89; Hd of Geog., Bristol GS, 1990–95; Dep. Headmaster, King Edward VI Camp Hill Sch. for Boys, 1995–2003; Asst Headmaster, King Edward's Sch., Birmingham, 2003–08; Headmaster, King Edward VI Camp Hill Sch. for Boys, Birmingham, 2008–14. Pres., Camp Hill Old Edwardian's Assoc., 2009–14. *Recreations*: golf, reading crime novels, running, Rugby, travel, ski-ing. *Address*: 84 Green Lanes, Wylde Green, Birmingham B73 5JJ. *E*: mroden2018@gmail.com. *Clubs*: Marston Lakes Golf (Sec., 2004–08, Captain, 2007); Whittington Heath Golf; Camp Hill Rugby Football (Pres., 2008–14), Camp Hill Old Edwardian's Cricket (Pres., 2008–14).

**RODENBURG, Prof. John Marius,** PhD; FRS 2019; CPhys, FInstP; Professor, Department of Electronic and Electrical Engineering, University of Sheffield, since 2003; *b* Bromley, Kent, 19 May 1960; *s* of Marius, (Max), Rodenburg and Margaret Edna Rodenburg (*née* Moody); *m* 2003, Cornelia, (Conny), Schonjahn; one *s* one *d*. *Educ*: Tonbridge Sch.; Univ. of Exeter (BSc 1st Cl. Hons Physics and Electronics 1982); Univ. of Cambridge (PhD Detection and Interpretation of electron microdiffraction patterns 1986). FRMS 2002; CPhys 2003; FInstP 2003. University of Cambridge: Res. Asst, 1986–88; Royal Soc. Res. Fellow, 1988–99; Res. Fellow, 1986–88, Fellow, 1988–99, New Hall; Prof. of Materials Analysis, Sheffield Hallam Univ., 1999–2003. Director: Redcastle Exchange Ltd, 1997–99; Phase Focus Ltd, 2006–15. *Publications*: contrib. scientific papers. *Recreations*: listening to music (favourite composers include Mahler, Sibelius and Prokofiev), walking, reading, especially Russian literature and books that attempt to explain macroeconomics, thinking in the bath. *Address*: Sheffield, S Yorks. *E*: J.M.Rodenburg@shef.ac.uk.

*See also* P. A. Rodenburg.

**RODENBURG, Prof. Patricia Anne, (Patsy),** OBE 2005; Head of Voice, since 1981, and Professor, since 2014, Guildhall School of Speech and Drama; Head of Voice, Royal National Theatre, 1990–2006; *b* 2 Sept. 1953; *d* of late Marius Rodenburg and Margaret Edna Rodenburg (*née* Moody). *Educ*: St Christopher's Sch., Beckenham; Central Sch. of Speech and Drama. Voice Tutor, Royal Shakespeare Co., 1981–90; Head of Voice, Stratford Fest. Theatre, Canada, 1984–85; Associate: Michael Howard Studios, NY, 1994–; Royal Court Theatre, 1999–; Founding Dir, Voice and Speech Centre, London, 1989–; works regularly with Almeida Theatre, Shared Experience, Cheek-by-Jowl, Théâtre de Complicité, Donmar Warehouse; works extensively in theatre, TV and radio throughout Europe, N America, Australia, Africa and Asia with major theatre and opera cos. Presenter, writer and producer, DVD, Shakespeare in the Present, 2011. Distinguished Vis. Prof., Southern Methodist Univ., Dallas, 1987–. Mem. Bd, RSC, 2014–. Dir, Cicero Project, Laurus Trust. *Publications*: The Right to Speak, 1992; The Need for Words, 1993; The Actor Speaks, 1997; Speaking Shakespeare, 2002; Presence, 2007; Power, Presentation, 2009; Shakespeare in the present, 2012. *Recreations*: travelling, reading. *Address*: c/o Guildhall School of Music and Drama, Silk Street, Barbican, EC2Y 8DT.

**RODERICK, Edward Joseph;** Co-Chairman, Envestors (MENA) Ltd, 2008–13; Group Chief Executive, Christian Salvesen PLC, 1997–2004; *b* 23 Oct. 1952; *s* of late Edward Deakin Roderick and Joan Roderick; *m* 1974, Denise Ann Rowan; two *s*. *Educ*: De La Salle Grammar Sch., Liverpool. National/International CPC, FCIL (FILog 1992). B&I Line, 1972–87 (Head, UK Freight Ops, 1984–87); Man. Dir, Alexandra Molyneux Transport, 1987–88; BET plc, 1988–90: Man. Dir, IFF, 1988–90; Gp Dir, UTCH Ltd, 1988–90; Director: UTL Ltd, 1988–90; Seawheel, 1988–90; Gen. Manager, UK and Iberia, Bell Lines, 1990–92; Divl Man. Dir, Hays Network Distribn and other directorships in Hays plc, 1992–95; Man. Dir, Industrial Div., 1996–97, Man. Dir, Logistics UK and Europe, 1997, Christian Salvesen PLC. Dir, Heywood Williams Gp plc, 2002–07. Non-executive Director: Liquid of Life Dubai, 2009–; Cash For Mobiles Dubai, 2010–11. Chairman: Passim Internat. Ltd, 2005–07; Truck Project Ltd, 2005–08. Director: Road Haulage

Assoc., 1998–2000; Freight Transport Assoc., 2000–07. Sen. Vice-Pres., Global Logistics Agility Inc., 2007–08. Dir, Northern Ballet Theatre, 1997–2000. MInstD 1987; CCMI (CIMgt 2000). Distinguished Fellow, Hult Internat. Business Sch., 2011. Hon. LLD De Montfort, 2001. *Recreations:* golf, opera, ballet, swimming, wife and family. *Address:* Campbell House, Northampton Road, Higham Ferrers, Rushden, Northants NN10 6AL. *T:* (01933) 419148. *Clubs:* Royal Automobile; Wellingborough Golf.

**RODERICK, Lindsey Ruth;** *see* George, L. R.

**RODGER, Prof. Albert Alexander,** DSc, PhD; FICE; FREng; FRSE; FGS; Professor of Civil Engineering, University of Aberdeen, 1995–2014 (Personal Chair of Civil Engineering, 1995–97), now Emeritus; *b* Greenock, Renfrewshire, 12 May 1951; *s* of Alexander Rodger and Grace Rodger; *m* 1973, Jane Helen Whyte; two *d*. *Educ:* Duncanrig Sch., East Kilbride; Univ. of Aberdeen (BSc 1st Cl. Engrg 1973; PhD 1976; DSc 2014). FGS 1975; CEng 1983; FICE 2001; FREng 2010. Res. Scientist, Cementation Research Ltd, 1977–79; University of Aberdeen: Lectr, 1979–89; Sen. Lectr, 1989–95; Dean, Sci. and Engrg, 2001–03; Vice Principal and Hd, Coll. of Physical Scis, 2003–11; Vice Principal, External Affairs, 2011–14. Vis. Prof. of Civil and Envmtl Engrg, Univ. of Strathclyde, 2015–17. Dir, Northern Res. Partnership of Univs, 2005–10. Mem. Bd, SFC, 2009–17. CEO, Nat. Subsea Res. Inst., 2009–11. Hon. Citizen, Hadong County, Rep. of Korea, 2014. FRSE 2016. (Jtly) Halcrow Premium, ICE, 1997; Silver Medal, RAEng, 2000. *Recreation:* photography. *Address:* 7 Mill Lade Wynd, Aberdeen AB22 8QN. *T:* (01224) 820761. *E:* a.a.rodger@abdn.ac.uk.

**RODGER, Martin Owen;** QC 2006; Deputy President, Upper Tribunal (Lands Chamber), since 2013; a Recorder, since 2003; a Deputy High Court Judge, since 2016; *b* 11 Feb. 1962; *s* of William Rodger and Elizabeth Rodger (*née* Tunney); *m* 1991, Catherine Murphy; two *s* one *d*. *Educ:* St Aloysius Coll., Glasgow; University Coll., Oxford (BA 1983). Called to the Bar, Middle Temple, 1986. *Address:* Upper Tribunal (Lands Chamber), 5th floor, Rolls Building, 7 Rolls Buildings, Fetter Lane, EC4A 1NL. *T:* (020) 7612 9700. *E:* deputychamberpresident.rodger.qc@ejudiciary.net.

**RODGER, Mary Elizabeth;** *see* Francis, M. E.

**RODGER, Prof. Nicholas Andrew Martin,** DPhil; FBA 2003; FSA, FRHistS; Senior Research Fellow, All Souls College, Oxford, 2008–17, now Emeritus Senior Research Fellow; *b* 12 Nov. 1949; *s* of Lt Comdr Ian Rodger and Sara Rodger; *m* 1982, Susan Eleanor Farwell; three *s* one *d*. *Educ:* Ampleforth Coll., York; University Coll., Oxford (BA 1971, MA; DPhil 1974). FRHistS 1980; FSA 1985. Asst Keeper, PRO, 1974–91; Anderson Sen. Res. Fellow, Nat. Maritime Mus., 1992–99; Sen. Lectr in Hist., 1999–2000, Prof. of Naval Hist., 2000–08, Exeter Univ. Lees-Knowles Lectr, Trinity Coll., Cambridge, 2018. Hon. PhD Thessaly, 2006; Hon. DLitt Buckingham, 2016. *Publications:* The Admiralty, 1979; (ed with G. A. Osbon) The Black Battlefleet, by G. A. Ballard, 1980; Exchequer Ancient Deeds DD Series, 1101–1645 (E211), 1983; Naval Records for Genealogists, 1985, 3rd edn 1998; (ed) The Naval Miscellany, Vol. V, 1985; The Wooden World: an anatomy of the Georgian Navy, 1986, 2nd edn 1988; (ed with G. J. A. Raven) The Anglo-Dutch Relationship in War and Peace 1688–1988, 1990; The Insatiable Earl: a life of John Montagu, Fourth Earl of Sandwich, 1718–1792, 1993; (ed jtly) British Naval Documents 1204–1960, 1993; (ed) Naval Power in the Twentieth Century, 1996; The Safeguard of the Sea: a naval history of Britain, Vol. I, 660–1649, 1997; (ed) Memoirs of a Seafaring Life: the narrative of William Spavens, 2000; The Command of the Ocean: a naval history of Britain, Vol. II, 1649–1815, 2004; (ed with R. Cock) A Guide to the Naval Records in the National Archives, 2006; Essays in Naval History, from Medieval to Modern, 2009; (ed) The Sea in History, Vol. IV, The Modern World, 2017. *Address:* All Souls College, Oxford OX1 4AL. *T:* (01865) 279379, *Fax:* (01865) 279299. *E:* Nicholas.Rodger@all-souls.ox.ac.uk.

**RODGERS,** family name of **Baron Rodgers of Quarry Bank**.

**RODGERS OF QUARRY BANK,** Baron *cr* 1992 (Life Peer), of Kentish Town in the London Borough of Camden; **William Thomas Rodgers;** PC 1975; Chairman, Advertising Standards Authority, 1995–2001; Leader, Liberal Democrats, House of Lords, 1998–2001; *b* 28 Oct. 1928; *s* of William Arthur and Gertrude Helen Rodgers; *m* 1955, Silvia (*d* 2006), *d* of Hirsch Szulman; three *d*. *Educ:* Sudley Road Council Sch.; Quarry Bank High School, Liverpool; Magdalen College, Oxford (Open Exhibnr in Modern History). General Secretary, Fabian Society, 1953–60; publisher's editor, 1961–64, 1970–72; management recruiter, 1972–74. Contested: (Lab) Bristol West, March 1957; (SDP) Stockton N, 1983; (SDP/Alliance) Milton Keynes, 1987. MP (Lab 1962–81, SDP 1981–83) Stockton-on-Tees, 1962–74; Teesside, Stockton, 1974–83; Parly Under-Sec. of State: Dept of Econ. Affairs, 1964–67, Foreign Office, 1967–68; Leader, UK delegn to Council of Europe and Assembly of WEU, 1967–68; Minister of State: BoT, 1968–69; Treasury, 1969–70; MoD, 1974–76; Sec. of State for Transport, 1976–79. Chm., Expenditure Cttee on Trade and Industry, 1971–74. Vice-Pres., SDP, 1982–87. Dir-Gen., RIBA, 1987–94. Borough Councillor, St Marylebone, 1958–62. Hon. FRIBA 1994; Hon. FIStructE 1993. Hon. Fellow, Liverpool John Moores Univ., 2008. Hon. LLD Liverpool, 2008. *Publications:* Hugh Gaitskell, 1906–1963 (ed), 1964; (jt) The People into Parliament, 1966; The Politics of Change, 1982; (ed) Government and Industry, 1986; Fourth Among Equals, 2000; pamphlets, etc. *Address:* 43 North Road, N6 4BE.

**RODGERS, Sir (Andrew) Piers (Wingate),** 3rd Bt *cr* 1964, of Groombridge, Kent; Secretary, Royal Academy of Arts, London, 1982–96; *b* 24 Oct. 1944; second *s* of Sir John Rodgers, 1st Bt and Betsy (*d* 1998), *y d* of Francis W. Aikin-Sneath; *S* brother, 1997; *m* 1st, 1979, Marie Agathe Houette (marr. diss. 2004); two *s*; 2nd, 2004, Ilona Medvedeva; two *d*. *Educ:* Eton Coll.; Merton Coll., Oxford (BA 1st Cl. Honour Mods, Prox. acc. Hertford and De Paravicini Prizes). J. Henry Schroder Wagg & Co. Ltd, London, 1967–73: Personal Asst to Chairman, 1971–73; Director, International Council on Monuments and Sites (ICOMOS), Paris, 1973–79; Consultant, UNESCO, Paris, 1979–80; Member, Technical Review Team, Aga Khan Award for Architecture, 1980, 1983; Secretary, UK Committee of ICOMOS, 1981. Trustee, The Type Mus., London, 1991–2004 (Dir, 2001–04). Mem. Bd, Warburg Inst., Univ. of London, 1993–98. FRSA 1973. Mem., Court of Assts, Masons' Co., 1982–. Chevalier de l'Ordre des Arts et des Lettres (France), 1987; Chevalier de l'Ordre National du Mérite (France), 1991; Cavaliere dell'Ordine al Merito della Repubblica Italiana, 1992. *Publications:* articles on protection of cultural heritage. *Recreations:* books, music, Real tennis, Islamic art. *Heir: s* Thomas Rodgers, *b* 18 Dec. 1979. *Address:* Peverell, Bradford Peverell, Dorset DT2 9SE. *Club:* Brooks's.

**RODGERS, Bríd;** Director, Bord Bia, 2004–10; *b* 20 Feb. 1935; *d* of Tom Stratford and Josephine (*née* Coll); *m* 1960, Antoin Rodgers; three *s* three *d*. *Educ:* St Louis Convent, Monaghan; University Coll., Dublin (BA Hons Mod. Langs; Higher DipEd). Exec. Mem., NI Civil Rights Assoc., 1970–71. Mem., Irish Senate, 1983–87. Mem. (SDLP), Craigavon BC, 1985–93. Social Democratic and Labour Party: Vice Chair, 1976–78; Chair, 1978–80; Gen. Sec., 1981–83; Delegate to Brooke/Mayhew Talks, 1991–92; elected in Upper Bann to Negotiations, 1996, Chair, Negotiating Team, 1996–98; Dep. Leader, 2001–04. Mem. (SDLP) Upper Bann, NI Assembly, 1998–2003. Minister of Agriculture & Rural Develt, NI, 1999–2002. Contested (SDLP) Tyrone West, 2001. Hon. LLD NUI, 2003; Hon. DLitt Harper Adams, 2009. *Recreations:* reading, music, golf. *Address:* 34 Kilmore Road, Lurgan, Co. Armagh BT67 9BP.

**RODGERS, Derek;** *see* Rodgers, His Honour R. F.

**RODGERS, Joan,** CBE 2001; soprano; *b* 4 Nov. 1956; *d* of Thomas and Julia Rodgers; *m* 1st, 1988, Paul Daniel, *qv* (marr. diss. 2005); two *d*; 2nd, 2013, Alan Samson. *Educ:* Univ. of Liverpool (BA Hons Russian); RNCM. FRNCM. Kathleen Ferrier Meml Scholarship, 1981. Début, Aix-en-Provence, 1982; Covent Garden début, 1984; NY Met. début, 1995; has appeared with all major British opera cos; has worked with many conductors, incl. Barenboim, Solti, Abbado, Rattle, Gardiner, Colin Davis, Andrew Davis, Salonen, Mehta, Harnoncourt; Mozart rôles incl. Susanna, Zerlina, Ilia, Fiordiligi, Elvira, Sandrina, Countess; other rôles incl. Cleopatra in Giulio Cesare, Ginevra in Ariodante, Tatyana in Eugene Onegin, Mélisande, Theodora, Governess in The Turn of the Screw, Marschallin in Der Rosenkavalier, Blanche in The Carmelites; regular recitals and concert performances in London, Australia, Vienna, Madrid, Los Angeles, New York, Chicago, Paris and Brussels; many recordings. Hon. DMus Liverpool, 2005. Evening Standard Award for outstanding perf. in opera, 1997. *Recreations:* walking, spending time with my family, birdwatching, gardening, supporting Arsenal FC. *Address:* c/o Groves Artists, 7 St George's Court, 131 Putney Bridge Road, SW15 2PA.

**RODGERS, Dr Patricia Elaine Joan;** Permanent Secretary, Ministry of Tourism, Commonwealth of the Bahamas, 2013; *b* 13 July 1948; *d* of late Dr Kenneth V. A. Rodgers, OBE and Anatol C. Rodgers, MBE. *Educ:* Univ. of Aberdeen (MA Hons English, 1970); Inst. of Internat. Relations, St Augustine, Trinidad (Dip. in Internat. Relns (Hons) 1972); Inst. Univ. des Hautes Etudes Internationales, Geneva (PhD 1977). Joined Ministry of Foreign Affairs, Nassau, Bahamas, 1970; Minister-Counsellor, Washington, 1978–83; Actg High Comr to Canada, 1983–86, High Comr, 1986–88; High Comr to UK, 1988–92, also Ambassador (non-resident) to: FRG and Belgium, 1988–92, to EC and France, 1989–92; Perm. Rep. to IMO, 1991–92; Chief of Protocol, Min. of For. Affairs, 1993–94; Permanent Secretary: Min. of Tourism, 1995–2003; Min. of For. Affairs, 2003–07; Cabinet Office, 2007–08; Min. of For. Affairs, 2008–12. Janet Bostwick Medal for Women in Foreign Service (Bahamas), 2014. *Publications:* Mid-Ocean Archipelagos and International Law: a study of the progressive development of international law, 1981. *Recreations:* folk painting, gourmet cooking, theatre.

**RODGERS, Paul David;** Group Commercial Director, Department for Transport, since 2018; *b* Manchester, 21 June 1962; *s* of John Rodgers and Lillian Rodgers; *m* (marr. diss.); one *s* one *d*. *Educ:* Univ. of Southampton (BA Hons Archaeol.). MCIPS 2010. Shell UK, 1989–99; Regl Commercial Manager, Great Western, 1999–2003; Hd, Passenger Business, Network Rail, 2003–04; Department for Transport: Divl Manager, Midlands, 2004–08; Prog. Dir, 2008–11; Director: Rail Commercial, 2011–14; HS2 Commercial Ops, 2014–18. Trustee Dir, Mus. of London Archaeology, 2019–. *Recreations:* hillwalking, beekeeping. *Address:* Department for Transport, 33 Horseferry Road, SW1P 4DR. *T:* 07769 960269, *Fax:* (020) 7944 2446. *E:* paul.rodgers@dft.gov.uk.

**RODGERS, Sir Piers;** *see* Rodgers, Sir A. P. W.

**RODGERS, His Honour Robert Frederick, (Derek);** a County Court Judge, Northern Ireland, 1997–2012; *b* 10 June 1947; *s* of Fred and Peggy Rodgers; *m* 1973, Kathleen Mary Colling; one *s* one *d*. *Educ:* Royal Belfast Academical Instn; Queen's Univ., Belfast (LLB 1970). J. C. Taylor & Co., solicitors, 1970–89; a Dep. District Judge, 1986–89; a District Judge, 1989–97. Parole Comr for Northern Ireland (formerly Life Sentence Review Comr), 2002–15. Mem., Legal Adv. Cttee, C of I, 2002–. Chancellor, Diocese of Connor, 2007–. *Recreations:* reading, music, Rugby. *Club:* Ulster Reform.

**RODHAM, Ven. Morris;** Priest-in-charge, Patterdale, since 2019; *b* 1959. *Educ:* Hatfield Coll., Durham (BA 1981); St John's Coll., Durham (PGCE 1985); Trinity Coll., Bristol (MA 1993). Ordained deacon, 1993, priest, 1994; Asst Curate, St Mark, New Milverton, 1993–97; Vicar, St Mary's, Leamington Priors, 1997–2010; Rural Dean, Warwick and Leamington, 2006–09; Archdeacon of Warwick, and Archdeacon Missioner, Dio. of Coventry, 2010–19.

**RODHOUSE, Paul Gregory Kenneth,** PhD, DSc; FLS; British Antarctic Survey Emeritus Fellow, since 2013; *b* Bromley, Kent, 13 Feb. 1951; *s* of Kenneth Frederick Rodhouse and Eileen Frances Rodhouse; *m* 1991, Laura Matthews; two *s* one *d*. *Educ:* St Mary's Coll., Southampton; Westfield Coll., Univ. of London (BSc Hons 1972); Univ. of Southampton (MSc 1973; PhD 1977; DSc 1995). Cambridge and London Galapagos Is Expedn, 1972; Res. Scientist, University Coll., Galway/NUI, 1977–82; Res. Associate and Lectr, SUNY at Stony Brook, 1982–84; British Antarctic Survey: Res. Scientist, 1985–2000; Hd, Biol Scis Div. and Mem. Bd, 2000–10; Student Registrar, 2010–13; Principal Scientist, S Georgia Govt Lab. at King Edward Point, 2001–13. Hon. Prof., Univ. of Aberdeen, 2001–16. Mem., Innovation and Strategy Bd, NERC, 2010–13. Pres., Cephalopod Internat. Adv. Council, 1997–2000. Chair, Scientific Cttee for Antarctic Res. prog. on evolution in the Antarctic, 1999–2004. Sen. Mem., St Edmund's Coll., Cambridge, 2003–. Mem. Exec. Cttee, S Georgia Assoc., 2014–. Trustee, Gilbert White's House and the Oates Collection, 2010–. FLS 1988. *Publications:* (with M. Drummond) The Yachtsman's Naturalist, 1980; (ed jtly) Squid Recruitment Dynamics, 1998; (with P. R. Boyle) Cephalopods: ecology and fisheries, 2005; contrib. papers to learned jls. *Recreations:* yachting, painting, natural history, angling, photography. *Address:* British Antarctic Survey, High Cross, Madingley Road, Cambridge CB3 0ET. *E:* p.rodhouse@bas.ac.uk.

**RODNEY,** family name of **Baron Rodney**.

**RODNEY,** 11th Baron *cr* 1782; **John George Brydges Rodney;** Bt 1764; *b* 5 July 1999; *o s* of 10th Baron Rodney and of Jane, *d* of Hamilton Rowan Blakeney; *S* father, 2011. *Educ:* Eton. *Heir:* kinsman Nicholas Simon Harley Rodney, *b* 20 Dec. 1947.

**RODNEY, Philip Emanuel;** Chairman, Burness Paull LLP, 2012–18 (Chairman, Burness LLP, 2005–12); *b* Glasgow, 25 Aug. 1953; *s* of Peter Rodney and Joan Rodney; *m* 1993, Cherie Lisus; three *s*. *Educ:* Giffnock Primary Sch.; High Sch., Glasgow; Univ. of Strathclyde (LLB). Partner: Alexander Stone & Co., 1979–98; Burness, 1998–2004. Chm. of Govs, Glasgow Sch. of Art, 2010–13. *Recreations:* music, cars, travel.

**RODRIGUES, Christopher John,** CBE 2007; Chairman: British Bobsleigh & Skeleton Association Ltd, since 2013; Openwork Ltd, since 2014; Port of London Authority, since 2016; British Council, since 2016; *b* 24 Oct. 1949; *s* of late Alfred John Rodrigues and of Joyce Margaret Rodrigues (*née* Farron-Smith); *m* 1973, Priscilla Purcell Young; one *s* one *d*. *Educ:* University College Sch.; Jesus Coll., Cambridge (BA Econs and Hist.; Pres., Cambridge Univ. Boat Club, 1971; rowing Blue, 1970 and 1971); Harvard Business Sch. (Baker Scholar; MBA 1976). With Spillers Foods, London, 1971–72; Foster Turner & Benson, London, 1972–74; McKinsey & Co., London, 1976–79; American Express, NY and London, 1979–88; Thos Cook Gp, 1988–95 (Chief Exec., 1992–95); Gp Chief Exec., Bradford & Bingley Bldg Soc., subseq. plc, 1996–2004; Chief Exec., Visa Internat., San

Francisco, 2004–06. Chm., Internat. Personal Finance, 2007–15; non-executive Director: Energis PLC, 1997–2002; Hilton Gp, 2003–06; Ladbrokes plc, 2006–13. Non-exec. Dir, FSA, 1997–2003. Chm., VisitBritain, 2007–17; Exec. Cttee Mem., World Travel and Tourism Council, 2007–17 (Vice Chm., 2016–17; Global Ambassador, 2018–). Chm., Almeida Th., 2008–16. National Trust: Mem. Council (formerly Exec. Cttee), 1994–2004, 2010–16; Trustee, 2012–16. Chm., Windsor Leadership Trust, later Windsor Leadership, 2007–15. FRSA 1994. Steward, Henley Royal Regatta, 1998–. *Recreations:* cooking, skiing, rowing, shooting, opera, ballet. *Address:* c/o Port of London Authority, Pinnacle House, 23–26 St Dunstan's Hill, EC3R 8HN. *Clubs:* Garrick; Leander Rowing (former Chm.) (Henley); Hawks (Cambridge); Century (Harvard); Brook (NY).

**RODRÍGUEZ IGLESIAS, Gil Carlos;** Arbitrator, 20 Essex Street Chambers; *b* 26 May 1946; *m* 1972, Teresa Díez Gutiérrez; two *d. Educ:* Oviedo Univ. (LLL 1968); Madrid Autonomous Univ. (doctorate 1975). Internat. law asst, then Lectr, Oviedo, Freiburg, Madrid Autonomous and Madrid Complutense Univs, 1969–82; Professor: Madrid Complutense Univ., 1982–83; Granada Univ., 1983–2003 (on leave 1986–2003); Judge, EC Court of Justice, 1986–2003; Pres., Court of Justice of Eur. Communities, 1994–2003. Prof. of Internat. Public Law, Madrid Complutense Univ., 2003. Dir, Real Instituto Elcano, Madrid, 2005–12. Hon. Bencher: Gray's Inn, 1995; King's Inns, Dublin, 1997. Hon. Dr: Univ. of Turin, 1996; Univ. of Babes-Bolyai' Cluj-Napoca, Romania, 1996; Univ. of Saarbrücken, Germany, 1997; Univ. of Oviedo, 2001; St Clement of Ohrid Univ. of Sofia, 2002; Univ. of Cádiz, 2010; Univ. of Granada, 2012; Hon. Dip. Romanian Acad., 2002. Walter-Hallstein Prize, City of Frankfurt, Johann-Wolfgang-Goethe Univ. of Frankfurt, and Dresdner Bank, 2003. Encomienda de la Orden de Isabel la Católica (Spain), 1976; Cruz de Honor de la Orden de San Raimundo de Peñafort (Spain), 1986; Gran Cruz, Orden del Mérito Civil (Spain), 1999; Grand Cross: Order of the Phoenix (Greece), 2001; Nat. Order of Star (Romania), 2002; Order of Merit (Luxembourg), 2004; Order of Isabel la Católica (Spain), 2005; Grande Ufficiale, Ordine al Merito (Italy), 2002. *Publications:* El régimen jurídico de los monopolios de Estado en la Comunidad Económica Europea, 1976; various articles and studies on EC law and internat. law.

**RODRÍGUEZ-MÚNERA, (José) Mauricio;** Ambassador of Colombia to the Court of St James's, 2009–13; *b* Bogotá, 5 March 1958; *s* of Jorge Rodríguez and Cecilia Múnera; *m* 2009, Sugey Pinzón-Alonso; two *s. Educ:* Colegio de Estudios Superiores de Administration, Bogota (BA Business Admin). Founder and Dir, Portafolio newspaper, 1993–2007; journalist for Caracol Radio, El Tiempo, El Espectador and Poder Magazine, 2007–09. Professor, Universidad de Los Andes, Bogota, 1982–2009; Professor, 1982–2009, Pres., 2007–09, Colegio de Estudios Superiores de Administration, Bogota. *Publications:* Brujulas Empresariales, I, 2004, II, 2005, III, 2007; Brujulas Curiosas, 2006; Geografía Económica de Colombia, 2006; Perfiles Empresariales, 2007. *Recreations:* reading, writing, enjoying art and classical music.

**RODRÍGUEZ-POSE, Prof. Andrés,** PhD; Professor of Economic Geography, London School of Economics and Political Science, since 2004; *b* Madrid, 9 June 1966; *s* of José Luis Rodríguez and Josefina Pose; *m* 1997, Leticia Verdú; one *s* one *d. Educ:* Complutense Univ. of Madrid (BA Geog. and Hist. 1989; PhD *summa cum laude* Geog. 1993); Universidad Nacional de Educación a Distancia (LLB Law 1991); Inst. of European Studies, Brussels (MSc dist. Eur. Studies 1991); European University Inst., Florence (PhD with dist. Soc. and Pol Scis 1996). Res. Dir, Cabinet for Planning and Spatial Develt, Galician Regl Govt, 1994–95; Lectr, 1995–2000, Sen. Lectr, 2000–02, Reader, 2002–04, in Econ. Geog., LSE. Vis. Prof. on Growth and Cohesion, College of Europe, Bruges, 2004–; Professorial Res. Fellow, Social Scis, Instituto Madrileño de Estudios Avanzados, 2009–; Leverhulme Trust Major Res. Fellow, 2009–. Vice Pres., Eur. Regl Sci. Assoc., 2012–17 (Sec., 2001–06); Vice Pres., 2014, Pres., 2015–16, Regl Sci. Assoc. Internat. Member, Board of Trustees: Internat. Centre for Advanced Econ. and Soc. Studies, Madrid, 2005–; Madrid Inst. for Advanced Studies, 2006–; Enterprise LSE Ltd, 2006–. Man. Ed., Envmt and Planning C: Govt and Policy, 2008–. Gill Meml Award, RGS, 2001. *Publications:* Reestructuración socioeconómica y desequilibrios regionales en la Unión Europea, 1995; The Dynamics of Regional Growth in Europe: social and political factors, 1998; The European Union: economy, society, and polity, 2002 (L'Unione Europea: economia, politica e società, 2003); (jtly) Local and Regional Development, 2006; (jtly) Handbook of Local and Regional Development, 2010; Innovation and Regional Growth in the European Union, 2011; more than 70 articles in learned jls. *Recreations:* reading, spending time with family and friends, swimming, listening to music (especially classical, R&B, rock, disco, funk). *Address:* Department of Geography and Environment, London School of Economics, Houghton Street, WC2A 2AE. *T:* (020) 7955 7971, *Fax:* (020) 7955 7412. *E:* a.rodriguez-pose@lse.ac.uk.

**RODRÍGUEZ ZAPATERO, José Luis;** Member, Council of State, Spain, since 2012; former President, Advisory Board, Institute for Cultural Diplomacy, Berlin; *b* 4 Aug. 1960; *m*; two *d. Educ:* Univ. of León (Law Degree). Mem. (PSOE) for León, Congress of Deputies, 1986–2011. Sec. Gen., Socialist Fedn of León, 1988–2000; Pres., Socialist Parly Gp, Congress of Deputies, 2000–04; Vice-Pres., Socialist Internat., 2003. Prime Minister of Spain, 2004–11. Mem., PSOE, 1979–, Sec. Gen., 2000–12.

**RODWAY, Susan Caroline;** QC 2002; two *s* two *d. Educ:* Cheltenham Ladies' Coll.; King's Coll., London (BA Hons); City Univ. (Dip. in Law). Accredited Mediator, 2000. Called to the Bar, Middle and Inner Temple, 1981, Bencher, 2009. Lay Mem., Clinical Standards Cttee, Guy's and St Thomas's NHS Trust, 1998–2001. Dep. Chm., NHS Tribunals, 2000–04. Mem., Professional Negligence Cttee, 2001–, and Personal Injuries Cttee, Bar Assoc. *Publications:* (contrib.) Application of Neural Networks in Clinical Practice, 2000; numerous articles and lectures. *Recreations:* motorcycling, riding. *Address:* 39 Essex Chambers, 81 Chancery Lane, WC2A 1DD. *E:* susan.rodway@39essex.com.

**RODWELL, His Honour Daniel Alfred Hunter;** QC 1982; a Circuit Judge, 1986–2002; *b* 3 Jan. 1936; *s* of late Brig. R. M. Rodwell, AFC, and Nellie Barbara Rodwell (*née* D'Costa); *m* 1967, Veronica Ann Cecil; two *s* one *d. Educ:* Munro Coll., Jamaica; Worcester Coll., Oxford, 1956–59 (BA Law). National service, 1954–56; 2/Lieut 1st West Yorks, PWO, 1955; TA, 1956–67: Captain and Adjt 3 PWO, 1964–67. Called to Bar, Inner Temple, 1960. A Deputy Circuit Judge, 1977 and 2002–05; a Recorder, 1980–86. *Recreations:* gardening, sailing. *Address:* The Old Surgery, 16 West Street, Buckingham MK18 1HP.

**RODWELL, Dr Warwick James,** OBE 2009; FSA, FSAScot, FRHistS; consultant archaeologist and architectural historian; *b* 24 Oct. 1946; *s* of late George and Olive Rodwell; *m* 1st, 1972, Kirsty Gomer (marr. diss. 1983); 2nd, 1984, Christine Bensted (marr. diss. 1999); 3rd, 2004, Diane Marie Gibbs. *Educ:* Southend High Sch. for Boys; Univ. of Nottingham (teaching cert. and dip. 1968); Univ. of London (BA Hons 1972; DLit 1998); Worcester Coll., Oxford (DPhil 1976; DLitt 1992); Univ. of Birmingham (MA 1979). FSAScot 1965; FSA 1977; FRHistS 1992. Res. Asst, MPBW, 1968–69; Dir, Cttee for Rescue Archaeol. in Avon, Glos and Somerset, 1975–81. Vis. Prof. in Archaeol., Univ. of Reading, 2002–. Consultant Archaeologist: Glastonbury Abbey, 1976–2005; Bristol Cath., 1976–2010; Wells Cath., 1977–2014; Lichfield Cath., 1982–2009; Westminster Abbey, 2004–. Directed major res. projs and/or excavations at Westminster Abbey, Dorchester Abbey, Lichfield Cath., Wells Cath. and parish churches at Barton-upon-Humber, Hadstock, Kellington and Rivenhall; directed res. and excavation campaigns in Jersey at Mont Orgueil Castle, Elizabeth Castle, Les Ecréhous Priory, St Lawrence Ch, St Helier Ch, Fishermen's Chapel and Hamptonne Farm. Member: Council for the Care of Churches, 1976–86; Cathedrals Adv. Commn, 1981–90; Cathedrals Fabric Commn for England, 1991–96; Member, Fabric Advisory Committee: Salisbury Cath., 1987–2006; Exeter Cath., 1999–2006. Mem., Coll. of Westminster Abbey, 2008–. Pres., Bristol and Gloucester Archaeol. Soc., 1999–2000. Trustee, Bath Archaeol. Trust, 1976–2005. Hon. Mem., La Société Jersiaise, 1998. Hon. BSc Loughborough, 2009. Frend Medal, Soc. of Antiquaries, 1988. *Publications:* Small Towns of Roman Britain (with T. Rowley), 1975; Historic Churches: a wasting asset, 1977; Temples, Churches and Religion in Roman Britain, 1980; Archaeology of the English Church, 1981, 3rd edn 2005; (with J. Bentley) Our Christian Heritage, 1984; (with K. Rodwell) Rivenhall: investigations of a villa, church and village, vol. 1 1985, vol. 2 1993; The Fishermen's Chapel, Jersey, 1990; Origins and Early Development of Witham, Essex, 1993; Les Ecréhous, Jersey, 1996; (with M. Paton and O. Finch) La Hougue Bie, Jersey, 1999; Archaeology of Wells Cathedral, 2001; Westminster Abbey Chapter House and Pyx Chamber, 2002; Church Archaeology, 2005; Mont Orgueil Castle, Jersey, 2006; (with G. Leighton) Architectural Records of Wells by John Carter 1784–1808, 2006; Dorchester Abbey, Oxfordshire, 2009; Jersey's Houses, Castles and Churches, 2009; (with R. Mortimer) Westminster Abbey Chapter House, 2010; The Lantern Tower of Westminster Abbey, 1060–2010, 2010; St Peter's, Barton-upon-Humber: a parish church and its community, 2011; The Archaeology of Churches, 2012; The Coronation Chair and Stone of Scone, 2013; (with T. Tatton-Brown) Westminster: the art, architecture and archaeology of the Royal Abbey and Palace, 2015; (with D. S. Neal) The Cosmatesque Mosaics of Westminster Abbey, 2019; numerous contribs to learned jls and multi-author vols. *Recreations:* visiting historic buildings, horology, bibliophilia, family history. *Address:* 2c Little Cloister, Westminster Abbey, SW1P 3PA.

**ROE, Maj. Gen. Andrew Michael,** PhD; Chief Executive, Defence Academy, and Commandant, Joint Services Command and Staff College, since 2019; *b* Keighley, 23 Oct. 1971; *s* of Michael and Susan Roe; *m* 1995, Philippa. *Educ:* US Army Comd and Gen. Staff Coll. (Master of Mil. Art and Sci., Gen. Studies 2005, Theatre Ops 2006); King's Coll. London (PhD 2009). Commnd Yorks Regt (Green Howards), 1992; operational tours in NI, Bosnia, Afghanistan and Iraq; SO, 3rd UK Div., 2006–08; OC, C Co., 2nd Bn, 2008–10, Yorks Regt; MA to Sgt, 2010–11; CO, 2nd Bn, 2011–13, Yorks Regt (Green Howards); Commander: Operational Trng and Adv. Gp, 2013–15; 38 (Irish) Bde, 2015–17; Dir, Higher Comd and Staff Course, 2017–19. *Publications:* Waging War in Waziristan: the British struggle in the land of Bin Laden, 1849–1947, 2010; From Fabric Wings to Supersonic Fighters and Drones: a history of military aviation on both sides of the North-West Frontier, 2015. *Recreations:* fly fishing, anything to do with the great outdoors, Indian history, walking.

**ROE, Catherine Mary;** Director, CMR Consult Ltd, since 2006; *b* Dar Es Salaam, Tanzania, 13 April 1961; *d* of Michael and Nancy Roe; one *d. Educ:* Wycombe High Sch.; Balliol Coll., Oxford (BA Hist. 1983); London Business Sch. (MBA 2005); Sch. of Oriental and African Studies, Univ. of London (MA Near and Middle Eastern Studies 2015). FCO, 1983–91; Pres. Dir Gen., Safinvest France (SA), 1992–94; Chief Exec., Saïd Foundn, 1992–2004; Dir, Saïd Business Sch. Foundn, 1998–2004; Associate, 2009–15, Strategic Advr, 2015–, More Partnership. Mem. Bd, 2012–18, Mem., Global Leadership Council, 2017–, Saïd Business Sch., Univ. of Oxford. Trustee: Prisoners of Conscience Appeal Fund, 1993–2000; Saïd Foundn, 2008–; Doorstep Library Network, 2009–15; Beanstalk, 2011–17; Internat. Inst. for Strategic Studies, 2016–; Horizon Foundn, 2016–. *Recreations:* theatre, opera, Muslim arts, walking my dog, reading, cooking. *E:* catherine.roe@cmrconsult.co.uk.

**ROE, Chang Hee;** Senior Advisor, Federation of Korean Industries, 1998–2003; *b* 25 Feb. 1938; *m* 1963, Chung Ja Lee; one *s* one *d. Educ:* Seoul Nat. Univ., Korea (BA Econ 1960). Joined Min. of Foreign Affairs, 1960: Instructor ROK Air Force Acad., 1962–66; Dir of Legal Affairs, 1968–69; First Sec., Korean Embassy, Canada, 1969–72; Private Sec. to Minister of Foreign Affairs, 1972–73; Dir, Treaties Div., 1973–75; Counsellor, Sweden, 1975–78; Dep. Dir-Gen., American Affairs Bureau, 1978–80; Dir-Gen., Treaties Bureau, 1980–82; Minister and Dep. Chief of Mission, USA, 1982–85; Ambassador to Nigeria, 1985–88; Sen. Protocol Sec. to Pres., 1988–91; Ambassador and Perm. Rep. to UN, 1991–92; Vice Minister of Foreign Affairs, 1992–93; Ambassador to UK, 1993–96; Ambassador at Large, 1996–98. Guest Prof., Hanseo Univ., Korea, 1998–2001. Gov., Asia Europe Foundn, 2001–05. *Recreations:* golf, ski-ing. *Address:* Hanyang Apt 62–606, Apkujong-dong, Kangnam-gu, Seoul 135–110, Korea.

**ROE, David John,** CBE 2001; organisation and leadership consultant, since 2011; Director, Innovation Capability (formerly Public Sector Innovation), Department for Business, Innovation and Skills, 2009–11; *b* 26 Nov. 1958; *s* of Malcolm Roe and late Pauline Roe (*née* Baker); partner, Alison Mary Sharpe; one *s. Educ:* Selwyn Coll., Cambridge (BA 1981); Queen Mary Coll., London (MA 1983); Roffey Park Inst. (MSc 2012). Export Credits Guarantee Dept, 1983–85; DTI, 1985–92; HM Treasury, 1992–2000: Hd, Internat. Financial Instns, 1994–97; Hd, Financial Regulatory Reform, 1997–2000; on secondment to Charities Aid Foundn, 2001–02; Prime Minister's Strategy Unit, 2002–03; Department for Culture, Media and Sport: Hd, Strategy, Policy and Delivery, 2003–05; Dir, Strategy, 2005–07; Dir, Change, 2007–08; Dir, Corporate Services, 2008–09. UK Alternate Dir (pt-time), EBRD, 1995–97. Parent Gov., Fielding Primary Sch., 2005–12. Chair, Brentham Colts FC, 2015–18. *Recreations:* playing golf, watching Brentford Football Club, being at the seaside, books, football management.

**ROE, Geoffrey Eric,** FRAeS; Director, Air Tanker Ltd, 2000–03 (Chairman, 2002–03); *b* 20 July 1944; *s* of Herbert William Roe and Florence Roe (*née* Gordon); *m* 1968, Elizabeth Anne Ponton; one *s* one *d. Educ:* Tottenham Grammar Sch. FRAeS 1996. Min. of Aviation, 1963; Finance (R&D) Br., 1963–67; Asst Private Sec. to Sir Ronald Melville, 1967–69; Exports and Internat. Relations Div., Min. of Technology, 1969–74; Guided Weapons Contracts Branch, 1974–76; seconded British Aerospace, 1976–78; Rocket Motor Exec., 1978–81; Asst Dir Contracts (Air), 1981–86; Dir of Contracts (Underwater Weapons), 1986–89; Head, Material Co-ord. (Naval), 1989–90; Principal Dir, Navy and Nuclear Contracts, 1990–91; Director-General: Defence Contracts, MoD, 1991–95; Commercial, MoD, 1995; Aircraft Systems 2, 1995–96. Man. Dir, FR Aviation Gp (formerly FR Aviation Ltd), 1997–2002; Director: Cobham plc, 1997–2002; FR Aviation Services Ltd, 2000–02; FBS Ltd, 2000–02; FBH Ltd, 2000–02; Brown Shutters Farm Airfield Ltd, 2016–. Chm., Nat. Jet Systems, Australia, and Nat. Air Support, Australia, 2000–02. Dir, SBAC, 1998–2000. Mem., Light Aircraft Assoc., 1990–. *Recreations:* ski-ing, sailing, flying and maintaining a homebuilt aircraft (Jodel D18). *Address:* Pond Barton, Norton St Philip, Bath BA2 7NE.

**ROE, Prof. Howard Stanley James,** DSc; Director, Southampton Oceanography Centre, NERC and the University of Southampton, 1999–2005; Professor, University of Southampton, 2000–05, now Emeritus; *b* 23 May 1943; *s* of Eric James Roe and Freda Mary Roe (*née* Perkins); *m* 1970, Heather Anne Snelling (*d* 2015); one *s* two *d. Educ:* Bedford

Sch.; University Coll. London (BSc 1st Cl. Hons Zool. 1965; DSc Biol Oceanography 1998). Natural Environment Research Council: Scientific Officer, Whale Res. Unit, 1965–68; transferred to Biol. Dept, Nat. Inst. Oceanography, 1968; Project Co-ordinator for develt of Southampton Oceanography Centre, 1989–95; Hd, George Deacon Div., Inst. Oceanographic Scis, later Southampton Oceanography Centre, 1993–99 (Dep. Dir, 1997–99). Public Orator, Univ. of Southampton, 2008–10. Chairman: NERC Project Bd, RRS James Cook, 2002–07; Partnership for Observing the Global Ocean, 2003–05; DEFRA Science Audit of CEFAS, 2005–06. Member: Council for Ocean Policy Studies, Ship and Ocean Foundn, Japan, 2003–13; Natural Scis Adv. Gp, English Nature, 2003–05; Exec. Cttee, Sargasso Sea Alliance, 2010–14 (Mem. Bd, 2011–14); Sargasso Sea Commn, 2014– (Chair, 2014–16); Search and Evaluation Cttee, Inst. for Basic Sci., Korea, 2014–16. Non-exec. Mem., Marine Sci. Co-ordination Cttee, DEFRA, 2009–13. Chm., Ext. Rev. Cttee, Seoul Nat. Univ., 2002–15. Mem., Challenger Soc. for Marine Sci. FIMarEST, 2003. Member: Lymington Naturalists Soc., 2017–; New Forest Probus Club. POGO Award, 2008. *Publications:* (ed jtly) Of Seas and Ships and Scientists, 2010; contrib. numerous papers and reports to jls, etc, dealing with whale biology, biological oceanography and develt of sampling technol., conservation and biology of the Sargasso Sea. *Recreations:* fishing, gardening, travel, theatre, sailing. *Address:* National Oceanography Centre Southampton, Empress Dock, Southampton SO14 3ZH; Barton Mere, Barton Court Avenue, New Milton, Hants BH25 7HD. *T:* (01425) 622092. *Clubs:* Christchurch Angling; Ringwood Fly Dressers; Hurst Castle Sailing.

**ROE, Dame Marion (Audrey),** DBE 2004; *b* 15 July 1936; *d* of William Keyte and Grace Mary (*née* Bocking); *m* 1958, James Kenneth Roe (*d* 2017); one *s* two *d*. *Educ:* Bromley High Sch. (GPDST); Croydon High Sch. (GPDST); English Sch. of Languages, Vevey, Switzerland. Member: London Adv. Cttee, IBA, 1978–81; Gatwick Airport Consultative Cttee, 1979–81; SE Thames RHA, 1980–83. Member (C): Bromley Borough Council, 1975–78; for Ilford N, GLC, 1977–86 (Cons. Dep. Chief Whip, 1978–82). Contested (C) Barking, 1979; MP (C) Broxbourne, 1983–2005. Parly Private Secretary to: Parly Under-Secs of State for Transport, 1985; Minister of State for Transport, 1986; Sec. of State for Transport, 1987; Parly Under Sec. of State, DoE, 1987–88. Member, Select Committee: on Agriculture, 1983–85; on Social Services, 1988–89; on Procedure, 1990–92; on Sittings of the House, 1991–92; Chairman: Select Cttee on Health, 1992–97 (Mem., 1988–89, 2000–01); H of C Admin. Cttee, 1997–2005 (Mem., 1991–97); Mem., Speaker's Panel of Chairmen, 1997–2005. Vice Chairman: All-Party Fairs and Showgrounds Gp, 1992–2005 (Jt Chm., 1989–92); All-Party Parly Garden Club, 1995–2005; All-Party Gp on Alcohol Misuse, 1997–2005; All-Party Gp on Domestic Violence, 1999–2005; Chairman: All-Party Hospice Gp, 1992–2005 (Sec., 1990–92); Jt Chm., All-Party Gp on Breast Cancer, 1997–2005; Member: H of C Liaison Cttee, 1992–2005; H of C Finance and Services Cttee, 1997–2005; UNICEF Parly Adv. Cttee, 2002–05. Chairman: Cons. Back bench Horticulture and Markets Sub-Cttee, 1989–97 (Sec., 1983–85); Cons. Back bench Social Security Cttee, 1990–97 (Vice-Chm., 1988–90); Vice-Chairman: Cons. Back bench Environment Cttee, 1990–97; Cons. Parly Health Cttee, 1997–99; 1922 Cttee, 2001–05 (Mem. Exec., 1992–94; Sec., 1997–2001); Sec., Cons. Back bench Horticulture Cttee, 1983–85; Jt Sec., Cons. Back bench Party Orgn Cttee, 1985; Vice-Chm., British-Canadian Parly Gp, 1997–2005 (Sec., 1991–97); Mem., Adv. Cttee on Women's Employment, Dept of Employment, 1989–92; Substitute Mem., UK Delegn to Parly Assemblies of Council of Europe and WEU, 1989–92; Mem., Exec. Cttee, UK Br., CPA, 1997–2005 (Vice Chm., 2002–03); Inter-Parliamentary Union: Mem. Exec. Cttee, British Gp, 1997–98, 2001–05 (Vice-Chm., 1998–2001); Mem., Internat. Panel on Prohibition of Female Genital Mutilation, 2002–05. Chm., Nat. Council for Child Health and Well-being (formerly Child Health Gp), 2001–; Vice-Pres., Women's Nationwide Cancer Control Campaign, 1985–87, 1988–2001; Patron: UN Women UK (formerly UK Nat. Cttee for UN Develt Fund for Women), 2004–15 (Mem., 1985–87); Hospice of Hope, Romania, Serbia and Moldova, 2005–; Gov., Research into Ageing Trust, 1988–97; Managing Trustee, Parly Contributory Pension Fund, 1990–97; Mem., Internat. Women's Forum, 1992–2005; Trustee, Nat. Benevolent Fund for the Aged, 1999–2016 (Chm., 2010–16). Vice-President: Capel Manor Horticultural and Envmtl Centre, 1994– (Chm., Trust Fund, 1989–94). Hoddesdon Soc., 2005–16. Pres., Broxbourne Parly Cons. Assoc., 2013– (Pres., Women's Section, 1983–2015; Patron, 2006–13). Mem. Council, Wine Guild of the UK, 2007–17 (Companion, 2017). Hon. Life Mem., Showmen's Guild of GB, 2005–. Fellow, Industry and Parlt Trust, 1990. Freeman: City of London, 1981; Borough of Broxbourne, 2005; Liveryman, Gardeners' Co., 1993–. Hon. MIHort 1993. *Recreations:* family, theatre, ballet, opera, travel.
*See also* Baroness Couttie.

**ROE, Prof. Nicholas Hugh,** DPhil; FBA 2017; Wardlaw Professor of English Literature, University of St Andrews, since 2017 (Professor of English Literature, 1996–2017); *b* Fareham, 14 Dec. 1955; *s* of Dennis Roe and Stella Mary Roe; *m* 1990, Susan Jane Stabler; one *s*. *Educ:* Royal Grammar Sch., High Wycombe; Trinity Coll., Oxford (BA 1978; DPhil 1985). Lectr in English, QUB, 1982–85; University of St Andrews: Lectr in English, 1985–93; Reader, 1993–96; Founder and Dir, St Andrews Poetry Festival, 1986–92. Visiting Professor: Univ. of São Paulo, 1988; Victoria Univ., Wellington, NZ, 2011, 2012; Univ. of Malta, 2015–18; Ashoka Univ., New Delhi, 2016; Leverhulme Res. Fellow, 1993–94; Joan Nordell Fellow, Harvard Univ., 2009. Director: Coleridge Summer Conf., 1994–2010; Wordsworth Summer Conf., 2010–; Trustee: Keats-Shelley Meml Assoc., 1997–2015; Wordsworth Conf. Foundn, 2007–; Wordsworth Trust, 2011–18; Chm., Keats Foundn, 2011–. Hon. Life Mem., Japan Soc. for English Romanticism, 2018. Hon. FEA 2006; FRSE 2009. Editor: Romanticism, 1995–; Keats-Shelley Review, 2008–15. Dist. Schol. Award, Keats-Shelley Assoc. of America, 2014. *Publications:* (ed jtly) Coleridge's Imagination, 1986; Wordsworth and Coleridge: the radical years, 1988; (ed) William Wordsworth: selected poetry, 1992; The Politics of Nature, 1992, 2nd edn 2002; (ed) Keats and History, 1995; (ed) Selected Poems of John Keats, 1995; John Keats and the Culture of Dissent, 1997; (ed) Samuel Taylor Coleridge and the Sciences of Life, 2002; (ed) Leigh Hunt: life, poetry, politics, 2003; Fiery Heart: the first life of Leigh Hunt, 2005; (ed) Romanticism: an Oxford guide, 2005; (ed) English Romantic Writers and the West Country, 2010; John Keats: a new life, 2012; (ed) John Keats and the Medical Imagination, 2018. *Recreations:* walking, railways, aircraft, Scottish Borders, Malta. *Address:* School of English, University of St Andrews, St Andrews, Fife KY16 9AR. *T:* (01334) 462666. *E:* nhr@st-and.ac.uk.

**ROE, Thomas Idris;** QC 2014; *b* St Albans, 3 June 1972; *s* of Philip Roe and Joy Roe; *m* 2002, Helen Berry; three *s* one *d* (and one *s* decd). *Educ:* St Albans Sch.; Downing Coll., Cambridge (BA 1994). FCIArb 2010. Called to the Bar, Middle Temple, 1995; in practice as barrister, 1996–; Jun. Counsel to the Crown, 2010–14. Member: British-German Jurists' Assoc.; Commonwealth-in-England Barristers' Assoc. *Publications:* (with M. Happold) Settlement of Investment Disputes under the Energy Charter Treaty, 2011; (contrib.) International Investment Law: sources of rights and obligations, 2012; various contribs to Cambridge Law Jl, Modern Law Rev., New Law Jl, Turkish Commercial Law Rev. *Recreations:* family, reading, classical music, travel, foreign languages. *Address:* 3 Hare Court, Temple, EC4Y 7BJ. *T:* (020) 7415 7800. *E:* thomasroe@3harecourt.com.

**ROE, William Deas,** CBE 2010; Chairman: Highlands and Islands Enterprise, 2004–12; Skills Development Scotland, 2008–10; *b* Perth, Scotland, 9 July 1947. *Educ:* Edinburgh Univ. (BSc). Chm., Rocket Sci. UK Ltd, 2004–09. Scotland Comr, UK Commn for Employment and Skills, 2008–12. Non-exec. Dir, Deptl Bd, DWP, 2011–15. Chair: British Council Scotland, 2015–19; Grameen Scotland Foundn, 2015–18; Dir, Highland Hangout Ltd, 2019–; Trustee, British Council, 2017–19. FRSA. DUniv Open, 2009. *Recreations:* sailing, ski-ing, hill-walking, visual arts, music, travel, restoring a garden. *Address:* Duirinish Oaks, Duirinish, Wester Ross IV40 8BE. *T:* 07771 930880. *E:* willyroe@gmail.com.

**ROEBUCK, Roy Delville;** barrister-at-law; *b* Manchester, 25 Sept. 1929; *m* 1957, Dr Mary Ogilvy Adams (*d* 1995); one *s*. *Educ:* various newspapers; Inns of Court Sch. of Law; Univ. of Leicester (LLM 1997; MA 2000). Called to the Bar, Gray's Inn, 1974. Served RAF (National Service), 1948–50 (wireless operator, FEAF). Journalist, Stockport Advertiser, Northern Daily Telegraph, Yorkshire Evening News, Manchester Evening Chronicle, News Chronicle, Daily Express, Daily Mirror and Daily Herald, and Asst Ed., Forward, 1950–66; freelance journalist, 1966–; columnist, London Evening News, 1968–70. Contested (Lab): Altrincham and Sale, 1964 and Feb. 1965; Leek, Feb. 1974. MP (Lab) Harrow East, 1966–70; Member, Select Committee: on Estimates, 1968–70; on Parly Comr, 1968–70; aide to Rt Hon. George Wigg, Paymaster-Gen., 1966–67, to Lord Wigg, Pres. of Betting Office Licensees Assoc., 1975–83. Founder Mem., Labour Common Market Safeguards Cttee, 1967. Member: Islington CHC, 1988–92; Bd of Governors, Moorfields Eye Hospital, 1984–88. Fellow, Atlantic Council, 1993–. Governor, Thornhill Sch., Islington, 1986–88. *Recreations:* tennis, ski-ing, music, reading Hansard and the public prints. *Address:* 12 Brooksby Street, N1 1HA. *T:* (020) 7607 7057. *Clubs:* Royal Automobile, Victory Services, Union Jack.

**ROFE, Christopher Henry;** Secretary and Chief Executive, Reform Club, since 2017; *b* London, 16 Jan. 1965; *s* of late Brian Henry Rofe and of Margaret Anne Rofe; *m* 1991, Julie; one *d* (one *s* decd). *Educ:* Royal Shrewsbury Sch.; Loughborough Univ. (BSc Hons Recreation Mgt 1987); Kingston Univ. (MBA 1997). Visitor Ops Manager, Science Mus., 1993–98; Dep. Dir Ops, New Millennium Experience Co. (The Dome), 1999–2001; Gen. Manager, Bourne Leisure, 2001–03; Dir of Ops, BM, 2003–08; CEO, Royal Instn of GB, 2009–17. Mem., Grocers' Co. *Recreations:* golf, football, sailing. *Address:* Banstead, Surrey. *T:* 07764 761372. *E:* chris.rofe@btinternet.com. *Club:* Royal Automobile.

**ROFF, Derek Michael,** OBE 1972; HM Diplomatic Service, retired; *b* 1 Aug. 1932; *m* 1957, Diana Susette Barrow; three *s*. *Educ:* Royal Grammar Sch., Guildford; St Edmund Hall, Oxford (BA). National Service with The Cameronians (Scottish Rifles) and King's African Rifles, 1952–54. ICI Ltd, 1958–67; entered Foreign Office, 1967; Consul (Economic), Frankfurt, 1968; First Sec., UK Delegn to the European Communities, Brussels, 1970; Consul (Economic), Düsseldorf, 1973; First Sec., FCO, 1977; Counsellor, FCO, 1981–92. Regl Dir, BESO, 1993–97. Mem., Internat. Cttee, Leonard Cheshire, 1997–2005.

**ROFFE, Melvyn Westley;** Principal, George Watson's College, Edinburgh, since 2014; *b* Derby, 15 June 1964; *s* of late Brian Roffe and of Vera Roffe (*née* Hickinbotham); *m* 1988, Catherine Stratford; one *s* one *d*. *Educ:* Noel-Baker Sch., Derby; Univ. of York (BA Eng. and Related Lit. 1985); Univ. of Durham (PGCE 1986). English Master, Oundle Sch., 1986–93; Monmouth School: Hd of English, 1993–97; Dir of Studies, 1997–2001; Headmaster, Old Swinford Hosp., Stourbridge, 2001–07; Principal, Wymondham Coll., 2007–14. Chairman: State Boarding Schs' Assoc., 2004–06; Boarding Schs' Assoc., 2008–09. Chm., Lay Adv. Panel, 2001–06, Lay Trustee, 2001–06, Coll. of Optometrists. Member: Corp., City Coll., Norwich, 2009–13; Royal Merchants' Co. (formerly Merchants' Co.), City of Edinburgh, 2015–; Adv. Cttee, Duke of Edinburgh's Award in Scotland, 2015–. Trustee: Thetford Learning Trust, 2010–13; ESU Scotland, 2014–19; Director: SCIS, 2015–17; Scottish Parent Teaching Council, 2017–. Hon. Pres., Norwich and Norfolk ESU, 2011–14. FRSA 2001. Hon. FCOptom 2008. Mem., E Northants DC, 1991–93; Mayor of Oundle, 1993; Burgess, City of Edinburgh, 2019. Contested (Lib Dem) Corby, 1992. *Recreations:* travel, cultural pursuits, historic transport, observing politics. *Address:* George Watson's College, Colinton Road, Edinburgh EH10 5EG. *T:* (0131) 446 6000. *E:* melvynroffe@hotmail.com. *Clubs:* National Liberal, Caledonian, Lansdowne.

**ROGAN,** family name of **Baron Rogan**.

**ROGAN,** Baron *cr* 1999 (Life Peer), of Lower Iveagh in the county of Down; **Dennis Robert David Rogan;** Leader, Ulster Unionist Party in House of Lords, since 2001; President, Ulster Unionist Party, 2004–06 (Chairman, 2000–04); *b* 30 June 1942; *s* of Robert Henderson Rogan and Florence Rogan; *m* 1968, Lorna Elizabeth Campbell; two *s*. *Educ:* Wallace High Sch., Lisburn; Belfast Inst. of Technol.; Open Univ. (BA). Moygashel Ltd, 1960–69; Wm Ewart & Co., 1969–72; Lamont Holdings plc, 1972–78; Chairman: (exec.) Associated Processors Ltd, 1985–; Stakeholder Communications Ltd, 2005–; Stakeholder Events Ltd, 2005–; Dep. Chm., Ind. News & Media (NI) Ltd, 2000–08. Member, International Advisory Board: Ind. Newspapers, 2001–08; Parker Green Internat., 2008–. Chm., Lisburn Unit of Mgt, Eastern Health Bd, 1984–85. Dep. Chm. of Cttees, 2017–, Dep. Lord Speaker, 2018–, H of L. Chairman: Ulster Young Unionist Council, 1968–69; S Belfast UU Constituency Assoc., 1992–96. Member: UK Br., CPA, 1999–; IPU, 2002–. Gov., Westminster Foundn for Democracy, 2005–08. Mem., Council, RFCA (NI), 2002–. Patron, Somme Assoc., 2000–. Hon. Col, 40 (Ulster) Signals Regt, 2006–10. *Recreations:* Rugby football, oriental carpets, shooting, gardening. *Address:* 31 Notting Hill, Belfast BT9 5NS. *T:* (028) 9066 2468. *Clubs:* Army and Navy; Ulster Reform (Belfast).

**ROGAN, Prof. Eugene Lawrence,** PhD; FBA 2017; Professor of Modern Middle Eastern History, University of Oxford, since 2015; Fellow, St Antony's College, Oxford, since 1991; *b* Burbank, Calif, 31 Oct. 1960; *s* of Richard Grant Rogan and Margaret Jane Rogan; *m* 1995, Prof. Ngaire Tui Woods, *qv*; one *s* one *d*. *Educ:* Columbia Univ. (BA Econs 1982); Harvard Univ. (MA Middle Eastern Studies 1984; PhD Hist. and Middle Eastern Studies 1991). Univ. Lect in Mod. Hist. of Middle East, Faculty of Oriental Studies, Univ. of Oxford, 1991–2015. *Publications:* Frontiers of the State in the late Ottoman Empire: Transjordan, 1850–1921, 1999; (ed with Avi Shlaim) The War for Palestine, 2001, 2nd edn 2007; The Arabs: a history, 2009, 2nd edn 2017; The Fall of the Ottomans: the Great War in the Middle East, 1914–1920, 2015. *Recreations:* sailing, ski-ing. *Address:* St Antony's College, Oxford OX2 6JF. *T:* (01865) 284773, *Fax:* (01865) 274529. *E:* eugene.rogan@sant.ox.ac.uk.

**ROGAN, Rev. Canon John;** Chaplain of St Mark's, Lord Mayor's Chapel, Bristol, 1999–2008; Canon Residentiary, 1983–93, and Chancellor, 1989–93, Bristol Cathedral (Precentor, 1983–89), Canon Emeritus since 1993; *b* 20 May 1928; *s* of William and Jane Rogan; *m* 1953, Dorothy Margaret Williams (*d* 2016); one *s* one *d*. *Educ:* Manchester Central High School; St John's Coll., Univ. of Durham. BA 1949, MA 1951; DipTheol with distinction, 1954; BPhil 1981. Education Officer, RAF, 1949–52. Asst Curate, St Michael and All Angels, Ashton-under-Lyne, 1954–57; Chaplain, Sheffield Industrial Mission, 1957–61; Secretary, Church of England Industrial Cttee, 1961–66; Asst Secretary, Board for Social Responsibility, 1962–66; Vicar of Leigh, Lancs, 1966–78; Sec., Diocesan Bd for Social Responsibility, 1967–74, Chm. 1974–78; Rural Dean of Leigh, 1971–78;

Hon. Canon of Manchester, 1975–78; Provost, St Paul's Cathedral, Dundee, 1978–83; Bishop's Adviser in Social Responsibility, dio. Bristol, 1983–93. *Publications:* (ed jtly) Principles of Church Reform: Thomas Arnold, 1962; (ed) Bristol Cathedral: history and architecture, 2000; Reading Roman Inscriptions, 2006; Roman Provincial Administration, 2011; Mysterious Deaths, 2012. *Recreations:* music, reading. *Address:* 84 Concorde Drive, Bristol BS10 6PX.

ROGÉ, Pascal; pianist; *b* Paris, 6 April 1951; two *s*. *Educ:* Paris Conservatoire. Débuts in Paris and London, 1969. Soloist with leading orchestras worldwide. Specialist in music of Ravel, Poulenc, Debussy and Satie. Piano duo with wife, Ami Rogé. Numerous recordings. *Address:* Rue du Château 7, 1354 Montcherand, Switzerland.

ROGERS, family name of Barons Lisvane and Rogers of Riverside.

ROGERS OF RIVERSIDE, Baron *cr* 1996 (Life Peer), of Chelsea in the Royal Borough of Kensington and Chelsea; **Richard George Rogers**, CH 2008; Kt 1991; RA 1984 (ARA 1978); RDI 2014; RIBA; architect; Senior Partner, Rogers Stirk Harbour + Partners LLP (formerly Richard Rogers Architects Ltd), UK, Sydney and Shanghai; Director, River Cafe Restaurant, London; *b* 23 July 1933; *s* of Dada Geiringer and Nino Rogers; *m* 1st, 1961, Su Rogers; three *s*; 2nd, 1973, Ruth Elias (*see* Lady Rogers of Riverside); one *s* (and one *s* decd). *Educ:* Architectural Assoc. (AA Dipl.); Yale Univ. (MArch; Fulbright and Yale Scholar). Reith Lectr, 1995. Winner of numerous internat. competitions incl. for Centre Pompidou, Paris, 1971–77; Lloyd's HQ, City of London, 1978. Major internat. work includes: *masterplanning:* River Arno, Florence, 1983; Royal Docks, London, 1984–86; Potsdamer Platz, Berlin, 1991; Shanghai, 1992; Shanghai Pu Dong District, 1994; Parc BIT, Mallorca, 1994; South Bank, 1994–95; Dunkirk, 1998; E Manchester, 1999; Greenwich Peninsula, 2000; Bankside, 2000–05; Singapore, 2001; Almada, Portugal, 2002; Woolston Shipyard, Southampton, 2003–05; Wembley, London, 2003–06; Granada, Spain, 2004–; Wood Wharf, London, 2004–08; Valladolid Alta Velocidad, Spain, 2005–08; *buildings:* PA Technology, Cambridge, 1975–83; Centre Pompidou, Paris, 1977; IRCAM, Paris, 1977; Fleetguard Manufacturing Centre, Quimper, France, 1981; PA Technology, Princeton, NJ, 1984; Patscentre, Princeton, 1985; Linn Products, Glasgow, 1987; Inmos Microprocessor Factory, Newport, 1987; Billingsgate Securities Market, London, 1988; Thames Wharf Studios and Thames Reach Housing, 1989; Marseille Airport, 1992; Reuters Data Centre, London, 1992; Europier, Terminal 1, Heathrow Airport, 1993; Kabuki-Cho, Tokyo, 1993; Channel 4 HQ, London, 1994; European Court of Human Rights, Strasbourg, 1995; Thames Valley Univ., Slough, 1996; VR Techno offices and lab., Gifu, Japan, 1998; Bordeaux Law Courts, 1998; Amano Res. Labs, Gifu, Japan, 1999; Daimler Chrysler, Berlin, 1999; Law Courts, Bordeaux, 1999; Millennium Dome, Greenwich, 1999; 88 Wood Street, London, 2000; Ashford Retail Designer Outlet, 2000; Lloyd's Register of Shipping, London, 2000; Montevetro Residential, London, 2000; Broadwick Street, London, 2002; Minami Yamashiro Sch., Kyoto, 2003; First Base Housing, 2004; Paddington Waterside, London, 2004; Nat. Assembly for Wales, Cardiff, 2005; Terminal 4, Barajas Airport, Madrid, 2005 (Stirling Prize, 2006); Paddington Basin, London, 2005; Mossbourne Community Acad., Hackney, 2005; Law Courts, Antwerp, 2005; Birmingham City Library, 2005; Roppongi GRIPS campus, Tokyo, 2005; Hesperia Hotel and Conference Centre, Barcelona, 2006; R9 Station, Kaohsiung, Taiwan, 2007; Ching Fu HQ, Kaohsiung, Taiwan, 2007; Terminal 5, Heathrow Airport, 2008; Cambridge Station area redevelt, 2008; Jacob Javits Convention Center, NY, 2008; Bodegas Protos, Peñafiel, 2008; Maggie's Centre, London, 2008 (Stirling Prize, RIBA, 2009); 300 New Jersey Avenue, Washington DC, 2009; Campus Palmas Atlas/HQ for Abengoa, Seville, 2009; Oxley Wood Housing, Milton Keynes, 2010 (Manser Medal, 2008); Las Arenas, Barcelona, 2011; One Hyde Park, Knightsbridge, 2011; Bullring, Barcelona, 2011; NEO Bankside, London, 2012; Up at the O₂, London, 2012; 8 Chifley Sq., Sydney, 2013; Nuovo Centro Civico, Scandicci, Italy, 2013; World Conservation and Exhibns Centre, British Mus., 2014; Extension to British Mus., 2014; Leadenhall Building, London, 2015; Y:CUBE, London, 2015; Chiswick Business Park, 2016; BBVA Bancomer HQ, Mexico City, 2016. *Current projects include:* The Berkeley Hotel, London; Capodichino Tube Station, Naples; Tower 3 on World Trade Centre site, NY; Future of Paris Agglomeration; Port Authority Bus Terminal and Tower, NY; 1201 K Street, Washington DC; P7 - Campus de la Justicia de Madrid; Santa Maria del Pianto Underground Station, Naples; White City Health Centre, London; Sewoon Sang Ga, Seoul; Heron Quays, Canary Wharf; Parc1, Yeouido, Seoul; Canary Riverside South; Barangaroo Masterplan, Sydney; Lok Wo Sha residential, Hong Kong; Beirut Grand Hotel; Ladywell, Lewisham. *Exhibitions worldwide include:* Royal Acad.; Mus. of Modern Art, NY; Louisiana Mus., Copenhagen; Richard Rogers + Architects touring exhibn, Paris 2007, London 2008, Madrid, Barcelona 2009, Taipei 2010, Singapore 2011. Teaching posts include: AA, London; Cambridge Univ.; Yale; UCLA. Chairman: Nat. Housing Tenants Resource Centre; Architecture Foundn, 1991–2001; Tate Gall. Trust, 1984–88; Govt Urban Task Force, 1998–2001; Vice-Chm., Arts Council of England, 1994–97; Mem., UN Architects' Cttee; Mem., Urban Strategies Adv. Council, Barcelona; Mem., Internat. Business Adv. Council for London, 2008–; UK Business Ambassador, 2008–; Trustee: London First; UK Bd, Médecins du Monde. Hon. Mem., Royal Inst. of Architects, Scotland, 1999; Hon. FAIA 1986. Hon. Dr RCA. Royal Gold Medal for Arch., 1985; Thomas Jefferson Meml Foundn Medal in Architecture, 1999; Praemium Imperiale, 2000; Pritzker Prize, 2007. Chevalier de la Légion d'Honneur, France, 1986. Subject of several television documentaries and jl articles on architecture. *Publications:* Richard Rogers + Architects, 1985; A+U: Richard Rogers 1978–1988, 1988; Architecture: a modern view, 1990; (jtly) A New London, 1992; Cities for a Small Planet (Reith Lectures), 1997; Richard Rogers: the complete works, vol. 1, 1999, vol. 2, 2001, vol. 3, 2006; (with Anne Power) Cities for a Small Country, 2000; Richard Rogers + Architects: from the house to the city, 2010; (with Richard Brown) A Place for All People, 2017; *relevant publications:* Richard Rogers, a biography, by Bryan Appleyard, 1986; Richard Rogers, by Kenneth Powell, 1994; The Architecture of Richard Rogers, by Deyan Sudjic, 1994; Richard Rogers Partnership, by Richard Burdett, 1995; Richard Rogers: architect of the future, by Kenneth Powell, 2006. *Recreations:* friends, art, architecture, travel, food. *Address:* (office) Rogers Stirk Harbour + Partners, The Leadenhall Building, 122 Leadenhall Street, EC3V 4AB. *T:* (020) 7385 1235.
See also P. W. Rogers.

ROGERS OF RIVERSIDE, Lady; **Ruth Rogers**, MBE 2010; Chef and owner, River Cafe Restaurant, since 1987; *b* 2 July 1948; *d* of Frederick and Sylvia Elias; *m* 1973, Richard George Rogers (*see* Baron Rogers of Riverside); one *s* (and one *s* decd), and three step *s*. *Educ:* Bennington Coll., NY; London Coll. of Printing (BA Hons Design). Penguin Books, 1970–73; Richard Rogers & Partners, 1973–87. *Publications:* with Rose Gray: River Cafe Cook Book, 1995; River Cafe Cook Book Two, 1997; Italian Kitchen, 1998; River Cafe Cook Book Green, 2000; River Cafe Cook Book Easy, 2003; River Cafe Two Easy, 2005; River Cafe Pocket Books, 2006; River Cafe Classic Italian Cookbook, 2009; (jtly) River Cafe 30, 2017. *Address:* River Cafe, Thames Wharf, Rainville Road, W6 9HA. *T:* (020) 7386 4200.

ROGERS, **Alan James**, MA; freelance journalist; Headmaster, Wellington School, Somerset, 1990–2006; Principal, Lodge International School, Kuching, Sarawak, Malaysia, 2007–09; *b* 30 March 1946; *s* of William James Albert Rogers and Beatrice Gwendolyn Rogers (*née* Evans); *m* 1968, Sheila Follett; one *s* two *d*. *Educ:* Humphry Davy Grammar Sch., Penzance; Jesus Coll., Oxford (MA; PGCE (Dist.)). Asst Master, Pangbourne Coll., 1969–73; Head of Geography and Geology, Arnold Sch., Blackpool, 1973–78; Head of Geography, Wellington Coll., 1978–82; Second Master and Dep. Headmaster, Wellington Sch., Som, 1982–90. Mem., Governing Body, Borneo Internat. Sch., Kuching, Sarawak, 2017–. Weekly columnist on nature matters, Borneo Sunday Post. *Publications:* articles on geographical educn in UK and Commonwealth jls and in various books and newspapers. *Recreations:* tropical rainforest environments, house restoration, dog walking, weather watching, writing, watching sport of all types.

ROGERS, Prof. **Alex David**, PhD; Science Director, REV Ocean, since 2018; Visiting Professor, Department of Zoology, University of Oxford, since 2018 (Professor of Conservation Biology, 2010–18); Senior Research Fellow, Somerville College, Oxford, since 2018; *b* Walthamstow, London, 21 Jan. 1968; *s* of David Rogers and Anne Rogers; *m* 1996, Candida Michaela Reed; two *d*. *Educ:* St Edmund Campion Sch., Hornchurch; Univ. of Liverpool (BSc Hons 1st Cl. Marine Biol. 1989; PhD 1993). Res. Fellow, Marine Biol Assoc. of UK, Plymouth, 1992–97; NERC Advanced Res. Fellow, Univ. of Southampton, 1997–2001; Principal Investigator in Biodiversity Res., British Antarctic Survey, 2001–06; Sen. Res. Fellow, 2006–09, Reader, 2009–10, Inst. of Zool., Zool Soc. of London; Res. Fellow, 2010–18, Dir, Oxford India Centre for Sustainable Develt, 2016–17, Somerville Coll., Oxford. Co-Dir, Internat. Prog. on State of the Ocean, 2006–; Chief Scientist, Nekton Foundn, 2016–18 (Trustee, 2016–18). Mem., Prog. Cttee, WWF, 2014–19 (Fellow, 2019). Zoological Society of London: Conservation Fellowship, 2011; Marsh Award for Marine and Freshwater Conservation, 2013. *Publications:* (jtly) Photographic Guide to the Sea and Shore Life of Britain and North-West Europe, 2001; (ed jtly) Antarctic Ecology: from genes to ecosystems part 1, 2007; (ed jtly) Antarctic Ecology: from genes to ecosystems part 2: evolution, diversity and functional ecology, 2007; (ed jtly) Antarctic Ecosystems: an extreme environment in a changing world, 2012; The Deep: the hidden wonders of our oceans and how we can protect them, 2019; 145 papers; 24 chapters in books; 69 reports and policy communications. *Recreations:* writing about science and policy, walking, reading science fiction and fantasy, collecting books on marine biology and zoology (antiquarian), home brewing, allotment growing. *Address:* REV Ocean, Oksenøyveien 10, 1366 Lysaker, Norway. *T:* 07927 645546. *E:* alex.rogers@revocean.org.

ROGERS, Alice; *see* Rogers, F. A.

ROGERS, **Allan Ralph**, FGS; *b* 24 Oct. 1932; *s* of John Henry Rogers and Madeleine Rogers (*née* Smith); *m* 1955, Ceridwen James; one *s* three *d*. *Educ:* University College of Swansea (BSc Hons Geology). Geologist, UK, Canada, USA, Australia, 1956–63; Teacher, 1963–65; Tutor-organiser, WEA, 1965–70, District Sec., 1970–79. Vis. Prof., Univ. of S Wales (formerly Univ. of Glamorgan), 1997–. MP (Lab) Rhondda, 1983–2001. Opposition spokesman: on defence, 1987–92; on foreign affairs, 1992–94. Mem., Intelligence and Security Cttee, 1994–2001. European Parliament: Mem. (Lab) SE Wales, 1979–84; Vice-Pres., 1979–82. Non-exec. Dir, Buy As You View, 2001–03. Bd Mem., British Geol Survey, 2001–05. Chm., Earth Sci. Educn Forum for England and Wales, 2002–10. *Recreation:* all sports. *Address:* 2 Dilwyn Avenue, Hengoed, Caerphilly CF82 7AG. *Clubs:* Workmen's (Treorchy); Penallta Rugby Football (Pres.).

ROGERS, **Anthony Gordon**, GBS 2011; QC (Hong Kong) 1984; JP; arbitrator, mediator, independent executor and expert witness; *b* 16 Feb. 1946; *s* of late Gordon Victor Rogers and Olga Elena Rogers; *m* 1970, Barbara Ann Zimmern; one *s* two *d*. *Educ:* Beaumont Coll. Called to the Bar, Gray's Inn, 1969; practised at the Bar: London, 1970–76; Hong Kong, 1976–93; Judge of the High Court, 1993–97, Judge of the Court of Appeal, 1997–2000, Vice-Pres. of the Court of Appeal, 2000–11, Hong Kong; Judge of Court of Appeal, Brunei Darussalam, 2010–11. Chm., Clearing and Settlements Systems Appeals Tribunal, 2013–. Arbitrator, Court of Arbitration for Sport, 2015–. Chm., Hong Kong Anti-Doping Disciplinary Panel, 2009–. Chm., Hong Kong Bar Assoc., 1990, 1991. Mem., Basic Law Consultative Cttee, 1985–90; Chm., Standing Cttee on Company Law Reform, 1994–2004. JP Hong Kong 1988. Dir, 1992–2010, Sec., 1995–, Hong Kong China Rowing Assoc. *Recreations:* rowing, golf, music, keeping the family happy. *Address:* 9C Jonsim Place, 228 Queen's Road East, Hong Kong. *T:* 92882910. *E:* agr@anthonyrogers.com. *Clubs:* Thames Rowing, Sloane; Hong Kong, Hong Kong Country, Shek-O, Lion Rock Rowing, Victoria Recreation (Hong Kong).

ROGERS, **Brett**, OBE 2014; Director, Photographers' Gallery, London, since 2005; *b* 22 Dec. 1954; *d* of Bob and Jerry Rogers; *m* 1982, Alan Lowery (marr. diss. 2007); one *s* one *d*. *Educ:* Univ. of Sydney (BA Hons 1976); Courtauld Inst. of Art, Univ. of London (MA 1981). Exhibns Officer, 1976–78, Hd of Exhibns, 1978–80, Australian Gall. Dirs Council; Exhibns Officer, 1982–95, Hd of Exhibns and Dep. Dir, 1996–2005, Fine Arts Dept, British Council. Vis. Fellow, UAL, 2014–. *Publications:* Madame Yevonde: Be Original or Die, 1998; Reality Check: recent developments in British photography, 2003; To be continued……aspects of recent British and Finnish photography, 2005. *Recreations:* visual arts, theatre, swimming. *Address:* Photographers' Gallery, 16–18 Ramillies Street, W1F 7LW. *T:* (020) 7087 9310. *E:* Brett.rogers@tpg.org.uk.

ROGERS, Catherine W.; *see* Wyn-Rogers.

ROGERS, Christopher; *see* Rogers, L. C. G.

ROGERS, **Dafydd Harries**; theatre producer; *b* London, 5 May 1969; *s* of Mac and Maggie Rogers; *m* 2002, Colleen Brown; one *s* one *d*. *Educ:* St Paul's Sch., Barnes; King's Coll. London (BD Hons Theol.). Productions include: Art, Wyndham's, 1996, transf. NY, 1998; Rebecca, UK tour, 2001; The Play What I Wrote, Wyndham's, 2001; Heroes, Wyndham's, 2005; Equus, Gielgud, 2007, transf. NY, 2009; God of Carnage, Gielgud, 2008, transf. NY, 2009; Noël Coward's Brief Encounter, Cinema Haymarket, 2008, transf. NY, 2009; Calendar Girls, Chichester, 2008, transf. Noël Coward, 2009; Deathtrap, Noël Coward, 2010; The Full Monty, Sheffield, transf. Noël Coward and UK tours, 2013; Rebecca, UK tour, 2015; The Girls, Leeds and Manchester, 2015, transf. Phoenix, 2017; The Band, UK tour, 2017. *Recreations:* sculling, harp, capoeira. *Address:* 9 Meard Street, W1F 0EP. *T:* (020) 7292 0390. *E:* dafydd@davidpughltd.com.

ROGERS, Dr **David Andrew**; Director, Constitution and Cabinet (formerly Strategy and Constitution), Scottish Government, since 2012. *Educ:* St Peter's Coll., Oxford (MA); Sidney Sussex Coll., Cambridge (PhD 1988). Post-doctoral Res. Fellow, Univ. of Oxford, 1988–89; geologist, oil industry, 1989–93; Scottish Office, 1993–99; Scottish Exec., later Scottish Govt, 1999–. *Address:* Scottish Government, St Andrew's House, Regent Road, Edinburgh EH1 3DG. *T:* (0131) 244 5210. *E:* david.rogers@gov.scot.

ROGERS, Ven. **David Arthur**; Archdeacon of Craven, 1977–86; *b* 12 March 1921; *s* of Rev. Canon Thomas Godfrey Rogers and Doris Mary Cleaver Rogers (*née* Steele); *m* 1951, Joan Malkin; one *s* three *d*. *Educ:* Saint Edward's School, Oxford (scholar); Christ's College, Cambridge (exhibitioner). BA 1947, MA 1952. War service with Green Howards and

RAC, 1940–45; Christ's Coll. and Ridley Hall, Cambridge, 1945–49; Asst Curate, St George's, Stockport, 1949–53; Rector, St Peter's, Levenshulme, Manchester, 1953–59; Vicar of Sedbergh, Cautley and Garsdale, 1959–79; Rural Dean of Sedbergh and then of Ewecross, 1959–77; Hon. Canon of Bradford Cathedral, 1967. *Address:* Sharnbrook House, High Street, Sharnbrook, Bedford MK44 1PB. *T:* (01234) 782650.

**ROGERS, Dr David P.;** President and Chair of the Board, Health and Climate Foundation, 2007–18; Advisor, World Bank, since 2007; *b* 20 March 1957. *Educ:* UEA (BSc Hons); Univ. of Southampton (PhD). Navigating Officer, British MN; res. appts, Desert Res. Inst., Univ. of Nevada; Scripps Institution of Oceanography, University of California, San Diego: res. scientist; Associate Dir, Calif Space Inst.; Dir, Physical Oceanography Res. Div. and Dir, Jt Inst. for Marine Observations, 1989–2000; Dir, Office of Weather and Air Quality Res. and Associate Dir of Res., Nat. Oceanographic and Atmospheric Admin, USA, 2000–03; Vice Pres., Meteorol and Oceanographic Services, Sci. Applications Internat. Corp., Virginia, 2003–04; Chief Exec., Met Office, 2004–05. *E:* drogers@bluewin.ch.

**ROGERS, Prof. (Frances) Alice,** OBE 2016; PhD; Professor of Mathematics, King's College London, 2007–14, now Emeritus; *b* 13 Sept. 1947; *d* of John George Monroe and Jane Monroe (*née* Reynolds); *m* 1970, Richard Ian Rogers (*d* 2009); one *s* one *d*. *Educ:* Cranborne Chase Sch.; New Hall, Cambridge (BA Maths 1968); Hughes Hall, Cambridge (PGCE 1969); Imperial Coll., London (PhD 1981). Secondary sch. teacher, 1969–76; SERC Res. Fellow, Imperial Coll., London, 1981–83; Department of Mathematics, King's College London: Res. Associate, 1983–84; SERC Adv. Res. Fellow, 1984–89; Royal Soc. Univ. Res. Fellow, 1989–94; Lectr, 1994–96; Reader, 1996–2007. Mem., Adv. Cttee on Maths Educn, 2007–11. Trustee and Educn Sec., LMS, 2012–17. FKC 2015. Kavli Educn Medal, Royal Soc., 2018. *Publications:* Supermanifolds: theory and applications, 2007; articles on mathematical physics in scientific jls. *Recreations:* gardening, history, hills, choral singing. *Address:* Department of Mathematics, King's College London, Strand, WC2R 2LS. *E:* alice.rogers@kcl.ac.uk.

**ROGERS, (George) Stuart L.;** *see* Lawson-Rogers.

**ROGERS, Hayley,** CB 2018; Parliamentary Counsel, since 2007; Project Lead, Good Law initiative, since 2013; *b* 16 July 1967; *d* of Peter Jordan and Ann Catherine Jordan (*née* Newman); *m* 1990, Steven Alexander Rogers. *Educ:* Univ. of Reading (LLB 1988); Coll. of Law, Guildford. Articled clerk, then solicitor, Boys and Maughan Solicitors, Margate, 1989–93; Asst Parly Counsel, 1993–98; Sen. Asst Parly Counsel, 1998–2002; Dep. Parly Counsel, 2002–07; Head Drafter, Tax Law Rewrite Project, HM Revenue and Customs, 2005–07. Associate Res. Fellow, Inst. of Advanced Legal Studies, 2013–. *Recreations:* walking, painting, gardening. *Address:* Parliamentary Counsel Office, 1 Horse Guards Road, SW1A 2HQ. *E:* hayley.rogers@cabinetoffice.gov.uk.

**ROGERS, Ian Paul;** QC 2014; *b* Newport, S Wales, 2 Jan. 1973; *s* of late Neil Rogers and of Denise Rogers. *Educ:* Hertford Coll., Oxford (BA 1st Cl. Hons 1994); Eur. Inst., Florence (LLM Comparative Eur. and Internat. Law 2007). Called to the Bar, Gray's Inn, 1995. Member: Attorney Gen.'s A Panel of Treasury Counsel, until 2014; Welsh Govt A Panel of Treasury Counsel, until 2014. Mem., RFU Judiciary, 2014–. *Publications:* (contrib.) Oliver & Dingeman's Employer's Liability Cases, 2003; contribs to jls incl. Solicitors' Jl, Legal Week, Eur. Human Rights Law Rev. *Recreations:* hiking, travel, theatre, cinema. *Address:* Monckton Chambers, 1 & 2 Raymond Buildings, Gray's Inn, WC1R 5NR. *T:* (020) 7405 7211. *E:* irogers@monckton.com.

**ROGERS, Prof. Jane Rosalind,** FRSL; novelist; Professor of Writing, Sheffield Hallam University, 2005–15, now Professor Emerita; *b* London, 21 July 1952; *d* of Andrew Walton Rogers and Margaret Kathleen Rogers (*née* Farmer); *m* 1981, Michael Harris; one *s* one *d*. *Educ:* Oxford High Sch. for Girls; New Hall, Cambridge (BA Hons English 1974); Univ. of Leicester (PGCE 1976). Writer of novels, scripts and short stories, 1981–. Lectr (pt-time), Sheffield Hallam Univ., 1987–. Teacher of writing: Arvon Foundn; British Council, Open Coll. of the Arts, 2010–12; mentor, Good Dust; writer, teacher and project co-ordinator, Radio Mifumi, Uganda, 2010. Scriptwriter: *television:* Dawn and the Candidate (play), 1989 (Samuel Beckett Award for best first television drama, 1989); Mr Wroe's Virgins (series), 1993; *radio:* adaptations: Diary of a Provincial Lady, 1999; Shirley, 2002; Lorna Doone, 2004; The Age of Innocence, 2008; The Custom of the Country, 2010; The Chrysalids, 2012; The Testament of Jessie Lamb, 2013; R. L. Stevenson, Terror in the South Seas, 2017; Real Worlds, 2017; *plays:* Island, 2002; The Inland Sea, 2004; Meanwood, 2005; Dear Writer, 2008; Red Enters the Eye, 2011. FRSL 1994. *Publications: fiction:* Separate Tracks, 1983; Her Living Image (Somerset Maugham Award), 1984; The Ice is Singing, 1987; Mr Wroe's Virgins, 1991; Promised Lands, 1995 (Writers' Guild Best Fiction Book award, 1996); Island, 1999; The Voyage Home, 2004; The Testament of Jessie Lamb, 2011 (Arthur C. Clarke Award, 2012); Hitting Trees with Sticks (collected stories), 2012; Conrad and Eleanor, 2016; *non-fiction:* (ed) The Good Fiction Guide, 2001, 2nd edn 2005. *Recreations:* walking, reading. *Address:* c/o Charles Walker, United Agents, 12–26 Lexington Street, W1F 0LE. *T:* (020) 3214 0800. *E:* jane.rogers@btinternet.com, CWalker@unitedagents.co.uk. *W:* www.janerogers.info

**ROGERS, Very Rev. John;** Dean of Llandaff, 1993–99, now Emeritus; *b* 27 Nov. 1934; *s* of William Harold and Annie Mary Rogers; *m* 1972, Pamela Mary Goddard (*d* 2003); one *s* one *d*. *Educ:* Jones' W Monmouth Sch., Pontypool; St David's Coll., Lampeter (BA 1955); Oriel Coll., Oxford (BA 1957; MA 1960); St Stephen's House, Oxford, 1957–59. Ordained deacon, 1959, priest, 1960; Assistant Curate: St Martin's, Roath (dio. of Llandaff), 1959–63; St Sidwell's, Lodge, with Holy Redeemer, Ruimveldt, Guyana, 1963–67; Vicar: Holy Redeemer, Ruimveldt, Guyana, 1967–69; Wismar and Lower Demerara River Missions, 1969–71; Caldicot, 1971–77; Monmouth, 1977–84; Rector, Ebbw Vale, 1984–93. Rural Dean: Monmouth, 1981–84; Blaenau Gwent, 1986–93; Canon of St Woolos Cathedral, 1988–93. *Recreations:* reading, listening to music. *Address:* 14 Dolau Brân, Llandovery SA20 0DF. *T:* (01550) 720089.

**ROGERS, Prof. (John) Michael,** DPhil; FSA; FBA 1988; Khalili Professor of Islamic Art, School of Oriental and African Studies, University of London, 1991–2000, now Emeritus; Hon. Curator, Nasser D. Khalili Collection of Islamic Art, Nour Foundation, since 2001; *b* 25 Jan. 1935. *Educ:* Ulverston Grammar Sch.; Corpus Christi Coll., Oxford (MA, DPhil). FSA 1974. Robinson Sen. Student, Oriel Coll., Oxford, 1958–61; Tutor in Philosophy, Pembroke and Wadham Colls, Oxford, 1961–65; Asst, then Associate, Prof. of Islamic Art and Archaeol., Center for Arabic Studies, Amer. Univ. in Cairo, 1965–77; Dep. Keeper, Dept of Oriental Antiquities, BM, 1977–91. Vis. Sen. Res. Fellow, Merton Coll., Oxford, 1971–72; Vis. Res. Fellow, New Coll., Oxford, 1998; Slade Prof. of Fine Art, Oxford Univ., 1991–92. Pres., British Inst. of Persian Studies, 1993–96. Corresp. Mem., Deutsches Archäologisches Inst., Berlin, 1988. Order of the Egyptian Republic, 2nd cl., 1969. *Publications:* The Spread of Islam, 1976; Islamic Art and Design 1500–1700, 1983; (with R. M. Ward) Süleyman the Magnificent, 1988; Mughal Painting, 1993, 2nd edn 2006; Empire of the Sultans: Ottoman art in the Khalili collection, 1995; (with M. B. Piotrovsky) Heaven on Earth: art from Islamic lands, 2004; Sinan, 2006; *translations:* Adamova, Persian Manuscripts, Paintings and Drawings: from the 15th to the early 20th Century, 2012; Ivanov, Copper, Brass and Bronze of Iran: from the late 14th to the mid-18th century in the Hermitage Collection, 2019; numerous articles on hist. and archaeol. of Islamic Turkey, Egypt, Syria, Iran and Central Asia. *Recreations:* walking, music, botany. *Address:* The Nour Foundation, Unit 24, Victoria Industrial Estate, W3 6UU.

**ROGERS, His Honour John Michael Thomas;** QC 1978; a Circuit Judge, 1998–2010; *m* 2006, Mrs Angela Victoria Galaud (*née* Ginders); one step *s* one step *d*, and one *d* from a former marriage. *Educ:* Rydal Sch.; Birkenhead Sch.; Fitzwilliam House, Cambridge (MA, LLB). Called to Bar, Gray's Inn, 1963, Bencher 1991. A Recorder, 1976–98; Pres., Mental Health Rev. Tribunal (NW), 1982–98; Dep. High Court Judge, 1990–2010. Chancellor, Dio. of St Asaph, 1982–2010. Leader, Wales and Chester Circuit, 1990–92. *Recreations:* farming, gardening. *Clubs:* Reform; Pragmatist's (Wirral); Barbarians Rugby Football.

**ROGERS, Air Chief Marshal Sir John (Robson),** KCB 1982; CBE 1971; FRAeS; Executive Chairman, RAC Motor Sports Association, 1989–98; *b* 11 Jan. 1928; *s* of B. R. Rogers; *m* 1955, Gytha Elspeth Campbell; two *s* two *d*. *Educ:* Brentwood Sch.; No 1 Radio Sch., Cranwell; Royal Air Force Coll., Cranwell. OC 56(F) Sqdn, 1960–61; Gp Captain, 1967; OC RAF Coningsby, 1967–69; Air Commodore, 1971; Dir of Operational Requirements (RAF), 1971–73; Dep. Comdt, RAF Coll., 1973–75; RCDS, 1976; Air Vice-Marshal, 1977; Dir-Gen. of Organisation, RAF, 1977–79; AOC Training Units, RAF Support Comd, 1979–81; Air Mem. for Supply and Organisation, MoD, 1981–83; Controller Aircraft, MoD PE, 1983–86, retired. Director: British Car Auctions, 1986–90; First Technology Gp, 1986–93. Pres., Internat. Historic Commn, Fedn Internat. de l'Automobile, 1995–2004. Chm., Children's Fire and Burn Trust, 2000–04. FRAeS 1983. *Recreation:* motor racing. *Address:* c/o Lloyds Bank, 27 High Street, Colchester, Essex. *Clubs:* Royal Automobile (Vice-Chm., 1990–98; Life Vice Pres., 1999), Royal Air Force.

**ROGERS, Prof. (Leonard) Christopher (Gordon),** PhD; Professor of Statistical Science, University of Cambridge, 2002, now Emeritus. *Educ:* St John's Coll., Cambridge (BA 1975; PhD 1980). Lecturer: Univ. of Warwick, 1980–83; Univ. Coll. of Swansea, 1983–85; Univ. of Cambridge, 1985–91; Fellow of St John's Coll., Cambridge, 1985–91; Prof. of Math. Statistics, QMW, 1991–94; Prof. of Probability, Univ. of Bath, 1994–2002. *Publications:* (with David Williams) Diffusions, Markov Processes, and Martingales, vol. 1, Foundations, 1979, vol. 2, Itô calculus, 1987; articles in learned jls. *Address:* Department of Pure Mathematics and Mathematical Statistics, Centre for Mathematical Sciences, Wilberforce Road, Cambridge CB3 0WB.

**ROGERS, Lucy Ellen;** *see* Musgrave, L. E.

**ROGERS, Malcolm Austin,** CBE 2004; DPhil; FSA; Ann and Graham Gund Director, Museum of Fine Arts, Boston, Mass, 1994–2015, now Emeritus; *b* 3 Oct. 1948; *s* of late James Eric Rogers and Frances Anne (*née* Elsey). *Educ:* Oakham School; Magdalen College, Oxford (Open Exhibnr); Christ Church, Oxford (Senior Scholar). Violet Vaughan Morgan Prize, 1967; BA (Eng. Lang. and Lit. 1st cl.), 1969; MA 1973; DPhil 1976. National Portrait Gallery: Asst Keeper, 1974–83; Dep. Keeper, 1983–85; Keeper, 1985–94; Dep. Dir, 1983–94. Trustee, Assoc. of Art Mus. Dirs, 2010–14. Mem., Amer. Acad. Arts and Scis, 2011. Humanitas Vis. Prof. in Museums, Galleries and Libraries, Univ. of Oxford, 2012. Trustee: Auckland Project, UK, 2015–; Worcester Art Mus., USA, 2016–; Internat. Mus. of World War II, 2016–; Fidelity Foundn (UK), 2018–; Watts Gall., 2019–; Chm., Trustees, Broadway Mus. and Art Gall., 2018–; Freeman, City of London, 1992; Liveryman, Girdlers' Co., 1992. Hon. DFA Emmanuel Coll., Boston, 2011; Hon. DHL Boston Architectural Coll., 2014. Excellency Award, Foundn for Italian Art and Culture, 2010; Award of Merit, British Assoc., 2012. Chevalier de l'Ordre des Arts et des Lettres (France), 2007; Commendatore al Merito della Repubblica Italiana, 2009; Encomienda de la Orden de Isabel la Católica (Spain), 2010. *Publications:* Dictionary of British Portraiture, 4 vols (ed jtly), 1979–81; Museums and Galleries of London, 1983, 3rd edn 1991; William Dobson, 1983; John and John Baptist Closterman: a catalogue of their works, 1983; Elizabeth II: portraits of sixty years, 1986; Camera Portraits, 1989; Montacute House, 1991; (with Sir David Piper) Companion Guide to London, 1992; (ed) The English Face, by Sir David Piper, 1992; Master Drawings from the National Portrait Gallery, 1993; articles and reviews in Burlington Magazine, Apollo, TLS. *Recreations:* food and wine, opera, travel. *Address:* Russell House, Lower Green, Broadway, Worcs WR12 7BU. *T:* (01386) 854828. *Clubs:* Beefsteak; Wednesday Evening Club of 1777 (Boston).

**ROGERS, Mark Nicholas; His Honour Judge Mark Rogers;** a Circuit Judge, since 2009; a Deputy High Court Judge (Queen's Bench and Family Divisions), since 2011; Nominated Judge, Court of Protection, since 2011; *b* High Wycombe, 10 Dec. 1955; *s* of late Leslie Paul and Mabel Rogers; *m* 1979, Valerie Ann Haynes; one *s* one *d*. *Educ:* Royal Grammar Sch., High Wycombe; Brasenose Coll., Oxford (BA); Poly. of Central London. Called to the Bar, Middle Temple, 1980; in practice as barrister, 1980–2006; Dep. Dist Judge, 2000–06, Dist Judge, 2007–09; Recorder, 2001–09. *Recreations:* music, watching men's and women's cricket, theatre, food and drink. *Address:* Leicester Combined Court, 90 Wellington Street, Leicester LE1 6HG. *T:* (0116) 222 5800.

**ROGERS, Michael;** *see* Rogers, J. M.

**ROGERS, Nicholas Martin,** CEng; FIMechE, FREng; Executive Director, Product Engineering, Jaguar Land Rover, since 2015; *b* Wallingford, 25 Dec. 1967; *s* of Martin Rogers and Patricia Rogers; one *d*; partner, Natascha Wolber. *Educ:* Coventry Univ. (BEng Hons Mech. Engrg 1993). FIMechE 2015; FREng 2018. Jaguar Land Rover Ltd: apprentice technician, 1984–88; Body Res. and Develt Engr, 1988–90; Proj. Engr, Body Engrg, 1990–91; Proj. Leader, Mini Convertible Body in White Facility, 1992–94; Proj. Team Leader, Rover 200 Body Structures, 1994–95; Chief Engineer: Body Structures Design, 1995–98; Re-engrg, BMW-Rover, 1998–99; Proj. Leader, new platform concept for Land Rover vehicles, 2000–03; Chief Prog. Engrg, Land Rover Discovery 3 and Range Rover Sport, 2003–05; Lean Manufg Manager, Range Rover, Land Rover Defender and Powertrain Ops, 2005–07; Dir, Global Vehicle Architecture, 2007–15. Led delivery of first all-electric performance SUV, Jaguar I-PACE, and new Range Rover Evoque, 2018. *Recreations:* classic cars, property development. *Address:* Jaguar Land Rover Ltd, Banbury Road, Gaydon, Warwickshire CV35 0RR. *T:* (01926) 649416. *E:* nick.m.rogers@jaguarlandrover.com. *Club:* Jaguar Drivers'.

**ROGERS, Prof. Nicholas William,** PhD; Professor of Earth Sciences, Open University, 2015–18, now Emeritus; President, Geological Society of London, 2018–June 2020; *b* Bishop Stortford, 12 March 1953; *s* of Leonard Alfred Rogers and Daphne Rogers (*née* Gayler); partner, 1991, Anne Margaret Holland; two *s*. *Educ:* Hertford Grammar Sch.; Bedford Coll., Univ. of London (BSc 1st Cl. Geol. with Chem. 1974); Univ. of Leeds (MSc Geochem. 1975); Imperial Coll. London (PhD 1980). NERC Post-doctoral Res. Fellow, Imperial Coll. London and Open Univ., 1980–83; Open University: Res. Officer, 1983–92; Res. Fellow in Geochem., 1992–98; Sen. Res. Fellow in Geochem., 1998–2004; Sen. Lectr, 2004–15; Hd, Dept of Earth and Envmt Scis, 2008–11; Sci. Prog. Dir and

Associate Dean, 2012–18. *Publications:* (ed) An Introduction to Our Dynamic Planet, 2007; contrib. papers to jls incl. Nature; book chapters. *Recreations:* the theatre, art, reading, gardening, walking. *Address:* 32 Church Street, Baldock, Herts SG7 5AF. *T:* 07821 506120. *E:* Nick.rogers@open.ac.uk.

**ROGERS, Nigel David;** free-lance singer, conductor and teacher; Professor of Singing, Royal College of Music, 1978–2000; *b* 21 March 1935; *m* 1961, Frederica Bement Lord (*d* 1992); one *d*; *m* 1999, Lina Zilinskyte; one *d*. *Educ:* Wellington Grammar Sch.; King's Coll., Cambridge (MA). Studied in Italy and Germany. Professional singer, 1961–; began singing career in Munich with group Studio der frühen Musik. Is a leading specialist in field of Baroque music, and has made over 70 recordings from Monteverdi to Schubert; gives concerts, recitals, lectures and master classes in many parts of world; most acclaimed role in opera as Monteverdi's Orfeo. Formed vocal ensemble Chiaroscuro, to perform vast repertory of Italian Baroque music, 1979, later extended to include Chiaroscuro Chamber Ensemble and Chiaroscuro Baroque Orch. Has lectured and taught at Schola Cantorum Basiliensis, Basle, Switzerland. Hon. RCM 1981. *Publications:* chapter on Voice, Companion to Baroque Music (ed J. A. Sadie), 1991; articles on early Baroque performance practice in various periodicals in different countries. *Address:* Wellington House, 13 Victoria Road, Deal, Kent CT14 7AS. *T:* and *Fax:* (01304) 379249.

**ROGERS, Parry;** *see* Rogers, T. G. P.

**ROGERS, Patricia Maureen S.;** *see* Shepheard Rogers.

**ROGERS, Sir Peter,** Kt 2009; Chairman, New West End Company, since 2013; *b* Wolverhampton, Sept. 1949. *Educ:* Wednesfield Grammar Sch. Accountancy and financial roles with local authorities; joined Westminster CC, 1996, Chief Exec., 2000–08; Chief Exec., London Develt Agency, 2008–11. Advr to Mayor of London for Regeneration, Growth and Enterprise, 2011–12. Mem. Bd, Housing Corp., 2004–08. Non-exec. Dir, Liberata UK Ltd, 2012– (Chm., CapacityGRID, 2012–). Dir, Rogers' Performance Mgt Consultancy, 2008–. Chm., PeopleToo, 2011–. Dir, Regents Park Open Air Th., 2010–. *Address:* New West End Company, 3rd Floor, Heddon House, 149–151 Regent Street, W1B 4JD.

**ROGERS, Peter Brian,** CBE 2001; Chief Executive, Independent Television Commission, 1996–2000; *b* 8 April 1941; *s* of late William Patrick Rogers and Margaret Elizabeth Rogers; *m* 1966, Jean Mary Bailey (*d* 2014); one *s* two *d*. *Educ:* De La Salle Grammar Sch., Liverpool; Manchester Univ. (1st Cl. Hons BAEcon; Cobden Prize); London Sch. of Econs and Pol Science, London Univ. (MSc Econs). Tax Officer, Inland Revenue, 1959–67; Res. Associate, Manchester Univ., 1967–68; Econ. Adviser, HM Treasury, 1968–73; Sen. Econ. Adviser, Central Policy Review Staff, Cabinet Office, 1973–74; Dir of Econ. Planning, Tyne and Wear CC (on secondment from Central Govt), 1974–76; Sen. Econ. Adviser, DoE, 1976–79; Dep. Chief Exec., Housing Corp., 1979–82; Dir of Finance, IBA, 1982–90; Dep. Chief Exec. and Dir of Finance, ITC, 1991–96. Dir, Channel Four Television Co., 1982–92. Trustee and Hon. Treas., Lakeland Arts Trust, 2006–13. *Address:* 6 Parklands, 8 Carrwood Road, Bramhall, Stockport, Cheshire SK7 3GR. *T:* 07788 582576. *E:* pbrogers@icloud.com.

**ROGERS, Peter Lloyd,** CBE 2011; Chairman, OCS Group, since 2017; *b* Rugby, 29 Dec. 1947; *s* of Arnold Rogers and Ivy Rogers; *m* 2006, Stephanie Corrigan. *Educ:* Wymondham Coll.; Manchester Univ. (LLB Hons 1968). FCA 1971. Ford Motor Co., 1972–84; Director: Imagination Ltd, 1984–85; Sperry UK, 1985–86; Courtaulds plc, 1996–98; Dep. Chief Exec., Acordis Gp, 1998–2000; Chief Operating Officer, 2000–03, Chief Exec., 2013–16, Babcock Internat. plc. Non-executive Director: Galliford Try plc, 2008–15; InvestIndustrial SA, 2017–; Dir, Aston Martin Lagonda. *Recreations:* golf, scuba diving, reading.

**ROGERS, Peter Standing;** JP; Member (C) North Wales, National Assembly for Wales, 1999–2003; *b* 2 Jan. 1940; *s* of late Harold Rogers and of Joan Thomas; *m* 1973, Margaret Roberts; two *s*. *Educ:* Prenton Secondary Sch., Birkenhead; Cheshire Sch. of Agriculture. Farm Manager, 1962–65; Sales Manager, Ciba Geigy UK, 1965; self-employed farmer, 1965–. Mem. (Ind) Isle of Anglesey CC, 2004–. Contested: (C) Ynys Môn, Nat. Assembly for Wales, 2003; (Ind) Ynys Môn, 2005, 2010. JP Ynys Môn, 1990; High Sheriff, Gwynedd, 2008. *Recreations:* sports, all rural activities. *Address:* Bodrida, Brynsiencyn, Anglesey LL61 6NZ. *Clubs:* Old Birkonians (Birkenhead); Welsh Crawshays Rugby.

**ROGERS, Peter William,** CBE 2007; Eur Ing, FREng; director of property companies; Founding Partner, Lipton Rogers Developments, since 2013; *b* 25 Oct. 1946; *s* of Dr Nino Rogers and Dada (*née* Geiringer); *m* 1971, Hélène Tombazis (marr. diss.); one *s* one *d*; *m* 1988, Barbara Peters; two *s*. *Educ:* Portsmouth Poly. (BSc). CEng 1975, FREng 2005; MICE 1975; Eur Ing 1989. Various construction industry appts, UK, USA, France, Holland and ME, 1970–84; Dir, Stanhope Plc (formerly Stanhope Properties Plc), 1985–2013, resp. for construction of Broadgate, 1985–91. Advr on arts projects, incl., Nat. Gall., Glyndebourne Opera House, Royal Opera House, Tate Modern, Royal Academy, Serpentine Gall. and RSC, 1986–. Non-exec. Dir, Firstbase, 2006– (Exec. Dir, 2004–06). Mem., Construction Industry Sector Gp, NEDO, 1988–92. Mem., Foresight Panel, DTI, 1994–95 and 2000–01. Advr, Heritage Lottery Fund, 1995–2000. Advr to Mayor of London, and Chm., Olympic Orbit, 2010–12. Dir, Reading Construction Forum, 1994–99; Chairman: Strategic Forum for Construction, 2002–06 (Chm., 2012 Task Gp, 2005–12); Constructing Excellence, 2003–08; DCLG (formerly ODPM) Steering Cttee for Sustainable Bldgs, 2005–07; Founding Chm., UK Green Bldg Council, 2006–14; Mem., Bldgs Steering Cttee, Courtauld Inst. of Art, 2014–. Trustee and Founder Chm., Buildings Strategy Cttee, V&A Mus., 1999–2008; Trustee, Serpentine Gall., 2010–11. Visitor, Ashmolean Mus., 2007–09. FRSA 2001. Hon. FRIBA 2004. *Recreations:* theatre, ballet, art, music, travel, sailing, ski-ing. *Address:* Lipton Rogers Developments LLP, 33 Cavendish Square, W1G 0PW. *T:* (020) 3757 0566. *E:* rogers@liptonrogers.com. *Club:* Royal Yachting Association.
*See also* Baron Rogers of Riverside.

**ROGERS, Philip John,** MBE 1990; FREng, FInstP; Optical Design Consultant, VNF Ltd, since 2006; *b* 4 Oct. 1942; *s* of late John William Rogers and Lilian (*née* Fleet); *m* 1979, Wendy Joan Cross; one *s* two *d*. *Educ:* Burnley Grammar Sch.; North London Poly. (HNC Applied Physics 1965). CPhys 1990; CEng 1993. Optical Designer, Hilger & Watts, London, 1960–66; Pilkington PE, subseq. Pilkington Optronics, then Thales Optics Ltd: Optical Designer, 1966–69; Chief Optical Designer, 1969–2005; Chief Optics Engr, 3 sites, Pilkington Optronics Gp, 1994–2000. Visiting Professor: Cranfield Univ., 2007–13; Glyndwr Univ., 2012–; lecturing activities incl. OU TV broadcast, 1977. Mem., Thomson Coll., Paris, 1992–98. FInstP 1992; FREng 1998; Fellow: Internat. Soc. for Optics and Photonics (formerly Optical Engrg), 1991 (Dir, Bd, 1995–97); Optical Soc. of America, 1998. A. E. Conrady Award, Internat. Soc. for Optics and Photonics, 2018. *Publications:* (contrib.) Electro Optical Displays, 1992; (contrib.) Optical Society of America Handbook of Optics, Vol. 1, 2nd edn 1995, Vol. 2, 3rd edn 2009; conf. procs papers; contrib. 6 articles in jls; 27 patents covering infrared, night vision, avionic, visual and miscellaneous optics. *Recreations:* listening to music, armchair astronomy, reading (history and science particularly), messing about on computers, lazing in S of France. *Address:* 24 Cilgant Eglwys Wen, Bodelwyddan, Denbighshire LL18 5US. *T:* (01745) 582498.

**ROGERS, Raymond Thomas,** CPhys, FInstP; Managing Director, Dragon Health International (formerly Ray Rogers Associates), 1997–2008; *b* 19 Oct. 1940; *s* of late Thomas Kenneth Rogers and of Mary Esther Rogers (*née* Walsh); *m* 1964, Carmel Anne Saunders; two *s* one *d*. *Educ:* Gunnersbury Grammar Sch.; Birmingham Univ. (BSc). CPhys, FInstP 1962. Basic Med. Physicist, London Hosp., 1962–66; Sen. Med. Physicist, Westminster Hosp., 1966–70; Department of Health and Social Security, later Department of Health: PSO, Scientific and Tech. Br., 1970; Supt Engr, then Dir 1984; Asst Sec., Health Inf. Br., 1984–91; Under Sec., and Exec. Dir Information Mgt Gp, 1991–97. FRSA 1997. *Publications:* contribs to scientific jls and books. *Recreations:* trekking, opera, science, peace. *Address:* 7 Pilgrims View, Ash Green, Surrey GU12 6HU. *T:* (01252) 650138.

**ROGERS, Ruth;** *see* Rogers of Riverside, Lady.

**ROGERS, Sheila;** equality, diversity and human rights consultant in public and voluntary sectors, since 2005; *b* 29 March 1947; *d* of Charles Rogers and Peggy Baird; *m* (marr. diss.); one *d*. *Educ:* Univ. of Winnipeg (BA 1976); Univ. of Manitoba (LLB 1979); CIPFA (AdvDip 1999). Legal Aid Manitoba, 1980–86, Dep. Dir, 1986; Equal Opportunities Commn for NI, 1989–98, Dir of Finance and Admin, 1993–98; Chief Exec., Commn for Racial Equality for NI, 1998–99; Dir of Race Unit, 1999–2002, and Asst Chief Exec., 2000–01, Equality Commn for NI; Commission for Racial Equality (on secondment): Hd, Community Policy and Progs, 2002–04; Dir, Strategy and Delivery, 2004; Chief Exec., 2004–05. Member: Ind. Assessment Panel for the Equality Standard, Premier League, 2015–; Equality and Inclusion Adv. Gp, British Sci. Assoc., 2019–. Trustee: Dance Resource Base NI, 2009–15; Disability Law Service, 2014–16. *Publications:* (contrib.) Equal Opportunities: women's working lives, 1993; (contrib.) Workplace Equality: an international perspective on legislation, policy and practice, 2002. *E:* rogers.sheila@gmail.com.

**ROGERS, Shirley Denise, (Mrs A. A. Gordon);** Chief People Officer, NHS Scotland and Director of Workforce, Leadership and Service Reform (formerly Director of Health Workforce, then Health Workforce and Health Strategy), Scottish Government, since 2016; *b* Whitchurch, Shropshire, 3 Sept. 1964; *d* of George and Eve Rogers; *m* 1999, Andrew Alexander Gordon. *Educ:* Sir John Talbot's Grammar Sch., Whitchurch; Newcastle upon Tyne Univ. (BA Hons; MA). HR Manager, English Heritage, 1986–89; Personnel Manager, J Sainsbury plc, 1989–91; Force Trng Manager, Northumbria Police, 1991–96; Dir, HR and Orgn Develt, Scottish Ambulance Service, 1996–2012. FCIPD 2000. *Recreations:* writing, watercolour painting, cooking, singing. *Address:* Health and Social Care, Scottish Government, St Andrew's House, Regent Road, Edinburgh EH1 3DG. *T:* (0131) 244 1826. *E:* shirley.rogers@gov.scot.

**ROGERS, (Thomas Gordon) Parry,** CBE 1991; Director, The Plessey Co. plc, 1976–86; *b* 7 Aug. 1924; *s* of late Victor Francis Rogers and Ella (*née* May); *m* 1st, 1947, Pamela Mary (*née* Greene) (marr. diss. 1973); one *s* seven *d*; 2nd, 1973, Patricia Juliet (*née* Curtis); one *s* one *d*. *Educ:* West Hartlepool Grammar Sch.; St Edmund Hall, Oxford (MA). Served RAC and RAEC, 1944–47. Procter & Gamble Ltd, 1948–54; Mars Ltd, 1954–56; Hardy Spicer Ltd, 1956–61 (Dir, 1957–61); IBM United Kingdom Ltd, 1961–74 (Dir, 1964–74); The Plessey Co. plc, 1974–86; Chairman: Percom Ltd, 1984–94; ECCTIS 2000 Ltd, 1989–97; Director: MSL Gp Internat. Ltd, 1970–78; ICL plc, 1977–79; Hobsons Publishing plc, 1985–90; Butler Cox plc, 1985–91; Norman Broadbent Internat. Ltd, 1985–90; Ocean Group plc, 1988–94; Future Perfect (Counselling) Ltd, 1986–92; PRIMA Europe Ltd, 1987–93; BNB Resources plc, 1990–94. Chm., Plessey Pension Trust, 1978–86; Trustee, BNB Resources Pension Trust, 1991–94. Chairman: BTEC, 1986–94; SW London Coll. HEC, 1989–91; IT Skills Agency, 1984–96; Salisbury HA, 1986–90; Commn on Charitable Fundraising, NCSS, 1970–76; Member: Employment Appeal Tribunal, 1978–87; Standing Cttee on Pay Comparability, 1980–81; Nat. Steering Gp, Trng and Vocational Educn Initiative, MSC, 1983–86; CBI/BIM Panel on Mgt Educn, 1968–78; CBI Employment Policy Cttee, 1980–86; Rev. Team, Children and Young Persons Benefits, DHSS, 1984–85; Oxford Univ. Appts Cttee, 1972–87; Member Council: CRAC, 1965–94; ISCO, 1988–95; Inst. of Manpower Studies, 1970–86; Indust. Participation Assoc., 1972–86; Inst. of Dirs, 1980–95 (Chm., 1985–88; Vice Pres., 1988–95); Inst. of Personnel Management, 1954– (Pres., 1975–77); EEF, 1980–86; Econ. League, 1982–86; E Europe Trade Council, 1982–85. Governor: Ashridge Management Coll., 1985–94; Warminster Sch., 1989–99; St Mary's Sch., Shaftesbury, 1991–94. Patron, Dorset Chamber Orch. Freeman, City of London, 1987; Mem., Information Technologists' Co., 1987–. CCIPD; CCMI. *Publications:* The Recruitment and Training of Graduates, 1970; contribs on management subjects to newspapers and jls. *Recreations:* birdwatching, tennis, photography, listening to music. *Address:* St Edward's Chantry, Bimport, Shaftesbury, Dorset SP7 8BA. *T:* (01747) 852789.

**ROGERSON, Rt Rev. Barry;** Bishop of Bristol, 1985–2002; an Assistant Bishop, Diocese of Bath and Wells, 2003–16, Hon. Assistant Bishop, since 2016; *b* 25 July 1936; *s* of Eric and Olive Rogerson; *m* 1961, Olga May Gibson; two *d*. *Educ:* Magnus Grammar School; Leeds Univ. (BA Theology); Wells Theol Coll. Midland Bank Ltd, 1952–57; Curate: St Hilda's, South Shields, 1962–65; St Nicholas', Bishopwearmouth, Sunderland, 1965–67; Lecturer, Lichfield Theological Coll., 1967–71, Vice-Principal, 1971–72; Lectr, Salisbury and Wells Theol Coll., 1972–75; Vicar, St Thomas', Wednesfield, 1975–79; Team Rector, Wednesfield Team Ministry, 1979; Bishop Suffragan of Wolverhampton, 1979–85. Chm., ABM (formerly ACCM), 1987–93; Mem. Central Cttee, WCC, 1991–2002 (Mem., Faith and Order Commn, 1987–98); Pres., CTBI, 1999–2002. Chm., Melanesian Mission, 1979–2002. Hon. Freeman, City and County of Bristol, 2003. Hon. LLD Bristol, 1993; Hon. DLitt UWE, 2003. *Recreations:* cinema, stained glass windows. *Address:* Flat 2, 30 Albert Road, Clevedon, N Somerset BS21 7RR. *E:* barry.rogerson@blueyonder.co.uk.

**ROGERSON, Bernadette;** *see* Baxter, B.

**ROGERSON, Daniel John;** Chairman, Wessex Water Partnership, since 2016; *b* 23 July 1975; *s* of late Stephen John Rogerson and of Patricia Anne Rogerson (*née* Jones); *m* 1999, Heidi Lee Purser; two *s* one *d*. *Educ:* St Mary's Sch., Bodmin; Bodmin Coll.; Univ. of Wales, Aberystwyth (BSc Econ Pols 1996). Local govt officer, Bedford BC, 1996–98; admin. officer, De Montfort Univ., 1998–2002. Mem., Bedford BC, 1999–2002. MP (Lib Dem) N Cornwall, 2005–15; contested (Lib Dem) same seat, 2015, 2017. Parly Under-Sec. of State, DEFRA, 2013–15. Dir, Plymouth CAST Multi-Academy Trust; Trustee, Bewnans Kernow. *Recreations:* listening to blues music, reading, travel. *Club:* Camelford Liberal.

**ROGERSON, Paul,** CBE 2007; DL; Chief Executive, Leeds City Council, 1999–2010; Consultant, Walton & Co., Planning Lawyers, Leeds, since 2010; *b* 10 June 1948; *s* of late John Rogerson and Hilda Rogerson (*née* Hepworth); *m* 1971, Eileen Kane; four *s* two *d*. *Educ:* De La Salle Coll., Sheffield; Manchester Univ. (LLB, MA Econ). Called to the Bar,

Gray's Inn, 1971; Lectr, Univ. of Leeds, 1969–75; Principal Legal Officer: Barnsley MBC, 1975–78; Kirklees MDC, 1978–89; Asst Dir/Chief Legal Officer, 1989–95, Exec. Dir, 1995–99, Leeds CC. Dir, Northern Gas Networks, 2014–. Vis. Prof., Univ. of Louisville, USA, 1972–73. Trustee: Lineham Farm Children's Centre, 2010– (Chair, 2012–); Heart Research UK, 2012– (Vice Chair, 2017–); Unipol Student Homes, 2014–18; Dio. of Leeds Trustee, 2017–. Gov., Leeds Trinity Univ., 2013– (Chair, Govs, 2019–). DL W Yorks, 2010. Jt Gen. Ed., Local Govt Law Reports, 1999–2001. *Recreations:* family, friends, travel. *Address:* 12 Oakwood Lane, Leeds LS8 2JQ. *T:* (0113) 368 9146.

**ROGERSON, Philip Graham;** Chairman: Bunzl, 2010–April 2020; De La Rue, 2012–19 (non-executive Director, 2012–19); *b* 1 Jan. 1945; *s* of Henry and Florence Rogerson; *m* 1968, Susan Janet Kershaw; one *s* two *d*. *Educ:* William Hulme's Grammar Sch., Manchester. FCA 1968. Dearden, Harper, Miller & Co., Chartered Accountants, 1962–67; Hill Samuel & Co. Ltd, 1967–69; Thomas Tilling Ltd, 1969–71; Steetley Ltd, 1971–72; J. W. Chafer Ltd, 1972–78; with ICI plc, 1978–92 (General Manager, Finance, 1989–92); British Gas, later BG plc: Man. Dir, Finance, 1992–94; Exec. Dir, 1994–98; Dep. Chm., 1996–98. Non-executive Chairman: Pipeline Integrity Internat., 1998–2002; Bertram Gp Ltd, 1999–2001; United Engineering Forgings Ltd, 1999–2001; KBC Advanced Technologies plc, 1999–2004; Viridian Gp plc, 1999–2005 (Dep. Chm., 1998); Project Telecom plc, 2000–03; Aggreko, 2002–12 (Dep. Chm., 1997–2002); Thus Gp plc, 2004–08; Carillion, 2005–14 (Dep. Chm., 2004–05); Northgate plc, 2007–09 (non-exec. Dir, 2003–07); non-executive Director: Leeds Permanent Bldg Soc., then Halifax Bldg Soc., now Halifax plc, 1994–98; Limit plc, 1997–2000; Internat. Public Relations, 1997–98; Wates City of London Properties, 1998–2001; British Biotech, 1999–2003; Octopus Capital plc, 2000–01; CopperEye Ltd, 2001–03; Celltech Gp plc, 2003–04; Davis Service Gp, 2004–10; Sen. Ind. Dir, Blancco Technol. Gp plc, 2017–. Chm. Adv. Bd, NE London Commng Support Unit, 2013–19. Chm., Central YMCA, 2011–. Trustee, Changing Faces, 1997–2011. *Recreations:* golf, tennis, theatre.

**ROGERSON, Dr Philippa Jane;** Reader in Private International Law, University of Cambridge, since 2017; Fellow, since 1989, and Master, since 2018, Gonville and Caius College, Cambridge; *b* Woodbridge, 24 Sept. 1961; *d* of Martin Jeremy Rogerson and Anne Theresa Rogerson (*née* Crimmin); *m* 1989, Gerard Fitzsimons (*d* 2007); five *d*. *Educ:* New Hall Sch.; Colchester Inst.; Newnham Coll., Cambridge (BA 1983; MA 1987; PhD 1990). Admitted Solicitor, 1986. Lectr, 1990–2001, Sen. Lectr, 2001–17, Univ. of Cambridge; Dir of Studies in Law, Gonville and Caius Coll., Cambridge, 1990–2018. *Publications:* Collier's Conflict of Laws, 2012; contribs on private internat. law. *Recreations:* family, singing, dog walking. *Address:* Gonville and Caius College, Cambridge CB2 1TA. *T:* (01223) 332400. *E:* pjr1000@cam.ac.uk.

**ROGG, Lionel;** organist and composer; Professor of Organ and Improvisation, Geneva Conservatoire de Musique, 1961–2002; Professor of Improvisation, Royal Academy of Music, 2004–09; *b* 1936; *m* Claudine Effront; three *s*. *Educ:* Conservatoire de Musique, Geneva (1st prize for piano and organ). Concerts or organ recitals on the five continents. Records include: 3 versions of complete organ works of J. S. Bach (Grand Prix du Disque, 1970, for The Art of the Fugue); works by Buxtehude (complete organ works; Deutscher Schallplatten Preis, 1980); Couperin, Grigny, Handel, Mozart, Liszt, Reger; transcriptions and own compositions. *Compositions:* Acclamations, 1964; Chorale Preludes, 1971; Partita, 1975; Variations on Psalm 91, 1983; Cantata "Geburt der Venus", 1984; Introduction, Ricerare and Toccata, 1985; Two Etudes, 1986; Monodies, 1986; Psalm 92, 1986; Piece for Clarinette, 1986; Face-à-face for two pianos, 1987; Organ Concerto, 1991. DèsL Univ. de Genève, 1989. *Publications:* Eléments de Contrepoint, 1969. *Address:* 38A route de Troinex, 1234 Vessy-Genève, Switzerland.

**ROH, Tae Woo,** Hon. GCMG 1989; President of Republic of Korea, 1988–93; *b* 4 Dec. 1932; *m* 1959, Kim-Ok-Sook; one *s* one *d*. *Educ:* Korean Military Academy; Republic of Korea War College. Commander, Capital Security, 1978, Defence Security, 1980; retd as Army General; Minister of State for Nat. Security and Foreign Affairs, 1981; Minister of Sports, and of Home Affairs, 1982; President: Seoul Olympic Organizing Cttee, 1983; Asian Games Organizing Cttee, 1983; Korean Olympic Cttee, 1984. Mem., Nat. Assembly and Pres., Ruling Democratic Justice Party, 1985. Hon. Dr George Washington Univ., 1989. Order of Nat. Security Merit (Sam Il Medal) (Korea), 1967; Grand Order of Mugunghwa (Korea), 1988; foreign decorations, incl. France, Germany, Kenya, Paraguay. *Publications:* Widaehan pot'ongsaram ui shidae (A great era of the ordinary people), 1987, trans. Japanese, 1988; Korea: a nation transformed, 1990. *Recreations:* tennis, swimming, golf, music, reading.

**ROITH, Oscar,** CB 1987; FREng, FIMechE; Deputy Chairman, British Maritime Technology, 1997–2002 (Director, 1987–2002); Chief Engineer and Scientist, Department of Trade and Industry, 1982–87; *b* London, 14 May 1927; *s* of late Leon Roith and Leah Roith; *m* 1950, Irene Bullock; one *d*. *Educ:* Gonville and Caius Coll., Cambridge (minor schol.; Mech. Scis Tripos; MA). FIMechE 1967; FREng (FEng 1983); Eur Ing 1988. Research Dept, Courtaulds, 1948; Distillers Co. Ltd: Central Engrg Dept, 1952; Engrg Manager, Hull Works, 1962; Works Manager, 1968, Works Gen. Manager, 1969, BP Chemicals, Hull; General Manager: Engrg and Technical, BP Chemicals, 1974; Engrg Dept, BP Trading, 1977; Chief Exec. (Engrg), BP Internat., 1981. Dir, Trueland Ltd, 1987–2004. Mem., Yorks and Humberside Economic Planning Council, 1972–74. Comr, Royal Commn for Exhibition of 1851, 1988–98. Chm., Mech. and Electrical Engrg Requirements Bd, 1981–82; Member: Mech. Engrg and Machine Tools Requirements Bd, 1977–81; (non-exec.) Res. Cttee. British Gas, 1987–96; ACORD, 1982–87; ACARD, 1982–87; Process Plant EDC, NEDO, 1979–82; SERC, 1982–87; NERC, 1982–87; Bd (part-time), LRT, 1988–95; Chm., Res. Adv. Gp, PCFC, 1989–92. Pres., IMechE, 1987–88 (Dep. Pres., 1985–87; Mem. Council, 1981–92; Mem., Process Engrg Gp Cttee, 1962–68); Dep. Chm. Council, Foundn for Science and Technol., 1988–95; Hon. Sec., Mech. Engrg, Council of Fellowship of Engrg, 1988–91. Hon. Prof., Dept of Mgt Sci., Univ. of Stirling, 1992–95; Hon. Fellow, Univ. of Brighton, 1992. Governor: Brighton Polytechnic, 1988–91; ICSTM, 1990–98. CCMI; FRSA. Hon. DSc West of England, 1993. *Recreations:* cricket, gardening, walking. *Address:* 12 Linden Court, Lesbourne Road, Reigate, Surrey RH2 7AB. *T:* (01737) 240187. *Club:* Athenæum.

**ROITT, Prof. Ivan Maurice,** FRS 1983; Emeritus Professor of Immunology, University College London, 1992–2009; Professor, 1969–92, and Head of Department of Immunology, 1969–92, and of Rheumatology Research, 1984–92, University College and Middlesex School of Medicine (formerly Middlesex Hospital Medical School); Chief Scientist, NALIA Systems Ltd, since 2005; Hon. Director, Middlesex University Centre for Investigative and Diagnostic Oncology, since 2009; *b* 30 Sept. 1927; *e s* of Harry Roitt; *m* 1953, Margaret Auralie Louise, *d* of F. Haigh; three *d*. *Educ:* King Edward's Sch., Birmingham; Balliol Coll., Oxford (exhibnr; BSc 1950; MA 1953; DPhil 1953; DSc 1968; Hon. Fellow 2004). FRCPath 1973. Res. Fellow, 1953, Reader in Immunopathol., 1965–68, Middlesex Hosp. Med. Sch. Chm., WHO Cttee on Immunol Control of Fertility, 1976–79; Mem., Biol. Sub-Cttee, UGC. Mem., Harrow Borough Council, 1963–65; Chm., Harrow Central Lib. Assoc., 1965–67. Vis. Prof., Middx Univ., 2006. Florey Meml Lectr, Adelaide Univ., 1982. Trustee, RSocMed, 2010–. Hon. FRCP 1995. Hon. Dr Middx, 2007. (Jtly) Van Meter Prize, Amer. Thyroid Assoc., 1957; Gairdner Foundn Award, Toronto, 1964. *Publications:* Essential Immunology, 1971, 12th edn 2011; (jtly) Immunology of Oral Diseases, 1979; (jtly) Immunology, 1985, 8th edn 2013; (jtly) Current Opinion in Immunology (series), 1989–93; (jtly) Clinical Immunology, 1991; Slide Atlas of Essential Immunology, 1992; (with Peter J. Delves) Encyclopedia of Immunology, 1992, 2nd edn 2006; (ed jtly) Medical Microbiology, 1993, 5th edn 2013; 283 contribs to learned scientific jls. *Recreations:* tennis, golf, clarinet (modest), piano (very modest), banjo (subliminal), the contemporary novel, models of public debate. *Address:* Department of Biomedical Sciences, Middlesex University, Hatchcroft Building, Room H115, The Burroughs, Hendon, NW4 4BT.

**ROJO, Tamara,** CBE 2016; ballerina; Artistic Director, English National Ballet, since 2012; *d* of Pablo Rojo and Sara Diez. *Educ:* Centro de Danza de Victor Ullate; Conservatorio Profesional de Danza Mariemma, Madrid (Bachelor of Dance and Choreog.); Univ. Rey Juan Carlos (Master of Scenic Arts); DA *magna cum laude* 2016). Compañía de Danza Victor Ullate, 1991–96; Guest Dancer, Scottish Ballet, 1996–97; Principal, English Nat. Ballet, 1997–2000; Principal Dancer, Royal Ballet, 2000–12. Guest Dancer: Birmingham Royal Ballet; Kirov Ballet; La Scala Ballet; Nat. Ballet of China; English Nat. Ballet; Tokyo Ballet; New Nat. Tokyo Ballet; Mikhailovsky Ballet; Royal Swedish Ballet; Nat. Ballet of Finland; Ballet Nat. de Cuba; Deutsche Oper Ballet Berlin; Ballet de La Opera de Niza; Ente Publico Arena di Verona; Scottish Ballet; Ballet Victor Ullate, Madrid. Resident Guest Teacher, Royal Ballet Sch. Advr, Superior Counsel of Artistic Studies, Spain. Member, Board: Dance UK; Arts Council East. Patron, DanceEast Acad., Norwich. Grand Prix Femme, Concours Internat. de Danse de Paris, 1994; Best Dancer of Year, Italian Critics, 1996; Award for Outstanding Achievements in Dance, Barclay's Th. Awards, 2000; Best Female Dancer of Year 2001, Critic's Circle Dance Awards, 2002; Leonid Massine Premio al Valore, 2004; Internat. Medal for the Arts, Madrid, Interpretation Award, Villa de Madrid, 2007; Prince of Asturias Arts Award, Benois de la Danse Award, 2008; Dancer Revelation of Year Award, The Times; Possitano Dance Award. Medalla de Oro al Mérito en las Bellas Artes (Spain), 2002. *Address:* c/o English National Ballet, Markova House, 39 Jay Mews, SW7 2ES. *W:* www.tamara-rojo.com.

**ROKISON, Kenneth Stuart;** QC 1976; a Judge of the Courts of Appeal of Jersey and Guernsey, 2000–07; a former Deputy High Court Judge; *b* 13 April 1937; *s* of late Frank Edward and late Kitty Winifred Rokison; *m* 1973, Rosalind Julia (*née* Mitchell); one *s* two *d*. *Educ:* Whitgift School, Croydon; Magdalene College, Cambridge (BA 1960). Called to the Bar, Gray's Inn, 1961, Bencher, 1985–2003; in practice as a barrister, 1961–97; a Recorder, 1989–94; an arbitrator and mediator, 1997–2018. *Recreations:* theatre, tennis. *Address:* Brettenden Barn, Gadbrook, Betchworth, Surrey RH3 7AH. *T:* (01306) 611244.
See also A. *Rokison-Woodall*.

**ROKISON-WOODALL, Dr Abigail;** Senior Lecturer in Shakespeare and Theatre, Shakespeare Institute, University of Birmingham, since 2013; *b* Epsom, 23 Sept. 1975; *d* of Kenneth Stuart Rokison, *qv*; *m* 2015, Andrew Woodall; one *s*. *Educ:* Croydon High Sch.; LAMDA (Dip. Acting 1996); Open Univ. (BA Hons 1st Cl. Humanities with Lit. 2001); King's Coll. London (MA Shakespeare Text and Playhouse (Dist.) 2002); Trinity Hall, Cambridge (PhD 2006). Actor, 1992–2000; Lectr in Eng. and Drama, Faculty of Educn, Univ. of Cambridge, 2006–12; Fellow, and Dir, Studies in Eng. and Drama, Homerton Coll., Cambridge, 2006–12. Chm., Trustees, British Shakespeare Assoc., 2008–10. Gen. Ed., Arden Shakespeare Performance Editions, 2017–. *Publications:* Shakespearean Verse Speaking, 2010 (Shakespeare's Globe Book Award, 2012); Shakespeare for Young People: productions, versions and adaptations, 2013; Shakespeare in the Theatre: Nicholas Hytner, 2017; (ed) Hamlet: Arden performance editions, 2017; (ed) A Midsummer Night's Dream: Arden performance editions, 2017; articles in Shakespeare Jl, Literature Compass. *Recreations:* theatre, ballet, music, singing, cooking, tap dancing. *Address:* Shakespeare Institute, Church Street, Stratford-upon-Avon CV37 6HP. *T:* (0121) 414 9511. *E:* a.rokison@bham.ac.uk.

**ROLAND, Prof. Martin Oliver,** CBE 2003; DM; FRCP, FRCGP; FMedSci; Professor of Health Services Research, University of Cambridge, 2009–16, now Emeritus; Professorial Fellow, 2014–18, now Emeritus, and Chairman, Art Committee, since 2014, Murray Edwards College, Cambridge; *b* 7 Aug. 1951; *s* of Peter Ernest Roland and Margaret Eileen Roland; *m* 1st, 1971, Gillian Chapman; one *s*; 2nd, 1979, Rosalind Thorburn; two *s* one *d*. *Educ:* Rugby Sch.; Merton Coll., Oxford (BA 1972; BM BCh 1975; DM 1989). MRCP 1978, FRCP 2001; FRCGP 1994. Lectr in Gen. Practice, St Thomas's Hosp. Med. Sch., 1979–83; Dir of Studies in Gen. Practice, Cambridge Univ. Sch. of Clinical Medicine, 1987–92; Prof. of General Practice, Univ. of Manchester, 1992–2009; Director: Nat. Primary Care Res. and Develt Centre, 1999–2009; NIHR Sch. for Primary Care Res., 2006–09. Mem., MRC Health Services Research Bd, 1992–96 (Chm. and Mem. MRC Council, 1994–96). FMedSci 2000. *Publications:* contribs on gen. practice, hosp. referrals, back pain, quality of care and out of hours care. *Recreations:* walking, opera, contemporary women's art. *E:* mr108@cam.ac.uk.

**ROLFE;** *see* Neville-Rolfe.

**ROLFE, Mervyn James,** CBE 2000; DL; Chairman, ESEP Ltd, 1999–2014; *b* 31 July 1947; *s* of late Raymond Rolfe and Margaret Rolfe; *m* 1977, Christine Margaret Tyrell (decd); one *s*. *Educ:* Buckhaven High Sch., Fife; Dundee Univ. (MEd Hons); Abertay Dundee Univ. (MSc). FSAScot 1993. Civil servant, MSC, 1977–83; Co-ordinator, Dundee Resources Centre for Unemployed, 1983–87. Tayside Regional Council: Councillor, 1986–96; Convener of Educn, 1986–94; Depute Leader, 1990–94; Opposition Leader, 1994–96; Dundee City Council: Mem., 1995–2003; Convener of Econ. Develt and Depute Leader, 1999–2003; Lord Provost and Lord-Lieut of Dundee, 1996–99. Chief Exec., Dundee and Tayside Chamber of Commerce and Industry, 2002–06; Dir, Scottish Enterprise Tayside, 1992–96, 1999–2003. Convenor, Scottish Police Services Authy, 2007–08. Lectr in Econs and Mgt, Univ. of Abertay, Dundee, 2008–13. Member: General Teaching Council Scotland, 1986–96; Exec., COSLA, 1990–96. Mem. Court, Dundee Univ., 1986–2000. Vice Chm. of Govs, HM Frigate Unicorn Preservation Soc., 1998–2014; Hon. Col, 2 (City of Dundee) Signals Sqn, TA, 2003–10. Hon. Fellow, Univ. of Abertay Dundee, 1999. FRSA 1992. JP 1988–2008, DL 1999, Dundee. OStJ 1997. *Recreations:* reading, music, local history. *Address:* 17 Mains Terrace, Dundee DD4 7BX. *T:* (01382) 450073.

**ROLFE, Richard B.;** *see* Boggis-Rolfe.

**ROLFE, William David Ian,** PhD; FRSE, FGS, FMA; Keeper of Geology, National Museums of Scotland, 1986–96; *b* 24 Jan. 1936; *s* of late William Ambrose Rolfe and Greta Olwen Jones; *m* 1960, Julia Mary Margaret, *d* of late Capt. G. H. G. S. Rayer, OBE; two *d*. *Educ:* Royal Liberty Grammar Sch., Romford; Birmingham Univ. (BSc 1957; PhD 1960). FGS 1960; FMA 1972; FRSE 1983. Demonstrator in Geol., UC of N Staffs, 1960; Fulbright Schol., and Asst Curator, Mus. of Comparative Zool., Harvard Coll., Cambridge, Mass, 1961–62; Geol. Curator, Univ. Lectr, then Sen. Lectr in Geol., Hunterian Mus., Univ. of Glasgow, 1962–81; Dep. Dir, 1981–86. Vis. Scientist, Field Mus. of Natural Hist., Chicago, 1981. Mem., Trng Awards Cttee, NERC, 1980–83. President: Palaeontol. Assoc.,

1992–94 (Vice-Pres., 1974–76); Soc. Hist. Natural Hist., 1996–99 (Vice-Pres., 1987). Geological Society of Glasgow: Ed., Scottish Jl of Geol., 1967–72; Pres., 1973–76; Geological Society: Editl Chm., Journal, 1973–76; Chm., Conservation Cttee, 1980–85; Murchison Fund, 1982; Tyrrell Res. Fund, 1982; Coke Medal, 1984; Edinburgh Geological Society: Pres., 1989–91; Clough Medal, 1997. FRSA 1985. *Publications:* (ed) Phylogeny and Evolution of Crustacea, 1963; Treatise on Invertebrate Paleontology, part R, 1969; Geological Howlers, 1980; (ed and contrib.) The Paper Museum of Cassiano dal Pozzo, vols B IV–V, Natural Curiosities, 2017; papers on fossil phyllocarid crustaceans and palaeontol., esp. other arthropods, and hist. of 18th century natural sci. illustration. *Recreations:* visual arts, walking, music. *Address:* 4A Randolph Crescent, Edinburgh EH3 7TH. *T:* (0131) 226 2094.

**ROLLAND, Lawrence Anderson Lyon,** PPRIBA; PPRIAS; FRSE; Senior Partner, Hurd Rolland Partnership (formerly L. A. Rolland & Partners and Robert Hurd and Partners), 1959–97; President of Royal Institute of British Architects, 1985–87; *b* 6 Nov. 1937; *s* of Lawrence Anderson Rolland and Winifred Anne Lyon; *m* 1960, Mairi Melville; two *s* two *d*. *Educ:* George Watson's Boys' College, Edinburgh; Duncan of Jordanstone College of Art. Diploma of Art (Architecture) 1959. ARIBA 1960; FRIAS 1965 (Pres., RIAS, 1979–81); FRSE 1989. Founder Mem., Scottish Construction Industry Group, 1979–81; Mem., Bldg EDC, NEDC, 1982–88. Mem. Bd, Architects' Registration Bd, 1996–2004 (Chm., Qualifications Adv. Gp, 2000–04). Architect for: The Queen's Hall, concert hall, Edinburgh; restoration and redesign of Bank of Scotland Head Office (original Architect, Sibbald, Reid & Crighton, 1805 and later, Bryce, 1870); much housing in Fife's royal burghs; British Golf Museum, St Andrews; General Accident Life Assurance, York; redesign, Council Chamber, GMC. Chairman: RIBA Educn Trust Fund, 1996–2003; RIBA Educn Funds Cttee, 1996–2003; Gen. Trustee, Church of Scotland, 1979–2014 (Chm., Adv. Cttee on Artistic Matters, 1975–81); Mem. of Council and Bd, Nat. Trust for Scotland, 2005–11. Chm. Bd of Govs, Duncan of Jordanstone Coll. of Art, 1993–94; Chm. Court, Univ. of Dundee, 1997–2004 (Mem., 1993–2009; Chancellor's Assessor, 2005–10). FRSA 1988. Hon. LLD Dundee, 2004. Winner of more than 20 awards and commendations from Saltire Soc., Stone Fedn, Concrete Soc., Civic Trust, Europa Nostra, RIBA, and Times Conservation Award. *Recreations:* music, fishing, food, wine, cars. *Address:* Blinkbonny Cottage, Newburn, nr Upper Largo, Leven, Fife KY8 6JF. *T:* (01333) 360383.

**ROLLINS, Marva,** OBE 2017; Headteacher, Raynham Primary School, Edmonton, since 2000; *b* St Andrews, Barbados, 14 Dec. 1951; *d* of Franklyn and Myrtle Hurst; *m* (marr. diss.); three *s*; partner, Eric Parke. *Educ:* Poly. of N London (BEd 1986); Open Univ. (MA Educn 1990). Comptometer operator, 1968–72; class teacher, Kensington, Salisbury and Sandringham Primary Schs, Newham, 1986–92; Dep. Headteacher, Cleves Primary Sch., Newham, 1992–95; Headteacher, Godwin Jun. Sch., Newham, 1995–2000. Lecturer (pt-time): Newham Coll., 1990–95; Inst. of Educn, Univ. of London, 2003– (Vis. Fellow, 2011–). Educn Advr, Barbadian Overseas Nationals Orgn, 1998–2004. Founder Member: Sickle Cell Soc., 1979; E London Black Women Orgn, 1979–; Newham African Caribbean Assoc., 1984–. Keynote speaker and trainer in educn leadership and personal develt. Hon. Licentiate, Coll. of Preceptors, 1996. Windrush Educn Champion, 2004. 50th Year of Independence Award, Barbados Govt, 2016. *Recreations:* travelling, reading, walking. *Address:* Raynham Primary School, Raynham Avenue, Edmonton, N18 2JQ. *T:* (020) 8807 4726, *Fax:* (020) 8807 8013. *E:* Headteacher@raynham.enfield.sch.uk.

**ROLLINSON, Timothy John Denis,** CBE 2012; Director-General and Deputy Chairman, Forestry Commission, 2004–13; *b* 6 Nov. 1953; *s* of William Edward Denis Rollinson and Ida Frances Rollinson (*née* Marshall); *m* 1st, 1975 (marr. diss.); one *s* two *d*; 2nd, 2013, Frances Isabel Smith. *Educ:* Chigwell Sch.; Edinburgh Univ. (BSc Hons). MICFor 1978, FICFor 1995; FIAgrE 2004; CEnv 2005. Forestry Commission: District Officer: Kent, 1976–78; New Forest, 1978–81; Head of: Growth and Yield Studies, 1981–88; Land Use Planning, 1988–90; Parly and Policy Div., 1990–93; Sec., 1994–97; Chief Conservator, England, 1997–2000; Head of Policy and Practice Div., 2000–03; Dir, Forestry Gp, 2003–04. Chairman: Forest Res. Co-ordination Cttee, 2000–04; Global Partnership on Forest Landscape Restoration, 2002–; Pres., Inst. of Chartered Foresters, 2000–02. Trustee: Royal Botanic Gardens, Edinburgh, 2009–17; Woodland Trust, 2013–18. Patron, Tree Aid, 2008–. CCMI 2006. *Publications:* Thinning Control in British Woodlands, 1985; articles in forestry jls. *Recreations:* golf, food. *Clubs:* Craigmillar Park Golf (Edinburgh); Dunbar Golf.

**ROLLO,** family name of **Lord Rollo.**

**ROLLO, 14th Lord** *cr* 1651; **David Eric Howard Rollo;** Baron Dunning 1869; *b* 31 March 1943; *s* of 13th Lord Rollo and Suzanne Hatton; *S* father, 1997; *m* 1971, Felicity Anne Christian, *o d* of Lt-Comdr J. B. Lamb; three *s*. *Educ:* Eton. Late Captain Grenadier Guards. *Heir: s* Master of Rollo, *qv*. *Address:* Pitcairns House, Dunning, Perthshire PH2 9BX. *Clubs:* Cavalry and Guards, Turf.

**ROLLO, Master of; Hon. James David William Rollo;** *b* 8 Jan. 1972; *s* and *heir* of Lord Rollo, *qv*; *m* 2001, Sophie Sara, *d* of Hubert de Castella; one *s* three *d*. *Educ:* Eton; Edinburgh Univ.

**ROLLO, Prof. James Maxwell Cree,** CMG 1998; Director, InterAnalysis Ltd, since 2008; Professor of European Economic Integration, University of Sussex, and Co-Director, Sussex European Institute, 1999–2011, now Professor Emeritus; Deputy Director and Fellow, UK Trade Policy Observatory, University of Sussex and Royal Institute of International Affairs, since 2016; *b* 20 Jan. 1946; *s* of late James Maxwell Cree Rollo and Alice Mary (*née* Killen); *m* 1st, 1970, Sonia Ann Halliwell (marr. diss. 2008); one *s* one *d*; 2nd, 2008, Rachel Ann Thompson. *Educ:* Gourock High Sch.; Greenock High Sch.; Glasgow Univ. (BSc); London School of Economics (MSc Econ). Asst Economist, 1968–75, Economic Advr, 1975–79, MAFF; Economic Advr, FCO, 1979–81; Sen. Economic Advr, ODA, 1981–84; Dep. Head, Economic Advrs, FCO, 1984–89; Dir, Internat. Econs Programme, RIIA, 1989–93; Chief Economic Advr, FCO, 1993–98. Dir, ESRC Res. Prog., One Europe or Several?, 2001–03. Special Prof., Univ. of Nottingham, 1996–99. Associate Fellow, Internat. Econs Prog., RIIA, 2001–; Associate Res. Fellow, Centre for Analysis of Regl Integration at Sussex, Univ. of Sussex, 2006–. Trustee, Mus. of Migration and Diversity, Spitalfields, 2001–. FAcSS (AcSS 2009). Ed., Jl of Common Market Studies, 2003–10. *Publications:* The New Eastern Europe: Western responses, 1990; (with John Flemming) Trade, Payments and Adjustment in Central and Eastern Europe, 1992; articles in learned jls. *Recreation:* having fun. *Address:* InterAnalysis Ltd, Sussex Innovation Centre, University of Sussex, Brighton BN1 9SB. *T:* (01273) 234641. *E:* j.rollo@sussex.ac.uk.

**ROLLS, Charles T.;** Co-founder, 2005, and non-executive Deputy Chairman, since 2017, Fever-Tree Drinks plc (Chief Executive Officer, 2005–14; Executive Deputy Chairman, 2014–17); *b* London, 1957. *Educ:* Imperial Coll. London (BSc); INSEAD (MBA). Man. Dir, Plymouth Gin, 1997–2001. Chm., Outside In Art, 2017–.

**ROLLS, Prof. Edmund Thomson,** DPhil, DSc; Director, Oxford Centre for Computational Neuroscience, since 2008; Professor of Computational Neuroscience, University of Warwick, since 2013; *b* 4 June 1945; *s* of Eric Fergus Rolls and May Martin Rolls (*née* Thomson); *m* 1969, Barbara Jean Simons (marr. diss. 1983); two *d*. *Educ:* Hardye's Sch., Dorchester; Jesus Coll., Cambridge (BA Preclinical Medicine 1967; MA); Queen's Coll., Oxford (Thomas Hardy Schol.); Magdalen Coll., Oxford (DPhil 1971); DSc Oxon 1986. Fellow by Exam., Magdalen Coll., Oxford, 1969–73; Lectr in Exptl Psychol., 1973–96, Prof. of Exptl Psychol., 1996–2008, Oxford Univ.; Fellow and Tutor in Psychol., 1973–2008, Vice Pres., 2003–06, Corpus Christi Coll., Oxford. Principal Res. Fellow, Univ. of Warwick, 2008–13. Associate Dir, MRC Oxford IRC for Cognitive Neurosci., 1990–2003. Member: Soc. for Neurosci.; Physiological Soc.; Exptl Psychol. Soc. Secretary: Eur. Brain and Behaviour Soc., 1973–76; Council, Eur. Neurosci. Assoc., 1985–88; Membre d'Honneur, Société Française de Neurologie, 1994; Mem., Academia Europaea. Canadian Commonwealth Fellow, 1980–81. Hon. DSc Toyama, 2005. Spearman Medal, BPsS, 1977. *Publications:* The Brain and Reward, 1975; (with B. J. Rolls) Thirst, 1982; (with A. Treves) Neural Networks and Brain Function, 1998; (jtly) Introduction to Connectionist Modelling of Cognitive Processes, 1998; The Brain and Emotion, 1999; (with G. Deco) Computational Neuroscience of Vision, 2002; Emotion Explained, 2005; Memory, Attention and Decision-Making, 2008; (with G. Deco) The Noisy Brain: stochastic dynamics as a principle of brain function, 2010; Neuroculture: on the implications of brain science, 2012; Emotion and Decision-Making Explained, 2014; Cerebral Cortex: principles of operation, 2016; The Brain, Emotion, and Depression, 2018; The Orbitofrontal Cortex, 2019; over 600 scientific papers. *Recreations:* yachting, windsurfing, music, including opera. *W:* www.oxcns.org.

**ROMAIN, Rabbi Dr Jonathan Anidjar,** MBE 2004; Minister, Maidenhead Synagogue, since 1980; Chairman, Assembly of Rabbis, 2007–09; *b* 24 Aug. 1954; *s* of Daniel and Gabrielle Romain; *m* 1981, Sybil Sheridan; four *s*. *Educ:* University Coll. London (BA Hons); Univ. of Leicester (PhD 1990). Semicha/Rabbinic Ordination, Leo Baeck Coll., London. Chaplain, Jewish Police Assoc., 2003–. Chm., Accord Coalition, 2009–18; Member, Board: CCJ, 1989–2017; St George's Hse, Windsor Castle, 2015–; Vice-Chm., Dignity in Dying, 2018–. *Publications:* Signs and Wonders, 1985; The Jews of England, 1988; Faith and Practice, 1991; Tradition and Change, 1995; Till Faith us to Part, 1996; Renewing the Vision, 1996; Your God Shall Be My God, 2000; (ed) Reform Judaism and Modernity, 2004; God, Doubt and Dawkins, 2008; Really Useful Prayers, 2009; (ed) Great Reform Lives, 2010; (ed) A Passion for Judaism, 2011; Royal Jews, 2013; (ed) Assisted Dying—Rabbinic Responses, 2014; (ed) Terror, Trauma and Tragedy, 2016; Rabbi, I Have a Problem, 2016; Confessions of a Rabbi, 2017; Inclusive Judaism, 2020. *Recreations:* tennis, completing a never-ending family tree, preaching what I think I ought to practise. *Address:* Grenfell Lodge, Ray Park Road, Maidenhead, Berks SL6 8QX. *T:* (01628) 673012.

**ROMAINE, Prof. Suzanne,** PhD; Merton Professor of English Language, and Fellow of Merton College, Oxford University, 1984–2015. *Educ:* Bryn Mawr Coll., Penn (AB); Edinburgh Univ. (MLitt); PhD Birmingham Univ. Lectr in Linguistics, Birmingham Univ., 1979–84. Marie Curie Fellow of EU and Ext. Sen. Fellow, Freiburg Inst. of Advanced Studies, 2015–16. Fellow: Finnish Acad. of Sci. and Letters, Helsinki, 2010; Norwegian Acad. of Sci. and Letters, Oslo, 2016. PhD *hc*: Tromsø 1998; Uppsala 1999. *Publications:* Socio-historical Linguistics: its status and methodology, 1982; Sociolinguistic Variation in Speech Communities, 1982; Language of Children and Adolescents, 1984; Pidgin and Creole Languages, 1988; Bilingualism, 1989; (ed) Language in Australia, 1991; Language Education and Development, 1992; Language in Society: introduction to sociolinguistics, 1994; (ed) Cambridge History of the English Language, vol. IV, 1998; Communicating Gender, 1999; (with D. Nettle) Vanishing Voices, 2000; (jtly) Linguistic Diversity in High Biodiversity Regions, 2014.

**ROMAN, Stephan,** CMG 2011; Regional Director, South Asia, British Council, 2011–16; writer and researcher, since 2016; *b* 29 March 1953; *s* of Victor and Muriel Roman; *m* 1986, Dorcas Pearmaine; one *s* two *d*. *Educ:* St Peter's Coll., Oxford (BA Hons Mod. Hist. 1974, MA); Univ. of Sheffield (MA Librarianship and Inf. Studies 1976). Libraries, Arts and Mus Dept, Coventry CC, 1974–78; British Council: Sudan and Yemen, 1979–82; Saudi Arabia and Gulf, 1983–86; Indonesia, 1986–91; Dir, Information Services, 1992–2001; Regl Dir, SE Europe, 2001–05; Regl Dir, W Europe and N America, 2005–11. Founding Mem., Armant de Brezilhac Associates, 2016–. Member, Board: Council for At-Risk Academics, 2012–; NATANDA Dance Th. Foundn, Sri Lanka, 2016–. FLA 1978; FRSA. Order of Merit (Romania), 2004. *Publications:* The Development of Islamic Library Collections in Western Europe and North America, 1990; Supporting Libraries under Pressure: the British Council experience 1934–2015, 2016. *Recreations:* history, philosophy, current affairs, arts, theatre.

**ROMAN, Stephen Thomas B.;** *see* Braviner Roman.

**ROMANIUK, Paula Shane;** *see* Pryke, P. S.

**ROMANOVITCH, Sacha Veronica;** Co-Chair, Inclusive Economy Partnership, since 2018; *b* Barnet, 14 March 1968; *d* of André Romanovitch and Margaret Elizabeth Romanovitch; *m* 2002, Neil Pemberthy; two *s*. *Educ:* Somerville Coll., Oxford (BA Chem. 1990; MA). ACA 1993, FCA 2003. Joined Grant Thornton LLP, 1990: Partner, 2001–18; Partner, Leading on People and Culture, Nat. Leadership Bd, 2008–15; CEO, 2015–18. Chm., Patron Gp, Access Accountancy, 2015–. Member: UK Nat. Adv. Bd, Global Impact Investing Steering Gp, 2016–; Bd, London and Partners, 2017–. Cert. in Coach Mentoring, Eur. Mentoring and Coaching Council, 2011; Neuro-linguistic Programming Practitioner, 2013. Yoga teacher trng, Sivananda, 1999. DUniv York, 2018. *Recreations:* family, travel, diving, yoga.

**ROMANOW, Hon. Roy John,** OC 2003; PC (Can.) 2003; QC (Sask.); Senior Fellow in Public Policy, Department of Political Studies, University of Saskatchewan, Canada, since 2001 (Chancellor, 2016–19); Senior Policy Fellow, Saskatchewan Institute of Public Policy, University of Regina, since 2001; *b* 1939; *s* of Mike and Tekla Romanow; *m* 1967, Eleanore Boykowich. *Educ:* Univ. of Saskatchewan (Arts and Law degrees). First elected to Saskatchewan Legislative Assembly, 1967; MLA (NDP) Saskatoon-Riversdale, 1967–82, 1986–2001; Dep. Premier, 1971–82; Attorney General, 1971–82; Minister of Intergovtl Affairs, 1979–82; Opposition House Leader for NDP Caucus, 1986; Leader, Saskatchewan NDP, 1987–2001; Premier, Saskatchewan, 1991–2001. Hd, Commn on Future of Health Care in Canada, 2001–02; Mem., Security Intelligence Rev. Cttee, 2003–08. Vis. Fellow, Sch. of Policy Studies, Queen's Univ., 2001–. *Publications:* (jtly) Canada Notwithstanding, 1984. *Address:* c/o Department of Political Studies, University of Saskatchewan, 9 Campus Drive, 919 Arts Building, Saskatoon, SK S7N 5A5, Canada.

**ROMEO, Antonia;** Permanent Secretary, Department for International Trade, since 2017; *b* London, 20 Oct. 1974; *d* of Prof. Peter Rice-Evans and Prof. Catherine Rice-Evans; *m* 1999, John Romeo; two *s* one *d*. *Educ:* N London Collegiate Sch.; Westminster Sch.; Brasenose Coll., Oxford (MA PPE 1996); London Sch. of Econs and Pol Sci. (MSc Econs 2000); Columbia Business Sch. (AMP 2015). Strategy Consultant, Oliver Wyman and Co.,

1996–99; Lord Chancellor's Department, then Department for Constitutional Affairs, later Ministry of Justice: economist, 2000–04; Hd of Inf., Rights Div., Constitution Directorate, 2004–06; Principal Private Sec. to Lord Chancellor and Sec. of State for Constitutional Affairs, then for Justice, 2006–08; Dir, FCO, 2008–10; Exec. Dir, Governance Reform, Cabinet Office, 2010–11; Dir Gen., Transforming Justice, 2011–13, Criminal Justice, 2013–15, MoJ; Dir Gen., Econ. and Domestic Affairs Secretariat, Cabinet Office, 2015; HM Govt Envoy to United States' Communications Service Providers, Cabinet Office, 2015–16; HM Consul Gen. in NY, 2016–17; Dir Gen., Econ. and Commercial Affairs USA, DIT, 2016–17. *Recreations:* arts, fashion, family, ski-ing, London life. *Address:* Department for International Trade, King Charles Street, Whitehall, SW1A 2AH. *Clubs:* Athenæum, Groucho.

**ROMEO, Lyn**; Chief Social Worker for Adults, Department of Health and Social Care (formerly Department of Health), since 2013; *b* Griffith, NSW, 8 Sept. 1955; *d* of Domenico and Mary Romeo. *Educ:* Univ. of NSW (BSW 1978); Univ. of Leeds (MBA 1995). Hosp. Social Worker, St Vincent's Hosp., Sydney, 1977–79; Residential Social Worker, Leeds CC, 1980–81; Bradford Metropolitan District Council: Social Worker, 1981–86; Social Work Team Leader, 1986–90; Area Social Services Manager, 1990–92; Principal Care Manager, 1992–2000; Area Manager, 2000–02; Social Services Inspector, DoH, 2002–05; Asst Dir, Adult Social Care, London Bor. of Camden, 2005–13. Hon. DLitt Manchester Metropolitan, 2017. *Recreations:* hill walking, cycling, dancing, theatre. *Address:* Department of Health and Social Care, 39 Victoria Street, SW1H 0EU. *E:* ChiefSocialWorkerforAdults@dhsc.gov.uk.

**ROMETTY, Virginia M., (Ginni)**; President, Chief Executive Officer and Chairman, IBM Corporation, since 2012. *Educ:* Northwestern Univ. (BSc Computer Sci. and Electrical Engrg). Joined IBM Corporation, 1981; posts include: Gen. Manager, Global Services, Americas; Gen. Manager, Global Insce and Financial Services Sector; Sen. Vice Pres., Global Business Services; Sen. Vice Pres. and Gp Exec., Sales, Mktg and Strategy. Mem., Council on Foreign Relations. Member: Bd of Trustees, Northwestern Univ.; Bd of Managers, Memorial Sloan-Kettering Cancer Center. *Address:* IBM Corporation, 1 New Orchard Road, Armonk, NY 10504–1722, USA.

**ROMINGER, Rev. Roberta Carol Sears**; Pastor, Mercer Island United Church of Christ, Washington, USA, since 2015; General Secretary, United Reformed Church, 2008–14; *b* USA, 30 Aug. 1955; *d* of Robert Alden Sears and Janet Carol Sears (*née* Graef); *m* 1990, Rev. Dale Rominger. *Educ:* Univ. of California, Berkeley (BA 1977); Pacific Sch. of Religion, Berkeley (MDiv 1982). Ordained Minister, 1982; Minister: Tombstone Community Church, United Church of Christ, Arizona, 1982–85; York Rd URC, Woking, 1985–90; Worplesdon URC, Guildford, 1987–90; Wideopen URC, Newcastle upon Tyne, 1991–98; Kingston Park Ecumenical Church, Newcastle upon Tyne, 1993–98; Moderator, Thames North Synod, URC, 1998–2008. *Recreation:* playing the cello.

**ROMNEY, 8th Earl of**, *cr* 1801; **Julian Charles Marsham**; Bt 1663; Baron of Romney, 1716; Viscount Marsham, 1801; *b* 28 March 1948; *s* of late Col Peter William Marsham, MBE and Hersey Marsham (*née* Coke); *S* cousin, 2004; *m* 1975, Catriona Ann Stewart (*see* Countess of Romney); two *s* one *d*. *Educ:* Eton. High Sheriff, Norfolk, 2007. *Heir:* *s* Viscount Marsham, *qv*.

**ROMNEY, Countess of; Catriona Ann Marsham**; Vice Lord-Lieutenant of Norfolk, since 2012; *b* Edinburgh, 10 March 1954; *d* of Lt-Col Sir Robert (Christie) Stewart, *qv*; *m* 1975, Julian Charles Marsham (*see* Earl of Romney); two *s* one *d*. Trustee, Westacre Arts Foundn; Dir, Fine Art Commns. Former Chair, Gayton Parish Council. Chair, NSPCC, W Norfolk, and involved with other local organisations and charities. DL Norfolk, 2005. *Recreations:* gardening, cooking, walking, grandchildren. *Address:* Wensum Farm, West Rudham, King's Lynn, Norfolk PE31 8SZ. *T:* (01485) 528432. *E:* ciciromney@icloud.com.

**ROMNEY, Daphne Irene**; QC 2009; *b* London, 29 July 1955; *d* of Dr David Romney and Olga Romney (*née* Lempert). *Educ:* Camden Sch. for Girls; Newnham Coll., Cambridge (BA 1978). Called to the Bar, Inner Temple, 1979; in practice as barrister specialising in employment law. Chm., Employment Law Bar Assoc., 2007–09. Fawcett Society: Mem., Rev. Panel of Sex Discrimination Laws, 2017; Chair, Cttee on Reforming Equal Pay Laws, 2018. Trustee, Save-A-Child, 2009–. *Publications:* Equal Pay: law and practice, 2018. *Recreations:* watching Arsenal, gym and pilates, cooking, eating, travel. *Address:* Cloisters, 1 Pump Court, EC4Y 7AA. *T:* (020) 7827 4000, *Fax:* (020) 7827 4100. *E:* dr@cloisters.com.

**ROMNEY, (Willard) Mitt**; US Senator from Utah, since 2019; *b* Detroit, 12 March 1947; *s* of George and Lenore Romney; *m* 1969, Ann Davies; five *s*. *Educ:* Brigham Young Univ. (BA 1971); Harvard Univ. (JD, MBA 1975). Consultant, Boston Consulting Gp, 1975–77; Consultant, 1977–78, Vice-Pres., 1978–84, Bain & Co.; Man. Partner and CEO, Bain Capital Inc., 1984–99; interim CEO, Bain & Co., 1990–92; Pres. and CEO, Salt Lake Organizing Cttee, 2002 Winter Olympics, 1999–2002; Gov., Massachusetts, 2003–07. Dir, Marriott Internat. Inc., 1993–2002, 2009–11, 2012–19; Exec. Partner and Gp Chm., Solamere Capital, 2012–19. Republican Candidate for Presidency of USA, 2012. *Publications:* Turnaround: crisis, leadership and the Olympic Games (with T. Robinson), 2004; No Apology: the case for American greatness, 2010.

**RON, Prof. David**, MD; FRS 2014; FMedSci; Professor of Cellular Pathophysiology and Clinical Biochemistry, University of Cambridge, since 2009; Fellow, Churchill College, Cambridge, since 2011. *Educ:* Technion-Israel Inst. Technol., Haifa (MD 1980). Internship, 1980, then residency trng in internal medicine, Mount Sinai Med. Center, NYC; Clin. Fellow in Endocrinol. and Metabolism, Massachusetts Gen. Hosp., Boston, 1989; faculty post, New York Univ. Sch. of Medicine and estabd Skirball Inst. of Biomolecular Medicine, 1992; Julius Raynes Prof. of Cell Biol. and Medicine, New York Univ., until 2009. Adjunct Prof., Dept of Cell Biol., Skirball Inst., NY Univ. Sch. of Medicine; Wellcome Trust Principal Res. Fellow, 2009–. FMedSci 2013. *Address:* Cambridge Institute for Medical Research, University of Cambridge, Cambridge Biomedical Campus, Wellcome-MRC Building, Hills Road, Cambridge CB2 0XY.

**RONALDSHAY, Earl of; Robin Lawrence Dundas**; Director, Zetland Estates Ltd (formerly Dundas Estates Ltd), since 1999; *b* 5 March 1965; *s* and *heir* of Marquess of Zetland, *qv*; *m* 1997, Heather, *d* of late Robert Hoffman, Maryland, USA and of Mrs Richard Cazenove, Cottesbrooke, Northants; four *d* (incl. twins). *Educ:* Harrow; Royal Agricl Coll., Cirencester. Director: Catterick Racecourse Co., 1988–2006; Redcar Racecourse Ltd (formerly Redcar Race Co.), 1989–2006; Fine Art Commissions Ltd, 1997–2016; Zetland Estates (Shetland) Ltd, 2004–10; Man. Dir, Musks Ltd, 1993–99. Dir, Stronghill Develts Ltd, 2004–11. Member: Richmond Burgage Pastures Cttee, 2000– (Chm., 2005–); Yorks Cttee, CLA, 2001–05. Chm., Yorks HHA, 2008–13 (Treas., 2000–05; Dep. Chm., 2005–08). Trustee, Trebetherick Estate Club, 1995–2017. Chm., Aske Parish Meeting, 1998–. *Club:* Slainte Mhah.

**RONAYNE, Prof. Jarlath**, AM 2002; PhD; FRSC, FTSE; Tan Sri Jeffrey Cheah Distinguished Professor, Sunway University (formerly University College), Malaysia, since 2009 (Academic Director, 2004–06; Vice-Chancellor, 2006–09; Director, Manchester Business School Centre, 2010–14); Senior Associate, Ronayne Francis International, Melbourne, since 2005; International Academic Director, Le Cordon Bleu, London, since 2012; Director, Cambridge-Sunway Collaboration in Biomedical Science; *b* 3 Sept. 1938; *s* of late Michael Ronayne and Anne Ronayne (*née* Kenny); *m* 1st, 1965, Rosalind Hickman (decd); two *s*; 2nd, 1995, Margaret Francis. *Educ:* Trinity Coll., Dublin (BA 1965; MA 1968; Hon. Fellow 1997); St John's Coll., Cambridge (PhD 1968). FRSC 1988; FTSE 1995. Lecturer: Dept of Applied Sci., Wolverhampton Poly., 1968–70; Dept of Sci. and Technol. Policy, Manchester Univ., 1970–74; Sen. Lectr, then Dir, Sci. Policy Res. Centre, Sch. of Sci., Griffith Univ., Brisbane, 1974–77; University of New South Wales: Prof. of Hist. and Philosophy of Sci., 1977–91; Hd of Dept of Hist. and Philosophy of Sci., 1977–83; Dean, Faculty of Arts, 1983–84; Pro-Vice-Chancellor, 1984–88; Dep. Vice-Chancellor, 1988–91; Prof. Emeritus, 1991; Vice-Chancellor and Pres., 1991–2003, Distinguished Professorial Fellow, 2004–08, Victoria Univ. of Technol., later Victoria Univ. Hon. Prof., Shanghai Inst. Tourism, 1993; Vis. Prof., Dept of Chem., TCD, 2010–; Visiting Fellow: Oriel Coll., Oxford, 1999; Wolfson Coll., Cambridge, 2004; President's Guest, St John's Coll., Cambridge, 2004; Jeffrey Cheah Scholar in Residence, Brasenose Coll., Oxford, 2016. Member: Internat. Council on Sci. Policy Studies, 1984–; Exec. Cttee, Australian Higher Educn Industrial Assoc., 1996–99; Bd, Communications Law Centre, Sydney, 1996–2003; Standing Cttee on Internat. Matters, AVCC, 1998– (Leader, AVCC Delegn to India, 1998); Bd Dirs, Sunway Univ. (formerly Coll.) Sdn Bhd, 2004–; Advr to Chm., Sunway Gp. Consultant to Commonwealth Dept of Employment, Educn and Youth Affairs, 1998. Mem., Victorian Educn Ministry Delegns to SE Asia and S America, 1998. Member Board: Melba Conservatorium of Music, Melbourne, 1995–; Playbox Theatre Co., Melb., 2000–03; Member: Academic Adv. Bd, Hong Kong Inst. of Technol., 2003–. Dir of Admissions (Australia), RCSI, 2003–13. Hon. Consul for Ireland in Victoria, 2002–09. Manoel de Vilhena Award, Malta, 1999. *Publications:* Guide to World Science: Australia and New Zealand, 1975; (jtly) Science, Technology and Public Policy, 1979; Science in Government: a review of the principles and practice of science policy, 1983; Science and Technology in Australasia, Antarctica and Pacific Islands, 1989; First Fleet to Federation: Irish supremacy in colonial Australia, 2001, republd as The Irish in Australia: rogues and reformers, First Fleet to Federation, 2003; contrib. numerous jl articles in chemistry and sci. policy, and book chapters in chemistry, hist. of sci. and sci. policy, and Irish history. *Recreations:* reading, especially Irish history. *Address:* PO Box 656, Williamstown, Vic 3016, Australia.

**RONEY, Joanne Lucille**, OBE 2009; FCIH; Chief Executive, Manchester City Council, since 2017; *b* 13 Sept. 1961; *d* of John William Roney and Grace (*née* Darnley). *Educ:* Univ. of Birmingham (MBA Public Admin 1996). Housing, Birmingham CC, 1977–89; Regl Dir, Sanctuary Housing Assoc., 1989–91; Dir of Housing, Kirklees MBC, 1991–99; Exec. Dir for Housing and Direct Services Orgn, 1999–2005, Exec. Dir for Neighbourhoods and Community Care, 2005–08, Sheffield CC; Chief Exec., Wakefield Council, 2008–17. FCIH 2000 (Chm. Policy Bd, 2000–06). *Recreations:* travel, reading, music. *Address:* Manchester City Council, Town Hall, Manchester M60 2LA.

**RONSON, Dame Gail**, DBE 2004; Board Member, since 1992, and Deputy President, since 2010, Jewish Care (Deputy Chairman, 2002–10); Ambassador, Royal Opera House, since 2014 (Director, 2001–14); President, Royal National Institute of Blind People, since 2012; *b* 3 July 1946; *d* of Joseph and Marie Cohen; *m* 1967, Gerald Maurice Ronson, *qv*; four *d*. *Educ:* Clarke's Coll. Co-Chm., St Mary's Hosp. Save the Baby Fund, 1985–96; Vice-Pres., Assoc. for Res. into Stammering in Childhood, 1991–. Jt Chm., Council for a Beautiful Israel, 1987–94. Trustee: Ronson Foundns, 1980–95; Royal Opera House Trust, 1985–2014 (Hon. Trustee, 2014–); Home Farm Develt Trust, 1991–94; Gerald Ronson Foundn, 2005– (Dep. Chm., 2005–). *Recreation:* opera and ballet lover. *Address:* Heron House, 4 Bentinck Street, W1U 2EF. *T:* (020) 7486 4477, *Fax:* (020) 7487 2970. *E:* gailronson@heron.co.uk.

**RONSON, Gerald Maurice**, CBE 2012; Chief Executive: Heron Corporation PLC; Heron International PLC; Chairman and Chief Executive, Snax 24 Corporation Ltd; Chairman: Ronson Capital Partners; Rontec; *b* 27 May 1939; *s* of Henry and Sarah Ronson; *m* 1967, Gail (*see* Dame G. Ronson); four *d*. Chief Executive: Heron Corp. PLC, 1976– (Chm., 1978–93); Heron International PLC, 1983– (Chm., 1983–93). Chm. and Trustee, Gerald and Gail Ronson Family Foundn, 2005–; Trustee, Holocaust Meml Charitable Foundn, 2018– (Co-Chm., 2019–). Ambassador of Druse community on Mount Carmel. Hon. DCL Northumbria, 2009; Hon. PhD Hebrew Univ. of Jerusalem, 2014. Encomienda de Numero of the Order of Civil Merit (Spain), 2009. *Recreation:* work. *Address:* Heron House, 4 Bentinck Street, W1U 2EF. *T:* (020) 7486 4477.

**RONSON, Jon**; writer, screenwriter and documentary maker; *b* Cardiff, 10 May 1967; *s* of David and Paula Ronson; *m* 1995, Elaine; one *s*. *Educ:* Cardiff High Sch.; Poly. of Central London. Columnist: The Guardian, 1990–; Time Out, 1990–94; keyboard player, Frank Sidebottom Band, 1988–91; documentary maker, BBC TV and Channel 4, 1994–; screenwriter, 2011–, incl. Frank, 2014, Okja, 2017. *Publications:* Then: adventures with extremists, 2001; Men Who Stare at Goats, 2004; The Psychopath Test, 2011; Lost at Sea, 2012; Frank: the true story that inspired the movie, 2014; So You've Been Publicly Shamed, 2015. *Recreations:* walking, coffee, anxiety, dogs. *Address:* c/o United Agents, 12–26 Lexington Street, W1F 0LE.

**ROOCROFT, Amanda Jane**; soprano; *b* 9 Feb. 1966; *d* of Roger Roocroft and Valerie Roocroft (*née* Metcalfe); *m* 1999; three *s*. *Educ:* Southlands High Sch.; Runshaw Tertiary Coll.; Royal Northern Coll. of Music. Début as Sophie in Der Rosenkavalier, WNO, 1990; has sung at Glyndebourne, Royal Opera House, English Nat. Opera, Bayerische Staatsoper, BBC Promenade Concerts, Edinburgh Internat. Fest.; rôles include: Fiordiligi in Così fan Tutte; Donna Elvira in Don Giovanni; Pamina in Die Zauberflöte; Giulietta in I Capuleti e I Montecchi; Mimi in La Bohème; Amelia in Simon Boccanegra; Jenifer in The Midsummer Marriage; Eva in Die Meistersinger; Desdemona in Otello; Tatyana in Eugene Onegin; Marschallin in Der Rosenkavalier; Duchess of Argyll in Powder Her Face; title rôles: in Katya Kabanova; in Jenufa; in The Merry Widow. FRNCM. Vis. Tutor of Singing, Royal Birmingham Conservatoire, Birmingham City Univ., 2018–. Hon. DMus Manchester, 2003.

**ROOK, His Honour Peter Francis Grosvenor**; QC 1991; a Senior Circuit Judge, Central Criminal Court, 2005–17; *b* 19 Sept. 1949; *s* of Dr Arthur James Rook and Frances Jane Elizabeth Rook (*née* Knott); *m* 1978, Susanna Marian Tewson; one *s* two *d*. *Educ:* Charterhouse; Trinity College, Cambridge (Open Exhibnr; MA Hist.); Bristol Univ. (Dip. Soc. Studies). Called to the Bar, Gray's Inn, 1973, Bencher, 2000; 2nd Standing Counsel to Inland Revenue at Central Criminal Court and Inner London Courts, 1981, 1st Standing Counsel, 1989; Asst Recorder, 1990–95; a Recorder, 1995–2005; Hd of Chambers, 18 Red Lion Court, 2002–05. Asst Coroner for Surrey, 2018–19. Chm., Criminal Bar Assoc. of England and Wales, 2002–03 (Dir of Educn, 2003–05). Course Dir, Serious Sexual Offences Seminar, Judicial Studies Bd, 2006–09. Judicial Fellow, Judicial Inst., UCL,

2017–. *Publications:* Rook and Ward on Sexual Offences, 1990, 5th edn 2016, supplement 2019. *Recreations:* tennis, cricket, theatre, devising theatrical productions about history of the Old Bailey and Newgate for charity, growing tropical plants. *Clubs:* MCC; Coolhurst Lawn Tennis and Squash.

**ROOKE, Rt Rev. Patrick William;** *see* Tuam, Killala and Achonry, Bishop of.

**ROOKER, Baron** *cr* 2001 (Life Peer), of Perry Barr in the County of West Midlands; **Jeffrey William Rooker;** PC 1999; CEng; Chairman, Food Standards Agency, 2009–13; *b* 5 June 1941; *m* 1st, 1972, Angela Edwards (*d* 2003); 2nd, 2010, Helen M. Hughes. *Educ:* Handsworth Tech. Sch.; Handsworth Tech. Coll.; Warwick Univ. (MA); Aston Univ. (BScEng). CEng, FIET; MCMI. Apprentice toolmaker, King's Heath Engrg Co. Ltd, Birmingham, 1957–63; student apprentice, BLMC, 1963–64; Asst to Works Manager, Geo. Salter & Co., West Bromwich, 1964–65, Assembly Manager, 1965–67; Prodn Manager, Rola Celestion Ltd, Thames Ditton and Ipswich, 1967–70; Industrial Relations and Safety Officer, Metro-Cammell, Birmingham, 1971; Lectr, Lanchester Polytechnic, Coventry, 1972–74. MP (Lab) Birmingham, Perry Barr, Feb. 1974–2001. Opposition spokesman on social services, 1979–80, on social security, 1980–83, on treasury and economic affairs, 1983–84, on housing, 1984–87, on local government, 1987–88, on health and social services, 1990–92, on higher educn, 1992–93; Dep. Shadow Leader of H of C, 1994–97; Minister of State: MAFF, 1997–99; DSS, 1999–2001; Home Office, 2001–02; for Housing, Planning and Regeneration, ODPM, 2002–05; NI Office, 2005–06; DEFRA, 2006–08. Mem., Public Accounts Cttee, 1989–91. Chair, Labour Campaign for Electoral Reform, 1989–95. Mem. Council, Instn of Prodn Engrs, 1975–81. Lay Gov., Aston Univ., 2008–10. Chair, Motor Sports Trng Trust, 2010–19; Chm., Nat. Envmtl Bd, 2014–16. Hon. DSc Aston, 2001; DUniv UCE, 2002. *Address:* House of Lords, SW1A 0PW. *T:* (020) 7219 6469.

**ROOKES, Caroline Mary,** CBE 2010; Chief Executive, Money Advice Service, 2013–17; *b* 28 Oct. 1954; *d* of late James Harold Hartley and Mary Irene Hartley; *m* 1975, John William Rookes (marr. diss. 1986); partner, Michael Pearce. *Educ:* Fleetwood Grammar Sch.; Downer Grammar Sch.; Univ. of Lancaster (BA Hons English 1975). Civil Service, 1975–2013: various postings in DHSS, subseq. DSS; Inland Revenue, then HM Revenue and Customs: Head, Review of Analytical Services, 1999; Dir of Charities, 2000; Head, Share Scheme, 2000–02; Director: Savings, Pensions, Share Schemes, 2002–05; Individuals, 2005; Department for Work and Pensions: Dir, Private Pensions, Retirement Planning and Older People, 2005–07; Dir, Workplace Pension Reform, later Private Pensions, 2007–13. Trustee, Pension Scheme: Nat. Employment Savings Trust, 2015–; Civil Service Sports Council, 2015–; Trustee, Pension Superfund, 2019–. Vice Chair, Vinspired, 2017–19. *Recreations:* opera, fell walking, friends, family, good food and wine, all things Italian.

**ROOKS, Robert John;** *b* 20 Nov. 1948; *s* of Ronald Sidney Rooks and Daisy Rooks; *m* 1970, Elizabeth Lewis; one *s* one *d*. *Educ:* Hardye's Sch., Dorchester; Liverpool Univ. (BEng Hons). Spacecraft Design Engr, BAC, 1970–72; Ministry of Defence: Admin. Trainee, Chief Exec. Dockyards, 1972–73; Adjutant Gen. Secretariat, 1973–74; Size, Shape and Cost of RAF Prog., Defence Secretariat, 1974–75; Private Sec. to Chief of Defence Procurement, 1975–78; Fighting Vehicles and Engrg, Equipment Secretariat, 1978–80; RAF Ops, Defence Secretariat, 1980–83; Mgt Services Orgn, 1983–85; Finance Mgt and Planning, 1985–88, Head, 1988–90, Controller Aircraft Secretariat; Head of: Adjutant Gen. Secretariat 2, 1990–93; Civilian Mgt (Personnel) 1, 1993–97; Dir of Orgn and Mgt, 1998–99; Comd Sec., RAF PTC, 1999–2003; Fellow, Weatherhead Center for Internat. Affairs, Harvard Univ., 2003–04; Dir Gen., Security and Safety, MoD, 2004; Dir, Business Resilience, MoD. *Recreations:* sailing, travel, IT. *Club:* Royal Air Force.

**ROOLEY, Anthony;** lutenist; Artistic Director, The Consort of Musicke, since 1969; *b* 10 June 1944; *s* of Madge and Henry Rooley; *m* 1967, Carla Morris; three *d*; one *s* by Emma Kirkby (*see* Dame Emma Kirkby); *m* 2014, Evelyn Tubb. *Educ:* Royal Acad. of Music. LRAM (Performers). Recitals in Europe, USA, Middle East, S America, New Zealand, Australia; radio and TV in UK, Europe and USA; numerous recordings, British and German. Vis. Prof., York Univ., 1998–; Vis. Prof., 1999–2007, Prof., 2007–, Dir, Advanced Vocal Ensemble Studies Practical Masters Prog., 2010–, Lectr in performance, repertoire and presentation, 2007–18, Schola Cantorum Basiliensis, Basle, Switzerland; Vis. Orpheus Scholar, Florida State Univ., Tallahassee, 2003–05, 2007–. Researcher, dir or producer of sound recording projects available in CD format, 1972–2016. Hon. FRAM 1990. Lifetime Achievement Award, York Early Music Fest., 2016. *Publications:* Penguin Book of Early Music, 1982; Performance—revealing the Orpheus within, 1990. *Recreations:* food, wine, gardening, philosophy. *Address:* Bwlch y Ddinas, Llansawel, Llandeilo, Carmarthenshire SA19 7PQ.

**ROOM, Maxine,** CBE 2012; educational consultant; Director, MG Consultancy (London) Ltd, since 2014; *b* London, 26 Jan. 1956; *d* of Arthur and Vera Johnson; *m* (marr. diss.); one *d*; *m* 2017. *Educ:* Skinners' Co. Sch. for Girls; Bath Coll. of Higher Educn (Cert Ed 1978); Bristol Univ. (BEd Hons 1979; MEd 1992). Joined Bridgwater Coll., Somerset, as Lectr, 1979; various posts, 1979–95, incl. Hd, Care, Public Services, Complementary Therapies; Filton College, Bristol: Team Leader, Care and Child Care, 1995–97; Dir, Progs and Planning, 1997–98; Dir, Curriculum, 1998–2001; Vice Principal, Curriculum, 2001–03; Principal and Chief Executive Officer: Swansea Coll., 2003–07; Leeds Park Lane Coll., 2007–09; Principal and CEO, LeSoCo (formerly Lewisham Coll.), 2009–14. Board Member: Northern Ballet; Women's Leadership Network; Helena Kennedy Foundn. MInstD 2007. Freeman: City of London, 2015; Mgt Consultants' Co., 2015. Hon. LLD Bristol, 2012. *Recreations:* gym junkie, travelling, writing short stories. *Address:* MG Consultancy (London) Ltd, Wellesley House, Duke of Wellington Avenue, SE18 6SS. *T:* 07507 525100. *E:* maxine.room@mgcll.com.

**ROONEY, Dougie;** energy consultant, since 2011; National Officer, responsible for Energy and Utilities, AEEU, later Amicus, then Unite the Union, 1997–2010; President, Trades Union Congress, 2010–11; *b* Edinburgh, 12 Oct. 1947. *Educ:* Balgreen Primary Sch., Edinburgh; Tynecastle Secondary Sch., Edinburgh. Ferranti: apprenticeship as mechanical fitter; craftsman, 1970 and Shop Steward for AEU, 1970, Sen. Shop Steward, 1974–85; Divl Organiser, AEU, 1985–97. Mem., Gen. Council, TUC, 1998–. *Recreations:* walking, golf. *Address:* 41 Baberton Mains Lea, Edinburgh EH14 3HB. *T:* 07531 911666. *E:* dougie.rooney@gmail.com.

**ROONEY, Fiona;** *see* Fox, F.

**ROONEY, Michael John,** RA 1991 (ARA 1990); Head of Painting, Royal Academy Schools, 1991–95; *b* 5 March 1944; *s* of Elisabeth and John Rooney; *m* 1st, 1967, Patricia Anne Lavender (marr. diss. 1984); one *s* one *d*; 2nd, 1988, Alexandra Grascher, Vienna; one *s*. *Educ:* primary and secondary schools; Sutton Sch. of Art; Wimbledon Sch. of Art (NDD); Royal Coll. of Art (MA RCA, ARCA); British Sch. at Rome (Austin Abbey Major Award). Part-time lectr, various art colls; artist-in-residence, Towner Art Gall., Eastbourne, 1983; one man exhibns in Holland, London, Edinburgh and other UK locations; jt exhibns in Chicago, NY, Portland (Oregon), and throughout Europe and UK; commissions include: painting for FT Centenary, 1988; London Transport Poster, 1990; tapestry for TSB Ltd, Birmingham, 1991; work in public collections: Sussex; Cumbria; Birmingham; Punta del Este, Uruguay; London; Govt Art Collection. Chm., Soc. of Painters in Tempera. Prizes include: Calouste Gulbenkian Printmakers' Award, 1984; John Player Portrait Award, Nat. Portrait Gallery, 1985; RA Summer Exhibn Awards, 1986, 1988, 1989; Chichester Arts Prize, 1995. *Recreations:* cooking, travel. *Club:* Chelsea Arts.

**ROONEY, Terence Henry;** *b* 11 Nov. 1950; *s* of Eric and Frances Rooney; *m* 1969, Susanne Chapman; one *s* two *d*. *Educ:* Buttershaw Comprehensive Sch.; Bradford Coll. Formerly: commercial insurance broker; Welfare Rights Advice Worker, Bierley Community Centre. Councillor, Bradford City, 1983–91 (Dep. Leader, 1990). MP (Lab) Bradford N, Nov. 1990–2010; contested (Lab) Bradford E, 2010.

**ROOSE-EVANS, James Humphrey;** freelance theatre director and author; non-stipendiary Anglican priest; *b* 11 Nov. 1927; *s* of Jack Roose-Evans and Catharina Primrose Morgan. *Educ:* St Benet's Hall, Oxford (MA). Started career in repertory, as an actor; Artistic Dir, Maddermarket Theatre, Norwich, 1954–55 (dir. English première of The Language of Flowers, 1955); Faculty of Juilliard Sch. of Music, NY, 1955–56; on staff of RADA, 1956–; founded Hampstead Theatre, 1959; Resident Dir, Belgrade Theatre, Coventry, 1961. Regularly tours USA, lecturing and leading workshops. Productions directed include: *Hampstead Theatre:* The Square, 1963; The Little Clay Cart (also adapted), 1964; Adventures in the Skin Trade, world première, The Two Character Play, world première, Letters from an Eastern Front (also adapted), 1966; An Evening with Malcolm Muggeridge (also devised), 1966; *West End:* Cider with Rosie (also adapted), 1963; Private Lives, 1963; An Ideal Husband, 1966; The Happy Apple, 1967; 84 Charing Cross Road (also adapted), 1981, NY 1982 (awards for Best Play and Best Dir, 2001), tour 2004, Salisbury Playhouse, 2015; Seven Year Itch, 1986; The Best of Friends, 1988 (also prod Comédie des Champs-Elysées, Paris, 1989), Hampstead and tour, 2006; Temptation, 1990; Irving (also jt author with Barry Turner), 1995; Legend of Pericles, 1996; *other productions:* Venus Observed, Chichester, 1992; Pericles, 2000, Macbeth, 2001, Ludlow Fest.; The Lovers of Viorne, Theatre Room, London, 2016. Author, Re: Joyce!, West End, 1991; The Bargain, Th. Royal, Bath and tour, 2007. Consultant, Theatre Mus. Founder and Chm., Bleddfa Trust-Centre for Caring and the Arts, subseq. Bleddfa Centre for Creative Spirit, Powys, 1974–; Bleddfa Lect., 2007. Columnist (Something Extra), Woman, 1986–88. Trng at Glasshampton Monastery, Worcs; ordained priest, 1981. *Publications:* adaptation of The Little Clay Cart, by King Sudraka, 1965; Directing a Play, 1968; Experimental Theatre, 1970, 4th rev. edn, 1988; London Theatre, 1977; play version of 84 Charing Cross Road, by Helene Hanff, 1983; Inner Journey, Outer Journey, 1987, rev. edn 1998 (US as The Inner Stage, 1990), new edn, 2019; (introd and ed) Darling Ma: the letters of Joyce Grenfell, 1988; The Tale of Beatrix Potter, 1988; (with Maureen Lipman) Re:Joyce!, 1988; (introd and ed) The Time of My Life: wartime journals of Joyce Grenfell, 1989; (trans.) Obey, On the Edge of Midnight, 1989; Passages of the Soul: ritual today, 1994; Cider with Rosie (stage adaptation), 1994; One Foot on the Stage (biog. of Richard Wilson), 1996; Eminently Victorian: the story of Augustus Hare (play), 1996; Loving without Tears (stage adaptation of Molly Keane novel), 1996; The Christ Mouse, 2004; (devised and ed) The Cook-a-Story Book, 2005; What is Spirituality?, 2005; Holy Theatre, 2005; Opening Doors and Windows: a memoir in four acts, 2009; Finding Silence: 52 meditations for daily living, 2009; Blue Remembered Hills: a Radnorshire journey, 2018; A Life Shared, 2018; Odd: a day by day journal in the author's 91st year, 2019; *for children:* The Adventures of Odd and Elsewhere, 1971; The Secret of the Seven Bright Shiners, 1972; Odd and the Great Bear, 1973; Elsewhere and the Gathering of the Clowns, 1974; The Return of the Great Bear, 1975; The Secret of Tippity-Witchit, 1975; The Lost Treasure of Wales, 1977. *Recreations:* gardening, writing. *Address:* c/o Sheil Land Associates, 52 Doughty Street, WC1N 2LF. *W:* www.jamesrooseevans.co.uk. *Club:* Garrick.

**ROOT, Jane;** Founder and Chief Executive, Nutopia, since 2010; *b* 18 May 1957; *e d* of James William Root and Kathleen Root; *m* 2003, Ray Hill; one *d*. *Educ:* Sussex Univ.; London Coll. of Printing. Manager, Cinema of Women (Film Distribn Co.), 1981–83; freelance journalist and film critic, 1981–83; Lectr in Film Studies, UEA, 1981–84; Researcher, Open the Box, Beat Productions, 1983; Co-Creator, The Media Show, 1986; Jt Founder and Jt Man. Dir, Wall to Wall Television, 1987–96; Head of Independent Commng Gp, BBC, 1997–98; Controller, BBC2, 1999–2004; Discovery Channel: Exec. Vice-Pres., 2004–06; Gen. Manager, 2004–07; Pres., 2006–07. Theme Leader, Connecting With Audiences, BBC, 2001. Mem., Exec. Cttee, Edinburgh TV Fest. (Chair, 1995). *Publications:* Pictures of Women: sexuality, 1981; Open the Box: about television, 1983. *Address:* 4209 Thornapple Street, Chevy Chase, MD 20815–5116, USA.

**ROOTES,** family name of **Baron Rootes.**

**ROOTES, 3rd Baron** *cr* 1959; **Nicholas Geoffrey Rootes;** author and copy-writer; business owner, Nick Rootes Associates; *b* 12 July 1951; *s* of 2nd Baron Rootes and of Marian, *d* of Lt-Col H. R. Hayter, DSO and widow of Wing Comdr J. H. Slater, AFC; *S* father, 1992; *m* 1976, Dorothy Anne Burn-Forti (née Wood); one step *s* one step *d*. *Educ:* Harrow Sch. Trustee, Rootes Charitable Trust, 1992–; Patron, Assoc. of Rootes Car Clubs, 1993–. *Publications:* The Drinker's Companion, 1987; Doing a Dyson, 1996. *Recreations:* ski-ing, fly-fishing. *Heir: cousin* William Brian Rootes [*b* 8 Nov. 1944; *m* 1969, Alicia, *y d* of Frederick Graham Roberts, OBE; two *d*]. *Address:* Harbour View, 82 High Street, Bembridge, Isle of Wight PO35 5SF. *Club:* Ski of Great Britain.

**ROOTS, Guy Robert Godfrey;** QC 1989; *b* 26 Aug. 1946; *s* of late William Lloyd Roots, QC and Elizabeth Colquhoun Gow (née Gray); *m* 1975, Caroline (née Clarkson); three *s*. *Educ:* Winchester College; Brasenose College, Oxford (MA). Called to the Bar, Middle Temple, 1969, Harmsworth Scholar, 1970, Bencher, 2000. Asst Boundary Comr, 2011–12. Chm., Planning and Envmt Bar Assoc., 2000–04. Fellow, Soc. of Advanced Legal Studies, 1998–. Liveryman, Drapers' Co., 1972. General Editor: Ryde on Rating and the Council Tax, 1986–2016; Compulsory Purchase and Compensation Service, 1999–2019. *Publications:* Law of Compulsory Purchase, 2011–19. *Recreations:* sailing, fishing, ski-ing, photography, woodworking. *Address:* Francis Taylor Building, Temple, EC4Y 7BY. *T:* (020) 7353 8415. *E:* clerks@ftbchambers.co.uk. *Club:* Itchenor Sailing.

**ROOTS, Paul John;** Director of Industrial Relations, Ford Motor Co. Ltd, 1981–86, retired; *b* 16 Oct. 1929; *s* of John Earl and Helen Roots; *m* 1950, Anna Theresa Pateman (*d* 2017); two *s* two *d*. *Educ:* Dormers Wells Sch.; London Sch. of Economics; Open Univ. BA Hons 1993; Cert. in Personnel Admin. CCIPD; CCMI. RN, 1947–54: service in Korean War. Personnel Officer, Brush Gp, 1955; Labour Officer, UKAEA, 1956, Labour Manager, 1959; Ford Motor Co. Ltd: Personnel Manager, Halewood, 1962; Forward Planning Manager, 1966; Labour Relations Manager, 1969; Dir of Employee Relations, 1974. Vice-Pres., IPM, 1981–83. Chairman: CBI Health and Safety Policy Cttee, 1984; CBI Health and Safety Consultative Cttee, 1984; Member: Council of Management, CBI Educn Foundn, 1981; CBI Working Party on the Employment of Disabled People, 1981; CBI Employment Policy Cttee, 1983; CBI Council, 1984; Engrg Industry Training Bd, 1985. *Publications:* (jtly) Communication in Practice, 1981; (jtly) Corporate Personnel Management, 1986; Financial Incentives for Employees, 1988; articles in personnel management jls. *Recreations:* riding, theatre, music.

**ROOTS, William;** Chief Executive and Director of Finance, City of Westminster, 1994–2000; *b* 12 April 1946; *s* of William Roots and Violet (*née* Frost); *m* 1st, 1963, Norma Jane Smith (marr. diss.); one *s* one *d*, 2nd 1980, Susan Grace Sharratt; two *s*. *Educ:* Wandsworth Sch. Sun Life Assce Soc., 1962–64; joined GLC as trainee, 1964; Hd of Budget, 1980; London Borough of Southwark: Head of: Exchequer, 1980–81; Finance, 1982; Director of Finance: London Borough of Bexley, 1982–90; City of Westminster, 1990–94. Mem., CIPFA 1970. *Recreations:* sport (esp. Rugby), relaxing with friends, films. *E:* billroots245@gmail.com.

**ROP, Anton;** Honorary Vice-President and Director, European Investment Bank, 2013–18 (Vice-President, 2010–13); *b* 27 Dec. 1960. *Educ:* Univ. of Ljubljana (MA). Asst Dir, Slovene Inst. for Macroecon. Analysis and Develt, 1985–92. Former Mem., Nat. Assembly, Slovenia (Lib Dem, until 2007, Soc Dem, 2007–10); State Sec., Min. of Econ. Relations and Develt, 1993–96; Minister of Labour, Family and Social Affairs, 1996–2000, of Finance, 2000–02; Prime Minister, 2002–04. Former Leader, Parly Gp, Liberal Democratic Party, until 2005.

**ROPER, Brian Anthony;** Chief Executive, 2002–09, and Vice Chancellor, 2004–09, London Metropolitan University; *b* 15 Dec. 1949; *s* of Harold Herbert Albert Roper and Elizabeth Roper (*née* Rooney); *m* 1971, Margaret Patricia Jones; one *s* one *d*. *Educ:* UWIST (BSc Hons Econs 1971); Univ. of Manchester (MA Econs 1973); Swansea Metropolitan Univ. (DipAD 2012); Swansea Univ. (MA Creative Writing (Dist.) 2015; PhD 2018). Tutor in Econs, UWIST, 1971–72; Lectr in Econs, Teesside Poly., 1973–75; Sen. Lectr, then Principal Lectr, Leicester Poly., 1975–80; Hd, Sch. of Econs, Dean, Faculty of Social Scis and Asst Dir, Resources, Newcastle upon Tyne Poly., 1980–90; Dep. Vice Chancellor Acad. Affairs and Dep. Chief Exec., Oxford Poly., subseq. Oxford Brookes Univ., 1991–94; Vice-Chancellor and Chief Exec., Univ. of N London, 1994–2002. DUniv Chelyabinsk State, Russia, 2001; Hon. DLitt Pennsylvania, 2004; Hon. DTech Nizhni Novgorod, Russia, 2007. *Publications:* Archaeological Phenomenology; contrib. Econ. Theory and Policy, Higher Educn Policy and Mgt; contrib. haiku to Blythe Spirit, poetry to Cardiff Women's Aid Anthology, and theatre reviews to New Welsh Rev., Buzz Mag. *Recreations:* thoughtful art, observing nature, haiku, haibun, writing creatively, trowelling the past.

**ROPER, Rev. Geoffrey Edward Hodgess;** Associate General Secretary (Free Churches), and Secretary, Free Churches Group, Churches Together in England, 2001–05; Company Secretary, Council for World Mission (UK), 2011–16; *b* 24 April 1940; *y* s of late Rev. Frederick Mabor Hodges Roper and Ellen Frances (*née* Brockway); *m* 1967, Janice Wakeham; one *s* one *d*. *Educ:* Christ's Hosp.; Magdalen Coll., Oxford (PPE); Mansfield Coll., Oxford (Theol.); MA Oxon. Ordained 1965. Minister: Trinity Congregational Church, Ifield, Crawley, 1965–71; Streatham Congregational Church, 1971–78 (URC from 1972); Seaford URC, 1978–85; Christ Church, Chelmsford, 1985–95; Gen. Sec., Free Church Fed. Council, later Free Churches' Council, 1996–2001; various tasks in connection with Council for World Mission, 2005–19; Cataloguing Asst (LMS archives), SOAS, 2006–07. Sec., URC Deployment Cttee, 1978–84; Convenor, URC Maintenance of Ministry Sub-Cttee, 2005–09; URC Ecumenical Officer: Sussex East, 1979–85; Essex, 1986–95; Dir, URC Ministers Pension Fund, 2005–09. Vice-Chm., Churches Main Cttee, 2004–05. Sec., Gen. Body of Dissenting Ministers and Deputies of the Three Denominations, 1998–2005. Chm., Churches Cttee for Hospital Chaplaincy, 2001–04; Mem., Eastbourne CHC, 1980–85 (Vice-Chm., 1983–84). British Isles Mem., Exec. Cttee, Leuenberg Doctrinal Conversations of Reformed and Lutheran Churches in Europe, subseq. Leuenberg Fellowship, 1987–94. Chair, King's Cross Develt Forum, 2006–10. Director: Highway Trust, 1977–94; Farthing Trust, 1985–95; British and Internat. Sailors' Soc., 1999–2006. Secretary: Lumen United Reformed Church, 2009–14; Chair, United Reformed Church History Soc., 2012–17; Vice-Pres., Friends of Dr Williams's Library, 2014– (Chm. of Cttee, 1991–2005; Sec., 2005–14); Compliance Project Analyst, Turn2us (Elizabeth Finn Care), 2014–17. Trustee: St George's Chapel, Heathrow Airport, 1999–2005; Congregational Fund, 2007– (Chair, 2014–); Project for Seniors and Lifelong Ministry, 2008–13. Pres., Mansfield Coll. Assoc., 2005–08. Hon. Treas., Soc. for Ecumenical Studies, 2012–17. Guide, Westminster Abbey, 2009–14. *Address:* 25 Witley Court, Coram Street, WC1N 1HD.

**ROPER, Joanna Louise, (Mrs Thomas Drew),** CMG 2016; HM Diplomatic Service; Special Envoy for Gender Equality, Foreign and Commonwealth Office, since 2017; *b* Hampshire, 20 Feb. 1969; *d* of Robert Edward Wardale and Elizabeth Anne Roper; *m* 2016, Thomas Drew, *qv*. *Educ:* Univ. of Kent at Canterbury (BA Hons Social Anthropol. with Linguistics 1991); Sch. of Oriental and African Studies, Univ. of London (MA Japanese Studies 2001). Home Office, 1992–2000; entered FCO, 2001; Resource and Financial Mgt, FCO, 2001–03; First Sec., Hd of Press and Public Affairs, Tokyo, 2003–07; Dep. Hd, Drugs and Internat. Crime Dept, FCO, 2007–08; Dep. Hd, then Interim Hd, Counter-Terrorism Dept, FCO, 2008–10; Political Counsellor, Islamabad, 2010–11; Head: Somalia Conf. Unit, FCO, 2011–12; China Dept, FCO, 2012–14; Dir, Consular Services, FCO, 2014–16; Actg Dir Gen. for Trade and Investment, Beijing, 2016–17. DUniv Kent, 2019. *Recreations:* travelling, outdoor pursuits, theatre, cinema. *Address:* c/o Foreign and Commonwealth Office, King Charles Street, SW1A 2AH. *E:* joanna.roper@fco.gov.uk.

**ROPER, Prof. Lyndal Anne,** PhD; FBA 2011; Regius Professor of History, University of Oxford, since 2011; Fellow of Oriel College, Oxford, since 2011; *b* Melbourne, 1956; *m* 2002, Prof. E. Nicholas R. Stargardt; one *s*, and one step *s*. *Educ:* Univ. of Melbourne (BA Hons Hist. with Philos. 1978); Univ. of London (PhD 1985). Jun. Res. Fellow, Merton Coll., Oxford, 1983–86; Lectr, KCL, 1986–87; Royal Holloway and Bedford New College, later Royal Holloway, University of London: Lectr in Hist., 1987–93; Reader in Hist., 1993–99; Prof. of Early Mod. Hist., 1999–2002; Lectr, 2002–04, Prof., 2004–11, Univ. of Oxford; Fellow and Tutor, Balliol Coll., Oxford, 2002–11. FAHA 2007. Jt Editor, Past & Present, 2000–12. *Publications:* The Holy Household, 1989 (German 1995); Oedipus and the Devil, 1993; Witch Craze: terror and fantasy in Baroque Germany, 2005; The Witch in the Western Imagination, 2011; Imagination, 2012; Martin Luther, 2016. *Address:* Oriel College, Oxford OX1 4EW.

**ROPER, Martyn Keith,** OBE 2013; HM Diplomatic Service; Governor, Cayman Islands, since 2018; *b* Halifax, W Yorks, 8 June 1965; *s* of Keith Roper and Sandra Heaton (*née* Parsisson); *m* 1989, Elisabeth Melanie Harman; one *s* one *d*. *Educ:* Heath Grammar Sch.; Hull Univ.; Open Univ. (BSc Hons 1999). Joined FCO, 1984; Middle East Dept, 1984–86; Tehran, 1986–87; Maputo, 1988–90; Vice Consul, Kuwait, 1990; Third Sec., Karachi, 1991–93; Second, then First Sec., FCO, 1994–98; First Sec., UK Delegn to OECD, 1999–2003; Dep. Hd, UN Dept, FCO, 2004–07; Dep. Hd of Mission, Brasilia, 2007–10; Ambassador to Algeria, 2010–14; Minister and Dep. Hd of Mission, Beijing, 2015–18. *Recreations:* cycling, tennis, keeping fit, reading. *Address:* c/o Foreign and Commonwealth Office, King Charles Street, SW1A 2AH.

**ROPER, Michael,** CB 1992; FRHistS; Keeper of Public Records, 1988–92; *b* 19 Aug. 1932; *s* of Jack Roper and Mona Roper (*née* Nettleton); *m* 1957, Joan Barbara Earnshaw; one *s* one *d*. *Educ:* Heath Grammar Sch., Halifax; Univ. of Manchester (BA, MA; Langton Fellow). Registered Mem., Soc. of Archivists, 1987. Public Record Office: Asst Keeper, 1959–70; Principal Asst Keeper, 1970–82; Records Admin Officer, 1982–85; Dep. Keeper of Public Records, 1985–88. Lectr (part time) in Archive Studies, UCL, 1972–87, Hon. Res. Fellow, 1988–; Dist. Visitor, Univ. of BC, 1994; Vis. Prof., Surugadai Univ., Japan, 1999. Sec., Adv. Council on Public Records, 1963–68; Vice-President: Soc. of Archivists, 1992– (Vice-Chm., 1983–84); Chm., 1985–86; Pres., 1989–92); British Records Soc., 1988–; RHistS, 1989–93 (Hon. Treas., 1974–80); Sec.-Gen., Internat. Council on Archives, 1988–92 (Sec. for Standardization, 1984–88; Hon. Mem., 1992); Hon. Sec., Assoc. of Commonwealth Archivists and Records Managers, 1996–2000 (Hon. Life Mem., 2017). Chairman: Voices from the Past, 1992–95; English Record Collections, 1994–2018. Ext. Examr, Nat. Univ. of Ireland, 1982–86, Univ. of Liverpool, 1986–89, Univ. of London, 1988–93. Chm., Judy Segal Trust, 1990–98; Hon. Treasurer, Bethlem Art & Hist. Collections Trust, 1995–2007. Hon. DLitt Bradford, 1991. *Publications:* Yorkshire Fines 1300–1314, 1965; Records of the Foreign Office 1782–1939, 1969; (with J. A. Keene) Planning, Equipping and Staffing a Document Reprographic Service, 1984; Guidelines for the Preservation of Microforms, 1986; Directory of National Standards Relating to Archives Administration and Records Management, 1986; Planning, Equipping and Staffing an Archival Preservation and Conservation Service, 1989; Geresye to Jersey: the record endures, 1991; Records of the War Office and Related Departments 1660–1964, 1998; Records of the Foreign Office 1782–1968, 2002; (with C. Kitching) Yorkshire Fines 1314–1326, 2006; contribs to learned jls. *Recreations:* listening to music, choral singing, local history. *Address:* Sherwood House, Vicarage Road, Roxwell, Chelmsford, Essex CM1 4NY. *T:* (01245) 249033. *E:* MRoper3784@aol.com.

**ROPER, Prof. Stephen Nicholas,** PhD; Professor of Enterprise, since 2008, and Director, Enterprise Research Centre, since 2013, Warwick Business School, University of Warwick; *b* Hong Kong, 27 June 1960; *s* of Norman Roper and Gillian Roper; *m* 1981, Marjorie Roberts; two *d*. *Educ:* Durham Univ. (BA Hons Econs 1981); St Peter's Coll., Oxford (MPhil 1983); London Sch. of Econs and Pol Sci. (PhD 1987). Res. Officer, thenسen. Res. Officer, 1986–98, Asst Dir, 1998–2003, NI Econ. Res. Centre; Prof. of Business Innovation, Aston Business Sch., 2003–07. FAcSS (AcSS 2010); FRSA 2012. *Publications:* Entrepreneurship: a global perspective, 2012; papers in Res. Policy, Technovation, Regl Studies, Industry and Innovation. *Recreations:* phillumeny, pottery, hoarding Japanese design. *Address:* Warwick Business School, University of Warwick, Coventry CV4 7AL. *T:* (024) 7652 2501. *E:* stephen.roper@wbs.ac.uk.

**ROPER, Prof. Warren Richard,** FRS 1989; FRSNZ 1984; Professor of Chemistry, University of Auckland, New Zealand, 1984–2007, now Emeritus; *b* 27 Nov. 1938; *m* 1961, Judith Delcie Catherine Miller; two *s* one *d*. *Educ:* Nelson Coll., Nelson, NZ; Univ. of Canterbury, Christchurch, NZ (MSc, PhD). FNZIC. Postdoctoral Res. Associate, Univ. of N Carolina, 1963–65; Lectr in Chemistry, Univ. of Auckland, 1966. Vis. Lectr, Univ. of Bristol, 1972; Pacific W Coast Inorganic Lectr, 1982; Brotherton Vis. Res. Prof., Univ. of Leeds, 1983; Visiting Professor: Univ. de Rennes, 1984, 1985; Stanford Univ., 1988; Sydney Univ., 2001. Mellor Lectr, NZ Inst. of Chemistry, 1985; Centenary Lectr and Medallist, RSC, 1988; Glenn T. Seaborg Lectr, Univ. of Calif., Berkeley, 1995; Gordon Stone Lectr, Univ. of Bristol, 2003; Arthur D. Little Lectr, MIT, 2005. Fellow, Japan Soc. for Promotion of Science, 1992. Hon. DSc Canterbury, 1999. RSC Award in Organometallic Chemistry, 1983; ICI Medal, NZ Inst. of Chemistry, 1984; Hector Medal, Royal Soc. of NZ, 1991; 12th Inorganic Award, Royal Australian Inst. of Chemistry, 1992; Dwyer Medallist, Univ. of NSW, 2000. *Publications:* 220 sci. papers in internat. jls. *Recreations:* music, espec. opera, walking. *Address:* 26 Beulah Avenue, Rothesay Bay, Auckland 0630, New Zealand. *T:* (9) 4786940.

**ROPER-CURZON,** family name of **Baron Teynham**.

**ROPNER, Sir Henry John William,** 3rd Bt *cr* 1952, of Thorp Perrow, N Riding of Yorkshire; *b* 24 Oct. 1981; *o s* of Sir John Bruce Woollacott Ropner, 2nd Bt and of Auriol Veronica Ropner (*née* Mackeson-Sandbach); *S* father, 2016, but his name does not appear on the Official Roll of the Baronetage; *m* 2012, Natasha Esmé Sinclair.

**ROPNER, Sir Robert (Clinton),** 5th Bt *cr* 1904; Director and Chairman, HR & F Management Services, 2004–10; *b* 6 Feb. 1949; *s* of Sir Robert Douglas Ropner, 4th Bt and Patricia Kathleen (*née* Scofield); *S* father, 2004; *m* 1978, Diana Felicia Abbott (*d* 2015); one *s* one *d* (twins). *Educ:* Harrow. FCA 1977. Global Funds Reporting Manager, Invesco Europe Ltd, 1999–2002. *Recreations:* motoring, ski-ing, gardening. *Heir: s* Christopher Guy Ropner, *b* 18 Jan. 1979. *Address:* 152 Bishops Road, SW6 7JG. *T:* (020) 7736 7482. *E:* robert.ropner@gmail.com.

**ROQUES, (David) John (Seymour);** Senior Partner and Chief Executive, Deloitte & Touche (formerly Touche Ross & Co.), 1990–99; *b* 14 Oct. 1938; *s* of late Frank Davy Seymour Roques and of Marjorie Mabel Hudson; *m* 1963, Elizabeth Anne Mallender; two *s* one *d*. *Educ:* St Albans Sch. Mem., Inst. of Chartered Accountants of Scotland, 1962. Touche Ross & Co., later Deloitte & Touche: Partner, 1967; Partner in charge, Midlands region, 1973; Partner in charge, Scottish region, 1978; Partner in charge, London office, 1984; Man. Partner, 1990. Chm., Portman Bldg Soc., 1999–2006 (Dir, 1995–2006). Non-executive Director: British Nuclear Fuels, 1990–2000; BBA Aviation plc, 1999–2010; Premier Farnell plc, 1999–2008; Chubb plc, 2003; Henderson Gp plc (formerly HHG plc), 2004–09. Member: Financial Reporting Review Panel, 1991–94; Financial Reporting Council, 1996–2001. Gov., Health Foundn, 2001–05. *Recreations:* Rugby football, racing, opera, gardening, golf. *Address:* High Down, Cokes Lane, Chalfont St Giles, Bucks HP8 4TQ. *Clubs:* Brooks's, MCC; Harewood Downs Golf.

**RORKE, Prof. John,** CBE 1979; PhD; FRSE; FIMechE; Professor of Mechanical Engineering, 1980–88, and Vice-Principal, 1984–88, Heriot-Watt University, now Professor Emeritus; *b* 2 Sept. 1923; *s* of John and Janet Rorke; *m* 1948, Jane Craig Buchanan; two *d*. *Educ:* Dumbarton Acad.; Univ. of Strathclyde (BSc, PhD). Lectr, Strathclyde Univ., 1946–51; Asst to Engrg Dir, Alexander Stephen & Sons Ltd, 1951–56; Technical Manager, subseq. Gen. Man., and Engrg Dir, Wm Denny & Bros Ltd, 1956–63; Tech. Dir, subseq. Sales Dir, Man. Dir, and Chm., Brown Bros & Co. Ltd (subsid. of Vickers Ltd), 1963–78; Man. Dir, Vickers Offshore Engrg Gp, 1978; Dir of Planning, Vickers Ltd, 1979–80. Chairman: Orkney Water Test Centre Ltd, 1987–94; Environment and Resource Technology Ltd, 1991–94. Pres., Instn of Engineers and Shipbuilders in Scotland, 1985–87. Hon. DEng Heriot-Watt, 1994. *Recreations:* golf, bridge. *Address:* Flat 23 Lyle Court, 25 Barnton Grove, Edinburgh EH4 6EZ. *T:* (0131) 339 6515. *Club:* Bruntsfield Links Golfing Society (Edinburgh).

**RORSMAN, Prof. Patrik,** PhD; FRS 2014; FMedSci; Professor of Diabetic Medicine, Oxford Centre for Diabetes, Endocrinology and Metabolism, University of Oxford, since 2003; Fellow, Harris Manchester College, Oxford, since 2003; Professor, Department of Physiology, University of Gothenburg, since 2012; *b* Lund, Sweden, 14 May 1959; *s* of Gunne Rorsman and Gun Rorsman; *m* 1983, Margareta Palm; two *s* two *d*. *Educ:* Uppsala Univ. (PhD 1986). Research assistant: Univ. of Gothenburg; lab. of Prof. Bert Sakmann, Univ. of Göttingen; Sen. Res. Asst, Novo Nordisk, Copenhagen, 1994–97; Prof. of Physiol., Lund Univ., 1997–2006; Canada Excellence Res. Chair, Univ. of Alberta, 2011–12. FMedSci 2010. Minkowski Prize, 1996, Albert Renold Prize, 2013, Eur. Assoc.

for Study of Diabetes. *Publications:* contribs to learned jls incl. Nature Cell Biol., Cell Metabolism, Jl Clin. Investigation, Nature, EMBO Jl. *Address:* Oxford Centre for Diabetes, Endocrinology and Metabolism, Churchill Hospital, University of Oxford, Oxford OX3 7LE.

**ROSBOROUGH, Dr Linda;** Chair, Scottish Wildlife Trust, since 2017; *b* Coleraine, NI; *d* of John and Elaine Rosborough; *m* Paul Stollard; two *s*. *Educ:* Coleraine High Sch.; Nottingham Univ. (BSc; PhD). Lectr, Leeds Poly.; Advr, Envmt Cttee, H of C; NI Office; Scottish Govt, latterly as Dir, Marine Scotland, 2012–16. Mem. Bd, Sea Fish Industry Authy, 2018–.

**ROSCOE, Alexis Fayrer;** *see* Brett-Holt, A. F.

**ROSCOE, Gareth;** *see* Roscoe, J. G.

**ROSCOE, Dame Ingrid (Mary),** DCVO 2017; PhD; FSA; Lord-Lieutenant, West Yorkshire, 2004–18 (Vice Lord-Lieutenant, 2001–04); *b* 27 May 1944; *d* of late Dr Arthur Allen and Else (*née* Markenstam) and adopted *d* of late Brig. Kenneth Hargreaves; *m* 1963, John Richard Marshall Roscoe; one *s* two *d*. *Educ:* St Helen's, Northwood; Univ. of Leeds (BA; PhD 1990). FSA 1998. Res. Fellow, Huntington Library, 1988; Lectr in Sculpture Hist., Univ. of Leeds, 1990–96. Co. Rep., NACF, 1972–93; Ed., Ch Monuments Jl, 1993–2000. Mem., Exec. Cttee, Walpole Soc., 2000–05. Chm. Trustees, 1996–2003, High Steward, 2000–08, Selby Abbey; Trustee: Martin House Children's Hospice, 1989–98; York Minster, 2005–11; Yorkshire Sculpture Park, 2006–17; Founding Trustee, Hepworth Wakefield Charitable Trust, 2006–; President: Calderdale Community Foundn, 2004–; Safe Anchor Trust, 2006–; Leeds Philharmonic Chorus, 2008–; Great Northern Art Show, 2008–14; ABF W Yorks; RBL W Yorks; W Yorks Scouts, 2012–; Together Women Project, 2013–. Patron: Nat. Mining Mus., 2004–; Yorks Volunteers Regtl Assoc., 2004–; Yorks Historic Churches, 2004–; W Yorks, Prince's Trust, 2005–; Nat. Heritage Trng Acad., Yorks and Humber, 2009–; Yorks Archaeol Soc.; W Riding Woodcarvers, 2010–; Huddersfield Choral Soc., 2013–. Mem. Council, Huddersfield Univ., 2010–. Hon. Col, Leeds Univ. OTC, 2007–14; Pres., Yorks RFCA, 2011–14. Hon. Fellow, Bradford Coll. of HE, 2014. Hon. DCL: Huddersfield, 2007; Leeds, 2010; Hon. LLD Leeds Metropolitan, 2008; Hon. DLitt Bradford, 2010. DStJ 2012 (OStJ 2006). *Publications:* (contrib.) The Royal Exchange, 1997; (jtly and Ed. in Chief) A Biographical Dictionary of British Sculptors, 2009; (contrib.) Durham Cathedral, 2014; contrib. articles to Apollo, Gazette des Beaux-Arts, Grove Dictionary of Art, Walpole Soc. Jl, Oxford DNB, etc. *Recreations:* the arts, British history, Shakespeare's plays, walking, grandchildren. *Address:* Church House, Nun Monkton, York YO26 8EW. *T:* (01423) 339145.

**ROSCOE, James Paul,** MVO 2017; Counsellor, UK Mission to the United Nations, New York, since 2019; *b* Bangor, Gwynedd, 29 June 1976; *s* of Meurig W. Roscoe and Eleri A. Roscoe; *m* 2008, Clemency Burton-Hill; two *s*. *Educ:* Diocesan Coll., Cape Town; Durham Univ. (BA Hons). Joined FCO, 2000; FCO, 2001–03; COS to Regl Co-ordinator, Coalition Provisional Authy, Basra, Iraq, 2003–04; Second Sec., Sierra Leone, 2004–06; Chief Press Officer, Foreign Affairs and Defence, Prime Minister's Office, 2006–09 (on secondment); First Sec., UK Mission to UN, 2009–12; Hd of News and Dep. Press Sec., 2012–13, Communications Sec. to the Queen, 2013–16, Buckingham Palace; Dir of Communications, Cabinet Office, 2016–17; Dir, Communications and Stakeholders, DExEU, 2017–19. *Recreations:* hiking, cricket, opera, music, reading. *Address:* UK Mission to the UN, 1 Dag Hammarskjold Plaza, New York, NY 10017, USA. *Clubs:* Travellers, Hurlingham.

**ROSCOE, (John) Gareth;** barrister; Legal Adviser, Competition Commission, 2002–04 and 2005–07; Lawyer, Department for Work and Pensions, 2004–05; *b* 28 Jan. 1948; *s* of late John Roscoe and Ann (*née* Jones); *m* 1st, 1970, Helen Jane Taylor (marr. diss. 1979; she *d* 2012); one *d*; 2nd, 1980, Alexis Fayrer Brett-Holt, *qv*; one *s* one *d*. *Educ:* Manchester Warehousemen and Clerks' Orphan Schools (now Cheadle Hulme Sch.); Stretford Tech. Coll.; London Sch. of Economics and Political Science (LLB); Univ. of Leicester (LLM 2003). Called to the Bar, Gray's Inn, 1972; in practice, 1972–75; Legal Asst 1975–79, Sen. Legal Asst 1979, DoE; Law Officers' Dept, Attorney-General's Chambers, 1979–83; Asst Solicitor, 1983–87, Dep. Solicitor, 1987–89, DoE; Dir, BBC Enterprises Ltd, 1989–96; Legal Advr to the BBC, 1989–98; Company Sec., BBC Worldwide Ltd, 1996–98; Consultant Advr, DTI, 1999–2001. Non-executive Director: Optimum NHS Trust, 1995–97; King's Coll. Hosp. NHS Trust, 2001–04. Mem., Gen. Council of the Bar, 1987–90. Member: Adv. Cttee, Centre for Communications and Information Law, UCL, 1991–98; Legal Cttee, EBU, 1989–98. Dir, John Peel Centre for Creative Arts, 2016–. Trustee and Dir, Anglia Care Trust, 2009– (Chm., 2011–14). *Recreations:* music, gardening and the company of friends.

**ROSE,** family name of **Baron Rose of Monewden**.

**ROSE OF MONEWDEN,** Baron *cr* 2014 (Life Peer), of Monewden in the County of Suffolk; **Stuart Alan Ransom Rose,** Kt 2008; Chairman: Ocado, since 2013 (non-executive Director, since 2013); Fat Face, since 2013; Zenith, since 2017; *b* 17 March 1949; *s* of late Harry Ransom Rose and Margaret Ransom Rose; *m* 1973, Jennifer Cook (marr. diss. 2010); one *s* one *d*. *Educ:* St Joseph's Convent, Dar-es-Salaam; Bootham Sch., York. Marks and Spencer plc, 1971–89; Chief Executive: Multiples, Burton Gp plc, 1989–97; Argos plc, 1998; Booker plc, 1998–2000; Iceland Group plc, 2000; Arcadia plc, 2000–02; Chief Exec., 2004–10, Exec. Chm., 2008–10, Marks and Spencer plc. Non-executive Director: Land Securities, 2003–13; Woolworths Hldgs, 2011–18; RM2 Internat., 2014–; Member: Eur. Adv. Cttee, Bridgepoint Capital, 2010–; Adv. Bd, Aldo, 2013–18. Chairman: British Fashion Council, 2003–08; BITC, 2008–10; Dressipi, 2012–; Retail Bd, Majid Al Futtaim Hldgs, 2015–; Time Out Markets, 2015–. Retail Advr, HSBC, 2013–. Chm., Healing Foundn, 2011–17. Trustee, RA, 2013–18. *Recreation:* wine. *Address:* Fulton Management Ltd, Mill House, 58 Guildford Street, Chertsey, Surrey KT16 9BE. *Club:* Groucho.

**ROSE, Alan Douglas,** AO 1994; Consultant, HWL Ebsworth Lawyers, 2011–17; *b* 3 May 1944; *s* of late Willfred Allen Rose and Hazel Agnes Rose (*née* Heinemann-Mirre); *m* 1966, Helen Elizabeth Haigh; two *d*. *Educ:* Univ. of Queensland (BA 1966; LLB Hons 1969); LSE, Univ. of London (LLM 1979). Barrister, Supreme Court of Queensland, 1973; Dep. Sec., Dept of Prime Minister and Cabinet, 1982–86; Sec. to Aust. Dept of Community Services, 1986–87; Associate Sec. and Sec. to Aust. Attorney-Gen. Dept, 1987–94; Pres., Aust. Law Reform Commn, 1994–99; Gen. Counsel, Phillips Fox Lawyers, 1999–2002; Consultant, DLA Phillips Fox Lawyers (formerly Phillips Fox Lawyers), 2002–11; Chm., Defence Honours and Awards Tribunal, 2011–14. *Publications:* articles in legal jls and works on public admin. *Recreations:* surfing, ski-ing, reading, travelling. *Address:* PO Box 3296, Manuka, ACT 2603, Australia.

**ROSE, Alison Jane;** Principal, Newnham College, Cambridge, since 2019; *b* Coventry. *Educ:* Barr's Hill Sch., Coventry; Newnham Coll., Cambridge (BA Modern Hist. 1983). Department of Employment: Jobcentre manager, MSC, 1983–88; Deputy Team Leader: EU Trng and Qualifs Policy, 1988–92; UK Health and Safety Policy, 1992–95; Team Leader: UK Health and Safety Finance and Ops, DETR, 1995–98; GLA Act team (Transport), Govt Office for London, 1998–99; First Sec. (regl funds, health, culture, media and sport), UK Perm. Repn to EU, Brussels, 1999–2003; Dep. Dir, Eur. Secretariat, Cabinet Office, 2003–06; Deputy Director: Change Mgt, DCLG, 2006–07; Equalities Strategy, Govt Equalities Office, 2007–08; Hd of Dept, EU Issues, EU Act 2011, FCO, 2008–12; Counsellor (EU and Global Issues), Paris, 2012–13; Dep. Dir, Heritage Policy, DCMS, 2013; Ambassador to Belgium, 2014–19. *Address:* Newnham College, Sidgwick Avenue, Cambridge CB3 9DF.

**ROSE, Alison Mary;** a District Judge (Magistrates' Courts), since 2002; *b* 31 May 1958; *d* of late Brian Henry Rose and of José Gwendoline Rose (*née* Rixon). *Educ:* Univ. of Exeter (LLB Hons 1979). Articled clerk, John H. Rosen & Co., 1980–82; admitted solicitor, 1983; Asst Solicitor, Rosen Hudson & Co., 1983–88; Partner, Hudson Freeman Berg, 1988–2000; Asst Solicitor, Farrell Matthews & Weir, 2000–02; Dep. Dist Judge (Magistrates' Courts), W Midlands, 1999–2002. *Address:* Thames Magistrates' Court, 58 Bow Road, E3 4DJ. *T:* (020) 8271 1219.

**ROSE, Anthea Lorrainne, (Mrs H. D. Rose);** Chief Executive, Association of Chartered Certified Accountants (formerly Chartered Association of Certified Accountants), 1993–2003; consultant to regulatory and professional organisations, now retired; *m* 1971, Hannan David Rose. *Educ:* St Hugh's Coll., Oxford (MA Mod. Hist.).

**ROSE, Sir (Arthur) James,** Kt 2007; CBE 1996; education consultant; President, National Foundation for Educational Research, since 2008; President, Education Development Trust (formerly CfBT Education Committee, then Trust), since 2015 (Chair, 2010–15); *m* 1960, Pauline; one *d*. *Educ:* Kesteven College; Leicester University. HM Chief Inspector for Primary Educn, DES, subseq. DFE, 1986–92; Dep. Dir of Inspection, 1992–94, Dir of Inspection, 1994–99, OFSTED. Leader: review of teaching of reading, DFES, 2006–; review of Primary Curriculum, DFES, 2008–; Ind. Review on Identifying and Teaching Children and Young People with Dyslexia and Literacy Difficulties, 2009. Chair, Dyslexia-Specific Learning Difficulties Trust, 2014–. Hon. DLaws Leicester, 2009; Hon. DEd Beds, 2009.

**ROSE, Aubrey,** CBE 1997 (OBE 1986); Deputy Chairman, Commission for Racial Equality, 1995 (Commissioner, 1991–95); *b* 1 Nov. 1926; *s* of Solomon Rosenberg and Esther Rosenberg (*née* Kurtz); *m* 1954, Sheila Ray Glassman (*d* 2007); one *s* one *d* (and one *s* decd). *Educ:* at various grammar schs incl. Central Foundn Sch., London. Admitted as solicitor, 1952; Sen. Partner, 1971–95. Chm., Legal Cttee, CRE, 1993–95. Founder Mem. and Treas., Commonwealth Human Rights Initiative, 1990–2003. Dep. Chm., British Caribbean Assoc., 1990–; Jt Chm., Indian-Jewish Assoc., 1996–2003 (Pres., 2008–). Sen. Vice-Pres., Bd of Deputies of British Jews, 1991–97; Chm., Jewish Wkg Gp on Envmt, 1991–; Jt Patron, New Assembly of Churches, 1993–. Trustee, Project Fullemploy, 1994–. Pres., Royal British Nurses' Assoc., 2009–. FRSA 1993. Freeman, City of London, 1965. DUniv N London, 2000. *Publications:* Judaism and Ecology, 1992; Jewish Communities of the Commonwealth, 1993; Journey into Immortality, 1997; Brief Encounters of a Legal Kind, 1997; The Rainbow Never Ends, 2005; Letters to My Wife: a tribute to Sheila Rose, 2007; Arich Handler: modern Jewish hero, 2010; Sea Olympics, 2013; Beyond the Rainbow, 2014. *Recreations:* gardening, walking, various sports, writing, reading, lecturing, listening to music. *Address:* 14 Pagitts Grove, Hadley Wood, Herts EN4 0NT. *T:* (020) 8449 2166.

**ROSE, Barry Michael,** OBE 1998; FRSCM; FRAM; Master of the Music, St Albans Abbey, 1988–97; *b* 24 May 1934; *s* of late Stanley George Rose and Gladys Mildred Rose; *m* 1965, Elizabeth Mary Ware; one *s* two *d*. *Educ:* Sir George Monoux Grammar Sch., Walthamstow; Royal Acad. of Music (ARAM). FRSCM 1973; FRAM 1989. First Organist and Master of the Choristers, new Guildford Cathedral, 1960–74; Sub-Organist, St Paul's Cath., 1974–77; Master of the Choir, 1977–84; Master of the Choirs, The King's School, Canterbury, 1985–88. Music Adviser to Head of Religious Broadcasting, BBC, 1970–90. Hon. FRCO 2003; Hon. FGCM 2004. Hon. DMus City, 1991; MUniv Surrey, 1992. *Recreation:* collecting and restoring vintage fountain-pens. *Address:* Level Crossing, Milking Lane, Draycott, Somerset BS27 3TL. *T:* and *Fax:* (01934) 744838. *E:* brose80648@aol.com. *W:* www.barryrose.co.uk.

**ROSE, Rt Hon. Sir Christopher (Dudley Roger),** Kt 1985; PC 1992; Chief Surveillance Commissioner, 2006–15; a Lord Justice of Appeal, 1992–2006; *b* 10 Feb. 1937; *s* of late Roger and Hilda Rose, Morecambe; *m* 1964, Judith, *d* of late George and Charlotte Brand, Didsbury; one *s* one *d*. *Educ:* Morecambe Grammar Sch.; Repton; Leeds Univ. (LLB and Hughes Prize, 1957); Wadham Coll., Oxford (1st cl. hons BCL 1959, Eldon Scholar 1959; Hon. Fellow, 1993). Lectr in Law, Wadham Coll., Oxford, 1959–60; called to Bar, Middle Temple, 1960 (Bencher, 1983; Treas., 2002); Bigelow Teaching Fellow, Law Sch., Univ. of Chicago, 1960–61; Harmsworth Scholar, 1961; joined Northern Circuit, 1961; QC 1974; a Recorder, 1978–85; a Judge of the High Court, QBD, 1985–92; Presiding Judge, Northern Circuit, 1987–90. Vice-Pres., Court of Appeal (Criminal Div.), 1997–2006. Chm., Criminal Justice Consultative Council, 1994–2000. Mem., Senate of Inns of Court and Bar, 1983–85. UK Trustee, Harold G. Fox Foundn, 1995–2005. Hon. LLD Leeds, 2008. *Recreations:* playing the piano, listening to music, travel. *Club:* Garrick.

**ROSE, Dinah Gwen Lison;** QC 2006; barrister; *b* 16 July 1965; *d* of Michael and Susan Rose; *m* 1991, Peter Kessler; two *d*. *Educ:* City of London Sch. for Girls; Magdalen Coll., Oxford (BA Hons Mod. Hist. 1987); City Univ. (Dip. Law 1988). Called to the Bar, Gray's Inn, 1989, Bencher, 2009; in practice as barrister, 1989–, specialising in public law, human rights, competition and regulatory law; a Dep. High Court Judge, 2016–. *Address:* Blackstone Chambers, Blackstone House, Temple, EC4Y 9BW. *T:* (020) 7583 1770, *Fax:* (020) 7822 7350. *E:* dinahrose@blackstonechambers.com.

**ROSE, Prof. Francis Dennis,** LLD, DCL; Senior Research Fellow, Harris Manchester College, Oxford, since 2016; Fellow, Commercial Law Centre, University of Oxford, since 2016; *b* 11 Jan. 1950; *s* of Francis Joseph Rose and late Catherine Mary Rose; *m* 1974, Lynda Kathryn Banks; one *s* two *d*. *Educ:* Farnborough Grammar Sch.; Magdalen Coll., Oxford (BA 1972, BCL 1973, MA 1975, DCL 2007); UCL (PhD 1986); MA 1992, LLD 2006, Cantab. Called to the Bar, Gray's Inn, 1983; barrister; Associate Mem., Quadrant Chambers (formerly 2, then 4, Essex Court Chambers). Lecturer in Law: Liverpool Univ., 1973–75; Cardiff Law Sch., UWIST, 1975–77; UCL, 1977–85; Sen. Lectr, UCL, 1985–89; Lectr in Law, Univ. of Cambridge and Fellow, St John's Coll., Cambridge, 1989–92; Prof. of Commercial and Common Law, Univ. of Buckingham, 1993–99; Prof. of Commercial Law, Univ. of Bristol, 2000–12; Prof. of Maritime and Commercial Law, Univ. of Southampton, 2012–15 (Vis. Prof., 2015–). Visiting Professor: UCL, 1992–94; Univ. of Natal, 1996; Internat. Maritime Law Inst., Malta, 2001–07; Univ. of Auckland, 2002; Tulane Univ., 2005; Univ. of Queensland, 2007; Robert S. Campbell Vis. Fellow, Magdalen Coll., Oxford, 2012–13. Convener, Restitution Section, SLS (formerly SPTL), 1983–2008 (Mem. Council, 1986–99; Sections Sec., 1990–96). Associate Ed., Current Legal Problems, 1983–85; Ed., 1983–87, Gen. Ed., 1987–, Lloyd's Maritime and Commercial Law Qly; Gen. Ed., Restitution Law Review, 1993–; Ed.-in-Chief, Company, Financial and Insolvency Law Review, 1997–99. Editl Dir, Mansfield Press, 1993–2000; Ed., Internat. Maritime and Commercial Yearbook, 2002–. *Publications:* The

Modern Law of Pilotage, 1984; Kennedy and Rose, The Law of Salvage, 5th edn 1985 (jtly) to 9th edn 2017; (ed) New Foundations for Insurance Law, 1987; (ed) International Commercial and Maritime Arbitration, 1987; (ed) Restitution and the Conflict of Laws, 1995; (ed) Consensus Ad Idem, 1996; (ed) Failure of Contracts: contractual, restitutionary and proprietary consequences, 1997; General Average: law and practice, 1997, 3rd edn 2017; (ed) Restitution and Banking Law, 1998; (ed jtly) Lessons of the Swaps Litigation, 2000; (ed jtly) Restitution and Equity, vol. I, Resulting Trusts and Equitable Compensation, 2000; (ed) Lex Mercatoria, 2000; (ed) Restitution and Insolvency, 2000; Marine Insurance: law and practice, 2004, 2nd edn 2012; (ed jtly) English Private Law, 3rd edn, 2013; (ed jtly) Benjamin's Sale of Goods, 10th edn, 2017; contribs to legal jls and books. *Recreations:* family, music, photography, collecting. *Address:* Harris Manchester College, Oxford OX1 3TD. *E:* Francis.Rose@hmc.ox.ac.uk.

**ROSE, Graham Hunt;** a Master of the Senior Courts (formerly Supreme Court), Queen's Bench Division, 1992–2010; *b* 15 July 1937; *er s* of late William Edward Hunt Rose and Mary Musgrave Rose (*née* Kent); *m* 1st, 1962, Malvinia Ann Saunders (marr. diss. 1988); three *s*; 2nd, 2009, Sara Margaret Gibbon (*née* Comer). *Educ:* Canford Sch.; University Coll., Oxford (MA). Nat. Service, RA, 1955–57: commnd 1956; active service, 1957. Called to the Bar, Inner Temple, 1961; practised at the Bar, 1961–92, Western Circuit. Jt Editor, Civil Procedure (formerly Supreme Court Practice), 1992–2010. *Publications:* The Queen's Bench Guide, 2014, 6th edn 2018. *Recreations:* most ball games, walking, gardening, birdwatching. *Address:* c/o Royal Courts of Justice, Strand, WC2A 2LL. *Clubs:* Travellers; Parkstone Golf.

**ROSE, Gen. Sir (Hugh) Michael,** KCB 1994; CBE 1986; DSO 1995; QGM 1981; DL; Adjutant General, 1995–97; Aide de Camp General to the Queen, 1995–97; *b* 5 Jan. 1940; *s* of late Lt-Col Hugh Vincent Rose, IA and Mrs Barbara Phoebe Masters (*née* Allcard); *m* 1968, Angela Raye Shaw; two *s*. *Educ:* Cheltenham College; St Edmund Hall, Oxford (2nd Cl. Hons PPE; Hon. Fellow, 1995); Staff College; RCDS. Commissioned Gloucestershire Regt, TAVR, 1959; RAFVR, 1962; Coldstream Guards, 1964; served Germany, Aden, Malaysia, Gulf States, Dhofar, N Ireland (despatches), Falkland Is (despatches); BM 16 Para. Bde, 1973–75; CO 22 SAS Regt, 1979–82; Comd 39 Inf. Bde, 1983–85; Comdt, Sch. of Infantry, 1987–88; DSF, 1988–89; GOC NE Dist and Comdr 2nd Inf. Div., 1989–91; Comdt, Staff Coll., 1991–93; Comdr, UK Field Army and Insp. Gen. of TA, 1993–94; Comdr, UN Protection Force, Bosnia-Herzegovina, 1994–95; Dep. C-in-C, Land Comd, 1995. Col, Coldstream Guards, 1999–2009. Hon. Col, Oxford Univ. OTC, 1995–2000. DL Somerset, 2003. Hon. DLitt Nottingham, 1999. Freeman, City of London, 1998; Liveryman, Drapers' Co., 1998. Comdr, Legion of Honour (France), 1995. *Publications:* Fighting for Peace, 1998; Washington's War, 2007. *Recreations:* sailing, hill walking. *Address:* c/o Regimental HQ Coldstream Guards, Wellington Barracks, Birdcage Walk, SW1E 6HQ. *Clubs:* Pratt's, Cavalry and Guards.

**ROSE, Prof. Jacqueline,** PhD; FBA 2006; Professor of Humanities, Birkbeck Institute for the Humanities, Birkbeck, University of London, since 2015; *b* 19 May 1949; *d* of Leslie David Stone and Lynn Rose; one *d*. *Educ:* St Hilda's Coll., Oxford (BA Hons English 1971); Paris-Sorbonne (MA Comparative and Gen. Lit. 1972); PhD London 1979. Lectr, 1976–88, Sen. Lectr, 1988–91, Reader, 1991–92, in English, Univ. of Sussex; Prof. of English, QMUL, 1992–2014; Diane Middlebrook/Carl Djerassi Prof. of Gender Studies, Univ. of Cambridge, 2014. Writer and presenter, TV prog., Dangerous Liaisons: Israel and America, 2002. Co-founder, Independent Jewish Voices, 2007. *Publications:* The Case of Peter Pan, or, The Impossibility of Children's Fiction, 1984, 2nd edn 1993; Sexuality in the Field of Vision, 1986, 2nd edn 2005; The Haunting of Sylvia Plath, 1991, 2nd edn 1996; Why War?: psychoanalysis, politics and the return to Melanie Klein, 1993; States of Fantasy, 1995; Albertine (novel), 2001; On Not Being Able to Sleep: psychoanalysis in the modern world, 2003; The Question of Zion, 2005; The Last Resistance, 2007; Conversations with Jacqueline Rose, 2010; The Jacqueline Rose Reader, 2011; Proust Among the Nations: from Dreyfus to the Middle East, 2011; Women in Dark Times, 2014; Mothers: an essay on love and cruelty, 2018. *Address:* Birkbeck Institute for the Humanities, Birkbeck, University of London, 43 Gordon Square, WC1H 0PD. *T:* (020) 7631 6153. *E:* j.rose@bbk.c.uk.

**ROSE, Sir James;** *see* Rose, Sir A. J.

**ROSE, Jeffrey David,** CBE 1991; Chairman of the Royal Automobile Club, 1981–98 (Deputy Chairman, 1979–81); *b* 2 July 1931; *s* of late Samuel and Daisy Rose; *m* 1st, 1958, Joyce (*née* Clompus) (marr. diss. 1999); one *s* two *d*; 2nd, 1999, Helga Maria Wiederschwinger Dusauzay (marr. diss. 2001). *Educ:* Southend High Sch.; London Sch. of Econs and Pol Science. Nat. Service, RA, 1950–52 (Lieut). Exec. Chm., RAC Motoring Services, 1980–98; Vice Chm., British Road Fedn, 1982–98; Vice President: Fédn Internationale de l'Automobile, 1983–93 and 1994–96 (Hon. Vice Pres., 1996–); Inst. of the Motor Industry, 1992–98; RAC Motor Sports Council, 1994–98; Chm., Commonwealth Motoring Conf., 1988–98; Member: Council, Inst. of Advanced Motorists, 1987–94; Adv. Council, Prince's Youth Business Trust, 1992–2000. Chm., Trustees, Brain and Spine Foundn, 1995–2005; Trustee, Brooklands Mus., 1991–2001. FIMI 1989. Liveryman, Worshipful Co. of Coachmakers and Coach Harness Makers, 1981– (Master, 2006–07). *Recreations:* dining, music. *Address:* Albany, Piccadilly, W1J 0AX. *Clubs:* Royal Automobile (Vice-Pres., 1998–), Brooks's, MCC, Pilgrims; Automobile de France.

**ROSE, Sir John (Edward Victor),** Kt 2003; FIMechE; Deputy Chairman, Rothschild Group, since 2011; *b* 9 Oct. 1952; *s* of (Wentworth) Victor Rose and late Doris Rose (*née* Bridge); *m* 1979, Emma Felicity Granville; two *s* one *d*. *Educ:* Charterhouse Sch.; Univ. of St Andrews (MA Hons Psychology). FRAeS 1993. Rolls-Royce, 1984–2011: Board Mem., 1992–2011; Chief Exec., 1996–2011. Hon. FREng 2009. Commander, Légion d'Honneur (France), 2008; Public Service Star (Singapore), 2008. *Recreations:* ski-ing, sailing, scuba-diving, tennis, theatre, arts. *Club:* Hurlingham.

**ROSE, Maj. Gen. John Gordon,** CB 2009; MBE 1991; Director General, Intelligence Collection, Ministry of Defence, 2006–09; *b* 30 May 1955; *s* of Charles and Yvonne Rose; *m* 1982, Mandie Jones; one *s*. *Educ:* Kitale Primary Sch., Kenya; Lenana Sch., Kenya; Dollar Acad. Royal Marines: joined, 1974, young officer trng; Troop Comdr 40 Commando, 1975–76; Ops Officer, Desert Regt, Sultan of Oman Land Forces (on secondment), 1976–78; Instructor, SNCO Tactics Wing (Army) and RM Officers Trng, 1979–82; Adjutant 40 Commando, 1982–83; SO HQ 3 Commando Bde, 1984–87; Army staff course, Camberley, 1988; COS Logistics HQ UK Mobile Force, 1989–90; Company Comdr 42 Commando, 1990–92; SO Directorate of Naval Staff Duties, MoD, 1992–93; COS 3 Commando Bde, 1994–96; Staff of C-in-C Fleet, 1996; Asst Dir, Middle East, MoD, 1997–98; CO 40 Commando, 1999–2000; Dir, Intelligence Ops MoD Defence Intelligence Staff, 2000–03; Chief of Defence Staff Liaison Officer, Pentagon, 2003; hcsc, 2004; Comdr 3 Commando Bde, 2004–06. Rep. Col Comdt, RM, 2009–12. Project Dir, African Union/UN Inf. Support Team for Somalia, 2012–13. *Recreations:* golf, photography, motor bike touring. *Address:* c/o Royal Marines Secretary, Whale Island, Portsmouth PO1 3LS.

**ROSE, John Raymond;** Clerk of Standing Committees, House of Commons, 1987–91; *b* 22 April 1934; *s* of late Arthur Raymond Rose and Edith Mary Rose, Merstham, Surrey and Minehead, Somerset; *m* 1st, 1961, Vivienne (marr. diss. 1991), *d* of late Charles Dillon Seabrooke, IoW; one *s* one *d*; 2nd, 1991, Dr Betty Webb, *d* of late Ernest Julian Webb, Statesville, NC, USA. *Educ:* Marlborough; Trinity Hall, Cambridge (Major Scholar in Classics; Law Tripos 1st Cl. Hons, Pts I and II). 2nd Lieut DCLI, Belize and Jamaica, 1953–55. Clerk's Department, House of Commons, 1958–91: Clerk of Select Cttees on Estimates (Sub-Cttee), Public Accounts, Violence in the Family, Race Relations, Abortion, European Community Secondary Legislation, Foreign Affairs, 1959–87. Vis. Kenan Prof., 1981, Adjunct Prof., 1991–, Meredith Coll., NC, USA. Fellow, Industry and Parlt Trust, 1987. Freeman, City of London, 1959; Liveryman, Salters' Co., 1959. *Recreations:* travel, walking, cycling, gardening, bridge. *Address:* 1612 Oberlin Road, Raleigh, NC 27608, USA. *T:* (919) 8283443; 4 St James's Square, Bath BA1 2TR. *T:* (01225) 481115. *E:* johnrrose34@gmail.com.

**ROSE, Jonathan Lee; His Honour Judge Rose;** a Circuit Judge, since 2008; *b* Leeds, 29 Oct. 1958; *s* of Malcolm and Shirley Rose; *m* 1990, Philippa, *d* of Eric and Pearl Green; one *s* one *d*. *Educ:* Roundhay Sch., Leeds; Preston Poly. (BA Hons); Keble Coll., Oxford. Called to the Bar, Middle Temple, 1981; barrister, N Eastern Circuit, 1983–2008; Recorder, 2000–08. Legal Mem., Mental Health Rev. Tribunal, 2002–08. Vice Pres., 2005–06, Pres., 2006–11, United Hebrew Congregation, Leeds. Hon. Fellow, Univ. of Central Lancs, 2016. *Publications:* Innocents: how justice failed Stefan Kisko and Lesley Molseed, 1997. *Recreations:* music, scuba diving, cycling, natural history, history. *Address:* Bradford Combined Court Centre, Exchange Square, Bradford BD1 1JA. *T:* (01274) 840274, *Fax:* (01274) 840275.

**ROSE, Ven. Judith;** *see* Rose, Ven. K. J.

**ROSE, Judith Ann;** *see* Goffe, J. A.

**ROSE, Sir Julian (Day),** 4th Bt *cr* 1909, of Hardwick House, and 5th Bt *cr* 1872, of Montreal; President, International Coalition to Protect the Polish Countryside, since 2000; *b* 3 March 1947; 3rd and *o* surv. *s* of Sir Charles Henry Rose, 3rd Bt and of Phoebe, *d* of 2nd Baron Phillimore (*d* 1947); *S* father, 1966, and cousin, Sir Francis Cyril Rose, 4th Bt, 1979; *m* 1976, Elizabeth Goode Johnson, Columbus, Ohio, USA (marr. diss. 2002); one *s* one *d*. *Educ:* Stanbridge School. Actor/asst dir, Players' Theatre of New England, 1973–79; Co-founder, Inst. for Creative Develt, Antwerp, 1978–83. Co-ordinator, Organic Farming practice, Hardwick Estate, 1975–. Chm., Assoc. of Rural Businesses in Oxfordshire, 1995–2001; Member: Council, Soil Assoc., 1984–96; Agricl Panel, Intermediate Technology Develt Gp, 1984–87; Bd, UK Register of Organic Food Standards, Food From Britain, 1987–90; BBC Rural and Agricl Affairs Adv. Cttee, 1991–93; Adv. Cttee, Food and Farming, Univ. of W London (formerly Thames Valley Univ.), 1994–2000; Agricl and Rural Economy Cttee, CLA, 1999–2002. Rural Economy Advr, SE of England Develt Agency, 1999–2002. Pres., Internat. Coalition to Protect the Polish Countryside, 2004–; Patron: Family Farmers Assoc., 2004–; Natural Food Finders, 2009–; Bees Action Network, 2010–. Trustee: SAFE Alliance, 1995–2000; Dartington Trust, 1996–2000. Agricl Correspondent, Environment Now, 1989–90; Presenter, Letter from Poland, Farming Today, BBC Radio 4, 2007–08. Chair, The Future of Agriculture, St George's House consultation, 1999–. Food Award, 1986, Best Dairy Produce, 1998, Soil Assoc. *Publications:* (contrib.) Town and Country, 1999; Changing Course for Life: local solutions to global problems, 2009; Back to our Roots, Resurgence, 2010; In Defence of Life: essays on a radical reworking of green wisdom, 2013; Overcoming the Robotic Mind, 2019; contrib. Fourth World Rev. *Heir: s* Lawrence Michael Rose, *b* 6 Oct. 1986. *Address:* Hardwick House, Whitchurch-on-Thames, Oxfordshire RG8 7RB. *W:* www.changingcourseforlife.info.

**ROSE, Ven. (Kathleen) Judith;** Archdeacon of Tonbridge, 1996–2002; *b* 14 June 1937; *d* of Cuthbert Arthur Rose and Margaret Rose; *m* 1991, David Ernest Gwyer (*d* 2000); two step *d*. *Educ:* Sexey's Grammar Sch., Blackford; Seale Hayne Agricl Coll. (NDD 1960); St Michael's House Theol Coll., Oxford (DipTh 1966); London Bible Coll. (BD(Hons)). Agriculture, 1953–64; Parish Worker, Rodbourne Cheney Parish Church, 1966–71; ordained deaconess, 1976, deacon, 1987, priest, 1994; Parish Worker, then Deaconess, St George's Church, Leeds, 1973–81; Chaplain, Bradford Cathedral, 1981–85; Minister responsible for St Paul's Parkwood, Gillingham, 1986–90; Chaplain to Bishop of Rochester, 1990–95. Rural Dean of Gillingham, 1988–90. *Publications:* Sunday Learning for All Ages, 1982; (contrib.) Women in Ministry, 1991; (contrib.) Women Priests: the first years, 1996; (contrib.) A Time and A Season, 2000; (contrib.) Voices of this Calling, 2002; Sow in Tears, Reap in Joy, 2007. *Recreations:* gardening, home-making. *Address:* 47 Hill Lea Gardens, Cheddar, Somerset BS27 3JH.

**ROSE, Lindsey Maxine; Her Honour Judge Lindsey Rose;** a Circuit Judge, since 2019; *b* Brighton, 27 July 1973; *d* of A. Rose and H. Rose; *m* 2004; two *s*. *Educ:* Univ. of Hull (LLB Hons); Inns of Court Sch. of Law (BVC). Called to the Bar, Middle Temple, 1996; a Recorder, 2009–19. *Recreations:* reading, travel, family. *Address:* Isleworth Crown Court, 36 Ridgeway Road, Isleworth TW7 5LP.

**ROSE, Martin Tristram;** consultant and writer, since 2018; Senior Adviser, British Council, 2014–18; *b* 3 Dec. 1954; *s* of late Geoffrey Rose and Jocelyn Rose (*née* Briggs); *m* 1984, Georgina Benson; one *s* three *d*. *Educ:* Bradfield Coll.; Magdalen Coll., Oxford (BA Hons Mod. Hist. 1976; MA 1984); St Antony's Coll., Oxford (MPhil Mod. Mid. Eastern Studies 1984). Sub-ed., The Egyptian Gazette, 1976–78; Sales exec., later ELT Sales, Macmillan Press, S Africa and Mid East, 1979–82; Mid East Dept, Mellon Bank NA, 1984–88; British Council, 1988–: Asst Rep., Baghdad, 1989–90; Asst Dir, Rome and founding Dir, Pontignano Conf., 1991–96; Hd, Eur. Series, London, 1996–99; Dir, Brussels and Cultural Counsellor, HM Embassies, Belgium and Luxembourg, 1999–2002; Dir, Counterpoint, 2002–06; Dir, Canada, and Cultural Counsellor, High Commn, Ottawa, 2006–10; Dir, Morocco, and Cultural Attaché, HM Embassy Rabat, 2010–14. Shaikh Zaki Badawi Meml Lect., Assoc. of Muslim Social Scientists UK, 2009. Vis. Fellow, Prince Waleed bin Talal Centre for Islamic Studies, Cambridge Univ., 2014–18. Trustee, BAX British-Arab Exchanges, 2014–18 (Chm., 2016–18). Fellow, Royal Canadian Geographical Soc., 2009. *Publications:* (with N. Wadham-Smith) Mutuality, Trust and Cultural Relations, 2004; (with M. Leonard) British Public Diplomacy in an Age of Schisms, 2005; The Affair of the Emerods, 2009; (ed with A. Hussey) The Challenge of North Africa, 2014; Education in North Africa, 2014; Immunizing the Mind, 2016; There and Back by Candle-light, 2016; A Morocco Anthology: travel writing through the centuries, 2018. *Recreations:* history, literature, language, memory, Middle East, gravestones. *Address:* Ridings, Catmere End, Saffron Walden, Essex CB11 4XG. *T:* 07880 932604. *E:* martin.rose@magd.oxon.org.

**ROSE, Martyn Craig;** Chairman: English National Opera, 2013–15; DanceEast, 2010–13; Floreat Education, since 2013; *b* Llandrindod Wells, 27 May 1948; *s* of Charles Rose and Margaret Rose; *m* 1990, Philippa Savill; one *s* one *d*. *Educ:* Malvern Coll.; Inns of Court Sch. of Law. Called to the Bar, Inner Temple, 1972. Chairman: Cherry Blossom Ltd, 1977–; Grangers Internat. Ltd, 1977–; Macaw Soft Drinks, 1990–2005; Minster

Sound Radio plc, 1992–2000; Frost and Reed Ltd, 1993–; Publishing Technology plc, 2005–; Dir, Dentons Pension Mgt Ltd, 2000–. Co-chair: Nat. Citizen Service, 2007–10; Get Britain Working, 2009–10; Chm., Society Network Foundn, 2011–14. Mem., Honours Cttee, Sci. and Technol., 2013–16. Chm., Trustees, UK Onward Thinktank Ltd, 2018–; Trustee: Cystic Fibrosis Trust, 2004–14; Cystic Fibrosis Care, 2015–. Gov., Orwell Park Sch., 2001–17. *Recreations:* Wimbledon, golf, shooting, performing arts both classical and modern, fine art collecting and dealing, struggling to beat my son at tennis. *Address:* 7 Trebeck Street, W1J 7LU. *T:* (020) 7408 0792, *Fax:* (020) 7408 0783. *E:* mcr@martynrose.com.

**ROSE, Gen. Sir Michael;** *see* Rose, Gen. Sir H. M.

**ROSE, Norman John,** FRICS; Member, Upper Tribunal (Lands Chamber) (formerly Lands Tribunal), 1998–2013; *b* 22 Oct. 1943; *s* of late Jack Rose and Margaret Rose (*née* de Groot); *m* 1968, Helena de Mesquita; three *s*. *Educ:* Christ's Coll., Finchley; Coll. of Estate Management (BSc (Est. Man.); Valuation Prize). FRICS 1976. Gerald Eve & Co., 1964–71; Partner, de Groot Collis, 1971–91; Dir of Valuation, Chesterton, 1992–98. *Address:* 22 Cholmeley Crescent, N6 5HA.

**ROSE, Paul Telfer;** QC 2002; *b* 18 Nov. 1958; 3rd *s* of late Ian Alexander Rose and of Pamela Margaret Rose (*née* Paisley); *m* 1986, Sara Jane Herbert; three *s* one *d*. *Educ:* University Coll. Sch., Hampstead; Reading Univ. (LLB 1980). Called to the Bar, Gray's Inn, 1981; in practice as barrister, specialising in employment law and personal injury law, 1983–. Fee-paid Judge (formerly Chairman), Employment Tribunals, 2003–18. *Recreations:* travel, Rugby, cricket, golf, walking with friends and family. *Address:* Old Square Chambers, 10–11 Bedford Row, WC1R 4BU. *T:* (020) 7269 0300. *E:* roseqc@oldsquare.co.uk.

**ROSE, Prof. Richard,** FBA 1992; FRSE; Professor of Politics, 1966–2005 and since 2012, and Founder and Director, Centre for the Study of Public Policy, since 1976, University of Strathclyde; *b* 9 April 1933; *o s* of late Charles Imse and Mary C. Rose, St Louis, Mo, USA; *m* 1956, Rosemary J., *o d* of late James Kenny, Whitstable, Kent; two *s* one *d*. *Educ:* Clayton High Sch., Mo; Johns Hopkins Univ., BA (Double distinction, Phi Beta Kappa) comparative drama, 1953; London Sch. of Economics, 1953–54; Oxford University, 1957–60, DPhil (Lincoln and Nuffield Colls). Political public relations, Mississippi Valley, 1954–55; Reporter, St Louis Post-Dispatch, 1955–57; Lecturer in Govt, Univ. of Manchester, 1961–66; Prof. of Politics and Public Policy, Strathclyde Univ., 1966–2005; Sen. Fellow, Oxford Internet Inst., 2003–05; Sixth Century Prof. of Politics and Public Policy, Univ. of Aberdeen, 2005–11. Consultant Psephologist, The Times, Independent Television, Daily Telegraph, STV, UTV etc., 1964–. American SSRC Fellow, Stanford Univ., 1967; Vis. Lectr in Political Sociology, Cambridge Univ., 1967; Dir, ISSC European Summer Sch., 1973. Sec., Cttee on Political Sociology, Internat. Sociological Assoc., 1970–85; Founding Mem., European Consortium for Political Res., 1970; Member: US/UK Fulbright Commn, 1971–75; Eisenhower Fellowship Programme, 1971. Guggenheim Foundn Fellow, 1974; Visiting Scholar: Woodrow Wilson Internat. Centre, Washington DC, 1974; Brookings Inst., Washington DC, 1976; Amer. Enterprise Inst., Washington, 1980; Fiscal Affairs Dept, IMF, Washington, 1984; Vis. Prof., 1976–78, Vis. Fellow, 2011–, European Univ. Inst., Florence; Vis. Fellow, Central European Univ., Prague, 1992–95; Vis. Prof., Instituto Ortega y Gasset, Madrid, 2000; Visitor, Japan Foundn, 1984; Hinkley Prof., Johns Hopkins Univ., 1987; Vis. Fellow, 1988–90, 2006–11, Vis. Res. Prof., 2015–, Wissenschaftszentrum, Berlin; Research Associate: UN Eur. Centre for Social Welfare Policy and Res., 1992–; Centre for Study of Democracy, Univ. of Westminster, 1998–2000; Fellow, Max-Planck Transformation Process Gp, Berlin, 1996; Wei Lun Prof., Chinese Univ. of Hong Kong, 2000. Ransone Lectr, Univ. of Alabama, 1990. Consultant Chm., NI Constitutional Convention, 1976; Mem., Home Office Working Party on Electoral Register, 1975–77. Co-Founder: British Politics Gp, 1974; Global Barometer Survey Network, 2001–05; Convenor, Work Gp on UK Politics, Political Studies Assoc., 1976–88; Mem. Council, Internat. Political Science Assoc., 1976–82; Keynote Speaker, Aust. Inst. of Political Science, Canberra, 1978; Steering Cttee, World Values Study, 1995; Transparency Internat. Res. Adv. Cttee, 1998–. Technical Consultant: OECD; World Bank; Internat. Inst. for Democracy and Electoral Assistance, Stockholm; Council of Europe; Dir, ESRC (formerly SSRC) Res. Programme, Growth of Govt, 1982–86; UNDP Cons. to Pres. of Colombia, 1990; Scientific Advr, Paul Lazarsfeld Soc., Vienna, 1991–. Mem. Council, Scottish Opera Ltd, 1992–. Hon. Vice-Pres., Political Studies Assoc., UK, 1986. Editor, Jl of Public Policy, 1985–2012. FRSE 2019. Foreign Member: Finnish Acad. of Science and Letters, 1985; Amer. Acad. of Arts and Scis, 1994. Hon. Dr: Orebru, 2005; European Univ. Inst., 2010. Amex Internat. Econs Prize, 1992; Lasswell Prize for Public Policy, Policy Studies Orgn, USA, 1999; Lifetime Achievement Award, UK Pol Studies Assoc., 2000; Lifetime Achievement Award, Council for Comparative Study of Electoral Systems, 2008; Dogan Foundn Award, Eur. Consortium for Pol Res., 2009; Sir Isaiah Berlin Lifetime Achievement Award, Pol Studies Assoc. of the UK, 2010; Lifetime Achievement Award, Internat. Public Policy Assoc., 2019. Subject of prog. in Man of Action series, BBC Radio 3, 1974. *Publications:* The British General Election of 1959 (with D. E. Butler), 1960; Must Labour Lose? (with Mark Abrams), 1960; Politics in England, 1964, 5th edn 1989; (ed) Studies in British Politics, 1966, 3rd edn 1976; Influencing Voters, 1967; (ed) Policy Making in Britain, 1969; People in Politics, 1970; (ed, with M. Dogan) European Politics, 1971; Governing Without Consensus: an Irish perspective, 1971; (with T. Mackie) International Almanack of Electoral History, 1974, 3rd edn 1991; (ed) Electoral Behavior: a comparative handbook, 1974; (ed) Lessons from America, 1974; The Problem of Party Government, 1974; (ed) The Management of Urban Change in Britain and Germany, 1974; Northern Ireland: a time of choice, 1976; Managing Presidential Objectives, 1976; (ed) The Dynamics of Public Policy, 1976; (ed, with D. Kavanagh) New Trends in British Politics, 1977; (ed with J. Wiatr) Comparing Public Policies, 1977; What is Governing?: Purpose and Policy in Washington, 1978; (ed, with G. Hermet and A. Rouquié) Elections without Choice, 1978; (with B. G. Peters) Can Government Go Bankrupt?, 1978; (ed with W. B. Gwyn) Britain: progress and decline, 1980; Do Parties Make a Difference?, 1980, 2nd edn 1984; (ed) Challenge to Governance, 1980; (ed) Electoral Participation, 1980; (ed with E. Suleiman) Presidents and Prime Ministers, 1980; Understanding the United Kingdom, 1982; (with I. McAllister) United Kingdom Facts, 1982; (ed with P. Madgwick) The Territorial Dimension in United Kingdom Politics, 1982; (ed with E. Page) Fiscal Stress in Cities, 1982; Understanding Big Government, 1984; (with I. McAllister) The Nationwide Competition for Votes, 1984; Public Employment in Western Nations, 1985; (with I. McAllister) Voters Begin to Choose, 1986; (with D. Van Mechelen) Patterns of Parliamentary Legislation, 1986; (ed with R. Shiratori) The Welfare State East and West, 1986; Ministers and Ministries, 1987; (with T. Karran) Taxation by Political Inertia, 1987; The Post-Modern President: the White House meets the world, 1988, 2nd edn 1991; Ordinary People in Public Policy, 1989; (with I. McAllister) The Loyalty of Voters: a lifetime learning model, 1990; Lesson-Drawing in Public Policy: a guide to learning across time and space, 1993; (with P. L. Davies) Inheritance in Public Policy: change without choice in Britain, 1994; What is Europe?, 1996; (with S. White and I. McAllister) How Russia Votes, 1997; (with W. Mishler and C. Haerpfer) Democracy and Its Alternatives, 1998; (ed jtly) A Society Transformed?: Hungary in time-space perspective, 1999; International Encyclopedia of Elections, 2000; The Prime Minister in a Shrinking World, 2001; (with Neil Munro) Elections Without Order: Russia's challenge to Vladimir Putin, 2002; (with Neil Munro) Elections and Parties in New European Democracies, 2003; Learning from Comparative Public Policy, 2005; (with W. Mishler and Neil Munro) Russia Transformed, 2006; Understanding Post-Communist Transformation, 2009; (with Neil Munro) Parties and Elections in New European Democracies, 2009; (jtly) Popular Support for an Undemocratic Regime, 2011; Representing Europeans: a pragmatic approach, 2013, 2nd edn 2015; Learning about Politics in Time and Space: a memoir, 2014; (with C. Peiffer) Paying Bribes for Public Services, 2015; (with C. Peiffer) Bad Governance and Corruption, 2018; How Referendums Challenge European Democracy, 2019; numerous contribs to academic journals in Europe and America; trans. into eighteen foreign languages; broadcasts on comparative politics and public policy. *Recreations:* architecture, textiles, music, writing. *Address:* 1 East Abercromby Street, Helensburgh, Scotland G84 7SP. *T:* (01436) 672164. *W:* www.profrose.eu. *Clubs:* Reform; Cosmos (Washington, DC).

**ROSE, Prof. Steven Peter Russell,** PhD; Professor of Biology and Director, Brain and Behaviour Research Group, Open University, 1969–2006, now Emeritus Professor of Neuroscience; *b* 4 July 1938; *s* of Lionel Sydney Rose and Ruth Rose (*née* Waxman); *m* 1961, Hilary Ann Chantler; two *s*. *Educ:* Haberdashers' Aske's Sch., Hampstead; King's Coll., Cambridge (BA); Inst. of Psychiatry, Univ. of London (PhD). FRSB (FIBiol 1970). Beit Meml and Guinness Res. Fellow, New Coll., Oxford, 1961–63; NIH Res. Fellow, Istituto Superiore di Sanità, Rome, 1963–64; MRC Res. Staff, Dept of Biochem., Imperial Coll., London, 1964–69. Vis. Sen. Res. Fellow, ANU, 1977; Vis. Schol., Harvard Univ., 1980; Distinguished Res. Prof., Univ. of Minn, 1992; Osher Fellow, Exploratorium, San Francisco, 1993; Vis. Prof., UCL, 1999–; Jt Gresham Prof. of Physic, 1999–2002. FRSA 1980. Life Mem., British Neurosci. Assoc., 2017. Anokhin Medal, Russia, 1990; Sechenov Medal, Russia, 1992; Ariens Kappers Medal, Netherlands Royal Acad. of Sci., Amsterdam, 1999; Biochem. Soc. Prize, 2002; Edinburgh Medal, 2004; Lifetime Award for Outstanding Contributions to Neuroscience, British Neurosci. Assoc., 2012. *Publications:* The Chemistry of Life, 1966, 4th edn 1999; (with Hilary Rose) Science and Society, 1969; The Conscious Brain, 1973; No Fire No Thunder, 1984; (jtly) Not in our Genes, 1984; The Making of Memory, 1992, new edn 2003 (Science Book Prize, COPUS, 1993); Lifelines, 1997; (ed) From Brains to Consciousness?, 1998; (ed with Hilary Rose) Alas, Poor Darwin, 2000; The 21st Century Brain: explaining, mending and manipulating the mind, 2005; (with Hilary Rose) Genes, Cells and Brains: the Promethean promises of the new biosciences, 2012; (with Hilary Rose) Can Neuroscience Change Our Minds?, 2016; numerous edited books, res. papers and scholarly articles. *Address:* Department of Life, Health and Chemical Sciences, The Open University, Milton Keynes MK7 6AA.

**ROSE, Timothy John; His Honour Judge Timothy Rose;** a Circuit Judge, since 2018; *b* London, 27 Jan. 1958; *s* of Victor and Elsie Rose; partner, Helen Mott; four *s*. *Educ:* Vyners Sch., Ickenham; Univ. of Bristol (LLB 1979); Coll. of Law, Lancaster Gate. Admitted as solicitor, 1982; a Dep. Dist Judge (Magistrates' Courts), 2006–18; a Recorder, 2016–18; a Dist Judge (Magistrates' Courts), 2018. *Recreations:* music, film, theatre, walking, family, tennis.

**ROSE, Rt Hon. Dame Vivien (Judith),** DBE 2013; PC 2019; **Rt Hon. Lady Justice Rose;** a Lady Justice of Appeal, since 2019; *b* London, 13 April 1960; *d* of late Eric Rose and Jacqueline Rose (*née* Sugarman); *m* 2002, Dr Bernard Joseph Bulkin, OBE. *Educ:* Kingsbury High Sch.; Newnham Coll., Cambridge (BA Law 1982); Brasenose Coll., Oxford (BCL 1983). Called to the Bar, Gray's Inn, 1984, Bencher, 2013; in practice as a barrister, Monckton Chambers, Gray's Inn, 1985–95; Standing Counsel to Dir Gen. of Fair Trading, 1992–95; Advr, Legal Dept, HM Treasury, 1996–2002; apptd to Sen. Civil Service, 2000; Dir, Operational and Internat. Humanitarian Law, MoD, 2002–05; Dep. Counsel, Office of Counsel to the Speaker of the H of C, 2005–08; Chm., Competition Appeal Tribunal, 2005–13, 2015–19; Judge, First-tier Tribunal, Charity Jurisdiction, 2005–13, Envmt Jurisdiction, 2010–13; a Recorder, 2009–13; a Dep. High Court Judge, Chancery Div., 2012–13; a Judge of the High Court of Justice, Chancery Div., 2013–19; Pres., Upper Tribunal Tax and Chancery Chamber, 2015–18. *Publications:* (ed) Bellamy and Child, 4th edn, Common Market Law of Competition, 1993; (ed with Hon. Mr Justice Roth) Bellamy and Child, 6th edn, European Community Law of Competition, 2007; (ed with David Bailey) Bellamy and Child, 7th edn, European Union Law of Competition, 2013. *Recreations:* theatre and cinema, choral singing. *Address:* Royal Courts of Justice, Strand, WC2A 2LL.

**ROSEBERY, 7th Earl of,** *cr* 1703; **Neil Archibald Primrose;** DL; Bt 1651; Viscount of Rosebery, Baron Primrose and Dalmeny, 1700; Viscount of Inverkeithing, Baron Dalmeny and Primrose, 1703; Baron Rosebery (UK), 1828; Earl of Midlothian, Viscount Mentmore, Baron Epsom, 1911; *b* 11 Feb. 1929; *o surv. s* of 6th Earl of Rosebery, KT, PC, DSO, MC, and Eva Isabel Marian (Eva Countess of Rosebery, DBE) (*d* 1987), *d* of 2nd Baron Aberdare; *S* father, 1974; *m* 1955, Alison Mary Deirdre, *d* of late Ronald William Reid, MS, FRCS; one *s* four *d*. *Educ:* Stowe; New Coll., Oxford. DL Midlothian, 1960. *Heir:* s Lord Dalmeny, *qv*. *Address:* Dalmeny House, South Queensferry, West Lothian EH30 9TQ.

**ROSEBY, Paul Robert,** OBE 2018; broadcaster; Chief Executive Officer and Artistic Director, National Youth Theatre, since 2004; *b* Leigh-on-Sea, Essex, 6 Aug. 1966; *s* of Albert Edward Roseby and Margaret Lillian Roseby (*née* Mitchell); *m* 2008, James Tod. *Educ:* Smithdon High Sch., Hunstanton, Norfolk; Norwich City Coll. Broadcaster, BBC Radio; television presenter: 5's Company, C5, 1998; Backstage, BBC, 1999; Great Food Live, UK TV Food, 2003–05; BBC: Heaven and Earth, 2004; Culture Show, 2008; Bite Size R and J, 2008; The Making of the Merchant of Venice, 2008; When Romeo Met Juliet, 2010; radio presenter and writer, BBC Radio 4: Fabulous Flops, 2005; More Fabulous Flops, 2006; Pilots That Never Flew, 2009. Director: The Merchant of Venice, Royal Opera Hse, 2005, Beijing, 2008; Relish, Tramshed Th., 2010; Story of Our Youth, Shaftesbury, 2016. *Publications:* White Van Wit Book, 2007; Producers' Choice: six plays for young performers, 2014; National Youth Theatre Monologues, 2018; 100 Acting Exercises for 8–18 Year Olds, 2019. *Address:* National Youth Theatre, 443–445 Holloway Road, N7 6LW. *T:* (020) 3696 7066. *E:* info@nyt.org.uk. *Club:* Soho House.

**ROSEN, Alan Peter;** Headteacher, Aylesbury High School, since 2005 (Deputy Headteacher, 1995–2005); *b* Edgware, Middx, 27 June 1955; *s* of M. and R. Rosen; *m* 1977, Janet; one *s* one *d*. *Educ:* Haberdashers' Aske's Sch., Elstree; Univ. of Wales, Aberystwyth (BSc Hons Maths and Computer Sci. 1976; PGCE 1977); Hatfield Poly. (MEd Classroom Processes 1989). NPQH 2001. Teacher, Hatfield Sch., Hatfield, 1977–83; Hd of IT, Astley Cooper Sch., Hemel Hempstead, 1983–89; Curriculum Manager, Maths, Sci. and Technol., Westfield Sch., Watford, 1989–95. *Recreations:* World Challenge Expedition Leader, orienteering—national and international competitor, controller (referee) of 1999 World Championships and 2005 World Cup. *Address:* c/o Aylesbury High School, Walton Road, Aylesbury, Bucks HP21 7SX. *T:* (01296) 388222, *Fax:* (01296) 388200. *E:* secretary@ahs.bucks.sch.uk.

**ROSEN, Howard John**, CBE 2003; Founder and Principal, Howard Rosen Solicitors, since 1989; Managing Director, Rosetrust AG, since 1993; *b* London, 14 April 1955; *s* of Leonard Sidney Rosen and Betty Clarissa Rosen; *m* 1985, Michelle Anne Oberman; two *s*. *Educ*: Braintcroft Primary Sch.; City of London Sch.; Exeter Coll., Oxford (BA Juris. 1978; MA). Admitted solicitor, 1980; Asst Solicitor, Tarlo Lyons & Aukin, 1980; UK Counsel, United Leasing plc, 1980–82; European Gen. Counsel, Equilease Gp, 1982–88. Chm., Rail Wkg Gp, 1995–; Corresp., UNIDROIT, 2001–. President: British-Swiss Chamber of Commerce, 1998–2003 (Hon. Life Councillor, 2013); Council of British Chamber of Commerce in Europe, 2005–12 (Chm., Public Affairs Commn, 2006–12). Member: Law Soc. of England and Wales; Internat. Bar Assoc.; Soc. of Trust and Estate Practitioners; MInstD. Ambassador at Large, Commonwealth Jewish Council, 2016–. Pres., Swiss Friends of Oxford Univ., 2017–. *Publications*: (ed) Leasing Law in the European Union, 1994; Disputes Involving Trusts, 1999; Implementing the Cape Town Convention and Domestic Laws on Secured Transactions, 2017; contribs to Asset Finance and Leasing Digest, Leasing World, Internat. Financial Law Rev., UK Law Soc. Gazette, Private Client Business, Uniform Law Rev., Trust and Trustees, Railways of the World, Eur. Rev. of Private Law, Cape Town Academic Protect Jl, Disputes Involving Trusts, Implementing the Cape Town Convention, Domestic Laws on Secured Transactions. *Recreations*: ski-ing, singing, football, aquarist. *Address*: Howard Rosen Solicitors, Baarerstrasse 98, PO Box 7262, 6302 Zug, Switzerland. *T*: (41) 7602888, *Fax*: (41) 7602909. *E*: howard.rosen@legalease.ch. *Club*: Baur au Lac (Zurich).

**ROSEN, Rabbi Jeremy**; Professor of Jewish Studies, Faculty for Comparative Study of Religions, Wilrijk, Belgium, 1991–2015 (President, 1994–2015); Rabbi, Persian Jewish Community, New York, since 2009; *b* 11 Sept. 1942; *s* of Rabbi Kopul Rosen and Bella Rosen; *m* 1st, 1971, Vera Giuditta Zippel (marr. diss. 1987); two *s* two *d*; 2nd, 1988, Suzanne Kaszirer. *Educ*: Carmel Coll.; Pembroke Coll., Cambridge (MA); Mir Academy, Jerusalem; Faculty for Comparative Study of Religions, Wilrik, Antwerp (PhD). Minister, Bulawayo Hebrew Congregation, Rhodesia, 1966; Minister, Giffnock Hebrew Congregation, Scotland, 1968–71; Headmaster, 1971–84, Principal, 1983–84, Carmel Coll.; Minister, Western Synagogue, subseq. (following amalgamation in 1990 with Marble Arch Synagogue) Marble Arch Western Synagogue, 1985–93; Principal, Yakar Study Centre, London, 1999–2007. Scholar in Residence, Jewish Community Center, NY, 2008–09. Chief Rabbi's Rep. on Inter-Faith Affairs, 1987–91. Mem. Bd, Centre Européen Juif d'Information, Brussels, 1991–97. Trustee, Yakar Educn Foundn, 1990–2000. *Publications*: Exploding Myths that Jews Believe, 2001; Understanding Judaism, 2003; Beyond the Pulpit, 2005; Kabbalah, 2005; Right or Right: how to reconcile religion with rationality, 2013; Can We Talk About God, 2015; Can We Talk About Religion, 2015; Commitment and Controversy: living in two worlds, vol. 1, 2015, vol. 2, 2017, vol. 3, 2018; Varieties of Jewish Religious Thought, 2016. *Address*: 1965 Broadway, Apt 30e, New York, NY 10023, USA. *T*: (212) 7217502. *E*: jeremyrosen@msn.com. *W*: www.jeremyrosen.com.

**ROSEN, Michael Wayne**, PhD; FRSL; poet and author; Children's Laureate, 2007–09; BBC Radio presenter, since 1989; *b* 7 May 1946; *s* of Harold Rosen and Connie Ruby Isakofsky; *m* 1st, 1976, Susanna Steele (marr. diss. 1987); one *s* (and one *s* decd); 2nd, 1987, Geraldine Clark (marr. diss. 1997); one *s*, and two step *d*; 3rd, 2003, Emma-Louise Williams; one *s* one *d*. *Educ*: Wadham Coll., Oxford (BA); Reading Univ. (MA); Univ. of N London (PhD 1997). BBC general trainee, 1969–73; freelance, 1973–, incl. BBC Radio 4, World Service, Radio 3; Word of Mouth, Radio 4, 1998–; On Being Selfish, Radio 4, 2004; Dons and Dragons, Radio 4, 2006; The People in the Playground Revisited, Radio 4, 2018. Guest Dir, Brighton Fest., 2013. Prof. of Children's Lit., Goldsmiths, Univ. of London, 2013–. Film, Under the Cranes, 2011. FEA 2006. DUniv Open, 2005; Hon. DLitt: Exeter, 2007; Tavistock and Portman NHS Foundn Trust/UEL, 2008. Sunday Times NUS Drama Fest. Award for Best New Play, 1968; Glenfiddich Award for Best Radio Programme on subject of food, 1996; Eleanor Farjeon Award for Distinguished Services to Children's Literature, 1997; Sony Radio Acad. Short Form Award for On Saying Goodbye, 2003. Chevalier, Ordre des Arts et des Lettres (France), 2008. *Publications*: include: Backbone, 1968; Mind Your Own Business, 1974; Quick, Let's Get Out of Here, 1983; Don't put Mustard in the Custard, 1985; The Hypnotiser, 1988; We're Going on a Bear Hunt, 1989 (Smarties Award for Best Children's Book of Year, 1990); You Wait Till I'm Older Than You, 1996; Michael Rosen's Book of Nonsense, 1997; (ed) Classic Poetry, 1998; Rover, 1999; Centrally Heated Knickers, 2000; Shakespeare, His Work and His World, 2001; Carrying the Elephant, 2002; Oww!, 2003; This Is Not My Nose, 2004; Howler, 2004; Michael Rosen's Sad Book, 2004 (Exceptional Award, English Assoc.); Shakespeare's Romeo and Juliet, 2004; Totally Wonderful Miss Plumberry, 2006; Mustard, Custard, Grumble Belly and Gravy, 2006; Fighters for Life, 2007; Selected Poems, 2007; What's so Special about Shakespeare?, 2007; What's so Special about Dickens?, 2007; The Bear in the Cave, 2007; Dear Mother Goose, 2008; Tiny Little Fly, 2010; Even My Ears Are Smiling, 2011; Fantastic Mr Dahl, 2012; Alphabetical, 2013; Good Ideas: how to be your child's (and your own) best teacher, 2014; A Great Big Cuddle: poems for the very young, 2015; Uncle Gobb and the Dread Shed, 2015; The Disappearance of Émile Zola: love, literature and the Dreyfus case, 2017; So They Call You Pisher!: a memoir, 2017. *Recreations*: Arsenal Football Club, politics, general arts. *Address*: c/o United Agents, 12–26 Lexington Street, W1F 0LE.

**ROSEN, Miriam Catherine**, CB 2012; Executive Director, 2009–10, HM Chief Inspector, 2011, Office for Standards in Education, Children's Services and Skills; Consultant, Ark Schools, 2012–15; *b* Manchester, 24 July 1949; *d* of late Charles Bescoby and Bessie Bescoby; *m* 1976, David Leon Rosen. *Educ*: Friends' Sch., Ackworth; Bangor Univ. (BSc Hons 1970); Univ. of Bath (PGCE 1973); Thames Poly. (Postgrad. Cert. Physics for Teachers). VSO teacher, Kenya, 1970–72; Science Teacher, Wheatley Park Sch., 1973–76; Hd of Biology, St Paul's Way Sch., 1976–79; Hd of Biology, then Actg Hd of Sci., Haverstock Sch., 1980–86; Hd, Sci. Faculty, Morecambe High Sch., 1986–89; Sci. Adv. Teacher, Lancs, 1989–90; HMI, DES, then Ofsted, 1991–2010; Dir, Educn, Ofsted, 2004–09. *Recreations*: running, orienteering, theatre, natural history. *Address*: 27 Beech Road, Halton, Lancaster LA2 6QQ. *T*: (01524) 811553. *Club*: Thames Hare and Hounds.

**ROSEN, Murray Hilary**; QC 1993; a Recorder, since 2000; a Deputy High Court Judge, Chancery Division, since 2014; arbitrator and mediator; *b* 26 Aug. 1953; *s* of Joseph and Mercia Rosen; *m* 1975, Lesley Samuels; one *s* three *d*. *Educ*: St Paul's Sch.; Trinity Coll., Cambridge (MA); Courtauld Inst. (Postgrad. Dip. History of Art, 2015). FCIArb 1999. Called to the Bar, Inner Temple, 1976; Mem., Lincoln's Inn *ad eundem*, Bencher, 2004; Head of Chambers, 11 Stone Buildings, 2000–04; admitted Solicitor, 2005; Partner, Herbert Smith Freehills (formerly Herbert Smith), 2005–14 (Hd, Advocacy Unit, 2005–13). Panel Arbitrator, Sports Resolution, 1997–; Panel Deemster, Isle of Man, 2012–. Accredited mediator (ADR Gp, 1989, CEDR, 2013). Mem., Court of Arbitration for Sport, 2016–. Chair: Bar Sports Law Gp, 1998–2001; British Assoc. for Sport and Law, 2003–06; Table Tennis England Bd of Appeal, 2017–. *Recreations*: books, arts, sports. *Address*: 4 New Square, Lincoln's Inn, WC2A 3RJ.

**ROSENBAUM, Martin George**; Executive Producer, BBC Political Programmes, since 2004; radio documentary maker; specialist in freedom of information; *b* London, 29 July 1959; *s* of Laurie Rosenbaum and Olga Rosenbaum (née Kochan); *m* 1992, Jane Ashley; two *s* one *d*. *Educ*: University College Sch., London; King's Coll., Cambridge (BA Maths, Philos. 1981); Univ. of Warwick (MA Philos. 1982); Green Coll., Oxford (Reuters Fellow 2004). Social action campaigner, 1983–90; freelance journalist and author, 1990–98; Radio Producer, BBC News, 1998–2003. Mem., ESRC, 2012–18. *Publications*: From Soapbox to Soundbite: party political campaigning in Britain since 1945, 1997; Britain and Europe: the choices we face, 2001. *Recreation*: thinking. *Address*: BBC Political Programmes Department, 4 Millbank, SW1P 3JQ. *T*: (020) 7973 6132. *E*: martin.rosenbaum@bbc.co.uk.

**ROSENBERG, Michael Anthony**; a District Judge (Magistrates' Courts) (formerly Provincial Stipendiary Magistrate), South Yorkshire, 1993–2011; *b* 6 March 1943; *s* of late Harry Rosenberg and Gertrude Rosenberg (née Silver); *m* 1969, Gillian Anne Wolff; two *s*. *Educ*: Hymers Coll., Hull; Law Soc. Joined Myer Wolff & Co., Hull, 1961: articled clerk, 1963–68; qualified as solicitor, 1969; Asst Solicitor, 1970–73; Jt Sen. Partner, 1973–93. *Recreations*: sport, gardening, music, humour. *Address*: Westfield House, 14 Manor Fields, West Ella, E Yorks HU10 7SG.

**ROSENBERG, Pierre Max**; Commandeur de la Légion d'honneur, 2014 (Officier, 2005); Member, Académie française, since 1995; President-Director, Louvre Museum, Paris, 1994–2001; *b* Paris, 13 April 1936; *s* of Charles Rosenberg and Gertrude (née Nassauer); *m* 1981, Béatrice de Rothschild; one *d*. *Educ*: Lycée Charlemagne, Paris; Law Faculty, Paris (Licence); Louvre Sch., Paris (Dip.). Chief Curator, Dept of Paintings, Louvre Mus., 1982–94. Member: Hist. of French Art Soc. (Pres., 1982–84); French Hist. of Art Cttee (Pres., 1984–96). *Publications*: Chardin, 1979, 2nd edn 1999; Peyron, 1983; Watteau, 1984; Fragonard, 1987; La Hyre, 1988; Les frères Le Nain, 1993; Poussin, 1994; Watteau: catalogue raisonné des dessins, 1996; Georges de la Tour, 1997; Dictionnaire amoureux du Louvre, 2007; Nicolas Poussin, les tableaux du Louvre, 2015; exhibn catalogues. *Address*: 35 rue de Vaugirard, 75006 Paris, France.

**ROSENBERG, Richard Morris**; Chairman and Chief Executive Officer, BankAmerica Corporation and Bank of America NT&SA, 1990–96; *b* 21 April 1930; *s* of Charles Rosenberg and Betty (née Peck); *m* 1956, Barbara C. Cohen; two *s*. *Educ*: Suffolk Univ. (BS 1956); Golden Gate Univ. (MBA 1962; LLD 1966). Served from Ensign to Lieut, USNR, 1953–59. Publicity Assistant, Crocker-Anglo Bank, San Francisco, 1959–62; Wells Fargo Bank: Banking Services Officer, 1962–65; Asst Vice Pres., 1965–68; Vice Pres., Marketing Dept, 1968; Vice Pres., Dir of Marketing, 1969; Sen. Vice Pres., Marketing and Advertising Div., 1970–75; Exec. Vice Pres., 1975–80; Vice Chm., 1980–83; Vice Chm., Crocker Nat. Corp., 1983–85; Pres., Chief Op. Officer and Dir, Seafirst Corp., 1986–87; Pres. and Chief Op. Officer, Seattle-First Nat. Bank, 1985–87; Vice Chm., BankAmerica Corp., 1987–90. Past Director: Airborne Express; Northrop Corp.; SBC Communications; past Chm., Mastercard Internat. Director: Buck Inst. for Age Res.; Health Care Property Investors Inc.; San Francisco Symphony; Naval War Coll. Foundn; Pacific Life Insurance Co.; Chronicle Publishing Co.; Potlatch Corp. Chairman: UCSF Foundn; Exec. Council, Univ. of Calif Med. Center. Mem., Bd of Trustees, CIT. Mem., State Bar of Calif. Jewish. Mem., Amer. Acad. of Arts and Scis. Horatio Alger Award, Horatio Alger Assoc. Distinguished Americans, 2007. *Recreation*: avid reader of history. *Address*: BankAmerica Corporation, 555 California Street CA5–705–11–01, San Francisco, CA 94104, USA. *T*: (415) 9133795. *Clubs*: Villa Taverna, St Francis Yacht (San Francisco).

**ROSENBLATT, Ian Isaac**, OBE 2016; Founder and Senior Partner, Rosenblatt Solicitors, since 1989; Co-Founder, Redleaf Communications, since 2000; *b* Liverpool, 2 Nov. 1959; *s* of Elliot and Ruth Rosenblatt; *m* 2007, Emma Kane; two *s* one *d*, and one step *s* one step *d*. *Educ*: Liverpool Coll.; London Sch. of Econs and Pol Sci. (LLB Hons). Articled clerk, Collyer-Bristow, 1981–83; admitted Solicitor, 1983; Sheridans, 1983–89 (Partner, 1985). Hon. Co-Treas., Royal Philharmonic Soc., 2008–17. Founder: Rosenblatt Recital Series, 1999–2017; Branscombe Fest., 2013–17. Trustee: Susan Chilcott Scholarship, 2007–17; Nat. Mus of Liverpool, 2016–; Ronson Family Foundn, 2017. Owner, Les Aldrich Music Shop, 2013–. *Recreations*: opera, art, family, working in Les Aldrich. *Address*: 9–13 St Andrew Street, EC4A 3AF. *T*: (020) 7955 1462. *E*: ianr@rosenblatt-law.co.uk.

**ROSENCRANTZ, Claudia Emma, (Mrs Daniel Abineri)**; Co-Chief Executive Officer, Studio 1, since 2019; *b* 23 June 1959; *d* of late Alfred Rosenkranz and Leonore (née Meyer); *m* 1998, Daniel Abineri; one *d*. *Educ*: Queen's Coll., London; French Inst., London. Picture editor and journalist, The Telegraph Sunday Mag., Sunday Mag., and Elle, 1979–86; TV Researcher, LWT, An Audience with Victoria Wood, Dame Edna Experience, 1986; Producer: Dame Edna Experience, 1989; Incredibly Strange Film Shows, A Late Lunch with Les, An Audience with Jackie Mason, A Night on Mount Etna, 1990 (Golden Rose of Montreux, 1991); Dame Edna's Hollywood, Edna Time, Tantrums and Tiaras; Creator and Producer, Dame Edna's Neighbourhood Watch, 1992; Exec. Producer, Don't Forget Your Toothbrush, 1994; Exec. Producer, BBC, 1994–95; Controller of Entertainment, ITV Network, 1995–2006; Director of Programming: Living TV, 2006–11; FTN, 2006–07; Dir of Television, Living TV Gp (formerly Virgin Media TV), 2007–11; Dir of Progs, Fresh One Prodns, 2012–15; CCO, then CEO, Jamie Oliver Media Gp, 2015–17. Responsible for commissioning over 600 progs a year, incl. Who Wants to be a Millionaire (Best Light Entertainment Prog., BAFTA, 1999 and 2000), Popstars (Silver Rose of Montreux, 2001), Pop Idol (Best Entertainment Prog., TRIC Awards, 2002; Lew Grade Award for Entertainment Prog. or Series, BAFTA 2002), I'm a Celebrity... Get Me Out of Here! (BAFTA 2003), Ant and Dec's Saturday Night Takeaway, The X Factor, Hell's Kitchen, Dancing on Ice, TV Burp, Dating in the Dark (Best Multi-Channel Prog., RTS Award, 2009). FRTS 2004. Woman of the Year, 2003.

**ROSENFELD, Alfred John**, CB 1981; Deputy Secretary, 1979–82, and Principal Finance Officer, 1976–82, Department of Transport; *b* 27 Feb. 1922; *s* of late Ernest Rosenfeld and late Annie Jeanette Rosenfeld (née Samson); *m* 1955, Mary Elisabeth (née Prudence); two *s* one *d*. *Educ*: Leyton County High Sch. Entered Public Trustee Office, 1938. Served War, Fleet Air Arm, 1942–46. Min. of Civil Aviation, 1947 (later, Min. of Transport, and Dept of Environment); Private Sec. to Jt Parliamentary Sec., 1958–59; Asst Sec., 1967; Under-Sec., 1972. Special Advr to Envmt Cttee, H of C, 1983–96. Mem., Shoreham Port Authority, 1983–92 (Dep. Chm., 1984–89; Chm., 1990–92). *Recreations*: puzzle solving, chess, gardening, cherishing grand- and great-grandchildren. *Address*: 33 Elmfield Road, Chingford, E4 7HT. *T*: (020) 8529 8160.

**ROSENKRANZ, Franklin Daniel, (Danny)**; Chief Executive, BOC Group plc, 1996–99; Chairman, 4C Associates, since 2010; *b* 28 May 1945; *s* of Manfred and Hendel Rosenkranz; *m* 1990, Catherine Ann Eisenklam. *Educ*: UMIST (BSc Chem. Engrg 1967); Univ. of Waterloo, Canada (MASc 1969); Manchester Business Sch. (DipBA 1970). Plessey Radar, 1970–73; BOC, later BOC Group plc: Monitoring Manager, 1973–74; Business Manager, Industrial, Sparklets, 1974–76; UK Manager, 1976–78, Gen. Manager, 1978–81,

BOC Sub Ocean Services; Business Develt Dir, 1982–83, Man. Dir, 1983–90, Edwards High Vacuum; Chief Exec., Vacuum Technology and Distribution Services, 1990–94; Man. Dir, 1994–96; Dir, 1994–99. Non-exec. Dir, 3i, 2000–07. *Recreations:* reading, music, theatre, sport, gardening.

**ROSENTHAL, Jim;** presenter, ITV Sport, 1980–2012; lead presenter, Box Nation, 2011–17; *b* 6 Nov. 1947; *s* of late Albi and Maud Rosenthal; *m* 1987, Chrissy (*née* Smith); one *s. Educ:* Magdalen College Sch., Oxford. Oxford Mail and Times, 1968–72; BBC Radio Birmingham, 1972–76; BBC Radio Sports Unit, 1976–80; presenter: Sport on Two; Sports Report; World Cup, and Wimbledon, 1978; host, FA Cup draw, 2008–12; award-winning Formula One coverage, ITV Sport, 1997–2005; Rugby World Cup, 1999, 2003 and 2007; ITV Boxing and World Cup, 2006 and 2010; eight football World Cups; Five Europa League coverage, 2010–12; presenter: Rugby World Cup, OSN Sports, Dubai, 2011, 2015; British Lions tests, Australia, OSN, 2013; Matchday Live Football League Files (series), MUTV, 2013–19; ICC World Twenty20, OSN Sports, 2016; OSN Sports Dubai ICC Champions Trophy, 2017; commentator, Crufts, Channel 4, 2015, 2017, 2018, 2019. Dir, Oxford United FC, 2011–12; Pres., Cookham Dean CC, 2016–. Sports Presenter of the Year, TRIC, 1990, RTS, 1997, 1999. *Address:* Saxons Productions, 714 Balmoral, 2 Praed Street, W2 1JL. *E:* Jim.Rosenthal@btinternet.com. *Clubs:* Lord's Taverners, Ivy.

**ROSENTHAL, Maureen Diane, (Mrs J. M. Rosenthal);** *see* Lipman, M. D.

**ROSENTHAL, Sir Norman Leon,** Kt 2007; freelance curator and art consultant; Exhibitions Secretary, Royal Academy of Arts, 1977–2008; *b* 8 Nov. 1944; *s* of Paul Rosenthal and Kate Zucker; *m* 1989, Manuela Beatriz Mena Marques, *d* of Francisco Mena and Manuela Marques de Mena, Madrid; two *d. Educ:* Westminster City Grammar School; University of Leicester. BA Hons History. Librarian, Thomas Agnew & Sons, 1966–68; Exhibitions Officer, Brighton Museum and Art Gallery, 1970–71; Exhibition Organiser, ICA, 1974–76; organiser of many exhibns worldwide including: Art into Society, ICA, 1974; A New Spirit in Painting, RA, 1981; Zeitgeist, West Berlin, 1982; German Art of the Twentieth Century, RA, London and Staatsgalerie, Stuttgart, 1985–86; Italian Art of the Twentieth Century, RA, 1989; Metropolis, Berlin, 1991; American Art in the Twentieth Century, Martin-Gropius Bau, Berlin, and RA, 1993; at Royal Academy: Charlotte Salomon, 1998; Apocalypse, 2000; Frank Auerbach, The Genius of Rome 1592–1628, Botticelli's Dante, 2001; Paris: capital of the arts 1900–1968, Return of the Buddha, The Galleries Show, The Aztecs, 2002; Masterpieces from Dresden, Kirchner: expressionism and the city, 2003; Illuminating the Renaissance: the triumph of Flemish manuscript painting in Europe, The Art of Philip Guston 1913–1980, 2004; Turks: a journey of a thousand years 600–1600, Edvard Munch by Himself, China: the three emperors 1662–1795, 2005; Jacob van Ruisdael: master of landscape, Modigliani and His Models, USA Today: new American art from the Saatchi Gallery, 2006; Georg Baselitz Retrospective, 2007; Empire State: New York Art Now, PalaExpo, Rome, 2013; Anish Kapoor, Martin-Gropius Bau, Berlin, 2013. Associate Curator, Sabanci Mus., Istanbul. TV and radio broadcasts on contemporary art. Member: Opera Bd, Royal Opera House, 1994–98; Bd, Palazzo Grassi, Venice, 1995; Comité Scientifique, Réunion des Musées Nationaux, Paris, 2005; Bd, English Nat. Ballet; Bd of Trustees, Hall Art Foundn; Trustee, Thyssen Bornemisza Foundn, 2002–12; Baltic Centre for Contemporary Art, Gateshead, 2004–. Hon. Fellow RCA, 1987. Hon. DLitt: Southampton, 2003; Leicester, 2006. German British Forum Award, 2003. Cavaliere Ufficiale, Order of Merit (Italy), 1992; Cross, Order of Merit (Germany), 1993; Officier, l'Ordre des Arts et des Lettres (France), 2003 (Chevalier, 1987); Order of Aztec Eagle (Mexico), 2006. *Publications:* The History of the Saatchi Gallery, 2011; Jeff Koons: conversations with Sir Norman Rosenthal, 2014; contribs to exhibn catalogues worldwide. *Recreations:* classical and contemporary music, particularly opera, the English countryside.

**ROSER, Air Vice-Marshal Phillip Wycliffe,** CB 2003; MBE 1983; Senior Directing Staff, Royal College of Defence Studies, 1999–2003, retired; *b* 11 July 1948; *s* of George Alfred Roser and Margaret Elizabeth Roser; *m* 1974, Andrea Jean Dobbin; one *s* one *d. Educ:* Thetford Grammar Sch.; RAF Coll., Cranwell; RAF Staff Coll., Bracknell. Qualified Weapons Instructor, 1974; Fighter Pilot, Lightning, Phantom, Tornado F3, 1970–94; on staff, MoD, 1979–83; MA to Minister for Armed Forces, MoD, 1983–85; OC 111(F) Sqdn, 1985–87; Operational Staff, Strike Comd, 1987–91; OC RAF Leeming, N Yorks, 1992–94; UK Liaison Officer, HQ US European Comd, Stuttgart, 1994–95; rcds 1996; Air Ops Staff, NATO, Sarajevo, 1996–97; NATO Staff, Heidelberg and Ramstein, Germany, 1997–98; Dep. UK Mil. Rep., HQ NATO, Brussels, 1998–99. Trustee, RAF Benevolent Fund, 2000–03; President: Friends of RAF Leeming Aviation Gp, 2015–; 111 (Fighter) Sqdn Assoc., 2018–. *Recreations:* golf, hill-walking, home maintenance, gardening, photography, woodwork, Rotary (Past Pres.). *Address:* c/o Lloyds Bank, Cox's and King's Branch, 8–10 Waterloo Place, SW1Y 4BE. *Club:* Royal Air Force (Chm., 2000–03).

**ROSEVEARE, Nicholas William,** MBE 1997; executive leadership and advisory consultancy, since 2016; *b* Washington, DC, 3 May 1961; *s* of late Robert William Roseveare, CBE and of Patricia Elizabeth Roseveare; *m* 1999, Caroline Mary Allison; two *s. Educ:* Bedford Sch., Bedford; Univ. of Newcastle upon Tyne (BA Hons Combined Arts 1982). Performing arts mgt, 1982–88; Oxfam: various internat. positions, Sudan, Ethiopia, Mozambique, 1988–2004; Humanitarian Dir, 2004–08; Chief Executive: British Overseas NGOs in Development, 2008–11; Mines Adv. Gp (MAG), 2011–16; Dir, Internat. Progs, Oxfam, 2018. *Recreations:* hill walking, theatre, film, poetry, France.

**ROSEWELL, Bridget Clare,** CBE 2019 (OBE 2013); economist; Senior Adviser, Volterra Partners, since 2014 (Chairman, 2011–14); *b* 19 Sept. 1951; *d* of Geoffrey Noel Mills and Helen Handescombe Mills; divorced; one *s* one *d. Educ:* Wimbledon High Sch.; St Hugh's Coll., Oxford (MA, MPhil). Tutor and Lectr in Econs, St Hilda's and Oriel Colls, Oxford, 1976–84; Dep. Dir, Econs, CBI, 1984–86; Chief European Economist, Wharton Econometric Forecasting Associates (WEFA), 1986–88; Founder and Chm., Business Strategies Ltd, 1988–2000; Chm., Volterra Consulting, 1999–2011. Consultant Chief Economist, GLA, 2002–08. Non-executive Director: Britannia Building Soc., 1999–; DWP, 2003–05; Network Rail, 2011– (Sen. Ind. Dir); Ulster Bank Gp, 2012–16; Atom Bank, 2014– (Chm., 2018–). Mem., Nat. Infrastructure Commn, 2015–; Chair, Driver and Vehicle Standards Agency, 2017–. Member: Forum UK, 1990–; Internat. Women's Forum, 1990–. FRSA 1991; FICE 2013. *Publications:* Reinventing London, 2013; pamphlets and contribs on econs to press and econ. jls. *Recreations:* hill walking, picture framing, yoga, curiosity. *Address:* Volterra Partners LLP, 56-58 Putney High Street, SW15 1SF. *T:* (020) 8878 6333, *Fax:* (020) 8878 6685. *E:* bridget@bridgetrosewell.com.

**ROSIN, (Richard) David,** FRCS, FRCSE; Consultant in General Surgery and Surgical Oncology, St Mary's Hospital, London, 1979–2007, now Honorary; Honorary Consultant, Imperial College School of Medicine, since 2007; Professor of Surgery, University of the West Indies, Cavehill Campus, Barbados, since 2008; *b* 29 April 1942; *s* of late Isadore Rowland Rosin and Muriel Ena Rosin (*née* Wolff); *m* 1st, 1971, Michele Shirley Moreton (marr. diss. 2009); one *s* two *d*; 2nd, 2017, Janet Mary Power. *Educ:* St George's Jesuit Coll., Zimbabwe; Westminster Hosp. Sch. of Medicine, Univ. of London (MB, MS); DHMSA 2003. Westminster Hospital: House Physician, subseq. House Surg., 1966–67; Sen. House Officer in Clin. Pathology, 1968, Surgical Rotation, 1969–71; Sen. Registrar, 1975–79; Ship's Surg., P & O Lines, 1967; Sen. House Officer, Birmingham Accident Hosp., 1969; Registrar: Sutton Hosp., Surrey, 1971–73; St Helier's Hosp., Carshalton, 1973–74; Clin. Asst, St Mark's Hosp., London, 1974–75; Sen. Registrar, Kingston Hosp., 1975–77; Vis. Lectr, Univ. of Hong Kong, 1978–79; Clin. Dir of Surgery, St Charles' Hosp., 1990–92; Chm., Div. of Surgery, St Mary's Hosp., London, 1992–96. Consultant Surg., King Edward VII's Hosp. for Officers, 1995–96. Chm. DTI Cttee, Operating Room of Year 2010, 1995–2000. Regl Advr, NW Thames Region, RCSE, 1990–; Member: Council, RCS, 1994–2006 (Vice-Pres., 2004–05; Sen. Vice-Pres., 2005–06; Penrose-May Tutor, 1985–90; Hunterian Prof., 1987; Lectures: Arris and Gale, 1978; Arnott, 1991; Gordon Gordon Taylor, 2005; Vicary, 2006; Stanford Cade, 2006; Zachary Cope, 2008); RSM, 1975 (Pres., Clin. Section, 1982–83, Surgery Section, 1992–93; Mem. Council, 2002–); Surgical Res. Soc., 1980; British Assoc. of Surgical Oncology, 1980 (Hon. Sec., 1983–86, Vice Pres., 2000–01, Pres., 2002–03); British Soc. of Gastroenterology, 1980; Melanoma Study Gp, 1988 (Hon. Sec., 1986–89, Pres., 1989–92); Soc. of Minimally Invasive Gen. Surgs, 1991 (Founder and Hon. Sec.); Hunterian Soc., 1994; Internat. Coll. of Surgs, 1992–. Chm., Intercollegiate Bd of Surgical Examinations, 2003–. First Pres., Caribbean Soc. Endoscopic Surgeons, 2013–; first Vice Pres., Barbados Cancer Soc. Fellow: Assoc. of Surgs of GB and Ire., 1975; Assoc. of Endoscopic Surgs of GB and Ire. (Mem. Council, 1995–); Assoc. of Upper Gastro-Intestinal Surgs of GB and Ire., 1997. Mem. Council, Marie Curie Foundn, 1984–92. Sir Ernest Finch Meml Lectr, Sheffield, 2000; G. B. Ong Lectr, Hong Kong Coll. of Surgeons, 2007; British Jl of Surgery Lectr, 2008; Moynihan Lectr, 2012; Lettsomian Lect., London Med. Soc., 2018. Freeman, City of London, 1972; Liveryman: Soc. of Apothecaries, 1971; Co. of Barber Surgeons, 1978. Series Ed., Minimal Access textbooks, 1993–; Editor-in-Chief: Internat. Jl of Surgery, 2007–17, now Emeritus; Internat. Jl of Surgery: Case Reports, 2010–; Open, 2015–; Oncology, 2016–; Short Reports, 2016–; Global Health, 2018–. *Publications:* (ed jtly) Cancer of the Bile Ducts and Pancreas, 1989; (ed jtly) Head and Neck Oncology for the General Surgeon, 1991; (ed jtly) Diagnosis and Management of Melanoma in Clinical Practice, 1992; (ed) Minimal Access Medicine and Surgery: principles and practice, 1993; (ed) Minimal Access General Surgery, 1994; (ed) Minimal Access Surgical Oncology, 1995; (co-ed) Minimal Access Thoracic Surgery, 1998; The Rhino Trail, 2019; papers in jls and contribs to books. *Recreations:* all sport, particularly golf; opera, music, theatre, history of medicine and surgery, travelling. *Address:* 302 Westcliffe, 1 South Wharf Road, W2 1JB. *T:* (020) 7087 4260; Middle Earth, Richmond, St Joseph, Barbados, West Indies; Queen Elizabeth Hospital, Martindales Road, Bridgetown, Barbados, West Indies. *E:* rdavidrosin@gmail.com, david.rosin@cavehill.uwi.edu. *Clubs:* Garrick, MCC, Royal Society of Medicine; New Zealand Golf (Weybridge); Barbados Cricket Assoc., Barbados Gold, Barbados Turf, Barbados Golf.

**ROSINDELL, Andrew;** MP (C) Romford, since 2001; *b* Romford, 17 March 1966; *s* of late Frederick William Rosindell and of Eileen Rosina Rosindell (*née* Clark). *Educ:* Rise Park Jun. and Infant Sch.; Marshalls Park Secondary Sch. Researcher and freelance journalist, and Res. Asst to Vivian Bendall, MP, 1986–97; Dir, 1997–99, Internat. Dir, 1999–2005, Eur. Foundn. Mem., London Accident Prevention Council, 1990–95. Mem. (C) Havering BC, 1990–2002 (Vice-Chm., Housing Cttee, 1996–97; Hon. Alderman, 2007–); Chm., N Romford Community Area Forum, 1998–2002. Contested (C): Glasgow Provan, 1992; Thurrock, 1997. An Opposition Whip, 2005–07; Shadow Home Affairs Minister and spokesman on Animal Welfare, 2007–10; Member: Deregulation and Regulatory Reform Select Cttee, 2001–05; Constitutional Affairs Select Cttee, 2004–05; Foreign Affairs Select Cttee, 2010–; Jt Cttee on Statutory Instruments, 2002–04; NI Grand Cttee, 2006–07; All Party Parliamentary Groups: Sec., Falkland Is, 2001–; Jt Chm., then Chm., British-Swiss, 2010–; Vice-Chairman: Bermuda, 2005–; Gibraltar, 2010– (Sec., 2001–02); Queen's Diamond Jubilee, 2010–13; Danish, 2015– (Jt Treas., 2001–15); Catalonia, 2015–; Vice Chm. and Sec., Cayman Is, 2010–; Chairman: Montserrat, 2005–; British-Manx (formerly Anglo-Manx), 2005–; Greyhound, 2006–; St George's Day, 2007–; Flags and Heraldry, 2008–; Australia/NZ, 2010– (Sec., 2001–10); Zoos and Aquariums, 2010– (Sec., 2007–10); Canada, 2010– (Sec., 2008–10); British Overseas Territory, 2010– (Sec., 2005–10); S Pacific Is, 2010– (Sec., 2009–10); Central America, 2011– (Sec., 2010–11); Channel Is, 2015– (Vice-Chm., 2006–15); British Indian Ocean Territory (Chagos Is), 2015– (Vice-Chm., 2008–15); Commonwealth, 2017–; Founding Chm., Polar Regs (Arctic and Antarctic), 2011–14; Co-Chairman: Mongolia, 2010–15; St Lucia, 2012–15; Secretary: Norfolk Is., 2016–; Caribbean, 2017–; Mem., Panel of Chairs, 2010–; Chairman, Parliamentary Support Group: for Campaign for Right of Abode for British-Hong Kong Ex-Servicemen, 2015–; for UK Victims of Libyan/UK Terrorism, 2016–. Member: Commonwealth Parly Assoc., 2001– (Mem. Exec. Cttee, 2010–); Vice-Chm., 2015–17); Inter-Parly Union, 2001– (Mem. Exec. Cttee, 2010–); British-American Parly Gp, 2001–; Adv. Bd, Commonwealth Exchange, 2013–; Parly Delegn to Commonwealth Heads of Govt, 2018. Fellow, Industry and Parlt Trust India Fellowship, 2009; Mem., British-Irish Parly Assembly, 2010– (Vice-Chm., 2015–); Vice-Chm., NATO Parly Assembly, 2015–; Co-Chm., British-Irish Parly Assembly, 2016–. Armed Forces Parly Scheme (RM), 2002–03, (RAF), 2005–07, (Army), 2009–13. Chairman: Royal Soc. of St George, Houses of Parlt Br., 2009–; Palace of Westminster Philatelic Soc., 2010–. Sec., Cons. 92 Gp, 2003–06, 2017–; Mem., No Turning Back Gp. Parly Advr, Guild of Travel and Tourism, 2008–. Joined Cons. Party and Young Conservatives, 1981; Chairman: Romford YC, 1983–84 (Pres., 2006–); Gtr London YC, 1987–88; Nat. YC, 1993–94; Eur. YC, 1993–97; Conservative Party: Mem., Nat. Union Exec. Cttee, 1986–88 and 1992–94; Vice-Chm., 2004–05; Pres., Gibraltar Br., 2004–; Chm., Romford Cons. Assoc., 1998–2001; Dep. Chm., Cons. Party Internat. Office, 2014–15. Chm., Cons. Friends of Gibraltar, 2002–; Pres., Cons. Friends of Taiwan, 2011–; Member: Cons. Middle East Council, 2005–; Cons. Friends of Israel, 2001–, India, 2005–, America, 2008–; Pres., Cons. Commonwealth Assoc., 2013. Chairman: Internat. Young Democrat Union, 1998–2002; UK-Norfolk Island Friendship Gp, 2009–; Zimbabwe-Rhodesia Relief Fund, 2010–. Pres., Caribbean Young Democrat Union, 2001–. Vice-Pres., Constitutional Monarchy Assoc. Member: Council, Freedom Assoc., 2005–; Flag Inst., 2008–; Bd of Govs, Westminster Foundn for Democracy, 2010–; Council, Canada UK Colloquium, 2010–; Hon. Bd Mem., Iman Foundn, 2011–. Pres., Romford Sqdn ATC, 2002–; Hon. Member: HMS Antrim Assoc., 2008–; Romford Lions Club, 2008– (Vice-Pres., 2010–); Burma Star (SW Essex Br.), 2010–; Romford Cons. and Constitutional Club, 2001–; Falkland Is Assoc., 2001–; Pitcairn and Norfolk Is. Soc., 2014–; Vice President: Romford and Dist Scout Assoc., 1995–; Romford RBL Band and Corps of Drums, 2010–; Romford Rotary Club, 2010–; Flag Inst., 2014–. Member: Salvation Army, Romford Citadel, 1973–82; St Edward the Confessor Ch, Romford Market, 1988–; St Alban Protomartyr Ch, Romford, 2001–. Member: RAFA; RBL; Essex Wildlife Trust, 2008–; British Overseas Territories Conservation Forum, 2003–; Adv. Bd, Polar Res. and Policy Initiative, 2016–; Parly Advr, Friends of British Overseas Territories, 2014–. Governor: Bower Park Sch., Romford, 1989–90; Dame Tipping C of E Sch., Havering-atte-Bower, 1990–2002. Vice-Pres., Romford FC; Hon. Mem., Havering-atte-Bower CC. Trustee, Retired Greyhound Trust, 2010–15 (Vice-Pres., 2015–); Chm. Trustees, Margaret Thatcher House Fund, 2013–. Patron: Justice for Dogs; Remus Meml Horse Sanctuary, 2005–; Assoc. of British Counties, 2007–; Lennox Children's Cancer Fund, 2009–; Romford Cons. Business and Enterprise Club, 2012–; British Monarchist Soc., 2013–. Hon. Member: Staffs Bull Terrier Club; E

Anglian Staffs Bull Terrier Club; Romford Lions, 2007; Hon. Associate, BVA, 2015–. Mayor's Award for Community Action, 1978. Freeman, City of London, 2003. *Publications:* (jtly) Defending Our Great Heritage, 1993. *Recreations:* Staffordshire bull terriers, travel, philately, history. *Address:* House of Commons, SW1A 0AA. *T:* (020) 7219 8475; (constituency office) Margaret Thatcher House, 85 Western Road, Romford, Essex RM1 3LS. *T:* (01708) 766700, (home) (01708) 761186. *E:* andrew@rosindell.com, andrew.rosindell.mp@parliament.uk. *Clubs:* Romford Conservative and Constitutional; Iona (Hornchurch); Romford Golf (Hon.).

**ROSLING, Derek Norman,** CBE 1988; FCA; Vice-Chairman, Hanson PLC, 1973–93; *b* 21 Nov. 1930; *s* of Norman and Jean Rosling; *m* 1st (marr. diss. 1982); two *s* one *d*; 2nd, 2000, Julia Catherine Crookston; one step *s*. *Educ:* Shrewsbury Sch. ACA 1955, FCA 1962. Professional practice, 1956–65; Hanson PLC, 1965–94. *Recreations:* golf, sailing, theatre. *Address:* South Hayes, Grove Road, Lymington, Hants SO41 3RN. *T:* (01590) 670201. *Clubs:* Royal Yacht Squadron (Cowes); Royal Southampton Yacht; Brokenhurst Manor Golf; Royal Lymington Yacht.

**ROSOFF, Margaret Jill, (Meg);** writer, since 2003; *b* Boston, USA, 16 Oct. 1956; *d* of late Dr Chester Rosoff and Lois Friedman (*née* Goldman); *m* 1990, (David) Paul Hamlyn; one *d*. *Educ:* Harvard Univ. (BA 1979); St Martin's Coll. of Art (Adv. Sculpture course 1978). Editorial Asst, People mag., 1980–82; Copywriter: New York Times, 1982–85; Backer & Spielvogel, 1985–89; Dep. Press Sec., NY State, Democratic presidential campaign, 1988; Copywriter: Young & Rubicam, 1990–93; Ogilvy & Mather, 1994–97; J. Walter Thompson, 1998–2003. FRSL 2014 (Mem., RSL, 2016); Fellow, Homerton Coll., Cambridge, 2016. Astrid Lindgren Meml Award, Swedish govt, 2016. *Publications:* How I Live Now, 2004 (Guardian Children's Fiction Prize, 2004; Michael L. Printz Award (US), 2005; Branford Boase Award, 2005; Der Luchs des Jahres, 2005; filmed, 2013); Meet Wild Boars, 2005; Just In Case, 2006 (Carnegie Medal, 2007; Deutscher Jugendliteraturpreis, 2008); What I Was, 2007 (Der Luchs des Jahres, 2009); Jumpy Jack and Googily, 2007; Wild Boars Cook, 2008; The Bride's Farewell, 2009 (Alex Award, Amer. Liby Assoc., 2010); Vamoose, 2010; There Is No Dog, 2011; Moose Baby, 2012; Picture Me Gone, 2013; Jonathan Unleashed, 2016; (with Mal Peet) Beck, 2016; Good Dog McTavish, 2017; McTavish Goes Wild, 2018; McTavish Takes the Biscuit, 2019. *Recreations:* horse riding, misplacing things. *Address:* 2 Rushworth Studios, 63 Webber Street, SE1 0QW. *T:* 07766 087257. *E:* meg@megrosoff.co.uk.

**ROSPIGLIOSI,** family name of **Earl of Newburgh**.

**ROSS, Rt Hon. Lord; Donald MacArthur Ross;** PC 1985; a Senator of the College of Justice, Scotland, and Lord of Session, 1977–97; Lord Justice-Clerk and President of the Second Division of the Court of Session, 1985–97; Lord High Commissioner, General Assembly, Church of Scotland, 1990 and 1991; *b* 29 March 1927; *s* of late John Ross, solicitor, Dundee; *m* 1958, Dorothy Margaret (*d* 2004), *d* of late William Annand, Kirriemuir; two *d*. *Educ:* Dundee High School; Edinburgh University. MA (Edinburgh) 1947; LLB with distinction (Edinburgh) 1951. National Service with The Black Watch (RHR), 2nd Lt, 1947–49. Territorial Service, 1949–58, Captain. Advocate, 1952; QC (Scotland) 1964; Vice-Dean, Faculty of Advocates of Scotland, 1967–73; Dean, 1973–76; Sheriff Principal of Ayr and Bute, 1972–73. Dep. Chm., Boundary Commn for Scotland, 1977–85. Member: Scottish Cttee of Council on Tribunals, 1970–76; Cttee on Privacy, 1970; Parole Bd for Scotland, 1997–2002; Chm., Judicial Studies Cttee, Scotland, 1997–2001. Mem. Court, Heriot-Watt Univ., 1978–90 (Chm., 1984–90). FRSE 1988 (Mem. Council, 1997–99, Vice Pres., 1999–2002). Hon. LLD: Edinburgh, 1987; Dundee, 1991; Abertay Dundee, 1994; Aberdeen, 1998. DUniv Heriot-Watt, 1988. Bicentenary Medal, RSE, 2004. *Recreations:* gardening, walking, travelling. *Address:* 7/1 Tipperlinn Road, Edinburgh EH10 5ET. *T:* (0131) 447 6771. *E:* RosD33@aol.com. *Club:* New (Edinburgh).

**ROSS, Rear Adm. Alastair Boyd,** CB 1999; CBE 1995; Clerk to Worshipful Company of Drapers, 2000–12; *b* 29 Jan. 1947; *s* of Joseph Charles Patrick Ross and Shirley Carlile (*née* Stoddart); *m* 1977, Heather Judy Currie; two *d*. *Educ:* Radley Coll.; BRNC, Dartmouth. Joined RN, 1965; commnd 1968; specialised in aviation; flew as Anti-Submarine Warfare helicopter observer, 1970–80; commanded: HMS Brinton, 1977–79; HMS Falmouth, 1983–85; HMS Edinburgh, 1988–89; RCDS 1990; Capt., HMS Osprey, 1991–93; Comdr, NATO Standing Naval Force, Mediterranean (Adriatic Ops), 1993–94; Dir Overseas (ME and Africa), MoD, 1994–96; Asst Dir Ops, Internat. Mil. Staff, NATO HQ, 1996–99. Mem., RNSA, 1984–. Trustee, Portman Estate, 2011–. Freeman, City of London, 2004; Liveryman, Drapers' Co., 2008. Honorary Fellow: Univ. of Wales, Bangor, 2005; QMUL, 2009. *Recreations:* sailing, golf. *Address:* Barn Cottage, Vosporth Hill, Crantock, Newquay, Cornwall TR8 5RQ. *Clubs:* Farmers, Royal Navy of 1765 and 1785, Pratt's.

**ROSS, Alastair Ian;** political consultant, since 2017; Member (DemU) East Antrim, Northern Ireland Assembly, May 2007–2017; *b* Belfast, 4 March 1981; *s* of Ian and Jennifer Ross; *m* 2010, Shakheera Lee. *Educ:* Friends Grammar Sch., Lisburn; Univ. of Dundee (MA Political Sci.); Queen's Univ., Belfast (MA Irish Politics). Policy Officer, DUP, 2005; Parly researcher for Sammy Wilson, MP, 2005–07. Jun. Minister, Office of First and Dep. First Minister, NI, 2016–17. Northern Ireland Assembly: Chm., Cttee for Standards, 2010–14; Private Sec. to Minister for Enterprise, Trade and Investment, 2011–14; Chair, Justice Cttee, 2014–16. Member: NI Policing Bd, 2010–11; Probation Bd for NI, 2018–; Electoral Commn, 2018–. *Recreations:* hockey, travel.

**ROSS, Alexander, (Sandy);** freelance television producer; media consultant; Managing Director, Murrayfield Media Ltd, since 2007; *b* 17 April 1948; *s* of late Alexander Coutts Ross and Charlotte Edwards (*née* Robertson); *m* 1992, Alison Joyce Fraser; two *s* one *d*. *Educ:* Edinburgh Univ. (LLB); Moray House Coll., Edinburgh (Pres., Students' Union, 1977–78; Cert. Youth and Community Work). Articled Solicitor, 1971; Solicitor, 1971–73; Lectr in Law, Paisley Coll., 1975–77; Researcher and Producer, Granada Television, 1978–86; Scottish Television: Controller Entertainment, 1986–97; Dep. Chief Exec., Scottish TV Enterprises, 1997–98; Controller Regional Production, Scottish TV and Grampian TV, Scottish Media Gp, 1998–2000; Controller, 2000; Man. Dir, 2000–04; Man. Dir, Internat. Develt Div., 2004–07. Councillor, Edinburgh Corp., 1971–74; Mem., Edinburgh DC, 1974–78. Dir, Assembly Th., 2004–; Chm., Salford Conf. on Television from Nations and Regions, 2005–15. Associate, Adam Smith Coll., Fife, 2010–12; Rector's Assessor, Edinburgh Univ., 2015–18. Mem., BAFTA, 1990 (Mem., Scotland Cttee, 2004–14; Chm., 2004–08, Vice-Chm., 2008–10, BAFTA Scotland). *Recreations:* golf, theatre, music, reading, curling, ski-ing (but never doing the Vallée Blanche run again!), looking after granddaughter. *Address:* 64 Glasgow Road, Edinburgh EH12 8LN. *T:* (0131) 539 1192, 07803 970107. *E:* sandy.ross@murrayfieldmedia.com. *Clubs:* Oyster (Edinburgh); Haunted Major Golf Society (N Berwick) (Correspondent, 2002–); Glen Golf, Prestonfield Golf, Edinburgh Corporation Golf (Capt., 2012–14); East Linton Curling (Pres., 2016–18); Vets Curling (Edinburgh).

**ROSS, Amanda;** Co-Founder and Chief Executive Officer, Cactus TV, since 1994; *b* 4 Aug. 1962; *m* 1990, Simon Ross; two *s*. *Educ:* Univ. of Birmingham (BA Hons Drama and Theatre Arts). Freelance TV producer and presenter, 1984–94; Founder, with Simon Ross, Cactus TV, 1994; programmes produced include: The Roux Scholarship; Roux Legacy; Madhur Jaffrey's Curry Nation; Richard and Judy Live, 2001– (numerous awards incl. Bookseller Expanding Mkt Award, 2007, for Richard and Judy Summer Read; RTS Award for Best Campaign, Lost for Words Season, Channel 4, 2008); Saturday Kitchen Live, 2006– (Best TV Cookery Show, Olive mag., 2007; Best Food Show, TV Choice Awards, 2015); The TV Book Club; Galaxy Nat. Book Awards; ITV Crime Thriller Season; Ten Mile Menu; Munch Box; Weekend; Spring Kitchen; Christmas Kitchen; Music and Entertainment Specials; Zoe Ball Show, 2018; The Sara Cox Show, 2019–; numerous cookery series and chat shows. Opened Cactus Kitchens Cookery Sch. with Michel Roux Jr, 2013. Member: BAFTA; RTS. Trustee: Kidscape, 1993–2014 (Ambassador, 2014–); UK Adv. Bd, Room to Read, 2008–14; Ambassador: Wellbeing of Women, 2010–; Nat. Literary Trust, 2010–. Award for Outstanding Contribution to Bookselling, Bookseller, 2009. *Publications:* (ed) Richard and Judy Wine Guide, 2005; Saturday Kitchen Cookbook, 2007, 2013; Saturday Kitchen: best bites, 2008; Saturday Kitchen at Home, 2010; Saturday Kitchen Cooking Bible, 2013; Saturday Kitchen Suppers, 2014. *Recreations:* my two boys, my dog Lulu, Italy. *Address:* c/o Cactus, 1 St Luke's Avenue, Clapham, SW4 7LG. *T:* (020) 7091 4900.

**ROSS, Lt-Col Sir Andrew (Charles Paterson),** 3rd Bt *cr* 1960, of Whetstone, Middlesex; RM; *b* 18 June 1966; *s* of Sir James Keith Ross, 2nd Bt, RD, FRCS, FRCSE and Jacqueline Annella Ross (*née* Clarke); *S* father, 2003; *m* 1997, Surg. Comdr Sarah Joanne Murray, RN; one *s* one *d*. *Educ:* Sherborne; Plymouth Poly. (BSc). Joined RM, 1988; left RM 2007. Cyber Assurance Dir, Wartsila, 2017–. *Recreations:* sailing, hill walking, Telemark ski-ing. *Heir:* *s* James Ross, *b* 21 May 1999.

**ROSS, Anthony Lee, (Tony);** author and illustrator; *b* 10 Aug. 1938; *s* of Eric Turle Lee Ross and Effie Ross (*née* Griffiths); *m* 1st, 1961, Carole D'Arcy (marr. diss. 1971); 2nd, 1971, Joan Spokes (marr. diss. 1976); 3rd, 1979, Zoe Goodwin; partner, Wendy Finney. *Educ:* Helsby Grammar Sch.; Liverpool Art Sch. (NDD, ATD). Advertising work, 1962–65; Sen. Lectr, Manchester Poly., 1965–86; children's author, illustrator and film-maker, 1972–; TV animated films: Towser, 1985; Horrid Henry, 2006; Little Princess, 2007; books published in UK, Europe, USA, Japan, Australia, Korea and S America. *Publications:* picture books include: Towser (series), 1984; I'm Coming to Get You, 1984; I Want My Potty (series), 1986; Oscar Got The Blame, 1987; Super Dooper Jezebel, 1988; I Want a Cat, 1989; A Fairy Tale, 1991; Don't Do That, 1991; Through the Looking Glass, 1992, and Alice's Adventures in Wonderland, 1993, abridged from Lewis Carroll; The Shop of Ghosts, from G. K. Chesterton, 1994; Three Little Kittens and Other Favourite Nursery Rhymes, 2007; My First Nursery Collection, 2009; My Favourite Fairy Tales, 2010; I Want To Do It By Myself, 2010; *books illustrated include:* Eric Morecambe, The Reluctant Vampire, 1982; Willis Hall, Vampire Park, 1983; Michael Palin, Limericks, 1985; Roald Dahl, Fantastic Mr Fox, 1988; Simon Brett, How to be a Little Sod, 1992; Michael Morpurgo, Red Eyes at Night, 1998; Oscar Wilde, The Picture of Dorian Gray, 2000; Jeanne Willis, Flabby Cat and Slobby Dog, 2009; David Walliams: Billionaire Boy, 2010; Fing, 2019; Jeanne Willis, I'm Going to a Party, 2011; Gervase Phinn, Who Am I?, 2011; series: Ian Whybrow, Little Wolf, 1985; Jeanne Willis, Dr Xargle, 1988; Richmal Crompton, Meet Just William, 1999; Astrid Lindgren, Pippi Longstocking, 2000; Francesca Simon, Horrid Henry, 2003. *Recreations:* sailing, gentle sports, keeping unfit. *Address:* c/o Andersen Press, 20 Vauxhall Bridge Road, SW1V 2SA. *Club:* Chelsea Arts.

**ROSS, Catherine Ruth;** see Schenk, C. R.

**ROSS, Cathryn Elizabeth;** Director of Regulatory Affairs, BT Group, since 2018; *b* Davyhulme, Manchester, 15 April 1972; *d* of David Henderson Ross and Pamela Jean Ross; *m* 1999, Piotr Jasinski. *Educ:* Altrincham Grammar Sch. for Girls; University Coll. London (BScEcon Economics); London Sch. of Economics and Pol Sci. (MSc Econ. Eur. Studies). Res. Asst, Regulatory Policy Inst., Oxford, 1997–2000; Econ. Advr, Oftel, 2000–01; Hd, Competition Econs, Office of the Rail Regulator, 2001–03; Dir, Remedies and Business Analysis, Competition Commn, 2003–08; Executive Director: Mkts and Econs, Ofwat, 2008–11; Railway Mkts and Econs, Office of Rail Regulation, 2011–13; Chief Exec., Ofwat, 2013–17. Member: Expert Adv. Gp on Nat. Lottery Competition, Gambling Commn, 2018–19; Adv. Gp, Office for Product Safety and Standards, BEIS, 2019–. Non-exec. Dir, Inst. of Customer Service, 2018–. Independent Director: National Grid Gas plc, 2019–; National Grid Electricity Transmission plc, 2019–. *Publications:* several articles in Communist Economies and Economic Transformation. *Recreations:* golf, gardening, crosswords, classical music, jazz. *Address:* BT Group plc, BT Centre, 81 Newgate Street, EC1A 7AJ. *Club:* Frilford Heath Golf.

**ROSS, David Peter John;** Chairman, David Ross Foundation, since 2007; Co-Founder, 1991, and Deputy Chairman, 2003–08, The Carphone Warehouse (Chief Operating Officer, 1996–2003); Chairman of Trustees, National Portrait Gallery, since 2017 (Trustee, since 2006); *b* 10 July 1965; *s* of late John Malcolm Thomas and Linda Susan Ross; one *s*. *Educ:* Uppingham Sch.; Univ. of Nottingham (BA Hons Law 1987). Chartered accountant; with Arthur Andersen, 1988–91; Finance Dir, Carphone Warehouse plc, 1991–96. Non-exec. Chairman: Nat. Express Gp, 2001–08; Gondola Hldgs plc, 2005–06; non-executive Director: Big Yellow Self Storage, 2000–08; Wembley Nat. Stadium Ltd, 2002–07; Trinity Mirror plc, 2004–07; Cosalt plc, 2005–15 (Chm., 2005–08, 2009–15). Mem., Audit Cttee, Home Office, 2004–07. Mem. Council, Sport England, 2001–05. Dir, LOCOG, 2008; Member, Board: BOA, 2011–; London Legacy Develt Corp., 2012–. Trustee, Uppingham Sch., 2001–; Chm. Trustees, New Schs Network, 2016–. Founder and Chm., David Ross Educn Trust, 2007–15; Member, Council: Serpentine Gall., 2008–; Univ. of Nottingham, 2009–. Founder, Nevill Holt Opera, 2013–. Liveryman, Co. of Chartered Accountants. *Recreations:* opera, sport, shooting. *Address:* 10 St James's Place, SW1A 1NP. *E:* eci@10sjp.co.uk. *Clubs:* Royal Automobile, Carlton, Beefsteak, Pratt's, Oswald's.

**ROSS, Donald Grant,** OBE 2005; Lord Lieutenant of Dunbartonshire, 2007–08; *b* 24 June 1946; *s* of John Sutherland Ross and Catherine Grant Ross; *m* 1974, Doreen Colina; two *s* one *d*. *Educ:* High Sch. of Glasgow; King Edward VI Grammar Sch., Chelmsford; Army Staff Coll., Camberley. Commnd Argyll and Sutherland Highlanders, 1967; i/c British Contingent, Multi-nat. Force and Observers, Sinai, 1987–88; i/c 3/51 Highland Volunteers, 1988–90; COS British Rear Combat Zone, Germany, 1990–93; Comdr, Recruiting and Liaison Staff, Scotland, 1993–96; retd 1996; Comdt, Garelochhead Trng Area, 1996. Member: Exec. Cttee, Erskine Hosp., 1997–2008; C of S Cttee on Chaplains to the Armed Forces, 1996–99. Comdt, Argyll and Sutherland Highlanders Army Cadets, 1998–2003; Hon. Pres., Lennox and Argyll Boys' Bde, 2007–08. Chairman: Grangemouth Br., RBL, 2002; Argyll and Sutherland Highlanders Regtl Assoc., 2011–; Hon. Pres., Dunbartonshire Br., SSAFA, 2007–08. Trustee, Tullochan Trust, 2007–08; Chm., Friends of St Modan's, 2012–. *Recreations:* sailing, hill-walking, gardening. *Address:* Cruachan, Shore Road, Cove, Helensburgh, Dunbartonshire G84 0NX. *T:* (01436) 842555, *Fax:* (01436) 810369. *E:* donalddanddoreen@hotmail.com.

**ROSS, Rt Hon. Donald MacArthur;** see Ross, Rt Hon. Lord.

**ROSS, Prof. Douglas Alan,** DPhil; FRS 2005; Professor of Physics, University of Southampton, 1993–2013, now Emeritus; *b* 9 May 1948; *s* of late Arnold Ross and Odette Ross; *m* 1973, Jacqueline Nahoum; two *s*. *Educ*: New Coll., Oxford (MA 1969; DPhil 1972). Postdoctoral Fellow: Imperial Coll., London, 1972–74; Rijksuniversiteit Utrecht, 1974–76; Fellow, CERN, 1976–78; Sen. Res. Fellow, CIT, 1978–80; Lectr, Univ. of Southampton, 1980–93. *Publications*: (with J. R. Forshaw) Quantum Chromodynamics and the Pomeron, 1997. *Recreations*: singing in choir (bass), learning modern languages, playing clarinet. *Address*: 242 Hill Lane, Southampton SO15 7NT. *T*: (023) 8078 7711. *E*: doug@soton.ac.uk.

**ROSS, Douglas Baird;** QC (Scot.) 2016; *b* Glasgow, 15 Oct. 1963; *s* of Malcolm and Isabella Ross; *m* 1997, Annabel King; three *d*. *Educ*: Hutchesons' Grammar Sch.; Univ. of Glasgow (LLB Hons); Queen's Coll., Cambridge (LLM 1985). Lectr in Law, Univ. of Dundee, 1985–87; Res. Asst, Res. Centre for Internat. Law, Univ. of Cambridge, 1987–88; Legal Officer, UN (UNRWA and UN Protection Force), 1988–96; Advocate, 1998–2016; First Standing Jun. Counsel to Scottish Govt, 2012–16. *Recreations*: music, family, golf, cricket. *Address*: Advocates Library, Parliament House, Edinburgh EH1 1RF. *T*: 07739 639257. *E*: douglas.ross@advocates.org.uk.

**ROSS, Douglas Gordon;** MP (C) Moray, since 2017; *b* Aberdeen, 27 Jan. 1983; *s* of Sandy and Lesley Ross; *m* 2015, Krystle Bentley. *Educ*: Alves Primary Sch.; Forres Acad.; Scottish Agricl Coll. (BTech Hons Agric.). Dairyman, various dairy farms, 2004–07; researcher, Scottish Parlt, 2007–16. Mem. (C), Moray Council, 2001–17. MSP (C) Highlands and Islands, 2016–17. Shadow Cabinet Sec. for Justice, Scottish Parlt, 2016–17; Mem., Home Affairs Cttee, 2017–. Contested (C) Moray, 2010, 2015. *Recreation*: football referee (Specialist Asst Referee, Scottish Professional Football League and for UEFA and FIFA). *Address*: House of Commons, SW1A 0AA; (office) 63 High Street, Forres IV36 3PB. *T*: (01309) 679253. *E*: douglas.ross.mp@parliament.uk.

**ROSS, Duncan Alexander,** CBE 1993; CEng, FIET; Chairman, Southern Electric plc (formerly Southern Electricity Board), 1984–93, retired; *b* 25 Sept. 1928; *s* of William Duncan Ross and Mary Ross; *m* 1958, Mary Buchanan Clarke Parsons; one *s* one *d*. *Educ*: Dingwall Academy; Glasgow Univ. (BSc Elec. Engrg). Various engineering posts, South of Scotland Electricity Board, 1952–57; engineering, commercial and management posts, Midlands Electricity Board, 1957–72; Area Manager, South Staffs Area, 1972–75, Chief Engineer, 1975–77; Dep. Chm., 1977–81, Chm., 1981–84, South Wales Electricity Bd. Mem., Electricity Council, 1981–90. CCMI. *Recreations*: golf, ski-ing. *Address*: Winterfold, Dovers Orchard, Hoo Lane, Chipping Campden, Glos GL55 6AZ. *T*: (01386) 841797.

**ROSS, Ernest;** *b* Dundee, July 1942; *m*; two *s* one *d*. *Educ*: St John's Jun. Secondary Sch. Quality Control Engineer, Timex Ltd. Mem., MSF (formerly AUEW (TASS)). MP (Lab) Dundee W, 1979–2005. Mem., Select Cttee on Foreign Affairs, 1997–99; Chm., All-Party Poverty Gp, 1997–2005. Chm. Bd of Govs, Westminster Foundn for Democracy, 1997–2002. Mem. Bd, Claverhouse Gp, 2002–. Mem. Council, Al-Maktoum Coll. (formerly Al-Maktoum Inst.), 2001–.

**ROSS, Prof. Fiona Mary,** CBE 2015; Professor of Health Research, Kingston University and St George's, University of London, since 2014 (Executive Dean, Faculty of Health and Social Care Sciences, 2006–14); Director of Research, Leadership Foundation for Higher Education, 2014–17; *b* London, 23 Oct. 1951; *d* of Dr Michael Stuart Ross and Margaret Lois Ross; *m* 1982, John C. Tatam; two *s* one *d*. *Educ*: James Allen's Girls' Sch., Dulwich; Univ. of Edinburgh (BSc 1973; RGN 1975); King's Coll. London (PhD 1987). Clin. nursing posts in community and palliative care, 1976–79; Dist Nursing Sister/Res. (jt appt), Dept of Gen. Practice, St Thomas' Hosp. Med. Sch., 1980–83; Queen's Nursing Inst. Lectr, Dept of Nursing Studies, KCL, 1983–89; St George's Hospital Medical School: Sen. Lectr, Div. of Gen. Practice, 1990–95 (Sub-Dean, 1993–95); Prof. of Primary Care Nursing, Faculty of Health and Social Care Scis, 1996–2002; Dir, DoH Nat. Nursing Res. Unit, KCL, 2002–05. Sen. Responsible Officer, Educn, Acad. Health Scis Network (pt-time secondment), 2013–16. Vis. Prof., Chinese Univ. of Hong Kong, 2015. Expert Advr, Prime Minister's Commn on Future of Nursing and Midwifery, 2009–10. Chair, Nursing and Midwifery Gp, Nat. Co-ordinating Centre Service Delivery and Orgn R&D Commng, 2005–06; Mem., NIHR Health Services and Delivery Res./Service Delivery and Orgn Commng Bd, 2009–15. Chair, London Higher Healthcare Educn Gp, 2010–14 (Trustee). Advr to Bd, Hounslow and Richmond Community Health Trust, 2014–16. Pres., Internat. Collaboration of Community Health Nursing Res., 2011–18. Trustee, Bd of Princess Alice Hospice, Esher, 2011– (Chair, 2016–). Ind. Gov., Court, Westminster Univ., 2019–. Ed.-in-Chief, Jl Interprofessional Care, 2005–10 (Emeritus Ed., 2010). Fellow, Eur. Acad. Nursing Scis 2005. *Publications*: (ed with S. Redfern) Nursing Older People, 2006; (jtly) Handbook of Service User Involvement in Nursing and Health Care Research, 2012; (jtly) Researching Critical Reflection: multidisciplinary perspectives, 2016; contribs to jls incl. British Jl Nursing, Nursing Times, Jl Interprofessional Care, Jl Advanced Nursing, Internat. Jl Nursing Studies, BMJ Quality and Safety, Higher Educn Qly, Jl of Widening Participation and Lifelong Learning. *Recreations*: house in France, gardening, cycling for travel, two grandchildren, volunteer for Nightstop London. *Address*: 19 Leyborne Park, Kew Gardens, Surrey TW9 3HB. *T*: (020) 8940 3739. *E*: fionamaryross@gmail.com.

**ROSS, Gail Elizabeth;** Member (SNP) Caithness, Sutherland and Ross, Scottish Parliament, since 2016; *b* Wick, 30 March 1977; *d* of Raymond George Macdonald and Moira Macdonald; *m* 2008, Stewart Ferguson Ross; one *s*. *Educ*: Wick High Sch.; Central Coll. of Commerce (HND Advertising and PR); Open Univ. Pharmacy Asst, Boots the Chemist Ltd, 1999–2001; Mktg Manager, Grey Coast Theatre Co., 2001–02; Advertising Field Sales, Scotsman Publications Ltd, 2003–05; Sales Exec., Football Aid Ltd, 2005–06; Officer Manager for Robert Gibson, MSP, 2007–16. Mem. (SNP), Highland Council, 2011– (Civic Leader, Caithness, 2012–16). *Recreations*: gardening, cooking, wheel glass engraving, animal welfare. *Address*: Scottish Parliament, Edinburgh EH99 1SP. *E*: gail.ross.msp@parliament.scot.

**ROSS, Graham Alexander Charles;** conductor and composer; Director of Music, Clare College, Cambridge, since 2010; *b* Frimley, Surrey, 29 April 1985; *s* of David and Linda Ross; *m* 2019, Richard Houston. *Educ*: Clare Coll., Cambridge (BA 2006); Royal Coll. of Music (MMus 2008). Freelance conductor, 2008–: Aalborg SO; Australian Chamber Orch.; Aurora Orch.; Orch. of Age of Enlightenment; BBC Concert Orch.; BBC Singers; DR VokalEnsemblet; London Mozart Players; LPO; Malaysian Philharmonic Orch.; Co-founder and Principal Conductor, Dmitri Ensemble, 2004–. *Recreations*: music, arts, travel, food, architecture, people. *Address*: Clare College, Trinity Lane, Cambridge CB2 1TL. *T*: (01223) 333264. *E*: gr267@cam.ac.uk.

**ROSS, Prof. Graham Garland,** PhD; FRS 1991; Professor of Theoretical Physics, Oxford University, 1992–2011, now Emeritus; Fellow of Wadham College, Oxford, 1983–2011, now Emeritus. *Educ*: Aberdeen Univ. (BSc); Durham Univ. (PhD); MA Oxon. Rutherford Atlas Res. Fellow, Pembroke Coll., Oxford, 1981–83; Lectr, 1983–90, Reader and SERC Sen. Res. Fellow in Theoretical Physics, 1990–92, Oxford Univ. *Address*: Rudolf Peierls Centre for Theoretical Physics, 1 Keble Road, Oxford OX1 3RH. *T*: (01865) 273999; Woodcock Cottage, Lincombe Lane, Boars Hill, Oxford OX1 5DX.

**ROSS, Hilary Anne, (Mrs C. M. Hix);** Partner, since 2011, Sector Group Head of Retail, Food and Hospitality, since 2012 and Executive Partner for London, since 2015, DWF Law LLP (formerly DWF LLP) (Member, Strategy Board, 2016–19); *b* Kilwinning, Scotland, 25 April 1969; *d* of David Stewart Ross and Amy Urquhart Ross (*née* McCreadie); *m* 2002, Christopher Martin Hix; one *s*. *Educ*: Winton Primary Sch.; Ardrossan Acad.; Glasgow Univ. (LLB; Dip. Legal Studies). Admitted solicitor: Scotland, 1993; England and Wales, 1994. Trainee, Hughes Dowdall, 1992–94; Associate: McKenna & Co., 1994–96; Sonnenschein Nath & Rosenthal, 1996–98; Partner: Berwin Leighton Paisner, 1998–2008; Bond Pearce, 2008–12. Mem. Cttee, Food Law Gp, 1998–. Chm., Eur. Food Law Assoc. (UK), 2008–11. *Recreation*: walking. *Address*: DWF Law LLP, 20 Fenchurch Street, EC3M 3BY. *T*: (020) 7645 9587, *Fax*: (020) 7645 9501. *E*: hilary.ross@dwf.co.uk.

**ROSS, Hugh Robert;** Director, Hehir-Ross Partnership Ltd, 2011–14; consultant, 2011–14; *b* 21 April 1953; *s* of Robert James Ross and Marion Bertha Ross (*née* Maidment); *m* 1981, Margaret Catherine Hehir; one *s* one *d*. *Educ*: Univ. of Durham (BA Pol. and Sociol.); London Business Sch. (MBA). Fellow, IHSM, 1987. Admin. Trainee, NHS, 1976–78; Asst Adminr, Princess Margaret Hosp., Swindon, 1978–80; Asst Adminr, 1980–81, Patient Services Officer, 1981–83, Westminster Hosp.; Dep. Adminr, 1983–84, Dir of Operational Services, 1984–86, St Bartholomew's Hosp.; Unit General Manager: City Unit, Coventry, 1986–90; Leicester Gen. Hosp., 1990–92; Chief Executive: Leicester Gen. Hosp. NHS Trust, 1993–95; Utd Bristol Healthcare NHS Trust, 1995–2002; Prog. Dir, Bristol Health Services Plan, 2002–04; Chief Exec., Cardiff and Vale NHS Trust, 2004–09; Dir, NHS Wales Health Strategy Unit, 2009–11. Member: Bd, HEFCE, 2011–18; Ind. Reconfiguration Panel, 2011–17. *Recreations*: Southampton FC, golf, travel, real ale, rock music. *Address*: 40 Alma Road, Clifton, Bristol BS8 2DB. *T*: (0117) 974 4987.

**ROSS, Ian;** *see* Ross, W. J.

**ROSS, James Hood,** OBE 2011; Deputy Chairman, National Grid Transco plc, 2002–04 (Chairman, National Grid Group plc, 1999–2002); *b* 13 Sept. 1938; *s* of Thomas Desmond Ross and Lettice Ferrier Ross (*née* Hood); *m* 1964, Sara Blanche Vivian Purcell; one *s* two *d*. *Educ*: Sherborne Sch.; Jesus Coll., Oxford (BA Hons Modern Hist.); Manchester Business Sch. (Dip. with distinction). British Petroleum, 1962–92: Gen. Manager, Corporate Planning, 1981–85; Chief Exec., BP Oil Internat., 1986–88; Chm. and Chief Exec., BP America, 1988–92; a Man Dir, BP, 1991–92; Chief Exec. and Dep. Chm., Cable and Wireless, 1992–96; Chm., Littlewoods Orgn, 1996–2002. Non-executive Director: McGraw Hill; Datacard; Schneider Electric; Prudential, 2004–11. Chm., Leadership Foundn for Higher Educn, 2003–10; Mem., Marshall Commn, 2005–10. Hon. LLD: Manchester, 2001; Liverpool, 2001. *Recreations*: gardening, travel, swimming, golf.

**ROSS, Jane Angharad;** *see* Watts, Jane A.

**ROSS, John Alexander,** CBE 1993; FRAgS; Chairman, Dumfries and Galloway NHS Board, 2001–08; Lord-Lieutenant for Wigtown, since 2015 (Vice Lord-Lieutenant for Dumfries and Galloway (District of Wigtown), 2014–15); *b* 19 Feb. 1945; *m* 1967, Alison Jean Darling; two *s* one *d*. *Educ*: Mahaar Primary Sch., Stranraer; George Watson's Coll., Edinburgh. FRAgS 1993. National Farmers' Union of Scotland: Convener, Hill Farming Sub-cttee, 1984–90; Wigtown Area Pres., 1985–86; Convener, Livestock Cttee, 1987–90; Vice-Pres., 1986–90; Pres., 1990–96. Comr, Meat & Livestock Commn, 1996–2002; Chm., Scotch Quality Beef and Lamb Assoc. Ltd, 1997–2000. Bd Dir, 1996–2007, Chm. Regl Bd, Scotland, 2007–12, NFU Mutual Insurance Soc. Dir, Animal Diseases Res. Assoc., 1986–2012; Chairman: Moredun Res. Inst., 2002–04; Moredun Res. Foundn, 2004–12; Care Farming Scotland, 2011–. Chairman: Dumfries and Galloway Health Bd, 1997–2000; Dumfries and Galloway Primary Care NHS Trust 2000–01; Nat. Prog. Bd for Prisoners' Healthcare, 2009–11; Care Farming Scotland, 2012–; Ind. Chair, Wigtownshire Health and Social Care Project, 2018–. Comr, Northern Lighthouse Bd, 2008–. Chm., Stranraer Sch. Council, 1980–89. Session Clerk, Portpatrick Parish Church, 1975–80; Elder, C of S. DL Wigtown 2010. Hon. Fellow, Scottish Agricl Coll., 2010. Hon. DVMS Glasgow, 2014. *Recreations*: golf, curling. *Address*: Low Auchenree, Portpatrick, Stranraer DG9 8TN. *T*: (01776) 810259. *Club*: Farmers.

**ROSS, John Graffin;** QC 2001; a Recorder, since 1994; *b* 9 March 1947; *er s* of late James Ross, MRCVS and of Eileen Ross; *m* 1973, Elizabeth Patricia Alexandra Layland. *Educ*: Umtali Boys' High Sch., Southern Rhodesia; University Coll. of Rhodesia and Nyasaland (LLB (ext.) London Univ.); University College London (LLM). Called to the Bar, Inner Temple, 1971, Bencher, 2006; Asst Recorder, 1990–94; Hd of Chambers, 1 Chancery Lane, 2007–17. Legal Assessor, RCVS, 2007–. Chairman: Professional Negligence Bar Assoc., 2011–13 (Vice-Chm., 2009–11; Mem. Cttee, 2006–13); Cttee, London Common Law and Commercial Bar Assoc., 2006–11. *Publications*: (contrib.) Pittaway and Hammerton, Professional Negligence Cases, 1998. *Recreations*: music, bridge, riding, golf, ski-ing. *Address*: c/o 1 Chancery Lane, WC2A 1LF. *T*: (020) 7092 2900. *Clubs*: Denham Golf; Real Valderrama (Golf).

**ROSS, Jonathan Steven,** OBE 2005; broadcaster; *b* 17 Nov. 1960; *m* 1988, Jane Goldman; one *s* two *d*. *Educ*: Sch. of Slavonic and E European Studies, Univ. of London (BA History). Formerly researcher, Channel 4; founding co-Producer, Channel X. Television includes: chat shows: The Last Resort (deviser and associate producer with Alan Marke), 1987; One Hour with Jonathan Ross, 1990; Tonight with Jonathan Ross, 1990; The Late Jonathan Ross, 1996; Friday Night with Jonathan Ross, 2001–10; The Jonathan Ross Show, 2011–; presenter: The Incredibly Strange Film Show, 1988–89; Jonathan Ross Presents; For One Week Only, 1991; Gag Tag; In Search Of…; The Big Big Talent Show; Film 1999–2010; Secret Map of Hollywood, 2005; Pinewood: 80 Years of Movie Magic, 2015; panel games: (host) It's Only TV… But I Like It, 1999–2002; (team mem.) They Think It's All Over, 1999–2006. Radio presenter, 1987–. Gov., BFI, 2014–. *Publications*: Why Do I Say These Things?, 2008; (jtly) Turf, 2011. *Address*: c/o Off the Kerb Productions, 44 Clerkenwell Close, EC1R 0AZ.

**ROSS, Kenneth Alexander;** Sheriff of South Strathclyde, Dumfries and Galloway at Dumfries, 2000–14; President, Law Society of Scotland, 1994–95 (Vice-President, 1993–94); *b* 21 April 1949; *s* of Alexander Cree Ross and Mary Hamilton Ross (*née* M'Lauchlan); *m* 1972, Morag Laidlaw; one *s* one *d*. *Educ*: Hutchesons' GS, Glasgow; Edinburgh Univ. (LLB (Hons) 1971). Pres., Edinburgh Univ. Union, 1970–71. Partner, M'Gowans, later Gillespie, Gifford & Brown, solicitors, Dumfries, 1975–97. Temp. Sheriff, 1987–97; Sheriff of Lothian and Borders at Linlithgow, 1997–2000. Member: Scottish Legal

Aid Bd, 2004–09; Judicial Appointments Bd for Scotland, 2008–12. Mem. Council, Law Soc. of Scotland, 1987–96. Contested (C): Kilmarnock, Feb. 1974; Galloway, Oct. 1974. *Recreations:* gardening, golf, beekeeping, curling. *Address:* Slate Row, Auchencairn, Castle Douglas, Kirkcudbrightshire DG7 1QL; 70 Orchard Brae Avenue, Edinburgh EH4 2GA.

**ROSS, Leslie Samuel,** CB 2006; Managing Director, Business International, Invest Northern Ireland, 2002–05; advisor on economic development, since 2005; *b* 5 July 1944; *s* of Herbert Ross and late Gretta Ross; *m* 1969, Violet Johnston; one *s* one *d*. *Educ:* Portora Royal Sch.; Open Univ. (BA Hons). Dep. Chief Exec. and other sen. positions, 1982–2000, Chief Exec., 2000–02, Industrial Develt Bd, NI. *Recreations:* sport, gardening, travel. *Address:* 5 Belmont Drive, Belfast BT4 2BL.

**ROSS, Lt-Col Sir Malcolm;** *see* Ross, Lt-Col Sir W. H. M.

**ROSS, Margaret Beryl C.;** *see* Clunies Ross.

**ROSS, Michael David,** CBE 2001; Chief Executive, Scottish Widows plc (formerly Managing Director, then Group Chief Executive, Scottish Widows' Fund and Life Assurance Society), 1991–2003; Joint Deputy Group Chief Executive, Lloyds TSB Group plc, 2000–03; *b* 9 July 1946; *s* of Patrick James Forrest Ross and Emily Janet; *m* 1973, Pamela Marquis Speakman. *Educ:* Daniel Stewart's Coll., Edinburgh. FFA 1969–2012. Joined Scottish Widows', 1964, as Trainee Actuary; Asst Gen. Manager, 1986–88; Actuary, 1988; Gen. Manager, 1988–90; Dep. Man. Dir. 1990–91. Non-executive Director: Phoenix Life, 2005–16; mform Ltd, 2005–10; Principle Insce Hldgs Ltd (formerly British Islamic Insce Hldgs), 2006–11. Chm., Scottish Financial Enterprise, 1999–2004 (Dep. Chm., 1998). Mem., Investment Cttee, 2005–16, Audit and Risk Mgt Cttee, 2008–16, Nat. Trust for Scotland. Association of British Insurers: Chm., 2001–03; Chm., Customer Impact Panel, 2006–11. CCMI until 2016 (CBIM 1991). *Publications:* contrib. Trans. Faculty of Actuaries. *Recreations:* golf, ski-ing, gardening.

**ROSS, Moira;** Chief Creative Officer, Panda Television, since 2016; *b* Wallasey, Merseyside; *d* of Keith Ross and Eileen Ross. *Educ:* Royal Scottish Acad. of Music and Drama (BA Hons Drama Studies); Drama Studio, London. ABC: Sen. Producer, Dancing with the Stars, 2007–08; Co-Exec. Producer, Dance War, 2008; BBC: Executive Producer: Last Choir Standing, 2008; Eurovision: Your Country Needs You, Tonight's the Night, 2009; So You Think You Can Dance, 2010; Strictly Come Dancing, 2010–11; Editor of Format Entertainment, 2011; Wall to Wall: Hd of Entertainment, 2012–16; Exec. Producer, The Voice UK, 2012–16. *Recreations:* theatre, concerts. *Club:* Soho House.

**ROSS, Nicholas David, (Nick Ross);** broadcaster and journalist; *b* 7 Aug. 1947; *s* of late John Caryl Ross and of Joy Dorothy Ross; *m* 1985, Sarah Caplin; three *s*. *Educ:* Wallington County Grammar Sch.; Queen's Univ., Belfast (BA Hons Psychol). Broadcaster, BBC N Ireland, 1971–72; Radio 4: reporter, Today, World at One, 1972–75; presenter, The World Tonight, Newsdesk, 1972–74, World at One, 1982, Call Nick Ross, 1986–97, Gulf News, 1991, The Commission, 1998–2005, documentaries, 2005–; producer and dir, TV documentaries, 1979–81; presenter, BBC TV: Man Alive, Man Alive Debates, Out of Court, 1975–82; Breakfast Time, Fair Comment, Star Memories, 60 Minutes, 1982–85; Watchdog, 1985–86; Crimewatch UK, 1984–2007; Westminster with Nick Ross, 1994–97; political party confs, 1996; Campaign Roadshow, 1997; So You Think You're A Good Driver, 1999–2002; The Syndicate, 2000; Nick Ross debates, 2000; The Truth About Crime with Nick Ross, 2009; ind. TV incl. A Week in Politics, Ch 4, 1986–88, Crime Museum, 2008. Member: COPUS, 1991–96; Cttee on the Ethics of Gene Therapy, DoH, 1991–93; Gene Therapy Adv. Cttee, DoH, 1993–96; Wider Working Gp on Health of the Nation, DoH, 1992–94; Nuffield Council on Bioethics, 1999–2005; NHS Action Team, 2000–01; RCP Cttee on Ethics in Medicine, 2004–14; Acad. of Med. Scis inquiry into use of non-human primates in res., 2005–06; Clin. Initiative Steering Cttee, RCS, 2016–; Ethics Cttee, UK Biobank, 2019–. Non-exec. Dir, Imperial Coll. NHS Healthcare Trust, 2016–; Trustee, Imperial Coll. Hosp. Charity Bd, 2016–; Dir, ICH Charity Ltd, 2016–. Member: Nat. Bd for Crime Prevention, 1993–96; Crime Prevention Agency, 1996–99; Property Crime Task Force, 1999–2002; Victim Support Adv. Bd, 1991–2008; Crime Concern Adv. Bd, 1991–2003; Learning Leaders Sen. Oversight Gp, Nat. Police Chiefs' Council, 2017–. President: SANEline, 1990–2010; Tacade, 1996–2011; Healthwatch, 1990–; London Accident Prevention Council, subseq. London Road Safety Council, 2007–15; Vice-President: Patients' Assoc., 1991–93; IAM RoadSmart, 2010– (Mem. Council, 2002–10); Chm., Adv. Bd, Wales Cancer Bank, 2010–18 (Vice-Chm., 2008–10); Vice-Chm., Nat. Road Safety Campaign, RoSPA, 1990–93. Chm., Evidence Matters, 2015–16. Chm., Rhône-Poulenc, then Aventis, Prize for Sci. Books, 1993, 2006. Guest Dir, Cheltenham Sci. Festival, 2008. Trustee: UK Stem Cell Foundn, 2005–; Crimestoppers, 2007–; Sense About Science, 2008–; Dfuse, 2011–17. Chm., Jill Dando Inst. of Crime Sci., UCL, 2000–. Vis. Prof., UCL, 2006– (Hon. Fellow, 2006). Fellow, WWF, 2011– (Ambassador, 2010–11). Pres., Kensington Soc., 2011–. Patron of various charities. FRSA 1994; FRSocMed 1998. Hon. Fellow, Acad. of Experimental Criminology, 2007; Hon. FRCP, 2015. DUniv QUB, 2002. *Publications:* Crime: how to solve it and why so much of what we're told is wrong, 2014. *Recreations:* ski-ing, scuba diving, influencing public policy. *Address:* PO Box 999, London, W2 4XT. *E:* nick@nickross.com. *W:* www.nickross.com.

**ROSS, Peter Michael; His Honour Judge Peter Ross;** a Circuit Judge, since 2004; *b* 24 June 1955; *s* of Michael and Colleen Ross; *m* 1979, Julie Anna Ibbetson; two *s* one *d*. *Educ:* John Hampden GS, High Wycombe; Venerable English Coll., Gregorian Univ., Rome (PhB 1975); Coll. of Law. Admitted solicitor, 1980; called to the Bar, Inner Temple, 2000. Articles of clerkship, Allan Janes & Co., 1976–79; Court Clerk, High Wycombe Magistrates' Court, 1979–81; Thames Valley Police: Asst Prosecuting Solicitor, 1981–82; Sen. Prosecuting Solicitor, 1982–84; Principal Prosecuting Solicitor, 1984–86; Sen. Crown Prosecutor, 1986–87, Br. Crown Prosecutor, 1987–90, CPS Aylesbury; Br. Crown Prosecutor, N London CPS, 1990–93; Asst Chief Crown Prosecutor (Ops), CPS London, 1993–96; Dir, Office for Supervision of Solicitors, 1996–99; an Asst Recorder, 1999–2000; a Recorder, 2000–04. *Recreations:* gardening, hedge laying, orchards, cider making, bee keeping.

**ROSS, Prof. Richard Lawrence;** screenwriter, since 2007; Research Professor, Norwegian Film School, 2001–07; Head of Diploma Course and Deputy to Director, National Film and Television School, 1998–2000; *b* 22 Dec. 1935; *s* of Lawrence Sebley Ross and Muriel Ross; *m* 1957, Phyllis Ellen Hamilton (*d* 2014); one *d* (one *s* decd). *Educ:* Westland High School, Hokitika, NZ; Canterbury University College, NZ. Exchange Telegraph, 1958–60; Visnews Ltd, 1960–65; BBC TV News, 1965–80; Prof. of Film and TV, then of Film, RCA, 1980–89; Co-Chm. (with Milos Forman) Grad. Film Dept, Columbia Univ. NY, 1989–90; Chm., Grad. Film Dept, NY Univ., 1990–92; Sen. Lectr in Film, 1995–96, Hd, Curriculum Planning, 1996–98, Nat. Film and TV Sch. Hon. Prof. of Film, Hochschule für Fernsehen und Film, Munich, 1992–2004; Visiting Professor: Jerusalem Film and TV Sch., 1992–2005; Deutsche Film- und Fernsehakad., Berlin, 1993–2003. Consultant Dir, Film Educn, 1986–89; Dir, Nat. Youth Film Foundn, 1988–89. Consultant: Univ. Sains, Penang, Malaysia, 1984–86; Calouste Gulbenkian Foundn, Lisbon, 1983–85. Chm., Educn Cttee, British Film Year, 1985–86; Exec. Mem., Centre Internat. de Liaison des Ecoles de Cinéma et de Télévision, 1990–95 (Chm., Short Film Project, 1990–95; Hon. Mem., 2004). Fellow in Fine Arts, Trent Polytechnic, 1970–72. Fellow, RCA, 1981–89. *Publications:* Strategy for Story-Telling (2 vols), 1992; Triangle (The Creative Partnership), vol. 1, 1998, vol. 2, 2001, vol. 3, 2002; Training the Trainers (11 manuals for film educn teachers), 2007; (contrib.) Hanly. *Recreations:* walking in London, eating in France, talking and drinking anywhere. *E:* dickross@dircon.co.uk.

**ROSS, Richard Y.;** *see* Younger-Ross.

**ROSS, Sir Robert;** *see* Ross, Sir W. R. A.

**ROSS, Lt-Gen. Sir Robert (Jeremy), (Sir Robin),** KCB 1994 (CB 1992); OBE 1978; Chairman, SSAFA Forces Help, 2000–10; *b* 28 Nov. 1939; *s* of Gerald and Margaret Ross; *m* 1965, Sara (*née* Curtis); one *s* one *d*. *Educ:* Wellington Coll.; Corpus Christi Coll., Cambridge (MPhil). Entered RM, 1957; Commando and Sea Service, 1959–69; Army Staff Coll., 1970; Commando Service, 1971–78; Instr, Army Staff Coll., 1978–79; CO 40 Commando RM, 1979–81; RCDS 1982; MoD, 1984–86; Comdr 3 Commando Bde, 1986–88; Maj.-Gen. RM Trng, Reserve and Special Forces, 1988–90; Maj.-Gen. RM Commando Forces, 1990–93; CGRM, 1993–96. Liveryman, Plaisterers' Co., 1996. Comdr, Legion of Merit (USA), 1993. *Recreation:* fishing.

**ROSS, Sandy;** *see* Ross, Alexander.

**ROSS, Sophie, (Mrs R. P. Ross);** *see* Mirman, S.

**ROSS, Tessa Sarah,** CBE 2010; Joint Chief Executive Officer, House Productions, since 2016; *b* 26 July 1961; *d* of E. Leonard Ross and Sharon F. Ross (*née* Kingsley), MBE; *m* 1987, Mark Scantlebury; two *s* one *d*. *Educ:* Somerville Coll., Oxford (BA Hons Oriental Studies (Chinese)). Literary Agent, Anthony Shiel Associates, 1986–88; Script Editor, BBC Scotland, 1988–89; Hd of Develt, British Screen Finance, 1990–93; Independent Commng Exec., 1993–97, Hd of Independent Commng, 1997–2000, BBC TV Drama; Channel 4: Hd of Drama, 2000–03; Hd of FilmFour, 2003–05; Hd of FilmFour and Drama, then Controller, Film and Drama, 2005–14; Chief Exec., 2014–15, consultant, 2015, Nat. Theatre. Mem., Nat. Council, Arts Council England, 2017–. Outstanding British Contribn to Cinema Award, BAFTA, 2013. *Address:* House Productions, 14a Clerkenwell Green, EC1R 0DP. *Club:* Union.

**ROSS, Thomas Leonard;** QC (Scot.) 2017; *b* Glasgow, 25 Oct. 1963; *s* of Thomas Ross and Frances Ross (*née* Dickson); *m* 1987, Alison Laurie; two *d*. *Educ:* Univ. of Strathclyde (LLB; DipLP); Univ. of Glasgow (Cert. Forensic Medicine). Solicitor, 1986–99; Advocate, 1999–. President: Glasgow Bar Assoc., 1995–96; Scottish Criminal Bar Assoc., 2015–16. *Recreations:* photography, diy-ing. *Address:* 7 Buchlyvie Road, Ralston, Renfrewshire PA1 3AD. *E:* TLRQC@benchmarkadvocates.co.uk. *Club:* Glasgow Arts (Glasgow).

**ROSS, Sir Timothy David M.;** *see* Melville-Ross.

**ROSS, Ven. Vernon;** Archdeacon of Westmorland and Furness, since 2017; *b* Willesden, 13 April 1957; *s* of Jack Ross and Margarette Ross; *m* 1980, Susan Francesca; two *s*. *Educ:* St John the Baptist Primary Sch., Findon; St Andrews C of E Secondary Modern Sch., Worthing; Portsmouth Poly. (BSc Hons Biol. 1979); Royal Naval and SE Hants Sch. of Nursing, Portsmouth (RGN 1986); Trinity Coll., Bristol (DipHE; PGCTh); York St John's Univ. (MA Theology 2013). Staff Nurse, St Mary's Hosp., Portsmouth, 1986–87; Research Nurse, Countess Mountbatten Hospice, Southampton, 1987–89; ordained deacon, 1991, priest, 1992; Curate, St John's, Fareham, 1991–94; Priest-in-charge, Witheridge Benefice, 1994–2000; Team Rector, Barnstaple, 2000–08; Priest-in-charge, Fyfield Benefice, 2008–16; Mission and Ministry Advr, Barking Episcopal Area, 2012–17. *Recreations:* walking, photography, current affairs, time with family and friends. *Address:* The Vicarage, Windermere Road, Lindale, Grange over Sands, Cumbria LA11 6LB.

**ROSS, Victor;** Chairman, Reader's Digest Association Ltd, 1978–84; *b* 1 Oct. 1919; *s* of Valentin and Eva Rosenfeld; *m* 1st, 1944, Romola Wallace; two *s*; 2nd, 1970, Hildegard Peiser. *Educ:* schs in Austria, Germany and France; London Sch. of Economics. Served in Army, 1942–45. Journalist and writer, 1945–55; joined Reader's Digest, 1955; Man. Dir and Chief Exec., 1972–81. Dir, Folio Soc., 1985–89. Pres., Assoc. of Mail Order Publishers, 1979–80, 1983–84; Mem., Data Protection Tribunal, 1985–95. Hon. Fellow, Inst. of Direct Marketing, 1995. Mackintosh Medal for Advertising, Advertising Assoc., 1989. *Publications:* A Stranger in my Midst, 1948; Tightrope, 1952; Basic British, 1956. *Recreations:* collecting books, fishing.

**ROSS, Lt-Col Sir (Walter Hugh) Malcolm,** GCVO 2005 (CVO 1994; KCVO 1999); OBE 1988; Lord-Lieutenant, Stewartry of Kirkcudbright (Dumfries and Galloway Region), 2006–18; *b* 27 Oct. 1943; *s* of Col Walter John Macdonald Ross, CB, OBE, MC, TD and Josephine May (*née* Cross); *m* 1969, Susie, *d* of Gen. Sir (James) Michael Gow, GCB; one *s* two *d*. *Educ:* Eton Coll.; Royal Military Acad., Sandhurst. Served in Scots Guards, 1964–87; Asst Comptroller, 1987–91, Comptroller, 1991–2006, Lord Chamberlain's Office; Management Auditor, The Royal Household, 1987–89; Master, Household of the Prince of Wales and Duchess of Cornwall, 2006–08. Sec., Central Chancery of the Orders of Knighthood, 1989–91. Chm., Westminster Gp plc, 2007–17. An Extra Equerry to the Queen, 1988–. Mem., Queen's Body Guard for Scotland, Royal Company of Archers, 1981– (Brigadier, 2003; Ensign, 2012; Lieut, 2016; Capt., 2018). Stewartry of Kirkcudbright (Dumfries and Galloway): DL 2003; JP 2006. Freeman, City of London, 1994. Order of St John: Prior of Scotland, 2009–15; Lord Prior, 2017–19 (GCStJ 2016; KStJ 2009; CStJ 2007). *Address:* Netherhall, Bridge of Dee, Castle Douglas, Kirkcudbrightshire DG7 2AA. *Clubs:* Cavalry and Guards, Pratt's; New (Edinburgh).
*See also* Sir W. R. A. Ross.

**ROSS, Sir (Walter) Robert (Alexander),** KCVO 2012 (CVO 2006); FRICS; Secretary and Keeper of the Records, Duchy of Cornwall, 1997–2013; Consultant, Savills, since 2014; *b* 27 Feb. 1950; *s* of Col Walter John Macdonald Ross, CB, OBE, MC, TD and Josephine May Ross (*née* Cross); *m* 1985, Ingrid Wieser; one *s* one *d*. *Educ:* Eton Coll.; Royal Agricl Coll., Cirencester. FRICS 1982. Chartered Surveyor, Buccleuch Estates Ltd, Selkirk, 1972–73; joined Savills, 1973: Partner, 1982–86; Dir, 1986–97. Director: OMS Co., 1998–; R. W. R. Consultants Ltd, 2014–. Director Trustee: Pirbright Inst., 2014–; Red Squirrel Survival Trust, 2014–; Trustee, Ernest Cook Trust, 2015–. *Club:* Boodle's.

**ROSS, William;** *b* 4 Feb. 1936; *m* 1974, Christine; three *s* one *d*. MP (UU) Londonderry, Feb. 1974–83, Londonderry East, 1983–2001 (resigned seat Dec. 1985 in protest against Anglo-Irish Agreement; re-elected Jan. 1986); contested (UU) Londonderry E, 2001. *Recreations:* fishing, shooting. *Address:* Hillquarter, Turmeel, Dungiven, Northern Ireland BT47 4SL. *T:* (028) 7774 1428.

**ROSS, William John, (Ian),** OBE 2007; Chairman, Scottish Natural Heritage, 2014–17; *b* Inverness, 6 March 1957; *m* 1987, Dr Lindsey Crum; one *s* one *d*. *Educ:* Fortrose Acad.; Univ. of Aberdeen (BSc Hons Forestry). FICFor 2001. Forest Officer, Forestry Commn, 1979–82; Scottish School of Forestry: Lectr, 1982–88; Sen. Lectr, 1988–95; pt-time Lectr, 1995–2014. Mem., Highland Council, 1999–2012 (Chairman: Sustainable Develt,

2001–07; Planning, Envmt and Develt, 2008–12; Vice-Convenor, Northern Jt Police Bd, 2007–12). Member, Board: Scottish Police Authy, 2012–16; Scotland's Rural Coll., 2017–. Ind. Chm., Caithness and N Sutherland Partnership, 2018–. FRSA. *Recreations:* family, reading, cycling, Rotary Club, travel. *E:* w.j.ross@btinternet.com.

**ROSS RUSSELL, Graham;** Founder Chairman, Securities Institute, 1992–2000; *b* 3 Jan. 1933; *s* of Robert Ross Russell and Elizabeth Ross Russell (*née* Hendry); *m* 1963, Jean Margaret Symington; three *s* one *d*. *Educ:* Loretto; Trinity Hall, Cambridge (MA; Hon. Fellow, 2001); Harvard Business School (MBA; Frank Knox Fellow, 1958–60). Sub Lieut, RNVR, 1951–53 (Mediterranean Fleet). Merchant banking: Morgan Grenfell & Co. and Baring Brothers, 1956–58; Philip Hill Higginson Erlanger, 1960–63; Stockbroker, Laurence Prust & Co., 1963–90, Partner, 1965; Chm., Laurence Prust & Co. Ltd, 1986–88. Chairman: Braham Miller Group, 1981–84; C. C. F. Hldgs, 1988–90; EMAP, 1990–94 (Dir, 1970–94); Tunnel Services Ltd, 1991–2002; F & C Capital and Income (formerly F & C Pep and Isa) Investment Trust plc, 1993–2005; Advent, then Foresight 3, Venture Capital Trust plc, 1996–2014; Enterprise Panel, 1997–2011; UK Business Incubation, 1997–2011; non-executive Director: UK Select Investment Trust (formerly Investment Trust of Guernsey) plc, 1995–2013; Fordath, 1971–84; Foster Braithwaite, 1988–96; Nasdaq (Europe) (formerly EASDAQ) SA, 1995–98 (Pres., 2000–01, Mem., Market Authy, 1999–2003); Barloworld plc, 2008–2003; Bamboo Investments plc, 2000–06; Barloworld Ltd, 2001–03; Averon Park, 2017–. Dir, SIB, 1989–93; Mem. Council, Internat. Stock Exchange, subseq. London Stock Exchange, 1973–91 (Dep. Chm., 1984–88; Chairman: Pre-emption Gp, 1987–2000; Rev. Cttee on Initial Public Offers, 1989–90). Comr, Public Works Loan Bd, 1980–95; Chm., Domestic Promotions Cttee, British Invisible Exports Council, 1987–91. Chm. Trustees, F & C Asset Mgt Pension Fund, 2004–07; Mem., Investment Cttee, RBK&C Pension Fund, 2004–14. Trustee: NESTA, 2001–07; Richmond Univ., 2017–. Mem. Council, Crown Agents Foundn, 1997–2002. Chm. Govs, Sutton's Hosp., Charterhouse, 1996–2006. Pres., Trinity Hall Assoc., 1994–95. Co-founder, retirementreinvented.com website, 2009. Hon. FCSI 2000. FRSA 1989. *Publications:* occasional articles in esoteric financial and fiscal jls. *Recreations:* tennis, golf, reading, 11 grandchildren. *Address:* 30 Ladbroke Square, W11 3NB. *T:* (020) 7727 5017. *Clubs:* Athenæum; Hawks (Cambridge); Woodpeckers (Oxford and Cambridge).

**ROSS-WAWRZYNSKI, Dame Dana,** DBE 2013; Executive Headteacher (formerly Headmistress), Altrincham Grammar School for Girls, 1999–2017; Company Member, Bright Futures Educational Trust, since 2011 (Chief Executive Officer, 2011–16); Chief Executive Officer, Great British Elite Schoolstrust, since 2012; *b* 24 March 1951; *d* of Richard and Pauline Ross; *m* 1974, Jack Wawrzynski (*d* 2017); two *s*. *Educ:* Glasgow Univ. (BSc Hons 1975); Strathclyde Univ. (MSc 1976); Manchester Univ. (NPQH 1999). Teacher, Loreto Sixth Form Coll., Manchester, 1977–81; Hd of Lower Sch. Sci., Central High Sch. for Boys, Manchester, 1981–82; Hd of Sci., St Joseph's High Sch. for Girls, Manchester, 1982–84; Dep. Headteacher, Abraham Moss High Sch. and N Manchester Coll., 1984–90; Dep. Headteacher, All Hallows High Sch., Macclesfield, 1990–98. Educnl expert consultant, Centre for Social Justice, 2012–14. Chair, Headteachers' Standards in England, DFE, 2014–15. Board Member: Ofqual, 2013–16; Regent Gp, 2016–; Nahda Internat. Sch., Saudi Arabia, 2017–. *Publications:* sex educn booklet, contrib. to educnl papers. *Recreations:* classical music, hill walking, reading, ski-ing. *Address:* Great British Elite Schoolstrust, 2A Wych Lane, Adlington, Cheshire SK10 4NB. *T:* (01625) 828801.

**ROSSANT, Dr Janet,** CC 2015; FRS 2000; FRSC; Professor, Department of Molecular Genetics (formerly Department of Molecular and Medical Genetics), since 1988, University Professor, since 2001, University of Toronto; Senior Scientist, Developmental and Stem Cell Biology Program, Hospital for Sick Children, Toronto, since 2015 (Chief of Research, 2005–15, now Emeritus); President and Scientific Director, Gairdner Foundation, since 2014; *b* 13 July 1950; *d* of Leslie and Doris Rossant; *m* 1977, Alex Bain (*d* 2016); one *s* (one *d* decd). *Educ:* St Hugh's Coll., Oxford (BA, MA 1972); Darwin Coll., Cambridge (PhD 1976; Hon. Fellow, 2017). Beit Meml Fellow, Univ. of Oxford, 1975–77; Asst Prof., 1977–82, Associate Prof., 1982–85, Brock Univ., St Catharines, Ont.; Associate Prof., Univ. of Toronto, 1985–88; Sen. Scientist, 1985–2005, and Co-head, 1998, Prog. in Develt and Fetal Health, Samuel Lunenfeld Res. Inst., Toronto; Pres. and Scientific Dir, Ontario Inst. for Regenerative Medicine, 2014–16. FRSC 1996. For. Associate, NAS, USA, 2008. Hon. LLD: Dalhousie, 2005; Acadia, 2013; Windsor, 2014; Hon. DSc: British Columbia, 2014; Cambridge, 2017. *Publications:* (with R. A. Pedersen) Experimental Approaches to Mammalian Development, 1986; (with P. L. M. Tam) Mouse Development, 2002; contrib. numerous articles to peer-reviewed jls. *Recreations:* walking, cooking, theatre. *Address:* Peter Gilgan Centre for Research and Learning, 686 Bay Street, Toronto, ON M5G 0A4, Canada.

**ROSSDALE, Rt Rev. David Douglas James;** Bishop Suffragan of Grimsby, 2000–13; an Honorary Assistant Bishop, Diocese of Lincoln, since 2013; *b* 22 May 1953; *m* 1982, Karen; two *s*. *Educ:* St John's Sch., Leatherhead; King's Coll., London; Westminster Coll., Oxford (MA 1990); Roehampton Inst. (MSc 2000); King's Coll., London (MSc 2010). Ordained deacon, 1981, priest, 1982; Curate, Upminster, 1981–86; Vicar: St Luke, Moulsham, 1986–90; Cookham, 1990–2000; Area Dean of Maidenhead, 1994–2000. Hon. Canon, Christ Church, Oxford, 1999–2000; Canon and Preb., Lincoln Cathedral, 2000–; Mem. Gen. Synod, 2010–13. Non-executive Director: Reach2 Ltd, 2013–16; Lincs Refugee Doctor Project CIC, 2017–19. Vice Chair, Nat. Soc., 2010–13. Trustee and Treas., Sons and Friends of the Clergy, 2007–18; Trustee, Blue Cross, 2015–18. Gov., Wellington Coll., 2004–10. *Recreations:* travel, cookery, DIY, microlights. *Address:* Home Farm, Fen Lane, East Keal, Spilsby, Lincs PE23 4AY. *T:* (01790) 752163. *Club:* Farmers.

**ROSSDALE, Peter Daniel,** OBE 1996; PhD; FRCVS; Editor, 1980–2010, Editor Emeritus, 2011, Equine Veterinary Journal, Editor-in-Chief, Equine Veterinary Education, 1979–2003, and Chairman, Equine Veterinary Journal Ltd, 1985–2005; *b* 8 Sept. 1927; *s* of George and Kate Rossdale; *m* 1st, 1954, Jillian Ruth Clifton (*d* 1999); two *s* one *d*; 2nd, 2003, Mary Annette Sharkey (*née* Lawrence). *Educ:* Egerton House; Stowe Sch.; Trinity Coll., Cambridge (MA, PhD 1985); RVC. FRCVS 1967. Founding Partner, Rossdale and Partners, Newmarket, 1959–2002, now Consultant. Dir, Romney Publications Ltd, 2010–. British Equine Veterinary Association: Treas., 1960–65; Pres., 1976–77; Chm., BEVA Trust, 1978–82; Chm., 1980–84, Treas., 1984–90, Internat. Equine Reproduction Symposia Cttee; Member: Veterinary Adv. Cttee, Wellcome Trust, 1975–79; Sci. Adv. Cttee, Animal Health Trust, 1978–90; Veterinary Adv. Cttee, Horserace Betting Levy Bd, 1983–96; Chm., Internat. Veterinary Perinatology Soc., 1992–95. Mem., 1957–2003, Hon. Mem., 2003–, Neonatal Soc. (Vickers Lecture); Frank Milne Lecture, American Assoc. of Equine Practitioners, 2004. FACVSc 1973; Dip. of Equine Stud Medicine, 1986. Hon. FRVC 2010. Dr *hc*: Berne, 1987; Edinburgh, 2001; Sydney, 2007. William Hunting Prize, Vet. Record, 1973; George Fleming Prize, British Vet. Jl, 1974; John Henry Steel Meml Medal, RCVS, 1978; Hochmoor Prize, Tierklinik Hochmoor, 1987; Equestrian Award, Animal Health Trust, 1992; Dalrymple Champneys Award, BVA, 1996; Duke of Devonshire Award, 2004; Merial Lifetime Achievement Award, World Equine Veterinary Assoc., 2008; Equine Welfare Award, BEVA, 2018. *Publications:* (jtly) The Practice of Equine Stud Medicine, 1974, revd edn 1980; (jtly) The Horse's Health from A–Z, 1974, revd edn 1998; The Horse from Conception to Maturity, 1975, revd edn 2003; Inside the Horse, 1975; Seeing Equine Practice, 1976; Horse Ailments Explained, 1979; Horse Breeding, 1981 (trans. French, Japanese, German, Swedish); (ed) Veterinary Notes for Horse Owners, 1987; (ed jtly) Equine Medical Veterinary Encyclopedia, 2010; (contrib. and ed jtly) The History of Veterinary Practice in Newmarket 1831–2011, 2011; (with Julie Galliard) The Power of Whitby, 2013; Canon George Austen Remembered in a Personal Perspective of Today, 2015; The Moral Mind, 2016; Knowing That We Know: the burden of human consciousness, 2019; A Veterinary Life in Newmarket, 2019; contrib. peer reviewed jls inc. Vet. Rec., EVJ, Jl Reprod. Fert., Res. Vet. Sci., Lancet, Nature, etc and jls of educn. *Recreations:* contract bridge, music, opera, horseracing and breeding, photography, travel. *T:* (01638) 663639. *E:* pd.rossdale@btinternet.com.

**ROSSE, 7th Earl of,** *cr* 1806; **(William) Brendan Parsons;** Bt 1677; Baron Oxmantown 1792; *b* 21 Oct. 1936; *s* of 6th Earl of Rosse, KBE, and Anne (*d* 1992), *o d* of Lt-Col Leonard Messel, OBE; *S* father, 1979; *m* 1966, Alison Margaret, *er d* of Major J. D. Cooke-Hurle, Startforth Hall, Barnard Castle, Co. Durham; two *s* one *d*. *Educ:* Aiglon Coll., Switzerland; Grenoble Univ.; Christ Church, Oxford (MA 1964). 2nd Lieut, Irish Guards, 1955–57. UN Official 1963–80, appointed successively to Ghana, Dahomey, Mid-West Africa, Algeria, as first UN Volunteer Field Dir (in Iran) and UN Disaster Relief Co-ordinator (in Bangladesh). Govt of Ireland: Mem., Adv. Council on Develt Co-operation, 1984–89; Dir, Agency for Personal Service Overseas, 1986–90. Founder and Dir, Birr Scientific and Heritage Foundn (resp. for creation of Ireland's Historic Science Centre), 1985–; Director: Historic Irish Tourist Houses and Gardens Assoc., 1980–91; Lorne House Trust, 1993–2001; Trustee, The Tree Register, 1989–. Lord of the Manor: Womersley, Yorks; Newtown and Parsonstown, Ireland. FRAS; FTCD 2014; Hon. FIEI. Hon. LLD Dublin, 2005. *Heir: s* Lord Oxmantown, *qv*. *Address:* (home) Birr Castle, Co. Offaly, Ireland. *T:* (57) 912 0023.

**ROSSEINSKY, Prof. Matthew Jonathan,** DPhil; FRS 2008; FRSC; Professor of Inorganic Chemistry, since 1999, and Royal Society Research Professor, since 2013, University of Liverpool; *m*; three *c*. *Educ:* St John's Coll., Oxford (BA Hons Chem. 1987); Merton Coll., Oxford (DPhil 1990). FRSC 1997. Postdoctoral mem., tech. staff, A T & T Bell Labs, Murray Hill, NJ, 1990–92; Lectr, Dept of Chem., Univ. of Oxford, 1992–99. Mem., UKRI-EPSRC (formerly EPSRC), 2015–19. De Gennes Prize in Materials Chem., RSC, 2009; Hughes Medal, Royal Soc., 2011; Davy Medal, Royal Soc., 2017. *Publications:* contribs to jls incl. Applied Physics Letters, Jl Amer. Chem. Soc., Science, Advanced Materials, Chem. of Materials, Nature, Nature Materials. *Address:* Department of Chemistry, University of Liverpool, Liverpool L69 7ZX.

**ROSSER,** family name of **Baron Rosser**.

**ROSSER, Baron** *cr* 2004 (Life Peer), of Ickenham in the London Borough of Hillingdon; **Richard Andrew Rosser;** JP; General Secretary, Transport Salaried Staffs' Association, 1989–2004; *b* 5 Oct. 1944; *s* of Gordon William Rosser and Kathleen Mary (*née* Moon); *m* 1973, Sheena Margaret (*née* Denoon); two *s* one *d*. *Educ:* St Nicholas Grammar Sch., Northwood. BScEcon London (external degree), 1970. CMILT (MCIT 1968). Clerk, London Transport, 1962–65; PA to Operating Man. (Railways), LTE, 1965–66; joined full staff of TSSA, 1966: Res. Officer, 1966–74; Asst, London Midland Div. Sec., 1974–76; Finance and Organising Officer, 1976–77; London Midland Region Div. Sec., 1977–82; Asst Gen. Sec., 1982–89. Non-exec. Dir, Nat. Offender Mgt Bd (formerly Correctional Services Bd), 2000–09; non-exec. Chm., National Offender Management Service (formerly Prison Service) Audit Cttee, 2003–09. Councillor, London Bor. of Hillingdon, 1971–78 (Chm., Finance Cttee, 1974–78); contested (Lab) Croydon Central, Feb. 1974. Mem., NEC, Labour Party, 1988–98; Vice-Chair, 1996–97, Chair, 1997–98, Labour Party. House of Lords: an Opposition Whip, 2010–11; opposition front bench spokesperson: on defence, 2011–15; Home Office and Transport, 2015–; Mem., opposition front bench team, Home Office, 2011–15, Transport, 2011–15. Mem. General Council, TUC, 2000–04. Hon. Vice-Pres., Ryman Isthmian Football League, 2008–; Vice-Pres., Level Playing Field (formerly Nat. Assoc. of Disabled Supporters) (Football), 2009–. JP Middlesex, 1978 (Chm., Uxbridge Bench, 1996–2000). *Recreations:* walking, music, reading The Guardian, and watching non-league football. *Address:* House of Lords, SW1A 0PW.

**ROSSI, Sir Hugh (Alexis Louis),** Kt 1983; farmer and arboriculturalist, Dordogne, since 1991; consultant in environmental law with Simmons and Simmons, solicitors, 1991–97; *b* 21 June 1927; *m* 1955, Philomena Elizabeth Jennings (*d* 2018); one *s* three *d* (and one *d* decd). *Educ:* Finchley Catholic Gram. Sch.; King's Coll., Univ. of London (LLB; FKC 1986). Solicitor with Hons, 1950. Member: Hornsey BC, 1956–65; Haringey Council, 1965–68; Middlesex CC, 1961–65. MP (C) Hornsey, 1966–83, Hornsey and Wood Green, 1983–92; Govt Whip, Oct. 1970–April 1972; Europe Whip, Oct. 1971–1973; a Lord Comr, HM Treasury, 1972–74; Parly Under-Sec. of State, DoE, 1974; opposition spokesman on housing and land, 1974–79; Minister of State: NI Office, 1979–81; for Social Security and the Disabled, DHSS, 1981–83. Chm., Select Cttee on the Environment, 1983–92. Dep. Leader, UK Delegn to Council of Europe and WEU, 1972–73 (Mem., 1970–73). Non-exec. Dir, Iveco NV, 1989–2003; Consultant, Wimpey Environmental Ltd, 1993–95. Vice President: (UK), Adv. Cttee on Protection of the Seas, 1992–2002; Nat. Soc. for Clean Air, 1985–. Chairman: UNA (UK), 1992–96; Italian Hosp., London, 1988–89, Italian Hosp. Fund, 1990–2002; Assoc. of Papal Orders in GB of Pius IX, St Gregory and St Sylvester, 1989–99; Historic Chapels Trust, 1992–2002 (Hon. Pres., 2002–14); Trustee, Trusthouse Charitable Foundn (formerly Mem., Forte Council), 1992–. Pres., KCL Assoc., 2004–06 (Vice Pres., 2003). Hon. FCIWEM 1990; Hon. Fellow, Inst. Wastes Management, 1993. Knight of Holy Sepulchre, 1966; KCSG 1985. *Publications:* Guide to the Rent Act, 1974; Guide to Community Land Act, 1975; Guide to Rent (Agriculture) Act, 1976; Guide to Landlord and Tenant Act, 1987; Guide to Local Government Acts 1987 and 1988, 1988. *Club:* Athenæum.

**ROSSINGTON, (Timothy) David,** CB 2018; Senior Lead (part-time), Blythe House cultural project, Department for Digital, Culture, Media and Sport, 2018–19; *b* 9 Feb. 1958; *s* of late Peter Gilman Rossington and of Freda Elizabeth (*née* Moseley); one *s* one *d*. *Educ:* Balliol Coll., Oxford (BA 1980); Kennedy Sch. of Govt, Harvard (Masters Public Policy 1982); Birkbeck Coll., London (MSc Econ 1985). Joined Civil Service, 1982; Private Sec. to Lord Belstead, 1986; seconded to UK Repn, Brussels, and EC, 1988–91; Private Sec. to Minister of Agriculture, 1991–93; Hd of Div., MAFF, 1993–2000 (Project Dir, IT system to trace cattle in GB, 1996–99); e-Business Dir, DEFRA, 2000–04 (Ops Dir in Cumbria during foot and mouth outbreak, 2001); Dir, Efficiency Team, OGC, 2004–07; Department for Communities and Local Government: Dir, Local Democracy, 2007–08; Acting Dir Gen., Communities, 2008–09; Dir, Strategy, Performance and Delivery, 2009–10; Acting Dir Gen., Finance and Corporate Services, 2010–11; Finance Dir, 2011–15; Department for Culture, Media and Sport, later for Digital, Culture, Media and Sport: Finance and Commercial Dir, 2015–16; Acting Dir Gen., Strategy and Performance, 2016–17; Dir, Office for Civil Soc., 2017. Trustee: Stoll veterans' charity, 2018–; Oxford Community Foundn, 2018–; Earth Trust, 2019–; Arts at the Old Fire Station, 2019–. ACMA 2013. *Recreations:* hill walking, gardening, music, history, running, contemporary art, French and Spanish language and culture. *T:* 07896 679857.

**ROSSITER, Ann Helen;** Executive Director, Society of College, National and University Libraries, since 2010; *b* 18 May 1966; *d* of Charles and Averil Rossiter. *Educ:* Birkbeck Coll., Univ. of London (BA Philosophy). Researcher, BBC Political Res. Unit, 1988–90; Asst Producer, BBC/C4, 1990–92; Researcher: John Denham, MP, 1992–94; Glenda Jackson, MP, 1994–96; Consultant, 1996–99, Dir, 1999–2001, Fishburn Hedges; Dir, Lexington Communications, 2001–02; Dir of Res. and Dep. Dir, 2003–05, Dir, 2005–08, Social Mkt Foundn; Special Adviser: to Sec. of State for Innovation, Univs and Skills, 2008–09; to Sec. of State for Communities and Local Govt, 2009–10. FRSA. *Publications:* The Future of the Private Finance Initiative, 2004; Choice; the evidence, 2004; News Broadcasting in the Digital Age, 2005; Road User Charging: a map, 2007; The Future of Healthcare, 2007; (contrib.) Public Matters: the renewal of the public realm, ed Patrick Diamond, 2007. *Recreations:* exploring Cornwall, contemporary art, bending the ear of politicians, gardening, serial music, film. *Address:* Society of College, National and University Libraries, 94 Euston Street, NW1 2HA. *T:* (020) 7387 0317.

**ROSSITER, Rt Rev. (Anthony) Francis,** OSB; Abbot President of the English Benedictine Congregation, 1985–2001 (Second Assistant, 1976–85); *b* 26 April 1931; *s* of Leslie and Winifred Rossiter. *Educ:* St Benedict's, Ealing; Sant Anselmo, Rome (LCL). Priest, 1955; Second Master, St Benedict's School, 1960–67; Abbot of Ealing, 1967–91; Vicar for Religious, Archdiocese of Westminster, 1969–88; Pres., Conf. of Major Religious Superiors of England and Wales, 1970–74; Pro-Primate, Benedictine Confedn, 1995–96 (Mem., Abbot Primate's Council, 1988–98). Hon. DD St Vincent Coll., Pa, 1988. *Address:* Ealing Abbey, W5 2DY. *T:* (020) 8862 2110.

**ROSSLYN,** 7th Earl of, *cr* 1801; **Peter St Clair-Erskine,** CVO 2014; QPM 2009; Bt 1666; Baron Loughborough, 1795; Master of the Household to the Prince of Wales and the Duchess of Cornwall, since 2014; *b* 31 March 1958; *s* of 6th Earl of Rosslyn, and of Athenais de Mortemart, *o d* of late Duc de Vivonne; *S* father, 1977; *m* 1982, Helen, *e d* of Mr and Mrs C. R. Watters, Christ's Hospital, Sussex; two *s* two *d. Educ:* Eton; Bristol Univ. (BA); Univ. of Cambridge (MSt). Metropolitan Police, 1980–94; Thames Valley Police, 1994–2000; a Comdr, Metropolitan Police, 2000–; Comdr, Royalty and Diplomatic Protection Dept, 2003–14. Elected Mem., H of L, 1999. Mem., Queen's Body Guard for Scotland, Royal Company of Archers, 2005–. Dir, A. G. Carrick, 2014–. Trustee, Dunimarle Museum. Commandeur, Légion d'Honneur (France), 2014. *Heir:* s Lord Loughborough, *qv. Address:* House of Lords, SW1A 0PW. *Club:* White's.

**ROSSMORE,** 7th Baron *cr* 1796; **William Warner Westenra;** *b* 14 Feb. 1931; *o s* of 6th Baron Rossmore and Dolores Cecil (*d* 1981), *d* of late Lieut-Col James Alban Wilson, DSO, West Burton, Yorks; *S* father, 1958; *m* 1982, Valerie Marion, *d* of Brian Tobin; one *s. Educ:* Eton; Trinity Coll., Cambridge (BA). 2nd Lieut, Somerset LI. Co-founder, Coolemine Therapeutic Community, Dublin, 1973. *Recreations:* drawing, painting. *Heir:* s Hon. Benedict William Westenra, *b* 6 March 1983.

**ROSSOR, Prof. Martin Neil,** MD, FRCP, FMedSci; Professor of Neurology, 1998–2015, now Professor Emeritus and Principal Research Associate, and Chairman, Division of Neurology, 2002–12, Institute of Neurology, University College London; Hon. Consultant Neurologist: St Mary's Hospital, London, 1986–2010; National Hospital for Neurology and Neurosurgery, since 1998; *b* 24 April 1950; *s* of late Bruce Rossor and Eileen Rossor; *m* 1973, Eve Lipstein; two *s* one *d. Educ:* Watford Boys' Grammar Sch.; Jesus Coll., Cambridge (MA, MD); King's College Hosp. Med. Sch. (MB BChir). FRCP 1990. Clinical Scientist, MRC Neurochemical Pharmacology Unit, 1978–82; Registrar, 1982–83, Sen. Registrar, 1983–86, Nat. Hosp. for Nervous Diseases and King's Coll. Hosp.; Clinical Dir, Medical Specialities, St Mary's Hosp., 1989–92; Sen. Lectr, Inst. of Neurology, 1992–98; Clin. Dir for Neurology, Nat. Hosp. for Neurology and Neurosurgery, 1994–98; NIHR Nat. Dir for Dementia Res., 2014–. Director: NIHR Clin. Res. Network for Dementia and Neurodegenerative Diseases, 2005–14; NIHR Queen Sq. Dementia Biomedical Res. Unit, 2012–16. Pres., Assoc. of British Neurologists, 2011–13. FMedSci 2002. FRSA. Liveryman, Soc. of Apothecaries, 1978– (Mem., Ct of Assistants, 1999–; Master, 2018–19). Ed., Jl of Neurology, Neurosurgery and Psychiatry, 2004–09. *Publications:* Unusual Dementias, 1992; (with J. Growdon) Dementia, 1998, 2nd edn 2007; (with C. Clarke, R. Howard and S. Shorvon) Neurology: a Queen Square textbook, 2009; papers on Alzheimer's disease and related dementias. *Recreations:* English literature, equestrian sports, sailing. *Address:* The National Hospital for Neurology and Neurosurgery, Queen Square, WC1N 3BG. *T:* (020) 3448 4773. *Club:* Athenæum.

**ROSSWALL, Prof. Thomas;** Professor, Swedish University of Agricultural Sciences, 2000–09, now Emeritus; Chairman: Mistra Urban Futures, 2014–17; Mistra Centre on Evidence-based Environmental Management, 2011–15; Sida, Science Advisory Council, 2016–19; *b* 20 Dec. 1941; *s* of Axel Rosswald and Britta (*née* Lindroth). *Educ:* Univ. of Uppsala (BSc 1966). Asst, Dept of Biochemistry, Univ. of Uppsala, 1967–70; Res. Asst, Dept of Microbiol., Swedish Univ. of Agricl Scis, 1970–76; Programme Officer, Swedish Council for Planning and Co-ordination of Research, 1976–80; Researcher, 1980–82, Asst Prof., 1982–84, Associate Prof., 1984, Dept of Microbiol., Swedish Univ. of Agricl Research; Prof., Dept of Water and Envmtl Studies, Univ. of Linköping, 1984–92; Exec. Dir, Internat. Geosphere-Biosphere Prog., 1987–94; Rector, Swedish Univ. of Agricl Scis, 1994–2000. Prof., Stockholm Univ., 1992–2000; Dir, Internat. Secretariat, System for Analysis, Res. and Trng, Washington, 1992–93; Dir, Internat. Foundn for Science, Stockholm, 2000–01; Exec. Dir, Internat. Council for Sci., 2002–09. Chm., Remote Sensing Cttee, Nat. Swedish Space Bd, 2015–16. Chair, Consultative Gp on Internat. Agricultural Res., Res. (formerly Challenge) Prog. on Climate Change, Agriculture and Food Security, 2009–14. MAE 1989; Fellow: Royal Swedish Acad. of Scis, 1989; Royal Swedish Acad. of Agric. and Forestry, 1995; Royal Acad. of Arts and Scis of Uppsala, 1999; World Acad. of Arts and Scis, 2005; Fellow, World Acad. of Scis (formerly Third World Acad. of Sci., then Acad. of Scis for the Developing World), 2015 (Associate Fellow, 2002). *Publications:* edited: Systems Analysis in Northern Coniferous Forests, 1971; (jtly) IBP Tundra Biome Procs 4th International Meeting on Biological Productivity of Tundra, 1971; Modern Methods in the Study of Microbial Ecology, 1973; (jtly) Structure and Function of Tundra Ecosystems, 1975; Nitrogen Cycling in West African Ecosystems, 1980; (jtly) Terrestrial Nitrogen Cycles: processes, ecosystems strategies and management impacts, 1981; (jtly) Nitrogen Cycling in South-East Asian Wet Monsoonal Ecosystems, 1981; (jtly) The Nitrogen Cycle, 1982; (jtly) Nitrogen Cycling in Ecosystems of Latin America and the Caribbean, 1982; (jtly) Scales and Global Change: spatial and temporal variability of biospheric and geospheric processes, 1988; (jtly) Ecology of Arable Land: the role of organism in carbon and nitrogen cycling, 1989; 100 papers in scientific jls. *Address:* Bellmansgatan 5, 11820 Stockholm, Sweden. *T:* 760191678. *E:* thomas.rosswall@gmail.com.

**ROST, Peter Lewis;** energy consultant, retired; *b* 19 Sept. 1930; *s* of Frederick Rosenstiel and Elisabeth Merz; *m* 1961, Hilary Mayo; two *s* two *d. Educ:* various primary schs; Aylesbury Grammar Sch. National Service, RAF, 1948–50; Birmingham Univ. (BA Hons Geog.), 1950–53. Investment Analyst and Financial Journalist with Investors Chronicle, 1953–58; firstly Investment Advisor, 1958, and then, 1962, Mem. London Stock Exchange, resigned 1977. MP (C) Derbys SE, 1970–83, Erewash, 1983–92. Secretary: Cons. Parly Trade and Industry Cttee, 1972–73; Cons. Parly Energy Cttee, 1974–77; Select Cttee on Energy, 1979–92. Treasurer, Anglo-German Parly Gp, 1974–92; Jt Chm., Alternative and Complementary Medicine Parly Gp, 1989–92. Chairman: Major Energy Users' Council, 1992–95; Utility Buyers' Forum, 1995–98; Vice-Pres., Combined Heat and Power Assoc. (Hon. Life Mem.). FRGS (Mem. Council, 1980–83); Fellow, Industry and Parlt Trust, 1987; Companion, Inst. of Energy, 1992. Freeman, City of London. Grand Cross, Order of Merit, Germany, 1979. *Publications:* Weimar to Westminster (autobiog.), 2010; papers on Recent Events. *Recreations:* tennis, ski-ing, gardening, antique map collecting. *Address:* Norcott Court, Berkhamsted, Herts HP4 1LE. *T:* (01442) 866123, 07818 007236, *Fax:* (01442) 865901; 629 Chemin de la Gipiere, 83440 Montauroux, Var, France. *T:* 494477067.

**ROSTRON, Martin Keith;** Principal, Greenhead College, Huddersfield, 2002–13; educational adviser, Alkemygold Ltd (Alps), 2013–18; *b* 10 Sept. 1953; *s* of Harold and Lucy Rostron; *m* 1976, Linda Potts; two *s* one *d. Educ:* Liverpool Univ. (BA Hons English 1974; PGCE 1977). Teacher: Knutsford High Sch., 1977–84; Priestley Coll., Warrington, 1984–91; Vice Principal, Greenhead Coll. (Sixth Form Coll.), 1991–2002. FRSA 2005. *Recreations:* walking, reading, cookery, classical music, watching sport, travel, visits to children and grandchildren overseas.

**ROTH, Prof. Alvin Elliot,** PhD; Craig and Susan McCaw Professor of Economics, Stanford University, since 2013 (McCaw Senior Visiting Professor of Economics, 2012); *b* New York, 18 Dec. 1951; *s* of Ernest and Lillian Roth; *m* 1977, Emilie; two *s. Educ:* Columbia Univ. (BS Ops Res. 1971); Stanford Univ. (MS Ops Res. 1973; PhD Ops Res. 1974). University of Illinois at Urbana-Champaign: Asst Prof., 1974–77, Associate Prof., 1977–79, Prof., 1979–82, Dept of Business Admin and Dept of Econs; Beckman Associate, Center for Advanced Study, 1981–82; University of Pittsburgh: A. W. Mellon Prof. of Econs, 1982–98; Fellow, Center for Philosophy of Sci., 1983–98; Prof. of Business Admin, Grad. Sch. of Business, 1985–98; George Gund Prof. of Econs and Business Admin, Harvard Univ., 1998–2012, now Emeritus. Pres., Econ. Sci. Assoc., 2011–13; Mem. Council, Econometric Soc., 2003–05, 2007–09, 2013–15. Fellow: Econometric Soc., 1983; Amer. Acad. Arts and Scis, 1998; FAAAS 2012; Econ. Theory Fellow, Soc. for Advancement of Econ. Theory, 2013; Charter Fellow, Soc. for Econ. Measurement, 2014. Mem., NAS, 2013. (Jtly) Nobel Prize in Econs, 2012; (jtly) Golden Goose Award, USA, 2013. Dr *hc:* Technion-Israel Inst. Technol., 2013; Amsterdam, 2014; Hon. DHL Pittsburgh, 2014; Hon. Dr Econs and Mgt Lund, 2014. *Publications:* Axiomatic Models of Bargaining, 1979; (ed) Game-Theoretic Models of Bargaining, 1985; (ed) Laboratory Experimentation in Economics: six points view, 1987; (ed) The Shapley Value: essays in honor of Lloyd S. Shapley, 1988; (with M. Sotomayor) Two-sided Matching: a study in game-theoretic modeling and analysis, 1990 (Frederick W. Lanchester Prize, Ops Res. Soc. of America); (ed with J. Kagel) Handbook of Experimental Economics, 1997; (ed jtly) Game Theory in the Tradition of Bob Wilson, 2002; Who Gets What—And Why: the new economics of matchmaking and market design, 2015; contribs to learned jls incl. Jl Political Econ., Maths Ops Res., Econ. Theory, Amer. Econ. Rev., Games, Amer. Jl Transplantation. *Address:* Department of Economics, Landau Economics Building, 579 Serra Hall, Stanford University, Stanford, CA 94305-6072, USA.

**ROTH, Hon. Sir Peter Marcel,** Kt 2009; **Hon. Mr Justice Roth;** a Judge of the High Court of Justice, Chancery Division, since 2009; President, Competition Appeal Tribunal, since 2013; *b* 19 Dec. 1952; *s* of Stephen Jeffery Roth and Eva Marta Roth; *m* 2010, Tessa Margaret Fras; one *d,* and one step *s* one step *d. Educ:* St Paul's Sch.; New Coll., Oxford (Open Schol.; BA 1974; MA 1986); Law Sch., Univ. of Pennsylvania (Thouron Fellow; LLM 1977). Called to the Bar, Middle Temple, 1977 (Harmsworth Schol.), Bencher, 2008; in practice at the Bar, 1979–2009; QC 1997; Recorder, 2000–09; Deputy High Court Judge, 2008–09. Vis. Associate Prof., Law Sch., Univ. of Pennsylvania, 1987; Vis. Prof., KCL, 2003–09. Chm., Tribunal Procedure Cttee, 2016–. Mem., Incorporated Council of Law Reporting, 2010–. Jt Chair, Bench and Bar Cttee, United Jewish Israel Appeal, 1997–2003. Chair, Competition Law Assoc., 2003–09. Chairman: Lawyers' Adv. Cttee, Peace Brigades Internat. UK, 2007–18; Exec. Cttee, Alliance for Lawyers at Risk, 2018–. Trustee: British Inst. of Internat. and Comparative Law, 2006–09; New Coll. Develt Fund, 2014–16. Chair, Insurance Wkg Party, Terrence Higgins Trust, 1989–94. Gov., Tel Aviv Univ., 2006–09. *Publications:* (Gen. Ed.) Bellamy & Child's European Community Law of Competition, 5th edn 2001, 6th edn 2008; articles in legal jls. *Recreations:* travel, music. *Address:* Competition Appeal Tribunal, Victoria House, Bloomsbury Place, WC1A 2EB.

**ROTHERAM, Steven Philip;** Mayor of Liverpool City Region (Lab), since 2017; *b* 4 Nov. 1961; *s* of Harry and Dorothy Rotheram; *m* 1989, Sandra; one *s* two *d. Educ:* Ruffwood Comprehensive Sch.; Kirkby Further Educn Coll.; Liverpool John Moores Univ. (MA Urban Renaissance). Work in construction sector, 1978–89; instructor, 1989–2001; Director: SIP Property Develt LLP, 2006–; SPR Consultants. Dir, Liverpool Inst. for Performing Arts, 2004–10. Mem. (Lab) Liverpool CC, 2002–11 (Lord Mayor, 2008). MP (Lab) Liverpool Walton, 2010–17.

**ROTHERMERE,** 4th Viscount *cr* 1919, of Hemsted, co. Kent; **Jonathan Harold Esmond Vere Harmsworth;** Bt 1910; Baron 1914; Chairman, Daily Mail and General Trust plc, since 1998; *b* 3 Dec. 1967; *s* of 3rd Viscount Rothermere and his 1st wife, Patricia Evelyn Beverley (*née* Matthews; *d* 1992); *S* father, 1998; *m* 1993, Claudia, *d* of T. J. Clemence; two *s* three *d. Heir: s* Hon. Vere Richard Jonathan Harold Harmsworth, *b* 20 Oct. 1994. *Address:* (office) Northcliffe House, 2 Derry Street, W8 5TT.

**ROTHERWICK,** 3rd Baron *cr* 1939, of Tylney, Southampton; **Herbert Robin Cayzer;** 6th Bt *cr* 1904, of Gartmore and 3rd Bt *cr* 1924, of Tylney; *b* 12 March 1954; *s* of 2nd Baron Rotherwick and Sarah-Jane (*d* 1978), *o d* of Sir Michael Nial Slade, 6th Bt; *S* father, 1996; *S* kinsman, Sir James Cayzer, 5th Bt, 2012; *m* 1st, 1982, Sara Jane (marr. diss. 1994), *o d* of Robert James McAlpine; two *s* one *d*; 2nd, 2000, Tania, *d* of Christopher Fox; one *s* one *d* (and one *s* decd). *Educ:* Harrow; RAC, Cirencester. Lieut, Life Guards. Elected Mem., H of L, 1999; Opposition Whip, H of L, 2001–05; Opposition spokesperson for Educn and Skills, Work and Pensions, 2001–03, for DEFRA, 2003–05. Mem., Council of Europe, 2000–01. Fellow, Industry and Parlt Trust, 2005. Mem., Armed Forces Parly Scheme, 2010–12. Pres., Gen. Aviation Awareness Council, 1997–. Director: PFA (Ulair) Ltd, 1999–2003; Cayzer Continuation PCC Ltd, 2004–; Cornbury Estates Co. Ltd, 2006–; Light Aircraft Assoc. Ltd, 2008–16; Cornbury Maintenance Co. Ltd, 2012–; Bygone Engrg Ltd, 2013–14; Spring Housing Co. Ltd, 2014–; Wild Cat WP Ltd, 2016–. Chm., Air Touring Ltd, 2006–10. Hon. Gp Capt., RAF 601 Sqn, 2017–. *Heir: s* Hon. Herbert Robin Cayzer [*b* 10 July 1989; *m* 2015, Allison Boynton; one *s*]. *Address:* The Estate Office, Ranger's Lodge, Cornbury Park, Charlbury, Oxford OX7 3HL.

**ROTHES,** 22nd Earl of, *cr* before 1457; **James Malcolm David Leslie;** Lord Leslie 1445; Baron Ballenbreich 1457; *b* 4 June 1958; *s* of 21st Earl of Rothes and of Marigold, *o d* of Sir David Evans Bevan, 1st Bt; *S* father, 2005. *Educ:* Eton. Graduated Parnham House, 1990. *Heir: b* Hon. Alexander John Leslie [*b* 18 Feb. 1962; *m* 1st, 1990, Tina Gordon (marr. diss.); 2nd, 2008, Mrs Francesca Clare MacManaway (marr. diss.); 3rd, 2014, Miranda Grant]. *Address:* Little Croft, West Milton, Bridport, Dorset DT6 3SL.

**ROTHMAN, Prof. James Edward,** PhD; Professor of Chemistry, Chairman, Department of Cell Biology and Founding Director, Nanobiology Institute, since 2011, and Sterling Professor of Cell Biology, since 2017, Yale University; Professorial Research Associate, Institute of Neurology, University College London; b Haverhill, Mass, 3 Nov. 1950; s of late Martin Rothman and of Gloria Rothman (née Hartnick); one s one d; m Prof. Joy Hirsch. Educ: Yale Univ. (BA Physics 1971); Harvard Univ. Med. Sch. (PhD Biol Chem. 1976). Damon Runyan Postdoctoral Fellow, Dept of Biol., MIT, 1976–78; Asst Prof., 1978–81, Associate Prof., 1981–84, Prof., 1984–88, Dept of Biochem., Stanford Univ.; Squibb Prof. of Molecular Biol., Princeton Univ., 1988–91; Paul Marks Prof. and Founder and Chm., Dept of Cellular Biochem. and Biophysics, and Vice-Chm., Meml Sloan-Kettering Cancer Center, 1991–2004; Prof., Dept of Physiol. and Cellular Biophysics, and Clyde and Helen Wu Prof. of Chem. Biol. and Dir, Sulzberger Genome Center, Columbia Univ. Coll. of Physicians and Surgeons, 2004–08; Wallace Prof. of Biomed. Scis, Yale Univ., 2008–17. Member: NAS, 1993; Inst. of Medicine, NAS, 1995. Foreign Mem., Royal Soc., 2019. For. Associate, EMBO, 1995. Fellow, Amer. Acad. Arts and Scis, 1994; FAAAS 2007. Hon. Dr: Regensburg, 1995; Geneva, 1997. Eli Lilly Award for Fundamental Res. in Biol Chem., USA, 1986; Alexander von Humboldt Award, Germany, 1989; Rosentiel Award in Biomed. Scis, USA, 1994; King Faisal Internat. Prize in Sci., Saudi Arabia, 1996; Gairdner Foundn Internat. Award, Canada, 1996; Lounsbery Award, NAS, 1997; Harden Medal, British Biochem. Soc., 1997; Heineken Prize for Biochem., Netherlands, 2000; Otto-Warburg Medal, German Biochem. Soc., 2001; Lasker Award for Basic Med. Res., USA, 2002; E. B. Wilson Medal, Amer. Soc. for Cell Biol., 2010; Kavli Prize for Neurosci., Kavli Foundn, 2010; (jtly) Nobel Prize in Physiol. or Medicine, 2013. Publications: contribs to scientific jls. Address: Rothman Laboratory, Sterling Hall of Medicine, Yale School of Medicine, PO Box 208002, New Harvey, CT 06520–8002, USA.

**ROTHNIE, Iain Andrew;** Partner, Real Estate, Herbert Smith LLP, international law firm, 2008–11; b 14 Nov. 1955; s of late Norman George Rothnie and Margaret Venables Rothnie; m 2003, Julie Fewtrell. Educ: Reading Sch.; Pembroke Coll., Cambridge (BA 1978); Univ. of Westminster (BA Photography 2018). Admitted solicitor, 1981; Herbert Smith: Partner, 1988–2011; Hd, Real Estate, 2000–02; Exec. Partner, subseq. Chief Operating Officer, 2002–06; Global Hd, Real Estate, 2006–08. Recreations: travel, art, theatre, photography.

**ROTHSCHILD,** family name of **Baron Rothschild**.

**ROTHSCHILD, 4th Baron** cr 1885; **Nathaniel Charles Jacob Rothschild,** Bt 1847; OM 2002; GBE 1998; President, RIT Capital Partners plc, since 2019 (Chairman, 1988–2019); President, Five Arrows Ltd, since 2010 (Chairman, 1980–2010); b 29 April 1936; e s of 3rd Baron Rothschild, GBE, GM, FRS and Barbara, o d of St John Hutchinson, KC; S father, 1990; m 1961, Serena Mary (d 2019), er d of late Sir Philip Gordon Dunn, 2nd Bt; one s three d. Educ: Eton; Christ Church, Oxford (BA 1st cl. hons History; Hon. Student, 2006). Chairman: Bd of Trustees, Nat. Gallery, 1985–91; Nat. Heritage Meml Fund, 1992–98, administering Heritage Lottery Fund, 1995–98. Dep. Chm., BSkyB Gp plc, 2003–08. Fellow, Ashmolean Mus., Oxford, 2006; Hon. Fellow, Courtauld Inst. of Art, 2008; Hon. FKC 2002; Hon. FBA 1998; Hon. FRIBA 1998; Hon. FRAM 2002. Hon. PhD Hebrew Univ. of Jerusalem, 1992; Hon. DLitt: Newcastle, 1998; Warwick 2003; Hon. LLD Exeter, 1998; DUniv Keele, 2000; Hon. DCL Oxon, 2002; Hon. DSc (Econs) London, 2004. Hon. Fellow, City of Jerusalem, 1992. Weizmann Award for Humanities and Scis, 1997; J. Paul Getty Medal, 2014. Comdr, Order of Henry the Navigator (Portugal), 1985. Heir: s Hon. Nathaniel Philip Victor James Rothschild, qv. Address: The Pavilion, Eythrope, Aylesbury, Bucks HP18 0HS. T: (01296) 748337.
See also E. Rothschild, Hon. H. M. Rothschild.

**ROTHSCHILD, Emma,** CMG 2000; Knowles Professor of History, since 2008, and Affiliated Professor, Harvard Law School, since 2013, Harvard University (Professor of History, 2007–08); Co-Director, Joint Centre for History and Economics, Magdalene College and King's College (formerly at King's College), Cambridge, since 1991, and Harvard University, since 2007; Fellow, Magdalene College, Cambridge, since 2010; b 16 May 1948; d of 3rd Baron Rothschild, GBE, GM, FRS and Lady Rothschild, MBE (née Teresa Mayor); m 1991, Prof. Amartya Kumar Sen, qv. Educ: Somerville Coll., Oxford (MA; Hon. Fellow, 2012); Massachusetts Inst. of Technology (Kennedy Schol. in Econs). Associate Professor: of Humanities, MIT, 1978–80; of Science, Technology and Society, MIT, 1979–88; Dir de Recherches Invité, Ecole des Hautes Etudes en Sciences Sociales, Paris, 1981–82. Fellow, King's College, Cambridge, 1988–2010; Hon. Prof. of Hist. and Econs, Univ. of Cambridge, 2010–. Mem., OECD Gp of Experts on Science and Technology in the New Socio-Economic Context, 1976–80; OECD Sci. Examiner, Aust., 1984–85. Member: Govg Bd, Stockholm Internat. Peace Res. Inst., 1983–93; Govg Bd, Stockholm Envmt Inst., 1989–93; Bd, Olof Palme Meml Fund (Stockholm), 1986–2007; Royal Commn on Environmental Pollution, 1986–94; Bd, British Council, 1993–98; Bd, UN Foundn, 1998–; Council for Sci. and Technol., 1998–2001; Chairman: UN Res. Inst. for Social Develt, 1999–2005; Kennedy Meml Trust, 2000–09. Internat. Mem. (formerly Foreign Mem.), Amer. Philosophical Soc., 2002. Hon. DLitt: Edinburgh, 2013; St Andrews, 2016. Publications: Paradise Lost: the Decline of the Auto-Industrial Age, 1973; Economic Sentiments, 2001; The Inner Life of Empires: an eighteenth-century history, 2011; articles in learned and other jls. Address: Department of History, Harvard University, 1730 Cambridge Street, Cambridge, MA 02138, USA.

**ROTHSCHILD, Baron Eric Alain Robert David de;** Chairman, Rothschild Bank AG, since 2000; Partner, Rothschild et Compagnie Banque, since 1982; b NY, 3 Oct. 1940; French nationality; m 1983, Maria Béatrice Caracciolo di Forino; two s one d. Educ: Ecole Polytechnique Fédérale, Zürich (Engr 1963). Chairman: Paris Orléans, 1974; Soc. du Château Rieussec, 1999; Managing Partner: Soc. Civile de Château Lafite Rothschild, 1974; Soc. Civile de Duhart Milon Rothschild, 1975; Partner, Rothschild et Cie Gestion, 1998; Board Member: Los Vascos, 1993; Christie's France, 1994. Chairman: Fondation de Rothschild, 1982; Mémorial du Martyr Juif Inconnu, 1984; Fondation Casip-Cojasor, 1989; Fondation Rothschild, 1993; Rothschild Private Mgt Ltd, 2003; Vice Chm., Fondation pour la Mémoire de la Shoah, 2001; Bd Mem., Alliance Israélite Universelle, 1994. Address: (office) 3 rue de Messine, 75008 Paris, France. T: (1) 40744006, Fax: (1) 40749816.

**ROTHSCHILD, Sir Evelyn de,** Kt 1989; Chairman, E. L. Rothschild Ltd; b 29 Aug. 1931; s of late Anthony Gustav de Rothschild; m 1973, Victoria Schott (marr. diss. 2000); two s one d; m 2000, Lynn Forester. Educ: Harrow; Trinity Coll., Cambridge. Chm., N. M. Rothschild and Sons Ltd, 1976–2003. Chairman: Economist Newspaper, 1972–89; St Mary's Hosp. Med. Sch., London, 1977–88; United Racecourses Ltd, 1977–94; former Chm., Concordia BV. Chm., British Merchant Banking and Securities Houses Assoc. (formerly Accepting Houses Cttee), 1985–89. Gov., LSE, 1968–. Chairman: ERANDA Foundn, 1967–; Cambridge Business Sch. Appeal; Hon. Life Pres., Norwood and Ravenswood Children's Charity. Recreations: art, racing.

**ROTHSCHILD, Hon. Hannah Mary,** CBE 2018; author; b London, 22 May 1962; d of 4th Baron Rothschild, qv; three d. Educ: St Paul's Girls' Sch.; Marlborough Coll.; St Hilda's Coll., Oxford (BA Mod. Hist.). Writer, filmmaker and freelance journalist; profiles and interviews for Vanity Fair, Vogue, House & Gardens, W mag., Independent, The Times, 1985–; Sen. Editor, Harpers Bazaar, 2012–. Television includes: Keeping up with the Medici (dir and writer), 1998; The Jazz Baroness (dir and writer), 2009; Hi Society: The Wonderful World of Nicky Haslam (dir, prod. and writer), 2009; Mandelson - The Real PM? (dir and prod.), 2010; film: Eddie Loves Mary (dir and writer), 2002. Non-executive Board Member: RIT Capital Partners; Windmill Hill Asset. Vice Pres., Hay Literary Fest., 2000–; Trustee: Rothschild Foundn, 2008–; Nat. Gall., 2009–19 (Chm. Trustees, 2015–19); Waddesdon Manor, 2010–; Tate Gall., 2013–17; Illuminated River Foundn (Chair, 2016–17). Co-founder, Artist on Film Trust. Publications: The Baroness: the search for Nica, the rebellious Rothschild, 2012; The Improbability of Love (novel), 2015. Recreations: art, film, books, charity. E: h.rothschild@jrsl.co.uk.
See also Hon. N. P. V. J. Rothschild.

**ROTHSCHILD, Hon. Nathaniel Philip Victor James;** Chairman, JNR Ltd, since 2002; Executive Chairman, Volex plc, since 2015; b London, 12 July 1971; o s and heir of 4th Baron Rothschild, qv; m 2016, Loretta Basey. Educ: Eton Coll.; Wadham Coll., Oxford (BA Hist.; Foundn Fellow, 2018); King's Coll. London (MSc). Co-Chm., Atticus Capital LP, 1996–2009; Founder, Co-Chm. and non-exec. Dir, Vallar plc, later Bumi plc, 2009–12; Director: RIT Capital Partners plc, 2002–10; Rothschild Foundn. Non-executive Director: Barrick Gold Corp., 2010–13; Genel Energy, 2011–17. Mem., Internat. Adv. Council, Brookings Inst. Mem., Belfer Center for Sci. and Internat. Affairs, Harvard Univ. Recreations: ski-ing, horseracing. Address: Riedweg 11A, Klosters 7250, Switzerland. Club: White's.

**ROTHSCHILD AGIUS, Kate Juliette de;** Trustee, Wallace Collection, since 2013; b London, 11 July 1949; d of late Edmund Leopold de Rothschild, CBE, TD and Elizabeth Edith de Rothschild; m 1971, Marcus Ambrose Paul Agius, qv; two d. Educ: Courtauld Inst. of Art, Univ. of London (BA Hons 1971). Curatorial asst, Fogg Art Mus., Cambridge, Mass, 1971–72; intern, Sotheby's, London, 1972–74; dealer (sole trader) in master drawings, 1974–2007; Chm., Patrons of BM, 2008–13. Member, vetting committees: Grosvenor Hse Antiques Fair, London, 1990–; Fine Art and Antique Dealers Fair, NY, 1996–. Dir, Exbury Gardens, 2016–. Recreations: visiting museums and galleries, visiting gardens, looking after Exbury Gardens, travel, being with my family. Address: 25 Chelsea Square, SW3 6LF. T: (020) 7351 7868, Fax: (020) 7351 7475. E: kate@katederothschild.co.uk.

**ROTHWELL, Margaret Irene,** CMG 1992; HM Diplomatic Service, retired; Ambassador to Côte d'Ivoire, 1990–97, and concurrently to the Republic of Niger, the People's Democratic Republic of Burkina and Liberia; b 25 Aug. 1938; d of Harry Rothwell and Martha (née Goedecke). Educ: Southampton Grammar School for Girls; Lady Margaret Hall, Oxford (BA LitHum). Foreign Office, 1961; Third, later Second Secretary, UK Delegn to Council of Europe, Strasbourg, 1964; FO, 1966; Second Sec. (Private Sec. to Special Representative in Africa), Nairobi, 1967; Second, later First Sec., Washington, 1968; FCO, 1972; First Sec. and Head of Chancery, Helsinki, 1976; FCO, 1980; Counsellor and Hd of Trng Dept, FCO, 1981–83; Counsellor, Consul-Gen. and Head of Chancery, Jakarta, 1984–87; Overseas Inspectorate, FCO, 1987–90. Reviewer, Quinquennial Review of the Marshall Aid Commemoration Commn, 1998; UK Rep., Jt US/UK Commn on Student Travel Exchanges, 1998; voluntary work for Govt of Rwanda, 2001. Mem. Cttee, Password, 2007–. Lay Rep., Council of Inns of Court, 2004–12. Trustee, Pimpernel Trust, 2007–16. Hon. LLD Southampton, 1994. Recreations: travel, gardening, cooking, tennis. Address: Hill House, Knapp, Ampfield, Romsey, Hants SO51 9BT.

**ROTHWELL, Dame Nancy (Jane),** DBE 2005; DL; PhD, DSc; FMedSci; FRS 2004; FRSB; Professor of Physiology, since 1994, and President and Vice-Chancellor, since 2010, University of Manchester (Vice President for Research, 2004–07; Deputy President and Deputy Vice-Chancellor, 2007–10). Educ: Univ. of London (BSc, PhD, DSc). Royal Soc. Res. Fellow, 1987, then Reader in Physiol Scis, and formerly Res. and Graduate Dean for Biol Scis, Univ. of Manchester. Chm., MRC Neurosci. and Mental Health Bd, 2002–04; Member, Council: MRC, 2000–04; BBSRC, 2005–08; Cancer Res. UK, 2002–08; NESTA, 2002–06; Council for Sci. and Technol., 2011– (Co-Chm., 2012–); Industrial Strategy Council, 2018–; Member: Bd, Greater Manchester LEP, 2011–; Bd, Northern Powerhouse Partnership, 2016–; Chair, Oxford Road Corridor Bd, 2015–. Chm., Wellcome Trust Public Engagement Strategy Gp, 2005–08. President: British Neurosci. Assoc., 2000–03; Soc. of Biology (formerly Bioscis Fedn), 2008–14; British Sci. Assoc., 2016–17. Mem. Council, Royal Soc., 2013–16; Mem. Bd, UK Dementia Res. Inst. Royal Instn Christmas Lectures, 1998. FMedSci 1999; Hon. FRCP 2006; FRSA. DL Gtr Manchester, 2010. Publications: over 300 research papers and several books. Address: Office of the President and Vice-Chancellor, University of Manchester, Oxford Road, Manchester M13 9PL.

**ROUCH, Ven. Peter Bradford;** Archdeacon of Bournemouth, since 2011; b Rochester, 22 April 1966; s of Victor Maurice Rouch and Esmée Edith May Rouch; m 1994, Tracey Michelle Hemmerdinger; two d. Educ: Sir Joseph Williamson's Math. Sch., Rochester; Brasenose Coll., Oxford (BA Hons Zool. 1987); Peterhouse, Cambridge (MA 1998); Univ. of Manchester (PhD 2005). Ordained deacon, 1999, priest, 2000; Asst Curate, St John the Evangelist, East Dulwich, 1999–2002; Junior Res. Fellow, St Stephen's House, Oxford, 2002–04; Chaplain, St John's Coll., Oxford, 2003–04; Priest-in-charge, Church of the Apostles', Manchester, with St Cuthbert, Miles Platting, 2005–11. Address: Glebe House, 22 Bellflower Way, Chandlers Ford, Hants SO53 4HN. T: (023) 8026 0955. E: peter.rouch@winchester.anglican.org.

**ROUCH, Peter Christopher;** QC 1996; b 15 June 1947; s of Rupert Trevelyan Rouch and Doris Linda Rouch; m 1980, Carol Sandra Francis; one s one d. Educ: UCW, Aberystwyth (LLB). Called to the Bar, Gray's Inn, 1972. Recreations: golf, ski-ing, fishing, cinema, music. Address: Church View, 9 Mayals Road, Mayals, Swansea SA3 5BT; 20 Archery Close, W2 2BE.

**ROUGIER, Maj.-Gen. Charles Jeremy,** CB 1986; FICE; Director, Royal Horticultural Society's Garden, Rosemoor, 1988–95; b 23 Feb. 1933; s of late Lt-Col and Mrs C. L. Rougier; m 1964, Judith Cawood Ellis (d 2013); three s one d. Educ: Marlborough Coll.; Pembroke Coll., Cambridge (MA). FICE 1986. Aden, 1960; Instructor, RMA Sandhurst, 1961–62; psc 1963; MA to MGO, 1964–66; comd 11 Engineer Sqn, Commonwealth Bde, 1966–68; jssc 1968; Company Comd, RMA Sandhurst, 1969–70; Directing Staff, Staff Coll., Camberley 1970–72; CO 21 Engineer Regt, BAOR, 1972–74; Staff of Chief of Defence Staff, 1974–77; Commandant, Royal Sch. of Military Engineering, 1977–79; RCDS 1980; COS, Headquarters Northern Ireland, 1981; Asst Chief of General Staff (Trng), 1982–83; Dir of Army Training, 1983–84; Chm., Review of Officer Training and Educn Study, 1985; Engr-in-Chief (Army), 1985–88, retd. Col Comdt, RE, 1987–92. Mem. (part-time), Lord Chancellor's Panel of Ind. Inspectors, 1988–2003. Gold Veitch Meml Medal, RHS, 1995. Recreations: mainly gardening, nowadays rather less hill walking and DIY! Address: c/o Lloyds Bank plc, PO Box 99 BX1 1LT.

**ROULSTONE, Brig. Joan Margaret;** Director, Women (Army), 1992–94; Aide-de-Camp to the Queen, 1992–95; *b* 7 Nov. 1945; *d* of Eric Laurie Frank Tyler and Jessie Tyler (*née* Louise); *m* 1971, Peter John Roulstone. *Educ*: seven schools worldwide. Commnd, WRAC, 1964; UK and BAOR, 1965–78; resigned 1978, reinstated, 1980; UK, 1980–86; Corps Recruiting and Liaison Officer, WRAC, 1986–87; Chief G1/G4 NE Dist and 2nd Inf. Div., 1988–89; Comd WRAC, UKLF, 1990–92. *Address*: c/o Barclays Bank, Priestpopple, Hexham, Northumberland NE46 1PE.

**ROUND, Prof. Nicholas Grenville,** FBA 1996; Hughes Professor of Hispanic Studies, University of Sheffield, 1994–2003, now Emeritus; *b* 6 June 1938; *s* of Isaac Eric Round and Laura Christabel (*née* Poole); *m* 1966, Ann Le Vin; one *d. Educ*: Boyton CP Sch., Cornwall; Launceston Coll.; Pembroke Coll., Oxford. BA (1st cl. Hons, Spanish and French) 1959; MA 1963; DPhil 1967. MITI 1990. Lecturer in Spanish, Queen's Univ. of Belfast, 1962–71, Reader, 1971–72; Warden, Alanbrooke Hall, QUB, 1970–72; Stevenson Prof. of Hispanic Studies, Glasgow Univ., 1972–94. Mem., Exec. Cttee, Strathclyde Region Labour Party, 1986–94; Chm., Cornwall Labour Party, 2007–10. Trustee, Morrab Library, Penzance, 2011–19. Pres., Assoc. Internat. de Galdosistas, 1999–2001. Officer, Order of Isabel the Catholic (Spain), 1990. *Publications*: Unamuno: Abel Sánchez: a critical guide, 1974; The Greatest Man Uncrowned: a study of the fall of Alvaro de Luna, 1986; trans., Tirso de Molina, Damned for Despair, 1986; (ed) Re-reading Unamuno, 1989; On Reasoning and Realism: three easy pieces, 1991; Libro llamado Fedrón, 1993; (ed) Translation Studies in Hispanic Contexts, 1998; (ed) New Galdós Studies, 2003; Occasion for All (poems), 2018; The Histories (poems), 2018; contribs to: Mod. Lang. Review, Bulletin Hispanic Studies, Proc. Royal Irish Academy, etc. *Recreations*: reading (music, all aspects of Cornwall. *Address*: 10 King's Road, Penzance, Cornwall TR18 4LG. *Club*: (Hon. Life Mem.) Students' Union (Belfast).

**ROUNDHILL, Rt Rev. (Andrew) John;** an Assistant Bishop, Diocese of Brisbane (Bishop of the Southern Region), since 2018; *b* Harrogate, 4 July 1965; *s* of Robert and Patricia Roundhill; *m* 1995, Frances Thompson; one *s* one *d. Educ*: Leeds Grammar Sch.; Corpus Christi Coll., Cambridge (BA Natural Scis 1987; MA); Ripon Coll., Cuddesdon (BTh). Ordained deacon, 1993, priest, 1994; Asst Curate, Dio. Blackburn, 1993–97; Chaplain, Loretto Sch., Musselburgh, 1997–2002; Chaplain, 2002–04, Subdean, 2004–06, St John's Cathedral, Hong Kong; Rector, Aspley Albany Creek, Dio. Brisbane, 2006–12; Dean, St Paul's Cathedral, Bendigo, 2012–18. *Recreations*: running, hill walking, travel. *Address*: St Martin's House, Anglican Church of Southern Queensland, Ann Street, Brisbane, Qld 4000, Australia. *E*: jroundhill@anglicanchurchsq.org.au.

**ROUNDS, Helen;** *see* Edwards, Helen.

**ROUNTREE, His Honour Peter Charles Robert;** a Circuit Judge, 1986–2001; *b* 28 April 1936; *s* of late Francis Robert George Rountree, MBE and Mary Felicity Patricia Rountree, MBE (*née* Wilson); *m* 1st, 1968, Nicola Mary (*née* Norman-Butler) (marr. diss. 1996); one *s*, and one step *d*; 2nd, 2004, Shirley Murray (*née* Arbuthnot); one step *s* one step *d. Educ*: Uppingham School; St John's College, Cambridge (MA). Called to the Bar, Inner Temple, 1961; a Recorder, April–July 1986. *Recreations*: sailing, golf, tennis. *Clubs*: Boodle's, Pratt's, Royal Yacht Squadron; Rye Golf, New Zealand Golf.

**ROUQUIER, Prof. Raphaël Alexis Marcel,** PhD; Professor of Mathematics, University of California, Los Angeles, since 2012; *b* Etampes, France, 9 Dec. 1969; *s* of Pierre Rouquier and Danièle Rouquier (*née* Raynaud); *m* 2003, Dr Meredith Cohen. *Educ*: Lycée Saint-Louis, Paris; Ecole Normale Supérieure, Paris; Université Paris 7 (PhD 1992). Chargé de Recherches, 1992–2002, Dir de Recherches, 2002–05, CNRS; Prof. of Representation Theory, Univ. of Leeds, 2005–06; Waynflete Prof. of Pure Maths, Univ. of Oxford, 2007–12; Fellow of Magdalen Coll., Oxford, 2007–12. *Address*: Department of Mathematics, University of California, Los Angeles, CA 90095–1555, USA.

**ROURKE, Josephine Frances;** Artistic Director, Donmar Warehouse, 2012–19; *b* Salford, Gtr Manchester, 3 Sept. 1976; *d* of Sean Rourke and Vivienne Rourke (*née* Perrin). *Educ*: St Patrick's RC High Sch.; Eccles Coll. of Further Educn; New Hall, Cambridge (BA Hons English 1998). Trainee Resident Asst Dir, Donmar Warehouse, 2000–01; Trainee Associate Dir, Royal Court Theatre, 2002–03; Associate Dir, Sheffield Theatres, 2005–06; Artistic Dir, Bush Theatre, 2007–11. *Productions include*: King John, RSC, 2006; Men Should Weep, NT, 2010; Much Ado About Nothing, Wyndham's, 2011; Donmar Warehouse: The Recruiting Officer, Berenice, The Physicists, 2012; The Weir, Coriolanus, 2013; Privacy, 2014, NY, 2016; City of Angels, 2014; The Vote, Les Liaisons Dangereuses, 2015, NY 2016; Elegy, Saint Joan, 2016; Measure for Measure, 2018; Sweet Charity, 2019; Dir, The Machine, Manchester Internat. Fest., 2013. Dir, film, Mary Queen of Scots, 2019. Non-exec. Mem. Bd, Channel 4, 2012–17. *Recreations*: cooking, walking and reading, rarely at the same time. *Address*: c/o John Buzzetti, WME, 11 Madison Avenue, New York, NY 10010, USA.

**ROUS,** family name of **Earl of Stradbroke.**

**ROUS, Matthew James;** HM Diplomatic Service; Group Chief Executive, China-Britain Business Council, since 2017; *b* 29 June 1964; *s* of late Ronald Frank Rous and of Florence Mary (*née* Woodward); *m* 1989, Beryl Ann Scott; one *s* two *d. Educ*: Burnt Mill Sch., Harlow; Churchill Coll., Cambridge (BA 1986; MA 1989). Chugai Pharmaceutical Co. Ltd, Tokyo, 1986–88; Asahi Shimbun European Gen. Bureau, London, 1989–91; joined HM Diplomatic Service, 1991; Second Sec., FCO, 1991–92; First Secretary: (Chancery), Beijing, 1994–97; (Commercial), Tokyo, 1998–2001; Dep. Hd of Mission and Consul-Gen., Brussels, 2002–05; Dep. Hd of Mission, 2005–10 and Consul-Gen., 2008–10, Jakarta; Portfolio Dir, FCO, 2010–13; Interim Hd of Mission, Baku, 2013; Consul-Gen., Guangzhou, China, 2014–17. *Recreations*: globetrotting, stargazing. *Address*: China-Britain Business Council, 3rd Floor, Portland House, Bressenden Place, SW1E 5BH.

**ROUS, Robert Charles;** farmer, Dennington Hall Farm, Suffolk, since 1979; Vice Lord-Lieutenant of Suffolk, since 2015; *b* Dennington, 30 July 1953; *s* of Major Hon. George Rous and Joyce Rous; *m* 1976, Teresa Heathcote; one *d* (and one *s* decd). *Educ*: Harrow Sch.; Trinity Coll., Cambridge (BA 1975). MRICS 1979. Land agent, 1975–78. Dir, Framlingham Farmers Ltd, 1998–2010 (Chm., 2005–10). Mem., Exec. Bd, Suffolk Agricl Assoc., 2008–17 (Chm., 2013–17). Hon. Lay Canon, St Edmundsbury Cath., 1993–99. Chm. Council, St Edmundsbury Cath., 2005–14. DL 1992, High Sheriff, 2002–03, Suffolk. *Recreations*: Suffolk, country sports, hill walking. *Address*: Dennington Hall, Woodbridge, Suffolk IP13 8AU. *T*: (01728) 638712. *E*: robert@denningtonhall.co.uk. *Club*: Farmers.

**ROUSE, Jonathan Mark,** CBE 2018; Chief Officer, Greater Manchester Health and Social Care Partnership, since 2016; *b* 23 May 1968; *s* of James Clement Rouse and Barbara Jean Rouse (*née* Fowler); *m* 1991, Heulwen Mary Evans; two *d. Educ*: Univ. of Manchester (LLB); Univ. of Nottingham (MBA Finance Dist.); Univ. of N London (MA Dist.). Principal Policy Officer, Ealing BC, 1992–93; Policy Analyst, Energy Saving Trust, 1993–94; Private Sec. to Housing Minister, 1994–95; Policy and Communications Manager, English Partnerships, 1995–98; Sec., Govt Urban Task Force, 1998–99; Chief Executive: CABE, 2000–04; Housing Corp., 2004–07; London Borough of Croydon, 2007–13; Dir-Gen., Social Care, Local Govt and Care Partnerships, DoH, 2013–16. Non-exec. Dir, English Partnerships, 2004–07. Chm., Shaw Educn Trust, 2018–; Trustee: Homeless Internat., 2005–08; SICK! Festival, 2018–. Hon. Prof., Univ. of Manchester, 2018–. Hon. RIBA 2001; Hon. RTPI 2002. DUniv Oxford Brookes, 2003. *Recreation*: hiking. *Address*: Greater Manchester Health and Social Care Partnership, 4th Floor, 3 Piccadilly Place, Manchester M1 3BN. *Club*: Queen's Park Rangers Football.

**ROUSE, Justin Clive Douglas;** QC 2015; a Recorder, since 2004; *b* Horndean, Hants, 21 May 1958; *s* of Lt Comdr D. Malcolm Rouse, MBE and Patricia Eileen Rouse; *m* 1989, Hilary Jane Brader; one *s* four *d. Educ*: Ryde Sch.; City of London Poly. (BA Hons Law); Inns of Court Sch. of Law. Called to the Bar, Lincoln's Inn, 1982; in practice as barrister, specialising in criminal law, 1983–. Advocacy trainer, Lincoln's Inn, 2005–. Member: South Eastern Circuit; Criminal Bar Assoc. Mem., BASC. *Recreations*: fishing, countryside, family, Rugby coach, school governor, travel, reading, gardening. *Address*: 9 Bedford Row, WC1R 4AZ. *T*: (020) 7484 2727, *Fax*: (020) 7489 2828. *E*: justin.rouse@9bedfordrow.co.uk. *Club*: Amersham and Chiltern Rugby Football.

**ROUSE, Ruth Elizabeth;** Permanent Secretary: Ministry of Legal Affairs, Grenada, since 2017; *b* 30 Jan. 1963. *Educ*: German Foundn for Internat. Develt, Berlin (Dip. Internat. Relns and Econ. Co-operation 1987); Diplomatic Acad. of London, PCL, (Post-Grad. Prog. in Diplomacy, Practice, Procedures, Dynamics 1989); Carleton Univ., Canada (BA French and Spanish 1996); Univ. of Westminster, London (MA Diplomatic Studies 2002). Ministry of Foreign Affairs, Grenada: Desk Officer (Africa and ME Affairs), Political and Economic Affairs Div., 1982–83; Protocol Officer, Protocol and Consular Div., 1983–90; Second Sec. (Protocol, Culture and Develt), Orgn of Eastern Caribbean States, High Commn, Ottawa, 1990–96; Chief of Protocol, 1996–99; High Comr in UK, 1999–2004; High Comr (non resident) to S Africa, 2000–05; Ambassador Designate to France, 2001–04; Perm. Rep. of Grenada to the UN, New York, 2004–07; High Comr for Grenada in UK, 2008–13 and (non-resident) to S Africa, 2012–13. Perm Rep., IMO, 2000–04, 2011–13; Perm. Sec., Min. of Educn and HR Develt, 2013–17 (with responsibility for Educn, 2015–17); Perm. Sec., Office of the Prime Minister, 2015–17. Mem., Nat. Celebrations Cttee, Grenada, 1996; Mem. Council, Royal Commonwealth Soc., 2010–13. Governor: Commonwealth Inst., 1999–2004; Commonwealth Foundn, 1999–2004, 2008–13; Advr, Commonwealth Business Council, 2010–13. Independence Award for Exemplary Public Service, 1998. *Recreations*: reading, travelling, Caribbean cooking, tennis, designing (art), photography, meeting people of different cultures, communications (radio/television), music (piano). *E*: ruth_elizabeth43@yahoo.com, ruthelizabethrouse@gmail.com. *Clubs*: Royal Over-Seas League, Women in Diplomatic Service; Commonwealth Countries League.

**ROUSSEAU, Prof. George Sebastian,** PhD; Professor, Faculty of History, 2003–15, now Emeritus, and Co-Director, Centre for the History of Childhood, 2003–14, University of Oxford; *b* 23 Feb. 1941; *s* of Hyman Victoire Rousseau and Esther (*née* Zacuto). *Educ*: Amherst Coll., USA (BA 1962); Princeton Univ. (MA 1964; PhD 1966). Princeton University: Osgood Fellow in English Lit., 1965–66; Woodrow Wilson Dissertation Fellow, 1966; Instructor, then Asst Prof., Harvard Univ., 1966–68; University of California, Los Angeles: Asst Prof. of English, 1968–69; Associate Prof., 1969–76; Prof., 1976–94; Regius Prof. of English Lit. and Dir, Thomas Reid Inst., Aberdeen Univ., 1994–98; Res. Prof. of English, De Montfort Univ., 1999–2003. Fulbright Res. Prof., W Germany, 1970; Cambridge University: Hon. Fellow, Wolfson Coll., 1974–75; Overseas Fellow, 1979; Vis. Fellow Commoner, Trinity Coll., 1982; Sen. Fulbright Res. Schol., Sir Thomas Browne Inst., Netherlands, 1983; Vis. Exchange Prof., King's Coll., Cambridge, 1984; Clark Liby Prof., Univ. of Calif, 1985–86; Sen. Fellow, NEH, 1986–87; Vis. Fellow and Waynflete Lectr, Magdalen Coll., Oxford, 1993–94; Visiting Fellow: Merton Coll., Oxford, 1998; New Coll., Oxford, 1999; Samkul Vis. Prof. of the Humanities, Univ. of Bergen, 2016–. Book reviewer, NY Times (Sunday), 1967–82. FRSocMed 1967; FRSA 1973. Dr *hc* Bucharest, 2007. *Publications*: (with M. Hope Nicolson) This Long Disease My Life: Alexander Pope and the sciences, 1968; (with N. Rudenstine) English Poetic Satire, 1969; (ed jtly) The Augustan Milieu: essays presented to Louis A. Landa, 1970; (ed jtly) Tobias Smollett: bicentennial essays presented to Lewis M. Knapp, 1971; (ed) Organic Form: the life of an idea, 1972; Goldsmith: the critical heritage, 1974; (with R. Porter) The Ferment of Knowledge: studies in the historiography of science, 1980; The Letters and Private Papers of Sir John Hill, 1981; Tobias Smollett: essays of two decades, 1982; (ed) Science and the Imagination: the Berkeley Conference, 1987; (with R. Porter) Sexual Underworlds of the Enlightenment, 1987; (with P. Rogers) The Enduring Legacy: Alexander Pope Tercentenary Essays, 1988; (with R. Porter) Exoticism in the Enlightenment, 1990; The Languages of Psyche: mind and body in enlightenment thought, 1990; Perilous Enlightenment: pre- and post-modern discourses - sexual, historical, 1991; Enlightenment Crossings: pre- and post-modern discourses - anthropological, 1991; Enlightenment Borders: pre- and post-modern discourses - medical, scientific, 1991; (jtly) Hysteria Before Freud, 1993; (with Roy Porter) Gout: the patrician malady, 1998; Framing and Imagining Disease in Cultural History, 2003; Yourcenar: a biography, 2004; Nervous Acts: essays on literature, culture and sensibility, 2004; Children and Sexuality: the Greeks to the Great War, 2007; The Notorious Sir John Hill: the man destroyed by ambition in the era of celebrity, 2012; Rachmaninoff's Cape: a nostalgia memoir, 2015; contrib. numerous articles to learned jls and mags. *Recreations*: chamber music, opera, walking, travel. *E*: george.rousseau@ntlworld.com.

**ROUSSEAU, Prof. Judith,** PhD; Professor, University Paris Dauphine, Ceremade, since 2004; Professor of Statistics, University of Oxford, since 2017; Fellow, Jesus College, Oxford, since 2017; *b* St Cloud, France, 28 May 1970; *d* of Philippe Rousseau and Martine Le Beire; partner, Thierry Brincourt; two *s* one *d. Educ*: Ecole Nat. de la Statistique et de l'admin économique; Univ. de Paris VII (DEA); Univ. de Paris VI (PhD). Maître de conference, Univ. de Paris V, 1998–2004. Medallion Lect., Inst. of Math. Scis, 2017. FIMS 2015; Fellow, Internat. Soc. for Bayesian Analysis, 2016. Ethel Newbold Prize, Bernoulli Soc., 2015. *Publications*: contribs to jls incl. Annals of Stats, Bernoulli, Electronic Jl Stats, Jl Royal Statistical Soc. - Series B, Biometrika. *Address*: Jesus College, Turl Street, Oxford OX1 3DW. *E*: Rousseau@ceremade.dauphine.fr.

**ROUT, Leslie;** Director General, National Kidney Research Fund and Kidney Foundation, 1992–97; *b* 5 Dec. 1936; *s* of James Rout and Ada Elizabeth Rout; *m* 1957, Josephine Goodley; one *s* one *d. Educ*: Queens, Wisbech. Police cadet, 1952–54; Nat. Service, 1954–56; Police Service, 1956–89: served in all depts; attained rank of Comdr Ops; awarded 6 commendations. FCMI. *Recreations*: music, history, travel.

**ROUT, Owen Howard;** Executive Director (UK Operations), Barclays PLC and Barclays Bank PLC, 1987–90; Chairman: Barclays Financial Services Ltd, 1988–90; Starmin plc, 1990–93 (Deputy Chairman, 1993–94); *b* 16 April 1930; *s* of Frederick Owen and Marion Rout; *m* 1954, Jean (*née* Greetham); two *d. Educ*: Grey High Sch., Port Elizabeth, SA. ACIS. Dir, Barclays Bank UK Ltd, 1977–87; Gen. Man., Barclays PLC and Barclays Bank PLC, 1982–87. Chairman: Barclays Insurance Services Co. Ltd, 1982–85; Barclays Insurance Brokers International Ltd, 1982–85; Mercantile Gp, 1989–92; Director: Spreadeagle Insurance Co. Ltd, 1983–85; Baric Ltd, 1982–84; Albaraka Internat. Bank,

1990–93. Chartered Institute of Bankers: Mem. Council, 1985–90; Treas., 1986–90. Mem., Supervisory Bd, Banking World Magazine, 1986–90. Mem., Bd of Govs, Anglia Polytechnic Univ., 1993–2001. *Recreations:* watching sport—Rugby and cricket, playing golf, listening to music, gardening. *Club:* Aldeburgh Golf.

**ROUTH, Donald Thomas;** Under Secretary, Department of the Environment, 1978–90; *b* 22 May 1936; *s* of Thomas and Flora Routh; *m* 1961, Janet Hilda Allum. *Educ:* Leeds Modern Sch. Entered WO, Northern Comd, York, as Exec. Officer, 1954; Nat. Service, RN, 1954–56; Higher Exec. Officer, Comd Secretariat, Kenya, 1961–64; Asst Principal, Min. of Housing and Local Govt, 1964–66; Asst Private Sec. to Minister, 1966–67; Principal, 1967; on loan to Civil Service Selection Bd, 1971; Asst Sec., DoE, 1972; Under Sec., 1978; Regional Dir, West Midlands, 1978–81; Hd of Construction Industries Directorate, 1981–85; Dir of Senior Staff Management, 1985–86; Controller, The Crown Suppliers, 1986.

**ROUTLEDGE, Dame (Katherine) Patricia,** DBE 2017 (CBE 2004; OBE 1993); actress; *b* 17 Feb. 1929; *d* of Isaac Edgar Routledge and Catherine (*née* Perry). *Educ:* Birkenhead High Sch.; Univ. of Liverpool (BA Hons English Lit. and Lang. 1951); Bristol Old Vic Theatre Sch. *Theatre* appearances include: A Midsummer's Night Dream, Liverpool Playhouse, 1952; The Duenna, Westminster, 1954; musical version, The Comedy of Errors, Arts, 1956; The Love Doctor, Piccadilly, 1959; revue, Out of My Mind, Lyric, Hammersmith, 1961; Little Mary Sunshine, Comedy, 1962; Virtue in Danger, Mermaid, transf. Strand, 1963; How's the World Treating You?, Hampstead Theatre Club, 1965, New Arts, transf. Wyndham's, Comedy and Broadway, 1966 (Whitbread Award); Darling of the Day, George Abbott, NY, 1967 (Antoinette Perry Award); The Caucasian Chalk Circle, The Country Wife, and The Magistrate, Chichester Fest., transf. Cambridge Th., 1969; Cowardy Custard, Mermaid, 1972; Dandy Dick, Chichester Fest., transf. Garrick, 1973; 1600 Pennsylvania Avenue, Mark Hellinger, NY, 1976; Pirates of Penzance, NY, 1980; Noises Off, Savoy, 1981; When the Wind Blows, Whitehall, 1983; Richard III, Henry V, RSC, 1984–85; Candide, Old Vic, 1988–89 (Laurence Olivier Award); Come for the Ride (one-woman show), Playhouse, nat. tour, 1989; Carousel, NT, 1992; The Corn is Green, Greenwich and tour, 1992; The Rivals, Chichester, transf. Albery, 1994; Beatrix, Chichester, 1996, tour and transf. Greenwich, 1997; The Importance of Being Earnest, Chichester, transf. Haymarket, 1999, Australian tour, Savoy, 2001; Wild Orchids, Chichester, 2002; The Solid Gold Cadillac, Garrick, 2004; The Best of Friends, Hampstead, 2006; Office Suite, A Visit from Miss Protheroe, Chichester, 2007; Crown Matrimonial, nat. tour, 2008; Admission: One Shilling, Nat. Gall., 2009, Cheltenham Music Fest., 2010, nat. and Eur. tour, 2010–14, Australian tour, 2014; Facing the Music: a life in musical theatre, Menier Chocolate Factory, 2010, nat. tour, 2010–17; An Ideal Husband, Chichester, 2014; *television* appearances include: A Visit from Miss Protheroe, 1978; Doris and Doreen, 1978; A Woman of No Importance, 1982; Victoria Wood As Seen on TV, 1983–86; Marjorie and Men, 1985; A Lady of Letters, 1988; Keeping Up Appearances (5 series), 1990–95 (Best Actress, British Comedy Awards, 1991); Hildegard of Bingen, 1994; Hetty Wainthropp Investigates (4 series), 1995–98; Miss Fozzard finds her Feet, 1998; Anybody's Nightmare, 2001; Beatrix Potter with Patricia Routledge, 2016; many radio plays. FGMS 2017. Hon. Mem. RNCM, 2017. Hon. DLitt: Liverpool, 1999; Lancaster, 2008. Grand Order of Water Rats Award, 1991; Variety Club of GB Award, 1993; 60th Anniv. Award, BBC, 1996; Gold Badge of Merit, Acad. of Songwriters, Composer and Authors, 1998. *Address:* c/o Penny Wesson Management, 26 King Henry's Road, NW3 3RP.

**ROUTLEDGE, Air Vice-Marshal Martin John,** CB 2009; independent consultant; Chairman, London Luton Airport Consultative Committee, since 2009; Assistant Chief of Staff Reserves, Headquarters Air Command, since 2010; *b* 22 Nov. 1954; *s* of James Routledge and Pamela Routledge (*née* Bangor-Ward); *m* 1981, Annette Powell; one *s* one *d*. *Educ:* St John's Sch., Episkopi; Glyn Sch.; Portsmouth Poly. (BSc Elec. Engrg); RAF Coll., Cranwell. Joined RAF, 1972; front-line service as navigator on Phantoms, 1977–89; commanded 29 (F) Sqdn equipped with Tornadoes, 1995–97; Comdr, British Air Forces Italy, 1999; Dep. Principal SO to Chief of Defence Staff, 1999–2001; AO Scotland and Comdr RAF Leuchars, 2001–03; staff duties, MoD, 2003–05; Nat. Mil. Rep. to SHAPE, 2006; COS Strategy, Policy and Plans, HQ Air Command, High Wycombe, 2007–09. RAF Vice-Pres., CCF Assoc., 2010–; Vice Chm. (Air), SE RFCA, 2019–. *Recreations:* conservation and the environment, watching wildlife, ornithology, walking, fighting the lawn, enjoying wine. *Club:* Royal Air Force.

**ROUTLEDGE, Dame Patricia;** *see* Routledge, Dame K. P.

**ROUX, Michel Albert;** Chef Patron, Le Gavroche, since 1991; *b* Kent, 23 May 1960; *s* of Albert and Monique Roux; *m* 1990, Gisele Malbos; one *d*. *Educ:* Highfield Sch. Apprenticeship in Paris, under Maître Pâtissier, Hellegouarche, 1976–79; commis chef de cuisine, with Alain Chapel at Mionay, 1980–82; mil. service, kitchens of Elysée Palace, Paris, 1982–83; sous chef, Gavvers Restaurant, London, 1983–84; commis de cuisine: Tante Claire, London, 1984; Mandarin Oriental, Hong Kong, 1984; Chef, Roux Restaurants, London, 1985–90. TV presenter: MasterChef: the professionals, 2008–13; Michel Roux's Service, 2010; Great British Food Revival, 2010–11; Michel Roux on Escoffier, 2012; Food & Drink, 2013; Patisserie, 2013; First Class Cooks, 2015; Kitchen Impossible, 2015; Hidden Restaurants, 2017. *Publications:* Le Gavroche Cookbook, 2001; The Marathon Chef, 2003; Matching Food and Wine, 2005; Vin de Constance, 2006; Michel Roux: a life in the kitchen, 2009; Cooking with the Master Chef, 2010; Les Abats, 2017; The French Revolution, 2018. *Recreations:* running marathons, Manchester United supporter, Harlequins Rugby Club supporter. *Address:* Le Gavroche, 43 Upper Brook Street, W1K 7QR. *T:* (020) 7408 0881, *Fax:* (020) 7491 4387.

**ROUX, Michel André,** Hon. OBE 2002; former Chef de cuisine; *b* 19 April 1941; *s* of late Henry Roux and Germaine Triger; *m* 1984, Robyn (Margaret Joyce); one *s* two *d* by previous marr. *Educ:* Ecole Primaire, Saint Mande; Brevet de Maîtrise (Pâtisserie). Apprenticeship, Pâtisserie Loyal, Paris, 1955–57; Commis Pâtissier-Cuisinier, British Embassy, Paris, 1957–59; Commis de Cuisine with Miss Cécile de Rothschild, Paris, 1959–60; Military service, 1960–62, at Versailles and Colomb Bechar, Sahara; Chef with Miss Cécile de Rothschild, 1962–67; came to England, 1967; restaurants opened: Le Gavroche, 1967; Le Poulbot, 1969; Waterside Inn, 1972; Gavvers, 1981. Mem., UK Br., Académie Culinaire de France, 1984–. TV series, At Home with the Roux Brothers, 1988. Numerous French and British prizes and awards, including: Médaille d'Or, Cuisiniers Français, 1972; Restaurateur of the Year, Caterer & Hotelkeeper, 1985; Personnalité de l'Année, Gastronomie dans le Monde, Paris, 1985; Culinary Trophy, Assoc. of Maîtres-Pâtissiers La Saint Michel, 1986; (with Albert Roux) Men of the Year (Radar), 1989; (with Albert Roux) Lifetime Achievement Award, Restaurant Magazine, 2006. Chevalier, National Order of Merit (France), 1987; Officer, Order of Agricultural Merit (France), 1987; Chevalier, Order of Arts and of Letters (France), 1990; Chevalier, Legion of Honour (France), 2004. *Publications:* Desserts: a lifelong passion, 1994; Sauces, 1996, rev. edn 2009; Life is a Menu (autobiog.), 2000; Only the Best, 2002; Eggs, 2006; Pastry, 2008; Desserts, 2011; Michel Roux: The Collection, 2012; The Essence of French Cooking, 2014; Cheese, 2017; with Albert Roux: New Classic Cuisine, 1983 (French edn 1985); The Roux Brothers on Pâtisserie, 1986; At Home with the Roux Brothers, 1988; French Country Cooking, 1989, rev. edn 2010; Cooking for Two, 1991. *Recreations:* shooting, walking, skiing. *Address:* Chalet Venus, Appartement 4, 10 Chemin du Mont Paisible, 3963 Crans Montana, Switzerland.

**ROWALLAN,** 4th Baron *cr* 1911; **John Polson Cameron Corbett;** Director, Rowallan Renewables (Scotland) Ltd, since 2016; *b* 8 March 1947; *s* of 3rd Baron Rowallan and of his 1st wife, Eleanor Mary Boyle; *S* father, 1993; *m* 1st, 1971, Jane Green (marr. diss. 1983); one *s* one *d*; 2nd, 1984, Sandrew Bryson (marr. diss. 1994); one *s* one *d*; 3rd, 1995, Claire Dinning; one step *s* one step *d*. *Educ:* Cothill House; Eton Coll.; RAC, Cirencester. Chartered Surveyor, 1972–; farmer, 1975–2014. British Show Jumping Association: Area Rep., 1982–2007; Judge, 1982–; Dir, 1998–2008, 2010–11; Jumping Judge, 2000–, Internat. Show Jumping Judge, 2003–, FEI; Show Jumping Judge, London Olympics, 2012. Commentator at equestrian events. Contested (C): Glasgow, Garscadden, Oct. 1974; Kilmarnock, 1979. Former Member All Party Groups on: Mental Health; Clinical Depression; Arts and Heritage; Alternative Medicine; Racing and Bloodstock; Rwanda and Genocide; Conservation; Advertising; Epilepsy; introduced Mental Health (Amendment) Act 1998 to H of L. Mem., Greenway Cttee. Dir, SANE, 1996–2007. Patron, Depression Alliance, 1998–. Chm., Fenwick and Lochgoin Covenanters Trust, 1977–. *Recreations:* commentating, ski-ing, travel, humanitarian projects. *Heir: s* Hon. Jason William Polson Cameron Corbett [*b* 21 April 1972; *m* 2000, Anna, *d* of Chris Smedley; two *s*]. *Address:* Ladeside House, Skeldon, Hollybush, Ayr KA6 7EB. *T:* (01292) 561839.

**ROWAN, David;** Co-Founder, Flow Journeys, since 2016; overtravelling speaker; technology investor and adviser; *b* 8 April 1965; *s* of Nigel Rowan and Iris Rowan; *m* 1995, Sarah Harris; two *s* one *d*. *Educ:* Haberdashers' Aske's Sch. for Boys; Gonville and Caius Coll., Cambridge (BA Hist. 1988). Trainee journalist, The Times, 1988–89; The Guardian, 1990–2000: Editor: EG and Education magazines, 1990–93; Outlook, Saturday section, 1993–94; Comment and letters, 1994–97; Analysis page, 1997–98; The Editor magazine, 1998–99; Guardian Unlimited websites, 1999–2000; freelance journalist and broadcaster, 2000–06: technology columnist, The Times; interviewer for Evening Standard; magazine writer, Sunday Times and Telegraph; film maker, Channel 4 News and More4 News; Editor: The Jewish Chronicle, 2006–08; Wired mag., 2008–17. *Publications:* A Glossary for the Nineties, 1998; Non-Bullshit Innovation: radical ideas from the world's smartest minds, 2019. *Recreations:* cycling past traffic, crashing into deadlines, collecting inspiring conferences, nurturing entrepreneurs' dreams, connecting good people through magical adventures.

**ROWAN, Patricia Adrienne,** (Mrs Ivan Rowan); journalist; Editor, The Times Educational Supplement, 1989–97; *d* of late Henry Matthew Talintyre and Gladys Talintyre; *m* 1960, Ivan Settle Harris Rowan; one *s*. *Educ:* Harrow County Grammar School for Girls. Time & Tide, 1952–56; Sunday Express, 1956–57; Daily Sketch, 1957–58; News Chronicle, 1958–60; Granada Television, 1961–62; Sunday Times, 1962–66; TES, 1972–97. Mem. Bd of Trustees, Nat. Children's Bureau, 1997–2003; Trustee, Stroud Valleys Project, 2001–10 (Chm., 2002–09). Hon. Fellow, Inst. of Educn, London Univ., 1997. Hon. FRSA 1989. *Publications:* What Sort of Life?, 1980; (contrib.) Education—the Wasted Years?, 1988. *Recreations:* cookery, gardening. *Club:* Reform.
*See also* D. G. Talintyre.

**ROWAN, Prof. Sheila,** MBE 2011; PhD; FRS 2018; FRSE; Professor of Experimental Physics, since 2006, and Director, Institute for Gravitational Research, since 2009, University of Glasgow; Chief Scientific Adviser to Scottish Government (part-time secondment), since 2016; *b* Dumfries, 25 Nov. 1969; *d* of Mark and Daisy Rowan. *Educ:* Maxwelltown High Sch., Dumfries; Univ. of Glasgow (BSc Hons Physics 1991; PhD 1996). Res. Asst, Univ. of Glasgow, 1995–98; Postdoctoral Res. Asst, 1998–2001, Staff Scientist/Res. Associate, 2001–03, Univ. of Glasgow and Stanford Univ.; Reader in Physics, Univ. of Glasgow, 2003–06. Helen Sawyer Hogg Dist. Visitor, Univ. of Toronto, 2016. Mem., STFC, 2018–. Chm., Gravitational Waves Internat. Cttee, 2015–19. Pres., Physics and Astronomy Section, British Sci. Assoc., 2012. FRSE 2008; Hon. FInstP 2018. Hon. DSc Robert Gordon, 2018. Phillip Leverhulme Prize for Astronomy and Astrophysics, 2005; Wolfson Res. Merit Award, Royal Soc., 2010; (jtly) President's Medal, RSE, 2016; Innovation Award: Scientific Breakthrough, Wired Mag./Audi, 2016; Kelvin Medal, Royal Philosophical Soc. of Glasgow, 2016; Hoyle Medal and Prize, Inst. Physics, 2016; Suffrage Sci. Award for Engrg and Physical Sci., London Inst. of Med. Scis/MRC, 2017. *Publications:* contribs to learned jls, books and conf. reports. *Recreations:* cooking, reading. *Address:* School of Physics and Astronomy, University of Glasgow, Glasgow G12 8QQ. *T:* (0141) 330 4701, *Fax:* (0141) 330 6833. *E:* sheila.rowan@glasgow.ac.uk.

**ROWAN-ROBINSON, Prof. (Geoffrey) Michael,** PhD; FInstP; Professor of Astrophysics, Blackett Laboratory, 1993–2012, now Emeritus, and Head, Astrophysics Group, 1993–2007, Imperial College, University of London; *b* 9 July 1942; *s* of John Christopher Rowan-Robinson and Audrey Christine (*née* Wynne); *m* 1978, Mary Lewin (*née* Tubb); one *d*, and two step *s*. *Educ:* Eshton Hall Sch., Gargrave, Yorks; Pembroke Coll., Cambridge (BA 1963); Royal Holloway Coll., London (PhD 1969). FInstP 1992. Queen Mary, later Queen Mary and Westfield College, London: Asst Lectr in Maths, QMC, 1967–69; Lectr, 1969–78; Reader in Astronomy, 1978–87; Prof. of Astrophysics, 1987–93. Royal Soc. and Academia dei Lincei Vis. Res. Fellow, Univ. of Bologna, 1969, 1971, 1976; Vis. Res. Fellow, Univ. of Calif, Berkeley, 1978–79. Member: Exec. Cttee, IAU Commn 47 on Cosmology, 1976–79; Sci. Team for Infrared Astronomical Satellite, 1977–84; Astronomy Wkg Gp, ESA, 1985–88; Space Sci. Prog. Bd, BNSC, 1988–91. Chairman, Time Allocation Committee: Isaac Newton Gp, 1988–91; Eur. Southern Observatory, 2011; Member, Time Allocation Committee: ESA's Infrared Space Observatory mission, 1993–96; Hubble Space Telescope, 1995 and 2000. Co-investigator: Herschel-SWIRE, 1993–2008; Planck-HFI, 1993–2013; Infrared Space Observatory Photometer, ESA, 1996–99; Principal Investigator, European Large Area ISO Survey, 1995–2000. Chm., Res. Assessment Panel for Astronomy, PPARC, 1994–97. Mem., RAS, 1965– (Pres., 2006–08). Mem., Scientists for Global Responsibility, 1992–95; Vice-Chm., Scientists Against Nuclear Arms, 1988–92. Chm., Hornsey Lab. Party, 1971–72. Governor: Creighton Comp. Sch., 1971–78; Fortismere Comp. Sch., 1985–88. Chm., Southwold and Reydon Soc., 2012–15. Hon. DSc Sussex, 2008. Daiwa Adrian Prize, Daiwa Anglo-Japanese Foundn, 2004; Hoyle Medal, Inst. of Physics, 2008. *Publications:* Cosmology, 1977, 4th edn 2004; Cosmic Landscape, 1979; The Cosmological Distance Ladder, 1985; Fire and Ice: the nuclear winter, 1985; Our Universe: an armchair guide, 1990; Ripples in the Cosmos, 1993; Nine Numbers of the Cosmos, 1999; Night Vision, 2013; Stars 'n Tides, 2014; numerous research papers in astronomical jls, articles and book reviews. *Recreations:* poetry, politics, going to the theatre, music, especially Liszt, golf. *Address:* Astrophysics Group, Blackett Laboratory, Imperial College, Prince Consort Road, SW7 2AZ. *T:* (home) (01502) 725223.

**ROWBOTHAM, Prof. Sheila;** writer; *b* 27 Feb. 1943; *d* of Lancelot and Jean Rowbotham; one *s* with Paul Atkinson. *Educ:* Hunmanby Hall Sch.; St Hilda's Coll., Oxford (BA Hons Hist. 1964); Chelsea Coll., London Univ. Lectr in Liberal Studies, Chelsea Coll. of Advanced Technol. and Tower Hamlets Coll. of Further Educn, 1964–68;

Extra-mural Lectr, WEA, 1968–80; Vis. Prof. in Women's Studies, Univ. of Amsterdam, 1981–83; Res. Officer, Industry and Employment Dept, GLC, 1983–86; Course Tutor, MA Women's Studies, Univ. of Kent, 1987–89; Res. Advr, World Inst. for Devlt and Econ. Res., Helsinki, UN Univ., 1987–91; Sociology Department, Manchester University: Simon Res. Fellow, 1993–94; Sen. Res. Fellow, 1995–2000; Sen. Lectr, 2000–01; Reader, 2001–03; Prof. of Gender and Labour History, 2003–08; Simon Res. Prof., 2008–11; Hon. Fellow, 2011. Writer-in-residence, Eccles Centre for Amer. Studies, British Liby, 2012. Hon. Fellow, Bristol, 2016–17. FRSA. Hon. DSSc N London, 1994; Hon. DLitt Sheffield, 2010. Eccles British Liby Writer's Award, 2012. *Publications:* Women, Resistance and Revolution, 1973; Woman's Consciousness, Man's World, 1973; Hidden from History, 1973; A New World for Women: Stella Browne, Socialist Feminist, 1977; Dreams and Dilemmas: collected writings, 1983; Friends of Alice Wheeldon, 1986; The Past is Before Us: feminism in action since the 1960s, 1989; Women in Movement: feminism and social action, 1993; Homeworkers Worldwide, 1993; A Century of Women, 1999; Threads Through Time, 1999; Promise of a Dream, 2000; Edward Carpenter: a life of liberty and love, 2008 (Lambda Literary Award, 2008); Dreamers of a New Day: women who invented the twentieth century, 2010; Rebel Crossings: new women, free lovers and radicals in Britain and the United States, 2016; *edited jointly:* Dutiful Daughters: women talk about their lives, 1977; Socialism and the New Life, 1977; Beyond the Fragments: feminism and the making of socialism, 1980; Dignity and Daily Bread: new forms of economic organisation among poor women, 1994; Women Encounter Technology, 1995; Women Resist Globalization, 2001; Looking at Class, 2001. *Recreations:* cinema, reading, swimming. *Address:* 102 Oxford Street, Bristol BS3 4RL.

**ROWE, Anthony George Edward,** OBE 2012; Chairman, South West Communications Group Ltd (formerly South West Telecoms), since 1983; Chairman and Chief Executive, Exeter Rugby Group plc, since 1998; *b* Portsmouth, 12 Sept. 1948; *s* of Reginald and Matilda Rowe; *m* 2005, Sharon Furzer; one *s* one *d*. Served Royal Marines, 1964–72. Establd power boat business, Exe Marine Services, 1972–83; power boat pilot, 1972–83 (British Champion, 1976). Chm., Exeter Estates Ltd, 2008–. Hon. LLD Exeter, 2014. *Recreations:* Rugby Union, collecting historical vehicles, philately. *Address:* c/o Exeter Rugby Club, Sandy Park Stadium, Sandy Park Way, Exeter EX2 7NN. *T:* (01392) 890900. *E:* tonyrowe@exeterchiefs.co.uk.

**ROWE, Bridget;** Senior Partner, African Strategic, since 2007; Proprietor, Zebra ZebR Womenswear Boutique, since 2010; Founder Partner, EU Referendum Campaign, 2010; *b* 16 March 1950; *d* of late Peter and Myrtle Rowe; *m*; one *s*. *Educ:* St Michael's School, Limpsfield. Editor, Look Now, 1971–76; Editor, Woman's World, 1976–81; Asst Editor, The Sun, 1981–82; Editor: Sunday Magazine, 1982–86; Woman's Own, 1986–90; TV Times, 1990–91; Sunday Mirror, 1991–92; Editor, 1992–96, Man. Dir, 1995–98, The People; Man. Dir, 1995–98, and Editor, 1997–98, Sunday Mirror; Dir of Communications, Nat. Magazines, 1998–99; Content Dir, Yava, 2000–01; Hd of Communications, Europe of Freedom and Democracy Gp, Eur. Parlt, 2009–10. Judge, Press Awards. *Recreations:* football, shopping.

**ROWE, Crispin;** Headmaster, St Paul's School, São Paulo, Brazil, 2008–14; *b* 28 May 1955; *s* of Peter Whitmill Rowe, *qv*; *m* 1977, Jillian Highton (*d* 2008); two *s* one *d*. *Educ:* Univ. of Newcastle upon Tyne (BA Hons; PGCE). Assistant Teacher: Watford Boys' Grammar Sch., 1978–80; Royal Grammar Sch., Newcastle upon Tyne, 1980–92; Dep. Hd, 1992–2004, Headmaster, 2004–08, King Edward's Sch., Bath. *Recreations:* sport, running, golf, music.

**ROWE, Jennifer, (Mrs J. Ellis),** CB 2013; Chief Executive, UK Supreme Court, 2009–15; *b* 2 Oct. 1955; *d* of Caryl Rowe and Beryl Rose Florence Rowe; *m* 1993, John Richard Ellis (*d* 2016). *Educ:* Sir James Smith's Sch., Camelford; King's Coll., London (BA Hons Hist. 1977); Coll. of Law, Lancaster Gate; Birkbeck Coll., London (MSc Policy Admin 1984). Principal Private Sec. to Lord Chancellor, 1990–93; Principal Estabt and Finance Officer, Serious Fraud Office, 1993–95; Lord Chancellor's Department: Hd, Criminal Policy, 1995–97; Principal Private Sec. to Lord Chancellor, 1997–99; Dir, Corporate Services, 1999–2002; Dir, Finance and Corporate Affairs, 2002–03; Sec., Butterfield Rev., 2003; Dir, Policy Admin, Attorney General's Office, 2004–08. Nat. Treas., Civil Service Retirement Fellowship, 2013–19. Non-exec. Mem., Audit and Risk Cttee, CPS, 2015–; non-exec. Mem., Audit and Risk Cttee, Govt Legal Dept, 2016–; Mem., State Honours Cttee, 2019–. Mem., Ind. Monitoring Bd, Exeter Prison, 2015–. Adv. Editor, Civil Procedure (The White Book), 2009–15. Mem., Council of Reference, Westminster Abbey Inst., 2013–16. Chm., Friends of Lanteglos Ch, 2011–. Mem., Girls' Cricket Bd, Chance to Shine, 2012–14. Trustee: RBL, 2005–13; RN and RM Charity, 2014–; Franciscan Servants of Jesus and Mary, 2019–. Lay Chapter Canon, Exeter Cathedral, 2017–; Gov., Exeter Cathedral Sch., 2018–. *Recreations:* reading, theatre, opera, gardening, cricket. *E:* jenny-rowe@outlook.com. *Clubs:* Royal Over-Seas League, Surrey CC.

**ROWE, Judith May;** QC 2003; **Her Honour Judge Rowe;** a Circuit Judge, since 2012; a Deputy High Court Judge, Family Division, since 2005; Designated Family Judge, West London, since 2014; *b* 7 Aug. 1957; *d* of David and Eileen Rowe; *m* 1989, Bill Waite; two *d*. *Educ:* Redrock Sch., Dursley; UCL (LLB Hons). Called to the Bar: Gray's Inn, 1979, Bencher, 2007; Lincoln's Inn, 1988. Recorder, 1999–2012. *Recreations:* ski-ing, scuba diving, gardening. *Address:* West London Family Court, Feltham, Middx TW14 0LR.

**ROWE, Kerry;** *see* Rowe, R. K.

**ROWE, Rear-Adm. Sir Patrick (Barton),** KCVO 2002 (LVO 1975); CBE 1990; Deputy Master and Chairman of the Board, Trinity House, 1996–2002; Chairman, General Lighthouse Authority, 1996–2002; *b* 14 April 1939; *e s* of Captain G. B. Rowe, DSC, RN and Doreen Rowe (*née* Robarts), Liphook, Hants; *m* 1964, Alexandra, *e d* of Alexander Mellor, OBE; one *s* one *d*. *Educ:* Wellington College; RNC Dartmouth. Served Far East Fleet, 1960–65; specialised in Navigation, 1966; navigation appts, 1966–70; Comd, HMS Soberton, 1970–71; Army Staff Coll., 1972; Navigation Officer, HM Yacht Britannia, 1973–75; Comd, HMS Antelope, 1977–79; Naval Staff appts, 1979–82; Comd, HMS Keren, 1983; Comd, HMS Liverpool, 1983–85; RN Presentation Team, 1985–86; Commodore, Clyde, 1986–88; RCDS 1989; Mil. Deputy, Defence Export Services, 1990–92; Clerk to the Worshipful Co. of Leathersellers, 1993–96. Liveryman: Shipwrights' Co., 1993–2008; Leathersellers' Co., 1996–2014. *Recreations:* sailing, travel, DIY. *Address:* Juniper Cottage, Meonstoke, Southampton, Hampshire SO32 3NA. *Clubs:* Army and Navy; Royal Yacht Squadron.

**ROWE, Peter Whitmill,** MA; Schoolteacher at Kent College, Canterbury, 1983–90, retired; *b* 12 Feb. 1928; British; *s* of Gerald Whitmill Rowe, chartered accountant, one-time General Manager of Morris Commercial Cars Ltd; *m* 1952, Bridget Ann Moyle; two *s* one *d*. *Educ:* Bishop's Stortford College; St John's College, Cambridge. BA 1950; MA (Hons) 1956. VI Form History Master, Brentwood School, Essex, 1951–54; Senior History Master, Repton School, Derbys, 1954–57; Headmaster: Bishop's Stortford Coll., Herts, 1957–70; Cranbrook Sch., Kent, 1970–81; teacher, Williston-Northampton Sch., Mass, USA, 1981–83. JP Bishop's Stortford, 1968–70, Cranbrook, 1971–81. *Recreations:* literature, music, woodland restoration, golf.
*See also* C. Rowe.

**ROWE, Prof. (Ronald) Kerry,** OC 2017; PhD, DEng; FRS 2013; FRSC; FREng, FCAE, FEIC; Professor and Canada Research Chair in Geotechnical and Geoenvironmental Engineering, Queen's University, Kingston, since 2010; *b* Australia, 1951; *s* of Ronald Rowe and Alma Rowe; *m* 1973, Kathryn; two *s* one *d*. *Educ:* Fort Street Boys High Sch., Sydney; Univ. of Sydney (BSc 1973; BE Hons I 1975; PhD 1979; DEng 1993). CPEng 1978; PEng 1980. Cadet Engr, 1971–74, Civil Engr, 1975–78, Dept of Construction, Australian Govt; University of Western Ontario: Asst Prof., 1979–82; Associate Prof., 1982–86; Prof., 1986–2000; Associate Dean (Res. and Graduate Affairs), Faculty of Engrg Sci., 1988–89; NSERC Steacie Fellow, 1989–91; Chair, Dept of Civil and Envmtl Engrg, 1992–2000; Vice-Principal (Res.), Queen's Univ., Kingston, 2000–10. Killam Fellow, 2012–14. Adjunct Professor: Dept of Civil Engrg, Royal Military Coll., Canada, 2008–; Dept of Civil Engrg, Monash Univ., 2011–. Foreign Mem., US NAE, 2016. FEIC 1993; FCAE 2001; FRSC 2001; FREng 2010. Hon. DSc Western Ontario, 2015. *Publications:* (jtly) Clayey Barrier Systems for Waste Disposal Facilities, 1995; (ed) Geotechnical and Geoenvironmental Engineering Handbook, 2001; (jtly) Barrier Systems for Waste Disposal Facilities, 2004; 14 book chapters; approx. 330 papers in jls; over 300 conf. papers. *Recreations:* canoeing, ski-ing. *Address:* Department of Civil Engineering, Queen's University, Kingston, ON K7L 3N6, Canada. *T:* (613) 5333113, *Fax:* (613) 5332128. *E:* kerry.rowe@queensu.ca.

**ROWE, Prof. William Walton,** PhD; FBA 2011; Anniversary Professor of Poetics, and Director, Contemporary Poetics Research Centre, Birkbeck, University of London, until 2017, now Professor Emeritus. *Educ:* Pembroke Coll., Cambridge (BA 1965); Univ. of London (PhD). Teacher: Univ. of Lambayeque, Peru; Univ. of Liverpool; Univ. of San Marcos, Peru; Univ. Católica, Peru; Univ. Iberoamericana, Mexico; Univ. Autónoma de Barcelona; Personal Chair in Latin Amer. Cultural Studies, KCL. Founding Ed., Jl Latin Amer. Cultural Studies: Travesia (Mem., Adv. Bd). Hon. Dr Católica, Peru, 2012. Congressional Medal of Honour (Peru), 2010. *Publications:* Juan Rulfo: el llano en llamas, 1987; (with V. Schelling) Memory and Modernity: popular culture in Latin America, 1991; Ensayos arguedianos, 1996; Hacia una poética radical: ensayos de hermenéutica cultural, 1996; Siete ensayos sobre poesía latinoamericana, 2003; Ensayos vallejianos, 2006; Three Modern Lyric Poets: Harwood, Torrance and MacSweeney, 2009; Cesar Vallejo: el acto y la palabra, 2010; (ed jtly) Huellas del mito prehispánico en la literatura latinoamericana, 2010. *Address:* Department of Iberian and Latin American Studies, Birkbeck, University of London, 43 Gordon Square, WC1H 0PD.

**ROWE-BEDDOE,** family name of **Baron Rowe-Beddoe**.

**ROWE-BEDDOE, Baron** *cr* 2006 (Life Peer), of Kilgetty in the County of Dyfed; **David Sydney Rowe-Beddoe,** Kt 2000; DL; Chairman: Wales Millennium Centre, 2001–10, now Life President; Cardiff International Airport Ltd, 2013–15; Deputy Chairman, Toye & Co. plc, 2003–14; *b* 19 Dec. 1937; *s* of late Sydney Rowe-Beddoe and Dolan Rowe-Beddoe (*née* Evans); *m* 1st, 1962, Malinda Collison (marr. diss. 1982); three *d*; 2nd, 1984, Madeleine Harrison. *Educ:* Cathedral Sch., Llandaff; Stowe Sch.; St John's Coll., Cambridge (MA); Harvard Univ. Grad. Sch. of Business Admin (PMD). Served RN, Sub-Lt, RNVR, 1956–58, Lieut, RNR, 1958–66. Thomas de la Rue & Company, 1961–76: Chief Executive, 1971–76; Exec. Dir, De la Rue Co. plc, 1974–76; Revlon Inc., NY, 1976–81; President: Latin America and Caribbean, 1976–77; Europe, ME and Africa, 1977–81; Pres. and Chief Exec. Officer, Ges. für Trendanalysen, 1981–87; Pres., Morgan Stanley-GFTA Ltd, 1983–91; Director: Development Securities plc, 1994–2000; EHC International Ltd and subsidiaries, 2001–13; Newport Networks Gp plc, 2004–09; Bd Mem., Mitel Inc., 2002–06; Chairman: Victoria Capital (UK) Ltd, 2007; GFTA - Euro/Dollar Technol. Co. Ltd (formerly GFTA Analytics Ltd), 2005–13; European Property Advisors Ltd, 2010– (Dir, 2010–). Member: Select Cttee on the EU, Sub-cttee B (Internal Mkt), H of L, 2007–12; Admin and Works Cttee, H of L, 2009–14; Econ. Affairs Cttee, H of L, 2012–15. Chairman: Welsh Development Agency, 1993–2001; Develt Bd for Rural Wales, 1994–98; N Wales Econ. Forum, 1996–2001; Mid Wales Partnership, 1996–2001; SE Wales Econ. Forum, 1999–2001; Cardiff Business Club, 2002–06 (Pres., 2006–); Member: Welsh Economic Council, 1994–96; UK Regl Policy Forum, 1999–2002; Dep. Chm., UK Statistics Authy, and Chm., ONS, 2008–12. Chm., Rep. Body, Church in Wales, 2002–12; Pres., Welsh Centre for Internat. Affairs, 1999–2005. Director: Welsh Internat. Film Fest. Ltd, 1998–2000; Cardiff Internat. Festival of Musical Theatre Ltd, 2000–04; City of London Sinfonia, 2000–03; President: Celtic Film Festival, 2000; Llangollen Internat. Musical Eisteddfod, 2000–05; Johnian Soc., Cambridge Univ., 2007. Mem., Prince of Wales' Cttee, 1994–97; Patron: Prince's Trust Bro, 1997–; Menuhin Competition, 2008; Chm., Aloud Charity, 2012–15; Trustee, Jeremy Winston Meml Fund, 2012–. Pro-Chancellor, Univ. of S Wales (formerly Glamorgan Univ.), 2007–. Pres., RWCMD (formerly WCMD), 2004– (Gov., 1993–2004; Chm., 2000–04). Freeman, City of London, 1993; Liveryman, 1993–, Mem. Ct of Assts, 2002–, Broderers' Co. DL Gwent, 2003. FRSA 1993. Hon. Fellow: Univ. of Wales Coll. Newport, 1998; Cardiff Univ., 1999; UWIC, 2002; Aberystwyth Univ., 2008. DUniv Glamorgan, 1997; Hon. DScEcon Wales, 2004. Order of Rising Sun, Gold Rays with Neck Ribbon (Japan), 2008. *Recreations:* music, theatre, country pursuits. *Clubs:* Garrick; Brook (New York).

**ROWE-HAM, Sir David (Kenneth),** GBE 1986; chartered accountant, since 1962; Lord Mayor of London, 1986–87; Consultant to Touche Ross & Co., 1984–93; *b* 19 Dec. 1935; *o s* of late Kenneth Henry and Muriel Phyllis Rowe-Ham; *m* Sandra Celia (*née* Nicholls), *widow* of Ian Glover; three *s*. *Educ:* Dragon School; Charterhouse. FCA. Commnd 3rd King's Own Hussars. Mem., Stock Exchange, 1964–84; Sen. Partner, Smith Keen Cutler, 1972–82. Chairman: Asset Trust plc, 1982–89; Jersey General Investment Trust Ltd, 1988–89; Olayan Europe Ltd, 1989–2018; Brewin Dolphin Hldgs PLC, 1992–2003; APTA Healthcare PLC, 1994–96; Coral Products PLC, 1995–2006; Peninsular S Asia Investment Co. (formerly BNP Paribas South Asia Investment Co.) Ltd, 1995–2008; Arden Partners PLC, 2006–10; Jt Chm., Gradus Group PLC, 1995–97; Regional Dir (London), Lloyds Bank plc, 1985–91; Director: W. Canning plc, 1981–86; Savoy Theatre Ltd, 1986–98; Williams PLC, 1992–2000; CLS Hldgs plc, 1994–99; Chubb plc, 2000–03; Hikma Pharmaceuticals plc, 2005–14. Pres., Crown Agents Foundn, 1996–2002. Chm., Adv. Panel, Guinness Flight Unit Trust Managers Ltd, 1987–99. Alderman, City of London, Ward of Bridge and Bridge Without, 1976–2004; Sheriff, City of London, 1984–85; HM Lieut, City of London, 1987–2004. Liveryman: Worshipful Co. of Chartered Accountants in England and Wales (Master, 1985–86); Worshipful Co. of Wheelwrights; Hon. Mem., Worshipful Co. of Launderers. Mem. Ct, 1981–86, Chancellor, 1986–87, City Univ. Gov., Royal Shakespeare Co., 1988–2003; former Trustee, Friends of D'Oyly Carte. Pres., Black Country Mus. Develt Trust, 1989–2010. Chm., Birmingham Municipal Bank, 1970–72; Mem., Birmingham CC, 1965–72. Chm., Political Council, Junior Carlton Club, 1977; Dep. Chm., Political Cttee, Carlton Club, 1977–79; Chm., 1900 Club, 2003–08. Mem., Pilgrims. JP City of London, 1976 (Chief Magistrate, 1986–87; Supp. List, 1994–). Hon. DLitt City Univ., 1986. KJStJ 1986. Commandeur de l'Ordre Mérite, France, 1984;

Commander, Order of the Lion, Malaŵi, 1985; Order of the Aztec Eagle (Cl. II), Mexico, 1985; Order of King Abdul Aziz (Cl. 1), 1987; Grand Officer, Order of Wissam Alouite, Morocco, 1987; Order of Diego Losada, Caracas, Venezuela, 1987; Pedro Ernesto Medal, Rio de Janeiro, 1987. *Recreation:* theatre. *Club:* Garrick.

**ROWELL, Anthony Aylett,** CMG 1992; occasional film consultant, since 2005; Founding Member, Advisory Council, and Senior Adviser (formerly Consultant), Good Governance Group (G3 UK), 2007–15; *b* 10 Jan. 1937; *s* of Geoffrey William and Violet Ella Aylett Rowell; *m* 1st, 1965, Bridget Jane Reekie (marr. diss. 1985); one *s* one *d*; 2nd, 1985, Caroline Anne Edgcumbe. *Educ:* Marlborough. With British American Tobacco, 1959–65; HM Diplomatic Service, 1966–93: 2nd Sec., Lusaka, 1968–69; 1st Secretary: FCO, 1969; Bucharest, 1970–73; FCO, 1974–78; Nicosia, 1979–80; FCO, 1981–85; Counsellor: Nairobi, 1985–90; Pretoria, 1990–93. Pol Advr (Southern Africa), Racal Radio Group UK, 1993; Dir, Racal Electronics SA Ltd, 1994; Pol Advr (Southern Africa), Racal Electronics PLC, 1996–97; Consultant (Africa), Kroll Associates, 1998–2005. *Recreations:* badminton, mountain and dog walking, international politics, photography, fine wines, cooking. *Address:* Bracken Cottage, Devauden, Monmouthshire NP16 6NS. *E:* anthonyarowell@gmail.com. *Club:* Muthaiga Country (Nairobi).

**ROWELL, Jack,** OBE 1998; Chairman: Turleigh Ltd, since 1995; Ukrainian Food Products plc, since 2005; *s* of late Edwin Cecil Rowell and Monica Mary Rowell (*née* Day); *m* 1969, Susan, *d* of Alan Cooper; two *s*. *Educ:* West Hartlepool Grammar Sch.; St Edmund Hall, Oxford (MA). FCA 1964. With Procter & Gamble to 1976; Finance Dir, then Chief Exec., Lucas Ingredients, Bristol, 1976–88; Chief Exec., Golden Wonder, 1988–92; Exec. Dir, Dalgety, 1993–94; Chairman: Lyon Seafoods Ltd, 1994–2003; Marlar Bennetts Internat. Ltd, 1994–99; Dolphin Computer Services Ltd, 1994–99; OSI Ltd, 1995–99; Pilgrim Foods Ltd, 1995–2004; Celsis plc, 1997–98, 2000–09 (Dir, 1995; Chief Exec., 1998–2000); Coppice Ltd, 2002–04; Dir, Oliver Ashworth Gp, 1997–98. Played for Gosforth RFC, later Newcastle Gosforth (Captain, later coach; Cup winners, 1976); coach, Bath RFC, 1977–94: Cup winners 8 times, League winners 5 times, Middlesex Sevens winners, 1994; Manager, England RFU Team, 1994–97 (winners two 5 Nations Championships and one Grand Slam); Dir, 1998–2000, Man. Dir, 2000–02, Bristol Rugby Ltd; Dir, 2002–07, Pres., 2007–09, Bath RFC (Chm. of Trustees, Bath Rugby, 2010–14). Advr, Sch. of Mgt, Univ. of Bath, 2009–14. Member: Bd, Sport England, 2006–09; Council, Prince's Trust (SW), 2008–13. Hon. LLD Bath, 1994.

**ROWELL, Prof. John Martin,** DPhil; FRS 1989; Professor, School of Materials, Arizona State University, 2002, now Distinguished Visiting Professor; *b* 27 June 1935; *s* of Frank L. and P. E. Rowell; *m* 1959, Judith A. Harte (*d* 2002); two *s* one *d*. *Educ:* Wadham Coll., Oxford (BSc, MA; DPhil 1961). Bell Telephone Labs, 1961–84; Bell Communications Research, 1984–89; Conductus Inc., 1989–95; Prof., Materials Res. Inst., Northwestern Univ., 1997. Chm., Sci. Adv. Bd, Hypres Inc. Member: Acad. of Scis, 1994; Acad. of Engrg, 1995. Fellow, Amer. Physical Soc., 1974. Fritz London Meml Low Temperature Physics Prize, 1978. *Publications:* about 100 pubns in jls.

**ROWEN, Paul John;** Director: Corinya (Uganda) Ltd, since 2004; Rochdale Reform Building Company, since 2010; Transport and Urban Transit Publishing, since 2014; Director, since 2010, and Vice Chairman, since 2014, Light Rapid Transit Association; *b* 11 May 1955. *Educ:* Bishop Henshaw RC Meml High Sch., Rochdale; Univ. of Nottingham (BSc 1976); PGCE 1977; NPQH 2004. Teacher of sci., Kimberley Comprehensive Sch., Nottingham, 1977–80; Hd of Chemistry, St Albans RC High Sch., Oldham, 1980–86; Hd of Sci., Our Lady's RC High Sch., Oldham, 1986–90; Dep. Headteacher, Yorkshire Martyrs Catholic Coll., Bradford, 1990–2005. Ind. consultant on educn and govt, 2010–. Mem. (Lib Dem), Rochdale MBC, 1983–2006. Contested (Lib Dem) Rochdale, 2001. MP (Lib Dem) Rochdale, 2005–10; contested (Lib Dem) same seat, 2010. Mem. Bd, Transport Focus (formerly Passenger Focus), 2013–17. Gov., St Cuthbert's RC High Sch., Rochdale, 2000–. Trustee, Arthritis Research UK, 2009–. *Address:* c/o 144 Drake Street, Rochdale OL16 1PZ. *Club:* Rotary (Rochdale).

**ROWLAND, Barry Alan;** Chief Executive, Falkland Islands Government, since 2016; *b* Co. Durham, 9 Aug. 1961; *m* 1985, Lynne; four *c*. *Educ:* Univ. of Durham Business Sch. (MBA 1997). Newcastle City Council: mgt trainee, 1979–82; Dist Inspector, 1982–85; Mgt Services Officer, 1985–86; Principal Ops Manager, 1986–89; Gen. Manager, Building Services, 1989–94; Divl Dir, 1994–95; Exec. Dir, 1995–2002; Dir, Strategic Change, 2002–03; Dep. Chief Exec., 2003–09; Chief Exec., 2009–12; Corporate Dir of Local Services, Northumberland CC, 2012–15.

**ROWLAND, Prof. Christopher;** Dean Ireland's Professor of the Exegesis of Holy Scripture, University of Oxford, 1991–2014, now Emeritus; Fellow of Queen's College, Oxford, 1991–2014; *b* Doncaster, 21 May 1947; *s* of late Eric Rowland and Frances Mary Lawson; *m* 1969, Catherine Rogers; three *s* one *d*. *Educ:* Doncaster Grammar Sch.; Christ's Coll., Cambridge; Ridley Hall, Cambridge; BA 1969, PhD 1975, Cantab. Ordained deacon, 1975, priest 1976. Lectr in Religious Studies, Univ. of Newcastle upon Tyne, 1974–79; Curate: St James', Benwell, 1975–78; All Saints', Gosforth, 1978–79; Asst Lectr in Divinity, 1983–85, Lectr in Divinity, 1985–91, Univ. of Cambridge; Fellow and Dean, Jesus Coll., Cambridge, 1979–91. Canon Theologian, Liverpool Cathedral, 2005–14. Hon. DD Liverpool Hope, 2019. Burkitt Medal for Biblical Studies, British Acad., 2018. *Address:* Queen's College, Oxford OX1 4AW.

**ROWLAND, Sir Geoffrey (Robert),** Kt 2009; Bailiff of Guernsey, 2005–12; President, Court of Appeal of Guernsey, 2005–12; a Judge of the Court of Appeal of Jersey, 2005–12; *b* 5 Jan. 1948; *s* of late Percy George Rowland and Muriel Florence (*née* Maunder); *m* 1972, Diana Janet Caryl; two *s*. *Educ:* Elizabeth Coll., Guernsey; Univ. of Southampton; Univ. of Caen. Called to the Bar, Gray's Inn, 1970, Hon. Bencher, 2008; called to the Guernsey Bar, 1971; QC (Guernsey) 1993. In private practice as advocate, Guernsey, 1971–91; Sen. Partner, Collas Day and Rowland, 1984–91; Solicitor General for Guernsey, 1992–99; Attorney-General for Guernsey, 1999–2002; HM Receiver General for Guernsey, 1999–2002; Dep. Bailiff of Guernsey, 2002–05. Vice-Chm., Guernsey Financial Services Commn, 1988–92. Chairman: Guernsey Press Co. Ltd, 1990–92; TSB Foundn for CI, 1990–92; Dir, Bailiwick Investments Ltd, 2016–. Chm., Guernsey Commonwealth Games Assoc. Appeal Bd, 2012–. President: Guernsey, Western Br., RBL, 2012–18; Guernsey Bn, Boys' Bde, 2012–; No 201 (Guernsey's Own) Sqn Assoc., 2016–; Comr, Guernsey Youth Commn, 2014–17. Trustee: Wessex Med. Trust, 2012–18; Ch of St John the Evangelist, 2017–; Patron: Guernsey FA, 2005–; Guernsey FC, 2011–; Elizabeth Coll. Foundn, 2011–; Bailiwick of Guernsey, BRCS, 2012–; Guernsey Eisteddfod Soc., 2012–; Founder Patron, Lihou Charitable Trust, 2017–. Provincial Grand Master, Guernsey and Alderney, United Grand Lodge of Freemasons of England, 2000–07. Hon. Fellow, Soc. for Advanced Legal Studies, 2001–. Hon. LLD: Bournemouth, 2006; Southampton, 2009. *Recreations:* charitable work, ski-ing, reading history, international travel. *Address:* Armorica, L'Ancresse, Guernsey, CI GY3 5JR. *T:* (01481) 247494. *E:* gdrowland@cwgsy.net. *Clubs:* United (Guernsey); Royal Guernsey Golf (Hon. Mem.).

**ROWLAND, John Peter;** QC 1996; *b* 17 Jan. 1952; *s* of Peter Rowland and Marion Rowland (*née* Guppy); *m* 1979, Juliet Hathaway; three *s* two *d*. *Educ:* Univ. of Western Australia (BEc Hons); King's Coll., London (LLB Hons). Pilot Officer, RAAF (Reserves), 1970–72; Sen. Tutor and Lectr in Econs, Univ. of Western Australia, 1973–74; Lectr in Economics, WA Inst. of Technology, 1974–75; called to the Bar, Middle Temple, 1979; admitted to practice, NSW, 2001, Victoria, 2001; Partner, Clayton Utz, Sydney, 2011–16. *Recreations:* cricket, walking, ski-ing. *Address:* 4 Pump Court, Temple, EC4Y 7AN. *Club:* Theberton Cricket.

**ROWLAND, Mark;** an Upper Tribunal Judge (Administrative Appeals Chamber) (formerly a Social Security Commissioner and Child Support Commissioner), 1993–2018; *b* 20 July 1953; *s* of late Sqdn Leader Bernard Rowland and Elizabeth Rowland (*née* Cuerden); *m* 1977, Eileen Cleary; two *d*. *Educ:* Ampleforth Coll.; Univ. of Warwick (LLB Hons). Called to the Bar, Gray's Inn, 1975; Welfare rights adviser, CPAG, 1975–78; private practice at the Bar, 1979–93; part-time Chm., social security, medical and disability appeal tribunals, 1988–93; Dep. Social Security Comr, 1992–93; Chairman: registered homes tribunal, 1995–2002; care standards tribunal, 2002–08; Mem., Tribunal Procedure Cttee, 2008–15; a Dep. Upper Tribunal Judge, 2019–. *Publications:* (ed jtly) Rights Guide to Non-means-tested Benefits, 2nd edn 1978, 14th edn 1991; The Industrial Injuries Scheme, 1983; Medical and Disability Appeal Tribunals: the Legislation, 1993, 3rd edn 1998; (ed jtly) Social Security Legislation, 2000, 20th edn 2019. *Recreations:* railways, military history, social history. *Address:* c/o Upper Tribunal, Administrative Appeals Chamber, 5th Floor, Rolls Building, 7 Rolls Buildings, Fetter Lane, EC4A 1NL.

**ROWLAND, Mark David;** Chief Executive Officer, Mental Health Foundation, since 2018; *b* Eastbourne, 25 Feb. 1977; *s* of Dr Richard Rowland and Prilla Rowland; *m* 2016, Josephine Lofthouse; one *s*. *Educ:* Liverpool Univ. (BA Hons); Open Univ. (MBA). Head: of Philanthropy, Christian Aid, 2006–11; of Fundraising, VSO, 2011–16; Dir, Communications, Mental Health Foundn, 2016–18. Chm. Trustees, Partners Relief and Develt, 2015–. Mem., St John's Ch, Farncombe. *Recreations:* marathon and ultra-marathons, meditation. *T:* 07717 350693. *E:* mrowland@mentalhealth.org.uk. *Club:* Waverley Harriers.

**ROWLAND, Rev. Mgr Phelim Christopher;** Rector, St Mary's, Holly Place, Hampstead, since 2006; *b* 9 Dec. 1949; *s* of Hugh and Ann Rowland. *Educ:* Tyburn Sch.; St George's Sch., London; Campion House; St Edmund's Coll., Ware. Ordained priest, 1975; Asst Priest, Holy Trinity, Brook Green, Hammersmith, 1975–79; commnd RN Chaplaincy Service, 1979–86: served in various estabts, incl. BRNC Dartmouth; served in Falkland Is, 1982; transf. RAChD, 1986: served Germany, NI, Cyprus, Bosnia, Kosovo and RMA Sandhurst; Principal RC Chaplain and VG for HM Land Forces, 2002–06. QHC 2004–06. Chair of Trustees, Catholic Children's Soc. (Westminster), 2009–; Administrator, Westminster Dio., Secular Clergy Common Fund, 2017–. Gov., St Edmund's Coll., Ware, 2001. KHS 2016. *Recreations:* cinema, military history. *Address:* 4 Holly Place, Hampstead, NW3 6QU. *T:* (020) 7435 6678. *Club:* Army and Navy.

**ROWLAND, His Honour Robert Todd;** QC 1969; County Court Judge of Northern Ireland, 1974–90; President, Lands Tribunal for Northern Ireland, 1983–90; part-time Chairman, Value Added Tax Tribunals, 1990–94; *b* 12 Jan. 1922; *yr s* of late Lt-Col Charles Rowland and Jean Rowland; *m* 1952, Kathleen (*d* 1991), *er d* of late H. J. Busby, Lambourn, Berks; two *s*. *Educ:* Crossley and Porter Sch., Halifax, Yorks; Ballyclare High Sch.; Queen's Univ. of Belfast (LLB 1948). Called to Bar of N Ireland, 1949; Mem., Bar Council, 1967–72. Served 2nd Punjab Regt, IA, in India, Assam, Burma, Thailand, Malaya, 1942–46. Counsel to Attorney-Gen. for N Ireland, 1966–69; Sen. Crown Prosecutor for Co. Tyrone, 1969–72; Vice-Pres., VAT Tribunal for N Ireland, 1972–74. Served on County Court Rules Cttee, 1965–72; Chairman: War Pensions Appeal Tribunal, 1962–72; Commn of Inquiry into Housing Contracts, 1978; Member: Bd of Governors, Strathearn Sch., 1969–89; Legal Adv. Cttee, Gen. Synod of Church of Ireland, 1975–89. Chancellor, dioceses of Armagh, and Down and Dromore, 1978–89. *Address:* The Periwinkle, 25 Back Lane, South Luffenham, Oakham, Rutland LE15 8NQ. *Club:* Flyfishers'.

**ROWLAND, Robin Frank; His Honour Judge Robin Rowland;** a Circuit Judge, since 2015; *b* Bedford, 17 July 1954; *s* of late David Rowland and Sheila Rowland; *m* 1980, Anne Elizabeth Smallwood; one *s* two *d*. *Educ:* St Bees Sch.; Univ. of Liverpool (LLB). Called to the Bar, Middle Temple, 1977; Lectr, Univ. of London, 1978–80; in practice as a barrister, 1980–2015; a Recorder, 2003–15; a Dep. High Court Judge (Family Div.), 2011–. *Recreations:* old buildings, art, Rugby. *Address:* c/o Birmingham Civil Justice Centre, 33 Bull Street, Birmingham B4 6DS.

**ROWLAND, Robin James Leslie,** OBE 2016; Operating Partner, TriSpan LLP, since 2018; *b* London, 9 March 1961; *s* of late Christopher Rowland and of Leslie Rowland; *m* 1997, Fiona Gillespie; two *s* one *d*. *Educ:* St Dunstan's Coll., London; Univ. of Kent (BA Hons American Studies); Univ. of S Carolina. Area Manager, Whitbread Inns, 1984–88; Old Orleans Ops Manager, Grand Metropolitan, 1988–92; Retail Dir, Scottish & Newcastle, 1992–95; Gp Franchise Dir, The Restaurant Gp, 1995–99; Yo! Sushi: Ops Dir, 1999–2000; Chief Exec., 2000–14 and 2016–17; Exec. Chm., 2015–16; non-exec. Dir, 2018–. Non-executive Director: Marston's plc, 2010–; Mexican Grill Ltd, 2012–15; Caffe Nero, 2012–; Eathos (formerly Masterfoods (Gulf)), 2014–; UK Hospitality (formerly Assoc. of Licensed Multiple Retailers), 2014–. *Recreations:* ski-ing, sailing, mountain biking, family trekking. *Address:* TriSpan LLP, 39 Sloan Street, SW1X 9LP. *E:* robin@robinrowland.co.uk.

**ROWLAND JONES, Very Rev. Dr Sarah Caroline,** LVO 1993; OBE 1997; Dean of St Davids, since 2018; *b* Stoke on Trent, 8 Sept. 1959; *d* of David Rowland Jones and Pearl Jones (*née* Jenkins); *m* 1st, 2002, Rt Rev. Justus Mauritius Marcus (*d* 2003); 2nd, 2011, (George) Peter Evans. *Educ:* Welshpool High Sch.; Shrewsbury High Sch.; Newham Coll., Cambridge (BA Maths 1980; MA 1984); St John's Coll., Nottingham (BTh Hons 1st cl. 1998; PhD 2011). Dep. Pres., Cambridge Students' Union, 1980–81; joined FCO, 1981; Third, later Second Sec., Amman, 1984–87; First Sec., Budapest, 1992–96; ordained deacon, 1999, priest, 2000; Asst Curate, Wrexham, 1999–2002; Res. and Ecumenical Advr to the Archbishop of Cape Town, 2003–13; Priest-in-charge, St John the Baptist City Parish, Cardiff, 2013–18. Hon. Canon, Anglican Church of Southern Africa, 2010–. Member: Inter-Anglican Standing Commn for Ecumenical Relations, 2000–08; Inter-Anglican Standing Commn for Unity, Faith and Order, 2009–; Church in Wales' Standing Doctrinal Commn, 2014–; Commn of Covenanted Churches' Faith and Order Panel, 2014–; Internat. Commn for Anglican Orthodox Theol Dialogue, 2016–. Res. Associate, Beyers Naudé Centre for Public Theology, Stellenbosch Univ., 2011–. OStJ 2015. *Publications:* (ed) Faith in Action: Njongonkulu Ndungane - Archbishop for the Church and the World, 2008. *Recreation:* poetry. *Address:* The Deanery, The Pebbles, St Davids, Haverfordwest, Pembrokeshire SA62 6RD. *T:* (01437) 720202. *E:* dean@stdavidscathedral.org.uk.

**ROWLAND-JONES, Prof. Sarah Louise, (Mrs R. T. Walton),** DM; FRCP, FMedSci; Professor of Immunology, University of Oxford, since 2000 (MRC Research Professor, 2008–14); Research Student, Christ Church, Oxford, since 1997; *b* 8 Nov. 1959; *d* of Timothy Louis Rowland-Jones and Kathleen Norah Rowland-Jones; *m* 1988, Prof. Robert Thompson Walton; one *d*. *Educ:* Girton Coll., Cambridge (BA 1st Cl. Hons 1980; MA 1984); Green Coll., Oxford (BM BCh 1983; DM 1995). MRCP 1986, FRCP 1999. Postgrad. med. trnng in gen. medicine and infectious diseases, Oxford, London (St George's and Brompton Hosps) and Sheffield, 1983–89; Molecular Immunology Group, Oxford: MRC Trng Fellow, 1989–92; MRC clinician scientist, 1992–95; MRC Sen. Fellow, 1995–2000; Dir, Oxford Centre for Tropical Medicine, 2001–04; Dir of Res., MRC Labs, The Gambia, 2004–08. Hon. Consultant in Infectious Diseases, Churchill Hosp., Oxford, 1995–. Pres., RSTM&H, 2018–19. FMedSci 2000. Elizabeth Glaser Scientist Award, Paediatric Aids Foundation, 1997. *Publications:* (ed with A. J. McMichael) Lymphocytes: a practical approach, 2000; contrib. papers to Nature, Nature Medicine, Immunity, The Lancet, Jl Exptl Medicine, Jl Immunology, Jl Virology, etc. *Recreations:* scuba diving, travel, gardening, collecting art deco, good wine and good company. *Address:* Nuffield Department of Medicine, NDM Research Building, Old Road Campus, Headington, Oxford OX3 7FZ. *T:* (01865) 612907; 53 Jack Straw's Lane, Headington, Oxford OX3 0DW.

**ROWLANDS,** family name of **Baron Rowlands**.

**ROWLANDS, Baron** *cr* 2004 (Life Peer), of Merthyr Tydfil and of Rhymney in the County of Mid-Glamorgan; **Edward Rowlands,** CBE 2002; *b* 23 Jan. 1940; *e s* of W. S. Rowlands; *m* 1968, Janice Williams (*d* 2004), Kidwelly, Carmarthenshire; two *s* one *d*. *Educ:* Rhondda Grammar Sch.; Wirral Grammar Sch.; King's Coll., London. BA Hons History (London) 1962. Research Asst, History of Parliament Trust, 1963–65; Lectr in Modern History and Govt, Welsh Coll. of Adv. Technology, 1965–66. MP (Lab): Cardiff North, 1966–70; Merthyr Tydfil, April 1972–1983, Merthyr Tydfil and Rhymney, 1983–2001. Parliamentary Under-Secretary of State: Welsh Office, 1969–70, 1974–75; FCO, 1975–76; Minister of State, FCO, 1976–79; Opposition spokesman on energy, 1980–87; Mem., Select Cttee on Foreign Affairs, 1987–2001; Chm., Jt Cttee (inquiring into strategic export controls) of Select Cttees on Defence, Internat. Develt, and Trade and Industry, 1999–2001. Trustee, History of Parliament Trust, 1991– (Chm., 1993–2001). Member: Governing Body, Commonwealth Inst., 1980–92; Academic Council, Wilton Park, 1983–92. A Booker Prize Judge, 1984. *Publications:* various articles. *Recreations:* music, golf. *Address:* House of Lords, SW1A 0PW; 42 Station Road, Kidwelly, Carms SA17 4UT.

**ROWLANDS, Prof. Brian James,** MD; Professor of Gastrointestinal Surgery, Queen's Medical Centre and University of Nottingham, 1997–2009, now Emeritus Professor of Surgery; *b* 18 March 1945; *s* of Arthur Leslie Rowlands and Lilian Grace Allan; *m* 1971, Judith Thomas (*d* 2008); one *d*; partner, Kalliope Valassiadou; one *d*. *Educ:* Wirral Grammar Sch. for Boys; Guy's Hosp., Univ. of London (MB BS 1968); Univ. of Sheffield (MD 1978). Surgical trng, Sheffield Hosps, 1971–77; Associate Prof. of Surgery, Univ. of Texas Health Sci. Center, Houston, 1977–86; Prof. of Surgery and Hd, Dept of Surgery, QUB, and Consultant Surgeon, Royal Victoria Hosp., Belfast, 1986–97. Pres., Assoc. of Surgeons of GB and Ireland, 2007–08. Dir of Professional Affairs, E Midlands Strategic HA, 2009–14, Vice-Chm., Dir of Professional Affairs Forum, RCS, 2009–12; Mem., E Midlands Clin. Senate Council, 2012–. *Publications:* Critical Care for Post Graduate Trainees, 2005; ABC of Tubes, Drains, Lines and Frames, 2008; numerous peer-reviewed contribs on surgical clinical practice, res., educn and trng. *Recreations:* the mountains and the sea, anything Greek, music and theatre, garden, golf, sailing. *Address:* Section of Surgery, Queen's Medical Centre/University Hospital, Nottingham NG7 2UH. *E:* bjr.surgery@nottingham.ac.uk; 96 Station Road, Cropston, Leicester LE7 7HE. *T:* (0116) 234 0074. *E:* b.rowlands364@btinternet.com.

**ROWLANDS, Christopher John,** FCA; Chief Operating Officer and Deputy Chairman, Apace Media plc, 2006–07; *b* 29 Aug. 1951; *s* of late Wilfrid John Rowlands and of Margaretta (*née* Roberts); *m* 1978, Alison Mary Kelly; twin *d*. *Educ:* Roundhay Sch., Leeds; Gonville and Caius Coll., Cambridge (MA Econ). FCA 1975. Peat Marwick Mitchell: articled clerk, 1973–75; CA, 1975; Manager, 1981; seconded as Partner, Zambia, 1981–83; Sen. Manager, London, 1983–85; Asda Group plc: Controller, business planning, Asda Stores, 1985–86; Divl Dir, Gp Finance, 1986–88; Dep. Man. Dir and Finance Dir, Asda Gp/Property Develt and Investment cos, 1988–92; Gp Finance Dir, 1992–93, Chief Exec., 1993–97, HTV Gp plc; Chief Exec., The Television Corporation, 1998–2001. Non-executive Director: iTouch plc, 2002–05; Standard Life (formerly Deutsche) Equity Investment Trust plc, 2003–12; Bristol & London plc, 2003–04. Mem. Council, ITVA, 1993–97 (Chm., Engrg Policy Gp, 1993–96). CCMI (CIMgt 1995); FRSA 1995. *Recreations:* family, theatre, church, reading, ski-ing, tennis, travel.

**ROWLANDS, Rev. John Henry Lewis;** Team Rector, Rectorial Benefice of Whitchurch, 2001–17 (Vicar, 1997–2001); Chaplain of Whitchurch Hospital, 1997–2016; Trust Chaplain, Cardiff and Vale University Health Board, 2016–17; Chancellor, Llandaff Cathedral, 2002–17; *b* 16 Nov. 1947; *s* of William Lewis and Elizabeth Mary Rowlands; *m* 1976, Catryn Meryl Parry Edwards; one *s* two *d*. *Educ:* Queen Elizabeth Grammar Sch., Carmarthen; St David's University Coll., Lampeter (BA); Magdalene Coll., Cambridge (MA); Durham Univ. (MLitt); Wescott House, Cambridge. Ordained deacon, 1972, priest, 1973 (St David's Cathedral); Curate, Rectorial Benefice of Aberystwyth, 1972–76; Chaplain, St David's University Coll., Lampeter, 1976–79; Youth Chaplain, dio. of St David's, 1976–79; Dir, Academic Studies, St Michael's Coll., Llandaff, 1979–84, Sub-Warden, 1984–88, Warden, 1988–97. Lectr, Faculty of Theology, University Coll., Cardiff, 1993–97. Diocesan Dir of Ordinands, Dio. Llandaff, 1985–88; Examng Chaplain to Archbishop of Wales, 1987–91; Sec., Doctrinal Commn of the Church in Wales, 1987–94. Hon. Canon, 1990–97, Residentiary Canon, 1997–2002, Llandaff Cathedral. Chaplain, Whitchurch Br., RBL, 1997–2017. Pres., Diwinyddiaeth (Soc. of Theol. Grads, Univ. of Wales), 1989–92. Member: (*ex officio*) Governing Body of the Church in Wales, 1988–97; Court, Univ. of Wales, 1988–94; Court, Univ. of Wales Coll. of Cardiff, 1988–97; Academic Bd, Univ. of Wales, 1991–94; Council, Llandaff Cathedral Sch., 1991–2017. Hon. Chaplain to High Sheriff of S. Glamorgan, 2017–18. Fellow, Woodard Corp., 1993–2017 (Hon. Fellow, 2017). *Publications:* (ed) Essays on the Kingdom of God, 1986; Church, State and Society 1827–45, 1989; Doing Theology, 1996. *Recreations:* beachcombing, auctioneering, antique markets. *Address:* Llys y Coed, Bwlchgwynt, New Quay, Ceredigion SA45 9QS. *T:* (01545) 560143, 07434 579466.

**ROWLANDS, Marc Humphreys;** QC 2012; *b* Den Haag, Netherlands, 8 Nov. 1967; *s* of Paul Rowlands and Alison Rowlands; *m* 1996, Amanda Jane Dixon; three *s* two *d*. *Educ:* Marlborough Coll.; Magdalen Coll., Oxford (BA). Called to the Bar, Gray's Inn, 1990. *Recreations:* French bureaucracy, child psychology, sexual politics. *Address:* Keating Chambers, 15 Essex Street, WC2R 3AA. *T:* (020) 7544 2600. *E:* mrowlands@keatingchambers.com.

**ROWLANDS, Rhys Price; His Honour Judge Rowlands;** a Circuit Judge, since 2010; Resident Judge, North Wales, since 2014; *b* Bangor, N Wales; *s* of Emyr Price Rowlands and Aileen Price Rowlands; *m* 1989, Kären Jayne Woolley; two *d*. *Educ:* Brynhyfryd Sch., Ruthin; University Coll. London (LLB Hons); Univ. of Wales, Cardiff (MSc). Admitted solicitor, 1982; in practice as a solicitor, 1982–86; called to the Bar, Gray's Inn, 1986; in practice as a barrister, 1986–2010; Recorder, 2000–10. Hon. Recorder, Caernarfon, 2015. *Recreations:* tennis, hill walking, gardening, local history. *Address:* Mold Crown Court, Mold CH7 1AE. *T:* (01352) 707300.

**ROWLATT, Amanda, (Mrs Heymann),** CBE 2011; Chief Analyst, Department for Transport, since 2014; *b* 21 Dec. 1962; *d* of Charles Rowlatt and Penelope Anne Rowlatt, *qv*; *m* 1995, Tim Heymann; two *s* one *d*. *Educ:* University Coll., Oxford (MA Maths); St Antony's Coll., Oxford (MPhil Econs). Economist, FCO and ODA, 1987–91; Econ. Advr, HM Treasury, 1991–98; Chief Economist: ONS, 1998–2002; Competition Commn, 2002–05; Dir, Internat. Finance and Europe (formerly Europe, Trade and Internat. Financial Instns), DFID, 2005–08; Associate, Oxera, 2007–08; Chief Economist and Dir for Families and Child Poverty, DWP, 2008–11; Chief Analyst, BIS, 2011–14 (interim Dir Gen., Econs and Mkts, 2013). Vice Chair, Care Internat. UK, 2003–05. Mem. Council, REconS, 2003–08. Board Member: VSO UK, 2011–15; Central and NW London NHS Foundn Trust, 2014–17; Brunel Univ., 2015–; Soc. of Business Economists, 2015–; VSO Internat., 2015–. Governor: Richmond Adult Community College, 2010–17; NIESR, 2014–.

**ROWLATT, Penelope Anne,** PhD; economist; *b* 17 May 1936; *d* of Theodore Alexander Maurice Ionides and Anne Joyce Ionides (*née* Cooke); *m* 1961, Charles Rowlatt (*d* 2017); one *s* three *d*. *Educ:* King Alfred Sch.; Somerville Coll., Oxford (BA 1959); Imperial Coll., London (PhD 1963); London Sch. of Economics (MSc 1973); University Coll. London (MPhil 2010; PhD 2018). Chief Economist, Economic Models Gp of Cos, 1975–76; Economist, NIESR, 1976–78; Economic Advr, HM Treasury, 1978–86; Sen. Economic Advr, Dept of Energy, 1986–88; Director: Nat. Economic Res. Associates, 1988–98; Europe Economics, 1998–2001. Publisher, Medicine Today, 2000–03. Member: Retail Prices Adv. Cttee, 1991–94; Royal Commn on Envmtl Pollution, 1996–2000; Steering Gp, Performance and Innovation Unit Project, Cabinet Office, 1999; Better Regulation Commn (formerly Task Force), 2000–07. Treas., REconS, 1999–2008. *Publications:* Group Theory and Elementary Particles, 1966; Inflation, 1992; Mind: a property of matter, 2018; papers in learned jls on nuclear physics, economics and philosophy. *Recreations:* walking, sailing, bridge, eating and drinking, debating current affairs with friends. *Address:* 10 Hampstead Hill Gardens, NW3 2PL.

*See also* A. Rowlatt.

**ROWLEY, Danielle;** MP (Lab) Midlothian, since 2017; *b* 1990; *d* of Alex Rowley. *Educ:* Dalkeith High Sch.; Edinburgh Telford Coll. (HNC Radio Broadcasting); Edinburgh Napier Univ. (BA 1st Cl. Hons Journalism 2014). Constituency Media Manager, Kirkcaldy and Cowdenbeath, 2014–15; E-Communications Officer, Scottish Parlt, 2015; Communications and Mktg Officer, Assoc. of Chief Officers of Scottish Voluntary Orgns, 2015–16; Campaigns and Public Affairs Officer, Shelter Scotland, 2016–17. Trustee Dir, Scottish Youth Parlt, 2009–11. Mem., Scottish Affairs Cttee, H of C, 2017–. *Address:* House of Commons, SW1A 0AA.

**ROWLEY, (John) James;** QC 2006; *b* 24 June 1964; *s* of late John Rowley and Gillian E. M. Rowley; *m* 1990, Clare Louise Brown; three *s*. *Educ:* Stonyhurst Coll.; Emmanuel Coll., Cambridge (BA Hons Classics 1985); Dip. Law. Called to the Bar, Lincoln's Inn, 1987 (Hardwicke Scholar); in practice as a barrister, Manchester, 1987– and London, 2004–; Counsel to Royal Liverpool Children's Inq., 2000–01; a Recorder, 2002–15. Chm., Personal Injuries Bar Assoc., 2010–12. Arbitrator, PIcARBS, 2016–. *Publications:* (contrib.) Personal Injuries Handbook, 1997, 3rd edn 2007; contrib. articles to Jl Personal Injuries Litigation. *Recreations:* cricketer, gardener, cook. *Address:* Byrom Street Chambers, 12 Byrom Street, Manchester M3 4PP. *T:* (0161) 829 2100.

**ROWLEY, Karl John;** QC 2013; a Recorder, since 2009; *b* Stoke-on-Trent, 16 Oct. 1969; *s* of John Rowley and Noreen Rowley; *m* 1994, Georgina Roberts. *Educ:* Oriel Coll., Oxford (BA Phil. and Theol.; DipLaw 1993). Called to the Bar, Middle Temple, 1994; in practice as a barrister, specialising in family law: Regent Chambers, 1995–97; Young St Chambers, 1997–2005, St John's Bldgs, 2005–. *Recreations:* walking, reading, cycling, fishing. *Address:* St John's Buildings, 24a–28 St John Street, Manchester M3 4DJ. *T:* (0161) 214 1500. *E:* clerks@stjohnsbuildings.co.uk.

**ROWLEY, Keith Nigel;** QC 2001; *s* of late James and Eva Rowley; *m* 1986, Chantal Anna Mackenzie; one *s* one *d*. *Educ:* King's Coll., London (LLB). Called to the Bar, Gray's Inn, 1979; Bencher, Lincoln's Inn, 2008; in practice at Chancery Bar, 1980–. Judge, First-tier Tribunal (formerly Chm., Consumer Credit Appeals Tribunal), 2008–. *Recreations:* classical music, gardening, theatre, wine. *Address:* Radcliffe Chambers, 11 New Square, Lincoln's Inn, WC2A 3QB. *T:* (020) 7831 0081. *Club:* Hurlingham.

**ROWLEY, Lee Benjamin;** MP (C) North East Derbyshire, since 2017; *b* Chesterfield, 11 Sept. 1980; *s* of Malcolm and Linda Rowley. *Educ:* Lincoln Coll., Oxford (BA Hons Modern Hist. 2002); Univ. of Manchester (MA Hist. 2004). Analyst, H. Clarkson & Co., 2004–07; Strategy Analyst, Barclays, 2007–08; Sen. Consultant, Santander, 2008–11; Manager, KPMG, 2011–12; Santander: Sen. Manager, 2012–14; Hd of Change, 2014–16; Hd, Risk Technol. and Ops, 2016–17; Hd of Change and Portfolio, Co-op Insce, 2017. Mem., Public Accounts Select Cttee, 2018–. Mem. (C), Westminster CC, 2006–14. *Address:* House of Commons, SW1A 0AA. *T:* (020) 7219 4197. *E:* lee.rowley.mp@parliament.uk.

**ROWLEY, Sir Richard (Charles),** 8th Bt *cr* 1836, of Hill House, Berkshire, and 9th Bt *cr* 1786, of Tendring Hall, Suffolk; *b* 14 Aug. 1959; *s* of Sir Charles Robert Rowley, 7th and 8th Bt and of Astrid Pennington Cleife, *d* of Sir Arthur Massey, CBE; *S* father, 2008; *m* 1st, 1989, Elizabeth Alison (*marr*. *diss*. 1999), *d* of late Henry Bellingham; two *s*; 2nd, 2013, Mrs Louise Gilks. *Educ:* Exeter Coll., Oxford (BA Metallurgy and Material Scis 1982); Open Univ. (BSc Psychol. 2005); Nottingham Univ. (MSc Occupational Psychol. 2006). CEO, Mansley Gp Hldgs Ltd, 2015–. *Heir:* s Joshua Andrew Rowley, *b* 5 Dec. 1989. *Address:* 21 Tedworth Square, SW3 4DR; Naseby Hall, Northants NN6 6DP.

**ROWLEY-CONWY,** family name of **Baron Langford**.

**ROWLING, Joanne Kathleen,** CH 2017; OBE 2000; FRSL; writer; *b* 31 July 1965; *d* of Peter John Rowling and late Anne Rowling; *m* 1st, 1992 (marr. diss.); one *d*; 2nd, 2001, Dr Neil Murray; one *s* one *d*. *Educ:* Univ. of Exeter (BA 1986). FRSL 2002. Author of the Year, British Book Awards, 2000. Chevalier de la Légion d'Honneur (France), 2009. *Publications:* Harry Potter and the Philosopher's Stone, 1997 (Smarties Prize, 1997; filmed, 2001); Harry Potter and the Chamber of Secrets, 1998 (Smarties Prize, 1998; Children's Book Award, Scottish Arts Council, 1999; filmed, 2002); Harry Potter and the Prisoner of Azkaban, 1999 (Smarties Prize, 1999; Whitbread Children's Book of the Year, 2000; filmed, 2004); Harry Potter and the Goblet of Fire, 2000 (WH Smith Children's Book of the Year, Children's Book Award, Scottish Arts Council, 2001; filmed, 2005); Fantastic

Beasts and Where to Find Them, 2001 (screenplay and script book, 2016); Quidditch Through the Ages, 2001; Harry Potter and the Order of the Phoenix, 2003 (filmed, 2007); Harry Potter and the Half-Blood Prince, 2005 (filmed, 2009); Harry Potter and the Deathly Hallows, 2007 (Part 1 filmed, 2010; Part 2 filmed 2011); The Tales of Beedle the Bard, 2008; The Casual Vacancy, 2012 (televised, 2015); Very Good Lives: the fringe benefits of failure and the importance of imagination, 2015; (with J. Tiffany and J. Thorne) Harry Potter and the Cursed Child (play and script book), 2016; Fantastic Beasts, The Crimes of Grindelwald (screenplay and script book), 2018; (as Robert Galbraith): The Cuckoo's Calling, 2013 (televised, 2017); The Silkworm, 2014 (televised, 2017); Career of Evil, 2015 (televised, 2018); Lethal White, 2018. *Address*: c/o Neil Blair, The Blair Partnership, Middlesex House, 4th Floor, 34–42 Cleveland Street, W1T 4JE.

**ROWLING, Sir John (Reginald)**, Kt 2003; educational consultant; Headteacher, Nunthorpe School, Middlesbrough, 1984–2003; *b* 8 Jan. 1941; *m* 1977, Sheila Elizabeth; one *s* one *d*. *Educ*: Durham Univ. (BSc Maths 1962; MSc Applied Maths 1963). Teacher, Royal GS, Newcastle, 1963–74; teacher, later Dep. Head, Hirst High Sch., Ashington, 1974–84. Vis. Prof., St Mary's UC, Twickenham, 2008–. Dir, PiXL Club, 2009– (Chm.). *Publications*: Heading Towards Excellence, 2002, 2nd edn 2003; Changing Towards Excellence, 2003; Climbing Towards Excellence, 2006; (ed) A String of Pearls, 2018. *Recreations*: golf, photography, walking, gardening. *Address*: Cromwell House, 38 College Square, Stokesley TS9 5DW. *T*: (01642) 712095. *E*: therowlings@hotmail.com.

**ROWNTREE, Phillip**; *see* Wright, P.

**ROWNTREE, Timothy John**; Director Engineering and Safety, Defence Equipment and Support, Ministry of Defence, since 2018; *b* 13 Sept. 1956; *s* of George Arthur and Cicely Beryl Rowntree; *m* 1982, Susan Margaret Jones; two *d*. *Educ*: Strensall Primary Sch.; Joseph Rowntree Secondary Modern Sch.; Univ. of Bradford (BTech Hons Electrical Engrg); King's Coll., London (MA Internat. Studies 2009). Systems Analyst, Army Electro Magnetic Compatibility Agency, Blandford, 1980–84; Sen. Engr, RAE, Farnborough, 1984–87; Attack and Identification System Manager, NATO Eur. Fighter Aircraft Mgt Agency, Munich, 1987–92; Head, RAF Signal Engrg Labs, RAF Henlow, 1992–96; Head, Tornado Mission Systems Support Authy, 1996–99, Dep. Tornado Integrated Project Team Leader, 1999–2001, RAF Wyton; Lynx Helicopter Integrated Project Team Leader, Yeovilton, 2001–04; Dep. Ops Dir, Air Systems, Defence Procurement Agency, Bristol, 2004–07; Dir Air Support, Defence Equipment and Support, MoD, 2007–13; Dir, Orgn Conjointe de Coopération en Matière d'Armement, 2013–17; Dir Air Projects, Defence Equipment and Support, MoD, 2017–18. *Recreations*: more than I can fit in my busy lifestyle, involving family and friends, including diving, gardening, theatre, music, boating, fishing, motorcycles. *Address*: Old Oaks, 2 Dod Lane, Glastonbury, Somerset BA6 8BZ. *Club*: Royal Air Force.

**ROWSELL, Edmund Charles P.**; *see* Penning-Rowsell.

**ROWSON, Martin George Edmund**; cartoonist, illustrator, writer, poetaster and broadcaster; *b* 15 Feb. 1959; adopted *s* of late K. E. K. Rowson, MD, PhD; *m* 1987, Anna Victoria Clarke; one *s* one *d*. *Educ*: Merchant Taylors' Sch., Northwood; Pembroke Coll., Cambridge (BA 1982). Cartoons contributed regularly to: New Statesman, 1982–84, 1985–86, 1995–98; One Two Testing/Making Music, 1983–91; Chartist, 1985–; Financial Weekly, 1985–90; Today, 1986–92; Sunday Today, 1986–87; Guardian, 1987–89, 1991–93, 1994–; Sunday Correspondent, 1989–91; Independent, 1989–; Time Out, 1990–2002; Sunday Tribune, 1991–2000; Independent on Sunday, 1991–; European, 1991–92; Modern Review, 1993–95; Tribune, 1994–; Daily Mirror, 1995–; Observer, 1996–98; Scotsman, 1998–2009; TES, 1998–2005; Irish Times, 1999–2000; Daily Express, 1999–2001; Red Pepper, 1999–; Erotic Review, 1999–; Index on Censorship, 2000–; The Times, 2001–05; Scotland on Sunday, 2002–04; New Humanist, 2002–; Spectator, 2007–; Morning Star, 2007–. Book reviews, Independent on Sunday, 1994–; Cult Books Expert, Mark Radcliffe Show, Radio 1, 1996–97; columnist, Tribune, 1998–, Dir, Tribune Publications, 2000–04. Vis. Fellow, Teesside Univ., 2015. Non-executive Director: Quex Park Estates, 2014–18; Goulash Co-operative, 2014–. Chm., British Cartoonists' Assoc., 2000. Vice-Pres., Zool Soc. of London, 2002–05, 2009–10, 2016– (Council Mem., 1991–2005, 2007–11, 2014–). Chm., Ken Sprague Trust, 2004–; Trustee: Cartoon Mus., 2003–; People's Trust for Endangered Species, 2013–17; Rep. Gov., Powell-Cotton Mus., 2007– (Chm. of Trustees, 2016–). Hon. Associate, Nat. Secular Soc.; Dist. Supporter, Humanists UK (formerly British Humanist Assoc.), 2009– (Trustee, 2011–15). Hon. Fellow, Goldsmiths, Univ. of London, 2014. Cartoonist Laureate to Mayor of London (in return for 1 pint of London Pride Ale per annum), 2001–. Political Cartoonist of the Year, 2000, 2003, Caricaturist of the Year, 2011, Cartoon Arts' Trust; Political Cartoon of the Year, 2002, 2007, Political Cartoonist of the Year, 2010, Political Cartoon Soc. Premio Satira Politica Award, Italy, 2007; Political Book Award for Humour and Satire, 2015. Hon. DLitt Westminster, 2007. *Publications*: Scenes from the Lives of the Great Socialists, 1983 (with Kevin Killane); Lower than Vermin: an anatomy of Thatcher's Britain, 1986; The Waste Land, 1990; (with Anna Clarke) The Nodland Express, 1994; (with Chris Scarre) Imperial Exits, 1995; (with Will Self) Sweet Smell of Psychosis, 1996; The Life and Opinions of Tristram Shandy, Gentleman, 1996; (with John Sweeney) Purple Homicide, 1997; Mugshots, 2005; Snatches, 2006; Stuff, 2007; The Dog Allusion, 2008; Fuck: the human odyssey, 2008; Giving Offence, 2009; The Limerickiad: vol. I: from Gilgamesh to Shakespeare, 2011; vol. II: John Donne to Jane Austen, 2012; vol. III, Byron to Baudelaire, 2013; vol. IV, from Tolstoy to Modernism, 2018; Gulliver's Travels, 2012; The Coalition Book, 2014 (Political Humour and Satire Book of Year, Political Book Awards, 2015); Carol Carnage, 2015; (illus.) Gimson's Kings and Queens, 2016; (illus.) Gimson's Prime Ministers, 2018; (with Karl Marx and Frederick Engels) The Communist Manifesto, 2018; The Pen is Mightier Than the Word, 2018; Pastrami Faced Racist and Other Verse, 2018. *Recreations*: cooking, drinking, ranting, atheism, zoos, collecting taxidermy, charity governance. *Address*: 46 Vicar's Hill, SE13 7JL. *T*: (020) 8244 7576, *Fax*: (020) 8244 7577. *E*: martin.rowson1@ntlworld.com. *Clubs*: Soho House, Chelsea Arts, Academy; Zoological.

**ROWTHORN, Prof. Robert Eric**; Professor of Economics, Cambridge University, 1991–2006, now Emeritus; Fellow, King's College, Cambridge, since 1991; *b* 20 Aug. 1939; *s* of Eric William Rowthorn and Eileen Rowthorn; *m* 1981, Amanda Jane Wharton; one *s* one *d*. *Educ*: Newport High Sch. for Boys; Jesus Coll., Oxford (BA, BPhil, MA). University of Cambridge: Res. Fellow, Churchill Coll., 1964–65; College Lectr, King's Coll., 1965–66; Asst Lectr, 1966–71; Lectr, 1971–82; Reader in Economics, 1982–91. *Publications*: International Big Business, 1971; Capitalism, Conflict and Inflation, 1980; (with J. Wells) De-industrialisation and Foreign Trade, 1987; (with N. Wayne) Northern Ireland: the political economy of conflict, 1988; (ed jtly) The Role of the State in Economic Change, 1995; (ed jtly) Democracy and Efficiency in the Economic Enterprise, 1996; (ed jtly) Transnational Corporations and the Global Economy, 1998; (ed with Antony Dnes) The Law and Economics of Marriage and Divorce, 2002. *Recreations*: swimming, reading, scuba-diving. *Address*: King's College, Cambridge CB2 1ST.

**ROXBEE COX, Philip Ardagh, (Philip Ardagh)**; children's author, poet, reviewer and commentator; *b* Shortlands, Kent, 11 Sept. 1961; *s* of late Hon. Christopher Withers Roxbee Cox and of Rosemary Joyce Roxbee Cox (*née* Ardagh); *m* 1994, Dr Héloïse Jeanne-Marie Coffey; one *s*. Literary prize judge for: Guardian Children's Book Award, 2003; Roald Dahl Funny Prize, 2010; Young Minds Book Award, 2010. Writer: Secret Undercover Vets on Ice, BBC Radio 7, 2004; Arthur Storms and the Department of Historical Correction (interactive drama), BBC Radio 7, 2005; Co-writer, The Gift (short film), 2013. On-line writer in residence, Booktrust, 2014–15. Guest Dir, Children's Prog., Stratford-upon-Avon Literary Fest., 2016. Patron: Stratford-upon-Avon Literary Fest., 2013–; Northern Children's Book Fest., 2015–. *Publications*: over 100 books, primarily for children, including: The Hieroglyphs Handbook, 1999; The Eddie Dickens Trilogy: Awful End, 2000 (Luchs Prize, 2002; Deutschen Jugendliteraturpreis, 2003), Dreadful Acts, 2001, Terrible Times, 2002; The Further Adventures of Eddie Dickens: Dubious Deeds, 2003, Horrendous Habits, 2005, Final Curtain, 2006; Unlikely Exploits: The Fall of Fergal, 2002, Heir of Mystery, 2003, The Rise of the House of McNally, 2004; The Green Men of Gressingham, 2002, The Red Dragons of Gressingham, 2008; Grubtown Tales: Stinking Rich and Just Plain Stinky (Roald Dahl Funny Prize), 2009, The Year that it Rained Cows, 2009, The Far From Great Escape, 2009, The Wrong End of the Dog, 2010, Trick Eggs and Rubber Chickens, 2010, Splash, Crash and Loads of Cash, 2010, The Great Pasta Disaster, 2010, When Bunnies Turn Bad, 2011; (with Sir Paul McCartney and G. Dunbar) High in the Clouds, 2005; Philip Ardagh's Book of Absolutely Useless Lists for Every Day of the Year, 2007; Philip Ardagh's Book of Howlers, Blunders and Random Mistakery, 2009; The Henry's House non-fiction series, 2009–; Philip Ardagh's Book of Kings, Queens, Emperors and Rotten Wart-Nosed Commoners, 2011; The Grunts in Trouble, 2012; The Grunts all at Sea, 2013; The Grunts in a Jam, 2014; The Grunts on the Run, 2015; The Black Knight of Gressingham, 2015; Unlikely Outlaws, 2015; for adults: The Not-So-Very-Nice Goings-on at Victoria Lodge: without illustrations by the author, 2004; The Silly Side of Sherlock Holmes: a brand new adventure using a bunch of old pictures, 2005; The Scandalous Life of the Lawless Sisters: criminally illustrated with what was to hand, 2008. *Recreations*: general beard maintenance, ducking through doorways, visiting historical and archaeological sites, Sherlock Holmes. *Address*: c/o Faber & Faber, Bloomsbury House, 74–77 Great Russell Street, WC1B 3DA.

**ROXBURGH, Charles Fergusson**; Second Permanent Secretary, HM Treasury, since 2016; *b* London, 25 Oct. 1959; *s* of Robert Roxburgh and Muriel Smith; *m* 1987, Karen Elizabeth Pierce (*see* Dame K. E. Pierce); two *s*. *Educ*: Stowe Sch., Buckingham; Trinity Coll., Cambridge (BA 1981); Harvard Business Sch. (MBA 1986). Associate, Arthur Andersen, 1981–84; McKinsey & Company, 1986–2013: Co-Hd, Global Strategy Practice, 1999–2003; Hd, UK Financial Instns Practice, 2003–05; Co-Hd, Corporate and Investment Banking Practice, 2005–09; Dir, McKinsey Global Inst., 2009–13; Dir Gen., Financial Services, HM Treasury, 2013–16. Chm., Financial Services Trade and Investment Bd, 2013–17; HM Treasury Rep., Financial Policy Cttee, 2013–; Mem. Bd, UK Govt Investments, 2016–. *Publications*: (jtly) The Emerging Equity Gap, 2012. *Recreations*: spending time with family, music, history. *Address*: HM Treasury, One Horse Guards Road, SW1A 2HQ. *E*: charles.roxburgh@hmtreasury.gov.uk. *Clubs*: Royal Automobile, Tuesday.

**ROXBURGH, Iain Edge**; advisor and commentator on local governance and public service management, since 2013 (consultant, 2001–13); *b* 4 Nov. 1943; *s* of John and Irene Roxburgh; *m* 1965, Tessa Breddy; two *s*. *Educ*: William Hulme's Grammar Sch. Manchester; Imperial Coll., London (BSc Eng, MSc, DIC). ACGI; CEng; MICE. Civil Engineer and transport planner, 1965–80; Greater London Council: Dep. Head of Personnel Services, 1981–83; Dir of Admin, 1983–85; Dep. Sec., AMA, 1985–89; Chief Exec. and Town Clerk, Coventry City Council, 1989–2001. Dir, Warwick Research Consortium, 2003–08. Sen. Res. Associate, 2003–13, Associate Fellow, 2006–13, Warwick Business Sch. Mem. Bd and Vice Chm., New Local Govt Network, 2013–17 (Chm., 2007–13). Trustee and Chm., Meriden Sports and Recreation Trust, 2015–. *Recreations*: photography, cycling, walking, ski-ing, golf. *Address*: Hill Rise, Leys Lane, Meriden, Coventry CV7 7LQ. *T*: (01676) 522496, 07971 780616.

**ROXBURGH, Prof. Ian Walter**; Professor of Mathematics and Astronomy, 1987–2001, Research Professor of Astronomy, 2001–11, Queen Mary, University of London (formerly Queen Mary College, later Queen Mary and Westfield College, University of London), now Emeritus Professor of Astronomy and Mathematics; *b* 31 Aug. 1939; *s* of Walter McRonald Roxburgh and Kathleen Joyce (*née* Prescott); *m* 1960, Diana Patricia (*née* Dunn); two *s* one *d*. *Educ*: King Edward VII Grammar Sch., Sheffield; Univ. of Nottingham (BSc Mathematics 1st Cl. Hons); Univ. of Cambridge (PhD); Elected Res. Fellow, Churchill Coll., Cambridge, 1963; Asst Lectr, Mathematics, 1963–64, Lectr, 1964–66, KCL; Reader in Astronomy, Univ. of Sussex, 1966–67; Queen Mary, later Queen Mary and Westfield College, London University: Prof. of Applied Maths, 1967–87; Hd, Dept of Applied Maths, 1978–84; Dir, Astronomy Unit, 1983–2001; Hd, Sch. of Math. Scis, 1984–95; Pro-Principal, 1987. Chm., Cttee of Heads of Univ. Depts of Maths and Stats, 1988–93. Chercheur associé, Observatoire de Paris, 2000–09. ESA scientist on COROT mission. Hon. Sen. Res. Fellow, Univ. of Birmingham, 2019–. Contested: (L) Walthamstow W, 1970; (SDP) Ilford N, 1983. *Publications*: (ed jtly) Physical Processes in Astrophysics, 1993; (ed jtly) Convection in Astrophysics, 2007; articles in Monthly Notices RAS, Astrophys. Jl, Astronomy and Astrophysics, Jl Geophysical Res., Phil. Trans Royal Soc., Gen. Relativity and Gravitation, Jl Physics A., Foundations of Physics, Nature, Solar Physics, Brit. Jl for the Philosophy of Science. *Recreations*: politics, economics, philosophy. *Address*: 37 Leicester Road, Wanstead, E11 2DW. *T*: (020) 8989 7117.

**ROXBURGH, Dame Karen Elizabeth**; *see* Pierce, Dame K. E.

**ROXBURGHE, 11th Duke of,** *cr* 1707; **Charles Robert George Innes-Ker**; Baron Roxburghe 1600; Earl of Roxburghe, Baron Ker of Cessford and Cavertoun, 1616; Bt (NS) 1625; Viscount Broxmouth, Earl of Kelso, Marquis of Bowmont and Cessford, 1707; Earl Innes (UK), 1837; *b* 18 Feb. 1981; *s* of 10th Duke of Roxburghe and of Lady Jane Dawnay, *qv*; *S* father, 2019; *m* 2011, Hon. Charlotte Susanna Aitken (marr. diss. 2013), *e d* of Baron Beaverbrook, *qv*. *Educ*: Eton Coll.; Newcastle Univ. (BSc); RMA Sandhurst. Commnd Blues and Royals (RHG and 1st Dragoons), 2004. *Recreations*: motor racing, golf, tennis, fishing. *Heir*: *b* Lord Edward Arthur Gerald Innes-Ker [*b* 1984; *m* 2017, Celia Margaret Brook]. *Address*: Floors Castle, Kelso TD5 7RW.

**ROY, Frank**; Campaign Director, Scotland Stronger in Europe, 2015–16; *b* 29 Aug. 1958; *s* of James Roy and Esther McMahon; *m* 1977, Ellen Foy; one *s* one *d*. *Educ*: St Joseph's High Sch.; Our Lady's High Sch., Motherwell; Motherwell Coll. (HNC Mktg); Glasgow Caledonian Univ. (BA Consumer and Mgt Studies 1994). Steelworker, Ravenscraig Steelworks, Motherwell, 1977–91; PA to Helen Liddell, MP, 1994–97. MP (Lab) Motherwell and Wishaw, 1997–2015; contested (Lab) same seat, 2015. An Asst Govt Whip, 2005–06; a Lord Comr, HM Treasury (Govt Whip), 2006–10; an Opposition Whip, 2010. *Recreations*: gardening, reading, football.

**ROY, Dr Helen Elizabeth**, MBE 2018; Principal Scientist-Ecologist, since 2007, and Individual Merit Scientist, since 2019, NERC Centre for Ecology and Hydrology; *b* Plymouth, 6 Nov. 1969; *d* of Alistair John Brown and Philippa Wendy Brown (*née* Richards, now Young); *m* 1994, David Brian Roy; two *d. Educ:* Cowes High Sch., IoW; Univ. of Southampton (BSc Hons Biol.); Univ. of Nottingham (MSc; PhD 1997). Lectr in Ecol., Anglia Ruskin Univ., 1997–2007. Vis. Prof. of Entomol., Univ. of Reading, 2015–. Member: British Ecol Soc., 1996; Royal Entomol Soc., 1996. Silver Medal, ZSL, 2013. *Publications: jointly:* From Biological Control to Invasion: the ladybird, *Harmonia axyridis*, as a model species, 2008; Provisional Atlas of the Aculeate Hymenoptera of Britain and Ireland, Part 7, 2009, Part 8, 2012, Part 9, 2016, Part 10, 2018; The Ecology of Fungal Entomopathogens, 2010; Ladybirds (Coccinellidae) of Great Britain and Ireland, 2011; Invasive Alien Arthropod Predators and Parasitoids: a ecological approach, 2012; Ladybirds (Naturalists' Handbook 10), 2013; Field Guide to Invasive Plants and Animals in Britain, 2015; Ladybirds, 2016; Field Guide to the Ladybirds of Britain and Ireland, 2018; contrib. papers. *Recreations:* entomology, science communication, family, swimming, diving, walking, UK ladybird survey. *Address:* Centre for Ecology and Hydrology, Maclean Building, Benson Lane, Crowmarsh Gifford, Wallingford, Oxon OX10 8BB.

**ROY, Lindsay Allan**, CBE 2004; *b* 19 Jan. 1949; *s* of John and Margaret Roy; *m* 1972, Irene Patterson; two *s* one *d. Educ:* Univ. of Edinburgh (BSc 1970). Principal Teacher of Mod. Studies, Queen Anne High Sch., 1974–83; Asst Rector, Kirkcaldy High Sch., 1983–86; Depute Rector, Glenwood High Sch., 1986–89; Rector, Inverkeithing High Sch., 1990–2008; Rector, Kirkcaldy High Sch., 2008. Associate Assessor, HM Inspectorate of Educn, 1996–2008. Pres., Headteachers' Assoc. of Scotland, 2004–05; Member: Jt Adv. Cttee, Scottish Credit and Qualifications Framework, 2003–07; Nat. Qualifications Steering Gp, 2003–08. Chm., Curriculum and Student Affairs Cttee, Lauder Coll., 1997–2006. Exec. Mem., Internat. Confederation of Principals, 2006–10. MP (Lab) Glenrothes, Nov. 2008–2015. FRSA 2004. *Recreations:* angling, mountain biking.

**ROY, Paul David**, BEM 2018; Founding Partner, NewSmith LLP (formerly NewSmith Capital Partners LLP), 2003–15; *b* 8 May 1947; *s* of Vernon Alfred Roy and Elsie Florence Roy; *m* 1985, Susan Mary Elkies; five *s* one *d. Educ:* Trinity Sch., Croydon; Liverpool Univ. (BA Hons Econs). Partner: Morton Bros (Stockbrokers), 1974–77; Kemp-Gee & Co., 1977–87; Jt Man. Dir, Citicorp Scrimgeour Vickers, 1987–89; Man. Dir, Smith New Court (UK), 1989–95; Chief Exec., Smith New Court plc, 1995; Merrill Lynch & Co.: Man. Dir of Equities, Europe, Middle East and Africa, 1995–98; Sen. Vice-Pres. and Head of Global Equities, 1998–2001; Exec. Vice-Pres. and Co-Pres., Investment Banking and Global Markets, 2001–03. Chairman: New River Retail Ltd, 2009–18; NS Asset Mgt (formerly NewSmith Asset Mgt) LLP, 2011. Chairman: British Horseracing Authy, 2007–13; Retraining of Racehorses. Mem. Bd, Horserace Betting Levy Bd, 2008–13. Vice Pres., Spinal Injuries Assoc. *Recreations:* art, golf, tennis, fishing, watching school matches.

**ROY, Sheila;** Group Director of Healthcare Services, Westminster Health Care, 2000–05; *b* 27 Feb. 1948; *d* of late Bertie and of Dorothy Atkinson; *m* 1970, Robert Neil Roy. *Educ:* BA Open Univ.; RGN; DN (London); Cert Ed Leeds Univ.; RNT; PMD Harvard Business Sch. Milton Keynes Health Authority: Dir, Nursing Studies, 1983–86; Actg Chief Nursing Officer and Dir, Nursing Studies, Feb.–May 1986; Dist Nursing Advr and Dir, Nurse Educn, Hillingdon HA, 1986–88; Dir of Nursing Management and Res., NW Thames RHA, 1988–91; Dir, Newchurch & Co., 1991–96; owner, Sheila Roy & Associates, 1996–2000. Non-exec. Dir, Meditech Gp Ltd, 1996–2001. Participant in Prosavin gene therapy trial for Parkinson's disease, 2011–. *Publications:* The Surprise Package, 2014. *Recreations:* gardening, writing, painting.

**ROYALL OF BLAISDON**, Baroness *cr* 2004 (Life Peer), of Blaisdon in the County of Gloucestershire; **Janet Anne Royall;** PC 2008; Principal, Somerville College, Oxford, since 2017; *b* 20 Aug. 1955; *d* of Basil Oscar Royall and Myra Jessie (*née* Albutt); *m* 1980, Stuart Henry James Hercock (*d* 2010); two *s* one *d. Educ:* Westfield Coll., Univ. of London (BA Hons). Flower importer, Covent Garden, 1978; Gen. Sec., British Labour Gp, European Parlt, 1979–85; Policy Advr/PA, 1985–92, Researcher/Press Officer, 1992–95, to Rt Hon. Neil Kinnock, MP; Mem., Cabinet of Mr Kinnock as Comr, then Vice-Pres., EC, 1995–2001; Parly Co-ordinator, Directorate Gen., Press and Communication, EC, 2001–03; Hd, EC Office in Wales, 2003–05. A Baroness in Waiting (Govt Whip), 2005–08; Captain of the Hon. Corps of Gentlemen at Arms (Govt Chief Whip in H of L), 2008; Leader of the House of Lords, 2008–10; Chancellor of the Duchy of Lancaster, 2009–10; Shadow Leader of the House of Lords, 2010–15. Vice Pres., Party of Eur. Socialists, 2012–18. Mem., Eur. Council on Foreign Relns. Chair, People's History Mus., 2016–. Trustee: Paladin, Nat. Stalking Advocacy Service, 2014–17; City Year UK, 2016–18. Pro-Chancellor, Univ. of Bath, 2014–17. Mem. Adv. Bd, Queen Mary Global Policy Inst., QMUL, 2018–. *Recreations:* reading, gardening, cooking, swimming. *Address:* Somerville College, Woodstock Road, Oxford OX2 6HD.

**ROYAN, James Fraser**, OBE 1986; FRAgS; Vice Lord-Lieutenant, Moray, since 2011; Master Butcher and Proprietor, Royan of Elgin, butchers, since 1972; *s* of James Fraser Royan; *m* Jean; one *s* one *d*. Joined family butchers, Royan of Elgin, 1964. Mem., MLC, 1978–95; Chm., Farm Assured Scotch Livestock, 1989–92. Dir, Highlands and Is Enterprise, 2008. Chair: Moray Health Services NHS Trust, 1996–99; Grampian Primary Care NHS Trust, subseq. Grampian NHS, 1998–2007. Chair, Spirit of Speyside Whisky Fest., 2009–12. Pres., Scottish Fedn of Meat Traders Assoc., 1973. Hon. Vice-Pres., Royal Highland Agricl Soc., 2005. Gov., Robert Gordon Univ., Aberdeen, 1998–2006. FRAgS 1993. DL Moray, 1991. *Address:* Royan of Elgin, 190 High Street, Elgin, Moray IV30 1BA.

**ROYCE, Felicity Ann Hope;** *see* Harvey, F. A. H.

**ROYCE, Hon. Sir (Roger) John**, Kt 2002; a Judge of the High Court, Queen's Bench Division, 2002–14; a Presiding Judge, Western Circuit, 2006–10; *b* 27 Aug. 1944; *s* of late J. Roger Royce and Margaret A. Royce (*née* Sibbald); *m* 1st, 1979, Gillian Wendy Adderley (marr. diss. 2013); two *s* one *d*; 2nd, 2013, Mary Teresa Pringle. *Educ:* The Leys Sch., Cambridge; Trinity Hall, Cambridge (BA). Qualified as Solicitor, 1969; called to the Bar, Gray's Inn, 1970, Bencher, 1997; a Recorder, 1986–2002; QC 1987; a Dep. High Ct Judge, QBD, 1993–2002; Leader, Western Circuit, 1998–2001. Jurist in Residence, Dayton Ohio Univ., 2017. Master, St Stephen's Ringers, 2002. Cambridge Hockey Blue, 1965, 1966; Captain Somerset Hockey, 1976; Austrian qualified ski instructor. Commandeur, Commanderie de Bordeaux (Bristol). Hon. LLD UWE, 2005. *Recreations:* cricket, ski-ing, golf, collecting corkscrews. *Clubs:* Hawks (Cambridge); Clifton (Bristol); St Enodoc Golf.

**ROYDEN, Sir John (Michael Joseph)**, 6th Bt *cr* 1905; Head of Research, JM Finn & Co., since 2010; *b* Santiago, Chile, 17 March 1965; *s* of Sir Christopher John Royden, 5th Bt and Diana Bridget Royden (*née* Goodhart); *S* father, 2017; *m* 1989, Lucilla Stourton (marr. diss. 2002); two *d*; one *d* by Maureen Prentice; partner, Sarah Elizabeth Bone (*née* Gaywood). *Educ:* Stowe Sch.; Univ. of Reading (LLB Hons); London Business Sch. (MBA). CFA. Consultant, ECU Gp plc, 1987–99; Merchant Adventurer, 1999–2010. *Recreations:* shooting, fishing, stalking, sailing, backgammon, bridge, walking, long distance swimming. *Heir: b* Richard Thomas Bland Royden [*b* 20 March 1967; *m* 1st, 1994, Annabel Julia Darling (marr. diss.); three *d*; 2nd, 2014, Alice Sibley]. *T:* 07854 092580. *E:* Sir.John@Royden.com. *Clubs:* Boodle's, Hurlingham.

**ROYLE, Catherine Jane;** Political Adviser, NATO, since 2015; *b* 17 Aug. 1963; *d* of Peter and Anne Royle; *m* 1991, Dr Marcelo Camprubi; two *s. Educ:* Somerville Coll., Oxford (MA 1985; Hon. Fellow 2007); Univ. of Wales, Aberystwyth (MScEcon 1990). Joined FCO, 1986; Third, then Second Sec., Chile, 1988–91; First Sec., FCO, 1992–97; First Sec., Dublin, 1997–2001; Policy Advr on European Constitution, FCO, 2001–03; Dep. Hd of Mission, Buenos Aires, 2003–06; Ambassador to Venezuela, 2007–10; Dep. Ambassador, Afghanistan, 2010–12; Hd of Secretariat, Internat. Police Co-ordination Bd, Afghanistan, 2012–13; Sen. Advr to Minister of Interior, Afghanistan, 2013–14. *Recreations:* reading, riding, sailing, cinema, politics, travelling.

**ROYLE, Rev. Canon Roger Michael;** freelance broadcaster and writer, since 1979; Hon. Canon and Chaplain, Southwark Cathedral, 1993–99; *b* 30 Jan. 1939; *s* of Reginald and Agnes Royle. *Educ:* St Edmund's Sch., Canterbury; King's Coll. London (AKC 2nd Class Hons). Curate, St Mary's, Portsea, Portsmouth, 1962–65; Sen. Curate, St Peter's, Morden, 1965–68; Succentor, Southwark Cathedral, 1968–71; Warden of Dorney Parish, Eton Coll. Project, 1971–74; Conduct, Eton Coll., 1974–79; Chaplain, Lord Mayor Treloar Coll., 1990–92; permission to officiate, dio. Southwark, 1999–. Hon. Chaplain, Entertainment Artistes' Benevolent Fund. Radio broadcasts incl. Sunday Half Hour, Radio 2, 1991–2007. MA Lambeth, 1990. Hon. Fellow, Harris Manchester Coll., Oxford, 2006. *Publications:* A Few Blocks from Broadway, 1987; Royle Exchange, 1989; To Have and to Hold, 1990; Picking up the Pieces, 1990; Mother Teresa: her life in pictures, 1992; Between Friends, 2001. *Recreations:* theatre, music, patience, cooking.

**ROYLE, Timothy Lancelot Fanshawe**, FCIM; Chairman, Cotswold Assistance, since 2005; *b* 24 April 1931; *s* of Sir Lancelot Carrington Royle, KBE, and Barbara Rachel Royle; *m* 1958, Margaret Jill Stedeford; two *s* one *d. Educ:* Harrow; Mons Mil. Acad. FCIM (FInstM 1977). Commnd 15th/19th King's Royal Hussars, 1949, Inns of Court Regt, TA, 1951–63. Joined Hogg Robinson Gp, 1951; Man. Dir, 1980–81. Chairman: Control Risks Group, 1972–91; Berry Palmer & Lyle, 1984–91; Hemotex Holdings, 1991–93; Director: Imperio Reinsurance Co. (UK), 1989–97; Imperio Holdings Ltd, 1995–97. Mem., Insce Brokers Regulatory Council, 1989–94. Lay minister, C of E, 1959–2019; Member: Church Assembly of C of E, 1965–70; Gen. Synod of C of E, 1985–2005; Church Comr, 1966–83. Director: Christian Weekly Newspapers, 1975–2002 (Chm., 1979–97); Lindley Educn Trust, 1970–2002 (Chm., 1970–98); Wellmarine Reinsurance Brokers, 1976–2002. Trustee: Ridley Hall, Cambridge, 1976–2003; Wycliffe Hall, Oxford, 1976–2003; Charinco, 1977–2002; Charishare, 1977–2002; Intercontinental Church Soc., 1977–2001. Freeman, City of London, 1976; Founder Member: Marketors' Co., 1977; Insurers' Co., 1979. Councillor (C) Cotswold DC, 1999–2007 (Chm. Council, 2001–04). Alphege Award for Evangelism and Witness, Lambeth Palace, 2016. *Recreations:* country pursuits, old age. *Address:* The Well House, Donnington, Moreton-in-Marsh, Glos GL56 0XZ. *Clubs:* Cavalry and Guards, MCC; St Moritz Tobogganing (St Moritz).

**ROYSTON, Viscount; Philip Alexander Joseph Yorke;** *b* 3 Dec. 2009; *s* and *heir* of Earl of Hardwicke, *qv*.

**ROZARIO, Patricia Maria**, OBE 2001; soprano; *b* Bombay; *m* Mark Troop; two *c. Educ:* Guildhall Sch. of Music (Gold Medal); Nat. Opera studio. Performances include: Sophie, Werther, Opera North, 1985; Pamina, Magic Flute, Kent Opera; Ilia, Idomeneo, Glyndebourne, 1985; Zerlina, Don Giovanni, Aix-en-Provence; première, Miriam, Golem, 1989; première, Belisa, The Nightingale's to Blame; première, Another America: Fire & Earth, Linbruy Studio, Royal Opera Hse; Tancredi and Clorinda, ENO; works written for her, incl. by Arvo Pärt, Roxanna Panufnik and John Tavener; numerous concerts and recitals in UK and worldwide. Recordings include Schubert songs, Tavener's Akhmatova songs. Prof. of Voice, RCM, 2006–. Co-Dir, Chamber Music Co. Co-Founder, Giving Voice Soc., 2009. FRCM 2014.

**ROZENBERG, Joshua Rufus;** legal journalist and commentator; *b* 30 May 1950; *s* of late Zigmund and Beatrice Rozenberg; *m* 1974, Melanie Phillips, *qv*; one *s* one *d. Educ:* Latymer Upper Sch., Hammersmith; Wadham Coll., Oxford (MA 1976). Solicitor's articled clerk, 1972; admitted Solicitor, 1976; trainee journalist, BBC, 1975; Legal Affairs Correspondent, 1985–97, Legal and Constitutional Affairs Correspondent, 1997–2000, BBC News; Legal Editor, Daily Telegraph, 2000–08. Hon. Bencher, Gray's Inn, 2003. Hon. QC 2016. Hon. LLD: Hertfordshire, 1999; Nottingham Trent, 2012; Lincoln, 2014; Univ. of Law, 2014. *Publications:* Your Rights and the Law (with Nicola Watkins), 1986; The Case for the Crown, 1987; The Search for Justice, 1994; Trial of Strength, 1997; Privacy and the Press, 2004. *Recreations:* reading, writing and wrestling with computers. *Address:* BCM Rozenberg, WC1N 3XX. *E:* joshua@rozenberg.net. *Club:* Garrick.

**ROZENBERG, Melanie;** *see* Phillips, Melanie.

**ROZENTAL, Andrés;** President: Rozental y Asociados, since 1997; Mexican Council on Foreign Relations, since 2001; Retired Eminent Ambassador of Mexico; *b* 27 April 1945; *s* of Leonid Rozental and Neoma Gutman; *m* 1971, Vivian Holzer; two *d. Educ:* Univ. of Bordeaux (Dip. French 1962); Univ. of the Americas (BA 1965); Univ. of Pennsylvania (MA 1966). Joined Foreign Service, 1967; Alternate Perm. Rep. to OAS, Washington, 1971–74; Counsellor, London, 1974–76; Prin. Advr to the Minister, 1977–79; Dir-Gen. of Diplomatic Service, 1979; Dir-Gen. for N American Affairs, 1979–82; Ambassador: to UN, Geneva, 1982–83; to Sweden, 1983–88; Sen. Vice-Pres., Banco Nacional de México, 1988; Dep. Foreign Minister, 1988–94; Amb. to Court of St James's, 1995–97; Amb. at Large, Mexico, 2000–01. Chm., Mittal Steel Mexico, later ArcelorMittal Mexico, 2000–17; Member, non-executive Board: ArcelorMittal Brazil, 2007–13; Ocean Wilson Hldgs, Wilson Sons Brazil, 2010–; HSBC Bank Mexico, 2013–; Mem., Strategy Cttee for Mexico, Airbus Gp, 2006–17 (formerly Mem., non-exec. Bd, EADS Mexico); Member, Advisory Board: Kansas City Southern de Mexico, 2009–14. Sen. Non-resident Fellow, Brookings Instn, 2007–14. Member: Internat. Bd of Governors, 2002–, Operating Bd, 2011–, Centre for Internat. Governance Innovation, Canada; Council, Internat. Inst. for Strategic Studies, London, 2015–. Gov., Internat. Develt Res. Centre, Canada, 2007–12. Trustee, Migration Policy Inst., 2008–15. Orders include: Polar Star (Sweden), 1983; Civil Merit (Spain), 1991; Order of Merit (France), 1993. *Publications:* (jtly) Paradoxes of a World in Transition, 1993; (jtly) The United Nations Today: a Mexican vision, 1994; Mexican Foreign Policy in the Modern Age, 1994; (jtly) Foreign Ministries: change and adaptation, 1997; (jtly) Mexico under Fox, 2004; (jtly) Canada Among Nations, 2009–2010: as others see us, 2009; (jtly) The Obama Administration and the Americas: agenda for change, 2010; (ed jtly) Canada Among Nations, 2011–2012: Canada and Mexico's unfinished agenda, 2012; (contrib.) The End of Nostalgia: Mexico confronts the challenges of global competition, 2013; (contrib.) Oxford Handbook of Modern Diplomacy, 2013. *Recreations:* swimming, sailing, hiking. *Address:* (home) Virreyes 1360, Col. Lomas de Chapultepec, 11000 México DF, México. *T:* (55) 52025347. *E:* mexconsult@gmail.com.

**RUANE, Caitríona;** Member (SF) South Down, Northern Ireland Assembly, 2003–17; *b* 19 July 1962; *d* of Michael Ruane and Nuala Gilmartin; *m* Brian McAteer; two *d*. *Educ:* St Angela's Nat. Sch., Mayo; St Joseph's Secondary Sch., Mayo. Former professional tennis player; human rights and develt worker, US aid foundn, Central America, 1983–87; Latin Amer. Project Officer, Trocaire, Dublin, 1987–88; Co-ordinator, Human Rights Centre, Centre for Res. and Documentation, Belfast, 1988–96; Dir, Féile an Phobail, W Belfast, 1997–2001. Minister for Educn, NI, 2007–11. Northern Ireland Assembly: Equality spokesperson, 2003–07; SF Chief Whip, 2011–16; Principal Dep Speaker, 2016–17; Member: Assembly Commn, 2011–16; N/S Interparly Exec., 2012–17; Chm., Women's Caucus, 2016. Mem., NI Policing Bd, 2011–16. Contested (SF) S Down, 2010.

**RUANE, Christopher Shaun;** MP (Lab) Vale of Clwyd, since 2017; *b* 18 July 1958; *s* of late Michael Ruane, labourer, and of Esther Ruane, dinner lady; *m* 1994, Gill, *d* of late Joe and of Phyl Roberts; two *d*. *Educ:* Blessed Edward Jones Comp. Sch., Rhyl; UCW Aberystwyth (BSc); Liverpool Univ. (PGCE). Teacher, Ysgol Mair RC Primary Sch., Rhyl, 1982–97 (Dep. Hd, 1991–97). Mem. (Lab) Rhyl Town Council, 1988–98. Contested (Lab) Clwyd NW, 1992. MP (Lab) Vale of Clwyd, 1997–2015; contested (Lab) same seat, 2015. PPS to Sec. of State for Wales, 2002–07, to Minister of State, DWP, 2007–08, to Minister for Housing, DCLG, 2008, to Foreign Sec., 2009–10, to Shadow Home Sec., 2010–11, to Shadow Chancellor, 2011; an Opposition Whip, 2011–13; Shadow Wales Minister, 2017–. Mem., Welsh Affairs Select Cttee, 1999–2002; Vice-Chm., 2007–08, Chm., 2008–15, PLP Welsh Regl Gp. Chairman: N Wales Gp of Labour MPs, 2002–15; All Party Gp on Heart Disease, 2002–15; All Party Gp on Irish in Britain, 2011–15. *Address:* House of Commons, SW1A 0AA.

**RUAUX, Her Honour Gillian Doreen, (Mrs W. D. Partington);** a Circuit Judge, 1993–2006; *b* 25 March 1945; *d* of late Charles Edward Ruaux and Denise Maud Ruaux (*née* Le Page); *m* 1968, William Derek Partington; one *d*. *Educ:* Bolton Sch.; Univ. of Manchester (LLB Hons, LLM). Called to the Bar, Gray's Inn, 1968; practised at the Bar, Manchester, 1968–93. *Recreations:* theatre, opera, horse-racing, cookery.

**RUBBIA, Prof. Carlo;** physicist; Senior Physicist, European Organisation for Nuclear Research, since 1993 (Director-General, 1989–93); Professor of Physics, University of Pavia, since 1997; Scientific Director, Institute for Advanced Sustainability Studies, Potsdam, 2010–15, now Honorary Senior Fellow; *b* 31 March 1934; *s* of Silvio and Bice Rubbia; *m* Marisa; one *s* one *d*. *Educ:* Scuola Normale Superiore, Pisa; Univ. of Pisa (Dr 1957). Research Fellow, Columbia Univ., 1958–59; Lectr, Univ. of Rome, 1960–61; CERN, 1960– (head of team investigating fundamental particles on proton-antiproton collider); scientist, Fermi Nat. Accelerator Lab., USA, 1969–73; Higgins Prof. of Physics, Harvard Univ., 1971–88. Pres., Agency for New Technology, Energy and the Envmt, Rome, 1999–2005; Mem., EU Adv. Gp on Energy and Climate Change, 2007–; Special Advr for Energy to Sec. Gen., ECLAC, 2009–. Member: Papal Acad. of Science, 1985–; Amer. Acad. of Arts and Sciences, 1985; Accademia dei XL; Accademia dei Lincei; European Acad. of Sciences; Ateneo Veneto; Foreign Member: Royal Soc.; Soviet Acad. of Scis, 1988; US Nat. Acad. of Scis; Polish Acad. of Scis. Senator for Life, Italian Senate, 2013. Hon. Doctorates: Boston, Chicago, Geneva, Genoa, Northwestern, Udine, Carnegie-Mellon, Loyola, Sofia, Moscow, Chile, Padova, Madrid, Rio de Janeiro, La Plata and Oxford Universities. Gold Medal, Italian Physical Soc., 1983; Lorenzo il Magnifico Prize for Sciences, 1983; Achille de Gasperi Prize for Sciences, 1984; Nobel Prize for Physics (jtly), 1984; Leslie Prize for exceptional achievements, 1986; Internat. Scientific and Technol Cooperation Award, China, 2016. Knight Grand Cross, Italy, 1985; Officer, Legion of Honour, France, 1989; Order of Merit (Poland), 1993. *Publications:* papers on nuclear physics: weak force quanta (W−, W+ and Z particles, intermediate vector bosons); proton-antiproton collision; sixth quark. *Address:* CERN, 1211 Geneva 23, Switzerland.

**RUBEN, Prof. David-Hillel;** Hon. Research Fellow, Birkbeck, University of London, 2011–20; Professor Emeritus, University of London; *b* 25 July 1943; *s* of Blair S. Ruben and Sylvia G. Ruben; *m* 1968, Eira (*née* Karlinsky); one *s* two *d*. *Educ:* Dartmouth Coll. (BA); Harvard Univ. (PhD). Tutor in Philosophy, Univ. of Edinburgh, 1969; Lecturer in Philosophy: Univ. of Glasgow, 1970–75; Univ. of Essex, 1975–79; Lectr, 1979–82, Sen. Lectr, 1982–84, City Univ.; Prof. of Philosophy, LSE, 1984–98; Director: Jews' Coll., London, later London Sch. of Jewish Studies, 1998–99; NY Univ. in London, 1999–2011; London Dir and Regl Dir for UK and Ireland, Arcadia Univ. in London, 2012–13; part-time Professor of Philosophy: SOAS, London, 2000–04; Birkbeck, Univ. of London, 2004–11; Prof. of Philosophy, Oxford Brookes Univ., 2013–14. Phi Beta Kappa, 1964. *Publications:* Marxism and Materialism, 1977, 2nd edn 1979; Metaphysics of the Social World, 1985; Explaining Explanation, 1990; (ed) Explanation, 1994; Action and its Explanation, 2003; The Metaphysics of Action: trying, doing, causing, 2018; articles in phil. jls.

**RUBENS, Prof. Robert David,** MD; FRCP; Professor of Clinical Oncology, Guy's, King's and St Thomas' School of Medicine of King's College London (formerly United Medical and Dental Schools of Guy's and St Thomas' Hospitals), University of London, 1985–2003; Consultant Physician in Medical Oncology, Guy's Hospital, 1975–2003; *b* 11 June 1943; *s* of Joel Rubens and Dinah Rubens (*née* Hasseck); *m* 1970, Margaret Chamberlin; two *d*. *Educ:* King's Coll., London (BSc); St George's Hosp. Med. Sch. (MB, BS); MD London. FRCP 1984. House and Registrar appts, St George's, Brompton, Hammersmith and Royal Marsden Hosps, 1968–72; Clin. Res. Fellow, ICRF Labs, 1972–74; Dir, ICRF Clinical Oncology Unit, Guy's Hosp., 1985–97. Chm., EORTC Breast Cancer Co-op. Gp, 1991–94. Examr, RCP, 1987–93. Pres., Assurance Medical Soc., 2003–05. Editor-in-Chief, Cancer Treatment Reviews, 1993–2001. *Publications:* A Short Textbook of Clinical Oncology, 1980; Bone Metastases: diagnosis and treatment, 1991; Cancer and the Skeleton, 2000; ed and contrib. books and papers on cancer and other med. subjects. *Recreations:* golf, bridge. *Address:* 5 Currie Hill Close, Wimbledon, SW19 7DX. *Club:* Royal Wimbledon Golf.

**RUBENSTEIN, Alan Martin,** FFA; Chief Executive, Pension Protection Fund, 2009–18; *b* Edinburgh, 3 Sept. 1956; *m* 1980, Beverley Glass; two *d*. *Educ:* Heriot-Watt Univ. (BSc Hons). FFA 1984. Scottish Widows, 1978–91; Dir, Barclays de Zoete Wedd, 1991–94; Chief Exec., Lucas Varity Fund Mgt Ltd, 1995–97; Managing Director: Morgan Stanley, 1997–2006; Lehman Bros, 2006–08. Mem., Takeover Panel, 2000–03. Mem., Supervisory Bd, Robeco Groep NV, 2014–16; non-exec. Dir, esure Gp plc, 2017–; Chm., Pembroke Heritage Fund, 2019–. Investment Advr, 2013–18, Trustee and Chair, Investment Sub-Cttee, 2018–, British Coal Staff Superannuation Scheme. Vice-Chm., Nat. Assoc. of Pension Funds, 2000–02. Member, Council: Faculty of Actuaries, 2004–09; Inst. and Faculty of Actuaries, 2012–15. Gov., Pensions Policy Inst., 2011–. Chm., Pension Scholarship Trust, 2019–.

**RUBERY, Dr Eileen Doris,** CB 1998; Senior Research Fellow and Registrar of the Roll, Girton College, Cambridge, 2000–13 (Visiting Senior Fellow, 1997–2000); Tutor in Art History, Institute of Continuing Education, University of Cambridge, since 2004; *b* 16 May 1943; *d* of James and Doris McDonnell; *m* 1969, Philip Huson Rubery; one *d*. *Educ:* Westcliff High Sch. for Girls; Sheffield Univ. Med. Sch. (MB ChB Hons); PhD Cambridge 1973; MA Art Hist. London Univ. 2004. FRCR 1976; FRCPath 1986; FFPH (FFPHM 1993). Royal Infirmary, Sheffield, 1966–67; MRC Res. Fellow, Dept of Biochem., Cambridge, 1967–71; Meres' Sen. Student, St John's Coll., Cambridge, 1971–73; Addenbrooke's Hospital, Cambridge: Registrar in Radiotherapy and Oncology, 1973–76; Sen. Registrar, 1976–78; Wellcome Sen. Clinical Res. Fellow, 1978–83; Hon. Consultant, 1978–83; Sen. Res. Fellow and Dir of Med. Studies, Girton Coll., 1981–83; SMO (Toxicology), DHSS, 1983–88; Department of Health: PMO, 1988–89; SPMO and Hd of Med. Div., Communicable Disease and Immunisation, 1989–91; SPMO and Hd of Health Promotion Med. Div., 1991–95; Under Sec. and Hd of Health Aspects of Envmtl and Food Div., 1995–97; Under Sec. and Hd of Protection of Health Div., 1996–99. Lectr in Public Policy, 1997–2004, Course Dir, Masters in Community Enterprise, 1997–2001, Sen. Associate, 2004–09, Judge Business Sch. (formerly Judge Inst. of Mgt Studies), Cambridge Univ.; Lectr, London Sch. of Mosaic, 2018–. Advr to Food Standards Agency and other public sector bodies on public health and public policy issues, 2000–07. Mem., Professional Conduct Cttee, 2000–06, Professional Performance Cttee, 2003–06, GMC. Chair, Sen. Fellows Special Interest Gp, Faculty of Public Health, 2015–; Co Chair, Cancer Patient Participation Gp, Addenbrooke's Hosp., 2017–; Mem., Clinical Bd, 2017–, Patient and Carers Bd, 2017–, East of England Cancer Alliance. QHP, 1993–96. *Publications:* (ed) Indications for Iodine Prophylaxis following a Nuclear Accident, 1990; (ed) Medicine: a degree course guide, 1974–83; papers on art history, especially on Byzantine Rome, the consequences of longevity, public health, food safety, health promotion, professionals and public sector incl. policy making, the management of uncertainty and leadership in community enterprise, in professional jls. *Recreations:* visiting Rome, reading Proust, Byzantine and Medieval art, opera, Wagner, Ruskin. *E:* edr1001@cam.ac.uk.

**RUBERY, Prof. Jill Christine,** PhD; FBA 2006; Professor of Comparative Employment Systems, since 1995 and Director, Work and Equalities Institute, since 2017, Alliance Manchester Business School (formerly Manchester Business School), University of Manchester (formerly University of Manchester Institute of Science and Technology) (Co-Director, European Work and Employment Centre, 1994–2004, 2011–12, and a Deputy Dean, 2007–12); *b* 4 Nov. 1951; *d* of late Austin Rubery and Gladys Mary Rubery (*née* Clueit); *m* 1974, Andrew Wilson; one *d*. *Educ:* Wintringham Grammar Sch., Grimsby; Newnham Coll., Cambridge (BA 1973, MA 1976); New Hall, Cambridge (PhD 1987). Res. Asst, Queen Elizabeth House, Oxford, 1973–75; Jun. Res. Officer, Res. Officer, then Sen. Res. Officer, Dept of Applied Econs, Univ. of Cambridge, 1978–89; Fellow and Dir of Studies in Econs, New Hall, Cambridge, 1977–89, Emeritus Fellow, 2006; Lectr, then Sen. Lectr, Manchester Sch. of Mgt, UMIST, 1989–95. Vis. Associate Prof., Univ. of Notre Dame, 1989; Visiting Fellow: Wissenschaftszentrum für Sozialforschung, Berlin, 1993; Inst. Industrial Relns, Univ. of Calif, Berkeley, 2002. Member: Bd of Arbitrators, ACAS, 1989–; Adv. Forum on Employment Regulations, DTI, 2005–09; High-Level Expert Gp on Social Investment, EC, 2012–. Co-ordinator, expert gp on gender and employment, EC, 1991–96, 2000–03 and 2004–07. *Publications:* (jtly) Labour Market Structure, Industrial Organisation and Low Pay, 1982; (ed) Women and Recession, 1988; (jtly) Women and European Employment, 1988; (ed) Equal Pay in Europe, 1988; (ed jtly) International Integration and Labour Market Organisation, 1992; (ed with F. Wilkinson) Employer Strategy and the Labour Market, 1994; (ed jtly) Occupation and Skills, 1994; (jtly) Women's Employment in Europe: trends and prospects, 1999; (jtly) Managing Employment Change: the new realities of work, 2002; (with D. Grimshaw) The Organization of Employment: an international perspective, 2003; (ed jtly) Systems of Production: markets, organizations and performance, 2003; (jtly) Fragmenting Work: blurring organisational boundaries and disordering hierarchies, 2005; (ed jtly) European Employment Models in Flux, 2009; (ed jtly) Welfare States and Life Transitions, 2010; (ed jtly) Women and Austerity, 2014; contribs to jls in econs, mgt, industrial relns and sociology. *Recreations:* cooking, holidays, reading. *Address:* Alliance Manchester Business School, University of Manchester, Booth Street West, Manchester M15 6PB. *T:* (0161) 306 3406, *Fax:* (0161) 306 3505. *E:* Jill.Rubery@manchester.ac.uk.

**RUBERY, His Honour Reginald John;** a Circuit Judge, 1995–2010; Member, Parole Board for England and Wales, since 2010; *b* 13 July 1937; *s* of Reginald Arthur Rubery and Phyllis Margaret (*née* Payne); *m* 1st, 1961, Diana Wilcock Holgate (marr. diss.); one *s*; 2nd, 1974, Frances Camille Murphy; one step *d*. *Educ:* Wadham House, Hale, Cheshire; King's Sch., Worcester. Admitted Solicitor, 1963; Partner: Whitworths, Manchester, 1966–72; Taylor Kirkman & Mainprice, 1972–78; County Court and Dist Registrar, then District Judge, 1978–95; Asst Recorder, 1987–91; a Recorder, 1991–95; Judge, St Helena Court of Appeal, 1997–2012; Justice of Appeal, Falkland Is, British Indian Ocean Territory, British Antarctic Territory. Chm. (pt-time) Immigration Appeal Tribunal, 1998–2005; Tribunal Judge (formerly Mem., Mental Health Review Tribunal), 2001–10. Mem., Manchester City Council, 1968–71. Hon. Sec., Manchester Law Soc., 1974–78. *Recreations:* golf, swimming, gardening. *Address:* Birkby, Charnes Road, Ashley, Market Drayton, Shropshire TF9 4LQ. *Club:* Lansdowne.

**RUBIDGE, Caroline Janet Pamela;** *see* Wright, C. J. P.

**RUBIN, Sir Peter (Charles),** Kt 2010; DM; FRCP; Professor of Therapeutics, University of Nottingham, 1987–2014, now Emeritus (Dean, Faculty of Medicine and Health Sciences, 1997–2003); *b* 21 Nov. 1948; *s* of late Woolf Rubin and Enis Rubin; *m* 1976, Dr Fiona Logan (marr. diss. 2006); one *s* one *d*. *Educ:* Redruth Grammar Sch.; Emmanuel Coll., Cambridge (MA; Hon. Fellow 2011); Exeter Coll., Oxford (DM 1980). FRCP 1989. Jun. hosp. posts, Stoke on Trent, 1974–77; American Heart Assoc. Fellow, Stanford Med. Center, 1977–79; Sen. Registrar (Medicine and Clinical Pharmacology), Glasgow, 1979–82; Wellcome Trust Sen. Fellow in Clinical Sci., Glasgow, 1982–87; University of Nottingham: Chairman: Dept of Medicine, 1991–97; Veterinary Sch. Project Bd, 2002–06. Mem., Nottingham HA, 1998–2002; Chairman: Specialist Adv. Cttee in Clinical Pharmacol. and Therapeutics, RCP, 1992–95; Steering Cttee, MAGPIE trial, MRC, 1998–2004; GMC Educn Cttee, 2002–08; Postgrad. Med. Educn and Trng Bd, 2005–08; GMC, 2009–14; Co-Chm., Dental Jt Implementation Gp, 2005–09; Member: Physiol Medicine and Infections Grants Cttee, MRC, 1992–96; Bd, HEFCE, 2003–09. Mem., Cttee on Standards, H of C, 2016–May 2020. Chairman: Bd for Acad. Medicine, Scotland, 2016–; Strategic Delivery Bd, Univ. of Nottingham, 2016–18. Hon. FRCGP 2006; Hon. FRCPE 2009; Hon. FRCPI 2012; Hon. FRCP Thailand 2015. Hon. DSc. Lincoln, 2004; Exeter, 2011; Hon. DM Plymouth, 2012. *Publications:* Lecture Notes on Clinical Pharmacology, 1981, 7th edn 2006; Prescribing in Pregnancy, 1987, 4th edn 2007; Hypertension in Pregnancy, 1988, 2nd edn 2000. *Recreations:* sport, walking, music, photography. *E:* peter.rubin@nottingham.ac.uk. *Clubs:* Oxford and Cambridge; Redruth.

**RUBIN, Robert E(dward);** Counselor, Centerview Partners LLC, since 2010; Chairman of the Executive Committee, Citigroup, 1999–2009; Secretary of the United States Treasury, 1995–99; *b* 29 Aug. 1938; *s* of Alexander Rubin and Sylvia Rubin (*née* Seiderman); *m* 1963, Judith Leah Oxenberg; two *s*. *Educ:* Harvard (AB *summa cum laude* 1960); LSE, London Univ.; Yale Univ. (LLB 1964). Admitted to NY Bar, 1965; Associate, Cleary, Gottlieb, Steen & Hamilton, 1964–66; Goldman, Sach & Co.: Associate, 1966–70; Partner, 1971; Mem. Mgt Cttee, 1980; Vice Chair and Co-Chief Operating Officer, 1987–90; Sen. Partner and Co-Chair, 1990–93; Asst to the Pres. on econ. policy and Head, Nat. Econ. Council, Exec. Office of US President, 1993–95. Chm., Local Initiatives

Support Corp., 1999–; Co-Chm., Council on Foreign Relations, 2007–17, now Co-Chm. Emeritus. Member, Board of Directors: Chicago Bd of Options Exchange, Inc., 1972–76; NY Futures Exchange, 1979–85; Center for Nat. Policy, 1982–93 (Vice Chair, 1984); NY Stock Exchange, Inc., 1991–93 (Mem., Regulatory Adv. Cttee, 1988–90); NYC Partnership Inc., 1991–93 (also Partner). Member: Adv. Cttee on Tender Offers, 1983, Adv. Cttee on Market Oversight and Financial Services, 1991–93, Securities and Exchange Commn; NY Adv. Cttee on Internat. Capital Markets, Federal Reserve Bank, 1989–93; Mayor's Council of Econ. Advrs, 1990. Trustee: Amer. Ballet Theatre Foundn, 1969–93; Mt Sinai Hosp., 1977 (Vice-Chm., 1986); Collegiate Sch., 1978–84; Station WNET-TV, 1985–93; Carnegie Corp., NY, 1990–93; Harvard Mgt Co. Inc., 1990–93; Mem., Harvard Corp., 2002–14. Hon. DHL Yeshiva, 1996. Nat. Assoc. of Christians and Jews Award, 1977; Dist. Leadership in Govt Award, Columbia Business Sch., 1996; Finance Minister of the Year Award, Euromoney mag., 1996. *Publications:* (with J. Weisberg) In an Uncertain World (memoirs), 2003. *Recreation:* fly fishing. *Clubs:* Harvard, Links (New York); Century Country (Purchase).

**RUBIN, Stephen Charles;** QC 2000; a Recorder, since 2004; *b* 14 March 1955; *s* of late Joseph Rubin and of Shirley Rubin (*née* Dank); *m* 1985, Jayne Anne Purdy; two *s* two *d*. *Educ:* Merchant Taylors' Sch., Northwood; Brasenose Coll., Oxford (Open Exhibnr; MA Jurisp.). Called to the Bar, Middle Temple, 1977, Bencher, 2014; in practice at the Bar, 1979–. Member: Professional Conduct and Complaints Cttee, Bar Council, 1994–99; Cttee, London Common Law and Commercial Bar Assoc., 2001–04; Chm., Bar Disciplinary Tribunal, 2013–16; Hon. Mem. Bd, UK Law Students' Assoc., 2011–. *Recreations:* contemporary art, tennis, ski-ing, golf. *Address:* Fountain Court Chambers, Temple, EC4Y 9DH.

**RUBINS, Jack,** FIPA; Chairman, Osprey Communications plc, 1993–2002 (non-executive Chairman, 1999–2000; Chief Executive, 1993–95); *b* 4 Aug. 1931; *m* 1962, Ruth Davids; three *s*. *Educ:* Northern Polytechnic (Architecture). Chm. and Chief Exec., DFS Dorland Advertising, 1976–87; Chm. and Chief Exec., McCann Erickson Gp UK, 1990–91; Chm., SMS Communications, 1991–93. Chairman: Nat. Advertising Benevolent Soc., 1987–90; History of Advertising Trust, 1990–96. *Recreations:* philately, golf, bridge. *Address:* 8 Portman Hall, Old Redding, Harrow Weald, Middx HA3 6SH.

**RUBINSTEIN, Mark Gabriel;** Theatre Producer and General Manager, since 2000; Director, Mark Rubinstein Ltd, since 2000; *b* London, 6 May 1961; *s* of Hilary and Helge Rubinstein; *m* 1987, Sue Johnston; one *s* one *d*. *Educ:* Latymer Upper Sch., Hammersmith; Kingsway Princeton Coll., London; Univ. of Sussex (BA Hons Soc. Anthropol. and Cognitive Studies 1985). Finance Dir, Royal Court Th., 1989–95; Gen. Manager, Inst. of Contemp. Arts, 1995–96; Producer, Bill Kenwright Ltd, 1996–99; Producer, Old Vic Productions Ltd, 1999–2002; ind. theatre producer, 2002–. Productions as Producer or General Manager include: Jesus Hopped the A Train, 2002; Sexual Perversity in Chicago, 2003; By the Bog of Cats, 2004; Otherwise Engaged, 2005; Whose Life is it Anyway, 2005; Bent, 2006; Sunday in the Park with George, 2006; Desperately Seeking Susan, 2007; Tintin, 2007; The Drowsy Chaperone, 2007; Glengarry Glen Ross, 2007; La Clique, 2008–10; Isango Portobello prodn of The Magic Flute, 2008; transfer of NT's War Horse, 2009 (UK tour, 2014–15); The Mysteries, 2009; La Soirée, 2010–; Butley, 2011; Fela! Eur. tour, 2011; Curious Incident of the Dog in the Night, 2013; The Drowned Man, 2013–14; A Doll's House, 2013; Jeeves and Wooster in Perfect Nonsense, 2013–16; ONCE, 2014–15; Beautiful—The Carole King Musical, 2015–17, tour, 2017–18; Billy Elliot, tour, 2016–17; The Dresser, 2016–17; The Miser, 2017; Heisenberg, 2017–18; Tina, 2018–; Company, 2018–19; Sweat, 2019. Trustee: Soc. of London Theatre, 2004–10, 2011– (Chm., Finance Cttee; Pres., 2011–14; Vice Pres., 2014–18); Theatre Develt Fund, 2004–10, 2011–; Complicite, 2006–13; Stage One (formerly Theatre Investment Fund), 2007–; Mousetrap Foundn for the Arts, 2007–11; League of Ind. Producers, 2012–. *Recreations:* paragliding (pilot level, recreational and competing in club competitions), cycling. *Address:* Mark Rubinstein Ltd, 25 Short Street, SE1 8LJ. *T:* (020) 7021 0787. *E:* info@mrluk.com.

**RUBINSZTEIN, Prof. David Chaim,** PhD; FRCPath, FMedSci; FRS 2017; Professor of Molecular Neurogenetics, since 2005, and Deputy Director for Medical Research, Cambridge Institute, since 2012, University of Cambridge; Academic Lead, Alzheimer's Research UK Cambridge Drug Discovery Institute, since 2015, and Professor, UK Dementia Research Institute, since 2017; *b* Cape Town, SA, 14 March 1963; *s* of Aron and Denise Rubinsztein; *m* 1988, Judy Kerbel; one *s* two *d*. *Educ:* Univ. of Cape Town (MB ChB 1986; BSc 1988; PhD 1993). Dip. RCPath 1996, MRCPath 1997, FRCPath 2005. Intern, Groote Schuur Hosp., Cape Town, 1987–88; Sen. Registrar in Genetic Pathol., Addenbrooke's Hosp., Cambridge, 1993–98; University of Cambridge: Glaxo Wellcome Res. Fellow, 1998–2002; Wellcome Trust Sen. Res. Fellow in Clin. Sci., 2002–11; Hon. Consultant in Med. Genetics, 1998–2011; Reader in Molecular Neurogenetics, 2003–05; Wellcome Trust Principal Res. Fellow, 2012–17. Kohn Lectr, RCPath, 2015. Mem., EMBO, 2011–. FMedSci 2004. Graham Bull Prize in Clin. Sci., RCP, 2007; Thudichum Medal, Biochem. Soc., 2017; Roger de Spoelberch Prize, 2017. *Publications:* (ed with M. R. Hayden) Analysis of Triplet Repeat Disorders, 1998; contrib. papers to scientific jls incl. Nature, Cell, Nature Cell Biol., Nature Medicine, Nature Genetics, Nature Chem. Biol. and Molecular Cell. *Recreations:* playing the cello and the piano, listening to music. *Address:* Department of Medical Genetics, Cambridge Institute for Medical Research, The Keith Peters Building, Cambridge Biomedical Campus, Hills Road, Cambridge CB2 0XY. *T:* (01223) 762608, *Fax:* (01223) 331206. *E:* dcr1000@cam.ac.uk.

**RUBLACK, Prof. Ulinka Christiane,** PhD; FBA 2017; FRHistS; Professor of Early Modern European History, University of Cambridge, since 2013; Fellow, St John's College, Cambridge, since 1994; *b* Tübingen, Germany, 14 April 1967; *d* of Hans-Christoph Rublack and Ursula Nelle; *m* 2002, Francisco Bethencourt; one *s* one *d*. *Educ:* Heinrich-Hertz Gymnasium, Hamburg (Arbitur); Hamburg Univ. (MA); Clare Coll., Cambridge (PhD 1995). FRHistS 1999. Jun. Res. Fellow, St John's Coll., Cambridge, 1994; University of Cambridge: Asst Lectr, Hist. Faculty, 1996–2000; Lectr, 2000–06; Sen. Lectr, 2006–10; Reader, 2010–13. *Publications:* The Crimes of Women in Early Modern Germany, 1999; Reformation Europe, 2005, 2nd edn 2017; Dressing Up: cultural identity in Renaissance Europe, 2010; The Astronomer and the Witch: Johannes Kepler's fight for his mother, 2015. *Recreations:* art, literature, theatre, yoga, walking, travel. *Address:* St John's College, Cambridge CB2 1TP. *T:* (01223) 338682. *E:* ucr10@cam.ac.uk.

**RUCKER, (Belinda) Christian,** OBE 2018 (MBE 2010); Founder, The White Company, since 1994; *b* 6 Nov. 1968; *d* of Anthony Rucker and Rosemary Calcutt; *m* 1995, Nicholas Charles Tyrwhitt Wheeler, *qv*; one *s* three *d*. *Educ:* Combe Bank Sch., Sevenoaks. Various asst roles, Condé Nast Pubns, 1987–90; PR Asst, Clarins UK Ltd, 1991; Asst Health and Beauty Asst, Harpers & Queen magazine, 1992–94. Veuve Clicquot's Tribute Award, 2019. *Recreation:* looking after four children in every spare moment! *Address:* The White Company, 2 Television Centre, 101 Wood Lane, W12 7FR.

**RUCKER, His Honour Jeffrey Hamilton;** a Circuit Judge, 1988–2007; a Resident Judge, Truro Crown Court, 2001–07; *b* 19 Dec. 1942; *s* of late Charles Edward Sigismund Rucker and Nancy Winifred Hodgson; *m* 1965, Caroline Mary Salkeld; three *s*. *Educ:* St Aubyn's, Rottingdean; Charterhouse. Called to the Bar, Middle Temple, 1967; a Recorder, 1984; a Circuit Judge, assigned to SE Circuit, 1988, transf. W Circuit, 2001. Legal Mem., Mental Health Rev. Tribunals, 1995–2017. Mem. Council of Govs, UMDS of Guy's and St Thomas', 1991–98. *Recreations:* sailing, ski-ing, music.

**RUCKER, William John;** Chairman, Lazard UK, since 2019 (Chief Executive Officer, 2004–19); *b* Cheam, Surrey, 18 June 1963; *s* of John and Natalie Rucker; *m* 1987, Angela Victoria Tollit; three *d*. *Educ:* Brockhurst Sch., Newbury; St Bartholomew's Sch., Newbury; Bristol Univ. (BSc Econs and Politics); Harvard Business Sch. (AMP 1998). Chartered Accountant, 1987; joined Lazard, 1987. Chairman: Quintain plc, 2009–15; Crest Nicholson plc, 2012–18; Marston's plc, 2018–. Chm., Dementia Res. Inst., 2016–. Mem. Cttee, Cheltenham Racecourse, 2014–. *Recreation:* horseracing. *Clubs:* Jockey; Royal Oddingley Tennis.

**RUDD, Rt Hon. Amber;** PC 2015; MP for Hastings and Rye, since 2010 (C, 2010–19; Ind, since 2019); *b* London, 16 Aug. 1963; *d* of late Anthony Rudd and of Ethne Rudd; *m* 1991, Adrian Anthony Gill (marr. diss.; he *d* 2016); one *s* one *d*. *Educ:* Queen's Coll., London; Edinburgh Univ. (MA Hons Hist. 1986). With J P Morgan, London and NY, 1986–87; Director: Lawnstone Ltd, 1988–97; MacArthur & Co., 1997–99; CEO, Investors Noticeboard Ltd, 1999–2001; Consultant, I-Search Ltd, 2001–03; Man. Dir and Sen. Consultant, Lawnstone Ltd, 2003–10. Columnist, Corporate Financier, 2003–10. Contested (C) Liverpool Garston, 2005. PPS to Chancellor of Exchequer, 2012–13; an Asst Govt Whip, 2013–14; Parly Under-Sec. of State, 2014–15, Sec. of State, DECC, 2015–16; Sec. of State for the Home Dept, 2016–18; Minister for Women and Equalities, 2018; Sec. of State for Work and Pensions, 2018–19. Mem., Envmt, Food and Rural Affairs Select Cttee, 2010–12. *Address:* House of Commons, SW1A 0AA.
*See also* R. D. Rudd.

**RUDD, Prof. Anthony George,** CBE 2013; FRCP; Professor of Stroke Medicine, King's College London, since 2010; Consultant Stroke Physician, Guy's and St Thomas' NHS Foundation Trust (formerly St Thomas' Hospital, then Guy's and St Thomas' Hospital Trust), since 1988; *b* Bolton, Lancs, 15 June 1954; *s* of Jack Rudd and Erica Rudd; *m* 1979, Lynne Simpson; three *s* one *d*. *Educ:* Haberdashers' Aske's Sch., Elstree; Jesus Coll., Cambridge (BA 1975; MB 1979); King's Coll. Med. Sch. (BChir 1978). FRCP 1994. Registrar, Hammersmith Hosp., 1982–83; Lectr, Geriatric Medicine, St George's Hosp. Med. Sch., 1983–88; London Stroke Clin. Dir, 2010–; Nat. Clin. Dir for Stroke, NHS England, 2013–. Pres., British Assoc. of Stroke Physicians, 2004–06; Trustee, Stroke Assoc., 2005–14 (Hon. Vice Pres., 2014–). Hon. MFPH 2015. *Publications:* A Strategy for Stroke Services and Research, 1996; Stroke at Your Fingertips, 2000, 2nd edn 2004; Measuring the Quality of Health Care, 2001; A Practical Guide to Stroke Care, 2011; articles in jls on stroke epidemiology, recovery, treatment and quality improvement. *Recreations:* flute playing, cooking, gardening, family. *Address:* Stroke Unit, St Thomas' Hospital, Westminster Bridge Road, SE1 7EH. *T:* (020) 7188 2515. *E:* anthony.rudd@kcl.ac.uk.

**RUDD, Sir (Anthony) Nigel (Russell),** Kt 1996; DL; Chairman: Heathrow (SP) Ltd (formerly BAA), 2007–16; BBA Aviation plc, since 2014 (non-executive Director, since 2013); *b* 31 Dec. 1946; *m* 1969, Lesley Elizabeth (*née* Hodgkinson); two *s* one *d*. *Educ:* Bemrose Grammar Sch., Derby. FCA. Qualified Chartered Accountant 1968; Divl Finance Dir, London & Northern Group, 1970–77; Chairman: C. Price & Son Ltd, 1977–82; Williams Holdings (later Williams plc), 1982–2000; Dep. Chm., Raine Industries, 1992–94 (non-exec. Chm., 1986–92); non-executive Chairman: Pendragon PLC, 1989–2010; East Midlands Electricity, 1994–97 (Dir, 1990–97); Pilkington plc, 1995–2006 (Dir, 1994–2006); Kidde, 2000–03; The Boots Co. plc, subseq. Alliance Boots plc, 2003–07 (non-exec. Dir, 1999–2007; Dep. Chm., 2001–03); Invensys plc, 2009–14; Meggitt plc, 2015–; Aquarius Platinum, 2015–; Dep. Chm., Barclays Bank plc, 2004–09 (non-exec. Dir, 1996–2009). Chm., UK Business Angels Assoc., 2012–. Member: European Round Table of Industrialists 1996–2001; Council, CBI, 1999–. Chancellor, Loughborough Univ., 2010–15. Freeman, City of London; Mem., Chartered Accountants' Co. DL Derbys, 1996. Hon. DTech Loughborough, 1998; DUniv Derby, 1998. *Recreations:* golf, ski-ing, theatre, field sports. *Clubs:* Brooks's, Royal Automobile.

**RUDD, Dominic;** international mountain leader, since 2009; Outdoor Learning and Forest School Leader, Brantridge Special School; *b* 4 Oct. 1958; *s* of William Rudd and Primrose (*née* Saddler Phillips; now Lady Lewis, widow of Adm. Sir Andrew Lewis, KCB); *m* 2004, Helena Clayton; two *s* by a previous marriage. *Educ:* Bedford Sch. Midshipman, RN, 1976–77; Officer, RM, 1977–89. Partner, Holley, Hextall & Associates, 1989–99; Manager for Wales, 1999–2001, Dir of Ops, 2001–07, RSPCA; CEO, Samaritans, 2007–09; interim CEO, Switchback, 2012. *Recreations:* rock climbing, Alpine mountaineering. *E:* dominic_rudd@hotmail.com.

**RUDD, Hon. Kevin Michael,** AC 2019; Senior Fellow, John F. Kennedy School of Government and Visiting Fellow, Institute of Politics, Harvard University, since 2014; Prime Minister of Australia, 2007–10 and 2013; *b* Nambour, Qld, 21 Sept. 1957; *s* of Bert and Margaret Rudd; *m* 1981, Thérèse Rein; two *s* one *d*. *Educ:* Marist Coll., Ashgrove; Nambour State High Sch.; Australian Nat. Univ. (BA 1st cl. Hons Asian Studies 1981). Diplomat, Aust. Dept of Foreign Affairs, 1981–88: served Stockholm, later First Sec., Beijing; Counsellor, 1988; COS to Hon. Wayne Goss, Leader of the Opposition, later Premier, of Qld, 1988–91; Dir-Gen., Office of the Cabinet, Qld, 1991–95; Sen. China Consultant, KPMG Australia, 1996–98. Contested (ALP) Griffith, Qld, 1996. MP (ALP) Griffith, Qld, 1998–2013. Chm., Parly ALP Cttee on Nat. Security and Trade, 1998; Shadow Minister: for Foreign Affairs, 2001–06; for Internat. Security, 2003–06; for Trade, 2005–06; Leader of the Opposition, Australia, 2006–07; Minister for Foreign Affairs, 2010–12. Leader, ALP, 2006–10 and 2013. Chm., Sanitation and Water for All, 2015–. Pres., Asia Soc. Policy Inst., NY, 2015–. *Publications:* Not For the Faint-Hearted, 2017; The PM Years, 2018; articles on Chinese politics, Chinese foreign policy, Australia-Asia relations and globalisation.

**RUDD, Sir Nigel;** *see* Rudd, Sir A. N. R.

**RUDD, His Honour Norman Julian Peter Joseph;** a Circuit Judge, 1988–2004; *b* 12 May 1943; *s* of Norman Arthur Rudd and Winifred Rudd; *m* 1968, Judith Margaret Pottinger; three *s*. *Educ:* Paston Sch., N Walsham, Norfolk; University Coll. London (LLB, LLM). Called to the Bar, Inner Temple, 1969; Asst Recorder, 1982–87, Head of Chambers, 1982–87; a Recorder, 1987. Trustee, New Forest Commoning Trust, 1993– (Chm., 1993–98, 2012–); Chm., Northern Commoners Assoc. (New Forest), 1999–. *Recreation:* farming.

**RUDD, Roland Dacre;** Founder and Chairman, Finsbury, since 1994; *b* London, 24 April 1961; *s* of late Anthony Rudd and of Ethne Rudd; *m* 1991, Sophie Alice Yarde Hale; two *s* one *d*. *Educ:* Millfield Sch.; Regent's Park Coll., Oxford (BA Hons Philos. and Theol. 1985; Hon. Fellow). Pres., Oxford Union, 1985. Policy Coordinator for David Owen, MP,

1985; Employment Corresp., The Times, 1985–89; Dep. City Ed., Sunday Correspondent, 1989–91; Financial and Political Writer, FT, 1991–94. Founding Chm., Business for New Europe, 2006–16; Chairman: Open Britain, 2016–; People's Vote, 2018–. Mem. Bd, Breakingviews, 1999–2009; non-exec. Dir, Exec. Cttee of the Army Bd, 2009–13. Trustee: Royal Opera House, 2011–17; Tate, 2017–. Vis. Fellow, Centre for Corporate Reputation, Univ. of Oxford, 2008–. Chm., Bd of Govs, Millfield Sch., 2017–. *Recreations:* Chelsea Football Club, Wagner, modern art. *Address:* Finsbury, The Adelphi, 1–11 John Adam Street, WC2N 6HT.

**RUDDOCK, Rev. Canon Bruce;** *see* Ruddock, Rev. Canon R. B.

**RUDDOCK, Joan Elizabeth,** CBE 2004 (OBE 1995); Parliamentary Boundary Commissioner for Northern Ireland, 2003–08; Independent Assessor for Public Appointments, 2004–09; *b* 22 May 1948; *d* of Robert John Boyle and Bertha Irene Boyle (*née* Johnston); *m* 1968, Alvin Ruddock. *Educ:* Trinity Coll., Dublin (BA 1970); Univ. of Ulster (Postgrad. DMS 1977); Open Univ. (BSc 1st Cl. Hons 2002). FCIM 1997. Mktg Manager, Conf. Div., FT, London, 1972–74; Redevelt Team Leader, NI Housing Exec., 1975–76; Corp. Finance Exec., NI Develt Agency, 1976–79; Mgt Consultant, Coopers & Lybrand, 1979–82; Sen. Exec., Industrial Develt Bd NI, 1982–84; Advr to European Pres. and Dir of Res., AVX Ltd, 1984–86; Gen. Manager, European Special Products Div., 1986–90; Man. Dir, Educational Company Ltd, 1990–99. Director: LEDU, 1984–98; Investment Belfast Ltd, 2000–06. Ind. Bd Mem., Dept of Agric. and Rural Develt, 2006–10. Chm., Belfast City Hosp. HSS Trust, 1999–2007; Dep. Chm., Gtr Village Regeneration Trust, 2000–06; Member: NIHEC, 1998–2005; Central Investment Trust for Charities, 1998–2004.

**RUDDOCK, Rt Hon. Dame Joan (Mary),** DBE 2012; PC 2010; *b* 28 Dec. 1943; *d* of Ken and Eileen Anthony; *m* 1st, 1963, Keith Ruddock (*d* 1996); 2nd, 2010, Frank Doran (*d* 2017). *Educ:* Pontypool Grammar Sch. for Girls; Imperial Coll., Univ. of London (BSc; ARCS). Worked for Shelter, national campaign for the homeless, 1968–73; Dir, Oxford Housing Aid Centre, 1973–77; Special Programmes Officer with unemployed young people, MSC, 1977–79; Organiser, CAB, Reading, 1979–86. Chairperson, CND, 1981–85, a Vice Chairperson, 1985–86. MP (Lab) Lewisham, Deptford, 1987–2015. Opposition spokesperson: on transport, 1989–92; on home affairs, 1992–94; on envmtl protection, 1994–97; Parliamentary Under-Secretary of State: for Women, DSS, 1997–98; DEFRA, 2007–08; DECC, 2008–09; Minister of State, DECC, 2009–10. Active in politics and pressure groups, and mem. of anti-racist concerns, throughout working life. Bd Mem., Trinity Laban, 2005–14. Chair, Board: Albany Th., 2016–; Lewisham Music, 2019–; Trustee, Blackheath Halls, London, 2016–. Hon. Fellow: Goldsmiths Coll., Univ. of London, 1996; Laban Centre, 1996; Hon. Companion, Trinity Laban, 2014. Frank Cousins' Peace Award, TGWU, 1984. *Publications:* CND Scrapbook, 1987; Going Nowhere (autobiog.), 2016; co-author of pubns on housing; (contrib.): The CND Story, 1983; Voices for One World, 1988. *Recreations:* music, travel, gardening.

**RUDDOCK, Sir Paul (Martin),** Kt 2012; FSA; Chief Executive and Co-Founder, Lansdowne Partners Ltd, 1998–2013; *b* 28 Aug. 1958; *s* of William Frederick Ruddock and Mary Eileen Ruddock; *m* 1991, Jill Ann Shaw (CBE 2016); two *d*. *Educ:* King Edward's Sch., Birmingham; Mansfield Coll., Oxford (BA 1st Cl. Law 1980, MA 1984; Bancroft Fellow, 2008). Goldman Sachs, 1980–84; Man. Dir, Hd of Internat., Schroder & Co. Inc., 1984–98. Dir, Alternative Investment Mgt Assoc., 2009–12. Member: Nat. Infrastructure Commn, 2015–16; President's Council, Getty Foundn, 2015–; Exec. Planning Cttee, Bard Graduate Inst., 2016–. Trustee: V&A Mus., 2002–15 (Chm., 2007–15; Chm., Finance Cttee, 2002–07; Chm., Develt Cttee, 2002–07; Mem., Collections Cttee, 2002); Burlington Mag. Foundn, 2005–12; Metropolitan Mus. of Art, NY, 2011– (Co-Chair, Internat. Council, 2017–); British Mus., 2016–. Chm., Gilbert Trust for the Arts, 2009–15. FSA 2010; Life Benefactor, Metropolitan Mus. of Art, 2014. Hon. DHL Bowdoin Coll., Maine, 2019; DUniv Birmingham, 2019. *Recreations:* tennis, mountain walking, medieval art, theatre. *Club:* Athenæum.

**RUDDOCK, Air Marshal Peter William David,** CB 2011; CBE 2001; FRAeS; FCMI; Chief Executive, Lockheed Martin UK, since 2016; *b* 5 Feb. 1954; *s* of William Ruddock and Evelyn (*née* Besanson); *m* 2001, Joanna Elizabeth Milford; one *s* one *d*. *Educ:* Grosvenor High Sch., Belfast. Joined RAF, 1974; Fighter Pilot, Qualified Weapons Instructor, to 1990; Advanced Staff Coll., Bracknell, 1990; Wing Comdr, MoD, 1991–93; OC Ops Wg, RAF Coningsby (Display Pilot, Battle of Britain Meml Flight), 1993–96; Gp Capt., MoD, 1996–99; Station Comdr, RAF Coningsby, 1999–2000; Air Cdre Defence Ops, HQ 1 Gp, 2000–02; Dir of Air Staff, 2002–04; Air Sec., 2004–06; Dir Gen., Saudi Armed Forces Project, 2006–11; Business Develt Dir, Lockheed Martin UK, 2011–15. Member: Ascent Bd, 2014–16; Defence Industries Council, 2016–; Defence Suppliers Forum, 2016–. FRAeS 2004. FCMI 2011. Freeman, City of London, 2018. Officer, Legion of Merit (USA), 2003. *Recreations:* golf, sailing, equestrian activities, most sports, military history. *Address:* Lockheed Martin UK, Cunard House, 15 Regent Street, SW1Y 4LR. *Club:* Royal Air Force.

**RUDDOCK, Rev. Canon (Reginald) Bruce;** Chaplain, Chichester Cathedral, and Custos of St Mary's Hospital, Chichester, since 2018; Chaplain to the Queen, since 2008; *b* 17 Dec. 1955; *s* of Reginald and Hilary Ruddock; *m* 1983, Vivien Chrismas. *Educ:* Hurstpierpoint Coll., Sussex; Guildhall Sch. of Music and Drama (AGSM); Chichester Theol Coll.; Southampton Univ. (Cert. Theol.). Ordained deacon, 1983, priest, 1984; Asst Curate, St Mary's, Felpham with St Nicholas, Middleton-on-Sea, 1983–86; Priest-in-Charge, St Wilfrid's Church, Parish of St Mary, Portsea, 1986–88; Vicar, St Michael's, Barnes, 1988–95; Dir, Anglican Centre in Rome, and Archbishop of Canterbury's Counsellor for Vatican Affairs, 1995–99; Residentiary Canon, Worcester Cathedral, 1999–2004; Diocesan Liturgical Officer, Peterborough, 2004–11; Residentiary Canon and Precentor, Peterborough Cathedral, 2004–17, now Canon Emeritus. Hon. Canon, Amer. Cathedral, Paris, 1996–. *Recreations:* music, cricket, art, theatre, visiting Italy and Ireland. *Address:* 6 Priory Road, Chichester, W Sussex PO19 1NS. *T:* 07919 092504.

**RUDENSTINE, Neil Leon;** President Emeritus, Harvard University, since 2001; *b* 21 Jan. 1935; *s* of Harry Rudenstine and Mae Esperito Rudenstine; *m* 1960, Angelica Zander; one *s* two *d*. *Educ:* Princeton Univ. (BA 1956); New Coll., Oxford (BA 1959; MA 1963; Hon. Fellow, 1992); Harvard Univ. (PhD 1964). Instructor, English and American Lit. and Lang., Harvard Univ., 1964–66, Asst Prof. 1966–68; Princeton University: Associate Prof., English Dept, 1968–73; Dean of Students, 1968–72; Prof. of English, 1973–88; Dean of College, 1972–77; Provost, 1977–88, Provost Emeritus, 1988–; Exec. Vice-Pres., Andrew W. Mellon Foundn, 1988–91; Pres., and Prof. of English and Amer. Lit. and Lang., Harvard Univ., 1991–2001. Chm., ARTstor, 2001–16. Chair: NY Public Liby Bd, 2011–14; Bd, Rockefeller Archive Center; Vice Chair, J. Paul Getty Trust; Member, Board: Courtauld Inst., 2004–16 (Hon. Fellow, 2016); Barnes Foundn. Member: Amer. Philosphical Soc.; Amer. Acad. of Arts and Scis. Hon. Fellow, Emmanuel Coll., Cambridge, 1991. Hon. DPhil: Princeton, 1989; Yale, 1992. Hon. DCL: Harvard, 1992; Oxford, 1998. *Publications:* Sidney's Poetic Development, 1967; (ed with George Rousseau) English Poetic Satire: Wyatt to Byron, 1972; (with William Bowen) In Pursuit of the PhD, 1992; Pointing Our Thoughts, 2001; The House of Barnes, 2012; Ideas of Order, 2014.

**RUDERS, Poul;** full-time composer, since 1991; *b* Ringsted, Denmark, 27 March 1949; *s* of late Poul Ruders and Inge Ruders; *m* 1995, Annette Gerlach. *Educ:* Royal Danish Conservatory (Organist's degree 1975). Self-taught composer. Guest Prof., Yale Music Sch., 1991; Distinguished Internat. Vis. Prof. of Composition, RAM, London, 2002–04. Composer in Residence, Aspen Music Fest., Colorado, 2003. Principal *compositions:* Symphony No 1, 1989; Solar Trilogy, 1992–95; Listening Earth, 2002; Final Nightshade, 2003; *operas:* The Handmaid's Tale, 1996–98; Kafka's Trial, 2001–03; Selma Jezková (formerly Dancer in the Dark), 2007–08; The Thirteenth Child: A Fairytale Opera, 2014–16. *Publications:* Tundra (orch.), 1990; Violin Concerto No 2, 1991; Anima (2nd 'cello concerto), 1993; Symphony No 2, 1997; Oboe Concerto, 1998; Horn Trio, 1998; Fairytale (orch.), 1999; Paganini Variations (2nd guitar concerto), 2000; The Handmaid's Tale, vocal score 2002, full score 2003; Kafka's Trial, 2004; Har man hørt så galt (autobiog.), 2019; *relevant publication:* Acoustical Canvases: the music of Poul Ruders, by Per Erland Rasmussen, 2007. *Recreations:* reading, DIY activities. *Address:* c/o Edition Wilhelm Hansen, 1 Bornholmsgade, 1266 Copenhagen K, Denmark. *T:* 33117888. *E:* ewh@ewh.dk. *W:* www.PoulRuders.net.

**RUDGE, Sir Alan (Walter),** Kt 2000; CBE 1995 (OBE 1987); PhD; FRS 1992; FREng; Chairman, ERA Technology Ltd, 1997–2003; President, ERA Foundation, since 2013 (Chairman, 2001–12); President, MSI Cellular (Celtel), 2002–04 (Chief Executive Officer, 2001–02); *b* 17 Oct. 1937; *s* of Walter Thomas Rudge and Emma (*née* McFayden); *m* 1969, Jennifer Joan Minott; one *s* one *d*. *Educ:* Hugh Myddelton Sch.; London Polytechnic; Univ. of Birmingham (PhD ElecEng). FIET, FIEEE; FREng (FEng 1984). Res. Engr, Illinois Inst. of Technol. Res. Inst., 1968–71; Lectr, Electronic and Elec. Engrg Dept, Univ. of Birmingham, 1971–74; Engrg Adviser, Illinois Inst. of Technol. Res. Inst., 1974–79; Man. Dir, Era Technology Ltd, 1979–86; BT (formerly British Telecom): Dir, Research and Technology, 1987–89; Group Technology and Develt Dir, 1989–90; Mem. Main Bd, 1989–97; Man. Dir, Develt and Procurement, 1990–95; Dep. Gp Man. Dir, 1995–96; Dep. Chief Exec., 1996–97; Chm., WS Atkins plc, 1997–2001. Non-executive Director and Member Board: British Maritime Technology Ltd, 1984–89; Ricardo Consulting Engrs PLC, 1985–89; BT&D Technologies Ltd, 1987–93; Telecom Securicor Cellular Radio, 1989–90; MCI (USA), 1995–96; LucasVarity plc, 1997–99; GEC, subseq. Marconi, plc, 1997–2002; GUS plc, 1997–2006; MSI Cellular Investment Hldgs BV, 1998–2002; non-exec. Chm., Metapath Software Internat. Inc., 1999–2000; Sen. Ind. Dir, Experian plc, 2006–14 (Dep. Chm., 2011–14). Vis. Prof., Queen Mary and Westfield Coll. (formerly QMC), Univ. of London, 1985–. Pres., AIRTO, 1986. Pres., IEE, 1993–94 (Vice Chm., 1989–91; Dep. Pres., 1991; Mem., Electronics Divl Bd, 1980–89, Chm., 1984; Faraday Medal, 1991); Chairman: Learned Soc. Bd, 1989–91; EPSRC, 1994–99; Senate, Engrg Council, 1996–99; Member: Systems and Electronics Bd, MoD Defence Scientific Adv. Council, 1981–87; CBI Res. and Technol. Cttee, 1980–86; ACOST, 1987–90; Council, DRA, then DERA, MoD, 1991–96; Council for Sci. and Technology, 1993–97. Chairman: Bd of Trustees, British Retinitis Pigmentosa Soc., 1996–2011 (Trustee, 1996–2012); Bd of Mgt, Royal Commn for Exhibn of 1851, 2001–12 (Mem., 1997–2012); Trustee, Civitas, 2015– (Chm., 2018–). Member, Council: QMW, 1991–93; Royal Instn, 1992–95. Pro-Chancellor, Univ. of Surrey, 2002–07. Freeman, City of London; Liveryman, Engineers' Co., 1998–. Hon. FIEE 2000. Hon. Fellow, UCL, 1998. Hon. DEng: Birmingham, 1991; Bradford, Portsmouth, 1994; Nottingham Trent, 1995; Hon. DSc: Strathclyde, 1992; Bath, Loughborough, 1995; Westminster, 1996; DUniv Surrey, 1994. Duncan Davies Meml Medal, R&D Soc., 1998; Founder's Medal, IEEE, 1998; Millennium Medal, IEEE, 2000; President's Medal, RAEng, 2009; 1851 Royal Commn Medal, Royal Commn for Exhibn of 1851, 2012. *Publications:* The Handbook of Antenna Design, vol. 1 1982, vol. 2 1983; papers in sci. and tech. jls on antennas, microwaves and satellite communications. *Recreations:* sailing, cycling, reading. *Address:* ERA Foundation, The IET, 2 Savoy Place, WC2R 0BL. *Clubs:* Athenæum, Royal Automobile, Royal Ocean Racing; Royal Southampton Yacht, Royal Southern Yacht.

**RUDGE, Christopher John,** CBE 2012; FRCS; *b* 1 Oct. 1948; *s* of Ben Rudge, DFC and Joan Rudge; *m* 1973, Elizabeth Mary Jameson; two *s*. *Educ:* Guy's Hosp. Medical Sch. (BSc 1969, MB BS 1972). FRCS 1976. Consultant Transplant Surgeon: Guy's Hosp., London, 1981–85; St Peter's Hosps, London, 1985–95; Royal London Hosp., 1995–2001, (part-time) 2001–11; Med. Dir, UK Transplant, 2001–05; Man. and Transplant Dir, UK Transplant, 2005–08; Nat. Clinical Dir for Transplantation, DoH, 2008–11. Patron, Live Life Then Give Life, 2012–. Kent Ambassador, 2016–. Freeman, Skinners' Co., 2016–. *Recreations:* Rugby Union, music, gardening, travel, cricket. *Address:* Pennis Farm, Fawkham, Kent DA3 8LZ. *T:* and *Fax:* (01474) 707522. *E:* cjrudge@btinternet.com. *Club:* MCC.

**RUDIN, Toni Richard Perrott;** Secretary, Magistrates' Association, 1986–93; *b* 13 Oct. 1934; *s* of Richard William Rudin and Sarah Rowena Mary Rudin (*née* Perrott); *m* 1958, Heather Jean (*née* Farley); one *s* three *d*. *Educ:* Bootham Sch.; Millfield Sch.; RMA Sandhurst; Army Staff Coll.; Univ. of London; Coll. of Law, Guildford. Commissioned Royal Artillery, 1954; served BAOR, Cyprus, 1957–60, and UK; MoD, 1967–69; Battery Comdr and 2 i/c 26th Field Regt, RA, BAOR, 1969–72; MoD, 1972–75; retired, 1975. Solicitor, 1978; private practice as solicitor, 1978–80; Press and Public Relations, Law Soc., 1980–86. Mem., Chartered Accountants Disciplinary Cttees, 1989–94. Pt-time Legal Chm., Pensions Appeal Tribunals, 1994–2007. Gen. Comr of Income Tax, 1995–97. Mem. Cttee, Rutland and Leics Army Benevolent Fund, 1997–2001. *Recreations:* 19th century history, house renovation, France, woodwork, bridge. *Address:* 2 Chapel Walk, Adderley Street, Uppingham, Rutland LE15 9NE. *T:* (01572) 822999. *Club:* Army and Navy.

**RUDKIN, David;** *see* Rudkin, J. D.

**RUDKIN, Duncan Hugh;** Chief Executive and Registrar, General Pharmaceutical Council, since 2010; *b* 2 Aug. 1966; *s* of Philip Rudkin and Peggy Rudkin (*née* Watts). *Educ:* Queen's Coll., Oxford (BA Mod. Langs 1989). Solicitor, City of London; General Dental Council: Dir, Legal Services, 1998; Dir, Professional Standards, 2001–06; Dep. Chief Exec., 2005–06; Chief Exec. and Registrar, 2006–09. Trustee, St Catherine's Hospice, Crawley, 2014–17. *Address:* General Pharmaceutical Council, 25 Canada Square, E14 5LQ.

**RUDKIN, (James) David;** dramatist, screenwriter and short-story writer; *b* 29 June 1936; *s* of David Jonathan Rudkin and Anne Alice Martin; *m* 1967, Alexandra Margaret Thompson; one *s* two *d* (and one *s* decd). *Educ:* King Edward's Sch., Birmingham; St Catherine's Coll., Oxford (MA). Judith E. Wilson Fellow, Cambridge Univ., 1984; Vis. Prof., Middlesex Univ., 2004–; Hon. Prof., Aberystwyth Univ. (formerly Univ. of Wales), 2006–. *Screenplays:* Testimony, 1987; December Bride, 1991; The Woodlanders, 1996; *opera libretti:* Broken Strings, 1992; (with Jonathan Harvey) Inquest of Love, 1993; Black Feather Rising, 2008; Awakening, 2020; *radio plays:* (trans.) The Persians, 1965; (trans.) Hecuba, 1976; The LoveSong of Alfred J. Hitchcock, 1993; The Haunting of Mahler, 1994; The Giant's Cause..., 2005; Macedonia, 2015. *Publications:* plays: Afore Night Come, 1963, 2nd edn 2000; (trans.) Moses and Aaron (opera libretto), 1965; The Grace of Todd (orig. opera libretto), 1969; Cries from Casement as his Bones are Brought to Dublin (radio), 1974; Penda's Fen (film), 1975; Burglars (for children), 1976; Ashes, 1978; (trans.)

Hippolytus, 1980; The Sons of Light, 1981; The Triumph of Death, 1981; (trans.) Peer Gynt, 1983; The Saxon Shore, 1986; (trans.) When We Dead Waken, 1989; (trans.) Rosmersholm, 1990; Vampyr (monograph), 2005; Red Sun, 2011; Merlin Unchained, 2011; The LoveSong of Alfred J. Hitchcock (stage version), 2014; (trans.) Deathwatch, 2016; articles, reviews etc. for Encounter, Drama, Tempo, Theatre Res. Internat. *Recreations:* piano, geology, anthropology, languages (now mainly Celtic), cliff-walking, bridge. *Address:* c/o Casarotto Ramsay and Associates Ltd, 3rd Floor, 7 Savoy Court, Strand, WC2R 0EX. *T:* (020) 7287 4450, *Fax:* (020) 7287 9128.

**RUDLAND, Margaret Florence;** Headmistress, Godolphin and Latymer School, 1986–2008; recruitment consultant, since 2010; *b* 15 June 1945; *d* of Ernest George and Florence Hilda Rudland. *Educ:* Sweyne School, Rayleigh; Bedford College, Univ. of London (BSc); Inst. of Education (PGCE). Asst Mathematics Mistress, Godolphin and Latymer Sch., 1967–70; VSO, Ilorin, Nigeria, 1970–71; Asst Maths Mistress, Clapham County Sch., 1971–72; Asst Maths Mistress and Head of Dept, St Paul's Girls' Sch., 1972–83; Deputy Headmistress, Norwich High Sch., GPDST, 1983–85. Pres., GSA, 1996 (Chm., Educn Cttee, 1993–94). Member: UCAS Bd, 2002–06; Gen. Teaching Council, 2002–06. Member Council: Nightingale Fund, 1989–2011 (Chm., 1998–2011); UCL, 1998–2006; Mem. Bd, Assoc. of Governing Bodies of Ind. Schs, 2009–. Governor: St Margaret's Sch., Bushey, 1997–2017; Merchant Taylors' Sch., Northwood, 2000–12; Redcliffe Sch., 2001–09; Glendower Prep. Sch., 2003–12; St Mary's, Ascot, 2003–13; British Sch. of Paris, 2007–; English Coll., Prague, 2008–; ESU, 2008–10; Headington Sch., 2009–; St Swithun's Sch., 2011–19; Channing Sch., 2011–14. *Recreations:* opera, cinema, travel. *Address:* 3 Langham Place, Chiswick, W4 2QL.

**RUDLAND, Martin William; His Honour Judge Rudland;** a Circuit Judge, Northern Circuit, since 2002; *b* 13 March 1955; *s* of late Maurice Rudland and Patricia Rudland (*née* Crossley); *m* 1st, 1980, Norma Jane Lee (marr. diss. 1989); two *s*; 3rd, 1997, Linda Sturgess Jackson (*née* Potter); one step *s* one step *d*. *Educ:* Rowlinson Sch., Sheffield; Sheffield Univ. (LLB Hons 1976). Called to the Bar, Middle Temple, 1977 (Harmsworth Schol. 1977); in practice at the Bar, North Eastern Circuit, 1977–2002; Circuit Jun., 1985; Asst Recorder, 1992–96; a Recorder, 1996–2002. *Recreations:* books, music, ukulele banjo, cinema, bridge, travel. *Address:* Manchester Crown Court, Courts of Justice, Crown Square, Manchester M3 3FL.

**RUDMAN, Michael Edward;** theatre director and producer; Artistic Director, Sheffield Theatres (Crucible and Lyceum), 1992–94; *b* Tyler, Texas, 14 Feb. 1939; *s* of M. B. Rudman and Josephine Davis; *m* 1963, Veronica Anne Bennett (marr. diss. 1981); two *d*; *m* 1983, Felicity Kendal, *qv* (marr. diss. 1994); one *s*. *Educ:* St Mark's Sch., Texas; Oberlin Coll. (BA *cum laude* Govt); St Edmund Hall, Oxford (MA). Pres., OUDS, 1963–64. Asst Dir and Associate Producer, Nottingham Playhouse and Newcastle Playhouse, 1964–68; Asst Dir, RSC, 1968; Artistic Director: Traverse Theatre Club, 1970–73; Hampstead Theatre, 1973–78 (Theatre won Evening Standard Award for Special Achievement, 1978); Associate Dir, Nat. Theatre, 1979–88; Dir, Lyttelton Theatre (National), 1979–81; Dir, Chichester Festival Theatre, 1990. Mem., Bd of Dirs, Hampstead Theatre, 1979–89. *Plays directed* include: *Nottingham Playhouse:* Changing Gear, Measure for Measure, A Man for All Seasons, 1965; Julius Caesar, She Stoops to Conquer, Who's Afraid of Virginia Woolf, Death of a Salesman, 1966; Long Day's Journey into Night, 1967; Lily in Little India, 1968; *RSC Theatregoround:* The Fox and the Fly, 1968; *Traverse Theatre:* Curtains (transf. Open Space, 1971), Straight Up (transf. Piccadilly, 1971), A Game called Arthur (transf. Theatre Upstairs, 1971), Stand for my Father, (with Mike Wearing) A Triple Bill of David Halliwell plays, 1970; The Looneys, Pantagleize, 1971; Caravaggio Buddy, Tell Charlie Thanks for the Truss, The Relapse, 1972; *Hampstead Theatre:* Ride across Lake Constance (transf. Mayfair), A Nightingale in Bloomsbury Square, 1973; The Black and White Minstrels, The Show-off, The Connection, The Looneys, 1974; Alphabetical Order (transf. Mayfair), 1975; Clouds, 1977 (transf. Duke of York's, 1978); Cakewalk, Beyond a Joke, Gloo-Joo (transf. Criterion), 1978; Making it Better (transf. Criterion), 1992; Benchmark (also cowriter), 2002; Berlin Hanover Express, 2009; *National Theatre:* For Services Rendered (televised, 1980), Death of a Salesman, 1979; Thee and Me, The Browning Version/Harlequinade, Measure for Measure, 1980; The Second Mrs Tanqueray, 1981; Brighton Beach Memoirs (transf. Aldwych), The Magistrate, 1986; Six Characters in Search of an Author, Fathers and Sons, Ting Tang Mine, Waiting for Godot, 1987; *Chichester:* The Merry Wives of Windsor, Rumours, 1990; Mansfield Park, 1996; The Admirable Crichton, 1997; Tallulah!, 1997; Our Betters, 1997; *Sheffield:* A Midsummer Night's Dream, 1992; Donkeys' Years, (with Robert Delamere) Jane Eyre, Hamlet, Mansfield Park, 1993; The Grapes of Wrath, 1994; *West End:* Donkeys' Years, Globe, 1976; Taking Steps, Lyric, 1980; Camelot, 1982; The Winslow Boy, 1983; The Dragon's Tail, Apollo, 1985; Exclusive, Strand, 1989; Fallen Angels, Apollo, 2000; A Man for all Seasons, Th. Royal, Haymarket, 2005; Mrs Warren's Profession, Comedy, 2010; *Rose Theatre, Kingston:* All My Sons, 2016, Hong Kong Arts Fest., 2017; *Gate Theatre, Dublin:* The Heiress, 1997; *New York:* The Changing Room, 1973 (Drama Desk Award); Hamlet, 1976; Death of a Salesman, 1984 (Tony Award for Best Revival); Measure for Measure, 1993; Have you spoken to any Jews lately?, 1995; The Old Masters, 2011; Chin-Chin, UK tour, 2013. *Publications:* I Joke Too Much: the theatre director's tale, 2014. *Address:* c/o Helen Mumby, MLR, 44 South Molton Street, W1K 5RT. *T:* (020) 7493 2444. *Clubs:* Royal Mid-Surrey Golf, Liphook Golf.

**RUDWICK, Prof. Martin John Spencer,** PhD, ScD; FBA 2008; Professor of History, University of California, San Diego, 1988–98, now Emeritus; Affiliated Research Scholar, History and Philosophy of Science, University of Cambridge, since 1998; *b* 26 March 1932; *er s* of Joseph Spencer Rudwick and Olivia Grace Rudwick (*née* Western); *m* 1st, 1965, Gillian Yendell (marr. diss. 1972); 2nd, 1974, Tricia MacColl (marr. diss. 1995). *Educ:* Harrow Sch.; Trinity Coll., Cambridge (BA 1953; PhD 1958; ScD 1976). Hon. Fellow 2017). University of Cambridge: Demonstrator, 1955–59; Sen. Asst in Res., 1960–65; Lectr, in Geol., 1965–67, in Hist. of Sci., 1967–74; Fellow, Trinity Coll., 1956–60, Corpus Christi Coll., 1962–74, Cambridge; Prof. of Hist. and Social Aspects of the Natural Scis, Vrije Univ., Amsterdam, 1974–80; Fellow-Commoner, Trinity Coll., Cambridge, 1983–85; Prof. of Hist., and Hist. of Sci., Princeton Univ., 1985–87. Vis. Fellow, Clare Hall, Cambridge, 1994–95. Visiting Professor of History of Science: Princeton Univ., 1981; Hebrew Univ., Jerusalem, 1982; Mem., Inst. for Advanced Study, Princeton, 1982–84; Maître de Recherche Associé, École des Mines de Paris, 1985; Vis. Prof. of Hist. of Scis Rijksuniversiteit Utrecht, 1993. Guggenheim Foundn Fellow, 1994–95. Tarner Lectr, Trinity Coll., Cambridge, 1994–97. Mem., Doctrine Commn, C of E, 1982–85. Mem., Acad. Internat. d'Histoire des Scis, 1980–; Pres., Hist. of Earth Scis Soc., 2005–06. Scientific Medal, Zool Soc. of London, 1973; Hist. of Geol. Award, Geol Soc. of America, 1987; Friedman Medal, Geol Soc. of London, 1988; Founder's Medal, Soc. for Hist. of Natural Hist., 1988; Bernal Prize, Soc. for Social Studies of Sci., 1999; Sarton Medal, 2007; Levinson Prize, 2012, Davis Prize, 2015, Hist. of Sci. Soc.; Prix Wegmann, Soc. Géologique de France, 2008; Dingle Prize, British Soc. Hist. of Sci., 2015; Vladimir Tichomirov Award, Internat. Union of Geol Scis, 2016. *Publications:* Living and Fossil Brachiopods, 1970; The Meaning of Fossils, 1972, 2nd edn 1985; The Great Devonian Controversy, 1985; Scenes from Deep Time, 1992; Georges Cuvier, 1997; The New Science of Geology, 2004; Lyell and Darwin Geologists, 2005; Bursting the Limits of Time, 2005; Worlds before Adam, 2008; Earth's Deep History, 2014; contrib. articles to learned jls on paleontology and hist. of earth scis. *Recreations:* early music, hill walking, woodturning, vernacular architecture. *Address:* Moat House, 2 Welsh Street, Bishop's Castle, Shropshire SY9 5BT.

**RUEBAIN, David Ezra;** Chief Executive, Conservatoire for Dance and Drama, since 2018; *b* London, 11 June 1962; *s* of Benny Menashi Ruebain and Yvette Chouéke. *Educ:* Hampstead Sch.; Oriel Coll., Oxford (BA Hons PPE 1984; MA 1989); Coll. of Law, London. Dep. Coordinator, Centre for Studies on Integration in Educn, 1986–87; articled clerk, Robin Thompson & Partners, 1987–89; admitted as solicitor, 1988; Solicitor, ILEA, 1989–90; Sen. Solicitor, London Bor. of Southwark, 1990–94; Partner, Levenes Solicitors, 1995–2007; Dir, Legal Policy, Equality and Human Rights Commn, 2007–10; Chief Exec., Equality Challenge Unit, 2010–18. Vis. Prof. of Law, Birkbeck, Univ. of London, 2019–. Mem., Diversity and Inclusion Strategic Adv. Bd, Wellcome Trust, 2017–. Ind. Mem., Adv. Gp to Office for Fair Access, 2013–17. Short-term Expert, EU, 2010–12. Equalities Advr, FA Premier League, 2005–. Person of Year Award, RADAR, 2002. *Publications:* (jtly) Atkins Encyclopaedia of Court Forms, Vol. 17 (2): Education Law, 2001; (jtly) Taking Action: appropriate education is every child's right: a guide for parents of children with Special Educational Needs, 2002; (jtly) Education Law and Practice, 2005; (jtly) Disabled Children and the Law, 2006; (ed jtly) Education, Disability and Social Policy, 2011; (ed jtly) Blackstone's Guide to the Equality Act, 2010, 3rd edn 2016. *Recreations:* exercise, watching Arsenal FC, TV, conversation, listening. *Address:* Conservatoire for Dance and Drama, The Energy Centre, Units 1–3, Bowling Green Walk, N1 6AL.

**RUF, Beatrix;** curator; Director, Stedelijk Museum, Amsterdam, 2014–18; *b* Singen, 14 Feb. 1960; *d* of Helmuth Ruf and Ruth Ruf. *Educ:* Konservatorium der Stadt Wien (MA 1987); Univ. of Zurich (Lic.phil 1991). Curatorial Asst, Haus für konstruktive und konkrete Kunst Zürich, 1992; freelance curator and publishing, 1993; Curator: Zeiträume für Kunst, Dresden, 1993–95; Kunstmuseum, Canton of Thurgau, Warth, 1994–98; Director and Chief Curator: Kunsthaus Glarus, 1998–2001; Kunsthalle Zürich, Zurich, 2001–14. Curator: Ringier Collection, Zürich, 1995–2014; Shed im Eisenwerk, Frauenfeld, 1995–98. Teaching position: Hochschule für Theater und Performance, Bern, 1995–99; Kunsthistorisches Institut, Univ. of Zurich, 2000; Curatorial Advr, Postgrad. Prog. in Curating MAS, 2009–12, Mentor, MA Fine Arts, 2013–, Zürcher Hochschule der Künste; Mentor, Universität St Gallen, 2006–14. Vis. Curator, MacDonald Art Centre, Guelph and Toronto, 1997; Curator/Moderator, Engadin Art Talks, 2010–15; Curatorial Educn Advr, deAppel Art Center, Amsterdam, 2015–. Member: Art Commn, Swiss Re, 1999–2015; Bd, Graphische Gesellschaft der Schweiz, 1999–2014; Bd of Dirs, JRP|Ringier, 2004–; Core Gp Think Tank for a Mus. of the 21st Century, LUMA Foundn, 2008–; Cultural Adv. Bd, CERN, Geneva, 2011–15; Prog. Cttee, Bundeskunsthalle, Bonn, 2015–; Supervisory Bd, MuMoK, Museum Moderne Kunst, Vienna, 2014–17; Bd, Foundn Mark Morrisroe Estate, 2015–. Co-Founder, POOL postgrad. curatorial prog., Zürich, 2013. Member: Adv. and Prog. Cttees incl. Istanbul Modern, Garage Moskow, MAXXI, Rome, Samdani Foundn, Bangladesh; Acquisition Cttee, La Caixa, Barcelona; Scientific Cttee, Fondazione per l'Arte Moderna e Contemporanea - CRT; frequent jury member in: award cttees incl. Guggenheim Mus. Hugo Boss Prize, Absolut Award, Han Nefkens/MACBA Award, Prix de Rome, Erasmus Prize, Turner Prize, Ars Fennica Award; numerous commns incl. Preis der Nationalgalerie Berlin; Vincent, Stedlijk Mus. Amsterdam; Beck's Futures, ICA London. Agnes Gund Curatorial Award, Ind. Curators Internat., NY, 2015. *Publications:* (ed) Peter Zimmermann, 1997; (ed) Roland Herzog, Balsam, 1998; (ed) Jeroen de Rijke and Willem de Rooij, 2004; (ed) Eva Rothschild, 2004; (ed) Richard Prince, Jokes and Cartoons, 2006; (ed) Laura Owens, 2006; (ed) Bekanntmachungen, 2006; (ed) Daria Martin, 2006; (ed jtly) Valentin Carron, 2007; (ed) Blasted Allegories: works from the Ringier Collection, 2008; (ed) Josh Smith, 2009; (ed jtly) Seth Price, 2010; (ed jtly) Mark Morrisroe, 2010; (ed jtly) Tris Vonna Michell, 2010; (ed jtly) Helen Marten, 2013; (ed jtly) Engadin Art Talks, 2013; (ed jtly) Imponderable: the archives of Tony Oursler, 2015; (ed jtly) Size Matters: (de)growth of the 21st century art museum, 2017; contrib. and ed exhibn catalogues. *Address:* Netherlands.

**RUFFER, Jonathan Garnier;** DL; Chair, Ruffer LLP, since 2011; *b* London, 17 Aug. 1951; *s* of Major John E. M. Ruffer and Dodo M. Ruffer; *m* 1982, Jane Sequeira; one *d*. *Educ:* Marlborough Coll.; Sidney Sussex Coll., Cambridge (BA 1972; MA). Myers & Co. Stock Exchange; called to the Bar, Middle Temple (Jun. Harmsworth Exhibnr; Hon. Bencher, 2015); Dunbar Gp Ltd, 1977–79; Exec., Corporate Finance Dept, J. Henry Schroder Wagg, 1980–85; Dir, CFS (Investment Mgt), 1985–88; Man. Dir, Rathbone Investment Mgt, 1988–94; Chief Exec., Ruffer LLP (formerly Ruffer Investment Mgt), 1994–2012. Non-executive Director: Odey Asset Mgt, 1992–2005; Electric and Gen. Investment Trust, 2000–11. Chm., Good Shepherd Mission, Bethnal Green, 1998–2008. Chm., Auckland Castle Trust, 2012–18. DL Co. Durham, 2013. Hon. DLit Durham, 2018; Hon. DLaw Northumbria, 2018. *Publications:* The Big Shots, 1977, 1989; Every Day is Christmas Day, 2005; Babel: the breaking of the banks, 2009. *Recreation:* seventeenth century Spanish pictures. *Address:* Castle Lodge, Market Place, Bishop Auckland, Co. Durham DL14 7NP; 10 Catherine Place, SW1E 6HF. *T:* (020) 7963 8169. *E:* jruffer@ruffer.co.uk. *Club:* Athenæum.

**RUFFLES, Philip Charles,** CBE 2001; RDI 1997; FRS 1998; FREng, FRAeS, FIMechE; Technical Advisor, Rolls-Royce plc, 2001–04; consultant, since 2001; *b* 14 Oct. 1939; *s* of Charles Richard Ruffles and Emily Edith Ruffles; *m* 1967, Jane Connor; two *d*. *Educ:* Sevenoaks Sch.; Bristol Univ. (BSc 1st Cl. Mech. Engrg 1961). FRAeS 1985 (Hon. FRAeS 2003); FREng (FEng 1988); FIMechE 1989. Rolls-Royce: trainee, 1961–63; technical appts, 1963–77; Chief Engr, RB211, 1977–81; Head of Engrg, Small Engines, 1981–84; Dir, Technol. & Design Engrg, 1984–89; Technical Dir, 1989–91; Dir of Engrg, Aerospace Gp, 1991–96; Dir, Engrg and Technol., 1997–2001. Non-exec. Dir, Domino Printing Science plc, 2002–14. Member: Defence Scientific Adv. Council, 1990–93; Technol. Foresight Defence and Aerospace Panel, 1994–97; LINK Bd (OST), 1995–98; Council for Central Lab. of Res. Councils, 1998–2004; Council for Sci. and Technol., 2007–10. Member Council: Royal Acad. Engrg, 1994–97, 2002–05; RAeS, 1995–2004; Royal Soc., 2010. FRSA 1998. Liveryman, Engineers' Co., 1998. Hon. FIC 2002. Hon. DEng: Bristol, 1995; Birmingham, 1998; Sheffield, 1999; Hon. DSc City, 1998. Ackroyd Stuart Prize, 1987, Gold Medal, 1996, RAeS; MacRobert Award, 1996, Prince Philip Medal, 2001, Royal Acad. of Engrg; James Clayton Prize, IMechE, 1998; Duncan Davies Meml Medal, R & D Soc., 2000; François-Xavier Bagnoud Aerospace Prize, Univ. of Michigan, 2001; R. Tom Sawyer Award, ASME, 2002; Premio Internazionale Barsanti e Matteucci, 2002; Glazebrook Medal, Inst. of Physics, 2011. *Publications:* History of the Rolls-Royce RB211 Turbofan Engine, 2014; contrib. to numerous learned jls on engrg and technol. topics. *Recreations:* Rugby, D-I-Y. *Address:* 5 Ford Lane, Allestree, Derby DE22 2EX.

**RUFFLEY, David Laurie;** *b* 18 April 1962; *s* of J. L. Ruffley, solicitor. *Educ:* Queens' Coll., Cambridge (Exhibnr, 1981, Foundn Scholar, 1983; Histl Tripos pt 1, Law Tripos pt 2, BA 1985, MA 1988). Articled clerk and Solicitor with Coward Chance, then Clifford Chance, 1985–91; Special Advr to Sec. of State for Educn and Science, 1991–92, to Home Sec., 1992–93, to Chancellor of the Exchequer, 1993–96. MP (C) Bury St Edmunds,

1997–2015. An Opposition Whip, 2004–05; Shadow Minister: for Work and Pensions, 2005–07; for Police Reform, 2007–10. Member: Select Cttee on Public Admin, 1997–99; Select Cttee on Treasury Affairs, 1998–2004 and 2010–15; Co-Chm., All Party Parly Gp on Qatar, 2013–15; Exec., 1922 Cttee, 2003–04; Secretary: Cons. Backbench Finance Cttee, 1999–2003; Parly Gp on Wholesale Financial Mkts and Services, 2010–15; Dep. Chm., Cons. Backbench Econ. Affairs Gp, 2010–15. US State Dept Internat. Visitor, res. prog. on econ. develt and trade, 2003; Fellow, British-American Project, 2002. *Recreations:* golf, thinking. *E:* druffley62@gmail.com. *Club:* Pratt's.

**RUGBY,** 3rd Baron *cr* 1947, of Rugby, Co. Warwick; **Robert Charles Maffey;** farmer; *b* 4 May 1951; *s* of 2nd Baron Rugby and of Margaret Helen, *d* of late Harold Bindley; *S* father, 1990; *m* 1974, Anne Penelope, *yr d* of late David Hale; two *s. Educ:* Brickwall House Sch., Northiam. *Recreations:* shooting, woodwork and metal work. *Heir: s* Hon. Timothy James Howard Maffey, *b* 23 July 1975.

**RUGG, Prof. Michael Derek,** PhD; FRSE, FAAAS; Distinguished Professor of Behavioral and Brain Sciences, since 2011 and Director, Center for Vital Longevity, since 2014, University of Texas, Dallas (Co-Director, 2011–14); Professor of Psychiatry, University of Texas Southwestern Medical Center, since 2010; Professor of Psychology, University of East Anglia, since 2019; *b* 23 Sept. 1954; *s* of Derek and Brenda Rugg; *m* 1976, Elizabeth Jackson; one *s. Educ:* Univ. of Leicester (BSc Psychol; PhD 1979). FRSE 1996. Res. Fellow, Dept of Psychology, Univ. of York, 1978–79; University of St Andrews: Lectr in Psychology, 1979–88; Reader, 1988–92; Prof., 1992–98; Head, Sch. of Psychology, 1992–94; Prof. of Cognitive Neurosci. and Wellcome Trust Principal Res. Fellow, UCL, 1998–2003; Prof. of Neurobiol. and Behavior, 2003–10, Dir, Center for Neurobiol. of Learning and Memory, 2004–10, Univ. of Calif, Irvine. Hon. Res. Fellow, Inst. of Neurology, 1994–98. Member: DoH Wkg Gp on Organophosphates, 1998–99; Govt Ind. Expert Gp on Mobile Phones, 1999–2000; Prog. mgt cttee, mobile telecomm. and health res. prog., 2000–03 and 2005–07; Adv. gp on non-ionising radiation, NRPB, 2001–03; Cognition Perception Study Section, 2007–11 (Chm., 2009–11), Neurobiology of Learning and Memory Study Section, 2014– (Chm., 2017–), NIH. FAAAS 2009; Fellow, Assoc. for Psychol Sci., 2009. *Publications:* (ed with A. D. Milner) Neuropsychology of Consciousness, 1991; (ed with M. G. H. Coles) Electrophysiology of Mind, 1995; (ed) Cognitive Neuroscience, 1996; over 250 articles in cognitive neuroscience and related fields in learned jls. *Recreations:* rock climbing, ski-ing, 20th century novels and visual arts, listening to and playing music. *Address:* Center for Vital Longevity, University of Texas at Dallas, 1600 Viceroy Drive, Suite 800, Dallas, TX 75235, USA.

**RUGGLES-BRISE, Sir Timothy (Edward),** 3rd Bt *cr* 1935, of Spains Hall, Finchingfield; owner, Spains Hall estate, since 1966; Partner, Spains Hall Partnership: Rural Estate Management and Hospitality, since 2011 (proprietor, 2006–11); *b* 11 April 1945; *s* of Guy Edward Ruggles-Brise, TD and Elizabeth Ruggles-Brise (*née* Knox); *S* uncle, 2007; *m* 1975, Rosemary Elizabeth (*née* Craig); three *s* two *d. Educ:* Eton Coll.; Regent St Polytechnic; RAC Cirencester. DipCE; DipAgr; CDipAF. CEng, MICE, now retired. 1964–78: Sen. Engr, Livesey & Henderson then Rendel Palmer & Tritton; civil engrg consultant. Sen. Partner, Whitehouse Farms Partnership, 1974–2001; estab. and Sen. Partner, Spains Hall Forest Nursery, 1979–2008. Chm., Forestry Gp, Horticultural Trades Assoc., and E Anglian Br., Timber Growers Assoc., 1993–97. Jt Master, East Essex Foxhounds, 1980–83. Mem., Finchingfield PCC; Churchwarden, St John the Baptist, Finchingfield, 2013–16. Master, Armourers' and Brasiers' Co., 2011–12; Chm., Armourers' and Brasiers' Gauntlet Trust, 2014–17. *Recreations:* country pursuits, food and wine. *Heir: s* Archibald Edward Ruggles-Brise [*b* 9 Dec. 1979; *m* 2007, Anna French; three *s*]. *Address:* Mill End Cottage, Spains Hall Road, Finchingfield, Braintree, Essex CM7 4NH. *T:* (01371) 810232. *E:* tim@rugglesbrise.co.uk. *Club:* Essex.

**RUGMAN, Jonathan Anthony;** Foreign Affairs Correspondent, Channel 4 News, since 2008; *b* London, 15 Nov. 1965; *s* of Roderick and Wendy Rugman; *m* 1995, Rachel Lewis; two *s* one *d. Educ:* Bradfield Coll.; Kent Sch., Connecticut; Churchill Coll., Cambridge (BA Hons English Lit. 1988). Turkey corresp., BBC World Service, 1991–92; Istanbul corresp., Guardian and Observer, 1993–96; reporter, File on 4, BBC Radio 4, 1996–98; associate producer, Lion Television, 1997–98; ITN Channel 4 News: Business corresp., 1999–2003; Washington corresp., 2003–06; Diplomatic corresp., 2006–08. Fellow Commoner, Corpus Christi Coll., Cambridge, 2017. Retail Business Award, 1999, Best Broadcast, 2000, 2001, Business Journalist of Year Awards; Business Broadcaster of Year, Harold Wincott Foundn, 2000; Midlands Current Affairs Award, RTS, 2000; British Envmt Award, 2006; Foreign Press Assoc. Award, 2009; Premio Luchetta Award, Fondazione Luchetta, Italy, 2015; BAFTA for TV News coverage (Paris terrorist attacks), 2016. *Publications:* Ataturk's Children: Turkey and the Kurds, 1996. *Recreation:* music. *Address:* ITN Channel 4 News, 200 Gray's Inn Road, WC1X 8XZ.. *T:* (020) 7430 4606. *E:* jonathan.rugman@itn.co.uk, jarugman@gmail.com. *Clubs:* West London Trades Union, Soho House.

**RUHNAU, Heinz;** consultant in strategic planning, since 1991; Professor of Business Administration, Technical University, Dresden, 1990; *b* Danzig, 5 March 1929; *m* Edith Loers; three *d. Educ:* Dip. in Business Administration, 1954. Asst to Chm., IG-Metall, Frankfurt; Regional Dir, IG-Metall, Hamburg, 1956–65; Mem., Senate of Free Hanseatic City of Hamburg (responsible for security and city admin.), 1965–73; Mem., Exec. Bd, COOP, 1973; State Sec., Ministry of Transport, 1974–82; CEO, Deutsche Lufthansa, 1982–91. Chairman: IATA, 1985; Assoc. of European Airlines, 1988. Federal Grand Cross of Merit, 1980, with Star, 1989, FRG; Officer, Légion d'Honneur (France), 1989; Cross of Merit (Spain), 1990. *Address:* Elsa Brändström Straße 213, 53227 Bonn, Germany.

**RUIZ, Cristina;** Editor-at-Large, The Art Newspaper, since 2009; *b* 16 Oct. 1971; *d* of Grazia and Domenico Ruiz. *Educ:* University Coll. London (BA Hons Ancient and Medieval Hist.); Courtauld Inst. of Art (MA Classical Art). Mem., British Drawings and Watercolours Dept, Christie's, London, 1994–95; The Art Newspaper: joined as staff reporter, 1995; Dep. Editor, 2000–03; Editor, 2003–08; Features Editor, 2009; Contributing Ed., The Gentlewoman, 2014–. *Recreations:* trash television, scuba-diving. *Address:* The Art Newspaper, 70 South Lambeth Road, SW8 1RL. *T:* (020) 7735 3331.

**RULE, Brian Francis;** Director General of Information Technology Systems, Ministry of Defence, 1985–94; Chairman, Emeritus Plus Ltd, 1994–98; *b* 20 Dec. 1938; *s* of late Sydney John Rule and Josephine Rule, Pen-y-ffordd, near Chester; *m* 1993, Irene M. Rees, Pembs. *Educ:* Daniel Owen Sch., Mold; Loughborough Univ. of Technology (MSc). Engineer, de Havilland Aircraft Co., 1955–59; Res. Assistant, Loughborough Univ., 1963–65; Lectr, Univ. of Glasgow, 1965–67; University of Aberdeen: Lectr, 1967–70; Sen. Lectr, 1970–72; Dir of Computing, 1972–78; Dir, Honeywell Information Systems Ltd, 1978–79; Dir of Scientific Services, NERC, 1979–85. *Publications:* various papers in scientific jls. *Recreations:* Boxer dogs, antique clocks. *Address:* c/o Lloyds Bank, 14 Castle Street, Cirencester, Glos GL7 1QJ.

**RULE, David Stephen;** Executive Director, Insurance Supervision, Bank of England, since 2016; *b* Poole, Dorset, 1 Jan. 1967; *s* of Dennis and Mary Rule; *m* 1997, Michelle Gillam; two *s* one *d. Educ:* Balliol Coll., Oxford (BA Modern Hist.); Univ. of Toronto (MA Pol Sci.); Queens' Coll., Cambridge (MPhil Econs 1996). Bank of England, 1990–2007; FSA, 2009–13; Bank of England, 2013–: Exec. Dir, Prudential Policy, 2014–16. *Address:* Bank of England, Threadneedle Street, EC2R 8AH. *E:* david.rule@bankofengland.co.uk.

**RUMALSHAH, Rt Rev. Munawar Kenneth, (Mano);** Bishop of Peshawar, 1994–98 and 2003–10, now Bishop Emeritus; Coordinator, Church of Pakistan, since 2013; *b* 16 June 1941; *s* of Ven. Inayat and Mrs Akhtar Rumalshah; *m* 1st, 1966, Rosalind Andrews; two *d*; 2nd, 1984, Sheila Benita Biswas; one *d. Educ:* Punjab Univ. (BSc 1960); Serampur Univ. (BD 1965); Karachi Univ. (MA 1968); Cambridge Univ. (PGCE 1986). Ordained deacon, 1965, priest, 1966; Curate: Holy Trinity Cathedral, Karachi, 1965–69; St Edmund Roundhay, Leeds, 1970–73; Area Sec., and Asst Home Sec., CMS, 1973–78; Educn Sec., BCC, 1978–81; Priest-in-charge, St George, Southall, 1981–88; Presbyter, St John's Cathedral, and Lectr, Edwarde's Coll., Peshawar, 1989–94; Gen. Sec., USPG, 1998–2003; and an Asst Bp, Southwark Dio., 1999–2003; Bishop in Residence, St John the Divine Episcopal Cath., NY, 2007. Member: Archbp of Canterbury's Commn on Urban Priority Areas, 1984–86; Archbp of Canterbury's Anglican Communion Fund, 2008–10. Ramsden Preacher, Cambridge Univ., 2003; Vis. Prof., Gen. Theol Seminary of Episcopal Church, NY, 2007–; Hon. Vis. Fellow, Yale Divinity Sch., Yale Univ., 2012–13. Jt Ed., Lambeth Conf., 1998. *Publications:* Focus on Pakistan, 1989, 4th edn 1999; Being a Christian in Pakistan, 1998. *Recreations:* watching cricket, music, reading, travel. *Address:* Diocesan Centre, 1 Sir Syed Road, Peshawar 25000, Khyber Pukhtunkhwa, Pakistan. *T:* (91) 5279094.

**RUMBELOW, His Honour (Arthur) Anthony;** QC 1990; a Circuit Judge, 2002–14; a Deputy High Court Judge (Family Division), 2000–14; Designated Family Judge, Northampton County Court, 2013–14; *b* Salford, Lancs, 9 Sept. 1943; *er s* of Arthur Rumbelow and Theresa (*née* Lucketti); *m* 1st; three *d*; 2nd, 2010, Vivienne Ashworth (*née* Fletcher); one *d. Educ:* Salford Grammar Sch.; Queens' Coll., Cambridge (Squire Schol.; BA 1966). Called to the Bar, Middle Temple, 1967 (Harmsworth Exhibnr, Astbury Schol.). Recorder, 1988–2002; Sen. Judge, British Sovereign Bases, Cyprus, 2008–13. Chairman: Medical Appeal Tribunal, 1988–2002; Mental Health Rev. Tribunal, 2000–13. Mem., Parole Bd, 2010–. Mem., Rochdale MBC, 1982–84. *Recreations:* wine, theatre, gardening.

**RUMBELOW, (Roger) Martin,** CEng; director and consultant, since 1996; *b* 3 June 1937; *s* of Leonard Rumbelow and Phyllis (*née* Perkins); *m* 1965, Marjorie Elizabeth Glover (*d* 2015). *Educ:* Cardiff High Sch.; Bristol Univ. (BSc); Cranfield Inst. of Technol. (MSc). CEng 1966. National Service, RAF Pilot, 1955–57. British Aircraft Corporation, 1958–74: Dep. Prodn Controller, 1967–73; Concorde Manufg Project Manager, 1973–74; Department of Trade and Industry, 1974–96: Principal, 1974–78; Asst Sec., 1978–86; Under Sec., 1987–96; Services Management Div., 1987–92; Head, Electronics and Engrg Div., 1992–96. Chm. and Dir, KPRA Ltd, 2001–. Dir and Trustee, Florestan Trust, 2006–12. *Recreations:* singing, opera, theatre, tennis. *Club:* Royal Air Force.

**RUMBLES, Michael John;** Member (Lib Dem) Scotland North East, Scottish Parliament, since 2016 (West Aberdeenshire and Kincardine, 1999–2011); *b* 10 June 1956; *s* of Samuel and Joan Rumbles; *m* 1985, Pauline Sillars; two *s. Educ:* Univ. of Wales (MSc Econ). Commissioned RAEC, 1979–94 (Major); Team Leader in Business Management, Aberdeen Coll., 1995–99. Contested (Lib Dem) Aberdeenshire W, Scottish Parlt, 2011. *Recreations:* family, hill walking. *Address:* Scottish Parliament, Edinburgh EH99 1SP.

**RUMBOLD, Sir Henry (John Sebastian),** 11th Bt *cr* 1779; Partner, Dawson Cornwell, 1991–2004; *b* 24 Dec. 1947; *s* of Sir Horace Anthony Claude Rumbold, 10th Bt, KCMG, KCVO, CB, and Felicity Ann Rumbold (*née* Bailey); *S* father, 1983; *m* 1978, Frances Ann (*née* Hawkes, formerly wife of Julian Berry). *Educ:* Eton College; College of William and Mary, Virginia, USA (BA). Articled Stileman, Neate and Topping, 1975–77; admitted solicitor, 1977; asst solicitor, Stileman, Neate and Topping, 1977–79; Partner, 1979–81; joined Stephenson Harwood, 1981, Partner, 1982–91. *Recreations:* shooting, reading. *Heir: cousin* Charles Anton Rumbold [*b* 7 Feb. 1959; *m* 1987, Susan, *er d* of J. M. Tucker; one *d*]. *Address:* 19 Hollywood Road, SW10 9HT. *T:* (020) 7352 9148; Hatch House, Tisbury, Wilts SP3 6PA. *T:* (01747) 870622. *Clubs:* Boodle's, Groucho.

**RUMFITT, Prof. Ian Patrick,** DPhil; FBA 2018; Professor of Philosophy, University of Oxford, since 2016; Senior Research Fellow, All Souls College, Oxford, since 2016; *b* 1 Dec. 1964; *s* of late Jurat Michael Rumfitt and of Dorothy Rumfitt (*née* Simpson); *m* 1999, Lucy Ranembe Baines; one *s* one *d. Educ:* Victoria Coll., Jersey; Balliol Coll., Oxford (BA 1st Cl. Maths and Philosophy 1986; DPhil 1991). Procter Fellow, Princeton Univ., 1986–87; Jun. Res. Fellow, Balliol Coll., Oxford, 1989–92; Lectr, Keele Univ., 1992–93; Asst Prof. of Philosophy, Univ. of Michigan at Ann Arbor, 1993–98; Fellow and Tutor in Philosophy, University Coll., Oxford, 1998–2005; Professor of Philosophy: Birkbeck Coll., Univ. of London, 2005–13; Univ. of Birmingham, 2013–16. *Publications:* The Boundary Stones of Thought: an essay in the philosophy of logic, 2015; contribs to Mind, Jl of Philosophy, Philosophical Rev. *Recreations:* playing the piano, listening to music. *Address:* All Souls College, Oxford OX1 4AL.

**RUMFITT, Nigel John;** QC 1994; *b* 6 March 1950; *s* of late Alan Regan Rumfitt and Dorothy Rumfitt (*née* Ackroyd); *m* 1984, Dorothy Pamela Pouncey. *Educ:* Leeds Modern Sch.; Pembroke Coll., Oxford (MA, BCL). Teaching Associate, Northwestern Univ. Sch. of Law, Chicago, 1972–73; called to the Bar, Middle Temple, 1974, Bencher, 2008; in practice as a barrister, 1974–2017; Asst Recorder, 1991–95; Recorder, 1995–2010. *Recreations:* ski-ing, travel, sailing, Francophilia. *Address:* c/o 7 Bedford Row, WC1R 4BS. *T:* (020) 7242 3555.

**RUMSEY, Rt Rev. Andrew Paul;** *see* Ramsbury, Bishop Suffragan of.

**RUMSFELD, Hon. Donald Henry;** Secretary of Defense, USA, 1975–77 and 2001–06; *b* Chicago, 9 July 1932; *s* of George Donald Rumsfeld and Jeannette Rumsfeld (*née* Husted); *m* 1954, Joyce Pierson; one *s* two *d. Educ:* New Trier High Sch., Ill; Princeton Univ. (AB 1954). Served US Navy, 1954–57. Admin. Asst, US House of Reps, 1957–59; investment broker, A. G. Becker & Co., Chicago, 1960–62. Mem., House of Reps, 1963–69; Dir, Office of Econ. Opportunity, and Asst to US Pres., 1969–70; Dir, Econ. Stabilization Prog., and Counsellor to the Pres., 1971–72; US Ambassador and Perm. Rep. to NATO, 1973–74; Chief of Staff, White House, and Asst to the Pres., 1974–75. Pres. and CEO, then Chm., G. D. Searle & Co., Ill, 1977–83 and 1984–85; special envoy to ME, 1983–84; Sen. Advr, William Blair & Co., 1985–90; Chm. and CEO, General Instrument Corp., Chicago, 1990–93; in private business, 1996–97; Chm., Gilead Sciences Inc., Calif, 1997–2000. US Presidential Medal of Freedom, 1977. *Publications:* Known and Unknown: a memoir, 2011; When the Center Held: Gerald Ford and the rescue of the American presidency, 2018.

**RUNACRES, Mark Alastair;** Associate, Ambassador Partnership, since 2019; Chair, Sustainability Advisors, since 2018 (Senior Advisor, 2017); Senior Adviser: International Affairs, Corporate Catalyst India, since 2016; International Business and and Diplomatic Exchange, since 2018; *b* 19 May 1959; *s* of late John Runacres and of Coral Runacres; *m*

1989, Shawn Reid; two s one d. *Educ*: St John's Coll., Cambridge (BA Hons). Entered FCO, 1981; FCO, 1981–83; New Delhi, 1983–86; Trade Relations Dept, 1986–88, and News Dept, 1988–90, FCO; First Sec. (Chancery), Paris, 1991–95; SE Asia Dept, FCO, 1995–97; Dir, Trade for S Asia and Africa, DTI, 1997–99 (on secondment); Counsellor (Economic and Social Affairs), UKMIS to UN, NY, 1999–2002; Minister and Dep. High Comr, New Delhi, 2002–06; on sabbatical from FCO, 2006–11. Sen. Vis. Fellow, Energy and Resources Inst., New Delhi, 2006–08. India Advr, CBI, 2009–16. Director: Business and Community Foundn (Delhi), 2006–17; Sheffield Haworth (India) Private Ltd, 2007–; Action for a Global Climate Community, 2008–10; SQN Partners, 2009–17; Canta Consultants, 2011–; Mass1 Engagement, 2011–16; SQN Partners Pte Ltd, Singapore, 2015–17; non-executive Director: Mind Tree Ltd, 2006–12; G4S (India) Ltd, 2006–15; Elara Capital (India) Pvt Ltd, 2007–16; Religare Capital Markets Europe, 2009–18; Religare Capital Markets Ltd, 2012–16; Elara Capital (Asia) Pvt Ltd, 2016–; non-exec. Chm., A4e India Pvt Ltd, 2012–14; Advisory Board: Avian Media Pvt Ltd, 2008–; Public Affairs Asia, 2008–; Liqvid eLearning Services Pvt. Ltd, 2011–12; Technovations Pvt Ltd, 2018; Cognito Edge PvT Ltd, 2018–; Mem. Bd, FCO Prosperity Fund, India, 2011–15. Chm., 2014–16, Internat. Advr, 2016–, British Business Gp, Delhi. Co-Founder, British Educn Centre, India, 2015–18. *Address*: 21 Enmore Road, SW15 6LL. *E*: mark@markrunacres.com. *Club*: MCC.

**RUNCIE, Hon. James Robert**, FRSL; writer; freelance director, since 2000; Commissioning Editor, Arts, BBC Radio Four, since 2016; *b* Cambridge, 7 May 1959; *s* of Baron Runcie, MC, PC and late Angela Rosalind Runcie (*née* Turner); *m* 1985, Marilyn Imrie; one d and one step d. *Educ*: Marlborough Coll.; Trinity Hall, Cambridge (BA 1981); Bristol Old Vic Th. Sch. Producer and dir, BBC, 1985–2000; Artistic Dir, Bath Lit. Fest., 2010–13; Hd of Literature and Spoken Word, Southbank Centre, 2012–15. Vis. Prof., Bath Spa Univ., 2013–16. FRSL 2016. *Publications*: The Discovery of Chocolate, 2001; The Colour of Heaven, 2002; Canvey Island, 2006; East Fortune, 2009; The Grantchester Mysteries: Sidney Chambers and the Shadow of Death, 2012; Sidney Chambers and the Perils of the Night, 2013; Sidney Chambers and the Problem of Evil, 2014; Sidney Chambers and the Forgiveness of Sins, 2015; Sidney Chambers and the Dangers of Temptation, 2016; Sidney Chambers and the Persistence of Love, 2017; The Road to Grantchester, 2019. *Recreations*: diligent indolence, the fortunes of Manchester City Football Club, cricket, patience with children. *Address*: c/o David Godwin Associates, 55 Monmouth Street, WC2H 9DG. *T*: (020) 7240 9992. *E*: David@DavidGodwinAssociates.co.uk. *Club*: Athenæum.

**RUNCIMAN**, family name of **Viscount Runciman of Doxford**.

**RUNCIMAN OF DOXFORD**, 3rd Viscount *cr* 1937; **Walter Garrison Runciman, (Garry)**, CBE 1987; FBA 1975; Bt 1906; Baron Runciman, 1933, of Shoreston; President, British Academy, 2001–05; Fellow, Trinity College, Cambridge, since 1971; *b* 10 Nov. 1934; *o s* of 2nd Viscount Runciman of Doxford, OBE, AFC, AE and Katherine Schuyler (*d* 1993), *y d* of late William R. Garrison, New York; *S* father, 1989; *m* 1963, Ruth (*see* Viscountess Runciman of Doxford); one s two d. *Educ*: Eton (Oppidan Schol.); Trinity Coll., Cambridge (Schol.; Fellow, 1959–63, 1971–). National Service, 1953–55 (2/Lt, Grenadier Guards); Harkness Fellow, 1958–60; part-time Reader in Sociology, Univ. of Sussex, 1967–69; Vis. Prof., Harvard Univ., 1970; Vis. Fellow, Nuffield Coll., Oxford, 1979–87 (Hon. Fellow, 1998). Lectures: Radcliffe-Brown, British Acad., 1986; Spencer, Oxford Univ., 1986; Chorley, London Univ., 1993; ESRC, 1993; T. H. Marshall, Southampton Univ., 1994; British Acad., 1998; Walters, Univ. of Bath, 2006. Chairman: Walter Runciman plc, 1976–90; Runciman Investments Ltd, 1990–2012; Andrew Weir & Co. Ltd, 1991–2005. Treas., Child Poverty Action Gp, 1972–97; Member: SSRC, 1974–79; Securities and Investments Board, 1986–97 (a Dep. Chm., 1990–97); British Library Bd, 1999–2002; Dep. Chm., FSA, 1997–98. Pres., Gen. Council of British Shipping, 1986–87 (Vice-Pres., 1985–86). Chm., Royal Commn on Criminal Justice, 1991–93. Hon. Foreign Mem., Amer. Acad. of Arts and Sciences, 1986. Hon. DSc (SocScis) Edinburgh, 1992; DUniv York, 1994; Hon. DLitt Oxford, 2000; Hon. DSc (Soc Sci) London, 2007; Hon. DCL Newcastle, 2012. *Publications*: Plato's Later Epistemology, 1962; Social Science and Political Theory, 1963, 2nd edn 1969; Relative Deprivation and Social Justice, 1966, 2nd edn 1972; Sociology in its Place, and other essays, 1970; A Critique of Max Weber's Philosophy of Social Science, 1972; A Treatise on Social Theory: vol. I, 1983, vol. II, 1989, vol. III, 1997; Confessions of a Reluctant Theorist, 1989; The Social Animal, 1998; The Theory of Cultural and Social Selection, 2009; Great Books, Bad Arguments, 2010; Very Different But Much the Same, 2015; articles in academic jls. *Heir*: *s* Prof. David Walter Runciman [*b* 1 March 1967; *m* 1997, Beatrice, (Bee), *yr d* of A. N. Wilson, *qv* and Katherine Duncan-Jones, *qv*; two s one d]. *Address*: 44 Clifton Hill, NW8 0QG. *Club*: Brooks's.

**RUNCIMAN OF DOXFORD, Viscountess**; Ruth Runciman, DBE 1998 (OBE 1991); Chairman, Central and North West London NHS Foundation Trust (formerly Central and North West London Mental Health NHS Trust), 2001–13; *b* 9 Jan. 1936; *o d* of Joseph Hellmann and Dr Ellen Hellmann; *m* 1st, 1959, Denis Mack Smith, CBE, FBA (marr. diss. 1962; he *d* 2017); 2nd, 1963, Viscount Runciman of Doxford, *qv*; one s two d. *Educ*: Roedean Sch., Johannesburg; Witwatersrand Univ. (BA 1956); Girton Coll., Cambridge (BA 1958; Hon. Fellow, 2001). Chairman: Mental Health Act Commn, 1994–98; Ind. Inquiry into Misuse of Drugs Act 1971, 1997–2000; Member: Adv. Council on Misuse of Drugs, 1974–95; Press Complaints Commn, 1998–2001 (Mem., Charter Compliance Panel, 2004–06). Council Mem., Nat. Assoc. of CAB, 1978–83; Outreach advice worker, Kensington CAB, 1988–2000; Chairman: Nat. AIDS Trust, 2000–06 (Trustee, 1989–93); UK Drug Policy Commn, 2007–13; Adv. Cttee, Miscarriages of Justice Support Service, 2002–; Dep. Chm., Prison Reform Trust, 1981–. Trustee: Prince's Trust Volunteers, 1989–94; Mental Health Foundn, 1990–96; Pilgrim Trust, 1999–2011; Sainsbury Centre for Mental Health, 2001–03. Dir, ENO, 1978–83. Hon. Fellow, Univ. of Central Lancs, 2000. Hon. LLD De Montfort, 1997. *Address*: 44 Clifton Hill, NW8 0QG.

**RUNCORN, Rt Rev. Jacqueline Ann**; *see* Searle, Rt Rev. J. A.

**RUNDELL, Dr Katherine**; writer; Fellow, All Souls College, Oxford, since 2008; *b* Kent, 10 July 1987; *d* of Peter and Barbara Rundell. *Educ*: Speciss Coll., Harare, Zimbabwe; British Sch. of Brussels; St Catherine's Coll., Oxford (MA English Lit.); All Souls Coll., Oxford (MSt; DPhil 2015). The Girl Savage, 2011, republd (jtly) as Cartwheeling in Thunderstorms, 2016; Rooftoppers, 2013 (Waterstone's Children's Book Prize, 2014); The Wolf Wilder, 2015; (jtly) One Christmas Wish, 2017; The Explorer, 2017 (Costa Children's Book Award, 2018); (jtly) Into the Jungle: stories for Mowgli, 2018; Why You Should Read Children's Books Even Though You Are So Old and Wise, 2019; The Good Thieves, 2019; contrib. essays to London Rev. of Books, TLS, NY Rev. of Books. *Recreation*: night climbing. *Address*: All Souls College, High Street, Oxford OX1 4AL.

**RUNDELL, His Honour Richard John**; a Circuit Judge, 2001–16; *b* 29 July 1948; *s* of Norman Henry Rundell and Pamela Anne Rundell; *m* 1969, Yvonne Doreen Lipinski; two s. *Educ*: Chelmsford Tech. High Sch.; Mid Essex Tech. Coll., Chelmsford (LLB London). Called to the Bar, Gray's Inn, 1971; barrister in practice, S Eastern Circuit, 1972–2001; a Recorder, 1996–2001. *Recreations*: cricket, choral music, opera, gardening.

**RUNDLE, Hon. Anthony Maxwell**, AO 2010; Treasurer, 1993–98, and Premier, 1996–98, Tasmania; *b* 5 March 1939; *s* of M. J. Rundle; *m* Caroline Watt; two d. *Educ*: Launceston Church Grammar Sch. Journalist, Australian Associated Press, London, 1961–62; Eric White & Associates Public Relns, London, 1963–68; journalist, Tasmanian TV, 1979. MHA (L) Braddon, Tasmania, 1986–2002; Govt Whip, 1986; Speaker, House of Assembly, 1988–89; Shadow Minister for Tourism and for Transport, 1989–92; Minister: for Forests and for Mines, 1992–93; assisting Premier on Econ. Develt, 1992–93; for Public Sector Mgt, 1993–96; for Finance, 1993–95; for Employment and for Racing and Gaming, 1993–95; assisting Premier on State Develt and Resources, 1993–96; for Energy, 1995–96; Leader of the Opposition, 1998–99; Shadow Minister: for Energy, 1998–2002; for Tourism, for Nat. Parks & Public Lands, and for Planning & Inland Fisheries, 1999–2001; for Small Business, 2001; for Planning, 2001–02. Chairman: Port Devonport Authy, 1982–87; Australian Fisheries Mgt Authy, 2004–09. *Recreations*: golf, Asia. *Address*: 8a Reid Road, Wongaling Beach, Qld 4852, Australia.

**RUSBRIDGE, Christopher Anthony**; Director, Digital Curation Centre, University of Edinburgh, 2005–10; consultant in data curation, digital preservation and project evaluation, 2010–13; *b* 25 Feb. 1946; *s* of Charles Edward Rusbridge and Elma May Rusbridge; *m* 1973, Sheila Margaret Stuart; one s two d. *Educ*: Imperial Coll., Univ. of London (BSc; ARCS). Programmer and Manager, ICT/ICL, 1967–74; Asst Dir, ADP, S Australian Public Service Hosps Dept, 1974–75; Programming Services Manager, 1975–83, Acad. Computing Services Manager, 1983–92, SA Inst. of Technol., then Univ. of S Australia; Dir, IT Services, Univ. of Dundee, 1992–94; Liby IT Co-ordinator, Univ. of S Australia, 1994; Dir, Jt Inf. Systems Cttee Electronic Libraries Prog., Univ. of Warwick, 1995–2000; Dir, Inf. Services, Glasgow Univ., 2000–05. *Recreations*: photography, music, walking.

**RUSBRIDGER, Alan Charles**; Principal, Lady Margaret Hall, Oxford, since 2015; *b* 29 Dec. 1953; *s* of late G. H. Rusbridger and B. E. Rusbridger (*née* Wickham); *m* 1982, Hon. Lindsay Mackie, *d* of Baron Mackie of Benshie, CBE, DSO, DFC; two d. *Educ*: Cranleigh Sch.; Magdalene Coll., Cambridge (MA). Reporter, Cambridge Evening News, 1976–79; reporter, columnist and feature writer, The Guardian, 1979–86; TV Critic, The Observer, 1986–87; Washington Corresp., London Daily News, 1987; Editor, Weekend Guardian, 1988–89; The Guardian: Features Editor, 1989–93; Dep. Editor, 1993–95; Editor, 1995–2015; Exec. Ed., The Observer, 1997–2015. Director: Guardian Newspapers Ltd, 1994–2015; Guardian Media Gp, 1999–2015. Chair, Reuters Inst. for Study of Journalism, 2016–. Vis. Fellow, Nuffield Coll., Oxford, 2004–12; Vis. Prof., QMC, London Univ.; Hon. Prof. of Journalism, Cardiff Univ., 2013. Mem., The Scott Trust, 1997–2016. Chairman: Photographer's Gall., 2001–04; NYO of GB, 2004–12; Director: RNT, 2015–; Cttee to Protect Journalists, NY, 2015–. Co-author (with Ronan Bennett), Fields of Gold, BBC TV, 2002. Hon. Dr: Lincoln, 2009; Kingston, 2010; Oslo, 2014; Roehampton, 2016; Open, 2016; Coventry, 2017; Hon. MA Oxford, 2015. Editor of the Year: Granada TV What the Papers Say Awards, 1996 and 2001; Newspaper Focus Awards, 1996; Nat. Newspaper Editor, Newspaper Industry Awards, 1996; Freedom of the Press Award, London Press Club, 1998; Judges Award, Granada TV What the Papers Say, 2005; Goldsmith Career Award, Harvard Univ., 2012; Media Soc. Award, 2012; Burton Benjamin Award, Cttee for Protection of Journalists, 2012; Pulitzer Prize for Public Service, 2014; European Press Prize, 2014; Ortega y Gasset Award, El Pais, 2014; Liberty Human Rights Award, 2014; Right Livelihood Award, Right Livelihood Award Foundn, Sweden, 2014; Outstanding Contribn to British Media Award, British Media Awards, 2016. *Publications*: Breaking News, 2018; Play it Again, 2013; *for children*: Coldest Day at the Zoo, 2004; Wildest Day at the Zoo, 2004. *Recreations*: chamber music, piano-playing, photography, golf. *Address*: Lady Margaret Hall, Oxford OX2 6QA. *Clubs*: Frontline, Oxford and Cambridge.

**RUSE, David John**; Tri-borough Director of Libraries and Archives, Westminster City Council, Royal Borough of Kensington and Chelsea and London Borough of Hammersmith and Fulham, 2011–13; *b* 24 Aug. 1951; *s* of Ronald Frank and Betty Irene Ruse; *m* 1975, Carole Anne Lawton; two d. *Educ*: Birmingham Coll. of Commerce. MCLIP (ALA 1973). Bath Municipal Libraries, 1969–70; Asst Librarian, London Borough of Havering, 1972–77; Branch Librarian, London Borough of Barking and Dagenham, 1977–81; Asst Dir, Library Assoc., 1981–89; Head, Planning and Review, Berks CC, 1989–93; Westminster City Council: Asst Dir, Leisure and Libraries, 1993–99; Asst Dir, Lifetime, then Lifelong Learning, later Dir of Libraries and Culture, 1999–2011. Member: Bd, Lifelong Learning UK, 2005–08; Adv. Council on Libraries, 2006–10. Mem., East Garston Parish Council. *Publications*: chapters in various librarianship books; various articles in professional library press. *Recreations*: social history of railways, reading, music, countryside matters. *E*: david.ruse@btinternet.com.

**RUSEDSKI, Gregory**; professional tennis player, retired 2007; media commentator; *b* Montreal, 6 Sept. 1973; *s* of Tom and Helen Rusedski; *m* 1999, Lucy Connor; one s one d. *Educ*: Lower Canada Coll. Mem., British Davis Cup Team, 1995–2007. Winner of 15 career titles including: singles: Newport, Rhode Is., 1993, 2004, 2005; Paris Indoor Open, 1998; Compaq Grand Slam Cup, 1999; Vienna Indoor Open, 1999; Sybase Open, San Jose, 2001; Indianapolis Open, 2002; Auckland, 2002. Recorded world record serve of 149 mph, 1998. LTA Talent Ambassador, 2007–. Sports Personality of the Year, BBC, 1997. *Recreations*: golf, chess, Arsenal Football Club, cinema, James Bond. *Address*: c/o Once Upon A Time, Golden House, 30 Great Pulteney Street, W1F 9NN.

**RUSH, Ann Patricia**; consultant, Archam, since 2002; *b* 17 March 1948; *d* of Peter Deshaw and Hanni Adele Gray; *m* 1969, Charles Anthony Rush; one s one d. *Educ*: Ursuline Convent; LSE (MSc). The Observer, 1966–68; RABI, 1969–76; CR Associates, 1974–89; Dep. Dir, 1990–92, Dir, Migraine Trust, 1992–2002. Trustee, Neurological Alliance, 1999–2001. *Publications*: Migraine, 1996. *Recreations*: family, reading, sailing. *E*: chanrush@live.co.uk.

**RUSH, Geoffrey Roy**, AC 2014; actor; *b* Toowoomba, Qld, 6 July 1951; *s* of Roy Baden Rush and Merle Kiehne (*née* Bischof); *m* 1988, Jane Menelaus; one s one d. *Educ*: Everton Park High Sch., Brisbane; Univ. of Queensland (BA); Jacques Lecoq Sch. of Mime, Movement and Th., Paris. Stage début in Wrong Side of the Moon, 1971; Mem., Qld Th. Co., 1971–74; Mem., Lighthouse State Th. Co., SA, 1982–83; Dir, Magpie Th., SA, 1984–86; Associate Artist, Qld Arts Council, 2003–. *Theatre* includes: The Diary of a Madman, 1989; The Government Inspector, 1991; Uncle Vanya, The Importance of Being Earnest, 1992; Oleanna, 1993; Hamlet, 1994; The Alchemist, 1996; The Marriage of Figaro, 1998; The Small Poppies, 2000; Exit the King, 2007 (Tony Award for Best Actor in a Play, 2009); also dir numerous prodns. *Films* include: Hoodwink, 1981; Twelfth Night, 1987; Children of the Revolution, Shine, 1996 (Academy, Golden Globe, BAFTA and Aust. Film Inst. Awards for Best Actor); Oscar and Lucinda (voice), 1997; Les Misérables,

Elizabeth, Shakespeare in Love (BAFTA Award for Best Supporting Actor), 1998; Mystery Men, House on Haunted Hill, 1999; The Tailor of Panama, Lantana, Quills, 2001; Swimming Upstream, 2002; The Banger Sisters, Frida, Ned Kelly, Intolerable Cruelty, Pirates of the Caribbean: The Curse of the Black Pearl, Finding Nemo (voice), 2003; The Life and Death of Peter Sellers, 2004 (Golden Globe, Screen Actors and Emmy Awards, 2005); Munich, Pirates of the Caribbean: Dead Man's Chest, 2006; Pirates of the Caribbean: At World's End, Elizabeth: The Golden Age, 2007; The King's Speech (BAFTA Award for Best Supporting Actor), 2011; Pirates of the Caribbean: On Stranger Tides, 2011; The Book Thief, The Best Offer, 2014; The Daughter, 2016; Final Portrait, 2017; *television* includes: Menotti, 1981; Mercury, 1996; Frontier, 1997; Genius, 2017. Inaugural Pres., Australian Acad. of Cinema and Television Arts, 2011–. Australian of the Year, Nat. Australia Day Council, 2012. Centenary Medal (Australia), 2001. *Publications:* (jtly) The Popular Mechanicals (play), 1992; (adapted with J. Clarke) Aristophanes' Frogs; (trans. jtly) The Government Inspector; (trans. jtly) Exit the King, 2008. *Address:* c/o Shanahan Management, PO Box 1509, Darlinghurst, NSW 1300, Australia.

**RUSHDIE, Sir (Ahmed) Salman,** Kt 2007; FRSL; writer; *b* 19 June 1947; *s* of Anis Ahmed Rushdie and Negin Rushdie (*née* Butt); *m* 1976, Clarissa Luard (marr. diss. 1987); one *s*; *m* 1988, Marianne Wiggins (marr. diss. 1993); *m* 1997, Elizabeth West (marr. diss. 2002); one *s*; *m* 2004, Padma Lakshmi (marr. diss. 2007). *Educ:* Cathedral Sch., Bombay; Rugby Sch.; King's Coll., Cambridge (MA (Hons) History). Hon. Prof., MIT, 1993; Dist. Fellow in Lit., UEA, 1995. Pres., PEN America Center, 2004–. Hon. DLitt Bard Coll., 1995; Hon. Dr: Amherst, Tromsø, 1997; Torino, UEA, Liège, Free Univ. of Berlin, 1999; Sorbonne, Albion Coll., 2003. Arts Council Literature Bursary Award; Kurt Tucholsky Prize, Sweden, 1992; Prix Colette, Switzerland, 1993; Austrian State Prize for European Literature, 1994; EU Aristeion Prize for Literature, 1996; London Internat. Writers' Award, 2002; PEN Pinter Prize for British Writers, 2014. Freedom of Mexico City, 1999. Commandeur, Ordre des Arts et des Lettres (France), 1999. *Films for TV:* The Painter and the Pest, 1985; The Riddle of Midnight, 1988. *Publications:* Grimus, 1975; Midnight's Children, 1981 (Booker Prize for Fiction, 1981; James Tait Black Meml Book Prize; ESU Literary Award; Booker of Bookers Prize, 1993; Best of the Booker award, 2008) (adapted for stage, 2003, for film, 2012); Shame, 1983 (Prix du Meilleur Livre Etranger, 1984); The Jaguar Smile: a Nicaraguan journey, 1987; The Satanic Verses, 1988 (Whitbread Novel Award; German Author of the Year Award, 1989); Haroun and the Sea of Stories, 1990 (Writers' Guild Award); Imaginary Homelands (essays), 1991; The Wizard of Oz, 1992; East, West, 1994; The Moor's Last Sigh (Whitbread Novel Award; British Book Awards Author of the Year), 1995; (ed with Elizabeth West) The Vintage Book of Indian Writing, 1947–97, 1997; The Ground Beneath Her Feet, 1999; Fury, 2001; Step Across This Line: collected non-fiction 1992–2002, 2002; Shalimar the Clown, 2005; The Enchantress of Florence, 2008; Luka and the Fire of Life, 2010; Two Years, Eight Months and Twenty-Eight Nights, 2015; Joseph Anton, 2012; The Golden House, 2017; Quichotte, 2019; contribs to many journals. *Address:* c/o Wylie Agency (UK) Ltd, 17 Bedford Square, WC1B 3JA.

**RUSHFORTH, Philip Christopher;** Director of Music, Chester Cathedral, since 2007; *b* Chester, 31 Dec. 1972; *s* of Christopher and Gillian Rushforth; *m* 2001, Louise Walker; two *s* one *d*. *Educ:* Abbey Gate Coll., Chester; Trinity Coll., Cambridge (BA 1994; MA 1998). ARCO 1993. Asst Organist, Southwell Minster, 1994–2002; Asst Dir of Music, Chester Cath., 2002–07. *Recreations:* Olympic class ships, horology, biography, coastal walking on Anglesey. *Address:* Chester Cathedral Office, 9 Abbey Square, Chester CH1 2HU. *T:* (01244) 500974. *E:* philip.rushforth@chestercathedral.com.

**RUSHTON, Prof. Julian Gordon,** DPhil; West Riding Professor of Music, University of Leeds, 1982–2002, now Emeritus; *b* 22 May 1941; *s* of Prof. William A. E. Rushton and Marjorie Rushton; *m* 1968, Virginia S. M. Jones (marr. diss. 2000); two *s*. *Educ:* Trinity Coll., Cambridge (BA 1963; BMus 1965; MA 1967); Magdalen Coll., Oxford (DPhil 1970). Lecturer in Music: UEA, 1968–74; and Fellow, King's Coll., Cambridge, 1974–81. Chm., Editl Bd, Musica Britannica, 1993–. Pres., Royal Musical Assoc., 1994–99. Corresp. Mem., Amer. Musicol Soc., 2000; Dir-at-large, Internat. Musicol Soc., 2007–17. MAE 2010. Berlioz Soc. Medal, 2015. *Publications:* Berlioz: Huit Scènes de Faust, 1970; La Damnation de Faust, vol. 1, 1979, vol. 2, 1986; W. A. Mozart: Don Giovanni, 1981, 2nd edn 1990; The Musical Language of Berlioz, 1983; Classical Music: a concise history, 1986; Berlioz: Choral Music I, 1991; W. A. Mozart: Idomeneo, 1993; Berlioz: Roméo et Juliette, 1994; Elgar: Enigma Variations, 1999; The Music of Berlioz, 2001; Potter: Symphony in G minor, 2001; (ed with D. M. Grimley) The Cambridge Companion to Elgar, 2004; Mozart: an extraordinary life, 2005; Mozart (Master Musicians series), 2006; (ed with R. Cowgill) Europe, Empire, and Spectacle in Nineteenth-Century British Music, 2006; (ed with J. P. E. Harper-Scott) Elgar Studies, 2007; (ed) Let Beauty Awake: Elgar, Vaughan Williams, and literature, 2010; Elgar Complete Edition: music for string orchestra, 2011; (ed) Cambridge Berlioz Encyclopedia, 2017; Elgar Complete Edition: songs with orchestra, 2012; Vaughan Williams: Serenade (1898) for small orchestra, 2012; Vaughan Williams: Bucolic Suite, 2012; Vaughan Williams, Flos Campi, rev. edn 2014; Vaughan Williams, Job: a masque for dancing, rev. edn 2018; contrib. to Music & Letters, Music Analysis, Cambridge Opera Jl, Musical Times, Elgar Soc. Jl, Early Music, Jl Amer. Musicological Soc. *Recreations:* literature and other reading, walking, gardening. *Address:* School of Music, University of Leeds, Leeds LS2 9JT. *E:* j.g.rushton@leeds.ac.uk; 362 Leymoor Road, Golcar, Huddersfield HD7 4QF.

**RUSHTON, Prof. Neil,** MD; FRCS; FIMMM; Professor of Orthopaedics, University of Cambridge, 2003–10, now Emeritus; Fellow of Magdalene College, Cambridge, 1984–2010, now Emeritus; *b* 16 Dec. 1945; *s* of John Allen Rushton and Iris Rushton; *m* 1971, Sheila Margaret Johnson; two *s* one *d*. *Educ:* Middlesex Hosp., London (MB BS 1970); Magdalene Coll., Cambridge (MA 1979; MD 1984). LRCP 1970; MRCS 1970, FRCS 1975; FIMMM 2008. Pre-Registration Sen. House Officer, Orsett Hosp., 1971–75; Registrar in Trauma and Orthopaedics, Royal Northern, Royal Free and Heatherwood Hosps, 1975–77; University of Cambridge: Sen. Registrar Orthopaedics, 1977–79; Clinical Lectr in Surgery, Cambridge and Black Notley, 1979–83; Lectr in Surgery, 1983–2000; Sen. Lectr, 2000–01, Reader, 2001–03, in Orthopaedics; Hon. Consultant in Orthopaedics, Addenbrooke's Hosp., 1983–2010; Hunterian Prof., RCSE, 1990–99. Dep. Ed. (Res.), Jl of Bone and Joint Surgery, 1996–2006; Editor: British Orthopaedic News, 2002–06; Magdalene Mag., 2014–18. Watson Jones Medal, RCSE, 2002; Chapman Medal, IMMM, 2012. *Publications:* Surgical Exposures of the Limbs, 1984; Classification of Limb Fractures in Adults, 2002; chapters in 8 books; articles on biocompatibility of materials used in orthopaedics, tissue engrg bone and cartilage, fractures of the proximal femur and the bone response to arthroplasty, in Jl of Bone and Joint Surgery, Acta Orthopaedica Scandinavica, Biomaterials and Jl of Materials Sci.: Materials in Medicine. *Recreations:* sailing, ski-ing, scuba diving, music, cycling, wine. *Address:* 37 Bentley Road, Cambridge CB2 8AW. *T:* (01223) 353624. *E:* nr10000@cam.ac.uk. *Clubs:* Athenæum; Ski of GB.

**RUSHTON, Nicola Jane;** QC 2018; *b* London, 27 Feb. 1970; *d* of David and Anne Rushton; *m* 2004, Jasper Warwick; two *d*. *Educ:* Tonbridge Grammar Sch. for Girls; St John's Coll., Cambridge (BA Hons Law 1991); Dalhousie Univ. (LLM 1992; BVC 1993). Called to the Bar, Gray's Inn, 1993; in practice as barrister, specialising in professional negligence and commercial; a Fee-paid Judge, First-tier Tribunal (Property Chamber), 2019–. *Recreation:* family. *Address:* Hailsham Chambers, 4 Paper Buildings, Temple, EC4Y 7EX. *T:* (020) 7643 5000. *E:* nicola.rushtonqc@hailshamchambers.com.

**RUSHTON, Ven. Samantha Jayne;** Archdeacon of Cleveland, since 2015; *b* 1965; *d* Peter Rushton; two *s*. *Educ:* St Hilda's Coll., Oxford (BA 1987); Trinity Coll., Bristol (BA 2005). Mgt Consultant, Lloyds TSB; ordained deacon, 2005, priest, 2006; Curate: St Michael, Highworth, 2005–08; St Leonard, Broad Blunsdon, 2005–08; St Paul, Chippenham with Hardenhuish and Langley Burrell, 2008–15; St Michael, Kington St Michael, 2008–15; Advr for Licensed Ministry, 2008–15, Warden of Readers, 2011–15, Diocese of Bristol; Area Dean, Chippenham, 2013–15. *Address:* 48 Langbaurgh Road, Hutton Rudby, Yarm TS15 0HL.

**RUSHWORTH, Dr (Frank) Derek;** Headmaster, Holland Park School, London, 1971–85; *b* 15 Sept. 1920; *s* of late Frank and Elizabeth Rushworth, Huddersfield; *m* 1941, Hamidah Begum, *d* of late Justice S. Akhlaque Hussain, Lahore, and Edith (*née* Bayliss), Oxford; two *d* (and one *d* decd). *Educ:* Huddersfield Coll.; St Edmund Hall, Oxford (Schol.: BA 1942, MA 1946); Doctorate of Univ. of Paris (Lettres), 1947. Served 6th Rajputana Rifles, Indian Army, 1942–45 (Major); began teaching, 1947; Head of Modern Languages: Tottenham Grammar Sch., 1953; Holland Park Sch., 1958; Head of Shoreditch Sch., London, 1965. Chairman: Associated Examining Board, French Committee, 1964–74; Schools Council, 16+ Examination Feasibility Study (French), 1971–75; Pres., London Head Teachers' Assoc., 1985. Governor, Holland Park Sch., 1990–95. *Publications:* Our French Neighbours, 1963, 2nd edn 1966; French text-books and language-laboratory books; articles in French Studies, Modern Languages, also educnl jls. *Recreation:* photography. *Address:* 25c Lambolle Road, NW3 4HS. *T:* (020) 7794 3691.

**RUSKELL, Mark Christopher;** Member (Green) Scotland Mid and Fife, Scottish Parliament, 2003–07 and since 2016; *b* 14 May 1972; *s* of David and Brenda Ruskell; *m* 1999, Melinda McEwen; two *s*. *Educ:* Edinburgh Acad.; Stevenson Coll., Edinburgh; Univ. of Stirling (BSc Hons Envmtl Sci. with Biol.); Scottish Agricl Coll., Univ. of Aberdeen (MSc Sustainable Agric.). Develt Worker, Falkirk Voluntary Action Resource Centre, 1997–2000; Regeneration Officer, Midlothian Council, 2000–02; Project Officer, Soil Assoc., 2002–03; Communications Manager, Scottish Renewables, 2008–10. Dir, Ruskell Communications, 2011–17. Mem. (Green) Stirling Council, 2012–17. Contested (Green) Stirling, 2001, 2010, 2015. *Address:* Scottish Parliament, Edinburgh EH99 1SP.

**RUSSELL;** see Hamilton-Russell, family name of Viscount Boyne.

**RUSSELL,** family name of **Duke of Bedford**, **Earl Russell**, and **Barons Ampthill**, **de Clifford** and **Russell of Liverpool**.

**RUSSELL, 7th Earl** *cr* 1861; **John Francis Russell;** Viscount Amberley 1861; *b* 19 Nov. 1971; *yr s* of 5th Earl Russell, FBA and Elizabeth Franklyn Russell (*née* Sanders); *S* brother, 2014; *m* 2002, Jane Elizabeth Swann; one *d*. *Heir:* none.

**RUSSELL OF LIVERPOOL, 3rd Baron** *cr* 1919; **Simon Gordon Jared Russell;** *b* 30 Aug. 1952; *s* of Captain Hon. Langley Gordon Haslingden Russell, MC (*d* 1975) (*o s* of 2nd Baron), and of Kiloran Margaret, *d* of late Hon. Sir Arthur Jared Palmer Howard, KBE, CVO; *S* grandfather, 1981; *m* 1984, Dr Gilda Albano, *y d* of late Signor F. Albano and of Signora Maria Caputo-Albano; two *s* one *d*. *Educ:* Charterhouse; Trinity Coll., Cambridge; INSEAD, Fontainebleau, France. Elected Mem., H of L, 2014. *Heir: s* Hon. Edward Charles Stanley Russell, *b* 2 Sept. 1985.

**RUSSELL, Sir (Alastair) Muir,** KCB 2001; FRSE; FInstP; *b* 9 Jan. 1949; *s* of Thomas Russell and Anne Muir; *m* 1983, Eileen Alison Mackay, *qv*. *Educ:* High Sch. of Glasgow; Univ. of Glasgow (BSc Nat. Phil.). FInstP 2003. Joined Scottish Office, 1970; seconded as Sec. to Scottish Development Agency, 1975–76; Asst Sec., 1981; Principal Private Sec. to Sec. of State for Scotland, 1981–83; Under Sec., 1990; seconded to Cabinet Office, 1990–92; Under Sec. (Housing), Scottish Office Envmt Dept, 1992–95; Dep. Sec., 1995; Sec. and Hd of Dept, Scottish Office Agric., Envmt and Fisheries Dept, 1995–98; Permanent Under-Sec. of State, Scottish Office, 1998–99; Permanent Sec., Scottish Exec., 1999–2003; Principal and Vice-Chancellor, Univ. of Glasgow, 2003–09. Chm., Judicial Appts Bd for Scotland, 2008–16. Non-exec. Director: Stagecoach Hldgs, 1992–95; National House-Building Council, 2012– (Chairman: Scottish Cttee, 2012–; Audit Cttee, 2014–17; Remuneration Cttee, 2018–). Dir, UCAS, 2005–09; Member, Council: ACU, 2006–10; RSE, 2012–16; Convener, Universities Scotland, 2006–08; Mem. Bd, Univs Superannuation Scheme, 2007–09. Council Mem., Edinburgh Festival Soc., 2004–09; Chm., Dunedin Consort, 2009–. Chm., Trustees, Royal Botanic Garden, Edinburgh, 2011–19. Member: Bd, Moredun Res. Inst., 2009–18; Adv. Bd, Leverhulme Res. Centre for Forensic Sci., Dundee, 2016–. Gov., Glasgow Sch. of Art, 2009–18 (Vice Chair, 2011–18). Freeman, City of London, 2006. DL Glasgow, 2004–09. FRSE 2000. Hon. FRCPSGlas 2005. Hon. LLD Strathclyde, 2000; DUniv Glasgow, 2001; Dhc Edinburgh, 2009. *Recreations:* music, food, wine. *E:* muir.russell@btinternet.com. *Club:* New (Edinburgh).

**RUSSELL, Alexander;** Chief Executive Officer, The London Clinic, since 2018 (Interim Chief Executive Officer, 2017–18); *b* Salisbury, 28 Dec. 1969; *s* of Michael Russell and Hon. Mrs M. Russell; *m* 1997, Rose Fairbairn; four *s* one *d*. *Educ:* Eton Coll.; Edinburgh Univ. (MA Hons). Dir, Vodafone UK, 2011–17. *Recreations:* cycling, outdoor pursuits, Norwich City Football Club. *Address:* Knighton Farm House, Ashbury, Swindon SN6 8NT.

**RUSSELL, Andrew Victor Manson;** Chief Executive (formerly Executive Director), Association for Spina Bifida and Hydrocephalus, 1991–2009; *b* 7 Dec. 1949; *s* of Manson McCausland Russell and Margaret Ivy Russell; *m* 1974, Susan Elizabeth Aykroyd; one *s* one *d*. *Educ:* Dartington Hall; Fitzwilliam Coll., Cambridge Univ. (MA). NSMHC, 1974–85; General Manager, Eastern Div., Royal MENCAP Soc., 1985–91. Member: Ethics and Governance Council, UK Biobank, 2008–; Bd, UK Clinical Res. Collaboration, 2009–13. *Recreations:* sailing, music.

**RUSSELL, Rt Rev. Anthony John,** DPhil; FRAgS; Bishop of Ely, 2000–10; an Honorary Assistant Bishop, Diocese of Oxford, since 2010; *b* 25 Jan. 1943; *s* of Michael John William and Beryl Margaret Russell; *m* 1967, Sheila Alexandra, *d* of Alexander Scott and Elizabeth Carlisle Ronald; two *s* two *d*. *Educ:* Uppingham Sch.; Univ. of Durham (BA); Trinity Coll., Oxford (DPhil; Hon. Fellow 2011); Cuddesdon Coll., Oxford. Deacon 1970, Priest 1971; Curate, Hilborough Group of Parishes, 1970–73; Rector, Preston on Stour, Atherstone on Stour and Whitchurch, 1973–88; Chaplain, Arthur Rank Centre (Nat. Agricl Centre), 1973–82, Director, 1983–88; Canon Theologian, Coventry Cathedral, 1977–88; Chaplain to the Queen, 1983–88; Area Bp of Dorchester, 1988–2000. Entered H of L, 2007. Hulsean Preacher, Cambridge Univ., 2004; Univ. Select Preacher, Oxford Univ., 2011. Mem.,

Gen. Synod, 1980–88. Royal Agricultural Society: Chaplain, 1982–91; Vice-Pres., 1991–2002; Vice-Patron, 2002; Pres., 2004–05; Hon. Trustee, 2018–; Hon. Chaplain, RABI, 1983–2002. ARAgS 2003, FRAgS 2008. Comr, Rural Develt Commn, 1991–99. Trustee, Rural Housing Trust, 1983–2006. President: Woodard Corp., 2003–17; E of England Agricultural Soc., 2007–08. Gov., Radley Coll., 2003–14. Visitor, Jesus Coll., St John's Coll., and Peterhouse, Cambridge, 2000–10. Hon. Fellow: St Edmund's Coll., Cambridge, 2000; Wolfson Coll., Cambridge, 2001; St Chad's Coll., Durham, 2007. *Publications:* Groups and Teams in the Countryside (ed), 1975; The Village in Myth and Reality, 1980; The Clerical Profession, 1980; The Country Parish, 1986; The Country Parson, 1993.

**RUSSELL, His Honour Anthony Patrick;** QC 1999; a Circuit Judge, 2004–15; a Senior Circuit Judge and Resident Judge, Lancashire Crown Courts, 2006–15; *b* 11 April 1951; *s* of late Dr Michael Hibberd Russell and Pamela Russell (*née* Eyre). *Educ:* King's Sch., Chester; Pembroke Coll., Oxford (MA). Called to the Bar, Middle Temple, 1974, Bencher, 2008; in practice at the Bar, Northern Circuit, 1974–2004; Junior, Northern Circuit, 1977; Standing Counsel to Inland Revenue, 1994–96; a Recorder, 1993–96, 2001–04; Hon. Recorder of Preston, 2006–15; Recorder, Preston Guild, 2012. Mem., Gen. Council of the Bar, 1987–94. Hon. Fellow, Univ. of Central Lancs, 2013. Hon. FGCM 2001 (Vice-Pres., 2005–). Hon. Burgess, City of Preston, 2012. *Publications:* I Think I Know Who I Am, 2016. *Recreations:* music, especially singing, the countryside, family history. *Address:* c/o Law Courts, Openshaw Place, Ringway, Preston PR1 2LL. *T:* (01772) 844700. *Club:* Oxford and Cambridge.

**RUSSELL, Ven. Brian Kenneth,** PhD; Senior Chaplain, St Edmund's, Oslo, 2014–17 (with oversight of the Anglican Church in Norway); Archdeacon of Aston, 2005–14, now Archdeacon Emeritus; *b* 1 Aug. 1950; *s* of William George Russell and Joan Russell; *m* 1976, Pamela Jean Gillard; one *s* one *d*. *Educ:* Bristol Grammar Sch.; Trinity Hall, Cambridge (BA 1973, MA 1976); Cuddesdon Coll., Oxford; Birmingham Univ. (MA 1977; PhD 1983). Ordained deacon, 1976, priest, 1977; Curate, St Matthew, Redhill, 1976–79; Priest-in-charge, St John, Kirk Merrington, and Dir of Studies, NE Ordination Course, 1979–83; Dir of Studies and Lectr in Christian Doctrine, Lincoln Theol Coll., 1983–86; Sec. to Cttee for Theol Educn, and Selection Sec., ACCM, subseq. ABM, 1986–93; Bishop's Dir for Ministries, Dio. Birmingham, 1993–2005. Hon. Canon, Birmingham Cathedral, 1999–. Mem., Bishops' Inspections Wkg Pty, 2003–08. Gov., Queen's Foundn for Theol Educn, Birmingham, 1994–2013. *Publications:* (ed jtly) Leaders for the 21st Century, 1993; (ed) Formation in a Changing Church, 1999; articles on theol educn in Theology and British Jl of Theol Educn, and reviews in Theology. *Recreations:* theatre, literature, National Hunt racing, links with Nordic and Baltic Churches. *Address:* 1 Plover Close, Stratford upon Avon, Warks CV37 9EN. *T:* (01789) 299923. *E:* B-Russell5@sky.com.

**RUSSELL, Sir Charles (Dominic),** 4th Bt *cr* 1916, of Littleworth Corner, Burnham, co. Buckingham; antiquarian bookseller, trading as Russell Rare Books, since 1978; *b* 28 May 1956; *o s* of Sir Charles Ian Russell, 3rd Bt and Rosemary Lavender Russell (*née* Prestige) (*d* 1996); *S* father, 1997; *m* 1st, 1986, Sarah Chandor (marr. diss. 1995); one *s*; 2nd, 2005, Wandee Ruanrakrao. *Educ:* Worth Sch. *Heir: s* Charles William Russell, *b* 8 Sept. 1988. *Club:* Chelsea Arts.

**RUSSELL, Christine Margaret;** *b* 25 March 1945; *d* of John Alfred William Carr and Phyllis Carr; *m* 1971, Dr James Russell (marr. diss. 1991); one *s* one *d*. *Educ:* Spalding High Sch.; London Sch. of Librarianship (ALA). PA to Brian Simpson, MEP, 1992–94. Mem. (Lab) Chester CC, 1980–97 (Chair, Develt). Co-ordinator, Mind Advocacy Scheme, 1995–97. MP (Lab) City of Chester, 1997–2010; contested (Lab) same seat, 2010. Chair, Bd, West Cheshire Coll., 2013–17; Mem. Bd, Cheshire Coll. - South and West, 2017–19. Chair, Chester Civic Trust, 2015–; Trustee, Chester Municipal Charities, 2012–. JP 1980. DLit Chester, 2011. *Recreations:* film, visual arts, walking, football. *E:* russellcm@hotmail.co.uk.

**RUSSELL, Christopher;** *see* Russell, R. C. G.

**RUSSELL, Clare Nancy,** CVO 2017; Lord-Lieutenant for Banffshire, 2002–19 (Vice Lord-Lieutenant, 1998–2002); estate owner and rural land manager, Ballindalloch, since 1979; *b* 4 Aug. 1944; *d* of Sir Ewan Macpherson-Grant, 6th Bt, and Lady Macpherson-Grant; *m* 1967, Oliver Henry Russell; two *s* one *d*. *Educ:* in Scotland. Professional florist, Head Decorator, Constance Spry, 1962–65; Sec. to Fourth Clerk at the Table, H of C, 1965–67; Dir, Craigo Farms Ltd, 1970–; living at Ballindalloch, 1978–; opened Ballindalloch Castle to public, 1993. Mem., Moray Health Council, 1986–91. Mem. Council, NT for Scotland, 1985–88; Dist Organiser, Moray and Banff, 1980–93; Mem. Exec. Cttee, 1987–93; Scotland's Garden Scheme. Chm., Queen Mary's Clothing Guild, 1990–93 (started Queen Mary's Clothing Guild in Scotland, 1986). Mem. Bd, Children's Hospice Assoc., Scotland, 1995–2002. Sunday Sch. teacher, Inveraven Ch, 1982–94. DL Banffshire, 1991–98. JP Aberdeenshire, 2003–07. Hon. MUniv Aberdeen, 2010. *Publications:* Favourite Recipes, Dried Flowers and Pot Pourri from Ballindalloch Castle, 1993; Favourite Puddings from Ballindalloch Castle, 1995; Favourite First Courses from Ballindalloch Castle, 1996; Favourite Recipes from Ballindalloch Castle, 1998; I Love Food, 2004; I Love Banffshire, 2009; I Love Food 2, 2012. *Recreations:* dog-handling, gardening, flower arranging, piano, tapestry, knitting, cooking, historic houses, antiques. *Address:* Pitchroy Lodge, Blacksboat, Ballindalloch, Banffshire AB37 9BQ. *Club:* Sloane.

**RUSSELL, Dan Chapman;** Sheriff of South Strathclyde, Dumfries and Galloway at Hamilton, 1992–2004; *b* 25 Dec. 1939; *s* of William Morris Russell and Isabella Ritchie Stein Scott; *m* 1969, Janet McNeil; three *d*. *Educ:* Airdrie Acad.; Glasgow Univ. (MA 1960; LLB 1963). Qualified as Solicitor, 1963; in private practice, 1963–92; Partner, Bell, Russell & Co., Solicitors, Airdrie, 1965–92; Temp. Sheriff, 1976–78 and 1985–92. Reporter, Airdrie Children's Panel, 1972–75. Mem. Council, Law Soc. of Scotland, 1975–84; Dean, Airdrie Soc. of Solicitors, 1986–88. *Recreations:* golf, bridge, walking.

**RUSSELL, David Norman;** Chief Executive Officer, Education and Training Foundation, since 2014; *b* Aberdeen, 6 May 1973; *s* of Norman George Fisher Russell and Margaret Jane Russell (*née* Dawson); *m* 2003, Zoe Elisabeth James; three *s*. *Educ:* Crieff Primary Sch.; Crieff High Sch.; St Andrews Univ. (MA Hons Ancient Hist. and Philosophy); Moray Hse Inst. of Educn (PGCE (Sec.)). Department for Children, Schools and Families, later Department for Education: Deputy Director: Adult Skills, 2004–08; Academies, 2008–09; Director: Apprenticeships, 2009–10; Curriculum and Behaviour Policy, 2010–11; Closing the Gap, 2012–14. *Recreations:* music, running and learning. *Address:* Education and Training Foundation, 157–197 Buckingham Palace Road, SW1W 9SP. *E:* david.russell@etfoundation.co.uk.

**RUSSELL, Prof. Donald Andrew Frank Moore,** FBA 1971; Fellow, St John's College, Oxford, 1948–88, now Emeritus; Professor of Classical Literature, Oxford, 1985–88; *b* 13 Oct. 1920; *s* of Samuel Charles Russell (schoolmaster) and Laura Moore; *m* 1967, Joycelyne Gledhill Dickinson (*d* 1993). *Educ:* King's College Sch., Wimbledon; Balliol Coll., Oxford (MA 1946); DLitt Oxon 1985. Served War: Army (R Signals and Intelligence Corps), 1941–45. Craven Scholar, 1946; Lectr, Christ Church, Oxford, 1947; St John's College, Oxford: Tutor, 1948–88; Dean, 1957–64; Tutor for Admissions, 1968–72; Reader in Class. Lit., Oxford Univ., 1978–85. Paddison Vis. Prof., Univ. of N Carolina at Chapel Hill, 1985; Vis. Prof. of Classics, Stanford Univ., 1989, 1991. Co-editor, Classical Quarterly, 1965–70. *Publications:* Commentary on Longinus, On the Sublime, 1964; Ancient Literary Criticism (with M. Winterbottom), 1972; Plutarch, 1972; (with N. G. Wilson) Menander Rhetor, 1981; Criticism in Antiquity, 1981; Greek Declamation, 1984; (ed) Antonine Literature, 1990; Commentary on Dio Chrysostom, Orations, 7, 12, 36, 1992; (trans.) Plutarch: selected essays and dialogues, 1993; (trans.) Libanius, Imaginary Speeches, 1996; (trans. and ed) Quintilian, 2001; (ed with D. Konstan) Heraclitus: Homeric problems, 2005; (trans. and ed with H. G. Nesselrath and others) Plutarch: on the daimonion of Socrates, 2010; (ed with R. Hunter) Plutarch: how to study poetry, 2011; (trans. and ed with H. G. Nesselrath and others) Synesius: de insomniis, 2014; articles and reviews in classical periodicals. *Address:* 36 Belsyre Court, Oxford OX2 6HU. *T:* (01865) 556135.

**RUSSELL, Eileen Alison, (Lady Russell);** *see* Mackay, E. A.

**RUSSELL, Sir George,** Kt 1992; CBE 1985; Deputy Chairman: Granada plc, 2002–04; ITV plc, 2004–09; *b* 25 Oct. 1935; *s* of William H. Russell and Frances A. Russell; *m* 1959, Dorothy Brown; three *d*. *Educ:* Gateshead Grammar Sch.; Durham Univ. (BA Hons). ICI, 1958–67 (graduate trainee, Commercial Res. Officer, Sales Rep., and Product Sales Man.); Vice President and General Manager: Welland Chemical Co. of Canada Ltd, 1968; St Clair Chemical Co. Ltd, 1968; Man. Dir, Alcan UK Ltd, 1976; Asst Man. Dir, 1977–81, Man. Dir, 1981–82, Alcan Aluminium (UK) Ltd; Man. Dir and Chief Exec., British Alcan Aluminium, 1982–86; Chief Exec., 1986–92, Chm., 1989–93, non-exec. Chm., 1993–97, Marley plc, Dir, 1992–2001, Chm., 1993–2001, 3i Gp plc; Chm., Camelot Gp plc, 1995–2002. Chairman: Luxfer Holdings Ltd, 1976–78; Alcan UK Ltd, 1978–82; Northern Develt Co., 1994–99; Director: Alcan Aluminiumwerke GmbH, Frankfurt, 1977–82; Northern Rock plc (formerly Bldg Soc.), 1985–2006; Alcan Aluminium Ltd, 1987–2000; Taylor Woodrow, 1992–2004; British Alcan plc, 1997–2001. Chairman: ITN, 1987–88; IBA, 1988–92 (Mem., 1979–86); ITC, 1991–96; Cable Authy, 1989–90; Dep. Chm., Channel Four TV, 1987–88. Visiting Professor, Univ. of Newcastle upon Tyne, 1978. Chm., IPPR North Commn on Public Sector Reform in NE, 2007–09; Member: Board, Northern Sinfonia Orchestra, 1977–80; Northern Industrial Development Board, 1977–80; Washington Development Corporation, 1978–80; Board, Civil Service Pay Research Unit, 1980–81; Megaw Inquiry into Civil Service Pay, 1981; Widdicombe Cttee of Inquiry into Conduct of Local Authority Business, 1985. Dir, 2002–08, Chm., 2011–15, Wildfowl and Wetlands Trust. Trustee, Beamish Develt Trust, 1985–90. Dir, Digital Theatre, 2011–. Hon. DEng Newcastle upon Tyne, 1985; Hon. DBA Northumbria, 1992; Hon. LLD: Sunderland, 1995; Durham, 1997. *Recreations:* tennis, bird watching. *Club:* Garrick.

**RUSSELL, George Thomas,** FIA; Chief Actuary (Scotland and Northern Ireland), Government Actuary's Department, since 2015; *b* Glasgow, 11 Feb. 1962; *s* of John and Anne Russell; *m* 1988, Pamela McLachlan; one *s*. *Educ:* Hermitage Acad., Helensburgh; Strathallan Sch., Perthshire; Churchill Coll., Cambridge (BA 1983; MA 1987). FIA 1990; ASA 2002. Actuarial Trainee, Coopers & Lybrand, 1983–84; Actuarial Trainee, then Consulting Actuary, Bacon & Woodrow, 1984–94; Government Actuary's Department: Actuary, 1994–99, Chief Actuary, 1999–2009, Pensions Policy, Demography and Stats Div.; Mem., Mgt Bd, 2008–15; Dep. Govt Actuary (Dir of Actuarial Ops), 2009–15. Hon. Treas., Inst. of Actuaries, 2005–08. *Recreations:* France, opera, cycling. *Address:* Government Actuary's Department, Elgin House, 20 Haymarket Yards, Edinburgh EH12 5WN. *T:* 07814 522498. *E:* george.russell@gad.gov.uk. *Clubs:* Caledonian, Actuaries'; Drumsheugh Baths (Edinburgh).

**RUSSELL, Gerald William,** FCA; President, Institute of Chartered Accountants in England and Wales, 2010–11 (Deputy President, 2009–10); *b* Twickenham, 21 May 1950; *s* of late Cyril and Elizabeth Russell; *m* 1976, Tessa (*d* 2009); one *s* four *d*. *Educ:* Ampleforth Coll. FCA 1973. With Ernst & Whinney, later Ernst & Young, 1969–2008: Partner, 1983–88; Man. Partner, S Reg., 1988–98; Man. Partner, London, 1998–2006; retd 2008. Trustee, Nat. Maritime Mus., 2014–. Chm. Govs, Notre Dame Sch., Cobham, 2014–. *Recreations:* sailing, classic cars. *Address:* The White House, Castle Road, Weybridge, Surrey KT13 9QN. *T:* (01932) 844498. *E:* gwrussell1@gmail.com. *Club:* Aldeburgh Yacht.

**RUSSELL, Gillian Erinna;** Director for Safer Communities, Scottish Government, since 2015; *b* Edinburgh, 20 Oct. 1967; *d* of John Albert Russell and Linda Margaret Russell; *m* Scott Webster; two *s*. *Educ:* Greenhall High Sch., Midlothian; Univ. of Edinburgh (MA Hons; LLB (Dist.); DipLP). Scottish Government: roles progressing to Sen. Lawyer, 1992–2010; Deputy Director: Safer Communities Div., 2010–13; Police Div., 2013–15. *Recreations:* art, travel, gardening, live music. *Address:* 7 Wilfrid Terrace, Edinburgh EH8 7DH. *T:* (0131) 661 3849. *E:* gillian.russell@gov.scot.

**RUSSELL, Graham;** *see* Russell, R. G. G.

**RUSSELL, Graham R.;** *see* Ross Russell.

**RUSSELL, Ven. (Harold) Ian (Lyle);** Archdeacon of Coventry, 1989–2000; Chaplain to the Queen, 1997–2004; *b* 17 Oct. 1934; *s* of Percy Harold and Emma Rebecca Russell; *m* 1961, Barbara Lillian Dixon; two *s* one *d*. *Educ:* Epsom College; London Coll. of Divinity (BD, ALCD). Shell Petroleum Co., 1951–53; RAF, Jan. 1953; RAF Regt, Nov. 1953–1956; London Coll. of Divinity, 1956–60; ordained, 1960; Curate of Iver, Bucks, 1960–63; Curate-in-charge of St Luke's, Lodge Moor, Parish of Fulwood, Sheffield, 1963–67; Vicar: St John's, Chapeltown, Sheffield, 1967–75; St Jude's, Mapperley, Nottingham, 1975–89. *Recreations:* walking, photography, sport, gardening. *Address:* Flat 28, Manormead, Tilford Road, Hindhead, Surrey GU26 6RA. *T:* (01428) 601528.

**RUSSELL, Prof. Ian John,** FRS 1989; FRSB; Professor of Neurobiology, University of Brighton, since 2011; *b* 19 June 1943; *s* of Philip William George Russell and Joan Lillian Russell; *m* 1968, Janice Marion Russell (marr. diss. 2006); one *s* one *d*. *Educ:* Chatham Technical Sch.; Queen Mary Coll., London (BSc Zoology); Univ. of British Columbia (NATO Student; MSc Zool.); Univ. of Cambridge (SRC Student; Trinity Hall Res. Student; PhD Zool.). FRSB (FSB 2012). Res. Fellowship, Magdalene Coll., Cambridge, 1969–71; SRC Res. Fellowship, Cambridge, 1969–71; Royal Soc. Exchange Fellowship, King Gustav V Res. Inst., Stockholm, 1970–71; University of Sussex: Lectr in Neurobiology, 1971–79; Reader in Neurobiology, 1979–80 and 1982–87; Prof. of Neurobiol., 1987–2011. MRC Sen. Res. Fellow, 1980–82, 1995–98. Award of Merit, Assoc. for Res. in Otolaryngology, 2010. *Publications:* on the neurobiology of hearing, in learned jls. *Recreations:* hockey, windsurfing, reading, music, gardening, walking, sailing. *Address:* Little Ivy Cottage, Waldron, Heathfield, East Sussex TN21 0QX. *T:* (01435) 813382.

**RUSSELL, Ian Simon MacGregor,** CBE 2007; CA; Chairman: Johnston Press, 2009–16 (non-executive Director, 2007–09); HICL Infrastructure Company Ltd, since 2016; *b* 16 Jan. 1953; *s* of James MacGregor Russell and Christine Russell (*née* Clark); *m* 1975, Fiona Brown; one *s* one *d*. *Educ:* George Heriot's Sch., Edinburgh; Univ. of Edinburgh (BCom). Mem., ICAS, 1977. Auditor, Thomson McLintock, 1974–78; accountant, Mars Ltd,

1978–81; Controller, Pentos plc, 1981–83; Finance Dir, HSBC, 1983–90; Financial Controller, Tomkins plc, 1990–94; Finance Dir, 1994–99, Dep. Chief Exec., 1999–2001, Chief Exec., 2001–06, Scottish Power plc. Chm., Remploy Ltd, 2007–15. Chm., Seeing is Believing Network, BITC, 2005–08. Chm., Russell Commn, 2004–05.

**RUSSELL, Jack;** *see* Russell, R. C.

**RUSSELL, Jenni Cecily;** newspaper columnist, since 2002; *b* Johannesburg, 16 July 1960; *d* of Martin Russell and Dr Margo Russell (*née* Phillips); *m* 1988, Stephen Lambert, *qv*; one *s* one *d*. *Educ:* City of Norwich Sch.; Maru-a-Pula Sch., Botswana; Wymondham Coll., Norfolk; St Catharine's Coll., Cambridge (BA Hons Hist. 1982). News trainee, 1985–87; Producer, World Service, 1987–88, BBC; Producer, 1989–92, Sen. Producer, 1992–94, Channel 4 News; Dep. Ed., Current Affairs, BBC Radio, 1994–97; Ed., The World Tonight, BBC Radio 4, 1997–2001; columnist on politics and social policy: Guardian, 2002–; Sunday Times, 2009–; Evening Standard, 2011–. Mem., Adv. Council, Demos, 2009–. Fellow, Young Foundn, 2006–. FRSA 2011. Orwell Prize for political journalism, 2011. *Recreations:* piano, ski-ing, entertaining friends. *E:* jennirussell01@gmail.com. *T:* 07711 032155.

**RUSSELL, Jeremy Jonathan;** QC 1994; *b* 18 Dec. 1950; *s* of Sidney Thomas Russell and Maud Eugenie Russell; *m* 1987, Gillian Elizabeth Giles; one *s* one *d*. *Educ:* Watford Boys' GS; City of London Poly. (BA); LSE (LLM). Lectr in Law, City of London Poly., 1973–80; called to the Bar, Middle Temple, 1975; in practice as barrister, 1977–2019. Lloyd's Salvage Arbitrator, 2000–05, 2009–16; Lloyd's Salvage Appeal Arbitrator, 2016–. CEDR accredited mediator, 2001; in practice as arbitrator and mediator, 2015–. *Recreations:* reading, gliding, classic cars. *Address:* Quadrant Chambers, Quadrant House, 10 Fleet Street, EC4Y 1AU.

**RUSSELL, Jonathan Michael,** CB 2017; Chief People Officer, Valuation Office Agency, since 2018; *b* Luton, 12 March 1963; *s* of David and Sue Russell; *m* 2003, Dawn Spence; two *s* one *d*. *Educ:* Harper Adams Univ. (HND 1985). Agricl sector, 1985; Civil Servant, 1985–: Health and Safety Executive: HM Inspector of Health and Safety, 1988–98; Principal Inspector, 1998–2005 (Hd, Business Engagement, 2002–05); Superintending Inspector and Hd of Enforcement, 2005–07; Dir, Health, Safety and Wellbeing, Dep. Dir, Employee Policy and Dir, HR Specialist Service, 2007–13, HR Dir, 2013–18, DWP. Mem. Bd, Civil Service Insce Soc., 2013–. Trustee, Charity for Civil Servants, 2014–. *Recreations:* literature, motor cycling, Rugby, outdoor pursuits, bovine photography. *Address:* Valuation Office Agency, Wingate House, 93–107 Shaftesbury Avenue, W1D 5BU. *T:* 03000 500031. *E:* jonathan.russell@voa.gsi.gov.uk.

**RUSSELL, Justin Nicholas;** HM Chief Inspector of Probation, since 2019; *b* London, 28 May 1965; *s* of Dr John Anderson Oliver Russell and Rosemary Russell; *m* 2003, Polly Shields; two *d*. *Educ:* Cotham Sch., Bristol; St John's Coll., Oxford (BA Hons Human Scis 1986); Univ. of Bristol (MSc Social Scis 1987). Res. Officer, Res. and Planning Unit, Home Office, 1987–91; Sen. Projects Officer, Mental Health Foundn, 1991–93; Harkness Fellow, Univ. of Calif, Berkeley, 1993–94; Policy Officer, Home Affairs, Labour Party Policy Unit, 1995–97; Sen. Manager, Audit Commn, 1997–98; Senior Policy Adviser: to Home Sec., 1998–2001; (Home Affairs) to Prime Minister, 2001–05; Dir, Strategy and Business Develt, Bazian Ltd, 2005–06; Sen. Policy Advr to Home Sec., 2006–07; Hd, Asylum Policy and Dir of Performance, UK Border Agency, 2007–08; Hd, Violent Crime Unit, Home Office, 2008–12; Dir, State Pension Policy, 2012–14, Dir, Disability Employment and Support, 2014–16, DWP; Dir Gen., Offender Reform and Commng Gp, then Justice Analysis and Offender Policy, MoJ, 2016–19. Trustee and non-exec. Dir, Turning Point, 2005–11. *Recreations:* cycling Kent country lanes, 1970s vinyl, Arsenal FC. *Address:* HM Inspector of Probation, 1st Floor, Manchester Civil Justice Centre, 1 Bridge Street West, Manchester M3 3FX.

**RUSSELL, Mark Francis,** CBE 2018; Chair, Defence Equipment and Support, Ministry of Defence, since 2019; *b* Manchester, 22 May 1960; *s* of Arthur Russell and Mary Russell; *m* 1991, Emma Wright; three *d*. *Educ:* Ampleforth Coll.; Univ. of Stirling (BA Hons Econs and Mgt Scis 1982); Cranfield Sch. of Mgt (MBA 1987). Associate, A. T. Kearney, 1982–85; Exec., Lazard Brothers & Co., 1985–86; Manager, Robert Fleming & Co., 1987–89; Dir, Coopers & Lybrand, later PricewaterhouseCoopers, 1989–2000; Partner, KPMG, 2000–04; Dir, 2004–07, Dep. Chief Exec., 2007–13, Chief Exec., 2013–19, Shareholder Executive, BERR, then BIS, later UK Govt Investments, HM Treasury. Non-exec. Dir, Submarine Delivery Agency, 2017–. Non-executive Director: Working Links (Employment) Ltd, 2005–12; Eurostar Internat. Ltd, 2010–15; London & Continental Railways, 2010–18; DP World, 2014–. *Recreations:* cycling, photography, italic handwriting. *Address:* Defence Equipment and Support, Ministry of Defence, Maple 0a, #2043, MoD Abbey Wood, Bristol BS34 8JH.

**RUSSELL, Mark Kenneth;** Chief Executive Officer, Children's Society, since 2019; *b* 25 June 1974; *s* of Kenneth and Elizabeth Russell. *Educ:* Portadown Coll.; Queen's Univ., Belfast (LLB 1995). Proj. Exec., W. D. Irwin & Sons Ltd, 1995–97; Youth Pastor, Lurgan Methodist Ch, 1997–2000; Youth Minister, Christ Ch, Chorleywood, 2000–06; Chief Exec. and Mem. Bd, Church Army, 2006–19. Member: Conf. of Methodist Ch in Ireland, 1996–98; Gen. Synod of C of E, 2005–11 and 2015–; Archbishops' Council, 2005–11 and 2015–; Marylebone Project Bd, 2006– (Chm., 2010–); Council, Evangelical Alliance, 2007–12; Coll. of Evangelists, 2008–; Mission and Public Affairs Council, C of E, 2011–; ACEVO, 2012–; Council of Reference for Youth for Christ, 2012–; Archbp's Task Gp, 2014–. Dir, Ecumenical Partnership Initiatives, 2017–. Hon. Canon, Worcester Cath., 2011–. Gov., Talbot Special Sch., Sheffield, 2012–; Dir, Eliot Smith Dance, 2017–. Member: Christians on the Left (formerly Christian Socialist Movement), 2008–; Amnesty Internat. FRSA 2016. *Recreations:* theatre, cinema, supporter of Tottenham Hotspur FC. *Address:* Children's Society, Edward Rudolf House, Margery Street, WC1X 0JL.

**RUSSELL, Michael William;** Member (SNP) Argyll and Bute, Scottish Parliament, since 2011 (Scotland South, 1999–2003 and 2007–11); Cabinet Secretary for Government Business and Constitutional Relations, since 2018; *b* 9 Aug. 1953; *s* of late Thomas Stevenson Russell and Jean Marjorie Russell (*née* Haynes); *m* 1980, Cathleen Ann Macaskill; one *s*. *Educ:* Marr Coll., Troon; Edinburgh Univ. (MA 1974). Creative Producer, Church of Scotland, 1974–77; Dir, Cinema Sgire, Western Isles Islands Council, 1977–81; Founder and Dir, Celtic Film and Television Fest., 1981–83; Exec. Dir, Network Scotland Ltd, 1983–91; Dir, Eala Bhan Ltd, 1991–2009; Chief Exec., SNP, 1994–99. Scottish Parliament: Opposition front bench spokesman for Parlt, 1999–2000, for children, educn and culture, 2000–03; Minister for Envmt, 2007–09, for Culture, External Affairs and Constitution, 2009; Cabinet Sec. for Educn and Lifelong Learning, 2009–14; Minister for UK Negotiations on Scotland's Place in Europe, 2016–18; Mem., Rural Affairs, Climate Change and Envmt Cttee, 2014–16; Convenor: Cross-Party Gp on Malawi, 2014–16; Finance and Constitution Cttee, 2016. Contested (SNP): Clydesdale, 1987; Cunningham South, 2003, Dumfries, 2007, Scottish Parlt. Prof. in Scottish Culture and Governance (pt-time), Univ. of Glasgow, 2015–16, Hon. Prof., Sch. of Arts, 2016. Culture columnist, The Herald, 1999–2006; political columnist: Holyrood Mag., 2003–07; Sunday National, 2019–; columnist, TES Scotland, 2004–07. Hon. Vice Pres., Eur. Movement (Scotland), 2014–; Hon. President: Scottish Creel Fishermen's Fedn, 2018–; Clyde Fishermen's Assoc., 2018–. Trustee: Scottish Futures Forum, 2014–16; Baird of Bute Foundn, 2016–. FRSA 2007. *Publications:* (ed) Glasgow: the book, 1990; (ed) Edinburgh: a celebration, 1992; A Poem of Remote Lives: the enigma of Werner Kissling, 1997; In Waiting: travels in the shadow of Edwin Muir, 1998; A Different Country, 2002; (ed) Stop the World, 2004; (with Dennis MacLeod) Grasping the Thistle, 2006; The Next Big Thing, 2007; (with Iain McKie) The Price of Innocence, 2007. *Recreations:* cooking, tending my garden. *Address:* Scottish Parliament, Edinburgh EH99 1SP; Feorlean, Glendaruel, Argyll PA22 3AH.

**RUSSELL, Sir Muir;** *see* Russell, Sir Alastair M.

**RUSSELL, Ven. Norman Atkinson;** Archdeacon of Berkshire, 1998–2013; *b* 7 Aug. 1943; *s* of Norman Gerald Russell and Olive Muriel Russell (*née* Williamson); *m* 1974, Victoria Christine Jasinska; two *s*. *Educ:* Royal Belfast Academical Instn; Churchill Coll., Cambridge (BA 1965; MA 1969); London Coll. of Divinity (BD London 1970). Articled Clerk, Coopers & Lybrand, 1966–67; ordained deacon, 1970, priest, 1971; Curate: Christ Church with Emmanuel, Clifton, Bristol, 1970–74; Christ Church, Cockfosters, and pt-time Chaplain, Middx Poly., 1974–77; Rector, Harwell with Chilton, 1977–84; Priest in Charge: St James, Gerrards Cross, 1984–88; St James, Fulmer, 1985–88; Rector, Gerrards Cross and Fulmer, 1988–98; RD, Amersham, 1996–98. Vice-Chm., Ecumenical Council for Corporate Responsibility, 1999–2002. Member: Gen. Synod, C of E, 2002–10; Archbishops' Council, C of E, 2005–10. Prolocutor, Lower House of the Convocation of Canterbury, 2005–10. *Publications:* Censorship, 1972. *Recreations:* walking, reading, watching Rugby football. *Address:* 47a Theobalds Way, Camberley, Surrey GU16 9RF. *T:* (01276) 64110.

**RUSSELL, Pam;** *see* Ayres, P.

**RUSSELL, Paul Anthony Wellington;** QC 2011; *b* London, 4 Dec. 1961; *s* of Anthony Russell, MRCOG, MRCS and Jilly Russell (*née* Pengilley); *m* 1989, Sara Young; two *d*. *Educ:* Taunton Sch.; Durham Univ. (BA Hons Law). Called to the Bar, Middle Temple, 1984. *Recreations:* family, golf, Rugby Union, Cornwall, Youth Offending Team of London Borough of Wandsworth. *Address:* 12 King's Bench Walk, Temple, EC4Y 7EL. *T:* (020) 7583 0811. *E:* russell@12kbw.co.uk. *Clubs:* Coombe Hill Golf, Rosslyn Park Rugby Football.

**RUSSELL, Prof. Philip St John,** DPhil; FRS 2005; Alfried Krupp von Bohlen und Halbach Professor, Institute for Optics, Information and Photonics, University of Erlangen-Nuremberg, since 2005; a Director, Max-Planck Institute for Science of Light, Erlangen, Germany, since 2009; *b* 25 March 1953; *s* of Edward Augustine Russell and Emily Frances Russell (*née* Stevenson); *m* 1981, Alison Rosemary Bennett (*d* 2017); two *s*. *Educ:* Royal Belfast Academical Instn; Magdalen Coll., Oxford (BA 1976; MA, DPhil 1979). Hayward Jun. Res. Fellow, Oriel Coll., Oxford, 1978–81; Alexander von Humboldt Fellow, Technische Universität Hamburg-Harburg, 1981–83; World Trade Vis. Scientist, IBM TJ Watson Res. Center, NY, 1983, 1985; Professeur Associé, Univ. de Nice, 1985, 1986; Lectr, then Reader, Univ. of Southampton, 1986–89, 1991–96; Reader, Univ. of Kent, 1989–90; Prof. of Physics, Univ. of Bath, 1996–2009. Chief Tech. Officer and Founder, BlazePhotonics Ltd, 2000–04. Hon. Dr Menéndez Pelayo Internat. Univ., Santander, 2016. Fellow, The Optical Soc. (formerly Optical Soc. of America), 2000 (Joseph Fraunhofer Award, Robert M. Burley Prize, 2000; Pres., 2015). Wolfson Res. Merit Award, Royal Soc., 2004–05; Dist. Lectr, IEEE Lasers and Electro-Optics Soc., 2004–06; signed Golden Book of Erlangen, 2006; Applied Optics Div. Prize, 2002, Thomas Young Prize, 2005, Inst. of Physics; Körber Prize for Eur. Sci., 2005; Prize for Res. into Science of Light, Eur. Phys. Soc., 2013; Zukunfts Prize, Berthold Leibinger Foundn, 2014; Photonics Award, IEEE, 2015; Rank Prize for Optoelectronics, 2017; Microoptics Conf. Award, Japanese Soc. Applied Physics, 2017; Prof. Maksymilian Pluta Award, Photonics Soc. of Poland, 2018. *Publications:* approaching 600 papers in learned jls and scientific confs. *Recreations:* classical and jazz piano playing, music composition and improvisation, art, reading. *Address:* Max-Planck Institute for Science of Light, Staudtstrasse 2, 91058 Erlangen, Germany. *E:* philip.russell@mpl.mpg.de.

**RUSSELL, Dame Philippa (Margaret),** DBE 2009 (CBE 2001; OBE 1998); Chair, Standing Commission on Carers, Department of Health, 2007–14; *b* Sheffield, 4 Feb. 1938; *d* of Garth Rivers Stoneham, FRCOG and Nancy Wooler Stoneham (*née* Leslie); *m* 1959, Dr Alan Keith Russell (*d* 2019); two *s* one *d*. *Educ:* Barrow-in-Furness Grammar Sch. for Girls; St Hilda's Coll., Oxford (BA Modern Hist.). Develt Officer, Council for Children's Welfare, 1968–76; Dir, Council for Disabled Children, 1976–2003; Disability Policy Advr, Nat. Children's Bureau, 2003–07; Disability Advr, DFES, 2003–05. Topic Advr for Guideline on Support for Adult Carers, NICE Nat. Guideline Alliance, 2017–. Member: Nat. Disability Council, 1996–2000; Disability Rights Task Force, 1997–99; Oversight Gp on Commitment to Carers, NHS England, 2015–; Ministerial Oversight Gp for Action Plan for Carers, 2019–. Mem. Bd, Think Local, Act Personal, 2016–. Nat. Affiliate, Doubleday Centre for Patient Experience, Univ. of Manchester Med. Sch., 2016–. Vice-Pres., Carers UK, 2016–. Trustee: Family Fund, 1998–2004; Nat. Develt Team for Inclusion, 2000–16; Mental Health Foundn, 2001–07; SE Forum on Ageing, 2016–; Chair of Trustees, MOVE, 2000–16. Hon. FRCPCH 1993; Hon. FRCPsych 2012; Hon. Fellow, Univ. of Central Lancs, 1988. Hon. Dr: York, 1998; Lincoln, 2013; Liverpool John Moores, 2017. Rose Fitzgerald Kennedy Centenary Internat. Award, 1990; Lifetime Achievement Award, RADAR, 2005. *Publications:* The Wheelchair Child, 1978 (Oddfellows Prize, Oddfellows Friendly Soc., 1979) (trans. 8 langs); articles and contribs on disabled children, family support, disability, social care and carers issues. *Recreations:* music, reading, the family. *Address:* c/o National Children's Bureau, 8 Wakley Street, EC1V 7QE. *T:* (020) 7843 9708.

**RUSSELL, Robert Charles, (Jack),** MBE 1996; cricketer; international artist; *b* 15 Aug. 1963; *s* of late Derek John Russell and of Jennifer Russell; *m* 1985, Aileen Ann Dunn; two *s* three *d*. *Educ:* Uplands Co. Primary Sch.; Archway Comprehensive Sch. Played for Glos CCC, 1981–2004; internat. début, England *v* Pakistan, 1987; played 54 Test Matches and 40 One-day Internationals; world record (11) for dismissals in a Test Match, England *v* SA, Johannesburg, 1995; record for dismissals (27) in a Test series for England, England *v* SA, 1995–96; retd from internat. cricket, 1998. Opened Jack Russell Gall., Chipping Sodbury, 1992; paintings sold and displayed in museums and collections worldwide; commissions include: We Will Remember Them, for RRF, in Tower of London; The Ten Field Marshals of the British Army, for Army Benevolent Fund, in Nat. Army Museum; Cricket World Cup Final, 1999, Australia *v* Pakistan, for NatWest Bank; Ashes Series 2005; Legal London series; portraits include: Duke of Edinburgh; Duke of Kent; Eric Clapton; Sir Norman Wisdom. *Publications:* A Cricketer's Art: sketches by Jack Russell, 1988; (illustr.) Sketches of a Season, 1989; Jack Russell's Sketch Book, 1996; Jack Russell: unleashed (autobiog.), 1997; The Art of Jack Russell: a collection of paintings, 1999; New Horizons: a collection of paintings, 2006; Eighteen Counties: a collection of cricket paintings and sketches, 2013, repr. 2019. *Address:* Jack Russell Gallery, 4 Russell Mews, 41 High Street, Chipping Sodbury, S Glos BS37 6BJ. *T:* (01454) 329583. *W:* www.twitter.com/jackrussellart, www.facebook.com/Jack Russell Gallery.

**RUSSELL, Sir Robert Edward, (Sir Bob)**, Kt 2012; *b* 31 March 1946; *s* of late Ewart Russell and Muriel Russell (*née* Sawdy); *m* 1967, Audrey Blandon; twin *s* one *d* (and one *d* decd). *Educ:* Myland Primary Sch., Colchester; St Helena Secondary Modern Sch., Colchester; NE Essex Technical Coll. Reporter, Essex County Standard and Colchester Gazette, 1963–66; News Editor, Braintree & Witham Times, 1966–68; Editor, Maldon & Burnham Standard, 1968–69; Sub-Editor, London Evening News, 1969–72; Sub-Editor, London Evening Standard, 1972–73; Press Officer, Post Office Telecommunications, subseq. British Telecom (Eastern Reg.), 1973–85; Publicity Officer, Univ. of Essex, 1986–97. Mem., Colchester BC, 1971–2002 (Lab 1971–81, SDP 1981–88, Lib Dem 1988–2002) (Mayor, 1986–87). MP (Lib Dem) Colchester, 1997–2015; contested (Lib Dem) same seat, 2015, 2017. High Steward, Colchester, 2015. *Recreation:* promoting the interests of the town of Colchester.

**RUSSELL, Prof. (Robert) Graham (Goodwin)**, PhD, DM; FRCP, FRCPath, FMedSci; FRS 2008; Professor of Musculoskeletal Pharmacology, Nuffield Department of Orthopaedics, Rheumatology and Musculoskeletal Sciences (formerly Nuffield Department of Orthopaedic Surgery), University of Oxford, 2006, now Professor Emeritus (Norman Collisson Professor of Musculoskeletal Science, 2000–06); Fellow of St Peter's College, Oxford, 2001–07, now Emeritus; Professor of Musculoskeletal Pharmacology, Mellanby Centre for Bone Research, University of Sheffield Medical School, since 2009; *b* 16 Feb. 1941; *s* of Charles Chambers Russell and Mary (*née* Goodwin); *m* 1960, Diana Mary (*née* Allfrey); one *s* three *d*. *Educ:* Clare Coll., Cambridge (BA 1962; MA 1966; MB BChir 1971); PhD Leeds 1967; DM Oxon 1975. MRCP 1974, FRCP 1981; MRCPath 1974, FRCPath 1986. MRC Unit, Leeds, 1962–65; Res. Fellow, Swiss Res. Inst., Davos, 1965–67; Med. Student, Clinical Sch., Oxford Univ., 1967–71; House Officer posts, Radcliffe Infirmary, Oxford, 1972–73; Med. Res. Fellow, St Peter's Coll., Oxford, 1973–76; Sen. Lectr, 1976–77, Prof. and Head of Dept of Human Metabolism and Clin. Biochemistry, 1977–2000, Sheffield Univ.; Dir, Botnar Res. Centre (Oxford Univ. Inst. of Musculoskeletal Scis), 2002–07; Head, Nuffield Dept of Orthopaedic Surgery, Oxford Univ., 2003–06. Sen. Lectr, Univ. Bern, 1970–71; Asst Prof. of Medicine, Harvard Med. Sch., 1974–75. Chm., Nat. Osteoporosis Soc., 2000–02 (Kohn Award, 2000). President: Internat. Bone and Mineral Soc., 1998–2001 (Gaillard Award, 2007); Paget's Assoc., 2009–. FMedSci 2001. Hon. MD Sheffield, 2003. John B. Johnson Award, Paget's Foundn, USA, 1997; Neuman Award, Amer. Soc. of Bone and Mineral Metabolism, 2000; Dent Award, Bone Res. Soc. UK, 2013; Rodan Award, Amer. Soc. of Bone and Mineral Metabolism, 2014; Horton Award, Eur. Soc. Calcified Tissues, 2015. *Publications:* contribs to learned jls and books. *Recreations:* fishing, ski-ing, nature, third generation. *Address:* Oxford University Institute of Musculoskeletal Sciences, Botnar Research Centre, Nuffield Department of Orthopaedics, Rheumatology and Musculoskeletal Sciences, Nuffield Orthopaedic Centre, Windmill Road, Headington, Oxford OX3 7LD; 20 Feilden Grove, Headington, Oxford OX3 0DU. *E:* graham.russell@ndorms.ox.ac.uk.

**RUSSELL, (Ronald) Christopher (Gordon)**, FRCS; Consultant Surgeon: Middlesex Hospital, 1975–2005; King Edward VII Hospital, since 1985; *b* 15 May 1940; *s* of Rognvald Gordon Russell, OBE and Doris Isa Russell (*née* Troup); *m* 1965, Ruth Pitcher; two *s* (and one *s* decd). *Educ:* Epsom College; Middlesex Hosp. Med. Sch. (MB BS, MS). Sen. Lectr in Surgery, St Mary's Hosp., 1973–75. Medical Advr, Nuffield Hosps, 1988–2003; Civilian Medical Advr, RN, 2002–08. Member Council: Med. Defence Union, 1996–; RCS, 1999–2008 (Chm., Ct of Examnrs, 1997–99; Vice-Pres., 2006–08); Pres., Assoc. of Upper Gastrointestinal Surgeons, 1998–2000; Pres., Assoc. of Surgeons of GB and Ire., 2001–02. Chm., Jt Cttee on Inter-Collegiate Examinations, 2000–04. Chm., British Jl of Surgery Soc. Ltd, 1996–2004; Associate Editor, 1978, Co-Editor, 1986–91, British Jl of Surgery; Gen. Editor, Operative Surgery, 1986–. Hon. FRCPSGlas 2005; Hon. FRCSI 2009; Hon. FFGDP(UK) 2009. Cheselden Medal, RCS, 2009. *Publications:* (ed) Recent Advances in Surgery, vol. XI 1982, vol. XII 1985, vol. XIII 1991; (ed jtly) Bailey & Love Textbook of Surgery, 1991–2005; numerous contribs to surgical and gastroenterological jls. *Recreation:* travel. *Address:* Grey Roofs, 34 West Common, Gerrards Cross SL9 7RE. *T:* (01753) 882264. *Club:* Royal Society of Medicine.

**RUSSELL, Sally Joy;** *see* Feldman, S. J.

**RUSSELL, Stephanie;** *see* Tozer, S.

**RUSSELL, Sir Stephen (Charles)**, 9th Bt *cr* 1812, of Swallowfield, Berkshire; *b* 12 Jan. 1949; *s* of Sir (Arthur) Mervyn Russell, 8th Bt and Ruth Russell (*née* Holloway); *S* father, 2014, but his name does not appear on the Official Roll of the Baronetage; *m* 1974, Dale Frances Markstein; one *d*. Heir: half-*b* Ian Mervyn Russell, *b* 8 Dec. 1956.

**RUSSELL, Stephen George;** Chief Executive, The Boots Co., 2000–03; *b* 13 March 1945; *s* of Llandel and Olive Russell; *m* 1969, Elizabeth Jane Brook; one *s* one *d*. *Educ:* Tiffin Sch., Kingston upon Thames; Trinity Hall, Cambridge (BA Hons Classics). Joined Boots 1967; Dir of Merchandise, Boots The Chemists, 1988–92; Managing Dir, Do It All Ltd, 1992–95; Man. Dir, Boots The Chemists, 1995–2000; Jt Gp Man. Dir, Boots Co., 1997–2000. Non-executive Director: Woolwich plc, 1998–2000; Barclays Bank plc, 2000–09; Business Control Solutions Gp, 2005– (Chm., 2007–); Network Rail Ltd, 2007–12. Trustee, Tommy's The Baby Charity, 2003–. Mem. Council, Nottingham Univ., 2003–13. *Recreations:* sport, classical music, opera, reading. *Club:* Hawks (Cambridge).

**RUSSELL, William Martin, (Willy);** author, since 1971; *b* 23 Aug. 1947; *s* of William and Margery Russell; *m* 1969, Ann Seagroatt; one *s* two *d*. *Educ:* St Katharine's Coll. of Educn, Liverpool, 1970–73 (Cert. of Educn). Ladies' Hairdresser, 1963–69; Teacher, 1973–74; Fellow in Creative Writing, Manchester Polytechnic, 1977–78. Founder Mem., and Dir, Quintet Films; Hon. Dir, Liverpool Playhouse. *Theatre:* Blind Scouse (3 short plays), 1971–72; When the Reds (adaptation), 1972; John, Paul, George, Ringo and Bert (musical), 1974; Breezeblock Park, 1975; One for the Road, 1976; Stags and Hens, 1978; Educating Rita, 1979; Blood Brothers (musical), 1983; Our Day Out (musical), 1983; Shirley Valentine, 1986; *television plays:* King of the Castle, 1972; Death of a Young, Young Man, 1972; Break In (for schools), 1974; Our Day Out, 1976; Lies (for schools), 1977; Daughters of Albion, 1978; Boy with Transistor Radio (for schools), 1979; One Summer (series), 1980; *radio play:* I Read the News Today (for schools), 1976; *screenplays:* Band on the Run, 1979 (not released); Educating Rita, 1981; Shirley Valentine, 1988; Dancing Through the Dark, 1989. Visual artist: solo exhibn, Kirkby Gall., Knowsley, 2017. Hon. MA Open Univ., 1983; Hon. DLit Liverpool, 1990. *Publications:* Breezeblock Park, 1978; One for the Road, 1980, rev. edn 1985; Educating Rita, 1981; Our Day Out, 1984; Stags and Hens, 1985; Blood Brothers, 1985 (also pubd as short non-musical version for schools, 1984); Shirley Valentine, 1989; The Wrong Boy (novel), 2000; several other plays included in general collections of plays; songs and poetry. *Recreations:* playing the guitar, composing songs, gardening, cooking. *Club:* Athenæum (Liverpool).

**RUSSELL BEALE, Sir Simon;** *see* Beale.

**RUSSELL-COBB, Piers Andrew Conrad;** Founder, Media Fund Ltd, since 1991; Publisher, Arcadia Books Ltd, since 2012; *b* Geneva, 14 Oct. 1953; *s* of Trevor Russell-Cobb and Nancy Florence Russell-Cobb (*née* Stanley-Hughes); *m* 1982, Sophia Melissa Jane, *d* of Sir Robin Chichester-Clark; two *s*. *Educ:* Westminster Sch.; New Coll., Oxford (BA 1975; MA 1980). Chatto, Bodley Head and Cape Services, 1975–77; writer and screenwriter, NY and LA; Exec. Ed., Marshall Editions, 1978; Internat. Mktg Manager, Thames and Hudson Ltd, 1979–87; Publicity and Promotions Dir, Reed Publishing Gp, 1987–90; Asst Dir, Ansbacher Media Ltd, 1990–91; Publisher, City Limits magazine, 1991. Non-exec. Chm., Bridgeman Images, 2019–. Ambassador, 2010–, Mem., Develt Cttee, 2011–14, RADA. Trustee, Music in Country Churches, 2000–11. Liveryman: Merchant Taylors' Co., 1990; Stationers' and Newspaper Makers' Co., 2009. *Publications:* Great Chefs of France (with Quentin Crewe), 1978; contrib. publishing and media mags; cookery book reviewer. *Recreations:* reading, music, fishing, food and drink, tennis. *Address:* Media Fund Ltd, 139 Highlever Road, W10 6PH. *T:* (020) 8960 4967. *E:* prc@mediafund.co.uk. *Clubs:* Academy, Blacks, Beefsteak, Century, Groucho, Soho House.

**RUSSELL FLINT, Simon Coleridge;** QC 2003; a Recorder of the Crown Court, since 2000; *b* 8 Oct. 1957; *s* of late Francis Murray Russell Flint and of Susan Mary Russell Flint (*née* Sumner); *m* 1983, Jacqueline Ann Verden; one *s* one *d*. *Educ:* Cranleigh Sch.; Polytechnic of Central London (BA Hons Law); Inns of Court Sch. of Law. Called to the Bar, Inner Temple, 1980; Asst Recorder, 1998–2000; Hd of Chambers, 2009. A Chm., Police Discipline Appeals Tribunal, 2003–. Chm., Kent Bar Mess, 2004. Gov., St George's Sch., Wrotham, 1996–. *Recreations:* tennis, ski-ing, Liverpool Football Club, armchair sport. *Address:* Reform Chambers, 1st Floor, The Cursitor Building, 38 Chancery Lane, WC2A 1EN.

**RUSSELL-JONES, Maj. Gen. (Peter) John**, OBE 1988; Army Adviser to BAE Systems, 2001–17; *b* 31 May 1948; *s* of Peter Rathbone Russell-Jones and Margaret Silis Russell-Jones; *m* 1976, Stella Margaret Barrett; one *s* one *d*. *Educ:* Wellington Coll.; RMCS (BScEng Hons 1972). Commnd RE, 1968; Regtl duty, 1972–79; Army Staff Coll., 1979–80; MA to Master Gen. of the Ordnance, 1986–88; CO 23 Engr Regt, 1988–90; Col, Defence Policy, MoD, 1990–91; Comdt, Royal Mil. Sch. of Engrg, 1992–95; rcds, 1995; Dir, Internat. Orgns, MoD, 1996–97; ACDS, Operational Requirements (Land Systems), MoD, 1997–99; Capability Manager (Manoeuvre), MoD, 1999–2001. *Recreations:* travel, rock and roll, family, golf. *Address:* Regimental HQ RE, Brompton Barracks, Chatham, Kent ME4 4UG.

**RUSSELL-MOYLE, Lloyd Cameron;** MP (Lab Co-op) Brighton Kemptown, since 2017; *b* Brighton, 1986; *s* of Brian Moyle and Sherry Russell. *Educ:* Wallands Primary Sch.; Priory Sch., Lewes; Sussex Downs Coll.; Univ. of Bradford (BA Hons; DipHE); Univ. of Sussex (LLM). Adminr, Youth Service, East Sussex CC, 2004–06; Trnr and Advr, Nat. Youth Agency, 2005–08; Union Sec. and Treas., Univ. of Bradford, 2007–09; Vice Pres., Eur. Youth Forum, 2010–14. Vice Chm., British Youth Council, 2006–08; Chm., Woodcraft Folk, 2009–11. Mem. (Lab and Co-op), Brighton and Hove CC, 2016–. Mem., Internat. Develt Cttee, H of C, 2017–; Chair, All Party Parly Gp for Youth, 2017–, for Northern Syria and the Kurds, 2017–; Mem., Parly Cttees on Arms Export Controls, 2017–. FRSA. *Recreations:* swimming, camping, theatre. *Address:* House of Commons, SW1A 0AA. *T:* (01273) 550121. *E:* lloyd@russell-moyle.co.uk.

**RUSSELL-SMITH, Penelope**, CVO 2007 (LVO 2000); voluntary worker, since 2007; Casual Celebrant and Registration Officer, Gloucestershire, since 2013; *b* 22 Oct. 1956; *d* of late Denham William Russell-Smith and Barbara Cynthia Russell-Smith. *Educ:* Sherborne Sch. for Girls; Girton Coll., Cambridge (MA). Dep. Editor, Whitaker's Almanack, 1980–81; Editor of Navy and Army publications, MoD, 1982–84; MoD Press Office (incl. Falkland Is, 1986), 1984–88; Chief Press Officer, Dept of Transport, 1988–90; EU Desk, News Dept, FCO, 1990–93; Asst Press Sec., 1993–97, Dep. Press Sec., 1997–2000, Press Sec., 2000–02, Communications and Press Sec., 2002–07, to the Queen; Dir of External Relations, AQ Research, 2007–08. Trustee, RBL Poppy Factory, 2008–10; Volunteer: Nat. Trust, 2009–; RVS (formerly WRVS), 2010–14. *Address:* Tree House, 2 Hetton Gardens, Charlton Kings, Glos GL53 8HU.

**RUSSEN, Jonathan Huw Sinclair;** QC 2010; **His Honour Judge Russen;** a Specialist Civil Circuit Judge (Commercial, Technology and Construction Court and Chancery), since 2017; *b* Newport, S Wales, 26 Feb. 1963; *s* of Peter John Sinclair Russen and Ruth Cecilia Russen (*née* Warren); *m* 1990, Gaynor Jacqueline Couch; one *s* one *d*. *Educ:* St Julian's Comp. Sch., Newport; University Coll. of Wales, Aberystwyth (LLB 1984); Sidney Sussex Coll., Cambridge (LLM 1985). Called to the Bar, Lincoln's Inn, 1986; in practice as barrister at Chancery Bar, 1988–2017. Mem., British Assoc. for Shooting and Conservation. *Publications:* Financial Services: a litigator's guide, 2006; (contrib.) Civil Fraud: law, practice and procedure, 2018. *Recreations:* my dogs, cycling, Rugby (especially Welsh hegemony thereof), fishing. *Address:* Bristol Civil and Family Justice Centre, 2 Redcliff Street, Bristol BS1 6GR.

**RUSSILL, Patrick Joseph;** Director of Music, London Oratory, since 1999; Head of Choral Conducting (formerly Choral Direction and Church Music), since 1997, and Professor of Organ, since 1999, Royal Academy of Music; *b* 9 Sept. 1953; *s* of John Leonard Russill and Vera Mary Russill (*née* Clarke); *m* 1979, Jane Mary Rogers; two *s* three *d*. *Educ:* Shaftesbury Grammar Sch.; New Coll., Oxford (Organ Schol.; BA 1st Cl. Hons 1975; MA). Asst Organist, 1976–77, Organist, 1977–99, London Oratory; Dir, Oxford Chamber Choir, 1976–79; organist for Papal Mass, Wembley Stadium, 1982; Prof. of Acad. Studies, 1982–87, Hd of Ch Music, 1987–97, RAM; Director: London Oratory Jun. Choir, 1984–2003; Europa Singers of London, 1985–89. RFH recital début, 1986; appearances as organist and conductor in UK, Europe, Near East and Asia; has made recordings. Visiting Lecturer: St George's Coll., Jerusalem, 1994–95; Malmö Coll. of Music, Sweden, 1994; Sibelius Acad., Helsinki, 2013; Royal Coll. of Music, Stockholm, 2015, 2019; Dusseldorf Hochschule für Musik, 2017; Strasbourg Conservatoire, 2019; Vis. Lectr, 1999, Vis. Prof. of Choral Conducting, 2001–, Leipzig Hochschule für Musik und Theater. External Examiner: UEA, 1991–97; Univ. of Leeds, 2003–05; Univ. of Sheffield, 2013; RWCMD, 2016–19; Univ. of Cambridge, 2017–19; Royal Birmingham Conservatoire, 2018–19; Ext. Moderator, Archbps' Cert., Guild of Ch Musicians, 1997–2002; Chief Examr, RCO, 2005–17; Adjudicator, Llangollen Internat. Eisteddfod, 2008–11. Gen. Ed., Church Music Soc., 2019–. Mem. Council, RCO, 1996–2009. Trustee: Ch Music Soc., 1990–; Organists Charitable Trust (formerly Organists' Benevolent League), 1994–; Nicholas Danby Trust, 1998–. Gov., RAM, 2014–. Organ restoration consultant, incl. St Dominic's Priory, London, 2001, Ely Cathedral, 1997–2001. Vice-Pres., Herbert Howells Soc., 2007– (Hon. Patron, 1993–2007). Hon. Mem., Cathedral Organists' Assoc., 2012. Hon. RAM 1993 (Hon. ARAM 1989); Hon. FGCM 1997; Hon. FRCO 2002; FRSCM 2017. Chair's Award for Choral Leadership, Assoc. of British Choral Dirs, 2015. *Publications:* (musical ed.) The Catholic Hymn Book, 1998; (contrib.) The Cambridge Companion to the Organ, 1998; (contrib.) Geschichte der Kirchenmusik, vol. 1, 2011, vol. 3, 2013; (ed) Sweelinck and Howells choral works; contrib. articles and reviews in Gramophone, Musical Times, Organists' Rev., Choir and Organ, British Inst. Organ Studies Jl, RCO Year Book. *Recreations:* family photography, rural open air. *Address:* 65 Sandford Avenue, Wood Green, N22 5EJ.

**RUSSON, David,** CPhys, FInstP; Deputy Chief Executive, British Library, 1996–2001; *b* 12 June 1944; *s* of Thomas Charles Russon and Violet Russon (*née* Jarvis); *m* 1967, Kathleen Mary Gregory; one *s* two *d. Educ:* Wellington Grammar Sch.; University College London (BSc); Univ. of York. CPhys, FInstP 2000. Various appts, Office for Scientific and Technical Information, DES, 1969–74; British Library: R & D Dept, 1974–75; Lending Div., 1975–85; Dir, Document Supply Centre, 1985–88; Dir Gen., Sci., Technol. and Industry, later Boston Spa, 1988–96; Mem., British Liby Bd, 1988–2001. Pres., Internat. Council for Scientific and Technical Information, 1995–2001 (Vice Pres., 1992–95). FCLIP. *Publications:* contribs to professional jls of library and inf. science. *Recreations:* golf, bridge. *Address:* March House, Tollerton, York YO61 1QQ. *T:* (01347) 838253.

**RUST, Prof. John Neville,** PhD; CPsychol; FSS, FBPsS; Director, Psychometrics Centre, Judge Business School (formerly in Psychology Department), University of Cambridge, 2008–19; Senior Member, Darwin College, Cambridge, since 2009; Associate Fellow, Leverhulme Centre for Future of Intelligence; *b* Scunthorpe, 25 Nov. 1943; *s* of John Cyprian Walcot Rust and Frances Mary Rust; *m* 1979, Prof. Susan Esther Golombok, *qv*; one *s*, and one *d* by a previous partner. *Educ:* Cirencester Grammar Sch.; Birkbeck Coll., Univ. of London (BSc 1st Cl. Hons Psychol., Statistics and Computer Sci. 1970; MA Philos. 1976); Inst. of Psychiatry, Univ. of London (PhD 1974). CPsychol 1982. University of London: Researcher and Lectr, Inst. of Psychiatry, 1972–76; Institute of Education: Lectr, then Sen. Lectr in Psychometrics, 1976–91; Hd, Dept of Child Develt and Educnl Psychol., 1984–87; Senator for Faculty of Educn, 1983–87; Sen. Lectr, then Reader in Psychometrics, Goldsmiths Coll., 1991–2002; Prof. of Psychometrics, City Univ., London, 2002–05; Dir, Psychometrics Centre, Cambridge Assessment, 2005–08. Visiting Academic: Univ. of Jos, 1979 and 1980; De La Salle Univ., Manila, 1986. Fellow, Amer. Acad. of Assessment Psychol., 1993. Freeman, City of London, 1986. Founder Editor, Philosophical Psychology, 1988. Author of and UK standardisations of psychometric tests. FSS 1976; FBPsS 1985. *Publications:* Modern Psychometrics (with S. E. Golombok), 1989, 3rd edn 2009; articles in learned jls. *Recreations:* astrophysics, promoting diversity and multiculturalism, genealogy, internet, cooking, films. *Address:* Psychometrics Centre, Judge Business School, Executive Education, University of Cambridge, Trumpington Street, Cambridge CB2 1AG. *T:* (01223) 769483. *E:* jnr24@cam.ac.uk.

**RUST, Nicholas John;** Chief Executive, British Horseracing Authority, since 2015; *b* Wallsend, Tyne and Wear, 14 June 1967; *s* of John Oubridge Rust and Carole Margaret Rust; *m* 1993, Margarita Victoria Shoebridge (*d* 2018); one *s. Educ:* Berwick upon Tweed Co. High Sch. Ladbrokes plc: Trainee Shop Manager, 1987–88; Shop Manager, 1988–89; District Supervisor, 1990–94; Area Manager, 1994–97; Regl Controller, 1997–98; Mktg Dir, 1998–99; Commercial Dir, eGaming, 2000–02; Managing Director: Sky Bet-BSkyB, 2002–07; Coral, 2007–10; Retail, Ladbrokes plc, 2010–14. Mem., Bookmakers' Cttee, Horserace Betting Levy Bd, 2007–10 and 2011–14. Mem., Mensa 2008. *Recreations:* golf, philately, racehorse ownership. *Address:* British Horseracing Authority, 75 High Holborn, WC1V 6LS. *T:* (020) 7152 0000. *E:* nrust@britishhorseracing.com.

**RUST, Susan Esther;** *see* Golombok, S. E.

**RUTHERFORD, Adam David,** PhD; scientist, writer, broadcaster; *b* 16 Jan. 1975; *m* 2011, Georgia Murray; one *s* two *d. Educ:* Ipswich Sch.; University Coll. London (BSc 1997); Inst. of Child Health, Univ. of London (PhD Genetics 2001). Video Editor, Nature, 2002–13; presenter: BBC Television: The Cell, 2009; The Gene Code, 2011; Horizon (episode), 2012; The Beauty of Anatomy, 2014; BBC Radio 4: Inside Science, 2013–; (with Hannah Fry), The Curious Cases of Rutherford and Fry, 2016–. Scientific consultant for films incl. Ex Machina, 2015, Life, 2017, Annihilation, 2018. Journalist, various publications incl. The Guardian. Hon. Fellow, British Sci. Assoc., 2017. *Publications:* Creation: the origin and future of life, 2013; A Brief History of Everyone Who Ever Lived, 2016; The Book of Humans, 2018; Genetics: a Ladybird Expert Book, 2018; How to Argue with a Racist, 2020. *Recreations:* cricket, cinema, eating and drinking. *E:* adam.rutherford@gmail.com. *Club:* Celeriac XI Cricket (Founder Mem.).

**RUTHERFORD, Prof. Alfred William, (Bill),** PhD; FRS 2014; Professor of Biochemistry of Solar Energy, Imperial College London, since 2011; *b* Morpeth, Northumberland, 2 Jan. 1955; *s* of Stanley Rutherford and Patricia Rutherford; *m* 1980, Agnes Vega (separated 2003); one *d. Educ:* King Edward VI Grammar Sch. for Boys, Morpeth; Univ. of Liverpool (BSc Hons Biochem. 1976); University Coll. London (PhD Microbiol. (Biophys) 1979). Post Grad. Student, Dept of Botany and Microbiol., UCL, 1976–79; Post Doctoral Associate, Dept of Biophys and Physiol., Univ. of Illinois, Urbana, 1979–81; CEN Saclay, then CEA Saclay: Post Doctoral Fellow, 1982–83, Gp Leader, 1985–2011, Dépt de Biologie, Service de Biophysique; Dir, Res. Unit 1290, Service de Bioénergétique, CNRS, 1992–96; Hd, Service de Bioénergétique, Dept Biologie Joliot-Curie; Dir, Nat. Res. Prog. on 'Photosynthèse Membranaire', 2000–04; Hd, Lab. of Biophys of Oxidative Stress Service de Bioénergétique, Dept Biologie Cellulaire et Moléculaire, 2001–07; Hd, Lab. of Molecular Bioenergetics and Photosynthesis, Inst. of Biol. and Technol. Saclay, 2007–11; Directeur de Recherche, CNRS, 2ème classe, 1988–92, 1ère classe, 1992–2009, Classe Exceptionelle, 2009–11 (en détachement, 2011–). Vis. Res. Scientist, Solar Energy Lab., RIKEN, Saitama, Japan, 1982, 1983; Vis. Prof. of Chem., 2005, Vis. Res. Fellow, 2006, 2007, 2008, ANU; Vis. Prof., QMC, 2007–11. Lectures: Craig Lect. of Chem., ANU, 2005; Total, Eur. Bioenergetics Conf., Dublin, 2008; Drummond, QMC, 2011; Sir Hans Krebs, Univ. of Sheffield, 2014. Mem., EMBO, 2001. Hon. Dr Uppsala, 2013. Silver Medal, CNRS, 2001; Wolfson Merit Award, Royal Soc., 2011. *Publications:* over 180 articles in learned jls; over 50 other articles and chapters. *Recreations:* musician: guitar, harmonica, vocals; genre: rock, blues, Americana, singer-songwriter; bands: Baskerville Willy (CD No Ordinary Hound, 2012, www.baskervillewilly.com), Baskervilles Blues Band (CD Elementary, 1997). *Address:* Department of Life Sciences, Sir Ernst Chain Building, Imperial College London, South Kensington Campus, SW7 2AZ. *E:* a.rutherford@imperial.ac.uk.

**RUTHERFORD, His Honour Andrew;** DL; a Circuit Judge, 1995–2018; *b* 25 March 1948; *s* of late Robert Mark Rutherford and Alison Wellington (*née* Clark); *m* 1994, Lucy Elizabeth Bosworth; two *d. Educ:* Clifton Coll.; Exeter Univ. (LLB). Called to the Bar, Middle Temple, 1970; Asst Recorder, 1990–93; Recorder, 1993–95. Chm., Fees Adv. Commn, 2006–11, Legal Aid Commn, 2011–, Gen. Synod of C of E. DL Somerset, 2000. *Club:* Bath and County.

**RUTHERFORD, Frederick John;** District Judge (Magistrates' Courts), Humberside, 2001–19; *b* Kelso, 6 Aug. 1954; *s* of late Frederick George Rutherford and Isabella Rutherford; *m* 1997, Jayne Louise Curry; one *s* two *d. Educ:* Heckmondwike Grammar Sch.; Leicester Univ. (LLB Hons). Articled Clerk, 1976–78, Asst Solicitor, 1978–80, Partner, 1980–89, Inesons, Solicitors, Cleckheaton; Partner, Jordans, Solicitors, Dewsbury, 1989–2000. *Recreations:* reading, walking, gardening, fly fishing.

**RUTHERFORD, Jessica Marianne Fernande,** FSA; Head of Libraries and Museums, and Director of the Royal Pavilion (Brighton and Hove), 1996–2005; *b* 7 Feb. 1949; *d* of Raymond Denys Rutherford and Simone Genvieve (*née* Michaud); *m* 2004, Nigel Pittman. *Educ:* Brighton and Hove High Sch.; Manchester Univ. (BA Hons Hist. of Art); Sussex Univ. (PGCE). V&A Mus., 1974; Royal Pavilion, Art Gallery and Museums, Brighton: Keeper of Decorative Art, 1974–85; Principal Keeper, Royal Pavilion, 1985–87; Asst Dir (Collections), 1987–92; Head of Mus and Dir, Royal Pavilion, 1992–96. Member: Steering Cttee, Nat. Report on Mus. Educn, Dept of Nat. Heritage, 1994–97; Bd, SE Museums Agency, 2001–02; Libraries, Museums & Archives Expert Panel, Heritage Lottery Fund, 2002–05 (Advr, Heritage Lottery Fund, 2005–). Decorative Arts Society: Sec., 1975–85; Trustee, 1992–2004; Mem. Council, Charleston Trust, 1992–2005; Sec. to Trustees and Governors, Friends of Royal Pavilion, Art Gall. and Museums, 1992–2004. Sussex University: Mem. Council, 1995–2001; Mem. Ct, 2002–; Dir, Gardner Arts Centre, 1996–98; Trustee, The Barlow Collection, 1996–2001. FRSA 1998. Hon. DLit Sussex, 2005. *Publications:* Art Nouveau, Art Deco and the Thirties: the furniture collections at Brighton Museum, 1983; (jtly) Art Nouveau, Art Deco and the Thirties: the ceramic, glass and metalwork collections at Brighton Museum, 1986; The Royal Pavilion: the palace of George IV, 1995; A Prince's Passion: the life of the Royal Pavilion, 2003; *chapters in:* James Tissot, 1984; The Crace Firm of Royal Decorators 1768–1900, 1990; Country House Lighting, 1992; articles and reviews for learned jls. *Recreations:* Spain, ceramics (Raku), horses. *Address:* 24 Clifton Hill, Brighton, E Sussex BN1 3HQ. *T:* (01273) 326718.

**RUTHERFORD, John Alexander;** Chairman, Fasfa Ltd, 2012–19 (Director, 2011–19); *b* 5 Dec. 1948; *s* of John and Pamela Gordon Rutherford; *m* 1970, Judith Ann Lodge; three *s. Educ:* Univ. of Birmingham (BCom). FCA 1972. Accountant, Cooper Bros & Co., 1969–72; Mgt Accountant, Procter & Gamble Ltd, 1972–75; Finance Dir, West of England Farmers Ltd, 1986–91; West Midland Farmers Ltd, subseq. WMF Ltd: Finance Dir, 1991–96; Man. Dir, 1996–99; Dep. Man. Dir, Countrywide Farmers, 1999–2001; Chief Exec., Sea Fish Industry Authy, 2002–10. Chm., Biggar Little Fest., 2011–. Treas., S Charlton PCC, 2013–; Treas./Trustee, N Northumberland Hospice Ltd, 2017–. *Recreation:* classic sports cars. *Address:* 4 Taylors Field, Alnwick NE66 2JN. *T:* (01665) 579316. *Clubs:* Farmers; Morgan Sports Car.

**RUTHERFORD-JONES, Maj. Gen. David John,** CB 2010; Clerk to the Trustees and Chief Executive, Morden College, since 2011; *b* Steamer Point, Aden, 11 Aug. 1958; *s* of Arthur and Penelope Rutherford-Jones; *m* 1985, Sarah Jane McNish; one *s* one *d. Educ:* Lancing Coll.; RMA Sandhurst. Commnd 15th/19th Hussars, 1977; COS 1st Mechanized Bde, 1993–95; Balkan Planning, HQ Allied Powers Europe, 1995–97; Comd Light Dragoons, 1997–2000; COS 3rd UK Div., 2000; Comd 20 Armoured Bde, Kosovo and Iraq, 2001–04; Dir Land Studies, UK Defence Acad., 2004–05; Dir RAC, 2005–07; Comdt, RMA Sandhurst, 2007–09; Military Secretary, 2009–11. Hon. Colonel: Corps of Army Music, 2009–12; Queen's Own Yeomanry, 2015–19; Light Dragoons: Trustee, 1999– (Chm. Trustees, 2013–); Col, 2013–. Trustee: RAC Benevolent Fund, 2010–13; Blind Veterans UK (formerly St Dunstan's), 2011–16; Chm., Hodson's Horse Meml Trust, 2012–. Fellow, Wellington Coll., 2009–12; Gov., Lancing Coll., 2011–17. Cdre, Army Sailing, 2007–11; Chm.; Services Telemark Skiing, 2007–11. Mem. Cttee, Grand Military Gold Cup, Sandown, 2011–13. Founder and Chm., Augustdorf Lunch Club, 2013–; Co-Founder and Co-Chair, CRAFT (Salcombe), 2013–. *Recreations:* sailing, ski-ing, fishing, reading, walking, Newcastle United FC. *Address:* Fugley, 15B Stockton, Warminster BA12 0SE.

**RUTHVEN;** *see* Hore-Ruthven, family name of Earl of Gowrie.

**RUTHVEN OF CANBERRA, Viscount;** Patrick Leo Brer Hore-Ruthven; Database Developer, Clyde & Co., since 2016; *b* 4 Feb. 1964; *s* and *heir* of 2nd Earl of Gowrie, *qv*; *m* 1990, Julie Goldsmith; one *s.* IT Consultant, Lloyds Banking Group, 2010–14; database application developer, 2015–16. *Heir:* s Hon. Heathcote Patrick Cornelius Hore-Ruthven, *b* 28 May 1990.

**RUTHVEN, Prof. Kenneth Borthwick Howard,** PhD; FAcSS; Professor of Education, University of Cambridge, 2005–17, now Emeritus; Fellow, Hughes Hall, Cambridge, since 1983; *b* 1 Feb. 1952. *Educ:* Corpus Christi Coll., Oxford (BA Hons Maths 1973, MA 1977); Moray House Coll., Edinburgh (PGCE 1974); Univ. of Edinburgh (DipEd 1974); Univ. of Stirling (PhD Educn 1980). MA Cantab 1983. Teacher of Maths and Computing, 1974–83: Broughton High Sch., Edinburgh; Brighton Hove & Sussex Sixth Form Coll.; Hills Road Sixth Form Coll., Cambridge; Lectr, 1983–98, Reader, 1998–2005, in Educn, Univ. of Cambridge. Guest Professor in Mathematics Education: Karlstad Univ., Sweden, 2017–; Univ. of Agder, Norway, 2017–. Mem., British Soc. for Res. into Learning Maths, 1983– (Chm., 2006–08). Trustee, Sch. Mathematics Proj., 1996– (Dep. Chm., 2004–05, Chm., 2006–, of Trustees). Adv. Editor, Educnl Studies in Maths, 2001– (Ed., 1994–95, Ed.-in-Chief, 1996–2000). FAcSS (AcSS 2011). *Publications:* Society and the New Technology, 1983; The Maths Factory, 1989; Learning from Computers: mathematics education and technology, 1993; The Didactical Challenge of Symbolic Calculators: turning a computational device into a mathematical instrument, 2005; Mathematical Knowledge in Teaching, 2011; Developing Research in Mathematics Education: twenty years of communication, cooperation and collaboration in Europe, 2018; around 100 res. papers in peer-reviewed jls. *Address:* University of Cambridge Faculty of Education, 184 Hills Road, Cambridge CB2 8PQ. *T:* (01223) 767600, *Fax:* (01223) 767602. *E:* kr18@cam.ac.uk.

**RUTHVEN, Hon. Malise Walter Maitland Knox Hore,** PhD; writer; *b* 14 May 1942; *s* of late Major Hon. Alexander Hardinge Patrick Hore-Ruthven and Pamela Margaret Hore-Ruthven (*née* Fletcher); *m* 1967, Ianthe Hodgkinson; two *d. Educ:* Eton Coll.; Trinity Coll., Cambridge (BA Eng. Lit. 1964; MA 1994; PhD Social and Pol Scis 2000). Writer and ed., BBC External Services, 1966–70, 1976–86; Lectr, Dept of Divinity with Religious Studies, Univ. of Aberdeen, 1994–99. Visiting Professor: Dartmouth Coll., NH, 1989–90; UCSD, 1990–91, 1999–2000; Colorado Coll., Colorado Springs, 2000–01. *Publications:* Torture: the grand conspiracy, 1978; Islam in the World, 1984, 3rd edn 2006; Traveller Through Time: a photographic journey with Freya Stark, 1986; The Divine Supermarket, 1989, repr. 2012; A Satanic Affair: Salman Rushdie and the wrath of Islam, 1990; Islam: a very short introduction, 1997, 2nd edn 2000; A Fury for God: the Islamist attack on America, 2002; Fundamentalism: the search for meaning, 2004; L'Arabie des Saouds - Wahhabisme, corruption et violence, 2019. *Recreations:* walking, basic cooking. *Address:* Hameau Travers, St Jacques de Néhou, 50390, France. *T:* (02) 33013849. *E:* maliseruthven@gmail.com.
*See also* Earl of Gowrie.

**RUTLAND,** 11th Duke of, *cr* 1703; **David Charles Robert Manners;** Marquess of Granby 1703; Earl of Rutland 1525; Baron Manners of Haddon 1679; Baron Roos of Belvoir 1896; *b* 8 May 1959; *er s* of 10th Duke of Rutland, CBE and of Frances Helen (*née* Sweeny); *S* father, 1999; *m* 1992, Emma, *d* of John Watkins; two *s* three *d.* Mem. Civilian Cttee, ATC Sqdn, Grantham. Mem., HHA (Chm., E Midlands Area, 1995–99). President: Notts Rifle Assoc.; Ex-Aircrew Assoc., Grantham and Dist Br.; Vice Pres., Buckminster Gliding Club, 2006–; Patron, Grantham to Nottingham Canal Preservation Trust.

Freeman, City of London; Liveryman, Gunsmiths' Co. *Publications:* (with Emma Ellis) Resolution, 2017. *Recreations:* shooting, fishing, flying when I can. *Heir: s* Marquis of Granby, *qv. Address:* Belvoir Castle, Grantham, Lincs NG32 1PE. *T:* (01476) 870246. *Clubs:* Turf, Annabel's.

**RUTLEDGE, Kelvin Albert;** QC 2013; *b* London, 14 April 1955; *s* of William Horace Sidney Rutledge and Dorothy Bessie Rutledge; one *s* two *d. Educ:* Mayflower Comp. Sch., Billericay; Univ. of Essex (LLB Hons); King's Coll. London (LLM). Called to the Bar, Middle Temple, 1989; in practice as a barrister, Cornerstone Barristers, 1990–. Vis. Fellow, Univ. of Essex, 1998–. Mem., Sheringham Soc. *Recreations:* angling, photography, cooking, reading history. *Address:* Cornerstone Barristers, 2–3 Gray's Inn Square, WC1R 5JH. *T:* (020) 7242 4986. *E:* kelvinr@cornerstonebarristers.com. *Club:* Amwell Magna Fly Fishing.

**RUTLEY, David Henry;** MP (C) Macclesfield, since 2010; a Lord Commissioner of HM Treasury (Government Whip), since 2017; *b* Gravesend, Kent, 7 March 1961; *s* of John Rutley and Birthe Rutley; *m* 1994, Rachel Faber; two *s* two *d. Educ:* Lewes Priory Sch.; London Sch. of Econs and Pol Sci. (BSc Econ 1985); Harvard Business Sch. (MBA 1989). Business Develt Dir, PepsiCo Internat., 1991–94; Special Advr to Cabinet Office, MAFF, HM Treasury, 1994–96; Dir, Business Effectiveness, Safeway Stores, 1996–2000; Dir, Financial Services and Dir, E-commerce, Asda Stores, 2000–05; Sales and Mktg Dir, Halifax Gen. Insce, 2005–07; Business Consultant, 2008–09, Mktg Dir, 2009–10, Barclays Bank. Contested (C) St Albans, 1997. Parliamentary Private Secretary: to Minister for Immigration, 2010–12; to Minister for Policing and Criminal Justice, 2012–14; to Minister for Europe, 2014–15; to Sec. of State for Work and Pensions, 2015–16; to Home Sec., 2016–17; Parly Under-Sec. of State, DEFRA, 2018–19. Mem., Treasury Select Cttee, 2010; Secretary: All Party Parly Gp on National Parks, 2012–16 (Vice-Chm., 2010–12); All Party Parly Gp for Mountain Rescue, 2012–16; Co-Chm., All Party Parly Gp on Mountaineering, 2010–17; Chm., British-Danish All Party Parly Gp, 2015–17. *Recreations:* family, walking in the Peak District, mountaineering, church. *Address:* House of Commons, SW1A 0AA. *T:* (020) 7219 7106. *E:* david.rutley.mp@parliament.uk.

**RUTNAM, Sir Philip (McDougall),** KCB 2018; Permanent Secretary, Home Office, since 2017; *b* Orpington, 19 June 1965; *s* of late Michael Donald Rutnam and Helen McDougall Rutnam (*née* Halliday); *m* 1996, Anna Frances Longman; one *s* two *d. Educ:* Dulwich Coll.; Trinity Hall, Cambridge (BA Hons Histl Tripos 1986); Harvard Univ. (Kennedy Scholar). Various posts, HM Treasury, 1987–2002, on secondment to Morgan Stanley Asia Ltd, Hong Kong, 1995–97; Dir, Regulatory Policy, Oftel, 2002–03; Partner, Competition and Mkts, 2003–07, Mem. Bd, 2007–09, Ofcom; Dir Gen., Business, then Business and Skills, BERR, later BIS, 2009–12, Actg Perm. Sec., BIS, 2010; Perm. Sec., DfT, 2012–17. *Recreations:* running, cycling, ski-ing, taking family up mountains, arts. *Address:* Home Office, 2 Marsham Street, SW1P 4DF.

**RUTOVITZ, Jeanne Elisabeth;** *see* Bell, J. E.

**RUTTER, Barrie Thomas,** OBE 2015; Founder and Artistic Director, Northern Broadsides Theatre Co., 1992–2018; *b* 12 Dec. 1946; *s* of Edward and Annie Rutter; one *d; m* 1978, Carol Chillington (marr. diss. 1997); two *d* (one *s* decd). *Educ:* Newton Hall, Hull; Nat. Youth Th. Professional actor, 1968–, mostly in theatre, but occasional TV, film and radio; *theatre* includes: Napoleon, in Animal Farm, 1984, and Silenus, in The Trackers of Oxyrhynchus, 1990, NT; Northern Broadsides Theatre Co., director: Richard III (also title rôle), 1992; A Midsummer Night's Dream (Shakespeare's Globe, Tyrone Guthrie Award for Best Production), 1995; Antony and Cleopatra (also title rôle), 1995; Samson Agonistes (also title rôle), 1998; King Lear (also title rôle), 1999; Alcestis (Ted Hughes' final play), 2000; Antigone, 2003; The Merchant of Venice (Shylock), 2004; Sweet William (Fat Jack), Comedy of Errors (Egeon), 2005; Wars of the Roses (also edited and acted, Duke of York), 2006; The Tempest (Prospero), 2007; Othello, 2009; Medea (Creon), 2010; Rutherford & Son (acted), 2013; The Merry Wives (Falstaff), When we are Married (acted), 2016; A Chorus of Disapproval (acted), Harold Pinter Th., 2012; Richard III, Hull Truck Th., 2017; The Captive Queen (acted), Sam Wanamaker Playhouse, 2018; director: The Two Noble Kinsmen, Shakespeare's Globe, 2018; Jack Lear (also acted), Hull Truck Th., 2019. Hon. DLitt: Hull, 2001; Bradford, 2005; Huddersfield, 2006; Lancaster, 2017. TMA Award for best dir, 1995; Overall Winner, Creative Briton Awards, Arts & Business/ Prudential, 2000; Sam Wanamaker Award, Shakespeare's Globe, 2003; Pragnell Shakespeare Award, 2010. *Recreations:* food and drink, sport, poetry. *Club:* Garrick.

**RUTTER, Dr (James) Michael,** CBE 2002; Consultant, JMR Consultancy, since 2002; Director of Veterinary Medicines, 1989–2002, and Chief Executive, Veterinary Medicines Directorate, 1990–2002, Department for Environment, Food and Rural Affairs (formerly Ministry of Agriculture, Fisheries and Food); *b* 20 Aug. 1941; *s* of late James and Lily Rutter; *m* 1967, Jacqueline Patricia Watson; one *d. Educ:* Kendal Grammar Sch.; Univ. of Edinburgh (BVM&S 1964; BSc 1965; PhD 1967). MRCVS 1964. Res. Schol., 1964–67, Res. Asst, 1967–69, Univ. of Edinburgh; Institute for Research on Animal Diseases, later Institute for Animal Health: Vet. Res. Officer, 1969–73; Principal Vet. Res. Officer, 1973–84 (on secondment to DES, 1975–78); Head: Dept of Microbiol., 1984–89; Compton Lab., 1986–89. Expert Consultant: ODA; FAO; WHO. Member: Cttee for Vet. Medicinal Products, EC, 1991–99; Mgt Bd, MAFF, 1992–99; Mgt Bd, Eur. Medicines Evaluation Agency, 1996–2002; Assessor, Animal Medicines Trng Regulatory Authy, 2007–. Chm., Poultry Res. Cttee, DEFRA/British Poultry Council, 2008–16. Dir, 2004–13, Sec., 2006–13, Vet. Benevolent Fund; Pres., Vet. Res. Club, 2007–08. FRSocMed 1985. *Publications:* Perinatal Ill Health in Calves, 1973; Pasteurella and Pasteurellosis, 1989; contrib. numerous papers to scientific jls. *Recreations:* gardening, outdoor sports, theatre, ballet, music.

**RUTTER, Jill Kathleen;** Programme Director, Institute for Government, since 2011; *b* 30 Oct. 1956; *d* of Derek John Rutter and June Kathleen Rutter. *Educ:* Somerville Coll., Oxford (BA PPE 1978). HM Treasury, 1978–97; BP plc, 1998–2004; Dir, Strategy and Sustainable Develt, DEFRA, 2004–09; Whitehall Fellow, Inst. for Govt, 2009–11. Harkness Fellow, Grad. Sch. of Public Policy, Univ. of Calif, Berkeley, 1988–89. *Address:* Institute for Government, 2 Carlton Gardens, SW1Y 5AA. *E:* jill.rutter@instituteforgovernment.org.uk.

**RUTTER, John Milford,** CBE 2007; composer and conductor; *b* 24 Sept. 1945; *s* of Laurence Frederick and Joan Mary Rutter (*née* Milford); *m* 1980, JoAnne Redden; one *s* (and one *s* decd), and one step *d. Educ:* Highgate Sch.; Clare Coll., Cambridge (MA, MusB; Hon. Fellow, 2001). Fellow and Director of Music, Clare Coll., Cambridge, 1975–79; Founder and Director, Cambridge Singers, 1981–. Hon. Freeman, Barbers' Co. 2008. Hon. FGCM 1988; Hon. Fellow, Westminster Choir Coll., Princeton, 1980; Hon. Bencher, Middle Temple, 2008. Hon. Life Mem., RPO, 2012. DMus Lambeth, 1996; Hon. Dr: Anglia Ruskin, 2004; Leicester, 2005; Hull, 2008; Durham, 2012; DUniv Open, 2014. Medal, RCO, 2014; European Church Music Prize, 2019. *Publications:* compositions include choral and orchestral works, anthems and carols, 1969–. *Address:* c/o Oxford University Press, Great Clarendon Street, Oxford OX2 6DP.

**RUTTER, Michael;** *see* Rutter, (James) M.

**RUTTER, Sir Michael (Llewellyn),** Kt 1992; CBE 1985; MD; FRCP, FRCPsych; FRS 1987; Professor of Child Psychiatry, 1973–98, Professor of Developmental Psychopathology, since 1998, Institute of Psychiatry, Psychology and Neuroscience, King's College London (formerly Institute of Psychiatry, University of London); *b* 15 Aug. 1933; *s* of Llewellyn Charles Rutter and Winifred Olive Rutter; *m* 1958, Marjorie Heys; one *s* two *d. Educ:* Moorestown Friends' Sch., USA; Wolverhampton Grammar Sch.; Bootham Sch., York; Birmingham Univ. Med. Sch. (MB ChB 1955, MD Hons 1963). MRCS 1955; LRCP 1955, MRCP 1958, FRCP 1972; FRCPsych 1971. Training in paediatrics, neurology and internal medicine, 1955–58; Maudsley Hosp., 1958–61; Nuffield Med. Travelling Fellow, Albert Einstein Coll. of Medicine, NY, 1961–62; Mem., Sci. Staff, MRC Social Psych. Res. Unit, 1962–65; University of London Institute of Psychiatry: Sen. Lectr, then Reader, 1966–73; Hon. Dir, MRC Child Psychiatry Unit, 1984–98; Dir, Social, Genetic and Develtl Psychiatry Res. Centre, 1994–98. Fellow, Center for Advanced Study in Behavioral Scis, Stanford, Calif, 1979–80. Lectures: Goulstonian, RCP, 1973; Salmon, NY Acad. of Medicine, 1979; Adolf Meyer, Amer. Psych. Assoc., 1985; Maudsley, RCPsych, 1986. Pres., Soc. for Res. in Child Devlt, 1999–2001 (Pres.-elect, 1997–99). Gov., 1996–2003, Dep. Chm., 1999–2003, Wellcome Trust; Trustee: Nuffield Foundn, 1992–; Jacobs Foundn, 1998–2004; Novartis Foundn, 1999–; One Plus One, 2001–. Founding Mem., Acad. Europaea, 1988; Founder FMedSci 1998; Foreign Associate Member: Inst. of Medicine, Nat. Acad. of Scis, USA, 1988; US Nat. Acad. of Educn, 1990; Foreign Hon. Mem., Amer. Acad. of Arts and Scis, 1989. FKC 1998. Hon. Prof., Amsterdam Univ., 2001. Hon. FBPsS 1978; Hon. Fellow: Amer. Acad. of Pediatrics, 1981; RSocMed 1996; Hon. FRCPCH 1996; Hon. FBA 2002. Hon. DSSc Univ. of Leiden, 1985; Hon. Dr Leuven, 1990; Hon. DSc: Birmingham, 1990; Chicago, 1991; Minnesota, 1993; Ghent, 1994; Warwick, 1999; E Anglia, 2000; Oxon, 2005; St Andrews, 2013; Sussex, 2014; Hon. MD Edinburgh, 1990; Hon. DPsych Jyväskylä, Finland, 1996; DUniv: N London, 2000; York, 2005. Numerous awards, UK and USA. *Publications:* Children of Sick Parents, 1966; (jtly) A Neuropsychiatric Study in Childhood, 1970; (ed jtly) Education, Health and Behaviour, 1970; (ed) Infantile Autism, 1971; Maternal Deprivation Reassessed, 1972, 2nd edn 1981; (ed jtly) The Child with Delayed Speech, 1972; Helping Troubled Children, 1975; (jtly) Cycles of Disadvantage, 1976; (ed jtly) Child Psychiatry, 1977, 2nd edn as Child and Adolescent Psychiatry, 1985, 4th edn 2002; (ed jtly) Autism, 1978; Changing Youth in a Changing Society, 1979; (jtly) Fifteen Thousand Hours: secondary schools and their effects on children, 1979; (ed) Scientific Foundations of Developmental Psychiatry, 1981; A Measure of Our Values: goals and dilemmas in the upbringing of children, 1983; (jtly) Lead Versus Health, 1983; (jtly) Juvenile Delinquency, 1983; (ed) Developmental Neuropsychiatry, 1983; (ed jtly) Stress, Coping and Development, 1983; (ed jtly) Depression in Young People, 1986; (jtly) Treatment of Autistic Children, 1987; (ed jtly) Language Development and Disorders, 1987; (ed jtly) Parenting Breakdown: the making and breaking of inter-generational links, 1988; (ed jtly) Assessment and Diagnosis in Child Psychopathology, 1988; (ed) Studies of Psychosocial Risk: the power of longitudinal data, 1988; (ed jtly) Straight and Devious Pathways from Childhood to Adulthood, 1990; (ed jtly) Biological Risk Factors for Psychosocial Disorders, 1991; (jtly) Developing Minds: challenge and continuity across the life span, 1993; (ed jtly) Development Through Life: a handbook for clinicians, 1994; (ed jtly) Stress, Risk and Resilience in Children and Adolescents: processes, mechanisms and interventions, 1994; (ed jtly) Psychosocial Disorders in Young People, 1995; (jtly) Behavioural Genetics, 3rd edn, 1997; (jtly) Antisocial Behaviour by Young People, 1998; (jtly) Sex Differences in Antisocial Behaviour: conduct disorder, delinquency and violence in the Dunedin longitudinal study, 2001; (ed jtly) Ethnicity and Causal Mechanisms, 2005; Genes and Behaviour, 2006; Genetic Effects on Environmental Vulnerability to Disease, 2008; (ed jtly) Policy and Practice Implications from the English and Romanian Adoptees Study, 2009; (ed jtly) Gene-environment Interactions in Developmental Psychopathology, 2011. *Recreations:* fell walking, tennis, wine tasting, theatre, family. *Address:* 190 Court Lane, Dulwich, SE21 7ED. *Club:* Royal Society of Medicine.

**RUTTER, Trevor John,** CBE 1990 (OBE 1976); Assistant Director General, British Council, 1990–91, retired; *b* 26 Jan. 1934; *s* of Alfred Rutter and Agnes Rutter (*née* Purslow); *m* 1959, Josephine Henson (*d* 2009); one *s. Educ:* Monmouth Sch.; Brasenose Coll., Oxford (BA). National Service, Army, 1955–57. British Council, Indonesia, W Germany (Munich), London, 1959–66; First Secretary, Foreign Office, 1967; British Council, 1968–91: Representative: Singapore, 1968–71; Thailand, 1971–75; various appointments, London, 1975–85, including: Head, Home Div., 1980; Asst Dir Gen., 1981–85; Rep. in W Germany, 1986–90. *Address:* 7 Grove Mews, Totnes, Devon TQ9 5GT. *E:* trevorintotnes@gmail.com.

**RUTTLE, (Henry) Stephen (Mayo);** QC 1997; *b* 6 Feb. 1953; *s* of His Honour Henry Samuel Jacob Ruttle and Joyce Mayo Ruttle (*née* Moriarty); *m* 1985, Fiona Jane Mitchell-Innes; two *s* two *d. Educ:* Westminster Sch. (Queen's Schol.); Queens' Coll., Cambridge (BA Hons Eng. Lit. and Law). Called to the Bar, Gray's Inn, 1976, Bencher, 2004; in practice at the Bar, 1976–; practising as commercial and community mediator, 2000– (CEDR accredited mediator, 1998); Chm. of Trustees, Wandsworth Mediation Service, 2005–. A Lieut Bailiff of Guernsey, 2008–. Fellow, Internat. Acad. of Mediators, 2005–. *Recreations:* Church, fly-fishing, the countryside, mountains, oak furniture. *Address:* Brick Court Chambers, 7–8 Essex Street, WC2R 3LD. *T:* (020) 7379 3550, *T:* (020) 7520 9871.

**RYALS, Prof. Lynette Joy,** OBE 2019; PhD; FCILT; Pro Vice-Chancellor, Cranfield University, since 2011, and Director, Cranfield School of Management, since 2017; Chief Executive, MK:U, since 2019 (Programme Director, 2018–19); *b* Sheffield, 13 July 1960; *d* of (Harry) Roy and Joy Evelyn Ryals. *Educ:* Sheffield High Sch. for Girls; St Hugh's Coll., Oxford (BA Hons PPE 1981); Internat. Mgt Centre Europe (MBA 1992); Cranfield Univ. (PhD 2002). FCILT 2014. Fund Manager, Manufacturers Life of Canada, 1982–84; stockbroker: Capel-Cure Myers, 1985–86; Citicorp, 1987–89; Management Consultant: Doctus, 1990–92; Strategic Centre, 1992–97; Lectr, 1997–2006, Prof., 2006–11, Cranfield Univ. FSIP 1986; PFHEA 2014. Trustee: The Stables; Women Leaders Milton Keynes. *Publications:* (jtly) Marketing Management, 2000; (jtly) Customer Relationship Management, 2003; (with Prof. M. McDonald) Key Account Plans, 2008; Managing Customers Profitably, 2008. *Recreations:* volunteer Ambassador for Willen Hospice and Milton Keynes College, swing dancing, singing, occasional dangerous sports, volunteering for Contact the Elderly. *Address:* Executive Office, Cranfield University, Kent House, Cranfield MK43 0AL. *T:* (01234) 758087. *E:* lynette.ryals@cranfield.ac.uk.

**RYAN, Prof. Alan James,** FBA 1986; Professor of Politics, University of Oxford, 1997–2010, now Emeritus; Fellow, New College, Oxford, 1969–2010 (Warden, 1996–2009); Senior Research Fellow in Politics, 2009–10; Hon. Fellow, 2010); *b* 9 May 1940; *s* of James William Ryan and Ivy Ryan; *m* 1971, Kathleen Alyson Lane; one *d. Educ:* Christ's Church; Balliol Coll., Oxford (Hon. Fellow, 2004). Lectr in Politics, Univ. of Keele, 1963–66, Univ. of Essex, 1966–69; Lectr in Politics, 1969–78, Reader, 1978–87, Univ. of Oxford; Prof. of Politics, Princeton Univ., 1988–96; Dir, Rothermere Amer. Inst., Univ. of Oxford, 1999–2002. Visiting Professor in Politics: City University of New York, 1967–68; Univs of Texas, 1972, California, 1977, the Witwatersrand, 1978; Vis. Schol., Princeton Univ., 2009–14; William H. Bonsall Vis. Prof. of Philosophy, Stanford Univ.,

2014–15; Vis. Fellow, ANU, 1974, 1979; Mellon Fellow, Inst. for Advanced Study, Princeton, 1991–92; Fellow, Center for Advanced Study, Stanford, 2002–03; de Carle Lectr, Univ. of Otago, 1983. Official Mem., CNAA, 1975–80. Delegate, Oxford Univ. Press, 1983–87. *Publications:* The Philosophy of John Stuart Mill, 1970, 2nd edn 1987; The Philosophy of the Social Sciences, 1970; J. S. Mill, 1975; Property and Political Theory, 1984; (ed jtly) The Blackwell Encyclopaedia of Political Thought, 1987; Property, 1987; Bertrand Russell: a political life, 1988; John Dewey and the High Tide of American Liberalism, 1995; Liberal Anxieties and Liberal Education, 1998; The Making of Modern Liberalism, 2012; On Politics, 2012; On Machiavelli, 2014; On Aristotle, 2014; On Tocqueville, 2014; On Marx, 2014; On Hobbes, 2015; On Augustine, 2015. *Recreations:* dinghy sailing, long train journeys. *Address:* 21 Cunliffe Close, Oxford OX2 7BJ. *Club:* Oxford and Cambridge.

**RYAN, Prof. Anthony John,** OBE 2006; PhD, DSc; Professor of Physical Chemistry, since 1997, and Director, Grantham Centre for Sustainable Futures, since 2014, University of Sheffield (ICI Professor of Physical Chemistry, 2002–08); *b* 20 March 1962; *s* of Anthony Ryan and Margaret Ryan; *m* 1990, Angela Potts; two *d*. *Educ:* Univ. of Manchester (BSc Hons 1983; PhD 1988); DSc UMIST 2004. Lectr, 1985–88 and 1990–94, Sen. Lectr, 1994–95, Reader, 1995–97, in Polymer Sci. and Technol., UMIST; NATO Res. Fellow, Univ. of Minnesota, 1988–89; Hd, Chemistry Dept, 1998–2003, Pro Vice Chancellor (Faculty of Sci.), 2008–16, Univ. of Sheffield. Mem., STFC, 2017–. Christmas Lectr, Royal Instn, 2002. *Publications:* Polymer Processing: structure development, 1998; Emerging Themes in Polymer Science, 2000; Project Sunshine: how science can use the sun to fuel and feed the world, 2013; (with S. McKevitt) The Solar Revolution: One World, One Solution: providing the energy and food for 10 billion people, 2014. *Recreations:* road and mountain biking, eating, drinking and being merry. *Address:* Department of Chemistry, University of Sheffield, Dainton Building, Sheffield S3 7HF. *T:* (0114) 222 9760, *Fax:* (0114) 222 9774.

**RYAN, Dame Christine,** DBE 2018; CBiol, FRSB; Chief Inspector and Chief Executive Officer, Independent Schools Inspectorate, 2005–17; Partner, Ryan and Grunsell Ltd, since 2017; *b* Kilnhurst, Yorks; *d* of William and Marjorie Parker; *m* 2000, Paul Steadman; one *d*. *Educ:* self-taught after primary sch.; Univ. of Liverpool (BA Chem.); Open Univ. (Cert Ed). CBiol 1982; FRSB 2011. Teacher, 1976–93; Ofsted Registered Inspector, 1993–2009; TV series advr and researcher, 1995–2007; Sci. and Educn Consultant, 2003–06; Chief Exec., ISI Consultancy Ltd, 2010–17. Mem. Bd, Ofqual, 2017–. Mem., Adv. Bd, Educn Investor Global, 2017–. Chair, TalentEd, 2017–. *Publications:* (contrib.) The Chemical Industry, 2nd edn 1994; The New Living Body (Teachers Guide), 1995; Phosgene and Related Carbonyl Halides, 1996; (contrib.) World Class: tackling the ten biggest challenges facing schools today, 2017; contribs to Coordination Chem. Rev. *Recreations:* theatre, movies but nothing that smacks of 'kitchen sink drama', gardening, fly-fishing, weight training, ballroom dancing, having fun with friends and family. *Address:* Ryan & Grunsell Ltd, 23 Telfords Yard, E1W 2BQ. *E:* christine@ryanandgrunsell.com.

**RYAN, David,** CBE 2003; Area Director Designate, Crime, London Region, HM Courts Service, 2004–05; *b* 7 Dec. 1948; *s* of Christopher and Ellen Ryan; *m* 1971, Anna Maria Scumaci; one *s* one *d*. *Educ:* City Grammar Sch., Lincoln. Personnel and Finance Officer, Midland and Oxford Circuit, 1987–92; Courts Administrator, Winchester, 1992–97; Circuit Administrator: Western Circuit, 1997–2003; S Eastern Circuit, 2003–04. *Recreations:* supporting Aston Villa and spectating sports generally, drinking the odd glass of red wine, holidays in Calabria. *Address:* 1 The Paddocks, Ampfield, Romsey, Hants SO51 9BG. *E:* daveandanna123@gmail.com.

**RYAN, Maj.-Gen. Denis Edgar,** CB 1987; Director of Army Education, 1984–87; *b* 18 June 1928; *s* of late Reginald Arthur Ryan and Amelia (née Smith); *m* 1955, Jean Mary Bentley; one *s* one *d*. *Educ:* Sir William Borlase School, Marlow; King's College, London (LLB). Commissioned RAEC, 1950; served BAOR, 1950–54; Instr, RMA Sandhurst, 1954–56; Adjt, Army Sch. of Educn, 1957–59; Staff Coll., 1960; served in Cyprus, Kenya and UK, 1961–67; CAES, HQ 4 Div., BAOR, 1968–70; Cabinet Office, 1970–72; TDA, Staff Coll., 1972–75; Col GS MoD, 1976–78; Chief Education Officer: HQ SE Dist, 1978–79; HQ BAOR, 1979–82; Comd, Education, UK, 1982–84. Col Comdt, RAEC, 1990–92; Dep. Col Comdt, AGC, 1992–93. *Recreations:* cricket, tennis, Rugby, music, theatre.

**RYAN, Sir Derek (Gerald),** 4th Bt *cr* 1919, of Hintlesham, Suffolk; architect; *b* 25 March 1954; *s* of Sir Derek Gerald Ryan, 3rd Bt and of Penelope Anne Hawkings; *S* father, 1990; *m* 1st (marr. diss.); 2nd, 1997, Roberta Tonn (marr. diss. 2000). *Educ:* Univ. of California at Berkeley (BAED 1977). Washington State Architect License #4296, 1984; NCARB Certificate #32,269, 1984; Idaho State Architect License #AR-2623. NBBJ architects and planners, Seattle, WA, 1980–99; Partner Architect, Williams Partners Architects (formerly Jeffrey Charles Williams Architects), Ketchum, ID, 1999–2014; Project Architect, dgrArchitect, 2014–. *Recreations:* ski-ing, guitar. *Heir:* cousin Barry Desmond Ryan [*b* 30 June 1943; *m* 1976, Evodia Massemola; one *s* one *d*]. *Address:* PO Box 6966, Ketchum, ID 83340–6966, USA. *T:* (208) 7204153.

**RYAN, Gerard Charles;** QC 1981; a Recorder of the Crown Court, 1984–98; *b* 16 Dec. 1931; *er s* of Frederick Charles Ryan, Hove, and Louie Violet Ryan (née Ball); *m* 1960, Sheila Morag Clark Cameron, *qv*; two *s*. *Educ:* Clayesmore Sch.; Brighton Coll.; Pembroke Coll., Cambridge (Exhibnr; MA); Inchbald Sch. of Design (Dip. Garden Design 2003). Served RA, 1955–57 (Lieut). Called to the Bar, Middle Temple, 1955, Bencher, 1988; Harmsworth Scholar, 1956; in practice at Common Law Bar, 1957–65, at Parly Bar and Planning and Envmt Bar, 1965–2001. Chm., Tribunal of Inquiry into Loscoe (Derbyshire) gas explosion, 1986–87. Chairman: Soc. of Sussex Downsmen, 1977–80; Murray Downland Trust, 1993–2001 (Jt Founder, 1993). *Publications:* (with A. O. B. Harris) Outline of the Law of Common Land, 1967. *Recreations:* conservation, growing trees and other plants, walking. *Address:* Bayleaves, Bepton, Midhurst, Sussex GU29 9RB.

**RYAN, Rt Hon. Joan (Marie);** PC 2007; MP for Enfield North, 1997–2010 and since 2015 (Lab, 1997–2010, 2015–19; Ind Gp for Change (formerly Change UK), since 2019); consultant in communications and strategy; *b* 8 Sept. 1955; *d* of late Michael Joseph Ryan and Dolores Marie Ryan (née Joyce); *m* 1998, Martin Hegarty; one *s* one *d*, and one step *s* one step *d*. *Educ:* City of Liverpool Coll. of Higher Educn (BA Hons 1979); South Bank Poly. (MSc 1983); Avery Hill Coll. (PGCE 1984). Sociology, Soc. Sci., Religious Studies and Eur. Politics Teacher, and Hd of Year, Hurlingham and Chelsea Secondary Sch., Fulham, 1984–89; Head of Pastoral Educn, Hawksmoor Sixth Form Coll., Fulham, 1989–94; Head of Humanities, William Morris Acad., Hammersmith, 1994–97. Mem. (Lab) Barnet LBC, 1990–98. Contested (Lab) Enfield N, 2010. An Asst Govt Whip, 2002–03; a Lord Comr of HM Treasury (Govt Whip), 2003–06; Parly Under-Sec. of State, Home Office, 2006–07; Special Rep. to Cyprus, 2007–08. Mem., Panel of Chairs, 2016–, Envmtl Audit Cttee, 2016–, H of C. Dir, Labour No 2 AV, 2010–12. CEO, 2010–12, Advr, 2012–15, Global Tamil Forum. Chair, Riders for Health, 2010–15. Oral history interviewer, Imperial War Mus., 1984–86. *Recreations:* visiting historic buildings, cinema, learning to sail. *Address:* House of Commons, SW1A 0AA.

**RYAN, Matthew Richard Goolden;** director and teacher; *b* London, 26 Jan. 1965; *s* of late Brian Tyler and Veronica Foley; partner, Ian Stephenson. *Educ:* Wanstead High Sch.; Sylvia Young Theatre Sch. Actor, theatre, film, TV and radio, 1974–90; theatre includes Peter Pan, Ardele, Cause Célèbre, Forty Years On, West End; Close of Play, NT. Resident/Associate Director, Les Misérables, Miss Saigon, Cameron Mackintosh Ltd, and Aspects of Love, Really Useful Group Ltd, 1988–99; Director: Miss Saigon, Aust. premiere, Netherlands premiere, 1st UK tour; Les Misérables, Australia, Asia, South African premiere, 2nd UK tour; Is There Life After High School?, Bridewell, 2001; Royal Academy of Music, 1999–: They Shoot Horses, Don't They?, Company, Cabaret, Sweeney Todd, Grand Hotel, Assassins, Promises Promises, A Doll's Life, Lady in the Dark, A Little Night Music, Sunday in the Park with George, The Light in the Piazza and Eur. premieres of Jane Eyre, A Man of No Importance, A Catered Affair; Mountview Academy of Theatre Arts, 2000–: Sweet Charity, Carousel, Oklahoma!, Nine, Songs for a New World, The York Realist, The Rink, Hello Again, A Winter's Tale, Pal Joey, First Lady Suite; Stage Entertainment, Netherlands, 2006–09: My Fair Lady (John Kraaijkamp Award for Best Dir), Evita, La Cage aux Folles; London School of Musical Theatre, 2009–: Violet, American Idiot, Carnival, Rent, The Wild Party, Bernarda Alba (Eur. premiere); William Finn's Elegies, Liverpool Inst. of Performing Art, 2011; The Importance of Being Earnest, English Th., Frankfurt, 2011; Dogfight, Southwark Playhouse, 2014; Dogfight in Concert, St James's, 2015; Stay Awake, Jake, Vaults 2016; Calendar Girls, nat. tour, 2018–19. Devised/directed entertainments for Philip Quast, Clare Burt and Frances Ruffelle. Hon. Mem., RAM, 2014. *Recreations:* theatre, reading, classic cinema, music, cooking and entertaining. *E:* mryanlondon@aol.com.

**RYAN, Michael James,** CBE 2005; FREng; Chief Operating Officer, Aerostructures, Bombardier Aviation, since 2018; *b* 14 Aug. 1959; *s* of Patrick and Maeve Ryan; *m* 1986, Mary Gibson; two *s* one *d*. *Educ:* Queen's Univ., Belfast (BSc Hons Aeronautical Engrg). CEng 1992; FRAeS 2003; FREng 2014. Joined Short Brothers, 1981: Develt Engr, 1981–84; Prodn Engr, 1985–87; Prodn Engrg Manager, 1988–89; Bombardier Aerospace, then Bombardier Aerostructures and Engineering Services: Ops Manager, 1990–93; Dir of Manufg, 1993–97; Procurement Dir, 1997–99; Gen. Manager Procurement, Montreal, 1999–2000; Vice Pres. and Gen. Manager, 2000–17; Pres., 2017–18. Council Mem., SBAC, 2000–09; Mem. Council and Operating Bd, ADS, 2009– (Vice Pres., Aero, 2016–). Chm., Belfast Citywide (formerly W Belfast/Gtr Shankhill) Employers' Forum, 2005–; Member: Bd, BITC, NI, 2000– (Chm., 2005–09); Bd, Centre for Competitiveness, 2000–13; Aerospace Growth Partnership Bd, 2011–. Pres. NI Br., RAeS, 2004–05. Hon. FRAeS 2016. Hon. DSc(Eng) QUB, 2009; Hon. DSc Ulster, 2015. *Recreations:* keeping fit, reading, music, art, travel. *Address:* Bombardier Aviation, Belfast, Airport Road, Belfast BT3 9DZ. *T:* (028) 9073 3553, *Fax:* (028) 9073 3143. *E:* michael.ryan@aero.bombardier.com.

**RYAN, Peter James,** QPM 1991; management consultant; Principal Security Advisor: International Olympic Committee, 2000–15; Athens 2004 Olympic Games, 2002–04; Turin, 2006, Beijing, 2008, Vancouver, 2010, London, 2012, Sochi, 2014; *b* 18 May 1944; *s* of late Lawrence Joseph Ryan and of Margaret Jane (née Stephenson); *m* 1985, Adrienne Margaret Butterworth; two *d*. *Educ:* Newman Coll., Preston; Univ. of Lancaster (BA Hons); Preston Poly. (DMS); Open Univ. (MSc). FIPM 1994. Lancs Constabulary, 1963–83; Metropolitan Police, 1983–84; Asst Chief Constable, N Yorks Police, 1984–88; Dep. Chief Constable, Durham Constabulary, 1988–90; Chief Constable, Norfolk, 1990–93; Nat. Dir of Police Trng and Comdt Police Staff Coll., 1993–96; Comr of Police for NSW, 1996–2002. Dir for Infrastructure and Resilience, Hyder Consulting, 2006–08; CEO, Crystal Professional Development, 2009–10. Advr, Bd, Canadian Centre for Emergency Preparedness, 2002–04; Member, Advisory Board: UN/WHO Pandemics and Mass Gatherings, 2010–12; Internat. Centre for Sports Security, 2010–16. Sec., 1991–92, Chm., 1992–93, Personnel & Trng Cttee, ACPO. Mem., BTEC, 1985–88. Vis. Fellow, UEA Sch. of Educn, 1993–96; Grad., FBI Nat. Exec. Inst., 1994. Pres., Assoc. of Eur. Police Colls, 1996; Vice Pres., Police Mutual Assurance Soc., 1994–96. Asst Dir Gen., St John Ambulance, 1995. FCMI (FIMgt 1980); FCIPD 1990; MAICD 2002. FRSA 1992. Hon. LLD Macquarie, 2000. OStJ 1995. *Publications:* (with Sue Williams) The Inside Story (autobiog.), 2002. *Recreations:* occasional golf, reading. *Address:* 2 Chopping Knife Lane, Marlborough, Wilts SN8 2FA. *Club:* Royal Sydney Yacht Squadron.

**RYAN, Sheila Morag Clark, (Mrs G. C. Ryan);** *see* Cameron, S. M. C.

**RYAN, Prof. Terence John,** DM; FRCP; Clinical Professor of Dermatology, Oxford University, 1992–97, now Emeritus Professor; Fellow, Green College, 1979–97, now Emeritus Fellow; *b* 24 July 1932; *s* of Gerald John Ryan and Kathleen May (née Knight); *m* 1968, Trudie Anne Merry; one *s* one *d*. *Educ:* numerous schs including: Michael Hall (Rudolf Steiner); Brickwall Sch., Northiam; Worcester Coll., Oxford (BM, BCh 1957; DM 1977). FRCP 1975. Capt. RAMC, 1955–60: Officer i/c Dept of Dermatol. and ENT Surgery, Colchester Mil. Hosp.; Radcliffe Infirmary, Oxford: Hse Officer, 1958; Registrar and Sen. Registrar in Dermatol., 1962–68; Lectr and Sen. Lectr, Inst. of Dermatol., London Univ., 1967–71; Dept of Dermatol., RPMS, 1968–71; Lectr in Dermatology, Oxford Univ., 1971–92. Cons. Dermatologist, 1969–97, Hon. Cons., 1997–, Oxon HA. Vis. Prof., Brookes Univ., Oxford, 1991–; Adjunct Professor: Jefferson Univ., Philadelphia, 1988–; Univ. of Limerick, 2007–; Univ. of Minneapolis, 2012–; Hon. Prof., Nanjing, 2003–. Med. Advr, St Francis Leprosy Guild, 1987–2012; Advr, Morbidity Control, Global Alliance to Eliminate Lymphatic Filariasis, 2003–. Promoter, Sine Lepra and Healthy Skin for All programmes, Internat. League of Dermatologists, 1987–2002; Dir, Fuel Initiatives Resources Strategies Technologies, 1988–; Chm., Skin Care for All Taskforce, 2008–. Pres., Section of Dermatol., RSocMed, 1990. Mem., Internat. Cttee of Dermatol., 1987–2002; Pres., Internat. Soc. for Dermatol., 1994–99 (Hon. Pres., 1999; Chm., Skin Care for All: Community Dermatol. Task Force, 2010–); Chm., Internat. Foundn for Dermatol., 1997–2002. Trustee: Oxford Internat. Biomedical Centre, 1999–; Arts Dyslexia Trust, 1999–2012; British Skin Foundn, 1999. Hon. Mem., various foreign nat. socs of dermatol. Hon. DM Martin Luther Univ., Halle-Wittenberg, 2007; Hon. DSc Hull, 2013. Gold Medal: Eur. Tissue Repair Soc., 1995; Brit. Assoc. Dermatology, 1997; Curatorium Angiologiae Internationalis, 2002; Brazilian Acad. Medicine, 2003. KStJ 1984 (County Surgeon Comr, then Comdr, SJAB, Oxon). *Publications:* (contrib.) Oxford Textbook of Medicine, 3rd edn 1995 to 5th edn 2002; (contrib.) White Paper Wounds and Lymphoedema, 2010; contrib. textbooks of dermatology and numerous in field of blood supply and lymphatics, dermatology and internat. dermatological policy. *Recreations:* painting water-colours, flowers, piano playing, foreign travel. *Address:* 7 Foxbury Place, Great Bedwyn, Marlborough, Wilts SN8 3PL.

**RYAN, Prof. William Francis,** DPhil; FSA; FBA 2000; Librarian, 1976–2002, Emeritus Professor, 2003, and Hon. Fellow, since 2003, Warburg Institute, and Professor of Russian Studies, School of Advanced Study, 2000–02, University of London; *b* 13 April 1937; *s* of William Gerard Ryan and Marjorie Ellen Ryan; *m* 1st, 1963, Marina Guterman (marr. diss. 1970); two *d*; 2nd, 1986, Janet Margaret Hartley; one *s* one *d*. *Educ:* Bromley GS for Boys; Oriel Coll., Oxford (MA; DPhil 1970). FSA 1972. Editor, Clarendon Press, Oxford, 1963–65; Asst Curator, Mus. of Hist. of Science, Oxford, 1965–67; Lectr in Russian Lang. and Lit., SSEES, London Univ., 1967–76. President: Folklore Soc., 2005–08; Hakluyt Soc.,

2008–11. Dhc Russian Acad. of Scis, 2007. *Publications:* (with Peter Norman) The Penguin Russian Dictionary, 1995; The Bathhouse at Midnight: an historical survey of magic and divination in Russia, Stroud and University Park PA, 1999. *Address:* Warburg Institute, Woburn Square, WC1H 0AB. *E:* will.ryan.home@gmail.com.

**RYCROFT, Matthew John,** CBE 2003; HM Diplomatic Service; Permanent Secretary, Department for International Development, since 2018; *b* 16 June 1968; *s* of Prof. Michael John Rycroft, *qv*; *m* 1997, Alison Emma Victoria Semple; three *d. Educ:* Merton Coll., Oxford (BA Maths and Philos. 1989). Joined FCO, 1989; Third Sec., Geneva, 1990; Third, then Second, Sec. (Chancery), Paris, 1991–95; First Sec., FCO, 1995–98; First Sec. (Political), Washington, 1998–2002; Private Sec. for Foreign Affairs to the Prime Minister, 2002–04; Ambassador to Bosnia and Herzegovina, 2005–08; Dir, EU, later Europe, FCO, 2008–11; Chief Operating Officer, FCO, 2011–14; Perm. Rep. and Ambassador to the UN, New York, 2015–18. *Address:* c/o Department for International Development, 22 Whitehall, SW1A 2EG. *E:* pspermsec@dfid.gov.uk.

**RYCROFT, Prof. Michael John,** PhD; Proprietor, Cambridge Atmospheric, Environmental and Space Activities and Research Consultancy, since 1998; Professor, International Space University, France, 1995–2014 (part-time, 1998–2014), now Emeritus; *b* 15 July 1938; *s* of late John Lambert Rycroft and Molly Elizabeth Rycroft (*née* Riglen); *m* 1967, Mary Cheeseright; three *s. Educ:* Merchant Taylors' School, Northwood; Imperial Coll., London (BSc Hons Physics); Churchill Coll., Cambridge (PhD Met. Physics). CPhys, MInstP; FIMA; FRAS. Lectr, Dept of Physics, Univ. of Southampton, 1966–79; Head, Atmospheric Scis Div., NERC British Antarctic Survey, Cambridge, 1979–90; Prof. of Aerospace, 1990–94, Hd, Coll. of Aeronautics, 1990–92, Cranfield Inst. of Technol., subseq. Cranfield Univ. Visiting Professor: Dept of Physics, Univ. of Houston, 1974–75; Cranfield Univ., 1995–2016; De Montfort Univ., 1998–2003); Vis. Sen. Fellow, Univ. of Bath, 2005–. Gen. Sec., Eur. Geophysical Soc., 1996–2003. Mem., Internat. Acad. of Astronautics, 1986; MAE 2000. Editor-in-Chief: Jl of Atmospheric and Solar-Terrestrial Physics, 1989–99; Surveys in Geophysics, 2001–. Hon. DSc De Montfort, 1998. *Publications:* (with D. Shapland) Spacelab: research in Earth orbit, 1984; (ed) Cambridge Encyclopedia of Space, 1990; (with G. Genta) Space, the Final Frontier?, 2003; (with V. Y. Trakhtengerts) Whistler and Alfvén Mode Cyclotron Masers in Space, 2008; 250 pubns on atmospheric and space sci. and related fields. *Recreations:* music, gardening, wining and dining. *Address:* Bassett Mead, 35 Millington Road, Cambridge CB3 9HW. *T:* (01223) 353839. *E:* michaelrycroft@btinternet.com.
See also M. J. Rycroft.

**RYCROFT, Philip John,** CB 2014; DPhil; Second Permanent Secretary and Head of UK Governance Group, Cabinet Office, 2015–19; Permanent Secretary, Department for Exiting the European Union, 2017–19 (Second Permanent Secretary, 2017); *b* 22 May 1961; *s* of John and Shirley Rycroft; *m* 1989, Kate Richards; two *s. Educ:* Leys Sch., Cambridge; Wadham Coll., Oxford (MA; DPhil 1988). Scottish Office: Res. Div., Agric. Dept, 1989–90; Private Sec. to Scottish Office Agric. and Fisheries Minister, 1990–91; Principal: European Support Unit, Industry Dept, 1992–94; Fisheries Gp, Fisheries Policy Branch, 1994; Cabinet of Sir Leon Brittan, EC, 1995–97; Scottish Office: Hd, Agricl Policy Co-ordination and Rural Develt Div. and IT Support Div., Agric., Envmt and Fisheries Dept, 1997–98; Hd, Mgt Gp Support Staff Unit, 1998–99; Dep. Hd, Scottish Exec. Policy Unit, 1999–2000; Public Affairs Manager, Scottish & Newcastle plc, 2000–02; Hd, Schs Gp, Scottish Exec. Educn Dept, 2002–06; Hd of Scottish Exec. Enterprise, Transport and Lifelong Learning Dept, 2006–07; Dir-Gen., Educn, Scottish Exec., later Scottish Govt, 2007–09; Dir-Gen., Business and Innovation, DIUS, later Dir-Gen., Innovation and Enterprise, and Chief Exec., Better Regulation Exec., BIS, 2009–11; Dir, Corporate Affairs, Hutchison Whampoa Ltd, 2011–12; Dir Gen., Dep. Prime Minister's Office, Cabinet Office, 2012–15. *Recreations:* hill-walking, woodwork, triathlon. *Address:* Lady's Field, Whitekirk, Dunbar, E Lothian EH42 1XS.

**RYCROFT, Sir Richard (John),** 8th Bt *cr* 1784, of Calton, Yorkshire; *b* 15 June 1946; *s* of Cdre Henry Richard Rycroft, OBE, DSC, RN, 4th *s* of 5th Bt, and Penelope Gwendoline Rycroft (*née* Evans-Lombe); *S* cousin, 1999. *Educ:* Sherborne. RNLI Burnham-on-Crouch: mem., inshore lifeboat crew, 1987–96; Dep. Launching Authy, 1996–2005; Lifeboat Operations Manager, 2005–16. Dep. Chm., Burnham-on-Crouch Br., RNLI, 2016–. *Recreations:* sailing, classic boats and cars, jazz music, Burmese cats. *Heir: cousin* Francis Edward Rycroft [*b* 4 Aug. 1950; *m* 1975, Cherry Willmott; one *s* one *d*]. *Club:* Royal Corinthian Yacht.

**RYDER,** family name of **Earl of Harrowby** and of **Baron Ryder of Wensum.**

**RYDER OF WENSUM,** Baron *cr* 1997 (Life Peer), of Wensum in the co. of Norfolk; **Richard Andrew Ryder,** OBE 1981; PC 1990; Chairman, Child Bereavement UK, since 2013; *b* 4 Feb. 1949; *s* of late Richard Stephen Ryder, JP, DL and Margaret MacKenzie; *m* 1981, Caroline Mary, CVO, MBE, *o d* of Sir David Stephens; one *d* (one *s* decd). *Educ:* Radley; Magdalene Coll., Cambridge (BA Hons History, 1971). Journalist. Chm., Eastern Counties Radio, 1997–2001; Vice-Chm., Bd of Govs, BBC, 2002–04 (Acting Chm., 2004). Dir, Great Bradley Farms Co. and other businesses, 2002–. Political Secretary: to Leader of the Opposition, 1975–79; to Prime Minister, 1979–81. Contested (C) Gateshead E, Feb. and Oct., 1974. MP (C) Mid Norfolk, 1983–97. Parliamentary Private Secretary: to Financial Sec. to the Treasury, 1984; to Sec. of State for Foreign and Commonwealth Affairs, 1984–86; an Asst Govt Whip, 1986–88; Parly Under-Sec. of State, MAFF, 1988–89; Econ. Sec. to HM Treasury, 1989–90; Paymaster General, 1990; Parly Sec. to HM Treasury and Govt Chief Whip, 1990–95. Chm., Cons. Foreign and Commonwealth Council, 1984–89. Chm., UCanDoIT, 2011–14. Chm., Bd of Mgt, Inst. of Cancer Res., 2005–13. Trustee: Estorick Foundn, 2000–12; Baroness Ryder of Warsaw Meml Trust, 2001–11. *Address:* House of Lords, SW1A 0PW.
See also C. B. Stephens.

**RYDER, Edward Alexander,** CB 1992; HM Chief Inspector of Nuclear Installations, Health and Safety Executive, 1985–91; Joint Chairman and Head of UK Delegation, Channel Tunnel Safety Authority, 1992–97; *b* 9 Nov. 1931; *s* of Alexander Harry and Gwendoline Gladys Ryder; *m* 1956, Janet (*d* 2005); one *s* one *d. Educ:* Cheltenham Grammar School; Bristol University (BSc). CPhys; FInstP. Flying Officer, RAF, 1953–55; Engineer, GEC Applied Electronics Labs, 1955–57; Control Engineer, Hawker Siddeley Nuclear Power Co., 1957–61; Sen. Engineer, CEGB, 1961–71; Principal Inspector, then Superintending Inspector, HM Nuclear Installations Inspectorate, 1971–80; Head of Hazardous Installations Policy Branch, 1980–85, Head of Nuclear Installations Policy Branch, 1985, HSE. Sec., Adv. Cttee on Major Hazards, 1980–85. Chairman: HSC Working Gp on Ionising Radiations, 1987–91; IAEA Nuclear Safety Standards Adv. Gp, 1988–93; Mem., Intergovtl Commn for Channel Tunnel, 1992–97. Organiser, Shiplake and Dunsden Area, RBL Poppy Appeal, 1996–2003. Mem., Shiplake Parish Council, 1999–2011 (Vice-Chm., 2000–03 and 2007–11; Chm., 2003–05). *Recreations:* golf—or is it nature study, concertgoing, bridge. *Address:* Pinewood, Baskerville Lane, Lower Shiplake, Henley on Thames, Oxon RG9 3JY.

**RYDER, Rt Hon. Sir Ernest (Nigel),** Kt 2004; PC 2013; TD 1996; **Rt Hon. Lord Justice Ryder;** DL; a Lord Justice of Appeal, since 2013; Senior President of Tribunals, since 2015; *b* 9 Dec. 1957; *s* of Dr John Buckley Ryder, TD and Constance Ryder; *m* 1990, Janette Lynn Martin; one *d. Educ:* Bolton Sch.; Peterhouse, Cambridge (MA 1983). Merchant banker, Grindley Brandt & Co., 1979; called to the Bar, Gray's Inn, 1981, Bencher, 2004; QC 1997; Asst Recorder, 1997–2000; a Recorder, 2000–04; a Dep. High Court Judge, 2001–04; a Judge of the High Ct of Justice, Family Div., 2004–13; Family Div. Liaison Judge, 2005–09; Presiding Judge, Northern Circuit, 2009–13; Judge in Charge of Modernisation of Family Justice, 2011–13. Associate WS, Scotland, 2017–. Counsel, N Wales Tribunal of Inquiry, 1996–99. Asst Boundary Comr, 2000–04. Commnd Duke of Lancaster's Own Yeomanry, 1981; Sqdn Leader, 1990; Sqdn Leader, Royal Mercian and Lancastrian Yeomanry, 1992. Chancellor, 2014–17, now Chancellor Emeritus, Prof. of Strategic Mgt of the Law, 2015–, Univ. of Bolton; Hon. Prof. of Law, Univ. of Lancaster, 2018–; Vis. Fellow, Nuffield Coll., Oxford, 2018–. Hon. Mem., Soc. of Legal Scholars, 2018–. Trustee, Nuffield Foundn, 2014–. DL Greater Manchester, 2009. FRSA 2010. Hon. LLD: Bolton, 2013; Lancaster, 2017. *Recreations:* listening, walking. *Address:* Royal Courts of Justice, Strand, WC2A 2LL.

**RYDER, Janet;** Member (Plaid Cymru) North Wales, National Assembly for Wales, 1999–2011; *b* Sunderland, 21 June 1955; *m* 1977, Peter Ryder (marr. diss. 2005); two *s* one *d. Educ:* Northern Counties Coll. of Educn (Teacher's Cert. (Dist.)); Open Univ. (BA Hist./Arts). Teacher: Little Weighton Co. Primary Sch., E Riding of Yorks, 1980–83; St Bede's Catholic Primary Sch., Hull, 1987–88; Coleford Primary Sch., Hull (i/c Religious and Moral Educn), 1988–89; Bransholme Youth Club, Hull. Member: N Wales Fire Authy, 1995–99; Bd, Denbighshire Voluntary Services Council, 1995–99. Mem., voluntary gps, incl. Strategic Planning Gp for People with a Learning Difficulty. Member (Plaid Cymru): Rhuthun Town Council, 1992–2003 (Mayor, 1998–2000); Denbighshire CC, 1994–99 (mem., various cttees; Chairman: Children and Families Sub-cttee, 1995–98; Denbigh Early Years Partnership, 1996–98; Denbigh Plan Partnership). National Assembly for Wales: Plaid Cymru spokesperson on local govt, planning, housing, envmt and transport, 1999–2001, on local govt and finance, 2001–03, on educn and life-long learning, 2003–09. Mem., Nat. Exec., Plaid Cymru, 1993–99, 2006–10.

**RYDER, John;** QC 2000; a Recorder, since 2000; *m* 1989, Carolyn Espley; one *d. Educ:* Monmouth Sch. Called to the Bar, Inner Temple, 1980; Asst Recorder, 1997–2000. *Recreations:* riding, ski-ing, opera. *Address:* 21 College Hill, EC4R 2RP. *Club:* Travellers.

**RYDER, Michael,** CMG 2007; HM Diplomatic Service, retired; Chief Executive, Royal Society for Asian Affairs, since 2017; *b* Manchester, 13 Nov. 1953; *s* of Bill and Vera Ryder; *m* Dr Frances Klemperer; one *s* one *d. Educ:* Marple Hall Grammar Sch. for Boys; Trinity Hall, Cambridge (BA 1976). Harkness Fellow, Johns Hopkins Univ., 1977–79; history supervisor, Cambridge Univ., 1979–82; Lectr, Osaka Gakuin Univ., 1982–84; entered FCO, 1984; various posts, FCO, 1984–97; Hd, Security Policy Dept, FCO, 1997; Special Rep. for Internat. Drug Issues, 1998–2003; Hd, Iraq Inquiry Unit, FCO and Dep. Sec., Butler Inquiry into Intelligence on Weapons of Mass Destruction in Iraq, 2003–04; Minister and Dep. Hd of Mission, Kabul, 2006–07; UK Sen. Civilian Rep. in Helmand, 2008; UK Special Envoy to Republic of Mali, 2009; Special Rep. for Sudan, 2010–12; UK Special Rep. for Deportations with Assurances, 2015–19. Dir, Avera Consulting Ltd, 2012–; non-executive Director: Knowledge Unlatched, 2013–18; KUResearch, 2018–. Chm., Peace Direct, 2013–. *Publications:* contrib. articles to Histl Jl, Notes and Queries. *Recreations:* mountain walking, reading.

**RYDER, Dr Peter,** CB 1994; FRMets; consultant in environmental information services, 1996–2018; *b* 10 March 1942; *s* of Percival Henry Sussex Ryder and Bridget (*née* McCormack); *m* 1965, Jacqueline Doris Sylvia Rigby; two *s* one *d. Educ:* Yorebridge Grammar Sch., Askrigg; Univ. of Leeds (BSc 1963; PhD 1966). FRMets 2004. Research Asst, Physics Dept, Univ. of Leeds, 1966–67; Meteorological Office, 1967–96: Asst Dir, Cloud Physics Res., 1976–82; Asst Dir, Systems Develt, 1982–84; Dep. Dir, Observational Services, 1984–88; Dep. Dir, Forecasting Services, 1988–89; Dir of Services, 1989–90; Dep. Chief Exec. and Dir of Ops, then Man. Dir (Ops), 1990–96. Royal Meteorological Society: Mem. Council, 1980–83; Mem., Qly Jl Editing Cttee, 1981–84; Gen. Sec., 2001–06; Hon. Mem., 2007. Chairman: Thames Regl Flood Defence Cttee, EA, 2003–09 (Mem., 1997–2003); EuroGOOS, 2003–08; Scientific Adv. Panel, Marine Protected Areas, DEFRA, 2009–12. William Gaskell Meml Medal, RMetS, 1981; L. G. Groves Meml Prize for Meteorology, MoD, 1982. *Publications:* papers in learned jls on experimental atmospheric physics and meteorology. *Recreations:* gardening, fishing, photography, grandchildren.

**RYDER, Dr Richard Hood Jack Dudley;** author, campaigner; *b* 3 July 1940; *s* of late Major D. C. D. Ryder, JP, Rempstone Hall, and Vera Mary (*née* Cook); *m* 1974, Audrey Jane Smith (marr. diss. 1999); one *s* one *d. Educ:* Sherborne Sch.; Cambridge Univ. (MA; PhD 1993); Edinburgh Univ. (DCP); Columbia Univ., NY (Fellow). AFBPsS; FZS. Sen. Clinical Psychologist, Warneford Hosp., Oxford, 1967–84; Principal Clin. Psychologist, St James Hosp., Portsmouth, 1983–84. Chm., Oxford Div. of Clin. Psych., 1981–83. Member: Oxford Regional Adolescent Service, 1971–84; DHSS Health Adv. Service, 1977–78. Dir, Radon Control Ltd, 1990–95; Chm., Animal Books and Media Ltd, 2012–. Royal Society for Prevention of Cruelty to Animals: Mem. Council, 1972– (Chm., 1977–79 and 2002–03); Vice-Chm., 1990–91); Dep. Treas., 2000–01; Chairman: Political Cttee, 1979–80; Animal Experimentation Adv. Cttee, 1983–85; Public Relns and Campaign Cttee, 1990–91; Scientific Cttee, 1992–; Internat. Cttee, 1999–. Dep. Chm., Cttee on Welfare of Animals in Psychology, BPsS, 2001–. Political Consultant, 1991–93, Dir, 1993–97, Political Animal Lobby Ltd. Founder Mem., Gen. Election Co-ordinating Cttee on Animal Protection, 1978; Founder, Eurogroup for Animal Welfare, 1979; Pres., British Union for Abolition of Vivisection, 1980; Prog. Organiser, 1984–91, Dir of Animal Welfare Studies, 1997–2000, IFAW; UK Delegate, Eurogroup, 1980, 2002. Chm., Liberal Animal Welfare Gp, 1981–88; Member: Liberal Party Council, 1983–87; Liberal Party Policy Panels on defence, health, home affairs, Eur. affairs, foreign affairs, environment, 1981–88; contested (L): Buckingham, 1983; Teignbridge, 1987. Pres., Lib Dems Animal Protection Gp, 1989–91. Chairman: Teignbridge NSPCC, 1984–87; Teignbridge Home Start, 1987–89; Strategic Animal Welfare Panel, RSPCA, 2009. Mellon Prof., Dept of Philosophy, Tulane Univ., New Orleans, 1996. Broadcaster and writer on psychological, ethical, political and animal protection subjects. Trustee, NT, 2001–04. Mem. Cttee, British Conifer Soc., 2005–11 (Chm., 2008–10). Co-founder of business, Psychoprofiles, 2005. FRSA 1992. *Publications:* Speciesism, 1970; Victims of Science, 1975, 2nd edn 1984; (ed) Animal Rights—a Symposium, 1979; Animal Revolution: changing attitudes to speciesism, 1989, 2nd edn 2000; Painism, 1990; (ed) Animal Welfare and the Environment, 1992; The Political Animal, 1998; Painism: a modern morality, 2001; The Calcrafts of Rempstone Hall, 2005; Putting Morality Back into Politics, 2006; Nelson, Hitler and Diana, 2009; Speciesism, Painism and Happiness: a morality for the twenty-first century, 2011; The Black Pimpernel, 2013; Inside Their Heads: psychological profiles of famous people, 2015; Appeasement and Revenge: the Cambridge spies and today's terrorism, 2018. *Recreations:* trees, opera, philosophy, psychobiography. *Address:* 11 The Imperial, Exeter EX4 4AJ. *T:* (01392) 426727. *Club:* National Liberal.

**RYDSTRÖM, Marilyn**, OBE 2009; Director General, People's Dispensary for Sick Animals, 1999–2008; *b* 24 Oct. 1947; *d* of Kenneth Oberg and Averil Irene Oberg (*née* Harding); *m* 1985, Björn Lennart Rydström. *Educ:* Guildford Co. Tech. Coll.; Bedford Coll., London Univ. (BSc Hons Sociol.). Churchill Fellow, 1984. Probation Officer, Surrey Probation Service, 1971–72; Social Worker, Surrey CC, 1972–74; Sen. Social Worker, Borough of Hillingdon, 1974–77; Hd of Community Projects, Capital Radio Plc, 1977–87; Dir, Fundraising, RNID, 1987–89; Consultant, Chapter One Ketchum Fundraising, 1989–92; Mktg/Commercial Dir, Stowe Sch., 1992–95; Dir, Client Services, Guide Dogs for the Blind, 1995–99. Mem., Crime Prevention Adv. Cttee, NACRO, 1979–83. Member: Grants Cttee, Help a London Child, 1977–84; Mgt Cttee, Piccadilly Advice Centre, 1978–82; Mgt Cttee, Alone in London, 1979–82. The Prince's Trust: Member: NW London Cttee, 1982–90 (Chm., 1987–90); Council, 1986–88; Strategy Gp for London, 1989–90. Member: Lord Chancellor's Adv. Cttee to appoint Shropshire JPs, 2010–12; Lord Chancellor's West Mercia Adv. Cttee, 2012–13; Shropshire Adv. Sub-Cttee, 2012–13. Dir, Severn Promotions Ltd, 2007–. Founding Trustee and Mem., Mgt Cttee, Artsline, 1983–85; Director and Trustee: Severn Hospice Ltd, 2007–16; Marine Conservation Soc., 2010–14. CCMI 2007. *Publications:* various articles/features of social/health interest in women's press. *Recreations:* marine biology and marine conservation, scuba diving, wildlife photography. *E:* marilynrydstrom@aol.com.

**RYKWERT, Prof. Joseph**, CBE 2014; MA (Cantab); DrRCA; Paul Philippe Cret Professor of Architecture, University of Pennsylvania, 1988–98, now Emeritus; *b* 5 April 1926; *s* of Szymon Rykwert and Elizabeth Melup; *m* 1st, 1960 (marr. diss. 1967); 2nd, 1972, Anne-Marie Sandersley; one *s* one *d*. *Educ:* Charterhouse; Bartlett Sch. of Architecture; Architectural Assoc. (Hon. Fellow 2013). Lectr, Hochschule für Gestaltung, Ulm, 1958; Librarian and Tutor, Royal Coll. of Art, 1961–67; Prof. of Art, Univ. of Essex, 1967–80; Lectr on Arch., 1980–85, Reader, 1985–88, Univ. of Cambridge. Bollingen Fellow, 1966; Inst. for Arch. and Urban Studies, NY, 1969–71; Sen. Fellow, Council of Humanities, Princeton Univ., 1971; Visiting Professor: Institut d'Urbanisme, Univ. of Paris, 1974–76; Princeton Univ., 1977; Andrew Mellon Vis. Prof., Cooper Union, NY, 1977; Slade Prof. of Fine Art, Cambridge Univ., 1979–80; Vis. Fellow, Darwin Coll., Cambridge, 1979–80; Mem., Trinity Hall, Cambridge, 1980–; Sen. Fellow, Center for the Advanced Studies in the Visual Arts. Nat. Gall. of Art, Washington; Vis. Prof., Univ. of Louvain, 1981–84; George Lurcy Vis. Prof., Columbia, 1986; Sen. Schol., Getty Res. Inst. in Hist. of Art and Humanities, 1992–93; British Acad. Vis. Prof., Univ. of Bath, 1998–99. Pres., Comité Internat. des Critiques d'Architecture, 1996–. Mem. Commn, Venice Biennale, 1974–78. Consultant, Min. of Urban Develt and Ecology, Republic of Mexico, 1986–88. Co-ed., RES (Anthropology and Aesthetics), 1981–. Member: Accademia Clementina, 1992; Accademia di S Luca, 1993; Polish Acad. of Arts and Scis, 1998. Hon. FRA 2011. Hon. DSc: Edinburgh, 1995; Bath, 2000; Hon. Dr: Córdoba, Argentina, 1998; Rome, 2005; Toronto, 2005; Trieste 2008; Bologna, 2016. Alfred Jurzykowski Foundn Award, 1990; Medalla de Oro en las Bellas Artes, Spain, 2009; Royal Gold Medal, RIBA, 2014. Chevalier des Arts et des Lettres, 1984. *Publications:* The Golden House, 1947; (ed) The Ten Books of Architecture, by L. B. Alberti (annotated edn of Leoni trans. of 1756), 1955, new translation from Latin, as On the Art of Building in Ten Books, 1988; The Idea of a Town, 1963, 3rd edn 1988; Church Building, 1966; On Adam's House in Paradise, 1972, 2nd edn 1982; (ed) Parole nel Vuoto, by A. Loos, 1972; The First Moderns, 1980; The Necessity of Artifice, 1981; (with Anne Rykwert) The Brothers Adam, 1985; The Dancing Column, 1996; The Seduction of Place, 2000, 2nd edn 2004; The Judicious Eye, 2008; contrib. Arch. Rev., Burlington Mag., Lotus. *Recreation:* rare. *Address:* 26A Wedderburn Road, NW3 5QG. *Club:* Savile.

**RYLANCE, His Honour John Randolph Trevor**; a Circuit Judge, 2003–14; a Deputy Circuit Judge, 2014–19; *b* 26 Feb. 1944; *s* of late Dr Ralph Curzon Rylance and Margaret Joan Clare Rylance (*née* Chambers); *m* 1974, Philippa Anne Bailey; two *d*. *Educ:* Shrewsbury Sch. Hon. Lieut, French Navy, 1962–63. Called to the Bar, Lincoln's Inn, 1968; Parly Res. Asst to Sir Edward Gardner, QC, MP, 1971–73; Asst Recorder, 1989–93; a Recorder, 1993–2003. Ind. Person pursuant to Localism Act 2011, Section 28, London Bor. of Hammersmith and Fulham, 2019–. Gov., Fulham Cross Sch., 1977–88. Mem. Exec. Cttee, Fulham Soc., 1988–2012. Trustee, Fulham Palace Trust, 1991–2012 (Chm., 1996–2011). *Address:* 28 Doneraile Street, SW6 6EN. *Club:* Hurlingham.

**RYLANCE, Prof. Richard William**, PhD; Dean and Chief Executive, School of Advanced Study, since 2017, and Pro-Vice Chancellor (Research), since 2017, University of London (Pro-Dean, 2016–17); Director, Institute of English Studies, 2016–17); *b* Manchester, 30 Jan. 1954; *s* of John and Doreen Rylance; *m*; one *d*. *Educ:* Bury Grammar Sch., Lancs; Univ. of Leicester (BA 1st Cl. English; PGCE 1981; PhD 1990). Lectr, Principal Lectr, Prof. and Dean, Anglia Poly. Univ., 1985–2002; Prof., 2003–15, now Hon. Prof., Hd of English, 2005, Hd, Sch. of Arts, Languages and Literatures, 2005–, Univ. of Exeter; Chief Exec., AHRC (on secondment), 2009–15. Chair: Council for Coll. and Univ. English, 2000–03; Sub-panel for English, RAE 2008; Exec., Res. Councils UK, 2011–15. *Publications:* Roland Barthes, 1994; Victorian Psychology and British Culture 1850–1880, 2000; Literature and the Public Good, 2016; contribs to jls and acad. books. *Recreations:* long distance hill walking, scuba diving, music, Manchester City Football Club. *Address:* School of Advanced Study, Senate House, Malet Street, WC1E 7HU. *E:* rick.rylance@sas.ac.uk.

**RYLAND, His Honour Timothy Richard Godfrey Fetherstonhaugh**; a Circuit Judge, 1988–2008; a Judge at Central London Civil Trial Centre (formerly Central London County Court), 1994–2008; *b* 13 June 1938; *s* of late Richard Desmond Fetherstonhaugh Ryland and Frances Katharine Vernon Ryland; *m* 1991, Jean Margaret Muirhead. *Educ:* St Andrew's Coll.; TCD (BA (Moderatorship), LLB). Called to Bar, Gray's Inn, 1961. Dep. Circuit Judge, 1978; a Recorder, 1983–88. *Recreations:* opera, wine. *Club:* Kildare Street and University (Dublin).

**RYLANDS, Rt Rev. Mark James**; Area Bishop of Shrewsbury, 2009–18; Priest-in-charge, Ashburton and Moorland Team Ministry, since 2018; an Honorary Assistant Bishop, Diocese of Exeter, since 2018; *b* 11 July 1961; *m* 1986, Amanda Byrom (Preb. Amanda Rylands); one *s* one *d*. *Educ:* Shrewsbury Sch.; St Hild and St Bede Coll., Durham Univ. (BA 1983); Trinity Coll., Bristol (BA 1987); Sheffield Univ. (MA 2006). Ordained deacon, 1987, priest, 1988; Asst Curate, St George's, Stockport, 1987–91; Vicar, Acton and Worleston, Church Minshull and Wettenhall, 1991–97; Team Rector, Langport Area Team Ministry, 1997–2002; Diocesan Missioner, Dio. of Exeter, 2002–09; Canon Residentiary, Exeter Cathedral, 2002–09. *Recreations:* cricket, fishing, butterflies. *Address:* The Rectory, Copperwood Close, Ashburton, Newton Abbot TQ13 7JQ. *T:* (01364) 716309. *E:* mark.rylands@mmuk.net.
See also P. C. Byrom.

**RYLE, Evelyn Margaret**; author, editor and consultant; *b* 26 March 1947; *d* of Paul and Emily Cassidy; *m* 1975, Anthony E. Ryle, OBE; one *s* one *d*. *Educ:* King's Park Sch., Glasgow; Univ. of Glasgow (MA Hons); Ealing Tech. Coll. (Dip. Management Studies). Dexion-Comino Internat., 1969; commnd WRAF; Flight Lieut, accountant officer, 1973; financial systems analyst: Dexion Gp, 1975; Southern Electricity, 1976; Departments of Trade and Industry, 1977–96; British Steel Corp. Finance; Commercial Relations and Exports; Consumer Affairs; Vehicles Div.; Dep. Dir, IT Services, 1987; Head, Educn and Trng Policy, 1990; seconded to Design Council as Dir-Gen., 1993; Dir, Business Competitiveness, Govt Office for London, 1995–96; Mem., CSSB Panel of Chairs, 1996–99. Mem., Finance Cttee, 1996–2002 (Chair, 2001–02), Mem., Exec., 1999–2002, Charter 88. Mem. Cttee, Romantic Novelists' Assoc., 2003–11 (Hon. Treasurer, 2004–08; Hon. Sec., 2008–11; Vice Pres., 2014–). *Recreations:* family, reading, music, gardening, needlework, walking. *E:* eryle@btinternet.com. *Club:* Royal Air Force.

**RYLEY, John Hamilton**; Head, Sky News, since 2006; *b* Chelmsford, 21 Dec. 1961; *s* of late Ted Ryley and of Wanda Ryley; *m* 1987, Harriet Constable; one *s* two *d*. *Educ:* Eastbourne Coll.; Durham Univ. (BA); Wharton Sch. of Business, Philadelphia (AMP). Freelance radio journalist, 1985–87; news trainee, BBC, 1987–89; news producer, 1990–92, prog. ed., 1992–95, News at Ten, ITN; Exec. Producer, 1995–2000, Exec. Ed., 2000–06, Sky News; producer, Sky Gen. Election results, Budget progs and breaking news specials, Sky Ocean Rescue campaign. Mem. Bd, NCTJ, 2010–. Mem. Bd, Media Trust, 2014–. Individual Achievement Award, Broadcast Digital Awards, for launching campaign for televised leaders debates, 2010. *Recreations:* cricket, cycling, fishing. *Address:* c/o Sky News, Isleworth, Middx TW7 5ED. *E:* john.ryley@BskyB.com.

**RYMER, Rear Adm. Alan Robert**; non-executive Director, South East Coast Ambulance Service NHS Foundation Trust, since 2015; *b* Southport, 2 April 1958; *s* of Robert Rymer and Muriel Rymer; *m* 1979, Janis Taylor; two *d*. *Educ:* King George V Grammar Sch., Southport; BRNC; Royal Naval Engrg Coll., Manadon (BSc Hons Mechanical Engrg 1979); Manchester Business Sch. (Chartered Mgt Inst. Strategic Direction and Leadership prog.). CEng 1994. HMS Blake, 1979; HMS Torquay, 1980–81; HMS Leander, 1981–83; HMS Sultan, 1983–86; HM Yacht Britannia, 1986–88; HMS Active, 1988–90; RN Staff Coll., Greenwich, 1991; Asst Defence Attaché, Bonn, 1992–94; HMS Marlborough, 1995–97; Naval Manning Agency, 1997–99; MoD, London, 1999–2000; CSO Engrg, 2000–03; Dir Naval Officer Appts (Engr), 2003; Dir of Ops, Warship Support Agency, 2003–05; Dir Naval Personnel, 2006–07; CO HMS Sultan and Comdt, Defence Coll. of Electro-Mechanical Engrg, 2007–10; Dir, Trng and Educn, MoD, 2010–12. Dir, Lune Consulting, 2012–18. Chm., C of E Soldiers', Sailors' and Airmen's Clubs Housing Assoc., 2014–. Vice Pres., Inst. of Marine Engrg, Sci. and Technol., 2008–13. Pres., Selsey RNLI Lifeboat Stn, 2012–. *Recreations:* family, golf, River Lune, guitar, triathlon. *Club:* Goodwood.

**RYRIE, Prof. Alexander Gray, (Alec)**, DPhil; FBA 2019; Professor of History of Christianity, Durham University, since 2007; *b* London, 20 Aug. 1971; *s* of Sir William (Sinclair) Ryrie, KCB and of Christine Ryrie, PhD; *m* 1995, Victoria Hufford; two *s*. *Educ:* Dulwich Coll.; Trinity Hall, Cambridge (BA Double 1st Hist. 1993); St Andrews Univ. (MLitt Reformation Studies 1999); St Cross Coll., Oxford (DPhil 2000). Lectr, 1999–2005, Sen. Lectr, 2005–06, Univ. of Birmingham. Prof. of Divinity, Gresham Coll., London, 2018–. Pres., Ecclesiastical Hist. Soc., 2019–20. Co-Ed., Jl Ecclesiastical Hist., 2014–. *Publications:* (ed with P. Marshall) The Beginnings of English Protestantism, 2002; The Gospel and Henry VIII: evangelicals in the early English Reformation, 2003; (ed with L. Racaut) Moderate Voices in the European Reformation, 2005; (ed) Palgrave Advances in the European Reformations, 2005; The Origins of the Scottish Reformation, 2006; The Sorcerer's Tale: faith and fraud in Tudor England, 2008; The Age of Reformation: the Tudor and Stuart realms 1485–1603, 2009, 2nd edn 2017; (ed with J. Martin) Private and Domestic Devotion in Early Modern Britain, 2012; (ed with N. Mears) Worship and the Parish Church in Early Modern Britain, 2013; Being Protestant in Reformation Britain, 2013; (ed with D. Wendebourg) Sister Reformations II - Schwesterreformationen II: reformations and ethics in Germany and in England, 2014; (ed with T. Schwanda) Puritanism and Emotion in the Early Modern World, 2016; Protestants: the radicals who made the modern world, 2017 (US and Dutch edns 2017); Unbelievers: an emotional history of doubt, 2019; The Reformation in England: a very short history, 2020. *Address:* Department of Theology and Religion, Durham University, Abbey House, Palace Green, Durham DH1 3RS. *E:* alec.ryrie@durham.ac.uk.

# S

**SAAKASHVILI, Mikheil**; Governor, Odessa Region, Ukraine, 2015–16; President of Georgia, 2004–13; *b* 21 Dec. 1967; *s* of Nokoloz Saakashvili and Giuli Alasania; *m* Sandra Elizabeth Roelofs; two *s*. *Educ*: Nat. Law Center, George Washington Univ.; Columbia Univ. (LLM); Internat. Inst. of Human Rights, France (Dip.); Dept of Internat. Law, Kiev State Univ. (law degree). Hd, Dept of Ethnic Relns, Georgian Cttee for Human Rights and Ethnic Relns, 1992–94; Foreign Lawyer, Patterson, Belknap, Webb & Tyler, NY, 1994–95; MP, Georgia, 1995–98; Chm., Cttee for Const., Legal Affairs and Rule of Law, Parlt of Georgia, 1995–98; Co-Chm., Council of Justice, Georgia, 1998; Vice-Pres., Parly Assembly of Council of Europe, 2000; Minister of Justice, 2000–01; Chm., Tbilisi City Council, 2002–03. Chm., Majority Faction of Union of Citizens, Parlt of Georgia, 1998.

**SAATCHI**, family name of **Baron Saatchi**.

**SAATCHI**, Baron *cr* 1996 (Life Peer), of Staplefield in the county of West Sussex; **Maurice Saatchi**; Partner, M & C Saatchi plc, since 1995; *b* 21 June 1946; *s* of late Daisy and Nathan Saatchi; *m* 1984, Josephine Hart (*d* 2011); one *s*, and one step *s*. *Educ*: London School of Economics and Political Science (1st class BSc Econ). Co-Founder of Saatchi & Saatchi Co., 1970, Chm., 1985–94. Chm. Finsbury Food Gp (formerly Megalomedia) PLC, 1995–2008. Opposition spokesman, H of L, on Treasury affairs, 1999–2003, on Cabinet Office affairs, 2001–03. Co-Chm., Conservative Party, 2003–05. A Trustee, Victoria and Albert Mus., 1988–96; Member: Council, RCA, 1997–2000; Westminster Abbey Inst.; Director: Centre for Policy Studies, 1999– (Chm., 2009–); Garden Mus. (formerly Mus. of Garden History), 2001–. Mem. Bd, Cons. Party Foundn. Governor, LSE, 1996–13. *Publications*: The Science of Politics, 2001; Brutal Simplicity of Thought, 2011; *pamphlets*: The War of Independence, 1999; Happiness Can't Buy Money, 1999; The Bad Samaritan, 2000; Poor People! Stop Paying Tax!, 2001; If This is Conservatism, I am a Conservative, 2005; In Praise of Ideology, 2006; Sleeping Beauty, 2007. *Address*: (office) 36 Golden Square, W1F 9EE. *T*: (020) 7543 4510.
See also C. Saatchi.

**SAATCHI, Charles**; Founder, Saatchi & Saatchi Co., 1970–93; Partner, M & C Saatchi plc, 1995–2006; *b* 9 June 1943; *m* 2003, Nigella Lucy Lawson, *qv* (marr. diss. 2013). *Educ*: Christ's Coll., Finchley. Founder, The Saatchi Gallery, 1985. *Publications*: My Name is Charles Saatchi and I am an Artoholic, 2009; Be The Worst You Can Be: life's too long for patience & virtue, 2012; Babble, 2013; Beyond Belief: racist, sexist, rude, crude and dishonest - the Golden Age of Madison Avenue, 2015. *Address*: Saatchi Gallery, Duke of York's HQ, King's Road, SW3 4RY.

**SABAPATHY, Paul Chandrasekharan**, CVO 2017; CBE 2004 (OBE 1995); Lord Lieutenant of West Midlands, 2007–15; *b* Madras, 26 Sept. 1942; *s* of John and Catherine Sabapathy; *m* 1969, Win White; one *s* one *d*. *Educ*: Lawrence Sch., Lovedale, India; Madras Christian Coll. (BSc Phys 1963); Aston Univ., Birmingham (MSc Industrial Admin 1968). ACMA 1994. IMI plc: Accountant, Eley Ltd, 1968–72; Cost Accountant, Enots Ltd, 1972–74; Finance Dir, IMI Refiners Ltd, 1974–88; IMI Gp Corporate Services Manager, 1988–92; Asst Man. Dir, IMI Titanium Ltd, 1992–96. Member Board: Black Country Develt Corp., 1987–89; Birmingham Heartland Develt Corp., 1992–98; Pres., Walsall Chamber of Commerce, 1988; Chm., W Midlands Industrial Develt Adv. Bd, 1997–2002. Chief Exec., N Birmingham Community NHS Trust, 1996–2000; Member Board: Nat. Blood Authy, 2000–05; N Birmingham PCT, 2001–03; Chairman: E Birmingham PCT, 2004–06; Birmingham E and N PCT, 2006–11; Vice Chm., NHS Confederation PCT Network, 2007–11. Trustee: New Walsall Art Gall., 1997–2003; Refugee Council, 2002–03; Bournville Village Trust, 2006–18. Chm., Birmingham City Univ., 2002–09; Dep. Chm., Cttee of Univ. Chairmen, 2004–05. FRSA; FRSocMed 2006. *Recreations*: travelling, gardening.

**SABBEN-CLARE, Rebecca Mary**; QC 2012; *b* Winchester, 13 June 1971; *d* of late James Paley Sabben-Clare; *m* 2008, William Howard; one *s* one *d*. *Educ*: St Swithun's Sch., Winchester; Winchester Coll.; New Coll., Oxford (BA). Called to the Bar, Gray's Inn, 1993; in practice as a barrister, 1993–. *Recreations*: scuba diving, cooking, building sandcastles. *Address*: 7 King's Bench Walk, Temple, EC4Y 7DS. *T*: (020) 7910 8300, *Fax*: (020) 7910 8400. *E*: rsabbenclare@7kbw.co.uk.

**SABIN, Paul Robert**; DL; Chairman, Veolia Water Southeast (formerly Folkestone and Dover Water Company), 2007–12 (non-executive Director, since 1998); Chief Executive, Leeds Castle Foundation and Leeds Castle (Enterprises) Ltd, 1998–2003; *b* 29 March 1943; *s* of Robert Reginald and Dorothy Maude Sabin; *m* 1965, Vivien Furnival; one *s* two *d*. *Educ*: Oldbury Grammar Sch. DMS Aston Univ.; CPFA (IPFA 1966). West Bromwich CBC, 1959–69; Redditch Develt Corp., 1969–81, Chief Finance Officer, 1975–81; City of Birmingham, 1981–86: City Treas., 1982–86; Dep. Chief Exec., 1984–86; Chief Exec., Kent CC, 1986–97. Hon. Citizen, City of Baltimore, Md, USA, 1985. Kent Ambassador, 2002–. DL Kent, 2001. *Recreations*: fine books, music.

**SABINE, Peter Aubrey**, DSc; FRSE; FIMMM; CEng, CGeol, CSci, FGS; Deputy Director (Chief Scientific Officer, Chief England), British Geological Survey (formerly Institute of Geological Sciences), 1977–84; *b* 29 Dec. 1924; *s* of late Bernard Robert and Edith Lucy Sabine; *m* 1946, Peggy Willis Lambert, MSc, FBCS, CITP, FRSA, FSS (*d* 2019); (one *s* decd). *Educ*: Brockley County Sch.; Chelsea Polytechnic; Royal Coll. of Science, Imperial Coll., London (BSc, ARCS (1st Cl. Geol.; Watts Medal) 1945); PhD 1951, DSc 1970, London. FRSE 1964 (Emeritus Fellow, 2017). Represented Youth of Empire, Westminster Abbey Empire Youth Service, 1940. Apptd Geological Survey of Gt Britain as Geologist, 1945; Geological Museum, 1946–50; in charge Petrographical Dept, Geol Survey and Museum, 1950, Chief Petrographer, 1959; Asst Dir, S England and Wales, 1970; Chief Geochemist, 1977; Dep. Dir, 1977–84. Sec., Geol. Soc. of London, 1959–66, Vice-Pres., 1966–67, 1982–84 (Lyell Fund, 1955; Sen. Fellow, 1994); International Union of Geological Sciences: Mem. Commn on Systematics of Igneous Rocks, 1969–2002; Mem. Commn on Systematics in Petrology, 1980–96 (Chm., 1984–92; Vice-Chm., 1992–96); Chief UK Deleg., 1980–84; Mem. Council, 1980–92; Member Council: Geologists' Assoc., 1966–70 (Life Mem., 1991); Mineralogical Soc., 1950–53; Instn of Mining and Metallurgy, 1976–80; Mineral Industry Res. Orgn, 1983–86; Member: DTI Chem. and Mineral Research Requirements Bd, 1973–82; Minerals, Metals Extraction and Reclamation Cttee, 1981–84; EEC Cttees on minerals and geochemistry; Cttee of Dirs of W European Geol Surveys, 1978–84; Chm., Sub-Cttee on geochem. and cosmochem. of British Nat. Cttee for Geology, 1977–86. Royal Institution: Visitor, 1979–82; Mem., Audit Cttee, 1987–90 (Chm., 1989–90). Life Fellow, Mineralogical Soc., 1999 (Mem., 1945; Mem. Council, 1950–53); FMSA 1959 (Sen. Fellow, 2003); FBCartS 1996. FRSA. *Publications*: Chemical Analysis of Igneous Rocks (with E. M. Guppy), 1956; (with D. S. Sutherland) Petrography of British Igneous Rocks, 1982; (jtly) Classification of Igneous Rocks, 1989, 2nd edn 2002 (trans. Chinese and Russian); numerous scientific contribs in Mem. Geol. Surv., Qly Jl Geol. Soc., Mineral. Mag., Phil. Trans Roy. Soc., etc. *Recreations*: gardening, genealogy. *Address*: Malmsmead, 12 Orchehill Avenue, Gerrards Cross, Bucks SL9 8PX. *T*: (01753) 891529. *Clubs*: Athenæum; Geological Society (Sen. Hon. Mem.); Royal Scots (Edinburgh); Gerrards Cross and Chalfont Probus (Hon. Life Mem.).

**SABOURIAN, Prof. Hamid**, PhD; FBA 2013; Professor of Economics and Game Theory, University of Cambridge, since 2005; Fellow, King's College, Cambridge, since 1985; *b* Tehran, 1 Jan. 1959; *s* of Eynollah Sabourian and Nosrat Zaman Sabourian (*née* Dashti); *m* 1998, Elisa May Sampson; one *s* three *d*. *Educ*: Safinia Primary Sch., Tehran; Alborz High Sch., Tehran; Clifton Coll., Bristol; King's Coll., Cambridge (BA 1st Cl. Econs 1980; MA Econs 1984; PhD 1987); London Sch. of Econs and Pol Sci. (MSc Math. Econs 1981). Asst Lectr, 1987–90, Lectr, 1990–2002, Reader, 2002–05, Univ. of Cambridge; Prof. of Econs, Birkbeck, Univ. of London, 2005–07; Chm., Faculty of Econs, Univ. of Cambridge, 2007–11. Visiting Professor: UCLA, 1992; Eur. Univ. Inst., Florence, 1995–96; NY Univ., 1999; Cowles Foundn, Yale Univ., 1999; CV Star Center, NY Univ., 2001, 2003; Birkbeck, Univ. of London, 2001–04, 2007–11; Univ. Carlos III Madrid, 2013 (Banco Santander Chair of Excellence, 2013); Singapore Mgt Univ., 2013; Fung Vis. Prof., Hong Kong Univ. of Sci. and Technol., 2011–14; Vis. Lectr, LSE, 1996. Fellow, Soc. for Advancement of Econ. Theory, 2011; Keynes Fellow, Univ. of Cambridge, 2011–. Associate Ed., Jl Econ. Theory, 2004–13; Mem., Editl Bd, Econ. Theory, 2009–. *Publications*: contribs to jls incl. Econometrica, Jl Econ. Theory, Games and Econ. Behavior, Econ. Jl, Eur. Econ. Jl, Jl Math. Econs, Math. Social Scis. *Recreations*: tennis, ski-ing, football. *Address*: Faculty of Economics, University of Cambridge, Sidgwick Avenue, Cambridge CB3 9DD. *T*: (01223) 335248, *Fax*: (01223) 335475. *E*: hs102@cam.ac.uk.

**SACHRAJDA, Prof. Christopher Tadeusz Czeslaw**, PhD; FRS 1996; Professor of Theoretical Physics, University of Southampton, 1990–2017, now Emeritus; *b* 15 Nov. 1949; *s* of Czeslaw Sachrajda and Hanna Teresa Sachrajda (*née* Grabowska); *m* 1974, Irena Czyzewska; two *s* one *d*. *Educ*: Ealing GS; Univ. of Sussex (BSc); Imperial Coll. of Sci. and Technol. (PhD 1974). CPhys, FInstP 1989. Harkness Fellow, Stanford Linear Accelerator Center, Stanford Univ., 1974–76; Fellow and Staff Mem., CERN, 1976–79 (Scientific Associate, 1986–87, 1995–96 and 2002); Department of Physics, University of Southampton: Lectr, 1979–86; Sen. Lectr, 1986–88; Reader, 1988–89; Hd of Dept of Physics and Astronomy, 1997–99. Leverhulme Trust Emeritus Fellow, 2018–20. Sen. Fellow, SERC and PPARC, 1991–96; Fellow, Winchester Coll., 2010–. Mem. Council, PPARC, 1998–2004. *Publications*: numerous research and review articles on theory of elementary particles. *Recreations*: family, tennis, philately (early Polish), walking. *Address*: Department of Physics and Astronomy, University of Southampton, Southampton SO17 1BJ. *T*: (023) 8059 2105. *E*: cts@soton.ac.uk; (home) 20 Radway Road, Southampton SO15 7PW. *Club*: Portswood Lawn Tennis (Southampton).

**SACKLER, Dame Jillian (Lesley)**, DBE 2005; President, AMS Foundation for the Arts, Sciences and Humanities, since 1980; *b* 17 Nov. 1948; *d* of Kenneth Herbert Tully and Doris Queenie Gillman Smith; *m* 1980, Arthur Mitchell Sackler (*d* 1987). *Educ*: Bromley Girls' High Sch.; New York Univ. Bd Mem., US Cttee for UNICEF, 1988–97. Chm., Cttee, Edinburgh Internat. Fest., 1985–90; Member: Vis. Cttee for Art Mus of Harvard Univ., 1983–; Bd, Metropolitan Opera, NY, 1986–2001; President's Circle, NAS, 1989–; Nat. Bd, Smithsonian Instn, 1989–; Bd, New York City Ballet, 1992–2001; Trustee: RA, 1988–; Council, Nat. Gall. of Art, Washington, 1986–94; American Film Inst., 1986–; Tufts Univ., 1986–98; Foundn for NIH, 2000–. Patron and Hon. Dir, Arthur M. Sackler Mus. of Art and Archaeol., New York, 1994–. Hon. FRIBA 2017. Dame with Crown, Order of Malta, 1994. *Address*: 660 Park Avenue, New York, NY 10065, USA. *T*: (212) 5178880, *Fax*: (212) 6282879. *Clubs*: Queen's; Pilgrims, Cosmopolitan, Town Tennis (New York).

**SACKLER, Dame Theresa (Elizabeth)**, DBE 2012; philanthropist; *b* Werrington, Staffs, 14 Sept. 1949; *d* of Maj. William Daniel Rowling and Margaret Mary Cecilia Rowling (*née* McKimmie); *m* 1980, Dr Mortimer David Sackler, Hon. KBE (*d* 2010); one *s* two *d*. *Educ*: Holt Hill Convent, Wirral, Cheshire; Maria Assumpta Coll. of Educn, London (Cert Ed 1971). Teacher, Sion Convent, Notting Hill, 1971–79. Dir, Sackler Trust, 2009–; Trustee: Dr Mortimer and Theresa Sackler Foundn, 1988–; Capital City Acad., Brent, N London; Dulwich Picture Gall., 2002–13; Tate Foundn; V&A Mus., 2011– (Mem., Learning and and Participation Cttee). Member: Chancellor's Ct of Benefactors, Univ. of Oxford; Bd of Hon. Dirs, ROH. Fellow, Ashmolean Mus., 2006. Hon. Fellow, St Peter's Coll., Oxford, 2016. Hon. FRCA 2012; Hon. FRIBA 2017. Prince of Wales Medal for Arts Philanthropy, 2011. Chevalier, Légion d'Honneur (France), 1999. *Recreations*: travel, gardens, natural history, arts. *Clubs*: Eagle Ski (Gstaad); Gstaad Yacht.

**SACKS**, family name of **Baron Sacks**.

**SACKS**, Baron *cr* 2009 (Life Peer), of Aldgate in the City of London; **Jonathan Henry Sacks**, Kt 2005; PhD; Chief Rabbi of the United Hebrew Congregations of the Commonwealth, 1991–2013; Professor of Law, Ethics and the Bible, King's College London, 2013–16, now Emeritus; *b* 8 March 1948; *s* of late Louis David Sacks and Louisa (*née* Frumkin); *m* 1970, Elaine (*née* Taylor); two *s* two *d*. *Educ*: Christ's Coll., Finchley; Gonville and Caius Coll., Cambridge (MA 1972; Hon. Fellow, 1993); New Coll., Oxford; PhD London, 1981. Rabbinic Ordination: Jews' Coll., London, 1976; Yeshivat Etz Hayyim, London, 1976. Lectr in Moral Philosophy, Middlesex Polytechnic, 1971–73;

Jews' College, London: Lectr in Jewish Philosophy, 1973–76; Lectr on the Talmud and in Phil., 1976–82; apptd (first) Sir Immanuel (later Lord) Jakobovits Prof. of Modern Jewish Thought, 1982–90; Dir, Rabbinic Faculty, 1983–90; Principal, 1984–90; Rabbi: Golders Green Synagogue, 1978–82; Marble Arch Synagogue, 1983–90. Member (Univ. of London): Bd of Phil., 1985–90; Bd of Studies in Oriental Languages and Literature, 1985–90; Bd of Studies in Theology and Religious Studies, 1986–90. Member: Theol. and Religious Studies Bd, CNAA, 1984–87; Central Religious Adv. Cttee, BBC and IBA, 1987–90. Visiting Professor: Univ. of Essex, 1989–90; Hebrew Univ. in Jerusalem, 1999–; KCL, 1999–. BBC Reith Lectr, 1990. Associate Pres., Conf. of European Rabbis, 2000–13. Editor, L'Eylah: A Journal of Judaism Today, 1984–90. Freeman, City of London and London Bor. of Barnet, 2006. FKC 1993. Hon. Bencher, Inner Temple, 2001. DD Lambeth, 2001; Hon. DD: Cantab, 1993; Heythrop Coll., London, 2006; DUniv Middlesex, 1993; Hon. PhD: Haifa, 1996; Glasgow, 2001; Hon. LLD Liverpool, 1997; Hon. Dr: Yeshiva, NY, 1997; St Andrews, 1998; Bar-Ilan, Leeds Metropolitan, 2004; Roehampton, 2009; Basel, 2010; Ben Gurion, Aberdeen, 2011; Salford, 2013; Liverpool Hope, 2013. Jerusalem Prize, 1995; Grawemayer Award, 2003; Guardian of Zion Award, Israel, 2014; Katz Prize, Israel, 2014; Canterbury Medal, Becket Law, 2014; Creativity Award, Moment Mag., 2015; Templeton Prize, 2016; Bradley Prize, Bradley Foundn, 2016; Irving Kristol Award, Amer. Enterprise Inst., 2017. *Publications:* Torah Studies, 1986; (ed) Tradition and Transition: essays presented to Sir Immanuel Jakobovits, 1986; Traditional Alternatives, 1989; Tradition in an Untraditional Age, 1990; The Persistence of Faith, 1991; Argument for the Sake of Heaven, 1991; (ed) Orthodoxy Confronts Modernity, 1991; Crisis and Covenant, 1992; One People? Tradition, Modernity and Jewish Unity, 1993; Will we have Jewish grandchildren?, 1994; Faith in the Future, 1995; Community of Faith, 1996; The Politics of Hope, 1997; Morals and Markets, 1999; Celebrating Life, 2000; Radical Then, Radical Now, 2001; The Dignity of Difference, 2002, 2nd edn 2003; The Passover Haggadah, 2003; From Optimism to Hope, 2004; To Heal a Fractured World, 2005; The Authorised Daily Prayer Book, 4th edn (new trans. and commentary), 2007; The Home We Build Together: recreating society, 2007; Future Tense: a vision for Jews and Judaism in the global culture, 2009; Covenant and Conversation: a weekly reading of the Jewish Bible, Genesis, 2009, Exodus, 2010, Leviticus, 2015, Numbers, 2017, Deuteronomy, 2019; The Great Partnership, 2011; Koren Sacks Yom Kippur Mahzor (trans. and commentary), 2011; Koren Sacks Rosh Hashana Mahzor (trans. and commentary), 2012; Koren Sacks Pesach Mahzor, 2013; Not in God's Name, 2015; The Koren Shavuot Mahzor (trans. and commentary), 2016; Ceremony and Celebration: introduction to the holidays, 2017; articles, booklets and book reviews.

**SACKS, Hon. Charlotte Mary;** *see* Hogg, Hon. C. M.

**SACKUR, Stephen John;** Presenter, HARDtalk, BBC World News, since 2005; *b* 9 Jan. 1964; *s* of Robert Neil Humphrys Sackur and Sallie Caley; *m* 1992, Zina Sabbagh; two *s* one *d*. *Educ:* Emmanuel Coll., Cambridge (BA Hons Hist. 1985). Reporter, Hebden Bridge Times, 1981–82; Henry Fellow, Harvard Univ., 1985–86; BBC: Producer, Current Affairs, 1986–89; Foreign Affairs Corresp., 1989–92; ME Corresp., Cairo, 1992–95; Jerusalem Corresp., 1995–97; Washington Corresp., 1997–2002; Europe Corresp., 2002–05. Hon. Dr Geneva Sch. of Diplomacy and Internat. Relns, 2017; Hon. DLitt Warwick, 2018. Internat. TV Personality of the Year Award, Assoc. of Internat. Broadcasters, 2010. *Publications:* On the Basra Road, 1991. *Recreations:* books, films, sports, family adventures. *Address:* c/o BBC World News, Broadcasting House, Portland Place, W1A 1AA.

**SACKVILLE,** family name of **Earl De La Warr**.

**SACKVILLE, 7th Baron** *cr* 1876; **Robert Bertrand Sackville-West;** DL; *b* 10 July 1958; *s* of Hugh Rosslyn Inigo Sackville-West, MC and Bridget Eleanor (*née* Cunliffe); *S* uncle, 2004; *m* 1st, 1985, Catherine Dorothea Bennett (marr. diss. 1992); 2nd, 1994, Margot Jane MacAndrew; one *s* two *d*. DL Kent, 2014. *Publications:* Inheritance: the story of Knole and the Sackvilles, 2010; The Disinherited, 2014. *Heir: s* Hon. Arthur George Sackville-West, *b* 25 Feb. 2000.

**SACKVILLE, Hon. Thomas Geoffrey, (Tom);** Chief Executive, International Federation of Health Plans (formerly International Federation of Health Funds), since 1998; *b* 26 Oct. 1950; 2nd *s* of 10th Earl De La Warr (*d* 1988) and of Anne Rachel, *o d* of Geoffrey Devas, MC, Hunton Court, Maidstone; *m* 1979, Catherine Theresa, *d* of Brig. James Windsor Lewis; one *s* one *d*. *Educ:* St Aubyn's, Rottingdean, Sussex; Eton Coll.; Lincoln Coll., Oxford (BA). Deltec Banking Corp., New York, 1971–74; Grindlays Bank Ltd, London, 1974–77; Internat. Bullion and Metal Brokers (London) Ltd, 1978–83. MP (C) Bolton West, 1983–97; contested (C) same seat, 1997. PPS to Minister of State at the Treasury, 1985, to Minister for Social Security, 1987–88; an Asst Govt Whip, 1988–90; a Lord Comr of HM Treasury (Govt Whip), 1990–92; Parliamentary Under-Secretary of State: DoH, 1992–95; Home Office, 1995–97. Sec., All-Party Cttee on Drug Misuse, 1984–88. Chm., Family Survival Trust, 2007–. *Address:* (office) 83 Victoria Street, SW1H 0HW. *E:* tom@ifhp.com.

**SACKVILLE-WEST,** family name of **Baron Sackville**.

**SACRANIE, Sir Iqbal (Abdul Karim Mussa),** Kt 2005; OBE 1999; Secretary General, The Muslim Council of Britain, 2002–06; Chairman, Muslim Aid, 2008–12 (Trustee, 1995–2016); *b* 6 Sept. 1951; *s* of Abdul Karim Mussa and Mariam Mussa; *m* 1976, Yasmin; three *s* two *d*. *Educ:* Kennington Coll.; Walbrook Coll. Fellow, Inst. of Financial Accountants, 1978; MInstAM 1978. Chm., Global Gp of cos (family business). Chm., Muslim Council of Britain Charitable Foundn, 2000–12; Chm. Bd of Trustees, Memon Assoc. UK, 1998–; Dep. Pres., World Memon Org., 2002–14; Vice Pres., Assoc. of Family Welfare, 1998–; Member: Rev. of Coroners' System, 2001–03; Race Equality Adv. Panel, 2003–05; Bd, World Islamic Economic Forum, 2005–15. Chairman Board of Trustees: Balham Mosque, 1986–; Al Risalla Sch. Trust, 2002–. Patron, Commn on Multi-Faith Britain, 2016–. Hon. DLaws Leeds Metropolitan, 2006. Award for Excellence, Muslim News, 2000; Award for commitment and dedication to community work, Memon Assoc. UK, 2001; Lifetime Achievement Award, Middle East Business Leaders Council, 2016. *Publications:* joint author and contributor: Need for Reform, 1992; Election 1997 and British Muslims, 1997; The Quest for Sanity, 2003; contrib. to Muslim News, News Internat., Daily Jang, Nation, Asian News and other ethnic media. *Recreations:* golf, cricket, volleyball. *T:* (020) 8974 2780, *Fax:* (020) 8974 2781. *E:* raheena@glotex.co.uk.

**SADDLER, Joan Angela,** OBE 2007; Associate Director, Patients and Communities, NHS Confederation, since 2013; *b* Leeds, 11 May 1962; *d* of Ashton Saddler and Bronte Saddler; one *s*. *Educ:* Jacob Krammer Coll. of Art, Leeds (Student Award 1979; Adv. Dip. Design 1981); Middlesex Poly. (Cultural Studies specialising in Race, Culture and Women's Liberation Movement); Southbank Univ. (Cert. Mgt 2000; Dip. Mgt 2006); INSEAD (Strategic Change Mgt 2006). Company Dir and Chief Exec., Haringey Women's Forum, 1997–2004; Dir, Direct Development Consultancy Ltd, 2007–; Nat. Dir, Patient and Public Affairs, DoH, 2008–13. Non-exec. Dir, Haringey Healthcare Trust, 1998–2000; Chm. Bd, Walthamstow Forest (formerly Walthamstow, Leyton and Leytonstone) PCT, 2001–08. Member: NHS Equality and Diversity Council, 2009– (Co-Chair, 2016–); Nat. Commissioning a Patient-Led NHS Expert Panel, 2005; Independent Inquiry into Access to Healthcare for People with Learning Disabilities, 2007–08. Mem. Bd, Adventist Develt Relief Agency UK, 2001–. Ambassador, Mary Seacole Meml Statue Appeal, 2014–. Black and Minority Ethnic Leader Award, Health Service Jl, 2014. *Publications:* contribs to Health Service Jl and Nursing Standard. *Recreations:* music (Mem., London Adventist Chorale, winner of Sainsbury's Choir of the Year, 1994), art and design (designer, Where are we now? exhibn, London's Living Room, City Hall, 2001), reading, black history.

**SADGROVE, Very Rev. Michael;** Dean of Durham, 2003–15, Dean Emeritus, 2016; *b* 13 April 1950; *s* of late Ralph Sadgrove and Dorothea Sadgrove; *m* 1974, (Elizabeth) Jennifer Suddes; one *s* three *d*. *Educ:* UCS; Balliol Coll., Oxford (BA (Maths and Philosophy) 1971; BA (Theology) 1973; MA 1975); Trinity Coll., Bristol. Ordained, deacon, 1975, priest, 1976; Lectr in OT studies, 1977–82, Vice-Principal, 1980–82, Salisbury and Wells Theol College; Vicar, Alnwick, Northumberland, 1982–87; Canon Residentiary and Vice-Provost, Coventry Cathedral, 1987–95; Provost, subseq. Dean, Sheffield, 1995–2003. Bishops' Sen. Inspector of Theol Educn, 1997–2010. Member: General Synod, 2003–10; Council for Ministry, 2005–10. Chm., Ethics Adv. Cttee, Univ. of Durham, 2004–14; Durham DAC, 2005–10; Mem., Cathedrals Fabric Commn for England, 1996–2006. Chm., Sheffield Common Purpose, 1996–99. Mem. Council, Univ. of Durham, 2003–15; Rector, St Chad's Coll., Durham, 2009–17 (Visitor, 2003–09). President: St Cuthbert's Hospice, Durham, 2003–15; MUSICON, Univ. of Durham, 2003–15. Hon. Pres., Durham City Trust, 2010–. FRSA 1997. DL Durham, 2011–15. *Publications:* A Picture of Faith, 1995; The Eight Words of Jesus, 2006; Wisdom and Ministry, 2008; I Will Trust in You: a companion to the evening psalms, 2009; Lost Sons: God's long search for humanity, 2012; Landscapes of Faith, 2013; (with P. Nixon) Durham Cathedral: a pilgrimage in photographs, 2013; Christ in a Choppie Box: sermons from North East England, 2015; contributor to: Studia Biblica, 1978; Reflecting the Word, 1989; Lion Handbook of the World's Religions, 1982, 2nd edn 1994; Rethinking Marriage, 1993; Coventry's First Cathedral, 1994; The Care Guide, 1995; Calling Time, 2000; Creative Chords, 2001; Dreaming Spires?, 2006; Treasures of Durham University Library, 2007; On Being Human, 2009; Reconciling People: Coventry Cathedral at fifty, 2011; Durham Cathedral: history, language, culture, 2015; Northern Gospel, Northern Church: reflections on identity and mission, 2016; articles and reviews in theol jls. *Recreations:* music, arts, literature, history, culture and landscapes of north-east of England, travels in France, European issues, photography, railways. *Address:* Burswell House, 27 Church Street, Haydon Bridge, Northumberland NE47 6JG. *E:* sadgrove@outlook.com.

**SADLER, John Stephen,** CBE 1982; Chairman, Argent Group PLC, 1997–2001; *b* 6 May 1930; *s* of late Bernard and Phyllis Sadler; *m* 1952, Ella (*née* McCleery); three *s*. *Educ:* Reading Sch.; Corpus Christi Coll., Oxford (MA 1st cl. PPE). Board of Trade, 1952–54; Treasury, 1954–56; Board of Trade, 1956–60; British Trade Commissioner, Lagos, Nigeria, 1960–64; Board of Trade, 1964–66. John Lewis Partnership Ltd, 1966–89: Finance Dir, 1971–87; Dep. Chm., 1984–89. Chairman: Water Res. Centre, subseq. WRC, 1989–93; West End Bd, Royal & Sun Alliance (formerly Sun Alliance) Insurance Gp, 1991–2001; UK Bd, Australian Mutual Provident Soc. and London Life, 1991–96; Pearl Gp PLC, 1994–96; Dir, Debenham Tewson & Chinnock Hldgs plc, 1987–2000. Dir, IMRO, 1987–94; Chm., Authorised Conveyancing Practitioners Bd, 1991–93; Mem., Monopolies and Mergers Commn, 1973–85. Special Advr, Ofgem, 1996–2001. Trustee, British Telecommunications Staff Superannuation Scheme, 1983–98. *Publications:* report of enquiry into cross media promotion. *Recreation:* boating. *Address:* Riverlea, The Warren, Caversham, Reading RG4 7TQ. *Club:* Leander.

**SADLER, Kevin Ian,** CBE 2018; Deputy Chief Executive, HM Courts and Tribunals Service, Ministry of Justice, since 2016; *b* 18 March 1962; *s* of Colin and Brenda Sadler; *m* 2004, Gillian (*née* Hazlehurst); two *d*. *Educ:* Leicester Polytechnic (BA Hons Law). DSS, 1984–93; Cabinet Office, 1993–95; DSS, subseq. DWP, 1995–2002; Dir, Tribunals, Unified Admin and Magistrates' Courts, LCD, subseq. DCA, 2002–05; Dir, Corporate Mgt, then Change Dir, DCA, subseq. MoJ, 2005–08; Ministry of Justice: Strategic Planning and Performance Dir, 2008–09; Chief Exec., Tribunals Service, 2009–11; Dir of Civil, Family and Tribunals, 2011–15, Dir of Develt, 2015–16, HM Courts and Tribunals Service, MoJ. Trustee, Charity for Civil Servants, 2013–. *Address:* Ministry of Justice, 102 Petty France, SW1H 9AJ. *T:* (020) 3334 3400, *Fax:* 0870 739 4486.

**SADLER, Prof. Peter John,** DPhil; FRS 2005; FRSE; Professor of Chemistry, University of Warwick, 2007–16 and since 2018 (Head, Department of Chemistry, 2007–10; Professorial Research Fellow, 2016–18); *b* 6 April 1946; *s* of Alfred George and Louisa Elsie Sadler; *m* 1972, Dr Tessa Elizabeth Halstead; two *s* one *d*. *Educ:* City of Norwich Sch.; Magdalen Coll., Oxford (MA 1972; DPhil Chemistry 1972). CChem, FRSC 1987; CSci 2004. MRC Res. Fellow, Univ. of Cambridge and NIMR, Mill Hill, 1971–73; Birkbeck College, London: Lectr in Chemistry, 1973–85; Reader in Biol Inorganic Chemistry, 1985–91; Prof. of Chemistry, 1991–96; Crum Brown Prof. of Chemistry, Univ. of Edinburgh, 1996–2007. Mok Hing Yiu Dist. Vis. Prof. in Chem., Univ. of Hong Kong, 2012–15. EPSRC Recognising Inspirational Scientists and Engrs Fellow, 2014. FRSE 1999. *Publications:* res. papers in jls, inc. Jl of ACS, Angewandte Chemie, Inorganic Chemistry, Chemical Communications, Dalton Transactions, Nature Structural Biology, Science, Jl of Medicinal Chemistry, Procs of NAS, Nature Communications, Amer. Chem. Soc. Chem. Biol., Chem. Sci., Nature Chem., Chem. Sci. *Recreations:* gardening, amateur dramatics and musical theatre, playing clarinet, guitar and piano, swimming, walking, painting. *Address:* Department of Chemistry, University of Warwick, Gibbet Hill Road, Coventry CV4 7AL. *T:* (024) 7652 3818, *Fax:* (024) 7652 3819.

**SAEED, Saleh,** OBE 2013; Chief Executive, Disasters Emergency Committee, since 2012; *b* Yafa, Yemen, 15 Jan. 1967; *s* of Saeed Abubakr Yafai and Razina Mohammed; *m* 1991, Roqaya Ahmed; two *s* three *d*. *Educ:* Univ. of Wolverhampton (BA Hons Business Enterprise 1991). Mktg and Fundraising Dir, Islamic Relief Worldwide, 1991–2000; Develt Manager, Sandwell HA, 2000–02; Policy and Communications Officer, W Midlands Regl Authy, 2002; Project Manager, Sandwell Council, 2002–07; Digital Inclusion Manager, Black Country Consortium, 2007–08; CEO, Islamic Relief Worldwide, 2008–12. *Recreations:* football, cycling. *Address:* Disasters Emergency Committee, 43 Chalton Street, NW1 1DU. *T:* (020) 7387 2000. *E:* info@dec.org.uk.

**SAFFMAN, Andrew Maurice; His Honour Judge Saffman;** a Circuit Judge, since 2013; *b* Leeds, 8 Feb. 1953; *s* of Leonard Saffman and Rita Saffman; *m* 1980, Andrea Jacqueline Spital; two *s* one *d*. *Educ:* Carmel Coll., Wallingford; Roundhay Grammar Sch., Leeds; Univ. of Leeds (LLB Hons 1974). Admitted solicitor, 1977; private practice, 1977–2001; a Dep. Dist Judge, 1995–2001; a Dist Judge, 2001–13; authorised to sit as a Judge of the High Ct, QBD and Chancery Div., Technology and Construction Ct and Mercantile Ct, 2013–, Admin. Court, 2016–, Business and Property Court, 2017–. An Election Comr, 2016–. *Recreations:* cycling, walking, travel, narrow boating, touring in my little convertible sports car. *Address:* Leeds Combined Court Centre, 1 Oxford Row, Leeds, W Yorks LS1 3BG.

**SAGE, Stephen Paul;** management consultant, since 2011; *b* 3 June 1953; *s* of late Ivor John Sage and Kathleen Gwendoline Sage (*née* Jeffrey); *m* 1982, Anne Jennifer Mickleburgh; two *s* one *d*. *Educ:* Bristol Grammar Sch.; Peterhouse, Cambridge (BA Hons Classics 1974; MA).

MCIPS 1993. John Henderson Sports, 1976–78; Crown Agents, 1978–80; Department of the Environment, 1980–93: Private Sec. to Housing Minister, 1984–85; Controller, Merseyside Task Force, 1989–93; Chief Exec., The Buying Agency, 1993–2000; Chief Exec., FCO Services, FCO, 2000–06; Dir, Trading Fund Programme, FCO, 2006–08; Dir, Stephen Sage Consulting Ltd, 2008–11. Member: Cttee, Pierhead Housing Assoc., 1994–2000; Cttee, Wirral and N Cheshire Prostate Cancer Support Gp, 2015–17. Trustee, Lancs W and Wigan (formerly Lancs W) Groundwork Trust, 2005–08. Captain: The Buying Agency Golf Soc., 2011–14; Mollington Golf Soc., 2017–18. *Recreations:* reading, music, Alfa Romeos, tennis, golf. *E:* sage247@hotmail.co.uk. *Clubs:* Bristol City Football; Oaks at Mollington Golf (Seniors Sec., 2015–16); Leasowe Golf.

**SAGGERSON, Alan David; His Honour Judge Saggerson;** a Circuit Judge, since 2009; a Deputy High Court Judge, since 2016; *b* Newcastle upon Tyne, 24 Dec. 1956; *s* of Graeme and Margaret Saggerson. *Educ:* Wilmslow Grammar Sch.; Hertford Coll., Oxford (BCL, MA Juris.); Inns of Court Sch. of Law. Called to the Bar, Lincoln's Inn, 1981, Bencher, 2007; Recorder, 2003–09. Member, Editorial Board: Internat. Travel Law Jl, 2002–; Travel Law Qly, 2009–. Chm., Travel and Tourism Lawyers' Assoc., 1997–2009. Trustee, St Giles Organ Project, 2009–. *Publications:* Travel Law and Litigation, 1998, 4th edn 2008; Package Travel Cases and Materials, 2008. *Recreations:* classical pipe organs (playing, listening, restoring), choral music. *Address:* Central London Civil Justice Centre, Thomas More Building, Royal Courts of Justice, Strand, WC2A 2LL.

**SAGOVSKY, Rev. Canon Nicholas,** PhD; Whitelands Professorial Fellow, Roehampton University, 2011–18; *b* 13 Aug. 1947; *s* of Vladimir Sagovsky and Hilary Douglas Sagovsky (*née* Taylor); *m* 1974, Ruth Scott; one *s* one *d*. *Educ:* Oundle Sch.; Corpus Christi Coll., Oxford (BA (English Lang. and Lit.) 1969); St John's Coll., Nottingham and Nottingham Univ. (BA (Theol.) 1973); St Edmund's Coll., Cambridge (PhD 1981). Ordained deacon, 1974, priest, 1975; Curate: St Gabriel's, Heaton, 1974–77; Gt St Mary's, Cambridge, 1981–82; Vice Principal, Edinburgh Theol Coll., 1982–86; Dean, Clare Coll., Cambridge, 1986–97; William Leech Prof. of Applied Christian Theol., Newcastle Univ., 1997–2002; Liverpool Prof. of Theol. and Public Life, Liverpool Hope UC, 2002–04; Canon Theologian, 2004–11, Sub-Dean, 2010–11, Westminster Abbey. Hon. Prof., Durham Univ., 1997–2000; Visiting Professor: Liverpool Hope Univ. (formerly University Coll.), 2004–15; KCL, 2016–. Mem., ARCIC, 1992–2018. *Publications:* Between Two Worlds: George Tyrrell's relationship to the thought of Matthew Arnold, 1983; On God's Side: a life of George Tyrrell, 1990; Ecumenism, Christian Origins and the Practice of Communion, 2000; Christian Tradition and the Practice of Justice, 2008. *Recreations:* rough gardening and other Northumbrian pursuits. *Address:* c/o Chapter Office, Dean's Yard, Westminster Abbey, SW1P 3PA. *T:* (020) 7654 4808.

**SAHAKIAN, Prof. Barbara Jacquelyn,** DSc; FBA 2017; FMedSci; Professor of Clinical Neuropsychology, University of Cambridge, since 2002; Fellow, Clare Hall, Cambridge, since 1997; *b* Boston, Mass, 17 March 1952; *d* of Prof. William S. Sahakian and Dr Mabel Lewis Sahakian; *m* 1979, Prof. Trevor William Robbins, *qv;* two *d*. *Educ:* Beaver Country Day Sch.; Mount Holyoke Coll. (BA *magna cum laude* 1973); Darwin Coll., Cambridge (PhD 1977); Dip. Clin. Psychol., BPsS, 1986; DSc Cantab 2015. Res. Associate, MIT, 1977–79; Asst Prof., Univ. of Mass Med. Center, 1978–79; MRC Res. Scientist, MRC Dunn Nutrition Unit, 1979–82; Res. Scientist, Inst. Neurol., London, 1983–85; probationer clin. psychologist, Northwest Thames RHA, 1983–85; Lectr, 1985–89, Sen. Lectr, 1989–91, Inst. of Psychiatry, London; Lectr, 1991–99, Reader, 1999–2002, Univ. of Cambridge; Bye Fellow, Christ's Coll., Cambridge, 1998–2007. Member: WEF Global Agenda Council on Brain Res., 2015–17; WEF on Future of Neurotechnologies and Brain Sci., 2017–; Clin. Adv. Bd, Human Brain Project, 2017–. FMedSci 2004. *Publications:* (ed jtly) Mental Capital and Wellbeing, 2009; (ed jtly) The Oxford Handbook of Neuroethics, 2011; (jtly) Bad Moves: how decision making goes wrong and the ethics of smart drugs, 2013; (jtly) Sex, Lies and Brain Scans: how fMRI reveals what really goes on in our minds, 2017. *Recreations:* communication of science and mental health to the public at science festivals and literary festivals; theatre, art, opera. *Address:* Department of Psychiatry and Behavioural and Clinical Neuroscience Institute, University of Cambridge, Herchel Smith Building for Brain and Mind Sciences, Forvie Site, Robinson Way, Cambridge CB2 0SZ. *T:* (01223) 768009. *E:* bjs1001@cam.ac.uk. *Club:* Oxford and Cambridge.

**SAHOTA, Onkar Singh;** Member (Lab) Ealing and Hillingdon, London Assembly, Greater London Authority, since 2012; *s* of Pargat Singh and Parminder Kaur; one *s* two *d*. *Educ:* Sheffield Univ. Med. Sch. (MB ChB 1983); London Business Sch. (MBA 1999). MRCS, LRCP 1984; DRCOG 1988; MRCGP 1989. Specialisation in family medicine, St Mary's Hosp. Med. Sch., London; hse surgeon, Royal Hallamshire Hosp., Sheffield, 1984; hse physician, Milton Keynes Gen. Hosp., 1985; gen. practice vocational trng scheme, 1986–89; GP, 1989–; est. own practice, Hanwell and Southall, 1994. Consultant, DFID and World Bank health projects, 1999–2003. Chm. and Mem., Southall and W Ealing PCG, 2001–05; Mem., Ealing PCT, 2005–12; Dir, Family Health Practices Gp, 2008–. Greater London Authority: Chair, Health Cttee, 2014–; Member: Regeneration Cttee, 2014–16; Envmt Cttee, 2014–16. JP Middx 1999. Trustee, Trust for London. *Address:* Greater London Authority, City Hall, Queen's Walk, SE1 2AA.

**SAÏD, Wafic Rida;** businessman, entrepreneur and philanthropist; Founder and Chairman, Saïd Foundation (formerly Karim Rida Saïd Foundation), since 1982; Founder, 1987, and Director, since 2017, Saïd Holdings Ltd (Chairman of the Board, 1987–2012; Chairman, Investment Committee, 2012–16); *b* Damascus, 21 Dec. 1939; *s* of Dr Rida Saïd and Kheire Mamiche Saïd; *m* 1969, Rosemary Thompson; one *s* one *d* (and one *s* decd). *Educ:* Coll. de Notre-Dame de Jamhour, Lebanon. Inst. of Bankers. Started investment banking career at Union Bank of Switzerland, Geneva, 1968; estd consultancy business for design and construction projects, Saudi Arabia, 1969; Co-Founder, Sagitta Asset Mgt Ltd, 1995. Mem., Bd, Banque Libano-Française, 2005–17. Benefactor and Founder Trustee, Saïd Business Sch. Foundn, 1998; Mem., Ct of Benefactors, Univ. of Oxford, 1992–. Hon. Fellow, Trinity Coll., Oxford, 2004; Foundn Fellow, Somerville Coll., Oxford, 2016. Ambassador of St Vincent and the Grenadines to UNESCO, 1996–2018, to the Holy See, 2012–18. Grand Commandeur: Ordre de Mérite du Cèdre (Lebanon); Ordre Chérifien (Morocco). *Recreations:* architecture, art, music. *Clubs:* White's, Royal Automobile; Monaco Yacht; Cercle de l'Union Interalliée (Paris); Eagle (Gstaad); Brook (New York).

**SAINI, Hon. Sir Pushpinder Singh,** Kt 2019; **Hon. Mr Justice Saini;** a Judge of the High Court, Queen's Bench Division, since 2019; *b* Nairobi, 26 Feb. 1968; *s* of late Surrinder Jit Singh Saini and Janak Dulari; *m* 1996, Gemma White; one *s* one *d*. *Educ:* Dormers Wells High Sch., Southall; Corpus Christi Coll., Oxford (MA, BCL). Called to the Bar, Gray's Inn, 1991, Bencher, 2012; barrister, Blackstone Chambers, 1992–2019; QC 2008; a Dep. High Court Judge, 2017–19. *Address:* Royal Courts of Justice, Strand, WC2A 2LL.

**SAINSBURY,** family name of **Barons Sainsbury of Preston Candover** and **Sainsbury of Turville**.

**SAINSBURY OF PRESTON CANDOVER,** Baron *cr* 1989 (Life Peer), of Preston Candover in the county of Hampshire; **John Davan Sainsbury,** KG 1992; Kt 1980; President, J Sainsbury plc, since 1992 (Vice-Chairman, 1967–69; Chairman, 1969–92; Director, 1958–92); *b* 2 Nov. 1927; *e s* of Baron Sainsbury; *m* 1963, Anya Linden, *qv;* two *s* one *d*. *Educ:* Stowe School; Worcester College, Oxford (Hon. Fellow 1982). Director: Royal Opera House, Covent Garden, 1969–85 (Chm., 1987–91; Hon. Vice Pres., 2009–; Hon. Dir, 2016–); Rambert Sch. of Ballet and Contemporary Dance, 2003–05; Chairman: Friends of Covent Garden, 1969–81; Benesh Inst. of Choreology, 1986–87; Bd of Trustees, Dulwich Picture Gall., 1994–2000 (Patron, 2004–); Govs, Royal Ballet, 1995–2003 (Gov., 1987–2003); Trustees, Royal Opera House Endowment Fund, 2001–05; Rambert Sch. Trust, 2005–10 (Chm., Develt Cttee, 2002–03, Steering Cttee, 2005–09); Gov., Royal Ballet Sch., 1965–76, and 1987–91. Director: The Economist, 1972–80; Royal Opera House Trust, 1974–84 and 1987–97; Jt Hon. Treas., European Movt, 1972–75; Pres., British Retail Consortium, 1993–97 (Mem. Council, Retail Consortium, 1975–79); Member: Nat. Cttee for Electoral Reform, 1976–85; President's Cttee, CBI, 1982–84; Jt Parly Scrutiny Cttee on Draft Charities Bill, 2004–05; Bd, Centre for Policy Studies, 2009–12. Contemporary Arts Society: Hon. Sec., 1965–71; Vice Chm., 1971–74; Vice Pres., 1984–96; Vice Patron, 1998–2006; Patron, Sir Harold Hillier Gardens and Arboretum, 2005–; Trustee: Nat. Gall., 1976–83; Westminster Abbey Trust, 1977–83; Tate Gall., 1982–83; Rhodes Trust, 1984–98; Saïd Business Sch. Foundn, 2003–15. Visitor, Ashmolean Mus., 2003–15. Dir, Friends of the Nelson Mandela Children's Fund, 1996–2000. Pres., Sparsholt Coll., Hants, 1993–2000. Hon. Bencher, Inner Temple, 1985. Hon. Fellow, British Sch. at Rome, 2002. Hon. DScEcon London, 1985; Hon. DLitt South Bank, 1992; Hon. LLD Bristol, 1993; Hon. DEconSc Cape Town, 2000. Albert Medal, RSA, 1989; Hadrian Award, World Monuments Fund, 2000; Prince of Wales Medal for Arts Philanthropy, 2008; Sheldon Medal, Univ. of Oxford, 2010; Gjergj Kastrioti-Skenderbeg Presidential Award, Albania, 2014. *Address:* c/o 33 Holborn, EC1N 2HT. *T:* (020) 7695 6000. *Clubs:* Garrick, Beefsteak.

See also Rt Hon. Sir T. A. D. Sainsbury.

**SAINSBURY OF PRESTON CANDOVER, Lady;** *see* Linden, Anya.

**SAINSBURY OF TURVILLE,** Baron *cr* 1997 (Life Peer), of Turville in the co. of Buckinghamshire; **David John Sainsbury;** Chancellor, University of Cambridge, since 2011; *b* 24 Oct. 1940; *s* of Sir Robert Sainsbury and Lisa Ingeborg (*née* Van den Bergh); *m* 1973, Susan Carroll Reid (CBE 2010); three *d*. *Educ:* King's Coll., Cambridge (BA); Columbia Univ., NY (MBA). Joined J. Sainsbury, 1963; Finance Dir, 1973–90; Dep. Chm., 1988–92; Chm., 1992–98; Chief Exec., 1992–97. Parly Under-Sec. of State, DTI, 1998–2006. Member: Cttee of Review of the Post Office (Carter Cttee), 1975–77; IPPR Commn on Public Policy and British Business, 1995–97. Founder, Gatsby Charitable Foundn, 1967. Trustee, Social Democratic Party, 1982–90; Mem. Governing Body, London Business Sch., 1985–98 (Chm., 1991–98); Chairman: Transition Bd, Univ. for Industry, 1998–99; Inst. for Govt, 2009–. Hon. FREng (Hon. FEng 1994); Hon. FRS 2008; Hon. FMedSci 2008; Hon. FBA 2016. Hon. doctorates from Cambridge, Oxford, Manchester, Imperial Coll. London and Rockefeller Univ. Andrew Carnegie Medal of Philanthropy (on behalf of Sainsbury family), Carnegie Inst., 2003. *Publications:* Government and Industry: a new partnership, 1981; (with Christopher Smallwood) Wealth Creation and Jobs, 1987; A Race to the Top: a review of Government's science and innovation policies, 2007; Progressive Capitalism: how to achieve economic growth, liberty and social justice, 2013.

**SAINSBURY, Alexander John;** Founder, and Director, Raven Row, since 2008; *b* London, 17 Jan. 1968; *s* of Rt Hon. Sir Timothy Alan Davan Sainsbury, *qv;* m 2003, Elinor Jansz; two *s*. *Educ:* Eton Coll.; New York Univ. Rear Window, contemp. art exhibns collective, 1993–95; Dir, 38 Langham St Art Gall., 2001–03. Settlor Trustee, Glass-House Trust, 1994–; Co-founder Trustee: Peer, 1998–2003; MayDay Rooms, 2013–; Founder: A Space, Children's Centre, Hackney, 1997; Glass-House Community Led Design, 1999; Chair of Bd, Whitechapel Gall., 2015–. *Publications:* (ed) Francesco Lo Savio, 2001. *Recreations:* cinema, architecture. *Address:* Sainsbury Family Charitable Trusts, The Peak, 5 Wilton Road, SW1V 1AP. *T:* (020) 7410 0330, *Fax:* (020) 7410 0332. *E:* info@ravenrow.org.

**SAINSBURY, Prof. (Richard) Mark,** FBA 1998; Professor of Philosophy, University of Texas at Austin, since 2002; *b* 2 July 1943; *s* of late Richard Eric Sainsbury and Freda Margaret Sainsbury (*née* Horne); *m* 1st, 1970, Gillian McNeill Rind (marr. diss. 2000); one *s* one *d*; 2nd, 2000, Victoria Goodman. *Educ:* Sherborne Sch.; Corpus Christi Coll., Oxford (MA, DPhil). Lecturer in Philosophy: Magdalen Coll., Oxford, 1968–70; St Hilda's Coll., Oxford, 1970–73; Brasenose Coll., Oxford, 1973–75; Univ. of Essex, 1975–78; Bedford Coll., Univ. of London, 1978–84; King's College London: Lectr in Philosophy, 1984–87; Reader in Philosophy, 1987–89; Stebbing Prof. of Philosophy, 1989–2008. Leverhulme Sen. Res. Fellow, 2000–02. Editor of Mind, 1990–2000. *Publications:* Russell, 1979; Paradoxes, 1988, 3rd edn 2009; Logical Forms, 1991, 2nd edn 2000; Departing From Frege, 2002; Reference Without Referents, 2005; Fiction and Fictionalism, 2009; (with Michael Tye) Seven Puzzles of Thought and How to Solve Them: an originalist theory of concepts, 2012; Thinking About Things, 2018. *Recreation:* baking bread. *Address:* Department of Philosophy, University of Texas, Austin, TX 78712, USA. *E:* marksainsbury@austin.utexas.edu. *W:* www.marksainsbury.net.

**SAINSBURY, Rt Rev. Dr Roger Frederick;** Chairman, Churches Together in England Urban Mission Group, 2011–13; an Assistant Bishop, Diocese of Bath and Wells, since 2003; *b* 2 Oct. 1936; *s* of Frederick William Sainsbury and Lillian Maude Sainsbury; *m* 1960, Jennifer Marguerite Carey. *Educ:* High Wycombe Royal Grammar School; Jesus Coll., Cambridge (MA); Clifton Theological Coll.; Seabury-Western Theol Seminary (DMin). Curate, Christ Church, Spitalfields, 1960–63; Missioner, Shrewsbury House, Liverpool, 1963–74; Warden, Mayflower Family Centre, Canning Town, 1974–81; Priest-in-Charge, St Luke, Victoria Dock, 1978–81; Vicar of Walsall, 1981–87; Rector, Walsall Team Ministry, 1987–88; Archdeacon of West Ham, 1988–91; Area Bp of Barking, 1991–2002. Alderman, London Borough of Newham, 1976–78. Moderator, Churches' Commn for Racial Justice, 1999–2003; Chairman: Frontier Youth Trustees, 1987–92; Barking Area Church Leaders Gp, 1994–2002; Urban Bishops Panel, 1996–2001; London Churches Gp, 1998–2002; Nat. Youth Agency, 2002–08; Trustees, Children in Distress, 1998–2000; Centre for Youth Ministry, 2004–07; UK Urban Congress Exec., 2005–; Co-Chair, Urban Mission Develt Adv. Project, 2004–10. Member: Coll. of Preachers, 2002–; Coll. of Evangelists, 2003–. Pres., Frontier Youth Trust, 2002–. Vice Chm., Trustees, Portishead Youth Centre, 2010–; Trustee, Evangelical Coalition for Urban Mission, 2002–. Tutor, Trinity Coll., Bristol, 2006–09. Mem., Friends of Sedgewick Mus., 2005–. *Publications:* From a Mersey Wall, 1970; Justice on the Agenda, 1985; Lifestyle, 1986; Rooted and Grounded in Love, 1988; God of New Beginnings, 1990; Young People as Prophets, 2006; Ten Commandments for Today, 2013. *Recreations:* geology, art, gardening. *Address:* (home) Abbey Lodge, Battery Lane, Portishead, Bristol BS20 7JD.

**SAINSBURY, Rt Hon. Sir Timothy (Alan Davan),** Kt 1995; PC 1992; b 11 June 1932; y s of Baron Sainsbury; m 1961, Susan Mary Mitchell; two s two d. Educ: Eton; Worcester Coll., Oxford (MA; Hon. Fellow 1982). Dir, J. Sainsbury, 1962–83; non-exec. Dir, J. Sainsbury plc, 1995–99; Chairman: Pendennis Shipyard (Hldgs) Ltd, 1999–2007; Marlborough Tiles Ltd, 1999–. Chm., Council for the Unit for Retail Planning Information Ltd, 1974–79. MP (C) Hove, Nov. 1973–1997. PPS to Sec. of State for the Environment, 1979–83, to Sec. of State for Defence, 1983; a Govt Whip, 1983–87; Parly Under-Sec. of State for Defence Procurement, 1987–89; Parly Under-Sec. of State, FCO, 1989–90; Minister of State, DTI, 1990–94 (Minister for Trade, 1990–92, for Industry, 1992–94). Pres., Cons. Friends of Israel, 1997–2005 (Parly Chm., 1994–97). Chm., Somerset House Ltd, then Somerset House Trust, 1997–2002. Mem. Council, RSA, 1981–83. Visitor, Ashmolean Mus., Oxford, 2000–06; Trustee, V&A Mus., 2003–11; Chm., V&A Foundn, 2012–. FSA 2009. Hon. FRIBA 1994; Hon. FRICS 1994.
See also P. Frankopan, Baron Sainsbury of Preston Candover, A. J. Sainsbury, Rt Hon. S. A. Woodward.

**SAINT, Prof. Andrew John;** General Editor, Survey of London, 2006–15; b 30 Nov. 1946; s of late Arthur James Maxwell Saint and Elisabeth Yvetta Saint (née Butterfield); three d. Educ: Christ's Hosp.; Balliol Coll., Oxford. Part-time Lectr, Univ. of Essex, 1971–74; Architectural Editor, Survey of London, 1974–86; Historian, London Div., English Heritage, 1986–95; Prof. of Architecture, Univ. of Cambridge, 1995–2006. Hon. FRIBA 1993. Publications: Richard Norman Shaw, 1976, 2nd edn 2010; The Image of the Architect, 1983; Towards a Social Architecture, 1987; (ed with D. Keene and A. Burns) St Paul's: the cathedral church of London 604–2004, 2004; Architect and Engineer: a study in sibling rivalry, 2007. Address: 14 Denny Crescent, SE11 4UY. T: (020) 7735 3863. E: ajs61@cam.ac.uk.

**ST ALBANS, 14th Duke of,** cr 1684; **Murray de Vere Beauclerk;** Earl of Burford, Baron of Heddington, 1676; Baron Vere of Hanworth, 1750; Hereditary Grand Falconer of England; Hereditary Registrar, Court of Chancery; Partner, Burford & Partners LLP (formerly Burford & Co.), chartered accountants, 1981–2015; b 19 Jan. 1939; s of 13th Duke of St Albans, OBE and Nathalie Chatham, d of P. F. Walker (later Mrs Nathalie C. Eldrid, d 1989); S father, 1988; m 1st, 1963, Rosemary Frances Scoones (marr. diss. 1974); one s one d; 2nd, 1974, Cynthia Theresa Mary (marr. diss. 2002; she d 2002), d of late Lt-Col W. J. H. Howard, DSO and formerly wife of Sir Anthony Robin Maurice Hooper, 2nd Bt; 3rd, 2002, Gillian Anita, d of late Lt-Col C. G. R. Northam and widow of Philip Nesfield Roberts. Educ: Tonbridge. Chartered Accountant, 1962. Gov.-Gen., Royal Stuart Soc., 1989–. Pres., Beaufort Opera, 1991–; Patron, Bestwood Male Voice Choir, 2001–. Liveryman, Drapers' Co., 1971–. Heir: s Earl of Burford, qv. Address: 16 Ovington Street, SW3 2JB.
See also D. C. S. Smellie.

**ST ALBANS, Bishop of,** since 2009; **Rt Rev. Alan Gregory Clayton Smith,** PhD; b 14 Feb. 1957; s of late Frank Eric Smith and of Rosemary Clayton Smith (née Barker). Educ: Trowbridge Grammar Sch.; Univ. of Birmingham (BA Theol. 1978; MA 1979; Hon. DD 2010); Wycliffe Hall, Oxford; Univ. of Wales, Bangor (PhD 2002). Ordained deacon, 1981, priest, 1982; Assistant Curate: St Lawrence, Pudsey, 1981–82; St Lawrence and St Paul, Pudsey, 1982–84; Chaplain, Lee Abbey Community, Devon, 1984–90; Diocesan Missioner, Lichfield, 1990–97; Team Vicar, St Matthew's, Walsall, 1990–97; Archdeacon, Stoke-upon-Trent, 1997–2001; Bishop Suffragan of Shrewsbury, 2001–09. Hon. Canon, Lichfield Cathedral, 1997–2009. Entered H of L, 2013. Chm., Shropshire Strategic Partnership, 2005–09. Vice Chm., Mission and Public Affairs, C of E, 2016–. Pres., Rural Coalition, 2016–; Vice Pres., LGA, 2017– Publications: Growing Up in Multifaith Britain, 2007; God-Shaped Mission, 2008; The Reflective Leader, 2011; Saints and Pilgrims in the Diocese of St Albans, 2013. Recreations: classical music, travel, ski-ing. Address: Abbey Gate House, 4 Abbey Mill Lane, St Albans AL3 4HD. T: (01727) 853305, Fax: (01727) 846715. E: bishop@stalbans.anglican.org.

**ST ALBANS, Dean of;** see John, Very Rev. J. P. H.

**ST ALBANS, Archdeacon of;** see Smith, Ven. J. P.

**ST ALDWYN,** 3rd Earl cr 1915; **Michael Henry Hicks Beach;** Bt 1619; Viscount St Aldwyn 1906; Viscount Quenington 1915; b 7 Feb. 1950; s of 2nd Earl St Aldwyn, GBE, TD, PC and Diana Mary Christian Smyly (d 1992), o d of Henry C. G. Mills; S father, 1992; m 1st, 1982, Gilda Maria, o d of Barão Saavedra, Copacabana, Rio de Janeiro (marr. diss. 2005); two d; 2nd, 2005, Louise Wigan (marr. diss. 2014). Educ: Eton; Christ Church, Oxford (MA). Heir: b Hon. David Seymour Hicks Beach [b 25 May 1955; m 1993, Kate, d of Michael Henriques; one s two d]. Address: The Mill House, Coln St Aldwyns, Cirencester, Glos GL7 5AJ. T: (01285) 750226.

**ST ANDREWS, Earl of; George Philip Nicholas Windsor;** b 26 June 1962; s of HRH the Duke of Kent and HRH the Duchess of Kent; m 1988, Sylvana Tomaselli; one s two d. Educ: Eton (King's Scholar); Downing College, Cambridge. Attached to FCO (UN, NY and Budapest), 1987–88. Specialist, Christie's (Books and Manuscripts Dept), 1996–98. Trustee: GB-Sasakawa Foundn, 1995– (Chm., 2005–); SOS Children's Villages UK, 1999–; Golden Web Foundn, 2003–12 (Chm., 2006–12); Prince George Galitzine Meml Library, 2005–; Global EHealth Foundn, 2013–; Mem., Adv. Bd, Next Century Foundn, 2012–. Patron: Worldwide Cancer Res. (formerly Assoc. for Internat. Cancer Res.), 1995–; Princess Margarita of Romania Trust, 1997–; Welsh Sinfonia, 2011–; Friends of Mongolia and Inner Asia Studies Unit, Univ. of Cambridge, 2012–; Centre for Islamic Finance, Univ. of Bolton, 2013–; Chancellor, Univ. of Bolton, 2017–. Heir: s Lord Downpatrick, qv. Address: York House, St James's Palace, SW1A 1BQ.
See under Royal Family.

**ST ANDREWS & EDINBURGH, Archbishop of, (RC),** since 2013; **Most Rev. Leo Cushley;** b Wester Moffat, 18 June 1961; s of William Cushley and Eileen Cushley (née Kane). Educ: All Saints Primary Sch., Coatdyke; St John Baptist's Primary Sch., Uddington; Holy Cross High Sch., Hamilton; St Mary's Coll., Blairs; Pontifical Scots Coll., Rome; Pontifical Gregorian Univ., Rome (PhB 1981; STB 1984; JCD 1997); Pontifical Liturgical Inst., Rome (Licence in Liturgy 1987). Ordained priest, 1985; Curate: Cath. Church of Our Lady of Good Aid, Motherwell, 1987–88; St Serf's Parish, Airdrie and Chaplain, St Margaret's High Sch., Airdrie, 1988–92; St Aidan's Parish, Wishaw, 1992–93; Chaplain: St Aidan's High Sch., Wishaw, 1992–93; Our Lady's High Sch., Motherwell, 1992–93; entered Dip. Service of Holy See, 1997; Second Secretary, Apostolic Nunciature in Burundi, 1997–2001; First Secretary: Portugal, 2001–04; Holy See Perm. Observer Mission to the UN, New York, 2004–07; Counsellor: S Africa, 2007–08; Botswana, 2008–09; Hd, English-lang. section, Vatican Secretariat of State, 2009–13; Prelate of the Anticamera, Apostolic Palace, 2012–13. Grand Cross, Conventual Chaplain ad honorem, SMHO of St John of Jerusalem, of Rhodes and of Malta, 2015. Recreations: hill-walking, music, films, books. Address: Archdiocesan Offices, 100 Strathearn Road, Edinburgh EH9 1BB.

**ST ANDREWS, DUNKELD AND DUNBLANE, Bishop of,** since 2018; **Rt Rev. Ian James Paton;** b Liverpool, 1957; m; one s. Educ: Jesus Coll., Cambridge (BA 1978; PGCE 1979); Westcott House, Cambridge (MA 1981); Edinburgh Univ. (MTh 2007). Ordained deacon, 1982, priest, 1983; Curate, Christ Church, Reading, 1982–84; Chaplain to Bishop of Oxford, 1984–86; Chaplain, Wadham Coll., Oxford and Asst Priest, University Church, Oxford, 1986–90; Canon and Vice Provost, St Mary's Cathedral, Edinburgh, 1990–94; Rector: Holy Trinity, Haddington and St Anne, Dunbar, 1994–97; Old St Paul's, Edinburgh, 1997–2018; Canon, St Mary's Cathedral, Edinburgh, 2004–18; Hon. Anglican Chaplain, Univ. of Edinburgh, 2013–18. Convenor, Liturgy Cttee, Scottish Episcopal Church, 1996–2002, 2011–14. Associate Tutor, Scottish Theol Inst., 1994–2014. Chair, Positive Help, 1992–94. Publications: contribs to Expository Times, Anaphora, Practical Theology. Recreations: reading and writing poetry, art, theatre, French culture and life; Scottish history, art and literature. Address: c/o The Diocese of St Andrews, Dunkeld and Dunblane, 28a Balhousie Street, Perth PH1 5HJ. T: (01738) 580426. E: bishop@standrews.anglican.org.

**ST ANDREWS, DUNKELD AND DUNBLANE, Dean of;** see Rathband, Very Rev. K. W.

**ST ASAPH, Bishop of,** since 2009; **Rt Rev. Gregory Kenneth Cameron;** b Tredegar, Monmouthshire, 6 June 1959; s of Kenneth Hughes Cameron and Irene Cameron; m 1995, Clare Margaret Lee; three s. Educ: Croesyceiliog Grammar, later Comprehensive Sch., Torfaen; Lincoln Coll., Oxford (MA 1984; Hon. Fellow 2010); Downing Coll., Cambridge (MA 1986); St Michael and All Angels Theol Coll., Llandaff (Dip. in Pastoral Studies 1983); Univ. of Wales Coll., Cardiff (MPhil 1990; LLM 1997). Ordained deacon, 1983, priest, 1984; Asst Curate, Parish of St Paul, Newport, 1983–86; Asst Priest/Team Vicar, Rectorial Benefice of Llanmartin, 1986–88; Chaplain and Hd of Religious Studies, Wycliffe Coll., Stonehouse, Glos, 1988–94 (Asst Housemaster, Haywardsfield, 1991–94); Dir, Bloxham Project, Oxford, 1994–2000; Chaplain to the Archbishop of Wales, 2000–03; Dep. Sec. Gen. and Dir of Ecumenical Affairs and Studies, Anglican Consultative Council, 2003–09. Anglican Co-Chair, Anglican Oriental Orthodox Internat. Commn, 2015–; Chm., Commn of Covenanted Churches in Wales, 2018–. Hon. Canon, Monmouth, 2003–09. Tutor, St Michael's Theol Coll., Llandaff, 1986–89; Lectr in Old Testament, Univ. Coll., Cardiff, 1986–89; Res. Fellow, 1998, Hon. Res. Fellow, 1999–, Centre for Law and Religion, Cardiff Univ. JP Glos, 1992–98. Hon. DD Episcopal Divinity Sch., Cambridge, Mass, 2007. Publications: (contrib.) Render Unto Caesar, 1999; (jtly) Christian Character, 2001; (contrib.) Faithful Discipleship, 2001; (ed jtly) Anglican-Lutheran Agreements, 2004; (co-ed) Mary, Grace and Hope in Christ: study guide, 2006; (contrib.) An Anglican Covenant, 2008; (contrib.) Faith in Action, 2008; (contrib.) Companion to the Anglican Communion, 2013; (contrib.) The Lambeth Conference, 2017. Recreations: art, ancient history, calligraphy, classical and film music, egyptology, heraldry, liturgy, reading, travel, world history, coin designer for Royal Mint and for London Mint Office. Address: Esgobty, Llanelwy, St Asaph LL17 0TW. T: (01745) 583503. E: bishop.stasaph@churchinwales.org.uk.

**ST ASAPH, Dean of;** see Williams, Very Rev. N. H.

**ST ASAPH, Archdeacon of;** see Grimwood, Ven. A. S.

**ST AUBIN de TERÁN, Lisa Gioconda;** writer; b London, 2 Oct. 1953; d of Cuthbert Jan Alwin Rynveld Carew and late Joan Mary St Aubin; m 1st, 1970, Jaime Terán (marr. diss. 1981); one d; 2nd, 1982, George Mann Macbeth (marr. diss. 1989; he d 1992); one s; 3rd, 1989, Robbie Charles Duff-Scott (marr. diss. 2004); one d; partner, Mees van Deth. Educ: James Allen's Girls' Sch., Dulwich. Sugar farmer and plantation manager, Venezuelan Andes, 1971–78. Founder, Teran Foundn, 2004; voluntary worker, Community Coll. of Tourism and Agriculture, Teran Foundn, Mossuril Dist, N Mozambique, 2005–. Writer of 3 film screenplays. John Llewellyn Rhys Prize, 1983; Eric Gregory Award for Poetry, 1983. Publications: Keepers of the House, 1982 (Somerset Maugham Award, 1983); The Slow Train to Milan, 1983; The Tiger, 1984; High Place (poetry), 1985; The Bay of Silence, 1986; Black Idol, 1987; Indiscreet Journeys, 1989; The Marble Mountain (short stories), 1989; Off the Rails: memoirs of a train addict, 1989; Joanna, 1990; Venice: the four seasons (essays), 1992; Nocturne, 1992; A Valley in Italy: confessions of a house addict, 1994; Distant Landscapes, 1995; The Hacienda (memoirs), 1997; The Palace, 1997; (ed) The Virago Book of Wanderlust and Dreams, 1998; Southpaw (short stories), 1999; Memory Maps (memoirs), 2001; Otto, 2005; Mozambican Mysteries, 2007. Address: Caixa Postal 81, Ilha de Moçambique, Provincia de Nampula, Mozambique.

**ST AUBYN,** family name of **Baron St Levan.**

**ST AUBYN, Edward;** writer; b London, 14 Jan. 1960; one s one d. Educ: Westminster Sch.; Keble Coll., Oxford. Publications: Patrick Melrose novels: Never Mind (Betty Trask Award), 1992; Bad News, 1992; Some Hope, 1994; Mother's Milk, 2006 (Prix Femina Etranger, 2007; South Bank Show Award for Literature, 2007; filmed, 2012); At Last, 2011; other novels: On the Edge, 1998; A Clue to the Exit, 2000; Lost for Words, 2014 (Bollinger Everyman Wodehouse Prize, 2014); Dunbar, 2017. Address: c/o Rogers Coleridge & White Ltd, 20 Powis Mews, W11 1JN. T: (020) 7221 3717. E: info@rcwlitagency.com.

**ST AUBYN, Nicholas Francis;** b 19 Nov. 1955; yr s of late Hon. Piers St Aubyn, MC, and Mary St Aubyn (née Bailey-Southwell); m 1980, Jane Mary, d of late William Frederick Brooks; two s three d. Educ: Eton; Trinity Coll., Oxford (MA PPE). With J. P. Morgan, 1977–86; Kleinwort Benson, 1986–87; American Internat. Gp, 1987–89; Gemini Clothescare, 1989–93; Chm., Fitzroy Gp, 1993. Contested (C) Truro, March 1987, gen. elecn 1987 and 1992. MP (C) Guildford, 1997–2001; contested same seat, 2001. Mem., Select Cttee on Educn and Employment, 1997–2001. Chm. Trustees, Arab-British Centre, 2005–13. Director: Project Trust, 2001–08; Zebra Housing Assoc., 2001–08. MInstD. Publications: Custom of the County, 2010. Recreations: riding, shooting, swimming, sailing. Address: Upper Ifold House, Dunsfold, Surrey GU8 4NX. T: (01483) 200213. Club: Brooks's.
See also Baron St Levan.

**ST AUBYN, Sir William M.;** see Molesworth-St Aubyn.

**ST CLAIR,** family name of **Lord Sinclair.**

**ST CLAIR, William Linn,** FBA 1992; FRSL; author; Senior Research Fellow: School of Advanced Study, University of London, since 2006; Centre for History and Economics, University of Cambridge, since 2007; Chairman, Open Book Publishers, since 2008; b 7 Dec. 1937; s of late Joseph and Susan St Clair, Falkirk; two d. Educ: Edinburgh Acad.; St John's Coll., Oxford. FRSL 1973. Admiralty and MoD, 1961–66; First Sec., FCO, 1966–69; transferred to HM Treasury, 1969, Under Sec., 1990–92; Consultant to OECD, 1992–95, to EC, 1997. Visiting Fellow: All Souls Coll., Oxford, 1981–82; Huntington Library, Calif, 1985; Fellow: All Souls Coll., Oxford, 1992–96; Trinity Coll., Cambridge, 1998–2006. Member: Cttee, London Liby, 1996–2000; Council, British Acad., 1996–2000. Internat. Pres., Byron Soc. Thalassa Forum award for culture, Greece, 2000. Publications:

Lord Elgin and the Marbles, 1967, 3rd edn 1998; That Greece Might Still Be Free, 1972 (Heinemann prize), rev. edn 2008; Trelawny, 1978; Policy Evaluation: a guide for managers, 1988; The Godwins and the Shelleys, 1989 (Time Life prize and Macmillan silver pen); Executive Agencies: a guide to setting targets and measuring performance, 1992; (ed with Irmgard Maassen) Conduct Literature for Women 1500–1640, 2000; Conduct Literature for Women 1640–1710, 2002; (ed with Peter France) Mapping Lives: the uses of biography, 2002; The Reading Nation in the Romantic Period, 2004; The Political Economy of Reading, 2005, rev. edn 2012; The Grand Slave Emporium: Cape Coast Castle and the British slave trade, 2006; The Door of No Return, 2007. *Recreations:* old books, Scottish hills. *Address:* 52 Eaton Place, SW1X 8AL. *Clubs:* Athenæum, PEN.

**ST CLAIR-ERSKINE,** family name of **Earl of Rosslyn**.

**ST CLAIR-FORD, Sir (William) Sam,** 10th Bt *cr* 1793, of Ember Court, Surrey; *b* 24 Jan. 1982; *er s* of Sir Robin Sam St Clair-Ford, 9th Bt and of Alison Frances St Clair-Ford (*née* Dickson); *S* father, 2016; *m* 2011, Kate Esther Anne, *d* of Brian Henderson; one *d*. *Educ:* Edinburgh Acad.; Univ. of Glasgow. *Heir: b* Peter James St Clair-Ford, *b* 17 Feb. 1984.

**ST CYRES, Viscount; Thomas Stafford Northcote;** *b* 5 Aug. 1985; *s* and *heir* of Earl of Iddesleigh, *qv*. *Educ:* Univ. of Exeter (BA Hons 2008; MA 2010). *Recreations:* cricket, cooking, shooting, Rugby, opera, ski-ing. *Address:* Hayne Barton, Newton St Cyres, Exeter, Devon EX5 5AH. *Clubs:* Brooks's, MCC.

**ST DAVIDS,** 4th Viscount *cr* 1918; **Rhodri Colwyn Philipps;** Baron Strange of Knokin, 1299; Baron Hungerford, 1426; Baron de Moleyns, 1445; Bt 1621; Baron St Davids, 1908; *b* 16 Sept. 1966; *s* of 3rd Viscount St Davids and Augusta Victoria Correa Larrain, *d* of late Don Estanislao Correa Ugarte; *S* father, 2009; *m* 2003, Sarah Louise, *o d* of late Dr Peter Butcher. *Educ:* Worth. *Heir: b* Hon. Roland Augusto Jestyn Estanislao Philipps [*b* 9 April 1970; *m* 1997, Jane Amber Robinson (marr. diss. 2004); two *d*].

**ST DAVIDS, Bishop of,** since 2016; **Rt Rev. Joanna Susan Penberthy;** *b* Swansea, 1960. *Educ:* Cardiff High Sch.; Newnham Coll., Cambridge (BA 1981); Cranmer Hall, Durham; St John's Coll., Nottingham (MTh 1984). Ordained deaconess, 1984, deacon, 1987, priest, 1997; Deaconess, St Andrew, Haughton Le Skerne, 1984–85; Deaconess, 1985–89, non-stipendiary Minister, 1987–89, St Isan, Llanishen; non-stipendiary Minister: St Wyddyn, Llanwddyn, 1989–93; St Sadwrn, Llansadwrn, 1993–95; Provincial Officer, Div. for Parochial Develt and Renewal, Church in Wales, 1994–99; Priest-in-charge, 1999–2001, Vicar, 2001–10, St Cynwyl, Cynwyl Gaeo; Priest-in-charge, 2010–11, Rector, 2011–15, St John, Charlton Musgrove, Wincanton; Rector, Glan Ithon, Llandrindod Wells, 2015–16. Adult Educn Officer, 2001–02, Warden of Readers, 2002–10, Dio. of St Davids; Canon, St Davids Cathedral, 2007–10. *Address:* Llys Esgob, Abergwili, Carmarthen SA31 2JG. *T:* (01267) 236597.

**ST DAVIDS, Dean of;** *see* Rowland Jones, Very Rev. S. C.

**ST EDMUNDSBURY, Dean of;** *see* Hawes, Very Rev. J. P.

**ST EDMUNDSBURY AND IPSWICH, Bishop of,** since 2015; **Rt Rev. Martin Alan Seeley;** an Honorary Assistant Bishop, Diocese of Ely, since 2015; *b* 29 May 1954; *s* of Alan and Joyce Seeley; *m* 1st, 1980, Cynthia McLean (marr. diss. 1989); 2nd, 1999, Rev. Jutta Brueck; one *s* one *d*. *Educ:* Jesus Coll., Cambridge (BA 1976, MA 1979); Ripon Coll., Cuddesdon, Oxford; Union Theol Seminary, NYC (STM 1978). Ordained deacon 1978, priest 1979; Curate: Bottesford with Ashby, Scunthorpe, 1978–80; Ch of the Epiphany, NYC, 1980–85; Asst Dir, Trinity Inst., Wall St, NYC, 1981–85; Exec. Dir, Thompson Center, St Louis, Mo, 1985–90; Sec. for Contg Ministerial Educn and Selection Sec., ABM, Gen. Synod of C of E, 1990–96; Vicar, Isle of Dogs, 1996–2006; Principal, Westcott House, Cambridge, 2006–15. Pres., Cambridge Theological Fedn, 2012–15. Hon. Canon, Ely Cathedral, 2007. Cheney Lectr, Yale Univ., 2018. Hon. DD Berkeley Divinity Sch., Yale, 2018. *Recreations:* cooking, playing tenor saxophone, cinema. *Address:* Bishop's House, 4 Park Road, Ipswich, Suffolk IP1 4ST. *T:* (01473) 252829. *E:* bishop.martin@ cofesuffolk.org.

**ST GEORGE, Sir John (Avenel Bligh),** 10th Bt *cr* 1766 (Ire.), of Athlone, co. Westmeath; *b* 18 March 1940; *s* of Sir George Bligh St George, 9th Bt and Mary Somerville St George (*née* Sutcliffe); *S* father, 1995; *m* (marr. diss.); two *d*; *m* 1981, Linda, *d* of Robert Perry; two *s*. *Heir: s* Robert Alexander Bligh St George [*b* 17 Aug. 1983; *m* 2014, Alison Conboy; one *d*].

**ST GEORGE-HYSLOP, Prof. Peter Henry,** OC 2018; MD; FRCPC; FRS 2004; FRSC 2002; FMedSci; Professor of Experimental Neuroscience, University of Cambridge, since 2007; University Professor, since 2003, Director, Tanz Centre for Research in Neurodegenerative Diseases, 1995–2019, University of Toronto; Consultant in Neurology, University Health Network, since 1990; *b* 10 July 1953; *s* of Noel St George-Hyslop and Daphne Bower Hyslop (*née* Tinker); *m* 1985, Veronika Andrea Fried; three *d*. *Educ:* Wellington Sch., Somerset; Univ. of Ottawa (MD *primum cum laude* 1976); Univ. of Toronto; Harvard Univ. FRCPC 1989. Instructor, Dept of Neurology, Harvard Med. Sch., 1987–90; Asst Prof., 1990–95, Prof., 1995–2003, Dept of Medicine, Univ. of Toronto. Director: Toronto Western Hospital Res. Inst., 2004–11; Univ. of Cambridge NIHR - Biomed. Res. Unit in Dementia, 2012–17. Samuel Rudin Dist. Vis. Prof., Columbia Univ., 2012. Foreign Mem., US Nat. Acad. Medicine, 2017. FMedSci 2009; Fellow, Amer. Neurol Assoc., 2013. Award for Med. Res., Metropolitan Life, 1987; Gold Medal in Medicine, Royal Coll. of Physicians Canada, 1993; Potamkin Award, Amer. Acad. Neurol., 1996; Michael Smith Gold Medal for Res. Excellence, MRC of Canada, 1997; F. E. Bennett Award, Amer. Neurol Assoc., 2000; BIAL Award in Med. Scis, 2013; Dan David Prize, Dan David Foundn, 2014; Ryman Prize, Ryman Foundn, 2017; Zenith Award, Alzheimer's Assoc., 2018. *Publications:* more than 425 peer-reviewed scientific articles and 20 book chapters. *Recreation:* vintage sports car racing. *Address:* Cambridge Institute for Medical Research, Cambridge Biomedical Campus, Wellcome-MRC Building, Addenbrooke's Hospital, Hills Road, Cambridge CB2 0XY. *E:* phs22@ cam.ac.uk; Tanz Centre for Research in Neurodegenerative Diseases, University of Toronto, Krembil Discovery Tower, 60 Leonard Avenue, 4th Floor - Reception, Toronto, ON M5T 2S8, Canada. *T:* (416) 978 7461, *Fax:* (416) 978 1878. *E:* CRND.secr@utoronto.ca.

**ST GERMANS,** 11th Earl of, *cr* 1815; **Albert Charger Eliot;** Baron Eliot 1784; *b* 2 Nov. 2004; *s* of Jago Nicholas Aldo Eliot, (Lord Eliot) (*d* 2006) and of Bianca Eliot (*née* Ciambriello); *S* grandfather, 2016. *Heir:* uncle Hon. Louis Robert Eliot [*b* 11 April 1968; partner, Murphy, *d* of Hugo Williams, *qv*; one *s* one *d*].

**ST GERMANS, Bishop Suffragan of;** *no new appointment at time of going to press.*

**ST HELENS,** 2nd Baron *cr* 1964; **Richard Francis Hughes-Young;** *b* 4 Nov. 1945; *s* of 1st Baron St Helens, MC, and Elizabeth Agnes (*d* 1956), *y d* of late Captain Richard Blakiston-Houston; *S* father, 1980; *m* 1983, Mrs Emma R. Talbot-Smith (*d* 2018); one *s* one *d*. *Educ:* Nautical College, Pangbourne. *Heir: s* Henry Thomas Hughes-Young, *b* 7 March 1986.

**ST HELENS AND WARRINGTON, Archdeacon of;** *no new appointment at time of going to press.*

**ST JOHN,** family name of **Earl of Orkney, Viscount Bolingbroke** and **Baron St John of Bletso**.

**ST JOHN, Lord; Michael John Paulet;** *b* 31 Aug. 1999; *s* and *heir* of Earl of Wiltshire, *qv*.

**ST JOHN OF BLETSO,** 21st Baron *cr* 1558; **Anthony Tudor St John;** Bt 1660; *b* 16 May 1957; *s* of 20th Baron St John of Bletso, TD, and of Katharine, *d* of late A. G. von Berg; *S* father, 1978; *m* 1994, Dr Helen Westlake (marr. diss. 2012); two *s* two *d*. *Educ:* Diocesan College, Cape Town; Univ. of Cape Town (BSocSc 1977, BA (Law) 1978); Univ. of S Africa (BProc 1982); London Univ. (LLM 1983). Solicitor. Financial consultant to Smith New Court plc, later Merrill Lynch, London, 1989–2008; Man. Dir, Globix Corp., 1998–2002; Consultant to Globix Europe, 2002–05. Non-executive Chairman: Estate & General (IOM Ltd), 1994–; Spiritel plc, 2004–10; Equest Balkan Properties plc, 2005–08; Strand Hanson, 2015–; non-executive Director: Regal Petroleum plc, 2005–10; Albion Ventures VCT, 2007–; Obtala Resources plc, 2009–. Strategic Adviser: 2e2 Gp plc, 2007–; Chayton Atlas Agriculture (formerly Chayton Capital), 2008–11. Chm., Governing Bd, Certification Internat., 1995–. An Extra Lord-in-Waiting to the Queen, 1998–. Crossbencher in House of Lords, specific interests foreign affairs, envmtl protection, sport, financial services, Africa, IT. Vice Chm., Parly South Africa Gp; Member: EU Select Cttee A on Trade, Finance and Foreign Affairs, 1996–99, 2001–; EU Sub Cttee B, 2003–08; H of L Information Cttee, 2009–16; H of L Select Cttee on Communications, 2009–14; Exec. Cttee, All Party Africa Gp; elected Mem., H of L, 1999. Trustee: Tusk; M'Afrika Tikkun; Coexistence Trust; Alexandra Rose charities (Chm., 2010–14; Life Vice Pres., 2014); Christel House, 2010–; Life Neurological Research Trust; Helen Feather Memorial Trust. Patron, Citizens online. *Recreations:* golf, tennis and ski-ing; bridge. *Heir: s* Hon. Oliver Beauchamp St John, *b* 11 July 1995. *Address:* 102 Cheyne Walk, SW10 0DQ. *Clubs:* Alfred's, Hurlingham; Sunningdale Golf, Beaverbrook Golf (Surrey); Royal Cape Golf (Cape Twon).

**ST JOHN, Rt Rev. Andrew Reginald;** Interim Rector, Church of Holy Apostles, New York, 2016–18; *b* 16 Feb. 1944; *s* of Reginald and Leila St John. *Educ:* Wesley Coll., Melbourne; Melbourne Univ. (LLB 1966); Trinity Coll., Melbourne (ThSchol 1971); Gen. Theol Seminary, New York (STM 1984). Barrister and solicitor, Supreme Court of Victoria, 1967. Ordained priest, 1972; Precentor, St Paul's Cathedral, Melbourne, 1975–78; Vicar: St Mary's, E Chadstone, 1978–84; Holy Trinity, Kew, 1984–95; an Asst Bp, dio. of Melbourne (Bp of the Western Region), 1995–2001; Rector, Ch of the Transfiguration, NY, 2005–16, now Rector Emeritus; Hon. Bp in Residence, St Thomas Ch, NY. Hon. DD Gen. Theol Seminary, NY, 1995. *Recreations:* reading, gardening, opera, travelling. *Address:* 333 East 43rd Street, #918, New York, NY 10017, USA. *T:* (917) 8229845. *Clubs:* Melbourne, Melbourne Cricket (Melbourne); Players (NY).

**ST JOHN, Lauren;** author and journalist, since 1987; *b* 21 Dec. 1966; *d* of Errol Antonie Kendall and Margaret May Dutton Kendall. *Educ:* Roosevelt High Sch., Harare, Zimbabwe; Harare Poly. (Dip. Journalism). Sub-editor, Resident Abroad magazine, 1987; journalist, Today's Golfer, 1988–89; Golf Correspondent, Sunday Times, 1994–98. Mem., Assoc. of Golf Writers, 1989–. *Publications:* Shooting at Clouds: inside the European golf tour, 1991; Seve: the biography, 1993, 2nd edn 1997; Out of Bounds: inside professional golf, 1995; Greg Norman: the biography, 1998; Walkin' After Midnight: a journey to the heart of Nashville, 2000; Hardcore Troubadour: the life and near death of Steve Earle, 2002; Rainbow's End: a memoir of childhood, war and an African farm, 2007; The Obituary Writer, 2013; The Glory, 2015; *for children:* The White Giraffe, 2006; Dolphin Song, 2007; The Last Leopard, 2008; The Elephant's Tale, 2009; Dead Man's Cove, 2010; Kidnap in the Caribbean, 2011; The One Dollar Horse, 2012; Kentucky Thriller, 2012; Rendezvous in Russia, 2013; Race the Wind, 2013; Fire Storm, 2014; Operation Rhino, 2015; The Secret of Supernatural Creek, 2017; The Snow Angel, 2017; Kat Wolfe Investigates, 2018. *Recreations:* music, painting, music, horse riding, saving wildlife, art.

**ST JOHN, Prof. Peter Rowland Tudor,** RA 2018; Partner, Caruso St John Architects, since 1991; Professor of Architecture, The Cass, London Metropolitan University, since 2018; *b* 27 June 1959; *s* of late Oliver Beauchamp St John and Eileen St John (*née* Morris); *m* 1988, Siw Thomas; two *s* one *d*. *Educ:* University Coll. London (BSc Hons); AA Dip. Hons 1984. Major projects include: New Art Gall., Walsall, 2000; extn to Hallfield Sch., Paddington, 2005; Gagosian Gall., King's Cross, 2005; extn to V&A Mus. of Childhood, 2006; Millbank Project, Tate Britain, 2006–13; Chiswick House Gardens Café, 2010; Nottingham Contemporary, 2010; Newport St Gall., Vauxhall, 2015 (RIBA Stirling Prize, 2016); Gagosian Gall., Mayfair, 2015. Sen. Lectr, Poly. of N London, 1990–97; Course Tutor, Grad. Sch. of Design, Harvard Univ., 2005–06. Visiting Professor: Acad. of Architecture, Mendrisio, 1999–2001; Dept of Architecture and Civil Engrg, Univ. of Bath, 2001–04; London Metropolitan Sch. of Architecture (formerly Cass Sch. of Architecture), 2012–18; Guest Prof., ETH Zurich, 2007–09. Jt Curator, British Pavilion, Venice Arch. Biennale, 2018. Hon. DDes Wolverhampton, 2001. *Recreations:* woodlands, swimming. *Address:* Caruso St John Architects, 1 Coate Street, E2 9AG.

**ST JOHN-MILDMAY, Sir Walter (John Hugh),** 11th Bt *cr* 1772, of Farley, Southampton; *b* 3 Sept. 1935; *s* of Michael Paulet St John-Mildmay (*d* 1993), *gggs* of Sir Henry Paulet St John-Mildmay, 3rd Bt, and Joan Elizabeth (*née* Stockley; *d* 1977); *S* kinsman, Rev. Sir (Aubrey) Neville St John-Mildmay, 10th Bt, who *d* 1955, after which Btcy was dormant until revived, 1998. *Educ:* Wycliffe Coll.; Emmanuel Coll., Cambridge (BA 1958); Hammersmith Coll. of Art and Building; RAC Cirencester. *Heir: b* Michael Hugh Paulet St John-Mildmay [*b* 28 Sept. 1937; *m* 1965, Mrs Crystal Margaret Ludlow; two *s* one *d*]. *Address:* 11 The Empire, Grand Parade, Bath BA2 4DF.

**ST JOHN PARKER, Dr Michael,** FSA; Headmaster, Abingdon School, Oxfordshire, 1975–2001; *b* 21 July 1941; *s* of Rev. Canon J. W. Parker; *m* 1965, Annette Monica Ugle; two *s* two *d*. *Educ:* Stamford Sch.; King's Coll., Cambridge (MA); Kellogg Coll., Oxford (MSc; DPhil). Asst Master: Sevenoaks Sch., 1962–63; King's Sch., Canterbury, 1963–69; Winchester Coll., 1969–75; Head of History Dept, Winchester Coll., 1970–75. Schoolmaster Student, Christ Church, Oxford, 1984. Member: Council, Hansard Soc., 1972–2003 (Exec. Cttee, 2001–03); Marsh Cttee on Politics and Industry, 1978–79. Chm., Midland Div., HMC, 1984; Member: Exec. Cttee, Assoc. of Governing Bodies of Ind. Schs, 2002–08; Stowe Adv. Cttee, 2002–; Council, Nat. Trust, 2008–17 (Mem., Governance Rev. Cttee, 2014–15). Governor: St Helen's Sch., 1975–83; Christ Church Cathedral Sch., 1981–2013; Cokethorpe Sch., 1985–2009 (Chm., 1990–2009; Gov. Emeritus, 2010); Josca's Sch., 1988–98; Hatherop Castle Sch., 2002–14 (Chm., 2003–14); Walsall Acad. (formerly Walsall City Acad.), 2003–17; Midhurst Rother Coll., 2008–15. Fellow, Winchester Coll., 2006–13. Chm., Cambridge Soc. of Oxfordshire, 2003–. Dir, Bampton Classical Opera, 2005–. Master, Civic Guild of Old Mercers, 2004–05; Liveryman, 2006, Hon. Archivist, 2007–, Masons' Co. FSA 2011. Contrib. Ed., Attain mag., 2007–12. *Publications:* The British Revolution—Social and Economic History

1750–1970, 1972; The Martlet and the Griffen, 1997; various pamphlets and articles, incl. contribs to Oxford DNB. *Recreations:* old buildings, music, books, gardens. *Address:* Exeter House, Cheapside, Bampton, Oxfordshire OX18 2JL. *Clubs:* Athenæum; Leander.

**ST JOHN-STEVENS, Philip Simeon; His Honour Judge St John-Stevens;** a Circuit Judge, since 2009; Acting Grand Court Judge, Cayman Islands, since 2016; *b* Herts, 10 March 1960; *s* of late Terence Stevens and of Betty Stevens; *m* 1990, Kathryn Jane Nightingale; two *s*. *Educ:* University Coll. Cardiff (LLB Hons). Called to the Bar, Inner Temple, 1985; Attorney Gen. of Montserrat, BWI, 2002; Liaison Judge, Kent Magistrates, 2010–13. Tutor Judge, Judicial Coll.; Mem., Internat. Judicial Coll. Ambassador, Anthony Nolan charity. *Recreations:* golf, cricket, cycling. *Address:* Maidstone Combined Courts, Law Courts, Maidstone ME16 8EQ. *Club:* Rye Golf.

**ST JOHNSTON, Colin David;** Director, Ocean Transport and Trading Ltd, 1974–88; *b* 6 Sept. 1934; *s* of Hal and Sheilagh St Johnston; *m* 1958, Valerie Paget; three *s* one *d*. *Educ:* Shrewsbury Sch.; Lincoln Coll., Oxford. Booker McConnell Ltd, 1958–70; Ocean Transport and Trading Ltd, 1970–88: Dep. Gp Chief Exec., 1985–88; Man. Dir, Ocean Cory, 1976–85; non-exec. Dir, FMC plc, 1981–83; Man. Dir, PRO NED, 1989–95. Mem. Council: Royal Commonwealth Society for the Blind, 1967–95; Industrial Soc., 1981–96; Trustee, Frances Mary Buss Foundn, 1981–95; Governor: Camden Sch., 1974–96; Arnold House Sch., 1993–2005 (Chm., 1995–2004). FRSA. *Recreations:* music, Real and lawn tennis. *Address:* 30 Fitzroy Road, NW1 8TY. *T:* (020) 7722 5932. *Club:* MCC.

*See also* R. D. St Johnston.

**ST JOHNSTON, Prof. (Robert) Daniel,** PhD; FRS 2005; Professor of Developmental Genetics, since 2003, and Director, Gurdon Institute, 2009–18, University of Cambridge; Bye Fellow, Peterhouse, Cambridge, since 1995; Wellcome Trust Principal Fellow, Wellcome Trust/Cancer Research UK Institute of Cancer and Developmental Biology, since 1997; *b* 24 April 1960; *s* of Colin St Johnston, *qv*; partner, Bénédicte Sanson; one *s* one *d*. *Educ:* Christ's Coll., Cambridge (BA 1st cl. (Natural Scis) 1981); Harvard Univ. (PhD (Cellular and Develtl Biol.) 1988). EMBO Post-doctoral Fellow, Max-Planck Inst., Tübingen, Germany, 1988–91; Wellcome Trust Sen. Fellow, Wellcome/CRC Inst. of Cancer and Develtl Biol., and Dept of Genetics, Cambridge Univ., 1991–97. Loeb Fellow, Woods Hole Marine Biol. Lab., 1982; Fellow, EMBO, 1997 (Gold Medal, 2000). Mem. Editl Adv. Bd, Development, 1999–. *Publications:* numerous papers in jls on anterior-posterior axis formation in Drosophila, how cells become polarized, and mechanism of messenger RNA localization. *Recreations:* cryptic crosswords, hill walking, cooking. *Address:* Wellcome Trust/Cancer Research UK Gurdon Institute, Tennis Court Road, Cambridge CB2 1QN. *T:* (01223) 334127.

**ST LEGER,** family name of **Viscount Doneraile**.

**ST LEVAN,** 5th Baron *cr* 1887; **James Piers Southwell St Aubyn;** Bt 1866; *b* 6 June 1950; *s* of Hon. Oliver Piers St Aubyn, MC (*d* 2006), *s* of 3rd Baron St Levan, and Mary Bailey Southwell (*d* 1987); *S* uncle, 2013; *m* 1981, Mary Caroline, *y d* of Peter Ward Bennett, OBE; two *s* two *d*. *Educ:* Eton; Magdalen Coll., Oxford. *Heir: s* Hon. Hugh James St Aubyn, *b* 14 June 1983.

*See also* N. F. St Aubyn.

**ST LOUIS, Brian Lloyd;** QC 2017; *b* London, 25 May 1969; *s* of Gittens James St Louis and Mable St Louis; *m* 2006, Nicola Howard, *qv*; one *s* one *d*. *Educ:* Liverpool Poly. (LLB Hons 1990); King's Coll. London (LLM Eur. Law 1991); Inns of Court Sch. of Law. Called to the Bar, Middle Temple, 1994 (Middle Temple Benefactor's Schol., 1992; Blackstone's Maj. Entrance Exhibn Award, 1992); in practice as barrister specialising in murder, civil and criminal fraud. Member: Criminal Bar Assoc., 1994; Bar Eur. Gp, 1994. Chm., Alcohol Recovery Project, 2000–03. Trustee, Pan Intercultural Arts, 2013–. *Recreations:* ballet, theatre, Arsenal Football Club, cricket, art. *Address:* New Bridge Chambers, 15 New Bridge Street, EC4V 6AU. *T:* (020) 7842 1900, *Fax:* (020) 7842 1901. *E:* brian.stlouis@15nbs.com.

**ST LOUIS, Nicola;** *see* Howard, N.

**ST OSWALD,** 6th Baron *cr* 1885, of Nostell, co. York; **Charles Rowland Andrew Winn;** DL; landowner; *b* 22 July 1959; *s* of 5th Baron St Oswald and of Charlotte Denise Eileen Winn, *d* of Wilfred Haig Loyd; *S* father, 1999; *m* 1985, Louise Alexandra, *yr d* of Stewart Mackenzie Scott; one *s* one *d*. *Educ:* New Sch., King's Langley. DL W Yorks, 2004. *Recreations:* shooting, walking. *Heir: s* Hon. Rowland Charles Sebastian Henry Winn, *b* 15 April 1986. *Address:* Nostell Priory Estate Office, Doncaster Road, Nostell, Wakefield, W Yorkshire WF4 1AB. *T:* (01924) 862221.

**ST PATRICK'S, Dublin, Dean of;** *see* Morton, Very Rev. W. W.

**ST PAUL'S, Dean of;** *see* Ison, Very Rev. D. J.

**ST VINCENT,** 8th Viscount *cr* 1801; **Edward Robert James Jervis;** *b* 12 May 1951; *er s* of 7th Viscount St Vincent and Phillida (*née* Logan); *S* father, 2006; *m* 1977, Victoria Margaret (*d* 2015), *o d* of Wilton Joseph Oldham; one *s* one *d*. *Educ:* Radley. *Heir: s* Hon. James Richard Anthony Jervis, *b* 1982.

**SAINTY, Christopher James;** HM Diplomatic Service; Ambassador to Portugal, since 2018; *b* London, 29 March 1967; *s* of Sir John Christopher Sainty, *qv*; *m* 1993, Sarah Helen Norris; one *s* one *d*. *Educ:* Westminster Sch.; New Coll., Oxford (BA Hons). Entered FCO, 1989; Hong Kong Dept, FCO, 1990–92; Second Sec. (Pol), New Delhi, 1992–96; Common Foreign and Security Policy Unit, FCO, 1996–98; Hd of Newsroom, Press Office, FCO, 1998–2000; First Sec. (Pol), Madrid, 2000–04; Hd, EU Presidency Dept, FCO, 2004–06; Dep. Hd of Mission, The Hague, 2006–08; Political Counsellor, Islamabad, 2008–10; Dep. Hd of Mission, Rome, 2011–15; Eur. Corresp. and Hd, Europe (South) Dept, Europe Directorate, FCO, 2015–17. *Recreations:* running, cycling, playing the piano, learning languages. *Address:* British Embassy, Rua de São Bernardo 33, 1249–082 Lisbon, Portugal. *T:* 213924000. *E:* chris.sainty@fco.gov.uk.

**SAINTY, Sir John Christopher,** KCB 1986; Clerk of the Parliaments, 1983–90, retired; *b* 31 Dec. 1934; *s* of late Christopher Lawrence Sainty and Nancy Lee Sainty (*née* Miller); *m* 1965, (Elizabeth) Frances Sherlock; three *s*. *Educ:* Winchester Coll.; New Coll., Oxford (MA). FSA; FRHistS. Clerk, Parlt Office, House of Lords, 1959; seconded as Private Sec. to Leader of House and Chief Whip, House of Lords, 1963; Clerk of Journals, House of Lords, 1965; Res. Asst and Editor, Inst. of Historical Research, 1970; Reading Clerk, House of Lords, 1974. Mem., Royal Commn on Historical MSS, 1991–2002. Institute of Historical Research: Sen. Res. Fellow, 1994; Hon. Fellow, 2000–. *Publications:* Treasury Officials 1660–1870, 1972; Officials of the Secretaries of State 1660–1782, 1973; Officials of the Boards of Trade 1660–1870, 1974; Admiralty Officials 1660–1870, 1975; Home Office Officials, 1782–1870, 1975; Colonial Office Officials 1794–1870, 1976; (with D. Dewar) Divisions in the House of Lords: an analytical list 1685–1857, 1976; Officers of the Exchequer, 1983; A List of English Law Officers, King's Counsel and Holders of Patents of Precedence, 1987; The Judges of England 1272–1990, 1993; (with R. O. Bucholz) Officials of the Royal Household 1660–1837, vol. 1 1997, vol. 2 1998; Peerage Creations 1649–1800, 1998; articles in Eng. Hist. Rev., Bull. Inst. Hist. Research. *Address:* 94 Ramillies Road, W4 1JA. *T:* (020) 8747 0988. *Club:* Brooks's.

*See also* C. J. Sainty.

**SAKER;** *see* Gordon-Saker.

**SAKMANN, Prof. Bert,** MD; Scientific Director, 2010–11, and Group Leader, Digital Neuroanatomy, since 2010, Max Planck Florida Institute; *b* Stuttgart, 12 June 1942; *m* 1970, Dr Christiane Wülfert; two *s* one *d*. *Educ:* Univ. of Tübingen; Univ. of Munich; University Hosp., Munich; Univ. of Göttingen (MD). Research Asst, Max-Planck-Institut für Psychiatrie, Munich, 1969–70; British Council Fellow, Dept of Biophysics, UCL, 1971–73; Max-Planck-Institut für biophysikalische Chemie, University of Göttingen: Res. Asst, 1974–79; Res. Associate, Membrane Biology Gp, 1979–82; Head, Membrane Physiology Unit, 1983–85; Dir 1985–87, Prof. 1987–89, Dept of Cell Physiology; Dir, Dept of Cell Physiology, Max-Planck-Institut für medizinische Forschung, Heidelberg, 1989–2008; Prof. of Physiology, Medical Faculty, Univ. of Heidelberg, 1990–2007; Gp Leader, Max-Planck-Institut für Neurobiologie, Martinsried, 2008–10. Lectures: Yale, 1982; Washington Univ., Seattle, 1986, 1990; Univ. of Miami, 1989; Liverpool Univ., 1990; Univ. of Rochester, NY, 1991. Foreign Member: Royal Soc., 1994; Nat. Acad., USA, 1993. Numerous prizes and awards; (jtly) Nobel Prize for Physiology, 1991. *Publications:* (contrib.) The Visual System: neurophysiology, biophysics and their clinical applications, 1972; (contrib.) Advances in Pharmacology and Therapeutics, 1978; (contrib. and ed with E. Neher) Single Channel Recording, 1983; (contrib.) Membrane Control of Cellular Activity, 1986; (contrib.) Calcium and Ion Channel Modulation, 1988; (contrib.) Neuromuscular Junction, 1989; numerous articles in jls incl. Annual Rev. Physiol., Jl Physiol., Nature, Proc. Nat. Acad. Scis, Pflügers Archiv, Jl Exptl Physiol., Neuron, FEBS Lett., Science, Eur. Jl Biochem., Proc. Royal Soc., Jl Cell Biol. *Recreations:* tennis, ski-ing, music, reading. *Address:* Max Planck Florida Institute, 1 Max Planck Way, Jupiter, FL 33458, USA.

**SAKO, Prof. Mari,** PhD; Professor of Management Studies, University of Oxford, since 1997; Fellow, New College, Oxford, since 2007; *b* Japan, 12 June 1960; *d* of Kanzo Sako and Akemi Sako; *m* 1983, Sumantra Chakrabarti (*see* Sir S. Chakrabarti); one *d*. *Educ:* Lady Margaret Hall, Oxford (BA Hons); London Sch. of Econs (MSc); PhD London 1990. Researcher, Technical Change Centre, London, 1984–86; London School of Economics and Political Science: Lectr in Modern Japanese Business, 1987–92; Lectr in Industrial Relns, 1992–94; Reader, 1994–97; Fellow, Templeton Coll., Oxford, 1997–2007. Fellow, Japanese Soc. for Promotion of Sci., Kyoto Univ., 1992; Japan Foundn Fellow, Tokyo Univ., 1997. *Publications:* (with R. Dore) How the Japanese Learn to Work, 1989, rev. edn 1998; Prices, Quality and Trust: inter-firm relations in Britain and Japan, 1992; (ed with H. Sato) Japanese Labour and Management in Transition, 1997; (jtly) Are Skills the Answer?, 1998; Shifting Boundaries of the Firm, 2006. *Recreation:* music. *Address:* Saïd Business School, University of Oxford, Park End Street, Oxford OX1 1HP. *T:* (01865) 288925.

**SAKORA, Hon. Sir Bernard Berekia,** KBE 2013 (CBE 2005); CSM; Judge, Supreme Court of Papua New Guinea, 1992–2018; *b* Tufi, Northern Province, PNG, 19 Nov. 1947; *s* of Korimaga and Gandai Sakora; *m* 1975, Roslyn Gay Cunningham; three *s* one *d*. *Educ:* Boys' Grammar Sch., Ipswich, Qld, Australia; Univ. of Papua New Guinea (LLB); University Coll. London (LLM). Barrister and solicitor, Supreme Court of PNG; Legal Officer, Crown Solicitor's Office, 1974–75; Sen. Legal Officer and Dep. State Solicitor, 1975–76; Principal Legal Officer and Asst Sec. for Justice, 1977–79; Dep. Sec., 1979–81; Sen. Lectr, Law Faculty, Univ. of PNG, 1982–92. Chm., Law Reform Commn, 1985–87. Chancellor, Anglican Ch of PNG, 2010–. *Recreations:* reading, watching Rugby and cricket on TV, swimming.

**SALA, Prof. Evis,** MD; PhD; Professor of Oncological Imaging, University of Cambridge, since 2018; Fellow, Girton College, Cambridge, since 2019; *b* Tirana, 5 July 1968; *s* of Bashkim Sala and Valdet Sala; *m* 1993, Dr Gezim Selenica; one *s*. *Educ:* Univ. of Tirana Med. Sch. (MD 1991); St John's Coll., Cambridge (MPhil 1998; PhD 2000). Lectr, Univ. of Cambridge, 2005–12; Chief, Body Imaging Service, Memorial Sloan Kettering Cancer Center, NY, 2012–17; Prof. of Radiol., Weill Cornell Med. Coll., NY, 2015–17. Fellow: Internat. Cancer Imaging Soc., 2013; Internat. Soc. Magnetic Resonance in Medicine, 2015. Honoured Educator Award, Radiol Soc. of N America, 2013, 2017. *Publications:* (ed with A. H. Freeman) Radiology of Stomach and Duodenum, 2007; (ed jtly) Diagnostic Imaging: gynaecology, 2007; (ed jtly) Radiology for Surgeons in Clinical Practice, 2008; Section Ed., Uterus, in Abdominal Imaging, 2013; contribs to peer-reviewed jls. *Address:* 81 Coton Road, Cambridge CB3 9NT. *T:* (01223) 746440. *E:* es220@cam.ac.uk.

**SALEM, Bridget Anne;** *see* O'Connor, B. A.

**SALES, Rt Hon. Lord; Philip James Sales,** Kt 2008; PC 2014; a Justice of the Supreme Court, since 2019; *b* 11 Feb. 1962; *s* of Peter and Janet Sales; *m* 1988, Miranda Wolpert; one *s* one *d*. *Educ:* Royal Grammar Sch., Guildford; Churchill Coll., Cambridge (BA 1983); Worcester Coll., Oxford (BCL 1984). Called to the Bar, Lincoln's Inn, 1985; barrister, 1986–2008; First Treasury Jun. Counsel (Common Law), 1997–2006; Asst Recorder, 1999–2001; Recorder, 2001–08; Dep. High Court Judge, 2004–08; QC 2006; First Treasury Counsel (Common Law), 2006–08; a Judge of the High Court of Justice, Chancery Div., 2008–14; a Lord Justice of Appeal, 2014–19. Mem., Panel of Chairmen, Competition Appeal Tribunal, 2008–19; Dep. Chm., Boundary Commn for England, 2009–14; Vice-Pres., Investigatory Powers Tribunal, 2014–15. *Publications:* (Asst Ed) Halsbury's Laws of England, Vol. I (I), Administrative Law, 4th edn 1989; articles in Cambridge Law Jl, Oxford Jl of Legal Studies, Law Qly Rev., Public Law, Judicial Rev. *Recreations:* theatre, film, reading, open water swimming, ultimate frisbee. *Address:* Supreme Court of the United Kingdom, Parliament Square, SW1P 3BD.

**SALES, (Donald) John;** gardens consultant; Chief Gardens Adviser, then Head of Gardens, The National Trust, 1974–98; *b* 1 May 1933; *s* of Frederic Donald Sales and Alice Elizabeth (*née* Burrell); *m* 1958, Lyn Thompson; three *s*. *Educ:* Westminster City Sch.; Kent Horticultural Coll.; Royal Botanic Gardens, Kew. MHort (RHS) 1957. Lectr in Horticulture, Writtle Agricl Coll., Chelmsford, 1958–70 (Fellow, 1998); Horticulturist (Asst to Gardens Advr), NT, 1971–74. Vice-President: Garden History Soc., 2004–; RHS, 2008–. Medal of Honour, Internat. Castles Inst., 1991; VMH, RHS, 1992; Inst. of Horticulture Award for Outstanding Services to Horticulture, 1996. *Publications:* West Country Gardens, 1980; A Year in the Garden, 2001; Shades of Green, 2018; contrib. articles in Country Life. *Recreations:* gardening, photography, walking, music, ballet, the arts generally. *Address:* Covertside, Perrott's Brook, Cirencester, Glos GL7 7BW. *T:* (01285) 831537.

**SALFORD, Bishop of, (RC),** since 2014; **Rt Rev. John Stanley Kenneth Arnold;** *b* 12 June 1953; *s* of late Stanley Kenneth Arnold and Mary Arnold (*née* Murray). *Educ:* Ratcliffe Coll., Leics; Trinity Coll., Oxford (MA Juris.); Council of Legal Educn, London; Gregorian Univ., Rome (DCL 1985). Called to the Bar, Middle Temple, 1976, Bencher, 2010; ordained priest, 1983; Chaplain, 1985–89, Sub-Adminr, 1989–93, Westminster

Cathedral; Parish Priest, Our Lady of Mt Carmel and St George, Enfield, 1993–2001; Westminster Diocese: VG and Chancellor, 2001–06; Moderator of the Curia, 2005–14 (Chancellor, 2005–10); Auxiliary Bishop of Westminster, (RC), 2006–14; Titular Bishop of Lindisfarne, 2006–14. *Publications:* Quality of Mercy: a fresh look at the Sacrament of Reconciliation, 1993. *Address:* Wardley Hall, Worsley, Manchester M28 2ND. *T:* (0161) 794 2825. *E:* bishop@dioceseofsalford.org.uk.

**SALFORD, Archdeacon of;** *see* Sharples, Ven. D. J.

**SALISBURY, 7th Marquess of,** *cr* 1789; **Robert Michael James Gascoyne Cecil,** KG 2019; KCVO 2012; PC 1994; DL; Baron Cecil, 1603; Viscount Cranborne, 1604; Earl of Salisbury, 1605; Baron Gascoyne-Cecil (Life Peer), 1999; *b* 30 Sept. 1946; *s* of 6th Marquess of Salisbury and Marjorie Olein, (Molly), *d* of Captain Hon. Valentine Wyndham-Quin, RN; *S* father, 2003; *m* 1970, Hannah Ann, *er d* of Lt-Col William Joseph Stirling of Keir; two *s* three *d*. *Educ:* Eton; Oxford. MP (C) Dorset South, 1979–87. Summoned to the Upper House of Parliament, 1992, as Baron Cecil, of Essendon in the County of Rutland; Mem., H of L, 1992–2017. Parly Under-Sec. of State for Defence, MoD, 1992–94; Lord Privy Seal and Leader of H of L, 1994–97; Leader of the Opposition, H of L, 1997–98. Chairman: Comparative Clinical Sci. Foundn, 2004–16; Friends of Lambeth Palace Liby, 2008–; Thames Diamond Jubilee Foundn, 2011–14; President: Friends of BL, 2005–; Game and Wildlife Conservation Trust, 2008–. Chm. Council, RVC, 1998–2007; Chancellor, Univ. of Herts, 2005–. Mem., Bd of Trustees, Hunterian Collection, 2014–. Governor, The Charterhouse, 2009–18. Chm., Ct of Patrons, Thrombosis Res. Inst., 2010–. DL Herts, 2007. *Heir: s* Viscount Cranborne, *qv. Address:* 2 Swan Walk, SW3 4JJ.

**SALISBURY, Bishop of,** since 2011; **Rt Rev. Nicholas Roderick Holtam;** *b* 8 Aug. 1954; *s* of late Sydney Holtam and Kathleen (*née* Freeberne); *m* 1981, Helen Harris; three *s* one *d*. *Educ:* Latymer Grammar Sch., Edmonton; Collingwood Coll., Univ. of Durham (BA Geog.; MA Theol.); King's Coll. London (BD, AKC; FKC 2005); Westcott House, Cambridge. Ordained deacon, 1979, priest, 1980; Asst Curate, St Dunstan and All Saints, Stepney, 1979–82; Tutor, Lincoln Theol Coll., 1983–87; Vicar, Christ Church and St John with St Luke, Isle of Dogs, 1988–95; Vicar, St Martin-in-the-Fields, 1995–2011. Took seat in H of L, 2014. Hon. DCL Durham, 2005. Patron, Mus. of Homelessness, 2017–. *Publications:* A Room With a View: ministry with the world at your door, 2008; The Art of Worship, 2011. *Recreations:* walking, cycling, reading, writing. *Address:* South Canonry, 71 The Close, Salisbury SP1 2ER. *T:* (01722) 334031. *E:* bishop.salisbury@salisbury.anglican.org.

**SALISBURY, Dean of;** *see* Papadopulos, Very Rev. N. C.

**SALISBURY, David Maxwell,** CB 2001; FRCP, FRCPCH, FFPH, FMedSci; Director of Immunisation, Department of Health, 2004–13; Associate Fellow, Centre on Global Health Security, Royal Institute for International Affairs, since 2013; *b* 10 Aug. 1946; *s* of Dr Steven Salisbury and Judith Grace Vivien Salisbury; *m* 1974, Anne Harvey; one *s* one *d*. *Educ:* Epsom Coll.; Royal London Hosp., Univ. of London (MB BS 1969). FRCP 1992; FRCPCH 1997; FFPH (FFPHM 1998). Sir William Coxen Res. Fellow, Dept of Paediatrics, Univ. of Oxford, 1973–75; Paediatric Registrar, John Radcliffe Hosp., Oxford, 1976–77; Sen. Registrar, Great Ormond Street Hosp. for Children, 1977–85; Consultant Paediatrician, New Cross Hosp., Wolverhampton, 1985–86; PMO, DoH, 1986–2004. Vis. Prof., Dept of Infectious Disease Epidemiology, Imperial Coll., London, 2007–. Chairman: Strategic Adv. Gp of Experts on Immunization, WHO, 2005–10; Commn for Certification of Poliomyelitis Eradication, European Region, WHO, 2007–; WHO Global Commn for Certification of Poliomyelitis Eradication, 2017–. Chm. Bd, Jenner Vaccine Foundn, 2012–. Freeman, City of London, 1980; Liveryman, Soc. of Apothecaries, 1980–. FMedSci 2014. *Publications:* contrib. jls and textbooks on immunisation, infectious disease, paediatrics and neonatology. *Recreations:* destructive gardening (lawns, logs and hedges), sailing. *Address:* Dobsons, Brightwell-cum-Sotwell, Wallingford OX10 0RH. *T:* (01491) 837209.

**SALISBURY, David Murray;** Chairman: Dimensional Fund Advisors Ltd, London, 2002–14 (Director, Dimensional Fund Advisors Inc., 1991–96); Dimensional Funds plc, Dublin, since 2004; *b* 18 Feb. 1952; *s* of late Norman Salisbury and of Isobel Sutherland Murray; *m* 1977, Lynneth Mary Jones; two *d*. *Educ:* Harrow Sch.; Trinity Coll., Oxford (MA). Joined J. Henry Schroder Wagg & Co. Ltd, 1974; Exec. Vice Pres., 1984–86; Chief Exec., 1986–96, Schroder Capital Management International Inc.; Jt Chief Exec., 1996–97, Chm., 1998–2000, Schroder Investment Management Ltd; Dir, Schroders PLC, 1998–2001; Chief Exec., Schroders, 2000–01. Gov., Harrow Sch., 1996–99, 2002–06. *Recreations:* tennis, ski-ing. *Address:* The Dutch House, West Green, Hartley Wintney, Hants RG27 8JN.

**SALISBURY, John;** *see* Caute, J. D.

**SALISBURY, Sir Robert (William),** Kt 1998; educational consultant, Northern Ireland; consultant to Department for Education and Skills, since 2001; Director of Partnerships, University of Nottingham, 1999–2004; *b* 21 Oct. 1941; *s* of Ernest Arthur Salisbury and Vera Ellen Salisbury; *m* 1975, Rosemary D'Arcy (former Principal, Drumragh Coll., Omagh, NI, now nat. educnl consultant); three *s*. *Educ:* Henry Mellish Sch., Nottingham; Kesteven Trng Coll., Lincs (Teacher's Cert.); Nottingham Univ. (CFPS); Loughborough Univ. (MA). Geography teacher, Holgate Sch., Hucknall, Notts, 1962–64; study in Europe, 1964–66; Second in English, Kimberley Comp. Sch., Notts, 1973–77; Head of Humanities and of 6th Form, Gedling Comp. Sch., Notts, 1977–83; Dep. Head, Alderman White Comp. Sch., Notts, 1983–89; Headteacher, Garibaldi Sch., Mansfield, 1989–99. Vis. Prof., Sch. of Educn, Nottingham Univ., 1998. Chairman: Educnl Funding Rev., Dept of Educn, NI, 2012–13; Further Educn Colls Rev., NI, 2013–14. Chief Examr, JMB/NEAB, 1979–90; tutor, Professional Qualification for Headship, 2000–; Co-Leader, Nat. Coll. of Sch. Leadership (Trainee Heads Scheme), 2000–. Formerly Ind. Chm., NE Lincs Educn Action Zone, 1998–99. Chm., Sherwood Partnership, 1998–2002; Vice-Chair, Integrated Educn Fund, NI, 2003–05. Associate Advr, Industrial Soc., 1992–; Mem. Adv. Council, Carlton Television, 2000–02; Educational Advisor: Centre for British Teaching, 1996–; CfBT Educn Trust, 2003–; QUB, 2006–. Regl Chairman: Teaching Awards Trust, 1998–; Literacy and Numeracy Task Force, NI, 2008–; Chairman, Trustees: Fathers Direct, 1998–2005; Sherwood Coalfield Develt Trust, 1999–2003. Patron, Drugs Abuse Resistance Educn, 2002–. Nat. and internat. speaker, 1992–. FRSA 1998. Award for best envmt project, Sustainable Ireland, 2019. *Publications:* Series Ed., Humanities textbooks, 1988; Marketing for Schools Guide, 1993; (contrib.) A River Never Sleeps, 2010; Days with Dog and Gun, 2012; A Wolf's Tale (for children), 2013; Bosie (for children), 2015; The Monk's Pond and other stories, 2016; Field of Dreams, 2018; contrib. numerous articles on educational issues, also on fishing and country matters to Irish Anglers Digest, Irish Shooter's Digest, Australian Hunter; freelance articles for The Times and TES. *Recreations:* trout and salmon fishing, travel, gardening and creating a wildlife area. *Address:* The Fod, 46 Drumconnelly Road, Omagh, Co. Tyrone BT78 1RT.

**SALJE, Prof. Ekhard Karl Hermann,** PhD; FRS 1996; FInstP, FGS; Professor of Mineralogy and Petrology, Cambridge University, 1994–2014, now Emeritus (Professor of Mineral Physics, 1992–94); Head of Department of Earth Sciences, 1998–2008); President, Clare Hall, Cambridge, 2001–08; *b* Hanover, Germany, 26 Oct. 1946; *s* of Gerhard Salje and Hildegard (*née* Drechsler); *m* 1980, Elisabeth Démaret; one *s* four *d*. *Educ:* Univ. of Hanover (PhD 1971); MA Cantab 1986. FInstP 1996; FGS 1997. University of Hanover: Lectr in Physics, 1972–75; Habilitation in Crystallography, 1975; Prof. of Crystallography, 1978–86; Hd, Dept of Crystallography and Petrology, 1983–86; Mem., Senate, 1980–82; Lectr, Cambridge Univ., 1987–92; Fellow, Darwin Coll., Cambridge, 1987–2001, Hon. Fellow, 2002. Programme Dir, Cambridge-MIT Inst., 2001–03; Chairman: Cambridge Envmtl Initiative, 2003–08; Mgt Cttee, Isaac Newton Inst., Cambridge, 2007–08. Chm., Eur. Network on Mineral Transformations, 1997–2001; Mem., Royal Soc. Cttee on Nuclear Waste, 2002. Associate Prof. of Physics, Univ. of Paris, 1981; Prof. invité in Physics, Grenoble Univ., 1990–91, 2011; Mombushu Vis. Prof., Nagoya, Japan, 1996; Visiting Professor: Le Mans Univ., France, 1998, 2000; Bilbao Univ., Spain, 1999; Leipzig, 2008; Max Planck Inst., Leipzig, 2009; Univ. of Paris, 2009; Ulam Scholar, Center for Nonlinear Studies, Los Alamos Nat. Lab, 2010; Hon. Prof., Xi'an Jintong Univ., China, 2012. Advr to British, French, German and EU scientific orgns incl. to Max Planck Soc., 1998–2010. Member: Wissenschaftsrat and German Sci. Foundn, 2006–12; Steering Cttee, Eur. Academies Adv. Council, 2006–08; Pres., Alexander von Humboldt Assoc., 2004–08. Member Board: Univ. of Hamburg, 2000–08; Max Planck Inst. of Maths, Leipzig, 2001–10; Univ. of Wurzburg, 2011–. Fellow, Leopoldina German Acad. of Natural Sci., 1994; For. Mem., Royal Soc. for Scis and Arts, Barcelona, 2010. Schlumberger Medal, 1988; G. Werner Medal, 1995, Agricola Medal, 2006, Mineralogical Soc., Germany; Humboldt Prize, Humboldt Foundn, Germany, 1999; Ernst Ising Prize for Physics, Univ. of Hamburg, 2002; Gold Medal for Internat. Relns, Univ. of Hamburg, 2002; Werner Heisenberg Medal, Humboldt Foundn, 2017. Chevalier, Ordre des Palmes Académiques (France), 2003. FRSA 1996. Cross, Order of Merit (Germany), 2007. *Publications:* Physical Properties and Thermodynamic Behaviour of Minerals, 1987; Phase Transitions in ferroelastic and co-elastic crystals, 1991; Application of Landau Theory for the Analysis of Phase Transitions in Minerals, 1992; numerous res. papers in solid state physics, crystallography and mineralogy. *Recreations:* painting, music. *Address:* 59 Glisson Road, Cambridge CB1 2HG.

**SALLON, Christopher Robert Anthony;** QC 1994; a Recorder, since 1996; *b* 3 May 1948; *s* of late Alexander and Alice Sallon; *m* 1971, Jacqueline Gould; two *s*. Called to the Bar: Gray's Inn, 1973, Bencher, 2002; Eastern Caribbean, 1994; Trinidad and Tobago, 2008. Bar Council: South Eastern Circuit Rep., 1992–94; Member: Professional Conduct Cttee, 1992–93; Public Affairs Cttee, 1994–97; Dir, Public Affairs, 1995–98. Fellow, American Bd of Criminal Lawyers, 1997. Member, Board: Counsel Magazine, 1995–2005; Nat. Campaign for the Arts, 2005–. *Publications:* (jtly) Bribery: a compliance handbook, 2014. *Recreations:* swimming, cycling, music. *Address:* Doughty Street Chambers, 53–54 Doughty Street, WC1N 2LS. *T:* (020) 7404 1313. *Club:* Garrick.

**SALMON, Maj. Gen. Andrew,** CMG 2009; OBE 2004; Founder and Director, Journey through Conflict, since 2016; *b* Wellington, Shropshire, 2 July 1959; *s* of Gordon John Grant Salmon and Margaret Salmon; *m* 1986, Elizabeth Jane Bolt; one *s* two *d*. *Educ:* Royal Grammar Sch., Guildford; Godalming Sixth Form Coll.; Univ. of Warwick (BA Hons Mod. Hist. 1980); King's Coll. London (MA Defence Studies 1993). Joined RM, 1977; Troop Comdr, 40 Cdo, 1981–83; OC RM, Ice Patrol Ship, 1984; Jun. Div., Staff Coll., 1985; Platoon Comdr, RMA, 1985–87; Batch Officer, Officer Trng Wing, 1987–88; Company Comdr, 45 Cdo, 1989–91; HQ Cdo Forces, 1992; psc 1993; Special Forces Requirements, MoD, 1994–95; HQ RM, 1995–97; COS Secretariat, MoD, 1997–99; CO, 42 Cdo, 2000–01; Dir Balkans, MoD, 2001–03; Dir Plans, Coalition Mil. Adv. Trng Team, Iraq, 2003; RCDS 2004; ACOS Plans and Resources, Fleet Comd, 2004–06; HCSC 2006; Comdt, Cdo Trng Centre, RM, 2006–08; Comdr, Multi Nat. Div. (SE), Iraq, 2008–09; Comdr UK Amphibious Forces, 2008–10; Comdt Gen., RM and Capt. of Deal Castle, 2009–10; Dep. Chief of Staff Force Readiness, SHAPE, 2010–13. London School of Economics and Political Science: Special Advr, Human Security Study Gp, 2004–18; Vis. Sen. Fellow, 2008–; Member, Advisory Board: Security in Transition prog., 2011–18; Conflict Res. Prog., 2018–. Practitioners' Adv. Bd, Jl of Global Policy, 2010–17. Owner, Andy Salmon Co. Ltd, 2013–. Vice President: RNRU, 2006–13; RNLTA, 2007–13; Pres., C Group, 2008–16. FRSA 2020. QCVS 2000. Bronze Star (USA), 2006; Legion of Merit (USA), 2009. *Recreations:* music, walking, cycling, swimming, mountains, ski-ing, tennis.

**SALMON, Charles Nathan;** QC 1996; *b* 5 May 1950; *s* of His Honour Judge Cyril Salmon, QC and of Patrice Salmon; *m* 1981, Vanessa Clewes; one *s*. *Educ:* Carmel Coll.; University Coll. London (LLB Hons 1971). Travelled through Asia and SE Asia, 1971–73, worked as rubber tapper in Malaysia; called to the Bar, Middle Temple, 1972; volunteer, ME war, 1973; in practice as barrister, 1974–2014; exclusively defending in substantial white collar fraud, 1996–2014. *Recreations:* reading about Middle East history, 2nd World War and Italian Risorgimento, travel, collecting 18th century Japanese woodcuts and modern British painting, painting land and seascapes in the naïve style.

**SALMON, Christopher Keith;** Global Chief Control Officer, Global Markets, HSBC Holdings plc, since 2018; *b* Stroud, 29 Aug. 1968; *s* of Tony and Jean Salmon; *m* 1999, Gina Hunt. *Educ:* Bristol Univ. (BSc Econs 1990); London Sch. of Econs and Pol Sci. (MSc Econometrics and Math. Econs 1991). Bank of England: various positions, Monetary Analysis Directorate, 1991–2000; IMF, 2000–02 (on secondment); Internat. Finance Div., 2002–04, Hd, 2004–06; Governor's Private Sec., 2006–09; Hd, Sterling Mkts Div., 2009–11; Exec. Dir, Banking Services and Chief Cashier, 2011–14; Exec. Dir, Markets, 2014–18. *Recreations:* running, tennis, family. *Address:* HSBC Holdings plc, 8 Canada Square, E14 5HQ.

**SALMON, Dr Frank Edwin,** LittD; FSA; Senior Lecturer in History of Art, University of Cambridge, since 2012; Fellow, St John's College, Cambridge, since 2006 (President, 2015–19); *b* Ipswich, 8 June 1962; *s* of Neil Salmon and Joyce Salmon (*née* Forrest); *m* 1990, Catharine Margaret MacLeod; one *s* one *d*. *Educ:* St Margaret's C of E Primary Sch., Ipswich; Northgate Grammar Sch. for Boys, Ipswich; Downing Coll., Cambridge (BA 1984; MA 1988; PhD 2001; LittD 2018); Courtauld Inst. of Art (MA 1986). Lectr in Architecture, 1989–97, Lectr in Hist. of Art, 1997–2002, Univ. of Manchester; Asst Dir for Academic Activities, Paul Mellon Centre for Studies in British Art, London, 2002–06 (Sen. Fellow, 2013–14); Adjunct Associate Prof. of Hist. of Art, Yale Univ., 2002–09; Lectr in Hist. of Art, Univ. of Cambridge, 2006–12 (Hd of Dept, 2009–12). Vis. Fellow, Yale Center for British Art, 1993; Hon. Res. Fellow, Dept of Hist. of Art, UCL, 2003–06. Mem., Adv. Cttee, 2012–18, Mem., Expert Adv. Gp, 2018–, Historic England (formerly English Heritage). Member, Executive Committee: Soc. of Architectural Historians of GB, 1995–98 (Chm., 2003–06); Walpole Soc., 2003–06; Member, Council: Soc. of Antiquaries, 2003–06; British Sch. at Rome, 2007–11 (Chm., Faculty of Archaeol., Hist. and Letters, 2007–11). Gov., Stephen Perse Foundn, Cambridge, 2007–14. FSA 2000. *Publications:* Building on Ruins: the rediscovery of Rome and English architecture, 2000; (ed) Summerson and Hitchcock: centenary essays on architectural historiography, 2006; (ed) The Persistence of the Classical: essays on architecture presented to David Watkin, 2008; contribs to books, learned jls and exhibn catalogues; exhibn and book reviews, incl. to TLS. *Recreations:* Church music, travelling south to Italy and north to the Outer Hebrides, making Sunday lunch for family and friends. *Address:* St John's College, Cambridge CB2 1TP.

**SALMON, (Frank) Julian (Evèn);** farmer and landowner, since 1978; Vice Lord-Lieutenant of Powys, since 2016; *b* Rhiwderin, Monmouthshire, 1 June 1947; 3rd *s* of Frank Robert and Patricia Salmon; *m* 1974, Margaret Tangye; one *s* three *d*. *Educ*: Winchester Coll.; Trinity Coll. Dublin (BA Hons Econs and Pol Sci.); Royal Agricl Coll., Cirencester (Cert. Agric.; Dip. Advanced Farm Mgt). VSO, 1965–66. Charter Consolidated Ltd: Mgt trainee, 1970–71; Project Officer, Charter-Idro Exploration, S Iran, 1972–73; PA to Chm., 1973–74; Manager, Paris, 1974–76. Regl Sec., 1991–94, Dir, Wales, 1994–2010, CLA. Pres., Radnor Scouts Assoc., 1994–. Trustee, Worgan Trust and Mt Pleasant Sch. Farm (formerly Worgan Trust), 1996–. ARAgS 2008. DL Powys, 2012. *Recreations*: country life and country sports, wildlife, the arts, family, travel. *Address*: Hoddell Farm, Kinnerton, Presteigne, Powys LD8 2PD. *T*: (01547) 560345. *E*: julian.salmon@btconnect.com.

**SALMON, Jonathan Carl; His Honour Judge Salmon;** a Circuit Judge, since 2018; *b* Chester, 15 March 1965; *s* of Kathleen Ernill and adopted *s* of David John Salmon and Judith Page; *m* 1994, Patricia Sally-Ann Walters; one *s* one *d*. *Educ*: Jack Hunt Comprehensive Sch., Peterborough; Univ. of Nottingham (LLB Hons); Inns of Court Sch. of Law. Called to the Bar, Inner Temple, 1987; in practice as barrister, 1987–2014; Tutor in Land Law (pt-time), Birmingham City Univ., 1987–90; a Dep. Dist Judge, 2002–14; Judge of First Tier Tribunal (Social Security) (pt-time), 2013–14; Dist Judge (Civil and Chancery), 2014–18. Legal Assessor to GMC, 2010–14. *Recreations*: ski-ing, mountain biking, mountain walking, cinema, fine food and wine. *Address*: Stafford Combined Court Centre, Victoria Square, Stafford ST16 2QQ. *E*: hhj.jonathan.salmon@ejudiciary.net.

**SALMON, Michael John;** Vice Chancellor, Anglia Polytechnic University, 1992–95, now Emeritus Professor; Partner, Salmons Reach Consultancy, since 2008; Chairman, Postgraduate Medical Institute, Anglia Ruskin University, 2009–13; *b* 22 June 1936; *o s* of Arthur and May Salmon; *m* 1st, 1958, Angela Cookson (marr. diss. 1973); one *s*; 2nd, 1973, Daphne Bird (*d* 1996); one *s*; 3rd, 1998, Sheila Frances Sisto (*see* S. F. Salmon). *Educ*: Roundhay Sch., Leeds; Leeds Univ.; Leicester Univ. Served RAF, 1957–62; commnd 1957. Teaching posts: Letchworth Coll. of Technology, 1962–65; Leeds Coll. of Technology, 1965–68; Barking Regional Coll., 1968–71; Head of Dept, NE London Poly., 1971–77; Dep. Dir, Chelmer Inst., 1977–83; Dir, Essex Inst., 1983–89; Director: Anglia HEC, 1989–91; Anglia Poly., 1991–92. Member: CNAA, 1970–92; IBA Educn Adv. Council, 1973–81; Electricity Industry Trng Council, 1971–74; PCFC, 1989–91; CBI (Eastern Region) Council, 1990–93; Gen. Optical Council, 1999– (Vice-Chm., 2002–05). Dir, Essex TEC, 1990–93. Member: Court, Essex Univ., 1987–2006; Acad. Cttee, RCM, 1994–2000; Governor: Norwich Sch. of Art and Design, 1996–2001 (Chm. Govs, 1998–2001); King Edward VI GS, Chelmsford, 1995–2001. Director: Proshare, 1991–93; Mid-Essex NHS Hosp. Trust, 1993–95; Chm., Essex Rivers Healthcare NHS Trust, 1995–2005. Mem., Disciplinary Cttee, Royal Pharmaceutical Soc., 2005–11. Chm., Tendring Community Develt Forum, 1998–2001. Vice Patron, Helen Rollason Cancer Appeal, 2001–. Mem., Spectacle Makers' Co., 2005–. FCMI (FBIM 1983); FRSA 1984. Hon. Fellow: Limburg Poly., Netherlands, 1993; Fachhochschule für Wirtschaft, Berlin, 1994.

**SALMON, Nicholas;** Director, Playful Productions, since 2010; *b* London, 21 Nov. 1947; *s* of Brian Salmon and Annette Salmon (*née* Mackay); partner, Janey Sargent; two *s* one *d*. *Educ*: Wellington Coll.; Jesus Coll., Cambridge (BA 1969; MA 1970). Chief Executive Officer: Churchill Th., 1983–91; (pt-time) Stage One (formerly Th. Investment Fund), 1989–2012; Th. of Comedy, 1991–96; Act Prodns, 1997–2010. Playful Productions theatre productions include: Wicked, Apollo, 2006–; Sweeney Todd, Adelphi, 2012; The Audience, Gielgud, 2012, Apollo, transf. NY, 2015; Charlie and the Chocolate Factory, Th. Royal Drury Lane, 2012–16; Wolf Hall and Bring Up the Bodies, Aldwych, 2014; Wolf Hall Parts I and II, NY, 2015; Shrek the Musical, UK tour, 2015; American Buffalo, Wyndham's, 2015; Kinky Boots, Adelphi, 2015, UK tour, 2018–; Hangmen, No Man's Land, Wyndham's, 2016; Don Juan in Soho, Wyndham's, 2017; The Goat, or Who is Sylvia?, Theatre Royal Haymarket, 2017; Moderate Soprano, Duke of York's, 2018; Quiz, Noel Coward, 2018; Imperium, Gielgud, 2018; Come From Away, Phoenix, 2019. Pres., Soc. of London Th., 1993–96. *Recreations*: reading, films, theatre, photography, wine, cooking. *Address*: Playful Productions, 4th Floor, 41–44 Great Queen Street, WC2B 5AD. *T*: (020) 7811 4600. *E*: annie@playfuluk.com. *Club*: Garrick.

**SALMON, Nicholas Robin,** FREng, FIMechE; Chairman, South East Water, since 2015; *b* 13 June 1952; *s* of Keneth Salmon and Winifred Elsie Salmon; *m* 1976, Deirdre Ann Thompson Hardy; two *d*. *Educ*: Bristol Univ. (BSc (Hons) Mech. Engrg 1973). Grad. trainee, 1969–74, Project Engr, 1974–77, CEGB; Project Manager, China Light and Power Co. Ltd (Hong Kong), 1977–88; Dir and Gen. Manager, Power Station Projects Div., GEC Turbine Generators Ltd, 1988–89; Dep. Man. Dir, Power Stn Projects Div. and Gas Turbine and Diesel Div., GEC Alsthom, 1989–93; Chief Exec., Babcock Internat. Gp plc, 1993–97; Man. Dir, Power Generation Div., GEC Alsthom, 1997–99; Exec. Vice Pres., ABB ALSTOM, subseq. ALSTOM Power, then ALSTOM, 1999–2004; Chief Exec., Cookson Gp, 2004–12. Chm., SE Water Ltd, 2015–; non-executive Director: United Utilities Gp plc, 2005–14 (Sen. Ind. Dir, 2007–14); Interserve plc, 2014–; Scotia Gas Networks Ltd, 2019–; Sen. Ind. Dir, Elementis plc, 2014–. FREng (FEng 1995). *Recreations*: sailing, ski-ing, bridge. *Club*: Royal Hong Kong Yacht.

**SALMON, Paul Raymond,** FRCPE, FRCP; independent consultant Physician and Gastroenterologist, 1989–2004; *b* 11 July 1936; *s* of late Harold William Salmon and Blanche Percy Salmon (*née* Piper); *m* 1st, 1962 (marr. diss. 1980); one *s* one *d*; 2nd, 1984, Diana Frances Lawrence. *Educ*: Epsom Coll.; Middx Hosp. Sch. of Medicine, Univ. of London (BSc Hons Anatomy 1958; MB BS 1962). MRCS 1961; MRCPE 1966, FRCPE 1977; MRCP 1967, FRCP 1978. House Physician and House Surgeon, 1962, Casualty MO, 1963–64, Middlesex Hosp.; House Physician, London Chest Hosp., 1963; Sen. House Physician, Ipswich and E Suffolk Hosp., 1964–65; Med. Registrar, Princess Margaret Hosp., Swindon, 1965–66; Res. Registrar in Gastroenterology, Bristol Royal Infirmary, 1967–68; Lectr in Medicine, 1969–73, Sen. Lectr in Medicine, 1974–79, Univ. of Bristol; Hon. Sen. Registrar, United Bristol Hosps, 1969–73; Hon. Consultant Physician, Bristol Health Dist, 1974–79; Consultant Physician, UCH, and Sen. Clin. Lectr in Gastroenterology, Sch. of Medicine, UCL, 1978–89; Consultant Physician, Middlesex Hosp., 1985–89. Annual Foundn Lectr, British Soc. for Digestive Endoscopy, 1979; Poona Orator, Indian Gastroenterology Soc., 1984. FDS Examr, RCS, 1982–88. Pres., Eur. Laser Assoc., 1981–85; Member: British Soc. of Gastroenterology, 1969–2004; Chelsea Clin. Soc., 1986– (Mem. Council, 2000–04); Independent Doctors Forum, 1989–. FRSocMed 1986. Freeman, City of London, 1985; Liveryman: Co. of Farriers, 1986; Soc. of Apothecaries, 1993. Privilegiate *hc*, 1996, Hon. Fellow, 2008, St Hilda's Coll., Oxford. Several teaching films (Dip., Marburg Film Fest., 1977, Silver Award, BMA Film Competition, 1983). Mem., Chopin Soc. *Publications*: Fibreoptic Endoscopy, 1974; (ed) Topics in Modern Gastroenterology, 1976; (jtly) Radiological Atlas of Biliary and Pancreatic Disease, 1978; (ed) Ranitidine, 1982; (ed) Advances in Gastrointestinal Endoscopy, 1984; (ed) Key Developments in Gastroenterology, 1988; 200 contribs to books, scientific papers and review articles. *Recreations*: golf, music, reproducing pianos, ski-ing, travel, angling. *Address*: 2d Melbury Road, W14 8LP. *T*: (020) 7602 3311. *E*: paulsalmon@btinternet.com. *Clubs*: Athenæum; Sunningdale Golf.

**SALMON, Peter;** Chief Creative Officer, Endemol Shine Group, since 2016; *b* 15 May 1956; *s* of Patrick and Doreen Salmon; three *s*; *m* 2001, Sarah Jane Abigail Lancashire, *qv*; one *s*. *Educ*: Univ. of Warwick (BA English and European Lit.). VSO, 1977; Min. of Overseas Develt, 1978; Chatham News, 1979–81; BBC, 1981–93: Series Producer, Crimewatch UK; Editor, Nature; Exec. Producer, 999, and The Wrong Trousers; Head of TV Features, BBC Bristol; Controller of Factual Programmes, Channel 4, 1993–96; Dir of Programmes, Granada TV, 1996–97; Controller, BBC 1, 1997–2000; Dir of Sport, BBC, 2000–05; Chief Exec., Television Corp., 2005–06; Chief Creative Officer, BBC Vision Prodns, 2006–09; Director: BBC North, 2009–13; BBC England, 2013–15; BBC Studios, 2015–16. *Recreations*: music, football, cycling, museums.

**SALMON, Sarah Jane Abigail;** *see* Lancashire, S. J. A.

**SALMON, Prof. Sheila Frances,** FRSocMed; Chairman, Essex Partnership University NHS Foundation Trust, since 2017; *b* Middlesex, 1952; *d* of Edward and Daisy Patterson; *m* 1st, 1971, Francisco Sisto (marr. diss. 1989); two *s* one *d*; 2nd, 1998, Michael John Salmon, *qv*. *Educ*: Walpole Grammar Sch.; Univ. of Surrey (MSc; Postgrad. Cert. Educn of Adults 1989; Postgrad. Dip. Professional Educn 1993); Royal Coll. of Midwives; Inst. of Leadership and Mgt (Postgrad. Cert. Exec. Coaching and Leadership Mentoring 2007). Nat. Nursery Exam. Bd 1971; RM 1974; ADM 1987; RMT 1989. Trained in Kensington, Chelsea and Hammersmith Hosps, 1969–72, Plymouth Hosps, 1972–74; Clin. Practice Midwifery, Women's and Children's Services, 1975–87; Clin. Tutor, Obstetrics and Family Health Midwifery, Essex, Kent, London and Surrey, 1987–90; Sen. Midwife Teacher, 1990–92, Hd of Dept, Postgrad. and Professional Studies, 1992–94, S Essex Coll. of Nursing and Midwifery; Associate Dean, Faculty of Health and Social Work, 1994–95, Exec. Dean and Dir of Health Strategy, 1995–2006, Anglia Ruskin Univ. (formerly Anglia Poly. Univ.); Chairman: Essex Ambulance Service NHS Trust, 2005–06; NHS NE Essex, 2006–10; Mid Essex Hosps NHS Trust, 2010–17; Founding Chair, Jt Wkg Bd, Mid and S Essex Acute Hosps Gp, 2016–17. Lead Visitor, Nursing and Midwifery Council, 2002–06. Lay Partner, GMC (formerly PMETB), 2008–. Equality and Diversity Ambassador, 2010–. Founder, Salmons Reach Consultancy, 2006. Non-exec. Dir and Trustee, Essex Air Ambulance Charity, 2002–06. FRSocMed 2007. *Publications*: contribs to British Jl Midwifery, Adult Educn, Internat. Congress of Midwives Triennial Conf. Procs. *Recreations*: travel, family, fundraising charity events. *Address*: Barberries, 10 Runsell Lane, Danbury, Essex CM3 4NZ. *T*: (01245) 223734, 07940 512374. *E*: sheila.salmon@gmail.com, sheila.salmon@meht.nhs.uk.

**SALMOND, Rt Hon. Alexander Elliot Anderson;** PC 2007; *b* 31 Dec. 1954; *s* of Robert F. F. Salmond and late Mary S. Milne; *m* 1981, Moira F. McGlashan. *Educ*: Linlithgow Acad.; St Andrews Univ. (MA Hons). Govt Econ. Service, 1980; Asst Agricl and Fisheries Economist, DAFS, 1978–80; Energy Economist, Royal Bank of Scotland plc, 1980–87. Scottish National Party: Mem. Nat. Exec., 1981–2018; Vice-Chair (Publicity), 1985–87; Sen. Vice-Convener (Dep. Leader) (formerly Sen. Vice-Chair), 1987–90; Leader, 1990–2000 and 2004–14. MP (SNP): Banff and Buchan, 1987–2010; Gordon, 2015–17; contested (SNP) same seat, 2017. SNP parly spokesperson on energy, treasury and fishing, 1987–88, on economy, energy, environment and poll tax, 1988–97, on constitution and fishing, 1997–2005; on foreign affairs, 2015–17. Scottish Parliament: Member (SNP): Banff & Buchan, 1999–2001; Gordon, 2007–11; Aberdeenshire E, 2011–16; Ldr of the Opposition, 1999–2000; First Minister, 2007–14. Mem. Bd, UK Holocaust Meml Foundn, 2015–. Vis. Prof. of Economics, Univ. of Strathclyde, 2003–. DUniv Glasgow, 2015. *Publications*: The Dream Shall Never Die: 100 days that changed Scotland forever (autobiog.), 2015; articles and conference papers on oil and gas economics; contribs to Scottish Government Yearbook, Fraser of Allander Economic Commentary, Petroleum Review, Opec Bulletin, etc.

**SALMOND, Dame Anne;** *see* Salmond, Dame M. A.

**SALMOND, Prof. George Peacock Copland,** PhD; ScD; FRSB; FRSE; Professor of Molecular Microbiology, since 1996 and Deputy Head, Department of Biochemistry (Postgraduate Education and Training), since 2010, University of Cambridge; Fellow, Wolfson College, Cambridge, since 2000; *b* 15 Nov. 1952; *s* of John Brown Salmond and Joan Tennant Lambie Salmond (*née* Copland); *m* 1975, Christina Brown Adamson (marr. diss. 1985); partner, Carolyn Ann Alderson; one *d*. *Educ*: Whitburn Primary Sch.; Bathgate Acad.; Whitburn Acad.; Univ. of Strathclyde (BSc 1st cl. Hons Microbiology); Univ. of Warwick (PhD Bacterial Genetics); MA, ScD 2006, Cantab. FRSB (FSB 2009); FRSE 2012. Postdoctoral Res. Fellow, Dept of Molecular Biology, Univ. of Edinburgh, 1977–80; Lectr in Microbiology, Biological Lab., Univ. of Kent at Canterbury, 1980–83; Lectr in Microbiology, 1983–89, Sen. Lectr, 1989–93, Prof., 1993–96, Dept of Biological Scis, Univ. of Warwick. Biotechnology and Biological Sciences Research Council: Member: Plants and Microbial Scis Cttee, 1999–2002; Integration Panel, BBSRC Inst. Sci. Quality Assessment, 2001; Cross Cttee Gp on Antimicrobial Res., 2001; Sequencing Panel, 2002–; Plant and Microbial Metabolomics Initiative Sift Panel, 2002; Res. Cttee B, 2009–10; Chairman: Plant and Microbial Scis Cttee 'Natural Products Biology' Steering Gp, 2000–02; Res. Equipment Initiative Cttee, 2002–04; Mem., Plant Panel, 2002, Integration Panel, 2002, and Chm., Plant Panel for Scottish Res. Insts, 2002, Quality of Sci. Assessment Panels, Scottish Exec. Envmt and Rural Affairs Dept; Member: Adv. Bd, NSC Technologies, USA, 1996–2000; Panel for Jt Res. Councils Equipment Initiative, 2001; Pathogen Sequencing Adv. Gp, Wellcome Trust Sanger Inst., 2002–06; Scottish Science Adv. Council, 2010–15. Mem., Internat. Expert Rev. Panel (Medicine), Linnaeus Res. Centres, Swedish Res. Council, 2013–14; Ind. Expert Advr, Wellcome Trust Strategic Awards Cttee, 2015. Royal Society of Edinburgh: Member: Sectional Cttee A4 (Cell and Molecular Biol.), 2012–15 (Convener, 2015–18); Sectoral Gp A Cttee (Life Scis), 2015–18); Society for General Microbiology: Mem. Council, 1997–2001, 2004–09; Convener, Physiol., Biochem. and Molecular Genetics Gp Cttee, 2002–07; Internat. Sec., 2004–09; Colworth Prize Lect., 2011. Member Council: Fedn of Eur. Microbiol Socs, 2004–09; Sci. Unions Cttee, Royal Soc., 2005–09. Member, Governing Body: Wolfson Coll., Cambridge, 2000–; Scottish Crop Res. Inst., 2003–11 (Sci. Cttee, 2006–11); Member: Governing Council, Dir and Trustee, John Innes Centre, Norwich, 2003–10; Governing Bd and Adv. Cttee on Sci., James Hutton Inst., 2011–14. UK Sen. Ed., Jl of Molecular Microbiology and Biotechnology, 1998–2008; Member Editorial Board: Molecular Microbiology, 1988–97; Molecular Plant Pathology-On Line, 1996–99; Microbiology, 1999–2000; Molecular Plant Pathology, 1999–2002; Associate Editor: European Jl of Plant Pathology, 1992–98; Molecular Plant-Microbe Interactions, 1993–98; Editl Adv. Panel, Future Microbiology, 2006–. Member: Biochem. Soc.; Genetics Soc.; Amer. Soc. of Microbiol.; Soc. for Industrial Microbiol., USA; Soc. for Applied Microbiol.; British Soc. for Antimicrobial Chemotherapy; British Soc. for Plant Pathology (Vice-Pres., 2009; Pres. Elect, 2009–10; Pres., 2011–12); Governing Council, Dir and Trustee, Microbiol. Soc., 2017–19 (Mem., Finance and Ops Cttee, 2017–19). Founding Fellow, Inst. of Contemp. Scotland, 2001; Fellow: Cambridge Phil Soc.; Amer. Acad. Microbiol.

2013; Hon. Fellow, James Hutton Inst., 2014. FRSA 2001. Hon. DSc Strathclyde, 2010. *Publications:* many res. articles on molecular microbiology, incl. studies on bacterial cell div., molecular phytopathology, antibiotics, quorum sensing, bacterial virulence, protein secretion, gas vesicles, bacterial viruses, anti-viral abortive infection and toxin-antitoxin systems in learned jls. *Recreations:* philosophy, poetry, comedy. *Address:* Department of Biochemistry, University of Cambridge, Tennis Court Road, Cambridge CB2 1QW. *T:* (01223) 333650.

**SALMOND, Dame (Mary) Anne,** DBE 1995 (CBE 1988); PhD; FRSNZ; Distinguished Professor, University of Auckland, since 2001 (Professor of Social Anthropology and Maori Studies, 1992–2001; Pro Vice-Chancellor (Equal Opportunity), 1997–2006); *b* 16 Nov. 1945; *d* of Jack Thorpe and Joyce Thorpe; *m* 1971, Jeremy Salmond; two *s* one *d*. *Educ:* Univ. of Auckland (BA 1966; MA 1st cl. 1966); Univ. of Pennsylvania (PhD 1972). FRSNZ 1990. Post-grad. Schol., Univ. of Auckland, 1968; Fulbright Schol., 1969; Nuffield Fellow, 1980–81; Capt. James Cook Fellow, RSNZ, 1987; Caird Fellow, Nat. Maritime Mus., 2004. Cecil H. and Ida Green Vis. Prof., UBC, 2013. Henry Myers Lectr, RAI, 1996. Chm., NZ Historic Places Trust, 2002–07. Mem., Sustainability Adv. Gp, Air NZ, 2014–. Vice Pres. (Humanities and Social Scis), Royal Soc. of NZ Te Aparangi, 2016–. Internat. Mem., Amer. Philosophical Soc., 2015. Corresp. FBA 2008. Founding Fellow, NZ Acad. of Humanities, 2007. Foreign Associate, NAS, 2009. Elsdon Best Meml Gold Medal, Polynesian Soc., 1976; Wattie Book of Year Awards, 1977, 1981, 1991; Nat. Book Award (non-fiction), 1991, 2004; Ernest Scott Prize, Melbourne Univ., 1992, 1997; NZ Prime Minister's Award for Literary Achievement, 2004; Kea World Class New Zealander, 2011; New Zealander of Year, Kiwibank, 2013; Rutherford Medal, Royal Soc. NZ, 2013; Carl Friedrich von Siemens Res. Award, Alexander von Humboldt Foundn, Germany, 2018. *Publications:* Hui: a study of Maori ceremonial gathering, 1975, 7th edn 1994; Amiria: the life story of a Maori woman, 1976, 3rd edn 1994; Eruera: the teachings of a Maori Elder, 1980; Two Worlds: first meetings between Maori and Europeans 1642–1772, 1991, 2nd edn 1993; Between Worlds: early Maori-European exchanges 1773–1815, 1997; The Trial of the Cannibal Dog: Captain Cook in the South Seas, 2003; Aphrodite's Island: the European discovery of Tahiti, 2009; Bligh: William Bligh in the South Seas, 2011; Tears of Rangi: experiments across worlds, 2017. *Recreations:* ecological restoration, reading, gardening, family and friends. *Address:* 14 Glen Road, Devonport, Auckland, New Zealand. *T:* (9) 4452573.

**SALOLAINEN, Pertti Edvard,** Hon. CBE 2017; Grand Cross, Order of the Lion of Finland, 1994; MP (C) Helsinki, Parliament of Finland, 2007–19; Hon. Minister, since 2004; *b* 19 Oct. 1940; *s* of Edvard Paavali Salolainen and Ella Elisabet Salolainen; *m* 1964, Anja Sonninen (*d* 2005); one *s* one *d*. *Educ:* Helsinki Sch. of Economics (MSc Econ 1969). TV newsreader and editor, then producer, 1962–66, London Correspondent, 1966–69, Finnish Broadcasting Co.; London Editor, BBC Finnish Sect., 1966; Head of Dept, Finnish Employers' Confedn, 1969–89. Ambassador of Finland to UK 1996–2004. MP (C), Helsinki, 1970–96; Minister for Foreign Trade, Finland, 1987–95; Dep. Prime Minister of Finland, 1991–95; Ministerial Chm., Finland-EU membership negotiations, 1991–95; Vice Chm., Foreign Affairs Cttee, 2011–19 (Chm., 2007–11). Leader, Conservative Party of Finland, 1991–94. Hon. Founder, WWF Finland, 1972 (Pres., 2006). Major, Mil. Reserve. Freeman, City of London, 1998. Liveryman: Co. of Hackney Carriage Drivers; Co. of Horners. Internat. Conservation Award, WWF, 1990. Grand Cross, Nordstjerna Order (Sweden), 1996; Grand Cross, nat. orders of Germany, Austria, Hungary and Estonia. *Recreations:* nature conservation, nature photography, tennis. *Address:* Aurorankatu 17.A.8, 00100 Helsinki, Finland. *Clubs:* Athenæum, Travellers; Pressikubi, Suomalainen.

**SALOMON, Eve Coulter;** Chairman of Trustees, Horniman Museum and Gardens, since 2014; *b* Tokyo, 22 April 1957; *d* of Ernest Salomon and Ruth Salomon; *m* 1st, 1983, Stephen Moss (marr. diss. 2002); one *s* one *d*; 2nd, 2004, Stephen Charles Whittle, *qv*. *Educ:* Univ. of Bath (BSc Hons Sociol. 1978); City of London Poly. (Law Soc. Finals 1981). Admitted solicitor, 1983; solicitor: Bulcraigs, 1981–87; Colyer-Bristow, 1987–92; Sen. Advertising and Sponsorship Officer, 1992–96, Dep. Sec. to the Commn, 1996–98, ITC; Dir, Legal Services and Sec., Radio Authy, 1998–2003. Dir, Salomon Whittle Ltd, 2004–. Member: Gambling Commn, 2004–11; Press Complaints Commn, 2004–10; Chm., Regulatory Bd, RICS, 2009–15. Chm., Internet Watch Foundn, 2009–12. Trustee, Privacy Internat., 2016–17 (Chm., 2017–). FRSA. *Publications:* Guidelines on Broadcasting Regulation, 2006, 2nd edn 2009. *Recreations:* friends and family, music, Alexander Technique. *Address:* 4 Carmarthen Place, SE1 3TS. *T:* (020) 7407 2016. *E:* eve.salomon@btopenworld.com.

**SALOMONSEN, His Honour Victor Erik Stanhope;** DL; a Circuit Judge, 2008–18; *b* Guildford, 26 Jan. 1951; *s* of Victor and Kathleen Salomonsen; *m* 1976, Frances Mary Douthwaite; three *d*. *Educ:* Queen's Coll., Taunton; Queen's Coll., Oxford (BA 1972; MA 1978). Admitted Solicitor, 1975; Partner, Bond Pearce LLP, 1979–2008; Asst Recorder, 1996–2000; Recorder, 2000–08. Judicial Mem., Parole Bd, 2018–. DL Devon, 2018. *Recreations:* sailing, choral music, walking. *Club:* Royal Cruising.

**SALONEN, Esa-Pekka;** conductor and composer; Principal Conductor and Artistic Adviser, Philharmonia Orchestra, London, since 2008; *b* 30 June 1958; *s* of Raimo Salonen and Pia Salonen; *m* 1991, Jane Price; one *s* two *d*. *Educ:* Sibelius Acad., Helsinki. Principal Conductor, Swedish Radio Symphony Orch., 1985–95; Principal Guest Conductor, Philharmonia Orch., 1985–94; Music Dir, Los Angeles Philharmonic Orch., 1992–2009, now Conductor Laureate. Artistic Dir, Helsinki Fest., 1995–96; Co-founder and Artistic Dir, Baltic Sea Fest., 2003–. Mem., Royal Swedish Music Acad., 1991; FRCM 1995. Hon. Dr: Hong Kong Acad. of Performing Arts, 2009; S Calif, 2010; Hon. DMus RAM, 2011. Opera Award, 1995, Conductor Award, 1997, Royal Philharmonic Soc.; numerous record and composition awards. Pro Finlandia Medal (Finland), 1992; Litteris et Artibus Medal (Sweden), 1996; Helsinki Medal (Finland), 2005. Officier de l'ordre des Arts et des Lettres (France), 1998. *Compositions include:* Saxophone Concerto, 1980; Floof, 1982; Giro, 1982–97; YTA I, 1982, II, 1985 and III, 1986; MIMO II, 1992; LA Variations, 1996; Gambit, 1998; Five Images after Sappho, 1999; Mania, 2000; Concert Etude, 2000; Two Songs to Poems of Ann Jäderlund, 2000; Dichotomie, 2000; Foreign Bodies, 2001; Insomnia, 2002; Wing on Wing, 2004; Piano Concerto, 2007; Homunculus (string quartet), 2008; Violin Concerto, 2009; Nyx, 2011; Dona Nobis Pacem, 2011; Karawane, 2014; Lachen Verlernt, 2016. *Address:* c/o Philharmonia Orchestra, 6 Chancel Street, SE1 0UX. *T:* (020) 7921 3900.

**SALOP, Archdeacon of;** *see* Thomas, Ven. P. W.

**SALT, Christine Anne, (Chrys),** MBE 2014; poet, writer; Artistic Director: The Bakehouse, Galloway, since 2005; BIG LIT Literature Festival, since 2011; *b* Birmingham, 15 May 1944; *d* of Frederick Arthur Salt and Joyce Winifred Salt; *m* 1997, Richard Macfarlane; two *s* one *d* by a previous marriage. *Educ:* Erdington Grammar Sch.; Birmingham Th. Sch.; Birmingham Rep. Th. Freelance writer and performer, 1962–2015; Parly Res. Asst, 1970–82; Tutor, London Actors Centre, 1982–2015; Artistic Dir, Bare Boards and Passion Th. Co., 1995–2006. Mem., London Actors Centre, 1981–. *Publications:* (ed) Of Whole Heart Cometh Hope, 1983; (with J. Layzell) Here We Go! Women's Memories of the 1984/85 Miners' Strike, 1985; (with M. Wilson) We Are of One Blood: memories of the first 60 years of the Woodcraft Folk, 1985; (with E. Bennett) College Lives, 1986; Inside Out, 1989; Daffodils at Christmas, 1998; Make Acting Work, 1997, 2nd rev. edn 2003; The Methuen Book of Contemporary Monologues for Men, 2003; The Methuen Book of Contemporary Monologues for Women, 2003; Collateral Damage, 2004; The Methuen Book of Modern Monologues for Men, 2004; The Methuen Book of Modern Monologues for Women, 2004; The Methuen Book of Classical Monologues for Men, 2005; The Methuen Book of Classical Monologues for Women, 2005; Greedy for Mulberries, 2009; (ed with J. Hudson) Adrian: Scotland celebrates Adrian Mitchell, 2009; Old Times, 2009; Grass, 2012; Home Front/Front Line, 2013; Weaver of Grass, 2014; Dancing on a Rock, 2015; The Punkawallah's Rope, 2017. *Recreations:* theatre, travel, family, cinema, art, books, politics. *Address:* 149 Chamberlayne Road, NW10 3NT. *T:* 07891 803027; The Bakehouse, 44 High Street, Gatehouse of Fleet, Kirkcudbrightshire DG7 2NP. *W:* www.chryssalt.com.

**SALT, Sir Michael;** *see* Salt, Sir T. M. J.

**SALT, Sir Patrick (Macdonnell),** 7th Bt *cr* 1869, of Saltaire, Yorkshire; *b* 25 Sept. 1932; *s* of Sir John Salt, 4th Bt and Stella Houlton Jackson (*d* 1974); *S* brother, 1991; *m* 1976, Ann Elizabeth Mary Kilham Roberts, *widow* of Denys Kilham Roberts, OBE. *Educ:* Summer Fields, Oxford; Stowe Sch. Dir, Cassidy Davis Members Agency Ltd, 1983–92. *Recreation:* fishing. *Heir: cousin* Daniel Alexander Salt [*b* 15 Aug. 1943; *m* 1968, Merchide, *d* of Dr Ahmad Emami; two *d*]. *Address:* Hillwatering Farmhouse, Langham, Bury St Edmunds, Suffolk IP31 3ED. *T:* (01359) 259367.

**SALT, Sir (Thomas) Michael (John),** 4th Bt *cr* 1899; *b* 7 Nov. 1946; *s* of Lt-Col Sir Thomas Henry Salt, 3rd Bt, and Meriel Sophia Wilmot, *d* of late Capt. Berkeley C. W. Williams and Hon. Mrs Williams, Herringston, Dorchester; *S* father, 1965; *m* 1971, Caroline, *er d* of Henry Hildyard; two *d*. *Educ:* Eton. *Recreations:* cricket, shooting. *Heir: b* Anthony William David Salt [*b* 5 Feb. 1950; *m* 1978, Olivia Anne, *yr d* of Martin Morgan Hudson; two *s*]. *Address:* Shillingstone House, Shillingstone, Blandford Forum, Dorset DT11 0QR.

**SALTER,** family name of **Baroness Wheatcroft**.

**SALTER, Ian George,** Consultant, Deutsche Bank Private Wealth Management, 2008–10; *b* Hobart, Tasmania, 7 March 1943; *s* of Desmond and Diane Salter. *Educ:* Hutchins Sch., Hobart, Tasmania. AASA. Member: Hobart Stock Exchange, 1965–69; London Stock Exchange, 1970–2000; Principal, Strauss Turnbull, subseq. Société Générale Strauss Turnbull (Investment Advisers Ltd), then SG (formerly Socgen) Investment Management Ltd, 1978–2003, Man. Dir, 2001–03; Dir, Tilney Private Wealth Mgt (formerly Tilney Investment Mgt), 2003–07; Chm., EmdexTrade, subseq. CCH International plc, 2001–09; non-executive Director: Plus Markets Gp plc, 2007–09; Pan Hldgs, 2008–12. Mem., Stock Exchange Council, 1980–91, subseq. London Stock Exchange Bd, 1991–2004, a Dep. Chm., 1990–2004. DTI Inspector, 1984–87. Mem., Bd, British Youth Opera, 1998–2000. *Recreations:* opera, travel, gardening. *Address:* Flat 2, 34 St Leonards Terrace, SW3 4QQ.

**SALTER, Martin John;** Chief Policy Advisor (formerly National Campaigns Co-ordinator), Angling Trust, since 2011; *b* 19 April 1954; *s* of Raymond and Naomi Salter. *Educ:* Univ. of Sussex. Co-ordinator, Reading Centre for Unemployed, 1986; Regl Manager, Co-operative Home Services Housing Assoc., 1987–96. Mem., Reading BC, 1984–96 (Dep. Leader, 1987–96). Contested (Lab) Reading E, 1987. MP (Lab) Reading W, 1997–2010.

**SALTER, Nicholas John Howard;** Senior Partner, Barnett Waddingham, since 2012; *b* Cobham, 4 Nov. 1956; *s* of James Salter and Violet Salter; *m* 1986, Susie; one *s* one *d*. *Educ:* Eton; Trinity Hall, Cambridge (BA Econs 1978). FIA 1986. Founding Partner, Barnett Waddingham, 1989. Pres., Inst. and Faculty of Actuaries, 2014–15. Master, Actuaries' Co., 2018–19. *Recreations:* cycling, ski-ing, tennis. *Address:* Little Chartridge House, 120 Chartridge Lane, Chesham, Bucks HP5 2RH. *T:* (01494) 788127. *E:* nick.j.h.salter@barnett-waddingham.co.uk. *Clubs:* Royal Automobile, MCC.

**SALTER, Rebecca Margaret,** RA 2014; artist, since 1981; Keeper of the Royal Academy, since 2017; *b* Middleton-on-Sea, 24 Feb. 1955; *d* of Rev. Samuel Salter and Margaret Salter; *m* 1991, Geoffrey Winston. *Educ:* Pate's Grammar Sch. for Girls, Cheltenham; Bristol Poly. (BA 1977); Kyoto City Univ. of Arts, Japan. Freelance work, 1981–96; Associate Lectr, 1996–, Res. Fellow, 2002–11, Camberwell Coll. of Arts, Univ. of the Arts, London. *Solo exhibitions* include: Inner Eye, 2004, The Unquiet Gaze, 2007, and 2011, First Light, 2015, Howard Scott Gall., NY; Bliss of Solitude, 2006, Pale Remembered, 2009, Drawn, 2011, Beyond, 2013, Along These Lines, 2015, New Work, 2016, Beardsmore Gall., London; into the light of things: Rebecca Salter 1981–2011, Yale Center for British Art, Conn, 2011; *work in collections* including: Tate Gall.; BM; V&A Mus.; British Council; Govt Art Collection; Cambridge Inst. for Med. Res.; Frechen Kunstverein, Germany; Graphotek, Stadtbucherei, Stuttgart; Yale Center for British Art, New Haven, Conn; Yale Univ. Art Gall.; Liby of Congress, Washington. *Publications:* Japanese Woodblock Printing, 2001, 2nd edn 2013; Japanese Popular Prints, 2006. *Recreations:* outdoor swimming, cookery, things Japanese, dogs. *Address:* c/o Royal Academy of Arts, Piccadilly, W1S 3ET. *T:* (020) 7300 8000. *E:* info@rebeccasalter.com.

**SALTER, Richard Stanley;** QC 1995; a Recorder, since 2000; a Deputy High Court Judge, Queen's Bench Division, since 2010, and Commercial Court, since 2016; *b* 2 Oct. 1951; *s* of late Stanley James Salter and Betty Maud Salter (*née* Topsom); *m* 1991, Shona Virginia Playfair Cannon. *Educ:* Harrow County Sch. for Boys; Balliol Coll., Oxford (MA); Inns of Court Sch. of Law. Called to the Bar, Inner Temple, 1975, Bencher, 1991; pupil to Sir Henry Brooke, 1975–76; in practice at Commercial Bar, 1976–; an Asst Recorder, 1997–2000. Chm., London Common Law and Commercial Bar Assoc., 2004–05 (Mem. Cttee, 1986–2001; Vice-Chm., 2002–03). Member: Council of Legal Educn, 1990–96; Advocacy Studies Bd, 1996–2000; (ex-officio) 2004–05, (elected) 2006–08, (nominated) 2009–13, Bar Council; Chairman: Bd of Examnrs for Bar Vocational Course, 1992–93; Scholarships Cttee, Inner Temple, 2002–09; Bar Council Legal Services Cttee, 2010–13. Vis. Fellow in Financial Law, Faculty of Law, 2013–16, Vis. Prof., 2016–, Univ. of Oxford. Gov., Inns of Court Sch. of Law, 1996–2001; Member: Adv. Bd, City Univ. Inst. of Law, 2001–07; Develt Bd, Centre for Commercial Law Studies, 2012–17. Liveryman, Musicians' Co., 2016 (Freeman, 2013–16). Trustee: Oxford Univ. Law Foundn, 2011–17; English Touring Opera Ltd, 2015–; Les Azuriales Opera Trust, 2019–. Consulting Ed., All England Commercial Cases, 1999–; Legislation Ed., Encyclopedia of Insurance Law, 2001–04. Dist. Friend of Oxford Award, 2014. *Publications:* (contrib.) Banks, Liability and Risk, 1991, 3rd edn 2001; (contrib.) Banks and Remedies, 1992, 2nd edn 1999; Guarantee and Indemnity, Halsbury's Laws of England, Vol. 20, 4th edn 1993; (ed) Legal Decisions Affecting Bankers, vols 12–14, 2001; (contrib.) Law of International Finance, 2017; (contrib.) Intermediation and Beyond, 2019; articles on financial law. *Recreations:* books, music, theatre, cricket. *Address:* 3 Verulam Buildings, Gray's Inn, WC1R 5NT. *T:* (020) 7831 8441. *Clubs:* Savile, Shoscombe Village Cricket.

**SALTHOUSE, Edward Charles,** PhD; CEng, FIET; Master of University College, Durham University, 1979–98; b 27 Dec. 1935; s of Edward Salthouse, MBE, and Mrs Salthouse (née Boyd); m 1961, Denise Kathleen Margot Reid; two s. Educ: Campbell Coll., Belfast; Queen's University of Belfast (BSc, PhD). Lecturer in Electrical Engrg, Univ. of Bristol, 1962–67; University of Durham: Reader in Elec. Engrg Science, 1967–79; Chairman, Board of Studies in Engrg Science, 1976–79; Dean, Faculty of Science, 1982–85; First Chm., School of Applied Science and Engrg, 1985–87; Pro-Vice-Chancellor, 1985–88. Sec., Scottish Industrial Heritage Soc., 1998–2008. *Publications:* papers on electrical insulation in Proc. IEE and other appropriate jls. *Recreations:* industrial archaeology, photography. *Address:* Shieldaig, Hume, Kelso TD5 7TR.

**SALTOUN, Lady** (20th in line), cr 1445, of Abernethy (by some reckonings 21st in line); **Flora Marjory Fraser;** Chief of the name of Fraser; b 18 Oct. 1930; d of 19th Lord Saltoun, MC, and Dorothy (d 1985), e d of Sir Charles Welby, 5th Bt; S father, 1979; m 1956, Captain Alexander Ramsay of Mar, Grenadier Guards retd (d 2000), o s of late Adm. Hon. Sir Alexander Ramsay, GCVO, KCB, DSO, and The Lady Patricia Ramsay, CI, VA, CD; three d. Elected Mem., H of L, 1999–2014. *Heiress:* d Hon. Katharine Ingrid Mary Isabel Fraser [b 11 Oct. 1957; m 1980, Captain Mark Malise Nicolson, Irish Guards; one s two d].

**SALUSBURY-TRELAWNY, Sir John William Richard;** see Trelawny, Sir J. W. R. S.

**SALVAGE, Jane Elizabeth;** author, nursing and health consultant; b 6 Aug. 1953; d of Robert Salvage and Patricia Grutchfield; m 1995, Nareman Taha Wahab. *Educ:* Newnham Coll., Cambridge (BA Hons); Royal Holloway and Bedford New Coll., London (MSc). RGN 1978; Staff Nurse, London Hosp., 1978–80; worked on British nursing jls, and Ed., Sen. Nurse, 1980–88; Dir, Nursing Develt Prog., King's Fund, London, 1988–91; Regl Advr for Nursing and Midwifery, European Reg., WHO, 1991–95; Editor, 1996–97, Editor-in-Chief, 1997–99, Nursing Times; Nursing Dir, Emap Healthcare, 2000–02; Ed., Nursing and Midwifery Council Review, 2011–12. Mem. Bd, Geneva Initiative on Psychiatry, 2001–04. Jt Lead, Support Office, Prime Minister's Commn on the Future of Nursing and Midwifery in England, 2009–10; Ind. Advr and report author, Willis Commn on Nursing Educn, 2012; Policy Advr, All-Party Parly Gp on Global Health, 2012–. Associate, Newnham Coll., Cambridge, 1993–2004 (Hon. Associate, 2012–); Visiting Professor: Sheffield Univ., 1999–2004; Florence Nightingale Sch. of Nursing and Midwifery, KCL, 2007–13; ESEnfC, Sch. of Nursing, Coimbra, Portugal, 2017–; Vis. Prof. and Writer-in-Residence, Kingston Univ. and St George's, Univ. of London, 2013–. Prog. Dir, Global Nursing Leadership Inst. (formerly Policy Leadership Inst.), Internat. Council of Nurses, 2016–. Trustee, Queen's Nursing Inst., 2011–14. First Hon. Mem., Romanian Nurses Assoc., 1992. FRCN 2012. Hon. Fellow, Queen's Nursing Inst., 2009. Hon. LLD Sheffield, 1996; Hon. DSc Kingston and St George's, 2011; DUniv Middlesex, 2016. *Publications:* The Politics of Nursing, 1985; (ed) Models for Nursing, Vol. 1 1986, Vol. 2 1990; Nurses at Risk, 1988, 2nd edn 1999; (ed) Nurse Practitioners, 1991; (ed) Nursing in Action, 1993; (ed) Nursing Development Units, 1995; (ed) Nursing in Europe, 1997; Now More Than Ever: nurses, midwives and primary health care—past and present, 2010; Skyros: island of dreams, 2011; contrib. numerous articles. *Recreations:* friendship, travel, reading, swimming, cooking and eating, walking, theatre, watching football, cloudspotting. *Address:* 18 Leicester Road, Lewes, E Sussex BN7 1SX. *W:* www.janesalvage.com.

**SALVESEN, (Charles) Hugh,** PhD; Ambassador to Uruguay, 2005–08; b 10 Sept. 1955; s of late John and Eelin Salvesen; m 1983, Emilie Maria Ingenhousz (marr. diss. 2012); two s (one d decd). *Educ:* Loretto Sch., Musselburgh; Christ's Coll., Cambridge (MA, PhD). Joined Diplomatic Service, 1982; FCO, 1982–84; First Sec., BMG, Berlin, 1984–85; Bonn, 1985–88; FCO, 1988–93; Argentina, 1993–96; Dep. High Comr, NZ, 1996–2000; Dep. Hd, Econ. Policy Dept, FCO, 2000–02; Hd, Mgt Consultancy, FCO, 2002–05. Trustee: Drumduan Trust, 2014–15; John Muir Trust, 2016–18.

**SALVIDGE, Paul;** Member, Consumer Panel, Financial Services Authority, 2000–06; b 22 Aug. 1946; s of Herbert Stephen and Winifred Alice Elisabeth Salvidge; m 1972, Heather Margaret (née Johnson); one d. *Educ:* Cardiff High School; Birmingham Univ. (LLB). Ministry of Power, 1967; Dept of Trade and Industry, 1972–2000: Asst Secretary, 1982; Under Sec., 1989; Dir, Employment Relations, 1998–2000; Acting Legal Services Ombudsman, 2002–03. Dir, Saffron Walden Museum Soc. Ltd, 2008–.

**SALWAY, Francis William;** Chairman, Town and Country Housing Group, since 2012; b 5 Oct. 1957; m 1985, Sarah Peplow; one s one d. *Educ:* Rugby Sch.; Christ's Coll., Cambridge (BA 1979; MA 1983). Richard Ellis, 1979–82; Abacus Develts Ltd, 1982–85; Coll. of Estate Management, 1985–86; Standard Life, 1986–2000; Land Securities Gp plc, 2000–12: Dir, 2001–12; Chief Operating Officer, 2003–04; Chief Exec., 2004–12. Non-executive Director: Next plc, 2010–; Investment Property Databank, 2012; Cadogan Gp Ltd, 2012–. Vis. Prof., LSE, 2012–. Chm., Property Adv. Gp, TfL, 2015–. Chairman: The London Community Foundn, 2012–; Crossrail 2 Funding Taskforce, London First, 2013–14. Pres., British Property Fedn, 2008–09. *Publications:* Depreciation of Commercial Property, 1986. *Recreations:* walking, climbing, swimming, bridge.

**SALZ, Sir Anthony (Michael Vaughan),** Kt 2013; Executive Vice Chairman, N. M. Rothschild & Sons Ltd, 2006–17; b 30 June 1950; s of Michael H. Salz and Veronica Edith Dorothea Elizabeth Salz (née Hall); m 1975, Sally Ruth Hagger; one s two d. *Educ:* Summer Fields Sch., Oxford; Radley Coll.; Exeter Univ. (LLB Hons). Admitted Solicitor, 1974; Kenneth Brown Baker Baker, 1972–75; joined Freshfields, 1975, Partner, 1980, Sen. Partner, 1996–2000; seconded to Davis Polk & Wardwell, NY, 1977–78; Jt Sen. Partner, Freshfields Bruckhaus Deringer, 2000–06. Chairman: Bloomsbury Publishing plc, 2013–17; Freeformers Hldgs Ltd, 2016–. Vice-Chm., Bd of Govs, BBC, 2004–06. Ind. Reviewer of Barclays business practices, 2013. Chm., Adv. Bd, Hambro Perks Ltd, 2018–. Advr, Teach First, Business Leaders Council, 2012–17. Chm., Forward Inst., 2014–. Chm., Adv. Council, Tate St Ives, 2018–; Member: Tate Gall. Corporate Adv. Gp, 1997– (Chm., 1997–2002); Adv. Bd, Sch. of Business and Econs, Univ. of Exeter, 2003–17; Adv. Panel, Swiss Re Centre for Global Dialogue, 2006–11; Adv. Bd, Financial Services Knowledge Transfer Network, 2010–14; Adv. Council, Carnegie Endowment Internat. Peace, 2016–; lead non-exec. Bd Mem., DfE, 2010–12. Director: Tate Foundn, 2000–; Habitat for Humanity GB, 2004–10; Royal Opera Hse Covent Gdn Foundn, 2008–16; Scott Trust, 2009–. Trustee: Eden Trust, 2002–15 (Chm., 2009–15); Paul Hamlyn Foundn, 2005–; Conran Foundn, 2007–; Media Standards Trust, 2008–15; SHINE: Support and Help in Educn, 2008–10; Reprieve, 2011–17; High Street Fund, 2011–13; Foundn for FutureLondon, 2015–18; Supreme Court of the UK Arts Trust, 2016–18. Chairman: London Higher Skills Bd, 2008–10; Ind. Commn on Youth Crime and Antisocial Behaviour, 2008–10; Co-Chm., Educn and Employers Taskforce, 2009–10. Gov., Wellington Acad., 2008–18. FRSA 1996. Hon. LLD: Exeter, 2003; Coll. of Law, 2008. *Publications:* contrib. to various legal books and jls. *Recreations:* golf, fly-fishing, watching sports (including Southampton FC), tennis, walking, theatre, contemporary art. *E:* anthony@northhoughton.com. *Clubs:* Garrick; MCC; Berkshire Golf, Trevose Golf.

**SALZEDO, Simon Lopez;** QC 2011; b London, 4 Jan. 1968; s of Maurice Salzedo and Marion Leighton; m 1992, Catherine Jane Dundon; two s two d. *Educ:* Trinity Sch., Croydon; Lowlands Sixth Form Coll., Harrow; Keble Coll., Oxford (BA PPE 1990); City Univ. (DipLaw 1994). ACA 1993, FCA 2011. Tax consultant, Price Waterhouse, 1990–93; called to the Bar, Lincoln's Inn, 1995; in practice as a barrister, Brick Court Chambers, 1995–. *Publications:* (with R. D. Lord, QC) Guide to the Arbitration Act 1996, 1996; (with C. Hollander, QC) Conflicts of Interest, 2000, 5th edn 2016; (with T. Singla) Accountants' Negligence and Liability, 2016. *Address:* Brick Court Chambers, 7–8 Essex Street, WC2R 3LD. *T:* (020) 7379 3550.

**SAMAAN, Alice Thomas;** Ambassador of Bahrain to the Court of St James's, 2011–15, to Republic of Ireland, 2012–15, and to the Netherlands, 2014–15; b Manama, Bahrain. *Educ:* British Lebanese Trng Coll., Beirut; BBC Broadcasting Hse, London (Dip. Radio Prodn and Directing); Dip. Hosp. Admin, London; Dip. Supervisory Mgt, Bahrain; Univ. of Southern Calif (Dip. Trng of Trainers). Teacher, Amer. Mission Sch., Bahrain; producer, presenter and dir of radio progs for religious radio stn, Beirut, Lebanon; Hd, Overseas and Local Trng, Min. of Health, Bahrain; Internat. Prog. Officer in Bahrain and Oman, UNICEF; ed., producer and presenter of news, Bahrain Radio and TV Stn. Mem., Shura Council (Second Dep. Chm.; Mem., Adv. Council, 2000–02; Mem., Services Cttee (Vice Chm.); Mem., Ad-hoc Cttee for women and children). Former Mem., Exec. Bd, American Mission Hosp.; Mem., Bd of Dirs, Al-Raja Sch. Member: Supreme Council for Vocational Trng, Bahrain; Bd, Coll. of Health Scis, Min. of Health, Bahrain; Exec. Cttee, Nat. Prog. for Mother and Child Care, Oman. *Clubs:* Mark's, Mosimann's.

**SAMANI, Prof. Sir Nilesh (Jayantilal),** Kt 2015; DL; MD; FRCP, FMedSci; Professor of Cardiology, University of Leicester, since 1997; Medical Director, British Heart Foundation, since 2016; Hon. Consultant Cardiologist, Glenfield Hospital, Leicester, since 1993; b Nanyuki, Kenya, 19 July 1956; s of Jayantilal and Kantaben Samani; m 1984, Varsha Raja; two s. *Educ:* Lenana Sch., Nairobi; Charles Keene Coll., Leicester; Univ. of Leicester (BSc 1978; MB ChB 1981; MD 1994). FRCP 1994. HO, Medicine and Surgery, 1981–82; SHO, Medicine, 1982–85; University of Leicester: MRC Clin. Trainee Fellow, 1985–88; Lectr in Medicine, 1988–93; Sen. Lectr in Cardiol., 1993–97. FMedSci 2002. DL Leics, 2010. *Publications:* contribs to jls incl. Nature, Nature Genetics, Lancet, New England Jl Medicine. *Recreations:* sports, reading, family. *Address:* Department of Cardiovascular Sciences, University of Leicester, BHF Cardiovascular Research Centre, Glenfield Hospital, Leicester LE3 9QP. *T:* (0116) 204 4758, *Fax:* (0116) 287 5792. *E:* njs@le.ac.uk.

**SAMARAWEERA, Hon. Mangala Pinsiri;** MP Matara, Sri Lanka, since 1989 (Freedom, 1989–2007; United Nat., since 2007); Minister of Finance and Mass Media, Sri Lanka, since 2017; b Matara; s of Mahanama and Khema Samaraweera. *Educ:* Royal Coll., Colombo; Central Sch. of Art and Design (BA Hons Fashion and Textile Design). Minister: of Posts and Telecommunications, 1994–2000; of Urban Develt and Housing, 2000–01; Chief Opposition Whip, 2001–04; Minister: of Ports, Aviation and Media, 2004–07; of Foreign Affairs, 2005–07; of Foreign Affairs, Telecommunications and IT, 2015–17. *Address:* Ministry of Finance and Mass Media, The Secretariat, Lotus Road, Colombo 01, Sri Lanka. *T:* 0777576495.

**SAMBLES, Prof. (John) Roy,** PhD; FRS 2002; CPhys; Professor of Physics, Exeter University, since 1991; b 14 Oct. 1945; s of Charles Henry Sambles and Georgina (née Deeble); m 1966, Sandra Elizabeth Sloman; two s one d. *Educ:* Callington Grammar Sch., Cornwall; Imperial Coll., London Univ. (BSc 1st Cl. Hons Physics 1967; ARCS; PhD 1970; DIC). CPhys 1988; FInstP 1988, Hon. FInstP 2018. Fellow, Imperial Coll., London, 1970–72; Exeter University: Lectr in Physics, 1972–85; Sen. Lectr, 1985–88; Reader, 1988–91. Mem., EPSRC, 2008–14. Pres., Inst. of Physics, 2015–17. George Gray Medal, British Liquid Crystal Soc., 1998; Thomas Young Medal and Prize, 2003, Faraday Medal, 2012, Inst. of Physics. *Publications:* numerous papers in learned scientific jls, incl. works on liquid crystals, melting, electron microscopy, resistivity of thin samples, spin waves in metals, molecular electronics, surface plasmons, structural colour in nature, microwave metasurfaces and acoustic metamaterials. *Recreations:* writing poetry, local Methodist preacher. *Address:* School of Physics, University of Exeter, Exeter, Devon EX4 4QL. *T:* (01392) 264103.

**SAMBROOK, Prof. Joseph Frank,** PhD; FRS 1985; FAA; Distinguished Fellow, Peter MacCallum Cancer Institute, Melbourne, since 2003 (Director of Research, 1995–2000; Director, Familial Cancer Centre, 2000–05); Executive Scientific Director, Australian Stem Cell Centre, 2006–07 and 2009–11; b 1 March 1939; s of Thomas Sambrook and Ethel Gertrude (née Lightfoot); m 1st, 1960, Thelma McGrady (marr. diss. 1984); two s one d; 2nd, 1986, Mary-Jane Gething; one d. *Educ:* Liverpool Univ. (BSc 1962); Australian Nat. Univ. (PhD 1965). FAA 2000. Res. Fellow, John Curtin Sch. of Med. Res., ANU, 1965–66; Postdoctoral Fellow, MRC Lab. of Molecular Biol., 1966–67; Jun. Fellow, Salk Inst. for Biol Studies, 1967–69; Sen. Staff Investigator, 1969–77, Asst Dir, 1977–85, Cold Spring Harbor Lab.; Prof. and Chm., Dept of Biochemistry, Southwestern Medical Center, Dallas, 1985–91; Dir, McDermott Center for Human Growth and Develt, Southwestern Med. Sch., Dallas, 1991–94. Hon. DSc: Watson Sch. of Biol Scis, 2007; Liverpool, 2007. *Publications:* contribs to learned jls. *Recreation:* music. *Address:* PO Box 3254, East Melbourne, Vic 3002, Australia. *T:* (3) 94157323.

**SAMBROOK, Prof. Richard Jeremy;** Professor of Journalism, and Director, Centre for Journalism, Cardiff University, since 2012; b 24 April 1956; s of Michael Sambrook and Joan Sambrook (née Hartridge); m 1987, Susan Fisher; one s one d. *Educ:* Maidstone Sch. for Boys; Reading Univ. (BA); Birkbeck Coll., London Univ. (MSc). Trainee journalist, Thomson Newspapers, 1977–80; joined BBC, 1980: Radio News, 1980–84; TV News, 1984–87; Dep. Ed., Nine O'Clock News, 1988–92; News Editor, BBC News, 1992–96; Head, Newsgathering, 1996–99; Dep. Dir, 1999–2001, Dir, 2001–04, BBC News; Dir, BBC Global News, 2004–10; Global Vice Chm., Edelman, 2010–12. Vis. Fellow, Reuters Inst. for the Study of Journalism, 2010–12. FRTS 1992; FRSA. *Publications:* (ed) Global Voice: Britain's future in international broadcasting, 2007; (jtly) Reporting Dangerously: journalist killings, intimidation and security, 2016; (ed jtly) The Future of TV News, 2016. *Recreations:* walking, photography, music. *Address:* Cardiff School of Journalism, Media and Cultural Studies, Cardiff University, Two Central Square, Central Square, Cardiff CF10 1FS.

**SAMEK, Charles Stephen;** QC 2009; b London, 4 July 1965; o s of Major Herbert Samek, OBE, REME, and Terry Samek (née Nash); m 2005, Maria Pierfederici; one s one d. *Educ:* St Paul's Sch., Barnes; Oriel Coll., Oxford (MA Lit. Hum.); City Univ. (DipLaw). Called to the Bar, Middle Temple, 1989 (Astbury Schol., 1988); in practice as barrister, specialising in commercial litigation, civil fraud and internat. arbitration and private internat. law, 1989–; Mem., Inner Temple (ad eundem), 1997. Member: Commercial Bar Assoc., 1993–; Chancery Bar Assoc., 2007–; Internat. Bar Assoc., 2009–; British-Italian Law Assoc., 2009–; Commercial Fraud Lawyers Assoc., 2010–. Mem., Lord Mayor's Big Curry Cttee, ABF The Soldiers' Charity (formerly ABF), 2009–13. Freeman, City of London, 2012; Liveryman, Feltmakers' Co., 2012. *Recreations:* opera, ballet, chess, watching Arsenal FC, ski-ing, wine. *Address:* Littleton Chambers, 3 King's Bench Walk, Temple, EC4Y 7HR. *T:* (020) 7797 8600. *E:* clerks@littletonchambers.co.uk. *Club:* Athenæum.

**SAMMONS, Prof. Pamela**, PhD; Professor of Education, University of Oxford, since 2009; Senior Research Fellow, Jesus College, Oxford, 2010–18, now Emeritus Fellow; *b* 6 April 1956; *d* of Albert Edward Henry Sammons and Violet Ruth Sammons; *m* 1st, 1984, David Michael Greet (*d* 2003); two *d*; 2nd, 2011, John Allen Lerwill. *Educ*: Nower Hill High Sch.; Harrow County Girls' Sch.; Univ. of Bristol (BSocSci Geog. with Econs); CNAA (PhD 1986). Sen. Res. Officer, Res. and Stats Br., ILEA, 1981–90; Res. Fellow, Centre for Educnl Res., LSE, 1990–93; Institute of Education, London: Sen. Researcher, 1993–98; Reader in Educn, 1998; Prof. of Educn, and Co-ordinating Dir, Internat. Sch. Effectiveness and Improvement Centre, 1999–2004; Prof. of Educn, Univ. of Nottingham, 2004–09. *Publications*: (jtly) School Matters: the junior years, 1988; (jtly) Forging Links: effective schools and effective departments, 1997; School Effectiveness: coming of age in the 21st century, 1999; (jtly) Teachers Matter, 2007; (jtly) Methodological Advances in Educational Effectiveness Research, 2010; (jtly) Early Childhood Matters, 2010; (jtly) Successful School Leadership, 2011; (ed jtly) School Effectiveness and Improvement Research, Policy and Practice: challenging the orthodoxy?, 2012; (jtly) Effective Classroom Practice, 2014; (ed jtly) Routledge International Handbook of Educational Effectiveness, 2016; articles, etc in area of school effectiveness and improvement. *Recreations*: walking, visiting museums and art galleries. *Address*: Department of Education, University of Oxford, 15 Norham Gardens, Oxford OX2 6PY. *E*: pamela.sammons@education.ox.ac.uk.

**SAMMUT ALESSI, Charles;** *see* Alessi, C.

**SAMPAIO, Jorge Fernando Branco de,** Hon. GCMG 2002; Hon. GCVO 1993; Special Envoy of the UN Secretary-General to Stop Tuberculosis, 2006–13; High Representative of the UN Secretary-General for the Alliance of Civilisations, 2007–13; Counsellor of State, Portugal, since 2006; *b* Lisbon, 18 Sept. 1939; *s* of António Arnaldo de Carvalho Sampaio and Fernanda Bensaúde Branco de Sampaio; *m* Maria José Ritta; one *s* one *d*. *Educ*: Law Sch., Univ. of Lisbon. Practised as a lawyer, specialising in defending political prisoners. Sec. of State for External Co-operation, 1975; MP, Lisbon, 1979–84; Speaker, Socialist Parly Gp, 1987–88; Mem., Council of State, 1989–92; Mayor of Lisbon, 1989–95; Pres. of Portugal, 1996–2006. Founder, Intervenção Socialista, 1975; joined Socialist Party, 1978: Mem., Nat. Secretariat, 1979–92; Dir, Internat. Dept, 1986–87; Sec. Gen., 1989–92. Mem., European Human Rights Commn, Council of Europe, 1979–84. Mem. Bd, Carnegie Corp., NY. Nelson Mandela Prize, UN, 2015. Numerous decorations, including: Grand Officer, Order of Prince Henry (Portugal), 1983; Grand Collar: Order of Southern Cross (Brazil), 1997; Orders of the Tower and Sword, of Valour, Loyalty, Merit, and of Liberty (Portugal), 2006; Collar: Order of Charles III (Spain), 1996; Order of Isabel la Católica (Spain), 2000; Grand Cross: Order of Orange Nassau (Netherlands), 1990; Order of White Eagle (Poland), 1997; Order of Merit (Germany), 1998; Légion d'Honneur (France), 1999. *Publications*: A Festa de um Sonho, 1991; A Look on Portugal, 1995; Os Portugueses, vols I-IX, 1997–2005; Com os Portugueses: dez anos na Presidência da República, 2005; numerous articles on political issues. *Recreations*: music, golf. *Address*: Casa do Regalo, Tapada das Necessidades, 1350–213 Lisbon, Portugal.

**SAMPRAS, Peter;** tennis player; *b* 12 Aug. 1971; *s* of Sam and Georgia Sampras; *m* 2000, Bridgette Wilson; two *s*. Professional tennis player, 1988–2003; won US Open, 1990 (youngest winner), 1993, 1995, 1996, 1999, 2002; Australian Open, 1994, 1997; Wimbledon, 1993, 1994, 1995, 1997, 1998, 1999, 2000; ATP World Champion, 1991, 1994, 1996, 1997, 1999; Davis Cup player. Co-Founder, Pure Sports Mgt LLC, 2007. Member: American Cancer Soc. Public Awareness Council; Board, Tim and Tom Gullikson Foundation; Founder, Aces for Charity Fund. *Publications*: (with Peter Bodo) A Champion's Mind: lessons from a life in tennis, 2008. *Recreations*: golf, basketball, Formula 1 racing. *Address*: c/o 200 ATP Tour Boulevard, Ponte Vedra Beach, FL 32082, USA. *T*: (904) 2858000.

**SAMPSON, Adam;** Managing Partner, DNGG Ltd, since 2016; *b* 13 June 1960; *s* of Derek and Janet Sampson; *m* 2000, Siobhan Grey, QC; one *s* one *d*. *Educ*: Brasenose Coll., Oxford (BA; MSc). Jun. Dean, Brasenose Coll., Oxford, 1986–87; Probation Officer, Tottenham, 1987–89; Dep. Dir, Prison Reform Trust, 1989–94; Asst Prisons Ombudsman, Home Office, 1994–97; CEO, RAPt, 1998–2002; Dir, then Chief Exec., Shelter, 2003–09; Chief Ombudsman, Office for Legal Complaints, 2009–14. Consultant: Which?, 2015; Sense About Science, 2015–16; Centre for Socio-Legal Studies, Oxford Univ., 2015–; Exec. Chair, C4H, 2014–. *Publications*: Acts of Abuse, 1993. *Recreation*: sleeping.

**SAMPSON, Prof. Fiona Ruth,** MBE 2017; FRSL; writer; Professor of Poetry and Poetry Centre Director, University of Roehampton, since 2013; *b* London, 7 Oct. 1963; *d* of Aylwin Arthur Sampson and Pamela Mary Sampson; *m* Peter William Perry Salmon. *Educ*: Penglais Comprehensive Sch.; Pates Grammar Sch. for Girls; Royal Acad. of Music (Foundn Schol.; John Waterhouse Prize); Manchester Coll., Oxford (Newdigate Prize; MA PPE 1992); Catholic Univ. of Nijmegen (PhD 2001). ARCM 1980. Writing residencies in health and social care, incl. Isle of Wight HA, Dyfed Probation Service, Age Concern Swindon, Addenbrooke's Hosp., Cambridge, 1992–2005. Founder Dir, Aberystwyth Internat. Poetry Fest., 1995–99; Dir, Stephen Spender Meml Trust, 1999–2001; Founder Ed., Orient Express, 2002–05; Ed., Poetry Review, 2005–12. Visiting Research Fellow: Univ. of Sussex, 2000–03; Inst. of English Studies, Sch. of Advanced Study, Univ. of London, 2011, 2012–13; Inst. of Musical Res., Univ. of London, 2012–15; Inst. of Modern Langs Res., 2018–19; AHRC Fellow in Creative and Performing Arts, Oxford Brookes Univ., 2002–05; Fellow in Creativity, Univ. of Warwick, 2007–08; Dist. Writer, 2009–13, Prof. of Poetry, 2013, Kingston Univ.; Writer's Fellowship: Hawthornden Castle, 2001; Fundación Valparaiso, 2002; Heinrich Böll Hse, 2005; Estonian Writers' Union Hse, 2009; Arts Council of England Grant, 2012; Keats-Shelley Mus., Rome, 2015; Vuk Karadzic Cultural Centre, 2018; Baltic Writers' Centre, 2018; Prague UNESCO City of Lit., 2019. FRSL 2009; FEA 2009. FRSA 2013; Fellow, Wordsworth Trust, 2016. Member, Board: Poetry Translation Centre, 2006–11; Wasafiri, 2008–. Mem., Council, RSL, 2011–17. Judge: Foyle Young Poets, 2003; IMPAC Award, Irish Times, 2006; Ind. Foreign Fiction Prize, 2009; Forward Prizes, Soc. of Authors Eric Gregory Awards, 2011; Griffin Prizes, Canada, 2012; Cholmondeley Awards, Soc. of Authors, 2012–; T. S. Eliot Prize, 2015; Ondaatje Prize, 2015; Chairman of Judges: Roehampton Prize, 2015–; Eur. Lyric Atlas Prize, 2016–. Patron, Anglo-Russian Cultural Assoc., 2016–. Southern Arts Writer's Award, 1993; Oppenheimer-John Downes Award, 1998; Writer's Award, Arts Council of Wales, 1999; Kathleen Blundell Trust Award, 2002; Zlaten Prsten Prize, Macedonia, 2003; Charles Angoff Award, USA, 2006; Cholmondeley Award, Soc. of Authors, 2009; Povelji za med?unarodnu saradnju, Bosnia, 2015; Slovo Podgorica, Bosnia, 2016. *Publications*: (ed jtly) The Self on the Page, 1998 (Hebrew edn 2002); The Healing Word, 1999; Folding the Real, 2001 (Romanian edn 2004); Patuvachki Knevnik, 2004; (trans.) Evening Brings Everything Back, by Jaan Kaplinski, 2004; (ed jtly) A Fine Line: new poetry from Central and Eastern Europe, 2004; (ed) Creative Writing in Health and Social Care, 2004; (jtly) Writing: self and reflexivity, 2005; The Distance Between Us, 2005 (Romanian and Macedonian edns 2005, Albanian edn 2006, Bulgarian edn 2009); (trans.) Day, by Amir Or, 2006; On Listening, 2007; Selected Poems in Hebrew Translation, 2007; Common Prayer, 2007; Zweimal sieben Gedichte, 2009; Poetry Writing, 2009; (ed) A Century of Poetry Review, 2009 (Special Commendation, Poetry Book Soc.); Poljupci I Molitva, 2010; Rough Music, 2010; (trans. jtly) Selected Poems, by Jaan Kaplinski, 2011; Music Lessons, 2011; (ed) Percy Bysshe Shelley, 2011 (On-line Choice, Poetry Book Soc.); Beyond the Lyric, 2012; Coleshill, 2013 (Recommendation, Poetry Book Soc.); Night Fugue: selected poems, 2013; Revenant (Chinese trans.), 2014; Volta, 2015; Marevo, 2015; Kolshil, 2016; The Catch, 2016; Lyric Cousins: musical form in poetry, 2016; Do Potopa, 2017; Limestone Country, 2017; In Search of Mary Shelley: the girl who wrote Frankenstein, 2018; Klopka, 2019; Kolshil, 2019. *Recreations*: string chamber music, English parish churches, Balkan train journeys. *Address*: c/o Sarah Chalfant, Wylie Agency, 17 Bedford Square, WC1B 3JA. *E*: mail@wylieagency.co.uk. *Club*: Athenæum.

**SAMPSON, James; His Honour Judge Sampson;** a Circuit Judge, since 2010; *b* Driffield, 15 Sept. 1962; *s* of James and Mary Sampson; *m* 1987, Helen Hewitt; one *s* two *d*. *Educ*: Bransholme High Sch.; Univ. of Nottingham; Inns of Court Sch. of Law. Called to the Bar, Inner Temple, 1985; in practice as barrister specialising in crime; Recorder, 2003–10. *Recreations*: cycling, swimming, running, ski-ing. *Clubs*: Barracuda Triathlon, City of Hull Athletic.

**SAMPSON, Mark Geraint;** First Team Coach, Stevenage Football Club, since 2019; *b* Bridgend; *s* of Derek and Tracy Sampson; *m* Gemma Doyle. *Educ*: Univ. of Wales Inst., Cardiff (BSc Sports Develt). UEFA Pro Licence, 2016. Coach: Swansea City Acad. team, 2008–10; Bristol Acad. Women FC, 2010–13; Head Coach, England Women Football, 2013–17. Patron, Women in Sport, 2016–17. *Address*: 54B Stephendale Road, SW6 2PG. *T*: 07957 441391.

**SAMPSON, Nicholas Alexander,** MA; Headmaster, Cranbrook School, Sydney, since 2012; *b* 27 Aug. 1958; *s* of Charles and Patricia Sampson; *m* 1981, Nancy Threlfall (marr. diss. 2014); two *d*. *Educ*: Gillingham Grammar Sch.; Howard Sch., Kent; Selwyn Coll., Cambridge (MA); Westminster Coll., Oxford (PGCE). Teacher of English and Housemaster, Wells Cathedral Sch., 1984–94; Headmaster, Sutton Valence Sch., 1994–2000; Principal, Geelong Grammar Sch., Australia, 2001–04; Master, Marlborough Coll., 2004–12. Member: Bd, Assoc. of Ind. Schs of Vic, 2003–04; Council, Marcus Oldham Coll., 2001–04; Council, Janet Clarke Hall, 2002–04. Governor: King's Sch., Rochester, 2006–12; St Andrew's Sch., Pangbourne, 2006–12; Swindon Acad., 2007–12; Marlborough Coll., Malaysia, 2012–. *Recreations*: family, literature, history, sport. *Address*: Cranbrook School, 5 Victoria Road, Bellevue Hill, NSW 2023, Australia. *Club*: Athenæum.

**SAMS, Craig Lynn;** Co-founder, 2007, and Executive Chairman, Carbon Gold Ltd; Director, Soil Association Certification Ltd, since 2007 (Chairman, 2007); President, Green & Black's, since 1999; *b* 17 July 1944; *s* of Kenneth Sams and Margaret Sams; *m* 1991, Josephine Fairley, *qv*; one *s* one *d* by a previous marriage. *Educ*: Wharton Sch., Univ. of Pennsylvania (BSc Econs). Co-founded Whole Earth Foods, 1967; estabd Ceres Bakery, 1972 (Chm.); co-founded Green & Black's Chocolate, 1991, created Maya Gold Chocolate, 1993; Director: Judges Bakery Ltd, 2004–13; Duchy Originals Ltd, 2009–; Gusto Organic Ltd, 2013– (Chm.); Wellington Natural Health. Hon. Treas., 1990–2001, Chm., 2001–07, Soil Assoc. Co-Publisher, Seed: the jl of organic living, 1972–77. Mem., Guild of Food Writers. Trustee: SEM Trust, 2015–; Stonelynk Valley Nature Reserve. *Publications*: About Macrobiotics, 1972; The Macrobiotic Brown Rice Cookbook, 1993; The Little Food Book, 2003; (with Jo Fairley) Sweet Dreams: the story of Green & Black's, 2008. *Recreations*: allotment gardening, orchardist, cliff walking, propcycling. *Address*: 106 High Street, Hastings, E Sussex TN34 3ES. *T*: (01424) 430016. *E*: craig@craigsams.com. *Club*: Groucho.

**SAMS, Jeremy Charles;** composer, translator, director; *b* 12 Jan. 1957; *s* of late Eric Sams and Enid Sams (*née* Tidmarsh); one *s*. *Educ*: Magdalene Coll., Cambridge (BA); Guildhall Sch. of Music. Freelance pianist, 1977–82; director: *theatre* includes: Entertaining Mr Sloane, Greenwich, 1992; Wind in the Willows, Tokyo, 1993, Old Vic, 1995; Neville's Island, Apollo, 1994; Wild Oats, RNT, 1995; Passion, Queen's, 1996; Marat/Sade, RNT, 1997; Enter the Guardsman, Donmar, 1997; Two Pianos, Four Hands, Birmingham Rep., and Comedy, 1999; Spend! Spend! Spend!, Piccadilly, 1999; Noises Off, RNT, 2000, transf. Piccadilly and NY, 2001; What the Butler Saw, Theatre Royal, Bath, and tour, 2001; Benefactors, Albery, and tour, 2002; The Water Babies, Chichester, 2003; Little Britain, UK tour, 2005; Donkeys' Years, Comedy, 2006; The Sound of Music, Palladium, 2006, UK tour, 2009; 13 The Musical, Broadway, 2008; The King and I, Royal Albert Hall, 2009; Educating Rita, Menier Chocolate Factory, transf. Trafalgar Studios, 2010; The Wizard of Oz, Palladium, 2011, Toronto, 2013, US tour, 2013; Monsieur Popular (also trans.), Theatre Royal, Bath, 2015; What's In a Name (also trans.), Birmingham Rep., 2016; Oklahoma!, Chichester, 2019; *opera*: The Reluctant King, Opera North, 1994; (libretto) The Enchanted Island, Metropolitan Opera, NY, 2012; La Périchole (also trans.), Garsington, 2012; Peter Grimes, Grange Park, 2014; *translations* include: The Rehearsal, Almeida and Garrick, 1991 (Time Out Award), Minerva, Chichester (also dir), 2015; Becket, Theatre Royal Haymarket, 1991; The Miser, NT; Les Parents Terribles, RNT and NY, 1990; Mary Stuart, RNT, 1996; Merry Widow, Royal Opera, 1997; A Fool and His Money, Nottingham Playhouse and Birmingham Rep., 1998; Colombe, Salisbury Playhouse, 1999; Twilight of the Gods (The Rheingold, The Valkyrie, Siegfried), 2001, Così fan tutte, 2002, and The Magic Flute, Macbeth, Figaro's Wedding, La Bohème, in repertory, ENO; Scapino, Chichester, 2005; Arms and the Cow, Opera North, 2006; Don Giovanni, ENO, 2010; Die Fledermaus, Metropolitan Opera, NY, 2014; Exit the King (Ionesco), Ustinov. Th., Bath, 2014; Rise and Fall of the City of Mahagonny, Royal Opera, 2015; Die schöne Müllerin (The Fair Maid of the Mill), Holywell Music Room, 2015; Schubert's Song Cycle, Die schöne Müllerin, Winterreise, Schwanengesang, Ryedale Fest. and Wigmore Hall, 2016; Edmond de Bergerac, Birmingham Rep. and tour, 2019; Fantasio, Garsington Opera, 2019; *adaptations* include: Waiting in the Wings, NY, 1999; Chitty Chitty Bang Bang, Palladium, 2002, transf. NY; Amour, NY, 2002; A Damsel in Distress, Chichester, 2015; composer of numerous scores: *theatre* includes: Kean, Old Vic, 1990; for RSC: Temptation, The Tempest, Measure for Measure, Merry Wives of Windsor, Midsummer Night's Dream; for RNT: Ghetto (also lyrics); Wind in the Willows (also lyrics); Arcadia; Honour, 2003; *television*: Persuasion, 1996 (BAFTA Award for Original TV Music); Have Your Cake, 1997; *films*: The Mother, 2003; Enduring Love (Ivor Novello Award), 2004; Hyde Park on Hudson, 2013; Le Weekend, 2013; My Cousin Rachel, 2017. Hon. FRAM 2013. DUniv Birmingham City, 2013. *Publications*: (ed) Wild Oats, 1995; *translations*: Molière, The Miser, 1991; Anouilh, The Rehearsal, 1991; Cocteau, Les Parents Terribles, 1995; Schiller, Mary Stuart, 1996; Anouilh, Becket, 1997; Lehár, The Merry Widow, 2000; Antigone, 2002; Eric Emmanuel Schmitt, Plays: 1, 2002; Enigma Variations, 2003. *Address*: c/o The Agency, 24 Pottery Lane, W11 4LZ.

**SAMSON, Polly,** FRSL; writer and lyricist; *b* London, 29 April 1962; *d* of Lance Samson and Esther Samson (*née* Cheo Ying); *m* 1994, David Jon Gilmour, *qv*; three *s* one *d*. *Educ*: Newton Abbot Grammar Sch. Publicity Dir, Jonathan Cape, 1986–89; journalist and columnist, Sunday Times, 1990–93. FRSL 2018. *Publications*: Lying in Bed, 1999; Out of the Picture, 2000; Perfect Lives, 2010; The Kindness, 2015; A Theatre of Dreamers, 2020. *Recreations*: music, books, dogs, photography. *Address*: 8 Medina Terrace, Brighton BN3 2WL. *T*: 07768 018009. *E*: polly@pollysamson.com. *Club*: Groucho.

**SAMSON, Prof. Thomas James, (Jim),** PhD; FBA 2000; Professor of Music, Royal Holloway, University of London, 2002–11, now Emeritus; *b* 6 July 1946; *s* of Edward Samson and Matilda Jayne (*née* Smyth). *Educ:* Queen's Univ., Belfast (BMus); UC, Cardiff (MMus; PhD 1972). LRAM 1972. Res. Fellow in Humanities, Univ. of Leicester, 1972–73; University of Exeter: Lectr in Music, 1973–87; Reader in Musicology, 1987–92; Prof. of Musicology, 1992–94; Stanley Hugh Badock Prof. of Music, Univ. of Bristol, 1994–2002. Vis. Prof., Univ. of Trondheim, 2004–07. Ed.-in-Chief, Grove Music Online Revisions, Eastern Europe, 2012–. Hon. Dr Ionian Univ. of Corfu, 2016. Harrison Medal for Musicology, Irish Res. Council, 2018. Order of Merit, Ministry of Culture (Poland), 1990. *Publications:* Music in Transition: a study of tonal expansion and early atonality 1900–1920, 1977, 3rd edn 1993; The Music of Szymanowski, 1980; The Music of Chopin, 1985, 2nd edn 1994 (trans. German 1991); (ed) Chopin Studies, 1988; (ed) The Late Romantic Era: Vol. VII, Man and Music, 1991; Chopin: the Four Ballades, 1992 (trans. Polish 2012); (ed) The Cambridge Companion to Chopin, 1992; (ed with J. Rink) Chopin Studies 2, 1994; Master Musicians Chopin, 1996 (trans. Japanese 2012); (ed) The Cambridge History of Nineteenth-Century Music, 2002; (ed with Bennett Zon) Nineteenth Century Music: selected proceedings of the Tenth International Conference, 2002; Virtuosity and the Musical Work: the Transcendental Studies of Liszt, 2003 (Royal Philharmonic Bk Prize, 2004); The Complete Chopin: a new critical edition, Ballades, 2006 (Internat. Piano Award, 2009); (ed with P. J. E. Harper-Scott) Introduction to Music Studies, 2008 (trans. Korean 2014); Music in the Balkans, 2013; (ed with M. Milin) Serbian Music: Yugoslav contexts, 2014; (ed with N. Demetriou) Music in Cyprus, 2015. *Recreation:* astronomy. *Address:* 81 Gainsborough Road, Kew, Richmond TW9 2ET; 19 Odos Kyknou, Kallithea, 21060 Drepano, Nafplio. Greece. Via Cesare Biondi 33, 55051 Barga (Lucca), Italy.

**SAMSON-BARRY, Hilary Alice;** executive coach; Director, Koru Leadership Ltd, since 2012; *b* 16 Aug. 1958; *d* of Dr Mattanja Erasmus Richard Samson and Dr Margaret Noel Samson (*née* Williams); *m* 1989, Desmond Neville Barry; one *s* one *d*. *Educ:* Sch. of St Mary and St Anne, Abbots Bromley; Ellesmere Coll.; Univ. of Exeter (BA Hons (Econs and Geog.) 1980); Cranfield Univ. (MBA 1986). Personnel Manager, Securiguard Services Ltd, 1980–85; Mgt Consultant, Towers Perrin, 1986–91; Project Manager, London Implementation Gp, DoH, 1992–95; Dir, Camden and Islington HA, 1995–96; Head: Health Develt, NHS London Region, 1997–2000; Policy Integration and Health, GLA, 2000–01; Dir, Productivity and Diversity, Women and Equality Unit, Cabinet Office and DTI, 2001–04; Hd of Children, Families and Maternity, DoH, 2004; Dir, Turning Point, 2010. Chm., Bipolar UK, 2019– (Vice Chm., 2016–19); Ind. Mem., Network Cttee, Mind, 2015–. Trustee, Scope, 2009–16. Gov., Francis Combe Sch. and Community Coll., 2003. Hon. DSc Greenwich, 2001. *Recreations:* personal and spiritual development, travel, family and community. *Address:* Highclere, 34 Abbots Road, Abbots Langley, Herts WD5 0AZ. *E:* HSamsonBarry@aol.com.

**SAMSOVA, Galina;** producer, teacher; *b* Stalingrad, 1937; *d* of a Byelorussian; *m* 1st, Alexander Ursuliak; 2nd, André Prokovsky. *Educ:* the Ballet Sch., Kiev (pupil of N. Verekundova). Joined Kiev Ballet, 1956 and became a soloist; Canadian Ballet, 1961; created chief rôle in Cendrillon, Paris 1963 (Gold Medal for best danseuse of Paris Festival). Ballerina, Festival Ballet, 1964–73; headed the group of André Prokovsky, The New London Ballet, (disbanded in 1977, revived for 3 new productions, The Theatre Royal, York, 1979); a Principal Dancer, Sadler's Wells Royal Ballet, subseq. Birmingham Royal Ballet, 1980–91; Artistic Dir, Scottish Ballet, 1991–97; has danced principal rôles in Sleeping Beauty, Nutcracker, Giselle, Swan Lake, Anna Karenina, and other classical ballets; danced in Europe, Far East and USA. Produced: Sequence from Paquita, Sadler's Wells, 1980; (with Peter Wright) Swan Lake, Sadler's Wells, 1983, Covent Garden, 1991, Royal Swedish Ballet, 2001; Giselle, London City Ballet, 1986, Birmingham Royal Ballet, 2013; Les Sylphides, Birmingham Royal Ballet, 1992; Sleeping Beauty, Scottish Ballet, 1994, Tulsa Ballet, USA, 2000; Swan Lake, Scottish Ballet, 1995, Rome Opera House, 2003, NBA Ballet Co., Japan, 2006.

**SAMUEL,** family name of **Viscounts Bearsted** and **Samuel**.

**SAMUEL, 5th Viscount** *cr* 1937, of Mount Carmel and of Toxteth, Liverpool; **Jonathan Herbert Samuel;** *b* 17 Dec. 1965; *s* of 4th Viscount Samuel (who had succeeded to the title in Oct. 2014) and Nonni Esther Samuel (*née* Gordon); *S* father, Nov. 2014; *m* 1995, Bridget Elizabeth, *d* of late Prof. Michael Mahoney, Princeton, USA; two *d*. *Heir:* half-b Hon. Benjamin Angus Samuel, *b* 29 Dec. 1983.

**SAMUEL, Andrew;** see Samuel, M. A.

**SAMUEL, Gillian Patricia;** Director (formerly General Manager) of Corporate Communications, P&O Nedlloyd Ltd, 1998–2005; *b* 19 Oct. 1945; *d* of Harry Martin Samuel and Kathleen Joyce Samuel (*née* Drake). *Educ:* Edmonton Co. Grammar Sch.; Exeter Univ. (BA Hons Hist.). Current Affairs Gp, BBC TV, 1968–70; Plessey Co., 1970–72; Department of: Nat. Savings, 1972–75; Industry, later DTI, 1975–87; Dir of Information, Dept of Transport, 1987–92; Press Sec. and Chief of Information, 1992–97, Sen. Advr, Internal Communications Develt, 1997–98, MoD. JP E Dorset, 2008–15. *Recreations:* golf, walking, choral singing, modern jazz.

**SAMUEL, Sir John (Michael Glen),** 5th Bt *cr* 1898; Chartered Engineer, Business Development, RedT Energy plc (formerly Renewable Energy Dynamics Technology Ltd), since 2009; *b* 25 Jan. 1944; *o s* of Sir John Oliver Cecil Samuel, 4th Bt and Charlotte Mary, *d* of late R. H. Hoyt, Calgary, Canada; *S* father, 1962; *m* 1st, 1966, Antoinette Sandra, *d* of late Captain Antony Hewitt, RE, 2nd SAS Regt, and Mrs K. A. H. Casson, Frith Farm, Wolverton, Hants; two *s*; 2nd, 1982, Mrs Elizabeth Ann Molinari, *y d* of late Major R. G. Curry, Bournemouth, Dorset. *Educ:* Radley; London Univ. Director: Enfield Automotive, 1967–70; Advanced Vehicle Systems Ltd, 1971–78; Chairman: Electric Auto Corp. (USA), 1978–83; Synergy Management Services Ltd, 1983–; Founder and Tech. Dir, RE-Fuel Technol. Ltd, 2001–09 (Chm., 2008). *Recreation:* motor racing. *Heir: s* Anthony John Fulton Samuel [*b* 13 Oct. 1972; *m* 2004, Gemma Chloe Rose Gubbins; three *s*].

**SAMUEL, Dr (Marcus) Andrew;** Chief Executive, Oil and Gas Authority, since 2015; *b* Lusaka, Zambia, 7 July 1969; *s* of Marcus, (Jimmy), Samuel and Heather Samuel; *m* 1999, Sue Entwistle; two *s*. *Educ:* Stowe Sch.; Sidney Sussex Coll., Cambridge (BA Hons Nat. Scis 1990); Birkbeck Coll., Univ. of London (PhD 1993). Postdoctoral Fellowship, Birkbeck Coll., Univ. of London; BG Group: UK-based geologist, 1994–99; Sen. Geologist, BG Egypt and Rashpetco JV Cairo, 1999–2002; UK Exploration Manager, 2003–06; North Sea High Pressure, High Temperature Asset Manager, 2006–08; Dep. Asset Gen. Manager, Trinidad and Tobago, 2008–10; Pres. and Gen. Manager, Appalachia shale gas Jt Venture, BG Gp and EXCO, 2010–12; Man. Dir, Europe Exploration and Prodn, BG Gp, 2012–14. *Publications:* articles in Jl of Amer. Assoc. of Petroleum Geologists, Marine and Petroleum Geol. and Jl of Geol Soc. *Recreations:* keen on variety of sports and outdoor pursuits including hiking, surfing, yoga, sailing, loves travel. *Address:* Oil and Gas Authority, AB1 Building, 48 Huntly Street, Aberdeen AB10 1SH. *T:* 0300 0201004. *E:* andy.samuel@ogauthority.co.uk.

**SAMUEL, Martin;** Chief Sports Writer, Daily Mail, since 2009; *b* 25 July 1964; *s* of Arthur Samuel and Rita Samuel; *m* 1994, Deborah Edmead; three *s*. *Educ:* Fairlop Jun. Sch.; Ilford Co. High Sch. Hayters Sports Agency, 1982–84; The People, 1984–87; The Sun, 1987–97, Chief Football Writer, 1994–97; The Express: Football Editor, 1997–2000; Chief Sports Writer and Columnist, 2000–02; Chief Sports Writer, News of the World, 2002–07; Columnist, 2002–09, Chief Football Corresp., 2007–09, The Times. Sports Writer of the Year: What the Papers Say, 2002, 2005, 2006; Sports Journalists' Assoc., 2005, 2006, 2007, 2010, 2013, 2014; British Press Awards, 2008, 2013; Sports Commentator of Year, Editl Intelligence Comment Awards, 2014. *Address:* Daily Mail, Northcliffe House, 2 Derry Street, W8 5TT.

**SAMUELS, Rev. Canon Christopher William John;** Rector of St Mary without-the-walls, Handbridge, Chester, 1983–2005; Chaplain to the Queen, 2001–12; *b* 8 Oct. 1942; *s* of John Bernard Boniface Samuels and Ethel Samuels (*née* Bamford); *m* 1967, Sarah Parry (*née* Irving); one *s* one *d*. *Educ:* Denstone Coll., Uttoxeter; KCL (AKC 1966); St Boniface, Warminster. Ordained deacon, 1967, priest, 1968; Curate, St Thomas, Kirkholt, Rochdale, 1967–72; Priest i/c, St Thomas, Parkside, Houghton Regis, 1972–76; Rector, St Helen's, Tarporley, 1976–83; Rural Dean of Chester, 1997–2005. Hon. Canon, Chester Cathedral, 1997–2005, now Emeritus. Nat. Chaplain, Dunkirk Veterans' Assoc., 1996–2000. Chm. of Trustees, Children in Distress, 2007–18. Chm. of Govs, King's Sch., Chester, 2002–05. Freeman, City of London, 1996. Paul Harris Fellow, Rotary Club, 1997. *Recreations:* book collecting, Scottish islands, travel. *Address:* Long View, Mannings Lane, Chester CH2 2PB. *T:* 07929 420423. *Club:* Rotary (Chester) (Pres., 2014–15).

**SAMUELS, Jeffrey Keith;** QC 2009; a Recorder, since 2012; *b* Manchester, 9 July 1965; *s* of Michael and Brenda Samuels; *m* 2000, Andrea Cowen; three *s* one *d*. *Educ:* Leeds Univ. (LLB Hons); Inns of Court Sch. of Law. Called to the Bar, Middle Temple, 1988; in practice as barrister specialising in crime.

**SAMUELS, His Honour John Edward Anthony;** QC 1981; a Circuit Judge, 1997–2006; a Deputy Circuit Judge, 2006–10; Chairman, Criminal Justice Alliance, 2012–17; *b* 15 Aug. 1940; *s* of late Albert Edward Samuels, solicitor, Reigate, Surrey, and Sadie Beatrice Samuels; *m* 1967, Maxine (*née* Robertson), JP; two *s*. *Educ:* Charterhouse; Perugia; Queens' Coll., Cambridge (MA). Commnd, Queen's Royal Regt (TA), 1959; Lieut, Queen's Royal Surrey Regt (TA), 1961–67. Chairman, Cambridge Univ. United Nations Assoc., 1962. Called to Bar, Lincoln's Inn, 1964 (Mansfield Schol., 1963; Bencher, 1990); South Eastern Circuit; a Dep. High Court Judge, 1981–97; a Recorder, 1985–97. Asst Parly Boundary Comr, 1992–95. Judicial Mem., Parole Bd, 2005–15. Mem. Bd (rep. England and Wales), Internat. Assoc. of Drug Treatment Cts, 2007–. Mem., Wkg Gp to plan introduction of Problem-Solving Courts, MoJ, 2016–. Member: Senate of the Inns of Court and the Bar, 1983–86; Bar Council, 1992–97; Council of Legal Educn, 1983–90; Adv. Panel, Inside Justice, 2017–; Chm., Jt Regulations Cttee, Inns' Council and Bar Council, 1987–90. Mem. Cttee, Council of HM Circuit Judges, 2001–12 (Chm., Criminal Sub-Cttee, 2002–06; Representative of retired judiciary, 2006–12). Co-opted Mem., ILEA Education Cttee, 1964–67; Jt Chm., ILEA Disciplinary Tribunals, 1977–87; Alternate Mem., Burnham Cttee, 1981–87; Lay Chm., NHS Complaints Panels, 1996–97; Dep. Chm., Disciplinary Cttee, RPSGB, 2006–10; Mem., Criminal Injuries Compensation Appeal Panel, 1997; Mem., Nat. Sentencer Probation Forum (representing Crown Court judges), 2004–12. Member: Richmond, Twickenham and Roehampton HA, 1982–86; Kingston and Richmond FPC, 1982–86. Vice-Pres., Assoc. of Members of Ind. Monitoring Bds, 2015–. Trustee: Richmond Parish Lands Charity, 1986–96 (Chairman: Educn Cttee, 1987–89; Property Cttee, 1987–95); Prisoners' Educn Trust, 2000– (Chm., 2006–12; Pres., 2012–); Centre for Crime and Justice Studies, 2002–13; Howard League for Penal Reform, 2007–16 (Chm. Legal Cttee, 2009–15). Vice-President: Unlock (Nat. Assoc. for Reformed Offenders), 2006–; Tempus Novo (prisoner rehabilitation charity), 2016–. Patron, Prisoners' Advice Service, 2015–. Vis. Prof., Nottingham Law Sch., 2012–18; Hon. Professorial Fellow, Roehampton Univ., 2018–. Occasional broadcaster. FRSA 2012. *Publications:* Action Pack: counsel's guide to chambers' administration, 1986, 2nd edn 1988; (with J. Aitken) What Happened to the Rehabilitation Revolution?, 2017; contributor to Halsbury's Laws of England, 4th edn. *Recreations:* conservation, restoration, serendipity. *Address:* c/o Treasury Office, Lincoln's Inn, WC2A 3TL. *T:* (020) 7405 1393. *Club:* Garrick.

**SAMUELSON, Sir James Francis,** 6th Bt *cr* 1884, of Bodicote, Banbury, Oxfordshire; *b* Hartfield, Sussex, 20 Dec. 1956; *er s* of Sir (Bernard) Michael (Francis) Samuelson, 5th Bt, and of Janet Amy, *yr d* of Lt-Comdr L. G. Elkington; *S* father, 2008; *m* 1987, Caroline Anne Woodley; two *d*. *Educ:* Hailsham Sch. *Heir: b* Edward Bernard Samuelson, *b* 30 June 1967. *Address:* Brookside, Kings Court Road, Gillingham, Dorset SP8 4LD. *T:* (01747) 833772.

**SAMUELSON, Sir Sydney (Wylie),** Kt 1995; CBE 1978; first British Film Commissioner, 1991–97; President, 1990–95, Senior Consultant, 1998–2000, Samuelson Group PLC (Chairman and Chief Executive, 1966–90); *b* 7 Dec. 1925; 2nd *s* of G. B. and Marjorie Samuelson; *m* 1949, Doris (*née* Magen); three *s*. *Educ:* Irene Avenue Council Sch., Lancing, Sussex. Served RAF, 1943–47. From age 14, career devoted to various aspects of British film industry: cinema projectionist, 1939–41; asst film editor, 1942–43; asst film cameraman, cameraman and dir of documentary films and television, 1947–59; founded Samuelson Gp, company to service film, TV and, later, audio-visual prodn organisations, supplying cameras and other technical equipment, with purchase of first camera, 1954; continued filming as technician on locations throughout world until 1959, when activities concentrated on developing the company. Mem., BAFTA, 1965– (Vice-Chm. Film, 1971–73; Chm. of Council, 1973–76; Trustee, 1974–2009; Chm., Bd of Mgt, 1976–2001; Mem., Business Bd, 1994–2001; Michael Balcon Award, 1985; Fellow, 1993); Chm., BAFTA-Shell UK Venture, 1988–91; Member: BECTU History Project, 1995–2002; Exec. Cttee, Cinema and Television Veterans, 1978– (Pres., 1980–81); Council and Exec. Cttee, Cinema and TV Benevolent Fund, 1969–92 (Trustee, 1982–89; Pres., 1983–86). Pres., Projected Picture Trust, 2002–. Hon. Mem., Brit. Soc. of Cinematographers (Governor, 1969–79; 1st Vice-Pres., 1976–77; award for Outstanding Contribution to British Film Industry, 1967; special award for services to UK film prodn sector as British Film Comr, 1997); Associate Mem., Amer. Soc. of Cinematographers, 1981–96; Hon. Life Mem., BECTU, 1990 (Mem., ACTT, 1947); Fellow, BFI, 1997; Life Fellow, BKSTS - The Moving Image Soc., 1995 (Patron, 1997–; Award of Merit, 2002; Lifetime Achievement Award, 2015); Hon. Mem., Guild of British Camera Technicians (Founder Trustee, 1993–). Hon. Technical Advr, Royal Naval Film Corp.; Member: Adv. Bd, Northern Media Sch., 1996–2001; Assoc. of Film Comrs Internat., 1999–. Pres., UK Friends of Akim (Israel Assoc. for Mentally Handicapped); Vice Pres., Muscular Dystrophy UK (formerly Muscular Dystrophy Campaign); Patron, Young Persons Concert Foundn. Freeman, City of London, 1987. Dr (*hc*) Sheffield Hallam, 1996. Britannica Award for Television News Film, BBC Sportsview, 1961; Award of Merit, Guild of Film Prodn Execs, 1986; Lifetime achievement award, Birmingham Internat. Film and TV Festival, 1997; Howard Dutch Horton Award, Assoc. of Film Comrs Internat., 1997; Friese Greene Award for outstanding career in cinema and television, 2011. *Recreations:* listening to music, vintage motoring, veteran jogging (finished a mere 13,006 places behind the winner, London Marathon 1982). *Address:* 31 West Heath Avenue, NW11 7QJ. *T:* (020) 8455 6696.

**SAMUELSSON, Prof. Bengt Ingemar;** Professor of Medical and Physiological Chemistry, Karolinska Institutet, Stockholm, 1972–99, now Emeritus; Chairman, Nobel Foundation, Stockholm, 1993–2005; *b* Halmstad, Sweden, 21 May 1934; *s* of Anders and Stina Samuelsson; *m* 1958, Inga Karin Bergstein; one *s* one *d* (and one *d* decd). *Educ:* Karolinska Institutet (DMedSci 1960, MD 1961). Res. Fellow, Harvard Univ., 1961–62; Asst Prof. of Med. Chemistry, Karolinska Inst., 1961–66; Prof., Royal Vet. Coll., Stockholm, 1967–72; Chm., Dept of Chemistry, 1973–83, Dean of Med. Faculty, 1978–83, Pres., 1983–95, Karolinska Inst., Stockholm. Vis. Prof., Harvard, 1976; T. Y. Shen Vis. Prof. in Med. Chem., MIT, 1977; Walker-Ames Prof., Washington Univ., 1987. Lectures include: Shirley Johnson Meml, Philadelphia, 1977; Sixth Annual Marrs McLean, Houston, 1978; Harvey, NY, 1979; Lane Medical, Stanford Univ., 1981; Eighth Annual Sci. in Med., Univ. of Washington, 1981; Arthur C. Corcoran Meml, Cleveland, Ohio, 1981; Kober, Assoc. of Amer. Physicians, 1982; Brown-Razor, Rice Univ., Houston, 1984; Solomon A. Berson Meml, Mount Sinai Sch. of Medicine, NY, 1984; Angelo Minich, Venice, 1988; Hans Neurath, Univ. of Washington, 1990; Dunham, Harvard Med. Sch., 1990; First Fogarty Internat., NIH, 1992. Member: Nobel Assembly, Karolinska Inst., 1972–99 (Chm., 1990); Nobel Cttee for Physiol. or Medicine, 1984–89 (Chm., 1987–89); Swedish Govt Res. Adv. Bd, 1985–88; Nat. Commn on Health Policy, 1987–90; ESTA, 1995–97. Member: Royal Swedish Acad. of Scis, 1981–; Mediterranean Acad., Catania, 1982–; US Nat. Acad. of Scis, 1984; French Acad. of Scis, 1989; Royal Soc., 1990; Royal Nat. Acad. of Medicine, Spain, 1991; Hon. Prof., Bethune Univ. of Med. Scis, China, 1986; Hon. Member: Amer. Soc. of Biological Chemists, 1976; Assoc. of American Physicians, 1982; Swedish Med. Assoc., 1982; Italian Pharmacological Soc., 1985; Acad. Nac. de Medicina de Buenos Aires, 1986; Internat. Soc. of Haematology, 1986; Spanish Soc. of Allergology and Clinical Immunology, 1989; Foreign Hon. Member: Amer. Acad. of Arts and Scis, 1982–; Internat. Acad. of Science, ICSD; Founding Mem., Academia Europaea, 1988. Hon. DSc: Chicago, 1978; Illinois, 1983; DUniv: Rio de Janeiro, 1986; Buenos Aires, 1986; Complutense, Madrid, 1991; Milan, 1993; Louisiana State, 1993; Uppsala, 2007. Nobel Prize in Physiology or Medicine (jtly), 1982; numerous awards and prizes. *Publications:* papers on biochemistry of prostaglandins, thromboxanes and leukotrienes. *Address:* Department of Medical Biochemistry and Biophysics, Karolinska Institutet, 17177 Stockholm, Sweden. *T:* (8) 52487600.

**SAMWORTH, Sir David (Chetwode),** Kt 2009; CBE 1985; DL; President, Samworth Brothers (Holdings) Ltd (formerly Gorran Foods Ltd), since 2005 (Director since 1981; Chairman, 1984–2005); *b* 25 June 1935; *s* of Frank and Phyllis Samworth; *m* 1969, Rosemary Grace Cadell; one *s* three *d*. *Educ:* Uppingham Sch. Chm., Pork Farms Ltd, 1968–81; Dir, Northern Foods Ltd, 1978–81. Non-executive Director: Imperial Gp, 1983–85; Thorntons plc, 1988–93. Chm., Meat and Livestock Commn, 1980–84. Member: Leicester No 3 HMC, 1970–74; Trent RHA, 1974–78, 1980–84. President: RASE, 2000–01; Leics Agricl Soc., 1996–99; Young Enterprise, Leics, 2001–04. Pres., Coll. of Canons, Leicester Cathedral, 2013–16. Chm. Trustees, Uppingham Sch., 1995–99 (Trustee, 1976–93). DL Leics, 1984, High Sheriff, Leics, 1997. Hon. LLD Leicester, 2012. *Recreation:* fishing. *Address:* Samworth Brothers (Holdings) Ltd, Chetwode House, Samworth Way, Melton Mowbray, Leics LE13 1GA.

**SAMWORTH, Prof. Richard John,** PhD; Professor of Statistical Science and Director, Statistical Laboratory, University of Cambridge, since 2017; Fellow, St John's College, Cambridge, since 2003; *b* Newport Pagnell, 6 May 1978; *s* of Peter and Anne Samworth. *Educ:* St John's Coll., Cambridge (BA Maths 1999; Part III Maths 2000; MMath (retrospective) 2011; PhD Stats 2004). Lectr, St John's Coll., Cambridge, 2005–; Lectr in Stats, 2005–10, Reader in Stats, 2010–13, Prof. of Stats, 2013–17, Univ. of Cambridge. *Publications:* contribs to stats jls. *Recreation:* sport. *Address:* Statistical Laboratory, University of Cambridge, Wilberforce Road, Cambridge CB3 0WB. *T:* (01223) 337950. *E:* r.samworth@statslab.cam.ac.uk.

**SANDARS, Christopher Thomas;** Director General (Central Budget) (formerly Assistant Under-Secretary of State (General Finance), Ministry of Defence, 1997–2002; *b* 6 March 1942; *s* of late Vice-Adm. Sir Thomas Sandars, KBE, CB and Lady Sandars; *m* 1966, Elizabeth Anne Yielder; three *s* one *d*. *Educ:* Oundle Sch.; Corpus Christi Coll., Cambridge (Trevelyan Schol.; Foundation Schol.). Joined MoD, 1964; Asst Private Sec. to Minister of State, 1967–69; Central Policy Review Staff, Cabinet Office, 1971–74; Private Sec. to Minister of State, 1975–77; Hd, General Finance Div. 1, 1977–80; Hd, Defence Secretariat 13, 1980–84; RCDS, 1985; Hd, Secretariat 9 (Air), 1986–90; Asst Under-Sec. of State, MoD, 1990–95; Fellow, Center for Internat. Affairs, Harvard Univ., 1995–96. *Publications:* America's Overseas Garrisons: the leasehold empire, 2000. *Recreations:* painting, gardening, theatre. *Address:* 10 Crescent Grove, SW4 7AH.

**SANDBACH, Antoinette;** *see* Mackeson-Sandbach.

**SANDBY-THOMAS, Rachel Mary,** CB 2012; Registrar, University of Warwick, since 2016; *b* 25 May 1963; *d* of Dr Paul and Mary Sandby-Thomas; *m* 1999, Richard Gough; two *s*. *Educ:* St Catharine's Coll., Cambridge (BA Law (double 1st) 1985). Admitted solicitor, 1989; Linklaters & Paines, 1987–92; Legal Adviser: Legal Advrs, HM Treasury, 1993–95; Legal Advrs, Cabinet Office, 1995–97; Attorney General's Chambers, 1997–99; DoH, 1999–2004; Legal Advrs, Cabinet Office, 2004; Dir, Legal Services B, DTI, 2004–07; Dir, Tax Law Gp, HMRC, 2007–08; Solicitor and Dir Gen., Legal Services, then Dir Gen., Legal, People and Communications, BERR, later BIS, 2008–12; Dir Gen., Skills, Deregulation and Local Growth and Legal Services (formerly Legal Business and Skills, then Enterprise, Skills and Legal Services), BIS, 2012–16; Shadow CEO, Inst. for Apprenticeships, BIS, 2016. *Recreations:* reading, socialising, family. *Address:* University of Warwick, Coventry CV4 7AL. *T:* (024) 7652 3704. *E:* R.sandby-thomas@warwick.ac.uk.

**SANDELL, Terence, (Terry),** OBE 1991; consultant and researcher, since 2010; Director, Cultural Futures LLP, 2010–14 and since 2016; *b* 8 Sept. 1948; *s* of James William Sandell and Helen Elizabeth McCombie; *m* 1984, Kate Ling; two *s*. *Educ:* Watford Grammar Sch. for Boys; Univ. of Nottingham (BA Hons); Univ. of Edinburgh; City Univ. (MA with Dist.). VSO, Berber, N Sudan, 1970–72. Joined British Council, 1974: Asst Rep. Dir, Omdurman Centre, Sudan, 1974–78; Regional Officer, Soviet Union and Mongolia, London, 1978–81; 1st Sec. (Cultural), British Embassy, Moscow, 1981–83; Asst Rep., Vienna, 1983–86, Rep. 1986–89; Projects Manager, Soviet Union, London, 1989; Dir, Soviet Union/CIS, and Cultural Counsellor, British Embassy, Moscow, 1989–92; attachment to Dept of Arts Policy and Management, City Univ., 1992–93; Consultant, Arts Policy Develt, British Council, 1993–94; Dir, Visiting Arts Office of GB and NI, subseq. Visiting Arts, 1994–2005; Dir, Ukraine, British Council, and Cultural Counsellor, British Embassy, Kyiv, 2005–08; Special Advr (Arts), British Council, 2008–10. Sen. Associate, St Antony's Coll., Oxford, 2010–15. Chairman, Council of Europe Review of Cultural Policy: Russian Fedn, 1995–96 and 2011–13; Romania, 1998–99; Georgia, 2000–02; Azerbaijan, 2000–02; Armenia, 2003; Ukraine, 2005–07; Consultant/Advr, Azerbaijan Cultural and Creative Industries State Prog., 2010–20; Co-Dir, Nat. Cultural Policy Review of Russian Fedn, 2011–13; Sen. Expert, 2011–14, Hd, 2015, EU-Eastern Partnership Culture and Creativity Prog., Kyiv; Hd, EU-Russia Cultural and Creative Industries and Tourism Innovation (Northern Dimension Countries) Project, 2016–17; Team Mem., EU-Algeria Heritage Support Project, 2017–18; Cultural Policy Advr, EU-Georgia Assoc. Agreement Facility, 2017–18; Consultant, Georgian Film Industry Cluster, 2018–19; Consultant and Developer, EU-Eastern Partnership Prog., 2019–. Dir, British-Ukrainian Soc., 2008–14. Trustee, Academia Rossica, 2000–. Hon. Doktor Nauk Ukrainian Acad. of Pedagog. Scis, 2008. *Recreation:* appreciation of beauty, life and cultures and encouraging others in this direction. *E:* terry.sandell@gmail.com.

**SANDER, Her Honour Audrey Olga Helen;** a Circuit Judge, 1995–2003; *b* 10 Nov. 1936; *d* of Ernest Sander and Marian Sander; *m* 1963, Prof. Adrian Gale; one *s* two *d*. *Educ:* St Paul's Girls' Sch.; Somerville Coll., Oxford (MA Jurisprudence). Called to the Bar, Gray's Inn, 1960; in practice at the Bar, 1960–77; Editl Asst, Legal Action Gp, 1978–83; admitted solicitor, 1986; practised as solicitor, 1986–95 (at Gill Akaster, 1989–95); Asst Recorder, 1990–94; Recorder, 1994–95. Legal Mem., Mental Health Rev. Tribunals, 1992–2011; Mem., Parole Bd of England and Wales, 2000–06. Civil and Family Mediator. *Address:* c/o Clerksroom, Equity House, Blackbrook Park Avenue, Taunton, Som TA1 2PX.

**SANDERS, Adrian Mark;** Secretary General, Parliamentary Diabetes Global Network, since 2016; *b* 25 April 1959; *s* of late John Sanders and Helen Sanders; *m* 1992, Alison Nortcliffe. *Educ:* Torquay Boys' Grammar Sch. Vice Pres., Nat. League of Young Liberals, 1985. Campaigns Officer, Assoc. of Liberal Councillors, 1986–89; Parly Officer, Lib Dem Whips' Office, 1989–90; Res. Officer, Assoc. of Lib Dem Councillors, 1990–92; Project Officer, Paddy Ashdown, MP, 1992–93; Policy Officer, NCVO, 1993–94; Grants Advr, Southern Assoc. of Voluntary Action Gps for Europe, 1994. Mem. (L) Torbay BC, 1984–86. Contested (Lib Dem): Torbay, 1992; Devon and Plymouth East, EP elecn, 1994. MP (Lib Dem) Torbay, 1997–2015; contested (Lib Dem) same seat, 2015. Lib Dem spokesman: on local govt and housing (on housing, 1997–2001, and on local govt, 1999–2001); on tourism, 2001–05; a Lib Dem Whip, 1997–2001; Lib Dem Dep. Chief Whip, 2006–10. Member: DCMS Select Cttee, 2005–15; Transport Select Cttee, 2012–15; Chairs Panel, 2014–15. Chm., All Pty Diabetes Gp, 1997–2015; Pres., Parly Diabetes Global Network, 2013–15. Mem. (Lib Dem), Torbay Council, 2015–19. Vice President: League Against Cruel Sports, 2013–19; JDRF UK, 2015–. Chm., Soc. of Ticket Agents and Retailers, 2015–18. Trustee, ABCD Diabetes Care Trust, 2019–.

**SANDERS, Prof. Dale,** PhD, ScD; FRS 2001; Director, John Innes Centre, since 2010; *b* 13 May 1953; *s* of Leslie G. D. Sanders and Daphne M. Sanders; *m* 1983, Marcelle Mékiès (*d* 2005); three *d*. *Educ:* Hemel Hempstead Grammar Sch.; Univ. of York (BA); Darwin Coll., Cambridge (PhD 1978, ScD 1993). James Hudson Brown Res. Fellow, 1978–79, Post-doctoral Res. Associate, 1979–83, Sch. of Medicine, Yale Univ.; Department of Biology, University of York: Lectr, 1983–89; Reader, 1989–92; Prof., 1992–2010; Hd of Dept, 2004–10; Hon. Vis. Prof., 2010–. Hon. Prof., UEA, 2010–. Nuffield Foundn Sci. Res. Fellow, 1989–90; Royal Soc./Leverhulme Trust Sen. Res. Fellow, 1997–98. President's Medal, Soc. for Exptl Biol., 1987; Körber Eur. Sci. Award, 2001. *Publications:* numerous refereed articles in learned jls. *Recreations:* early music, literature, talking and walking with family and friends, cooking. *Address:* John Innes Centre, Norwich Research Park, Colney, Norwich NR4 7UH. *T:* (01603) 450000.

**SANDERS, Prof. David John,** PhD; FBA 2005; Professor of Government, 1993–2017, now Emeritus, and Regius Professor of Political Science, 2014–17, University of Essex; *b* 19 Dec. 1950; *s* of John Sanders and Nora Sanders; *m* 2001, Gillian Wills; three *s* one *d*. *Educ:* John Port Sch., Etwall; Loughborough Univ. (BSc); Univ. of Essex (MA; PhD). University of Essex: Lectr, 1975–88, Sen. Lectr, 1988–90, Reader, 1990–93, in Government; Pro Vice Chancellor for Res., 1997–2001 and 2011–16. Vis. Prof., Univ. of Wisconsin-Madison, 1981–82. *Publications:* Patterns of Political Instability, 1981; Lawmaking and Co-operation in International Politics, 1986; Losing an Empire, Finding a Role, 1990; (jtly) On Message, 1997; Political Choice in Britain, 2004; Performance Politics, 2009; Affluence, Austerity and Electoral Change in Britain, 2013; The Political Integration of Ethnic Minorities in Britain, 2013; over 70 articles in learned jls. *Recreations:* playing folk music in pubs, walking, cycling. *Address:* Department of Government, University of Essex, Wivenhoe Park, Colchester CO4 3SQ. *T:* (01206) 872759. *E:* sanders@essex.ac.uk.

**SANDERS, Donald Neil,** AO 1994; CB 1983; Chief Executive, 1987–92 and Managing Director, 1991–92, Commonwealth Bank of Australia; *b* Sydney, 21 June 1927; *s* of L. G. and R. M. Sanders; *m* 1952, Betty Elaine, *d* of W. B. and E. M. Constance; four *s* one *d*. *Educ:* Wollongong High Sch.; Univ. of Sydney (BEc). Commonwealth Bank of Australia, 1943–60; Australian Treasury, 1956; Bank of England, 1960; Reserve Bank of Australia, 1960–87: Supt, Credit Policy Div., Banking Dept, 1964–66; Dep. Manager: Banking Dept, 1966–67; Res. Dept, 1967–70; Aust. Embassy, Washington DC, 1968; Chief Manager: Securities Markets Dept, 1970–72; Banking and Finance Dept, 1972–74; Adviser and Chief Manager, Banking and Finance Dept, 1974–75; Dep. Governor and Dep. Chm., 1975–87; Man. Dir, Commonwealth Banking Corp., 1987–91. Chm., H-G Ventures Ltd, 1995–2000; Director: Queensland Investment Corp., 1992–98; Lend Lease Corp. Ltd, 1992–99; Australian Chamber Orch. Ltd, 1993–99; MLC Ltd, 1994–99 (Chm., 1998–99). *Address:* 106 Blaxland Road, Wentworth Falls, NSW 2782, Australia.

**SANDERS, Prof. Ed Parish,** FBA 1989; Arts and Sciences Professor of Religion, Duke University, 1990–2005; *b* 18 April 1937; *s* of Mildred Sanders (*née* Parish) and Eula Thomas Sanders; *m* 1st, 1963, Becky Jill Hall (marr. diss. 1978); one *d*; 2nd, 1996, Rebecca N. Gray. *Educ:* Texas Wesleyan College (BA); Southern Methodist Univ. (BD); Union Theological Seminary, NY (ThD). Asst Prof. of Religious Studies, McMaster Univ., 1966–70, Associate Prof., 1970–74, Prof., 1974–88; Dean Ireland's Prof. of Exegesis of Holy Scripture, Oxford Univ., 1984–89. Visiting Professor: Jewish Theol. Seminary, 1980; Chair of Judeo-Christian Studies, Tulane Univ., 1980; Walter G. Mason Dist. Vis. Prof., Coll. of William and Mary in Virginia, 1981; Vis. Fellow Commoner, Trinity Coll., Cambridge, 1982; Kraft-Hiatt Vis. Prof., Brandeis Univ., 1999. Donnellan Lectr, TCD, 1982. Fellow, Amer. Acad. of Arts and Scis, 2003. *Publications:* The Tendencies of the Synoptic Tradition, 1969; Paul and Palestinian Judaism, 1977, 2nd edn 1981; (ed) Jewish and Christian Self-Definition, vol. I, The Shaping of Christianity in the Second and Third Centuries, 1980, vol. II, Aspects of Judaism in the Graeco-Roman Period, 1981, vol. III, Self-Definition in the Graeco-Roman World, 1982; Paul, The Law and the Jewish People, 1983; Jesus and Judaism, 1985, 3rd edn 1987; (ed) Jesus, The Gospels and the Church, 1987; (with Margaret Davies) Studying the Synoptic Gospels, 1989; Jewish Law from Jesus to the Mishnah, 1990; Paul, 1991; Judaism: practice and belief 63 BCE to 66 BCE, 1992; The Historical Figure of Jesus, 1993; Paul: a very short introduction, 2001; Paul: the Apostle's life, letters and thought, 2015; Comparing Judaism and Christianity, 2016; articles in NT Studies, Jl of Biblical Literature, Harvard Theol. Review, Jewish Quarterly Review.

**SANDERS, Prof. Jeremy Keith Morris,** CBE 2014; FRS 1995; Professor, Department of Chemistry, 1996–2015, now Emeritus, and Pro-Vice-Chancellor for Institutional Affairs, 2011–15, University of Cambridge; Fellow of Selwyn College, Cambridge, since 1976; *b* 3 May 1948; *s* of Sidney Sanders and Sylvia (*née* Rutman); *m* 1972, Louise Elliott; one *s* one *d*. *Educ:* Imperial Coll., London (BSc, ARCS Chem. 1969); PhD 1972, MA 1974, ScD 2001, Cantab. FRSC, CChem. Junior Res. Fellow, Christ's Coll., Cambridge, 1972;

NATO/EMBO Fellow, Stanford Univ., 1972–73; Cambridge University: Demonstrator, 1973–78; Lectr in Chemistry, 1978–92; Reader in Chemistry and Asst Hd, Dept of Chemistry, 1992–96; Dep. Hd, 1998–2000, Hd, 2000–06, Dept of Chem.; Dep. Vice-Chancellor, 2006–10; Hd, Sch. of Physical Scis, 2009–11; Mem. Council, 1999–2002; Chm., Allocations Cttee, 1999–2000; Chm., Bd of Mgt, Cambridge Prog. for Industry, 2003–07. Chm., Chem. sub-panel, 2008 RAE, 2004–08. Chm., Athena Forum, 2019– (Dep. Chm., 2017–19). Trustee, Cambridge Foundn, 2007–13; Dep. Chm., NW Cambridge Syndicate, 2011–15; Syndic, Fitzwilliam Mus., 2012–14. Mem. Council, Imperial Coll., London, 2016–. Pres., Bürgenstock Conf., Switzerland, 2011. Mem., Internat. Adv. Bd for Gender and Diversity, Univ. of Southern Denmark, 2018–. Chm., Storey's Field Community Trust, 2016–. FRSA 1997. Associate Ed., New Jl of Chemistry, 1998–2000; Chm. Editl Bd, Chem. Soc. Reviews, 2000–02; Ed.-in-Chief, Royal Soc. Open Sci., 2016–. Pfizer Awards, Pfizer plc, 1984, 1988; Royal Society of Chemistry: Meldola Medal, 1975; Hickinbottom Award, 1981; Josef Loschmidt Prize, 1994; Pedler Lect. and Medal, 1996; Fellow, Japan Soc. for the Promotion of Science, 2002; Izatt-Christensen Award for Macrocyclic Chemistry, USA, 2003; Davy Medal, Royal Soc., 2009. *Publications:* (with B. K. Hunter) Modern NMR Spectroscopy, 1987, 2nd edn 1993; contribs to chem. and biochem. jls. *Recreations:* family, cooking, music. *Address:* University Chemical Laboratory, Lensfield Road, Cambridge CB2 1EW. *T:* (01223) 336411.

**SANDERS, Rear-Adm. Jeremy Thomas,** CB 1994; OBE 1982; Commander British Forces, Gibraltar, 1992–94; *b* 23 Nov. 1942; *s* of late Thomas Sanders and Pauline (*née* Woodfield-Smith); *m* 1st, 1966, Judith Rosemary Jones (*d* 2003); two *d*; 2nd, 2005, Jane Elizabeth Cambrook. *Educ:* Norwood Sch., Exeter; Pangbourne Coll. BRNC, Dartmouth, 1960; appts include: Lieut i/c HMS Chilcompton and Kellington, 1968–69; long communications course, HMS Mercury, 1970; Lt Comdr on staff of Flag Officer, Submarines, 1974–76; Comdr i/c HMS Salisbury, 1977–78; ndc 1979; SO Ops to Flag Officer, 1st Flotilla, 1981–83; Capt., 8th Frigate Sqdn and i/c HMS Andromeda, 1985–87; Dir, Maritime Tactical Sch., 1987–89; Chief Naval Signal Officer, 1989–90; Dir, Naval Warfare, 1990–92. Trustee: Falkland Islands Memorial Chapel, 2003–12 (Chm., 2006–12); RN Submarine Mus., 2004–06. JP S Hants 1997–2006 (Dep. Chm. Bench, 2003, 2004). *Recreations:* countryside, family and travel. *Clubs:* MCC, Anchorites; Exeter Flotilla.

**SANDERS, John Leslie Yorath;** HM Diplomatic Service, retired; *b* 5 May 1929; *s* of late Reginald Yorath Sanders and Gladys Elizabeth Sanders (*née* Blything); *m* 1953, Brigit Mary Lucine Altounyan (*d* 1999); one *s* two *d*. *Educ:* Dulwich Coll. Prep. Sch.; Cranleigh School. Higher Dip. in Furniture Prodn and Design, London Coll. of Furniture, 1982. Nat. Service in HM Forces (RA), 1948–50; entered HM Foreign Service, 1950; FO, 1950–52; MECAS, Lebanon, 1953; Damascus, 1954–55; Bahrain, 1955–56; Vice-Consul, Basra, 1956–60; Oriental Sec., Rabat, 1960–63; FO, 1964–67; 1st Sec., Beirut, 1968–70; 1st Sec. and Head of Chancery, Mexico City, 1970–73; Counsellor, Khartoum, 1973–75; Counsellor, Beirut, 1975–76; Dir of Res., FCO, 1976–78; Ambassador to Panama, 1978–80. *Publications:* contrib. to Archaeologia Aeliana. *Recreations:* genealogy, music.

**SANDERS, Michael David,** FRCS, FRCP, FRCOphth; Consultant Ophthalmologist, National Hospital for Neurology and Neurosurgery, 1969–99; *b* 19 Sept. 1935; *s* of Norris Manley Sanders and Gertrude Florence Sanders (*née* Hayley); *m* 1969, Thalia Margaret Garlick; one *s* one *d*. *Educ:* Tonbridge Sch.; Guy's Hosp., Univ. of London (MB BS). DO RCS/RCP; FRCS 1967; FRCP 1977; FRCOphth 1990 (Hon. FRCOphth 2001). Guy's Hosp., 1954–60; Moorfields Eye Hosp., 1964–67; Univ. of California, San Francisco, 1967–68; Consultant Ophthalmologist, St Thomas' Hosp., 1972–96. Civilian Consultant, RAF, 1975–2000; Dep. Hospitaller, St John Ophthalmic Hosp., Jerusalem, 1992. Visiting Professor: Mayo Clinic, 1979; Univ. of New South Wales, 1982; NY Eye and Ear Infirmary, 1995. Lectures: Middlemore, Birmingham and Midlands Eye Hosp., 1985; Percival J. Hay Meml, N of England Ophthalmol Soc., 1986; Ida Mann, Oxford Univ., 1987; Sir Stewart Duke Elder, Ophthalmol. Soc. UK, 1987; Lettsomian, Med. Soc. London, 1988; Sir William Bowman, RCOphth, 1996; Montgomery, Irish Coll. of Ophthalmologists, 1997. Trustee, Frost Charitable Trust, 1974–96 (Chm., 1996–); Med. Advr, Iris Fund for Prevention of Blindness, 1982–97 (Mem. Council, 1997–2003); Pres., Internat. Neuro-Ophthalmology Soc., 1990– (Mem. Council, 1974–97); Mem. Council, Gift of Sight, 2009–17. Chm., Friends of Chawton Ch, 2003–19. *Publications:* Topics in Neuro-Ophthalmology, 1978; Computerised Tomography in Neuro-Ophthalmology, 1982; Common Problems in Neuro-Ophthalmology, 1997. *Recreations:* golf, collecting. *Address:* Chawton Lodge, Chawton, near Alton, Hants GU34 1SL. *T:* (01420) 86681. *Clubs:* Royal Air Force; Hankley Common Golf (Farnham).

**SANDERS, Neil John Tait; His Honour Judge Sanders;** a Circuit Judge, since 2010; *b* Suva, Fiji, 17 April 1953; *s* of Sir Robert Tait Sanders, KBE, CMG and of Barbara Sanders; *m* 1984, Frances Ann Spencer; two *s* one *d*. *Educ:* Fettes Coll., Edinburgh; Pembroke Coll., Cambridge (BA 1974); Coll. of Law. Called to the Bar, Inner Temple, 1975; a Recorder, 2001–10. *Recreations:* golf, sailing, tennis, theatre, music. *Address:* Snaresbrook Crown Court, 75 Hollybush Hill, Snaresbrook, E11 1QW. *Clubs:* Royal Solent Yacht, Yarmouth Sailing, Clapham Common All Weather Tennis.

**SANDERS, Nicholas John,** CB 1998; PhD; Higher Education Adviser, Department for Education and Skills, 2004–05; *b* 14 Sept. 1946; *s* of Ivor and Mollie Sanders; *m* 1971, Alison Ruth Carter; one *s* one *d*. *Educ:* King Edward's Sch., Birmingham; Magdalene Coll., Cambridge (MA, PhD). Joined DES, 1971, subseq. Dept for Educn, then DFEE, then DFES; Principal Private Sec. to Sec. of State, 1974–75; Private Sec. to Prime Minister, 1978–81; Prin. Finance Officer, 1989–93; Hd, Teachers Br., 1993–95; Dir, Teachers, Funding and Curriculum, 1995–99; Dir for Higher Education, 1999–2003. Mem. Council, Univ. of Warwick, 2004–10 and 2011–14. Hon. LLD Manchester, 2004. Chancellor's Medal, Univ. of Warwick, 2016.

**SANDERS, Nicholas Paul Martin;** a District Judge (Magistrates' Courts), Cheshire, 2007–13 and since 2018 (Merseyside, 2004–13, Greater Manchester, 2013–18); *b* 25 Feb. 1958; *s* of late Oswald Sanders and Betty Sanders (*née* Hooper); *m* 1981, Alexandra (*née* Langham); two *d*. *Educ:* Exeter Sch.; Britannia Royal Naval Coll.; Univ. of Exeter (LLB Hons). RN officer, 1976–89. Called to the Bar, Middle Temple, 1987; admitted solicitor, 1990; Solicitor: Linford Brown, Exmouth, 1989–94; Rundle Walker, Exeter, 1994–2001; Sen. Magistrate and HM Coroner, Falkland Is and British Antarctic Territory, 2001–04; Sen. Magistrate, Ascension Is., 2004–06. Dep. Chm., Adv. Cttee on Conscientious Objectors, 2014–. Reader, C of E, 2013–. *Recreations:* English canals, pottering in the garden, occasionally knocking a golf ball around, anything with an engine, association croquet. *Address:* c/o Chester Magistrates' Court, Grosvenor Street, Chester CH1 2XA.

**SANDERS, Oliver Tschanz;** QC 2017; *b* Rochford, Essex, 8 Aug. 1972; *s* of Barry Billington Sanders and Margaret Jean Sanders (*née* Coole, now Finlayson); partner, Jessica Lauren Elliott; one *s*. *Educ:* Church Stretton Comprehensive Sch., Shropshire; Adams' Grammar Sch., Newport, Shropshire; Queen Mary and Westfield Coll. (LLB Hons 1993); Inns of Court Sch. of Law; St Anne's Coll., Oxford (BCL Hons 1995). Called to the Bar, Inner Temple, 1995; Lawyer: Treasury Solicitor's Dept, 1997–98; Legal Advr's Br., Home Office, 1998–99; Treasury Solicitor's Dept, 2000–04; Mem. Chambers, 1 Crown Office Row, 2004–. Member: Attorney Gen.'s B Panel of Jun. Counsel (Civil and EU), 2005–12; Attorney Gen.'s A Panel of Jun. Counsel (Civil and EU), 2012–17. Visiting Fellow, Faculty of Laws: QMW, 1993–94; Brunel Univ., 1997–98. *Publications:* (contrib.) Information Rights, 2004, 5th edn 2019; contrib. articles to Judicial Rev. *Recreations:* books, cricket, films, football, theatre, trees. *Address:* 1 Crown Office Row, EC4Y 7HH. *T:* (020) 7797 7500, *Fax:* (020) 7797 7550. *E:* oliver.sanders@1cor.com.

**SANDERS, Gen. Patrick Nicholas Yardley Monrad,** CBE 2012 (OBE 2004); DSO 2008; Commander Joint Forces Command, since 2019; Aide-de-Camp General to the Queen, since 2019; *b* Tidworth, Hants, 6 April 1966; *s* of John Sanders and Marianne Sanders (*née* Monrad); *m* 1992, Fiona Bullen; one *s*. *Educ:* Worth Abbey; RMA Sandhurst; Cranfield Univ. (MA Defence Technol.). Commnd 3RGJ, 1986; acsc 1997–99; COS 1st Mech. Bde, 2001–03; CO 2RGJ, then 4 Rifles, 2004–07; Col Army Strategy, 2008–09; Comd 20 Armoured Bde, 2009–12; CDS Liaison Officer to Chm. Jt Chiefs of Staff, 2012; Hd, Overseas Ops, 2012–13; ACDS (Ops), 2013–15; GOC 3rd (UK) Div., 2015–16; Comdr Field Army, 2016–19. Col Comdt, Rifles, 2019– (Dep. Col, 2012–16; Asst Col Comdt, 2016–19); Hon. Col, Manchester Univ. OTC, 2013–18; Col Comdt, Small Arms Sch. Corps, 2014–19; Ext. Col Comdt, REME, 2016–18. President: Army Rifle Assoc., 2013–; Army Winter Sports Assoc., 2016–. *Publications:* articles in RUSI Jl, BAR and Defence Acad. Yearbook. *Recreations:* ski-touring, jagd, Spurs, whisky, cycling, Burgundy wines (Chevalier de Tastevin). *Address:* c/o Regimental Headquarters The Rifles, Peninsula Barracks, Romsey Road, Winchester, Hants SO23 8TS. *T:* (01962) 828527.

**SANDERS, Peter Basil,** CBE 1993; Chief Executive, Commission for Racial Equality, 1988–93 (Director, 1977–88); *b* 9 June 1938; *s* of Basil Alfred Horace Sanders and Ellen May Sanders (*née* Cockrell); *m* 1st, 1961, Janet Valerie (*née* Child) (marr. diss. 1984); two *s* one *d*; 2nd, 1988, Anita Jackson (*d* 2006). *Educ:* Queen Elizabeth's Grammar Sch., Barnet; Wadham Coll., Oxford (MA, DPhil). Administrative Officer, Basutoland, 1961–66; Research in Oxford for DPhil, 1966–70; Officer, Min. of Defence, 1971–73; Race Relations Bd: Principal Conciliation Officer, 1973–74; Dep. Chief Officer, 1974–77. Chm., Stop Stansted Expansion, 2004–. *Publications:* Lithoko: Sotho Praise-Poems (ed with M. Damane and trans. with an Introd. and Notes), 1974; Moshoeshoe, Chief of the Sotho, 1975; The Simple Annals: the history of an Essex and East End family, 1989; (ed jtly) Race Relations in Britain: a developing agenda, 1998; The Last of the Queen's Men: a Lesotho experience, 2000; (with C. Murray) Medicine Murder in Colonial Lesotho: the anatomy of a moral crisis, 2005; 'Throwing Down White Man': Cape rule and misrule in colonial Lesotho, 1871–1884, 2011; On the Beaten Track: a history of Stansted Mountfitchet, 2016. *Address:* 31D Church Street, Saffron Walden, Essex CB10 1JW. *T:* (01799) 520411.

**SANDERS, His Honour Roger Benedict;** a Circuit Judge, 1987–2005; Resident Judge, Harrow Crown Court, 1999–2005; *b* 1 Oct. 1940; *s* of late Maurice and Lilian Sanders; *m* 1st, 1969, Susan Brenner (marr. diss. 1992); two *s* (one *d* decd); 2nd, 1998, Dee Connolly, *e d* of John and Mary Connolly. *Educ:* Highgate School. Co-founder, Inner Temple Debating Soc., 1961, Chm. 1962. Called to the Bar, Inner Temple, 1965; South Eastern Circuit. Metropolitan Stipendiary Magistrate, 1980–87; a Recorder, 1986–87. A Chm., Inner London Juvenile Courts, 1980–87; Chm., Legal Cttee, Inner London Juvenile Panel, 1983–86; First Chm., No 1 (London S) Regional Duty Solicitor Cttee, 1984–85; Chm., NW London Adv. Cttee (Magistrates), 2008–10 (Dep. Chm., 2004–08); Member: Inner London Magistrates' Training Panel, 1983–87; Mental Health Review Tribunal, 1990–2000, 2006–10; Middx Probation Cttee, 1999–2001; Restorative Justice Panel, 2003–05; occasional facilitator and assessor for intermediaries and professional witnesses, City Law Sch., City Univ. London, 2007–. Hon. Pres., Middx Br., Magistrates' Assoc., 2009–10. Chairman, Walker School Assoc. (Southgate), 1976, 1977; Schools' Debating Assoc. Judge, 1976–93. Mem., Haringey Schools Liaison Group, 1979. Hon. Fellow, Univ. of E London, 1993. *Recreations:* painting, writing, travel.

**SANDERS, Sir Ronald (Michael),** KCMG 2002 (CMG 1997); KCN 2001; Hon. AM 2012; international consultant and writer; Ambassador for Antigua and Barbuda to United States of America and to Organisation of American States, since 2015; High Commissioner (non-resident) for Antigua and Barbuda in Canada, since 2017; *b* Guyana, 26 Jan. 1948; *m* 1975, Susan Indranij (*née* Ramphal). *Educ:* Sacred Heart RC Sch., Guyana; Boston Univ., USA; Sussex Univ., UK. Gen. Man., Guyana Broadcasting Service, 1973–76; Communication Cons. to Pres., Caribbean Develt Bank, Barbados, 1977; Cons. to Govt of Antigua, 1977–81; Advr to For. Minister of Antigua and Barbuda, 1981–82; Dep. Perm. Rep. to UN, 1982–83; Ambassador to UNESCO and EEC, 1983–87, to FRG, 1986–87; High Comr for Antigua and Barbuda in London, 1984–87 and 1995–2004; Vis. Fellow, Oxford Univ., 1988–89; Ambassador (non-resident) to France and Germany, 1996–2004; Sen. Ambassador with Ministerial rank, Antigua and Barbuda, 1999–2004; Ambassador: to WTO, 2000–04. Director: Swiss Amer. Nat. Bank, Antigua, 1990–97; Guyana Telephone and Telegraph Co., 1991–97; Innovative Communications Corp., USA, 1998–2008; US Virgin Islands Telephone Co., 2003–08; Belize Telephone Ltd, 2004–05; consultant, Internat. Relns, Atlantic Tele Network, USA, 1989–97; Advr to Commonwealth Secretariat and World Bank on Small States, 2002. Dep. Chm., 2002–03, Chm., 2003–04, Caribbean Financial Action Task Force. Member: Inter-Govtl Council, Internat. Prog. for Develt of Communications, UNESCO, 1983–87; Exec. Bd, UNESCO, 1985–87; RIIA, 1987–; Internat. Inst. of Communications, 1984–2009; Caribbean Adv. Bd to FCO, 2007–08; and Rapporteur, Eminent Persons Gp advising Commonwealth Hds of Govt on reform of Commonwealth, 2010–11; Friends of Democratic Charter, 2011–. Pres., Permanent Council, OAS, 2016 (Chief, Special Mission to Haiti to resolve conflict and end constitutional impasse). Sen. Res. Fellow, Inst. of Commonwealth Studies, Univ. of London, 2012–; Sen. Associate Fellow, Massey Coll., Univ. of Toronto, 2015–. Hon. DLitt W Indies, 2014. *Publications:* Broadcasting in Guyana, 1977; Antigua and Barbuda: transition, trial, triumph, 1984; (ed) Inseparable Humanity—an anthology of reflections of Shridath Ramphal, Commonwealth Secretary-General, 1988; (ed) Antigua Vision, Caribbean Reality: perspectives of Prime Minister Lester B. Bird, 2002; Crumbled Small: the Commonwealth Caribbean in world politics, 2005; contrib. chapters in several books; several contribs to internat. jls on the Commonwealth, the Caribbean, and the Small States, also political commentaries in weekly leading newspapers in Caribbean and on internet news websites. *Recreations:* reading, cinema, music. *Clubs:* Royal Automobile, St James's.

**SANDERS, Prof. Roy,** FRCS; consultant plastic surgeon, 1974–2006; former Consultant: Mount Vernon Centre for Plastic Surgery; BUPA Hospital Harpenden; BUPA Hospital Bushey; Humana Hospital; Bishops Wood Hospital, Northwood; *b* 20 Aug. 1937; *s* of Leslie John Sanders and Marguerite Alice (*née* Knight); *m* 1st, 1961, Ann Ruth Costar (marr. diss.); two *s* one *d*; 2nd, 1984, Fleur Annette Chandler, Baroness von Balajthy (*d* 2011). *Educ:* Hertford Grammar Sch.; Charing Cross Hosp. Med. Sch. (BSc Hons Anatomy, MB, BS). LRCP 1962; FRCS 1967. Various hosp. appts; Sen. Lectr in Plastic Surgery, London Univ. and Hon. Cons. Plastic Surgeon, Mt Vernon Centre for Plastic Surgery, 1972–74; Cons. Plastic Surgeon, St Andrew's Hosp., Billericay and St Bart's Hosp., 1974–76; Hon. Sen. Lectr, London Univ., 1976–93; Hd, Service Dept, Plastic Maxillo-Facial and Oral Surgery, Mt Vernon Hosp., 1986–2003; Hon. Prof., UCL, 1993–. Non-exec. Dir, Burnt Mill Multi-Acad. Trust, 2016– (Vice-Chm., 2016–). Sec., Brit. Assoc. Aesthetic Plastic Surgeons, 1984–87; Pres., Brit. Assoc. Plastic Surgeons, 1993 (Sec., 1987–90); Mem. Senate, RCS, 1994–96. OC Light Cavalry, HAC, 1996–2004. *Publications:* scientific pubns in med. jls and textbooks. *Recreations:* equestrian pursuits, watercolour painting, books. *Address:* 77 Harley Street, W1G 8QN. *T:* (020) 7935 7417; Upper Rye Farmhouse, Moreton-in-Marsh, Glos GL56 9AB. *T:* (01608) 650542. *Clubs:* Garrick, Honourable Artillery Company.

**SANDERS, Sebastian;** Stable Jockey to Sir Mark Prescott, 1997; *b* 25 Sept. 1971; *s* of Kevin Sanders and Jean Sanders (now Cooper); *m* 1998, Leona Robertson; one *d. Educ:* Lakeside Sch., Tamworth, Staffs. Champion Apprentice, 1995; winner: July Cup, on Compton Place, 1997; Irish 2000 Guineas, on Bachelor Duke, 2004; Preis von Europa, on Albanova, 2004; Nunthorpe, on Bahamian Pirate, 2004; French Prix de Diane Hermes, on Confidential Lady, 2006; Oaks, on Look Here, 2008. (Jt) Champion Flat Jockey, 2007. *Recreations:* golf, scuba diving.

**SANDERS, Prof. Thomas Andrew Bruce,** PhD, DSc; Professor of Nutrition and Dietetics, 1994–2014, now Emeritus, and Head, Diabetes and Nutritional Sciences Division, 2010–14, School of Medicine, King's College London; *b* Eastbourne, 29 Dec. 1949; *s* of John Bruce Sanders and Annie Sanders; *m* 1973, Linda Marie Fassbender; one *s* one *d. Educ:* Eastbourne Coll.; Queen Elizabeth Coll., Univ. of London (BSc Nutrition 1971; PhD 1977; DSc 1996). Registered Public Health Nutritionist 2001. Prog. Associate, UNICEF, 1971–73; Res. Asst, Kingston Hosp., 1973–77; Queen Elizabeth College: Rank Prize Funds Fellow, 1977–79; Res. Fellow, 1979–82; Lectr in Nutrition, 1982–84; King's College London: Lectr in Nutrition, 1984–91; Reader, 1991–94; Head: Dept of Nutrition and Dietetics, 1995–2001; Div. of Nutritional Scis, Sch. of Biomed. and Health Scis, 2003–10. Member: UK Scientific Adv. Cttee on Novel Foods and Processes, 1994–2001; UK Scientific Adv. Cttee, Jt Health Claims Initiative, 2001–08; WHO/FAO Expert consultation on role of fats and fatty acids in human nutrition, 2008. Hon. Nutritional Dir, HEART UK, 2005–. Scientific Gov., 2000–, Trustee, 2005–14, British Nutrition Foundn. MRSocMed 1986, FRSocMed 2014; Member: Nutrition Soc., 1971; Internat. Atherosclerosis Soc., 1983; British Atherosclerosis Soc., 1993; Biochemical Soc., 1994; Amer. Heart Assoc., 1995; Assoc. for Nutrition, 2012; Amer. Soc. for Nutrition, 2012. FHEA 2007; Fellow, Assoc. for Nutrition, 2013. *Publications:* The Vegetarian's Healthy Diet Book, 1986; The Food Revolution, 1991; You Don't Have to Diet!, 1994; Dietary Fats, 1994, 2nd edn 1999; Foods that Harm, Foods that Heal, 1999; The Molecular Basis of Human Nutrition, 2003; Nutrition and Development: short and long-term consequences for health, 2014; Functional Dietary Lipids: food formulation, consumer issues and innovation for health, 2016; over 350 articles in scientific jls. *Recreations:* theatre, opera, cinema, walking, surfing, sailing, diving, watching wildlife, travel. *Address:* Department of Nutritional Sciences, King's College London, Franklin Wilkins Building, 150 Stamford Street, SE1 9NH. *T:* (020) 7848 4273, *Fax:* (020) 7848 4171. *E:* tom.sanders@kcl.ac.uk.

**SANDERS, William George,** CB 1991; CEng, FRINA; RCNC; Head of Royal Corps of Naval Constructors, 1986–91; Director General, Submarines, Ministry of Defence (PE), 1985–91; *b* 22 Jan. 1936; *s* of George and Alice Irene Sanders; *m* 1956, Marina Charlotte Burford; two *s* one *d. Educ:* Public Secondary Sch., Plymouth; Devonport Dockyard Tech. Coll.; RN Coll., Greenwich. Asst Constructor, Ship Dept, Admiralty, 1961–68; FNCO Western Fleet, 1968–70; Constructor, Ship Dept, MoD (Navy), 1970–77; Principal Naval Overseer, Scotland, 1977–79; Marconi Space and Defence Systems, 1979–81; Project Director, Type 23, 1981–83; DG Future Material Projects (Naval), MoD (PE), 1983–85. *Recreations:* golf, painting, gardening. *Address:* 12 New Lawns, Melksham, Wilts SN12 7UB.

**SANDERSON,** family name of **Baron Sanderson of Bowden**.

**SANDERSON OF AYOT;** 2nd Baron *cr* 1960, title disclaimed by the heir, Dr Alan Lindsay Sanderson, 1971.

**SANDERSON OF BOWDEN, Baron** *cr* 1985 (Life Peer), of Melrose in the District of Ettrick and Lauderdale; **Charles Russell Sanderson,** Kt 1981; Chairman, Clydesdale Bank PLC, 1998–2004 (Director, 1986–87 and since 1994; Deputy Chairman, 1996–98); Vice Lord-Lieutenant, Borders Region (Roxburgh, Ettrick and Lauderdale), 2003–08; *b* 30 April 1933; *s* of Charles Plummer Sanderson and Martha Evelyn Gardiner; *m* 1958, Frances Elizabeth Macaulay; one *s* two *d* (and one *s* decd). *Educ:* St Mary's Sch., Melrose; Trinity Coll., Glenalmond; Scottish Coll. of Textiles, Galashiels; Bradford Coll. (now Bradford Univ.). Commnd Royal Signals, 1952; served: 51 (Highland) Inf. Div. Signal Regt TA, 1953–56, KOSB TA, 1956–58. Partner, Chas P. Sanderson, Wool and Yarn Merchants, Melrose, 1958–87; Chairman: Edinburgh Financial Trust (formerly Yorkshire & Lancashire Investment Trust), 1983–87; Shires Investment Trust, 1984–87; Scottish Mortgage & Trust, 1993–2003 (Mem. Bd, 1991–); Scottish Pride plc, 1994–97; Director: Hawick Cashmere, 1991– (Chm., 1991–2014); United Auctions, 1992–99; Edinburgh Woollen Mills, 1993–97; Watson & Philip, 1993–99; Morrison Construction Group, 1995–2000; Nat. Australia Gp Europe, 1998–2004; Develica Deutschland plc, 2006–10; Accsys Technologies plc, 2007–14. Mem., H of L, 1985–2018. Minister of State, Scottish Office, 1987–90. Chairman, Roxburgh, Selkirk and Peebles Cons. and Unionist Assoc., 1970–73; Scottish Conservative Unionist Association: Chm. Central and Southern Area, 1974–75; Vice-Pres. 1975–77; Pres. 1977–79; Vice-Chm. Nat. Union of Cons Assocs, 1979–81 (Mem. Exec. Cttee, 1975–); Chm. Exec. Cttee, Nat. Union of Cons. Assocs, 1981–86; Member: Cons. Party Policy Cttee, 1979–86; Standing Adv. Cttee of Parly Candidates, 1979–86 (Vice-Chm. with responsibility for Europe, 1980–81); Chm., Scottish Cons. Party, 1990–93. Chm., Scottish Peers Assoc., 1998–2000. Pres., RHASS, 2002–03. Deacon, Galashiels Manufrs Corp., 1976; Chm., Eildon Housing Assoc., 1978–82. Trustee, Abbotsford Trust, 2008–16 (Chm., 2008–15). Mem. Court, Napier Univ., 1994–2001; Governor, St Mary's Sch., Melrose, 1977–87 (Chm., 1998–2004); Mem. Council, Trinity Coll., Glenalmond, 1982–2000 (Chm., 1994–2000). Comr, Gen. Assembly of Ch of Scotland, 1972. Mem. Court, Framework Knitters' Co., 2000– (Master, 2005–06). DL Roxburgh, Ettrick and Lauderdale, 1990. *Recreations:* golf, fishing, amateur operatics (Past Pres., Producer and Mem. Melrose Amateur Operatic Soc.). *Address:* Becketts Field, Bowden, Melrose, Roxburgh TD6 0ST. *T:* (01835) 822756. *Clubs:* Caledonian; Hon. Co. of Edinburgh Golfers (Muirfield).

**SANDERSON, Prof. Alexis Godfrey James Slater;** Spalding Professor of Eastern Religions and Ethics, University of Oxford, 1992–2015; Fellow of All Souls College, Oxford, 1992–2015, now Emeritus; *b* 28 June 1948; *e s* of J. J. Sanderson, Houghton-le-Spring. *Educ:* Royal Masonic Sch., Watford; Balliol Coll., Oxford (BA 1971). Oxford University: Domus Sen. Schol., Merton Coll., 1971–74; Platnauer Jun. Res. Fellow, Brasenose Coll., 1974–77; Univ. Lectr in Sanskrit, 1977–92; Fellow of Wolfson Coll., 1977–92, Fellow Emeritus, 1992. Petra Kappert Fellow, Centre for Study of Manuscript Cultures, Hamburg Univ., 2012; Vis. Prof., Kyoto Univ., 2012. *Address:* All Souls College, Oxford OX1 4AL.

**SANDERSON, Bryan Kaye,** CBE 1999; Chairman, Florence Nightingale Foundation, 2008–18; *b* 14 Oct. 1940; *s* of Eric and Anne Sanderson; *m* 1966, Sirkka Kärki; one *s* one *d. Educ:* Dame Allan's Sch., Newcastle upon Tyne; LSE (BSc Econ.); Dip. Business Studies, IMEDE Lausanne, 1973. VSO Peru, 1962–64; British Petroleum, 1964; Chief Exec. Officer, BP Nutrition, 1987–90; CEO, BP Chemicals, then Chief Exec., BP Amoco Chemicals, 1990–2000; Man. Dir, British Petroleum, then BP Amoco, 1992–2000. Chm., Low Pay Commn, 2019– (Interim Chm., 2017–18). Chairman: BUPA, 2001–06; Standard Chartered plc, 2003–06 (non-exec. Dir, 2002–06); Northern Rock plc, 2007–08; non-executive Director: Corus (formerly British Steel), 1994–2001; Six Continents plc, 2001–03; Sunderland FC plc, 1997–2004 (Chm., 1998–2004); Argus Media Ltd, 2012–16; Chm., Sunderland Area Regeneration Co., 2001–09. Chm., LSC, 2000–04. Mem., DTI Co. Law Steering Gp, 1998–2001. Chm., Home Renaissance Foundn, 2006–. Dir, Durham CCC, 2005–16. Gov., LSE, 1997–2009, now Emeritus (Vice-Chm. Govs, 1998–2003). Trustee, Economist, 2006–17. Hon. FIChemE 2002. Hon. DBA: Sunderland, 1998; York, 1999. *Recreations:* reading, golf, walking, gardening. *Address:* 40 Netherhall Gardens, Hampstead, NW3 5TP. *T:* (020) 7794 2488.

**SANDERSON, Charles Denis;** HM Diplomatic Service, retired; Fellow, St Peter's College, Oxford, 1985–96, now Emeritus; *b* 18 Dec. 1934; *s* of Norman and Elsie Sanderson; *m* 1960, Mary Joyce Gillow; one *s* two *d. Educ:* Bishopshalt Sch., Hillingdon, Middx; Pembroke Coll., Oxford (MA). National Service, 1953–55; Oxford, 1955–58; British Petroleum Co. Ltd, 1958–64; Second, later First Secretary, Commonwealth Relations Office, 1964–67; First Sec., Kingston, and concurrently, Haiti, 1967–70; Acting Consul, Port au Prince, 1969; First Sec., Head of Chancery and Consul, Panama, 1970–73; First Sec., FCO, 1973–75; Consul (Commercial), British Trade Development Office, New York, 1975–77; Dep. Consul General and Director Industrial Development, New York, 1977–79; Counsellor, Caracas, 1979–84; Hd, W Indian and Atlantic Dept, FCO, 1984–85. Domestic Bursar, 1985–92, Bursar, 1992–96, St Peter's Coll., Oxford. *Address:* Reskajeage Farm, Gwithian, Hayle, Cornwall TR27 5EF. *T:* (01209) 712512.

**SANDERSON, Eric Fenton;** Chairman: MWB Group Holdings PLC (formerly Marylebone Warwick Balfour plc), 2005–12 (non-executive Director, 2002–12); Schroder UK Mid Cap Fund plc, since 2014 (non-executive Director, since 2011); Black Rock Greater Europe Investment Trust plc, since 2016 (non-executive Director, since 2013); *b* 14 Oct. 1951; *s* of Francis Kirton Sanderson and Margarita Shand (*née* Fenton); *m* 1975, Patricia Ann Shaw; three *d. Educ:* Morgan Acad., Dundee; Univ. of Dundee (LLB); Harvard Business Sch. (AMP). FCIBS (MCIBS 1991). Touche Ross & Co., CA, 1973–76; CA 1976; British Linen Bank Group Ltd, 1976–97: Corporate Finance Div., 1976–84; Dir, British Linen Bank and Head, Corporate Finance Div., 1984–89; Chief Exec., 1989–97; Chief Exec., Bank of Scotland Treasury Services PLC, 1997–99; Chm., Kwik-Fit Insurance Services Ltd, 2002–03 (Dir, 1999–2002); Man. Dir, 2000–01). Non-executive Director: MyTravel Group (formerly Airtours) plc, 1987–2004 (Dep. Chm., 2001–02; Chm., 2002–04); DLR Ltd, 1999–2001 (Chm., Quality Panel, 2001–05); First Milk Ltd, 2006–12; MWB Malmaison Hldgs Ltd, 2012 (Chm., 2012); MWB Business Exchange plc, 2012. Mem., BRB, 1991–94. Graduates Assessor and Mem. Court, Univ. of Dundee, 2005–16 (Chm. Court, 2010–16). *Recreations:* tennis, photography, gardening. *E:* ericsanderson@blueyonder.co.uk. *Club:* New (Edinburgh).

**SANDERSON, Sir Frank (Linton),** 3rd Bt *cr* 1920, of Malling Deanery, South Malling, Sussex; OBE 2005; *b* 21 Nov. 1933; *s* of Sir Bryan Sanderson, 2nd Bt and Annette Korab Laskowska (*d* 1967); *S* father, 1992; *m* 1961, Margaret Ann, *o d* of late John Cleveland Maxwell, New York, USA; two *s* three *d* (incl. twin *d*). *Educ:* Stowe; Univ. of Salamanca. RNVR, 1950–65. J. H. Minet & Co. Ltd, 1956–93 (Dir, 1985); Dir, Knott Hotels Co. of London, 1965–75; Dir and Chm., Humber Fertilisers plc, 1972–88. Underwriting Mem. of Lloyd's, 1957–88. Mem., Chichester Dio. Synod, 1980–93. Chm., Thiepval Project, 1999–2006. Master, Worshipful Co. of Curriers, 1993–94. *Heir: s* David Frank Sanderson [*b* 26 Feb. 1962; *m* 1990, Fiona Jane Ure; one *d*]. *Address:* Grandturzel Farm, Burwash, East Sussex TN19 7DE. *Clubs:* Naval, City of London, Farmers.

**SANDERSON, Guy Rory;** Headmaster, Eltham College, since 2014; *b* Kitwe, Zambia, 27 May 1972; *s* of Malcolm and Linda Sanderson; *m* 2001, Laura Prideaux; three *d. Educ:* Spalding Grammar Sch.; Trinity Coll., Oxford (MA); Inst. of Educn (PGCE). Stockbroker, Kemper Financial, 1994–95; Strategy Relief Asst, UNHCR, 1995–96; Teacher of History: St Paul's Sch. for Boys, 1996–97; Whitgift Sch., 1997–2000; Fundraising Dir, City of London Sch. for Boys, 2000–03; Reigate Grammar School: Hd of Fundraising and Hd of Dept, 2003–07; Hd of Sixth Form, 2007–10; Dep. Hd, 2010–14. FRSA. *Recreations:* theatre, art, opera, travel, sailing, ski-ing. *Address:* Eltham College, Grove Park Road, SE9 4QF. *T:* (020) 8857 1455. *E:* Headmaster@eltham-college.org.uk. *Club:* Lansdowne.

**SANDERSON, Lt-Gen. John Murray,** AC 1994 (AO 1991; AM 1985); ActionAid Australia Ambassador for Cambodia, 2006–12; Chairman, Indigenous Implementation Board, Department of Indigenous Affairs, Western Australia, 2008–11; Governor of Western Australia, 2000–05; *b* 4 Nov. 1940; *s* of John Edward, (Jack), Sanderson and (Dorothy) Jean Sanderson; *m* 1962, Viva Lorraine; one *s* two *d. Educ:* Bunbury High Sch., WA; Royal Mil. Coll., Duntroon; Royal Melbourne Inst. of Technol. (Fellow 1964). Australian Army: Comdr of Sqdn, Vietnam, 1970–71; Sen. Instructor, Sch. of Mil. Engrg, 1972; Instructor, Staff Coll., Camberley, UK, 1976–78; Comdr, 1st Field Engrg Regt, 1979–80; MA to CGS, 1982; Dir of Army Plans, 1982–85; Comdr, 1st Bde, 1986–88; Chief of Staff, Land HQ, 1989; Asst Chief, Defence Forces Develt, 1989–91; Mil. Comdr, UN Transitional Authy, Cambodia, 1992–93; Comdr, Jt Forces Aust., 1993–95; CGS, 1995–97; Chief of Aust. Army, 1997–98. Adjunct Professor: Murdoch Univ., 2006–; Griffith Univ., 2006–. Mem. Bd, Australian Centre for Christianity and Culture, 2007–. Fellow, Aust. Inst. of Internat. Affairs, 2008. Hon. FIEAust 2000. Comdr, Legion of Merit, USA, 1997; Grand Cross, Royal Cambodian Order, 2006.

**SANDERSON, Kerry Gaye,** AC 2016 (AO 2004); Governor of Western Australia, 2014–18; *b* Perth, WA, 21 Dec. 1950; *d* of late Stanley Thomas Smith and Valma June Smith; *m* 1972, Lancelot John Sanderson (*d* 2007); two *s. Educ:* Univ. of Western Australia (BSc, BEc). FCILT. Treasury, WA, 1971–87, incl. Dir, Econ. and Financial Policy, 1980–87; Dep. Dir Gen., Transport, WA, 1987–91; CEO, Fremantle Ports, 1991–2008. Dir, AWB Ltd, 1995–2005. Mem. Bd, Australian Trade Commn, 2005–06. Pres., Ports Australia, 2007–08; Agent Gen. for WA in London, 2008–11. Chm., State Emergency Mgt Cttee, WA, 2012–14. Co-Chair, First Murdoch Commn, 2013. Adjunct Prof., Curtin Univ., 2013–14. Chancellor, Edith Cowan Univ., 2018–. Chm., Gold Corp., 2012–14; Ind. non-exec. Dir, Atlas Iron Ltd, 2012–14; non-executive Director: Downer EDI Ltd, 2012–14; St John of God Healthcare, 2012–14 (Chair, 2018–); Internat. Centre for Radio-Astronomy Res., 2013–14; Mem. Bd, Rio Tinto WA Future Fund, 2002–08; Trustee, Fremantle Hosp. Med. Res. Foundn, 1998–2008; Director: Senses Foundn, 2012–14; Paraplegic Benefit Fund, 2012–14; Chm., WA Parks Foundn, 2016–. FAIM; FAICD. Hon. LittD WA, 2005. Centenary Medal, 2001. Telstra Businesswoman of Year, WA, 1996. *Recreations:* hiking, swimming.

**SANDERSON, Dr Michael David;** Chairman, Third Wave Enterprise Ltd, 2007–10; *b* 7 June 1943; *s* of Arthur Joseph Sanderson and Betty (*née* Potter); *m* 1967, Mariana Nelly Madinaveitia; one *s* one *d. Educ:* Strode's Sch., Egham; Univ. of Reading (BSc Hons Chem. 1964); Univ. of Leeds (PhD 1968). With Wilkinson Sword: Research Scientist, 1968–71; Technical Manager, 1971–73; Technical Dir, 1973–79; Internat. Marketing Dir, 1979–82; Engrg Dir, AMF Legg, 1982–84; with Lansing Bagnall: Export Dir, 1984–87; Gp Dir, UK Market, 1987–89; Jt Man. Dir, Lansing Linde, 1989–90; Man. Dir, AWD Bedford, 1990–91; Chief Executive: BSI, 1991–93; Nat. Assoc. of Goldsmiths and Sec. Gen.,

Internat. Confedn of Jewellers, 1994–95; Engrg and Marine Trng Authy, subseq. Sci., Engrg and Manufacturing Technologies Alliance, 1995–2004; Man. Dir, Technical Qualifications Validation Ltd, 2005–07. Pres., Inst. of Supervision and Mgt, 1995–99; Chairman: Action for Engrg, Task Force 3, 1995–96; Output Standards Adv. Cttee, Engrg Professors Council, 2000–05; Res. Div., Inst. of Continuing Professional Develt, 2004–06; Nat. Chm., Women into Sci. and Engrg Campaign, 2001–03; Dep. Nat. Chm., Inst. Materials Management, 1991–93; Member Council: Inst. of Materials, 1993–96; Inst. of Logistics, 1988–94; Inst. of Quality Assurance, 1997–2001; Foundn for Sci. and Technol., 2000–04; Dir, Engrg and Technol. Bd, 2001–02. Consultant, Engrg Council, 2005–. Mem., Benchmarking Forum, Amer. Soc. for Trng and Develt, 1999–2004. Trustee: Enterprise Education Trust (formerly Understanding Industry, subseq. Business Dynamics), 1998–2014; Scottish Council of NTOs, 1999–2004; EdExcel Foundn, 2001–04; Sci., Engrg Technol. and Math. Network, 1999–2004; E Midlands Leadership Centre, 2004–11. Chm. and Trustee, Young Electronic Designer of the Year Award, 2002–05; Trustee, Nat. Exam. Bd in Occupational Health and Safety, 2005–10. Member Court: Cranfield Univ., 1996–2005; Imperial Coll. London, 2002; City Univ., 2004. Mem., Editorial Bd, TQM Magazine, 1993–. Chm., Childs Hill Allotment Soc., 2006–07 (Dep. Chm., 2005–06). Freeman: City of London, 1995; City of Glasgow, 2001; Incorp. of Hammermen of City of Glasgow, 2001; Freeman, 1994–96, Liveryman, 1996–, Mem. Court, 2000–, Master, 2008–09, Clockmakers' Co.; Freeman, 2002–03, Liveryman, 2003–, Engrs' Co. Hon. FIET (Hon. FIIE 2003). *Publications*: contribs to learned jls on surface chemistry, thin surface films, materials management, quality and general management topics. *Recreation*: books. *Address*: 31 Murray Mews, NW1 9RH. *T*: (020) 7284 3155, *Fax*: (020) 7267 9453. *Clubs*: Athenæum, Carlton.

**SANDERSON, Rev. Canon Peter Oliver;** Supply Priest, Diocese of the Rio Grande, New Mexico, 2010–13; *b* 26 Jan. 1929; *s* of Harold and Doris Sanderson; *m* 1956, Doreen Gibson (*d* 2013); one *s* one *d* (and one *s* decd). *Educ*: St Chad's College, Durham Univ. (BA, DipTh). Asst Curate, Houghton-le-Spring, Durham Diocese, 1954–59; Rector, Linstead and St Thomas Ye Vale, Jamaica, 1959–63; Chaplain, RAF, 1963–67; Vicar, Winksley-cum-Grantley and Aldfield-with-Studley, Ripon, 1967–74; Vicar, St Aidan, Leeds, 1974–84; Provost of St Paul's Cathedral, Dundee, 1984–91; Vicar, All Saints' Episcopal Ch, Storm Lake, Iowa, 1991–2000; Asst Priest, Trinity Episcopal Church, Iowa City, 2000–05; Interim Dean, Trinity Cathedral, Davenport, Iowa, 2005–06; Interim Priest-in-Charge, Lincoln County, Dio. of the Rio Grande, New Mexico, 2008–10. Hon. Canon, St Paul's Cath., Des Moines, Iowa, 2004. *Recreations*: music, reading.

**SANDERSON, Roy,** OBE 1983; National Secretary, Federation of Professional Associations Section, Amalgamated Engineering and Electrical Union, 1992–93; *b* 15 Feb. 1931; *s* of George and Lillian Sanderson; *m* 1951, Jean (*née* Booth); two *s* (and one *s* decd). *Educ*: Carfield Sch., Sheffield. Electrical, Electronic Telecommunication & Plumbing Union: Convenor, Lucas Aerospace, Hemel Hempstead, 1952–67; Asst Educn Officer, 1967–69; Nat. Officer, 1969–87; Nat. Sec., Electrical and Engrg Staff Assoc., 1987–92. Non-exec. Dir, UKAEA, 1987–96. Member: Armed Forces Pay Review Body, 1987–95; Economic and Social Cttee, EU, 1990–98; Industrial Tribunals, 1992–99; Employment Appeal Tribunal, 1995–2002. *Recreations*: golf, snooker; supporter of Watford Football Club. *Address*: 24 Harborough Road North, Kingsthorpe, Northampton NN2 8LU.

**SANDERSON, Theresa Ione, (Tessa),** CBE 2004 (OBE 1998; MBE 1985); former athlete; Founder, Tessa Sanderson Foundation and Academy, 2009; *b* 14 March 1956; *m* 2010, Design White; one adopted *s* one adopted *d* (twins). *Educ*: Wards Bridge Comprehensive Sch., Wednesfield, Wolverhampton; Bilston Coll. of Further Educn. Javelin thrower; represented GB, 1974–96: Olympic Games: Gold Medal, Los Angeles, 1984 (Olympic record); finalist, Barcelona, 1992; competitor, Atlanta, 1996 (record 6th Olympic Games); Gold Medal, Commonwealth Games, 1978, 1986, 1990; Silver Medal, European Championships, 1978; Gold Medal, World Cup, Cuba, 1992. Set UK record, javelin, 1976 and 1983; UK record, heptathlon, 1981. Sports presenter, Sky News, 1989–92; presenter of own Sunday radio show for Colourful Radio. Mem., 1998–2005, Vice-Chm., 1999–2005, Sport England; Mem., Sports Honours Cttee, 2005–; Ambassador for London 2012, 2005–12; Hd of Talent Develt for 2012, Newham Council, 2005–12. Founder, Newham Classic 10K, 2009–. Patron: Disabled Olympics; Adoption UK. Hon. MA Birmingham. Difference Award, St John Ambulance, 2010. *Publications*: Tessa: my life in athletics (autobiog.), 1985.

**SANDFORD, 3rd Baron** *cr* 1945, of Banbury; **James John Mowbray Edmondson;** private counselling practice, Sand Tray Therapy, since 2017; President, Surrey School Counsellors Association, British Columbia, 2001–07; *b* Winchester, England, 1 July 1949; *er s* of 2nd Baron Sandford, DSC and Catharine Mary, *d* of Rev. Oswald Andrew Hunt; *S* father, 2009; *m* 1st, 1973, Ellen Sarah Shapiro (marr. diss. 1985); one *d*; 2nd, 1985, Linda (marr. diss. 2014; she *d* 2015), *d* of Mick and Betty Wheeler, Nova Scotia; one *s*. *Educ*: York Univ., UK (BA Hons Political Sci.); Univ. of British Columbia (MEd Counselling Psychol.). Elementary sch. teacher, 1974–81; elementary school counsellor, 1981–2017. Pres., Vancouver-Kensington NDP, 2005–11. Pres., Vancouver Folk Song Soc., 1988–92. Member: singing and recording gp, Three Strong Winds, 1989–99; singing gp, Lemon Gin with Lyn Pinkerton, 2005–15; singing gp, with Dr Madeleine De Little, 2015–. *Heir*: *s* Hon. Devon John Wheeler Edmondson [*b* 15 April 1986; *m* 2016, Stephanie Devlin]. *Address*: 404–908 West 7th, Vancouver, BC V5Z 1C3, Canada. *T*: (778) 2290594. *E*: jimedmondson@telus.net.

**SANDFORD, Arthur;** DL; Chairman, Trent Strategic Health Authority, 2002–06; *b* 12 May 1941; *s* of Arthur and Lilian Sandford; *m* 1963, Kathleen Entwistle; two *d*. *Educ*: Queen Elizabeth's Grammar Sch., Blackburn; University Coll., London (LLB Hons (Upper 2nd Class)). Preston County Borough Council: Articled Clerk to Town Clerk, 1962–65; Asst Solicitor, 1965–66; Sen. Asst Solicitor, 1966–68; Asst Solicitor, Hants CC, 1969–70; Nottinghamshire County Council: Second Asst Clerk, 1970–72; First Asst Clerk, 1972–74; Dep. Dir of Admin, 1973–75; Dir of Admin, 1975–77; Dep. Clerk and County Sec., 1977–78; Clerk and Chief Exec., 1978–89; Chief Executive: Football League, 1990–92; Manchester CC, 1992–98. Chm., Christie Hosp. NHS Trust, 1999–2002. Consultant: Pannone & Partners, 1998–2002; Amey plc, 1998–2002. DL Notts, 1990. *Recreations*: watching sport, gardening, golf. *Address*: 4 Wentworth Way, Edwalton, Nottingham NG12 4DJ. *T*: (0115) 914 9854.

**SANDHURST,** 6th Baron; *see* Mansfield, G. R. J.

**SANDIFORD, Rt Hon. Sir Lloyd Erskine,** KA 1999; PC (Barbados); PC 1989; JP; Ambassador of Barbados to the People's Republic of China, 2009–13; Prime Minister of Barbados, 1987–94; *b* 24 March 1937; *s* of Cyril and Eunice Sandiford; *m* 1963, Angelita P. Ricketts; one *s* two *d*. *Educ*: Coleridge/Parry Sec. Sch.; Harrison Coll.; Univ. of WI, Jamaica (BA Hons English); Univ. of Manchester (MAEcon). Assistant Master: Modern High Sch., Barbados, 1956–57; Kingston Coll., Jamaica, 1960–61; Asst Master, 1963–64, Sen. Graduate Master, 1964–66, Harrison Coll., Barbados; part-time Tutor and Lectr, Univ. of the WI, Barbados, 1963–65; Asst Tutor, Barbados Community Coll., 1976–86. Democratic Labour Party, Barbados: Mem., 1964–; Asst Sec., 1966–67; Gen. Sec., 1967–68; (first) Vice-Pres., 1972–74; Pres., 1974–75; Vice-Pres., 1975–76; Founder, Acad. of Politics. Member: Senate, 1967–71; House of Assembly, St Michael South, 1971–99; Personal Asst to the Prime Minister, 1966–67; Minister: of Educn, 1967–71; of Educn, Youth Affairs, Community Develt and Sport, 1971–75; of Health and Welfare, 1975–76; Dep. Leader of Opposition, 1978–86; Dep. Prime Minister and Minister of Educn and Culture, 1986–87; Minister: for Civil Service, 1987–94; of Finance and Economic Affairs, 1987–93; of Economic Affairs, 1993–94; of Tourism and Internat. Transport, 1994. Dist. Fellow, Univ. of WI, Barbados. Order of the Liberator (Venezuela), 1987. *Publications*: Books of Speeches 1987–1994; The Essence of Economics, 1997; Politics and Society in Barbados and the Caribbean, 2000; Fighting for the Just Society: an autobiographical note, 2011; *poems*: Ode to the Environment; When She Leaves You; (contrib.) Business, Government and Society, ed Monya Anyadike-Danes. *Address*: Hillvista, Porters, St James, Barbados, West Indies.

**SANDIFORD, Peter,** OBE 1992; Director, Spain, British Council, 1999–2003; *b* 23 May 1947; *s* of Jack Sandiford and Joan Mary Sandiford; *m* 1st, 1970, Yvonne Kay Haffenden (marr. diss. 2005); one *s* one *d*; 2nd, 2006, Victoria Francesca Cornwell-García. *Educ*: Watford Grammar Sch. for Boys; University College London (BSc Hons Anthropology 1969). VSO Volunteer, Malawi, 1965–66; Archaeologist, MPBW, 1969–70; British Council: Asst Dir, Singapore, 1971–75; Regl Dir, Munich, 1975–82; Dir, Mgt Services Dept, London, 1982–86; Dir, Israel, 1986–94; Regl Dir, East and Southern Europe, 1994–96, Americas, 1996–98, London. *Recreations*: amateur radio, sailing, hiking.

**SANDILANDS,** family name of **Baron Torphichen**.

**SANDIS, Alexandros C.;** Director, Diplomatic Office of the Prime Minister, Athens (with rank of Ambassador), 2004–09; *b* Alexandria, Egypt, 29 Aug. 1947; *s* of Constantinos and Maria Sandis; *m* 1969, Anastasia Tsagarakis; one *s* one *d*. *Educ*: Univ. of Athens (BA Pol and Econ. Scis). Joined Ministry of Foreign Affairs, Athens, 1971: Attaché, 1971–73; 2nd Sec., New Delhi, 1973–77; Counsellor, Nicosia, 1977–83; Counsellor, Perm. Delegn to EC, Brussels, 1983–88; Dir, EU Affairs Dept, Athens, 1989–91; Ambassador to: Zimbabwe, 1991–93; Cyprus, 1993–97; Italy, 1997–2000; UK, 2000–03. Greek Govt Rep. at Cyprus Talks, 1997–2001. Grand Cross: Order of Makarios III (Cyprus), 1993; Norwegian Order of Merit (Norway), 2004; Order of the Phoenix (Greece), 2005; Order of the Honour in Gold, First Class (Austria), 2007; Comdr, Order of Greek Orthodox Patriarchate of Alexandria, 1995; Grand Comdr, Order of Dannebrog (Denmark), 2006. *Recreations*: history, music, theatre, football.

**SANDIS, Aristidis C.;** Ambassador of Greece to the Court of St James's, 2010–12; Permanent Representative to the International Maritime Organization, 2010; *b* Alexandria, Egypt, 1 Dec. 1951; *s* of Constantinos and Maria Sandis; *m* Ekaterini Simopoulou; three *d*. *Educ*: Univ. of Athens (Public Law and Pol Scis degree 1973). Joined Greek Diplomatic Service as Attaché, 1974; 2nd Pol Directorate, Min. of For. Affairs, 1974–76; Second Sec., Bonn, 1976–80; Consul of Greece, Cape Town, 1981–87; Minister-Counsellor, Moscow, 1987–91; Hd, Diplomatic Cabinet of Dep. Minister of For. Affairs, Min. of For. Affairs, 1991–93; Dep. Perm. Rep. to OSCE, Vienna, 1993–96; Ambassador to Jordan, 1996–99; Hd, A6 Directorate for Arab Countries and Middle East, Min. of For. Affairs, 1999–2001; Perm. Rep. to OSCE, Vienna, 2001–05; Ambassador to Rep. of SA, and concurrently to Botswana, Lesotho, Mozambique, Namibia and Swaziland, 2005–09; Sec. Gen., Min. of For. Affairs, 2009. Grand Cross, Order of Phoenix (Greece), 2007 (Grand Comdr, 1999); Cross, 1st Cl., Order of Merit (Germany), 1981; Grand Cordon, Order of Independence (Jordan), 1999; Comdr, Order of Cedar (Lebanon), 2001.
*See also* Alexandros C. Sandis.

**SANDISON, Alexander, (Alec),** FCCA; charity governance and management consultant, 1994–2013; *s* of late Alexander and Mary Sandison; *m* Judy Hamilton (*née* Evans). *Educ*: Cambs High Sch.; Trinity Sch. of John Whitgift, Croydon. Commercial Union Assce Co., 1962–63; John Mowlem PLC, 1964–71 (Gp Financial Accountant, 1970–71); Chief Accountant: and Co. Sec., J. E. Freeman & Co., 1972–73; Wings Ltd, 1973–78; Divl Financial Dir, Doulton Glass Inds, 1978–80; Sec. for Finance and Corporate Controller, RICS, 1980–90; Chief Exec., Surveyors Holdings Ltd, 1985–89; Chm., Imaginor Systems Ltd, 1989–90; Director: Cruse-Bereavement Care, 1990–91; Finance and Admin, Prince's Trust and Royal Jubilee Trusts, 1992–94; Co. Sec., Who Cares? Trust, 1995–2008. Mem., Charities Tech. Adv. Gp, Chartered Assoc. of Certified Accountants, 1998–2012. Trustee: Chartered Certified Accountants Benevolent Fund, 1999–; Islington Volunteer Centre, 1999–2002; Charity Appointments, 2002–; Dystonia Soc., 2012–16; Co-Founder, SpeakersBank, 2002–05. Chm., Finance Cttee, Lutheran Council of GB, 2010–11 (Mem., 1998–2011). Chm., LCGB Trading Ltd, 2008–12. *Publications*: People to People: course notes, 1985; Watton-at-Stone Village Guide, 1989; contribs to learned jls, brainteasers and poetry. *Recreations*: family, voluntary social work; reading, writing; avoiding involvement with and conversations about sport.

**SANDISON, Craig Robert Kindness;** QC (Scot.) 2009; *b* Falkirk, 30 May 1966; *s* of late George Edward Grant Sandison and Margaret Sandison (*née* Kindness). *Educ*: Queens' Coll., Cambridge (Schol.; LLM 1990); Magdalene Coll., Cambridge (PhD 1994). Advocate, 1996, specialising in commercial law. *Recreation*: international affairs. *Address*: 29 Northumberland Street, Edinburgh EH3 6LR. *T*: (0131) 226 2881. *E*: crks@cantab.net.

**SANDISON, James Sinclair,** FCA; freelance financial and management consultant, 1998–2000; *b* 22 June 1936; *s* of William Robert Sandison and Evelyn Gladys Sandison; *m* 1978, Jeannette Avery Keeble; one *s* one *d*. *Educ*: John Lyon Sch., Harrow. FCA 1958. Nat. Service, 2nd Lt, 1958–60. Franklin, Wild & Co., 1953–58; Touche Ross & Co., 1960–62; British Relay Wireless and Television Ltd, 1962–66; joined Dexion Gp, 1966: Gp Controller, 1975–76; Finance Dir, Dexion Ltd, 1977–91; Royal Society for Encouragement of Arts, Manufactures and Commerce: Dir of Finance and Admin, 1991–96; Acting Dir, 1996–97. Treas., London Soc., 2005–08. FRSA 1998. *Recreations*: tennis, silent and world cinema, film noir, London, European history, British and European Art 1850–1950. *Address*: 33 Montagu Road, Highcliffe, Christchurch, Dorset BH23 5JT.

**SANDLE, Prof. Michael Leonard,** DFA; RA; FRSS; sculptor; Professor of Sculpture, Akademie der Bildenden Künste, Karlsruhe, Germany, 1980–99; *b* 18 May 1936; *s* of Charles Edward Sandle and Dorothy Gwendoline Gladys (*née* Vernon); *m* 1971, Cynthia Dora Koppel (marriage annulled 1974); *m* 1988, Demelza Spargo (marriage annulled 2004); one *s* one *d*. *Educ*: Douglas High Sch., IOM; Douglas Sch. of Art and Technol.; Slade Sch. of Fine Art (DFA 1959). ARA 1982, RA 1989, resigned 1997, rejoined 2004; FRSS (FRBS 1994). Studied painting and printmaking, Slade Sch. of Fine Art, 1956–59; changed to sculpture, 1962; various teaching posts in Britain, 1961–70, including Lectr, Coventry Coll. of Art, 1964–68; resident in Canada, 1970–73; Vis. Prof., Univ. of Calgary, Alberta, 1970–71; Vis. Associate Prof., Univ. of Victoria, BC, 1972–73; Lectr in Sculpture, Fachhochschule für Gestaltung, Pforzheim, W Germany, 1973–77, Prof., 1977–80. Sen. Res. Fellow, De Montfort Univ., 1996–2001; Fellow, Kenneth Armitage Foundn, 2004–06. Has participated in exhibns in GB and internationally, 1957–, including: V Biennale, Paris, 1966; Documenta IV, Kassel, W Germany, 1968 and Documenta VI, 1977. Work in public collections, including: Arts Council of GB, Tate Gall.; Australian Nat. Gall., Canberra; Met. Mus., NY; Stzüki Mus., Lodz; Nat. Gall., Warsaw; Wilhelm Lehmbruck

Mus., Duisburg, W Germany. Designed: Malta Siege Bell Meml, Valetta, 1992; Seafarers Meml, for Internat. Maritime Orgn's HQ, London, 2001. Nobutaka Shikanai Special Prize, Utsukushi-Ga-Hara Open-Air Mus., Japan, 1986; Henry Hering Meml Medal, Nat. Sculpture Soc. of Amer., 1995. *Address*: c/o The Royal Society of Sculptors, 108 Brompton Road, SW7 3RA.

**SANDLER, Prof. Mark Brian,** PhD; FREng, FIET, FIEEE; Professor of Signal Processing, since 2001, and Director, Centre for Digital Music, 2003–10 and since 2014, Queen Mary University of London; *b* London, 11 Dec. 1955; *s* of late Alfred (*né* Abraham) Sandler and of Ruth Doris Sandler (*née* Coffman); *m* 1991, Valerie Susan Smith (marr. diss. 2012); one *s* two *d*. *Educ*: Christ's Coll., Finchley; Univ. of Essex (BSc Hons Electronic Engrg 1978; PhD Electrical Engrg Sci. 1984). FIET 1994; FIEEE 2014; FREng 2016. King's College London: Lectr, 1982–92; Reader in Signal Processing, 1992–95; Prof. of Signal Processing, 1995–2001; Hd, Dept of Electronic Engrg, 1996–97; Queen Mary University of London: Founder Dir, RCUK/EPSRC/AHRC Centre for Doctoral Trng in Media and Arts Technol., 2009–16; Hd, Sch. of Electronic Engrg and Computer Sci., 2010–14. Fellow, Audio Engrg Soc., 2000. Founder Editor, Eurasip (formerly Springer) Jl of Applied Signal Processing, 1992–2001. *Publications*: articles primarily in IEEE Trans of Acoustics Speech and Lang. Processing and Jl of Audio Engrg Soc. *Recreations*: cricket, swimming, cycling, tai chi chu'an, playing congas, singing, concerts, movies, cooking, jam making. *Address*: School of Electronic Engineering and Computer Science, Queen Mary University of London, Mile End Road, E1 4NS. *T*: (020) 7882 7680. *E*: mark.sandler@qmul.ac.uk. *Clubs*: Crouch End Cricket, Unison Staff Society Cricket.

**SANDLER, Ronald Arnon,** Hon. CBE 2004; Chairman: Towry, 2014–16; Centaur Media, 2015–18; *b* 5 March 1952; *s* of Bernard Maurice Sandler and Carla Sandler; *m* 1977, Susan Lee; two *s*. *Educ*: Milton Sch., Bulawayo; Queens' Coll., Cambridge (MA); Stanford Univ., USA (MBA). Boston Consulting Gp Inc., 1976–84, Dir 1983–84; Sen. Vice Pres., Booz Allen & Hamilton Inc., 1984–88; Chm., Chalcon Ltd, 1989–93; Chm. and Chief Exec., Martin Bierbaum Gp plc, 1990–93; Chief Executive: Exco plc, 1993–94; Lloyd's of London, 1995–99; Chief Operating Officer, NatWest Gp, 1999–2000. Chairman: Computacenter plc, 2001–08; Kyte Gp, 2000–08; Oxygen Gp plc, 2004–08; Paternoster Ltd, 2006–11; Ironshore Inc., 2007–15; Northern Rock plc, 2008–12; Phoenix Gp (formerly Pearl), 2009–12; non-executive Director: Greenalls Gp plc, 1998–2000; Fortis, 2004–09. Pres., CIB, 2004–05. Special Advr, RIIA, 2014–. Mem., Partnership Council, Herbert Smith, 2001–06. Chm., Personal Finance Educn Gp, 2003–08. Trustee, Royal Opera House, 1999–2001. Hon. DSc City, 2012. *Recreations*: golf, ski-ing, guitar playing, fly fishing. *Address*: 5 Southside, Wimbledon, SW19 4TG. *T*: (020) 8946 1179. *Clubs*: MCC; Sunningdale Golf (Trustee, 2019–); Lloyd's Fly Fishing.

**SANDON, Viscount;** Dudley Anthony Hugo Coventry Ryder; *b* 5 Sept. 1981; *s* and heir of Earl of Harrowby, *qv*. *Educ*: Eton Coll.; Edinburgh Univ. (MA). *Address*: Sandon Estate Office, Sandon, Stafford ST18 0DA.

**SANDON, Henry George,** MBE 2008; antiques expert and broadcaster; *b* London, 4 Aug. 1928; *s* of Augustus Sandon and Clara Sandon; *m* 1956, Barbara Sophia (*d* 2013); three *s*. *Educ*: High Wycombe Royal Grammar Sch.; Guildhall Sch. of Music. FLCM; ARCM. Music Master, Worcester Royal Grammar Sch., 1953–59; Curator, Royal Worcester Porcelain, and Dyson Perrins Mus., subseq. Museum of Royal Worcester, 1966–83, Patron, 1999–. Lay Clerk, Worcester Cathedral, 1953–82. Regular expert, BBC Antiques Roadshow, 1978–. Mem., Cttee of Mgt, Choir Benevolent Fund; Chm., Commemorative Collectors' Soc.; President: Pershore, St John's Ambulance; City of Worcester Decorative and Fine Arts Soc. Mem., Claines, Worcester Br., RBL. Freedom, City of London, 2006. Hon. MA Worcester, 2009. Police Long Service (Specials) Medal. *Publications*: British Pottery and Porcelain, 1969, 1980; Worcester Porcelain 1751–1793, 1969, 2nd edn 1974; Coffee Pots and Teapots, 1973; Royal Worcester Porcelain, 1973, 3rd edn 1978; Flight and Barr Worcester Porcelain, 1978; Sandon Guide to Worcester Figures, 1987; Living with the Past (autobiog.), 1997. *Recreation*: giving pots a good home and love. *Address*: c/o Museum of Royal Worcester, Severn Street, Worcester WR1 2ND. *T*: (01905) 21247.

**SANDON, Susan;** Managing Director, Cornerstone Division, Penguin Random House UK, since 2007 (Deputy Managing Director, 2003–07); *b* Camberley, Surrey, 4 June 1959; *d* of Frederick Donald Peace Weaver and Doris Lilian Weaver; one *s*; *m* Richard Hamilton Cable. *Educ*: Frimley and Camberley Grammar Sch.; Broadmoor Sch. of Nursing (RMN); Univ. of Sussex (BA 1st Cl. Hons); Univ. of E Anglia (MA). Headline, 1987–89; Publicity Manager, then Mktg Dir, Virago Press, 1989–92; Publicity Dir, Penguin, 1992–95; Gp Publicity and Mktg Dir, Random House, 1995–2003. *Recreations*: books, music, travel. *Address*: Penguin Random House UK, 20 Vauxhall Bridge Road, SW1V 2SA. *T*: (020) 7840 8622. *E*: ssandon@penguinrandomhouse.co.uk.

**SANDS, Catherine K.;** *see* Knight-Sands.

**SANDS, Jonathan Peter,** OBE 2011; Chairman, Elmwood Design, brand design consultancy, since 1989; *b* 27 March 1961; *s* of Peter and Viveanne Sands; *m* 1983, Carolyn Fletcher; two *s* one *d*. *Educ*: Normanton Boys' Sch.; Stockport Coll. of Technol. Council Mem., Design Council, 2000–10; Vis. Prof. of Innovation, Huddersfield Univ., 2014–. Former Mem., Arts Council Yorkshire. Trustee, Royal Armouries, 2018–. Regular speaker at internat. confs on design worldwide. FRSA (Council Mem., 1997–2000). Hon. DSc Huddersfield, 2002. *Publications*: regular contribs to design jls and media. *Recreation*: long-suffering Derby County supporter. *Address*: Elmwood, 105 Water Lane, Leeds LS11 5WD. *Clubs*: Groucho; Moortown Golf, Pannal Golf, Gullane Golf.

**SANDS, Peter Alexander;** Executive Director, Global Fund to Fight AIDS, Tuberculosis and Malaria, since 2018; *b* 8 Jan. 1962; *s* of Martin and Susan Sands; *m* 1989, Mary Elizabeth, (Betsy), Tobin; one *s* three *d*. *Educ*: Brasenose Coll., Oxford (BA PPE); Kennedy Sch. of Govt, Harvard Univ. (MPA). Asst Desk Officer for Afghanistan and Pakistan, and Desk Officer for Libya, FCO, 1984–86; McKinsey & Co.: Associate, 1988–96; Principal, 1996–2000; Dir, 2000–02; Gp Finance Dir, 2002–06, Gp CEO, 2006–15, Standard Chartered plc. Lead non-exec. Dir, DoH, 2011–17. Res. Fellow, Mossavar-Rahmani Center for Business and Govt, Harvard Kennedy Sch., Harvard Univ. (Sen. Fellow, 2015). Chm., Commn on Global Health Risk Framework, Nat. Acad. of Medicine, Washington, 2015–. *Recreations*: reading, music, riding, football.

**SANDS, Prof. Philippe Joseph;** QC 2003; Professor of Laws, and Director, Centre on International Courts and Tribunals, University College London, since 2002; *b* 17 Oct. 1960; *s* of Alan Sands and Ruth (*née* Buchholz); *m* 1993, Natalia Schiffrin; one *s* two *d*. *Educ*: Corpus Christi Coll., Cambridge (BA 1982; LLM 1983). Res. Fellow, St Catharine's Coll., Cambridge, 1984–88; called to the Bar, Middle Temple, 1985, Bencher, 2009; Lectr, Faculty of Law, KCL, 1988–92; Lectr, then Reader, subseq. Prof. of Internat. Law, SOAS, 1993–2001. *Publications*: Chernobyl: law and communication, 1988; (ed and contrib.) Greening International Law, 1993; Principles of International Environmental Law, 1995, 4th edn 2017; Manual of International Courts and Tribunals, 1999, 2nd edn 2010; (jtly) Bowett's Law of International Institutions, 6th edn 2009; From Nuremburg to The Hague, 2003; Lawless World, 2005; Torture Team: deception, cruelty and the compromise of law, 2008; East West Street: on the origins of genocide and crimes against humanity, 2016 (Non-Fiction Book of Year, British Book Awards, 2017); City of Lions, 2016. *Address*: Matrix Chambers, Gray's Inn, WC1R 5LN. *T*: (020) 7404 3447, *Fax*: (020) 7404 3448. *E*: philippesands@matrixlaw.co.uk.

**SANDS, Sir Roger (Blakemore),** KCB 2006; Clerk and Chief Executive of the House of Commons, 2003–06; *b* 6 May 1942; *s* of late Thomas Blakemore Sands and Edith Malyon (Betty) Sands (*née* Waldram); *m* 1966, Jennifer Ann Cattell; one *d* (and one *d* decd). *Educ*: University Coll. Sch., Hampstead; Oriel Coll., Oxford (scholar; MA LitHum). A Clerk, House of Commons, 1965–2006; Sec. to H of C Commn and Clerk to H of C (Services) Cttee, 1985–87; Clerk of Overseas Office, 1987–91; Clerk of Select Cttees and Registrar of Members' Interests, 1991–94; Clerk of Public Bills, 1994–97; Clerk of Legislation, 1998–2001; Clerk Asst, 2001–02. Chm., Study of Parlt Group, 1993–95. Chm., Standards Cttee, Mid Sussex DC, 2007–12; ind. advr on standards matters, 2012–16. Ind. Mem., UK Public Affairs Council, 2010–14. *Recreations*: listening to music, walking, incompetent golf. *Address*: No 4 (Ashurst Suite), Woodbury House, Lewes Road, East Grinstead, W Sussex RH19 3UD. *T*: (01342) 315118. *Club*: Holtye Golf.

**SANDS SMITH, David,** CBE 2002; development administrator; *b* 19 April 1943; *s* of late Arthur S. Smith and Eileen Annie Smith; *m* 1966, Veronica Harris; one *s* one *d*. *Educ*: Brighton Coll. of Technology, Dept of Technical Co-operation, 1963–71. 2nd Sec., British High Commn, Kuala Lumpur, 1971–75; Overseas Development Administration: Principal, European Community Dept, 1975–80; Zimbabwe Desk, 1980–85; Asst Head, 1985–88, Head, 1988–90, European Community Dept; Head, British Develt Div. in Eastern Africa, 1990–93; UK Perm. Rep., FAO, World Food Programme and IFAD, 1993–97; Head: Procurement, Appts and NGOs Dept, DFID, 1997–99; Develt Policy Dept, DFID, 1999–2001. Consultant to FAO, 2003–06. Trustee, Sightsavers Internat., 2006–11.

**SANDWICH, 11th Earl of,** *cr* 1660; John Edward Hollister Montagu; Viscount Hinchingbrooke and Baron Montagu of St Neots, 1660; editor and researcher; *b* 11 April 1943; *er s* of (Alexander) Victor (Edward Paulet) Montagu (who disclaimed his peerages for life) and Rosemary Peto; *S* father, 1995; *m* 1968, Caroline, *o d* of late Canon P. E. C. Hayman, Beaminster, Dorset; two *s* one *d*. *Educ*: Eton; Trinity College, Cambridge. Inf. Officer, 1974–85, Res. Officer, 1985–86, Mem., Bd, 1999–2004, Christian Aid; Editor, Save the Children Fund, 1987–92; Consultant, CARE Britain, 1987–93; Mem. Council, Anti-Slavery Internat., 1997–2006. Chm., Britain Afghanistan Trust, 1995–2000; Trustee, TSW Telethon Trust, 1987–91; Gov. Beaminster Sch., 1996–2004. Pres., Earl of Sandwich, 2001–. Jt Administrator, Mapperton Estate, 1982–. Crossbencher, H of L, 1995–; elected Mem., H of L, 1999; Member: Information Cttee, 2001–04; Constitution Cttee, 2004–06; Ind. Asylum Commn, 2006–08; EU Sub-Cttee E, 2009–13; EU Select Cttee, 2010–15; EU Sub-Cttee C, 2013–15 and 2019–. Mem., Adv. Panel, British Coll., Kathmandu, 2012–. Pres., Samuel Pepys Club, 1985–. *Publications*: The Book of the World, 1971; Prospects for Africa's Children, 1990; Children at Crisis Point, 1992; (ed jtly) Hinch: a celebration of Viscount Hinchingbrooke, MP 1906–1995, 1997; (ed) Rosemary Peto Illustrated Letters, 2009; Sandwich Man, 2015; Mapperton (guidebook), 2018. *Heir*: *s* Viscount Hinchingbrooke, *qv*. *Address*: House of Lords, SW1A 0PW.

**SANDYS, Laura Jane;** Chief Executive Officer, Challenging Ideas, since 2017; *b* 5 June 1964; *d* of Baron Duncan-Sandys, CH, PC and of Marie-Claire (*née* Schmitt); *m* 2007, Dr Randolph Kent. *Educ*: Univ. of Cambridge (MSt Internat. Relns 2003). Founded and sold two companies specialising in communications and mktg, 1993–99; led Parly Unit, Consumers' Assoc., 1986–87; former Sen. Research Associate, Centre for Defence Studies, KCL; former journalist and commentator. Vis. Sen. Fellow, KCL, 2014–; Mem., Carbon Capture and Storage Adv. Gp, Imperial Coll. London, 2012–. MP (C) S Thanet, 2010–15. PPS to Minister for Energy and Climate Change, 2012–13. Member: Energy and Climate Change Select Cttee, 2010–12; Jt Cttee on Draft H of L Reform Bill, 2011–12; Eur. Main Team; Chairman: All-Party Parly Gp for Epilepsy; All-Party Gp for Civic Voice; Vice Chm., All-Party Parly Gp for Carers. Co-Chair, Justice and Envmt Commn, IPPR. Member: Govt's Cost of Energy Rev., 2017; Carbon Capture, Utilisation and Storage Council and Taskforce, 2017–; Chair, Govt's Energy System Data Taskforce. Chair, Eur. Movt, 2015–16. Ind. Dir, SGN, 2018–. Co-Founder, Powerful Women Gp, 2014; Founder, Food Foundn, 2014 (Dep. Chair, 2017–); Dep. Chair, Food Standards Agency Bd, 2017–19. Former Chm., OpenDemocracy.net; former Dep. Chm., Civic Trust; former Trustee, Open Univ.

**SANÉ, Pierre Gabriel;** Founder and President, Imagine Africa Institute, 2010; *b* 7 May 1948; *s* of Nicolas Sané and Therese Carvalho; *m* 1981, Ndeye Sow; one *s* one *d*. *Educ*: London Sch. of Econs and Pol Sci. (MSc in Public Admin and Public Policy); Ecole Supérieure de Commerce, Bordeaux (MBA); Carleton Univ., Canada (doctoral studies in pol scis). Regl Dir, Internat. Develt Research Centre, Ottawa, Canada, 1978–92; Sec.-Gen., Amnesty Internat., 1992–2001; Asst Dir-Gen. for Social and Human Scis, UNESCO, 2001–10; Mem., Bd of Dirs, West Africa Inst.

**SANGHERA, Jasvinder,** CBE 2013; Founder and Chief Executive Officer, Karma Nirvana, since 1993; *b* Derby, 28 Sept. 1965; *d* of Chanan Singh and Jagir Kaur; marr. diss. 1998; one *s* two *d*; partner, Jonathan Agyeman. *Educ*: Littleover Sch., Derby; Univ. of Derby (BA 1st Cl. Hons Social and Cultural Studies). Non-exec. Dir, Derby PCT, 1998–2006. Ind. Mem., Derbys Police Authy, 2003–07. Expert witness to courts on forced marriages and honour-based violence, 2009–; Chair, Domestic Homicide Reviews, 2004–17. Mem., RSA. Hon. Mem., Rotary Amber Valley, 2014. Paul Harris Fellow, Rotary Internat., 2014. DUniv Derby, 2009; Hon. LLD De Montfort, 2018. Women of the Year Window to the World Award, 2007; Pride of Britain Award, 2009; Ultimate Woman of Year, Cosmopolitan mag., 2011; Global Punjabi Award, Global Punjabi Soc., 2012; Legal Campaigner of Year, Soc. of Asian Lawyers, 2014. *Publications*: Shame (autobiog.), 2007; Daughters of Shame, 2009; Shame Travels, 2011. *Address*: PO Box 515, Leeds LS6 9DW. *E*: jsa@jasvindersanghera.com. *W*: www.jasvindersanghera.com.

**SANGHERA, Sathnam Singh,** FRSL; writer and columnist, The Times, since 2007; author; *b* Wolverhampton, 12 Oct. 1976; *s* of Jagjit Singh and Surjit Kaur. *Educ*: Wolverhampton Grammar Sch.; Christ's Coll., Cambridge (BA 1st Cl. English Lang. and Lit. 1998; MA). News reporter, specialising in media reporting, UK and USA, 1998–2004, Chief Feature Writer, 2004–06, FT. Trustee and Chm., Creative Access charity, 2005–07. Presenter, TV documentary, The Massacre that Shook the Empire, Channel 4, 2019. FRSL 2016. Hon. DLitt Wolverhampton, 2009. Young Journalist of Year, British Press Awards, 2002; Media Commentator of Year, Editl Intelligence Comment Awards, 2015; Edgar Wallace Trophy, London Press Club Awards, 2017. *Publications*: If You Don't Know Me By Now: a memoir of love, secrets and lies in Wolverhampton, 2009 (pbk edn as The Boy With The Topknot) (Book of Year Award, Mind, 2009) (televised, 2017); Marriage Material: a novel, 2013. *Recreations*: motoring, music, literature. *Address*: The Times, 1 London Bridge Street, SE1 9GF. *E*: sathnam@thetimes.co.uk.

**SANGSTER, Nigel;** QC 1998; a Recorder, since 2000; *s* of Dr H. B. Singh and Irene Singh (*née* Carlisle), JP. *Educ*: Repton; Leeds Univ. (LLB Hons). Called to the Bar, Middle Temple, 1976, Bencher, 2008; criminal defence barrister specialising in fraud cases; Head of

Chambers, St Pauls Chambers, Leeds, 1995–2005; joined 25 Bedford Row, 2005. Leader, North Eastern Circuit, 2017–19. Member: Bar Council, 1994–2004 and 2017–; Criminal Bar Assoc.; Fraud Lawyers Assoc. *Address:* 25 Bedford Row, WC1R 4HD. *T:* (020) 7067 1500. *E:* mail@nigelsangsterqc.com.

**SANIN POSADA, Noemi;** Ambassador of Colombia to the Court of St James's, 1994–95 and 2008–09; *b* Bogotá, 10 June 1949; *d* of Jaime Sanin Echeverri and Noemi Posada de Sanin; one *d. Educ:* Univ. Javeriana, Bogota; postgrad. studies in financial and commercial law. Pres., Colmena, Colombia, 1980–84; Minister of Communications, 1984–86; Pres., Corp. Financiera Colombiana, 1988–90; Ambassador to Venezuela, 1990–91; Minister of Foreign Relns, 1991–94; Fellow, Harvard Univ., 1999–2001; Ambassador to Spain, 2002–08. Presidential candidate, 1998, 2002, 2010. Mem., Peace Commn, Colombia. Hon. Dr: Soka Gakkai Univ. of Japan; Autonoma of Bucaramanga, Colombia. Gran Cruz Extraordinaria, Orden de Boyacá (Colombia); holds numerous foreign decorations, including: Orden de Isabel la Católica, Orden Civil al Merito (Spain); Orden del Sol, 1st Cl. (Peru); Orden de Cruceiro del Sur, 1st Cl. (Brazil). *Recreations:* walking, reading.

**SANKEY, John Anthony,** CMG 1983; PhD; HM Diplomatic Service, retired; Secretary General, Society of London Art Dealers, 1991–96; *b* 8 June 1930; *m* 1958, Gwendoline Putman; two *s* two *d. Educ:* Cardinal Vaughan Sch., Kensington; Peterhouse, Cambridge (Classical Tripos Parts 1 and 2, Class 1; MA); Univ. of Leeds (PhD 2002). 1st (Singapore) Regt, RA (2nd Lieut), 1952. Colonial Office, 1953–61; UK Mission to United Nations, 1961–64; Foreign Office, 1964–68; Guyana, 1968–71; Singapore, 1971–73; NATO Defence Coll., Rome, 1973; Malta, 1973–75; The Hague, 1975–79 (Gov., British Sch. in the Netherlands); FCO, 1979–82; High Comr, Tanzania, 1982–85; UK Perm. Rep. to UN Office, Geneva, 1985–90. Leader, British Govt Delegn to Internat. Red Cross Conf., 1986. Dir, Internat. Art and Antiques Loss Register Ltd, 1993–96. Chm., Tanzania Develt Trust, 1997–2004; Legacies Officer, St Francis Leprosy Guild, 2005–14. Sir Evelyn Wrench Lectr, ESU, 1990. KCHS 2003 (KHS 1996). *Publications:* (contrib.) The United Kingdom—the United Nations, 1990; The Conscience of the World, 1995; (ed) Thomas Brock, Forgotten Sculptor of the Victoria Memorial: a memoir by Frederick Brock, 2012. *Address:* 108 Lancaster Gate, W2 3NW.

**SANKEY, Vernon Louis;** Chairman, Firmenich SA, 2008–13 (Director, since 2005); *b* 9 May 1949; *s* of late Edward Sankey and Marguerite Elizabeth Louise (*née* van Maurik); *m* 1976, Elizabeth, *d* of Tom Knights; three *s* one *d* (of whom one *s* one *d* are twins). *Educ:* Harrow School; Oriel Coll., Oxford (MA Mod. Langs). Joined Reckitt & Colman, 1971: Mgt Trainee, 1971–74; Asst Manager, Finance and Planning, 1974–76; Dir, Planning and Develt, Europe, 1976–78; General Manager, Denmark, 1978–80; PA to Chm. and Chief Exec., 1980–81; Man. Dir, France, 1981–85; Man. Dir, Colman's of Norwich, 1985–89; Chm. and Chief Exec. Officer, Reckitt & Colman Inc., USA, 1989–92; Chief Exec., 1992–99. Chairman: The Really Effective Develt Co. Ltd, 2000–05; Thomson Travel Gp, 2000; Gala Gp Holdings, 2000–03; Photo-Me Internat. plc, 2005–07 (Dir and Dep. Chm., 2000–05); Dep. Chm., Beltpacker plc, 2000–04; non-executive Director: Pearson, 1993–2000; Allied Zurich plc, 1998–2000; Zurich Allied AG, 1998–2000; Zurich Financial Services AG, 2000–12; Cofra AG, 2001–07; Taylor Woodrow plc, 2004–07; Zurich Insurance Co. AG, 2004–12; Atos SE (formerly Atos Origin SA), 2005– (Chm., Audit Cttee, 2014–); Vividas plc, 2005–07. Member: Internat. Adv. Bd, Korn/Ferry Internat., 1994–2005; Adv. Bd, Proudfoot UK, 2000–06; Adv. Bd, GLP LLP, 2005–. Mem. Bd, Grocery Manufacturers of Amer., 1995–99. Member: Listed Cos Adv. Cttee, London Stock Exchange, 1997–99; Bd, Food Standards Agency, 2000–05. FRSA 2000. *Recreations:* fitness, tennis. *Address:* c/o Corporate Affairs, Atos SE, River Ouest, Quai Voltaire, 95877 Bezons, France. *Club:* Leander (Henley).

**SANKEY, William Patrick F.;** *see* Filmer-Sankey.

**SANSOM, Bruce Edward;** freelance ballet coach, repetiteur and teacher; *b* 8 Sept. 1963; *s* of Dr Bernard Sansom and Prudence Sansom. *Educ:* Royal Ballet Sch. Joined Royal Ballet Co., 1982; Soloist, 1985; Principal Dancer, 1987–2000; also danced with San Francisco Ballet Co., 1991–92 season; has danced principal rôles in all major ballets, incl. La Fille Mal Gardée, Swan Lake, Giselle, The Nutcracker, Manon, Sleeping Beauty, La Bayadère, Cinderella, The Dream, Romeo and Juliet, Scènes de Ballet, Manon; leading rôles created for him in a number of ballets including Galanteries, Still Life at the Penguin Café, Pursuit, Piano, Prince of the Pagodas, Tombeaux; Dir, Central Sch. of Ballet, 2006–09; Ballet Master and Asst to Artistic Dir, San Francisco Ballet, 2009–13. Time Out Award for performances with Royal Ballet, 1990. *Recreations:* opera, contemporary art, Parson Jack Russell terriers, working Cocker Spaniels, shooting and farming.

**SANT, Hon. Dr Alfred;** Member (Lab) Malta, European Parliament, since 2014; *b* 28 Feb. 1948; *s* of Joseph and Josephine Sant; one *d. Educ:* Univ. of Malta (BSc, MSc); Inst. Internat. d'Admin Publique, Paris (Dip.); Boston Univ. (MBA); Harvard Univ. (DBA). Res. Fellow, Harvard Business Sch. First Sec., Malta Mission to EEC, Brussels, 1970–75; Man. Dir, Medina Consulting Gp, 1979–80; Dep. Chm., Malta Develt Corp., 1980–82. MP (Lab) Malta, 1987–2013; Leader, Labour Party, 1992–2008; Prime Minister of Malta, 1996–98; Leader of Opposition, 1998–2008. *Publications:* Malta's European Challenge, 1995; Memoires: confessions of a European Maltese, 2003; Malta and the euro, 2012; *novels:* L-Ewwel Weraq tal-Bajtar, 1968; Silg fuq Kemmuna, 1982; Bejgh u Xiri, 1984; La Bidu, La Tmiem, 2001; L-Ghalqa tal-Iskarjota, 2009 (The Iscariot Field, 2011); Bhal f'Dizzjunarju, 2011; George Bush in Malta, 2013; *dramas:* Min hu Evelyn Costa?, 1982; Fid-Dell tal-Katidral, 1994; Qabel Tiftah l-Inkjesta - u drammi ohra, 1999. *Recreations:* listening to classical music, walking. *Address:* 18A Victory Street, B'Kara, Malta.

**SANTANA CARLOS, António Nunes;** Diplomatic Adviser to the Mayor of Lisbon, since 2011; Ambassador of Portugal to the Court of St James's, 2006–10; *b* Lisbon, 20 March 1945; *s* of Victor Santana Carlos and Maria N. C. Santana Carlos; *m* 1982, Maria Pena Escudeiro; one *s. Educ:* Univ. of Lisbon (Soc. and Pol Scis). Joined Foreign Service, 1971, Attaché of Embassy; Third Sec., 1973–74; Second Sec., Tokyo, 1974–76; Hd, Cipher Dept, Foreign Office, 1976–79; First Sec., Dept of Internat. Econ. Orgns, Foreign Office, 1979–82; Perm. Mission of Portugal in Geneva, 1982–86; Minister Counsellor, Portuguese Embassy, Luanda, 1986–90; Dir, Multilateral Affairs Dept, Foreign Office, 1990–93; Minister Plenipotentiary and Dep.-Dir Gen. of Pol and Econ. Affairs, 1993–94; Dir, Office of Econ. Affairs, 1994, Chargé de Mission to the Minister of Foreign Affairs for promotion of Expo 98, Lisbon World Exhibn, 1995; Sen. Rep. to Sino-Portuguese Jt Liaison Gp and Pres., Interministerial Commn on Macau, 1996–2000; rank of Ambassador, 2000; Chargé de Mission to Minister of Foreign Affairs for East Timor Affairs, 2000; Dir-Gen. of Foreign Policy (Pol Dir), 2000–02; Ambassador to the People's Republic of China, 2002–06. Grand Cross, Order of Christ (Portugal); Grand Cross, Order of Merit (Portugal); Grand Officer, Order of Infante Dom Henrique (Portugal); Grand Officer, Order of Wissan Alouite (Morocco); Knight, Order of Rio Branco (Brazil). *Recreations:* golf, sailing, cinema. *Clubs:* Athenæum, Travellers, Royal Automobile; Royal Mid-Surrey Golf.

**SANTER, Jacques;** Chairman, CLT-UFA, 2004–17; Member of the Board, RTL Group, 2004–17; Chairman, UniCredit International Bank, Luxembourg, 2005–15; *b* 18 May 1937; *m* Danièle Binot; two *s. Educ:* Athénée de Luxembourg; Paris Univ.; Strasbourg Univ.; Inst. d'Etudes Politiques, Paris. DenD. Advocate, Luxembourg Court of Appeal, 1961–65; Attaché, Office of Minister of Labour and Social Security, 1963–65; Govt Attaché, 1965–66; Christian Social Party: Parly Sec., 1966–72; Sec.-Gen., 1972–74; Pres., 1974–82; Sec. of State for Cultural and Social Affairs, 1972–74; Mem., Chamber of Deputies, 1974–79; MEP, 1975–79 (a Vice-Pres., 1975–77); Minister of Finance, Labour and Social Security, Luxembourg, 1979–84; Prime Minister of Luxembourg, 1984–95; Pres. of Govt, Minister of State and Minister of Finance, 1984–89; Minister for Cultural Affairs, 1989–94; Pres., EC, 1995–99; MEP (EPP), 1999–2004.

**SANTER, Rt Rev. Mark;** Bishop of Birmingham, 1987–2002; an Hon. Assistant Bishop: Diocese of Worcester, since 2002; Diocese of Birmingham, since 2003; *b* 29 Dec. 1936; *s* of late Rev. Canon Eric Arthur Robert Santer and Phyllis Clare Barlow; *m* 1st, 1964, Henriette Cornelia Weststrate (*d* 1994); one *s* two *d;* 2nd, 1997, Sabine Böhmig Bird. *Educ:* Marlborough Coll.; Queens' Coll., Cambridge (MA; Hon. Fellow, 1991); Westcott House, Cambridge. Deacon, 1963; priest 1964; Asst Curate, Cuddesdon, 1963–67; Tutor, Cuddesdon Theological Coll., 1963–67; Fellow and Dean of Clare Coll., Cambridge, 1967–72 (and Tutor, 1968–72; Hon. Fellow, 1987); Univ. Asst Lectr in Divinity, 1968–72; Principal of Westcott House, Cambridge, 1973–81; Hon. Canon of Winchester Cathedral, 1978–81; Area Bishop of Kensington, 1981–87. Co-Chm., Anglican Roman Catholic Internat. Commn, 1983–98. Hon. DD Birmingham, 1998; DD Lambeth, 1999; DUniv UCE, 2002. *Publications:* (contrib.) The Phenomenon of Christian Belief, 1970; (with M. F. Wiles) Documents in Early Christian Thought, 1975; Their Lord and Ours, 1982; (contrib.) The Church and the State, 1984; (contrib.) Dropping the Bomb, 1985; contrib. Jl of Theological Studies, Ecclesiology, Theology. *Address:* 81 Clarence Road, Birmingham B13 9UH. *T:* (0121) 441 2194.

**SANTOMARCO,** family name of **Baroness King of Bow**.

**SANTOS-NEVES, Carlos Augusto Rego;** Consul-General for Brazil in Porto, 2010; *b* Rio de Janeiro, 26 Jan. 1944; *m* Mary Joan Hershberger; two *s* one *d. Educ:* Colégio Pedro II, Rio de Janeiro; Inst. Rio Branco (Brazilian Diplomatic Acad.) (*summa cum laude;* doctorate); Fundação Getúlio Vargas (MBA Finance); Columbia Univ. (postgrad. pol sci.). Ministry of External Affairs, Brazil: Asst to Foreign Minister, 1977–79; COS to Sec. Gen., 1985–88; Consul Gen., NY, 1988–92; Ambassador: to Mexico, 1992–96; (non-resident) to Belize, 1995–96; to Canada, 1996–99; Sec., Policy Planning, 1999–2001; Consul Gen., Houston, 2001–03; Ambassador: to Russian Fedn, 2003–08; (non-resident) to Belarus, Georgia, Turkmenistan and Uzbekistan, 2003–08 and Kazakhstan, 2003–06; to the Court of St James's, 2008–10. Order of Rio Branco, Order of the Navy, Order of the Army, Order of the Air Force (Brazil); holds numerous foreign decorations incl. Chevalier, Légion d'Honneur, Ordre du Mérite (France); Simon Bolívar, Orden de Francisco de Miranda (Venezuela).

**SANTS, Sir Hector (William Hepburn),** Kt 2013; Chairman, Julius Baer International, 2015–18; Chair, Money and Pensions Service, since 2018; *b* 15 Dec. 1955; *s* of Hector John Sants and late Elsie Ann Watt Sants (*née* Hepburn); *m* 1987, Caroline Jane Mackenzie; three *s. Educ:* Clifton Coll.; Corpus Christi Coll., Oxford (MA PPP). Phillips & Drew, stockbrokers: joined as grad. trainee res., 1977; Partner, 1984–89; Hd, European Equities, Union Bank of Switzerland, 1989–97; Hd, Internat. Equities, Donaldson, Lufkin and Jenrette, 1997–2000; European Chief Exec., Credit Suisse First Boston, 2001–04; Man. Dir, Wholesale and Instnl Mkts, 2004–07, Chief Exec., 2007–12, FSA; Hd of Compliance and Govt Affairs, and Mem., Gp Exec. Cttee, Barclays Bank, 2013–14; Chief Advr to Abu Dhabi Global Market, 2014–15; Vice Chm., Oliver Wyman, 2015–17. Non-executive Director: London Stock Exchange, 1996–2001; LCH.Clearnet, 2009–11. Mem., Interim Financial Policy Cttee, Bank of England, 2011–12. Chm., Archbp's Task Gp on credit and savings, 2014–17. Chm. Bd, Saïd Business Sch., Oxford Univ., 2010–13 (Mem., Adv. Bd, 2001–10); Mem. Bd, Nuffield Orthopaedic Centre, 2002–07. Chm., Step Change, 2015–19.

**SAPERSTEIN, Rabbi Prof. Marc Eli,** PhD; Professor of Jewish History and Homiletics, Leo Baeck College, London, since 2011 (Principal, 2006–11); *b* 5 Sept. 1944; *s* of Harold Irving Saperstein and Marcia Belle Saperstein (*née* Rosenblum); *m* 2007, Tamar de Vries Winter; two *d* from former marriage. *Educ:* Harvard Coll. (AB English Lit. 1966); Hebrew Univ. of Jerusalem (MA Jewish Hist. 1971); Hebrew Union Coll.-Jewish Inst. of Religion, NY (MA 1972); Harvard Grad. Sch. of Arts and Scis (PhD Jewish Hist., Lit. and Thought 1977). Ordained Rabbi, 1972; Lectr on Hebrew Lit., Harvard Faculty of Arts and Scis, 1977–79; Asst Prof. of Jewish Studies, 1979–83, Associate Prof. of Jewish Studies, 1983–86, Harvard Divinity Sch.; Goldstein Prof. of Jewish Hist. and Thought, Washington Univ. in St Louis, 1986–97; Charles E. Smith Prof. of Jewish Hist. and Dir of Prog. in Judaic Studies, George Washington Univ., 1997–2006. Visiting Professor: Columbia Univ., 1980; Univ. of Pennsylvania, 1995; Revel Grad. Sch., Yeshiva Univ., 2002; KCL, 2009–; Harvard, 2012; Yale, 2013; Visiting Fellow: Inst. for Advanced Studies, Jerusalem, 1989; Center for Advanced Judaic Studies, Univ. of Pennsylvania, 1995–96; Centre for Jewish-Christian Relns, Cambridge, 2002; Harvard Center for Jewish Studies, 2005. Mem. Bd of Dirs, Assoc. for Jewish Studies, 1983–99; Vice Pres., Amer. Acad. for Jewish Res., 2004–06. Book Rev. Ed., Assoc. for Jewish Studies Rev., 1997–2002. *Publications:* Decoding the Rabbis: a thirteenth-century commentary on the Aggadah, 1980; Jewish Preaching 1200–1800, 1980; Moments of Crisis in Jewish-Christian Relations, 1989; Your Voice Like a Ram's Horn: themes and texts in traditional Jewish preaching, 1996; Exile in Amsterdam: Saul Levi Morteira's sermons to a congregation of New Jews, 2005; Jewish Preaching in Times of War 1800–2001, 2008; Leadership and Conflict: tensions in medieval Jewish history and culture, 2014; editor: Essential Papers on Messianic Movements and Personalities in Jewish History, 1992; Harold I. Saperstein: Witness from the Pulpit: topical sermons 1933–1980, 2000; Agony in the Pulpit: Jewish preaching in response to Nazi persecution and mass murder, 1933–1945, 2018; articles and reviews on Jewish hist., lit. and thought. *Recreation:* classical piano. *Address:* 21 Owlstone Road, Cambridge CB3 9JH. *T:* (01223) 312082. *E:* msaper@gwu.edu.

**SAPHIR, Nicholas Peter George;** Chairman: OMSCo, The Organic Milk Suppliers Co-operative, since 2003; Epicore Health Ltd, since 2015; *b* 30 Nov. 1944; *s* of Emanuel Saphir and Ann (*née* Belikoff); *m* 1971, Ena Bodin; one *s. Educ:* City of London Sch.; Manchester Univ. (LLB Hons). Called to the Bar, Lincoln's Inn, 1967. Chm., Hunter Saphir, 1987–97; Director: Bodin & Nielsen Ltd, 1975–; Albert Fisher Gp PLC, 1993–97; City Food Centres Ltd, 2011–16; Chairman: Coressence, 2006–14; New Israel Fund, 2009–14; non-executive Director: Dairy Crest Ltd, 1987–93; San Miguel SA (Argentina), 1993–98, 2001–07. Chairman: CCAHC, 1980–83; Agricultural Forum, 2001–04; Rural Revival, 2004–07; Founder Chm., Food From Britain, 1983–87; Mem., Food and Drink EDC, 1984–87; Chm., British Israel Chamber of Commerce, 1991–94. Pres., Fresh Produce Consortium, 1997–2000. *Recreation:* sailing. *Address:* Combe Manor Farm, Coombe Lane, Wadhurst, E Sussex TN5 6NU. *T:* (01892) 785111. *Clubs:* Farmers; Royal Cinque Ports Yacht.

**SAPIN, Michel Marie;** Deputy (Soc.) for Indre, National Assembly, France, 2007–17; Minister of Finance, France, 2014–17; Minister of the Economy, 2016–17; *b* 9 April 1952; *m* 1982, Yolande Millan (marr. diss.); three *s. Educ:* Ecole Normale Supérieure de la rue d'Ulm (MA Hist., post-grad. degree Geog.); Institut d'Etudes Politiques de Paris; Ecole

Nationale d'Administration. Joined Socialist Party, 1975; National Assembly: Socialist Deputy of the Indre, 1981–86, of Hauts-de-Seine, 1986–91; Sec., 1983–84; Vice-Pres., 1984–85, 1988; Vice-Chm., Socialist Gp, 1987–88; Pres., Commn of Law, 1988–91. Minister-Delegate of Justice, 1991–92; Minister of the Economy and Finance, 1992–93, for the Civil Service and Admin. Reform, 2000–02; Minister of Labour, Employment and Social Dialogue, 2012–14. Mem., Monetary Policy Council, Bank of France, 1994–95. City Cllr, Nanterre, 1989–94; Regl Cllr, Ile de France, 1992–94; Gen. Cllr of the Indre, 1998–2004; Pres., 1998–2000, 2004–07, Vice-Pres., 2000–01, Centre Regl Council. Mayor, Argenton-sur-Creuse (Indre), 1995–2014. First Vice-Pres., Assoc. of Regions of France, 1998–2000. *Address*: 9 bis rue Dupertuis, 36200 Argenton-sur-Creuse, France.

SAPNARA, Khatun; Her Honour Judge Sapnara; a Circuit Judge, since 2014; *b* Sylhet, Bangladesh, 29 April 1967; *d* of Mimbor Ali and Sufia Khanam; *m* 2000, Simon Stanley, JP; two *s*. *Educ*: Chadwell Heath Sch., Essex; London Sch. of Econs and Pol Sci. (LLB Hons); Inns of Court Sch. of Law. Called to the Bar, Middle Temple, 1990, Bencher, 2015; in practice as barrister, specialising in family law, 1990–2014; a Recorder, 2006–14. Mem., Family Justice Council, 2004–10. Chair, Ashiana Network, 2003–14. Mem. Bd, Rights of Women, 2009–14. Gov., Chadwell Heath Sch., 1992–2008. Hon. LLD RHUL, 2018. *Publications*: (contrib.) Re-Rooted Lives, 2007; (contrib.) Forced Marriage: social justice and human rights, 2011. *Recreations*: foreign travel, cooking and world cuisine, antique Indian textiles. *Address*: East London Family Court, 11 Westferry Circus, Canary Wharf, E14 8RP.

SAPSTEAD, Nicole Zoe Selina; Chief Executive, UK Anti-Doping, since 2015; *b* London, 18 April 1974; *d* of Gordon and Jill Sapstead; one *s*. *Educ*: Univ. of West of England (LLB Hons). Asst to Dir, then Legal Associate, Drug Control Centre, KCL, 2001–04; UK Sport: Policy Advr, Drug-Free Sport, 2004–05; Prog. Manager, 2006–07; Compliance Manager, 2007–09; Hd of Ops, 2009; Dir of Ops, UK Anti-Doping, 2010–15. *Recreations*: cinema, cooking, reading, family, fitness. *Address*: UK Anti-Doping, Fleetbank House, 2–6 Salisbury Square, EC4Y 8AE. *T*: (020) 7842 3467. *E*: nicole.sapstead@ukad.org.uk.

SARDAR, Ziauddin; writer, critic, broadcaster; Director, Center for Postnormal Policy and Futures Studies, since 2014; *b* 31 Oct. 1951; *s* of late Salahuddin Sardar and of Hamida Bagum; *m* 1978, Saliha Basit; two *s* one *d*. *Educ*: Brooke House Sec. Sch., London; City Univ., London (BSc Hons 1974, MSc Inf. Sci. 1975). Inf. Consultant, Hajj Res. Centre, King Abdul Aziz Univ., Jeddah, 1975–79; Reporter, LWT, 1981–83; Dir, Centre for Policy and Future Studies, East West Univ., Chicago, 1985–88; Advr to Dep. Prime Minister of Malaysia, 1988–97. Member: Commn for Equality and Human Rights, 2006–09; Interim Nat. Security Forum, 2009–. Prof. of Law and Society, Middlesex Univ., 2011–14. Editor, Futures, 1997–2012; Co-editor: Third Text, 1999–2006; Critical Muslim, 2012–. *Publications*: Science, Technology and Development in the Muslim World, 1977; (jtly) Hajj Studies, 1978; Muhammad: aspects of his biography, 1978; Science Policy and Developing Countries, 1978; Islam: outline of a classification scheme, 1979; The Future of Muslim Civilization, 1979, 1987; Science and Technology in the Middle East, 1982; (ed) Touch of Midas: science values and environment in Islam and the West, 1984, 1999; Islamic Futures: the shape of ideas to come, 1986; (ed) The Revenge of Athena: science, exploitation and the Third World, 1988; Information and the Muslim World: a strategy for the twenty-first century, 1988; (ed) Building Information Systems in the Islamic World, 1988; (ed) An Early Crescent, 1989; Explorations in Islamic Science, 1989; (jtly) Distorted Imagination: lessons from the Rushdie affair, 1990; (jtly) Christian-Muslim Relations: yesterday, today, tomorrow, 1991; (ed) How We Know, 1991; Introducing Islam, 1992; Barbaric Others, 1993; (ed jtly) Muslim Minorities in the West, 1995; (ed jtly) Cyberfutures, 1996; Postmodernism and the Other, 1998; (ed) Futures Studies; Orientalism, 1999; Introducing Muhammad, 1999; Introducing Mathematics, 1999; The Consumption of Kuala Lumpur, 2000; Thomas Kuhn and the Science Wars, 2000; Introducing Media Studies, 2000; Introducing Chaos, 2001; Introducing Cultural Studies, 2001; (jtly) Introducing Learning and Memory, 2002; Introducing Science, 2002; Aliens R Us, 2002; The A to Z of Postmodern Life, 2002; (jtly) Why Do People Hate America?, 2002; (ed jtly) The "Third Text" Reader on Art, Culture and Theory, 2002; (jtly) The No-Nonsense Guide to Islam, 2003; Islam, Postmodernism and other Futures, 2003; Desperately Seeking Paradise, 2004; (jtly) American Dream, Global Nightmare, 2004; (jtly) What is British?, 2004; American Terminator: myths, movies and global power, 2004; How Do We Know?: reading Ziauddin Sardar on Islam, science and cultural relations, 2005; What Do Muslims Believe?, 2006; Balti Britain: a journey through the British Asian experience, 2008; (jtly) Will America Change?, 2008; Reading the Qur'an, 2011; Muhammad: all that matters, 2012; (ed jtly) Muslims in Britain: making social and political space, 2012; Future: all that matters, 2013; Mecca: the Sacred City, 2014; Islam Beyond Violent Jihadis, 2016; (with J. Henzell-Thomas) Rethinking Reform in Higher Education: from Islamization to the integration of Knowledge, 2017 (ed) The Postnormal Times Reader, 2017; A Person of Pakistani Origins, 2018. *Recreation*: promoting critical thought and engaging with young scholars and thinkers. *E*: zsardar51@gmail.com. *Club*: Athenæum.

SARGEANT, Rt Rev. Frank Pilkington; an Hon. Assistant Bishop, Diocese of Manchester, since 1999; *b* 12 Sept. 1932; *s* of John Stanley and Grace Sargeant; *m* 1958, Sally Jeanette McDermott; three *s* two *d*. *Educ*: Boston Grammar School; Durham Univ., St John's Coll. and Cranmer Hall (BA, Dip Theol); Nottingham Univ. (Diploma in Adult Education). National Service Commission, RA (20th Field Regt), 1955–57. Assistant Curate: Gainsborough Parish Church, 1958–62; Grimsby Parish Church, and Priest-in-Charge of St Martin's, Grimsby, 1962–67; Vicar of North Hykeham and Rector of South Hykeham, 1967–73; Residentiary Canon, Bradford Cathedral, 1973–77; Archdeacon of Bradford, 1977–84; Bishop Suffragan of Stockport, 1984–94; head of the Archbishop of Canterbury's staff (with title of Bishop at Lambeth), 1994–99, and Asst Bishop, dio. of Canterbury, 1995–99; retired 1999. Hon. Asst Bishop, Dio. in Europe, 1999–2008. Pres., Actors' Church Union, 1995–2007; Chm., Retired Clergy Assoc., 2003–07. *Publications*: A Complete Parish Priest: Peter Green 1871–1961, 2011; Dispatches from the Home Front, 2015. *Address*: 32 Brotherton Drive, Trinity Gardens, Salford M3 6BH. *T*: (0161) 839 7045. *E*: frankpsargeant68@gmail.com.

SARGEANT, Jack; Member (Lab) Alyn and Deeside, National Assembly for Wales, since 2018; *b* Bodelwyddan, Wales, 9 April 1994; *s* of late Carl Sargeant and of Bernie Sargeant. *Educ*: Wrexham Glyndwr Univ. (BEng Industrial Engrg 2016). Apprentice mechanical engr, 2011–15, Planning Engr, 2015–16, DRB Gp; Develt Engr, Atlas Copco, 2016–18. *Recreations*: music, football, travel. *Address*: National Assembly for Wales, Cardiff CF99 1NA.

SARGENT, Anthony; *see* Sargent, D. A.

SARGENT, Dick; *see* Sargent, J. R.

SARGENT, (Donald) Anthony, CBE 2013; Chief Executive Officer, Luminato Festival, Toronto, since 2015; *b* 18 Dec. 1949; *s* of Sir (Sidney) Donald Sargent, KBE, CB and Dorothy Mary (*née* Raven); *m* 1st, 1978, Sara Gilford (marr. diss.); 2nd, 1986, Caroline Gant; one *d*. *Educ*: King's Sch., Canterbury; Oriel Coll., Oxford (Open Exhibnr; MA Hons PPE); Magdalen Coll., Oxford (Lay Clerk); Christ Church, Oxford (Choral Schol.). Various prodn and presentation posts, BBC Radio and TV, 1974–86 (Manager, BBC Concert Planning, 1982–86); Artistic Projects Dir, S Bank Centre, London, 1986–89; Hd of Arts, Birmingham CC, 1989–99; Partnerships and Prog. Develt Manager, BBC Music Live, 1999–2000; Founding Gen. Dir, Sage Gateshead (formerly Music Centre Gateshead) and North Music Trust, 2000–15. Chairman: NewcastleGateshead Cultural Venues, 2009–12; Fest. of the NE, 2011–13. Member, Board: Internat. Soc. for Performing Arts, 2005–17 (Chm., 2013–16); Toronto Arts Council, 2015–; Council for Canadian American Relns, 2015–. Freeman, Bor. of Gateshead, 2015. FRSA 1999. Hon. Fellow: Birmingham Conservatoire, 1999; Sunderland Univ., 2005. Hon. DMus Newcastle, 2015. Hotspur Award, Northumbrian Assoc., 2008. *Publications*: (with K. Zeserson) Beginning at the Beginning: the creativity gap, 2007; contrib. miscellaneous periodical and professional articles, incl. to Eur. Jl Cultural Policy, and reports. *Recreations*: problem solving, fresh air, laughing. *Address*: (home) 99 Stafford Street, Toronto, ON M6J 3R1, Canada; 6 Winchester Terrace, Summerhill Square, Newcastle upon Tyne NE4 6EH; Luminato Festival, 180 Shaw Street, Suite 301, Toronto, ON M6J 2W5, Canada.

SARGENT, John Richard, (Dick); *b* 22 March 1925; *s* of John Philip Sargent and Ruth (*née* Taunton); *m* 1st, 1949, Anne Elizabeth Haigh (marr. diss. 1980; *d* 2012); one *s* two *d*; 2nd, 1980, Hester Mary Campbell (*d* 2004). *Educ*: Dragon Sch., Oxford; Rugby Sch.; Christ Church, Oxford (MA). Fellow and Lectr in Econs, Worcester Coll., Oxford, 1951–62; Econ. Consultant, HM Treasury and DEA, 1963–65; Prof. of Econs, Univ. of Warwick, 1965–73 (Pro-Vice-Chancellor, 1971–72), Hon. Prof., 1974–81 and 2007–. Vis. Prof. of Econs, LSE, 1981–82; Gp Economic Adviser, Midland Bank Ltd, 1974–84; Houblon-Norman Res. Fellow, Bank of England, 1984–85. Member: Doctors and Dentists Rev. Body, 1972–75; Armed Forces Pay Rev. Body, 1972–86; Channel Tunnel Adv. Gp, 1974–75; SSRC, 1980–85; Pharmacists Review Panel, 1986–; Pres., Société Universitaire Européenne de Recherches Financières, 1985–88. Editor, Midland Bank Rev., 1974–84. *Publications*: British Transport Policy, 1958; (ed with R. C. O. Matthews) Contemporary Problems of Economic Policy, 1983; To Full Employment: the Keynesian Experience and After, 2007; articles in various economic jls, and in vols of conf. papers etc. *Recreation*: work. *Address*: 1 Carlton Court, Knole Road, Bexhill-on-Sea, E Sussex TN40 1LG. *T*: (01424) 214849. *Club*: Reform.

SARGENT, Robert John; independent consulting hydrologist, since 2012; *b* Hove, Sussex, 17 Oct. 1952; *s* of Reginald and Patricia Sargent; *m* 1978, Elizabeth Mutch; two *d*. *Educ*: Hove Grammar Sch.; Univ. of Lancaster (BA 1974); Internat. Mgt Coll. (MBA 1985). CSci 2005; CEnv 2005. Chief Hydrologist, Forth River Bd, 1976–96; Hd, Envmtl Services, SEPA, 1996–2003; Principal Hydrologist, Marcus Hodges Envmt, 2003–04; Dir, Water Envmt, Hyder Consulting, 2005–11; Water Envmt Dir, Envmtl Gain Ltd, 2011–12. *Publications*: book chapters; contrib. papers to learned jls. *Recreations*: running, cycling, gardening and plant propagation. *Address*: Brook House, Mead Lane, Wanstrow, Som BA4 4TF. *E*: bobjsargent@msn.com.

SARGENT, Prof. Thomas John, PhD; Senior Fellow, Hoover Institution, Stanford University, since 1987; William R. Berkley Professor of Economics and Business, Leonard W. Stern School of Business, New York University, since 2002; *b* Pasadena, Calif, 19 July 1943; *s* of Charles R. Sargent; *m* Carolyn. *Educ*: Univ. of Calif, Berkeley (BA Econs 1964); Harvard Univ. (PhD Econs 1968). First Lieut, then Captain, US Army, 1968–69. Associate Prof. of Econs, Univ. of Pennsylvania, 1970–71; Associate Prof. of Econs, 1971–75, Prof. of Econs, 1975–87, Univ. of Minnesota; David Rockefeller Prof. of Econs, Univ. of Chicago, 1991–98; Donald Lucas Prof. of Econs, Stanford Univ., 1998–2002. Res. Associate, Nat. Bureau of Econ. Res., 1970–73, 1979–. Advr, Fed. Reserve Bank of Minneapolis, 1971–87. President: Soc. for Econ. Dynamics and Control, 1989–92; Amer. Econ. Assoc., 2007. Fellow: Econometric Soc., 1976 (Pres., 2005); NAS, 1983; Amer. Acad. Arts and Scis, 1983. Corresp. FBA, 2011. Mary Elizabeth Morgan Prize for Excellence in Econs, Univ. of Chicago, 1979; Erwin Nemmers Prize for Econs, Northwestern Univ., 1996; (jtly) Nobel Prize in Econ. Scis, 2011; NAS Award for Scientific Reviewing, 2011. *Publications*: (with N. Wallace) Rational Expectations and the Theory of Economic Policy, 1975, 3rd edn 2013; Macroeconomic Theory, 1979, 2nd edn 1987; (ed with R. Lucas) Rational Expectations and Econometric Practice, 1981; (ed) Energy, Foresight and Strategy, 1985; Rational Expectations and Inflation, 1986, 3rd edn 2013; Dynamic Macroeconomic Theory, 1987; Bounded Rationality in Macroeconomics, 1993; The Conquest of American Inflation, 1999; (with F. Velde) The Big Problem of Small Change, 2002; (with L. Ljungqvist) Recursive Macroeconomic Theory, 2004, 3rd edn 2012; (with L. P. Hansen) Robustness, 2008; (with L. P. Hansen) Recursive Models of Dynamic Linear Economies, 2013. *Address*: Department of Economics, New York University, 19 W Fourth Street, New York, NY 10012–1119, USA.

SARIN, Arun, Hon. KBE 2010; Chief Executive, Vodafone plc, 2003–08; *b* 21 Oct. 1954; *s* of Lt Col Krishan Sarin and Romilla Sarin; *m* 1980, Rummi Anand; one *s* one *d*. *Educ*: Indian Inst. of Technol., Kharagpur (BS Engrg); Univ. of California, Berkeley (MS Engrg; MBA). Various positions, Pacific Telesis Gp Inc., 1984–94; Vice Pres., Human Resources, Corporate Strategy and Develt, AirTouch Communications, 1994–95; Pres. and Chief Exec., AirTouch Internat., 1995–97; Pres. and Chief Operating Officer, AirTouch Communications, 1997–99; Chief Executive Officer: US/Asia Pacific Reg., Vodafone AirTouch, 1999–2000; Infospace, 2000; Accel-KKR Telecom, 2001–03. Non-executive Director: Cisco Systems Inc., 1998–2003 and 2009–; Bank of England, 2005–09; Safeway Inc., 2009–15; Aricent Inc., 2010–14; Accenture LLP, 2015–; Sen. Advr, KKR, 2009–14. *Recreations*: golf, tennis, running.

SARKAR, Bidesh; Director, Finance and Business Services, Department for International Trade, since 2019; *b* Leicester, 1 June 1969; *s* of Bibhuti Kumar Sarkar and Jharna Sarkar; *m* 1995, Emma Louise; two *s* one *d*. *Educ*: Univ. of Sussex (BSc Hons Maths and Econs); INSEAD (MBA). ACA 1994. Kimberly-Clark Europe, 1997–2005, Divl Finance Dir, 2003–05; Gp Finance Dir, Plan Internat., 2005–07; Chief Financial Officer, British Council, 2007–13; Gp Finance Dir, Academies Enterprise Trust, 2015–17; Dir, New Educn Ventures, Blenheim Chalcot, 2017–18. Dir and Chm., Pinkham Way Alliance, 2011–12. Gov., Hollickwood Primary Sch., N London, 2010–16. *Recreations*: running (London Marathon, 2009, 2014, 2016, Paris Marathon, 2015, Leicester Marathon, 2017), yoga, cycling.

SARKIS, Angela Marie, CBE 2000; Member, Youth Justice Board, 2009–15; *b* 6 Jan. 1955; *d* of Rupert Sadler and Hazel Sadler (*née* McDonald); *m* 1980, Edward Tacvor Sarkis; one *s* one *d*. *Educ*: Cottesmore Sch., Nottingham; Clarendon Coll. of Further Educn, Nottingham; Leeds Univ. (BA Theol./Sociol.); Leicester Univ. (Dip. Social Work and CQSW). Probation Officer, Middx Probation Service, 1979–89; Unit Manager, Brent Family Services Unit, 1989–91; Asst Dir, Intermediate Treatment Fund, 1991–93; Dir, DIVERT Trust, 1993–96; Chief Exec., Church Urban Fund, 1996–2001; a Governor, BBC, 2002–06; Nat. Sec., YMCA England, 2006–08; Chief Exec., Nurture Group Network, 2009–11. Advr, Social Exclusion Unit, Cabinet Office, 1997–2000; Mem., H of L Appts Commn, 2000–08; a Civil Service Comr, 2012–17. Mem. Council, Howard

League for Penal Reform, 1998–2002. Member: Housing and Neighbourhood Cttee, Joseph Rowntree Foundn, 1997–2002; Bd, Capacitybuilders, 2008–11. Mem. Council, Evangelical Alliance, 1995–99; Vice-Pres., African and Caribbean Evangelical Alliance, 1996–2009; Mem., Leadership Team, Brentwater Evangelical Ch, NW2, 1990–94. Mem. Cttee, Assoc. Charitable Foundns, 1995–99; Trustee: BBC Children in Need, 1995–2002; Inst. Citizenship Studies, 1995–97; Notting Hill Housing Trust, 1995–97. Trustee: Single Homeless Housing Project, NW10, 1980–87; Learie Constantine Youth Club, NW2, 1980–90; Single Mothers Project, NW10, 1984–90; Tavistock Youth Club, NW10, 1985–90. *Recreations:* gardening, family, singing.

**SARKOZY DE NAGY-BOCSA, Nicolas Paul Stéphane**; Grand Croix de la Légion d'Honneur, 2007; Hon. GCB 2008; President of the French Republic, 2007–12; Member, Constitutional Council of France, 2012–13; *b* 28 Jan. 1955; *s* of Pal Sarkozy de Nagy-Bocsa and Andrée (*née* Mallah); *m* 1996, Cécilia Ciganer-Albeniz (marr. diss. 2007); one *s*, and two *s* from previous marriage; *m* 2008, Carla Bruni; one *d*. *Educ:* Maîtrise de droit privé, 1978; Cours St-Louis de Monceau; Inst d'Études Politiques, Paris (Cert d'aptitude à la profession d'avocat, 1981); Univ. Paris X-Nanterre. Lawyer, 1981–87. Neuilly-sur-Seine: Municipal Councillor, 1977–83; Mayor, 1983–2002; Dep. Mayor, 2002; Conseil Général des Hauts-de-Seine: Mem., 1985–88 and 2004; Vice-Pres., 1986–88; Pres., 2004–07; Deputy (RPR) Hauts-de-Seine, 1988, re-elected 1993, 1995, 1997, 2002. Minister: of the Budget, 1993–95; of Communication, 1994–95; of the Interior, Interior Security and Local Freedom, 2002–04; of State, and Minister of the Economy, Finance and Industry, 2004; of the Interior and Regional Develt, 2005–07. Rassemblement pour la République: Nat. Sec., 1988–92; Dep. Sec.-Gen., 1990–93; Mem., Political Office, 1993; Sec. Gen., then interim Pres., 1998–99; Pres., Deptl Cttee, Hauts-de-Seine, 2000; Pres., UMP, later Les Républicains, 2004–07 and 2014–16. Ind. Dir, Accor Hotels, 2017–. *Publications:* Georges Mandel: le moine de la politique, 1994; (with M. Denisot) Au bout de la passion, l'équilibre, 1995; Libre, 2001; La République, les Réligions, l'Espérance, 2004; Témoignage, 2006; Ensemble, 2007; Passions, 2019. *Address:* 77 rue de Miromesnil, 75008 Paris, France.

**SARMADI, Morteza**; Deputy Foreign Minister, Iran, since 2013; *b* July 1954; *m* 1982, Fatemeh Hosseini; four *d*. *Educ:* Sharif Univ. (BS Metallurgy); Tehran Univ. (Internat. Relns). Joined Ministry of Foreign Affairs, Tehran, 1981: Dir Gen., Press and Inf., 1982–89; Deputy Foreign Minister: for Communication, 1989–97; Eur. and American and CIS Countries' Affairs, 1997–2000; Iranian Ambassador to UK, 2000–04; Dep. Foreign Minister for European and American Affairs, Iran, 2004–05; Advr to Foreign Minister for Political and Internat. Studies, 2005–08; Sec. Gen. (formerly Exec. Dir), Indian Ocean Rim Assoc. for Regl Co-operation, 2008–11. Special Rep. to Caspian Sea Legal Regime; Sen. Mem., Delegn for Iran and Iraq Peace Negotiation. Has participated in numerous confs internationally. Trustee Member: Islamic Thought Foundn; Islamic Republic News Agency; Islamic High Council of Propagation Policy; Inst. for Political and Internat. Studies. *Recreations:* reading, watching TV, swimming, spending time with the family.

**SARNAK, Prof. Peter**, PhD; FRS 2002; Eugene Higgins Professor of Mathematics, since 2002, and Professor, Institute for Advanced Study, since 2007, Princeton University; *b* Johannesburg, 18 Dec. 1953. *Educ:* Univ. of Witwatersrand (BSc 1975); Stanford Univ. (PhD 1980). Asst Prof., 1980–83, Associate Prof., 1983–84, Prof., 2001–05, Courant Inst. of Math. Scis, NY Univ.; Associate Prof., 1984–87, Prof., 1987–91, Stanford Univ.; Princeton University: Prof., 1991–; H. Fine Prof., 1995–96; Chm., Dept of Maths, 1996–99; Mem., Inst. for Advanced Study, 1999–2002 and 2005–07. *Publications:* Some Applications of Modular Forms, 1990; (jtly) Extremal Riemann Surfaces, 1997; (ed jtly) Random Matrices, Frobenius Eigenvalues and Monodromy, 1998; articles in jls. *Address:* Department of Mathematics, Princeton University, Fine Hall, Washington Road, Princeton, NJ 08544–1000, USA.

**SARNO, Prof. Lucio**, PhD; Professor of Finance, and Keynes Fellow, University of Cambridge, since 2019; *b* Vallo della Lucania, Italy, 10 Dec. 1970; *s* of Raffaele Pompilio Sarno and Teresa Sarno (*née* Sangiovanni); *m* 2008, Dr Yulia Igonina; one *s*. *Educ:* Univ. of Liverpool (MSc Econs 1995; PhD Econs 1997). Post-doctoral Schol., Columbia Univ., 1997–98; Schröder Fellow in Econs, Univ. of Oxford, 1998–2000; Prof. of Finance, Univ. of Warwick, 2000–08; Dir of Res., AXA Investment Managers, 2007–08; Prof. of Finance, Cass Business Sch., City, Univ. of London, 2009–19. *Publications:* The Economics of Exchange Rates, 2003; The Handbook of Exchange Rates, 2012; contrib. articles on asset pricing, internat. finance and macro policy. *Recreations:* tennis, musicals, opera. *Address:* Cambridge Judge Business School, University of Cambridge, Trumpington Street, Cambridge CB2 1AG. *T:* 07903 458000. *E:* luciosarno@hotmail.com.

**SAROOP, Narindar**, CBE 1982; Senior Adviser, Gow & Partners, 2005–07; *b* 14 Aug. 1929; *e s* of late Chaudhri Ram Saroop, Ismaila, Rohtak, India and Shyam Devi; *m* 1st, 1952, Ravi Gill (marr. diss. 1967), *o* surv. *c* of the Sardar and Sardarni of Premgarh, India; one *d* (and one *s* one *d* decd); 2nd, 1969, Stephanie Denise, *yr d* of Alexander and Cynthia Amie Cronopulo, Zakynthos, Greece. *Educ:* Aitchison Coll. for Punjab Chiefs, Lahore; Indian Military Acad., Dehra Dun. Served as regular officer, 2nd Royal Lancers (Gardner's Horse) and Queen Victoria's Own The Poona Horse; retired, 1954. Management Trainee, Yule Catto, 1954; senior executive and Dir of subsidiaries of various multinationals, to 1976; Hon. Administrator, Oxfam Relief Project, 1964; Director: Devi Grays Insurance Ltd, 1981–84; Capital Plant International Ltd, 1982–86. Adviser: Develt, Clarkson Puckle Gp, 1976–87; Banque Belge, 1987–91; Cancer Relief Macmillan Fund, 1992–95; Nat. Grid plc, 1993; Coutts & Co., 1995–98. Mem., BBC Adv. Council on Asian Programmes, 1977–81. Pres., Indian Welfare Soc., 1983–92. Member Council: Freedom Assoc., 1978–86; Internat. Social Services, 1981–91; Inst. of Directors, 1983–93; Founder Mem., Tory Asians for Representation Gp, 1984–85; Mem. Adv. Council, Efficiency in Local Govt, 1984. Contested (C) Greenwich, 1979 (first Asian Tory Parliamentary candidate this century); Founder and 1st Chm., UK Anglo Asian Cons. Soc., 1976–79, 1985–86; Vice Chm., Cons. Party Internat. Office, 1990–92. Councillor (C), Kensington and Chelsea, 1974–82; initiated Borough Community Relations Cttee (Chm., 1975–77, 1980–82); Chm., Working Party on Employment, 1978; Founder and Chm., Durbar Club, 1981–2014. Mem., V & A Mus. Appeal Cttee, 1994–95. Patron, Conservative World, 2003–05. Hon. Mem., Clan Moncreiffe, 2000. *Publications:* In Defence of Freedom (jtly), 1978; A Squire of Hindoostan, 1983; The Last Indian (autobiog.), 2005. *Recreation:* keeping fools, boredom and socialism at bay. *Clubs:* Beefsteak, Cavalry and Guards, Pratt's; Puffin's (Edinburgh); Imperial Delhi Gymkhana; Royal Bombay Yacht, Royal Calcutta Golf.

**SAROOSHI, Prof. Dan**, PhD; QC 2018; Professor of Public International Law, University of Oxford, since 2006; Senior Research Fellow, Queen's College, Oxford, since 2012 (Fellow, 2003); barrister, since 2005; *b* 3 March 1968; *s* of R. and R. Sarooshi; *m* 1997, Mary Huddleston; two *s*. *Educ:* Univ. of New South Wales (LLB/BComm 1991); King's Coll., London (LLM 1992); London Sch. of Econs (PhD 1997). Lectr, Sen. Lectr then Reader in Public Internat. Law, UCL, 1997–2003; Lectr, then Herbert Smith Reader in Public Internat. Law, Univ. of Oxford, 2003–06. Emile Noël Fellow, Sch. of Law, New York Univ., 2002. Of Counsel, Tite & Lewis, in assoc. with Ernst & Young, 2001–04; called to the Bar, Middle Temple, 2005; barrister, Essex Court Chambers, 2006–. Member: List of Panellists, World Trade Orgn Dispute Settlement, 2006–; Attorney-Gen.'s Panel (A) of Public Internat. Law Counsel, 2013–. Mem., Exec. Council, Amer. Soc. of Internat. Law, 2008–11 (Counsellor, 2018–). Hague Acad. Internat. Law Lectr, 2018. Hon. MA Oxon, 2003. *Publications:* The United Nations and the Development of Collective Security: the delegation by the United Nations Security Council of its Chapter VII powers, 1999 (Guggenheim Book Prize, Swiss Guggenheim Foundn, 1999; Book Prize, Amer. Soc. of Internat. Law, 2001); (ed with M. Fitzmaurice) Issues of State Responsibility before International Judicial Institutions, 2004; International Organizations and their Exercise of Sovereign Powers, 2005 (Myres S. McDougal Book Prize, Amer. Soc. for the Policy Scis, 2006; Book Prize, Amer. Soc. of Internat. Law, 2006); Responsibility, Immunities and Remedies for the Acts of International Organizations, 2014. *Recreations:* opera, jazz. *Address:* Essex Court Chambers, 24 Lincoln's Inn Fields, WC2A 3EG. *T:* (020) 7813 8000. *E:* Dan.Sarooshi@law.ox.ac.uk.

**SARSFIELD, Brendan**; Chief Executive, Peabody, since 2017; *b* Romford, 3 Sept. 1960; *s* of Patrick Sarsfield and Annie-Bernadette Sarsfield; *m* 1986, Hilary Chamberlain; four *d*. *Educ:* Campion High Sch., Essex; Leeds Univ. (BSc Hons Architectural Engrg). Chartered Inst. of Housing Qualif. 1986. Castle Point DC, 1982–83; Hillingdon BC, 1983–85; Barnet BC 1985–88; New Business Manager, L&Q housing assoc., 1988–94; Dir, Family Housing Assoc., 1994–2001; Chief Executive Officer: Mosaic Homes, 2001–06; Family Mosaic, 2006–17. Chair, g15 London Housing Assocs, 2013–15. *Recreations:* golf, music. *Address:* Peabody, 45 Westminster Bridge Road, SE1 7JB. *T:* (020) 3828 4142. *E:* brendan.sarsfield@peabody.org.uk.

**SARUM, Archdeacon of;** *see* Jeans, Ven. A. P.

**SARWAR, Anas**; Member (Lab) Glasgow, Scottish Parliament, since 2016; *b* Glasgow, 14 March 1983; *s* of Mohammad Sarwar, *qv*; *m* 2006, Furheen Ashrif; two *s*. *Educ:* Hutchesons' Grammar Sch.; Sch. of Dentistry, Univ. of Glasgow (BDS Dentistry 2005). NHS Dentist, 2005–10. MP (Lab) Glasgow Central, 2010–15; contested (Lab) same seat, 2015. Mem., Internat. Develt Select Cttee, 2010–12. *Recreations:* current affairs, sport, reading, travelling, spending time with family. *Address:* Scottish Parliament, Edinburgh EH99 1SP.

**SARWAR, Mohammad**; Governor of Punjab, Pakistan, 2013–15 and since 2018; *b* 18 Aug. 1952; *s* of Mohammed and Rashida Abdullah Sarwar; *m* 1976, Perveen Sarwar; three *s* one *d*. *Educ:* Government Coll., Faisalabad (FSC; BA). Shopkeeper, 1976–83; Dir, United Wholesale Ltd, 1983–97. Member (Lab): Glasgow DC, 1992–96; Glasgow CC, 1995–97. MP (Lab) Glasgow Govan, 1997–2005, Glasgow Central, 2005–10. First ethnic minority MP in Scotland; first Muslim MP in Britain. *Publications:* My Remarkable Journey (autobiog.), 2016. *Recreation:* relaxing with family and friends.
*See also* A. Sarwar.

**SASSOON**, family name of **Baron Sassoon**.

**SASSOON**, Baron *cr* 2010 (Life Peer), of Ashley Park in the County of Surrey; **James Meyer Sassoon**, Kt 2008; FCA; Executive Director, Jardine Matheson Holdings, since 2013; *b* 11 Sept. 1955; *s* of Hugh Meyer Sassoon and Marion Julia Sassoon (*née* Schiff); *m* 1981, Sarah Caroline Ray Barnes, *d* of Sir (Ernest) John Ward Barnes; one *s* one *d*. *Educ:* Eton Coll.; Christ Church, Oxford (MA). ACA 1980, FCA 1991. Thomson McLintock & Co., 1977–86; SG Warburg & Co. Ltd, 1987–95 (Dir, 1991–95); Warburg Dillon Read, subseq. UBS Warburg: Man. Dir, 1995–2002; Vice Chm., Investment Banking, 2000–02; Man. Dir, Finance, Regulation and Industry, 2002–06; Chancellor's Rep. for Promotion of City, 2006–08; HM Treasury. Pres., Financial Action Task Force, 2007–08. Author of The Tripartite Review, 2009. Mem., Econ. Recovery Cttee, Shadow Cabinet, 2009–10; Commercial Sec. to HM Treasury, 2010–13. Director: Partnerships UK, 2002–06; Nuclear Liabilities Fund, 2008–10. Dir, Hackney Business Venture, subseq. HBV Enterprise, 2000–02. Director: Dairy Farm Internat. Hldgs, 2013–; Hongkong Land Hldgs, 2013–; Mandarin Oriental Internat., 2013–; Jardine Lloyd Thompson, 2013–19. Chairman: ifs Sch. of Finance, 2009–10; Merchants Trust, 2010 (Dir, 2006–10); China-Britain Business Council, 2013–; Member: Adv. Bd, Resolution Foundn, 2007–10; Global Adv. Bd, Mitsubishi UFJ Financial Gp, 2013–; Cttee, Hong Kong Assoc., 2013–. Trustee: Gerald Coke Handel Foundn, 2001–10; Nat. Gall. Trust, 2002–09; British Mus., 2009–10 and 2013–. Governor, Ashdown House Sch., 2001–06. *Publications:* articles in art and financial jls. *Recreations:* travel, the arts, watching sport. *Address:* Jardine Matheson Holdings, 3 Lombard Street, EC3V 9AQ. *Club:* MCC.
*See also* A. D. Sassoon.

**SASSOON, Adrian David**; dealer in 18th century French porcelain and contemporary British studio ceramics, glass and silver, since 1992; *b* 1 Feb. 1961; *s* of Hugh Meyer Sassoon and Marion Julia Sassoon (*née* Schiff). *Educ:* Sunningdale Sch.; Eton Coll.; Inchbald Sch. of Design, London; Christie's, London (fine arts diploma). Asst Curator of Decorative Arts, J. Paul Getty Mus., Malibu, 1980–84; ind. researcher, 1984–87; Dir, Alexander & Berendt Ltd, London, 1987–92; private dealer and art advr, 1992–. Trustee: Hermitage Mus. Foundn UK (formerly UK Friends of Hermitage Mus., St Petersburg), 2006–; Wallace Collection, 2007–15; The Silver Trust, 2013–19. Member: Council, Furniture History Soc., 2010–13; Internat. Council, Metropolitan Museum of Art, NY, 2017–. *Publications:* Decorative Arts: a handbook catalogue of the collection of the J. Paul Getty Museum (with Gillian Wilson), 1986; Catalogue of Vincennes and Sèvres Porcelain in the J. Paul Getty Museum, Malibu, 1991; Vincennes and Sèvres Porcelain from a European Private Collector, 2001; Jewels by JAR, 2013. *Recreations:* museums, beaches. *E:* email@adriansassoon.com. *Clubs:* Brooks's; Lyford Cay (Nassau).
*See also* Baron Sassoon.

**SASSOON, Prof. Donald**, PhD; Professor of Comparative European History, Queen Mary, University of London, 1997–2012, now Emeritus; *b* 25 Nov. 1946; *s* of Joseph Isaac Sassoon and Doris Sassoon (*née* Bardak); *m* 1973, Anne Showstack (marr. diss. 1987); one *d*. *Educ:* schools in Paris, Milan and Tunbridge Wells; University Coll. London (BSc Econ 1969); Pennsylvania State Univ. (MA 1971); Birkbeck Coll., Univ. of London (PhD 1977). Lectr in Hist., 1979–89, Reader in Hist., 1989–97, Westfield Coll., then QMW, Univ. of London. Nuffield Social Sci. Fellow, 1997–98; Vis. Prof., Univ. of Trento, 1999; Leverhulme Maj. Res. Fellow, 2000–03; Sen. Res. Fellow, New York Univ., 2001; Samuel Wood Brooks Vis. Prof. of English Lit., Univ. of Qld, 2009; Vis. Prof., Univ. of Padua, 2017. Mem., Comité Scientifique (formerly Comité d'Orientation), Maison de l'Histoire de France, 2011–12. Literary Ed., Political Qly, 2000–. Premio Napoli Internazionale, Fondazione Premio Napoli, 2017. *Publications:* The Strategy of the Italian Communist Party, 1981; Contemporary Italy: politics, economy and society since 1945, 1986, 2nd edn 1997; One Hundred Years of Socialism: the West European Left in the Twentieth Century, 1996 (Deutscher Meml Prize 1997); Mona Lisa: the history of the world's most famous painting, 2001; Leonardo and the Mona Lisa Story, 2006; The Culture of the Europeans, 2006 (Premio Alassio Internazionale, 2009); Mussolini and the Rise of Fascism, 2007; The Anxious Triumph: a global history of capitalism, 1860–1914, 2019; Sintomi Morbosi, 2019; contribs to jls. *Recreations:* travel, classical music, country walking. *Address:* School of History, Queen Mary, University of London, Mile End Road, E1 4NS. *E:* d.sassoon@qmul.ac.uk.

**SATCHELL, Keith;** Group Chief Executive, Friends Provident plc (formerly Friends Provident Life Office), 1997–2007; *b* 3 June 1951; *s* of Dennis Joseph Satchell and Joan Betty Satchell; *m* 1972, Hazel Burston; two *s* one *d*. *Educ:* Univ. of Aston (BSc). FIA 1976. With Duncan C. Fraser, 1972–75; UK Provident, 1975–86; Friends Provident, 1986–2007: Gen. Manager, 1987–97; Dir, 1992–2007. Chairman: ABI, 2005–07; Rothesay Life, 2007–16; Barnett Waddingham, 2007–18. *Recreations:* soccer, golf, ski-ing, theatre.

**SATCHWELL, Sir Kevin (Joseph),** Kt 2001; Headmaster, Thomas Telford School, since 1991; *b* 6 March 1951; *e s* of late Joseph and Pauline Satchwell; *m* 1975, Maria Bernadette Grimes; one *s* one *d*. *Educ:* Wodensborough High Sch.; Wednesbury Boys' High Sch.; Shoreditch Coll. of Technology (Cert Ed London Univ. 1973); Open Univ. (BA 1977; AdvDip Educn Mgt 1978). Teacher, Cantril High Sch., Liverpool, 1973–79; Dep. Head, Brookfield Sch., Liverpool, 1979–87; Headteacher, Moseley Park Sch., Wolverhampton, 1987–90. Dir, London Qualifications, 2003–05. Exec. Advr, Thomas Telford Multi Acad. Trust, 2017–. Member: NCET, 1994–96; City Technology Colls Principals' Forum, 1991 (Chm., 1997); Chm., W Midlands Consortium for School Centred Initial Teacher Trng, 1993–. Trustee: Edge Foundn, 2010–; Baker Dearing Educnl Trust, 2014–. *Recreations:* family, football coaching, tennis, golf. *Address:* Thomas Telford School, Old Park, Telford TF3 4NW. *T:* (01952) 200000.

**SATER,** family name of **Baroness Sater**.

**SATER, Baroness** *cr* 2018 (Life Peer), of Kensington in the Royal Borough of Kensington and Chelsea; **Amanda Jacqueline Sater;** JP; *b* 21 June 1963; *d* of John and Jacqueline Hamilton-Jones; *m* 1988, Roisen Mark Sater; one *s* one *d*. Man. Dir, Control Promotions Ltd, 1989–97; Dir, Inst. of Sales Promotion, 1996–97. Conservative Party: Mem. Bd, 2016–; Dep. Chm., 2016–18; Vice Chm., Responsibilities for Women, 2014–15; Co. Chm., Candidates Cttee, 2015–. Member, Board: Metropolitan Police Authy, 2010–12; Youth Justice Bd, 2013–17. Chm., Queen's Club Foundn, 2015–; Vice Chm. and Trustee, Queen's Club, 2009–15. Trustee: Addaction, 2002–05; British Lung Foundn, 2005–11; Chm., StreetGames UK, 2015–18 (Patron, 2019–). JP Inner London, 1995–2018, Supplemental List, 2019–. Freedom, City of London. FRSA. *Address:* House of Lords, SW1A 0PW.

**SATSANGI, Prof. Jyoti, (Jack),** DPhil; FRCP, FRCPE, FMedSci; FRSE; Lee Placito Professor of Gastroenterological Disease, University of Oxford, since 2018; Fellow, Green Templeton College, Oxford, since 2018; *b* Yorks, 8 May 1963; *s* of Prem Nath Satsangi and Nirmal Satsangi; *m* 2008, Patricia Moore; one *s* one *d*. *Educ:* Brentwood Sch.; St Thomas's Hosp. Med. Sch., London (BSc 1984; MB BS (Dist.) 1987); Worcester Coll., Oxford (DPhil 1996). MRCP 1990, FRCP 2005; FRCPE 2002. Hse Physician, St Thomas's Hosp., London, 1987–88; SHO, Oxford Radcliffe Hosps., 1988–90; University of Oxford: Registrar in Medicine, Nuffield Dept of Medicine, 1990–92; MRC Clinical Fellow, 1992–96; MRC Clinician Scientist and Hon. Consultant Physician, 1997–2000; Prof. of Gastro-enterology, Univ. of Edinburgh, 2000–18; Hon. Consultant Physician, Western General Hosp., Edinburgh, 2000–18. FMedSci 2009; FRSE 2010. *Publications:* articles in many jls incl. Nature, Nature Genetics, Lancet, New England Jl. *Recreations:* tennis, running, cycling, reading, playing with my children. *Address:* Nuffield Department of Clinical Medicine, University of Oxford, Old Campus Road, Headington, Oxford OX3 7DQ. *E:* jack.satsangi@ndm.ox.ac.uk.

**SATTERTHWAITE, Christopher James,** CBE 2017; Group Chief Executive, Chime Communications plc, 2003–17 (non-executive Director, since 2017); Chairman, Access Intelligence plc, since 2018; *b* 21 May 1956; *s* of Col Richard George Satterthwaite and Rosemary Ann Satterthwaite; *m* 1988, Teresa Mary Bailey; two *s* one *d*. *Educ:* Ampleforth Coll.; Lincoln Coll., Oxford (MA Mod. Hist.). Graduate trainee, H. J. Heinz, 1978–81; IMP Ltd, 1981–98, Chief Exec., 1990–98; Chief Executive: HHCL Ltd, 1998–2000; Bell Pottinger Ltd, 2000–02. Chm., Roundhouse, 2010–17; Sen. Ind. Dir, Centaur Media, 2011. *Recreations:* Parson Woodforde Society, marathon running, bombology. *Address:* Tuesley Manor, Tuesley Lane, Godalming, Surrey GU7 1UD. *T:* (01483) 429336.

**SATYANAND, Rt Hon. Sir Anand,** GNZM 2009 (PCNZM 2006; DCNZM 2005); QSO 2007; Governor-General of New Zealand, 2006–11; Chairman, Royal Commission into Historical Abuse in State Care, since 2018; *b* 22 July 1944; *s* of Dr Mutyala Satyanand and Tara Satyanand; *m* 1970, Susan Jean Sharpe; one *s* two *d*. *Educ:* Univ. of Auckland (LLB). Barrister and solicitor, 1970–82; Dist Court Judge with Jury Trial Warrant, 1982–2005; Parly Ombudsman, 1995–2005. Registrar, Pecuniary Interests of MPs, 2005. Chm., Commonwealth Foundn, 2013–16. Chm., Commonwealth Observation Gp on Nat. Elections in Ind. State of PNG, 2017. Chairman: Confidential Forum for Former In Patients of Psychiatric Hosps, 2005–06; Aegis Study of Govt Information Sharing, 2013–16; Member: Adv. Council, Transparency Internat., 2015– (Patron, Transparency Internat. NZ 2012–13); Internat. Anti-Corruption Council, 2018–. Mem., Standing Cttee, NZ Inst. Internat. Affairs, 2017–. Hon. LLD Auckland, 2006. KStJ 2006. Pravasi Bharatiya Samman (India), 2011; Mem., Royal Order of the Crown of Tonga, 2011. *Publications:* contrib. jls and legal pubns on legal educn, trial skills enhancement, ombudsman and governor-general office studies. *Recreations:* reading, writing, sport, sporting administration. *Address:* PO Box 9062, Marion Square, Wellington 6141, New Zealand. *T:* (2) 1586409. *E:* anand.satyanand@gmail.com. *Clubs:* Wellington, Royal Commonwealth (Wellington); Northern (Auckland).

**SAUER, Fernand Edmond;** Honorary Director General, European Commission, since 2006; *b* 14 Dec. 1947; *s* of Ferdinand Sauer and Emilie Scherer Sauer; *m* 1971, Pamela Sheppard; one *s* two *d*. *Educ:* Univ. of Strasbourg (pharmacist, 1971); Paris II Univ. (Masters in European Law, 1977). Hosp. Pharmacist, Reunion Island, 1972–73; Pharmaceutical Insp., Health Min., France, 1974–79; European Commission: Adminr, 1979–85; Head of Pharmaceuticals, 1986–94; Exec. Dir, Eur. Agency for the Evaluation of Medicinal Products, 1994–2000; Dir, Public Health Policy, DG for Health and Consumer Protection, EC, 2000–05. Member: Faculty of Pharmacy, London Univ., 1996–; High Council for Public Health (France), 2007–11. Mem., French Acad. of Pharmacy, 2000. Hon. Fellow, RPSGB, 1996. Chevalier de l'Ordre du Mérite (France), 1990; Chevalier de la Légion d'Honneur (France), 1998. *Publications:* various articles and publications on pharmaceutical regulation. *Recreation:* jogging. *Address:* 12 avenue de la Marne, 13260 Cassis, France.

**SAUL, Christopher Francis Irving;** Senior Partner, Slaughter and May, 2008–16; Founder, Christopher Saul Associates, 2016; *b* Carlisle, 1955; *s* of Irving and Greta Saul; *m* 1985, Anne Cartier; one *s* one *d*. *Educ:* Tiffin Sch.; St Catherine's Coll., Oxford (BA Juris.). Joined Slaughter and May, 1977; Partner, 1986–2016. *Recreations:* motor cars, contemporary music, reading, cinema.

**SAUL, Prof. Nigel Edward,** DPhil; FSA, FHA; Professor of Medieval History, Royal Holloway, University of London, 1997–2015, now Emeritus; *b* 20 June 1952; *s* of Edward Thomas Saul and Marion Saul (*née* Duffy); *m* 1983, Jane Melanie Nichols; one *s* one *d*. *Educ:* King Edward VI Sch., Stratford-upon-Avon; Hertford Coll., Oxford (BA 1974; MA, DPhil 1978). FRHistS 1984–2015; FSA 1988; FHA 2012. Royal Holloway, University of London: Lectr in Medieval Hist., 1978–88; Reader in Medieval Hist., 1988–97; Hd, Dept of History, 2002–05. Vice-Pres., Monumental Brass Soc., 2002– (Pres., 1995–2002). Lectures: Bond Meml, St George's Chapel, Windsor, 2008; Cantilupe, Hereford Cathedral, 2011. Trustee, Victoria County History, 2009–. Series Editor, Hambledon and London Books, 1998–2007; Mem., Editorial Adv. Bd, History Today, 1987–2017. *Publications:* Knights and Esquires: the Gloucestershire gentry in the fourteenth century, 1981; Scenes from Provincial Life: knightly families in Sussex 1280–1400, 1986; (ed and contrib.) Historical Atlas of Britain: prehistoric to medieval, 1994; Richard II, 1997; (ed and contrib.) Oxford Illustrated History of Medieval England, 1997; Companion to Medieval England 1066–1400, 2000; (ed) Fourteenth Century England, vol. I, 2000; Death, Art and Memory: the Cobham family and their monuments 1300–1500, 2001; The Three Richards, 2005; (ed) St George's Chapel, Windsor, in the Fourteenth Century, 2005; Fourteenth Century England, vol. V, 2008; English Church Monuments in the Middle Ages: history and representation, 2009; (ed jtly) St George's Chapel, Windsor: history and heritage, 2010; For Honour and Fame: chivalry in England, 1066–1500, 2011; Lordship and Faith: the English gentry and the parish church, 2017; articles in learned jls. *Recreations:* church crawling, lepidoptera, gardening, walking. *Address:* Gresham House, Egham Hill, Egham, Surrey TW20 0ER. *E:* n.saul@rhul.ac.uk.

**SAUL, Roger John;** Owner, Sharpham Park, since 2004; Executive Chairman, Kilver Court Designer Village and Gardens, since 2016 (Chief Executive Officer, 2008–16); *b* 25 July 1950; *s* of late Michael and Joan Saul; *m* 1977, Monty Cameron; three *s*. *Educ:* Kingswood Sch., Bath; Westminster Coll., London. Founded Mulberry Co. 1971 (Queen's Award to Industry for Export, 1979, 1989 and 1996); Chm. and Chief Exec., 1971–2002; Pres., 2002–03; launched Mulberry at Home, 1991; opened Charlton House Hotel and Mulberry Restaurant, 1997 (Michelin Star, annually, 1997–2003); launched Sharpham Park (rare breed meat) and Spelt Flour (bread, pasta and cereal range), 2005; built first organic spelt flour mill in UK, 2006; created Feastival, eco/sustainability event, 2009; curated Eco Car event, London, 2010; creator and Exec. Chm., Kilver Court Designer Outlet Village, 2011–; Kilver Court Garden Nursery, 2016–. Chm., London Designer Collections, 1976–80; Dir, Monty's, 2004–09. Dir, EV Cup, 2011–19. Trustee and Chm., Bottletop, 2003–09. Mem., RHS. Gov., Kingswood Sch., 2006–10. Classic Designer of Year, British Fashion Council, 1992. *Publications:* Mulberry at Home, 1992; Spelt Recipe Book, 2015. *Recreations:* garden design, tennis, tai chi, historic car racing (winner: Brooklands Trophy, 2006; Porto GP, Irish GP, Donnington Legends, 2006; Brighton Speed Trials Pre '59 Trophy, 2007), 6m yacht racing. *Address:* Kilver Court, Shepton Mallet, Somerset BA4 5NF.

**SAULTER, Paul Reginald;** Managing Director, 1989–2012, Hon. Chairman, 2012–16, Heritage of Industry (formerly Cornwall of Mine) Ltd; *b* 27 Aug. 1935; *s* of Alfred Walter Saulter and Mabel Elizabeth Oliver. *Educ:* Truro Sch.; University Coll., Oxford (MA). Admin. Asst, Nat. Council of Social Service, 1960–63; Sen. Asst and Principal, CEGB, 1963–65; Dep. Head, Overseas Div., BEAMA, 1965–69; Dir, Internat. Affairs, ABCC, 1969–73; Sec.-Gen., British Chamber of Commerce in France, 1973–81; Chief Executive: Manchester Chamber of Commerce and Industry, 1981–85; Assoc. of Exhibn Organisers, 1985–86; Administrator, St Paul's, Knightsbridge, 1987–95. Mgt consultant, 1986–89; Exhibn Advr, London Chamber of Commerce, 1986–88. Secretary: For. Trade Working Gp, ORGALIME, 1967–69; Council of British Chambers of Commerce in Continental Europe, 1977–80; Member: Export Promotion Cttee, CBI, 1983–86; Bd, Eur. Fedn of Assocs of Industrial and Technical Heritage, 1999–2014 (Vice-Pres., 2002–11; Pres., 2011–13). Member: RHS; Trevithick Soc., 1986–; Assoc. for Industrial Archaeology; Newcomen Soc., 1995– (Mem. Council, 1995–98, 1999–2002). Trustee: Kirkaldy Testing Mus. Southwark Ltd, 2014–16; A4Altruistic, 2015–. *Recreations:* walking, music, theatre, researching Cornish mining history, industrial archaeology. *Address:* Rye, Sussex.

**SAUMAREZ,** family name of **Baron de Saumarez**.

**SAUMAREZ SMITH, Sir Charles (Robert),** Kt 2018; CBE 2008; PhD; FSA; Senior Director, Blain|Southern, since 2019; *b* 28 May 1954; *s* of late William Hanbury Saumarez Smith, OBE and of Alice Elizabeth Harness Saumarez Smith (*née* Raven); *m* 1979, Romilly Le Quesne Savage; two *s*. *Educ:* Marlborough Coll.; King's Coll., Cambridge (BA 1st Cl. Hist., Pt 1, 1974, 1st Cl. History of Art 1976; MA 1978); Henry Fellow, Harvard, 1977; Warburg Inst. (PhD 1986). FSA 1997. Christie's Res. Fellow in Applied Arts, Christ's Coll., Cambridge, 1979–82 (Hon. Fellow, 2002); Asst Keeper with resp. for V&A/RCA MA course in history of design, 1982–90, Head of Res., 1990–94, V & A (Emeritus Sen. Res. Fellow, 2018); Dir, NPG, 1994–2002; Slade Prof., Univ. of Oxford, 2001–02; Dir, National Gallery, 2002–07; Sec. and Chief Exec., RA, 2007–18. Vis. Fellow, Yale Center for British Art, 1983; Benno Forman Fellow, Winterthur Mus., 1988; South Square Fellow, RCA, 1990; Vis. Prof., QMUL, 2007–. Member, Executive Committee: Design History Soc., 1985–89; Soc. of Architectural Historians, 1987–90; Assoc. of Art Historians, 1990–94; London Library, 1992–96; Member, Advisory Council: Paul Mellon Centre for British Studies, 1995–99; Warburg Inst., 1997–2003; Inst. of Historical Research, 1999–2003; Sch. of Advanced Study, 2003–07; Mem. Council, Museums Assoc., 1998–2001 (Vice-Pres., 2002–04; Pres., 2004–06). Gov., Univ. of the Arts, London (formerly London Inst.), 2001–13. Trustee: Soane Monuments Trust, 1988–2006; Charleston, 1993–2015 (Trustee Emeritus, 2016); Royal Drawing Sch. (formerly Prince's Drawing Sch.), 2003–16; Public Catalogue Foundn, 2003–15; Watercolour World, 2017–; Garden Mus., 2018–. FRSA 1995. Hon. Fellow, RCA, 1991; Hon. FRIBA 2000. Hon. DLitt: UEA, 2001; Westminster, 2002; London, 2003; Sussex, 2003; Essex, 2005. *Publications:* The Building of Castle Howard, 1990 (Alice Davis Hitchcock Medallion); Eighteenth Century Decoration, 1993; The National Portrait Gallery, 1997; The National Gallery: a short history, 2009; The Company of Artists: the origins of the Royal Academy of Arts in London, 2012; New Annals of The Club, 2014; East London, 2017. *Address:* Blain|Southern, 4 Hanover Square, W1S 1BP.

**SAUNDERS, Alison Margaret,** CB 2013; Partner, Linklaters, since 2018; *b* Aberdeen, 14 Feb. 1961; *d* of Hugh Colin Brown and Margaret Bennett Brown; *m* 1986, Neil Saunders; two *s*. *Educ:* St Teilo's Church in Wales Sch., Cardiff; Runshaw 6th Form Coll., Leyland, Lancs; Univ. of Leeds (LLM Hons). Called to the Bar, Inner Temple, 1983; Lloyd's of London, 1984–86; Crown Prosecution Service: joined, 1986; Policy Directorate, 1991; London, 1997; Dep. Chief Crown Prosecutor London, 1999–2002; Chief Crown Prosecutor Sussex, 2002–04; Dep. Legal Sec., Attorney Gen.'s Office, 2004–06; Hd, Organised Crime Div., CPS, 2006–10; Chief Crown Prosecutor for London, 2010–13; Dir of Public Prosecutions, 2013–18. Gov., Eastbourne Coll., 2009–14. *Recreations:* cooking, theatre, reading, family. *Address:* Linklaters, One Silk Street, EC2Y 8HQ.

**SAUNDERS, Andrew William,** CB 1998; Director, Communications-Electronics Security Group, 1991–98; *b* 26 Oct. 1940; *s* of late Joseph and Winifred Saunders; *m* 1964, Josephine Sharkey; one *s* two *d*. *Educ:* Wolverhampton Grammar Sch.; Christ Church, Oxford (MA). Joined Civil Service, GCHQ, 1963: Principal, 1968; Asst Sec., 1978; Counsellor, Washington, 1983–86 (on secondment); Under Sec., 1991. *Recreations:* outdoor pleasures and practicalities, genealogy, history. *Address:* c/o Barclays Bank PLC, 128 High Street, Cheltenham, Glos GL50 1EL.

**SAUNDERS, Ann Loreille**, MBE 2002; PhD; FSA; historian; Lecturer in History of London, University of Connecticut Programme, City University, London, 1982–2007; *b* 23 May 1930; *d* of George and Joan Cox-Johnson; *m* 1960, Bruce Kemp Saunders; one *s* (and one *d* decd). *Educ*: Henrietta Barnett Sch., London; Queen's Coll., London; UCL (BA); Leicester Univ. (PhD 1965). FSA 1975. Asst, City of York Art Gall., 1951–52; Dep. Librarian, Lambeth Palace, 1952–55; Temp. Asst Keeper, BM, 1955–56; Borough Archivist, Marylebone Public Library, 1956–63; freelance writing, lecturing and editing, 1965–; Lectr in Hist. of London, Richmond Coll., London, 1979–94; Fellow and Hon. Res. Fellow, UCL, 1992–95. Mem. Council, Soc. of Antiquaries of London, 1989–91; President: Camden History Soc., 1984–89; St Marylebone Soc., 1985–89; Regent's Park DFAS, 1989–95. Governor, Bedford Coll., 1982–85. Asst to Hon. Editor, Jl of British Archaeol Assoc., 1963–75; Honorary Editor: Costume Soc., 1967–2008; London Topographical Soc., 1975–2015. *Publications*: Regent's Park: a study of the development of the area from 1066 to the present day, 1969, 2nd edn 1981; (ed) Arthur Mee's London North of the Thames, 1972; (ed) Arthur Mee's London: the City and Westminster, 1975; The Art and Architecture of London: an illustrated guide (Specialist Guide Book of the Year Award, London Tourist Bd), 1984, 3rd edn 1992; (ed and contrib.) The Royal Exchange, 1997; St Paul's: the story of the cathedral, 2001, 2nd edn as St Paul's: 1,400 years at the heart of London, 2012; (jtly) The History of the Merchant Taylors' Company, 2004; (ed) The London County Council Bomb Damage Maps, 2005; Historic Views of London: photographs from the collection of B. E. C. Howarth-Loomes, 2008; contribs to Burlington Mag., London Jl, Geographical Mag., Dome, LAMAS, etc. *Recreations*: reading, walking, embroidery, cooking, studying London, going to exhibitions and theatres, visiting churches.

**SAUNDERS, Sir Bruce (Joshua),** KBE 2012 (OBE 2003); Managing Director, BJS Group of Companies, 1980; *b* Port Pirie, SA, 20 Dec. 1941; *s* of Edward Hugh Saunders and Grace Olive Saunders; *m* 1966, Keithie Wilma Blum, OBE; three *d*. *Educ*: Sch. Leaving Cert. Trained as chef, William Angliss Trade Sch., Melbourne; managed: catering facilities, Sydney, 1961–66; Hotel Rarotonga, Cook Is, 1966–68; family business of A. J. and G. Blum, Solomon Is, 1968. Member: Tourist Authy, 1972–75; Govt of Solomon Is Think Tank, 1996–98; Civil Society Network, 2000–04; Vice Chm., Solomon Is Chamber of Commerce, 1998–2013 (Exec. Mem.); Mem. Bd, Central Bank of Solomon Is, 2005–07; Mem. Bd, Pacific Is Private Sector Orgn, 2012–. Proj. Manager to Trustee Bd, Solomon Scouts and Coastwatchers Memorial, 2009–; Trustee, Blue Light Police Youth Assoc., 2012–. Mem., Baha'i World Faith, 1956–. *Recreations*: tennis, squash, reading, community service reading. *T*: 7496448. *Club*: Rotary (Honiara) (Paul Harris Fellow).

**SAUNDERS, Christopher John,** MA; Headmaster, Lancing College, 1993–98; *b* 7 May 1940; *s* of R. H. Saunders and G. S. Saunders (née Harris); *m* 1973, Cynthia Elizabeth Stiles; one *s* one *d*. *Educ*: Lancing Coll.; Fitzwilliam Coll., Cambridge (MA); PGCE Wadham Coll., Oxford. Assistant Master, Bradfield College, 1964–80 (Housemaster, 1972–80); Headmaster, Eastbourne Coll., 1981–93. Life Vice-Pres., FA, 2012 (Vice-Pres., 2002–12). *Recreations*: music, bridge, theatre, gardening, soccer (Oxford Blue 1963), cricket (Oxford Blue 1964), golf, people. *Address*: Folly Bottom, Scottalls Lane, Hampstead Norreys, Thatcham, Berks RG18 0RT. *T*: (01635) 200222. *Clubs*: MCC; Hawks (Cambridge).

**SAUNDERS, David,** DPhil, FIIC, FSA; Keeper of Conservation and Scientific Research (formerly Conservation, Documentation and Science), British Museum, 2005–15, now Honorary Research Fellow; *b* 10 Oct. 1959; *s* of Morris and Gwen Saunders; *m* 1984, Alison Hesketh. *Educ*: Harrow Co. Sch. for Boys; Univ. of York (BSc Chem. 1981; DPhil Chem. 1984). FIIC 1993. Post-doctoral Researcher, Univ. of Bristol, 1984–85; Scientist, Nat. Gall., London, 1985–2005. Vice Pres., Internat. Inst. for Conservation, 2013–18 (Dir, Pubns, 2003–09). Visiting Professor: UCL, 2016–; NY Univ., 2018. Syndic, Fitzwilliam Mus., 2016–. Getty/Rothschild Fellow, 2017. FSA 2013. Editor: Studies in Conservation, 1990–2009; BM Technical Res. Bulletin, 2007–16. *Publications*: 100 articles incl. in Nat. Gall. Technical Bulletin, Studies in Conservation and Jl of Chemical Soc. *Recreations*: cooking for friends, Italian and Scandinavian cities, hill-walking, orienteering, selected opera, other people's museums. *Address*: British Museum, Great Russell Street, WC1B 3DG.

**SAUNDERS, David; His Honour Judge Saunders;** a Circuit Judge, since 2018; *b* Ramsgate, 22 June 1958; *s* of Reginald Walter Saunders and Hilary Anne Saunders; one *s* one *d*; *m* 2018, Justina Jang. *Educ*: Chatham House Grammar Sch., Ramsgate; Birmingham City Univ. (BA Hons Law 1979); Chester Coll. of Law. Admitted solicitor, 1984; solicitor in private practice, Canterbury, 1984–2006; Fee-paid Chm., Social Security Appeals, 1993–2006; Tribunal Judge, Social Entitlement Chamber, 2006–18; a Dep. Dist Judge, 2006–18; Diversity and Community Judge, 2014–. *Recreations*: Taekwondo (2nd Dan Black Belt), guitar, cricket, Rugby, football, travel, Korean studies (Mem., British Korean Soc.). *Address*: Central London County Court, Thomas More Building, Royal Courts of Justice, Strand, WC2A 2LL. *Club*: Phyllis Court (Henley-on-Thames).

**SAUNDERS, Air Vice-Marshal David John,** CBE 1986; FIMechE; FRAeS; FCILT; Advisor, Airinmar Group, 2011–12 (Director of Logistics, 1997–99; Senior Vice President, 1999–2011); *b* 12 June 1943; *s* of John Saunders and Nina Saunders (née Mabberley); *m* 1966, Elizabeth Jane Cairns; one *s* one *d*. *Educ*: Commonweal Grammar Sch.; RAF College; Cranfield Inst. of Technology. BSc, MSc; CEng, FRAeS 1993; FCILT (FILog 1997). Joined RAF 1961; management appts, 1966–85; Station Comdr, RAF Sealand, 1983; ADC to HM the Queen, 1984–86; Command Mechanical Engineer, HQ RAF Germany, 1986; Dir of Engineering Policy (RAF), MoD, 1989–91; ACDS (Logistics), 1991–93; Hd of RAF Mobility Study, 1993; AO Engrg and Supply, 1993–97. Director: Airinmar Gp Ltd, 2000–11; Airinmar UK Ltd, 2000–11; Airinmar Inc., 2000–11. *Recreations*: rowing, off-road cycling, horse riding, season ticket holder Swindon Town FC. *Address*: The Hermitage, 150 Above Town, Dartmouth, Devon TQ6 9RH. *Club*: Royal Air Force.

**SAUNDERS, David John;** Senior Advisor, Financial Conduct Authority, since 2014; Special Advisor, Europe Economics, since 2014; *b* 4 Aug. 1953; *s* of James and Margaret Saunders; *m* 1975, Elizabeth Jean Hdgson; two *s* two *d*. *Educ*: Royal Grammar Sch., Guildford; Kingston Poly. (BSc Chemistry and Business Studies); Aston Univ. (PhD Applied Business Studies 1978). Joined DTI, 1978; Private Sec. to Sec. of State, 1981–82, to Parly Under Sec. of State, 1982–84; seconded to OFT, 1984–87; British Steel privatisation, 1987–88; Export Promotion, 1988–95; Sec., BOTB, 1990–95; Director: Nuclear Power Privatisation Team, 1995–96; Oil and Gas Directorate, 1996–98; Regl Dir, Govt Office for SE, 1998–2002; Dir, Business Support, DTI, 2002–04; Dir, Consumer and Competition Policy, DTI, later BERR, 2004–09; Chief Exec., Competition Commn, 2009–14. *Recreations*: swimming, cycling, diving, photography, ballet, music. *Address*: Financial Conduct Authority, 12 Endeavour Square, E20 1JN. *T*: (020) 7066 9668. *Club*: Reform.

**SAUNDERS, David William,** CB 1989; Counsel to the Chairman of Committees, House of Lords, 1999–2005; *b* 4 Nov. 1936; *s* of William Ernest Saunders and Lilian Grace (née Ward); *m* 1963, Margaret Susan Rose Bartholomew. *Educ*: Hornchurch Grammar Sch.; Worcester Coll., Oxford (MA). Admitted solicitor, 1964. Joined Office of Parly Counsel, 1970; Dep. Parly Counsel, 1978–80; Parly Counsel, 1980–94 and 1996–99; Second Parly Counsel, 1994–96; with Law Commn, 1972–74, 1986–87. *Recreations*: golf, bridge. *Address*: Highfields, High Wych, Sawbridgeworth, Herts CM21 0HX. *T*: (01279) 724736. *Club*: Oxford and Cambridge.

**SAUNDERS, Ernest Walter,** MA; President, Stambridge Management (formerly Associates), 1992; *b* 21 Oct. 1935; *m* 1963, Carole Ann Stephings; two *s* one *d*. *Educ*: Emmanuel Coll., Cambridge (MA). Man. Dir, Beecham Products Internat., and Dir, Beecham Products, 1966–73; Chm., European Div., Great Universal Stores, 1973–77; Pres., Nestlé Nutrition SA, and Mem. Worldwide Management Cttee, Nestlé SA, Vevey, Switzerland, 1977–81; Chm., Beechnut Corp., USA, 1977–81; Chief Exec., 1981–87, Chm., 1986–87, Arthur Guinness & Sons plc, later Guinness PLC; Chairman: Arthur Guinness Son & Co. (Great Britain), 1982–87; Guinness Brewing Worldwide, 1982–87. Dir, Brewers' Soc., 1983. Dir, Queens Park Rangers Football & Athletic Club, 1983. *Recreations*: ski-ing, tennis, football.

**SAUNDERS, Dame Frances (Carolyn),** DBE 2018; CB 2011; PhD, CEng, FREng; CPhys, FInstP; Chief Executive, Defence Science and Technology Laboratory, Ministry of Defence, 2006–12; *b* Cambridge, 28 June 1954; *d* of Archibald John Christopher Reger, MBE and Joyce Anne Reger (née Wood); *m* 1977, Martin Vernon Saunders. *Educ*: Portsmouth High Sch.; Nottingham Univ. (BSc, PhD 1984). CPhys, FInstP 1999 (Hon. FInstP 2016); CEng, FREng 2011. Electronics engr, British Leyland, 1975–78; Res. Scientist, RSRE, 1978–92; Hd, Tech. Policy, Defence Res. Agency, 1992–95; rcds 1995; Director: Defence Test and Evaluation Orgn, 1995–97; Centre for Defence Analysis, DERA, 1997–2000; Res. Councils, OST, DTI, 2000–03; Tech./Ops Dir, DSTL, 2003–06. Non-executive Director: Becatech Systems Ltd, 2013–14; Sentinor Ltd, 2014–16. Mem., UK Space Agency Steering Bd, 2015–; Chair, Bd, Cockcroft Inst., 2016–. Member: REF 2014 Physics Panel, 2012–14; STFC, 2018–. Pres., Inst. of Physics, 2013–15; Trustee: Engrg Develt Trust, 2012–18; RAEng, 2015–18. Mem. Council, Cranfield Univ., 2009–16. Hon. DSc: Nottingham, 2015; Cranfield, 2017; DUniv Open, 2016. *Recreations*: cycling, walking, music, playing guitar, travel. *E*: francessaunders@hotmail.com.

**SAUNDERS, Grace Augustina;** *see* Amakye, G. A.

**SAUNDERS, Jennifer;** actress, writer; *b* 6 July 1958; *m* Adrian Edmondson; three *d*. *Educ*: Central Sch. of Speech and Drama. *Theatre*: An Evening with French and Saunders (nat. tour), 1989; Me and Mamie O'Rourke, Strand, 1993; French and Saunders Live - 2000, Apollo Hammersmith, 2000; French and Saunders: Still Alive (nat. tour), 2008; Lady Windermere's Fan, Vaudeville Th., 2018; Blithe Spirit, Th. Royal Bath, 2019; writer, Viva Forever!, Piccadilly Th., 2012; *television*: actor and co-writer: Ab Fab The Last Shout, 1996; Mirrorball, 2000; actor: The Boy in the Dress, 2014; Grandpa's Great Escape, 2018; *series*: The Comic Strip Presents…, 1982–90; Girls on Top, 1985–87; French and Saunders (5 series); Absolutely Fabulous, 1992–96, 2001–03, 2011 (Emmy Award, 1993; BAFTA Award, 2012); Jam and Jerusalem, 2006, 2008, 2009; The Life and Times of Vivienne Vyle, 2007; (actor) Let Them Eat Cake, 1999; (documentary) Jennifer Saunders: Back in the Saddle, 2012; (actor) Five Go To Rehab, 2012; (actor) Blandings, 2013–14; *films*: The Supergrass, 1984; Muppet Treasure Island, 1996; In the Bleak Midwinter, 1996; Fanny and Elvis, 1999; (actor and writer) Absolutely Fabulous: the Movie, 2016; Patrick, 2018; Isn't It Romantic, 2019. Fellow, BAFTA, 2009. *Publications*: (with Dawn French) A Feast of French and Saunders, 1992; Absolutely Fabulous: the scripts, 1993; Absolutely Fabulous: Continuity, 2001; Bonkers: my life in laughs, 2013. *Address*: c/o United Agents, 12–26 Lexington Street, W1F 0LE.

**SAUNDERS, Hon. Sir John Henry Boulton,** Kt 2007; a Judge of the High Court of Justice, Queen's Bench Division, 2007–16; *b* 15 March 1949; *s* of Kathleen Mary Saunders and Henry G. B. Saunders; *m* 1975, Susan Mary Chick; one *s* two *d*. *Educ*: Uppingham School; Magdalen College, Oxford (BA). Called to the Bar, Gray's Inn, 1972; a Recorder, 1990–2004; QC 1991; a Senior Circuit Judge, 2004–07; Recorder of Birmingham, 2004–07. Mem., Sentencing Council for England and Wales, 2013–16; a Surveillance Comr, 2016–; Judicial Mem. and Vice Chm., Parole Bd, 2016–. Vis. Fellow, Magdalen Coll., Oxford, 2016–17. Hon. DLaws Birmingham, 2008. *Publications*: (ed) Paterson's Licensing Acts, 2004–. *Recreation*: music.

**SAUNDERS, Prof. Kenneth Barrett,** MD, DSc; FRCP; Professor of Medicine, St George's Hospital Medical School, 1980–95, now Emeritus; *b* 16 March 1936; *s* of Harold N. Saunders and Winifred F. Saunders (née Gadge); *m* 1961, Philippa Mary Harrison; one *s* one *d*. *Educ*: Kingswood Sch., Bath; Trinity Hall, Cambridge (MB BChir 1961; MA 1966; MD 1966); St Thomas's Hosp. Med. Sch.; DSc London 1995. FRCP 1978. Sen. Lectr, then Reader in Medicine, Middx Hosp. Med. Sch., 1972–80; Dean, Fac. of Medicine, London Univ., 1990–94. Member: GMC, 1992–95; Jt Planning and Adv. Cttee, 1990–94; Jt Cttee on Higher Med. Trng, 1990–94. Hon. Consultant Physician to the Army, 1994–97. Chm., Assoc. of Clinical Profs of Medicine, 1993–95. Royal College of Physicians: Tudor Edwards Lectr, 1987; Procensor, 1986–87; Censor, 1987–88. Member: Governing Body, BPMF, 1990–96; Council, Sch. of Pharmacy, London Univ., 1990–96. Vice-Pres., Hellenic Soc., 2005– (Hon. Treas., 1998–2005). *Publications*: Clinical Physiology of the Lung, 1977; various papers on respiratory science and medicine, and on Homer. *Recreations*: English, classical and Egyptian literature, gardening, golf. *Address*: 77 Lee Road, Blackheath, SE3 9EN. *T*: (020) 8852 8138. *Clubs*: Royal Automobile, Academy, Royal Society of Medicine; Royal Blackheath Golf.

**SAUNDERS, Matthew John,** MBE 1998; FSA; Secretary, Ancient Monuments Society, 1977–2018; *b* 12 April 1953; *s* of John William Saunders and Joyce Mary Saunders. *Educ*: Latymer Sch., Edmonton; Corpus Christi Coll., Cambridge (MA Hist. and Hist. of Architecture 1974). FSA 1980. Editorial Asst, Whitaker's Almanack, 1975; Sec., SAVE Britain's Heritage, 1976–77; Asst Sec., Ancient Monuments Soc., 1976. Sec., Jt Cttee of Nat. Amenity Socs, 1982–2005; Dir, Friends of Friendless Churches, 1993–2018; Trustee: Historic Chapels Trust, 1993–95; Heritage Lottery Fund, 2005–11 (Member: Places of Worship Adv. Cttee, 1995–98; Historic Bldgs and Land Panel, 1999–2005); John Coales Charitable Trust, 2014–. Member: Fabric Adv. Cttee, St Paul's Cathedral, 2001–03; Church Bldgs Council, 2016–. Pres., Men of the Stones, 2015– (Vice Pres., 2000–15); Vice President: Ecclesiological Soc., 1994–; Enfield Preservation Soc., 1999–. IHBC 1998. *Publications*: (contrib.) Railway Architecture, 1979; (contrib.) The Architectural Outsiders, 1985; The Historic Home Owner's Companion, 1987; (contrib.) Concerning Buildings, 1996; Saving Churches: the first 50 years of the Friends of Friendless Churches, 2010. *Recreations*: music, travel, photography, good food.

**SAUNDERS, Michael Potter;** Chief Executive, Bibendum PLB Group, 2014–16 and since 2018; *b* Bath, 20 Aug. 1963; *s* of Peter Saunders and Didi Saunders; *m* 1992, Katherina Peyton-Jones; two *s* one *d*. *Educ*: Eton Coll. Bibendum Wine Ltd, 1982–2016: Sales Dir, 1989–2001; Jt Man. Dir, 2001–16; Man. Dir, 2006–16; Business Develt Dir, Conviviality plc, 2016–17. Chairman: Wine and Spirit Trade Assoc., 2019–; The Benevolent, 2019–. *Recreations*: golf, ski-ing. *Address*: Bibendum PLB Group, 109a Regents Park Road, NW1 8UR. *Club*: White's.

**SAUNDERS, Dr Nicholas Thomas**; QC 2018; *b* London, 27 June 1974; *s* of John and Jeanne Saunders; *m* 2001, Nicola; three *d*. *Educ*: Dulwich Coll.; Magdalene Coll., Cambridge (BA 1996; MA; PhD); City Univ. (Postgrad. DipLaw); Inns of Court Sch. of Law (BVC). With CERN, Geneva, 1995–96; Associate Lectr, Cambridge Univ., 1999–2006; called to the Bar, 2001; Mem., Attorney Gen.'s Panel of Counsel, 2011–14; Standing Counsel to Comptroller Gen. of Patents, Designs and Trade Marks, 2014–18. *Publications*: Divine Action and Modern Science, 2001; (contrib.) Copinger and Scone James on Copyright, 15th edn 2004, 16th edn 2010; (contrib.) Modern Law of Patents, 2nd edn, 2010. *Recreations*: family, sport, classical music, opera. *Address*: Brick Court Chambers, 7–8 Essex Street, WC2R 3LD. *T*: (020) 7379 3550. *E*: clerks@brickcourt.co.uk. *Club*: Leander (Henley-on-Thames).

**SAUNDERS, Nigel James**, MD; FRCOG; Consultant Obstetrician, Southampton University Hospitals, 1992–2014; *b* 9 May 1955; *s* of Peter St John and Eileen Saunders; *m* 1988, Deborah Sanderson; three *d*. *Educ*: Manchester Grammar Sch.; Manchester Univ. (MB ChB; MD 1989). FRCSE 1983; FRCOG 1983. Lectr in Obstetrics and Gynaecol., Sheffield Univ., 1985–89; Consultant and Sen. Lectr, St Mary's Med. Sch., Paddington, 1989–92; Med Dir, Southampton Univ. Hosps NHS Trust, 2001–07. *Publications*: articles and editorials relating to labour ward mgt and minimally invasive surgery in BMJ, Lancet. *Recreations*: cycling, reading, songwriting, blues guitar. *Address*: 420 Fulwood Road, Sheffield S10 3GH. *E*: nigelsaunders@gmail.com.

**SAUNDERS, Peter Gordon**; Editor, The Birmingham Post, 1986–90; *b* 1 July 1940; *s* of late Gordon and Winifred Saunders; *m* 1964, Teresa Geraldine Metcalf; two *d*. *Educ*: Newport High Sch. for Boys, Gwent; London Sch. of Econs and Pol Science (BScEcon 1961). Reporter, Gloucestershire Echo, 1961–63; Sports Reporter, Sunderland Echo, 1963–64; Sub-Editor: Yorkshire Post, 1964; The Birmingham Post, 1964–69; Lectr in Journalism, Cardiff Coll. of Commerce, 1969–70; The Birmingham Post, 1971–90: successively Dep. Chief Sub-Editor, Chief Sub-Editor, Asst Editor, Exec. Editor; media consultant, 1991–2005. *Recreations*: Rugby Union, reading, rhythm and blues, golf. *Address*: 3 Carpenter Close, Langstone, Newport, South Wales NP18 2LF. *T*: and *Fax*: (01633) 411688. *E*: petesaund@sky.com. *Club*: Newport High School Old Boys.

**SAUNDERS, Prof. Philippa Tansy Kemp**, PhD; FMedSci; Professor of Reproductive Steroids, MRC Centre for Inflammation Research, and Dean, Postgraduate Research, College of Medicine and Veterinary Medicine, since 2012, University of Edinburgh; *d* of late Christopher and of Hazel Saunders; *m* 1989, William Byers; one *s* one *d*. *Educ*: Bristol Univ. (BSc Hons); Darwin Coll., Cambridge (PhD 1982). Postdoctoral Associate, Univ. of Florida, 1981–84; Res. Associate, Inst. of Zool., Zool Soc. of London, 1984–87; University of Edinburgh: Res. Fellow, Dept of Obstetrics and Gynaecol., 1987–89; Prog. Leader, MRC Human Reproductive Scis Unit, 1989–2011; granted tenured post with MRC, 1993; Hon. Res. Fellow, 1998–2005; Hon. Prof., 2005–11; Hd, Centre for Reproductive Biol., 2007–11; Dir, MRC Centre for Reproductive Health, 2011–12. Registrar, Acad. Med. Scis, 2016–20. *Publications*: contribs to learned jls related to field of reproductive health. *Recreations*: jogging, pilates, theatre, city breaks. *Address*: MRC Centre for Inflammation Research, Queen's Medical Research Institute, 47 Little France Crescent, Edinburgh EH16 4TJ. *T*: (0131) 242 6388, *Fax*: (0131) 242 6441. *E*: p.saunders@ed.ac.uk.

**SAUNDERS, Raymond**; Secretary, British Museum (Natural History), 1976–87; *b* 24 July 1933; *s* of late Herbert Charles Saunders and Doris May (*née* Kirkham-Jones); *m* 1959, Shirley Marion Stringer (*d* 2017); two *s*. *Educ*: Poole Grammar Sch. WO, 1950; Air Min., 1956; Min. of Land and Natural Resources, 1966; Land Commn, 1967; Treasury, 1968; CSD, 1969. *Recreations*: reading biographies, gardening, sport (now as spectator). *Address*: 24 Landguard Manor Road, Shanklin, Isle of Wight PO37 7HZ.

**SAUNDERS, Richard**; Partnership Consultant, Christ's Hospital, 1993–96; *b* 4 July 1937; *s* of late Edward E. Saunders and Betty Saunders; *m* 1st, 1961, Suzannah Rhodes-Cooke (marr. diss.); one *s*; 2nd, 1970, Alison Fiddes. *Educ*: St Edmund's Sch., Hindhead; Uppingham. FRICS 1965. National Service, commnd The Life Guards, 1958–60. Jun. Partner, Richard Ellis, Chartered Surveyors, 1966–69; formed Richard Saunders & Partners, 1969; Baker Harris Saunders, 1977; Chm., Baker Harris Saunders Group, 1986–92; Director: Herring Baker Harris, 1992–93; (non-exec.) Herring Baker Harris Gp, 1992–93. Chm., City Br., RICS, 1979–80; Pres., Associated Owners of City Properties, 1985–87; Member: Council, British Property Fedn, 1979–90 (Hon. Treas., 1974–85); Bd, Gen. Practice Finance Corp., 1984–89. Chairman: Barbican Residential Cttee, 1981–83; Barbican Centre Cttee, 1983–86; Metropolitan Public Gardens Assoc., 1984–90; Governor: Bridewell Royal Hosp. and King Edward's Sch., Witley, 1976–93; St Edmund's Sch., Hindhead, 1979–93 (Chm., 1979–87); (also Almoner), Christ's Hosp., 1980–93; Royal Star and Garter Home, 1984–2007. Mem., Court of Common Council, Corp. of London, 1975–2000; Deputy for Ward of Candlewick, 1983–2000; Liveryman: Clothworkers' Co., 1960– (Warden, 1989; Master, 2001–02); Co. of Chartered Surveyors, 1979–93; Church Warden, St Lawrence Jewry-by-Guildhall, 1984–2004; Sheriff, City of London, 1987–88. *Recreations*: instant gardening, music, golf, tennis. *Address*: The Old Rectory, Bagendon, Cirencester, Glos GL7 7DU. *Club*: MCC.

**SAUNDERS, Steven Michael**; Creative Director and Founding Partner, Fabled Studio, since 2011; *b* Reading, 28 June 1982; *s* of Michael Trevor and Susan Saunders; partner, Carolyn Sophie Kelly; one *s*. *Educ*: Arts Inst., Bournemouth (BA Hons 3D Design 2004). Jun. designer, GMP Design Associates, 2004–07; middle weight designer, United Designers, 2007; Sen. Interior Designer, David Collins Studio, 2007–11. *Publications*: Room: inside contemporary interiors, 2014. *Recreation*: sharpening knives and pretending to be a chef! *Address*: Fabled Studio, 116 Commercial Street, E1 6NF. *T*: (020) 7269 9900. *E*: steven@fabledstudio.com.

**SAUNDERS, Prof. William Philip**, PhD; Professor of Endodontology, University of Dundee, 2000–13, now Emeritus; Hon. Consultant in Restorative Dentistry: Greater Glasgow Health Board, 1988–2000; Tayside Health Board, 2000–13; Dean, Dental Faculty, Royal College of Surgeons Edinburgh, 2014–17; *b* 12 Oct. 1948; *s* of late William Walton Saunders and Elva Doreen Saunders; *m* 2009, Jennifer Anne, *d* of Alexander Birrell Wilkinson, *qv*; one *s* one *d* from a previous marriage. *Educ*: RAF Changi Grammar Sch., Singapore; Maidstone Grammar Sch.; Royal Dental Hosp. of London (BDS 1970); Univ. of Dundee (PhD 1986). FDSRCSE 1982; FDSRCPSGlas 1993; MRD 1994; FDS RCS *ad eundem* 2001; FCDSHK 2009. Dental Officer, RAF, 1971–75; gen. dental practice, 1975–81; Lectr, Dept of Conservative Dentistry, Univ. of Dundee, 1981–88; University of Glasgow: Sen. Lectr in Clinical Practice, 1988–93; Personal Chair in Clinical Practice, 1993–95; Personal Chair in Endodontology, 1995–2000; Dean and Hd of Dept, Univ. of Dundee Dental Sch., 2000–11. Postgrad. Dental Hosp. Tutor, Glasgow Dental Hosp., 1992–95. Chairman: Council of Heads and Deans of Dental Schs, later Dental Schs Council, 2008–11; Dental Cttee, NHS Educn for Scotland, 2013–19. Pres., British Endodontic Soc., 1997–98; Chm., Assoc. of Consultants and Specialists in Restorative Dentistry, 1999–2002; Mem., Dental Council, 2000–17, Chm., Speciality Adv. Bd in Restorative Dentistry, 2006–12, RCSE. Chm. Educn Cttee, 1996–2009, Congress Pres., 2007–09, Eur. Soc. of Endodontology. FHEA (ILTM 2000); Fellow, Faculty of Dental Trainers, RCSE, 2017; Hon. FRCSE 2018. Hon. Diplomate, Indian Bd of Endodontics, 2017. DSc (ad hominem) Aberdeen, 2011. *Publications*: chapters in textbooks; res. papers on endodontics and applied dental materials. *Recreations*: ornithology (a bird ringer), natural history, golf (badly), Scottish art. *Address*: University of Dundee Dental School, Park Place, Dundee DD1 4HN. *T*: (01382) 635977, *Fax*: (01382) 225163. *E*: w.p.saunders@dundee.ac.uk, williamphilipsaunders@gmail.com. *Clubs*: Royal Air Force; New (Edinburgh).

**SAUNDERS WATSON, Comdr (Leslie) Michael (Macdonald)**, CBE 1993; RN (retired); Chairman: British Library Board, 1990–93; Kettering General Hospital NHS Trust, 1993–99; *b* 9 Oct. 1934; *s* of Captain L. S. Saunders, DSO, RN (retd), and Elizabeth Saunders (*née* Culme-Seymour); *m* 1958, Georgina Elizabeth Laetitia, *d* of Adm. Sir William Davis, GCB, DSO; two *s* one *d*. *Educ*: Eton; BRNC, Dartmouth. Joined Royal Navy, 1951; specialised in Communications (Jackson Everett Prize); Comdr 1969; retired, 1971, on succession to Rockingham Castle Estate. Pres., Historic Houses Assoc., 1982–88 (Dep. Pres., 1978–82; Chm., Tax and Parly Cttee, 1975–82); Chairman: Northamptonshire Assoc. Youth Clubs, 1977–91 (Pres., 1997–2008); Heritage Educn Year, 1977; Corby Community Adv. Gp, 1979–86; Ironstone Royalty Owners Assoc., 1979–91; Nat. Curriculum History Wkg Gp, 1988–90; Heritage Educn Trust, 1988–99; Modern Records Centre Adv. Cttee, Warwick Univ., 1993–98; Public Affairs Cttee, ICOMOS UK, 1994–98; Friends of British Library, 1994–2000; Vice-Chm., Northamptonshire Small Industries Cttee, 1974–79; Member: British Heritage Cttee, BTA, 1978–88; Northamptonshire Enterprise Agency, 1986–90; Country Landowners' Association: Member: Taxation Cttee, 1975–90; Exec. Cttee, 1977–82, 1987–92; Legal and Land Use Cttee, 1982–87; F and GP Cttee, 1994–98; Chairman: Northamptonshire Branch, 1981–84; Game Fair Local Cttee, 1997. Director: Lamport Hall Preservation Trust, 1978–91; English Sinfonia, 1981–2000. Trustee: Royal Botanic Gdns, Kew, 1983–91 (Chm., Bldgs and Design Cttee, 1985–91); Nat. Heritage Meml Fund, 1987–96. Chm., Governors Lodge Park Comprehensive Sch., 1977–82; Trustee, Oakham Sch., 1975–77. FSA 2001; FRSA 1986. High Sheriff, 1978–79, DL 1979–2009, Northamptonshire. Hon. DLitt: Warwick, 1991; Leicester, 1997. *Publications*: I Am Given A Castle: a memoir, 2008. *Recreations*: sailing, music, gardening, painting. *Address*: The Manor House, Ashley Road, Stoke Albany, Market Harborough, Leicestershire LE16 8PL.

**SAUVAIN, Stephen John**; QC 1995; *b* 1949; *s* of Alan Sauvain and Norah Sauvain; *m* 1980, Christine McLean; two *s*, and one step *s*. *Educ*: King Edward VII Grammar Sch., King's Lynn; Sidney Sussex Coll., Cambridge (MA, LLB). Lectr in Law, Univ. of Manchester, 1971–78; called to the Bar, Lincoln's Inn, 1977; in practice as barrister, 1978–2019. Gen. Ed., Encyclopedia of Highway Law and Practice, 4 vols, 1965–2018 (Consultant Ed., 2018–). *Publications*: Highway Law, 1988, 5th edn 2013. *Address*: Marconnelle, Spring Grove, Milverton, Taunton, Som TA4 1NL.

**SAUVEN, John Bernard**; Executive Director, Greenpeace, since 2007; *b* London, 6 Sept. 1954; *s* of late Maurice Oswald Sauven and of Helen Mary Orpin; *m* 1990, Janet Helene Convery; two *s*. *Educ*: University Coll., Cardiff (BSc Econ). Actg Gen. Sec., CND, 1989; Campaign and Communications Dir, Greenpeace, 2001–07. *Recreations*: photography, poetry, sailing. *Address*: Greenpeace, Canonbury Villas, N1 2PN. *T*: 07929 638296. *E*: john.sauven@greenpeace.org.

**SAVAGE, Caroline Le Quesne**; *see* Lucas, C.

**SAVAGE, Francis Joseph**, CMG 1996; LVO 1986; OBE 1989; HM Diplomatic Service, retired; Adviser to Foreign and Commonwealth Office, since 2003; Principal, FS Associates, since 2004; Chairman, Commonwealth Disaster Management Agency, since 2015; *b* Preston, Lancs, 8 Feb. 1943; *s* of late Francis Fitzgerald Savage and Mona May Savage (*née* Parsons); *m* 1966, Veronica Mary McAleenan; two *s*. *Educ*: Holy Cross Convent, Broadstairs; St Stephen's Sch., Welling, Kent; NW Kent Coll., Dartford. Joined FO, 1961; served in: Cairo, 1967–70; Washington, 1971–73; Vice-Consul, Aden, 1973–74; FCO, 1974–78; Vice-Consul, then Consul (Commercial), Düsseldorf, 1978–82; Consul, Peking, 1982–86; First Sec. (Consular), Lagos, and Consul for Benin, 1987–90; First Sec., FCO, 1990–93; Counsellor, FCO, 1993; Governor: Montserrat, 1993–97; British Virgin Islands, 1998–2002. Member: Catenian Assoc., 1991–; Montserrat Nat. Trust, 1993–97; Montserrat Cricket Assoc., 1993–97; London Soc. of Ragamuffins, 2002– (Pres., 2008–09). Trustee: Virgin Islands Search and Rescue, UK, 2002–; Montserrat Foundn, 2008–. Chm., Friends of the BVI, 2005–. Ambassador, MISSIO, 2016–. Montserrat Badge of Honour, 2001. KCSG 2002. *Recreations*: cricket, volcano watching, hurricane dodging, travel, meeting people. *Address*: Commonwealth Disaster Management Agency, Cornhill House, 59–60 Cornhill, EC3V 3PD; FS Associates, 19 Cleeve Park Gardens, Sidcup, Kent DA14 4JL. *Clubs*: Royal Over-Seas League; Peking Cricket; Royal British Virgin Islands Yacht (Life Mem.).

**SAVAGE, Gary John**, MA, PhD; Head Master, Alleyn's School, since 2010; *b* Oulton Broad, Suffolk, 5 Dec. 1970; *s* of Keith Savage and Doreen Savage; *m* 1992, Natalie Watts. *Educ*: Bungay High Sch.; Sidney Sussex Coll., Cambridge (BA Hist. 1992; MA 1995; PhD 2005). Eton College: Asst Master, 1996–2000; Hd of Hist., 2000–02; Master-in-Coll., 2002–06; Under Master, Westminster Sch., 2006–10. Chm., London Div., HMC, 2014–15. Trustee, Dulwich Picture Gall., 2014–18. Governor: Notting Hill Prep. Sch., 2004–14; Roedean Sch., 2016–19; London Acad. Excellence, Tottenham, 2017–. FRSA. *Publications*: (contrib.) Cultures of Power in Europe During the Long Eighteenth Century, 2007. *Recreations*: German, Ipswich Town FC, the Arts. *Address*: Alleyn's School, Townley Road, Dulwich, SE22 8SU. *T*: (020) 8557 1500. *E*: headmaster@alleyns.org.uk.

**SAVAGE, Prof. Michael**, PhD; FBA 2007; Martin White Professor of Sociology, London School of Economics and Political Science, since 2014 (Professor of Sociology, 2012–14); *b* 20 June 1959; *s* of Dennis Savage and Margaret Savage; one *s*. *Educ*: Univ. of York (BA 1980); Univ. of Lancaster (MA 1981; PhD 1984). Res. Asst, Univ. of Lancaster, 1984–85; Res. Fellow in Urban Studies, 1985–87, British Acad. Post-doctoral Res. Fellow, 1988–89, Univ. of Sussex; Temp. Lectr, Univ. of Surrey, 1987–88; Keele University: Lectr, 1989–93; Sen. Lectr, 1993–94; Reader, 1994–95; University of Manchester: Prof. of Sociol., 1995–2010; Hd, Dept of Sociol., 1999–2001; Dir, ESRC Centre for Res. on Socio-Cultural Change, 2003–10 (Vis. Fellow, 2010–); University of York: Prof. of Sociol., 2010–12; Hd of Dept, 2011–12; Vis. Prof., 2012–. Visiting Professor: Univ. of N Carolina at Chapel Hill, 1995–96; Sciences Po, Paris, 2004; Adjunct Prof., Bergen, 2010–11. FAcSS (AcSS 2003). Managing Ed., Sociol. Rev., 2001–07. *Publications*: (jtly) Localities, Class and Gender, 1985; The Dynamics of Working-class Politics: Labour movement in Preston, 1880–1940, 1987; (ed jtly) Gender and Bureaucracy, 1992; (jtly) Property, Bureaucracy and Culture: middle class formation in contemporary Britain, 1992; (with A. Wardle) Urban Sociology, Capitalism and Modernity, 1993, 2nd edn (with K. Ward) 2003 (trans. Portuguese, Arabic, Chinese, 2003); (with A. Miles) The Remaking of the British Working Class 1840–1940, 1993; (ed jtly) Social Change and the Middle Classes, 1995; (jtly) Gender, Organisations and Careers, 1997; Class Analysis and Social Transformation, 2000; (ed jtly) Renewing Class Analysis, 2000; (jtly) Globalisation and Belonging, 2004; (ed jtly) Rethinking Class, Identities, Cultures and Lifestyles, 2004; (ed jtly) Remembering Elites, 2008; (ed jtly) Networked Urbanism, 2008; (jtly) Culture, Class Distinction, 2009; Identities and Social Change in Britain since 1940, 2010; Social Class in the 21st Century,

2015; contribs to jls incl. Sociol., Cultural Sociol., Contemp. British Hist., Sociol Rev., British Jl Sociol. *Address:* Department of Sociology, London School of Economics and Political Science, Houghton Street, WC2A 2AE.

**SAVAGE, Prof. (Richard) Nigel,** PhD; Chairman, Savage Hutchinson Consulting Ltd, since 2014; Chief Executive, 1996–2013, President, 2013–14, now Emeritus President, University of Law (formerly College of Law of England and Wales); *b* 27 May 1950; *s of* Jack and Joan Savage; *m* 1st, 1976, Linda Jane Sherwin (marr. diss. 2006); two *s*; 2nd, 2010, Sarah Hutchinson. *Educ:* Edward Cludd Sch., Southwell; Newark Tech. Coll.; Manchester Poly. (BA 1st cl. 1972); Univ. of Sheffield (LLM 1974); Univ. of Strathclyde (PhD 1980). Lectr, Univ. of Strathclyde, 1974–83; Principal Lectr, Nottingham Poly., 1983–85; Prof., 1985–96, and Dean and Founding Man. Dir, 1989–96, Nottingham Law Sch. Mem., HEFCE, 2002–09. Consultant, Nat. Centre for Citizenship and the Law, 2014–. Non-exec. Dir, Fletchers Solicitors Ltd, 2014–. Hon. LLD Univ. of Law, 2015. *Publications:* Business Law, 1987, 2nd edn (with R. Bradgate) 1993; (with R. Bradgate) Commercial Law, 1991; articles in business and legal jls. *Recreation:* cricket. *Address:* 3 Foxhill Court, Tarporley, Cheshire CW6 0FA. *Club:* Reform.

**SAVAGE, Thomas Hixon,** CBE 1990; Chairman: North American Trust Co., 1992–95; A. G. Simpson Automotive Inc., 1996–2000; *b* Belfast, 21 Nov. 1928; *s of* Thomas Hixon Savage and Martha Foy Turkington; *m* 1st, 1950, Annie Gloria Ethel Gilmore (marr. diss. 1975); one *s* two *d*; 2nd, 1976, Evelyn Phyllis Chapman. *Educ:* Belfast High Sch.; Indian Army Officers' Trng Coll.; Univ. of Toronto Dept of Extension (Indust. Management). Supervisor, Methods & Standards, W. J. Gage, 1953–58; Manager, Process Engrg, Hallmark Greeting Cards, 1958–63; Manager, Ops Improvements, Union Carbide (Canada) 1963–68; ITT Canada Ltd: Dir, Ops Staffs, 1968–73; Chm. and Pres., 1973–93; Sen. Officer (Canada), ITT Corp., NY, 1984–93. Dir, Samuel Manu-Tech Inc., 1994–2010. Chm., Abbey Life Insurance Co., Canada; formerly Chief Industrial Engineer: Dunlop Canada; Electric Reduction Co.; Dir, Acklands; Mem. Adv. Bd, Accenture (formerly Andersen Consulting). Former Mem., Policy Cttee, Business Council on Nat. Issues; Business Co-Chm., Canadian Labour Market & Productivity Center, 1990. Director: Nat. Retinitis Pigmentosa Eye Res. Foundn, Canada; Ireland Fund of Canada, 1979–95 (Chm., 1996–98). Mem., Bd of Trustees, 1995–99, Heritage Gov., 2000–05, Royal Ontario Mus. Chairman: Bd of Govs, West Park Hosp., 1991–94; Adv. Bd, Canadian Inst. of Management, 1971 (Life Mem.); Adv. Bd, Boys' and Girls' Clubs of Canada; NI Partnership in Canada. *Recreation:* golf. *Address:* 15 Prince William Way, Barrie, ON L4N 0Y9, Canada. *Clubs:* Ontario (Toronto); Lambton Golf and Country (Islington).

**SAVAGE, (Thomas) William,** CMG 1993; HM Diplomatic Service, retired; Senior Duty Officer, Cabinet Office, 1996–2001; *b* Knockloughrim, Co. Derry, 21 Nov. 1937; *s of* late Hugh Murray Savage and Anna Mary Savage (*née* Whyte); *m* 1966, Gloria Jean Matthews; three *d*. *Educ:* Sullivan Upper Sch., Holywood, Co. Down; Queen's Univ., Belfast (BA (Hons), DipEd); LSE. Vice-Pres. and Sec., 1961–64, Pres., 1964–66, Nat. Union of Students; journalist, ITN, 1967; joined Diplomatic Service, 1968; Dar es Salaam, 1970–73; First Sec., FCO, 1973; Counsellor, on loan to Cabinet Office, 1981; Counsellor, FCO, 1984–93. *Recreations:* amateur drama, golf, topiary. *Clubs:* Wimbledon Park Golf, Tanganyika Golfing Society.

**SAVAGE, Wendy Diane,** FRCOG; Senior Lecturer in Obstetrics and Gynaecology, St Bartholomew's and the Royal London School of Medicine and Dentistry, Queen Mary, University of London (formerly London Hospital Medical College. then Queen Mary and Westfield College), 1977–2000; *b* 12 April 1935; *d of* William George Edwards and Anne (*née* Smith); *m* 1960, Miguel Babatunde Richard Savage (marr. diss. 1973); two *s* two *d*. *Educ:* Croydon High School for Girls; Girton Coll., Cambridge (BA); London Hosp. Med. Coll. (MB BCh); London Sch. of Hygiene and Tropical Medicine (MSc (Public Health) 1997). MRCOG 1971, FRCOG 1985. Res. Fellow, Harvard Univ., 1963–64; MO, Nigeria, 1964–67; Registrar: Surgery and Obst. and Gynaec., Kenya, 1967–69; Obst. and Gynaec., Royal Free Hosp., 1969–71; venereology, abortion work, family planning, Islington, 1971–73; Specialist in obst. and gynaec., family planning and venereology, Gisborne, NZ, 1973–76; Lectr, London Hosp., 1976–77. Queen Mary, University of London: Hon. Sen. Clinical Lectr, Wolfson Inst. of Preventive Medicine, Bart's and The London Sch. of Medicine and Dentistry, 2002–05; Hon. Sen. Res. Fellow, Centre for Envmtl and Preventative Medicine and Dentistry, 2005–. Hon. Vis. Prof., Middx Univ., 1991–. Contract as Hon. Cons. suspended for alleged incompetence, April 1985 - reinstated by unanimous vote of DHA after exoneration by HM61/112 Enquiry, July 1986. Member: GMC, 1989–2005; Council, BMA, 2016–. Public Gov., Camden and Islington NHS Foundn Trust, 2012–. Pres., Keep Our NHS Public, 2013–. Hon. DSc Greenwich, 2001. Lifetime Achievement Award in Sexual Health, Brook/FPA, 2013; Award for Outstanding Contribution to Health, BMJ, 2018. *Publications:* Hysterectomy, 1982; (with Fran Reader) Coping with Caesarean Section and other difficult births, 1983; A Savage Enquiry - who controls childbirth?, 1986; (jtly) Caesarean Birth in Britain, 1993; (jtly) Birth and Power, 2008; papers on abortion, sexually transmitted disease, ultrasound, sex in pregnancy, cervical cytology, medical education. *Recreations:* playing piano duets, reading, fell-walking. *Address:* Flat 11, Galileo Apartments, 48 Featherstone Street, EC1Y 8RT. *E:* wd.savage@qmul.ac.uk, wdsavage@doctors.org.uk.

**SAVAGE, William;** *see* Savage, T. W.

**SAVAGE-SMITH, Prof. Emilie,** PhD; FBA 2010; former Professor of the History of Islamic Science, University of Oxford; Fellow, since 2004, and Archivist, St Cross College, Oxford. Sen. Res. Consultant, Bodleian Liby. Co-Pres., Soc. for Hist. of Medieval Technol. and Sci. Former Mem. Council, British Inst. for Study of Iraq (formerly British Sch. of Archaeol. in Iraq). *Publications:* Science, Tools and Magic, Pt I (with F. Maddison), Body and Spirit, Mapping the Universe, Pt II, Mundane Worlds, 1997; (with E. Edson) Medieval Views of the Cosmos, 2004; A Descriptive Catalogue of Oriental Manuscripts at St John's College, Oxford, 2005; (with P. Pormann) Medieval Islamic Medicine, 2007; A New Catalogue of Arabic Manuscripts in the Bodleian Library, University of Oxford, Vol. 1: Medicine, 2011; (ed with Y. Rapoport) An Eleventh-Century Egyptian Guide to the Universe: the Book of Curiosities, 2014; (ed) St Cross at Fifty, 2014; (with Y. Rapoport) Lost Maps of the Caliphs, 2019. *Address:* c/o Oriental Institute, University of Oxford, Pusey Lane, Oxford OX1 2LE.

**SAVARESE, Signora Fernando;** *see* Elvin, Violetta.

**SAVÉN, Bjorn;** Chairman, IK Investment Partners Ltd, since 2010; *b* Stockholm, 29 Sept. 1950; *s of* Karlerik Savén and Eivor Savén; *m* 1979, Inger; two *s* one *d*. *Educ:* Karolinska Skolan; Stockholm Sch. of Econs (MSc Econ 1972); Harvard Business Sch. (MBA 1976). Financial Analyst, Gulf Oil Nordic, Stockholm, 1972–74; Esselte AB, Stockholm: Planning Associate, 1976; Treas. Internat., 1977–79; Dir, Esselte Meto, London, 1979–84; CFO and Vice Pres., Esselte Business Systems, London, 1984–85; Pres., Esselte Pendaflex, NY, 1986–88; Founder and Chief Exec., Enskilda Ventures, London, 1988–93; Industri Kapital, subseq. IK Investment Partners Ltd: Chief Exec., 1993–2008; Exec. Chm., 2008–10. Member, Board: Finnish-Swedish Chamber of Commerce; German-Swedish Chamber of Commerce; Dep. Chm., Swedish-UK Chamber of Commerce, 2012–. Mem., Supervisory Bd, Heart-Lung Foundn of Sweden. Trustee: Tommy's, 2015–; NPG, 2017–. Mem., Royal Swedish Engrg Scis Acad., 2003– (Dep. Chm., 2008–11). Hon. Fellow, Harris Manchester Coll., Oxford, 2016 (Hon. MA 2017). Dr *hc*: Swedish Sch. of Econs and Business, Helsinki, 1999; Stockholm Sch. of Econs and Business, 2011; Lund, 2013; Sci. Acad. of Bulgaria (and Mem.), 2015. HM the King's Gold Medal, 12th size in seraphim ribbon (Sweden), 2008; Knight 1st Cl., Order of Merit (Germany), 2007; Commander: Order of Lion (Finland), 2008; Order of Merit (Belgium), 2012; Order of Merit (Poland), 2013; Chevalier, Légion d'Honneur (France), 2015. Medal of Honour, Swedish-Finnish Culture Fund, 2012. *Recreations:* golf, shooting, ski-ing. *Address:* IK Investment Partners Ltd, The Adelphi, 1–11 John Adam Street, WC2N 6HT. *T:* (020) 7304 4300. *E:* bjorn.saven@ikinvest.com. *Clubs:* Brooks's, Oxford and Cambridge; Queenwood Golf.

**SAVERNAKE, Viscount; Thomas James Brudenell-Bruce;** *b* 11 Feb. 1982; *s* and *heir* of Earl of Cardigan, *qv*. *Educ:* Radley Coll.; Univ. of Edinburgh.

**SAVIĆ, Prof. Dragan,** PhD; FREng, FICE; Professor of Hydroinformatics, University of Exeter, since 2001 (Head of Engineering, 2010–14); *b* Belgrade, 22 April 1960; *s of* Aleksander and Danica Savić; *m* 2006, Alison; one *s* one *d*. *Educ:* Univ. of Belgrade (Dip. Ing. 1983; MSc Civil Engrg 1987); Univ. of Manitoba (PhD Civil Engrg). CEng, FREng 2013; FCIWEM. Hydraulic Engineer: Energoprojekt, Belgrade, Yugoslavia, 1983–90; KGS Gp, Winnipeg, Canada, 1990–91; Lecturer: Univ. of Novi Sad, Yugoslavia, 1991–95; Univ. of Exeter, 1995–2001. CEO, KWR Watercycle Res. Inst., 2018–. Visiting Professor: Harbin Inst. of Technol., China; Tech. Univ. of Bari, Italy; UNESCO-IHE, Delft, Netherlands; Univ. of Novi Sad; Univ. of Belgrade. Ed.-in-Chief, Internat. Water Assoc. Jl Hydroinformatics. *Publications:* Water Distribution Modeling, 2001; Advanced Water Distribution Modeling and Management, 2003; Water Distribution Systems, 2011. *Recreation:* running. *Address:* Engineering Department, College of Engineering, Mathematics and Physical Sciences, University of Exeter, Harrison Building, Exeter EX4 4QF. *T:* (01392) 723637, *Fax:* (01392) 217965. *E:* d.savic@exeter.ac.uk.

**SAVIDGE, Malcolm Kemp;** Senior Fellow in Nuclear Non-Proliferation and Disarmament, David Davies Memorial Institute of International Studies, Aberystwyth University, since 2009 (Hon. Departmental Fellow in International Politics, 2009–12); *b* 9 May 1946; *s of* late David Gordon Madgwick Savidge and Jean Kirkpatrick Savidge (*née* Kemp). *Educ:* Wallington County Grammar Sch., Surrey; Aberdeen Univ. (MA); Aberdeen Coll. of Educn (Teaching Cert.). Production Control and Computer Asst, Bryans Electronics Ltd, 1970–71; Teacher: Greenwood Dale Secondary Sch., Nottingham, 1971; Peterhead Acad., 1972–73; Teacher of Maths, Kincorth Acad., Aberdeen, 1973–97. Mem. (Lab) Aberdeen City Council, 1980–96 (Dep. Leader, 1994–96). Contested (Lab) Kincardine and Deeside, Nov. 1991 and 1992. MP (Lab) Aberdeen N, 1997–2005. Convener, All Party Parly Gp on Global Security and Non-Proliferation, 2000–05. Parly Consultant, Oxford Res. Gp, 2005–08. Advr, British American Security Inf. Council, 2011– (Mem. Bd, 2005–11). Vice-President: UNA (UK), 2003–; One World Trust, 2005–; Hon. Pres., UNA-Scotland, 2008–12. Governor: Robert Gordon's Inst. of Technol., 1980–88; Aberdeen Coll. of Educn, 1980–87. Member: IISS; RIIA; RUSI. Hon. Fellow, Robert Gordon Univ., 1997. *Recreation:* exploring "life, the Universe and everything". *Address:* Flat 1, 5 Ridgeway Road, Redhill, Surrey RH1 6PQ. *E:* mksavidge@aol.com.

**SAVILE,** family name of Earl of Mexborough.

**SAVILE, 4th Baron** *cr* 1888; **John Anthony Thornhill Lumley-Savile;** *b* 10 Jan. 1947; *s* of late Hon. Henry Leoline Thornhill Lumley-Savile and of Presiley June, *o d of* Geoffrey Herbert Elliot Inchbald; *S* uncle, 2008; *m* 1986, Barbara Ann Holmes, *d of* Anthony Henry Toms. *Educ:* Aiglon Coll., Switzerland. *Heir: half b* Hon. James George Augustus Lumley-Savile [*b* 30 April 1975; *m* 2005, Stephanie, *d of* Dr A. Barba Mendoza].

**SAVILL, Sir John Stewart,** Kt 2008; PhD; FRCP, FRCPE, FMedSci; FRS 2013; FRSE; Regius Professor of Medical Science, University of Edinburgh, since 2017; Hon. Consultant Physician in Renal and General Medicine, Royal Infirmary of Edinburgh, since 1998; *b* 25 April 1957; *s of* Peter Edward Savill and Jean Elizabeth Savill (*née* Garland); *m* 1979, Barbara Campbell; two *s*. *Educ:* St Catherine's Coll., Oxford (BA 1st cl. Hons Physiol Scis 1978); Sheffield Univ. Med. Sch. (MB ChB Hons 1981; Hon. MD 2010); Royal Postgrad. Med. Sch., London (PhD 1989). MRCP 1984, FRCP 1994; FRCPE 2000; FRSE 2005. Jun. med. posts in Sheffield, Nottingham and London, 1981–85; Department of Medicine, Royal Postgraduate Medical School, Hammersmith Hospital: Registrar in Renal Medicine, 1985–86; MRC Training Fellow, 1986–89; Sen. Registrar in Renal Medicine 1989–90; Wellcome Trust Sen. Res. Fellow in Clin. Sci., Hon. Sen. Lectr and Consultant Physician, 1990–93; Prof. in Medicine and Hd, Div. of Renal and Inflammatory Disease, 1993–98, Hd of Sch., 1997–98, Sch. of Med. and Surgical Scis, Univ. of Nottingham Faculty of Medicine and Health Scis; Edinburgh University: Prof. of Medicine, 1998–2005; Prof. of Exptl Medicine, 2005–17; Dir, Univ. of Edinburgh/MRC Centre for Inflammation Res., 2000–02; Vice-Principal, and Head, Coll. of Medicine and Vet. Medicine, 2002–17; Chief Scientist, Scottish Govt Health Directorates, 2008–10; Chief Exec. and Dep. Chm., MRC, 2010–18. Mem., MRC, 2002–08 (Chair: Physiol Med. and Infections Bd, 2002–04; Physiol Systems and Clinical Scis Bd, 2004–07). Chm., Progs and Chairs Cttee, British Heart Foundn, 2007–10. Non-exec. Dir, NHS Lothian, 2002–10. Gov., Health Foundn, 2002–10. Founder FMedSci 1998 (Chm., Wkg Party on Career Structure and Prospects for Clinical Scientists in UK, 1999–2000); Fellow, Amer. Soc. of Nephrology, 2004. Hon. FRCSE 2012; Hon. FRCPCH 2017. Presidential Award, Soc. of Leukocyte Biology of USA, 1989, 1990; Milne-Muehrcke Award, Nat. Kidney Foundn, USA, 1992; Lifetime Achievement Award, European Cell Death Orgn, 2004. *Publications:* papers on cell death in inflammation. *Recreations:* hockey, cricket, Rugby Union, football, literature. *Address:* College of Medicine and Veterinary Medicine, University of Edinburgh, Queen's Medical Research Institute, Edinburgh EH16 4TJ. *T:* (0131) 242 9313. *Club:* Wollaton Cricket (Pres., 2011–).

**SAVILL, Mark Ashley; His Honour Judge Savill;** a Circuit Judge, since 2015; *b* Eastbourne, E Sussex, 17 May 1969; *s of* Brian and Claire Savill; *m* 1997, Rachel Shenton; one *s* one *d*. *Educ:* Eton; Durham Univ. (BA Hons Law). Called to the Bar, Inner Temple, 1993; in practice as barrister: Fenners Chambers, Cambridge, 1993–94; Deans Court Chambers, Manchester, 1994–2015. Fee-paid Judge, Mental Health Rev. Tribunal, 2004–; First Jun. Counsel to Rosemary Nelson Inquiry, 2005–10. Lead Asst Parly Boundary Comr, NW Reg., 2011–12. *Recreations:* golf, yoga, tennis. *Clubs:* MCC; Hale Golf, Rye Golf, Bowdon Lawn Tennis.

**SAVILL, Peter David;** Chairman, British Horseracing Board, 1998–2004; *b* 30 July 1947; *s of* late Harry and Betty Savill; *m* 1996, Ruth Pinder (marr. diss. 2011); two *s* four *d*. *Educ:* Ampleforth Coll.; Downing Coll., Cambridge (LLB 1969). Trainee, Doyle Dane Bernbach, Advertising Agency, 1969–70; Special Projects Manager, Admaster Corp., 1970–71; Asst to Chm., Barclay Securities, 1971–75; President: P & D International, 1975–91; International Voyager Publications, 1980–91; Shorex International, 1991–95; Chm., North South Net,

1985–98. Chm., Plumpton Racecourse, 1998–. Director: Horserace Totalisator Bd, 1998–2002; Horserace Betting Levy Bd, 1998–99; Atheraces, 2001–04. *Recreations:* cricket, golf, horse racing, sport. *Clubs:* Residence (Dublin); K; Gleneagles.

**SAVILL, Dame Rosalind (Joy),** DBE 2009 (CBE 2000); FBA 2006; FSA; Director, The Wallace Collection, 1992–2011, now Curator Emeritus; *b* 12 May 1951; *d* of late Dr Guy Savill and Lorna (*née* Williams); one *d*. *Educ:* Wycombe Abbey Sch.; Châtelard Sch., sur-Montreux; Univ. of Leeds (BA Hons 1972); Study Centre, London (Dip in Fine and Decorative Arts 1973). Ceramics Dept, V&A Mus., 1973–74; The Wallace Collection: Museum Asst, 1974–78; Asst to Dir, 1978–92. Guest Scholar, J. Paul Getty Mus., 1985. Mem. Council, Attingham Trust, 1980–92; Member: Nat. Trust Arts Panel, 1995–2015; Art Adv. Cttee, Nat. Mus and Galls of Wales, 1997–2003; Museums and Collections Adv. Cttee, English Heritage, 1998–2003; Accreditation Panel, MLA (formerly Registration Cttee, Museums and Galls Commn), 1999–2007; Adv. Cttee, Royal Mint, 1999–2007; Expert Panel, NHMF, 2006–13; Academic Cttee, Waddesdon Manor, 2012–. Conseiller d'Administration, Sèvres: Cité de la Céramique, 2010–12. Trustee: Somerset House Trust, 1997–2004; Campaign for Museums, 1999–2008; Samuel Courtauld Trust, 2008–; Holburne Museum, Bath, 2003–07; Buccleuch Living Heritage Trust, 2009–; Wallace Collection Foundn (formerly Hertford House Trust), 2012–19; Royal Collection Trust, 2012–18. Pres., French Porcelain Soc., 1999– (Chm., 1988–94). Governor: Camden Sch. for Girls, 1996–2009; Alpha Plus Schs, 2012– (non-exec. Dir, Alpha Plus Hldgs, 2012–). Vis. Prof., Univ. of Arts, London, 2008–11; Professorial Res. Fellow, History of the Decorative Arts, Univ. of Buckingham, 2011–. FSA 1990; FRSA 1990. Hon. PhD Bucks and Chiltern UC, 2005; Hon. DLitt Buckingham, 2013. Officier, l'Ordre des Arts et des Lettres (France), 2013. Nat. Art Collections Award for Scholarship, 1990; European Woman of Achievement Arts and Media Award, EUW, 2005; Iris Foundn Award for Outstanding Contribution to Decorative Arts, Bard Graduate Center, NY, 2014. *Publications:* The Wallace Collection Catalogue of Sèvres Porcelain, 3 vols, 1988; (contrib.) Treasure Houses of Britain, 1985; Boughton House, 1992; Versailles: tables royales, 1993; articles in Apollo, Burlington Mag., Antologia di Belle Arti, J. Paul Getty Mus. Jl, Ars Ceramica, Antique Collector, French Porcelain Soc. Jl. *Recreations:* music, birds, wildlife, Sèvres patrons and collectors.

**SAVILLE,** family name of **Baron Saville of Newdigate**.

**SAVILLE OF NEWDIGATE,** Baron *cr* 1997 (Life Peer), of Newdigate in the co. of Surrey; **Mark Oliver Saville,** Kt 1985; PC 1994; a Justice of the Supreme Court of the United Kingdom, 2009–10 (a Lord of Appeal in Ordinary, 1997–2009); *b* 20 March 1936; *s* of Kenneth Vivian Saville and Olivia Sarah Frances Gray; *m* 1961, Jill Gray; two *s*. *Educ:* St Paul's Primary Sch., Hastings; Rye Grammar Sch.; Brasenose Coll., Oxford (BA, BCL; Hon. Fellow, 1998). Nat. Service, 2nd Lieut Royal Sussex Regt, 1954–56; Oxford Univ., 1956–60 (Vinerian Schol. 1960); called to Bar, Middle Temple, 1962 (Bencher, 1983); QC 1975; Judge of the High Court, QBD, 1985–93; a Lord Justice of Appeal, 1994–97. Chm., Bloody Sunday Inquiry Tribunal, 1998–2010. Hon. LLD: London Guildhall, 1997; Nottingham Trent, 2008. *Recreations:* sailing, flying, computers. *Address:* House of Lords, SW1A 0PW. *Club:* Garrick.

**SAVILLE, Clive Howard;** Chief Executive, UKCOSA: Council for International Education, 1997–2004; *b* 7 July 1943; *m* 1967, Camille Kathleen Burke. *Educ:* Bishop Gore Grammar Sch., Swansea; University Coll., Swansea (BA). Joined DES as Asst Principal, 1965; Cabinet Office, 1975; Private Sec. to Leader of H of C and Lord Pres. of Council, 1975–77; Grade 3, DES, then DFE, later DFEE, 1987–97. Member: Exec. Cttee, Nat. Literary Trust, 1997–2007; British Accreditation Council for Ind. Further and Higher Educn, 1998–2004; Adv. Panel, Office of Immigration Services Comr, 2001–05. Governor: Morley Coll., 1999–2002; UCL Hosps Foundn Trust, 2004–09. *E:* savilleclive@aol.com.

**SAVILLE, Jenny,** RA 2007; painter; *b* Cambridge, 1970. *Educ:* Glasgow Sch. of Art (BA 1992). Lectr, Slade Sch. of Fine Arts, London, 2000–06. *Solo exhibitions* include: Place McGill Gall., NY, 1996; Gagosian Gall., NY, 1999, 2003, 2018; Gagosian Gall., Beverly Hills, 2002; Univ. of Massachusetts, 2004; Museo d'Arte Contemporanea, Rome, 2005; Gagosian Gall., London, 2010, 2014; Modern Art Oxford, 2012, 2014; Scottish Nat. Gall. of Modern Art, Edinburgh, 2018; *group exhibitions* include: RA, London, 1990, 1997, 2017; Saatchi Gall., London, 1994; McLellan Galls, Glasgow, 1995; NPG, 2000; Kunsthalle Emden, 2002; 50th Biennale di Venezia, 2003; Frist Center for Arts, Nashville, 2009; Gagosian Gall., London, 2010; Tate Britain, 2018.

**SAVILLE, John Donald William;** HM Diplomatic Service; Consul General, Chicago, since 2017; *b* 29 June 1960; *s* of Donald and Elizabeth Saville; *m* 1992, Fabiola Moreno de Alboran; one *d*. *Educ:* Hitchin Boys' Grammar Sch.; Jesus Coll., Oxford (MA). Joined FCO, 1981; Third, then Second Sec., Jakarta, 1982–85; FCO, 1985–88; Second, then First Sec., Warsaw, 1988–91; First Secretary: FCO, 1991–95; Vienna, 1995–98; Hd, Commonwealth and Burma Section, SE Asia Dept, FCO, 1998–2000; Dep. Hd of Mission, Havana, 2000–03; Hd, Weapons of Mass Destruction Review Unit (Butler Review of Iraq Intelligence), FCO, 2004; High Comr, Brunei, 2005–09; Counsellor, FCO, 2009; Hd, Foreign Policy Climate Change Adaptation Proj., FCO, 2009–10; Dir, Asia, 2010–14, Acting Man. Dir, 2013–14, UKTI; Ambassador to Venezuela, 2014–17. *Recreations:* fishing, pulling sofas from the River Wandle. *Address:* c/o Foreign and Commonwealth Office, King Charles Street, SW1A 2AH. *Clubs:* Travellers, Royal Geographical Society.

**SAVILLE, Peter Andrew,** RDI 2011; designer; *b* 9 Oct. 1955; *s* of Lionel Stuart Saville and Dorothy Mabel Saville (*née* Foley). *Educ:* St Ambrose Coll., Altrincham; Manchester Poly. (BA 1st Cl. Hons Graphic Design 1978). Founding Partner, Factory Records, 1979, created album covers for Joy Division and New Order, etc; Art Dir, Dindisc Records, 1979–82; founded Peter Saville Associates design studio, 1983; Partner, Pentagram, 1990–92; Art Dir, Frankfurt Balkind, LA, 1993–94; founded: The Apartment, with Meiré and Meiré, advertising and design agency, 1995; with Nick Knight, SHOWstudio.com, 1999; Consultant Creative Dir to Manchester CC, 2004–. Vis. Prof., Univ. of the Arts, London, 2008. *Exhibitions* include: major retrospective, Design Mus., London, 2003, transf. Tokyo and Manchester; ESTATE, Migros Mus., Zurich, 2005. MInstD. Hon. DArts Manchester Metropolitan, 2005. *Publications:* Designed by Peter Saville, 2003; (jtly) Peter Saville Estate, 2007. *E:* mail@petersavillestudio.com. *Club:* Groucho.

**SAVILLE ROBERTS, Rt Hon. Elizabeth, (Rt Hon. Liz);** PC 2019; MP (Plaid Cymru) Dwyfor Meirionnydd, since 2015; *b* London, 16 Dec. 1964; *d* of Nicholas and Nancy Saville; *m* 1994, Dewi Wyn Roberts; twin *d*. *Educ:* Univ. of Wales, Aberystwyth (BA Hons Celtic Studies 1987); Bi-lingual Postgrad. Cert. for Personal Assts 1988; NCTJ 1991; Coleg Meirion-Dwyfor, Dolgellau (PGCE 1996). Sec., French and Russian Depts, QMC, 1988–89; staff reporter, Retail Newsagent, 1989–90; news reporter, Herald Newspapers, 1990–92; Lectr, 1993–2001, Hd, Canolfan Sgiliaith, 2001–12, Coleg Meirion-Dwyfor; Dir of Bilingualism, Grŵp Llandrillo, Menai, 2012–14. Mem. (Plaid Cymru) Gwynedd CC, 2004–15. *Recreations:* horse riding, hill walking, art, history, poetry. *Address:* Angorfa, Heol Meurig, Dolgellau, Gwynedd LL40 1LN. *T:* (01341) 422661. *E:* liz.savilleroberts.mp@parliament.uk.

**SAVORY, Sir Michael Berry,** Kt 2006; Managing Partner, Muckleburgh Collection, since 1989; Lord Mayor of London, 2004–05; *b* 10 Jan. 1943; *s* of late Claude Berry Savory and Irene Anne Parker; *m* 1992, Fiona Anne Macrae; two *d*. *Educ:* Whitestones, Bulawayo, Zimbabwe; Harrow Sch. Partner, Foster & Braithwaite Stockbrokers, 1967–89; Chm., BT Batsford, 1981–90; Dir, Terrafix, 1985–90. Chairman: HSBC Bank plc Stockbroker Services, 2001–05; ProShare, 2003–05. Chief Exec., Young Enterprise, 2006–09. Mem. Council, SSAFA-Forces Help, 1972–2006; Treas., Royal Nat. Mission to Deep Sea Fishermen, 1985–2006; Trustee: Hull Fishermen's Widows and Orphans Trust, 1985–2006; John Rice Charity, 1991–2003; Adm. Arthur Phillip Meml Trust, 1996–; Lord Mayor's 800th Anniversary Trust, 2000–; Britain-Australia Bicentennial Trust, 2001–14; John Carpenter Trust, 2002–. Hon. FCSI. Hon. Col, London Regt, TA, 2007–11. Churchwarden, St Margaret, Lothbury, 1987–2003; Freeman, City of London, 1964; Corporation of London: Mem., Court of Common Council, 1981–96; Alderman, 1996–2013; Sheriff, 2001–02; Freeman, Co. of Goldsmiths, 1984; Liveryman: Co. of Poulters (Master, 1996); Co. of Clockmakers (Master, 1998); Co. of Information Technologists, 2004. *Recreation:* military vehicle collection (Muckleburgh Collection, Weybourne, Norfolk). *Address:* 8 Beaumaris Court, Sheringham, Norfolk NR26 8HB. *E:* mbsavory@aol.com.

**SAVOURS;** see Campbell-Savours, family name of Baron Campbell-Savours.

**SAVULESCU, Prof. Julian,** PhD; Uehiro Professor of Practical Ethics, since 2002, Director, Oxford Uehiro Centre for Practical Ethics, since 2003, and Director, Oxford Centre for Neuroethics, since 2009, University of Oxford; Fellow of St Cross College, Oxford, since 2002; *b* 22 Dec. 1963; *s* of Radu Ion and Valda Jean Savulescu. *Educ:* Monash Univ., Australia (BMedSci 1st cl. Hons 1985; MB BS 1st cl. Hons 1988; PhD 1994). Sir Robert Menzies Med. Scholar, Oxford Univ., 1994–97; Clinical Ethicist, Oxford Radcliffe Hosps, 1995–97; Logan Res. Fellow, Monash Univ., 1997–98; Director: Bioethics Prog., Centre for Study of Health and Society, Univ. of Melbourne, 1998–2002; Ethics of Genetics Prog., Murdoch Children's Res. Inst., Royal Children's Hosp., Melbourne, 1998–2002. Louis Matheson Vis. Prof., Monash Univ., 2010–. Chm., Dept of Human Services, Victoria Ethics Cttee, 1998–2002. Editor: Jl of Med. Ethics, 2001–04, 2011–; Jl of Practical Ethics, 2013–. *Publications:* (jtly) Medical Ethics and Law: the core curriculum, 2003; over 240 articles in BMJ, Lancet, Australasian Jl of Philosophy, Bioethics, Jl of Med. Ethics, American Jl of Bioethics, Med. Jl of Australia, Philosophy, Psychiatry and Psychology and New Scientist. *Recreations:* ski-ing, surfing, cycling, swimming, roller blading, film, wine. *Address:* Oxford Uehiro Centre for Practical Ethics, Littlegate House, St Ebbe's Street, Oxford OX1 1PT. *T:* (01865) 286888, *Fax:* (01865) 286886. *E:* ethics@philosophy.ox.ac.uk.

**SAWATZKY, Prof. George Albert,** PhD; FRS 2008; FRS(Can) Professor of Applied and Solid State Physics, University of Groningen, since 1985; Professor of Physics and Chemistry of Nanostructured Materials, University of British Columbia, since 2001. *Educ:* Univ. of Manitoba (PhD). University of Groningen: NRC postdoctoral res. in solid state physics, 1969–71; Associate Prof., Physical Chem. Dept, 1971–79; Prof. of Physical Chem., 1979–85; Dir, Materials Sci. Centre, 1986–97. Member: Sci. Adv. Cttee, Eur. Synchrotron Radiation Facility, Grenoble, 1997–98; Sci. Technol. Adv. Cttee, Synchrotron Radiation Facility of China, 1998; Dutch Forum for Technol. and Sci., 1999–2002; Adv. Bd, Dutch Res. Sch. of Theoretical Physics, Utrecht Univ., 1999. Mem., Royal Dutch Acad. of Scis, 1991; Associate Mem., Canadian Inst. for Advanced Res., 1998. FRS(Can) 2002. NWO-Spinoza Award, Netherlands Orgn for Scientific Res., 1996; Nieuwsblad van het Noorden Prize, 1997; Henry Marshall Tory Medal, Royal Soc. of Canada, 2007. *Address:* Department of Physics and Astronomy, University of British Columbia, 6224 Agricultural Road, Vancouver, BC V6T 1Z1, Canada.

**SAWER, Dr David Peter;** composer; Professor of Composition, Royal Academy of Music, since 2008; *b* Stockport, 14 Sept. 1961; *s* of Brian and Mavis Sawer; civil partnership 2008, Jesus Jimenez Jimenez. *Educ:* Ipswich Sch.; Univ. of York (BA Hons, DPhil 1988); Staatliche Hochschule für Musik Rheinland, Köln. DAAD Schol., 1984–85; Fulbright-Chester-Schirmer Fellow in Composition, 1992–93. *Publications: compositions:* Cat's-eye, 1986; Songs of Love and War, 1990; Byrnan Wood, 1992; Trumpet Concerto, 1994; Hollywood Extra, 1996; Tiroirs, 1996; the greatest happiness principle, 1997; From Morning to Midnight, 2001; Piano Concerto, 2002; Rebus, 2004; Skin Deep, 2008; Rumpelstiltskin, 2009; Flesh and Blood, 2011; The Lighthouse Keepers, 2013; Bronze and Iron, 2013; Coachman Chronos, 2014; Caravanserai, 2015; April\March, 2016; The Skating Rink, 2018; Blue Moon, 2019. *Address:* c/o Allied Artists, Southbank House, Black Prince Road, SE1 7SJ. *T:* (020) 7589 6243.

**SAWERS, David Richard Hall;** environmental campaigner and writer; *b* 23 April 1931; *s* of late Edward and Madeline Sawers; unmarried. *Educ:* Westminster Sch.; Christ Church, Oxford (MA). Research Asst to Prof. J. Jewkes, Oxford Univ., 1954–58; Journalist, The Economist, 1959–64; Vis. Fellow, Princeton Univ., 1964–65; Econ. Adviser, Min. of Aviation and of Technology, 1966–68; Sen. Econ. Adviser, Min. of Technology, Aviation Supply, and DTI, 1968–72; Under-Sec., Depts of Industry, Trade and Prices and Consumer Protection, 1972–76; Under-Sec., Depts of Environment and Transport, 1976–83; Principal Res. Fellow, Technical Change Centre, 1984–86. Chairman: Forum of Arun Dist Amenity Gps, 1998–; E Preston and Kingston Preservation Soc., 2000–. *Publications:* (with John Jewkes and Richard Stillerman) The Sources of Invention, 1958; (with Ronald Miller) The Technical Development of Modern Aviation, 1968; Competition in the Air, 1987; Should the Taxpayer Support the Arts, 1993; (contrib.) Markets and the Media, 1996; (contrib.) Does the Past Have a Future?: the political economy of heritage, 1998; articles in daily press and journals. *Recreations:* listening to music, watching ballet and opera, looking at pictures, gardening. *Address:* 10 Seaview Avenue, East Preston, Littlehampton BN16 1PP. *T:* (01903) 779134.

**SAWERS, Dr Lesley,** OBE 2018; Commissioner for Scotland, Equality and Human Rights Commission, since 2016; Executive Chair, GenAnalytics Ltd, since 2016; *b* Glasgow, 8 Jan. 1959; *d* of John and May Sawers; *m* 1990, William Allan McKechnie. *Educ:* Our Lady's High Sch., Cumbernauld; Univ. of Glasgow (MA Hons); Univ. of Stirling (PhD 1986). Sen. Consultant, Mgt Horizons Ltd, 1985–87; Regl Dir Scotland, CACI Ltd, 1987–92; Dir of Communications, Scottish Power plc, 1992–2001; Dir of Scottish Affairs, and Chair, Adv. Bd Scotland, Royal Mail, 2001–03; Bd Strategic Advr, Visit Scotland, 2003–04; Chief Executive: Glasgow Chamber of Commerce, 2004–08; Scottish Council for Develt and Industry, 2008–13; Vice Principal and Pro Vice-Chancellor, Glasgow Caledonian Univ., 2013–15. Hon. Prof., Glasgow Caledonian Univ., 2015–. Non-exec. Dir, Visit Scotland, 2006–12; Leadership Gp Chair, Scottish Cities Alliance, 2010–14; Dep. Chair, Scottish Envmtl Protection Agency, 2012–. Trustee: Action for Children, 2008–10; Glasgow Life, 2012–. Hon. DBA Strathclyde, 2009; DUniv Glasgow Caledonian, 2012. *Recreations:* reading, travel. *E:* lesley.sawers@equalityhumanrights.com.

**SAWERS, Sir (Robert) John,** GCMG 2015 (KCMG 2007; CMG 1996); Chairman, Macro Advisory Partners, since 2015; *b* 26 July 1955; *s* of Colin Simon Hawkesley Sawers and Daphne Anne Sawers; *m* 1981, Avril Helen Shelley Lamb; two *s* one *d*. *Educ:* Beechen Cliff Sch., Bath; Univ. of Nottingham (BSc Hons Physics and Philosophy). FCO 1977;

served Sana'a, 1980; Damascus, 1982; FCO, 1984; Pretoria/Cape Town, 1988; Head, EU Presidency Unit, 1991; Principal Private Sec. to Sec. of State for Foreign and Commonwealth Affairs, 1993–95; Career Develt Attachment, Harvard Univ., 1995–96; Counsellor, Washington, 1996–99; For. Affairs Private Sec. to the Prime Minister, 1999–2001; Ambassador to Egypt, 2001–03; Special Rep. for Iraq, 2003; Political Dir, FCO, 2003–07; UK Perm. Rep. to UN, 2007–09; Chief, Secret Intelligence Service (MI6), 2009–14. Non-exec. Dir, BP, 2015–. Vis. Prof., KCL, 2015–; Sen. Fellow, RUSI, 2015–; Sen. Advr, RIIA, 2018. Gov., Ditchley Foundn. *Recreations:* sport, the arts.

**SAWFORD, Andrew;** Chief Executive, Connect Communications, since 2015; *b* Desborough, Northants, 15 March 1976; *s of* Philip Andrew Sawford, *qv*; *m* 2000, Joanna Veevers; one *s* one *d*. *Educ:* Durham Univ. (BA Hist. 1997). Worked for Philip Hope, MP, H of C, 1997; work in business and public service; Dir, Connect Public Affairs, 2003–07; Chief Exec., Local Govt Information Unit, 2008–12. Mem. (Lab) Dartford BC, 1999–2003. MP (Lab) Corby, Nov. 2012–2015; contested (Lab) same seat, 2015. Shadow Minister for Local Govt, 2013–15. Mem., Communities and Local Govt Select Cttee, 2012–13; All Party Parly Gps on steel making, local govt and local growth, 2012–15. *Address:* Connect Communications, Third Floor, Millbank Tower, SW1P 4QP.

**SAWFORD, Philip Andrew;** *b* 26 June 1950; *s of* John and Audrey Sawford; *m* 1971, Rosemary Stokes; two *s*. *Educ:* Ruskin Coll., Oxford (Dip. Soc.); Univ. of Leicester (BA Hons). Manager, training orgn, Wellingborough, 1985–97 and 2007–09; Northamptonshire Enterprise Ltd, 2009–10. Member (Lab): Desborough Town Council, 1977–97 and 2018–; Kettering BC, 1979–83, 1986–97, 1991–97 (Leader). Contested (Lab): Wellingborough, 1992; Kettering, 2005, 2010. MP (Lab) Kettering, 1997–2005. *Recreations:* playing guitar, reading. *Address:* 46 Federation Avenue, Desborough, Northants NN14 2NX.

*See also* A. *Sawford*.

**SAWYER,** Baron *cr* 1998 (Life Peer), of Darlington in the co. of Durham; **Lawrence Sawyer, (Tom);** *b* 12 May 1943. *Educ:* Eastbourne Sch., Darlington; Darlington Tech. Sch. Dep. Gen. Sec., NUPE, later UNISON, 1981–94; Gen. Sec., Labour Party, 1994–98. Mem., NEC, Labour Party, 1981–94 and 1999–2001; Chm., Labour Party, 1990–91. Non-exec. Chm., Reed Health Gp, 2001–03; Chairman: Royal Mail Partnership Bd, 2001–07; Norlife, 2004–; non-exec. Dir, Investors in People UK, 1998–2005. Chairman: Notting Hill Housing Gp, 1998–2005; Supervisory Bd, Thompsons, Solicitors, 2001–11; Union Insurance (formerly Union Income Benefit), 2003–. Vis. Prof., Cranfield Sch. of Mgt, 1999–2013. Chancellor, Univ. of Teesside, 2005–17. Pres., William Morris Soc., 2018–. *Address:* House of Lords, SW1A 0PW.

**SAWYER, Anthony Charles,** CB 1999; fiscal expert, International Monetary Fund, 1999–2007 (expert missions to Bulgaria, Egypt, Jordan, Kenya, Kyrgyzstan, Nigeria, Pakistan, Romania, Tajikistan, Tanzania and the Philippines); *b* 3 Aug. 1939; *s of* Charles Bertram and Elizabeth Sawyer; *m* 1962, Kathleen Josephine McGill; two *s* one *d*. *Educ:* Redhill Tech. Coll., Surrey. RAEC; Nat. Service, RA, 1960. Underwriter, Northern Assurance Group, 1962; Customs and Excise, 1964–99: Collector, Edinburgh, 1984; Dep. Dir, 1988; Comr, 1991–99; Director: Outfield, 1991–94; Enforcement, 1994–99. Dir, Customs Annuity and Benevolent Fund, 1998–2004. Non-exec. Dir, Retail Banking Bd, Royal Bank of Scotland, 1994–97; fiscal adviser: Kyrgyzstan, 2000; Egypt, 2003; Ethiopia, 2004; Kenya, 2005. FRSA 1994; FCMI (FIMgt 1996); FInstD 1997; FRMetS 2001. *Recreations:* walking, cricket, poetry. *Clubs:* National Liberal; Royal Scots (Edinburgh); Sussex County Cricket.

**SAWYER, Rt Hon. Dame Joan (Augusta),** DBE 1997; PC 2004; President, Bahamas Court of Appeal, 2001–10; *b* 26 Nov. 1940; *m* 1962, Geoffrey Sawyer (*d* 2004); one *s*. *Educ:* London Univ. (LLB 1973). Clerk, 1958–68; HEO (Public Service), 1968–73; called to the Bar, Gray's Inn, 1973; Asst Crown Counsel, 1973–78; acting Stipendiary and Circuit Magistrate, 1978; Sen. Counsel, 1979–83; acting Dir, Legal Affairs, 1983; Counsel, Central Bank of the Bahamas, 1984–88; Justice, 1988–95, Sen. Justice, 1995–96, Supreme Court of Bahamas; Chief Justice of the Bahamas, 1996–2001. *Publications:* articles in Bahamian Review. *Recreations:* reading, sewing, serious theatre, gardening, embroidering. *Address:* PO Box N-1733, Nassau, Bahamas. *T:* 3943055.

**SAWYER, Miranda Caroline;** journalist, author and broadcaster; *b* Bristol, 7 Jan. 1967; *d of* Richard and Jennifer Sawyer; *m* 2007, Michael Smiley; one *s* one *d*. *Educ:* Cheadle Hulme Sch., Cheadle Hulme; Pembroke Coll., Oxford (BA Juris.). Writer: Smash Hits, 1988–90; Select, 1990–95; The Face, 1994–98; columnist, Time Out, 1993–96; Feature Writer, 1993–, Radio Critic, 2005–, The Observer; presenter: The Culture Show, BBC TV, 2008–; Sound and Vision, BBC 6 Music, 2017–. Member: Council, Tate Members, 2008–17 (Dep. Chm.); Bd, South London Gallery, 2014–. Writer of the Year, PPA, 1993; Record of the Day Award for Music Journalism, 2012. *Publications:* Park and Ride, 1999; Out of Time, 2016. *Recreations:* reading, writing, pop music, art, theatre, second-hand shops, outdoor swimming pools, chatting, going out, running very slowly, walking the dog. *E:* mail@mirandasawyer.com.

**SAWYER, Priti;** *see* Patel, P.

**SAWYER, Timothy Charles,** CBE 2016; Chief Investment Officer, UK Research and Innovation, since 2017; *b* Plymouth, 2 Feb. 1962; *s of* Frank and Patricia Sawyer; *m* 1990, Sheila Pollock; one *s* one *d*. *Educ:* Wellington Coll.; St John's Coll., Oxford (BA Hist. 1984; MA). Lloyds Bank, 1984–91; Abbey National, 1991–2002; Chief Executive Officer: Cahoot Bank, 2002–05; Ivobank, 2005–10; Chief Operating Officer, One Savings Bank, 2010–11; Chm., Banque Dubois, Zurich, 2010–14; CEO, Start Up Loans, 2012–17; Chm., Folk2Folk, 2012–. Mem., Competition Appeal Tribunal, 2018–; Mem., Legal Services Bd, 2019–. Chm. Govs, Univ. of Beds, 2018–. *Recreations:* travel, theatre, literature. *T:* 07917 457618. *E:* tim.sawyer@talk21.com. *Club:* Army and Navy.

**SAWYERS, Bridget Truus;** Director, Bridget Sawyers Ltd, public art and cultural consultancy, since 2002; *b* Dover, 31 May 1965; *d of* David Sawyers and Truus Sawyers. *Educ:* Kingston Poly. (BA Hons Arch. 1986); Poly. of Central London, later Univ. of Westminster (DipArch 1986; RIBA Pt III 1991; MA Urban Design 1995). Architect, Building Design Partnership, 1989–96; Sen. Officer, Architecture, Arts Council of England, 1996–2000; Hd, Regions, CABE, 2000–02; Chief Exec., Architecture Centre Network, 2009–12. Dir, Project Compass CIC, 2013–. Mem., Nat. Panel, Civic Trust Awards, 2011–15; Prize Manager, Queen Elizabeth Prize for Engrg, 2013–14. FRSA 2015. Academician, Acad. of Urbanism, 2012–14. *Publications:* (ed jtly) International Architecture Centres, 2003; contribs to architecture and public art publns and reports. *Recreations:* visual arts, architecture, art in the public realm, travel, Wicks Vintners wine tasting. *Address:* 19 Windmill House, Windmill Walk, SE1 8LX. *T:* (020) 7928 7131. *E:* bridgetsawyerslimited@gmail.com. *W:* www.bridgetsawyers.com.

**SAXBEE, Rt Rev. John Charles,** PhD; Bishop of Lincoln, 2001–11; Assistant Bishop, Diocese of St David's, since 2011; *b* 7 Jan. 1946; *s of* Charles Albert Saxbee and Florence Violet Saxbee (*née* Harris); *m* 1965, Jacqueline Margaret Carol Skym; one *d*. *Educ:* Cotham Grammar Sch., Bristol; Bristol Univ. (BA 1968); Durham Univ. (DipTh 1969; PhD 1976); Cranmer Hall, Durham. Ordained deacon, 1972, priest, 1973; Asst Curate, Emmanuel with St Paul, Plymouth, 1972–77; Vicar of St Philip, Weston Mill, Plymouth, 1977–81; Team Vicar, Central Exeter Team Ministry, 1981–87; Dir, SW Ministry Training Course, 1981–92; Priest-in-Charge of Holy Trinity, Wistanstow with St Michael, Cwm Head and St Margaret, Acton Scott, 1992–94; Archdeacon of Ludlow, 1992–2001, Bishop Suffragan of Ludlow, 1994–2001. Prebendary of Exeter Cathedral, 1988–92; of Hereford Cathedral, 1992–2001. Chm., C of E Bd of Educn, 2008–11. Pres., Modern Churchpeople's Union, 1997–2011; Chm., Rural Theology Assoc., 2011–14. Religious Advr, Central TV, 1997–2006. Member: Exec., Springboard, 1998–2004; Coll. of Evangelists, 1999–2012. Hon. Dr Bishop Grosseteste UC Lincoln, 2010. *Publications:* Liberal Evangelism: a flexible response to the decade, 1994; No Faith in Religion: some variations on a theme, 2009; Waymarkers: a route map through Lent to Easter, 2013; What Happens When We Pray? 2014. *Recreations:* televised sport, most kinds of music. *Address:* 22 Shelley Road, Priory Park, Haverfordwest, Dyfed SA61 1RX.

**SAXBY, Oliver Charles John;** QC 2013; a Recorder, since 2019; *b* London, 10 Nov. 1969; *s of* Marygold Saxby (now Turner) and step *s of* late Dr Colin Turner; *m* 1996, Rebecca Helen Leighton; one *d*. *Educ:* Eton Coll.; Univ. of Southampton (LLB (Hons) Law). Called to the Bar, Inner Temple, 1992; in practice as a criminal barrister, 1992–. Chm., Kent Bar Mess, 2013–16 (Jun., 2001–03); Captain., Bar Golfing Soc., 2019; Capt., Inner Temple Golfing Soc., 2012. *Recreations:* football, golf, ski-ing, shooting, fishing, opera. *Address:* 6 Pump Court, Temple, EC4Y 7AR. *T:* (020) 7797 8400, *Fax:* (020) 7797 8401. *E:* oliver.saxbyqc@6pumpcourt.co.uk. *Clubs:* Garrick; Rye Golf; Eton Ramblers, Band of Brothers.

**SAXBY, Sir Robin (Keith),** Kt 2002; FRS 2015; FREng; CEng; engineer, entrepreneur, investor and mentor; *b* 4 Feb. 1947; *s of* Keith William Saxby and Mary Saxby; *m* 1970, Patricia Susan Bell; one *s* one *d*. *Educ:* Univ. of Liverpool (BEng Electronics 1968). CEng 2002. R&D engr, Rank Bush Murphy, 1968–72; Sen. Engr, Pye TMC, 1972–73; Sales Engr, then System Strategy Manager, Europe, Motorola Semiconductors, 1973–84; Chief Exec., Henderson Security Systems, 1984–86; Man. Dir, ES2 Ltd, 1986–91; Chief Exec. and Chm., 1991–2001, Chm., 2001–06, Emeritus Chm., 2006–07, Advanced RISC Machines Ltd, later ARM Hldgs plc. Angel investor and advr to UK HQ technol. start ups, 2007–. Non-exec. Dir, Glotel, 1999–2007. Vis. Prof., Dept of Electronics, Univ. of Liverpool. Pres., IET, 2006–07. FREng 2002. FRSA; CCMI. Hon. FIET. Hon. DEng Liverpool, 2000; Hon. DTech: Loughborough, 2001; Anglia Ruskin, 2010; Nottingham Trent, 2012; DU: Essex, 2003; York, 2009. Faraday Medal, IET, 2002; Global Semiconductor Alliance Leadership Award, 2012. *Publications:* (contrib.) Electronic Engineers' Reference Book, 1983; Microcomputer Handbook, 1985; (contrib.) Advances in Information Technology, 1998. *Recreations:* ski-ing, tennis, music, painting, nature, birdwatching, genealogy, restoration of old technology, keeping fit.

**SAXON, Prof. David Harold,** OBE 2005; DPhil, DSc; CPhys, FInstP; FRAS; FRSE; Kelvin Professor of Physics, 1990–2008, now Professor Emeritus, Dean, Physical Sciences, 2002–08, University of Glasgow; *b* 27 Oct. 1945; *s of* late Rev. Canon Eric Saxon and Ruth (*née* Higginbottom); *m* 1968, Margaret Flitcroft; one *s* one *d*. *Educ:* Manchester Grammar Sch.; Balliol Coll., Oxford (MA, DSc); Jesus Coll., Oxford (DPhil). CPhys 1985; FInstP 1985; FRSE 1993; FRAS 2004. Jun. Res. Fellow, Jesus Coll., Oxford, 1968–70; Res. Officer, Nuclear Physics Dept, Oxford, 1969–70; Res. Associate, Columbia Univ., NY, 1970–73; Rutherford Appleton Laboratory, Oxford: Res. Associate, 1974–75; SSO, 1975–76; PSO, 1976–89; Grade 6, 1989–90; Glasgow University: Hd, Dept of Physics and Astronomy, 1996–2001; Vice-Dean, Physical Scis, 2000–02. Member, SERC Committees: Particle Physics Experiment Selection Panel, 1989–92; Particle Physics, 1991–94 (Chm., 1992–94); Nuclear Physics Bd, 1992–93; Particles, Space & Astronomy Bd, 1993–94. Member Council: PPARC, 1997–2001 (Chairman: Particle Physics Cttee, 1994–95; Public Understanding of Sci. Panel, 1997–2001); CCLRC, 2000–01, 2005–07 (Chm., Particle Physics Users Adv. Cttee, 1998–2004). Chairman: 27th Internat. Conf. on High Energy Physics, 1994; Scottish Univs Summer Schs in Physics, 1997–2003; Member: Scientific Policy Cttee, 1993–98, External Rev. Cttee, 2001–02, CERN, Geneva; Physics Res. Cttee, Deutsches Elektronen Synchrotron, Hamburg, 1993–99; MRC Scientific Adv. Gp on Technology, 1999; MRC Discipline Hopping Panel, 2000–01 and 2006–08; Eur. Cttee on Future Accelerators, 2003–05; Commn C11, Internat. Union of Pure and Applied Physics, 2006–08; Chm., STFC CALICE Oversight Cttee, 2006–08. Member: Physics Panel, 1996 RAE, HEFC; Physics Benchmarking Panel, QAA, 2000–01; Res. Exchange Panel, British Council, 2006–08. Mem. Council, 2001–04, Res. Convener, 2002–05, RSE; Chm., Inst. of Physics in Scotland, 2003–05. Mem., Scientific Adv. Panel, Univ. Trento, Italy, 2001–05. FRSA 1997. *Recreations:* staying close to home, visiting grandchildren. *Address:* c/o Miss V. Flood, School of Physics and Astronomy, University of Glasgow, Glasgow G12 8QQ. *T:* (01788) 832225.

*See also* R. G. *Saxon*.

**SAXON, Richard Gilbert,** CBE 2001; Client and Business Adviser for construction projects, Consultancy for the Built Environment, since 2005; *b* 14 April 1942; *s of* late Rev. Canon Eric Saxon and Ruth Saxon (*née* Higginbottom); *m* 1968, Elizabeth Anne Tatton. *Educ:* Manchester Grammar Sch.; Univ. of Liverpool (BArch 1st cl. Hons 1965; MCD 1966). RIBA 1970, FRIBA 2016; FRICS 2013. Joined Building Design Partnership, 1966: Partner, 1977–2005; Mem., Mgt Gp, 1984–86; Project Dir, J. P. Morgan HQ, AELTC Masterplan, Adam Opel HQ, 1986–93; Chm., London Office, 1993–99; Practice Chm., 1996–2002; Dir, Strategic Marketing, 1999–2005. Non-exec. Dir, BLP Insurance, 2013–19; Associate Dir, Deploi BIM Strategies, 2015–. BIM Ambassador for Growth, 2012–13. Consultant to EC Harris LLP, 2007–10. Pres., British Council for Offices, 1995–96; Vice-Pres., RIBA, 2002–08. Chairman: Reading Construction Forum, 1999–2002; Be (Collaborating for the Built Environment), 2002–04; City Architecture Forum, 2005–15; Jt Contracts Tribunal, 2015–; Member: Exec. Bd, Construction Industry Council, 2006–14; Ind. Dispute Avoidance Panel for the London Olympics, 2008–12; Res. Reference Gp, CABE, 2008–11; Cross-Cutting Issues Gp, Low-Carbon Construction Innovation and Growth Team, 2010. Member, Advisory Board: Ecodomus Inc., 2017–; Construction Manager Mag., 2017–. Mem., Bldg Cttee, Univ. of Cambridge, 2004–16. MCIM 1990. FRSA 1987. Liveryman, Co. of Chartered Architects, 1988 (Master, 2005–06). *Publications:* Atrium Buildings: development and design, 1983, 2nd edn 1986 (also USA, Japan, Russia); The Atrium Comes of Age, 1993 (also USA, Japan); Be Valuable, 2005; City Architecture: redesigning the City of London 1991–2011, 2011; Growth through BIM, 2013; BIM for Construction Clients, 2016; Going Digital: a guide for construction clients, building owners and their advisers, 2018; articles in Building Res. and Inf., Architects Jl, Building Design and Building, RIBA Jl, Architecture Today, Public Service Review. *Recreations:* travel, early music, theatre, film, birds, enjoying London. *Address:* Consultancy for the Built Environment, 9 Whistlers Avenue, SW11 3TS. *T:* (020) 7585 1976, 07768 482838. *E:* Richard@saxoncbe.com. *W:* www.saxoncbe.com.

*See also* D. H. *Saxon*.

**SAXTON, Jonathon Hugh Christopher, (Joe);** Driver of Ideas, nfpSynergy, since 2003 (Head, Not for Profit, Future Foundation, 2000–03); *b* Bristol, 6 Feb. 1962; *s of* Hugh Michael Saxton and Barbara Bevil Saxton; *m* 1990, Julie Margaret Evans; two *s* one *d*. *Educ:*

Leigh Prim. Sch.; Downsend Sch.; Bedales Sch.; Robinson Coll., Cambridge (BA Nat. Sci. 1984); Univ. of E Anglia (MA Develt Studies 1986); Henley Management Coll. (MBA 1995). Co-ordinator, Harambee Centre, Cambridge, 1986–88; Fundraising Dept, Oxfam, Oxford, 1988–91; Account Dir and Dep. Client Services Dir, Brann Ltd, Cirencester, 1991–96; Dir of Communications, RNID, 1997–2000. Chm., Fedn of Small Business Cttee on Northern Powerhouse, 2016–18. Trustee: RSPCA, 1994–2001; Inst. of Fundraising, 2002–08 (Chm., 2005–08); Chm. and Co-founder, CharityComms, 2007–13; Chairman: People & Planet, 2005–15; Parentkind (formerly PTA UK), 2015–. Trustee and Dir, Pemberton Barnes Trust, 2015–. *Publications*: It's Competition, but not as we know it?, 1997; What are Charities For?, 1998; Polishing the Diamond, 2002; Mission Impossible, 2004; (as J. B. Browne) Secrets of the Flock, 2019; numerous reports on charity strategy. *Recreations*: DIY, reading, fell walking, karaoke with the team, snuggling with my wife. *Address*: nfpSynergy, 2–6 Tenter Ground, Spitalfields, E1 7NH. *T*: (020) 7426 8888. *E*: joe.saxton@nfpsynergy.net.

**SAXTON, Prof. Robert Louis Alfred,** DMus; FGS; Professor of Composition, Oxford University, since 2008 (University Lecturer, 1999–2008); Tutor and Fellow in Music, Worcester College, Oxford, since 1999; Director, University of York Music Press, since 2004; Composer in Association, Purcell School for Young Musicians, since 2012; *b* 8 Oct. 1953; *s* of late Ian Sanders Saxton and Jean Augusta Saxton (*née* Infield); *m* 2005, Teresa Cahill, *qv. Educ*: Bryanston Sch.; St Catharine's Coll., Cambridge (MA; Hon. Fellow, 2015); Worcester Coll., Oxford (BMus; DMus 1992). FGS (FGSM 1987). Lectr, Bristol Univ., 1984–85; Fulbright Arts award, 1985; Vis. Fellow, Princeton Univ., 1986; Head of Composition: GSMD, 1990–98; RAM, 1999–99; Vis. Fellow in Composition, Bristol Univ., 1995–2001. Artistic Dir, Opera Lab, 1994–2000; Associate Dir, Performing Arts Labs, 1998–2001; Pres., Brunel Ensemble, 1995–. Hon. Pres., Assoc. of English Singers and Speakers, 1997–. Dir, South Bank Centre, 1998– (Mem., Site Develt Bd, 1997–). Patron, Bristol Univ. Music Soc., 1997–2008; Trustee, Mendelssohn/Boise Foundn, 2010– (Trustee, Mendelssohn Scholarship, 2012–). Advr, Orchestra Europa, 2006–. Finalist, BBC Young Composers' Comp., 1973; First Prize, Gaudeamus Music Fest., Holland, 1975; early works at ISCM Fest., Bonn, 1977, Royan Fest., 1977; later works, majority recorded, include: The Ring of Eternity, 1983; Concerto for Orchestra, 1984; The Circles of Light, 1985; The Child of Light (carol), 1985; The Sentinel of the Rainbow, 1984; Viola Concerto, 1986; Night Dance, 1986–87; I Will Awake the Dawn, 1987; In the Beginning, 1987; Elijah's Violin, 1988; Chacony, 1988; Music to celebrate the Resurrection of Christ, 1988; Violin Concerto, Leeds Fest., 1990; Caritas (opera with libretto by Arnold Wesker), 1990–91; Paraphrase on Mozart's Idomeneo, 1991; At the Round Earth's Imagined Corners (anthem), 1992; 'Cello Concerto, 1992; Psalm—a song of ascents, 1992; O Sing unto the Lord a new song (anthem), 1993; Fantazia, 1993; Canticum Luminis, 1994; A Yardstick to the Stars, 1994; Ring, Time, 1994; Songs, Dances, Ellipses, 1997; Prayer before Sleep, 1997; Music for St Catharine, 1998; Miniature Dance for a Marionette Rabbi, 1999; Sonata for solo 'cello on a theme of Sir William Walton, 1999; The Dialogue of Zion and God, 2000; Alternative Canticles, 2002; Five Motets, 2003; Was It Winter? (carol), 2005; Song Without Words, 2005; There and Back, 2005; O Living Love (anthem), 2007; The Beach in Winter: Scratby (for Tess), 2008; The Wandering Jew (radio opera), 2010; String Quartet No 3, 2011; Hortus Musicae, 2012; Time and the Seasons, 2013; Shakespeare Scenes, 2012–13; Sonata for brass band on a Prelude of Gibbons, 2014; Vexilla Regis, 2014; Chorale Prelude: Wo Gott zum Haus, 2014; The Legend of King Herla, 2015; Passacaglia for organ on the name of John McCabe, 2015; Hortus Musicae Book 2, 2016; The Resurrection of the Soldiers, 2016; String Quartet No 4, 2018; Suite for violin and piano, 2019; Chorale prelude in memory of Oliver Knussen for organ, 2019; works commissioned by: Fires of London, London Sinfonietta, BBC, LSO, ECO, Aldeburgh Fest., Cheltenham Fest., Opera North, LPO, RPO, City of London Fest./St Paul's Cathedral, Leeds Fest. *Publications*: contributor to: Composition-Performance-Reception, 1998; Cambridge Companion to the Orchestra, 2003; Composing Music for Worship, 2003; all compositions; contribs TLS, Musical Times, etc. *Recreations*: theatre, cinema, studying history, reading philosophy. *Address*: c/o Music Sales, 14/15 Berners Street, W1T 3LJ. *T*: (020) 7612 7400; University of York Music Press, Department of Music, University of York, Heslington, York YO10 5DD. *T*: (01904) 432434, *Fax*: (01904) 432450. *E*: lizwebbmanagement@gmail.com. *W*: www.robertsaxton.net.

**SAYCE, Lucy Elizabeth, (Liz),** OBE 2009; Chief Executive, Disability Rights UK (formerly Royal Association for Disability and Rehabilitation, then Royal Association for Disability Rights), 2007–17; *b* 12 Jan. 1954; *d* of late Dr Richard Sayce and Dr Olive Sayce; partner, Dr Rachel Perkins. *Educ*: Kent Univ. (BA English and French 1976); Bedford Coll., London Univ. (MSc Soc. Work and Soc. Policy, CQSW, 1985). Policy Dir, Mind, 1990–98; Director: Lambeth, Southwark and Lewisham Health Action Zone, 1998–2000; Policy and Communications, Disability Rights Commn, 2000–07. Harkness Fellow, Washington, 1995–96; Vis. Sen. Fellow, LSE, 2018–. Member: Mental Health Task Force, 1994; Disability Rights Task Force, 1997–99; Commn for Health Improvement Investigation Team, N Lakeland NHS Trust, 2000; Disability Cttee, 2007–10, Disability Adv. Cttee, 2018–, Equality and Human Rights Commn; UK Commn for Employment and Skills, 2007–16; Cttee, Healthwatch England, 2014–; SSAC, 2016–; Bd, Care Quality Commn, 2018–. FRSA. Trustee, Stonewall, 2005–11. DUniv Kent, 2014. *Publications*: From Psychiatric Patient to Citizen, 2000; From Psychiatric Patient to Citizen Revisited 2016; contrib. numerous chapters; papers in disability and mental health jls, reports pubd by Mind, Research and Develt for Psychiatry. *Recreation*: walking the Thames and other waterways.

**SAYE AND SELE,** 21st Baron *cr* 1447 and 1603; **Nathaniel Thomas Allen Fiennes;** DL; chartered surveyor, retired; *b* 22 Sept. 1920; *s* of Ivo Murray Twisleton-Wykeham-Fiennes, 20th Baron Saye and Sele, OBE, MC, and Hersey Cecilia Hester, *d* of late Captain Sir Thomas Dacres Butler, KCVO; *S* father, 1968; *m* 1958, Mariette Helena, DL, *d* of Maj.-Gen. Sir Guy Salisbury-Jones, GCVO, CMG, CBE, MC; two *s* one *d* (and two *s* decd). *Educ*: Eton; New College, Oxford. Served with Rifle Brigade, 1941–49 (despatches twice). Partner in firm of Laws and Fiennes. Regl Dir, Lloyds Bank, 1982–90. Trustee, Ernest Cook Trust, 1960–95 (Chm. Trustees, 1965–92). DL Oxfordshire, 1979. Fellow, Winchester Coll., 1967–83. *Heir*: *s* Hon. Martin Guy Fiennes [*b* 27 Feb. 1961; *m* 1996, Pauline Kang Chai Lian, *o d* of Kang Tiong Lam; three *s*]. *Address*: 8 Godswell Park, Bloxham, Banbury, Oxon OX15 4ES. *T*: (01295) 720142.

**SAYED, Bethan Maeve;** Member (Plaid Cymru) South Wales West, National Assembly for Wales, since 2007; *b* 9 Dec. 1981; *d* of Mike Jenkins and Marie Jenkins; *m* 2018, Rahil Sayed. *Educ*: Ysgol Gyfun Rhydfelen, Pontypridd; Univ. of Wales, Aberystwyth (BScEcon Internat. Pol. and Internat. Hist.). Equal Opportunities Officer, 2003–04, Pres., 2004–05, Aberystwyth Guild of Students; Youth Organiser, Plaid Cymru, 2005–07. Plaid Cymru spokesperson on Welsh language, heritage and sport; Mem., Communities, Equality and Local Govt Cttee. *Recreations*: playing viola, swimming, travelling, Nordic Noir. *Address*: Unit 2, Brunel Way, Baglan Energy Park, Port Talbot SA11 2FP. *T*: (01639) 820530. *E*: bethan.sayed@assembly.wales.

**SAYEED, Jonathan;** Chairman, Ranelagh Ltd, since 2016 (Chairman, Ranelagh International Ltd, 2005–16); *b* 20 March 1948; *m* 1980, Nicola Anne Parkes Power; two *s*. *Educ*: Britannia Royal Naval Coll., Dartmouth; Royal Naval Engrg Coll., Manadon. Chairman, Ranelagh Ltd, 1992–96; Trng Div., Corporate Services Group plc, 1996–97. MP (C) Bristol E, 1983–92; contested (C) same seat, 1992; MP (C) Mid Bedfordshire, 1997–2005. PPS to Paymaster General and Minister of State for NI, 1991–92; Opposition frontbench spokesman on the environment, 2001–03. Vice-Chm., 1987–91, Chm., 1991–92, Cons. Backbench Shipping and Shipbuilding Cttee; Dep. Chm., All Party Maritime Group, 1987–92; Member: Environment Select Cttee, 1987–92; Defence Select Cttee, 1988–91; Chairman's Panel, 1999–2001, 2003–05. Pres., Bristol E Cons. Assoc., 1995–. Pres., Bristol West Indian Cricket Club, 1986–. Mem., RNSA. *Recreations*: painting, golf, yachting, riding, classical music. *Clubs*: Carlton; Royal Naval Sailing Assoc.; Royal Thames Yacht; Highgate Golf.

**SAYER, John Raymond Keer,** MA; Research Fellow, Department of Educational Studies, University of Oxford, since 1991; *b* 8 Aug. 1931; *s* of Arthur and Hilda Sayer; *m* 1955, Ilserose (*née* Heyd); one *s* one *d*. *Educ*: Maidstone Grammar Sch.; Brasenose Coll., Oxford (Open Scholar; MA). Taught languages, 1955–63; Dep. Head, Nailsea Sch., Somerset, 1963–67; Headmaster, Minehead Sch., Somerset, 1967–73; Principal, Banbury Sch., 1973–84; Vis. Fellow, Univ. of London Inst. of Educn, 1985–92 (Dir, Educn Management Unit, 1987–90); Dir, E. C. Tempus Projects: Developing Schs for Democracy in Europe, Oxford Univ., 1991–2000; Co-Dir, European Sch. of Educnl Mgt, 1991–96; Dir, Developing Services for Teaching in Europe, 1997–2012. Chairman: Reform of Assessment at Sixteen-Plus, 1972–75; External Relations Cttee, Headmasters' Assoc., 1974–77; Secondary Heads Association: Mem. Exec., 1978–86; Press and Publications Officer, 1978–79, 1982–84; Pres., 1979–80. Chm., Jt Council of Heads, 1981; Member: Exec., UCCA, 1975–84; Schools Panel, CBI, 1975–82; Heads Panel, TUC, 1975–80; National Adv. Council on Educn for Industry and Commerce, 1974–77; Adv. Cttee on Supply and Educn of Teachers, 1982–85. Hon. Sec., 1990–94, Vice-Chm., 1994–2000, Chm., 2000–02, GTC (England and Wales) Trust. Trustee and Mem. Exec., Education 2000, 1983–89 (Hon. Sec., 1987–89); Trustee, English Trust for European Educn, 2006–11 (Patron, 2012–). Mem. Exec., Schools Curriculum Award, 1986–91. Hon. Prof., Russian Fedn Min. of Educn (Perm State Humanitarian-Pedagogical Univ.), 1998–. *Publications*: (ed) The School as a Centre of Enquiry, 1975; (ed) Staffing our Secondary Schools, 1980; (ed) Teacher Training and Special Educational Needs, 1985; What Future for Secondary Schools?, 1985; Secondary schools for All?, 1987, 2nd edn 1994; (ed) Management and the Psychology of Schooling, 1988; Schools and External Relations, 1989; Managing Schools, 1989; Towards the General Teaching Council, 1989; The Future Governance of Education, 1993; Developing Schools for Democracy in Europe, 1995; (ed) Developing Teaching for Special Needs in Russia, 1999; (ed with K. Van der Wolf) Opening Schools to All, 1999; (ed with J. Vanderhoeven) School Choice, Equity and Social Exclusion, 2000; (ed with J. Vanderhoeven) Reflection for Action, 2000; The General Teaching Council, 2000; (ed) Opening Windows to Change, 2002; Jean Racine: life and legend, 2006; (ed with L. Erler) Schools for the Future Europe, 2012; Wolf Graf Baudissin: life and legacy, 2015 (trans. German 2016). *Recreation*: postal history. *Address*: 8 Northmoor Road, Oxford OX2 6UP. *T*: (01865) 556932.

**SAYER, Ven. Penelope Jane;** Archdeacon of Sherborne, since 2018; *b* 1959. *Educ*: Newcastle Univ. (BA 1980); Open Univ. (BA 1993); South East Inst. for Theol Educn. Ordained deacon, 2007, priest, 2008; non-stipendiary Minister, St John the Evangelist, St Leonards, 2007–10; Team Rector, St Alban's, Becontree South, Dagenham, 2010–16; Turnaround Minister, Bradwell Area, 2016–18; non-stipendiary Minister, St Margaret's, Woodham Mortimer and St Michael's, Woodham Walter, Maldon, 2016–18. *Address*: c/o Sherborne Office, St Nicholas' Church Centre, 30 Wareham Road, Corfe Mullen, Dorset BH21 3LE.

**SAYER, Robert;** Senior Partner, Sayer Moore & Co., since 1983; President, Law Society, 1999–2000 (Vice-President, 1995–96 and 1998–99); *b* 16 Jan. 1952; *s* of Kenneth Albert Ernest Sayer and Ellen Sayer; *m* 1997, Cathy Hunt. *Educ*: Salvatorian Coll., Harrow Weald, Middx; Swansea Univ. (BA Hons). Admitted Solicitor, 1979. Law Society: Dep. Vice Pres., 1997–98; Treas., 1997–99. Hon. Mem., Inst. of Advanced Legal Studies, 2000. *Publications*: numerous articles in legal jls. *Recreations*: sailing, walking. *Address*: (office) 190 Horn Lane, W3 6PL. *T*: (020) 8993 7571. *Club*: Naval and Military.

**SAYER, Roger Martin;** Organist and Director of Music, Temple Church, London, since 2013; *b* Portsmouth, 1 May 1961; *s* of Dennis and Barbara Sayer; one *s* one *d*. *Educ*: Royal Coll. of Music (Dip. RCM 1st Cl.; ARCM). FTCL; LRAM. Organist, Woodford Parish Church, 1981–89; Rochester Cathedral: Asst Organist, 1989–94; Dir of Music, 1994–2008; Organist, 2008–13. London Symphony Chorus: Accompanist, 2005–; Deputy Chorus Dir, 2012–. *Recreations*: travel, aircraft, cats, football. *Address*: 2 King's Bench Walk, 1st Floor, Temple, EC4Y 7DE. *E*: roger@templechurch.com.

**SAYER, Susan Joscelyn,** CBE 2013 (OBE 2000); Vice President, United Response, since 2015 (Co-founder and Chief Executive, 1972–2014); Chair, Campaign to Protect Rural England, since 2014; *b* Chichester, W Sussex, 7 Feb. 1947; *d* of Charles Edmund Johnson and Joscelyn Fay Johnson; *m* 1972, Richard John Sayer (marr. diss. 2000); two *s*. *Educ*: Hollington Park Sch.; Seaford Coll.; Reading Univ. (BSc Hons Chem. Physics 1969). Chair, ACEVO (formerly ACENVO), 1991–94; Chair, Mem. Bd, and Mem. Develt Cttee, Southern Housing Gp, 1994–99. Hon. Sen. Vis. Fellow, Faculty of Mgt, 2005–, Ambassador, 2015–, Cass Business Sch., City Univ. Non-exec. Dir, Hounslow and Richmond Community Healthcare NHS Trust, 2013–17 (Sen. Indep. Dir, 2015–17). Member, Board: Council for Professions Supplementary to Medicine, 1999–2001; Nat. Care Standards Commn, 2001–04. Mem. Bd, Silver Line, 2012–16. Vice Chair: Bath Univ. Students' Union, 2009–11; Seaford Coll., 2013–. Chair of Judges, Charity Awards, 2019–. Trustee: NCVO, 1996–99; Save the Children, 1998–2004; Trustee and Vice Chair, Prostate Cancer UK, 2002–12. Outstanding Achievement, Charity, Finance Charity Awards, 2003; Lifetime Achievement, Charity Times UK Charity Awards, 2004. *Publications*: Playing Safe: a parents' guide to keeping children safe, 1989. *Recreations*: family, countryside, walking, theatre, cinema. *Address*: c/o Campaign to Protect Rural England, 5–11 Lavington Street, SE1 0NZ. *E*: susayercbe@gmail.com.

**SAYER, William Laurence L.;** *see* Latimer-Sayer.

**SAYERS, Michael Patrick;** QC 1988; a Recorder of the Crown Court, 1986–2005; *b* 28 March 1940; *s* of Major Herbert James Michael Sayers, RA (killed on active service, 1943) and late Joan Sheilah de Courcy Holroyd (*née* Stephenson); *m* 1976, Mrs Moussie Brougham (*née* Hallstrom); one *s* one *d*, and one step *s*. *Educ*: Harrow School; Fitzwilliam College, Cambridge (Evelyn Rothschild Scholar; MA). Called to the Bar, Inner Temple, 1970, Bencher, 1994; Junior, Central Criminal Court Bar Mess, 1975–78; Supplementary Prosecuting Counsel to the Crown, Central Criminal Court, 1977–88; a Dep. Circuit Judge, 1981–82; Asst Recorder, 1982–86. Mem. Cttee, Barristers' Benevolent Assoc., 1991–2007. Vice-Pres., Harrow Assoc., 1999– (Chm., 1992–97). Vice-Chm., Anglo-

Swedish Council, 2016– (Hon. Sec., 2006–15). *Recreations:* shooting, sculpture, theatre, Sweden. *Address:* 26 King's Quay, Chelsea Harbour, SW10 0UX. *T:* (020) 7351 6003. *Clubs:* Garrick, Pratt's; Swinley Forest Golf.

**SAYLE, Alexei David;** actor, comedian, writer; *b* 7 Aug. 1952; *s* of Joseph Henry Sayle and Malka Sayle; *m* 1974, Linda Rawsthorn. *Educ:* Alsop GS, Liverpool; Southport Coll. of Art; Chelsea Sch. of Art (DipAD); Garnett Coll. (CertEd). Compère: Comedy Store Club, 1979–80; Comic Strip Club, 1980–81; live stand-up comedy, Soho Th., Edinburgh Fringe and nat. tour, 2013; *television series:* Young Ones, 1982–84; Alexei Sayle's Stuff (also writer), 1988–89, 1991; The Gravy Train, 1990; All New Alexei Sayle Show (also writer), 1994–95; Alexei Sayle's Merry-go-round, 1998; Arabian Nights, 2000; Alexei Sayle's Liverpool, 2008; *radio series,* Alexei Sayle's Imaginary Sandwich Bar, BBC Radio 4, 2016, 2017, 2019; *films include:* Gorky Park, 1983; Indiana Jones and the Last Crusade, 1989; Swing, 1998; Sometimes Always Never, 2019. Columnist: Independent; Daily Telegraph; formerly on Observer, Time Out, Car, Sunday Mirror. Hon. Prof., Thames Valley Univ., 1995. *Publications:* Train to Hell, 1982; Geoffrey the Tube Train and the Fat Comedian, 1987; Great Bus Journeys of the World, 1988; Barcelona Plates (short stories), 2000; The Dog Catcher (short stories), 2001; Overtaken (novel), 2003; The Weeping Women Hotel (novel), 2006; Mister Roberts (novel), 2008; Stalin Ate My Homework (memoir), 2010; Alexei Sayle's Imaginary Sandwich Bar, 2017. *Recreation:* walking. *Address:* c/o Cassie Mayer, 5 Old Garden House, The Lanterns, Bridge Lane, SW11 3AD. *T:* (020) 7350 0880. *Club:* Chelsea Arts.

**SAZANOV, Prof. Leonid,** PhD; FRS 2019; Professor, Institute of Science and Technology, Austria, since 2015; *b* Brest, Belarus, 22 Oct. 1960; *s* of Alexey Sazanov and Alexandra Sazanova; *m* 2002, Elena Sokolova; one *s* one *d. Educ:* Belarus State Univ. (MSc 1982); Moscow State Univ. (PhD 1990). Research Fellow: Moscow State Univ., 1990–92; Univ. of Birmingham, 1992–94; Imperial Coll. London, 1994–97; MRC Lab. of Molecular Biol., Cambridge, 1997–2000; Gp Leader, MRC Dunn Human Nutrition Unit, 2000–06, Prog. Leader, MRC Mitochondrial Biol. Unit, 2006–15, Univ. of Cambridge. Mem., EMBO, 2018. *Publications:* (ed) A Structural Perspective on Complex I, 2012; (jtly) Cellular Bioenergetics, 2016. *Recreations:* art, opera, hiking, ski-ing. *Address:* Institute of Science and Technology, Am Campus 1, 3400 Klosterneuburg, Austria. *E:* sazanov@ist.ac.at.

**SCACCHI, Greta;** actress. *Films* include: Heat and Dust, 1983; The Coca Cola Kid, 1985; Burke & Wills; Defence of the Realm, 1986; Good Morning Babylon, 1987; A Man in Love, 1988; White Mischief, 1988; Love and Fear (Les Trois Soeurs), 1990; Presumed Innocent, 1990; Fires Within, 1991; Shattered, 1991; Turtle Beach, 1992; The Player, 1992; Salt on our Skin; The Browning Version, 1994; Jefferson in Paris, 1994; Country Life, 1994; Emma, 1996; The Serpent's Kiss; The Red Violin, 1999; Cotton Mary, 1999; Tom's Midnight Garden, 2000; Beyond the Sea, 2004; Shoot on Sight, 2007; Brideshead Revisited, 2008; The Falling, 2015; North v South, 2015; The White King, 2017; *television:* The Ebony Tower, 1984; Dr Fischer of Geneva; Waterfront (Best Actress, Penguin and Golden Logie Awards, Australia); Rasputin (Emmy for best-supporting actress), 1996; The Odyssey, 1997; Macbeth, 1997; Daniel Deronda, 2002; Miss Austen Regrets, 2008; A. D. The Bible Continues, 2015; War and Peace, 2016; Versailles, 2017; *radio:* Life and Fate, 2011; *stage:* Cider with Rosie, Phoenix Arts, Leicester, 1982; Times Like These, Bristol Old Vic, 1985; Airbase, Oxford Playhouse, 1986; Uncle Vanya, Vaudeville, 1988; The Doll's House, Fest. of Perth, 1991; Miss Julie, 1992, Simpatico, 1996, Sydney Theatre Co.; The Guardsman, Albery, 2000; The True Life Fiction of Mata Hari Palace Theatre, Watford, 2002; Private Lives, Th. Royal, Bath, 2005; The Deep Blue Sea, Vaudeville, 2008; Bette and Joan, Arts Th., 2011; The Glass Menagerie, W Yorkshire Playhouse, 2015; The Entertainer, Garrick Th., 2016. *Address:* c/o Conway van Gelder Grant Ltd, 8–12 Broadwick Street, W1F 8HW.

**SCADDING, Dr John William,** OBE 2015; FRCP; Consultant Neurologist, National Hospital for Neurology and Neurosurgery, 1982–2008, now Honorary Consultant Emeritus (Medical Director, 1993–96); *b* 17 June 1948; *s* of late Prof. John Guyett Scadding, FRCP. *Educ:* University College London and UCH Med. Sch. (BSc 1st Cl. Hons, MB BS, MD). Jun. hosp. posts at UCH, Hammersmith, Brompton, Royal Free and National Hosps, 1972–82; Res. Fellow, UCL and Royal Free Hosp. Sch. of Medicine, 1978–80. Hon. Sen. Lectr, Inst. of Neurology, 1982–2008. Consultant Neurologist, Whittington Hosp., 1982–2003; Hon. Neurologist: St Luke's Hosp. for the Clergy, 1983–2002; Royal Soc. of Musicians, 1996–2008; Civilian Consultant Adviser, MoD, 1983–; Civilian Consultant Neurologist to RN, 1993–2003, to RAF, 1997–2003. Royal Society of Medicine: Associate Dean, 2002–06; Dean, 2006–08; Emeritus Dean, 2008–; Vice Pres., 2010–12. Chm., RSocMed Press, 2008–15. Trustee: Royal Hosp. for Neurodisability, 2004–16; Cure Parkinson's Trust, 2008–11 (Chm., Res. Cttee, 2009–19); CORDA, 2009–14; Chm. and Trustee, Neuro-disability Res. Trust, 2012–13. Gov., Yehudi Menuhin Sch., 2011–19. RSM Medal, 2013. *Publications:* research papers on mechanisms of pain in neurological disease; contribs to learned jls. *Recreations:* music (pianist), mountain walking. *Address:* National Hospital for Neurology and Neurosurgery, Queen Square, WC1N 3BG. *T:* (020) 7837 3611.

**SCALES, Dr Helen Joanna;** writer and marine biologist; Tutor, Madingley Hall, University of Cambridge, since 2013; *b* Surrey, 23 April 1977; *d* of Tom and Diana Hendry; *m* 2004, Ivan Scales. *Educ:* St John's Coll., Cambridge (BA 1999); Newcastle Univ. (MSc 2000); PhD Cantab 2006. Marine Biologist, WWF, Malaysia, 2000–01; freelance consultant and Ocean Conservation Expert, IUCN and Natural England, 2006–10. Freelance writer and radio presenter, 2010–. *Publications:* Poseidon's Steed, 2009; Spirals in Time, 2015; 11 Explorations into Life on Earth, 2017; Eye of the Shoal, 2018; Octopuses, 2019. *Recreations:* surfing, fish watching, free diving, dress making. *Address:* Madingley Hall, University of Cambridge, Madingley, Cambridge CB23 8AQ. *E:* helen@helenscales.com.

**SCALES, Neil,** OBE 2005; Director-General, Department of Transport and Main Roads, Australia, since 2013; *b* 24 June 1956; *s* of Gordon and Joyce Scales; *m* 1983, June Bradley; one *s* one *d. Educ:* Sunderland Poly. (BSc 1981; MSc 1984; DMS 1986); Open Univ. (MBA 1991). Apprentice, Sunderland Corp. Transport, 1972–76; engrg posts, Tyne & Wear PTE, 1976–86; Chief Engr, 1986–88, Dir of Engrg, 1988–90, Greater Manchester Buses; Man. Dir, Northern Counties, 1990–96; Greater Manchester PTE, 1996; consultant, private sector, 1997–99; Dir of Customer Services, 1999, CEO and Dir Gen., 1999–2012, Merseytravel; CEO, TransLink Authy, Australia, 2012–13. Hon. Fellow, Liverpool John Moores Univ., 2011. *Recreations:* Sunderland AFC, tutoring with Open University. *Clubs:* Reform; Brisbane.

**SCALES, Prunella, (Prunella Margaret Rumney West),** CBE 1992; actress; *d* of John Richardson Illingworth and Catherine Scales; *m* 1963, Timothy Lancaster West, *qv*; two *s. Educ:* Moira House, Eastbourne; Old Vic Theatre School, London; Herbert Berghof Studio, New York (with Uta Hagen). Repertory in Huddersfield, Salisbury, Oxford, Bristol Old Vic, etc; seasons at Stratford-on-Avon and Chichester Festival Theatre; plays on London stage include: The Promise, 1967; Hay Fever, 1968; It's a Two-Foot-Six-Inches-Above-The-Ground-World, 1970; The Wolf, 1975; Breezeblock Park, 1978; Make and Break, 1980; An Evening with Queen Victoria, 1980; The Merchant of Venice, 1981; Quartermaine's Terms, 1981; Big in Brazil, 1984; When We Are Married, 1986; Single Spies (double bill), 1988; The School for Scandal, 1990; Long Day's Journey into Night, 1991; Mother Tongue, 1992; The Birthday Party, 1999; A Day in the Death of Joe Egg, 2001; A Woman of No Importance, 2003; Carrie's War, 2009; regional theatre: Happy Days, Leeds, 1993; The Matchmaker, Chichester, 1993; Staying On, nat. tour, 1997; The Cherry Orchard, Oxford Playhouse, 2000; Gertrude's Secret, Apollo Th. and nat. tour, 2006–08; *films include:* Howard's End, 1992; Second Best, 1993; Wolf, 1994; An Awfully Big Adventure, 1994; An Ideal Husband, 1999; Ghost of Greville Lodge, 2001; *television:* Fawlty Towers (series), 1975, 1978; Grand Duo, The Merry Wives of Windsor, 1982; Mapp and Lucia (series), 1985–86; Absurd Person Singular, 1985; The Index Has Gone Fishing, What the Butler Saw, 1987; After Henry (series), 1988, 1990; The Rector's Wife, Fair Game, 1994; Dalziel & Pascoe, 1996; Signs and Wonders, Lord of Misrule, Breaking the Code, 1997; Midsomer Murders, 2001; Looking for Victoria, 2003; Casualty, 2004; Where the Heart Is, 2005; Great Canal Journeys, 2014–19; frequent broadcasts, readings, poetry recitals and fringe productions. Has directed plays at Bristol Old Vic, Arts Theatre, Cambridge, Billingham Forum, Almost Free Theatre, London, Nottingham Playhouse, Palace Theatre, Watford, W Yorks Playhouse, Leeds, Nat. Theatre of WA, Perth, and taught at several drama schools. Pres., CPRE, 1997–2002. Hon DLitt: Bradford, 1995; East Anglia, 1996. *Publications:* (with Timothy West) So You Want to be an Actor?, 2005. *Recreation:* gardening. *Address:* c/o Conway van Gelder Grant Ltd, 3rd Floor, 8–12 Broadwick Street, W1F 8HW.

*See also* S. A. J. West.

**SCALES, Sheila Lesley, (Mrs Roger Harris);** Director, Early Years, Extended Schools and Special Educational Needs Group (formerly Sure Start Extended Schools and Childcare Group), Department for Children, Schools and Families (formerly Department for Education and Skills), 2006–09; *b* Leeds, 22 Aug. 1949; *d* of Lesley and Hilda Scales; *m* 1973, Dr Roger Harris; three *s* one *d. Educ:* New Hall, Cambridge (BA 1970). Joined DES, 1970; Private Sec. to Perm. Under-Sec. of State, DES, 1973–75; Develt Planner, Kiribati, 1977–79; various posts, DES, then DfE, later DfEE, 1979–97; Asst Chief Exec., Surrey CC, 1997–98; Dep. Dir, Standards and Effectiveness Unit, DfEE, then DfES, 1998–2001; on secondment to Ofsted, 2001–02; Dep. Dir, Improving Behaviour and Attendance, 2002–04, Dir, Local Transformation Gp, 2004–06, DfES. Governor: City Acad., Hackney, 2008–; CoLA Shoreditch Park, 2017–. Advr, East End CAB, 2010–. *T:* 07850 169467.

**SCALLY, Dr Gabriel John,** FFPH; Chair, Soil Association, since 2017; *b* 24 Sept. 1954; *s* of Bernard Gabriel Scally and Maureen Scally (*née* Hopkins); *m* 1990, Rona Margaret Campbell; two *d. Educ:* St Mary's Grammar Sch., Belfast; Queen's Univ., Belfast (MB, BCh, BAO 1978); London Sch. of Hygiene and Tropical Medicine, Univ. of London (MSc 1982). MFPHM 1984, FFPH (FFPHM 1991); MFPHMI 1992; MRCGP 1993; FRCP 2004. Trainee in Gen. Practice, 1980–81; Sen. Tutor, Dept of Community Medicine, QUB, 1984–86; Consultant in Public Health Medicine, 1986–88, Chief Admin. MO and Dir of Public Health, 1989–93, Eastern Health and Social Services Bd, Belfast; Regional Director of Public Health: SE Thames RHA, 1993–94; South and West RHA, 1994–96; SW Region, DoH, 1996–2012; Dir, WHO Collaborating Centre for Healthy Urban Envmts, UWE, 2012–14. Member: NI Bd for Nursing, Health Visiting and Midwifery, 1988–93; Council, BMA, 1985–86, 1988–89 (Chm., Jun. Mems Forum, 1988–89); GMC, 1989–99. Pres., Sect. of Epidemiology and Public Health, RSocMed, 2017–. Hon. DSc UWE, 2012. *Publications:* papers on med. res. and health policy in med. jls. *Recreations:* sailing, traditional and contemporary Irish music, London Irish RFC. *Address:* 11 Dowry Square, Bristol BS8 4SH. *T:* (0117) 926 8510.

**SCAMPION, John,** CBE 2001; DL; Chairman, Determinations Panel, Pensions Regulator, 2005–13; *b* 22 Aug. 1941; *s* of John William and Rosa Mary Scampion; *m* 1995, Jennifer Mary Reeves; two *s,* and two step *d. Educ:* Queen Elizabeth's Grammar Sch., Alford, Lincs; Downing Coll., Cambridge (MA). Admitted solicitor, 1966; Town Clerk and Chief Exec., Solihull MBC, 1977–95; Social Fund Comr for GB and NI, 1995–2000; Comr for Immigration Services, 2000–05; Chm., Immigration Adv. Service, 2007–11. Tribunal Judge (formerly Mem.), Criminal Injuries Compensation Tribunal (formerly Appeals Panel), 1997–2012; Mem., Healthcare Commn (formerly Commn for Health Audit and Improvement), 2003–09. Chm., Stratford-upon-Avon Soc., 2016– (Vice Chm., 2013–16). Trustee, Arts in Minds Foundn, Worcester, 2015–17. FRSocMed 2008. DL W Midlands, 1992. *Recreations:* theatre-going, directing plays - occasionally, watching football, reading, hill walking, music listening. *Address:* 4 Hill House, 16/18 Welcombe Road, Stratford-upon-Avon, Warwicks CV37 6UJ.

**SCANLAN, Dorothy, (Mrs Charles Denis Scanlan);** *see* Quick, Dorothy.

**SCANLON, Mary Elizabeth,** CBE 2017; Member (C) Highlands and Islands, Scottish Parliament, 1999–2006 and 2007–16; *b* 25 May 1947; *d* of John Charles Campbell and Anne Campbell (*née* O'Donnell); *m* 1970, James Scanlon; one *s* one *d. Educ:* Univ. of Dundee (MA Econ/Pol 1982). Civil Service Administrator; Lecturer: Dundee Inst. of Technology, 1982–85; Perth Coll., 1985–88; Lectr in Econs, Dundee Coll. of Technology, 1988–94; Lectr in Econs and Business Studies, Inverness Coll., 1994–99. Contested (C) Moray, Scottish Parlt, April 2006. *Recreations:* walking, yoga, pilates, knitting. *Address:* 5 Broughton Place, Edinburgh EH1 3RL.

**SCARBOROUGH, Vernon Marcus;** HM Diplomatic Service, retired; Deputy High Commissioner, Tarawa, Republic of Kiribati, 2000–04; *b* 11 Feb. 1940; *s* of George Arthur Scarborough and Sarah Florence Scarborough (*née* Patey); *m* 1966, Jennifer Bernadette Keane; three *d. Educ:* Brockley County Grammar Sch.; Westminster Coll. Passport Office, FO, 1958–61, CRO 1961; served Dacca, Karachi, Brussels (Vice Consul, 1969–71), Bathurst, later Banjul, FCO, Muscat, Lagos and El Salvador; Kuala Lumpur, 1983–86 (First Sec., 1983); FCO, 1986; Chargé d'Affaires, San Salvador, 1987–90; Dep. Consul Gen. and Trade Comr, Auckland, 1990–94; Dep. High Comr, Suva, Tuvalu, Nauru and Ambassador to Palau, Federated States of Micronesia and Marshall Is, 1995–2000. Mem. Council, Pacific Is Soc. of UK, 2004–. *Recreations:* photography, antiques, grandchildren. *Address:* 2 Willow Place, Barns Green, Horsham, W Sussex RH13 0BA. *Clubs:* Fiji, Defence, Returned Servicemen's and Ex-Servicemen's Association (Suva).

**SCARBROUGH, 13th Earl of,** *cr* 1690; **Richard Osbert Lumley;** DL; Viscount Lumley (Ire.), 1628; Baron Lumley, 1681; Viscount Lumley, 1690; *b* 18 May 1973; *s* of 12th Earl of Scarbrough, and of Lady Elizabeth Ramsay, LVO, *d* of 16th Earl of Dalhousie, KT, GCVO, GBE, MC; S father, 2004; *m* 2007, Mrs Henrietta Elfrida Helen Scherman (*née* Boyson). DL S Yorks, 2011. *Heir: b* Hon. Thomas Henry Lumley [*b* 6 Feb. 1980; *m* 2016, Charan, *d* of late Pritpal Sohanpawl].

**SCARD, Dennis Leslie;** General Secretary, Musicians' Union, 1990–2000; *b* 8 May 1943; *s* of late Charles Leslie Scard and Doris Annie (*née* Farmer); *m* 1st (marr. diss.); two *s;* 2nd, 1993, Linda Perry. *Educ:* Lascelles Co. Secondary Sch.; Trinity Coll. of Music, London (Hon. Fellow, 1997). Professional horn player, 1962–85, performed with leading symphony and chamber orchestras. Part-time instrumental teacher, London Borough of Hillingdon, 1974–85. Musicians' Union: Chm., Central London Br., 1972–85; Mem., Exec. Cttee, 1979–85; full-time Official, Birmingham, 1985–90. Mem., TUC Gen. Council, 1990–2001. Bd Mem., 2002–, Dep. Chm., 2003–06, Chm., 2007–11, Shoreham Port

Authy. Worker Rep., BIS (formerly DTI, then BERR) Central Arbitration Cttee, 2002–14; Lay Mem., Employment Tribunal Service, 2005–13. Mem. Bd, Trinity Coll. of Music, 1998–2006. Trustee, Performances (Birmingham) Ltd (Symphony Hall and Town Hall Birmingham), 1996–2017. Chair, Henry Wood Accommodation Trust (formerly Music Students Hostel Trust), 2003–. *Recreations:* music, walking, theatre, lawn bowls. *Address:* 6 Cranborne Avenue, Meads, Eastbourne BN20 7TS. *T:* (01323) 648364.

**SCARDINO, Dame Marjorie (Morris),** DBE 2002; DJur; Chief Executive, Pearson plc, 1997–2012; *b* 25 Jan. 1947; *d* of Robert Weldon and Beth Morris (*née* Lamb); adopted dual American-British nationality, 2002; *m* 1974, Albert James Scardino; two *s* one *d. Educ:* Baylor Univ. (BA); Univ. of San Francisco (DJur). Partner, Brannen Wessels & Searcy, 1976–85; Pres., Economist Newspaper Gp Inc., 1985–93; Chief Exec., Economist Gp, 1993–97. Non-executive Director: Nokia, 2001–13 (Vice Chm., 2007–13); Twitter, 2013–18; Internat. Airlines Gp, 2013–. Trustee: Carter Center, 2003–; MacArthur Foundn, 2005– (Chm., 2012–17); Oxfam, 2010–15. Chm., Council, LSHTM, 2015–. Fellow, Amer. Acad. of Arts and Scis, 2010.

**SCARFE, Gerald Anthony,** CBE 2008; RDI 1989; artist; *b* 1 June 1936; *m* Jane Asher, *qv*; two *s* one *d. Educ:* scattered (due to chronic asthma as a child). Punch, 1960; Private Eye, 1961; Daily Mail, 1966; Sunday Times, 1967–2017; London Evening Standard, 2017–; cover artist to illustrator, Time Magazine, 1967; animation and film directing for BBC, 1969–; artist, New Yorker, 1993–. Has taken part in exhibitions: Grosvenor Gall., 1969 and 1970; Pavilion d'Humour, Montreal, 1967 and 1971; Expo '70, Osaka, 1970; six sculptures of British Character, Millennium Dome, 2000; Pink Floyd - Their Mortal Remains, V&A, 2017, Madrid, 2019. One-man exhibitions of sculptures and lithographs: Waddell Gall., New York, 1968 and 1970; Grosvenor Gall., 1969; Vincent Price Gall., Chicago, 1969; National Portrait Gall., 1971; retrospective exhibn, Royal Festival Hall, 1983; drawings: Langton Gall., 1986; Chris Beetles Gall., 1989; Gerald Scarfe Meets Walt Disney, MOMI, 1997; Gerald Scarfe, The Art of Hercules, Z Gall., NY, 1997; Nat. Portrait Gall., 1998, 2003; Cleveland Gall., 1998; Millennium Galls, Sheffield, 2005; Fine Arts Soc., London, 2005; Portcullis House, Westminster, 2008–09; Halle, 2009; Hanover, 2010; Cesky Krumlov, Czech Republic, 2012; Prague, 2013; Milk Snatcher, Bowes Mus., Co. Durham, 2015; Scarfe & Music, Barbican Music Library, 2016; Scarfe Stage & Screen, King's Cross, 2017–18, Beaney Hse of Art and Knowledge, Canterbury, Kirkcudbright Art Gall., 2019; Retrospective, Hanover, 2018; perm. display, Scarfes Bar, Rosewood, London, 2014–. Animated film for BBC, Long Drawn Out Trip, 1973 (prizewinner, Zagreb); title sequence of TV series: Yes Minister, 1980; Yes Prime Minister, 1986; New Yes Prime Minister, 2013; Dir, Scarfe by Scarfe, BBC (BAFTA Award, 1987); Designer and Dir, animated sequences in film, The Wall, 1982; designer: Who's A Lucky Boy?, Royal Exchange, Manchester, 1984; Orpheus in the Underworld, ENO, 1985; Born Again, Chichester, 1990; The Magic Flute, Los Angeles, 1993, Houston, Texas, 1997, Seattle, 1999, San Francisco, 2007, Los Angeles, 2009; An Absolute Turkey, Globe, 1994 (Olivier Award for best costumes); Mind Millie For Me, Haymarket, 1996; Fantastic Mr Fox, Los Angeles Opera, 1998; The Nutcracker, English Nat. Ballet, 2002; production designer, Hercules (Walt Disney film), 1995–97; costume designer, Peter and the Wolf, Holiday on Ice and world tour, 2000; animation sequence, Miss Saigon, UK and internat. tour, 2004; animation, The Wall by Roger Waters, internat. tour, 2011. Hon. DLitt Kent, 2003; Hon. DArts: Liverpool, 2005; Lincoln, 2018; Hon. LLD Dundee, 2007. *Publications:* Gerald Scarfe's People, 1966; Indecent Exposure (ltd edn), 1973; Expletive Deleted: the life and times of Richard Nixon (ltd edn), 1974; Gerald Scarfe, 1982; Father Kissmass and Mother Claws, 1985; Scarfe by Scarfe (autobiog.), 1986 (televised, 1987); Scarfe's Seven Deadly Sins, 1988; Scarfe's Line of Attack, 1988; Scarfeland: a lost world of fabulous beasts and monsters, 1989; Scarfe on Stage, 1992; Scarfeface, 1993; Hades: the truth at last, 1997; Heroes and Villains, 2003; Gerald Scarfe: drawing blood - 40 years of Scarfe uncensored, 2005; Monsters: how George Bush saved the world and other tall stories, 2008; The Making of Pink Floyd The Wall, 2011; Long Drawn Out Trip (autobiog.), 2019; Scarfe (large format retrospective), 2019. *Recreations:* drawing, painting and sculpting.

**SCARFE, Jane;** *see* Asher, J.

**SCARGILL, Arthur;** General Secretary, Socialist Labour Party; Honorary President, National Union of Mineworkers, since 2002 (General Secretary, 1992; President, 1981–2002); *b* 11 Jan. 1938; *oc* of Harold and Alice Scargill; *m* 1961, Anne, *d* of Elliott Harper; one *d. Educ:* Worsbrough Dale School; White Cross Secondary School; Leeds Univ. Miner, Woolley Colliery, 1953; Mem., NUM branch cttee, 1960; Woolley branch deleg. to Yorks NUM Council, 1964; Mem., Nat. Exec., 1972, Pres., 1973, Yorks NUM. Mem., TUC Gen. Council, 1986–88. Member: Young Communists' League, 1955–62; Co-op Party, 1963; Labour Party, 1966–95; Socialist Labour Party, 1996; CND. Contested (Socialist Lab): Newport East, 1997; Hartlepool, 2001; London, Eur. Parlt, 2009. *Address:* c/o Socialist Labour Party, 9 Victoria Road, Barnsley, S Yorks S70 2BB.

**SCARLETT,** family name of **Baron Abinger**.

**SCARLETT, Sir John (McLeod),** KCMG 2007 (CMG 2001); OBE 1987; Senior Adviser, Morgan Stanley, since 2010; Chairman: Strategy Advisory Council, Statoil ASA, since 2012; SC Strategy Ltd, since 2013; International Adviser's Group, Equinor ASA, since 2018; *b* 18 Aug. 1948; *s* of late Dr James Henri Stuart Scarlett and Clara Dunlop Scarlett; *m* 1970, Gwenda Mary Rachel Stilliard; one *s* three *d* (and one *s* decd). *Educ:* Epsom Coll.; Magdalen Coll., Oxford (MA). Secret Intelligence Service, 1971–2001: Nairobi, 1973–74; lang. student, 1974–75; Second, later First, Sec., Moscow, 1976–77; First Secretary: London, 1977–84; Paris, 1984–88; London, 1988–91; Counsellor: Moscow, 1991–94; London, 1994–2001 (Dir of Security and Public Affairs, 1999–2001); Chm., Jt Intelligence Cttee, and Intelligence Co-ordinator, then Head of Intelligence and Security Secretariat, Cabinet Office, 2001–04; Chief, SIS, 2004–09. Advr, Swiss Re Zurich, 2010–; Dir, Times Newspaper Hldgs, 2010–. Chm., Bletchley Park Trust, 2012–18; Trustee: Imperial War Mus., 2010–17; RUSI, 2010– (Vice Chm., 2016–); Friends of the French Inst., UK, 2012–; Co-Chair, Global Adv. Council, Woodrow Wilson Center, Washington, 2017–. MInstD 2016. Officier, Légion d'Honneur (France), 2011. *Recreation:* family. *Club:* Oxford and Cambridge.

**SCARLETT, Liam;** Artist in Residence, Royal Ballet, since 2012; *b* Ipswich, 8 April 1986; *s* of Laurence Stephen and Deborah Frances Scarlett. *Educ:* Royal Ballet Sch. Artist, 2005–07, First Artist, 2007–12, Royal Ballet; has worked with NYC Ballet, San Francisco Ballet, American Ballet Th., Miami City Ballet, K-Ballet, Ballet Boyz, English Nat. Ballet; choreographed for Royal Opera House: The Age of Anxiety, 2014; Frankenstein, 2015; Swan Lake, 2018; Asphodel Meadows, The Cunning Little Vixen, 2019; film, The Nutcracker and the Four Realms, 2018. *Recreations:* theatre, ballet, cinema, art, poetry, family, cooking, reading. *Address:* Royal Ballet, Royal Opera House, Covent Garden, WC2E 9DD. *T:* (020) 7212 9685. *E:* liam.scarlett@roh.org.uk.

**SCARONI, Paolo,** Cavaliere del Lavoro, 2004; Chief Executive, Eni, 2005–14; Deputy Chairman, Rothschild Group, since 2014; *b* 28 Nov. 1946; *s* of Bruno and Clementina Boniver Scaroni; *m* 1974, Francesca (*née* Zanconato); two *s* one *d. Educ:* Luigi Bocconi Commercial Univ., Milan (Dr Econs 1969); Columbia Univ., NY (MBA). Chevron,

1968–71; Associate, McKinsey & Co., 1972–73; Saint-Gobain, 1973–85: Financial Dir, Italy, 1973–78; General Delegate: Venezuela, Colombia, Ecuador, and Peru, 1978–81; Italy, 1981–84; Pres., Flat Glass Div. (world-wide), France, 1984–85; Exec. Vice-Pres., Techint, Italy, 1985–96; Pilkington plc: Pres., Automotive Products Worldwide, 1996–98; Gp Chief Exec., 1997–2002; Dep. Chm., 2002; Chief Exec., Enel SpA, 2002–05. Non-executive Director: Burmah Castrol plc, 1998–2000; BAE SYSTEMS, 2000–04; Alliance UniChem, 2003–06 (Chm., 2005–06); London Stock Exchange Gp, 2007–14 (Dep. Chm., 2010–14); Generali, 2007–; Mem., Supervisory Bd, ABN AMRO Bank NV, 2003. Mem., Bd of Overseers, Columbia Business Sch., 1996–. Commandeur, Légion d'Honneur (France), 2013 (Officier, 2007). *Publications:* (jtly) Professione Manager, 1985. *Recreations:* reading, ski-ing, golf. *Address:* Rothschild Group, New Court, St Swithin's Lane, EC4N 8AL. *Club:* Royal Automobile.

**SCARRATT, Richard John; His Honour Judge Scarratt;** a Circuit Judge, since 2009; a Deputy High Court Judge, since 2014; Designated Family Judge for Kent, since 2014; *b* Leicester, 21 Aug. 1955; *s* of late Richard Geoffrey Lawrence Scarratt and June Scarratt (*née* Beck); *m* 1989, Sarah Jane May; three *s. Educ:* Ryde Sch., IoW; Birmingham Univ. (LLB Hons 1978); Inns of Court Sch. of Law. Called to the Bar, Lincoln's Inn, 1979; Dep. Dist Judge, Principal Registry of Family Div., 2003–09; Recorder, Western Circuit, 2005–09. *Recreations:* family, sailing, ski-ing, gardening, music, keeping busy. *Address:* The Law Courts, Chaucer Road, Canterbury, Kent CT1 1ZA. *T:* (01227) 819283, *Fax:* (01227) 819283. *E:* hhj.richard.scarratt@ejudiciary.net. *Clubs:* Hurlingham; Rock Sailing (Cornwall).

**SCARSDALE,** 4th Viscount *cr* 1911; **Peter Ghislain Nathaniel Curzon;** Bt (Scot.) 1636, (Eng.) 1641; Baron Scarsdale 1761; *b* 6 March 1949; *s* of 3rd Viscount Scarsdale and his 1st wife, Solange Yvonne Palmyre Ghislaine Curzon (*née* Hanse); *S* father, 2000; *m* 1st, 1983, Mrs Karen Osborne (marr. diss. 1996); one *d*; 2nd, 1996, Michelle Reynolds. *Educ:* Ampleforth. *Heir: b* Hon. David James Nathaniel Curzon [*b* 3 Feb. 1958; *m* 1981, Ruth Linton (*d* 2010); one *s* one *d*; *m* 2015, Martine Mansourian (*née* Joyce)].

**SCATTERGOOD, Andrew Edward;** Chief Executive, Royal Parks, since 2015; *b* Meriden, Warwickshire, 8 Sept. 1975; *s* of Edward and Margaret Scattergood; *m* 2003, Emma Robertson; two *s* one *d. Educ:* Arden Sch.; Bristol Univ. (BA Hons Hist. 1998). Travelling, 1998–99; Fast Stream, DCMS, 1999–2003; Hd, Culture and Sport, FCO, 2003–06; Dep. Dir, Planning, 2006–11, Dir of Ops, 2012, Govt Olympic Exec.; Dir, Spectrum Release, Ofcom, 2013–15. Mem., Crown Estate Paving Commn, 2015–. *Recreations:* Rugby (including coaching), ski-ing, walking, mountain biking. *Address:* Royal Parks, The Old Police House, Hyde Park, W2 2UH. *T:* 07828 314915. *E:* ascattergood@royalparks.org.uk.

**SCHAFF, Alistair Graham;** QC 1999; *b* 25 Sept. 1959; *s* of John Schaff and Barbara Schaff (*née* Williams); *m* 1991, (Marie) Leona Burley; one *s* one *d. Educ:* Bishop's Stortford Coll.; Magdalene Coll., Cambridge (MA 1st Cl. Jt Hons History and Law). Called to the Bar, Inner Temple, 1983; in practice at the Bar, 1983–. *Recreations:* family life, foreign travel, history, spectator sport, opera. *Address:* 7 King's Bench Walk, Temple, EC4Y 7DS. *T:* (020) 7583 0404.

**SCHALLER, George Beals;** Senior Conservationist, Wildlife Conservation Society, New York, since 2008; Vice President, Panthera, New York, 2008–16; *b* 26 May 1933; *m* 1957, Kay Morgan; two *s. Educ:* Univ. of Alaska (BA, BS 1955); Univ. of Wisconsin (PhD 1962). Fellow, Center for Advanced Study in the Behavioral Sciences, Stanford Univ., 1962–63; Res. Associate, Johns Hopkins Univ., 1963–66; Wildlife Conservation (formerly NY Zoological) Society, 1966–: Dir of Internat. Progs, 1972–88; Dir for Sci., 1988–2001; Vice Pres., 2001–08. *Publications:* The Mountain Gorilla, 1963; The Year of the Gorilla, 1964; The Deer and the Tiger, 1967; The Serengeti Lion, 1972; Serengeti: a kingdom of predators, 1972; Golden Shadows, Flying Hooves, 1973; Mountain Monarchs: wild sheep and goats of the Himalaya, 1977; Stones of Silence, 1980; (with Chinese co-authors) The Giant Pandas of Wolong, 1985; The Last Panda, 1993; Tibet's Hidden Wilderness, 1997; Wildlife of the Tibetan Steppe, 1998; (ed jtly) Antelopes, Deer and Relatives, 2000; A Naturalist and other Beasts, 2007; Tibet Wild, 2012; Into Wild Mongolia, 2020; *books for children:* (with M. Selsam) The Tiger: its life in the wild, 1969; (with K. Schaller) Wonders of Lions, 1977; The Good Pika (in Chinese), 2012; Deki, the Adventures of a Dog and a Boy in Tibet, 2014; 120 scientific articles and 105 popular articles about wildlife and conservation in various jls and mags. *Recreations:* watching wildlife, photography. *Address:* Wildlife Conservation Society, 2300 Southern Boulevard, Bronx, NY 10460, USA; 8 Arbor Court, West Lebanon, NH 03784, USA.

**SCHALLY, Dr Andrew Victor;** Distinguished Medical Research Scientist, Veterans Affairs Department, and Chief of Endocrine, Polypeptide and Cancer Institute, Veterans Affairs Medical Center, Miami, since 2006; Professor, University of Miami, Miller School of Medicine, since 2006; *b* Wilno, Poland, 30 Nov. 1926; US Citizen (formerly Canadian Citizen); *s* of Casimir and Maria Schally; *m* 1st, 1956, Margaret White (marr. diss.); one *s* one *d*; 2nd, 1976, Ana Maria Comaru (*d* 2004); 3rd, 2011, Maria Rasmussen. *Educ:* Bridge of Allan, Scotland (Higher Learning Cert.); London (studied chemistry); McGill Univ., Montreal, Canada (BSc Biochem., 1955; PhD Biochem., 1957). Res. Assistant: Dept of Biochem., Nat. Inst. for Med. Res., MRC, Mill Hill, 1949–52; Endocrine Unit, Allan Meml Inst. for Psych., McGill Univ., Montreal, 1952–57; Baylor University Coll. of Medicine, Texas Med. Center: Res. Associate, Dept of Physiol., 1957–60; Asst Prof. of Physiol., Dept of Physiol., and Asst Prof. of Biochem., Dept of Biochem., 1960–62; Chief, Endocrine, Polypeptide and Cancer Inst., Veterans Admin Hosp., then Veterans Affairs Med. Center, New Orleans, 1962–2006, Sen. Med. Investigator, 1973–99; Tulane University School of Medicine, New Orleans: Associate Prof., 1962–67; Prof. of Medicine, 1967–2006; Head, Section of Experimental Medicine, 1978–2006. Member: Endocrine Soc., USA; AAAS; Soc. of Biol Chemists; Amer. Physiol Soc.; Soc. for Experimental Biol. and Med.; Amer. Assoc. for Cancer Res.; Amer. Soc. for Reproductive Medicine; Internat. Brain Res. Org.; Nat. Acad. of Medicine, Mexico; Nat. Acad. of Medicine, Brazil; Nat. Acad. of Medicine, Venezuela; Nat. Acad. of Scis (US); Hungarian Acad. of Scis; Acad. of Scis, Russia, 1991; Acad. of Medicine, Poland, 1995; Royal Acad. of Medicine, Spain, 2004. Hon. Member: Chilean Endocrine Soc.; Mexican Soc. of Nutrition and Endocrinol.; Acad. of Med. Sciences of Cataluna and Baleares; Endocrine Soc. of Madrid; Polish Soc. of Internal Med.; Endocrine Soc. of Ecuador; Endocrine Soc. of Peru. Member, Editorial Board: Life Sciences, 1980–; Peptides, 1980–; The Prostate, 1985–. Dr *hc* State Univ. of Rio de Janeiro, 1977; Rosario, Argentina, 1979; Univ. Peruana Cayetano Heredia, Lima, 1979; Univ. Nat. de San Marcos, Lima, 1979; MD *hc* Tulane, 1978; Cadiz, 1979; Univ. Villareal-Lima, 1979; Copernicus Med. Acad., Cracow, 1979; Chile, 1979; Buenos Aires, 1980; Salamanca, 1981; Complutense Univ., Madrid, 1984; Pécs Univ., 1986; Autónoma, Madrid, 1994; Alcalá, Madrid, 1996; Malaga, 2002; Milan, 2005; Hon. DSc McGill, 1979; Hon. Dr Université René Descartes, Paris, 1987; Hon. Dr rer. nat. Regensburg Univ., 1992; Hon. Dr Nat. Sci. Salzburg, 1997; Hon. Dr: Federal Univ. Porto Alegre, Brazil, 1998; Univ. Nacional Autónoma de México, 2001; Rio de Janeiro, 2003; Athens, 2003; Szeged, 2012; Debrecen, 2012. Nobel Prize in Physiology or Medicine, 1977. Veterans Administration: William S. Middleton Award, 1970; Exceptional Service Award and

Medal, 1978. Van Meter Prize, Amer. Thyroid Assoc., 1969; Ayerst-Squibb Award, US Endocrine Soc., 1970; Charles Mickle Award, Faculty of Med., Univ. of Toronto, 1974; Gairdner Foundn Internat. Award, Toronto, 1974; Edward T. Tyler Award, 1975; Borden Award, Assoc. of Amer. Med. Colls, 1975; Albert Lasker Basic Med. Res. Award, 1975; Spanish Pharmaceutical Soc., 1977; Laude Award, 1978; Heath Meml Award from M. D. Anderson Tumour Inst., 1989. Chevalier, Légion d'Honneur (France), 2004. *Publications*: (compiled and ed with William Locke) The Hypothalamus and Pituitary in Health and Disease, 1972; over 2500 other pubns (papers, revs, books, abstracts). *Address*: Research Service (151), Veterans Administration Medical Center, 1201 NW 16th Street, Miami, FL 33125, USA. *T*: (305) 5753477.

**SCHAMA, Sir Simon (Michael),** Kt 2018; CBE 2001; FRSL; University Professor, Department of History, Columbia University, since 1997; writer, New Yorker (art critic, 1995–98); *b* 13 Feb. 1945; *s* of Arthur Osias Schama and Gertrude Steinberg Schama; *m* 1983, Virginia Papaioannou; one *s* one *d*. *Educ*: Christ's Coll., Cambridge (BA 1966; MA 1969; Hon. Fellow, 1995). Fellow and Dir of Studies in History, Christ's Coll., Cambridge, 1966–76; Fellow and Tutor in Modern History, Brasenose Coll., Oxford, 1976–80; Mellon Prof. of History, 1980–90, and Kenan Prof., 1990–93, Harvard Univ.; Old Dominion Foundation Prof. in the Humanities, Columbia Univ., 1993–96. Writer and presenter: A History of Britain, BBC TV Series, 2000, 2001, 2002; Simon Schama's Power of Art, BBC2, 2006; The American Future: A History, 2008; Simon Schama's John Donne, BBC2, 2009; Simon Schama on Obama's America, BBC2, 2010; Simon Schama's Shakespeare, BBC2, 2012; The Story of the Jews, BBC2, 2013; Schama on Rembrandt, BBC2, 2014; The Face of Britain, 2015; Civilisations, 2018. Corresp. FBA 2015; FRSL 2016. *Publications*: Patriots and Liberators: revolution in the Netherlands 1780–1813, 1978; Two Rothschilds and the Land of Israel, 1979; The Embarrassment of Riches: an interpretation of Dutch culture in the Golden Age, 1987; Citizens: a chronicle of the French Revolution, 1989; Dead Certainties (Unwarranted Speculations), 1991; Landscape and Memory, 1995; Rembrandt's Eyes, 1999; A History of Britain, vol. 1, 3000 BC–AD 1603, 2000, vol. 2, The British Wars 1603–1776, 2001, vol. 3, The Fate of Empire 1776–2000, 2002; Hang-Ups: essays on painting (mostly), 2004; Rough Crossings, 2005; Power of Art, 2006; The American Future: a history, 2008; Scribble, Scribble, Scribble: writings on ice cream, Obama, Churchill and my mother, 2010; The Story of the Jews: finding the words (1000 BCE–1492 CE), 2013; The Face of Britain: the nation through its portraits, 2015; Belonging: the story of the Jews 1492–1900, 2017. *Recreations*: Bordeaux wine, gardening, Brazilian music. *Address*: Department of History, Fayerweather Hall, Columbia University, New York, NY 10027, USA. *T*: (212) 8544593. *Club*: Century (New York).

**SCHAPIRA, Prof. Anthony Henry Vernon,** MD; DSc; FRCP, FMedSci; Chairman and Professor of Neurology, University Department of Clinical and Movement Neurosciences, Institute of Neurology, University College London, and Professor of Neurology, National Hospital for Neurology and Neurosurgery, Queen Square, and Royal Free Hospital, London, since 1990; Vice-Dean, University College London and Director of Royal Free Campus, since 2009; *b* 3 Sept. 1954; *s* of Markus and Constance Schapira; *m* 2003, Laura Jean Johnson; one *d*. *Educ*: Bradford Grammar Sch.; Westminster Med. Sch., London Univ. (BSc Hons, AKC; MB BS, MD, DSc). MRCP, FRCP 1992; FMedSci 1999. House Physician to Chief Physician to the Queen, 1979; med. trng, Hammersmith and Whittington Hosps, Nat. Hosp. for Neurology and Neurosurgery and St Thomas' Hosp., 1980–84; trng in neurology, Royal Free Hosp. and Nat. Hosp. for Neurology and Neurosurgery, 1983–88; Wellcome Res. Fellow, 1985–87; Sen. Lectr and Consultant in Neurology, Royal Free Hosp. and UC Med. Sch., and Inst. of Neurology, London, 1988–90; Consultant Neurologist, Royal Free Hosp. and Nat. Hosp. for Neurology and Neurosurgery, 1988–. Sen. Investigator, NIHR, 2012–. Hon. Prof. of Neurology, Mount Sinai Med. Sch., NY, 1995; Visiting Professor: Harvard, 2009; Yale, 2010. Non-executive Director: Royal Free London Foundn Trust, 2009–; Office of the Public Guardian, MoJ, 2012–18; NHS Ind. Reconfiguration Panel, 2019–. Member: Movement Disorders Soc., 1992–; Harveian Soc., 1994–. Co-Ed.-in-Chief, 2006–12, Ed.-in-Chief, 2012–, Eur. Jl of Neurology. Queen Square Prize, Inst. of Neurology, 1986; Graham Bull Prize for Clinical Sci., RCP, 1995; European Prize for Clinical Sci., Eur. Soc. Clin. Sci., 1998; Buckston Browne Medal, Harveian Soc., 1995; Opprecht Prize, Neurol. Soc. Switzerland, 1999; Duchenne Prize, German Neurol. Soc., 2005. *Publications*: (ed jtly) Mitochondrial Disorders in Neurology, 1994, 2nd edn 2002; Mitochondria: DNA, protein and disease, 1994; (ed jtly) Muscle Diseases, 1999; (ed jtly) Clinical Cases in Neurology, 2001; (ed) Mitochondrial Function and Dysfunction, 2002; Treatment of Parkinson's Disease, 2005; Understanding Parkinson's Disease, 2005; Neurology and Clinical Neuroscience, 2007; Parkinsonian Disorders, 2008; Neurodegeneration, 2017. *Recreations*: chess (Yorkshire champion, 1966), European history, international affairs. *Address*: University Department of Clinical Neurosciences, University College London, Rowland Hill Street, NW3 2PF. *T*: (020) 7830 2012. *E*: anthony.schapira@nhs.net. *Club*: Athenæum.

**SCHARPING, Rudolf;** Founder and Managing Partner, RSBK GmbH, since 2004; *b* Niederelbert, Westerwald, 2 Dec. 1947. *Educ*: Univ. of Bonn. State Chm. and Nat. Dep. Chm., Jusos (Young Socialists), 1966; joined SPD, 1966; Rhineland-Palatinate: Mem., State Parlt, 1975–94; Leader, SPD, 1985–91; Leader of Opposition, 1985–91; Minister-Pres., 1991–94; Mem., Bundestag, 1994–2005; Leader of Opposition, 1994–98; Minister of Defence, 1998–2002; Dep. Chm., SPD, 1995–2003 (Chm., 1993–95); Pres., SDP of Europe, 1994–2001. Vis. Prof., Fletcher Sch., Tufts Univ., USA, 2004–06. Pres., Fedn of German Cyclists, 2005–. *Address*: RSBK GmbH, Freiherr-vom-Stein-Str. 11, 60323 Frankfurt am Main, Germany.

**SCHATZ, Meryl Jane;** *see* Halls, M. J.

**SCHÄUBLE, Dr Wolfgang;** Member, since 1972, and President, since 2017, of Bundestag; Deputy Chairman, CDU/CSU Parliamentary Group, Germany, 2002–05 (Chairman, 1991–2000); *b* 18 Sept. 1942; *s* of Karl Schäuble and Gertrud (*née* Göhring); *m* 1969, Ingeborg Hensle; one *s* three *d*. *Educ*: Univ. of Freiburg; Univ. of Hamburg (Dr jur 1971). Tax Revenue Dept, State of Baden-Württemberg, 1971–72; solicitor, 1978–84; Parly Sec., CDU/CSU, 1981–84; Federal Minister with special responsibility and Head of Federal Chancellery, 1984–89; Federal Minister of the Interior, 1989–91 and 2005–09, of Finance, 2009–17. Chm., 1998–2000, Mem. Governing Bd, 2000–, CDU, Germany. Chairman: CDU Cttee on Sports, 1976–84; Working Gp, European Border Regions, 1979–82. Grosskreuz des Verdienstordens der Bundesrepublik Deutschland, 1990; Internationaler Karlspreis zu Aachen, 2012. *Publications*: Der Vertrag, 1991; Und der Zukunft zugewandt, 1994; Mitten im Leben, 2000; Scheitert der Westen?, 2003; Braucht unsere Gesellschaft Religion?, 2009; Zukunft mit Maß, 2009. *Recreation*: classical music. *Address*: (office) c/o Deutscher Bundestag, Platz der Republik 1, 11011 Berlin, Germany. *E*: wolfgang.schaeuble@bundestag.de. *W*: www.wolfgang-schaeuble.de.

**SCHAUFUSS, Peter;** ballet dancer, producer, choreographer, director; Founder, Edinburgh Festival Ballet School, 2019; *b* 26 April 1950; *s* of late Frank Schaufuss and Mona Vangsaae, former solo dancers with Royal Danish Ballet. *Educ*: Royal Danish Ballet School. Apprentice, Royal Danish Ballet, 1965; soloist, Nat. Ballet of Canada, 1967–68; Royal Danish Ballet, 1969–70; Principal, London Festival Ballet, 1970–74; NY City Ballet, 1974–77; Principal, National Ballet of Canada, 1977–83; Artistic Dir, London Fest. Ballet, later English Nat. Ballet, 1984–90; Dir of Ballet, Deutsche Oper, Berlin, 1990–93; Ballet Dir, Royal Danish Ballet, 1994–95; Founder Dir, Peter Schaufuss Ballet, 1997–. Guest appearances in Austria, Canada, Denmark, France, Germany, Greece, Israel, Italy, Japan, Norway, S America, Turkey, UK, USA, USSR; Presenter, Dancer, BBC, 1984; numerous TV appearances. Roles created for him in: Phantom of the Opera; Orpheus; Verdi Variations; The Steadfast Tin Soldier; Rhapsodie Espagnole. Produced ballets: La Sylphide (London Fest. Ballet, Stuttgart Ballet, Roland Petit's Ballet de Marseille, Deutsche Oper Berlin, Teatro Comunale, Florence, Vienna State Opera, Opernhaus Zurich, Teatro dell' Opera di Roma, Hessisches Staatstheater, Wiesbaden, Ballet du Rhin, Royal Danish Ballet, Ballet West); Napoli (Nat. Ballet of Canada, Teatro San Carlo, English Nat. Ballet); Folktale (Deutsche Oper Berlin); Dances from Napoli (London Fest. Ballet); Bournonville (Aterballetto); The Nutcracker (English Nat. Ballet, Deutsche Oper, Berlin); Giselle, Sleeping Beauty, Swan Lake, Tchaikovsky Trilogy (Deutsche Oper, Berlin). Staging for Ashton's Romeo and Juliet, and prod. and choreog. Hamlet, Royal Danish Ballet, 1996; produced and/or choreographed, for Peter Schaufuss Ballet, new versions of: Swan Lake, Sleeping Beauty, The Nutcracker, 1997; Hamlet, Romeo and Juliet, 1998; The King, Manden der Onskede Sig en Havudsigt, 1999; Midnight Express, The Three Presents, 2000; Hans Christian Andersen, 2001; Satisfaction, 2007; Divas, 2008; Marilyn. Solo award, 2nd Internat. Ballet Competition, Moscow, 1973; Star of the Year, Munich Abendzeitung, 1978; Evening Standard and SWET ballet award, 1979; Manchester Evening News theatre award, 1986; Lakerolprisen, Copenhagen, 1988; Berlin Co. award, Berlinerzeitung, 1991; Edinburgh Festival Critics' Prize, 1991. Knight of the Dannebrog (Denmark), 1988; Officier de l'Ordre de la Couronne (Belgium), 1995. *Recreation*: boxing.

**SCHEER, Hon. Andrew James;** PC (Can.) 2017; MP (C) Regina-Qu'Appelle, since 2004; Leader of the Opposition, Canada, since 2017; *b* Ottawa, 20 May 1979; *s* of James Scheer and Mary Scheer (*née* Enright); *m* 2003, Jillian Ryan; two *s* three *d*. *Educ*: Immaculata High Sch., Ottawa; Univ. of Ottawa (BA Hist.). Canadian Accredited Insce Broker Level 1. Insce agent, Regina, Saskatchewan, 2003–04. Dep. Speaker, 2008–11, Speaker, 2011–15, House Leader, 2015–16, H of C, Canada. Leader, Cons. Party of Canada, 2017–. Saskatchewan Centennial Medal, 2005. *Recreations*: Roman history, golf, tennis. *Address*: House of Commons, Ottawa, ON K1A 0A6, Canada. *T*: (613) 9924593, *Fax*: (613) 9954253; (office) 984 Albert Street, Regina, SK S4R 2P7, Canada. *T*: (306) 7904727, *Fax*: (306) 7904728.

**SCHEKMAN, Prof. Randy Wayne,** PhD; Professor of Cell and Developmental Biology, University of California, Berkeley, since 1989; Investigator, Howard Hughes Medical Institute, since 1991; *b* St Paul, Minn, 30 Dec. 1948; *s* of Alfred Schekman and late Esther Schekman (*née* Bader); *m* 1973, Nancy Walls; one *s* one *d*. *Educ*: Univ. of Calif, Los Angeles (BA Molecular Biol. 1970); Stanford Univ. (PhD Biochem. 1975). Postdoctoral res., Univ. of Calif., San Diego, 1974–76; University of California, Berkeley: Asst Prof., Associate Prof., then Prof. of Biochem., 1976–89; Co-Chm., Dept of Molecular and Cell Biol., 1997–2000; Founding Dir, Stem Cell Center, 2005. Adjunct Prof. of Biochem. and Biophysics, UCSF. Editor-in-Chief: Annual Rev. Cell and Develtl Biol., 1999–; Proc. NAS, 2006–11; eLife, 2011–19. Chair, Adv. Council, Aligning Sci. Against Parkinson's. Member: NAS, 1992; Amer. Acad. Arts and Scis, 2000. Foreign Associate: EMBO, 2001; Royal Soc., 2013. Hon. Dr: Geneva, 1997; Regensburg, 2005. Eli Lilly Res. Award, Amer. Soc. for Microbiol., 1987; Gairdner Foundn Internat. Award, Canada, 1996; Albert Lasker Basic Med. Res. Award, 2002; E. B. Wilson Award, Amer. Soc. for Cell Biol., 2010; Otto Warburg Prize, German Biochem. Soc., 2013; (jtly) Nobel Prize in Physiology or Medicine, 2013. *Address*: Schekman Laboratory, Department of Molecular and Cell Biology, University of California, Berkeley, Berkeley, CA 94720–3370, USA.

**SCHELLNHUBER, Prof. Hans Joachim, (John),** Hon. CBE 2004; PhD; Professor for Theoretical Physics, Potsdam University, since 1993 (Director, Potsdam Institute for Climate Impact Research, 1993, now Emeritus); Distinguished Science Advisor, Tyndall Centre for Climate Change Research, 2005–09; *b* 7 June 1950; *s* of Gottlieb and Erika Schellnhuber; *m* 1981, Petra (d 2001); *m* 2003, Margret Boysen; one *s*. *Educ*: Regensburg Univ. (MSc; PhD); Univ. of California, Santa Barbara and Santa Cruz; Oldenburg Univ. (Habitation). Heisenberg Fellow, 1987–89; Prof. for Theoretical Physics, Oldenburg Univ., 1989–93; Res. Dir, Tyndall Centre for Climate Change Res., and Prof. for Envmtl Scis, UEA, 2001–05. Vis. Prof. of Physics, Oxford Univ., 2005–09. Mem., German Adv. Council on Global Change, 1992– (Chm.); Chm., Global Change Adv. Gp, EC, 2002–06; Chief Govt Advr on Climate to German EU/G8 Presidency, 2007; Mem., High-Level Adv. Gp on Energy and Climate to Pres. EU Commn, 2007–11. Scientific Mem., Max Planck Soc., 2002–. Member: NAS, 2005; German Nat. Acad. (formerly German Acad. of Scis) Leopoldina, 2007. Wolfson Res. Merit Award, Royal Soc., 2002; German Envmt Prize, Deutsche Bundesstiftung Umwelt, 2007; Envmt Prize, Bundesdeutsche Arbeitskreis für Umweltbewusstes Mgt, 2008. Order of Merit: State of Brandenburg, 2008; FRG, 2011. *Publications*: author or editor of about 40 books on complex systems theory and environmental analysis; over 200 articles in Nature, Science, Physical Rev. Letters, etc. *Recreations*: Romanesque art, philosophy of science, reading about history, mountain hiking. *Address*: Potsdam Institute for Climate Impact Research, PO Box 601203, 14412 Potsdam, Germany. *T*: (331) 2882501, *Fax*: (331) 2882600. *E*: emdirector@pik-potsdam.de.

**SCHENK, Prof. Catherine Ruth,** PhD; FRHistS; Professor of Economic and Social History, University of Oxford, since 2017; Fellow, St Hilda's College, Oxford, since 2017; *b* Halifax, NS, 2 Sept. 1964; *d* of Paul and Margot Schenk; *m* 1994, Duncan Ross; one *s* one *d*. *Educ*: Queen Elizabeth High Sch., Halifax, NS; Univ. of Toronto (BA Hons 1986; MA Econs 1987); London Sch. of Econs and Pol Sci. (PhD Econ. Hist. 1991). FRHistS 1998. Lecturer: Victoria Univ., Wellington, NZ, 1990–92; RHBNC, Univ. of London, 1992–96; Lectr, 1996–2004, Prof. of Internat. Econ. Hist., 2004–17, Univ. of Glasgow. Vis. Prof., Univ. of Hong Kong, 2005; Guest Prof., Nankai Univ., Tianjin, 2017. IMF Res. Fellow, 2009; Associate Fellow, Chatham Hse, 2014. FRSA 2017. *Publications*: Britain and the Sterling Area, 1994; Hong Kong as an International Financial Centre, 2001; Hong Kong SAR's Monetary and Exchange Rate Challenges, 2009; The Decline of Sterling, 2010; International Economic Relations since 1945, 2011; Oxford Handbook of Banking and Financial History, 2016. *Recreations*: playing violin, swimming, slowly running short distances, collecting Scottish and Canadian art and 18th century manuscripts. *Address*: St Hilda's College, Cowley Place, Oxford OX4 1DY. *T*: (01865) 276884.

**SCHIEMANN, Rt Hon. Sir Konrad Hermann Theodor,** Kt 1986; PC 1995; a Judge of the Court of Justice of the European Union (formerly European Communities), 2004–12; *b* 15 Sept. 1937; *s* of Helmuth and Beate Schiemann; *m* 1965, Elisabeth Hanna Eleonore Holroyd-Reece; one *d*. *Educ*: King Edward's Sch., Birmingham; Freiburg Univ.; Pembroke Coll., Cambridge (Schol.; MA, LLB; Hon. Fellow, 1998). Served Lancs Fusiliers, 1956–58 (commnd, 1957). Called to Bar, Inner Temple, 1962 (Bencher, 1985; Reader, 2002; Treas., 2003); Junior Counsel to the Crown, Common Law, 1978–80; QC 1980; a Recorder of the Crown Court, 1985–86; a Justice of the High Court, QBD, 1986–95; a Lord Justice of Appeal, 1995–2004. Chairman of panels conducting Examinations in Public of: North-East Hants and Mid Hants Structure Plans, 1979; Merseyside Structure Plan, 1980; Oxfordshire Structure Plan, 1984. Mem., Parole Bd, 1990–92 (Vice-Chm.,

1991–92). Member, Advisory Board: Centre for Eur. Legal Studies, Cambridge Univ., 1996–; Eur. Law Rev., 2007–. Mem. Council of Mgt, British Inst. of Internat. and Comparative Law, 2000–06. Patron, Busoga Trust, 1999– (Chm., 1989–99); Trustee, St John's, Smith Square, 1990–2004 (Chm., 1994–2004). Dir, Acad. of Ancient Music, 2001–04 (Mem. Council, 2012–); Gov., English Nat. Ballet, 1995–2001. *Publications:* contrib. English and German legal books and jls. *Recreations:* music, reading. *Address:* 1 Temple Gardens, EC4Y 9BB. *Club:* Athenæum.

**SCHIFF, Sir András,** Kt 2014; concert pianist and conductor; *b* Budapest, 21 Dec. 1953; *s* of Odon Schiff and Klara Schiff (*née* Csengeri); *m* 1987, Yuuko Shiokawa. *Educ:* Franz Liszt Academy of Music, Budapest; with Prof. Pal Kadosa, Ferenc Rados and Gyorgy Kurtag; private study with George Malcolm. Artistic Dir, September Chamber Music Fest., Mondsee, Austria, 1989–98; Co-founder, Ittinger Pfingstkonzerte, Switzerland, 1995; Founder, Homage to Palladio Fest., Vicenza, Italy, 1998; Artist in Residence, Kunstfest, Weimar, 2004–. Hon. Prof., Music Schs in Budapest, Detmold and Munich; Supernumerary Fellow, Balliol Coll., Oxford, 2009. Concerts as soloist with orchestras including: NY Philharmonic, Chicago Symphony, Vienna Phil., Concertgebouw, Orch. de Paris, London Phil., London Symph., Philharmonia, Royal Phil., Israel Phil., Philadelphia, Washington Nat. Symph., Hallé; orchestras conducted include: Baltimore Symphony, Chamber Orch. of Europe, City of Birmingham Symphony, Danish Radio, LA Philharmonic, Philadelphia and Philharmonia; major festival performances include: Salzburg, Lucerne, Edinburgh, Aldeburgh, Tanglewood, Feldkirch Schubertiade, Lucerne. Created Cappella Andrea Barca orch., 1999. Recordings include: extensive Bach repertoire (Grammy Award for recording of English Suites, 1990); all Mozart Piano Sonatas; all Mozart Piano Concertos; all Schubert Sonatas; all Bartok Piano Concertos; all Beethoven Piano Concertos; Lieder records with Peter Schreier, Robert Holl and Cecilia Bartoli. Hon. Member: Beethoven House, Bonn, 2006; Vienna Konzerthaus, 2012. Prizewinner, Tchaikovsky competition, Moscow, 1974 and Leeds comp., 1975; Liszt Prize, 1977; Premio, Accademia Chigiana, Siena, 1987; Wiener Flotenuhr, 1989; Bartok Prize, 1991; Instrumentalist of the Year, Internat. Classical Music Awards, 1993; Claudio Arrau Meml Medal, 1994; Instrumentalist of the Year, Royal Philharmonic Soc., 1994; Kossuth Prize, 1996; Deutsche Schallplattenkrik, 1996; Leonie Sonnings Music Prize, Copenhagen, 1997; Palladio d'Oro, Citta di Vicenza, 2003; Musikfest Preis, Bremen, 2003; Abbiati Prize, Italian Critics' Assoc., 2007; Bach Prize, RAM, 2007; Wigmore Hall Medal, 2008; Ruhr Piano Fest. Prize, 2009; Schumann Prize, City of Zwickau, 2011; Golden Mozart-Medaille, Internat. Stiftung Mozarteum, 2012; Gold Medal, Royal Philharmonic Soc., 2013. Order of Merit (FRG), 2012. *Recreations:* literature, languages, soccer, theatre, art, cinema. *Address:* c/o Askonas Holt Ltd, 15 Fetter Lane, EC4A 1BW.

**SCHIFFRIN, Prof. David Jorge,** PhD; FRSC; Brunner Professor of Physical Chemistry, University of Liverpool, 1990–2004, now Emeritus, and Senior Fellow, since 2004 (Director, Centre for Nanoscale Science, 1998–2004); *b* 8 Jan. 1939; *s* of Bernardo Schiffrin and Berta Kurlat Schiffrin; *m* 1965, Margery Watson; one *s* one *d*. *Educ:* Univ. of Buenos Aires (BSc); Univ. of Birmingham (PhD). FRSC 1997. Lectr in Physical Chemistry, Univ. of Buenos Aires, 1966; Asst Technical Manager, CIABASA, Buenos Aires, 1967–68; Lectr in Physical Chemistry, Chemistry Dept, Univ. of Southampton, 1968–72; Head of Applied Electrochemistry Div., Nat. Inst. of Technology, Buenos Aires, 1972–77; Asst Technical Manager, R. Kurlat, Buenos Aires, 1977–79; Manager and Dir, Wolfson Centre for Electrochemical Science, 1979–90, Sen. Lectr, Chemistry Dept, 1988–90, Univ. of Southampton; participated in and organised Eur. res. projects. Mem., Dept of Energy Adv. Cttee on impact of hydrogen on greenhouse gas abatement, 1990–91; Titular Mem., IUPAC Electrochemistry Commn, 1995–2001. Project assessor for numerous internat. organisations; ext. PhD examr, 28 univs. Vis. Prof., Helsinki Univ. of Technol., 2004–08. Presented exhibits on electroluminescence sensors and nanoscale sci, Royal Soc. Summer Sci. Exhibns, London, 1996, 2001. Chm., EU Marie Curie Chem. Panel, 2009 (Vice Chm., 2005–08); Ind. Observer, EU Marie Curie Fellowship Prog., 2011. Foreign Mem., Finnish Soc. of Scis and Letters, 1996; Member: Internat. Selection Cttee, Fellowship Panel, Finnish Acad. of Scis, 2006; Internat. Fellowship Selection Cttee, COFUND prog., Denmark, 2016–19. Chm., Faraday Discussion, Nanoparticle Assemblies, Liverpool, 2003; Member, Scientific Committee: Faraday Discussion Molecular Wires and Nanoscale Conduction, Manchester, 2005; Faraday Discussion, Cambridge, 2017. Fellow, Internat. Soc. of Electrochem., 2005. Dr *hc* Buenos Aires, 2016. Electrochemistry Medal and Prize, RSC, 2001; RAICES Prize for Internat. Collaborations, Min. of Sci., Argentina, 2013. Member: Editorial Bd, Jl of Electroanalytical Chemistry, 1997–; Adv. Editl Bd, Physical Chemistry Chemical Physics, 2005–. *Publications:* over 270 articles in jls; chapters in books; over 170 conf. papers. *Recreations:* hill walking, music, photography. *Address:* Chemistry Department, University of Liverpool, Liverpool L69 7ZD. *T:* (0151) 794 3574.

**SCHILLING, Keith;** Co-Founder, Chairman and Senior Partner, Schillings (formerly Schilling, Gleadow and Lom, later Schilling and Lom), since 1984; *b* Orpington, 25 July 1956. *Educ:* City of London Poly. (MA Eur. Business Law 1982). Articled Wright Webb Syrett; admitted as solicitor, 1978; specialises in libel, privacy and family law; landmark decisions include first-time recovery of 50% of assets by wife in big money divorce (Lambert v Lambert, 2002), re-introduction to English law of John Doe injunction (J. K. Rowling v persons unknown, 2003), first-time establishment of right of privacy in English law (Naomi Campbell v Mirror Gp Newspapers, 2004), first-time use of video link in libel trial (Roman Polanski v Vanity Fair, 2005); Solicitor-Advocate (Higher Civil Courts, England and Wales), 2008–. Lectr on legal topics. *Publications:* contrib. articles to legal and non-legal jls. *Recreations:* reading, trekking, sailing, climbing, sports. *Address:* Schillings, 41 Bedford Square, Bloomsbury, WC1B 3HX. *T:* (020) 7034 9000, *Fax:* (020) 7034 9200. *E:* keith.schilling@schillingspartners.com.

**SCHINDLER, Prof. David William,** OC 2004; AOE 2008; DPhil; FRS 2001; FRSC 1983; Killam Memorial Professor of Ecology, University of Alberta, 1989–2013, now Emeritus. *Educ:* N Dakota State Univ. (BSc 1962); St Catherine's Coll., Oxford (Rhodes Schol.; DPhil 1966). Asst Prof., Trent Univ., 1966–68; Prog. Leader, then Res. Scientist, Experimental Limnology Prog., Freshwater Inst., and Founder and Dir, Experimental Lakes Project, Dept of Fisheries and Oceans, Canada, 1968–89. Adjunct Prof., Univ. of Manitoba, 1971–89. *Publications:* contrib. learned jls. *Address:* Department of Biological Sciences, University of Alberta, Edmonton, AB T6G 2E9, Canada.

**SCHLAGMAN, Richard Edward;** Owner and Publisher, Cahiers du cinéma, since 2009; *b* 11 Nov. 1953; *s* of Jack Schlagman and late Shirley Schlagman (*née* Goldston); partner, Mia Hågg; two *s*. *Educ:* University Coll. Sch., Hampstead; Brunel Univ. Co-Founder, Jt Chm., and Man. Dir, Interstate Electronics Ltd, 1973–86; purchased Bush from Rank Orgn, renamed IEL Bush Radio Ltd, 1981, floated on London Stock Exchange, 1984; sold as Bush Radio Plc, 1986; acquired Phaidon Press Ltd, 1990; Owner and Publisher, Phaidon Press Ltd, 1990–2012; President: Phaidon Press Inc., 1998–2012; Phaidon SARL, 1999–2012; Phaidon Verlag, 2000–12; Phaidon KK, 2004–12. Mem., Exec. Cttee, Patrons of New Art, Tate Gall., 1994–97. Mem., Judd Foundn, Marfa, Texas, 1999–2009 (Pres., 1999–2001); Jury Mem., City of Ascona Concert Hall Architecture Comp., 2004. Member: Glyndebourne Fest. Soc.; Freunde der Bayreuther Festspiele; Freunde der Salzburger Festspiele. Patron: Bayreuther Festspiele; Salzburger Festspiele; Salzburger Osterfestspiele; Schubertiade; Bayerische Staatsoper. FRSA 1994. *Recreations:* music, art, architecture. *Address:* Piazza Grande 26, 6600 Locarno, Switzerland. *T:* (91) 7596000. *Clubs:* Chelsea Arts, Annabel's.

**SCHLEE, Clive Edward Benedict;** Chief Executive, Pret A Manger, 2003–19 (non-executive Director, since 2019); *b* London, 17 March 1959; *s* of Robin and Rosemary Schlee; *m* 1987, Eileen Conley; one *s* two *d*. *Educ:* Rugby Sch., Warks; University Coll., Oxford (BA 1st Cl. Hons Modern Hist.). Jardine Matheson, 1980–97; Partner, ITSU, 1998–. *Recreations:* hill walking, ski-ing, sailing, chess. *Address:* The Crooked House, Bromeswell, Suffolk IP12 2PQ. *T:* (020) 7827 8000. *E:* clive.schlee@pret.com. *Club:* Waldringfield Sailing.

**SCHLESINGER, David Adam;** Founder and Managing Director, Tripod Advisors, since 2012; *b* 15 April 1960; *s* of Ernest Carl and Gabriella Pintus Schlesinger; *m* 1987, Rachel Shiu-Ping Wong. *Educ:* Oberlin Coll. (BA 1982); Harvard Univ. (AM 1986). Freelance journalist, 1986–87; Reuters: correspondent, Hong Kong, 1987–89; Bureau Chief: Taiwan, 1989–91; China, 1991–94; Ed., Greater China, 1994–95; Financial Ed., 1995–97, Man. Ed., 1997–2000, Ed., 2000–03, Americas; Global Man. Ed., News, 2003–06; Ed.-in-Chief, News, 2006–11. Board Member: Internat. News Safety Inst., 2005–11; 1World Online, 2019–. Hon. Pres., Internat. Network of Street Papers, 2009–14. Chairman: Danenberg Oberlin-in-London Prog., 2008–11 (Dir, 2007–08, 2019–); Thomson Reuters China, 2011–12; Poseidon Research Ltd, 2012–14; Director: Thomson Reuters Foundn (formerly Reuters Foundn), 2008–11; Cttee to Protect Journalists, 2009–19; ChinaWeb, 2011–12; Index on Censorship, 2012–. Hon. Fellow, Reuters Inst. for Journalism, Oxford, 2012–. FRSA. *Address:* D. A. Schlesinger Ltd, 28/F AIA Central Building, 1 Connaught Road Central, Hong Kong. *T:* 28248727. *E:* das@daschlesinger.com. *Clubs:* House of St Barnabas; Foreign Correspondents (Hong Kong).

**SCHLUTER, Prof. Dolph,** PhD; FRS 1999; FRSC 2001; Professor of Zoology, University of British Columbia, since 1996 (Director, Biodiversity Research Centre, 2003–07); *b* 22 May 1955; *s* of Antoine Schluter and Magdalena Schluter; *m* 1993, Andrea Lawson; one *d*. *Educ:* Univ. of Guelph, Ont (BSc Wildlife Biol. 1977); Univ. of Michigan (PhD Ecol. and Evolution 1983). NSERC Postdoctoral Fellow, Zool. Dept, UBC and Univ. of Calif, Davis, 1983–85; Zoology Department, University of British Columbia: NSERC Univ. Res. Fellow, 1985–89; Asst Prof., 1989–91; Associate Prof., 1991–96. E. W. R. Steacie Meml Fellow, NSERC, 1993; Izaak Walton Killam Meml Faculty Res. Fellow, UBC, 1996; Scholar-in-Residence, Peter Wall Inst. of Advanced Studies, UBC, 1999; Canada Res. Chair, 2001–; Guggenheim Fellow, 2003–04; Killam Sen. Res. Fellow, Canada Council, 2011–13. Pres., American Soc. of Naturalists, 2013 (Vice-Pres., 1999; President's Award, 1997); Pres., Soc. for Study of Evolution, 2005. Foreign Mem., Amer. Acad. of Arts and Scis, 2012; For. Fellow, US NAS, 2017. Charles A. McDowell Medal, 1995, Killam Res. Prize, 2008, Killam Mentoring Award, 2010, UBC; Rosenblatt Award, Scripps Inst. of Oceanography, 2006; Sewall Wright Award, Amer. Soc. of Naturalists, 2007; Darwin-Wallace Medal, Linnean Soc., 2014. *Publications:* (ed with R. Ricklefs) Species Diversity in Ecological Communities: historical and geographical perspectives, 1993; The Ecology of Adaptive Radiation, 2000; (with M. C. Whitlock) The Analysis of Biological Data, 2008, 2nd edn 2015; (ed jtly) Speciation and Patterns of Diversity, 2009; contrib. chapters in books; contrib. numerous articles to Science, Nature, Evolution, American Naturalist, Ecology, Proc. Royal Soc., Philosophical Trans Royal Soc. *Address:* Zoology Department, University of British Columbia, 6270 University Boulevard, Vancouver, BC V6T 1Z4, Canada. *T:* (604) 8222387, *Fax:* (604) 8222416. *E:* schluter@zoology.ubc.ca.

**SCHMIDHUBER, Peter Michael;** Member, Commission of the European Communities, 1987–94; attorney in Munich; *b* 15 Dec. 1931; *s* of Jakob Schmidhuber and Anna (*née* Mandlmayr); *m* 1960, Elisabeth Schweigart; one *d*. *Educ:* Univ. of Munich (MA Econs 1955). Qualified as lawyer, 1960. Member: Man. Bd, Deutsche Bundesbank, 1995–. Member: Bundestag, 1965–69 and 1972–78; Bundesrat, Bavarian Parliament, 1978–87 (Bavarian Minister of State for Federal Affairs). Mem., CSU. *Address:* Wiesengrund 1b, 81243 Munich, Germany.

**SCHMIDT, Benno Charles,** Jr; Chairman, Avenues: The World School, 2011; *b* 20 March 1942; *s* of Benno Charles Schmidt and Martha Chastain; *m* 2001, Anne McMillen; one *s* two *d* from previous marriage. *Educ:* Yale Univ. (BA 1963; LLB 1966). Mem., DC Bar, 1968; Law Clerk to Chief Justice Earl Warren, 1966–67; Special Asst AG, Office of Legal Counsel, US Dept of Justice, Washington, 1967–69; Harlan Fiske Stone Prof. of Constitutional Law, Columbia Univ., 1969–86, Dean of Law School, 1984–86; Professor of Law, and President, Yale Univ., 1986–92; Pres. and Chief Exec., The Edison Project, 1992–98; Chm. Bd, 1998–2007, Vice-Chm., 2007–, Edison Schs, later Edison Learning; Vice Chm., 1999–2003, Chm., Bd of Trustees, 2003–16, City Univ. of NY. Hon. Bencher, Gray's Inn, 1988. Hon. degrees: LLD Princeton, 1986; DLitt Johns Hopkins, 1987; LLD Harvard, 1987. Hon. AO 1991 (Hon. AM 1989). *Publications:* Freedom of the Press Versus Public Access, 1974; (with A. M. Bickel) The Judiciary and Responsible Government 1910–1921, 1985.

**SCHMIDT, Prof. Brian Paul,** AC 2013; PhD; FRS 2012; FAA; Vice-Chancellor and President, Australian National University, since 2016; *b* Missoula, Montana, USA, 24 Feb. 1967; *s* of Dana C. Schmidt and Donna P. Schmidt (*née* Pentz); *m* 1992, Jennifer Gordon; two *s*. *Educ:* Univ. of Arizona (BS Astronomy and Physics 1989); Harvard Univ. (AM Astronomy 1992; PhD 1993). FAA 2008. CFA Postdoctoral Fellow, Harvard Smithsonian Center for Astrophysics, 1993–94; Australian National University: Postdoctoral Fellow, 1995–96; Lectr in Introductory Astrophysics, 1996–98; Res. Fellow, 1997–99; Fellow, 1999–2002; Lectr in Observational Astronomy, 1999; ARC Professorial Fellow, 2003–05; Lectr in Observational Cosmol., 2004–; ARC Fedn Fellow, 2005–09; ARC Australian Laureate Fellow, 2009, Dist. Prof., 2010–, Res. Sch. of Astronomy and Astrophysics. Non-exec. Dir, Astronomy Australia Ltd, 2007–. Member: Anglo Australian Telescope Bd, 2004–08; Australia Telescope Steering Cttee, 2010–; Adv. Cttee, Australia Astronomical Observatory, 2010–; Adv. Bd, Questacon, 2012–. Member, Council: Astronomical Soc. of Australia, 2001–03; Australian Acad. Sci., 2012– (Mem., Nat. Cttee of Astronomy, 2010–). Vigneron and grape grower, Maipenrai Vineyard and Winery. Fellow: Japanese Soc. for Promotion of Sci., 1999; NAS, USA, 2008. Hon. DLitt Macquarie, 2012; Dr *hc* Chile, 2012; Hon. Dr Arizona, 2012. Pawsey Medal, Australian Acad. Sci., 2001; Vainu Bappu Medal, Astronomical Soc. India, 2002; (jtly) Shaw Prize, Shaw Foundn, 2006; (jtly) Gruber Prize for Cosmol., Gruber Foundn, 2007; Peter Baume Award, ANU, 2010; (jtly) Nobel Prize in Physics, 2011; Dirac Medal, Univ. of NSW, 2012. *Address:* Office of the Vice-Chancellor, Chancelry Building 10, Australian National University, Acton, ACT 2601, Australia.

**SCHMIDT, Helle T.;** *see* Thorning-Schmidt.

**SCHMIDT, Prof. Michael Norton,** OBE 2006; FRSL; Professor of English, University of Manchester, since 2018; Founder, and Editorial and Managing Director, Carcanet Press Ltd, since 1969; *b* 2 March 1947; *s* of Carl Bernhardt Schmidt and Elizabeth Norton Schmidt (*née* Hill); *m* 1979, Claire Harman (marr. diss. 1989); two *s* one *d*; civil partnership

2010, Angel Garcia-Gomez. *Educ:* Harvard Univ.; Wadham Coll., Oxford (BA 1969; MA); Univ. of Cambridge (MA 2015). Manchester University: Gulbenkian Fellow of Poetry, 1970–73; Special Lectr, 1973–92; Sen. Lectr in Poetry, 1992–98; Dir, Writing Sch., 1998–2005, and Prof. of English, 2000–05, Manchester Metropolitan Univ.; Prof. of Poetry, Glasgow Univ., 2006–15; Writer in Residence, St John's Coll., Cambridge, 2012–15. Vis. Prof. Univ. of Bolton, 2013–; Vis. Fellow Commoner, Trinity Coll., Cambridge, 2016–17. Founder and Ed., PN Rev. (formerly Poetry Nation), 1971–; Poetry Ed., Grand Street (NY), 1998–2000. Librarian, Apollo Series, Head of Zeus, 2013–. FRSL 1994. Hon. Dr Bolton, 2006. *Publications: criticism:* Fifty Modern British Poets: an introduction, 1979; Fifty English Poets 1300–1900: an introduction, 1979; Reading Modern Poetry, 1989; Lives of the Poets, 1998; The Story of Poetry: from Caedmon to Caxton, 2001; The Story of Poetry: from Skelton to Dryden, 2002; The First Poets: lives of the ancient Greek poets, 2004; The Story of Poetry: from Pope to Burns, 2007; The Novel: a biography, 2014; Gilgamesh: the life of a poem, 2019; *translations:* (with E. Kissam) Flower and Song: Aztec poetry, 1977; On Poets and Others, by Octavio Paz, 1986; *poetry anthologies* include: Eleven British Poets, 1980; The Harvill Book of 20th Century Poetry in English, 1999; The Great Modern Poets, 2006; Five American Poets, 2010; New Poetries V, 2011; New Poetries VI, 2014; New Poetries VII, 2018; *fiction:* The Colonist, 1983; The Dresden Gate, 1988; *poetry* includes: New and Selected Poems, 1997; The Resurrection and the Body, 2007; Collected Poems, 2009; The Stories of My Life, 2013. *Address:* Carcanet Press Ltd, Alliance House, 30 Cross Street, Manchester M2 7AQ. *Club:* Savile.

**SCHMIDT-GARRÉ, Philomene Korinna Kornelia;** *see* Magers, P. K. K.

**SCHOFIELD, Prof. Andrew Noel,** MA, PhD (Cantab); FRS 1992; FREng, FICE; Professor of Engineering, Cambridge University, 1974–98, now Professor Emeritus; Fellow of Churchill College, Cambridge, 1963–66 and since 1974; *b* 1 Nov. 1930; *s* of late Rev. John Noel Schofield and Winifred Jane Mary (*née* Eyles); *m* 1961, Margaret Eileen Green; two *s* two *d. Educ:* Mill Hill Sch.; Christ's Coll., Cambridge. John Winbolt Prize, 1954. Asst Engr, in Malawi, with Scott Wilson Kirkpatrick and Partners, 1951. Cambridge Univ.: Demonstrator, 1955, Lectr, 1959, Dept of Engrg. Research Fellow, California Inst. of Technology, 1963–64. Univ. of Manchester Inst. of Science and Technology: Prof. of Civil Engrg, 1968; Head of Dept of Civil and Structural Engrg, 1973. Chm., Andrew N. Schofield & Associates Ltd, 1984–2000. Rankine Lecture, ICE British Geotechnical Soc., 1980. Chm., Tech. Cttee on Centrifuge Testing, Internat. Soc. for Soil Mech. and Foundn Engrg, 1982–85. FREng (FEng 1986). James Alfred Ewing Medal, ICE, 1993; Sir Frank Whittle Award Medal, RAEng, 2017. US Army Award, Civilian Service 1979. *Publications:* (with C. P. Wroth) Critical State Soil Mechanics, 1968; (ed with W. H. Craig and R. G. James and contrib.) Centrifuges in Soil Mechanics, 1988; (ed with J. R. Gronow and R. K. Jain and contrib.) Land Disposal of Hazardous Waste, 1988; Disturbed Soil Properties and Geotechnical Design, 2005, 2nd edn (with S. Haigh), 2017; papers on soil mechanics and civil engrg. *Address:* 1 Old School Court, Cambridge CB22 5FF. *E:* ans10@cam.ac.uk.

**SCHOFIELD, Prof. Christopher Joseph,** DPhil; FRS 2013; FRSC; Professor of Chemistry, since 1998, and Head of Organic Chemistry, since 2011, University of Oxford; Fellow of Hertford College, Oxford, since 1990; *b* Barnston, 17 June 1960; *s* of Anthony Schofield and Bridget Ann Schofield (*née* Smith); *m* 1987, Pauline Poh Lin Tan; three *s* one *d. Educ:* Barnston Co. Primary Sch.; St Anselm's Coll., Birkenhead; Univ. of Manchester Inst. of Sci. and Technol. (BSc 1st Cl. 1982); St John's Coll., Oxford (DPhil 1985). FRSC 2005. Deptl Demonstrator, 1985–90, Lectr, 1990–98, Univ. of Oxford. Mem., EMBO, 2014. Jeremy Knowles Award, 2011, Interdisciplinary Prize, 2019, RSC. *Publications:* articles in scientific jls. *Recreations:* sport, 'gardening'. *Address:* Chemistry Research Laboratory, Department of Chemistry, University of Oxford, Mansfield Road, Oxford OX1 3TA. *T:* (01865) 265725. *E:* christopher.schofield@chem.ox.ac.uk; Rivendell, Old Boars Hill, Oxford OX1 5JJ.

**SCHOFIELD, Derek;** a Recorder, 2000–15; *b* 20 Feb. 1945; *s* of John Schofield and Ethelena Schofield (*née* Calverley); *m* 1st, 1967, Judith Danson (marr. diss.); one *s* one *d*; 2nd, 1983, Anne Wangeci Kariuki; one *s* one *d. Educ:* Morecambe Grammar Sch.; NAJCA Dip. in Magisterial Law, 1966; Mediation Trng Inst. Internat. (Cert. Professional Mediation 2012). English Magisterial Service, 1961–74; called to the Bar, Gray's Inn, 1970; Kenya: Resident Magistrate, 1974–78; Sen. Resident Magistrate, 1978–82; Puisne Judge, 1982–87; Judge of Grand Court, Cayman Islands, 1988–96; Chief Justice of Gibraltar, 1996–2009; Asst Recorder, 1997–2000. *Recreations:* travel, reading, bird watching.

**SCHOFIELD, John Allen,** PhD; FSA; archaeologist and architectural historian, since 2008; Curator, Architecture, Museum of London, 1998–2008; *b* 23 Aug. 1948; *s* of Jack and Edna Schofield. *Educ:* Christ Church Coll., Oxford (BA 1970); Univ. of Edinburgh (MPhil 1974); Royal Holloway Coll., Univ. of London (PhD 1989). FSA 1981; MCIfA (MIFA 1983). Museum of London: Field Officer, Dept of Urban Archaeol., 1977–87; Actg Chief Urban Archaeologist, 1987–90; Hd of Pubns, Archaeol. Service, 1991–98. Archaeol. Advr, Dio. of London, 1985–2007. Cathedral Archaeologist, St Paul's Cathedral, 1990–. Chm., Assoc. of Diocesan and Cathedral Archaeologists, 2000–06; Hon. Sec., City of London Archaeol. Trust, 1990–. Reviews Ed., Trans, 2002–, Chm., Pubns Cttee, 2005–, Series Ed., Special Papers, 2013–15, London and Middx Archaeol. Soc.; Series Ed., Studies in the Archaeology of Medieval Europe, 2003–13. *Publications:* Building of London from the Conquest to the Great Fire, 1984, 3rd edn 1999; The London Surveys of Ralph Treswell, 1987; (with A. Vince) Medieval Towns, 1994, 2nd edn 2003; Medieval London Houses, 1995, rev. edn 2003; (ed with C. Maloney) Archaeology in the City of London 1907–91: a guide to records of excavations by the Museum of London, 1998; (ed with A. Saunders) Tudor London: a map and a view, 2001; (with R. Lea) Holy Trinity Priory Aldgate, City of London, 2005; London 1100–1600: the archaeology of a capital city, 2011; St Paul's Cathedral Before Wren, 2011; (with H Pearman) One Tower Bridge: a living history, 2013; St Paul's Cathedral: archaeology and history, 2016; (jtly) London's Waterfront 1100–1666: excavations in Thames Street London, 1974–84, 2018. *Recreations:* travel, jazz. *Address:* 2 Carthew Villas, W6 0BS.

**SCHOFIELD, Kenneth Douglas,** CBE 1996; Executive Director, European Golf Tour, Professional Golfers' Association, (PGA European Tour), 1975–2004, now Consultant; *b* 3 Feb. 1946; *s* of late Douglas Joseph and Jessie Schofield (*née* Gray); *m* 1968, Evelyn May Sharp; two *d. Educ:* Auchterarder High Sch. Associate, Savings Bank Inst., 1966. Joined Trustee Savings Bank, Perth, 1962, Br. Manager, Dunblane, 1969–71; Media and PR Exec. to Dir-Gen., PGA Tournament, 1971–74; Sec., PGA European Tour, 1975. Order of Merit, Royal Spanish Golf Fedn, 1993; Christer Lindberg Award, PGA of Europe, 2002. *Publications:* Pro Golf: the official PGA European Tour Media Guide, 1972–1975. *Recreations:* golf, cricket, soccer, walking. *Address:* European Tour, Wentworth Drive, Virginia Water, Surrey GU25 4LX. *T:* (01344) 840452. *Clubs:* Caledonian; Wentworth Golf; Crieff Golf; Auchterarder Golf; Royal and Ancient Golf (St Andrews).

**SCHOFIELD, Prof. Malcolm,** FBA 1997; Professor of Ancient Philosophy, University of Cambridge, 1998–2009, now Emeritus; Fellow, St John's College, Cambridge, since 1972; *b* 19 April 1942; *er s* of Harry Schofield and Ethel Schofield (*née* Greenwood); *m* 1970, Elizabeth Milburn (*d* 2005); one *s. Educ:* St Albans Sch.; St John's Coll., Cambridge; Balliol Coll., Oxford. Asst Prof. of Classics, Cornell Univ., 1967–69; Dyson Res. Fellow in Greek Culture, Balliol Coll., Oxford, 1970–72; Cambridge University: Lectr in Classics, 1972–89; Reader in Ancient Philosophy, 1989–98; Dir of Research, Faculty of Classics, 2009–11; Mem., Gen. Bd, 1991–94 and 1999–2003; Chm. Council, Sch. of Arts and Humanities, 1993–94; Chm. Faculty Bd of Classics, 1997–98, 2009–10; Mem., Univ. Council, 1997–2003; Chm., Liby Syndicate, 1998–2003; St John's College: Praelector, 1975–76, 1977–80, 2006–11; Dean, 1979–82; Tutor, 1982–89; Pres., 1991–95; Fellows' Steward, 2014–. Chm., Benchmarking Gp for Classics and Ancient History, QAA, 1999–2000. Editor, Phronesis, 1987–92. Hon. Sec., Classical Assoc., 1989–2003 (Pres., 2006–07); Pres., Soc. for Promotion of Hellenic Studies, 2008–11. Carlyle Lectr, Univ. of Oxford, 2012; J. H. Gray Lectr, Univ. of Cambridge, 2015. Chm. Council, British Sch. at Athens, 2010–16. Hon. Mem., Amer. Acad. Arts and Scis, 2018. Hon. Citizen, Rhodes, 1992. Gold Medal, TCD Histl Soc., 2017. *Publications:* (ed jtly) Articles on Aristotle, 4 vols, 1975–79; (ed jtly) Doubt and Dogmatism, 1980; An Essay on Anaxagoras, 1980; (ed with M. Nussbaum) Language and Logos, 1982; (ed jtly) Science and Speculation, 1982; (with G. S. Kirk and J. E. Raven) The Presocratic Philosophers, 2nd edn, 1983; (ed with G. Striker) The Norms of Nature, 1986; The Stoic Idea of the City, 1991; (ed with A. Laks) Justice and Generosity, 1995; Saving the City, 1999; (ed jtly) The Cambridge History of Hellenistic Philosophy, 1999; (ed with C. J. Rowe) The Cambridge History of Greek and Roman Political Thought, 2000; Plato: political philosophy, 2006; (ed with T. Griffith) Plato: Gorgias, Menexenus, Protagoras, 2010; (ed) Aristotle, Plato and Pythagoreanism in the First Century BC, 2013; (ed with T. Griffith) Plato: Laws, 2016. *Address:* St John's College, Cambridge CB2 1TP. *T:* (01223) 338644.

**SCHOFIELD, Michael,** CBE 1999; Chairman, Dorset Community NHS Trust, 1996–2001; *b* 30 Jan. 1941; *s* of Edward Ronald Schofield and Edna Schofield (*née* Davies); *m* 1st, 1971, Patricia Ann Connell (marr. diss. 1982); two *s*; 2nd, 1989, Angela Rosemary Tym. *Educ:* Manchester Grammar Sch.; Exeter Coll., Oxford (BA Mod. Hist. 1962); Manchester Univ. (Dip. Social Admin). Asst House Gov., General Infirmary, Leeds, 1969–72; Asst Sec., United Liverpool Hosps, 1972–74; Dep. Dist Administrator, Liverpool Central and Southern NHS Dist, 1974–76; Area Administrator, 1976–86, and Chief Exec., 1985–86, Rochdale HA; Dir, Health Services Mgt Unit, Univ. of Manchester, 1987–95; Chm., Bradford Community NHS Trust, 1992–96. Vis. Prof., Bournemouth Univ., 1999–2007. Mem., EOC, 1997–2000. Chm., Nat. Assoc. of Health Authorities and Trusts, 1995–97. Pres., IHSM, 1990–91; Mem. Council, RPSGB, 1999–2007. *Publications:* (jtly) The Future Healthcare Workforce, First Report, 1996, Second Report, 1999, Final Report, 2002. *Recreations:* golf, music, gardening. *Address:* 17 West Court, Hollins Hall, Hampsthwaite, Harrogate HG3 2WY. *T:* (01423) 502463. *Club:* Oakdale Golf (Harrogate).

**SCHOFIELD, Naomi Wendy;** *see* Climer, N. W.

**SCHOFIELD, Neill;** DoE, 1970–78; Dept of Energy, 1978–82; Department of Employment, later Department for Education and Employment, 1982–96: Director: Business and Enterprise, 1990–92; Quality Assurance, 1992–93; Training, Infrastructure and Employers Div., 1994–96. *Recreations:* walking, German language, history and culture, politics.

**SCHOFIELD, Peter Hugh Gordon,** CB 2017; Permanent Secretary, Department for Work and Pensions, since 2018; *b* Redhill, 27 April 1969; *s* of John Michael Stuart Schofield and Bridget Merrilyn Schofield; *m* 2001, Sarah-Louise Prime; two *s* one *d. Educ:* Whitgift Sch.; Gonville and Caius Coll., Cambridge (BA 1991; MA 1994). HM Treasury: Public Enterprises Team, 1991–93; Educn Team, 1993–94; Privatisation Team, 1994–96; Private Sec. to Chief Sec., 1996–98; Hd of Public Enterprises, 1998–2002; Investment Exec., London Buy-out Team, 3i Gp plc, 2002–04 (on secondment); Dir, Shareholder Exec., 2004–08 (Mem. Bd, 2009–12); Dir, Enterprise and Growth Unit, HM Treasury, 2008–12; Dir Gen., Neighbourhoods Gp, DCLG, 2012–16; Dir Gen., Finance, DWP, 2016–18. Non-executive Director: Partnerships UK, 2006–15; Local Partnerships, 2011–16. *Address:* Department for Work and Pensions, Caxton House, Tothill Street, SW1H 9NA.

**SCHOFIELD, Rosalyn Sharon;** Director, Company Secretariat, Associated British Foods plc, since 2001; *b* London, 18 Sept. 1956; *d* of Jack and Sonia Schofield; one *s* one *d. Educ:* Henrietta Barnett Sch.; Univ. of Hull (LLB Hons); Coll. of Law, Chester. Admitted as solicitor, 1982; commercial property lawyer in private practice 1982–90; J. D. Wetherspoon plc: Sen. Legal Advr, 1990–95; Co. Sec., 1995–97; Legal Dir and Co. Sec., 1997–2001. Mem., Adaptation Sub-cttee of Cttee on Climate Change, 2015–. Mem., Law Soc., 1981. Trustee, Regent's Univ., 2016–. *Recreations:* theatre, travel, arts. *Address:* Hampstead, London. *T:* 07809 698098. *E:* Rosalynschofield@gmail.com. *Club:* Royal Over-Seas League.

**SCHOLAR, Sir Michael (Charles),** KCB 1999 (CB 1991); President, St John's College, Oxford, 2001–12; Pro-Vice-Chancellor, University of Oxford, 2005–12; *b* 3 Jan. 1942; *s* of Richard Herbert Scholar and Mary Blodwen Scholar; *m* 1964, Angela Mary (*née* Sweet); three *s* (one *d* deed). *Educ:* St Olave's Grammar School, Bermondsey; St John's College, Cambridge (PhD, MA; Hon. Fellow, 1999). ARCO. Teaching asst, Univ. of California at Berkeley, 1964–65; Loeb Fellow, Harvard Univ., 1967; Asst Lectr in Philosophy, Leicester Univ., 1968; Fellow, St John's College, Cambridge, 1969; HM Treasury, 1969; Private Sec. to Chief Sec., 1974–76; Barclays Bank International, 1979–81; Private Sec. to Prime Minister, 1981–83; Under Secretary, HM Treasury, 1983–87; Dep. Sec., 1987–93; Permanent Secretary: Welsh Office, 1993–96; DTI, 1996–2001. Chm., UK Statistics Authy, 2008–12. Non-exec. Dir, Legal & Gen. Investment Mgt (Hldgs), 2002–07. Chm., Civil Service Sports Council, 1998–2001 (Chm., Staff Pension Fund, 2006–12); Mem., Council of Mgt, NIESR, 2001–05. Chm., Benton Fletcher Trust, 2004–11. Fellow: Univ. of Wales, Aberystwyth, 1996; Cardiff Univ., 2003. Freeman: Merchant Taylors' Co., 2012; City of London, 2013. Hon. Dr Glamorgan, 1999. *Recreations:* playing the piano and organ, making long journeys by foot. *Address:* 9 Stanley Road, Oxford OX4 1QY.
*See also* Sir T. W. Scholar.

**SCHOLAR, Sir Thomas Whinfield,** KCB 2017; Permanent Secretary, HM Treasury, since 2016; *b* 17 Dec. 1968; *s* of Sir Michael Charles Scholar, *qv. Educ:* Trinity Hall, Cambridge (MA); LSE (MSc). HM Treasury, 1992–2007: Principal Private Sec. to Chancellor of the Exchequer, 1997–2001; UK Exec. Dir, IMF and World Bank, and Minister (Econ.), British Embassy, Washington, 2001–07; Chief of Staff and Principal Private Sec. to the Prime Minister, 2007–08; Man. Dir, Internat. and Finance Directorate, 2008–09, Second Perm. Sec., 2009–13, HM Treasury; Prime Minister's Advr on European and Global Issues, 2013–16. *Address:* HM Treasury, 1 Horse Guards Road, SW1A 2HQ.

**SCHOLEFIELD, Susan Margaret,** CMG 1999; JP; Chair, Competition Appeal Tribunal and Competition Service, since 2013; *b* 9 May 1955; *d* of John and Millicent Scholefield; *m* 1977 (marr. diss. 1981); one *s. Educ:* Blackheath High Sch.; Somerville Coll., Oxford (MA); Univ. of Calif, Berkeley (MA). Joined MoD, 1981; on secondment to Ecole Nationale d'Admin, Paris, 1985–86; Principal, MoD, 1986–92 (Private Sec. to Chief of Defence Procurement, 1990–92); Asst Sec., Efficiency Unit, Cabinet Office (on secondment), 1992–95; Head, Balkans Secretariat, MoD, 1995–98; Asst Sec., NI Office (on secondment), 1998–2000; Under Sec., 2000, Finance and Exec. Dir, 2000–02, Defence Procurement Agency, MoD; Head, Civil Contingencies Secretariat, Cabinet Office (on secondment),

2002–04; Comd Sec., Permt Jt HQ, Northwood, MoD, 2004–07; Dir Gen. for Equalities, 2007, for Cohesion and Resilience, 2007–08, DCLG; Dir Gen. for HR and Corporate Services, MoD, 2008–12; Sec. and Chief Legal Officer, LSE, 2012–14. Non-exec. Dir, Surrey and Borders Partnership NHS Foundn Trust, 2018–. JP Kent, 2014, Sussex, 2015 (Dep. Chair, Sussex Family Panel, 2018–). *Recreations:* reading, music, theatre, gardening. *Address:* c/o Competition Service, Victoria House, Bloomsbury Place, WC1A 2EB.

**SCHOLES, Prof. Gregory Denton**, PhD; FRS 2019; FRS(Can); FRSC; William S. Tod Professor of Chemistry, Princeton University, since 2014; *b* Melbourne, Australia, 7 Sept. 1967; *s* of Robert Morley Scholes and Jennifer Margaret Davis Scholes; *m* 2018, Carolyne Murff; one *s* one *d* and two step *d*. *Educ:* Camberwell Grammar Sch., Melbourne; Univ. of Melbourne (BSc Hons Chem. 1990; PhD 1994). FRSC 2015. Ramsay Meml Postdoctoral Fellow, Imperial Coll., London, 1995–97; Postdoctoral Fellow, Univ. of Calif, Berkeley, 1997–2000; University of Toronto: Asst Prof. of Chemistry, 2000–05; Associate Prof. of Chemistry, 2005–10; D. J. LeRoy Dist. Prof., 2011–14. Professorial Fellow, Sch. of Chemistry, Univ. of Melbourne, 2015–20; Adjunct Prof., Beijing Inst. of Technol., 2016–20. Dep. Ed., Jl Physical Chemistry Letters, 2016–. FRS(Can) 2009. *Publications:* contribs to jls incl. Jl of ACS, Nature. *Recreation:* woodworking. *Address:* Department of Chemistry, Princeton University, Washington Road, Princeton, NJ 08544, USA. *T:* (609) 2580729. *E:* gscholes@princeton.edu. *Club:* Melbourne Cricket.

**SCHOLES, Mary Elizabeth, (Mrs A. I. M. Haggart)**, OBE 1983; SRN; Chief Area Nursing Officer, Tayside Health Board, 1973–83; *b* 8 April 1924; *d* of late John Neville Carpenter Scholes and Margaret Elizabeth (*née* Hines); *m* 1983, Most Rev. Alastair Iain Macdonald Haggart (*d* 1998). *Educ:* Wyggeston Grammar Sch. for Girls, Leicester; Leicester Royal Infirmary and Children's Hosp. (SRN 1946); Guy's Hosp., London (CMB Pt I Cert. 1947); Royal Coll. of Nursing, London (Nursing Admin (Hosp.) Cert. 1962). Leicester Royal Infirmary and Children's Hospital: Staff Nurse, 1947–48; Night Sister, 1948–50; Ward Sister, 1950–56; Night Supt, 1956–58; Asst Matron, 1958–61; Asst Matron, Memorial/Brook Gen. Hosp., London, 1962–64; Matron, Dundee Royal Infirm. and Matron Designate, Ninewells Hosp., Dundee, 1964–68; Chief Nursing Officer, Bd of Mgt for Dundee Gen. Hosps and Bd of Mgt for Ninewells and Associated Hosps, 1968–73. Pres., Scottish Assoc. of Nurse Administrators, 1973–77. Member: Scottish Bd, Royal Coll. of Nursing, 1965–70; Gen. Nursing Council for Scotland, 1966–70, 1979–; Standing Nursing and Midwifery Cttee, Scotland, 1971–74 (Vice-Chm., 1973–74); UK Central Council for Nursing, Midwifery and Health Visiting, 1980–84; Mgt Cttee, State Hosp., Carstairs, 1983–92; Scottish Hosp. Endowments Res. Trust, 1986–96; Chm., Scottish National Bd for Nursing, Midwifery and Health Visiting, 1980–84. *Recreations:* travel, music. *Address:* 14/2 St Margaret's Place, Edinburgh EH9 1AY. *Club:* Royal Over-Seas League.

**SCHOLES, Prof. Myron Samuel**, PhD; Chairman, Platinum Grove Asset Management (formerly Oak Hill Platinum Partners), 1999–2009; Frank E. Buck Professor of Finance, Graduate Business School, Stanford University, 1983–95, now Emeritus; Chief Investment Strategist, Janus Henderson Investors (formerly Janus Capital Group), since 2014; *b* 1 July 1941; *m*; two *d*; *m* 1998, Jan Blaustein. *Educ:* McMaster Univ.; Univ. of Chicago. Instr, Univ. of Chicago Business Sch., 1967–68; Asst Prof., 1968–72, Associate Prof., 1972–73, MIT Mgt Sch.; University of Chicago: Associate Prof., 1973–75; Prof., 1975–79; Dir, Center for Res. in Security Prices, 1975–81; Edward Eagle Brown Prof. of Finance, 1979–82; Prof. of Law, 1983–87, and Sen. Res. Fellow, Hoover Inst., 1988–93, Stanford Univ. Man. Dir, Salomon Bros, 1991–93; Partner, Long-Term Capital Management, 1994–98; Man. Partner, Oak Hill Capital Mgt, 1999–2005; Chm., Bd of Economic Advrs, Sterling Stamos Capital Mgt. (Jtly) Nobel Prize for Economics, 1997. *Publications:* (jtly) Taxes and Business Strategy: a planning approach, 1992, 5th edn 2015.

**SCHOLEY, Sir David (Gerald)**, Kt 1987; CBE 1976; Senior Advisor, UBS Investment Bank (formerly SBC Warburg, then Warburg Dillon Read, later UBS Warburg), since 1997; *b* 28 June 1935; *s* of Dudley and Lois Scholey; *m* 1960, Alexandra Beatrix, *d* of Hon. George and Fiorenza Drew, Canada; one *s* one *d*. *Educ:* Wellington Coll., Berks; Christ Church, Oxford (Hon. Student, 2003). Nat Service, RAC, 9th Queen's Royal Lancers, 1953–55; TA Yorks Dragoons, 1955–57; 3/4 CLY (Sharpshooters), 1957–61; Metropolitan Special Constabulary (Thames Div.), 1961–65. Thompson Graham & Co. (Lloyd's brokers), 1956–58; Dale & Co. (Insce brokers), Canada, 1958–59; Guinness Mahon & Co., 1959–64; joined S. G. Warburg & Co., 1965, Dir, 1967–95, Dep. Chm., 1977, Jt Chm., 1980–84, Chm., 1985–95; Chm., SBC Warburg, July–Nov. 1995; Sen. Advr, IFC, Washington, 1996–2005. Director: Mercury Securities, 1969–86 (Chm., 1984–86); Orion Insurance Co., 1963–87; Stewart Wrightson Holdings Ltd, 1972–81; Union Discount Co. of London, 1976–81; Bank of England, 1981–98; British Telecom, 1986–94; Chubb Corp. (USA), 1991–2008; General Electric Co., 1992–95; J. Sainsbury, 1996–2000; Vodafone Group, 1998–2005; Close Bros, 1999–2006 (Chm., 1999–2006); G3 Good Governance Gp Ltd, 2012–13; Cranemere Gp, 2014–; non-exec. Dir, Anglo-American, 1999–2005; Chm., UBS Pension Trustee Co., 2004–17; Advisor: Vice Chief of Defence Staff, MoD, 1997–2001; Capgemini Financial Services UK, 2005–10; Longreach Gp, 2006–; MDM Bank (Moscow), 2008–12; Senior Adviser: FSA, 2010–13; Good Governance Gp G3, 2013–. Mem., Export Guarantees Adv. Council, 1970–75 (Dep. Chm. 1974–75); Chm., Construction Exports Adv. Bd, 1975–78; Member: Inst. Internat. d'Etudes Bancaires, 1976–94 (Pres., 1988); Cttee on Finance for Industry, NEDO, 1980–87; Council, IISS, 1984–93 (Hon. Treas., 1984–90); President's Cttee, BITC, 1988–91; Industry and Commerce Gp, SCF, 1989–95; Ford Foundn Adv. Gp on UN Financing, 1992–93; London First, 1993–96; Bd of Banking Supervision, 1996–98; Mitsubishi Internat. Adv. Cttee, 2001–07; Sultanate of Oman Financial Adv. Gp, 2002–06; Fitch Internat. Services Adv. Cttee, 2002–07; Develt Bd, Christ Church, Oxford, 2002–15; Clinical Governance Cttee, King Edward VII Hosp. (Sister Agnes), 2009–15. Dir, INSEAD, 1989–2005 (Chairman: UK Council, 1994–97; Internat. Council, 1995–2003 (Hon. Chm., 2005); Hon. Alumnus, 2000). Gov., BBC, 1994–2000; Dir, LSO, 2012–16 (Mem. Adv. Council, 1998–2016); Advisor: BBC Philharmonic Orch., 2006–13; Royal Opera House Muscat, 2011–. Trustee: Glyndebourne Arts Trust, 1989–2002; Nat. Portrait Gallery, 1992–2005 (Chm., 2001–05); Barbican Centre, 2010–12. Governor: Wellington Coll., 1978–88, 1996–2004 (Vice-Pres., 1998–2004); NIESR, 1984–2014; LSE, 1993–96. FRSA. Dist. Friend of Oxford Univ., 2011. Hon. DLitt London Guildhall, 1993; Hon. DSc UMIST, 1999. *Address:* (office) 5 Broadgate, EC2M 2QS.

**SCHOLEY, Dr Keith Douglas**; Director: Wild Horizons Ltd, since 2008; Big Cat Ltd, since 2008; Silverback Films Ltd, since 2013; *b* 24 June 1957; *s* of Douglas and Jeannie Scholey; *m* 1985, Elizabeth Sara Potter; two *s*. *Educ:* Reed's Sch., Surrey; Univ. of Bristol (BSc Hons (PhD 1982). Postgrad. res., Bristol Univ., 1978–81; joined BBC, 1982: researcher, 1982–85; TV asst producer, 1985–88; TV producer, 1989–93; editor, TV series, Wildlife on One and Wildlife specials, 1993–98; Head, Natural Hist. Unit, 1998–2002; Controller: Specialist Factual, 2002–06; Factual Production, 2006; Controller, Content Prodn and Dep. Chief Creative Officer, BBC Vision Studios, 2006–08. Hon. DSc Bristol, 2001. *Recreations:* flying (private pilot's licence), scuba diving, sailing, photography. *Address:* 59 Cotham Hill, Cotham, Bristol BS6 6JR.

**SCHOLL, Andreas**; countertenor; *b* Germany, 1967. *Educ:* Schola Cantorum Basiliensis, Switzerland (Dip. in Ancient Music). Former chorister, Kiedricher Chorbuben, Germany. Début internat. recital, Théâtre de Grévin, Paris, 1993; opera début in Handel's Rodelinda, Glyndebourne, 1998; appears regularly in recitals and concerts at all major European venues, and in N America. Teacher, Schola Cantorum Basiliensis, 2000–. Composes and records pop music; prizewinning recordings include works by Vivaldi and Caldara, and English folk and lute songs. *Address:* c/o HarrisonParrott Ltd, The Ark, 201 Talgarth Road, W6 8BJ.

**SCHOLL, Prof. Anthony James**, DPhil; Kuwait Professor of Number Theory and Algebra, University of Cambridge, since 2001; *b* 18 Dec. 1955; *s* of late William Howard Scholl and Barbara Russell Beilby; *m* 1st, 1980, Caroline Somerville-Large (marr. diss. 2000); three *s*; 2nd, 2002, Gülsin Onay. *Educ:* Worth Sch., Sussex; Christ Church, Oxford (MA, MSc; DPhil 1980). University of Oxford: SRC Res. Fellow, 1980–81; Jun. Lectr, 1981–84; University of Durham: Lectr, 1984–89; Prof. of Pure Mathematics, 1989–2001. Mem., Inst. for Advanced Study, Princeton, 1989–90; Prof. Associé, Univ. Paris-Sud, 1992; Leverhulme Trust Res. Fellow, 2001–02. *Recreation:* music (listening, playing and composing). *Address:* Department of Pure Mathematics and Mathematical Statistics, Centre for Mathematical Sciences, Wilberforce Road, Cambridge CB3 0WB. *T:* (01223) 765889. *E:* a.j.scholl@dpmms.cam.ac.uk.

**SCHOLTE, Nicholas Paul**; Chief Executive, NHS Business Services Authority, 2006–17; *b* 6 May 1959; *s* of Christiaan and Sylvia Joyce Scholte; one *s* one *d* (by Iris Esters (*d* 2003); *m* 2006, Claire Louise Emmerson, BEM. *Educ:* Chesterfield Grammar Sch.; Manchester Univ. (BA Hons Politics). Law Society: Exec. Officer, 1981–85; Sen. Exec. Officer, 1985–86; Finance Manager, 1986–89; Legal Aid Board: Gp Manager (NE), 1990–96; Business Systems Dir, 1996–99; Chief Exec., Prescription Pricing Authy, 1999–2006. Non-exec. Dir, Supporta plc, 2005–10. *Recreations:* ballet, literature, football, jazz. *Club:* Cullercoats Crescent.

**SCHOLTEN, Stephanus Cornelis Gerardus Tarcisius**; Director, The Hunterian, University of Glasgow, since 2017; *b* Amsterdam, 19 Sept. 1961; *s* of Joop Scholten and Diny Aggenbach; *m* 1993, José Steer; two *d*. *Educ:* Univ. of Amsterdam (MA Art Hist. 1990). Policy Advr, Min. of Educn, Culture and Sci., Netherlands, 1989–97; Policy Advr, 1997–2000, Hd of Res., 2000–02, Project Manager, 2002–05, Netherlands Inst. for Cultural Heritage; Hd, Collections Dept, 2002–09, Dep. Dir, 2007–09, Nat. Mus. of Antiquities, Leiden; Dir, Heritage Collections, Univ. of Amsterdam, 2009–17. *Address:* The Hunterian, University of Glasgow, Glasgow G12 8QQ. *T:* (0141) 330 3711. *E:* steph.scholten@glasgow.ac.uk.

**SCHOLZ, Prof. Dr Rupert**; Professor of Public Law, Institut für Politik und öffentliches Recht, University of Munich, 1981–2005, now Emeritus; Of Counsel, Gleiss Lutz, since 2005; *b* 23 May 1937; *s* of Ernst and Gisela Scholz (*née* Merdas); *m* 1971, Dr Helga Scholz-Hoppe. *Educ:* Abitur, Berlin; studied law and economics, Berlin and Heidelberg; Dr Jur., Univ. of Munich. Prof., Univ. of Munich, taught in Munich, Berlin, Regensburg, Augsburg; Public Law Chair, Berlin and Munich, 1978. Senator of Justice, Land Berlin, 1981; Acting Senator for Federal Affairs; Mem., Bundesrat, 1982; Mem., N Atlantic Assembly, 1982; Senator for Federal Affairs, Land Berlin, 1983; MHR, Berlin, and Senator for Justice and Federal Affairs, 1985; Federal Minister of Defence, FRG, 1988–89; Mem. (CDU), German Bundestag, 1990–2002. *Publications:* numerous papers in jurisp., German policy, foreign policy, economic policy. *Address:* Gleiss Lutz, Friedrichstrasse 71, 10117 Berlin, Germany.

**SCHÖNBERGER, Viktor M.**; *see* Mayer-Schönberger.

**SCHOPPER, Prof. Herwig Franz**; Professor of Physics, University of Hamburg, 1973–89, now Emeritus; *b* 28 Feb. 1924; *s* of Franz Schopper and Margarete Hartmann; *m* 1949, Dora Klara Ingeborg (*née* Stieler); one *s* one *d*. *Educ:* Univ. of Hamburg. Dip. Phys. 1949, Dr rer. nat. 1951. Asst Prof. and Univ. Lectr, Univ. of Erlangen, 1954–57; Prof., Univ. of Mainz, 1957–60; Prof., Univ. of Karlsruhe and Dir of Inst. for Nuclear Physics, 1961–73; Chm., Scientific Council, Kerforschungszentrum, Karlsruhe, 1967–69; Chm., Deutsches Elektronen Synchrotron particle physics Lab., Hamburg, 1973–80; European Organisation for Nuclear Research (CERN): Res. Associate, 1966–67; Head, Dept of particle physics and Mem., Directorate for experimental prog., 1970–73; Chm., Intersecting Storage Ring Cttee, 1973–76; Mem., Sci. Policy Cttee, 1979–80; Dir-Gen., 1981–88. Chm., Assoc. of German Nat. Research Centres, 1978–80; Mem., Scientific Council, IN2P3, Paris; Advr, UNESCO, 1994–2009; Chm., Scientific Bd, Internat. Basic Sci. Prog., UNESCO, 2003–12. Mem., Steering Cttee, SE Eur. Internat. Inst. for Sustainable Technologies, 2018–. President: German Physical Soc., 1992–94; European Physical Soc., 1995–97; Internat. Council, Centre of Res. for Synchrotron Radiation in Jordan, 1999–2008; Council, Synchrotron-light for Exptl Sci. and Applications in Middle East, 2003–08. Member: Akad. der Wissenschaften Leopoldina, Halle; Joachim Jungius Gesellschaft, Hamburg; Sudetendeutsche Akad. der Wissenschaft, 1979; Acad. Scientiarium et Artium, Vienna, 1993; Portuguese Acad. of Scis; Bd of Trustees, Cyprus Inst., 2002– (Chm., Scientific Council, 2002–); MAE 1992; Corresp. Mem., Bavarian Acad. of Scis, 1981; Hon. Member: Hungarian Acad. of Scis, 1995; Eur. Physical Soc., 2011; Deutsche Physikalische Gesellschaft, 2013; Swiss Physical Soc., 2015; Polish Acad. of Scis and Arts, 2015. Fellow, APS, 2006; Foreign FInstP 1996. Dr *hc*: Erlangen, 1982; Moscow, 1989; Geneva, 1989; London, 1989; Jt Inst. of Nuclear Res., Dubna, 1998; Inst. of High Energy Physics, Russia, 1999; Cyprus Inst., 2018. Physics Award, Göttinger Akad. der Wissenschaft, 1957; Carus Medal, Akad. Leopoldina, 1958; Ritter von Gerstner Medal, 1978; Sudetendeutscher Kulturpreis, 1984; Golden Plate Award, Amer. Acad. of Achievement, 1984; Gold Medal, Weizmann Inst., 1987; Wilhelm Exner Medal, Gewerbeverein, Austria, 1991; Purkyne Meml Medal, Czech Acad. of Scis, 1994; 650 Years Jubilee Medal, Charles Univ., Prague, 1998; Tate Medal, Amer. Inst. Physics, 2004; Einstein Gold Medal, UNESCO, 2004; Bohr Gold Medal, UNESCO-Denmark, 2005; Medal of Honour, Portuguese Minister for Higher Educn and Res., 2009; Medal of Honour, Lanskroun, Czech Republic, 2010; Physics Medal, First Grade, Czech Physical Soc., 2010. Grosses Bundesverdienstkreuz (FRG), 1989; Friendship Order of Russian Pres., 1996; Grand Cordon, Order of Independence (Jordan), 2003; Grosses Verdienstkreuz (Cyprus), 2012; Goldene Ehrenmedal, Deutsches Elektronen-Synchrotron, 2013; Award for Sci. Diplomacy, AAAS, 2019. Editor, data on Nuclear and Particle Physics, Elementary Particles, Nuclei and Atoms in Springer Materials: The Landoldt Börnstein Database. *Publications:* Weak Interactions and Nuclear Beta Decay, 1966; (ed) Investigation of Nuclear Structure by Scattering Processes, 1975; Matter—Antimatter, 1989; (ed) Advances of Accelerator Physics and Technologies, 1993; (ed with M. Jacob) Large Facilities in Physics, 1995; LEP - The Lord of the Collider Rings at CERN, 2009; (ed with L. Di Lella) 60 Years of Experiments and Discoveries at CERN, 2015; papers on elementary particle physics, high energy accelerators, relation of science and society. *Recreations:* music, gardening. *Address:* c/o CERN, 1211 Geneva 23, Switzerland. *T:* (22) 7675350.

**SCHORI, Most Rev. Katharine J.**; *see* Jefferts Schori.

**SCHREIBER**, family name of **Baron Marlesford**.

**SCHREMPP, Jürgen E.;** Chairman, Board of Management, DaimlerChrysler AG, 2000–05 (Joint Chairman, 1998–2000); b 15 Sept. 1944; m 2000, Lydia Deininger; one s one s, and two s from previous marriage. *Educ:* Univ. for Applied Scis, Offenburg. Apprentice motor mechanic, Mercedes-Benz Dealership, Freiburg, 1961–64; joined Daimler-Benz AG, 1967; Mercedes-Benz of South Africa: Manager, Service Div., 1974–80; Mem., Bd of Mgt, 1980–82, 1984–87; Vice Pres., 1984; Pres., 1985–87, now non-exec. Chm.; Pres., Euclid Inc., USA (subsidiary of Daimler-Benz AG), 1982–84; Daimler-Benz Board of Management: Dep. Mem., 1987–89; Mem., 1989–95; Chm., 1998; Pres. and CEO, Daimler-Benz Aerospace AG, 1989–95. Non-executive Director: Sasol Ltd, 1997–2015 (Lead Ind. Dir, 2008–15); Vodafone Gp plc, 2000; Cie Financière Richemont SA, 2003–17 (Mem., Internat. Adv. Council, 2017–); Jonah Capital (Pty) Ltd. Partner, Cie Financière Rupert, 2006–. Mem., President's Internat. Investment Council, SA. Chm., Sub-Saharan Africa Initiative of German Business. Cross, Order of Merit (Germany); Order of Good Hope (SA). *Address:* PO Box 200651, 80006 Munich, Germany.

**SCHREUDER, Prof. Deryck Marshall Van der Heyde,** DPhil; FAHA; FRHistS; historian and educationalist; Emeritus Professor, Macquarie University and University of Western Sydney, 1998, and University of Western Australia, 2004; Visiting Professor, School of Education and Social Work (formerly College of Humanities and Social Sciences), Faculty of Arts, University of Sydney, since 2004; Adjunct Professor, Australian National University, since 2005; b 19 Jan. 1942; s of Pieter Jurian and Jean Margaret Schreuder; m 1965, Patricia Anne Pote; three s. *Educ:* Llewellin High Sch., Zambia; Univ. of Rhodes, S Africa (BA Hons; Beit Meml Hist. Prize, 1963); DPhil Oxon 1964. FAHA 1985; FRHistS 1988. Rhodes Schol. from Central Africa, 1964–67; Kennedy Fellow of Modern Hist., New Coll., Oxford, 1967–69; Prof. of Hist., and Hd of Dept, Trent Univ., Ontario, 1970–79; Challis Prof. of Hist., Univ. of Sydney, 1980–93 (Dep. Chm., Acad. Bd, 1984–85); on secondment as Associate Dir, Humanities Res. Centre, ANU, 1992–93; Dep. Vice-Chancellor (Acad.), Macquarie Univ., 1993–95; Vice-Chancellor, Univ. of Western Sydney, 1995–98, now Vice-Chancellor Emeritus; Vice-Chancellor, and Principal, subseq. Pres., Univ. of WA, 1998–2004. Res. Fellow, Res. Sch. of Social Scis, ANU, 1976–77. Pres., Aust. Vice-Chancellors' Cttee, 2002–03; Chm., Aust. Univs Quality Agency, 2004–09; Member: Aust. Res. Grants Cttee, 1986–92; Commn on Commonwealth Studies, 1995–97; Dir, Aust. Scholarship Foundn, 2008–. President: Aust. Hist. Assoc., 1985–86; Aust. Acad. Humanities, 1992–95 (Vice-Pres., 1989–90). Associate Ed., Oxford DNB, 1995–2000. Hon. LLD Rhodes, 2004. Centenary Medal (Australia), 2001. *Publications:* Gladstone and Kruger: Liberal Government and Colonial Home Rule (1880–85), 1969; The Scramble for Southern Africa (1877–95): the politics of partition reappraisal, 1981, 2nd edn 2010; (jtly) The Rise of Colonial Nationalism: Australia, New Zealand, Canada and South Africa first assert their nationality 1880–1914, 1988; (ed jtly) The Commonwealth and Australia in World Affairs, 1990; (ed jtly) History and Social Change: the G. A. Wood Memorial Lectures 1949–91, 1991; (ed) Imperialisms, 1991; A Letter from Sydney: history and the post-Colonial society (J. M. Ward Memorial Lecture), 1991; (ed jtly) History at Sydney, 1992; (ed) The Humanities and the Creative Nation, 1995; (ed jtly) Africa Today, 1997; (ed jtly) The State and the People: Australian federation 1870–1901, 2002; (ed jtly) Sir Graham Bower's Secret History of the Jameson Raid and the South African Crisis 1895–1902, 2002; Who Killed Newman?: the ideal of a university and its enemies, 2007; (ed jtly) Australia's Empire, 2008, in The Oxford History of the British Empire Companion Series; (ed) Universities for a New World: making a global network in higher education, 1913–2013, 2013; chapters in major scholarly volumes incl. Cambridge History of Australia, 2014. *Recreations:* writing history, cycling, community work, life with 7 grandchildren. *Address:* School of Education and Social Work, Faculty of Arts, University of Sydney, Sydney, NSW 2006, Australia.

**SCHREYER, Rt Hon. Edward Richard,** CC 1979; CMM 1979; CD 1979; OM 2000; PC (Can.) 1984; High Commissioner for Canada in Australia, and concurrently Ambassador to Vanuatu, 1984–88; b Beausejour, Man, 21 Dec. 1935; s of John and Elizabeth Schreyer, a pioneer family of the district; m 1960, Lily, d of Jacob Schulz, MP; two s two d. *Educ:* Beausejour, Manitoba; United Coll., Winnipeg; St John's Coll., Winnipeg, Univ. of Manitoba (BA, BEd, MA). While at university served as 2nd Lieut, COTC, Royal Canadian Armored Corps, 1954–55. Member, Legislative Assembly of Manitoba, 1958; re-elected, 1959 and 1962; MP: for Springfield, 1965; for Selkirk, 1968; chosen as Leader of New Democratic Party in Manitoba, 1969, and resigned seat in House of Commons; MLA for Rossmere and Premier of Manitoba, 1969–77; Minister of: Dominion-Provincial Relns, 1969–77; Hydro, 1971–77; Finance, 1972–74; re-elected MLA, 1977; Governor-Gen. and C-in-C of Canada, 1979–84. Prof. of Political Science and Internat. Relns, St John's Coll., Univ. of Manitoba, 1962–65. Distinguished Vis. Prof., Univ. of Winnipeg, 1989–90; Vis. Prof., Simon Fraser Univ., Vancouver, 1991; Distinguished Fellow, Inst. for Integrated Energy Systems, Univ. of Victoria, 1992–94; Univ. of BC, 1995–96. Director: Perfect Pacific Investments, 1989–96; China International Trade and Investment Corp., Canada, 1991–98; Saskatchewan Energy Conservation and Develt Authy, 1993–96; Alternative Fuel Systems Inc. (Calgary), 1994–99; Cephalon Oil & Gas Resource Corp. (Calgary), 1994–95. Chancellor, Brandon Univ., 2002–08. Chm., Canadian Shield Foundn, 1984–; Member: Internat. Assoc. of Energy Economists; CPA; IPU. Hon. LLD: Manitoba, 1979; Mount Allison, 1983; McGill, 1984; Simon Fraser, 1984; Lakehead, 1985; Hon. Dr Sci. Sociale Ottawa, 1980. *Recreations:* reading, golf, sculpting, woodworking. *Address:* 250 Wellington Crescent, Unit 401, Winnipeg, MB R3M 0B3, Canada. *T:* (204) 9897580, *Fax:* (204) 9897581. *Clubs:* Rideau (Ottawa); York, Upper Canada (Toronto).

**SCHREYER, Michaele,** PhD; Member, European Commission, 1999–2004; b Cologne, 9 Aug. 1951. *Educ:* Univ. of Cologne (Dip. Econs and Sociology 1976); Univ. of Berlin (PhD 1983). Res. Asst, Inst. for Public Finances and Social Policy, Free Univ. of Berlin, 1977–82; Green Party Advr, Bundestag, 1983–87; Researcher, Inst. for Econ. Res., 1987–88. Mem., Green Party, 1987–; Minister for Urban Develt and Envmtl Protection, State Govt (Senate) of Berlin, 1989–90; Mem., State Parlt of Berlin (Green Party), 1991–99 (Chair, Green Party Gp, 1998–99). Vice-Pres., European Movt, Germany, 2006–18. Lectr on European Politics, Free Univ. of Berlin, 2004–18 (Hon. Prof., 2018) and Univ. of Bonn, 2004–. Mem., Adv. Council, Transparency Internat., Germany, 2005–09; Co-Chair, Supervisory Bd, Heinrich Böll Stiftung, Germany, 2009–14. Member, Foundation Council: European Univ. Viadrina Frankfurt (Oder), 2008–12; Georg-August Univ. Göttingen, 2009–15.

**SCHROCK, Prof. Richard Royce,** PhD; Frederick G. Keyes Professor of Chemistry, Massachusetts Institute of Technology, 1989–2018, now Professor Emeritus; George K. Helmkamp Professor in Chemistry, University of California at Riverside, since 2018; b Berne, Indiana, 4 Jan. 1945; s of late Noah J. Schrock and Martha A. Schrock (née Habegger); m 1971, Nancy F. Carlson; two s. *Educ:* Mission Bay High Sch.; Univ. of Calif, Riverside (AB 1967); Harvard Univ. (PhD 1971). Postdoctoral Fellow, Univ. of Cambridge, 1971; Res. Chemist, Central Res. and Develt Dept, E. I. duPont de Nemours and Co., Wilmington, Delaware, 1972–75; joined MIT, 1975, Prof., 1980–89. Foreign Mem., Royal Soc., 2008. (Jtly) Nobel Prize for Chemistry, 2005. *Publications:* articles in jls. *Address:* Department of Chemistry, Massachusetts Institute of Technology, 77 Massachusetts Avenue, Cambridge, MA 02139–4307, USA.

**SCHRÖDER, Gerhard;** Member, Bundestag, 1980–86 and 1998–2005; Chancellor, Federal Republic of Germany, 1998–2005; Chairman, Social Democratic Party, Germany, 1999–2004; b Mossenberg, 7 April 1944; *Educ:* Univ. of Göttingen. Apprentice retailer, 1959–61; qualified as lawyer, 1976; in practice, Hannover, 1978–90 and 2005–. Joined SPD, 1963; Mem. for Lower Saxony Landtag, 1986–98; Chm., SPD Gp, 1986–90; Prime Minister, Lower Saxony, 1990–98. Sozialdemokratische Partei Deutschlands: Chm., Young Socialists, Göttingen, 1969–70; Nat. Chm., Young Socialists, 1978–80; Member: Exec. Cttee, Hannover, 1977 (constituency Chm., 1983–93); Party Council, 1979–2005; NEC, 1986–2005; Presiding Council, 1989–2005; Chm., Lower Saxony Br., 1994–98. Advr, Ringier AG, 2005–; Chm., Shareholders' Cttee, Nord Stream AG, 2006–; Mem., Eur. Adv. Council, Rothschild Gp, 2006–16; Dir, TNK-BP, 2009–11; Chm., Rosneft, 2017–. Hon. Chairman: German Near and Middle East Assoc.; Emirati-German Friendship Soc. Patron, Gesicht Zeigen. *Publications:* Entscheidungen: mein leben in der politik, 2007; Klare Worte, 2014. *Address:* Deutscher Bundestag, Platz der Republik 1, 11011 Berlin, Germany.

**SCHRÖDER, Prof. Martin,** PhD, DIC; CChem, FRSC; FRSE; Vice President, and Dean, Faculty of Science and Engineering (formerly of Engineering and Physical Sciences), University of Manchester, since 2015; b Taplow, Berks, 14 April 1954; s of Herman and Edith Schröder; m 1985, Dr Leena-Kreet Kore; one s. *Educ:* Univ. of Sheffield (BSc Special Hons in Chem. 1975); Imperial Coll. of Sci., Technol. and Medicine (PhD 1978; DIC). CChem 1975; FRSC 1994. Royal Soc./Swiss Nat. Foundn Postdoctoral Fellow, Laboratorium für Organische Chemie, ETH, Zürich, 1978–79; Postdoctoral Res. Asst, Univ. Chem. Labs, Univ. of Cambridge, 1980–82; Department of Chemistry, University of Edinburgh: Sen. Demonstrator, 1982–83; Lectr, 1983–91; Reader in Inorganic Chem., 1991–94; Personal Chair in Inorganic Chem., 1994–95; University of Nottingham: Prof. of Inorganic Chem., 1995–2015; Hd, Sch. of Chem., 1999–2005; Exec. Dean, Faculty of Sci., 2011–15. Vis. Prof., Lash Miller Labs, Univ. of Toronto, 1990; Mellor Vis. Prof., Dept of Chem., Univ. of Dunedin, NZ, 1995; Vis. Prof., Sch. of Chem., Univ. Louis Pasteur, Strasbourg, 2004. Support Res. Fellow, RSE, 1991–92; Leverhulme Trust Sen. Res. Fellow, 2005–06; ERC Advanced Grant Awardee, 2008, 2017. Member: Rev. Panel for Commonwealth Scholarships, 2001–06; Strategic Adv. Team for EPSRC Chem. Prog., 2002–04; Inorganic and Physical Rev. Panel for Sci. Foundn Ireland, 2003; Sen. Jury, Review Panel, Inst. Universitaire de France, 2011–12, 2014. Royal Society of Chemistry: Member: Dalton Div., Standing Cttee on Confs, 1997–99 (Chm., 1999–2001); Dalton Council, 1998–2001; Nat. Organising Cttee of Annual Conf., 1999–2002; Chm., Macrocyclic and Supramolecular Chem. Subject Gp, 2000–05. FRSE 1994. MAE 2016. Hon. Dr Chem: Tech. Univ. of Tallinn, 2005; Nikolaev Inst. of Chemistry, Russian Acad. of Scis, Novosibirsk, 2017. Royal Society of Chemistry: Corday Morgan Medal and Prize, 1989; Tilden Lectr and Medal, 2001–02; Award for Chem. of Transition Metals, 2003; Award for Chem. of Noble Metals and their Compounds, 2008; Wolfson Merit Award, Royal Soc., 2005–10. *Publications:* 500 publications, patents and book chapters. *Recreations:* opera, music, travel. *Address:* Faculty of Science and Engineering, Room B1, Sackville Street Building, University of Manchester, Manchester M13 9PL.

**SCHRODER, Dr Timothy Bruno,** FSA; freelance lecturer, curator and advisor; b Ascot, Berks, 12 Aug. 1953; s of John and Joan Schroder; m 1987, Ellen Laskey; one s three d. *Educ:* St Edward's Sch., Oxford; Christ Church, Oxford (BA Philosophy and Theol.; MA; DLitt 2013). Technical Asst, 1976–80, Dir, Silver Dept, 1981–84, Christie's; Curator, Decorative Arts, Los Angeles Co. Mus. of Art, 1984–89; Dir, Partridge Fine Arts, 1991–96; Keeper, Gilbert Collection, 1996–2000; Consultant Curator, V&A Mus., 2000–09. Mem., Westminster Abbey Fabric Commn, 2017–. Chm., Prostate Cancer Res. Centre, 2008–18. Pres., Silver Soc., 2018– (Chm., 2011–16); Trustee: Silver Trust, 2012–19; Wallace Collection, 2013–. Liveryman: Goldsmiths' Co., 1993 (Prime Warden, 2015–16 and 2019–20); Art Scholars' Co., 2014–. FSA 1997. *Publications:* English Domestic Silver, 1988; The Gilbert Collection of Gold and Silver, 1988; Renaissance Silver from the Schroder Collection, 2007; (ed) Treasures of the English Church: a thousand years of sacred gold and silver, 2008; British and Continental Gold and Silver in the Ashmolean Museum, 2009; The Zilkha Collection, 2012; English Silver Before the Civil War, 2015; contrib. articles to jls incl. Apollo, Burlington Mag., Silver Soc. Jl. *Recreations:* punning, collecting and listening to Beethoven. *Address:* 32 Steeles Road, NW3 4RE. *T:* (020) 7722 5937. *E:* tim@schroder.uk.com. *Club:* Brooks's.

**SCHROEDER, Dominic Sebastian;** HM Diplomatic Service; Ambassador to Denmark, since 2016; b London, 13 Nov. 1965; s of late Hermann Schroeder and of Isobel Schroeder (née Allen); m 1997, Susan Caroline Kerr; one s one d. *Educ:* Highgate Wood Sch.; St Anne's Coll., Oxford (BA Mod. Hist.). Asst Desk Officer, NATO, FCO, 1988–89; Third, then Second Sec., Kinshasa, 1989–91; Asst Desk Officer, Middle E Peace Process, FCO, 1992–93; Second Sec., UK Mission to the UN, NY, 1993; Sen. Press Officer, News Dept, 1994–96, Hd, Iran Section, 1996–97, FCO; Chargé d'Affaires (temp.), Tehran, 1997; First Sec. and Hd, Commercial Section, Berlin, 1997–2001; Dep. Hd, Eastern Dept, 2001–04, Hd, Common Foreign and Security Policy, 2004–06, FCO; Counsellor, EU/Econ., 2006–10 and Dep. Hd of Mission, 2009–10, Berlin; Hd of Mission, Bratislava, 2011; Hd of Delegation to OSCE (with personal rank of Ambassador), Vienna, 2011–15. *Address:* c/o Foreign and Commonwealth Office, King Charles Street, SW1A 2AH.

**SCHÜELEIN-STEEL, Danielle Fernande Dominique, (Danielle Steel);** writer; b 14 Aug. 1947; d of John and Norma Schüelein-Steel; m Claude-Eric Lazard; one d; m John Traina (marr. diss.); one s four d (and one s decd). *Educ:* Lycée Français, NYC; Parsons Sch. of Design, NY; New York Univ. Vice-Pres. of Public Relations and New Business, Supergirls Ltd, 1968–71; copywriter, Grey Advertising Agency, 1973–74. Officier, Ordre des Arts et des Lettres (France), 2002. *Publications: fiction:* Going Home, 1973; Passion's Promise, 1977; Now and Forever, 1978; The Promise, 1978; Season of Passion, 1980; Summer's End, 1980; The Ring, 1980; To Love Again, 1981; Palomino, 1981; Loving, 1981; Remembrance, 1981; A Perfect Stranger, 1982; Once in a Lifetime, 1982; Crossings, 1982; Changes, 1983; Thurston House, 1983; Full Circle, 1984; Secrets, 1985; Family Album, 1985; Wanderlust, 1986; Fine Things, 1987; Kaleidoscope, 1987; Zoya, 1988; Star, 1989; Daddy, 1989; Message from Nam, 1990; Heartbeat, 1991; No Greater Love, 1991; Jewels, 1992; Mixed Blessings, 1992; Vanished, 1993; Accident, 1994; The Gift, 1994; Wings, 1994; Lightning, 1995; Five Days in Paris, 1995; Malice, 1996; Silent Honor, 1996; The Ranch, 1997; The Ghost, 1997; Special Delivery, 1997; The Long Road Home, 1998; The Klone and I, 1998; Mirror Image, 1998; Bittersweet, 1999; Granny Dan, 1999; Irresistible Forces, 1999; The Wedding, 2000; The House on Hope Street, 2000; Journey, 2000; Lone Eagle, 2001; Leap of Faith, 2001; The Kiss, 2002; The Cottage, 2003; Sunset in St Tropez, 2002; Answered Prayers, 2002; Dating Game, 2003; Johnny Angel, 2003; Safe Harbour, 2003; Ransom, 2004; Second Chance, 2004; Echoes, 2004; Impossible, 2005; Miracle, 2005; Toxic Bachelors, 2005; The House, 2006; Coming Out, 2006; HRH, 2006; Sisters, 2007; Bungalow 2, 2007; Amazing Grace, 2007; Rogue, 2008; Honor Thyself, 2008; A Good Woman, 2008; One Day at a Time, 2009; Matters of the Heart, 2009; Southern Lights, 2009; Big Girl, 2010; Family Ties, 2010; Legacy, 2010; 44 Charles Street,

2011; Happy Birthday, 2011; Hotel Vendome, 2011; Betrayal, 2012; Friends Forever, 2012; The Sins of the Mother, 2012; Until the End of Time, 2013; First Sight, 2013; Winners, 2013; Power Play, 2014; Pegasus, 2014; A Perfect Life, 2014; Prodigal Son, 2015; Country, 2015; Undercover, 2015; Precious Gifts, 2015; Blue, 2016; Property of a Noblewoman, 2016; The Apartment, 2016; Magic, 2016; Rushing Waters, 2016; The Award, 2016; The Mistress, 2017; Dangerous Games, 2017; Against All the Odds, 2017; The Duchess, 2017; The Right Time, 2017; Fairytale, 2017; Past Perfect, 2017; Fall From Grace, 2018; Accidental Heroes, 2018; The Cast, 2018; The Good Fight, 2018; In His Father's Footsteps, 2018; Beauchamp Hall, 2018; Turning Point, 2019; Silent Night, 2019; Blessing in Disguise, 2019; Lost and Found, 2019; The Dark Side, 2019; Child's Play, 2019; *non-fiction:* (contrib.) Having a Baby, 1984; His Bright Light: the story of Nick Traina, 1998; A Gift of Hope, 2012; Pure Joy, 2013; *poetry:* Love, 1981; several children's books incl. Pretty Minnie in Paris, 2014; Pretty Minnie in Hollywood, 2016. *Address:* c/o Janklow and Nesbit Associates, 285 Madison Avenue, 21st Floor, New York, NY 10017, USA.

**SCHULTZ, Prof. Wolfram**, MD; FRS 2009; Wellcome Trust Principal Research Fellow, and Professor of Neuroscience, University of Cambridge, since 2001; Fellow, Churchill College, Cambridge, since 2004; *b* 27 Aug. 1944; *s* of Robert and Herta Schultz; *m* 1972, Gerda Baumann; two *s* one *d*. *Educ:* Heidelberg (MD 1972); Univ. of Fribourg (Habilitation 1981). Postdoctoral work, 1973–77: MPI, Goettingen; NY State Univ., Buffalo, NY; Karolinska Inst., Stockholm; Asst, Associate, then full Prof. of Neurophysiology, Univ. of Fribourg, 1977–2001. Vis. Prof., Tamagawa Univ., Japan, 2001–; Vis. Res. Associate, CIT, 2004–. Sabbaticals: Univ. of Cambridge, 1993; Tokyo Metropolitan Inst. for Neurosci., 1997; Moore Fellow, CIT, Pasadena, 2005. Ellermann Prize, Swiss Socs for Neurology, Neurosurgery and Neuropathology, Bern, 1984; (jtly) Theodore-Ott Prize, Swiss Acad. of Medical Scis, 1997; Golden Brain Award, Minerva Foundn, Berkeley, Calif, 2002; (jtly) Ipsen Prize for Neuronal Plasticity, 2005; Eur. Jl of Neurosci. Award, Fedn of Eur. Neurosci. Socs, 2010; (jtly) Zülch Prize, Gertrud Reemtsma Foundn, 2013; Brain Prize, Lundbeck Foundn, 2017; Gruber Prize for Neurosci., Gruber Foundn, 2018; Lashley Award, APS, 2019. *Publications:* articles in learned jls. *Recreations:* sailing, scuba diving, snowboarding. *Address:* Department of Physiology, Development and Neuroscience, University of Cambridge, Downing Street, Cambridge CB2 3DY. *T:* (01223) 333779. *E:* ws234@cam.ac.uk.

**SCHUMACHER, Diana Catherine Brett**, OBE 2011; Director, Work Structuring Ltd, 2002–16; *b* 8 April 1941; *d* of Clarence Edward Brett Binns and Phyllis Mary Brett Binns; *m* 1966, Christian Schumacher; two *d*. *Educ:* St Hilda's Coll., Oxford (MA Mod. Hist.). British Council, 1964–66; Internat. Survey Res., Univ. of Chicago, 1969–73; Partner, Schumacher Projects Consultancy, 1979–2002; Co-Founder, Green Books, 1986. Founder Mem. and Trustee, Schumacher Soc., 1978–2001 (Pres., 1991–2000); Advr, Schumacher Coll., 1991–93; Founder Mem., Schumacher Inst., 2005. Member: Exec. Cttee, Green Alliance, 1982–92; Mgt Bd, Centre for Internat. Peacebuilding, 1985–; Founder Member and Trustee: Gandhi Foundn, 1983–98; New Econs Foundn, 1986–98; Founder Member: Envmtl Law Foundn, 1987– (Vice Chm., 1987–95; Life Vice-Pres., 1995–); SPES Forum, 2005–; Trustee: India Develt Gp, 1980–2005; Ecological Action Gp for Europe, 1984– (Vice Pres., 2005–); Themba Trust, 2005–. Patron: UK Social Investment Forum; Green Network; Peace Child Internat.; Tree Aid; Member: Soil Assoc. Gov., St Stephen's C of E and Middle Sch., S Godstone, 1970–90. FRSA. *Publications:* (jtly) Going Solar, 1977, 2nd edn 1979; (jtly) Solar Flatplate Collectors for Developing Countries, 1979; Energy: crisis or opportunity, 1985; Our Human Shelter Within the Global Shelter, 1987; Ten Principles for an Organic Energy Policy, 1992; Small is Manageable: from theory to practice, 2003; Small is Beautiful in the 21st Century: the legacy of E. F. Schumacher, 2011; *contributions to:* Habitat un ambiente per Vivere, 1994; This I Believe, 1997; Cuba Verde, 1999; The Council of Europe as the Conscience of Europe, 1999; Spirituality as a Public Good, 2007; contribs to jls incl. European Business Review, Resurgence, etc. *Recreations:* walking, the arts, organic gardening and food, making incomprehensible lists. *Address:* Cross Green Cottage, Berwick, near Shrewsbury, Shropshire SY4 3HU.

**SCHUMACHER, Michael;** professional racing driver, 1983–2006 and 2010–12; *b* 3 Jan. 1969; *s* of Rolf and late Elisabeth Schumacher; *m* 1995, Corinna Betsch; one *s* one *d*. Formula 3, 1989–90; European and World Champion, 1990; Formula 1, 1991–2006; Jordan-Ford team, 1991; Benetton-Ford team, 1991–95; Ferrari team, 1996–2006; Mercedes GP, 2010–12; Drivers' World Champion, 1994, 1995, 2000, 2001, 2002, 2003, 2004. *Publications:* (jtly) Formula for Success, 1996; (jtly) Michael Schumacher: driving force, 2003. *Address:* The MS Office, Avenue du Mont-Blanc 14B, 1196 Gland, Switzerland.

**SCHÜSSEL, Dr Wolfgang;** MP (People's Party), Austria, 1979–2011; Chancellor of Austria, 2000–07; *b* Vienna, 7 June 1945; *m*; two *c*. *Educ:* Vienna Univ. (DJur). Sec., Austrian People's Party, 1968–75; Sec.-Gen., Austrian Econ. Fedn, 1975–89. Minister of Econ. Affairs, Austria, 1989–95; Vice-Chancellor and Minister of Foreign Affairs, 1996–2000. Chm., 1995–2006, Leader, Parly Gp, 2006–08, Austrian People's Party. Dir, and Chm., Bd of Trustees, Konrad Adenauer Foundation; Mem., Bd of Trustees, Bertelsmann Stiftung, Bertelsman Foundn, 2007.

**SCHWAB, Dr Klaus**, Hon. KCMG 2006; Founder and Executive Chairman, World Economic Forum, since 1971; *b* 30 March 1938; *s* of Eugen and Erika Schwab; *m* 1971, Hilde Stoll; one *s* one *d*. *Educ:* Humanistisches Gymnasium, Ravensburg; Swiss Fed. Inst. of Technology (Dip. ing 1962; Dr ing 1966); Univ. of Fribourg (Lic.ès.sc.écon 1963; Dr rer. pol. 1967); John F. Kennedy Sch. of Govt, Harvard (MPA 1967). Experience on shop floor of several cos, 1958–62; Asst to Dir Gen. of German Machine-building Assoc., Frankfurt, 1963–65; Mem., Managing Bd, Sulzer Escher Wyss AG, Zurich, 1967–70. Prof. for Business Policy, Geneva Univ., 1973–2003, Hon. Prof., 2003. Co-founder and Mem. Foundn Bd, Schwab Foundn for Social Entrepreneurship, Geneva, 1998–; Founder: Forum of Young Global Leaders, 2004; Global Shapers Community, 2011. Trustee, Peres Center for Peace, Tel Aviv, 1997–; Mem. Adv. Bd, Foreign Policy, Washington, 1997–. Mem. Vis. Cttee, JFK Sch. of Govt, Harvard Univ., 1996–; Hon. Prof., Ben-Gurion Univ. of the Negev, Israel, 2003–; Mem. President's Council, Univ. of Tokyo, 2006–. Mem. Bd, Lucerne Fest., 2007–. Freedom, City of London, 2006. Twelve hon. doctorates. Grand Cross, Nat. Order of Merit (Germany), 1995; Knight, Légion d'Honneur (France), 1997; Golden Grand Cross, Nat. Order (Austria), 1997; Medal of Freedom (Slovenia), 1997; Comdr's Cross with Star, Nat. Order (Poland), 2002; Decoration of 1st Degree for Outstanding Giving (Jordan), 2005; Comdr's Cross (Lithuania), 2008; Grand Cross, OM (Germany), 2012; Grand Cordon, Order of Rising Sun (Japan), 2013; Friendship Medal (China), 2018. *Publications:* Modern Enterprise Management in Mechanical Engineering, 1971; Global Competitiveness Report (annually), 1979–; The Fourth Industrial Revolution, 2016; Shaping the Future of the Fourth Industrial Revolution: a guide to building a better world, 2018; numerous articles. *Recreations:* cross-country ski marathon, high mountain climbing. *Address:* (office) World Economic Forum, 91–93 route de la Capite, 1223 Cologny, Switzerland. *T:* (22) 8691212, *Fax:* (22) 7862744. *E:* contact@weforum.org.

**SCHWARTE, Maria;** *see* Adebowale-Schwarte, M.

**SCHWARTZ, Prof. Steven**, AM 2013; PhD; Chairman, Australian Curriculum, Assessment and Reporting Authority, 2015–18; Consultant, Department of Health, Australia; *b* New York, 5 Nov. 1946; *s* of Robert and Frances Schwartz; *m* 2001, Claire Mary Farrugia; one *s* three *d* (and one *s* decd). *Educ:* Brooklyn Coll., City Univ. of New York (BA); Syracuse Univ., New York (MSc, PhD). FASSA 1991; FAICD 2001; FAIM 2001. Res. Scientist, Dept of Psychiatry, Community and Public Health, Med. Br., Univ. of Texas, 1975–79; Sen. Lectr, Dept of Psychology, Univ. of Western Australia, Perth, 1978–79; University of Queensland: Prof. and Hd, Dept of Psychology, 1980–90; Pres., Academic Bd, 1991–93; Exec. Dean, Faculty of Medicine and Dentistry, Univ. of WA, 1994–95; Vice-Chancellor and Pres., Murdoch Univ., 1996–2001; Vice-Chancellor and Principal, Brunel Univ., 2002–05; Vice-Chancellor and Pres., Macquarie Univ., Sydney, 2006–12; CEO, Council for Humanities, Arts and Social Scis, Australia, 2013–15. Royal Soc. Anglo-Australian Exchange Fellow, ICRF Labs, London, 1988. Leader, Admissions to Higher Educn Review, 2003–04; Mem. and Sen. Fellow, Adv. Bd, Centre for Ind. Studies, 1997–; Member: Bd, Council for Internat. Educn Exchange, 1997–2009; Nat. Panel, Student Aptitude Test for Tertiary Admission, Aust. Govt, 2007–; Bd, Univs Australia, 2009–12; Internat. Adv. Cttee, Zhejiang Univ., 2014–; Adv. Bd, Acquire Educn, 2015–; Chm., Bologna Process Steering Gp, Dept of Educn, Employment and Workplace Relns, 2007–12. Mem., London Production Industries Commn, 2004–05; Director: Australia-America Fulbright Commn, 2007– (Chm., 2011–); Teach for Australia, 2013–; NSW Library Foundn, 2013–. Sen. Advr, Nous Gp, 2012–. Gov., Richmond, Amer. Internat. Univ. in London, 2004–05; Australian Govt Rep., Council, Univ. of South Pacific, 2007–. Mem. Adv. Council, Reform, 2004–. Oliver Smithies Fellow, Balliol Coll., Oxford, 2013; Hon. Sen. Fellow, Univ. of Melbourne, 2014–. *Publications:* (jtly) Psychopathology of Childhood, 1981, 2nd edn 1995; Measuring Reading Competence, 1984; Classic Studies in Psychology, 1986 (trans. German 1991); (with T. Griffin) Medical Thinking: the psychology of medical judgement and decision-making, 1986; Pavlov's Heirs, 1987; Classic Studies in Abnormal Psychology, 1993; Abnormal Psychology, 2000; *edited:* (jtly) Human Judgement and Decision Processes, 1975; (jtly) Human Judgement and Decision Processes in Applied Settings, 1977; Language and Cognition in Schizophrenia, 1978; Case Studies in Abnormal Psychology, 1992; contrib. books and learned jls. *Recreations:* bushwalking, reading, writing. *Address:* Centre for Independent Studies, Level 1, 131 Macquarie Street, Sydney, NSW 2000, Australia; Apartment 802, 45 Bowman Street, Pyrmont, Sydney, NSW 2009, Australia.

**SCHWARTZMAN, Arnold Martin**, OBE 2002; RDI 2006; President, Arnold Schwartzman Productions, Los Angeles, since 1985; *b* Wapping, London, 6 Jan. 1936; *s* of David and Rose Schwartzman; *m* 1st, 1958, Marilyn Bild (marr. diss. 1979); one *d*; 2nd, 1980, Isolde Weghofer. *Educ:* Shoreham Grammar Sch.; Thanet Sch. of Art and Crafts, Margate; Canterbury Coll. of Art (NDD 1955). Served Royal Sussex Regt, Germany and Korea, 1955–57. Graphic Designer: Southern TV, Southampton, 1959–60; Associated-Rediffusion Television, London, 1960–66; Concept Planning Executive, Erwin Wasey Advertising, London, 1966–69; Dir, Conran Design Gp, 1969; Principal, Arnold Schwartzman Prodns, London, 1970–78; Design Dir, Saul Bass & Associates, LA, 1978–79; Producer/Dir, Genocide, 1981 (Acad. Award for Best Documentary Feature); Dir of Design, 1984 Los Angeles Olympic Games, 1982; Creative Dir, Voices and Visions, 2011–12. Other documentary feature films as prod. and dir include: Building a Dream, 1989; Echoes that Remain, 1991; Liberation, 1994. Muralist, London Time and Golden Age of Transportation, Cunard's Queen Elizabeth, 2010; T. S. Eliot tiled mural, Margate, Kent, 2018; designer, UN Peace Bell Meml, Korean War Meml Mus., Seoul, 2013. Hon Design Consultant, Projected Picture Trust Mus., Elstree Studios, 2016. Exhibn, Schwartzman's Six Decades of Graphic Art and Film, CG Showroom, W Hollywood, 2015. First Co-Chm., 1997–98, Chm. Bd, 1999–2000, Gov., 2000–, BAFTA/LA; Chm. Documentary Exec. Cttee, Acad. of Motion Picture Arts and Scis, 2000–01; Mem. Jury, Premios Platino Film Fest., Panama City, 2014, Marbella, 2015, Montevideo, 2016, Madrid, 2017; Member, Jury: Guadalajara Film Fest., 2017; SE Europe Film Fest., 2017; Pres., Documentary Jury, Fest. De Cine Global Dominicano, 2017. Mem., Bd of Govs, Univ. for the Creative Arts, 2008–16. Patron: UK Nat. Defence Medal Campaign, 2010–; Margate Clock Tower Time Ball Restoration Project, 2014–; Margate Sch., 2015–. Mem., AGI, 1974–. FRSA 1998. Global Award, Fest. De Cine Global Dominicano, 2017. *Publications:* (with Len Deighton) Airshipwreck, 1978; Graven Images, 1993; Phono-Graphics, 1993; Liberation, 1994; Designage, 1998; (with Michael Webb) It's a Great Wall, 2000; Flicks: how the movies began, 2000; Deco Landmarks, 2005; London Art Deco, 2007; Griffith Observatory 80th Anniversary: a celebration of its architectural splendour, 2015; (with Stephen Gee) Los Angeles Central Library: its art and architecture, 2016; Art Deco City: the world's most beautiful buildings, 2018; Arnold Schwartzman: a masterclass on the graphic art and work of the left-handed polymath, 2018; Art Nouveau City: the world's most beautiful buildings, 2019; Arts & Crafts City: the world's most beautiful buildings, 2020. *Recreations:* cinema, photography, drawing. *Address:* 317½ North Sycamore Avenue, Los Angeles, CA 90036, USA. *T:* (323) 9381481. *E:* arnold@schwartzmandesign.com.

**SCHWARZ, Cheryl Lynn;** *see* Studer, C. L.

**SCHWARZ, Gerard;** conductor and composer; Music Director: Eastern Music Festival, since 2008; The All-Star Orchestra, since 2013; The Mozart Orchestra of New York, since 2015; Palm Beach Symphony Orchestra, since 2019; Distinguished Professor of Music, Frost School of Music, University of Miami, since 2019; *b* NJ, 19 Aug. 1947; *m* 1984, Jody Greitzer; two *s* two *d*. *Educ:* Juilliard Sch., NYC. Conductor, 1966–; Music Director: Erick Hawkins Dance Co., 1967–72; SoHo Ensemble, 1969–75; Eliot Field Dance Co., NYC, 1972–78; NY Chamber SO, 1977–2002; LA Chamber Orch., 1976–86; Music Advr, 1983–84, Principal Conductor, 1984–85, Seattle SO; Music Director: Royal Liverpool Philharmonic Orch., 2001–06; Seattle SO, 1985–2011, now Conductor Laureate. Estabd Music Today, 1981, Music Dir, 1981–89; Music Advr, Mostly Mozart Fest., NYC, 1982–84 (Music Dir, 1984–2001); Artistic Advr, Tokyo Bunkamura's Orchard Hall, 1994–97; operatic conducting début with Washington Opera, 1982, with Seattle Opera, 1986. Guest Conductor with major orchestras in N America, Europe, Australia and Japan. Has made over 350 recordings, incl. The Gerard Schwarz Collection, 2017. Hon. DMus: Juilliard Sch.; Puget Sound; Hon. DFA: Farleigh Dickinson; Seattle. Ditson Conductor's Award, Columbia Univ. 1989; ASCAP Awards: for adventurous programming, 1990, 1994, 2001, 2006; for strongest commitment to new Amer. music, 1991; for programming of contemp. music, 1996; 2004; Concert Music Award, 2002; Conductor of Year, Musical America Internat. Directory of Performing Arts, 1994; Emmy Awards, 2006, 2007, 2013, 2014, 2016, 2017. *Publications:* Behind the Baton (memoir), 2017. *Address:* c/o AOR Management Inc., 6910 Roosevelt Way NE, PMB 221, Seattle, WA 98115, USA.

**SCHWARZ, Michael Robert;** Senior Consultant, Bindmans LLP, since 2018 (Partner, 1995–2018; Member until 2018); *b* 16 July 1963. *Educ:* Lancaster Royal Grammar Sch.; Hertford Coll., Oxford (BA Juris.); Coll. of Europe, Bruges (Dip. Adv. European Legal Studies). Admitted as solicitor, 1992; Bindmans LLP, specialising in criminal and human rights law, 1990–. Vis. Lectr, Univ. of Westminster, 2007–12. Mem., Policy Council, Liberty. Chm., Trustees, Sheila McKecknie Foundn, 2013–16. *Publications:* (jtly) The Law of Public Order and Protest, 2010. *Recreation:* species survival. *Address:* Bindmans LLP, 236 Gray's Inn Road, WC1X 8HB. *T:* (020) 7833 4433, *Fax:* (020) 7837 9792. *E:* m.schwarz@bindmans.com.

**SCHWARZ, Sebastian F.;** General Director, Glyndebourne, 2016–17; *b* Rostock, Germany, 5 March 1974; *s* of Lothar Pichl and Cornelia Schwarz; *m* 2017, Ladislav Elgr. *Educ:* Univ. Ca' Foscari, Venice; Freie Univ., Berlin. Co. mgt, Wexford Fest. Opera, 2004–07; asst to Dir of Opera, Hamburg State Opera, 2007; Dir, Artistic Admin and Casting, Theater an der Wien, Vienna, 2008–16. Member, Board of Directors: Nat. Opera Studio, 2016; Opera Europa, 2017. Mem., juries of internat. opera competitions, 2005–. Kt, Order of the Star (Italy), 2015. *Publications:* contrib. articles in programme books. *Recreations:* bee keeping, rowing, theatre, anatomy, ice cream critic, cross country ski-ing.

**SCHWARZENEGGER, Arnold Alois;** actor; Governor of California, 2003–11; Co-founder, Chair and Governor Downey Professor of State and Global Policy, Schwarzenegger Institute for State and Global Policy, University of Southern California, since 2012; *b* Graz, Austria, 30 July 1947; *s* of late Gustav Schwarzenegger and Aurelia Schwarzenegger (*née* Jedrny); arrived in USA 1968, naturalized citizen of USA, 1983; *m* 1986, Maria Owings Shriver (marr. diss. 2011); two *s* two *d*; one *s* by Mildred Baena. *Educ:* Univ. of Wisconsin-Superior (BA 1980). Weightlifter and bodybuilder, 1965–75; Jun. Mr Europe, 1965; Best Built Man of Europe, 1966; Mr Europe, 1966; Internat. Powerlifting Champion, 1966; Mr Universe, Nat. Amateur Body Builders' Assoc., (amateur) 1967, (professional) 1968, 1969, 1970; German Powerlifting Champion, 1968; Mr International, 1968, Mr Universe (amateur), 1969, Mr Olympia, annually, 1970–75, 1980, Internat. Fedn of Body Building; Mr World, 1970. *Films include:* Stay Hungry, 1976; Pumping Iron, 1977; The Villain, 1979; The Jayne Mansfield Story, 1980; Conan the Barbarian, 1982; Conan the Destroyer, 1983; The Terminator, 1984; Commando, 1985; Raw Deal, 1986; Predator, Running Man, 1987; Red Heat, Twins, 1988; Total Recall, Kindergarten Cop, 1990; Terminator 2: Judgement Day, 1991; The Last Action Hero (also prod.), 1993; True Lies, Junior, 1994; Jingle All the Way, Eraser, 1996; Batman and Robin, With Wings of Eagles, 1997; End of Days, 1999; The Sixth Day (also prod.), 2000; Collateral Damage, 2002; Terminator 3: Rise of the Machines, 2003; The Expendables 2, 2012; The Last Stand, 2013; Sabotage, 2014; Terminator Genysis, Maggie, 2015; Aftermath, 2017. Host, TV series, The New Celebrity Apprentice, 2017. Chm., US President's Council on Physical Fitness and Sports, 1990–93. *Publications:* (jtly) Arnold: the education of a bodybuilder, 1977; Arnold's Bodyshaping for Women, 1979; Arnold's Bodybuilding for Men, 1981; Arnold's Encyclopedia of Modern Bodybuilding, 1985, 2nd edn 1998; (jtly) Arnold's Fitness for Kids, 1993; Total Recall (memoir), 2012.

**SCHWEBEL, Stephen Myron;** President, Administrative Tribunal, World Bank, 2010–17 (Member, 2007–17); international arbitrator; *b* 10 March 1929; *s* of Victor Schwebel and Pauline Pfeffer Schwebel; *m* 1972, Louise Killander; two *d*. *Educ:* Harvard Coll. (BA); Trinity Coll., Cambridge (Frank Knox Meml Fellow; Hon. Fellow, 2005); Yale Law Sch. (LLB). Attorney, White & Case, 1954–59; Asst Prof. of Law, Harvard Law Sch., 1959–61; Asst Legal Advr, State Dept, 1961–66; Exec. Dir, Amer. Soc. of Internat. Law, 1967–73; Dep. Legal Advr, State Dept, 1973–81; Judge, 1981–2000, Pres., 1997–2000, Internat. Court of Justice. Pres., Admin. Tribunal, IMF, 1993–2010. Burling Prof. of Internat. Law, Sch. of Advanced Internat. Studies, Johns Hopkins Univ., 1967–81. Member: UN Internat. Law Commn, 1977–81; Panel of Arbitrators, ICSID, 2001–; Perm. Court of Arbitration, The Hague, 2006–. Hon. Bencher, Gray's Inn, 1998. Weill Medal, NY Univ. Sch. of Law, 1992; Medal of Merit, Yale Law Sch., 1997; Manley O. Hudson Medal, Amer. Soc. of Internat. Law, 2000. *Publications:* The Secretary-General of the United Nations, 1952; International Arbitration: three salient problems, 1987, 2nd edn 2019; Justice in International Law, 1994; Justice in International Law: further selected writings, 2011. *Recreations:* music, walking. *Address:* Cady Brook Farm, PO Box 356, South Woodstock, VT 05071, USA. *T:* (802) 4571358. *Clubs:* Athenæum; Harvard (New York); Cosmos, Metropolitan (Washington).

**SCHWEITZER, Louis;** Chairman, Renault, 1992–2009, now Hon. Chairman (Chief Executive Officer, 1992–2005); Special Representative of Minister of Foreign Affairs to Japan, since 2012; Chairman, Council of Foreign Affairs, 2013–18; General Commissioner for Investment, 2014–18; *b* Geneva, 8 July 1942; *s* of late Pierre-Paul Schweitzer; *m* 1972, Agnès Schmitz; two *d*. *Educ:* Institut d'Etudes Politiques, Paris; Faculté de Droit, Paris; Ecole Nationale d'Administration, Paris. Inspectorate of Finance, 1970–74; special assignment, later Dep. Dir, Min. of Budget, 1974–81; Chief of Staff: to Minister of Budget, 1981–83; of Industry and Research, 1983; to Prime Minister, 1984–86; Régie Renault: Vice-Pres. for Finance and Planning, 1986–90; Chief Finance Officer, 1988–90; Exec. Vice-Pres., 1989–90; Pres. and Chief Operating Officer, 1990–92. Prof., Inst d'Etudes Politiques de Paris, 1982–86. Director: Inst Français des Relations Internats, 1989–; BNP, 1993–2013; Philips, 1997–2008; EDF, 1999–2008; Volvo, 2001–12 (Chm., 2010–12); Veolia Environnement, 2003–; L'Oréal, 2005–16; BPI France, 2014–; non-exec. Chm., AstraZeneca, 2005–12. Chm., Supervisory Bd, Le Monde, 2008–10. Chm., Haute Autorité de Lutte contre les Discriminations et pour l'Égalité, 2005–10; Pres., France Initiative, 2011–. Grand Officier, Ordre National du Mérite (France), 2007 (Officier, 1992, Comdr, 2002); Grand Croix, Légion d'Honneur (France), 2016 (Officier, 1998; Comdr, 2005; Grand Officier, 2013). *Address:* 27 Rue des Abondances, Boulogne-Billancourt, 92100 Paris, France.

**SCHWEITZER, Prof. Miguel;** Dean, Finisterrae University Law School, 2003–18; Senior Partner, Schweitzer & Co., law firm, since 1970; *b* 22 July 1940; *s* of Miguel Schweitzer and Cora Walters; *m*; three *s* two *d*. *Educ:* The Grange School, Santiago (preparatory and secondary schooling); Law School, Univ. of Chile (law degree). Doctorate in Penal Law, Rome, 1964–65; Professor of Penal Law: Law Sch., Univ. of Chile, 1966; High Sch. of Carabineros (Police), 1968, 1970 and 1974–80; Director, Dept of Penal Sciences, Univ. of Chile, 1974–76; Chile's Alternate Representative with the Chilean Delegn to UN, 1975, 1976, 1978; Ambassador on special missions, 1975–80; Chilean Delegate to OAS, 1976–78; Ambassador to UK, 1980–83; Minister for Foreign Affairs, Chile, 1983. *Publications:* El Error de Derecho en Materia Penal (Chile), 1964; Sull elemento soggettivo nel reato di bancarotta del l'imprenditore (Rome), 1965; Prospectus for a Course on the Special Part of Penal Law (USA), 1969. *Recreations:* music, reading, golf, ski-ing. *Address:* Floor 15, Miraflores 178, Santiago, Chile. *E:* msw@schweitzer.cl. *Clubs:* Prince of Wales Country (Santiago); Marbella Country (Valparaiso).

**SCICLUNA, Martin Anthony;** Chairman: Great Portland Estates, 2009–19 (Director, since 2008); RSA Insurance Group, since 2013; J. Sainsbury plc, since 2019 (Director, since 2018); *b* 20 Nov. 1950; *s* of late William Scicluna and Miriam Scicluna; *m* 1979 (marr. diss. 2000); two *s* one *d*. *Educ:* Berkhamsted Sch., Herts; Univ. of Leeds (BCom). Joined Deloitte & Touche (formerly Touche Ross & Co.), 1973; Partner, 1982–2008; Head, London Audit, 1990–95; Mem., Bd of Partners, 1991–2007; Chm., 1995–2007; Mem. Bd Dirs and Governance Cttee, 1999–2007, Managing Partner, Global Strategic Clients, 2001–03, Deloitte Touche Tohmatsu. Dir, Lloyds Banking Gp, 2008–13 (Chm., Audit Cttee, 2009–13); non-exec. Dir, Worldpay plc, 2013–18 (Chm. Audit Cttee, 2013–18; Sen. Ind. Dir, 2015–18). Mem., Financial Services Trade and Investment Bd, 2013–15. Chm., Accounting and Reporting Working Gp, and Mem., Steering Gp, Company Law Review, 1999–2001. Chm., London Soc. Chartered Accountants in England and Wales, 1989–90; Institute of Chartered Accountants in England and Wales: Mem. Council, 1990–95; Chm. Auditing Cttee, 1990–95. Chm., Chairmen's Business Forum, Leeds Univ. Bus. Sch., 2002–06; Mem. Council, Leeds Univ., 2008–11. Trustee, Understanding Industry, 1999–2003; Mem. Bd of Trustees, WellBeing, 2000–03. Vice Patron, businessdynamics, 2003–06. Member: Sailability Develt Bd, RYA, 2000–03; Adv. Council, Cancer Res. UK (formerly CRC), 1999–2003; Finance Cttee, V&A Mus., 2007–08. Governor: NIESR, 2002–17; Berkhamsted Sch., 2008–16. Freeman, City of London, 1993. Hon. LLD Leeds, 2008. *Recreations:* Arsenal FC, tennis, gardening, wine. *Address:* Parkways, Little Heath Lane, Potten End, Herts HP4 2RX.

**SCICLUNA, Martin Leonard Andrew;** Director General, Today Public Policy Institute, 2007–17; Chairman, National Commission for Further and Higher Education, Malta, 2013–16; Council Member for Life, Din l-Art Helwa (National Trust of Malta) (Council Member, 1996–2014; Executive President, 2001–05; Vice-President, 2005–13); *b* 16 Nov. 1935; *s* of Richard Hugh Scicluna and Victoria Mary (*née* Amato-Gauci); *m* 1st, 1960, Anna Judith Brennand (marr. diss. 1988); one *s*; 2nd, 1989, Loraine Jean Birnie; two step *d*. *Educ:* St Edward's Coll., Cottonera, Malta; RMA, Sandhurst. Royal Malta Artillery, 1953–65 (commnd 1955); transferred to RA, 1965–74 (Army Staff Coll., 1965). Joined Civil Service, MoD, 1974; Principal: Naval Personnel Div., 1974–76; Naval and Army Defence Secretariats, 1976–80; Asst Sec., 1980; Hd, Air Force Logistics Secretariat, 1980–83; Dep. Chief, Public Relns, 1983–85; Hd, Gen. Staff Secretariat, 1985–89; RCDS, 1989; Hd, Manpower Resources and Progs, 1990–91; Hd, Resources and Progs (Management Planning), 1991; Asst Under Sec. of State (Adjt Gen.), MoD, 1992; on secondment to FCO, UK delegn to NATO, 1993–95; Ambassador of Malta to NATO, 1996; Advr on Defence Policy to the PM of Malta, 1996–99; Dir of Finance and Infrastructure, PricewaterhouseCoopers, Malta, 1999–2002. Advr on Illegal Immigration to Minister of Home Affairs and Nat. Security (formerly of Justice and Home Affairs), Malta, 2005–13. Director: HSBC Cares for Heritage Fund, 2007–10; HSBC Malta Heritage Foundn, 2010–14. Co-Chm., St Paul's Anglican Pro-Cathedral Restoration Appeal, Valletta, 2017–. 1992–93: Chm. of Comrs, Duke of York's Royal Mil. Coll.; Comr, Royal Hosp., Chelsea; Commissioner: Queen Victoria Sch., Dunblane; Welbeck Coll., Notts; Chm., of Trustees, Army Welfare Fund; Trustee: Nat. Army Mus.; Army Benevolent Fund. Member: Council, 2003–09, Bd, 2009–12, Europa Nostra; Cttee of Guarantee of Malta's Cultural Heritage, 2003–05; Nat. Commn for Sustainable Develt, 2003–08; Bd, Internat. Nat. Trusts Orgn, 2005–12; Pres., European Network of Nat. Heritage Orgns, 2003–04; Chm., ESU Malta, 2009–11 (Mem. Cttee, ESU Malta, 2011–); Co-Chm., St Paul's Anglican Pro-Cathedral Restoration Appeal, 2016–. Chm. Bd of Govs, St Edward's Coll., 2000–05; Trustee, Lady Strickland's Trust for St Edward's Coll., 2000–14. *Recreations:* painting, theatre, watching sport, other sedentary pursuits. *Address:* c/o Barclays Bank plc, 212 Regent Street, W1A 4BP; Dar San Martin, Triq Il-Bali Guarena, Qrendi QRD 1350, Malta. *T:* 21689532.

**SCIVER, Julia Margaret;** *see* Longbottom, J. M.

**SCLATER, Prof. John George,** PhD; FRS 1982; Professor of Marine Geophysics, Scripps Institution of Oceanography, University of California at San Diego, since 1991; *b* 17 June 1940; *s* of John George Sclater and Margaret Bennett Glen; *m* 1st, 1968, Fredrica Rose Felcyn; two *s*; 2nd, 1985, Paula Ann Edwards (marr. diss. 1991); 3rd, 1992, Naila Gloria Cortez; one *d*. *Educ:* Carlekemp Priory School; Stonyhurst College; Edinburgh Univ. (BSc); Cambridge Univ. (PhD 1966). Research Scientist, Scripps Instn of Oceanography, 1965; Massachusetts Institute of Technology: Associate Prof., 1972; Professor, 1977; Dir, Jt Prog. in Oceanography and Oceanographic Engrg with Woods Hole Oceanographic Instn, 1981; Prof., Dept of Geol Scis, and Associate Dir, Inst. for Geophysics, 1983–91, Shell Dist. Prof., 1983–88, Univ. of Texas at Austin. Guggenheim Fellow, 1998–99. Fellow Geological Soc. of America; Fellow Amer. Geophysical Union; Mem., US Nat. Acad. of Scis, 1989. Rosenstiel Award in Oceanography, Rosenstiel Sch., Univ. of Miami, 1979; Bucher Medal, Amer. Geophysical Union, 1985. *Recreations:* running, swimming, golf. *Address:* Scripps Institution of Oceanography, 9500 Gilman Drive, La Jolla, CA 92093–0220, USA.

**SCLATER, John Richard,** CVO 1999; Managing Partner, Sutton Hall Farms, since 2002; Chairman, Sclater Estates Ltd (formerly Berner, Nicol & Co. Ltd), 2002–04 and since 2005 (Director, 1968–2004); *b* 14 July 1940; *s* of late Arthur William Sclater and Alice Sclater (*née* Collett); *m* 1st, 1967, Nicola Mary Gloria Cropper (marr. diss.); one *s* (one *d* decd); 2nd, 1985, Grizel Elizabeth Catherine Dawson, MBE. *Educ:* Charterhouse; Gonville and Caius Coll., Cambridge (schol., 1st Cl. Hons History Tripos, BA, MA); Commonwealth Fellow, 1962–64; Yale Univ. (MA 1963); Harvard Univ. (MBA 1968). Glyn, Mills & Co., 1964–70; Dir, Williams, Glyn & Co., 1970–76; Chief Exec., Nordic Bank, 1976–85 (Chm., 1985); Dir, 1985–87, Jt Dep. Chm., 1987, Guinness Peat Gp PLC; Dir and Dep. Chm., 1985–87, Chm., 1987, Guinness Mahon & Co. Ltd; Chairman: Foreign & Colonial Investment Trust PLC, 1985–2002 (Dir, 1981–2002); Graphite (formerly Foreign & Colonial) Enterprise Trust Plc, 1986–2009; Foreign & Colonial Ventures Ltd, 1989–98; Berisford plc, 1990–2000 (Dir, 1986–2000); Hill Samuel Bank Ltd, 1992–96 (Dir, 1990–96; Vice-Chm., 1990–92); Graphite (formerly Foreign & Colonial) Private Equity Trust PLC, 1994–2002; Union (formerly Union Discount Co. of London) plc, 1996 (Dir, 1981–96, Dep. Chm., 1986–96); Biotech Growth Trust plc (formerly Reabourne Merlin, then Finsbury, Life Scis Investment Trust, subseq. Finsbury Emerging Biotechnol. Trust plc), 1997–2012; Argent Gp Europe Ltd, 1998–2012; Infinity Christmas Trees Ltd, 2017–. Pres., Equitable Life Assce Soc., 1994–2001 (Dir, 1985–2002); Deputy Chairman: Yamaichi International (Europe) Ltd, 1985–97; Millennium & Copthorne Hotels PLC, 1996–2007; Grosvenor Gp Ltd (formerly Grosvenor Estate Hldgs), 1999–2005 (Dir, 1989–); Director: James Cropper PLC, 1972–2008; Holker Estates Co. Ltd, 1974–2013; F & C Group (Hldgs) Ltd, 1999–2001; Fuel Tech (Europe), 1990–98; Angerstein Underwriting Trust PLC, 1995–96; Wates Group Ltd, 1999–2004; Member, London Bd of Halifax Building Soc., 1983–90. Trustee, Grosvenor Estate, 1973–2005. Mem., City Taxation Cttee, 1973–76. Chm., Assoc. of Consortium Banks, 1980–82. Mem., City Adv. Gp, CBI, 1988–99. Mem. Council, Duchy of Lancaster, 1987–2000. First Church Estates Comr, 1999–2001; Mem., Archbishops' Council and Gen. Synod, C of E, 1999–2001. Governor: Internat. Students House, 1976–99; Brambletye Sch. Trust, 1976–2006. Freeman, City of London, 1992; Liveryman, Goldsmiths' Co., 1992–. *Recreation:* country pursuits. *Address:* Sutton Hall, Barcombe, near Lewes, Sussex BN8 5EB. *T:* (01273) 400450, *Fax:* (01273) 401086. *Clubs:* Brooks's; University Pitt (Cambridge); Sussex.

**SCLATER-BOOTH,** family name of **Baron Basing**.

**SCOBIE, James Timothy Norman;** QC 2010; *b* Dhekelia, Cyprus, 7 Sept. 1960; *s* of Col F. H., (Jim), Scobie and Goodeth Scobie; *m* 1995, Sophie; two *d*. *Educ:* Eton Coll.; Univ. of Exeter (BA Gen. Hons 1982); City Univ. (DipLaw 1983). Called to the Bar, Gray's Inn, 1984; in practice as a barrister, specialising in crime, Francis Taylor Bldg, 1985–91, Garden Court Chambers, 1991–. *Recreations:* follower of all sports, especially cricket and football, lifelong supporter of Manchester United Football Club. *Address:* Garden Court Chambers, 57–60 Lincoln's Inn Fields, WC2A 3LJ. *Clubs:* MCC (Mem., 1979–); Surrey County Cricket (Internat. Mem.); Old Etonian Association Football (Sec.).

**SCOBIE, Kenneth Charles,** CA; Chairman, Chemring, 1997–2010; *b* 29 July 1938; *s* of Charles Scobie and Shena (*née* Melrose); *m* 1973, Adela Jane Hollebone; one *s* one *d*. *Educ:* Daniel Stewart's Coll., Edinburgh; Edinburgh Univ. CA 1961. Romanes-Munro, CA, 1956–61; BMC (Scotland) Ltd, 1961–63; Rolls-Royce Ltd, 1963–66; Robson Morrow & Co., 1966–70; Black & Decker, 1971–72; Vavasseur South Africa Ltd, 1972–76; H. C. Sleigh Ltd, 1979–83; Blackwood Hodge plc, 1984–90; Dep. Chm. and Chief Exec., Brent Walker Group, 1991–93; Chairman: Lovells Confectionery Ltd, 1991–98; William Hill Group, 1992–93; Allied Leisure, 1994–2000; Dep. Chm., Addis, 1993–94; Dir, Postern Exec. Gp, 1991–97. Non-exec. Director: Albrighton plc, 1990–93; Gartmore Venture Capital, 1993–98. Chm. Exec. Bd, Scottish Rugby Union, 2000–03. CCMI (CBIM 1987). *Recreations:* sport, Bridge. *Address:* Path Hill House, Path Hill, Goring Heath, Oxon RG8 7RE. *T:* (0118) 9842417. *Clubs:* London Scottish Football (Pres., 1997–2001); Huntercombe Golf; Durban (S Africa).

**SCOBLE, Christopher Lawrence;** Assistant Under-Secretary of State, Home Office, 1988–95; *b* 21 Nov. 1943; *s* of Victor Arthur Oliphant Scoble and Mabel Crouch; *m* 1st, 1972, Florence Hunter (*d* 2001); one *s* one *d*; 2nd, 2012, Sheelagh Hunter. *Educ:* Kent Coll., Canterbury; Corpus Christi Coll., Oxford. Asst Principal, Home Office, 1965; Private Sec. to Minister of State, Welsh Office, 1969–70; Home Office: Principal, 1970; Sec. to Adv. Council on the Penal System, 1976–78; Asst Sec., 1978; Asst Under-Sec. of State, Broadcasting and Miscellaneous Dept, 1988–91, Establishment Dept, 1991–94, Police Dept, 1994–95. Vice-Chm., Media Policy Cttee, Council of Europe, 1985–87. CS (Nuffield and Leverhulme) Travelling Fellowship, 1987–88. *Publications:* Fisherman's Friend: a life of Stephen Reynolds, 2000; (ed) A Poor Man's House, by Stephen Reynolds, 2001; Colin Blythe: lament for a legend, 2005; Letters from Bishopsbourne: three writers in an English village, 2010; Under Shrub Hill: a Chestfield childhood, 2012; Julliberrie's Grave: the biography of a long barrow, 2018. *Address:* The School House, Church Lane, Sturminster Newton, Dorset DT10 1DH. *T:* (01258) 473491.

**SCOBLE, Malcolm John,** PhD, DSc; Scientific Associate, Department of Life Sciences (formerly Entomology Department), Natural History Museum, since 2010 (Keeper of Entomology, 2006–10); *b* Buckfastleigh, Devon, 6 July 1950; *s* of George Luis Evan, (Dick), Scoble and Edith Maud, (Babs), Scoble; *m* 1982, Theresa Jean Smuts. *Educ:* Kelly Coll., Tavistock; Portsmouth Poly. (BSc Zool., London ext., 1972; MPhil 1974); Rhodes Univ. (PhD 1982); DSc London 2002. MRSB (MIBiol 1982); CBiol 1982; FLS 1995; FRES 1987. Res. Asst, Portsmouth Poly., 1972–74; Professional Officer, then Sen. Professional Officer in Entomol., Transvaal Mus., Pretoria, 1975–82; Asst Curator/Actg Curator, Hope Entomological Collections, University Mus., Univ. of Oxford, 1982–85; Res. Entomologist, 1985–2002, Associate Keeper, 2002–06, Natural Hist. Mus. Member Council: Systematics Assoc., 1986–89; Brit. Entomol and Natural Hist. Soc., 1997–98 (Vice Pres., 1994–95, 1996–97; Pres., 1995–96); Mem. Council, 1995–98, 2007–, Zoological Sec., 2009–12, Scientific Sec., 2012–, Linnean Soc. of London (Vice-Pres., 1997–98, 2009–10, 2011–12, 2013–14, 2015–16, 2016–17, 2017–18, 2018–19). Karl Jordan Medal, Amer. Lepidopterists' Soc., 2002. *Publications:* The Lepidoptera: form, function and diversity, 1992; (ed) A taxonomic catalogue to the Geometridae of the world (Insecta: Lepidoptera), 1999; (ed) ENHSIN: the European natural history specimen information network, 2003; (ed jtly) Digital Imaging of Biological Type Specimens: a manual of best practice, 2005; articles in learned jls on Lepidoptera taxonomy (incl. Linnaeus's butterflies), natural history museum resources and information access, biodiversity informatics, esp. internet-based taxonomy. *Recreations:* natural history, music, theatre, Devon. *Address:* Holybrook, Grange Road, Buckfast, Buckfastleigh, Devon TQ11 0EH. *T:* (01364) 643274. *E:* m.scoble@nhm.ac.uk.

**SCOLDING, Fiona Kate;** QC 2017; a Deputy District Judge, since 2010; a Judge of the Upper Tribunal, since 2018; *b* London, 8 March 1973; *d* of Peter and Pamela Scolding; *m* 2002, James Anderson; one *d*. *Educ:* Coopers' Co. Coborn Sch.; Downing Coll., Cambridge (BA Hist. 1994); City Univ. (DipLaw 1995; BVC 1996). Called to the Bar, Gray's Inn, 1996; in practice as barrister, specialising in public and administrative law, 1996–. Gov., Winton Primary Sch., 2005–15. Mem., London Library. *Publications:* (contrib.) Health and Social Care Handbook, 2006; (contrib.) NHS and the Law, 2018. *Recreations:* singing show tunes, learning languages, theatre, ballet, cinema, community activism, decluttering. *Address:* Landmark Chambers, 180 Fleet Street, EC4A 2HG. *T:* (020) 7430 1221. *E:* fscolding@landmarkchambers.co.uk.

**SCOLES, Prof. Giacinto,** FRS 1997; Donner Professor of Science, Princeton University, 1987–2008, now Emeritus; Professor of Biophysics and Condensed Matter, International School for Advanced Studies, Trieste, since 2004; Distinguished Adjunct Professor of Biology, Temple University, Philadelphia, since 2008; *b* 2 April 1935; *m* 1964, Giok-Lan Lim; one *d*. *Educ:* Univ. of Genova (DChem 1959; Libera docenza 1968). Asst Prof., 1960–61 and 1964–68, Associate Prof., 1968–71, Physics Dept, Univ. of Genova; Res. Associate, Kamerlingh-Onnes Lab., Univ. of Leiden, 1961–64; Prof. of Chemistry and Physics, Univ. of Waterloo, Canada, 1971–86. Sen. Consultant for Nanotechnol., UNIDO Internat. Center for Sci. and High Technol., Trieste. Hon. DPhys Genova, 1996; Hon. DSc Waterloo, Canada, 2000. Peter Debye Award, ACS, 2002; Benjamin Franklin Medal, Franklin Inst., 2006. *Publications:* Atomic and Molecular Beam Methods, vol. 1, 1988, vol. 2, 1992; The Chemical Physics of Atomic and Molecular Clusters, 1990; contribs to learned jls. *Address:* Biology Department, Temple University, Biology Life Sciences Building, Room 449A, N 12th Street, Philadelphia, PA 19122, USA; International School for Advanced Studies, Via Bonomea 265, Trieste 34136, Italy.

**SCOONES, Andrew Geoffry;** Director, Ngenuity Ltd, since 2013; *b* Shrewsbury, 1 Oct. 1959; *s* of Kenneth Geoffry Scoones and Anne Elizabeth Scoones; *m* 1990, Kwee; one *s* one *d*. *Educ:* Univ. of Leeds (BA Hons Eng. and French); Birkbeck Coll., London (MSc Computer Sci.). Manager, Building Centre Trust, 1994–2013; Dir, Building Centre, 2005–13. Dir, Italian Wine Club. Hon. FRIBA 2008. *Publications:* Renewable Energy in the Built Environment, 2003; Prefabulous Homes, 2005. *Recreations:* tennis, Italian wine, gardening.

**SCOPELITIS, Anastase;** Ambassador Emeritus, Greece, since 2012; *b* Port Said, 1944; *s* of late Evangelos Scopelitis and Rhodesia Scopelitis (*née* Antoniadis); *m* 1971, Hélène Lolos; three *s*. *Educ:* Univ. of Athens (Master in Politics and Econs). Lectr in Public Finance, Univ. of Athens, 1969–71; Ministry of Foreign Affairs: Attaché, 1971; Third Sec., Cairo, 1973; Second Sec., 1976–79, First Sec., 1979, London; Dep. Hd of Mission, The Hague, 1980; First Counsellor, 1982; First Counsellor, 1985; Hd, EC Ext. Relns and EC New Policies Units, 1987; European Correspondent and Actg Dir of European Political Cooperation, 1989; Minister Plenipotentiary 2nd Cl. and Dir of European Political Cooperation, 1991; Minister and Dep. Hd of Mission, London, 1993, Minister Plenipotentiary 1st Cl., 1994; Ambassador to Denmark, 1996–99; Dir Gen. for Political Affairs and Political Dir, 1999, promoted to Ambassador, 2001; Sec. Gen., 2002–03; Ambassador to Court of St James's and Permanent Rep. to IMO, 2003–06; Special Advr to Minister of Foreign Affairs, Greece, 2006–12. Hd, Working Gp for 2009 Greek Chair of Global Forum on Migration and Develt, Athens, 2008–10. Grand Cross, Order of Phoenix (Greece), 2003. Commander: Order of Merit (Egypt), 1976; Order of Oranje-Nassau (Netherlands), 1987; Grand Cross: Order of White Star (Estonia), 1999; Order of Dannebrog (Denmark), 1999; Order of Merit (Germany), 2001; Order of Leopold II (Belgium), 2001; Order of Infante Dom Henrique (Portugal), 2002; Order of Merit (Italy), 2003; Order of Merit (Cyprus), 2003; Grand Cross, Order of Phoenix (Greece), 2003. *Address:* 6 Panagouli Street, 190 09 Rafina, Greece.

**SCOREY, David William John;** QC 2015; *b* Manchester, 27 Oct. 1973; *m* 2004, Katie Renwick; two *s* one *d*. *Educ:* St John's Coll., Oxford (BA Juris.); Leiden Univ. (LLM EU Law). Called to the Bar, Lincoln's Inn, 1997, Bencher, 2018; Mem., Essex Court Chambers, in practice at commercial and revenue bars, 1998–. Consultant Ed., De Voil Indirect Tax Intelligence, 2015–. *Publications:* (with Tim Eicke) Human Rights Damages, 2001; (jtly) The Bermuda Form: interpretation and dispute resolution of excess liability insurance, 2011. *Recreations:* wine, reading. *Address:* Essex Court Chambers, 24 Lincoln's Inn Fields, WC2A 3EG. *T:* (020) 7813 8000, *Fax:* (020) 7813 8080. *E:* dscorey@essexcourt.com. *Club:* Garrick.

**SCORSESE, Martin;** American film director; *b* 17 Nov. 1942; *s* of Charles Scorsese and Catherine (*née* Cappa); *m* 1st, 1965, Laraine Marie Brennan (marr. diss.); one *d*; 2nd, Julia Cameron (marr. diss.); one *d*; 3rd, 1979, Isabella Rosellini (marr. diss. 1983); 4th, 1985, Barbara DeFina; *m* 1999, Helen Morris; one *d*. *Educ:* Univ. of New York (BS 1964; MA 1966). Faculty Asst, 1963–66, Lectr, 1968–70, Dept of Film, Univ. of New York; dir and writer of documentaries, incl. No Direction Home - Bob Dylan, 2005; George Harrison: living in the material world, 2011; Rolling Thunder Revue: a Bob Dylan story, 2019. Films include: Who's That Knocking At My Door? (also writer), 1968; Mean Streets (also co-writer), 1973; Alice Doesn't Live Here Any More, 1974; Taxi Driver (Palme d'Or, Cannes Film Fest.), 1976; New York, New York, 1977; The Last Waltz (also actor), 1978; Raging Bull, 1980; After Hours, 1985 (Best Dir Award, Cannes Film Fest., 1986); The Color of Money, 1986; acted in 'Round Midnight, 1986; The Last Temptation of Christ, 1988; Goodfellas, 1990; Cape Fear, 1992; The Age of Innocence, 1993; Bringing out the Dead, 1999; Gangs of New York, 2002; The Aviator, 2005; The Departed, 2006 (Acad. Award, Best Dir, 2007); Shine a Light, 2008; Shutter Island, 2010; Hugo, 2011; The Wolf of Wall Street, 2014; Silence, 2017; The Irishman (also prod.), 2019; producer: Mad Dog and Glory, 1993; Naked in New York, 1994; Casino, 1996; Kundun, 1998; The Young Victoria, 2009; The Ciambra, 2017; The Snowman, 2017; Abundant Acreage Available, 2018; Happy as Lazaro, 2018; Diane, 2019. Co-Prod. and Co-Dir, TV series, Vinyl, 2016. Fellow, BAFTA, 2012.

**SCOTFORD, Garth Barrie,** OBE 1994; QFSM 1982; County Manager, Berkshire County Council, 1993–96; *b* 28 Oct. 1943; *s* of Albert Edward Scotford and Louisa Emily Jane Scotford (*née* Leach); *m* 1st, 1964, Gillian Avril Patricia Constable (*d* 1999); one *s* two *d*; 2nd, 2000, Caroline Susan James. *Educ:* Reading Grammar Sch. Joined Fire Service, 1961: served in Reading, Liverpool, Hants and Gtr Manchester; Chief Fire Officer, Berks, 1984–93, retd. FIFireE 1977 (Pres., 1985). *Recreations:* opera, bridge. *Address:* 34 Napier Street, Nedlands, WA 6009, Australia. *T:* (8) 93866738.
*See also* J. E. Scotford.

**SCOTFORD, John Edward,** CBE 1993; Treasurer, Hampshire County Council, 1983–97; *b* 15 Aug. 1939; *s* of Albert and Louisa Scotford; *m* 1st, 1962, Marjorie Clare Wells (marr. diss. 2001); one *s*; 2nd, 2001, Alison Cawley. *Educ:* Reading Grammar Sch. CPFA. Reading County Borough Council, 1955–62; Coventry County Borough Council, 1962–65; Hampshire CC, 1965–97; Dep. County Treasurer, 1977–83. Public Works Loan Comr, 1992–96. Pres., CIPFA, 1996–97. Freeman, City of London, 1995. *Address:* Manor House Barn, Petherton Park, North Petherton, Bridgwater, Somerset TA7 0DT.
*See also* G. B. Scotford.

**SCOTHERN, Mark Francis;** freelance psychotherapist, since 2010; *b* 2 July 1960; *s* of late Norman Scothern and of Joan Scothern; *m* 1998, Caroline Fiske. *Educ:* Austin Friars Sch., Carlisle; MBA Warwick Univ. Business Sch., 2000. Co-ordinator, Thamesdown Housing Link, 1984–88; Policy Officer, CHAR (Housing Campaign for Single People), 1988–91; Dir, Crisis (formerly Crisis at Christmas), 1991–96; Develt Man., Shelter, 1997–98; Associate, Rho Delta, mgt consultancy, 1998–99; Director: Derby CVS, 1999–2005; Cornwall Foundn of Promise, 2006–07; Psychotherapist: Cornwall PCT, 2007–08; Outlook South West, 2008–10. *Recreations:* film, contemporary music, food, biographies, cycling.

**SCOTLAND OF ASTHAL,** Baroness *cr* 1997 (Life Peer), of Asthal in the co. of Oxfordshire; **Patricia Janet Scotland;** PC 1991; Commonwealth Secretary-General, since 2016; *b* 19 Aug. 1955; *m* 1985, Richard Mawhinney; two *s*. *Educ:* London Univ. (LLB). Called to the Bar, Middle Temple, 1977, Bencher, 1997; Member: Antigua and Barbuda Bar; Dominica Bar; a Recorder, 2000. Parly Under-Sec. of State, FCO, 1999–2001; Parly Sec., LCD, 2001–03; Minister of State (Minister for Criminal Justice System and Law Reform, subseq. for Criminal Justice and Offender Mgt), Home Office, 2003–07; Attorney General, 2007–10; Shadow Attorney Gen., 2010–11. Former Mem., Commn for Racial Equality; Mem., Millennium Commn, 1994–99; Chm., National Catholic Safeguarding Commn, 2011–12. Chancellor, Univ. of Greenwich, 2014–19. Alderman, Bishopsgate Ward, City of London, 2015–. *Address:* Commonwealth Secretariat, Marlborough House, Pall Mall, SW1Y 5HX.

**SCOTLAND, Alastair Duncan,** OBE 2012; FRCSE, FRCP, FRCGP, FFPH; Medical Director, National Clinical Assessment Service, 2005–11; *b* 19 Aug. 1951; *s* of James Scotland and Jean (*née* Cowan). *Educ:* Glasgow High Sch.; Aberdeen Grammar Sch.; Aberdeen Univ. (MB ChB 1975). FRCSE 1980; MFPHM 1987, FFPH (FFPHM 1993); FRCP 1999; FRCGP 2008. House Surgeon/House Physician, Aberdeen Royal Infirmary, 1975–76; training prog. in surgery specialising in plastic surgery, Aberdeen, Inverness, Dundee and Perth Hosps, 1976–83; training prog. in public health medicine, SE and NW Thames RHAs, 1983–88; Consultant in Public Health Medicine, then Regl MO, NE Thames RHA, 1988–94; Trust Unit Med. Dir, N Thames RHA, 1994–96; Dir of Med. Educn and Res. and Postgrad. Clinical Tutor, Chelsea and Westminster Hosp., 1996–2001; Chief Exec. and Med. Dir, Nat. Clin. Assessment Authy, NHS, 2001–05. Associate Consultant, Edgecumbe Gp, Bristol, 2011–. Hon. Senior Lecturer in Public Health Medicine: ICSM, 2000–01; KCL Sch. of Medicine (formerly GKT), 2001–; Vis. Prof. in Public Health, KCL Sch. of Medicine (formerly GKT), 2004–. Advr, Med. Educn, Training and Staffing, London Implementation Gp, 1993–95; Chairman: Clinical Disputes Forum for England and Wales, 1996–2002; Health of Health Professional Staff Wkg Gp, 2007–10; Member: Ministerial Gp on Jun. Doctors' Hours of Work, 1990–95; Jt Cttee, Funding of Postgrad. Med. and Dental Educn in NHS, 1991–96; CMO's Cttee on Specialist Med. Training, 1992–95; Jt Cttee, NHS Consultant Appointment Procedures, 1992–94. FRSocMed 1981. FRSA 1992. Member Editorial Boards: Hospital Medicine, 1989–2008; Clinical Risk, 2000–12. *Publications:* (with L. Swift) Disciplining and Dismissing Doctors in the NHS, 1995; (ed) Clinical Governance One Year On, 2000;

(contrib.) Clinical Negligence, 4th edn 2008; (contrib) The Intoxication of Power, 2016; orig. papers on medical professional and public health issues. *Recreations:* theatre, music, antique conservation and restoration. *Address:* Cobham, Surrey. *Club:* Reform.

**SCOTT**; *see* Hepburne Scott, family name of Lord Polwarth.

**SCOTT**; *see* Maxwell Scott and Maxwell-Scott.

**SCOTT**; *see* Montagu Douglas Scott, family name of Duke of Buccleuch.

**SCOTT**; *see* Stedman-Scott.

**SCOTT**, family name of **Earl of Eldon, Baron Scott of Foscote** and **Baroness Scott of Needham Market**.

**SCOTT OF BYBROOK**, Baroness *cr* 2015 (Life Peer), of Upper Wraxall in the County of Wiltshire; **Jane Antoinette Scott**, OBE 2010; Member (C) and Leader, Wiltshire Council, since 2009. *Educ:* Lancs Coll. of Agric. Mem. (C), Wilts CC, 1997–2009 (Leader, 2003–09). *Address:* House of Lords, SW1A 0PW.

**SCOTT** *cr* 2000 (Life Peer), of Foscote in the county of Buckinghamshire; **Richard Rashleigh Folliott Scott**, Kt 1983; PC 1991; a Lord of Appeal in Ordinary, 2000–09; Judge, 2003–11, Justice, 2011–13, Qatar Civil and Commercial Court; *b* Dehra Dun, India, 2 Oct. 1934; *s* of Lt-Col C. W. F. Scott, 2/9th Gurkha Rifles and Katharine Scott (*née* Rashleigh); *m* 1959, Rima Elisa, *d* of Salvador Ripoll and Blanca Korsi de Ripoll, Panama City; two *s* two *d*. *Educ:* Michaelhouse Sch., Natal; Univ. of Cape Town (BA); Trinity Coll., Cambridge (BA Hons; LLB). Bigelow Fellow, Univ. of Chicago, 1958–59. Called to Bar, Inner Temple, 1959, Bencher, 1981. In practice, Chancery Bar, 1960–83; QC 1975; Attorney Gen., 1980–83, Vice-Chancellor, 1987–91, Duchy and County Palatine of Lancaster; Judge of the High Court of Justice, Chancery Div., 1983–91; a Lord Justice of Appeal, 1991–2000; Vice-Chancellor, Supreme Court, 1994–2000; Head of Civil Justice, 1995–2000; a non-permanent Judge, Hong Kong Court of Final Appeal, 2003–11. Inquiry into defence related exports to Iraq and related prosecutions, 1992–96. Chm. of the Bar, 1982–83 (Vice-Chm., 1981–82). Editor-in-Chief, Supreme Court Practice, 1996–2000. Mem., H of L, 2000–16; Member, House of Lords Select Committee: on EU, 2002–05 (Chm., Sub-Cttee E (Law and Instns), 2009–14); for Privileges, 2010–14; on Merits of Statutory Instruments, 2009–14. Hon. Member: Amer. Bar Assoc., 1983; Canadian Bar Assoc., 1993; Soc. of Legal Scholars, 2005; Amer. Coll. of Trial Lawyers, 2006. Hon. LLD: Birmingham, 1996; Buckingham, 1999. *Publications:* articles in legal jls. *Recreations:* horse riding, hunting (Chm., Grafton Hunt, 1989–94, 2011–14), tennis, bridge, twelve grandchildren, formerly Rugby (Cambridge Blue, 1957). *Club:* Hawks (Cambridge).

**SCOTT OF NEEDHAM MARKET**, Baroness *cr* 2000 (Life Peer), of Needham Market in the co. of Suffolk; **Rosalind Carol Scott**; President, Liberal Democrat Party, 2009–10; *b* 10 Aug. 1957; *d* of Kenneth Vincent and Carol Jane Leadbeater; *m* 1st (marr. diss.); one *s* one *d*; 2nd, 2008, Mark Valladares. *Educ:* Whitby Grammar Sch.; Univ. of East Anglia. Member (Lib Dem) Mid Suffolk DC, 1991–94; Suffolk CC, 1993–2005 (Gp Leader, 1997–2000). Member: UK delegn to EU Cttee of the Regions, 1998–2002; Commn for Integrated Transport, 2001–07. Chm., Transport Cttee, LGA, 2002–04 (Vice-Chair, 1996–2002). Mem., H of L Appts Commn, 2010–. Contested (Lib Dem) Eastern Region, EP elecns, 1999. Non-executive Director: Entrust, 2000–07; Anglia TV, 2002–05; Lloyds Register, 2004–08. Chm., England Volunteering Develt Council, 2011; Mem. Bd, Harwich Haven Authy, 2013. *Recreations:* walking, travel, genealogy. *Address:* House of Lords, SW1A 0PW.

**SCOTT, Hon. Lady; Margaret Elizabeth Scott;** a Senator of the College of Justice in Scotland, since 2012; partner, Frank Richard Crowe, *qv*; one *s*. *Educ:* Univ. of Edinburgh (LLB Hons); Univ. of Strathclyde (DipLP). Admitted: solicitor, 1989; to Faculty of Advocates, 1991; QC (Scot.) 2002; pt-time Sheriff, 2003–12. *Address:* Court of Session, Parliament House, Parliament Square, Edinburgh EH1 1RQ.

**SCOTT, Alan James**, CVO 1986; CBE 1982; Governor, Cayman Islands, 1987–92; *b* 14 Jan. 1934; *er s* of Rev. Harold James Scott and Mary Phyllis Barbara Scott; *m* 1st, 1958, Mary Elizabeth Ireland (*d* 1969); one *s* two *d*; 2nd, 1971, Joan Hall; one step *s* two step *d*. *Educ:* King's Sch., Ely; Selwyn Coll., Cambridge. Suffolk Regt, Italy and Germany, 1952–54. HMOCS, 1958–87: Fiji: Dist Officer, 1958; Estabts Officer, 1960; Registry of Univ. of S Pacific, 1968; Controller, Organisation and Estabts, 1969; Hong Kong: Asst Financial Sec., 1971; Prin. Asst Financial Sec., 1972; Sec. for CS, 1973; MLC, 1976–85; Sec. for Housing, and Chm. Hong Kong Housing Authy, 1977; Sec. for Information, 1980; Sec. for Transport, 1982; Dep. Chief Sec., 1985–87. Vice. later Chm., Home Farm Residents Assoc., 2013–. President: Fiji AAA, 1964–69; Hong Kong AAA, 1978–87. Chm., Château de Bon Vivant, 1983–87; Chevalier, Confrérie des Chevaliers de Tastevin, 1989. Hon. Kentucky Col, 1990. *Recreations:* Western history, writing, rueing the sad decline of GB. *Address:* 6 Home Farm, Iwerne Minster, Dorset DT11 8LB.

**SCOTT, Hon. Alexander;** *see* Scott, Hon. W. A.

**SCOTT, Allan;** *see* Shiach, A. G.

**SCOTT, Prof. Andrew**, DPhil; Professor of Economics, London Business School, since 2005; Fellow, All Souls College, Oxford, 2011–17; *b* London, 12 May 1965; *s* of John Scott and Ray Scott (*née* Palmer); two *s* one *d*. *Educ:* Trinity Coll., Oxford (BA 1987); London Sch. of Econs and Pol Sci. (MSc 1991); All Souls Coll., Oxford (DPhil 1994). Fellow, All Souls Coll., Oxford, 1991–2005; Res. Officer, LSE, 1991–94; Lectr, Oxford Univ., 1994–96; Associate Prof. of Econs, 1996–2005, Dep. Dean, 2010–15, London Business Sch. Vis. Asst Prof., Harvard Univ., 1996. Ed., Econ. Jl, 2003–10. Non-exec. Dir, FSA, 2009–13. Chm., Longevity Forum, 2018–. Trustee, NIESR, 2018–. *Publications:* (with Ramon Marimon) Computational Methods for Dynamic Economies, 1999; (with David Miles) Macroeconomics, 2001, 3rd edn 2012; (with Lynda Gratton) The Hundred Year Life: living and working in an age of longevity, 2016. *Recreations:* reading, idle contemplation, Tottenham Hotspur FC. *Address:* Department of Economics, London Business School, Sussex Place, Regents Park, NW1 4SA. *T:* (020) 7000 8416. *E:* ascott@london.edu.

**SCOTT, Andrew John**, CBE 2006; FMA; CEng; Director, National Railway Museum, 1994–2009; Acting Director, National Museum of Science and Industry, 2009–10; *b* 3 June 1949; *s* of late Cyril John Scott and Gertrude Ethel (*née* Miller); *m* 1972, Margaret Anne Benyon, JP, MA. *Educ:* Bablake Sch., Coventry; Univ. of Newcastle upon Tyne (BSc Civil Engrg 1970; MSc Mining Engrg 1971). CEng, MICE 1976. AMA 1987, FMA 1993. Practising civil engr, 1972–84; Actg Dir, W Yorks Transport Mus., 1984–86; Keeper of Technol., Bradford City Museums, 1986–87; Dir, London Transport Mus., 1988–94. Member: North Eastern Locomotive Preservation Gp, 1967– (Pres., 2009–); Bd, N Yorks Moors Historical Railway Trust, 2010– (Vice Chm., 2016–); Bd, N Yorks Moors Nat. Park Authy, 2012–; Council Member: Assoc. of Ind. Museums, 1991–2003; Internat. Assoc. of Transport Museums, 1992–2011 (Vice Pres., 1999–2011); Vice Chairman: Assoc. of British Transport and Engrg Museums, 1992–; Ffestiniog Railway Heritage Ltd, 2010–18. Dir, York Tourism Bureau, 1995–2008 (Chm., 1999–2008). Trustee: Friends of Nat. Railway Mus., 1994–; York Civic Trust, 2013– (Chm., 2015–). Pres., London Underground Railway Soc., 1995–96. *Publications:* North Eastern Renaissance, 1991; (with C. Divall) Making Histories in Transport Museums, 2001; contrib. to railway and museological jls and books. *Recreations:* travel, railways, ecclesiastical architecture. *Address:* 14 New Walk Terrace, York YO10 4BG.

**SCOTT, Anthony Douglas**, TD 1972; chartered accountant in public practice, 1988–2005; *b* 6 Nov. 1933; *o s* of Douglas Ernest and Mary Gladys Scott; *m* 1962, Irene Robson; one *s* one *d*. *Educ:* Gateshead Central Technical Secondary Sch. Articled to Middleton & Middleton, also J. Stanley Armstrong, Chartered Accountants, Newcastle upon Tyne, 1952–57; National Service, WO Selection Bd, 1957–59; Accountant with Commercial Plastics Ltd, 1959; joined ICI Ltd (Agricl Div), 1961; seconded by ICI to Hargreaves Fertilisers Ltd, as Chief Accountant, 1966; ICI Ltd (Nobel Div.) as Asst Chief Acct, 1970; seconded by ICI to MoD as Dir-Gen. Internal Audit, 1972–74. Dir of Consumer Credit, Office of Fair Trading, 1974–80. Chief Exec. and Dir, CoSIRA, 1981–88. Chm., Teesside Soc. of Chartered Accts, 1969–70; Mem. Cttee, London Chartered Accountants, 1974–79. Chm., Jt Working Party on Students' Societies (ICAE&W), 1979–80. Mem., Smaller Firms Council, CBI, 1983–86. TA (17th (later 4th) Bn Para. Regt (9 DLI) TA, 44 Para. Bde (TA) and 6th (V) Bn Royal Anglian Regt), 1959–91, Major. *Publications:* Accountants Digests on Consumer Credit Act 1974, 1980; Accountants Digest on Estate Agents Act 1979, 1982. *Recreations:* antiquary, walking, gardening. *Address:* 9 The Foresters, Harpenden, Herts AL5 2FB. *T:* (01582) 763067.

**SCOTT, Brough;** *see* Scott, J. B.

**SCOTT, Charles Thomas**, FCA; Chairman, William Hill, 2004–10; *b* 22 Feb. 1949. FCA 1979. Binder Hamlyn, 1967–72; ITEL Internat. Corp., 1972–77; IMS Internat. Inc., 1978–89; Saatchi & Saatchi Co. plc, later Cordiant plc, 1990–97: Chief Exec., 1993–95; Chm., 1995–97; Chm., Cordiant Communications Group plc, 1997–2003. *Recreations:* golf, tennis, sport in general.

**SCOTT, Christina Martha Elena;** Minister and Deputy Head of Mission, Beijing, China, since 2018; *b* London; *d* of Preb. Allan G. Scott and Elena Delcheva-Scott. *Educ:* Francis Holland Sch., Clarence Gate; Christ Church, Oxford (BA (Hons) PPE). Various graduate develt posts with Civil Service, 1996–99; Office of the Dir Gen., Envmt, EC, 1999–2000; Hd, EU Enlargement Team, DfT, 2000–01; Asst Dir, Eur. Secretariat, Cabinet Office, 2001–03; Asst Dir, Corporate and Private Finance Team, HM Treasury, 2003–04; Dep. Dir, West Midlands and SW Div., 2004–05, Principal Private Sec. to Sec. of State, 2005–06, DfT; Private Sec. to the Prime Minister, 10 Downing St, 2006–09; Dir, Civil Contingencies Secretariat, Cabinet Office, 2009–13; Gov., Anguilla, 2013–17. *Recreations:* cycling along canal paths, good food with friends, opera, travel, cooking. *Address:* c/o Foreign and Commonwealth Office, King Charles Street, SW1A 2AH.

**SCOTT, Sir Christopher James**, 4th Bt *cr* 1909 of Yews, Undermillbeck, Cumbria; *b* 16 Jan. 1955; *s* of Sir Oliver Christopher Anderson Scott, 3rd Bt and Phoebe Ann Scott (*née* Tolhurst); S father, 2016; *m* 1988, Emma Jane, *o d* of Michael Boxhall; two *s* two *d*. *Educ:* Bryanston Sch.; Trinity Coll., Cambridge (BA 1976); INSEAD. *Recreations:* singing, travelling. *Heir: s* Edward James Saim Scott, *b* 25 Oct. 1990.

**SCOTT, Prof. Clive**, DPhil; FBA 1994; Professor of European Literature, University of East Anglia, 1991–2007, now Emeritus; *b* 13 Nov. 1943; *s* of Jesse Scott and Nesta Vera Scott (*née* Morton); *m* 1st, 1965, Elizabeth Anne (*née* Drabble) (marr. diss.); one *s* one *d*; 2nd, 1984, Marie-Noëlle Guillot; two *s*. *Educ:* St John's Coll., Oxford (MA, MPhil, DPhil). University of East Anglia: Asst Lectr, 1967–70; Lectr, 1970–88; Reader, 1988–91; Hd, Sch. of Literature and Creative Writing, 2004–05. Clark Lectr, Trinity Coll., Cambridge, 2010. Pres., Modern Humanities Res. Assoc., 2014. Officier, Ordre des Palmes Académiques (France), 2008. *Publications:* French Verse-Art: a study, 1980; Anthologie Eluard, 1983; A Question of Syllables: essays in nineteenth-century French verse, 1986; The Riches of Rhyme: studies in French verse, 1988; Vers Libre: the emergence of free verse in France 1886–1914, 1990; Reading the Rhythm: the poetics of French free verse 1910–1930, 1993; The Poetics of French Verse: studies in reading, 1998; The Spoken Image: photography and language, 1999; Translating Baudelaire, 2000; Channel Crossings: French and English poetry in dialogue 1550–2000, 2002 (R. H. Gapper Book Prize, Soc. for French Studies, 2004); Translating Rimbaud's Illuminations, 2006; Street Photography: from Atget to Cartier-Bresson, 2007; Translating the Perception of Text: literary translation and phenomenology, 2012 (R. H. Gapper Book Prize Commendation, Soc. for French Studies, 2013); Literary Translation and the Rediscovery of Reading, 2012; Translating Apollinaire, 2014; The Work of Literary Translation, 2018. *Address:* School of Literature, Drama and Creative Writing, University of East Anglia, Norwich NR4 7TJ.

**SCOTT, Craig Alexander Leslie;** QC (Scot.) 2012; Sheriff Principal of Glasgow and Strathkelvin, 2011–16; *b* Edinburgh, 10 May 1961; *s* of Leslie Scott and Evelyn Scott (*née* Thomson); *m* 1987, Elizabeth Nicola Annand (*d* 2013); two *s* one *d*. *Educ:* Royal High Prep. Sch., Edinburgh; George Watson's Coll., Edinburgh; Aberdeen Univ. (LLB, DipLP). Trainee and Qualified Asst, Biggart, Baillie & Gifford, WS, 1982–85; pupil of Malcolm G. Thomson and Donald R. Findlay, 1985–86; admitted Faculty of Advocates, 1986; Standing Jun. Counsel, Scottish Office Envmt Dept, 1993–94 and 1997–99; Advocate Depute, 1994–97; Temp. Sheriff, 1997–99; Sheriff of Glasgow and Strathkelvin, 1999–2011; Vice Pres., Sheriff Appeal Court, 2015–16. *Recreations:* golf, walking, music. *Clubs:* New (Edinburgh); Luffness New Golf.

**SCOTT, Prof. Dana Stewart**, FBA 1976; Hillman University Professor of Computer Science, Philosophy and Mathematical Logic, Carnegie Mellon University, 1981–2003, now Emeritus; *b* Berkeley, Calif, 11 Oct. 1932; *m* 1959, Irene Schreier; one *d*. *Educ:* Univ. of Calif, Berkeley (BA 1954); Princeton Univ. (PhD 1958). Instructor, Univ. of Chicago, 1958–60; Asst Prof., Univ. of Calif, Berkeley, 1960–63; Associate Prof. and Prof., Stanford Univ., 1963–69; Prof., Princeton, 1969–72; Prof. of Mathematical Logic, Oxford Univ., 1972–81. Visiting Professor: Amsterdam, 1968–69; Linz, 1992–93; Institut Mittag-Leffler, Sweden, 2001; Vis. Scholar, Univ. of Calif, Berkeley, 2004–. Guggenheim Fellow, 1978–79; Humboldt Stiftung Sen. Vis. Scientist, Munich, 2003. Winchester Lectr, Univ. of Oxford, 2010. Member: US Nat. Acad. of Scis, 1988; Amer. Assoc. for Advancement of Sci.; Amer. Acad. of Arts and Scis; Amer. Math. Soc.; Assoc. for Computing Machinery; Finnish Acad. of Scis and Letters; NY Acad. of Scis; MAE. Hon. Fellow, Merton Coll., Oxford, 2014. Hon. Dr: Rijksuniversiteit Utrecht, 1986; Tech. Univ. of Darmstadt, 1995; Edinburgh, 1995; Ljubljana, 2003; St Andrews, 2014. Leny P. Steele Prize, Amer. Math. Soc., 1972; Harold Pender Award, Univ. of Pennsylvania, 1990; Rolf Schock Prize in Logic and Philosophy, Royal Acad. of Scis, 1997; Bolzano Medal for Merit, Czech Acad. of Scis, 2001; Gold Medal, Sobolev Inst. of Maths, 2009. *Publications:* papers on logic and mathematics in technical jls. *Address:* 1149 Shattuck Avenue, Berkeley, CA 94707–2609, USA.

**SCOTT, David Gordon Islay**, MD; FRCP, FRCPE; Consultant Rheumatologist, Norfolk and Norwich University Hospital NHS Trust, 1988–2011, now Honorary Consultant; *b* Elgin, 8 July 1948; *s* of late Gordon Islay Scott and Mora Joan Scott (*née* Craig); *m* 1976, Daphne Bellworthy, (Dee); three *s*. *Educ*: Trinity Coll., Glenalmond; Univ. of Bristol Med. Sch. (MB ChB 1973; MD 1982). MRCP 1977, FRCP 1994; FRCPE 2007. Lectr in Rheumatol., Univ. of Birmingham, 1981–88. Hon. Sen. Lectr in Rheumatol., Royal London Hosp. Med. Sch., 1988–96; Hon. Sen. Lectr in Rheumatol., 1995–98, Hon. Prof., Norwich Medical Sch. (formerly Sch. of Medicine, Health Policy and Practice), 1998–, UEA. Pres., British Soc. for Rheumatol., 2002–04; Chief Med. Advr, Nat. Rheumatoid Arthritis Soc., 2007–15 (Patron, 2016–); Patient Involvement Officer, RCP, 2007–11; Clinical Dir, Norfolk and Suffolk Comp. Local Res. Network, 2007–11; Secondary Care Rep., Gt Yarmouth and Waveney CCG, 2012–17. Non-exec. Dir, James Paget Univ. Hosps NHS Foundn Trust, 2017– (Sen. Ind. Dir, 2019–). *Publications*: contrib. chapters in medical textbooks on clinical aspects, epidemiology and outcome of systemic vasculitis; over 300 reviews, editorials and papers. *Recreations*: hockey—(ex) player, now watching, running—marathons/half marathons (Great North Run x 14 so far), now Park Runs! *Address*: 443 Unthank Road, Norwich, Norfolk NR4 7QN. *T*: (01603) 259389. *E*: dscott443@btinternet.com.

**SCOTT, David Maxwell**, FREng; FRSE; Director, Engineering Excellence Group, Laing O'Rourke, since 2012; *b* Glasgow, 11 March 1956; *s* of Archibald and Grietje Scott; *m* 1984, Marion Mapstone; two *c*. *Educ*: Bearsden Acad.; Edinburgh Univ. (BSc 1977). FREng 2014. Engr, Arup Hong Kong, 1984–98; Associate Dir, then Dir, Arup NY, 1998–2009; Americas Building Practice Leader, Arup, 2010–12. Chm., Council on Tall Buildings and Urban Habitat, 2006–09. FRSE 2010. Hon. AIA 2009. *Recreations*: walking, sailing, bad golf, theatre, food, fun and family. *Address*: Laing O'Rourke, Bridge Place 1 & 2, Anchor Boulevard, Crossways, Dartford, Kent DA2 6SN. *T*: 07771 885996. *E*: davidscott@laingorourke.com. *Club*: Caledonian.

**SCOTT, Sir David (Richard Alexander)**, Kt 2013; CBE 2006; FCA; business consultant; Chief Executive, Digital UK (formerly SwitchCo) Ltd, 2008–13 (Director, 2005–13); *b* 25 Aug. 1954; *s* of R. I. M. Scott, OBE and Daphne Scott (*née* Alexander); *m* 1981, Moy Barraclough; one *s* one *d*. *Educ*: Wellington Coll. FCA 1979. Chartered Accountant, Peat Marwick Mitchell & Co., 1972–81; Channel Four Television, subseq. Channel Four Television Corporation: Controller of Finance, 1981–88; Dir of Finance, 1988–97; Man. Dir, 1997–2005; Dep. Chief Exec., 2002–05; Consultant, 2005–08. Dir, Digital Television Gp Ltd, 2006–19. FRTS 2004. *Recreations*: sailing, walking, film, opera, bridge, ballet. *Clubs*: Boodle's; Guards' Polo, Royal Thames Yacht.

**SCOTT, Dermot;** *see* Scott, W. D.

**SCOTT, Douglas Keith, (Doug Scott)**, CBE 1994; *b* Nottingham, 29 May 1941; *s* of George Douglas Scott and Edith Joyce Scott; *m* 1st, 1962, Janice Elaine Brook (marr. diss. 1988); one *s* two *d*; 2nd, 1993, Sharavati, (Sharu), Prabhu (marr. diss. 2003); two *s*; 3rd, 2007, Patricia Lang. *Educ*: Cottesmore Secondary Modern Sch.; Mundella Grammar Sch., Nottingham; Loughborough Teachers' Trng Coll. (Teaching Certificate). Began climbing age of 12; first ascent, Tarso Teiroko, Tibesti Mts, Sahara, 1965; first ascents, Cilo Dag Mts, SE Turkey, 1966; first ascent, S face Koh-i-Bandaka (6837 m), Hindu Kush, Afghanistan, 1967; first British ascent, Salathé Wall, El Capitan, Yosemite, 1971; 1972: Spring, Mem., European Mt Everest Expedn to SW face; Summer, first ascent, E Pillar of Mt Asgard, Baffin Island Expedn; Autumn, Mem., British Mt Everest Expedn to SW face; first ascent, Changabang (6864 m), 1974; first ascent, SE spur, Pic Lenin (7189 m), 1974; reached summit of Mt Everest, via SW face, with Dougal Haston, as Members, British Everest Expedn, 24th Sept. 1975 (first Britons on summit); first Alpine ascent of S face, Mt McKinley (6226 m), via new route, British Direct, with Dougal Haston, 1976; first ascent, East Face Direct, Mt Kenya, 1976; first ascent, Ogre (7330 m), Karakoram Mountains, 1977; first ascent, N Ridge route, Kangchenjunga (8593 m), without oxygen, 1979; first ascent, N Summit, Kussum Kangguru, 1979; first ascent, N Face, Nuptse, 1979; Alpine style, Kangchungtse (7640 m), 1980; first ascent Shivling E Pillar, 13-day Alpine Style push, 1981; Chamlang (7366 m) North Face to Central Summit, with Rheinhold Messner, 1981; first ascent, Pungpa Ri (7445 m), 1982; first ascent Shishapangma South Face (8046 m), 1982; first ascent, Lobsang Spire (Karakoram), and ascent Broad Peak (8047 m), 1983; Mt Barunste (7143 m), first ascent, East Summit Mt Chamlang (7287 m), and traverse over unclimbed central summit Chamlang, Makalu SE Ridge, Alpine Style, to within 100 m of summit, 1984; first Alpine style ascent, Diran (7260 m), 1985; first ascent of rock climbs in S India, 1986; first ascent of rock climbs, Wadi Rum, Jordan, 1987; Mt Jitchu Drake (Bhutan) (6793 m), South face first ascent of peak, Alpine style, 1988; first ascent, Indian Arete Latok III, 1990; first ascent, Hanging Glacier Peak South (6294 m), via South Ridge, 1991; first British ascent of Chimtarga (5482 m), Fanskiye Mountains, Tadzhikistan, 1992; first ascent, Central Mazeno Peaks (6970 m) of Nanga Parbat, 1992; first ascent, Mt Pelagic (2000 m), Tierra del Fuego, 1993; first ascent Carstensz Pyramid North Face, 1995; first ascent, Chombu East (5745 m), NE Sikkim, 1996; first ascent Drohmo Central summit (6855 m), via South pillar, Alpine style, with Roger Mear, 1998; first ascent, Targo Ri (6650 m), Central Tibet, 2000. Pres., Alpine Climbing Gp, 1976–82; Vice-Pres., British Mountaineering Council, 1994–97. Hon. MA: Nottingham, 1991; Loughborough, 1993; Hon. MEd Nottingham Trent, 1995; Hon. Dr Derby, 2007. *Publications*: Big Wall Climbing, 1974; (with Alex MacIntyre) Shishapangma, Tibet, 1984; Himalayan Climber, 1992; Up and About: the hard road to Everest, 2015; The Ogre, 2017; contrib. to Alpine Jl, Amer. Alpine Jl, Mountain Magazine and Himal Magazine. *Recreations*: rock climbing, photography, organic gardening. *Address*: Stewart Hill Cottage, Hesket Newmarket, Wigton CA7 8HX. *T*: (01768) 484841, 07752 251256, (office) (01768) 484842. *E*: dougscott25@hotmail.com. *Clubs*: Alpine (Pres., 1999–2001); Alpine Climbing Group; Nottingham Climbers'.

**SCOTT, Edward McM.;** *see* McMillan-Scott.

**SCOTT, Eleanor Roberta;** Member (Green) Highlands and Islands, Scottish Parliament, 2003–07; *b* 23 July 1951; *d* of late William Ettles and Roberta Ettles (*née* Reid); *m* 1977, David Scott (marr. diss. 1995); one *s* one *d*; partner, Robert McKay Gibson, *qv*. *Educ*: Bearsden Acad.; Glasgow Univ. (MB ChB 1974). Jun. doctor posts, 1974–80; Clin. Med. Officer, Community Paediatrics, Inverness, 1980–87; Sen. Clin. Med. Officer, Community Paediatrics, Dingwall, Ross-shire, 1987–2003. *Recreations*: traditional music, gardening. *Address*: Tir Nan Oran, 8 Culcairn Road, Evanton IV16 9YT. *T*: (01349) 830388. *E*: eleanorsco@googlemail.com.

**SCOTT, Emma Jane;** Chief Executive Officer, Beano Studios, since 2015; *b* 21 May 1968; *d* of Michael Bryan Scott and late Jennifer Scott (*née* Birtwistle); *m* 2003, James Tatam (marr. diss. 2010); two *d*. *Educ*: Hatfield Sch.; Univ. of Hull (BA Hons Pols and Legislative Studies); Bradford Management Sch. (MBA with distinction). Researcher to Austin Mitchell, MP, 1989 and 1990–91; Strategy Analyst, Optus Communications, Sydney, 1992–95; Cogent Consulting, Nortel, 1996; BBC: Sen. Advr, Corporate Strategy, 1997; Hd, Dir Gen.'s Office, 1999–2004; Freeview Launch Dir, 2002–03; Hd, Partnership Strategy, 2005; Launch Dir, 2006, Man. Dir, 2007–14, Freesat. Mem., Adv. Panel, RTS, 2010– (Vice Chm.); Trustee, Bd, Ovarian Cancer Action, 2010–. FRSA. *Address*: Beano Studios Ltd, 185 Fleet Street, EC4A 2HS.

**SCOTT, Finlay McMillan**, CBE 2009; TD 1984; Chief Executive and Registrar, General Medical Council, 1994–2009; *b* 25 May 1947; *s* of Finlay McMillan Scott and Anne Cameron Robertson Coutts Scott; *m* 1st, 1969, Eileen Frances Marshall (marr. diss. 2001); one *s* one *d*; 2nd, 2002, Prof. Elizabeth Susan Perkins. *Educ*: Greenock High Sch.; Open Univ. (BA Hons; LLB Hons); Durham Univ. (MSc). Department of Education and Science, subseq. Department for Education, 1975–94: Head of Pensions Br. and Controller, Darlington, 1983–86; Head of Inf. Systems Br., 1986–90; on secondment: to UFC, 1990–93; to PCFC, 1992–93; to HEFCE, 1992–94; Under Sec., 1990–94. Lt-Col, RAOC, 1989–93, RLC, 1993–95, RARO, 1995–, TA. Member: NIHEC, 1993–2001; Medical Workforce Standing Adv. Cttee, 1996–2001; Postgrad. Med. Educn and Trng Bd, 2003–10. Governor: London Guildhall Univ., 1996–2002; London Metropolitan Univ., 2003–09. *Recreations*: horse riding, learning to be a farmer. *E*: finlayscott@kilnfarm.org.

**SCOTT, Sir (George) Peter**, Kt 2007; Professor of Higher Education Studies, Institute of Education, University College London (formerly Institute of Education, University of London), 2011–18, now Emeritus Professor; Commissioner for Fair Access, Scottish Government, since 2016; *b* 1 Aug. 1946; *s* of George Edward Grey Scott and Evelyn Mary Scott (*née* Robb); *m* 1968, Cherill Andrea Williams; one *d*. *Educ*: Merton Coll., Oxford (BA 1st cl. Hons Modern History 1967). Journalist: TES, 1967–69; The Times, 1969–71; Dep. Editor, THES, 1971–73; Vis. Scholar (Harkness Fellow), Grad. Sch. of Public Policy, Univ. of Calif at Berkeley, 1973–74; leader writer, The Times, 1974–76; Editor, THES, 1976–92; Prof. of Education, 1992–97, Pro-Vice-Chancellor, 1996–97, Univ. of Leeds; Vice-Chancellor, Kingston Univ., 1998–2010. Mem. Bd, HEFCE, 2000–06. Chm. Council, Univ. of Glos, 2011–15. Trustee, LAMDA, 2015–18. Hon. Fellow, UMIST, 1992. Hon. LLD Bath, 1992; Hon. DLitt: CNAA, 1992; Grand Valley State Univ., 1999; St George's, Univ. of London, 2012; Leicester, 2013; Glos, 2016; Hon. PhD Anglia Polytech. Univ., 1998. *Publications*: The Crisis of the University, 1986; Knowledge and Nation, 1990; The New Production of Knowledge, 1994; The Meanings of Mass Higher Education, 1995; Governing Universities, 1996; Re-thinking Science, Knowledge and the Public in an age of uncertainty, 2001; (with C. Callender) Browne and Beyond: the reform of English higher education, 2013; (with L. Engwall) Trust in Universities, 2013; (with Jim Gallacher and Gareth Parry) New Languages and Landscapes of Higher Education, 2016. *Address*: UCL Institute of Education, 20 Bedford Way, WC1H 0AL. *T*: (020) 7612 6048.

**SCOTT, Prof. Hamish Marshall**, PhD; FBA 2006; FRSE, FSAScot; Professor of International History, 2000–06, Wardlaw Professor of International History, 2006–09, University of St Andrews, now Emeritus; Senior Research Fellow, Jesus College, Oxford, since 2017; *b* 12 July 1946; *s* of James Donaldson Scott and Elizabeth Levack Scott (*née* Dalrymple); *m* 2005, Julia Mary Howard Smith, *qv*. *Educ*: George Heriot's Sch., Edinburgh; Univ. of Edinburgh (MA 1968); London Sch. of Econs (PhD 1978). Lectr, Univ. of Birmingham, 1970–78; Lectr, then Sen. Lectr, Univ. of St Andrews, 1979–2000; Hon. Sen. Res. Fellow, Dept of Hist., then Sch. of Humanities (Hist.), Univ. of Glasgow, 2009–17. Vis. Fellow, Oriel Coll., Oxford, 2016–17. Vice-Pres. (Pubns), British Acad., 2019–; Pres., Royal Philosophical Soc. of Glasgow, 2012–14. FRSE 2008; FSAScot 2010. MAE 2009. *Publications*: (with D. McKay) The Rise of the Great Powers 1648–1815, 1983; British Foreign Policy in the Age of the American Revolution, 1990; (ed) Enlightened Absolutism: reform and reformers in later eighteenth-century Europe, 1990; (ed) The European Nobilities in the Seventeenth and Eighteenth Centuries, 2 vols, 1995, 2nd edn 2007; (ed jtly) Royal and Republican Sovereignty in Early Modern Europe: essays in memory of Ragnhild Hatton, 1997; The Emergence of the Eastern Powers 1756–1775, 2001; The Birth of a Great Power System 1740–1815, 2006; (ed jtly) Cultures of Power in Europe during the Long Eighteenth Century, 2007; (ed) The Oxford Handbook of Early Modern European History, 2 vols, 2015; contrib. to learned jls and collected vols. *Recreations*: music, sport, hill-walking, cooking. *Address*: 3 Abberbury Road, Iffley Village, Oxford OX4 4ET. *E*: hamish.scott@history.ox.ac.uk.

**SCOTT, Sir Henry (Douglas Edward)**, 4th Bt *cr* 1913, of Witley; *b* London, 26 March 1964; *s* of Sir Anthony Percy Scott, 3rd Bt and of Caroline Theresa Anne Scott; *S* father, 2018; *m* 1993, Carole Ruth Maddick. *Educ*: Harrow Sch. Philipp Brothers Ltd, 1985–93; Euromin SA, 1993–2002; Louis Dreyfus, 2002–04; MRI Trading AG, 2004–. *Heir*: *b* Rev. Simon James Scott [*b* 31 March 1968; *m* 2003, Susanna Rhoads Cook; two adopted *d*]. *Address*: Baarerstrasse 55, 6300 Zug, Switzerland. *T*: 793356402. *E*: henry.scott@bluewin.ch.

**SCOTT, Hilary;** independent consultant, retired; *b* 9 June 1954; *d* of Stephen and late June Scott; civil partnership 2007, Linda Charlton. *Educ*: Camden Sch. for Girls; Poly. of Central London (BA Hons Social Sci. 1978); Poly. of South Bank (MSc Sociol. of Health and Illness 1986); DipHSM 1983. Nat. Admin. Trainee, NHS, 1978–81; Asst House Gov., St Stephen's Hosp., 1981–83; Dep. Administrator, Brook Gen. Hosp., 1983–86; Outpatient and Diagnostic Services Manager, Northwick Park Hosp., 1986–89; Chief Exec., Enfield & Haringey FHSA, 1989–93; Project Dir, City and E London Family and Community Health Services, 1993–95; Chief Exec., Tower Hamlets Health Care NHS Trust, 1995–99; Dep. Health Service Ombudsman, 1999–2003; Complaints and Clin. Negligence Prog. Manager, DoH, 2003–04. Chm., Action on Elder Abuse, 2004–07; Trustee, Action against Medical Accidents, 2010–18. Vice Chm., Gwynedd Cttee, North Wales Community Health Council, 2012–13. Middlesex University Business School: Vis. Prof., 2002–07; Associate Prof., 2007–10; Vis. Prof., 2010–18; Vis. Sen. Fellow, Birmingham Univ., 2004–18. Mem. Ct of Govs, Univ. of Westminster, 2002–09. FIHM 1997. *Recreations*: family, friends, gardening, sewing.

**SCOTT, Prof. Ian Richard**, PhD; Barber Professor of Law, 1978–2000, Professor of Law (personal chair), 2001–05, University of Birmingham, Emeritus Professor, since 2006; *b* 8 Jan. 1940; *s* of Ernest and Edith Scott; *m* 1971, Ecce Cole; two *d*. *Educ*: Geelong Coll.; Queen's Coll., Univ. of Melbourne (LLB); King's Coll., Univ. of London (PhD). Barrister and Solicitor, Supreme Court of Victoria; called to Bar, Gray's Inn, 1995. Dir, Inst. of Judicial Admin, 1975–82. Exec. Dir, Victoria Law Foundn, 1982–84; Dean, Faculty of Law, Univ. of Birmingham, 1985–94. Member: Lord Chancellor's Civil Justice Review Body, 1985–88; Policy Adv. Gp, NHS Litigation Authy, 1996–2000; Alternative Dispute Resolution sub-cttee, Civil Justice Council, 1998–2002; Chm., N Yorks Magistrates' Courts Inquiry, 1989. Non-exec. Dir, Royal Orthopaedic Hosp. NHS Trust, 1995–2000. Hon. Bencher, Gray's Inn, 1988. Hon. QC 2016. Life Mem., Aust. Inst. of Judicial Admin, 1990. An Ed., 1989–2006, Gen. Ed., 2007–19, Emeritus Ed., 2019, Civil Procedure (the White Book). *Recreation*: law. *Address*: School of Law, University of Birmingham, Birmingham B15 2TT.

**SCOTT, Irene Elizabeth;** *see* Gray, I. E.

**SCOTT, Prof. James**, FRCP; FRS 1997; Professor of Medicine, since 1997 and Deputy Principal for Research, since 2000, Imperial College London (Deputy Vice-Principal, 1997–2000); Director, Imperial College Genetics and Genomics Research Institute, 2000;

b 13 Sept. 1946; s of Robert Bentham Scott and Iris Olive Scott (née Hill); m 1976, Diane Marylin Lowe; two s one d. Educ: London Univ. (BSc 1968); London Hosp. Med. Coll. (MB, BS 1971; MSc Biochem. 1978). MRCP 1974, FRCP 1986. House Officer: London Hosp., 1971–72; Hereford Co. Hosp., 1972; Sen. House Officer, Midland Centre for Neurosurgery and Neurol., and Queen Elizabeth Hosp., Birmingham, 1972–73; Registrar in Medicine: General Hosp., Birmingham, 1973–74; Acad. Dept of Medicine, Royal Free Hosp., 1975–76; MRC Res. Fellow and Hon. Sen. Registrar, RPMS and Hammersmith Hosp., 1977–80; European Molecular Biol. Fellow, Dept of Biochem., Univ. of Calif, San Francisco, 1980–83; MRC Clinical Scientist and Hon. Consultant Physician, MRC Clinical Res. Centre and Northwick Park Hosp., 1983–91; Prof. and Chm. of Medicine, RPMS, 1992–97; Dir of Medicine and Chief of Service Med. Cardiology, Hammersmith Hosps NHS Trust, 1994–97; Hon. Consultant Physician, Hammersmith Hosp., 1992–; Hon. Dir, MRC Molecular Medicine Gp, 1992–. Member: RCP Res. Cttee, 1988–91; Assoc. of Physicians of GB and Ireland, 1987; European Molecular Biol. Orgn, 1993–; RSocMed Adv. Cttee, 1999–; Chm., N Thames Higher Merit Award Adv. Cttee, 1996–2000. Lectures include: Humphrey Davy Rolleston, RCP, 1989; Simms, RCP, 1995; Pfizer, Clin. Res. Inst., Montreal; Guest, Japan Atherosclerosis Soc., 1992; Dolan Boyd Pritchett Meml, Perelman Sch. of Medicine, Univ. of Pennsylvania, 2008; Crisps/Cas 9 Technol., St Hilda's Coll., Oxford, 2015. Founder FMedSci 1998. Graham Bull Prize, RCP, 1989; Squibb Bristol Myers Award for Cardiovascular Res., 1993. Publications: numerous on molecular medicine, molecular genetics, atherosclerosis, RNA modification, RNA editing and gene expression. Recreations: family and friends, the twentieth century novel, British Impressionists and modern painting, long distance running, swimming. Address: National Heart and Lung Institute, Imperial College London, Hammersmith Campus, W12 0HS.

**SCOTT, James Alexander,** OBE 1987; FCA; Partner, Binder Hamlyn, Chartered Accountants, 1969–98; Chairman, Schroder Exempt Property Unit Trust, 2010–12 (Director, 1994–2012); b 30 April 1940; s of Douglas McPherson Scott and Mabel Mary (née Skepper); m 1965, Annette Goslett; three s two d. Educ: Uppingham Sch.; Magdalene Coll., Cambridge (Schol.; MA); London Business Sch. (MSc). Joined Binder Hamlyn, 1961; Man. Partner, London Region, 1980–88; Nat. Man. Partner, 1988–89. Dir, Vestey Hldgs (formerly Gp) Ltd, 1992–. Chm. Trustees, Lonmin Superannuation Scheme, 2000–09; Trustee, Western Utd Gp Pension Scheme, 2009–16. Mem., Agricl Wages Bd for England and Wales, 1971–86; Sec., Review Bd for Govt Contracts, 1969–98; Member: NHS Pharmacists Remuneration Review Panel, 1982; Restrictive Practices Court, 1993–2000. DTI Inspector, Atlantic Computers plc, 1990. Recreations: walking, golf, tennis, bridge. Clubs: Berkshire Golf; St Enodoc Golf.

**SCOTT, James Archibald,** CB 1988; LVO 1961; FRSE; Deputy Spokesman on trade and industry, Scottish National Party, 1997–99; b 5 March 1932; s of late James Scott, MBE, and Agnes Bone Howie; m 1957, Elizabeth Agnes Joyce Buchan-Hepburn; three s one d. Educ: Dollar Acad.; Queen's Univ. of Ont.; Univ. of St Andrews (MA Hons). FRSE 1993. RAF aircrew, 1954–56. Asst Principal, CRO, 1956; served in New Delhi, 1958–62, and UK Mission to UN, New York, 1962–65; transf. to Scottish Office, 1965; Private Sec. to Sec. of State for Scotland, 1969–71; Asst Sec., Scottish Office, 1971; Under-Sec., Scottish Economic Planning Dept, later Industry Dept for Scotland, 1976–84; Sec., Scottish Educn Dept, 1984–87; Sec., Industry Dept for Scotland, 1987–90; Chief Exec., SDA, 1990–91; Exec. Dir, Scottish Financial Enterprise, 1991–94. Non-exec. Director: Scottish Power plc, 1992–96; Dumyat Investment Trust plc, 1995–2000. Fellow, SCOTVEC, 1990. Chevalier, Ordre National du Mérite (France), 1995. Recreations: travel, golf. Address: Flat 38, 4 Simpson Loan, Edinburgh EH3 9GY. T: (0131) 228 3606.

**SCOTT, Prof. James Floyd,** PhD; FRS 2008; Professor of Physics, and Research Director, Department of Physics, Cavendish Laboratory, University of Cambridge, 2009, now Professor Emeritus; b 4 May 1942; s of William Burgess Scott and Isabel Miles; m 1982, Galina Alexeevna Dergilyova; one d. Educ: Harvard (AB 1963); Ohio State Univ. (PhD 1966). Prof. (Physics) and Asst Vice Chancellor, Univ. of Colorado, 1971–92; Professor and Dean: RMIT, Melbourne, 1992–95; Univ. of New South Wales, 1995–99. Chm. Bd, 1986–90, Dir, 1986–99, Symetrix Corp., USA; Prof. of Ferroics, 1999–2009, Symetrix Professor of Ferroics, 1999–2004, Univ. of Cambridge. Fellow, APS, 1974. Mem., Acad. of Scis, Slovenia, 2011. Humboldt Prize, Germany, 1997; Monkasho Prize, Japan, 2001; Gold Medal, Materials Res. Soc., 2008; Jozef Stefan Gold Medal, Slovenia, 2009. Publications: Ferroelectric Memories, 2000; over 700 articles in learned jls. Recreations: travel, gardening. Address: Thorndyke, Huntingdon Road, Cambridge CB3 0LG. T: (01223) 277793, Fax: (01223) 333450. E: jfs32@hermes.cam.ac.uk.

**SCOTT, Sir James (Jervoise),** 3rd Bt cr 1962, of Rotherfield Park, Alton, Hants; DL; b 12 Oct. 1952; e s of Lt-Col Sir James Walter Scott, 2nd Bt, and Anne Constantia (née Austin); S father, 1993; m 1982, Judy Evelyn, d of Brian Trafford and Hon. Mrs Trafford; one s one d. Educ: Eton; Trinity Coll., Cambridge (MA). Agricultural journalist, 1977–88. Chm., Taxation and Political Cttee, Historic Houses, 2007–19. Mem., Hampshire CC, 2001–05. Pres., Royal Forestry Soc., 2019–. High Sheriff, Hants, 2004–05. DL Hants, 2013. Recreation: shooting. Heir: s Arthur Jervoise Trafford Scott [b 2 Feb. 1984; m 2011, Emily Helen Wahlberg, d of David George Fossett Thompson, qv; three s]. Clubs: White's, Travellers.

**SCOTT, Jane Elizabeth, (Mrs Justin Byam Shaw);** Member, International Advisory Board, Professional Boards Forum, since 2016 (UK Director, 2009–16); b Theydon Bois, 21 Aug. 1960; d of Dr Sydney Scott and Dr Margaret Scott (née Barrie); m 1991, Justin David Elliott Byam Shaw, qv; one s (and one s decd). Educ: City of London Sch. for Girls; Trinity Coll., Oxford (BA Modern Langs 1983; MA); London Business Sch. (MBA 1996). Mktg Manager, 1986–91, Mktg Dir, 1991–92, Wolff Olins; ind. mgt consultant, 1992–2008. Founder Mem., Steering Cttee, 30% Club, 2010–. Vice Pres., Muscular Dystrophy UK (formerly Muscular Dystrophy Campaign), 2009–. Trustee: Felix Byam Shaw Foundn, 2014–; Felix Project, 2017–. Gov., Byam Shaw Sch. of Art, 1994–99. Recreations: tennis, yoga, ski-ing. Clubs: Holland Park Lawn Tennis, Campden Hill Lawn Tennis.

**SCOTT, Janet Howard;** see Darbyshire, J. H.

**SCOTT, Janys Margaret;** QC (Scot.) 2007; Advocate, since 1992; part-time Sheriff, since 2005; b Radcliffe, 28 Aug. 1953; d of John and Dylys Allen; m 1974, Dr Kevin F. Scott; two s one d. Educ: Newnham Coll., Cambridge (BA 1974). Articled clerk, Oxford, 1974–76; Asst Lectr, Sulaimaniyah Univ., Iraq, 1976–78; Solicitor, Oxford, 1978–86, Edinburgh, 1987–91. Hon. Lectr, Dundee Univ., 1989–94. Convener, Scottish Child Law Centre, 1992–97; Chairman: Stepfamily Scotland, 1998–2002; Scottish Legal Gp, Brit. Assoc. for Adoption and Fostering, 2004–10; Advocates Family Law Assoc., 2013–18; UK Deleg., Family and Succession Cttee (formerly CCBE Family and Succession Working Gp), 2012–. Chair, Bd of Trustees, Adoption and Fostering Alliance Scotland, 2016–; Trustee, Lawyers' Christian Fellowship, 2018–. Vice-Pres., 2014–17, Pres., 2018–, Part-time Sheriffs' Assoc. Publications: Education Law in Scotland, 2003, 2nd edn 2016. Recreations: growing vegetables, cooking, reading. Address: Westwater Advocates, Parliament House, Edinburgh EH1 1RF.

**SCOTT, Jean Grant, (Mrs Donald Macleod);** Chairman, Independent Schools Council, 2001–06; Headmistress, South Hampstead High School GDST, 1993–2001; b 7 Oct. 1940; d of Dr Duncan W. D. MacLaren and Etta M. MacLaren (née Speirs); m 1st, 1964, John Scott (d 1979); two s; 2nd, 2000, Donald Macleod. Educ: George Watson's Ladies' Coll., Edinburgh; Wellington Sch., Ayr; Univ. of Glasgow (BSc Hons Zool.); Univ. of London Inst. of Educn (PGCE). Research Biologist: Glaxo Labs Ltd, 1962–65; ICI, Alderley Edge, 1966–67; part-time Lectr in Biol., Newcastle-under-Lyme Coll. of FE, 1969–70; Teacher of Biology: (part-time) Dr Challoner's High Sch., 1970–76; Northgate Grammar Sch., Ipswich, 1976–77; Hd of Biol. and Sen. Mistress, Ipswich High Sch. (GPDST), 1977–86; Headmistress, St George's Sch. for Girls, Edinburgh, 1986–93. Trustee, American Sch. in London, 1997–2005. Governor: Central Sch. of Speech and Drama, 1998–2006; Downe Hse Sch., 2001–10; Haileybury Coll., 2001–15; Haileybury Almaty Sch., Kazakhstan, 2008–15; Haileybury Astana Sch., Kazakhstan, 2011–15; Edge Grove Sch., Aldenham, 2011– (Chm., 2014–18). Recreations: concerts, theatre, film, swimming, ski-ing, golf, loch fishing, travel abroad. Address: 3 Merton Rise, NW3 3EN.

**SCOTT, Prof. Joanne,** FBA 2013; FRSE; Professor of European Law, University College London, since 2005 (on leave); Professor of European Law, European University Institute, Florence, since 2017; b Edinburgh, 17 Dec. 1965; d of Terence Scott and late Jean Isabella Scott (née Meikle); partner, Ferguson Morton Murray. Educ: Madras Coll., St Andrews; Univ. of Aberdeen (LLB 1987); European University Inst., Florence (LLM 1989). Lectr, Univ. of Kent at Canterbury, 1988–93; Lectr, 1994–98, Reader, 1998–2000, QMW, then QMUL; Lectr, 2000–02, Reader, 2002–05, Law Faculty, Univ. of Cambridge; Fellow, Clare Coll., Cambridge, 2000–05. Visiting Professor: Columbia Law Sch., 2002–03; Harvard Law Sch., 2005–06. Mem., Royal Commn on Envmtl Pollution, 2009–11. Leverhulme Major Res. Fellow, 2009–12. FRSE 2012. Publications: EC Environmental Law, 1997; (ed with G. de Burca) Constitutional Change in the EU: from uniformity to flexibility, 2000; (ed with G. de Burca) The EU and the WTO: legal and constitutional aspects, 2001; European Regional Development Policy: confusing quantity with quality, 2005; (ed with G. de Burca) Law and New Approaches to Governance in the EU and US, 2006; Commentary on the Sanitary and Phytosanitary Measures Agreement, 2007; articles in jls incl. Eur. Jl of Internat. Law, Amer. Jl of Comparative Law, Common Mkt Law Rev., Eur. Law Jl. Recreations: walking, birdwatching, travelling, opera. Address: Faculty of Laws, University College London, Bentham House, Endsleigh Gardens, WC1H 0EG. T: (020) 7699 1408. E: joanne.scott@eui.eu.

**SCOTT, Sir John;** see Scott, Sir W. J.

**SCOTT, John;** see Scott, W. J. G.

**SCOTT, Prof. John Anthony Gerard,** FRCP, FMedSci; Professor of Vaccine Epidemiology, London School of Hygiene and Tropical Medicine, since 2013; Wellcome Trust Senior Research Fellow in Clinical Science, Kenya Medical Research Institute-Wellcome Trust Research Programme, Kenya, since 2008; b Liverpool, 6 Nov. 1962; s of John Scott and Mary Scott (née McCabe); m 1985, Louise M. M. Leahy; two s two d. Educ: Churchill Coll., Cambridge (BA Psychol. 1984); Merton Coll., Oxford (BM BCh 1987); London Sch. of Hygiene and Tropical Medicine, Univ. of London (MSc Epidemiol. 1993). MRCP 1990, FRCP 2004; DTM&H 1991. Clin. trng, in Medicine, Newcastle, 1988–90, in Infectious Diseases, Northwick Park Hosp., 1991–92; Wellcome Trust Res. Trng Fellow, 1992–96, Tropical Res. Fellow, 1998–2000, Career Develt Fellow, 2001–07, Kenya Med. Res. Inst. – Wellcome Trust Res. Prog., Kilifi, Kenya and Univ. of Oxford; Co-Dir, Kilifi Health and Demographic Surveillance System, 2000–; Prof. of Epidemiol., Univ. of Oxford, 2010–12. Vis. Prof., Univ. of Oxford, 2013–. Associate, Johns Hopkins Sch. of Public Health, 2011–14. Hon. Consultant Physician, Oxford Univ. Hosps Trust, 2000–. Mem., Jt Cttee on Vaccination and Immunisation, 2013–. FMedSci 2013. Publications: (contrib.) Oxford Textbook of Medicine, 5th edn 2010, 6th edn 2012; (contrib.) Principles of Medicine in Africa, 3rd edn 2004, 4th edn 2011; contrib. res. papers on infectious disease epidemiol., pneumococcal disease and vaccines. Recreations: hiking, mountain biking, swimming, photography. Address: Department of Infectious Disease Epidemiology, London School of Hygiene and Tropical Medicine, Keppel Street, WC1E 7HT. T: (020) 7927 2827. E: anthony.scott@lshtm.ac.uk.

**SCOTT, (John) Brough;** Founding Director, Racing Post, 1986–2007; journalist and broadcaster; b 12 Dec. 1942; s of Mason Hogarth Scott and Irene Florence Scott, Broadway, Worcs; m 1973, Susan Eleanor MacInnes; two s two d. Educ: Radley College; Corpus Christi, Oxford (MA History). Amateur, then professional, Nat. Hunt jockey, 1962–71 (100 winners, incl. Imperial Cup and Mandarin Chase). ITV presenter, sports programmes and documentaries, 1971–; chief racing presenter, ITV, 1979–85; chief presenter, Channel 4 Racing, 1985–2001. Evening Standard sports correspondent, 1972–74; sports journalist: Sunday Times, 1974–90, 1993–94; The Independent on Sunday, 1990–92; Sports Writer, Sunday Telegraph, 1995–2008. Vice-Pres., Jockeys' Assoc., 1969–71; Trustee: Injured Jockeys Fund, 1978– (Chm., 2007–); Moorcroft Racehorse Welfare Centre, 2003–; Internat. Concussion and Head Injury Res. Foundn, 2016–. Lord Derby Award, 1978 (racing journalist of the year); Clive Graham Trophy, 1982; Sports Feature Writer of the Year, 1985, 1991, 1992. Publications: World of Flat Racing, 1983; On and Off the Rails, 1984; Front Runners, 1991; Up Front—Willie Carson, 1994; Racing Certainties, 1995; Galloper Jack, 2003; Of Horses and Heroes, 2008; (ed) McCoy, 2010; Warrior, 2011; Henry Cecil: trainer of genius, 2013. Recreation: making bonfires. Address: Meadow House, Coneyhurst Lane, Ewhurst, Surrey GU6 7PL. T: 07860 258881.

**SCOTT, Prof. John Donald,** PhD; FRS 2003; Edwin G. Krebs-Speights Professor of Cell Signaling and Cancer Biology, Department of Pharmacology, University of Washington, since 2008; Investigator, Howard Hughes Medical Institute, 2004 (Associate Investigator, 1997–2003); b 13 April 1958; m Shonnie; one s one d. Educ: Heriot-Watt Univ., Edinburgh (BSc Hons (Biochem.) 1980); Univ. of Aberdeen (PhD Biochem.). Med. Endowments Hon. Scholar, Univ. of Aberdeen, 1980–83; NIH Postdoctoral Fellow, Dept of Pharmacol., 1983–86, Res. Asst Prof., Dept of Biochem., 1986–88, Univ. of Washington, Seattle; Sen. Associate, Howard Hughes Med. Inst., 1986–88; Asst Prof., Dept of Physiol., Univ. of Calif, Irvine, 1988–89; Asst Scientist, 1990–92, Scientist, 1993–96, Sen. Scientist, 1997–2008, Vollum Inst., Oregon Health and Sciences Univ. Consultant, ICOS Corp., Seattle, 1992–2000; Scientific Adv. Bd, Upstate Biotechnology, Lake Placid, 1995–; Trellis Bioscience Inc., Mountain View, 2003–. Member NIH Study Section: Med. Biochem., 1993–96; Biochem., 1998–2002. Member: Biochemical Soc., 1981–; Amer. Soc. for Biochem. and Molecular Biol., 1990– (Mem. Program Cttee, 2000–); Endocrine Soc., 1997– (Ernst Oppenheimer Award, 2001); Amer. Soc. for Pharmacol. and Experimental Therapeutics, 1997– (Mem., 1999–2001, Chm., 2001–, John Jacob Abel Award Selection Cttee; John J. Abel Award in Pharmacol., 1996). Mem. Edtl Bd, Jl of Biological Chemistry, 1993–98; Review Ed., Biochemical Jl, 2002–. D'Agrosa Meml Lecture, St Louis Univ., 2001. Discovery Award, Med. Res. Foundn, 2003. Publications: many articles in learned jls. Address: Department of Pharmacology, University of Washington, 1959 Pacific Avenue NE, Box 357750, Seattle, WA 98195, USA. T: (206) 6163340, Fax: (206) 6163386. E: scottjdw@u.washington.edu.

**SCOTT, Rev. Prof. John Fraser,** AO 1990; Associate Priest, St George's, Malvern, since 1992; b 10 Oct. 1928; s of Douglas Fraser Scott and Cecilia Louise Scott; m 1956, Dorothea Elizabeth Paton Scott; one s three d. Educ: Bristol Grammar Sch.; Trinity Coll., Cambridge (MA); Melbourne Coll. of Divinity (BD 1994). FIS. Research Asst, Univ. of Sheffield, 1950–53; Asst, Univ. of Aberdeen, 1953–55; Lectr in Biometry, Univ. of Oxford, 1955–65; University of Sussex: Reader in Statistics, 1965–67; Prof. of Applied Statistics, 1967–77; Pro-Vice-Chancellor, 1971–77; Vice-Chancellor, La Trobe Univ., Melbourne, 1977–90. Adv. Prof., E China Normal Univ., 1988. Visiting Consultant in Statistics: Nigeria, 1961, 1965; Sweden, 1969; Kuwait, 1973, 1976; Iraq, 1973; Malaysia, 1976. Reader, Church of England, 1971–77; Examining Chaplain to Bp of Chichester, 1974–77; Diocesan Lay Reader, Anglican Dio. of Melbourne, 1977–90; ordained deacon, then priest, 1990; Asst Curate, St George's, E Ivanhoe, 1990–91. Chairman: Jt Cttee on Univ. Statistics, 1978–86; Cttee of Review of Student Finances, 1983; Aust. Univs Industrial Assoc., 1986–88; AVCC, 1986–88 (Dep. Chm., 1986, Chm., Wkg Party on Attrition, 1981–86); Council for Chaplains in Tertiary Instns, 1990–94; Member: Grad. Careers Council of Aust., 1980–86; Council, 1986–89, Exec. Cttee, 1986–88, ACU; ABC Victorian State Adv. Cttee, 1978–81; Ethics Cttee, Victorian State Dept of Health, 1990–2004; Pres., Victorian State Libraries Bd, 1990–96. Dir, La Trobe Univ. Credit Union, 2001–05. Chieftain, Ringwood Highland Games, 2003. Editor, Applied Statistics, 1971–76; Mem., Editl Bd, The Statistician, 1987–. DUniv La Trobe, 1990. Publications: The Comparability of Grade Standards in Mathematics, 1975; Report of Committee of Review of Student Finances, 1983; papers in JRSS, Lancet, BMJ, Chemistry and Industry, Statistician, etc. Recreations: wine, women and song; canals. Address: 1/18 Riversdale Road, Hawthorn, Victoria 3122, Australia. T: (3) 98191862. Club: Melbourne.

**SCOTT, Sir John (Hamilton),** KCVO 2011; Lord-Lieutenant for Shetland, 1994–2011; farming in Bressay and Noss; b 30 Nov. 1936; s of Dr Thomas Gilbert Scott and Elizabeth M. B. Scott; m 1965, Wendy Ronald; one s one d. Educ: Bryanston; Cambridge Univ.; Guy's Hosp., London. Shepherd, Scrabster, Caithness, 1961–64. Chm., Woolgrowers of Shetland Ltd, 1981–. Pres., Shetland NFU, 1976; Chairman: Shetland Crofting, Farming and Wildlife Adv. Gp, 1984–95; Shetland Arts Trust, 1993–98; Sail Shetland Ltd, 1997–2002; Belmont Trust, 1997–2012; Member: Nature Conservancy Council Cttee for Scotland, 1984–91; NE Regl Bd, Nature Conservancy Council for Scotland, 1991–92, Scottish Natural Heritage, 1992–97. Trustee, Shetland Charitable Trust, 1994–2011. Recreations: mountain climbing, Up-Helly-Aa, music. Address: Keldabister Banks, Bressay, Shetland ZE2 9EL. T: (01595) 820281. E: scott.gardie@virgin.net. Clubs: Alpine, Farmers.
See also T. H. Scott.

**SCOTT, (John) Michael,** CMG 2003; independent rural livelihoods consultant, since 2003; b 18 Feb. 1943; s of late Harold Scott and Joan Winifred Scott (née Holroyd); m 1967, Pauline Rachel Wright; one d. Educ: Boston Grammar Sch., Lincs; Royal Veterinary Coll., London Univ. (BVetMed 1967); Royal (Dick) Sch. of Vet. Studies, Univ. of Edinburgh. MRCVS 1967. Vet. Surgeon, Whittle, Taylor and Chesworth, Rochdale, 1967–69; Vet. Officer, Govt of Botswana, Mahalapye and Francistown, 1969–71; Veterinary Investigation Officer (funded as UK Government Technical Co-operation Officer): Ethiopia, 1972–77; El Salvador, 1977–79; Overseas Development Administration: Animal Health and Prodn Advr, 1979–82; Sen. Animal Health and Prodn Advr, 1982–86; Sen. Natural Resources Advr, Fiji, 1987–90; Hd, Natural Resources Policy and Adv. Dept, 1990–97; Department for International Development: Hd, Rural Livelihoods Dept, 1997–2003; Chief Natural Resources Advr, 2002–03; Sen. Rural Livelihoods Advr, Southern Africa, 2003–04, Bangladesh, 2004–07; short-term consultancies, 2007–09; Natural Resource Mgt Advr, DFID/Danida, Cambodia, 2009–10; short assignments, DFID, 2011–14; Sen. Mgt Team, BRACED, 2014–. Publications: contrib. learned jls on animal trypanosomiasis and fascioliasis. Recreations: international affairs, cricket, ornithology, wildlife. Address: 63 Oxford Road, Wokingham, Berks RG41 2YH. T: (0118) 978 6603. E: jm.vets@btinternet.com.

**SCOTT, Prof. John Peter,** CBE 2013; PhD; FBA 2007; sociologist; Professor of Sociology, 2008–13, and Pro Vice-Chancellor (Research), 2010–13, University of Plymouth; b 8 April 1949; s of Philip Charles Scott and Phyllis Scott (née Bridges); m 1971, Gillian Wheatley; one s one d. Educ: Kingston Coll. of Technol. (BScSoc London 1971); London Sch. of Econs; Univ. of Strathclyde (PhD 1976). Lectr in Sociol., Univ. of Strathclyde, 1972–76; University of Leicester: Lectr, 1976, Reader, 1987–91, in Sociol.; Prof. of Sociol., 1991–94; Prof. of Sociol., Univ. of Essex, 1994–2008. Adjunct Prof., Bergen Univ., Norway, 1997–2005; Hon. Prof., Univ. of Copenhagen, 2012–; Honorary Visiting Professor: Exeter Univ., 2014–; Essex Univ., 2016–. Mem. Council, British Acad., 2017– (Chm., Section S4, 2016–18). British Sociological Association: Mem., 1970–; Chm., 1992–93; Pres., 2000–02; Hon. Vice Pres., 2002–. FAcSS (AcSS 2003); FRSA 2005. DUniv Essex, 2016. Dist. Services to British Sociology Award, British Sociological Assoc., 2014. Editor: Network, 1984–87; Sociology Review, 1986–2002; European Societies, 2006–10. Publications: Corporations, Classes and Capitalism, 1979, 2nd edn 1985; The Anatomy of Scottish Capital, 1980; The Upper Classes: property and privilege in Britain, 1982; (with C. Griff) Directors of Industry, 1984; (ed jtly) Networks of Corporate Power, 1985; Capitalist Property and Financial Power, 1986; A Matter of Record: documentary sources in social research, 1990; (ed) The Sociology of Elites, three vols, 1990; Who Rules Britain?, 1991; Social Network Analysis, 1992, 4th edn 2017; (ed jtly) Reviewing Sociology, 1993; (with M. Nakata and H. Hasegawa) Kigyo to kanri no kokusai hikaku (An International Study of Enterprise and Administration), 1993; Poverty and Wealth: citizenship, deprivation and privilege, 1994; (ed) Power, three vols, 1994; Sociological Theory: contemporary debates, 1995, 2nd edn 2012; Stratification and Power: structures of class, status and domination, 1996; (ed) Class, four vols, 1996; Corporate Business and Capitalist Classes, 1997; (with Masao Watanabe and John Westergaard) Kaikyu genron no genzai igirisu to Nihon (Debates on Class in Contemporary Britain and Japan), 1998; (with James Fulcher) Sociology, 1999, 4th edn 2011; (with José López) Social Structure, 2000; (ed jtly) Renewing Class Analysis, 2000; Power, 2001; (ed) Social Networks: critical concept, four vols, 2002; (ed jtly) Rethinking Class: culture, identities, and lifestyle, 2004; (ed jtly) Models and Methods in Social Network Analysis, 2005; (ed with G. Marshall) Oxford Dictionary of Sociology, 3rd edn 2005; Social Theory: central issues in sociology, 2006; (ed) Documentary Research, four vols, 2006; (ed) Sociology: the key concepts, 2006; (ed) Fifty Key Sociologists: the formative theorists, 2007; (ed) Fifty Key Sociologists: the contemporary theorists, 2007; (ed with P. Carrington) The Sage Handbook of Social Network Analysis, 2011; Conceptualising The Social World, 2011; (ed with G. Murray) Financial Elites and Transnational Business, 2012; What is Social Network Analysis?, 2012; (with G. Letherby and M. Williams) Objectivity and Subjectivity in Social Research, 2013; (with R. Bromley) Envisioning Sociology: Victor Branford, Patrick Geddes and the quest for social reconstruction, 2013; (ed with A. Nilsen) C. Wright Mills and the Sociological Imagination, 2013; (ed with J. Holmwood) The Palgrave Handbook of Sociology in Britain, 2014; British Social Theory: recovering lost traditions before 1950, 2018; The Emerald Guide to Max Weber, 2019; contribs to many learned jls inc. British Jl of Sociol., Sociol Rev., Sociology, Sociol Analysis and Theory, etc. Recreations: listening to music, reading. W: www.johnscottcbe.com.

**SCOTT, Jonathan Willoughby;** Senior Partner, Herbert Smith Freehills (formerly Herbert Smith) LLP, 2010–15, now Consultant. Educ: St Catharine's Coll., Cambridge (BA 1978). Herbert Smith, later Herbert Smith Freehills: joined as trainee, 1979; Partner, 1988–2015; Head: Brussels office, 1989; EU and Competition Practice, until 2007. Mem., Gambling Commn, 2015–. Non-exec. Dir, CMA, 2016–.

**SCOTT, Judith Margaret,** CEng, FBCS; Chief Executive, British Computer Society, 1995–2002; b 4 Oct. 1942; d of Robert Wright and Marjorie Wood; m 1972, Gordon Robert Scott; two d. Educ: St Andrews Univ. (BSc Hons); Cambridge Univ. (Dip. Computer Sci.). Various posts, Computel Systems Ltd (Canada), 1968–79; seconded to Computer/Communications Policy Task Force, Govt of Canada, 1971–72; Manager, Product Mktg, Gandalf Data Inc. (Canada), 1979–82; Dir Corporate Planning, Gandalf Technologies Inc. (Canada), 1982–87; Man. Dir, Gandalf Digital Communications Ltd, UK, 1987–95. Mem., PPARC, 2001–06. Mem. Council, Reading Univ., 2003–13 (Vice Pres., 2007–13). Dist. Fellow, Reading Univ., 2014. DUniv Staffs, 2002. Recreation: orchid growing. Address: 4 Crescent Road, Wokingham, Berks RG40 2DB.

**SCOTT, Keith John;** HM Diplomatic Service; High Commissioner to Papua New Guinea, since 2018; b Aberdeen, 19 Feb. 1969; s of John and Evelyn Scott; m 2013, Carly Hore; one s one d. Educ: Robert Gordon's Coll., Aberdeen; Univ. of Aberdeen (MA 1st Cl. Jt Hons French-German). Policy Officer (Maastricht Treaty), EC Dept (Internal), FCO, 1991–93; Desk Officer, Transcaucasus/Central Asia Section, Eastern Dept, FCO, 1993–94; Second Sec. (Political), Abuja, 1994–95; Desk Officer, Eastern Adriatic Dept, FCO, 1995–98; on secondment to Exec. Office of UN Sec. Gen., NY, 1998–99; Regl Manager for W and Central Africa, Trade Partners UK, DTI, 1999–2002; Temp. Duty as First Sec. (Political), Kabul, 2002; Hd, N Africa and Maghreb Team, Near East and N Africa Dept, FCO, 2002–04; First Secretary: (Energy), Baghdad, 2004–05; (Political), Kabul, 2005–07; Head: Political and Communications Section, Harare, 2007–12; Network Dept, Finance Directorate, FCO, 2012–15; Dep. Migration Envoy, Mediterranean Migration Unit, Econ. Diplomacy Directorate, FCO, 2016–18. Recreations: sport, especially football, cricket, Rugby Union - heartache of following Scotland. Address: British High Commission Port Moresby, BFPO 5617, BF1 9PW. E: keith.scott@fco.gov.uk.

**SCOTT, Lee;** b 6 April 1956; s of late Sidney and Renne Scott; m 1987, Estelle Dombey; two s three d. Educ: Clarks Coll., Ilford; Coll. for Distributive Trades, London. Worked for: Scott & Fishell (Leather Goods); Selfridges, 1975–80; Tatung, 1980–82; Toshiba, 1982–84; ITT, 1984–86; NFR Office Furniture, 1986–88; Campaign Dir, Utd Jewish Israel Appeal, 1988–98; Scott Associates (consultancy working with charities), 1998–2005. Contested (C) Waveney, 2001. MP (C) Ilford N, 2005–15; contested (C) same seat, 2015, 2017. Recreations: music, travel, football (Leyton Orient supporter), tennis.

**SCOTT, Linda Valerie;** see Agran, L. V.

**SCOTT, Malcolm Charles Norman;** QC (Scot.) 1991; b 8 Sept. 1951; s of James Raymond Scott and Marjorie Stewart Simpson. Educ: Trinity Coll., Glenalmond; Gonville and Caius Coll., Cambridge (BA 1972). Glasgow Univ. (LLB 1975). Advocate 1978. Dir, Mid Wynd International Investment Trust plc, 1990– (Chm., 2016–). Recreations: fishing, ski-ing, hill walking. Club: New (Edinburgh).

**SCOTT, Margaret Elizabeth;** see Scott, Hon. Lady.

**SCOTT, Matthew Paul Noy;** composer and musician; Head of Music, 2006–16, Music Consultant, 2016–19, Royal National Theatre; b 19 Sept. 1956; s of David and Elizabeth Scott. Educ: Caldicott Sch.; Eton Coll. (Chorister Schol.); Epsom Coll. (Music Schol.); City Univ./Guildhall Sch. of Music and Drama (BSc 1979). Freelance composer, 1979–; Tutor, RADA, 1984–; Lectr, Univ. of Reading, 1996–2000; Lectr, 1996–2013, Prof. of Composition, 2013–18, Univ. of Southampton, now Prof. Emeritus (Mem. of Senate, 2015–17); Associate Artist, Birmingham Rep Th., 1997–; Associate Composer, Chichester Fest. Th., 2006–16. Many theatre and television credits as composer incl. Drop the Dead Donkey, 1990; Mother Clap's Molly House, Aldwych, 2002; Goodnight Mr Tom; films including: Lord of Misrule, 1996; The Landgirls (co-composer), 1998. Publications: A New Orpheus, 1985; composition: Four Bars of Agit, 1983. Recreations: architecture, surrealism, surrealist architecture, stationery and gadgets, detecting scepticism in others. Address: Music Department, National Theatre, SE1 9PX. T: (020) 7452 3390. E: matthewscott128@gmail.com. W: www.matthewscott.net.

**SCOTT, Michael;** see Scott, J. M.

**SCOTT, Prof. Michael,** PhD; DL; Vice-Chancellor, Glyndŵr University, 2008–15. Educ: Univ. of Wales, Lampeter; Univ. of Nottingham; De Montfort Univ. (PhD). Prof. of English and Hd, Sch. of Humanities, Sunderland Poly., until 1989; Pro Vice-Chancellor, De Montfort Univ., 1989–2008. Formerly Vis. Prof. of English, Georgetown Univ. (Centennial Award for Dist. Teaching and Scholarship, 1989). Dir, UK Nat. Commn for UNESCO, 2005–09; Chm., UNESCO Cymru. Formerly: Mem., Broadcasting Council for Wales; Chm., N Wales Film Commn. Mem. Council, CBI. Vice-Chair, Clwyd Th., Cymru. FRSA; FHEA. DL Clwyd, 2008. Publications: Antony and Cleopatra, 1983; Renaissance Drama and a Modern Audience, 1985; (ed) Harold Pinter, The Birthday Party, The Caretaker and The Homecoming, 1986; Shakespeare and the Modern Dramatist, 1993; (ed jtly) Talking Shakespeare, 2001; Shakespeare's Comedies: all that matters, 2014; Shakespeare's Tragedies: all that matters, 2015; Shakespeare: a complete introduction, 2016.

**SCOTT, Maj.-Gen. Michael Ian Eldon,** CB 1997; CBE 1987; DSO 1982; author; Complaints Commissioner, Bar Council, 1997–2006; b 3 March 1941; s of Col Eric Scott and Rose-Anne Scott; m 1968, Veronica Daniell; one s one d. Educ: Bradfield Coll. Commnd Scots Guards, 1960; Regtl service in UK, E Africa, N Ireland, BAOR; Staff Coll., Camberley, 1974; 2nd MA to CGS, 1975; COS Task Force Delta, 1979; Armed Forces Staff Coll., USA, 1981; CO, 2nd Bn Scots Guards, London, Falklands War and Cyprus, 1981–84; Comd 8th Inf. Bde, N Ireland, 1984–86; RCDS 1987; Dep. Mil. Sec., 1988–93; GOC Scotland and Gov., Edinburgh Castle, 1993–95; Mil. Sec., 1995–97. Pres., Third Guards Club, 1999–2018. Publications: (with David Rooney) In Love and War: the lives of Sir Harry and Lady Smith, 2008; Scapegoats: thirteen victims of military injustice, 2013; Royal Betrayal: the great Baccarat scandal of 1890, 2017. Recreations: travel, visual arts. Clubs: Pratt's, Garrick.

**SCOTT, Sir Peter;** see Scott, Sir G. P.

**SCOTT, Peter Anthony;** Managing Director, Peel Holdings plc, 1985–2007 (non-executive Director, 2007–12); b 24 April 1947; s of Barclay and Doris Scott; m 1969, Lynne Smithies; one s one d. Educ: Heywood Grammar Sch.; Littleborough High Sch.; Manchester Poly. ACCA 1979. Financial Accountant: Fothergill & Harvey Ltd, 1962–75; Crane Fruehauf Trailers (Oldham) Ltd, 1975–77; Co. Sec., 1977–81, Financial Dir, 1981–85, Peel Hldgs plc. Address: 11 Lakeside, Hollingworth Lake, Littleborough, Rochdale, Lancs OL15 0DD.

**SCOTT, Peter Denys John**, CBE 2008; QC 1978; Chairman, City Panel on Takeovers and Mergers, 2000–10; *b* 19 April 1935; *s* of John Ernest Dudley Scott and Joan G. Steinberg. *Educ*: Monroe High Sch., Rochester, NY, USA; Balliol Coll., Oxford (MA). Second Lieut, RHA, Lieut (TA), National Service, 1955. Called to the Bar, Middle Temple (Harmsworth Scholar), 1960, Bencher, 1984; Standing Counsel: to Dir, Gen. of Fair Trading, 1973–78; to Dept of Employment, 1974–78. Member: Home Sec.'s Cttee on Prison Disciplinary System, 1984; Interception of Communications Tribunal, 1986–2002; Lord Chancellor's Adv. Cttee on Legal Educn and Conduct, 1991–94; Investigatory Powers Tribunal, 2000–10; Investigatory Powers Guernsey Tribunal, 2006–; conducted Attorney Gen.'s rev. of Northern Irish judicial proceedings, 2006–07; Chm., Appeal Bd, Inst. of Actuaries, 1995–2001; a Judicial Tribunal Chm., City Disputes Panel, 1997–. Vice-Chm., Senate of the Inns of Court and the Bar, 1985–86; Chm., General Council of the Bar, 1987; Mem., Senate and Bar Council, 1981–87; Chm., London Common Law Bar Assoc., 1983–85. Hon. Mem., Canadian Bar Assoc., 1987. Mem. Adv. Council, Centre for Commercial Law Studies, QMW, 1990–2006; former Chm., Dame Colet House and Tower Hamlets Law Centre. Chm., Bd of Trustees, Nat. Gall., 2000–08. Chairman: N Kensington Amenity Trust, 1981–85; Kensington Housing Trust, 1999–2002. *Recreations*: gardening, theatre. *Address*: 4 Eldon Road, W8 5PU. *T*: (020) 7937 3301; Château Bellegarde, 32140 Masseube, France. *T*: (5) 62660027.

**SCOTT, Air Vice-Marshal Peter John**, CB 2003; CEng, FIMechE; Air Officer Logistics and Communications Information Systems, HQ Strike Command, 1998–2004; *b* 4 April 1949; *s* of John and Kathleen Scott; *m* 1973, Carolyn Frances, (Chips), Barrett; one *d*. *Educ*: Bromley Grammar Sch.; RAF Coll. Cranwell (BSc Hons 1971); Cranfield Inst. of Technol. (MSc 1979). Joined RAF, 1967; 96C Entry Cranwell, tours at Chivenor, Honington, Abingdon; OC Engineering and Supply Wing, RAF Germany Wildenrath, 1985–87; OC Engineering Wing, Falkland Islands, 1987–88; rcds 1995; Station Comdr and AO Wales, RAF St Athan, and ADC to the Queen, 1995–97. Patron, Univ. of Wales Air Sqn, 2004–09. *Recreations*: golf, model railways, hill walking. *Address*: Princes Risborough. *Clubs*: Royal Air Force; Ellesborough Golf (Capt., 2012–13).

**SCOTT, Primrose Smith**; Head of Quality Review, Institute of Chartered Accountants of Scotland, 1999–2002; Senior Partner, The McCabe Partnership (formerly Primrose McCabe & Co.), 1987–99; *b* 21 Sept. 1940. *Educ*: Ayr Acad. Trained with Stewart Gilmour, Ayr; qualified as CA, 1963; joined Romanes & Munro, Edinburgh, 1964; progressed through manager ranks to Partner, Deloitte Haskins & Sells, 1981–87; set up own practice, Linlithgow, 1987; moved practice to Edinburgh, 1997. Dep. Chm., Dunfermline Building Soc., 1998–2006; non-exec. Dir, Northern Venture Trust PLC, 1995–2010; Dir, Ecosse Unique Ltd, 2004–. Pres., Institute of Chartered Accountants of Scotland, 1994–95. Trustee, New Lanark Conservation Trust, 2002–06. Comr, Queen Victoria Sch., Dunblane, 1998–2016. Hon. Treas., Hospitality Industry Trust Scotland, 1994–2002; Treasurer: Age Scotland (formerly Age Concern Scotland), 2004–14; Borders Youth Th., 2007–14. Fellow, SCOTVEC, 1994. *Recreation*: walking dogs in Scottish Borders. *Address*: The Cleugh, Redpath, Earlston, Berwicks TD4 6AD. *T*: (01896) 849042.

**SCOTT, Richard John Dinwoodie**; Sheriff of Lothian and Borders at Edinburgh, 1986–2004; *b* 28 May 1939; *s* of late Prof. Richard Scott and Mary Ellen Maclachlan; *m* 1969, Josephine Moretta Blake; two *d*. *Educ*: Edinburgh Academy; Univ. of Edinburgh (MA, LLB) (Vans Dunlop Schol. in Evidence and Pleading, 1963). Lektor in English, British Centre, Sweden, 1960–61; Tutor, Faculty of Law, Univ. of Edinburgh, 1964–72; admitted to Faculty of Advocates, 1965; Standing Jun. Counsel to Min. of Defence (Air) in Scotland, 1968–77. Sheriff of Grampian, Highland and Islands, at Aberdeen and Stonehaven, 1977–86. Mem., Parole Bd for Scotland, 2003–09. Convenor, Additional Support Needs Tribunals for Scotland, 2005–10. Chm., Scottish Assoc. for Study of Delinquency, 1996–2001 (Chm., Aberdeen Branch, 1978–86, Edinburgh Branch, 1993–96); Mem., Working Party on Offenders aged 16–18, 1991–93; Chm., Grampian Victim Support Scheme, 1983–86; Pres., Sheriffs' Assoc., 2002–04 (Mem. Council, 1979–82 and 1994–2004; Vice-Pres., 2001–02); Mem., Sheriff Court Rules Council, 1995–98. Chm., Birthlink, 2008–14. Hon. Lectr, Univ. of Aberdeen, 1980–86. *Publications*: various articles in legal jls. *Recreations*: golf, curling, traditional music of Scotland. *Address*: c/o Sheriff Court House, 27 Chambers Street, Edinburgh EH1 1LB.

**SCOTT, Sir Ridley**, Kt 2003; film director and producer; *b* S Shields, 30 Nov. 1937. *Educ*: Royal Coll. of Art. *Films include*: director: The Duellists, 1976; Alien, 1978; Black Rain, 1989; director and producer: Blade Runner, 1980; Someone to Watch over Me, 1987; Thelma and Louise, 1991; 1492: Conquest of Paradise, 1992; White Squall, 1996; GI Jane, 1997; Gladiator, 2000; Hannibal, 2001; Black Hawk Down, 2002; Matchstick Men, 2003; Kingdom of Heaven, 2005; A Good Year, 2006; American Gangster, 2007; Body of Lies, 2008; Robin Hood, 2010; Prometheus, 2012; Life in a Day (documentary), 2011; The Grey, 2012; The Counsellor, 2013; Exodus, 2014; The Martian, 2015; All the Money in the World, 2018; prod., Child 44, 2015; *for television*: Churchill - The Gathering Storm, 2002; Gettysburg (drama documentary), 2011. BAFTA Fellowship, 2018. *Address*: Scott Free, 42–44 Beak Street, W1F 9RH. *T*: (020) 7437 3163.

**SCOTT, Robert Avisson**, CBE 2002; *b* 6 Jan. 1942; *s* of Robert Milligan Scott and Phyllis Winifred Scott; *m* 1979, Joanne Rose Adams; two *d*. *Educ*: Scots Coll., Wellington, NZ. Associate: Australian Insce Inst.; Insce Inst. NZ; FCIBS 2004. South British Insce Co. Ltd, later NZI Corp. Ltd, then General Accident plc, subseq. CGU plc, then CGNU plc, 1959–2001: Asst Gen. Manager, NZ, 1981–83; Australia: Asst Gen. Manager, 1983–85; Gen. Manager, 1985–87; Chief Gen. Manager, 1987–90; Dep. Gen. Manager, UK, 1990–91, Gen. Manager, 1991–94; Dep. Chief Exec., 1994–96; Gp Chief Exec., 1996–2001. Hon. FCII 2005. *Recreations*: sporting interests, walking, do it yourself. *Address*: 51 Great Pulteney Street, Bath, Som BA2 4DP. *T*: (01225) 313308.

**SCOTT, Sir Robert (David Hillyer)**, Kt 1994; Chairman, South London Business Council (formerly South London Economic Development Alliance), 1999–2014; *b* 22 Jan. 1944; *s* of Sir David Aubrey Scott, GCMG; *m* 1st, 1972, Su Dalgleish (marr. diss. 1995); two *s* one *d*; 2nd, 1995, Alicia Tomalino; two step *d*. *Educ*: Haileybury; Merton Coll., Oxford (Pres., OUDS, 1965–66). Actor, 1966–67; Administrator: 69 Theatre Co., Manchester, 1968–74; Royal Exchange Theatre Trust, 1974–77; Man. Dir, Manchester Theatres Ltd, 1978–96; Chairman: Manchester Olympic Bid Cttee, 1985–93; Manchester Commonwealth Games Bid Cttee, 1993–95; Chief Exec., Greenwich Millennium Trust, 1995–2001; Chief Exec., 2000–03, Chm., 2003–05, Internat. Ambassador, 2005–09, Liverpool Culture Co. Chm., EC Panel for choosing and monitoring European Capitals of Culture, 2008–11. Mem., Central Manchester Develt Corp., 1988–96. Special Projects Dir, Apollo Leisure Gp, 1994–99. Chairman: Cornerhouse Manchester, 1984–95; Granada Foundn, 1993–; Piccadilly Radio, 1993–2001; Tour East London, 1998–2001; City Bars and Restaurants, 1999–2003; Greenwich Theatre, 1999–2008; Bexley Heritage Trust, 1999–2007; Greenwich Peninsula Partnership, 2001–08; Trinity Laban, 2005–12; City Screen Ltd, 2006–12. Director: Royal Exchange Theatre, 1976–94; Hallé Concerts Soc., 1989–94; White Horse Fast Ferries, 1998–2002; London First, 1999–2003. Mem. Cttee, Whitworth Art Gall., 1989–95. DL Greater Manchester, 1988–97. Hon. RNCM 1990. Hon. Fellow: Manchester Poly., 1987; UMIST, 1989; Liverpool John Moores Univ., 2003.

Hon. MA: Manchester, 1988; Salford, 1991; Hon. LLD Greenwich, 2003; Hon. DArts Leeds Metropolitan, 2010. Officier de l'Ordre des Arts et des Lettres (France), 1991. *Publications*: The Biggest Room in the World, 1976. *Recreations*: food, travel, talking, sport, theatre. *Address*: 62 Crooms Hill, Greenwich, SE10 8HG.

**SCOTT, Robert William Lowry**, OBE 2005; JP; Lord Lieutenant of County Tyrone, since 2009; *b* Oakham, Rutland, 17 June 1951; *s* of Robert Irwin Maddin Scott and Margaret Sylvia Daphne (*née* Alexander); *m* 1978, Marie-Christine Cormerais; two *d*. *Educ*: Wellington Coll., Berks; Royal Agricl Coll., Cirencester. FRICS 1988. Agent and Factor, Abercorn Estates, 1977–2013. Dir, Balcas Ltd, 2005–15. Chairman: Forestry and Timber Assoc., 2002–04; Pro Silva Ireland, 2004–07; Tyrone Electric Ltd, 2014–; Dep. Chm., Confedn of Forest Industries (UK) Ltd, 2004–05. Trustee, Scottish Forestry Trust, 2002–12 (Chm., 2010–12). Hon. Col, 152 (N Irish) Regt RLC, 2014–. JP 1990, Sheriff 1992, Co. Tyrone. *Recreations*: silviculture, ski-ing. *Address*: Ballyrenan, Newtownstewart, Co. Tyrone, Northern Ireland BT78 4HB.

**SCOTT, Prof. Roger Davidson**, PhD; CPhys, FInstP; FRSE; Director, Scottish Universities Research and Reactor Centre, 1991–98; Professor of Nuclear Science, University of Glasgow, 1994–98; *b* 17 Dec. 1941; *s* of Alexander N. Scott and Jessie H. Scott (*née* Davidson); *m* 1965, Marion S. McCluckie; two *s* one *d*. *Educ*: Anderson Inst., Lerwick; Univ. of Edinburgh (BSc 1st Cl. Hons Physics; PhD Nuclear Physics). University Demonstrator, Univ. of Edinburgh, 1965–68; Lectr, 1968–88, Depute Dir, 1988–91, Scottish Univs Res. and Reactor Centre. Non-exec. Dir, Nuclear Decommissioning Authy, 2004–08. FRSE 1995. *Publications*: articles on nuclear physics and envmtl radioactivity; contribs to learned jls. *Recreations*: watching football, walking wife and dogs, home maintenance. *Address*: 6 Downfield Gardens, Bothwell, Glasgow G71 8UW. *T*: (01698) 854121.

**SCOTT, Sheila Margaret**, OBE 2007; Chief Executive, National Care Association (formerly National Care Homes Association), 1993, now Advisor to Board; *b* 18 Dec. 1948; *d* of G. W. Brownlow and late Audrey Brownlow (*née* Louth); *m* 1973, A. L. Scott (marr. diss. 1996); one *s* one *d*. *Educ*: Wisbech High Sch.; Addenbrooke's Hosp., Cambridge (RGN 1971). Sister, Springdene Gp, N London, 1975–83; care home proprietor, N London, 1983–88; with Nat. Care Homes Assoc. (later Nat. Care Assoc.), 1988–; Office Manager/Company Sec., 1988–93; on secondment to DoH, 1992–93. *Recreations*: travel, cinema, cycling, gardening. *Address*: 1 Westwater Crescent, Hampton Vale, Peterborough PE7 8LT. *E*: sheilamscott@hotmail.com.

**SCOTT, Sionaidh D.**; *see* Douglas-Scott.

**SCOTT, Prof. Sophie Kerttu**, PhD; FBA 2016; FMedSci; Professor of Cognitive Neuroscience, University College London, since 2016; *b* London, 16 Nov. 1966; *d* of Colin Mountford Scott and Christine Winnifred Scott; partner, Dr Tom Manly; one *s*. *Educ*: Westholme Sch., Blackburn; Queen Elizabeth's Grammar Sch., Blackburn; Poly. of Central London (BSc Hons Life Scis 1990); University Coll. London (PhD Cognitive Sci. 1994). SO, MRC Applied Psychol. Unit, Cambridge, 1995–98; University College London: Res. Fellow, 1998–2001; Wellcome Trust Career Develt Fellow, 2001–05, Wellcome Trust Sen. Fellow, 2005–16, Inst. of Cognitive Neurosci., UCL. Royal Instn Christmas Lectr, 2017. FMedSci 2012. *Publications*: over 90 papers. *Recreation*: watching and performing stand-up comedy. *Address*: Institute of Cognitive Neuroscience, University College London, 17 Queen Square, WC1N 3AR. *T*: (020) 7679 1144. *E*: sophie.scott@ucl.ac.uk. *Club*: Groucho.

**SCOTT, Prof. Stephen Basil Cuthbert**, CBE 2014; PhD; FRCP, FRCPsych; FMedSci; Professor of Child Health and Behaviour, and Director, National Academy for Parenting Research, King's College London, since 2007; Consultant Child and Adolescent Psychiatrist, Maudsley Hospital; *b* Cambridge, 28 Sept. 1951; *s* of John and Eleanor Scott; *m* 1990, Penelope Susan Titman; three *s*. *Educ*: Leys Sch., Cambridge; King's Coll., Cambridge (MB BChir 1980; PhD). MRCP 1988; MRCPsych 1990. Hd, Nat. Adoption and Fostering Clinic and Nat. Conduct Problems Clinic, Maudsley Hosp., London, 1995–. Chair, NICE Guideline on Antisocial Behaviour, 2012. Chair, Assoc. for Child and Adolescent Mental Health, 2015. FMedSci 2017. *Publications*: (with R. Goodman) Child and Adolescent Psychiatry, 1997, 3rd edn 2012 (trans. 7 langs); Fostering Changes, 2000, 2nd edn 2005; over 100 scholarly papers on how to help disruptive children. *Recreations*: cycling in Provence, tennis, ski-ing. *Address*: Box P85, Department of Child and Adolescent Psychiatry, Institute of Psychiatry, Psychology and Neuroscience, King's College London, 16 De Crespigny Park, SE5 8AF. *T*: (020) 7848 0746. *E*: Stephen.Scott@kcl.ac.uk.

**SCOTT, Tavish Hamilton**; farmer; Head of External Affairs, Scottish Rugby, since 2019; *b* 6 May 1966; *s* of Sir John Hamilton Scott, *qv*; three *s* one *d*. *Educ*: Napier Coll., Edinburgh (BA Hons Business Studies). Research Asst to J. R. Wallace, MP, 1989–90; Press Officer, Scottish Lib Dem Party, 1990–92. Mem. (Lib Dem) Shetland Islands Council, 1992–99. Mem. (Lib Dem) Shetland, 1999–2011, Shetland Islands, 2011–19, Scottish Parlt. Scottish Executive: Dep. Minister for Parlt, 2000–01, for Parly Business and for Finance and Public Services, 2003–05; Minister for Transport, 2005–07; Opposition front bench spokesman on finance and sustainable growth, Scottish Parlt, 2007–08. Leader, Scottish Lib Dems, 2008–11. Chm., Lerwick Harbour Trust, 1997–99. *Recreations*: football, golf, cinema, reading, current affairs, Up Helly Aa. *Address*: Scottish Rugby, BT Murrayfield, Edinburgh EH12 5PJ.

**SCOTT, Tiffany Anne**; QC 2018; *b* Swindon, 8 June 1974; *d* of Derek and Vanessa Scott. *Educ*: Farnborough Hill Coll., Farnborough; Strodes Coll., Egham; Oriel Coll., Oxford (BA Lit.Hum. 1996); Coll. of Law, Guildford (DipLaw 1997); Inns of Court Sch. of Law (BVC 1998). Called to the Bar, Middle Temple, 1998; in practice as chancery and commercial barrister, 1998–. *Recreations*: cinema, playing piano, walking, travel, ski-ing. *Address*: Wilberforce Chambers, 8 New Square, Lincoln's Inn, WC2A 3QP. *T*: (020) 7306 0102. *E*: tscott@wilberforce.co.uk.

**SCOTT, Timothy John Whittaker**; QC 1995; a Recorder, since 1999; *b* 19 July 1949; *s* of late John Dick Scott and Helen Scott (*née* Whittaker); *m*; one *s* two *d*. *Educ*: Westminster Sch. (Queen's Schol.); New Coll., Oxford (Exhibnr; MA). Journalist, 1970–72; called to the Bar, Gray's Inn, 1975; Asst Recorder, 1995–99. *Publications*: articles on family law topics in specialist jls. *Recreations*: fishing, reading, travel. *Address*: 29 Bedford Row, WC1R 4HE. *T*: (020) 7404 1044. *Club*: Garrick.

**SCOTT, Sir (Walter) John**, 5th Bt *cr* 1907, of Beauclerc, Bywell St Andrew, Northumberland; countryside campaigner, farmer, author, broadcaster and snuff manufacturer; *b* 24 Feb. 1948; *s* of Sir Walter Scott, 4th Bt and Diana Mary (*d* 1985), *d* of J. R. Owen; *S* father, 1992; *m* 1st, 1969, Lowell Patria (marr. diss. 1971), *d* of late Gp Capt. Pat Vaughan Goddard, Auckland, NZ; one *d*; 2nd, 1977, Mary Gavin, *d* of Alexander Fairley Anderson, Gartocharn, Dunbartonshire; one *s* one *d*. Chm., Sir Walter Scott's Fine Border Snuff, 2012–. Chm., N Pennine Hunt, 2008– (Jt Master, 2009–); President: Union of Country Sports Workers, 2000–; Tay Valley Wildfowlers' Assoc., 2001–; Gamekeepers Welfare Trust, 2009–; Newcastle upon Tyne Wildfowlers' Assoc., 2009–; Member Board: Heather Trust, 2004–; Eur. Squirrel Fedn, 2004–; Patron: Sporting Lucas Terrier Assoc.,

2004–; Nat. Orgn of Beaters and Pickers Up, 2007–; Wildlife Ark Trust, 2008–; Centenary Patron, British Assoc. for Shooting and Conservation, 2008–; Pres., Assoc. of Working Lurcher/Longdog, 2015–. Writer and co-presenter, Clarissa and the Countryman, TV series, 2000–03. Founder Mem., Cholmondeley Coursing Club, 1995. *Publications*: (jtly) Clarissa and the Countryman, 2000; (jtly) Clarissa and the Countryman Sally Forth, 2001; (jtly) A Sunday Roast, 2002; (jtly) The Game Cookbook, 2004; (jtly) A Greener Life, 2005; A Book of Britain, 2010. *Recreation*: field sports. *Heir*: s Walter Samuel Scott, b 6 Dec. 1984. *Address*: Old Mill Cottage, Cornhill-on-Tweed, Northumberland TD12 4RA. *Club*: Pratt's.

**SCOTT, Hon. (William) Alexander,** CBE 2013; JP; MP (PLP) Warwick South East, 1993–2012; Premier of Bermuda, 2003–06; b 12 June 1940; s of Willard Alexander Scott and Edith Lucille Scott; m 1972, Olga Lawrence; one s one d. *Educ*: Temple Univ., Philadelphia (BA Fine Arts). Graphic designer and design consultant; owner, Scotts Crafts Ltd, 1964–97. Founding Mem. and former Chm., Big Brothers. Mem., Pitt Commn, 1978. Mem. (PLP), 1985–93, and Leader of the Opposition, 1989–93, Senate, Bermuda; Minister of Works and Engrg, 1998–2003. JP Bermuda, 1985.

**SCOTT, (William) Dermot;** Head, European Parliament Office for the United Kingdom, 2002–09; b 19 Sept. 1943; s of Rev. Dr Eric Scott and Bee Scott (née Knight); m 1970, Susan Burdon Davies; one s one d. *Educ*: Campbell Coll., Belfast; Trinity Coll., Dublin (BA Mod., MSc Econ); Sch. of Public Admin, Dublin. Institute of Public Administration, Dublin, 1967–79; European Parlt Office in Ireland, 1979–98; Hd, European Parlt Office in Scotland, 1998–2002. Life Member: NUJ; Irish Inst. of Internat. and European Affairs. Member: Royal Dublin Soc. (Member: Council, 2012–17; Bd of Mgt, 2016–17); Bd, Irish Georgian Soc., 2016–. Silver Medal, Fondation du Mérite européen, 2011. *Publications*: Caisleán Eireannacha, 1972; (contrib.) Ireland and EU Membership Evaluated, 1991; Ireland's Contribution to the European Union, 1994; Ireland and the IGC, 1996; (ed) Europe is Our Story: towards a new narrative for the European Union, 2014; numerous articles on European affairs. *Recreations*: trout fishing, putting on recitals, looking at ruins. *Address*: 29 Wellington Road, Ballsbridge, Dublin 4, Ireland. *T*: (1) 6684652. *Clubs*: Reform; Kildare Street and University (Dublin).

**SCOTT, (William) John (Graham);** Member (C) Ayr, Scottish Parliament, since March 2000; b 7 June 1951; s of William Scott and Elizabeth Haddow Scott; m 1975, Charity Nadine Mary Bousfield (d 2000); one s one d; m 2015, Sheila Marguerite Belcher (née Georgeson). *Educ*: Barrhill Primary Sch.; George Watson's Coll.; Edinburgh Univ. (BSc Civil Engrg 1973). Farming in family partnership, 1973–; Partner, family catering business, 1985–2000. Founder Dir, Ayrshire Country Lamb Ltd, 1988–93; created Ayrshire Farmers' Mkts, 1999 (Chm., 1999–2005). Convenor, Hill Farming Cttee, NFU Scotland, 1993–99; Chairman: S of Scotland Regl Wool Cttee, 1996–2000; Ayrshire and Arran Farming Wildlife Adv. Gp, 1993–99. Scottish Parliament: Cons. Shadow Cabinet Sec. for Rural Affairs and Envmt, 2007–11, for Sustainable Develt, 2016–; Dep. Presiding Officer, 2011–16; Member: Transport and Envmt Cttee, 2001–03; Corporate Body, 2003–07; Vice-Chm., Petitions Cttee, 2003–07 (Mem., 2000–01); Vice Chm., Rural Affairs and Envmt Cttee, 2007–11; Chm., Delegated Powers and Law Reform Cttee, 2016–. Chm., Hill Sheep and Native Woodland Project, Scottish Agricl Coll., 1999–2009. Founder Chm., Scottish Assoc. of Farmers' Markets, 2001–05. FRASE 2016. Hon. Mem., BVA. JP Girvan, 1997–99. Elder, Ballantrae Ch, 1985–. Hon. Fellow, Moredun Inst. *Recreations*: curling, geology, bridge. *Address*: Scottish Parliament, Edinburgh EH99 1SP. *T*: (0131) 348 5664; (constituency office) 17 Wellington Square, Ayr KA7 1EZ. *T*: (01292) 286251, *Fax*: (01292) 280480.

**SCOTT, Rev. Preb. William Sievwright,** CVO 2014; Sub-Dean of Her Majesty's Chapels Royal, Deputy Clerk of the Closet, Sub-Almoner and Domestic Chaplain to the Queen, 2007–15; a Chaplain to the Queen, 2003–15; an Extra Chaplain to the Queen, since 2015; b 1 Feb. 1946; s of David Anderson Harper Scott and Amelia Scott (née Sievwright). *Educ*: Harris Acad., Dundee; Edinburgh Theol Coll. Ordained deacon 1970, priest 1971; Curate: St Ninian's, Glasgow, 1971–73; St Francis, Bridgwater, 1973–77; Rector: Shepton Beauchamp, Barrington, Puckington and Stocklinch, 1977–82; Woolavington and Cossington, 1982–84; Chaplain, Community of All Hallow's, Ditchingham, 1984–91; Vicar, St Mary's, Bourne St, SW1, 1991–2002; Area Dean, Westminster (St Margaret), 1997–2004; Preb., St Paul's Cathedral, 2000–15, now Preb. Emeritus; Chaplain of the Queen's Chapel of the Savoy and of the Royal Victorian Order, 2002–07. Chaplain, Priory of Our Lady of Walsingham, 1991–2007. *Recreations*: music making and listening, reading novels and poetry, conducting retreats. *Address*: 13 Kylestrome House, Cundy Street, SW1W 9JT. *Clubs*: National Liberal, Savile.

**SCOTT CATO, Molly;** Member (Green) South West Region, European Parliament, since 2014; b Wrexham, 21 May 1963; d of David Brian Curtis and Mary Curtis (née French); m 1987, Raymond Alexander Scott (marr. diss. 1996); two s one d. *Educ*: Bath High Sch.; St Hugh's Coll., Oxford (MA PPE); Univ. of Wales, Aberystwyth (PhD 2001). Desk ed., OUP, 1988; Lectr, Mgt Sch., 2001–12, Dir, Cardiff Inst. for Cooperative Studies, 2008–12, Univ. of Wales Inst., Cardiff, later Cardiff Metropolitan Univ.; Prof. of Green Economics, Univ. of Roehampton, 2012–14. Mem. (Green) Stroud DC, 2011–14 (Leader, Green Gp, 2012–14). Contested (Green) Bristol W, 2017. *Publications*: The Pit and the Pendulum, 2004; Market Schmarket, 2006; Green Economics: theory, policy and practice, 2009; Environment and Economy, 2011; The Bioregional Economy, 2012. *Recreations*: choral singing, basket-making, bodging. *Address*: European Parliament, 60 Rue Wiertz, Brussels 1047, Belgium. *E*: molly.scottcato@europarl.europa.eu.

**SCOTT-GALL, His Honour Anthony Robert Gall;** a Circuit Judge, 1996–2016; b 30 March 1946; s of Robert and Daphne Scott-Gall; m 1973, Caroline Anne Scott; one s one d. *Educ*: Stowe Sch.; New Coll., Oxford (BA). Called to the Bar, Middle Temple, 1971; Recorder, 1993. *Recreations*: cricket, Rugby football, gardening, travel, ornithology, history, music, five grandchildren and the dog. *Clubs*: Richmond Football; Armadillos Cricket.

**SCOTT-KERR, William Andrew;** Publisher, Transworld Publishers Ltd, since 2005; b Stoke on Trent, 27 April 1964; s of Robert James Scott-Kerr and Ann Alexandra (née Sagar); m 1995, Joanna Frank (marr. diss. 2010); three s. *Educ*: Sedbergh Sch.; Southampton Univ. (BA English and Hist. 1985). Bookseller, Hatchards Booksellers, 1985–87; Fiction Buyer, Pan Bookshop, 1987–88; Jun. Ed. to Editl Dir, Pan Macmillan Ltd, 1988–94; Editl Dir, Transworld Publishers Ltd, 1994–2005. *Recreations*: photography, music, walking, cookery. *Address*: Transworld Publishers Ltd, 61–63 Uxbridge Road, W5 5SA. *T*: (020) 8579 2652. *E*: b.scott-kerr@transworld-publishers.co.uk.

**SCOTT-LEE, Sir Paul (Joseph),** Kt 2007; QPM 1997; DL; Chief Constable, West Midlands Police, 2002–09; b 25 July 1953; s of Hubert George Scott-Lee and Decima Florence Scott-Lee (née Hancorn); m 1975, Rosemary Susan Hargreaves. *Educ*: Whitley Abbey Comprehensive Sch., Coventry; Police Staff Coll., Bramshill. Joined Warwickshire and Coventry Constabulary from Cadet Corps, 1972; Sergeant to Chief Inspector, W Midlands Police, 1978–88; Superintendent to Chief Superintendent, Northants Police, 1988–92; Asst Chief Constable, Kent Co. Constabulary, 1992–94; Dep. Chief Constable, 1994–98, Chief Constable, 1998–2002, Suffolk Police. Ind. Assessor, Leveson Inquiry into culture, practice and ethics of the press, 2011–. Trustee, Police Arboretum Meml Trust, 2014–. Patron, St Paul's Community Trust, Balsall Heath, Birmingham, 2010–. DL W Midlands, 2003. Hon. DLaws Wolverhampton, 2009. *Recreations*: fly fishing, golf, reading.

**SCOTT-MANDERSON, Marcus Charles William;** QC 2006; b 10 Feb. 1956; s of late Dr William Scott-Manderson, MB ChB, MRCGP and Pamela Scott-Manderson; m 2003, Melinda Penelope Tillard. *Educ*: Harrow Sch.; Christ Church, Oxford (BCL, MA); Hague Acad. of Internat. Law; Glasgow Univ. Called to the Bar, Lincoln's Inn, 1980; in practice, specialising in internat. cases relating to children, until 2019. *Recreations*: archaeology, travel. *Club*: Lansdowne.

**SCOTT-MONCRIEFF, Lucy Ann,** CBE 2014; a Mental Health Tribunal Judge, since 2008; Managing Director, Scott-Moncrieff and Associates Ltd, since 2011; Commissioner for Standards, House of Lords, since 2016; b England, 26 March 1954; d of late William Scott-Moncrieff and (Dora) Rosemary Scott-Moncrieff (née Knollys); two s by John Dowie. *Educ*: St Mary's, Calne; Guildford Tech. Coll.; Univ. of Kent (BA 1975). Admitted as solicitor, 1978; Asst Solicitor, Offenbach and Co. and Bradbury's, 1979–86; Partner, Offenbach's, 1986–87; Partner, Scott-Moncrieff Harbour and Sinclair, 1987–2011. Mental Health Act Comr, 1987–89; Postcomm Comr, 2008–11; Comr, Judicial Appts Commn, 2014–17. Law Society of England and Wales: Mem. Council, 2002–; Vice Pres., 2011–12; Pres., 2012–13; Chair, Equality, Diversity and Inclusion Cttee, 2013–. Co-Chair, Access to Justice and Legal Aid Cttee, Internat. Bar Assoc., 2013–17; Chair, Adv. Panel, UK Admin. Justice Inst., 2015–. Mem., QC Appts Panel, 2005–11. Hon. LLD Kent, 2009. *Recreations*: gardening, reading, ignoring housework, enthusing about new ways of doing things (not housework).

**SCOTT-SPICER, Gail;** Chief Executive Officer, King's College Hospital Charity, since 2018; b Chertsey, 1 June 1974; d of John Spicer and Hils Jago (née Cox); m 2010, Bruce McKay; two c. *Educ*: Middlesex Univ. (MA Mktg Mgt 1997); Inst. of Dirs (Dip. Co. Direction 2007). Mkt develt, media relns and advertising campaign roles, London Transport and London Underground, 1990–97; Head: Mktg and Student Recruitment, Univ. of N London, 1997–2000; Mktg Communications, Audit Commn, 2000–03; Dep. Chief Exec., Assoc. of Chief Execs of Voluntary Orgns, 2004–06; Director: Communications, Catch 22, 2006–08; Mktg and Communications, Scout Assoc., 2009–15; Chief Executive Officer: Carers Trust, 2015–17; Dame Kelly Holmes Trust, 2017–18. Non-exec. Dir, Scout Shops Ltd, 2012–15. Trustee: CharityComms, 2011–17 (Vice Chm., 2014–17); Money Advice Trust, 2013– (Dep. Chm., 2017–); Premier League Charitable Fund, 2017–; Adv. Mem., Charity Bank, 2017–. *Recreations*: performing arts, gardening, walking, wildlife.

**SCOTT THOMAS, Dame Kristin,** DBE 2015 (OBE 2003); actress; b 24 May 1960; m 1981, François Olivennes (marr. diss.); two s one d. *Educ*: Cheltenham Ladies' Coll.; Central Sch. of Speech and Drama; École Nationale des Arts et Technique de Théâtre, Paris. *Theatre includes*: Bérénice, Paris, 2001; The Three Sisters, 2003, As You Desire Me, 2005, Playhouse Th.; The Seagull, Royal Court, 2007 (Best Actress, Laurence Olivier Award, 2008); Betrayal, Comedy Th., 2011; Old Times, Harold Pinter Th., 2013; Electra, Old Vic, 2014; The Audience, Apollo Th., 2015. *Films include*: Under the Cherry Moon, 1986; A Handful of Dust, 1988; Bitter Moon, 1992; Four Weddings and a Funeral, 1994 (Best Supporting Actress Award, BAFTA); Angels and Insects, 1995 (Best Actress Award, BAFTA); Richard III, The Confessional, Mission Impossible, 1996; The English Patient, 1997; The Horse Whisperer, 1998; Random Hearts, 1999; Up at the Villa, Play, 2000; Gosford Park, Life as a House, 2002; Petites Coupures, 2003; Man to Man, The Adventures of Arsène Lupin, Keeping Mum, 2005; The Walker, 2007; Il y a longtemps que je t'aime, Easy Virtue, 2008; Nowhere Boy, 2009; Partir, 2010; Sarah's Key, 2011; The Woman in the Fifth, Bel Ami, Salmon Fishing in the Yemen, In Your Hands, 2012; In the House, Only God Forgives, 2013; The Invisible Woman, Before the Winter Chill, My Old Lady, 2014; Suite Française, 2015; The Party, 2017; Darkest Hour, 2018. *Television includes*: The Tenth Man, 1988; Endless Game, Framed, 1990; Titmuss Regained, 1991; Look At It This Way, 1992; Body and Soul, 1994; Fleabag, 2019.

**SCOURSE, Rear-Adm. Frederick Peter,** CB 1997; MBE 1972; FREng, FIET; Acting Controller of the Navy, 1996–97; b 23 June 1944; s of late Frederick David John Scourse and Margaret Elaine Scourse; m 1967, Nicolette Jean Somerville West; one s. *Educ*: Wells Cathedral Sch.; RN Coll., Dartmouth; Churchill Coll., Cambridge (MA Mech Sci., Elect. Sci.). Served HM Ships: Dido, 1963–64; Warspite, 1969–72; Renown, 1974–77; MoD (PE), 1979–82; NDC, 1982–83; MoD (PE), 1983–89; Dir-Gen., Surface Weapons (Navy), 1989–94; Dir-Gen., Surface Ships, 1994–97. Nuclear Weapons Safety Advr, MoD, 1997–2003. Industry Advr, Churchill Coll., Cambridge, 1998–2007. Dir, Wild Trout Trust, 2002–04; Sec., Five Valleys Trust, 2004–19. Vice Chm., Regular Forces Employment Assoc., 1999–2002. FREng 2000. *Recreations*: fly fishing, singing. *Address*: Valley View, 278a Turleigh, Bradford on Avon BA15 2HH.

**SCOWCROFT, Gen. Brent,** Hon. KBE 1993; President: Forum for International Policy, since 1993; Scowcroft Group, since 1993; b 19 March 1925; s of James Scowcroft and Lucile (née Ballantyne); m 1951, Marian (Jackie) Horner (d 1995); one d. *Educ*: Ogden City Schs; US Mil. Acad.; Columbia Univ. (MA 1953; PhD 1967); Lafayette Coll.; Georgetown Univ. Joined Army 1943; qualified pilot 1948; Prof. of Russian History, US Mil. Acad., 1953–57; service in Washington, Yugoslavia, Colorado, Western Hemisphere Region; with Jt Chiefs of Staff, 1970; MA to President, 1972–73; Dep. Asst, 1973–75, and Asst 1975–77 and 1989–93, to successive Presidents, for Nat. Security Affairs; retired from mil. service, 1975; Dir, Council on Foreign Relations, 1983–89; served on major US cttees, commns and bds, 1977–89. Vice-Chm., Kissinger Associates, 1982–89. Chm., CSIS/Pacific Forum, 1993–; Co-Chm., Blue Ribbon Commn on America's Nuclear Future, 2010–12. Mem. Bd of Visitors, USAF Acad., 1993–99. US Medal of Freedom, 1991; Grand Cross, OM (Germany), 2009; numerous Service medals and awards. *Publications*: (with George H. W. Bush) A World Transformed, 1998; (jtly) America and the World: conversations on the future of American foreign policy, 2008; (jtly) US Nuclear Weapons Policy, 2009. *Recreation*: ski-ing.

**SCRAFTON, Douglas,** CMG 1998; Member (Lib Dem) Cornwall Council, 2013–17; b 14 July 1949; s of late Douglas Scrafton and Irene Hilda Kirk (formerly Scrafton, née Hammett); m 1975, Carolyn Patricia Collison; one s one d. HM Diplomatic Service, 1967–2001: Mem., UK Delegn (later UK Perm. Repn) to EC, 1970–73; Kampala, 1973–74; Mbabane, 1975–77; FCO, 1977–80; Jedda, 1980–82; British Liaison Office, Riyadh, 1982–84; Cairo, 1984–85; FCO, 1985–87; on loan to Cabinet Office, 1987–88; Ottawa, 1989–92; FCO, 1992–94; Ambassador: to Yemen Republic, 1995–97; to Democratic Republic of the Congo, 1998–2000; Foreign Sec.'s Special Rep. for the Great Lakes region, 2000–01. Member: St Blaise Town Council, 2007–15; Tywardreath and Par Parish Council, 2014–19. Director: St Austell Bay Economic Forum CIC, 2015–17; Roundhouse Cornwall Ltd, 2015–18; non-exec. Dir, Corserv, 2016–17; Chm., Par Track Ltd, 2016–. Volunteer, CAB, 2003–10. *Recreations*: photography, reading, gardening. *Address*: Reynards Rest, The Mount, Par, Cornwall PL24 2BZ.

**SCRASE-DICKINS, Mark Frederick Hakon,** CMG 1991; DL; HM Diplomatic Service, retired; *b* 31 May 1936; *s* of late Alwyne Rory Macnamara Scrase-Dickins and Ingeborg Oscara Frederika Scrase-Dickins; *m* 1969, Martina Viviane Bayley; one *s* one *d* (and one *d* decd). *Educ:* Eton Coll.; RMA, Sandhurst. Commnd Rifle Bde (later Royal Green Jackets), 1956; Malaya, 1956–57 (despatches); ADC to GOC Ghana Army, 1958–59; ADC to Chief of Imperial Gen. Staff, 1959–60; SE Asia, 1962–65; Army Staff Coll., 1967; Hong Kong, 1968–70; transferred to FCO, 1973; Vientiane, 1975; Muscat, 1976; Counsellor: Jakarta, 1983; Riyadh, 1990. Pres., St John Ambulance Sussex, 2005–11. Chm. Trustees, John Bodley Trust, 2004–; Trustee, Lodge Hill Trust, 2006–11. High Sheriff, 2003–04, DL 2004, West Sussex. OStJ 2013 (SBStJ 2008). *Recreation:* field sports. *Address:* Coolhurst Grange, Horsham, West Sussex RH13 6LE. *T:* (01403) 252416. *Club:* White's.

**SCREECH, Rt Rev. Royden;** Bishop Suffragan of St Germans, 2000–11; *b* 15 May 1953; *s* of Raymond Kenneth Screech and Gladys Beryl Screech; *m* 1988, Angela May Waring; no *c. Educ:* Cotham Grammar Sch.; King's Coll. London (BD 1974, AKC 1974); St Augustine's Coll., Canterbury; London South Bank Univ. (MSc 2015). Ordained deacon, 1976, priest, 1977; Curate, St Catherine, Hatcham, 1976–80; Vicar, St Antony, Nunhead, 1980–87; Priest-in-charge, St Silas, Nunhead, 1982–87; Rural Dean, Camberwell, 1984–87; Vicar, St Edward, New Addington, 1987–94; Selection Sec., 1994–97, Sen. Selection Sec., 1997–2000, ABM, subseq. Ministry Div., Archbishops' Council. *Recreations:* opera, holidays in Italy, Coronation Street.

**SCRIVEN, Baron** *cr* 2014 (Life Peer), of Hunters Bar in the City of Sheffield; **Paul James Scriven;** Managing Partner, Scriven Consulting; *b* 7 Feb. 1966. Former NHS manager. Mem. (Lib Dem) Sheffield CC, 2000–12 (Leader, 2008–11). Contested (Lib Dem) Sheffield Central, 2010. *Address:* House of Lords, SW1A 0PW.

**SCRIVEN, Rt Rev. Henry William;** Mission Director for Latin America, Church Mission Society, 2009–17; an Honorary Assistant Bishop: Diocese of Oxford, since 2010; Diocese of Winchester, since 2013; *b* 30 Aug. 1951; *s* of late William Hamilton Scriven and Jeanne Mary Edwards; *m* 1975, Catherine Rose Ware; one *s* one *d. Educ:* Repton Sch.; Sheffield Univ. (BA Hons); St John's Theol Coll., Nottingham. Ordained deacon, 1975, priest, 1976; Asst Curate, Holy Trinity, Wealdstone, Harrow, 1975–79; Missionary with S American Missionary Soc., N Argentina, 1979–82; Educn Associate Rector, Christ Church, Little Rock, Arkansas, 1982–83; Missionary, S American Missionary Soc., Spain, 1984–90; Chaplain, British Embassy Church of St George, Madrid, 1990–95; Suffragan Bp of Gibraltar in Europe, 1995–2002; Asst Bp of Pittsburgh, USA, 2002–08; Hon. Asst Bp, Dio. of Chichester, 2010–14. *Recreations:* reading, walking, cycling, music. *Address:* 16 East St Helen Street, Abingdon, Oxon OX14 5EA. *T:* (01235) 536607, 07789 635260. *E:* henry.scriven@gmail.com.

**SCRIVEN, Pamela;** QC 1992; a Recorder, since 1996; *b* 5 April 1948; *d* of Maurice Scriven and Evelyn Scriven (*née* Stickney); *m* 1973; two *s. Educ:* University College London (LLB Hons). Called to the Bar, Inner Temple, 1970 (Bencher, 1995). Chm., Family Law Bar Assoc., 1999–2001. Mem. Bd, Ofsted, 2018–. *Address:* 1 King's Bench Walk, Temple, EC4Y 7DB. *T:* (020) 7583 6266.

**SCRIVENER, Christiane;** Commandeur de la Légion d'Honneur, 2001 (Officier, 1995); Médiateur, Société Générale, since 1996; Member, Commission of the European Communities, 1989–95; *b* 1 Sept. 1925; *m* 1944, Pierre Scrivener; one *s* decd. *Educ:* Lycée de Grenoble; Faculté de lettres et de droit de Paris. Dip. Psychol.; Dip. Harvard Business Sch. Directeur Général: l'Assoc. pour l'organisation des Stages en France, 1958–69; l'Assoc. pour l'organisation des missions de coopération technique, 1961–69; l'Agence pour la coopération technique industrielle et économique, 1969–76; Sec. d'Etat à la Consommation, 1976–78; Pres., la Commission chargée d'étudier les problèmes éthiques de la publicité, 1978; Sec. Gen. Adj. du parti républicain, 1978–79; Mem., Parlement européen (UDF), 1978–89; Mem., Conseil d'admin des Assurances Générales de France, 1986–89. Alumni Achievement Award (Harvard Business Sch.), 1976. Officier, Polonia Restituta, 1968; Médaille d'Or du Mérite Européen, 1990; Grand Croix de l'Ordre de Léopold II (Belgium), 1995; Grand Croix de Mérite du Grand Duché de Luxembourg, 1996. *Publications:* L'Europe, une bataille pour l'avenir, 1984; (pour les enfants) L'histoire du Petit Troll, 1986. *Recreations:* ski-ing, tennis, classical music. *Address:* 21 avenue Robert-Schumann, 92100 Boulogne-Billancourt, France.

**SCRIVER, Prof. Charles Robert,** CC 1997 (OC 1986); GOQ 1997; FRS 1991; FRSC 1973; Alva Professor of Human Genetics, 1994–2002, Professor of Pediatrics, Faculty of Medicine, and Professor of Biology, Faculty of Science, 1969–2002, McGill University, Montreal, now Professor Emeritus; *b* 7 Nov. 1930; *s* of Walter DeMoulpied Scriver and Jessie Marion (*née* Boyd); *m* 1956, Esther Katharine Peirce; two *s* two *d. Educ:* McGill Univ., Montreal (BA *cum laude* 1951, MD, CM *cum laude* 1955). Intern, Royal Victoria Hosp., Montreal, 1955–56; Resident: Royal Victoria and Montreal Children's Hosps, 1956–57; Children's Med. Center, Boston, 1957–58; McLaughlin Travelling Fellow, UCL, 1958–60; Chief Resident in Pediatrics, Montreal Children's Hosp., 1960–61; Asst, Associate Prof., Pediatrics 1961–69, Markle Schol., 1962–67, McGill Univ. Rutherford Lectr, RSCan, 1983. Associate, 1968–95, Dist. Scientist, 1995–, MRC; Dir, MRC Gp (Med. Genetics), 1982–94; Associate Dir, Can. Genetic Diseases Networks (Centers of Excellence), 1989–98. President: Can. Soc. Clinical Investigation, 1974–75; Soc. Pediatric Res., 1975–76; Amer. Soc. Human Genetics, 1986–87; Amer. Pediatric Soc., 1994–95. FAAAS 1992; Member: Amer. Soc. Clinical Investigation; Assoc. Amer. Physicians; Hon. Member: Brit. Paediatric Assoc.; RCPI; Soc. Française de Pédiatrie. Hon. DSc: Manitoba, 1992; Glasgow, 1993; Montreal, 1993; Utrecht, 1999; UBC, 2002; Western Ontario, 2007; McGill, 2007. Wood Gold Medal, McGill Univ., 1955; Mead Johnson Award, 1968, Borden Award 1973, Amer. Acad. Pediatrics; Borden Award, Nutrition Soc. Can., 1969; Allan Award, 1978, Excellence in Human Genetics Educn Award, 2001, Amer. Soc. Human Genetics; G. Malcolm Brown Award, Can. Soc. Clin. Invest., 1979; Gairdner Internat. Award, Gairdner Foundn, 1979; McLaughlin Medal, RSC, 1981; Ross Award, Can. Pediatric Soc., 1990; Award of Excellence, Genetic Soc. of Canada, 1992; Prix du Québec (Wilder Penfield), 1995; Lifetime Achievement Award in Genetics, Birth Defects Foundn, 1997; Querci Prize, Italy, 2001; McGill Alumni Global Lifetime Achievement Award, 2009; Folling Award, Eur. Phenylketonuria Gp, 2010; Pollin Prize, Columbia Univ. and NY Presbyterian Hosp., 2010; Howland Medal, Amer. Pediatric Soc., 2010; McKusick Leadership Award, Amer. Soc. of Human Genetics, 2015; F. Clarke Fraser Award for Excellence in Mentorship and Teaching, Canadian Coll. of Medical Geneticists, 2017. *Publications:* (jtly) Amino Acid Metabolism and its Disorders, 1973; (ed) The Metabolic Basis of Inherited Disease, 6th edn 1986, 7th edn as The Metabolic and Molecular Bases of Inherited Disease, 1995, 8th edn 2001; numerous res. pubns. *Recreations:* history, music, photography, literature. *Address:* 232 Av. Strathearn N, Montreal West, QC H4X 1Y2, Canada. *T:* (514) 4860742. *E:* charles.scriver@sympatico.ca.

**SCROPE, Major Peter Geoffrey;** Vice Lord-Lieutenant of North Yorkshire, since 2015; Chairman, NYnet Ltd, since 2018; *b* Yarm, N Yorks, 3 Jan. 1955; *s* of Ralph Henry Scrope and Lady Beatrice Scrope (*née* Savile), 2nd *d* of 6th Earl of Mexborough; *m* 1983, Penelope Eldrydd, 3rd *d* of Hon. E. D. G. Davies; two *s* three *d. Educ:* Ampleforth Coll.; RMA, Sandhurst; Essex Univ. (BA Hist. and Politics). 2nd Lieut, latterly Major, 13th/18th Royal Hussars (Queen Mary's Own), 1974–84. Man. Dir, Millicom Cellular (UK) Ltd, 1987–91; Dir, Millicom Internat. Cellular, 1991–2003; Director: Tele 2, 2009–; OnePhone AB, 2010–. DL 2010, High Sheriff, 2012–13, N Yorks. OStJ 2011. *Recreations:* ski-ing, gadgets. *E:* peterscrope@yahoo.com. *Clubs:* Cavalry and Guards, Pitt.

**SCRUTON, Sir Roger (Vernon),** Kt 2016; FBA 2008; FRSL; writer and philosopher; *b* 27 Feb. 1944; *s* of John Scruton and Beryl C. Haynes; *m* 1st, 1973, Danielle Laffitte (marr. diss. 1979); 2nd, 1996, Sophie Jeffreys; one *s* one *d. Educ:* Jesus Coll., Cambridge (MA, PhD). FRSL 2004. Called to the Bar, Inner Temple, 1978; Bencher, 2015. Res. Fellow, Peterhouse, 1969–71; Lectr in Philosophy, Birkbeck Coll., London, 1971–79, Reader, 1979–85, Prof. of Aesthetics, 1985–92; Prof. of Philosophy, Boston Univ., Mass, 1992–95. Res. Prof., Inst. of Psychological Scis, Arlington, Va, 2007–09; Sen. Res. Fellow, Blackfriars Hall, Oxford, 2008–; Vis. Prof. in Philosophy, Univ. of Oxford, 2010–; Professorial Fellow in Moral Philosophy, Univ. of St Andrews, 2011–14. Founder and Dir, The Claridge Press, 1987–. Chair, Building Better, Building Beautiful Commn, 2018–19. Medal for Merit (1st Cl.) (Czech Republic), 1998. Editor, Salisbury Review, 1982–2000. *Publications:* Art and Imagination, 1974, 2nd edn 1982; The Aesthetics of Architecture, 1979; The Meaning of Conservatism, 1980, 3rd edn 2001; From Descartes to Wittgenstein, 1981, 2nd edn 1995; Fortnight's Anger (novel), 1981; The Politics of Culture, 1981; Kant, 1982; A Dictionary of Political Thought, 1982, 2nd edn 1996; The Aesthetic Understanding, 1983; (with Baroness Cox) Peace Studies: a critical survey, 1984; Thinkers of the New Left, 1985; (jtly) Education and Indoctrination, 1985; Sexual Desire, 1986; Spinoza, 1986; A Land held Hostage, 1987; Untimely Tracts, 1987; The Philosopher on Dover Beach (essays), 1990; Francesca (novel), 1991; A Dove Descending and Other Stories, 1991; (ed) Conservative Texts: an anthology, 1991; Xanthippic Dialogues (novel), 1993; Modern Philosophy, 1994; The Classical Vernacular, 1994; An Intelligent Person's Guide to Philosophy, 1996; The Aesthetics of Music, 1997; On Hunting, 1998; (ed with Anthony Barnett) Town and Country, 1998; An Intelligent Person's Guide to Modern Culture, 1998; Animal Rights and Wrongs, 2000; England: an elegy, 2000; The West and the Rest: globalisation and the terrorist threat, 2002; Death-devoted Heart: sex and the sacred in Wagner's Tristan and Isolde, 2004; News from Somewhere, 2004; Gentle Regrets, 2005; A Political Philosophy, 2006; Culture Counts, 2008; Beauty, 2009; The Uses of Pessimism and the Danger of False Hope, 2010; Green Philosophy: how to think seriously about the planet, 2012; The Face of God, 2012; Our Church: a personal history of the Church of England, 2012; Notes from Underground (novel), 2014; The Soul of the World, 2014; How to be a Conservative, 2014; The Disappeared (novel), 2015; Fools, Frauds and Firebrands: thinkers of the new left, 2015; Where We Are: the state of Britain now, 2017; Conservatism: ideas in profile, 2017; Music as an Art, 2018; contribs to The Times, Guardian, etc. *Recreations:* music, architecture, literature, hunting. *Address:* Sunday Hill Farm, Brinkworth, Wilts SN15 5AS.
*See also* E. Hodder.

**SCRYMGEOUR,** family name of **Earl of Dundee**.

**SCRYMGEOUR, Lord; Henry David Wedderburn of that Ilk;** *b* 20 June 1982; *s* and heir of 12th Earl of Dundee, *qv*; *m* 2005, Eloise, *d* of Ludovic van der Heyden, Fontainebleau; one *s. Heir: s* Tassilo Alexander Robert Scrymgeour, Master of Scrymgeour, *b* 16 Dec. 2005.

**SCUDAMORE, Prof. James Marfell,** CB 2004; consultant, since 2004; Professor of Livestock and Veterinary Public Health, University of Liverpool, since 2004; *b* 24 March 1944; *s* of Leonard John Scudamore and Joan Kathleen Scudamore; *m* 1968, Alison Ceridwen Foulkes. *Educ:* Chester City Grammar Sch.; Liverpool Univ. (BVSc 1967; BSc 1st cl. Hons 1968). Qualified as vet. surg., 1967; Dist Vet. Officer, Kenya, 1968–71; Vet. Res. Officer, Kenya, 1971–74; joined MAFF, 1974: Vet. Investigation Service, 1974–80; Divl Vet. Officer, Tolworth, 1980–84, Taunton, 1984–87; Regl Vet. Officer, S Scotland, 1987–90; Asst Chief Vet. Officer, Edinburgh, 1990–96, Tolworth (Meat Hygiene), 1996–97; Chief Vet. Officer, 1997–2004, and Dir Gen., Animal Health and Welfare, 2001–04, MAFF, subseq. DEFRA. *Recreations:* reading, swimming, gardening. *Address:* 56 Horseshoe Lane East, Guildford, Surrey GU1 2TL. *T:* (01483) 572706.

**SCUDAMORE, Peter Michael,** MBE 1990; National Hunt jockey, 1979–93; Assistant Trainer at Arlary House Stables, Kinross, since 2007; *b* 13 June 1958; *s* of late Michael and Mary Scudamore; two *s. Educ:* Belmont Abbey, Hereford. Champion Jockey, 1981–82 and annually, 1986–93; rode for British Jump Jockeys; winners in Australia, Belgium, Germany, New Zealand, Norway; Leading Jockey, Ritz Club Charity Trophy, Cheltenham Festival, 1986; leading jockey, Cheltenham, 1986, 1987; set new record for number of winners ridden in career, 1989, for number in one season (221), 1989; rode 1,500th winner, 1992; record 1,678 wins on retirement. Asst Trainer at Bromsash, Herefordshire, with son, Michael Scudamore, 2003–06. Racing journalist, Daily Mail, 1993–; Commentator for Nat. Hunt racing, Grandstand, BBC TV, 1993–2012. *Publications:* Scu: the autobiography of a champion, 1993; (jtly) The Scudamores: three of a kind, 2018. *Recreations:* golf, watching sport. *E:* p.scu13@googlemail.com.

**SCUDAMORE, Richard Craig,** CBE 2019; Executive Chairman (formerly Chief Executive), Premier League (formerly Football Association Premier League), 1999–2018; *b* 11 Aug. 1959; *s* of late Kenneth Ronald Scudamore and of Enid Doreen Scudamore (*née* Selman); *m* 1999, Catherine Joanne Ramsey; three *s* two *d. Educ:* Kingsfield Sch., Bristol; Nottingham Univ. Regl Dir, BT Yellow Pages, ITT World Directories, 1981–89; Man. Dir, Newspaper and Media Sales Ltd, Ingersoll Publications, 1989–90; Thomson Corporation: Newspaper Gp Sales and Mktg Dir, 1991–94; Asst, then Man. Dir, Scotsman Publications, 1994–95; Sen. Vice Pres., N America, 1995–98; Chief Exec. and Dir, Football League Ltd, 1998–99. Co-chair, Sports Business Council, 2017–; Mem. Cttee, Ryder Cup, 2019–. *Recreations:* golf, music, children, and of course football.

**SCULLY, Paul Stuart;** MP (C) Sutton and Cheam, since 2015; *b* Rugby, 29 April 1968; *s* of Basil and Joan Scully; *m* 1999, Emma May; one *s* one *d. Educ:* Bedford Sch.; Univ. of Reading. Political Assistant: office of Andrew Pelling, MP, 2005–07; office of Shailesh Vara, MP, 2007–09; office of Alok Sharma, MP, 2010–12; Partner, Nudge Factory Ltd, 2011–17. Mem. (C) Sutton LBC, 2006–10 (Leader of Opposition, 2007–10). Prime Minister's Trade Envoy to Brunei, Burma and Thailand, 2017–. Member: Petitions Cttee, 2015–; Internat. Develt Cttee, 2016–. Dep. Chm., Cons. Party, 2019– (Vice-Chm. for London, 2017–19). *Address:* (office) Donnington House, 2a Sutton Court Road, Sutton, Surrey SM1 4SY. *T:* (020) 8661 9900. *E:* info@scully.org.

**SCULLY, Sean Paul,** RA 2013; artist; *b* Dublin, 30 June 1945; *s* of John Anthony Scully and Holly Scully; *m* 1st, 1978, Catherine Lee (marr. diss.); (one *s* decd); *m* 2nd, 2007, Liliane Tomasko; one *s. Educ:* Croydon Coll. of Art; Newcastle Univ.; Harvard Univ. Became American citizen, 1983. Lecturer: Harvard Univ., 1972–73; Chelsea Sch. of Art, and Goldsmiths' Sch. of Art, 1973–75; Princeton Univ., 1978–83; Parsons Sch. of Design, NY, 1983–; Prof. of Painting, Acad. of Fine Arts, Munich, 2002–07. *Solo exhibitions* include: Rowan Gall., London, 1973, 1975, 1977, 1979, 1981; Tortue Gall., Calif, 1975–76; Nadin Gall., NY, 1979; Mus. für (Sub-) Kultur, Berlin, 1981; retrospective, Ikon Gall., Birmingham, and tour, 1981; David McKee Gall., NY, 1983, 1985–87; Art Inst. of

Chicago, 1988; University Art Mus., Univ. of Calif at Berkeley, 1988; Paintings and Works on Paper 1982–88, Whitechapel Art Gall., Neubachhaus, Munich, Palacio Velázquez, Madrid, 1989; Waddington Gall., 1992, 1995; The Catherine Paintings, Mus. of Modern Art, Fort Worth, 1993, Palais de Beaux-Arts, Belgium, 1995, Galerie Nat. de Jeu de Paume, Paris, 1996; Haus der Kunst, Munich, 2001; Abbot Hall Gall., Cumbria, 2005; Timothy Taylor Gall., London, 2004, 2006, 2009, 2010, 2012, 2014, 2015, 2016, 2017, 2018; Fundacio Joan Miro, Barcelona, 2007; Ingleby Gall., Carlow Centre for Contemp. Art, Leeds Art Gall., Künstammlungen Chemnitz, 2010; Chazen Mus. of Art, Madison, 2011; Granada Palacio Carlos V, Athens Benaki Mus., Kunstmuseum Bern, 2012; Galleria Nazionale d'Arte Moderna, Rome 2013; Triptychs, Pallant House Gall., Chichester, 2013–14; Follow the Heart: the art of Sean Scully 1964–2014, Shanghai, 2014; Against Landscape, Reid Gall., Glasgow Sch. of Art, 2017; Facing East, Multimedia Art Mus., Moscow, 2017; Standing on the Edge of the World, Hong Kong Arts Centre, 2018; Nat. Gall., 2019; *works in public collections include*: Mus. of Modern Art, NY; Tate Gall.; V & A Mus.; Aust. Nat. Gall., Canberra; Art Gall. of NSW, Sydney; Guggenheim Mus., NY; Centro de Arte Reina Sofia, Madrid. *Address*: c/o Timothy Taylor Gallery, 15 Carlos Place, W1K 2EX; c/o Neo Neo Inc., 447 West 17th Street, New York, NY 10011, USA.

**SCURR, Dr Ruth Ginette,** FRSL; Fellow, and Director of Studies in Human, Social and Political Sciences, Gonville and Caius College, Cambridge, since 2006; *b* London, 6 July 1971; *d* of John Henry Scurr and Gillian Margaret Scurr (*née* Mason); *m* 1997, Prof. John Montfort Dunn, *qv* (marr. diss. 2013); two *d* and one step *s*. *Educ*: St Bernard's Convent, Slough; Mansfield Coll., Oxford (BA Hons); École Normale Supérieure, Paris; New Hall, Cambridge (MPhil 1994); King's Coll., Cambridge (PhD 2000). British Acad. Post-doctoral Fellow, 2000–05. Consultant Ed., TLS, 2015–. Judge: Man Booker Prize, 2007; Samuel Johnson Prize, 2014. FRSL 2016. *Publications*: Fatal Purity: Robespierre and the French Revolution, 2006; John Aubrey: my own life, 2015. *Recreations*: yoga, gardening. *Address*: Gonville and Caius College, Cambridge CB2 1TA. *E*: rs10032@cam.ac.uk.

**SCUTT, Thomas Crisford;** production designer and director; *b* Epsom, 21 Oct. 1983; *s* of Simon and Susan Scutt; partner, Jordan Fein. *Educ*: Royal Welsh Coll. of Music and Drama (BA Hons Theatre Design 2006; Hon. Fellow, 2016). Production designer, NT, Royal Court, Almeida, RSC, Lyric Hammersmith, ROH, ENO, Opera North, Scottish Opera, 2007–; productions include: Constellations, Royal Court, transf. Duke of York's, 2012, NY, 2015; King Charles III, Almeida, transf. Wyndham's, 2014, NY, 2015; Summer and Smoke, Almeida, transf. Duke of York's, 2018; A Very Expensive Poison, Old Vic, 2019; production designer, MTV Video Music Awards, 2015, 2016; Resident, Somerset Hse Studios, 2016–; Associate Artist, Donmar Warehouse, 2016–; Creative Dir to Christine and the Queens, Sam Smith, Liam Gallagher, Ben Platt, 2018–. Linbury Biennale Prize for Stage Design, 2007. *Recreations*: theatre, cinema, drawing, walking. *T*: 07813 660273. *E*: tscutt@gmail.com.

**SEABECK, Alison Jane;** *see* Raynsford, A. J.

**SEABORN, Hugh Richard,** CVO 2014; Chief Executive Officer, Cadogan Estates Ltd, since 2008; *b* 24 May 1962; *s* of Richard Anthony Seaborn and Wendy Nora Seaborn (*née* Punt); *m* 2000, Michaela Louise Scanlon; three *s*. *Educ*: Pocklington Sch.; Newcastle upon Tyne Poly. (BSc 1984). FRICS 1999. Landmark Property Consultants, Cape Town, 1985–88; Richard Ellis Fleetwood-Bird, Gaborone, 1988–91; Dir and Hd, Investment Mgt Dept, Richard Ellis, 1991–2000; CEO and Agent to Trustees, The Portman Estate, 2000–08. Mem. Council and Audit Cttee, Duchy of Lancaster, 2005–13. Chairman: Westminster Property Owners Assoc., 2008 (Dep. Chm., 2006–08); Estate Business Gp, 2012–15; Knightsbridge Business Gp, 2015–. Non-exec. Dir, TR Property Investment Trust, 2007– (Chm., 2015–). *Recreations*: family, cycling, fly fishing. *Address*: (office) 10 Duke of York Square, SW3 4LY. *Club*: Sloane.

**SEABROOK, Graeme;** Director (non-executive): P. Cleland Enterprises Ltd, Australia, 1997–2003; Country Road Ltd, 1997–2003; *b* 1 May 1939; *s* of Norman and Amy Winifred Seabrook; *m* 1967, Lorraine Ellen Ludlow; one *s* one *d*. G. J. Coles & Co. (later Coles Myer), Australia, 1955; Chief Gen. Manager, G. J. Coles, 1982; acquisition of Myer, 1985; Man. Dir, Discount Stores Group, 1985; Jt Man. Dir, Coles Myer, 1987, resigned 1988; joined Dairy Farm International, Hong Kong and seconded to Kwik Save Group, 1988: Man. Dir, 1988–93, Chief Exec., 1989–93, non-exec. Dir, 1993–96; Man. Dir, Dairy Farm Internat., Hong Kong, 1993–96. Non-exec. Dir, Woolworths Hldgs Ltd, S Africa, 1997–2000. *Recreations*: lawn bowls, photography.

**SEABROOK, Peter John,** MBE 2005; VMH; consultant horticulturist, since 1971; *b* 2 Nov. 1935; *s* of Robert Henry Seabrook and Emma Mary Seabrook (*née* Cottey); *m* 1960, Margaret Ruth Risbey; one *s* one *d*. *Educ*: King Edward VI Grammar Sch., Chelmsford; Essex Inst. of Agric., Writtle (Dip. Hort, MHort). Cramphorn Ltd, 1952–66; Bord Na Mona, 1966–70; Gardening Corresp., Sun, 1977–; Director: Wm Strike Ltd, 1972–95; Roger Harvey Ltd, 1981–99. TV presenter: WGBH TV, Boston, USA, 1975–97; Pebble Mill At One, 1975–86; Gardeners' World, 1976–79; Chelsea Flower Show, (annually) 1976–89; Gardeners' Direct Line, 1982–90; Peter Seabrook's Gardening Week, 1996; This Week in the Garden (podcast), 2017–. Hon. Fellow, Writtle Coll., 1997. Pearson Meml Medal, Horticultural Trades Assoc., 1985; Associate of Honour, 1996, VMH 2003, RHS; Prince Edward Award, Gardeners' Co., 2019. *Publications*: Shrubs for Your Garden, 1973, 10th edn 1991; Plants for Your Home, 1975; Complete Vegetable Gardener, 1976, 4th edn 1981; Book of the Garden, 1979, 2nd edn 1984; Good Plant Guide, 1981; Good Food Gardening, 1983; Shrubs for Everyone, 1997. *Recreation*: gardening. *Address*: (office) 212A Baddow Road, Chelmsford, Essex CM2 9QR. *T*: (01245) 354870. *Club*: Farmers.

**SEABROOK, Robert John;** QC 1983; a Recorder, 1985–2007; a Deputy High Court Judge, 1991–2010; *b* 6 Oct. 1941; *s* of late Alan Thomas Pertwee Seabrook, MBE and Mary Seabrook (*née* Parker); *m* 1st, 1965, Liv Karin Djupvik, Bergen, Norway (marr. diss. 2008); two *s* one *d*; 2nd, 2016, Sarah Bird (*d* 2016), Greenwich, London. *Educ*: St George's Coll., Salisbury, Southern Rhodesia; University Coll., London (LLB). Called to the Bar, Middle Temple, 1964, Bencher, 1990, Treas., 2007. Leader, SE Circuit, 1989–92; Chm., Bar Council, 1994. Member: Criminal Justice Consultative Council, 1995–2003; Interception of Communications Tribunal, 1996–2000; Investigatory Powers Tribunal, 2000–16; Regulation of Investigatory Powers Tribunal for Guernsey, 2006–11. Member: Brighton Fest. Cttee, 1976–86; Court, Univ. of Sussex, 1988–93. Vice Pres., Brighton Coll., 2005– (Gov., 1993–2004; Chm. of Govs, 1998–2004). Liveryman, Curriers' Co., 1972–2016 (Master, 1995–96). *Recreations*: travel, walking, listening to music, wine, ski-ing. *Address*: (chambers) 1 Crown Office Row, Temple, EC4Y 7HH. *T*: (020) 7797 7500. *Clubs*: Athenæum (Trustee, 2015–), Les Six.

**SEAFIELD,** 13th Earl of, *cr* 1701; **Ian Derek Francis Ogilvie-Grant;** Viscount Seafield, Baron Ogilvy of Cullen, 1698; Viscount Reidhaven, Baron Ogilvy of Deskford and Cullen, 1701; *b* 20 March 1939; *s* of Countess of Seafield (12th in line), and Derek Studley-Herbert (who assumed by deed poll, 1939, the additional surnames of Ogilvie-Grant; he *d* 1960); S mother, 1969; *m* 1st, 1960, Mary Dawn Mackenzie (marr. diss. 1971), *er d* of Henry Illingworth; two *s*; 2nd, 1971, Leila, *d* of Mahmoud Refaat, Cairo. *Educ*: Eton. *Recreations*: shooting, fishing, tennis. *Heir*: *s* Viscount Reidhaven, *qv*. *Address*: Old Cullen, Cullen, Banffshire AB56 4XW. *T*: (01542) 840221. *Club*: White's.

**SEAFORD,** 6th Baron *cr* 1826, of Seaford, co. Sussex; **Colin Humphrey Felton Ellis;** *b* 19 April 1946; *o s* of Major William Felton Ellis and Edwina (*née* Bond); S to Seaford Barony of cousin, 9th Baron Howard de Walden, 1999; *m* 1st, 1971, Susan Magill (marr. diss. 1992); two *s* two *d*; 2nd, 1993, Penelope Mary Bastin. *Educ*: Sherborne; RAC, Cirencester (MRAC 1968). MRICS (ARICS 1970). Hon. Sec., British Bison Assoc., 1991–2019. *Publications*: Bison Farming Handbook, 1992; Arthur's Pheasant: a short story, 2014. *Heir*: *s* Hon. Benjamin Felton Thomas Ellis [*b* 17 Dec. 1976; *m* 2017, Josephine Goodbody; one *s*]. *Address*: Bush Farm, West Knoyle, Warminster, Wilts BA12 6AE.

**SEAFORD, Very Rev. John Nicholas Shtetinin;** Dean of Jersey and Rector of St Helier, 1993–2005; *b* 12 Sept. 1939; *s* of Nicholas Shtetinin Seaford and Kathleen Dorothy (*née* Longbotham); *m* 1967, Helen Marian Webster; two *s* one *d*. *Educ*: Radley Coll.; St Chad's Coll., Durham Univ. (BA 1967; DipTh 1968). Ordained deacon, 1968, priest, 1969; Assistant Curate: St Mark, Bush Hill Park, Enfield, 1968–71; St Luke, Winchester, 1971–73; Vicar: Chilworth and North Baddesley, 1973–78; Highcliffe and Hinton Admiral, 1978–93. Hon. Canon, Winchester Cathedral, 1993–2005, now Canon Emeritus. Chm., Cttee for the Care of Churches, Dio. of Salisbury, 2017–. Chaplain, HM Prison La Moye, Jersey, 2003–05. Religious Broadcasting Advr, Channel TV, 1993–2005. Mem., States of Jersey, 1993–2005. *Recreation*: walking.

**SEAGER,** family name of **Baron Leighton of Saint Mellons**.

**SEAGER-SMITH, Lauren Mary;** Chief Executive Officer, Kidscape, since 2017; *b* Reading, 1 July 1978; *d* of Anthony and Marie Seager; *m* 2010, Jermaine Smith; one *s* one *d*. *Educ*: Univ. of Sheffield (BA Hons English Lit.); Goldsmiths Coll., Univ. of London (MA Educn: Culture, Lang. and Diversity). Project Coordinator, 2000–02, Global Develt Manager, 2002–04, GAP Activity Projects; Connexions Intensive Personal Advr, Reading BC, 2004–06; Develt Officer, Save the Children, 2006–08; Regl Strategy Coordinator, 2008–12, Nat. Coordinator, 2012–16, Anti-Bullying Alliance, Nat. Children's Bureau. Trustee, Woodley Pilot Light Trust, 2011–. *Recreations*: a good book, haphazard gardening and lover of roses, laughing with my children, philosophy and faith. *Address*: Kidscape, 2 Grosvenor Gardens, SW1W 0DH. *E*: lauren@kidscape.org.uk.

**SEAGER BERRY, Thomas Henry Seager;** Deputy Costs Judge, 2005–08; Master (Costs Judge) of the Supreme Court Costs (formerly Taxing) Office, 1991–2005; *b* 29 Jan. 1940; *s* of late Thomas Geoffrey Seager Berry, CBE and Ann Josephine Seager Berry; *m* 2002, Agnes Christine Thomson. *Educ*: Shrewsbury Sch. Admitted solicitor, 1964; Sherwood & Co., 1964–69 (Partner, 1966–69); Partner, Boodle Hatfield, 1969–91. Pres., London Solicitors Litigation Assoc., 1982–84; Mem. Cttee, Media Soc., 1985–91; Mem. Council, Feathers Clubs Assoc., 1986–2007. Liveryman, Merchant Taylors' Co., 1967. *Publications*: Longman's Litigation Practice, 1988. *Recreations*: croquet, gardening, wine-tasting, walking. *Clubs*: Hurlingham, MCC.

**SEAGROATT, Hon. Conrad;** a Judge of the High Court (formerly a Judge of the Supreme Court), Hong Kong, 1995–2003; a Recorder of the Crown Court, 1980–2004; Deputy High Court Judge, Hong Kong, 2011–18; Judicial Commissioner, Court of Appeal, Brunei Darussalam, since 2016; *s* of late E. G. Seagroatt, Solicitor of the Supreme Court and Immigration Appeals Adjudicator, and of Gray's Inn, and of Barbara C. Seagroatt; *m* Cornelia Mary Anne Verdegaal; five *d*. *Educ*: Solihull Sch., Warwicks; Pembroke Coll., Oxford (MA Hons Modern History). Admitted Solicitor of the Supreme Court, 1967; called to the Bar, Gray's Inn, 1970, Bencher, 1991; Jun., Midland and Oxford Circuit, 1974–75; QC 1983; Dep. High Court Judge, 1993–2004; Judge i/c of Hong Kong Personal Injury List, 1998–2003. Member: Senate of the Inns of Court and the Bar, 1980–83; Criminal Injuries Compensation Bd, 1986–94. Mem., Hong Kong Chief Justice's Wkg Party on Civil Reform Process, 2000–03. Mem., Editl Adv. Bd, Hong Kong Court Forms, 2000–03; Adv. Ed., Hong Kong Civil Procedure, (The White Book), 2000–03. *Publications*: (contrib.) The Reform of the Civil Process in Hong Kong, 1999; contrib. Hong Kong Law Jl. *Recreations*: running, fairweather ski-ing.

**SEAGROVE, Jennifer Ann;** actress, since 1979; Trustee, Born Free, since 2002; Founding Trustee, Mane Chance Sanctuary, since 2011; *b* 4 July 1957; *d* of late Derek and Pauline Seagrove; *m* 1984, Madhav Sharma (marr. diss. 1988); partner, William Kenwright, *qv*. *Educ*: St Hilary's Sch., Godalming; Queen Anne's Sch., Caversham; Kirby Lodge, Cambridge; Bristol Old Vic Theatre Sch. *Theatre includes*: Jane Eyre, Chichester, 1986; King Lear in New York, Chichester, 1992; Present Laughter, Globe, 1993; The Miracle Worker, Comedy, 1994; Dead Guilty, Apollo, 1995; Hurlyburly, Queen's, 1997; Brief Encounter, Lyric, 2000; The Female Odd Couple, Apollo, 2001; The Constant Wife, Apollo, 2002; The Secret Rapture, Lyric, 2003; The Night of the Iguana, Lyric, 2005; The Letter, Wyndhams, 2007; Absurd Person Singular, Garrick, 2007; Pack of Lies, UK tour, 2009; A Daughter's a Daughter, Trafalgar Studios, 2009; Bedroom Farce, Duke of Yorks, 2010; The Country Girl, Apollo, 2010; Volcano, UK tour and Vaudeville, 2012; The Governess, UK tour, 2013; Fallen Angels, UK tour, 2014; Brief Encounter on air, 2015; How the Other Half Loves, Haymarket Th., 2016; The Exorcist, Birmingham Rep, 2016, transf. Phoenix, 2017; *films include*: Local Hero, 1982; A Shocking Accident, 1982; Savage Islands, 1982; Appointment with Death, 1987; A Chorus of Disapproval, 1988; The Guardian, 1989; Miss Beatty's Children, 1992; Don't Go Breaking My Heart, 1997; Zoe, 1999; (short film) Pranks, 2011; Another Mother's Son, 2017; Peripheral, 2018; *television includes*: The Woman in White, 1982; A Woman of Substance, 1984; Diana, 1984; Judge John Deed, 2000–07; Lewis, 2012; Endeavour, 2013; Camp X, 2014. Founder, Springing Dog Prodns, film prodn co., 2008–. FRSA. Michael Elliott Award for Best Actress, 2006. *Recreations*: dog handling, tennis, running, cycling, promoting organic farming and animal welfare, trying to save the planet! *Address*: c/o Duncan Heath, Independent Talent Group, 40 Whitfield Street, W1T 2RH. *T*: (020) 7636 6565.

**SEAL, Dr Barry Herbert;** Chairman: U Can Recycling CiC, since 2010; Age UK Leeds, since 2013; *b* 28 Oct. 1937; *s* of Herbert Seal and Rose Anne Seal; *m* 1963, Frances Catherine Wilkinson; one *s* one *d*. *Educ*: Heath Grammar Sch., Halifax; Univ. of Bradford (MSc, PhD); European Business Sch., Fontainebleau. CEng. Served RAF, 1955–58. Trained as Chem. Engr, ICI Ltd, 1958–64; Div. Chem. Engr, Murex Ltd, 1964–68; Sen. Engr, BOC Internat., 1968–71; Principal Lectr in Systems, Huddersfield Polytechnic, 1971–79. Contested (Lab) Harrogate, Oct. 1974; Leader, Bradford MDC Labour Gp, 1976–79. MEP (Lab) Yorks W, 1979–99. European Parliament: Leader, British Lab. Gp, 1988–89; Chm., Econ., Monetary and Industrial Policy Cttee, 1984–87; Pres., delegn to USA, 1998–99. Chairman: N Kirklees PCT, 2002–07; Bradford District Care Trust, 2007–12. Hon. Freeman, Borough of Calderdale, 2000. *Publications*: papers on computer and microprocessor applications. *Recreations*: walking, reading, films, bridge. *Address*: Brookfields Farm, Brookfields Road, Wyke, Bradford, West Yorks BD12 9LU. *E*: barryseal@btinternet.com.

**SEAL, (Karl) Russell**, OBE 2013; Joint Managing Director, British Petroleum Co. plc, 1991–97; *b* 14 April 1942; *m* 1966, Pauline Hilarie (*née* Edwards); three *s*. *Educ:* Keele Univ. Joined BP, 1964; NY, 1970–72; Rotterdam, 1976–78; Asst Gen. Manager, Gp Corporate Planning, 1978–80; Chief Exec., Mktg and Refining, Singapore, Malaysia, and Hong Kong, and Sen. Rep., SE Asia, 1980–84; Gen. Manager, BP Oil Trading & Supply Dept, 1984; Chief Exec. and Man. Dir, BP Oil, 1988–95. Non-executive Director: Commonwealth Develt Corp., 1996–2001; Blue Circle plc, 1996–2001. Sen. Exec. Prog., Stanford Univ., 1984. Pro-Chancellor and Chm. Council, Exeter Univ., 2005–12. *Recreations:* jogging, walking, golf.

**SEAL, Richard Godfrey**, FRCO; FRSCM; Organist of Salisbury Cathedral, 1968–97; *b* 4 Dec. 1935; *s* of late William Godfrey Seal and of Shelagh Seal (*née* Bagshaw); *m* 1975, Dr Sarah Helen Hamilton; two *s*. *Educ:* New Coll. Choir Sch., Oxford; Cranleigh Sch., Surrey; Christ's Coll., Cambridge (MA). FRCO 1958; FRSCM 1987; FGCM 2008. Assistant Organist: Kingsway Hall, London, 1957–58; St Bartholomew the Great, London, 1960–61; Chichester Cathedral (and Dir of Music, Prebendal Sch.), Sussex, 1961–68. DMus Lambeth, 1992. *Address:* The Bield, Flamstone Street, Bishopstone, Salisbury, Wilts SP5 4BZ. *Club:* Crudgemens (Godalming).

**SEAL, Russell**; *see* Seal, K. R.

**SEALE, Sir (Clarence) David**, Kt 2000; JP; Chairman and Managing Director, R. L. Seale & Co., since 1969; *b* 11 Dec. 1937; *m* 1961, Margaret Anne Farmer; one *s* three *d*. *Educ:* Harrison Coll., Barbados. Airline Clerk, 1956–62; Gen. Manager, R. L. Seale & Co., 1962–69. JP Bridgetown, 1978. *Recreation:* horse racing. *Address:* Hopefield Manor, Hopefield, Christ Church, Barbados. *T:* 4280065. *Club:* Barbados Turf (Bridgetown).

**SEALE, Sir (John) Robert (Charters)**, 6th Bt *cr* 1838; *b* Christchurch, NZ, 17 Aug. 1954; *s* of Sir John Henry Seale, 5th Bt and Ray Josephine Seale (*née* Charters); *S* father, 2017; *m* 1996, Michelle Judith, *d* of Kevan William Taylor; twin *s*. *Educ:* Eton; University Coll. of N Wales, Bangor (BSc Chem. and Biochem.). *Heir: s* Christopher Charles Seale, *b* 16 March 2002. *Address:* Slade, Kingsbridge, Devon.

**SEALEY, Barry Edward**, CBE 1990; Director, Archangel Informal Investments Ltd, 2000–11 (Chairman, 2005–07); *b* 3 Feb. 1936; *s* of Edward Sealey and Queenie Katherine Sealey (*née* Hill); *m* 1960, Helen Martyn; one *s* one *d*. *Educ:* Dursley GS; St John's Coll., Cambridge (BA 1958; MA 1991); Harvard Business Sch. (PMD 1968). Christian Salvesen plc, 1958–90: Dir, 1969–90; Man. Dir, 1981–89; Chm., Optos plc (formerly Besca Ltd), 1992–2006. Director: Scottish American Investment Co. plc, 1983–2001; Morago Ltd, 1989–2011; Queen's Hall (Edinburgh) Ltd, 1990–99; Caledonian Brewing Co. Ltd, 1990–2004; Wilson Byard plc, 1992–2003; Interface Graphics Ltd, 1992–99; Stagecoach Hldgs plc, 1992–2001; Scottish Equitable Policy Holders Trust Ltd, 1993–2006; Scottish Equitable, 1993–99; ESI Investors Ltd, 1999–2008; Northern 3 VCT plc, 2001–07; CXR Biosciences Ltd, 2001–09 (Chm., 2001–07); Scottish Health Innovations Ltd, 2002–07 (Chm., 2002–07); Lab 901 Ltd, 2002–08 (Chm., 2002–08); Dundas Commercial Property (Gen. Partner), Ltd, 2002–11; Earlsgate Hldgs Ltd, 2004–06; Indigo Lighthouse Gp, 2004–14 (Chm., 2004–14); EZD Ltd, 2005–09; Landmark Trustee Co. Ltd, 2006–11. Chairman: Edinburgh Healthcare NHS Trust, 1993–99; Lothian Univ. Hosps NHS Trust, 1999–2002; Dir, Lothian Health Bd, 1999–2001. Mem. Council and Policy Cttee, Industrial Soc., 1990–2001. Dep. Chm. of Court, Napier Poly., subseq. Univ., 1987–98. *Recreations:* walking, music. *Address:* Flat 5, 2 The Cedars, Colinton Road, Edinburgh EH13 0PL. *T:* (0131) 441 2802. *E:* bes@morago.co.uk. *Club:* New (Edinburgh).

**SEALEY, Jennifer**, MBE 2009; Chief Executive Officer and Artistic Director, Graeae Theatre Company, since 1997; *b* Masham Green, Birmingham, 17 Sept. 1963; *d* of Robert and Patricia Sealey; one *s*. *Educ:* Haywood Comprehensive Sch., Nottingham; Clarendon Coll.; Middlesex Poly. (BA Hons Performing Arts 1986). Freelance actor, 1986–94 (Theatre Centre, Half Moon Young People's Th., Graeae Th., Red Ladder Th. Co.); freelance dir, 1994–97 (Roundabout, Interplay Th., Gazebo). Fellow: Central Sch. of Speech and Drama; Rose Bruford Coll. Hon. Dr of Drama Royal Conservatoire Scotland; Hon. Dr of Performance Middx. *Address:* Graeae Theatre, Bradbury Studios, 138 Kingsland Road, E2 8DY. *T:* (SMS only) 07780 672741. *E:* jenny@graeae.org.

**SEALY, Sir Austin (Llewellyn)**, Kt 2015; Managing Partner, A. Sealy & Co., international business consultancy and management services, since 1996; *b* 17 Sept. 1939; *s* of Kenneth Llewellyn Sealy and Gerdsene Elaine Sealy (*née* Crawford); *m* 1964, Rita Anita Pilgrim; three *s*. *Educ:* St Mary's Boys' Sch., Barbados; Harrison Coll., Barbados. Banker, 1958–93: Sen. Mgt Official with Barclays Bank PLC in Caribbean; High Comr for Barbados in UK, and Ambassador to Israel, 1993–94. Founder, Caribbean Free Trade Assoc. Games, 1972; Pres., Nat. Olympic Cttee of Barbados, 1982–96; Hon. Treas., Commonwealth Games Fedn, 1986–2015 (Hon. Life Vice-Pres.); Member: IOC, 1994– ; Exec. Council, Assoc. of Nat. Olympic Cttees, 1995–2002. Silver Crown of Merit (Barbados), 1985; Merit Award, Assoc. of Nat. Olympic Cttees, 2012. *Recreations:* cricket, tennis, golf. *Address:* Crestview, 35 Highgate Gardens, St Michael, Barbados. *T:* 4272256; A. Sealy & Co., Leamington House, 4th Avenue, Belleville, St Michael, Barbados. *E:* austinsealy@sealygroup.com.

**SEALY, Prof. Leonard Sedgwick**, PhD; S. J. Berwin Professor of Corporate Law, University of Cambridge, 1991–97, now Emeritus; Life Fellow, Gonville and Caius College, Cambridge, since 1997 (Fellow, 1959–97); *b* 22 July 1930; *s* of Alfred Desmond Sealy and Mary Louise Sealy, Hamilton, NZ; *m* 1960, Beryl Mary Edwards; one *s* two *d*. *Educ:* Stratford High Sch.; Auckland Univ. (MA, LLM); Gonville and Caius Coll., Cambridge (PhD). Barrister and solicitor, NZ, 1953; in practice at NZ Bar, 1953–55 and 1958–59. Faculty of Law, University of Cambridge: Asst Lectr, 1959–61; Lectr, 1961–91; Tutor, 1961–70, Sen. Tutor, 1970–75, Gonville and Caius Coll. Gen. Ed., British Co. Law and Practice, 1989–2014. *Publications:* Cases and Materials in Company Law, 1971, 12th edn (with S. Worthington) 2016; Company Law and Commercial Reality, 1984; Disqualification and Personal Liability of Directors, 1986, 5th edn 2000; (with D. Milman) Guide to the 1986 Insolvency Legislation, 1987, (with D. Milman and P. Bailey) 20th edn as Annotated Guide to the Insolvency Legislation, 2017, 22nd edn 2019; (with R. Hooley and others) Cases and Materials in Commercial Law, 1994, 5th edn 2017; (ed with A. G. Guest *et al.*) Benjamin's Sale of Goods, 1974, 7th edn 2006; (General Editor): British Company Law and Practice, 1989–2014; International Corporate Procedures, 1992–2005; Commonwealth Editor, Gore-Browne on Companies, 1997–2005. *Address:* Gonville and Caius College, Cambridge CB2 1TA. *T:* (01223) 332400.

**SEAMAN, Christopher**; international conductor; Music Director, Rochester Philharmonic Orchestra, New York, 1998–2011, now Conductor Laureate for Life; *b* 7 March 1942; *s* of late Albert Edward Seaman and Ethel Margery Seaman (*née* Chambers). *Educ:* Canterbury Cathedral Choir Sch.; The King's Sch., Canterbury; King's Coll., Cambridge. MA, double first cl. Hons in Music; ARCM, ARCO. Principal Timpanist, London Philharmonic Orch., 1964–68 (Mem., LPO Bd of Dirs, 1965–68); Asst Conductor, 1968–70, Principal Conductor, 1971–77, BBC Scottish Symphony Orchestra; Principal Conductor and Artistic Dir, Northern Sinfonia Orch., 1974–79; Principal Guest Conductor, Utrecht Symphony Orch., 1979–83; Principal Conductor, BBC Robert Mayer concerts, 1978–87; Conductor-in-Residence, Baltimore SO, 1987–98; Music Dir, Naples Phil. Orch., Florida, 1993–2004; also works widely as a guest conductor, and appears in America, Holland, France, Germany, Belgium, Italy, Norway, Spain, Portugal, Czechoslovakia, Israel, Hong Kong, Japan, Australia, New Zealand and all parts of UK. FGS (FGSM 1972). Hon. DMus Rochester, NY, 2009. *Recreations:* people, reading, walking, theology. *Address:* 70 Belgarum Place, Staple Gardens, Winchester, Hants SO23 8SL.

**SEAMMEN, Diana Jill;** *see* Hansen, D. J.

**SEAR, Prof. John William**, PhD; Professor of Anaesthetics, University of Oxford, 2002–10, now Emeritus; Fellow, Green Templeton College (formerly Green College), Oxford, 1982–2010, now Emeritus; *b* 3 Sept. 1947; *e s* of late Lionel and Ethel Alice Moore, and adoptive *s* of late Frederick Carl William Sear; *m* 1978, Yvonne Margaret Begley; three *s*. *Educ:* Enfield Grammar Sch.; London Hosp. Med. Coll. (BSc, MBBS); Univ. of Bristol (PhD); MA Oxford. FFARCS, FANZCA. Posts in London Hosp., 1972–75; Registrar in Anaesthetics, Royal Devon & Exeter Hosp. and United Bristol Hosps, 1975–77; University of Bristol: MRC Res. Training Fellow and Hon. Sen. Registrar, 1977–80; Lectr in Anaesthetics, 1980–81; University of Oxford: Clin. Reader in Anaesthetics, 1982–2002; Dir of Clinical Studies, 1995–98; Vice Warden, Green Coll., Oxford, 2002–07. Hon. Consultant Anaesthetist, Oxford Radcliffe Hosp. NHS Trust, 1982–2010; non-exec. Dir, Nuffield Orthopaedic Centre NHS Trust, 1993–2002. Member, Editorial Board: British Jl of Anaesthesia, 1989–2009; Jl of Clinical Anesthesia, USA, 1989– ; Anesthesia and Analgesia, 2006– (Pharmacology Section Sen. Ed., 2016– ); Current Anaesthesiology Reports, 2014– . Hon. Fellow, Colleges of Medicine, S Africa, 2009. *Publications:* papers in learned jls. *Recreations:* sport, music, writing. *Address:* 6 Whites Forge, Appleton, Abingdon, Oxon OX13 5LG. *T:* (01865) 863144.

**SEARBY, Maj. Gen. Robin Vincent**, CB 2002; Arab affairs and security consultant, since 2007; *b* 20 July 1947; *s* of late John Henry Searby and Eva Searby; *m* 1976, Caroline Angela Beamish; one *s* two *d*. *Educ:* Leasam House; RMA Sandhurst. Commissioned 9th/12th Royal Lancers, 1968; Directing Staff, Camberley, 1984–87; CO, 9th/12th Royal Lancers, 1987–89; COS to HQ Dir, RAC, 1989–91; Comdr, Armoured 1st (Br) Corps, 1991–93; Comdr, British Forces Bosnia-Hercegovina, 1993; Pres., Regular Commissions Bd, 1994; Chief, Jt Ops (Bosnia), HQ Allied Forces Southern Europe, 1995; GOC 5th Div., 1996–2000; Sen. British Loan Service Officer, Sultanate of Oman, 2000–04; UK Defence Co-ordinator for Libya, 2004–10. Prime Minister's Counter Terrorist Advr for N Africa and the Sahel, 2009–12. Hon. Col, 9th/12th Lancers, 2003–08; Hon. Chm., London Central, SSAFA, 2012– . Distinguished Service Medal for Gallantry, Sultanate of Oman, 1975; QCVS 1994. *Recreations:* walking, country sports, reading. *Clubs:* Cavalry and Guards, Beefsteak.

**SEARLE, Corinne Louise Teague; Her Honour Judge Searle;** a Circuit Judge, since 2016; *b* Portsmouth, 9 May 1959; *d* of Dr John Stanley Teague Searle and Dr Gwenllian Searle; *m* 1988, Stephen Fisher Crouch; one *s* two *d*. *Educ:* Edgehill Coll.; North Devon Coll.; Queen Mary Coll., Univ. of London (LLB Hons). Called to the Bar, Gray's Inn, 1982; in practice as barrister, 1982–2016, specialising in family law, 1990–2016; a Recorder, 2005–16. Liverywoman, Skinners' Co., 1995. *Recreations:* family, theatre, topiary, all things Jane Austen. *Address:* Exeter Combined Court Centre, Southernhay Gardens, Exeter EX1 1UH.

**SEARLE, Prof. Geoffrey Russell**, PhD; FBA 2005; FRHistS; Professor of Modern British History, University of East Anglia, 1993–2001, now Emeritus; *b* 3 Oct. 1940; *s* of George William, (Bill), Searle and Winifred Alice Searle (*née* Chapman); *m* 1994, Barbara Elisabeth Caroline Rahn. *Educ:* St Dunstan's Coll., Catford; Peterhouse, Cambridge (BA 1962; PhD 1966). FRHistS 1977. Lectr in Hist., 1962–81, Sen. Lectr, 1981–93, Univ. of East Anglia. *Publications:* The Quest for National Efficiency 1899–1914, 1971; Eugenics and Politics in Britain 1900–1914, 1976; Corruption in British Politics 1895–1930, 1987; The Liberal Party: triumph and disintegration 1886–1929, 1992, 2nd edn 2001; Entrepreneurial Politics in mid-Victorian Britain, 1993; Country Before Party 1885–1987, 1995; Morality and the Market in Victorian Britain, 1998; A New England?: peace and war 1886–1918, 2004; Miles Edmund Cotman, 2014. *Recreations:* music, art, literature, supporter of local football team. *Address:* School of History, University of East Anglia, Norwich, Norfolk NR4 7TJ.

**SEARLE, Rt Rev. Jacqueline Ann;** *see* Crediton, Bishop Suffragan of.

**SEARS, David;** *see* Sears, R. D. M.

**SEARS, Hon. Raymond Arthur William;** Judge of the Court of First Instance of the High Court (formerly a Judge of the Supreme Court), Hong Kong, 1986–99; Commissioner of the Supreme Court of Brunei Darussalam, 1987–99; *b* 10 March 1933; *s* of William Arthur and Lillian Sears; *m* 1960 (marr. diss. 1981); one *s* one *d*. *Educ:* Epsom Coll.; Jesus Coll., Cambridge. BA 1956. Lieut RA (TA) Airborne, 1953. Called to Bar, Gray's Inn, 1957. QC 1975; Recorder of the Crown Court, 1977–86. Vice-Chm., Judges' Forum, Internat. Bar Assoc., 1993. Dir, South China Financial Hldgs Ltd (formerly South China Brokerage Ltd), 2000– . *Recreations:* watching horse-racing, music. *Address:* 3A Ewan Court, 54–56 Kennedy Road, Hong Kong. *Clubs:* Hong Kong, Hong Kong Jockey (Hong Kong); Sydney Turf (Sydney).

**SEARS, (Robert) David (Murray);** QC 2003; barrister; *b* 13 Dec. 1957; *s* of Robert Murray and Janet Leslie Sears; *m* 1984, Victoria Morlock (marr. diss. 2007); one *s* one *d*. *Educ:* Eton Coll.; Trinity Coll., Oxford (MA Jurisprudence 1979). Called to the Bar, Middle Temple, 1984; in practice, specialising in professional negligence and construction law, 1985– . *Recreations:* sailing, motorcycling, supporting Ipswich Town FC, working with heavy horses (Suffolk Punches). *Address:* Crown Office Chambers, 2 Crown Office Row, Temple, EC4Y 7HJ. *E:* sears@crownofficechambers.com. *Clubs:* Bucks; Leander (Henley-on-Thames); Vincent's (Oxford).

**SEATON, Andrew James;** Executive Director, British Chamber of Commerce in Hong Kong, since 2015; *b* 20 April 1954; *s* of Albert William Seaton and Joan Seaton (*née* Mackenzie); *m* 1983, Helen Elizabeth Pott; three *s*. *Educ:* Royal Grammar Sch., Guildford; Univ. of Leeds (BA Hons); Beijing Univ. Joined FCO, 1977; Third, later Second, Sec., Dakar, 1979–81; Hd, China Trade Unit, British Trade Commn, Hong Kong, 1982–86; FCO, 1987–92; Asst Hd, Aid Policy Dept, ODA, 1992–95; Trade Counsellor, British Trade Commn, Hong Kong, 1995–97; Dep. Consul-Gen., Hong Kong, 1997–2000; Hd, China Hong Kong Dept, FCO, 2000–03; Consul-General: Chicago, 2003–07; Hong Kong and Macau, 2008–12; FCO, 2012–13. Non-exec. Dir, Wharf REIC Ltd, 2017– . *Recreations:* family, wine, walking. *Address:* British Chamber of Commerce, 1201 Emperor Group Centre, 288 Hennessy Road, Hong Kong, Oriental.
*See also* J. A. Seaton.

**SEATON, Prof. Anthony**, CBE 1997; MD; FRCP, FRCPE, FMedSci; Professor of Environmental and Occupational Medicine, Aberdeen University, 1988–2003, now Emeritus; Hon. Consultant, Institute of Occupational Medicine, Edinburgh, since 2003; *b* 20 Aug. 1938; *s* of late Douglas Ronald Seaton and Julia Seaton; *m* 1962, Jillian Margaret Duke; two *s*. *Educ:* Rossall Sch.; King's Coll., Cambridge (BA, MB, MD); Liverpool Univ.

FRCP 1977; FFOM 1982; FRCPE 1985. Jun. med. posts, Liverpool and Stoke-on-Trent, 1962–69; Asst Prof. of Medicine, W Virginia Univ., 1969–71; Consultant Chest Physician, Cardiff, 1971–77; Dir, Inst. of Occupational Medicine, Edinburgh, 1978–90. Chairman: Expert Panel on Air Quality Standards, DoE, 1992–2002; Res. Adv. Cttee, NERC, 2006–08; Member: Cttee on Med. Effects of Air Pollution, DoH, 1992–2003; Wkg Gp on Nanotechnol., Royal Soc./Royal Acad. Engrg, 2003–04; Industrial Injuries Adv. Council, 2013–19; EU Scientific Cttee on Occupational Exposure Limits, 2015–17. Lectures: Tudor Edwards, RCP, 1996; Baylis, PPP, 1997; Warner, British Occupational Hygiene Soc., 1998; Hunter, FOM, 2000; Gehrmann, Amer. Coll. of Occupational and Envmtl Medicine, 2001; Thackrah, SOM, 2010. President: British Thoracic Soc., 1999; Harveian Soc., 2007. Founder FMedSci 1998. Editor, Thorax, 1977–81. Hon. DSc Aberdeen, 2007. Medal, British Thoracic Soc., 2006. *Publications*: jointly: Occupational Lung Diseases, 1975, 3rd edn 1995; Crofton and Douglas's Respiratory Diseases, 1989, 2nd edn 2000; Practical Occupational Medicine, 1994, 2nd edn 2004; Farewell, King Coal: from industrial triumph to climate disaster, 2018; papers in med. literature and essays in Scottish Review. *Recreations*: opera, painting, sculpture. *Address*: 8 Avon Grove, Cramond, Edinburgh EH4 6RF. *T*: (0131) 336 5113. *Club*: St Andrew Boat.

**SEATON, Prof. Jean Ann;** Professor of Media History, University of Westminster, since 2002; Official Historian of the BBC, since 2003; Director, Orwell Prize for Political Writing and Journalism, since 2007; *b* 6 March 1947; *d* of late Albert William Seaton and Joan Seaton (*née* MacKenzie); *m* 1977, Benjamin John Pimlott (*d* 2004); three *s*; *m* 2016, David George Loyn. *Educ*: Grey Coat Hosp. for Girls; Univ. of Leicester (BSc); Univ. of Essex (MA). Lecturer: Holloway Prison for Women, 1971; Birkbeck Coll., Univ. of London, 1972–73; Oxford Poly., 1973–74; Sen. Lectr, 1974–90, Hd of Dept, 1990–96, South Bank Poly., later Univ.; Reader, 1996–2002, Hd, Grad. Prog., 1998–2001, Westminster Univ. British Acad. Thank-Offering to Britain Res. Fellow, 1981–82; Vis. Fellow, Griffiths Univ., Australia, 1982–83; Leverhulme Res. Fellow, 2008–09. Ed., Political Qly, 2003–. *Publications*: Power Without Responsibility: the press and broadcasting in Britain (with James Curran), 1981, 7th edn as Power Without Responsibility: press, broadcasting and the internet in Britain, 2009; The Media in British Politics, 1984; The Media of Conflict, 1995; Harlots and Prerogatives: the media and politics, 2000; What Can be Done?: making the media and politics better, 2005; Carnage and the Media, 2005; Pinkoes and Traitors: the BBC and the nation 1974–1987, 2015; numerous articles. *Recreations*: books, art, suppers, sons. *Address*: 9 Milner Place, Islington, N1 1TN. *T*: (020) 7609 1793. *E*: j.seaton@theorwellprize.co.uk. *Club*: Frontline.

*See also* A. J. Seaton.

**SEATON, Prof. Nigel Anthony,** PhD; CEng, FREng; FIChemE; Principal and Vice-Chancellor, Abertay University (formerly University of Abertay Dundee), since 2012; *b* Falkirk, 27 Aug. 1960; *s* of Denis and Daphne Seaton; *m* 1985, Roxana Jiménez Eguiluz; three *s*. *Educ*: Linlithgow Primary Sch.; Linlithgow Acad.; Univ. of Edinburgh (BSc Chem. Engrg 1982); Univ. of Pennsylvania (MSE 1984; PhD 1986). CEng 1995; FIChemE 2000; FREng 2012. Research Engineer: Atkins R&D, 1986–87; BP, 1987–89; Lectr, Univ. of Cambridge, 1989–97; University of Edinburgh: Prof. of Interfacial Engrg, 1997–2008; Head: Div. of Engrg, 1999–2002; Inst. for Materials and Processes, 2002–03; Dean, Undergrad. Studies, 2003–07; Asst Principal, 2007–08; Dep. Vice-Chancellor (Acad. Develt), 2008–09, Sen. Dep. Vice-Chancellor, 2009–12, Univ. of Surrey. *Publications*: res. papers. *Recreations*: family, walking, cycling, sailing. *Address*: Abertay University, Dundee DD1 1HG. *T*: (01382) 308016. *E*: n.seaton@abertay.ac.uk.

**SEAWARD, Tracey;** film producer, since 1992; *b* Hull, 5 March 1964; partner, Mark Tildesley. Films: producer: Nora, 2000; Dirty Pretty Things, 2002 ((jtly) Best Brit. Film, BIFA, Best Film, Evening Standard Brit. Film Awards, 2003); The Queen, 2006 ((jtly) Best Film, BAFTA Awards, 2007); Chéri, 2009; Tamara Drewe, 2010; Philomena, 2013; Victoria and Abdul, 2017; co-producer: The Good Thief, 2002; Millions, 2004 ((jtly) Christopher Award, 2006); The Constant Gardener, 2005; Eastern Promises, 2007; War Horse, 2012 ((jtly) Christopher Award, 2011); The Program, 2015; Florence Foster Jenkins, 2016; Genius, 2016; Producer, Opening Ceremony, London Olympic Games 2012. Member: BAFTA; Acad. for Motion Picture Arts and Scis; Eur. Film Acad. Advisor: Project Everyone, 2015–; UN Sustainable Develt Goals, 2015–. Trustee: S.A.F.E., Kenya, 2013–; Choose Love. Hon. DLitt Hull, 2008. Envy Producer Award, Sky Women in Film and TV Awards, 2012. *Address*: c/o Sue Greenleaves, Independent Talent, 40 Whitfield Street, W1T 2RH. *T*: (020) 7636 6565. *E*: suegreenleaves@independenttalent.com. *Club*: Groucho.

**SEAWRIGHT, Prof. Paul,** PhD; FRPS; Head, Belfast School of Art, since 2012 and Executive Dean, Faculty of Arts, Humanities and Social Sciences, since 2016, Ulster University (formerly University of Ulster); *b* Belfast, 20 Aug. 1965; *s* of William J. Seawright and Isobel Seawright; *m* 1988, Sarah Homan; three *s*. *Educ*: W Surrey Coll. of Art and Design (BA 1st Cl. Hons Film and Photography 1988); Univ. of Wales, Newport (PhD 2006). FRPS 2006. Lectr in Art and Design, Univ. of Ulster, 1991–94; University of Wales College, Newport, later University of Wales, Newport: Lectr in Photography, 1994–96; Hd of Res. - Art and Design, 1996–2002; Dean, Sch. of Art and Design, 2002–06; Prof. of Photography, Univ. of Ulster, 2007–12. Hon. Prof., Luxun Acad. of Fine Arts, China, 2019. Artworks in collections incl. Tate, Irish MOMA, Internat. Center of Photography, NY, Govt Art Collection, San Francisco MOMA, Imperial War Mus., Ulster Mus. Mem. Bd, Arts Council, NI, 2007–15. Vice-Pres., Royal Ulster Acad., 2012– (Fellow). Hon. Fellow, Cardiff Metropolitan Univ., 2008. FRSA. *Publications*: Inside Information, 1995; The Forest, 2001; Hidden, 2003; Invisible Cities, 2007; Volunteer, 2013; Things Left Unsaid, 2014. *Address*: Executive Dean, Ulster University, BA–04–002, York Street, Belfast BT15 1ED. *E*: p.seawright@ulster.ac.uk.

**SEBAG-MONTEFIORE, Charles Adam Laurie;** Trustee, National Gallery, since 2012; *b* London, 25 Oct. 1949; *s* of late Denzil Sebag-Montefiore and Ruth Sebag-Montefiore (*née* Magnus); *m* 1979, Pamela Mary Diana Tennant; one *s* two *d*. *Educ*: Eton Coll.; Univ. of St Andrews (MA). FCA 1974; FSA 1995. With Touche Ross & Co., 1971–76: articled clerk, 1971; Tax Supervisor, 1976; Partner, Grieveson Grant and Co., 1981–86; Dir, Kleinwort Benson Securities Ltd, 1986–94; Dep. Chm., Harvill Press Ltd, 1994–2002. Director: Euclidian plc, 1994–99; Elderstreet Corporate Finance Ltd, 1997–99; IDJ Ltd, 1999–2004; Govett European Enhanced Investment Trust plc, 1999–2004 (Chm., 2003–04); Kiln plc, 2001–06; Ludgate Investments Ltd, 2004–13 (non-exec. Dir, 2013–); Chm., Community Careline Services Ltd, 2001–02; non-exec. Dep. Chm., West 175 Media Gp, 2001–06 (Dir, 2000–06); non-executive director: Hightex Gp plc, 2006–14; Scholium Gp plc, 2014–; Trustee, HSBC Common Funds for Growth and Income, 1994–2002. Chm., Projects Cttee, 1977–86, Trustee, 2000–11, Nat. Art Collections Fund; Chm., London Historic House Mus Trust, 1992–2009 (Trustee, 1987–2009); Trustee: Samuel Courtauld Trust, 1992–2007; Nat. Manuscripts Conservation Trust, 2000–; Montefiore Endowment, 2004–07; Oxford Centre for Hebrew and Jewish Studies, 2004–18; Strawberry Hill Trust, 2004–07; Wordsworth Trust, 2013–18; Harewood House Trust, 2014–; Hon. Treasurer: Friends of Nat. Libraries, 1990–; Friends of BL, 1990–95; Friends of Lambeth Palace Liby, 1990–; London Liby, 1991–2003; Walpole Soc., 1992–2017; Gov., Patrons, Nat. Gall. of Scotland, 1992–2010; Treas., Roxburghe Club, 2002–; Jt Sec., Soc. of Dilettanti, 2002–. FRSA 1980; FSA 1995. Liveryman, Spectacle Makers' Co., 1973. *Publications*: The British as Art Collectors: from the Tudors to the present (jtly), 2012; A Dynasty of Dealers: John Smith and successors 1801–1924, 2013; (ed) Brooks's 1764–2014: the story of a Whig club, 2013. *Recreations*: reading, visiting bookshops and picture galleries, opera. *Address*: 21 Hazlewell Road, SW15 6LT. *T*: (020) 8789 5999. *E*: csmontefiore@gmail.com. *Clubs*: Brooks's, Beefsteak, Roxburghe.

**SEBAG-MONTEFIORE, Rupert Owen,** FAAV; Consultant, Savills (UK) Ltd, since 2015 (Head of Global Residential, 2012–15); *b* London, 11 Nov. 1953; *s* of late Stephen Sebag-Montefiore and of April Sebag-Montefiore (*née* Jaffe); *m* 1979, Charlotte Anne Sain-Ley-Berry; one *s* two *d*. *Educ*: Wellington Coll., Berks; Magdalene Coll., Cambridge (BA 1975; MA); Reading Univ. (BSc Surveying). Dir, Savills plc, 1995–2010; Chm. and Chief Exec., Savills (L&P) Ltd, 2000–12. Non-executive Director: Bournemouth Univ., 1999–2007; Fastcrop plc, 2001–08; Adventis plc, 2004–06; Pigeon Land, 2012–; Penhurst Properties Ltd, 2013–17; Prime Purchase Ltd, 2015–; Clarion Housing Assoc., 2017–. Chairman: Develt Council, Regent's Park Open Air Th., 2009–11; Investment Cttee, Winchester Coll., 2009–; Investment Gp, Christ Church, Oxford, 2012–. *Recreations*: riding, tennis, walking, tree-planting, hobby farming, opera, theatre, books. *Address*: Savills (UK) Ltd, 33 Margaret Street, W1G 0JD. *T*: (020) 7499 8644.

*See also* S. J. Sebag-Montefiore.

**SEBAG-MONTEFIORE, Simon Jonathan,** FRSL; writer; historian; novelist; *b* London, 1965; *s* of late Dr Stephen Sebag-Montefiore and of April Jaffe; *m* 1998, Santa Palmer-Tomkinson; one *s* one *d*. *Educ*: Harrow Sch.; Gonville and Caius Coll., Cambridge (BA Hist. 1987, PhD 2013). Presenter, TV series: Jerusalem: the making of a Holy City, 2011; Rome: a history of the Eternal City, 2012; Byzantium: a tale of three cities, 2013; Blood and Gold, 2015; Vienna: empire, dynasty and dream, 2016. *Publications*: Catherine the Great and Potemkin, 2000; Stalin: the Court of the Red Tsar, 2003 (History Book of the Year, British Book Awards, 2004); Young Stalin, 2007 (Costa Biography Prize, LA Times Book Prize in Biography, Bruno Kreisky Prize for Political Lit., 2007; Le Grand Prix de la Biographie Politique, 2008); Heroes: great men and women for an unheroic age, 2007; Monsters: history's most evil men and women, 2008; Jerusalem: the biography, 2011 (WenJin Book of the Year, Liby of China; Best Book of the Year, Jewish Book Council USA); Titans of History, 2012; The Romanovs 1613–1918, 2016 (Lupicaia del Terriccio Book Prize); Written in History: letters that changed the world, 2018; Voices of History: speeches that changed the world, 2019; *novels*: King's Parade, 1991; My Affair With Stalin, 1997; Moscow Trilogy: Sashenka, 2008; One Night in Winter, 2013 (Political Novel of the Year Prize); Red Sky at Noon, 2017; *for children*: (with Santa Montefiore) The Royal Rabbits of London (series), 2016. *Address*: c/o Georgina Capel, Georgina Capel Associates Ltd, 29 Wardour Street, W1D 6PS. *T*: (020) 7734 2414. *W*: www.simonsebagmontefiore.com. *Club*: Literary Society.

*See also* R. O. Sebag-Montefiore.

**SEBAN, Alain Pierre;** Chevalier de la Légion d'Honneur, 2011; Councillor of State, France, since 2015; *b* Toulouse, 15 July 1964; *s* of Roger Seban and Andrée Moure. *Educ*: Pamiers High Sch.; Pierre de Fermat High Sch., Toulouse; Ecole Polytechnique; Institut d'études politiques de Paris; Ecole nationale de la statistique et de l'administration économique; Ecole nationale d'admin. Jun. Judge, 1991, Master of the Roll, 1994, Conseil d'Etat, France; Mem., Picq Cttee on responsibility and orgn of the State, 1993–94; Sec. Gen., Cttee for creation of a Nat. Inst. of Hist. of Art, 1994–95; Personal Advr to Cabinet Minister of Culture, 1995–97; Legal Advr to Assoc. for creation of Quai Branly Mus., 1997–2002; Special Personal Advr to Minister of Foreign Affairs, 2002; Dir of Media, Prime Minister's Office, 2002–05; Personal Advr for Educn and Culture to Pres. of the Republic of France, 2005–07; Chm., Dir and CEO, Centre national d'Art et de Culture Georges Pompidou, 2007–15. Professor: Ecole Polytechnique, 1993; Ecole nationale d'admin, 1996–99. Chairman, Board: Bibliothèque publique d'information, 2007–15; Institut de recherche et de coordination acoustique-musique, 2007–15; Centre Pompidou-Metz, 2010–15. Comdr, Ordre des Arts et des Lettres (France), 2002; Comdr, Royal Order of Merit (Norway), 2015. *Publications*: (contrib.) Bilan de la France 1981–93, 1993. *Recreations*: art, opera, literature. *E*: alain.seban@yahoo.fr.

**SEBASTIAN, Timothy;** freelance writer, broadcaster and consultant; *b* 13 March 1952; *s* of late Peter Sebastian, CBE and Pegitha Saunders; *m* 1977, Diane Buscombe (marr. diss. 1995); one *s* two *d*. *Educ*: Westminster School; New College, Oxford. BA (Hons) Mod. Lang. BBC Eastern Europe correspondent, 1979–82; BBC TV News: Europe correspondent, 1982–84; Moscow correspondent, 1984–85; Washington correspondent, 1986–89. Presenter: Hardtalk, BBC TV, 1997–2004; Conflict Zone, DW TV, 2015–. Fellow Commoner, Corpus Christi Coll., Cambridge, 2015–16. Chairman: Doha Debates, 2004–12; New Arab Debates, 2011–15. TV journalist of the year, 1982, Interviewer of the Year, 2000, 2001, RTS; Richard Dimbleby Award, BAFTA, 1982. *Publications*: Nice Promises, 1985; I Spy in Russia, 1986; *novels*: The Spy in Question, 1988; Spy Shadow, 1989; Saviour's Gate, 1990; Exit Berlin, 1992; Last Rights, 1993; Special Relations, 1994; War Dance, 1995; Ultra, 1997.

**SEBBA, Anne Marietta;** biographer, lecturer and journalist; *b* London, 31 Dec. 1951; *d* of Eric Rubinstein, MBE and Joan Rubinstein; *m* 1975, Mark Jonathan Sebba (*d* 2018); one *s* two *d*. *Educ*: King's Coll. London (BA Hons Hist. 1972). Trainee, BBC World Service, 1972; Foreign Corresp., London and Rome, Reuters, 1972–78. Mem. Exec. and Mem., Writers in Prison Cttee, PEN, 1993–2003; Chm., Mgt Cttee, 2012–14, Mem. Council, 2015–, Soc. of Authors. Sen. Res. Fellow, Inst. of Histl Res., 2017–18. *Publications*: Samplers: five centuries of a gentle craft, 1980; Enid Bagnold, 1986, 3rd edn 2013; Laura Ashley: a life by design, 1990, 3rd edn 2013; Battling for News: the rise of the woman reporter, 1994, 4th edn as Battling for News from the Risorgimento to Tiananmen, 2013; Mother Teresa Beyond the Image, 1997; The Exiled Collector: William Bankes and the making of an English country house, 2004, 3rd edn 2013; Jennie Churchill, Winston's American Mother, 2007, 5th edn 2011; That Woman: the life of Wallis Simpson, Duchess of Windsor, 2011; Les Parisiennes: how the women of Paris lived, loved and died in the 1940s, 2016 ((jtly) Franco-British Soc. Book Prize, 2016). *Recreations*: cooking, grandchildren, learning Greek. *Address*: c/o Clare Alexander, Aitken Alexander Associates, 291 Gray's Inn Road, WC1X 8EB. *E*: anne@annesebba.com.

**SEBBA, Prof. Judith Carmel, (Judy),** OBE 2018; FAcSS; Professor of Education, Rees Centre for Research in Fostering and Education, University of Oxford (Director, 2012–17); *b* London, 9 Dec. 1952; *d* of Samuel Sebba and Isabella Sebba (*née* Schalit); *m* 1st, 1986, John Clarke (marr. diss. 2007); two *s*; 2nd, 2010, Brian Parkinson; two step *d*. *Educ*: Univ. of Sussex (BA Psychol.); Univ. of Manchester (MPhil). Res. Fellow, Univ. of Manchester, 1976–87; Lectr in Educn, Univ. of Cambridge, 1988–97; Sen. Advr, DFEE, 1997–2003; Prof. of Educn, Univ. of Sussex, 2004–12. Member: Dignity in Dying, 2008–; Jews for Justice for Palestinians, 2009–. FAcSS 2011. DUniv Sussex, 2016. *Publications*: (with J. Hogg) Profound Retardation and Multiple Impairment, vol. I: Development and Learning, 1986, vol. II: Education and Therapy, 1986, vol. III (ed with J. Hogg and L. Lambe): Medical and Physical Care Management, 1990; (jtly) In-Service Training and Special Educational Needs: running short, school-focused courses, 1988; (jtly) Redefining the

Whole Curriculum for Pupils with Learning Difficulties, 1993, rev. edn 1996; (with D. Sachdev) What Works in Inclusive Education?, 1997; (jtly) Improving Research Through User Engagement, 2011; contrib. res. reports and jl articles on SEN, inclusion, sch. improvement, teacher develt and children in care. *Recreations:* family, walking, yoga, folk music, travel. *Address:* Department of Education, University of Oxford, 15 Norham Gardens, Oxford OX2 6PY. *T:* (01865) 274050.

**SEBER, Andrew James,** CBE 2004; consultant in leadership, education and public services, since 2006; *b* 18 Sept. 1950; *s* of Philip George Seber and Helen Kathleen Seber (*née* Medhurst); *m* 1972, Sally Elizabeth Tyrrill (*d* 2016); one *s* one *d. Educ:* East Barnet Grammar Sch.; Hertford Coll., Oxford (MA Biochemistry); Univ. of York; Middlesex Poly. (PGCE dist. 1977). Science Teacher: City of Leeds Sch., 1973–74; Hayes Manor Sch., 1974–79; Education Officer: Ealing LBC, 1979–81; Bucks CC, 1981–83; Hants CC, 1983–98; City Educn Officer, Portsmouth CC, 1998; County Educn Officer, Hants CC, 1998–2005; Dir, Andrew Seber Ltd Consultancy, 2006–13. Director: Southern Careers Ltd, 1996–2005; South Central Connexions, 2001–05; Chm., Hants and Portsmouth Learning Partnership, 2002–04; Advr, Service Children's Educn, 2000–02; Mem., local LSC, 2001–05. Mem. and Vice-Pres., Nat. Council, Soc. of Educn Officers, 2000–02; Pres., Confedn of Educn Service Managers, 2002–04. Mem., Governing Council, 2006–12, and Chm., Strategy Cttee, 2007–12, Nat. Coll. for Sch. Leadership; Observer, Bd, Training and Develt Agency for Schs, 2007–12. Member: Educn Adv. Cttee, St John Ambulance, 2013–18; Cttee, Oxford Educn Soc., 2014–18 (Chm., 2017). Trustee, Helena Kennedy Foundn, 2014–17. *Publications:* contribs to educnl jls. *Recreations:* university of the third age, biochemistry, genetics, guitar, ukulele, cycling, rambling, grandsons. *E:* andrewseber@yahoo.co.uk.

**SEBRIGHT, Sir Rufus Hugo Giles,** 16th Bt *cr* 1626, of Besford, Worcestershire; *b* 31 July 1978; *s* of Sir Peter Giles Vivian Sebright, 15th Bt and his 1st wife, Regina Maria (*née* Clarebrough); *S* father, 2003, but his name does not appear on the Official Roll of the Baronetage.

**SECCOMBE,** family name of **Baroness Seccombe**.

**SECCOMBE,** Baroness *cr* 1991 (Life Peer), of Kineton in the County of Warwickshire; **Joan Anna Dalziel Seccombe,** DBE 1984; an Extra Baroness in Waiting to the Queen, since 2004; *b* 3 May 1930; *d* of Robert John Owen and Olive Barlow Owen; *m* 1950, Henry Lawrence Seccombe (*d* 2008); two *s. Educ:* St Martin's Sch., Solihull. Member: Heart of England Tourist Bd, 1977–81 (Chm., Marketing Sub-Cttee, 1979–81); Women's Nat. Commn, 1984–90; Chm., Lord Chancellor's Adv. Cttee, 1975–93. Mem. Exec., 1975–97, Vice-Chm., 1984–87, Chm., 1987–88, Nat. Union of Cons. and Unionist Assocs.; Chairman: W Midlands Area Cons. Women's Cttee, 1975–78; Cons. Women's Nat. Cttee, 1981–84; Cons. Party Social Affairs Forum, 1985–87; Dep. Chm., W Midlands Area Cons. Council, 1979–81; Vice-Chm., with special responsibility for women, Cons. Party, 1987–97. Mem., W Midlands CC, 1977–81 (Chm., Trading Standards Cttee, 1979–81). House of Lords: An Opposition Whip, 1997–2001; Dep. Opposition Chief Whip, 2001–10; Cons. Party Whip, 2010–. Governor, 1988–2001, Dep. Chm., 1994–2001, Nuffield Hosps; Chm. Trustees, Nuffield Hosps Pension Scheme, 1992–2000. Pres., Govs of St Martin's Sch., Solihull, 1990–2011 (Patron, 2011–16). Patron, W Midlands Youth Ballet, 1998–2010. JP Solihull, 1968–2000 (Chm., 1981–84). *Recreations:* family, canvassing (especially for the family!), enjoying each day. *Address:* House of Lords, SW1A 0PW. *Club:* St Enodoc Golf (Pres., 1992–).

**SECKER-WALKER, Prof. Lorna Margaret,** PhD; Professor of Cancer Cytogenetics, Royal Free Hospital School of Medicine, 1993–97, Emeritus since 1997; *b* 17 Nov. 1933; *d* of late William Elmer Lea and Margaret Violet Lea (*née* Rees); *m* 1957, David Secker-Walker; one *s* three *d. Educ:* numerous schs; St Anne's Coll., Oxford (BA 1955; MA 1959); Inst. of Orthopaedics, London Univ. (PhD 1961). FRCPath 1996. Res. Fellow, MRC Unit for bone seeking isotones, Oxford, 1955–56; Post-grad. Scholarship, Louvain Univ., Belgium, 1956–57; Royal Marsden Hospital, 1967–84; Non-clinical Lectr in cytogenetics of leukaemia; Gordon Jacobs, MRC and Leukaemia Res. Fund Fellowships; Royal Free Hospital School of Medicine: Lectr, 1984–85; Sen. Lectr, 1985–93. Member Editorial Board: Acta Haematologica, 1988–2000; Cancer Genetics and Cytogenetics, 1987–97; Leukemia, 1994–2001. Chm., UK Cancer Cytogenetics Gp, 1988–97; Dir, Leukaemia Res. Fund Leukaemia Cytogenetics Gp and UK Cancer Cytogenetics Gp Karyotype Database in Acute Lymphoblastic Leukaemia, 1992–97; Mem. Fac., European Sch. of Haematol., 1986–95. Advr to MRC on cytogenetics of leukaemia, 1985–97. Member: Brit. Soc. Haematol., 1975–97; Internat. Soc. Hematol., 1976–97; Genetical Soc., 1976–97; RSocMed, 1984– (Life Fellow, 2013); Assoc. of Clin. Cytogeneticists, 1984–97; Amer. Soc. Hematol., 1994–97; European Haematol. Assoc., 1994–97; European Soc. Human Genetics, 1994–97. Dir, Mount Vernon Freehold Ltd, 2014–. *Publications:* Chromosomes and Genes in Acute Lymphoblastic Leukemia, 1997; chapters in: Postgraduate Haematology, 3rd edn 1989, 4th edn 1998; Haematological Oncology, 1994; over 100 articles in scientific and med. jls. *Recreations:* theatre, opera, travel, jigsaw puzzles, Sudoku, swimming. *Address:* 18 Pavilion Court, Frognal Rise, NW3 6PZ. *T:* (020) 7722 6467.

**SECKERSON, Edward Stuart;** music critic, writer and broadcaster; *s* of William Douglas Seckerson and Daphne Lilian (*née* Beard). *Educ:* Spender Park Sch.; private studies music and drama. BBC Gramophone Liby, 1966–69; Marketing Assistant, Decca Record Co., 1969–72; professional actor, 1972–80; music journalist, 1980–; contributor to: music mags incl. Classical Music, Hi-Fi News & Record Rev., BBC Music Mag., Gramophone; newspapers: The Guardian; The Times; Chief Music Critic, Sunday Correspondent, 1989–90; Chief Classical Music Critic, Independent, 1991–2012. Founder, ArtsPod audio podcasts, 2010. Presenter: Singular Sensations, Charing Cross Theatre, 2013–16; Comparing Notes, Pizza Express Live Holborn, 2016–; Conversations with Maureen Lipman, Patricia Hodge, Dame Diana Rigg, St James Th., 2014–, Claude-Michel Schönberg, Bridge Th., and Patti LuPone, Th. Royal Haymarket; Facing the Music With Patricia Routledge; co-host: Rodgers Revealed; Bernstein Revealed. Radio and TV: contrib. BBC Radio 2, 3, 4 and World Service; commentator, Cardiff Singer of the World, BBC TV, 1991, 1993, 1995, 1997, 2004, 2007. Founder Mem., theartsdesk.com, 2009–. *Publications:* Mahler: his life and times, 1984; Viva Voce: conversations with Michael Tilson Thomas, 1994. *Recreations:* music, literature, cinema, theatre. *W:* www.edwardseckerson.biz.

**SECOMBES, Prof. Christopher John,** PhD, DSc; FRSE; FRSB; Regius Professor of Natural History, University of Aberdeen, since 2014 (Established Professor of Zoology, 2004–14); *b* London, 1 April 1956; *s* of Alfred Robert Secombes and Joan Helena Secombes; *m* 1982, Karen Ruth Misseldine; two *s* one *d. Educ:* Longdean Sch., Hemel Hempstead; Univ. of Leeds (BSc 1977); Univ. of Hull (PhD 1981); Univ. of Aberdeen (DSc 1997). FRSB (FIBiol 1998). University of Aberdeen: Lectr, 1984–91; Sen. Lectr, 1991–97; Personal Chair, 1997; Head: Dept of Zoology, 2001–02; Scottish Fish Immunol. Res. Centre, 2001–; Sch. of Biol Scis, 2002–11; Chairman: Genetically Modified Organisms Cttee, 2002–; DSc Cttee, 2012–. Adjunct Prof., Univ. of Tromso, 2003–06. Member: Marine Scis Peer Rev. Cttee, NERC, 2001–03; BBSRC Panel of Experts, 2014–17. Mem., Exec. Cttee, 1990–2009, Pres., 2003–06, Internat. Soc. for Develtl and Comparative Immunol.; Life Mem., Internat. Soc. of Fish and Shellfish Immunol., 2013. Chm., Aquaculture grant round, Norwegian Res. Council, 2009–11, 2013–15; Member: Sci. Adv. Bd, Sea Lice Res. Center, Bergen, 2013–; Sci. Adv. Bd, Centre for Res.-Based Innovation in Closed-Containment Aquaculture, Norway, 2015–. Ed., Fish and Shellfish Immunol., 1995–; Member: Editl Bd, Veterinary Immunol. and Immunopathol., 2001–; Editl Adv. Bd, Molecular Immunol., 2009–. FRSE 2007. Hon. DSc Hull, 2014. Alexander Ninian Bruce Prize, RSE, 2007. *Publications:* over 400 res. papers and articles in jls. *Address:* School of Biological Sciences, University of Aberdeen, Zoology Building, Tillydrone Avenue, Aberdeen AB24 2TZ. *T:* (01224) 272872, *Fax:* (01224) 272396. *E:* c.secombes@abdn.ac.uk.

**SECRETAN, Lance Hilary Kenyon;** corporate coach and adviser to leaders, author and keynote speaker; Founder and President, The Secretan Center Inc., since 1972; Founder, The Higher Ground Community; President, Thaler Resources Ltd, since 1981; *b* Amersham, 1 Aug. 1939; *s* of late Kenyon Secretan and Marie-Therese Secretan (*née* Haffenden); *m* 1st, 1961, Gloria Christina (marr. diss. 1990; she *d* 2000); two *d* (and one *d* decd); 2nd, 1993, Patricia Edith Sheppard (*d* 2014). *Educ:* Los Cocos, Argentina; Italia Conti, London; St Peters, Bournemouth; Univ. of Waterloo, Canada; Univ. of Southern California (MA in International Relations, *cum laude*, 1980); LSE (PhD in International Relations 1984). Emigrated to Canada, 1959; Sales Manager, J. J. Little and Ives, Toronto, 1959–60; Analyst, Toronto Stock Exchange, 1960; Sales Manager, Office Overload Co. Ltd, 1960–67; Man. Dir, Manpower Ltd Gp of Cos, UK, Ireland, Middle East and Africa, 1967–81. Prof. of Entrepreneurship, McMaster Univ., 1981–82; Vis. Prof., York Univ., Toronto, 1983–84; Special Goodwill Ambassador for Canada, UNEP, 1989–93; Chm. Adv. Bd, 1997 Special Olympics World Winter Games; Chm., Pay It Forward Foundn, 2017. Internat. Caring Award, US Senate, 1999; McFeely Award, Internat. Mgt Council, 2002. *Publications:* How to be an Effective Secretary, 1972; From Guns to Butter, 1983; Managerial Moxie, 1986, rev. edn 1993; The State of Small Business in Ontario, 1986; The Masterclass, 1988; The Way of the Tiger, 1989; The Personal Masterclass, 1992; Living the Moment, 1992; Reclaiming Higher Ground, 1996; Inspirational Leadership, 1999, repr. 2003; (contrib.) Imagine: what America could be in the 21st century, 2000; Spirit@Work Cards, 2002; !Inspire! What Great Leaders Do, 2004; One: the art and practice of conscious leadership, 2006; The Spark, the Flame, and the Torch, 2010; A Love Story: an intensely personal memoir, 2015; (jtly) Peak Performers: the remarkable history and adventures of a senior skiing program in America, 2018; The Bellwether Effect: stop following, start inspiring, 2018. *Recreations:* life, music, ski-ing, Mother Earth, kayaking. *T:* (Canada) (519) 3060393. *E:* info@secretan.com. *Club:* Mensa.

**SEDAT, Elizabeth Helen, (Mrs J. W. Sedat);** *see* Blackburn, E. H.

**SEDDON, Catharine Jane;** JP; Commissioner, since 2016, and Senior Independent Director, since 2017, Gambling Commission; *b* Cheadle, Cheshire, 1962; *d* of Ron and Sylvia Seddon; two *s* two *d* by Patrick Deane. *Educ:* Manchester High Sch.; Somerville Coll., Oxford (Exhibnr; MA 1st Cl. Psychol. and Philosophy). BBC TV: grad. trainee, 1984–86; Asst Producer, 1987; Producer/Dir, 1988–94; Series Producer, 1995–97; Founder and Man. Dir, Cat's Eye Ltd, 1997–2007; Member: Human Tissue Authy, 2008–16 (Chm., Audit and Risk Assurance Cttee, 2012–16); Ind. Appeals Cttee, HFEA, 2009–15. Member: Determinations Panel, Pensions Regulator, 2013–; Legal Services Bd, 2016– (Chm., Audit and Risk Assurance Cttee, 2019–). Tribunal Mem., Social Entitlement Chamber, 2007–16; Mem., Employment Tribunal, 2009–; Specialist Mem., Mental Health Tribunal, 2012–. Lay Assessor to county courts under Equality Act, 2015–. Trustee, CPotential (formerly London Centre for Children with Cerebral Palsy, 2009–). JP Central London, 2002. *Recreations:* museums, theatre, fiction. *Address:* c/o Determinations Panel, Pensions Regulator, Napier House, Trafalgar Terrace, Brighton BN1 4DW. *T:* (01273) 811881. *E:* laseddongb@aol.com.

**SEDGMAN, Francis Arthur,** AO 2019 (AM 1980); Lawn Tennis Champion: Australia, 1949, 1950; USA, 1951, 1952; Wimbledon, 1952; Italy, 1952; Asia, 1952; Professional Tennis Player, since 1953; *b* Victoria, Australia, 29 Oct. 1927; *m* 1952, Jean Margaret Spence; four *d. Educ:* Box Hill High School, Vic, Australia. First played in the Australian Davis Cup team, 1949; also played in winning Australian Davis Cup team, 1950, 1951, 1952. With John Bromwich, won Wimbledon doubles title, 1948; with Kenneth McGregor, won the Australian, French, Wimbledon and American doubles titles in the same year (1951), the only pair ever to do so; with Kenneth McGregor also won Australian, French and Wimbledon doubles titles, 1952; with Doris Hart, won French, Wimbledon and US mixed doubles titles, 1952. Last male player to win three titles at Wimbledon in one year, 1952. Director of many private companies. USA Hall of Fame, 1987; Australian Hall of Fame, 1988. *Publications:* Winning Tennis, 1955; Game, Sedge and Match, 2015. *Recreations:* golfing, racing. *Clubs:* All England Lawn Tennis and Croquet, Queen's; Melbourne Cricket (Melbourne); Kooyong Tennis; Grace Park Tennis; Carbine (Melbourne); Mornington Racing (Life Mem.).

**SEDGMORE, Lynne,** CBE 2004; Executive Director, 157 Group, 2008–15; *b* 23 Oct. 1955; *d* of Mansel Sedgmore and Vera Sedgmore; *m* 1975, John Capper; one *d*, and two step *d. Educ:* Clayton Hall Grammar Sch.; Univ. of Kent (BA Hons); Madeley Coll. (PGCE 1980); Univ. of Surrey (MSc 1995). Lectr in further educn colls, 1979–86; Hd of Dept, Hackney Coll., 1986–88; Croydon College: Dir of Mktg, 1988–90; Hd, Croydon Business Sch., 1990–94; Vice Principal, 1994–98; Principal, Guildford Coll., 1998–2004; Chief Exec., Centre for Excellence in Leadership, 2004–08. Non-exec. Dir of several Bds; Dir, Talent Foundn, 2008–. MCIM 1989; MInstD 1998; FRSA 2002. *Publications:* Marketing for College Managers, 1992. *Recreations:* comparative religion, grandchildren, travel to Far East/India.

**SEDGWICK, (Ian) Peter;** Chairman, Schroders, 2000–02 (Deputy Chairman, 1995–2000); *b* 13 Oct. 1935; *m* 1956, Verna Mary Churchward; one *s* one *d*. National Westminster Bank, 1952–59; Ottoman Bank, 1959–69; J. Henry Schroder Wagg & Co., 1969–89; Chief Exec., Schroder Investment Management, 1985–95; Chm., Schroders plc, 1987–2002; Pres. and CEO, Schroders Inc., NY, 1996–2000; Chm., Schroder & Co. Inc., NY, 1996–2000; Vice Pres., Equitable Life Assurance Soc., 1995–2001. Dir, Frimley Park Hosp. Trust, 1992–96; Vice-Pres., Queen Elizabeth's Foundn for disabled people, 2010– (Chm., 2006–10). Mem., Global Adv. Bd, J. E. Robert Property Co., Washington, 2002–06. *Recreations:* golf, theatre, grandchildren.

**SEDGWICK, Rev. Canon Peter Humphrey,** PhD; Principal, St Michael's College, Llandaff, 2004–14; Metropolitan Canon, Province of Wales, Llandaff Cathedral, since 2006; *b* 13 Dec. 1948; *s* of Oliver George Humphrey Sedgwick and Cathleen Winifred Sedgwick; *m* 1st, 1973, Helena Elizabeth Cole (marr. diss. 1995); one *s* two *d*; 2nd, 1996, Rev. Janet Gould. *Educ:* Trinity Hall, Cambridge (BA (Hist.) 1970; BA (Theol.) 1973); Durham Univ. (PhD 1983). Ordained deacon, 1974, priest, 1975; Curate, St Dunstan's, Stepney, 1974–77; Priest-in-charge, St Lawrence, Pittington, Durham, 1977–79; Lectr in Theol., Birmingham Univ., 1979–82; Theol Consultant, NE Churches, 1982–88; Lectr in Theol., Hull Univ., 1988–94; Fellow, Center for Theol Inquiry, Princeton, 1991; Vice Principal, Westcott House, Cambridge, 1994–95; Policy Officer (Home Affairs), C of E Bd for Social Responsibility, 1996–2004; Ministry Officer, 2006–14, Permission to officiate, 2014–,

Church in Wales. Vis. Schol., Faculty of Divinity, Univ. of Cambridge, 2011; Alan Richardson Fellow, Dept of Theol., Durham Univ., 2014. Member: Anglican-Roman Catholic Internat. Commn, 2011–; English Anglican-Roman Catholic Cttee, 2014–16; Chm., Church in Wales Standing Doctrinal Commn, 2013–16. Moderator, Church and Society, CTBI, 2007–10. Trustee, William Temple Foundn, Manchester, 2015–18. *Publications:* Mission Impossible?: a theology of the local church, 1990; The Enterprise Culture, 1992; (ed) The Weight of Glory: the future of liberal theology, 1992; (ed) God in the City, 1996; The Market Economy and Christian Ethics, 1999; (ed) The Future of Criminal Justice, 2002; (with A. Britton) Economic Theory and Christian Belief, 2003 (trans. German 2009); (ed) Rethinking Sentencing, 2004; The Origins of Anglican Moral Theology, 2018. *Recreations:* gardening, walking, dogs. *Address:* Church House, Grand Avenue, Ely, Cardiff CF5 4HX. *T:* (029) 2067 9833, 07743 314899. *E:* peter.sedgwick2@btinternet.com.

**SEDGWICK, Peter Norman;** Chairman, Guernsey Financial Stability Advisory Committee, since 2016; *b* 4 Dec. 1943; *s* of late Norman Victor Sedgwick and Lorna Clara (*née* Burton); *m* 1984, Catherine Jane, *d* of Mr and Mrs B. D. T. Saunders; two *s* two *d*. *Educ:* Westminster Cathedral Choir Sch.; Downside; Lincoln Coll., Oxford (MA PPE, BPhilEcon). HM Treasury: Economic Asst, 1969; Economic Adviser, 1971; Sen. Economic Adviser, 1977; Under Sec., 1984; Hd of Internat. Finance Gp, 1990–94; Hd of Educn, Trng and Employment Gp, 1994–95; Dep. Dir, Public Services (formerly Public Spending) Directorate, 1995–99; Vice-Pres., and Mem. Mgt Cttee, European Investment Bank, 2000–06; Dir, European Investment Fund, 2002–06; Chm., 3i Infrastructure plc, 2007–15. Chm. 1979–84, Mem. Develt Cttee 1984–93, London Symphony Chorus; Trustee, London Symphony Chorus Endowment Fund, 1993– (Chm., 2016–); Trustee and Dir, Dyslexia Action, 2007–11 (Chm., Governance Cttee, 2007–11); Chm., Bowel Cancer UK, 2013–17. *Recreations:* singing, walking, gardening. *Address:* 20 Skeena Hill, SW18 5PL.

**SEDLEY, Prof. David Neil,** PhD; FBA 1994; Laurence Professor of Ancient Philosophy, University of Cambridge, 2000–14, now Emeritus; Fellow, Christ's College, Cambridge, since 1976; *b* 30 May 1947; *s* of William Sedley and Rachel Sedley (*née* Seifert); *m* 1973, Beverley Anne Dobbs; two *s* one *d*. *Educ:* Westminster Sch.; Trinity Coll., Oxford (BA Lit. Hum. 1969; MA 1973; Hon. Fellow 2003); University Coll. London (PhD 1974). Dyson Jun. Res. Fellow in Greek Culture, Balliol Coll., Oxford, 1973–75; University of Cambridge: Asst Lectr in Classics, 1975–78; Lectr, 1978–89; Reader in Ancient Philosophy, 1989–96; Prof. of Ancient Philosophy, 1996–2000. Townsend Lectr, Cornell Univ., 2001; Sather Prof., Univ. of California, Berkeley, 2004. Foreign Hon. Mem., Amer. Acad. of Arts and Scis, 1998. Editor: Classical Qly, 1986–92; Oxford Studies in Ancient Philosophy, 1998–2007. *Publications:* (with A. A. Long) The Hellenistic Philosophers, 2 vols, 1987; Lucretius and the Transformation of Greek Wisdom, 1998; (ed) The Cambridge Companion to Greek and Roman Philosophy, 2003; Plato's Cratylus, 2003; The Midwife of Platonism: text and subtext in Plato's Theaetetus, 2004; Creationism and its Critics in Antiquity, 2007; articles in classical and philosophical jls and collaborative vols. *Recreations:* cinema, vegetable growing. *Address:* Christ's College, Cambridge CB2 3BU. *T:* (01223) 334910; 97 Hills Road, Cambridge CB2 1PG. *T:* (01223) 368845.
*See also Rt Hon. Sir S. J. Sedley.*

**SEDLEY, Rt Hon. Sir Stephen (John),** Kt 1992; PC 1999; a Lord Justice of Appeal, 1999–2011; *b* 9 Oct. 1939; *s* of William and Rachel Sedley; *m* 1st, 1968, Ann Tate (marr. diss. 1995); one *s* two *d*; 2nd, 1996, Teresa, (Tia) (*née* Chaddock). *Educ:* Mill Hill Sch. (entrance schol.); Queens' Coll., Cambridge (open schol./exhibnr; BA Hons 1961). Musician, translator, 1961–64; called to the Bar, Inner Temple, 1964, Bencher, 1989; QC 1983; a Judge of the High Court of Justice, QBD, 1992–99; Pres., Nat. Reference Tribunals for the Coalmining Industry, 1983–88. Chm., Sex Discrimination Cttee, Bar Council, 1992–95; Mem., Judicial Cttee, Privy Council, 2000–13. President: British Inst. of Human Rights, 2000–12; British Tinnitus Assoc., 2006–15. Ad hoc judge, European Court of Human Rights, 2000. Vis. Professorial Fellow, Warwick Univ., 1981; Vis. Fellow, 1987, Vis. Prof., 1997, Osgoode Hall Law Sch., Canada; Distinguished Visitor, Hong Kong Univ., 1992; Hon. Professor: Univ. of Wales, Cardiff, 1993–; Univ. of Warwick, 1994–; Vis. Fellow, Victoria Univ. of Wellington, NZ, 1998; Judicial Visitor, UCL, 1999–; Vis. Prof., Univ. of Oxford, 2011–15. Lectures: Bernard Simons Meml, 1994; Paul Sieghart Meml, 1995; Radcliffe (with Lord Nolan), 1996; Laskin, 1997; Hamlyn, 1998; Lord Morris of Borth-y-Gest, 1999; MacDermott, 2001; Atkin, 2001; Pilgrim Fathers, 2002; Leicester Univ., 2004; Holdsworth, 2005; Blackstone, 2006; Mishcon, 2007; Ruth Adler, 2015; David Williams, 2016; Neill, 2016. A Dir, Public Law Project, 1989–93; Hon. Vice-Pres., Administrative Law Bar Assoc., 1992–. Mem., Internat. Commn on Mercenaries, Angola, 1976; Chair, Hammarskjold Commn of Inquiry, 2012–13. Chm., British Council Adv. Cttee on Governance, 2002–05. Sec., Haldane Soc., 1964–69. Hon. Fellow: Inst. for Advanced Legal Studies, 1997; Mansfield Coll., Oxford, 2012. Hon. Dr N London, 1996; Hon. LLD: Nottingham Trent, 1997; Bristol, 1999; Warwick, 1999; Durham, 2001; Hull, 2002; Southampton, 2003; Exeter, 2004; Essex, 2007. *Publications:* (trans.) From Burgos Jail, by Marcos Ana and Vidal de Nicolas, 1964; (ed) Seeds of Love (anthology), 1967; Whose Child? (report of inquiry into death of Tyra Henry), 1987; (ed) A Spark in the Ashes: writings of John Warr, 1992; (with Lord Nolan) The Making and Remaking of the British Constitution (Radcliffe Lectures), 1997; Freedom, Law and Justice (Hamlyn Lectures), 1999; Ashes and Sparks, 2011; Lions Under the Throne, 2015; Law and the Whirligig of Time, 2018; contributed: Orwell: inside the myth, 1984; Civil Liberty, 1984; Police, the Constitution and the Community, 1986; Challenging Decisions, 1986; Public Interest Law, 1987; Civil Liberties in Conflict, 1988; Law in East and West, 1988; Citizenship, 1991; Administrative Law and Government Action, 1994; Frontiers of Legal Scholarship, 1995; Law Society and Economy, 1997; Human Rights for the 1990s, 1997; The Golden Metwand and the Crooked Cord (essays for Sir William Wade), 1998; Freedom of Expression and Freedom of Information (essays for Sir David Williams), 2000; Judicial Review in International Perspective (essays for Lord Slynn of Hadley), 2000; Discriminating Lawyers, 2000; The New Brain Sciences, 2004; Le Conseil d'Etat et le Code Civil, 2004; Liber amicorum (essays for Luzius Wildhaber), 2007; A Simple Common Lawyer (essays for Michael Taggart), 2009; contrib. DNB: Missing Persons; Oxford DNB; London Review of Books, Public Law, Modern Law Review, Jl of Law and Soc., Civil Justice Qly, Law Qly Review, Industrial Law Jl, Eur. Human Rights Law Rev., NI Law Qly, Jl of Legal Ethics, Aust. Jl of Administrative Law; Edinburgh Law Rev. *Recreations:* carpentry, music, walking, changing the world. *Address:* c/o Cloisters, Temple, EC4Y 7AA.
*See also D. N. Sedley.*

**SEDWILL, Sir Mark (Philip),** KCMG 2018 (CMG 2008); Cabinet Secretary and Head of the Civil Service, Cabinet Office, since 2018; National Security Adviser, since 2017; *b* 21 Oct. 1964; *s* of late Edward Peter Sedwill and of Mary June Sedwill; *m* 1999, Sarah-Jane Lakeman; one *d*. *Educ:* Univ. of St Andrews (BSc Hons); St Edmund Hall, Oxford (MPhil). Joined FCO, 1989; Second Secretary: Security Coordination Dept, FCO, 1989–91; Cairo, 1991–94; First Secretary: Resource Mgt Dept, 1994–96, ME Dept, attached to UN Special Commn, 1996–98, FCO; Nicosia, 1998–2000; Press Sec., FCO, 2000; Private Sec. to Sec. of State for Foreign and Commonwealth Affairs, 2000–02; Dep. High Comr, Islamabad, 2003–05; Dep. Dir, Middle East and N Africa, FCO, 2005; Director: UK Visas, 2006–08; Internat. Gp, UK Border Agency, 2008–09; Ambassador to Afghanistan, 2009–10; NATO Sen. Civilian Rep. in Afghanistan, 2010–11; UK Special Rep. for Afghanistan and Pakistan, 2011–13; Dir Gen., Political, FCO, 2012–13; Perm. Sec., Home Office, 2013–17. UK Dir, American Acad. of Overseas Studies, 1987. Chm., Lifeboat Fund, 2015–19; Trustee: HALO Trust, 2015–17; Team Rubicon UK, 2015–. FInstD 2011. FRGS 2010. DSM (USA) 2011; MSM (NATO) 2011. *Recreations:* golf, squash, scuba diving, windsurfing, hill-walking, history, family and friends. *Address:* Cabinet Office, 70 Whitehall, SW1A 2AS. *Clubs:* Special Forces (Pres., 2018–); Kate Kennedy (St Andrews); Vincent's (Oxford).

**SEED, Rev. Michael Joseph Steven Wayne,** SA; STD; Chaplain of Westminster Cathedral, 1985–2008; *b* Manchester, 16 June 1957; *né* Godwin; adopted *s* of late Joseph Seed and Lillian Seed (*née* Ramsden). *Educ:* St Mary's Coll., Aberystwyth; St Joseph's Coll., Cork; Missionary Inst., Mill Hill; Washington Theol Inst., Md; Catholic Univ. of America, Washington (MDiv. 1984); Heythrop Coll.; Pontifical Lateran Univ., Rome (STL 1987; STD 1989); Polish Univ., London (PhD 1991). Entered Franciscan Friars of the Atonement, 1979; final profession, 1985; ordained deacon, 1985, priest, 1986; Chaplain, Westminster Hosp., 1986–90; Officiating Chaplain to the Forces, Wellington Barracks, 1990–2000. Sec., Ecumenical Commn (formerly Ecumenical Officer), Archdio. of Westminster, 1988–2008 (on sabbatical, 2009). Hon. Prof., Polish Univ., London, 1991. Chaplain: Soc. of Useless Information, 1998; St Mary's Sch., Ascot, 2010–11. For. Corresp. Academician, Historical Inst. of Dom Luiz I (Portugal), 1998. Mem., Zwingli Soc., Zurich, 2009–. Freeman, City of London, 2005. Hon. Chaplain: Internat. Cttee for the Promotion of Human Dignity, Rome (formerly Eur. Parlt), 2009–; to Archbishop of Cardiff, 2013–. Cross of Merit in Gold (Poland), 1988; Order of Orthodox Hospitallers (Cyprus), 1988; Ecclesiastical Kt Comdr of Grace, Sacred and Mil. Constantinian Order of St George (Naples), 1989; Knight of Justice with Grand Cross, Military Order of the Collar of St Agatha of Paternò, 2001 (Titular Abbot of Brontë, 2007–); Cross Pro Ecclesia et Pontifice (Holy See), 2004; Three Faiths Forum Interfaith Gold Medallion, 2006. *Publications:* I Will See You in Heaven, 1991; (contrib.) Sons and Mothers, 1996; (contrib.) Faith, Hope and Chastity, 1999; Will I See You in Heaven?, 1999; Assurance, 2000; Letters from the Heart, 2000; (contrib.) Catholic Lives, 2001; The Gift of Assurance, 2003; Nobody's Child (autobiog.), 2007; Thinking of Becoming a Catholic?, 2007; (contrib.) C4 x 25, 2007; Sinners and Saints (memoir), 2009; contribs to various publications. *Recreations:* politicians, pizza, Zwingliana. *Address:* Flat 6, 40 Buckingham Gate, SW1E 6BS. *T:* (020) 3490 9302, 07944 286287. *Clubs:* Beefsteak, Nicolson Toynbee.

**SEED, Nigel John;** QC 2000; **His Honour Judge Seed;** a Circuit Judge, since 2010; *b* 30 Jan. 1951; *s* of late Thomas Robinson Seed and of Joan Hall Seed (*née* Evison). *Educ:* Ellesmere Port Grammar Sch. for Boys; St Chad's Coll., Durham (BA 1972). Called to the Bar, Inner Temple, 1978, Bencher, 2008; Mem., Western Circuit, 1981–2010; Asst Recorder, 1995–2000; Recorder, 2000–10. Special Adjudicator, Immigration and Asylum Appeals, 1997–98. Chancellor: Dio. of Leicester, 1989–2002; Dio. of London, 2002–; Deputy Chancellor: Dio. of Salisbury, 1992–97; Dio. of Norwich, 1992–98. Freeman, City of London, 2009. *Recreations:* walking, cooking, eating and drinking. *Address:* Inner London Crown Court, Sessions House, Newington Causeway, SE1 6AZ. *Club:* Athenæum.

**SEED, Ven. Richard Murray Crosland;** Residentiary Canon and Prebendary, York Minster, 2011–15; Archdeacon of York, 1999–2012, now Archdeacon Emeritus; *b* 9 May 1949; *s* of Denis Briggs Seed and Mary Crosland Seed (*née* Barrett); *m* 1974, Jane Margaret Berry; one *s* three *d*. *Educ:* St Philip's Sch., Burley-in-Wharfedale; Edinburgh Theol Coll.; Leeds Univ. (MA). Ordained deacon 1972, priest 1973; Asst Curate, Christ Church, Skipton, 1972–75, Baildon, 1975–77, Dio. of Bradford; Team Vicar, Kidlington, Oxford, 1977–80; Chaplain, HM Detention Centre, Campsfield House, 1977–80; Vicar of Boston Spa, Dio. of York, 1980–99; Priest-in-charge: Clifford, 1989–99; Thorp Arch with Walton, 1998–99; Priest-in-charge, St Mary, Bishophill Junior, 2000–04; Rector, Holy Trinity, Micklegate, 2000–12. Mem., Gen. Synod of C of E, 2000–10. Chairman: Diocesan Redundant Churches Cttee, 1999–2013; Diocesan Pastoral Cttee, Dio. of York, 2003–13. Founder Chm., 1980–2012, Chaplain, 1980–99, Martin House Hospice for Children. Life Mem., Friends of Mount Athos. *Publications:* (contrib.) Appointed for Growth, 1994. *Recreations:* swimming, travel, Byzantine studies, monastic spirituality, walking dogs, iconography, gardening. *Address:* Mill Cottage, Main Street, Allerston, Pickering, N Yorks YO18 7PG.

**SEEISO, HRH Prince Seeiso Bereng;** High Commissioner of Lesotho to the United Kingdom, 2005–11; *b* 16 April 1966; *s* of HM King Bereng Seeiso; *m* HRH Princess Mabereng Seeiso; two *s* one *d*. *Educ:* Gilling Castle; Ampleforth Coll.; Nat. Univ. of Lesotho; Birmingham Univ.; Guyana. Principal Chief, Matsieng, 1991. Member: Senate, 1992–; Nat. Constituent Assembly, 1993–. Patron, Sentebale. *Recreations:* horse-riding, theatre, reading, football, Rugby.

**SEEL, Derek,** FDSRCS; FRCS; FRCA; Dental Postgraduate Dean, University of Bristol, 1986–98; *b* 2 April 1932; *s* of William Alfred and Olive Seel; *m* 1960, Gillian Henderson. *Educ:* Stockport Sch.; Manchester Univ. Inst. of Dental Surgery (BDS). MOrthRCS; FRCS 1994; FRCA 1995. General dental practice, 1956–62; orthodontic trainee, 1962–68; Lectr in Orthodontics, Bristol Univ., 1967–69; Consultant Orthodontist, Univ. of Wales Coll. of Medicine, 1969–94; Consultant in Orthodontics, Welsh RHA, 1969–94. Dean, Faculty of Dental Surgery, RCS, 1990–92. LRPS 1991. Hon. Diploma in Gen. Dental Practice, RCS 1994. C. F. Ballard Medal, Consultant Orthodontists' Gp, 1992; Colyer Gold Medal, RCS 1994. *Recreations:* golf, music, reading, photography. *Address:* 20 Blenheim Road, Bristol BS6 7JP. *T:* (0117) 973 6635. *E:* seelderek@gmail.com.

**SEELEIB-KAISER, Prof. Martin,** Dr phil; Professor of Comparative Public Policy, Institute of Political Science, University of Tübingen, since 2017; *b* 13 Feb. 1964. *Educ:* Ludwig-Maximilians Univ. (MA Politics 1989; Dr phil Politics 1992); Univ. of Bremen (Habil. Politics 2000). Res. Fellow, Univ. of Bremen, 1993–99; Deutscher Akademischer Austauschdienst Associate Prof. of Pol Sci. and Sociol., Duke Univ., 1999–2002; Sen. Res. Fellow, Univ. of Bremen, 2002–04; Interim Prof. of Social Policy, Univ. of Bielefeld, 2003–04; University of Oxford: Lectr, 2004–06; Reader, 2006–09; Prof. of Comparative Social Policy and Politics, 2009–12; Hd, Dept of Social Policy and Intervention, 2011–15; Barnett Prof. of Comparative Social Policy and Politics, 2013–17; Associate Fellow, Dept of Social Policy and Intervention, 2018–; Fellow, Green Coll., subseq. Green Templeton Coll., Oxford, 2004–13; Fellow, St Cross Coll., Oxford, 2013–17; Associate Mem., Nuffield Coll., Oxford, 2015–19. Co-ed., Jl of European Social Policy, 2018–. *Publications:* The Dual Transformation of the German Welfare State, 2004; (jtly) Party Politics and Social Welfare, 2008; (ed) Welfare State Transformations: comparative perspectives, 2008; (ed jtly) The Age of Dualization, 2012; (ed jtly) EU Citizenship and Social Rights, 2018; (ed jtly) Youth Labor in Transition, 2019. *Address:* Institut für Politikwissenschaft, Universität Tübingen, Melanchthonstrasse 36, 72074 Tübingen, Germany.

**SEELEY, Rt Rev. Martin Alan;** *see* St Edmundsbury and Ipswich, Bishop of.

**SEELY,** family name of **Baron Mottistone**.

**SEELY, Jonathan Sebastian; His Honour Judge Seely;** a Circuit Judge, since 2016; *b* Portsmouth, 11 Dec. 1962; *s* of James Richard Francis Seely and Wendy Mary Seely (*née* Hutchinson); one *s*. *Educ:* Harrow Sch.; Univ. of E Anglia (BA Hons History and Norwegian 1984); Poly. of Central London (DipLaw 1986). Called to the Bar, Inner Temple, 1987; a Recorder, 2013–16. *Recreations:* motorcycling, languages. *Address:* Chelmsford Crown Court, New Street, Chelmsford CM1 1EL.

**SEELY, Robert William Henry,** MBE 2016; MP (C) Isle of Wight, since 2017; *b* London, 1 June 1966; *s* of Richard and Helga Seely. *Educ:* Arnold Hse Prep. Sch.; Harrow Sch.; Birkbeck, Univ. of London (MA). Corresp. for The Times and Special Corresp. for Washington Post in Soviet Union, then Kiev, Ukraine, 1990–94; Advr to Shadow Foreign Sec., Leader of Cons. Party and opposition front bench spokesman on work and pensions, Cons. Campaign HQ, 2000–05; MTV, 2005–08. Served Full Time Reserve Service, 2008–17. *Publications:* Russo-Chechen Conflict, 1800–2000: a deadly embrace, 2001; contribs to RUSI Jl, Defence in Depth (KCL blog). *Recreations:* walking, keeping fit, research into modern warfare and Russian warfare, occasionally keeping bees. *Address:* House of Commons, SW1A 0AA. *E:* bob.seely.mp@parliament.uk. *Clubs:* Island Sailing, Yarmouth Sailing.

**SEELY, Sir William Victor Conway,** 6th Bt *cr* 1896; *b* 16 Sept. 1983; *s* of late Victor Ronald Seely and Annette Seely; *S* uncle, 2019, but his name does not appear on the Official Roll of the Baronetage.

**SEEYAVE, Sir René (Sow Choung),** Kt 1985; CBE 1979; Chairman: Altima Group, since 2004; Innodis (formerly Mauritius Farms, then Happy World Foods) Ltd, 1974–2013; *b* 15 March 1935; *s* of late Antoine Seeyave, CBE and Lam Tung Ying; *m* 1961, Thérèse How Hong; one *s* four *d*. *Educ:* Royal College, Port Louis, Mauritius. Gp Man. Dir, 1968–86, Gp Chm., 1986–2004, Happy World Ltd. Chm., Electricity Adv. Cttee, 1972–76. Vice Chairman: Mauritius Employers' Fedn, 1972; Mauritius Broadcasting Corp., 1980–81. Director: Mauritius Development Investment Trust Ltd, 1968–2000; Swan Insurance Co. Ltd, 1969–2003; Mauritius Marine Authority, 1980–95. Mauritius Res. Council, 1997–2000; Vice-Chm. Council, Univ. of Mauritius, 1985–87. Chm., Sui Loong Elders Centre, 1997–. Hon. Pres., Heen Foh Soc., 1991–. *Address:* Altima Ltd, Level 10, Ebène Heights, 34 Ebène Cybercity, Ebène, Mauritius. *T:* 4016363, *Fax:* 4542828. *E:* sir.rene@altima.mu. *Clubs:* Royal Over-Seas League; Mauritius Gymkhana, Port Louis City.

**SEFI, Michael Richard,** LVO 2013; FCA; FRPSL; Keeper of the Royal Philatelic Collection, 2003–18 (Deputy Keeper, 1996–2002); *b* 11 Dec. 1943; *s* of Antony Michael Sefi and Judith Sefi (*née* Hull); *m* 1968, Harriet Mary Davidson; one *s* two *d*. *Educ:* Downside Sch. Chartered Accountant 1970; FCA 1975. Partner, Mann Judd, then Touche Ross, 1975–83; Dir, Noble Lowndes Personal Financial Services Ltd, then Noble Lowndes & Partners Ltd, 1983–92. FRPSL 1990 (Council Mem., 1990–2005); Pres., GB Philatelic Soc., 1998–2000 and 2012–14. Fellow, Royal. Philatelic Soc. of Canada, 2012. Signatory, Roll of Distinguished Philatelists, 2012. *Publications:* contrib. to London Philatelist, GB Jl, Crosspost. *Recreations:* philately, ski-ing, diving, naval history, classical ballet. *Address:* Highfield House, Crossbush, Arundel, West Sussex BN18 9PQ. *E:* m.sefi@btinternet.com. *Club:* Army and Navy.

**SEFTON, Dr Allan Douglas;** Director, Rail Safety, and HM Chief Inspector of Railways, Health and Safety Executive, 2001–05; *b* 15 April 1945; *s* of James and Alice Sefton; *m* 1968, Jennifer Elizabeth Pratt; two *s*. *Educ:* UCNW, Bangor (BSc; PhD 1970). FIOSH 1990. Trainee, HM Insp. of Factories, Dept of Employment, Scotland, 1969–73; HM Insp. of Factories, Dept of Employment and HSE, Scotland, 1973–81; Health and Safety Executive: HM Insp., Hazardous Substances Div., 1981–86; Principal Insp., Field Ops Div., 1986–87; Hd, Hazardous Installation Nat. Interest Gp, 1987–90; Dir, W and N Yorks, 1990–92; Dir of Ops, 1992–96, Hd, 1996–2000, Off-shore Safety Div.; Dir, Scotland, 2000–01. Non-exec. Dir, Angel Trains Gp, 2006–12. *Publications:* Getting Started at Fly Fishing for Trout, 2013; Fly Fishing for Salmon, 2015; Get Fishing, 2019. *Recreations:* fishing, game shooting. *Address:* 4 Barnfield, Common Lane, Hemingford Abbots, Cambs PE28 9AX.

**SEFTON, Mark Thomas Dunblane;** QC 2018; *b* Beverley, 24 Jan. 1973; *s* of Graham and Jan Sefton; *m* 2006, Elizabeth Fitzgerald; one *s* two *d*. *Educ:* Leeds Grammar Sch.; Trinity Coll., Cambridge (MA Hons); City Univ. (DipLaw); Inns of Court Sch. of Law (BVC). Called to the Bar, Middle Temple, 1996. *Recreations:* mountains, cities, walking, cycling, wine, investing, all things Japanese. *Address:* Falcon Chambers, Falcon Court, EC4Y 1AA. *T:* (020) 7353 2484. *E:* clerks@falcon-chambers.com.

**SEGAL, Prof. Anthony Walter,** MD; PhD, DSc; FRCP, FMedSci; FRS 1998; Charles Dent Professor of Medicine, University College London, since 1986; *b* 24 Feb. 1944; *s* of late Cyril Segal and Doreen (*née* Hayden); *m* 1966, Barbara Miller; three *d*. *Educ:* Univ. of Cape Town (MB, ChB; MD 1974); PhD 1979, DSc 1984, London. FRCP 1987. Internship, Groote Schuur Hosp., SA, 1968–69; Sen. House Officer, Registrar and Sen. Registrar in Medicine, Hammersmith Hosp., 1970–76; Registrar and Clinical Scientist, Northwick Park Hosp. and Clinical Res. Centre, 1971–79; Wellcome Trust Sen. Clinical Fellow, UCL, 1979–86; Hon. Consultant Physician, UCH, 1979–. Fellow, UCL, 2002. MAE; Founder FMedSci 1998. *Publications:* contribs on biochemistry, cell biology, immunology and gastroenterology. *Recreations:* golf, sculpture, painting, theatre, music, dining. *Address:* Rayne Building, Centre for Molecular Medicine, 5 University Street, WC1E 6JJ. *T:* (020) 7679 6175. *Clubs:* Garrick; Highgate Golf.

**SEGAL, Graeme Bryce,** DPhil; FRS 1982; Senior Research Fellow, All Souls College, Oxford, 1999–2009, now Emeritus; *b* 21 Dec. 1941; *s* of Reuben Segal and Iza Joan Harris; *m* 1962, Desley Rae Cheetham (marr. diss. 1972); partner, 1978–2000, Helen Elizabeth Phillips; partner, 2002, *m* 2015, Marina Sarah Warner (*see* Dame M. S. Warner). *Educ:* Sydney Grammar School; Univ. of Sydney (BSc 1962); Univ. of Cambridge; Univ. of Oxford (MA, DPhil 1967). Oxford University: Junior Res. Fellow, Worcester Coll., 1964–66; Junior Lectr in Mathematics, 1965–66; Fellow, St Catherine's Coll., 1966–90; Reader in Maths, 1978–89; Prof. of Maths, 1989–90; Lowndean Prof. of Astronomy and Geometry, and Fellow, St John's Coll., Cambridge, 1990–99. Mem., Inst. for Advanced Study, Princeton, 1969–70. Pres., LMS, 2011–13. Editor, Topology, 1970–90. *Publications:* (with A. Pressley) Loop Groups, 1986; articles in learned jls. *Address:* c/o All Souls College, Oxford OX1 4AL. *E:* graeme.segal@all-souls.ox.ac.uk; 1 Beechcroft Road, Oxford OX2 7AY. *T:* (01865) 558016.

**SEGAL, Michael Giles,** PhD; consultant; Director, Strategy and Evidence Group, Department for Environment, Food and Rural Affairs, 2009–11; *b* 31 July 1950; *s* of late Paul and Hanna Maria Segal; *m* 1972, Agnes Henderson; one *s* (and one *s* decd). *Educ:* St Paul's Sch.; King's Coll., Cambridge (BA 1972; PhD 1975). MRSC, 1983–2011. Res. Officer, CEGB, 1978–88; Civil Servant: MAFF, 1988–99, variously Hd, Food Safety (Radiation) Unit, Hd, Radiological Safety Div. and Chief Nuclear Inspector, and Hd, Radiological Safety and Nutrition Div.; Dir of Corporate Strategy and Sec. to the Bd, Food Standards Agency, 2000–01; Department for Environment, Food and Rural Affairs: Hd, Livestock Strategy Div., 2001–04; Dir, Food Chain Analysis and Farming Regulation, 2004–06; Dir, Sustainable Farming Strategy, 2006–07; Dir, Food and Farming Gp, 2007–09. Mem., Ethical Adv. Gp, Standard Life Investments, 2016–. *Publications:* approx. 70 articles in learned jls, conf. procs, etc. *Recreations:* sports—cricket, badminton, ski-ing and scuba diving, photography (incl. underwater), dancing, travel.

**SEGAL, Michael John;** District Judge (formerly Registrar), Principal Registry, Family Division, 1985–2010; *b* 20 Sept. 1937; *s* of Abraham Charles Segal and Iris Muriel (*née* Parsons); *m* 1963, Barbara Gina Fluxman; one *d*. *Educ:* Strode's Sch., Egham; Birkbeck, Univ. of London (BA 2014; MA 2016; MRes 2018). Served 7th RTR, 1955–56. Called to the Bar, Middle Temple, 1962. Practised at Bar, Midland and Oxford Circuit, 1962–84. Mem., Civil and Family Cttee, Judicial Studies Bd, 1990–94. Editor, Family Div. section, Butterworth's Cost Service, 1987–2008; Jt Editor, Supreme Court Practice, 1991–94; contributor: Protecting Children Update, 2003–; Education Law Update, 2006–. FLS 2004. *Publications:* Costs Advocacy, 2002; contribs to New Law Jl, Family Law. *Recreations:* living in the past, reading philosophy. *Address:* 28 Grange Road, N6 4AP. *T:* (020) 8348 0680. *Clubs:* Garrick, Savage.

**SEGAL, Prof. Naomi Dinah,** PhD; Visiting Professor, School of Arts, Birkbeck, University of London, since 2014 (Professorial Fellow, 2011–13); *b* 6 Oct. 1949; *d* of Prof. Judah Benzion Segal, MC, FBA and Leah Segal (*née* Seidemann); marr. diss.; one *d* one *s*. *Educ:* Newnham Coll., Cambridge (BA 1972); King's Coll. London (PhD 1978). Fellow, Tutor and Lectr, Queens' Coll., Cambridge, 1980–86; Fellow, Tutor and Lectr, St John's Coll., Cambridge, 1986–93; Prof. of French Studies, Univ. of Reading, 1993–2004; Dir, Inst. of Germanic & Romance Studies, Sch. of Advanced Study, Univ. of London, 2004–11. Convenor, Panel 5, Advanced Res., and Mem. Bd, AHRB, then AHRC, 1999–2005; UK Rep., Standing Cttee for Humanities, ESF, 2005–11. Chair or Mem., nat. and internat. panels, incl. AHRC, Humanities in European Res. Area, IUF, RAE, and in Bulgaria, Latvia, Czech Republic; organised numerous internat. confs. Chair, Cultural Literacy in Europe, 2007–. Academic Associate, British Psychoanalytical Soc., 2012–. Hon. Fellow, Queens' Coll., Cambridge, 2018. MAE 2013. Chevalier, l'Ordre des Palmes académiques, 2005. *Publications:* The Banal Object, 1981; The Unintended Reader, 1986; Narcissus and Echo, 1988; (ed jtly) Freud in Exile, 1988; The Adulteress's Child, 1992; (ed jtly) Scarlet Letters: fictions of adultery from antiquity to the 1990s, 1997; André Gide: pederasty and pedagogy, 1998; (ed jtly) Coming Out of Feminism, 1998; Le Désir à l'œuvre, 2000; (ed jtly) Indeterminate Bodies, 2003; Consensuality, 2009; (ed jtly) When familiar meanings dissolve…: essays in French studies in memory of Malcolm Bowie (1943–2007), 2011; (ed jtly) Vicissitudes: histories and destinies of psychoanalys, 2013; (ed jtly) From Literature to Cultural Literacy, 2014; (ed jtly) Opera, Exoticism and Visual Culture, 2015; (trans.) Didier Anzieu, The Skin-Ego, 2016; (ed jtly) On Replacement: cultural, social and psychological representations, 2018; numerous articles. *Recreations:* friendship, Hebrew, singing, knitting. *Address:* Department of Cultures and Languages, Birkbeck, University of London, 43 Gordon Square, WC1H 0PD. *E:* n.segal@bbk.ac.uk.

**SEGAL, Oliver Leon;** QC 2011; *b* London, 18 April 1963; *s* of Ronald and Susan Segal; *m* 1992, Lesley Mitchell; one *s* one *d*. *Educ:* Corpus Christi Coll., Oxford (MA Lit.Hum. 1985). Called to the Bar, Middle Temple, 1992. *Publications:* Partnership Bidding at Bridge, 1991. *Recreations:* meditation, bridge. *Address:* Old Square Chambers, 10–11 Bedford Row, WC1R 4PU. *E:* segal@oldsquare.co.uk.

**SEGALL, Anne Celia, (Mrs D. H. Evans),** freelance journalist; Economics Correspondent, Daily Telegraph, 1985–2001; *b* 20 April 1948; *d* of John Segall and Marsha (*née* Greenberg); *m* 1973, David Howard Evans, *qv*; two *s*. *Educ:* St Paul's Girls' Sch., London; St Hilda's Coll., Oxford (BA Hons PPE 1969). Banking correspondent: Investors' Chronicle, 1971–76; The Economist, 1976–80; Daily Telegraph, 1981–85. Wincott Award for Financial Journalism, 1975. *Recreations:* swimming, reading, languages, historical research. *Address:* 24 Pembroke Gardens, W8 6HU.

**SEGAR, Christopher Michael John,** CMG 2004; HM Diplomatic Service, retired; Programme Manager (formerly Energy Analyst), Europe, Middle East and North Africa, International Energy Agency, Paris, 2008–15; *b* 25 Nov. 1950; *s* of Cyril John Segar and Margery (*née* Angliss). *Educ:* Sevenoaks Sch.; Sidney Sussex Coll., Cambridge (BA Hons). VSO, Cameroun, 1969; joined FCO, 1973; MECAS, 1974–76; Third, later Second Sec., Dubai, 1976–79; FCO, 1979–84; Head of Chancery and Consul, Luanda, 1984–87; UK Delegn to OECD, Paris, 1987–90; Dep. Head of Mission and Consul Gen., Baghdad, 1990–91; on secondment to MoD, 1991–94; Commercial Counsellor: Riyadh, 1994–97; Peking, 1997–2001; Head of Aviation, Maritime, Sci. and Energy Dept, subseq. Aviation, Maritime and Energy Dept, FCO, 2001–03; Head of British Office, Baghdad, 2003–04. Dep. Dir, Centre for Studies in Security and Diplomacy, Univ. of Birmingham, 2006–08. Chm., Arab-British Centre, 2006–10; Trustee, Foundn for Relief and Reconciliation in the Middle East (formerly Foundn for Reconciliation in the Middle East), 2006– (Chm. Trustees, 2005–06). *Recreations:* music, travel. *Club:* Royal Over-Seas League.

**SEGARS, Joanne,** OBE 2003; Chair, LGPS Central Ltd, since 2017; *b* 5 Dec. 1964; *d* of Terry and Jean Segars; *m* David Coats. *Educ:* Liverpool Poly. (BA Hons Econs 1986); Univ. of Warwick (MA Industrial Relns 1987). Sen. Policy Officer (Pensions), TUC, 1987–2001; Hd, Pensions and Savings, ABI, 2001–05; Dir of Policy, 2005–06, Chief Exec., 2006–17, Nat. Assoc. of Pension Funds, then Pensions and Lifetime Savings Assoc. Member, Board: Occupational Pensions Regulatory Authy, 1987–2002; Envmt Agency, 2017–18; Chm., Envmt Agency Pension Fund, 2017–18. Trustee Dir, NOW: Pensions, 2017–; Mem., Ind. Governance Cttee, Legal & General. Mem. Council and Gov., Pensions Policy Inst., 2001–; Chm., Shadow Scheme Adv. Bd, Local Govt Pension Scheme, 2013–16. Dir, PensionsEurope (formerly Eur. Fedn of Retirement Provision), 2007–17 (Chm., 2012–16). *Recreations:* travel, photography. *E:* joanne@thesegars.com.

**SEGHATCHIAN, Tanya;** film and television producer; *b* 17 April 1968. *Educ:* Gonville and Caius Coll., Cambridge (BA 1st Cl. Hons Hist. 1990). Researcher, then Producer, South Bank Show and BBC Documentary Features and Music and Arts, 1990–95; Script Editor, BBC Drama, 1995–96; Hd of Develt, Heyday Films, 1997–2001; film producer: Harry Potter and the Philosopher's Stone, 2001; Harry Potter and the Chamber of Secrets, 2002; Harry Potter and the Prisoner of Azkaban, 2004; My Summer of Love, 2004; Harry Potter and the Goblet of Fire, 2005; Angel, 2007; Cold War, 2018; producer, TV series, The Crown, 2016. Head: Develt Fund, 2007–10, Film Fund, 2010–11, UK Film Council; Film Fund, BFI, 2011. Hon. Prof., Manchester Univ., 2014–. Mem. Bd, Almeida Th., 2015–; Trustee: BAFTA, 2013–15; Literature Prize Foundn, 2013–.

**SÉGUIN, Yannick N.;** *see* Nézet-Séguin.

**SEIF EL NASR, Hatem;** Ambassador of Egypt to the Holy See, since 2015; *b* Cairo, 30 July 1957; *s* of Nevine Adly Yassine; one *s* one *d*. *Educ:* Cairo Univ. (BA Econs and Political Scis). Cabinet, Dep. Prime Minister and Minister of Foreign Affairs, Cairo, 1979–82; Mem., Egyptian Perm. Mission to UN, 1982–86; Cabinet, Dr Boutrous Boutrous-Ghali, Minister of State for Foreign Affairs, 1986–88; Pol Counsellor, Egyptian Embassy, Washington, 1988–93; Hd, UN Dept, Ministry of Foreign Affairs, 1993–96; Minister Plenipotentiary, Dep. Chief of Mission, Egyptian Embassy, Paris, 1996–2000; Ambassador of Egypt: to Brazil, 2000–01; to Lebanon, 2001–02; to France, 2002–06; Asst Minister of Foreign Affairs for the Americas and the Orgn of American States, 2006–08; Ambassador of Egypt to the Court of St James's, 2008–12; Perm. Rep. of Egypt to IMO, 2010–12; Asst Minister for Eur. Affairs and Security and Strategic Orgns in Europe, Egyptian Min. of Foreign Affairs, 2013–15. *E:* hatemseifelnasr@gmail.com.

**SEIFTER, Pavel,** PhD; Ambassador of the Czech Republic to the Court of St James's, 1997–2003; Distinguished Visiting Fellow, Civil Society and Human Security Research Unit, Department of International Development (formerly Centre for the Study of Global Governance, then LSE Global Governance), London School of Economics and Political Science, 2003; *b* 27 May 1938; *s* of Karel and Anna Seifter; *m* 1st, 1966, Jana Macenauerová; one *d*; 2nd, 1986, Lenka Urbanová; 3rd, 1999, Lesley Chamberlain. *Educ:* Charles Univ., Prague (Hist., Czech Lang. and Lit. degree 1961; PhD Hist. 1968); Centre Universitaire Européen, Nancy, France (postgrad. study). Lectr in Hist., Charles Univ., Prague, 1964–68; translator, window cleaner, editor of dissident histl publications, 1969–89; Deputy Director: Inst. of Contemporary Hist., Prague, 1990–91; Inst. of Internat. Relns, Prague, 1991–92; Dir, Foreign Policy Dept, Office of Pres. of Czech Republic, 1993–97. Visiting Fellow: CISAC, Stanford Univ., 1992; Uppsala Univ., 1992.

**SEIKEN, Jason;** Chief Executive Officer, QCatalyst, since 2015; Chief Content Officer and Editor in Chief, Telegraph Media Group, 2013–15; *b* Michigan, USA; *s* of Arnold and Ione Seiken; *m* 2005, Juyoung Seo; one *s* one *d*. *Educ:* Union Coll., NY (BA Pol Sci.); Stanford Univ. Reporter, 1983–86, Ed., City and West Edns, 1986–93, Quincy Patriot Ledger; Ed. in Chief, washingtonpost.com, 1994–97; Vice President: AOL, 1997–2001; AOL Europe, 2001–06; Sen. Vice Pres. and Gen. Manager, Public Broadcasting Service Digital, 2006–13. *E:* seikenj@gmail.com.

**SEITLER, Jonathan Simon;** QC 2003; barrister; *b* 11 June 1961; *s* of Benjamin and Sandra Seitler; *m* 2012, Fiona Fishman; one *s* one *d* from a previous marriage. *Educ:* Stand Grammar Sch., Whitefield, Manchester; Pembroke Coll., Oxford (BA Hons PPE); City Univ., London (Dip Law). Called to the Bar, Inner Temple, 1985; in practice, specialising in law of property and related professional negligence. *Publications:* Property Finance Negligence: claims against solicitors and valuers, 1995; Commercial Property Disputes: law and practice, 1999; Leases: covenants and consents, 2009. *Address:* Wilberforce Chambers, 8 New Square, Lincoln's Inn, WC2A 3QP. *T:* (020) 7306 0102. *E:* JSeitler@wilberforce.co.uk.

**SEITZ, Raymond George Hardenbergh;** Ambassador of the United States of America to the Court of St James's, 1991–94; *b* Honolulu, 8 Dec. 1940; *s* of Maj. Gen. John Francis Regis Seitz and Helen Johnson Hardenbergh; one *s* one *d*; *m* 1985. *Educ:* Yale University (BA History 1963). Joined Foreign Service, Dept of State, 1966; served Montreal, Nairobi, Bukavu, Zaire, 1966–72; Staff Officer, later Director, Secretariat Staff, Washington, Special Asst to Dir Gen., Foreign Service, 1972–75; Political Officer, London, 1975–79; Dep. Exec. Sec., Washington, 1979–81; Senior Dep. Asst Sec., Public Affairs, Washington, 1981–82; Exec. Asst to Secretary George P. Shultz, Washington, 1982–84; Minister and Dep. Chief of Mission, US Embassy, London, 1984–89; Asst Sec. for European and Canadian Affairs, State Dept, Washington, 1989–91. A Sen. Man. Dir, 1995–96, Vice Chm., 1996–2003, Lehman Brothers; Chm., Sun-Times Media Gp, 2006–09. Trustee: Nat. Gall., 1996–2001; Royal Acad., 1996. Gov., Ditchley Foundn, 1995. Contrib. Ed., Condé Nast Traveller mag., 1997–2004. Freedom, City of London, 1998. Hon. Dr: Bath; York; Durham; Leeds; Reading; Heriot-Watt; Open. Benjamin Franklin Medal, RSA, 1996. Kt Comdr's Cross (Germany), 1991. *Publications:* Over Here (memoir), 1998. *Address:* PO Box 22, 159 Norris Road, Orford, NH 03777, USA.

**SEKERS, David Nicholas Oliver,** OBE 1986; FMA, FSA; author and consultant for heritage, museums and charities; *b* 29 Sept. 1943; *s* of Sir Nicholas Sekers, MBE and Lady Sekers; *m* 1965, Simone, *er d* of late Moran Caplat, CBE; one *d*. *Educ:* Eton; Worcester College, Oxford (BA). Dir, Gladstone Pottery Museum (Museum of the Year 1976), 1973–78; Museum Dir, Quarry Bank Mill (Museum of the Year 1984), 1978–89; Dir, Southern Reg., 1989–98, Dir of the Regions, 1998–2001, Nat. Trust; Specialist Advr, DCMS Select Cttee, 2005–. FSA 2010. *Publications:* The Potteries, 2009; (ed) The Diary of Hannah Lightbody 1786–1790, 2009; A Lady of Cotton: Hannah Greg, mistress of Quarry Bank Mill, 2013. *Recreations:* growing vegetables, fell-walking. *Address:* Cross House, Henstridge BA8 0QZ. *Club:* Garrick.

**SEKIMIZU, Koji;** Secretary-General, International Maritime Organization, 2012–15; Distinguished Visiting Fellow, S. Rajaratnam School of International Studies and Maritime and Port Authority of Singapore, 2016–18; *b* Yokohama, Japan, 3 Dec. 1952; *m* 1976, Chiho; one *s* one *d*. *Educ:* Elementary and secondary schs, Yokohama; Osaka Univ. (BEng 1975; MEng 1977). Ministry of Transport, Japan: ship inspector, 1977; Chief Officer in charge of IMO regulations, Safety Planning Section, Ship Bureau, 1979; Shipbuilding Res. Assoc. of Japan, 1980; Dep. Dir, Envmt Div., Min. of Transport, 1982–84; Dep. Dir, Second Internat. Orgns Div., Econ. Affairs Bureau, Min. of Foreign Affairs, 1984–86; Dep. Dir, Safety Standards Div., Maritime Technol. and Safety Bureau, 1986–89; International Maritime Organization: Tech. Officer, Sub-Div. for Technol., 1989–92, Hd, Technol. Section, 1992–97, Maritime Safety Div.; Sen. Dep. Dir, 1997–2000, Dir, 2000–04, Marine Envmt Div.; Dir, Maritime Safety Div., 2004–11. Chancellor, World Maritime Univ., 2012–15; Chm., Governing Bd, Internat. Maritime Law Inst., 2012. Mem., Japan Soc. of Naval Architects, 1975–; Councillor, Alumni Soc. of Naval Architects of Osaka Univ. (Kousi Zosen Kai), 1985–. Internat. Maritime Prize, IMO, 2016. *Recreations:* plays golf, playing guitar and composing songs.

**SELBORNE, 4th Earl of,** *cr* 1882; **John Roundell Palmer,** GBE 2011 (KBE 1987); FRS 1991; DL; Baron Selborne, 1872; Viscount Wolmer, 1882; Vice-President, Foundation for Science and Technology, 1994–2006 and since 2019 (Chairman, 2006–19); *b* 24 March 1940; *er s* of William Matthew, Viscount Wolmer (killed on active service, 1942), and Priscilla (who *m* 1948, Hon. Peter Legh, later 4th Baron Newton (*d* 1992); she *m* 1994, Frederick Fryer; she *d* 2010), *d* of late Captain John Egerton-Warburton; *S* grandfather, 1971; *m* 1969, Joanna Van Antwerp, PhD, *yr d* of late Evan Maitland James; three *s* one *d*. *Educ:* Eton; Christ Church, Oxford (MA). Chm., AFRC, 1983–90 (Mem., 1975–90); Vice-Chm., 1980–83; Vice-Chm., Apple and Pear Develt Council, 1969–73; Mem., Hops Mkting Bd, 1972–82 (Chm., 1978–82); Pres., British Crop Protection Council, 1977–80; Chm., SE Regl Panel, MAFF, 1979–83. Member: Royal Commn on Environmental Pollution, 1993–98; Govt Panel on Sustainable Develt, 1994–97. Chm., UK Chemical Stakeholder Forum, 2000–04. Chairman: H of L Select Cttee on Sci. and Technol., 1993–97 and 2014–17; Sub-Cttee D (Agric. and Food), H of L Select Cttee on European Communities, 1991–93; Sub-Cttee D (Agric., Food, Envmt and Consumer Affairs), H of L Select Cttee on EU, 1999–2003; elected Mem., H of L, 1999; Pres., Parly and Scientific Cttee, 1997–2000. Director: Agricl Mortgage Corp., 1990–2002 (Chm., 1995–2002); Lloyds Bank, 1994–95; Lloyds TSB Gp, 1995–2004. Chm., Jt Nature Conservation Cttee, 1991–97. President: South of England Agric. Soc., 1984; RASE, 1988; Royal Bath & West Agricl Soc., 1995; RGS (with IBG), 1997–2000; Vice-Pres., RSPB, 1996–2007; Chm., Trustees, Royal Botanic Gdns, Kew, 2003–09 (Trustee, 1993–98). Chancellor, Southampton Univ., 1996–2006. Treas., Bridewell Royal Hosp. (King Edward's Sch.,

Witley), 1972–83. Mem., Hampshire County Council, 1967–74. FRSB (FIBiol 1984); FRAgS 1986; FLS, 1994. Master, Mercers' Co., 1989–90. JP Hants 1971–78; DL Hants 1982. Hon. LLD Bristol, 1989; Hon. DSc: Cranfield, 1991; UEA, 1996; Southampton, 1996; Birmingham 2000. *Heir: s* Viscount Wolmer, *qv*. *Address:* Temple Manor, Selborne, Alton, Hants GU34 3LR. *T:* (01420) 473646. *Club:* Travellers.

**SELBOURNE, David Maurice;** author; *b* 4 June 1937; *s* of Hugh Selbourne, MD and Sulamith Amiel; *m* 1963, Hazel Savage; one *s* one *d*. *Educ:* Manchester Grammar Sch.; Balliol Coll., Oxford (Winter Williams Law Schol., Hon. Exhibnr, Paton Studentship, Jenkins Law Prize, BA Hons, MA). Called to the Bar, Inner Temple, 1960. British Commonwealth Fellow, Univ. of Chicago, 1959; Tutor, Ruskin Coll., Oxford, 1966–86 (Mem. Governing Body, 1973–75). Freelance journalist, 1975–: New Society, New Statesman, Spectator, Independent, Guardian, Tribune, The Times, Sunday Times, Daily Telegraph, Sunday Telegraph, India Today (Delhi), Sunday (Calcutta), *etc.* Member: Chief Minister's Cttee on Human Rights in Sri Lanka, Madras, 1984; Steering Cttee on Ethnic Violence, Dutch Inst. of Human Rights, 1984–85. Vis. Fellow, Europa Inst., Univ. of Leiden, 1964; Aneurin Bevan Meml Fellow, Govt of India, 1975–76; Indian Council of Social Sci. Res. Fellow, New Delhi, 1979–80. Lectures: The Times-Dillon's, LSE, 1994; Geraldine Aves Meml, H of C, 1994; Spectator Debates, 2010; Visiting Lectures, 1975–2005: RIIA; Inst. Commonwealth Studies, Oxford; Jawaharlal Nehru Univ., New Delhi; Aligarh Muslim Univ.; Czech Underground Univ., Prague and Bratislava, 1987, 1989; Berkeley; UCSD; Notre Dame Univ., Indiana, *etc.* Mem., Accademia Rubiconia, Savignano, Italy, 1993. *Plays* performed, 1968–83: Traverse Th., Edinburgh; Everyman Th., Liverpool; Northcott Th., Exeter; Crucible Th., Sheffield; Soho Th., London; People's Th., Calcutta, *etc.* Officer, Order of Merit of the Italian Republic, 2001. *Publications:* The Play of William Cooper and Edmund Dew-Nevett, 1968; The Two-backed Beast, 1969; Samson, 1971; The Damned, 1971; An Eye to China, 1975, 2nd edn 1978; An Eye to India, 1977; Through the Indian Looking-Glass, 1982; The Making of A Midsummer Night's Dream, 1982, 3rd edn 2010; (ed) In Theory and in Practice, 1985; Against Socialist Illusion, 1985; Left Behind: journeys into British politics, 1987; (ed) A Doctor's Life: the diaries of Hugh Selbourne, MD 1960–64, 1989, 2nd edn 2009; Death of the Dark Hero: Eastern Europe 1987–1990, 1990, 2nd edn 2009; The Spirit of the Age, 1993; Not an Englishman: conversations with Lord Goodman, 1993; The Principle of Duty: an essay on the foundations of the civic order, 1994, 4th edn 2009; Moral Evasion, 1998; The City of Light, 1997, 2nd edn 1998, other edns in translation, incl. Catalan, Chinese, French, German, Hebrew, Hungarian, Korean, Norwegian, Polish, Portuguese and Spanish, 1997–2002; The Losing Battle with Islam, 2005; The Free Society in Crisis, 2019; contribs to learned jls, incl. Bull. Concerned Asian Scholars, Critique, Electoral Studies, Hist. Workshop Jl, Monthly Review, Social Scientist and Third World Qly. *Recreations:* listening to music, reading, walking, talking. *Address:* c/o Christopher Sinclair-Stevenson, 3 South Terrace, SW7 2TB. *Club:* Oxford and Cambridge.

**SELBY, 6th Viscount** *cr* 1905, of the City of Carlisle; **Christopher Rolf Thomas Gully;** *b* 18 Oct. 1993; *s* of 5th Viscount Selby and of his 1st wife, Charlotte Cathrine Brege; *S* father, 2001. *Educ:* Glenalmond Coll. *Heir: great-uncle* Hon. James Edward Hugh Grey Gully [*b* 17 March 1945; *m* 1971, Fiona Margaret Mackenzie (*d* 2012); two *s*].

**SELBY, Bishop Suffragan of,** since 2014; **Rt Rev. Dr John Bromilow Thomson;** *b* Edinburgh, 1 July 1959; *s* of David and Betty Thomson; *m* 1986, Susan Clare Wade; two *d*. *Educ:* Edinburgh Acad.; Haberdashers' Aske's Sch., Elstree; Univ. of York (BA Hons Hist. 1981); Wycliffe Hall, Oxford (MA Theol. 1991); Univ. of Nottingham (PhD Theol. 2001). Ordained deacon, 1985, priest, 1986; Asst Curate and Youth Chaplain, All Saints, Ecclesall, Sheffield, 1985–89; Tutor, St Paul's Coll., Grahamstown, SA, 1989–92; Asst Lectr, Rhodes Univ., Grahamstown, SA, 1991–92; Vicar, St Mary, Wheatley, Doncaster, 1993–2001; Dir of Ministry, Dio. of Sheffield, 2001–14. *Publications:* The Ecclesiology of Stanley Hauerwas: a Christian theology of liberation, 2003; Church on Edge? Practising Christian Ministry Today, 2004; Doxa: a discipleship course, 2007; Living Holiness: Stanley Hauerwas and the church, 2010; Sharing Friendship: exploring Anglican character, vocation, witness and ministry, 2015. *Recreations:* cycling, choral singing, walking, reading, gardening, cooking. *Address:* Bishop's House, York Road, Barlby, Selby YO8 5JP. *T:* (01757) 429982. *E:* bishopofselby@yorkdiocese.org.

**SELBY, Dona Pamela;** consultant on fundraising and market research, since 2009; *d* of Donald and Sybil Davis; *m* 1981, Peter Selby. *Educ:* Bexleyheath Technical High Sch. Royal Mail: Marketing Asst, 1971–76; Marketing Exec., 1976–81; Marketing Manager, 1981–86; Sen. Corporate Manager, WWF, 1989–92; Great Ormond Street Hospital Children's Charity: Head of Commercial and Direct Marketing, then Dir of Fundraising, 1992–2001; Exec. Dir, 2001–06; Dir of Fundraising and Dep. CEO, Jeans for Genes, 2006–08. Trustee, Orchid Cancer Appeal, 2008–17. *Recreations:* keep fit, travel, motor racing. *E:* dona.selby21@gmail.com.

**SELBY, Jonathan Lee;** QC 2018; *b* Liverpool, 26 Aug. 1977; *s* of Brian and Linda Selby; *m* 2006, Lucy Needleman; one *s* one *d*. *Educ:* Liverpool Coll.; St Catharine's Coll., Cambridge (BA 1st Cl. Law 1998; MA). Called to the Bar, Gray's Inn, 1999; Res. Asst, Law Commn of England and Wales, 1999–2000; in practice as barrister, specialising in construction and engrg, 2000–. Accredited Adjudicator, Technol. and Construction Bar Assoc., 2007. Lay Mem., RIBA Professional Conduct Panel, 2017–. *Recreations:* football, cricket, tennis, swimming, food, cinema, ski-ing. *Address:* Keating Chambers, 15 Essex Street, WC2R 3AA. *T:* (020) 7544 2600. *E:* jselby@keatingchambers.com.

**SELBY, Prof. Peter John,** CBE 2001; MD, DSc; FMedSci; Professor of Cancer Medicine, since 1988, and Associate Dean, 2017–19, University of Leeds; Consultant Physician, St James's University Hospital, Leeds, since 1988; *b* 10 July 1950; *s* of Joseph Selby and Dorothy Selby (*née* Cross); *m* 1972, Catherine Elisabeth, *d* of Peter Thomas and Vera Thomas (*née* Wilson); one *s* one *d*. *Educ:* Lydney Grammar Sch.; Christ's Coll., Cambridge (MA; MB BChir; MD 1980); Univ. of Leeds (DSc 2011). FRCP 1990; FRCR 1994. Registrar, Fellow and Sen. Lectr (Consultant), Royal Marsden Hosp. and Inst. Cancer Res., 1977–88; Director: Cancer Res. UK Clinical Centre (formerly ICRF Cancer Medicine Res. Unit), Leeds, 1993–2010; Clin. Res., ICRF, 1997–2001; Lead Clinician, then Clin. Dir, Leeds Cancer Centre, 1997–2005. Dir, Nat. Cancer Res. Network, 2001–05; Foundn Dir, Leeds Inst. of Molecular Med. and Cancer Res., 2003–06; Jt Dir, UK Clinical Res. Network, 2005–10; Sen. Investigator, NIHR, 2010–. President: British Oncol Assoc., 1992–94; Assoc. of Cancer Physicians, 2008–18 (Fellow, 2017); Eur. Cancer Concord, 2014–17 (Mem., Steering Gp, 2013–); Mem. Council, Res. Strategy Cttee. Trustee, CRUK, 2012–16. FMedSci 1998. Pfizer Prize for Excellence in Oncology, British Oncol Soc., 2008. *Publications:* Hodgkin's Disease, 1987; Confronting Cancer: care and prevention, 1993; Cancer in Adolescents, 1995; Malignant Lymphomas, 2000; Cell and Molecular Biology of Cancer, 2005; Problem Solving in Oncology, 2007; Problem Solving in Acute Oncology, 2014; Problem Solving for Older Cancer Patients, 2015; Problem Solving through Precision Oncology, 2017; Problem Solving through Patient Centred and Integrated Care, 2018. *Recreations:* reading, music, watching sport, boating. *Address:* 18 Marine Approach, Burton Waters, Lincoln LN1 2WW.

**SELBY, Rt Rev. Peter Stephen Maurice**, PhD; Bishop of Worcester, 1997–2007; *b* 7 Dec. 1941. *Educ*: St John's Coll., Oxford (BA 1964; MA 1967); Episcopal Theol Sch., Cambridge, Mass (BD 1966); Bishops' Coll., Cheshunt; King's Coll. London (PhD 1975). Asst Curate, Queensbury, 1966–68; Associate Dir of Training, Southwark, 1969–73; Asst Curate, Limpsfield with Titsey, 1969–77; Vice-Principal, Southwark Ordination Course, 1970–72; Asst Missioner, Dio. Southwark, 1973–77; Canon Residentiary, Newcastle Cathedral, 1977–84; Diocesan Missioner, Dio. Newcastle, 1977–84; Suffragan Bishop, 1984–91, Area Bishop, 1991–92, of Kingston-upon-Thames; William Leech Professorial Fellow in Applied Christian Theol., Univ. of Durham, 1992–97; Bishop to HM Prisons, 2001–07; Hon. Asst Bishop, dios of Durham and Newcastle, 1992–97, dio. of Portsmouth, 2008–11, dio. of Southwark, 2011–. Interim Co-Dir, St Paul's Inst., 2012–14. Visitor Gen., Community of Sisters of the Church, 1991–2001. Vis. Prof., Internat. Centre for Prison Studies, 2008–11, Dept. of Theol. and Religious Studies, 2008–, KCL; Hon. Prof., Univ. of Worcester, 1998–. Charles Gore Lectr, Westminster Abbey, 2006; Eric Symes Abbott Lectr, Westminster Abbey and Keble Coll., Oxford, 2012; Hugh Price Hughes Lectr, 2013. Mem., Doctrine Commn, 1991–2003. Pres., Nat. Council for Ind. Monitoring Bds, 2008–13. President: Modern Churchpeople's Union, 1990–96; Soc. for Study of Theology, 2003–04. Hon. DD Birmingham, 2007. *Publications*: Look for the Living, 1976; Liberating God, 1983; BeLonging, 1991; Rescue, 1995; Grace and Mortgage, 1997; An Idol Unmasked, 2014.

**SELBY, Sarah Jayne;** *see* Buckingham, S. J.

**SELDON, Sir Anthony (Francis),** Kt 2014; PhD; FRHistS; Vice-Chancellor, University of Buckingham, since 2015; *b* 2 Aug. 1953; *s* of late Arthur Seldon, CBE and (Audrey) Marjorie Seldon (*née* Willett); *m* 1982, Joanna Pappworth (*d* 2016); one *s* two *d*. *Educ*: Tonbridge Sch.; Worcester Coll., Oxford (MA 1980); London School of Economics (PhD 1981); KCL (PGCE 1983); MBA Poly. of Central London 1989. FRHistS 1992. Res. Fellow and Tutor, London School of Economics, 1980–81; Consultant Historian, Rio Tinto Zinc, 1981–83; Head of Politics, Whitgift Sch., 1983–86; Co-founder, 1987, and first Dir, 1987–89, Inst. of Contemporary British History; Head of History and Gen. Studies, Tonbridge Sch., 1989–92; Dep. Headmaster, 1993–97, acting Headmaster, 1997, St Dunstan's Coll.; Headmaster, Brighton Coll., 1997–2005; Master, Wellington Coll., 2006–15; Exec. Head, Wellington Acad., 2013–15. Prof. of Educn, Coll. of Teachers, 2009–. Member: Bd, RSC, 2012–; Social Integration Commn, 2014–. Chair: Comment Awards, 2015–17; Nat. Archives Trust, 2019–. FRSA 1990; FKC 2013. Hon. DLitt Buckingham, 2013. Series Ed., Making Contemporary Britain, 1988. Co-founder: Contemporary Record, 1987 (Ed., 1987–95); Modern Hist. Rev., 1988 (Ed., 1989–92); Twentieth Century British Hist., 1989 (Consulting Ed., 1989–91); Contemp. European Hist., 1989 (Consulting Ed., 1989–90). Hon. DLitt Brighton, 2004. *Publications*: Churchill's Indian Summer, 1981; (jtly) By Word of Mouth, 1983; (ed) Contemporary History, 1987; (ed jtly) Ruling Performance, 1987; (ed) Political Parties since 1945, 1988; (ed jtly) Thatcher Effect, 1989; (jtly) Politics UK, 1991; (ed jtly) Conservative Century, 1994; (ed jtly) Major Effect, 1994; (ed jtly) The Heath Government 1970–74, 1996; (ed jtly) Contemporary History Handbook, 1996; (ed jtly) Ideas That Shaped Postwar Britain, 1996; (ed) How Tory Governments Fall: the Conservative Party in power since 1783, 1996; Major: a political biography, 1997; 10 Downing Street: the illustrated history, 1999; (jtly) Britain under Thatcher, 1999; (jtly) The Powers Behind the Prime Minister, 1999; The Foreign Office: an illustrated history of the place and the people, 2000; (ed) The Blair Effect, 2001; (jtly) A New Conservative Century?, 2001; Public and Private Education, 2001; Brave New City, 2002; Partnership not Paternalism, 2002; Blair: the biography, 2004; (ed jtly) Governing or New Labour, 2004; (jtly) The Conservative Party: an illustrated history, 2004; (ed jtly) Recovering Power: the Conservatives in Opposition since 1867, 2005; (ed) The Blair Effect 2, 2001–05: a wasted term?, 2005; Blair Unbound: 2001–07, 2007; (ed) Blair's Britain 1997–2007, 2007; Autonomy Lost, Autonomy Regained, 2009; Trust: how we lost it and how to get it back, 2009; An End to Factory Schools: an education manifesto 2010–2020, 2010; (jtly) Brown At 10, 2010; Why Schools? Why Universities?, 2011; The Politics of Optimism, 2011; The Great War and Public Schools, 2013; (jtly) The Architecture of Diplomacy, 2014; Schools United, 2014; Beyond Happiness, 2015; (ed jtly) The Coalition Effect 2010–2015, 2015; (jtly) Cameron at 10: the inside story 2010–15, 2015; (jtly) Cameron at 10: the verdict, 2016; The Cabinet Office 1916–2016, 2016; The Positive University, 2017; The Fourth Education Revolution, 2018; May at 10, 2019. *Recreations*: drama, sport, writing, walking, running. *Address*: University of Buckingham, Hunter Street, Buckingham MK18 1EG. *T*: (01280) 814080. *Club*: Royal Over-Seas League.

**SELF, Deborah Jane;** *see* Orr, D. J.

**SELF, Heather,** FCA; Tax Partner, Blick Rothenberg Ltd, since 2018; Founder, Women in Tax, 2015; *b* Chelsea, 16 Sept. 1959; *d* of late Alan Robert Dowdeswell and of Audrey Dowdeswell; *m* 1982, Howard John Self; one *s* one *d*. *Educ*: Manchester High Sch. for Girls; Newnham Coll., Cambridge (BA Maths 1980; MA 1983). CTA (Fellow) 2003; FCA 2004. Ernst & Young: trainee, 1980–83; Tax Dept, 1983–92; Tax Partner, 1992–2001; Gp Tax Dir, Scottish Power plc, 2002–06; Partner, Grant Thornton LLP, 2006–08; Anti-Avoidance Advr, HMRC, 2008–11; Partner (non lawyer), Pinsent Masons LLP, 2011–17. Mem. Council, Chartered Inst. of Taxation, 1993–2004. FRSA. *Publications*: contribs to tax tech. press, incl. Tax Jl. *Recreations*: walking, singing, Shakespeare, the restoration of an ex-BR 9F steam engine. *Address*: Blick Rothenberg Ltd, 16 Great Queen Street, Covent Garden, WC2B 5AH. *T*: (020) 7544 8752. *E*: heather.self@blickrothenberg.com.

**SELF, William Woodard;** writer, since 1990; Professor of Contemporary Thought, Brunel University, since 2012; *b* 26 Sept. 1961; *s* of late Prof. Peter John Otter Self and of Elaine Self (*née* Rosenbloom); *m* 1st, 1989, Katharine Sylvia Chancellor (marr. diss. 1997); one *s* one *d*; 2nd, 1997, Deborah Jane Orr, *qv* (marr. diss. 2018); two *s*. *Educ*: Exeter Coll., Oxford (BA Hons). Freelance cartoonist, 1982–88; Publishing Dir, Cathedral Publishing, 1988–90; contributing editor, London Evening Standard mag., 1993–95; columnist: Observer, 1995–97; The Times, 1998–99; Independent on Sunday, 1999–2001; London Evening Standard, 2002–09; New Statesman, 2009–. *Publications*: The Quantity Theory of Insanity, 1991; Cock & Bull, 1992; My Idea of Fun, 1993; Grey Area, 1994; Junk Mail, 1995; The Sweet Smell of Psychosis, 1996; Great Apes, 1997; Tough Tough Toys for Tough Tough Boys, 1998; Sore Sites, 2000; How the Dead Live, 2000; Perfidious Man, 2000; Feeding Frenzy, 2001; Dorian, 2002; Dr Mukti and Other Tales of Woe, 2004; The Book of Dave, 2006; PsychoGeography, 2007; The Butt, 2008; Liver, 2008; Psycho Too, 2009; Walking to Hollywood, 2010; Umbrella, 2012; Shark, 2014; Phone, 2017. *Recreation*: walking. *Address*: The Wylie Agency, 17 Bedford Square, WC1B 3JA. *T*: (020) 7908 5900.

**SELINGER, Gregory F.;** MLA (NDP) Saint-Boniface, Manitoba, 1999–2018; Premier of Manitoba, 2009–16; *b* Regina, Saskatchewan, 16 Feb. 1951; *s* of late Margaret E. Crawford; *m* 1976, Claudette Toupin; two *s*. *Educ*: Univ. of Manitoba (Bachelor Social Work); Queen's Univ. (MPA); London Sch. of Econs and Pol Sci. (PhD). Associate Prof., Faculty of Social Work, Univ. of Manitoba, 1984–99. Former Mem., St Boniface CC (Chm., Finance and Admin Cttee). Legislative Assembly of Manitoba: Minister: of Finance, 1999–2009; responsible for Francophone Affairs (formerly French Lang. Services), 1999–; charged with admin of Crown Corporations Public Rev. and Accountability Act, 1999–2009; charged with admin of Manitoba Hydro Act, 1999–2002, 2006–09; responsible for Civil Service, 2001–09; charged with admin of Liquor Control Act, 2002–03, 2007–08; charged with admin of Manitoba Lotteries Corp. Act, 2007–08; resp. for Skills Strategy; of Federal-Provincial Relns; Pres., Exec. Council, 2009–16. Former Board Member: St Boniface Hosp.; St Boniface Mus.; former Pres., Old St Boniface Residents' Assoc. Coach, YMCA. *Recreations*: cycling, fishing, outdoor activities.

**SELKIRK,** Earldom of (*cr* 1646); title disclaimed by 11th Earl (*see under* Selkirk of Douglas, Baron).

**SELKIRK OF DOUGLAS,** Baron *cr* 1997 (Life Peer), of Cramond in the City of Edinburgh; **James Alexander Douglas-Hamilton;** PC 1996; QC (Scot.) 1996; Lord High Commissioner, General Assembly, Church of Scotland, 2012 and 2013; *b* 31 July 1942; 2nd *s* of 14th Duke of Hamilton, and *b* of 15th Duke of Hamilton; disclaimed Earldom of Selkirk, 1994, prior to succession being determined in his favour, 1996; *m* 1974, Hon. Priscilla Susan Buchan, *d* of 2nd Baron Tweedsmuir, CBE, CD, and late Baroness Tweedsmuir of Belhelvie, PC; four *s* (incl. twins). *Educ*: Eton College; Balliol Coll., Oxford (MA, Mod. History; Oxford Boxing Blue, 1961; Pres., Oxford Univ. Cons. Assoc., 1963; Pres., Oxford Union Soc., 1964); Edinburgh Univ. (LLB, Scots Law). TA Officer, 6th/7th Bn of Cameronians (Scottish Rifles), 1961–66; Cameronian Co. 2nd Bn of Lowland Vols, 1972–74, Capt., 1973. Advocate at Scots Bar and Interim Procurator Fiscal Depute, 1968–74. Town Councillor, Murrayfield-Cramond, Edinburgh, 1972–74. MP (C) Edinburgh West, Oct. 1974–1997; contested (C) same seat, 1997. Scottish Conservative Whip, 1977; a Lord Comr of HM Treasury, and Govt Whip for Scottish Cons. Mems, 1979–81; PPS to Foreign Office Minister, 1983–86, to Sec. of State for Scotland, 1986–87; Parly Under-Sec. of State for Home Affairs and the Envmt, 1987–92, for Educn and Housing, 1992–95, Scottish Office; Minister of State for Home Affairs and Health, Scottish Office, 1995–97. MSP (C) Lothians, 1999–2007. Scottish Parliament: Business Manager and Chief Whip, Conservative Gp, 1999–2001; spokesman on home affairs, 2000–03, on education, 2003–07. Captain Cameronian Co., 2 Bn Low Vols RARO, 1972–74. Hon. Air Cdre, No 2 (City of Edinburgh) Maritime HQ Unit, 1994–99; Hon. Air Cdre, 603 (City of Edinburgh) Sqn, RAAF, 1999–2015; Pres., Internat. Rescue Corps, 1995. Hon. Pres., Scottish Amateur Boxing Assoc., 1975–99; President: Royal Commonwealth Soc. in Scotland, 1979–87; Scottish Council, UNA, 1981–87. Chm., Scottish Adv. Cttee, Skillforce, 2009–. Mem. Royal Co. of Archers, Queen's Body Guard for Scotland. Patron, Hope and Homes for Children, 2002– (Chm., Edinburgh Support Gp, 2002–07); President: Scottish Veterans Garden City Assoc. Inc., 2003–; Trefoil House Charity, 2008–18. *Publications*: Motive for a Mission: The Story Behind Hess's Flight to Britain, 1971; The Air Battle for Malta: the diaries of a fighter pilot, 1981, 2nd edn 1990; Roof of the World: man's first flight over Everest, 1983; The Truth About Rudolf Hess, 1993, new edn 2016; After You, Prime Minister, 2009. *Recreations*: golf, forestry, modern history. *Heir*: (to Earldom of Selkirk): *s* Hon. John Andrew Douglas-Hamilton, Master of Selkirk [*b* 8 Feb. 1978; *m* 2015, Marleen van Baal; twin *d*]. *Address*: House of Lords, SW1A 0PW. *Clubs*: Sloane; Royal Scots (Hon. Mem.) (Edinburgh); Hon. Company of Edinburgh Golfers.

*See also* Duke of Hamilton.

**SELLA, Prof. Andrea,** DPhil; Professor of Chemistry, University College London, since 2012; *b* Milan, 20 Feb. 1961. *Educ*: Trinity Coll., Univ. of Toronto (BSc Chem. 1984; MSc Chem. 1986); Balliol Coll., Oxford (DPhil Inorganic Chem. 1990). Lectr, 1990–96, Sen. Lectr, 1996–2012, in Inorganic Chemistry, UCL. EPSRC Sen. Media Fellow, 2007–12. Founder and Mem., Gillespie Sci. Club, 2006–. Columnist, Classic Kit series, Chemistry World, 2007–. Contrib./consultant on TV progs incl. Secret Life of Chaos, 2010, Chemistry: A Volatile History, 2010, The Story of Science, 2010, Everything and Nothing, 2011, Order and Disorder, 2012; consultant and contributor, Elemental Economics, BBC World Service, 2014–. Michael Faraday Prize, Royal Soc., 2014. *Publications*: articles in acad. jls. *Recreation*: playing. *Address*: Department of Chemistry, University College London, 20 Gordon Street, WC1H 0AJ. *E*: a.sella@ucl.ac.uk. *Club*: Cycling (Hackney).

**SELLARS, John Ernest,** CBE 1994; Chief Executive, Business and Technology (formerly Business and Technician) Education Council, 1983–94; *b* 5 Feb. 1936; *s* of late Ernest Buttle Sellars and Edna Grace Sellars; *m* 1958, Dorothy Beatrice (*née* Morrison); three *d*. *Educ*: Wintringham Grammar Sch., Grimsby; Manchester Univ. (BSc, MSc). Research Engineer, English Electric (GW) Ltd, 1958–61; Lectr, Royal College of Advanced Technology (now Univ. of Salford), 1961–67; Head of Mathematics, Lanchester College of Technology, Coventry, 1967–71; Head of Computer Science, Lanchester Polytechnic, Coventry/Rugby, 1971–74; Chief Officer, Business Educn Council, 1974–83. Member: Bd, Nat. Adv. Body for Public Sector Higher Educn, 1982–88; BBC School Broadcasting Council for UK, 1982–87; City Technology Colls Trust, 1989–94; Engrg and Technol. Adv. Cttee, British Council, 1990–95; Engrg Council, 1994–95 (Mem., Standing Cttee for Engrg Profession, 1994–95); British Accreditation Council for Ind., Further and Higher Educn, 1999–2002. Mem. Exec. Cttee, RoSPA, 1994–2002. Governor, London Guildhall Univ., 1994–2000. Trustee, Gatsby Technical Educn Projects, 1999–2005. Hon. FCP 1989. DUniv Sheffield Hallam, 1994; Hon. DTech London Guildhall, 2001. *Publications*: papers on mathematics, computer science and business educn. *Recreation*: walking. *Clubs*: Reform, MCC.

**SELLARS, Peter;** American opera and theatre director; *b* 27 Sept. 1957. *Educ*: Phillips Acad., Mass; Harvard Univ. (BA 1980). Artistic Director: Boston Shakespeare Co., 1983–84; American Nat. Theater at Kennedy Center for the Performing Arts, 1984; LA Fest., 1990, 1993. Prof. of World Arts and Cultures, UCLA. *Productions* include: Armida, Monadnock Music Fest., 1981; The Mikado, Lyric Opera of Chicago, 1983; Così fan tutte, Castle Hill Fest., Mass, 1984; The Electrification of the Soviet Union, Glyndebourne Touring Opera, 1987; Nixon in China, Houston, 1987, ENO, 2000; Die Zauberflöte, Glyndebourne, 1990; The Death of Klinghoffer, Théâtre Royal de la Monnaie, Brussels, 1991; The Persians, Edinburgh Fest., 1993; Pelléas and Mélisande, Amsterdam, 1993; The Merchant of Venice, Barbican, 1994; Mathis der Maler, Royal Opera House, 1995; Theodora, Glyndebourne, 1996; The Rake's Progress, 1996, El Niño, 2000, L'Amour de Loin, 2001, Châtelet, Paris; Idomeneo, Glyndebourne, 2003; Tristan und Isolde, Opéra Nat. de Paris, 2005; Dr Atomic, San Francisco, 2005; Zaïde, Barbican, 2006; Othello, NY, 2009; Desdemona, Barbican, 2012; The Gospel According to the Other Mary, Coliseum, 2014; Bach's St John Passion, Berlin, 2014; The Indian Queen, Coliseum, 2015.

**SELLARS, Wendy Jane;** *see* Lloyd, W. J.

**SELLERS, Ann H.;** *see* Henderson-Sellers.

**SELLERS, Basil Alfred,** AM 2003; Chairman, Sellers Group, since 1987; *b* 19 June 1935; *s* of William Alfred Sellers and Irene Ethel Sellers (*née* Freemantle); *m* 2nd, 1980, Gillian Clare Heinrich; two *s* one *d* from previous marr. *Educ*: King's College, Adelaide, SA. Clerk, State Bank of SA, 1952; Clerk, Cutten & Harvey, Adelaide, 1954–69 (Investment Advr, 1969); owner, Devon Homes, SA, 1970; bought Ralph Symonds Ltd, 1975 (Man. Dir);

Chm., Gestetner plc, 1987–94. *Recreations:* cricket, art, music. *Address:* 43 William Street, Double Bay, NSW 2028, Australia. *Clubs:* MCC, Cricketers'; University (Australia).
*See also* E. *Sellers.*

**SELLERS, Elizabeth, (Libby);** Director, Libby Sellers Office, since 2015 (Founder and Director, Gallery Libby Sellers, 2007); *b* Adelaide, Australia, 1972; *d* of Basil Alfred Sellers, *qv* and Beverley Maizie Daw (*née* Addicott). *Educ:* Badminton Sch., Bristol; Univ. of East Anglia (BA Hons Hist. of Art 1994); Central St Martins (MA Journalism 1996); Royal Coll. of Art (MA Hist. of Design 1998). Asst Curator, Glasgow 1999, City of Architecture and Design, 1998; Partner, Restructure Ltd, 1999–2001; Curator, Design Mus., London, 2001–07. Patron: Rambert Dance Co., 2010–; Michael Clark Co.; South London Gall. *Publications:* Why What How: collecting design in a contemporary market, 2010; Women Design, 2018. *E:* office@libbysellers.com.

**SELLERS, Geoffrey Bernard,** CB 1991; Parliamentary Counsel, 1987–2010; *b* 5 June 1947; *s* of late Bernard Whittaker Sellers and Elsie (*née* Coop); *m* 1971, Susan Margaret Faulconbridge (*d* 1995); two *s* two *d*. *Educ:* Manchester Grammar Sch. (Scholar); Magdalen Coll., Oxford (Mackinnon Scholar; BCL 1st Cl. Hons; MA). Called to the Bar, Gray's Inn, 1971 (Macaskie Scholar). Legal Assistant: Law Commn, 1971; Commn on Industrial Relations, 1971–74; Office of Parly Counsel, 1974–2010; with Law Commn, 1982–85, and 1991–93; with Inland Revenue, 1996–99. *Address:* 53 Canonbury Road, N1 2DG.
*See also* J. M. *Sellers.*

**SELLERS, John Marsland,** CB 2005; Parliamentary Counsel, 1998–2010; *b* 15 July 1951; *s* of late Bernard Whittaker Sellers and Elsie (*née* Coop); *m* 1975, Patricia Susan Burns; two *s*. *Educ:* Manchester Grammar Sch.; Magdalen Coll., Oxford (BA, BCL). Lecturer: Lincoln Coll., Oxford, 1973–75; LSE, 1975–77; Articled Clerk, 1977–80, Solicitor, 1980–83, Freshfields; Asst Parly Counsel, 1983–88; Sen. Asst Parly Counsel, 1988–91; Dep. Parly Counsel, 1991–98; on secondment to Law Commn, 1998–2001, to Tax Law Rewrite Project, 2007–09, to Law Commn, 2010. *Address:* Crestover, Horsell Rise, Woking, Surrey GU21 4BA. *T:* (01483) 770559.
*See also* G. B. *Sellers.*

**SELLERS, Libby;** *see* Sellers, E.

**SELLERS, Philip Edward,** CBE 2001; Director C4MA, Climate Change Capital, 2007–13; *b* 20 March 1937; *s* of George Edward and Helen Sellers; *m* 1962, Brenda Anne Bell; two *s*. *Educ:* Ernest Bailey Grammar School, Matlock; CIPFA. Local Govt, 1953–72; Controller of Audit, British Gas Corp., 1972–76; Finance Dir, North Thames Gas, 1976–80; Dir of Finance and Planning, British Rail Board, 1980–84; Board Mem. for Corporate Finance and Planning, Post Office, 1984–89. Mem., Postel Property Cttee, 1992–94; non-exec. Dir, Postel Investment Management, 1994–95; Trustee, Post Office Pension Funds, 1985–99; Chm., Audit Cttee, DTI, 1994–2003; Chm., Nuclear Decommng Prog. Bd, DTI, 2003–05. Non-executive Chairman: CSL Group, 1989–93; ICL Outsourcing Ltd (formerly CFM Group Ltd, then ICL/CFM), 1989–99; Pegasus Group plc, 1992–2000; Inner City Enterprises, 1992–98; Powerleague Soccer Centres Ltd (formerly Powerplay Supersoccer Ltd), 1995–99; Workplace Technologies plc, 1995–99; Alexander Mann Associates Ltd, 1997–2000; Dep. Chm., Powerleague Ltd, 1999–2001; non-exec. Dir, Etam Gp, 1991–98; Advr, Nomura Asset Mgt, 2002–07. UK rep., IFAC Public Sector Cttee, 1987–90; Philip Sellers Communications and Consultancy, 1989–2010. Mem., NCC Impact Adv. Bd, 1989–92. Pres., CIPFA, 1985–86; Chm., Nationalised Industries Finance Panel, 1986–89. Non-exec. Dir, London Festival Orch., 1994–98. *Recreations:* tennis, ski-ing. *Address:* Magnolia, School Lane, Seer Green, Bucks HP9 2QJ.

**SELLEY, Elaine;** *see* Logan, E.

**SELLIER, Robert Hugh,** FICE; Chief Executive, Y. J. Lovell, 1991–95; *b* 15 Nov. 1933; *s* of Major Philip Joseph Sellier and Lorna Geraldine Sellier (*née* Luxton); *m* 1st, 1963, Cynthia Ann Dwelly (*d* 1985); one *d*; 2nd, 1987, Gillian Dalley (*née* Clark). *Educ:* St Joseph's Coll., Oxford; King's Coll., Durham Univ. (BScCivEng). FCIHT. Man. Dir, New Ideal Homes, 1972–74; Dep. Man. Dir, Cementation International, 1974–79; Man. Dir, Cementation Construction, 1979–83; Chm., Cementation Gp of Companies, 1983–86; Gp Man. Dir, George Wimpey, 1986–91. Non-exec. Dir, Hyder plc, 1993–2000. *Recreations:* ski-ing, shooting, scuba, flying.

**SELLS, (Edward) Andrew (Perronet),** FCA; Chairman, Natural England, 2014–19; *b* 30 Nov. 1948; *s* of Sir David Perronet Sells and Beryl Cecilia Sells (*née* Charrington); *m* 1st, 1997, Kate Hatch (marr. diss.); one *d* (one *s* decd); 2nd, 2015, Marina, (Mini), Dumas, *d* of late Allan Heyman, QC and Anne-Marie Castenschiold, of Denmark. *Educ:* St Peter's, Seaford; Wellington Coll.; London Business Sch. (MSc 1988). FCA 1972. With Schroders Gp, 1972–82; Man. Dir, venture capital funds, 1983–2000, incl. Man. Dir, Sovereign Capital Ltd, 1990–2000. Chairman: Linden plc, 1992–2007; Westerleigh Gp, 1992–2003; Garden Centre Gp (Wyevale), 2009–13. Advr on Work Prog. to Minister of State, DWP, 2013–15 (Chair, Best Practice Gp, 2013–15). Trustee: RHS, 2003–10 (Hon. Treas., 2008–10); Policy Exchange, 2007–13; Open Europe, 2011–13. Co-Treas., No2AV Campaign, 2011. Chair, Isles of Scilly Partnership, 2019. *Recreations:* cricket, travel, trees. *Address:* Sandy Farm, Sopworth, Chippenham, Wilts SN14 6PP.
*See also* O. M. *Sells.*

**SELLS, Oliver Matthew;** QC 1995; a Recorder of the Central Criminal Court, since 2008 (Crown Court, 1991–2008); *b* 29 Sept. 1950; *s* of Sir David Perronet Sells and Beryl Cecilia Sells (*née* Charrington); *m* 1986, Lucinda Jane, *d* of late Gerard William Mackworth-Young and Lady Eve Mackworth-Young; one *s* one *d*. *Educ:* St Peter's, Seaford; Wellington Coll.; Coll. of Law, London. Mem., Hon. Soc. of Inner Temple, 1969–; called to the Bar, Inner Temple, 1972, Bencher, 1996; SE Circuit, 1974–; Supplementary Counsel to the Crown, 1981–86. Chm., SE Circuit Liaison Cttee, 1998–2007. Member: Gen. Council of the Bar, 1977–80 and 1986–91; Commonwealth Law Assoc. (Legal Advr, 2008–); Chair: Symposium on Economic Crime, Cambridge Univ., 2008–; Open Europe, 2008. Mem. Council, Conservative Policy Forum, 2011–16; Legal Advr, Red Tape Initiative, 2017–. Mem., City of London Council, 2017–. Hon. Mem., Amer. Bar Assoc.; Dir, Music for Charity. Trustee, Breckland Soc. *Recreations:* mediaeval wall paintings, travel, dendrology. *Address:* 5 Paper Buildings, Temple, EC4Y 7HB. *T:* (020) 7583 6117. *Clubs:* Boodle's, Garrick, MCC; Norfolk (Norwich); Royal West Norfolk Golf.
*See also* E. A. P. *Sells.*

**SELLS, Robert Anthony,** FRCS, FRCSE; Consultant Surgeon, Royal Liverpool University Hospital (formerly Liverpool Royal Infirmary), 1970–2005; *b* 13 April 1938; *s* of late Rev. William Blyth Sells and Eleanor Mary Sells; *m* 1st, 1964, Elizabeth Lucy Schryver (marr. diss. 1976); two *s* one *d*; 2nd, 1977, Pauline Gilchrist Muir; two *s*. *Educ:* Christ's Hosp. Sch., Horsham; Guy's Hosp. Med. Sch., Univ. of London (MB BS). FRCS 1966; FRCSE 1966. Lecturer, Department of Surgery: Guy's Hosp. Med. Sch., 1966–67; Univ. of Cambridge, 1967–69; MRC Travelling Schol., Univ. of Harvard, 1969–70; Dir of Transplantation, 1970–97, Dir of Surgery, 1997–99, Royal Liverpool Univ. Hosp.; Hon. Prof. of Surgery and Immunology, Univ. of Liverpool, 1998–. Vis. Professor: Detroit Univ., 1977; Adelaide Univ., 1984; Minnesota Univ., 1984–85; London Univ., 1998. Gen. Sec. and Pres., British Transplantation Society, 1978–86; Mem. Council, Chm. of Ethics Cttee and Vice Pres., The Transplantation Soc., 1986–94; Vice Pres., Inst. of Med. Ethics, 1986–2007; Co-Founder and Chm., Internat. Forum for Transplant Ethics, 1995–; Pres., Liverpool Med. Instn, 1997–98 (Mem., 1972–). Expert Witness, 1982–. Principal Conductor and Musical Dir, Crosby SO, 1982–2014, now Conductor Laureate; Founder and Dir, Vale of Clwyd Singers, 2010–; Hon. Pres., Aberwheeler Show, 1995. Mem., Noblemen's and Gentlemen's Catch Club, 2017–. Hon. Fellow, Amer. Soc. of Transplant Surgeons, 1978–. Liveryman, Livery Co. of Wales (formerly Welsh Livery Guild), 2009–. *Publications:* (ed jtly) Transplantation Today, 1983; (ed jtly) Organ Transplantation: current clinical and immunological concepts, 1989; papers on transplantation and bioethics in med. jls. *Recreations:* collecting Victorian pickle jars, orchestral and choral conducting. *Address:* Cil Llwyn, Llandyrnog, Denbighshire LL16 4HY. *T:* (01745) 710296. *Clubs:* Moynihan Chirurgical Travelling (Pres., 2000–01), Twenty (Liverpool); Cheshire Pitt.

**SELLWOOD, Philip Henry George;** Chief Executive, Energy Saving Trust, since 2003; *b* 10 Jan. 1954; *s* of Albert Edward Sellwood and Irene Sellwood; *m* 1977, Lynn Ann Harris (marr. diss. 2005); one *s* one *d*; partner, Susan Hollis; one *d*. *Educ:* Nottingham Univ. (BEd); Univ. of Westminster (MBA Dist.). Marks & Spencer plc, 1977–2000: Commercial Exec.; Dir, Gp Strategy, 1998–2000; Man. Dir, Thresher Gp, 2000–02. Non-executive Director: Veos plc, 1999–2002; Marks & Spencer Financial Services, 1998–2001; Criminal Records Bureau, 2000–03; Local Govt Improvement and Innovation (formerly Improvement and Develt Agency), 2002–; LGA IDeA Co., 2010–; Renewable Energy Assurance Ltd, 2013–; Tevva Motors (Jersey), 2018–. Dir, Low Carbon Vehicle Partnership, 2005– (Dep. Chair, 2013); Member: Adv. Bd, Nat. Consumer Council, 2003–09; Sustainable Bldgs Task Force, 2004–05; UK Energy Res. Council, 2005–; LGA Climate Commn, 2007–09; Govt Zero Carbon Task Force, 2008–15; European Energy Network, 2011–; Adv. Bd, Nat. House Building Council, 2012–; Energy Res. Partnership, 2013–; Adv. Bd, Twenty65, 2016–. Trustee, Ellen Macarthur Foundn, 2009–. FCMI; FRSA; FInstD; FInstE. *Recreations:* reading, wine, cricket, the arts. *Address:* The Beach House, 30 Val Prinseps Road, Pevensey Bay, E Sussex BN24 6JG. *T:* (01323) 762064, 07831 829888. *E:* philip_sellwood@hotmail.com.

**SELOUS, Andrew Edmund Armstrong;** MP (C) South West Bedfordshire, since 2001; *b* 27 April 1962; *s* of late Gerald M. B. Selous, OBE, VRD, and Miranda Selous (*née* Casey); *m* 1993, Harriet Marston; three *d*. *Educ:* London Sch. of Econs (BSc Econ). ACII 1993. Great Lakes Re (UK) PLC, 1991–2001. An Opposition Whip, 2004–06; Shadow Minister for Work and Pensions, 2006–10; Parly Under-Sec. of State, MoJ, 2014–16; an Asst Govt Whip, 2014–16. Member: Work and Pensions Select Cttee, 2001–05; Health and Social Care (formerly Health) Select Cttee, 2016–. Contested (C) Sunderland N, 1997. Served TA, HAC and RRF, 1981–94. *Recreation:* family life. *Address:* House of Commons, SW1A 0AA. *Clubs:* Leighton Buzzard Conservative, Dunstable Conservative.

**SELSDON,** 3rd Baron *cr* 1932, of Croydon; **Malcolm McEacharn Mitchell-Thomson;** Bt 1900; banker; Exploitant Vini-Viticole, Provence, France, since 1987; *b* 27 Oct. 1937; *s* of 2nd Baron Selsdon (3rd Bt, *cr* 1900), DSC; S father, 1963; *m* 1st, 1965, Patricia Anne (marr. diss.; she *d* 2018), *d* of Donald Smith; one *s*; 2nd, 1995, Gabrielle Tesseron (*née* Williams). *Educ:* Winchester College. Sub-Lieut, RNVR. Deleg. to Council of Europe and WEU, 1972–78. C. T. Bowring Gp, 1972–76; Midland Bank Group, 1976–90: EEC Advr, 1979–85; Public Finance Advr, 1985–90. Dir of various companies. Chm., Committee for Middle East Trade (COMET), 1979–86; Member: BOTB, 1983–86; E European Trade Council, 1985–87. Pres., British Exporters Assoc., 1990–98. Elected Mem., H of L, 1999. Chm., Greater London and SE Regional Council for Sport and Recreation, 1977–83. *Recreations:* rackets, squash, tennis, lawn tennis, ski-ing, sailing. *Heir: s* Hon. Callum Malcolm McEacharn Mitchell-Thomson [*b* 7 Nov. 1969; *m* 1999, Vanessa, *d* of Stefan Glasmacher; one *s* one *d*]. *Address:* c/o House of Lords, SW1A 0PW. *Club:* MCC.

**SELVANAYAGAM, Rev. Dr Israel;** Methodist Minister, South Worcestershire (formerly Stratford-upon-Avon and Evesham) Circuit, since 2016; *b* 10 March 1951; *s* of Samuel and Nallathai Selvanayagam; *m* 1977, Gnana Leelal; two *d*. *Educ:* Kerala Univ. (MA); Serampore Coll. (BD 1978; DTh 1990); Tamilnadu Theol Seminary. Probationer in church ministry, Kanyakumari dio., Ch of S India, 1969–73; ministerial training, 1973–77; on staff of Tamilnadu Theol Seminary, Madurai, S India, teaching religions, mission and inter-faith dialogue with special responsibilities in lay theol educn, prog. on dialogue and editing Tamil theol books, 1977–96; ordained deacon, 1980, presbyter, 1981; World Ch Tutor, World Ch in Britain Partnership, Wesley Coll., Bristol, 1996–2000; Principal, United Coll. of the Ascension, Birmingham, 2001–06; Interfaith Consultant, Heartlands Team of Elmdon Circuit, Birmingham Dist of Methodist Ch, 2006; Principal, United Theol Coll., Bangalore, 2008–09; Prof. of Religions, Gurukul Lutheran Theol Coll., Chennai, 2010–16. Advr for Inter-faith Dialogue, WCC, 1991–98. *Publications:* A Dialogue on Dialogue, 1995; The Dynamics of Hindu Religious Traditions, 1996; Gospel and Culture in Tamilnadu, 1996; Vedic Sacrifice, 1996; A Second Call: ministry and mission in a multifaith milieu, 2000; (ed) Moving Forms of Theology, 2002; Relating to People of Other Faiths, 2004; Being Evangelical and Dialogical: healthy balance in a multifaith context, 2012; (jtly) Glimpses of Life through the Bible (booklets), 2012–; The Last Week of Jesus (in Tamil), 2015; Kristu Bhakti and Krishna Bhakti: a Christian-Hindu dialogue contributing to comparative theology, 2017; (ed) Religion, Spirituality and Secularity in India, 2017; (with G. Mithra) The Challenge of Fundamentalism and Response of Theological Education in India, 2017; The Newness of Jesus, Birth: 20 sermons in Tamil, 2017; Religion and Religions: an interfaith perspective, 2018; Interreligious Life Issues, 2019; Waves of God's Love: 100 tiny drops (in Tamil), 2019; contribs to learned jls incl. Asian Jl Theol., Current Dialogue. *Recreations:* music, composing Tamil songs, swimming, early morning fast walking 6 days a week, gardening.

**SELVARATNAM, Vasanti Emily Indrani, (Mrs P. Capewell);** QC 2001; a Recorder, 2000–18; *b* 9 April 1961; *d* of late George H. Selvaratnam and Wendy L. Selvaratnam (*née* Fairclough); *m* 1989, Phillip Capewell; one *s*. *Educ:* King's Coll., London (AKC 1982; LLB Hons 1982, LLM 1st Cl. 1984); Inns of Court Sch. of Law. Called to the Bar, Middle Temple, 1983, Bencher, 2011; in practice as barrister, specialising in commercial and shipping law, 1985–. *Recreations:* fine dining, foreign travel, horse riding. *Address:* (chambers) 36 Stone, 4 Field Court, Gray's Inn, WC1R 5EF. *T:* (020) 7440 6900. *Clubs:* Royal Automobile; Phyllis Court (Henley-on-Thames); Royal Solent Yacht.

**SELVEY, Michael Walter William;** Cricket Correspondent, The Guardian, 1987–2016; *b* 25 April 1948; *s* of late Walter Edwin Selvey and Edith Milly Selvey; *m* 1st, 1970, Mary Evans (marr. diss. 1991); one *d*; 2nd, 1992, Sarah (*née* Taylor); two *s* one *d* (triplets). *Educ:* Battersea Grammar Sch.; Univ. of Manchester (BSc Geog.); Emmanuel Coll., Cambridge (Cert Ed). Professional cricketer: Middlesex, 1972–82; Glamorgan, 1983–84 (Capt.); played 3 Tests for England: two *v* West Indies, 1976; one *v* India, 1977. Journalist, Guardian, 1985–2016. *Publications:* The Ashes Surrendered, 1989. *Recreations:* golf, fitness, cooking, real ale, crosswords, garden, children, guitar. *Club:* Woburn Golf and Country.

**SELWAY, Mark Wayne**; Chief Executive, IMI plc, 2014–19; b Adelaide, Australia, 2 June 1959; s of Vernon and Dawn Selway; m 1985, Catherine Piper (marr. diss.); twin s one d. Educ: Westminster Sch., Adelaide. Pres., Britax Rainsfords Inc., USA, 1989–94; Board Member: Britax Rear Vision Systems, 1995–96; Britax Internat. Plc, 1996–2000; Shefenacker Internat. AG, 2000–01; Chief Executive: Weir Group plc, 2001–09; Boral Ltd, 2010–13. Non-exec. Dir, Lend Lease, 2008–10. Mem., Efficient Govt Adv. Bd, Scottish Enterprise, 2003–06.

**SELWOOD, His Honour Maj.-Gen. David Henry Deering**; a Circuit Judge, 1992–2004; Resident Judge, Portsmouth Crown Court, 1996–2004; b 27 June 1934; s of late Comdr George Deering Selwood, RN, and Enid Marguerite Selwood (née Rowlinson); m 1973, Barbara Dorothea (née Hütter); three s one d. Educ: Kelly Coll., Tavistock; University College of the South-West; Law Society's School of Law. Articled to G. C. Aldhouse, Esq., Plymouth, 1952–57; admitted Solicitor 1957; National Service, RASC 2/Lieut, 1957–59; private practice, Plymouth, 1959–61; TA 4 Devons, Lieut, 1959–61; commnd Army Legal Services Staff List, 1961; service on legal staffs, MoD, Headquarters: BAOR, MELF, FARELF, UKLF, Land Forces Cyprus, 1961–85; Brig., Legal, HQ BAOR, 1986–90; Dir of Army Legal Services, MoD, 1990–92. Asst Recorder, SE Circuit, 1980, Recorder, 1985–92. Dep. Col Comdt, AGC, 1996–2003. Hon. Advocate, US Court of Military Appeals, 1972. Publications: (jtly) Criminal Law and Psychiatry, 1987; (ed jtly) Crown Court Index, 1996–2004.

**SELWOOD, Prof. Sara Michel**, PhD; independent cultural analyst, since 2008; b 3 Aug. 1953; d of Maurice David Selwood and Cordelia Selwood; m 1994, Russell Southwood. Educ: Putney High Sch.; Univ. of Newcastle (BA 1st cl. Hons Fine Arts 1974); Univ. of Essex (MPhil Hist. and Theory of Art 1979); Univ. of Westminster (PhD 2005). Director: AIR Gall., London, 1986–89; Art & Society, London, 1989–91; Res. Fellow, 1991–95, Hd of Cultural Prog., 1995–98, Policy Studies Inst.; Quintin Hogg Res. Fellow, then Principal Lectr, Sch. of Media, Arts and Design, Univ. of Westminster, 1998–2005; Prof. of Cultural Policy and Mgt, 2005–08, Hon. Prof., 2010–13, City Univ. Hon. Prof., Inst. of Archaeology, UCL, 2009–. Partner, Pomegranate, 2012–19. Trustee, NPG, 2002–10; Bd Mem., MLA, 2006–07; Chm., Portrait Trust, 2012–; Mem., Cttee for Res., Learning and Access, Nat. Mus of RN, 2014–. Editor, Cultural Trends, 1996–. Publications: The Benefits of Public Art: the polemics of permanent art in public places, 1995; The UK Cultural Sector: profile and policy issues, 2001; frequent contribs to books and learned jls incl. Cultural Trends. Recreations: cooking, films, visiting museums and galleries, travel, citizen scientist and domestic goddess. Address: 54 Walnut Tree Walk, SE11 6DN. E: s.selwood@city.ac.uk.

**SEMMENS, Victor William**; Partner, Eversheds Solicitors, until 2002 (Chairman, 1989–96; Director of International Business, 1998–2002); b 10 Oct. 1941; s of Ronald William Semmens and Cecile Maude Semmens; m 1964, Valerie Elizabeth Norton; two s. Educ: Blundell's. Qualified Solicitor, 1964; Partner, Wells & Hind, subseq. Eversheds, Nottingham, 1968–2002. Various non-exec. directorships, 2002–. Chm., Nottingham Library, Bromley House, 2002–. Recreations: golf, tennis, ski-ing, bowls. Address: 12 Park Valley, Nottingham NG7 1BQ.

**SEMPER, Very Rev. Colin (Douglas)**; Canon of Westminster, 1987–97; House for Duty Priest, Parish of Frensham, 2003–06; b 5 Feb. 1938; s of William Frederick and Dorothy Anne Semper; m 1962, Janet Louise Greaves (d 2011); two s. Educ: Lincoln School; Keble College, Oxford (BA); Westcott House, Cambridge. Curate of Holy Trinity with St Mary, Guildford, 1963–66; Recruitment and Selection Sec., ACCM, 1966–69; Head of Religious Programmes, BBC Radio, and Deputy Head of Religious Broadcasting, BBC, 1969–82; Provost of Coventry Cathedral, 1982–87. Hon. Chaplain, 1985–, Freeman, 1991, Liveryman, 1991–, Feltmakers' Co. Recreations: travel, reading modern novels, canals. Address: 9 St Marys Cottages, Frensham, Surrey GU10 3EA.

**SEMPILL**, family name of **Baron Sempill**.

**SEMPILL, 21st Baron** cr 1489; **James William Stuart Whitemore Sempill**; tour guide, since 2012; Director, Clan Chief Tours, since 2013; b 25 Feb. 1949; s of Lady Sempill (20th in line), and Lt-Col Stuart Whitemore Chant-Sempill (d 1991); S mother, 1995; m 1977, Josephine Ann Edith, e d of J. Norman Rees, Kelso; one s one d. Educ: The Oratory School; St Clare's Hall, London (BA Hons History, 1971); Hertford Coll., Oxford. Gallaher Ltd, 1972–80; PA to Man. Dir, Sentinel Engineering Pty Ltd, Johannesburg, 1980–81; Manager, TWS Public Relations Company, Johannesburg, 1981–83; investment manager, Alan Clarke and Partners, 1982–83; Marketing Manager, S African Breweries, 1983–86; Account Director: Bates Wells (Pty), 1986; Partnership in Advertising, Johannesburg, 1988–90; Client Service Dir, Ogilvy & Mather, Cape Town, 1990–92; Trade Marketing Dir, 1993–95, Dir, Special Projects, 1995, Scottish & Newcastle; Sales and Marketing Manager, Angus Distillers plc, 2001–03; Dir of Marketing, Caledonian Brewing Co. Ltd, Edinburgh, 2003–06. Dir, Panalba.Ltd, 2009–11. Chm., Edinburgh N and Leith Cons. Assoc., 1999–2001. Contested (C) Edinburgh N and Leith, Scottish Parly elecn, 1999; Prosp. Scottish Parly Cand. (C) Edinburgh Central, 2006–07. Member: Standing Council of Scottish Chiefs, 1996– (Vice-Convenor, 2005–11); Bd, American Scottish Foundn, 2011–. Moderator, High Constabulary of Port of Leith, 2015–16. Heir: s Master of Sempill, qv.

**SEMPILL, Master of; Hon. Francis Henry William Forbes Sempill**; Investment Manager and Head of Client Service (formerly Investment Manager), Walter Scott & Partners Ltd, Edinburgh, since 2001; b 4 Jan. 1979; s and heir of Baron Sempill, qv; m 2010, Robin Anna, e r d of Donald Strathairn, Aberfeldy; one s one d. Educ: Western Province Prep. Sch., Cape Town; Merchiston Castle Sch., Edinburgh; Napier Univ., Edinburgh. Recreations: shooting, golf, travel, cooking, wine. Address: Kevock Bank House, Kevock Road, Lasswade EH18 1HX.

**SEMPLE, Andrew Greenlees**; b 16 Jan. 1934; s of late William Hugh Semple and Madeline, d of late E. H. Wood, Malvern, Worcs; m 1st, 1961, Janet Elizabeth Whates (d 1993); one s one d; 2nd, 2000, Susan Lucy Jacobs. Educ: Winchester Coll.; St John's Coll., Cambridge (MA). Entered Min. of Transport and Civil Aviation, 1957; Private Sec. to Permanent Sec., 1960–62; Principal, 1962; Asst Sec., 1970; Private Sec. to successive Secs of State for the Environment, 1972–74; Under Sec., DoE, 1976; Principal Finance Officer, PSA, DoE, 1980–83; Sec., Water Authorities Assoc., 1983–87; Man. Dir, Anglian Water Authority, 1987–89; Gp Man. Dir, 1989–90, Vice-Chm., 1990–92, Anglian Water plc. Mem., Bd, Eureau, 1983–92. Chm., Huntingdonshire Enterprise Agency, 1990–2001. Governor: Huntingdonshire Regl Coll., 1992–2002; Kimbolton Sch., 2001–08. Trustee, Plumstead Almshouses, 2001–13. Hon. Mem., IWO (AWO, 1988). FCIWEM 1994. Recreations: reading, gardens, watching cricket. Address: 14 Druce Road, SE21 7DW. T: (020) 8693 8202. Club: Surrey CC.

**SEMPLE, Sir John (Laughlin)**, KCB 2000 (CB 1993); Head of Northern Ireland Civil Service, 1997–2000; Director, Northern Ireland Affairs for Royal Mail Group (known as Consignia, 2001–02), 2001–06; b 10 Aug. 1940; s of late James E. Semple and Violet E. G. Semple; m 1970, Maureen Anne Kerr; two s one d. Educ: Campbell Coll., Belfast; Corpus Christi Coll., Cambridge (MA); BScEcon London. Joined Home CS as Asst Principal, Min. of Aviation, 1961; transf. to NI CS, 1962; Asst Principal, Mins of Health and Local Govt, Finance, and Health and Social Services, 1962–65; Dep. Principal, Min. of Health and Social Services, 1965; Principal: Min. of Finance, 1968; Min. of Community Relations, 1970–72; Asst Sec. (Planning), Min. of Develt, 1972; Asst Sec. (Housing), DoE, 1977–79; Under Sec. (Housing), DoE for N Ireland, 1979–83; Under Sec., 1983–88, Permanent Sec., 1988–97, Dept of Finance and Personnel for NI; Second Perm. Under-Sec. of State, NI Office, 1998–99; Sec. to Exec. Cttee, NI Assembly, 1999–2000. Recreations: golf, gardening, reading.

**SEMPLE, Margaret Olivia, (Maggie)**, OBE 2000; Chief Executive and Director, The Experience Corps, since 2001; owner, Maggie Semple Ltd, since 2010; b 30 July 1954; d of Robert Henry Semple and Olivia Victorine Semple. Educ: Shelborne High Sch. for Girls; Worcester Coll. of Higher Educn (BEd); Univ. of London (Advanced Dip.); Univ. of Sussex (MA). Teacher, Hd of Performing Arts, Inspector, ILEA, 1975–88; Dir, Educn and Trng, Arts Council of GB, 1989–97; Dir, Learning Experience, New Millennium Experience Co., 1997–2001. Civil Service Comr, Cabinet Office, 2001–07. Non-executive Director: HM Court Service, 2007–08; Criminal Cases Rev. Commn, 2011–17; Mem., QC Selection Panel, 2017–. Member: DfES Nat. Curriculum PE Working Gp, 1989–90; DfES Widening Participation Cttee, 1995–97; DfES Lifelong Learning Cttee, 2001–02; DfES e-learning Task Gp, 2002–03. Fellow, British American Project, 1992; Expert: EC Cttee, 1994–97; European Cultural Centre, Delphi, 1997–2000; Council of Europe Young People's Cttee, 1998–2000. Member: Commonwealth Inst. Educn Cttee, 1992–94; All Souls Educn Gp, All Souls Coll., Oxford, 1994–; TTA, 2000–03; Women's Liby, 2000–04; De Montfort Univ., 2000–11; Inst. of Educn, London, 2003–11; Adv. Bd, Arts Council London, 2003–06; Council, C&G, 2006–16; Pres., Laban Guild, 1994–2000; Chairman: Nat. Youth Music Th., 2002–12; Nat. Res. and Develt Centre, 2004–11; Wolfson Welcome Dana Centre, 2004–11. Ext. Examr, Liverpool Inst. for Performing Arts, 1997–2000. Trustee: Barnardo's, 1997–2000; RSA, 1998–2003 (Council Mem., 1992–98); Rambert Dance Th., 1998–2006; Roundhouse Trust, 2000–06; Arts Educnl Schs Trust, 2000–10; Nat. Mus of Sci. and Ind., 2003–11; Balance Foundn for Unclaimed Assets, 2004–07; British Library, 2007–15. Mem. Bd, South Bank Arts Centre, 2011–. Sen. Associate, King's Fund, 2001–04. Governor: Brit Sch., 2003–07; Sadler's Wells Th., 2005–11. Mem. Bd, South Bank Univ., 2011–12. FCGI 2005. Hon. DEd De Montfort, 2000. Recreations: being an entrepreneur, reading. Address: The Experience Corps Ltd, 4 Goodwins Court, WC2N 4LL. E: maggie.semple@experience-corps.co.uk.

**SEMPLE, Maj. Gen. Richard James**, CBE 2014; Chief Executive Officer, UK Shared Business Services Ltd, since 2018; b Plymouth, 26 Aug. 1964; s of William John Semple and Judith Mary Semple; m 1992, Hilary Wylie; one s one d. Educ: Sir Roger Manwood's Sch., Sandwich; Hatfield Poly. (BSc); RMA Sandhurst; Cranfield Univ. (MBA). Commnd RE, 1986; CO 32 Engr Regt, 2003–06; DACOS Commnd Battlespace Management HQ Land Forces, 2006–08; ACOS J6 PJHQ, 2008–11; Brig. Gen. Staff, 2011–13; Dir Gen. Logistic Support and Equipment, 2013–15; Dir Information, Army HQ, 2015–18. Recreations: walking, running, ski-ing, field sports. E: richardsemple@live.co.uk.

**SEN, Prof. Amartya Kumar**, Bharat Ratna, 1999; Hon. CH 2000; FBA 1977; Professor of Economics and Philosophy and Lamont University Professor, Harvard University, 1988–98 and since 2004 (Emeritus Professor, 1998–2003); b 3 Nov. 1933; s of late Dr Ashutosh Sen, Dhaka, and of Amita Sen, Santiniketan, India; m 1st, 1960, Nabaneeta Dev (marr. diss. 1975); two d; 2nd, 1978, Eva Colorni (d 1985); one s one d; 3rd, 1991, Emma Rothschild, qv. Educ: Calcutta Univ.; Trinity Coll., Cambridge (MA, PhD; Hon. Fellow, 1991). Prof. of Economics, Jadavpur Univ., Calcutta, 1956–58; Trinity Coll., Cambridge: Prize Fellow, 1957–61; Staff Fellow, 1961–63; Professor of Economics: Delhi Univ., 1963–71 (Chm., Dept of Economics, 1966–68, Hon. Prof., 1971–); LSE, 1971–77; Oxford Univ., 1977–80; Fellow, Nuffield College, Oxford, 1977–80 (Associate Mem., 1980–89; Hon. Fellow, 1998); Drummond Prof. of Political Economy, and Fellow, All Souls Coll., Oxford, 1980–88 (Distinguished Fellow, 2005); Sen. Fellow, Harvard Soc. of Fellows, 1989–98; Master, Trinity Coll., Cambridge, 1998–2004; Chancellor and Chm. Bd of Governors, Nalanda Univ., 2012–15. Hon. Dir, Agricultural Economics Research Centre, Delhi, 1966–68 and 1969–71. Res. Advr, World Inst. for Develt Econ. Res., Helsinki, Finland, 1985–93; Special Advr to Sec. Gen. of UN, 2001–. Visiting Professor: MIT, 1960–61; Univ. of Calif at Berkeley, 1964–65; Harvard Univ., 1968–69; Andrew D. White Professor-at-large, Cornell Univ., 1978–84. Chm., UN Expert Gp Meeting on Role of Advanced Skill and Technology, New York, 1967. President: Develt Studies Assoc., 1980–82; Econometric Soc., 1984 (Fellow 1968–, Vice-Pres. 1982–83); Internat. Economic Assoc., 1986–89 (Hon. Pres., 1989); Indian Econ. Assoc., 1989; Amer. Econ. Assoc., 1994; Soc. for Social Choice and Welfare, 1993–94; Vice-Pres., Royal Economic Soc., 1988– (Mem. Council, 1977–87); Hon. Advr, Oxfam, 2002– (Hon. Pres., 2000–02); Trustee: Inst. for Advanced Study, Princeton, 1987–94; British Mus., 2010–18. Member: Accademia Nazionale dei Lincei; Amer. Philos. Assoc.; Foreign Hon. Mem., Amer. Acad. of Arts and Sciences, 1981; Hon. Mem., Amer. Econ. Assoc., 1981. Hon. FRSE; Hon. FMedSci; Hon. Fellow: Inst. of Social Studies, The Hague; LSE, 1984; IDS, Sussex Univ., 1984; SOAS, London Univ., 1998; Darwin Coll., Cambridge, 1998; LSHTM; St Edmund's Coll., Cambridge, 2004; Frances Perkins Fellow, Amer. Acad. of Political and Social Sc., 2003. Hon. DLitt: Saskatchewan, 1980; Visva-Bharati, 1983; Georgetown, 1989; Jadavpur, Kalyani, 1990; Williams Coll., City of London Poly., 1991; New Sch. for Social Res., NY, 1992; Calcutta, 1993; Syracuse, 1994; Oxford, 1996; Bard Coll., 1997; Leicester, Kingston, Columbia, Chhatrapati Shahu Ji Maharaj, 1998; UEA, Nottingham, Heriot-Watt, 1999; Allahabad, Assam, Strathclyde, Kerala, 2000; Mumbai, 2002; N Bengal, 2002; Cambridge, 2009; Hon. DHumLit: Oberlin Coll., 1993; Wesleyan, 1995; McGill, 1998; Mass, Lowell, 2006; Hon. DSc: Bath, 1984; Edinburgh, 1995; Dhaka, 1999; Assam Agricl, Birmingham, London, 2000; Sussex, 2003; Michigan, 2006; Hon. DSocSc: Chinese Univ. of HK, 1999; Yale, 2003; DU: Essex, 1984; Rabindra Bharati, 1998; Dr hc: Caen, 1987; Bologna, 1988; Univ. Catholique de Louvain, 1989; Athens Univ. of Econs and Business, 1991; Valencia, Zurich, 1994; Antwerp, 1995; Stockholm, 1996; Kiel, 1997; Padua, 1998; Athens, Méditerranée (Marseille), Delhi, 1999; Tech. Univ. of Lisbon, Univ. Jaume I de Castellón, Spain, 2001; Tokyo, Clark Univ. (Worcester, USA), Southampton, 2002; Univ. Pierre Mendès France, Grenoble, 2002; Santa Clara Univ., Calif, 2002; Bidhan Chandra Krishi Viswavidyalaya, 2003; Ritsumeikan, Japan, 2003; York, 2004; Koç, Turkey, 2004; Rhodes, S Africa, 2004; York, Canada, 2004; Rovira I Virgili, Tarrogona, 2004; Simmons Coll., Boston, 2005; Göttingen, 2005; Hon. LLD: Tulane, 1990; Queen's Univ., Kingston, Ont., 1993; Harvard, 2000; Mount Holyoke Coll., USA, 2003; Toronto, 2004; Connecticut, 2006; Hon. Dr Ph Jawaharlal Nehru, 1998; Hon. DSc Econs: London, 2000; Cape Town, 2006; Laurea hc: Florence, 2000; Turin, 2004; Pavia, 2005; DUniv Open, 2002; Hon. DCL Durham, 2002. Mahalanobis Prize, 1976; Frank E. Seidman Dist. Award in Pol Econ., 1986; Agnelli Internat. Prize, 1990; Alan Shawn Feinstein World Hunger Award, 1990; Jean Mayer Global Citizenship Award, 1993; Indira Gandhi Gold Medal Award, Asiatic Soc., 1994; Edinburgh Medal, 1997; Catalonia Internat. Prize, 1997; Nobel Prize for Economics, 1998; Leontief Prize, 2000; Ayrton Senna Grand Prix of Journalism, 2002; Medal of Distinction, Barnard Coll., USA, 2005; Silver Banner, Florence, 2005; George C. Marshall Award, USA, 2005. Eisenhower Medal, USA, 2000; Presidency of Italian Republic Medal, 2000. Grand Cross, Order of Scientific Merit (Brazil), 2000.

*Publications:* Choice of Techniques, 1960, 3rd edn 1968; Growth Economics, 1970; Collective Choice and Social Welfare, 1971; On Economic Inequality, 1973; Employment, Technology and Development, 1975; Poverty and Famines: an essay on entitlement and deprivation, 1981; (ed with Bernard Williams) Utilitarianism and Beyond, 1982; Choice, Welfare and Measurement, 1982; Resources, Values and Development, 1984; Commodities and Capabilities, 1985; On Ethics and Economics, 1987; The Standard of Living, 1987; (with Jean Drèze) Hunger and Public Action, 1989; (ed with Jean Drèze) The Political Economy of Hunger, 3 vols, 1990–91; Inequality Re-examined, 1992; (with Jean Drèze) India: economic development and social opportunity, 1995; Development as Freedom, 1999 (Bruno-Kreisky Award for Political Book of the Year, 2001; European Economics Book Prize, 2002); Rationality and Freedom, 2002; The Argumentative Indian, 2005; Identity and Violence: the illusion of destiny, 2006; The Idea of Justice, 2009; (with Jean Drèze) An Uncertain Glory: India and its contradictions, 2013; articles in various jls in economics, philosophy, political science, decision theory, demography and law. *Address:* Harvard University, University Hall, Cambridge, MA 02138, USA.

**SEN, Emma;** *see* Rothschild, Emma.

**SEN, Ranendra, (Ronen);** Ambassador for India to the United States of America, 2004–09; *b* 9 April 1944; *s* of late Satyendra Mohan Sen and Shrimati Suniti Rani; *m* 1970, Kalpana Chowdhury; one *d*. *Educ:* Calcutta Univ. (BA Hons). Joined Indian Foreign Service, 1966; served: Moscow, 1968–71; San Francisco, 1972–74; Dhaka, 1974–77; Dep. Sec., Min. of External Affairs, 1977; Dep. Sec., Dept of Atomic Energy, and Sec., Atomic Energy Commn, 1978–80; Counsellor, then Minister, Moscow, 1981–84; Jt Sec., Min. of External Affairs, 1984–85; Jt Sec. to Prime Minister of India, 1986–91; Ambassador: to Mexico, 1991–92; to Russia, 1992–98; to Germany, 1998–2002; High Comr in UK, 2002–04. Non-executive Director: Tata Motors Ltd, 2010–12; Tata Sons, 2015–. *Recreations:* music, reading, travel. *Clubs:* Delhi Gymkhana; Cosmos (Washington).

**SEN, Prof. Samita,** PhD; Vere Harmsworth Professor of Imperial and Naval History, University of Cambridge, since 2018; Fellow, Trinity College, Cambridge, since 2018; *b* Calcutta, 31 Oct. 1962; *d* of late Sandip Kumar Sen and of Joyanti Sen. *Educ:* Calcutta Univ. (BA Hons; MA); Trinity Coll., Cambridge (PhD Hist. 1992). Fellow, Trinity Coll., Cambridge, 1990–94; Lectr, 1994–99, Reader, 1999–2006, Calcutta Univ.; Prof., 2006–18, Dir, Sch. of Women's Studies, 2006–13 and 2016–17, and Dean, Faculty of Interdisciplinary Studies, Law and Mgt, 2017–18, Jadavpur Univ.; First Vice Chancellor, Diamond Harbour Women's Univ., India, 2013–15. *Publications:* Women and Labour in Late Colonial India: the bengal jute industry, 1999; (ed with A. de Haan) A Case for Labour History: the jute industry in Eastern India, 1999; (ed jtly) Intimate Others: marriage and sexuality in India, 2010; (ed jtly) Mapping the Field: gender relations in contemporary India, vol. 1, 2011, vol. 2, 2012; (jtly) Domestic Days: women, work and politics in contemporary Kolkata, 2016; (ed) Passage to Bondage: labour in the Assam tea plantations, 2016; (ed jtly) Accumulation in Post Colonial Capitalism, 2016; contribs to jls incl. Modern Asian Studies, Jl Women's Studies, Internat. Rev. Social Hist., Gender and Hist. *Recreations:* crafts and needlework, music and poetry, cooking. *Address:* Trinity College, Cambridge CB2 1TQ. *T:* (01223) 761 891. *E:* ss162@cam.ac.uk; 403 Srishti, P-10 Regent Estate, Kolkata 700029, India.

**SENEWIRATNE, Kshenuka Dhireni;** Ambassador of Sri Lanka to Thailand, since 2015; *b* 20 July 1960; *d* of late Deutram de Silva and of Githa de Silva; *m* 1998, Surendra Senewiratne. *Educ:* Univ. of Salford (BSc Econs 1982); Corpus Christi Coll., Oxford (Chevening Schol.; Foreign Affairs Study Prog.); Univ. of Colombo (MA Internat. Relns 1992). Asst Dir, Bureau of the Minister of Foreign Affairs, Min. of Foreign Affairs, Sri Lanka, 1985–88; diplomatic posting, Perm. Mission of Sri Lanka to the UN, NY, 1988–90; Ministry of Foreign Affairs: Deputy Director: Publicity Div., 1990–91; UN and Multilateral Affairs Div., 1991–93; diplomatic posting, Brussels, 1993–96; Ministry of Foreign Affairs: Dir, UN and Multilateral Div., 1997–98; Dir, 1998–2001, Actg Dir Gen., 2001–02, Econ. Affairs Div.; Dep. High Comr, London, 2002–04; Additional Dir Gen., Econ. Affairs Div., Min. of Foreign Affairs, 2004–05; High Comr in UK, 2005–08; Dir Gen. for Europe and CIS, Min. of Foreign Affairs, Sri Lanka, 2008–09; Ambassador and Perm. Rep. to UN Office at Geneva, and Consul Gen. in Switzerland, 2009–11; Additional Sec., Min. of Foreign Affairs; Perm. Sec., Min. of External Affairs, 2014–15. *Recreations:* reading, cycling, music, travelling. *Address:* Embassy of Sri Lanka, 13th Floor, 75/6–7 Ocean Tower 2, Sukhumvit Soi 19, Wattana, Bangkok 10110, Thailand.

**SEN GUPTA, Diya;** QC 2019; *b* London, 2 Jan. 1978; *d* of Dipak and Jayasree Sen Gupta; *m* 2003, Rory Mullan; two *s* one *d*. *Educ:* N London Collegiate Sch.; Magdalene Coll., Cambridge (MA Hons Law). Called to the Bar, Inner Temple, 2000; in practice as barrister, 2001–. *Address:* Blackstone Chambers, Blackstone House, EC4Y 9BW. *T:* (020) 7583 1770. *E:* diyasengupta@blacstonechambers.com.

**SENIOR, Gary;** Managing Director, Helix Insight, since 2018; *b* Leeds, 23 May 1962; *s* of Harry Fern Senior and Anne Senior; *m* 1988, Sarah Gibson; one *s* one *d*. *Educ:* Cross Green Sch., Leeds; Durham Univ. (BA Law). Admitted as solicitor, 1986; Baker & McKenzie, later Baker McKenzie: articled clerk, 1984; Associate, 1986; Partner, 1992–2018; Man. Partner, 2003–13; Chm., Global Policy Cttee, 2011–13; Mem., Global Exec. Cttee, 2013–18; Chair, EMEA Reg., 2014–17. *Recreations:* chess, Leeds United, family, cricket, history. *Address:* Helix Management Services, 181 Queen Victoria Street, EC4V 4EG. *Club:* MCC.

**SENIOR, Nora Margaret,** CBE 2017; Chair, UK Regions and Ireland, Weber Shandwick, since 2009 (Managing Director, 1998–2009); *b* St Andrews, Scotland; *d* of Peter and Norah Mary Connelly; *m* 1999, Stuart Senior; one *s* one *d*. *Educ:* Glasgow Univ. (MA Hons). Exec., Marley Tile Co., Sevenoaks; Managing Director: Saatchi & Saatchi Hall Associates, 1987–90; PR Centre, 1990–98. Non-exec. Chm., Enterprise and Skills Strategic Bd, Scottish Govt, 2017–. President: British Chambers of Commerce, 2013–16; Scottish Chambers of Commerce, 2013–17; Mem., Internat. Chambers of Commerce, 2016–. Mem. Council, Univ. of Nottingham, 2016– (Vice Chm., 2019–). FCIPR 2003. *Recreations:* ski-ing, cycling, running, art. *Address:* Weber Shandwick, 9 York Place, Edinburgh EH1 3EB; Weber Shandwick, 2 Waterhouse Square, 140 Holborn, EC1N 2AE. *T:* 07770 886921. *E:* nsenior18@outlook.com.

**SENNITT, His Honour John Stuart;** a Circuit Judge, 1994–2007; *b* Cambridge, 5 March 1935; *s* of late Stuart Osland Sennitt and Nora Kathleen Sennitt; *m* 1966, Janet Ann; one *s* two *d*. *Educ:* Culford Sch., Bury St Edmunds; St Catharine's Coll., Cambridge (MA, LLB). Admitted Solicitor, 1961; Partner, Wild, Hewitson & Shaw, Cambridge, 1963–83; County Court Registrar, then Dist Judge, 1983–94; Asst Recorder, 1988–92; a Recorder, 1992–94. *Address:* c/o Cambridge County Court, 197 East Road, Cambridge CB1 1BA.

**SENTAMU, Most Rev. and Rt Hon. John Tucker Mugabi;** *see* York, Archbishop of.

**SENTANCE, Dr Andrew William,** CBE 2012; independent business economist, since 2018; Senior Economic Adviser, PricewaterhouseCoopers LLP, 2011–18; Professor of Practice, Warwick Business School, University of Warwick, since 2012 (Professorial Fellow (part-time), 2006–12); *b* 17 Sept. 1958; *s* of late William Thomas Wulfram Sentance and of Lillian Sentance (*née* Bointon); *m* 1985, Anne Margaret Penfold; one *s* one *d*. *Educ:* Eltham Coll., London; Clare Coll., Cambridge (BA Hons, MA); London Sch. of Econs (MSc Econ; PhD 1988). Manager, Petrocell Ltd, 1980–81; with NCB, 1982–83; Confederation of British Industry: Head, Econ. Policy, 1986–89; Dir, Econ. Affairs, 1989–93; London Business School: Sen. Res. Fellow, 1994–95; Dir, Centre for Economic Forecasting, 1995–98; British Airways: Chief Economist, 1998–2006; Head of Envmtl Affairs, 2003–06; Mem., Monetary Policy Cttee, Bank of England, 2006–11. Chief Economic Advr, British Retail Consortium, 1995–98. Member: HM Treasury Panel of Independent Forecasters, 1992–93; various statistical adv. cttees, 1988–99. Comr, Commn for Integrated Transport, 2006–10. Vis. Prof. of Econs, Royal Holloway, Univ. of London, 1998–; Vis. Prof., Cranfield Univ., 2001–08. Fellow, Soc. of Business Economists (Mem. Council, 1991–2003; Chm., 1995–2000; Dep. Chm., 2000–03; Vice Pres., 2013–17). Trustee: Anglo-German Foundn, 2001–09; British Airways Pension Funds, 2002–06; BuildIT Internat., 2012–. Chm., Templefield Multi-Acad. Trust, 2017–. Organist and Dir of Music, Parish of Bengeo, 2019–. Ed., London Business Sch. Econ. Outlook, 1994–98. *Publications:* Rediscovering Growth: after the crisis, 2013; numerous articles in books and jls on current economic issues. *Recreations:* playing piano, guitar and organ, listening to music. *E:* andrewsentance@aol.com.

**SEOKA, Rt Rev. Dr Johannes Thomas;** Bishop of Pretoria, 1998–2015; *b* 29 Aug. 1948; *s* of Isaac and Margaret Seoka; *m* 1980, Sybil Elizabeth Nomathonya; two *s*. *Educ:* school in Stanger; Eshowe Coll. of Educn, Zululand (grad. as teacher, 1971); St Bede's Coll., Umtata; Chicago Theol Seminary, Ill, USA (MTh); Univ. of Chicago (DMin); studies in industrial mgt, W Germany and USA. Ordained deacon 1974, priest 1975, Natal; Curate, St Augustine, Umlazi, Natal, 1976–78; Rector, St Peter's, Greytown, 1978–80; Rector, St Hilda's, Senaoane, Soweto, 1980; seconded as Dir of Industrial Mission, 1981; Priest-in-Charge: Trinity Episcopal Church, Chicago, Ill, 1986; St James's, Diepkloof, Soweto, 1993–95; Church of the Good Shepherd, Tladi, Soweto, 1995–96; Dean of Pretoria and Rector, St Alban's Cathedral, 1996–98. Pres., SA Council of Churches, 2010–. Continuing urban and industrial work, including: Dir, Agency for Industrial Mission; Dir, Urban and Industrial Mission, 1994. CPSA Rep., Faith and Order Commn, WCC; Mem., WCC Adv. Gp on Urban and Rural Mission, 1983–. Hon. DD Gen. Theol Seminary, NY, 2006. *Publications:* The Experiential Meaning of Spirituality and the Theology of Work, 2010; contribs to books and magazines.

**SEPHTON, Craig Gardner;** QC 2001; **His Honour Judge Sephton;** a Circuit Judge, since 2018; a Deputy High Court Judge, since 2010; *b* 7 Dec. 1957; *s* of Bruce and Betty Sephton; *m* 1st, 1985, Colette (marr. diss.); three *s*; 2nd, 2008, Tanya Anne Mackenzie. *Educ:* Ecclesbourne Sch., Duffield; Lincoln Coll., Oxford (MA, BCL). Called to the Bar, Middle Temple, 1981; a Recorder, 2002–18; Hd of Chambers, Deans Court Chambers, 2013–18. Sometimes Treas., Personal Injuries Bar Assoc.; Treas., Northern Circuit, 2010–18. *Recreations:* swimming, mountaineering, music, cycling. *Address:* Manchester County Court, Manchester Civil and Family Justice Centre, 1 Bridge Street West, Manchester M60 9DJ.

**SEPHTON, Prof. Mark Andrew,** PhD; Professor of Organic Geochemistry and Meteoritics, since 2007, and Head, Department of Earth Science and Engineering, since 2016, Imperial College London; *b* St Helens, Merseyside, 1966; *m* 1996, Sarah Victoria Rogers: two *s* one *d*. *Educ:* Univ. of Durham (BSc Hons 1991); Univ. of Newcastle (MSc 1992); Open Univ. (PhD 1997). Post Doctoral Researcher, Netherlands Inst. for Sea Res. and Univ. of Utrecht, 1996–98; Post Doctoral Researcher, 1998–2000, Lectr, 2000–05, Open Univ.; Reader, Imperial Coll. London, 2005–07. Chair, Space Exploration Adv. Cttee, UK Space Agency, 2013–16; Mem., Planetary Protection Wkg Gp, ESA, 2014–. Asteroid 7552 named 'Sephton' by IAU, 2006. *Publications:* (with I. Gilmour) An Introduction to Astrobiology, 2004, 3rd edn (with I. Gilmour and D. A. Rothery) 2018; over 200 scientific articles. *Recreations:* running, hillwalking. *Address:* Department of Earth Science and Engineering, South Kensington Campus, Imperial College London, SW7 2AZ. *T:* (020) 7594 6542. *E:* m.a.sephton@imperial.ac.uk.

**SEPÚLVEDA-AMOR, Bernardo,** Hon. GCMG 1985; Of Counsel, and Head of Arbitration and International Dispute Resolutions, Creel, Garcia-Cuellar, Aiza y Enriquez S.C, since 2015; Ambassador Emeritus of Mexico; *b* 14 Dec. 1941; *s* of Bernardo Sepúlveda and Margarita Amor; *m* 1970, Ana Yturbe; three *s*. *Educ:* Univ. of Mexico (Law Degree *magna cum laude*, 1964); Queens' Coll., Cambridge (LLB 1966; Hon. Fellow, 1990). Prof. of Internat. Law, El Colegio de México, 1967–81; Dep. Dir Gen. for Legal Affairs to Secretary of the Presidency, 1968–70; Asst Sec. for Internat. Affairs, Min. of the Treasury, 1976–80; Principal Advisor on Internat. Affairs to the Minister of Planning and Budget, 1981; Ambassador to USA, 1982; Minister of Foreign Relations, Mexico, 1982–88; Ambassador to UK, 1989–93; Foreign Affairs Advr to Pres. of Mexico, 1993. Member: UN Internat. Law Commn, 1996–2006; Inst. de Droit Internat. Bencher, Middle Temple, 2011. Judge, 2006–15, Vice Pres., 2012–15, Internat. Court of Justice, The Hague. Gen. Counsel, Empresas ICA, 1997–2005 (Ind. Mem., Bd of Dirs, 2015–); Chm. Bd, ALTÁN Redes S.A.P.I. de C.V, 2017–. Dr *hc*: Univ. of San Diego, Calif, 1982; Univ. of Leningrad, 1987. Príncipe de Asturias Prize, Spain, 1984; Simón Bolívar Prize, UNESCO, 1985. Grand Cross, Order of: Civil Merit (Spain), 1979; Isabel the Catholic (Spain), 1983; Southern Cross (Brazil), 1983; Boyacá (Colombia), 1984; Merit (FRG), 1984; Liberator San Martín (Argentina), 1984; Vasco Núñez de Balboa (Panama), 1984; Manuel Amador Guerrero (Panama), 1985; Christ (Portugal), 1985; Crown (Belgium), 1985; Quetzal (Guatemala), 1986; Prince Henry the Navigator (Portugal), 1986; Sun (Peru), 1987; Rio Branco (Brazil), 1988; Grand Officier, Nat. Order of Legion of Honour (France), 1985; also orders and decorations from Korea, Venezuela, Poland, Yugoslavia, Greece, Japan, Egypt and Jamaica. *Publications:* The United Nations: dilemma at 25, 1970; Foreign Investment in Mexico, 1973; Transnational Corporations in Mexico, 1974; articles on internat. law in prof. jls. *Recreations:* reading, music.

**SERAFÍN, David;** *see* Michael, I. D. L.

**SERGEANT, Emma;** artist; *b* 9 Dec. 1959; *d* of Sir Patrick John Rushton Sergeant, *qv*; *m* 2001, Count Adam Zamoyski. *Educ:* Channing Sch.; Camden High Sch.; Camberwell Sch. of Arts and Crafts; Slade Sch. of Fine Art. Commnd by NPG to paint portraits of Lord David Cecil and Lord Olivier, 1981; Official Royal Tour Artist to Prince of Wales: Egypt and Morocco, 1995; Ukraine and Central Asian Republics of Turkmenistan, Kazakhstan, Kyrgyzstan and Uzbekistan, 1996. Exhibitions include: Drinks at Milapote: friends and family, 1984, Afghanistan, in aid of UNICEF, 1986, Faces from Four Continents, 1988, Orpheus and the Underworld, 1994, Agnew's, London; Retour en Afghanistan, in aid of Médecins du Monde, Mona Bismarck Foundn, Paris, 1987; Gods, Newhouse Gall., NY, and Agnew's, London, 1996; Dolphins, 1998, From the Sea, 1999, Shades of Grey, 2004, Ali Baba's Mausoleum, 2008, Fine Art Soc.; Scenes from a Hittite Court, Prince's Foundn, 2001; Touch the Spirit (retrospective), Museo della Contrada della Tartuca, Siena, 2018; Touch the Spirit II, The Gall. at Green & Stone, 2018; portrait commissions include: the Duke of York, Sir Christopher Cockerell, Lord Carrington, Imran Khan, Lord Todd, Sir William Deacon, Paul Dacre, Padraic Fallon, Lord Rothermere, Trudie Styler, Earl of Radnor, Sir Rocco Forte, Jeremy Paxman, Michael Portillo, Jerry Hall. NPG Award, 1981. *Recreation:* horses. *E:* emma@emmasergeant.com.

**SERGEANT, John**; broadcaster and journalist; Chief Political Correspondent, BBC, 1988–2000; Political Editor, ITN, 2000–03; *b* 14 April 1944; *s* of Ernest Sergeant and late Olive Sergeant (then Stevens); *m* 1969, Mary Smithies; two *s*. *Educ*: Millfield Sch., Street; Magdalen Coll., Oxford (BA Hons PPE). Appeared in On the Margin, BBC TV, 1966–67; Reporter, Liverpool Daily Post and Echo, 1967–70; BBC: Reporter, 1970–81: reported from 25 countries, incl. conflicts in Vietnam, Cyprus, Israel, Lebanon, Rhodesia and NI; acting Corresp., Dublin, Paris and Washington; Presenter, current affairs progs, Radio 4, incl. Today, World at One, PM; Political Corresp., 1981–88; Lobby Chm., 2000–01. Mem., Hansard Soc. Commn on Communication of Parly Democracy, 2004–05. Has appeared on numerous TV and radio progs, incl. Have I Got News for You, Room 101, Call My Bluff, News Quiz, Quote Unquote, Strictly Come Dancing, One Show, Argumental, QI, John Sergeant on the Tourist Trail, John Sergeant on Tracks of Empire, Britain's Flying Past: the Spitfire, Britain's Flying Past: the Sea King, Britain's Flying Past: the Lancaster, Britain's First Photo Album, Sergeant on Spike, Royal Greenwich, Barging Round Britain, Pompeii's Final Hours: new evidence; Britain by Boat, etc.; regular contributor to BBC One Show; UK theatre tour, An Audience with John Sergeant, 2003–09. Pres., Johnson Soc., 2003–04. Hon. DLitt: Teesside, 2010; Lincoln, 2013. Most Memorable TV Broadcast award, BPG, 1991; Best Individual TV Contributor, Voice of the Listener and Viewer, 1999. *Publications*: Give Me Ten Seconds (memoirs), 2001; Maggie: her fatal legacy, 2005; (with David Bartley) Barging Round Britain, 2015. *Recreations*: sailing, listening to classical music. *Address*: c/o Anita Land Ltd, 10 Wyndham Place, W1H 2PU.

**SERGEANT, Sir Patrick (John Rushton)**, Kt 1984; City Editor, Daily Mail, 1960–84; Founder, 1969, and Chairman, 1985–92, Euromoney Publications (Managing Director, 1969–85); *b* 17 March 1924; *s* of George and Rene Sergeant; *m* 1952, Gillian Anne Wilks, Cape Town; two *d*. *Educ*: Beaumont Coll. Served as Lieut, RNVR, 1945. Asst City Editor, News Chronicle, 1948; Dep. City Editor, Daily Mail, 1953. Director: Associated Newspapers Group, 1971–83; Daily Mail General Trust, 1983–2004; (non-exec.) Euromoney Institutional Investor plc (formerly Euromoney Publications), 1992–. Domus Fellow, St Catherine's Coll., Oxford, 1988. Freeman, City of London, 1987. Wincott Award, Financial Journalist of the Year, 1979. *Publications*: Another Road to Samarkand, 1955; Money Matters, 1967; Inflation Fighters Handbook, 1976. *Recreations*: tennis, swimming, talking. *Address*: One The Grove, Highgate Village, N6 6JU. *T*: (020) 8340 1245. *Clubs*: Royal Automobile, Garrick; All England Lawn Tennis and Croquet, Queen's. *See also* E. Sergeant.

**SERHAL, Paul**; Medical Director, Centre for Reproductive and Genetic Health (formerly Assisted Conception Unit), since 1990; Honorary Consultant in Reproductive Medicine, University College Hospital, since 1990; *b* Lebanon, 18 Sept. 1954; *s* of Farid Serhal and Lili Serhal; *m* Claude; one *s* two *d*. *Educ*: MB BS. MRCOG. University College Hospital, London: Clin. Res. Fellow in Reproductive Medicine, Dept of Obstetrics and Gynaecol., 1985–87; Clin. Lectr and Sen. Registrar, 1987–90. Grand Officer, Nat. Order of the Cedar (Lebanon). *Publications*: (ed with Caroline Overton) Good Clinical Practice in Assisted Reproduction, 2004; contrib. learned jls incl. Lancet, Jl for Sterility and Fertility and Human Reproduction. *Recreations*: horse riding, sailing. *Address*: Centre for Reproductive and Genetic Health, 230–232 Great Portland Street, W1W 5QS. *T*: (020) 7837 2905, *Fax*: (020) 7278 5152. *E*: info@crgh.co.uk.

**SERIES, Prof. Caroline Mary**, PhD; FRS 2016; Professor of Mathematics, University of Warwick, 1992–2014, now Emeritus; *b* Oxford, 24 March 1951; *d* of George William Series, FRS and Annette Series. *Educ*: Oxford High Sch. for Girls, GPDST; Somerville Coll., Oxford (Schol.; BA 1st Cl. Maths 1972; Hon. Fellow 2017); Harvard Univ. (Kennedy Schol.; PhD Maths 1976). Lectr, Univ. of Calif, Berkeley, 1976–77; Res. Fellow, Newnham Coll., Cambridge, 1977–78; Lectr, 1978–87, Reader, 1987–92, Maths Dept, Univ. of Warwick. Founder Mem., Eur. Women in Maths, 1986–; Vice-Chair, Cttee for Women in Maths, IMU, 2014–18. Pres., London Mathematical Soc., 2017–19. MAE 2017; FIMA 2011; FAMS 2013. Hon. Dr Duke Univ., USA, 2019. Univ. Mathematical Prize, Oxford, 1972; Jun. Whitehead Prize, 1987, Sen. Anne Bennett Prize, 2014, London Mathematical Soc. *Publications*: (jtly) Indra's Pearls, 2002, rev. edn 2015; contrib. papers to learned mathematical jls and popular articles. *Recreations*: reading, gardening, walking. *E*: c.m.series@warwick.ac.uk.

**SERJEANT, Graham Roger**, CMG 1981; MD; FRCP; Chairman, Sickle Cell Trust of Jamaica, since 1986; *b* 26 Oct. 1938; *s* of Ewart Egbert and Violet Elizabeth Serjeant; *m* 1965, Beryl Elizabeth, *d* of late Ivor Edward King, CB, CBE. *Educ*: Sibford Sch., Banbury; Bootham Sch., York; Clare Coll., Cambridge (BA 1960, MA 1965); London Hosp. Med. Sch.; Makerere Coll., Kampala. MB BChir 1963, MD 1971, Cantab. MRCP 1966, FRCP 1977. House Physician: London Hosp., 1963–64; Royal United Hosp., Bath, 1965–66; RPMS, 1966; Med. Registrar, University Hosp. of WI, 1966–67; Wellcome Res. Fellow, Dept of Medicine, Univ. of WI, 1967–71; Medical Research Council: Mem., Scientific Staff, Abnormal Haemoglobin Unit, Cambridge, 1971–72; Epidemiology Res. Unit, Jamaica, 1972–74; Dir, MRC Labs, Jamaica, 1974–99. Hon. Prof. of Clin. Epidemiology, Univ. of WI, 1981–99, now Emeritus. Pres., Caribbean Orgn of Sickle Cell Assocs, 1997–2000. Gold Musgrave Medal, Inst. of Jamaica, 1995; Pelican Award, Univ. of WI, 1995; Vice-Chancellor's Award for Excellence, 1999. Dist. Res. Award, Caribbean Health Res. Council, 1999. Hon. CD (Jamaica), 1996; Commander, Mérite Congolais, 2005; Hon. OJ 2015. *Publications*: The Clinical Features of Sickle Cell Disease, 1974; Sickle Cell Disease, 1985, 3rd edn 2001; Guide to Sickle Cell Disease, 2001; approx. 500 papers on the nat. hist. of sickle cell disease, in med. jls. *Recreations*: theatre, art, Greek peasant life, travel. *Address*: Sickle Cell Trust, 14 Milverton Crescent, Kingston 6, Jamaica, WI. *T*: 9272300, *Fax*: 9700074. *E*: grserjeant@gmail.com.

**SERJEANT, William Ronald**, FRHistS; County Archivist, Suffolk, 1974–82, retired; Vice-President, Society of Archivists, since 1988 (President, 1982–88); Hon. Archivist to British Association for Local History, 1982–2011; *b* 5 March 1921; *s* of Frederick William and Louisa (*née* Wood); *m* 1961, Ruth Kneale (*née* Bridson); one *s*. *Educ*: Univ. of Manchester (BA Hons History); Univ. of Liverpool (Dip. Archive Admin. and Study of Records). Archivist/Librarian: Univ. of Sheffield, Sheffield City Library, Liverpool Record Office, 1952–56; Librarian/Archivist, Manx Nat. Library and Archives, Dep. Dir, Manx Mus. and Nat. Trust, 1957–62; County Archivist, Notts, 1962–70; Jt County Bor. and County Archivist, Ipswich and E Suffolk, 1970–74. Hon. Archivist: to Lord de Saumarez, 1982–2007; to Lord Tollemache, 1983–2013. Member: Lord Chancellor's Adv. Council on Public Records, 1982–88; Suffolk Heraldry Soc., 1982–; Member, Executive Committee: Suffolk Local History Council, 1970–2001; Ipswich Film Soc., 1974–2013; Council Member: Suffolk Inst. of Archeology and History, 1970–90; Suffolk Records Soc., 1970–2009; British Records Soc., 1974–2001; Ipswich Building Preservation Trust, 1988–2009; British Assoc. for Local History, 1994–97 (Mem. Publications Cttee, 1982–2010 (Chm., 1988–92)); Trustee, 1983–2005, Patron, 2005–, Leiston Long Shop (formerly Steam) Museum. Editor: Jl of the Manx Museum, 1957–62; The Suffolk Review, 1970–82; The Blazon (Suffolk Heraldry Soc.), 1984–88. *Publications*: The History of Tuxford Grammar School, 1969; (ed) Index to the Probate Records of the Court of the Archdeacon of Suffolk 1444–1700, 1979–80; (ed) Index to the Probate Records of the Court of the Archdeacon of Sudbury 1354–1700, 1984; articles in county and other local history periodicals. *Recreations*: walking, participation in local historical and heraldic studies and activities, theatre and cinema going; any gaps filled by reading novels. *Address*: 23 Dalton Road, Ipswich, Suffolk IP1 2HT. *T*: (01473) 221219.

**SEROTA, His Honour Daniel**; QC 1989; a Circuit Judge, 1999–2015; *b* 27 Sept. 1945; *s* of Louis and N'eema Serota; *m* 1970; two *d*. *Educ*: Carmel Coll.; Jesus Coll., Oxford (MA). Called to the Bar, Lincoln's Inn, 1969; a Recorder, 1989–99. Former Consulting Ed., Civil Practice Law Reports.

**SEROTA, Sir Nicholas (Andrew)**, CH 2013; Kt 1999; Chairman, Arts Council England, since 2017; *b* 27 April 1946; *s* of Stanley Serota and Beatrice Serota (Baroness Serota, DBE); *m* 1st, 1973, Angela Beveridge (marr. diss. 1995); two *d*; 2nd, 1997, Teresa Gleadowe; two step *d*. *Educ*: Haberdashers' Aske's Sch., Hampstead and Elstree; Christ's Coll., Cambridge (BA; Hon. Fellow, 2002); Courtauld Inst. of Art, London (MA). Regional Art Officer and Exhibn Organiser, Arts Council of GB, 1970–73; Director: Museum of Modern Art, Oxford, 1973–76; Whitechapel Art Gallery, 1976–88; Tate Gall., 1988–2017. Chm., Visual Arts Adv. Cttee, British Council, 1992–98 (Mem., 1976–98); Comr, Commn for Architecture and the Built Envmt, 1999–2006; Mem. Bd, Olympic Delivery Authy, 2006–12. Member: Exec. Bd, BBC, 2016–17; BBC Bd, 2017–. Trustee: Architecture Foundn, 1991–99; Little Sparta Trust, 1995–2007; Chinati Foundn, 1999–; Cy Twombly Foundn, 2018–; Moontower Foundn (Rebecca Horn), 2018–. Sen. FRCA 1996. Hon. Fellow: QMC 1988; Goldsmiths' Coll., Univ. of London, 1994. Hon. FRIBA 1992. Hon. DLitt: Keele, 1994; South Bank, 1996; Surrey, 1997; Exeter, 2000; London Inst., 2001; Cambridge, 2016; Hon. Dr Arts: City of London Polytechnic, 1990; Plymouth, 1993; DU Essex, 2002. Audrey Irmas Award for Curatorial Excellence, Bard Coll., USA, 2017. Officier de l'Ordre des Arts et des Lettres (France), 2003; Légion d'Honneur (France), 2012. *Publications*: Experience or Interpretation: the dilemma of museums of modern art, 1996. *Address*: Arts Council England, 21 Bloomsbury Street, WC1B 3HF.

**SERRA, Davide**; Founding Partner and Chief Executive, Algebris Investments LLP, since 2006; *b* Genoa, 19 Jan. 1971; *m* 1998; two *s* two *d*. *Educ*: Bocconi Univ. (BA Hons Econs and Finance *cum laude* 1994); Univ. Catholique de Louvain and NHH, Norway (Community of Eur. Mgt Schs Master 1995). Sen. Financial Analyst, UBS, Italy, 1995–2000; Co-Hd, Eur. Banks, Morgan Stanley Internat. Ltd, London, 2001–06. Mem., Industry Partnership, WEF. Designated Young Global Leader, 2010. *Recreations*: climbing, mountaineering, off-piste ski-ing in the Alps and mountains, sailing. *Address*: Algebris Investments LLP, 1 St James's Market, SW1Y 4AH. *E*: info@algebris.com. *Club*: Ambrosetti (Italy).

**SERRANO-QUEVEDO, Rafael**; Founder and Chief Executive, Prime Investors Capital Ltd, since 2009; *b* Madrid, 9 Aug. 1966; *s* of Ramon Serrano-Garcia and Cristina Serrano-Quevedo; *m* 2009, Marije Visser; one *s* one *d*. *Educ*: London Business Sch. (Postgrad. Cert. Finance and Investment Portfolio); Univ. of Oxford (Dip. Business and Mgt); Faculty of Law, Univ. of Madrid (MA Hons). Investment Banker, Capital Mkts and Internat. Fund Mgt, JP Morgan, 1991–99; Man. Dir, Focus Investment Gp, Europe, 2000–09. Prime Investors Capital Ltd projects include restoration and development of Bvlgari Hotel and Residences, Knightsbridge and of Admiralty Arch, Westminster. *Recreations*: arts, opera, classical music, history, property, hotels, tennis, charity work. *Address*: 4 Elm Park Road, SW3 6BB. *T*: (020) 3178 4660. *E*: rserrano@primeinvestors.com. *Clubs*: Arts, Queen's; Travellers (Paris).

**SERSALE di CERISANO, (Renato) Carlos**, PhD; Ambassador of Argentina to the Court of St James's, since 2016; *b* Buenos Aires, Argentina, 21 March 1950; *s* of Luigi Sersale di Cerisano and Rita Croci; *m* 1978, Liliana Scocozza (marr. diss. 2006); two *s* one *d*; partner, Linette de Jager. *Educ*: Univ. of Buenos Aires (Licenciado en Economia); Columbia Univ. of New York (Master in Internat. Affairs); Univ. of El Salvador (Dr Political Scis 1984). Joined Argentine Diplomatic Service, 1979; Rep. of Argentina to FAO, UN World Food prog., IFAD, Rome, 1982–86; UN Rep. to Econ. and Social Council and UN progs and UNDP and UNIDO Sen. Official, 1998–99; Director General: Human Rights, 2001–03; Internat. Security, Nuclear and Space Affairs; Ambassador to SA and Southern African Develt Community countries, 2006–15. Freeman, City of London, 2018; Hon. Freeman, Butchers' Co., 2018. Konex Award for Diplomats, 2018. Order of Merit (Italy), 1987; Kt of Justice, Constantine Order of St George, 1996. *Publications*: contrib. articles to specialised jls on foreign policy and institutional issues. *Recreations*: sports, cinema, reading. *Address*: Argentine Embassy, 65 Brook Street, W1K 4AH. *T*: (020) 7318 1321, *Fax*: (020) 7318 1305. *E*: ambassadors-office@argentine-embassy-uk.org. *Clubs*: Canning, Travellers, Naval and Military, Turf; Jockey, Circulo de Armas (Buenos Aires).

**SERVICE, Louisa Anne**, OBE 1997; Joint Chairman: The Hemming Group (formerly The Municipal Group) of Companies, 1976–2011 (non-executive Director, 2011–15); Hemming Publishing Ltd, 1987–2011; *d* of late Henry Harold Hemming, OBE, MC, and Alice Louisa Weaver, OBE; *m* 1959, Alastair Stanley Douglas Service, CBE, MVO (marr. diss. 1984; he *d* 2013); one *s* one *d*. *Educ*: private and state schs, Canada, USA and Britain; Ecole des Sciences Politiques, Paris; St Hilda's Coll., Oxford (BA and MA, PPE). Export Dir, Ladybird Appliances Ltd, 1957–59; Municipal Journal Ltd and associated cos: Financial Dir, 1966; Dep. Chm., 1974; Chm., Merchant Printers Ltd, 1975–80; Dir, Brintex Ltd, 1965–; Dir, Glass's Information Services Ltd, 1971, Dep. Chm. 1976–81, Chm., 1982–95. Member: Dept of Trade Consumer Credit Act Appeals Panel, 1981–2006; Cttee of Magistrates, 1985–88; FIMBRA Appeals Panel, 1988–92; Solicitors Complaints Bureau, 1992–93. JP Inner London Juvenile Courts, 1969–2001; Chm., Hackney Youth Court, 1975–82, Westminster Juvenile Ct, 1982–88, Hammersmith and Fulham Juvenile Court, 1988–94, Camden Youth and Family Proceedings Ct, 1994–2002; JP Inner London (5) PSD, 1980–; Chairman: Exec. Cttee, Inner London Juvenile Courts, 1977–79; Inner London Juvenile Liaison Cttee, 1986–88 (Mem., 1980–86); Member: working party on re-org. of London Juvenile Courts, 1975; Inner London Family Proceedings Courts, 1991–2002; Inner London Youth Courts, 1992–2002; Inner London Magistrates' Cts Cttee, 1995–2001; Vice-Chm., Paddington Probation Hostel, 1976–86. Corresp. mem., SDP Policy Gp on Citizens' Rights, 1982–89. Mem., Develt Adv. Cttee, 1996–2012, 125 Campaign Bd, 2016–, St Hilda's Coll., Oxford; Dir, 1997–2001, Chm., 2001–06, Jacqueline du Pré Music Building Ltd. Dir, Opera Circus Ltd, 2000–04. Chm. Council, Mayer-Lismann Opera Workshop, 1976–91; Hon. Sec., Women's India Assoc. of UK, 1967–74. Director: Arts Club Ltd, 1981–84; 9 Avenue Road Ltd, 2019–; Member Council: Friends of Covent Garden, 1982–2005; Haydn-Mozart Soc., 1988–93; Chm., Youth & Music, 1990–2001 (Dir, 1988–90); Mem., E-SU Music Cttee, 1984–91, 1997–2001. Mem. Adv. Bd, Rudolf Kempe Soc., 2000–03. Trustee, Performing Arts Labs, 1996–99. Pres., Commonwealth Countries League, 2009–14, now Patron (Vice Pres., 1994–2009; Trustee, Educn Fund, 1994–2004); Trustee, Commonwealth Girls Educn Fund, 2014–. Judge, Historical Dagger, Crime Writers' Assoc., 2013–. Distinguished Friend of Oxford, Oxford Univ., 2012. *Publications*: articles on a variety of subjects. *Recreations*: travel, and attractive and witty people including my family. *Club*: Athenæum (Member: Gen. Cttee, 2003–09; Exec. Cttee, 2004–09; Talk Dinner Cttee, 2010–16; Music Cttee, 2014–19). *See also* J. H. Hemming.

**SERVICE, Prof. Robert John**, PhD; FBA 1998; Professor of Russian History, Oxford University, 2002–13, now Emeritus; Fellow, St Antony's College, Oxford, 1998–2014, now Emeritus; *b* 29 Oct. 1947; *s* of Matthew Service and Janet Service (*née* Redpath); *m* 1975, Adele Biagi; two *s* two *d*. *Educ:* Northampton Town and County Grammar Sch. for Boys; King's Coll., Cambridge (Douton Open Schol. in Classics; BA 1970; MA 1971); Univ. of Essex (MA Govt and Politics 1971; PhD 1977). British Council Exchange Res. Student, Leningrad, 1973–74; Lectr in Russian Studies, Univ. of Keele, 1975–84; School of Slavonic and East European Studies, University of London: Lectr in Hist., 1984–87; Reader in Soviet Hist. and Politics, 1987–91; Prof. of Russian Hist. and Politics, 1991–98; Chairman: Hist. Dept, 1987–90; Acad. Assembly, 1990–92; Grad. Studies, 1993–97; Oxford University: Dir, Grad. Studies in Russian and E European Studies, 2000–02; Dean, St Antony's Coll., 2003. *Publications:* The Bolshevik Party in Revolution, 1979; Lenin: a political life, Vol. 1 1985, Vol. 2 1991, Vol. 3 1995; The Russian Revolution 1900–1927, 1986, 3rd rev. edn 1999; A History of Twentieth-Century Russia, 1997; Lenin: a biography, 2000; Russia: experiment with a people, from 1991 to the present, 2002; A History of Modern Russia from Nicholas II to Putin, 2003; Stalin: a biography, 2004; Comrades: Communism, a world history, 2007; Trotsky: a biography, 2009; Spies and Commissars, 2011; The End of the Cold War: 1985–1991, 2015; Kremlin Winter: Russia and the second coming of Vladimir Putin, 2019. *Recreations:* walking, bicycling, singing. *Address:* St Antony's College, Oxford OX2 6JF. *T:* (01865) 284747.

**SERWOTKA, Mark Henryk**; General Secretary, Public and Commercial Services Union, since 2002 (General Secretary elect, 2001–02); *b* 26 April 1963; *s* of Henryk Josef Serwotka and Audrey Phylis Serwotka; *m* 2001, Ruth Louise Cockroft; one *s* one *d*. *Educ:* St Margaret's RC Primary Sch., Aberdare; Bishop Hedley RC Comprehensive Sch., Merthyr Tydfil. Admin Officer, DHSS, subseq. DSS, 1980–2001. Pres., TUC, 2018–19. *Recreations:* sport (golf, football), reading, walking. *Address:* (office) 160 Falcon Road, SW11 2LN; 132 Portnalls Road, Chipstead, Coulsdon, Surrey CR5 3DX. *T:* (01737) 554545.

**SESHADRI, Prof. Conjeevaram Srirangachari**, PhD; FRS 1988; Director, Chennai Mathematical Institute (formerly Dean, School of Mathematics, SPIC Science Foundation, then SPIC Mathematic Institute), 1989–2010, now Director Emeritus; *b* 29 Feb. 1932; *s* of C. Srirangachari and Chudamani; *m* 1962, Sundari; two *s*. *Educ:* Loyola College, Madras (BA Hons Maths Madras Univ. 1953); PhD Bombay Univ. 1958. Tata Institute of Fundamental Research: Student, 1953; Reader, 1961; Professor, 1963; Senior Professor, 1975–84; Sen. Prof., Inst. of Math. Scis, Madras, 1984–89. *Publications:* Fibres Vectorials sur les courtes algébriques, Asterisque, 96, 1982; Introduction to the Theory of Standard Monomials, 1985. *Recreation:* south Indian classical music. *Address:* Chennai Mathematical Institute, Plot H1, SIPCOT IT Park, Padur PO, Siruseri 603103, India.

**SESHMI, Uanu**, MBE 2008; Co-Founder, and Creative Director, since 2008, From Boyhood to Manhood Foundation (Director, 1996–2008); male therapist, since 2009; filmmaker, since 2009; *b* Kingston, Jamaica, 8 Dec. 1959; one *d*. *Educ:* London Sch. of Business and Finance (HND Creative Media Production 2015); Southbank Univ. (BA Film Practice 2018; MA Editing and Post-production, 2019). Graphic designer; creator and author of Calling the Shots curriculum concept, anti-knife and gun educn and information resource. Anne Frank Award, Anne Frank Trust UK, 2007. *Recreations:* yoga, meditation, nutrition, jazz, drumming. *E:* uanu_seshmi@yahoo.co.uk.

**SESSIONS, John;** see Marshall, J. G.

**SETCH, Terence Frank**, RA 2009; RWA; professional artist (painter), since 1960; *b* London, 11 March 1936; *s* of Frank Arthur Setch and Florence Beatrice Setch; *m* 1967, Dianne Shaw; one *d*. *Educ:* Sutton and Cheam Sch. of Art; Slade Sch. of Fine Art; University Coll. London (DFA 1959). Lectr, Leicester Coll. of Art, 1960–64; Principal Lectr in Painting, Cardiff Coll. of Art, 1964–2001. Vis. Lectr, Emily Carr Coll. of Art, Vancouver, 1981; Artist in Residence, Victorian Coll. of the Arts, Melbourne. External Examiner BA: Slade Sch. of Fine Art, UCL, 1989–92; Faculty of Art, Univ. of Reading, 1989–92. Artist Advr, Derek Williams Trust Cttee, Nat. Mus. of Wales, 1996–2005. *Solo exhibitions include:* Grabowski Gall., 1967, 1968, 1970, 1973; Serpentine Gall., 1980; Nigel Greenwood Gall., 1982, 1985, 1987; Welsh Arts Council, Nat. Mus. of Wales, Cardiff, Camden Arts Centre, Talbot Rice Arts Centre, 1992; retrospective, RWA, Univ. of Wales Inst., Howard Gdns Gall., Cardiff, Glynn Vivian Art Gall., Swansea, 2001; retrospective, Collins Gall., Glasgow, 2002; Art Space Gall., Islington, 2008–10; Flowers Gall., 2012, 2014, 2016; Bay Art, Cardiff, 2017. Elected to Faculty of Painting, British Sch. at Rome, 1987; RWA 2002. *Relevant publications:* Terry Setch, by Paul Moorhouse, 1992; Terry Setch: a retrospective (essays), by Michael Tooby and Martin Holman, 2001; Terry Setch, by Martin Holman, 2009. *Recreations:* watching films, listening to music. *E:* setch@terrysetch.co.uk. *W:* www.terrysetch.co.uk. *Clubs:* Chelsea Arts, Arts.

**SETCHELL, Sir Marcus (Edward)**, KCVO 2014 (CVO 2004); FRCSE, FRCS, FRCOG; Surgeon-Gynaecologist to the Queen, 1990–2014; Consultant Obstetrician and Gynaecologist: London Clinic, 1975–2014; Portland Hospital, 1980–2014; *b* 4 Oct. 1943; *s* of late Eric Hedley Setchell and Barbara Mary (*née* Whitworth); *m* 1973, Dr Sarah French; two *s* two *d*. *Educ:* Felsted Sch.; Gonville and Caius Coll., Cambridge (MA, MB BChir); St Bartholomew's Hosp. Consultant Obstetrician and Gynaecologist: St Bartholomew's and Homerton Hosps, 1975–2000, now Hon. Consultant; Whittington Hosp. NHS Trust, 2000–08; Consultant Gynaecologist: King Edward VII Hosp. (formerly King Edward VII Hosp. for Officers), 1982–2014 (Chm. Med. Cttee, 1998–2005); St Luke's Hosp. for Clergy, 1983–2009. Advr in Gynaecology, Nat. Patient Safety Agency, 2003–06. Convener, Scientific Meetings, 1989–92, Mem. Council, 1994–2000, Chm., Consumers' Forum, 1995–98, RCOG; Mem., Council, 1990–94, Pres., Section of Obstetrics and Gynaecology, 1994–95, RSocMed. Chm. of Govs, Voluntary Hosp. of St Bartholomew, 2007–. Pres., WellBeing of Women, 2014– (Trustee, 2004–11). *Publications:* (with R. J. Lilford) Multiple Choice Questions in Obstetrics and Gynaecology, 1985, 3rd edn 1996, 4th edn (with B. Thilaganathan) 2001; (contrib.) Ten Teachers in Obstetrics and Gynaecology, 13th edn 1980 to 16th edn 1995; (with E. E. Philipp) Scientific Foundations of Obstetrics and Gynaecology, 1991; (with C. N. Hudson Shaw) Shaw's Textbook of Operative Gynaecology, 5th edn, 2001 to 7th edn (with J. H. Shepherd) 2012. *Recreations:* tennis, ski-ing, gardening, walking. *Address:* 64 Wood Vale, N10 3DN. *T:* (020) 8444 5266. *Clubs:* Royal Society of Medicine, St Albans Medical, Garrick; All England Lawn Tennis.

**SETH, Prof. Catriona Jane**, PhD; FBA 2017; Marshal Foch Professor of French Literature, University of Oxford, since 2015; Fellow, All Souls College, Oxford, since 2015; *b* Worsthorne, 30 Aug. 1964; *d* of Alasdair Seth and Susan Seth (*née* Mackrell). *Educ:* Colegio Francia, Caracas; Lycée Sainte-Croix, Fribourg; Lycée français de Belgique); Magdalen Coll., Oxford (BA 1986; MA 2001); Univ. de Paris-Sorbonne (Maîtrise, 1987; DEA 1988; PhD 1995; Agrégation 1995; HDR 2004). Translator and interpreter, 1986–89; mgt consultant, 1989–94; Prof. agrégé, Académie de Rouen, 1995–2000; Lectr, Univ. de Rouen, 2000–06; Prof. of 18th Century French Lit., Univ. de Nancy 2/Univ. de Lorraine, 2006–. Visiting Professor: Indiana Univ., Bloomington, 2010; Jakob-Fugger-Zentrum, Univ. of Augsburg, 2017. World Leading Researcher, QUB, 2013–14. Pres., Société française d'Étude du XVIII$^e$ siècle, 2015–. Mem., Académie Royale de Belgique, 2018. Hon. DSSc QUB, 2018. *Publications:* Les poètes créoles du XVIII$^e$ siècle, 1998; (jtly) Anthologie de la poésie française, 2000, 7th edn 2015; (ed jtly) Voltaire en Europe: hommage à Christiane Mervaud, 2000; (ed jtly) Sade en toutes lettres: Autour d'Aline et Valcour, 2004; André Chénier: le miracle du siècle, 2005; Marie-Antoinette: anthologie et dictionnaire, 2006; (ed jtly) Destins romanesques de l'émigration, 2007; Les Rois aussi en mouraient: les Lumières en lutte contre la petite vérole, 2008; (ed jtly) Parny, Le Paradis perdu, 2009; (ed jtly) Les Discours du corps au XVIII$^e$ siècle: littérature - philosophie - histoire - science, 2009, 2nd edn 2015; (ed) Imaginaires gothiques: aux sources du roman noir français, 2010; (ed) Laclos, Les Liaisons dangereuses, 2011; (ed jtly) Autour de Bernardin de Saint-Pierre: les écrits et les hommes des Lumières à l'Empire, 2011; Nobody's Children? Enlightenment Foundlings, Identity and Individual Rights, Burgerhart Lecture, 2012; (ed jtly) Le Tournant des Lumières Mélanges en l'honneur du professeur Malcolm Cook, 2012; La Fabrique de l'intime: mémoires et journaux de femmes du XVIII$^e$ siècle, 2013; (ed jtly) Marie Leprince de Beaumont: de l'éducation des filles à La Belle et La Bête, 2013; (ed jtly) Le temps des femmes: textes mémoriels des Lumières, 2013; Évariste Parny (1753–1814): Créole révolutionnaire, académicien, 2014; (ed) Lettres à Sade, 2014; (ed) Polier de Bottens, Mémoires d'une famille émigrée, 2015; (ed) Laclos après Laclos, 2016; (ed) Madame de Staël, Œuvres, 2017; (ed jtly) L'Idée de l'Europe au siècle des Lumières, 2017 (trans. English, German, 2017); (ed jtly) Une Éducatrice des Lumières: Marie Leprince de Beaumont, 2017. *Address:* All Souls College, Oxford OX1 4AL. *T:* (01865) 279379. *E:* Catriona.Seth@all-souls.ox.ac.uk.

**SETH, Vikram**, Hon. CBE 2001; writer; *b* 20 June 1952; *s* of Premnath and Leila Seth. *Educ:* Doon Sch., Dehra Dun, India; Tonbridge Sch., Kent; Corpus Christi Coll., Oxford (MA Hons PPE; Hon. Fellow 1994); Stanford Univ., Calif (MA Econs); Nanjing Univ., China. Sen. Editor, Stanford Univ. Press, 1985–86. Trustee, British Mus., 2004–08. Officier, Ordre des Arts et des Lettres (France), 2010 (Chevalier, 2001); Padma Shri (India), 2007. *Publications:* Mappings (poems), 1982; From Heaven Lake: travels through Sinkiang and Tibet, 1983; The Humble Administrator's Garden (poems), 1985; The Golden Gate (novel in verse), 1986; All You Who Sleep Tonight (poems), 1990; Three Chinese Poets: translations of Wang Wei, Li Bai and Du Fu, 1992; Beastly Tales From Here and There (fables in verse), 1992; A Suitable Boy (novel), 1992; Arion and the Dolphin (libretto), 1994; An Equal Music (novel), 1999; Two Lives (memoir), 2005; The Rivered Earth (libretti), 2011; Summer Requiem (poems), 2015. *Recreations:* music, Chinese calligraphy, swimming. *Address:* c/o David Godwin Associates, 55 Monmouth Street, WC2H 9DG.

**SETHIA, Anjum;** see Anand, A.

**SETHIA, Babulal**; DL; FRCP, FRCS; Consultant Cardiac Surgeon, Royal Brompton Hospital, since 1999; President, Royal Society of Medicine, 2014–17; *b* Edinburgh, 9 Feb. 1951; *s* of Babulal and Joan Sethia; *m* 1978, Nicola Jane Austin; one *s* three *d*. *Educ:* Rugby Sch.; St Thomas's Hosp. Med. Sch., London Univ. (BSc 1972; MB BS 1975). FRCS 1981; FRCP 2014. Surgical Registrar, Bournemouth and Southampton Hosps, 1976–80; Registrar, then Sen. Registrar, Cardiac Surgery, Glasgow Royal Infirmary, 1980–85; Sen. Registrar, Hosp. for Sick Children, Great Ormond St, London, 1985–87; Consultant Cardiac Surgeon, Birmingham Univ. and Children's Hosp., 1987–99. Hon. Sen. Lectr, Imperial Coll. London, 2012–. DL Gtr London, 2016. *Publications:* contribs on congenital heart surgery to internat. jls. *Recreations:* classical music, opera, wine. *Address:* Royal Society of Medicine, 1 Wimpole Street, W1G 0AE. *T:* (020) 7290 2902. *E:* B.Sethia@rsm.ac.uk.

**ŠETINC, Marjan;** Ambassador of Slovenia to Poland, 2009–14; *b* 15 May 1949; *s* of late Martin Šetinc and Ana Šetinc; *m* 1973, Marta Bartol; one *s* one *d*. *Educ:* Atlantic Coll., S Wales; Univ. of Ljubljana (BA Psychol.); London Sch. of Econs (MSc). Researcher, TUC of Slovenia, 1974–80; Sen. Researcher, Educnl Res. Inst., Ljubljana, 1980–92. MP (Liberal Democracy) Brezice, Slovenia, 1992–96; Mem., Culture and Educn, Sci. and Technol. and Foreign Affairs Select Cttees; Chm., EU Affairs Select Cttee. Rep. of Slovenia, OSCE Parly Delegn, IPU Delegn and Delegn to EU Parlt; Chm., Parly delegns to various bilateral confs; Ambassador to UK and to Ireland, 1998–2002; Dir Gen., Develt Co-operation, 2002–06, Ambassador Responsible for Relns with Multi-Lateral Econ. Orgns, 2006–09, Min. of Foreign Affairs. Member: Gen. Assembly for Slovenia, Internat. Assoc. for Evaluation of Educnl Achievement, 1989–96; Exec. Cttee, Eur. Educnl Res. Assoc., 1996–2001; Nat. Stats Council, 1996–2000. Mem., London Diplomatic Assoc., 1998–2002. Pres., Slovene Assoc. for Internat. Relns 2019–. Founder Ed., Theory and Res. in Educn jl (formerly School Field), 1989–. *Publications:* Social Conflicts and Strikes, 1975; Public Opinion on Political Decision-Making, 1980; The Averageachieving Curriculum: comparative assessment of pre-university mathematics in Slovenia, 1991; (jtly) Knowledge for Entering the 21st Century, Maths and Natural Sciences: comparison of the achievements of school children aged 14 to 15, in 45 countries, 1997; (jtly) Slovenian International Development Cooperation 2002–04, 2005; contrib. numerous articles and papers to scientific jls. *Recreations:* tennis, mountain walking, chess. *Address:* Mestni trg 17, 1000 Ljubljana, Slovenia.

**SETON, Sir Charles Wallace**, 13th Bt *cr* 1683 (NS), of Pitmedden, Aberdeenshire; *b* 25 Aug. 1948; *s* of Charles Wallace Seton (*d* 1975) and of Joyce (*née* Perdunn); *S* uncle, 1998, but his name does not appear on the Official Roll of the Baronetage; *m* 1st, 1974, Rebecca (marr. diss. 1994), *d* of Robert Lowery; one *d*; 2nd, 2000, Cindy, *d* of Billy Lee Smith. *Heir:* *b* Bruce Anthony Seton [*b* 29 April 1957; *m* 1991, Paula Harper; one *s* one *d*].

**SETON, Sir Iain (Bruce)**, 13th Bt *cr* 1663 (NS), of Abercorn; *b* 27 Aug. 1942; *s* of Sir (Christopher) Bruce Seton, 12th Bt and Joyce Vivien (*d* 2005), *d* of late O. G. Barnard; *S* father, 1988; *m* 1963, Margaret Ann, *d* of Walter Charles Faulkner; one *s* one *d*. *Educ:* Colchester and Chadacre. Farming until 1972; mining, 1972–2004. *Heir:* *s* Laurence Bruce Seton [*b* 1 July 1968; *m* 1990, Rachel, *d* of Jeffery Woods (marr. diss. 2019); one *s* two *d*]. *Address:* 16 Radiata Drive, Albany, WA 6330, Australia. *T:* (8) 98415667.

**SEVER, (Eric) John;** *b* 1 April 1943; *s* of Eric and Clara Sever; *m* Patricia; one *d*. *Educ:* Sparkhill Commercial School. Travel Executive with tour operator, 1970–77. MP (Lab) Birmingham, Ladywood, Aug. 1977–1983; PPS to the Solicitor General, 1978–79. Contested (Lab) Meriden, 1983. *Recreations:* theatre, cinema, reading. *Address:* 16 The Chase, Sutton Coldfield, West Midlands B76 1JS.

**SEVERIN, Prof. Dorothy Virginia Sherman**, Hon. OBE 2003; PhD; FSA; Gilmour Professor of Spanish, University of Liverpool, 1982–2008, now Professor Emerita; *b* 24 March 1942; *d* of Wilbur B. and Virginia L. Sherman; marr. diss.; one *d*. *Educ:* Harvard Univ. AB 1963; AM 1964; PhD 1967. FSA 1989. Teaching Fellow and Tutor, Harvard Univ., 1964–66; Vis. Lectr, Univ. of W Indies, 1967–68; Asst Prof., Vassar Coll., 1968; Lectr, Westfield Coll., London Univ., 1969–82; Pro-Vice-Chancellor, Univ. of Liverpool, 1989–92. Member: NI Higher Educn Council, 1993–2001; Res. Panel, British Acad. Humanities Res. Council, 1994–96; Iberian sub-panel, 2008 RAE, HEFCE, 2005–08; Peer Review Coll., AHRC, 2006–09. Vis. Associate Prof., Harvard Univ., 1982; Visiting Professor: Columbia Univ., 1985; Yale Univ., 1985; Univ. of Calif, Berkeley, 1996. Past Pres., British Br., Internat. Courtly Lit. Soc.; Member: Cttee, Asociación Hispánica de Literatura Medieval, 1997–99; Cttee, Asociación Internacional de Hispanistas, 2004–10; Cttee, Convivio, 2004–09; Trustee, 1979–2013, Hon. Treas., 2009–13, MHRA. Corresp. Mem. for UK, Real Academia Española, 2009–. Editor, Bulletin of Hispanic Studies,

1982–2008; Mem. Editl Bd, Hispanic Rev., Celestinesca, Boletín de Real Academia Española. *Publications:* (ed) de Rojas, La Celestina, 1969; Memory in La Celestina, 1970; (ed) Diego de San Pedro, La pasión trobada, 1973; (ed) La Lengua de Erasmo romançada por muy elegante estilo, 1975; The Cancionero de Martínez de Burgos, 1976; (ed with K. Whinnom) Diego de San Pedro, Poesía (Obras completas III), 1979; (ed with Angus MacKay) Cosas sacadas de la Historia del rey Juan el Segundo, 1982; (ed) Celestina, trans. James Mabbe (Eng./Spanish text), 1987; (ed) Celestina (Spanish edn), 1987; Tragicomedy and Novelistic Discourse in Celestina, 1989; Cancionero de Oñate-Castañeda, 1990; ADMYTE: The Paris Cancioneros, 1993, 2nd edn 1999 (PN2 with M. Garcia, PN9, PN13 with F. Maguire); Witchcraft in Celestina, 1995; Animals in Celestina, 1999; Two Spanish Songbooks: The Colombina (LB3) and Egerton (SV2), 2000; Del manuscrito a la imprenta en la época de Isabel la Católica, 2004; Religious Parody and the Spanish Sentimental Romance, 2005; An Electronic Corpus of 15th Century Castilian Cancionero Manuscripts, 2007; Religious Piety and Religious Parody: lives of Christ in late fifteenth-century Castile, 2013; contribs to learned jls incl. Hispanic Rev., Romance Philology, Medium Aevum, MLR and THES. *Address:* Department of Modern Languages and Cultures, The University, Abercromby Square, Liverpool L69 3BX.

**SEVERIN, (Giles) Timothy;** author, traveller and historian; *b* 25 Sept. 1940; *s* of Maurice Watkins and Inge Severin; *m* 1966, Dorothy Virginia Sherman (marr. diss. 1979); one *d*. *Educ:* Tonbridge School; Keble Coll., Oxford. MA, BLitt. Commonwealth Fellow, USA, 1964–66. Expeditions: led motorcycle team along Marco Polo route, 1961; R. Mississippi by canoe and launch, 1965; Brendan Voyage from W Ireland to N America, 1977; Sindbad Voyage from Oman to China, 1980–81; Jason Voyage from Iolkos to Colchis, 1984; Ulysses Voyage from Troy to Ithaca, 1985; first Crusade route by horse to Jerusalem, 1987–88; travels by horse in Mongolia, 1990; N Pacific voyage by bamboo sailing raft, 1993; Moluccan Islands voyage by traditional sailing prahu, 1996; Pacific and Indonesian island travels, 1998; Caribbean rim travels, 2000. Hon. DLitt Dublin, 1997; Hon. LLD NUI, 2003. Founders Medal, RGS; Livingstone Medal, RSGS; Sykes Medal, RSAA. *Publications:* Tracking Marco Polo, 1964; Explorers of the Mississippi, 1967; The Golden Antilles, 1970; The African Adventure, 1973; Vanishing Primitive Man, 1973; The Oriental Adventure, 1976; The Brendan Voyage, 1978; The Sindbad Voyage, 1982; The Jason Voyage, 1985; The Ulysses Voyage, 1987; Crusader, 1989; In Search of Genghis Khan, 1991; The China Voyage, 1994; The Spice Islands Voyage, 1997; In Search of Moby Dick, 1999; Seeking Robinson Crusoe, 2002; *fiction:* Viking trilogy: Odinn's Child; Sworn Brothers; King's Man, 2005; Pirate series: Corsair, 2007; Buccaneer, 2008; Sea Robber, 2009; Privateer, 2014; Freebooter, 2017; Saxon trilogy: The Book of Dreams, 2012; The Emperor's Elephant, 2013; The Pope's Assassin, 2015. *Address:* Timoleague, Co. Cork, Eire. *E:* severin.tim@gmail.com.

**SEVERN, Viscount; James Alexander Philip Theo Mountbatten-Windsor;** *b* 17 Dec. 2007; *s* of TRH the Earl and Countess of Wessex.
*See under Royal Family.*

**SEVILLE, Prof. Jonathan Peter Kyle,** PhD; CEng, FREng, FIChemE; Professor of Formulation Engineering, and Academic Director, Collaborative Teaching Laboratory, University of Birmingham, since 2017; *b* 5 Feb. 1956; *s* of Peter Linton Seville and Joan Kathleen Seville (*née* Monks); *m* 1984, Elizabeth Jane Pope; two *d*. *Educ:* Gonville and Caius Coll., Cambridge (BA 1979, MA 1983; MEng 1994); Univ. of Surrey (PhD 1987). FIChemE 1997; FREng 2004. Chemical engr, Courtaulds Ltd, 1979–81; Lectr, 1984–91, Sen. Lectr, 1991–94, Univ. of Surrey; Prof. of Chemical Engrg, 1994–2008, Hd, Dept of Chemical Engrg, 1998–2008, Univ. of Birmingham; Dean of Engrg, Univ. of Warwick, 2008–11; Dean, Faculty of Engrg and Physical Scis, 2011–16, Prof. of Chemical Engrg, 2016–18, Univ. of Surrey. Visiting Professor: Univ. of BC, 1989; Tech. Univ. of Denmark, 1997. Ed.-in-Chief, Powder Technol., 1995–2014. Mem. Council, 2003–10, 2015–, Dep. Pres., 2015–16, Pres., 2016–17, IChemE; Mem. Bd, Engrg Council, 2013–. *Publications:* (ed jtly) Gas Cleaning at High Temperatures, 1993; (jtly) Processing of Particulate Solids, 1997; (ed) Gas Cleaning in Demanding Applications, 1997; (ed jtly) Granulation, 2007; (jtly) Particle Technology and Engineering, 2016. *Recreation:* theatre. *Address:* 33 Franklin Court, Wormley, Godalming, Surrey GU8 5US. *E:* j.p.k.seville@bham.ac.uk.

**SEWARD, Dame Margaret (Helen Elizabeth),** DBE 1999 (CBE 1994); Chief Dental Officer, Department of Health, 2000–02; *b* 5 Aug. 1935; *d* of Dr Eric Oldershaw and Gwen Oldershaw; adopted, 1938, by John Hutton Mitchell and Marion Findlay Mitchell; *m* 1962, Prof. Gordon Seward, CBE; one *s* one *d*. *Educ:* Latymer Sch., Edmonton; London Hosp. Med. Coll. Dental Sch. (BDS Hons 1959; MDS 1970). FDSRCS 1962; MCCDRCS 1989. Dental practice: Highlands Hosp., 1962–64; Cheshunt Community Clinic, 1969–75; Royal London Hosp., 1980–94. Sen. Res. Fellow, BPMF, Univ. of London, 1975–77. Member: GDC, 1976–99; Bd, Faculty of Dental Surgery, RCS, 1980–94 (Vice-Dean, 1990). President: Section of Odontology, RSM, 1991; BDA, 1993–94; GDC, 1949–99. Editor: Brit. Dental Jl, 1979–92; Internat. Dental Jl, 1990–2000. Dir, Teamwork Project, DoH, 1991–95; Ind. Dir, Quality Assessment Agency, 1997–2000. Chm., Communication Cttee, FDI, 1984–89. Hon. Pres., Women in Dentistry, 1989–92; Hon. Member: Amer. Dental Assoc., 1992; Amer. Coll. of Dentists, 1994. Chm. Govs, Latymer Sch., 1984–94. Hon. FDSRCSE 1995; Hon. Fellow, QMW, 1997. Hon. DDSc: Newcastle, 1995; Sheffield, 2002; Hon. DDS Birmingham, 1995; Hon. DSc: Portsmouth 2005; Plymouth 2011. List of Honour, FDI World Dental Federation, 2008. *Publications:* Disturbances Associated with the Eruption of the Primary Dentition, 1969; Provision of Dental Care by Women Dentists in England and Wales, 1975, 2nd survey 1985; Better Opportunities for Women Dentists, 2001; Open Wide: memoir of the dental dame, 2009; numerous articles in learned jls, UK and internationally. *Recreations:* cooking, entertaining, house-work! *Address:* 1 Wimpole Street, W1G 0AE. *Club:* Royal Society of Medicine.

**SEWEL,** family name of **Baron Sewel**.

**SEWEL, Baron** *cr* 1995 (Life Peer), of Gilcomstoun in the District of the City of Aberdeen; **John Buttifant Sewel,** CBE 1984; PhD; *b* 15 Jan. 1946; *s* of late Leonard Buttifant Sewel and of Hilda Ivy Sewel (*née* Brown); *m* 2005, Jennifer Ann (*née* Lindsay). *Educ:* Hanson Boys' Grammar Sch., Bradford; Univ. of Durham (BA 1967); UC, Swansea (MSc (Econ) 1970); Univ. of Aberdeen (PhD 1977). Res. Asst, Dept of Sociology and Anthropology, UC, Swansea, 1967–69; University of Aberdeen: Res. Fellow, Dept of Politics, 1969–72, Depts of Educn and Political Economy, 1972–75; Lectr, 1975; Sen. Lectr, 1988; Prof., Regl Centre for Study of Econ. and Social Policy, 1991–97; Dean: Econ. and Social Scis, 1988–95; Social Scis and Law, 1995–96; Vice-Principal, 1994–96 and 1999–2001; Sen. Vice-Principal, 2001–04. Mem., City of Aberdeen DC, 1974–84 (Leader, 1977–80). Mem., H of L, 1995–2015. Parly Under-Sec. of State, Scottish Office, 1997–99. Chm. of Cttees and Principal Dep. Speaker, H of L, 2012–15. Mem., NATO Parly Assembly, 2000–12. Pres., COSLA, 1982–84. Member: Accounts Commn for Scotland, 1987–96; Scottish Constitutional Commn, 1994–95. Hon. LLD: Aberdeen, 2008; Swansea, 2012. *Publications:* Colliery Closure and Social Change, 1975; Education and Migration, 1976; (with F. W. Bealey) The Politics of Independence: a study of a Scottish town, 1981; (jtly) The Rural Community and the Small School, 1983; articles and chapters on sociology and politics. *Recreations:* hill walking, ski-ing, watching cricket.

**SEWELL, Prof. Herbert Fitzgerald,** PhD; FRCP, FRCPGlas, FRCPath, FMedSci; Professor of Immunology, and Consultant Immunologist, Faculty of Medicine, University of Nottingham, 1990–2019, now Emeritus; *b* 19 May 1949; *s* of late Wilfred Sewell and Maud Sewell; two *s*. *Educ:* King Edward's Grammar Sch., Aston, Birmingham; Univ. of Birmingham (BDS 1973, MSc 1975, PhD 1978); Univ. of Leicester (MB ChB 1983). MRCPath 1980, FRCPath 1992; MRCPGlas 1987, FRCPGlas 1989; FRCP 1998. Jun. dental posts, Birmingham Dental and Gen. Hosp., 1974–75; MRC Student and Res. Fellow, Dept Exptl Pathol., Univ. of Birmingham, 1974–78; jun. med. posts, East Birmingham Hosp., 1983–84; Consultant Immunologist, Glasgow Royal Infirmary, 1984–85; Sen. Lectr and Hon. Consultant, Dept of Pathology, Univ. of Aberdeen, 1985–90; Pro-Vice-Chancellor Res., Univ. of Nottingham, 2002–07. Non-exec. Dir, Nottingham Univ. Hosps Trust, 2013–19 (Vice Chm., 2016–19). Chairman: Jt Commn on Immunology and Allergy, RCP and RCPath, 1994–98; Quality and Assurance Cttee, Nottingham Univ. Hosps Trust, 2015–19; Member: UK Xenotransplantation Interim Regulatory Authy, 1997–2001; UK Medicines Commn, 1998–2004; Nuffield Council on Bioethics, 2002–06; Medical Research Council: Council Mem., 2004–11; Member: Clinical Trng and Career Develt Panel, 1998–2001; subgp on Inflammatory Bowel Disease and Autism, Strategy Develt Gp, 1998–2000. Founder FMedSci 1998. Hon. DDS Birmingham 2001; Hon. DSc West Indies, 2003. *Publications:* (ed jtly) Essential Immunology for Surgeons, 2011; papers on mechanisms in allergy and on basic and clinical immunology, auto-antibodies (immuno-biomarkers) used in early detection and diagnosis of human solid cancers, such as lung (clinical test, Early CDT-Lung), breast and colorectal tumours. *Recreations:* road jogging, Chinese and African cultural studies, sampling rums of the world. *Address:* A Floor West Block, Queen's Medical Centre, Notts NG7 2UH. *T:* (0115) 823 0001. *E:* herb.sewell@nottingham.ac.uk.

**SEWELL, James Reid,** OBE 2001; FSA; City Archivist (formerly Deputy Keeper of Records), Corporation of London, 1984–2003; *b* 12 April 1944; *s* of late James Campbell Sewell and Iris Eveleen Sewell (*née* Reid). *Educ:* High Sch., Glasgow; Univ. of Glasgow (MA Hons Hist.); University Coll. London (Dip. Archive Admin). FSA 1979. Asst Archivist, Durham Co. Record Office, 1967–70; Asst Dep. Keeper, Corp. of London Records Office, 1970–84. Chm. and Pres., Section of Municipal Archives, Internat. Council on Archives, 1992–2000 (Mem. Cttee, 1986–92). Chm., Morley Coll. Ceramic Circle, subseq. London Ceramic Circle at Morley Coll., 2010–. Fellow, Guildhall Wine Acad., 1993. *Publications:* (with W. A. L. Seaman) The Russian Journal of Lady Londonderry 1836–37, 1973; The Artillery Ground and Fields in Finsbury, 1977; contrib. articles to various professional jls. *Recreations:* tennis, orchid growing, wine. *Address:* 120 Addiscombe Road, Croydon, Surrey CR0 5PQ. *T:* (020) 8656 4046. *Club:* Shirley Park Lawn Tennis (Hon. Sec., 1983–98).

**SEWELL, Rufus Frederick;** actor; *b* 29 Oct. 1967; *s* of late Bill Sewell and of Jo Sewell; *m* 1999, Yasmin Abdallah (*see* Y. Sewell) (marr. diss.); partner, Amy Gardener; one *s*. Theatre includes: As You Like It, The Government Inspector, The Seagull, Crucible, Sheffield, 1989; Royal Hunt of the Sun, Comedians, Compass, 1989; Pride and Prejudice, Royal Exchange, Manchester, 1991; Making It Better, Hampstead and Criterion, 1992; Arcadia, NT, 1993; Translations, Plymouth Th., NY, 1995; Rat in the Skull, Duke of York's, 1995; Macbeth, Queen's, 1999; Luther, NT, 2001; Rock 'n' Roll, Royal Court, 2006 (Best Actor: London Evening Standard Th. Awards, 2006; Critics' Circle Th. Awards, 2006; Laurence Olivier Awards, 2007); Old Times, Harold Pinter Th., 2013; Closer, Donmar, 2015; Art, Old Vic, 2016. *Films include:* Twenty-One, 1991; Dirty Weekend, 1993; A Man of No Importance, 1994; Carrington, Victory, 1995; Hamlet, 1997; Dark City, The Woodlanders, At Sachem Farm, Martha Meet Frank Daniel and Laurence, Illuminata, 1998; The Honest Courtesan, In a Savage Land, 1999; Bless the Child, A Knight's Tale, 2001; Extreme Ops, 2003; The Legend of Zorro, 2005; Tristan & Isolde, The Holiday, 2006; The Illusionist, Amazing Grace, 2007; All Things to All Men, 2013; The Sea, 2014; Hercules 3D, 2014; Gods of Egypt, 2016; Judy, 2019. *Television includes:* The Last Romantics, 1991; Gone to Seed, 1992; Dirty Something, 1993; Citizen Locke, Middlemarch, 1994; Cold Comfort Farm, Henry IV, 1995; Arabian Nights, 2000; She-Creature, 2001; Helen of Troy, 2003; Charles II: The Power and the Passion, 2003; The Pillars of the Earth, 2010; Zen, 2011; Parade's End, Restless, 2012; Killing Jesus, The Man in the High Castle, 2015, 2016, 2018; Victoria, 2016, 2017. *Address:* c/o Julian Belfrage Associates, 3rd Floor, 9 Argyll Street, W1F 7TG.

**SEWELL, Maj.-Gen. Timothy Patrick T.;** *see* Toyne Sewell.

**SEWELL, Yasmin;** Founder and Director, Yasmin Sewell Ltd, since 2008; Vice President of Style and Creative, Farfetch, since 2017; *b* Sydney, 22 Jan. 1976; *d* of Robert Abdallah and Joyce Abdallah; *m* 1999, Rufus Frederick Sewell, *qv* (marr. diss.); *m* 2012, Kyle Robinson; one *s*. *Educ:* St Catherine's Sch., Waverly. Founder and Dir, Yasmin Cho Boutique, London, 1998–2001; Buying Dir, Browns, London, 2005–08; Chief Creative Consultant, Liberty, London, 2008–09; Fashion Dir, Style.com, 2016–17. Young Australian of the Year Award, 2012. *Publications:* (contrib.) Pattern, 2013. *Address:* Yasmin Sewell Ltd, 26 Cross Street, N1 2BG. *T:* (020) 7613 2766. *E:* you@yasminsewell.com.

**SEXTON, David Howard;** Literary Editor, since 1997, and Lead Film Reviewer, 2010–17 and since 2019, Evening Standard (formerly Evening Standard, then London Evening Standard); *b* 2 Aug. 1958; *s* of late Richard Herbert Sexton and of Margaret Laura Sexton (*née* Page); *m* 1988, Emma Crichton-Miller (marr. diss. 1997); one *d* by Catherine Bennett; one *s* by Catherine Shoard. *Educ:* Colchester Royal Grammar Sch.; Trinity Coll., Cambridge (BA 1980). Literary Ed., Sunday Correspondent, 1990–91; columnist, TLS, 1991–97; radio critic, Sunday Telegraph, 1991–2007. Critic of the Year, British Press Awards, 2015. *Publications:* The Strange World of Thomas Harris, 2001. *Recreations:* food, wine, books, trees, France. *Address:* Evening Standard, Northcliffe House, 2 Derry Street, W8 5EE. *E:* David.Sexton@standard.co.uk; Saint Caprais, 82110 Bouloc, France.

**SEYCHELLES, Bishop of;** *see* Indian Ocean, Archbishop of.

**SEYFRIED HERBERT,** family name of **Baron Herbert**.

**SEYMOUR,** family name of **Duke of Somerset**, and **Marquess of Hertford**.

**SEYMOUR, Lord; Sebastian Edward Seymour;** *b* 3 Feb. 1982; *s* and heir of 19th Duke of Somerset, *qv*; *m* 2006, Arlette Lafayeedney (marr. diss. 2013). *Educ:* Marlborough Coll.; RAC Cirencester. MRICS. *Recreations:* Middle East and African business, politics, travel, food and wine, sports. *Address:* The Estate Office, Shadrack, Berry Pomeroy, Totnes, Devon TQ9 6NJ.

**SEYMOUR, Anya;** *see* Hindmarch, A.

**SEYMOUR, Prof. Carol Anne, (Mrs Carol Seymour-Richards),** PhD; FRCP, FRCPath, FFFLM; Professor of Clinical Biochemistry and Metabolic Medicine, St George's Hospital Medical School, 1991–2004, now Emeritus; Senior Medico-legal Adviser, Medical Protection Society, since 2016 (Medico-legal Adviser, 2003–16); *b* 19 March 1945; *d* of Raymond and Erica Seymour; *m* 1987, Prof. Peter Richards (*d* 2011). *Educ:* Badminton Sch.; St Anne's Coll., Oxford (MA, BM BCh); RPMS (MSc, PhD);

Holborn Coll., Univ. of Wolverhampton (Postgrad. DipLaw 1998); Inns of Court Sch. of Law (Postgrad. DipLS 2001). MRCP 1972, FRCP 1985; FRCPath 1993; FFFLM 2006. Lectr in Medicine and Hon. Consultant Physician, Univ. of Cambridge Sch. of Clinical Medicine/Addenbrooke's Hosp., 1977–91; Fellow, and Dir of Med. Studies, Trinity Coll., Cambridge, 1981–91. Dir of Med. Advice to Parly and Health Service Comr, 1997–2003; Royal College of Physicians: Academic Registrar, 1987–91; Examiner for MRCP, 1991–; Mem. Council, 1996–2000, 2003–05; Examiner for MRCPath, RCPath, 1993–2005; Mem., GMC, 1987–91 (Lead Performance Assessor, 1999–2003). Pres., Faculty of Forensic and Legal Medicine, 2017–19 (Vice Pres., 2014–16). Trustee, Acad. of Royal Med. Colls 2017–19. Called to the Bar, Gray's Inn, 2001. *Publications:* (contrib.) Oxford Textbook of Medicine, 1983, 3rd edn 1995; Clinical Clerking, 1984, (jtly) 3rd edn 2003; many articles on liver disease and metabolic aspects of clinical medicine. *Recreations:* music (clarinet and organ), walking, cycling. *Address:* Barefords, 78 Commercial End, Swaffham Bulbeck, Cambs CB25 0NE. *T:* (01223) 812007. *E:* (work) carol.seymour@medicalprotection.org, (personal) carolrichards2010@hotmail.co.uk.

**SEYMOUR, David,** CB 2005; Independent Reviewer, Justice and Security (Northern Ireland) Act 2007, since 2014; Legal Adviser to the Home Office and Northern Ireland Office, 2000–12; *b* 24 Jan. 1951; *s* of late Graham Seymour and Betty (*née* Watson); *m* 1972, Elisabeth Huitson; one *s* two *d*. *Educ:* Trinity Sch., Croydon; Queen's Coll., Oxford (Open Exhibn; BA Jurisprudence 1972; MA 1977); Fitzwilliam Coll., Cambridge (LLB 1974). Law clerk, Rosenfeld, Meyer & Susman (Attorneys), Beverly Hills, Calif, 1972–73; called to the Bar: Gray's Inn (Holt Schol.), 1975, Bencher, 2001; NI, 1997; pupillage, 1975–76; Legal Advr's Br., Home Office, 1976–97; Principal Asst Legal Advr, 1994; Dep. Legal Advr, 1996; Legal Sec. to the Law Officers, 1997–2000. Vis. Lectr in European Human Rights Law, Univ. of Conn Sch. of Law, 1986. Mem., Review of Criminal Justice System in NI, 1998–2000. Master of Estates and Mem., Mgt Cttee, Gray's Inn, 2012–14. Governor: Trinity Sch., Croydon, 2010– (Chm. Govs, 2015–); Court, Whitgift Foundn, 2015–. Chm., Reigate Squash Club, 2007–11. *Recreations:* watching cricket, gardening, walking, golf. *Address:* c/o Home Office, 2 Marsham Street, SW1P 4DF. *Clubs:* MCC; Reigate Heath Golf.

**SEYMOUR, Gillian Elizabeth, (Jill);** Member (UK Ind) West Midlands Region, European Parliament, 2014–19; *b* Cosford, Shropshire, 8 May 1958; *m* 1985, Brian Seymour; one *s*. *Educ:* Trinity Sch., Croydon; Queen's Coll., Oxford (Open PR exec., Aga-Rayburn; sales exec., American Express and Thomson Internat.; Seymour Manufg Internat. Ltd. Contested (UK Ind) Wrekin, 2015. Former Mem., UKIP NEC.

**SEYMOUR, Sir Julian (Roger),** Kt 2014; CBE 2001; *b* 19 March 1945; *s* of Evelyn Roger Seymour and Rosemary Evelyn Seymour (*née* Flower); *m* 1984, Diana Elizabeth Griffith; one *s* one *d*. *Educ:* Eton. Director: Collett, Dickinson, Pearce Ltd, 1969–79; Robert Fox Ltd, 1980–85; Dir, Corporate Finance, Lowe Gp PLC, 1985–91; Dir, Lady Thatcher's Private Office, 1991–2000. Non-executive Director: Chime Communications PLC, 1990–2007; Vanderbilt Homes, 2014–. Comr, English Heritage, 1992–98; Chm., Margaret Thatcher Archive Trust, 2005–. *Recreations:* gardening, shooting. *Address:* 37 Surrey Lane, SW11 3PA.

**SEYMOUR, Prof. Leonard William,** PhD; Professor of Gene Therapies, University of Oxford, since 2002 (Head, Department of Clinical Pharmacology, 2009–10); *b* 4 Sept. 1958; *s* of Percy and Daisy Seymour. *Educ:* Plymouth Coll.; Univ. of Manchester (BSc Hons 1980); Keele Univ. (PhD 1985). Lectr, 1993–99, Reader in Molecular Therapy, 1999–2002, CRC Inst. for Cancer Studies, Univ. of Birmingham. Pres. (first), British Soc. for Gene Therapy, 2004–09; Gen. Sec., European Soc. for Gene and Cell Therapy, 2009–14. Co-founding Scientist: Psioxus Therapeutics (formerly Hybrid Systems Ltd), 1998 (Chair, Scientific Adv. Bd); Oxford Genetics Ltd, 2010 (non-exec. Dir); Theolytics Ltd, 2018; MacrophOx Ltd, 2018 (Chief Scientific Officer, 2018–). *Publications:* over 200 primary scientific papers in fields of gene therapy and immunotherapy/virotherapy of cancer. *Recreations:* all forms of music, playing keyboard, hill walking and trekking through remote areas. *Address:* Department of Oncology, University of Oxford, Old Road Campus Research Building, Old Road Campus, off Roosevelt Drive, Headington, Oxford OX3 7DQ. *T:* (01865) 617020.

**SEYMOUR, Lynn,** CBE 1976; ballerina; *b* Wainwright, Alberta, 8 March 1939. *Educ:* Vancouver; Sadler's Wells Ballet School. Joined Sadler's Wells Ballet Company, 1957; Deutsche Oper, Berlin, 1966; Artistic Director: Ballet of Bavarian State Opera, Munich, 1979–80; Greek National Opera Ballet, 2006–07; has danced with Royal Ballet, English Nat. Ballet, Berliner Ballet, and Adventures in Motion Pictures. *Roles created:* Adolescent, in The Burrow, Royal Opera House, 1958; Bride, in Le Baiser de la Fée, 1960; Girl, in The Invitation, 1960; Young Girl, in Les Deux Pigeons, 1961; Principal, in Symphony, 1963; Principal, in Images of Love, 1964; Juliet, in Romeo and Juliet, 1964; Albertine, BBC TV, 1966; Concerto, 1966; Anastasia, 1966; Flowers, 1972; Side Show, 1972; A Month in the Country, 1976; Five Brahms Waltzes in the manner of Isadora Duncan, 1976; mother, in Fourth Symphony, 1977; Mary Vetsera, in Mayerling, 1978; Take Five, 1978. *Other appearances include:* Danses Concertantes; Solitaire; La Fête Etrange; Sleeping Beauty; Swan Lake; Giselle (title-role); Cinderella; Das Lied von der Erde; The Four Seasons; Voluntaries; Manon; Dances at a Gathering; The Concert; Pillar of Fire; Romeo and Juliet (Tudor, Nureyev and Cranko); Las Hermañas; Moor's Pavane; Auriole; Apollon; Le Corsaire; Flower Festival; La Sylphide (Sylph and Madge); A Simple Man; Onegin. *Choreography for:* Rashomon, for Royal Ballet Touring Co., 1976; The Court of Love, for SWRB, 1977; Intimate Letters, 1978 and Mac and Polly, for Commonwealth Dance Gala, 1979; Boreas, and Tattoo, for Bavarian State Opera Ballet, 1980; Wolfi, for Ballet Rambert, 1987; Bastet, for SWRB, 1988. A Time to Dance (film), 1986.

**SEYMOUR, Sir Michael Patrick Culme-,** 6th Bt *cr* 1809, of Highmount, co. Limerick and Friery Park, Devonshire; consultant, entrepreneur, photographer; Vice President, Asia Pacific, Marken Ltd, Singapore, since 2015; *b* 28 April 1962; *s* of Major Mark Charles Culme-Seymour and of his 3rd wife, Patricia June, *d* of Charles Reid-Graham; *S* cousin, 1999; *m* 1st, 1986, Karin Fleig (marr. diss. 2007); two *s*; 2nd, 2008, Christin Kaufmann; one *d*. Regl Vice-Pres., Asia, Pacific and India, Swisscargo, 1998–2003; CEO, Asia, Pacific and EMEA, DHL Global Mail, 2003–08; Owner: MCS Lifestyle Photography, Singapore, 2008–; Fischer Road Express Asia Pte Ltd, Singapore, 2012–13; Partner, Competitive Capital Ltd, Singapore, 2009–11. *Heir:* s Michael Culme-Seymour, *b* 5 Oct. 1986. *E:* mcslifestyle@gmail.com.

**SEYMOUR, His Honour Richard William;** QC 1991; a Senior Circuit Judge, 2000–15; *b* 4 May 1950; *e s* of late Albert Percy and Vera Maud Seymour; *m* 1971, Clare Veronica, BSS, MSc, *d* of Stanley Victor Peskett; one *s* one *d*. *Educ:* Brentwood Sch.; Royal Belfast Academical Instn; Christ's Coll., Cambridge (schol.; BA 1971; MA 1975). Holker Jun. Exhibn, 1970, Holker Sen. Schol., 1972, Gray's Inn; called to the Bar, Gray's Inn, 1972. Asst Recorder, 1991–95; Recorder, 1995–2000; a Judge of the Technology and Construction Court, 2000–05; assigned to Queen's Bench Div. of High Court, 2005–15. Pres., Mental Health Review Tribunals, 2000. Gov., Anglia Ruskin Univ., 2011–17. Mem., Chapter, Chelmsford Cath., 2015–. *Publications:* (ed jtly) Kemp and Kemp, The Quantum of Damages, 4th edn 1975; legal chapters in: Willis and Willis, Practice and Procedure for the Quantity Surveyor, 8th edn 1980; Willis and George, The Architect in Practice, 6th edn 1981; with Clare Seymour: Courtroom Skills for Social Workers, 2007; Courtroom and Report Writing Skills for Social Workers, 2011; Practical Child Law for Social Workers. 2013. *Recreations:* archaeology, military history, phaleristics.

**SEYMOUR, Richard William;** Founder and Director, Seymour Powell, 1984–2017; *b* 1 May 1953; *s* of Bertram Seymour and Annie Irene (*née* Sherwood); *m* 1980, Anne Margaret Hart; one *s* one *d*. *Educ:* Central Sch. of Art & Design (BA); Royal Coll. of Art (MA; Sen. Fellow, 2005). Advertising Creative Dir, Blazelynn Advertising, London, 1978–81; film prodn designer, with Anton Furst, later Seymour Furst, 1981–83; freelance designer working on advertising and new product develt projects, 1982–83; Founder, with D. Powell, Seymour Powell (product and transportation design consultancy), 1984 (clients incl. Nokia, Ford, Aqualisa). Vis. Prof. of Product and Transportation Design, RCA, 1995–. Trustee, Design Mus., London, 1994–2011. Contrib. to TV progs and children's progs featuring design and future thinking. Pres., D&AD, 1999 (Mem., Exec. Cttee, 1997–). FRSA 1993; FCSD 1993. Hon. DDes Centre of Creative Studies, Michigan, 2002. Awards include: Best Overall Design and Product Design (for Norton F1 motorcycle), Design Week Awards, 1990; Silver Awards (for Technophone Cellular Phone), 1991, and (for MuZ Scorpion motorcycle), 1993, and President's Award (for outstanding contribn to design), 1995, D&AD; Product Design Award, BBC Design Awards, 1994; Design Effectiveness Award, Design Business Assoc. (for SEB appliances), 1995, 2002, 2003; Special Commendation, Prince Philip Designers Prize, 1997; Janus award, France, 2002; Gerald Frewer Meml Trophy, Inst. of Engrg Designers, 2003; Star Pack Award, 2003; Best Corporate Film, Golden Camera Awards: for Samsung European Premium Design, 2003; for Unilever, 2005; Lifetime Achievement Award, FX Mag., 2010. *Publications:* (with M. Palin) The Mirrorstone (Smarties Design Award, Hatchard's Top Ten Author's Award), 1986. *Recreations:* Early English music, cello, motorcycling. *Clubs:* Bluebird, Chelsea Arts.

**SEYMOUR, Urmila;** see Banerjee, U.

**SEYMOUR-JACKSON, Ralph;** Chief Executive Officer, Student Loans Company Limited, 2003–10; *b* 11 May 1963; *s* of Alan and Arabella Seymour-Jackson; *m* 1993, Angela Fenn; one *s* one *d*. *Educ:* Wadham Coll., Oxford (BA Maths 1984). FIA 1991. Pilot, RAF, 1980–88; Actuary, Norwich Union, 1988–92; Chief Exec., Scoplife Insce Co., Athens, 1992–96; Scottish Provident Institution (Mutual Life Insurer): Gp Corporate Develt and Mktg Manager, Gp Hd Office, Edinburgh, 1996–98; Hd, UK Ops, 1998–2000; IT Dir, Abbey National Finance and Investment Services, 2001–03. *Recreations:* skydiving, cooking, children.

**SEYMOUR-RICHARDS, Carol Anne;** see Seymour, C. A.

**SEYS LLEWELLYN, His Honour Anthony John;** QC 2003; a Senior Circuit Judge and Designated Civil Judge for Wales, 2008–16; *b* 24 April 1949; *s* of late His Honour John Desmond Seys-Llewellyn and Hilda Elaine (*née* Porcher); *m* 1975, Helen Mary Manson; two *s* two *d*. *Educ:* King's Sch., Chester; Jesus Coll., Oxford (1st cl. Hons Law 1970; BCL 1st cl. Hons 1971). Called to the Bar, Gray's Inn, 1972 (scholarships; Bencher, 2006); Recorder of the Crown Court, Wales and Chester Circuit, 1990–2008. Asst Comr, Parly Boundary Commns for England and Wales, 1991–2008. *Recreations:* sports including rowing (now viewed from river banks), art, music, family man.

**SHACKERLEY, Very Rev. Dr (Albert) Paul;** Dean of Brecon, since 2014; *b* Tredegar, S Wales, 16 Aug. 1956. *Educ:* Chichester Theol Coll.; King's Coll. London (MA 1997); Sheffield Univ. (PhD 2007). Served Royal Army Medical Corps, 1977–80; Church Army Officer, 1980–97; ordained deacon, 1993, priest, 1994; Asst Curate, All Souls, Harlesden, 1993–96; Priest-in-charge, 1996–98, Vicar, 1998–2002, All Saints, Chelmsford; Canon Residentiary, 2002–09, Vice-Dean, 2005–10, Hon. Canon, 2010–14, Sheffield Cathedral; Vicar, Doncaster Minster, 2010–14. *Address:* The Deanery, Cathedral Close, Brecon LD3 9DP.

**SHACKLE, Prof. Christopher,** PhD; FBA 1990; Professor of Modern Languages of South Asia, University of London, 1985–2007, now Emeritus; *b* 4 March 1942; *s* of late Francis Mark Shackle and Diana Margaret Shackle (*née* Harrington, subseq. Thomas); *m* 1st, 1964, Emma Margaret Richmond (marr. diss.); one *s* two *d*; 2nd, 1988, Shahrukh Husain; one *s* one *d*. *Educ:* Haileybury and ISC; Merton College, Oxford (BA 1963); St Antony's College, Oxford (DipSocAnthrop 1965; BLitt 1966); PhD London, 1972. School of Oriental and African Studies, University of London: Fellow in Indian Studies, 1966; Lectr in Urdu and Panjabi, 1969; Reader in Modern Languages of South Asia, 1979; Pro-Dir for Academic Affairs, 1997–2002 (Acting Dir, Jan.–April 2001); Pro-Dir, 2002–03; Res. Prof., 2007–08. British Academy: Mem. Council, 1995–96, 2001–04; Chm., Sect. H3 Oriental and African Studies, 1999–2003. Medal, Royal Asiatic Soc., 2006. Sitara-i-Imtiaz (Pakistan), 2005. *Publications:* Teach Yourself Punjabi, 1972; (with D. J. Matthews) An Anthology of Classical Urdu Love Lyrics, 1972; The Siraiki Language of Central Pakistan, 1976; Catalogue of the Panjabi and Sindhi Manuscripts in the India Office Library, 1977; A Guru Nanak Glossary, 1981; An Introduction to the Sacred Language of the Sikhs, 1983; The Sikhs, 1984; (with D. J. Matthews and S. Husain) Urdu Literature, 1985; (with R. Snell) Hindi and Urdu since 1800, 1990; (with Z. Moir) Ismaili Hymns from South Asia, 1992; (with R. Snell) The Indian Narrative, 1992; (with S. Sperl) Qasida Poetry in Islamic Asia and Africa, 1996; (with J. Majeed) Hali's Musaddas, 1997; (with N. Awde) Treasury of Indian Love Poetry, 1999; (with G. Singh and A. Mandair) Sikh Religion, Culture and Ethnicity, 2001; (with D. Arnold) SOAS Since the Sixties, 2003; (with A. Mandair) Teachings of the Sikh Gurus, 2005; (with L. Lewisohn) Attar and the Persian Sufi Tradition, 2006 (Internat. Book of the Year Award, Iran, 2008); (trans.) Mazhar ul Islam, The Season of Love, Bitter Almonds and Delayed Rains, 2006; (ed and trans.) Bullhe Shah, Sufi Lyrics, 2015; (ed and trans.) Shah Abdul Latif, Risalo, 2018; numerous articles.

**SHACKLETON,** family name of **Baroness Shackleton of Belgravia**.

**SHACKLETON OF BELGRAVIA,** Baroness *cr* 2010 (Life Peer), of Belgravia in the City of Westminster; **Fiona Sara Shackleton,** LVO 2006; Personal Solicitor to Prince William of Wales and Prince Harry of Wales, since 1996; Partner, Payne Hicks Beach, since 2001; *b* 26 May 1956; *d* of late Jonathan Philip Charkham, CBE and Moira Elizabeth Frances Charkham; *m* 1985, Ian Ridgeway Shackleton; two *d*. *Educ:* Francis Holland Sch.; Benenden Sch.; Univ. of Exeter (LLB 1977). Articled Clerk, Herbert Smith, 1978–80; admitted solicitor, 1980; Partner, Brecher & Co., 1981–84; Farrer & Co., 1984–2000 (Partner, 1987–2000); Personal Solicitor to Prince of Wales, 1996–2005. Inaugural Mem., Internat. Acad. of Matrimonial Lawyers, 1986–2016. Mem., Adv. Council, IEA, 2013–. Founding Trustee, Royal Foundn, 2010–17; Trustee, Endowment Fund, ROH, 2013–. Gov., Benenden Sch., 1986–2007. Freeman, City of London, 2019. Hon. LLD Exeter, 2010. *Publications:* (with Olivia Timbs) The Divorce Handbook, 1992. *Recreations:* listening to music, particularly opera, cooking, calligraphy, bridge. *Address:* 10 New Square, Lincoln's Inn, WC2A 3QG. *T:* (020) 7465 4300.
See also Rev. R. A. Charkham.

**SHACKLETON, Margaret;** Principal, Abbots Bromley School, 2017–19; *b* Solihull, 1 Sept. 1969; *d* of Anne Corkery; *m* 1999, Paul Shackleton. *Educ:* Univ. of East Anglia (BA Hons; PGCE). NPQH 2010. Teacher of Hist. and Eng., and Hd of Year, Acle High Sch., 1993–96; Hd of Hist., Pingle Sch., 1997–2001; Asst Headteacher, George Spencer Technology Coll., 2001–07; Dep. Headteacher, 2007–10, Headteacher, 2010–17, Sutton Coldfield Grammar Sch. for Girls. *Recreations:* reading, cinema, theatre, walking with Paul and our dogs in the Yorkshire Dales, watching 'The West Wing'.

**SHADAREVIAN, Paul;** QC 2017; *b* London, 18 July 1958; *s* of Sarkis Shadarevian and Jean Shadarevian (*née* West); *m* 1988, Elizabeth Ann Williams; one *s*, and two step *s*. *Educ:* Univ. of Essex (BA Hons); City Univ. (DipLaw). Sen. Res. Officer, Univ. of Essex, 1981–83; called to the Bar, Gray's Inn, 1984; Partner, Norton Rose, solicitors, 1986–98; in practice as a barrister, specialising in planning and envmtl law, Cornerstone Barristers, 2000–. *Publications:* (Ed.) Butterworths Planning Law Service, 1988–98. *Recreations:* fly fishing, cycling, sailing, drawing, reading. *Address:* Cornerstone Barristers, 2–3 Gray's Inn Square, WC1R 5JH. *E:* ps@cornerstonebarristers.com.

**SHADBOLT, Sir Nigel (Richard),** Kt 2013; PhD; FRS 2017; CEng, FREng; CPsychol; Professorial Research Fellow in Computer Science, University of Oxford, since 2015; Principal, Jesus College, Oxford, since 2015; Chairman and Co-Founder, Open Data Institute, London, since 2012; *b* 9 April 1956; *s* of Douglas William Robert and Audrey Shadbolt; *m* 1992, Beverly Saunders; one *s* one *d*. *Educ:* Univ. of Newcastle upon Tyne (BA 1st cl. Hons Philosophy and Psychol.); Univ. of Edinburgh (PhD Artificial Intelligence 1983). CPsychol 1990; CITP 2004; CEng 2005, FREng 2006. Res. Fellow, Univ. of Edinburgh, 1982–83; University of Nottingham: Lectr, 1983–90; Reader, 1990–92; Allan Standen Prof. of Intelligent Systems, 1992–99; University of Southampton: Prof. of Artificial Intelligence, 2000–15; Dep. Hd, Sch. of Electronics and Computer Sci., 2000–11; Hd, Web and Internet Sci. Gp, 2011–15; Vis. Prof., 2015–. Chief Technol. Officer, 2006–10, Chief Scientific Officer, 2010–11, Garlik Ltd. UK Information Advr, 2009–10; Chairman: Local Public Data Panel, DCLG, 2010; MiData Prog., BIS, 2011–16. Member: Public Sector Transparency Bd, 2010; Sci. Adv. Bd, Home Office, 2010–; Res. Sector Transparency Bd, DoH, 2012–; Health and Social Care Transparency Panel; Inf. Economy Council, BIS, 2013–16. Dir, World Wide Web Foundn, 2009–13; Dir and Trustee, Web Science Trust, 2009–. FBCS 2002 (Vice Pres., 2003–05; Dep. Pres., 2005–06; Pres., 2006–07). Hon. DSc Nottingham, 2011. *Publications:* (jtly) POP-11 Programming for Artificial Intelligence, 1987; Research and Development in Expert Systems VI, 1989; (jtly) Advances in Knowledge Acquisition, 1996; (jtly) Knowledge Engineering and Management, 2000; (jtly) The Spy in the Coffee Machine: the end of privacy as we know it, 2008; (with Roger Hampson) The Digital Ape, 2018; over 500 articles on facets of artificial intelligence, psychology, web science, open data and computing. *Recreations:* my family, sailing, reading, collecting - ranging from space memorabilia to fossils! *Address:* Jesus College, Turl Street, Oxford OX1 3DW.

**SHAFER, Prof. Byron Edwin,** PhD; Glenn B. and Cleone Orr Hawkins Professor of Political Science, University of Wisconsin, Madison, since 2001; *b* 8 Jan. 1947; *s* of Byron Henry Shafer and Doris Marguerite (*née* Von Bergen); *m* 1981, Wanda K. Green; one *s*. *Educ:* Yale Univ. (BA Magna Cum Laude, Deptl Hons in Pol Sci. with Excep. Dist. 1968); Univ. of California at Berkeley (PhD Pol Sci. 1979). Resident Scholar, Russell Sage Foundn, USA, 1977–84; Associate Prof. of Pol Sci., Florida State Univ., 1984–85; Andrew W. Mellon Prof. of American Govt, Univ. of Oxford, 1985–2001; Fellow, 1985–2001, now Emeritus, and Actg Warden, 2000–01, Nuffield Coll., Oxford. John G. Winant Vis. Prof. of American Govt, Univ. of Oxford, 2015. Editor, The Forum: a Jl of Applied Res. in Contemporary Politics, 2007–. Hon. MA Oxford, 1985. E. E. Schattschneider Prize, 1980, Franklin L. Burdette Prize, 1990, Jack L. Walker Award, 1997, Amer. Pol Sci. Assoc.; V. O. Key Award, Southern Pol Sci. Assoc., 2007. *Publications:* Presidential Politics, 1980; Quiet Revolution: the struggle for the Democratic Party and the shaping of post-reform politics, 1983; Bifurcated Politics: evolution and reform in the National Party Convention, 1988; Is America Different?, 1991; The End of Realignment?: interpreting American electoral eras, 1991; The Two Majorities: the issue context of modern American politics, 1995; Postwar Politics in the G-7, 1996; Present Discontents: American politics in the very late twentieth century, 1997; Partisan Approaches to Postwar American Politics, 1998; Contesting Democracy: substance and structure in American political history 1775–2000, 2001; The State of American Politics, 2002; The Two Majorities and the Puzzle of Modern American Politics, 2003; The End of Southern Exceptionalism, 2006; The American Public Mind: the issue structure of mass politics in the postwar United States, 2010; The American Political Landscape, 2014; The American Political Pattern: stability and change 1932–2016, 2016; The Long War Over Party Structure, 2019; articles in learned jls. *Recreations:* furniture restoration, gardening, livestock management. *Address:* Department of Political Science, University of Wisconsin, 110 North Hall, 1050 Bascom Mall, Madison, WI 53706, USA.

**SHAFFER, Elinor Sophia,** PhD; FBA 1995; Senior Research Fellow, School of Advanced Study, Institute of Modern Languages Research (formerly Institute of Germanic Studies, then Institute of Germanic and Romance Studies), University of London, since 1998 (Fellow, 1997–98); *b* 6 April 1935; *d* of Vernon Cecil Stoneman and Helene Dorothy Stoneman (*née* Nieschlag); *m* 1964, Brian M. Shaffer; two *s*. *Educ:* Chicago Univ. (BA 1954); St Hilda's Coll., Oxford (BA 1958; MA 1962); PhD Columbia Univ., NY, 1966; MA Cantab 1968. Fellow, Columbia Univ., 1961–63; Instr, Dept of English, Univ. of Calif, Berkeley, 1963–64; Res. Fellow, Clare Hall, Cambridge, 1968–71; Lectr, 1971–77, Reader in English and Comparative Lit., 1977–97, UEA. Visiting Professor: Brown Univ., 1983–84; Zurich Univ., 1986; Stanford Univ., 1988; Vis. Lectr, Free Univ., Berlin, 1979; Study Fellow, ACLS, 1971; Leverhulme Fellowship, 1976; Research Fellow: Humanities Res. Centre, ANU, 1982; Humanities Res. Inst., Univ. of Calif, 1991; Dist. Fellow, Eur. Humanities Res. Centre, Oxford, 1995–; Vis. Fellow, All Souls Coll., Oxford, 1996; Hon. Prof., UCL, 2013–. Editor: Comparative Criticism, 1979–2004; inaugural issue (with A. Brady), 2004, special issue on reception studies, 2006, Comparative Critical Studies; Series Editor, The Reception of British and Irish Authors in Europe (contrib. preface and/or introduction to all vols), 1997–. Hon. Dr Bucharest, 2013. *Publications:* 'Kubla Khan' and The Fall of Jerusalem: the mythological basis of Biblical criticism and secular literature 1770–1880, 1975; Erewhons of the Eye: Samuel Butler as painter, photographer and art critic, 1988; The Third Culture: literature and science, 1998; (ed jtly and introd.) The Reception of S. T. Coleridge in Europe, 2007; (ed jtly and introd.) The Reception of Charles Darwin in Europe, vols III and IV, 2013; (ed jtly and introd.) The Reception of George Eliot in Europe, 2016; Coleridge's Literary Theory, 2019; (ed) Peter Shaffer, Memoir, 2019; *chapters in*: The Coleridge Connection, 1990; Romanticism and the Sciences, 1990; Aesthetic Illusion: theoretical and historical approaches, 1990; Reflecting Senses: perception and appearance in literature, culture and the arts, 1994; Milton, the Metaphysicals and Romanticism, 1994; Apocalypse Theory and the Ends of the World, 1995; Boydell's Shakespeare Gallery, 1996; Transports: imaginative geographies 1600–1830, 1996; (contrib.) Oxford Encyclopedia of Aesthetics, 1998, 2nd edn 2014; The Cambridge History of Literary Criticism, vol. V, Romanticism, 2000; Coleridge and the Science of Life, 2001; Mapping Lives: the uses of biography, 2001; Goethe in the English-speaking World, 2002; (contrib.) Oxford Companion to Photography, 2003; Anglo-German Affinities and Antipathies in the Nineteenth Century, 2004; Samuel Butler: Victorian against the grain, 2007; Oxford Handbook of Coleridge, 2008; contrib. to Oxford DNB; catalogues for exhibns about Samuel Butler, 1989, 2002; many lectures, reviews and contribs to learned jls. *Recreations:* theatre, travelling, photography, wine. *Address:* 9 Cranmer Road, Cambridge CB3 9BL.

**SHAFIK, Dame Nemat, (Minouche),** DBE 2015; DPhil; Director, London School of Economics and Political Science, since 2017; *b* 13 Aug. 1962; *d* of Dr Talaat Shafik and Maissa Hamza; *m* 2002, Dr Raffael Jovine; one *s* one *d*, and three step *c*. *Educ:* Univ. of Massachusetts, Amherst (BA *summa cum laude* Pols and Econs 1983); London Sch. of Econs (MSc Econs 1986); St Antony's Coll., Oxford (DPhil Econs 1989). World Bank: joined 1990, as economist in Res. Dept; Country Economist, Central Europe, 1992–94; Dir, Private Sector and Finance, ME and N Africa, 1997–99; Vice-Pres., Private Sector and Infrastructure, 1999–2004; Dir Gen., Country (formerly Regl) Progs, 2004–08, Perm. Sec., 2008–11, DFID; Dep. Man. Dir, IMF, 2011–14; a Dep. Gov. and Mem., Monetary Policy Cttee, Mem., Financial Policy Cttee and Mem., Prudential Regulation Authy, Bank of England, 2014–17. Adjunct Prof., Econs, Georgetown Univ., 1989–94; Vis. Associate Prof., Wharton Business Sch., Univ. of Pennsylvania, 1996. Non-exec. Dir, Mgt Bd DFID, 2002–04. Chairman: Consultative Gp to Assist the Poorest, 1999–2004; Infodev, 1999–2004; Global Water and Sanitation Prog., 1999–2004; Private Participation in Infrastructure Adv. Facility, 1999–2004; Treas., Our Place DC, 2001–04; Bd Mem., Operating Council, Global Alliance for Workers and Communities, 1999–2003. Trustee, British Mus., 2016–. Bd Mem., Middle East Jl, 1996–2002. Hon. Bencher, Middle Temple, 2018. Woman of the Year, GG2, 2009; 100 Women in Finance European Industry Leadership Award, 2019. *Publications:* Reviving Private Investment in Developing Countries, 1992; Globalization Regionalism and Growth, 1996; Challenges Facing Middle Eastern and North African Countries: alternative futures, 1998; Prospects for Middle East and North African Economies: from boom to bust and back?, 1998; articles in Jl of Develt Economics, Oxford Economic Papers, World Develt, Columbia Jl of World Business, Middle East Jl. *Address:* London School of Economics and Political Science, Houghton Street, WC2A 2AE.

**SHAFTESBURY,** 12th Earl of, *cr* 1672; **Nicholas Edmund Anthony Ashley-Cooper;** Bt 1622; Baron Ashley 1661; Baron Cooper 1672; DL; *b* 3 June 1979; *yr s* of 10th Earl of Shaftesbury and of Christina Eva (*née* Montan); *S* brother, 2005; *m* 2010, Dinah Streifeneder; one *s* two *d*. *Educ:* Eton; Manchester Univ.; London Business Sch. (MBA). DL Dorset, 2019. *Publications:* (jtly) The Rebirth of an English Country House: St Giles House, 2018. *Heir: s* Anthony Francis Wolfgang Ashley-Cooper, Lord Ashley, *b* 24 Jan. 2011.

**SHAH, Akhil;** QC 2010; *b* Nairobi, Nov. 1965; *s* of Jayu Shah and Sibylle Shah; *m* 1993, Sarah Anderson; one *s* one *d*. *Educ:* Haberdashers' Aske's Sch., Elstree; St John's Coll., Cambridge (BA 1989). Called to the Bar, Inner Temple, 1990; in practice as a barrister, specialising in commercial law, 1990–. *Publications:* (jtly) Carriage by Air, 2000; (contrib.) Bullen and Leake and Jacobs Precedents of Pleadings, 15th edn 2009 to 18th edn 2015; (consultant ed.) Halsbury's Laws of England, vol. 2, Aviation, 5th edn 2017. *Recreations:* cricket, tennis, travel, music. *Address:* Fountain Court, Temple, EC4Y 9DH. *T:* (020) 7583 3335. *Club:* MCC.

**SHAH, Bharat Chimanlal;** Chairman: ABS/BCS Business Consultants, since 2001; Nijjar Holdings Ltd, since 2010; Alderbrooke Ltd, since 2015; *b* Jinja, Uganda, 8 Dec. 1953; *s* of Chimanlal Shankerlal Shah and Lalitaben Chimanlal Shah; *m* 1982, Asha Bharat Shah (marr. diss.); one *s* one *d*. *Educ:* FCCA 1987. Eastman Kodak Company, 1973–2001: Finance Dir, EMEA Reg., Kodak Consumer Imaging, 1992–95; Chm. and Man. Dir, Kodak Processing Cos, 1995–97; Man. Dir, UK, Ire., Nordic and Baltics, Kodak Consumer Imaging, 1997–2000; CEO, EMEA Reg., Kodak Consumer Imaging, and Vice Pres., Eastman Kodak Co., 2000–01. Chairman: Picdar Gp, 2002–05; West Bromwich Building Soc. Staff Retirement Scheme, 2006–; Sure Gp, 2008–10; Smart-Sal Ltd, 2012–16; Places for People Pension Trustee Ltd, 2016–18; Antler Ltd, 2017; non-executive Director: West Bromwich Building Soc., 2004–10; Places for People Gp Ltd, 2010–16; Vice Pres., EMEA, SVP Worldwide, 2006; Ind. Mem., Audit Cttee, Local Pensions Partnership, 2016–18. Dep. Chm., Audit Commn, 2007–15. Ind. Mem., Remuneration Cttee, ACCA, 2005–06. Trustee, Paul Strickland Scanner Centre, 2010–14. *Recreations:* family, dining out, tennis, gym, travelling.

**SHAH, Dipesh Jayantilal,** OBE 2007; Chairman: ANHD International Advisory Services, since 2007; Notting Hill Genesis (formerly Genesis Housing Association), since 2017; a Crown Estate Commissioner, since 2011; *b* 11 May 1953; *s* of Jayantilal S. Shah and Sumati J. Shah; *m* 1983, Annie Therese Duchesne; one *s* one *d*. *Educ:* Warwick Univ. (BA Hons Econs); Birkbeck Coll., London (MSc Distn Econs); Harvard Business Sch. (Prog. for Mgt Develt); Templeton Coll., Oxford (Strategic Leadership Prog.). Various roles in planning, Shell-Mex and BP, 1974–75; BP plc, 1976–2002: Chief Economist, BP Oil UK, 1977–79; Commercial Dir, Natural Resources, NZ, 1985–87; Man. Dir and CEO, BP Solar Internat., 1991–97; Chief Exec., Forties Pipeline System, and Gen. Manager, Grangemouth, 1998–99; Global Hd, Acquisitions and Divestments, 2000–02; Chief Exec., and Bd Mem., UKAEA, 2003–06. Non-exec. Chm., IT Power Ltd, 2002–05; Chairman: Viridian Gp plc, 2005–06 (non-exec. Dir, 2003–04); Hg Capital Renewable Power Partners LLP, 2002–08; Jetion Holdings Ltd, 2007–08; non-executive Director: Babcock Internat. Gp plc, 1999–2009; Kemble Gp of Cos, 2007–14; Thames Water Gp of Cos, 2007–17; Lloyd's of London Franchise Bd, 2008–10; JKX Oil and Gas plc, 2008–15 (Sen. Ind. Dir, 2012–15); Cannacord Genuity Inc. (formerly Canaccord Financial Inc.), 2012–; non-exec. Dir and Sen. Ind. Dir, Equus Petroleum plc, 2013–15. Mem., Renewable Energy Adv. Cttee, DTI, 1994–2002. Bd Advr, Crown Estate, 2009–10. Chm., European Photovoltaics Industry Assoc., Brussels, 1992–97; Mem., UK Panel, European Awards for Envmt, 2000. Mem. Bd and Chm., Investment Cttee, EU Marguerite Fund, 2010–, Marguerite Fund II, 2017–. Trustee, British Youth Opera, 2010–. Gov., Merchant Taylors' Sch., 2009–. MInstD; FRSA. *Recreations:* sports, travel (with family), reading. *Club:* Harvard Business School Alumni (London).

**SHAH, Hetan;** Executive Director, Royal Statistical Society, since 2011; *b* London, 1975; *s* of Vinod Depar Parbat Shah and Usha Dharamshi Pancha Shah; *m* 2007, Mahua Nandi; one *s* one *d*. *Educ:* Langdon Comprehensive Sch.; Wadham Coll., Oxford (BA PPE 1996); Nottingham Law Sch. (Postgrad. DipLaw 1998; Legal Practice course, 1999); Birkbeck, Univ. of London (MA Contemp. Hist. and Politics 2002; Postgrad. Cert. Econs 2003). Chief Exec., Think Global, 2007–11. Vis Prof., Policy Inst., KCL, 2017–. Dep. Chair, Ada Lovelace Inst., 2018–. Hon. Vice Pres., Geographical Assoc., 2011–18. Trustee, Higher Educn Statistics Agency, 2014–16. Trustee: Friends Provident Foundn, 2015– (Chm., 2016–); St George's House Trust (Windsor Castle), 2019–. *Address:* Royal Statistical Society, 12 Errol Street, EC1Y 8LX.

**SHAH, Monisha;** Managing Director, Hogerty Hill Ltd, since 2010; Chair, Rose Bruford College of Theatre and Performance, since 2015; *b* Bombay, India, 11 Sept. 1969; *d* of Amrit Shamji Shah and Rekha Shah (*née* Pavagadhi); partner, Mark Young; one *s*. *Educ:* Univ. of Bombay (BA Pol Sci. 1989); Sch. of Oriental and African Studies, Univ. of London (MSc Politics of Asia and Africa 1991); London Business Sch. (MBA 2002). Dir, BBC

World India, 2001–10. BBC Worldwide Bd Rep., Radio Mid-Day West, India, 2006–10; Dir, Emerging Markets, 2005–08, Dir, Developed and Emerging Markets, EMEA, 2008–10, BBC Worldwide; Dir, Worldwide Media, India, 2008–10. Member: Cttee on Standards in Public Life, 2015–; Content Bd, Ofcom, 2017–; Bd, Office for Students, 2018–; QC Selection Panel, 2018–. Trustee: Tate, 2007–15; Nat. Gall., 2013–15; Foundling Mus., 2014–16; Art Fund, 2017–; Donmar Warehouse, 2018–; Mem., Adv. Council, Tate Modern 2008–17; non-executive Director: Tate Enterprises, 2008–15; Next MediaWorks plc, 2012–19; Imagen Ltd (formerly Cambridge Imaging Systems), 2015–18. Young Global Leader, World Econ. Forum, 2009. *Recreations:* art, television, books, dogs, family. *Address:* Hogerty Hill, Lunghurst Road, Woldingham, Caterham, Surrey CR3 7HE. *E:* hogerty.hill@live.co.uk.

**SHAH, Naseem Akhter;** MP for Bradford West, since 2015 (Lab, 2015–16 and since 2016, Ind, 2016); *b* 13 Nov. 1973; *d of* Zoora Shah; two *s* one *d*. Carer for children with disabilities; advocate for women with disabilities and their carers; work for Samaritans; work with NHS in commng services; Chm., Sharing Voices Bradford, mental health charity, 2012–15. Mem., Home Affairs Cttee, H of C, 2015–17, 2017–18. *Address:* House of Commons, SW1A 0AA.

**SHAH, Navin;** Member (Lab) Brent and Harrow, London Assembly, Greater London Authority, since 2008; *b* Ahmedabad, India; *m* Rekha; one *s* one *d*. *Educ:* Acad. of Architects, Bombay; University Coll. London. Formerly in private practice as architect and develt planner. Mem. (Lab) Harrow LBC, 1994–2014 (Leader, 2004–06). Contested (Lab) Harrow E, 2017. *Address:* Greater London Authority, City Hall, Queen's Walk, SE1 2AA.

**SHAH, Samir,** CBE 2019 (OBE 2000); DPhil; Chief Executive, Juniper, since 2006 (Managing Director, 1998–2006); *b* 29 Jan. 1952; *s of* Amrit Shah and Uma Bakaya (*née* Chaudhary); *m* 1983, Belkis Bhegani; one *s*. *Educ:* Latymer Upper Sch.; Univ. of Hull (BSc Hons 1973); St Catherine's Coll., Oxford (DPhil 1978). Res. Officer, Home Office, 1978–79; London Weekend Television, 1979–87: Producer, Eastern Eye, 1982–84; Editor: Credo, 1984–86; The London Programme, 1986–87; British Broadcasting Corporation, 1987–98: Head: Current Affairs, TV, 1987–94; Political Programming, TV and Radio, 1994–98. Non-exec. Dir, BBC, 2007–10. Special Prof., Centre for Study of Post Conflict Cultures, Univ. of Nottingham, 2006–18; Vis. Prof. of Creative Media, Oxford Univ., 2019. Chairman: Runnymede Trust, 1999–2009; Screen West Midlands, 2009–11; Geffrye Mus., 2014–; Trustee: Med. Foundn for Victims of Torture, 2004–06; V&A Mus., 2005–15 (Dep. Chair, 2013–15); Reprieve, 2014–; BAFTA, 2015–17. FRTS 2002; FRSA 2008. *Recreations:* Manchester United, movies, music. *Address:* Juniper, 52 Lant Street, SE1 1RB. *T:* (020) 7407 9292. *Clubs:* Groucho, Chelsea Arts.

**SHAIKH, Dr Abdul Hafeez;** General Partner, New Silk Route Partners LLC, New York, 2006–10 and since 2013; *b* Jacobabad, 26 Dec. 1954; *s of* Abdul Nabi Shaikh and Afroze Nabi Shaikh; *m* Nadene Nichols; three *d*. *Educ:* Boston Univ. (PhD Econs). On faculty staff, Harvard Univ., 1989–92; Country Hd, Saudi Arabia, World Bank, 1992–2000; Minister for Finance, Planning and Develt, Sindh, 2000–02; Mem. (Pakistan People), Senate of Pakistan; Chm., Senate Cttee on WTO; Federal Minister for Investment and Privatization, 2003–06; Mem., Senate of Pakistan, 2010–13; Advr to Prime Minister of Pakistan on Finance, Revenue, Econ. Affairs, Stats, and Planning and Develt, 2010; Minister for Finance, Revenue, Econ. Affairs, Stats, and Planning and Develt, 2010–13.

**SHAKER, Mohamed Ibrahim,** PhD; Order of the Arab Republic of Egypt (Second Grade), 1976; Order of Merit (Egypt) (First Grade), 1983; Chairman, Egyptian Council for Foreign Affairs, 1999–2003 and 2009–15 (Vice Chairman, 2003–09); Chairman of Trustees: Sawiris Foundation for Social Development, since 2001; Magdi Yacoub Foundation for Heart Research, since 2008; National Centre for Middle East Studies, since 2006; *b* 16 Oct. 1933; *s of* Mahmoud Shaker and Zeinab Wasef; *m* 1960, Mona El Kony; one *s* one *d*. *Educ:* Cairo Univ. (Lic. en Droit); Inst. of Internat. Studies, Geneva (PhD). Representative of Dir-Gen. of IAEA to UN, New York, 1982–83; Amb. and Dep. Perm. Rep. of Egypt to UN, New York, 1984–86; Amb. to Austria, 1986–88; Hd of Dept of W Europe, Min. of For. Affairs, Cairo, 1988; Ambassador of the Arab Republic of Egypt to UK, 1988–97. President: Third Review Conf. of the Parties to the Treaty on Non-Proliferation of Nuclear Weapons, Geneva, 1985; UN Conf. for the Promotion of Internat. Co-operation in the Peaceful Uses of Nuclear Energy, Geneva, 1987; Member: UN Sec. General's Adv. Bd on Disarmament, 1993–98 (Chm., 1995); Core Gp of Prog. for Promotion of Non-Proliferation of Nuclear Weapons, 1987–97; Court on Values, Arab Rep. of Egypt, 2004–06. Advr, Regl Information Technol. and Software Engrg Centre, Cairo, 1997–. *Publications:* The Nuclear Non-Proliferation Treaty: origin and implementation 1959–1979, 1980; The Evolving Regime of Nuclear Non-proliferation, 2006; several articles. *Recreations:* tennis, music. *Address:* 9 El Aziz Osman Street, Zamalek, Cairo, Egypt; Regional Information Technology and Software Engineering Centre, 11A Hassan Sabry Street, Zamalek, Cairo, Egypt; Egyptian Council for Foreign Affairs, Osman Towers No 2, 12th Floor, Kornish El Nile, Maadi, Cairo, Egypt; Magdi Yacoub Foundation, 22 Montazah Street, Zamalek, Cairo, Egypt. *Clubs:* Royal Automobile; Guizera Sporting (Cairo).

**SHAKERLEY, Sir Nicholas Simon Adam,** 7th Bt *cr* 1838, of Somerford Park, Cheshire; *b* 20 Dec. 1963; *s of* Sir Geoffrey Adam Shakerley, 6th Bt and Virginia Elizabeth (*née* Maskell); *S father,* 2012; *m* 2018, Caroline Rosamund McAfee, *d of* late Alexander Forrest Harper. *Heir: b* Jonathan Peter Shakerley [*b* 9 Feb. 1966; *m* 1995, Meii-Jung, (Sonia) Sung; two *d*].

**SHAKESPEARE, John William Richmond,** CMG 1985; LVO 1968; HM Diplomatic Service, retired; *b* 11 June 1930; *s of* late Dr W. G. Shakespeare; *m* 1955, Lalage Ann, *d of* late S. P. B. Mais; three *s* one *d*. *Educ:* Winchester; Trinity Coll., Oxford (Scholar, MA). 2nd Lieut Irish Guards, 1949–50. Lectr in English, Ecole Normale Supérieure, Paris, 1953–54; on editorial staff, Times Educational Supplement, 1955–56 and Times, 1956–59; entered Diplomatic Service, 1959; Private Sec. to Ambassador in Paris, 1959–61; FO, 1961–63; 1st Sec., Phnom-Penh, 1963–64; 1st Sec., Office of Pol Adviser to C-in-C Far East, Singapore, 1964–66; Dir of British Information Service in Brazil, 1966–69; FCO, 1969–73; Counsellor and Consul-Gen., Buenos Aires, 1973–75; Chargé d'Affaires, Buenos Aires, 1976–77; Head of Mexico and Caribbean Dept, FCO, 1977–79; Counsellor, Lisbon, 1979–83; Ambassador to Peru, 1983–87, to Kingdom of Morocco, 1987–90. Mem., Sensitivity Review Unit, FCO, 1991–2002. Chm., Morgan Grenfell Latin American Cos Trust, 1994–2000; Latin Amer. Consultant, Clyde & Co., 1991–2002. Chm., Anglo-Portuguese Soc., 1994–97; Mem., Exec. Cttee, S Atlantic Council, 1998–2013. Hon. Vice Pres., Anglo-Peruvian Soc., 1991–. Officer, Order of Southern Cross (Brazil), 1968; Commander, Alaouite Order (Morocco), 1990. *Recreations:* gardening, music (light), travel. *Address:* Townsend Wood, Sutton Mandeville, Salisbury SP3 5ND. *Club:* Garrick.
See also N. W. R. Shakespeare.

**SHAKESPEARE, Nicholas William Richmond;** novelist and biographer; *b* 3 March 1957; *s of* J. W. R. Shakespeare, *qv*; *m* 1999, Gillian Johnson; two *s*. *Educ:* Dragon Sch., Oxford; Winchester Coll.; Magdalene Coll., Cambridge (MA English). BBC TV, 1980–84; Dep. Arts and Literary Editor, The Times, 1985–87; Literary Editor: London Daily News, 1987–88; Daily Telegraph, 1988–91; Sunday Telegraph, 1989–91; film critic, Illustrated London News, 1989; Chief book reviewer, Daily Telegraph, 2009–16. Associate Mem., Exeter Coll., Oxford, 2012–; Vis. Fellow, All Souls Coll., Oxford, 2016. Work for TV includes: writer and narrator: The Evelyn Waugh Trilogy; Mario Vargas Llosa; Iquitos; For the Sake of the Children (Christopher Award, USA); Return to the Sacred Ice; In the Footsteps of Bruce Chatwin; The Private Dirk Bogarde (BAFTA and RTS awards, 2001); presenter, Cover to Cover. Patron, Anita Goulden Trust, 2000–. FRSL 1999. Borges Lect., Anglo-Argentine Soc., 2010. Hon. Fellow, Australian Acad. of Humanities, 2018. *Publications:* The Men who would be King, 1984; Londoners, 1986; The Vision of Elena Silves, 1989 (Somerset Maugham Award, Betty Trask Award, 1990); The High Flyer, 1993; The Dancer Upstairs, 1995 (American Liby Assoc. Award, 1997; adapted for film, 2002); Bruce Chatwin, 1999; Snowleg, 2004; In Tasmania, 2004 (Tasmania Book Prize, 2007); Secrets of the Sea, 2007; Inheritance, 2010; (ed with Elizabeth Chatwin) Under the Sun: the letters of Bruce Chatwin, 2010; Priscilla: the hidden life of an Englishwoman in wartime France, 2013; Stories from Other Places, 2015; Six Minutes in May: how Churchill unexpectedly became Prime Minister, 2017. *Recreations:* travelling, drawing. *Address:* Miles Cottage, Sutton Mandeville, Wilts SP3 5LX. *Club:* Beefsteak.

**SHAKESPEARE, Stephan;** Co-Founder, 2000, and Chief Executive Officer, YouGov plc; Founder, PoliticsHome.com; Owner, ConservativeHome.com; *b* Mönchengladbach, 9 April 1957; *s of* Karl-Heinz Kukowski and Lina Kukowski; *m* 1984, Rosamund Shakespeare; two *d*. *Educ:* Christ's Hospital, Horsham; St Peter's Coll., Oxford (BA Eng. Lang. and Lit.). Chm., Data Strategy Bd, BIS. Trustee, NPG, 2012–16. *Recreations:* art, music, Arsenal. *Address:* YouGov plc, 50 Featherstone Street, EC1Y 8RT. *E:* Stephan.Shakespeare@YouGov.com.

**SHAKESPEARE, Sir Thomas William,** 3rd Bt *cr* 1942, of Lakenham, City of Norwich; FBA 2018; (known professionally as Prof. Tom Shakespeare); Professor of Disability Research, London School of Hygiene and Tropical Medicine, since 2018; *b* 11 May 1966; *er s of* Sir William Geoffrey Shakespeare, 2nd Bt and of Susan Mary Shakespeare (*née* Raffel); *S father,* 1996; one *d* by Lucy Ann Broadhead; one *s* by Judy Brown; *m* 2002, Caroline Emily (*née* Bowditch) (marr. diss. 2018). *Educ:* Pembroke Coll., Cambridge (BA (Hons) 1987); King's Coll., Cambridge (PhD 1994). Printer, Cambridge Free Press, 1987–88; Administrator, The Works Theatre Co-operative, 1988–89; Lectr, Univ. of Sunderland, 1993–95; Res. Fellow, Univ. of Leeds, 1996–99; Newcastle University: Dir of Outreach, 1999–2005; Res. Fellow, Policy, Ethics and Life Scis Res. Inst., 2005–08; NESTA Fellow, 2005–08; Consultant, 2008–10, Tech. Officer, 2010–13, WHO; Sen. Lectr, 2013–16, Prof. of Disability Res., 2016–18, UEA. Mem., Working Party on the ethics of res. on genes and behaviour, 2000–02, Mem. Council, 2014–, Nuffield Council on Bioethics. Vice-Chair, Gateshead Voluntary Orgns Council, 1993–96; Chair, Northern Disability Arts Forum, 1993–95. Vice-Chm., Northern Arts Bd, 1998–99 (Mem., 1995–99 and 2000–02); Member: Tyneside Cinema Bd, 1995–97; Arts Council England, 2004–10 (Chm., NE Regl Arts Council, 2004–10). Vice Chair, Light for the World, 2018– (Chair, 2016–18); Trustee, Equal Lives, 2013–. *Publications:* (jtly) The Sexual Politics of Disability, 1996; The Disability Reader, 1998; (jtly) Exploring Disability, 1999; Help, 2000; (jtly) Disability and Postmodernism, 2002; (jtly) Genetic Politics, 2002; Disability Rights and Wrongs, 2006; Disability Rights and Wrongs Revisited, 2013; Disability Research Today, 2015; Disability: the basics, 2017; various articles in academic jls. *Recreations:* arts and culture, gardening, cooking. *Heir: b* James Douglas Geoffrey Shakespeare [*b* 12 Feb. 1971; *m* 1996, Alison (*née* Lusby)]. *Address:* 2 Kilner House, Clayton Street, SE11 5SE; London School of Hygiene and Tropical Medicine, Keppel Street, WC1E 7HT.

**SHALIT, Jonathan Sigmund,** OBE 2014; Chairman, InterTalent Rights Group (formerly ROAR and Cole Kitchenn), since 1994; *b* London, 17 April 1962; *s of* David Manuel Shalit and Sophie Shalit, JP (*née* Gestetner); *m* 2010, Katrina; two step *d*. *Educ:* City of London Sch. Account Manager, Saatchi and Saatchi Gp, 1981–87; Managing Director: ROAR Global (formerly Shalit Global), 1994–; FAB, 1997–2004. Hon. Prof., Henley Business Sch., Univ. of Reading, 2012. Trustee: REGAIN the Trust for Sports Tetraplegics, 1992–2010; Chicken Shed Theatre Co., 1996–; Variety Club of GB, 2005– (Vice-Pres., 2005–). Freeman, City of London, 1987; Liveryman, Coachmakers' and Coach Harness Makers' Co., 1987. Mem., BAFTA. Hon. Dr 2017. *Recreations:* sailing, music, theatre, family, television, film. *Address:* InterTalent Group, InterTalent House, 46 Charlotte Street, W1T 2GS. *E:* jonathan@intertalentgroup.com. *Clubs:* Annabel's, Ivy, Royal Automobile, Groucho, Soho House, 5 Hertford St, Arts.

**SHALLICE, Prof. Timothy,** PhD; FRS 1996; FBA 2013; Professor of Psychology, University College London, 1990–2005, now Emeritus (Director, Institute of Cognitive Neuroscience, 1996–2004); *b* 11 July 1940; *s of* Sidney Edgar Shallice and Doris Dronsfield Shallice; *m* 1987, Maria Anna Tallandini. *Educ:* St John's Coll., Cambridge (BA 1961); University Coll. London (PhD 1965; Fellow, 2010). Asst Lectr in Psychol., Univ. of Manchester, 1964–65; Lectr in Psychol., UCL, 1966–72; Sen. Res. Fellow in Neuropsychol., Inst. Neurology, London, 1972–77; Scientist, MRC Applied Psychol. Unit, 1978–90. Prof. of Cognitive Neurosci., Scuola Internazionale Superiore di Studi Avanzati, Trieste, 1994–2010. MAE 1996. Founder FMedSci 1998. Hon. Dr: Univ. Libre de Bruxelles, 1992; London Guildhall, 1999; Trinity Coll., Dublin, 2005. President's Award, BPsS, 1991; Mind and Brain Prize, Univ. Torino, 2013; British Acad. Medal, 2013. *Publications:* From Neuropsychology to Mental Structure, 1988; (with D. Plaut) Connectionist Modelling in Cognitive Neuropsychology, 1994; (with R. Cooper) The Organisation of Mind, 2011. *Recreations:* e-mail chess, mountain walking, cinema, theatre. *Address:* Institute of Cognitive Neuroscience, University College London, Gower Street, WC1E 6BT.

**SHAND, His Honour John Alexander Ogilvie;** DL; a Circuit Judge, 1988–2005; *b* 6 Nov. 1942; *s of* late Alexander Shand and Marguerite Marie Shand; *m* 1st, 1965, Patricia Margaret (*née* Toynbee) (marr. diss.); two *s* one *d*; 2nd, 1990, Valerie Jean (*née* Bond). *Educ:* Nottingham High Sch.; Queens' Coll., Cambridge (MA, LLB; Chancellor's Medal for Law 1965); Centre for Reformation and Early Modern Studies, Univ. of Birmingham (MA 2008). Called to the Bar, Middle Temple, 1965 (Harmsworth Scholarship); practised on Midland and Oxford Circuit (Birmingham), 1965–71 and 1973–81 (Dep. Circuit Judge, 1979); a Recorder, 1981–88. Chm. of Industrial Tribunals (Birmingham Reg.), 1981–88. Fellow and Tutor, Queens' Coll., Cambridge, 1971–73. Chancellor: Dio. Southwell, 1981–2004; Dio. Lichfield, 1989–2005 (Licensed Reader, 2014–). Mem., House of Laity, Gen. Synod of C of E, 2010–15. DL Staffs, 1998. *Publications:* (with P. G. Stein) Legal Values in Western Society, 1974; contrib. various articles in Cambridge Law Jl. *Address:* c/o Stafford Combined Court Centre, Victoria Square, Stafford ST16 2QQ. *T:* (01785) 610801.

**SHAND, Lesley Munro;** QC (Scot.) 2005; *b* 9 Feb. 1960; *d of* Alexander Dewar Shand and Isabella Shand (*née* Irving); *m* 1988; two *s* one *d*. *Educ:* Lenzie Acad.; Edinburgh Univ. (LLB Hons; DipLP). Admitted solicitor, 1985; in practice, 1985–89; Advocate, 1990–; ad hoc Advocate Depute, 1995–2000; Sen. Advocate Depute, 2010–13; Mem., Rules Council, Court of Session, 2000–11; Convenor, Standing Sub-Cttee on Reparation, Law Reform

Cttee, Faculty of Advocates, 2013–; Fee-paid Judge, Immigration and Asylum Chamber, 2014–. *Recreations:* reading, cycling, walking. *Address:* Faculty of Advocates, Parliament House, Edinburgh EH1 1RQ. *T:* (0131) 226 5071.

**SHAND, William Stewart,** MD; FRCS, FRCSE; Hon. Consulting Surgeon to St Bartholomew's Hospital and The Royal London Hospital, since 1997; *b* 12 Oct. 1936; *s* of William Paterson Shand and Annabella Kirkland Stewart Shand (*née* Waddell); *m* 1972, (Anne) Caroline Dashwood (*née* Charvet) (*d* 2005); two *s*, and one step *s* two step *d*. *Educ:* Repton Sch.; St John's Coll., Cambridge (BA 1958, MA 1962; MB BChir 1962; MD 1970); Medical Coll. of St Bartholomew's Hosp. LRCP; MRCS; FRCS 1970; FRCSE 1970. Consultant Surgeon: St Bartholomew's, Hackney and Homerton Hosps, London, 1973–96; King Edward VII's Hosp. for Officers, London, 1995–97. Hon. Consultant Surgeon: St Luke's Hosp. for the Clergy, London, 1982–97; St Mark's Hosp. for Diseases of Colon and Rectum, London, 1986–96. Senior Fellow: Assoc. of Surgeons of GB and Ireland, 2001–; Assoc. of Coloproctology of GB and Ireland, 2001–. Penrose May Tutor, 1980–85, Penrose May Teacher, 1985–, RCS. Member: Ct of Examrs, RCS, 1985–91; Bd of Examrs, RCSE, 1986–96; Examiner: Professional and Linguistic Assessment Bd for GMC, 1983–98; Univ. of London, 1990–96; Univ. of Liverpool, 1991–96. FRSocMed 1967. Fellow: Hunterian Soc., 1971–; Harveian Soc. of London, 1972–. Vice-Pres., Phyllis Tuckwell Hospice, Farnham, 2001– (Trustee, 1995–2000). Governor: Med. Coll. of St Bartholomew's Hosp., 1987–96; Sutton's Hosp. in Charterhouse, 1989–2009; BPMF, 1991–96. Member: Ct of Assts, Soc. of Apothecaries, 1990 (Master, 2004–05); Ct of Assts, Barbers' Co., 1992 (Master, 2001–02); Travelling Surgical Soc. of GB and NI, 1982 (Pres., 1994–97). Member: Cambridge Med. Graduates' Club, subseq. Cambridge Graduates' Med. Soc., then Cambridge Med. Graduates' Soc. (Pres., 1993–2006); Hon. Med. Panel, Artists' Gen. Benevolent Instn, 1979–. Chm., Homerton Hosp. Art Work Cttee, 1988–92; Hon. Curator of Ceramics, RCS, 1980–. Reader, C of E, 1996–. NACF Award, 1992. *Publications:* (jtly) The Art of Dying: the story of two sculptors' residency in a hospice, 1989; contribs to books and articles in jls on surgery, colorectal disease, chronic inflammatory bowel disease in children and oncology. *Recreations:* maker of stained glass windows, water-colour painting, ski-ing, dry-fly fishing, walking. *Address:* 14a St George's Square, Stamford, Lincs PE9 2BN. *T:* (01780) 239541.

**SHAND SMITH, Rev. Lewis;** Chief Ombudsman, and Chief Executive, Ombudsman Services, 2009–18; *b* Lerwick, 16 March 1952; *s* of Lewis Shand Smith and Jessie Shand Smith (*née* Marshall); *m* 1974, Annette Bald; one *d*. *Educ:* Anderson Educnl Inst., Lerwick; Aberdeen Univ. (MA Hons); Edinburgh Univ. (BD); Edinburgh Episcopal Theol Coll. (GOE); Inst. of Dirs (Cert. Co. Direction). Ordained deacon, 1977, priest, 1978; Priest-in-charge, Holy Trinity, Motherwell and St Andrew, Wishaw, 1979–80; Officiating Chaplain, RAF Saxavord, 1980–95; Rector: St Magnus Episcopal Ch, Lerwick, 1980–2000; St John's Episcopal Ch, Dumfries, 2000–05; Canon, St Andrew's Cath., Aberdeen, 1993–2000; Dep. Ombudsman, Scottish Public Services, 2002–07; leadership coach, Potent 6, 2007–09. Non-executive Director: UHI Ltd, 1993–97; Shetland Towage, 1994–99; Scottish Homes, 1999–2002. Convener, Shetland Is Council, 1994–99 (Mem., 1990–99). Vice-Pres., COSLA, 1998–99. Mem., Eur. Cttee of the Regions, 1998–99. Chm., Ombudsman Assoc., 2014–16. Pres., Eur. Nat. Energy Ombudsman, 2014–18. Chair: Rev. of Consumer Rights in Private Rented Sector, 2018; Funeral Services Consumer Standards Rev., 2019; Implementation Steering Gp, Dispute Resolution Service for UK Finance, 2019; Member: Scottish Govt Expert Gp on Mediation, 2018–19; Western Power Networks Consumer Engagement Gp, 2019. Convener, Home Mission Cttee, Scottish Episcopal Ch, 2001–10. Chair: Shetland Cell., 1990–94; Sullam Voe Assoc. Ltd, 1994–99. Chair and Trustee, Shetland Churches Council Trust, 1986–95; Trustee: Shetland Charitable Trust, 1990–99; Lerwick Harbour Trust, 1994–99. FRSA 1999. *Recreations:* gym, cooking, ballet, theatre. *Address:* Sandvive Cottage, Bigton, Shetland ZE2 9JA. *E:* lewis@shand.smith.com. *Club:* Royal Air Force.

**SHANKS, Duncan Faichney,** RSA 1990 (ARSA 1972); RGI 1982; RSW 1987; artist; *b* 30 Aug. 1937; *s* of Duncan Faichney Shanks and Elizabeth Clark; *m* 1966, Una Brown Gordon. *Educ:* Glasgow School of Art; DA (Post Diploma) 1960. Travelling scholarship to Italy, 1961; part-time teacher, Glasgow Sch. of Art, 1963–79; full-time artist, 1979–. *Recreation:* classical and contemporary music.

**SHANKS, Fiona;** *see* Shanks, W. F.

**SHANKS, Ian Alexander,** OBE 2012; PhD; FRS 1984; FREng; FRSE; Vice President, Physical and Engineering Sciences (formerly Head of Engineering Sciences), Unilever plc, 2001–03; *b* 22 June 1948; *s* of Alexander and Isabella Affleck (*née* Beaton); *m* 1971, Janice Smillie Coulter; one *d*. *Educ:* Dumbarton Acad.; Glasgow Univ. (BSc); Glasgow Coll. of Technology (PhD). CEng, MIEE 1983, FIET (FIEE 1990); FREng (FEng 1992). Projects Manager, Scottish Colorfoto Labs, 1970–72; Research Student, Portsmouth Polytechnic, 1972–73 (liquid crystal displays); RSRE, Malvern, 1973–82 (displays and L–B films); Unilever Research, 1982, Principal Scientist, 1984–86 (electronic biosensors); Chief Scientist, THORN EMI plc, 1986–94; Divl Sci. Advr, Unilever Res., 1994–2000. Vis. Prof. of Electrical and Electronic Engrg, Univ. of Glasgow, 1985–. Chm., Inter-Agency Cttee for Marine Sci. and Technol., 1991–93; Member: Opto-electronics Cttee, Rank Prize Funds, 1985–2016; Science Consultative Gp, BBC, 1989–91; ABRC, 1990–93; Sci. Adv. Gp, NPL, 1998–2007 (Chair, 2008–14); Sci. Adv. Bd, Inst. of Nanotechnology, 2001–06; Strategic Adv. Bd, Photonics Explorer, 2009–. A Vice-Pres. and Mem. Council, Royal Soc., 1989–91; Vice-Pres., Industrial Trust, 1999–; Pres., Assoc. for Science Educn, Scotland, 2007–08. Founder and Chm., Optoelectronics Coll., 2006–14. FRSA 1993; FRSE 2000. Hon. Fellow, Inst. of Nanotechnology, 2005. Hon. DEng Glasgow, 2002. Paterson Medal and Prize, Inst. of Physics, 1984; Best Paper Award, Soc. for Inf. Display, 1983. *Publications:* numerous sci. and tech. papers; numerous patents. *Recreations:* music, horology, Art Deco sculpture. *Address:* 23 Reres Road, Broughty Ferry, Dundee DD5 2QA.

**SHANKS, Murray George; His Honour Judge Shanks;** a Circuit Judge, since 2009; *b* Windsor, 19 June 1960; *s* of Paul and Maggie Shanks. *Educ:* Worth Abbey; Trinity Coll., Cambridge (BA 1983). Called to the Bar, Middle Temple, 1984; Acting High Court Judge: Belize, 2000; Eastern Caribbean Supreme Court, 2003–05; Recorder, 2004–09; Dep. Chm., Information Tribunal, 2007–10. *Publications:* (contrib.) Information Rights, 2004, 2nd edn 2007. *Clubs:* Groucho, Soho House.

**SHANKS, Prof. Robert Gray, (Robin),** CBE 1997; MD, DSc; FRCP, FRCPI, FRCPE, FACP; Whitla Professor of Therapeutics and Pharmacology, 1977–98, now Emeritus, and Pro-Vice-Chancellor, 1991–98, Queen's University, Belfast; *b* 4 April 1934; *s* of Robert Shanks and Mary Anne Shanks (*née* Gray); *m* 1960, Denise Isabelle Sheila Woods (*d* 1998); four *d*. *Educ:* Queen's Univ., Belfast (MD; DSc). FRCPE 1977; FRCP 1987; FRCPI 1987; FACP 1998. MRIA. RMO, Royal Victoria Hosp., Belfast, 1958–59; Res. Fellow, Medical Coll. of Georgia, 1959–60; Lectr in Physiology, QUB, 1960–62; Pharmacologist, ICI, 1962–66; Queen's University, Belfast: Sen. Lectr, Therapeutics and Pharmacology, 1967–72; Prof., Clinical Pharmacology, 1972–77; Dean, Faculty of Medicine, 1986–91; Consultant Physician, Belfast City and Royal Victoria Hosps, 1967–98. Hon. LLD QUB, 1999. *Publications:* papers in scientific jls. *Recreations:* cooking, walking, gardening. *Address:* 16 Grange Road, Bangor, Northern Ireland BT20 3QQ. *Club:* Royal County Down Golf.

**SHANKS, Sharon;** *see* Heal, S.

**SHANKS, (Wilhelmina) Fiona; Her Honour Judge Fiona Shanks;** a Circuit Judge, since 2018; Designated Family Judge for Norfolk, since 2019; *b* Willingham by Stow, Lincs, 14 July 1955; *d* of Dr James Shanks and Dr Wilhelmina Shanks. *Educ:* Cheltenham Ladies' Coll.; University Coll., Cardiff (LLB Hons). Admitted as solicitor, 1980; Dep. Dist Judge, 1991–98; Dist Judge, 1998–2018. *Recreations:* cooking, travel, films, reading, gardening.

**SHANNON, 10th Earl of,** *cr* 1756 (Ire.); **Richard Henry John Boyle;** Viscount Boyle, Baron Castle Martyr, 1756; Baron Carleton (GB), 1786; *b* 19 Jan. 1960; *s* of 9th Earl of Shannon and Susan Margaret (*née* Hogg); S father, 2013. *Heir:* cousin Robert Francis Boyle [*b* 15 Aug. 1930; *m* 1956, Janet Eleanor Ashley Cooper; two *s* one *d*]. *Address:* Edington House, Edington, Bridgwater, Somerset TA7 9JS.

**SHANNON, Alan David,** CB 2012; Permanent Secretary, Department for Employment and Learning, Northern Ireland, 2010–13; Chair, Northern Ireland Federation of Housing Associations, 2014–19; *b* 11 Jan. 1949; *s* of Samuel and Florence Shannon; *m* 1972, Christine Montgomery; one *s* two *d*. *Educ:* Belfast Royal Acad.; Queen's Univ., Belfast (BA Hons 1971). Joined NI Civil Service as Asst Principal, 1971; Min. of Agriculture (NI), 1971–82; Cabinet, British Mem. of European Court of Auditors, Luxembourg, 1982–85; Hd of Efficiency Scrutiny, Health Service, NI Dept of Finance and Personnel, 1985–86; Northern Ireland Office: Hd of Police Div., 1986–90; Hd of Probation, Juveniles and Compensation Div., 1990–92; Chief Exec., NI Prison Service, 1992–98; Principal Estabt and Finance Officer, NI Office, 1998–99; Permanent Secretary: Dept of Higher and Further Educn, Training and Employment, subseq. Dept for Employment and Learning, NI, 1999–2003; Dept for Social Develt, NI, 2003–10. Mem. Bd, Civil Service Healthcare, 2004–14. Trustee: Marie Curie, 2014–16; British Council, 2016–17 (Chair, NI Adv. Cttee, 2015–). Mem. Senate, QUB, 2014–. *Recreations:* tennis, golf, local history, travel.

**SHANNON, David William Francis,** PhD; Chief Scientist, Department of Environment, Food and Rural Affairs (formerly Ministry of Agriculture, Fisheries and Food), 1986–2001; *b* 16 Aug. 1941; *s* of late William Francis Shannon and Elizabeth (*née* Gibson); *m* 1967, Rosamond (*née* Bond); one *s* one *d*. *Educ:* Wallace High Sch., Lisburn, NI; Queen's Univ., Belfast (BAgr, PhD); DMS Napier Coll., Edinburgh, 1976. Poultry Res. Centre, ARC, Edinburgh, 1967; study leave; Dept of Animal Science, Univ. of Alberta, Edmonton, 1973–74; Hd of Nutrition Sect., Poultry Res. Centre, AFRC, 1977, Dir, 1978. Member: AFRC, 1986–94; BBSRC, 1995–2001; NERC, 1995–2001; Pres., UK Br., World's Poultry Science Assoc., 1986–90. Chm., Exec. Council, CAB Internat., 1988–91. Director: The Perry Foundn, 2002–; David Shannon Ltd, 2002–11. Mem. Court, Cranfield Univ., 1996–2001. FRSA 1996. *Publications:* contribs to learned jls on poultry science and animal nutrition. *Recreations:* golf, bridge. *Address:* 4 Old Court, Ashtead, Surrey KT21 2TS. *T:* (01372) 813096.

**SHANNON, James;** *see* Shannon, R. J.

**SHANNON, Keith;** HM Diplomatic Service; Ambassador to Latvia, since 2017; *b* Edinburgh, 17 Sept. 1966; *s* of Andrew Graeme Shannon and Catherine Lavin Shannon (*née* Sutherland); *m* 2002, Catherine Maria Levesley. *Educ:* Craigmount High Sch., Edinburgh; Univ. of St Andrews (MA Hons Modern Hist. with Internat. Relns). Entered HM Diplomatic Service, 1988; Asst Desk Officer, EC Dept (Internal), FCO, 1989–90; Desk Officer, Latin America Dept, FCO, 1990–91; Third Sec. (Aid/Commercial), Maputo, 1991–94; Second Sec. (Technol.), Paris, 1995–99; Head of Section: Drugs and Internat. Crime Dept, FCO, 1999–2002; Financial Planning and Performance Dept, FCO, 2002–03; Dep. Hd of Mission and Consul, Vilnius, 2004–08; Ambassador to Moldova, 2009–13; Dep. Dir, Foreign Policy, Nat. Security Secretariat, Cabinet Office (on secondment), 2013; Dep. Dir, Eastern Europe and Central Asia Directorate, FCO, 2014–17. *Recreations:* travel, literature, history, sport (especially football, cricket and golf), rock music. *Address:* c/o Foreign and Commonwealth Office, King Charles Street, SW1A 2AH. *E:* Keith.Shannon@fco.gov.uk.

**SHANNON, (Richard) James,** MP (DemU) Strangford, since 2010; *b* Omagh, 25 March 1955; *s* of Richard James Shannon and Mona Rebecca Rhoda Shannon; *m* 1987, Sandra George; three *s*. *Educ:* Ballywalter Primary Sch.; Coleraine Academical Instn. Served UDR, 1974–75 and 1976–77; 102 Light Air Defence Regt, RA, 1978–89. Ards Borough Council: Mem. (DemU), 1985–2010; Mayor, 1991–92; Alderman, 1997–2010. Mem., NI Forum, 1996–98; Mem. (DemU) Strangford, NI Assembly, 1998–2010. Member: Defence Cttee, 2015–16; NI Affairs Cttee, 2016–. GSM (NI) 1974. *Recreations:* field sports, football, Ulster-Scots language and culture. *Address:* (office) 34a Frances Street, Newtownards, Co. Down BT23 7DN. *T:* (028) 9182 7990.

**SHANT, Nirmal Kanta;** QC 2006; **Her Honour Judge Shant;** a Circuit Judge, since 2015; *b* 2 July 1962; *d* of Chaman Lal Shant and Santosh Lakhanpal; *m* 1992, Narinder Sharma; two *d*. *Educ:* Univ. of Leicester (LLB Hons 1983); Council of Legal Educn. Called to the Bar, Gray's Inn, 1984, Bencher, 2010; in practice as a barrister specialising in criminal law; a Recorder, 2001–15. *Recreations:* tennis, theatre, reading, cooking.

**SHAPCOTT, Jo A.;** poet; *b* 24 March 1953; *d* of Frank William Gordon Shapcott and Josephine Cann; *m* 1995, Simon Andrew James Hainault Mundy. *Educ:* Cavendish Sch., Hemel Hempstead; TCD (BA 1st cl. Hons, MA); Bristol Univ. (DipEd); Harvard Univ. (Harkness Fellowship). Lectr in English, Rolle Coll., Exmouth, 1981–84; Educn Officer, South Bank Centre, 1986–92. Judith E. Wilson Vis. Fellow, Cambridge Univ., 1991; Penguin Writers' Fellow, BL, 1996–97; Northern Arts Literary Fellow, 1998–2000; Visiting Professor: Newcastle Univ., 2000–; Univ. of the Arts, London (formerly London Inst.), 2003–; Royal Literary Fund Fellow, Oxford Brookes Univ., 2003–05. Mem., Yr Academi Cymreig (Welsh Acad.). FRSL. First Prize, Nat. Poetry Competition, 1985, 1991; Queen's Gold Medal for Poetry, 2011. *Publications: poetry:* Electroplating the Baby, 1988 (Commonwealth Poetry Prize); Phrase Book, 1992; (ed with Matthew Sweeney) Emergency Kit: poems for strange times, 1996; Motherland, 1996; Penguin Modern Poets 12, 1997; My Life Asleep, 1998 (Forward Poetry Prize); (ed with Don Paterson) Last Words: poetry for the new century, 1999; Her Book: poems 1988–1998, 2000; Tender Taxes, 2002; The Transformers, 2007; Of Mutability, 2010 (Costa Book of the Year, 2010); *essay collection:* (ed with Linda Anderson) Elizabeth Bishop: poet of the periphery, 2002. *Address:* c/o Faber & Faber, Bloomsbury House, 74–77 Great Russell Street, WC1B 3DA.

**SHAPER, Prof. (Andrew) Gerald,** FRCP; FRCPath; FFPH; Professor of Clinical Epidemiology and Head of Department of Primary Care and Population Sciences, Royal Free Hospital School of Medicine, University of London, 1975–92, now Professor Emeritus, University College Medical School, Royal Free Campus; *b* 9 Aug. 1927; *s* of Jack and Molly Shaper; *m* 1952, Lorna June Clarke; one *s*. *Educ:* Univ. of Cape Town (MB ChB); DTM&H with Milne Medal (Liverpool). Ho. Phys./Surg., Harare, 1952; SHO, Trop. Diseases Unit, Sefton Gen. Hosp., Liverpool, and Res. Asst, Liverpool Sch. of Trop.

Med., 1953–54; Registrar: Clatterbridge Gen. Hosp., 1954–55; Hammersmith Hosp. and Post Grad. Med. Sch., 1955–56; Lectr, Sen. Lectr, Reader in Medicine and Prof. of Cardiovascular Disease, Makerere Univ. Med. Sch., Kampala, 1957–69; Mem. Sci. Staff, MRC Social Medicine Unit, LSHTM, 1970–75; Hon. Cons. Phys. (Cardiology), UCH, 1975–87; Hon. Consultant in Community Medicine, subseq. Public Health Medicine, Hampstead HA, 1975–92. RCP Milroy Lectr, 1972; Pickering Lectr, British Hypertension Soc., 1993. Chm., Jt Wkg Party of RCP and Brit. Cardiac Soc. on Prevention of Coronary Heart Disease, 1976; Member: DHSS Cttee on Med. Aspects of Water Quality, 1978–84; DHSS Cttee on Med. Aspects of Food Policy, 1979–83; Chairman: MRC Health Services Res. Panel, 1981–86; Heads of Academic Depts of Public Health (formerly Community) Medicine, 1987–90; Vice-Chm., Nat. Heart Forum, 1995–98; Member: WHO Expert Adv. Panel on Cardiovascular Disease, 1975–; DHSS Central Health Monitoring Unit Steering Gp, 1989–91. Elected Mem., Commonwealth Caribbean MRC, 1986–98. Alwyn Smith Prize Medal, FPHM, 1991. *Publications:* (ed) Medicine in a Tropical Environment, 1972; (ed) Cardiovascular Disease in the Tropics, 1974; Coronary Heart Disease: risks and reasons, 1988. *Recreations:* walking, second-hand/antiquarian books, theatre, golf. *Address:* 12 Greenholme Farm, Leather Bank, Burley in Wharfdale, Ilkley, W Yorks LS29 7HP. *T:* (01943) 865675. *E:* agshaper@wentworth.u-net.com.

**SHAPIRO, Dr Bernard Jack**, OC 1999; Principal and Vice-Chancellor, McGill University, Montreal, 1994–2002, now Emeritus; first Ethics Commissioner of Canada, 2004–07; *b* 8 June 1935; *s* of Maxwell Shapiro and Mary Tafler; *m* 1957, Dr Phyllis Schwartz (*d* 2004); one *s* one *d*. *Educ:* McGill Univ. (Schol.; BA Hons Econs and Pol Sci. 1956); Harvard Univ. (MAT Social Sci.; EdD Measurement and Stats 1967). Vice-Pres., William Barbara Corp., 1956–61; Res. Fellow, Educnl Testing Service, 1963; Res. Asst/Associate, Educnl Res. Council of America, 1965–67; Boston University: Asst Prof., 1967–71; Associate Prof., 1971–76; Chm., Dept of Humanistic and Behavioral Studies, 1971–74; Associate, Sch. of Educn, 1974–76; University of Western Ontario: Dean, Faculty of Educn and Prof. of Educn, 1976–78; Vice-Pres. (Academic) and Provost, 1978–80; Dir, Ont Inst. for Studies in Educn, 1980–86; Deputy Minister, Ontario: of Educn, 1986–89; of Skills Develt, 1988–89; Dep. Sec. of Cabinet, Ont, 1989–90; Deputy Minister: and Sec., Mgt Bd, 1990–91; of Colls and Univs, 1991–93; Prof. of Educn and Public Policy, Univ. of Toronto, 1992–94. Co-Chm., Nat. Adv. Cttee on Educn Stats, 1987–89. Chm., Governing Bd, OECD Centre for Educnl Res. and Innovation, 1984–86. President: Canadian Soc. for Study of Educn, 1983–84; Social Sci. Fedn of Canada, 1985–86; Conf. of Rectors and Principals of Quebec Univs, 1997–99. Hon. LLD: McGill, 1988; Toronto, 1994; Ottawa, 1995; Yeshiva, 1996; McMaster, 1997; Montreal, 1998; Edinburgh, 2000; Glasgow, 2001; Bishop's, 2001.
*See also* H. T. Shapiro.

**SHAPIRO, Dr Harold Tafler**; Professor of Economics and Public Affairs, Woodrow Wilson School, since 2001, and President, 1988–2001, now President Emeritus, Princeton University; *b* Montreal, 8 June 1935; *s* of Maxwell Shapiro and Mary Tafler; *m* Vivian; four *d*. *Educ:* McGill Univ. (Lieut Governor's Medal; BA 1956); Graduate Sch., Princeton (PhD Econ 1964). University of Michigan: Asst Prof. of Economics, 1964; Associate Prof., 1967; Prof., 1970–88; Vice-Pres. for Acad. Affairs and Chm., Cttee on Budget Admin, 1977; President, 1980–88. Dir, Nat. Bureau of Economic Research. Member: Conference Board Inc.; Govt-Univ.-Industry Res. Round-table; Inst. of Medicine, Nat. Acad. of Scis; Council of Advrs to Pres. Bush on Sci. and Technology, 1990–92; Bd, Robert Wood Johnson Med. Sch., 2000–; Bd, DeVry Inst., 2001–; Bd, Hastings Center, 2001–; Bd of Dirs, Reading is Fundamental, 2001–04; Knight Foundn Cttee on Intercollegiate Athletics, 2004–; Merck Vaccine Adv. Bd, 2004–; Stem Cell Inst. of NJ Jt Bd Managers, 2005–; Adv. Cttee, Human Embryonic Stem Cell Res., 2006–; Cttee on America's Energy Future, NAS, 2007–. Mem., Amer. Philosophical Soc.; Fellow, Amer. Acad. of Arts and Scis. Trustee: Alfred P. Sloan Foundn; Univs Res. Assoc.; Univ. of Pa Med. Center; Educnl Testing Service; Amer. Jewish Cttee, 2002–; Princeton Healthcare Systems, 2006–; Univ. of Med. and Dentistry of NJ, 2006–. William D. Carey Lectureship Award, 2006. *Publications:* (ed jtly) Universities and their Leadership, 1998; A Larger Sense of Purpose: higher education and society, 2005; (ed jtly) Belmont Revisited: ethical principles for research with human subjects, 2005. *Address:* Woodrow Wilson School, Princeton University, 427 Robertson Hall, Princeton, NJ 08544–0015, USA.
*See also* B. J. Shapiro.

**SHAPIRO, Leonard Melvyn**, MD; FRCP, FACC; Consultant Cardiologist, with special interest in non-coronary intervention and valve disease, Royal Papworth (formerly Papworth) Hospital, Cambridge, since 1988; *b* 9 March 1951; *s* of Joseph and Stella Shapiro. *Educ:* Manchester Univ. (BSc 1st Cl.; MB ChB Hons 1976). MD 1981; FRCP 1994; FACC 1994. Senior Registrar: Brompton Hosp., 1982–84; Nat. Heart Hosp., 1984–88. Medical Advr, FA, 1997–. Founding Pres., British Soc. of Echocardiography, 1994–96. *Publications:* (jtly) A Colour Atlas of Hypertension, 1985, 2nd edn 1992; (jtly) A Colour Atlas of Angina Pectoris, 1986; (jtly) A Colour Atlas of Heart Failure, 1987, 2nd edn 1995; (jtly) A Colour Atlas of Physical Signs in Cardiovascular Disease, 1988; (jtly) A Colour Atlas of Palpitations and Syncope, 1990; (jtly) A Colour Atlas of Congenital Heart Disease in the Adult, 1990; A Colour Atlas of Coronary Atherosclerosis, 1992, 2nd edn 1993; (jtly) Mitral Valve Disease Diagnosis and Treatment, 1995; (jtly) An Atlas of Cardiac Ultrasound, 1998. *Recreations:* sport, triathlon. *Address:* Royal Papworth Hospital, Cambridge CB23 3RE. *T:* 07442 502602. *E:* sec@lmshapiro.com. *W:* www.lmshapiro.com.

**SHAPLAND, Prof. Joanna Mary**, DPhil; Professor of Criminal Justice, since 1993 and Edward Bramley Professor of Criminal Justice, since 2013, University of Sheffield; *b* 17 Feb. 1950; *d* of late Brig. John C. C. Shapland and Mary W. Shapland (*née* Martin, then Moberly); *m* 1978, Dr John Patrick George Mailer; one *s*. *Educ:* Croydon High Sch.; St Hilda's Coll., Oxford (BA 1971); Darwin Coll., Cambridge (Dip. Criminol. 1972); Wolfson Coll., Oxford (DPhil 1975). CPsychol 1989; Chartered Forensic Psychologist, 1993. Home Office Res. Fellow in Criminology, KCL, 1975–78; Res. Fellow, Centre for Criminol. Res., Oxford Univ., 1978–88; Jun. Res. Fellow, 1979–83, Res. Fellow, 1983–88, Wolfson Coll., Oxford; Sheffield University: Sen. Res. Fellow, Centre for Criminol. and Socio-Legal Studies, 1988–89; Lectr, 1989–91, Sen. Lectr, 1991–93, Dept of Law; Director: Inst. for the Study of the Legal Profession, 1993–2005; Centre for Criminological Res., 2005–10 and 2014–; Hd, Sch. of Law, 2009–13. Chm., Restorative Justice Forum (Scotland), 2014–. Cons. Expert, Select Cttee on Victim and Criminal and Social Policy, Council of Europe, 1982–87; Ind. Assessor, Review of Criminal Justice in NI, 1998–2000. Co-Ed., 1989–2002, Exec. Ed., 2002–, Internat. Review of Victimology; Ed., British Jl of Criminology, 1990–98. Outstanding Achievement Award, British Soc. of Criminology, 2013. *Publications:* Between Conviction and Sentence: the process of mitigation, 1981; *jointly:* Victims in the Criminal Justice System, 1985; Policing by the Public, 1988; Developing Vocational Legal Training for the Bar, 1990; Violent Crime in Small Shops, 1993; Arson in Schools, 1993; Drug Usage and Drugs Prevention, 1993; Organising UK Professions: continuity and change, 1994; Studying for the Bar, 1995; Starting Practice, 1995; Pupillage and the Vocational Course, 1995; Milton Keynes Criminal Justice Audit: the detailed report, 1996; Professional Bodies' Communications with Members and Clients, 1996; Affording Civil Justice, 1998; Good Practice in Pupillage, 1998; Social Control and Policing: the public/private divide, 1999; A Civil Justice Audit, 2002; The Informal Economy: threat and opportunity in the City, 2003; Evaluation of Statutory Time Limit Pilot Scheme in the Youth Court, 2003; The Junior Bar in 2002, 2003; Restorative Justice in Practice, 2006; Justice, Community and Civil Society, 2008; Urban Crime Prevention, Surveillance and Restorative Justice, 2009; Restorative Justice in Practice: evaluating what works for victims and offenders, 2011; (ed) Getting By or Getting Rich?: the formal, informal and criminal economies in a globalised world, 2013; (ed) Global Perspectives on Desistance, 2016. *Recreations:* gardening, music, tapestry. *Address:* School of Law, University of Sheffield, Bartolomé House, Winter Street, Sheffield S3 7ND. *T:* (0114) 222 6712.

**SHAPPS, Rt Hon. Grant**; PC 2010; MP (C) Welwyn Hatfield, since 2005; Secretary of State for Transport, since 2019; *b* 14 Sept. 1968; *s* of Tony and Beryl Shapps; *m* 1997, Belinda Goldstone; two *s* one *d* (of whom one *s* one *d* are twins). *Educ:* Watford Grammar Sch.; Cassio Coll., Watford (business and finance); Manchester Polytech. (HND Business and Finance). Founded Printhouse Corp. (design, web and print co.), 1990, Chm., 2000–. Contested (C) Welwyn Hatfield, 2001. Shadow Housing Minister, 2007–10; Minister of State, DCLG, 2010–12; Minister of State (Minister without Portfolio), Cabinet Office, 2012–15; Minister of State: DFID, 2015; FCO, 2015. Mem., Public Admin Select Cttee, 2005–07. Vice Chm. (Campaigning), 2005–07, Chm., 2012–15, Cons. Party. *Recreation:* private pilot with IMC and night qualifications. *Address:* House of Commons, SW1A 0AA. *T:* (020) 7219 8497, *Fax:* (020) 7219 0659. *E:* grant@shapps.com.

**SHAPS, Simon**; Chairman, Simon Shaps Ltd, since 2015; Film, Television and Radio Consultant, Georgina Capel Associates Ltd, since 2015; *b* 10 Sept. 1956; *m*. *Educ:* Magdalene Coll., Cambridge (BA 1979). Researcher, Thames TV, 1982–83; London Weekend Television: researcher, 1983–90; Head of Current Affairs, 1990–93; Controller, Factual Progs, 1993–96; Dir of Progs, 1996–97; Dir of Progs, Granada TV, 1997–2000; Managing Director: Granada Prodns, 2000; Granada Broadband, 2000–01; Man. Dir, then Chief Exec., Granada Content, 2001–04; Chief Exec., Granada, 2004–05; Dir of Television, ITV, 2005–08; Chairman: A Brand Apart TV, 2009–13; MercuryMedia, 2010–14; Man. Dir, Internat. Content and Prodn, Core Media Gp, 2013–14. Chm., Nat. Film and TV Sch., 2009–13.

**SHARDLOW, Matthew Edward Ambrose**; Chief Executive Officer, Buglife - The Invertebrate Conservation Trust, since 2002; *b* London, 13 Jan. 1971; *s* of Michael and Anne Shardlow; *m* 2001, Helen Vine; one *s* one *d*. *Educ:* Chichester High Sch. for Boys; Univ. of E Anglia (BSc Envmtl Sci.; MPhil Restoration Ecology). Invertebrate ecologist, 1995–96, biodiversity ecologist, 1996–99, Biodiversity Reserves Ecologist, 2000–02, RSPB. Country Diary columnist, The Guardian, 2011–. Chairman: Riverfly Partnership, 2003–06; Legal Strategy Gp, Wildlife and Countryside Link, 2010–17; Committee Member: UK Biodiversity Reporting and Information Gp, 2006–11; Eur. Habitats Forum, 2008–; Mem., BBC Rural Affairs Cttee, 2015–. Mem., UK Sheep-dip Steering Gp, 2005–10. Trustee: Wildlife and Countryside Link, 2004–07; Friends of Gondwana Rainforest, 2014–. *Publications:* contrib. chapters in books: Ecology and Geomorphology of Coastal Shingle, 2001; Insect Conservation: past, present and prospects, 2012; The Management of Insects in Recreation and Tourism, 2013; contribs to guides and reports; contrib. to Jl Applied Ecol., Atropos, Tentacle. *Recreations:* walking, natural history, cricket, snorkelling. *Address:* Buglife - The Invertebrate Conservation Trust, The Lindens, 86 Lincoln Road, Peterborough PE1 2SN. *T:* (01733) 201210. *E:* matt.shardlow@buglife.org.uk. *Club:* Benefield Cricket (Cambs).

**SHARIF, Mohammad Nawaz**; Prime Minister of Pakistan, 1990–93, 1997–99 and 2013–17; *b* 25 Dec. 1949; *m* 1971, Kalsoom Nawaz Sharif (*d* 2018); two *s* two *d*. *Educ:* St Anthony Sch., Lahore; Government Coll., Lahore; University Law Coll., Lahore. Finance Minister, Govt of Punjab, 1981–85; Chief Minister, Punjab, 1985–90; Leader of the Opposition, Nat. Assembly of Pakistan, 1993–97. *Recreations:* sports, especially cricket.

**SHARKEY**, family name of **Baron Sharkey**.

**SHARKEY**, Baron *cr* 2010 (Life Peer), of Niton Undercliff in the County of the Isle of Wight; **John Kevin Sharkey**; Director, Sharkey Associates Ltd; *b* 24 Sept. 1947; *m* Astrid; three *d*. Jt Man. Dir, Saatchi & Saatchi UK; Dep. Chm., Saatchi Internat.; Chief Operating Officer, Blue Arrow plc; Chm., BDDP Hldgs Ltd; Co-Chm. and Proprietor, Bainsfair Sharkey Trott, 1990–97; Co-Chm., BDDP GGT, 1997–98. Chairman: Highland Partners Europe; Ad-Air. Advr on Strategic Communications, Leader of Lib Dems, 2008; Chm., Lib Dem Gen. Election Campaign, 2010. Mem., EU Sub Cttee, Home Affairs, Health and Educn, H of L, 2012–15, Draft Deregulation Bill Jt Cttee, 2013, Inf. Cttee, 2014–16, Select Cttee on Econ. Affairs, 2015–, H of L. Director: New City Agenda Thinktank, 2015–; Full Fact, 2015–. Chair: Assoc. of Med. Res. Charities, 2015–; Specialised Healthcare Commissioning Alliance, 2017–. Mem., Hansard Soc., 2004– (Hon., Treas., 2007–10; Chair, 2016–). Gov., Inst. for Govt, 2013–18. Mem. Council, UCL, 2017–. Trustee, Turn2Us. *Address:* House of Lords, SW1A 0PW.

**SHARKEY, Annette**, CBE 2004; Chief Operating Officer, Technology, Department for Work and Pensions, 2015–17; *b* 4 May 1963; *d* of David Richard Willacy and Edith Willacy; *m* 2014, Peter Francis Sharkey. *Educ:* Preston Poly. (HND Business Studies (Dist.)). Joined DHSS, 1984; various information technol. and business change roles until 1999 (incl. secondment to Australian DSS, 1992–93); Lord Chancellor's Department, subseq. Department for Constitutional Affairs: IT Dir, Court Service, 1999–2002; Chief Inf. Officer, 2002–06; Interim Dir, Criminal Justice IT, 2003–04; Home Office: Chief Inf. Officer, Identity and Passport Service, 2006–08; Chief Inf. Officer, 2008–10; on sabbatical, 2010–15. Dir, MTC Educn and Glasstastik, 2011–16. Mem., Contemporary Glass Soc., 2011–. Mem. Cttee, Newton Residents Assoc., 2012–. FBCS 2010. *Recreations:* glass artist, gardening, travel.

**SHARKEY, Georgina Emma**; *see* Gibbs, G. E.

**SHARLAND, Andrew James**; Partner, Clintons, since 1990; *b* Chandlers Ford, Hants, 24 Nov. 1963; *s* of Ian James and Margaret Sharland; *m* 2005, Corrina Ann; two *d*. *Educ:* Winchester Coll.; Jesus Coll., Cambridge (BA 1985; MA). Called to the Bar, Lincoln's Inn, 1986; admitted as solicitor, 1988; Partner, D. M. Landsman & Co., 1988–90. *Recreations:* contemporary music, analogue synthesizers, football, yoga. *Address:* Clintons, 55 Drury Lane, WC2B 5RZ. *T:* (020) 7379 6080, *Fax:* (020) 7240 9310. *E:* asharland@clintons.co.uk.

**SHARLAND, Andrew John**; QC 2018; a Recorder, since 2018; *m* 2006, Anna Brown; one *s* one *d*. *Educ:* Skinners' Sch., Tunbridge Wells; Queen Mary Coll., Univ. of London (LLB Hons); Leiden Univ., Netherlands; Worcester Coll., Oxford (BCL); William and Mary Coll., Virginia, USA (LLM). Called to the Bar, Gray's Inn, 1996. *Publications:* (jtly) Media Law and Human Rights, 2001, 2nd edn 2009; (jtly) Judicial Review: Principles and Procedure, 2013. *Recreations:* dog walking, table tennis, 5-a-side football. *Address:* 11 KBW, 11 King's Bench Walk, Temple, EC4Y 7EQ. *T:* (020) 7632 8500. *E:* andrew.sharland@11kbw.com. *Clubs:* Haywards Heath Table Tennis; Mid Sussex Galaxy Football.

**SHARLAND, (Edward) John**; HM Diplomatic Service, retired; High Commissioner, the Seychelles, 1992–95; *b* 25 Dec. 1937; *s* of late William Rex Sharland and Phyllis Eileen Sharland (*née* Pitts); *m* 1970, Susan Mary Rodway Millard; four *d*. *Educ*: Monmouth Sch.; Jesus Coll., Oxford. BA Hons History; MA. FO, 1961–62; Bangkok, 1962–67; Far Eastern Dept, FCO, 1967–69; Dep. Perm. Rep. to UNIDO and Dep. Resident Rep. to IAEA, Vienna, 1969–72; Bangkok, 1972–75; Montevideo, 1976–79; Cultural Relations Dept, FCO, 1979–82; Consul-Gen., Perth, 1982–87; Consul-Gen., Cleveland, 1987–89; High Comr, PNG, 1989–91. *Recreations*: bridge, stamp collecting.

**SHARLAND, Susan Margaret, (Mrs D. Woodwark)**, PhD; Chief Executive, Transport Research Foundation and TRL Ltd, 2001–13; *b* 26 Aug. 1961; *d* of Ian and Margaret Sharland; *m* 2005, Dr David Woodwark. *Educ*: St Swithun's Sch., Winchester; New Hall, Cambridge (BA (Maths) 1983); Imperial Coll., London (PhD 1988). Res. Scientist/Dept Manager, UKAEA, 1983–96; Gen. Manager, AEA Technology plc, 1996–98; Man. Dir, AEA Technology Consulting/Engineering Software, 1998–2001. Non-executive Director: MGM Assurance, 2003–09; HR Wallingford Gp Ltd, 2008– (non-exec. Chair, 2016–); LUC Ltd, 2013–; Transport Systems Catapult Ltd, 2014–; non-executive Advisory Director: CEFAS, 2010–15; Vehicle Certification Agency, 2013–. Pres., Chartered Instn of Highways and Transportation, 2015–16. Trustee, Road Safety Foundn, 2017–. *Recreations*: gardening, travelling, walking, gym. *E*: susan.sharland@icloud.com.

**SHARMA, Rt Hon. Alok**; PC 2019; MP (C) Reading West, since 2010; Secretary of State for International Development, since 2019; *b* 7 Sept. 1967; *m*; two *d*. *Educ*: Blue Coat Sch., Reading; Salford Univ. (BSc Applied Physics with Electronics 1988). CA. Accountancy and corporate finance advr. Parly Under-Sec. of State, FCO, 2016–17; Minister of State, DCLG, 2017–18; Minister of State (Minister for Employment), DWP, 2018–19. *Address*: House of Commons, SW1A 0AA.

**SHARMA, Kamalesh**, Hon. GCVO 2016; Commonwealth Secretary-General, 2008–16; *m* Babli; one *s* one *d*. *Educ*: Modern Sch. and St Stephen's Coll., Delhi; King's Coll., Cambridge (Eng. Lit.). Lectr in English, Delhi Univ.; Indian Foreign Service, 1965–2002: Hd of Divs, Technical Co-opn, Econ. Relns, Internat. Orgns and Policy Planning, Min. of External Affairs; Oil Sector and Develt Assistance from Europe, Treasury; served in Bonn, Hong Kong, Saudi Arabia and Turkey; Ambassador: to GDR; to Republics of Kazakhstan and Kyrgyzstan; Ambassador and Perm. Rep. of India to the UN, Geneva, 1988–90, NY, 1997–2002; Special Rep. of Sec.-Gen. of the UN to E Timor, as Under-Sec.-Gen., 2002–04; High Comr for India in the UK, 2004–08. Formerly Mem. Bd, Internat. Peace Acad., NY. Chancellor, QUB, 2009–15, now Chancellor Emeritus. Gov., Ditchley Foundn. Fellow, Weatherhead Center for Internat. Affairs, Harvard Univ. Dir, Centre for Respect and Understanding, Cordia Educnl Instns, Sanghol, Punjab, 2018–. Hon. Dr: Middx; London; De Montfort; Nat. Univ. of Rwanda; Glasgow, 2014. Medal, Foreign Policy Assoc., USA, 2001. *Publications*: (ed) Imagining Tomorrow: rethinking the global challenge, 1999; (ed) Milles Fleurs: poetry from around the world, 2000. *Recreations*: literature, religious and mystical traditions, cosmology, development, global affairs, human society, cricket, Indian classical music, jazz. *Clubs*: Travellers, National Liberal; Gymkhana, India Internat. Centre, Habitat Centre (New Delhi).

**SHARMA, Murari Raj**; Ambassador of Nepal to the Court of St James's, 2007–09; *b* Dingla, Bhojpur, Nepal, 16 April 1951; *s* of Dina Raj Adhikari and Padma K. Adhikari; *m* 1989, Nila Koirala Adhikari; two *s*. *Educ*: Univ. of Pittsburgh (MPIA 1983); Tribhuvan Univ. (MA Econs 1975; MCom 1978; BL 1990). Asst Lectr, Tribhuvan Univ., 1974–76; Jt Accounts Officer, Nat. Commercial Bank, Nepal, 1976–77; Officer, Nepal Food Corp., 1977–78; Section Officer, Min. of Finance, 1978–83; Under Sec., Min. of Gen. Admin., 1983–88; Under Sec., Min. of Home, 1988–90; Jt Sec. (Dir-Gen.), Ministries of Finance and of Foreign Affairs, 1991–97; Foreign Sec., 1997–2000; Ambassador of Nepal to the UN, NY, 2000–04; Mem., Adv. Cttee on Admin. and Budgetary Questions, UN, 2004–06. Consultant, Admin. Reform Commn, 1991; Convener, High-level Foreign Policy Rev. Cttee of Nepal, 2006. Columnist, República, Nepal, 2011–. Educnl consultant, 2012–. Gorkha Dakshin Bahu (Nepal), 1999. *Publications*: Murari Adhikari's Short Stories, 2000; (jtly) Reinventing the United Nations, 2007; (jtly) United Nations International Civil Service, 2009; (jtly) The Rise of Communists and Fall of the Monarchy, 2018; papers and articles on topical issues in reputed daily newspapers, weekly magazines and e-magazines. *Recreations*: reading, writing, travel, volleyball, tennis. *Address*: 110/49 Janasahayog Marg, New Baneshwar, Kathmandu-34, Nepal. *T*: 4474048. *E*: murari.sharma@gmail.com. *Club*: Lions (Dingla, Bhojpur).

**SHARMA, Surinder Mohan**; DL; JP; Co-Director, Unit for Diversity, Inclusion and Community Engagement, Department of Media, Communication and Sociology (formerly of Sociology), University of Leicester, since 2015; *s* of Daulat Ram Sharma and Raksha Vati Sharma; *m* 1976, Vijay; one *s* one *d*. *Educ*: Univ. of Kent, Canterbury (BA Hons Law). Joined CRE, 1978; work at BBC TV; Corporate Equal Opportunities Manager, Littlewoods, until 2000; Dir, Diversity, Ford of Europe, 2000–04; Dir Gen., then Nat. Dir, Equality and Human Rights, DoH, 2004–12. Diversity and Inclusion Consultant, 2005–08, Mem., Diversity and Inclusion Global Adv. Council, 2008–12, Novartis Internat. AG, Basel. Member: EOC, 2000–07; Diversity Panel, MoD, 2008–; Ind. Advr for BIS, Diversity and Equality Council, 2011–16; Chm., NHS and Social Care Black and Minority Ethnic Networks, 2013–. Board Member: Race for Health, 2006–12; Race for Opportunity Campaign, 2008–12; Chm., Leicester Racial Equality Council. Mem., Leicester CC, 1983–91 (Hon. Alderman, 2013); Ind. Person, Leicestershire CC, 2013. Shadow Gov., Leics Partnership NHS Trust, 2012–15. Trustee: Nat. Space Centre, 2003–; UNICEF UK, 2013–. JP, 1983, High Sheriff, 2016–17, Leicester; DL Leics 2017. Hon. Professor: Wolverhampton, 2010; Manchester Univ. Business Sch., 2013. Mem. Council, Aston Univ., 2012– (Mem., Audit Cttee, 2012–; Chair, Ethics Sub Cttee, 2012–; Mem., Nominations Cttee, 2013–). Hon. Dr Central England, 2006; Hon. DLitt De Montfort, 2007; Hon. LLD Leicester, 2017; Hon. DSc Aston, 2018. *Recreations*: gardening, holidays, playing cricket.

**SHARMA, Virendra**; MP (Lab) Ealing and Southall, since July 2007; *b* 5 April 1947; *s* of Dr Lekh Raj Sharma and R. P. Sharma; *m* 1968, Nirmala; one *s* one *d*. Started working life as bus conductor; subseq. in voluntary sector; Day Services Manager for people with learning disabilities, Hillingdon, 1996–2007. Mem. (Lab) Ealing BC, 1982–2010. Member: Jt Cttee on Human Rights, 2007–15; Internat. Develt Cttee, 2009–10, 2015–; Health Select Cttee, 2010–15; Panel of Chairs, 2017–; Parly Assembly, Council of Europe, 2010–14, 2015–. Chm., Indo-British All Party Parly Gp. Nat. Ethnic Minorities Officer, Lab Party, 1986–92. *Recreations*: reading, walking. *Address*: House of Commons, SW1A 0AA. *T*: (020) 7219 6080. *E*: sharmav@parliament.uk.

**SHARMAN**, family name of **Baron Sharman**.

**SHARMAN**, Baron *cr* 1999 (Life Peer), of Redlynch in the county of Wiltshire; **Colin Morven Sharman**, OBE 1979; FCA; Chairman, Aviva plc, 2006–12; *b* 19 Feb. 1943; *s* of late Col Terence John Sharman and Audrey Emmiline Sharman (*née* Newman); *m* 1966, Angela M. Timmins; one *s* one *d*. *Educ*: Bishop Wordsworth's Sch., Salisbury. FCA 1977. Qualified as Chartered Accountant with Woolgar Hennel & Co., 1965; joined Peat Marwick Mitchell, later KPMG Peat Marwick, then KPMG, 1966; Manager, Frankfurt office, 1970–72; The Hague, 1972–81 (Partner 1973, Partner i/c, 1975); London, 1981–99; Sen. Partner (Nat. Mkting and Industry Gps), 1987–90; Sen. Mgt Consultancy Partner, 1989–91; Sen. Regl Partner (London and SE), 1990–93; Sen. Partner, 1994–98; Chm., KPMG International, 1997–99. Chm., Aegis Gp plc, 2000–08 (Dep. Chm., 1999–2000); Chm., then Dep. Chm., Securicor plc, later Group 4 Securicor, 2003–05; non-executive Director: BG Gp plc, 2000–11; Reed Elsevier plc, 2001–11; Supervisory Dir, ABN Amro NV, 2003–07; Chm., Le Gavroche Restaurant. Mem., H of L, 1999–2015. Conducted review of audit and accountability for Central Govt (report published, 2001). Pres., GamCare, 2011–17. Chm., Salisbury Cath. Council, 2010–. Mem., Industrial Soc. CCMI. Liveryman, Co. of Gunmakers, 1992 (Master, 2010–11). *Publications*: (jtly) Living Culture, 2001. *Recreations*: fishing, shooting, sailing, opera, wine and food. *Clubs*: Reform; Royal Yacht Squadron.

**SHARMAN, Maj.-Gen. Alan George**, CBE 2002; CEng, FIMechE; non-executive Director, Aspire Defence Holdings Ltd, since 2006; *b* 14 May 1942; *s* of late Major Frederick Sharman and Margaret (*née* Watkins); *m* 1st, 1967, Caroline Anne Lister (marr. diss.); one *d*; 2nd, 1977, Juanita Jane Lawson; one *s* one *d*. *Educ*: Hutton Grammar Sch.; Welbeck Coll.; RMA, Sandhurst; Reading Tech. Coll.; Army Staff Coll. CEng, FIMechE 1989. Commnd REME, 1962; served Aden and Oman, 1963; Elec. and Mech. Engr, The Life Guards, Singapore, 1967–68; psc, 1974–75; Signals Res. and Develt Establishment, 1976–77; Comd Allied Comd Europe Mobile Force (Land) Workshop, 1978–79; Mil. Sec's Dept, MoD, 1979–80; REME Combat Develt, 1981–83; Comdr Maintenance, 1 (Br) Corps Troops, 1984; Col Elec. and Mech. Engr 7, 1985–87; Project Manager, Logistic Vehicles, MoD (PE), 1987–89; Dir Elec. and Mech. Engr (Orgn and Trng), 1990–91; Prog. Dir, Tank Systems, MoD (PE), 1991–95; Dir Gen. Land Systems, MoD (PE), 1995–96. Dir Gen., Defence Manufrs Assoc., 1997–2007. Non-exec. Dir, MIRA Ltd, 2006–15. Member: DTI Defence and Aerospace Cttee, 1998–2002; Defence Industries Council, 1997–2007; Vice Pres., Eurodefense UK, 2012–. Col Comdt, REME, 1996–2002; Pres., Bordon Br., REME Assoc., 1998–. Chm., Auto. Div., IMechE, 1996. *Recreations*: yachting, gardening, travel, family, military history. *Address*: c/o Regimental HQ REME, MoD Lyneham, Lyneham, Chippenham SN15 9HB. *Clubs*: Army and Navy; Royal Southern Yacht (Southampton) (Dir, 2012–15); Aston Martin Owners.

**SHARMAN, Evelyn Janet, (Jane)**, CBE 1998; *b* 5 July 1943; *d* of Kenneth Blair Austin Dobson and Evelyn Barbara Dobson (*née* Phillips); *m* 1972, John Matthew Reid Sharman; two *s*. *Educ*: St Andrews Univ. (MA 1st Cl. Hons Mod. and Med. History); Bryn Mawr Coll., USA. Asst Principal, MPBW then DoE, 1968–72; Principal, DoE, 1972–85 (incl. secondment to Cabinet Office and Royal Commn on Envmtl Pollution); English Heritage: Head, Ancient Monuments Div., 1985–89; Actg Dir of Conservation, 1989–91; Dir of Conservation, 1991–96; Acting Chief Exec., 1996–97. Sec., Historic Buildings Council, 1981–84. Chm., Architectural Heritage Fund, 2001–07. Trustee: Chatham Historic Dockyard Trust, 1997–2008; Royal Artillery Museums, 1998–2009; Bexley Heritage Trust, 2001–13; Greenwich Foundn for Old Royal Naval Coll., 2002–10. *Recreations*: reading, travelling.

**SHARMAN, Helen Patricia**, CMG 2018; OBE 1993; speaker and science communicator, since 1991; UK Outreach Ambassador, Imperial College London, since 2019 (Departmental Operations Manager, 2015–18); *b* Sheffield, 30 May 1963; *d* of John David Sharman and Lyndis Mary Sharman. *Educ*: Jordanthorpe Comprehensive Sch., Sheffield; Univ. of Sheffield (BSc Chem.); University Coll. London (MA Central and SE Eur. Studies). Engr and Dep. Hd of Coatings, M-O Valve Co., 1985–87; Res. Technologist, Mars Confectionery, 1987–89; astronaut, Antequerra Ltd, 1989–91; Consultant, Serco Space, 1992–93; Gp Leader, Nat. Physical Lab., 2010–13; Tech. Manager, Kingston Univ., 2013–15. Pres., Inst. of Sci. and Technol., 2015–. Patron, Spacelink Learning Foundn, 1999–. *Publications*: Seize the Moment (autobiog.), 1994; The Space Place (for children), 1997. *Recreations*: mountain walking, fitness, music. *Address*: c/o DBA Speakers, Landmark House, Station Road, Hook, Hants RG27 9HA. *T*: (01932) 228544. *E*: info@dbaspeakers.com.

**SHARMAN, Mark Brian**; Chairman, S3Media Ltd, 2009–17; *b* 2 Jan. 1950; *s* of Stanley Sharman and Beryl Sharman; *m* 1981, Patricia; two *s*. *Educ*: John Port Grammar Sch., Etwall, Derby. Reporter, Derby Evening Telegraph, 1967–71; Sports Sub-Editor, Birmingham Evening Mail, 1971–76; Asst Producer, ATV Birmingham, 1976–77; Prog. Ed., Sport, LWT, 1977–81; Controller of News and Sport, TVS, Southampton, 1981–88; Man. Dir, Chrysalis Television, 1988–92; Dir of Progs, London Network, 1992–94; Dep. Man. Dir, Sky Sports, 1994–98; Controller of Sport, Channel 4, 1998–2000; Dir of Broadcasting, 2000–03, Dep. Man. Dir, 2003–04; Sky Networks, BSkyB Ltd; Dir (formerly Controller), Sport, 2005–08, and Dir, News, 2007–08, ITV.

**SHARMAN, Peter William**, CBE 1984; Director, 1974–95 and Chief General Manager, 1975–84, Norwich Union Insurance Group; *b* 1 June 1924; *s* of William Charles Sharman and Olive Mabel (*née* Burl); *m* 1946, Eileen Barbara Crix; one *s* two *d*. *Educ*: Northgate Grammar Sch., Ipswich; Edinburgh Univ. MA 1950; FIA 1956. War service as Pilot, RAF. Joined Norwich Union Insce Gp, 1950; Gen. Man. and Actuary, 1969. Chairman: Life Offices' Assoc., 1977–78; British Insurance Assoc., 1982–83. *Recreation*: golf. *Address*: 28B Eaton Road, Norwich NR4 6PZ. *T*: (01603) 451230.

**SHARP**, family name of **Baroness Sharp of Guildford**.

**SHARP OF GUILDFORD**, Baroness *cr* 1998 (Life Peer), of Guildford in the co. of Surrey; **Margaret Lucy Sharp**; *b* 21 Nov. 1938; *d* of Osmund and Sydney Mary Ellen Hailstone; *m* 1962, Thomas Sharp, *qv*; two *d*. *Educ*: Tonbridge Girls' Grammar Sch.; Newnham Coll., Cambridge (BA 1960; MA 1962; Associate Fellow, 2007–10). Asst Principal, Bd of Trade and HM Treasury, 1960–63; Lectr in Economics, LSE, 1963–72; (pt-time) Guest Fellow, Brookings Instn, Washington, DC, 1973–76; Econ. Advr, NEDO, 1977–81; Res. Fellow, Sussex European Res. Centre, 1981–84, Sen. Fellow, Sci. Policy Res. Unit, 1984–99, Vis. Fellow, 1999–, Univ. of Sussex. Mem., Lib Dem Federal Policy Cttee, 1992–2003. Contested: (SDP/Alliance) Guildford, 1983 and 1987; (Lib Dem) Guildford, 1992 and 1997. Mem., H of L, 1998–2016; Lib Dem front bench spokesman on educn, H of L, 2000–09. Mem., Corp., Guildford Coll. for Further and Higher Educn, 2005–13 (Chm., Curriculum Standards Cttee, 2008–13); Gov., Weyfield Community Primary Sch., 2005–; Chm., Colleges in their Communities Commn, NIACE/Assoc. of Colleges/157 Gp, 2010–12. Chm., Age Concern Surrey, 2004–08; Patron, Surrey Law Centre, 2010–14. Trustee, Transformation Trust, 2009–. Hon. FCGI 2004. Hon. Fellow, Birkbeck Coll., London, 2006. Hon. Liveryman, Plumbers' Co., 2013. Hon. LLD Sussex, 2005; Hon. DAppSc South Bank, 2017. *Publications*: The State, the Enterprise and the Individual, 1974; The New Biotechnology: European Governments in search of a strategy, 1985; (ed) Europe and the New Technologies, 1985; (with Geoffrey Shepherd) Managing Change in British Industry, 1986; (ed with Peter Holmes) Strategies for New Technologies, 1987; (with Claire Shearman) European Technological Collaboration, 1987; (ed jtly) Technology and the Future of Europe, 1992; (with John Peterson) Technology Policy in the European

Union, 1998; many articles in learned jls dealing with science and technology policy. *Recreations:* reading, walking, theatre. *Address:* 96 London Road, Guildford GU1 1TH. *T:* (01483) 572669. *E:* margaretsharp96@gmail.com.

**SHARP, Sir Adrian,** 4th Bt *cr* 1922, of Warden Court, Maidstone, Kent; *b* 17 Sept. 1951; *s* of Sir Edward Herbert Sharp, 3rd Bt and of Beryl Kathleen, *d* of Leonard Simmons-Green; *S* father, 1986; *m* 1st, 1976, Hazel Patricia Bothwell (marr. diss. 1986), *o d* of James Trevor Wallace; 2nd, 1994, Denise, *o d* of Percy Edward Roberts; one *s*. *Heir: s* Hayden Sean Sharp, *b* 27 Aug. 1994. *Address:* 9–1610 Crawforth Street, Whitby, ON L1N 9B1, Canada.

**SHARP, Ann Elizabeth;** *see* Hussey, A. E.

**SHARP, Christopher Francis;** QC 1999; a Recorder, since 2005; a Deputy High Court Judge, Family Division, since 2011; *b* 17 Sept. 1952; *s* of late (Charles Vyvyan) Peter Sharp and (Lilian) Corona Sharp (*née* Bradshaw); *m* 1978, Sarah Margot Cripps, LLB, JP; one *s* one *d*. *Educ:* Canford Sch., Dorset; Worcester Coll., Oxford (MA). Called to the Bar, Inner Temple, 1975, Bencher, 2016; Mem., Western Circuit; founder mem., St John's Chambers, Bristol, 1978 (Dep. Hd, 1988–2000, Hd of Chambers, 2000–08). Founder Chm., Bristol Family Law Bar Assoc., 1990–96. Vis. Fellow, Faculty of Law, UWE, 2003–. Mem. Adv. Council, Worcester Coll., Oxford, 2006–15. Trustee, Quartet Community Foundn, 2011–17 (Mem. Cttee, 2010). *Publications:* articles in legal jls; idle random poetry. *Recreations:* walking, ski-ing, sailing, theatre, Dorset, and (increasingly) grandchildren. *Address:* St John's Chambers, 101 Victoria Street, Temple, Bristol BS1 6PU. *Clubs:* Bar Yacht, Bristol and Bath Tennis.

**SHARP, Sir Fabian Alexander Sebastian,** 5th Bt *cr* 1920, of Heckmondwike, W Riding, co. York; *b* 5 Nov. 1973; *o s* of Sir Sheridan Christopher Robin Sharp, 4th Bt and Anna Maria Sharp (*née* Rossi); *S* father, 2014, but his name does not appear on the Official Roll of the Baronetage; *m* 2006, Marcia Debbie Gordon, *d* of Wentworth Williams. *Educ:* University Coll. London (BA 1997); Westminster Univ. (MA 2002). *Heir:* cousin John Henry Edward Sharp [*b* 1965; *m* 1994, Sally Anne Sayer (marr. diss.); one *d*].

**SHARP, Howard;** QC (Jersey) 2010; Advocate, Ardent Chambers (formerly Central Chambers), since 2015; *b* Cambridge, 19 Dec. 1975; *s* of John and Barbara Sharp. *Educ:* Warwick Univ. (BA Hons Hist.); Coll. of Law, London (CPE, BVC). Called to the Bar, Inner Temple, 2001; in practice as barrister, specialising in crime, internat. money laundering and corruption, 2001–08; Crown Advocate, Jersey, 2008–10; Solicitor Gen. for Jersey, 2010–15. *Recreation:* scuba diving. *Address:* Ardent Chambers, 14 Hill Street, St Helier, Jersey JE2 4UA.

**SHARP, Isobel Nicol,** CBE 2009; Partner, Deloitte (formerly Deloitte & Touche) LLP, 2002–12; President, Institute of Chartered Accountants of Scotland, 2007–08; *d* of late Alexander and of Catherine Sharp. *Educ:* Kirkcaldy High Sch.; Univ. of Edinburgh (BSc 1976). CA 1980; ACIS 1986. Member: Financial Reporting Rev. Panel, 1994–99; Accounting Standards Bd, 2000–05; Ind. Parly Standards Authy, 2009–13; non-executive Member: Audit and Assurance Bd, Scottish Parlt Corporate Body, 2014–17; HM Passport Office, 2014–15. Hon. Prof., Edinburgh Univ. Business Sch., 2008– (Mem., Internat. Adv. Bd, 2010–). Non-executive Director: Green Investment Bank plc, 2012–17; Winton Group Ltd (formerly Winton Capital Ltd), 2013–; IMI plc, 2015–; Bankers Investment Trust plc, 2017–. *Publications:* Stock Exchange Reporting, 1994; Financial Statements for Smaller Companies, 1997, 4th edn 2002; Financial Statements for UK Listed Groups, 2004, 9th edn as Annual Report Disclosures for UK Listed Groups, 2012; Financial Statements for UK Unlisted Groups, 2007, 3rd edn 2010.

**SHARP, James Lyall;** HM Diplomatic Service; Ambassador to the Republic of Azerbaijan, since 2019; *b* 12 April 1960; *s* of Sir Richard Lyall Sharp, KCVO, CB; *m* 1992, Sara Essam El-Gammal; two *s*. *Educ:* Queen Elizabeth's Boys' Sch., Barnet; Durham Univ. (BA Hons Modern Middle Eastern Studies 1982). Customer Relations, British Aerospace, Riyadh, 1983–86; entered FCO, 1987; S America Dept, 1987–88; lang. trng, 1988–89, 2nd Sec., Chancery/Inf., 1989–92, Cairo; Hd of Section, Eastern Dept, 1992–95, Hong Kong Dept, 1995–96, FCO; 1st Sec., OSCE, Vienna, 1996–98; Hd of Section, NE Asia and Pacific Dept, FCO, 1998–2000; Dep. Hd, Security Policy Dept, FCO, 2000–01; lang. trng, 2002; Ambassador to Kazakhstan, 2002–05; Hd, Western Mediterranean/Justice and Home Affairs Gp, FCO, 2006–08; Regl Dir Asia-Pacific, UK Border Agency, Hong Kong, 2008–12; Dir, Migration, FCO, 2013–15; Policy Advisor, Mediterranean Migration Unit, 2015–17; Eastern Europe and Central Asia Directorate, 2017–18, FCO; lang. trng, 2018–19. *Address:* c/o Foreign and Commonwealth Office, King Charles Street, SW1A 2AH.

**SHARP, Sir Leslie,** Kt 1996; QPM 1986; Chief Constable of Strathclyde Police, 1991–95; *b* 14 May 1936; *s* of George James Sharp and Lily Mabel (*née* Moys); *m* 1st, 1956, Maureen (*née* Tyson) (decd); two *d*; 2nd, 1985, Audrey (*née* Sidwell); two *d*. *Educ:* University Coll. London (LLB). MRC, 1952–54; Nat. Service, Middx Regt, 1954–56; Metropolitan Police, 1956–80; Asst Chief Constable, 1980–83, Dep. Chief Constable, 1983–88, W Midlands Police; Chief Constable, Cumbria Constab., 1988–91. Hon. LLD Strathclyde, 1995. *Recreations:* home computing, genealogy.

**SHARP, Dr Lindsay Gerard;** museum consultant, since 2005; Director, National Museum of Science & Industry, 2000–05; *b* 22 Aug. 1947; *s* of late Clifford Douglas Sharp and Olive Dora Sharp; *m* 1st, 1968, Margaret Mary Sommi (marr. diss. 1979); one *s*; 2nd, 1981, Robyn Catherine Peterson; one *d*. *Educ:* Wadham Coll., Oxford (BA 1st cl. Hons 1969); Queen's Coll., Oxford (DPhil 1976). Clifford Norton Res. Fellow, Queen's Coll., Oxford, 1972–75; Asst Keeper, Pictorial Collection, Science Mus., 1976–78; Dep. Dir, then Dir, Mus. of Applied Arts and Scis, Sydney, 1978–88; Director: Entertainment and Leisure, Merlin Internat. Properties, Sydney, 1988–90; The Earth Exchange, Sydney, 1990–93; consultant, Asia and Australasia, 1990–93; Sen. Mus. Consultant and Dep. Dir, Mus. of Creativity Project, Milken Family Foundn, Santa Monica, 1993–96; Pres. and CEO, Royal Ontario Mus., Toronto, 1996–2000. *Recreations:* reading, garden design, music, opera, film, wine collection, travel, cultural and architectural history, bio-diversity, sustainability and cultural diversity issues.

**SHARP, Michael John Todkill;** Chief Executive Officer, Debenhams plc, 2011–16; *b* Stamford, Lincs, 22 March 1957; *s* of Sqdn Leader Joseph Todkill Sharp and Doreen Mary Sharp; *m* 1985, Elaine Agnes Walsh; five *d*. *Educ:* Bartholomew Sch., Eynsham; Oxford Coll. of Further Educn. Sears Hldgs, 1976–81; Littlewoods Orgn, 1982–85; Burton Gp, 1985–92; Buying and Merchandising Dir, Topshop/Topman, 1992–96; Man. Dir, Principles and Racing Green, 1996–97; Chief Operating Officer, 2003–08, Dep. Chief Exec., 2008–11, Debenhams plc. Hon. Prof. in Fashion Business, Glasgow Caledonian Univ., 2013. *Recreations:* travelling, playing guitar, classic cars, my lovely family.

**SHARP, Prof. Paul Martin,** PhD; FRS 2013; FRSE; MRIA; Alan Robertson Professor of Genetics, Institute of Evolutionary Biology, University of Edinburgh, since 2007; *b* 12 Sept. 1957; *s* of late Maurice Hicking and Wendy Griffiths. *Educ:* Univ. of Edinburgh (BSc 1st Cl. Hons Biol Scis (Genetics); PhD 1982). Lectr in Genetics, 1982–92, Associate Prof. of Genetics, 1992–93, TCD; Prof. of Genetics, Univ. of Nottingham, 1993–2007. Vis. Asst Prof., Univ. of Texas at Houston, 1985–87. Mem., EMBO, 1992. Pres., Soc. for Molecular Biol. and Evolution, 2008. FRSE 2010. MRIA 1993. *Publications:* contribs to learned jls incl. Science, Cell, Jl Virology, Nature, Proc. Nat. Acad. of Scis, USA. *Recreations:* hill walking, pteridology, supporter of Nottingham Forest Football Club since 1967. *Address:* Institute of Evolutionary Biology, University of Edinburgh, Ashworth Laboratories, Kings Buildings, West Mains Road, Edinburgh EH9 3FL. *E:* paul.sharp@ed.ac.uk.

**SHARP, Peter Marjoribanks;** freelance consultant and trainer, health, social care and education, since 2015; *b* Aberdeen, 12 March 1955; *s* of Harold Sharp and Isobel Sharp; *m* 1987, Lindsey May Darking; two *d*. *Educ:* Kings Norton Grammar Sch.; Poly. of Central London (BSc Life Scis 1977); Southlands Coll., London (PGCE 1978); Inst. of Educn, Univ. of London (DipEd 1983; MA Child Develt 1986); Tavistock Clinic (Cert Ed Psych. 1987). CPsychol 1991; CSci 2007; AFBPsS 2010. Teacher, Langdon Sch., 1978–80; Hd of Sci., Park High Sch., 1980–86; Psychologist, 1988–90, Sen. Psychologist, 1990–92, Divisional Sen. Psychologist, 1992–94, Asst Principal Educnl Psychologist, 1994–97, Hants; Principal Educnl Psychologist, Southampton CC, 1997–2002; Mouchel: Principal Consultant, 2002–05; Director: Children's Services, 2005–07; Learning, 2007–09; Wellbeing, 2009–13; Chief Exec., Centre for Workforce Intelligence, 2010–13; Hd, Wellbeing, Cordis Bright, 2013–15. *Publications:* (jtly) Anger Management, 1998, 3rd edn 2017; (contrib.) Clinical Counselling in Schools, 2000; Nurturing Emotional Literacy, 2001. *Recreations:* family, photography, Francophile, reading, travel, social media @ Peter_M_Sharp, Italian language, woodturning, watercolour painting, genealogy. *T:* (01579) 351948, 07966 310691. *E:* petersharp12@gmail.com.

**SHARP, Prof. Phillip Allen,** PhD; Institute Professor, David H. Koch Institute for Integrative Cancer Research (formerly Center for Cancer Research), Massachusetts Institute of Technology, since 1999 (Salvador E. Luria Professor, 1992–99); *b* 6 June 1944; *s* of Joseph W. Sharp and Katherin (*née* Colvin); *m* 1964, Ann Christine Holcombe; three *d*. *Educ:* Union Coll., Barbourville, Ky (BA 1966); Univ. of Illinois (PhD 1969). NIH Postdoctoral Fellow, CIT, 1969–71; Sen. Res. Investigator, Cold Spring Harbor Lab., NY, 1972–74; Massachusetts Institute of Technology: Associate Prof., 1974–79; Prof. of Biol., 1979–86; Class of '41 Prof., 1986–87; John D. MacArthur Prof., 1987–92; Associate Dir, 1982–85, Dir, 1985–91, Center for Cancer Res.; Hd, Dept of Biol., 1991–99; Dir, McGovern Inst., 2000–04. Co-founder, and Mem. Director Bd, 1978–2009; Chm., Scientific Bd, 1987–2002, Biogen IDEC (formerly Biogen, Inc.); Co-founder, and Mem., Scientific and Director Bds, Alnylam Pharmaceuticals Inc., 2002–. Chm., General Motors Cancer Res. Foundn Awards Assembly, 1994–2006. Member: Cttee on Sci., Engrg and Public Policy, 1992–95; President's Cttee of Advrs on Sci. and Technol., 1994–97; Scientific Cttee, Ludwig Inst. for Cancer Res., 1998–; Bd of Scientific Govs, Scripps Res. Inst., 1999–; Bd of Advrs, Polaris Venture Partners, 2002–; Adv. Bd, Verastem, 2010–; Bd of Dirs, Syros Pharmaceuticals, 2012–. Advr, Longwood Fund, 2010–. Mem., Alfred P. Sloan Foundn, 1995–2004; Mem. Bd of Trustees, Massachusetts Gen. Hosp., 2002–11. Member: American Acad. of Arts and Scis, 1983; NAS, 1983; Inst. of Medicine, 1991; American Philosophical Soc., 1991 (Benjamin Franklin Medal, 1999). FAAAS 1987 (Pres., 2013–14). Hon. FRSE 2002. Hon. Mem., NAS, Republic of Korea, 2004; Foreign Mem., Royal Soc., 2011. Hon. Dr: Union Coll., Ky, 1991; Univ. of Ky, 1994; Bowdoin Coll., Maine, 1995; Univ. of Tel Aviv, 1996; Albright Coll., Penn, 1996; Univ. of Glasgow, 1998; Thomas Moore Coll., Ky, 1999; Uppsala Univ., 1999; Univ. of Buenos Aires, 1999; Northern Ky Univ., 2001; Rippon College, Wis, 2006. Alfred P. Sloan Jr Prize for Cancer Res., Gen. Motors Res. Foundn, 1986; Gairdner Foundn Internat. Award, Canada, 1986; Albert Lasker Basic Med. Res. Award, 1988; Nobel Prize in Physiology or Medicine, 1993; Nat. Medal of Sci., 2004; Double Helix Medal for Sci. Res., Cold Spring Harbor Lab., NY, 2006; Othmer Gold Medal, Chemical Heritage Foundn, 2015. *Publications:* numerous scientific articles in jls and other pubns. *Address:* The Koch Institute, Room 76–461A, Massachusetts Institute of Technology, 77 Massachusetts Avenue, Cambridge, MA 02139–4307, USA. *T:* (617) 2536421.

**SHARP, Robin John Alfred,** CB 1993; Director, Global Environment, Department of the Environment, 1994–95; *b* 30 July 1935; *s* of Robert Arthur Sharp and Yona Maud (*née* Brazier); *m* 1963, Anne Elizabeth Davison. *Educ:* Brentwood Sch.; Brasenose Coll., Oxford (MA). Wesley House, Cambridge (BA). Methodist Minister, West Mersea, 1960–62; Theol Colls Sec., SCM, 1962–65; Minister, Paddington, 1965–66. Principal, Min. of Housing and Local Govt and DoE, 1966–72; Asst Sec., 1972; Special Advr to Chancellor of Duchy of Lancaster, Cabinet Office, 1972; Department of the Environment: Road Safety Div., 1972–75; Housing Div., 1975–81; Under Sec., 1981; Public Housing and Right to Buy, 1981–86; Local Govt, 1986–91; Dir of Rural Affairs, 1991–94. Chairman: European Sustainable Use Gp, IUCN, 1997–2007, now Emeritus; New Renaissance Gp, 1997–2002; Brent Fairtrade Network, 2012–; Kilburn Locality Patient Participation Gp, NHS Brent Commng Gp, 2013–16; Brent Patient Voice, 2014–; Vice Pres., BTCV, 1997–2007. Trustee, Fauna and Flora Internat., 1995–2004 (Company Sec., 2000–04). Harry Messel Award for Conservation Leadership, IUCN Species Survival Commn, 2006; Brent Community Champion of Year Award, 2017. *Publications:* (jtly) Preparing for the Ministry of the 1970s, 1964; (jtly) Worship in a United Church, 1964; (contrib.) British Environmental Policy and Europe, 1998; (jtly) Freshwater Fisheries in Central and Eastern Europe, 2004; (contrib.) Recreational Hunting: conservation and livelihoods, 2009; (contrib.) Silent Summer: the state of the nation's wildlife, 2010; (contrib.) Transitional Environmental Support Systems Design: global solutions, 2013. *Recreations:* bird-watching, walking, concert-going, travel. *Address:* 30 Windermere Avenue, NW6 6LN. *T:* (020) 8969 0381.

**SHARP, Dr Roy Martin;** Chief Executive, Tertiary Education Commission, 2008–11; *b* 3 April 1946; *s* of Leonard and Freda Sharp; *m* 1971, Beverley Davison; two *s* one *d*. *Educ:* Dame Allan's Sch., Newcastle-on-Tyne; St Peter's Coll., Oxford (MA; DPhil). Dist. FIPENZ (FIPENZ 1992). University of Auckland: Lectr, 1973–75; Sen. Lectr, 1975–89; Prof., 1989–97; Dean of Engrg, 1992–97; Asst Vice-Chancellor, 1993–94; Dep. Vice-Chancellor, 1995–96; Dep. Vice-Chancellor, Victoria Univ. of Wellington, 1997–2003; Vice-Chancellor, Univ. of Canterbury, NZ, 2003–08. *Recreations:* walking, music.

**SHARP, Dr Sonia,** CPsychol; Partner, EY, Melbourne, since 2018; *b* Sheffield, 22 Oct. 1961; *d* of Dr Mike Sharp and Beryl Sharp; partner, Edwin; two *d*. *Educ:* Univ. of Aston in Birmingham (BSc Hons, PGCE); Univ. of Sheffield (MSc; PhD 1998). CPsychol 1990. NPQH 2001. Teaching posts in Derbys, Leeds and Barnsley, 1984–88; Educational Psychologist, Barnsley, 1989–94; Lincs, 1994–97; Chief Educnl Psychologist, Bucks, 1997–99; Asst Dir of Educn, Birmingham CC, 1999–2003; Dep. Chief Exec., Educn Leeds, 2003–05; Dir of Children's Services, Rotherham MBC, 2005–08; Exec. Dir, Children and Young People's Services, Sheffield CC, 2008–12; Dep. Sec., Early Childhood Develt Gp, 2012–13, Early Child and Sch. Educn Gp, 2013–15, Dept of Educn and Early Childhood Develt, Vic, Australia; Principal, Nous Gp, 2015–18. Chm., Yorks and Humber Br., Assoc. of Dirs of Children's Services, 2007–09. British Psychological Society: Chm., Div. of Child and Educnl Psychol., 1996–98; Associate Fellow, 1998. *Publications:* (with D. A. Thompson) Improving Schools: establishing and integrating whole school behaviour policies, 1994; (ed with P. K. Smith) How to Tackle Bullying in your School, 1994; (with

H. Covie) Peer Counselling in Schools, 1996; (with H. Covie) Supporting and Counselling Children in Distress, 1998; (jtly) Bullying Behaviour: a long term perspective, 2002. *Recreations:* walking, fell-running, dance.

**SHARP, Thomas, (Tom),** CBE 1987; retired; General Manager, Names' Interests, Lloyd's of London, 1987–91; *b* 19 June 1931; *s* of late William Douglas Sharp and Margaret Sharp (*née* Tout); *m* 1962, Margaret Lucy Hailstone (*see* Baroness Sharp of Guildford); two *d. Educ:* Brown Sch., Toronto; Abbotsholme Sch., Derbys; Jesus Coll., Oxford. BoT and DTI (with short interval HM Treasury), 1954–73; Counsellor (Commercial), British Embassy, Washington, 1973–76; Dept of Trade, 1976–79; Dept of Industry, 1979–83; DTI, 1983–87. Member (Lib Dem): Surrey CC, 1989–2005 (Chm., Social Services Cttee, 1993–95); Guildford BC, 1991–99. Chm., Guildford CAB, 2004–07. *Publications:* (ed jtly) Just a Larger Family: letters of Marie Williamson from the Canadian Home Front, 1940–1944, 2011. *Address:* 96 London Road, Guildford, Surrey GU1 1TH. *T:* (01483) 572669. *E:* tomsharp96@ntlworld.com.

**SHARP, Rt Hon. Dame Victoria (Madeleine),** DBE 2009; PC 2013; **Rt Hon. Lady Justice Sharp;** a Lady Justice of Appeal, since 2013; President, Queen's Bench Division, since 2019 (Vice-President, 2016–19); *b* 8 Feb. 1956; *d* of Lord Sharp of Grimsdyke, CBE and of Marion (*née* Freedman); *m* 1986; three *s* one *d. Educ:* N London Collegiate Sch.; Univ. of Bristol (LLB). Called to the Bar, Inner Temple, 1979, Bencher, 2009; a Recorder, 1998–2008; a Judge of the High Ct of Justice, QBD, 2009–13; a Presiding Judge, Western Circuit, 2012–13. QC 2001.

**SHARPE, Prof. David Thomas,** OBE 1986; FRCS; Consultant Plastic Surgeon, Bradford Royal Infirmary, 1985–2014; Director, Plastic Surgery and Burns Research Unit, 1986–2014, and Professor in Plastic and Reconstructive Surgery, 1996–2014, University of Bradford; *b* 14 Jan. 1946; *s* of Albert Edward Sharpe and Grace Emily Sharpe; *m* 1st, 1971, Patricia Lilian Meredith (marr. diss. 2002); one *s* two *d;* 2nd, 2004, Tracey Louise Bowman. *Educ:* Grammar School for Boys, Gravesend; Downing Coll., Cambridge (MA); Clin. Med. Sch., Oxford (MB BChir); FRCS 1975. Ho. Surg., Radcliffe Inf., Oxford, 1970–71; Senior House Officer: Plastic Surgery, Churchill Hosp., Oxford, 1971–72; Accident Service, Radcliffe Inf., 1972; Pathology, Radcliffe Inf., 1972–73; Gen. Surgery, Royal United Hosp., Bath, 1973–75; Plastic Surgery, Welsh Plastic Surgery Unit, Chepstow, 1976; Registrar, Plastic Surgery: Chepstow, 1976–78; Canniesburn Hosp., Glasgow, 1978–80; Sen. Registrar, Plastic Surgery, Leeds and Bradford, 1980–84; Visiting Consultant Plastic Surgeon: Yorkshire Clinic, Bradford, 1985–2014; BUPA Hosp., Elland, W Yorks, 1985–2011; Cromwell Hosp., London, 1985–2006. Chm., Breast Special Interest Gp, British Assoc. of Plastic Surgeons, 1997–99. Pres., British Assoc. of Aesthetic Plastic Surgeons, 1997–99. Chm., Yorks Air Ambulance, 2001–03. Inventor and designer of med. equipment and surgical instruments and devices; exhibitor, Design Council, London, 1987. Hon. DSc Bradford, 2011. British Design Award, 1988; Prince of Wales Award for Innovation and Production, 1988. *Publications:* chapters, leading articles and papers on plastic surgery topics, major burn disaster management, tissue expansion and breast reconstruction. *Recreations:* painting, shooting, flying. *Address:* Danby Low Mill, near Middleham, N Yorks DL8 4PX. *T:* (01969) 625795. *E:* profsharpe@hotmail.com.

**SHARPE, John Herbert S.;** *see* Subak-Sharpe.

**SHARPE, Malcolm David; His Honour Judge Sharpe;** a Circuit Judge, since 2014; Designated Family Judge, Mid and West Wales, since 2014; a Deputy High Court Judge (Family Division), since 2014; *b* Liverpool, 6 July 1966; *s* of Barrie Ronald Walter Sharpe and Joan Sharpe (*née* Waters); *m* 2006, Stephanie Phyllis Davidson; one *s. Educ:* St Edward's Coll., Liverpool; Univ. of Sheffield (LLB); Queen's Univ., Belfast (LLM); Inns of Court Sch. of Law. Called to the Bar, Lincoln's Inn, 1989; a Recorder, 2010–14. *Publications:* (contrib.) Child Care Management Practice, 2010, 3rd edn 2018. *Recreations:* football, cycling, technology. *Address:* c/o Swansea Civil and Family Justice Centre, Caravella House, Quay West, Quay Parade, Swansea SA1 1SP.

**SHARPE, Prof. Richard,** PhD; FBA 2003; FSA, FRHistS; Professor of Diplomatic, University of Oxford, since 1998, and Fellow, Wadham College, Oxford, since 1990; *b* 17 Feb. 1954; *s* of John Maden Sharpe and Dorothy Sharpe (*née* Lord). *Educ:* St Peter's Sch., York; Trinity Coll., Cambridge (BA, MA, PhD). FRHistS 1988; FSA 1990. Asst Warden, YHA Lakeland Reg., 1973; Asst Editor, Dictionary of Medieval Latin from British Sources, 1981–90; University of Oxford: Reader in Diplomatic, 1990–98; Sen. Tutor, Wadham Coll., Oxford, 1997–2000; Jun. Proctor, 2000–01. O'Donnell Lectr in Celtic Studies, Oxford, 2004, Univ. of Wales, 2007. Res. Assoc., Sch. of Celtic Studies, Dublin Inst. of Adv. Studies, 1988–2010; Mem., Sch. of Historical Studies, IAS, Princeton, 1997. Mem., Oxford CC, 1987–95. Mem., Commn internat. de diplomatique, 2008–. Member: Oxford Archaeol Adv. Cttee, 1987–2000 (Chm., 1995–2000); Council, Oxford Historical Soc., 1990–; Pres., Surtees Soc., 2002–. Hon. MRIA 2018. Gen. Editor, Corpus of British Medieval Library Catalogues, 1990–. *Publications:* Raasay: a study in island history, vol. 1 1977, vol. 2 1978, 2nd edn 1982; (with M. Lapidge) A Bibliography of Celtic-Latin Literature 400–1200, 1985; (contrib. with D. R. Howlett) Dictionary of Medieval Latin from British Sources, fasc. III 1986, fasc. IV 1989, fasc. V 1997; Medieval Irish Saints' Lives, 1991; (with J. Blair) Pastoral Care before the Parish, 1992; Adomnán of Iona: Life of St Columba, 1995; (with R. G. Eales) Canterbury and the Norman Conquest, 1995; (jtly) English Benedictine Libraries, 1996; A Handlist of the Latin Writers of Great Britain and Ireland before 1540, 1997; (with A. T. Thacker) Local Saints and Local Churches in the Early Medieval West, 2002; Titulus: identifying Medieval Latin texts, 2003; Norman Rule in Cumbria 1092–1136, 2006; Roderick O'Flaherty's Letters, 2013; (with R. Easting) Peter of Cornwall's Book of Revelations, 2013; contribs to books and learned jls. *Recreations:* exploring Britain, working out, piano. *Address:* Old Indian Institute, Broad Street, Oxford OX1 3BD. *E:* richard.sharpe@history.ox.ac.uk.

**SHARPE, Robert James,** FRCO; Director of Music, York Minster, since 2008; *b* 14 Nov. 1971; *s* of Nigel and Carole Sharpe; *m* 1998, Mary, (Polly), Proctor; one *s* one *d. Educ:* Lincoln Christ's Hosp. Sch.; Exeter Coll., Oxford (Organ Schol.); BA Music 1994; MA 1998). FRCO 1993. Asst Organist, Lichfield Cathedral, 1994–2002. Asst Conductor, Birmingham Bach Choir, 1996–2002; Dir of Music, Truro Cath., 2002–08; Conductor, Three Spires Singers and Orch., 2002–08. FRSA. Hon. FGCM 2008. Cornish Gorsedd Cornwhylen Cross, 2008. *Recreations:* wine, cooking, interior design, colour, furniture, architecture, technology, people. *Address:* 1 Minster Court, York YO1 7JJ. *E:* robert@robertsharpe.org.uk.

**SHARPE, Rosemary Helen,** CMG 2011; HM Diplomatic Service; Counsellor, Foreign and Commonwealth Office, since 2003; *b* 11 March 1956. *Educ:* Lady Margaret Hall, Oxford (BA Juris. 1974). Second Secretary: FCO, 1982–85; (Inf.), New Delhi, 1985–87; First Secretary: UK Repn, Brussels, 1987–88; FCO, 1988–91; (Econ.), Berlin, 1991–96; FCO, 1996–2000; Counsellor, Madrid, 2000–03.

**SHARPE, Samuel John;** Chief Financial Officer, Save the Children UK, since 2014; *b* London, 4 May 1962; *s* of Anthony John Sharpe and late Monica Margaret Sharpe (*née* Vincent); *m* 1997, Tansy Stephané Jessop; two *s. Educ:* University Coll., Oxford (BA Classics 1985); Birkbeck Coll., Univ. of London (MSc Econs 1988); Univ. of Warwick (MSc Mgt 2014). CPFA 2008. Various posts, ODA, 1985–97; Department for International Development: India, 1997–2000; South Africa, 2000–04; Policy Div., 2004–07; Finance Dir, 2007–10; Hd of India Office, 2010–14. *Address:* Save the Children UK, 1 St John's Lane, EC1M 4AR.

**SHARPE, Thomas Anthony Edward;** QC 1994; *b* 21 Dec. 1949; *e s* of late James Sharpe, MC, Maxwelltown, Dumfriesshire and Lydia de Gegg, Donauwörth, Germany; *m* 1988, Phillis M. Rogers, *y d* of late W. P. Rogers and Mrs M. Rogers, Warlingham, Surrey; one *s* one *d;* one *s* one *d* by previous marriage. *Educ:* Trinity Hall, Cambridge (MA). Called to the Bar: Lincoln's Inn, 1976 (Bencher, 2004); St Kitts and Nevis, 2002; Fellow in Law, Wolfson and Nuffield Coll., Oxford, 1979–88; in practice at the Bar, 1987–. Comr, Commn of Inquiry into Maladministration, St Kitts and Nevis, 2009–12. Exec. Dir (part-time), Inst. for Fiscal Studies, 1981–87. Member: Adv. Bd, Centre for Competition Policy, UEA, 2005– (Chm., 2012–); Editl Bds, European Competition Jl and Concurrences, 2005–. Chm., New London Orch., 1998–2000; Trustee: Help Musicians UK (formerly Musicians' Benevolent Fund), 1999–2017; Awards for Young Musicians, 2019–; Mem. Council, LPO, 2014–. Chm., Foundn for Family Medicine in Palestine, 2018–. FRSA. *Publications:* monographs and articles in law jls on competition law, utility regulation and EC law. *Recreations:* music, travel, history, wine, grandchildren. *Address:* 1 Essex Court, Temple, EC4Y 9AR. *T:* (020) 7583 2000, *Fax:* (020) 7583 0118. *Clubs:* Reform, Beefsteak.

**SHARPE, Prof. William Forsyth;** STANCO 25 Professor of Finance, Stanford University, 1995–99, now Emeritus (Timken Professor of Finance, 1970–89; Professor of Finance, 1993–95); *b* 16 June 1934; *s* of Russell Thornley Sharpe and Evelyn Jillson Maloy; *m* 1st, 1954, Roberta Ruth Branton; one *s* one *d;* 2nd, 1986, Kathryn Peck. *Educ:* UCLA (AB 1955; MA 1956; PhD 1961). Economist, Rand Corp., 1957–61; University of Washington: Asst Prof. of Economics, 1961–63; Associate Prof., 1963–67; Prof., 1967–68; Prof., Univ. of California, Irvine, 1968–70. Pres., William F. Sharpe Associates, 1986–92. Chm., Financial Engines Inc., 1996–2003. Hon. DHumLit De Paul, 1997; Dr *hc* Alicante, 2003; Dr Econs *hc* Vienna, 2004; Hon. DSc(Econ) London Business Sch., 2008. Graham and Dodd Award, 1972, 1973, 1986, 1988, 1998, 2007, 2010, Nicholas Molodovsky Award, 1989, Financial Analysts Fedn; (jtly) Nobel Prize in Economics, 1990; UCLA Medal, 1998. *Publications:* Economics of Computers, 1969; Portfolio Theory and Capital Markets, 1970; Investments, 1978, 6th edn 1999; Fundamentals of Investments, 1989, 3rd edn 2000; Investors and Markets, 2007; Selected Works, 2012. *Recreations:* sailing, opera, music. *Address:* Graduate School of Business, Stanford University, Stanford, CA 94305–5015, USA. *T:* (650) 7254876.

**SHARPLES,** family name of **Baroness Sharples**.

**SHARPLES,** Baroness *cr* 1973 (Life Peer); **Pamela Sharples;** Director, TVS, 1981–90 and 1991–93; *b* 11 Feb. 1923; *o d* of late Lt-Comdr K. W. Newall and Violet (who *m* 2nd, Lord Claud Hamilton, GCVO, CMG, DSO); *m* 1st, 1946, Major R. C. Sharples, MC, Welsh Guards (later Sir Richard Sharples, KCMG, OBE, MC, assassinated 1973); two *s* two *d;* 2nd, 1977, Patrick D. de Laszlo (*d* 1980); 3rd, 1983, Robert Douglas Swan (*d* 1995). *Educ:* Southover Manor, Lewes; Florence. WAAF, 1941–46. Mem., H of L, 1973–2017. Mem., Review Body on Armed Forces Pay, 1979–81. Trustee, Wessex Med. Trust, 1997–. *Address:* 60 Westminster Gardens, SW1P 4JG. *T:* (020) 7821 1875.
*See also* Hon. C. J. Sharples.

**SHARPLES, Adam John,** CB 2007; Chairman, Money Advice Trust, since 2016; *b* 1 Feb. 1954; *s* of Frederick Sharples and Margaret (*née* Robertson); *m* 1982, Barbara Bleiman; one *s* one *d. Educ:* Corpus Christi Coll., Oxford (BA PPE 1975); Queen Mary Coll., London Univ. (MSc Econs 1977). Economist, Labour Party, 1978–83; Head of Res., NUPE, 1983–88; HM Treasury: Principal, 1988; Head: Tax Policy Team, 1992–96; Transport Team, 1996–97; Public Enterprise Partnerships Team, 1997–98; Dep. Dir, Public Services Directorate, then Dir, Public Spending, 1998–2003; Dir, Internat., Bd of Inland Revenue, 2003–04; Dir Gen., Work, Welfare and Equality Gp, 2004–09, Employment, 2009–11, DWP; Dir of Policy, Which?, 2012. Chm., Ixion Gp, 2012–17. FRSA 2000. *Recreations:* family, football, guitar, cooking. *Address:* Money Advice Trust, 21 Garlick Hill, EC4V 2AU.

**SHARPLES, Hon. Christopher John;** Chairman, Wheatley Associates, since 2010; *b* 24 May 1947; *s* of Sir Richard Sharples, KCMG, OBE, MC and of Baroness Sharples, qv; *m* 1st, 1975, Sharon Joanne (marr. diss. 2009), *d* of late Robert Sweeny, DFC and Joanne Sweeny; one *s* two *d;* 2nd, 2010, Gaynor Malet, *d* of late Major Rhydian Llewellyn MC and of Lady Honor Llewellyn. MCSI (MSI 1992). VSO, India, 1965–66; C. Czarnikow Ltd (commodity brokers), 1968–72; Co-founder and Dir, Inter-Commodities Ltd, 1972 (renamed GNI Ltd, 1984; Chm., 1994–96); Director: GNI Holdings Ltd, 1984–2000; GNI Wallace Ltd, 1986–97; Founder Director and Chairman: ICV Ltd, 1981–98; Intercom Data Systems (renamed RoyalBlue Ltd), 1982–90; Chairman: GH Asset Management Ltd, 1991–94; Datastream Internat. Ltd, 1996–98; Lombard Street Research, 1997–2000; Membertrack Ltd, 1999–2000; Director: Gerrard Vivian Gray, 1994–98; Hiscox Dedicated Insurance Fund, 1995–96; Digital River Inc., 1998–2000; Unigestion (UK) Ltd, 2000–17; Grandeye Ltd, 2004–08; Seeker Wireless Ltd, 2006–12. Member: Adv. Panel to SIB, 1986–87; City Panel on Takeovers and Mergers, 1991–95; Association of Futures Brokers and Dealers, 1987–92: Chairman: Rules Cttee, 1987–91; F and GP Cttee, 1987–91; Chm., Securities and Futures Authority, 1991–95 (Chairman: Exec. Cttee, 1991–95; Capital Rules Cttee, 1991–95; Finance Cttee, 1991–95). International Petroleum Exchange: Dir, 1981–87; Dep. Chm., 1986–87; Mem., Public Relns Cttee, 1981–87; Member: Public Relns Cttee, London Commodity Exchange, 1983–96; Clearing Cttee, LIFFE, 1982–87; Taxation Cttee, British Fedn of Commodity Assocs, 1985–87; London Markets Adv. Gp on Regulation, 1986–87. Mem., Royal Air Sqdn (formerly Air Sqdn), 1993– (Chm., 1998–2005); Chm., Yacht Squadron Racing Ltd, 2014– (Mem., America's Cup Wkg Cttee, 2017–); Trustee, Royal Yacht Squadron Foundn, 2018–. Mem., Younger Brethren, Trinity House, 2014–. *Recreations:* sailing, flying light aircraft. *Address:* 39 Rose Square, SW3 6RS. *Clubs:* Pratt's, White's; Royal Yacht Squadron (Cdre, 2013–17); Royal Bermuda Yacht.

**SHARPLES, Ven. David John;** Archdeacon of Salford, since 2009; *b* Manchester, 17 March 1958; *s* of Eric and Jean Sharples; *m* 1982, Elaine Maria Cottrell; two *s. Educ:* King's Coll., London (BD 1981; AKC 1981); Coll. of the Resurrection, Mirfield. Ordained deacon 1982, priest 1983; Asst Curate, St Mary the Virgin, Prestwich, 1982–87; Vicar, St Anne's, Royton, 1987–2002; Area Dean, Tandle, 1994–2002; Dir of Ordinands, Dio. of Manchester, 2002–. Chaplain, Dr Kershaw's Hospice, 1989–2002. Hon. Canon, Manchester Cathedral, 2006–. *Recreation:* Manchester City FC. *Address:* c/o Church House, 90 Deansgate, Manchester M3 2QH. *T:* (0161) 828 1423.

**SHARPLES, Sir James,** Kt 1996; QPM 1989; DL; Chief Constable, Merseyside Police, 1989–98. Lancashire Constabulary, 1964–74; Greater Manchester Police, 1974–82; Asst Chief Constable, 1982–85, Dep. Chief Constable, 1985–88, Avon and Somerset

Constabulary; Dep. Chief Constable, Merseyside Police, 1988–89. Mem., ESRC, 1996–98. Non-exec. Chm., Countess of Chester NHS Trust, 2005–12 (non-exec. Dir, 2001–12). DL Merseyside, 1997.

SHARPLES, Hon. Sir Pita Russell, KNZM 2015; CBE 1990; PhD; Director, Tū Māori Mai Ltd, consultancy business; *b* Waipawa, NZ, 20 July 1941; *s* of Paul Massey Sharples and Ruiha Karani Niania; *m* 1990, Arapera Wikitoria Hineamaru; three *s* two *d*. *Educ*: Waituna W Primary Sch.; Takapau Primary Sch.; Waipukurau Dist High Sch.; Te Aute Coll.; Auckland Teachers' Coll. (Dip. Teaching 1966); Univ. of Auckland (BA 1967; MA; PhD Anthropol. and Linguistics 1977). Prof. of Educn, Auckland Univ. MP (Māori Party) Tāmaki Makaurau, New Zealand, 2005–14; Minister of Māori Affairs, 2008–14; Associate Minister of Educn and Corrections, 2008–14. Founding CEO, Race Relns Office, 1981–90. Estabd Māori Taskforce. Co-Leader, Māori Party, 2004–13. Tohunga Huarewa, Takitimu Māori Performing Arts Sch. and Massey Univ., 2001. *Publications*: contrib. articles and papers on educn, race relns, Māori culture and lang., Māori hist. and the justice system of NZ. *Recreations*: Rugby, Māori fighting arts, Māori performing arts. *Address*: 52 San Marino Drive, Western Heights, West Auckland 0612, New Zealand. *T*: 212446950. *E*: drpitasharples@gmail.com.

SHARPLES, Prof. Sarah Catherine, PhD; Professor of Human Factors, since 2012, and Pro-Vice-Chancellor, since 2018, University of Nottingham; *b* Kingston-upon-Thames, 1 Nov. 1972; *d* of Barry and Anne Nichols; *m* 2004, Craig Sharples; one *s* one *d*. *Educ*: Maple Infants; St Andrew and St Mark C of E Jun. Sch., Surbiton; Wimbledon High Sch.; Univ. of Nottingham (BSc Psychol. 1994; MSc Human Factors in Manufacturing Systems 1995; PhD Engrg 1999). University of Nottingham: Lectr, 1999–2007; Associate Prof. of Mechanical, Materials and Manufacturing Engrg, 2007–12; Associate Pro-Vice-Chancellor for Res. and Knowledge Exchange, 2015–18. Member: Catapult Bd, Transport Systems/ Connected Places, 2015–; Sci. Adv. Council, DfT, 2017–; UKRI-EPSRC, 2018–. Pres., Chartered Inst. of Ergonomics and Human Factors, 2015–16. *Publications*: (ed with J. R. Wilson) Evaluation of Human Work, 4th edn, 2015. *Recreations*: spending time with my family and friends, gardening, cooking, AFC Wimbledon and as many other armchair sports as possible. *Address*: University of Nottingham, University Park, Nottingham NG7 2RD. *T*: (0115) 823 2467. *E*: sarah.sharples@nottingham.ac.uk. *W*: www.twitter.com/@ scsharples.

SHARPLESS, Prof. Karl Barry, PhD; W. M. Keck Professor of Chemistry, The Scripps Research Institute, since 1990, and Skaggs Institute for Chemical Biology, La Jolla, California, since 1996; *b* 28 April 1941; *m* 1965, Jan Dueser; two *s* one *d*. *Educ*: Dartmouth Coll. (BA 1963); Stanford Univ. (PhD 1968). Postdoctoral Associate: Stanford Univ., 1968; Harvard Univ., 1969; Chemistry Faculty, MIT, 1970–77; Stanford Univ., 1977–80; Prof., 1980–90, Arthur C. Cope Prof., 1987–90, Chemistry Faculty, MIT. Fellow: Nat. Sci. Foundn, 1963; NIH, 1968; Foundation Fellow: A. P. Sloan, 1973; Camille and Henry Dreyfus, 1973; Sherman Fairchild, CIT, 1987; Simon Guggenheim, 1987. FAAAS 1984; Fellow: American Acad. Arts and Sci., 1984; NAS, 1985 (Chemical Scis Award, 2000); Hon. MRSC 1998. Honorary Doctorate: Dartmouth Coll., 1995; Royal Inst. of Technology, Stockholm, 1995; Technical Univ., Munich, 1995; Catholic Univ. of Louvain, 1996; Wesleyan Univ., 1999. Janssen Prize, 1986; Chemical Pioneer Award, Amer. Inst. of Chemists, 1988; Prelog Medal, ETH, Zurich, 1988; Scheele Medal, Swedish Acad. of Pharm. Scis, 1991; Tetrahedron Prize, 1993; King Faisal Prize for Sci., 1995; Microbial Chemistry Medal, Kitasato Inst., Tokyo, 1997; Harvey Sci. and Tech. Prize, Israel Inst. of Tech., 1998; Chirality Medal, Italian Chemical Soc., 2000; (jtly) Nobel Prize for Chemistry, 2001; Wolf Prize in Scis, Israel, 2001; Rhône Poulenc Medal, UK, 2001; Benjamin Franklin Medal, 2001, John Scott Prize and Medal, 2001, Philadelphia. American Chemical Society: Award for Creative Work in Organic Synthesis, 1983; Arthur C. Cope Scholar, 1986; Arthur C. Cope Award, 1992; Roger Adams Award in Organic Chemistry, 1997. *Address*: The Scripps Research Institute, 10550 North Torrey Pines Road, La Jolla, CA 92037, USA. *T*: (858) 784 7505, *Fax*: (858) 784 7562. *E*: sharpless@scripps.edu.

SHARPLING, Drusilla Hope, CBE 2007; HM Inspector of Constabulary, since 2009, and HM Inspector of Fire and Rescue Services, since 2017; *b* London, 7 Aug. 1955; *d* of James and Dulcie Sharpling; one *s*. *Educ*: City of London Sch. for Girls; Birmingham Univ. (LLB). Called to the Bar; various roles, incl. Hd of Casework and Crown Prosecutor, CPS, 1987–99; Associate, Penningtons, 1999–2002; Chief Crown Prosecutor, London Area, CPS, 2002–09. Mem., Ind. Panel Inquiry into Child Sexual Abuse, 2014–. *Recreation*: music. *Address*: HM Inspectorate of Constabulary and Fire and Rescue Services, 6th Floor, Globe House, 89 Eccleston Square, SW1V 1PN.

SHARPSTON, Eleanor Veronica Elizabeth; QC 1999; Advocate General, Court of Justice of the European Union (formerly Communities), since 2006; Fellow in Law, King's College, Cambridge, 1992–2010, Emeritus Fellow, 2011; *b* 13 July 1955; *d* of late Charles Sharpston and Pauline Sharpston (*née* Bryant); *m* 1991, David John Lyon (*d* 2000). *Educ*: St Paul's Girls' Sch. (Schol.); Bedales Sch. (Schol.); Konservatorium der Stadt Wien, Vienna; King's Coll., Cambridge (BA 1st Cl. Hons 1976; Schol. 1976; MA 1979); Corpus Christi Coll., Oxford (Squash Blue, 1978; Rowing Blue, 1978, 1979, 1980; Pres., Oxford Univ. Women's Boat Club, 1978–79 and 1979–80; Hon. Fellow, 2010); Inns of Court Sch. of Law. Called to the Bar: Middle Temple, 1980 (Bencher, 2005); Republic of Ireland, 1986; Gibraltar, 1999; Hong Kong, 2001; in practice as barrister, specialising in EU and ECHR law, Brussels, 1981–87, London, 1990–2005; référendaire (judicial asst) to Advocate Gen. (later Judge) Sir Gordon Slynn at Court of Justice of EC, Luxembourg, 1987–90; Lectr and Dir of Eur. Legal Studies, UCL, 1990–92; Univ. Lectr, 1992–98, Affiliated Lectr, 1998–2006, Sen. Fellow, Centre for Eur. Legal Studies, 1998–2005, Yorke Dist. Vis. Fellow, 2006–, Cambridge. Hon. Prof., Riga Grad. Sch. of Law, 2011–. Hon. FBA 2019. Hon. LLD: Glasgow, 2010; Nottingham Trent, 2011; Stockholm, 2014; Edinburgh, 2017. *Publications*: Interim and Substantive Relief in Claims Under Community Law, 1993; contrib. articles to Eur. Law Rev., Common Market Law Rev. and other books and jls on EU law. *Recreations*: theatre, classical music, European literature, sailing square riggers, karate, ski-ing. *Address*: Court of Justice of the European Union, L-2925 Luxembourg. *T*: 43032215. *Clubs*: Athenæum; Leander (Henley); Remenham (Henley).

SHARRATT, Steven, OBE 2009; Chief Executive Officer, IBMS Group Ltd (and subsidiary companies), since 2017; *b* Nottingham, 20 Aug. 1964; *s* of late Ian Sharratt and of Brenda Sharratt; *m* 1989, Sarah Mason; one *s* one *d*. *Educ*: Univ. of Kent (BA Hons Law); Chester Coll. of Law. Articled Clerk and Solicitor, Edge & Ellison, 1987–90; Solicitor, BP plc, 1990–91; Dir, Neville Gp and Subsidiaries, 1991–92; Solicitor, Gepp and Sons, 1992–94; Partner, Connolly Sharratt, 1994–97; Partner and Consultant, Taylor Vinters, 1997–2002; Gp Man. Dir, Chameleon Gp, 2000–02; non-exec. Chm., Cambridge Recycling Services Ltd, 2002–06; Gp Chief Exec., Bio Gp Ltd, 2006–17. Chm., Business Challenge Panel, BIS, 2011–15; Member: Small Business Investment Taskforce, DTI, 2004–07; Admin. Burdens Adv. Bd, HMRC, 2006–14; Climate Change Taskforce, 2007; Adv. Council, BASE, 2010–15; Bd, Green Economy Pathfinder, New Anglia LEP, 2011–17; Employment Sector Champion, Red Tape Challenge, 2011–17. Confederation of British Industry: Chairman: Small and Medium Enterprises Council, 2006–08; Eastern Reg., 2008–10 (Vice Chm., 2010–11); Climate Change Bd, 2008–; Climate Change Policy Cttee, 2013–; Mem., Mayday (formerly Envmtl) Leadership Gp, 2008–12, Regl Leadership Team, 2009–12, BITC. Founder, Mayday East of England (formerly Carbon Coalition), 2008–12; Founder and Co-Chair, East of England Space 4 Ideas Forum, 2010–12. Mem., Adv. Gp, Prince of Wales Mayday Network, 2007–10; Chm., Prince's Trust, Suffolk, 2009–11. FRSA 2008. *Recreations*: my family, occasional guitar, keyboard and drums, now driving zero emission cars, motorbikes to follow, so still on Ducatis, MUFC and MotoGP.

SHARROCK, Christopher Duncan; UK Permanent Representative to the Organisation for Economic Cooperation and Development (with rank of Ambassador), since 2016; *b* Reading, Berks, 4 Jan. 1975; *s* of Colin and Lesley Elizabeth Sharrock; partner, Bérengère Cecile Decroux; one *s* one *d*. *Educ*: Reading Sch.; Univ. of Manchester (BA Hons English 1996); Univ. of Bristol (PGCE 1998); Birkbeck, Univ. of London (MSc Econs 2011). Teacher, Katharine Lady Berkeley's Sch., 1998–2003; HM Treasury: Policy Advr, 2003–04; Asst Private Sec. to Chancellor of Exchequer, 2004–06; Sen. Policy Advr, 2006–12; Chief Economist, DCMS, 2012–13; Dep. Dir, HM Treasury, 2013–15. *Recreations*: books, films, music, walking, running, tennis, Reading FC, cricket. *Address*: c/o Foreign and Commonwealth Office, King Charles Street, SW1A 2AH.
*See also* J. O. Sharrock.

SHARROCK, Jonathan Owen; Chief Executive, Coast to Capital, since 2016; *b* Reading, 28 Oct. 1971; *s* of Colin Sharrock and Lesley Elizabeth Sharrock; *m* 2002, Tracey Pennyfather; two *d*. *Educ*: Reading Sch.; Bristol Univ. (BA Hons 1st Cl. Pols and French 1994). Eur. fast-stream, 1994–99, Policy Manager, Rough Sleepers Unit, 1999–2001, DoE, later DETR; desk officer, Eur. Secretariat, Cabinet Office, 2001–03; Department for Transport: Hd, Airspace Div., 2003; Hd, Airports Policy Div., 2004–07; Hd, Aviation Security, 2007–09; Director: London and Road Demand Mgt, 2009–11; London and Olympics, 2011–12; High Speed Two Strategy and Engagement, 2013–15. *Recreations*: my family, road running. *Address*: Coast to Capital, Arun House, Horsham RH12 2DN. *Club*: Collingwood Athletic.
*See also* C. D. Sharrock.

SHARWOOD-SMITH, Col Christopher Hugh, MBE 2016; Managing Director, CSS Global Consulting Ltd, since 2010; Vice Lord-Lieutenant for Bedfordshire, since 2018; *b* Barnet, 4 Aug. 1960; *s* of John and Felicity Sharwood-Smith; *m* 1990, Karen Lealand; one *d*. *Educ*: University Coll. Sch.; Univ. of Greenwich (Cert Ed 2000); Univ. of Hertfordshire (MSc 2003). Metropolitan Police: Cadet, 1976–79; Constable, 1979–93; Acting Sgt, 1994–95; Herts Constabulary: Sgt, 1995–2003; Inspector, 2003–09; seconded to UK Mission to the UN, FCO, 2008–10; Chief Inspector, 2009–10. Instructor, Middlesex & NW London ACF, 1986–93; Herts ACF: Detachment Comdr, 1993–94; Asst County Trng Officer, 1994–97; County Trng Officer, 1997–2001; Co. Comdr, 2001–04; Dep. Comdt, 2004–08; Beds & Herts ACF: Dep. Comdt (Admin), 2008–11; Comdt, 2011–15; Col, Cadets (E Anglia), 7 Infantry Brigade, 2015–18; Nat Trng Advr (Col), 2019–. Mem., Asst Directing Staff, Cadet Trng Centre, Frimley Park, 1994–. Mem. for Beds, St John Ambulance, 2007– (MStJ 1993). DL Beds, 2014. *Publications*: (contrib. jtly) Police Organization and Training: innovations in research and practice, 2011. *Recreations*: assisting charitable organisations, walking, gardening. *Address*: Lieutenancy Office, Priory House, Monks Walk, Chicksands, Shefford, Beds SG17 5TQ. *T*: (0300) 300 6090. *Club*: Victory Services.

SHATTOCK, David John, CBE 1995; QPM 1985; Personal Advisor to Prime Minister of Mauritius, 1998–2000; Chief Constable, Avon and Somerset Constabulary, 1989–98; *b* 25 Jan. 1936; *s* of Herbert John Shattock and Lucy Margaret Shattock; *m* 1973, Freda Thums; three *s*. *Educ*: Sir Richard Huish's Sch., Taunton. Joined as Constable, final post Asst Chief Constable, Somerset and Bath, later Avon and Somerset Constabulary, 1956–82; Deputy Chief Constable: Wilts Constab., 1983–85; Dyfed-Powys Police, 1985–86; Chief Constable, Dyfed-Powys Police, 1986–89. Hon. MA Bristol, 1998; Hon. LLD UWE, 1999. OStJ 1989. *Recreations*: racket sports, particularly badminton, antique restoration, keeping fit, horse riding. *Club*: Bristol Savages (Bristol).

SHAUGHNESSY, family name of Baron Shaughnessy.

SHAUGHNESSY, 5th Baron *cr* 1916, of Montreal and of Ashford, Limerick; **Charles George Patrick Shaughnessy**; actor; *b* 9 Feb. 1955; *s* of late Capt. Alfred James Shaughnessy and of Jean Margaret (*née* Lodge); S cousin, 2007; *m* 1983, Susan Rachael, *d* of Sydney Fallender; two *d*. *Educ*: Eton; Magdalene Coll., Cambridge (BA Hons Law 1977); Central Sch. of Speech and Drama. Theatre includes Salisbury Repertory, 1981–83 and stage appearances in USA; television in UK and USA incl. Days of Our Lives (series), 1984–91; The Nanny (series), 1992–99; also many film credits. Co-Founder, Bus Stop 31 Prodns, 2005. *Heir*: *b* David James Bradford Shaughnessy [*b* 3 March 1957; *m* 1985, Anne-Marie, *d* of Thomas Schoettle; three *d*]. *Address*: 3631 Barry Avenue, Los Angeles, CA 90066, USA. *E*: chucker22@mac.com.

SHAVE, Alan William, CVO 1994; OBE 1991; HM Diplomatic Service, retired; *b* 3 Nov. 1936; *s* of late William Alfred Shave and Emily Shave; *m* 1961, Lidia Donoso Bertolotto; one *s* one *d*. *Educ*: George Green's Grammar Sch., Poplar. Cert., Nat. Council of Journalists. Journalist, E London Advertiser, 1953–57; Nat. Service, RAF, 1957–59; Journalist: Greenock Telegraph, 1960; Bristol Evening World, 1961; Asst Information Officer, COI, 1961; joined CRO, 1961; Salisbury, Rhodesia, 1961–62; Dar es Salaam, 1962–64; Sydney, 1964–66; La Paz, 1966–70; FCO, 1970–72; Santiago, 1972–76; Consul (Commercial): Barcelona, 1977–81; Milan, 1981–84; First Sec., FCO, 1984–88; Dep. Hd of Mission and Consul, La Paz, 1988–92; Governor of Anguilla, 1992–95. Representative: for Bolivia, BESO, 1996–2005; for Bolivia, British Consultancy Charitable Trust, 2005–13; for La Paz, PUM Netherlands Sen. Experts, 2006–10; for Bolivia, Confedn of European Sen. Expert Services, 2006–10. *Recreations*: track cycling, ornithology, travel. *Address*: Casilla 3–35183, San Miguel (Calacoto), La Paz, Bolivia. *E*: awshave@gmail.com.

SHAW; *see* Byam Shaw.

SHAW, family name of Barons Craigmyle and Shaw of Northstead.

SHAW OF NORTHSTEAD, Baron *cr* 1994 (Life Peer), of Liversedge in the County of West Yorkshire; **Michael Norman Shaw**, Kt 1982; JP; DL; *b* 9 Oct. 1920; *e s* of late Norman Shaw; *m* 1951, Joan Mary Louise, *o d* of Sir Alfred L. Mowat, 2nd Bt; three *s*. *Educ*: Sedbergh. Chartered Accountant. MP (L and C) Brighouse and Spenborough, March 1960–Oct. 1964; MP (C) Scarborough and Whitby, 1966–74, Scarborough, 1974–92. Mem., H of L, 1994–2015. Mem., UK Delegn to European Parlt, 1974–79. FCA. JP Dewsbury, 1953; DL W Yorks, 1977. *Address*: Sunrise Senior Living, Stockbridge Road, Winchester, Hants SO22 5JH. *Club*: Carlton.

SHAW, Rt Rev. (Alexander) Martin; Bishop of Argyll and the Isles, 2004–09; an Honorary Assistant Bishop, Diocese of Exeter, since 2010; *b* 22 Sept. 1944; *s* of James D. D. Shaw, MBE and Jean Shaw; *m* 1971, Elspeth Longden; one *s* one *d* (and one *s* decd). *Educ*: Trinity Coll., Glenalmond; KCL (AKC 1967); Glasgow Univ. (Dip. Social Psych. 1969). Ordained deacon, 1968, priest, 1969; Curate: St Oswald's, Glasgow, 1968–70; Old St Paul's, Edinburgh, 1970–75; Chaplain, King's Coll., Cambridge, 1975–77; Principal,

Inst. of Christian Studies, All Saints, Margaret St, W1, 1977–78; Rector, Holy Trinity, Dunoon, 1978–81; Succentor, Exeter Cathedral, 1981–83; Diocesan Missioner, Exeter Dio., 1983–89; Res. Canon, Precentor and Sub-Dean, St Edmundsbury Cathedral, 1989–2004; Temp. Dean, King's Coll., Cambridge, 2002. Actg Precentor, Exeter Cathedral, 2017–18. Broadcaster on radio and television; writer of poetry; singer (baritone), song recitals and oratorios. *Publications:* First Light, 2001; My Father's Arms, song cycle for soprano and string trio, 2002; Christ's Winter Pilgrimage, 2006; Matthew in Your Pocket, 2017. *Recreations:* walking, movies, photography, opera, reading, avoiding gardening. *Address:* 11 Russell Terrace, Exeter EX4 4HX. *E:* amartinshaw@gmail.com.

**SHAW, Alison;** Founder and Chief Executive, Bristol University Press, since 2016; *b* High Wycombe, 26 March 1962; *d* of Alan and Patricia Shaw; *m* 1990, Prof. Richard Apps; two *s. Educ:* Lord William's Sch., Thame; Bristol Poly. (BA Hons Humanities). Publicity Asst, Bloomsbury Publishing, 1987–88; University of Bristol: Pubns Manager, SAUS Pubns, and Mktg and Ext. Relns Manager, Sch. for Advanced Urban Studies, 1989–95; Founder and Dir, Policy Press, 1995–2016. *Publications:* contribs to Learned Publishing jl. *Recreations:* cooking and eating, walking, family and friends, gardening, travel. *Address:* Bristol University Press, 1–9 Old Park Hill, Bristol BS2 8BB. *T:* (0117) 954 5940. *E:* ali.shaw@bristol.ac.uk.

**SHAW, Andrew David; His Honour Judge Shaw;** a Circuit Judge, since 2018; *b* Clatterbridge, Wirral, 30 July 1973; *s* of Malcolm Arthur and Kaye Isabel Shaw; *m* 1st, 2007, Shona Julie Harvey (marr. diss. 2017); three *s* one *d*; 2nd, 2017, Kelly Victoria Macdonald; one *d. Educ:* Wirral Grammar Sch. for Boys; Selwyn Coll., Cambridge (BA 1995). Called to the Bar, Lincoln's Inn, 1998; a Recorder, 2016–18. *Address:* Norwich Combined Court Centre, The Law Courts, Bishopsgate, Norwich NR3 1UR.

**SHAW, Andrew Jeremy;** a District Judge (Magistrates' Courts), since 2004; *b* 2 Feb. 1956; *s* of late Geoffrey James Shaw and of Noelle Shaw; *m* 2004, Miriam Jane Taylor; one *s. Educ:* Bromsgrove Sch.; Berkhamsted Sch.; Staffordshire Univ. (BA Hons Law). Admitted solicitor, 1981; joined Walker Smith & Way, 1981; Partner and Hd of Criminal Dept; Higher Courts Advocate (Criminal), 1999–2004. *Recreations:* golf, ski-ing, mountaineering.

**SHAW, Angela Brigid L.;** *see* Lansbury, A. B.

**SHAW, Antony Michael Ninian;** QC 1994; a Recorder, 2000–07; *b* 4 Oct. 1948; *s* of late Harold Anthony Shaw and Edith of Beatrice Sandbach (*née* Holmes); *m* 1983, Louise Göta Faugust (*d* 2006); one *s* two *d. Educ:* King's Sch., Canterbury; Trinity Coll., Oxford (Schol.; BA Juris. 1969). Researcher in Law, Bedford Coll., London, 1972–74; called to the Bar, Middle Temple, 1975 (Astbury Scholar, 1975; Bencher 2003); an Asst Recorder, 1997–2000. Head of Chambers, 4 Brick Court, 1988–99. Major cases: Guinness; Eagle Trust; Polly Peck; BCCI; Butte Mining; Alliance; VHS; Holbein; VHP; Operation Aloof (insider trading); Operation Amazon (carbon credits/tax relief); Innospec 2 (corruption); LIBOR. Vice Chm., Fees and Legal Aid Cttee, 1995–97, Chm., Remuneration Cttee, 2010–11, Gen. Council of the Bar. Gov., Internat. Students House, 1999–2003. *Publications:* contrib. Halsbury's Laws of England, 1977; (ed jtly) Archbold: Criminal Pleading, Evidence and Practice, 1991–; (Dep. Ed.) Fraud: Criminal Law and Procedure, 2010–; contrib. various law jls and Practical Law. *Recreations:* history, most literature. *Address:* 18 Red Lion Court, EC4A 3EB. *T:* (020) 7520 6000.

**SHAW, Prof. Bernard Leslie,** FRS 1978; FRSC; Professor of Chemistry, 1971–94, Research Professor, 1995–2005, now Emeritus Professor, University of Leeds; *b* Springhead, Yorks, 28 March 1930; *s* of Thomas Shaw and Vera Shaw (*née* Dale); *m* 1951, Mary Elizabeth Neild; two *s* (and one *s* decd). *Educ:* Hulme Grammar Sch., Oldham; Univ. of Manchester (BSc 1st cl. Hons Chem.; PhD). Sen. DSIR Fellow, Torry Research Station, Aberdeen, 1953–55; Scientific Officer, CDEE, Porton, 1955–56; Technical Officer, ICI Ltd, Akers Research Labs, Welwyn, 1956–61; Lectr, Reader, and Prof., Univ. of Leeds, 1962–. Consultant for large-scale petrochemical industry, USA. Visiting Professor: Univ. of Western Ontario, 1969; Carnegie Mellon Univ., 1969; ANU, 1983; Univ. of Auckland, 1986; Univ. of Strasbourg, 1993. Liversidge Lectr, 1987–88, Ludwig Mond Lectr, 1992–93, Sir Edward Frankland Prize Lectr, 1996, RSC. Member: Royal Soc. Cttees; RSC Cttees; SERC (formerly SRC) Chem. Cttee, 1975–78, 1981–84 (and Inorganic Panel, 1977–78, Co-operative Grants Panel, 1982–84); Tilden Lectr and Prizewinner, 1975; Chem. Soc. Medal and Prize for Transition Metal Chem., 1975; Premo Calabria Prize for Sci., 2001. *Publications:* Transition Metal Hydrides, 1967; (with N. Tucker) Organotransition Metal Chemistry, and Related Aspects of Homogeneous Catalysis, 1973; over 400 original papers and reviews in chem. jls, several patents. *Recreations:* pottery, music, walking, gardening. *Address:* Department of Chemistry, The University of Leeds, Leeds LS2 9JT. *T:* (0113) 343 6465.

**SHAW, Brian Hamilton;** Director and Chief Executive, Britannic Group plc (formerly Britannic Assurance plc), 1997–2001; *b* 26 April 1942; *s* of late Dennis Hamilton Shaw and Peggy Shaw (later Dolan). *Educ:* King Edward's Sch., Birmingham. FIA 1966. Nat. Farmers' Union Mutual Insurance Soc., 1960–63; joined Britannic Assurance, 1963: Dir and Gen. Manager, 1979–86; Dir, Gen. Manager and Actuary, 1986–97. *Recreation:* sports. *Address:* 15 Saturn Way, Stratford on Avon CV37 7NE. *T:* (01789) 299202. *Club:* Royal Automobile.

**SHAW, Carolyn Janet;** Headmistress, Roedean School, 2003–08; *b* 24 April 1947; *d* of Norman and Mary Carey; *m* 1974, Dr Charles Drury Shaw; one *s* one *d. Educ:* Goldsmiths' Coll., Univ. of London (BA Hons 1970); Liverpool Univ. (PGCE 1971). English Teacher, La Sainte Union Convent, Bath, 1972–74; Head of English, Mount Saint Agnes Acad., Bermuda, 1974–77; English Teacher and Univ. Advr, Cheltenham Ladies' Coll., 1989–96; Headmistress, St Mary's Sch., Calne, 1996–2003. Chm. Govs, Amberley C of E First Sch., 2010–16. Chm., Chichester Singers, 2018– (Hon. Treas., 2011–17). Trustee, Southern Pro Musica, 2012–. *Recreations:* reading, gardening, music, travel.

**SHAW, Sir Charles (de Vere),** 8th Bt *cr* 1821, of Bushy Park, Dublin; Chief Executive Officer: Leadership Dynamics Oman LLC; Bondoni; *b* 1 March 1957; *s* of John Frederick de Vere Shaw, *yr s* of 6th Bt and of Penelope Ann Shaw (*née* Milbank, now Mills); *S* uncle, 2002; *m* 1st (marr. diss. 2013); one *s* one *d*; 2nd, 2017, Doria (*née* Michaelides). *Educ:* Michaelhouse, Natal; RMA Sandhurst. Officer, 5th Royal Inniskilling Dragoon Guards, 1976–87 (Major, retd). Dir, Safetynet plc, 1987–94; Gp Man. Dir, Morgan Lovell plc, 1994–2000; CEO, IntelliSpace, 2001–05. Country Dir and Chm., TQ Oman, 2013–. Non-executive Director: Shaw Travel Co. Ltd, 2002–10; Interiors Gp, 2008–13; Hurley Palmer Flatt, 2008–12. Expedition leader: Geographic North Pole, Aconcagua, Kilimanjaro, Himalayas, South China Seas. FRGS 2003. *Recreations:* shooting, fishing, photography, active Rugby supporter, cycling, scuba diving. *Heir: s* Robert Jonathan de Vere Shaw, *b* 7 Aug. 1988. *Address:* Bondoni, PO Box 34, PC 104, CPU Al Bahjah, Seeb, Muscat, Sultanate of Oman. *T:* 24514101, 93227010. *E:* cdvshaw@gmail.com.

**SHAW, Prof. Christopher Edward Dennistoun,** MD; FRCP, FRACP; Professor of Neurology and Neurogenetics, King's College London, since 2004; *b* 27 March 1960; *s* of Roger and Helen Shaw; *m* 1988, Pinar Bagci; one *s* one *d. Educ:* Burnside High Sch.; Otago Medical Sch. (MB ChB 1984); MD 1997. FRACP 1993; FRCP 2000. Med. trng, Northland Hosp., 1985, and Wellington Hosp., 1986–92; Wellcome Trust-HRCNZ Res. Fellow, Univ. of Cambridge, 1992–95; Institute of Psychiatry, King's College London: Lectr, 1995–98; Sen. Lectr, 1998–2004; Director: KHP Centre for Neurogeneration Res., 2009–; Maurice Wohl Clinical Neuroscience Inst., 2013–. FMedSci 2010. *Publications:* 70 scientific articles; res. interest includes genetic and molecular basis of motor neuron disorders, use of cloning technologies in discovery of novel therapies. *Recreations:* house building, watching old films, dancing with family, slow meals with extended family, holidays in Turkey. *Address:* Clinical Neuroscience PO 41, Institute of Psychiatry, Psychology and Neuroscience, King's College London, De Crespigny Park, SE5 8AF. *T:* (020) 7848 5180, *Fax:* (020) 7848 0988. *E:* Chris.shaw@kcl.ac.uk.

**SHAW, Christopher Thomas;** Editorial Director, ITN, since 2019; *b* 19 June 1957; *s* of John Denis Bolton Shaw and Isabel Shaw (*née* Loewe); *m* 2001, Martha Catherine Kearney, *qv. Educ:* Westminster Sch.; Balliol Coll., Oxford (BA Hons Modern Hist.). Independent Radio News, 1980–85; ITN, 1985–89; Sen. Prog. Ed., Sky News, 1989–91; Foreign Ed., Channel 4 News, 1991–93; Programme Ed., News At Ten, 1993–95; Exec. Producer, ITN Factual, 1995–96; Ed., Channel 5 News, 1996–98; Controller, News, Current Affairs and Documentaries, Channel 5, 1998–2000; Sen. Programme Controller, Five (formerly Channel 5), 2000–10; Editl Dir, 2010–18, Creative Dir, 2018–19, ITN Productions. Dir, Edinburgh TV Fest., 2006– (Chm., 2014–). FRTS 2008. BAFTA Award for Best Current Affairs; two Emmy Awards for Best Internat. Current Affairs. *Recreations:* travel, watching football, archaeology. *Address:* c/o ITN, 200 Gray's Inn Road, WC1X 8XZ.

**SHAW, Prof. David Aitken,** CBE 1989; FRCP, FRCPE; Professor of Clinical Neurology, University of Newcastle upon Tyne, 1976–89, now Emeritus; *b* 11 April 1924; *s* of John James McIntosh Shaw and Mina Draper; *m* 1960, Jill Parry; one *s* two *d. Educ:* Edinburgh Academy; Edinburgh Univ. MB ChB (Edin) 1951; FRCPE 1968; FRCP (Lond.) 1976. Served in RNVR, 1943–46, demobilised in rank of Lieut. Jun. hospital appts, Edinburgh Royal Infirmary, 1951–57; Lectr, Inst. of Neurology, Univ. of London, 1957–64; Mayo Foundation Res. Fellow, 1962–63; University of Newcastle upon Tyne: Sen. Lectr, 1964–76; Public Orator, 1976–77; Dean of Medicine, 1981–89. Hon. FRCSLT (Hon. FCST 1988). *Publications:* (with N. E. F. Cartlidge) Head Injury, 1981; chapters in books and scientific articles in medical jls. *Recreations:* literature, music. *Address:* 5 Little Dene, Lodore Road, High West Jesmond, Newcastle upon Tyne NE2 3NZ. *T:* (0191) 285 2029.

**SHAW, Maj. Gen. David Anthony Hirst,** CBE 2012; Founder and Chief Executive Officer, The Veterans' Foundation, since 2016; Founder, and Chief Executive Officer, since 2017, AF&V Launchpad (Chairman, Trustees, 2013–16); *b* Ceylon, 19 Feb. 1957; *m* 1985, Verity Jane Negus; two *s. Educ:* Haileybury, Hertford; RMA Sandhurst; Cranfield Univ. (MDA). Dip. CIM. Commnd RA, 1976; served 3 Regt RHA and 40 Regt, RA; CO 40 Regt RA, 1995–98; Comdr, 15 NE Bde, 2002–04; COS, Regl Forces, HQ Land Comd, 2004–07; Dir, Army Media and Communication, 2007–09; GOC 2nd Div. and Gov., Edinburgh Castle, 2010–12. Vis. Prof., Robert Gordon Univ., Aberdeen, 2010–. HM Comr, Queen Victoria Sch., 2009–15. FCIPD 2006; CIPR 2008. *Recreations:* painting, sailing, ski-ing. *Clubs:* Royal Scots; Royal Artillery Yacht, Bembridge Sailing.

**SHAW, David Lawrence,** FCA; chartered accountant; Founder, Chairman and Director, Sabrelance Ltd, corporate finance advisers, 1983–2013; *b* 14 Nov. 1950; *m* 1986, Dr Lesley Brown; one *s* one *d. Educ:* King's Sch., Wimbledon; City of London Polytechnic. FCA 1974. Coopers & Lybrand, 1971–79; County Bank, 1979–83. Chairman: RRI PLC, 1994–2000; 2020 Strategy Ltd, 1997–2012; Dep. Chm., The Adscene Group PLC, 1986–99; Dir, Nettec plc, 2003–05. Mem., Political, Communications and Marketing Cttee, Quoted Cos Alliance (formerly City Gp for Smaller Quoted Cos), 1997–2006. Mem., Royal Borough of Kingston upon Thames Council, 1974–78. Contested (C) Leigh, 1979; MP (C) Dover, 1987–97; contested (C) same seat, 1997; contested (C) Kingston and Surbiton, 2001. Chm., Bow Gp, 1983–84 (Founder, Transatlantic Conf., 1982); Mem., Social Security Select Cttee, 1991–97; Jt Chm., All Party Cttee on Dolphins, 1989–97; Chm., Cons. Backbench Smaller Businesses Cttee, 1990–97 (Sec., 1987–90); Vice Chm., Cons. Backbench Finance Cttee, 1991–97 (Hon. Sec., 1990–91). Vice-Chm., Kingston and Malden Cons. Assoc., 1979–86. Director: Business Council for Internat. Understanding (Europe) Ltd, 2002–16; Internat. Trade and Investment Center, 2010–16. Mem., Bd of Sen. Advrs, Center for Global Econ. Growth, Washington DC, 2005–18. Founder and Dir, David Shaw Charitable Trust, 1994–2017. Vice-Pres., Inst. of Patentees and Inventors, 1996–2016.

**SHAW, David Lewis,** OBE 2014; Head, Regent Street Portfolio, The Crown Estate, 2002–17; Chairman, The Pollen Estate, 2015–19; *b* Cheadle, Cheshire, 20 July 1947; *s* of Joseph Lewis Shaw and Sarah Eirwen Mary Shaw (*née* Jenkins); *m* 1972, Heather Anne Johnson; two *s. Educ:* Wellington Sch., Somerset; Bristol Tech. Coll. FRICS 1981. Dir, Arrowcroft Investments Ltd, 1971–79; Partner, Richard Main & Co., 1979–82; Dir, Crouch Gp plc, 1982–84; Dir, Shearwater Hldgs, Rosehaugh Gp, 1984–92; Man. Dir, Burton Property Trust, 1992–95; Dir, Mgt Bd, Burton Gp, 1995–99; Property Dir, Servus Hldgs, Nomura Gp, 1999–2001. Director: New West End Co., 2002–19; Mayfair Art Weekend, 2016. Chm., Orpheus Sinfonia Foundn, 2007–. Mem., Property Investment Bd, City of London, 2018–. Gov., ESU, 2017–. Hon. DLitt Westminster, 2016. *Recreations:* walking, classical music, gadgets. *Address:* 9 Hamilton House, Vicarage Gate, W8 4HL. *T:* 07773 335569. *E:* dls.user@gmail.com.

**SHAW, Donald,** WS, NP; Partner, CMS Cameron McKenna Nabarro Olswang (formerly CMS Cameron McKenna) LLP, since 2014; *s* of D. B. Shaw, DSC, BL, NP and P. E. Shaw; *m* Susan; two *d. Educ:* Univ. of Aberdeen (LLB). NP; WS. Dundas & Wilson: Partner, 1985–2014; Real Estate Industry Leader, 2003–06; Man. Partner, 2006–12. Leader Real Estate Law, Andersen Worldwide, 1998–2002. Fellow, Soc. for Advanced Legal Studies, 1999. *Recreations:* history, music, travel, family, wine. *Address:* CMS Cameron McKenna Nabarro Olswang LLP, Cannon Place, 78 Cannon Street, EC4N 6AF. *E:* donald.shaw@cms-cmno.com.

**SHAW, Rev. Prof. Douglas William David,** OBE 2009; Professor of Divinity, 1979–91, and Principal, St Mary's College, 1986–92, University of St Andrews; *b* 25 June 1928; *s* of William David Shaw and Nansie Smart. *Educ:* Edinburgh Acad.; Loretto; Ashbury Coll., Ottawa; Univs of Cambridge and Edinburgh. MA (Cantab), BD (Edin.), LLB (Edin.). WS. Practised law as Partner of Davidson and Syme, WS, Edinburgh, 1953–57. Ordained Minister of Church of Scotland, 1960; Asst Minister, St George's West Church, Edinburgh, 1960–63; Official Observer of World Alliance of Reformed Churches at Second Vatican Council, Rome, 1962. University of Edinburgh: Dean, Faculty of Divinity, and Principal, New College, 1974–78; Lectr in Divinity, 1963–79; Dean, Faculty of Divinity, Univ. of St Andrews, 1983–86. Croall Lectr, New Coll., Edinburgh, 1983; Alexander Robertson Lectr, Univ. of Glasgow, 1991–92. Editor, Theology in Scotland, 1994–2002. Hon. DD: Glasgow, 1991; St Andrews, 2005. *Publications:* Who is God? 1968, 2nd edn 1970; The Dissuaders, 1978; trans. from German: F. Heyer: The Catholic Church from 1648 to 1870, 1969; (ed) In Divers Manners—a St Mary's Miscellany, 1990; Dimensions—Literary and Theological, 1992; various articles in Festschrifts and theological jls. *Recreations:* squash

(Scottish Amateur Champion, 1950–51–52), golf, mountaineering. *Address:* 4/13 Succoth Court, Edinburgh EH12 6BZ. *T:* (0131) 337 2130. *W:* www.dwdshaw.co.uk. *Clubs:* New (Edinburgh); Royal and Ancient (St Andrews); Edinburgh Sports; Jesters.

**SHAW, Elizabeth Angela;** Chair, Members Allowance Panel, South Somerset District Council, 2003–10; *b* 5 June 1946; *d* of John Edward Comben and Irene (*née* Thomson); *m* 1st, 1970, Graham Shaw (marr. diss. 1985); two *s* one *d*; 2nd, 1993, Adrian Carter. *Educ:* Sydenham High Sch.; Open Univ. (BA 2003). Executive Officer: Home Office, 1965–68; FCO, 1968–70; DSS, 1970–72; Department of Health and Social Security: HEO (Develt), 1972–77; Principal, 1977–84; Asst Sec., 1984–87; Dir of Finance, Planning and Marketing, Civil Service Coll., 1987–90; Head of Staff Develt, DoH, 1990–91; Exec. Dir, Charity Commn, 1991–96. Chair: COMPAID Trust, 1997–99; St Michael's Fellowship, 1997–99; Dir, Musikansky Theatre Co., 1998–2003. Chair, Spectra Musica chamber choir, 2011–16. *Recreations:* music, literature, walking, riding, family.

**SHAW, Fiona Mary,** Hon. CBE 2001; actress; *b* 10 July 1958; *d* of Dr Denis Joseph Wilson and Mary Teresa Wilson (*née* Flynn), MSc; adopted Shaw as stage name; *m* 2018, Sonali Deraniyagala. *Educ:* University Coll. Cork (BA); Royal Acad. of Dramatic Art (Hons Dip.; Bancroft Gold medal; Tree Prize; Ronson Award). *Theatre* includes: The Rivals, 1983; RSC, 1985–88: Philistines; As You Like It; Les Liaisons Dangereuses; Mephisto; Much Ado About Nothing; The Merchant of Venice; Hyde Park; The Taming of the Shrew; New Inn; Electra (title rôle); Mary Stuart, Greenwich, 1988; As You Like It, Old Vic, 1989; The Good Person of Sichuan, NT, 1989; Hedda Gabler (title rôle), Dublin and Playhouse, 1991; Machinal, NT (Best Actress, Evening Standard Awards), 1993; Footfalls, Garrick, 1994; The Way of the World, RNT, 1995; Richard II, RNT, 1995, Salzburg Fest., 1996; The Waste Land, Brussels, Perth and Dublin Fests, NY (Drama Desk Award), Toronto, Paris, 1996, Wilton's Music Hall, London, 1997, 2009, Adelaide, 1998; The Prime of Miss Jean Brodie, RNT, 1998; Medea, Abbey Th., Dublin, 2000, Queen's (Best Actress, Evening Standard Awards), 2001, NY 2002; The PowerBook, NT, 2002; The Seagull, Edinburgh, 2004; My Life as a Fairy Tale, NY, 2005; Julius Caesar, Barbican, 2005; Woman and Scarecrow, Royal Ct, 2006; Happy Days, NT, 2007; Mother Courage and Her Children, NT, 2009; London Assurance, NT, 2010; John Gabriel Borkman, Abbey Th., Dublin, 2010, NY, 2011; Scenes from an Execution, NT, 2012; The Rime of the Ancient Mariner, Athens Fest., Old Vic Tunnels, 2012, Bouffes du Nord, Paris, 2014; Testament of Mary, NY, 2013, Barbican, 2014; Director: Riders to the Sea, London Coliseum, 2008; Elegy for Young Lovers, Young Vic, 2010; The Marriage of Figaro, ENO, 2011; The Rape of Lucretia, Glyndebourne, 2013, 2015; Cendrillon, Glyndebourne, 2018. *Films* include: My Left Foot, 1988; The Mountains of the Moon, 1988; Three Men and a Little Lady, 1990; London Kills Me, 1991; Super Mario Brothers, 1993; Undercover Blues, 1993; Jane Eyre, 1994; Anna Karenina, 1996; The Butcher Boy, 1996; The Avengers, 1997; The Last September, 2000; Harry Potter and the Philosopher's Stone, 2001; Harry Potter and the Chamber of Secrets, 2002; The Triumph of Love, 2004; The Black Dahlia, 2006; Catch and Release, 2007; Fracture, 2007; Harry Potter and the Order of the Phoenix, 2007; Dorian Gray, 2009; Harry Potter and the Deathly Hallows, Pt 1, 2010; The Tree of Life, 2011; The White King, 2016; Lizzie, 2018; Colette, 2019; *television* includes: Fireworks for Elspeth, 1983; Persuasion, 1994; The Waste Land, 1995; Gormenghast, 2000; Mind Games, 2000; True Blood, 2011; Marple: Greenshaw's Folly, 2013; Lumen, 2015; (documentary) The British Face, 2011; Maigret Sets a Trap, 2016; Killing Eve, 2018, 2019 (BAFTA Award for Best Supporting Actress, 2019); Mrs Wilson, 2018; Fleabag, 2019. Hon. Prof. of Drama, TCD, 1997. Hon. LLD NUI, 1996; DUniv Open, 1998; Hon. DLitt: TCD, 2001; Ulster, 2004. London Theatre Critics' Award, 1989, 1992; Best Actress, Olivier Awards, 1989, 1994. Officier, Ordre des Arts et des Lettres (France), 2003. *Publications:* contributor to: Players of Shakespeare, 1987; Clamorous Voices, 1988; Conversations with Actresses, 1990. *Recreations:* travel, reading, walking, thinking, painting. *Address:* c/o Independent Talent Group Ltd, 40 Whitfield Street, W1T 2RH.

**SHAW, Howard;** see Shaw, J. H.

**SHAW, Prof. Jane Alison,** PhD; FRHistS; Principal, Harris Manchester College, Oxford, since 2018; Pro Vice-Chancellor and Professor of the History of Religion, University of Oxford, since 2018; *b* 28 April 1963; *d* of Jack Davies Shaw and Joyce Shaw. *Educ:* Norwich High Sch., GPDST; Regent's Park Coll., Oxford (BA; MA); Harvard Univ. (MDiv); Univ. of Calif, Berkeley (PhD 1994). FRHistS 2019. Fellow and Tutor, Regent's Park Coll., Oxford, 1994–2001; Res. Lectr, 1997–2007, Reader in Church Hist., 2007–10, Univ. of Oxford; Dean of Divinity, Chaplain and Fellow, New Coll., Oxford, 2001–10; ordained deacon, 1997, priest, 1998; Dean, Grace Cathedral, San Francisco, 2010–14; Prof. of Religious Studies, and Dean for Religious Life, Stanford Univ., 2014–18. Vis. Prof., Univ. of Calif, Berkeley, 2009, 2013, 2014; Vis. Schol., 2012–14, Res. Affiliate, 2018–20, Center for Advanced Study in Behavioural Scis, Stanford Univ. Lectures: MacCandless, Georgetown Coll., 2000; Marshall, Melbourne Univ., 2006; Hensley Henson, Univ. of Oxford, 2006; Eric Abbot Meml, Westminster Abbey and Keble Coll., Oxford, 2008; Pierce, Emory Univ., 2010; Cheney, Yale Univ., 2016; Sarum, Sarum Coll. and Salisbury Cathedral, 2017; Bell, Univ. of Tulsa, 2019. Mem., Calif Cttee, Human Rights Watch, 2013–18. Fellow (Gov.), Winchester Coll., 2004–10. Hon. Fellow: Regent's Park Coll., Univ. of Oxford, 2018; Homerton Coll., Univ. of Cambridge, 2019; Kellogg Coll., Univ. of Oxford, 2019. Hon. Canon, Christ Ch Cathedral, Oxford, 2005–10; Canon Theologian, Salisbury Cathedral, 2008–12, Canon Emerita, 2014. Hon. DD Episcopal Divinity Sch., Cambridge, Mass, 2006; Hon. DLitt Colgate, 2013. *Publications:* (ed jtly) Culture and the Non-Conformist Tradition, 1999; (ed jtly) The Call for Women Bishops, 2004; Miracles in Enlightenment England, 2006; Octavia, Daughter of God: the story of a female messiah and her followers, 2011; A Practical Christianity, 2012; (ed jtly) The History of a Modern Millennial Movement, 2017; Pioneers of Modern Spirituality, 2018. *Recreations:* the arts, reading. *Address:* Principal's Lodgings, Harris Manchester College, Mansfield Road, Oxford OX1 3TD. *T:* (01865) 271006. *E:* jane.shaw@hmc.ox.ac.uk.

**SHAW, Sir John (Calman), (Jack),** Kt 1995; CBE 1989; CA; FRSE; Governor, Bank of Scotland, 1999–2001 (non-executive Director, 1990–2001; Deputy Governor, 1991–99); *b* 10 July 1932; *m* 1960, Shirley Botterill; three *d*. *Educ:* Strathallan Sch.; Edinburgh Univ. BL; JDipMA. National Service, RAF, 1955–57. Partner in Graham, Smart & Annan (later Deloitte, Haskins & Sells), 1960, Sen. Edinburgh Partner, 1980–87. Pres., Inst. of Chartered Accountants of Scotland, 1983–84. Johnstone Smith Prof. of Accountancy (pt-time appt), Glasgow Univ., 1977–82. Chairman: Scottish American Investment Co. PLC (formerly Trust), 1991–2001 (Dir, 1986–2003); US Smaller Cos Investment Trust, 1991–99 (Dir, 2000); TR European Growth Trust PLC, 1998–2002 (Dir, 1992); Director: Scottish Metropolitan Property plc, 1994–2000; Scottish Mortgage and Trust PLC, 1982–2001; Templeton Emerging Markets Investment Trust plc, 1994–2003. Chairman: SHEFC, 1992–98; Scottish Financial Enterprise, 1995–99 (Exec. Dir, 1986–90); Scottish Science Trust, 1998–2002; Edinburgh Technology Fund, 1999–2001; Member: Bd, Scottish Enterprise, 1990–98; Financial Reporting Council, 1990–96. Chm., David Hume Inst., 1995–2002. Dep. Chm., Edinburgh Fest. Soc., 1991–2000. Mem. Court, Univ. of Edinburgh, 1998–2003. Dr *hc* Edinburgh, 1998; Hon. LLD: Glasgow, 1998; Abertay Dundee, 1998; St Andrews, 1999; Hon. DEd Napier, 1999. Receiver General, The Priory of Scotland of Most Venerable Order of St John, 1992–2002; KStJ 1992. *Publications:* (ed) Bogie on Group Accounts (3rd edn), 1973; The Audit Report, 1980; (jtly) Information Disclosure and the Multinational Corporation, 1984; numerous articles in accountancy and res. jls. *Recreations:* opera, theatre, walking. *Club:* New (Edinburgh).

**SHAW, John Campbell;** Managing Director: Amberton Shaw, 1997–2004; Stannifer Group Holdings, 1998–2004; *b* 2 Aug. 1949; *s* of late John C. B. Shaw and of May B. Shaw; *m*; two *d*. *Educ:* Grosvenor High Sch., Belfast; QUB (BSc Hons in Urban Geography); Heriot-Watt Univ. (MSc in Town & Country Planning). Lanarkshire CC, 1973–75; Motherwell DC, 1975–78; East Kilbride Development Corporation, 1978–95: Head of Planning, 1982; Tech. Dir, 1986; Man. Dir, 1990–95; Bd Mem., Lanarkshire Develt Agency, 1991–95. Director: Ramoyle Gp, 2008–10; Total Retail Concepts, 2010–15; Shaw Sandison Ltd, 2010–. *Recreation:* sport.

**SHAW, John Frederick,** CB 1996; Director of Corporate Affairs, National Health Service Executive, 1993–96; *b* 7 Dec. 1936; *s* of James Herbert and Barbara Shaw; *m* 1964, Ann Rodden (*d* 2017); two *s* one *d*. *Educ:* Loretto Sch., Musselburgh; Worcester Coll., Oxford (MA). National Service, 2/Lieut KOYLI, 1955–57. Church Comrs, 1960–62; Industrial Christian Fellowship, 1962–63; HQ Staff, VSO, 1963–73; Principal (Direct Entry), DHSS, 1973, Asst Sec. 1978; Under Sec., DHSS, then DoH, 1987–93. Chairman: REACH, 1988–92; Nat. Family Mediation, 1996–2001; Rickmansworth Waterways Trust, 1997–2006; UK Transplant Support Services Authority, 1998–2001; Nat. Centre for Volunteering, 1999–2004 (Trustee, 1996–2004, Chm. Trustees, 1998–2004); Member Council: Patients' Assoc., 1996–99 (Vice-Chm., 1996–98); British Assoc. of Day Surgery, 1998–2005; Lay Mem., 1996–2003, Associate Mem., 2003–06, GMC; Lay Mem., Jt Cttee on Postgrad. Training for General Practice, 1997–2005. Mem. Cttee, 2007–17, Trustee, 2016–, Watford and Three Rivers Refugee Partnership. *Recreations:* church activities, singing, gardening. *Address:* Hyde House, West Hyde, Rickmansworth, Herts WD3 9XH.

**SHAW, (John) Howard;** QC 2011; arbitrator, since 2013; *b* Oldham, 6 Sept. 1948; *s* of Arthur Shaw and Edith Shaw; *m* 1972, Mary; two *s*. *Educ:* Hulme Grammar Sch., Oldham; Univ. of London (LLB). Called to the Bar, Inner Temple, 1973, Ire., 1998; Hd of Chambers, 3 Dr Johnson's Bldg, 1990–96. Qualified collaborative lawyer, 2009. MCIArb 2013. *Recreations:* theatre, travel, reading, walking the dogs, watching the tortoises, sport. *Address:* 29 Bedford Row, WC1R 4HE. *T:* (020) 7404 1044, *Fax:* (020) 7831 0626. *E:* hshaw@29br.co.uk. *Club:* Wimbledon Village.

**SHAW, Jonathan Rowland;** Chief Executive Officer, Policy Connect, since 2016; *b* 3 June 1966; *s* of Alan James Shaw and Lesbia Virginia Percival Shaw; *m* 1990, Susan Lesley Gurmin; one *s* one *d*. *Educ:* Vinters Boys' Sch., Maidstone; Bromley Coll., Kent (Cert. in Social Services). Social Worker, Kent Social Services, 1990–97. MP (Lab) Chatham and Aylesford, 1997–2010; contested (Lab) same seat, 2010. An Asst Govt Whip, 2006–07; Minister for the SE, 2007–10; Parly Under-Sec. of State, DEFRA, 2007–08, DWP, 2008–10. Dir, Shaw Business Partnership Ltd, 2010–16. *Recreations:* walking, cooking, reading.

**SHAW, Prof. Josephine, (Jo),** LLD; AcSS; Salvesen Professor of European Institutions, University of Edinburgh, since 2005 (Director, Institute for Advanced Studies in the Humanities, 2014–17); *b* Shipley, W Yorks, 17 Sept. 1961; *d* of Robert Shaw and Freda Shaw (*née* Baxter); partner, 2001, Alf Thomas; one *s*. *Educ:* Bradford Girls' Grammar Sch.; Trinity Coll., Cambridge (BA 1982); Université Libre de Bruxelles (Licence en droit européen 1983); Univ. of Edinburgh (LLD 2008). Lectr in Law, Univ. of Exeter, 1984–90; Lectr, then Sen. Lectr in Law, Keele Univ., 1990–95; Professor of European Law: Univ. of Leeds, 1995–2001; Univ. of Manchester, 2001–04. Vis. Prof., Harvard Law Sch., 1998; Eur. Insts for Advanced Study Fellow, Helsinki Univ., 2017–18. AcSS 2005. FRSA 2001; FRSE 2018. *Publications:* The Transformation of Citizenship in the European Union, 2007; (jtly) Economic and Social Law and Policy in the European Union, 2007. *Recreations:* music, galleries, photography, Blipfoto. *Address:* Edinburgh Law School, Old College, South Bridge, Edinburgh EH8 9YL. *T:* (0131) 650 9587. *E:* jo.shaw@ed.ac.uk.

**SHAW, Prof. Kenneth Martin,** MD, FRCP; consultant physician; Visiting Professor of Medicine, Portsmouth University, 1996–2008, now Emeritus; *b* 20 April 1943; *s* of late Frank Shaw and Gwen (*née* Mosson); *m* 1968, Phyllis Dixon; two *s*. *Educ:* City of Norwich Sch.; Downing Coll., Cambridge (BA 1965, MA 1969; BChir 1968, MB 1969; MD 1979); University Coll. Hosp., London. FRCP 1985. MRC Res. Fellow, Dept of Clin. Pharmacol., UCH Med. Sch., 1971–72; Sen. Registrar, 1973–77, Resident Asst Physician, 1977–78, UCH, London; Portsmouth and SE Hants Health Dist, later Portsmouth Hosps NHS Trust: Associate Clin. Dir, Medicine, and Dir, 1979, Clin. Dir, then Hd of Service, 1979–2008, Dept of Diabetes and Endocrinol.; Sen. Consultant Physician, 1979–2008; Hon. Consultant, 2008–; Postgrad. Clin. Tutor, Univ. of Southampton, 1983–90; Dir, R&D, Portsmouth Hosps NHS Trust, and R&D Support Unit and Portsmouth R&D Consortium, Sch. of Postgrad. Medicine, Univ. of Portsmouth (at Queen Alexandra Hosp.), 1995–2008; Clin. Lead (Diabetes/Metabolic and Endocrine), Hants and IoW Comprehensive Local Res. Network, 2008–09. Arnold Bloom Lect., Diabetes UK, 2011; James Lind Lect., Inst. of Naval Medicine, 2016. Editor-in-Chief, Practical Diabetes Internat., 1992–2014. External Examiner: Sch. of Medicine, Univ. of Cardiff, 2008–11; Coll. of Medicine, Univ. of Leicester, 2012–17; Ext. Consultant Reviewer, Standards of Acute Medical Care, Univ. Hosp. Southampton NHS Foundn Trust, 2014–15. Royal College of Physicians: Hon. Sec., Jt Specialty Cttee for Endocrinol. and Diabetes, 2001–08 (Mem., 1998–2009); Mem., Adv. Panel for Service Rev. Visits, 2000–08; Diabetes UK (formerly British Diabetic Association): Mem., Med. Adv. Cttee, 1982–86; Vice Chm., Specialist Care Cttee, 1998–2002; Mem., 2002–, Mem. Exec., 2006–11, Professional Adv. Council; Chm., Professional Support and Develt Cttee, 2006–11; Chm., Wessex Diabetes and Endocrinol. Assoc., 1989–96; Mem., Med. Panel (Diabetes), DVLA, 2005–15; Ind. Specialist Consultant (Diabetes), CAA, 2010–; Member: Healthcare Professionals' Wkg Party, EMEA, 2013–15; Transparency of Doctors' Interests Wkg Gp, RCP/BMA, 2014–. Member: Eur. Assoc. for Study of Diabetes, 1980–; Amer. Diabetes Assoc., 1995–2008; Internat. Diabetes Fedn, 1995–; Founding Mem. and Trustee, Assoc. of British Clin. Diabetologists, 1996– (Hon. Treas., 1996–2006; Hon. Chm., 2006–08; Hon. Trustee, Diabetes Care Trust (formerly Charitable Trust), 1996–). Hon. Trustee, Solent Diabetes Charitable Trust, 2007–13, 2015–. FRSocMed 1972; Scientific FZS 1974. Mem., Harveian Med. Soc. of London, 1969–. UK Hosp. Diabetes Team Award, 1998. *Publications:* Complications of Diabetes, 1996, 3rd edn 2012; The Life and Legacy of Doctor James Lind, 2019; contrib. chapters in books; contrib. numerous rev. articles and peer-reviewed original scientific articles. *Recreations:* golf, opera. *Address:* Castle Acre, Hospital Lane, Portchester, Hants PO16 9QP. *W:* www.profkenshaw.com.

**SHAW, (Lucy) Nicola,** CBE 2016; Executive Director, UK National Grid plc, since 2016; *b* Crockham Hill, Kent, 21 May 1969; *d* of Stephen John and Helen Caroline Shaw; *m* 2012, Andrew Lang; two step *s*. *Educ:* King's Sch., Canterbury; Lincoln Coll., Oxford (BA Hons Modern Hist. and Econs; Hon. Fellow 2018); Massachusetts Inst. of Technol. (MSc Transportation). FCILT 2014; FIET 2016. Planner, London Transport, 1990–93; Transport Specialist, World Bank, 1995–97; Associate, Halcrow Fox, 1997–99; Office of Rail Regulator: Economist, 1999–2000; Dep. Chief Economist, 2000–01; Dep. Dir, Access,

Competition and Licensing, 2001–02; Man. Dir, Ops, Strategic Rail Authy, 2002–05; Exec. Dir, First Gp, 2005–10; CEO, High Speed 1, 2011–16. Non-executive Director: Aer Lingus, 2009–15; Ellevio AB, 2015–17; IAG plc, 2018–. Author, Shaw Report on Future Shape and Financing of Network Rail, 2016. Patron, Garsington Opera; Mem., Blue Plaques Club. *Recreations:* playing tennis, hill walking, rose cultivation, riding, reading novels, listening to opera, travelling. *Address:* National Grid plc, One Strand, WC2H 5EH. *T:* (01926) 653085. *E:* nicola.shaw@nationalgrid.com. *Club:* Widnes Rugby Union Football.

**SHAW, Prof. Malcolm Nathan;** QC 2002; PhD; Sir Robert Jennings Professor of International Law, University of Leicester, 1994–2011, now Professor Emeritus; Senior Fellow, Lauterpacht Centre for International Law, University of Cambridge, since 2010; *b* 8 July 1947; *s* of late Benjamin Shaw, CBE, and Paulette Shaw; *m* 1974, Judith Freeman; one *s* two *d*. *Educ:* Liverpool Univ. (LLB Hons); Hebrew Univ., Jerusalem (LLM with distinction); Keele Univ. (PhD). Called to the Bar, Gray's Inn, 1988; Lectr, then Principal Lectr, Liverpool Poly., 1972–81; Sen. Lectr and Reader in Law, 1981–89, Founder, Human Rights Centre, 1983, Essex Univ.; Ironsides, Ray and Vials Prof. of Law, Leicester Univ., 1989–94. Hebrew University of Jerusalem: Forcheimer Vis. Prof., 1986–87; Lady Davis Vis. Prof., 2009; Dist. Vis. Prof., 2013–16; Vis. Fellow, Lauterpacht Res. Centre for Internat. Law, Cambridge Univ., 2000–01 and 2005; Acad. of Internat. Law, Xiamen, China, 2006; Vis. Prof., Univ. of Paris Ouest, Nanterre-La Défense, 2009. Hersch Lauterpacht Meml Lectr, Univ. of Cambridge, 2010. Mem., Law Assessment Panel, 1996 and 2001 RAE, HEFCE. Trustee, British Inst. of Internat. and Comparative Law, 2010–16. Associate Mem., Institut de Droit Internat., 2013–. Co-ed. in Chief, Israel Law Rev., 2017–; Member: Hon. Bd, Cambridge Law Rev., 2018–; Editl Cttee, British Year Book of International Law. Officier de l'Ordre de la Valeur (Cameroon), 2003. *Publications:* International Law, 1977, 8th edn 2017 (trans. Polish, Hungarian, Chinese, Portuguese, Turkish, Kazakh); Title to Territory in Africa, 1986; (ed) Rosenne's Law and Practice of International Court of Justice, 5th edn, 2016; contrib. British Yr Book of Internat. Law, Finnish Yr Book of Internat. Law, Internat. and Comparative Law Qly, European Jl of Internat. Law, Collected Courses of Xiamen Acad., China. *Recreations:* reading, listening to music, watching TV, maps. *Address:* 50 Carisbrooke Road, Leicester LE2 3PB. *E:* shawmalcolm@hotmail.com; Essex Court Chambers, 24 Lincoln's Inn Fields, WC2A 3EG. *T:* (020) 7813 8000, *Fax:* (020) 7813 8080. *E:* mshaw@essexcourt.net.

**SHAW, Mark Richard;** QC 2002; *b* 6 June 1962; *s* of Dennis Ronald Shaw and Jill Merilyn Shaw. *Educ:* St Peter's Sch., Bournemouth; Durham Univ. (BA 1984); Gonville and Caius Coll., Cambridge (LLM 1985). Called to the Bar, Inner Temple, 1987; in practice, specialising in public law, human rights, professional discipline/regulation and mediation; Jun. Counsel to the Crown, Common Law, 1992–2002; Special Advocate, 1998–. CEDR Accredited Mediator, 2008; Mem., Mediation Chambers, 2012–. Fellow, Internat. Acad. of Trial Lawyers, 2008–. Member: Cttee, Constitutional and Admin. Law Bar Assoc., 1995–98; Adv. Bd, Judicial Rev., 1996–2016; Cttee, Assoc. of Regulatory and Disciplinary Lawyers, 2009–12. *Publications:* (jtly) Immigration and Nationality, in Halsbury's Laws of England: vol. 4, 1992; (contrib.) Human Rights Law and Practice, 1999, and Supplement, 2000. *Recreations:* golf, scuba diving, running, wine, travel (especially in Italy). *Address:* Blackstone Chambers, Temple, EC4Y 9BW. *T:* (020) 7583 1770. *Clubs:* Athenæum; Royal St George's Golf.

**SHAW, Dr Mark Robert,** FRSE; Keeper of Geology and Zoology, 1996–2005, now Hon. Research Associate, National Museums of Scotland; *b* 11 May 1945; *s* of William Shaw and Mabel Courtenay Shaw (*née* Bower); *m* 1970, Francesca Dennis Wilkinson; two *d*. *Educ:* Dartington Hall Sch.; Oriel Coll., Oxford (BA 1968; MA, DPhil 1972). FRSE 2004. Res. Assistant, Manchester Univ., 1973–76; Univ. Res. Fellow, Reading Univ., 1977–80; Asst Keeper, Dept of Natural History, 1980–83, Keeper of Natural History, 1983–96, Royal Scottish Mus., subseq. Nat. Museums of Scotland. *Publications:* contribs (mainly on parasitic wasps) to entomological jls. *Recreations:* field entomology, family life. *Address:* 48 St Albans Road, Edinburgh EH9 2LU. *T:* (0131) 667 0577.

**SHAW, Martin;** actor; *b* 21 Jan. 1945; two *s* one *d*. *Educ:* Great Barr Sch., Birmingham; LAMDA. *Stage* includes: appearances at Royal Court and National Theatre; West End: Are You Lonesome Tonight, Phoenix, 1985; The Big Knife, Albery, 1987; Other People's Money, Lyric 1990; Betrayal, 1991; An Ideal Husband, Globe, 1992, Haymarket, 1996 (Best Actor Award, NY Drama Desk, 1996), 1997, transf. Gielgud, and Albery, 1998, Haymarket, and Lyric, 1999; Rough Justice, Apollo, 1994; A Man for All Seasons, Haymarket, 2006; The Country Girl, Apollo, 2010; Twelve Angry Men, Garrick, 2013; The Best Man, Playhouse Th., 2018; Hobson's Choice, Th. Royal, Bath, 2016; *television* includes, 1968–: The Professionals; The Chief, 1994; title rôle in Rhodes, 1996; The Scarlet Pimpernel, 1999; Always and Everyone, later A & E, 1999–2002; Judge John Deed, 2001–07; Death in Holy Orders, 2003; The Murder Room, 2004; Cranford, 2007; Inspector George Gently, 2007–17; Apparitions, 2008; Strike: The Cuckoo's Calling, 2017. Hon. Bencher, Gray's Inn. *Recreation:* flies own antique biplane.

**SHAW, Rt Rev. Martin;** *see* Shaw, Rt Rev. A. M.

**SHAW, Group Captain Mary Michal,** RRC 1981; Director and Matron-in-Chief, Princess Mary's Royal Air Force Nursing Service, and Deputy Director, Defence Nursing Services, 1985–88; *b* 7 April 1933; *d* of Ven. Archdeacon Thorndike Shaw and Violet Rosario Shaw. *Educ:* Wokingham Grammar School for Girls. SRN 1955, Royal Berkshire Hosp., Reading; SCM 1957, Central Middlesex Hosp., London and Battle Hosp., Reading; PMRAFNS, 1963–88; QHNS, 1985–88. OStJ 1974. *Recreations:* gardening, home crafts.

**SHAW, Michael Hewitt,** CMG 1990; foreign affairs adviser and consultant; HM Diplomatic Service, retired; *b* 5 Jan. 1935; *s* of late Donald Shaw and Marion (*née* Hewitt); *m* 1963, Elizabeth Rance; two *d* (and two *d* decd). *Educ:* Sedbergh; Clare College, Cambridge (MA); UCL (MA 1992). HM Forces, 1953–55. HMOCS Tanganyika, 1959–62; joined Diplomatic Service, 1963; served The Hague, FCO and Vientiane, 1964–68; First Sec., FCO, 1968–72, Valletta, 1972–76, FCO, 1976–82, Brussels, 1982–84; Counsellor, Brussels, 1984–86, FCO, 1986–95. Chm., Lynchmere Soc., 2007–12. *Recreations:* cricket, theatre, travel, historical research, preservation of the countryside. *Address:* The Close, Marley Common, Haslemere, Surrey GU27 3PT. *E:* michael@mhshaw.co.uk. *Clubs:* Army and Navy, MCC; Ashton Lacrosse.

*See also* R. O. Shaw.

**SHAW, Sir Neil (McGowan),** Kt 1994; Chairman: Tate & Lyle PLC, London, 1986–98 (Director, 1975–98); Chief Executive, 1986–92); Tate & Lyle Holdings, 1981–98; Tate & Lyle Industries, 1981–98; Tunnel Refineries, 1982–98 (Director, 1981–98); Vice-Chairman: Redpath Industries, 1981–98 (Director, 1972–98); A. E. Staley Manufacturing Co., 1988–98; *b* 31 May 1929; *s* of late Harold LeRoy Shaw and Fabiola Marie Shaw; *m* 1952, Audrey Robinson (marr. diss.); two *s* three *d*; *m* 1985, Elizabeth Fern Mudge-Massey. *Educ:* Knowlton High Sch.; Lower Canada Coll., Canada. Trust Officer, Crown Trust Co., Montreal, 1947–54; Exec. Asst, Redpath Industries, 1954–58; Merchandising Manager, 1958–63, Vice Pres. and Gen. Manager, 1967–72, Canada & Dominion Sugar Co., Toronto; Export Sales Manager, Tate & Lyle PLC, 1963–68; Pres., Redpath Industries Ltd, 1972–80; Gp Man. Dir, Tate & Lyle PLC, 1980–86. Director: Americare Corp. 1980–96; Alcantara, 1983–98; Canadian Imperial Bank of Commerce (Toronto), 1986–2000; United Biscuits (Hldgs), 1988–97; M & G Investment Income Trust, 1991–95; Medcan (Toronto), 2001–10. Non-executive Director: Texaco Canada Inc., 1974–89; Smiths Industries, 1986–96; Scottish and Newcastle Breweries, 1986–92. Dir, World Sugar Res. Orgn, 1982–97 (Chm., 1994–96); Gov., World Food and Agro Forum, 1988–96. Chairman: BITC, 1991–94; Assoc. of Lloyd's Members, 1992–94; E London Partnership, 1989–91; Member: Food Assoc., 1989–95; Church Urban Fund Council, 1989–91; Canadian Univs Soc. of GB, 1989–2001; Adv. Council, PYBT, 1990–98; Listed Cos Adv. Cttee, Stock Exchange, 1991–97; Chm. and Dir, Federal Security Agency, Toronto, 2008–. Trustee, Royal Botanic Gardens, Kew, 1990–98 (Chm., Trustees and Friends, 1994–2000). Dir, Inst. of Dirs, 1986–97. Dir and Gov., United World Coll. of Atlantic, 1997–2000. Gov., Montreal Gen. Hosp. Jt Chm., Percent Club, 1992–97. CIMgt, 1981–98; Fellow, Inst. of Grocery Distribn, 1989–2000 (Mem., British N American Cttee, 1991–97). Hon. Fellow, RHBNC, 1995. Hon. LLD E London, 1997. *Recreations:* dogs, golfing.

**SHAW, Nicola;** *see* Shaw, L. N.

**SHAW, Nicola Jane;** QC 2012; *b* Bishop's Stortford; *d* of Michael John Shaw and Christine Shaw. *Educ:* Pembroke Coll., Oxford (BA Hons Juris.; BCL). Called to the Bar, Inner Temple, 1995; Attorney Gen.'s Panel of Jun. Counsel to the Crown, C Panel, 2001, B Panel, 2006. Chair, Revenue Bar Assoc., 2016–19. *Recreations:* parties, screenwriting, downhill ski-ing, cooking, eating, racquet sports, creative retreats, sailing, restaurants, theatre, Scrabble. *Address:* Gray's Inn Tax Chambers, 36 Queen Street, EC4R 1BN. *T:* (020) 7242 2642, *Fax:* (020) 7831 9017. *E:* ns@taxbar.com.

**SHAW, Peter Alan,** PhD, DCL; CB 2000; Partner, Praesta Partners, since 2005; *b* 31 May 1949; *s* of late Frank Shaw and Ursula Lister Shaw (*née* Dyson); *m* 1975, Frances Willcox; two *s* one *d*. *Educ:* Bridlington Sch.; Durham Univ. (BSc Geography); Bradford Univ. (MSc Traffic Eng. and Planning); Regent Coll., Univ. of British Columbia (Master in Christian Studies); Chester Univ. (PhD Leadership Develt 2011); Acad. of Exec. Coaching (Adv. Dip. Exec. Coaching). FCIHT. Department of Education and Science, subseq. Department for Education, then Department for Education and Employment, then Department for Education and Skills, 1972–2003: Private Sec. to Perm. Sec., 1975–76; Principal Private Sec. to Sec. of State, 1979–81; Asst Sec., 1981–91; on loan to HM Treasury, 1985–86; Press Sec. to DES Sec. of State, 1988–89; Grade 3, 1991–98; on loan to Depts of the Envmt and Transport as Regl Dir, Northern Reg., 1991–93; Dir of Estabts and Personnel, 1993–94; Dir of Services (personnel, analytical and inf. systems), 1994–95; Leader, Sen. Mgt Review, 1995; Dir, Sch. Places, Buildings and Governance, 1995–97; Dir, Finance, 1997–98; Grade 2, 1998–2003; Director-General: Finance and Analytical Services, 1998–2000; Employment, Equality and Internat. Relations, 2000–01; Youth Policy, 2001–03; Partner, Change Partnership, 2003–05. Hon. Visiting Professor: Educn Dept, Univ. of Durham, 1997–2000; of Leadership Develt, Newcastle Univ. Business Sch., 2008–; Univ. of Chester Business Faculty, 2011–; De Montfort Univ., 2017–; Vis. Lectr, Regent Coll., UBC, 2008–; Visiting Professor: Surrey Univ., 2018–; Huddersfield Univ., 2019–; Victoria Judicial Coll., Melbourne, 2019. Trustee, Christian Assoc. of Business Execs, 2005–11. Member: Council, St John's Coll., Durham Univ., 1993–2008 (Hon. Fellow, 2009–14, now Hon. Professorial Fellow); Ct, Univ. of Newcastle upon Tyne, 2005–12; Governing Body, Godalming Sixth Form Coll., 1996–2008; Chm. of Trustees, Friends of Regent Coll., UBC, 2010–. Mem., RIIA, 2018–. Anglican Lay Reader, 1972–, Chm. of Selectors for Lay Readers in Trng, 1999–, Mem., Ministerial Adv. Council, 1999–2004, dio. of Guildford; Lay Canon, 2016–, Chair, Council, 2016–, Guildford Cathedral. FRSA. Hon. DCL Durham, 2015; DUniv Huddersfield, 2018. *Publications:* Mirroring Jesus as Leader, 2004; Conversation Matters, 2005; The Vs of Leadership: vision, values, value added and vitality, 2006; Finding Your Future: the second time around, 2006; (with Robin Linnecar) Business Coaching: achieving practical results through effective engagement, 2007; Making Difficult Decisions: how to be decisive and get the business done, 2008; Deciding Well: a Christian perspective on making decisions as a leader, 2009; Raise Your Game: how to succeed at work, 2009; Effective Christian Leaders in the Global Workplace, 2010; Defining Moments, 2010; (with Alan Smith) The Reflective Leader, 2011; Thriving in Your Work, 2011; Getting the Balance Right, 2012; (with Graham Shaw) Leading in Demanding Times, 2013; (with Colin Shaw) The Emerging Leader: stepping up in leadership, 2013; 100 Great Personal Impact Ideas, 2013; Celebrating Your Senses, 2014; 100 Great Coaching Ideas, 2014; Sustaining Leadership, 2014; 100 Great Team Effectiveness Ideas, 2015; Wake up and Dream, 2015; 100 Great Building Success Ideas, 2016; (with Hilary Douglas) The Reluctant Leader, 2016; 100 Great Leading Well Ideas, 2017; (with Graham Shaw) Living With Never Ending Expectations, 2017; 100 Great Leading through Rapid Change Ideas, 2018; The Mindful Leader: embodying Christian principles, 2018; 100 Great Leading Through Frustration Ideas, 2019; Leadership to the Limits: freedom and responsibility, 2020; articles on exec. coaching, leadership and spirituality. *Recreations:* long-distance walking (completed 34 UK long distance walks), travelling, bus rides with grandchildren. *Address:* Praesta Partners, 43 Berkeley Square, W1J 5AP. *T:* (020) 7907 2473. *E:* peter.shaw@praesta.com.

**SHAW, Dr Richard Oliver;** Interim Chief Executive, South Downs National Park Authority, 2009–12; *b* 20 Jan. 1949; *s* of Donald Smethurst Shaw and Marion Clarissa Shaw; *m* 1983, Poorna Charles; three *s*. *Educ:* Sedbergh Sch.; Univ. of Sussex (BA 1st cl. Hons); Univ. of Exeter (PGCE 1973); UCL (PhD 1981). Teacher: Lycée el Hourriya, Algeria, 1971–72; Rishi Valley Sch., India, 1974–76; Sen. Educn Officer, then Field Dir, PNG, VSO, 1976–81; Head Teacher, Pahadi Sch., India, 1981–87; teacher, ILEA, 1987–88; Hd, Rural Affairs, then Hd, Global Atmosphere, DoE, 1988–97; Dir for the Envmt, Surrey CC, 1997–2001; Chief Executive: Oxfordshire CC, 2001–04; Surrey CC, 2005–09. Non-exec. Dir, Surrey and Sussex Healthcare NHS Trust, 2012– (Chm., 2018–). Chm., UK Local Govt Alliance for Internat. Develt, 2009–; Associate, Nat. Sch. of Govt, 2009–11. Mem. Council, Univ. of Surrey, 2005–09 (Mem., Audit Cttee, 2006–09). *Publications:* English lang. school textbooks for India. *Recreations:* tennis, PADI Master scuba diver, travel, family, music.

*See also* M. H. Shaw.

**SHAW, Prof. Richard Wright,** CBE 1997; Vice-Chancellor and Principal, University of Paisley, 1992–2001 (Principal, Paisley College, 1987–92); *b* 22 Sept. 1941; *s* of late George Beeley Shaw and Bella Shaw; *m* 1965, Susan Angela Birchley; two *s*. *Educ:* Lancaster Royal Grammar Sch.; Sidney Sussex Coll., Cambridge (MA). Leeds University: Asst Lectr in Management, 1964–66; Lectr in Econs, 1966–69; Stirling University: Lectr in Econs, 1969–75; Sen. Lectr, 1975–84; Head of Dept of Econs, 1982–84; Paisley College: Head, Dept of Econs and Management and Prof., 1984–86; Vice Principal, 1986–87. Convenor, Cttee of Scottish Higher Educn Principals, 1996–98. Member: Scottish Economic Council, 1995–98; Scottish Business Forum, 1998–99; Chm., Lead Scotland, 2001–07. Fellow, SCOTVEC, 1995; FRSA. DUniv: Glasgow, 2001; West of Scotland, 2008. *Publications:* (with C. J. Sutton) Industry and Competition, 1976; articles in Jl Industrial Econs, Scottish Jl Pol Econ., Managerial and Decision Econs. *Recreations:* walking, listening to music, sketching and painting. *Address:* Drumbarns, 18 Old Doune Road, Dunblane, Perthshire FK15 9AG.

**SHAW, Prof. Robert Wayne,** CBE 2002; MD; FRCSE, FRCOG; Professor of Obstetrics and Gynaecology, Nottingham University, 2002–12, now Emeritus; *b* 25 June 1946; *s* of Arthur Stanley Shaw and Margery Maude Shaw (*née* Griffiths); *m* 1980, Mary Philomena McGovern; one *s* one *d. Educ:* Priory Grammar Sch., Shrewsbury; Birmingham Univ. Med. Sch. (MB ChB 1969; MD 1975). FRCSE 1978; MRCOG 1977, FRCOG 1993. Lectr, 1975–79, and Sen. Lectr, 1979–81, in Obstetrics and Gynaecology, Birmingham Univ.; Sen. Lectr, Edinburgh Univ., 1981–83; Prof., Royal Free Hosp. Sch. of Medicine, 1983–92; Prof. and Head of Acad. Dept of Obstetrics and Gynaecology, Univ. of Wales Coll. of Medicine, 1992–2001; Postgrad. Dean, Med. and Dental Educn, Eastern Deanery, Univ. of Cambridge, 2001–02. Vice-Pres., 1995–98, Pres., 1998–2001, RCOG. Chm. Bd, Nat. Collaborating Centre for Women's and Children's Health (producing clinical guidelines for NICE), 2007–11. Founder FMedSci 1998; FRCPI 2000; FACOG 2000. Hon. FFSRH (Hon. FFFP 2002); Hon. Fellow, Finnish Gynaecological Soc., 1992. *Publications:* (ed jtly) Gynaecology, 1992, 4th edn, 2010; (ed) Endometriosis: current management, 1995; (ed jtly) Atlas of Endometriosis, 3rd edn 2008; over 320 articles on gynaecological reproductive medicine. *Recreations:* sailing, hill walking, gardening, music. *Address:* Grosvenor House, Weaverlake Drive, Yoxall, Staffs DE13 8AD. *Club:* Athenæum.

**SHAW, Prof. Rory James Swanton,** MD; FRCP; Director, London Healthcare Consultancy Ltd, since 2018; Medical Director, Feedback plc, since 2018; *b* 5 Jan. 1954; *s* of late Dr James Brian Shaw, OBE and Irma Valerie Shaw, JP; *m* 1991, Sarah Margaret Foulkes (*d* 2011); two *d. Educ:* Bedford Sch.; St Bartholomew's Hosp. Med. Sch. (BSc 1974; MB BS 1977); MD 1985, MBA 1995, London. MRCP 1979, FRCP 1993. Sen. Lectr, St Mary's Hosp. Med. Sch., Imperial Coll., and Consultant Physician in Respiratory Medicine, 1989–97; Prof. of Respiratory Med., Imperial Coll. Sch. of Med., 1997–; Medical Director: Hammersmith Hosps NHS Trust, 1998–2006; Royal Berkshire NHS Foundn Trust, 2007–09; NW London Hosps NHS Trust, 2009–13; Med. Dir and Clinical Lead, Healthcare UK, 2013–18. Chm., Nat. Patient Safety Agency, 2001–03; non-exec. Dir, NHS Litigation Authy, 2007–15. *Publications:* (jtly) Management Essentials for Doctors, 2011; articles on tuberculosis and asthma in learned jls.

**SHAW, Stephen Arthur,** CBE 2004; PhD; Independent Assessor of Complaints, Crown Prosecution Service, since 2013; *b* 26 March 1953; *s* of late Walter Arthur Shaw and Gwendolyn Primrose Shaw (*née* Cottrell); *m* 1977, Christine Elizabeth Robinson; partner, Jane Angela Skinner; two *s. Educ:* Rutlish Sch., Merton; Univ. of Warwick (BA 1974); Univ. of Leeds (MA 1976); Univ. of Kent (PhD 1979). Lectr in Further Educn, Mid-Kent Coll. of Technology, 1977–79; Researcher, NACRO, 1979–80; Research Officer, Home Office, 1980–81; Dir, Prison Reform Trust, 1981–99; Prisons Ombudsman, 1999–2001; Prisons and Probation Ombudsman, 2001–10; Chief Exec., Office of the Health Professions Adjudicator, 2010–12; Ind. Complaints Assessor, DfT, 2013–19. Chair: Ind. Adv. Panel on Non-Compliance Mgt, Home Office, 2013–14; Ind. Review into Welfare in Detention of Vulnerable Persons, Home Office, 2015 and 2017–18. Dir, Procordia Ltd, 2012–; Sen. Associate, Verita Consultants LLP, 2015–. Mem., Disciplinary Panel, Propertymark (formerly Nat. Fedn of Property Professionals), 2012–. *Publications:* numerous contribs to books and jls. *Recreations:* family, sport, gardening, collecting antiques, watching Fulham FC. *E:* stephen.shaw999@gmail.com.

**SHAW, Sir Thomas Joshua B.;** *see* Best-Shaw.

**SHAW, Tim,** RA 2013; FRSS; sculptor and installation artist; *b* Belfast, 1964. *Educ:* Portora Sch., Enniskillen; Manchester Poly. (Art Foundn (Dist.)); Falmouth Coll. of Art and Design (BA 1st Cl. Hons Fine Art 1989). FRSS (FRBS 2013). Work on architectural and sculptural restoration progs, then Sculpture Shed studio, Bristol, 1989–91. Vis. Lectr, Falmouth Coll. of Art and Design, subseq. Coll. of Arts, 1991–2007. Artist-in-Residence: Delfina Studio Trust, Spain, 1996; British Sch. at Athens (Prince's Bursary), 2005; Kenneth Armitage Foundn Sculpture Fellow, 2006; Artist Fellow, Kate Hamburger Centre for Advanced Study in the Humanities, Bonn, 2015. Hon. Fellow, Falmouth Univ., 2013. *Solo exhibitions* include: Duncan Campbell Gall., London, 1995, 1997; Falmouth Coll. of Art Gall., 1995, 1999; Truro Cathedral, 2005; Goldfish Contemp. Fine Art, Penzance, 2006, 2008; Kenneth Armitage Foundn, London, 2008, 2009; Millennium Gall., St Ives, 2011; Riflemaker Contemp. Art Gall., London, 2012; MAC Birmingham, Aberystwyth Arts Centre, 2014; Kappatos Gall., Athens, 2014; F. E. McWilliam Gall., Banbridge, NI, 2015; The Exchange, Penzance, 2018; Beyond Reason, San Diego Mus. of Art, 2018–19; *group exhibitions* include: Newlyn Art Gall., Cornwall, 1992, 2004, 2011, 2013; St Paul's Cathedral, 1993; Contemp. Art Fair, London, 1994, 1998; Mall Galls, London, 1997, 2008; Lemon St Gall., Truro, 2000, 2001, 2002, 2003, 2004, 2005; Newlyn Soc. of Artists, 2001, 2003, 2005, 2006; Badcocks Gall., Newlyn, 2001, 2002; Millfield Open, 2003, 2004; SW Acad. Summer Open, 2003, 2004; Mullan Gall., Belfast, 2005, 2009, 2011; Goldfish Contemp. Art, Penzance, 2005, 2006, 2007, 2008; Royal Ulster Acad., Ulster Mus., 2005; Falmouth Art Gall., 2006, 2007; Summer Exhibn, Royal Acad. of Arts, 2007, 2011, 2012, 2014, 2015 (Jack Goldhill Prize for Sculpture, 2015); Millennium Gall., St Ives, 2010; Threadneedle Space, London, 2012; Flowers Gall., London, 2014; RWA, 2014; *public commissions* include: The Rites of Dionysos for Eden Project, Cornwall, 2004; The Minotaur for Royal Opera Hse, 2008; The Drummer, Lemon Quay, Truro, 2011; The Green Man, Antony Hse, Cornwall, 2012. Hon. RWA. Prince's Trust Award, 1990; Mullan Prize, Royal Ulster Acad. Annual Exhibn, 2005; FBA Selectors' Choice, Threadneedle Prize, Mall Galls, 2008. *Address:* c/o Anima-Mundi, Street-an-Pol, St Ives, Cornwall TR26 2DS.

**SHAW, Prof. Timothy Milton,** PhD; Visiting Adjunct Research Professor and Foundation Graduate Program Director, since 2015, PhD in Global Governance and Human Security, University of Massachusetts Boston (Visiting Professor, 2012–June 2020); *b* 27 Jan. 1945; *s* of Arnold and Margaret Shaw; *m* 1983, Jane Little Parpart; one *s* one *d*, and two step *d. Educ:* Univ. of Sussex (BA 1967); Univ. of East Africa (MA Internat. Relns 1969); Princeton Univ. (MA Politics 1971, PhD Politics 1975). Teaching Fellow, Dept Political Sci., Makerere UC, Kampala, 1968–70; Dalhousie University, Canada, 1971–2001: Asst Prof., then Assoc. and Full Prof. of Political Sci.; Dir, Centre for African Studies, 1977–78, 1983–89; Exec. Dir, Pearson Inst. for Internat. Develt, 1985–88; Prof. in Internat. Develt Studies, 1990–2000; Dir, Centre for Foreign Policy Studies, 1993–2000; Dir, Inst. of Commonwealth Studies and Prof. of Commonwealth Governance and Develt, Sch. of Advanced Study, Univ. of London, 2001–06; Dir and Prof., Inst. of Internat. Relns, Univ. of West Indies, 2007–11. Vis. Lectr, Univ. of Zambia, 1973–74; Vis. Assoc. Prof., Carleton Univ., 1978–80; Vis. Sen. Lectr, Univ. of Ife, Nigeria, 1979–80; Visiting Professor: Univ. of Zimbabwe, 1989; Univs of Stellenbosch and Western Cape, South Africa, 1998–2015; Aalborg Univ., Denmark, 2000–01 and 2012–; Makerere Univ. Business Sch., 2006–15; Bank of Uganda Vis. Prof., Mbarara Univ. of Sci. and Tech., 2000–15; Adjunct Research Professor: Carleton Univ., 2015–; Univ. of Ottawa, 2015–. Editor: Internat. Political Economy Series, Palgrave Macmillan, 1983–; Internat. Political Economy of New Regionalism Series, Routledge, 1998–. Hon. DLitt St Andrews, 2014. *Publications:* Commonwealth, 2008; *edited jointly and contributed:* Africa's Challenge to International Relations Theory, 2001; Crises of Governance in Asia and Africa, 2001; Theories of New Regionalism, 2003; Twisting Arms and Flexing Muscles: humanitarian intervention and peacebuilding in perspective, 2005; The Political Economy of Regions and Regionalisms, 2005; The Diplomacies of Small States, 2009, 2nd edn 2013; Inter-American Cooperation at a Crossroads, 2011; Africa and International Relations in the Twenty-First Century: still challenging theory?, 2011; Ashgate Research Companion to Regionalisms, 2011; Rethinking Development Challenges for Public Policy: insights from contemporary Africa, 2012; Comparative Regionalisms for Development in the 21st Century, 2013; Development in Africa: refocusing the lens after the MDGs, 2015; African Foreign Policy and International Institutions, 2017; From MDGs to SDGs: rethinking African development, 2017; (with Jason Warner) African Foreign Policies in International Institutions, 2018; The Palgrave Handbook of Contemporary IPE, 2019; Development and Sustainable Growth of Mauritius, 2019. *Recreations:* jogging, swimming, tennis, cycling, travelling, cooking. *Address:* 318 Selby Avenue, Ottawa, ON K1Z 6R1, Canada.

**SHAW STEWART, Sir Ludovic (Houston),** 12th Bt *cr* 1667 (NS), of Greenock and Blackhall, Renfrewshire; *b* 12 Nov. 1986; *s* of Sir Houston Shaw-Stewart, 11th Bt, MC, TD and of Lucinda Victoria (*née* Fletcher, later Hon. Mrs Christopher Chetwode); *S* father, 2004. *Educ:* Belhaven; Eton; Edinburgh Univ. *Recreation:* finding silver linings of clouds and promptly unthreading them.

**SHAWCROSS, Conrad,** RA 2013; artist; sculptor; *b* London, 26 April 1977; *s* of Hon. William (Hartley Hume) Shawcross, *qv* and Dame Marina (Sarah) Warner, *qv*; *m* 2013, Carolina Mazzolari; one *s. Educ:* Westminster Sch.; Chelsea Sch. of Art (Foundn 1996); Ruskin Sch. of Drawing and Fine Art, Oxford (BA Hons Fine Art 1999); Slade Sch. of Art, University Coll. London (MFA Fine Art 2001). *Solo exhibitions* include: Sci. Mus., 2011–12; Victoria Miro Gall., 2011, 2015, 2018; Mudam Luxembourg, 2011; Palais de Tokyo, Paris, 2013; Roundhouse, 2013; Artmia Foundation, Beijing, 2014; Careyes Foundn, Mexico, 2015; New Art Centre, Wilts, 2015; The Peninsula, Hong Kong, 2016; Tucci Russo Studio per l'Arte Contemporanea, Torino, 2016; Ivorypress, Madrid, 2016; Wadsworth Atheneum Mus. of Art, Conn, 2018; *group exhibitions* include: Mus. of Old and New Art, Tasmania, 2011, 2014; Nat. Gall. and ROH, 2012; KW Inst. for Contemp. Art, Berlin, 2012; Grand Palais, Paris, 2013; RA, 2014–18; Imma, Dublin, 2014; ArtScience Mus., Singapore, 2014, 2017; Mudam Luxembourg, 2015; Palazzo Fortuny, Venice, 2015; Sharjah Art Centre, UAE, 2015; ZKM, Karlsruhe, 2015, 2019; Musée des arts et métiers, Paris, 2016; Mori Art Mus., Tokyo, 2016; Herning Mus. of Contemp. Art, Denmark, 2017; Barbican, London, 2017; Whitechapel Gall., London, 2018; Harbour Arts Sculpture Park, Hong Kong, 2018; Frieze Sculpture Park, London, 2018; *commissions* include: Three Perpetual Chords, Dulwich Park, 2015; Paradigm, Francis Crick Inst., 2016; The Optic Cloak, Greenwich Peninsula, 2016; The Interpretation of Movement, St Pancras, 2017; Exploded Paradigm, Comcast Technol. Center, 2018; Manifold 5:4, Liverpool St Station, Elizabeth line, 2018. *Recreation:* trapeze.

**SHAWCROSS, His Honour Roger Michael;** a Circuit Judge, 1993–2008; Deputy Designated Family Judge, Hampshire and Isle of Wight, 2006–08; *b* 27 March 1941; *s* of Michael and Friedel Shawcross; *m* 1969, Sarah Broom; one *s* one *d. Educ:* Radley Coll.; Christ Church, Oxford (MA). Called to the Bar, Gray's Inn, 1967; a Recorder, 1985–93; Res. Judge, Newport, IoW, 1994–99. Member: Ancillary Relief Adv. Cttee, Family Justice Council, 1994–2005; Family Appeals Review Gp, 1998–2005; Magistrates' Area Trng Cttee (Hants and IoW), 2005–08; Chm., Hants and IoW Family Justice Council, 2006–08. *Recreations:* growing vegetables, reading, history, music, cinema, travel, admiring my wife's gardening skills, playing golf.

**SHAWCROSS, Valerie,** CBE 2002; Deputy Mayor for Transport, Greater London Authority, and Deputy Chair, Transport for London, 2016–18 (Member, 2018–19); *b* 1958; *d* of Alfred and Florence Shawcross; *m* 1st, 1983, Alan Frank Neil Parker, *qv* (marr. diss. 2002); 2nd, 2005, Michael John Anteney. *Educ:* Univ. of Liverpool (BA Hons Pol Theory and Instns 1980); Inst. of Education, Univ. of London (MA Educn 1986). Sabbatical Officer, Liverpool Univ. Guild of Undergraduates, 1980–81; UK Council for Overseas Students' Affairs, 1981–84; ILEA, 1984–86; World Univ. Service (UK), 1986; Commonwealth Secretariat, 1987–91; freelance appointments, 1992–: NFWI, Labour Party. Mem. (Lab), Croydon LBC, 1994–2000 (Chair of Educn, 1995, Dep. Leader, 1997, Leader, 1997–2000). Mem., Labour Party, 1979–. London Assembly, Greater London Authority: Mem. (Lab), Lambeth and Southwark, 2000–16; Chm., Transport Cttee, 2008–11, 2013–14 and 2015–16. Chm., London Fire and Emergency Planning Authy, 2000–08 (Mem., 2013–16); Mem., Metropolitan Police Authy, 2009–12. Contested (Lab) Bermondsey and Old Southwark, 2010. *Recreation:* poetry.

**SHAWCROSS, Hon. Mrs William;** *see* Polizzi, Hon. Olga.

**SHAWCROSS, Hon. William (Hartley Hume),** CVO 2011; writer and broadcaster; Chairman, Charity Commission, 2012–18; Special Representative for the Foreign Secretary on UK Victims of Qadhafi-sponsored IRA Terrorism, since 2019; *b* 28 May 1946; *s* of Baron Shawcross, GBE, PC, QC; *m* 1st, 1971, Marina Sarah Warner (*see* Dame M. S. Warner); one *s*; 2nd, 1981, Michal Levin; one *d*; 3rd, 1993, Hon. Olga Polizzi, *qv. Educ:* Eton; University Coll., Oxford. Chm., Article 19, Internat. Centre on Censorship, 1986–96; Mem. Bd, Internat. Crisis Gp, 1995–2006; Member: Informal Adv. Gp, High Comr for Refugees, 1996–2001; BBC Govs World Service Consultative Gp, 1997–2004; Council, Disasters Emergency Cttee, 1998–2002; Exec. Cttee, Anglo-Israel Assoc., 2011–12. Presenter and Assoc. Producer, Queen and Country, BBC TV, 2002. Mem. Bd, Henry Jackson Soc., 2011–12. Patron, Weiner Liby, 2007–12. *Publications:* Dubcek, 1970; Crime and Compromise, 1974; Sideshow: Kissinger, Nixon and the destruction of Cambodia, 1979; The Quality of Mercy: Cambodia, holocaust and modern memory, 1984; The Shah's Last Ride, 1989; Kowtow: a plea on behalf of Hong Kong, 1989; Murdoch, 1992; Cambodia's New Deal, 1994; Deliver Us from Evil, 2000; Queen and Country, 2002; Allies, 2003; Queen Elizabeth, the Queen Mother: the official biography, 2009; Justice and the Enemy: Nuremberg, 9/11 and the trial of Khalid Sheikh Mohammed, 2012; Counting One's Blessings: the selected letters of Queen Elizabeth, the Queen Mother, 2012. *Recreations:* walking, sailing. *Address:* c/o Janklow and Nesbit, 13a Hillgate Street, W8 7SP. *E:* william.shawcross@gmail.com. *Clubs:* Special Forces; Royal Yacht Squadron; St Mawes Sailing.

*See also* C. Shawcross.

**SHAWE-TAYLOR, Desmond Philip,** LVO 2011; Surveyor of the Queen's Pictures, since 2005; *b* 30 Sept. 1955; *s* of late Brian Newton Shawe-Taylor and Jocelyn Cecilia Shawe-Taylor; *m* 1987, Rosemary Gillian North; two *s* one *d. Educ:* Shrewsbury Sch.; University Coll., Oxford; Courtauld Inst. of Art, London. Lectr, History of Art Dept, Nottingham Univ., 1979–96; Dir, Dulwich Picture Gall., 1996–2005. *Publications:* Genial Company: the theme of genius in eighteenth-century British portraiture, 1987; The Georgians: eighteenth-century portraiture and society, 1990; Dramatic Art: theatrical paintings from the Garrick Club, 1997; Rembrandt to Gainsborough: masterpieces from Dulwich Picture Gallery, 1999; Shakespeare in Art, 2003; Bruegel to Rubens: masters of Flemish painting, 2007; The Conversation Piece: scenes of fashionable life, 2009; Dutch Landscapes, 2010; The First Georgians: art and monarchy 1714–1760, 2014; Masters of the Everyday: Dutch artists in the Age of Vermeer, 2015; (ed) Charles I: King and collector, 2018. *Recreation:* playing the piano. *Address:* Flat 1, 20 Tregothnan Road, SW9 9JX. *T:* 07710 376667.

**SHAWYER, Eric Francis,** CBE 1998; FICS; Chairman, E. A. Gibson Shipbrokers Ltd, 1988–2000; Chairman, Baltic Exchange, 1996–98 (Director, 1991–98); *b* 17 July 1932; *m* 1956, Joyce Patricia Henley; one *s* one *d*. Joined E. A. Gibson Shipbrokers, 1948; Dir, 1963–; Man. Dir, 1969–98. Chairman: Worldscale Assoc. (London) Ltd, 1979–96; London Tanker Brokers Panel Ltd, 1990–96; Director: Maersk Air Ltd, 1994–2003; Maersk Air Hldg Ltd, 1994–2003; Corda, 2003–14. Trustee: Old Royal Naval Coll. Chapel Fund, 2005–16; Wellington Trust, 2009–. Gov., George Green's Sch., 2000–13. FICS 1994 (Pres., 1996). Freeman, City of London, 1980; Liveryman: Co. of Shipwrights, 1981 (Mem., Ct of Assts); Co. of Master Mariners, 2015; Freeman, Co. of Watermen and Lightermen, 1989. *Address*: Souvenir, Woodlands Road, Bromley, Kent BR1 2AE.

**SHAWYER, Peter Michael;** Chairman, Ingenious Media plc, since 2007; *b* 11 Sept. 1950; *s* of Edward William Francis Shawyer and Marjorie Josephine Shawyer; *m* 1979, Margot Bishop (*d* 2015); one *s* one *d*; *m* 2018, Kim McDermott Brown. *Educ*: Enfield GS; Univ. of Sheffield (BA Hons). FCA 1975. Touche Ross & Co., subseq. Deloitte & Touche, 1972–2004: admitted Partner, 1982; Tax Partner, 1982–84; Group Partner, a Tax Group, 1984–93; Partner in charge of Tax Dept, 1993–95; Partner in charge of London Office, 1995–99; Man. Partner, 1999–2004; Mem. Bd, Deloitte & Touche, UK. Chm., British Internat. Ltd, 2006–14; non-executive Director and Member, Audit Committee: HSBC Bank, 2004–14; HSBC France, 2005–14. *Recreation*: golf. *Address*: c/o Janice Aminoff, Deloitte, Stonecutter Court, 1 Stonecutter Street, EC4A 4TR. *Club*: Hadley Wood Golf.

**SHCHASNY, Uladzimir;** Chairman, National Commission of Republic of Belarus for UNESCO, 2001–13; Ambassador at Large, Ministry of Foreign Affairs, Belarus, 2001–13; *b* 25 Nov. 1945; *s* of Ryhor and Nadzeya Shchasny; *m* 1972, Lyudmila Kazakova (marr. diss. 1993). *Educ*: Minsk State Linguistic Univ. (grad. 1972). Interpreter for USSR Min. of Geology, Pakistan, 1969–70, 1972–74; Lectr, Minsk State Inst. of Foreign Languages, 1975–77; Translation Service, UN Secretariat, NY, 1978–82; joined Min. of Foreign Affairs, Belarus, 1983; Press Dept and Dept of Internat. Orgns, 1983–91; Asst to Minister for Foreign Affairs, 1991–92; Dir, Dept of Bilateral Co-operation, 1992–93; Chargé d'Affaires, 1993–94, Counsellor Minister, 1994–95, Lithuania; Ambassador of the Republic of Belarus to the UK and to the Republic of Ireland, 1995–2000; Dir, Dept of Bilateral Relations with CIS Countries, Min. of For. Affairs, 2000–01; Belarus Rep., Exec. Bd, UNESCO, 2001–05, 2009–13. Frantsysk Skaryna Medal (Belarus), 2009. *Publications*: Artists of Paris School from Belarus, 2010; Léon Bakst: life by firebird's feather, 2016; numerous translations of works of English and Urdu writers into Belarusian; articles in Belarusian jls. *Recreation*: antique map collecting.

**SHEA, Caroline Mary;** QC 2016; *b* Sussex, 22 Jan. 1961; *d* of Charles Shea and Julia McDonald Shea; *m* 1986, Alan Roberts; one *s* two *d*. *Educ*: Haberdashers' Aske's Sch. for Girls, Elstree; Robinson Coll., Cambridge (BA 1983; MA 1987); City Univ. (DipLaw 1993). Management Consultant: Andersen Consulting, 1983–86; Berkeley Partnership, 1986–90; called to the Bar, Middle Temple, 1994; in practice as barrister, specialising in property litigation, 1994–. FCIArb 2014. *Publications*: (contrib.) The Law and Practice of Charging Orders on Land, 2013; (contrib.) Muir Watt & Moss on Agricultural Holdings, 15th edn 2018. *Recreations*: walking on Dartmoor, playing cello, theatre, poetry, damson vodka. *Address*: Falcon Chambers, Falcon Court, EC4Y 1AA. *T*: (020) 7353 2484, *Fax*: (020) 7353 1261. *E*: clerks@falcon-chambers.com. *Club*: Blacks.

**SHEADER, Timothy;** Artistic Director, Open Air Theatre, Regent's Park, since 2008; *b* Scarborough, 23 Nov. 1971; *s* of Harry and Carol Sheader. *Educ*: Univs of Birmingham and Limoges (LLB Law with French). Freelance theatre dir, until 2008, working at RSC, West End and regl theatres; director of productions, Open Air Theatre, Regent's Park: Crazy for You, 2011, transf. Novello Th., 2011; All My Sons, 2014; Porgy and Bess, 2014; Peter Pan, 2015, revival, 2018; Lord of the Flies, 2015, then Edinburgh Fest., 2015; (with Dale Rooks) Running Wild, 2016; A Tale of Two Cities, 2017; The Turn of the Screw, 2018; Hansel and Gretel, 2019. *Recreations*: dance, yoga, voluntary work. *Address*: Regent's Park Open Air Theatre, Inner Circle, Regent's Park, NW1 4NU.

**SHEAR, Graham Julian;** Partner, Litigation and Corporate Risk, and Head, International Litigation and Corporate Risk, Bryan Cave Leighton Paisner LLP (formerly Berwin Leighton Paisner LLP), since 2009 (Partner, Corporate and Commercial Disputes, 2009–18; Head of Corporates and Private Wealth Group, 2010–18); *b* London, 19 June 1963; *s* of Ronald and Frula Shear; *m* 1991, Dalya Freedman; three *s*. *Educ*: Seaford Coll., Sussex; City of London Sch. for Boys; Poly. of N London (LLB Hons); Lancaster Gate Coll. of Law. Admitted Solicitor, 1989; joined Teacher Stern Selby, subseq. Teacher Stern as trainee solicitor, 1986; specialised in commercial entertainment and music law, 1986–91; Litigation Dept, 1991–2009; Man. Partner, 2001–09; founder, Media and Reputation Protection practice gp, 1999; established Sports practice gp, 2000. Mem., Law Panel, The Times, 2008–. *Publications*: contrib. The Times Law Supplement. *Recreations*: contemporary and modern art, Latin music and culture, especially Cuban, lifelong fan of West Ham United FC. *Address*: Bryan Cave Leighton Paisner LLP, Adelaide House, London Bridge, EC4R 9HA. *T*: (020) 3400 4191, *Fax*: (020) 3400 1111. *E*: graham.shear@bclplaw.com. *Club*: Soho House.

**SHEARD, Rodney Kilner;** Senior Principal, Populous (formerly HOK sport architecture), 1999; *b* 11 Sept. 1951; *s* of Saville Kilner Sheard and Margaret Helen Sheard; *m* 1989, Catherine Elisabeth Nouqueret; two *s*. *Educ*: Queensland Univ. of Technol. (DipArch 1975). RIBA 1977; ARAIA 1979. Partner, LOBB Architectural Practice, 1981; changed from partnership to co., 1993; merged with HOK, 1999. Architect for: Alfred McAlpine Stadium, Huddersfield, 1996; Millennium Stadium, Cardiff, 1998; Telstra Stadium (Sydney Olympic Stadium), 2000; Ascot Racecourse, 2006; Emirates Stadium, 2006; Wembley Stadium, 2007; Wimbledon Centre Court, 2009; London Olympic Stadium, 2012. Initiator of concept 'Generations of Stadia'. FRSA. Hon. DSc Luton, 2002. *Publications*: Stadia: a design and development guide, 1998 (jtly); Sport Architecture, 2000; numerous articles in sports jls. *Recreations*: flyfishing, tennis, sailing. *Address*: Populous, 14 Blades Court, 121 Deodar Road, Putney, SW15 2NU. *T*: (020) 8874 7666, *Fax*: (020) 8874 7470. *E*: rod.sheard@populous.com. *Club*: Royal Automobile.

**SHEARER, Alan,** CBE 2016 (OBE 2001); DL; football commentator, BBC Television; *b* 13 Aug. 1970; *s* of Alan Shearer and Anne Shearer (*née* Collins); *m* Lainya; one *s* two *d*. *Educ*: Gosforth High Sch. Professional footballer, scoring 409 goals, with: Southampton FC, 1988–92; Blackburn Rovers, 1992–96; Newcastle United FC, 1996–2006, Captain, 1997–2006; played for England, 1992–2000, Captain, 1996–2000 (63 caps; 30 goals). Manager, Newcastle United FC, 2009. DL Northumberland, 2009. *Publications*: The Story So Far (autobiog.), 1998.

**SHEARLOCK, Very Rev. David John;** Dean and Rector of St Mary's Cathedral, Truro, 1982–97, now Dean Emeritus; *b* 1 July 1932; *s* of Arthur John Shearlock and Honora Frances Hawkins; *m* 1959, Jean Margaret Marr; one *s* one *d*. *Educ*: Univ. of Birmingham (BA); Westcott House, Cambridge. Assistant Curate: Guisborough, Yorks, 1957–60; Christchurch Priory, Hants, 1960–64; Vicar: Kingsclere, 1964–71; Romsey Abbey, 1971–82; Diocesan Director of Ordinands (Winchester), 1977–82; Hon. Canon of Winchester, 1978–82. Chm., Beaminster Arts Festival, 1998–2003. FRSA 1991; FRGS 1992; ARSCM 1998. *Publications*: The Practice of Preaching, 1990; When Words Fail: God and the world of beauty, 1996. *Address*: 3 The Tanyard, Shadrack Street, Beaminster, Dorset DT8 3BG. *T*: (01308) 863170. *E*: davidshearlock@gmail.com.

**SHEARMAN, Prof. Clifford Paul,** FRCS; Professor of Vascular Surgery, University of Southampton, 1999–2016, now Emeritus; Consultant Vascular Surgeon, 1994–2016, and Associate Medical Director, 2008–16, University Hospital Southampton NHS Foundation Trust (formerly Southampton University Hospitals NHS Trust); *b* Ramsgate, 28 April 1955; *s* of Douglas Shearman and Dorothy Shearman; *m* 1982, Susan Mary Robinson; one *s* two *d*. *Educ*: Worthing High Sch. for Boys; Guy's Hosp. Med. Sch., London (BSc 1st Cl. Hons 1976; MB BS 1979; MS 1989). FRCS 1983. Sen. Lectr, and Hon. Consultant Vascular Surgeon, Queen Elizabeth Hosp., Birmingham, 1990–94; Sen. Lectr, Southampton Univ. Hosps NHS Trust, 1994–99; Head, Postgrad. Sch. of Surgery, Wessex Deanery, 2007–12. Non-exec. Dir, Royal Bournemouth and Christchurch NHS Foundn Trust, 2017–. President: Vascular Soc. of GB and Ire., 2009–10; Soc. of Academic and Res. Surgery, 2013–; Chair, Vascular Surgery Specialist Adv. Cttee, 2012–15; Dir, Professional Affairs, Assoc. of Surgeons of GB and Ire., 2011–12; Mem. Council, RCS, 2015– (Vice-Pres., 2018–). *Publications*: (jtly) MCQs in Surgery, 1994; (jtly) Chronic Wound Healing, 1999; (jtly) Vascular Surgery, 1999; Management of Diabetic Foot Complications, 2015. *Recreations*: running, long distance walking in the UK, Shakespearean theatre, art, live music.

**SHEARMAN, Donald Norman;** *b* 6 Feb. 1926; *s* of late S. F. Shearman, Sydney; *m* 1952, Stuart Fay, *d* of late Chap. F. H. Bashford; three *s* three *d*. *Educ*: Fort St and Orange High Schools; St John's Theological College, Morpeth, NSW. Served War of 1939–45: air crew, 1944–46. Theological College, 1948–50. Ordained deacon, 1950; Priest, 1951. Curate: of Dubbo, 1950–52; of Forbes, and Warden of St John's Hostel, 1953–56; Rector of Coonabarabran, 1957–59; Director of Promotion and Adult Christian Education, 1959–62; Canon, All Saints Cathedral, Bathurst, 1962; Archdeacon of Mildura and Rector of St Margaret's, 1963; Bishop of Rockhampton, 1963–71; Chairman, Australian Board of Missions, Sydney, 1971–73; Bishop of Grafton, 1973–85; Asst Bishop, dio. of Brisbane, 1989–91; resigned Holy Orders, 2003.

**SHEARMAN, James Robert,** FRAM; conductor, orchestrator and composer; *b* S Benfleet, Essex, 23 March 1970; *s* of David Robert Shearman and Georgina Eunice Shearman. *Educ*: St Margaret's C of E Primary Sch., Benfleet; Appleton Sch., Benfleet; Army Jun. Sch. of Music, Dorset; Royal Acad. of Music (BMus Hons). ARAM 2004, FRAM 2015. Conductor and orchestrator; *film scores* include: Shakespeare in Love, 1998; Mansfield Park, 1999; Gosford Park, Bridget Jones's Diary, Lara Croft: Tomb Raider, 2001; Harry Potter and the Goblet of Fire, 2005; The Other Boleyn Girl, 2008; Rise of the Planet of the Apes, Thor, 2011; Jack Ryan: Shadow Recruit, 2014; Cinderella, 2015; Manchester by the Sea, Beauty and the Beast, 2017. Début as conductor, Royal Fest. Hall, 2014; Guest Conductor: London SO; Philharmonia Orch.; London Studio Orch.; Hollywood Studio Symphony; City of Birmingham SO; Qatar Philharmonic Orch. *Recreations*: fitness, reading. *E*: info@james-shearman.com.

**SHEARMAN, Martin James,** CVO 2003; HM Diplomatic Service; Ambassador to Belgium, since 2019; *b* 7 Feb. 1965; *s* of John Christopher Shearman and Barbara Wendy Shearman; *m* 1996, Miriam Elizabeth Pyburn; two *s*. *Educ*: Skinners' Sch., Tunbridge Wells; Trinity Coll., Oxford (BA Hons). Joined FCO, 1989; Third, then Second Sec., FCO, 1989–91; Second, then First, Sec., Tokyo, 1993–96; on secondment to DTI, 1996–98, to Cabinet Office, 1998; NATO Secretariat, 1999; FCO, 1999–2003; Dep. High Comr, Abuja, 2003–06; Hd, Common Foreign and Security Policy Gp, Europe Directorate, FCO, 2006–08; High Comr, Uganda, 2008–12; Hd, Develt and Human Rights, UK Mission to the UN, NY, 2013–17.

**SHEARS, Philip Peter;** QC 1996; a Recorder, since 1990; *b* 10 May 1947; *m* 1990, Sarah; two *s* one *d* by previous marriage. *Educ*: Leys Sch., Cambridge; Nottingham Univ. (LLB); St Edmund's Coll., Cambridge (LLB). Called to the Bar, Middle Temple, 1972; Mem., Midland Circuit. Liveryman, Fletchers' Co., 2011–. *Recreations*: sailing, France. *Address*: 7 Bedford Row, WC1R 4BS. *T*: (020) 7242 3555. *Clubs*: Royal London Yacht (Trustee; former Cdre), Royal Yacht Squadron; Bar Yacht (Vice Cdre).

**SHEARSMITH, Reeson Wayne, (Reece);** actor, writer, producer and director; *b* Kingston-upon-Hull, 27 Aug. 1969; *s* of Reece Shearsmith and Christine Shearsmith (*née* Don); *m* 2001, Jane Welch; one *s* one *d*. *Educ*: Bretton Hall. Coll. (BA Hons). Theatre: A Local Show for Local People, Theatre Royal and UK tour, 2000–01; Art, Whitehall, 2002; As You Like It, Wyndham's, 2005; The Producers, Theatre Royal, 2006; The Common Pursuit, Menier Chocolate Factory, 2008; Comedians, Lyric Hammersmith, 2009; Rocky Horror Show, Hull New and nat. tour, 2010; Betty Blue Eyes, Novello, 2011; Ghost Stories, Duke of York's, 2010; Absent Friends, Harold Pinter, 2012; Hangmen, Royal Court, 2015, transf. Linda Gross Th., NY, 2018; The Dresser, Duke of York's, 2016; The League of Gentlemen (also writer), nat. tour, 2018; A Very Expensive Poison, Old Vic, 2019; television includes: In the Red, 1998; Spaced, 1999; The League of Gentlemen (also writer), 1999–2002, 2017; TLC, 2002; Catterick, 2004; The Abbey, Ladies and Gentlemen, Christmas at the Riviera, 2007; Mid Life Christmas, 2009; Psychoville (also writer), 2009–11; Eric and Ernie, 2011; Bad Sugar, 2012; An Adventure in Space and Time, 2013; Psychobitches, 2013–14; The Widower, Chasing Shadows, House of Fools, 2014; Inside No. 9 (also writer), 2014– (Best Comedy, Rose d'Or, 2016; (jtly) Writers' Guild of GB award for Best TV Situation Comedy, BAFTA award for Writer - Comedy, 2018); Hunderby, 2015; Stag, 2016; films: This Year's Love, 1999; Birthday Girl, 2001; Shaun of the Dead, 2004; The League of Gentlemen's Apocalypse, 2005; The Cottage, 2008; Burke & Hare, 2010; A Field in England, 2013; The World's End, 2013; High Rise, 2015; Home, 2019 ((jtly) Best Comedy Performance, RTS Awards, 2019); radio: On the Town with the League of Gentlemen, 1997; Self Storage, Reece Shearsmith's Haunted House, 2009; Bird Island, 2012; Aonach Hourn, 2014. Hon. DLitt Huddersfield, 2013; DUniv Hull, 2013. (Jtly) Best Comedy Perf., RTS Awards, 2014. *Publications*: (jtly) A Local Book for Local people, 2000; (jtly) The League of Gentlemen: scripts and that, 2003; (jtly) The League of Gentlemen's Book of Precious Things, 2007. *Recreations*: drawing (caricatures, cartoons), magic, conjuring. *Address*: c/o Nick Forgacs, Independent Talent Group Ltd, 40 Whitfield Street, W1T 2RH. *T*: (020) 7636 6565; c/o Daisy Skepelhorn, PBJ Management, 22 Rathbone Street, W1T 1LG. *T*: (020) 7287 1112. *W*: www.twitter.com/reeceshearsmith. *Club*: Soho House.

**SHEBBEARE, Sir Thomas Andrew, (Sir Tom),** KCVO 2003 (CVO 1996); DL; Chairman: Virgin StartUp, since 2013; Virgin Money Giving, since 2012 (Director, since 2008); Spring Films Ltd, since 2012; *b* 25 Jan. 1952; *s* of late Robert Austin Shebbeare and Frances Dare Graham; *m* 1976, Cynthia Jane Cottrell; one *s* one *d*. *Educ*: Malvern Coll.; Univ. of Exeter (BA Politics). World University Service (UK), 1973–75; Gen. Sec., British Youth Council, 1975–80; Administrator, Council of Europe, 1980–85; Exec. Dir, European Youth Foundn, 1985–88; Exec. Dir, The Prince's Trust and Sec., The Royal Jubilee Trusts, 1988–99; Chief Exec., The Prince's Trust, 1999–2004; Dir of Charities to the Prince of Wales, then Dir, The Prince's Charities, 2004–11. Director: CIM Asset Mgt, 2007–17; Delphis-Eco Ltd, 2011–17. Chm., Royal Parks Foundn, 2014–17; Trustee:

Nations Trust (S Africa), 1995–2008; Sentebale—The Princes' Fund for Lesotho, 2005–09; Turquoise Mountain Foundn (Kabul), 2005–; Prince's Charities Foundn (China), 2009–17; Dir, Gifts in Kind UK, 1994–2011. DL Oxfordshire, 2018. Fellow, Green Templeton Coll., Oxford, 2012–. Hon. LLD Exeter, 2005. *Recreations:* family, cooking, garden, food and drink. *E:* tom@shebbeare.com.

**SHECHTMAN, Prof. Daniel,** PhD; Philip Tobias Professor of Materials Science, since 1989, and Distinguished Professor, since 1998, Technion-Israel Institute of Technology; Professor of Materials Science and Engineering, Iowa State University, since 2004; Senior Chemist, Materials Chemistry and Biomolecular Materials, Ames Laboratory, Iowa, since 2004; *b* Tel Aviv, British Mandate of Palestine, 24 Jan. 1941; *m* Tzipora; one *s* three *d*. *Educ:* Technion-Israel Inst. of Technol. (BSc Mech. Engrg 1966; MSc Materials Engrg 1968; PhD 1972). Nat. Res. Council postdoctoral res. associate, Aerospace Res. Labs, Wright Patterson AFB, Ohio, 1972–75; Department of Materials Engineering, Technion-Israel Institute of Technology: Lectr, 1975–77; Sen. Lectr, 1977–84; Associate Prof., 1984–86; Prof., 1986–98; on sabbatical at Johns Hopkins Univ., 1981–83, at Nat. Inst. Standards Technol., Md, 1992–94. Visiting Professor: Dept of Materials Engrg, 1981–89, Physics and Astronomy, 1989–97, Johns Hopkins Univ.; Univ. of Maryland, Baltimore, 1997–2004; Tohoku Univ., Japan, 2006–. Member: Israel Acad. Scis, 1996; NAE, USA, 2000; Eur. Acad. Scis, 2004. Hon. Dr Ben Gurion, 2002. Awards include: Internat. Award for New Materials, Amer. Physical Soc., 1988; Rothschild Prize in Engrg, Rothschild Prizes Foundn, 1990; Weizmann Sci. Award, Weizmann Inst., 1993; Israel Prize in Physics, 1998; Wolf Prize in Physics, Wolf Foundn, 1999; Gregori Aminoff Prize, Royal Swedish Acad. of Scis, 2000; EMET Prize in Chem., AMN Foundn, Israel, 2002; 25th Anniv. Award, Eur. Materials Res. Soc., 2008; Nobel Prize in Chem., 2011. *Publications:* contribs to jls incl. Nature, Jl de Physique, Jl Materials Res., Jl Materials Sci., Materials Sci. Forum. *Address:* Department of Materials Science and Engineering, Technion-Israel Institute of Technology, Technion City, Haifa 32000, Israel; College of Engineering, Iowa State University, 342 Spedding, Ames, IA 50011–3020, USA.

**SHEDDEN, Alfred Charles,** OBE 2008; Director, Centre for Confidence and Wellbeing Ltd, since 2005 (Chairman, 2005–16); *b* 30 June 1944; *s* of Alfred Henry Shedden and Jane Murray Shedden; *m* 1st, 1968, Rosalyn Terris; one *s*; 2nd, 1979, Irene McIntyre; one *d*. *Educ:* Aberdeen Univ. (MA, LLB). Mem., Law Soc. of Scotland. McGrigor Donald: apprentice, 1967; Partner, 1971; Managing Partner, 1985–92; Sen. Partner, 1993–2000. Chm., Halladale Gp plc, 2001–07; Vice-Chm., Glasgow Housing Assoc. Ltd, 2003–05; non-executive Director: Standard Life Assurance Co., 1992–99; Scottish Financial Enterprise, 1988–99; Martin Currie Japan Investment Trust plc, 1996–2005; Scottish Metropolitan Property plc, 1998–2000; Burn Stewart Distillers plc, 2000–03; Iomart Group plc, 2000–11; Murray Internat. Trust plc, 2000–14; Equitable Life Assurance Soc., 2002–09. Mem., Scottish FEFC, 1999–2005. Gov., Glasgow Sch. of Art, 2002–10. *Recreations:* contemporary Scottish art, wine, travel, being a grandfather. *Address:* 17 Beaumont Gate, Glasgow G12 9ED. *T:* (0141) 339 4979, 07810 553672.

**SHEDDEN, Rev. John,** CBE 1998; Minister, Fuengirola, Costa del Sol, 2005–08; *b* 23 June 1943; *s* of Robert Blair Arnott Shedden and Grace Roberts (*née* Henderson); *m* 1965, Jeannie Lillian Gilling; one *s* one *d*. *Educ:* Johnstone High Sch.; Univ. of St Andrews (BD Hons; Dip. in Pastoral and Social Studies). Asst Minister, Paisley Abbey, 1970–72; ordained 1971; Parish Minister, Thornhill, Dumfries, 1972–75; Social Welfare Officer, Salisbury, Rhodesia, 1975–76; Chaplain, RN, 1977–84; Minister, St Mark's, Moose Jaw, Sask., 1984–86; Chaplain, RAF, 1986–98; Principal Chaplain, Church of Scotland and Free Churches, RAF, 1994–98; Minister: Hawick Wilton with Teviothead, 1998–2001; Glenorchy Innishael with Strathfillan, 2001–05 (Locum Minister, 2013–15). QHC 1994–98. Vol. warden, Cotswolds AONB, Cotswolds Conservation Bd, 2017–. *Recreations:* hill-walking, D-I-Y, reading, radio.

**SHEEHAN,** family name of **Baroness Sheehan**.

**SHEEHAN,** Baroness *cr* 2015 (Life Peer), of Wimbledon in the London Borough of Merton and of Tooting in the London Borough of Wandsworth; **Shaista Ahmad, (Shas) Sheehan;** *m* Patrick Sheehan; three *c*. *Educ:* Rosa Bassett Grammar Sch.; University Coll. London (BSc Hons 1978); Imperial Coll. London (MSc Dist. Envmtl Technol. 1990). Teacher, auxiliary nurse at New Cross Hosp. and sen. planner and buyer in advertising, 1981–2005; Hd of Office and Sen. Caseworker for Susan Kramer, MP, 2005–08; charity worker, Wimbledon Guild Daycentre and Faith in Action project for homeless people, 2010. Mem. (Lib Dem), Richmond upon Thames LBC, 2006–10. Contested (Lib Dem) Wimbledon, 2010. *Address:* House of Lords, SW1A 0PW.

**SHEEHAN, Albert Vincent;** Sheriff of Tayside, Central and Fife, 1983–2005; *b* 23 Aug. 1936; *s* of Richard Greig Sheehan and May Moffat; *m* 1965, Edna Georgina Scott Hastings (*d* 2000); two *d*. *Educ:* Bo'ness Acad.; Edinburgh Univ. (MA 1957; LLB 1959). Admitted as solicitor, 1959. 2nd Lieut, 1st Bn The Royal Scots (The Royal Regt), 1960; Captain, Directorate of Army Legal Services, 1961. Depute Procurator Fiscal, Hamilton, 1961–71; Sen. Depute Procurator Fiscal, Glasgow, 1971–74; Depute Crown Agent for Scotland, 1974–79; Asst Solicitor, Scottish Law Commn, 1979–81; Sheriff of Lothian and Borders, 1981–83. Leverhulme Fellow, 1971. *Publications:* Criminal Procedure in Scotland and France, 1975; Criminal Procedure, 1990, 2nd edn 2003. *Recreations:* naval history, travel, legal history.
See also W. A. Sheehan.

**SHEEHAN, Antony;** President and Chief Executive Officer, South Shore Mental Health, since 2017; *b* 10 Sept. 1964; *s* of late Thomas Sheehan and Mary Kerr Sheehan; *m* 2001, Andrea Coleman; one *s* one *d*. *Educ:* Manchester Metropolitan Univ. (BEd Hons 1992); Nottingham Univ. (MPhil 1998); RN 1986. Nurse Manager; Chief Exec., Nat. Inst. for Mental Health in England, 2001–03; Dir Gen. for Care Services, 2003–06, for Health and Care Partnerships, 2006–07, DoH; Prof. of Health and Social Care Strategy, Univ. of Central Lancs, 2006; Chief Exec., Leics Partnership NHS Trust, 2007–13; Pres., Church Health Center, Memphis, Tenn, 2013–16; Sen. Advr, Methodist Le Bonheur Healthcare, 2016–17. Chm., Internat. Initiative for Mental Health Leadership, 2005–08. Patron, AS-IT (IT consultancy for people with Asperger Syndrome), 2007–09. Hon. DSc Wolverhampton, 2003; DUniv Staffordshire, 2006. *Publications:* more than 50 articles and book chapters. *Recreations:* walking (with two very big labradors), Manchester United, travel (in particular the USA), goalkeepers' gloves (and other paraphernalia), coffee (especially latte).

**SHEEHAN, Gerald;** Chief Executive (Deputy Master and Comptroller), Royal Mint, 2001–06; *b* 20 March 1950; *s* of Edmund and Morfydd Sheehan; *m* 1987, Jacqueline Marian; two *s* one *d*. *Educ:* Univ. of Nottingham (BSc Hons); Univ. of Sheffield (MSc); Harvard Business Sch. (AMP). ASW Holdings plc, 1981–2001: Bd Mem., 1996–2001; Ops Dir, 1999–2001. Mem. Business Leaders Gp, Prince's Trust. *Recreations:* squash, boating, fishing.

**SHEEHAN, Gen. John Joseph,** USMC; Senior Vice President for Europe, Africa, Middle East and Southwest Asia, Bechtel Group Inc., 2001; Supreme Allied Commander, Atlantic and Commander-in-Chief, US Atlantic Command, 1994–97; *b* 23 Aug. 1940; *s* of John J. Sheehan and Ellen Sheehan; *m* Margaret M. Sullivan; one *s* three *d*. *Educ:* Boston Coll. (BA English 1962); Georgetown Univ. (MA Govt 1985). Joined USMC, 1960; various postings, incl. Vietnam; Amphibious Warfare Sch., 1969–70; Airborne Corps, 1970–71; 2nd Marine Div., 1971–73; Naval War Coll., 1974–75; HQ USMC, 1975–78; 1st Marine Air Wing, 1978–79; Nat. War Coll., 1979–80; 1st Marine Bde, 1980–83; Jt Staff, 1983–84; Office of Sec. of Defense, 1984–86; 2nd Marine Div., 1986–88; 4th Marine Exped. Bde, 1988–89; HQ USMC, 1989–91; US Naval Forces Central Comd, 1991; US Atlantic Comd, 1991–93; Jt Staff, 1993–94. Joined Bechtel Gp Inc., 1998. Numerous gallantry and other Service awards. Grand Cross, Norwegian Order of Merit, 1996. *Publications:* contribs to Joint Forces Qly. *Recreations:* golf, tennis, gardening. *Clubs:* Military Order of the Carabao, Ancient and Honorable Artillery Company of Massachusetts.

**SHEEHAN, Malcolm Peter;** QC 2015; a Recorder, since 2019; *b* London, 28 June 1968; *s* of John and Mary Josephine Sheehan; partner, Alexis Roberts. *Educ:* All Saints' High Sch., Bradley Bar; Oriel Coll., Oxford (BA 1st Cl. Hons Modern Hist. 1989; MA 1993). Called to the Bar, Lincoln's Inn, 1993; in practice as barrister, 1993–. Judicial Asst to Court of Appeal, 1997; Judge (pt-time) of First-tier Tribunal (Property Chamber), 2009–. Mem., Attorney Gen.'s Panel of Jun. Counsel to the Crown, 2006–15. *Publications:* contributor: Civil Practitioner's Guide to the Human Rights Act 1998, 1999; Halsbury's Laws of England, 4th edn reissue, Appeals; Butterworth's Civil Court Precedents, 2009–; Kluwer International Product Law Manual, 2011. *Recreations:* tennis, swimming, theatre, running, cycling. *Address:* Henderson Chambers, 2 Harcourt Buildings, Temple, EC4Y 9DB. *T:* (020) 7583 9020, *Fax:* (020) 7583 2686. *E:* msheehan@hendersonchambers.co.uk.

**SHEEHAN, Wendy Anne;** Sheriff of Lothian and Borders at Edinburgh, since 2014; *b* Glasgow, 26 Dec. 1968; *d* of Albert Vincent Sheehan, *qv*. *Educ:* St George's Sch. for Girls; Univ. of Aberdeen (LLB 1989; DLP 1990). Accredited Family Law Mediator 1996; Accredited Family Law Specialist 1998. Admitted solicitor, 1991; Solicitor, Russel + Aitken, 1990–96; Associate, Balfour & Manson, 1996–2000; Partner, Mowat Hall Dick, 2000–06; Hd, Family Law, Pagan Osborne, 2006–08; Dir, Sheehan Kelsey Oswald Solicitors, accredited family law specialists, 2008–11; Sheriff of Glasgow and Strathkelvin at Glasgow, 2011–14. Chm., Lothian, Couple Counselling, 1996–2005; former Convenor, CALM; Sec., Family Law Arbitration Gp, Scotland; Vice Pres., Sheriffs' Assoc. *Publications:* (contrib.) Butterworths Family Law Service; (contrib.) Butterworths Elderly Client Service; (contrib.) The Art of Family Law. *Recreations:* Director of Licketyspit Ltd (early years theatre company), scuba diving, water ski-ing, art, cinema. *Address:* Edinburgh Sheriff Court, 27 Chambers Street, Edinburgh EH1 1LB. *T:* (0131) 225 2525. *E:* sheriffwsheehan@scotcourts.gov.uk.

**SHEEHY, Rev. Jeremy Patrick,** DPhil; Rector, Swinton and Pendlebury, since 2006; *b* 31 Oct. 1956; *s* of late Eric Sheehy and Noreen Patricia Sheehy. *Educ:* Trinity Sch. of John Whitgift; Bristol Grammar Sch.; King Edward's Sch., Birmingham; Magdalen Coll., Oxford (BA (Jurisprudence Cl. 1)); St Stephen's House, Oxford (BA (Theol. Cl. 1)); MA 1981, DPhil 1990, Oxon. Ordained deacon 1981; priest 1982; Assistant Curate: St Barnabas, Erdington, 1981–83; St Gregory, Small Heath, 1983–84; Dean of Divinity, Chaplain and Fellow, New Coll., Oxford, 1984–90; Vicar, St Margaret, Leytonstone, 1990–96; Priest in charge, St Andrew, Leytonstone, 1993–96; Principal, St Stephen's House, Oxford, 1996–2006. Area Dean, Eccles, 2011–13. Mem., Gen. Synod, C of E, 2018–. Chm., Oxford Partnership for Theol Educn and Trng, 1999–2001. Examining Chaplain to Bishop of Manchester, 2008–. Vis. Lectr, Nashotah House, Wis, USA, 2006. Guardian, Shrine of Our Lady of Walsingham, 1997–. Gov., Quainton Hall Sch., Harrow, 1998–2007. Hon. DD: Grad. Theol Foundn, Indiana, 2004; Nashotah House, Wisconsin, 2009. *Recreations:* hill-walking, cooking. *Address:* St Peter's Rectory, Vicarage Road, Swinton, Manchester M27 0WA. *T:* (0161) 794 1578.

**SHEEN, Michael Christopher,** OBE 2009; actor; *b* Newport, S Wales, 5 Feb. 1969; *s* of Meyrick and Irene Sheen; one *d* by Kate Beckinsale. *Educ:* Glan Afan Comprehensive Sch., Port Talbot; Royal Acad. of Dramatic Art. Theatre includes: When She Danced, Globe, 1991; Romeo and Juliet, Manchester Royal Exchange, 1992; Don't Fool with Love, Donmar Warehouse, 1993; Peer Gynt, Oslo, Tokyo and Barbican, 1994; Charley's Aunt, Manchester Royal Exchange, 1994; The Seagull, Theatre Royal, Bath, 1995; The Homecoming, NT, 1997; Henry V, RSC, Stratford, 1997; Amadeus, Old Vic, trans. NY, 1998; Look Back in Anger, NT, 1999; Caligula, Donmar Warehouse, 2003 (Evening Standard and London Th. Critics Awards for Best Actor); The UN Inspector, NT, 2005; Frost/Nixon, Gielgud, 2006; The Passion (also dir), NT of Wales, 2011 (jtly) Theatre UK Award for Best Dir), filmed version as The Gospel of Us, 2012; Hamlet, Young Vic, 2011; *films* include: Othello, 1995; Mary Reilly, 1996; Wilde, 1997; The Four Feathers, Heartlands, Bright Young Things, Underworld, Timeline, 2003; Laws of Attraction, 2004; Kingdom of Heaven, 2005; Underworld: Evolution, The Queen, Dead Long Enough, Blood Diamonds, 2006; Music Within, 2007; Frost/Nixon, 2008; Underworld: the Rise of the Lycans, The Damned United, My Last Five Girlfriends, The Twilight Saga: New Moon, 2009; Unthinkable, Tron: Legacy, 2010; Midnight in Paris, The Twilight Saga: Breaking Dawn, Resistance, 2011; Kill the Messenger, Far from the Madding Crowd, 2015; Passengers, 2016; Brad's Status, Slaughterhouse Rulez, 2018; *television* includes: Gallowglass, 1993; The Deal, 2003; Dirty Filthy Love, 2004; H. G. Wells: War with the World, Kenneth Williams: Fantabulosa!, 2006 (RTS Award for Best Actor), Ancient Rome: the Rise and Fall of an Empire, 2006; 30 Rock, The Special Relationship, 2010; Masters of Sex, 2013–16; Good Omens, 2019. Variety Award, BIFA, 2008; BAFTA Britannia Award for British Artist of Year, 2010. *Address:* c/o Roxanne Vacca Management, 61 Judd Street, WC1H 9QT.

**SHEEPSHANKS, David Richard,** CBE 2013; DL; Chairman: UK Community Foundations, since 2013; Technical Advisory Board, Football Association, since 2016; *b* London, 30 Oct. 1952; *s* of Robin Sheepshanks and Lilias Sheepshanks; *m* 1978, Mona Ullbin; one *s* one *d*. *Educ:* Eton Coll. Chm. and Man. Dir, Starfish Ltd, 1980–89; Chm., Suffolk Foods Ltd, 1990–2004. Chairman: Ipswich Town FC, 1995–2009; Football League, 1996–98; St George's Park (formerly Nat. Football Centre), FA, 2008–15. Regl Chm., Coutts Bank, 2009–. Chm., Suffolk Foundn, 2005–13. DL Suffolk, 2005. Hon. DCL UEA, 2004. *Recreations:* playing golf, swimming, gardening, flower arranging, watching football, cricket and golf. *Address:* The White Lodge, Eyke, Woodbridge, Suffolk IP12 2RP. *T:* (01394) 461540. *E:* dsheep@whitelodge.biz. *Clubs:* White's, MCC.

**SHEERMAN, Barry John;** MP (Lab) Huddersfield, since 1983 (Huddersfield East, 1979–83); *b* 17 Aug. 1940; *s* of late Albert William Sheerman and Florence Sheerman (*née* Pike); *m* 1965 Pamela Elizabeth (*née* Brenchley); one *s* three *d*. *Educ:* Hampton Grammar Sch.; LSE (BSc (Econs) Hons; MSc Hons). Lectr, Univ. Coll. of Swansea, 1966–79. Visiting Professor: of Social Enterprise, Huddersfield Univ.; Inst. of Educn, London Univ. 2004–, Policy Connect, 1995–. An opposition front bench spokesman on: employment, dealing with training, small business and tourism, 1983–88; home affairs, dealing with police, prisons, crime prevention, drugs, civil defence and fire service, 1988–92; disabled people's rights, 1992–94. Mem., Public Accounts Cttee, 1981–83; Co-Chm., Educn and Employment Select Cttee, 1999–2001 (Chm., Sub-Cttee on Educn, 1999–2001); Chm., Select Cttee on Educn and Skills, 2001–10; Chairman: Parly Adv. Council on Transport Safety, 1981–; Labour Campaign for Criminal Justice, 1989–92; Labour Party Commn on Sch.-to-Work; Parly Labour Party Backbench DEFRA Cttee, 2016–; Co-Chm., Parly Manufg Industry Gp, 1993–; Vice-Chm., Parly Univ. Gp, 1994–2012; Chair: Westminster Crowdfunding Forum, 2014–; Westminster Commn on Autism, 2016–. Chm., Parly Gps for Sustainable Waste Mgt, 1995–, and for Manufg, Design and Innovation, 1999–; Chm., Cross-Party Adv. Gp on Preparation for EMU, 1998–, on European Economic Reform, 2005–. Mem., Sec. of State for Trade and Industry's Manufg Task Force, 1999–2002. Chairman: World Bank Business Partnerships for Develt Cttee, 2001–03; Global Road Safety Partnership, 2001–; UN-WHO Global Network for Road Safety Legislators, 2017–; Adv. Bd, Sutton Trust, 2015–. Chm., John Clare Trust. FRSA; FRGS 1989; FCGI 2005. Hon. Dr: Kingston, 2007; Bradford, 2007. *Publications:* (jtly) Harold Laski: a life on the Left, 1993; pamphlets on education and training, tourism, and justice. *Address:* House of Commons, SW1A 0AA. *W:* www.twitter.com/barrysheerman.

**SHEFFIELD, Bishop of,** since 2017; **Rt Rev. Dr Peter Jonathan Wilcox;** *b* 1961; *m* 1984, Catherine Fox; two *s. Educ:* St John's Coll., Durham (BA 1984; MA 1990); Ridley Hall, Cambridge (BA 1986); St John's Coll., Oxford (DPhil 1993). Ordained deacon, 1987, priest, 1988; Curate, Preston on Tees, 1987–90; Non-stipendiary Minister, St Margaret with St Philip and St James with St Giles, Oxford, 1990–93; Team Vicar, St Edmund's Chapel, Gateshead, 1993–98; Dir, Urban Mission Centre, Cranmer Hall, 1993–98; Priest-in-charge, St Paul's at the Crossing, Walsall, 1998–2006; Canon Residentiary, Lichfield Cath., 2006–12; Dean of Liverpool, 2012–17. *Publications:* Living the Dream: Joseph for today, 2007; Walking the Walk: the rise of King David for today, 2009; Talking the Talk: the fall of King David for today, 2011. *Address:* Bishopscroft, Snaithing Lane, Sheffield S10 3LG. *T:* (0114) 230 2170.

**SHEFFIELD, Dean of;** see Bradley, Very Rev. P. E.

**SHEFFIELD AND ROTHERHAM, Archdeacon of;** see Chamberlain, Ven. M. L.

**SHEFFIELD, Graham Edward,** CBE 2010; Director, Arts, British Council, 2011–18; *b* 12 Feb. 1952; *s* of Gordon and Jacqueline Sheffield; *m* 1979, Ann Roberta Morton (marr. diss. 2019); two *s. Educ:* Tonbridge Sch.; Edinburgh Univ. (BMus Hons 1975). Producer, then Sen. Producer, Music Dept, BBC Radio 3, 1976–90; Music Dir, South Bank Centre, 1990–95; Artistic Dir, Barbican Centre, 1995–2010; CEO, W Kowloon Cultural Dist Authy, Hong Kong, 2010–11. Dir, City Arts and Culture Forum, 2007–10; Consultant, Luminato Fest., Toronto, 2007–10; Advr, Arts and Creative Economy, British Council, 2009–10. Mem. Council, Arts Council England (London), 2002–08. Mem. Council, 1999–, Chm., 2006–10, Royal Philharmonic Soc.; Chairman: Internat. Soc. for Performing Arts, 2004–06 (Sec., 2000–01; Chm.-elect, 2002–03; Internat. Citation of Merit, 2015); Help Musicians UK, 2014–. Trustee, Rambert, 2019–. FRSA 2016. Hon. FGSM 2010. Hon. DArts City, 2004. Chevalier, Tastevin de Bourgogne, 2005. Chevalier, Ordre des Arts et des Lettres (France), 2005. *Recreations:* piano, golf, ski-ing, travel, fine wine. *Address:* 107 Breton House, Barbican, EC2Y 8PQ. *Club:* MCC.

**SHEFFIELD, (John) Julian (Lionel George);** DL; Chairman, North Hampshire Medical Fund, 2002–09; *b* 28 Aug. 1938; *s* of late John Vincent Sheffield, CBE and Anne Margaret, *d* of Sir Lionel Faudel-Phillips, 3rd Bt; *m* 1961, Carolyn Alexander Abel Smith; three *s* one *d. Educ:* Eton Coll.; Christ's Coll., Cambridge. Joined Portals Ltd, 1962; Dir, 1969–95, Chm., 1979–95, Portals Hldgs, then Portals Gp. Director: Norcros, 1974–96 (Chm., 1989–93); Tex Hldgs, 1985–93; Guardian Royal Exchange, 1981–99 (Dep. Chm., 1988–99); Newbury Racecourse, 1988–2005; Inspec, 1994–99. Chm., Axa UK Gp Pension Scheme, 1993–2008. Mem., Economic and Commercial Cttee, EEF, 1974–90. Member: Council, St John's Sch., Leatherhead, 1966–96; Bd of Govs, N Foreland Lodge, 1987–97 (Chm., 1992–97). Trustee: Henry Smith's, subseq. Henry Smith Charity, 1971–2007 (Chm., 1997–2007); Winchester Cathedral Trust, 1984–2014; Hosp. of St Cross and Almshouse of Noble Poverty, 1996–2010 (Chm., 2005–06). High Sheriff, 1998, DL 2001, Hants. *Recreations:* outdoor sports, collecting. *Address:* Spring Pond, Laverstoke, Whitchurch, Hants RG28 7PD. *T:* (01256) 895130. *Clubs:* White's, MCC.

**SHEFFIELD, Sir Reginald (Adrian Berkeley),** 8th Bt *cr* 1755; DL; Director, Normanby Estate Co. Ltd, since 1983, and other companies; *b* 9 May 1946; *s* of Edmund Charles Reginald Sheffield, JP, DL (*d* 1977) and Nancie Miriel Denise (*d* 1997), *d* of Edward Roland Soames; *S* uncle, 1977; *m* 1st, 1969, Annabel Lucy Veronica Jones (*see* Viscountess Astor) (marr. diss. 1975); two *d*; 2nd, 1977, Victoria Penelope, *d* of late R. C. Walker, DFC; one *s* two *d. Educ:* Eton. Member of Stock Exchange, 1973–75. Vice-Chm., S Humberside Business Advice Centre Ltd, 1984–2010. Pres., S Humberside CPRE, 1985–96; Member: Cttee, Lincs Br., CLA, 1987–99; Taxation Cttee, CLA, 1989–95; Central Transport Consultative Cttee (NE Reg.), 1988–94; Rail Users Consultative Cttee for NE England, 1994–97. Mem. (C) for Ermine Ward, Humberside County Council, 1985–93. Chm., Brigg and Goole Cons. Assoc., 2007–09. Pres., Scunthorpe United Football Club, 1982–94. Pres., Scunthorpe and Dist, Victim Support Scheme, 1989–2003; Vice-Pres., Victim Support Humber, 2003–08. DL Humberside, now Lincs, 1985. *Heir: s* Robert Charles Berkeley Sheffield, *b* 1 Sept. 1984. *Address:* Estate Office, Normanby, Scunthorpe, N Lincs DN15 9HS. *E:* norestate@btconnect.com. *Clubs:* Beefsteak, White's, Pratt's; Lincolnshire.

**SHEGOG, Rev. Preb. Eric Marshall;** Director of Communications, Church of England, 1990–97; *b* 23 July 1937; *s* of late George Marshall Shegog and Helen (*née* Whitefoot); *m* 1961, Anne Thomas; two *s* one *d. Educ:* Leigh Grammar School; College of St Mark and St John; Whitelands College; Lichfield Theol College; City Univ. (MA). CertEd London; DipTh London. Asst Master, Holy Trinity Primary Sch., Wimbledon, 1960–64; Asst Curate, All Saints, Benhilton, 1965–68; Asst Youth Adviser, Dio. of Southwark, 1968–70; Vicar, St Michael and All Angels, Abbey Wood, 1970–75; Town Centre Chaplain, Sunderland, 1976–83; Head of Religious Broadcasting, IBA, 1984–90; Dir of Communications, 1997–2000 and Acting Gen. Sec., 1999–2000, Dio. of London; Communications Advr, Dio. of Europe, 2000–02; Prebendary, St Paul's Cathedral, 1997–2000, now Emeritus. Chm., BBC Adv. Cttee for NE, 1980–83 (Mem., Gen. Adv. Cttee, 1980–83); Dir and Chm. Mgt Cttee, Churches TV Centre, 1997–2007; Dir, World Assoc. for Christian Communication, 1990–93 (Vice-Chm., Eur. Region, 1990–93). Chm., Age Concern Sunderland, 1980–83. *Publications:* (jtly) Religious Television: controversies and conclusions, 1990; (jtly) Religious Broadcasting in the 90s, 1991; (contrib.) Elvy, Opportunities and Limitations in Religious Broadcasting, 1991; (contrib.) The Communication of Values, 1993. *Recreation:* gardening. *Address:* The Coach House, 7A High Street, Clophill, Beds MK45 4AB. *T:* (01525) 864868.

**SHEIKH, Baron** *cr* 2006 (Life Peer), of Cornhill in the City of London; **Mohamed Iltaf Sheikh;** Chairman: Courtlands Property & Investments Ltd (Director, since 2009); Lygon Property Investments Ltd (Director, since 2008); *b* 13 June 1941; *s* of late Mohamed Abdullah Sheikh and Kalsum Ara Sheikh; *m* 1986, Shaida Begum (marr. diss.), *d* of Mohamed Lateef Thantrey; one *d* from previous *m. Educ:* Mbale Secondary Sch., Uganda; Holborn Coll.; City of London Coll. ACII 1966, FCII 1968; FPC 1998. With Sun Alliance Insurance Co., 1962–66; Household and General Insurance Co., 1966–69; Guardian Royal Exchange, 1969–78; Camberford Law plc, 1978–2008. Dir, Silk Route Global Ltd, 2017–. Dir, BIBA (Regl Chm., 1998–2002). Pres., Insce Inst. of Croydon, 1981–82 (Chm., Life and Pensions Gp, 1989–90). Member: Nat. Council, Chartered Insce Inst., 1985–87; Cttee, FIMBRA, 1991, 1996. Chairman: Sheikh Abdullah Foundn, 2003–; Conservative Muslim Forum, 2003–14 (Pres., 2014–); Conservative Ethnic Diversity Council, 2005–10. Freeman, City of London, 1995. Hon. Fellow, BICSc. *Recreations:* walking, countryside, keeping fit, travelling. *Address:* House of Lords, SW1A 0PW.

**SHEIKH, Prof. Aziz,** OBE 2014; MD; FRCP, FRCPE, FRCGP, FFPH, FMedSci, FRSE; Professor of Primary Care Research and Development, since 2003, and Director, Usher Institute of Population Health Sciences and Informatics, since 2017, University of Edinburgh (Co-Director: Centre for Population and Health Studies, 2012–15; Centre of Medical Informatics, 2015–17); *b* Karachi, 15 Dec. 1968; *s* of Hafeez Sheikh and Kausar Sheikh; *m* 1991, Dr Sangeeta Dhami; three *s* one *d. Educ:* Bancroft's Sch., Woodford Green; University Coll. London (BSc Hons Physiol. 1990; MB BS Medicine 1993); Imperial Coll. London (MD 2001); London Sch. of Hygiene and Tropical Medicine, Univ. of London (MSc Epidemiol. 2002). DRCOG 1995; DCH 1996; MRCP 1996, FRCP 2006; MRCGP 1997, FRCGP 2004; FRCPE 2013; FFPH 2015. Imperial College of Science, Technology and Medicine, London: London Acad. Trng Scheme, 1997–98; Clin. Res. Fellow, 1998–99; NHS R&D Nat. Primary Care Trng Fellow, 1999–2002; NHS/PPP Nat. Primary Care Post-Doctoral Researcher, St George's Hosp. Med. Sch., London, 2002–03. Harkness Fellow in Health Care Policy and Practice, Brigham and Women's Hosp., Boston, 2013–14. Hon. Consultant in Paediatric Allergy, Royal Hosp. for Sick Children, Edinburgh, 2008–. Visiting Professor: Care and Public Health Res. Inst., Faculty of Medicine, Univ. of Maastricht, 2009–; Univ. of Birmingham, 2011–; Barts and The London Sch. of Medicine and Dentistry, QMUL, 2012–; of Medicine, Harvard Med. Sch., Boston, 2014–. FRSE 2015; FMedSci 2015; Fellow, American Coll. of Med. Informatics, 2015; Founding Fellow, Faculty of Clinical Informatics, 2017. *Publications:* (ed with A. R. Gatrad) Caring for Muslim Patients, 2000, 2nd edn 2007; (ed with A. R. Harnden) Key Topics in Child Health Promotion, 2002; (ed jtly) Basic Skills in Statistics: a guide for healthcare professionals, 2004; (ed with A. R. Gatrad) Palliative Care for South Asians: Muslims, Hindus and Sikhs, 2006; (ed jtly) Caring for Hindu Patients, 2008; (ed with B. Hurwitz) Health Care Errors and Patient Safety, 2009; (jtly) Landmarks in Allergy, 2013; (ed jtly) Healthcare Improvement and Safety at a Glance, 2014; (ed with R. E. O'Hehir and S. T. Holgate) Middleton's Allergy Essentials, 2016; (ed with D. Bates, A. Wright and K. Cresswell) Key Advances in Clinical Informatics, 2017; over 900 articles in learned internat. jls incl. Lancet, BMJ, PLOS Medicine, Jl of Allergy and Clin. Immunol., Thorax, Allergy and Jl of Amer. Med. Informatics Assoc. *Recreations:* table tennis, travelling, reading. *Address:* Usher Institute of Population Health Sciences and Informatics, University of Edinburgh, Medical School, Doorway 3, Teviot Place, Edinburgh EH8 9AG. *T:* (0131) 651 4151, *Fax:* (0131) 650 9119. *E:* aziz.sheikh@ed.ac.uk.

**SHEIKH, Saira Kabir;** QC 2014; *b* Kensington, 29 July 1969; *d* of Salim Kabir Sheikh and Latifa Kabir Sheikh; *m* 1996, Paul David Jennings (marr. diss. 2017); one *s* one *d. Educ:* St Swithun's Sch., Winchester; Kinnaird Coll., Lahore (BA); Univ. of the Punjab (LLB); University Coll. London (LLM); Lewis and Clark North Western Sch. of Law, Portland, Oregon (LLM). Advocate, Lahore High Court, 1995; called to the Bar, Inner Temple, 2000, Bencher, 2016; in practice as barrister, 2002–. *Recreations:* travel, reading. *Address:* Francis Taylor Building, Temple, EC4Y 7BY. *T:* (020) 7353 8415, *Fax:* (020) 7353 7622. *E:* clerks@ftbchambers.co.uk.

**SHEIKH, Tasmina;** see Ahmed-Sheikh.

**SHEIL, Brenda Margaret Hale, (Lady Sheil);** barrister; Member, Radio Authority, 1994–99; *o d* of late Rev. Forde Patterson and Elizabeth Bell Patterson (*née* Irwin); *m* 1979, John Joseph Sheil (*see* Rt Hon. Sir J. J. Sheil); one *s. Educ:* Armagh Girls' High Sch.; Trinity Coll., Dublin (BA (Mod) Legal Science; LLB 1966; MA 1990). Called to the Bar, NI, 1976, Ireland, 1995; Government Service (Legal): Min. of Home Affairs, NI, 1967–72; NI Office, 1972–79; Head, Legal Div., NI Court Service, Lord Chancellor's Dept, 1979–80. Chm. (part time), Industrial Tribunals, 1984–87. Member: Secretariat of Anglo-Irish Law Commn, 1973–74; Ind. Commn for Police Complaints, 1988–90. Mem., Gen. Consumer Council, NI, 1985–88. Mem., Standing Cttee, Gen. Synod of Church of Ireland, 1988–2011 (Lay Hon. Sec., 1999–2011); Lay Rep., Ch of Ireland, ACC, 1994–2000; Lay Canon, St Patrick's Cathedral, Armagh, 2008–. Governor, Royal Sch., Armagh, 1992–2017; Trustee, Irish Sch. of Ecumenics Trust, 2004–. *Recreations:* horses (Hon. Sec., Tynan and Armagh Hunt, 1973–), gardening, travel, golf. *Address:* Bar Library, Royal Courts of Justice, Belfast BT1 3JF.

**SHEIL, Rt Hon. Sir John (Joseph),** Kt 1989; PC 2005; a Surveillance Commissioner, 2010–17; a Lord Justice of Appeal, Supreme Court of Judicature, Northern Ireland, 2004–06; *b* 19 June 1938; *yr* twin *s* of late Hon. Mr Justice (Charles Leo) Sheil and Elizabeth Josephine Sheil (*née* Cassidy); *m* 1979, Brenda Margaret Hale Patterson (*see* B. M. H. Sheil); one *s. Educ:* Clongowes Wood Coll.; Queen's Univ. Belfast (LLB); Trinity Coll., Dublin (MA). Called to Bar: NI, 1964 (Bencher 1988), QC 1975; Gray's Inn, 1974 (Hon. Bencher, 1996); Ireland, 1976. A Judge of the High Court, NI, 1989–2004. Chairman: Mental Health Rev. Tribunal, 1985–87; Fair Employment Appeals Bd, 1986–89; Mem., Standing Adv. Commn on Human Rights, 1981–83. Mem., NI Cttee, British Council, 2002–06. Senator, QUB, 1987–99. Hon. Bencher, Middle Temple, 2005. *Recreations:* theatre, golf, travel. *Address:* c/o Royal Courts of Justice, Belfast BT1 3JY.

**SHEINWALD, Sir Nigel (Elton),** GCMG 2011 (KCMG 2001; CMG 1999); HM Diplomatic Service, retired; Ambassador to the United States of America, 2007–12; *b* 26 June 1953; *s* of late Leonard and Joyce Sheinwald; *m* 1980, Dr Julia Dunne; three *s. Educ:* Harrow Co. Sch. for Boys; Balliol Coll., Oxford (BA Classics 1976; Hon. Fellow 2014). Joined HM Diplomatic Service, 1976; Japan Desk, FCO, 1976–77; Russian lang. trng, 1977–78; Third, later Second Sec., Moscow, 1978–79; Rhodesia/Zimbabwe Dept, FCO, 1979–81; E European and Soviet Dept, FCO, 1981–83; First Sec., Washington, 1983–87; Deputy Head: Policy Planning Staff, FCO, 1987–89; European Community Dept (Internal), FCO, 1989–92; Counsellor and Hd of Chancery, UK Perm. Rep. to EU, Brussels, 1993–95; Hd of News Dept, FCO, 1995–98; Dir, EU, FCO, 1998–2000; Ambassador and UK Perm. Rep. to EU, Brussels, 2000–03; Foreign Policy and Defence Advr to the Prime Minister, 2003–07. Prime Minister's Special Envoy on intelligence and law enforcement data sharing, 2014–15. Non-executive Director: Royal Dutch Shell, 2012–; Innovia Gp, 2015–17; Invesco Ltd, 2015–; Raytheon UK, 2017–; Sen. Advr, Universal Music Gp, 2012–. Vis. Prof., 2012–, Mem., Governing Council, 2014–, KCL. Member: Adv. Bd, Centre for European Reform, 2012–; British American Business, 2012–; Governing Council, Ditchley Foundn, 2012–; UK-US Fulbright Commn, 2015– (Chm., 2016–). Hon. Bencher, Middle Temple, 2011. *Recreations:* theatre, music. *Address:* c/o Department of War Studies, King's College London, Strand, WC2R 2LS.

**SHEKERDEMIAN, Marcia Anna-Maria;** QC 2015; *b* London, 16 Nov. 1963; *d* of Hrant and Loretta Shekerdemian; *m* 1993, Roland Higgs (*d* 2009); one *s* one *d. Educ:* Notting Hill and Ealing High Sch.; Trinity Hall, Cambridge (BA 1986; MA). Called to the Bar, Middle

Temple, 1987; in practice as a barrister, 11 Stone Bldgs, 1989–2015, Wilberforce Chambers, 2015–; a Dep. Insolvency and Companies Court Judge of High Court (formerly Dep. Registrar of High Court in Bankruptcy), 2002–. Chair, Equality and Diversity Cttee, Chancery Bar Assoc., 2016–19. *Publications:* (contrib.) Kerr & Hunter on Receivers and Administrators, 20th edn 2018; articles in legal jls. *Recreations:* family life, dogs, cinema, theatre, fashion, listening to live music, cooking, walking on Exmoor. *Address:* Wilberforce Chambers, 8 New Square, Lincoln's Inn, WC2A 3QP. *T:* (020) 7306 0102. *E:* mshekerdemian@wilberforce.co.uk. *Clubs:* Athenæum, Allbright.

**SHELBROOKE, Rt Hon. Alec (Edward);** PC 2019; MP (C) Elmet and Rothwell, since 2010; *b* 10 Jan. 1976; *s* of Derek and Patricia Shelbrooke; *m* 2011, Susan Spencer. *Educ:* St George's C of E Comp. Sch., Gravesend; Brunel Univ. (BEng Hons 1998). Project mgt, Univ. of Leeds, 1999–2010. Mem. (C), Leeds CC, 2004–10. Contested (C) Wakefield, 2005. *Address:* House of Commons, SW1A 0AA.

**SHELDON,** family name of **Baron Sheldon.**

**SHELDON,** Baron *cr* 2001 (Life Peer), of Ashton-under-Lyne in the County of Greater Manchester; **Robert Edward Sheldon;** PC 1977; *b* 13 Sept. 1923; *m* 1st, 1945, Eileen Shamash (*d* 1969); one *s* one *d*; 2nd, 1971, Mary Shield. *Educ:* Elementary and Grammar Schools; Engineering Apprenticeship; Technical Colleges in Stockport, Burnley and Salford; WhSch 1944. Engineering diplomas; external graduate, London University. Contested (Lab) Withington, Manchester, 1959; MP (Lab) Ashton-under-Lyne, 1964–2001. Chm., Labour Parly Economic Affairs and Finance Group, 1967–68; Opposition front bench spokesman on Civil Service and Machinery of Govt, also on Treasury matters, 1970–74; Minister of State, CSD, March–Oct. 1974; Minister of State, HM Treasury, Oct. 1974–June 1975; Financial Sec. to the Treasury, 1975–79; Opposition front bench spokesman on Treasury matters, 1981–83; Chairman: Public Accounts Cttee, 1983–97 (Mem., 1965–70, 1975–79); Standards and Privileges Cttee, 1997–2001; Liaison Cttee, 1997–2001; Public Accounts Commn, 1997–2001; Dep. Chm., All Party Arts and Heritage Gp, 1997–2001; Member: Public Expenditure Cttee (Chm. Gen. Sub-Cttee), 1972–74; Select Cttee on Treasury and Civil Service, 1979–81 (Chm., Sub-Cttee); Econ. Affairs Cttee, 2003–07. Mem., Fulton Cttee on the Civil Service, 1966–68. Chm., NW Gp of Labour MPs, 1970–74. Mem., H of L, 2001–15. *Address:* 2 Ryder Street, SW1Y 6QA.

**SHELDON, Clive David;** QC 2011; a Deputy High Court Judge, since 2018; *b* London, 13 Oct. 1966; *s* of Jack Cecil Sheldon and Jacqueline Sheldon (*née* Anisfeld); *m* 1993, Jean Horowitz; one *s* two *d*. *Educ:* Latymer Sch., Edmonton; Gonville and Caius Coll., Cambridge (BA 1989); Univ. of Pennsylvania (LLM). Called to the Bar, Inner Temple, 1991; in practice as barrister specialising in public and employment law; Lectr (pt-time) in Labour Law, 1991–92; Mem., NY State Bar, 1992–; Associate, Cleary, Gottlieb, Steen & Hamilton, NY, 1992–94; barrister, 11 King's Bench Walk Chambers, 1995–. Mem., Complaints Cttee, Bar Standards Bd, 2010–12. Co-Chm., Masorti Judaism (formerly Assembly of Masorti Synagogues), 2012–15 (Vice Chm., 2011–12); Mem. Council, Jewish Leadership Council, 2013–15; Chm., New Israel Fund, 2015–. Vice Chm., Govs, Akiva Sch., 2008–10. *Recreations:* cycling, swimming. *Address:* 11 King's Bench Walk Chambers, Temple, EC4Y 7EQ. *T:* (020) 7632 8500, *Fax:* (020) 7583 9123. *E:* sheldon@11kbw.com.

**SHELDON, David Henry;** QC (Scot.) 2013; *b* Dundee, 22 April 1965; *s* of Henry Duncan, (Harry), Sheldon and Muriel Sheldon. *Educ:* High Sch. of Dundee; Univ. of Aberdeen (LLB 1st Cl. Hons; DipLP). University of Edinburgh: Lectr in Law, 1990–98; Associate Dean, 1994–98; Advocate, 1998–2013. *Publications:* Scots Criminal Law (with R. A. A. McCall Smith), 1992, 2nd edn 1997; Evidence: cases and materials, 1996, 2nd edn 2002; (contrib.) Stair Memorial Encyclopaedia of Scots Law, 1995–; (contrib.) Court of Session Procedure, 2002–; articles in legal jls incl. Criminal Law Rev., Scots Law Times, Edinburgh Law Rev. *Recreations:* cycling, running, rock climbing, choral singing, music. *Address:* Advocates Library, Parliament House, Edinburgh EH1 1RF. *T:* 07780 483910. *E:* david.sheldon@compasschambers.com. *Club:* Edinburgh Road.

**SHELDON, John Denby,** OBE 2000; Joint General Secretary, Public and Commercial Services (formerly Public Services, Tax and Commerce) Union, 1996–2000; *b* 31 Jan. 1941; *s* of Frank and Doreen Sheldon; *m* 1976; two *s*. *Educ:* Wingate County Primary Sch.; West Leeds High Sch.; Oxford Univ. Diploma in Social Studies. Post Office Engineer, 1957–68; student, Ruskin Coll., 1968–70; full time Trade Union Official, Instn of Professional Civil Servants, 1970–72; Civil Service Union: National Officer, 1972–78; Deputy Gen. Sec., 1978–82; Gen. Sec., 1982–88; Dep. Gen. Sec., 1988–93, Gen. Sec., 1993–96, Nat. Union of Civil and Public Servants. *Recreations:* cricket, Rugby League as spectator, family. *Address:* 20 Clifton Park Road, Caversham, Reading, Berks RG4 7PD.

**SHELDON, Michael John;** Member, Agriculture and Horticulture Development Board, since 2017 (Chairman, Pork Board, since 2017); *b* Brighton, 19 Jan. 1959; *s* of Conway and Dilys Sheldon; *m* 2014, Judith Alesbury; one *s* one *d*. *Educ:* Magdalen Coll., Oxford (BA Jt Hons Classics and Modern Langs 1982). PIC Ltd: graduate trainee, 1982–84; Farm Manager, 1985–86; Prodn Controller, 1987; UK Prodn Manager, 1988–92; UK Sales and Mktg Manager, 1992–95; Eur. Mktg Manager, 1995–96; Man. Dir, Greenway Farms Ltd, 1996–2014. Chm., Meadow Quality Ltd, 2012–13; Dir, Assured Food Standards Bd, 2012– (Chm., Pig Sector, 2012–). Chief Exec., Nat. Pig Assoc., 1999–2000; Mem., British Pig Exec., 2001–12; Dep. Chair, Sea Fish Industry Authy, 2019–. *Recreations:* ski-ing, theatre, writing. *Address:* c/o Agriculture and Horticulture Development Board, Stoneleigh Park, Kenilworth CV8 2TL. *T:* (024) 7669 2051. *E:* mike.sheldon@ahdb.org.uk.

**SHELDON, Neil John;** QC 2019; *b* Brighton, 20 June 1974; *s* of Robert and Penelope Sheldon; *m* 2004, Caroline; two *s* one *d*. *Educ:* Lancing Coll.; Trinity Hall, Cambridge (BA 1995; MA 1999). Called to the Bar, Gray's Inn, 1998; in practice as barrister, 1998–; Jun. Counsel to the Crown, 2002–19. *Recreations:* cricket, Burgundy. *Address:* 1 Crown Office Row, Temple, EC4Y 7HH. *T:* (020) 7797 7500. *E:* neil.sheldon@1cor.com.

**SHELDON, Peter,** OBE 2010; FCA; Chairman, Kardan NV, since 2012; *b* 11 June 1941; *s* of Izydor Schuldenfrei and Regina Schuldenfrei; surname changed to Sheldon by Deed Poll, 1964; *m* 1965, Judith Marion Grunberger; two *s* one *d*. *Educ:* Kilburn Grammar Sch. FCA 1969. Partner: Alfred N. Emanuel & Co., Chartered Accountants, 1963–70; Bright, Grahame Murray, Chartered Accountants, 1970–71; Director: UDS Gp Plc, 1971–83; Hambros Bank, 1983–85; World of Leather Plc, 1985–97; Geo Interactive Media Gp Ltd, 1996–98. Chairman: Stirling Gp Plc, 1990–94; BATM Advanced Communications Ltd, 1999–2014 (Dir, 1998–99); Video Domain Technologies Ltd, 2001–07; Dir, Kindertec Ltd, 1994–2000. Pres., United Synagogue, 1999–2005. JP Haringey, 1979–90 and 1997–2011. *Recreations:* theatre, travel, walking, grandchildren. *Address:* Jabotinsky 13/3, Jerusalem 9214101, Israel. *T:* (020) 8346 5155.

**SHELDON, Richard Michael;** QC 1996; a Deputy High Court Judge, 2003–15; *b* 29 Sept. 1955; *s* of Ralph Maurice Sheldon and Ady Sheldon (*née* Jaudel); *m* 1983, Helen Mary Lake; two *s* one *d*. *Educ:* Maidenhead Grammar Sch.; Jesus Coll., Cambridge (MA). Called to the Bar, Gray's Inn, 1979, Bencher, 2004. Vis. Prof., Nottingham Trent Univ. *Publications:* Gen. Ed., Cross-Border Insolvency, 3rd edn, 2012, 4th edn, 2015; contrib. Halsbury's Laws of England. *Recreations:* music, bassoon.

**SHELDON, Susan Jean;** Lord Lieutenant, Isle of Wight, since 2019; *b* Peaslake, 29 Sept. 1958; *m* 1984, Timothy James Sheldon; two *s* one *d*. *Educ:* West Heath Sch.; Exeter Univ. (BA Hons Hist.). ACA 1982. KPMG, 1979–87; SJS, 1987–93; Harry Ferguson Hldgs, 1990–. Chairman: IoW Sports Foundn, 2011–19; Royal Yacht Sqdn Foundn, 2019–. High Sheriff, IoW, 2011–12. Master, IoW Hunt, 2000–03, 2008–11. *Recreations:* sailing, riding, ski-ing, country sports, tennis, music, environmental projects. *Address:* Kings Manor, Freshwater, Isle of Wight PO40 9TL. *T:* (01983) 756050. *E:* susiesheldon@hotmail.com. *Clubs:* Royal Yacht Squadron; Royal Solent Yacht, Yarmouth Sailing.

**SHELDRAKE, Prof. Philip Farnsworth;** Senior Research Fellow, Westcott House Cambridge Theological Federation, since 2010; Senior Research Associate, Von Hugel Institute, St Edmund's College, Cambridge, since 2016; Moulsdale Fellow, St Chad's College, University of Durham, since 2003; Professor and Director, Institute for the Study of Contemporary Spirituality (formerly Professor of Christian Spirituality), Oblate School of Theology, San Antonio, Texas, since 2013; *b* 22 Nov. 1946; *s* of Archibald Douglas Farnsworth Sheldrake, MC and Ann Mary Sheldrake (*née* Fitzgibbon). *Educ:* Heythrop Pontifical Athenaeum (Phil. Bac. 1969); Campion Hall, Oxford (MA 1976; BD 1995; DD 2015); Univ. of London (PGDPT 1977; MTh 1977). Dir, Inst. of Spirituality, Heythrop Coll., London, 1983–92; Dir of Pastoral Studies, Westcott House, Cambridge, 1992–97; Sen. Res. Fellow, Queen's Foundn, Birmingham, 1997–98; Academic Dir and Vice-Principal, Sarum Coll., Salisbury, 1998–2003; William Leech Professorial Fellow in Applied Christian Theol., Univ. of Durham, 2003–08. Hon. Prof. of Theol., Univ. of Wales, Lampeter, later Univ. of Wales Trinity St David, 1998–2013; Hon. Res. Fellow, Centre for Study of Cities and Regions, Univ. of Durham, 2008–13; Dist. Res. Fellow, Global Cities Initiative, Georgetown Univ., Washington DC, 2018–19. Sen. Mem., St Edmund's Coll., Cambridge, 1999–) Hulsean Lectr, Univ. of Cambridge, 1999–2000. Visiting Professor: Univ. of Notre Dame, Indiana, 1995–2010; Boston Univ., 2002; Boston Coll., Chestnut Hill, 2005–13; Bellarmine Univ., 2012; Joseph Vis. Prof., Boston Coll., 2008–09; Veale Prof., Milltown Inst., Dublin, 2010–11. FRSA 1998; FRHistS 2005. *Publications:* Images of Holiness, 1987; Spirituality and History, 1991, 2nd edn 1996; Befriending our Desires, 1994, 3rd edn 2016 (trans. Polish 2019); Living Between Worlds: place and journey in Celtic Christianity, 1995; Spirituality and Theology, 1998; Love Took My Hand: the spirituality of George Herbert, 2000; Spaces for the Sacred: place, memory, identity, 2001; (ed) New Dictionary of Christian Spirituality, 2005; A Brief History of Spirituality, 2006, 2nd edn as Spirituality: a brief history, 2013; Heaven in Ordinary: George Herbert and his writings, 2009; Explorations in Spirituality, 2010; Spirituality: a very short introduction, 2012 (trans. Italian 2016); The Spiritual City: theology, spirituality and the urban, 2014 (trans. Korean 2018); Spirituality: a guide for the perplexed, 2014; Julian of Norwich: in God's sight—her theology in context, 2018; (ed) Surrender to Christ for Mission: French spiritual traditions, 2018. *Recreations:* music, art, contemporary literature, international affairs, wine (Mem., Wine Soc.), travel, history and culture of Italy, family and friends. *Address:* Westcott House, Jesus Lane, Cambridge CB5 8BP. *T:* (01223) 741000. *E:* ps220@cam.ac.uk. *Clubs:* House of St Barnabas, Oxford and Cambridge.

**SHELDRICK, Prof. George Michael,** PhD; FRS 2001; Professor of Structural Chemistry (formerly of Inorganic Chemistry), University of Göttingen, 1978–2011, now Emeritus; *b* 17 Nov. 1942; *s* of George and Elizabeth M. Sheldrick; *m* 1968, Katherine E. Herford; two *s* two *d*. *Educ:* Huddersfield New Coll.; Jesus Coll., Cambridge (MA; PhD 1966). University of Cambridge: Demonstrator, 1966–71, Lectr, 1971–78, Dept of Inorganic, Organic and Theoretical Chm.; Fellow, Jesus Coll., 1966–78. Mem., Akademie der Wissenschaften zu Göttingen, 1989. Mineral Sheldrickite named after him, 1996. Meldola Medal, 1970, Corday-Morgan Medal, 1978, Award for Structural Chem., 1981, RSC; Leibniz Prize, Deutsche Forschungsgemeinschaft, 1987; Patterson Prize, Amer. Crystallographic Assoc., 1993; Carl-Hermann Medal, Deutsche Ges. für Kristallographie, 1999; Hodgkin Prize, British Crystallographic Assoc., 2004; Perutz Prize, Eur. Crystallographic Assoc., 2004; Gregori Aminoff Prize, Royal Swedish Acad. of Sci., 2009; Ewald Prize, Internat. Union of Crystallography, 2011. *Publications:* numerous papers in scientific jls. *Recreations:* tennis, chess. *Address:* Institut für Anorganische Chemie, Tammannstrasse 4, 37077 Göttingen, Germany. *T:* (551) 3933021. *E:* gsheldr@shelx.uni-ac.gwdg.de.

**SHELFORD, William Thomas Cornelius;** DL; *b* 27 Jan. 1943; *s* of late Cornelius William Shelford and Helen Beatrice Hilda (*née* Schuster); *m* 1971, Annette Heap Holt; two *s* one *d*. *Educ:* Eton Coll.; Christ Church, Oxford (MA Jurisprudence). Partner, 1970–2002, Sen. Partner, 1990–2002, Cameron Markby Hewitt, later Cameron McKenna; Consultant, CMS Cameron McKenna, 2002–07. Chm. Govs, 2004–14, Chm. Trustees, 2014–18, Chailey Heritage Foundn (formerly Sch.). Vice Chm., Friends of the Keep, E Sussex archival services, 2014–. High Sheriff 2009–10, DL 2011, E Sussex. *Recreations:* gardening, walking, ski-ing, golf. *Club:* City of London.

**SHELLAM, Fiona Juliet;** *see* Stanley, F. J.

**SHELLARD, Dr Dominic Marcus;** Vice-Chancellor and Chief Executive, De Montfort University, 2010–19; *b* Farnborough, Kent, 24 April 1966; *s* of Marcus Reginald Shellard and Christine Jean Shellard; civil partnership 2010, John Walker. *Educ:* Crofton Infants and Jun. Sch.; Dulwich Coll.; St Peter's Coll., Oxford (MA English and German 1989; DPhil English Lit. 1993). Researcher for Ann Clwyd, MP, Shadow Sec. of State for Nat. Heritage, 1993; Lectr in English, Univ. of Salford, 1993–96; University of Sheffield: Lectr in English Lit., 1996–99; Reader in English Lit., 1999–2003; Prof. of English Lit., 2003–10; Hd, Sch. of English, 2004–07; Pro-Vice-Chancellor for Ext. Affairs, 2008–10. *Publications:* Harold Hobson: the complete catalogue 1922–1988, 1995; Harold Hobson: witness and judge, 1995; Shakespeare: a writer's life, 1998; British Theatre Since the War, 2000; (ed) British Theatre in the 1950s, 2000; Kenneth Tynan: a life, 2003; (with S. Nicholson) The Lord Chamberlain Regrets... A History of British Theatre Censorship, 2004; An Economic Impact Study of UK Theatre, 2004; (with W. McDonnell) A Social Impact Study of UK Theatre, 2006; Kenneth Tynan theatre writings, 2007; (ed) The Golden Generation: new light on British theatre 1945–1968, 2008. *Recreations:* supporting QPR, reading, current affairs, convivial meals, travelling, going to the theatre, attending sports events.

**SHELLARD, Maj.-Gen. Michael Francis Linton,** CBE 1989; Comptroller, Royal Artillery Institution, 2001–08; *b* 19 Aug. 1937; *s* of Norman Shellard and Stella (*née* Linton); *m* 1960, Jean Mary Yates; one *s* one *d*. *Educ:* Queen's Coll., Taunton; RMA, Sandhurst. Commnd, RA, 1957; Staff Coll., Camberley, 1969; NDC, Latimer, 1974; GSO1 MO4, MoD, 1975–76; CO 22 AD Regt, 1977–79; Col, 1983; Brig., 1985; Comd 1st Artillery Bde and Dortmund Garrison, 1985–88; Comdr Artillery, 1st British Corps, 1990–92. Dir, NATO Area, Short Brothers plc, 1992–94; Chief Exec., Regular Forces Employment Assoc., 1994–2001. Col Comdt, RA, 1993–2002; Hon. Col 22nd Regt, RA, 1993–2000. Chairman: RA Historical Affairs Cttee, 1994–2002; RA Historical Trust, 1994–2002. Dir, RA Museums Ltd, 1997–2004. Mem., Army Benevolent Fund Grants Cttee, 2002–14. Chm., Confedn of British Service and Ex-Service Orgns, 2003–06. Chm., Andover Talking Newspaper, 2014–. Gov., Queen's Coll., Taunton, 1989–2012. *Recreations:* golf, gardening, Hawk Conservancy Trust, Samaritans, volunteer at Andover Hospital. *Address:* c/o HSBC, 19 Minster Street, Salisbury, Wilts SP1 1TE. *Club:* Army and Navy (Chm., 2000–03; Trustee, 2004–18).

**SHELLEY, David Richard;** Chief Executive, Hachette UK, since 2018; *b* Dusseldorf, 1976; *s* of Alan and Jennifer Shelley; civil partnership 2005, Chris Gardner. *Educ:* Priory Sch., Lewes; Varndean Coll., Brighton; New Coll., Oxford (BA English). Editor, 1997–99, Publisher, 2000–05, Allison & Busby; Editl Dir, Little, Brown, 2005–07; Publisher, Sphere, 2007–09; Dep. Publisher, Hachette Book Gp, 2009–10; Publisher, Little, Brown Book Gp, 2010–15; Chief Exec., Little, Brown Book Gp and Orion Publishing Gp, 2015–17. *Recreations:* hiking, swimming, reading, gardening. *Address:* Hachette, Carmelite House, 50 Victoria Embankment, EC4Y 0DZ. *T:* (020) 3122 6942. *E:* david.shelley@hachette.co.uk.

**SHELLEY, Howard Gordon,** OBE 2009; concert pianist and conductor; *b* 9 March 1950; *s* of Frederick Gordon Shelley and Katharine Anne Taylor; *m* 1975, Hilary Mary Pauline Macnamara; one *s*, and one step *s*. *Educ:* Highgate Sch.; Royal College of Music (ARCM Hons 1966; Foundn Schol. 1967–71); Boise Schol. 1971–72; ARCO 1967. Studied with Vera Yelverton, Harold Craxton, Kendall Taylor, Lamar Crowson and Ilona Kabos. Recital début, Wigmore Hall, 1971; televised Henry Wood Prom début, 1972; conducting début, London Symphony Orch., Barbican, 1985; Associate Conductor, 1990–92, Principal Guest Conductor, 1992–98, Conductor Laureate, 2014–, London Mozart Players; Music Dir and Principal Conductor, Uppsala Chamber Orch., Sweden, 2000–03. Internat. solo career extending over five continents; performed world's first complete exposition of solo piano works of Rachmaninov, Wigmore Hall, 1983; soloist, 100th anniv. of Henry Wood Proms, 1995. Discography of over 160 recordings includes: Rachmaninov solo works (8 vols), Rachmaninov two-piano works, Rachmaninov Complete Piano Concertos, Mozart, Hummel (9 vols) and Mendelssohn Piano Concertos, and contribs to Hyperion's Romantic Piano series, including Concertos by Moscheles, Herz, Hiller and Kalkbrenner; Chopin, Schumann recitals, Schubert recital on fortepiano, piano concertos of Alwyn, Gershwin, Tippett, Vaughan Williams, Howard Ferguson, Szymanowski, Korngold, Rubbra, Carwithen, Balakirev, Messiaen and Peter Dickinson; Mozart and Schubert symphonies (conductor); Haydn's London and Cycle of Spohr symphonies; complete Clementi sonatas (6 double CD vols); 4 CDs of complete works of Beethoven for piano and orch. (conductor/soloist). 2 piano partnership with Hilary Macnamara, 1976–2001. Presenter, conductor and pianist, TV documentary on Ravel (Gold Medal, NY Fests Awards), 1998. Chappell Gold Medal and Peter Morrison Prize, 1968, Dannreuther Concerto Prize, 1971, RCM; Silver Medal, Co. of Musicians, 1971. *Address:* c/o Caroline Baird Artists, Stable Cottage, High Street, Culham, Oxon OX14 4NA. *E:* caroline@carolinebairdartists.co.uk.

**SHELLEY, Sir John (Richard),** 11th Bt *cr* 1611; (professionally Dr J. R. Shelley); general medical practitioner; farmer; *b* 18 Jan. 1943; *s* of John Shelley (*d* 1974), and Dorothy, *d* of Arthur Irvine Ingram; *S* grandfather, 1976; *m* 1965, Clare, *d* of late Claud Bicknell, OBE; two *d*. *Educ:* King's Sch., Bruton; Trinity Coll., Cambridge (BA 1964, MA 1967); St Mary's Hosp., London Univ. MB, BChir 1967; DObstRCOG 1969; MRCGP 1978; Exeter Univ. (MA Theol. 2009). Mem., Exeter Diocesan Synod for South Molton Deanery, 1976–79, for Cadbury Deanery, 2002–15 (Lay Chair, 2007–15); Mem., Gen. Synod, C of E, 2009–. Member: CLA; NFU. *Heir:* *b* Thomas Henry Shelley [*b* 3 Feb. 1945; *m* 1st, 1970, Katherine Mary Holton (marr. diss. 1992); three *d*; 2nd, 1994, Linda Joyce Wallis (*née* Poole)]. *Address:* Shobrooke Park, Crediton, Devon EX17 1DG.

**SHELTON, Gordon Edward; His Honour Judge Shelton;** a Circuit Judge, since 2018. *Educ:* Ashville Coll., Harrogate; Univ. of Leicester (LLB). Called to the Bar, Inner Temple, 1981; a Recorder, 1999–2018. *Recreations:* family, sport, travel. *Address:* Sheffield Family Hearing Centre, 48 West Bar, Sheffield S3 8PH.

**SHELTON, Gen. (Henry) Hugh;** Chairman, Joint Chiefs of Staff, USA, 1997–2001; *b* 2 Jan. 1942; *s* of late Hugh Shelton and of Sarah Shelton (*née* Laughlin); *m* 1963, Carolyn L. Johnson; three *s*. *Educ:* N Carolina State Univ. (BS Textiles 1963); Auburn Univ., Alabama (MS Pol Sci.); Harvard Univ.; Air Comd and Staff Coll., Alabama; Nat. War Coll., Washington. Entered US Army, 1963: active duty assignments in US, Hawaii and Vietnam (2 tours), 1963–87; Dep. Dir for Ops, Nat. Mil. Comd Center, Jt Chiefs of Staff, Washington, 1987–88; Chief, Current Ops, Jt Chiefs of Staff, 1988–89; Assistant Division Commander, 101st Airborne Division (Air Assault): Fort Campbell, Kentucky, 1989–90; Operations Desert Shield and Desert Storm, Saudi Arabia, 1990–91; Fort Campbell, March–May 1991; Commanding General: 82nd Airborne Div., Fort Bragg, NC, 1991–93; XVIII Airborne Corps and Fort Bragg, 1993–96 (i/c Jt Task Force, Operation Uphold Democracy, Haiti, 1994); Lt-Gen. 1993; Gen. 1996; C-in-C, US Special Ops Comd, MacDill Air Force Base, Fla, 1996–97. Mem., Council on Foreign Relns, 1998–. Mem., Assoc. of US Army, 1983–. Gov., American Red Cross, 1998–. Purple Heart, 1967; Bronze Star Medal: (with V device), 1967; (with three Oak Leaf Clusters), 1968, 1969, 1991; MSM (with two Oak Leaf Clusters), 1979, 1982, 1983; Legion of Merit (with Oak Leaf Cluster), 1985, 1991; DSM 1994; Defense DSM (with two Oak Leaf Clusters), 1989, 1994, 1997. *Publications:* Without Hesitation: the odyssey of an American warrior, 2010; contrib. to Harvard Internat. Rev., Armed Forces Jl, Nat. Defense, Special Warfare, Jt Force Qly, Qly Mil. Rev. *Recreations:* jogging, woodworking, reading, playing guitar. *Address:* c/o The Pentagon, Room 2E872, Washington, DC 20318–9999, USA. *T:* (703) 6979121.

**SHENG, Prof. Morgan Hwa-Tze,** PhD; FRS 2007; Core Institute Member, and Co-Director, Stanley Center for Psychiatric Research, Broad Institute, Massachusetts Institute of Technology and Harvard University, since 2019; Professor of Neuroscience, Department of Brain and Cognitive Sciences, Massachusetts Institute of Technology, since 2019; *b* London; *m*; one *s* one *d*. *Educ:* Corpus Christi Coll., Oxford (BA Physiol. 1979); Guy's Hosp. Med. Sch., Univ. of London (MB BS 1982); Harvard Univ. (PhD Molecular Genetics 1990). MRCP. Internship and residency in gen. medicine, London, 1982–86; Postdoctoral Fellow in Neurosci., UCSF, 1990–94; Asst Prof., 1994–98, Associate Prof., 1998–2001, Dept of Neurobiol., Massachusetts Gen. Hosp. and Harvard Med. Sch., Boston; Asst Investigator, then Associate Investigator, Howard Hughes Med. Inst., Mass Gen. Hosp., 1994–2001; Massachusetts Institute of Technology: Principal Investigator, RIKEN-MIT Neurosci. Res. Center, 2001–08; Investigator, Howard Hughes Med. Inst., 2001–08; Menicon Prof. of Neurosci., Picower Inst. for Learning and Memory, Dept of Brain and Cognitive Scis and Dept of Biol., 2001–08; Vice Pres., Neurosci. and Molecular Biol., Genentech Inc., 2008–19. FAAAS 2004; FMedSci 2009. Member: Soc. for Neurosci.; Amer. Soc. for Cell Biol.; Soc. Chinese Bioscientists of America. *Publications:* contribs to jls incl. Cell, Neuron, Jl Neurosci.

**SHENKIN, Prof. Alan,** PhD; FRCP, FRCPath, FRCPGlas; Professor of Clinical Chemistry, University of Liverpool, 1990–2007, now Emeritus; Hon. Consultant and Clinical Director, Royal Liverpool and Broadgreen University Hospitals NHS Trust, 1990–2007 (Director of Research and Development, 1998–2004); *b* 3 Sept. 1943; *m* 1967, Leonna Estelle Delmonte; one *s* one *d*. *Educ:* Hutchesons' Boys' Grammar Sch.; Univ. of Glasgow (BSc Hons 1965; MB ChB 1969; PhD 1974). FRCPath 1990; FRCPGlas 1990; FRCP 1993. Lectr in Biochem., Univ. of Glasgow, 1970–74; Sen. Registrar in Clinical Biochem., Glasgow Royal Infirmary, 1974–78; Royal Soc. Eur. Exchange Fellow, Karolinska Inst., Stockholm, 1976–77; Consultant in Clinical Biochem., Glasgow Royal Infirmary, 1978–90. Chm., Specialty Adv. Cttee on Chemical Pathology, RCPath, 1995–98; Chairman: Royal Med. Colls Intercollegiate Gp on Nutrition, 1996–2006; Sub-Cttee on Metabolic Medicine, Jt Cttee on Higher Med. Trng, 2001–04. Pres., Assoc. Clinical Biochemists, 2000–03; Hon. Treas., Eur. Soc. Parenteral and Enteral Nutrition, 1988–92 (Vice-Pres., 2002–03; Hon. Mem., 2010); Scientific Vice-Pres., British Nutrition Foundn, 2005–10 (Hon. Pres., 2010–). Hon. Associate, British Dietetic Assoc., 1989; Hon. Member: Czechoslovakian Med. Soc., 1990; Czechoslovakian Soc. for Parenteral and Enteral Nutrition, 1990; Assoc. for Clin. Biochem., 2007. Trustee, Alkaptonuria Soc., 2006–. Trustee and Mem. Council, Royal Philosophical Soc. of Glasgow, 2013– (Vice Pres., 2016–19). 650th Anniversary Jubilee Medal, Charles Univ., 1998. *Publications:* contrib. res. papers, book chapters and reviews on trace elements and vitamins in health and disease, nutritional support, metabolic response to illness, and role of laboratory in assessing nutritional status. *Recreations:* golf, word games, malt whisky, travel. *Address:* 9/3 Barcapel Avenue, Newton Mearns, Glasgow G77 6QJ. *Club:* Glasgow Golf.

**SHENNAN, Robert Duncan James;** Group Managing Director, and Member, Executive Committee, BBC, since 2019; *b* 18 March 1962; *s* of Joseph and Margaret Shennan; *m* 1987, Joanne Margaret Melford; two *s* one *d*. *Educ:* Lancaster Royal Grammar Sch.; Corpus Christi Coll., Cambridge (BA Hons English Lit. 1984). Journalist, Hereward Radio, 1984–87; BBC: Radio Sport: Producer, 1987–90; Asst Editor, 1990–92; Editor, 1992–94; Head, 1994–97; Head of Sport (TV and Radio), 1997–2000; Controller: BBC Radio Five Live, 2000–08; Five Live Sports Extra, 2002–08; BBC Asian Network, 2004–08; Dir of Radio, Channel 4, 2008–09; Controller: BBC Radio 2 and 6 Music, 2009–16; BBC Asian Network, 2011; Director: BBC Music, 2014–16; Radio and Music, BBC, 2016–19. *Recreations:* sport, music, my children. *Address:* BBC, Broadcasting House, Portland Place, W1A 1AA; Fairbanks, 30 Amersham Road, High Wycombe, Bucks HP13 6QU. *T:* (01494) 459216.

**SHENNAN, Prof. Stephen James,** PhD; FBA 2006; Professor of Theoretical Archaeology, University College London, since 1996 (Director, Institute of Archaeology, 2005–14); *b* 9 May 1949; *s* of James Francis Shennan and Martha Shennan (*née* Elias); *m* 2006, Lúcia Nagib; one *s* one *d* from former marriage. *Educ:* Becket Sch., Nottingham; Fitzwilliam Coll., Cambridge (BA 1971, MA 1974; PhD 1977). University of Southampton: Lectr in Archaeol., 1978–90; Reader, 1990–95; Prof. of Archaeol., 1995–96. MAE 2013. Rivers Meml Medal, RAI, 2010; Shanghai Forum Archaeological Res. Award, 2015. *Publications:* (ed with C. Renfrew) Ranking, Resource and Exchange, 1982; (jtly) Prehistoric Europe, 1984; The East Hampshire Survey, 1985; Quantifying Archaeology, 1988, 2nd edn 1997; (ed) Archaeological approaches to Cultural Identity, 1989; (with C. W. Beck) Amber in Prehistoric Britain, 1991; Bronze Age Copper Producers of the Eastern Alps, 1995; (ed with J. Steele) The Archaeology of Human Ancestry: power, sex and tradition, 1996; Genes, Memes and Human History: Darwinian archaeology and cultural evolution, 2002; (ed jtly) The Explanation of Culture Change, 2004; (ed jtly) The Evolution of Cultural Diversity: a phylogenetic approach, 2005; (ed jtly) Mapping Our Ancestors: phylogenetic methods in anthropology and prehistory, 2006; (ed jtly) A Future for Archaeology: the past in the present, 2006; (ed) Pattern and Process in Cultural Evolution, 2009; (ed jtly) Innovation in Cultural Systems: contributions from evolutionary anthropology, 2010; (ed jtly) The Origins and Spread of Domestic Animals in Southwest Asia and Europe, 2013; The First Farmers of Europe: an evolutionary perspective, 2018; monographs; contrib. numerous acad. papers. *Recreations:* rock climbing, walking, classical music (especially opera), cinema. *Address:* Institute of Archaeology, University College London, 31–34 Gordon Square, WC1H 0PY. *T:* (020) 7679 4739, *Fax:* (020) 7387 2572. *E:* s.shennan@ucl.ac.uk.

**SHENTON, Caroline,** DPhil; FSA, FRHistS; historian and archivist; *b* Evesham, Worcs, 16 Nov. 1965; *d* of Peter Shenton and Gillian Shenton; *m* 1994, Mark Purcell. *Educ:* Univ. of St Andrews (MA (Hons) Medieval Hist. 1989); Worcester Coll., Oxford (DPhil 1996); University Coll. London (Dip. Archives and Records Mgt 1997). Registered Archivist 2000. FSA 2007; FRHistS 2009. PR Account Exec., Lindy Beveridge Public Relns, 1989–90; Archive Cataloguer, 1993–96, Sen. Archivist, 1996–99, PRO; Asst Clerk of the Records, Parly Archives, 1999–2008; Director: Parly Archives, 2008–14; Parly Archives Accommodation Prog., 2014–17. Hon. Teaching Fellow, Centre for Archive and Information Studies, Univ. of Dundee, 2011–. Sec. to Council, Girton Coll., Cambridge, 2017–; Tutor, Inst. for Contg Educn, Univ. of Cambridge, 2018–. Member: Lindley Liby and Arts Cttee, RHS, 2011–16; Cttee, Section of Archives of Parliaments and Political Parties, Internat. Council on Archives, 2012–14. Trustee: H of L Collection Trust, 2008–14; Parly History Yearbook Trust, 2018–. Accredited Lectr, Arts Soc., 2013–. *Publications:* Victoria Tower Treasures from the Parliamentary Archives (ed jtly), 2010; The Day Parliament Burned Down, 2012 (Political Book of the Year, Paddy Power and Total Politics Political Book Awards, 2013); Mr Barry's War, 2016 (Book of the Year, Daily Telegraph and BBC Hist. Mag., 2016); historical and inf. mgt articles in learned jls. *Recreations:* historical research, Italian language and culture, early music, Twitter, foreign travel. *Address:* c/o Bill Hamilton, A. M. Heath Ltd, 6 Warwick Court, WC1R 5DJ.

**SHEPHARD OF NORTHWOLD,** Baroness *cr* 2005 (Life Peer), of Northwold in the county of Norfolk; **Gillian Patricia Shephard;** PC 1992; JP; DL; *b* 22 Jan. 1940; *d* of Reginald and Bertha Watts; *m* 1975, Thomas Shephard; two step *s*. *Educ:* North Walsham High Sch. for Girls; St Hilda's Coll., Oxford (MA Mod. Langs; Hon. Fellow, 1991). Educn Officer and Schools Inspector, 1963–75; Lectr, Cambridge Univ. Extra-Mural Bd, 1965–87. Councillor, Norfolk CC, 1977–89 (Chm. of Social Services Cttee, 1978–83, of Educn Cttee, 1983–85); Chairman: W Norfolk and Wisbech HA, 1981–85; Norwich HA, 1985–87; Co-Chm., Women's Nat. Commn, 1990–91. MP (C) SW Norfolk, 1987–2005. PPS to Economic Sec. to the Treasury, 1988–89; Parly Under Sec. of State, DSS, 1989–90; Minister of State, HM Treasury, 1990–92; Sec. of State for Employment and Minister for Women, 1992–93; Minister of Agric., Fisheries and Food, 1993–94; Sec. of State for Educn, later Educn and Employment, 1994–97; Shadow Leader, H of C, 1997; Opposition front bench spokesman on the envmt, transport and the regions, 1997–99. Mem., Procedure Cttee, H of L, 2007–09. Dep. Chm., Cons. Party, 1991–92 and 2002–03; Chm., Assoc. of Conservative Peers, 2007–12. Member: Cttee on Standards in Public Life, 2003–08; Jt Cttee on Reform of H of L, 2011–12; Pres., Video Standards Council, 2006–14; Dep. Chm., Commn on Social Mobility, 2013–17. Vice Pres., Hansard Soc., 1997–2004. Mem., Franco-British Council, 1997–2006; Chairman: Cons. Friends of Israel, 1997–2001; E of England Bio-Fuels Forum, 2004–12; Franco-British Soc., 2005–11; Patron, WEA, 2006–. Comr, Fawcett Soc., 2005–. Mem. Council, 2000–06, Mem., Bd of Continuing Educn, 2005–12, Univ. of Oxford; Chairman, Council: RVC, 2008–12; Inst. of Educn, Univ. of London, 2010–15. Vis. Prof., Public Policy Unit, KCL, 2014–. Gov., NIESR, 2014–18. President: Royal Norfolk Agricl Assoc., 2000–01; Norfolk Assoc. of Local Councils, 2008–14; Chm., Oxford Univ. Soc., 2007–14 (Pres., Norfolk Br., 2007–); Vice Patron, Norfolk Community Foundn, 2006–. JP Norwich, 1973; DL Norfolk, 2003. FRVC 2012. Hon. Fellow, QMUL, 2008. Chevalier, Légion d'Honneur (France), 2009. *Publications:* The Future of Local Government, 1999; Shephard's Watch, 2000; Knapton Remembered,

2007; Knapton: 20th century village voices, 2011; The Real Iron Lady: working with Margaret Thatcher, 2013. *Recreations:* music, gardening, France. *Address:* House of Lords, SW1A 0PW.
*See also N. Shephard.*

**SHEPHARD, Jonathan;** Chief Executive, Autism West Midlands, 2010–16; *b* 20 March 1949; twin *s* of Grey and Mollie Shephard; *m* 1985, Penelope Guest (marr. diss. 2000); two *s* one *d* (triplets). *Educ:* Sir Thomas Rich's Sch., Gloucester; St Catherine's Coll., Oxford (BA (English) 1971; BA (Law) 1973; Chancellor's English Essay Prize, Matthew Arnold Meml Prize). Called to the Bar, Inner Temple, 1977; with Which?, 1979–94: Financial Researcher, 1979–83, Financial Res. Manager, 1983–86; Editor: Holiday Which?, 1986–90; Health Which?, 1988–90; Project Dir, 1990–92; Dir of Mgt Inf., 1992–94; Mktg Dir, 1994–95; Man. Dir, 1995–97, Newhall Gp; Man. Dir, Southern Magazines, 1997–2002; Gen. Sec., subseq. Chief Exec., Independent Schs Council, 2004–08; Chief Exec., PPA, 2008–09. Director: Audit Bureau of Circulations, 2008–09; Advertising Standards Bd of Finance, 2008–09; Copyright Licensing Agency, 2008–09; Eur. Fedn of Mag. Publishers, 2008–09; Internat. Fedn of Periodical Press, 2008–09; Publishers Licensing Soc., 2008–09; Press Standards Bd of Finance, 2008–09. Dir and Trustee, Autism Alliance, 2011–15; Dir, SPARC Autism, 2013–16; Trustee, Physics Partners (formerly Success in Shortage Subjects), 2007–17 (Advr, 2017–). *Publications:* (ed) Which? Book of Tax, 1986. *Recreations:* music, architecture, writing novels. *E:* jonathanshephard@btinternet.com.

**SHEPHARD, Prof. Neil,** PhD; FBA 2006; Professor of Economics and of Statistics, since 2013, and Chair, Department of Statistics, since 2015, Harvard University; *b* 8 Oct. 1964; *s* of Dr Thomas F. Shephard (who *m* 1975, Gillian Watts (*see* Baroness Shephard of Northwold)) and late Tydfil Shephard; *m* 1998, Dr Heather Bell; two *d*. *Educ:* Univ. of York (BA Hons Econs and Stats 1986); London Sch. of Economics (MSc Stats 1987; PhD 1990). Lectr, LSE, 1988–93; Gatsby Res. Fellow in Econometrics, 1991–93, Official Fellow in Econs, 1993–2006, Professorial Fellow, 2006–13, Nuffield Coll., Oxford; Titular Prof. of Econs, 1999–2006, Prof. of Econs, 2006–13, Res. Dir, Oxford-Man Inst., 2007–11, Univ. of Oxford. Fellow, Econometric Soc., 2004. Hon. DEcon, Aarhus Univ., 2009. Richard Stone Prize, Soc. for Applied Econometrics, 2012; Guy Medal in Silver, Royal Statistical Soc., 2017. *Publications:* scientific papers in Econometrica, Rev. of Econ. Studies, Jl of Amer. Stat. Assoc., Biometrika, etc. *Recreations:* reading, cricket, family. *Address:* Department of Economics, Harvard University, Littauer Center, 1802 Cambridge Street, Cambridge, MA 02138, USA. *E:* shephard@fas.harvard.edu.

**SHEPHARD, Capt. Samuel John,** GC 2014; Chief of Staff, CQS, 2017–18; *b* Craigavon, 20 July 1987; *s* of John Shephard, MBE and Grace Shephard; partner, Victoria Gass. *Educ:* Royal Sch., Armagh; Queen's Univ., Belfast (BSc Marine Biol.; MSc Fisheries and Aquaculture). Joined Royal Marines, 2011; Officer-in-Comd 5 Troop, Bravo Co., 40 Cdo (Herrick 17), 2013; Second-in-Comd, Bravo Co., 40 Cdo, 2013–15; Flag Lieut to First Sea Lord, 2015–16; Tactical Team Comdr, Mission Trng and Mobilisation Centre, 2016–17.

**SHEPHEARD ROGERS, Patricia Maureen;** leader of teachers' professional development in Pakistan and Uganda; Mathematics Educator: Open University, 1972–2017; National Centre for Excellence in the Teaching of Mathematics, 2010–17; numeracy support, Blackfriars settlement, since 2018; *b* Colchester, 18 May 1947; *d* of Maj. Gen. Joseph Kenneth Shepheard, CB, DSO, OBE and Maureen E. H. Shepheard (*née* Bowen-Colthurst); *m* 1969, David Rogers (marr. diss. 2004); two *s*. *Educ:* New Hall, Cambridge (BA Hons 1968); Inst. of Educn, London Univ. (PGCE); Univ. of Greenwich (DMS). Lecturer in Mathematics: West Kent Coll., 1968–69; Univ. of Lagos Coll. of Educn, 1969–71; King's Coll., Lagos, 1971–72; Foreman Christian Coll., Univ. of Punjab, 1975–78; Founder and Dir, Computer Materials Prog., Centre for World Develt Educn, 1979–85; broadcaster and newspaper columnist, S Korea, 1985–89; develt educn researcher and writer, 1981–90; Chief Executive: Council for Educn in World Citizenship, 1990–99; Pestalozzi Internat. Village, 1999–2005; Jubilee Debt Campaign, 2005–08. Director: RIIA, 2007–10 (Mem., 1990–2015); UN Assoc.-UK, 2007–12; Humanists UK (formerly British Humanist Assoc.), 2008– (Vice Chair, 2010–17); Cttee, Central London Humanists Gp, 2018–. *Publications:* Sand Harvest, 1985; Let's Visit South Korea, 1988. *Recreation:* active supporter of four grandchildren. *Address:* 27 River Court, Upper Ground, SE1 9PE. *T:* (020) 7928 3667. *E:* trisha_rogers@yahoo.com.

**SHEPHERD,** family name of **Baron Shepherd**.

**SHEPHERD, 3rd Baron** *cr* 1946, of Spalding, co. Lincoln; **Graeme George Shepherd;** Founder, 1986, and Chairman, Anglo Sterling Ltd; Director, Star Material Solutions Ltd, Hong Kong, since 2005; *b* 6 Jan. 1949; *er s* of 2nd Baron Shepherd, PC and Allison (*née* Redmond); *S* father, 2001; *m* 1st, 1971, Eleanor Philomena (marr. diss. 2002), *d* of Patrick Glynn; one *s*; 2nd, 2005, Evelyn Cortes; two *s*. *Heir:* s Hon. Patrick Malcolm Shepherd [*b* 10 July 1980; *m* 2007, Laura, *d* of Tim Street; one *s* one *d*]. *Clubs:* Oriental; Hong Kong, Shek O Golf and Country (Hong Kong).

**SHEPHERD, Rev. Canon Anthony Michael,** MBE 2017; Vicar, St Peter's, Harrogate, 1987–2015; Chaplain to the Queen, 2009–15; *b* Broadstairs, 8 July 1950; *s* of Alfred Shepherd and Betty Shepherd; *m* 1978, Ann Elisabeth Gilbert-Trujols; one *s* one *d*. *Educ:* Chatham House Grammar Sch., Ramsgate; Emmanuel Coll., Cambridge (BA 1972; MA 1976). Ordained deacon, 1974, priest, 1975; Curate, Folkestone Parish Church, 1974–79; Bishop's Chaplain, Dio. of Ripon, 1979–87. Hon. Canon, Ripon Cathedral, 1989, Canon Emeritus, 2015. *Recreations:* golf, old postcards. *Address:* 3 Heatherdale, Summerbridge, Harrogate, N Yorks HG3 4BQ. *E:* ashepherd@talktalk.net.

**SHEPHERD, Sir Colin (Ryley),** Kt 1996; Director of Parliamentary Studies, Centre for Political and Diplomatic Studies, 1999–2010; *b* 13 Jan. 1938; *s* of late T. C. R. Shepherd, MBE; *m* 1966, Louise, *d* of late Lt-Col E. A. M. Cleveland, MC; three *s*. *Educ:* Oundle; Caius Coll., Cambridge; McGill Univ., Montreal. Nat. Service, RN, 1956–58; RCN 1960–63; Dir, Haigh Engineering Co. Ltd, 1963–2010. MP (C) Hereford, Oct. 1974–1997; contested (C) same seat, 1997. PPS to Sec. of State for Wales, 1987–90. Jt Sec., Cons. Parly Agr. Fish. and Food Cttee, 1975–79, Vice-Chm., 1979–87, 1991–92; Member: Select Cttee on H of C Services, 1979–92; Select Cttee on H of C Finance and Services, 1993–97; Sec., Cons. Parly Hort. Sub-Cttee, 1976–87; Chairman: Library Sub-Cttee, 1983–91; Catering Cttee, 1991–97. Chm., UK Br., CPA, 1991–94 (Mem. Exec. Cttee, 1986–97; Treas., 1991–93, Chm., 1993–96, Internat. Exec. Cttee). Council Mem., RCVS, 1983–99 (Hon. ARCVS 2001); Governor, Commonwealth Inst., 1989–97; Chm., Trustees, Friends of the Commonwealth Foundn, 1998–2014. Fellow, Industry and Parlt Trust, 1985. *Address:* Manor House, Ganarew, Monmouth NP25 3SU. *T:* (01600) 890220.

**SHEPHERD, Prof. James,** PhD; FRCPath, FRCPGlas, FMedSci; FRSE; Professor, and Head of Department of Pathological Biochemistry, University of Glasgow and Glasgow Royal Infirmary, 1988–2006, now Professor Emeritus; *b* 8 April 1944; *s* of James Bell Shepherd and Margaret McCrum Shepherd (*née* Camick); *m* 1969, Janet Bulloch Kelly; one *s* one *d*. *Educ:* Hamilton Acad.; Glasgow Univ. (BSc Hons 1965; MB ChB Hons 1968; PhD 1972). MRCPath 1982, FRCPath 1994; FRCPGlas 1990. Lectr in Biochemistry, Univ. of Glasgow, 1969–72; Lectr, 1973–77, Sen. Lectr and Hon. Consultant, 1977–88, Dept of Pathological Biochemistry, Univ. of Glasgow and Glasgow Royal Infirmary; Clin. Dir, Labs, Glasgow Royal Infirmary, 1993–2004. Asst Prof. of Medicine, Methodist Hosp., Houston, Texas, 1976–77; Vis. Prof. of Medicine, Cantonal Hosp., Geneva, 1984. Dir, W Scotland Coronary Prevention Study, 1989–96; Chairman: European Atherosclerosis Soc., 1993–96 (Chm., Congress, 2001); Prospective Study of Pravastatin in the Elderly at Risk, 1997–2002; Mem., Exec. Cttee, Treating to New Targets Study, 2001–06; UK Principal Investigator: Justification for the Use of Statins in Primary Prevention, 2005–08; JUPITER (Mem., Internat. Cttee). Mem., Internat. Atherosclerosis Soc., 1977–. FRSE 1996; Founder FMedSci, 1998. *Publications:* (jtly) Lipoproteins in Coronary Heart Disease, 1986; (jtly) Atherosclerosis: developments, complications and treatment, 1987; Lipoprotein Metabolism, 1987; (ed jtly) Coronary Risks Revisited, 1989; (ed jtly) Human Plasma Lipoproteins, 1989; (ed jtly) Preventive Cardiology, 1991; (ed jtly) Lipoproteins and the Pathogenesis of Atherosclerosis, 1991; (ed jtly) Cardiovascular Disease: current perspectives on the Asian-Pacific region, 1994; (jtly) Clinical Biochemistry, 1995, 4th edn 2008; (jtly) Lipoproteins in Health and Disease, 1999; (jtly) Statins in Perspective, 1999, 2nd edn 2004; (jtly) Atherosclerosis Annual, 2001; Lipids and Atherosclerosis Annual, 2003. *Recreations:* travel, walking, art appraisal. *Address:* (home) 17 Barriedale Avenue, Hamilton ML3 9DB. *T:* (01698) 428259.

**SHEPHERD, James Rodney;** Under-Secretary, Department of Trade and Industry (formerly Department of Industry), 1980–89, retired; *b* 27 Nov. 1935; *s* of Richard James Shepherd and Winifred Mary Shepherd. *Educ:* Blundell's; Magdalen Coll., Oxford (PPE; Diploma in Statistics). National Inst. of Economic and Social Res., 1960–64; Consultant to OECD, 1964; HM Treasury, 1965–80 (Under-Sec., 1975–80). *Publications:* articles in technical jls.

**SHEPHERD, Sir John (Alan),** KCVO 2000; CMG 1989; Director, Global Leadership Foundation, since 2007; *b* 27 April 1943; *s* of William (Mathieson) Shepherd and (Elsie) Rae Shepherd; *m* 1st, 1969, Jessica Mary Nichols (*d* 2011); one *d*; 2nd, 2015, Alison Mairi Sephton (*née* Forsyth). *Educ:* Charterhouse; Selwyn Coll., Cambridge (MA); Stanford Univ., Calif (MA). Merchant Navy, 1961; HM Diplomatic Service, 1965–2003: CO, 1965–66; MECAS, Lebanon, 1966–68; 3rd Sec., Amman, 1968–70; 2nd Sec., Rome, 1970–73; 1st Secretary: FCO, 1973–76; The Hague, 1977–80; First Sec., 1980–82, Counsellor and Hd of Chancery, 1982–84, Office of UK Rep. to EEC, Brussels; Head of European Community Dept (External), FCO, 1985–87; Ambassador to Bahrain, 1988–91; Minister, Bonn, 1991–96; Dir, Middle East and North Africa, FCO, 1996–97; Dep. Under-Sec. of State, FCO, 1997–2000; Ambassador to Italy, 2000–03; Sec.-Gen., Global Leadership Foundn, 2003–06. Chm., Norbert Brainin Foundn, 2003–; Deputy Chairman: Trustees, Prince's Sch. of Traditional Arts, 2004–10; Bahrain Soc., 2009–; Trustee, Music at Paxton, 2015–. President: Selwyn Assoc., 2011–12; FCO Assoc., 2015–19. *Recreations:* hills, birds, tennis. *Club:* Oxford and Cambridge.

**SHEPHERD, Prof. John Graham,** CBE 2010; PhD; FRS 1999; CMath, FIMA; Professorial Research Fellow in Earth System Science, University of Southampton, 2006–16, now Emeritus Professor (Professor of Marine Sciences, 1994–2006); *b* 24 Aug. 1946; *s* of Ian Alastair Shepherd and Eileen Alice Mary Shepherd; *m* 1968, Deborah Mary Powney; two *s*. *Educ:* Pembroke Coll., Cambridge (MA); Cavendish Lab., Cambridge (PhD 1971). FIMA 1989; CMath 1991. Res. Officer, CEGB, 1970–74; MAFF Fisheries Lab., Lowestoft, 1974–94, Dep. Dir and Hd, Fish Stock Mgt Div., 1989–94; Director: Southampton Oceanography Centre, NERC, 1994–99; Earth System Modelling Initiative, Univ. of Southampton, 1999–2006. Vis. Sen. Res. Associate, Lamont-Doherty Geol Observatory, Columbia Univ., NY, 1978–79. Pres., Challenger Soc., 2000–02. *Publications:* numerous professional articles on marine science, climate change, fish stock assessment and fishery mgt. *Recreations:* rowing, music, walking, beekeeping. *Address:* National Oceanography Centre, European Way, Southampton SO14 3ZH. *Club:* Lowestoft Rowing.

**SHEPHERD, Prof. John Henry,** FRCS, FRCOG, FACOG; Professor of Surgical Gynaecology, Barts and the London School of Medicine and Dentistry, Queen Mary University of London (formerly St Bartholomew's and the Royal London Hospital School of Medicine and Dentistry, then Barts and the London, Queen Mary's School of Medicine and Dentistry), 1999–2008, now Emeritus; Consultant Surgeon and Gynaecological Oncologist, Royal Marsden Hospital, London, 1983–2015; *b* 11 July 1948; *s* of late Dr Henry Robert Shepherd, DSC and of Mimika Matarki; *m* 1972, Alison Brandram Adams; one *s* two *d*. *Educ:* Blundell's Sch., Tiverton; St Bartholomew's Hosp. Med. Coll. (MB BS 1971). LRCP 1971; FRCS 1976; MRCOG 1978 (Gold Medal), FRCOG 1996; FACOG 1981. Fellow in Gynaecol Oncology, Univ. of S Florida, Tampa, 1979–81; Sen. Registrar, Queen Charlotte's Hosp., 1978–79; Consultant Surgeon and Gynaecological Oncologist, St Bartholomew's Hosp., 1981–2008; Consultant Surgeon, Chelsea Hosp. for Women, 1983–84; Consultant: London Clinic, 1994–2015; King Edward VII Hosp., London, 1995–2015. Hunterian Prof., RCS, 2006–07. *Publications:* (jtly) Gynaecological Oncology, 1985, 2nd edn 1990; (jtly) Ovarian Cancer, 2002; (jtly) Gynaecological Surgery, 2013; numerous articles on gynaecol cancer and pelvic surgery. *Recreations:* sailing (offshore ocean racing), ski-ing, opera. *Address:* Claremont House, Market Hill, Cowes, Isle of Wight PO31 7TR. *Clubs:* MCC, Royal Ocean Racing.

**SHEPHERD, Prof. Jonathan Paul,** CBE 2008; PhD, DDSc; FDSRCS, FMedSci; FLSW; Professor of Oral and Maxillofacial Surgery, since 1991, and Director, Crime and Security Research Institute, 2015, now Emeritus Director, Cardiff University (formerly University of Wales College of Medicine, later Wales College of Medicine, Cardiff University) (Vice-Dean, 2004–17); *b* 25 Sept. 1949; *s* of Paul Richard Shepherd and Heather Mary Shepherd (*née* Gifford); *m* 1980, Daphne Elizabeth Bird; three *s* one *d*. *Educ:* Bideford Grammar Sch.; King's Coll. London (BDS); Wolfson Coll. (MSc); PhD Bristol 1988; DDSc Wales 2000. FDSRCS 1977; FRCEM (FFAEM 2001). House Surgeon: KCH, 1974; Queen Victoria Hosp., E Grinstead, 1974–75; Registrar, Royal Infirmary, Cardiff, 1975–80; Res. Fellow, Univ. of Oxford, 1978–79; Sen. Registrar in Oral and Maxillofacial Surgery, Yorks RHA, and Hon. Lectr, Univ. of Leeds, 1980–83; Sen. Lectr in Oral and Maxillofacial Surgery, 1983–88, Reader, 1988–91, Univ. of Bristol; Hd, Dept of Oral Surgery, Medicine and Pathol., UWCM, Cardiff Univ., 1991–2004. Hon. Consultant Oral and Maxillofacial Surgeon: Bristol and Weston HA, 1983–91; Cardiff and Vale Univ. Health Bd (formerly University Hosp. of Wales/Cardiff and Vale NHS Trust), 1991–. King James IV Prof., RCSE, 2006–08; Bradlaw Orator, RCS, 2014. Chm., WHO Violent Crime Task Gp, 1996–; author of reports for Home Office on violence prevention, 2010, and hate violence, 2011, for Cabinet Office on effectiveness, 2014; Member: Faculty of Dental Surgery, RCS, 2002–12 (Vice-Dean, 2009–11); Council, Acad. of Med. Scis, 2011–14; Sci. Adv. Council, Home Office, 2012–; What Works Council, Cabinet Office, 2013–; Public Services Leadership Bd, Welsh Govt, 2014–17; Mem. Council and Trustee, RCS, 2009–12, Chm., Welsh Bd, 2010–13, RCS, Dir, Violence and Society Res. Gp, 1996–. Trustee: Victim Support, 1998–2006 (Vice Chair, 2000–03); Hunterian Mus., RCS, 2013–; Chartered Coll. of Teaching, 2015–. Mem. Governing Body, Church in Wales, 2014–. Author, Declaration on Evidence, signed by 27 professional bodies across medicine, educn and policing, 2017. FMedSci 2002; FLSW 2011. Hon. FDSRCSE 1996; Hon. FFPH 2001; Hon. FRCPsych 2008; Hon. FFGDP 2008; Hon. FRCS 2012; Hon. FRCPSGlas 2018. Hon. Dr Odontol.

Malmö, 2005. Stockholm Criminology Prize, 2008; Colyer Gold Medal, RCS, 2014; Down Surgery Prize, BAOMS, 2014. *Publications:* Slide Interpretation in Oral Diseases and the Oral Manifestations of Systemic Diseases, 1986; Violence in Healthcare, 1994, 2nd edn 2001; contributions: on decision-making and cost effectiveness in surgery and anaesthesia to surgery, dentistry, anaesthesia and clin. decision-making jls; on psycho-social causes and sequelae and epidemiol. of violence to med. and social sci. jls; on the effectiveness and orgn of res. for public services and social policy; series of randomised controlled expts in epidemiol., psychiatry and emergency medicine jls; res. discoveries to BMJ and Lancet editls; policy guidelines for medical Royal Colls. *Recreations:* industrial archaeology (Mem., Trevithick Soc.), walking, 19th century history. *Address:* Crime and Security Research Institute, Cardiff University, Friary House, Greyfriars Road, Cardiff CF10 3AE. *T:* and *Fax:* (029) 2087 5440. *E:* shepherdjp@cardiff.ac.uk.

SHEPHERD, Louise Claire, CBE 2017; Chief Executive, Alder Hey Children's NHS Foundation Trust, since 2008; *b* Derby, 26 Aug. 1964; *d* of Leslie Reginald and Joan Kirk; *m* 1991, Keith Andrew Shepherd; one *s* one *d. Educ:* Clare Coll., Cambridge (BA Hons 1985; MA); Warwick Business Sch. (MBA 1997); Inst. of Public Finance and Accountancy (CPFA 1989). Trainee accountant, Dudley MBC, 1985–89; Sen. Manager, KPMG, 1989–93; Dir, Business Develt, Birmingham Heartlands and Solihull NHS Trust, 1993–97; Finance Dir, Countess of Chester NHS Foundn Trust, 1997–2003; Chief Exec., Liverpool Women's NHS Foundn Trust, 2003–08. Trustee, Royal Liverpool Philharmonic Soc., 2004–10. *Recreations:* favourite challenges: playing the violin, climbing the Scottish Munros, following Derby County FC, bringing up two children. *Address:* Alder Hey Children's NHS Foundation Trust, Eaton Road, West Derby, Liverpool L12 2AP. *T:* (0151) 252 5412. *E:* louise.shepherd@alderhey.nhs.uk.

SHEPHERD, Sister Margaret Ann; Member, Religious Congregation (RC) of Our Lady of Sion, and Province Leader of UK/Ireland Province, 2005–08; Secretary, Bishops' Committee for Catholic Jewish Relations, since 2011, and Advisor on Catholic Jewish Relations, since 2016, Catholic Bishops' Conference of England and Wales; Director, Sion Centre for Dialogue and Encounter, since 2013; *b* 26 April 1944; *d* of Alfred and Alice Shepherd. *Educ:* Maria Assumpta Coll. of Educn (DipEd); Open Univ. (BA); Leo Baeck Coll. (Dip. Jewish Studies 1980); King's Coll., London (MTh Biblical Studies). Teacher of English (part time) during noviciate period; teacher, English and religious studies: Our Lady of Sion Boarding Sch., Shropshire, 1969–70; Our Lady of Sion Sen. Sch., Worthing, 1970–77; full time rabbinical studies, 1977–80; Study Centre for Christian Jewish Relations: Team Mem., 1980–86; Dir, 1986–89; Council of Christians and Jews: Educn Officer, 1989–93; Dep. Dir, 1993–98; Dir, 1999–2003; Mem. Exec. Bd, Internat. CCJ, 2002–08; State Coordinator for Mississippi, 2008–, and Texas, 2010–, Lifelines. Trustee, 2005–15, Hon. Vice Pres., 2015–, Ammerdown Centre. Gov., St Mary's Sch., Battersea, 2009–11. *Publications:* contributor: Dialogue with a Difference, ed Tony Bayfield and Marcus Braybrooke, 1992; Splashes of Godlight, ed Terence Copley, 1997; The Holocaust and the Christian World, 2000; Jews and Christians: making theological space for each other, 2000; He Kissed Him and They Wept: towards a theology of Jewish-Catholic partnership, ed Tony Bayfield, Sidney Brichto and Eugene Fisher, 2002; Public Life and the Place of the Church, ed Michael Brierley, 2006; The Legacy of John Paul II, ed Gerald O'Collins and Michael A. Hayes, 2008; contrib. to The Month. *Recreations:* visiting art galleries and exhibitions, music, painting, poetry, browsing in second hand bookshops, spending time with friends. *Address:* 35 Gilbert Close, Shooters Hill Road, SE18 4PT. *T:* (020) 8319 1930. *E:* margaretashepherd@gmail.com.

SHEPHERD, Mike; actor and director; Founder and Artistic Director, Kneehigh, since 1980; *b* London, 25 May 1953; *s* of Fred and Phyllis Shepherd; *m* Sarah Wright; one *d. Educ:* St Austell Grammar Sch.; Balls Park Coll.; Hertford Teacher Trng Coll. Teacher in Inner London; specialist primary teacher, Mevagissey, Cornwall. *Director:* Dead Dog in a Suitcase (and other love songs); Tin Drum (opera); The Very Old Man with Enormous Wings; Blast; The Dancing Frog; Zog; *actor:* Red Shoes; Tristan and Iseult; Wooden Frock; Bacchae; A Matter of Life and Death; Don John; Steptoe & Son; 946; Wise Children, Old Vic, 2018; actor in films: Anna Karenina, 2012; Pan, 2015. Trelawny Plate for service to Cornwall, 2015. *Publications:* Kneehigh Book. *Address:* Kneehigh Theatre, 15 Walsingham Place, Truro, Cornwall TR1 2RP. *T:* (01872) 267911. *E:* chloe@kneehigh.co.uk.

SHEPHERD, Nicholas José, FRICS; Chairman, Property Income Trust for Charities, since 2013; *b* London, 29 Nov. 1958; *s* of Ian Shepherd and Sylvia Shepherd; *m* 1984, Deborah Weller; one *s* two *d. Educ:* Royal Grammar Sch., High Wycombe; Sidney Sussex Coll., Cambridge (BA Geog. 1980); MA). FRICS 1990. Drivers Jonas, later Drivers Jonas Deloitte, 1984–2012; Partner, 1988–2012; Managing Partner, 2001–11; Mem. Exec. Bd, 2010–12, Vice Chm., 2012–13, Deloitte LLP; Consultant, Deloitte Real Estate, 2013–14. Chairman: Riverside Capital, 2015–19 (Dir, 2013–19); Hectare Agritech Ltd, 2016–; non-exec. Dir, McKay Securities plc, 2015–. Surveyor to Skinners' Co., 1991–2014. Member: Surveyors' Assoc.; Skinners' Co. *Recreations:* golf, horse riding, ski-ing, walking. *Address:* Hanger Lodge, Frensham Lane, Churt, Surrey GU10 2QG. *T:* 07771 798852. *E:* nick.shepherd999@gmail.com. *Club:* Liphook Golf.

SHEPHERD, Philip Alexander; QC 2003; a Recorder of the Crown Court, since 2000; *b* 1 May 1950; *s* of John and Eve Shepherd; *m* 1984 (marr. diss. 2013); two *s*; *m* 2014, Francesca Kate Liebling; three *s. Educ:* St George's Coll., Weybridge; Monash Univ., Melbourne; LSE (BSc Econ). Inns of Court Sch. of Law. Called to the Bar, Gray's Inn, 1975; barrister specialising in commercial litigation and aviation law. MCIArb 1997; Member: Commercial Bar Assoc.; British-Italian Law Assoc.; Internat. Bar Assoc.; Chancery Bar Assoc. MRAeS. *Recreations:* Rugby, theatre, opera. *Address:* 24 Old Buildings, Lincoln's Inn, WC2A 3UP. *T:* (020) 7691 2424, *Fax:* (020) 7405 1360. *E:* philip.shepherd@xxiv.co.uk. *Club:* Royal Automobile.

SHEPHERD, Sir Richard (Charles Scrimgeour), Kt 2013; *b* 6 Dec. 1942; *s* of late Alfred Reginald Shepherd and Davida Sophia Wallace. *Educ:* LSE; Johns Hopkins Univ. (Sch. of Advanced Internat. Studies). Director: Shepherd Foods (London) Ltd, 1970–; Partridges of Sloane Street Ltd, 1972–. Mem., SE Econ. Planning Council, 1970–74. Underwriting Mem. of Lloyds, 1974–94. MP (C) Aldridge-Brownhills, 1979–2015. Member: Treasury and Civil Service Select Cttee, 1979–83; Modernisation Select Cttee, 1997–2010; Jt Cttee on Human Rights, 2001–15; Secretary: Cons. Parly Industry Cttee, 1980–81; Cons. Parly European Cttee, 1980–81. Parly Co-Vice Chm., Campaign for Freedom of Inf., 1989–2015. Sponsor, Liberty, 2001–14. Mem., Court of Govs, LSE, 1996–. Backbencher of the Year, Spectator, 1987; Special Award, Campaign for Freedom of Information, 1988; Parliamentarian of the Year, Spectator, 1995. *Recreations:* book collecting; searching for the Home Service on the wireless. *Clubs:* Garrick, Beefsteak, Pratt's, Chelsea Arts.

SHEPHERD, Richard Thorley, FRCPath, FFFLM; Senior Lecturer in Forensic Medicine and Head of Forensic Medicine Unit, St George's Hospital Medical School, 1996–2010; Hon. Consultant, Forensic Pathology, Royal Liverpool Hospital, since 2007; *b* 20 Sept. 1952; *s* of George and Lucy Shepherd; *m* 1st, 1978, Jane Caroline Malcolm (marr. diss. 2007); one *s* one *d*; 2nd, 2008, Linda Evelyn Teebay. *Educ:* University Coll. London (BSc Hons); St George's Hosp. Med. Sch. (MB BS 1977). DMJ 1984; MRCPath 1987, FRCPath 1997; FFFLM 2006. Lectr in Forensic Medicine, St George's Hosp. Med. Sch., 1981–86; Lectr in Forensic Medicine, 1986–88, Sen. Lectr, 1988–96, UMDS of Guy's and St Thomas' Hosps. Visiting Professor: City Univ., 2007–13; Chester Univ., 2013–16. Civilian Consultant to RAF, 2006–12. Asst Ed., Medico-Legal Jl, 1986–97. President: Sect. of Clin. Forensic and Legal Medicine, RSocMed, 2003–05; British Assoc. in Forensic Medicine, 2004–06. Member: Tribunal Service, Criminal Injuries Compensation (formerly Criminal Injuries Compensation Appeals Panel), 2000–10; Ind. Adv. Panel on Non-Compliance Mgt, UK Border Agency, Home Office, 2013–14. Expert Advisor: Bloody Sunday Inquiry, 1998–2002; Operation Paget (inquiry into the death of Diana, Princess of Wales), 2004–08; Attorney Gen.'s Rev. concerning reopening of inquest into death of Dr David Kelly, 2010–11; Member: Ministerial Ind. Adv. Gp on Deaths in Custody, 2009–; Restraint Adv. Bd (formerly Accreditation Panel), 2010–12; Ind. Review into Self-Inflicted Deaths in Custody of 18–24 year-olds (Harris Review), MoJ, 2014–15; Registrar, Faculty of Forensic and Legal Medicine, RCP, 2018– (Mem. Bd, 2010–14). Presenter, TV series: Death Detective, 2006; Autopsy (4 series), 2014–15. *Publications:* Simpson's Forensic Medicine, 12th edn 2003; (contrib.) A Physician's Guide to Clinical Forensic Medicine, 2000, 3rd edn 2011; (contrib.) Fire Toxicity, 2011; Unnatural Causes, 2018. *Recreations:* flying light aircraft, keeping bees. *Address:* PO Box 498, Northwich, Cheshire CW9 9BE. *Clubs:* Athenæum, Lansdowne.

SHEPHERD, Prof. Theodore Gordon, PhD; FRS 2016; Grantham Professor of Climate Science, University of Reading, since 2012; *b* Saskatoon, Canada, 6 Aug. 1958; *s* of Gordon and Marian Shepherd; *m* 2009, Michaela Hegglin; one *s* one *d. Educ:* Univ. of Toronto (BSc Maths and Physics 1979); Massachusetts Inst. of Technol. (PhD Meteorol. 1984). Asst Prof., 1988–93, Associate Prof., 1993–96, Prof. of Physics, 1996–2012, Univ. of Toronto. Thomson Reuters highly-cited researcher in geoscis. *Recreations:* choral singing, walking. *Address:* Department of Meteorology, University of Reading, Earley Gate, Whiteknights, Reading, Berks RG6 6BB. *T:* (0118) 378 8957. *E:* theodore.shepherd@reading.ac.uk.

SHEPHERD-BARRON, Prof. Nicholas Ian, PhD; FRS 2006; Professor of Geometry, King's College London, since 2013; *b* 17 March 1955; *s* of late John Adrian Shepherd-Barron, OBE and (Jane Patricia) Caroline Shepherd-Barron; *m* 1988, Michelle Stern (marr. diss. 2016); one *d. Educ:* Winchester; Jesus Coll., Cambridge (BA 1976); Warwick Univ. (PhD 1981). Bonn Univ., 1981–82; Asst Prof., Columbia Univ., NY, 1982–86; Asst, then Associate, Prof., Univ. of Illinois, Chicago, 1986–93; University of Cambridge: Lectr, 1990–97; Reader, 1997–2000; Prof. of Algebraic Geometry, 2000–13; Fellow, Trinity Coll., Cambridge, 1990–. *Publications:* papers in mathematical jls. *Recreation:* learning the piano. *Address:* Department of Mathematics, Strand, King's College London, WC2R 2LS. *T:* (020) 7848 7126. *E:* nicholas.shepherd-barron@kcl.ac.uk.

SHEPLEY, Christopher John, CBE 2002; Principal, Chris Shepley Planning Consultancy; *b* 27 Dec. 1944; *s* of George Frederick Shepley and Florence Mildred Shepley (née Jepson); *m* 1st, 1967, Jennifer Webber (marr. diss. 1992); one *s* one *d*; 2nd, 1998, Janet Winifred Molyneux. *Educ:* Stockport Grammar Sch.; LSE (BA Hons Geography); Univ. of Manchester (DipTP). MRTPI. Manchester City Council, 1966–73; Greater Manchester County Council, 1973–85 (Dep. County Planning Officer, 1984–85); Plymouth City Council: City Planning Officer, 1985–92; Dir of Develt, 1992–94; Chief Planning Inspector and Chief Exec., Planning Inspectorate Agency, DoE, then DETR, then DTLR, then ODPM and Welsh Office, then Nat. Assembly for Wales, 1994–2002. Mem., Architecture Adv. Gp, Arts Council England (formerly Arts Council of England), 1992–2003. Chm., Bath Festivals Trust, 2003–06; Trustee, Theatres Trust, 2003–12. Chm., Nat. Retail Planning Forum, 2013–16. Pres., RTPI, 1989. Honorary Visiting Professor: Univ. of Manchester Dept of Planning and Landscape, 1990–94; Univ. of Westminster, 2007–. Hon. DSc West of England, 2001. *Publications:* The Grotton Papers, 1979; (contrib.) Plymouth: a maritime city in transition, 1990; Grotton Revisited, 2010; articles in planning and local govt jls. *Recreations:* music, watching sport, travel, walking. *Address:* Greenleas, Perrymead, Bath BA2 5AX. *T:* (01225) 834499.

SHEPPARD, Andy; jazz saxophonist and composer; *b* 20 Jan. 1957; *s* of Philip Charles Sheppard and Irene Sheppard (née Rhymes); *m* Rebecca Sian, *d* of Rod Allerton (marr. diss.); one *s* one *d*; *m* 2013, Sara Da Costa. *Educ:* Bishop Wordsworth Grammar Sch. Performances with bands incl. Urban Sax, In Co Motion, Big Co Motion, Inclassificable, Moving Image (tours of UK, Europe, world). Composer for TV, film, theatre and dance. Recordings incl. Introductions in the Dark, Soft on the Inside, In Co Motion, Rhythm Method, Inclassificable, Songs with Legs, Moving Image, Delivery Suite, Learning to Wave, Nocturnal Tourist, Music for a New Crossing, PS, Deep River, The Lost Chords find Paolo Fresu, On the Edge of a Perfect Moment, Movements in Colour, Trio Libero, Surrounded by Sea. *Address:* c/o Serious Ltd, 51 Kingsway Place, Sans Walk, EC1R 0LU.

SHEPPARD, Audley William; QC 2015; Partner, Clifford Chance LLP, since 1995; *b* Hastings, NZ, 19 Aug. 1960; *s* of William Searle Sheppard and Joyce Marion Sheppard (née Audley); *m* 1997, Amanda Caroline Carter; one *s* one *d. Educ:* Hereworth Sch., Havelock North, NZ; Lindisfarne Coll., Hastings, NZ; Victoria Univ. of Wellington (LLB Hons 1983; BCA 1984); Sidney Sussex Coll., Cambridge (LLM 1986). With Bell Gully, NZ, 1984–85; admitted as barrister and solicitor, NZ, 1985; joined Coward Chance, subseq. Clifford Chance LLP, 1986; admitted as solicitor, England and Wales, 1990. Chm., Bd, London Court of Internat. Arbitration, 2017– (Vice-Pres., 2012–16). Vis. Prof., Sch. of Internat. Arbitration, QMUL, 2011–. Co-Chair, Arbitration Cttee, Internat. Bar Assoc., 2006–08. *Recreations:* family, Rugby, sailing. *Address:* Clifford Chance LLP, 10 Upper Bank Street, Canary Wharf, E14 5JJ. *T:* (020) 7006 1000, *Fax:* (020) 7006 5555. *E:* audley.sheppard@cliffordchance.com. *Club:* Garrick.

SHEPPARD, Maurice Raymond, RWS, painter; President, Royal Society of Painters in Water-Colours, 1984–87; *b* 25 Feb. 1947; *s* of late Wilfred Ernest Sheppard and of Florence Hilda (née Morris). *Educ:* Loughborough; Kingston upon Thames (DipAD Hons 1970); Royal College of Art (MA 1973). ARWS 1974, RWS 1977, Vice-Pres., 1978–83, Trustee, 1983–95, Hon. Retired Mem., 2002; NEAC 2000–17, Hon. Retired Mem., 2018. One man exhibitions: New Grafton Gallery, 1979; Christopher Wood Gall., 1989; inaugural exhibn of L'Institut Européen de l'Aquarelle, Brussels, 1986; Casgliad Maurice Sheppard Collection, Nat. Library of Wales, 2007; group exhibns include Celebration of Welsh Contemp. Painting, Cyfartha Castle Mus. and Art Gall., 2019; works in: Royal Library, Windsor; BM; Contemporary Art Soc. for Wales; V&A; Nat. Museum of Wales; Beecroft Museum and Art Gallery, Southend; Birmingham City Mus. and Art Gallery; Glynn Vivian Mus., Swansea; Towner Art Gall., Eastbourne; Nat. Library of Wales; Tullie House, Carlisle; Topsham Mus., Devon; watercolour: The Golden Valley (for film, Shadowlands, 1993). British Instn Award, 1971; David Murray Landscape Award, 1972; Geoffrey Crawshay Meml Travelling Schol., Univ. of Wales, 1973. *Publications:* articles and essays in jls and catalogues; *relevant publication:* Maurice Sheppard, RWS, by Felicity Owen (Old Watercolour Society Club, vol. 59, 1984). *Recreations:* cycling, a small garden, the pursuit of quiet. *Address:* 33 St Martins Park, Haverfordwest, Pembrokeshire SA61 2HP. *T:* (01437) 762659.

**SHEPPARD, Prof. Michael Charles,** PhD; FRCP; Professor of Medicine, University of Birmingham, since 1986 (William Withering Professor of Medicine, 2000–08; Provost and Vice-Principal, 2008–13); *b* 24 Jan. 1947; *s* of Kenneth Alfred and Eileen Maude Sheppard; *m* 1973, Judith Elaine James; two *s* one *d*. *Educ:* Univ. of Cape Town (MB, ChB; PhD 1979). MRCP 1974, FRCP 1985. University of Birmingham: Wellcome Trust Sen. Lectr, Dept of Medicine, 1982–86; Hd, Dept of Medicine, 1992–2006; Vice Dean, 2000–07, Dean and Hd, 2007, Med. Sch.; Pro-Vice-Chancellor, 2007–08; Hon. Consultant Physician, Queen Elizabeth Hosp., Birmingham, 1982–2013. Pres., Assoc. of Physicians of GB and Ireland, 2009–10. Founder FMedSci, 1998. *Publications:* numerous contribs to learned jls and works on clinical and experimental endocrinology. *Recreations:* coastal walking, sport, glass and porcelain collecting. *Address:* University of Birmingham, Edgbaston, Birmingham B15 2TT. *T:* (0121) 414 5938. *Club:* Edgbaston Priory (Birmingham).

**SHEPPARD, Maj.-Gen. Peter John,** CB 1995; CBE 1991 (OBE 1982); Controller (Chief Executive), Soldiers, Sailors, Airmen and Families Association—Forces Help, 1996–2004; *b* 15 Aug. 1942; *s* of Kenneth Wescombe Sheppard and Margaret Sheppard; *m* 1964, Sheila Elizabeth Bell; one *s* one *d*. *Educ:* Welbeck Coll.; RMA Sandhurst; RMCS (BScEng 1st Class Hons London Univ.). Commnd Royal Engineers, 1962; Staff Coll., 1974 (psc); British Embassy, Washington, 1975; OC 29 Field Sqn, 1977 (despatches 1978); GSO1 Mil. Ops, MoD, 1980; CO 35 Engineer Regt, 1982; ACOS, HQ 1st (BR) Corps, 1984; Comdr Corps RE, 1st (BR) Corps, 1986; Dir, Army Plans and Programmes, MoD, 1989; COS HQ BAOR, 1991; Dir Gen. Logistic Policy (Army), MoD, 1993; COS HQ QMG, 1994. Special Advr, H of C Defence Select Cttee, 1997–2001. Dir, Army Charitable Adv. Co., 2004–08. Chairman: RE Officers Widows Soc., 2000–06; REACH Volunteering, 2009–12. Chm., ABF The Soldiers Charity (formerly Army Benevolent Fund), 2011–16 (Trustee, 2006–16). Gov., Royal Sch., Hampstead, 1997–2004 (Chm., Bd of Govs, 1999–2004). *Publications:* contribs to RE Jl, NATO's 16 Nations, Officer mag. *Recreations:* golf, philately, travel. *Address:* c/o Lloyds, 3 Allendale Place, Tynemouth, Tyne and Wear NE30 4RA. *Club:* Army and Navy.

**SHEPPARD, Thomas;** MP (SNP) Edinburgh East, since 2015; *b* Coleraine, NI, 6 March 1959; partner, Catherine Louise Burton; two step *d*. *Educ:* Aberdeen Univ. (MA Sociol. and Politics 1982). Vice Pres., NUS, 1982–84; work in PR and campaigns: Capa Ltd, 1984–86; Camden LBC, 1986–88; Islington LBC, 1988–93; Edinburgh DC, 1993–94; Asst Gen. Sec., Labour Party in Scotland, 1994–97; Dir, Stand Comedy Club, 1998–2015. Mem. (Lab) Hackney LBC, 1986–94 (Dep. Leader, 1990–94). *Address:* House of Commons, SW1A 0AA. *E:* tommy.sheppard.mp@parliament.uk.

**SHEPPERSON, Prof. George Albert,** CBE 1989; William Robertson Professor of Commonwealth and American History, University of Edinburgh, 1963–86, now Emeritus; *b* 7 Jan. 1922; *s* of late Albert Edward Shepperson and Bertha Agnes (*née* Jennings); *m* 1952, Joyce Irene (*née* Cooper) (*d* 2006); one *d*. *Educ:* King's Sch., Peterborough; St John's Coll., Cambridge (Schol.; 1st Class Hons: English Tripos, Pt I, 1942; Historical Tripos, Pt II, 1947); 1st Cl. CertEd (Cantab), 1948. Served War, commnd Northamptonshire Regt, seconded to KAR, 1942–46. Edinburgh University: Lectr in Imperial and American History, 1948, Sen. Lectr, 1960, Reader, 1961; Dean of Faculty of Arts, 1974–77. Visiting Professor: Roosevelt and Chicago Univs, 1959; Makerere Coll., Uganda, 1962; Dalhousie Univ., 1968–69; Rhode Is Coll., 1984; Vis. Scholar, W. E. B. DuBois Inst. for Afro-American Res., Harvard Univ., 1986–87; Lectures: Herskovits Meml, Northwestern Univ., 1966 and 1972; Livingstone Centenary, RGS, 1973; Soc. of the Cincinnati, State of Virginia, 1976; Sarah Tryphena Phillips, in Amer. Lit. and Hist., British Acad., 1979; Rhodes Commem., Rhodes Univ., 1981; Alan Graham Meml, Queen's Univ., Belfast, 1992. Chairman: British Assoc. for American Studies, 1971–74; Mungo Park Bicentenary Cttee, 1971; David Livingstone Documentation Project, 1973–89; Commonwealth Inst., Scotland, 1973–89; Mem., Marshall Aid Commemoration Commn, 1976–88. Hon. Life Mem., 2011, Hd of Roll of Honour, 2011, Soc. of Malawi. FEIS 1990. DUniv: York, 1987; Edinburgh, 1991; Hon. DLitt Malawi, 2002. Jt Editor, Oxford Studies in African Affairs, 1969–85. Dist. Africanist Award, African Studies Assoc. UK, 2008. *Publications:* Independent African: John Chilembwe, 1958, 6th edn 2000; David Livingstone and the Rovuma, 1964; many articles and chapters in learned jls, collaborative vols and encycs. *Recreations:* reading, music. *Address:* 15 Farleigh Fields, Orton Wistow, Peterborough PE2 6YB. *T:* (01733) 238772.

**SHER, Sir Antony,** KBE 2000; actor, writer, artist; *b* 14 June 1949; *s* of late Emmanuel and Margery Sher; civil partnership 2005, *m* 2015, Gregory Doran, *qv*. *Educ:* Sea Point Boys' Junior and High Schools, Cape Town; Webber-Douglas Acad. of Dramatic Art, London, 1969–71. Repertory seasons at Liverpool Everyman, Nottingham Playhouse and Royal Lyceum, Edinburgh; John, Paul, George, Ringo and Bert; Teeth and Smiles; Goose-Pimples; Torch Song Trilogy, Albery, 1985; National Theatre: True West; The Trial, The Resistible Rise of Arturo Ui, 1991; Uncle Vanya, 1992; Stanley, 1996 (also NY, 1997); Primo, 2004 (also Cape Town, and NY, 2005); Royal Shakespeare Co.: Associate Artist, 1984–2014; Hon. Associate Artist, 2014–; Richard III, Merchant of Venice, Twelfth Night, The Revenger's Tragedy, Molière, Tartuffe, Hello and Goodbye, Maydays, Red Noses, Singer, Tamburlaine the Great, Travesties, Cyrano de Bergerac, The Winter's Tale, Macbeth, The Roman Actor, The Malcontent, Othello, (co-prodn with Baxter Th., Cape Town) The Tempest, (dir) Breakfast with Mugabe, Henry IV Parts 1 and 2, Death of a Salesman, King Lear, Kunene and the King; Titus Andronicus, Johannesburg and RNT, 1995; Mahler's Conversion, Aldwych, 2001; (also writer) I.D., Almeida, 2003; Kean, Apollo, 2007; An Enemy of the People, Sheffield Crucible, 2010; Broken Glass, Tricycle Th., 2010, transf. Vaudeville, 2011; Travelling Light, NT, 2012; Hysteria, Theatre Royal, Bath, 2012, Hampstead Th., 2013; The Captain of Köpenick, NT, 2013; One for the Road, Harold Pinter Th., 2018; *films:* Shadey, 1986; The Young Poisoner's Handbook, 1995; Alive and Kicking, 1996; Mrs Brown, 1997; Shakespeare in Love, 1999; Churchill the Hollywood Years, 2004; *television series:* The History Man, 1980; The Jury, 2002; *television films:* The Land of Dreams, 1990; Genghis Cohen, 1994; Macbeth, 2001; Home, 2003; Primo, 2007; God on Trial, 2008; Joe Orton Laid Bare, 2017. Art exhibitions: Barbican, 1985; NT, 1996, 2009; London Jewish Cultural Centre, 2007; Sheffield Crucible Th., 2010; Coventry Herbert Gall., 2010; Royal Shakespeare Th., 2018. Hon. DLitt: Liverpool, 1998; Exeter, 2003; Warwick, 2007; Cape Town, 2010. Best Actor Awards: Drama Magazine, 1984; Laurence Olivier, 1985, 1997; Evening Standard, 1985; TMA, 1995; Evening Standard Peter Sellers Film Award, 1998; Best Solo Performance Awards, NY Drama Desk and Outer Critics Circle, 2006; Best Shakespearean Performance, Critics Circle, 2014. *Publications:* Year of the King, 1985; Middlepost (novel), 1988; Characters (paintings and drawings), 1989; Changing Step (TV filmscript), 1989; The Indoor Boy (novel), 1991; Cheap Lives (novel), 1995; (with Greg Doran) Woza Shakespeare!, 1996; The Feast (novel), 1998; Beside Myself (memoir), 2001; I.D. (stageplay), 2003; Primo (stageplay), 2005; Primo Time, 2005; The Giant (stageplay), 2007; Year of the Fat Knight: the Falstaff diaries, 2015; Year of the Mad King: the Lear diaries, 2018. *Address:* c/o Paul Lyon-Maris, Independent Talent Group Ltd, 40 Whitfield Street, W1T 2RH. *T:* (020) 7636 6565.

**SHER, Samuel Julius, (Jules);** QC 1981; a Deputy High Court Judge, Chancery Division and Commercial Court, 1989–2010; *b* 22 Oct. 1941; *s* of Philip and Isa Phyllis Sher; *m* 1965, Sandra Maris; one *s* two *d*. *Educ:* Athlone High Sch., Johannesburg; Univ. of the Witwatersrand (BComm, LLB); New Coll., Oxford (BCL). Called to the Bar, Inner Temple, 1968, Bencher, 1988; Hd of Chambers, Wilberforce Chambers, 2006–10. Special Advr to Attorney-Gen. of Singapore on Mgt of Complex Disputes, 2012–. Mem., Ethics Cttee, Tate, 2007–. Qualified Mediator, 2012; Arbitrator, Wilberforce Chambers, 2014–; Acting Judge, High Ct, Eastern Caribbean Supreme Court, 2016. *Recreation:* tennis. *Address:* 12 Constable Close, NW11 6TY. *T:* (020) 8455 2753.
*See also V. H. Sher.*

**SHER, Victor Herman, (Harold),** CA (SA); Executive Chairman, Amalgamated Metal Corporation Plc, since 2015 (Chief Executive, 1992–2015); *b* 13 Jan. 1947; *s* of Philip Sher and Isa Phyllis Sher; *m* 1979, Molly Sher; one *s* three *d*. *Educ:* King Edward VII Sch., Johannesburg; Univ. of the Witwatersrand, Johannesburg (BComm). Chartered Accountant, Fuller, Jenks Beechcroft, 1972–73; Amalgamated Metal Corporation: Taxation Manager, 1973; Finance Manager, 1977; Dir of Corporate Finance, 1978; Dir of Corporate Treasury, 1981; Finance Dir, 1983; Finance and Trading Dir, 1986; Gp Man. Dir, 1988–92. Chm. of Trustees, Amalgamated Metal Corp. Pension Scheme, 1983–91 (Trustee, 1978). *Recreation:* golf.
*See also S. J. Sher.*

**SHERATON, Kenneth Frederick;** a District Judge (Magistrates' Courts) for Cambridgeshire, since 2006; *b* 23 July 1955; *s* of Antony and Marian G. Sheraton; *m* 2003, Jayne Claire, *d* of Peter and Audrey Bustin; one *s* one *d* from a previous marriage. *Educ:* Kingsbury County Grammar Sch.; Bristol Poly. (Dip Magisterial Law 1980); Inns of Court Sch. of Law. Called to the Bar, Gray's Inn, 1983; admitted solicitor, 1991. Magistrates' Court Clerk, then Principal Court Clerk, 1976–90; Solicitor, Messrs Hodders, London, 1990–2000; freelance solicitor, 2000–06. Committee Member: Central and S Middx Law Soc., 1994–96; London Criminal Courts Solicitors Assoc., 2003–06. *Recreations:* most sports, watching Queens Park Rangers Football Club, travel, walking. *Address:* c/o Peterborough Magistrates' Court, The Court House, Bridge Street, Peterborough PE1 1ED. *T:* 0845 310 0575, *Fax:* (01733) 313749.

**SHERBOK, Dan C.;** *see* Cohn-Sherbok.

**SHERBORNE, Bishop Suffragan of,** since 2016; **Rt Rev. Karen Marisa Gorham;** *b* 24 June 1964. *Educ:* Mayflower Sch., Billericay; Trinity Coll., Bristol (BA 1995). Administrator: BTEC, 1982–86; RSA, 1986–88; ordained deacon, 1995, priest, 1996; Asst Curate, All Saints, Northallerton with Kirby Sigston, 1995–99; Priest-in-charge, St Paul's, Maidstone, 1999–2007; Area Dean, Maidstone, 2003–07; Asst Dir of Ordinands, Dio. of Canterbury, 2002–07; Archdeacon of Buckingham, 2007–16. Canon, Salisbury Cathedral, 2016–; Hon. Canon, Canterbury Cathedral, 2006–07. Mem., Gen. Synod of C of E, 2003–07 and 2010–16. FRSA 2011. *Recreations:* walking, travel, reading, theatre. *Address:* Sherborne House, Tower Hill, Iwerne Minster, Blandford Forum DT11 8NH. *T:* (01747) 811960.

**SHERBORNE, Archdeacon of;** *see* Sayer, Ven. P. J.

**SHERBORNE, Montague;** QC 1993; *b* 2 Dec. 1930; *s* of Abraham and Rose Sherborne; *m* 1963, Josephine Valerie Jay; two *s* one *d*. *Educ:* East Ham Grammar Sch.; New Coll., Oxford (BA Hons PPE); London Univ. (PGCE). Teaching, E London, 1954–58; called to the Bar, Middle Temple, 1960 (Harmsworth Schol.). *Recreations:* bridge, my grandchildren. *Address:* 47 Shirehall Park, NW4 2QN.

**SHERBOURNE OF DIDSBURY,** Baron *cr* 2013 (Life Peer), of Didsbury in the City of Manchester; **Stephen Ashley Sherbourne,** Kt 2006; CBE 1988; *b* 15 Oct. 1945; *s* of late Jack and Blanche Sherbourne. *Educ:* Burnage Grammar Sch., Manchester; St Edmund Hall, Oxford (MA PPE). Hill Samuel, 1968–70; Conservative Research Dept, 1970–75: Head of Economic Section, 1973–74; Asst Dir, 1974–75; Head of Rt Hon. Edward Heath's Office, 1975–76; Gallaher, 1978–82; Special Adviser to Rt Hon. Patrick Jenkin, (then) Sec. of State for Industry, 1982–83; Political Sec. to the Prime Minister, 1983–88; Sen. Corporate Communications Consultant, Lowe Bell Communications, 1988–92; Man. Dir, Lowe Bell Consultants, subseq. Bell Pottinger Consultants, 1992–99; Chm., Lowe Bell Political, subseq. Bell Pottinger Public Affairs, 1994–2001; Dir, Chime Communications plc, 2001–03; Chief of Staff to Leader of the Opposition, 2003–05. Director: Newscounter, 2007–10; Smithfield Consultants, 2006–15; Trufflenet, 2010–14; Chm., Interel Consulting UK, 2012–13. Member: Policy Adv. Bd, Social Mkt Foundn, 2007–; Edelman Adv. Bd, 2016–18. Trustee, China Oxford Scholarship Fund, 2006–11. *Recreations:* cinema, tennis, music, theatre. *Address:* House of Lords, SW1A 0PW. *E:* sherbournes@parliament.uk. *Clubs:* Reform, Beefsteak, Garrick.

**SHERCLIFF, Simon,** OBE 2004; HM Diplomatic Service; Director of National Security, Foreign and Commonwealth Office, since 2018; *b* 23 Dec. 1972; *s* of Robin Frank Shercliff and Judith Shercliff; *m* 2002, Emma Louise Cole; one *s* one *d*. *Educ:* High Ham Primary Sch.; Wells Cathedral Sch.; St Catharine's Coll., Cambridge (BA Hons Nat. Scis 1995). Chemistry teacher, VSO, Tanzania, 1995–97; FCO, 1998; Pol Officer, Tehran, 2000–03; Private Sec. to Prime Minister's Special Rep. for Iraq, Baghdad, 2003–04; Press Officer, FCO, 2004–06; Actg Press Sec. for Foreign Sec. and Dir Commns, 2006; Pol Officer, Kabul, 2007–08; First Sec., Washington, 2006–11; Dep. Hd, S Asia Dept, 2011–12, Hd, Counter-Terrorism Dept, 2012–14, FCO; Dep. High Comr, Abuja, 2014–16; Ambassador to Yemen, 2017–18. Trustee, Orphans in the Wild charity, Tanzania, 2005–. *Recreations:* biking, running and outdoor pursuits, cricket, Rugby, mountains, Tanzania, gardening. *Address:* c/o Foreign and Commonwealth Office, King Charles Street, SW1A 2AH. *T:* (020) 7008 2181. *E:* simon.shercliff@fco.gov.uk. *Clubs:* Hawks, Vann (Cambridge); 1890.

**SHERFIELD,** 3rd Baron *cr* 1964, of Sherfield-on-Loddon, Southampton; **Dwight William Makins;** *b* 2 March 1951; *yr s* of 1st Baron Sherfield, GCB, GCMG, FRS and Alice Brooks (*d* 1985), *e d* of Hon. Dwight Davis; *S* brother, 2006; *m* 1st, 1983, Penelope Massy Collier (marr. diss.); 2nd, 2010, Jennifer Rolls. *Educ:* Winchester; Christ Church, Oxford (MA). Man. Dir, John Govett & Co. Ltd, 1984–88; Chairman: Cadiz Inc., 1992–2002; Greenway plc, 1997–99; Dir, Ruffena Capital Ltd, 2013–. *Recreation:* National Hunt racing. *Heir:* none. *Club:* Boodle's.

**SHERGOLD, Peter Roger,** AC 2007 (AM 1996); PhD; Chancellor and Chairman, Board of Trustees, Western Sydney University (formerly University of Western Sydney), since 2011; *b* 27 Sept. 1946; *s* of Archibald Amos Shergold and Kathleen Dora Shergold; *m* Carol Green; one *d*. *Educ:* Univ. of Hull (BA 1967); Univ. of Illinois (MA 1968); LSE (PhD 1976). Hd, Dept of Econ. Hist., Univ. of NSW, 1985–87; Dir, Office of Multicultural Affairs, 1987–90; Chief Executive Officer: Aboriginal and Torres Strait Islander Commn, 1991–94; Comcare Australia, 1994–95; Comr, Public Service and Merit Protection Commn, 1995–98; Secretary: Dept of Employment, Workplace Relns and Small Business, 1998–2002; Dept of Educn, Sci. and Trng, 2002–03; Dept of the Prime Minister and Cabinet, 2003–08. Macquarie Gp Foundn Prof. (formerly Chief. Exec.), Centre for Social Impact, Univ. of NSW, 2008–12. Sen. Vis. Fellow, Singapore Civil Service Coll., 2008–.

**SHERIDAN**

Director: AMP Ltd, 2008–17; AMP Life Ltd, 2008–17; QuintessenceLabs, 2008–18; Corrs Chambers Westgarth, 2009–16; Veda Gp, 2013–16. Chairman: Australian Rural Leadership Foundn, 2008–11; Nat. Centre for Vocational Educn Res., 2009–18; NSW Public Service Commn Adv. Bd, 2011–; Aged Care Sector Cttee, 2014–15; Tertiary Educn Quality Standards Agency Adv. Council, 2014–15; Opal Aged Care, 2014–; Higher Educn Standards Panel, 2015–18; Centre for Social Impact, 2018–; Forum on Western Sydney Airport, 2016–; AMP Foundn, 2018–; Joblife, 2018–; Scanlon Inst. for Applied Cohesion Res. Member: Prime Minister's Indigenous Adv. Council, 2013–15; Council, State Library of NSW, 2015–. NSW Coordinator Gen. for Refugee Resettlement, 2017–. Director: Nat. Centre for Indigenous Excellence, 2008–12; Sir John Monash Foundn, 2009–14; Public Sector Renewal Bd, Qld, 2011–15; Chair, Ethics Cttee, Fundraising Inst. of Australia, 2009–11; Dep. Chair, Sydney Writers' Fest., 2011–14. Pres., Inst. of Public Admin Australia, 2017–. FASSA 2005. Centenary Medal, Australia, 2003. *Publications:* Working Class Life, 1982. *Recreations:* history, tennis, ski-ing. *T:* (2) 96787848. *E:* p.shergold@westernsydney.edu.au. *Club:* Commonwealth (Canberra).

**SHERIDAN, Christopher Julian;** Chairman, Yorkshire Building Society, 2001–06 (non-executive Director, 1995–2006); *b* 18 Feb. 1943; *s* of late Mark Sheridan and Olive Maud Sheridan (*née* Hobbs); *m* 1972, Diane Virginia (*née* Wadey); one *d*. *Educ:* Berkhamsted School. Joined Samuel Montagu & Co., 1962; Dir, 1974; Managing Dir, 1981; Chief Exec., 1984–94; Dep. Chm., 1988–94. Mem., Internat. Exec. Cttee, Lovells (formerly Lovell White Durrant), 1996–2006. Non-executive Director: Hanover Acceptances Ltd, 1995–; Prudential Bache International Bank, 1996–2004; Minerva plc, 1996–2008; Willmott Dixon Ltd, 1999–2003; ICBC Standard Bank Plc (formerly Standard Bank Ltd), 1999–2016; Alpha Bank London, 2004–18 (Chm., 2015–18); Willmott Dixon Hldgs Ltd, 2008–; Dep. Chm., Inspace plc, 2005–08. Mem., Adv. Bd, Alexander Proudfoot, 2010–12. *Recreations:* theatre, travel.

**SHERIDAN, Prof. Desmond John,** MD, PhD; FRCP; ARPS; Professor of Clinical Cardiology, Imperial College London Faculty of Medicine (formerly St Mary's Hospital School of Medicine), 1985–2009, now Emeritus; Consultant Cardiologist: St Mary's Hospital, 1985–2009 (Head of Academic Cardiology, 1985–2006); The Royal Brompton Hospital, 2006–09; *b* 10 Feb. 1948; *s* of Bernard Sheridan and Maureen Sheridan (*née* Kelly); *m* 1971, Jacqueline Hirschfeld; two *s*. *Educ:* Patrician Coll., Ballyfin; Trinity Coll. Dublin (MB, BAO, BCh 1971; MD 1974); Univ. of Newcastle upon Tyne (PhD 1982). MRCP 1974, FRCP 1987; LRPS 2013, ARPS 2015. British-American Fellow, Washington Univ., St Louis, 1978–79; Sen. Lectr in Cardiology, Univ. of Wales Coll. of Medicine, 1981–85; Consultant Cardiologist, UCH, Cardiff, 1981–85; Clinical Dean, ICSM, 1998–2001. Member: Nat. Forum for Prevention of Coronary Heart Disease, 1991–98; Physiology, Medicine and Infections Bd, MRC, 1997–2001. Principal Advr, Cardiovascular Science, Global R&D, Pfizer, 2002–05. John Banks Medal and Travelling Fellow, 1974. *Publications:* (contrib.) Early Arrhythmias from Myocardial Ischaemia, 1982; (contrib.) Autonomic Failure, 1988; (contrib.) Clinical Aspects of Cardiac Arrhythmias, 1989; (contrib.) Cerebrovascular Ischaemia: investigation and management, 1996; Left Ventricular Hypertrophy, 1998; Innovation in the Biopharmaceutical Industry, 2007; Medical Science in the 21st Century: sunset or new dawn, 2012; Evidence Based Medicine; best practice or restrictive dogma, 2016; peer reviewed articles relating to disturbances in heart rhythm and normal and abnormal growth of heart muscle. *Recreations:* country walking, making furniture, letter writing, photography. *Address:* 28 Chestnut View, Chilton Road, Chearsley, Bucks HP18 0DN. *E:* d.sheridan@imperial.ac.uk.

**SHERIDAN, Francis Anthony; His Honour Judge Sheridan;** DL; a Circuit Judge, since 2009; Resident Judge, Aylesbury and Amersham Crown Courts, since 2014; *b* Belfast, 24 Jan. 1957; *s* of Maurice Joseph Sheridan and Kathleen Sheridan (*née* O'Hare); *m* 1987, Colette Maggs; three *s* two *d*. *Educ:* Chelmer Inst. of Higher Educn (BA Hons; BL). Called to the Bar: Inner Temple, 1980; Ireland, 1991; NI, 1994; Recorder, 2005–09. Gov., Chesham Prep. Sch., 2001–14 (Chm., 2010–14). Hon. Recorder of Aylesbury, 2011–. DL Bucks, 2018. *Publications:* (contrib.) Inns of Court Advocacy Manual, 1987; (contrib.) Criminal Plea Bargains in the English and Polish Administration, 2011. *Recreations:* farming, power boating, gardening, sub-aqua diving. *Address:* Aylesbury Crown Court, County Hall, 38 Market Square, Aylesbury HP20 1XD.

**SHERIDAN, James;** *b* 24 Nov. 1952; *s* of Frank and Annie Sheridan; *m* 1977, Jean McDowell; one *s* one *d*. *Educ:* St Pius Secondary Sch., Drumchapel, Glasgow. Worked in manufacturing industry since leaving school, 1967; full-time Trade Union Official, TGWU, 1998–99. Mem. (Lab), Renfrewshire Council, 1999–2003, 2017–. MP (Lab) W Renfrewshire, 2001–05, Paisley and Renfrewshire N, 2005–15; contested (Lab) same seat, 2015. *Recreations:* leisure activities, current affairs.

**SHERIDAN, Prof. Lionel Astor,** PhD, LLD; Professor of Law, University College, Cardiff, 1971–88 (Acting Principal, 1980 and 1987); retired; *b* 21 July 1927; *s* of Stanley Frederick and Anne Agnes Sheridan; *m* 1948, Margaret Helen (*née* Béghin) (*d* 2017); one *s* (one *d* decd). *Educ:* Whitgift Sch., Croydon; University College London (LLB 1947; LLD 1969); Queen's Univ., Belfast (PhD 1953). Called to the Bar, Lincoln's Inn, 1948. Part-time Lectr, Univ. of Nottingham, 1949; Lectr, QUB, 1949–56; Prof. of Law, Univ. of Singapore (formerly Univ. of Malaya in Singapore), 1956–63; Prof. of Comparative Law, QUB, 1963–71. Hon. LLD Univ. of Singapore, 1963. *Publications:* Fraud in Equity, 1957; Constitutional Protection, 1963; Rights in Security, 1974; Injunctions and Similar Orders, 1999; *jointly:* The Cy-près Doctrine, 1959; Constitution of Malaysia, 1961, 5th edn 2004; Malaya, Singapore, The Borneo Territories, 1961; Equity, 1969, 3rd edn 1987; Survey of the Land Law of Northern Ireland, 1971; The Modern Law of Charities, 1971, 4th edn 1992; The Law of Trusts, 10th edn 1974, 12th edn 1993; The Comparative Law of Trusts in the Commonwealth and the Irish Republic, 1976; Digest of the English Law of Trusts, 1979; papers in jls. *Recreations:* reading, theatre-going. *Address:* 9 Warwick House, Westgate Street, Cardiff CF10 1DH. *Club:* Athenæum.

**SHERIDAN, Susan Elizabeth;** *see* Norman, S. E.

**SHERIDAN, Tommy;** Member for Glasgow, Scottish Parliament, 1999–2007 (Scot Socialist, 1999–2006, Solidarity Group, 2006–07); Co-Convenor, Solidarity (Scotland), 2006–16; *b* 1964; *m* 2000, Gail; one *d*. *Educ:* Lourdes Secondary Sch., Glasgow; Univ. of Stirling. Former Columnist: Daily Record; Sunday Herald; Scottish Socialist Voice. Mem. (Scot Mil Lab) Glasgow Council, 1992–2007. Nat. Convenor, Scottish Socialist Party, 1999–2004. Contested: (Scot Mil Lab) Glasgow Pollok, 1992; (Solidarity) Glasgow NE, Nov. 2009; (Trade Unionist and Socialist Coalition) Glasgow NE, 2010. Contested (No2EU) Scotland, Eur. Parlt, 2009. Pres., Anti-Poll Tax Fedn, 1989–92. *Publications:* (jtly) A Time to Rage, 1994; (with Alan McCombes) Imagine, 2000. *Address:* 2005 Paisley Road West, Glasgow G52 3TD.

**SHERLOCK,** family name of **Baroness Parminter**.

**SHERLOCK,** Baroness *cr* 2010 (Life Peer), of Durham in the County of Durham; **Maeve Christina Mary Sherlock,** OBE 2000; an Opposition Whip, and Opposition Spokesperson on Work and Pensions, House of Lords, since 2013; *b* 10 Nov. 1960; *d* of William and Roisin Sherlock. *Educ:* Our Lady's Convent, Abingdon; Univ. of Liverpool (BA Hons Sociol. 1984); Open Univ. (MBA 1997); Durham Univ. (MA 2007). Treas., Univ. of Liverpool Guild, 1984–85; National Union of Students: Exec. Officer, 1985–86; Treas., 1986–88; Pres., 1988–90; Dep. Dir, 1990–91, Dir, 1991–97, UKCOSA; Dir, NCOPF, 1997–2000; Advr to the Chancellor of the Exchequer, 2000–03; Chief Exec., British Refugee Council, 2003–06. Chair: Nat. Student Forum, 2008–10; Chapel Street Gp, 2011–. Member: Adv. Bd on Naturalisation and Integration, 2004–; Nat. Refugee Integration Forum, 2006–; Equality and Human Rights Commn, 2007–10. Non-executive Director: Financial Ombudsman Service, 2008–; Child Maintenance and Enforcement Commn, 2008–10. Mem., Exec. Bd, Eur. Assoc. for Internat. Educn, 1994–97. Dir, Endsleigh Insce, 1986–90. Member: Court, Univ. of Warwick, 1993–95; Assembly, Greenwich Univ., 1995–97; Mem. Council and Dir, St John's Coll., Durham Univ., 2008–; Gov., Sheffield Hallam Univ., 1997–2000. Trustee: Nat. Family and Parenting Inst., 1999–2000; Demos, 2004–07. Hon. Fellow, St Chad's Coll., Durham, 2006. DUniv Sheffield Hallam, 2000. *Recreations:* politics, theology, music, books, cooking. *Address:* c/o House of Lords, SW1A 0PW.

**SHERLOCK, David Christopher,** CBE 2006; FCGI, FCIFE; Chair, Prospects College of Advanced Technology, 2013–19; Partner, Beyond Standards Partnership, since 2018 (Director, Beyond Standards Ltd, 2007–18); *b* 6 Nov. 1943; *s* of Frank Ernest Sherlock and Emily Edna (*née* Johnson); *m* 1st, 1970, Jean Earl; 2nd, 1976, Cynthia Mary (*née* Hood); one *s* one *d*. *Educ:* Rutlish Sch., Merton; Newcastle upon Tyne College of Art and Industrial Design; Univ. of Nottingham (BA, MPhil). Nottingham Coll. of Art, 1966–70; Trent Polytechnic, 1970–74; Dep. Dir, Nat. College of Art and Design, Dublin, 1975–80; Principal, Winchester Sch. of Art, 1980–87; Exec. Chm., Hampshire Consortium for Art, Design and Architecture, 1985–87; Head of Central Saint Martin's Coll. of Art and Design and Asst Rector, London Inst., 1988–91; Dir of Develt, RCA, 1991–93; Sen. Inspector, Art, Design and Performing Arts, and for SE England, FEFCE, 1993–97; Chief Inspector and Chief Exec., Training Standards Council, 1997–2001; Chief Inspector of Adult Learning and Chief Exec., Adult Learning Inspectorate, 2000–07. Dep. Comr for Further Educn, 2015–16. Chm., GTA England, 2009–13. City and Guilds of London Institute: Mem., Fellowship Adv. Cttee for Educn, Health and Social Care, 2010–15; Chm., Quality and Standards Cttee, 2015–; Professional Lead, Rev. of Professionalism in Further Educn, 2012. Mem., QCA, 2006–09. Pres., NIACE, 2006–12 (Life Mem., 2012); Vice Chm., Inst. for FE, 2013–15. Chm., Nat. Skills Acad. for Social Care, 2008–12. FCGI 2006; FCIFE 2018. FRSA. Award for Services to Lifelong Learning, Assoc. of Coll. Mgt, 2007. *Publications:* (with N. Perry) Quality Improvement in Adult Vocational Education and Training: transforming skills for the global economy, 2008; (contrib.) Further Education: coming of age, 2015. *Address:* Poplar Farm, West Tytherley, Salisbury SP5 1NR.

**SHERLOCK, Neil Roger,** CBE 2015; Senior Adviser, PwC, since 2018 (Partner and Head of Reputational Strategy, 2013–17; Partner, Corporate Affairs, 2017–18); *b* Windlesham, Surrey, 13 Aug. 1963; *s* of Roger Sherlock and late Susan Sherlock; *m* 1994, Kathryn Jane, (Kate), Parminter (*see* Baroness Parminter); two *d*. *Educ:* Esher Co. Grammar Sch.; Esher Coll.; Christ Church, Oxford (BA 1st Cl. Hons PPE 1984; Pres., Oxford Union Soc., 1985). Peat Marwick Mitchell, later KPMG Peat Marwick, then KPMG, 1985–2011; Partner, Public Affairs, KPMG, 1999–2011; Vice Chm., KPMG Foundn, 2000–11; Special Advr and Dir of Govt Relns for the Dep. Prime Minister, 2012–13. Contested (Lib Dem) SW Surrey, 1992, 1997. Speechwriter for Rt Hon. Paddy Ashdown, MP, 1988–99, Rt Hon. Charles Kennedy, MP, 2001, Rt Hon. Sir Menzies Campbell, MP, 2006–07; Hd, Communications, leadership campaign of Nick Clegg, MP, 2007; Advr, TV Debates for Rt Hon. Nick Clegg, MP, 2010. Member: Armed Forces' Pay Review Body, 2001–07; Adv. Gp, Russell Commn, 2004–05; Commn of Inquiry into Future of Civil Society, 2008–10; Panel on Fair Access to the Professions, 2009; Wkg Gp, Everyone's Business, Centre for Social Justice, 2015–16; Adv. Bd, NPC, 2017–; Trust Adv. Bd, City of London Corp., 2017–18; Co-Chair, French Chamber of Commerce, Brexit Forum, 2017–. Mem. Adv. Bd, Echo Research, 2018–. Chairman: Enterprise Europe, 1995–2001; Working Families, 2009–11; Trustee: CentreForum, 2003–11; Heart of the City, 2005–11; HTI, 2007–10; Demos, 2008–11 and 2014–; PwC Foundn, 2014–18; Nat. Literacy Trust, 2017–; Member: Adv. Bd, Giving Campaign, 2000–03; Bd, London First, 2003–06; Bd of Govs, Inst. for Govt, 2009–11; Speakers' Adv. Council on Public Engagement, 2010–11; Women's Justice Taskforce, Prison Reform Trust, 2010–11. Pres., SW Surrey Lib Dems, 2007–. *Publications:* (ed with Neal Lawson) The Progressive Century: the future of the Centre-Left in Britain, 2001. *Recreations:* cricket, golf, football, reading, theatre. *Address:* The Corner House, Grosvenor Road, Godalming, Surrey GU7 1PA. *Clubs:* National Liberal; Godalming Cricket.

**SHERLOCK, Sir Nigel,** KCVO 2014; OBE 2003; Lord-Lieutenant, County of Tyne and Wear, 2000–15; *b* 12 Jan. 1940; *s* of late Horace Sherlock and Dorothea Sherlock (*née* Robinson); *m* 1966, Helen Diana Frances Sigmund; two *s* one *d*. *Educ:* Barnard Castle Sch.; Univ. of Nottingham (BA Law). Chief Exec., 1993–2002, Chm., 2002–05, Wise Speke; Director: Ockham Hldgs, 1993–98; Brewin Dolphin Holdings plc, 1998–2002; Brewin Dolphin Securities, 1998–2005; non-executive Director: London Stock Exchange, 1995–2001; Skipton Bldg Soc., 1998–2007. Mem. Bd, Assoc. of Private Client Investment Managers and Stockbrokers, 1993–2003 (non-exec. Dep. Chm., 1995–2003). Mem. Council, NE Regl Chamber of Commerce, 1997–2004 (Pres., 2000–01). Member: Council, Nat. Assoc. of Pension Funds, 1988–90; C of E Pension Bd, 1998–2009. Chm., Crown Nominations Commn for appt of Archbp of York, 2005; Member: Bishop's Council, Dio. Newcastle, 1975–94; Financial Adv. Cttee, Dean and Chapter of Durham Cathedral, 1997–2014; Chm. Council, Newcastle Cathedral, 2002–05 (Hon. Lay Canon, 2007–10, now Emeritus Lay Canon). Patron, Northumbrian Coalition Against Crime, 2001–15 (Vice-Patron, 1995–2001). Founder Mem., Community Foundn of Tyne and Wear, 1988 (Vice-Pres., 2001–15; Vice-Patron, 2015). Member: Council, 1984–2002 (Pro Chancellor and Chm., 1993–2002), Court, 2002–09 (Emeritus Mem., 2009), Univ. of Newcastle upon Tyne; Council, St John's Coll., Univ. of Durham, 1984–95 (Hon. Fellow, 1997); Bd of Govs, Royal GS, Newcastle upon Tyne, 1998–2006 (Chm., 2000–05). Member: Bd, N Music Trust, 2000–05 (Chm., Sage Gateshead Fundraising Cttee, 2000–05); Bd, Northern Sinfonia Orchestral Soc., 1974–95 (Chm., 1990–95); Northern Sinfonia Develt Trust, 1980–2001 (Trustee, 1980–2001; Chm., 1981–2001). Pres., Northumberland Co. Scouts, 2000–12 (Mem. Council, 1980–98, Chm., 1990–97; Silver Wolf, 2007). Co-Pres., RFCA, N of England, 2001–14. Jt Pres., St John Ambulance, Northumbria, 2001–12. Trustee: Bede Monastery Mus. Trust, 1980–90 (Chm., 1985–90); William Leech Charity, 1990–2019. Hon. Mem., Trinity House, Newcastle upon Tyne, 1995–. CCMI (CIMgt 2000). Tyne and Wear: High Sheriff, 1990–91, DL, 1995–2000, JP 2001–15. Hon. Colonel: Royal Marines Reserve Tyne, 2003–12; Northumbrian Univs OTC, 2003–08. Freeman: City of London, 2000; City of Newcastle, 1985; Liveryman, Scriveners' Co. of Newcastle, 1985–. Hon. Winterbottom Fellow, S Tyneside Coll., 2015. Hon. DCL: Newcastle, 2002; Northumbria, 2006; Hon. DBA Sunderland, 2015. KStJ 2002. Lifetime Achievement Award: NE Businessman of the Year Awards, 2014; Univ. of Nottingham, 2017. *Recreations:* family, the countryside, listening to music, theatre. *Address:* 14 North Avenue, Gosforth, Newcastle upon Tyne NE3 4DS. *T:* (0191) 285 4379. *Club:* Northern Counties (Newcastle upon Tyne).

**SHERMAN, Prof. Lawrence William**, PhD; Wolfson Professor of Criminology, 2009–17, now Emeritus, Director, Jerry Lee Centre of Experimental Criminology, since 2008, Director, Cambridge Centre for Evidence-Based Policing, since 2014, and Chair, Cambridge Police Executive Programme, 2014–20 (Director, 2007–14), University of Cambridge (Director, Institute of Criminology, 2012–17); Fellow of Darwin College, Cambridge, 2009–17; *b* 25 Oct. 1949; *s* of Donald L. and Margaret H. Sherman; *m* 1st, 1973, Eva Fass (marr. diss. 2010); one *s* one *d*; 2nd, 2010, Heather Strang. *Educ:* Denison Univ. (BA High Hons Political Sci. 1970); Univ. of Chicago (MA Social Sci. 1970); Darwin Coll., Cambridge (Dip. Criminol. 1973); Yale Univ. (PhD Sociol. 1976); Univ. of Pennsylvania (MA Hons 1999); Univ. of Cambridge (MA Hons 2009). Sloan Foundn Urban Fellow, Office of the Mayor, NYC, 1970–71; Prog. Res. Analyst, NYC Police Dept, 1971–72; Ford Foundn Fellow, Cambridge Univ., 1972–73; Associate-in-Res., Yale Univ., 1974–76; Asst to Associate Prof. of Criminal Justice, SUNY at Albany, 1976–82; University of Maryland, College Park: Associate Prof., 1982–84; Prof., 1984–98; Dist. Univ. Prof., 1998–99 and 2010–; Chair, Dept of Criminol. and Criminal Justice, 1995–99; University of Pennsylvania: Albert M. Greenfield Prof. of Human Relns, 1999–2007; Prof. of Sociol., 1999–2009; Director: Fels Inst. of Govt, 1999–2005; Jerry Lee Center of Criminol., 2000–10; Prof. of Criminol., 2003–09. Seth Boyden Dist. Vis. Prof., Rutgers Univ., 1987; Adjunct Prof., Regulatory Institutions Network, ANU, 1994–. Dir of Res., Police Foundn, Washington, 1979–85; Pres., Crime Control Inst., Washington, 1985–95; Scientific Dir, Reintegrative Shaming Experiments, Australian Fed. Police, 1995–2000; Co-Dir, Justice Res. Consortium, UK, 2001–07; Co-Dir, Mid-Career Trng Prog. Phase IV, Nat. Police Acad. of India, 2010–12; non-exec. Dir, Coll. of Policing, 2013–. Mem., Adv. Bd, HM Inspectorate of Constabulary, 2014–. Co-Chm., Jury, Stockholm Prize in Criminol., 2006–. Founding Pres., Acad. Exptl Criminol., 1998 (Fellow 1999); McCord Award, 2006); President: Internat. Soc. of Criminol., 2000–05; Amer. Soc. of Criminol., 2001–02 (Fellow 1994; Sutherland Prize, 1999); Amer. Acad. Political and Social Sci., 2001–05 (Sellin Fellow, 2009); Hon. Pres., British Soc. of Evidence-Based Policing, 2010–. FRSA 2007 (Life Fellow 2011). Ed.-in-Chief, Cambridge Jl of Evidence-Based Policing, 2017–. Hon. PhD (Social Sci.) Stockholm, 2013; Hon. DHL Denison, 2014. Beccaria Medal, German Soc. of Criminol., 2009; Boruch Award, Campbell Collaboration, 2010; Benjamin Franklin Medal, RSA, 2011; Jerry Lee Lifetime Achievement Award in Experimental Criminol., 2012; Dist. Achievement in Evidence-Based Crime Policy, George Mason Univ., 2013; Outstanding Experiment Award, Div. of Experimental Criminol., 2014; Lifetime Achievement Award, Div. of Policing, Amer. Soc. Criminol., 2016; Wilbur Lucius Cross Medal, Yale Univ. Grad. Sch., 2017; Univ. Medal, Univ. of Bialystock, 2017. Knight Comdr, Order of the Polar Star (Sweden), 2016. *Publications:* Scandal and Reform: controlling police corruption, 1978; Policing Domestic Violence: experiments and dilemmas, 1992; (jtly) Preventing Crime: what works, what doesn't, what's promising, 1997; (ed jtly) Evidence-Based Crime Prevention, 2002; (with Heather Strang) Restorative Justice: the evidence, 2007; contribs to learned jls incl. Amer. Sociol. Rev., Criminology, Jl Amer. Med. Assoc. *Recreations:* running, walking, rowing, swimming, music. *Address:* Institute of Criminology, University of Cambridge, Sidgwick Avenue, Cambridge CB3 9DA. *Clubs:* Athenæum; Cosmos (Washington).

**SHERR, Prof. Avrom Hirsh**, PhD; Consultant Director, Independent Peer Review of Legal Aid Providers, Legal Aid Agency, since 2013; Woolf Professor of Legal Education, Institute of Advanced Legal Studies, University of London, 1995–2014, now Emeritus Professor (Director, 2004–14); *b* 28 March 1949; *s* of Louis Julian Sherr and Charlotte Maissel; *m* 1974, Lorraine Isaacs; three *s* one *d*. *Educ:* Carmel Coll. (Sch. Bursary); London Sch. of Econs (LLB 1971); Sch. of Law, Univ. of Warwick (PhD 1992). Admitted solicitor, 1974, Coward Chance; University of Warwick: Lectr in Law, Sch. of Law, 1974–90; Dir, Legal Practice, 1976–90; University of Liverpool: Alsop-Wilkinson Prof. of Law, 1990–95; Dir, Centre for Business and Professional Law, 1991–95; Associate Dean, 2010–12, Dep. Dean, 2011–12, Sch. of Advanced Study, Univ. of London. Dir of Trng, Macfarlanes, 1988–2013. Vis. Professor: Sch. of Law, Univ. of San Francisco, 1981; Sch. of Law, UCLA, 1984–85; Univ. of Essex, 1995–2000; Penn State Dickinson Sch. of Law, 2004–05; Univ. of Westminster, 2014–18; summer schools: Sch. of Law, Univ. of Bridgeport, 1984; New York Law Sch., 1985; Law Sch., Touro Coll., 1987; William Mitchell Law Sch., 1987, 1988; Hon. Prof., UCL, 1995–2013; Vis. Fellow, Law Sch., LSE, 2013–14. Adviser to: Amer. Bar Assoc., Central and Eastern Eur. Law Initiative on legal competence in Eastern Europe, 2003; EC on changes to the system of legal aid in Turkey, 2004; British Council and British Embassy on judicial corruption in Bulgaria, 2006; British Council, Santiago and Public Defender Office, Chile on monitoring professional competence, 2006–08; Korean Legal Aid Corp. on develt of legal aid, 2009; People's Republic of China, China-EU Access to Justice Prog., 2015–18; USAid PROLog project for Legal Aid in Georgia, 2015–18; European Council Working Gp on Legal Aid in Armenia, Azerbaijan, Georgia, Moldova and Ukraine, 2015–16; Architects Registration Bd 2015; British Acupuncture Council, 2016; Council of Europe - Ukrainian Legal Aid, 2019; Chairman: Adv. Bd and Strategy Cttee, UK Centre for Legal Educn, 2007–11; Adv. Panel, Office of the Adjudicator for Higher Educn, 2009–13; Advice Quality Standard Project Adv. Cttee, 2012–. Member: Exec. Cttee, Law Centres Fedn, 1979–83; Ethnic Minorities Adv. Cttee, Judicial Studies Bd, 1991–94; Lord Chancellor's Adv. Cttee on Legal Educn and Conduct, 1995–2000; Exec. Cttee, Soc. of Advanced Legal Studies, 1997–; Consumer Adv. Bd, Legal Services Complaints Comr, 2005–11; Save the Children Ethics Cttee, 2017–. Law Society of England and Wales: Member: Internat. Human Rights Gp, 1987–90; Trng Contracts Cttee, 1992–94; Equal Opportunities Cttee, 1994–2002; Ethics Forum, 2004. Gov., Heythrop Coll., Univ. of London, 2002–07. Chm., Hamlyn Trust, 2009–15, 2019–; Trustee, Jewish Law Pubn Fund, 1990–2011. Chm., London Jewish Chaplaincy Bd, 2001. Minister, Coventry Hebrew Congregation, 1976–90; Hon. Minister, Wembley United Synagogue, 1986–87. Chm., Ner Yisrael Community, 2005–07 (Gabay, 2002–05). Founder Ed., Internat. Jl of Legal Profession, 1993–. *Publications:* Client Interviewing for Lawyers: an analysis and guide, 1986, 2nd edn as Client Care for Lawyers: an analysis and guide, 1999; Freedom of Protest, Public Order and the Law, 1989; (jtly) Transaction Criteria: quality assurance standards in legal aid, 1992; Advocacy, 1993; (jtly) Lawyers—The Quality Agenda, 2 vols, 1994; (ed with I. Manley) Advising Clients with AIDS/HIV—A Guide for Lawyers, 1998; (jtly) Willing Blindness?: OSS complaints handling procedures, 2000; (jtly) Quality and Cost, Final Report on the Contracting of Civil, Non-Family Advice and Assistance Pilot, 2001; (jtly) Where Science Meets Law: an inquiry into training and qualification for patent agents and trade mark attorneys, 2003; The Other Side of the Mountain: an evaluation of the Overberg Access to Justice programme in South Africa, 2003; (jtly) The Regulation of Private English Language Teaching Institutions, 2004; (ed) Legal Aid, vol. 27 (3), in Halsbury's Laws of England, 4th edn, 2006 issue; (jtly) Evaluation of the Public Defender Service in England and Wales, 2007; Religion and Human Rights: redressing the balance, 2007; (jtly) Effectiveness of Online Dispute Resolution in the County Court, 2009; Decline of Legal Aid, Litigants in Person and Independence of the Judiciary, 2010; Policing the Conflict in South Africa: Tony Mathews and the Pietermaritzburg Conference, 2011; Setting Standards—The Legal Education and Training Review, 2013; Tesco Law and Tesco Lawyers: will our needs change if the market develops?, 2013; (jtly) Workforce Education and Training Arrangements in Regulated Entities, 2014; The Common Law in Europe—Legal Education in the Global Context, 2015; (ed jtly) Too Many Lawyers?, 2016; Legal Education at the Crossroads, 2017; numerous articles on legal profession, legal ethics, legal services and legal aid in learned jls. *Recreations:* wadi walking in Eilat mountains, tennis, scuba diving, entertaining grandchildren Zac, Lilia and Charlie Jack. *Address:* Institute of Advanced Legal Studies, Charles Clore House, 17 Russell Square, WC1B 5DR. *T:* (020) 7862 5859, *Fax:* (020) 7862 5850. *E:* Avrom.Sherr@sas.ac.uk, Avrom.Sherr@gmail.com. *Club:* Ner Yisrael Kiddush.

**SHERRARD, Charles Isaac**; QC 2012; a Recorder, since 2019; *b* London, 17 Feb. 1965; *s* of Barry Sherrard and Jean Sherrard; *m* 1991, Sara Melanie Tropp; one *s* two *d*. *Educ:* University College Sch., Hampstead; Univ. of East Anglia (LLB Hons). Called to the Bar, Middle Temple, 1986; in practice as a barrister, 1986–. *Recreations:* Hertfordshire League tennis player, Middlesex League cricketer, regular golfer. *Address:* 8 Sunnyfield, NW7 4RG. *T:* 07590 530243. *E:* charlie@sherrard.co.uk. *Club:* MAL Cricket.

**SHERRARD, Simon Patrick**; DL; Chairman, Bibby Line Group Ltd, 1999–2015; *b* 22 Sept. 1947; *s* of Patrick Sherrard and Angela Beatrice Sherrard (*née* Stacey); *m* 1975, Sara Anne Stancliffe; one *s* three *d*. *Educ:* Eton Coll. Samuel Montagu & Co. Ltd, 1968–74; Jardine Matheson & Co. Ltd, 1974–85; Man. Dir, Bibby Line Group Ltd, 1985–99; Mem., PLA, 2000–09 (Chm., 2001–09). Chairman: Abacus Syndicates Ltd, 1999–2002 (Dir, 1997–2002); A & P Group, 2002–09; Johnson Service Gp plc, 2004–08 (Dir, 2000–08); Cooke Bros (Tattenhall) Ltd, 2005 (Dir, 1991–2005). Dir and Trustee, Lloyds Register, 2005–08 (Dep. Chm., 2002–05); Pres., Chamber of Shipping, 2000–01; UK Rep. on Exec. Cttee, Internat. Chamber of Shipping, 1993–2001 (Vice Chm., 1999–2001). Elder Brother, Corp. of Trinity House, 2001–. Mem. Adv. Bd, Liverpool Business Sch., 1996–2001; Member Council: Liverpool Sch. of Tropical Medicine, 1998–2007 (Dep. Chm., 2002–07); Mission to Seafarers, 1999–2015; White Ensign Assoc., 2004–; RNLI, 2006–16 (Vice Pres., 2016–). Chm., Merlin MS Therapy Centre Ltd, 2009–19. Trustee: Royal Liverpool Philharmonic Hall Diamond Jubilee Foundn, 1996–2005; Plymouth Marine Lab., 2012–; Nat. Maritime Mus., Cornwall, 2014– (Dep. Chm., 2017–19; Chm., 2019–). Liveryman, Co. of Shipwrights, 1993– (Prime Warden, 2010); Freeman, Co. of Watermen and Lightermen, 2002–. High Sheriff, Cheshire, 2004; DL Cornwall, 2014. *Recreations:* golf, tennis, breeding rare sheep. *E:* simon@sherrard1.demon.co.uk. *Clubs:* Boodle's, Beefsteak, MCC.

**SHERRATT, Antoinette**; *see* Mackeson-Sandbach, A.

**SHERRATT, Brian Walter**, OBE 1995; PhD; researcher in political science, since 2010; Headmaster, Great Barr School, 1984–2005; *b* 28 May 1942; *er s* of Walter Eric Sherratt and Violet Florence Sherratt (*née* Cox-Smith); *m* 1966, (Pauline) Brenda Hargreaves; two *s* two *d*. *Educ:* Univ. of Leeds (BA Hons 1964, PGCE 1965); Inst. of Educn, Univ. of London (AcDipEd 1973, MA 1976); Univ. of Birmingham (PhD 2004). Asst Master, Normanton GS, 1965–67; Hd, Religious Studies Dept, Selby GS, 1967–70; Avery Hill College of Education: Sen. Lectr in Religious Studies and Warden, 1970–73 (Sen. Warden, 1972–73); Warden, Mile End Teachers' Centre, 1971–73; concurrently Asst Master, Kidbrooke Sch., London, 1970–71; Sen. Master, 1973–76, Dep. Headmaster, 1976–79, Sandown Court Sch., Tunbridge Wells; Headmaster and Warden, Kirk Hallam Sch. and Community Centre, Ilkeston, Derbys, 1979–84. Mem. Court, 1986–90, Hon. Lectr, Sch. of Educn, 1988–, Univ. of Birmingham; Mem., Academic Adv. Council, Univ. of Buckingham, 2005–; Visiting Lecturer: Univ. of Bristol, 2001–02; Univ. of Asmara, 2001–02. Member: Centre for Policy Studies, 1994–; Politeia, 1995–; Civitas, 2000–; Educn Commn, 2003–05. Chairman: Eco-Schs Adv. Panel, 1997–2001; Green Code for Schs Adv. Panel, 1998–2001; non-executive Director: Going for Green, 1994–98 (Mem., Organising Cttee, 1994–96); Envmtl Campaigns, 1998–2005 (Trustee, Pension Fund, 1999–2005; Mem., Resources Cttee, 2002–03, Audit Cttee, 2003–05; Vice-Chm., 2003–05; Chm., Devolution Cttee, 2004–05). Founder, Sherratt Sch. Leadership Lab. website, 2012. Chm., Nottingham Park Estate Ltd, 2008–11 (Dir, 2005–11). Mem., Magistrates' Assoc., 2006–; Magistrate Trng Observer, Nottingham Bench, 2008–12. Mem., T. S. Eliot Soc., 2012– FCMI (FIMgt 1984); FRSA 1984. Freeman: City of London, 2012; Liveryman, Educators' Co., 2013– (Freeman, Guild of Educators, 2003). JP Notts, 2006. Queen Mother's Birthday Award for the Envmt, 1999; Best Thesis Award, British Educnl Leadership Mgt and Admin Soc., 2005; George Cadbury Prize in Educn, 2005. *Publications:* Gods and Men: a survey of world religions, 1971; Local Education Authorities Project, 1988; Opting for Freedom: a stronger policy on grant-maintained schools, 1994; Grant-Maintained Status: considering the options, 1994; (jtly) A Structured Approach to School and Staff Development: from theory to practice, 1996; (jtly) Headteacher Appraisal, 1997; (jtly) Radical Educational Policies and Conservative Secretaries of State, 1997; (jtly) Policy, Leadership and Professional Knowledge in Education, 1999; Educational Leadership: effective use of resources in pursuit of leadership aims, 2008; contrib. to TES, etc. *Recreations:* opera, buildings, reading, antiques. *Club:* Athenaeum.

**SHERRATT, Prof. David John**, PhD; FRS 1992; FRSE; Professor of Biochemistry, University of Oxford, since 2010; Fellow, Linacre College, Oxford, since 1994; *b* 14 June 1945; *m* 1st, 1968, Susan Bates (marr. diss. 1992); one *s* two *d*; 2nd, 1992, Dr Lidia Kamilla Arciszewska; one *d*. *Educ:* Manchester Univ. (BSc 1st Cl. Biochem. 1966); Edinburgh Univ. (PhD Molecular Biol. 1969). FRSE 1984. Post-doctoral Fellow, Univ. of California, 1969–71; Lectr in Microbial Genetics, Univ. of Sussex, 1971–80; Prof. of Genetics, Inst. of Genetics, Glasgow Univ., 1980–93; Iveagh Prof. of Microbiol., 1994–2010, and Hd, Microbiol. Unit, Univ. of Oxford. Mem., EMBO, 1983. *Publications:* scientific papers and reviews; editor of several jls. *Recreations:* variety of outdoor pursuits. *Address:* Linacre College, Oxford OX1 3JA.

**SHERRIFF, Paula Michelle**; MP (Lab) Dewsbury, since 2015; *b* Alexandria, Scotland. Victim support rôle, Police Service, 1993–2003; community healthcare, NHS, 2003–13; private healthcare sector, 2013–15. Chair, Pontefract Business Forum. Mem. (Lab) Wakefield Council, 2012–15. Shadow Minister for Women and Equalities, 2016–17. *Address:* House of Commons, SW1A 0AA. *E:* paula.sherriff.mp@parliament.uk.

**SHERRINGTON, Prof. David**, PhD; FRS 1994; FInstP; Wykeham Professor of Physics, University of Oxford, 1989–2008, now Emeritus; Fellow, New College, Oxford, 1989–2008, now Emeritus (Sub-Warden, 2006–07); *b* 29 Oct. 1941; *s* of James Arthur and Elfreda Sherrington; *m* 1966, Margaret Gee-Clough; one *s* one *d*. *Educ:* St Mary's Coll.; Univ. of Manchester (BSc 1st Cl. Hons Physics, 1962; PhD Theoretical Physics, 1966). FInstP 1974. Asst Lectr in Theoretical Physics, 1964–67, Lectr, 1967–69, Univ. of Manchester; Asst Res. Physicist, UCSD, 1967–69, Lectr in Theor. Solid State Phys, 1969–74, Reader in Theor. Solid State Phys, 1974–83, Prof. of Phys, 1983–89, Imperial Coll., Univ. of London; Cadre Supérieur, Inst Laue Langevin, Grenoble, France, 1977–79; Ulam Scholar, Los Alamos Nat. Lab., USA, 1995–96. Bakerian Lect., Royal Soc., 2001; Scott Lectures, Cambridge, 2008. Delegate, OUP, 2001–06. MAE 2012. Fellow: Amer. Physical Soc., 1985; Eur. Acad. of Scis. Editor, Advances in Physics, 1984–; Hon. Editor, Jl of Physics A: Mathematical and General, 1989–93. Hon. MA Oxford, 1989. Dirac Medal and Prize, Inst. of Physics, 2007; Blaise Pascal Medal in Physics, Eur. Acad. of Scis, 2010. *Publications:* (ed jtly) Phase Transitions in Soft Condensed Matter, 1990; (ed jtly) Spontaneous Formation of Space-Time Structures and Criticality, 1991; (ed jtly) Phase

**SHERRINGTON**, *continued* Transitions and Relaxation in Systems with Competing Energy Scales, 1993; (ed jtly) Physics of Biomaterials: fluctuations, self-assembly and evolution, 1995; (ed jtly) Dynamical properties of unconventional magnetic systems, 1998; (ed jtly) Stealing the Gold, 2004; papers in learned jls. *Recreations:* wine tasting, travel, theatre, walking, ski-ing, gardening. *Address:* c/o Rudolf Peierls Centre for Theoretical Physics, Clarendon Laboratory, Parks Road, Oxford OX1 3PU.

**SHERRINGTON, Rt Rev. John Francis**; Auxiliary Bishop of Westminster, (RC), since 2011; Titular Bishop of Hilta, since 2011; *b* Leicester, 5 Jan. 1958; *s* of Frank and Catherine Sherrington. *Educ:* Wyggeston Boys' Grammar Sch., Leicester; Queens' Coll., Cambridge (BA Maths 1980); All Hallows Coll., Dublin; Gregorian Univ., Rome (STL 1990). Arthur Andersen Mgt Consultants, London, 1980–82; ordained priest, 1987; Asst Priest, St Anne's, Ratcliffe on Trent, 1987–88; Lecturer in Moral Theology, Director of Studies and Formation Director: All Hallows Coll., Dublin, 1990–98; St John's Seminary, Wonersh, 1998–2004; Parish Priest: Our Lady of Lourdes, Derby, 2004–09; Good Shepherd Parish, Nottingham, 2009; Mem., Bishop's Council and Episcopal Vicar for Derbyshire, 2008–11; Moderator of the Curia, 2016–. Chairman: Marriage and Family Life Commn, Archdio. of Nottingham, 2008–11; Educn Commn, Archdio. of Westminster, 2011–. Member: Bioethics Cttee, British Assoc. Sovereign Mil. Order of Malta, 2004–12; Bishops' Conf. Healthcare Ref. Gp, 2005; Internat. Methodist Roman-Catholic Dialogue, 2011–16 (Chair, 2017–); Mem., 2004–11, Co-Chair, 2011–14, British Methodist-Roman Catholic Cttee; Bishops' Conf. Dept for Catholic Educn and Formation, 2011–14; Catholic Bishops' Conf. Dept for Social Justice (formerly for Christian Responsibility and Citizenship), 2014–. Trustee and Mem., Mgt Cttee, Catholic Educn Service of Eng. and Wales, 2012–14; Trustee: Dio. of Westminster, 2011–; CAFOD, 2015–16; Beda Coll., 2016–; All Hallows Coll., Dublin, 2018–. Gov., Anscombe Bioethics Centre, 2015–. Pres., Nat. Bd of Religious Inspectors and Advrs, 2011–14. *Address:* Archbishop's House, Ambrosden Avenue, SW1P 1QJ. *T:* (020) 7798 9075. *E:* johnsherrington@rcdow.org.uk.

**SHERRINGTON, Patrick Philip**; Regional Managing Partner, Asia Pacific and Middle East, 2013–18, and Member, International Management Committee, 2010–18, Hogan Lovells International LLP, Consultant, 2018–19; *b* Portsmouth, 1 Nov. 1951; *s* of John Sherrington and Peggy Sherrington; *m* 1976, (Sheila) Joy Smallman; two *s* one *d. Educ:* St John's Coll., Southsea; Univ. of Exeter (LLB); Univ. of Illinois (LLM). Teaching Fellow, Univ. of Illinois Coll. of Law, 1975–76; Vis. Asst Prof. of Law, Depaul Univ., Chicago, 1976–77; admitted solicitor, England, 1980, Hong Kong, 1987, and Australia, 1990; Lovell White & King, then Lovell White Durrant, later Lovells, subseq. Hogan Lovells Internat. LLP: Partner, 1985–2018; seconded to Hong Kong office, 1989–96; Mem., Internat. Exec., 2000–10; Global Hd of Dispute Resolution, 2000–13. Member: Council, Law Soc. of Hong Kong, 1990–96 (Vice Pres., 1993–96); Council, Inter Pacific Bar Assoc., 1991–96, 2005–09. Chm., Pacific Rim Adv. Council, 2008–10; Mem. Bd, CEDR, 2002–17. Chm. Council, Wycombe Abbey Sch., 2010–; Gov., Sutton Valence Sch., 2018–. Director: Barefoot Coll. Internat., India, 2018–; Mother's Choice, Hong Kong, 2018–. *Recreations:* family first, keeping busy and staying relevant, education, art, opera, sport, Chelsea FC. *Address:* 12 St James's Gardens, W11 4RD; Benenden House, Rolvenden Road, Benenden, Kent TN17 4BU. *Clubs:* Carlton, Reform, Arts; Hong Kong.

**SHERRINGTON, Air Vice-Marshal Terence Brian**, CB 1997; OBE 1984; Air Officer Administration and Air Officer Commanding Directly Administered Units, Strike Command, 1994–97; *b* 30 Sept. 1942; *s* of Thomas and Edna Sherrington; *m* 1969, Anne Everall; one *s* one *d. Educ:* Ottershaw Sch.; Westminster Technical Coll. Commnd RAF, 1963; served Aden, Sharjah, Germany and UK, 1963–78; RAF Staff College, 1979; MoD, 1980–81; OC Admin Wing, RAF Leuchars, 1981–83; OC, RAF Hereford, 1983–85; RCDS, 1986; Sen. Officer Admin, HQ 11 Gp, 1987–88; Dir of Personnel (Ground), MoD, 1988–91; AOA and AOC Support Units, RAF Support Comd, 1992–93; Head, RAF Admin. Br., 1992–97. Dir Welfare, RAF Benevolent Fund, 1998–2006; Mem. Council, Wycombe Abbey Sch., 1998–2015; Gov., Duke of Kent Sch., 2003–08. Freeman, City of London, 2002; Liveryman, Tallow Chandlers' Co., 2002. *Recreations:* fishing, golf, Rugby. *Address:* c/o Lloyds, Shipston-on-Stour Branch, PO Box 99 BX1 1LT. *Club:* Royal Air Force.

**SHERSTON-BAKER, Sir Robert (George Humphrey)**, 7th Bt *cr* 1796, of Dunstable House, Richmond, Surrey; *b* 3 April 1951; *o s* of Sir Humphrey Sherston-Baker, 6th Bt and Margaret Alice (*m* 2nd, Sir Ronald Leach, GBE; she *d* 1994), *o d* of Henry William Binns; *S* father, 1990; *m* 1991, Vanessa, *y d* of C. E. A. Baird; one *s* one *d*. *Heir: s* David Arbuthnot George Sherston-Baker; *b* 24 Nov. 1992.

**SHERVAL, Rear-Adm. David Robert**, CB 1989; CEng; FIMechE; FIMarEST; Chief Surveyor and Deputy General Manager, The Salvage Association, 1990–98; *b* 4 July 1933; *s* of William Robert Sherval (HMS Hood, 1941), and Florence Margaret Sherval (*née* Luke); *m* 1961, Patricia Ann Phillips (*d* 2018); one *s* one *d. Educ:* Portsmouth Southern Grammar School. Artificer Apprentice, 1950; BRNC Dartmouth, 1951; Training: at sea, HM Ships Devonshire, Forth and Glasgow, 1951–52 and 1955; RNEC, 1952–54, 1956; served: HM Ships Eagle, Tiger, Hampshire, HM Dockyard Gibraltar and HMY Britannia, 1957–68; BRNC, 1968–70; HMS Juno, 1970–72; NATO Defence Coll., 1972–73; Naval Plans, MoD, 1973–75; Staff of FO Sea Training, 1975–76; Naval Op. Requirements, MoD, 1976–77; NATO Defence Coll., Rome, 1979; ACOS (Intell.) to SACLANT, 1979–82; Fleet Marine Engineer Officer, 1982–84; Dir, Naval Logistic Planning, 1984–85; ADC to the Queen, 1985; CSO (Engrg) to C-in-C Fleet, 1985–87; Dir Gen. Ship Refitting, 1987–89. *Recreation:* music.

**SHERWIN, Deborah Ann; Her Honour Judge Sherwin**; a Circuit Judge, since 2014; *d* of William Anthony and Dinah June Sherwin; *m* 1981, Stephen John Ashurst, *qv*; one *s* one *d. Educ:* Wycombe High Sch.; Exeter Univ. (LLB Hons). Called to the Bar, Inner Temple, 1979; in practice as barrister, 1980–2014; Asst Recorder, 1995–98, Recorder, 1998–2014. *Recreations:* relaxing with family, walking, running, cycling, ski-ing. *Address:* Teesside Combined Court Centre, Russell Street, Middlesbrough TS1 2AE. *T:* (01642) 340000.

**SHERWIN, Glynn George;** Head of Corporate Finance, Sheffield City Council, 1998–2001; *b* 27 Feb. 1948; *s* of George Sherwin and Lilian Sherwin (*née* Billingham); *m* 1969, Janet Heather Broomhead Ferguson; one *s* two *d. Educ:* Firth Park Grammar Sch., Sheffield; Chesterfield Coll. of Technol. CPFA (Hons Final) 1971. Various posts, Sheffield CBC, 1966–74; Sheffield City Council: Principal Accountant, 1974–79; Chief Develt Officer, 1979–88; Asst City Treas., 1988–94; Dep. City Treas., 1994–98. Project Examr, 1978–83, Sen. Project Examr, 1983–86, Chartered Inst. Public Finance and Accountancy. Non-executive Director: MFH Engrg (Hldgs) Ltd, 2006–17; Quoit Assets Ltd, 2006–18; Chm. and non-exec. Dir, Sheffield Internat. Venues Ltd, 2005–16. Dir and Trustee, Sheffield Carers Centre, 2009–17. Mem., Bd of Govs, Sheffield City Trust Ltd, 2003–16. *Recreations:* family, reading, travel, cinema, theatre, Sheffield Wednesday supporter.

**SHERWIN, Rt Hon. Dame Sarah Jane;** *see* Asplin, Rt Hon. Dame S. J.

**SHERWOOD, Bishop Suffragan of,** since 2006; **Rt Rev. Anthony Porter;** *b* 10 Feb. 1952; *s* of Sydney and Valerie Porter; *m* 1974, Lucille Joyce Roberts; two *s* two *d. Educ:* Don Valley High Sch.; Gravesend Sch. for Boys; Hertford Coll., Oxford (BA English 1974, MA); Ridley Hall, Cambridge (BA Theol. 1977). Ordained deacon, 1977, priest, 1978; Curate: Edgware, 1977–80; St Mary, Haughton, 1980–83; Priest-in-charge, Christ Ch, Bacup, 1983–87; Vicar, 1987–91, Rector, 1991–2006, Holy Trinity, Rusholme. Mem., Coll. of Evangelists, 2009–. Archbishops' Sport Ambassador, 2014–. *Publications:* Chips, 1979; Super Jack, 1983; Mission Countdown, 1986; Prince of Thieves, 2006; Seed Scattering, 2013. *Recreation:* sport. *Address:* Jubilee House, Westgate, Southwell, Notts NG25 0JH. *T:* (01636) 819133. *E:* bishopsherwood@southwell.anglican.org.

**SHERWOOD, Christopher Geoffrey;** Chief Executive, Royal Society for the Prevention of Cruelty to Animals, since 2018; *b* Kettering, 6 Aug. 1980; *s* of William and Sharon Sherwood. *Educ:* Univ. of Exeter (BA Hons Hist. and Society 2002); Inst. of Dirs (Dip. Co. Direction 2016). Business Develt Manager, Scope, 2005–09; Sen. Develt Manager, Nesta, 2009–11; Dir, Innovation and Develt, Scope, 2011–12; Dir, Policy, Communications and Digital Services, Relate, 2012–15; Chief Exec., Relate, 2015–18. Trustee, Spice UK, 2014–. *Recreations:* travel, politics, film, history. *Address:* Royal Society for the Prevention of Cruelty to Animals, Wilberforce Way, Southwater, Horsham, W Sussex RH13 9RS.

**SHERWOOD, James Blair;** Founder and President, Sea Containers Group, Bermuda and London, 1965–2005; Founder, 1976, and Chairman Emeritus, 2011, Belmond Ltd (formerly Orient-Express Hotels) (Chairman, 1987–2007; Director, 2007–11); Proprietor: Capannelle Wine Resort Srl (formerly Capannelle Vineyards), Tuscany, since 1997; Panorama Farms, Tulbagh, CP, South Africa, since 2014; *b* 8 Aug. 1933; *s* of William Earl Sherwood and Florence Balph Sherwood; *m* 1977, Shirley Angela Masser Cross; two step *s. Educ:* Yale Univ. (BA Economics 1955). Lieut US Naval Reserve, Far East service, afloat and ashore, 1955–59. Manager, French Ports, later Asst General Freight Traffic Manager, United States Lines Co., Le Havre and NY, 1959–62; Gen. Manager, Container Transport Internat. Inc., NY and Paris, 1963–64. In partnership with Mark Birley, established Harry's Bar Club in London, 1979. Restored, and brought into regular service, the Venice Simplon-Orient-Express, 1982. Dir, Save Venice Inc., 2000–. Non-exec. Dir, Casuarina Shipping Pte Ltd, Singapore, 2011–. Trustee: Solomon R. Guggenheim Foundn, 1989–; Oxford Philharmonic, 2009–. Mem. Internat. Council, Yale Univ., 2002–. Hon. Citizen of Venice, 1995; Grand Master, Nat. Order of the Southern Cross (Brazil), 2004; Comdr, Chevaliers de Tastevin, 2005. *Publications:* James Sherwood's Discriminating Guide to London, 1975, 2nd edn 1977; Orient-Express, a personal journey, 2012. *Recreations:* sailing, tennis, ski-ing. *Address:* Hinton Manor, Hinton Waldrist, Oxon SN7 8SA. *T:* (01865) 820260. *Clubs:* Garrick, Hurlingham, Pilgrims, Mark's, Harry's Bar.

**SHERWOOD, Katharine Ann;** *see* Bowyer, K. A.

**SHERWOOD, Prof. Thomas,** FRCP, FRCR; Professor of Radiology, 1978–94, Clinical Dean, 1984–96, University of Cambridge, now Professor Emeritus; Fellow of Girton College, Cambridge, since 1982; *b* 25 Sept. 1934; *m* 1961, Margaret Gooch; two *s* one *d. Educ:* Frensham Heights Sch.; Guy's Hospital, London. MA; DCH. Consultant Radiologist, Hammersmith Hospital and St Peter's Hospitals, 1969–77. Chm. Govs, Frensham Heights Sch., 1996–2000. Ombudsman, The Lancet, 1996–2001. *Publications:* Uroradiology, 1980; Roads to Radiology, 1983; Blow the Wind Southerly, 1988; Cutting Through the Colleges, 2010; Cutting Across Cambridge, 2011; Cutting Around Cambridgeshire, 2012; Cutting Into The Workshop, 2013; The Boy David Kindersley, 2015; The Man David Kindersley, 2016; I Ask About The Sky, 2016; papers in medical and radiological jls, 1964–2004. *Recreations:* music, reading and writing. *Address:* 19 Clarendon Street, Cambridge CB1 1JU.

**SHERWOOD LOLLAR, Prof. Barbara,** CC 2016; PhD; FRS 2019; FRSC; Director, Stable Isotope Laboratory, since 1992, Professor, Department of Earth Sciences, since 2001 and Canada Research Chair in Isotope Geochemistry, since 2007, University of Toronto; Fellow and Co-Director (Earth 4D), Canadian Institute for Advanced Research, since 2019; *b* Jersey City, 19 Feb. 1963; *d* of John M. Sherwood and Joan Sherwood (*née* Cavanagh). *Educ:* Harvard Univ. (BA Hons Geol Scis *summa cum laude* 1985); Univ. of Waterloo (PhD Earth Sci. 1990). NSERC Postdoctoral Fellow, Univ. of Cambridge, 1990–92; Department of Geology, University of Toronto: Asst Prof., 1992–96; Associate Prof., 1996–2001. Sen. Fellow, 2010–, Sci. Chair, 2016–20, Massey Coll., Univ. of Toronto; Helmholtz Internat. Fellow, 2014. Member: Space Studies Bd, Nat. Acads of Scis, 2016–20; Adv. Council to Gov. Gen. for Order of Canada, 2018–20. Dir, Earth, Oceans and Atmosphere Scis Div., Royal Soc. Canada, 2018–20. Pres., Geochemical Soc., 2014–15 (Vice-Pres., 2012–13). FRSC 2004; Fellow: Amer. Geophysical Union, 2015; Geochemical Soc., 2019; Eur. Assoc. Geochem., 2019. Award in Protection of Envmt, ENI, 2012; John C. Polanyi Award, 2016, Gerhard Herzberg Gold Medal, 2019, NSERC; Bancroft Medal, RSC, 2016; Logan Medal, Geol Assoc. Canada, 2018; C. C. Patterson Award, Geochemical Soc., 2019. *Address:* Earth Sciences Centre, University of Toronto, 22 Russell Street, Toronto, ON M5S 3B1, Canada. *T:* 9780770. *E:* barbara.sherwoodlollar@utoronto.ca.

**SHESTOPAL, Dawn Angela, (Mrs N. J. Shestopal);** *see* Freedman, Her Honour D. A.

**SHETTY, Rajeev Rama; His Honour Judge Shetty;** a Circuit Judge, since 2014; *b* London, 30 March 1973; *s* of Rama Bogu Shetty and Mahabando Shetty; *m* 2001, Dr Emma Jayne Watts; one *s* one *d. Educ:* Univ. of Southampton (LLB Hons). Called to the Bar, Inner Temple, 1996; barrister, 9 Gough Square, 1999–2014; a Recorder, 2009–14. Attorney Gen.'s List of Criminal Advocates Panel, 2002–07; Legal Assessor to GMC, 2010–14; Dir, Bar Mutual Indemnity Fund, 2011–14. Treas., Herts and Beds Bar Mess, 2005–12. *Publications:* (contrib.) APIL Guide to Evidence, 2012; (contrib.) APIL Guide to Industrial Disease Claims, 2013; (contrib.) APIL Guide to Road Traffic Accidents, 2013. *Recreations:* golf, football, films, greyhounds. *Address:* Chester Crown Court, The Castle, Chester, Cheshire CH1 2AN. *Club:* Woking Golf.

**SHETTY, Salil;** Secretary General, Amnesty International, 2010–18; *b* Bombay, 3 Feb. 1961; *s* of V. T. Rajashekar and Hamlatha Shetty; *m* 1984, Bina Rani; one *s* one *d. Educ:* Bangalore Univ.; Indian Inst. of Management, Ahmedabad (MBA); London Sch. of Econs and Pol Sci. (MSc). ActionAid: joined 1985; postings to Africa and India; CEO, 1998–2003; Dir, UN Millennium Campaign, 2003–10. Strategic Planning Gp, Amnesty Internat. Sen. Fellow, Carr Center for Human Rights Policy, Harvard Kennedy Sch., 2018–19.

**SHEWRY, Prof. Peter Robert;** Principal Investigator, Rothamsted Research, since 2012 (Associate Director, 2003–12); Professor of Crops and Health, University of Reading, 2012–18, now Emeritus; *b* 19 March 1948; *s* of late Robert Thomas Shewry and Mary Helen Shewry; *m* 1969, Rosemary Willsdon; one *s* one *d. Educ:* Bristol Univ. (BSc, PhD, DSc). Postdoctoral Res. Fellow, Westfield Coll., Univ. of London, 1972; Rothamsted Experimental Station: Res. Scientist, 1974; Head of Biochem. Dept, 1986; Dir, Long Ashton Res. Stn and Prof. of Agricl Scis, Univ. of Bristol, 1989–2003; Francqui Chair, KU Leuven, 2016. Dr *hc:* Swedish Univ. of Agricultural Scis, Uppsala, 2007; Budapest Univ. of Technol. and Econs, 2012. Rank Prize for Nutrition (with Donald D. Kasarda), 2002; Clyde H. Bailey Medal, ICC, 2016. *Publications:* (ed with Steven Gutteridge) Plant Protein

Engineering, 1992; (ed) Barley: genetics, biochemistry, molecular biology and biotechnology, 1992; (ed with A. K. Stobart) Seed Storage Compounds, 1993; (ed jtly) Protein Phosphorylation in Plants, 1996; (ed jtly) Engineering Crop Plants for Industrial End Uses, 1998; (ed with R. Casey) Seed Proteins, 1999; (ed with A. S. Tatham) Wheat Gluten, 2000; (ed jtly) Biotechnology of Cereals, 2001; (ed with G. Lookhart) Wheat Gluten Protein Analysis, 2003; (ed jtly) Elastomeric Proteins, 2003; (ed with E. N. C. Mills) Plant Protein Allergies, 2004; (ed with K. Khan) Wheat Chemistry and Technology, 4th edn, 2009; (ed with H. Jones) Transgenic Wheat, Barley and Oats: production and characterisation protocols, 2009; (ed with J. Ward) Healthgrain Methods: analysis of bioactive components in small grain cereals, 2009; (ed with S. Ullrich) Barley Chemistry and Technology, 2nd edn, 2014; numerous papers in sci. jls on plant genetics, biochem. and molecular biol. *Address:* Rothamsted Research, Harpenden, Herts AL5 2JQ. *T:* (01582) 763133.

**SHI JIUYONG;** a Judge, International Court of Justice, 1994–2010 (Vice-President, 2000–03; President, 2003–06); *b* 9 Oct. 1926; *m* 1956, Zhang Guoying; one *s*. *Educ:* St John's Univ., Shanghai (BA Govt and Public Law 1948); Columbia Univ., NY (MA Internat. Law 1951). Legal Advr, Min. of Foreign Affairs, People's Republic of China, 1980–93; Prof. of Internat. Law, Foreign Affairs Coll., Beijing, 1984–93. Hon. Prof. of Internat. Law, East China Coll. of Law and Political Sci., 2001–. Pres., Xiamen Acad. of Internat. Law, 2005–. Honorary President: Chinese Soc. of Internat. Law, Beijing, 2006–; Coll. of Internat. Law, Univ. of Foreign Relations, Beijing, 2007–. Mem., 1987–93, Chm., 1990, Internat. Law Commn, UN.

**SHIACH, Allan George;** film writer (as Allan Scott) and producer; Chairman: Macallan-Glenlivet plc, 1980–96; Rafford Films Ltd, since 1983; *b* Elgin; *er s* of late Gordon Leslie Shiach, WS and Lucy Sybil (*née* De Freitas); *m* 1966, Kathleen Swarbreck; two *s* one *d*. *Educ:* Gordonstoun Sch.; L'Ecole des Roches; McGill Univ. (BA). Writer of TV and radio drama, 1965–72; screenwriter and co-writer of films, including: Don't Look Now, 1975; Joseph Andrews, 1977; Martin's Day, 1980; D.A.R.Y.L., 1984; Castaway, 1985; A Shadow on the Sun, 1987; The Witches, 1989; Cold Heaven, 1990; Two Deaths, 1994; In Love and War, 1996; The Preacher's Wife, 1996; Regeneration, 1997; also Producer or Exec. Producer: Cold Heaven, 1991; Shallow Grave, 1994; Two Deaths, 1995; True Blue, 1996; Grizzly Falls, 1999; The Match, 1999; The Fourth Angel, 2001; (co-prod. and co-writer) Priscilla Queen of the Desert - The Musical, Palace Th., 2009–12, NY, 2011–, Brazil, 2012–, Milan, 2012–; Rome, 2013–; UK and US tours, 2013; (co-writer and script consultant) Kon Tiki, 2013; (prod.) Act 3, Laguna Playhouse, Calif, 2016. Dir, Scottish Media Group plc (formerly Scottish Television plc), 1993–2006. Mem., BBC Broadcasting Council (Scotland), 1987–90; Chairman: Writers' Guild of GB, 1989 and 1990; Scottish Film Council, 1991–97; Scottish Film Prodn Fund, 1992–97; Scottish Screen, 1997–98; Governor, BFI, 1993–2000. Mem., Amer. Acad. of Motion Picture Arts & Scis, 1991–. Mem. Council, Scotch Whisky Assoc., 1983–96. Liveryman, Distillers' Co., 1989–. Hon. DA Napier Univ., Edinburgh, 2007; Dr *hc* Aberdeen, 2009. *Recreations:* writing, cooking, tennis. *Address:* Rafford Ltd, 1st Floor, 19 Garrick Street, WC2E 9AX. *Clubs:* Savile, Garrick.

**SHIACH, Gordon;** Sheriff of Lothian and Borders, at Edinburgh, 1984–97, also at Peebles, 1996–97; *b* 1935; *o s* of late Dr John Shiach, FDS, QHDS; *m* 1962; one *d* (and one *d* decd). *Educ:* Lathallan Sch.; Gordonstoun Sch.; Edinburgh Univ. (MA 1957; LLB 1959); Open Univ. (BA Hons 1979); Rose Bruford Coll. (BA Hons in Opera Studies 2006; DipHE Theatre Studies 2012). Admitted to Faculty of Advocates, 1960; practised as Advocate, 1960–72; Tutor, Dept of Evidence and Pleading, Univ. of Edinburgh, 1963–66; Clerk to Rules Council of Court of Session, 1963–72; Standing Jun. Counsel in Scotland to Post Office, 1969–72; Sheriff of: Fife and Kinross, later Tayside, Central and Fife, at Dunfermline, 1972–79; Lothian and Borders at Linlithgow, 1979–84; Hon. Sheriff at Elgin, 1986–. Mental Welfare Comr for Scotland, 2001–05. Member: Council, Sheriffs' Assoc., 1989–95 (Pres., 1993–95); Bd, Lothian Family Conciliation Service, 1989–93; Standing Cttee on Criminal Procedure, 1989–93; Parole Bd for Scotland, 1990–99 (Vice-Chm., 1995–99); Council, Faculty of Advocates, 1993–95; Shrieval Training Gp, 1994–95; Review Gp on Social Work Nat. Standards for Throughcare, 1994–95. Chairman: The Scottish Soc., 1992–93; Edinburgh Sir Walter Scott Club, 1995–98. *Recreations:* hill-walking, travelling, reading, gym exercising, and enjoying music (especially opera), art, theatre, film. *Club:* New (Edinburgh).

**SHIELDS, Baroness** *cr* 2014 (Life Peer), of Maida Vale in the City of Westminster; **Joanna Shields,** OBE 2014; Chief Executive Officer, Benevolent AI, since 2018; *b* 12 July 1962; holds dual US/UK nationality; *m* Andrew Stevenson; one *s*. *Educ:* Pennsylvania State Univ.; George Washington Univ. (MBA). Man. Dir, Europe, RealNetworks International, 2001–03; Man. Dir, EMEA, Google Inc., 2005–07; CEO, Bebo Inc., 2007–08; Vice Pres., Aol, 2007–09; Vice Pres. and Man. Dir, EMEA, Facebook, 2010–12; Chief Exec., 2012–14, Chm., 2014–15, Tech City UK; Parly Under Sec. of State, DCMS, 2015–16, Home Office, 2015–17; Prime Minister's Special Representative: on Internet Crime and Harms, 2016–17; on Internet Safety, 2017–18. Non-exec. Dir, London Stock Exchange Gp 2014–15. UK Business Ambassador for Digital Industries, 2012. Trustee, American Sch. in London, 2013–.

**SHIELDS, Elizabeth Lois;** Lecturer, Medieval Studies Department, University of York, since 1995; *b* 27 Feb. 1928; *d* of Thomas Henry Teare and Dorothy Emma Elizabeth Roberts-Lawrence; *m* 1961, David Cathro Shields. *Educ:* Whyteleafe Girls' Grammar School; UCL (BA Hons Classics); Avery Hill College of Education (Cert Ed); MA York 1988. Asst Teacher, St Philomena's Sch., Carshalton, 1954–59; Head of Department: Jersey Coll. for Girls, 1959–61; Whyteleafe Girls' Grammar Sch., 1961–62; Trowbridge Girls' High Sch., 1962–64; St Swithun's, Winchester, 1964–65; Queen Ethelburga's, Harrogate, 1967–69; Malton Sch., N Yorks, 1976–86; Univ. of York (on secondment), 1985–86 (Medieval Studies). Mem., Ryedale DC, 1980– (Chm., 1989–2007; Chm., Community Services Cttee; Chm., Overview and Scrutiny Cttee, 2007); Mem. (Lib Dem) N Yorks CC, 2013–17 (Chm., Young People and Children Overview and Scrutiny Cttee, 2013–15). Contested (L) Howden, 1979, Ryedale, 1983, 1992; MP (L) Ryedale, May 1986–87. Lib Dem spokesman on envmt, Yorks and Humberside Reg., 1989–92; Chm., Yorks and Humberside Lib Dem Candidates' Assoc., 1992–97; President: Lib Dems in Ryedale Constituency, 1995–; Yorks and Humberside Lib Dem Regl Party, 1998–. Chm., Ryedale Housing Assoc., 1990–91; President: Ryedale Motor Neurone Disease Assoc., 1990–95; Ryedale Cats' Protection League, 1991–2002. *Publications:* A Year to Remember, 1996. *Recreations:* gardening, music, travel, Arsenal FC supporter 2004–. *Address:* Firby Hall, Kirkham Abbey, Westow, York YO60 7LH. *T:* (01653) 618474. *Club:* National Liberal.

**SHIELDS, (Robert) Michael (Coverdale),** CBE 2002; Deputy Chairman and Trustee, Manufacturing Institute, 2006–17; *b* 23 Jan. 1943; *s* of Thomas and Dorothy Shields; *m* 1965, Dorothy Jean Dennison; two *s* one *d*. *Educ:* Durham Johnston Grammar Tech. Sch.; Durham Univ. (BSc Hons); Newcastle Univ. (DipTP). MRTPI. Planning Departments: Newcastle upon Tyne, 1964–65; Durham CC, 1965–69; Nottingham, 1969–73; Dep. Dir of Planning, Leeds City Council, 1973–78; City Tech. Services Officer and Dep. Chief Exec., Salford City Council, 1978–83; Chief Executive: Trafford BC, 1983–87; Trafford Park Develt Corp., 1987–98; Northwest (formerly NW Regl) Develt Agency, 1998–2003; Manchester Knowledge Capital, 2003–05; Principal, URC Associates, 2003–11; Associate, AMION Consulting, 2004–11. Chm., Liverpool Land Develt Co., 2005–08 (Dep. Chm., 2004–05); non-exec. Dep. Chm., Merseycare NHS Trust, 2009–12. Non-exec. Dir, Innvotec North West Trust Ltd, 1998–2001. Chm., United Utilities Trust Fund, 2005–09. Salford University: Pro Chancellor, 1993–99; Chm. Council, 1997–99 (Dep. Chm., 1999–2003). Mem. Bd, Altrincham Forward, 2011–14; Chm., Altrincham Town Centre Neighbourhood Business Plan Forum Working Gp, 2013–18; Mem., Altrincham Neighbourhood Forum. Gov., Altrincham Grammar Sch., 1988–98 (Chm., 1988–93). Hon. DSc Salford, 2000; Hon. DLit UMIST, 2004; Hon. LLD Manchester, 2004. Howorth Medal for Enterprise and Innovation, RSA, 2004. *Recreations:* family, books. *Address:* 42 Crescent Road, Hale, Altrincham, Cheshire WA15 9NA. *E:* mike.shields@urca.co.uk.

**SHIFFNER, Rear-Adm. John Robert,** CB 1995; DL; Consultant, Newton Industrial Consultants, 2002–07; *b* 30 Aug. 1941; *s* of late Captain John Scarlett Shiffner, RN and Margaret Harriet Shiffner (*née* Tullis); *heir-presumptive* to Sir Michael George Shiffner, 9th Bt, *qv*; *m* 1969, Rosemary Tilly; two *s* one *d*. *Educ:* Sedbergh Sch.; BRNC Dartmouth; RNEC Manadon; RNC Greenwich (BSc). CEng, FIMarEST. Joined RN, 1959; served in HM Ships Centaur, Glamorgan, Andromeda, Zulu; Staff Marine Engineer Officer, CBNS Washington, 1980; RCDS 1983; MoD Procurement Executive: Project Manager, Type 42 Destroyer/Aircraft Carrier, 1984–86; Dir, Mechanical Engineering, 1987–88; Captain, Britannia RNC, Dartmouth, 1989–91; ADC to the Queen, 1989–91; COS to C-in-C Naval Home Comd, 1991–93; Dir Gen. Fleet Support (Equipment and Systems), MoD, 1993–95. Director: MSI-Defence Systems Ltd, 1996–2001; GEC Marine, 1996–98; Marconi Electronic Systems, 1997–99; Internat. Festival of the Sea Ltd, 2000–02. Chairman: Britannia Assoc., 2004–07; Dartmouth RNLI, 2007–15; Maritime Cttee, Dartmouth Mayflower 400, 2015–. DL Devon, 2005. *Recreations:* golf, sailing, country pursuits, garden taming, picture restoration. *Address:* West Holme, Dartmouth, S Devon TQ6 0JR. *Club:* Royal Yacht Squadron (Cowes).

**SHIFFNER, Sir Michael (George Edward),** 9th Bt *cr* 1818; *b* Chelmsford, 5 March 1963; *s* of George and Helena Shiffner; *S* cousin, 2018, but his name does not appear on the Official Roll of the Baronetage; *m* 1996, Suzanne E. Buss (marr. diss. 2007); one *d*. *Educ:* Gosfield Boys' Sch. Hotel owner, 1994–2016. *Recreations:* cycling, motorsport, horse racing, art. *Heir: cousin* Rear-Adm. John Robert Shiffner, *qv*. *Address:* Searles, Alderford Street, Sible Hedingham, Essex CO9 4EX. *E:* michaelshiffner@gmail.com. *Club:* Cambridge Oxford Owners'.

**SHIGEHARA, Kumiharu;** President, International Economic Policy Studies Association (formerly Head, International Economic Policy Studies Group), since 2001; *b* 5 Feb. 1939; *s* of Seizaburo Shigehara and Rutsu (*née* Tanabe); *m* 1965, Akiko Yoshizawa; one *s* one *d*. *Educ:* Law Sch., Univ. of Tokyo (Hozumi Hon. Award, 1960). Joined Bank of Japan, 1962; joined OECD, 1970: Principal Administrator, 1971–72; Hd, Monetary Div., 1972–74; Councillor on policy planning, and Advr on Internat. Finance, Bank of Japan, 1974–80; Dep. Dir, Gen. Econs Br., OECD, 1980–82; Bank of Japan: Manager of Res., 1982–83, Dep. Dir, 1987, Inst. for Monetary and Econ. Studies; Manager, Nagasaki Br., 1983–86; Bank Inspector, 1986–87; Dir, Gen. Econs Br., OECD, 1987–89; Dir, Inst. for Monetary and Econ. Studies, Bank of Japan, 1989–92; Hd, Econs Dept and Chief Economist, OECD, 1992–97; Dep. Sec.-Gen., OECD, 1997–99. Hon. Dr Econs Liège, 1998. *Publications:* The Role of Monetary Policy in Demand Management (with Niels Thygesen), 1975; Stable Economic Growth and Monetary Policy, 1991; New Trends in Monetary Theory and Policy, 1992; (with Paul Atkinson) Surveillance by International Institutions: lessons from the global financial and economic crisis, 2011; Japan at the OECD and the OECD in Japan, 2014; The Limits of Surveillance and Financial Market Failure, 2014. *Recreations:* art, hiking, classical music. *E:* shigehara.kumiharu@gmail.com.

**SHILLER, Prof. Robert James,** PhD; Professor of Economics, since 1982, and Sterling Professor of Economics, since 2013, Yale University; *b* Detroit, Michigan, 29 March 1946; *s* of Benjamin P. Shiller and Ruth R. Shiller (*née* Radzvill); *m* 1976, Virginia M. Faulstich; two *s*. *Educ:* Southfield High Sch., Michigan; Univ. of Michigan (BA 1967); Massachusetts Inst. of Technol. (SM 1968; PhD 1972). Asst Prof., Univ. of Minnesota, 1972–74; Associate Prof., Univ. of Pennsylvania, 1974–80; Vis. Schol., Harvard Univ. and Nat. Bureau of Econ. Res., 1980–81; Vis. Prof., Dept of Econs, MIT, 1981–82. Member: Amer. Acad. of Arts and Scis; Amer. Philosophical Soc. (Jtly) Nobel Prize in Econs, 2013. *Publications:* Market Volatility, 1989; Macro Markets, 1993; Irrational Exuberance, 2000, 2nd edn 2005; The New Financial Order, 2003; Subprime Solution, 2008; Animal Spirits, 2009; Finance and the Good Society, 2012; (with G. A. Akerlof) Phishing for Phools: the economics of manipulation and deception, 2015; Narrative Economics, 2019. *Address:* Cowles Foundation for Research in Economics, Yale University, 30 Hillhouse Avenue, New Haven, CT 06520–8281, USA. *T:* (203) 4323708, *Fax:* (203) 4326167. *E:* robert.shiller@yale.edu.

**SHILLING, Elizabeth Mary;** *see* Carter, E. M.

**SHILLING, (Hugh) David (V.);** artist, designer; President, David Shilling, since 1976; *b* 27 June 1954; *s* of late Ronald and Gertrude Shilling. *Educ:* Colet Court; St Paul's Sch., Hammersmith. Founded David Shilling, 1976. Sen. Consultant on design, ITC, UNCTAD and GATT, 1990. One person shows in UK and worldwide, 1979–, including: NT and Crafts Council, 1979; Ulster, Worthing, Plymouth, Leeds, Cheltenham, Durham, Salisbury, Chester and Edinburgh Museums; LA Co. Mus., 1982; Moscow, 1989; Sotheby's, Stockholm, 1992; Salama-Caro Gall., London, 1993; Rio de Janeiro, 1993; Manila, 1994; Brit. Embassy, Paris, 1995; British Council, Cologne, 1995, and Delhi and Bombay, 1996; War Child/Pavarotti, Modena, 1995; Royal Shakespeare Theatre, Stratford upon Avon, 1996; Dubai, 1999; Hatworks Mus., Stockport, 2001; Nat. Horseracing Mus., Newmarket, 2001; Internat. Mus. of the Horse, Lexington, Ky, 2002; Newmarket Racecourse, 2002; Nat. Mus. of Scotland Dumfries, 2003; Musée Chapeau, Lyon, 2004–05; Ferrero Gall., Nice, 2004, 2005; Regent's Park, London, 2005; Holdenby, Northampton, 2006; Museu da Chapeleria, Portugal, 2008; rue Princesse Caroline, Monaco, 2009; Beijing, 2009; Decoh Exhibn, Monaco, 2010; work in permanent collections: Metropolitan Mus., NY, LA Co. Mus., Philadelphia Mus. of Art, Musée des Arts Décoratifs, Paris, V&A Mus. Pres. for Life, Valdivia, Ecuador, 1993. Freeman, Gold and Silver Wyre Drawers, 1975. *Publications:* Thinking Rich, 1996. *Address:* 2 rue Basse, Monaco, MC 98000. *T:* 97770137. *Clubs:* City Livery; City Livery Yacht.

**SHILLITO, Mark Robert;** Partner, since 1996, and Global Head of Intellectual Property, since 2011, Herbert Smith Freehills (formerly Herbert Smith); *b* Sheffield, 29 Nov. 1964; *s* of George Edward Shillito and Jill Margaret Shillito (*née* Wattam, now Grove); *m* 1993, Leyla Daybelge; two *d*. *Educ:* Churston Grammar Sch.; University Coll. London (LLB); Queen Mary and Westfield Coll., Univ. of London (Dip. IP). Admitted as solicitor, 1989; Herbert Smith, then Herbert Smith Freehills: Solicitor, 1989–96; Dep. Hd, Disputes, 2008–12; Hd of Disputes, UK and US, 2012–18. *Recreations:* fly fishing, motorcycles, ski-ing, the arts, anything which involves hitting a target. *Address:* Herbert Smith Freehills, Exchange House, Primrose Street, EC2A 2EG. *T:* (020) 7466 2031, *Fax:* (020) 7374 0888. *E:* mark.shillito@hsf.com.

**SHILSON, Stuart James,** LVO 2004; DL; *b* 12 Feb. 1966. *Educ:* St Paul's Sch.; Balliol Coll., Oxford (BA 1st Cl. Hons 1988, MSc 1989); St John's Coll., Cambridge (MPhil 1990). Called to the Bar, Middle Temple, 1992; in practice at the Bar, 1992–97; McKinsey & Co., 1997–2001; Sen. Civil Servant, Cabinet Office, 1999–2000 (on leave of absence); Asst Pvte Sec. to the Queen, 2001–04, and Asst Keeper of the Queen's Archives, 2002–04; rejoined McKinsey & Co., 2005. FRGS 1989; FRSA 1996. DL Gtr London, 2019.

**SHILSTON, David Thomas;** Technical Director for Engineering Geology, since 2004, and Fellow, since 2014, Atkins Ltd, now Member of SNC-Lavalin Group; President: Geological Society of London, 2012–14; Earth Science Teachers' Association, 2016–18; *b* Staines, 1954; *s* of Michael Shilston, CEng, MICE; *m* Pauline, *d* of Dr Eric Meek; one *s* one *d*. *Educ:* King's College Sch., Wimbledon; Univ. of Nottingham (BSc Geol. 1975); St John's Coll., Cambridge (Post-grad. Cert. Prehistoric Archaeol. 1976); Imperial Coll. London (MSc and DIC Engrg Geol. 1980). Affiliate/Associate ICE 1976; FGS 1981; MIGeol 1983; CGeol 1990; Affiliate, Chartered Inst. for Archaeologists (Affiliate, Instn of Field Archaeologists, 1991); CSci 2005. Student engr, Sir William Halcrow & Partners, 1972–73; Geologist, Nuttall Geotechnical Services Ltd, 1976–79; Engrg Geologist, Soil Mechanics Ltd, 1980–88; Sen. Engrg Geologist, Principal Engrg Geologist, then Chief Engrg Geologist, Atkins Ltd, 1988–2004. Ground Engrg Advr, UK Register of Ground Engrg Professionals, 2011. FRSA 1996. Coke Medal, Geol Soc. of London, 2018. *Publications:* contrib. articles to tech. jls, conf. procs and tech. pubns. *Recreations:* hill walking, archaeology, rural and urban landscapes (ancient and modern). *Address:* Atkins Ltd, Woodcote Grove, Ashley Road, Epsom KT18 5BW. *T:* (01372) 754409.

**SHILTON, Peter,** OBE 1991 (MBE 1986); footballer; *b* 18 Sept. 1949; *s* of Les and May Shilton; *m* 1st, 1970, Sue; two *s*; 2nd, 2016, Stephanie Hayward. *Educ:* King Richard III Sch., Leicester. Goalkeeper; started playing, 1964, for Leicester City; scored a goal, 1967; Stoke City, 1974; Nottingham Forest, 1977; Southampton, 1982; Derby County, 1987; Plymouth Argyle, 1992–95 (player-manager); Leyton Orient, 1996; 1,000 League appearances (record), 1996; first played for England, 1970; 125 England caps (record); final appearance, World Cup, 1990. PFA Footballer of the Year, 1978. *Publications:* Peter Shilton: the autobiography, 2004.

**SHIMMON, Ross Michael,** OBE 2000; Secretary General, International Federation of Library Associations and Institutions, 1999–2004; *b* 10 Jan. 1942; *s* of late John Ross Shimmon and Eileen Margaret Shimmon; *m* 1967, Patricia, *d* of late Ronald George Hayward, CBE; one *s* two *d*. *Educ:* St John's Coll., Southsea; Poly. of North London; Coll. of Librarianship, Wales. FLA 1972; Hon. FCLIP (Hon. FLA 2000). Liby Assistant, Portsmouth City Libraries, 1960; Asst Librarian, 1962, Area Librarian, Havant, 1964, Hants County Liby; Lectr, Southampton Coll. of Technol., 1964; Librarian (Tech. Assistant), London Bor. of Bexley, 1966; Professional Assistant to Library Advisers, DES, 1968; Lectr, Coll. of Librarianship, Wales, 1970; Services Librarian, Preston Poly., 1975; Head, Liby Studies Dept, Admin. Coll. of PNG, 1979; Library Association: Sec. for Manpower and Educn, 1984; Dir, Professional Practice, 1988; Chief Exec., 1992–99. Member: Adv. Council, 1992–99; Adv. Cttee, 1994–99, British Council; BookAid Internat. Council, 1994–99; Adv. Cttee, Liby and Inf. Stats Unit, Univ. of Loughborough, 1997–99; Cttee on Freedom of Access to Information and Freedom of Expression, IFLA, 1998–99; Adv. Council on Libraries, 1999; Design Gp, Museums, Libraries and Archives Council, 1999. President: Eur. Bureau of Liby, Inf. and Documentation Assocs, 1992–95; Internat. Cttee of Blue Shield, 2003. Hon. Mem. PNG Liby Assoc., 1983; Hon. Life Mem., Liby and Inf. Assoc. of S Africa, 2007. Hon. Fellow, Univ. of Central Lancs, 2002. Trustee, Faversham Activity for Health (formerly Activity for Health), 2005–11 (Chm. Trustees, 2009–11). Publicity Officer, Col Stephens Soc., 2014–18. Member: Adv. Cttee, Internat. Jl on Recorded Information, 2001–03; Editl Adv. Bd, Information Develt, 2005–07; Ed., The Colonel, 2004–14. *Publications:* Reader in Library Management, 1976; (with Brian Janes) Colonel Stephens and his Railmotors, 2018; conf. papers and contribs to liby jls. *Recreations:* cricket, photography, railways (prototype and model). *Address:* 7 Nobel Court, Faversham, Kent ME13 7SD. *E:* pandrshimmon@btinternet.com.

**SHIN, Prof. Hyun Song,** DPhil; FBA 2005; Economic Adviser and Head of Research, Bank for International Settlements, since 2014; *b* 9 Aug. 1959. *Educ:* Magdalen Coll., Oxford (BA 1985); Nuffield Coll., Oxford (MPhil 1987); DPhil Oxon 1988. Lectr in Econs, Univ. of Oxford and Fellow, University Coll., Oxford, 1990–94; Prof. of Econs, Univ. of Southampton, 1994–96; Lectr in Public Econs, Univ. of Oxford and Fellow, Nuffield Coll., Oxford, 1996–2000; Prof. of Finance, LSE, 2000–05; Prof. of Econs, Princeton Univ., 2005–14. *Publications:* articles in learned jls. *Address:* Bank for International Settlements, Centralbahnplatz 2, 4051 Basel, Switzerland.

**SHINDLER, Nicola,** OBE 2019; television executive producer; Founder and Chief Executive, Red Production Company, since 1998; *b* Rochdale, 8 Oct. 1968. *Educ:* Bury Grammar Sch.; Gonville and Caius Coll., Cambridge (BA 1990). Began career at Granada TV; script editor, Cracker, 1993; BBC, until 1998. Television series: prod., Queer as Folk, 1999; executive producer: Bob and Rose, 2001; Linda Green, 2001–02; Clocking Off, 2000–02; Conviction, 2004; Mine All Mine, 2004; Casanova, 2005; New Street Law, 2006–07; Single Father, 2010; Exile, 2011; Bedlam, 2011–12; Scott and Bailey, 2011–16; Love Life, 2012; The Syndicate, 2012; Last Tango in Halifax, 2012–16; Happy Valley, 2014–16; Ordinary Lies, 2016; Trust Me, 2017; Come Home, Butterfly, 2018. *Address:* Red Production Company, MediaCityUK, Level 2, White, Salford M50 2NT.

**SHINE, Prof. Keith Peter,** PhD; FRS 2009; Regius Professor of Meteorology and Climate Science, University of Reading, since 2013; *b* Birmingham, 19 April 1958; *s* of Isaac and Sylvia Shine; two *s*. *Educ:* Halesowen Grammar Sch.; Imperial Coll. London (BSc Physics; ARCS); Univ. of Edinburgh (PhD Meteorol. 1981). Research scientist: Univ. of Liverpool, 1981–83; Univ. of Oxford, 1983–88; University of Reading: res. scientist, 1988–90; Lectr, 1990–94; Reader, 1994–98; Prof. of Physical Meteorology, 1998–2013. Lead Author, Sci. Assessment of Intergovtl Panel on Climate Change, 1990, 1995. *Publications:* contrib. papers to learned jls with h-index of 55. *Recreations:* season ticket holder, Reading FC, fan of McCartney, Monet and running. *Address:* Department of Meteorology, University of Reading, Earley Gate, Reading RG6 6BB. *T:* (0118) 378 8405. *E:* k.p.shine@reading.ac.uk.

**SHINE, Stephen Frank,** OBE 2011; Chairman: Anesco Ltd, since 2012; UKDN Waterflow Ltd, 2013–15; Chief Executive Officer, SSLS Ltd, since 2012; *b* Raynes Park, London, 20 March 1957; *s* of Dennis Arthur Shine and Sheila Mary Shine; *m* 1981, Janice Margaret Nolan; one *s* two *d*. *Educ:* South Thames Coll. (HNC Electrical Engrg); Croydon Coll. (DMS); DipM, MCIM; Southbank Univ. (MBA). Various positions incl. apprentice electrician, Principal Engr and Engrg Dir, London Electricity Bd, subseq. LEB, then London Electricity plc, 1973–95; Managing Director: London Electricity Contracting, 1995–2000; 24seven Utility Services Ltd, 2000–05; CEO, SGB Ltd, Harsco Corp., 2005–07; Chief Operating Officer, Thames Water Ltd, 2007–12. Non-exec. Dir, Veolia Water Outsourcing Ltd, 2012–14. Trustee, Canal and River Trust, 2012–. FInstD 2011; MCMI; MIET. *Recreations:* shooting, fishing, golf. *Address:* Surrey. *T:* 07739 923481. *E:* Steve@theShines.net.

**SHINER, Janice,** CB 2005; Chairman, National Youth Agency, 2009–12. *Educ:* PGCE. Private sector advertising; human resource and communication mgt in various cos incl. WH Smith and Chase Manhattan Bank; Vice-Pres. Human Resources, Chase Manhattan, 1987; Vice Principal, Yeovil Coll., 1989–93; Sen. Inspector, 1993–97, Dir of Educn and Instns, 1997–99, FEFC; Principal, Leicester Coll., 1999–2002; Dir Gen. for Lifelong Learning, DfES, 2002–05; Chief Exec., Tertiary Educn Commn, NZ, 2005–08.

**SHINER, Philip Joseph;** Head of Strategic Litigation, Public Interest Lawyers (International), 2014–16 (Principal, Public Interest Lawyers Ltd, 1999–2014); *b* Coventry, 25 Dec. 1956; *s* of Peter and Patricia Shiner; two *s* three *d*. *Educ:* Univ. of Birmingham (LLB 1978); Coll. of Law; Univ. of Warwick (LLM (by res.) 1985). Articled clerk, Needham and James, 1979–81; Solicitor: Robin Thompson and Partners, 1981–82; Small Heath Community Law Centre, 1982–84; Birmingham Council Estates Project, 1985–89; Thompsons, 1989–90; Community develt worker, Barnardo's, 1990–92; Solicitor, Birkenhead Resource Unit, 1992–95; Partner, Tyndallwoods, Solicitors, 1995–99. Hon. Prof. of Law, London Metropolitan Univ., 2005–13; Hon. Res. Fellow, Sch. of Law, Univ. of Warwick, 1999–2004; Vis. Fellow, Sch. of Law, LSE, 2005–13; Prof. in Practice Law, Middlesex Univ., 2014. Hon. LLD Kent, 2012. *Publications:* (ed with A. Williams) The Iraq War and International Law, 2008; contrib. Eur. Human Rights Law Rev., Local Econ., Judicial Rev., Mineral Planning, Legal Action Jl, Planning, Local Govt Chronicle. *Recreations:* running, cycling, contemporary music, comedy, hill walking, current affairs, religious affairs.

**SHINGLES, Godfrey Stephen, (Geoff),** CBE 1987; CEng, FIET; FBCS; Chairman, Imagination Technologies (formerly VideoLogic) Group PLC, 1995–2015; *b* 9 April 1939; *s* of Sidney and Winifred Shingles; *m*; two *s*; *m* 1997, Frances Margaret Mercer; one *d*. *Educ:* Paston Sch., N Walsham; Leeds Univ. (BSc). Digital UK, 1965–94; Chm., Digital Equipment Co. Ltd, 1991–94 (Man. Dir, 1983–91; Chief Exec., 1991–93). Vice-Pres., Digital Equipment Corp., 1981–92. Chm. and CEO, Celebrus Technologies Ltd (formerly Speed-Trap Hldgs Ltd), 2007–15 (non-exec. Dir, 2004–07); non-exec. Chm., Sarantel, 2006–14; non-exec. Dir, IS Solutions, 2015–16. FInstD. Freeman, City of London. *Recreations:* sailing, cricket, Rugby, golf, ski-ing. *Clubs:* Royal Ocean Racing, MCC.

**SHINKWIN,** Baron *cr* 2015 (Life Peer), of Balham in the London Borough of Wandsworth; **Kevin Joseph Maximilian Shinkwin.** *Educ:* Univ. of Hull (BA British Politics and Legislative Studies). Campaigning work with charities incl. RNID, 1999–2001; Parly Affairs Manager, Macmillan Cancer Support, 2001–05; Parliamentary Affairs Manager, CRUK, 2005–08; Head of Public Affairs, RBL, 2008–13; Parly Affairs and Campaigns Dir, Wine and Spirit Trade Assoc., 2013–15. Mem., Equality and Human Rights Commn, 2017–18. *Address:* House of Lords, SW1A 0PW.

**SHINNER, Thomas Patrick James;** Director, Cross-Government Policy Coordination, Department for Exiting the European Union, 2016–19; *b* Aylesbury, 18 Oct. 1985; *s* of Patrick and Stephanie Shinner. *Educ:* Dr Challoner's Grammar Sch., Amersham; Magdalen Coll., Oxford (MA Modern Hist. 2007). With McKinsey & Co., 2006–13; on sabbatical as Teacher of Hist., Dr Challoner's GS, 2009–11; Sen. Policy Advr to Sec. of State for Educn, 2013; Dir of Strategy, DfE, 2014–16. Lieut, RNR, 2004–. *Recreations:* sailing, ski-ing, running, walking, school governor (secondary).

**SHINWELL, Sir Adrian;** *see* Shinwell, Sir M. A.

**SHINWELL, Anne Hilary;** *see* Middle, A. H.

**SHINWELL, Sir (Maurice) Adrian,** Kt 1996; NP; solicitor, retired; Senior Partner, Kerr Barrie (formerly Kerr, Barrie & Duncan), Glasgow, 1991–2016; *b* 27 Feb. 1951; *s* of late Maurice Shinwell and Andrina (*née* Alexander); *m* 1973, Lesley McLean; one *s* one *d* (and one *s* decd). *Educ:* Hutchesons' Boys' Grammar Sch.; Glasgow Univ. (LLB). NP 1976. MCIArb 1999–2008 (ACIArb 1990). Admitted solicitor, 1975; Solicitor-Mediator, 1994–2004. Mem., Children's Panel, 1973–77. Part-time Tutor, Law Faculty, Glasgow Univ., 1980–84. Dir, Digital Animations Gp plc, 2002–07. Dir, Nat. Th. of Scotland, 2007–15. Scottish Conservative & Unionist Association: Mem., 1975–2014; Mem., Scottish Council, 1982–98; Chairman: Eastwood Assoc., 1982–85; Cumbernauld & Kilsyth Assoc., 1989–91; Scottish Cons. Candidates' Bd, 1997–2000; Vice-Pres., 1989–92; Pres., 1992–94; Member: Gen. Purposes Cttee, 1993–98; Scottish Exec. and Scottish Council, 1998–2000. Mem., Central Adv. Cttee on Justices of the Peace, 1996–99; Vice Chm., JP Adv. Cttee, E Renfrewshire, 2000–06. Dir, St Leonards Sch., St Andrews, 2000–03. DL Renfrewshire, 1999–2012. *E:* adrian.shinwell@btinternet.com.

**SHIPLEE, Howard John,** CBE 2012; Director General, Universal Credit, Department of Work and Pensions, 2013–14; *b* Liverpool, 21 Oct. 1946; *s* of William James Shiplee and Dorothy Elizabeth Shiplee; *m* 1968, Barbara Joan Callaghan; one *s* one *d*. *Educ:* Liverpool Coll. of Building (OND; HND Building 1966); Univ. of Liverpool (Postgrad. Dip. 1967). FCIOB 2002; FICE 2008. Engrg and mgt roles with Sir Alfred McAlpine, Cementation Construction, and John Howard and Co., 1968–75; sen. mgt roles, Middle East Construction Co., Qatar, 1975–84; Gen. Manager, Al Qahtari Gp, Saudi Arabia, 1984–86; Divl Dir, Boris Construction, 1986–88; Amec Construction: N Reg. Ops Dir, 1988–92; Proj. Dir, Manchester Airport Terminal 2, 1992–95; Proj. Dir, British-Chinese-Japanese Jt Venture, Hong Kong Airport, 1995–99; London Dir of Construction, Capitaland, 1999–2001; Dir of Carillion Bldg/Proj. Dir, GCHQ, 2001–02; Prog. Dir, Network Rail-Thameslink, 2002–04; Dir, High-Point Rendel, 2004–06 (Redevelt Chief Exec., Ascot Racecourse, 2004–06); Dir, Construction, Olympic Delivery Authy, 2006–11; Exec. Dir, Laing O'Rourke plc, 2011–13. Non-exec. Dir, HSE, 2012–14. *Recreations:* home, horticulture, vehicle renovation, labradors.

**SHIPLEY,** family name of **Baron Shipley.**

**SHIPLEY,** Baron *cr* 2010 (Life Peer), of Gosforth in the County of Tyne and Wear; **John Warren Shipley,** OBE 1995; Member (Lib Dem) Newcastle upon Tyne City Council, 1975–2003 and 2004–12 (Leader, 2006–10; Opposition Leader, 1988–98); *b* 5 July 1946; *m* 1969, Margaret Pattison; one *s* one *d*. *Educ:* University Coll., London (BA Hist. 1969). Brand mgt, Procter & Gamble Ltd, 1969–71; with Open Univ., 1971–2005 (Regl Dir, North and EU, 1997–2005). Mem., Tyne and Wear Passenger Transport Authy, 2004–06. Mem. Bd, One North East, 2005–12. Contested: (Lib) Blyth, Feb. and Oct. 1974, Hexham, 1979; (Lib/SDP) Newcastle N, 1983 and 1987. Mem., Select Cttee on Econ. Affairs, H of L, 2010–15. Dep. Chm., Ind. Adv. Panel, Regl Growth Fund, 2012–15. Chm., Prince's Trust NE, 2011–12. *Address:* House of Lords, SW1A 0PW.

**SHIPLEY, Debra Ann;** artist (painter); *b* 22 June 1957. *Educ:* Oxford Poly. (BA Hons); MA London. Writer and lecturer, history, critical studies and architecture. MP (Lab) Stourbridge, 1997–2005. Chm., Drinkaware, 2007. *Publications:* 17 books on subjects including architecture, museums, heritage, travel. *Recreations:* walking, reading, cooking.

**SHIPLEY, Rt Hon. Dame Jennifer (Mary),** DNZM 2009 (DCNZM 2003); PC 1998; Managing Director, Jenny Shipley New Zealand Ltd, since 2002; Prime Minister of New Zealand, 1997–99; *b* 4 Feb. 1952; *d* of Rev. Len Robson and Adele Robson; *m* 1973, Burton Shipley; one *s* one *d*. *Educ:* Marlborough Coll., NZ; Christchurch Coll. of Educn (Dip. Teaching). Primary Sch. Teacher, 1972–77; farmer in partnership, 1973–88. MP (Nat.) Ashburton, then Rakaia, NZ, 1987–2002; MEC, NZ, 1990–99; Minister: of Social Welfare, 1990–93; of Women's Affairs, 1990–99; of Health, 1993–96; of State Services, of Transport, i/c Accident Rehabilitation and Compensation Insurance, for State Owned Enterprises, and i/c Radio NZ, 1996–97; i/c Security Intelligence Service, 1997–99; Chair, Security and Intelligence Cttee, 1997–99; Leader of the Opposition, 1999–2001. Chairman: Mainzeal Property and Construction Ltd, 2004–13; Genesis Energy, 2009–18; Global Women NZ, 2012–15; Oravida NZ Ltd, 2015–; Seniors Money Internat. Ltd, 2007–16; Co-Chm., Champions for Change, 2015; Director: Richina Pacific, 2004–; Momentum, 2005–; China Construction Bank, 2007– (Chm., 2014–). *Recreations:* gardening, walking, water sports.

**SHIPLEY DALTON, Duncan Edward;** Member (UU) Antrim South, Northern Ireland Assembly, 1998–2003; barrister-at-law; *b* 7 Nov. 1970; *s* of Kenneth Shipley and Susan Iris Dalton, BSc, MSc, PhD. *Educ:* Carisbrooke, Isle of Wight; Univ. of Essex (LLB Hons); Queen's Univ., Belfast (CPLS 1996; LLM 2003); BL Inn of Court of NI 1996; Harvard Univ. (MPA 2007). Called to the Bar, N Ireland, 1996; Mem., Gray's Inn, 2017. 7th (City of Belfast) Bn, Royal Irish Regt, 1994–98. *Recreations:* reading (history and politics), karate, computers.

**SHIPMAN, Timothy James;** Political Editor, Sunday Times, since 2014; *b* Basingstoke, Hants, 13 May 1975; *s* of Richard Shipman and Jane Shipman (*née* Neighbour); *m* 2015, Charlotte Todman; one *d*. *Educ:* Queen Elizabeth's Grammar Sch., Horncastle, Lincs; Churchill Coll., Cambridge (BA Hist. 1996; MPhil Internat. Relns 1997). Dep. Foreign Ed., Daily Express, 1998–2001; Dep. Political Ed., Sunday Express, 2001–05; Political corresp., Daily Mail, 2005–07; Washington corresp., Sunday Telegraph, 2007–09; Dep. Political Ed., Daily Mail, 2009–14. Chm., Parly Press Gall., 2012. Press Journalist of the Year, London Press Club, 2017; Political Reporter of the Year, Political Commentator of the Year, British Press Awards, 2018. *Publications:* All Out War: the full story of Brexit, 2016; Fall Out: a year of political mayhem, 2017. *Recreations:* reading, travelling, cricket, gluttony and sloth. *Address:* Sunday Times, 1 London Bridge Street, SE1 9GF. *T:* 07841 156819. *E:* tim.shipman@sunday-times.co.uk. *Clubs:* Groucho; White City All Stars Cricket.

**SHIPPERLEY, (Reginald) Stephen;** Executive Chairman, Connells Group, since 2008 (Chief Executive, 1989); *b* 31 Oct. 1958; *s* of Reginald Scott Shipperley and Elizabeth May Shipperley; *m* Janet Frances; three *d*. *Educ:* Brill Primary Sch.; Aylesbury Grammar Sch. Connells Estate Agents, 1977–; Founding Dir, 2000, non-exec. Dir, 2006–10, Rightmove plc. *Recreations:* cricket (player and spectator), all other sports as spectator, golf.

**SHIPSTER, Michael David,** CMG 2003; OBE 1990; HM Diplomatic Service, retired; international adviser, since 2013; *b* 17 March 1951; *s* of late Col John Neville Shipster, CBE, DSO and Cornelia Margaretha Shipster (*née* Arends); *m* 1974, Jackie, *d* of late Norman Mann, SA Springbok cricketer; one *s* two *d*. *Educ:* Ratcliffe Coll., Leicester; St Edmund Hall, Oxford (MA 1972); Sch. of Develt Studies, UEA (MA 1977). Nuffield Fellow, ODI, in Botswana, 1972–74; worked for Botswana Develt Corp., 1972–75; joined HM Diplomatic Service, 1977: Second Sec., FCO, 1977–79; Army Sch. of Languages, Beaconsfield, 1979–80; First Sec. (Econ.), Moscow, 1981–83; FCO, 1983–86; First Secretary: New Delhi, 1986–89; Lusaka, 1990; Consul (Political), Johannesburg, 1991–94; Counsellor: FCO, 1994–2004; Washington, 2004–06. Chm., Jt Adv. Gp for Overseas Business Risk (formerly Security Inf. for Business), UK Trade and Industry and FCO, 2011–13. Dir, Internat., Rolls-Royce, 2008–13. *Recreations:* music, military history, messing about on bikes and boats. *Address:* Carman's House, Compton, Winchester, Hants SO21 2AR. *Clubs:* Vincent's (Oxford); Royal Naval Sailing Association, Royal Cruising.

**SHIPTON, Alyn Graham,** PhD; Presenter, Jazz Record Requests, BBC Radio 3, since 2012; *b* Guildford, 24 Nov. 1953; *s* of Donald Shipton and Catherine Mary Shipton (*née* O'Donnell); *m* 1977, Siobhan Fraser; one *s* two *d*. *Educ:* Farnham Grammar Sch.; St Edmund Hall, Oxford (BA 1975); Oxford Brookes Univ. (PhD 2004). Sch. Books Editor, Macmillan, 1975–81; Publisher, Grove's Dictionaries of Music, 1981–87; Reference Publisher, Blackwell, 1987–95, Dir, NCC Blackwell Publishing, 1991–95. Presenter, 1989–, Exec. Prod. (for Unique Prodn Co.), 2012–17, (for 7digital), 2017–, BBC Radio 3. Lectr in Music, Oxford Brookes Univ., 2003–04; Lectr in Jazz Hist., 2008–, Res. Fellow, 2013–, RAM; Lectr in Jazz, City Univ., London, 2012–13. Hon. ARAM 2012. *Publications:* (with Danny Barker) A Life in Jazz, 1986, 2nd edn 2016; Fats Waller: his life and times, 1988, 2nd edn 2002; (with Alan Groves) The Glass Enclosure; the life of Bud Powell, 1993; Making Music, vols 1–6, 1993; (with Doc Cheatham) I Guess I'll Get The Papers and Go Home, 1996; Groovin' High: the life of Dizzy Gillespie, 1999; (with Danny Barker) Buddy Bolden and the Last Days of Storyville, 2002; A New History of Jazz, 2001, 2nd edn 2007; Jazz Makers, 2002; Handful of Keys, 2004; (with George Shearing) Lullaby of Birdland, 2004; Out of the Long Dark, 2006; I Feel a Song Coming On, 2009; Hi-De-Ho: life of Cab Calloway, 2010; Nilsson, 2013; (with Chris Barber) Jazz Me Blues, 2013; (with Billy J. Kramer) Do You Want To Know A Secret?, 2016; (contrib.) Harlem à Limoges, 2018; (contrib.) A History of European Jazz, 2018. *Recreations:* gardening, living and travelling in France, art, music, Co-Leader of Buck Clayton Legacy Band (jazz). *Address:* c/o BBC Radio 3, Broadcasting House, Portland Place, W1A 1AA. *E:* alyn.shipton@bbc.co.uk.

**SHIRAKAWA, Prof. Hideki,** PhD; Professor, Institute of Materials Science, University of Tsukuba, 1982–2000, now Emeritus; *b* Tokyo, Aug. 1936; *s* of Hatsutarou and Fuyuno Shirakawa; *m* 1966, Chiyoko Shibuya; two *s*. *Educ:* Tokyo Inst. of Technol. (PhD 1966). Res. Associate, Tokyo Inst. of Technol., 1966–79; Associate Prof., Inst. of Materials Sci., Univ. of Tsukuba, 1979–82. Pioneered work on conductive polymers. (Jtly) Nobel Prize for Chemistry, 2000. Order of Culture (Japan), 2000. *Address:* c/o Institute of Materials Science, University of Tsukuba, Sakura-mura, Ibaraki 305, Japan.

**SHIRE, Rabbi Dr Michael Jonathan;** Chief Academic Officer, since 2016, and Dean, Shoolman Graduate School of Jewish Education, since 2011, Hebrew College, Boston; *b* 15 Dec. 1957; *s* of Dr Heinz Shire and Ruth Shire; *m* 1991, Rabbi Marcia Plumb; one *s* one *d*. *Educ:* George Dixon Sch., Birmingham; University Coll. London (BA Hons 1981); Hebrew Union Coll., USA (MA 1983; PhD 1996); Leo Baeck Coll. (MA 1995). Dir of Educn, Temple Beth Hillel, Calif, 1983–88; Dep. Dir, 1988–90, Dir, 1990–2002, Centre for Jewish Educn; Vice-Principal, Leo Baeck Coll. - Centre for Jewish Educn, later Leo Baeck Coll., 2002–11. Ordained, 1996. *Publications:* The Illuminated Haggadah, 1998; L'Chaim, 2000; The Jewish Prophet, 2002; Mazal-Tov, 2003. *Recreations:* theatre, contemporary architecture, the men's movement, modern fiction. *Address:* Hebrew College, 160 Herrick Road, Newton Centre, MA 02459, USA. *T:* (617) 6784951.

**SHIRLEY,** family name of **Earl Ferrers.**

**SHIRLEY, Martin William,** CBE 2010; PhD; FRSB; CBiol; Director, Institute for Animal Health, 2006–10; *b* Leighton Buzzard, 8 Dec. 1949; *s* of William Shirley and Pamela Shirley; *m* 1992, Fiona Clare Dunsdon; one *s* one *d*, and one step *s* one step *d*. *Educ:* Cedars Sch., Leighton Buzzard; Brunel Univ. (BSc 1974; PhD 1977). MIBiol 1974, FRSB (FSB 2009); CBiol 1994. Houghton Poultry Research Station: Technician, 1967–74; Res. Scientist, 1974–92; Institute for Animal Health: Principal Scientist, 1992–2003; Hd, Molecular Biol., 2003–04; Dep. Dir, 2004–06. Visiting Professor: Liverpool Univ., 2002; Guangdong Acad. of Agricultural Scis, 2003. Hon. Prof., RVC, 2007. Trustee: Houghton Trust, 1996–2014; British Egg Mktg Bd Trust, 2011–; Chairman: Chicken (formerly Poultry) Tech. Adv. Cttee, 2011–, Duck Tech. Adv. Cttee, 2013–, Turkey Tech. Adv. Cttee, 2015–, Red Tractor. Hon. Fellow, Liverpool Sch. of Tropical Medicine, 2003; Hon. Associate, RCVS, 2010. Tom Newman Meml Medal Internat. Award for Poultry Sci., British Poultry Council, 1989; Res. Medal, Royal Agricl Soc. of England, 2004. *Publications:* over 200 articles on biology of avian coccidial parasites, *Eimeria* spp. and coccidiosis. *Recreations:* golf, photography, computing, learning about wine, tackling a variety of Times puzzles, spending time with grandchildren, Ava, Lucas, Serennah, Imogen and Orla, following Rugby football. *Address:* 48 Vineyard Way, Buckden, St Neots, Cambs PE19 5SR. *Clubs:* Farmers; Brampton Park Golf; Hunstanton Golf.

**SHIRLEY, Dame (Vera) Stephanie, (Steve),** CH 2017; DBE 2000 (OBE 1980); FMedSci; FREng; FBCS CITP; philanthropist; UK Ambassador for Philanthropy, 2009–10; *b* 16 Sept. 1933; *d* of late Arnold Buchthal and Mrs Margaret Brook (formerly Buchthal, *née* Schick); name changed to Brook on naturalisation, 1951; *m* 1959, Derek George Millington Shirley; (one *s* decd). *Educ:* Sir John Cass Coll., London. BSc (Spec.) London 1956. FBCS CITP 2003 (FBCS 1971). PO Res. Stn, Dollis Hill, 1951–59; CDL (subsid. of ICL), 1959–62; F International Group, later F.I. Group, 1962–93 (Founder and Chief Exec., 1962–87; Settlor Xansa Employee (formerly FI Shareholders') Trust, 1981); Life Pres., Xansa (formerly F.I. Gp plc), 1993; Director: AEA Technology Plc, 1992–2000; Tandem Computers Inc., 1992–97; John Lewis Partnership plc, 1999–2001; European Adv. Bd, Korn/Ferry Internat., 2001–04; CSR Adv. Bd, Steria, 2008. Member: Computer, Systems and Electronics Requirements Bd, 1979–81; Electronics and Avionics Requirements Bd, 1981–83; Open Tech, MSC, 1983–86; Council, Industrial Soc., 1984–90; NCVQ, 1986–89; Strategy Bd, Oxford Internet Inst., 2000–11. Pres., British Computer Soc., 1989–90; Vice Pres., C&G, 2000–05. Consulting Editor on information processing, J. Wiley & Sons, 1978–87. Member: Council, Duke of Edinburgh's Seventh Commonwealth Study Conf., 1991–92; British-N American Cttee, 1992–2001. Chm., Women of Influence, 1993. President: Autistica (formerly Nat. Alliance for Autism Res. (UK), then Autism Speaks), 2009 (Founder, 2004); Autism Cymru, 2012 (Founder, 2001); Trustee: Help The Aged, 1987–90; Nat. Alliance for Autism Res. (USA), 2004–06. Patron: Disablement Income Gp, 1989–2001; Centre for Tomorrow's Co., 1997–2017; Fellow, Oxford Univ. Ct of Benefactors, 2001–; Companion, Guild of Cambridge Benefactors, 2006–; Univ. Benefactor, Edinburgh, 2013. Founder: The Kingwood Trust, later Autism at Kingwood, 1993; The Shirley Foundn, 1996–2019; Prior's Court Foundn, 1998. Master, Information Technologists' Co., 1992 (Liveryman, 1992); Freeman, City of London, 1987. CCMI (CBIM 1984); FREng 2001; FMedSci 2017. Hon. FCGI 1989. Hon. Fellow: Manchester Metropolitan Univ. (formerly Poly.), 1989; Staffordshire Univ. (formerly Poly.), 1991; Sheffield Hallam Univ., 1992; IMCB, 1999; Birkbeck, 2002; Murray Edwards Coll. (formerly New Hall), Cambridge, 2002; RCPsych, 2017; Foundn Fellow, Balliol Coll., Oxford, 2001. Hon. DSc: Buckingham, 1991; Aston, 1993; Nottingham Trent, 1994; Southampton Inst., 1994; Southampton, 2003; Brunel, 2005; Lincoln, 2014; Cambridge, 2017; Royal Holloway, 2018; Hon. DTech: Loughborough, 1991; Kingston, 1995; DUniv: Leeds Metropolitan, 1993; Derby, 1997; London Guildhall, 1998; Stirling, 2000; Strathclyde, 2014; Hon. DLitt: de Montfort, 1993; Bradford, 2017; Hon. DBA: West of England, 1995; City, 2000; Hon. Dr: Edinburgh, 2003; Open, 2009; Hon. LLD: Leicester, 2005; Bath, 2006; St Andrews, 2011; University Campus Suffolk, 2012; Hon. DEng Portsmouth, 2018. Recognition of Information Technology Achievement Award, 1985; Gold Medal, Inst. of Mgt, 1991; Mountbatten Medal, IEE, 1999. US Nat. Women's Hall of Fame, 1995; US Computer Hall of Fame, 2018. *Publications:* Let IT Go (memoir), 2012, republd 2019. *Recreation:* wishful thinking. *Address:* 47 Thames House, Phyllis Court Drive, Henley-on-Thames, Oxon RG9 2NA. *T:* (01491) 579004, *Fax:* (01491) 574995. *E:* steve@steveshirley.com. *Club:* Royal Society of Medicine.

**SHIRRAS, Ven. Edward Scott;** Priest-in-charge, Marcham with Garford, diocese of Oxford, 2002–09; *b* 23 April 1937; *s* of Edward Shirras and Alice Emma Shirras (*née* Morten); *m* 1962, Pamela Susan Mackenzie; two *s* three *d*. *Educ:* Sevenoaks School; St Andrews Univ. (BSc); Union Coll., Schenectady, NY, USA; Clifton Theol Coll., Bristol. Curate: Christ Church, Surbiton Hill, 1963–66; Jesmond Parish Church, Newcastle upon Tyne, 1966–68; Church Pastoral Aid Society: Youth Sec., 1968–71; Publications Sec., 1971–74; Asst Gen. Sec., 1974–75; Vicar of Christ Church, Roxeth, dio. London, 1975–85; Area Dean of Harrow, 1982–85; Archdeacon of Northolt, 1985–92; Vicar, Christ Church, Winchester, 1992–2001. *Recreations:* transport photography (Scottish), Aberdeen FC. *Address:* 4 Culham Close, Abingdon, Oxon OX14 2AS. *T:* (01235) 553129. *E:* epshirras@aol.com.

**SHIRREFF, Gen. Sir (Alexander) Richard (David),** KCB 2010; CBE 2001; Founder and Managing Partner, Strategia Worldwide Ltd, since 2016; *b* 21 Oct. 1955; *s* of late Alexander David Shirreff, MC and Dione Hilary Shirreff (*née* Wood-White); *m* 1980, Sarah-Jane Patrick; one *s* one *d*. *Educ:* Oundle Sch.; Exeter Coll., Oxford (BA, MA Mod. Hist.). Commnd 14th/20th King's Hussars, 1978; sc 1986–87; COS HQ 33 Armoured Bde, 1988–89; MA to C-in-C BAOR and Comdr Northern Army Gp, 1992–94; Comdg King's Royal Hussars, 1994–96; Col, Army Plans, MoD, 1996–98; Comdr 7th Armoured Bde, 1999–2000; Principal SO to CDS, 2000–02; rcds 2003; COS HQ Land Comd, 2003–05; GOC 3rd (UK) Div., 2005–07; Comdr Allied Rapid Reaction Corps, 2007–11; Dep. Supreme Allied Comdr Europe, 2011–14. Hon. Colonel: Oxford Univ. OTC, 2007–13; Royal Wessex Yeomanry, 2010–15; Col, King's Royal Hussars, 2013–17. Mem., Develt Bd, English Touring Opera, 2019–. *Publications:* 2017: War with Russia (fiction), 2016. *Recreations:* ski-ing, the country, walking, history. *Address:* c/o Home HQ, King's Royal Hussars, Peninsula Barracks, Winchester, Hants SO23 8TS. *T:* (01962) 828539. *Clubs:* Beefsteak, Cavalry and Guards, Pitt.

**SHIVJI, Rebecca;** *see* Stubbs, R.

**SHLAIM, Prof. Avi,** PhD; FBA 2006; Professor of International Relations, University of Oxford, 1996–2011; Fellow, St Antony's College, Oxford, 1987–2011, now Emeritus; *b* Baghdad, 31 Oct. 1945; *s* of Joseph and Aida Shlaim; *m* 1973, Gwyneth Daniel; one *d*. *Educ:* Jesus Coll., Cambridge (BA Hist. 1969); London Sch. of Econs (MSc(Econ.) Internat. Relns 1970); Reading Univ. (PhD Politics 1980). Lectr, 1970–86, Reader in Politics, 1986–87, Univ. of Reading; University of Oxford: Alastair Buchan Reader in Internat. Relns, 1987–96; Dir, Grad. Studies in Internat. Relns, 1993–95 and 1998–2001; Dir, Middle E Centre, 2007–08, Sub-Warden, 2008–10, St Antony's Coll., Oxford. Fellow, Woodrow Wilson Internat. Center for Scholars, Washington, 1980–81; British Acad. Res. Reader, 1995–97; British Acad. Res. Prof., 2003–06. Sir Percy Sykes Meml Medal, RSAA, 2011; British Acad. Medal for Lifetime Achievement, 2017. *Publications:* (jtly) British Foreign

Secretaries since 1945, 1977; The United States and the Berlin Blockade 1948–49: a study in crisis decision-making, 1983; Collusion across the Jordan: King Abdullah, the Zionist Movement, and the partition of Palestine, 1988; The Politics of Partition, 1990; War and Peace in the Middle East: a concise history, 1995; (ed jtly) The Cold War and the Middle East, 1997; The Iron Wall: Israel and the Arab world, 2000, rev. edn 2014; (ed jtly) The War for Palestine: rewriting the history of 1948, 2001; Lion of Jordan: the life of King Hussein in war and peace, 2007; Israel and Palestine: reappraisals, revisions, refutations, 2009; (ed jtly) The 1967 Arab-Israeli War: origins and consequences, 2012. *Recreations:* walking and talking. *Address:* St Antony's College, Oxford OX2 6JF. *T:* (01865) 274460. *E:* avi.shlaim@sant.ox.ac.uk.

**SHOEBRIDGE, Michele Indianna**; consultant in higher education, since 2015; Deputy Registrar (formerly Director, Academic Services), University of Exeter, 2006–15; *b* 7 Nov. 1954; *d* of Charles William Shoebridge and Maisie Indianna Shoebridge (*née* Wissenden); one *d*. *Educ:* Maidstone Tech. High Sch. for Girls; Univ. of Birmingham (BA Hons Medieval and Mod. Hist. 1976); City of Birmingham Poly. (Postgrad. DipLib 1977); Wolverhampton Univ. (MA 1982). University of Birmingham: various posts, University Library, 1979–95, Information Services, 1995–2002; Dir, Inf. Services, 2002–06; Interim Registrar: UWS, 2015–16; SOAS, 2016–17; Interim Dir of Campus Life, Ulster Univ., 2017–18; Interim Dep. Registrar, Univ. of Bristol, 2018–19. *Publications:* Women in Sport: a select bibliography, 1988; Union Catalogue of Periodicals in Sport and Recreation, 1988; Information Sources in Sport and Leisure, 1991; (jtly) A History of the Birmingham Athletic Institute, 1992; articles in jls on aspects of inf. mgt, teaching and learning. *Recreations:* family, cinema, travel, history of art.

**SHONE, Carole Gibson;** *see* Mundell, C. G.

**SHONE, Richard Noel**; Editor, The Burlington Magazine, 2003–15; *b* Doncaster, 8 May 1949; *s* of Dr Godfrey Noel Shone and Eleanor May Shone (*née* Clough). *Educ:* Wrekin Coll.; Clare Coll., Cambridge (BA 1971). Associate Ed., The Burlington Mag., 1979–2003. Exhibition Curator: Portraits by Duncan Grant, Arts Council, 1969; Duncan Grant: designer, 1980; Portraits by Walter Sickert, 1990; Sickert (co-selector), RA and Van Gogh Mus., Amsterdam, 1992–93; Head First, Arts Council tour, 1998–99; The Art of Bloomsbury, Tate Gall., London, Huntington Liby, San Marino, Calif, Yale Center for British Art, New Haven, Conn, 1999–2000. Mem., Adv. Cttee, Govt Art Collection, 1990–94. Member: Charleston Trust, 1981–2011; Jury, Turner Prize, 1988. *Publications:* Bloomsbury Portraits: Vanessa Bell, Duncan Grant and their circle, 1976, 2nd edn 1993; The Century of Change: British painting since 1900, 1977; Augustus John, 1979; The Post-Impressionists, 1980; Walter Sickert, 1988; Rodrigo Moynihan, 1988; Alfred Sisley, 1992; Damien Hirst, 2001; (ed jtly) The Books that Shaped Art History, 2013; numerous catalogue introductions. *Address:* 87 High Street, Hastings, E Sussex TN34 3ES. *Club:* Cranium.

**SHONIBARE, Yinka,** CBE 2019 (MBE 2004); RA 2013; visual artist, since 1991; *b* London, 9 Aug. 1962; *s* of Olatunji Shonibare and Laide Shonibare; one *s*. *Educ:* Redrice Sch.; Byam Shaw Sch. of Art; Goldsmiths Coll. (MA 1991; Hon. Fellow 2003). *Exhibitions include:* Sensation, RA, 1997; Documenta 11, Kassel, 2002; Nelson's Ship in a Bottle, Fourth Plinth, Trafalgar Square, 2010, Nat. Maritime Mus., 2013; Pop!, Stephen Friedman Gall., 2013; Fabric-Ation, Yorks Sculpture Park, 2013; William Morris Gall., 2015. Estabd Guest Projects, experimental project space, 2009–. FRSA 2010. Hon. Dr: Huron, 2007; RCA, 2010. Wollaston Award, RA, 2010. *Recreations:* opera, cinema, music, museums. *Address:* Sunbury House, 1 Andrews Road, E8 4QL. *T:* (020) 7249 1409. *E:* info@guestprojects.com. *Clubs:* Arts, Shoreditch House, Black's.

**SHOOTER, Adrian,** CBE 2010; FREng; FIMechE; Chairman: Vivarail Ltd, since 2012; SLC Ltd, since 2016; Vintage Trains Ltd; *b* London, 22 Nov. 1948; *s* of late Prof. Reginald Arthur Shooter, CBE and Jean Shooter (*née* Wallace); *m* 1st, 1970, Diana Crombie (marr. diss. 2002); one *s* one *d*; 2nd, 2006, Barbara Harding. *Educ:* Epsom Coll.; N Staffs Poly. (HND Mech. Engrg 1970). With British Railways, 1970–96: engrg grad. trainee, 1970–71; engrg mgt posts, 1971–84; Area Manager, St Pancras, 1984–87; Man. Dir, Red Star Parcels, 1987–89; Dir, Parcels Business, 1989–93; Man. Dir, 1993–2001, Chm., 2002–11, Chiltern Rlys. Chm., Oxon LEP, 2012–15. Non-executive Director: Railway Safety and Standards Bd, 2004–11; Wabtec UK Ltd, 2012–14. Chm., W Midlands Regl Council, CBI, 2011–13. Hon. Dr: Staffs, 2002; Birmingham, 2013. *Recreations:* restoring and driving vintage cars, running steam railways, helping develop communities. *E:* shooter.adrian@gmail.com.

**SHOOTER, Michael Stanhope,** CBE 2005; FRCPsych; President, Royal College of Psychiatrists, 2002–05; *b* 19 Sept. 1944; *s* of Arnold Shooter and Audrey Frances Shooter (*née* Stanhope); *m* 1967, Mary Davies; three *s* one *d*. *Educ:* Lady Manners Sch., Bakewell; St Catharine's Coll., Cambridge (MA Hist./Law); Clare Coll., Cambridge (MB BChir). FRCPsych 1994. Consultant: Child and Adolescent Psychiatry, S Glamorgan, 1982–94; and Clinical Dir, Child Psychiatry Service, Gwent Healthcare NHS Trust, 1994–2002. Dir of Public Educn, 1994–2002, Registrar, 1997–2002, RCPsych. Pres., British Assoc. for Counselling and Psychotherapy, 2012–16. Chairman: Young Minds, 2006–09; Children in Wales, 2006–12; Mental Health Foundn, 2008–11; Play Wales, 2015–. *Publications:* contrib. books and jls on all aspects of psychiatry and paediatric liaison in UK, USA and elsewhere. *Recreations:* horse-racing, poetry, late-night cards in isolated country pubs. *Address:* Ty Boda, Upper Llanover, Abergavenny, Gwent NP7 9EP. *E:* shootermary@yahoo.co.uk. *Club:* East India.

**SHORE OF STEPNEY, Lady;** *see* Shore, E. C.

**SHORE, Andrew;** freelance operatic baritone, since 1979; *b* Oldham, Lancs, 30 Sept. 1952; *s* of Frank and Edith Shore; *m* 1976, Fiona Mary Macdonald; three *d*. *Educ:* Counthill Grammar Sch., Oldham; Bristol Univ. (BA Theol. 1974); Royal Northern Coll. of Music; London Opera Centre. Débuts: Kent Opera, 1979; ENO, 1987; Glyndebourne Fest. Opera, 1988; Royal Opera, Covent Gdn, 1992; Paris Opera, 1995; Metropolitan Opera, NY, 2006; Bayreuth Fest., Germany, 2006; La Scala, Milan, 2009; rôles include: title rôles in Falstaff, Don Pasquale, Gianni Schicchi, King Priam, Wozzeck, Jakob Lenz; Papageno in Die Zauberflöte; Bartolo in Barbiere di Siviglia; Dulcamara in L'Elisir d'amore; Leporello in Don Giovanni; Alberich in Der Ring des Nibelungen; Pooh Bah in The Mikado; Major-General in The Pirates of Penzance; Beckmesser in Die Meistersinger; Fra Melitone in The Force of Destiny. FRNCM 2015. Hon. DMus Bristol, 2014. *Recreations:* theatre, art galleries, country-walking, fine wine, model railways. *Address:* c/o Groves Artists, 7 St George's Court, 131 Putney Bridge Road, SW15 2PA. *T:* (020) 8874 3222. *E:* jg@groveartists.co.uk. *Club:* Two Brydges.

**SHORE, Dr Elizabeth Catherine,** CB 1980; Chairman, St Ives University of the Third Age, 2004–07; *b* 19 Aug. 1927; *d* of Edward Murray Wrong and Rosalind Grace Smith; *m* 1948, Peter David Shore (later Baron Shore of Stepney, PC; he *d* 2001); one *s* two *d* (and one *s* decd). *Educ:* Newnham Coll., Cambridge; St Bartholomew's Hospital; BA Hons Open 1999. MRCP, FRCP; MRCS, FFCM, DRCOG. Joined Medical Civil Service, 1962; Dep. Chief Medical Officer, DHSS, 1977–85. Dean of Postgrad. Medicine, NW Thames Reg., 1985–93; Assoc. Dean of Postgrad. Med. Educn, N Thames Reg., 1993–95. Hon. Sen. Lectr, Charing Cross and Westminster Med. Sch., 1993–97. Mem., GMC, 1989–94 (Member: Standards Cttee, 1989–91; Professional Conduct Cttee, 1991–93; Educnl Cttee, 1992–93; Prelim. Proceeding Cttee, 1993). Pres., Med. Women's Fedn, 1990–92 (Chm., Careers Cttee, 1989–95); Chair: BMA Career Progress Cttee, 1994–96; BMA Working Party on Exodus of Doctors, 1996–97. Mem. Council, PSI, 1992–2001; Chm., Mgt Cttee, St Ives Archive Centre, 2005–07. Trustee, Child Accident Prevention Trust, 1985–91 (Chm., Council and Professional Cttee, 1985–90). Editor, Medical Woman, 1992–98. *Recreations:* reading, cookery, swimming in rough seas. *Address:* 3 Barnaloft, St Ives, Cornwall TR26 1NJ.

**SHORE, Prof. Paul Raymond,** PhD; FREng; Head, Engineering Measurement Division, National Physical Laboratory, since 2015; McKeown Professor of Ultra Precision Technologies, Cranfield University, since 2003 (Head, Precision Engineering Centre, 2003–15); *b* Chester, 5 Oct. 1962; *s* of John Shore and Eileen Shore (*née* Walker); *m* 1993, Siân Jones; one *s* two *d*. *Educ:* Liverpool Poly. (HND Mech. Engrg 1984); Cranfield Inst. of Technol. (MSc Machine Design 1986); Cranfield Univ. (PhD Ultra Precision Engrg 1995). FREng 2009. Process Develt Manager, Cranfield Unit for Precision Engrg, 1988–95; Sen. Engr, SKF (Netherlands), 1996–97; Tech. Develt Manager, Lidköping Machine Tools, 1997–2000; Gp Tech. Manager, SKF (Sweden), 2000–03. Pres., Eur. Soc. for Precision Engrg and Nanotechnol., 2011–13. *Publications:* contribs to jls incl. Wear, Advanced Engrg Materials, Key Engrg Materials, Ingenia. *Recreations:* classic motorcycling, football. *Address:* 29 The Mount, Aspley Guise, Beds MK17 8DZ. *T:* (01908) 582944. *E:* shores29@btinternet.com. *Club:* Brickhill Rangers Association Football.

**SHORLEY, Deborah Catherine,** FCLIP; Director of Library Services, Imperial College London, 2007–12; President, Chartered Institute of Library and Information Professionals, 2005–06; *b* 28 May 1950; *d* of late Dennis Randall and Monica (*née* Wilson); *m* 1976, Christopher Shorley (*d* 2007). *Educ:* Univ. of Durham (BA Hons French 1972); Queen's Univ., Belfast (DLIS 1977). FCLIP 2004. Librarian: Central Liby, Belfast, 1977–80; Ulster Polytechnic, subseq. Univ. of Ulster, 1980–2000; Univ. of Sussex, 2000–07. *Publications:* (ed with M. Jubb) The Future of Scholarly Communication, 2013; articles on liby and information issues to professional jls. *E:* dshorley@gmail.com.

**SHORROCK, (John) Michael;** QC 1988; a Recorder of the Crown Court, 1982–2015; *b* 25 May 1943; *s* of late James Godby Shorrock and Mary Patricia Shorrock (*née* Lings); *m* 1971, Marianne (*née* Mills); two *d*. *Educ:* Clifton College, Bristol; Pembroke College, Cambridge. MA. Called to the Bar, Inner Temple, 1966, Bencher, 1995; in practice as barrister, Manchester, 1966–2005, London, 2005–16; Junior, 1968, Sec., Exec. Cttee, 1981–85, Northern Circuit. Member: Criminal Injuries Compensation Bd, 1995–2000; Criminal Injuries Compensation Appeals Panel, 1996–2008; Tribunal Judge, Social Entitlement Chamber, Criminal Injuries Compensation, 2008–16. Gov., William Hulme's Grammar Sch., 1999–2005. *Recreations:* walking, gardening, opera, theatre, cinema, golf. *Address:* 2 Harcourt Buildings, Temple, EC4Y 9DB. *T:* (020) 7353 2112.

**SHORROCK, Philip Geoffrey; His Honour Judge Shorrock;** a Circuit Judge, since 2009; *b* 28 June 1956; *s* of Geoffrey and Jean Shorrock. *Educ:* King's Sch., Canterbury; Clare Coll., Cambridge (BA Hons Law 1977). Called to the Bar, Middle Temple, 1978, Bencher, 2005; in practice as barrister, 1978–2009; Recorder, 2002–09. *Recreations:* the turf, cricket, soccer, good food, drink and company. *Address:* Woolwich Crown Court, 2 Belmarsh Road, SE28 0EY. *T:* (020) 8321 7000. *Clubs:* Garrick, XII.

**SHORT, Alan;** *see* Short, C. A.

**SHORT, Andrew John;** QC 2010; *b* Sidcup, 30 March 1967; *s* of John Short and Shirley Short; *m* 1998, Frances Louise Tomlinson; one *d*. *Educ:* Dartford Grammar Sch.; Bristol Univ. (LLB Hons). Called to the Bar, Gray's Inn, 1990; in practice as barrister, specialising in employment, discrimination and pensions law. *Publications:* Disability Discrimination: law and practice, 1996. *Recreations:* triathlon, Arsenal, food (all aspects). *Address:* Outer Temple Chambers, The Outer Temple, 222 Strand, WC2R 1BA. *T:* (020) 7353 6381. *E:* andrew.short@outertemple.com. *Club:* East London Triathletes.

**SHORT, (Bernard) David,** CBE 1995; Head of Further Education Support Unit, Department for Education and Employment (formerly Department for Education), 1993–96; *b* 9 June 1935; *s* of late Bernard Charles and of Ethel Florence Short; *m* 1960, Susan Yvonne Taylor (*d* 2013); two *s* one *d*. *Educ:* St Edmund Hall, Oxford (MA). Served The Royal Scots, 1953–56 (commnd 1954). Taught at Ingiliz Erkek Lisesi, Istanbul, Turkey, 1960–63; Lectr, Univ. of Kyushu, Japan, 1963–65; Asst Lectr, Garretts Green Technical Coll., Birmingham, 1966–67; Lectr, Bournville Coll. of Further Educn, Birmingham, 1967–71; Sen. Lectr, Henley Coll. of Further Educn, Coventry, 1971–73; Head, Dept of Gen. Studies, Bournville Coll., Birmingham, 1973–76; HM Inspectorate of Schools, 1976–93: Inspector, 1976; Staff Inspector, 1984; Chief Inspector, Further Education, 1986. Chm. of Govs, Bournville Coll., Birmingham, 2000–06. FRSA 1991. *Publications:* A Guide to Stress in English, 1967; Humour, 1970. *Recreations:* music, gardening, seven grandchildren.

**SHORT, Prof. (Charles) Alan,** PhD; Professor of Architecture, University of Cambridge, since 2001 (Head, Department of Architecture, 2001–04); Fellow, since 2002 and Vice President, since 2018, Clare Hall, Cambridge; Principal, Short & Associates, since 1997; *b* 23 March 1955; *s* of C. R. and D. H. Short; *m* 2003, Slaine Catherine Campbell; one *d*. *Educ:* Trinity Coll., Cambridge (MA, DipArch); Univ. of Cambridge (PhD). RIBA 1981. Exchange Fellow, Harvard Grad. Sch. of Design, 1979–80; Partner: Edward Cullinan Architects, 1980–86; Peake Short and Partners, 1986–92; Short Ford & Associates, 1992–97; Dean, Faculty of Art and Design, De Montfort Univ., 1997–2001. George Collins Fellowship, Soc. of Architectural Historians, USA, 2014; Geddes Fellow, Univ. of Edinburgh, 2014. Dist. Prof., People's Republic of China, 2018–; Guest Prof., Zhejiang Univ., 2019–. Major projects include: Simonds Farsons Cisk Brewery, Malta (High Architecture, Low Energy Award, Architecture Today jl, 1994); Queen's Building, Leicester (Green Building of the Year Award, Independent/RIBA, 1995); Coventry Univ. Library (Public Building of Year award, Building mag., 2001); Poole Arts Centre, Dorset, 2002 (Project of Year Award, CIBSE, 2003); Lichfield Garrick Theatre, 2003 (Project of Year Award, CIBSE, 2004); new SSEES for UCL, 2005 (RIBA Award, 2006; Envmtl Initiative of the Year Award, CIBSE, 2006; Public Building of the Year, BDA, 2006;) Braunstone Integrated Health and Social Care Centre, 2005. President's Award for Res., 2007, President's Commendation for Res., 2009, RIBA. Mem., Editl Bd, Bldg Res. and Inf., 2011–. Global Sustainability Film Award, tv/e, 2013; Carter Bronze Medal, CIBSE, 2016. *Publications:* Geometry and Atmosphere, 2011; The Recovery of Natural Environments in Architecture, 2017; contrib. jls. *Recreations:* restoration of family home and gardens in Lincolnshire, historical and contemporary landscape. *Address:* Department of Architecture, University of Cambridge, 1–4 Scroope Terrace, Trumpington Road, Cambridge CB2 1PX. *T:* (01223) 332958, *Fax:* (01223) 307443. *E:* cas64@cam.ac.uk. *Clubs:* Chelsea Arts, Oxford and Cambridge.

**SHORT, Rt Hon. Clare;** PC 1997; *b* 15 Feb. 1946; *d* of late Frank Short and Joan Short; *m* 1981, Alexander Ward Lyon (*d* 1993), sometime MP for York; one *s* by previous marriage. *Educ:* Keele Univ.; Leeds Univ. (BA Hons Political Sci.). Home Office, 1970–75; Dir, All Faiths for One Race, Birmingham, 1976–78; Dir, Youth Aid and the Unemployment Unit, 1979–83. MP Birmingham, Ladywood, 1983–2010 (Lab, 1983–2006, Ind, 2006–10). Chm., All Party Parly Gp on Race Relations, 1985–86; Mem., Home Affairs Select Cttee, 1983–85; front bench spokesperson on employment, 1985–88, on social security, 1989–91, on envmtl protection, 1993, on women, 1993–95, on transport, 1995–96, on overseas develt, 1996–97; Sec. of State for Internat. Develt, 1997–2003. Mem., Labour Party NEC, 1988–98. Chair, Extractive Industries Transparency Initiative, 2011–16. Chair, Bd, Cities Alliance, 2016– (Sen. Policy Advr, 2006–16). Trustee, Hope Projects, W Midlands, 2011–; Patron, Israeli Cttee against House Demolitions, 2012–. *Publications:* Talking Blues: a study of young West Indians' views of policing, 1978; Handbook of Immigration Law, 1978; Dear Clare … this is what women think about Page 3, 1991; An Honourable Deception?: New Labour, Iraq and the misuse of power, 2004. *Recreations:* family and friends, swimming. *W:* www.clareshort.org.

**SHORT, Maj. Gen. James Henderson Terry,** CB 2005; OBE 1994; Director, AugMentor UK, 2006–15; Director, Joint Warfare Centre (formerly Chief of Staff, Joint Headquarters North), Norway, 2002–05; *b* 20 March 1950; *s* of Frederick Gordon Terry Short and Verona Margaret Terry Short (*née* Peters); *m* 1975, Claire Elizabeth Hedley (*née* Hooper); two *s*. *Educ:* Wellington Coll., Berks; RMCS, Shrivenham (BSc Hons Applied Sci.). Regtl Service, 9th/12th Royal Lancers, 1970–82; army staff course, 1982–83; MA to Comdr 1 (BR) Corps, 1984–86; Directing Staff, Staff Coll., Camberley, 1988–90; Procurement Exec., MoD, 1990–92; CO 9th/12th Royal Lancers, 1992–94; Cabinet Office Assessments Staff, 1994–95; Comdr 39 Infantry Bde, Belfast, 1995–97; Dir, RAC, 1997–2000; Special Advr to Macedonian Govt, 2000–02. Col, 9th/12th Royal Lancers, 2008–15. Chm., Jesse May Trust, 2008–13. FCMI (FIMgt 1997). *Recreations:* sailing (Atlantic crossing 2013 (Warrior 40—Ocean Rainbow); Caribbean/S and Central America 2014–17), ski-ing, tennis, windsurfing. *Address:* 11 Tansy Lane, Portishead, N Somerset BS20 7JL. *T:* 07818 054645. *E:* jhtshort@hotmail.com. *Club:* Cavalry and Guards.

**SHORT, Rt Rev. Mark Graham;** *see* Canberra and Goulburn, Bishop of.

**SHORT, Dr Mary Elizabeth;** Headmistress, St Helen's School, Northwood, 2011–19; *b* Gillingham, Kent, 2 Oct. 1958; *d* of Alexander Short and Joyce Short (*née* Taylor); *m* 2005, David Dyke. *Educ:* Chatham Grammar Sch. for Girls; University Coll. London (BA Hons Hist.); Inst. of Educn, Univ. of London (PGCE); St John's Coll., Cambridge (PhD 1986). Teacher of History and Politics, City of London Sch., 1987–95; Hd of Hist., St Paul's Girls' Sch., 1995–2004; Dep. Hd, Pastoral, Haberdashers' Aske's Sch. for Girls, 2004–11. Governor: Orley Farm Sch., 2015–; Ladies Coll., Guernsey, 2016–. Trustee, NFL Trust, 2019–. *Recreations:* walking, reading, history, pottering - gardening, cooking, drawing. *Address:* 58 Leicester Road, N2 9EA. *T:* (020) 8883 6611. *E:* maryeshort@gmail.com. *Club:* Royal Air Force.

**SHORT, Nigel David,** MBE 1999; professional chess player, commentator, coach and writer; *b* 1 June 1965; *s* of David Malcolm Short and Jean Short (*née* Gaskell); *m* 1987, Rhea Argyro, *d* of Nikolaos Karageorgiou; one *s* one *d*. *Educ:* Bolton Sch. British chess champion: 1979 (equal first), 1984, 1987, 1998; English Chess Champion, 1991; internat. master 1980; grandmaster 1984; world championship candidate, 1985–93 (finalist, 1992, defeating Anatoly Karpov in semi-final); Commonwealth Champion, 2004, 2006, 2008; EU Champion, 2006; Canadian Open Champion, 2013. Formed Professional Chess Assoc. with Garry Kasparov, 1993, Pres., 2005–08. Chess columnist: Sunday Telegraph, 1996–2005; The Guardian, 2005–06; New in Chess, 2011–. Chess Coach, Islamic Republic of Iran, 2006–07. Vice-Pres., World Chess Fedn, 2018–. Hon. ScD Bolton, 2010. *Recreations:* olive farming, cricket, swimming, guitar.

**SHORT, Norma Ann;** *see* Winstone, N. A.

**SHORT, Robin;** *see* Short, W. R.

**SHORT, Prof. Roger Valentine,** AM 2004; FRCOG; FRS 1974; FRSE; FRCVS; FAA; Hon. Professorial Fellow, Faculty of Medicine, University of Melbourne, since 2006; *b* 31 July 1930; *s* of F. A. and M. C. Short, Weybridge, Surrey; *m* 1st, 1958, Dr Mary Bowen Wilson (marr. diss. 1981); one *s* three *d*; 2nd, 1982, Prof. Marilyn Bernice Renfree; two *d*. *Educ:* Sherborne Sch.; Univs of Bristol (BVSc, MRCVS), Wisconsin (MSc) and Cambridge (PhD, ScD). FRSE 1974; FRCVS 1976; FAA 1984; FRCOG 1991. Mem., ARC Unit of Reproductive Physiology and Biochemistry, Cambridge, 1956–72; Fellow, Magdalene Coll., Cambridge, 1961–72; Lectr, then Reader, Dept of Veterinary Clinical Studies, Cambridge, 1961–72; Dir, MRC Unit of Reproductive Biology, Edinburgh, 1972–82; Prof. of Reproductive Biology, Monash Univ., Australia, 1982–95; Wexler Professorial Fellow, Dept of Perinatal Medicine, subseq. Obstetrics and Gynaecol., Univ. of Melbourne, 1996–2005. Hon. Prof., Univ. of Edinburgh, 1976–82. Chm., Bd of Dirs, Family Health Internat., NC, USA, 1984–90. Fellow, American Acad. of Arts and Scis. Hon. DSc: Guelph, 1988; Bristol, 1997; Edinburgh, 2002. *Publications:* (ed, with C. R. Austin) Reproduction in Mammals, vols 1–8, 1972–80, 2nd edn vols 1–5, 1982–86; (ed, with D. T. Baird) Contraceptives of the Future, 1976; (with M. Potts) Ever Since Adam and Eve, 1999; contrib. Jl Endocrinology, Jl Reproduction and Fertility, Jl Zoology, Lancet, Nature. *Recreations:* gardening, wildlife, history of biology, elephants. *Address:* The Dean's Ganglion, Level 4, 766 Elizabeth Street, University of Melbourne, Vic 3010, Australia.

**SHORT, Sonia Ruth Harris;** *see* Harris, S. R.

**SHORT, Maj.-Gen. William Robert, (Robin),** CB 1999; Operations Director, PHC Ltd, 1999–2007; *b* 30 March 1942; *s* of Dr Andrew Galbraith Short and Dr Helen Greig Short (*née* Dunlop); *m* 1st, 1967, Annette Pamela Barrow (*d* 2012); three *s*; 2nd, 2013, Sylvia Nina Quayle, OBE. *Educ:* Glasgow High Sch.; Glasgow Univ. (MB ChB). RMO, 1 Black Watch, RHR, 1969–72; 19 Field Ambulance, RAMC, 1972–73; RAMC Trng Centre, 1973–76; Army Staff Coll., 1976–77 (psc); SO2, Med. HQ 1 (BR) Corps, 1978–81; CO, 3 Armd Field Ambulance, RAMC, 1981–84; Chief Instr, RAMC Trng Centre, 1984–86; Comdr Med. 1 Armd Div., 1986–88; Col, Ops and Plans, 1988–91, Dir Med. Ops and Logistics, 1991–94, Defence Med. Services Directorate; Comdr, Med. HQ Land Comd, 1994–96; DGAMS, 1996–99. Chm., RAMC Assoc., 1999–2005. QHP, 1996–99. CStJ 1997 (OStJ 1971). *Recreations:* running a smallholding, collecting cigarette cards (cartophily).

**SHORTER, Hugo Benedict;** HM Diplomatic Service; Director, Americas, Foreign and Commonwealth Office, since 2019; *b* 11 Aug. 1966; *s* of Gervase Shorter and Charmian Shorter (*née* Stopford-Adams); *m* 2001, Laura Mercedes Lindon; two *s* one *d*. *Educ:* Lycée Molière, Rio de Janeiro; Queen's Coll., Oxford (BA 1988); Ecole Nat. d'Admin, Paris. Entered HM Diplomatic Service, 1990; FCO, 1990–92; Second Sec., on attachment to Ecole Nat. d'Admin, Paris, 1992–93; Second, later First, Sec., UK Delegn to NATO, 1994–98; FCO, 1998; Private Sec. to Minister of State, FCO, 2000–01; Dep. Hd, NE Asia and Pacific Dept, FCO, 2001–04; Dep. Hd of Mission, Brasilia, 2004–07; Counsellor (Global Issues), later Minister-Counsellor (Europe and Global Issues), Paris, 2007–12; Hd, Europe Directorate - External, FCO, 2012–15; Ambassador to Lebanon, 2015–18. *Recreations:* reading, travel. *Address:* Foreign and Commonwealth Office, King Charles Street, SW1A 2AH. *E:* hugo.shorter@fco.gov.uk.

**SHORTRIDGE, Sir Jon Deacon,** KCB 2002; Permanent Secretary, Welsh Office, then National Assembly for Wales, later Welsh Assembly Government, 1999–2008; *b* 10 April 1947; *s* of late Eric Creber Deacon Shortridge and Audrey Joan Shortridge (*née* Hunt); *m* 1972, Diana Jean Gordon; one *s* one *d*. *Educ:* Chichester High Sch.; St Edmund Hall, Oxford (MA; Hon. Fellow 2012); Edinburgh Univ. (MSc). Min. of Housing, then Countryside Commn, subseq. DoE, 1969–75; Shropshire County Planning Dept, 1975–84; Welsh Office: Principal, 1984–88, Pvte Sec. to Sec. of State for Wales, 1987–88; Asst Sec., 1988–92; G3, 1992–97; Dir of Economic Affairs, 1997–99; Perm. Sec., 1999; Interim Permanent Sec., DIUS, then BIS, 2009. Mem., UK Statistics Authy, 2010–12; Adv. Mem., Commn for Local Govt in England, 2012–18. Chair: Audit Cttee (formerly Audit Panel), Cardiff CC, 2009–15; Audit Cttee, Parly and Health Service Ombudsman, 2010–16 (Mem., Unitary Bd (formerly Adv. Bd), 2012–18); Audit Cttee, Commn for Local Govt in England, 2012–18; Member: Audit and Scrutiny Cttee, Oxford Univ., 2012–; Audit Cttee, Royal Soc., 2014–. Chair, Volunteering Matters (formerly Community Service Volunteers), 2010–16. Mem. Council, Cardiff Univ., 2008–12. Chancellor and Chm., Glyndŵr Univ., 2012–15. Hon. Fellow: Aberystwyth Univ., 2008; Univ. of Wales Inst., Cardiff, 2008; Glyndŵr Univ., 2011. DUniv Glamorgan, 2010. *Recreations:* gardening, tennis, walking, modern history. *Address:* Ebor House, 31 Kennedy Road, Shrewsbury, Shropshire SY3 7AB. *Club:* Oxford and Cambridge.

**SHORVON, Prof. Simon David,** MD; FRCP; Professor in Clinical Neurology, Institute of Neurology, University College London, since 1995; Hon. Consultant Neurologist, National Hospital for Neurology and Neurosurgery (formerly for Nervous Diseases), since 1983; *b* 17 June 1948; *s* of late Hyam Joseph Shorvon, DPM and of Mary Barbara Shorvon (*née* Bensusan Butt), MRCPsych; *m* 1st, 1984, Penelope Farmer (marr. diss.); 2nd, 1999, Dr Lynne Soon Li Low; one *s*. *Educ:* City of London Sch.; Trinity Coll., Cambridge (BA 1970; MB BChir 1974; MA 1974; MD 1983); St Thomas' Hosp. Med. Sch. MRCP 1975, FRCP 1990. Jun. med. and academic appts, Oxford, Manchester, KCH, Maudsley Hosp., and Nat. Hosp. for Nervous Diseases, 1973–83; Vis. Scientist, Univ. of Virginia, 1981; Sen. Lectr, 1983–92, Reader in Neurology, 1992–95, Chm., Dept of Clin. Neurology, 1998–2002, Inst. of Neurology, UCL; Dir, Nat. Neurosci. Inst., Singapore, 2000–03. Med. Dir, Nat. Soc. for Epilepsy, 1989–98. Member: Med. Panel, DVLA, 1987–2003; Disability Living Allowance Bd, 1994–96; Chm., Med. Commn, Nat. Hosp. for Neurology and Neurosurgery, 2010–15. Harveian Librarian and Mem. Council, RCP, 2012–16. Mem., Exec. Cttee, Internat. League Against Epilepsy (Vice-Pres., 1993–2013). Hon. Pres., Clinical Neurosciis Section, RSocMed, 2016–17. Mem., editl bds, internat. learned jls; Guarantor, Brain, 1998–2017; Ed.-in-Chief, Epilepsia, 1999–. Eur. Epileptology Award, Internat. League against Epilepsy, 2008; Lennox Award, Amer. Epilepsy Soc., 2010; T. S. Shrinivasan Award, 2010. *Publications:* Neurological Emergencies, 1989; Status Epilepticus: its clinical form and treatment in children and adults, 1994; (ed jtly) Magnetic Resonance Scanning and Epilepsy, 1994; (ed jtly) Epilepsy, 2nd edn 1995; Clinical Epilepsy, 1995; (ed jtly) The Treatment of Epilepsy, 1996, 4th edn 2015; Handbook of Epilepsy Treatment, 2000, 4th edn 2016; (ed jtly) Neurology: a Queen Square textbook, 2009, 2nd edn 2016; International League Against Epilepsy 1909–2009: a centenary history, 2009; The Causes of Epilepsy, 2011, 2nd edn 2019; The Beginning of the End of the Falling Sickness, 2012; Oxford Textbook of Epilepsy and Epileptic Seizures, 2013; The End of Epilepsy?, 2016; Physicians and War, 2016; 500 Years of the Royal College of Physicians, 2018; Queen Square: a history of the National Hospital and its Institute of Neurology, 2019; contribs to epilepsy, epidemiology and clin. neurology in learned jls. *Recreations:* the liberal arts, human rights and political freedom. *Address:* UCL Institute of Neurology, Box 5, National Hospital for Neurology and Neurosurgery, Queen Square, WC1N 3BG. *T:* (020) 3448 3422. *E:* s.shorvon@ucl.ac.uk. *Club:* Athenæum.

**SHOSTAK, Raymond Jon,** Hon. CBE 2005; international adviser to governments on education, effectiveness of government, delivery units and public sector reform, since 2013; *b* 2 July 1949; *s* of late Jerome M. Shostak and Alma (*née* Stern); *m* 1980, Gill Rivaz; one *s* one *d*. *Educ:* Nanuet Jun. Sen. High Sch.; Syracuse Univ. (BA Hons); Univ. of Southern Calif (MSc). Teacher: Isbell Jun. High Sch., Santa Paula, Calif, 1971–73; Leggatts Sch., Watford, Herts, 1973–74; Dep. Warden, 1974, Warden, 1975–83, SW Herts Teachers' Centre, Herts CC; Sen. Staff Inspector, Notts CC Adv. Inspection Service, 1983–86; Asst Dir of Educn and Chief Advr, W Sussex CC, 1989–96; Ofsted Inspector, 1993–99; Head, Pupil Performance Team, Sch. Effectiveness Div., DFEE, 1996–97; Dir of Educn, 1997–2001, Dir, Children, Schs and Families Service, 2001–03, Herts CC; Strategic Advr, Children's Services, Improvement and Develt Agency, 2003; Dir, Public Services, HM Treasury, 2003–07; Head, Prime Minister's Delivery Unit, 2007–10; Lead Exec., Core Assets Gp, 2011–13. Non-exec. Dir, Nat. Audit Office, 2015–. Dir, Herts TEC, 1997–2001; Board Member: QCA, 2001–03; Herts Learning and Skills Council, 2001–03; Chm., Wallenberg Centre for Improvement in Educn, Univ. of Cambridge, 1998–2001. Mem., Eastern Region NHS Children's Task Force, 2001–03. Sec., Soc. of Chief Inspectors and Advrs, 1992–96. Chm. Trustees, Consortium of Voluntary Adoption Agencies, 2014–; Trustee, Early Intervention Foundn, 2013–. Vis. Fellow (part-time), Sussex Univ., 1996–99; Hon. Norham Fellow, Oxford Univ., 2014–. Adv. Bd, Centre for Social Investigation, Oxford Univ., 2014–; Public Policy Cttee, British Acad., 2015–. FRSA 1993. *Recreations:* family, ski-ing, tennis, photography, woodturning.

**SHOTT, Ian Dermot,** CBE 2009; CEng, FREng, FIChemE, FRSC; Managing Partner, Shott Trinova, since 2011; Chairman and Managing Director, Arc Trinova Ltd, since 2016; Chairman, BPE Design Support Ltd, since 2014; *b* Tanga, Tanganyika, 26 Feb. 1957; *s* of Albert Shott and Mary Shott (*née* White); *m* 1985, Nicole Sara Poirier; one *s* one *d*. *Educ:* King Edward VI Grammar Sch., Southampton; Imperial Coll., London (BScEng Hons Chem. Engrg); INSEAD (Adv. Mktg Dip.). CEng 1984; FIChemE 2003; FRSC 2007; FREng 2008. Gen. Manager, Zeneca, 1990–93; Sen. Vice Pres., Lonza, 1993–98; Chief Operating Officer and Pres., Chirex, 1998–2000; Pres., Rhodia Chirex, 2000–03; Founder and CEO, Ian Shott Enterprises Ltd, subseq. Excelsyn, 2003–10; CEO, Shott Consulting Ltd, 2011–13. Chairman: Gap Technologies Ltd, 2011–13; GXPi Ltd, 2011–13; KFS Ltd, 2011–18; AM Technology Ltd, 2015–16; non-exec. Dir, Sterling Pharma Solutions Ltd, 2017–19. Chairman: Pharmaceutical and Specialty Cluster, 2001–04; RTC North, 2002–05; Centre of Excellence for Life Scis, 2006–12; UK Innovation and Growth Team for Industrial Biotechnol., 2007–10; Industrial Biotechnol. Leadership Forum, 2010–13; Industrial Biotechnol. Innovation Centre, 2014–18; Dep. Chm., NE Process Industry Cluster, 2004–05; Member: Ministerial Adv. Gp on Manuf. Strategy, 2008–10; Governing Bd, InnovateUK (formerly Technology Strategy Bd), 2011–16 (Chm., Catapult Cttee, 2014–16); Chemistry Growth Partnership, Govt Industrial Strategy, 2013–18; Specialist Advr to Sci. and Technol. Cttee, H of L, 2013–14; Chm., Strategic Adv. Bd (Chem. Engrg), Imperial Coll. London, 2014–. Vis. Prof., Newcastle Univ., 2004– (Mem. Council, 2004–12; Hon. Prof. 2007; Hon. Fellow, 2015); Vis. Prof., Oxford Univ., 2015–; Hon. Prof., Sustainable Process Technol., Nottingham Univ., 2014– (Chm., Strategic Adv. Bd, Synthetic Biol. Res. Centre, 2014–). Pres., IChemE, 2009–10. Royal Academy of

Engineering: Mem., Policy Cttee, 2010–13; Chairman: Enterprise Fellowship Cttee, 2010–13; Enterprise Hub Cttee, 2013; Enterprise Cttee, 2014–. Hon. DSc: Nottingham, 2010; Imperial Coll. London, 2019. Pres.'s Medal, RAEng, 2017. *Recreations:* motoring, squash, ski-ing, golf, food and wine.

**SHOTT, Nicholas Roland;** Vice Chairman, European Investment Banking and Head, UK Investment Banking, Lazard, since 2009; *b* Surrey, 22 Sept. 1951; *s* of Roland and Madeline Shott; *m* 2007, Melanie Sarah Hutton; two *s;* one *d* from previous marriage. *Educ:* Haileybury and ISC. Joined Beaverbrook Newspapers Ltd as exec., 1971; Gen. Manager, Evening Standard, 1981; Dir, Express Newspapers, 1981–87; Man. Dir, Express Newspapers (North), 1983; Chief Exec., Sunday Correspondent, 1987–90; Lazard: banker, 1991–; Dir, 1993–96; Man. Dir, 1996. Non-executive Director: Phoenix Gp Hldgs, 2016–; Home Office, 2017–. Hd of Inquiry into viability of local TV for Sec. of State, DCMS, 2010. MCSI (MSI 1992). *Recreations:* shooting, walking, sailing/boating, opera. *Address:* Lazard, 50 Stratton Street, W1J 8LL. *E:* nicholas.shott@lazard.com. *Club:* Thirty.

**SHOTTON, Dr Keith Crawford,** CEng, FIET; CPhys, FInstP; Head of Management and Technology Services Division, Department of Trade and Industry, 1994–96; *b* 11 Sept. 1943; *s* of William Crawford Shotton and Mary Margaret Shotton (*née* Smith); *m* 1969, Maria Elizabeth Gonszor; two *d. Educ:* Newcastle upon Tyne Royal Grammar Sch.; Trinity Coll., Cambridge (Schol.; MA, PhD). CPhys, FInstP 1982; CEng, FIET (FIEE 1988). Postdoctoral Fellow (laser physics and spectroscopy), NRCC, 1969–71; National Physical Laboratory: mem. team measuring speed of light, 1971–77; Head, Ultrasonics Metrology Unit, 1977–80; Head, Marketing and Inf. Services, 1980–84; DCSO, Supt, Div. of Radiation Sci. and Acoustics, 1984–87; Department of Trade and Industry: Dir, Radio Technology, Radio Communications Div., 1987–90; Hd, IT Div., 1990–92; Hd, Inf. and Manufg Technols Div., 1992–93; Hd, Technol. Progs and Services Div., 1993–94. *Publications:* papers in sci. jls, principally in spectroscopy, laser physics, ultrasonics and instrumentation. *Recreations:* family, walking, gardens, books, food.

**SHOULTS, Matthew Robert Charles;** Headmaster, Notting Hill and Ealing High School GDST, since 2017; *b* London, 5 Dec. 1974; *s* of Antony and Dinah Shoults. *Educ:* King's Coll. Sch., Wimbledon; Worcester Coll., Oxford (MA Lit. Hum.); Sidney Sussex Coll., Cambridge (PGCE). Asst trainee, DETR, 1997–99; teacher, King's Coll. Sch., 2000–04; North London Collegiate School: Hd of Classics, 2004–10; Academic Dep., 2010–12; Sen. Dep., 2012–16. *Recreations:* singing, violin, piano, hill-walking, crosswords. *Address:* Notting Hill and Ealing High School, 2 Cleveland Road, W13 8AX. *T:* (020) 8799 8400. *E:* enquiries@nhehs.gdst.net.

**SHOVE, Prof. Elizabeth,** PhD; FBA 2019; Professor of Sociology, Lancaster University, since 2005; *b* Guildford, 7 Nov. 1959; *d* of John and Jocelyn Shove. *Educ:* Godalming Grammar Sch.; York Univ. (BA; PhD 1986). Res. Fellow, Inst. of Advanced Architectl Studies, York Univ., 1986–92; Sen. Lectr, Univ. of Sunderland, 1992–95; Lancaster University: Dep. Dir, Centre for Study of Envmtl Change, 1995–98; Dir, Centre for Sci. Studies, 1998–2000; Dept of Sociol., 2000–. *Publications:* (with S. Guy) A Sociology of Energy, Buildings and the Environment, 2000; Comfort, Cleanliness and Convenience: the social organization of normality, 2003; (jtly) Infrastructures of Consumption, 2005; (jtly) The Design of Everyday Life, 2007; (ed jtly) Comfort in a Lower Carbon Society, 2009; (jtly) Time, Consumption and Everyday Life, 2009; (jtly) The Dynamics of Social Practice, 2012; (ed with N. Spurling) Sustainable Practices: social theory and climate change, 2013; (ed jtly) The Nexus of Practices: connections, constellations, practitioners, 2016; (ed with F. Trentmann) Infrastructures in Practice: the dynamics of demand in networked societies, 2018; (ed jtly) Energy Fables: challenging ideas in the energy sector, 2019. *Recreations:* floorball, cycling. *Address:* Department of Sociology, Lancaster University, Lancaster LA1 4YT.

**SHOVELTON, Dame Helena,** DBE 1999; Chair, 2020health, 2012–16, now Chair, Advisory Board; *b* 28 May 1945; *d* of late Denis George Richards, OBE and Barbara Smethurst; *m* 1968, Walter Patrick Shovelton, CB, CMG (*d* 2012). *Educ:* North London Collegiate Sch.; Regent St Poly. (HND Business Studies); Strathclyde Univ. (MBA 1998). Manager, Tunbridge Wells and Dist CAB, 1987–94; National Association of Citizens Advice Bureaux: Council Mem., 1989–90; Vice-Chm., 1990–94; Chm., 1994–99. Mem., 1995–98, Chair, 1998–2001, Audit Commn; Chief Exec., British Lung Foundn, 2002–12; Member: Local Govt Commn, 1995–98 (Dep. Chm., 1996–98); Banking Code Standards Bd (formerly Ind. Review Body for Banking and Mortgage Lending Codes), 1997–2000; Competition (formerly Monopolies and Mergers) Commn, 1997–2004; Better Regulation Task Force, 1997–99; Nat. Lottery Commn, 1999–2000; NHBC, 2009–18 (non-exec. Dir, 2012–18; Chair, Consumer Cttee, 2012–18). Chm., Independent Review Panel on Continuing Care, E Sussex, Brighton and Hove HA, 1996–97. Non-exec. Dir, Energy Saving Trust, 1998–2009. Trustee: RAF Benevolent Fund, 1997–2005; Independent Age, 2013– (Vice Chair); Street Games, 2017–19. FRSA 1995; CCMI 2001. Hon. FRCP 2006. British Thoracic Soc. Medal, 2011. *Recreations:* films, theatre, friends.

**SHOWALTER, Prof. Elaine,** PhD; FRSL; Professor of English and Avalon Foundation Professor of Humanities, Princeton University, 1984–2003, now Emerita; *b* 21 Jan. 1941; *d* of Paul Cottler and Violet Rottenberg; *m* 1963, English Showalter; one *s* one *d. Educ:* Bryn Mawr Coll. (BA 1962); Univ. of California, Davis (PhD 1970). Departments of English: Douglass Coll., 1966–78; Rutgers Univ., 1966–84. Pres., Modern Language Assoc. of America, 1998. FRSL 2012. *Publications:* A Literature of Their Own, 1977; The Female Malady, 1985; Sexual Anarchy, 1990; Sister's Choice: tradition and change in American women's writing, 1991; (jtly) Hysteria Beyond Freud, 1993; Hystories: hysterical epidemics and modern culture, 1997; Inventing Herself: claiming a feminist intellectual heritage, 2001; Teaching Literature, 2002; Faculty Towers, 2005; A Jury of Her Peers: American women writers from Anne Bradstreet to Annie Proulx, 2009; The Civil Wars of Julia Ward Howe, 2016. *Address:* 4620 North Park Avenue #405E, Chevy Chase, MD 20815–4579, USA. *T:* (301) 6563248.

**SHREEVE, Ven. David Herbert;** Archdeacon of Bradford, 1984–99, now Emeritus; *b* 18 Jan. 1934; *s* of Hubert Ernest and Ivy Eleanor Shreeve; *m* 1957, Barbara (*née* Fogden); one *s* one *d. Educ:* Southfield School, Oxford; St Peter's Coll., Oxford (MA); Ridley Hall, Cambridge. Asst Curate, St Andrew's Church, Plymouth, 1959–64; Vicar: St Anne's, Bermondsey, 1964–71; St Luke's, Eccleshill, 1971–84; RD of Calverley, 1978–84. Mem., Gen. Synod and Proctor in Convocation, 1977–90, 1993–98; Mem., Dioceses Commn, 1988–98. Hon. Canon of Bradford Cathedral, 1983–84. *Recreations:* choral singing, travel, photography. *Address:* 26 Kingsley Drive, Harrogate, N Yorks HG1 4TJ. *T:* (01423) 886479.

**SHRESTHA, Surya Prasad;** Ambassador of Nepal to the Court of St James's, 1992–97; *b* 1 March 1937; *s* of late L. P. Shrestha and Mrs G. K. Shrestha; *m* 1958, Ginni Baba Shrestha; two *s* two *d. Educ:* Tribhuvan Univ. (MA Pol Sci.); LSE (Dip. Econs and Social Admin). Joined HM Govt service, Nepal, 1958; Section Officer, Parlt Secretariat and Min. of Develt, 1958–63; Under Secretary: Min. of Home and Panchayat, 1963–65; Election Commn, 1965–66; Jt Zonal Comr, 1970–74, Zonal Comr, 1974–78, Bagmati Zone; Actg Sec., Home and Panchayat Min., 1978–79; Sec. of Industry and Commerce, 1979–83; Jt Mem., Nat. Planning Commn, 1983–85; Chief Election Comr, 1985–92. Prabal Gorkha Dakshin Bahu, III Cl. (Nepal), 1966, Prasiddha, II Cl., 1976; Trishakti Patta, Vikhyat, III Cl. (Nepal), 1973, Suvikhyat, II Cl., 1991. FRGS 1996. *Publications:* Democracy Prevails: general election in Nepal, 1991. *Recreations:* reading, gardening. *Address:* PO Box 2482, Jagaran Marg-130, Maharajgung (Chakrapath), Kathmandu, Nepal. *T:* (1) 4720708, 4721135.

**SHREWSBURY, Area Bishop of,** since 2019; **Rt Rev. Sarah Ruth Bullock;** *b* Manchester, 17 March 1964; *d* of Gerald Wheale and Jean Wheale; *m* 1992, Peter Bullock; one *s. Educ:* Fallowfield C of E High Sch.; Univ. of Surrey (BA Hons English 1986); Univ. of Manchester (Dip. Community Work); Univ. of Durham (BA Hons Theol. 1993; Postgrad. CTh 2012). Teacher, Cheadle Hulme Sch., 1986–90; Asst Diocesan Youth Officer, 1986–90; ordained deacon, 1993, priest, 1994; Asst Curate, St Paul, Kersal Moor and St Andrew, Carr Clough, 1993–98; Rector, St Edmund, Whalley Range and St James' with St Clement, Moss Side, 1998–2013; Area Dean of Hulme, 2012–13; Archdeacon of York, 2013–19. Chair, Discipleship and Ministry Trng Cttee, Dio. of Manchester, 2005–13; Bishops Advr for Women's Ministry, 2009–13; Borough Dean, City and Borough of Manchester, 2010–13; Proctor in Convocation, Gen. Synod, 2010–13 and 2015–20. Hon. Canon, Manchester Cath., 2007–. Chaplain to Lord Mayor of Manchester, 2002–03. *Publications:* (contrib.) Everybody Welcome, 2009. *Recreations:* family, reading, travel, cooking, walking, ski-ing, theatre. *Address:* Athlone House, 68 London Road, Shrewsbury SY2 6PG.

**SHREWSBURY, Bishop of, (RC),** since 2010; **Rt Rev. Mark Davies;** *b* Manchester, 12 May 1959. *Educ:* St Richard's Infant Sch., St Robert's Primary Sch., Manchester; Broadstone Hall Co. Primary Sch., St Anne's High Sch., Stockport; Ushaw Coll., Univ. of Durham. Ordained priest, 1984; Assistant Priest: Our Lady of Grace, Prestwich, 1984; St Mary's, Swinton, 1984–88; Private Sec. to RC Bishop of Salford, 1988–92; Parish Priest, St John Bosco, Blackley, 1992–2003; Vicar Gen., Diocese of Salford, 2003–09; Parish Priest: St Teresa's, Little Lever, 2003–05; St Joseph's, Longsight, 2005–07; Holy Family, Wigan, 2008–09. *Address:* Diocese of Shrewsbury, 2 Park Road South, Prenton, Wirral CH43 4UX.

**SHREWSBURY AND WATERFORD,** 22nd Earl of, *cr* 1442 and 1446; **Charles Henry John Benedict Crofton Chetwynd Chetwynd-Talbot;** DL; Baron Talbot, 1733; 7th Earl Talbot, Viscount Ingestre, 1784; Premier Earl on the Rolls of England and Ireland, Hereditary Great Seneschal or Lord High Steward of Ireland; Lord Dungarvan; *b* 18 Dec. 1952; *s* of 21st Earl of Shrewsbury and Waterford, and Nadine (*d* 2003), *yr d* of late Brig.-Gen. C. R. Crofton, CBE; *S* father, 1980; *m* 1974, Deborah, *o d* of late Noel Hutchinson; two *s* one *d. Educ:* Harrow. Director: Britannia Building Soc., 1984–92 (Dep. Chm., 1987–89); Jt Dep. Chm., 1989–92); Richmount Enterprise Zone Managers, 1988–94. Mem. Exec. Cttee, 1988–2004, Chm., 2000–04, Staffs Br., Game Conservancy Trust. Pres., Staffordshire Soc., 1989–91; Vice-Pres., Midland & West Assoc. of Building Socs, 1984–92; Pres., BSA, 1993–97. Chairman: Firearms Consultative Cttee, 1994–99; British Shooting Sports Council, 1996–2003 (Pres., 2003–09). Chancellor, Univ. of Wolverhampton, 1993–99. Elected Mem., H of L, 1999. President: British Inst. of Innkeeping, 1996–97; Staffs & Birmingham Agricl Soc., 2000–01; Vice-Pres., Staffs Assoc. of Clubs for Young People, 2000–. Patron, Staffs Br., BRCS, 1989–92. Hon. President: Lord Roberts Wkshops and SSAFA (Wolverhampton Br.), 1987–2010; Staffs Small Bore Rifle Assoc., 1988–; Gun Trade Assoc., 2000–18; Hon. Vice-Pres., Rugeley Rugby FC. Hon. Pres., Shropshire Hospice, 1983–88. Patron of 10 livings. Hon. Col, A Sqdn Royal Mercian and Lancastrian (formerly Staffs) Yeomanry, 2004–07. DL Stafford, 1994. Hon. LLD Wolverhampton, 1994. *Recreations:* shooting, fishing. *Heir: s* Viscount Ingestre, *qv. Address:* Throstles House, Birdsgrove Lane, Ashbourne, Derbys DE6 2BP.

**SHRIBMAN, Sheila Joan,** CBE 2011; FRCP, FRCPCH, FRCGP; Consultant Paediatrician, Northampton General Hospital, 1985–2011; National Clinical Director for Children, Young People and Maternity Services (formerly for Children), Department of Health, 2005–13; *b* 8 March 1951; *d* of Wilfred and Margaret Norval; *m* 1981, Dr Jonathan Shribman; two *s* one *d. Educ:* Girton Coll., Cambridge (BA 1972; MB BChir 1976); St George's Hosp., London. FRCP 1993; FRCPCH 1996; FRCGP 2010. Paediatric trng posts at St George's, Brompton, Queen Charlotte's and Gt Ormond St Hosps; Med. Dir, Northampton Gen. Hosp., 1995–2005. Registrar, RCPCH, 2003–05. Non-exec. Dir, Guys' and St Thomas's NHS Foundn Trust, 2013– (Vice Chm.). *Recreations:* travel, books, cookery, family, tennis. *Address:* Summer Hill, Kingston Lane, Dartmouth, Devon TQ6 9HB. *T:* (01803) 834651. *E:* sheila@shribman.co.uk. *Club:* Royal Society of Medicine.

**SHRIMPLIN, John Steven;** consultant, 1994–2011; UK Member, European Space Agency Appeals Board, 2000–10; *b* 9 May 1934; *s* of late John Reginald Shrimplin and Kathleen Mary (*née* Barnes); *m* 1957, Hazel Baughen; two *s. Educ:* Royal Grammar Sch., Colchester; King's Coll., London (BSc Maths). Joined RAE, Farnborough, 1956; Defence Operational Analysis Estabt, 1966; JSSC, 1970; Weapons Dept, RAE, 1971; Defence R&D Staff, British Embassy, Washington, 1972; Asst Dir, Future Systems, Air Systems Controllerate, MoD PE, 1974; Asst Chief Scientist, RAF, 1978; Head of Weapons Dept, RAE, 1983; Dep. Hd, British Defence Staff, and Minister/Counsellor, Defence Equipment, British Embassy, Washington, DC, 1985–88; Dir, Defence Science (Studies), MoD, 1988–91; Dep. Dir Gen. and Dir, Space Technol., BNSC, 1991–94. UK Rep., Eur. Space Policy Cttee, 1994–99. Pres., Old Colcerian Soc., 2010–11. FRAeS 1993. *Recreations:* travel, camping, walking. *Address:* c/o National Westminster Bank, 2 Alexandra Road, Farnborough, Hants GU14 6BZ.

**SHRIMSLEY, Robert Gideon;** Editorial Director and political columnist, Financial Times, since 2017; *b* 21 Sept. 1964; *s* of late Anthony Shrimsley and of Yvonne Shrimsley; *m* 1997, Reeve Lewis; one *s* one *d. Educ:* St Nicholas Preparatory Sch.; University College Sch.; London Sch. of Economics (BSc Econs 1985). Reporter: Darlington Evening Despatch, 1986; Kentish Times, 1986–88; Sunday Telegraph, 1988–89; Reporter, 1989–92, political staff, 1992–95, Daily Telegraph; Lobby Corresp., Financial Times, 1995–96; Chief Pol Corresp., Daily Telegraph, 1996–2000; Financial Times: Chief Pol Corresp., 2000–02; UK News Ed., 2002–04; columnist, 2004–05; News Ed., 2005–09; Managing Ed., FT.com, 2009–17. *Recreations:* cinema, reading, walking on Dartmoor, trying to persuade my children to watch QPR rather than Arsenal. *Address:* Financial Times, Bracken House, 1 Friday Street, EC4M 9BT. *T:* (020) 7873 3000.

**SHTAUBER, Dr Zvi;** Chairman, Israel Intelligence Heritage and Commemoration Center, since 2012; company director; *b* 15 July 1947; *m* Nitza Rousso; two *s* one *d. Educ:* Fletcher Sch. of Law and Diplomacy; Harvard Business Sch.; Hebrew Univ. of Jerusalem. Brig. Gen., Israel Defence Force, 1970–95; Vice-Pres., Ben Gurion Univ. of Negev, 1996–99; Foreign Policy Advr to Prime Minister of Israel, 1999–2000; Ambassador of Israel to the Court of St James's, 2001–04; Hd, Jaffee Center for Strategic Studies, Tel Aviv Univ., 2005–08; Dir, Inst. for Nat. Security Studies, Israel, 2006–08.

**SHUCKBURGH, Sir James Rupert Charles,** 14th Bt *cr* 1660, of Shuckburgh, Warwickshire; *b* 4 Jan. 1978; *er s* of Sir Rupert Charles Gerald Shuckburgh, 13th Bt and of Judith (*née* Mackaness); *S* father, 2012. *Heir: b* Peter Gerald William Shuckburgh, *b* 1982. *Address:* c/o Shuckburgh Hall, Daventry, Northants NN11 6DT.

**SHUCKSMITH, Prof. (David) Mark,** OBE 2009; PhD; FAcSS; Professor of Planning, University of Newcastle upon Tyne, since 2005 (Director, Institute for Social Renewal, 2012–18); *b* 25 Aug. 1953; *s* of Thomas David Shucksmith and Gwladys Inga Shucksmith; *m* 1979, Janet Susan Raper; two *d. Educ:* Sidney Sussex Coll., Cambridge (BA 1976); Univ. of Newcastle upon Tyne (MSc; PhD Agricl Econs 1987). University of Aberdeen: Lectr, 1981–87; Sen. Lectr, 1987–89; Reader, Dept of Land Econ., 1989–93; Prof. of Land Economy, 1993–2004; Dir, Arkleton Centre for Rural Develt Res., 1995–2004. Vis. Prof., Univ. of Trondheim, 2016–. Co-Dir, Scottish Centre for Res. on Social Justice, 2001–04. Joseph Rowntree Foundation: Advr, Action in Rural Areas prog., 1995–; Sec., Rural Housing Policy Forum, 2005–06. Member: Bd, Countryside Agency, 2005–06; Affordable Rural Housing Commn, 2005–06; Bd, Commn for Rural Communities, 2006–13. Chm., Cttee of Enquiry on Crofting, 2007–08. Programme Chairman: World Rural Sociol. Congress, 2004; European Soc. Rural Sociol. Congress, 2015; First Vice-Pres., Internat. Rural Sociol. Assoc., 2004–08 (Mem. Council, 2012–16); Mem., Exec. Cttee, Eur. Soc. of Rural Sociol., 2009–13. Specialist Advr, H of L Select Cttee, on Natural Envmt and Rural Communities Act, 2017–18, on Rural Economy, 2018–19. Trustee: Arkleton Trust, 2011–14; ACRE 2014–; Carnegie UK Trust, 2016– (Carnegie Fellow, 2015). FAcSS (AcSS 2010); FRSA 2015. *Publications:* No Homes for Locals?, 1981; Rural Housing in Scotland: recent research and policy, 1987; Housebuilding in Britain's Countryside, 1990; (jtly) Rural Scotland Today: the best of both worlds, 1996; Exclusive Countryside?: social inclusion and regeneration in rural Britain, 2000; (jtly) Housing in the European Countryside, 2003; (jtly) Young People in Rural Europe, 2004; (jtly) CAP and the Regions: the territorial impact of the Common Agricultural Policy, 2005; (jtly) Comparing Rural Development: continuity and change in the countryside of Western Europe, 2009; (jtly) From Community to Consumption: new and classical themes in rural sociological research, 2010; (jtly) Rural Transformations and Rural Policies in the US and UK, 2012; Future Directions in Rural Development, 2012; (jtly) Routledge International Handbook of Rural Studies, 2016; contrib. numerous articles to learned jls. *Recreations:* music, reading novels, hill-walking, finding coffee shops. *Address:* School of Architecture, Planning and Landscape, University of Newcastle upon Tyne, Claremont Tower, Newcastle upon Tyne NE1 7RU. *T:* (0191) 208 6808. *E:* mark.shucksmith@ncl.ac.uk.

**SHUE, Prof. Vivienne B.,** PhD; FBA 2008; Leverhulme Professor of Contemporary China, and Director, Contemporary China Studies Programme, University of Oxford, 2002, now Emeritus; Fellow of St Antony's College, Oxford, 2002, now Emeritus. *Educ:* Vassar Coll., NY (BA 1967); St Antony's Coll., Oxford (BLitt 1969); Harvard Univ. (PhD 1975). Asst Prof., 1976–81, Associate Prof., 1981–82, Dept of Pol Sci., Yale Univ.; Associate Prof., 1982–87, Prof. of Govt, 1987–95, Frank and Rosa Rhodes Prof. of Chinese Govt, 1995–2004, Cornell Univ. *Publications:* Peasant China in Transition, 1980; The Reach of the State, 1988; (ed jtly) State Power and Social Forces, 1994; (with Marc Blecher) Tethered Deer: government and economy in a Chinese county, 1996; (ed with C. Wong) Paying for Progress in China, 2007; (ed with Patricia M. Thornton) To Govern China: evolving practices of power, 2017; contrib. learned jls. *Address:* c/o St Antony's College, Oxford OX2 6JF.

**SHUKER, Gavin;** MP for Luton South, since 2010 (Lab and Co-op, 2010–19; Ind, since 2019); *b* 10 Oct. 1981; *m* 2007, Lucie Moore (marr. diss. 2016); one *d. Educ:* Icknield High Sch.; Luton Sixth Form Coll.; Girton Coll., Cambridge (BA Soc. and Pol Sci. 2003). Associate Pastor, Cambridge, 2003–06, Church Leader, Luton, 2006–, City Life Church; charity worker, Fusion UK, 2003–08; Endis Ltd, 2008–10. Shadow Minister for Water and Waste, 2011–13, for Internat. Develt, 2013–15. *Address:* House of Commons, SW1A 0AA.

**SHUKLA, (Amit) Nikesh;** author, since 2010; *b* Harrow, 8 July 1980; *s* of Situ and Jayshree Shukla. *Educ:* Queen Mary and Westfield Coll., Univ. of London (LLB). Ed., Rife Mag., 2014–; Global Thinker, Foreign Policy mag., 2016. *Publications:* Coconut Unlimited, 2010; Meatspace, 2014; (ed) The Good Immigrant, 2016; The One Who Wrote Destiny, 2018; Run, Riot, 2018; (ed) The Good Immigrant USA, 2019. *Recreations:* reading Spider-Man comics, eating dosas, punching heavy bags. *W:* http://nikesh-shukla.com.

**SHUKLA, Rashmita,** CBE 2007; Regional Director, Midlands and East, Public Health England, since 2013; *b* 4 July 1960; *d* of Himatlal Shukla and Mrudula Shukla; *m* 1992, Dr Vinod Patel. *Educ:* Univ. of Southampton Med. Sch. (BM 1984). MRCP 1988, FRCP 2007; FFPH 2001. Leicestershire Health Authority: Consultant in Communicable Disease/ Public Health Medicine, 1994–2001; Actg Dir of Public Health, 2000–01; Director of Public Health: Eastern Leicester PCT, 2001–04; Leicester City West PCT, 2004; Regl Dir of Public Health, W Midlands DoH, 2004–13. Hon. Sen. Lectr, Univ. of Leicester, 2003–. *Publications:* articles in Communicable Disease Review, Sexually Transmitted Infections, Jl of Public Health Medicine and Postgraduate Med. Jl. *Recreations:* cycling, ski-ing, reading, supporting local Rugby team (Leicester Tigers). *Address:* Public Health England, 1st Floor, 5 St Philip's Place, Birmingham B3 2PW. *T:* (0121) 232 9267. *E:* Rashmi.Shukla@ phe.gov.uk.

**SHUKMAN, David Roderick,** FRGS; Science Editor, BBC News, since 2012; *b* 30 May 1958; *s* of late Dr Harold Shukman and of Rev. Dr Ann Shukman; *m* 1988, Jessica Therese Pryce-Jones; two *s* one *d. Educ:* Eton Coll.; Durham Univ. (BA Hons Geog.). Reporter, Coventry Evening Telegraph, 1980–83; joined BBC, 1983: trainee, News, 1983–85; reporter, NI, 1985–87; Defence Corresp., TV News, 1987–95; Europe Corresp., Brussels, 1995–99; World Affairs Corresp., News, 1999–2003; Envmt and Sci. Corresp., News, 2003–12. FRGS 2007. *Publications:* (with B. Brown) All Necessary Means, 1991; The Sorcerer's Challenge: fears and hopes for the weapons of the next millennium, 1995; US edn as Tomorrow's War, 1996; Reporting Live from the End of the World, 2010; An Iceberg as Big as Manhattan, 2011; contribs to RUSI Jl, Brassey's Defence Yearbook. *Recreations:* cooking, diving, surfing. *Address:* BBC News Centre, Broadcasting House, Portland Place, W1A 1AA. *E:* david.shukman@bbc.co.uk. *Club:* Frontline.

**SHULMAN, Alexandra,** CBE 2018 (OBE 2005); Editor, British Vogue, 1992–2017; *b* 13 Nov. 1957; *d* of late Milton Shulman and of Drusilla Beyfus, *qv*; *m* 1994, Paul (marr. diss. 2005), *s* of late Rev. Dr Robert W. Spike, NY; one *s. Educ:* St Paul's Girls' Sch.; Sussex Univ. (BA Social Anthropology). Tatler: Commissioning Editor, 1982–84; Features Editor, 1984–87; Sunday Telegraph: Editor, Women's Page, 1987; Dep. Editor, 7 Days Mag., 1987–88; Features Editor, Vogue, 1988–90; Editor, GQ, 1990–92. Dir, Condé Nast Pubns, 1997–2002. Vis. Prof., Univ. of the Arts, London, 2003–. Trustee: Nat. Portrait Gall., 1999–2008; Arts Foundn, 2001–10; Royal Marsden Cancer Charity, 2009–15. Vice Pres., London Liby, 2017–. Hon. MA Univ. for Creative Arts, 2010. *Publications:* Can We Still Be Friends, 2012; The Parrots, 2015; Inside Vogue, 2016.

*See also* Marchioness of Normanby.

**SHULMAN, Drusilla Norman;** *see* Beyfus, D. N.

**SHULMAN, Neville,** CBE 2005 (OBE 1995); Director, International Institute of Dance and Theatre, since 2013. Vice Pres./Ambassador, Action for Children, 1989; Vice Chm., UK UNESCO Culture Cttee, 2005. Director: Theatre Forum, 2002; Shepperton Studios Ltd, 2003–. Freeman, City of London, 1992; Liveryman, Blacksmiths' Co., 1992. FRGS 1990. *Publications:* Exit of a Dragonfly, 1985; Zen in the Art of Climbing Mountains, 1992; On Top of Africa, 1995; Zen Explorations in Remotest New Guinea, 1997; Some Like it Cold, 2001; Climbing the Equator, 2003; Maybe Your Father's Inside Somewhere, 2016. *Recreations:* mountaineering, exploring, theatre, film. *Address:* 35A Huntsworth Mews, Gloucester Place, NW1 6DB. *Clubs:* Travellers, Explorers (Fellow, 1993).

**SHULTZ, George Pratt;** Secretary of State, United States of America, 1982–89; Distinguished Fellow, Hoover Institution, since 1989; *b* New York City, 13 Dec. 1920; *s* of Birl E. Shultz and Margaret Pratt; *m* 1946, Helena Maria O'Brien (*d* 1995); two *s* three *d*; *m* 1997, Charlotte Mailliard Swig (Hon. CVO 2007). *Educ:* Princeton Univ., 1942 (BA Econ); Massachusetts Inst. of Technology, 1949 (PhD Industrial Econ). Served War, US Marine Corps, Pacific, 1942; Major, 1945. Faculty, MIT, 1949–57; Sen. staff economist, President's Council of Economic Advisers, 1955–56 (on leave, MIT); Univ. of Chicago, Graduate Sch. of Business: Prof. of Industrial Relations, 1957–68; Dean, 1962–69; Prof. of Management and Public Policy, Stanford Univ., Graduate Sch. of Business, 1974. Secretary of Labor, 1969–July 1, 1970; Dir, Office of Management and Budget, 1970–72; Secretary of the Treasury, 1972–74; Exec. Vice-Pres., Bechtel Corp., 1974–75, Pres. 1975–77; Vice-Chm., Bechtel Corp., 1977–81 (Dir); Pres., Bechtel Group Inc., San Francisco, 1981–82. Chairman: President's Economic Policy Adv. Bd, 1981–82; Internat. Council, J. P. Morgan, 1989–2009; Adv. Council, Inst. of Internat. Studies, 1989–; Adv. Bd, Accenture Energy, 2002–07; Theranos Inc., 2011–18. Director: General Motors Corp., 1981–82, 1989–91; Boeing Corp., 1989–93; Bechtel Gp Inc., 1989–2009; Tandem Computers Inc., 1989–92; Chevron Corp., 1989–93; Gulfstream Aerospace Corp., 1992–99; AirTouch Communications, 1994–98; Gilead Scis, 1996–2006; Charles Schwab & Co. Inc., 1997–2004; Unext, 2000–03; Infrastructure World, 2000–03; Accretive Health Associates, 2004–11; Mem., GM Corporate Adv. Council. Chm., State of California Gov's Econ. Policy Adv. Bd, 1995–98, Council of Econ. Advrs, 2004–09. US Chm., N American Forum, 2005–09; Chairman: Adv. Council, Precourt Inst. for Energy, Stanford Univ., 2007–; Ext. Adv. Bd, MIT Energy Initiative, 2007–; Energy Taskforce, Hoover Inst., 2007–. Hon. Dr of Laws: Notre Dame Univ., 1969; Loyola Univ., 1972; Pennsylvania, 1973; Rochester, 1973; Princeton, 1973; Carnegie-Mellon Univ., 1975; Columbia, 2001; Williams Coll., 2008; Peking, 2009. *Publications:* Pressures on Wage Decisions, 1950; The Dynamics of a Labor Market (with C. A. Myers), 1951; Labor Problems: cases and readings (with J. R. Coleman), 1953; Management Organization and the Computer (with T. L. Whisler), 1960; Strategies for the Displaced Worker (with Arnold R. Weber), 1966; Guidelines, Informal Controls, and the Marketplace (with Robert Z. Aliber), 1966; Workers and Wages in the Urban Labor Market (with Albert Rees), 1970; Leaders and Followers in an Age of Ambiguity, 1975; Economic Policy Beyond the Headlines (with Kenneth W. Dam), 1977, 2nd edn 1998; Turmoil and Triumph: my years as Secretary of State, 1993; (with John Shoven) Putting Our House in Order: a guide to social security and healthcare reform, 2008; Ideas & Action, Featuring 10 Commandments for Negotiations, 2010; (ed jtly) Ending Government Bailouts as We Know Them, 2010; Issues on My Mind: strategies for the future, 2013; (ed jtly) Game Changers: energy on the move, 2014; (jtly) Nuclear Security: the problems and the road ahead, 2014; Learning from Experience, 2016; Thinking About the Future, 2019. *Recreation:* golf. *Address:* Hoover Institution, Stanford University, Stanford, CA 94305–6010, USA.

**SHUMAN, Karen Ann Elizabeth;** Master of the High Court, Chancery Division, since 2017; *b* Scotland, 24 Dec. 1967; *d* of John and Iris Shuman; *m* 1996, Paul Stewart; two *s. Educ:* Birmingham Univ. (LLB Hons). Called to the Bar, Lincoln's Inn, 1991, Bencher, 2015; in practice as barrister, 1993–2017. *Recreations:* wildlife, travel, opera, cinema. *Address:* Royal Courts of Justice, Business and Property Courts, Rolls Building, 7 Rolls Buildings, Fetter Lane, EC4A 1NL.

**SHUTER, Jo;** Headteacher, Quintin Kynaston School, Marlborough Hill, 2002–13; education consultant. *Educ:* Univ. of Bristol (BA Psychol. and Social Sci.); Univ. of Birmingham (PGCE Social Scis/Physical Educn). Asst Headteacher, Phoenix High Sch., Shepherds Bush, 1993–99; Dep. Headteacher, Broomfield Sch., N London, 1999–2000; Sen. Dep. Headteacher, Hertswood Sch., Borehamwood, 2000–01. Nat. Headteacher of Year (Secondary Sch.), Teaching Awards Trust, 2007.

**SHUTLER, (Ronald) Rex (Barry),** CB 1992; FRICS; FAAV; Chairman, Leasehold Valuation Tribunal and Rent Assessment Panel, 1994–2001 (Vice President, 1994–99); *b* 27 June 1933; *s* of Ronald Edgar Coggin Shutler and Helena Emily Shutler (*née* Lawes); *m* 1958, Patricia Elizabeth Longman; two *s. Educ:* Hardye's, Dorchester. Articled pupil and assistant, chartered surveyors, Dorchester, 1952–59; joined Valuation Office (Inland Revenue), 1959; District Valuer, Hereford and Worcester, 1970; Superintending Valuer, Wales, 1976; Dep. Chief Valuer, 1984–88; Chief Valuer, then Chief Exec., Valuation Office Agency, 1988–94. FRICS 1972; FAAV 1962; Hon. FSVA 1994. *Recreations:* golf, country pursuits, gardening, bridge. *Club:* Bank House Golf & Country.

**SHUTT,** family name of **Baron Shutt of Greetland**.

**SHUTT OF GREETLAND,** Baron *cr* 2000 (Life Peer), of Greetland and Stainland in the county of West Yorkshire; **David Trevor Shutt,** OBE 1993; PC 2009; FCA; *b* 16 March 1942; *s* of Edward Angus Shutt and Ruth Satterthwaite Shutt (*née* Berry); *m* 1965, Margaret Edith Pemberton; two *s* one *d. Educ:* Pudsey Grammar Sch. FCA 1969. Smithson Blackburn & Co., Leeds: Articled Clerk, 1959–64; Audit Clerk, 1964–66; Bousfield Waite & Co., Halifax: Taxation Asst, 1967–70; Partner, 1970–94; Consultant, 1994–2001. Mem. (L then Lib Dem) Calderdale MBC, 1973–90 and 1995–2003 (Mayor, 1982–83). Dir, Joseph Rowntree Reform Trust Ltd, 1975–2010 (Vice Chm., 1987–2005; Chm., 2007–10); Trustee, Joseph Rowntree Charitable Trust, 1985–2010. Treas., Inst. for Citizenship, 1995–2002. Contested: (L): Sowerby, 1970, Feb. and Oct. 1974, 1979; (L/Alliance): Calder Valley, 1983, 1987; (Lib Dem): Pudsey, 1992. House of Lords: Lib Dem Asst Whip, 2001–02, Dep. Chief Whip, 2002–05, Chief Whip, 2005–12; Coalition Dep. Chief Whip, 2010–12; Lib Dem spokesman on internat. develt, 2001–02, on NI, 2001–05; govt spokesman on culture, media and sport, on NI and on transport, 2010–12; Captain of the Yeomen of the Guard (Dep. Chief Whip, H of L), 2010–12. Freeman of Calderdale, 2000. Paul Harris Fellow, Rotary Club, 1999. Citoyen d'honneur, Commune de Riorges (France), 1983. *Recreations:* transport, travel. *Address:* Woodfield, 197 Saddleworth Road, Greetland, Halifax, West Yorkshire HX4 8LZ. *T:* (01422) 375276.

**SHUTT, Ven. Nicholas Stephen;** Archdeacon of Plymouth, since 2019; *b* Senghenydd, S Wales, 26 Sept. 1958; *s* of Arthur Shutt and Dorothy Margaret Shutt; *m* 1981, Corinne Dare; one *s* one *d* (and two *s* decd). *Educ:* Hampton Grammar Sch.; Queen Mary Coll., Univ. of London (LLB Hons 1980); Univ. of Wales, Cardiff (LLM Canon Law 2001); Plymouth Coll. of Art (BA Photography 2011). Admitted solicitor, 1983; Solicitor, Plymouth and Yelverton; ordained deacon, 1994, priest, 1995; Asst Curate, Yelverton Team Ministry, 1994–2008; Priest-in-charge, 2008–12, Rector, 2012–19, Yelverton Benefice; Rector, Sampford Spinney and Horrabridge, 2012–19;

Preb., Exeter Cathedral, 2011–19. *Recreations:* photography, music, motorbiking, dog walking. *Address:* St Mark's Church, 1 Sanctuary Close, Plymouth PL2 1EN. *T:* (01752) 858382. *E:* archdeacon.of.plymouth@exeter.anglican.org.

**SHUTTLE, Penelope (Diane);** writer and poet; *b* 12 May 1947; *d* of Jack Frederick Shuttle and Joan Shepherdess Lipscombe; *m* Peter Redgrove, FRSL (*d* 2003); one *d*. *Educ:* Staines Grammar Sch.; Matthew Arnold County Secondary Sch., Middx. Radio plays: The Girl who Lost her Glove, 1975 (Jt 3rd Prize Winner, Radio Times Drama Bursaries Comp., 1974); The Dauntless Girl, 1978. Poetry recorded for Poetry Room, Harvard Univ. Arts Council Awards, 1969, 1972 and 1985; Greenwood Poetry Prize, 1972; E. C. Gregory Award for Poetry, 1974. *Publications:* novels: An Excusable Vengeance, 1967; All the Usual Hours of Sleeping, 1969; Wailing Monkey Embracing a Tree, 1974; Rainsplitter in the Zodiac Garden, 1976; Mirror of the Giant, 1979; *poetry:* Nostalgia Neurosis, 1968; Midwinter Mandala, 1973; Photographs of Persephone, 1973; Autumn Piano, 1973; Songbook of the Snow, 1973; Webs on Fire, 1977; The Orchard Upstairs, 1980; The Child-Stealer, 1983; The Lion from Rio, 1986; Adventures with my Horse, 1988; Taxing the Rain, 1992; Building a City for Jamie, 1996; Selected Poems, 1998; A Leaf out of his Book, 1999; Redgrove's Wife, 2006; Sandgrain and Hourglass (new poems), 2010; Unsent: new and selected poems, 2012; In the Snowy Air (pamphlet), 2014; Four Portions of Everything on the Menu for M'sieur Monet (pamphlet), 2016; (with John Greening) Heath, 2016; Will You Walk a Little Faster?, 2017; *with Peter Redgrove:* The Hermaphrodite Album (poems), 1973; The Terrors of Dr Treviles (novel), 1974; The Wise Wound (psychology), 1978, 5th edn 1999; Alchemy for Women, 1995. *Recreations:* listening to music, Hatha Yoga, walking, reading, contemplation. *Address:* c/o David Higham Associates Ltd, 7th Floor, Waverley House, 7–12 Noel Street, W1F 8GQ.

**SHUTTLEWORTH,** 5th Baron *cr* 1902, of Gawthorpe; **Charles Geoffrey Nicholas Kay-Shuttleworth,** KG 2016; KCVO 2011; JP; Bt 1850; Lord-Lieutenant and Custos Rotulorum of Lancashire, since 1997; *b* 2 Aug. 1948; *s* of 4th Baron Shuttleworth, MC, and Anne Elizabeth (*d* 1991), *er d* of late Col Geoffrey Phillips, CBE, DSO; *S* father, 1975; *m* 1975, Mrs Ann Mary Barclay, *d* of James Whatman, MC; three *s*. *Educ:* Eton. Trainee Surveyor, Raby Estates, Co. Durham, 1966–70; Vigers, Chartered Surveyors, 1970–77; Partner, Burton, Barnes & Vigers, Chartered Surveyors, 1977–96; National & Provincial Building Society: Dir, 1983–96; Chm., 1994–96; Director: Burnley Bldg Soc., 1978–82 (Vice-Chm., 1982); Rank Foundn, 1993–2015; Abbey National plc, 1996–2004 (Dep. Chm., 1996–99); Rural Solutions Ltd, 1999–2007 (Chm., 2005–07); Chairman: Abbey National Gp Pension Funds Trustee Co., 2002–12; Santander UK Gp Pension Scheme Trustees Ltd, 2012–18. Chairman: Rural Develt Commn, 1990–97; Lancs Small Industries Cttee, COSIRA, 1978–83; Lancs Youth Clubs Assoc., 1980–86, Pres., 1986–2012; Member: Skelmersdale Develt Corp., 1982–85; NW Regional Cttee, National Trust, 1980–89; Council, CBI, 1993–96; Council, Duchy of Lancaster, 1998–2014 (Chm., 2006–14). Chm., Assoc. of Lord-Lieutenants, 2008–18. President: Royal Lancashire Agricl Soc., 1985–86, 2000–01; Assoc. of Lancastrians in London, 1986–87 and 1997. Pres., RFCA, NW, 2011–15 (Vice-Pres., 1997–2011, 2015–). Chm. of Trustees, Yorkshire Dales Millennium Trust, 2000–05. Mem. Council, Lancaster Univ., 1990–93; Governor, Giggleswick Sch., 1981–2006 (Chm., 1984–97). Hon. Fellow: Univ. of Central Lancs, 1996; Myerscough Coll., 2002. Hon. Colonel: 4th (V) Bn, Queen's Lancs Regt, 1996–99; Lancastrian and Cumbrian Vol., 1999–2005. FRICS, 1983–2002. JP 1997, DL Lancs, 1986. KStJ 1997 (Pres., Council for Lancs, 1997–2012). *Heir:* s Hon. Thomas Edward Kay-Shuttleworth [*b* 29 Sept. 1976; *m* 2002, Clare Barbara Tozer; one *s* two *d*]. *Address:* Heber House, Leck, Carnforth, Lancs LA6 2JG. *Clubs:* Brooks's, MCC.

**SHUTTLEWORTH, Kenneth Owen;** Chief Executive, Make Ltd, since 2004; Founder, Future Spaces Foundation, since 2013; *b* 10 Sept. 1952; *s* of Owen William Shuttleworth and late Ilene Doris; *m* 1987, Seana Ann Brennan (marr. diss. 2006); one *s* one *d*, *m* 2008, Claire Nicola Dexter; one *s*. *Educ:* Leicester Poly. (DipArch Dist. 1977). RIBA 1978. Registered architect, 1978; Dir, Foster and Partners, 1984–2003. Projects include: 30 St Mary Axe; City Hall, London; Nottingham Univ. Campus; St Paul's inf. kiosk; Grosvenor Waterside; 55 Baker Street; Cube Birmingham; Handball Arena (Copper Box); Dunbar Place, Ho Man Tin. Mem., CABE, 2003–11. Hon. DDes De Montfort 1994; Hon. DSc Westminster, 2007; Hon. DLit Nottingham, 2009; Hon. Dr UEL. FRSA. *Recreations:* painting, landscape drawing. *Address:* Make Ltd, 32 Cleveland Street, W1T 4JY. *T:* (020) 7636 5151, *Fax:* (020) 7636 5252. *E:* kenshuttleworth@makearchitects.com.

**SHUTTLEWORTH, Prof. Sally Ann,** PhD; FBA 2015; Professor of English Literature, University of Oxford, since 2005; Fellow, St Anne's College, Oxford, since 2005; *b* Sheffield, 5 Sept. 1952; *d* of Kenneth and Barbara Shuttleworth; *m* 1988, John Christie; two *d*. *Educ:* Univ. of York (BA 1st Cl. Hons English Lit. and Sociol. 1974); Darwin Coll., Cambridge (PhD English Lit. 1980). Asst Prof., English Dept, Princeton Univ., 1980–83; Lectr, 1983–91, Sen. Lectr, 1991–94, Sch. of English, Univ. of Leeds; University of Sheffield: Prof. of English Lit., 1994–2005; Hd of Dept, 1996–99; Dean of Arts, 1999–2003; Hd, Humanities Div., Univ. of Oxford, 2005–11. Frank Knox Fellow, Harvard Univ., 1978–79; Soc. for Humanities Fellow, Cornell Univ., 1986–87; Leverhulme Res. Fellow, 1994–95; British Acad. Readership, 2003–05. Member: Peer Rev. Coll., AHRC, 2004– (Strategic Reviewer, 2009–); Res. Awards Adv. Cttee, Leverhulme Trust, 2010– (Chair, 2018–). AHRC Science in Culture prog. award, 2013–19; Eur. Res. Council Advanced Investigator Award, 2014–19. *Publications:* George Eliot and Nineteenth-Century Science: the make-believe of a beginning, 1984; (ed with John Christie) Nature Transfigured: science and literature, 1700–1900, 1989; (ed jtly) Body/Politics: women and the discourses of science, 1990; Charlotte Brontë and Victorian Psychology, 1996; (ed with J. Bourne Taylor) Embodied Selves: an anthology of psychological texts, 1830–1890, 1998; (ed jtly) Memory and Memorials, 1789–1914: literary and cultural perspectives, 2000; (jtly) Science in the Nineteenth-Century Periodical: reading the magazine of nature, 2004; (ed jtly) Science Serialised: representations of the sciences in nineteenth-century periodicals, 2004; (ed jtly) Culture and Science in the Nineteenth-Century Media, 2004; The Mind of the Child: child development in literature, science and medicine, 1840–1900, 2010 (British Soc. for Lit. and Sci. Prize); (jtly) Anxious Times: medicine and modernity in nineteenth-century Britain, 2019. *Recreations:* family, walking on moors and mountains, wild swimming, citizen science. *Address:* St Anne's College, Woodstock Road, Oxford OX2 6HS. *T:* (01865) 274800. *E:* sally.shuttleworth@st-annes.ox.ac.uk.

**SIBBETT, Prof. Wilson,** CBE 2001; PhD; FRS 1997; FInstP; FRSE; Wardlaw Professor of Natural Philosophy, School of Physics and Astronomy, University of St Andrews, 1997–2014, now Emeritus; *b* 15 March 1948; *s* of John Sibbett and Margaret (*née* McLeister); *m* 1979, Barbara Anne Brown; three *d*. *Educ:* Ballymena Tech. Coll.; Queen's Univ., Belfast (BSc 1st Cl. Hons Physics); Imperial Coll., London (PhD Laser Physics 1973). FInstP 1986, Hon. FInstP 2016. Blackett Laboratory, Imperial College, London: Postdoctoral Res. Asst, 1973–77; Lectr in Physics, 1977–84; Reader, 1984–85; University of St Andrews: Prof., 1985–2014; Head, Physics Dept, 1985–88; Chm., 1988–94, Dir of Research, 1994–2005, Sch. of Physics and Astronomy. Mem., EPSRC, 1998–2001; Chm., Scottish Science Adv. Cttee, 2002–06. Mem. Council, Royal Soc., 2011–; Vice Pres., Physical Scis, RSE, 2011–. Mem., St Andrews Rotary Club. FRSE 1988; Fellow: Optical Soc. of America, 1998; Eur. Optical Soc., 2008. Hon. LLD Dundee, 2002; Hon. DSc: Dublin, 2005; Glasgow, 2012; DUniv Strathclyde, 2012. Hubert Schardin Gold Medal for Res. in Ultrafast Lasers and Diagnostics, 1978; C. V. Boys Prize and Medal for Exptl Physics, Inst. of Physics, 1993; Rank Prize for Optoelectronics, 1997; Rumford Medal, Royal Soc., 2000; Quantum Electronics Prize, European Physical Soc., 2002; Royal Medal, RSE, 2009; Charles Hard Townes Award, Optical Soc. of America, 2011. *Publications:* numerous on laser physics and related diagnostic techniques in internat. scientific jls. *Recreations:* golf, gardening, DIY. *Address:* School of Physics and Astronomy, University of St Andrews, North Haugh, St Andrews, Fife KY16 9SS. *T:* (01334) 463100. *Clubs:* Rotary (St Andrews); Royal and Ancient Golf, New Golf (St Andrews).

**SIBERRY, (William) Richard;** QC 1989; a Deputy High Court Judge, since 2002; *b* 11 Dec. 1950; *s* of late John William Morgan Siberry; *m* 1976, Julia Christine Lancaster. *Educ:* King's Coll., Taunton; Pembroke Coll., Cambridge (MA, LLB). Fellow, Pembroke Coll., Cambridge, 1973–75. Called to the Bar, Middle Temple, 1974, Bencher, 2002. Asst Recorder, 1997–2000; Recorder, 2000–10. Arbitrator, 2018–. *Recreations:* music, gardening, walking, photography, North West Highlands of Scotland. *Address:* 24 Lincoln's Inn Fields, WC2A 3EG. *T:* (020) 7813 8000. *Club:* Royal Automobile.

**SIBLEY, Dame Antoinette, (Dame Antoinette Corbett),** DBE 1996 (CBE 1973); Prima Ballerina, The Royal Ballet, Covent Garden; President, Royal Academy of Dance (formerly of Dancing), 1991–2012 (Vice-President, 1989–91); guest coach, Royal Ballet, since 1991; Governor, Royal Ballet Board, since 2000; *b* 27 Feb. 1939; *d* of late Edward G. Sibley and Winifred M. Sibley (*née* Smith); *m* 1964, Michael Somes, CBE (marr. diss. 1973; he *d* 1994); *m* 1974, Panton Corbett; one *s* one *d*. *Educ:* Arts Educational Sch. and Royal Ballet Sch. 1st performance on stage as Student with Royal Ballet at Covent Garden, a swan, Jan. 1956; joined company, July 1956; appeared with the company or as guest artist in most opera houses worldwide; iconic dancing partnership with Sir Anthony Dowell spanned three decades. Leading rôle in: Swan Lake, Sleeping Beauty, Giselle, Coppelia, Cinderella, The Nutcracker, La Fille Mal Gardée, Romeo and Juliet, Harlequin in April, Les Rendezvous, Jabez and the Devil (created the rôle of Mary), La Fête Etrange, The Rake's Progress, Hamlet, Ballet Imperial, Two Pigeons, La Bayadère, Symphonic Variations, Scènes de Ballet, Lilac Garden, Daphnis and Chloe, Pas de Quatre (Dolin's), Konservatoriet, A Month in the Country, Raymonda Act III, The Dream (created Titania), Laurentia, Good Humoured Ladies, Aristocrat in Mam'zelle Angot, Façade, Song of the Earth, Monotones (created rôle), Jazz Calendar (created Friday's Child), Enigma Variations (created Dorabella), Thais (created pas de deux), Anastasia (created Kshessinska), Afternoon of a Faun, Triad (created the Girl), Pavanne (created pas de deux), Manon (created title rôle), Soupirs (created pas de deux), L'invitation au voyage (created), Impromptu (created pas de deux), Varii Capricci (created La Capricciosa), Fleeting Figures (created rôle); retired from dancing, 1988. *Film:* The Turning Point (with Baryshnikov), 1978. *Relevant publications:* Classical Ballet—the Flow of Movement, by Tamara Karsavina, 1962; Sibley and Dowell, by Nicholas Dromgoole and Leslie Spatt, 1976; Antoinette Sibley, 1981, photographs with text by Mary Clarke; Reflections of a Ballerina, by Barbara Newman, 1986. *Recreations:* watching sport, opera, reading. *Address:* 24 Chapel Street, SW1X 7BY.

**SIBSON, Angela Margaret,** OBE 2010; Diocesan Secretary, Diocese of Lincoln, 2014–17; *b* 1 May 1949; *d* of Robert Sibson, Maryport, Cumbria and Joan Sibson (*née* Stafford); *m* 1971, Tom Ridler (*d* 2001); one *s* one *d*. *Educ:* Univ. of Birmingham (BA 1970); Queen Mary and Westfield Coll., London (MSc 2000). Chief Exec. Officer, Mothers' Union, 1993–99; Chief Executive: Relate, 2000–06; Commn for the Compact, 2007; Nat. Acad. for Parenting Practitioners, 2007–10; Diocesan Sec., Dio. of Chichester, 2011–14. *Recreations:* history, gardening, inter-generational studies and support.

**SIBSON, Clare Adele;** QC 2016; *b* Isle of Wight, 3 May 1975; *d* of G. E. Simms; *m* (marr. diss.), one *s* one *d*. *Educ:* Bishop Stopford C of E Sch., Kettering; Corpus Christi Coll., Cambridge (BA 1st Cl. Double Hons Law 1996; MA 1999); Inns of Court Sch. of Law. Called to the Bar, Middle Temple, 1997; in practice as barrister, 1997–. *Recreations:* choral singing, running. *Address:* Cloth Fair Chambers, 39–40 Cloth Fair, EC1A 7NT.

**SIBSON, Prof. Richard Hugh,** PhD; FRS 2003; FRSNZ; Professor of Geology, University of Otago, New Zealand, 1990–2009, now Emeritus (Head, Department of Geology, 1990–96); *b* 28 Nov. 1945; *s* of Richard Broadley Sibson and Joan Winifred Sibson (*née* Fleming); *m* 1999, Prof. Francesca Cancarini Ghisetti, Catania, Italy. *Educ:* King's Coll., Otahuhu, Auckland; Univ. of Auckland (BSc 1st Cl. Hons Geol. 1968; Dist. Alumnus 2010); Imperial Coll., London (MSc, DIC Structural Geol. 1970; PhD 1977). Jun. Scientific Officer, Geophysics Div., DSIR, NZ, 1969; Lectr in Structural Geol., Imperial Coll., London, 1973–81; Vis. Scientist, Office of Earthquake Studies, US Geol Survey, Menlo Park, Calif, 1981; Asst Prof., 1982–83, Associate Prof., 1984–87, Prof., 1988–90, Dept of Geol Scis, UCSB. Francis Birch Lectr, Amer. Geophysical Union, 2012; Umbgrove Lectr, Univ. of Utrecht, 2015. FGS 1973; FRSNZ 1993; FAAAS 2006; Fellow: Geol Soc. of America, 1991; American Geophysical Union, 1999; Soc. of Econ. Geologists, 2010. Dist. Res. Medal, Univ. of Otago, 2003; Wollaston Medal, Geol Soc. of London, 2010; Structural Geol. and Tectonics Career Contribn Award, Geol. Soc. of America, 2011. *Publications:* contrib. numerous scientific res. papers to geol and geophysical jls on earthquake source mechanics in relation to structure, mechanics and mineralisation of crustal fault zones. *Recreations:* recorded music, hill and coastal walking, sea-kayaking, fly-fishing. *Address:* 60 Brabant Drive, Ruby Bay, Mapua 7005, New Zealand. *T:* (3) 5403713. *E:* rick.sibson@otago.ac.nz.

**SIDDALL, Jonathan Charles;** Protector, Spirit of 2012, since 2014; *b* 6 July 1954; *s* of John Siddall and Joan Siddall; *m* 1988, Nicola Ann Glover; two *d*. *Educ:* Rugby Sch.; Univ. of Birmingham (LLB Hons 1976). Called to the Bar, Middle Temple, 1978; Accredited Mediator, CEDR, 1999. Pupillage, 1979–80; in-house Lawyer, Internat. Mgt Gp, 1980–83; Gen. Sec., British Univs Sports Fedn, 1984–86; Sec., Cumberland Lawn Tennis Club, 1987–90; Sec. and Campaign Co-ordinator, Law Aid Trust, 1990–91; Dep. Sec., LTA, 1992–98; Dir, Sports Dispute Resolution Panel Ltd, 1999–2006; Chief Exec., LandAid Charitable Trust, 2007–12; Dir, Commercial Educn Trust, 2012–15; Chief Exec., Civil Mediation Council, 2013–15; Interim Chief Operating Officer, Access to Justice Foundn, 2017–18. *Recreations:* golf, tennis, ski-ing, amateur dramatics. *Clubs:* Cumberland Lawn Tennis; Jesters; Highgate Golf.

**SIDDALL, Nicholas Michael;** QC 2019; *b* Scarborough, N Yorks, 30 Jan. 1975; *s* of Michael and Marjorie Siddall; *m* 2001, Karen Louise Pond; two *d*. *Educ:* Scalby Sch., Scarborough; Scarborough Sixth Form Coll.; Downing Coll., Cambridge (BA Law 1996); Inns of Court Sch. of Law. Called to the Bar, Middle Temple, 1997; in practice as a barrister, specialising in employment and industrial relations law. *Recreations:* Rugby Union (Bowdon Rugby Club 3rd XV and passionate follower of internat. Rugby and Sale Sharks RUFC), football (passionate follower of Manchester United FC). *Address:* Littleton Chambers, 3 Kings Bench Walk North, Temple, EC4Y 7HR. *T:* (020) 7797 8600. *E:* nsiddall@littletonchambers.co.uk.

**SIDDALL, Victoria May**; Director, Frieze Art Fairs (Frieze London, Frieze New York, Frieze Masters and Frieze Los Angeles), since 2014; *b* Belfast, 8 Dec. 1977; *d* of Stephen and Jill Siddall. *Educ:* Uppingham Sch.; Bristol Univ. (BA Hons). Proposals Writer, Christie's, London, 2000–04; Hd of Develt, Frieze, 2004–11; Dir, Frieze Masters, 2011–14. *Address:* Frieze, 1 Surrey Street, WC2R 2ND. *T:* (020) 3372 6111.

**SIDDELEY**, family name of **Baron Kenilworth**.

**SIDDELEY, Randle**; *see* Kenilworth, 4th Baron.

**SIDDIQ, Irfan**, OBE 2005; HM Diplomatic Service; Ambassador to Sudan, since 2018; *b* London, 27 Jan. 1977; *s* of late Mohammed Siddiq Noor and of Nusrat Siddiq; *m* 2012, Penelope Andre-Eklund; two *d*. *Educ:* University Coll., Oxford (BA Hons PPE 1998). Entered FCO, 1998; Second Sec. (Econ.), New Delhi, 1999–2000; Arabic Lang. Trng, 2000–02; Second Sec. (Pol), Cairo, 2002–03; First Sec. (Pol), Coalition Provisional Authy, Baghdad, 2003–04; on secondment to US State Dept, Washington, 2004–05; Private Sec. to Sec. of State for Foreign and Commonwealth Affairs, 2005–07; Dep. Hd of Mission, Syria, 2007–10, Iraq, 2010–11; Hd, Arab Partnership Dept, FCO, 2011–13; Ambassador to Azerbaijan, 2013–16; Hd, Secondment Unit, FCO, 2016–17; Internat. Advocacy Dir, Plan Internat. (on secondment), 2017–18. *Recreations:* football, literature, current affairs. *Address:* c/o Foreign and Commonwealth Office, King Charles Street, SW1A 2AH. *E:* irfan.siddiq@fco.gov.uk.

**SIDDIQ, Tulip**, (Mrs C. W. St J. Percy); MP (Lab) Hampstead and Kilburn, since 2015; *b* London, 16 Sept. 1982; *d* of Dr Shafiq Siddiq and Sheikh Rehana; *m* 2013, Christian William St John Percy; one *s* one *d*. *Educ:* University Coll. London (BA); King's Coll. London (MA); Birkbeck, Univ. of London (MSc). Work for Amnesty Internat.; researcher: Philip Gould Associates; GLA; Brunswick Gp LLP. Mem. (Lab) Camden LBC, 2010–14 (Cabinet Mem. for Culture and Communities, 2010–14). *Address:* House of Commons, SW1A 0AA. *T:* (020) 7219 3000.

**SIDDIQUI, Prof. Mona**, OBE 2011; PhD; FRSE; Professor of Islamic and Interreligious Studies, Edinburgh Divinity School, University of Edinburgh, since 2011 (Dean International for Middle East, 2016–17); *b* 3 May 1963; *d* of Abdul Ali and Hasina Khatoon; *m* 1991, Farhaj Ahmed Siddiqui; three *s*. *Educ:* Leeds Univ. (BA Hons Arabic and French); Manchester Univ. (MA; PhD 1992). Lectr in Islamic Law, Glasgow Caledonian Univ., 1993–95; University of Glasgow: Sen. Lectr in Arabic and Islamic Studies, 1995–2006; Hd, Dept of Theol. and Religious Studies, 2002–05; Prof. of Islamic Studies, 2006–11; Mem. Court, 2004. Member: Central Religious Adv. Council, BBC, 1998–2005; Chair: Scottish Religious Adv. Council, BBC, 2005–; Home Office Ind. Rev. into Sharia councils in England; Comr, Calman Commn on Scottish Devolution, 2008–09; Member: BMA Med. Ethics Cttee, until 2018; Nuffield Council on Bioethics, until 2018. FRSE 2005. FRSA 2005. Fellow, Amer. Acad. of Arts and Scis, 2019. Hon. DCL Huddersfield, 2009; Hon. DLitt: Leicester, 2009; Roehampton, 2014; Robert Gordon, 2018; Hon. Dr: Wolverhampton, 2002; KCL, 2016. *Publications:* How to Read the Qur'an, 2007; Islam (4 vols), 2010; The Good Muslim: reflections on classical Islamic law and theology, 2012; (ed) The Routledge Reader on Christian-Muslim Relations, 2012; Christians, Muslims and Jesus, 2013; My Way: a Muslim woman's journey, 2014; Hospitality and Islam: welcoming in God's name, 2015; contrib. articles on inter-religious dialogue and Islamic law to various internat. jls. *Recreations:* cooking, interior design. *Address:* Edinburgh Divinity School, Mound Place, Edinburgh EH1 2LX. *T:* (0131) 650 7912. *E:* mona.siddiqui@ed.ac.uk.

**SIDDLE, Anne Elizabeth**; *see* Willis, A. E.

**SIDDLE, Prof. Kenneth**, PhD; Professor of Molecular Endocrinology, University of Cambridge, 1990–2014, now Emeritus; Fellow, Churchill College, Cambridge, since 1982 (Vice-Master, 2012–19); *b* 30 March 1947; *s* of Fred and Vera Siddle; *m* 1st, 1971, Yvonne Marie Kennedy (marr. diss. 1994); one *s*; 2nd, 1996, Anne Elizabeth Willis, *qv*; one *s*. *Educ:* Morecambe Grammar Sch.; Downing Coll., Cambridge (BA 1969). MA, PhD 1973. Lectr, Dept Medical Biochemistry, Welsh Nat. Sch. Med., Cardiff, 1971–78; Meres Sen. Student for Med. Research, St John's Coll., Cambridge, 1978–81; Wellcome Lectr, Dept Clinical Biochem., Univ. of Cambridge, 1981–90. Vis. Scientist, Joslin Diabetes Center and Harvard Med. Sch., 1989–90. Chair, Council, Univ. of Buckingham, 2014–17. Hon. Treas., Cambridge Univ. CC, 1990–. Chm. Editl Bd, Biochemical Jl, 1995–99. *Publications:* articles in biochem. jls. *Recreations:* mountaineering (especially Munro bagging), cricket, bird watching, gardening. *Address:* 6 Church Street, Wing, Oakham, Rutland LE15 8RS. *T:* (01572) 737675. *Clubs:* MCC; Hawks (Cambridge); Lancashire County Cricket.

**SIDDONS, Michael Powell**; Wales Herald of Arms Extraordinary (Herodr Arbennig Cymru), 1994–2010; *b* 4 June 1928; *s* of Bertram Siddons and Enid Mary Powell; *m* 1951, Denise Maria Jacqueline Dambre; three *s* (and one *d* decd). *Educ:* Shrewsbury Sch.; Trinity Coll., Cambridge (MA, MB BCh); St Thomas' Hosp. MFOM 1983; Licence en médecine du Travail, Univ. Catholique de Louvain, 1980. Casualty and anaesthetics officer, then house physician, St Thomas' Hosp., London, 1952–53; Nat. Service, RAMC, Malaya, 1953–55; general medical practitioner, Pontypool, 1955–74; Commission of European Communities: MO, Med. Service, Brussels, 1974–78; Head, Medical Service, Brussels Staff, 1978–87. Mem., Académie Internat. d'Héraldique, 2000; FSA 1987; FHS 1996; FSG 1998. Hon. DLitt Wales, 1997. *Publications:* the Development of Welsh Heraldry, vol. I, 1991, vols II and III, 1993, vol. IV, 2006; Welsh Pedigree Rolls, 1996; Visitations by the Heralds in Wales, 1996; Visitation of Herefordshire 1634, 2002; Heraldic Badges in England and Wales, 2009; The Heraldry of Foreigners in England 1400–1700, 2010; A Dictionary of Mottoes in England and Wales, 2014; Welsh Genealogies AD 1500–1600, 2017; contribs to books on heraldic and genealogical subjects and articles in jls. *Recreations:* gardening especially magnolias, medieval Welsh heraldry, genealogy. *Address:* Castagnon, 32800 Eauze, France.

**SIDELL, Ron Daniel**; architect; Sidell Gibson Architects (formerly Sidell Gibson Partnership LLP) (private practice), since 1970; *b* 20 April 1941; *s* of Daniel Sidell and Dorothy Eady; *m* Sally Hodgson; one *d*. *Educ:* Canterbury Coll. of Architecture; York Univ. Projects in London and Germany include: Unilever, Lloyds, Cazenove, Prudential, Rothschilds, European Bank and Civic Bldgs; Crown Jewel House and Windsor Castle reconstruction; One New Change, St Paul's; masterplans: Paddington Central; Birmingham Snow Hill redevelt. Winner: Grand Buildings Trafalgar Square Internat. Competition, 1986; City of Winchester Central Redevelt Proposal Comp., 1989. *Recreations:* just about most things. *Address:* (office) Ground Floor, 46 Loman Street, SE1 0EH. *T:* (020) 3179 9000.

**SIDHU, Navjot, (Jo)**; QC 2012; *b* Perivale, 4 Nov. 1965; *s* of Pritam Singh Sidhu and Surjit Kaur Sidhu; *m* 1996, Luna Tiwana; two *d*. *Educ:* Villiers High Sch.; Wadham Coll., Oxford (BA Hons PPE 1987); London Sch. of Econs and Pol Sci. (MSc Politics of the World Economy 1989); Coll. of Law (CPE 1992); Inns of Court Sch. of Law (BVC 1993). Policy and Res. Officer, London Bor. of Ealing, 1988; Sen. Researcher, BBC, 1989; Tutor in Law (pt-time), 1989–91; called to the Bar, Lincoln's Inn, 1993, Bencher, 2014; in practice as a barrister, 1993–. Pres., Soc. of Asian Lawyers, 2014–16. Mem., Ealing LBC, 1994–98. Chm. of Govs, Beaconsfield Primary Sch., 1997–2017. Asian Professional of the Year,

2016. *Publications:* (contrib.) Cases that Changed our Lives, 2010; articles in Criminal Law and Justice Weekly, Criminal Bar Qly and The Guardian. *Recreations:* sport and fitness, travel, motoring, comedy, mentoring, TV and radio broadcasting on legal, political and cultural issues. *Address:* 25 Bedford Row, WC1R 4HD. *T:* (020) 7067 1500. *E:* jo.sidhu@sky.com.

**SIDI, Marianne**; *see* Elliott, Marianne.

**SIDMOUTH**, 8th Viscount *cr* 1805; **Jeremy Francis Addington**; *b* 29 July 1947; *s* of 7th Viscount and Barbara Mary Addington (née Rochford); *S* father, 2005; *m* 1st, 1970, Grete Henningsen (marr. diss.); one *s* one *d*; 2nd, 1986, Una Coogan (*d* 2009); one *s* two *d*. *Educ:* Ampleforth. *Heir: s* Hon. John Addington, *b* 29 Nov. 1990.

**SIDNEY**, family name of **Viscount De L'Isle**.

**SIDWELL, Dr Elizabeth Mary**, CBE 2009; FRGS; Schools Commissioner for England, 2011–13; *b* Johannesburg, 29 Sept. 1949; *d* of Richard Archibald Freeman and Mary Willmott Freeman (née Alderton); *m* (marr. diss. 1978); two *s*. *Educ:* Ursuline High Sch., Brentwood, Essex; Queen Mary Coll., Univ. of London (BSc Hons 1972); London Sch. of Econs and Political Sci. (PhD 1976); Hughes Hall, Cambridge (PGCE 1978). FRGS 1998. TEFL Teacher: Anglo World Lang. Sch., Cambridge, 1978–80; Forest Sch., E17, 1980–91, Dep. Hd, 1985–91; Principal: Haberdashers' Aske's Hatcham Girls' Sch., 1991–95; Haberdashers' Aske's Hatcham Coll., 1995–2005; CEO, Haberdashers' Aske's Fedn, 2005–11; Lead Educnl Consultant, Aske's Consultancy Services, 2005–11. OFSTED Inspector, 1995–. Exec. Coach, Specialist Schs and Acads Trust, 1995–2011 (Trustee, 2007–11); Sen. Educn Advr, Baker Dearing Trust, 2013–15; Member, Academic Advisory Board: Wey Educn Ltd, 2017–19; New City Coll., 2017–18. Mem., HMC, 1996–2011. Founder, Aske's Annual Educn Lecture series, 1995–. Trustee, Beacon Acad. Trust, 2015– (Chair, 2018–). Governor: Wellington Coll., 2008–15; Forest Sch., E17, 2012–17. MRI 2000; FRSA. Freeman, City of London, 2007; Liveryman, Haberdashers' Co., 2009–. *Recreations:* family, walking, theatre, travel, Hearing Dogs for the Deaf, Riding for the Disabled, painting. *Address:* 12 Forest Court, E11 1PL. *T:* (020) 8530 4773, 07798 791738. *E:* lizsidwell29@googlemail.com.

**SIEDENTOP, Sir Larry (Alan)**, Kt 2016; CBE 2004; DPhil; writer; Fellow, Keble College, Oxford, 1973–2003, now Emeritus; *b* Chicago, 24 May 1936; *s* of Russell and Dorothy Siedentop. *Educ:* Hope Coll. (BA 1957); Harvard Univ. (MA 1958); Oxford Univ. (Marshall Schol., 1960–63; DPhil 1966). Res. Fellow, Nuffield Coll., Oxford, 1965–68; Lectr in Intellectual Hist., Univ. of Sussex, 1972–73; Faculty Lectr in Political Thought, Oxford Univ., 1973–2003. Vis. Fellow, Netherlands Inst. for Advanced Study, 2003; Queen Victoria Eugenia Vis. Prof., Complutense Univ., Madrid, 2004; Vis. Fellow, Univ. of St Andrews, 2004. *Publications:* (with D. Miller) The Nature of Political Theory, 1985; Tocqueville, 1994; Democracy in Europe, 2000; Inventing the Individual, 2014. *Recreations:* walking, swimming, looking at old master paintings. *Address:* c/o Keble College, Oxford OX1 3PG. *Clubs:* Beefsteak, Turf.

**SIEGERT, Prof. Martin John**, PhD; FRSE; Co-Director, Grantham Institute, Imperial College London, since 2014; *b* Walthamstow, London, 19 Nov. 1967; *s* of David Alan Siegert and Kathleen May Siegert; *m* 2001, Maggie Robertson; one *s*. *Educ:* Sudbury Upper Sch.; Univ. of Reading (BSc Geol Geophysics 1989); Pembroke Coll., Cambridge (PhD 1993). Lectr in Phys. Geog., Univ. of Wales, Aberystwyth, 1994–98; University of Bristol: Lectr, 1999–2002, Reader, 2002–03, in Phys. Geog.; Prof. of Phys. Geog., 2003–06; Prof. of Geoscis, 2006–12, Hd, Sch. of GeoScis, 2006–11, Univ. of Edinburgh; Prof. of Geoscis, Univ. of Bristol, 2012–14. Chief Scientist, UK prog. investigating Lake Ellsworth, W Antarctica, 2009–14. FRSE 2007; FRGS 2015; FGS 2015. Martha T. Muse Prize, Tinker Foundn, 2013. *Publications:* Ice Sheets and Late Quaternary Environmental Change, 2001; over 240 papers in scientific jls, incl. Nature and Science, on Antarctic glaciol. and subglacial lake exploration. *Recreations:* running around Bristol Downs, walking in countryside, watching football (especially Leyton Orient), playing golf. *Address:* Grantham Institute, Imperial College London, South Kensington, SW7 2AZ. *T:* (020) 7594 9667, *Fax:* (020) 7594 9668. *E:* m.siegert@imperial.ac.uk.

**SIEGHART, Mary Ann Corinna Howard**; writer and broadcaster; *b* 6 Aug. 1961; *d* of late Paul Sieghart and Felicity Ann Sieghart (née Baer); *m* 1989, David Prichard; two *d*. *Educ:* Cobham Hall; Bedales Sch.; Wadham Coll., Oxford (MA). Occasional feature and leader writer (part-time), Daily Telegraph, 1980–82; Eurobond Correspondent and Lex Columnist, Financial Times, 1982–86; City Editor, Today, 1986; Political Correspondent, Economist, 1986–88; The Times: Asst Editor, 1988–2007; Opinion Page Editor, 1988–91; Arts Editor, 1989–90; Political Leader Writer, 1990–2007; acting Editor on Sundays, 1997–99; columnist, 1998–2007; Equity Partner, The Browser, 2008–12; columnist, The Independent, 2010–12. Television: presenter: The World This Week; The Brains Trust; The Big Picture Show; Powerhouse; radio: presenter, Start the Week, Newshour, Profile, The Week in Westminster, Beyond Westminster, One to One, Analysis, The Inquiry. Founding Cttee Mem., Women in Journalism, 1995–98; Member: Adv. Council and Steering Cttee, New Europe, 1999–2006; Steering Gp, "No" Campaign, 2000–04; Council, Tate Modern, 2008–17. Member: Social Studies Adv. Bd, Oxford Univ., 1999–2003; Adv. Panel, IntoUniversity, 2007–. Vis. Fellow, All Souls Coll., Oxford, 2018–19. Non-executive Director: Henderson Smaller Cos Investment Trust, 2008–18 (Sen. Ind. Dir, 2016–18); DLN Digital Ltd, 2011–17; The Merchants Trust plc, 2014–; Content Bd, Ofcom, 2014–17. Chm., Social Market Foundn, 2010–. Trustee: Nat. Heritage Meml Fund, 1997–2002; The Radcliffe Trust, 2006–16; Inst. of Art and Ideas, 2012–; Kennedy Meml Trust, 2015–. Vice Pres., Nat. Assoc. for Gifted Children, 1996–2010. Vice-Chair, New Deal for Communities, N Fulham, 2001–06. Laurence Stern Fellow, Washington Post, 1984. Harold Wincott Young Financial Journalist of the Year, 1983; Commended, Young Journalist of the Year, British Press Awards, 1983. *Recreations:* travel to remote places, singing in choirs, art, architecture, music, theatre, geometric doodling, reading fiction, convertible classic cars. *E:* sieghart@journalist.com. *W:* www.maryannsieghart.com. *Clubs:* Groucho, Chelsea Arts, Ivy.

*See also* W. M. T. S. Sieghart.

**SIEGHART, William Matthew Timothy Stephen**, CBE 2016; Chairman: Forward Thinking, since 2004; Somerset House Trust, since 2015; *b* 14 April 1960; *s* of late Paul Sieghart and Felicity Ann Sieghart (née Baer); *m* 1996, Molly Dineen; one *s* two *d*. *Educ:* Eton Coll.; St Anne's Coll., Oxford (MA Hons PPE). Founder and Chm., Forward Publishing, 1986–2001. Director: Groucho Club plc, 1995–2001; Hammer Films, 1998–2017; Elmovo, 2019–. Vice-Pres., Arts and Business, 2001–12; Dir, Index on Censorship, 1999–2000. Dir, Forward Gp, 1998–2006. Founder and Chm., Forward Arts Foundn, 1993–2017 (Trustee, 2017–); Chm., Arts Foundn, 2002–17. Mem. Council, Arts Council England (formerly Arts Council of England), 2000–06 (Chm., Lottery Panel, 2000–05); Author, ind. review for DCMS, E-Lending in Public Libraries in England, 2013; Chm., Govt Adv. Panel on public library service in England, 2014 (report publd 2014). Trustee: Citizenship Foundn, 1994–2011; and Mem. Council, RSA, 1995–99; Esmée Fairbairn Foundn, 1998–2017; YCTV, 1998–2001; Writer's and Scholar's Educnl Trust, 1999–2000; The Poetry Archive, 2001–05; Internat. Prize for Arab Fiction, 2007–14; Free

Word, 2008–16; Reprieve, 2008–16; Brit Docs, 2013–; Grenfell Foundn, 2018–. Sen. Adv. Fellow, UK Defence Acad., 2004–10. Founder and Chm., Streetsmart (Action for the Homeless), 1998–. Gov., British Inst. of Human Rights, 1998–2013. Founder: Nat. Poetry Day, 1995–; Bedtime Reading Week, 2000–05; Big Arts Week, 2001–08. FRSL 2019. *Publications:* (ed) The Forward Book of Poetry, annually 1993–; (ed) Poems of the Decade, 2001, 2nd edn 2011; The Swing Factory, 2004; Winning Words, 2012; The Poetry Pharmacy, 2017; The Poetry Pharmacy Returns, 2019; The Poetry Remedy, 2019. *Recreations:* travelling, playing and watching sport, poetry. *Address:* 50 Albemarle Street, W1S 4BD. *T:* (020) 7493 4361. *E:* sieghart1@mac.com. *Clubs:* Brooks's, Groucho, MCC; Queenwood Golf, Aldeburgh Golf.
See also M. A. C. H. Sieghart.

**SIGMON, Robert Leland;** lawyer; *b* Roanoke, Va, 3 April 1929; *s* of Ottis Leland Sigmon and Aubrey Virginia (*née* Bishop); *m* 1st, 1963, Marianne Rita Gellner (marr. diss.; she *d* 2005); 2nd, 1992, Jean Mary Anderson. *Educ:* Univ. of Virginia; Sorbonne; London Sch. of Economics. BA, DJur. Member of the Bar: US Supreme Court; Court of Appeals, District of Columbia Circuits; Virginia; District of Columbia. Vice-Pres., Pilgrims Soc. of GB, 1993– (Chm., Exec. Cttee, 1977–93); Founder Member: Associates of the Victoria and Albert Museum, 1976 (Dir, 1976–87); Amer. and Internat. Friends of V&A Mus. (Trustee, 1985–2000). Mem., Council of Management, British Inst. of Internat. and Comparative Law, 1982–2006. Trustee: American Sch. in London, 1977–91; Magna Carta Trust, 1984–94; Vice-Chm., Mid-Atlantic Club of London, 1977–96; Vice-Pres., European-Atlantic Gp, 1978–94; Member: Exec. Cttee, Amer. Soc. in London, 1969– (Chm. 1974); Amer. Soc. of Internat. Law; Selden Soc.; Guild of St Bride's Church, Fleet Street; Ends of the Earth; Gov., E-SU, 1984–90. Chevalier du Tastevin. *Publications:* contribs to legal periodicals. *Recreations:* collecting antiquarian books, oenology. *Address:* Flat 46, Queen Alexandra Mansions, Judd Street, WC1H 9DQ. *Club:* Reform.

**SIKORA, Prof. Karol,** FRCP, FRCR, FFPM; Dean, Buckingham Medical School, since 2007; Chief Medical Officer, Proton Partners International, since 2015; *b* 17 June 1948; *s* of Witold Karol Sikora and Thomasina Sikora; *m* 1974, Alison Mary Rice; one *s* two *d*. *Educ:* Dulwich Coll.; Corpus Christi Coll., Cambridge (MA, MB, BChir, PhD); Middlesex Hospital. FRCR 1980; FRCP 1988; FFPM 2002. Middlesex Hosp., 1972; Hammersmith Hosp., 1973; MRC Clinical Fellow, Lab. for Molecular Biol., Cambridge, 1974–77; Clinical Fellow, Stanford Univ., 1978–79; Dir, Ludwig Inst. for Cancer Research, Cambridge, 1980–86; Prof. of Clin. Oncol., RPMS, then ICSM, Hammersmith Hosp., 1986–2007; Dep. Dir (Clinical Res.), ICRF, 1995–97; Chief, WHO Cancer Prog., Lyon, France, 1997–99; Med. Dir, then Chief Med. Officer, Cancer Partners UK, 2006–15. Vis. Prof. of Cancer Medicine, Hammersmith Hosp., 1999–. Vice Pres., Global Clinical Res. (Oncology), Pharmacia Corp., 1999–2002; Special Advr on cancer services, HCA Internat., 2002–06. *Publications:* Monoclonal Antibodies, 1984; Interferon, 1985; Cancer: a student guide, 1988; (ed jtly) Treatment of Cancer, 1990, 6th edn 2015; Fight Cancer, 1990; Genes and Cancer, 1990; (with N. Bosanquet) The Economics of Cancer Care, 2006; The Streetwise Patients Guide to Surviving Cancer, 2017; contrib. Gene Therapy. *Recreations:* boating, travelling, rock climbing. *Address:* 21 Dorset Square, NW1 6QG. *T:* (020) 7724 8086. *Clubs:* Athenæum, Polish Hearth.

**SILBER, Dr Evelyn Ann,** FMA; freelance lecturer and cultural tour director, since 2006; Hon. Professorial Research Fellow, University of Glasgow, since 2006; *b* 22 May 1949; *d* of late Martin Helmut Silber and Mavis Evelyn (*née* Giles). *Educ:* Hatfield Girls' Grammar Sch.; New Hall, Cambridge (MA); Univ. of Pennsylvania (MA); Clare Hall, Cambridge (PhD). Guide, Hatfield House, 1965–70; Thouron Fellow, Univ. of Penn., 1972–73; copy-writer and media controller, Associated Book Publishers, 1973–74; publicity manager, Addison Wesley Publishers, 1974–75; Leverhulme Res. Fellow in Hist. of Art, 1975–76; Lectr, Hist. of Art, Glasgow Univ., 1978; Birmingham Museum and Art Gallery: Asst Keeper (Fine Art), 1979–82; Dep. Keeper (Painting and Sculpture), 1982–85; Birmingham Museums and Art Gallery: Asst Dir, Public Services, 1985–94; Head of Central Museums, 1994–95; Director: Leeds Mus and Galls, 1995–2001; Hunterian Mus. and Art Gall., Univ. of Glasgow, 2001–06. Mem. Council, Ikon Gall., 1981–88. Member: Bd, Cultural Heritage NTO (formerly Museums Trng Inst.), 1996–2003; Historic Envmt Adv. Council for Scotland, 2006–09. Chm., Scottish Archaeol Finds Allocation Panel, 2012–. Chm., Charles Rennie Mackintosh Soc., 2006–12. Chm., Queen's Park Arena Ltd, 2011–. FMA 1996; FRSA 2000. *Publications:* The Sculpture of Epstein, 1986; (with F. Friedman) Jacob Epstein Sculpture and Drawings, 1987; Gaudier-Brzeska: Life and Art, 1996. *Recreations:* travel, music, walking, gardening. *Address:* School of Culture and Creative Arts, University of Glasgow, 8 University Gardens, Glasgow G12 8QQ. *Club:* Royal Over-Seas League.

**SILBER, Hon. Sir Stephen (Robert),** Kt 1999; a Judge of the High Court of Justice, Queen's Bench Division, 1999–2014; *b* 26 March 1944; *s* of late J. J. Silber and Marguerite Silber; *m* 1982, Lucinda, *d* of late Lt-Col David St John Edwards; one *s* one *d*. *Educ:* William Ellis Sch.; University Coll. London; Trinity Coll., Cambridge. Called to Bar, Gray's Inn, 1968, Bencher, 1994 (Vice-Treas., 2013; Treas., 2014). QC 1987; a Recorder, 1987–99; a Dep. High Court Judge, 1995–99. A Judge, Employment Appeal Tribunal, 2004–14; Dep. Chm., Security Vetting Appeals Panel, 2009–18; Judicial Comr, Investigatory Powers Comr's Office, 2017–. Law Comr for England and Wales, 1994–99. Mem., Criminal Law Cttee, Judicial Studies Bd, 1994–99. Mem. Adv. Council, Inst. of Eur. and Comparative Law, Univ. of Oxford, 2004–; Distinguished Judicial Visitor, UCL, 2011–; Distinguished Judicial Mem., Commercial Law Centre, 2018–. Pres., Travel and Tourism Law Assoc., 2002–. Hon. Fellow, Harris Manchester Coll., Oxford, 2018. *Recreations:* walking, music, watching sport, theatre. *Address:* c/o Royal Courts of Justice, Strand, WC2A 2LL.

**SILBERT, Roxana Alba;** Artistic Director, Hampstead Theatre, since 2019; *b* La Plata, Argentina, 12 May 1964; *d* of Moises Silbert and Yolanda Silbert; *m* 2016, Chahine Yavroyan (*d* 2018). *Educ:* Eaton (City of Norwich) Comp. Sch.; New Hall, Cambridge (BA Hons Eng. Lit. 1986). Associate Dir, Royal Court Th., 1996–98; Literary Dir, Traverse Th., 2001–04; Artistic Dir, Paines Plough Theatre Co., 2005–09; Associate Dir, RSC, 2009–12; Artistic Dir, Birmingham Rep. Th., 2012–19.

**SILCOCK, David Thomas;** road safety consultant; Chief Executive, Global Road Safety Partnership, 2002–08; *b* 2 March 1945; *s* of John and Marjorie Silcock; *m* 1st, 1967, Lesley Maureen Reeves (marr. diss. 1994); three *d*; 2nd, 1996, Annette de Villiers Herholdt. *Educ:* Churchill Coll., Cambridge (BA 1966, MA 1970); Imperial Coll., London (MSc 1970). CEng, MICE, 1971. Engr, Canadian Pacific Railway Co. and Consultant, N. D. Lea and Assocs, Vancouver, 1967–69; various transport consultancy assignments, Halcrow Fox and Assocs, UK, 1969–74; Sen. Associate, Halcrow Fox and Assocs (London), and Man. Dir, Halcrow Fox and Assocs (Hong Kong), 1974–79; Dep. Dir, Transport Ops Res. Gp, Univ. of Newcastle upon Tyne, 1979–82; Ross Silcock, subseq. Babtie Group: Partner, Ross Silcock Partnership, 1986–96; Man. Dir, Ross Silcock Ltd, transportation and road safety consultants, 1996–2001; Divl Dir, Babtie Gp Ltd, 2001–02. Mem. Council, 1995–96, Dir, 1996–2001, British Consultants Bureau. Mem. Edtl Bd, Transport Reviews (internat. jl), 1989–92. *Publications:* over 90 tech. articles in fields of transport and road safety. *Recreations:* walking, music.

**SILJA, Anja;** German opera singer; *b* Berlin, 17 April 1940; parents both actors; *m* 1980, Christoph von Dohnányi, *qv* (marr. diss.); one *s* two *d*. Started career at age 10; first opera engagement, Staatstheater Braunschweig, 1956; débuts: Stuttgart State Opera, Frankfurt Opera, 1958; Bayreuth Fest. (Senta in The Flying Dutchman), 1960; has appeared widely in USA, Japan and Europe, in all major opera houses, incl. Salzburg, and Glyndebourne Fest. (début, 1989); repertoire includes: all major Wagner rôles, Salome, Lulu, Fidelio, Elektra, Jenůfa, The Makropulos Case, Erwartung, Pierrot Lunaire, Dialogues des Carmélites, etc. Has made recordings and videos. Bundesverdienstkreuz (Germany). *Address:* c/o Artists Management Zürich/Rita Schütz, Rütistrasse 52, 8044 Zürich-Gockhausen, Switzerland.

**SILK, Rev. Mgr David;** *see* Silk, Rev. Mgr R. D.

**SILK, Sir (Evan) Paul,** KCB 2015; *b* 8 Feb. 1952; *s* of late Evan Silk and Joan Silk (*née* King); *m* 1986, Kathryn Barnes; three *s*. *Educ:* Christ Coll., Brecon; Brasenose Coll., Oxford (John Watson Scholar; MA 1st Cl. Hons Lit.Hum.); Princeton Univ.; Open Univ. (Dip. French 2013). A Clerk in H of C, 1975–77 and 1979–2001: Energy Cttee, 1984–89; Home Affairs Cttee, 1989–93; Foreign Affairs Cttee, 1998–2001; NI Office, 1977–79; occasional work with Council of Europe Parly Assembly, 1976–99; Clerk to Nat. Assembly for Wales, 2001–07; Dir of Strategic Projects, H of C, 2007–10; Chair, Commn on Devolution to Wales, 2011–14. Member, Board of Visitors: HM Prison Ashford, 1981–90; HM Prison Belmarsh, 1991–93; Member: Ind. Reference Gp, Police Fedn of England and Wales, 2016; Parly and Political Service Hons Cttee, 2017–; Expert Panel on Assembly Electoral Reform, 2017; Chair: Bd of Finance, Dio. of Swansea and Brecon, 2017–; Membership Panel, Dwr Cymru/Welsh Water, 2018–; Dep. Chm., Rep. Body, Ch in Wales, 2019–. Associate: Global Partners Governance, 2013–; Westminster Foundn for Democracy, 2017– (occasional work, 2010–). Pres., Study of Parlt Gp, 2015–19. Hon. Prof., Wales Governance Centre, Sch. of Law and Politics (formerly Eur. Studies), Cardiff Univ., 2011–; Hon. Fellow, Aberystwyth Univ., 2016. Trustee: Oxford Univ. Student Union, 2011–15; Hansard Soc. for Parly Govt, 2017–. Patron: Tools for Self-Reliance Cymru, 2013–; Inst. for Welsh Affairs, 2019–. Dir, RWCMD, 2014–15; Gov., Univ. of S Wales, 2014–15; Chm. of Govs, Christ Coll., Brecon, 2014–. FLSW 2017. *Publications:* (with R. Walters) How Parliament Works, 1987, 4th edn 1998; (with P. Evans) Parliamentary Assembly of the Council of Europe: practice and procedure, 10th edn 2008, 11th edn 2013; contribs to other works on Parliament. *Recreation:* living in countryside. *Address:* Mill Cottage, Crickhowell NP8 1SA. *E:* evanpaulsilk@gmail.com. *Clubs:* Chelsea Arts; Ebbw Vale Rugby Football; Gwernyfed Rugby Football.

**SILK, Prof. Joseph Ivor,** PhD; FRS 1999; Research Professor and Homewood Professor of Physics and Astronomy, Johns Hopkins University, since 2010; Emeritus Professor and Research Scientist, Institut d'Astrophysique, Paris; *b* 3 Dec. 1942; *s* of Philip and Sylvie Silk; *m* 1st, 1968, Margaret Wendy Kuhn (marr. diss. 1998); two *s*; 2nd, 2001, Jacqueline Riffault. *Educ:* Clare Coll., Cambridge (MA 1963); Harvard Univ. (PhD 1968). Research Fellow: Inst. of Astronomy, Cambridge Univ., 1968–69; Princeton Univ. Observatory, 1969–70; University of California at Berkeley: Prof. of Astronomy, 1970; Miller Res. Prof., 1980–81; Prof. of Physics, 1988; Savilian Prof. of Astronomy, Oxford Univ., 1999–2011, now Emeritus; Fellow, New Coll., Oxford, 1999–2011, now Emeritus. Alfred P. Sloan Foundn Fellow, 1972–74; Guggenheim Fellow, 1975–76; Leon Lectr, Univ. of Penn, 1984; Hooker Dist. Vis. Prof., McMaster Univ., 1987; Bearden Vis. Prof., Johns Hopkins Univ., 1994; Sackler Fellow, Inst. Astronomy, Cambridge, 1997; Tercentenary Fellow, Emmanuel Coll., Cambridge, 1997; Blaise-Pascal Prof., Inst. d'Astrophysique, Paris, 1997–98; Biermann Lectr, Max-Planck Inst. für Astrophys., Garching, 1997; Prof. of Astronomy, Gresham Coll., 2015. FAAAS 1987; Fellow, APS, 1996. Hon. Mem., French Physical Soc., 1997. Henry Norris Russell Lectureship, AAS, 2018; (jtly) Gruber Cosmology Prize, Gruber Foundn, 2019. *Publications:* The Big Bang, 1980, 3rd edn 2001; (jtly) Star Formation, 1980; The Left Hand of Creation, 1983, rev. edn 1994; Cosmic Enigmas, 1994; A Short History of the Universe, 1994; Horizons of Cosmology: exploring worlds seen and unseen, 2009; contrib. numerous articles to refereed jls. *Recreation:* ski-ing. *Address:* Department of Physics and Astronomy, Bloomberg Center for Physics and Astronomy, Johns Hopkins University, 3400 N Charles Street, Baltimore, MD 21218, USA.

**SILK, Prof. Michael Stephen,** FBA 2009; Professor of Classical and Comparative Literature, King's College London, 2006–15, now Emeritus; *b* 11 June 1941; *s* of Norman and Ada Silk; *m* 1964, Laurel Evans; one *s* one *d*. *Educ:* King Edward's Sch., Birmingham; St John's Coll., Cambridge (BA 1964; MA 1967; PhD 1969). Res. Fellow, St John's Coll., Cambridge, 1967–70; King's College London: Lectr in Classics, 1970–85; Reader in Classics, 1985–91; Head, Dept of Classics, 1993–97; Prof. of Greek Lang. and Lit., 1991–2006. Leverhulme Major Res. Fellowship, 2000–03. Vis. Prof., Greek and Comparative Lit., 2003, 2005, 2007, Affiliated Faculty (Comparative and Creative Lit.), Dept of Classical Studies, 2014–, Boston Univ.; Adjunct Prof., Dept of English and Comparative Lit., Univ. of North Carolina, Chapel Hill, 2012–19. Co-founder and co-editor, Dialogos, 1994–99. FKC 2010. *Publications:* Interaction in Poetic Imagery, 1974; (with J. P. Stern) Nietzsche on Tragedy, 1981, rev. edn 1983; Homer: the Iliad, 1987, 2nd edn 2004 (trans. Greek 2009); (ed) Tragedy and the Tragic: Greek theatre and beyond, 1996; Aristophanes and the Definition of Comedy, 2000; (ed with A. Hirst) Alexandria, Real and Imagined, 2004; (ed with A. Georgakopoulou) Standard Languages and Language Standards: Greek, past and present, 2009; (with I. Gildenhard and R. Barrow) The Classical Tradition: art, literature, thought, 2014; articles and reviews in classical and literary jls and collections. *Recreations:* poetry, jazz, standard popular songs, cricket. *Address:* Department of Classics, King's College London, Strand, WC2R 2LS. *T:* (020) 7848 2627.

**SILK, Sir Paul;** *see* Silk, Sir E. P.

**SILK, Rev. Mgr (Robert) David;** Bishop of Ballarat, 1994–2003; Hon. Assistant Bishop: Diocese of Chichester, 2003–04: Diocese of Exeter, 2004–10; *b* 23 Aug. 1936; *s* of Robert Reeve Silk and Winifred Patience Silk; *m* 1957, Joyce Irene Bracey; one *s* one *d*. *Educ:* Gillingham Grammar School; Univ. of Exeter (BA Hons Theology 1958); St Stephen's House, Oxford. Deacon 1959, priest 1960, Rochester; Curate: St Barnabas, Gillingham, 1959–63; Holy Redeemer, Lamorbey, 1963–69; Priest-in-Charge of the Good Shepherd, Blackfen, 1967–69; Rector of Swanscombe, 1969–75; Rector of Beckenham, St George, 1975–80; Archdeacon of Leicester, 1980–94; Team Rector, Holy Spirit, Leicester, 1982–88; Priest i/c of Amberley with N Stoke, Parham, Greatham and Wiggonholt, 2003–04; received into RC Church and ordained deacon and priest, 2011. Proctor in Convocation, 1970–94; Prolocutor of Lower House of Convocation of Canterbury, 1980–94; Member of Liturgical Commn, 1976–91; Chm., Leicester Council of Faiths, 1986–93; Moderator, Churches Commn for Inter-Faith Relations (formerly Cttee for Relations with Peoples of Other Faiths), 1990–93; Pres., Victorian Council of Churches, 1995–97; Member: Anglican-Lutheran Commn, 1995–2003 (Chm., 2001–03); Liturgy Commn, 1996–2003; Chairman: Leaders of Faith Communities Forum, Victoria, 1996–2003; Glastonbury Pilgrimage Assoc., 2003–09. Chaplain of His Holiness Pope Benedict XVI, 2012. *Publications:* Prayers for Use at the Alternative

Services, 1980; Compline—an Alternative Order, 1980; In Penitence and Faith, 1988. *Recreations:* Richard III Society, Leicester FC, theatre. *Address:* 1 Centenary Way, Torquay TQ2 7SB. *E:* david.silk3@btopenworld.com.

**SILK, Robert K.;** *see* Kilroy-Silk.

**SILKIN,** Barony of (cr 1950); title disclaimed by 3rd Baron; *see under* Silkin, Christopher Lewis.

**SILKIN, Christopher Lewis;** b 12 Sept. 1947; s of Baron Silkin of Dulwich (Life Peer), PC, QC and his 1st wife, Elaine Violet (née Stamp); S uncle, 2001, as 3rd Baron Silkin, but disclaimed his peerage for life; one s one d by Carolyn Theobald. *Educ:* Dulwich; LLB London 1974. Admitted solicitor, 1977.

**SILLARS, James;** management consultant; Assistant to Secretary-General, Arab-British Chamber of Commerce, 1993–2002; b Ayr, 4 Oct. 1937; s of Matthew Sillars; m 1st, 1957; one s one d; 2nd, 1981, Mrs Margo MacDonald, MSP (d 2014). *Educ:* Newton Park Sch., Ayr; Ayr Academy. Former official, Fire Brigades Union; Past Member Ayr Town Council and Ayr County Council Educn Cttee. Head of Organization and Social Services Dept, Scottish TUC, 1968–70. Full-time Labour Party agent, 1964 and 1966 elections. Contested (SNP): Linlithgow, 1987; Glasgow, Govan, 1992. MP: (Lab) South Ayrshire, March 1970–1976, (SLP) 1976–79; (SNP) Glasgow, Govan, Nov. 1988–1992. Among the founders of the Scottish Labour Party, Jan. 1976. Man. Dir, Scoted Ltd, 1980–83. Especially interested in education, social services, industrial relations, development policies. *Publications:* Scotland—the Case for Optimism, 1986; Labour Party pamphlets on Scottish Nationalism; Tribune Gp pamphlet on Democracy within the Labour Party. *Recreations:* reading, golf. *Address:* 97 Grange Loan, Edinburgh EH9 2ED.

**SILLEM, Jeremy William;** Managing Partner, Spencer House Partners LLP, since 2005; b London, 4 July 1950; s of late Arthur and Patricia Sillem; divorced; two d. *Educ:* Downside Sch.; Brasenose Coll., Oxford (MA). Lazard Brothers, London, 1971–85, latterly Exec. Dir; Lazard Frères and Co., NY, 1985–95, latterly Gen. Partner and Hd of Corp. Finance; Chief Exec., Lazard Capital Mkts, London, 1995–2000; Chairman: Bear Stearns Internat., 2000–04; BioPharma Credit PLC, 2017–. Director: Martin Currie Hldgs, 2007–14; CDC Gp, 2011–14; RIT Capital Partners PLC, 2018–. Dir, Reform Res. Trust, 2010–. *Recreations:* fishing, shooting. *Address:* Spencer House Partners LLP, 15 St James's Place, SW1A 1NP. *T:* (020) 7647 8529. *E:* j.sillem@spencerhousepartners.com. *Club:* Brooks's.

**SILLERY, William Moore,** OBE 2002; DL; Headmaster, Belfast Royal Academy, 1980–2000; b 14 March 1941; s of William and Adeline Sillery; m 1963, Elizabeth Margaret Dunwoody; two d. *Educ:* Methodist Coll., Belfast; St Catharine's Coll., Cambridge. Head of Modern Languages, Belfast Royal Academy, 1968, Vice-Principal 1974, Deputy Headmaster 1976. Educnl Advr, Ulster Television, 1985–94. Chm., Ministerial Working Party on Modern Langs in NI Curriculum, 1991; Member: NI Cttee, UFC, 1989–93; Belfast Educn and Liby Bd, 1994–97; Cttee, HMC, 1998–99; Chm., Irish Div., HMC, 1998–99. Lay Mem., Solicitors' Disciplinary Tribunal, NI, 1999–2012. Chm., Arion Selection Panel, British Council, 2003–06. Gov., Methodist Coll., Belfast, 2007–14. DL Belfast, 1997. *Recreations:* golf, bridge. *Address:* Ardmore, 15 Saintfield Road, Belfast BT8 7AE. *T:* (028) 9064 5260. *Club:* Belvoir Park (Belfast).

**SILLITO, Prof. Adam Murdin,** PhD; FMedSci; Professor of Visual Science, 1987–2014, now Emeritus, and Director, 1991–2006, Institute of Ophthalmology, University College London; b 31 March 1944; s of Adam Cheswardine Sillito and Jean Mary Sillito, Amington, Tamworth; m Sharon Pascoe; one s one d. *Educ:* Univ. of Birmingham (MRC Schol.; BSc, PhD). Res. Fellow, Dept of Physiol., Univ. of Birmingham, 1968–70; Sir Henry Wellcome Travelling Fellow, Dept of Physiol., Johns Hopkins Med. Sch., Baltimore, 1970–71; Lectr, 1971–79, Wellcome Trust Sen. Lectr, 1979–82, Med. Sch., Birmingham; Prof. and Hd of Dept of Physiol., UC, Cardiff, 1982–87. Mem. Editl Bd, Jl Physiol., 1979–86; Co-Ed., Exptl Brain Res., 1989–; Mem., Adv. Cttee, Plenum Press Cerebral Cortex series, 1991–. Non-exec. Dir, Moorfields NHS Trust, 1994–2006 (Mem. Bd, Moorfields Eye Hosp., 1992–94). Medical Research Council: Member: Neurosci. Grants Cttee, 1982–86; Neurosci. Bd, 1991–95; Non-clinical Trng and Career Develt Panel, 1993–95. Chairman: Res. Cttee, BPMF, 1990–94; Electrophysiol. Panel, Prog. Cttee, ARVO, 1996–99; Member: Surgery Task Force—Technol. Transfer of Minimal Access Surgery, ACOST Med. Res. and Health Cttee, 1992; Human Frontiers Fellowship Panel, 1994–98. Chm., Brain Res. Assoc., 1980–83; Member: Physiol Soc. (Mem. Cttee, 1982–86); IBRO; British Neurosci. Assoc.; Soc. for Neurosci.; Assoc. for Res. in Vision and Ophthalmology (Mem., Prog. Cttee, 1996–99); Eur. Neurosci. Assoc. Founder FMedSci, 1998. Hon. Fellow, UCL. *Publications:* (ed jtly) Progress in Brain Research, 1990; Mechanisms of the GABA Action in the Visual System, 1992; (ed with G. Burnstock) Nervous Control of the Eye, 2000; numerous contribs to learned jls on mechanisms of vision. *Recreations:* dreaming of better things, learning and speculating, fine art photography. *Address:* UCL Institute of Ophthalmology, Bath Street, EC1V 9EL. *E:* a.sillito@ioores.co.uk.

**SILLITOE, Prof. Paul,** PhD, ScD; FBA 2006; Professor of Anthropology, Durham University, since 1997; s of Frank Arthur George Sillitoe and Doris Mary Sillitoe (née Graves); m 1972, Jacqueline Ann Bryan; two s. *Educ:* Durham Univ. (BA, MA Anthropol.); Trinity Coll., Cambridge (PhD 1976, ScD Social Anthropol. 2001); Open Univ. (BA Nat. Scis); Newcastle Univ. (MSc Soil Sci.); Wye Coll., London Univ. (MSc Agricl Scis). Field work in New Guinea and projects in S Asia and Gulf region. Work with internat. develt agencies. *Publications:* Give and Take, 1979; Roots of the Earth, 1983; Made in Niugini, 1988; The Bogaia of the Muller Ranges, 1994; A Place Against Time, 1996; An Introduction to the Anthropology of Melanesia, 1998; Social Change in Melanesia, 2000; (jtly) Horticulture in Papua New Guinea, 2002; Managing Animals in New Guinea, 2003; (jtly) Indigenous Knowledge Inquiries, 2005; (jtly) Grass-Clearing Man, 2009; From Land to Mouth, 2010 (ed) Sustainable Development, 2014; (ed) Indigenous Studies and Engaged Anthropology, 2015; Built in Niugini, 2017; (ed) Indigenous Knowledge: enhancing its contribution to natural resources management, 2017. *Recreation:* urban peasant occupations. *Address:* Anthropology Department, Durham University, Dawson Building, South Road, Durham DH1 3LE. *T:* (0191) 334 6190, *Fax:* (0191) 334 6101. *E:* paul.sillitoe@durham.ac.uk.

**SILLS, Dame Eileen,** DBE 2015 (CBE 2004); Chief Nurse and Director of Patient Experience, Guy's and St Thomas' NHS Foundation Trust, since 2005; b Stockport, 21 June 1962; d of William Henry McQuinn and Eileen Jenifer Ann McQuinn; m 1988, Michael David Sills; two d. *Educ:* Tottenham Technol. Coll. (Dip. Nursing); London Sch. of Hygiene and Tropical Medicine (MSc Health Services Mgt). RN 1983. Jun. and sen. nursing posts, Stepping Hill Hosp., Withington Hosp., N Middx Hosp., 1983–95; Sen. Nurse, then Dep. Gen. Manager, Royal Free NHS Trust, 1995–99; Dir of Nursing, Royal Nat. Orthopaedic Hosp., 1999–2001; Dir of Nursing and Dep. Chief Exec., Whipps Cross Hosp., 2001–05. Visiting Professor: KCL, 2005–; London South Bank Univ., 2005–. *Recreation:* keeping fit. *Address:* Guy's and St Thomas' NHS Foundation Trust, St Thomas' Hospital, Westminster Bridge Road, SE1 7EH.

**SILMAN, Prof. Alan Jonathan,** FRCP, FMedSci; Medical Director, Arthritis Research UK (formerly Campaign), 2007–14; Professor of Musculoskeletal Health, University of Oxford, since 2015; b 4 Dec. 1951; m 1979, Ruth Abrams; two s one d. *Educ:* Leeds Univ. (MB ChB); LSHTM (MScSocMed 1979); MD London 1985. MRCP 1977, FRCP 1992; MFCM 1980, FFCM 1988; FMedSci 2001. House Surgeon, then Houe Physician, St James Univ. Teaching Hosp., Leeds, 1974–75; SHO, Professorial Dept of Paediatrics, Royal Liverpool Children's Hosp., 1975–76; SHO/Registrar, N Manchester Gen. Hosp., 1976–77; Hon. Registrar, SE Thames RHA, 1977–79; Lectr, 1979–82, Sen. Lectr, 1982–88, in Clinical Epidemiology, London Hosp. Med. Coll.; Hon. Sen. Registrar, 1979–82, Hon. Consultant, 1982–88, Tower Hamlets Health Dist; ARC Prof. of Rheumatic Disease Epidemiology and Dir, ARC Epidemiology Res. Unit, Univ. of Manchester, 1989–2007. Hon. Consultant in Rheumatology, Manchester Royal Infirmary, 1989–2011. Chair, NICE Technol. Appraisals Appeal Panel, 2014–. Hon. DSc: E Anglia, 2009; Keele, 2012. *Publications:* (with M. Hochberg) Epidemiology of the Rheumatic Diseases, 2001; (ed jtly) Rheumatology, 3rd edn 2004 to 7th edn 2018; over 500 res. articles on rheumatic diseases.

**SILSOE,** 3rd Baron cr 1963, of Silsoe, co. Bedford; **Simon Rupert Trustram Eve;** Bt 1943; b 17 April 1966; o s of 2nd Baron Silsoe, QC and of Bridget Min (née Hart-Davis); S father, 2005; m Julie C. Legge. *Heir: uncle* Hon. Peter Nanton Trustram Eve, OBE [b 2 May 1930; m 1961, Petronilla Letiere Sheldon (née Elliott); two s].

**SILUNGWE, Hon. Annel Musenga; Hon. Mr Justice Silungwe;** Judge of the High Court and acting Judge of the Supreme Court, Namibia, 1999–2009; Judge, Court of Appeal, Seychelles, 1992; b 10 Jan. 1936; s of late Solo Musenga Silungwe and Janet Nakafunda Silungwe; m 1960, Abigail Nanyangwe; one s four d. *Educ:* Council of Legal Educn; Univ. of Zambia (LLM 1977). Called to the Bar, Inner Temple, 1966; State Counsel, Zambia, 1974; Judge of the High Court, Zambia, 1971–73; Minister of Legal Affairs and Attorney-General, 1973–75; Chief Justice of Zambia, 1975–92; Dir, Justice Trng Centre, Ministry of Justice, Namibia, 1994–99. Chairman: Judicial Services Commn, 1975–92; Council of Legal Educn, 1975–92; Council of Law Reporting, 1975–92; Technical Cttee on Drafting the Zambian Constitution, 2011–14. Award of Merit, Rotary Internat. Dist 9210, 1989. *Publications:* contrib. learned jls. *Recreations:* music, photography, reading, golf. *T:* and *Fax:* (home) (61) 242705.

**SILVER, Caroline Louise;** Partner and Managing Director, Moelis & Co., since 2009; b Wokingham, Berks, 30 Dec. 1962; d of Henry and Louise Nery; m 1986, Mark Silver; one s one d. *Educ:* Ranelagh Grammar Sch., Bracknell; Durham Univ. (BA Hons English with Spanish). ACA 1987. Price Waterhouse, 1984–88; Corporate Finance Exec., Morgan Grenfell & Co. Ltd, 1988–90; Dir, Internat., Deutsche Morgan Grenfell, 1990–94; Vice Chairman: Global Investment Banking, Morgan Stanley Inc., 1994–2007; Investment Banking, Merrill Lynch Inc./Bank of America, 2007–09. Non-executive Director: London Ambulance Service, 2005–14; PZ Cussons plc, 2014– (Chair, 2017–); BUPA, 2017–; Meggitt plc, 2019–; Sen. Ind. Dir, M&G Prudential, 2019–. Trustee, V&A Mus., 2014–. *Recreations:* opera, safaris, scuba diving, racehorse ownership, family, Africa, arts and design. *Address:* Moelis & Co., First Floor, Condor House, 10 St Paul Churchyard, EC4M 8AL. *T:* (020) 7634 3578. *E:* caroline.silver@moelis.com.

**SILVER, Prof. Ian Adair;** Professor of Comparative Pathology, University of Bristol, 1970–93, Emeritus Professor of Pathology, since 1993; Adjunct Professor of Neurology, University of Pennsylvania, 1977–2006; b 28 Dec. 1927; s of Captain George James Silver and Nora Adair Silver; m 1st, 1950, Dr Marian Scrase (d 1994), d of Dr F. J. Scrase; two s two d; 2nd, 1996, Prof. Maria Erecińska, d of Prof. K Erecińksi. *Educ:* Rugby School; Corpus Christi Coll., Cambridge (BA, MA); Royal Veterinary Coll. (BVetStuds). MRCVS 1952, FRCVS 1990. University of Cambridge: Univ. Demonstrator, Zoology, 1952–57; Univ. Lectr, Anatomy, 1957–70; Official Fellow and Coll. Lectr, Churchill Coll., 1965–70; Sen. Tutor for Advanced Students, Churchill Coll., 1966–70; University of Bristol: Hd, Dept of Path., later Path. and Microbiol., 1981–93; Dean, Faculty of Medicine, 1987–90; Sen. Res. Fellow, 1994–2017; Chm., Inst. of Clinical Neuroscience, 2000–15; Chm., Burden Neurological Inst., 2006–. Chm., Southmead Health Services NHS Trust, Bristol, 1992–99. Vis. Fellow, Weitzmann Inst., Rehovot, 1963; Vis. Prof., Louisiana Tech. Univ., 1973; Royal Soc. Vis. Prof., Fed. Univ. of Rio de Janeiro, 1977. Mem., SERC Biol. Scis Cttee, 1975–80; President: Internat. Soc. for O$_2$ Transport to Tissue, 1976 and 1986; RCVS, 1985–86 and 1987 (Sen. Vice-Pres., 1986–87 and 1987–88). Fellow, Anatomical Soc., 2012. RAgS Silver Medal, 1952; Sir Frederick Hobday Meml Medal, British Equine Vet. Assoc., 1982; Dalrymple-Champneys Medal, BVA, 1984. *Publications:* Editor of scientific books, 1971–; numerous articles in scientific jls, 1956–. *Recreations:* farming, exploring, fishing, DIY. *Address:* Centre for Applied Anatomy, Faculty of Health Sciences, School of Veterinary Sciences, University of Bristol, Bristol BS2 8EJ. *T:* (0117) 928 8362.

**SILVER, Dame Ruth (Muldoon),** DBE 2006 (CBE 1998); Principal and Chief Executive Officer, Lewisham College, London, 1991–2009; b 23 Jan. 1945; d of Francis Faughnan and Catherine Muldoon; m 1970, Anthony Silver (marr. diss. 1985); partner, Andrew Mingay; one d. *Educ:* Hamilton Acad.; Univ. of Glasgow (NUM schol.; MA Lit. and Psychol. 1966); Univ. of Southampton (Dip. Educn Psychol. 1968); Tavistock Inst. of Human Relations (clinical trng); Univ. of London (Dip. Educn Mgt 1978); Polytech. of Central London (MA 1983). Teaching in schs, Hackney, and Trng Psychologist, Woodberry Down Child Guidance Clinic, 1968–70; in training and work (pt-time), ILEA, 1970–75; BBC broadcaster and author in community youth develts, 1975–77; ILEA inspectorate, DES, 1977–80; Policy Principal in Youth Develt Team, MSC, 1980–82; academic consultant to MSC, 1982–83; Hd of Faculty, Southwark Coll., 1983–86; Vice Principal and actg Principal, Newham Community Coll., 1986–91. Vis. Scholar, Lucy Cavendish Coll. Centre for Women Leaders, Cambridge, 1988–. Broadcaster, lectr and author on equal opportunities and leading orgnl change. Member: Bd, British Trng Internat., 1997–99; Bd, Council for Ind. and Higher Educn, 1999– (Trustee, 1999–); Post 16 e-Learning Task Force, 2002–04; Standing Conf. of E London Principals, 2003–; Women and Work Commn, 2004–; Strategic Skills Commn, 2004–; Review Gp, students with learning difficulties and disabilities, LSC, 2004–; Nat. Skills Forum, 2005–; London Skills and Employment Bd, 2006–08; Chair, Bd, Learning and Skills Improvement Service (formerly Further Educn Improvement Agency), 2008–; Co Chair, Skills Commn; Chair, Widening Access Commn, 2014–16. Founder Member: Further Educn NTO, 1999–2001; Higher Educn Policy Inst., 1999–; Centre for Excellence in Leadership, 2001–05; Adv. Forum, Learning and Skills Res. Centre, 2002–; Acad. Adv. Bd, NHSU, 2004–05; EDGE, 2004–10; acted as Scrutineer to Cabinet Office's ministerial network on social exclusion, 2000–02; Chm., Wkg Gp on Faiths and Further Educn, LSC/Nat. Ecumenical Agency in Further Educn, 2005–. Chief Assessor, Trng of Principals' Qualifications in England, 2006–08. Trustee: Working Men's Coll., 1995– (Chm. Govs, 1995–2008); Laban Coll., 2000; Lottie Betts-Priddy Educn Trust, 2009–; Baker Dearing Educnl Trust, 2009; Jamie Oliver Foundn, 2010. Bd Mem., London Internat. Fest. of Theatre, 1999–2004. FRSA 1994; FCGI 2003. Hon. DSocSc Southampton, 2001; Hon. DEd London Southbank, 2005. *Publications:* Making a Living, 1977; Personal Effectiveness and Young People, 1983;

Guidance of Young People, 1984; Changing College Culture, 1984; (with Julian Gravatt) Further Education Re-formed, 2000; regular contribs to TES on further educn. *Recreations:* Martha, cinema, talking, reading, wondering. *Address:* 52 Fortess Road, NW5 2HG.

**SILVERMAN, Sir Bernard (Walter),** Kt 2018; FRS 1997; FAcSS; Professor of Modern Slavery Statistics, University of Nottingham, since 2018; Chief Scientific Adviser to the Home Office, 2010–17; Professor of Statistics, University of Oxford, 2003–15, now Emeritus; *b* 22 Feb. 1952; *s* of Elias Silverman and Chana Szajna Silverman (*née* Korn); *m* 1985, Dr Rowena Fowler; one *s. Educ:* City of London Sch.; Jesus Coll., Cambridge (BA 1973; PhD 1978; ScD 1989; Hon. Fellow, 2003; MMath 2011); Southern Theol Educn and Trng Scheme (BTh). CStat. Research Fellow, Jesus Coll., Cambridge, 1975–77; Calculator Develt Manager, Sinclair Radionics, 1976–77; Weir Fellow, University Coll., Oxford, and Jun. Lectr, Oxford Univ., 1977–78; University of Bath: Lectr, Reader, and Prof. of Statistics, 1978–93; Head, Sch. of Math. Scis, 1988–91; University of Bristol: Prof. of Stats, 1993–2003; Henry Overton Wills Prof. of Maths, 1999–2003, now Emeritus; Provost, Inst. for Advanced Studies, 2000–03; Master of St Peter's Coll., Oxford, 2003–09. Sen. Res. Fellow, Smith Sch. for Enterprise and Envmt, 2010, Professorial Res. Associate, Wellcome Trust Centre for Human Genetics, 2010–15, Univ. of Oxford; Vis. Prof., LSE, 2010–13; various vis. appts at foreign univs, 1978–; Fellow, Center for Advanced Study in Behavioral Scis, Stanford, 1997–98. Ed., Annals of Stats, 2007–09. Non-exec. Dir, Defence Analytical Services Agency, MoD, 2003–09. Mem., GM Sci. Rev. Panel, 2002–04; Chm., Peer Rev. Panel, Project for Sustainable Develt of Heathrow, 2005–06; Chm., UK Research Integrity Office, 2014–19; Mem. Bd, Parly Office of Sci. and Technol., 2017–; Chair: Technol. Adv. Panel to Investigatory Powers Comr, 2017–; Methodological Assurance Panel for Modernising the Census, ONS, 2018–. Mem., AHRC, 2012–17. Adv. Bd, Public Gp Internat. Ltd, 2018–. President: Inst. of Mathematical Stats, 2000–01; Royal Statistical Soc., 2010; Chairman: Jt Mathematical Council of UK, 2003–06; UK Maths Trust, 2004–10; Mem. Council, Royal Soc., 2009–10. MAE 2001; FAcSS (AcSS 2014). Ordained deacon, 1999, priest, 2000; Hon. Curate, 1999–2003, Associate Parish Priest, 2003–05, St Paul's Clifton, and St Mary's, Cotham, Bristol; Proctor in Convocation, Gen. Synod of C of E, 2000–03; Associate Priest, St Giles and St Margaret's, Oxford, 2009–15. Hon. Fellow, St Chad's Coll., Durham, 2010. Guy Medals in Bronze, 1984, and Silver, 1995, Royal Statistical Soc.; (N American) Cttee of Presidents of Statistical Socs' Award, 1991. Hon. DSc: St Andrews, 2014; Lancaster, 2016; Bath, 2017; Bristol, 2017. *Publications:* Density Estimation for Statistics and Data Analysis, 1986; (with P. J. Green) Nonparametric Regression and Generalized Linear Models, 1994; (with J. O. Ramsay) Functional Data Analysis, 1997, 2nd edn 2005; (with J. O. Ramsay) Applied Functional Data Analysis, 2002; numerous papers in learned jls.

**SILVERMAN, Prof. (Hugh) Richard,** OBE 2000; Professor of Architecture, University of Wales, Cardiff (formerly University of Wales College of Cardiff), 1986–99, now Emeritus (Head of Welsh School of Architecture, 1986–97); *b* 23 Sept. 1940; *m* 1963, Kay Sønderskov-Madsen; two *d. Educ:* Edinburgh Univ. (MSc Soc. Sci). Lectr, then Sen. Lectr, Univ. of Bristol, 1971–82. Partner, Alec French Partnership, Architects, Bristol, 1984–86. Built project, 1 Bridewell St, Bristol, 1985 (RIBA Regl Award). Mem. Board, Cardiff Bay Develt Corp., 1990–2000; Director: Edward Ware Homes, Bristol, 2002–03; Under the Sky Urban Renewal, 2004–13. FRSA 1989–2010.

**SILVERSTONE, Daniel William;** Chair, René Cassin, since 2014; *b* 29 Sept. 1951; *s* of Jack and Liesl Silverstone; *m* 1988, Judith Anne Hunt, *qv;* two step *d. Educ:* Univ. of Sussex (BA Hons Politics); Univ. of Manchester (MA Govt). Greater London Council: Prin. Race Relns Advr, 1982–84; Dep. Dir, Personnel, 1984–86; Dep. Dir, Personnel, ILEA, 1986–89; Dep. Dir, Educn, London Bor. of Hackney, 1989–95; Dir, London Boroughs Grants, 1995–2001; Chief Exec., CRE, 2001–04; Principal Associate, Global Diversity Practice, Norman Broadbent, 2004; CEO, London Remade, 2004–09; Exec. Dir, Interights, 2010–12. Mem., Commn for a Sustainable London 2012, 2008–10; Chair, Leadership Gp, Refugee Council, 2008–. Special Advr, England Cttee, Big Lottery Fund, 2014– (Mem., 2010–14). Chair, Host Nation, 2018–. Gov., Parliament Hill Sch., 2014– (Chair, 2016–). FRSA 1998. *Publications:* (jtly) The System, 1981. *Recreations:* modern jazz, saxophone, books, film, tennis, Tottenham Hotspur. *E:* daniel@dsilverstone.co.uk.

**SILVERSTONE, Judith Anne;** *see* Hunt, J. A.

**SILVERTON, Kate;** broadcaster and journalist with BBC, since 2003; *b* Waltham Abbey, Essex, 4 Aug. 1970; *d* of Terence George and Patricia Ann Silverton; *m* 2010, Mike Heron; one *s* one *d. Educ:* West Hatch High Sch., Chigwell; Univ. of Durham (BSc Psychol., and Arabic and Middle Eastern Studies). Volunteer, Operation Raleigh, 1990; Corporate Finance, Barclays de Zoete Wedd, 1994–96; with BBC, 1996–98: travel and traffic reporter, Breakfast Show, Radio Newcastle, 1997–98; reporter and presenter: Look North, 1997–98; Evening News, Tyne Tees Television, 1998–2000; The Wright Stuff, Channel 5, 2000–02; presenter: World Travel, Travel Channel, 2003; Third Degree, BBC 3, 2003; 3D, Sky News, 2003; BBC: co-presenter: Five Live Breakfast Show, Radio 5 Live, 2004; Weekend with Rod Liddle and Kate Silverton, 2004; reporter and presenter, News Channel, 2004–; reporter, Panorama, 2006–; News Foreign Corresp., Iraq, 2006, Afghanistan, 2009; reporter and presenter: Breakfast News, 2006–; One O'Clock News, 2008–; Six O'Clock News, 2008–; presenter: Ultimate Wild Water, 2007; Big Cat Live, 2008; Propertywatch, 2009; Ten O'Clock News, 2009; Kate Silverton Show, Radio 5 Live, 2009–11. Patron, Tusk Trust, 2014–; Ambassador, The Journalists' Charity. *Recreations:* outdoor pursuits, adventure sports, swimming, triathlon, travelling, specialising in field of mental health, training as a children's counsellor. *E:* enquiries@katesilverton.com. *W:* www.katesilverton.com.

**SILVESTER, Frederick John;** author; Chairman and Managing Director, Advocacy (formerly Advocacy Partnership) Ltd, 1986–2000; *b* 20 Sept. 1933; *s* of William Thomas Silvester and Kathleen Gertrude (*née* Jones); *m* 1971, Victoria Ann, *d* of James Harold and Mary Lloyd Davies; two *d. Educ:* Sir George Monoux Grammar Sch.; Sidney Sussex Coll., Cambridge. Called to the Bar, Gray's Inn, 1957. Teacher, Wolstanton Grammar School, 1955–57; Political Education Officer, Conservative Political Centre, 1957–60. Member, Walthamstow Borough Council, 1961–64; Chairman, Walthamstow West Conservative Association, 1961–64. MP (C): Walthamstow West, Sept. 1967–70; Manchester, Withington, Feb. 1974–1987; contested (C) same seat, 1987. An Opposition Whip, 1974–76; PPS to Sec. of State for Employment, 1979–81, to Sec. of State for NI, 1981–83. Member: Public Accounts Cttee, 1983–87; Procedure Cttee, 1983–87; Exec., 1922 Cttee, 1985–87; Vice-Chm., Cons. Employment Cttee, 1976–79. Sen. Associate Dir, J. Walter Thompson, 1970–88. *Publications:* The Northern Briton, 1984; Global Speak: the five untruths, 2005; Rape of democracy, 2008; Facing Up to Human Rights, 2012, 2nd edn as Facing Up to Human Rights: why Britain should leave the Strasbourg Court, 2013. *Address:* 27 King Edward Walk, SE1 7PR.

**SIM, Andrew Fraser;** Consultant, Kennedys, solicitors, 1999–2005; *b* 27 Nov. 1948; *s* of Donald Fraser Sim and Pamela Jean Sim; *m* 1975, Antonia Rolfe Tweedie Aitken; two *s* one *d. Educ:* Haileybury Coll., Herts; City of London Poly. (BA Business Law). Admitted Solicitor. British Railways Board: Asst Solicitor, 1975; Head of Litigation, 1982; Dep. Solicitor, 1986–93; Solicitor, 1993–99. *Recreations:* cricket, golf, fishing.

**SIMEON, Sir Stephen George Barrington,** 9th Bt *cr* 1815, of Grazeley, Berkshire; *b* 29 Oct. 1970; *s* of Sir Richard Edmund Barrington Simeon, 8th Bt and of Agnes Joan Simeon (*née* Weld); *S* father, 2013, but his name does not appear on the Official Roll of the Baronetage; *m* 1996, Michelle Owens; one *s* one *d. Heir: s* Ewan Barrington Harold Simeon, *b* 4 June 1998.

**SIMEONE, Reginald Nicola,** CBE 1985; FRMetS; Adviser to the Chairman, Nuclear Electric plc, 1990–96; *b* 12 July 1927; *s* of late Nicola Francisco Simeone, FCIS, and Phyllis Simeone (*née* Iles); *m* 1954, Josephine Frances Hope; two *s. Educ:* Raynes Park Grammar Sch.; St John's Coll., Cambridge (Schol.; MA). FRMetS 1993. Instructor Lieut (Meteorol), Royal Navy, 1947–50; Admiralty: Asst Principal, 1950–55; Principal, 1955–59; UKAEA: Finance Br., 1959–61; Economics and Programmes Br., 1961–65; Chief Personnel Officer, AWRE, 1965–69; Principal Estabts Officer, 1970–76; Authority Personnel Officer, 1976–84; Comptroller and Bd Mem. for Finance and Administration, 1984–88; Advr to the Chm., 1988–90. Chm., Atomic Energy Constabulary Police Cttee, 1985–90; Exec. Vice Pres., European Atomic Energy Soc., 1987–91. *Recreations:* European travel, theatre, opera, ballet, music, meteorology. *Address:* 31 Portsmouth Avenue, Thames Ditton, Surrey KT7 0RU.

**SIMINOVITCH, Dr Louis,** CC 1989 (OC 1980); PhD, FRS 1980; FRSC 1965; Director, Samuel Lunenfeld Research Institute of Mount Sinai Hospital (formerly Mount Sinai Hospital Research Institute), 1983–94, then Director Emeritus (University Professor Emeritus, 1985), and Senior Fellow, Massey College, since 2009, University of Toronto; *b* Montreal, PQ, 1 May 1920; *s* of Nathan Siminovitch and Goldie Watchman; *m* 1944, Elinore (*d* 1995), *d* of late Harry Faierman; three *d. Educ:* McGill Univ. (BSc 1941, PhD 1944; Arts and Sci. schol. 1939, Sir William McDonald schol. 1940, Anne Molson prize in Chem. 1941). With NRC at Ottawa and Chalk River, Ont., 1944–47; NRC Studentship and Fellowship, 1942–44; Canadian Royal Soc. Fellowship, 1947–49; with Centre Nat. de la Recherche Scientifique, Paris, 1949–53; Nat. Cancer Inst. Canadian Fellowships, 1953–55; Connaught Med. Res. Labs, Univ. of Toronto, 1953–56. Sen. Scientist, 1956–69 and Head, Div. of Biolog. Research, 1958–69, Ontario Cancer Inst., Univ. of Toronto; Chm., Dept of Med. Cell Biology, Univ. of Toronto, 1969–72; Chm., Dept of Med. Genetics, 1972–79, Univ. Prof., 1976–85, Special Advr to Dean on Res., 1994–, Toronto Univ.; Geneticist-in-Chief, Hosp. for Sick Children, Toronto, 1976–85. Founding Mem. and Pres., Editorial Bd, Science Forum, 1966–79; Pres., Canadian Cell Biology Soc., 1967. Member: Bd of Dirs, Nat. Cancer Inst. of Canada, 1975–85 (Pres., 1982–84); Nat. Bd of Dirs, Canadian Cancer Soc., 1981–84; Bd, Ontario Cancer Treatment and Res. Foundn, 1979–94; Scientific Adv. Cttee, Connaught Res. Inst., 1980–84; Alfred P. Sloan, Jr Selection Cttee, General Motors Cancer Res. Foundn, 1980–81, 1983–84; Health Res. and Develt Council of Ont, 1983–86. Chairman: Scientific Advisory Committee: Ontario Cancer Treatment and Res. Foundn, 1985–99; Loeb Inst. for Med. Res., Ottawa, 1988–99; Rotman Res. Inst., Toronto, 1988–; Phagetech, 1998–2005; Scientific Advisory Board: Bioniche Inc., 1996–98; Cytochroma Inc., 1999–2001; Member, Scientific Advisory Committee: Montreal Neurol Inst., 1992– (Mem., Neuro. Adv. Council, 1997–2001); Glycodesign, 1996–2001; Member, Scientific Advisory Board: Apoptogen Inc., 1995–2000; Univ. Medical Discoveries Inc., 1996–2006; GeminX, 1997–2000; Lorus (formerly Genesense) Technologies Inc., 1998–; Ottawa Gen. Hosp. Res. Inst., 1998–2000; Genetic Diagnostics, 2003–. Member: Hybrisens Ltd, 1995–98; Program Adv. and Sci. Adv. Cttee, Tanenbaum Chairs, Univ. of Toronto, 1995–2000; Scientific Adv. Bd, Canadian Med. Discoveries Fund, 1998–2002; Bd, Premier's Res. Excellence Awards Prog., 1998–2005; Bd, Viventia Biotech, 2000–06. Member: Bd of Dirs, Ottawa Civic Hosp. & Loeb Res. Inst. Corp., 1996–2000; Bd, Baycrest Centre for Geriatric Care, Toronto, 1998– (Consultant to Vice-Pres. Res. and Co-Chm. Res. Adv. Cttee, 1994–); Chm., Sci. Adv. Cttee, KLARU, 1997–). Founding Editor: Virology, 1960–80; Cell, 1973–81; Ed., Jl of Molecular and Cellular Biology, 1980–90; Member Editorial Board: Jl Cancer Surveys (London), 1980–89; Somatic Cell and Molecular Genetics, 1984–2005. Foreign Associate, NAS, 1999. Hon. DSc: Meml Univ., Newfoundland, 1978; McMaster Univ., 1978; Hon. Dr: Univ. of Montreal, 1990; McGill Univ., Montreal, 1990; Univ. of Western Ont, London, 1990; Univ. of Toronto, 1995; Univ. of Guelph, 2001. Flavelle Gold Medal, RSC, 1978; Univ. of Toronto Alumni Assoc. Award, 1978; Izaak Walton Killam Meml Prize, 1981; Gairdner Foundn Wightman Award, 1981; Medal of Achievement Award, Institut de Recherches Cliniques de Montreal, 1985; Environmental Mutagen Society Award, Baltimore, Maryland, 1986; R. P. Taylor Award, Canadian Cancer Soc., Nat. Cancer Inst., 1986; Distinguished Service Award, Canadian Soc. for Clinical Investigation, 1990; Toronto Biotechnol. Initiative Community Service Award, 1991; Canadian Medical Hall of Fame, 1997; Canadian Sci. and Engrg Hall of Fame, 2008. Silver Jubilee Medal, 1977; Gov.-Gen.'s Commemorative Medal for 125th Anniversary of Canadian Confedn, 1992; Lifetime Achievement Award, Toronto Biotechnol. Initiative, 2006. Has specialised in the study of bacterial and somatic cell genetics. *Publications:* many contribs to scientific and learned journals. *Address:* c/o Lunenfeld-Tanenbaum Research Institute of Mount Sinai Hospital, 600 University Avenue, Room 778D, Toronto, ON M5G 1X5, Canada; Apt 805, 130 Carlton Street, Toronto, ON M5A 4K3, Canada.

**SIMITIS, Konstantinos,** DJur; MP (PASOK) Piraeus, 1985–2009; Prime Minister of Greece, 1996–2004; Leader, Panhellenic Socialist Movement, 1996–2004; *b* Athens, 23 June 1936; *s* of George Simitis and Fani Cristopoulou; *m* Daphne Arkadiou; two *d. Educ:* Univ. of Marburg (DJur 1959); LSE. Lawyer of the Supreme Court, 1961; Reader in Law, Univ. of Konstanz, Germany, 1971; Prof. of Commercial Law and Civil Law, Justus Liebig Univ., Germany, 1971–75; Prof. of Commercial Law, Panteion Univ. of Political and Social Scis, Athens, 1977. Member: Nat. Council, Panhellenic Liberation Movt, 1970; PASOK, 1974–. Minister: of Agriculture, 1981–85; of Nat. Econ., 1985–87; of Educn and Religious Affairs, 1989–90; of Industry and Commerce, 1993–95. *Publications:* The Structural Opposition, 1979; Policy for Economic Stabilisation, 1989; Nationalistic Populism or National Strategy?, 1992; Towards a Vigorous Society, Towards a Vigorous Greece, 1995; Politics for a Creative Greece, 2005; Strategy and Perspectives, 2006; books and articles on legal and econ. matters. *Address:* Akademias 35, 10672 Athens, Greece.

**SIMLER, Rt Hon. Dame Ingrid (Ann),** DBE 2013; PC 2019; **Rt Hon. Lady Justice Simler;** a Lady Justice of Appeal, since 2019; *b* 17 Sept. 1963; *d* of Derek and Judy Simler; *m* 1991, John Bernstein; two *s* two *d. Educ:* Henrietta Barnett Sch.; Sidney Sussex Coll., Cambridge (BA 1985; MA); Europa Inst., Univ. of Amsterdam (Dip. EC Law 1986). Called to the Bar, Inner Temple, 1987, Bencher, 2008; a Recorder, 2002–13; Jun. Counsel to IR, 2002–06; QC 2006; a Dep. High Ct Judge, 2010–13; a Judge of the High Ct of Justice, QBD, 2013–19; Pres., Employment Appeals Tribunal, 2016–19. Chm., Equality and Diversity Cttee, Bar Council, 2003–11; Mem., Equal Treatment Adv. Cttee, Judicial Studies Bd, 2007–11. Gen. Editor, Jordans Employment Law Service, 2007–. *Publications:* (contrib.) Tottel Discrimination Law. *Recreations:* theatre, travel, being with my children. *Address:* Royal Courts of Justice, Strand, WC2A 2LL.

**SIMM, Ian Richard;** Chief Executive, Impax Asset Management Group plc, since 2005; *b* Ilkley, Yorks; *s* of John and Marjorie Simm; *m* 1999, Helen Dell; one *s* one *d. Educ:* St John's Coll., Cambridge (BA Natural Scis 1988); Harvard Univ. (MPA 1993). Consultant: EC, 1988–89; Envmtl Resources Ltd, 1990–91; McKinsey & Co., 1993–96; Dir, Impax Capital,

1996–98; Founder and Man. Dir, Impax Asset Mgt Ltd, 1998–2005. Non-exec. Dir, NERC, 2013–18. *Recreations:* sailing, tennis, family. *Address:* c/o Impax Asset Management, 30 Panton Street, SW1Y 4AJ. *T:* (020) 7434 1122. *E:* i.simm@impaxam.com.

**SIMMERS, Graeme Maxwell,** CBE 1998 (OBE 1982); Chairman, Scottish Sports Council, 1992–99; *b* 2 May 1935; *s* of W. Maxwell Simmers and Gwen Simmers; *m* 1965, Jennifer Roxburgh; two *s* two *d*. *Educ:* Glasgow Acad.; Loretto Sch. CA 1959. National Service, commnd Royal Marines, 1959–61. Sen. Partner, S. Easton Simmers & Co., 1960–86; Dir, Scottish Highland Hotels Gp, 1962–92 (Chm., 1972–92). Mem., Scottish Tourist Bd, 1979–86; British Hospitality Association (formerly British Hotels & Restaurants Association): Chm., Bd of Management, 1987–88; Mem. Nat. Exec., 1991–97. Chm., Forth Valley Acute Hosps NHS Trust, 2002–04; non-exec. Mem., Forth Valley Health Bd, 2002–10. Chm., British Golf Mus., 2010–. Governor: Loretto Sch., 1968–2000 (Chm., 1992–99); Queen's Coll., Glasgow, 1989–93; Mem. Court, Stirling Univ., 2000–10. DL Stirling and Falkirk, 2004. Hon. Col, RM Reserve, Scotland, 2000–06. Elder, Killearn Kirk. DUniv Stirling, 2012. *Address:* 11 Crawford Gardens, St Andrews, Fife KY16 8XG. *Clubs:* All England Lawn Tennis; Royal & Ancient Golf (Chm., Championship Cttee, 1988–91; Captain, 2001–02); Prestwick Golf, Loch Lomond Golf, Pine Valley Golf.

**SIMMONDS, Andrew John;** QC 1999; a Deputy High Court Judge, since 2006; *b* 9 May 1957; *s* of late Ernest Simmonds and of Sybil Simmonds; *m* 1981, Kathleen Moyse; one *d*. *Educ:* Sevenoaks Sch., Kent; St John's Coll., Cambridge (MA). Called to the Bar, Middle Temple, 1980, Bencher, 2012. *Recreations:* alpine ski-ing, running. *Address:* 5 Stone Buildings, Lincoln's Inn, WC2A 3XT. *T:* (020) 7242 6201.

**SIMMONDS, Brigid Mary,** OBE 2006; Chief Executive, British Beer and Pub Association, 2009–19; *b* 17 April 1958; *d* of Rev. Dermot Quinlan and Edna Quinlan; *m* 1984, Gavin Simmonds; two *s* one *d*. *Educ:* St Margaret's Sch., Bushey; WRAC Coll., Camberley. Short Service Commn, WRAC, 1978–86: Hong Kong, 1982–84; MoD, 1984–86. Dir, Mktg and PR, S & P Architects, 1986–91; Chief Exec., Business In Sport and Leisure, 1992–2009. Mem., then Chm., Lottery Panel, 1994–2000, Mem. Bd, 1998–2004, Sport England; Chm., Sport and Recreation Alliance (formerly CCPR), 2005–11 (Mem. Bd, 2000–12; Vice Pres., 2012–); Dir, Tourism Alliance, 2005– (Chm., 2005–06, 2011–12); Mem., Future High Streets Forum, 2015–. Trustee, GambleAware (formerly Responsible Gambling Trust), 2016–18; Chm., Betting and Gaming Council, 2019–. Dir, Leicester City FC, 2002–03. Non-exec. Dir, Quintus PA, 2006–08. Shine Industry Expert of the Year Award, 2007; Leisure Report Industry Individual Award, 2007. *Publications:* Developing Partnerships in Sport and Leisure, 1996. *Recreations:* sport (running and tennis), reading, music.

**SIMMONDS, Christopher Albert; His Honour Judge Simmonds;** a Circuit Judge, since 2018; *b* Chatham, Kent, 24 May 1973; *s* of late Albert Simmonds and of Ruth Simmonds; *m* 1999, Louise Hudson. *Educ:* Hertfordshire Univ. (LLB Hons); London Guildhall Univ. (Law Soc. Annual Prize for Outstanding Perf. 1997). Admitted as solicitor, 1999; with Stantons, Solicitors, Strood; Solicitor, later Partner, Stephens & Son, Chatham; Founder, Davis Simmonds & Donaghey Solicitors, Sen. Partner, 2004–10; a District Judge, Principal Registry of the Family Div., later Central Family Court, 2010–18. Comr, Judicial Appointments Commn, 2014–17. Course Dir (Family), Judicial Coll., 2016–17. *Recreations:* walking with my dogs, gardening, reading, caring for our chickens, sailing. *Address:* Bournemouth Courts of Justice, Deansleigh Road, Bournemouth, Dorset BH7 7DS.

**SIMMONDS, Rt Hon. Sir Kennedy (Alphonse),** KCMG 2004; PC 1984; Prime Minister, Federation of St Christopher (St Kitts) and Nevis, 1983–95; *b* 12 April 1936; *s* of Bronte Clarke and Arthur Simmonds; *m* 1976, Mary Camella (*née* Matthew); three *s* two *d*. *Educ:* St Kitts and Nevis Grammar School; Leeward Islands Scholar, 1954; Univ. of West Indies (studies in Medicine), 1955–62. Senior Bench Chemist, Sugar Assoc. Res. Lab., St Kitts, 1955; Internship, Kingston Public Hosp., 1963; medical practice, St Kitts, Anguilla and Nevis, 1964–66; postgrad. studies, Princess Margaret Hosp., Bahamas, 1966; Resident in Anaesthesiology, Pittsburgh, 1968–69; medical practice, St Kitts, 1969–80; Premier of St Christopher (St Kitts) and Nevis, 1980–83. Dir of Med. Services, Health Authy of Anguilla, 2008–13. Foundn Mem., People's Action Movement Opposition Party, 1965, Pres., People's Action Movement, 1976. Fellow, Amer. Coll. of Anaesthesiology, 1970. Medal of Honour, Anguilla, 2005; Order of Nat. Hero, St Kitts and Nevis, 2016. *Recreations:* tennis, cricket, football, video taping. *Address:* PO Box 167, Earle Morne Development, Basseterre, St Kitts, West Indies.

**SIMMONDS, Rt Hon. Mark (Jonathan Mortlock);** PC 2014; Senior Advisor, Kroll, since 2015; *b* 12 April 1964; *s* of Neil Mortlock Simmonds and Mary Griffith Simmonds; *m* 1994, Lizbeth Josefina Hanomancin; one *s* two *d*. *Educ:* Trent Poly. (BSc Hons). MRICS 1987. With Savills, 1986–88; Partner, Strutt & Parker, 1988–96; Dir, C. B. Hillier Parker, 1996–98; Man. Dir, 1998–2001, Chm., 2001–12, CEO, 2014–, Mortlock Simmonds Brown (formerly Mortlock Simmonds). MP (C) Boston and Skegness, 2001–15. Shadow Minister: for Public Services, Health and Educn, subseq. Educn, 2003–04; for Foreign Affairs, 2004–05; for Internat. Develt, 2005–07; for Health, 2007–10; PPS to Sec. of State, DEFRA, 2010–12; Parly Under-Sec. of State, FCO, 2012–14. Sen. Adv, Farallon Capital, 2016–; Chairman: Invest Africa, 2015–; Fincomeco, 2016–. Trustee, British Inst. of Eastern Africa, 2016–; Vice Pres., Flora and Fauna Internat., 2015–. *Recreations:* family, hockey, Rugby, tennis, history, reading.

**SIMMONDS, Michael George Edward;** Chief Executive, Populus Group, since 2014 (Director, 2003–14); *b* London, 27 May 1964; *s* of Keith and Patricia Simmonds; *m* 2015, Rt Hon. Nicolas John Gibb, *qv*. *Educ:* Internat. Sch. of London; Univ. of Leeds (BA Political Studies 1986). Researcher, Adam Smith Inst., 1986–89; Special Advr to Sec. of State for Trade and Industry, 1989–90; Asst to Rt Hon. Cecil Parkinson, MP, 1990–92; researcher, BBC Political Res. Unit, 1992–94; Special Adviser: to Sec. of State for Transport, 1994–95; to Chm., Cons. Party, 1995–97; Dep. Dir, Cons. Res. Dept, and Dir, Cons. Policy Forum, 1997–98; Director: Membership and Mktg, Cons. Party, 1998–99; Live Strategy, 2000–03. Dir, BrandCap Gp, 2013–. Gov., City Lit, 2016–. *Recreations:* Arsenal, running. *Address:* Populus, Northburgh House, 10 Northburgh Street, EC1V 0AT. *T:* (020) 7253 9900. *E:* msimmonds@populus.co.uk. *Club:* Ivy.

**SIMMONDS, Posy,** MBE 2002; FRSL; freelance illustrator/cartoonist, since 1969; *b* 9 Aug. 1945; *d* of late Reginald A. C. Simmonds and Betty Cahusac; *m* 1974, Richard Graham Hollis, *qv*. *Educ:* Queen Anne's Sch., Caversham; L'Ecole des Beaux Arts, Paris; Central Sch. of Art and Design, London (BA Art and Design). Cartoonist: The Guardian, 1977–87, 1988–90, 1992–; The Spectator, 1988–90. Exhibitions: The Cartoon Gall. (formerly the Workshop), 1974, 1976, 1979, 1981, 1982, 1984; Mus. of Modern Art, Oxford, 1981; Manor House Mus. & Art Gall., Ilkley, 1985; Belgian Comic Strip Centre, Brussels, 2012; Mercer Art Gall., Harrogate, 2018; Retrospective, Pulp Fest., La Ferme du Buisson, Paris, 2019; House of Illustration, London, 2019. TV documentary, Tresoddit for Easter, 1991. FRSL 2005. Hon. DArt Plymouth, 1993; Hon. DLitt Exeter, 2007. Cartoonist of the Year: Granada TV/What The Papers Say, 1980; British Press Awards, 1981; Nat. Art Liby Illustrations Award, 1998. *Publications:* Bear Book, 1978; Mrs Weber's Diary, 1979; True Love, 1981; Pick of Posy, 1982; (illustrator) Daisy Ashford, The Young Visiters, 1984; Very Posy, 1985; Fred, 1987 (filmed as Famous Fred, 1997); Pure Posy, 1987; Lulu and the Flying Babies, 1988; The Chocolate Wedding, 1990; (illustrator) Hilaire Belloc, Matilda, who told such Dreadful Lies, 1991; Mustn't Grumble, 1993; Bouncing Buffalo, 1994; F-Freezing ABC, 1995; (illustrator) Hilaire Belloc, Cautionary Tales, 1998; Gemma Bovery, 1999 (filmed, 2014); (illustrator) Folio Book of Humorous Verse, 2002; Lavender, 2003; Literary Life, 2003; Baker Cat, 2004; Tamara Drewe, 2007 (Grand Prix 2009 de la critique bande dessinée) (filmed, 2010); Mrs Weber's Omnibus, 2012; Literary Life Revisited, 2016; Cassandra Darke, 2018. *Address:* c/o United Agents, 12–26 Lexington Street, W1F 0LE. *T:* (020) 3214 0800.
*See also R. J. Simmonds.*

**SIMMONDS, Richard James,** CBE 1996; farmer and forester; Chairman, London and Economic Properties, 2002–13; *b* 2 Aug. 1944; *s* of late Reginald A. C. Simmonds and Betty Cahusac; *m* 1967, Mary (*née* Stewart); one *s* two *d*. *Educ:* Trinity Coll., Glenalmond. Councillor, Berkshire CC (Chm. of Environment, Property, Transport, and Development Cttees), 1973–79. National Vice-Chm. of Young Conservatives, 1973–75; Founding Vice-Chm. of Young European Democrats, 1974; Personal Asst to Rt Hon. Edward Heath, 1973–75; MEP (C) Midlands W, 1979–84, Wight and Hampshire E, 1984–94; PPS to Sir James Scott-Hopkins, Leader of European Democratic Gp, European Parlt, 1979–82; Cons. spokesman on youth and educn, European Parlt, 1982–84; on budget control, 1984–87; Whip, 1987–89; Chief Whip, 1992–94. Mem., Agric., Fisheries, Food and Rural Develt Cttee, 1992–94; Expert Advr, Eur. Commn, 1997–2010. Fellow of Parly & Industry Trust. Chairman: Countryside Commn, 1995–99; Ind. Transport Commn, 1999–2001. Pres., A>B Global Inc., 2005–. Mem. Council, PDSA, 1995–2001. Founding Pres., Mounted Games Assoc. of GB, 1984–; President: Royal E Berks Agricl Assoc., 1995; Jersey Cattle Soc., 1997. Fellow, Waitangi Foundn, NZ, 1996. Chm. of Governors, Berkshire Coll. of Agriculture, 1979–92; Mem. Adv. Cttee, Centre for Agric. Strategy, Reading Univ., 1998–2001. Churchwarden, St John the Baptist, Cookham Dean, 2015–; Licensed Lay Minister, Benefice of the Cookhams, 2017–. ARAgS 1997. Hon. Pres., Fair Weather Golfing Soc., 2011–. *Publications:* The Common Agricultural Policy—a sad misnomer, 1979; An A to Z of Myths and Misunderstandings of the European Community, 1981, 3rd edn 1993; (jtly) Cork Declaration on Rural Development, 1996; European Parliamentary report on farm animal welfare, 1985, 1987, 1990; report on prodn, processing, politics and potential of NZ meat (P4 report), 1996. *Recreations:* resisting bureaucracy, getting things done. *Address:* Dyars, Cookham Dean, Berkshire SL6 9PJ. *Clubs:* Royal Ascot Racing; Ancient Britons, Tamworth; OPB Sailing (Hon. Cdre, 1999–).
*See also Posy Simmonds.*

**SIMMONS, His Honour Alan Gerald;** a Circuit Judge, 1990–2006; *b* 7 Sept. 1936; *s* of late Maurice Simmons and Sophie Simmons (*née* Lasserson); *m* 1961, Mia, *d* of late Emanuel and Lisa Rosenstein; one *s* one *d*. *Educ:* Bedford Modern Sch.; Quintin Sch.; Inns of Court Sch. of Law. RAF, 1956–58. Director: Aslon Labs; Record Productions (Surrey); Ashcourt. Called to the Bar, Gray's Inn, 1968 (Lee Essay Prize); Holker Sen. Exhibn); SE Circuit; Assistant Recorder, 1985; Recorder, 1989. Mem., Mental Health Rev. Tribunal, 1993–2000. Member: Board of Deputies of British Jews, 1982–88; Council, United Synagogue, 1979–93. *Recreations:* music, reading, (formerly) fencing.

**SIMMONS, Sir David (Anthony Cathcart),** KA 2001; BCH 2001; QC 1984; Chief Justice of Barbados, 2002–10; Chairman, Integrity Commission of Turks and Caicos Islands, since 2010; *b* 28 April 1940; *s* of late Kenneth G. Simmons and of Sybil Louise Simmons; *m* 1966, Marie MacCormack, QC; one *s* one *d*. *Educ:* London Sch. of Econs and Pol Sci. (LLB Hons 1963; LLM 1965). Called to the Bar, Lincoln's Inn, 1968, Hon. Bencher, 2006; joined law chambers of Henry Forde, QC, Barbados, 1970; private law practice, 1970–85 and 1986–94; Lectr in Law (pt-time), Univ. of WI, 1970–75; Chairman: Nat. Housing Corp., 1976–79; Caribbean Broadcasting Corp., 1979–81; Nat. Sports Council, 1982–85. MP, Barbados, 1976–81, 1985–2001; Mem., Barbados House of Assembly, 1981–85; Attorney General, 1985–86 and 1994–2001. Caribbean Court of Justice: Chairman: Prep. Cttee for establishment, 1999–2001; Regl Judicial Legal Services Cttee, 2003–04; High Level Task Force for inauguration, 2004–05. Mem., Barbados Cricket Assoc. Hon. Fellow, Univ. of WI, 2003. Hon. LLD LSE, 2003. *Recreations:* reading, sports, collecting calypso music, playing trumpet. *Club:* Barbados Turf (Appellate Steward).

**SIMMONS, Fr Eric,** CR; Prior of St Michael's Priory, Burleigh Street, London, 1993–98; *b* 3 Aug. 1930. *Educ:* Univ. of Leeds (BA Phil 1951). Coll. of the Resurrection, Mirfield, 1951; deacon, 1953, priest, 1954; Curate of St Luke, Chesterton, 1953–57; Chaplain, University Coll. of N Staffordshire, 1957–61; licensed to officiate: Dio. Wakefield, 1963–65 and 1967–; Dio. Ripon, 1965–67; Warden and Prior of Hostel of the Resurrection, Leeds, 1966–67; subseq. Novice Guardian, CR, looking after young Community members; Superior, Community of the Resurrection, Mirfield, Yorks, 1974–87; permission to officiate, Dio. London, 1989–98; the Community is an Anglican monastic foundation engaged in evangelism and teaching work, based in Yorkshire. *Address:* House of the Resurrection, Mirfield, W Yorks WF14 0BN.

**SIMMONS, Guy Lintorn,** LVO 1961; HM Diplomatic Service, retired; *b* 27 Feb. 1925; *s* of late Captain Geoffrey Larpent Simmons, RN and Frances Gladys Simmons (*née* Wright); *m* 1951, Sheila Jacob; three *d*. *Educ:* Bradfield Coll.; Oriel Coll., Oxford. RAF, 1943–46; CRO, 1949; 2nd Sec., British High Commn: Lahore, 1950; Dacca, 1952; CRO, 1954–58 and 1964–66; 1st Sec.: Bombay, 1958; New Delhi, 1961; Commercial Counsellor: New Delhi, 1966–68; Cairo, 1968–71; Head of Trade Policy Dept, FCO, 1971–73; Diplomatic Service Inspectorate, 1973–76; Commercial Counsellor, Copenhagen, 1976–79; Consul-General: Karachi, 1979–82; Montreal, 1982–84; FCO, 1984–90. Chm., Crouch End Open Space, 1992–94. *Recreation:* awaiting publication of my letters to the Times. *Address:* 29 Wood Vale, N10 3DJ.

**SIMMONS, Prof. Ian Gordon,** PhD, DLitt; FSA; FBA 1997; Professor of Geography, University of Durham, 1981–2001, now Emeritus; *b* 22 Jan. 1937; *s* of Charles Frederick Simmons and Christina Mary Simmons (*née* Merrills); *m* 1962, Carol Mary Saunders; one *s* one *d*. *Educ:* UCL (BSc 1959; PhD 1962); Durham Univ. (DLitt 1990). CGeog 2002. Lectr, 1962–70, Sen. Lectr, 1970–76, Reader, 1976–77, in Geography, Univ. of Durham; Prof. of Geography, Univ. of Bristol, 1977–81. ACLS Postdoctoral Fellow, Univ. of Calif at Berkeley, 1964–65; Churchill Meml Travelling Fellow, 1970–71. Chm., Benchmarking Panel for Geography, QAA, 1999–2001; Mem. Geog. Panel, RAE, 1996–2001. FSA 1980; MAE 1994. Hon. DSc Aberdeen, 2005. Victoria Medal, RGS, 1998; Chancellor's Medal, Durham Univ., 2016. Writer on medieval and early modern landscape history of E Lincs at www.durham.ac.uk/east-lincs-history. *Publications:* Ecology of Natural Resources, 1974 (trans. Polish 1979, Spanish 1982); Biogeography, 1979 (trans. Spanish 1982); Changing the Face of the Earth, 1989, 2nd edn 1996; Earth, Air and Water, 1993 (trans. German 1983); Interpreting Nature, 1993; Environmental History, 1993 (trans. Swedish 1994); The Environmental Impact of Later Mesolithic Cultures, 1996; Humanity and Environment: a cultural ecology, 1997 (trans. Portuguese 2001, Japanese 2003); An Environmental History of Great Britain, 2001; An Environmental History of the Moorlands of England and Wales, 2003; A Global Environmental History, 2008 (trans. Croatian 2010); (with K. J. Gregory)

Environmental Sciences: a student's companion, 2009; 44 chapters in edited collections and about 115 papers in learned jls. *Recreations:* music, poetry, channel zapping. *Address:* Department of Geography, Lower Mountjoy, South Road, Durham DH1 3LE. *E:* i.g.simmons@durham.ac.uk.

**SIMMONS, John Barry Eves,** OBE 1987; VMH 1986; Curator: Castle Howard Arboretum Trust, 1997–2006; Royal Botanic Gardens, Kew, 1972–95; *b* 30 May 1937; *s* of Alfred John and Gladys Enid Simmons; *m* 1958, Valerie Lilian Dugan; two *s* one *d*. *Educ:* Harrow County Grammar Sch.; Herts Coll. of Agric. and Hort.; Regent Street Polytechnic; Sch. of Horticulture, Kew. MHort 1962, FIHort 1984; FIBiol 1988–2004; FLS 2004. Royal Botanic Gardens, Kew: Supervisor, Tropical Propagation Unit, 1961–64; Asst Curator, Temperate Section, 1964–68; Deputy Curator, 1968–72. Chm., Nat. Council for Conservation of Plants and Gardens, 1994–97 (Mem. Council, 1985–97; Vice-Chm., 1991–94; Pres., Norfolk Gp, 1993–2002); Member: RHS Award and Judging Cttees, 1969–2007; Longwood Gardens (Pennsylvania) Visiting Cttee, 1984–91; Westonbirt Arboretum Consultative Cttee, 1986–2004; Chm., Bedgebury Pinetum Consultative Cttee, 1992–2003; Dir, Flora for Fauna, 1997–2000; Trustee, Stanley Smith (UK) Horticultural Trust, 1994–. Pres., Inst. of Horticulture, 1987–88. Chm., N Norfolk Voluntary Gp, Diabetes UK, 2011–17. Gov., Writtle Agricl Coll., 1990–93. *Publications:* The Life of Plants, 1974, 2nd edn 1990; (series editor) Kew Gardening Guides, 1987–; (gen. editor) Kew Gardens Book of Indoor Plants, 1988; (jtly) The Gardens of William Morris, 1998; (jtly) English Plants for your Garden, 2000; Managing the Wet Garden, 2008; ed and contrib. to learned jls. *Recreations:* photography, walking, gardening (own garden!).

**SIMMONS, Melinda;** HM Diplomatic Service; Ambassador to Ukraine, since 2019; *b* London, 28 Jan. 1966; *d* of Cyril and Sylvia Simmons; *m* 1995, Stephen Bevan; two *c*. *Educ:* City of London Sch. for Girls; Exeter Univ. (BA Hons Modern Langs); Univ. of N London (MA Eur. Studies). Marketing Exec. then Associate Dir, The Register Gp Ltd, 1988–92; Marketing Manager, Primesight Internat., 1992–95; Public Affairs Officer, Internat. Alert, 1995–98; Department for International Development: Russia Desk Officer, 1998–99; Business Partnerships Dept, 1999–2000; Team Leader, Conflict Dept, 2000–02; Dep. Hd, Africa Policy Dept, 2002–03; Head: Africa Team, Gleneagles GB 2005 Unit, 2003–05; Southern Africa, 2005–08; Middle East Dept, 2008–09; Humanitarian Response Rev., 2009–10; Dep. Dir, Europe Dept, 2010–13; Foreign and Commonwealth Office: Dep. Dir, Conflict Dept, 2013–16; Dir, Jt Funds Unit, Nat. Security Secretariat, 2016–18. Associate Mem., CIPD, 2009. *Recreations:* singing, baking, gardening, walking, boot camp, nordic running. *Address:* c/o Foreign and Commonwealth Office, King Charles Street, SW1A 2AH.

**SIMMONS, Air Marshal Sir Michael (George),** KCB 1989 (CB 1988); AFC 1976; Member, Air Force Board, Defence Council, 1989–92; *b* 8 May 1937; *s* of George and Thelma Simmons; *m* 1964, Jean Aliwell; two *d*. *Educ:* Shrewsbury Sch.; RAF Coll., Cranwell. Commissioned 1958; No 6 Squadron, Cyprus, 1959–61; ADC to AOC-in-C FTC, 1961–64; No 39 Sqdn, Malta, 1964–66; No 13 Sqdn, Malta, 1966–67; No 51 Sqdn, Wyton, 1967–69; RN Staff Coll., 1970; MoD, 1971–72; OC No XV Sqdn, Germany, 1973–76; MoD, 1976–79; OC RAF Cottesmore, 1980–82; MoD, 1982–84; SASO, HQ Strike Comd, 1984–85; AOC No 1 Gp, RAF, 1985–87; ACAS, 1987–89; Dep. Controller Aircraft, MoD, 1989–92. ADC to the Queen, 1980–81; Air ADC to the Queen, 1981–82. Mem. Council, RAF Benevolent Fund, 1994–2006. Chm. Bd of Govs, Duke of Kent Sch., 1994–96. QCVS 1969. *Recreations:* clock repairing, gardening, golf. *Club:* Royal Air Force.

**SIMMONS, Richard John,** CBE 1995; FCA; Executive Chairman, BPP Education Group, since 2017 (Director, since 2010 and Chairman, 2010–17, BPP University of Professional Studies); Chairman: Inclusive Learning, since 2010; Skill Boosters, since 2010; Senior Partner, Andersen (formerly Arthur Andersen), 1996–2001, Senior Adviser, 2002; *b* 2 June 1947; *s* of John Eric Simmons and Joy Mary Simmons (*née* Foat); *m* 1983, Veronica Sinkins (marr. diss. 2016); one *s* one *d*. *Educ:* Moseley GS, Birmingham; London School of Economics (BSc Econs); Haas Business Sch., Univ. of California, Berkeley. FCA 1971. Joined Arthur Andersen, subseq. Andersen, 1968; Partner, 1979–2001. Asst Sec., Internat. Accounting Standards Cttee, 1973–75. Non-executive Director: Cranfield Information Technology Inst., 1987–89; Westminster Forum Ltd, 1999–2013; Chairman: Atticmedia Ltd, 2007–10; Shimmer Productions Ltd, 2008–10; Rewind Creative Media Ltd, 2008–10; CET Primary Schools Ltd, 2011–14; Director: GreenAcre Films Ltd, 2010–14; Mediacorp Online, 2017–18. Chairman: Bow Gp, 1980–81; CBlu Adv. Council, 2000–02; Member: Shadow Nat. Accounts Commn, 2000–01; Bd of Treasurers, Cons. Party, 2002–03. Mem., Develt Bd, Royal Acad. of Arts, 1995–2002. Dir, Constable Trust, 2003–14; Trustee, Foundn for Social and Econ. Thinking, 2003– (Chm., Governing Council, 2005–14). Gov., Moat Sch., 2003–14. FRSA 2004. *Recreations:* horse racing, gardening, walking. *Clubs:* Carlton (Hon. Treas., 1995–2001, Hon. Mem., 2006–, Political Cttee), United and Cecil; Royal Jersey Golf.

**SIMMONS, Richard Thomas,** PhD; FRGS; Chief Executive, Commission for Architecture and the Built Environment, 2004–11; *b* 17 Feb. 1953; *s* of Laurence and Audrey Simmons; *m* 1976, Elizabeth Mary; two *s* two *d*. *Educ:* Univ. of Sheffield (BA Hons 1974); South Bank Polytech. (BTP (Postgrad.) 1982); Univ. of Leicester (PhD 1995). MRTPI 1984; FRGS 2010. Town Planner, London Bor. of Hackney, 1978–85; Sen. Planning Officer, Inner Cities Directorate, DoE, 1985–87; Develt Manager, LDDC, 1987–93; Chief Exec., Dalston City Challenge, 1993–97; Dir of Develt and Envmt, Medway Council, 1997–2004. Vis. Prof. of City Design and Regeneration, Univ. of Greenwich, 2011–14; Vis. Lectr, Bartlett Sch. of Planning, UCL, 2015–. Mem., SE Design Review Panel, Design South East, 2015–. Mem., Acad. of Urbanism, 2006. FRSA. Hon. FRIBA 2011. DUniv Oxford Brookes, 2010. *Recreations:* climbing, scouting, DJing, reading science fiction and detective novels.

**SIMMONS, Prof. Robert Malcolm,** FRS 1995; Professor of Biophysics, King's College London, 1983–2001, now Emeritus; *b* 23 Jan. 1938; *s* of Stanley Laurence Simmons and Marjorie Amys; *m* 1967, Mary Ann (Anna) Ross; one *s* one *d*. *Educ:* King's College London (BSc Physics 1960; FKC 1996); Royal Institution (PhD London 1965); University College London (MSc Physiol. 1967). CBiol, FRSB (FIBiol 2000). Department of Physiology, University College London: Sharpey Scholar, 1967–70; Lectr, 1970–79; MRC Res. Fellow, 1979–81; King's College London: MRC Cell Biophysics Unit, 1981–83; Associate Dir, 1983–91; Head of Dept of Biophysics, 1983–88; Head of Div. of Biomolecular Sci, 1988–91; Hon. Dir, MRC Muscle and Cell Motility Unit, 1991–2001; Dir, Randall Centre (formerly Randall Inst.), 1995–2001. *Publications:* contribs on physiol. and biophys to learned jls. *Recreations:* music, fishing. *Address:* 1 Woodborough Road, Pewsey, Wilts SN9 5NH.

**SIMMONS, Rosemary Ann;** freelance artist, writer and curator, since 1975; *b* 19 Oct. 1932; *d* of Donald and Alys Simmons; *m* 1974, Anthony H. Christie (*d* 1994); two step *s* three step *d*. *Educ:* Chelsea Sch. of Art (NDD and Chelsea Dip. 1955). Graphic Designer, Curwen Press, 1955–58; Dir, Curwen Gall., 1965–71; Man. Dir, Curwen Prints Ltd, 1971–75. Chm., Combe Down Heritage Soc., 2004–14. President: Bath Artist Printmakers, 2006–; Combe Down Stone Legacy Trust, 2015–. Founder Ed., 1990–98, Consultant Ed., 1998–, Printmaking Today. Hon. RE 1990. *Publications:* Printmaking in Easy Steps, 1977; Collecting Original Prints, 1980; (with Katie Clemson) The Complete Manual of Relief Printmaking, 1988; A Dictionary of Printmaking Terms, 2002; Collecting Original Prints, 2005; Mr & Mrs Ralph Allen at home, 2015. *Recreations:* supporting Printmaking Today, art and science, gardens, the company of friends. *Address:* 12 Greendown Place, Combe Down, Bath BA2 5DD. *T:* (01225) 833301. *E:* rosyprint12@gmail.com.

**SIMMONS, Timothy Michael John,** CVO 2008; Senior Manager, Student Administration, Royal Holloway, University of London, since 2016 (Senior Faculty Administrator, Physics Department, 2011–14; Project Officer, 2015–16); *b* 8 April 1960; *m* 1989, Caroline Mary Radcliffe; two *s*. *Educ:* Univ. of East Anglia (BA Jt Hons 1981). Entered FCO, 1982; Nuclear Energy Dept, FCO, 1982–85; Third, later Second Sec., Warsaw, 1985–87; First Secretary: FCO, 1987–93; UK Mission to UN, Geneva, 1993–97; Price Waterhouse, subseq. PricewaterhouseCoopers, 1997–99 (on secondment); Asst Dir, Personnel Comd, FCO, 1999–2001; Dep. Hd of Mission, Warsaw, 2001–04; Ambassador to Slovenia, 2005–09; Asst Dir, HR Strategy, Talent and Perf. Mgt, FCO, 2009–10. *Recreations:* reading, music, miniature wargames.

**SIMMONS, Tom Christopher;** Town Clerk, Corporation of London, 1998–2003; *b* 29 Oct. 1942; *s* of Tom Francis Simmons and Mary Simmons; *m* 1971, Barbara Loxley (*d* 2009); one *s*. *Educ:* Nottingham Univ. (BA Law 1963). Admitted Solicitor, 1968. Borough Sec., Chelmsford BC, 1973–83; Dep. Town Clerk, 1983–95, City Sec., 1996–98, Corp. of London. Sec., Mus. of London, 1990–2003; Clerk: Nat. Crime Squad Authy, 1998–2003; Nat. Criminal Intelligence Service Authy, 1998–2003. Board Member: and Hon. Treas., Mosaic Housing Assoc. (formerly New Islington and Hackney Housing Assoc.), 2003–06; Family Mosaic Housing Assoc., 2006–08. *Recreations:* water colour and acrylic painting, gardening, walking. *Address:* 20 Great Oaks, Hutton, Brentwood, Essex CM13 1AZ.

**SIMMS, Andrew Mark;** author; campaigner; Fellow, New Economics Foundation, since 2011; Co-Director, New Weather Institute, since 2013; Coordinator, Rapid Transition Alliance, since 2018; Assistant Director, Scientists for Global Responsibility, since 2018; *b* Chelmsford, 23 April 1965; *s* of David Simms and June Simms; *m* 1995, Rachel Maybank; one *d*. *Educ:* Poly. of Central London (BA Hons Film and Photography); London Sch. of Econs (MSc Develt (Internat. Pol Econ.)). Campaigns officer, British Trust for Conservation Volunteers, 1987–88; freelance envmt writer and Green Party Nat. Youth Spokesperson, 1988–90; Co-ordinator, The Other Economic Summit, New Econs Foundn, 1991; Campaign and Press Officer, Oxfam, 1992–93; freelance researcher for Internat. Inst. for Envmt and Develt, Shadow Minister for Overseas Develt and World Develt Movement, 1993–95; Campaign Communications Manager, Christian Aid, 1995–99; New Economics Foundation: Hd, Global Econ. Prog., 1999–2001; Policy Dir, 2002–11; Hd, Climate Change Prog., 2002–10. Co-Founder, Green New Deal Gp, 2007. Advr on develt alternatives, Global Witness, 2015– (Hd of Envmtl Investigations, 2013–15). Res. Associate, Centre for Global Political Economy, Univ. of Sussex, 2016–. Trustee: Energy and Resource Inst., Europe, 2003–17; Greenpeace UK, 2004–12; 10:10 UK, 2010–12; 10:10 Internat., 2010–12; Transition Network, 2014–18. Associate Ed., Resurgence mag., 2002–. *Publications:* Ecological Debt: global warming and the wealth of nations, 2005, 2nd edn 2009; Tescopoly: how one shop came out on top and why it matters, 2007; (with Joe Smith) Do Good Lives have to Cost the Earth?, 2008; (with David Boyle) The New Economics: a bigger picture, 2009; (with David Boyle) Eminent Corporations, 2010; Cancel the Apocalypse, 2013; (ed) There Was a Knock At The Door: 23 modern folk tales for troubling times, 2016; (ed) Knock Twice: 25 modern folk tales for troubling times, 2017; (with David Boyle) Economics: a crash course, 2019. *Recreations:* coffee and conversation, trees (appreciating them), bicycles, film, photography, writing and drawing, paradigm shifting, running. *Address:* c/o New Economics Foundation, 10 Salamanca Place, SE1 7HB. *T:* (020) 7820 6300, *Fax:* (020) 7820 6301. *E:* andrewsimms.uk@gmail.com.

**SIMMS, Prof. Brendan Peter,** PhD; Professor of the History of European International Relations, University of Cambridge, since 2008; Fellow, Peterhouse, Cambridge, since 1993; *b* Dublin, 1967; *s* of David John Simms and Anngret Simms (*née* Erickson); *m* 1993, Anita Bunyan; one *s* two *d*. *Educ:* St Kilian's German Sch., Dublin; Trinity Coll. Dublin (BA 1989); Peterhouse, Cambridge (PhD 1993). Jun. Res. Fellow, Christ Church, Oxford, 1992–93; Lectr in Internat. Relns, 1998–2005, Reader, 2005–08, Univ. of Cambridge. *Publications:* Three Victories and a Defeat, 2007; Europe: the struggle for supremacy, 2013; The Longest Afternoon: the 400 men who decided the Battle of Waterloo, 2014; Britain's Europe: a thousand years of conflict and cooperation, 2016; (with C. Laderman) Donald Trump: the making of a world view, 2017; Hitler: only the world was enough, 2019. *Recreations:* walking, travelling, current affairs. *Address:* Peterhouse, Cambridge CB2 1RD. *T:* (01223) 338234, *Fax:* (01223) 337578. *E:* bps11@cam.ac.uk. *Club:* Athenæum.

**SIMMS, Sir Neville (Ian),** Kt 1998; FREng, FICE, FCIOB; Chairman, Thames Tideway Tunnel Ltd, since 2013; *b* 11 Sept. 1944; *s* of late Cdre Arthur Neville Simms, RN and Anne Davidson Simms (*née* McCulloch). *Educ:* Queen Elizabeth's GS, Crediton; Univ. of Newcastle upon Tyne (BSc 1st cl. Hons 1966); Univ. of Glasgow (MEng 1971). CEng 1970; FICE 1995; FCIOB 1995; FREng (FEng 1996). Structural Engr, Ove Arup and Partners, 1966–69; joined Tarmac plc as Sect. Engr, Roads Div., Tarmac Civil Engrg, 1970; Chief Exec., Tarmac Construction Ltd, 1988–92; Gp Chief Exec., 1992–99, Dep. Chm., 1994–99, Tarmac plc; Chief Exec., 1999–2000, Chm., 1999–2005, Carillion plc. Dir, Bank of England, 1995–2002; non-executive Director: Courtaulds, 1994–98; Private Finance Panel Ltd, 1994–99; National Power, 1998–2000; Operating Partner, Duke St Capital, 2006–08; Chm., 2000–11, Dep. Chm., 2011–15, Internat. Power plc, later GDF SUEZ Energy Internat.; Jt Chm., TML, 1992–95; Chairman: Equiniti Gp Ltd, 2009–11; OasisIP LLC (Abu Dhabi), 2009–14. Chairman: BITC (W Midlands), 1998–2001; BITC Solent Regl Leadership Team, 2006–07; Govt Sustainable Procurement Task Force, 2005–06; Member: Pres.'s Cttee, CBI, 1997–2010, 2012–15; New Deal Task Force, 1999–2001; Trade Partners UK-Business Adv. Panel, 2001–03. Trustee, BRE Trust (formerly Foundn for Built Envmt), 2002– (Chm., 2006–15). Gov., Ashridge Mgt Coll., 2000–11 (Dep. Chm., 2006–11). MInstD 1995; CCMI (CIMgt 1992); FRSA 1992. Hon. DTech Wolverhampton Univ., 1997; Dr *hc* Edinburgh, 2000; Dr Eng Glasgow, 2001. *Address:* Cottons Centre, Cottons Lane, SE1 2QG.

**SIMON,** family name of **Viscount Simon,** and of **Barons Simon of Highbury** and **Simon of Wythenshawe.**

**SIMON,** 3rd Viscount *cr* 1940; **Jan David Simon;** a Deputy Speaker, House of Lords, since 1999; *b* 20 July 1940; *o s* of 2nd Viscount Simon, CMG; *S* father, 1993; *m* 1969, Mary Elizabeth, *d* of late John J. Burns, Sydney, NSW; one *d*. *Educ:* Westminster; Sch. of Navigation, Univ. of Southampton; Sydney Tech. Coll. Dep. Chm. of Cttees, H of L, 1998–; Member, Select Committee: on Procedure of H of L, 1999–2002; on Personal Bills, 2004–; on Standing Orders (Private Bills), 2004–; elected Mem., H of L, 1999. Fellow, Univ. of Hertfordshire, 2013. Younger Brother, Trinity House, 2007. Awarded truncheon for roads policing work, Police Fedn of England and Wales, 2015. *Heir:* none. *Address:* House of Lords, SW1A 0PW.

**SIMON OF HIGHBURY**, Baron *cr* 1997 (Life Peer), of Canonbury in the London Borough of Islington; **David Alec Gwyn Simon**, Kt 1995; CBE 1991; *b* 24 July 1939; *s* of late Roger Albert Damas Jules Simon and Barbara (*née* Hudd); *m* 1st, 1964, Hanne (*née* Mohn) (marr. diss. 1987); two *s*; 2nd, 1992, Sarah (*née* Roderick Smith). *Educ*: Christ's Hospital; Gonville and Caius College, Cambridge (MA Hons; Hon. Fellow 2001); MBA INSEAD. Joined BP 1961; a Man. Dir, 1985–97, CEO, 1992–95 and Chm., 1995–97, BP. A Dir, Bank of England, 1995–97. Mem., H of L, 1997–2017. Minister of State, HM Treasury and DTI, 1997–99; Advr, Cabinet Office, 1999–2003. Mem., Prodi Gp advising on Enlargement Implications, EU, 1999. Sen. Advr (formerly Dir), Morgan Stanley Internat., 2000–; Director: Unilever, 2000–09 (Dep. Chm., 2006–09); Engie (formerly Suez) Gp, 2001–16; Sen. Advr, MWM, 2010–. Member: International Council and UK Adv. Bd, INSEAD, 1985–2008; Internat. Adv. Bd, Dana Gas, 2006–; Chm., Adv. Bd, Montrose Associates, 2009–; Vice Chm., European Round Table, 1993–97. Mem., Cambridge Univ. Council, 2005–10 (Dep. Chm., 2007–10). Gov., Inst. for Govt, 2009–. Cadman Medal, Inst. of Petroleum, 1997. Grand Officer, Order of Leopold (Belgium), 2005 (Comdr, 2001). *Recreations*: golf, books, music. *Address*: 1 St James's Square, SW1Y 4PD. *Clubs*: Athenæum, Brooks's.

**SIMON OF WYTHENSHAWE**, Barony of; *see* Simon, Matilda.

**SIMON, (Dominic) Crispin (Adam)**, CBE 2015; Deputy High Commissioner, Mumbai and West of India, since 2017; HM Trade Commissioner, South Asia, since 2018; *b* London, 25 March 1958; *s* of Baron Simon of Glaisdale, PC and of Fay Elizabeth Leicester (*née* Pearson); *m* 1983, Georgina Brown; one *s* one *d* (and one *s* decd). *Educ*: Westminster Sch.; Lincoln Coll., Oxford (BA PPE 1979; MA). NM Rothschild and Sons, 1979–85; McKinsey & Co., 1985–87; Division Dir, Bowater plc, 1987–95; Division Pres., Smith & Nephew plc, 1995–98; Chief Exec., Biocompatibles International plc, 1998–2011; Man. Dir, Trade Gp, UK Trade and Investment, 2012–14; CEO, Rex Bionics plc, 2014–17. Non-executive Director: Imperial Coll. Healthcare NHS Trust, 2005–08; NHS Trust Develt Authy, 2013–15. *Recreations*: Bath Rugby, theatre, Jack Russell terriers. *Address*: British Deputy High Commission, Naman Chambers, C–32, G-Block, Bandra Kurla Complex, Bandra East, Mumbai 400 051, India. *E*: Crispin.simon@fco.gov.uk. *Club*: Reform.
*See also* Rt Hon. Sir P. C. H. Simon.

**SIMON, Francesca Isabella**; writer; *b* St Louis, Missouri, 23 Feb. 1955; *d* of Mayo and Sondra Simon; *m* 1986, Martin Stamp; one *s*. *Educ*: Palisades High Sch.; Yale Univ. (BA Medieval Studies); Jesus Coll., Oxford (BA Old and Middle English). Freelance journalist, 1981–. *Publications*: Papa Forgot, 1993; Whoops-A-Daisy, 1993; Rosie's Swing, 1994; But What Does the Hippopotamus Say?, 1994; Higgledy-Piggledy: the hen who loved to dance, 1994; The Topsy-Turvies, 1995; Spider School, 1995; Big Class, Little Class, 1996; Café at the Edge of the Moon, 1996; What's That Noise?, 1996; Moo Baa Baa Quack, 1998; Calling All Toddlers, 1998; Don't Wake the Baby!, 1998; Where Are You?, 1998; Camels Don't Ski, 1998; Hugo and the Bullyfrogs, 1999; Helping Hercules, 1999; Toddler Times, 2000; Miaow Miaow Bow Bow, 2000; Three Cheers for Ostrich, 2001; Little Yellow Dog Says Look at Me, 2003; Little Yellow Dog Bites the Builder, 2003; Little Yellow Dog Meets His Match, 2003; Little Yellow Dog Gets a Shock, 2003; The Parent Swap Shop, 2011; The Sleeping Army, 2011; Do You Speak English, Moon?, 2013; The Lost Gods, 2013; The Monstrous Child, 2016; Hack and Whack, 2017; The Goat Café, 2018; *Horrid Henry series*: Horrid Henry, 1994; Horrid Henry and the Secret Club, 1995; Horrid Henry Tricks the Tooth Fairy, 1996; Horrid Henry's Nits, 1997; Horrid Henry Gets Rich Quick, 1998; Horrid Henry's Haunted House, 1999; Horrid Henry and the Mummy's Curse, 2000; A Handful of Horrid Henry, 2000; Don't Be Horrid, Henry, 2000; A Helping of Horrid Henry, 2001; Horrid Henry's Revenge, 2001; Horrid Henry and the Bogey Babysitter, 2002; Horrid Henry's Stinkbomb, 2002; A Triple Treat of Horrid Henry, 2002; Horrid Henry's Underpants, 2003; Horrid Henry's Joke Book, 2004; Horrid Henry Meets the Queen, 2004; Horrid Henry's Big Bad Book, 2004; Horrid Henry and the Mega-Mean Time Machine, 2005; Horrid Henry and the Football Fiend, 2006; Horrid Henry's Christmas Cracker, 2006; Horrid Henry and the Abominable Snowman, 2008; Horrid Henry Robs a Bank, 2008; Horrid Henry Wakes the Dead, 2009; Horrid Henry Rocks, 2010; Horrid Henry and the Zombie Vampire, 2011; Horrid Henry's Monster Movie, 2012; Horrid Henry's Nightmare, 2013; Horrid Henry's Krazy Ketchup, 2014; Horrid Henry's Cannibal Cruise, 2015; Horrid Henry Up Up and Away, 2019. *Recreations*: theatre, reading, discovering opera. *Address*: c/o Stephanie Thwaites, Curtis Brown Ltd, Haymarket House, 28–29 Haymarket, SW1Y 4SP. *Club*: 2 Brydges.

**SIMON, Jacob Michael Henry**, FSA; Editor, Walpole Society, 1981–89 and since 2013; Research Fellow, National Portrait Gallery, since 2011 (Chief Curator, 2001–11); *b* 29 Sept. 1946; *s* of John Eric Henry Simon and Josephine (*née* Sammone); partner, Jenny Bescoby; two *s*. *Educ*: Christ's Coll., Cambridge (BA 1969; MA 1972). FMA 1988; FSA 1992. Trainee Asst, Temple Newsam House, Leeds, 1971–73; Asst Curator, Iveagh Bequest, Kenwood, 1973–83; Curator, 18th century portraits, NPG, 1983–2001. Mem. Council and Cttee, NT, 1969–2000; Trustee, Grimsthorpe and Drummond Castle Trust, 1989–2005. *Publications*: (ed) Handel: a celebration of his life and times 1685–1759, 1985; The Art of the Picture Frame: artists, patrons and the framing of portraits in Britain, 1996; Thomas Johnson's The Life of the Author, 2003. *Recreations*: walking, book collecting. *Address*: National Portrait Gallery, WC2H 0HE. *T*: (020) 7306 0055, *Fax*: (020) 7306 0056. *E*: jsimon@npg.org.uk.

**SIMON, Josette Patricia**, OBE 2000; actor, since 1980; *b* Leicester; 24 March, *d* of Charles Simon and Precious Ilene Simon; *m* 1996, Mark Joseph Padmore, *qv* (marr. diss. 2004); one *d*. *Educ*: Alderman Newton's Sch. for Girls, Leicester; Central Sch. of Speech and Drama (Dip.). Associate Artist: RSC, 1982–; RNT, 1991–: actor: *theatre*: Royal Shakespeare Co.: Much Ado About Nothing, Macbeth, The Tempest, 1982; Cleopatra, 1982, 2017; The Custom of the Country, 1983 (Most Promising Newcomer, Plays and Players); Peer Gynt, 1983; The Merchant of Venice, Love's Labours Lost, 1984; After the Assassinations, The Party, Golden Girls, 1985; Measure for Measure, 1987; Henry IV, Pt One, The Taming of the Shrew, 1995; Don Carlos, A Midsummer Night's Dream, 1999; Royal National Theatre: After the Fall, 1990 (Best Actress, Evening Standard, Plays and Players, Drama Circle and Critics' Circle Awards); The White Devil, 1991; The Lady from the Sea, Lyric Hammersmith, 1994; The Maids, Donmar Warehouse, 1997; The Vagina Monologues, Old Vic, 2001; *films* include: Cry Freedom, 1987; Milk and Honey, 1988 (Best Actress, Paris Film Fest., Atlantic Film Fest.); Red Lights, 2012; Wonder Woman, 2017; Pokémon Detective Pikachu, 2019; *television* includes: Blake's 7, 1980–81; The Pyrates, 1986; Harem, 1988; Thompson, 1988; Somewhere to Run, 1989; Nice Town, 1992; Seekers, 1993; Silent Witness, 1998, 2011; Casualty, 2006 and 2009–10; Skins, 2008; Minder, 2009; The Silence, 2010; Merlin, 2012; NW, 2016; Broadchurch, 2017; Nightflyers, 2018; *radio* includes: Dictator Gal, 1980 (Best Actress (Radio), Prix Futura, Berlin, 1980); Mirandolina, BBC Radio 3, 1986; Nick Silver Can't Sleep, BBC Radio 3, 1990; Twelfth Night, BBC Radio 3, 1990. Co-signproducer, Kaos Signing Choir for Deaf and Hearing Children, 2009–. Trustee, Deaf Ethnic Women's Assoc., 2011–; Patron: Life and Deaf, 2012–; Active Deafness, 2015–; Adept UK, 2015–; Community Gov., Blanche Neville Secondary Sch. for Deaf Children, 2011–. Ambassador and Dementia Friends Champion, Alzheimer's Soc., 2011–; Ambassador, WRVS, 2012–. Hon. MA Leicester, 1996. Pioneers and Achievers Award, British Sign Lang., 2003; Learner of Year, Signature, 2013. *Recreations*: theatre, cinema, yoga, travel, cycling, walking, swing dancing. *Address*: c/o Scott Marshall Partners, Holborn Studios, 49/50 Eagle Wharf Road, N1 7ED. *T*: (020) 7637 4623.

**SIMON, Prof. Leon Melvyn**, PhD; FRS 2003; FAA; Robert Grimmett Professor of Mathematics, Stanford University, now Emeritus Professor; *b* 6 July 1945. *Educ*: Univ. of Adelaide (BSc 1967; PhD 1971). FAA 1983. Lectr in Math., Flinders Univ., 1972–73; Asst Prof., Stanford Univ., 1973–76; Vis. Prof., Univ. of Adelaide, 1976–77; Associate Prof., Univ. of Minnesota, 1977–78; Professor of Mathematics: Univ. of Melbourne, 1978–81; ANU, 1981. *Address*: Department of Mathematics, Stanford University, 450 Serra Mall, Building 380, Stanford, CA 94305–2125, USA.

**SIMON, Matilda**, PhD; artisan; Principal Lecturer, Sheffield Hallam University, 1998–2011; *b* 10 April 1955; *yr c* of 2nd Baron Simon of Wythenshawe and (Anthea) Daphne (*née* May); as Matthew Simon S father to Barony, 2002, but has not used the title; changed name and gender, 2016; *m* 1987, Sally Mitchell (*d* 2014); two *d*. *Educ*: St Paul's Sch.; Balliol Coll., Oxford (BA 1978); Manchester Poly. (PhD 1983). CEng; MIMechE 1991. Sen. Lectr, Dept Mech. Engrg, Manchester Metropolitan Univ. (formerly Manchester Poly.), 1983–98; Lectr, Univ. of Zimbabwe, Harare, 1988–90. *Heir*: (to Barony) *cousin* Michael Ben Simon, *b* 3 March 1970.

**SIMON, Michael Henry; His Honour Judge Simon**; a Circuit Judge, since 2016; *b* Dublin, 4 Dec. 1968; *s* of John Simon and Luise Simon (now Ross); *m* 1990, Hayley Jane Rosen; two *s* one *d* (and one *d* decd). *Educ*: Manchester Grammar Sch.; Univ. of Liverpool (LLB). Called to the Bar, Inner Temple, 1992, Bencher, 2012.

**SIMON, Paul**; American singer and songwriter; *b* 13 Oct. 1941; *s* of Louis and Belle Simon; *m* 1st, Peggy Harper (marr. diss.); one *s*; 2nd, 1983, Carrie Fisher (marr. diss.; she *d* 2016); 3rd, 1992, Edie Brickell; two *s* one *d*. *Educ*: Queens Coll. (BA Eng. Lit.). Mem., Simon and Garfunkel, 1964–71; solo performer, 1971–. *Songs* include: *with Art Garfunkel*: The Sounds of Silence; Homeward Bound; I Am a Rock; 59th Street Bridge Song (Feelin' Groovy); Scarborough Fair/Canticle; Mrs Robinson; The Boxer; Bridge Over Troubled Water; Cecilia; *solo*: American Tune; Loves Me Like a Rock; Still Crazy After All These Years; 50 Ways to Leave Your Lover; Slip Slidin' Away; Something So Right; Hearts and Bones; Graceland; You Can Call Me Al; Diamonds on the Soles of her Shoes; Under African Skies; The Rhythm of the Saints; albums include: (with Derek Walcott) Songs from The Capeman, 1997; You're the One, 2000; So Beautiful or So What, 2011; Stranger to Stranger, 2016; *films*: performer (with Art Garfunkel) and composer of soundtrack, The Graduate, 1967; actor, Annie Hall, 1977; writer of screenplay and score, One-Trick Pony, 1980; musical, The Capeman (lyrics with Derek Walcott), 1998. Numerous Grammy Awards. *Publications*: At the Zoo, 1991.

**SIMON, Rt Hon. Sir Peregrine (Charles Hugo)**, Kt 2002; PC 2015; FLS; **Rt Hon. Lord Justice Simon**; a Lord Justice of Appeal, since 2015; *b* 20 June 1950; *s* of Baron Simon of Glaisdale, PC and of Fay Elizabeth Leicester (*née* Pearson); *m* 1980, Francesca Fortescue Hitchins; two *s* two *d*. *Educ*: Westminster School; Trinity Hall, Cambridge (MA). Called to the Bar, Middle Temple, 1973, Bencher, 1999; QC 1991; a Recorder, 1998–2002; a Dep. High Court Judge, 1999–2002; a Judge of the High Court, QBD, 2002–15; Presiding Judge, North Eastern Circuit, 2006–08. Mem. Council, Zool Soc., 1992–96 (Vice-Pres., 1995–96). *Address*: Royal Courts of Justice, Strand, WC2A 2LL.
*See also* D. C. A. Simon.

**SIMON, Robin John Hughes**, FSA; art historian; Founder and Editor, The British Art Journal, since 1999; *b* 23 July 1947; *s* of Most Rev. (William) Glyn (Hughes) Simon, sometime Archbishop of Wales, and Sarah Sheila Ellen (*née* Roberts); *m* 1st, 1971, Jette Margaret Brooke (*see* J. M. Guillebaud) (marr. diss.); one *s* one *d*; 2nd, 1979, Joanna Christine Ross; one *d*. *Educ*: Cardiff High Sch.; Univ. of Exeter (BA Hons English; DLitt 2008); Courtauld Inst. of Art (MA Hist. European Art). FSA 1998. Lectr in Hist. of Art and English, Univ. of Nottingham, 1972–78; Historic Bldgs Rep., NT, 1979–80; Dir, Inst. European Studies, London, 1980–90; Editor, Apollo, 1990–97; Hd of Publications, NACF, and Ed., Art Qly, Annual Review, 1997–98. Vis. Lectr in Hist. of Art, Univ. of Warwick, 1978; Vis. Prof. in Hist. of Art and Architecture, Westminster Coll., Fulton, Mo, 1989; Vis. Prof., Dept of English, UCL, 2007–; Professorial Res. Fellow in Hist. of Art, Univ. of Buckingham, 2018–. Arts Corresp., 1987–90, Art Critic, 1990–, Daily Mail; columnist, Tatler, 1994–98. Delmas Foundn Fellow, Venice, 1978. Co-Curator, Richard Wilson and the Transformation of European Landscape Painting exhibn, Yale Center for British Art, Nat. Mus. of Wales, Cardiff, 2014. Paul Mellon Lectr in British Art, Nat. Gall., London and Yale Center for British Art, New Haven, 2013. Member: Council, 1991–96, Exec. and Editl Cttee, 1993–96, 2005–10, Walpole Soc.; Adv. Council, Paul Mellon Centre for Studies in British Art, 1993–98; Exec. Cttee, Assoc. of Art Historians, 1993–96; Cttee, Courtauld Assoc. (formerly Courtauld Assoc. of Former Students), 1992– (Chm., 1998–2010); Johnson Club, 1995–; Member, Advisory Committee: Battle of Britain Meml, 2001–02; Thomas Jones (1742–1803) Exhibn, 2001–03; Mem. Centenary Cttee, Nat. Mus. of Wales, 2006–07; Trustee, Foundling Mus., 2008–09. Creator of commissioned entertainments including: Hogarth versus Handel, perf. Middle Temple, 2000; Ruling Passions: Music and Monarchs, perf. Villa Decius, Cracow, 2002; From Pencerrig to Pozzuoli, perf. Swansea Arts Fest., 2003; Hogarth, Handel..., Stockholm, 2016. *Publications*: (with Alastair Smart) The Art of Cricket, 1983; The Portrait in Britain and America, 1987; Hogarth, France and British Art, 2007; *edited*: Buckingham Palace: a complete guide, 1993; The King's Apartments, Hampton Court Palace, 1994; (with Gervase Jackson-Stops) The National Trust 1895–1995: 100 great treasures, 1995; (with Christopher Woodward) A Rake's Progress: from Hogarth to Hockney, 1997; (with Rhian Harris) Enlightened Self-interest: the Foundling Hospital and Hogarth, 1997; Oxford: art and architecture, 1997; Somerset House: the building and collections, 2001; Public Artist, Private Passions: the world of Edward Linley Sambourne, 2001; (with Natasha McEnroe) The Tyranny of Treatment: Samuel Johnson, his friends, and Georgian medicine, 2003; Hogarth's Children, 2007; (with Martin Postle) Richard Wilson and the Transformation of European Landscape Painting, 2014; The Royal Academy of Arts: history and collections, 2018; contrib. Oxford DNB; articles in British Art Jl, Apollo, Burlington Mag., TLS, Papers of Brit. Sch. at Rome, Spectator, Tatler, Opera Now, Country Life, Sunday Times, Mail on Sunday, etc. *Recreations*: cricket, Rugby, music. *Address*: The British Art Journal, 46 Grove Lane, SE5 8ST. *Clubs*: Garrick, MCC.

**SIMON, Siôn Llewelyn**; Member (Lab) West Midlands Region, European Parliament, 2014–19; *b* 23 Dec. 1968; *s* of Jeffrey Simon and Anne Loverini Simon (*née* Jones; now Owen); *m* 1992, Elizabeth Jane Middleton (marr. diss. 2003); one *s* two *d*. *Educ*: Handsworth Grammar Sch., Birmingham; Magdalen Coll., Oxford (BA PPE 1990). Res. Asst to George Robertson, MP, 1990–93; Sen. Manager, Guinness plc, 1993–95; freelance writer, 1995–97; columnist: Daily Telegraph, 1997–2001; News of the World, 2000–01; Associate Ed., The Spectator, 1997–2002. MP (Lab) Birmingham, Erdington, 2001–10. Parly Under-Sec. of State, DIUS, 2008–09, DCMS, 2009–10. Contested (Lab) W Midlands Reg., EP, 2019.

**SIMON, Susannah Kate**; Director, Trade and Investment Negotiations (Services and Investment), Department for Business, Energy and Industrial Strategy, since 2019; *b* 7 June 1964; *d* of Peter and Sheila Simon; *m* 1994, Mikhail Kubekov; one *s*. *Educ*: Lady Eleanor Holles Sch., Hampton; St Hilda's Coll., Oxford (BA Hons Modern Langs). Entered FCO, 1988; Third, later Second Sec., Bonn, 1989–92; Second Sec., Almaty, 1992–93; FCO, 1994–99; First Sec. (EU), Berlin, 1999–2003; Dir, Eur. Policy, Immigration and Nationality Directorate, Home Office (on secondment), 2003–06; Hd, Climate Change and Energy Gp, FCO, 2006–09; Dir, Jt Internat. Unit for Educn, Employment and Social Affairs, DWP, BIS and DfE (on secondment), 2010–11; Dir, Migration Directorate, FCO, 2011–13; Dir, European Reform, BIS, subseq. Europe, BEIS, 2013–19. *Recreation*: gardening. *Address*: c/o Department for Business, Energy and Industrial Strategy, SW1H 0ET. *E*: susannah.simon@beis.gov.uk.

**SIMON, Tobias Robert Mark, (Toby)**; Secretary to London Probation Board, 2002–05; *b* 31 May 1948; *s* of A. P. W., (Tim), Simon and B. M. Simon; *m* 2001, Mrs Margaret Anne McAlpine; two step *s* one step *d*. *Educ*: Bryanston Sch., Dorset; Trinity Hall, Cambridge (MA); BA Open Univ. 1976. Department of Health and Social Security, 1969–87; Sen. Lectr, Civil Service Coll., 1984–87; Sec., Chartered Soc. of Physiotherapy, 1987–96. Gen. Manager, Assoc. of Anaesthetists of GB and Ireland, Jan.–Aug. 2000; Interim Chief Exec., 2001–02, Gov., 2004–10, Inst. of Optimum Nutrition. Chm. Scrutiny Commn, London Fire and Civil Defence Authy, 1999–2000; Mem., London Fire and Emergency Planning Authy, 2000–02; Member: Regl Legal Services Cttee for London, 2000–04; Professional Conduct Panel (formerly Investigating Cttee), Inst. of Legal Executives, 2002–11. A Gen. Comr of Income Tax, 2001–09; Mem., First-tier Tribunal (Tax), 2009–18. Mem. (Lab) Enfield LBC, 1998–2002 and 2006–18 (Chairman: Social Inclusion Scrutiny Panel, 2000–02; Overview and Scrutiny Cttee, 2010–14; Pension Cttee, 2010–18; Planning Cttee, 2014–18). Governor: Enfield County Sch., 1996–2004; Edmonton County Sch., 1999–2009; Gladys Aylward Sch., 2006–10; Chm. Govs, Brettenham Prim. Sch., 2010–18. JP North London and Family Courts, 1998–2018. *Address*: 2 Badminton Gardens, Bath BA1 2XS. *E*: trmsimon@gmail.com.

**SIMONDS, Gavin Napier**; Chairman, Voyage Care, since 2015; *b* 1 Jan. 1955; *s* of Duncan and Monica Simonds; *m* 1980, Venetia Steele; one *s* three *d*. *Educ*: Eton Coll. ACA 1980. Trainee, Peat Marwick Mitchell, 1975–81; Corporate Finance Exec., Rowe & Pitman, 1982–85; Corporate Finance Dir, UBS, 1985–88; Dir, Kleinwort Benson Ltd, 1988–93; Jt Man. Dir, Intercontinental Hotels Gp, 1993–96; Founding Dir, ResidenSea, 1997–2000; Consultant/Dir, various cos, 2000–04; Chairman: Peacock Gp plc, 2004–06; Jessops plc, 2004–07; Club Co., 2004–06; Red Funnel Gp, 2004–07; Craegmoor Healthcare, 2006–08; Classic Hospitals, 2006–08; Apollo Gp, 2006–09; Snell Gp, 2009–14; Ez Revenue Mgt Systems, 2011–12; non-executive Director: Sunseeker Internat. Hldgs, 2010; A-Gas Internat., 2011–15. *Recreations*: family, sailing, tennis. *Club*: Seaview Yacht.

**SIMONS, Joanna Lesley**, CBE 2011; Director, Beaumont Strategy Ltd, since 2016; *b* 16 Aug. 1959; *d* of late Frank Simons and Philippa Simons; *m* 1987, Richard John Robinson, *qv* (marr. diss. 2010). *Educ*: Lady Margaret Sch., Fulham; Open Univ. Business Sch. (MBA 2002); Henley Business Sch. (MSc 2018). FCIH 1987. Estates Officer, Hammersmith and Fulham LBC, 1980–83; Neighbourhood Manager, Newcastle CC, 1983–87; Dist Housing Officer, Barnet LBC, 1987–89; Asst Dir of Housing, Hounslow LBC, 1989–95; Dir of Housing, Greenwich LBC, 1995–2001; Chief Exec., Sutton LBC, 2001–05; Chief Exec., Oxfordshire CC and Clerk to the Lieutenancy, 2005–15; Chief Exec., Alcohol Concern, 2016–17. Non-executive Director: South London Business, 2003–05; Government Office for the South East, 2009–11. Chair, ACCE, 2013–15. Board Member: London Wildlife Trust, 1981–83, 1988–93; Notting Hill Housing Trust, 1996–2005; Trustee: Leadership Centre for Local Govt, 2010–13; Shelter, 2012–18; Berks, Bucks and Oxon Wildlife Trust, 2016; Chair, Experience Oxfordshire, 2017–. Mem. Ct, Oxford Brookes Univ., 2007– (Chm. of Govs, 2008–12; Pro-Chancellor, 2011–12). FRSA 2006. DUniv Oxford Brookes, 2014. *Recreations*: travel, cooking, entertaining, walking. *E*: info@beaumontstrategy.com.

**SIMONS, Prof. John Philip**, PhD, ScD; FRS 1989; CChem, FRSC; Dr Lee's Professor of Chemistry, Oxford University, 1993–99, now Emeritus; Professorial Fellow of Exeter College, Oxford, 1993–99, now Emeritus; *b* 20 April 1934; *s* of Mark Isaac Simons and Rose (née Pepper); *m* 1st, 1956, Althea Mary (née Screaton) (*d* 1989); three *s*; 2nd, 1992, Elizabeth Ann Corps. *Educ*: Haberdashers' Aske's Hampstead Sch.; Sidney Sussex Coll., Cambridge (BA; PhD 1958; ScD 1975). CChem, FRSC 1975. Chemistry Department, University of Birmingham: ICI Fellow, 1959; Lectr, 1961; Reader in Photochemistry, 1977; Prof. of Photochem., 1979; Prof. of Physical Chemistry, Univ. of Nottingham, 1981–93. JSPS Fellow, Univ. of Kyoto, 1992; Erskine Fellow, Univ. of Canterbury, NZ, 1996; Dist. Vis. Prof., Texas A&M Univ., 1995; Visiting Professor: Univ. of Pittsburgh, 1998; Univ. Paul Sabatier, Toulouse, 1998; Vis. Miller Prof., Univ. of Calif, Berkeley, 2000. Lectures: Tilden, RSC, 1983; Tri-Jt, Univ. of Southern Calif, UCLA, CIT, 1988; Pimentel, UC Berkeley, 1998; Spiers, RSC, 1999; Burton, KCL 2001; Humphry Davy, Royal Soc., 2001; Liversidge, RSC, 2007. Vice Pres. and Hon. Sec., 1981–93, Pres., 1993–95, Faraday Div., RSC. Member: Chemistry Cttee, 1983–85, Laser Facility Cttee, 1983–87, SERC; Comité de Direction, CNRS Lab. de Photophysique Moléculaire, Orsay, 1985–90, 2004–05; specially promoted scientific programme panel, NATO, 1985–88; Council, Royal Soc., 1999–2000; Scientific Adv. Cttee, FOM Inst., The Netherlands, 2004–06. Adv. Councillor, Ramsay Meml Fellowship Trust, 1991–2006. Ed., PhysChemComm, 1998–2002. Member Editorial Boards: Molecular Physics, 1980–96; Chemical Physics Letters, 1982–99; Jl Chem. Soc. Faraday Trans, 1990–98; Chemical Physics, 1994–2006; Phys Chem Chem Phys, 1998–2013 (Mem., Hon. Editl Bd, 2016–). Leverhulme Emeritus Fellow, 2009–10. Hon. DSc Birmingham, 2002. Chemical Dynamics Award, 1994, Polanyi Medal, 1996, RSC; Davy Medal, Royal Soc., 2007. Citoyen d'Honneur de la Ville de Toulouse, 1997. *Publications*: Photochemistry and Spectroscopy, 1970; research papers in learned jls of chemical/molecular/biophysics. *Recreations*: reading, walking, talking. *Address*: Physical and Theoretical Chemistry Laboratory, South Parks Road, Oxford OX1 3QZ. *T*: (01865) 275400.

**SIMONS, Prof. Peter Murray**, PhD; FBA 2004; Professor of Moral Philosophy, Trinity College Dublin, 2009–16, now Emeritus; *b* 23 March 1950; *s* of Jack Simons and Marjorie Nita Simons (née Brown); *m* 1973, Susan Jane Walker; one *s* one *d*. *Educ*: Univ. of Manchester (BSc (Maths) 1971; MA 1973, PhD 1975 (Philos.)); Univ. of Salzburg (Habilitation Philos. 1986). Asst Librarian, Univ. of Manchester, 1975–77; Lectr in Philos., Bolton Inst., 1977–80; Lectr, 1980–95, Hon. Prof., 1996–, in Philos., Univ. of Salzburg; Prof. of Philosophy, Univ. of Leeds, 1995–2009. British Acad. Reader, 2004–06. Consultant, Ontek Corp., 1989–2001. MAE 2006; MRIA 2013; Mem., Polish Acad. of Sci., 2018. FTCD 2010. Hon. PhD Bolton, 2012. *Publications*: Parts, 1987; Philosophy and Logic in Central Europe from Bolzano to Tarski, 1992; (with E. Morscher) Joint Ventures in Philosophy, 2014; about 280 articles in learned jls. *Recreations*: walking, choral singing, reading history, classical music. *Address*: 3 Tower House Gardens, Arundel, W Sussex BN18 9RU. *T*: (01903) 884850. *E*: psimons@tcd.ie.

**SIMONS, Richard Brian**; Lecturer in Broadcasting and Journalism, University of West Scotland, since 2013; Managing Director, Norbury Media Ltd, 2008–14; *b* 5 Nov. 1952; *s* of Harry Simons and Ann Lily Simons (née Gold); one *s* one *d*; *m* 2001, Lisa, *d* of late Ronald Hazlehurst and of Kathleen Hazlehurst; one *s* one *d*. *Educ*: Royal Grammar Sch., High Wycombe; Exeter Coll., Oxford (BA Hons PPE). Independent Television News Ltd: Trainee TV Journalist, 1974–75; Writer, News at Ten, and Reporter, News at One, 1976–78; Prog. Editor and News Editor, News At One, 1979; Special Progs Producer, Foreign News Editor and Home News Editor, 1980–84; Head of Investigative Unit, and Associate Producer, D-Day: 40 Years On, 1984; Associate Prod., VE Day: 40 Years On, 1985; Sports Editor, and Mem., ITV Sport Network Cttee, 1985; Editor, World Cup Mexico, 1986; News Editor, 'Vote '87', General Election Results Special, 1986; Special Productions Editor, 1988–90; Commissioning Editor, Factual Progs, 1992–94, Head of Features, 1995–96, Carlton TV; Dir of Progs, Meridian Broadcasting, 1994–2000; Develt Dir, New Media Productions, United Broadcasting & Entertainment, 2000; Dir of TV, CSS-Stellar plc, 2001; Hd of Develt, GMTV, 2002–04; Man. Dir, Banana Split Prodns, 2006–08. Dir, 2entertain Ltd, 2006–08. *Recreations*: my children, piano, papers and TV for pleasure, tennis.

**SIMOR, Jessica Margaret Poppaea**; QC 2013; *b* London, 1968; *d* of Peter Simor and Anne Simor; *m* 2000, Philippe Haag; one *s* one *d*. *Educ*: St Paul's Girls' Sch.; Bryanston Sch.; St Catherine's Coll., Oxford (MA 1986); City Univ., London (CPE 1992); King's Coll. London (Dip. EU Law 1993). Called to the Bar, Middle Temple, 1992, Bencher, 2016; in practice as barrister, Monckton Chambers, 1992–2000; Founder Mem., Matrix Chambers, 2000–. Lawyer, Eur. Commn of Human Rights, 1995–96; Legal Advr, Human Rights Ombudsman, Bosnia, 1996–97. Fellow, Bingham Centre for the Rule of Law, British Inst. Internat. and Comparative Law, 2015–. *Publications*: Human Rights Practice, 2000 (Gen. Editor, 2000–). *Recreations*: reading, music, dance, theatre. *Address*: 2 The Old Orchard, NW3 2TR; Matrix Chambers, Griffin Building, Gray's Inn, WC1R 5LN. *E*: jessicasimor@matrixlaw.co.uk.

**SIMPKINS, Christopher John**, CBE 2017; Director General, Royal British Legion, 2007–16; *b* Hornchurch, 28 Jan. 1952; *s* of Walter and Constance Simpkins; *m* 1974, Denise Dickens; one *s* one *d*. *Educ*: John Taylor High Sch.; Dovecliff Grammar Sch.; Birmingham Poly.; Stafford Coll. of Further Educn; Local Govt Trng Bd (Dip. Municipal Admin). Dep. Town Clerk, Tamworth BC, 1984–88; Chief Executive: South Holland DC, 1988–2003; Falkland Is Govt, 2003–07. Executive Vice Chairman: Falkland Is Develt Corp., 2003–07; Falkland Hldgs, 2003–07; Director: S Lincs Enterprise Agency and Venture Capital Ltd, 1993–99; Lincs Trng and Enterprise Council, 1996–98; Lincs and Rutland Connexions, 2001–03; Stanley Services, 2003–07; Member: Trent Reg. NHS Modernisation Bd, 2000–02 (Chm., Inequalities Task Force, 2000–02); Nat. Rural Affairs Forum, 2002–03. Chm., Corp., Stamford Coll. of Further Educn, 2000–03. Trustee: Officers' Assoc., 2007–12; Nat. Meml Arboretum, 2007–11 and 2014; Poppy Scotland, 2011; RBL Republic of Ireland, 2016–. FInstD 2014. DL Lincs, 2011–15. DUniv Loughborough, 2011. *Recreations*: good company, good food, good wine, motoring, gardening, cycling. *Club*: Royal Over-Seas League.

**SIMPKINS, Peter B.**; *see* Bowen-Simpkins.

**SIMPKISS, (Richard) Jonathan; His Honour Judge Simpkiss**; a Circuit Judge, since 2004; a Deputy High Court Judge and Designated Civil Judge for Kent, Surrey and Sussex, since 2005; a Senior Circuit Judge, since 2010; *b* 21 Oct. 1951; *s* of Dr Michael Simpkiss and late Eileen Simpkiss; *m* 1985, Elizabeth Anne Weaver; two *d*. *Educ*: Magdalene Coll., Cambridge (BA 1974). Called to the Bar, Middle Temple, 1975, Bencher of Lincoln's Inn, 2003; a Recorder, 2000–04. *Recreations*: salmon fishing, shooting, gardening, wine. *Club*: Flyfishers'.

**SIMPSON**, family name of **Baron Simpson of Dunkeld**.

**SIMPSON OF DUNKELD**, Baron *cr* 1997 (Life Peer), of Dunkeld in Perth and Kinross; **George Simpson**, FCCA; FIMI; FCIT; Chief Executive, Marconi (formerly General Electric Co.) plc, 1996–2001; *b* 2 July 1942; *s* of William Simpson and Elizabeth Simpson; *m* 1964, Eva Chalmers; one *s* one *d*. *Educ*: Morgan Acad., Dundee; Dundee Inst. of Technology. ACIS. Sen. Accountant, Gas Industry, Scotland, 1962–69; Central Audit Man., BLMC, 1969–73; Financial Controller, Leyland Truck and Bus Div., 1973–76; Dir of Accounting, Leyland Cars, 1976–78; Finance and Systems Dir, Leyland Trucks, 1978–80; Managing Director: Coventry Climax Ltd, 1980–83; Freight Rover Ltd, 1983–86; Chief Exec. Officer, Leyland DAF, 1986–88; Man. Dir, 1989–91, Chm., 1991–94, and Chief Exec., 1991–92, Rover Gp; Dep. Chief Exec., BAe, 1992–94 (Dir, 1990–94); Chairman: Ballast Nedam Construction Ltd, 1992–94; Arlington Securities, 1993–94; Chief Exec., Lucas Industries plc, 1994–96. Mem., H of L, 1997–2015. Non-executive Director: Pilkington plc, 1992–99; ICI plc, 1995–2001; Nestlé SA, 1999–2004; Alstom SA, 1998–2005; Triumph Gp Inc., 2000; HBOS, 2001–02; Member, Supervisory Board: Northern Venture Capital, 1992; Pro Share, 1992–94. Member: Exec. Cttee, SMMT, 1986 (Vice Pres., 1986–95, Pres., 1995–96, Council); Senate, Engrg Council, 1996–2002. Industrial Prof., Warwick Univ., 1991. *Recreations*: golf, squash and Rugby (now spectating). *Clubs*: Royal Automobile; Royal Birkdale Golf, New Zealand Golf (Weybridge), Gleneagles Golf, Rosemount Golf (Blairgowrie), Pine Valley Golf (NJ); Kenilworth RFC.

**SIMPSON, His Honour Alan**; a Circuit Judge, 1985–2000; *b* 17 April 1937; *s* of William Henry Simpson and Gladys Simpson; *m* 1965, Maureen O'Shea; one *s* one *d*. *Educ*: Leeds Grammar Sch.; Corpus Christi Coll., Oxford (MA). Called to the Bar, Inner Temple, 1962; a Recorder, 1975–85. Prosecuting Counsel to DHSS, North Eastern Circuit, 1977–85. Admin. Steward, 1994–, Vice-Chm., 2000–04, Chm., 2004, BBB of C. *Recreations*: music, books, sport. *Address*: Leeds Combined Court Centre, Oxford Row, Leeds LS1 3BG.

**SIMPSON, Alan Gordon**, OBE 2015; Lord-Lieutenant of Stirling and Falkirk, since 2017; *b* Edinburgh, 15 Feb. 1950; *s* of Gordon Russell Simpson and Marion Elizabeth Simpson; *m* 1977, Veronica Janet Carlyon Evans; one *s* one *d*. *Educ*: Rugby Sch.; Magdalen Coll., Oxford (BA). CEng, MICE 1977. Civil Engr, Brian Colquhoun and Partners, 1972–78; Civil Engr, 1979–89, Partner, 1989–2009, W. A. Fairhurst and Partners. Institution of Civil Engineers: Mem. Council, 2000–03; Chm., Glasgow and W of Scotland Br., 2006–07; Chm., Scotland, 2011–12. Chm., Lake of Menteith Fisheries Ltd, 2009; Tech. Advr, Caledonia Clean Energy Proj., 2012. Chairman: Nat. Youth Orchs of Scotland, 1998–2011; MacRobert Arts Centre, 2015. Chm. Court, Univ. of Stirling, 2007–15 (Mem. Court, 1996–2007). Officer, Royal Co. of Archers (Queen's Bodyguard for Scotland), 2007– (Mem., 1984–). DL Stirling and Falkirk, 2004. DUniv Stirling, 2016. *Recreations*: music, gardening, ski-ing, archery. *Address*: Arntomie, Port of Menteith, Stirling FK8 3RD.

**SIMPSON, Alan John**; writer; independent campaigner on energy and climate policy; Shadow Chancellor's Advisor on Sustainable Economics, since 2016; *b* 20 Sept. 1948; *s* of Reginald James and Marjorie Simpson; *m* (marr. diss.); one *d* two *s*; *m* 2005, Pascale Quiviger; one *d*. *Educ*: Bootle Grammar Sch.; Nottingham Poly. (BSc Econ). Asst Gen. Sec., Nottingham Council of Voluntary Service, 1970–72; Develt Officer, Home Office

Pilot Programme (Non Custodial Treatment of Offenders), 1972–74; Community Worker, Nottingham Areas Project, 1974–78; Res. and Inf. Officer, Nottingham Racial Equality Council, 1979–92. Cllr, Notts CC, 1985–93. MP (Lab) Nottingham S, 1992–2010. Advisor: on renewable energy to DECC Ministers, 2009–10; Friends of the Earth, 2010–13; End Fuel Poverty Coalition, 2013–14; Community Energy England, 2014; Expert Advr to Envmt and Sustainability Cttee, Nat. Assembly of Wales, 2015–16. Member: Meadows Ozone Energy Services, Nottingham; Schs Energy Co-Op. Member: CND; Action Aid. *Publications:* (contrib.) Issues in Community Education, 1980; Stacking the Decks: race, inequality and council housing, 1981; I'll Never Forget What's His Name: one year on from the Scarman Report, 1982; (contrib.) The Right to a Home, 1984; Cuckoos in the Nest—Task Forces and urban policy, 1988; (with M. Read, MEP) Against a Rising Tide—racism, Europe and 1992, 1991; Beyond the Famished Road—defence and common security, 1994; (contrib.) Football and Commons People, 1994; (contrib.) What the Three Main Parties Are Not Telling You, 2015; Transformation Moment: can Britain make it to the Age of Clean?, 2017; (contrib.) The Struggle for Labour's Soul, 2nd edn, 2018; (contrib.) The Local Energy Book: clean power for the many not the few, 2019. *Recreations:* tennis, football (lifelong supporter, Everton FC), vegetarian cooking, eclectic interest in music and reading.

**SIMPSON, Very Rev. Alison Jane;** Rector, St Columba's Episcopal Church, Nairn, since 2009; Dean of Moray, Ross and Caithness, since 2014; *b* Dumfries, 15 Sept. 1960; *d* of George Fazakerley and Daisy Clark; *m* 1992, Stephen William Simpson. *Educ:* Dumfries Acad.; St Andrews Univ. (BSc Marine Biol. 1983; BD 1986): Princeton Theol Seminary (MTh 1987). Associate Minister, Ellon, Aberdeenshire, 1988–90; Minister, Maud with Savoch Parish, Aberdeenshire, 1990–97; sabbatical study, 1997–99; ordained deacon and priest, 1999; Curate, St Mary-on-the-Rock, Ellon, 1999–2002; Rector, Holy Trinity, Keith, 2002–09. Synod Clerk, Dio. of Moray, Ross and Caithness, 2012–13. *Recreations:* hill-walking, climbing, canoeing, travel, theatre, playing bagpipes. *Address:* St Columba's Rectory, 3 Queen Street, Nairn IV12 4AA. *T:* (01667) 452458. *E:* revalison433@btinternet.com. *Club:* Scottish Midweek Mountaineering (Pres., 2010–12).

**SIMPSON, Anthony Maurice Herbert,** TD 1973; Manager, DAPHNE Programme, Justice and Home Affairs Task Force, later Directorate General, Justice and Home Affairs, European Commission, 1996–2000; *b* 28 Oct. 1935; *y s* of late Lt-Col Maurice Rowton Simpson, OBE, TD, DL and Mrs Renée Claire Simpson; *m* 1961, Penelope Gillian, *d* of late Howard Dixon Spackman; one *s* two *d*. *Educ:* Rugby; Magdalene College, Cambridge. BA 1959, LLM (LLB 1961), MA 1963. Leics and Derbys (PAO) Yeomanry, 1956–59; 21st and 23rd SAS Regts (TA), 1959–74, Major 1968. Called to Bar, Inner Temple, 1961; practised Midland and Oxford Circuit, 1961–75; Mem., Legal Service of European Commn, Brussels, 1975–79; MEP (C) Northamptonshire, later Northamptonshire and S Leics, 1979–94; contested (C) Northamptonshire and Blaby, Eur. Parly elecns, 1994; Quaestor of the European Parlt, 1979–87, and 1989–94; EDG spokesman on develt and co-operation, 1987–89; Mem., Inspectorate-Gen. of Services, Eur. Commn, 1994–96. Contested (C) West Leicester, Feb. and Oct. 1974. Treas., Eur. Foundn for Street Children Worldwide, 2003–11; Chm., AIACE-UK, 2005–09. Mem., Bd of Govs, De Montfort Univ., 2004–08. Common Market Law Editor, Current Law, 1965–72. *Recreations:* walking, travelling. *Address:* 17 Alderney Street, SW1V 4ES. *T:* (020) 7233 9344. *Club:* Travellers.

**SIMPSON, Brian,** OBE 2015; Member (Lab) North West England, European Parliament, 2006–14; *b* Leigh, Lancs, 6 Feb. 1953; *s* of late John Hartley Simpson and Freda Simpson; *m* 1975, Linda Jane Gwynn; one *s* two *d*. *Educ:* Golborne Comprehensive Sch., Wigan; W Midlands Coll. of Educn, Walsall (Cert Ed). Teacher, City of Liverpool, 1974–89. Member: Merseyside CC, 1981–85; Warrington BC, 1987–91. MEP (Lab) Cheshire E, 1989–99, NW Reg., England, 1999–2004. Chm., Transport and Tourism Cttee, EP, 2010–14. Campaign Dir, NW Rail Campaign, 1994–96; Chm., Heritage Railway Assoc., 2014– (Vice Pres., 2000–14); Vice Pres., Warrington RSPCA, 1996–; Pres., Warrington Rugby League Referees Soc., 1997–. *Recreations:* Rugby League, cricket, military history, heritage and modern railways. *Clubs:* Golborne Sports and Social (Wigan), Golborne Cricket (Pres., 1992–).

**SIMPSON, Claire Margaret;** *see* Ward, C. M.

**SIMPSON, David;** District Judge (Magistrates' Courts) (formerly Metropolitan Stipendiary Magistrate), 1993–2012; *b* 29 July 1947; *s* of Albert Edward Simpson and Lily Simpson; *m* 1975, Jane Richards; one *s*. *Educ:* N Cestrian GS, Altrincham; Worthing High Sch. for Boys; King's Coll., London (LLM 1987). Admitted a solicitor, 1974. British Bank of ME, 1966–67; Court Clerk, Magistrates' Court: Worthing, 1967–74; Mansfield, 1975–76; Dep. Clerk, 1976–82, Clerk, 1982–93, to the Justices, Uxbridge. Part-time Immigration Special Adjudicator, 1996–2000. Vice-Pres., Assoc. of Magisterial Officers, 1981–82; Member: Council, Justices' Clerks' Soc., 1987–93; Magisterial Cttee, Judicial Studies Bd, 1990–93, 2003–12; Inner London Magistrates' Courts' Cttee, 1998–2001; Youth Justice Bd, 2003–13; Local Safeguarding Children's Bd, Royal Borough of Windsor and Maidenhead, 2013–19; Safeguarding Cttee, C of E Dio. in Europe, 2013–. Member: Adv. Panel on Children's Viewing, BBFC, 1999–2010; Windsor Learning Partnership, 2015–; Lay Mem., Sec. of State for Transport's Medical Adv. Bd, 2012–17. Gov., Windsor Boys' Sch., 2002–15. Mem., Josephine Wolf Trust, 2016–.

**SIMPSON, David;** MP (DemU) Upper Bann, since 2005; *b* 16 Feb. 1959; *m* Elaine Elizabeth; one adopted *s* two adopted *d*. *Educ:* Killicomaine High Sch.; Coll. of Business Studies, Belfast. Businessman. Mem. (DemU), Craigavon BC, 2001–10; Mayor of Craigavon, 2004–05. Mem. (DemU) Upper Bann, NI Assembly, 2003–10. *Address:* (office) 13 Thomas Street, Portadown, Craigavon, Co. Armagh BT62 3NP; House of Commons, SW1A 0AA.

**SIMPSON, David Rae Fisher;** Economic Adviser, Standard Life Assurance Co., 1988–2001; Deputy Chairman, Water Industry Commission for Scotland, 2005–12; *b* 29 Nov. 1936; *s* of late David Ebenezer Simpson and Roberta Muriel Wilson; *m* 1st, 1980, Barbara Dianne Goalen (marr. diss. 2008), *d* of late N. and Mrs G. Inglis, Edinburgh; one *s* (and one step *s* one step *d*); 2nd, 2009, Judith Mary Riley, widow of Prof. E. C. Riley. *Educ:* Gordonstoun S.; Skerry's Coll.; Edinburgh and Harvard Univs. MA 1st cl. hons Econs Edinburgh; PhD Econs Harvard. Instr in Econs, Harvard Univ., 1963–64; Assoc. Statistician, UN HQ, NY, 1964–65; Res. Officer, Econ. Res. Inst., Dublin, 1965–67; Lectr in Pol Economy, UCL, 1967–69; Sen. Lectr in Econs, Univ. of Stirling, 1969–74; University of Strathclyde: Prof. and Dir, Fraser of Allander Inst., 1975–80, Res. Prof., 1980–85; Prof., Dept of Economics, 1985–88. Contested (SNP) Berwick and E Lothian Division, 1970 and Feb. 1974. *Publications:* Problems of Input-Output Tables and Analysis, 1966; General Equilibrium Analysis, 1975; The Political Economy of Growth, 1983; The Challenge of New Technology, 1987; The End of Macro Economics?, 1994; Regulating Pensions, 1996; Re-Thinking Economic Behaviour, 2000; The Rediscovery of Classical Economics, 2013; articles in Econometrica, Financial Times, Scientific American, Spectator. *Recreation:* tilting at windmills. *Address:* The Old Kitchen, Tyninghame House, East Lothian EH42 1XW.

**SIMPSON, David Richard Salisbury,** OBE 1989; Founder and Director, International Agency on Tobacco and Health, since 1991; *b* 1 Oct. 1945; *s* of late Richard Salisbury Simpson and Joan Margaret Simpson (*née* Braund). *Educ:* Merchiston Castle School, Edinburgh. ACA 1969; FCA 1979 (but resigned from Institute, 1981). Teacher at Cadet College, Hasan Abdal, West Pakistan, 1963–64 (VSO). Peat, Marwick, Mitchell & Co., Chartered Accountants, 1964–72; Scottish Director, Shelter, Campaign for the Homeless, 1972–74; Director: Amnesty International (British Section), 1974–79; ASH, 1979–90. Hon. Consultant, Clin. Trial Service Unit and Epidemiol Studies Unit, Oxford Univ., 1991–. Vis. Prof., LSHTM, 2000–17. News Ed., Tobacco Control, 1993–2012. Trustee, Pier Arts Centre, Stromness, 1994–2012. *Publications:* Doctors and Tobacco: medicine's big challenge, 2000; (with J. Crofton) Tobacco: a global threat, 2002. *Recreations:* friends, reading, music, hill-walking, Orkney. *Address:* Clinical Trial Service Unit, Richard Doll Building, Old Road Campus, Roosevelt Drive, Headington, Oxford OX3 7LF.

**SIMPSON, Lt-Col (Retd) David Sackville Bruce,** CBE 1990; Chief Executive, Civil Service Catering Organisation, 1981–91, retired; *b* 18 March 1930; *s* of Henry and Violet Simpson; *m* 1956, Margaret Elizabeth Goslin; two *s* three *d*. *Educ:* Brockley Grammar Sch.; Westminster Technical Coll. FIH. Regular Officer, Army Catering Corps (retd in rank of Lt-Col), 1950–75; Principal Education Catering Organiser, Inner London Education Authority, 1975–81. *Recreations:* golf, squash. *Address:* 1 Tavistock Road, Fleet, Hants GU51 4EH. *T:* (01252) 625795.

**SIMPSON, Dennis Charles;** business consultant and lecturer; Managing Director, Axtel (UK) Ltd, 1986–88; *b* 24 Oct. 1931; *s* of late Arthur and Helen Simpson; *m* 1st, 1964, Margery Bruce Anderson (marr. diss.); three *s* one *d*; 2nd, 1983, Susan Gaynor Conway-Williams. *Educ:* Manchester Univ. (BA). FInstPS. 2nd Lieut Royal Signals, 1952–54; commercial appts, Philips Electrical Industries, 1956–63; Group Purchasing Manager, STC Ltd, 1963–66; Gp Purchasing Controller, Rank Organisation, 1966–69; Gen. Man., Cam Gears (S Wales) Ltd, 1969–72; Industrial Dir for Wales, Dept of Industry, 1972–75; Industrial Dir for Wales, Welsh Office, 1975–76; Business Agent, Welsh Develt Agency, 1983–85. Chairman: Spencer Harris Ltd, 1976–81; Grainger Hydraulics Ltd, 1976–81; Wellfield Engineering, 1976–81; Director: Beechwood Holdings, 1976–81; Gower Technology Ltd, 1983–87; Video Interactive Systems Ltd, 1983–87; Gower Alarms Ltd, 1985–87; Video Interactive Teaching Aids Ltd, 1985–87. *Recreations:* golf, bridge, reading war histories.

**SIMPSON, Derek;** Joint General Secretary, Unite, 2007–10 (General Secretary, Amicus, 2004–07, on merger with Transport and General Workers' Union); *b* 23 Dec. 1944; *m* Freda; three *c*. *Educ:* Sheffield Central Tech. Sch.; Open Univ. (BA 1987). Engrg apprentice, Firth Brown Tools, 1960–66; with Balfour Darwin, 1966–81; full-time official, AEU, 1981–2002; elected Gen. Sec., Amicus-AEEU, 2002; Jt Gen. Sec., Amicus, 2002–04. *Address:* Unite, 128 Theobalds Road, Holborn, WC1X 8TN.

**SIMPSON, Edward Alexander,** CB 1993; Director, Northern Ireland Court Service, 1987–95; *b* 25 Dec. 1935; *s* of late Robert Simpson and Eva (*née* Graham); *m* 1960, Audrey Gordon; two *s*. *Educ:* Regent House Sch., Newtownards; Queen's Univ., Belfast (BSc Econ). Joined Ministry of Finance, 1953; various posts in Mins of Health and Local Govt and DoE, 1956–77; Asst Sec., Transportation and the Fire Service, 1977–81; Belfast Develt Officer, 1981–87. *Recreations:* golf, walking, gardening, wine, school governor. *Address:* 28 Londonderry Avenue, Comber, Newtownards BT23 5ES.

**SIMPSON, Prof. Elizabeth,** OBE 2004; FRS 2010; FMedSci; Professor of Immunogenetics, Imperial College London (formerly Royal Postgraduate Medical School, subsequently Imperial College School, then Faculty, of Medicine, London University), 1994–2004, now Emeritus Professor of Transplantation Biology; Head of Transplantation Biology Group, 1984–2004, and Deputy Director, 1994–2004, MRC Clinical Sciences Centre, Hammersmith Hospital (formerly Clinical Research Centre, Harrow); *b* 29 April 1939; *d* of J. H. G. Browne and O. R. Browne (*née* Wood); *m* 1963 (marr. diss. 1973); one *d* with Prof. Peter Charles Leonard Beverley, *qv*. *Educ:* Old Palace Sch. for Girls, Croydon; Girton Coll., Cambridge (BA Nat. Sci. 1960; VetMB 1963; MA 1964). Vet. Surg., private practice, Canada, 1963–65; Res. Virologist, Ottawa, 1965–66; Univ. Demonstrator in Animal Pathology, Cambridge Univ., 1966–69; Research Scientist: NIMR, 1969–71; Clin. Res. Centre, Harrow, 1971–84. Visiting Scientist: All India Inst. Med. Res., Delhi, 1971; Nat. Inst. Health, Bethesda, 1972–73; Jackson Lab., Maine, 1976–. Mem., peer review research funding cttees, MRC, AFRC, CRUK, Wellcome Trust, Royal Soc., ERC, 1983–. FMedSci 1999. Hon. FRCVS 2010. Hon. DSc Imperial Coll. London, 2015. *Publications:* (ed) T Cell Receptors, 1995; A Thousand Natural Shocks, 2011; reviews and scientific papers on transplantation, immunology and genetics in jls. *Recreations:* writing, reading, music, swimming. *Address:* Division of Immunology and Inflammation, Department of Medicine, Imperial College London, W12 0NN.

**SIMPSON, Frances Clare;** *see* Nash, F. C.

**SIMPSON, Sir Gilbert, (Sir Gil),** KNZM 2000; QSM 1986; Founder and Chief Executive, Jolly Good Software Pty Ltd, since 2006; *b* 5 April 1948; *m* 1998, Joyce Adele, (Joy) Reilly (CNZM 2016). *Educ:* Christchurch Boys' High Sch. Clerk, Nat. Bank of NZ, 1967–71; Sen. Programmer, NZ Aluminium Shelters, 1971–74; Data Processing Manager, Whitcoulls NZ, 1974–78; formed own co., 1978; CEO, Aoraki Corp. Ltd, 1982–2003; Dir, Jade Software Corp., 2003–06. Dir, Reserve Bank of NZ, 1997. Pres., Royal Soc. of NZ, 2000. Fellow: NZ Computer Soc., 1998; NZ Inst. Mgt, 1999; NZ Inst. Dirs, 2000. *Recreations:* tramping, flying, railway enthusiast, following cricket and Rugby.

**SIMPSON, James;** *see* Simpson, William J.

**SIMPSON, Very Rev. James Alexander;** an Extra Chaplain to the Queen in Scotland, since 2004 (Chaplain, 1992–2004); Moderator of the General Assembly of the Church of Scotland, 1994–95; *b* 9 March 1934; *s* of Robert and Marion Simpson; *m* 1960, Helen Gray McCorquodale; three *s* two *d*. *Educ:* Glasgow Univ. (BSc Hons 1955; BD 1958); Union Seminary, New York (STM 1959). Minister: Gramshorn Church, Falkirk, 1960–66; St John's Renfield Church, Glasgow, 1966–76; Dornoch Cathedral, 1976–97; Interim Minister: Almondbank Tibbermore, Perth, 1997–98; Brechin Cathedral, 1998–99. Hon. DD Aberdeen, 1995. *Publications:* There is a Time To, 1971; Marriage Questions Today, 1975; Doubts Are Not Enough, 1982; Holy Wit, 1986, 4th edn 2002; Laughter Lines, 1988, 2nd edn 1991; The Master Mind, 1989; History of Dornoch Cathedral, 1989; More Holy Wit, 1990; Keywords of Faith, 1992; Royal Dornoch Golf Club (a pictorial history), 1992; All about Christmas, 1994; The Laugh shall be First, 1998; Life, Love and Laughter, 2002, 2nd edn 2003; A Funny Way of Being Serious, 2005; At Our Age, 2010; The Magic of Words, 2013; Uncommon Sense and Comic Nonsense, 2016. *Address:* Dornoch, Perth Road, Bankfoot, Perth PH1 4ED. *Club:* Royal Dornoch Golf (Captain, 1993).

**SIMPSON, James Walter Thorburn,** OBE 2007; RIBA; FRIAS; Partner, Simpson & Brown, Architects, 1977–2010, Consultant, since 2010; *b* 27 July 1944; *s* of Robert Alison Crighton Simpson, TD, FRIBA, and Rosemary Euphemia (*née* Morrison); *m* 1968, Ann Mary Bunney; two *d*. *Educ:* Belhaven Hill Sch.; Trinity Coll., Glenalmond; Edinburgh Coll. of Art (BArch Hons). RIBA 1970; FRIAS 1985. Trained as architect with Ian G.

Lindsay and with Sir Bernard Feilden, 1972–77 (work on St Paul's, Norwich and St Giles' Cathedral, Edinburgh); estabd Simpson & Brown, with Stewart Brown, 1977. Building projects in Scotland and NE England, including: St Giles' Cathedral; Alderman Fenwick's House, Newcastle-upon-Tyne; Auchinleck House, Ayrshire; Kinlochmoidart House, Inverness-shire; Rosslyn Castle and Chapel, Midlothian; 26–31 Charlotte Square, Edinburgh. Curator, William Adam Exhibn, Scottish Nat. Portrait Gall., 1989. Surveyor of the Fabric, York Minster, 1994–95. Mem., Ancient Monuments Bd for Scotland, 1984–96. Comr, Royal Commn on Ancient and Historical Monuments of Scotland, 1997–2006. *Publications:* Vitruvius Scoticus, 1980, repr. 2011; The Care of Historic Buildings and Ancient Monuments by Government Departments in Scotland, 1995; The British Standard Guide to the Principles of the Conservation of Historic Buildings, 1998. *Recreations:* playing Scottish small pipes, Norfolk Terriers, thinking about architecture, learning Gaelic, India. *Address:* (office) with Addyman Archaeology, The Old Printworks, 77a Brunswick Street, Edinburgh EH7 5HS; 1 Belgrave Crescent, Edinburgh EH4 3HQ. *T:* (0131) 332 7294.

**SIMPSON, Dr Jennifer Linda,** OBE 2000; FRCPE; Founder, European Association of Medical Management (Acting Chairman, 2010); Clinical Director, Professional Standards and Revalidation, NHS England, 2013–15; *b* 18 April 1953; *d* of Dr I. M. Simpson and Janette Simpson; *m* 1981, Dr Gavin M. M. Thoms (marr. diss. 2010); one *s* two *d*; *m* 2011, Tim Scott. *Educ:* Univ. of Manchester Med. Sch. (MB ChB, DCH); Sheffield Business Sch. (MBA, DBA). Clinical posts in Manchester and Sheffield, 1976–80; clinical and managerial posts, Sheffield Children's Hosp., 1983–90; Dir, Resource Mgt, Mersey RHA, 1990–94. Clinical Advr, Resource Mgt Team, DoH, 1991–93; Associate Dir, Revalidation Support Team, DoH, 2011. Founder and Chief Exec., British Assoc. of Med. Managers, 1991–2010; Pres., Inst. of Healthcare Mgt, 2011–12. Vis. Prof., Centre for Leadership, York Univ.; Vis. Fellow, Cranfield Sch. of Mgt. *Publications:* Clinicians as Managers, 1994; Clinical Governance in the New NHS, 1997; Appraisal in Action, 1998; The Duties of the Medical Director, 2001; Consultant Careers: times of change, 2001; Making Sense: a career framework for medical management, 2003. *Recreations:* music, working with a talented group of musicians running an independent recording label, physical fitness, and sheer enjoyment of my three children. *E:* jenny@jennysimpson.com.

**SIMPSON, John Andrew,** OBE 2014; lexicographer, writer and researcher; Chief Editor, Oxford English Dictionary, 1993–2013; Fellow, 1991–2013, now Emeritus, and Dean of Degrees, since 2014, Kellogg College (formerly Rewley House), Oxford; *b* 13 Oct. 1953; *s* of Robert Morris Simpson and Joan Margaret (*née* Sersale); *m* 1976, Hilary Croxford; two *d*. *Educ:* Dean Close Sch., Cheltenham; Univ. of York (BA Hons English Literature); Univ. of Reading (MA Medieval Studies). Editorial Asst, Supplement to OED, 1976–79; Editor, Concise Oxford Dictionary of Proverbs, 1979–81; Sen. Editor, Supplement to OED, 1981–84; Editor (New Words), OED, 1984–86; Co-editor, OED, 1986–93. Mem., Faculty of English, Univ. of Oxford, 1993–. Editl Consultant, Australian National Dictionary, 1986–88. Mem. Adv. Cttee, Opera del Vocabolario Italiano, Florence, 2003–05. Vis. Asst Prof., Dept of English, Univ. of Waterloo, Ont, Canada, 1985. Mem., Philolog. Soc., 1994–; Founding Mem. and Mem. Exec. Cttee, European Fedn of Nat. Instns for Lang., 2003–18 (Hon. Advr, 2018–). BBC TV series, Balderdash & Piffle, 2006, 2007. Fellow, Dictionary Soc. of N America, 2015. FRSA 2007. Hon. LittD: ANU, 1999; Leicester, 2015. Editor (with Harald Beck), James Joyce Online Notes, 2011–; Project Leader, Pittville History Works, 2014–. *Publications:* (ed) Concise Oxford Dictionary of Proverbs, 1982, 3rd edn 1998; (contrib.) Oxford English, 1986; (contrib.) Words, 1989; (ed) Oxford English Dictionary, 2nd edn (with Edmund Weiner) 1989, 3rd edn (online) 2000–; (contrib.) Wörterbücher: ein internationales Handbuch zur Lexikographie, 1990; (ed with John Ayto) Oxford Dictionary of Modern Slang, 1992, 2nd edn 2008 as Stone the Crows: Oxford Dictionary of Modern Slang; (ed with Edmund Weiner) OED Additions series, vols 1 and 2, 1993, (Gen. Ed.) vol. 3, 1997; The First English Dictionary 1604, 2007; The First Dictionary of Slang 1699, 2010; Superstitions: omens, charms, cures 1787, 2011; Ware's Victorian Dictionary of Slang and Phrase, 2013; The Word Detective: searching for the meaning of it all at the Oxford English Dictionary, 2016; Ambrose Bierce, The Devil's Dictionary, 2018; Managing Poverty: Cheltenham settlement examinations and removal orders 1831–52, 2020; articles in Medium Aevum, English Today, Dublin James Joyce Qly, European Joyce Studies, and other lexicographical, linguistic and historical publications. *Address:* 67 Prestbury Road, Cheltenham, Glos GL52 2BY. *E:* john.simpson@kellogg.ox.ac.uk. *Club:* Athenæum.

**SIMPSON, John Anthony,** CVO 2002; RIBA; architect; Principal, John Simpson & Partners, since 1980; *b* 9 Nov. 1954; *s* of late John Simpson and of Lydia Simpson; *m* 1990, Erica; two *s* one *d*. *Educ:* Marlborough Coll.; UCL (BSc Hons; DipArch). RIBA 1981. Main commissions: Paternoster Square Develt, City of London, 1990–96 (AIA Honor Award for Urban Design); W Range of Gonville Court, Gonville and Caius Coll., Cambridge, 1993–98 (RICS Conservation Award); Brownsword Market Bldg, Poundbury, 1996–2000; Queen's Gallery, Buckingham Palace, 1998–2002 (RIBA and Royal Fine Art Commn Trust awards, 2003); St Mary's Ch Hall and Vicarage, Old Church St, Chelsea, 1998–2002 (RBKC Envmt Award); masterplan for 4500 new houses, Swindon Southern Develt Area, 2001–05; Carhart Mansion, 5th Avenue, NY, 2002–05 (Palladio Award, 2007; Stanford White Award, Inst. of Classical Architecture, 2012); redevelt of Rochester Row Police Stn site at 68 Vincent Square, Westminster, 2003–08; redevelt of Royal Worcester Porcelain Wks, Worcester, 2004; Stanhope redevelt, 5th Ave, NY, 2005–07; Pipe Partridge Bldg, Lady Margaret Hall, Oxford, 2005–10 (Classical Bldg of Yr Award, Georgian Gp, 2010); new public facilities, Kensington Palace for Queen's Diamond Jubilee, 2012; New Birley Schs, Elliott Schs, Lyttleton Schs, Jafar Debating Chamber, Museum of Antiquities and McCrum Yard, Eton Coll., 2015; Whittle Bldg, Gisborne Court, Peterhouse, Cambridge, 2015; current commissions: Forthergill Bldg and Duffield Graduate Centre, Lady Margaret Hall, Oxford; Sch. of Architecture, Univ. of Notre Dame, USA; Defence and Nat. Rehabilitation Centre, Stanford Hall; two music halls and museum, Royal Coll. of Music. Arthur Ross Award for Excellence in Classical Tradition, Inst. of Classical Architecture, 2008; Philippe Rotthier European Prize for the reconstruction of the City, 2008. *Recreations:* music, opera, swimming, vintage motor cars. *Address:* (office) 29 Great James Street, WC1N 3ES. *T:* (020) 7405 1285, *Fax:* (020) 7831 1781.

**SIMPSON, John (Cody Fidler-),** CBE 1991; World (formerly Foreign) Affairs Editor, BBC, since 1988; *b* 9 Aug. 1944; *s* of Roy Simpson Fidler-Simpson and Joyce Leila Vivienne Cody; *m* 1965, Diane Jean Petteys (marr. diss. 1995), El Cajon, California; two *d*; *m* 1996, Adèle Krüger; one *s*. *Educ:* St Paul's School; Magdalene Coll., Cambridge (MA; Hon. Fellow, 1999). FRGS 1990. Reporter, BBC Radio News, 1970; BBC correspondent, Dublin, 1972; Common Market correspondent (based in Brussels), 1975; Southern Africa correspondent (based in Johannesburg), 1977; Diplomatic correspondent, BBC Television News, 1978; BBC Political Editor, 1980; Presenter and Correspondent, BBC-TV News, 1981; Diplomatic Editor, BBC-TV, 1982–88. Associate Editor, The Spectator, 1991–96. Pres., Chelsea Soc., 2013–. Chancellor, Roehampton Univ., 2005–14. Freeman, City of London, 2011. Hon. DLitt: De Montfort, 1995; Nottingham, 2000; Dundee, Southampton, 2003; St Andrews, Roehampton, 2005. RTS Journalist of the Year, 1990, 2000; BAFTA Award, 1992, 2000; Peabody Award, USA, 1998; Internat. Emmy Award for reporting in Afghanistan, 2002; Bayeux War Correspondent's Award, 2002; RTS award for reporting in Afghanistan and Iraq, 2002; Mungo Park Medal, RSGS, 2004; Internat. Ischia Prize for journalism, Italy, 2010; Churchillian Award, Churchill Centre UK, 2012. *Publications:* (ed jtly) The Best of Granta, 1966; The Disappeared: voices from a secret war, 1985; Behind Iranian Lines, 1988; Despatches from the Barricades, 1990; From the House of War: Baghdad and the Gulf, 1991; The Darkness Crumbles: the death of Communism, 1992; In the Forests of the Night: drug-running and terrorism in Peru, 1993; (ed) The Oxford Book of Exile, 1995; (jtly) Lifting the Veil: life in revolutionary Iran, 1995; Wars Against Saddam, 2003; Unreliable Sources, 2010; *autobiography:* Strange Places, Questionable People, 1998; A Mad World, My Masters: tales from a traveller's life, 2000; News from No Man's Land, 2002; Days from a Different World, 2005; Not Quite World's End, 2007; We Chose to Speak of War and Strife: the world of the foreign correspondent, 2016; *novels:* Moscow Requiem, 1981; A Fine And Private Place, 1983; Moscow, Midnight, 2018. *Recreations:* collecting obscure books, travelling to obscure places, and returning to Suffolk. *Address:* c/o Kruger Cowne Ltd, Unit 7C, Chelsea Wharf, 15 Lots Road, SW10 0QJ. *Clubs:* Garrick, Travellers, Chelsea Arts.

**SIMPSON, Julia Elizabeth;** Chief of Staff, International Airlines Group, since 2011; *b* 18 May 1958; *d* of Jack Victor Simpson and Ellen Kathleen Simpson (*née* Powell); *m* 2002, Graham Hassell (*d* 2009); two *d*. *Educ:* Lady Margaret Sch., Fulham; Royal Acad. of Dancing; Univ. of Warwick (BA Spanish and European Studies); Salamanca Univ. (1978). News reporter, Iberia Daily Sun and Majorca Daily Bulletin, 1982–84; News Ed., Nat. Union of Civil and Public Servants, 1985–93; Hd of Communications, CWU, 1993–96; Asst Chief Exec., London Bor. of Camden, 1996–98; Head of News: DfEE, 1998–2001; Home Office, 2001–02; Dir of Communications, Home Office, 2002–06; Strategic Communications Advr to Prime Minister, 2006–07; Dir of Corporate Communications, British Airways, 2007–11. Mem. Bd, Iberia and British Airways, 2012–. Freelance subed. and reviewer, Egon Ronay's Guide: And Baby Comes Too, 1988–89. Gov., Robinsfield Infants Sch. and Barrow Hill Junior Sch., London, 1992–2001. *Recreations:* tennis, hispanophile, birds, dance, London, my lovely daughters. *Address:* International Airlines Group, 2 World Business Centre Heathrow, Newall Road, London Heathrow Airport, Hounslow TW6 2SF.

**SIMPSON, Rt Hon. Keith (Robert);** PC 2015; MP (C) Broadland, since 2010 (Mid Norfolk, 1997–2010); *b* 29 March 1949; *s* of Harry Simpson and Jean Simpson (*née* Day); *m* 1984, Pepita Hollingsworth; one *s*. *Educ:* Thorpe Grammar Sch.; Univ. of Hull (BA Hons 1970). Postgrad. res., KCL, 1970–72; Sen. Lectr in War Studies, RMA Sandhurst, 1973–86; Hd of Oversea and Defence Section, Cons. Res. Dept, 1986–88; Special Advr to Sec. of State for Defence, 1988–90; Dir, Cranfield Security Studies Inst., Cranfield Univ., 1991–97. Opposition front bench spokesman on defence, 1998–99 and 2002–05, on agriculture, 2001–02, on foreign affairs, 2005–10; an Opposition Whip, 1999–2001; PPS to Foreign Sec., 2010–14. Member: DEFRA Select Cttee, 2001–02; Parly Intelligence and Security Cttee, 2015–. Sec., Cons. backbench Defence Cttee, 1997–98; Mem., H of C Catering Cttee, 1997–98; Chm., Cons. History Gp, 2003–. Member: Lord Chancellor's Adv. Council on Nat. Records and Archives, 2006–08; Prime Minister's First World War Centenary Adv. Gp, 2014–15. Member: RUSI, 1970–; IISS, 1975–; British Commn for Mil. History, 1980–; Comr, Commonwealth War Graves Commn, 2008–18. Trustee, Hist. of Parlt Trust, 2005–10. *Publications:* The Old Contemptibles, 1981; (ed) A Nation in Arms, 1985; History of the German Army, 1985; (ed) The War the Infantry Knew 1914–1919, 1987; Waffen SS, 1990. *Recreations:* collecting books, cinema, visiting restaurants, walking battlefields, observing ambitious people. *Address:* House of Commons, SW1A 0AA. *T:* (020) 7219 4053.

**SIMPSON, Mark Taylor;** QC 2008; barrister; *b* Maidstone, 5 Jan. 1963; *s* of His Honour Keith Taylor Simpson and of Dorothy May Simpson; *m* 1987, Janet McDowell; two *s* one *d*. *Educ:* King's Sch., Canterbury; Oriel Coll., Oxford (BA Hons Classics 1986); Hughes Hall, Cambridge (PGCE 1987); City Univ., London (Dip. Law 1991); King's Coll. London (Dip. Eur. Law 1995). Teacher of Classics, St Paul's Sch., Barnes, 1987–90; called to the Bar, Middle Temple, 1992. *Publications:* (Gen. Ed.) Professional Negligence and Liability, 2000–; (Associate Ed.) Clerk & Lindsell on Torts, 19th edn, 2006, 20th edn, 2010. *Recreations:* golf, tennis, travel, reading. *Address:* Fountain Court Chambers, Temple, EC4Y 9DH. *T:* (020) 7583 3335, *Fax:* (020) 7353 0329. *E:* ms@fountaincourt.co.uk. *Club:* Rye Golf.

**SIMPSON, Meg;** *see* Hillier, M.

**SIMPSON, Morag;** *see* Macdonald, M.

**SIMPSON, Prof. Patricia Ann,** DèsSc; FRS 2000; Wellcome Trust Principal Fellow, 2000–10, and Professor of Comparative Embryology, 2003–11, now Emeritus, Department of Zoology, University of Cambridge; Fellow of Newnham College, Cambridge, 2000–11, now Emeritus (Honorary Fellow, 2014); *b* 9 Dec. 1945; *d* of James Alfred Simpson and Peggy Anderson Simpson. *Educ:* Univ. of Southampton (BSc Hons); Univ. Pierre et Marie Curie, Paris (DèsSc). Scientific research at: Inst. d'Embryologie et Tératologie Experimentale, Nogent sur Marne, Paris, 1968–72; Center for Pathobiol., Univ. of Calif, Irvine, 1972–74; Centre de Génétique Moléculaire, Gif sur Yvette, France, 1975–80; Inst. de Génétique et de Biologie Moléculaire et Cellulaire, Univ. Louis Pasteur, Strasbourg (Res. Dir, 1981–2000). Silver Medal, CNRS, France, 1993; Waddington Medal, British Soc. for Develtl Biol., 2008. *Publications:* The Notch Receptors, 1994. *Recreations:* hiking in remote corners of the world, woodwork, boating. *Address:* Department of Zoology, Downing Street, Cambridge CB2 3EJ. *T:* (01223) 336669.

**SIMPSON, Sir Peter (Austin),** Kt 2011; OBE 2006; education consultant, since 2013; Chief Executive Officer, Brooke Weston Trust, 2007–13; *b* North Shields, 27 April 1950; *s* of Henry and Dorothy Simpson; *m* 1972 (marr. diss. 1995); two *s*. *Educ:* Open Univ. (BA 1975); Univ. of Leicester (MA 1996). Science teacher: Waltham Forest, 1971; Northants, 1972–75; Sharnbrook Upper Sch., 1975–83; Dir of Electronics, Abergele High Sch., 1983–85; Inspector of Sci. and Technol., Walsall Local Authy, 1985–92; Vice Principal, 1992–99, Principal, 1999–2007, Brooke Weston. *Recreations:* amateur radio (callsign G3XQZ), sailing, walking. *Address:* Orchard House, 8 Church Road, Egleton, Oakham, Rutland LE15 8AD. *T:* (01572) 722300. *E:* sirpetersimpson@btinternet.com.

**SIMPSON, Sir Peter (Jeffery),** Kt 2006; MD; FRCA, FRCP; President, Royal College of Anaesthetists, 2003–06; Consultant Anaesthetist, Frenchay Hospital, Bristol, 1982–2007; *b* 17 Dec. 1946; *s* of Thomas Simpson and Barbara Josephine (*née* Greenwood); *m* 1969, Jane Carpenter-Jacobs; one *s* three *d*. *Educ:* Bryanston Sch., Blandford; St Bartholomew's Hosp. Med. Sch., London (MB BS 1970; MD 1978). MRCS 1970; LRCP 1970; FRCA (FFARCS 1975); FRCP 2005. Registrar and Lectr in Anaesthetics, St Bartholomew's Hosp., 1972–76; Sen. Registrar in Anaesthetics, Oxford, 1976–78; Consultant Sen. Lectr in Anaesthetics, Univ. of Bristol, 1978–82. Chairman: Nat. Confidential Enquiry into Patient Outcome and Death (formerly Nat. Confidential Enquiry into Perioperative Deaths), 2002–05; UK Donation Ethics Cttee, 2010–13; Mem. and Dep. Chm., Postgrad. Medical Educn and Trng Bd, 2004–06. Mem. Council, Royal Coll. of Anaesthetists, 1997–2007 (Vice Pres., 2001–03). Chm. Examination Cttee, European Acad. of Anaesthesiology, 1999–2005; Pres., European Soc. of Anaesthesiology, 2006–07.

MRSocMed 1994. Hon. Mem., German Soc. of Anaesthesiology, 2007–. Hon. FCARCSI 2006; Hon. FRCS 2007. *Publications:* Understanding Anaesthesia, 1982, 4th edn 2001; 600 MCQ's in Anaesthesia: basic science, 1985; 600 MCQ's in Anaesthesia: clinical practice, 1986. *Recreations:* golf, walking, choral singing, bird-watching, classical music, opera. *Address:* 2 St Hilary Close, Stoke Bishop, Bristol BS9 1DA. *T:* (0117) 968 1537, 07768 732373. *E:* pjsimpson@blueyonder.co.uk. *Clubs:* Bristol Savages; Clifton Down Probus; Bristol and Clifton Golf.

**SIMPSON, Philip James Dalrymple;** QC (Scot.) 2014; *b* Glasgow, 23 Feb. 1973; *s* of James Thomas Farquhar Simpson and Patricia Simpson; partner, Joya Van Hout; one *s* one *d*. *Educ:* Bearsden Acad.; Univ. of Aberdeen (LLB with German Law 1st Cl. Hons 1995); Univ. of Regensburg (LLM 1st Cl. 1996); Univ. of Edinburgh (DipLP 1997). Admitted Advocate, 2001; called to the Bar, Inner Temple, 2001; Chartered Tax Advr, 2006. *Publications:* contrib. articles on tax law. *Recreations:* languages, literature, piano, triathlon. *Address:* Old Square Tax Chambers, 15 Old Square, Lincoln's Inn, WC2A 3UE. *Club:* New (Edinburgh).

**SIMPSON, Richard John,** OBE 2017; FRCPsych, FRCGP; Member (Lab) Mid Scotland and Fife, Scottish Parliament, 2007–16; *b* 22 Oct. 1942; *s* of John and Norah Simpson; *m* 1967, Christine McGregor; two *s*. *Educ:* Edinburgh Univ. (MB ChB; DPM). FRCPsych 1994; MRCGP 1996, FRCGP 2013. Pres., Scottish Union of Students, 1967–69. GP, Stirling, 1970–99; psychiatrist, 1970–99; consultant addiction psychiatrist, 1970–99. MSP (Lab) Ochil, 1999–2003; Scottish Executive: Dep. Minister for Justice, 2001–02; Shadow Minister for Public Health, 2007–16. Hon. Prof. of Health Services and Sport, Stirling Univ., 1997–2003, 2016–; Vis. Prof., Med. Faculty, Univ. of St Andrews, 2017–. Mem., Bd of Dirs, St Andrews Clinics for Children, 2018–. Trustee: Thomas and Margaret Roddan Trust; Bowden Trust, 2017–. Patron, Trellis Scotland, 2018–. *Publications:* numerous papers and articles in medical research. *Recreations:* watching Rugby, golf.

**SIMPSON, Ven. Richard Lee;** Archdeacon of Auckland, since 2018; *b* 5 July 1966; *m* 1991, Rachel Lunney. *Educ:* St John's Coll., Leatherhead; Keble Coll., Oxford (BA 1988; MPhil 1991); Westminster Coll., Oxford (PGCE 1989); Wycliffe Hall, Oxford (DipMin 1991); York St John Univ. (MA 2010). Ordained deacon, 1993, priest, 1994; Curate, St Gabriel's, Heaton, 1993–97; Priest-in-charge: Holy Trinity, Jesmond, 1997–2006; St Barnabas and St Jude, Newcastle upon Tyne, 1997–2006; St Brandon, Brancepeth, 2006–18. Dir, Initial Ministerial Educn 4–7 for Durham and Newcastle Dioceses, 2006–09; Formational Tutor, Initial Ministerial Educn 4–7 Phase 2, Lindisfarne Regl Trng Partnership, 2009–18. *Publications:* Blasphemy and the Law, 1993; Abortion and the Law, 2002; The Supervision of Anglican Curates, 2011; contrib. Anvil jl. *Address:* 45 Milbank Road, Darlington DL3 9NL. *E:* Archdeacon.of.auckland@durham.anglican.org.

**SIMPSON, Robert Brian;** Chairman, Antenna Audio Ltd, 2001–03; *b* 12 Sept. 1944; *s* of Harold and Clara Simpson; *m* 1966, Vivienne Jones; three *s*. *Educ:* Liverpool Inst.; University Coll. London (BA 1966). Asst to Marketing Dir, Holt, Rinehart & Winston (Publishers) Ltd, 1966–68; Asst Develt Manager, later Develt Manager, and Dep. Hd of Inf. Services, Consumers' Assoc., 1968–73; Marketing Manager, Universal News Services Ltd, 1973–74; Marketing Dir, later Man. Dir, University Microfilms Internat. Ltd, 1974–79; Marketing and Develt Manager, later Commercial Manager, Press Assoc., 1979–86; Chief Exec., Universal News Services Ltd, 1986–90; Chm. and Chief Exec., PNA Ltd, 1989–90; Chief Exec., The Press Assoc. Ltd, 1990–2000 (Dir, 1989–2000). Chairman: Two-Ten Communications Ltd, 1990–99; Tellex Monitors Ltd, 1990–99; PA News Ltd, 1994–2000; PA Listings Ltd, 1996–2000; PA WeatherCentre Ltd, 1997–2000; Director: Canada NewsWire, 1986–2000; PA Sporting Life Ltd, 1996–2000; World Assoc. of Newspapers, 1997–2000. Pres., Eur. Alliance of Press Agencies, 1998–99 (Mem., 1990–2000); Mem. Council, CPU, 1995–2000. *Recreations:* music, walking, reading, gardening.

**SIMPSON, Robert Watson, (Robin);** Director, Brewers and Licensed Retailers Association (formerly Brewers' Society), 1993–98; *b* 14 June 1940; *s* of Robert Simpson and Susan Simpson (née Rolland). *Educ:* Perth Academy; University of St Andrews (BSc Hons). Board of Trade (Patent Office), 1962; Dept of Trade (Aviation), 1973; Dept of Industry (Indust. Develt Unit), 1976; Dept of Trade (Shipping), 1979; Department of Trade and Industry: (Management Services and Manpower), 1982; Under Sec., and NE Regl Dir, 1986; Head, Business Task Force Div. (incl. Envmt Unit), 1990–92; Head, Steel, Metals and Minerals Div., 1992. JP W London, 2001–07. *Recreations:* history, commemorative pottery.

**SIMPSON, Robin Muschamp Garry;** QC 1971; *b* 19 June 1927; *s* of Ronald Maitland Simpson, actor and Isla Maravan Simpson (née Muschamp); *m* 1st, 1956, Avril Carolyn Harrisson; one *s* one *d*; 2nd, 1968, Mary Faith Laughton-Scott; one *s* one *d*. *Educ:* Charterhouse; Peterhouse, Cambridge (MA). Called to Bar, Middle Temple, 1951, Bencher, 1979; SE Circuit; former Mem., Surrey and S London Sessions; a Recorder of the Crown Court, 1976–86. Mem., CCC Bar Mess. Appeal Steward, British Boxing Bd of Control. Mem., Friends of Hardwick. *Recreation:* Real tennis (Mem., Dedanists Club). *Address:* 116 Station Road, Barnes, SW13 0NB. *T:* (020) 8878 9898. *Clubs:* Pratt's, MCC.

**SIMPSON, Sir Roderick Alexander C.;** *see* Cordy-Simpson.

**SIMPSON, Sally Anne;** *see* Hatfield, S. A.

**SIMPSON, Prof. Stephen James,** AC 2015; PhD; FRS 2013; FAA; Professor, School of Life and Environmental Sciences (formerly of Biological Sciences), since 2005, and Academic Director, Charles Perkins Centre, since 2012, University of Sydney; Executive Director, Obesity Australia, since 2014; *b* 26 June 1957; *s* of Arthur Leonard and Patricia Simpson; *m* 1984, Lesley Kathryn Dowie; two *s*. *Educ:* C of E Grammar Sch., Brisbane; Univ. of Queensland (BSc Hons 1978); King's Coll., London (PhD 1982); MA Oxon 1986. FAA 2007. Univ. of Qld Travelling Schol., 1979–82; University of Oxford: MRC Post-doctoral Res. Associate, Dept of Exptl Psychol., 1982–83; Demonstrator, Dept of Zool., 1983–86; Lectr in Entomol., 1986–98 and Curator, 1986–2005, Hope Entomol Collections; Reader in Zool., 1996–98; Prof., 1998–2004; Vis. Prof., 2005–08; Associate Hd, Dept of Zool., 2000–04; Principal Curator, Univ. Mus. of Natural Hist., 1989–92; Fellow, Linacre Coll., 1986–88, Jesus Coll., 1988–2004, Oxford; Aust. Res. Council Federation Fellow, 2005–10, Aust. Res. Council Laureate Fellow, 2010–14, Sch. of Biol Scis, Univ. of Sydney. Guest Prof. in Animal Behaviour, Univ. of Basel, 1990; Dist. Vis. Prof., Univ. of Arizona, 1999. Fellow, Wissenschaftskolleg (Inst. for Advanced Study), Berlin, 2002–03. FRSN 2015. Hon. FRES 2013. NSW Scientist of Year, NSW State Govt, 2009; Wigglesworth Medal, Royal Entomological Soc. of London, 2011. *Publications:* The Right Fly, 1996 (US edn as Angler's Fly Identifier, 1996); Anglers' Flies, 1997; The Nature of Nutrition: a unifying framework from animal adaptation to human obesity, 2012; ed books and scientific papers. *Recreations:* fishing, cookery. *Address:* Charles Perkins Centre, D17, University of Sydney, NSW 2006, Australia.

**SIMPSON, Susan Margaret;** *see* Haird, S. M.

**SIMPSON, Prof. Thomas James,** PhD, DSc; FRS 2001; CChem, FRSC; FRSE; Professor of Organic Chemistry, since 1990, Alfred Capper Pass Professor of Chemistry, since 2005, University of Bristol; *b* 23 Feb. 1947; *s* of Thomas Simpson and Hughina Ross Hay; *m* 1st, 1972, Elizabeth Crosthwaite Nattrass; one *s* one *d*; 2nd, 1987, Prof. Mary Norval. *Educ:* Univ. of Edinburgh (BSc 1st Cl. Hons 1969; Macfarlan-Smith Prize; DSc 1986); Univ. of Bristol (PhD 1973). Sen. Univ. Demonstrator, Dept of Organic Chem., Univ. of Liverpool, 1973–74; Research Fellow: Res. Sch. of Chem., ANU, 1974–76; Dept of Organic Chem., Univ. of Liverpool, 1977–78; Lectr, Dept of Chem., Univ. of Edinburgh, 1978–88; Prof. of Organic Chem., Univ. of Leicester, 1988–89. Royal Society of Chemistry: Tilden Lectr, 2001; Simonsen Lectr, 2002; Hugo Müller Lectr, 2004; Mem., Perkin Council, 1989–96 (Vice-Pres., 1993–95); Mem., 1989–93, Chm., 1993–96, Perkin Div. Standing Cttee on Meetings; Chm., Internat. Adv. Bd, Natural Products Reports; Mem., Editl Bd, Chem. in Britain, 1994–2000. FRSE 2006. Hon. DSc Edinburgh, 2015. Corday-Morgan Medal and Prize, 1984; Natural Products Chemistry Medal, 2007, Rita and John Cornforth Award, 2013, RSC; Sir James Black Medal, RSE, 2017. *Publications:* contrib. numerous original papers and review articles. *Recreations:* mountain walking, food and wine. *Address:* School of Chemistry, University of Bristol, Bristol BS8 1TS. *T:* (0117) 928 7656.

**SIMPSON, William George;** international library and heritage consultant, since 2008; Director of the John Rylands Library and University Librarian, University of Manchester, 2002–07; *b* 27 June 1945; *s* of William Anion Simpson and Sarah Jane Simpson; *m* 1968, Margaret Lilian Pollard; two *d*. *Educ:* Liverpool Inst.; Univ. of Liverpool (BA); MA Dublin 1995. MCLIP. Gilroy Scholar in Semitic Languages, Univ. of Aberdeen, 1968; Asst Librarian, Univ. of Durham, 1969–73; Asst Librarian, Sub-Librarian and Senior Sub-Librarian, John Rylands Univ. Library of Manchester, 1973–85; University Librarian: Surrey, 1985–90; London, 1990–94; Librarian and Coll. Archivist, TCD, 1994–2002. Chairman: Guildford Inst., 1987–90; Amer. Studies Library Gp, 1992–94; Mem., Humanities and Social Scis Adv. Cttee, 1991–92, London Adv. Cttee, 1992–94, British Library; Dir, Consortium of University Res. Libraries, 1992–97 and 2003–05; Curator, Oxford Univ. Libraries, 2002–07. UK Advr to British Univ. in Egypt, 2008–11. Dir, IRIS, 1994–2003; Member: An Chomhairle Leabharlanna (Liby Council of Ireland), 1995–2002; Council for Library Co-operation, 1995–2002 (Chm., 1998–2000); Nat. Preservation Adv. Cttee, 1994–96; Nat. Preservation Office Mgt Cttee, 1996–2002 (Chm., 1999–2002); Working Gp on UK Literary Heritage, 2005–08; Chairman: CONUL, 1997–99; Standing Cttee on Legal Deposit, 1999–2001; Sec., Div. of Library Mgt and Admin, LIBER, 2002–07. Fellow, Salzburg Foundn, 2004–. Trustee: Worth Library, 1997–; The People's History Mus., 2003–05; Working Class Movement Library, 2007–17; Frome Heritage Mus., 2014–18 (Vice-Chm., 2015–18; Special Advr, 2018–). Mem., Internat. Editl Bd, Jl of Library Administration, 2004–12. FRSA 1988. Jubilee Medal, Charles Univ., Prague, 1998. *Publications:* Libraries, Languages and the Interpretation of the Past, 1988; articles in learned and professional jls and press. *Recreations:* astronomy, genealogy, languages, travel, Everton FC. *Address:* 1 Woolmer Villas, Petersfield Road, Greatham, Liss, Hants GU33 6AY.

**SIMPSON, Prof. (William) James,** PhD; Donald P. and Katherine B. Loker Professor of English and American Literature and Language, Harvard University, since 2006 (Professor of English and American Literature and Language, 2004–06); *b* 16 March 1954; *s* of R. C. Simpson and M. A. Simpson (née MacDougall); *m* 1982, Luisella Maria Brunetti; two *s* one *d*. *Educ:* Scotch Coll., Melbourne; Univ. of Melbourne (BA Hons); St Edmund Hall, Oxford (MPhil); Girton Coll., Cambridge (PhD 1996). Lectr in English Lit., Westfield Coll., Univ. of London, 1981–89; University of Cambridge: Fellow, Girton Coll., 1989–2003; Lectr in English, and Lectr, Girton Coll., 1989–99; Prof. of Medieval and Renaissance English, 1999–2003. *Publications:* Piers Plowman: an introduction to the B-text, 1990; Sciences and the Self in Medieval Poetry, 1995; Reform and Cultural Revolution 1350–1547, 2002; Burning to Read: English fundamentalism and its Reformation opponents, 2007; Under the Hammer: iconoclasm in the Anglo-American tradition, 2010; Permanent Revolution: the Reformation and the illiberal roots of Liberalism, 2019; contrib. articles to Medium Aevum, Rev. English Studies, Speculum, Traditio, Jl Medieval & Early Modern Studies, etc. *Recreation:* conversation. *Address:* Department of English and American Literature and Language, Harvard University, Barker Center, 12 Quincy Street, Cambridge, MA 02138, USA. *E:* jsimpson@fas.harvard.edu.

**SIMS, Prof. Andrew Charles Petter,** MD; FRCP, FRCPsych, FRCPE; Professor of Psychiatry, 1979–2000, Chairman, Division of Psychiatry and Behavioural Sciences in Relation to Medicine, 1994–97, University of Leeds; Consultant Psychiatrist, St James's University Hospital, 1979–2000; *b* 5 Nov. 1938; *s* of late Dr Charles Henry Sims and Dr Norah Winifred Kennan Sims (née Petter); *m* 1964, Ruth Marie Harvey; two *s* two *d*. *Educ:* Monkton Combe Sch.; Emmanuel Coll., Cambridge (MA; MD 1973); Westminster Hosp. DObstRCOG; FRCPsych 1979; FRCPE 1993; FRCP 1997. House Surgeon, Westminster Hosp., 1963–64; Registrar in Psychiatry, Manchester Royal Infirmary, 1966–69; Consultant Psychiatrist, All Saints Hosp., Birmingham, 1971–76; Sen. Lectr, Univ. of Birmingham, 1976–79; Head of Dept of Psychiatry, Univ. of Leeds, 1980–83, 1986–89, 1994–97. Royal College of Psychiatrists: Sub-Dean, 1984–87; Dean, 1987–90; Pres., 1990–93; Dir, Continuing Professional Develt, 1993–97; Chm., Spirituality and Psychiatry Special Interest Gp, 2003–05. Chairman: Confidential Inquiry into Homicides and Suicides by Mentally Ill People, 1993–96; Schizophrenia Cttee, Clinical Standards Adv. Gp, DoH, 1994–95; Health Adv. Service 2000, 1997–98. Mem., GMC, 1994–99. Lay Co-Chair, Bridgenorth Deanery, Dio. Hereford, 2014–17. Patron: John Young Foundation, 1991–2016; Assoc. for Pastoral Care in Mental Health, 1994–; Interhealth, 1998–; Leeds Faith in Schs, 2011–. Hon. FCPS (Pak) 1994; Hon. FCMSA 1997. MD Lambeth, 1995. Editor: Advances in Psychiatric Treatment, 1994–2003; Developing Mental Health, 2002–05. *Publications:* Neurosis in Society, 1983; Psychiatry (Concise Medical Textbooks), 5th edn (with Sir William Trethowan), 1983, 6th edn (with D. Owens), 1993; (with W. I. Hume) Lecture Notes in Behavioural Sciences, 1984; Symptoms in the Mind: introduction to descriptive psychopathology, 1988 (Italian edn 1993, Portuguese edn 2000, Korean edn 2008, Japanese edn 2009), 3rd edn 2002; (with R. P. Snaith) Anxiety in Clinical Practice, 1988 (German edn 1993); Speech and Language Disorders in Psychiatry, 1995; (with C. Williams) Disorders of Volition, 1999; Is Faith Delusion?, 2009 (Dutch edn 2010); (ed with C. C. H. Cook and A. Powell) Spirituality and Psychiatry, 2009; (ed with C. C. H. Cook and A. Powell) Spiritual Narrative in Psychiatric Practice, 2016; (with P. Martinez) Mad or God?: Jesus the healthiest mind of all, 2018. *Recreations:* gardening, music, theatre, walking. *Address:* Church Farm House, Alveley, Bridgnorth, Shropshire WV15 6ND. *Clubs:* Christian Medical Fellowship, Royal Society of Medicine.

**SIMS, Prof. Christopher A.,** PhD; Professor of Economics, since 1999, and John J. F. Sherrerd '52 University Professor of Economics, since 2012, Princeton University; *b* Washington, DC, 21 Oct. 1942; *s* of Albert Sims and Ruth Sims (née Leiserson); *m* 1967, Catherine Sears; one *s* two *d*. *Educ:* Harvard Coll. (BA Maths 1963); Univ. of Calif, Berkeley; Harvard Univ. (PhD Econs 1968). Instructor in econs, 1967–68, Asst Prof. of Econs, 1968–70, Harvard Univ.; Associate Prof. of Econs, 1970–74, Prof. of Econs, 1974–90, Univ. of Minnesota; Henry Ford II Prof. of Econs, Yale Univ., 1990–99; Harold

H. Helm '20 Prof. of Econs, Princeton Univ., 2004–12. Visiting Professor: Yale Univ., 1974; MIT, 1979–80; Visiting Scholar: Fed. Reserve Bank of Atlanta, 1995–; Fed. Reserve Bank of NY, 1994–97, 2004– (Resident Schol., 2012–13); Fed. Reserve Bank of Philadelphia, 2000–03; IMF, 2003–. Consultant: Fed. Reserve Bank of Minneapolis, 1983 and 1986–87; Fed. Nat. Mortgage Assoc., 1999–2002. President: Econometric Soc., 1995 (Fellow 1975); Amer. Econ. Assoc., 2012. Member: Amer. Acad. Arts and Scis, 1988; NAS, 1989. (Jtly) Nobel Prize in Econ. Scis, 2011. *Publications:* contribs to learned jls incl. Rev. Econs and Stats, Econometrica, Annals Math. Stats, Amer. Econ. Rev., Jl Amer. Statistical Assoc. *Address:* Department of Economics, Princeton University, 209 Julis Romo Rabinowitz Building, Princeton, NJ 08544–1021, USA.

**SIMS, Ven. Christopher Sidney;** Archdeacon of Walsall, 2009–14, now Archdeacon Emeritus; *b* Shipley, W Yorks, 9 Sept. 1949; *s of* Rev. Sidney Sims and Dorothy Sims; *m* 1972, Catherine Virginia Thomson; three *s*. *Educ:* Wycliffe Hall, Oxford (Cert. Theol.). Ordained deacon, 1977, priest, 1978; Asst Curate, St John the Evangelist, Walmley, Sutton Coldfield, 1977–80; Vicar: St Cyprian with St Chad, Hay Mill, Birmingham, 1980–88; St Michael, Stanwix, with St Mark, Belah, Carlisle, 1988–96; Rural Dean, Carlisle, 1990–95; Priest-in-charge, Allhallows and Torpenhow, Boltongate with Ireby and Uldale, Bassenthwaite with Isel and Setmurthy, 1996–2001; Team Rector, Binsey Team Ministry, Cumbria, 2001–03; Vicar, Shrewsbury Abbey and St Peter, Monkmoor, 2003–09; Rural Dean, Shrewsbury, 2008–09. Hon. Canon, Carlisle Cathedral, 1991–96. *Recreations:* cricket, football, self-confessed petrol head.

**SIMS, Prof. Mark Rayner,** PhD; Professor of Astrobiology and Space Instrumentation, University of Leicester, since 2008; *b* Bristol, 10 Feb. 1956; *s of* Norman and Sheila Sims. *Educ:* Wellsway Sch., Keynsham, Bristol; Univ. of Leicester (BSc Physics with Astrophysics 1977; PhD 1982). Res. Fellow, ESA, 1981–84; Res. Associate, 1984–91, Res. Fellow, 1991–2008, Beagle 2 (Mars Lander) Mission Manager, 2008–14, Space Res. Dir, 2014–, Univ. of Leicester. *Publications:* contribs to scientific and technical jls. *Recreations:* birdwatching, photography, walking, golf, dancing, badminton. *Address:* Space Research Centre, Department of Physics and Astronomy, University of Leicester, Leicester LE1 7RH. *T:* (0116) 252 3513. *E:* mrs@le.ac.uk.

**SIMS, Sir Roger (Edward),** Kt 1996; JP; *b* 27 Jan. 1930; *s of* late Herbert William Sims and Annie Amy Savidge; *m* 1957, Angela Mathews (*d* 2015); two *s* one *d*. *Educ:* City Boys' Grammar Sch., Leicester; St Olave's Grammar Sch., London. MCInstM. National Service, 1948–50. Coutts & Co., 1950–51; Campbell Booker Carter Ltd, 1953–62; Dodwell & Co. Ltd, 1962–90; Dir, Inchcape International Ltd, 1981–90. Contested (C) Shoreditch and Finsbury, 1966 and 1970. MP (C) Chislehurst, Feb. 1974–1997. PPS to Home Sec., 1979–83. Mem., Nat. Commn of Inquiry into the Prevention of Child Abuse, 1995–96. Mem., GMC, 1989–99. Mem., Central Exec. Cttee, NSPCC, 1980–93. Chm., Bromley Voluntary Sector Trust, 1997–2001. Mem. Chislehurst and Sidcup UDC, 1956–62. JP Bromley, 1960–72 (Dep. Chm. 1970–72); Chm., Juvenile Panel, 1971–72. *Recreations:* swimming; music, especially singing (Mem. Royal Choral Soc., 1950–2008). *Address:* 68 Towncourt Crescent, Petts Wood, Orpington, Kent BR5 1PJ.

**SIMS, Sonia Lisa;** a District Judge (Magistrates' Courts), since 2002; Designated District Judge for Stratford, since 2011, and for East London, since 2012; *b* 8 Jan. 1957; *d of* Beryl Leonora Sims (*née* Lang). *Educ:* St John of Jerusalem Primary Sch.; Dalston Co. Grammar Sch.; Kingsway Princeton Coll.; City of London Poly. Trainee legal executive: Richard Sandler & Co., 1975–77; Rance & Co., 1978–81; Legal Exec., then Asst Solicitor, 1981–88, Partner, 1988–98, Whitelock & Storr; Consultant, Traymans, 1998–2002. Dep. Dist Judge, 1998–2002. Member: London Criminal Courts Cttee, 1999–2003; Criminal Justice Council, 2011–. Mem., Legal Aid Rev. Cttee (formerly Legal Aid Bd), Legal Services Commn, 1989– (Chm., 1995–2002). Mem., Local Cttee, Highbury and City, 1989–2002, Regl Mem., City of London, 1999–2000, Duty Solicitor Schemes. Associate, 1978, and Fellow, 1984, Inst. Legal Execs. *Recreations:* dance, music, travelling, good food, good wine and song, humour, all things of a Latin flavour, friends, children, animals, a challenge. *Address:* c/o Thames Magistrates' Court, 58 Bow Road, E3 4DJ. *T:* (020) 8271 1252.

**SIMS-WILLIAMS, Prof. Nicholas John,** PhD; FBA 1988; Research Professor of Iranian and Central Asian Studies, School of Oriental and African Studies, University of London, 2004–07 and 2012–15, now Emeritus (Professorial Research Associate, 2008–12); *b* 11 April 1949; twin *s of* late Rev. M. V. S. Sims-Williams; *m* 1972, Ursula Mary Judith, *d of* late Prof. Hugh Seton-Watson, CBE, FBA; two *d*. *Educ:* Trinity Hall, Cambridge (BA, MA; PhD 1978). Res. Fellow, Gonville and Caius Coll., Cambridge, 1975–76; SOAS, University of London: Lectr in Iranian Langs, 1976–89; Reader in Iranian Studies, 1989–94; Prof. of Iranian and Central Asian Studies, 1994–2004. Visiting Professor: Collège de France, 1998–99; Macquarie Univ., 1998–2000; Univ. of Rome 'La Sapienza', 2001. British Acad. Res. Reader, 1992–94; Leverhulme Major Res. Fellow, 2002–04. MAE 2012. Corresp. Mem., Austrian Acad. of Scis, 1999; Associé Etranger, Acad. des Inscriptions et Belles Lettres, Inst de France, 2002; Mem., Amer. Philosophical Soc., 2014. Hon. Mem., Amer. Oriental Soc., 2011. Hirayama Prize for Silk Road Studies, 1996; Denis Sinor Medal for Inner Asian Studies, RAS, 2015; Farabi Internat. Award (Iran), 2019. *Publications:* The Christian Sogdian manuscript C2, 1985 (Prix Ghirshman, Inst. de France, 1988); Sogdian and other Iranian Inscriptions of the Upper Indus, vol. I, 1989, vol. II, 1992; (with James Hamilton) Documents turco-sogdiens du IXe–Xe siècle de Touen-houang, 1990, rev. edn in English as Turco-Sogdian documents from 9th–10th century Dunhuang, 2015; Partita, 1993; Serenade, 1997; New Light on Ancient Afghanistan: the decipherment of Bactrian, 1997; Bactrian Documents from Northern Afghanistan, vol. I, 2001, rev. edn 2012, vol. II, 2007 (World Prize for Book of the Year, Iran, 2009), vol. III, 2012; In Memoriam (string trio), 2002; Bactrian Personal Names, 2010; (with Judith A. Lerner) Seals, Sealings and Tokens from Bactria to Gandhara, 2011; (with D. Durkin-Meistererernst) Dictionary of Manichaean Sogdian and Bactrian, 2012; Iranian manuscripts in Syriac script in the Berlin Turfan collection, 2012; Biblical and Other Christian Sogdian Texts from the Turfan Collection, 2014; The Life of Serapion and other Christian Sogdian texts from the manuscripts E25 and E26, 2015; A Dictionary: Christian Sogdian, Syriac and English, 2016; An Ascetic Miscellany: the Christian Sogdian manuscript E28, 2017; (with F. de Blois) Studies in the Chronology of the Bactrian Documents from Northern Afghanistan, 2018; (with Bi Bo) Sogdian Documents from Khotan in the Museum of Renmin University of China, 2018; From Liturgy to Pharmacology: Christian Sogdian texts from the Turfan Collection, 2019; *festschrift:* Exegisti Monumenta, ed W. Sundermann, A. Hintze and F. de Blois, 2009; contrib. on Iranian and Central Asian langs and culture to learned jls. *Recreation:* music. *Address:* 11 Park Parade, Cambridge CB5 8AL. *E:* ns5@soas.ac.uk.

*See also* P. P. Sims-Williams.

**SIMS-WILLIAMS, Prof. Patrick Philip,** PhD; FBA 1996; Professor of Celtic Studies, Aberystwyth University (formerly University College of Wales, Aberystwyth, then University of Wales, Aberystwyth), 1994–2014, now Emeritus; *b* 11 April 1949; twin *s of* late Rev. Michael Sims-Williams and Kathleen (*née* Wenborn); *m* 1986, Prof. Marged Haycock; one *s* one *d*. *Educ:* Borden GS, Sittingbourne; Trinity Hall, Cambridge (BA 1972; MA 1975); PhD Birmingham 1980. Cambridge University: Lectr, Dept of Anglo-Saxon, Norse and Celtic, 1977–93; British Acad. Res. Reader, 1988–90; Reader in Celtic and Anglo-Saxon, 1993; Fellow, St John's Coll., 1977–93. O'Donnell Lectr, Oxford Univ., 1981–82, Edinburgh Univ., 1986, Univ. of Wales, 2000–01; Bergin Lectr, UCD, 2015. Leverhulme Major Res. Fellow, 2003–06. Dir, British Acad. proj., The Development of the Welsh Language, 2007–. Mem., Royal Commn on Ancient and Historical Monuments of Wales, 1998–2008. Council Member: Irish Texts Soc., 1991–97; Philological Soc., 1997–2000 and 2016–; British Acad., 2012–15; Pres., Internat. Congress of Celtic Studies, 2011–. Editor, Cambrian Medieval Celtic Studies, 1981–. Gollancz Prize, British Acad., 1992; Antiquity Prize, 1998; G. T. Clark Award, Cambrian Archaeol Assoc., 2007; Vernam Hull Prize, Univ. of Wales, 2011. *Publications:* Religion and Literature in Western England 600–800, 1990; Britain and Early Christian Europe, 1995; Ptolemy: towards a linguistic atlas of the earliest Celtic place-names of Europe, 2000; The Celtic Inscriptions of Britain, 2003; New Approaches to Celtic Place-names in Ptolemy's Geography, 2005; Ancient Celtic Place-names in Europe and Asia Minor, 2006; The Iron House in Ireland, 2006; (with Georges Cousin) Additions to Alfred Holder's Celtic Thesaurus, 2006; Studies on Celtic Languages Before the Year 1000, 2007; (with M. E. Raybould) The Geography of Celtic Personal Names in the Latin Inscriptions of the Roman Empire, 2007; (with M. E. Raybould) A Corpus of Latin Inscriptions of the Roman Empire Containing Celtic Personal Names, 2007, Introduction and Supplement, 2009; Irish Influence on Medieval Welsh Literature, 2010; Rhai Addasiadau Cymraeg Canol o Sieffre o Fynwy, 2011; Liber Coronacionis Britanorum, 2017; Liber Coronacionis Britanorum: a Welsh version of Geoffrey of Monmouth, II: introduction and commentary, 2017; Buchedd Beuno: the Middle Welsh life of St Beuno, 2018; The Book of Llandaf as a Historical Source, 2019. *Recreations:* music, sailing, carpentry. *Address:* Department of Welsh and Celtic Studies, Aberystwyth University, Aberystwyth SY23 3AJ.

*See also* N. J. Sims-Williams.

**SINCLAIR,** family name of **Earl of Caithness, Viscount Thurso** and **Baron Sinclair of Cleeve**.

**SINCLAIR,** 18th Lord *cr* 1449 (Scot.); **Matthew Murray Kennedy St Clair;** DL; Director, Saint Property Ltd, since 2001; *b* 9 Dec. 1968; *s of* 17th Lord Sinclair, CVO and of Anne Lettice, *yr d of* Sir Richard Cotterell, 5th Bt, CBE; *S* father, 2004; *m* 2005, Laura Cicely, *y d of* Jonathan Coode, DL; two *s*. *Educ:* Glenalmond; RAC Cirencester. MRICS. *Heir: s* Harry Murray Kennedy St Clair, Master of Sinclair, *b* 6 Oct. 2007. *Address:* Knocknalling, St Johns Town of Dalry, Castle Douglas DG7 3ST. *E:* mstc@saintproperty.com. *Club:* New (Edinburgh).

**SINCLAIR OF CLEEVE,** 3rd Baron *cr* 1957, of Cleeve, Somerset; **John Lawrence Robert Sinclair;** *b* 6 Jan. 1953; *s of* 2nd Baron Sinclair of Cleeve, OBE, and Patricia, *d of* late Major Lawrence Hellyer; *S* father, 1985; one *d*. *Educ:* Winchester College; Manchester Univ. Technical support and Gov., an Inner London comprehensive sch., 1984–94. Founding Mem. and Sec., Hackney Local Economic Trading System, 1992. Interest in archaeology and campaigning. *Recreations:* motor cycling, mime, music, construction, design, marathons.

**SINCLAIR, Angus Hugh;** Secretary to the Speaker, House of Commons, 2005–10; *b* 4 Nov. 1952; *s of* late Dr Hugh Melville Sinclair and Diana Grieve; *m* 1981 (marr. diss. 2002); one *s* one *d*. *Educ:* Merchiston Castle Sch.; Durham Univ. (BA Hons Geog. 1974). Asst Master, Wellingborough Sch., 1975; joined RN, 1975; served submarines and surface ships; Comdr (Trng) Britannia RNC, 1993–95; Sec. C-in-C Fleet, 1995–99; Naval Attaché, Rome, 1999–2002; Defence Attaché, Malta, 2001–02; Dir, RN Logistics, 2002–05. Editor: Encyclopaedia Britannica, 1993–95; Norsworthy's Epitome, 1996–97. *Recreations:* endeavouring to persevere, striving for parsimony. *Clubs:* Royal Navy of 1919, Naval; Moffat Cricket.

**SINCLAIR, Prof. Anthony Ronald Entrican,** DPhil; FRS 2002; FRSC; Professor of Zoology, University of British Columbia, 1987–2009, now Emeritus; *b* 25 March 1944; *s of* Sir Ronald Ormiston Sinclair, KBE and Ellen Isobelle Sinclair; *m* 1966, Anne Catherine Begbie; two *d*. *Educ:* Pembroke Coll., Oxford (BA 1966, MA 1970; DPhil 1970). Res. Officer, Animal Behaviour Res. Gp, Oxford Univ., 1970; Staff Ecologist, Serengeti Res. Inst., Tanzania, 1970–73; Res. Scientist, Div. of Ecol. and Wildlife, CSIRO, Australia, 1973–75; University of British Columbia: Asst Prof., 1975–81, Associate Prof., 1981–87, Dept of Zool.; Dir, Centre for Biodiversity Res., 1996–2002. FRSC 1996. Aldo Leopold Medal, Wildlife Soc., 2013. *Publications:* The African Buffalo, 1977; (ed with M. Norton-Griffiths) Serengeti, 1979, 2nd edn 1995; (with G. Caughley) Wildlife Ecology, 1994; (ed with P. Arcese) Serengeti II, 1995; (ed jtly) Conserving Nature's Diversity, 2000; (with J. Fryxell and G. Caughley) Wildlife Ecology, Conservation and Management, 2006, 3rd edn 2014; (ed with C. Packer, S. Mduma and J. Fryxell) Serengeti III, 2008; Serengeti Story, 2012; (ed jtly) Serengeti IV, 2015; contrib. scientific papers concerning ecology and conservation to leading jls, incl. Jl Animal Ecol., Ecol., Nature, Science. *Address:* Department of Zoology, University of British Columbia, 6270 University Boulevard, Vancouver, BC V6T 1Z4, Canada. *T:* (604) 2751563, *Fax:* (604) 8222416. *E:* sinclair@zoology.ubc.ca.

**SINCLAIR, Carolyn Elizabeth Cunningham, (Mrs S. J. Bowen);** Director, Constitutional and Community Policy Directorate, and Registrar of the Baronetage, Home Office, 1996–2001; *b* 13 July 1944; *d of* John Archibald Sinclair and Grace Margaret Stuart Sinclair (*née* Cunningham); *m* 1979, Stephen John Bowen. *Educ:* Laurel Bank Sch., Glasgow; Brown Univ., RI; Edinburgh Univ. (MA Hist.); Univ. of E Africa (Leverhulme Schol.; MA Pol Sci.). Joined FCO, 1968; Vienna, 1970–73; Private Sec. to Minister of State, 1977–78; transferred to HM Treasury, 1979; Prime Minister's Policy Unit, 1988–92; transf. to Home Office, as Asst Under-Sec. of State, 1992. *Recreations:* gardening, listening to music, reading, seeing friends.

**SINCLAIR, Charles James Francis,** CBE 2009; Warden, Winchester College, 2014–19 (Fellow, 2010); *b* 4 April 1948; *s of* Sir George (Evelyn) Sinclair, CMG, OBE and Katharine Jane Sinclair (*née* Burdekin); *m* 1974, Nicola Bayliss; two *s*. *Educ:* Winchester Coll.; Magdalen Coll., Oxford (BA). ACA 1974, FCA 1980. VSO, Zambia, 1966–67. Dearden Farrow, CA, 1970–75; joined Associated Newspapers Holdings, 1975; Asst Man. Dir and Mem. Main Bd, 1986; Man. Dir, 1988 (Associated Newspapers Holdings became the wholly-owned operating subsid. of Daily Mail and General Trust, 1988); Gp Chief Exec., Daily Mail and General Trust plc, 1988–2008. Non-executive Director: Euromoney Institutional Investor PLC, 1989–2008; Schroders plc, 1990–2004; Reuters Group plc, 1994–2005; SVG Capital plc, 2005–13; Associated British Foods plc, 2008–18 (Chm., 2009–18); Mem., UK Adv. Bd, Spencer Stuart, 2006–12 (Chm., 2009–12). Chm. of Trustees, Minack Theatre Trust, Porthcurno, Cornwall, 1985–; Mem., UK Cttee, VSO, 2006–11. Mem., Adv. Bd, Reuters Inst. for Study of Journalism, Univ. of Oxford, 2007–10. Gov., Courtauld Inst. of Art, 2011–14. *Recreations:* theatre, opera, fishing. *Clubs:* Athenæum; Vincent's (Oxford).

**SINCLAIR, Sir Clive (Marles),** Kt 1983; Chairman, Sinclair Research Ltd, since 1979; *b* 30 July 1940; *s of* late George William Carter Sinclair and Thora Edith Ella (*née* Marles); *m* 1st, 1962, Ann (*née* Trevor Briscoe) (marr. diss. 1985; she *d* 2004); two *s* one *d*; 2nd, 2010, Angie Bowness. *Educ:* Boxgrove Prep. Sch., Guildford; Highgate; Reading; St George's

Coll., Weybridge. Editor, Bernards Publishers Ltd, 1958–61; Chairman: Sinclair Radionics Ltd, 1962–79; Sinclair Browne Ltd, 1981–85; Cambridge Computer Ltd, 1986–90; Dir, Shaye Communications Ltd, 1986–91. Vis. Fellow, Robinson Coll., Cambridge, 1982–85; Vis. Prof., Dept of Elec. Engrg, Imperial Coll. of Science, Technol. and Medicine, London, 1984–92 (Hon. Fellow, 1984). Chm., British Mensa, 1980–97 (Hon. Pres., 2001–). Hon. Fellow UMIST, 1984. Hon. DSc: Bath, 1983; Warwick, 1983; Heriot-Watt, 1983. Mullard Award, Royal Soc., 1984. *Publications:* Practical Transistor Receivers, 1959; British Semiconductor Survey, 1963. *Recreations:* music, poetry, mathematics, science, poker. *Address:* 1A Spring Gardens, Trafalgar Square, SW1A 2BB. *T:* (office) (020) 7839 6868, *Fax:* (020) 7839 6622, *T:* (home) (020) 7839 7744. *Clubs:* National Liberal, Royal Automobile.

**SINCLAIR, Fiona Mary;** QC 2013; *b* Chester; *d* of John Mark Sinclair and Emily Georgina Sinclair; one *s. Educ:* Jesus Coll., Cambridge (BA 1987; LLM 1998). Called to the Bar, Inner Temple, 1989; Mem., Lincoln's Inn, 2000–; in practice as a barrister, specialising in internat. and domestic construction, professional liability and insurance dispute resolution. *Publications:* (ed) Jackson and Powell on Professional Negligence, 3rd edn 1992 to 8th edn, as Jackson and Powell on Professional Liability, 2016; (contrib.) Drawing the Thread Together: a festschrift for Lord Justice Jackson, 2018. *Recreations:* ski-ing, mountaineering, Italy. *Address:* 4 Pump Court, Temple, EC4Y 7AN. *T:* (020) 7842 5555. *E:* fsinclair@4pumpcourt.com.

**SINCLAIR, Maj.-Gen. George Brian,** CB 1983; CBE 1975; Engineer-in-Chief (Army), 1980–83; *b* 21 July 1928; *s* of Thomas S. Sinclair and Blanche Sinclair; *m* 1953, Edna Margaret Richardson (*d* 2011); two *s* one *d. Educ:* Christ's College, Finchley; RMA Sandhurst. Commissioned, Royal Engineers, 1948; served UK, BAOR, Korea, and Christmas Island, 1948–66; Directing Staff, Staff College, Camberley, 1967–69; CRE, Near East, 1970–71; Col GS, HQ 1st British Corps, 1972–74; Nat. Defence Coll., India, 1975; Commandant Royal School of Military Engineering, 1976–77; BGS, Military Operations, MoD, 1978–80. Col Comdt, RE, 1983–91; Hon. Col, Engineer and Transport Staff Corps, 1988–93. Vice Pres., Red R (formerly Register of Engrs for Disaster Relief), 1985–98; Trustee: Imperial War Mus., 1990–2000; RE Museum Foundn, 1993–2001. Mem., Smeatonian Soc. of Civil Engrs, 1985–. Governor, King's Sch., Rochester, 1984–97. Freeman, City of London, 1981. DL Kent, 1996–97. *Publications:* The Staff Corps: the history of the Engineer and Logistic Staff Corps RE, 2001, 2nd edn 2015. *Recreations:* bird watching and discussion. *Address:* Brockie's Hole, The Croft, St Boswells, Roxburghshire TD6 0AE. *Club:* Army and Navy (Chm., 1995–97; Trustee, 1999–2006).

**SINCLAIR, Rt Rev. (Gordon) Keith;** *see* Birkenhead, Bishop Suffragan of.

**SINCLAIR, Rt Hon. Ian (McCahon),** AC 2001; PC 1977; Chairman, Foundation for Rural and Regional Renewal, since 1999; *b* 10 June 1929; *s* of George McCahon Sinclair and Gertrude Hazel Sinclair; *m* 1st, 1956, Margaret Tarrant (*d* 1967); one *s* two *d;* 2nd, 1970, Rosemary Fenton; one *s. Educ:* Knox Grammar Sch., Wahroonga, NSW; Sydney Univ. BA, LLB. Barrister; grazier. Mem. Legislative Council, NSW, 1961–63; MP (Nat.) New England, NSW, 1963–98; Minister for: Social Services, 1965–68; Trade and Industry (Minister Assisting Minister), 1966–71; Shipping and Transport, 1968–71; Primary Industry, 1971–72; Leader of House for Opposition, 1974–75; Country Party spokesman for Defence, Foreign Affairs, Law and Agriculture, 1973; Opposition spokesman on primary industry, 1974–75; Leader of House, 1975–79, 1980–82; Minister for: Agriculture and N Territory, Nov.–Dec. 1975; Primary Industry, 1975–78; Special Trade Representations, 1980; Communications, 1980–82; Defence, 1982–83; Leader of the House for the Opposition, 1983–89; Shadow Minister: Defence, 1983–87; Trade and Resources, 1987–89; of State, Jan.–May 1994; Speaker, House of Reps, Australia, 1998. Member Committee: House of Reps Standing Orders, 1974–79, 1980–82, 1983–84; Privileges, 1980–82; Legal and Constitutional Affairs, 1990–98; Jt Foreign Affairs, Defence and Trade, 1990–98 (Chm., 1996–98); Nat. Crime Authority, 1990–98; Member: Jt Standing Cttee on Migration Regulations, 1990–98; Jt Cttee on Corps and Securities, 1990–98; Parly Code of Conduct Working Gp, 1994–96. Perm. Rep., Exec., IPU, 1996–98; Chm., Aust. Parly Gps for UK, PNG, Uruguay and Vietnam, 1996–98. Dep. Leader, 1971–84, Leader, 1984–89, Nat. Party of Australia. Dir, Farmers and Graziers Cooperative Ltd, 1962–65. Chairman: Australian Constitutional Convention, 1998; Australian Rural Summit, 1999; Australian Sheep Cooperative Res. Centre, 2002–07; Co-Chairman: NSW Drugs Summit, 1999; NSW Salinity Summit, 2000; SA Economic Summit, 2003; NSW Health Care Adv. Council, 2005–11. Chairman: Good Beginnings (Australia), 2000–10; Australia Taiwan Business Council, 2000–08; Dir, Regl Australia Inst., 2011–18. President: Austcare, 2000–09; Murray Darling Basin Commn, 2003–08; Scouts Australia (NSW), 2003–. Adjunct Prof. of Social Scis (Pol Sci.), Univ. of New England, 2000–. DUniv New England, 1999; Hon. DLitt Southern Cross, 2005. *Address:* Mulberry Farm, Dumaresq Island, NSW 2430, Australia. *T:* (2) 65538276. *E:* iansinclair@ozemail.com.au. *Clubs:* Australian, Union University and Schools (Sydney).

**SINCLAIR, James Boyd A.;** *see* Alexander-Sinclair.

**SINCLAIR, Rev. Canon Jane Elizabeth Margaret;** Canon of Westminster and Rector of St Margaret's, Westminster Abbey, since 2016; *b* 1956. *Educ:* St Hugh's Coll., Oxford (BA 1978; MA 1980); St John's Coll., Nottingham (BA Nottingham Univ. 1982). Ordained deaconess, 1983, deacon, 1987, priest, 1994; Deaconess, St Paul's, Herne Hill, London, 1983–86; Chaplain, and Lectr in Liturgy and Pastoral Studies, St John's Coll., Nottingham, 1986–93; Canon Residentiary and Precentor, 1993–2003, Hon. Canon, 2003–07, Sheffield Cathedral; Vicar, Rotherham, 2003–07; Sec., Convocation of York, 2005–07; Archdeacon of Stow and Lindsey, 2007–14; Canon Steward, Westminster Abbey, 2014–16. Member: Liturgical Commn of C of E, 1986–2001; Archbishop's Commn on Church Music, 1989–92; Gen. Synod of C of E, 1995–2007; Clergy Discipline Commn, 2013–; Comr, Cathedrals Fabric Commn for England, 2001–10. *Address:* 2 Little Cloister, SW1P 3PL. *E:* jane.sinclair@westminster-abbey.org.

**SINCLAIR, Jeremy Theodorson,** CBE 2017; Chairman, M & C Saatchi plc, since 2004 (Founder and Partner, since 1995); *b* 4 Nov. 1946; *s* of Lilian Theodora Sinclair and Donald Alan Forrester Sinclair; *m* 1976, Jacqueline Margaret Metcalfe; two *s* one *d. Educ:* Rannoch Sch., Perthshire; Watford Art Sch. Saatchi & Saatchi and Co.: Jt Founder, 1970; Dir, 1973–95; Head of Creative Dept, 1973–86; Chairman: Saatchi & Saatchi International, 1986–95. Pres., D&AD, 1987. Chm., Art Acad., 1999–2007; Mem., Exec. Cttee, Sch. of Econ. Sci., London, 1987–2007; Chm., Ind. Educnl Assoc. Ltd, 2007– (Gov., 1999–). Organiser, Art in Action, 2004–14. Trustee: Jyotirnidhi Nyasa Trust, 2000– (Chm., 2017–); Tony Blair Faith Foundn, 2008–18 (Chm., 2015–18). *Publications:* Brutal Simplicity of Thought, 2011; Faces, Faces, Faces, 2015. *Recreations:* philosophy, economics, Italy. *Address:* M & C Saatchi plc, 36 Golden Square, W1F 9EE. *T:* (020) 7543 4500.

**SINCLAIR, Jonathan William Rossiter,** LVO 2007; HM Diplomatic Service; Director, Human Resources, Foreign and Commonwealth Office, since 2018; *m* 2003, Helen Aiken; one *s* two *d. Educ:* Univ. of Oxford (BA PPE); Johns Hopkins Univ. (Masters in Internat. Relns). Entered FCO, 1996; EU Dept (Internal), FCO, 1996–98; Second Sec. (Political), 1999–2000, First Sec. (Political-Mil.), 2000–02, New Delhi; Hd, Eur. Communities Team, FCO, 2002; Private Sec. to Foreign Sec., 2002–04; Hd, Political Team, Washington, 2005–09; Dep. Hd, HR-Recruitment and Promotion, 2009–11, Hd, Intelligence Policy Dept, 2011–13, FCO; Nat. Policy Advr, UKTI, 2013–14; High Comr to NZ and non-resident Gov., Pitcairn, Henderson, Ducie and Oeno Is, 2014–18; Principal Private Sec. to Sec. of State for Foreign and Commonwealth Affairs, 2018. *Address:* c/o Foreign and Commonwealth Office, King Charles Street, SW1A 2AH.

**SINCLAIR, Karen;** Member (Lab) Clwyd South, National Assembly for Wales, 1999–2011; *b* 20 Nov. 1952; *m* 1973, Mike Sinclair; one *s* one *d. Educ:* Grove Park Girls' Sch., Wrexham; Cartrefle Coll., Wrexham. Worked for Youth Service, 1976–90; co-managed community home for learning disabled adults, Wrexham Social Services, 1990–99. CAB Advr, 1995–97. Member (Lab): Glyndwr DC, 1988–95; Denbighshire CC, 1997–99. Minister for Assembly Business, Nat. Assembly for Wales, 2003–05. Mem., N Wales Cancer Forum, 2010–. *Recreations:* reading, gentle walking, family.

**SINCLAIR, Rt Rev. Keith;** *see* Sinclair, Rt Rev. G. K.

**SINCLAIR, Lindsay Neil;** Group Chief Executive, NFU Mutual Insurance Society, since 2008; *b* Palmerston North, NZ, 19 Aug. 1956; *s* of Graeme Sinclair and Ann Sinclair (*née* O'Keeffe); *m* 1984, Janet Scholma; two *d. Educ:* Poole Grammar Sch. ACIB 1990. Bank Officer: Midland Bank, UK, 1974–76; Barclays Internat., UK, France and Netherlands Antilles, 1976–85; Standard Chartered Bank, Bahrain, San Francisco, Hong Kong, Sri Lanka, 1985–95; Sen. Manager, Commercial Banking, Amsterdam, 1996–98, Hd, Intermediary Banking, 1998–99, ING Gp; Hd, Business Develt, 1999–2002, CEO UK, 2002–07, ING Direct. Mem. Bd, Internat. Cooperative and Mutual Insce Fedn, 2008–. Trustee, NFU Mutual Charitable Trust, 2008–. *Recreations:* researching the Pratt family of Castlemartyr 1647–, reading (history and travel), listening to music, walking, the arts. *Address:* NFU Mutual, Tiddington Road, Stratford upon Avon CV37 7BJ. *T:* (01789) 265388. *Club:* Farmers.

**SINCLAIR, Marion Frances;** Chief Executive, Publishing Scotland, since 2008; *b* Glasgow, 17 Feb. 1963; *d* of Iain and Mary Sinclair; *m* 1997, Stephen Webster; three *s. Educ:* Castlebay Junior Secondary Sch., Isle of Barra; Nicolson Inst., Isle of Lewis; Glasgow Univ. (MA Hons English Lit. and French 1986); Stirling Univ. (MPhil Publishing Studies 1988); Edinburgh Univ. (MBA 1996). Editl and marketing asst, Edinburgh Univ. Press, then Polygon, 1988–90; Editl Dir, Polygon, 1990–97; Lectr, Edinburgh Napier Univ., 1997–2003; Business Develt Manager, Publishing Scotland, 2003–08. *Publications:* (ed) Hebridean Odyssey, 1996. *Recreations:* jazz, theatre, cooking, reading, Gaelic culture, history. *Address:* Publishing Scotland, Scott House, 10 South St Andrew Street, Edinburgh EH2 2AZ. *T:* (0131) 228 6866. *E:* marion@publishingscotland.org.

**SINCLAIR, Martin John;** Executive Leader (formerly Assistant Auditor General), National Audit Office, 1999–2015; *b* 24 April 1957; *s* of late Malcolm Sinclair and of Susan Sinclair; *m* 1996, Joke Pouw; one *s* one *d. Educ:* Glasgow Univ. (MPhil Town and Regl Planning). CPFA 1985. Joined Nat. Audit Office, 1981 (Mem., Mgt Bd, 1999–2015). *Recreations:* hill-walking, swimming, reading.

**SINCLAIR, Matthew John Hayes;** Assistant Director, Deloitte LLP, since 2017; *b* Reading, 10 Dec. 1983; *s* of Michael Paul and Michelle Anne Sinclair; *m* 2013, Arianna Capuani; two *s. Educ:* London Sch. of Econs and Pol Sci. (BSc Econs and Econ. Hist.; MSc Econ. Hist.). Taxpayers' Alliance: Policy Analyst, 2007–08; Res. Dir, 2008–12; Chief Exec., 2012–14; Sen. Consultant, Europe Economics, 2014–16; Account Dir, Westbourne Communications, 2016–17. *Publications:* (ed) How to Cut Public Spending and Still Win an Election, 2010; Let Them Eat Carbon: the price of failing climate change policies, and how governments and big business profit from them, 2011. *Address:* Deloitte LLP, 66 Shoe Lane, EC4A 3BQ. *E:* mjsinclair@deloitte.co.uk.

**SINCLAIR, Rt Rev. Maurice Walter;** an Hon. Assistant Bishop, Diocese of Birmingham, since 2002; *b* 20 Jan. 1937; *s* of Maurice and Dorothea Sinclair; *m* 1962, Gillian (*née* Spooner); four *s. Educ:* Chigwell Sch.; Nottingham Univ. (BSc 1959); Leicester Univ. (PGCE 1960); Tyndale Hall, Bristol. Asst Master, Brays Grove County Secondary Sch., Harlow, Essex, 1960–62. Ordained, 1964; Asst Curate, St John's Church, Boscombe, 1964–67; Missionary, South American Missionary Soc., serving in Argentina, 1967–78; Personnel Sec., 1979–83, Asst Gen. Sec., 1983–84, South American Missionary Soc.; Principal, Crowther Hall, Selly Oak Colls, 1984–90; Bp of Northern Argentina, 1990–2001 and Presiding Bp (Primate), Province of Southern Cone of America, 1995–2001. Dean, All Saints Cathedral, Cairo, 2004–05; Hon. Asst Bp, Dio. Egypt, 2009–. Faculty Mem., Alexandria Sch. of Theol., 2006–. Hon. DD Nashotah House Seminary, 2001. Ibo chief, Nigeria, 1987. *Publications:* Green Finger of God, 1980; Ripening Harvest Gathering Storm, 1988; Way of Faithfulness, 1999; To Mend the Net, 2001; Pathways of Wisdom, 2010; From Cradle to Crucible, 2016. *Recreations:* gardening, hill walking, running. *Address:* 55 Selly Wick Drive, Selly Park, Birmingham B29 7JQ. *T:* (0121) 471 2617.

**SINCLAIR, Moira Sarah;** Chief Executive, Paul Hamlyn Foundation, since 2015; *b* London, 11 March 1964; *d* of Harvey Sinclair and Maureen Sinclair (*née* Nelligan); *m* 1993, Julian Millard; one *d. Educ:* Manchester Univ. (BA Hons Drama 1985). Freelance stage manager, 1985–92; Th. Manager, Tricycle Th., 1992–96; Community Leisure Manager, S Beds DC, 1998–2000; Dir, Vital Arts, 2001–05; Arts Council England: Dir, 2005–08, Exec. Dir, 2008–14, London; Exec. Dir for Nat. Strategy and London and SE, 2014–15. Fellow, 2004–05, Chm., 2019–, Clore Leadership. Mem., Adv. Council, British Liby, 2015–. Vice Chm., Mayor's Cultural Leadership Bd, 2017–. Chm., E London Dance Co., 2015–. *Recreations:* theatre, cooking for friends and family, walking despite the rain. *Address:* Paul Hamlyn Foundation, 5–11 Leeke Street, WC1X 9HY. *T:* (020) 4812 3444. *E:* msinclair@phf.org.uk.

**SINCLAIR, Paul;** QC 2018; *b* Bromley, 19 Feb. 1973; *s* of Neil Sinclair and Susan Sinclair (*née* Frazer); *m* 2000, Samantha Louise Foster; two *s* one *d. Educ:* King's Coll. Sch., Wimbledon; Gonville and Caius Coll., Cambridge (BA 1995); Harvard Law Sch. (LLM). Called to the Bar, Middle Temple, 1997; in practice as barrister, specialising in commercial law, 1997–. *Publications:* (contrib.) Commercial Court Procedure, 2001; (contrib.) Bullen and Leake and Jacob's Precedents of Pleadings, 2001, 18th edn 2016; contribs to Jl Internat. Bank and Finance Law. *Recreations:* travel, reading, bridge, piano. *Address:* Fountain Court Chambers, Fountain Court, Temple, EC4Y 9DH. *T:* (020) 7583 3335.

**SINCLAIR, Rear-Adm. the Hon. Peter Ross,** AC 1992 (AO (mil.) 1986); Governor of New South Wales, 1990–96; farmer, Flagship Poll Hereford Stud; *b* 16 Nov. 1934; *s* of late G. P. Sinclair; *m* 1957, Shirley, *d* of J. A. McLellan; one *s* two *d. Educ:* North Sydney Boys' High Sch.; Royal Aust. Naval Coll.; Royal Coll. of Defence Studies. jssc. Joined RAN 1948; served HM Australian ships Australia, Tobruk, Vengeance, Arunta, Swan, Sydney, Vendetta, Vampire, Penguin, HMS Maidstone, HMS Jutland; CO HMAS Duchess, 1970–72; CO HMAS Hobart, 1974–77; Dir, Naval Plans, 1979–80; Dir-Gen., Mil. Staff Branch, Strategic and Internat. Policy Div., Defence Dept, 1980–82; Chief of Staff, 1983–84; First Comdt, Aust. Defence Force Acad., 1984–86; Maritime Comdr Australia, 1986–90 and Dep. Chief of Naval Staff, 1989. Chm. Council, Order of Australia,

1996–2002. Hon. FIEAust 1994; CPEng 1994. DUniv Sydney, 1992. KStJ 1991. *Recreations:* painting, sketching, whittling, reading, cricket, golf, tennis. *Address:* Post Office, Tea Gardens, NSW 2324, Australia.

**SINCLAIR, Sir Robert (John),** Kt 2001; Chairman: Lae Builders & Contractors Ltd, since 1974; Lae International Hotel Ltd, since 1977; *b* 21 Nov. 1943; *s* of William Arthur Sinclair; *m* 1985, Phuong Lan; three *s* two *d*. *Educ:* St Mary's Primary High Sch., PNG. Chm., PNG Post Ltd, 2000–. Chm., PNG Apprenticeship Bd, 1996–. *Recreation:* breeding thoroughbred horses. *Address:* PO Box 1730, Lae, Papua New Guinea. *T:* (675) 4724109, *Fax:* (675) 4725494. *Clubs:* Papua (Port Moresby); Royal Yacht (Lae).

**SINCLAIR, Sonia Elizabeth, (Mrs A. A. Sinclair);** Board Member, Royal Court Theatre, 1974–84; *b* 6 Sept. 1925; *d* of Col R. H. Graham; *m* 1st, 1947, Hon. Julian Mond, later 3rd Baron Melchett (*d* 1973); two *d* (one *s* decd); 2nd, 1984, Andrew Annandale Sinclair (*d* 2019). *Educ:* Royal School, Bath. Board Member: NSPCC, 1960–70; Nat. Theatre, then RNT, 1984–94. JP Marylebone, 1962–72. *Publications:* Tell Me, Honestly, 1964; Someone is Missing, 1987; Passionate Quests, 1991; From the Ganges to the Thames, 2017. *Recreations:* reading, walking, swimming, foreign travel. *Address:* Flat 20, Millennium House, 132 Grosvenor Road, SW1V 3JY. *T:* (020) 7976 6958.

**SINCLAIR, Susan Myraid;** Sheriff of North Strathclyde at Paisley, 2002; *b* 16 Sept. 1958; *d* of William Stevenson Sinclair and Myraid Elizabeth Sinclair; *m* 1983, David Robert Adie. *Educ:* Glasgow Univ. (MA Hons; LLB; DLP). Solicitor, 1983; Advocate, 1988; Pt-time Chm., Appeals Service, 1996–2001; Temp. Sheriff, 1998–99; Pt-time Sheriff, 2000–01; All Scotland Floating Sheriff, 2001–02. Pt-time tutor, Univ. of Glasgow, 1995–97. *Recreations:* sailing, scuba diving, walking, reading, theatre.

**SINCLAIR, Sir William (Robert Francis),** 11th Bt *cr* 1704 (NS), of Dunbeath, Caithness-shire; construction senior site engineer; *b* London, 27 March 1979; *s* of Sir Patrick Robert Richard Sinclair, 10th Bt and of Susan Catherine Beresford Davies, *e d* of Geoffrey Clive Davies, OBE; *S* father, 2011; *m* 2011, Piriyah Sivagnanam, MB BS, BSc, MRCS; one *s* one *d*. *Educ:* Winchester Coll.; Imperial Coll., London; South Bank Univ. (BEng Civil Engrg). Engrg Surveyor, MAL Ltd, 2006–11; Man. Dir, H2I Ltd, 2011–; Sen. Site Engr, Collen Construction Ltd (Ireland), 2018–19. *Recreations:* cricket, cycling, field sports, kites. *Heir: s* Robert (John Pulavan) Sinclair, *b* 6 March 2013. *Address:* Archer House, 209 Greenkeepers Road, Great Denham, Bedford MK40 4RQ.

**SINCLAIR-LOCKHART, Sir Simon (John Edward Francis),** 15th Bt *cr* 1636 (NS); *b* 22 July 1941; *s* of Sir Muir Edward Sinclair-Lockhart, 14th Bt, and of Olga Ann, *d* of late Claude Victor White-Parsons, Hawkes Bay, NZ; *S* father, 1985; *m* 1973, Felicity Edith, *d* of late I. L. C. Stewart, NZ; one *s* one *d* (and one *s* decd). *Heir: yr* twin *s* James Lachlan Sinclair-Lockhart, *b* 12 Sept. 1973. *Address:* 62 Muritai Crescent, Havelock North, Hawke's Bay, New Zealand.

**SINCLAIR-STEVENSON, Christopher Terence;** literary agent, since 1995; *b* 27 June 1939; *s* of late George Sinclair-Stevenson, MBE and Gloria Sinclair-Stevenson; *m* 1965, Deborah Susan (*née* Walker-Smith). *Educ:* Eton Coll.; St John's Coll., Cambridge (MA). Joined Hamish Hamilton Ltd, 1961, Dir, 1970, Man. Dir, 1974–89; Man. Dir, Sinclair-Stevenson Ltd, 1989–92; Publisher, Sinclair-Stevenson, and Editor-in-Chief, Reed Consumer Books, 1992–95; Consultant, Sinclair-Stevenson, 1995–96. *Publications:* The Gordon Highlanders, 1968; Inglorious Rebellion, 1971; The Life of a Regiment, 1974; Blood Royal, 1979; That Sweet Enemy, 1987; (ed) Enjoy!, 2000. *Recreations:* music, travel, food, the written word. *Address:* 3 South Terrace, SW7 2TB. *T:* (020) 7584 8087.

**SINCLAIR TAYLOR, (Robin) James;** Partner, Charity and Social Business Team, Russell-Cooke Solicitors, since 2004; Senior Consultant, Whitecliff Consultants, since 2011; *b* Hastings, 9 March 1948; *s* of Bob and Wendy Sinclair Taylor; *m* 2014, Semra Oreilly; two *d*. *Educ:* Univ. of Leicester (BA Social Sci.). Admitted as solicitor, 1976; Solicitor: N Kensington Law Centre, 1976–80; Sinclair Taylor and Martin Solicitors, 1981–2004. *Chair:* Shelterbox; Reside Housing Assoc.; Vice Chair: Swanage and Purbeck Develt Trust; Islington Play Assoc. *Publications:* Voluntary Sector Legal handbook, 1996, 3rd edn 2009. *Recreations:* sailing, gardening, the visual arts. *Address:* 2 Putney Hill, SW15 6AB. *T:* (020) 8394 6480. *E:* james.taylor@Russell-Cooke.co.uk. *Clubs:* London Corinthians Sailing, Swanage Sailing.

**SINCLAIRE, Nicole;** Member, West Midlands Region, European Parliament, 2009–14 (UK Ind, 2009–10, Ind, 2010–12, We Demand a Referendum, 2012–14); *b* London, 26 July 1968. *Educ:* Univ. of Kent. New Business Liaison Officer, Lloyds Blackhorse Life; Store Manager, Gateway Food Mkts; hospitality, Cyprus; Hd Office Manager, UKIP; Political Advr to Michael Nattrass, MEP. Contested (We Demand a Referendum) W Midlands, EP, 2014. *Publications:* Never Give Up: standing tall through adversity (autobiog.), 2013. *Recreations:* foreign travel, playing football, avid supporter of Liverpool FC.

**SINDALL, Adrian John,** CMG 1993; HM Diplomatic Service, retired; Chairman, Council for British Research in the Levant, 1997–2005; *b* 5 Oct. 1937; *s* of Stephen Sindall and Clare Mallet; *m* 1st, 1958; one *s* one *d*; 2nd, 1978, Jill Margaret Cowley. *Educ:* Battersea Grammar Sch. FO, 1956–58; ME Centre for Arab Studies, 1958–60; Third Sec. (Commercial), Baghdad, 1960–62; Second Sec., British Embassy, Rabat, 1962–67; First Secretary: FCO, 1967–70; Beirut, 1970–72; First Sec. and Head of Chancery, British Embassy, Lima, 1972–76; FCO, 1976–79; Counsellor, Head of Chancery and Consul-Gen., Amman, 1979–82; Hd of S America Dept, FCO, 1982–85; Consul-Gen., Sydney, 1985–88; ME Marketing Dir, Defence Export Services Orgn, MoD, on secondment, 1988–91; High Comr, Brunei, 1991–94; Ambassador to Syria, 1994–96. Sen. Diplomatic Consultant, Landair Internat. Chairman: Gtr London Fund for the Blind, 1997–99; Internat. Adv. Panel, Nat. Lottery Charities Bd, 1997–2003; Arab-British Centre, 1997–2001; Vice-Chm., Medical Aid for Palestinians, 1997–99; Mem. Adv. Council, London Middle East Inst., SOAS (formerly Mem. Adv. Bd, Centre for Near and Middle Eastern Studies), 1997–2010. Mem., RIIA. SPMB (Negara Brunei Darussalam), 1992. *Address:* 11 The Woodlands, Kings Worthy, Hants SO23 7QQ. *Club:* English-Speaking Union.

**SINDALL, Barry John;** Chief Executive, Grammar Schools Headteachers Association, 2008–16; Headmaster, Colyton Grammar School, Devon, 1990–2008; *b* 20 Oct. 1945; *s* of Reginald and Kathleen Sindall; *m* 1975, Margaret Eleanor Barker; one *s* one *d*. *Educ:* Univ. of Exeter (MEd). Teacher of Hist., Duncan Bowen Secondary Mod. Sch., Ashford, Kent, 1967–68; Hd of Humanities, R. M. Bailey High Sch., Nassau, Bahamas, 1968–76; Dir of Studies, Colyton GS, 1976–88; Dep. Headteacher, Torquay Boys' GS, 1988–90. Consultant Hd to Nat. Leading Edge prog., 2006–13. Chm. Trustees, Colyton GS, 2017–; Trustee, W of England Sch. for Young People with Little or No Sight, 2010–. FRSA 1994. *Recreations:* amateur dramatics, cricket, fell-walking, ski-ing, lifelong supporter of Tranmere Rovers. *Club:* Somerset County Cricket.

**SINES, Prof. David Thomas,** CBE 2010; PhD; FRCN; Pro Vice Chancellor and Executive Dean, Faculty of Society and Health, Buckinghamshire New University, 2009–14, now Emeritus Professor, Associate and Healthcare Provost; *b* Woking, 7 April 1954; *s* of Thomas Sines and Anne Patricia Sines; *m* (marr. diss.); one *s*. *Educ:* Brunel Univ. (BSc Hons Sociol./Psychol. with Nursing 1977); Univ. of Southampton (PhD 1990); Univ. of Ulster (PGCHE 1993). FRCN 1989. Community Charge Nurse, NW Surrey Dist Health Authy, 1977–79; Community Nursing Officer, Richmond, Twickenham and Roehampton Health Authy, 1979–85; Dir, Nursing and Gen. Manager, Winchester HA, 1985–90; Prof. of Community Health Nursing, and Hd, Sch. of Health Scis, Univ. of Ulster, 1990–99; Prof. of Community Health Care Nursing, and Exec. Dean, Health and Social Care, London South Bank Univ., 1999–2009. Ind. primary care workforce consultant, 2013–. Associate non-exec. Dir, Bucks Hosps NHS Trust, 2012–; non-exec. Dir, Central London Community Healthcare NHS Trust, 2012–. Chm., Jt Council for Cosmetic Practitioners, 2016–. Dir, British Sch. of Osteopathy, 2007–13. Trustee, Burdett Nursing Trust, 2014–. *Publications:* Community Health Care Nursing, 1995, 5th edn 2013. *Recreations:* walking, reading, theatre, cinema. *Address:* Arranmore, Sayes Court Farm Drive, Addlestone, Surrey KT15 1NB. *T:* 07787 002297. *E:* david.sines@icloud.com.

**SINGARES ROBINSON, Ariadne Elizabeth;** Ambassador of Panama to the Court of St James's, 2000–04; *b* Panama, 24 Sept. 1961; *m* Andrew Ian Robinson; one *d*. *Educ:* Knox Sch., Long Island, NY; Le Château Mont-Choisi, Geneva; Stony Brook Univ., NY; Parson Sch. of Design, Manhattan; New York Univ. A designer and personal asst to Gerald Franklin, Canadian designer of haute couture, NY, 1985–88. Member: Breast Cancer Assoc., Race for Life; City Harvest; Meals on Wheels; volunteer, St Lucas Hosp., Manhattan.

**SINGER, Andrew Michael;** QC 2018; a Recorder, since 2011; a Recorder of the Technology and Construction Court, since 2012; *b* Bury, Lancs, 22 July 1967; *s* of His Honour Harold Samuel Singer, *qv*; *m* 1994, Allison Moss. *Educ:* Bury Grammar Sch.; Fitzwilliam Coll., Cambridge (BA 1989). Called to the Bar, Gray's Inn, 1990; in practice as a barrister, Manchester, 1991–; Member: Bar of NI, 1996–; Bar of Irish Republic, 2014–. Chm. Trustees, Manchester Jewish Mus., 2015–. *Publications:* contrib. articles to Tecbar Rev. and Construction Engrg and Energy Law Jl. *Recreations:* peripatetic cricket watching, travel, wine collecting, Member of Whisky Club. *Address:* King's Chambers, 36 Young Street, Manchester M3 3FT. *T:* (0161) 832 9082. *E:* asingerqc@kingschambers.com; 4–5 Gray's Inn Square, WC1R 5AH. *T:* (020) 7404 5252. *E:* clerks@4-5.co.uk. *Clubs:* Lansdowne; Stand Cricket.

**SINGER, His Honour Harold Samuel;** a Circuit Judge, 1984–2003; *b* 17 July 1935; *s* of Ellis and Minnie Singer; *m* 1966, Adèle Berenice Emanuel; one *s* two *d*. *Educ:* Salford Grammar School; Fitzwilliam House, Cambridge (MA). Called to the Bar, Gray's Inn, 1957; a Recorder, 1981–84. *Recreations:* music, painting, books, photography.
*See also A. M. Singer.*

**SINGER, Norbert,** CBE 1990; PhD; FRSC; Vice Chancellor, University of Greenwich (formerly Director, Thames Polytechnic), 1978–93; *b* 3 May 1931; *s* of late Salomon Singer and Mina Korn; *m* Brenda Margaret Walter, *e d* of late Richard and Gladys Walter, Tunbridge Wells, Kent. *Educ:* Highbury County School; Queen Mary Coll., London (BSc, PhD). CChem, FRSC. Research Chemist and Project Leader, Morgan Crucible Co. Ltd, 1954–57; Lecturer, Senior Lectr, Principal Lectr and Dep. Head of Department, Dept of Chemistry, Northern Polytechnic, 1958–70; Head of Dept of Life Sciences 1971–74; Professor of Life Sciences 1972–74, Polytechnic of Central London; Asst Dir, then Dep. Dir, Polytechnic of N London, 1974–78. Vis. Prof., Univ. of Westminster, 1996–99. Council for National Academic Awards: Mem., 1982–88; Chm., Reviews Co-ordination Sub-Cttee, 1984–87; Vice Chm., Cttee for Academic and Institutional Policy, 1985–87. Mem., Accreditation Cttee, 1987–89; Chm., Cttee for CATs, 1990–93. Mem., MSC Nat. Steering Gp, TVEI, 1984–88 (Mem., Quality and Standards Gp, 1987–89). Chairman: Bexley HA, 1993–94; Oxleas (formerly Bexley Community Health) NHS Trust, 1994–2001. Chm., Governing Body, Rose Bruford Coll., 1994–99; Governor: London Inst., 1993–99; Nene Coll., Northants, 1993–97; St Peter's C of E Primary Sch., Tunbridge Wells, 1995–2004 (Chm., 2004–10). Fellow: QMW, 1993; Nene Coll., 1998. Hon. DSc Greenwich, 1993. *Publications:* research papers in electrochemistry, theoretical chemistry and surface chemistry in scientific jls. *Recreation:* reading. *Address:* Croft Lodge, Bayhall Road, Tunbridge Wells, Kent TN2 4TP. *T:* (01892) 523821.

**SINGER, Philip Francis;** QC 1994; a Recorder, 1989–2013; *b* 1 Dec. 1940; *s* of late Abraham Singer and Sylvia Singer (*née* Hyman); *m* 1978, Heather Angela Cutt. *Educ:* Bedford Modern Sch.; Bishop's Stortford Coll.; St John's Coll., Cambridge (MA, LLM). Called to the Bar, Inner Temple, 1964; Hd of Chambers, 2 Pump Court, Temple, 1994–2008.

**SINGER, Sara Catherine;** *see* Nathan, S. C.

**SINGER, Susan Honor;** educational consultant, since 2003; Headmistress, Guildford High School, 1991–2002; *b* 23 Feb. 1942; *d* of late Brig. John James McCully, DSO and Honor Goad McCully (*née* Ward, later Mrs E. B. Elliott); *m* 1964, Christopher Ronald Morgan Singer (*d* 2017); one *s* two *d*. *Educ:* St Mary's, Calne; Open Univ. (BA), Garnett Coll. (PGCE). Set up and ran pre-school playgroup, E Sheen, 1968–74; St Paul's Girls' School: maths teacher, 1980–91; Head of Middle School, 1988–91; Head of Maths, 1990–91. President: GSA, 2001; Mathematical Assoc., 2005–06. *Recreation:* transatlantic sailing 1907 gaff cutter. *Address:* 39 East Sheen Avenue, SW14 8AR. *T:* (020) 8876 4031.

**SINGH,** family name of **Baron Singh of Wimbledon**.

**SINGH OF WIMBLEDON,** Baron *cr* 2011 (Life Peer), of Wimbledon in the London Borough of Merton; **Indarjit Singh,** CBE 2009 (OBE 1996); JP; CEng; Director, Network of Sikh Organisations (UK), since 1995; *b* 17 Sept. 1932; *s* of Dr Diwan Singh and Kundan K. Singh; *m* 1962, Dr Kanwaljit Kaur; two *d*. *Educ:* Birmingham Univ. (MCom, MBA). CEng 1967; MIMinE 1967. Worked in sen. positions in mining and civil engrg, 1955–75: NCB, 1955–59, 1965–67; manager of mines, India, 1959–65; with Costain, 1967–75; mgt consultant in various areas of local govt, Gtr London, 1975–. Founder Mem., 1987–, Vice Chair, 2010–, Interfaith-Network UK (Co-Chair, 1989–92); hon. work for Sikh community and in promotion of inter-faith understanding, 1993–. Mem., All Party Parly Gp for Religious Educn, 2012–; Vice Chair, All Party Parly Gp for Freedom of Religion and Belief, 2013–. Editor, Sikh Messenger (qly mag.), 1984–. Has made broadcasts on religious and current affairs, incl. Any Questions, Thought for the Day. JP Wimbledon, 1984. UK Templeton Prize for the promotion of inter-faith understanding, 1989; Inter-faith Medallion for services to religious broadcasting, BBC and CCJ, 1991. Hon. DLitt: Coventry, 2002; York, 2014; Hon. DLaws Leicester, 2004; Hon. DArts Leeds, 2007. *Recreations:* writing, broadcasting, debating, grandchildren. *Address:* 43 Dorset Road, Merton Park, SW19 3EZ. *T:* (020) 8540 4148. *E:* sikhmessenger@aol.com.

**SINGH, Dapinderpaul;** QC 2017; a Recorder, since 2016; *b* 31 Dec. 1977; *s* of Parminder Singh and Kashmir Kaur; *m* 2008, Rebecca Smith-Bains. *Educ:* Univ. of Huddersfield (LLB Hons); Nottingham Trent Univ. (BVC). Called to the Bar, Middle Temple, 2000; in practice as a barrister specialising in criminal law. *Publications:* contrib. to New Law Jl. *Recreation:* world wide travel. *Address:* c/o Wilford Smith, MBP3, Carbrookhall Road, Sheffield S9 3EQ. *T:* 0808 169 5677. *E:* dsingh@wilfordsmith.com.

**SINGH, Darra,** OBE 2004; Partner, since 2013, and Head, Government and Public Sector, since 2016, Ernst & Young (Executive Director, 2012–13); *b* 26 July 1959; *s* of Lachsman Singh and Gurmit Kaur; *m* 1995, Monika Singh; one *d*. *Educ:* Fairfax Secondary Sch., Bradford; Newcastle upon Tyne Poly. (BA Hons Law 1981). Housing caseworker, Tyneside Housing Aid Centre, 1983; Housing Advr, London Housing Aid Centre, 1983–85; housing campaign worker, Housing Campaign for Single People, 1985–88; Sen. Policy and Res. Officer, London Housing Unit, 1988–90; Regl Dir, North British Housing Assoc., 1990–92; Chief Executive: Asra Greater London Housing Assoc., 1992–95; Hexagon Housing Assoc., 1995–2000; Regl Dir, Audit Commn, 2000–01; Chief Executive: Luton BC, 2001–05; Ealing LBC, 2005–09; Jobcentre Plus, DWP, 2009–11; Chair, Communities and Victims Panel, 2011–12. Mem., Balance of Funding Review Gp, ODPM, 2004. Chm., Commn of Integration and Cohesion, 2006–07. *Recreations:* motor bikes, guitar-based bands, films. *Address:* (office) 1 More London Place, SE1 2AF.

**SINGH, Deepak;** Group Chief Information Officer, Bunzl plc, since 2017; *b* Ethiopia, 1964; *s* of Surjan Singh and Suman L. Singh; *m* 1986, Sally Ruth Westwood; one *s* two *d*. *Educ:* Univ. of York (BA Hons Pols). Team Leader, Jaguar Cars Ltd, 1988–91; Application Services Manager, Facilities Technology Ltd, 1992–95; Sen. Proj. Manager, AstraZeneca plc, 1997–2000; Exec. Vice Pres., T-Mobile, 2001–06; Dir Gen. and Chief Inf. Officer, HMRC, 2006–09; Man. Dir, Cable & Wireless plc, 2009–10; Sen. Vice Pres., RR Donnelley & Sons, 2011–17. *Recreations:* investing in the stock market, golf, football, politics and current affairs.

**SINGH, Gurbux;** Strategic Account Director, Department for Work and Pensions, 2012–14; *b* Punjab, India, 4 Dec. 1950; *s* of Parkesh Singh and Shaminder Kaur; *m* 2001, Siobhan Maguire; three *s*. *Educ:* Univ. of Sussex (BA Hons Pol Sci.). Housing Specialist, CRC, 1972–77; housing and local govt, CRE, 1977–83; Housing Services, GLC, 1983–85; Dep. Dir of Housing, Brent BC, 1985–87; Dir of Housing, 1987–89, Chief Exec., 1989–2000, Haringey BC; Chair, CRE, 2000–02; Man. Dir, Diverse Solutions, Mgt Consultancy, 2005–10; Contract Dir, SERCO Civil Govt, 2008–11. Mem., Home Sec.'s Race Relns Forum, 1998; Dir, N London TEC, 1990–2000; Mem. Bd, Food Standards Agency, 2000–02; Nat. Dir, Civic Educn and Democracy, Research Triangle Inst., Iraq, 2003–04. *Recreations:* supporting Wolverhampton Wanderers and the Indian cricket team. *Address:* 6 Hollycroft Gardens, Tettenhall, Wolverhampton WV6 8FB. *T:* (01902) 755366, 07810 874189.

**SINGH, Kanwar N.;** *see* Natwar-Singh.

**SINGH, Karamjit Sukhminder,** CBE 2000; Northern Ireland Judicial Appointments Ombudsman, 2006–16; Chairman, University Hospitals of Leicester NHS Trust, since 2014; *b* 11 March 1950; *s* of Tara Singh and Chanan Kaur; *m* 1972, Jaswir Kaur (*d* 2014); one *s* (and one *s* decd). *Educ:* Univ. of Warwick (MA); Nottingham Law Sch. (PGDipLaw 1997). Res. Associate, Industrial Relns Res. Unit, Univ. of Warwick, 1971–75; Caseworker, Leicester CRC, 1975–78; Sen. Race Officer, CRE, 1978–82; Principal Officer, W Midlands CC, 1982–84; Asst Co. Clerk, Leics CC, 1984–87; Member: Police Complaints Authy for England and Wales, 1987–90 and 1991–94; Parole Bd for England and Wales, 1994–97. Harkness Fellow, US, 1990–91. Member: Data Protection Tribunal, 1997–2003; Criminal Cases Review Commn, 1997–2006; Regulatory Decisions Cttee, FSA, 2002–06; QC Selection Panel for England and Wales, 2005–11; Social Fund Commissioner for GB, 2009–13; for NI, 2009–15. Chm., Coventry and Warwicks NHS Partnership Trust, 2006–09. Member: Area Manpower Bd for Coventry and Warwicks, 1984–87; Industrial Tribunals Panel for England and Wales, 1986–96; Complaints Audit Cttee, Immigration and Nationality Dept, Home Office, 1994–97; Judicial Studies Bd, 1994–99; Ind. Mem., W Midlands Police Authy, 1994–96; Member: CS Commn, 1996–2000; UK Electoral Commn, 2001–10. FRSA 1995; CCMI 2002. Trustee: Citizenship Foundn, 1993–2000; Lloyds TSB Foundn for England and Wales, 2001–06; British Lung Foundn, 2007–09; Joseph Rowntree Foundn, 2014–16. *Recreations:* family, reading, charity work in India. *T:* (0116) 258 8940. *E:* karamjit.singh@uhl-tr.nhs.uk.

**SINGH, Laleshwar Kumar Narayan,** CCH 1996; High Commissioner for Guyana in London, 1993–2015; also non-resident Ambassador to The Netherlands, 1993–2015, the Republic of France, 1995–2015, the Russian Federation, 1995–2015, the Czech Republic, 1997–2015 and the Holy See, 1998–2015; *b* 2 April 1941; *s* of late Mr and Mrs Narayan, Windsor Forest, Guyana; *m* 1971, Latchmin Ramrattan; one *s* one *d*. *Educ:* Windsor Forest Govt Sch., Guyana; Indian Educn Trust Coll., Guyana. Left Guyana, 1961; Mem., Lincoln's Inn; Clerk to the Justices, Inner London Magistrates' Courts Service, 1971–93: Bow St, Marlborough St, Highbury Corner, Clerkenwell; Old St; Principal Chief Clerk's Office, Horseferry Rd; Personnel Officer, 1988–89.

**SINGH, Manmohan,** DPhil; Member, Rajya Sabha, since 1991; Prime Minister of India, 2004–14, and Finance Minister, 2012–14; *b* 26 Sept. 1932; *m* Gursharan Kaur; three *d*. *Educ:* Punjab Univ.; St John's Coll., Cambridge (BA 1957); Nuffield Coll., Oxford (DPhil 1962). Lectr, Punjab Univ., 1957–69; Prof., Delhi Sch. of Econs, 1969–71; Secretariat, UNCTAD; Econ. Advr, Min. of Foreign Trade, India, 1971–72; Chief Econ. Advr, 1972–76, Sec., 1976–80, Min. of Finance; Dir, 1976–80, Gov., 1982–85, Reserve Bank of India; Mem.-Sec., 1980–82, Dep. Chm., 1985–87, Planning Commn; Sec.-Gen. and Comr, South Commn, Geneva, 1987–90; Advr to Prime Minister, 1990–91; Union Finance Minister, 1991–96; Leader of the Opposition, 1998–2004. Chm., Univ. Grants Commn. Hon. DCL Oxon, 2005; Hon. LLD Cantab, 2006. Padma Vibhushan, 1987. *Publications:* India's Export Trends and Prospects for Self-Sustained Growth, 1964. *Address:* 3 Motilal Nehru Place, New Delhi 110011, India. *E:* manmohan@gov.in.

**SINGH, Margaret Stella, (Mrs Christopher Cook),** CBE 1996; Chair, Association of District Councils, 1993–95; *b* 10 Aug. 1945; *d* of Edward Richard Jones and Stella Jones; *m* 1st (marr. diss.); one *s* one *d*; 2nd, 2001, Christopher Cook; one step *d*. Working in and for local govt, 1962–; Mem. (Lab) Reading BC, 1976–95. Lay Mem., W Norfolk Primary Care Trust, 2000–06; Vice Chair, Norwich and W Norfolk CAB, 2009–. Bd Mem., Broadlands Housing Assoc., 2004–10. Trustee, Meridian East, 2008–. *Recreations:* reading, walking the dogs, listening to people. *Address:* Chiswick House, Creake Road, Burnham Market, Norfolk PE31 8EN.

**SINGH, Sir Pritpal,** Kt 2005; Head, Drayton Manor High School, since 1994; *b* 22 June 1953; *s* of Lt Col Dr Gurbuxsh Singh and Vidya Vati; *m* 1983, Elizabeth Szulc; two *s*. *Educ:* Chelsea Coll., Univ. of London (BSc (Hons) Chemistry 1975; PGCE 1979; MA 1986). Head of Chemistry, Feltham Sch., 1982–86; Head of Science, Vyne Sch., 1986–89; Dep. Head, Cranford Community Sch., 1989–94. Non-exec. Dir, E Berks NHS Trust, 1999–2001. Mem., Educn Cttee, Royal Soc., 2003–04; Jt Dir, London Leadership Strategy, 2005–06; Chm., Nat. Awards Panel, PTA-UK (formerly Nat. Confedn of PTAs), 2010–12. Mem. Council, Imperial Soc. of Knights Bachelor, 2011–. Promethean Award for Head Teacher of the Year, London, Teaching Awards Trust, 2004. *Recreations:* history, Rugby, sport, travel, music. *Address:* Drayton Manor High School, Drayton Bridge Road, W7 1EU. *T:* (020) 8357 1900, *Fax:* (020) 8357 1901.

**SINGH, Rt Hon. Sir Rabinder,** Kt 2011; PC 2017; **Rt Hon. Lord Justice Singh;** a Lord Justice of Appeal, since 2017; President, Investigatory Powers Tribunal, since 2018 (Member, since 2016); *b* 6 March 1964; *s* of late Lakhinder Singh and Swarn Kaur; *m* 1989, Alison Joy Baigent; two *s*. *Educ:* Bristol Grammar Sch.; Trinity Coll., Cambridge (BA Hons 1985; MA Hons 2013); Univ. of Calif, Berkeley (Harkness Fellow; LLM 1986). Lectr in Law, Univ. of Nottingham, 1986–88; called to the Bar, Lincoln's Inn, 1989, Bencher, 2009; QC 2002; in practice as barrister, 1989–2011; a Dep. High Court Judge, 2003–11; a Recorder, 2004–11; a Judge of the High Court, QBD, 2011–17; a Presiding Judge, S Eastern Circuit, 2013–16; Liaison Judge, Admin. Court for Wales and Midland and Western Circuits, 2017. Visitor, Brunel Univ., 2006–14; Vis. Fellow, LMH, Oxford, 2016–19. Hon. LLD: London Metropolitan, 2004; Nottingham, 2011. *Publications:* The Future of Human Rights in the United Kingdom, 1997; (jtly) Human Rights: judicial protection in the United Kingdom, 2008; contrib. articles to Public Law, Judicial Rev. and Eur. Human Rights Law Rev. *Recreations:* walking, drama, film, opera, saxophone. *Address:* Royal Courts of Justice, Strand, WC2A 2LL.

**SINGH, Rachim; His Honour Judge Singh;** a Circuit Judge, since 2019; *b* Birmingham; *s* of Faqiria Singh and Jeeto Kaur; *m* 1984, Sukhpal Kaur; one *s* one *d*. *Educ:* Bristnall Hall High Sch., Birmingham; Univ. of Glamorgan (BA Hons Law). Admitted as solicitor, 1987; Partner, 1987–94, Sen. Partner, 1994–2019, Petherbridge Bassra Solicitors, Bradford; a Recorder, 2008–19. *Recreation:* golf. *Address:* Wood Green Crown Court, Woodall House, Lordship Lane, Wood Green, N22 5LF. *T:* 07887 953982. *E:* hhj.rachim.singh@ejudiciary.net.

**SINGH, Rameshwar, (Ray),** CBE 2001; a District Judge, 1997–2010; Manager/Coordinator, Glamorgan House Family Development Centre, since 2011; *s* of late Brijmohan Singh and Ram Kumari; *m* Gwynneth, BSc; three *s*. *Educ:* Deenbandhu High Sch., Fiji; Council of Legal Educn. Called to the Bar, Middle Temple, 1969. In practice as barrister, Wales and Chester Circuit, 1969–97; Dep. Dist Judge, 1992–97. Chm. (pt-time), Child Support Appeals Tribunal, 1993–97; Ind. Chm. (pt-time), Complaints against Nat. Assembly for Wales, 2000. Mem., CRE for England and Wales, 1996–2002. Member: Adv. Cttee on Drugs and Alcohol Abuse to Sec. of State for Wales, 1996–2000; Nat. Assembly for Wales Adv. Cttee, 1999–2000. Mem., S Wales Criminal Justice Cttee, 1996. Chairman: Challenges for the Future, Birmingham, 2000–01; Formal Investigation into the Prison Service, 2000; Stephen Lawrence Inquiry Commn, 2002; Mem., Rees Rev.: student support system and tuition fee regime to Wales, 2004–05. Chair, Race Council, Cymru, 2010–. Non-exec. Dir, Gwalia Housing plc, 1999 (Chm., 2016–17). Mem., Family Mediators Assoc., 2011–. FLBA. Mem., Hon. Soc. of Middle Temple. Mem., Age Concern, Wales, 1999. Lay Mem. Council, Cardiff Univ., 2016; Governor: Swansea Inst. for Higher Educn, 2000–09; Swansea Coll., 2002–09; Gower Coll., 2010–. *Recreations:* mountain walking, cooking, watching cricket, Rugby. *Address:* Maranatha, Main Road, Cilfrew, Neath, West Glamorgan SA10 8NE. *Clubs:* Neath Cricket; Bonymaen Rugby Football.

**SINGH, Reuben;** Founder, 1999, and Chief Executive Officer, 1999–2004 and since 2015, alldayPA; Chairman, Reuben Singh Group of Companies, 2000; Founder, 2009, and Chief Executive Officer, since 2010, Isher Capital; *b* 20 Sept. 1976. *Educ:* William Hulme's Grammar Sch., Manchester. Founded first company, Miss Attitude, 1994; launched IT Golden Fund, 2001. Member: Competitiveness Council, DTI, 1999–2001; Small Business Council, DTI, 2000–02. British Ambassador for Entrepreneurship, 1999; Chm., Genesis Initiative, 2000–02. British Entrepreneur of the Year, 2002; Asian Entrepreneur of the Year, 2002; World Sikh Personality of the Year, 2003; listed as Youngest Self-made Millionaire, Guinness Book of World Records, 1998. *Recreation:* inspiring future entrepreneurs younger than myself.

**SINGH, Sarabjit;** QC 2018; *b* Gravesend, 4 Oct. 1978; *s* of late Ajaib Singh and Avtar Kaur. *Educ:* Stanground Coll., Peterborough; Corpus Christi Coll., Oxford (BA Juris. 2000; MA). Called to the Bar, Lincoln's Inn, 2001; in practice as barrister, 2001–. *Address:* 1 Crown Office Row, Temple, EC4Y 7HH. *T:* (020) 7797 7500, *Fax:* (020) 7797 7550. *E:* sarabjit.singh@1cor.com.

**SINGH, Simon Lehna,** MBE 2003; PhD; writer, journalist and television producer; *b* 19 Sept. 1964; *s* of Mengha and Sawarn Singh; *m* 2007, Anita Anand, broadcaster; two *s*. *Educ:* Imperial Coll., London (BSc Physics 1987); Emmanuel Coll., Cambridge (PhD Physics 1990). Joined Science Dept, BBC, 1991, producer, director and broadcaster, radio and TV; Dir, Fermat's Last Theorem (documentary), 1996 (BAFTA Award for best documentary); presenter, Science of Secrecy (series), Channel 4, 2001. Trustee, Science Mus., 2002–06. *Publications:* Fermat's Last Theorem, 1997; The Code Book, 1999; Big Bang, 2004; (with E. Ernst) Trick or Treatment?, 2008; The Simpsons and their Mathematical Secrets, 2013. *Recreations:* games of chance, observing solar eclipses. *Address:* Morley House, 36 Acreman Street, Sherborne, Dorset DT9 3NX.

**SINGH, Vijay;** golfer; *b* Fiji, 22 Feb. 1963; *m* Ardena Seth; one *s*. *Educ:* Univ. of N Carolina. Professional golfer, 1982–; joined PGA Tour, 1983; wins include: Malaysian Championship, 1984; Malaysian Open, 1992, 2001; Buick Classic, 1993, 1995, 2004, 2005; Toyota World Match Play Championship, 1997; Buick Open, 1997, 2004; US PGA Championship, 1998, 2004; US Masters, 2000; Singapore Masters, 2001; Tour Championship, 2002; Pebble Beach Nat. Pro-Am, 2004; Canadian Open, 2004; Sony Open, 2005; Chrysler Championship, 2005. Member: President's Cup Team, 1994, 1996, 1998, 2000, 2003; World Cup Team, 2002.

**SINGLA, Nikki Shailinder;** QC 2018; *b* London, 13 July 1977; *s* of Surjit Singla and Kamaldeep Singla; *m* 2009, Preeti Ahuja; one *s* one *d*. *Educ:* Caldicott Sch., Farnham Royal, Bucks; Winchester Coll.; New Coll., Oxford (BA Hons; BCL). Called to the Bar, Middle Temple, 2000; in practice as barrister, specialising in commercial and chancery litigation, 2001–. *Recreations:* cricket, tennis, walking. *Address:* Wilberforce Chambers, 8 New Square, Lincoln's Inn, WC2A 3QP. *T:* (020) 7306 0102. *E:* nsingla@wilberforce.co.uk.

**SINGLETON, Barry Neill;** QC 1989; *b* 12 April 1946; *s* of late Clifford and Moyna Singleton; *m* 1971, Anne Mary Potter; one *s* two *d*. *Educ:* Downside Sch.; Gonville and Caius Coll., Cambridge (MA). Called to the Bar, Gray's Inn, 1968.

**SINGLETON, Sir Roger,** Kt 2006; CBE 1997; Chief Executive, Barnardo's, 1984–2006; independent safeguarding consultant, government advisor and interim manager, since 2006; *b* 6 Nov. 1942; *s* of late Malcolm and Ethel Singleton, Nether Edge, Sheffield; *m* 1966, Ann Hasler; two *d*. *Educ:* City Grammar Sch., Sheffield; Durham Univ. (MA); Bath Univ. (MSc; Hon. LLD 2011); London Univ. (DipSocStud); Leeds (Cert. Ed.). Accredited Mediator. Appts in care and educn of vulnerable young people, 1961–71; professional adviser to Children's Regional Planning Cttee, 1971–74; Dep. Dir, Dr Barnardo's, 1974–84. Non-exec. Dir, Capacitybuilders, 2006–11. Chairman: Ind. Safeguarding Authy (formerly Ind. Barring Bd), 2007–12; Panel on Independence of Voluntary Sector, 2012–15; Govt Chief Advr on Safety of Children, 2009–10 (reported 2010). Dir, SafeguardingFirst Ltd, 2013–17. Mem., Nat. Safeguarding Panel, C of E, 2014–18; Chair, Safeguarding Ref. Gp, Dio. of Chelmsford, 2016–. Chm., Social Care Route, Inst. for Apprenticeships, then Inst. for

Apprenticeships and Tech. Educn, 2017–. Author, Drawing the Line, DFE report on Govt Vetting and Barring Scheme, 2009. Trustee, Nat. Council of Voluntary Child Care Organisations, 1984–2002 (Chm., 1990–92). Chair, Princess of Wales Meml Fund, 2006–13 (Trustee, 2001–13). Trustee, Lumos (formerly Children's High Level Gp), 2006–14. Pres., Friends of St Andrew's Ch, Shalford, 2006–; Vice-Pres., Perennial (Gardeners' Royal Benevolent Soc.), 2014– (Chm., 2006–14); Patron, Ann Craft Trust, 2012–. CCMI (FBIM 1982); FRSA 1991. *Publications*: contribs to professional jls. *Recreation*: timber framed buildings. *E*: rogersingleton42@gmail.com. *Club*: Reform.

**SINGLETON, Sarah Louise;** QC 2006; **Her Honour Judge Singleton;** a Circuit Judge, since 2012; *b* 9 March 1962; *d* of James and Beryl Singleton. *Educ*: Goff's Oak Primary Sch., Herts; Roedean; Lancaster Girls' Grammar Sch.; Hertford Coll., Oxford (BA Juris. 1982). Called to the Bar, Middle Temple, 1983, Bencher, 2010; barrister, 1983–2012; Recorder, 2000–12; a Deputy High Court Judge, 2011. Chancellor, Diocese of Sheffield, 2014– (Dep. Chancellor, 2013–14). *Recreations*: running, cycling, book clubs. *Address*: Sessions House, Lancaster Road, Preston, Lancs PR1 2PD.

**SINGLETON, Valerie,** OBE 1994; television broadcaster, travel writer for newspapers and magazines; with BBC, 1962–93; *b* 9 April 1937; *d* of late Wing Comdr Denis G. Singleton, OBE and Eileen Singleton, LRAM. *Educ*: Arts Educational Sch. (3 times Drama Cup); RADA (schol.). Bromley Rep.; commercial voice-overs; TV advertising magazines; joined BBC as announcer, 1962; presenter: Blue Peter, 1962–71; Blue Peter Special Assignments, covering capital cities, islands, famous houses, 1972–75, and Rivers Niagara and Yukon, 1980; Val Meets the VIPs, 1972–75; Nationwide, 1972–78; Tonight, and Tonight in Town, 1978–79; Echoes of Holocaust, documentary, BBC 2, Midweek, Radio 4, 1980; The Money Programme, BBC 2, 1980–88; Radio 4 PM, 1981–93; (jtly) Travel UK, Central TV, 1992; Backdate, Channel 4, 1996; Playback, History Channel, 2 series, 1998, 1999; numerous other radio and TV progs; corporate videos, business confs. Dir, simplicity Computers with Envelope software, 2008–15. *Recreations*: sailing, ski-ing, water ski-ing, photography, exploring London, travelling… especially cities, riding, pottering in museums and antique shops. *Address*: c/o Panmedia, 18 Montrose Crescent, N12 0ED. *Clubs*: Hurlingham, Chelsea Arts.

**SINGLETON, William Brian,** CBE 1974; FRCVS; retired; Director, Animal Health Trust, 1977–88; *b* 23 Feb. 1923; *s* of William Max Singleton and Blanche May Singleton; *m* 1947, Hilda Stott; two *s* one *d* (and one *s* decd). *Educ*: Queen Elizabeth Grammar Sch., Darlington; Royal (Dick) Sch. of Vet. Studies, Edinburgh. Vis. Prof. Surgery, Ontario Vet. Coll., Guelph, Canada, 1973–74; Hon. Vet. Advr to Jockey Club, 1977–88. Member: Govt Cttee of Inquiry into Future Role of Veterinary Profession in GB (Chm., Sir Michael Swann), 1971–75; UGC Wkg Pty on Vet. Educn into the 21st Century (Chm., Sir Ralph Riley, FRS), 1987–89. President: British Small Animal Vet. Assoc., 1960–61; RCVS, 1969–70; World Small Animal Vet. Assoc., 1975–77; BEVA, 1988–89. Hon. Diplomate, Amer. Coll. of Vet. Surgeons, 1973; Hon. DVM & S Edinburgh, 1993. ARPS 2001. Dalrymple-Champneys Award, 1987. *Publications*: (contrib.) Canine Medicine and Therapeutics, 1979; numerous papers on veterinary orthopaedics and comparative medicine. *Recreations*: gardening, photography, bird watching. *Club*: Farmers.

**SINHA,** 6th Baron *cr* 1919, of Raipur; **Arup Kumar Sinha;** *b* 23 April 1966; *er s* of 5th Baron Sinha and of Lolita, *d* of Deb Kumar Das; *S* father, 1999; *m* 1st, 1993, Deborah Jane Tidswell (marr. diss. 1995); 2nd, 2002, Penny Askins. *Heir: b* Hon. Dilip Kumar Sinha, *b* 28 May 1967.

**SINKER, Isabel Margaret;** *see* Dedring, I. M.

**SINKINSON, Philip Andrew,** OBE 2006; HM Diplomatic Service, retired; High Commissioner to The Gambia, 2006–11; *b* 7 Oct. 1950; *m* 1971, Clare Maria Catherine Jarvis; one *s*. Bd of Inland Revenue, 1967–70; entered FCO, 1970; Warsaw, 1973–74; FCO, 1974; E Berlin, 1974–75; Rome, 1975–76; FCO, 1976–78; Rio de Janeiro, 1978; Quito, 1978–79; Prague, 1979–81; FCO, 1981–82; Blantyre, 1982–85; Lilongwe, 1985–86; FCO, 1986–92; Second Sec. (Commercial), São Paulo, 1992–95; on secondment to British Olympic Assoc., Atlanta, 1995–96; First Sec. (Commercial), Lisbon, 1996–2001; Dep. High Comr, Jamaica, 2001–05. Chm., Bournemouth RFC, 2014–. Patron, Bansang Hosp. Appeal, 2012–.

**SINNATT, Maj.-Gen. Martin Henry,** CB 1984; *b* 28 Jan. 1928; *s* of Dr O. S. Sinnatt and Mrs M. H. Sinnatt (*née* Randall); *m* 1957, Susan Rosemary Clarke; four *d*. *Educ*: Hitchin Grammar School; Hertford College, Oxford (1 Year Army Short Course); RMA Sandhurst. Commissioned RTR, 1948; served Germany, Korea, UK, Hong Kong, 1948–58; psc 1959; Aden, 1959–62; Germany and UK, 1962–64; MA to C-in-C AFNE, Norway, 1964–66; jssc 1967; Germany and UK, 1967–69; CO 4 RTR, BAOR, 1969–71; Nat. Defence Coll., 1971–72; Comdr RAC, 1 (BR) Corps, BAOR, 1972–74; Dir Operational Requirements MoD, 1974–77; rcds 1978; Dir, Combat Development (Army), 1979–81; Chief of Staff to Live Oak, SHAPE, 1982–84; completed service, 1984. Sen. Exec. and Sec., Kennel Club, 1984–93. *Address*: Meadowside Farmhouse, Tulls Lane, Standford, Bordon, Hants GU35 8RB.

**SINNOTT, John Brian,** CBE 2010; MVO 2019; Chief Executive, Leicestershire County Council and Clerk of Lieutenancy, since 1994; *s* of William John Sinnott and Mary Josephine Sinnott (*née* Foley); *m* 1970, Helen Mary Turner; two *s* two *d*. *Educ*: St Mary's Coll., Crosby; Univ. of Liverpool (MA, Dip. Public Admin). Liverpool CC, 1970–74; PA to Chm. and Leader of Council, Head of Leader's office, Merseyside CC, 1974–86; Management Consultant, Coopers and Lybrand Associates, 1986–87; Leicestershire County Council: Asst, then Sen. Asst, County Clerk, 1987–90; Asst Chief Exec., 1990–92 Dir, Corporate Management, 1992–94. Director: Leics TEC, 1994–2001; Leics Business Point (Business Link), 1995–2001; Leics Develt Agency, 1998–2003; Heart of the Nat. Forest Foundn, 1998–2004; Leics and Rutland Sport, 2005–; Leics Econ. Partnership, 2007–09; Prospect Leics, 2009–11. Mem. Council, Loughborough Univ., 2015–. Chm., ACCE, 2001–02. Chairman: Leics Cricket Bd, 2001–06; Everton FC Shareholders' Assoc., 2003–04. Hon. LLD: Leicester, 2010; De Montfort, 2015. *Publications*: papers in local govt jls. *Recreations*: sport, cricket literature, history of rock music. *Address*: County Hall, Glenfield, Leicester LE3 8RA. *T*: (0116) 305 6000. *Club*: Everton Football.

**SINOUSSI, Françoise Claire;** *see* Barré-Sinoussi, F. C.

**SINTON, William Baldie,** OBE 1999; HM Diplomatic Service, retired; *b* 17 June 1946; *s* of late John William Sinton and Isabella McCrae Sinton (*née* Baldie); *m* 1995, Jane S. B. Aryee. *Educ*: Bristol Cathedral Sch.; Kirkcaldy High Sch.; Edinburgh Univ. (MA 1968). Third Sec., FCO, 1968; Third later Second Sec., Prague, 1970; Second later First Sec., UK Delegn to NATO, Brussels, 1973; FCO, 1977–81; First Sec. (Commercial), Algiers, 1981; FCO, 1985–96; Ambassador to Panama, 1996–99; Ambassador to Algeria, 1999–2001; Ambassador to Bolivia, 2001–05. Clerk, Cttee Office, H of L, 2006–14. *Address*: 22 Fairburn Court, St John's Avenue, SW15 2AU. *Clubs*: Reform; Lundin Golf.

**SINYOR, Joseph, (Joe);** Chairman, Stiga Sarl, 2014–18; *b* 16 Aug. 1957; *s* of Samuel Joseph Sinyor and Claire Sinyor; *m* 1987, Pamela Caroline Neild Collis; two *s* one *d*. *Educ*: Jesus Coll., Cambridge; London Business Sch. (MBA). Corporate Finance Exec., J. Henry Schroder Wagg, 1983–85; Sen. Engagement Manager, McKinsey & Co. Inc., 1985–90; Gp Chief Exec., Pepe Gp plc, 1990–93; Man. Dir, Dillon's Bookstores Ltd, 1994–98; Man. Dir, Sony UK Ltd, 1998–2000; Chief Exec., Newspapers, Trinity Mirror plc, 2000–03; Man. Dir, Terra Firma Capital Partners, 2003–06; Operating Partner (formerly Man. Dir), Strategic Value Partners LLP, 2007–11; Hd, Value Creation Gp, Actis, 2011–14. Non-executive Director: Channel 4 TV Corp., 1998–2004; Ideal Standard Internat., 2014–15. *Recreations*: opera, ski-ing, walking. *Address*: 70 Sheldon Avenue, N6 4ND.

**SIPPINGS, Gwenda Margaret;** Head, Knowledge and Information Management, Medical Defence Union, 2011–16; *b* London, 20 April 1957; *d* of late David Hughes and Dr Joan Hughes (*née* Isaac); *m* 1984, Andrew John Sippings. *Educ*: Dame Alice Harpur Sch., Bedford; Univ. of Wales, Aberystwyth (BLib 1978; MLib 1986). FCLIP 2002. Reference Librarian Reader Services Team, Bedford Central Liby, 1978–84; Asst Database Adminr, BT Prestel, 1984–86; Inf. Specialist, 1987–88, Trng Manager, 1989, ASLIB; Hd, Accommodation Information Unit, BTA, 1989–94; Hd, Information, Clifford Chance, 1994–2002; Dir, Information Resources, Bd of Inland Revenue, subseq. Dir, Knowledge Resources, HMRC, 2002–06; Ind. Records Consultant, London Bor. of Southwark, 2007–09; Hd, Information and Res., Linklaters LLP, 2009–11. Hon. Deptl Fellow of Information Studies, Univ. of Aberystwyth, 2010–16. Trustee, Cymmrodorion Soc., 2003–17 (Chm. Council, 2003–16). Trustee and Archivist, Old Students Assoc., Aberystwyth, 2012–18 (Pres., 2018–19). FIRM 2016. FRSA 2002–14. Editor, Business Information Review, 2008–10. *Publications*: articles in professional information jls. *Address*: Cysgod y Llyfrgell, 5 Bryn Ardwyn, Aberystwyth SY23 1ED. *T*: 07877 803252. *E*: gwendasippings@gmail.com.

**SIRKS, Prof. (Adriaan Johan) Boudewijn;** Regius Professor of Civil Law, University of Oxford, and Fellow of All Souls College, Oxford, 2006–14, now Emeritus. *Educ*: Leyden Univ. (LLM 1972); Univ. of Amsterdam (PhD 1984). Formerly: Lectr, Hist. of Roman Law, Utrecht State Univ.; Associate Prof. of Legal Techniques, Univ. of Amsterdam; Prof. of Legal Hist. and Private Law, Johann Wolfgang Goethe Univ., Frankfurt am Main, 1998–2006. Corresp. Mem., Koninklijke Nederlandse Akademie van Wetenschappen, 2002. Kt, Order of the Lion (Netherlands), 2014. *Publications*: Food for Rome, 1991; (jtly) Ein früh-byzantinisches Szenario für die Amtswechslung in der Sitonie, 1996; The Theodosian Code: a study, 2007; (ed jtly) Papyri in Memory of P. J. Sijpesteijn, 2007; (ed) Nova Ratione: change of paradigms in Roman law, 2014. *Address*: All Souls College, Oxford OX1 4AL. *E*: boudewijn.sirks@law.ox.ac.uk.

**SIRLEAF, Ellen Eugenia J.;** *see* Johnson Sirleaf.

**SIRR, Stephanie Ann;** Chief Executive, Nottingham Playhouse, since 2001; *b* Bristol, 1965; *d* of Christine Haydn Thomas and Chris Denys; *m* 1996, Mark Grabiec; two *s*. *Educ*: Southgate Comprehensive Sch.; Univ. of Kent at Canterbury (BA Hons Drama and Th. Studies 1988); Univ. of Central Lancs (MBA 2002). Prog. Co-ordinator, Sadler's Wells, 1991–95; Dir, Merlin Th., Frome, 1995–97; CEO, Blackpool Grand Th., 1997–2001. Chair, Dance Touring Partnership, 2005–18. Director: Ticketing Network E Midlands, 2009–; UK Theatre, 2015–; Parents and Carers in Performing Arts, 2017–; One Nottingham, 2018–. FRSA. *Publications*: (contrib.) The Business Growth Benefits of Higher Education, 2014; (contrib.) Reflections on Resilience and Creative Leadership, 2019. *Recreations*: reading, Scrabble, tennis, Candy Crush. *Address*: Nottingham Playhouse, Wellington Circus, Nottingham NG1 5AL. *T*: (0115) 873 6201. *E*: stephanies@nottinghamplayhouse.co.uk.

**SIRRINGHAUS, Prof. Henning,** PhD; FRS 2009; Hitachi Professor of Electron Device Physics, University of Cambridge, since 2004; Fellow, Churchill College, Cambridge, since 1999. *Educ*: Eidgenössische Technische Hochschule Zürich (BSc; PhD). Postdoctoral Res. Fellow, Princeton Univ., 1995–96; Univ. of Cambridge, 1997–. Co-founder and Chief Scientist, Plastic Logic Ltd, 2000–. Mullard Award, Royal Soc., 2003. *Publications*: contribs to jls incl. Nature Nanotechnol., Nature Materials, Nature. *Address*: Microelectronics Research Centre, Cavendish Laboratory, Department of Physics, University of Cambridge, J J Thomson Avenue, Cambridge CB3 0HE.

**SISSLING, David Anthony;** Senior Leadership Advisor, NHS Improvement and NHS England, since 2017; *b* St Albans, 5 Nov. 1957; *s* of Brian Sissling and late Moira Sissling; *m* 2007, Caroline Angelina Godfrey; two *s*. *Educ*: Thornbury Grammar Sch., subseq. Marlwood Comp. Sch.; Univ. of Birmingham (BA Geog. 1978). Merchant seaman, Blue Star Ship Mgt, 1978–80; Personnel Manager, Northern Foods, 1980–85; Personnel Manager, 1985–89, Gen. Manager, 1989–93, Robinson & Sons Ltd; Leicester Royal Infirmary NHS Trust: Business Manager, 1993–96; Dir, Contracts, 1996–98; Chief Exec., 1998–2000; Chief Executive: Northampton HA, 2000–02; Leicestershire, Northamptonshire and Rutland Strategic HA, 2002–06; NI Health and Social Care Authy, 2006–08; Prog. Dir, Healthcare for London, 2008–09; Chief Exec., Abertawe Bro Morgannwg Univ. Health Bd, 2009–11; Chief Executive: NHS Wales and Dir Gen., Dept of Health, Social Services and Children, Welsh Govt, 2011–14; Kettering Gen. Hosp. NHS Foundn Trust, 2014–17; Prog. Dir, NICE, 2017–19. Mem., Sen. Salaries Rev. Body, 2019–. *Recreations*: golf, running, ski-ing, football (Leicester City), Rugby (Leicester Tigers), dining out, cookery.

**SISSONS, Peter George;** journalist, broadcaster and writer; *b* 17 July 1942; *s* of late George Robert Percival Sissons and Elsie Emma Evans; *m* 1965, Sylvia Bennett; two *s* one *d*. *Educ*: Liverpool Inst. High Sch. for Boys; University Coll., Oxford (MA PPE). Independent Television News: graduate trainee, 1964; general reporter, 1967; industrial corresp., 1970; indust. editor, 1972–78; presenter, News at One, 1978–82; presenter: Channel Four News, 1982–89; BBC TV 6 o'clock news, 1989–93; BBC TV 9 o'clock news, 1993–2000; BBC TV 10 o'clock news, 2000–03; presenter, BBC News 24, 2003–09; Chm., BBC TV Question Time, 1989–93; occasional presenter, Breakfast with Frost, 2002–05. Mem., Hillsborough Ind. Panel, 2010–12. Vice Pres., Liverpool Sch. of Tropical Medicine, 2013–. Hon. Fellow, Liverpool John Moores Univ., 1997. Hon. LLD Liverpool, 2002. Broadcasting Press Guild Award, 1984; RTS Judges' Award, 1988; Newscaster of the Year, TRIC, 2001. *Publications*: When One Door Closes (memoir), 2011. *Recreations*: relaxing, supporting Liverpool FC.

**SITWELL, Sir George (Reresby Sacheverell),** 8th Bt *cr* 1808, of Renishaw, Derbyshire; *b* London, 22 April 1967; *er s* of late Francis Trajan Sacheverell Sitwell, *yr s* of 6th Bt, and of Susanna Carolyn, *d* of Rt Hon. Sir Ronald Hibbert Cross, 1st Bt, KCMG, KCVO; *S* uncle, 2009, but his name does not appear on the Official Roll of the Baronetage; *m* 2008, Martha Louise, 2nd *d* of late Justin Robert de Blank. *Educ*: Eton Coll.; Edinburgh Univ. (MA Hons). Merchant banker, 1990–98; J & M Entertainment, 1998–2000; Co-founder and Director: Interquest Gp plc, 2000–06; Crossover Capital Ltd, 2001–. *Recreations*: travel, reading, dogs. *Heir*: *b* William Ronald Sacheverell Sitwell [*b* 2 Oct. 1969; *m* 1st, 1999, Laura Barbara (marr. diss. 2017), *d* of Euan Norman Jersey McCorquodale; one *s* one *d*; 2nd, 2017, Emily Jane Lopes, *d* of 3rd Baron Roborough; one *s*]. *Clubs*: Brooks's, Pratt's.

**SIU, Gordon Kwing-Chue,** GBS 2002; CBE 1997; JP; Secretary for Planning and Lands, Hong Kong, 1999–2002; *b* 29 Nov. 1945; *s* of Siu Wood-chuen and Chan Shuk-ming; *m* 1999, Cynthia Wong Kuk-yee; two *s* by a previous marriage. *Educ:* Birmingham Univ. (MSocSci). Joined Hong Kong Civil Service, 1966; Sec.-Gen., Office of Members of Exec. and Legislative Councils, 1985; Postmaster Gen., 1988; Comr for Transport, 1989; Dir, New Airport Projects Co-ordination Office, 1992; Secretary for: Economic Services, 1993; Transport, 1996; Hd, Central Policy Unit, 1997. Founder, 2009, now Dir of Training, Music For Our Young Foundn (Chm., 2009–15; Dir, 2015–). *Recreations:* reading, swimming, golf. *Clubs:* Hong Kong Golf, Hong Kong Jockey.

**SIXSMITH, Martin;** author and broadcaster, since 2002; *b* Warrington, 24 Sept. 1954; *s* of George Sixsmith and Joyce Sixsmith (*née* Sutton); *m* 1976, Mary Cooney; two *s* two *d*. *Educ:* Manchester Grammar Sch.; Sorbonne Univ., Paris; New Coll., Oxford (MA Hons); Leningrad State Univ.; Harvard Univ. Grad. student, St Antony's Coll., Oxford, 1979–80; trainee, BBC News, 1980–82; BBC Correspondent: Brussels, 1982–86; Warsaw, 1986–88; Moscow, 1988–91; Washington, 1991–95; Moscow, 1995–97; Dir of Communications, Govt Information Service, 1997–99; Communications Dir, Marconi plc, 1999–2001; Dir of Communications, Govt Information Service, 2001–02. Television: writer and presenter: No, Minister: an Uncivil Service, 2004; Ireland's Lost Children, 2015; consultant: The Thick of It, 2005–12; film, In the Loop, 2010. Member: Mensa; Barbirolli Soc. *Publications:* Vladislav Khodasevich, poet of emigration, 1980; Moscow Coup: the death of the Soviet system, 1991 (German and Dutch edns); Spin, a novel, 2003; I Heard Lenin Laugh, 2005; The Litvinenko File: politics, polonium and Russia's war with itself, 2008 (American, Dutch, Portuguese, Polish, Czech and Bulgarian edns); The Lost Child of Philomena Lee, 2009 (filmed 2013); Putin's Oil: the oligarchs and the struggle for Russia, 2010 (Russian, Chinese, Israeli, Latvian and Lithuanian edns); Russia: a 1,000-year chronicle of the wild east, 2011 (American, Romanian, Chinese and Taiwanese edns); (ed and introd.) Vladimir the Russian Viking, 2012; (contrib.) Historically Inevitable? Turning Points in Russian History, 2016; Ayesha's Gift, 2017. *Recreation:* good living. *Address:* c/o Rogers, Coleridge and White Ltd, 20 Powis Mews, W11 1JN. *Club:* Liverpool Football.

**SIZELAND, Paul Raymond,** CMG 2006; HM Diplomatic Service, retired; Director, Economic Development, City of London Corporation, 2008–15 (Assistant Director, City, European and International Affairs, 2006–08); *b* 19 Feb. 1952; *s* of Raymond Sizeland and Patricia Sizeland (*née* Dudley); *m* 1976, Vasantha, *d* of late James Kanaka and Nancy Jesudasan; two *d*. *Educ:* Dulwich Coll.; Bradford Univ. (BTech Hons Applied Biol. 1975). MIPD 1995. VSO teacher, St Stephen's Coll., Trinidad, 1970–71; Res. Student, Rowett Res. Inst., Aberdeen, 1973–74; CMS volunteer teacher, Ida Scudder Sch., Vellore, S India, 1976–78; Med. Rep. for Essex and Suffolk, Merrell Pharmaceuticals, 1978–80; joined HM Diplomatic Service, 1980; Third Sec., UK Delegn to NATO, Brussels, 1981–84; Commercial Attaché, Doha, 1985–86; Second Sec., FCO, 1986–88; First Sec., Political/Develt, Lagos, 1988–91; Private Sec. to Lord Carrington, Chm., EU Conf. on former Yugoslavia, 1991–92; Head, Career Develt Unit, FCO, 1992–95; Dep. Head, Personnel Mgt Dept, FCO, 1995–96; Dep. Hd of Mission, Bangkok, 1996–2000; Consul Gen., Shanghai, 2000–03; Dir, Consular Services, FCO, 2003–06. Dir, Internat. Business and Diplomatic Exchange, 2016–19; Sen. Advr, Internat. Affairs, Corporate Catalyst India, 2016–; Advr, Accenture, 2015–. Hon. Sen. Vis. Fellow, Cass Business Sch., 2014–; coach, Teach First, 2014–17. Trustee: Prisoners Abroad, 2006–17 (Vice Chm., 2016–17); Dorset Community Foundn, 2017–. Gov., Twynham Primary Sch., 2019–. *Recreations:* family, Millwall FC supporter, travel, books, music, Kipling Society.

**SKAISGIRYTĖ LIAUŠKIENĖ, Asta;** Political Director, Ministry of Foreign Affairs, Lithuania, since 2017; *b* 20 March 1966; *m*; one *c*. *Educ:* Vilnius Univ. (MA Romanic-Germanic Philology 1989); Internat. Inst. of Public Admin, France (Internat. Relns). Correspondent, Atgimimas, weekly newspaper, 1989–90; Hd, Inter-Parliamentary Relns Dept, Supreme Council, Rep. of Lithuania, 1990–92; First Sec., 1993–94, Hd, 1994–95, W Eur. Div., Political Dept, Min. of Foreign Affairs; Advr for Internat. Relns, Govt of Lithuania, 1995–98; Ambassador to France, 1998–2003; non-resident Ambassador to Tunisian Republic, 2002–03; Ambassador-at-Large, Eur. Affairs Dept, 2003, Hd, Personnel Dept, 2003–06, Min. of Foreign Affairs; Ambassador to Israel, 2006–09; non-resident Ambassador to S Africa, 2007–09; Vice Minister of Foreign Affairs, 2009–12; Ambassador to the Court of St James's, 2012–17. Comdr, Légion d'Honneur (France), 2001; Commemorative Medal for 13th Jan. (Lithuania), 2003; Comdr Cross, Order of Merit (Lithuania), 2003; Grand Officer, Order of Merit (France), 2004.

**SKARBEK, Marjorie Shiona Douglas, (Countess Skarbek);** *see* Wallace, M. S. D.

**SKATES, Kenneth Christian;** Member (Lab) Clwyd South, National Assembly for Wales, since 2011; Minister for Economy and Transport (formerly Cabinet Secretary for Economy and Infrastructure, then Economy and Transport), since 2016; *b* Wrexham, 2 April 1976; *s* of Kenneth and Mary Skates. *Educ:* Alun Sch., Mold; Sidney Sussex Coll., Cambridge (BA Hons Social and Political Sci. 1997). Chief Reporter, N Wales Newspapers, 1998–2001; freelance journalist, 2001; Office Manager for Mark Tami, MP, 2001–11. Dep. Minister for Skills and Technol., 2013–14, for Culture, Sport and Tourism, 2014–16, Welsh Govt. *Recreations:* theatre, running, golf, ski-ing, cycling, cinema, climbing, gym, family, gardening, drawing, walking, travel, architecture, cars. *Address:* National Assembly for Wales, Cardiff Bay, Cardiff CF99 1NA. *T:* (029) 2089 8768. *E:* ken.skates@gov.wales.

**SKEA, Prof. James Ferguson,** CBE 2013 (OBE 2004); Professor of Sustainable Energy, Centre for Environmental Policy, Imperial College London, since 2009; *b* 1 Sept. 1953; *s* of Colin Hill Skea and Margaret Ferguson Skea; *m* 1976, Jane Howley (marr. diss. 2001); one *s* one *d*. *Educ:* Grove Acad., Broughty Ferry; Univ. of Edinburgh (BSc 1st cl. Hons); Clare Coll., Cambridge (PhD 1979). Res. Asst, Cavendish Lab., 1978–81; Vis. Res. Associate, Carnegie-Mellon Univ., 1981–83; Res. Fellow, 1983–94, Professorial Fellow, 1994–98, Science Policy Res. Unit; Director: Global Envmtl Change Prog., ESRC, 1995–98; PSI, 1998–2004; UK Energy Res. Centre, 2004–12. Member: UK Climate Change Cttee, 2008–18; Bureau of the Intergovernmental Panel on Climate Change, 2008–15 (Co-Chair, Wkg Gp III, 2015–); Chair, Scottish Just Transition Commn, 2018–. Pres., Energy Inst., 2015–17. FRSA 2000; FEI 2005. Hon. FSE 2011. Melchett Award, Energy Inst., 2010. *Publications:* Acid Politics, 1991; Standards, Innovation, Competitiveness and Policy, 1995; Clean and Competitive, 1997; Pollution for Sale, 1998; Energy 2050, 2011; Energy Innovation for the 21st Century, 2019. *Recreations:* walking the South Downs, mountain biking, losing keys. *Address:* Flat 13, 17–19 Nevern Place, SW5 9NR. *T:* (020) 3581 7688. *E:* j.skea@ic.ac.uk.

**SKEAPING, Lucie, (Lucie Finch);** musician, writer and broadcaster; Presenter, The Early Music Show, BBC Radio 3, since 1995; Co-Founder, 1973, and Director, since 1978, The City Waites; Founder and Director, The Burning Bush, since 1992; *d* of Dr Bernard Finch, GP and Patricia Finch, sculptor; *m* 1974, Roderick Skeaping; one *s*. *Educ:* King Alfred Sch., London; Henrietta Barnett Sch., London; Arts Educnl Sch., London; RCM. Performances of early and trad. English and Jewish music with ensembles, The City Waites and The Burning Bush, 1973–; presenter: music and children's programmes, BBC TV, 1980–85; performances with Michael Nyman Band, Sadista Sisters, Martin Best Consort, 1980–90; music documentaries and features for radio. Artistic Dir, Windsor Fest., 1995–99. Producer, historical recordings for Soundalive Music, 1994–96; collaborations include: projects and performances for RNT, Rambert Dance Co., RSC, Cultural Co-operation, Shakespeare's Globe; vocal soundtracks include: History of Britain, BBC TV; The Pianist (film), 2002. Numerous recordings, 1972–. Mem. Judging Panel, Live Music Now, 2006– (Ambassador, 2009–); contrib. to govt singing in schools initiative 'Sing Up', 2008. Patron, Finchley Children's Music Gp, 1995–. Mem., Samuel Pepys Club, 2006–. *Publications:* Let's Make Tudor Music, 1999; Broadside Ballads, 2005 (Best Classical Music Pubn, Music Industry Awards, 2006); (ed jtly) Singing Simpkin and other Bawdy Jigs: musical comedy on the Shakespearean stage, 2014; contribs to BBC Music Magazine, BBC History Magazine, Early Music Today. *Address:* 19 Patshull Road, NW5 2JX. *T:* 07931 373133. *E:* lucieskeaping@hotmail.com. *W:* www.lucieskeaping.co.uk.

**SKEFFINGTON,** family name of **Viscount Massereene and Ferrard**.

**SKEGG, Sir David (Christopher Graham),** KNZM (DCNZM 2009); OBE 1990; DPhil; FRSNZ; Vice-Chancellor, University of Otago, 2004–11, now Emeritus Professor; President, Royal Society of New Zealand, 2012–15; *b* 16 Dec. 1947; *s* of Donald and Margaret Skegg; *m* 1973, Dr Keren Mary Cargo; two *d*. *Educ:* King's Coll., Auckland; Univ. of Auckland; Univ. of Otago (BMedSc 1970; MB ChB 1972); Univ. of Oxford (DPhil 1979). FAFPHM 1994; FFPHM 1999. Rhodes Scholar, Balliol Coll., Oxford, 1973, 1975–76. House Physician, Waikato Hosp., NZ, 1974; Lectr in Epidemiology, Univ. of Oxford, 1976–79; University of Otago: Prof. of Preventive and Social Medicine, 1980–2004; Fellow, Knox Coll., 1980– (Life Fellow, 2009). Vis. Fellow, Wolfson Coll., Oxford, 1986. Consultant to WHO, Geneva, 1984–2004 and 2009– (Chm., Scientific and Tech. Adv. Gp, WHO Dept of Reproductive Health and Res., 2011–16); Chairman: Health Res. Council of NZ, 1991–94; Public Health Commn, 1992–95; BSE Expert Sci. Panel, 1996–2011; Res. Cttee, Universities NZ, 2004–10; Matariki Network of Univs, 2010–11; NZ Sci. Bd, 2011–12. Sec., Rhodes Scholarships in NZ, 2004–13. Trustee: NZ Antarctic Res. Inst., 2012–18; Antarctic Heritage Trust, 2012–18. FRSNZ 1992; Life FRACP 2017. Hon. Life Mem., Otago Inst., 2010. Hon LLD Otago, 2011; Hon. DSc Queen's, Canada, 2017. NZ Commem. Medal, 1990; Sir Charles Hercus Medal, Royal Soc. of NZ, 1999; Dist. Res. Medal, Univ. of Otago, 2003. *Publications:* The Health of the People, 2019; scientific articles on cancer causes and control, contraceptive and drug safety and epidemiology of multiple sclerosis and AIDS. *Recreations:* books, art history, walking. *Address:* PO Box 6023, Dunedin 9059, New Zealand. *T:* (3) 4795774.

**SKEGGS, Sir Clifford (George),** Kt 1987; JP; FNZIM; Founder, 1952, and former Chairman and Chief Executive, Skeggs Group; Director of various public and private companies; Mayor, Dunedin City, 1978–89; *b* 19 March 1931; *s* of George Henry Skeggs and Beatrice Hannah (*née* Heathcote); *m* 1952, Marie Eleanor Ledgerwood; three *s*. *Educ:* Southland Technical Coll., New Zealand. Mem., 1968–80, Chm., 1973–77, Otago Harbour Bd. City Councillor, Dunedin, 1972–77. Mem. Council, Univ. of Otago, 1981–89. FNZIM 1985; Mem., Inst. of Dirs, 1984. JP Dunedin, 1978. OStJ 1987. *Publications:* contrib. fishing and general business publications. *Recreations:* yachting, golf, flying, power boating, squash, keen follower of Rugby. *Club:* Dunedin (Dunedin).

**SKEHEL, Sir John (James),** Kt 1996; PhD; FRS 1984; Director, MRC National Institute for Medical Research, 1987–2006, then Visiting Scientist, now Emeritus Scientist, Francis Crick Institute; *b* 27 Feb. 1941; *s* of Joseph and Annie Josephine Skehel; *m* 1962, Anita Varley; two *s*. *Educ:* St Mary's Coll., Blackburn; University College of Wales, Aberystwyth (BSc); UMIST (PhD). Post-doctoral Fellow, Marischal Coll., Aberdeen, 1965–68; Fellow, Helen Hay Whitney Foundn, 1968–71; MRC National Institute for Medical Research: Mem., Scientific Staff, 1971–2006; Head of Div. of Virology, 1984–87. Dir, World Influenza Centre, 1975–93. Leeuwenhoek Lecture, Royal Soc., 1990. Hon. Professor: Liverpool John Moores Univ. (formerly Liverpool Poly. Sch. of Nat. Sci.), 1990–; Div. of Virology, UCL, 2003–; Vis. Prof. of Virology, Glasgow Univ., 1997–. Biol Sec. and Vice-Pres., Royal Soc., 2013–. Mem., EMBO, 1983; MAE, 1992. Founder FMedSci 1998 (Vice-Pres., 2001–07). Hon. Mem., Soc. for Gen. Microbiol., 2004. Foreign Associate, NAS, 2014–. Hon. Fellow, Univ. of Wales, 2004. Hon. DSc: CNAA, 1990; London, 2004; Liverpool John Moores, 2007; La Laurea *hc* Medicina E Chirurgia, Univ. of Padua, 2010. Wilhelm Feldberg prize, Feldberg Foundn, 1986; Robert Koch prize, Robert Koch Foundn, 1987; Prix Louis Jeantet de Médecine, Jeantet Foundn, 1988; Internat. Prize in Virology, ICN Pharmaceuticals, 1992; Royal Medal, Royal Soc., 2003; Ernst Chain Prize, Imperial Coll., London, 2004; Grand Prix, Louis D Foundn, Institut de France, 2007. *Publications:* numerous scientific articles in various jls. *Address:* Francis Crick Institute, 1 Midland Road, NW1 1AT.

**SKELLETT, Colin Frank,** OBE 2012; CChem, FRSC; FCIWEM; Chief Executive, Wessex Water, since 1988; *b* 13 June 1945; *s* of Harry and Ivy Skellett; *m* 1st, 1963, Jennifer Trout (marr. diss.); two *s* one *d*; 2nd, 2010, Theresa McDermott. *Educ:* City Univ. (MSc Water Engrg). CChem 1971, FRSC 1990. Chemist, Nottingham CC, 1961–69; Sen. Chemist, Bath CC, 1970–74; operational and mgt posts, Wessex Water, 1974–88. Non-executive Chairman: Jarvis plc, 2000–02; Regen South West Ltd, 2002–07; European Connoisseurs Travel, 2006–; Bath Hotel & Spa Ltd, 2013–; Vice-Chm., Azurix Services, 1999–2001; Director: YTL Utilities UK Ltd, 2002–; GWE/Business West, 2008– (Jt Chm., 2008–13); Chairman: Future Bath Plus, 2008–12; Bd, West of England LEP, 2011–15; Thermae Bath Spa, 2013–; YTL Develts (UK) Ltd, 2017–. Bd Mem., SW RDA, 2001–07. Trustee: WaterAid, 1995–2003; Money Advice Trust, 2000–02; Dir, Venturers Trust, 2017–. Chm. Govs, Merchants' Acad., 2016–. Churchill Fellow, 1983. Master, Soc. of Merchant Venturers, 2009–10. Hon. DEng: West of England, 2014; Bristol, 2019. *Publications:* various technical papers on water and waste water treatment. *Recreations:* walking, theatre, music, charity fundraising. *Address:* (office) Wessex Water, Claverton Down, Bath BA2 7WW. *T:* (01225) 526000.

**SKELLORN, Kathryn Mair;** QC 2014; a Recorder, since 2018; *b* Cardiff, 4 June 1971; *m* 2004; three *d*. *Educ:* Heaton Grammar Sch., Newcastle upon Tyne; Clifton High Sch., Bristol; Magdalen Coll., Oxford (MA Juris. 1992); Inns of Court Sch. of Law. Gray's Inn Jun. Schol., 1992–93; called to the Bar, Gray's Inn, 1993; in practice as a barrister, 1993–; Children Act specialist. Trustee, Nonita Glenday Fund, 2013–. *Recreations:* running, cookery, writing. *Address:* St John's Chambers, 101 Victoria Street, Bristol BS1 6PU. *E:* Kathryn.skellornqc@stjohnschambers.co.uk.

**SKELLY, Michael Anthony;** Headmaster, Westcliff High School for Boys, since 2012 (Deputy Headmaster, 2010–12); *b* Dublin, 1 Nov. 1971; *s* of Michael and Mary Skelly; partner, Maria Morris. *Educ:* Patrician Coll.; St Patrick's Coll., Maynooth (BA Econs and Music 1992); Open Univ. (MA Open and Distance Educn). Asst Choir Dir, Palestrina Choir, Dublin Pro-Cathedral, 1992–93; Teacher of Econs, 1994–2000, Dir, Sixth Form Studies, 2000–03, Westcliff High Sch. for Boys; Dep. Headmaster, 2003–09, Actg Headmaster, 2009–10, Calday Grange GS. Gov., Chalkwell Hall Infant Sch., 2013–. *Recreations:* theatre, concerts, opera, economic literature. *Address:* Westcliff High School for Boys, Kenilworth Gardens, Westcliff on Sea, Essex SS0 0BP. *T:* (01702) 475443. *E:* skellym@whsb.essex.sch.uk.

**SKELLY, William Alan**; Chief Constable, Lincolnshire Police, since 2017; *b* Dundee, 29 Nov. 1966; *s* of William Skelly and Gladys Emily Skelly (*née* Wood); *m* Alison Margaret Dobbie (marr. diss.); two *d*; *m* Jane Wilkin. *Educ*: Auchterhouse Primary Sch., Angus; Newtyle Secondary Sch., Angus; Harris Acad., Dundee; Edinburgh Univ. (BSc Maths 1988; MBA 1997); Cambridge Univ. (Dip. Criminol. 2004); Inst. of Dirs (Cert. and Dip. 2016). Joined Lothian and Borders Police, 1990; plain clothed and uniformed roles, 1990–99; Project Officer, Local Govt Section, Audit Scotland (on secondment), 1999–2000; Inspector, 1999–2001; Chief Inspector, 2001–02; Temp. Supt, then Supt, later Chief Supt, 2002–07; Strategic Comd Course, Bramshill, 2004; on secondment to Metropolitan Police, 2005, as Leader, Immigration Crime Team, then i/c UK Campaign targeting criminals involved in trafficking women for sexual exploitation; Asst Chief Constable (Crime and Operational Support), 2007–08; Temp. Dep. Chief Constable, 2008–09; HM Inspector of Constabulary for Scotland (on secondment), 2009–10; Asst Chief Constable, Lothian and Borders Police, 2011–13; Dep. Chief Constable, Devon and Cornwall Police, 2013–17. Internat. Visitor Leadership Prog., US State Dept, 2007. Mem. Bd, Scottish Inst. of Policing Res., 2009. Mem., Adv. Gp, Place2Be (children's charity), 2010–. Chm., volleyball section, Police Sport UK. Hon. Col, Kentucky, 2007. Queen's Golden Jubilee Medal, 2002. *Publications*: Public Servant Scotland, 2010. *Recreations*: volleyball (played European match as mem., GB Police team competing against Finland, 2009, Turkey, 2013, Greece, 2017), learning the guitar (consistently guilty of terrible crimes against many respected songs).

**SKELMERSDALE**, 8th Baron *cr* 1828; **Andrew Bootle-Wilbraham**; *b* 9 Aug. 1977; *s* of 7th Baron Skelmersdale and of Christine Joan (*née* Morgan); *S* father, 2018; *m* 2005, Fenella Jane, *yr d* of Jonathan Richmond Edwards; two *s*. *Heir*: *s* Hon. Daniel Peter Bootle-Wilbraham, *b* 7 June 2007.

**SKELTON, Nicholas David, (Nick)**, CBE 2017 (OBE 2012); show jumper; *b* 30 Dec. 1957; *s* of David Frank Skelton and Norma Skelton (*née* Brindley); *m* 1982, Sarah Poile; two *s*. Jun. European Champion, 1975; British Champion, 1981, on St James; European Championships: team gold medal, 1985, 1987, 1989, team silver medal, 1991, 1993, 1995, team bronze medal, 2011, individual bronze medal, on Apollo, 1987, on Carlo, 2011; World Championships: team bronze medals, 1982, 1990, 1998, team silver medal, and individual bronze medal, on Apollo, 1986; winner: King George V Gold Cup, on St James, 1984, on Limited Edition, 1993, 1996, on Hopes Are High, 1999; Hickstead Derby, on J Nick, 1987, on Apollo, 1988, 1989; Grand Prix in Britain, Canada, France, Germany, Ireland, USA; Member: Nations Cup team, 1978; British Team, 1978; Olympic team, 1988, 1992, 1996, 2004, 2008, 2012 (Gold Medal, team jumping); Gold Medal, individual jumping, Olympic Games, Rio de Janeiro, 2016. Chef d'équipe, British team, Nations Cup, Lisbon, 2001. *Publications*: Only Falls and Horses (autobiog.), 2001; Gold: my autobiography, 2017.

**SKELTON, Peter**; QC 2016; *b* Sheffield, 5 Oct. 1971; *s* of Roger Edward Skelton and Christine Mary Skelton; *m* 2004, Justine Leah Walton; two *s*. *Educ*: Trent Coll.; Univ. of York (BA English Lit. 1994); Univ. of California, San Diego; Trinity Hall, Cambridge (MPhil 1996). Called to the Bar, Middle Temple, 1997; in practice as barrister, specialising in human rights, public inquiries and inquests. *Publications*: (jtly) Public Inquiries, 2011; (jtly) The Inquest Book, 2016. *Recreations*: watching films, making my children laugh, swimming in the sea. *Address*: 1 Crown Office Row, Temple, EC4Y 7HH. *T*: (020) 7797 7500, *Fax*: (020) 7797 7550. *E*: peter.skelton@1cor.com. *Club*: Soho House.

**SKELTON, Peter John**, OBE 1997; Director, Tunisia, 2005–09, and Director, Business Support Services, Near East and North Africa Region, 2008–09, British Council; Volunteer, Refugee Support Devon (Ltd), since 2013; *b* 24 Sept. 1949; *s* of John Frederick and Gwendoline Mabel Skelton; *m* 1st, 1971, Heather Morrison (marr. diss. 2009); one *s* one *d*; 2nd, 2009, Trupti Desai; one *s*. *Educ*: Queen Elizabeth's Grammar Sch., Barnet; Durham Univ. (BA Hons Modern Arabic Studies 1971); UCNW, Bangor (PGCE (TEFL) 1973). Desk Officer, FCO, 1971; British Council: Asst Rep., Jordan, 1977–81, Peru, 1982–84; Dep. Rep., Wales, 1984–86, Zambia, 1986–88; Dir, Hamburg, 1989–93, E Jerusalem (West Bank and Gaza), 1993–98; Regl Dir, Eastern and Central Africa, and Dir, Kenya, 1998–2000; Dir, Cyprus, 2000–05. CSV Volunteer Co-ordinator, BBC Radio Devon, 2010–13. Parent Gov., Clyst St Mary Primary Sch., Devon, 2014–16. *Recreations*: family, Tottenham Hotspur, all sport, cycling, playing guitar, Hospital Radio Exeter, editing the Clyst Valley News. *Address*: c/o British Council Association, 10 Spring Gardens, SW1A 2BN. *T*: (020) 7930 8466.

**SKELTON, Robert William**, OBE 1989; Keeper, Indian Department, Victoria and Albert Museum, 1978–88; *b* 11 June 1929; *s* of John William Skelton and Victoria (*née* Wright); *m* 1954, Frances Aird; three *s*. *Educ*: Tiffin Boys' Sch., Kingston-upon-Thames. Joined Indian Section of Victoria and Albert Museum, 1950; Asst Keeper, 1960; Dep. Keeper, 1972; Nuffield Travelling Fellow in India, 1962. Mem. Council: Royal Asiatic Soc., 1970–73, 1975–78, 1988–92; Soc. for S Asian Studies, 1984–94; Trustee: Asia House Trust (London), 1977–2008; Indian Nat. Trust for Art and Cultural Heritage, UK, 1991–2008. *Publications*: Indian Miniatures from the XVth to XIXth Centuries, 1961; Rajasthani Temple Hangings of the Krishna Cult, 1973; (jtly) Islamic Painting and Arts of the Book, 1976; (jtly) Indian Painting, 1978; (jtly) Arts of Bengal, 1979; (jtly) The Indian Heritage, 1982; (jtly) Islamic Art in the Keir Collection, 1988; (jtly) The Indian Portrait 1560–1860, 2010; (jtly) Ragamala Paintings from India, 2011; (jtly) Beyond Extravagance: a Royal collection of gems and jewels, 2013; various contribs to art periodicals and conf. proc., 1956–. *Recreations*: chamber music, walking. *Address*: 10 Spencer Road, South Croydon CR2 7EH. *E*: robertskelton@blueyonder.co.uk.

**SKEMPTON, Howard While**; composer; *b* Chester, 31 Oct. 1947; *s* of late Ivor Skempton and Leslie Skempton; *m* 1984, Susan Lordon (*d* 2008); one *s*. *Educ*: Birkenhead Sch.; Ealing Technical Coll. Composition Tutor, Birmingham Conservatoire, 2005–. *Compositions include*: Lento, 1991; Six Figures, for solo cello, 1998; Five Preludes, for guitar, 1999; Chamber Concerto, for 15 players; Concerto for Hurdy-Gurdy and Percussion; Tendrils, for string quartet; The Moon is Flashing, song cycle for tenor and orch.; Only the Sound Remains, for viola and ensemble; Song's Eternity, choral; Five Rings Triples, for eight church bells, 2012; Piano Concerto, 2015; The Rime of the Ancient Mariner, 2015; Ave Maria, choral, 2016; Man and Bat, 2017. Hon. RAM 2012. *Recreations*: art, theatre, friendship. *Address*: 4 Pleasant Way, Leamington Spa CV32 5XA. *T*: (01926) 338739. *E*: howardskempton@aol.com.
*See also Maj. Gen. K. Skempton.*

**SKEMPTON, Maj. Gen. Keith**, CBE 1997; DL; independent consultant, since 2016; Defence Sector Lead (formerly defence consultant), Capita Property and Infrastructure Ltd (formerly Capita Symonds), 2010–16; *b* 22 Feb. 1949; *s* of late Dr Ivor Skempton and Leslie Skempton; *m* 1971, Susan Lawrence; one *d*. *Educ*: Birkenhead Sch.; Liverpool Coll. of Building; Mons OCS; Army Staff Coll., Camberley. Commnd Cheshire Regt, 1969; served UK, ME and FE; COS, 33 Armd Bde, 1982–83; MA to GOC NI, 1986–88; CO, 1st Bn Cheshire Regt, 1988–91 (mentioned in despatches, 1988, 1990, NI); Dep. COS, 1st Armd Div., 1991–93; DACOS, G4 Ops and Plans, HQ Land Comd, 1993–96; COS, HQ British Forces Cyprus, 1996–98; Dep. COS, Support, HQ ARRC, 1998–2001 (QCVS 1999, Kosovo op.); ACOS, HQ AFSOUTH, 2001–03; Col, 22nd (Cheshire) Regt, 1999–2006. Business Develt Dir, Denis Ferranti Gp, 2006–07; Operations Dir, Chester Cathedral, 2007–08. Pres., SSAFA (Cheshire Br.), 2011–. Trustee, Cheshire Military Mus., 1998–. FCMI 2003–13. DL Cheshire, 2006. *Recreations*: sailing, game shooting, ski-ing, motor vehicles. *Address*: Regimental Headquarters, Mercian Regiment (Cheshire), The Castle, Chester CH1 2DN. *T*: (01244) 327617, (mobile) 07795 476172. *E*: keithskempton@hotmail.com, keith@skempton.co.uk. *Clubs*: Army and Navy; Chester City, Cheshire Pitt.
*See also H. W. Skempton.*

**SKENE, Alison Jean Katherine**, MBE 2015; Director, Skene Group, since 1972; Vice Lord-Lieutenant of Aberdeen City, 2007–14; *b* 26 May 1939; *d* of Alexander Lamont and Alexa Lee Lamont (*née* Will); *m* 1964, Charles Pirie Skene; one *s* two *d*. *Educ*: High Sch. for Girls, Aberdeen; Univ. of Aberdeen (MA); Aberdeen Trng Coll. Teacher of French, 1961–65. Pres., Jun. Chamber Wives Gp, 1970–71; Committee Member: St John Assoc., 1984–90; Queens Cross/Harlaw Community Council, 1987–94; Grampian/Houston Assoc., 1989–2002. Mem., Gen. Council, Business Cttee, 1980–2007, Court, 1990–2002, Aberdeen Univ. Mem. Cttee, Elphinstone Inst. Friends' Assoc., 1996–2005. Burgess of Guild, City of Aberdeen, 1998. DL Aberdeen, 1999. Pres., St Nicholas Probus Club, 2006–07. MUniv Aberdeen, 2016. OStJ 2000 (SSStJ 1987). *Recreations*: spending time with grandsons, Hamish, Cameron, Charlie and Oscar, walking, travelling, golfing, reading, crosswords. *Address*: 21 Rubislaw Den North, Aberdeen AB15 4AL. *T*: (01224) 317517. *E*: alison.skene@theskenegroup.com. *Clubs*: Aberdeen Ladies' Golf; St Nicholas Probus (Aberdeen).

**SKENE, Prudence Patricia**, CBE 2000; Governance Associate, Clore Leadership Programme, since 2009; *b* 9 Jan. 1944; *d* of Robert Worboys Skene and Phyllis Monica Skene (*née* Langley); *m* 1986, Brian Henry Wray (*d* 2002); one step *s* one step *d*. *Educ*: Francis Holland Sch., London; Open Univ. (BA Hons. 1st Cl. 2009). Dep. Administrator, The Round House, Chalk Farm, 1973–75; Ballet Rambert: Administrator, 1975–78; Admin. Dir, 1978–84; Exec. Dir, 1984–86; Exec. Producer, English Shakespeare Co., 1987–90 and 1992; Dir, The Arts Foundn, 1993–98. Non-executive Director: Theatre Royal, Bath, 1998–2003; Royal United Hosp. Bath NHS Trust, 1999–2003; Chairman: Arvon Foundn, 2000–05; Rambert Dance Co., 2000–09; Free Word, 2010–14. Mem., Arts Council of England (formerly Arts Council of GB), 1992–2000 (Chairman: Dance Panel, 1992–96; Lottery Panel, 1996–2000). Vice-Pres., 1985–89, Pres., 1991–92, Theatrical Management Assoc.; Chm., Dancers Resettlement Trust and Vice-Chm., Dancers Resettlement Fund, 1988–92. Chm., Cardboard Citizens, 2016–; Trustee: Cardiff Old Liby Trust, 1996–2000; Stephen Spender Trust (formerly Meml Fund), 2000–17 (Chm., 2013–17); Friends of the V&A, 2004–10; NESTA, 2006–07; Nureyev Foundn, 2007–; Ambit, 2014–17; Rosie Kay (formerly Athena Contemp.) Dance Trust, 2016–19. FRSA 1992. *Publications*: Capital Gains: how the National Lottery transformed England's arts, 2017. *Recreations*: travel, food, the performing arts. *Address*: 19a Eccleston Street, SW1W 9LX.

**SKENE CATLING, Charlotte Merilyn, (Mrs Adam Lowe)**, RIBA; architect; Co-Founder and Director, Skene Catling de la Peña, since 2003; *b* London; *b* 27 Oct.; *d* of Patrick Skene Catling and Diane Skene Catling (*née* Wheeler-Nicholson); *m* 2016, Adam Lowe; one step *s*. *Educ*: Univ. of Westminster (BA Hons Arch. (RIBA Pt I) 1992; MArch (Dist.) (RIBA Pt II) 1996); Architectural Assoc. (RIBA Pt III 2014). RIBA 2014; Mem., ARB 2014. Studio Axel Kufus, Berlin, 1993; collaboration with Malcolm McLaren on writing projects, 1994–2000 (and on design for men's and women's wear fashion collection, 1999); Dir, Eco Lab plc, 2000–01; designer of architectural/brand identity for Agent Provocateur (incl. shops, 50 sites in UK and abroad), 2001–08; designed sets/architectural interventions for Beethoven's Fidelio, with Perm State P. I. Tchaikovsky Opera Theatre, former Gulag Perm36, Perm, Russia, 2010. Hd, Postgrad. Architecture Unit, RCA, 2007–12; Lectr, postgrad. architecture, Karlsruhe Inst. Technol., 2015–16; res. project, RCA/Rothschild Foundn, on representation in architecture, 2013–16. Maker of architectural films; Co-Founder, Architecture Film Fest., London, 2016. An Ambassador, London Sch. of Architecture, 2014–. *Publications*: contrib. articles to Burlington Mag., Sunday Telegraph, Architectural Rev., Architecture Today, ARCH+. *Recreations*: escaping with Adam Lowe on his Factum adventures, drifting through cities, dreaming over atlases, old book catalogues, architecture and geology (geo-archaeology), architectural film and images of the intangible: music, electricity and the moon. *Address*: 3, 71 Elm Park Gardens, SW10 9QE. *T*: (020) 7262 2806. *E*: charlotte@scdlp.net; Calle Albarracin 28, 28037 Madrid, Spain. *Clubs*: Chelsea Arts, Academy, 5 Hertford Street, Union; National Arts (New York).

**SKEOCH, (Norman) Keith**; Chief Executive, Standard Life Aberdeen, since 2019 (Co-Chief Executive, 2017–19); *b* Ouston, 5 Nov. 1956; *s* of Norman and Audrey Skeoch; *m* 1981, Andrea Ball; two *s*. *Educ*: Prior Pursglove Coll.; Univ. of Sussex (BA Hons); Univ. of Warwick (MA). Govt Econ. Service, 1979–80; James Capel: Internat. Economist, 1980–99; Chief Economist and Associate Partner, 1984–99; Sen. Exec. (Partner), 1986–99; Dir, Econs and Strategy and Mem., James Capel & Co. Bd, 1993–99; Man. Dir, Internat. Equities, 1998–99; Exec. Dir, 1999–2017, Chief Investment Officer, 1999–2004, CEO, 2004–17, Standard Life Investments Ltd; Exec. Dir, 2006–17, CEO, 2015–17, Standard Life plc. Director: HDFC Asset Mgt Co. Ltd, 2005–; HDFC Standard Life Insce Co. Ltd, 2005–; Standard Life Investments (Hldgs) Ltd, 2006–; Aida Capital Ltd, 2010–15; Standard Life Assurance Ltd, 2015–; Standard Life Employee Services Ltd, 2015–; Standard Life Foundn, 2015–. Mem., Chancellor's Wkg Gp on Rights Issues, 2007. Mem., Sen. Practitioner Panel, FSA, 2006–; Mem., Adv. Panel on impact of financial crisis, 2010–, Dir, and Mem., Codes and Standards Cttee, 2012–, Financial Reporting Council. Dir, ABI, 2007 (Chm., Investment Cttee); Director: Investment Mgt Assoc., 2007 (Chm., Asset Mgt Cttee); Investment Assoc., 2019–. Chm., Instnl Shareholders Cttee, 2009. Mem., Adv. Council, Instnl Investor Cttee, 2011–14. FCSI 2005; Fellow, Soc. of Business Economists, 2012. Hon. DBA Teesside, 2011; DUniv Sussex, 2015. *Recreations*: fly fishing, music, watching Rugby. *Address*: Standard Life Aberdeen, 6 St Andrew Square, Edinburgh EH2 2AH. *T*: (0131) 245 5046. *Club*: Reform.

**SKERRIT, Hon. Roosevelt**; MHA (Lab) Vieille Case, Dominica, since 2000; Prime Minister of Dominica, since 2004; Minister for Finance, since 2004, and for Foreign Affairs and Information Technology, since 2010; *b* 8 June 1972; one *s*; *m* 2013, Melissa Poponne; one *s*. *Educ*: New Mexico State Univ. (Dip. Secondary Educn 1995); Univ. of Mississippi (BA Hons Psychol. and English 1997). Quality Assce Officer, JUC Factory, Dominica; teacher, Portsmouth Secondary Sch.; Supervisor, Student Activity Center, Univ. of Mississippi; Database Manager/Advr, Offshore Firm; Lectr, Dominica State Coll., 1997–99. Minister: for Sports and Youth Affairs, 2000; for Educn, Sports and Youth Affairs, 2000–04. Mem., Exec. Bd, UNESCO. Mem. Council, Univ. of WI (Member: F and GP Cttee; Strategy Cttee). Leader, Dominica Labour Party, 2004–.

**SKEWIS, (William) Iain**, PhD; FTS; FCILT; Principal Consultant, Maldwyn Development Consultancy (trading as Action with Impact) (formerly Maldwyn Development Consultancy and Rural Development Solutions), since 2009; *s* of John Jamieson and Margaret Middlemass Skewis; *m* 1963, Jessie Frame Weir; two *s* one *d*. *Educ*:

Hamilton Academy; Univ. of Glasgow (BSc, PhD). FTS 1987. British Rail, 1961–63; Transport Holding Co., 1963–66; Highlands and Islands Develt Bd, 1966–72; Yorkshire and Humberside Develt, 1973–77; Chief Executive: Develt Bd for Rural Wales, 1977–90; Enterprise SW Shropshire, 1998–2009. Consultant, Develt Consultancy, 1995–2009. Chm., Regl Studies Assoc., 1990–93. Dir/Coordinator, Soccer Destinations, 1984–2012; Chairman: British Isles Soccer Tournaments Assoc., 1996–2010; Football Assoc. of Wales Premier Cup, 1998–2008. *Recreation:* soccer. *Address:* 6 Heritage Green, Forden, Welshpool SY21 8LH. *T:* (01938) 580695. *E:* iain.skewis@gmail.com.

**SKIDELSKY,** family name of **Baron Skidelsky**.

**SKIDELSKY,** Baron *cr* 1991 (Life Peer), of Tilton in the County of East Sussex; **Robert Jacob Alexander Skidelsky,** DPhil; FRSL; FRHistS; FBA 1994; Professor of Political Economy, Warwick University, 1990–2007, now Emeritus; *b* 25 April 1939; *s* of late Boris Skidelsky and Galia Sapelkin; *m* 1970, Augusta Mary Clarissa Hope; two *s* one *d. Educ:* Brighton Coll.; Jesus Coll., Oxford (BA and MA Mod. Hist.; DPhil; Hon. Fellow, 1997). FRHistS 1973; FRSL 1978. Res. Fellow: Nuffield Coll., Oxford, 1965–68; British Acad., 1968–70; Associate Prof. of History, Sch. of Advanced Internat. Studies, Johns Hopkins Univ., Washington, DC, 1970–76; Head, Dept of History, Philosophy and Eur. Studies, Polytechnic of N London, 1976–78; Prof. of Internat. Studies, Warwick Univ., 1978–90. Director: Stilwell Financial Inc., 2001–03; Janus Capital, 2003–11; Gtr Europe Fund, 2005–09; Sistema, 2008–10; Rusnano Capital, 2010–. Dir, 1999–91, Chm., 1991–2001, Social Market Foundn; Mem., Policy Cttee, SDP, 1988–90. Opposition Spokesman on: Culture, Media and Sport, H of L, 1997–98; Treasury affairs, 1998–99. Chairman: Charleston Trust, 1987–92; Hands Off Reading Campaign, 1994–98. Member: Adv. Council on Public Records, 1988–93; Schools Examinations and Assessment Council, 1992–93; Council, Royal Economic Soc., 2007–; Adv. Council, Inst. for New Economic Thinking, 2010–. Mem., Bd of Dirs, Moscow Sch. of Pol Studies, 1999–; Exec. Sec., UK/Russia Roundtable, 2005–07. Governor: Portsmouth Univ., 1994–97; Brighton Coll., 1998–2004 (Chm. of Govs, 2004–17); Wilton Park Academic Council, 2003–09. Hon. DLitt: Buckingham, 1997; Rome, 2010; Warwick, 2011. *Publications:* Politicians and the Slump, 1967, 2nd edn 1994; English Progressive Schools, 1969; Oswald Mosley, 1975; (ed) The End of the Keynesian Era, 1977; (ed, with Michael Holroyd) William Gerhardie's God's Fifth Column, 1981; John Maynard Keynes, vol. 1 1883–1920, Hopes Betrayed, 1983, vol. 2 1921–1937, The Economist as Saviour (Wolfson History Prize), 1992, vol. 3 1937–1946, Fighting for Britain (Duff Cooper, Lionel Gelber, James Tait Black Meml and Council on Foreign Relations Prizes), 2000, abridged edn in one vol. 2003; (ed) Thatcherism, 1988; Interests and Obsessions, 1993; The World After Communism, 1995; Keynes, 1996; Keynes: return of the master, 2009; (with Edward Skidelsky) How Much is Enough?: the love of money, and the case for the good life, 2012; Britain in the 20th Century: a success?, 2014; (ed) The Essential Keynes, 2015; (with Nicolò Fraccaroli) Austerity vs Stimulus: the political future of economic recovery, 2017; Money and Government, 2018. *Recreations:* music, travelling, sport, conversation. *Address:* Aberdeen House, 41 Steyne Road, Seaford, East Sussex BN25 1HU. *T:* (01323) 890941.

**SKIDMORE, Rt Hon. Christopher (James),** FRHistS, FSA; PC 2019; MP (C) Kingswood, since 2010; Minister of State, Department for Education and Department for Business, Energy and Industrial Strategy, since 2019; author, since 2004; *b* Bristol, 17 May 1981; *s* of Robert and Elaine Skidmore; *m* 2014, Lydia Wilson; one *s* one *d. Educ:* Bristol Grammar Sch.; Christ Church, Oxford (BA Hons Double First; MSt). FRHistS 2010; FSA 2014. Advr, Cons. Party, 2006–09; Tutor, 2009–10, Hon. Res. Fellow, 2012–, Bristol Univ. PPS to Chancellor of the Duchy of Lancaster, 2015, to Chancellor of the Exchequer, 2015–16; Parly Sec., Cabinet Office, 2016–18; Minister of State, DfE and BEIS, 2018–19, DHSC, 2019. Member: Health Select Cttee, 2010–13; Educn Select Cttee, 2012–14; Policy Bd, No 10 Downing St, 2013–15 (Dep. Chm., 2014–15). FRSA. *Publications:* Edward VI: the lost king, 2007; Death and the Virgin, 2010; After the Coalition, 2011; Britannia Unchained, 2012; Bosworth: the birth of the Tudors, 2013; Richard III: brother, protector, king, 2017. *Address:* House of Commons, SW1A 0AA. *T:* (020) 7219 7094. *E:* chris.skidmore.mp@parliament.uk.

**SKIDMORE, Jeffrey,** OBE 2015; Artistic Director and Conductor, Ex Cathedra, since 1969; *b* 27 Feb. 1951; *s* of Ernest and Lily Mary Skidmore; *m* 1974, Janet Mary Moore; two *s* one *d. Educ:* Magdalene Coll., Oxford (BA). Head of Music: Hagley Park Sch., Rugeley, 1978–80; John Wilmott Sch., Birmingham, 1980–92. Hon. Res. Fellow, Univ. of Birmingham, 1998–; Hon. Fellow, Birmingham Conservatoire, 2001. Has made recordings. Hon. DMus Birmingham, 2017. *Address:* Ex Cathedra, CBSO Centre, Berkley Street, Birmingham B1 2LF. *T:* (0121) 616 3411. *E:* info@excathedra.co.uk.

**SKILBECK, Diana Margaret,** MBE 2012; Headmistress, The Queen's School, Chester, 1989–2001; *b* 14 Nov. 1942; *d* of late William Allen Skilbeck and Elsie Almond Skilbeck. *Educ:* Wirral County Grammar School for Girls, Cheshire; Furzedown Coll., London (Teacher's Cert.); BA Hons London (External). Assistant Teacher: Mendell Primary Sch., 1964–67; Gayton Primary Sch., 1967–69; Wirral County Grammar Sch., 1969–74; Head of Geography, Wirral County Grammar Sch., 1974–78; Dep. Headmistress, West Kirby Grammar Sch., 1978–83; Headmistress, Sheffield High School, GPDST, 1983–89. Hon. MA Chester, 2015. *Recreations:* inland waterways, walking, singing, reading, industrial archaeology.

**SKILBECK, Prof. Malcolm,** AO 2014; education consultant and writer; Emeritus Professor, Deakin University, Australia, 1986; *b* 22 Sept. 1932; *s* of Charles Harrison Skilbeck and Elsie Muriel Nash Skilbeck; *m* Helen Connell. *Educ:* Univ. of Sydney (BA); Acad. DipEd London, PhD London; MA Illinois. Secondary school teacher and adult educn teacher, 1958–63; Lectr, Univ. of Bristol, 1963–71; Prof., New Univ. of Ulster, 1971–75; Dir, Australian Curriculum Develt Centre, 1975–81; Dir of Studies, Schs Council for Curriculum and Exams for England and Wales, 1981–83; Prof. of Education, Univ. of London, 1981–85; Vice-Chancellor and Pres., Deakin Univ., Australia, 1986–91; Dep. Dir (Educn), Directorate of Educn, Employment, Labour and Social Affairs, OECD, 1991–97. Active in voluntary organizations concerned with educn for internat. understanding, e.g. Chm., World Educn Fellowship, 1981–85. Currently researching history of nature ideas in art, religion, science and educn. Hon. DLitt NUI, 2000. *Publications:* John Dewey, 1970; (jtly) Classroom and Culture, 1976; (jtly) Inservice Education and Training, 1977; A Core Curriculum for the Common School 1982; (ed) Evaluating the Curriculum in the Eighties, 1984; School Based Curriculum Development, 1984; Readings in School-Based Curriculum Development, 1984; Curriculum Reform, 1990; The Vocational Quest, 1994; (jtly) Redefining Tertiary Education, 1998; Access and Equity in Higher Education, 2000; Education for All: 2000 assessment, 2000; numerous contribs to jls, project reports, etc. *Recreations:* landcare, winemaking, reading.

**SKILTON, Ven. Christopher John;** Archdeacon of Croydon, 2013–Feb. 2020; *b* 19 March 1955; *s* of John Hampsheir Skilton and Kathleen Ada Skilton; *m* 1980, Barbara Kilgour; one *s* two *d. Educ:* Magdalene Coll., Cambridge (BA 1976, MA 1980); Wycliffe Hall, Oxford; St John's Coll., Nottingham (MA in Mission/Ministry 1996). Ordained deacon, 1980, priest, 1981; Curate: St Mary, Ealing, 1980–84; Newborough and Leigh St John, Wimborne, 1984–88; Team Vicar, St Paul, Great Baddow, 1988–95; Team Rector, Sanderstead, 1995–2003; RD, Croydon S, 2000–03; Archdeacon of Lambeth, 2004–13; Priest-in-charge, St Mark's, Kennington, 2008–09. *Recreations:* gardening, cricket, recent British politics, The Archers, classical music, classic and contemporary fiction, walking. *Address:* 6 St Peter's Road, Croydon CR0 1HD; (until Feb. 2020) (office) St Matthew's House, 100 George Street, Croydon CR0 1PE. *T:* (020) 8256 9633. *E:* chris.skilton@southwark.anglican.org.

**SKILTON, Prof. David John;** Professor of English, 1988–2009, now Emeritus, and Research Professor, 2002–11, Cardiff University (formerly University of Wales College of Cardiff); *b* July 1942; *s* of Henry C. S. Skilton and Iris F. M. Skilton; *m* 1st, 1976, Marvid E. G. Kennedy-Finlayson (marr. diss.), 2nd, 1984, Joanne V. Papworth; one *s* one *d. Educ:* Tollington Grammar Sch., London; King's Coll., Cambridge (MA, MLitt); Univ. of Copenhagen. Lectr, Glasgow Univ., 1970–80; Professor of English: St David's University Coll., Lampeter, 1980–86; UWIST, 1986–88; Head of School of English, Communication and Philosophy, UWCC, then Cardiff Univ., 1988–2002; Pro Vice-Chancellor, UWCC, 1992–96; Dean, Faculty of Humanities, Cardiff Univ., 1997–99. Mem., Nat. Curriculum English Working Group, 1988–89; Trustee, Brainwave Project Trust (formerly Roald Dahl Arts Project), 1996–2016 (Chair, 2011–16). Literary Adviser to Trollope Soc., 1988–; Editor, Trollope Soc. edn of novels of Anthony Trollope, 1988–99; Founding Ed., Jl of Illustration Studies, 2007–18; co-author, Database of Mid-Victorian Illustration, 2007–. *Publications:* Anthony Trollope and his Contemporaries, 1972, 2nd edn 1996; Defoe to the Victorians, 1977, 2nd edn 1985; The Early and Mid-Victorian Novel, 1993. *Recreations:* music, Scandinavian culture, anticipated ruins, art and literature of London and Paris. *Address:* School of English, Communication and Philosophy, Cardiff University, Cardiff CF10 3EU.

**SKINGLE, Diana;** HM Diplomatic Service, retired; High Commissioner to Seychelles, 2004–07; *b* 3 May 1947; *d* of Eric Barry Skingle and Joyce Ada Skingle; *m* 2011, Christopher John Marshall Carrington. *Educ:* Chatham Grammar Sch. for Girls; Open Univ. (BSc Hons; Dip Env and Dev); Birkbeck Coll., London (MSc Merit Pols and Sociol.). Joined Commonwealth Office, subseq. FCO, 1966; Kampala, 1970; FCO, 1972; Abidjan, 1974; Vila, 1975; Prague, 1977; Casablanca, 1979; Second Secretary: FCO, 1982; (Aid/Commercial) Georgetown, 1985; (Develt) Bridgetown, 1986; First Secretary: (Information) UK Delegn to NATO, Brussels, 1988; FCO, 1993; Dep. Hd of Mission, Addis Ababa, 2001–04. *Recreations:* cats, walking.

**SKINNER, Angus Mackinnon Cumming;** writer; *b* 4 Jan. 1950; *s* of Dr Theodore Skinner, OBE and Morag Mackinnon Skinner; *m* (marr. diss. 2001); one *s* two *d. Educ:* Univ. of Edinburgh (BSc 1971); London Univ. (CQSW 1973); Strathclyde Univ. (MBA 1988); Pennsylvania Univ. (Master of Applied Positive Psychol., 2006); Univ. of Oxford (Dip. Local History, 2002); Open Univ. (MA Art History, 2015). Social Worker, Cheshire and Kent, 1971–75; Social Work Manager, Lothian and Borders, 1975–91; Chief Social Work Advr, Scottish Office, 1991–92; Chief Insp. of Social Work Services for Scotland, Scottish Office, subseq. Scottish Exec. Educn Dept, 1992–2005. Founding Fellow: Inst. of Contemp. Scotland, 2000; Internat. Positive Psychol Assoc., 2006; FRSA. *Publications:* Gratitude, 2008. *Recreations:* family, friends, learning.

**SKINNER, Charles Edward;** reputation management consultant and trainer, since 2014; *b* 27 July 1951; *s* of late Charles John Henry Skinner and Nell Skinner (*née* Seward); *m* 1973, Caroline Mary Gregory; one *d. Educ:* Nightingale Sch., Wanstead, London. Editorial Trainee, Industrial Daily News, 1968; Editorial Asst, Maclean-Hunter News Publishing, 1969–71; Asst Ed., IPC Business Press, 1971–75; Central Office of Information: Information Officer, N Amer. Desk, Overseas Press and Radio, 1975; Sen. Press Officer, ME Desk, and Defence Correspondent, 1981; Hd, UK and Overseas Radio, 1985; Dir, Films, Television and Radio, 1988–90; Hd, Mktg and Corporate Communication, Home Office, 1990–97; Dir, Govt Information and Communication Service Develt Centre, Cabinet Office, 1997–99; Hd of Mktg, DETR, 1999–2002; Dir of Communication, DfT, 2002–04; Head of Communication, Tower Hamlets Council, 2007–09; of Communications and Consultation, Haringey Council, 2005–07 and 2009–12. Founder and Dir, Your Reputation Matters, 2014–17. Chm., Whitehall Hds of Marketing, 2000–04. FRSA 1993; FCIPR (FIPR 2004). *Publications:* (ed) MI5 - The Security Service, 1993. *Recreations:* opera, political biography, horology, naval history, cycling, old friends.

**SKINNER, Prof. Christopher John,** CBE 2010; PhD; FBA 2004; Professor of Statistics, London School of Economics and Political Science, since 2011; *b* 12 March 1953; *s* of Richard Skinner and Daphne Skinner; two *s*; *m* 2018, Sandra Jones. *Educ:* Trinity Coll., Cambridge (BA 1975); LSE (MSc 1976); Univ. of Southampton (PhD 1982). Lectr, 1982–89, Sen. Lectr, 1989–94, Prof., 1994–2011, Univ. of Southampton. *Publications:* (ed jtly) Analysis of Complex Surveys, 1989; (ed with R. Chambers) Analysis of Survey Data, 2003. *Recreations:* cinema, music. *Address:* Department of Statistics, London School of Economics and Political Science, Houghton Street, WC2A 2AE. *T:* (020) 7405 7686.

**SKINNER, David;** Chief Executive, Co-operative Wholesale Society Ltd, 1992–96; *b* 27 Oct. 1931; *s* of late David Skinner and Mary (*née* Davidson); *m* 1st, 1956, Elizabeth Vera Harben (marr. diss. 1976); one *s* one *d*; 2nd, 1996, Morag J. L. Mar (*née* Busby). *Educ:* Gateshead Grammar Sch.; Nottingham Univ. (BSc). Nat. Service, RNVR, 1953–55. Mgt Trainee, Yorkshire Imperial Metals, 1955–57; Productivity Services Manager, Distillers' Co., 1957–60; Mgt Consultant, 1960–68; Food Divl Manager, Scottish CWS, 1969–73; Co-operative Wholesale Society Ltd: Non Food Controller, 1974–83; Retail Controller and Dep. Chief Exec. (Retail & Services), 1983–92. *Recreations:* comfortable travelling, easy gardening.

**SKINNER, David Victor,** FRCS, FRCSE, FRCSGlas, FRCEM, FIMCRCSE; Consultant, Emergency Department, John Radcliffe Hospital, Oxford, 1981–2011, now Emeritus; Dean, Faculty of Accident and Emergency Medicine, 2000–04; *b* 6 May 1948; *s* of Victor and Joan Skinner; *m* 1975, Alison Rosemary (*née* Earley); one *s* one *d. Educ:* Haberdashers' Aske's Sch.; Royal Free Hosp., London (MB BS 1975). FRCSE 1981; FRCS 1990; FRCSGlas 1993; FIMCRCSE 2004. Consultant, Emergency Dept, St Bartholomew's Hosp., London, 1986–93; Founder Trustee, Bart's City Lifesaver, 1986–; Hon. Sen. Lectr, Oxford Med. Sch. Chair, project exec. team, trauma guidelines, NICE, 2013–16. Gov., RNLI. Trustee, Maternal and Childhealth Advocacy Internat., 2013–16. Service Medal, OStJ, 2003; Royal Coll. of Emergency Medicine Medal, 2011. *Publications:* (ed jtly) Cambridge Textbook of Accident and Emergency Medicine, 1997; (ed jtly) Trauma Care, 1998; (ed jtly) Trauma (A Companion to Bailey and Love's Short Practice of Surgery), 1999; (ed jtly) ABC of Major Trauma, 4th edn 2013. *Recreations:* family, home, Portugal, Scottish Highlands, the Swan yacht Red Beauty, the Scuderia and vintage British motorcycles. *Address:* Northcott, Chiltern Road, Chesham Bois, Amersham, Bucks HP6 5PH. *E:* mvf4312r@gmail.com.

**SKINNER, Dennis Edward;** MP (Lab) Bolsover, since 1970; *b* 11 Feb. 1932; good working-class mining stock; *m* 1960; one *s* two *d. Educ:* Tupton Hall Grammar Sch.; Ruskin Coll., Oxford. Miner, Parkhouse Colliery and Glapwell Colliery, 1949–70. Mem., Nat. Exec. Cttee of Labour Party, 1978–92, 1994–98, 1999–; Vice-Chm., Labour Party, 1987–88, Chm., 1988–89; Pres., Derbyshire Miners (NUM), 1966–70; Pres., NE Derbys

Constituency Labour Party, 1968–71; Derbyshire CC, 1964–70; Clay Cross UDC, 1960–70. *Publications:* Sailing Close to the Wind: reminiscences, 2014. *Recreations:* tennis, cycling, walking. *Address:* House of Commons, SW1A 0AA. *T:* (01773) 581027. *Clubs:* Miners' Welfares in Derbyshire; Bestwood Working Men's.

SKINNER, Frank; entertainer, since 1987; *b* 28 Jan. 1957; *s* of John and Doris Collins; *né* Chris Collins, changed name to Frank Skinner, 1987. *Educ:* Birmingham Polytech. (BA Hons English 1981); Univ. of Warwick (MA English 1982). Numerous stand-up performances incl. London Palladium, 1996, and Battersea Power Station, 1997; UK tour, 2007; Showbiz, UK and Ireland tour, 2019; appearances in West End include: Art, 1999; Cooking with Elvis, 2000; Baddiel & Skinner Unplanned, 2001; Credit Crunch Cabaret (host), Lyric, 2009; Frank Skinner & Friends, Noel Coward Th., 2012; Frank Skinner: Man In A Suit, Soho Th., 2013, Leicester Sq. Th. and UK tour, 2014; Frank Skinner: The Man With No Show, Soho Th., 2016; Frank Skinner: Showbiz Tour, Leicester Sq. Th. and UK and Ireland tour, 2019; *television:* Fantasy Football League (with David Baddiel), 5 series, 1994–2005 (VHE Award of Excellence for Top Comedy Prog., 1994); The Frank Skinner Show, 8 series, 1995–2005; Baddiel & Skinner Unplanned (with David Baddiel), 5 series, 2000–05; (writer and star) Shane, 2 series, 2004–05; Frank Skinner's Opinionated, 3 series, 2010–11; Frank Skinner on George Formby, 2011; Room 101, 7 series, 2012–18; I Love My Country, 2013; Sky Arts Portrait Artist of the Year, 4 series, 2013–18; Sky Arts Landscape Artist of the Year, 2015–17; Taskmaster, 2015; What a Performance!, 2015; Don't Ask Me Ask Britain, 2017; Frank Skinner on Muhammed Ali, 2017; Urban Myths: Johnny Cash and the Ostrich, 2018; *radio:* Saturday morning show for Absolute Radio, 2009– (Sony Award for Best Entertainment Prog., 2011); Don't Start, 2011, 2012, 2015, 2016; The Rest is History, Radio 4, 2014–16; *stage play:* (writer) Nina's Got News, Edinburgh Fest., 2019. Number one single (with David Baddiel and The Lightning Seeds), Three Lions, 1996, 1998 and 2018. Columnist, The Times, 2009–11. Pres., Dr Johnson Soc., 2010–11. In Conversation with Archbishop of Canterbury, Dr Rowan Williams, Canterbury Cath., 2011. DUniv: UCE, 2006; Wolverhampton, 2009. Perrier Comedy Award, 1991; Best Comedy Entertainment Personality, British Comedy Awards, 2001; Variety Club Award for Comedy, 2001; London's Favourite Comedy Act, Capital Awards, 2005; Radio Academy Award, 2014; Gold Award for Best Entertainment/Comedy Prodn, Audio Radio Industry Awards, 2017; Baird Medal, RTS Midlands, 2018. *Publications:* Frank Skinner on Frank Skinner, 2001; Frank Skinner on the Road, 2008; Dispatches from the Sofa: the collected wisdom of Frank Skinner, 2011. *Recreations:* watching football, playing ukulele, visiting art galleries. *Address:* Avalon Management Group Ltd, 4A Exmoor Street, W10 6BD.

SKINNER, Air Vice-Marshal Graham, CBE 1999 (MBE 1982); CEng, FIMechE, FRAeS; non-executive Director, Short Brothers plc, Belfast, Bombardier Aerostructures and Engineering Services (formerly Bombardier Aerospace), 2000–16; *b* 16 Sept. 1945; *s* of late Frederick and Phyllis Skinner; *m* 1969, Margaret Christine Hacon; one *s* one *d*. *Educ:* Hampton Sch.; RAF Tech. Coll., Henlow; Bristol Univ. (BSc); Loughborough Univ. (MSc). CEng 1972; MRAeS 1980, FRAeS 2003; FIMechE 1990; FCILT (FILT 1997). Commnd Engr Br., RAF, 1964; served at Odiham, Sharjah, Coltishall, Leconfield, Kemble, 1967–78; RAF Staff Coll., Bracknell, 1978; air weapons staff, MoD, London, 1979–83; OC Engrg Wing, RAF Valley, 1983–85; various engrg posts and SO Engrg and Supply, HQ 38 Gp, Strike Comd, 1986–95; Air Cdre, Policy and Plans, HQ Logistics Comd, 1996–97; Dir, Support Mgt (RAF), 1997–99; COS, 1999–2000; last AOC-in-C Logistics Comd, 1999; Mem. Mgt Bd, Defence Logistics Orgn, 1999–2000; retd RAF, 2000. Vis. Prof, Acquisition and Logistics Unit, RMCS, Shrivenham, at Cranfield Univ., 2000–05. Mil. Advr, Marshall Aerospace, Cambridge, 2000–09; Defence Advr, Symbia, 2002–09 (non-exec. Dir, 2003–09). Hon. Pres., 606 (Beaconsfield) Sqdn, ATC, 2017–. Dir, Insight Publishing Ltd, 2003–13. Vice-Pres., RedRUK, 2015–18. Freeman, City of London, 2000–; Liveryman, Engineers' Co., 2000– (Clerk, 2003–09; Master, 2013–14). Gov., Hampton Sch., Middx, 2001–18; Trustee, Fitzwygram Foundn for Hampton Sch., 2018–. *Publications:* contrib. various articles to professional jls on aerospace engrg and defence logistics. *Recreations:* golf, watercolour painting. *Address:* Rokesly, 63 Sandelswood End, Beaconsfield, Bucks HP9 2AA. *T:* (01494) 672350. *Club:* Royal Air Force.

SKINNER, Sir Keith; *see* Skinner, Sir T. K. H.

SKINNER, Paul David, CBE 2014; Group Managing Director, Royal Dutch/Shell Group of Companies, 2000–03; Chairman, Rio Tinto plc and Rio Tinto Ltd, 2003–09 (non-executive Director, 2001–09); *b* 24 Dec. 1944; *s* of William Stanley Skinner and Elizabeth Ann Skinner; *m* 1971, Rita Jacqueline Oldak; two *s*. *Educ:* Palmer's Boys' Sch., Grays; Pembroke Coll., Cambridge (BA Law; Fellow Commoner); Manchester Business Sch. (Univ. of Manchester Dist. Alumnus, 2009). Royal Dutch/Shell Group of Companies, 1963–2003: sen. appts in UK and Greece, 1974–76, Nigeria, 1976–78, NZ, 1984–87, Norway, 1987–91; Pres., Shell Internat. Trading and Shipping Co. Ltd, 1991–96; Man. Dir, Shell Transport and Trading Co. plc, 2000–03; Chm., Shell Canada, 2001–03. Non-executive Director: Standard Chartered plc, 2003–15; Tetra Laval Gp, 2005–15; Air Liquide SA, 2006–15; PricewaterhouseCoopers LLP, 2010–19; Mem., Adv. Bd, Norton Rose Fulbright LLP, 2014–17. Chairman: Infrastructure UK, HM Treasury, 2009–13; Defence Equipment and Support, MoD, 2014–19. Pres., UK Chamber of Shipping, 1997–98; Chairman: ICC UK, 2005–08; Commonwealth Business Council, 2007–09. UK Business Ambassador, 2008–12. Member: Bd, Eur./Asian Business Sch., INSEAD, 1999–2011; Eur. Round Table of Industrialists, 2005–09; Defence Bd (formerly Mgt Bd), MoD, 2006–09, 2014–19; Defence Adv. Forum, 2009–10. Liveryman, Co. of Shipwrights, 2000–. *Recreations:* opera, ski-ing, fly-fishing, boating. *Address:* PO Box 65129, SW1P 9LY. *E:* paul@skinnerlondon.com. *Clubs:* Royal Automobile; Hawks (Cambridge).

SKINNER, Peter William; Member (Lab) South East Region, England, European Parliament, 1999–2014 (Kent West, 1994–99); Director of Political Affairs, Allianz Group, Munich, 2014; *b* 1 June 1959; *s* of William James Skinner and Jean Theresa Skinner; *m* 1st, 1990, Julie Doreen (marr. diss. 2006); one *d*, and one step *s* one step *d*; 2nd, 2006, Kimberly Strycharz; two *s*. *Educ:* Bradford Univ. (BSc); Warwick Univ. (Post Grad. Cert. in Industl Relns); Greenwich Univ. (PGCE 1992). Industrial Relations Officer, 1982; Course Dir for HNC in Business and Finance, North West Kent Coll. of Technol., 1989–94. European Parliament: Member: Employment and Social Affairs Cttee, 1994–99; Educn, Culture, Media and Youth Cttee, 1997–99; Economic and Monetary Affairs Cttee, 2000–14; Internat. Trade Cttee, 2011–14; Rapporteur on: Health and Safety Rapporteur, 1995–2014; Solvency II and Reinsurance Directive; liaison with HM Treasury EP Delegn, 2002–10; Lab. spokesman on employment and social affairs, 1996–2000, on economic and monetary affairs, 2002–14. Mem., Transatlantic Economic Council, 2005–09. Mem., Educn and Employment Policy Commn, Lab Party, 1995. Fellow, Univ. of Sunderland, 2003.

SKINNER, Prof. Quentin Robert Duthie, FRHistS; FBA 1981; Barber Beaumont Professor of the Humanities, Queen Mary University of London, since 2008; *b* 26 Nov. 1940; 2nd *s* of late Alexander Skinner, CBE, and Winifred Skinner (*née* Duthie), MA; *m* 2nd, 1979, Susan Deborah Thorpe James, MA, PhD; one *s* one *d*. *Educ:* Bedford Sch.; Gonville and Caius Coll., Cambridge (BA 1962, MA 1965; Hon. Fellow, 1997). FRHistS 1971. Cambridge University: Lectr in History, 1967–78; Prof. of Political Sci., 1978–96; Chm., Faculty of Hist., 1993–95; Regius Prof. of History, 1996–2008; Pro-Vice-Chancellor, 1999; Fellow, 1962–2008, now Hon. Fellow, Vice Master, 1997–99, Christ's Coll., Cambridge. Visiting Fellow: Research Sch. of Social Science, ANU, 1970, 1994; Humanities Res. Centre, ANU, 1989, 1994, 2006; Institute for Advanced Study, Princeton: Mem., School of Historical Studies, 1974–75; longer-term Mem., School of Social Science, 1976–79; Professeur invité, Collège de France, 1997; Vis. Schol., Center for Eur. Studies, Harvard Univ., 2008; Dist. Vis. Prof., Northwestern Univ., 2011; Rockefeller Vis. Prof., Princeton Univ., 2013–14; Spinoza Prof., Univ. of Amsterdam, 2014; Visiting Professor: Global Fellowship Prog., Peking Univ., 2017; Cttee of Social Thought, Univ. of Chicago, 2017. Member: Council, British Acad., 1987–90; Res. Council, Eur. Univ. Inst., Florence, 2003–08; Prize Cttee, Balzan Foundn, 2009–. Lecture series: Gauss Seminars, Princeton Univ., 1980; Carlyle, Oxford Univ., 1980; Messenger, Cornell Univ., 1983; Tanner, Harvard Univ., 1984; T. S. Eliot Meml, Univ. of Kent, 1995; Ford, Oxford Univ., 2003; Adorno, Univ. of Frankfurt, 2005; Clarendon, Oxford Univ., 2011; Clark, Trinity Coll., Cambridge, 2012; Academia Sinica, Taiwan, 2013. Fellow, Wissenschaftskolleg zu Berlin, 2003–04; Corresp. Fellow, Österreichische Akademie der Wissenschaften, 2009. Foreign Hon. Mem., Amer. Acad. of Arts and Sciences, 1986; Foreign Member: Amer. Phil Soc., 1997; Accademia Nazionale dei Lincei, 2007; Royal Danish Acad. of Scis and Letters, 2015; Hon. Mem., Univ. Adolfo Ibáñez, Santiago, 2009. MAE 1989. FRSA 1996. Hon. MRIA 1999. Hon. Fellow, QMW, 1999. Hon. LittD: Chicago, East Anglia, 1992; Helsinki, 1997; Leuven, 2004; Harvard, St Andrews, 2005; Aberdeen, Athens, 2007; Oslo, 2011; Copenhagen, 2014; Kent, 2017; Hon. DLitt Oxford, 2000; Hon. Dr Uppsala, 2018. Benjamin Lippincott Award, Amer. Pol Sci. Assoc., 2001; Sir Isaiah Berlin Prize, British Pol Studies Assoc., 2006; Balzan Foundn Prize, 2006; David Easton Award, Amer. Pol Sci. Assoc., 2007; Bielefelder Wissenschaftspreis, 2008. *Publications:* (ed jtly and contrib.) Philosophy, Politics and Society, Series 4, 1972; The Foundations of Modern Political Thought, Vol. 1, The Renaissance, 1978; Vol. 2, The Age of Reformation, 1978 (Wolfson History Prize, 1979); Machiavelli, 1981; (ed jtly and contrib.) Philosophy in History, 1984; (ed and contrib.) The Return of Grand Theory in the Human Sciences, 1985; (ed jtly and contrib.) The Cambridge History of Renaissance Philosophy, 1988; Meaning and Context: Quentin Skinner and his critics, ed J. H. Tully, 1988; (ed and introd) Machiavelli: The Prince, 1988, 2nd edn 2019; (ed jtly and contrib.) Machiavelli and Republicanism, 1990; (ed jtly and contrib.) Political Discourse in Early-modern Britain, 1992; (ed jtly) Milton and Republicanism, 1995; Reason and Rhetoric in the Philosophy of Hobbes, 1996; Liberty Before Liberalism, 1998; Machiavelli: a very short introduction, 2000, 2nd edn 2019; Visions of Politics, Vol. 1, Regarding Method, 2002, Vol. 2, Renaissance Virtues, 2002, Vol. 3, Hobbes and Civil Science, 2002; (ed jtly and contrib.) Republicanism: a shared European heritage, 2 vols, 2002; (ed jtly and contrib.) States and Citizens, 2003; (ed jtly) Thomas Hobbes: writings on common law and hereditary right, 2005; Hobbes and Republican Liberty, 2008; (ed jtly and contrib.) Sovereignty in Fragments, 2010; (ed) Families and States in Western Europe, 2011; (ed jtly and contrib.) Freedom and the Construction of Europe, 2 vols, 2013; Forensic Shakespeare, 2014; (ed jtly) Popular Sovereignty in Historical Perspective, 2016; From Humanism to Hobbes: studies in rhetoric and politics, 2018. *Address:* School of History, Queen Mary University of London, Mile End Road, E1 4NS.

SKINNER, Rachel Susan, CEng, FICE; UK Head of Transport, WSP, since 2019; Vice President, Institution of Civil Engineers, since 2016; *b* Reading, 11 Dec. 1976; *d* of Geoffrey Mark Bass and Dr Catherine Jennifer Bass (*née* Orbell); *m* 2006, Robert James Skinner; one *s* two *d*. *Educ:* Univ. of Durham (BSc 1st Cl. Hons Geog. 1998); Univ. of Leeds (MSc(Eng) Transport Planning and Engrg (Dist.) 2001). CEng 2003; MICE 2003, FICE 2013. Kennedy & Donkin, then Parsons Brinckerhoff, later WSP: grad. transport planner to Dir, 1998–2007; UK Hd of Transport Planning, 2007–11; Eur. Mktg and Communications Dir, 2011–14; Dir of Develt, 2014–17; UK Hd of Develt, 2017–18. Comr, Infrastructure Commn for Scotland, 2018–. Women's Transportation Seminar, later Women in Transport: Treas., 2005–07; Vice Pres., 2007–09; Pres., 2009–13; Patron, 2017–. *Publications:* contrib. articles on transport and mobility futures to New Civil Engr. *Recreations:* family, friends, ski-ing, home renovation and gardening. *Address:* WSP, WSP House, 70 Chancery Lane, WC2A 1AF. *T:* (020) 7314 5000. *E:* rachel.skinner@wsp.com.

SKINNER, Robert George; Chief Executive, Lending Standards Board, 2009–16; *b* 8 Aug. 1955; *s* of George and Mary Patricia Skinner; *m* 1974, Sheila White; one *s* one *d* (and one *d* decd). *Educ:* St Peter's Coll., Oxford (MA Physics). ACIB 1979. Barclays Bank Plc, 1976–2003: Mgt Develt Prog., 1976–80; Assistant Manager: Sunbury Br., 1981–82; Hounslow Br., 1982–84; Manager, Energy Dept, 1984–87; PA to Gp Chm., 1987–89; Man. Dir, Swaziland, 1989–92; Corporate Dir, Energy Finance Team, 1992–93; UK Personal Sector Network Dir, 1993–98; Mktg Dir, Private Banking Div., 1998–2003; Dir Gen., Money Advice Trust, 2003–06; Chief Exec., Banking Code Standards Bd, 2006–09. Non-executive Director: Money Advice Service, 2012–18; Money Advice Liaison Gp, 2017–; Totemic Ltd, 2018–. Fellow, Inst. Financial Services, 1998. *Recreations:* triathlons, photography, travel. *E:* robert.skinner1@ntlworld.com.

SKINNER, Sir (Thomas) Keith (Hewitt), 4th Bt *cr* 1912; Director, Reed International, 1980–90; Chairman and Chief Executive, Reed Publishing and Reed Regional Publishing, 1982–90, and other companies; *b* 6 Dec. 1927; *s* of Sir (Thomas) Gordon Skinner, 3rd Bt, and Mollie Barbara (*d* 1965), *d* of Herbert William Girling; *S* father, 1972; *m* 1959, Jill, *d* of Cedric Ivor Tuckett; two *s*. *Educ:* Charterhouse. Managing Director, Thomas Skinner & Co. (Publishers) Ltd, 1952–60; also Director, Iliffe & Co. Ltd, 1958–65; Director, Iliffe-NTP Ltd; Chairman: Industrial Trade Fairs Holdings Ltd, 1977–92; Business Press Internat., 1970–84. *Recreations:* publishing, shooting, fishing, gardening, golf. *Heir: s* Thomas James Hewitt Skinner, *b* 11 Sept. 1962. *Address:* Wood Farm, Reydon, near Southwold, Suffolk IP18 6SL.

SKINNER, Zoe Ann; *see* Billingham, Z. A.

SKIPPER, Mark David; DL; Chief Executive, Northern Ballet, since 1996; *b* Brighton, 23 July 1961; *s* of David and Diane Skipper; civil partnership 2006, *m* 2014, Neil Jarman. *Educ:* Kings Manor Sch., Shoreham. Barclays Bank, 1979–84; freelance stage manager, 1984–87; Northern Ballet: Dep. Stage Manager, 1987; Co. Manager, 1988–95; Hd of Planning, 1995–96. DL W Yorks, 2010. *Recreations:* all types of theatre, fine dining, travel. *Address:* c/o Northern Ballet, Quarry Hill, Leeds LS2 7PA. *T:* (0113) 220 8000. *E:* mark.skipper@northernballet.com.

SKIPWITH, Sir Alexander Sebastian Grey d'Estoteville, 13th Bt *cr* 1622; Co-founder and Director, Studio White Group, since 2010; *b* 9 April 1969; *s* of Sir Patrick Alexander d'Estoteville Skipwith, 12th Bt and Gillian Patricia Skipwith (*née* Harwood); *S* father, 2016; *m* 2006, Anne, *d* of late Paul Tolstoy Miloslavsky; one *s* one *d*. *Educ:* Harrow Sch.; Univ. of Kent; Kingston Univ. (BA 1998). Man. Dir, Pepper Head Design (Hot Ideas) Ltd, 1997–99; Design and Develt Dir, Kapok 2050 Ltd, 1999–2000; Man. Partner, Laughing Lemon, 2001–06; Man. Dir, Logichound Ltd, 2006–; Co-founder, Feefo.com, 2005–

*Recreations:* theatre, squash, scuba diving, in-line skating, bicycle polo, ski-ing. *Heir:* s Constantine Alexander Paul d'Estoteville Skipwith, *b* 30 July 2006. *Address:* 26 Archel Road, W14 9QH. *Club:* Chelsea Arts.

**SKIPWORTH, Kevin Leslie,** CVO 2011 (LVO 2000); JP; Chairman, Perth Convention Bureau, since 2016; Agent General for Western Australia, London, 2012–15; *b* Kalgoorlie, WA, 27 July 1947; *s* of late Donald John Skipworth and Sheila Edith Skipworth (*née* McAlister); *m* 1970, Edith Ann True; one *s* three *d*. *Educ:* CBC Leederville; Perth Technical Coll. (Dip. Public Admin; Cert. Personnel Mgt). Private Sec. to Ministers of the Crown, Govt of WA, 1977–83; Exec. Officer to Premier of WA, 1983–85; Dir, Office of Agent Gen. for WA, London, 1986–88; Chief of Protocol, Min. of the Premier and Cabinet, WA, 1988–90; Official Sec. and CEO, Governor's Establishment, WA, 1991–2011. Chm., Govt Domain Reserve Bd, 1991–2011; Mem. Council, Govt House Foundn of WA, 1991–2011. Mem., Royal Assoc. of Justices of WA, 1986–. Patron, UK tour, Youth Theatre Perth, Australia, 2012–15. Dep. Chm., Perron Inst. for Neurological and Translational Sci. Ltd (formerly WA Neurosci. Res. Inst.) Breakthrough and Beyond Capital Funding Campaign, 2015–. Member: Govt Hse Foundn, WA, 1991–2017 (Hon. Life Mem., 2017); Britain–Australia Soc., 2012–15 (Hon. Life Mem., 2015); Cook Soc., UK, 2012–15, Perth Br., 2016–, WA Cttee, 2016–. Member: Planning, Bldg and Finance Cttee, WA Historical Soc., 2014–; Finance and Membership Cttee, Perth Convention Bureau. Mem. Bd, Men's Sheds of WA (formerly WA Men's Shed Assoc.), 2016–. Friend, Perth Internat. Arts Fest. JP W Australia, 1986. Freeman, City of London, 2015. *Recreations:* tennis, golf, family and grandchildren, theatre arts, fishing, reading, walking, cycling. *Address:* 38 Marbella Drive, Hillarys, WA 6025, Australia. *T:* 452402085. *E:* skipwest38@gmail.com. *Clubs:* Royal Over-Seas League; University of Western Australia.

**SKIPWORTH, Mark;** writer, since 2016; Deputy Editor, Telegraph Media Group, 2014–16; *b* Kingston upon Hull, 27 Jan. 1959; *s* of late George and Jean Marjorie Skipworth; *m* 1981, Julie Alison Patricia Deegan; two *s* one *d*. *Educ:* Sydney Smith Sch., Hull; St John's Coll., Oxford (BA Modern Hist.). Reporter, Sheffield Star, 1980–84; writer, Which? mag., 1984–89; reporter, Daily Telegraph, 1989; Sunday Times: consumer affairs corresp., 1990–93; Dep. Insight Ed., 1994–95; News Ed., 1995–97; Man. Ed. (News), 1998–2008; Exec. Ed. (Sport), 2008, Exec. Ed., 2009–14, Telegraph Media Gp. *Publications:* (with A. Billen) Oxford Type: the best of Isis, 1984; The Scotch Whisky Book, 1987; (with G. Hadfield) Class, 1994; The Illinois Chronicles, 2018; The Texas Chronicles, 2019. *Recreations:* piano and piano accordion. *E:* markskipworth27@gmail.com.

**SKLYANIN, Prof. Evgeny Konstantinovich,** PhD; FRS 2008; Professor of Mathematics, University of York; *b* Leningrad. *Educ:* Steklov Inst., St Petersburg (MSc, PhD). Formerly Reader in Maths, Univ. of York. *Publications:* contribs to jls incl. Contemporary Maths, Phil Trans Royal Soc., Sigma, Indagationes Mathematicae. *Address:* Department of Mathematics, University of York, Heslington, York YO10 5DD.

**SKOLL, Lindsay Samantha,** CMG 2019; HM Diplomatic Service; Minister and Deputy Head of Mission, Moscow, since 2018; *b* 26 Sept. 1970; *d* of Gordon Stent and Linda Stent; *m* 2005, Richard Skoll; one *s*, and one step *s* one step *d*. *Educ:* Queen's Sch., Chester; Univ. of Nottingham (BA Hons 1st Cl. Hist. with Russian); Edinburgh (TEFL Dip). Counsellor, Internat. Relns, JET Prog., Japan, 1992–95; Lewis Communications, Internat. PR, 1996; joined FCO, 1996; Information Dept, 1996–97; Media Services Officer, G8 and EU Presidency, 1997–98; Hd, VIP Visits Section, Conf. and Visits Gp, 1999–2001; Hd, Korea and Mongolia Section, NE Asia Pacific Dept, 2001–02; Japanese lang. trng, 2002; on secondment to Cabinet Office, 2002–04; Dep. Hd of Mission, Pyongyang, 2004–06; Whitehall Liaison Dept, FCO, 2006–07; Middle East Dept, FCO, 2010; Dep. Hd (Climate), Climate Change and Energy Dept, FCO, 2010–12; High Comr to the Seychelles, 2012–15; UK Zika Coordinator, FCO, 2016; Minister-Counsellor, FCO, 2016–17; full time lang. trng, 2017. *Recreations:* food and wine, travel and languages, country pursuits, singing, piano, beachcombing. *Address:* c/o Foreign and Commonwealth Office, King Charles Street, SW1A 2AH. *E:* lindsay.skoll@fco.gov.uk.

**SKOLNICK, Prof. Maurice,** PhD; FRS 2009; Professor of Condensed Matter Physics, since 1991, and Co-Director, EPSRC National Centre for III-V Technologies, University of Sheffield. *Educ:* Univ. of Oxford (PhD 1975). Postdoctoral res., Max-Planck Inst., Grenoble, 1976–77; RSRE, Malvern, 1978–91 (SPSO, 1988–91). EPSRC Sen. Res. Fellow, 2001–06. Chm., Semiconductor Gp, Inst. of Physics, 2006–09. Chm., Semiconductor Commn, and a Vice Pres., IUPAP, 2002–05. Mott Medal and Prize, Inst. of Physics, 2002. *Publications:* contribs to jls incl. Physics Rev. Letters, Physics Rev., Applied Physics Letters. *Address:* Department of Physics and Astronomy, Hicks Building, Hounsfield Road, Sheffield S3 7RH.

**SKOTT, Maria;** *see* Nikolajeva, M.

**SKOURIS, Prof. Vassilios;** Judge, 1999–2015, President, 2003–15, Court of Justice of the European Union (formerly Communities); Affiliate Professor, Bucerius Law School, Hamburg, since 2016; *b* 6 March 1948; *s* of Panagiotis and Katerina Skouris; *m* Vassiliki Papaïoannou; one *s* one *d*. *Educ:* Free Univ. of Berlin; Univ. of Hamburg (Dr jur 1973). Asst Prof. of Constitutional and Admin. Law, Univ. of Hamburg, 1978; Professor of Public Law: Dimokriteio Univ. of Thrace, 1977–80; Bielefeld Univ., Germany, 1980–82; Prof., Aristoteleio Univ. of Thessaloniki, 1982–; Dir of Res., 1985–90, Sec., 1990–97, Centre for Internat. and Eur. Econ. Law, Thessaloniki. Minister for Internal Affairs, Greece, 1989 and 1996. Mem., Higher Selection Bd for Greek Civil Servants, 1994–96. Mem., Acad. Council, Acad. Eur. Law, Trier, 1995–. Pres., Greek Assoc. for Eur. Law, 1992–94. Chm., Ind. Ethics Cttee (Adjudicatory Chamber), FIFA, 2017–. Hon. LLD: Thrace, 2004; Vilnius, 2005; Münster, 2007; Bucharest, 2009; Paris II Panthéon-Assas, 2010; Deutsche Hochschule für Verwaltungswissenschaften, 2005. Grand Officier, Ordre of Merit (Italy), 2005; Ehrenkreuz für Wissenschaft und Kunst, 1st Cl. (Austria), 2005; Grand Cross, Order of Makarios III (Cyprus), 2006; Commandeur de la Légion d'Honneur (France), 2008. *Publications:* (contrib.) Constitutional Review and Legislation: an international comparison, ed C. Landfried, 1988; (contrib.) Advertising and Constitutional Rights in Europe: a study in comparative constitutional law, 1994; (contrib.) Verfassung im Diskurs der Welt, 2004; (contrib.) The Future of the European Judicial System: the constitutional role of European courts, 2005; contribs to Eur. Business Law Rev.

**SKUDDER, Taryn Jane;** *see* Lee, T. J.

**SKUSE, Prof. David Henry,** MD; FRCP, FRCPsych, FRCPCH; Professor of Behavioural and Brain Sciences, since 1994, and Deputy Director, Population, Practice and Policy Programme, Great Ormond Street Institute of Child Health (formerly Institute of Child Health), since 2016, University College London; Hon. Consultant in Child and Adolescent Psychiatry, Great Ormond Street Hospital for Children since 1985; *b* Bristol, 25 Jan. 1949; *s* of Henry Lawrence Skuse and Kathleen Mary Skuse (*née* Holten); *m* 1993, Linda Rose Dowdney; one step *s* one step *d*. *Educ:* Manchester Univ. (MB, ChB 1973; MD 1985). FRCP 1991; FRCPsych 1993; FRCPCH 1997. SHO, Oxford United Hosps (Gen. Medicine), 1974–76; Registrar, 1976–78, Sen. Registrar, 1979–85, Maudsley Hosp.; Lectr, Inst. of Psychiatry, KCL, 1979–85; Wellcome Trust Sen. Lectr, Inst. of Child Health, 1985–90, Sen. Lectr, 1990–94, UCL. Vis. Prof., Mayo Clinic, 2001–. Ed., Jl Child Psychol. and Psychiatry, 1992–2001; Ed., British Jl of Psychiatry Internat. (formerly Internat. Psychiatry), 2013– (Co-Ed., 2009–13). Treas., British Neuropsychiatry Assoc., 1998–2015. *Publications:* (ed jtly) Motherhood in Human and Nonhuman Primates: biosocial determinants, 1994; (jtly) Schedule for Oral-Motor Assessment, 2000; (ed jtly) Child Psychology and Psychiatry: frameworks for practice, 2011, 3rd edn as Child Psychology and Psychiatry: frameworks for Clinical training and practice, 2017; contrib. papers to scientific jls on child neuropsychiatry, theory and practice. *Recreations:* cycling, walking, running, travel. *Address:* Great Ormond Street Institute of Child Health, 30 Guilford Street, WC1N 1EH. *T:* (020) 7905 2168. *E:* d.skuse@ucl.ac.uk.

**SLACK, Prof. Jonathan Michael Wyndham,** PhD; FMedSci; Tulloch Professor of Stem Cell Biology, Genetics and Genomics, University of Minnesota, 2007–13, now Emeritus Professor (Director, Stem Cell Institute, 2007–12); Emeritus Professor, University of Bath, 2009; *b* 10 Sept. 1949; *s* of Ronald Slack and Pamela Zoe Slack (*née* Gregory); *m* 1980, Janet Elizabeth Blaker; two *d*. *Educ:* Balliol Coll., Oxford (BA 1st cl. Hons (Biochem.) 1971); Edinburgh Univ. (PhD 1974). Res. Fellow, Middlesex Hosp. Med. Sch., 1974–76; Res. Scientist, later Sen. and Principal Scientist, ICRF, 1976–95; Prof. of Develtl Biol., 1995–2007, Hd, Dept of Biol. and Biochem., 2000–06, Univ. of Bath. SW Regl Champion, Acad. of Med. Scis, 2014–. Mem., EMBO, 1993. FMedSci 2004. Waddington Medal, British Soc. Develtl Biol., 2002; Rank Prize, Biochem. Soc., 2009. *Publications:* From Egg to Embryo, 1983, 2nd edn 1991; Egg and Ego, 1999; Essential Developmental Biology, 2001, 3rd edn 2013; Stem Cells: a very short introduction, 2012; Genes: a very short introduction, 2014; The Science of Stem Cells, 2018; numerous scientific papers. *Recreations:* walking, travelling in Turkey, playing the melodeon, Morris dancing, amateur astronomy and geology. *Address:* Department of Biology and Biochemistry, University of Bath, Bath BA2 7AY.

**SLACK, Michael Dennis;** Founder and Chairman, Saxon Klassik Group, since 2013; *b* Sudbury, 20 Oct. 1942; one *s*. *Educ:* Kent Coll., Canterbury. Various posts, insce industry, 1960–80; Founder, Stuart Fyfe & Partners Ltd, 1980; Founder and Chm., Road Runner Gp, subseq. Fyfe Gp, 1989–2008. Founder and Chm., Temporary Cover Ltd, 2002–17. Mem., Insce Brokers' Registration Council, 1989–2002; Founder Dir, Gen. Insce Standards Council, 1999–2003; non-exec. Dir, FSA, 2004–09. Dir, Inst. of Insce Brokers, 1992–97; Founder Chm., Assoc. of Insce Intermediaries and Brokers, 1997; Mem. Main Bd, Brit. Insce Brokers' Assoc., 2002–09. FCMI. Mem., Co. of Insurers. Mem., RYA. *Recreations:* sailing, boating. *Clubs:* Royal London Yacht; Royal Thames Yacht; City Livery Yacht.

**SLACK, Prof. Paul Alexander,** DPhil, DLitt; FBA 1990; FRHistS; Principal of Linacre College, Oxford, 1996–2010; Titular Professor of Early Modern Social History, University of Oxford, 1999–2010, now Emeritus; *b* 23 Jan. 1943; *s* of Isaac Slack and Helen (*née* Firth); *m* 1965, Diana Gillian Manby (*d* 2003); two *d*. *Educ:* Bradford Grammar Sch.; St John's Coll., Oxford (Casberd Exhibnr and Schol.; 1st cl. Hons Mod. Hist. 1964; MA; DPhil 1972; DLitt 2010; Hon. Fellow, 1998). FRHistS 1972. A. M. P. Read Schol., Oxford Univ., and Harmsworth Sen. Schol., Merton Coll., Oxford, 1965–66; Jun. Res. Fellow, Balliol Coll., Oxford, 1966–9; Lectr in Hist., York Univ., 1969–72; Oxford University: Fellow and Tutor, 1973–96 (Emeritus Fellow, 1996–), Sub-Rector, 1983, Sen. Tutor, 1984–86 and 1991–92, Exeter Coll.; Reader in Modern Hist., 1990–96; Jun. Proctor, 1986–87; Mem., Hebdomadal Council, 1987–2008; Chm., Gen. Bd of Faculties, 1995–96; Pro-Vice-Chancellor, 1997–2000; Pro-Vice-Chancellor (Acad. Services and Univ. Collections), 2000–05; Delegate, OUP, 2000–13. Vis. Prof., Univ. of S Carolina, 1980; Vis. Res. Associate, Rikkyo Univ., Tokyo, 1988. Ford's Lectr in British History, Oxford, 1994–95; Aylmer Memorial Lectr, York, 2003; Stenton Lectr, Reading, 2010. Member: Internat. Commn for Hist. of Towns, 1976–; Humanities Res. Bd, 1994–95. Pres., Soc. for Social Hist. of Medicine, 1991; Member, Council: RHistS, 1984–87; British Acad., 1994–95. Editor, Past and Present, 1985–94. Hon. Fellow: Balliol Coll., Oxford, 2009; Linacre Coll., Oxford, 2010. DUniv York, 2005. *Publications:* (ed with Peter Clark) Crisis and Order in English Towns 1500–1700, 1972; (ed) Poverty in Early Stuart Salisbury, 1975; (with P. Clark) English Towns in Transition 1500–1700, 1976 (Japanese edn 1989); (ed) Rebellion, Popular Protest and the Social Order in Early Modern England, 1984; The Impact of Plague in Tudor and Stuart England, 1985; Poverty and Policy in Tudor and Stuart England, 1988; The English Poor Law 1531–1782, 1990; (ed with T. Ranger) Epidemics and Ideas, 1992; (ed jtly) Public Duty and Private Conscience in Seventeenth-Century England, 1993; From Reformation to Improvement: public welfare in early modern England, 1999; (ed) Environments and Historical Change, 1999; (ed jtly) Civil Histories: essays presented to Sir Keith Thomas, 2000; (ed jtly) The Peopling of Britain, 2002; Plague: a very short introduction, 2012; The Invention of Improvement: information and material progress in seventeenth-century England, 2015 (Samuel Pepys Award, 2015); contribs to learned jls. *Recreations:* opera, fell-walking. *Address:* Linacre College, Oxford OX1 3JA. *T:* (01865) 271650.

**SLACK, Stephen;** Head, Legal Office of the Church of England and Chief Legal Adviser to the Archbishops' Council, 2001–19; Chief Legal Adviser and Registrar, General Synod of the Church of England, 2001–19; Joint Registrar of the Provinces of Canterbury and York, 2001–19; Official Solicitor to the Church Commissioners, 2009–19; *b* 29 Dec. 1954; *s* of Thomas and Ada Genary Slack; *m* 1982, Georgiana Sophia (*née* Shaw); one *s* two *d*. *Educ:* Aylesbury Grammar Sch.; Christ Church, Oxford (MA). Solicitor in private practice, 1979–84; Charity Commission: Sen. Lawyer, Liverpool, 1984–89; Hd, Legal Sect., Taunton, 1989–2001. *Recreations:* gardening, music, historic buildings. *Address:* 6 Dyers Hill, Charlbury, Oxon OX7 3QD. *Club:* Athenæum.

**SLADE, Adrian Carnegie,** CBE 1988; PR and TV training consultant, 1991–2002; political journalist, 2002–12; *b* 25 May 1936; *y s* of late George Penkivil Slade, KC and Mary Albinia Alice Slade; *m* 1960, Susan Elizabeth Forsyth; one *s* one *d*. *Educ:* Eton Coll.; Trinity Coll., Cambridge (BA Law). Pres., Cambridge Footlights, 1959. Writer, J. Walter Thompson, 1959–64; S. H. Benson, 1964–71, Dir, 1970–71; Co-Founder and Managing Director: Slade Monico Bluff Ltd, 1971–75; Slade Bluff & Bigg Ltd, 1975–86; Slade Hamilton Fenech Ltd, 1986–91. Director: Orange Tree Th., Richmond, 1986–98 (Chm., 1991–98); Adzido, 1998–2004 (Chm., 2001–04). Trustee, One plus One, 1987–97 (Chm., 1990–97). Mem. (L) Richmond, GLC, 1981–86 (Leader, L/SDP Alliance Gp, 1982–86). Contested: (L) Putney, 1966, Feb. and Oct. 1974; (L/SDP Alliance) Wimbledon, 1987. Pres., Liberal Party, 1987–88; Jt Pres., 1988, Vice-Pres., 1988–89, Liberal Democrats. *Publications:* contrib. Jl of Liberal History. *Recreations:* music, theatre, films, piano playing, song writing, golf, photography. *Address:* 28 St Leonard's Road, SW14 7LX. *T:* (020) 8876 8712.
*See also* Rt Hon. Sir C. J. Slade.

**SLADE, Sir Benjamin Julian Alfred,** 7th Bt *cr* 1831; Chairman: Shirlstar Holdings Ltd, since 1992; Pyman Bell (Holdings) Ltd, since 1991; *b* 22 May 1946; *s* of Sir Michael Slade, 6th Bt and Angela (*d* 1959), *d* of Captain Orlando Chichester; *S* father, 1962; *m* 1977, Pauline Carol (marr. diss. 1991), *er d* of Major Claude Myburgh. *Educ:* Millfield Sch. Chm., Shirlstar Container Transport Ltd, 1973–95. Chm., Wilshaw Plc, 2005–09. Mem., Worshipful Co. of Ironmongers. Freeman, City of London, 1979. *Recreations:* racing, polo, bridge. *Heir*: none. *Address*: Maunsel House, North Newton, North Petherton, Bridgwater, Somerset TA7 0BU. *T*: (01278) 661076, (Sec.) (01278) 663107. *E*: events@maunselhouse.co.uk; (office) Woodlands Castle, Ruishton, Taunton, Somerset TA3 5LU. *T*: (01823) 444955. *E*: events@woodlandscastle.co.uk. *Club*: White's.

SLADE, Prof. Christina Mary, (Mrs Robert Hamilton), PhD; Vice-Chancellor, Bath Spa University, 2012–17, now Emeritus Professor; *b* Adelaide, SA, 29 June 1953; *d* of John Slade and Gwenyth Slade; *m* 1976, Robert Hamilton; one *s* one *d*. *Educ*: Presbyterian Girls' Coll., Adelaide; Australian National Univ. (BA 1st Cl. 1974; PhD 1982); Univ. of New England (DipEd 1986). Lectr, then Sen. Lectr, Univ. of Canberra, 1990–96; Harkness Fellow, New York Univ., 1996–97; Vis. Prof., Univ. Iberoamericana, Mexico and Instituto Tecnológico de Monterrey, Mexico City, 1997–2001; Hd, Sch. of Creative Communications, Univ. of Canberra, 2001–03; Dean, Humanities, Macquarie Univ., Sydney, 2003–08; Prof. of Media Theory, 2004–10, Vis. Prof., 2010–11, Univ. of Utrecht; Dean, Arts and Soc. Scis, City Univ., London, 2009–12. *Publications*: The Real Thing: doing philosophy with media, 2002; A Tale of Two Women, 2008; (ed with M. Möllering) From Migrant to Citizen, 2010; Watching Arabic Television in Europe: from diaspora to hybrid citizens, 2014. *Clubs*: Athenæum; Queen Adelaide (Adelaide).

SLADE, Rt Hon. Sir Christopher John, Kt 1975; PC 1982; a Lord Justice of Appeal, 1982–91; *b* 2 June 1927; *e s* of late George Penkivil Slade, KC, and Mary Albinia Alice Slade; *m* 1958, Jane Gwenllian Armstrong Buckley, *d* of Rt Hon. Sir Denys Buckley, PC, MBE; one *s* three *d*. *Educ*: Eton (Scholar); New Coll., Oxford (Scholar). Eldon Law Scholar, 1950. Called to Bar, Inner Temple, 1951; joined Lincoln's Inn *ad eundem*, 1954, Bencher, 1973 (Treas., 1994). In practice at Chancery Bar, 1951–75; QC 1965; Attorney General, Duchy of Lancaster and Attorney and Serjeant Within the County Palatine of Lancaster, 1972–75; a Judge of the High Ct, Chancery Division, 1975–82; a Judge of Restrictive Practices Ct, 1980–82, Pres., 1981–82. Member: Gen. Council of the Bar, 1958–62, 1965–69; Senate of Four Inns of Court, 1966–69; Lord Chancellor's Legal Educn Cttee, 1969–71. Master, Ironmongers' Co., 1973. *Address*: 40 Rivermead Court, Ranelagh Gardens, SW6 3RX. *Club*: Garrick.
See also A. C. Slade.

SLADE, Hon. Dame Elizabeth Ann, DBE 2008; a Judge of the High Court of Justice, Queen's Bench Division, 2008–19; *b* 12 May 1949; *d* of late Dr Charles and Henriette Slade; *m* 1975 (*d* 2015); two *d*. *Educ*: Wycombe Abbey Sch.; Lady Margaret Hall, Oxford (Exhibnr, MA; Hon. Fellow, 2009). Called to the Bar, Inner Temple, 1972, Bencher, 1990. QC 1992; Asst Recorder, 1995–98; Recorder, 1998–2008; Dep. High Court Judge, 1998–2008; additional pt-time Judge, Employment Appeal Tribunal, 2000–03. Member, Administrative Tribunal: Bank for Internat. Settlement, 1999–2008 (Vice Pres., 2008); EBRD, 2008. Chm., Sex Discrimination Cttee, Bar Council, 2000–02. Hon. Vice Pres., Employment Law Bar Assoc., 1998– (Chm., 1995–97). Trustee, Free Representation Unit, 1998–2002. *Publications*: Tolley's Employment Handbook, 1978, to 7th edn (ed jtly) 1991. *Recreations*: theatre, art, music.

SLADE, Prof. Gordon Douglas, PhD; FRSC 2000; FRS 2017; Professor, Department of Mathematics, University of British Columbia, since 1999; *b* Toronto, 14 Dec. 1955; *s* of Douglas Gordon Slade and Madeleine Marie Yvonne Slade; partner, Joanne Nakonechny. *Educ*: Univ. of Toronto (BASc Engrg Sci. 1977; MSc Maths 1979); Univ. of British Columbia (PhD Maths 1984). Lectr, Univ. of Virginia, Charlottesville, 1985–86; Asst Prof., 1986–90, Associate Prof., 1990–95, Prof., 1995–99, McMaster Univ. *Publications*: (with N. Madras) The Self-Avoiding Walk, 1993, repr. 2013; The Lace Expansion and Its Applications, 2006. *Recreations*: literature, walking, gardening, travel, wilderness. *Address*: Department of Mathematics, University of British Columbia, Vancouver, BC V6T 1Z2, Canada. *T*: (604) 8223781. *E*: slade@math.ubc.ca.

SLADE, Laurie George; Insurance Ombudsman, 1994–96 and 1999–2000; *b* Nairobi, 12 Feb. 1944; *yr s* of Humphrey Slade and Constance Laing Gordon. *Educ*: Duke of York Sch., Nairobi; Magdalen Coll., Oxford (MA); London Univ. Inst. of Educn (PGCE). Called to the Bar, Lincoln's Inn, 1966. Stage management and acting in professional theatre and TV, Kenya and UK, 1967–70; teaching, 1972–75; Advocate, Kenya High Court, 1975–81; Legal Advr, CIArb and Dep. Registrar, London Court of Internat. Arbitration, 1982–88; Dep. Insurance Ombudsman, 1988–94; Independent Investigator, SIB, then FSA, 1996–99. Mem., Insurance Brokers' Registration Council, 1997–98. Mem., British and Irish Ombudsman Assoc., 1993–2008; Chm., FSA Ombudsman Steering Gp, 1998. Voluntary counsellor, Hounslow Social Services, 1988–94; counselling and psychotherapy practice and consultancy, 1991–; UKCP Registered Psychoanalytic Psychotherapist, 1999; Hon. Psychotherapist, Charing Cross Hosp., 2000–05; social dreaming practitioner, 2002–. Mem., Guild of Psychotherapists, 1999–; Founder Mem., Internat. Neuro-Psychoanalysis Soc., 2000–; Mem., Confedn for Analytical Psychology (formerly Confedn of Analytical Psychologists), 2002–; Founder Associate, Gordon Lawrence Foundn for Promotion of Social Dreaming, 2013–19; Mem., Internat. Assoc. for Study of Dreams, 2019–. Wrote plays: Out of Africa, 1988 and Karen's Tale, 1996 (both after Karen Blixen); Joe & I, 2005; The Father, 2012 (after August Strindberg), BBC Radio 3, 2013; Marriage, 2013 (after Nikolai Gogol); The Liberty Truck, 2018; operetta libretto: (with composer, Joseph Phibbs) Juliana, 2018 (after August Strindberg). *Publications*: professional papers and contribs to learned jls. *Recreations*: theatre, painting (2 solo exhibns in Kenya, 1974, 1979).

SLADE, Patrick Buxton M.; *see* Mitford-Slade.

SLADE, William Charles; Vice-Principal, 1998–2000, Consultant, 2000–02, King's College London; *b* 20 June 1939; *s* of late Charles Slade and Phyllis (*née* Littlejohns); *m* 1961, Elizabeth Lyn Roberts; two *d*. *Educ*: St Julian's High Sch., Newport, Gwent; UC of Swansea (BSc; Pres., Students' Union, 1960–61). ACMA 1966. Guest Keen Iron and Steel Ltd, 1961–66; Management Accountant: Tunnel Cement Ltd, 1966–71; Pye TMC Ltd, 1971–75; Finance Officer, 1975–77, Sec., 1977–85, Chelsea Coll., Univ. of London; Sec., 1986–98, Mem. Council, 1998–2000, KCL (FKC 1989). Chm., Univ. of London Purchasing Consortium, 1991–94. Mem. Council, Greenacre Sch. for Girls, 1980–95. Member: NADFAS (Epsom branch), 2002–, (Ashtead branch), 2014–; Epsom Literary Soc., 2003–13 (Cttee Mem., 2005–12; Chm., 2009–12); 1964 Club (Epsom and Ewell), 2015– (Cttee Mem., 2015–). *Recreations*: theatre, golf, Rugby football. *Address*: 1b The Murreys, Ashtead, Surrey KT21 2LU. *T*: (01372) 273847. *Club*: Royal Automobile.

SLADEK, Nancy; Editor, since 1999, and Proprietor, since 2005, Literary Review; *b* London, 7 Dec. 1960; *d* of Milan Sladek and Hana Sladek (*née* Kozeluhova); one *s* by Andrea Chiari-Gaggia. *Educ*: Heathfield Sch., Ascot; Univ. of Geneva (LèsL). Dep. Ed., Literary Rev., 1989–99. Benson Medal, RSL, 2015. *Address*: Literary Review, 44 Lexington Street, W1F 0LW. *T*: (020) 7437 9392, *Fax*: (020) 7734 1844. *E*: nancy@literaryreview.co.uk. *Club*: Academy.

SLADEN, Teresa; Secretary of the Victorian Society, 1987–93; *b* 16 Sept. 1939; *d* of Robert John Fawcett and Anne (*née* Fairlie Clarke); *m* 1961, David Sladen; one *s* two *d*. *Educ*: Birkbeck Coll., London Univ. (BA Hons Hist. of Art/Italian); Courtauld Inst. (MA Medieval Art and Architecture, 1978). Royal Commn on Historical Monuments, 1978–79; part-time lectr and freelance researcher, 1980–82; Architectural Advr, Victorian Soc., 1983–87. Trustee and Cttee Mem., Mausolea & Monuments Trust, 1997–2008 (Chm., 1998–2000); Vice-Chm., Victorian Soc., 1998–2001; Member: Southwark DAC, 1993–2002; Adv. Bd for Redundant Churches, 1999–2008; Trustee, Highgate Cemetery, 2016–. Compiler, Gazetteer of English Mausoleums, 2005. *Publications*: (contrib.) The Albert Memorial, 2000; (contrib.) St Paul's Cathedral, 2004; contrib. to Jl of Garden History. *Recreations*: drawing and printmaking, biography.

SLANE, Viscount; Rory Nicholas Burton Conyngham; *b* 28 Feb. 2010; *s* and *heir* of Earl of Mount Charles, *qv*.

SLANEY, (William) Simon (Rodolph) K.; *see* Kenyon-Slaney.

SLATER, Dr David Homfray, CB 1996; Director, Cambrensis Ltd, since 2001; Chief Scientist, Willworth Enterprises Ltd, since 2008; *b* 16 Oct. 1940; *m* 1964, Edith Mildred Price; four *d*. *Educ*: University College of Wales Aberystwyth (BSc, PhD). CChem, FRIC, FIChemE, CEng, FInstE. Research Associate, Ohio State Univ., 1966–69; Sen. Res. Fellow, Dept of Chemistry, Univ. of Southampton, 1969–70; Lectr in Combustion, Dept of Chem. Engineering and Chem. Technology, Imperial College London, 1970–75; Cremer and Warner: Sen. Scientist, 1975; Partner, 1979–81; Founding Dir, Technica, 1981–91; Chief Inspector, HM Inspectorate of Pollution, 1991–96; Dir, Pollution Prevention and Control, Envmt Agency, 1996–98; Dir, Oxera Envmtl, 1998–2001; Principal Partner, Acona Gp, 2001–05; Chairman: RLtec, 2003–09; NIREX CLG Ltd, 2005–07; non-executive Director: Alsitek Ltd, 2010–16; Tidal Lagoon (Swansea Bay) plc, 2012–. Specialist Advr to Envmt, Transport and Regl Affairs Select Cttee, H of C, 1999–2000; Envmtl Advr, Better Regulation Task Force, Cabinet Office, 2000. Chm., Envmtl Gp, Regulatory Policy Inst., Oxford, 2001–03. Associate, Envmtl Change Unit, Oxford Univ., 1999–2001; Royal Acad. of Engrg Vis. Prof., UMIST, 2002–06; Adjunct Prof., Industrial Adv. Panel, KCL, 2002. Hon. Professor: of Life Sciences, Univ. of Wales, Aberystwyth, 1991; Sch. of Engrg, Cardiff Univ., 2009–. Chm. and Trustee, SEE – I t Working. Mem. Court, Cranfield Univ., 1997–2001. *Publications*: numerous contribs to sci. jls and conference procs. *Recreations*: music, horses. *Club*: Athenæum.

SLATER, Francesca; *see* Wiley, F.

SLATER, Prof. Gillian Lesley, (Mrs Ian Huntley); DL; DPhil; Vice-Chancellor, Bournemouth University, 1994–2005; *b* 13 Jan. 1949; *d* of Leonard William Henry Filtness and Adeline Mary Filtness; *m* 1st, 1970, John Bruce Slater (marr. diss. 1983); two *d*; 2nd, 1988, Ian David Huntley. *Educ*: Sutton High Sch. for Girls; St Hugh's Coll., Oxford (BA 1970; MSc 1971; MA, DPhil 1973). FIMA 1982; CMath 1991. Lectr, Poly. of South Bank, 1973–79; Sen. Lectr, 1979–84, Prin. Lectr, 1984–86, Sheffield City Poly., 1979–86; Head of Dept of Math. and Physics, 1986–89, Asst Dir and Dean of Science and Engrg, 1989–92, Manchester Poly.; Pro-Vice-Chancellor, Manchester Metropolitan Univ., 1992–94. Governor: UEL, 2006–08; Talbot Heath Sch. (Dep. Chm.), 2006–09; Sherborne Sch., 2009–13. DL Dorset, 2006. *Publications*: Essential Mathematics for Software Engineers, 1987; (with A. Norcliffe) Mathematics for Software Construction, 1991; numerous articles in learned jls. *Recreations*: listening to classical orchestral music, handweaving. *Address*: 2 Strata, 150 Canford Cliffs Road, Poole BH13 7ER.

SLATER, Adm. Sir John Cunningham Kirkwood, (Sir Jock), GCB 1992 (KCB 1988); LVO 1971; DL; First Sea Lord and Chief of Naval Staff, and First and Principal Naval Aide-de-Camp to the Queen, 1995–98; *b* 27 March 1938; *s* of late Dr James K. Slater, OBE, MD, FRCPE and M. C. B. Slater (*née* Bramwell); *m* 1972, Ann Frances, *d* of late Mr and Mrs W. P. Scott of Orkney; two *s*. *Educ*: Edinburgh Academy; Sedbergh. BRNC Dartmouth, 1956–58; served HM Ships Troubridge, Yaxham, HM Yacht Britannia, Cassandra, 1959–64; Comd HMS Soberton, 1965; specialised in navigation, HMS Dryad, 1965–66; HM Ships Victorious and Scarborough (Dartmouth Training Sqdn), 1966–68; Equerry to HM the Queen, 1968–71; Comdr 1971; Comd, HMS Jupiter, 1972–73; Directorate of Naval Ops, MoD, 1973–75; Captain 1976; Comd, HMS Kent, 1976–77; RCDS 1978; Asst Dir of Naval Warfare, MoD, 1979–81; Comd, HMS Illustrious, 1982–83; Captain, Sch. of Maritime Ops and Comd, HMS Dryad, 1983–85; Rear Adm. 1985; ACDS (Policy and Nuclear), 1985–87; Vice-Adm., 1987; Flag Officer, Scotland and NI, and NATO Comdr Northern sub area Eastern Atlantic, Comdr Nore sub area Channel and Naval Base Comdr, Rosyth, 1987–89; Chief of Fleet Support (Mem., Admiralty Bd), 1989–91; Adm. 1991; C-in-C, Fleet, Allied C-in-C, Channel, and Eastern Atlantic, 1991–92; VCDS, 1993–95. Non-executive Director: VTGp (formerly Vosper Thornycroft Hldgs) plc, 1999–2004; Lockheed Martin UK Ltd, 2000–08; Consultant, Bristow Helicopters, 2001–04. Vice Pres., RUSI, 1995–98 (Vice Chm., 1993–95); Chm., RNLI, 2004–08 (Council, 1999–2008; Chm., Ops Cttee, 2001–02; Dep. Chm., 2002–04; Chm. Emeritus, 2008); Mem., Bd of Mgt, BNSC, 1986–87. Chm., Royal Navy Club of 1765 and 1785, 2001–04; Chm., White Ensign Assoc., 2002–05 (Mem. Council, 1999–2008; Vice Pres., 2008–); Vice-Pres., British Forces Foundn, 2002– (Vice-Chm., 1999–2002); President: RM Assoc. Concert Band, 2007–; Royal Navy and Royal Marines Charity, 2008–11. Chm., Imperial War Mus., 2001–06 (Trustee, 1999–2006); Pres., Amer. Air Mus. in Britain, 2001–06. Mem., Nat. Youth Orchestra of GB, 1955. Gov., Sedbergh Sch., 1997–2002. Elder Brother, Trinity Hse, 1995 (Younger Brother, 1978–95). Freeman, City of London, 1989; Liveryman, Shipwrights' Co., 1991– (Mem. Ct of Assts, 2005–; Prime Warden, 2011, 2012). DL Hants, 1999. Hon. DSc: Cranfield, 1998; Southampton, 2008. Comdr Legion of Merit (US), 1997. *Recreation*: outdoor. *Address*: c/o Naval Secretary, Fleet Headquarters, Whale Island, Portsmouth PO2 8BY. *Clubs*: Army and Navy; Liphook Golf.
See also P. J. B. Slater.

SLATER, Dr John Morton; agricultural economic consultant, since 1998; *b* 21 Aug. 1938; *s* of Rev. Percy William Slater and Evelyn Maude Morton Slater; *m* 1972, Susan Mary Black, *d* of Rev. Dr John Ferguson Park and Mary Davis McCaughey Park; two *s* one *d*. *Educ*: Durham Sch.; Univ. of Nottingham (BSc Agric. Sc 1961); Univ. of Toronto (MS Agric. Econ. 1963); Univ. of Illinois (L. J. Norton Meml Fellow; PhD 1965). Lectr, Univ. of Manchester, 1965–70; Consultant, FAO, 1966–67; Ministry of Agriculture, Fisheries and Food: Economic Advr, 1970–84; Head of Econs and Stats (Food) Div., 1984–92; Head of Econs (Internat.) Div., 1992–96; Head of Econs and Stats Gp, 1996–98, Special Advr, H of L Select Cttee on Science and Technol., 1999–2000. Master, Worshipful Co. of Turners, 1999–2000; Chm., Millennium Masters Assoc., 2003–06. MRI. *Publications*: (ed) Fifty Years of the National Food Survey 1940–1990, 1991. *Recreations*: cricket, golf, bridge. *Address*: 28 Swains Lane, N6 6QR. *T*: (020) 7485 1238. *E*: slaterconsult@gmail.com. *Clubs*: City Livery (Hon. Sec., 2002–03), United Wards, MCC.

SLATER, Jonathan; Permanent Secretary, Department for Education, since 2016; *b* London, 29 Nov. 1961; *s* of Christopher and Julia Slater; *m* 2001, Jane Ramsey; two *s* one *d*. *Educ*: Univ. of York (BSc Maths); Univ. of Sussex (MSc Operational Res.). Operational Res. Analyst, British Rlys Bd, 1985–88; Sen. Policy Analyst, Newham BC, 1988–90; Islington Borough Council: Prin. Policy Develt Officer, 1990–93; Contract Services Manager, 1993–95; Asst Chief Exec., 1995–98; Exec. Dir, 1998–2000; Dep. Chief Exec. and Dir of Educn, 2000–01; Director: Cabinet Office, 2001–05; Prime Minister's Delivery Unit, 2005–06; Performance and Improvement, Nat. Offender Mgt Service, 2006–08;

Chief Exec., Office for Criminal Justice Reform, 2008–09; Director General: Transforming Justice, MoJ, 2009–11; Transformation and Corporate Strategy, MoD, 2011–14; Head Office and Commissioning Services, MoD, 2014–15; Econ. and Domestic Secretariat, Cabinet Office, 2015–16. *Recreations:* piano playing, tennis, musical theatre. *Address:* Department for Education, Sanctuary Buildings, Great Smith Street, SW1P 3BT.

**SLATER, Judith Mary**; HM Diplomatic Service; Consul-General, Istanbul, since 2016; HM Trade Commissioner, Eastern Europe and Central Asia, since 2018; *b* 26 June 1964; *d* of George Norris Stewart Slater and Valerie Mary Slater (*née* Pratt); *m* 1998, Philip Frederick de Waal; one *s* one *d*. *Educ:* Howell's Sch., Denbigh; St John's Coll., Cambridge (BA 1987). Joined HM Diplomatic Service, 1988; Third, then Second Sec. (Political), Canberra, 1989–93; First Sec., FCO, 1993; Private Sec. to Minister of State, 1994; First Sec. (Press and Public Affairs), New Delhi, 1997–2001; Asst Dir, Personnel Policy, FCO, 2001–04; Consul-Gen., Houston, 2004–07; Dep. High Comr, Pretoria, 2007–11; Dep. High Comr and Dir, UK Trade and Investment, Singapore, 2011–15; Dir Gen., Trade and Investment for Turkey, Central Asia and S Caucasus, 2016. *Recreations:* golf, tennis, cinema. *Address:* c/o Foreign and Commonwealth Office, King Charles Street, SW1A 2AH.

**SLATER, Keith Francis**; Bishop of Grafton, NSW, 2003–13; *b* 13 Dec. 1949; *s* of George Richard Slater and Edna May Slater (*née* Eriksen); *m* 1969, Lorraine Margaret Halvorson; two *s*. *Educ:* Univ. of Qld (BA); St Francis Theol Coll., Brisbane (ThL); Kelvin Grove Teachers' Coll., Brisbane (Dip. Teaching); Brisbane Coll. of Theology (MMin 2007). Ordained deacon and priest, 1975; Asst Curate, St Saviour's, Gladstone, 1975–78; Priest i/c, 1978–80, Rector, 1980–82, St Peter's, Springsure; Rector: St Luke's, Ekibin, Brisbane, 1982–87; St Saviour's, Gladstone, 1987–94; St Clement's-on-the-Hill, Stafford, Brisbane, 1994–2003; Archdeacon of Lilley, Brisbane, 1996–2003. Provincial Minister (Aust. Province), 1993–99, Minister Gen., 1999–2005, Third Order of Soc. of St Francis; Episcopal Advr, Nat. Secretariat Anglican Cursillo Movt of Australia, 2009–13. Mem. Bd, Foundn of St George's Coll., Jerusalem, 2008–15.

**SLATER, Prof. Michael Derek**, MBE 2014; DPhil; Professor of Victorian Literature, Birkbeck College, University of London, 1991–2001, now Emeritus; *b* 29 Dec. 1936; *s* of Jesse Slater and Valentine Blanche (*née* Clément). *Educ:* Reading Sch.; Balliol Coll., Oxford (Goldsmith Schol., Charles Oldham Schol., MA, DPhil 1965). Birkbeck College, University of London: Res. Asst, 1962–65; Asst Lectr in English, 1965–67; Lectr in English, 1967–79; Sen. Lectr, 1979–83; Reader, 1983–91. Dist. Vis. Prof., Ohio State Univ., 1975–76; Visiting Professor: Univ. of Debrecen, Hungary, 1992; Univ. of Kyoto, Japan, 1995, 2005; Evelyn Wrench Lectr, English-Speaking Union of USA, 2011. Tennyson Soc. annual Lect., 1997; Lee Seng Tee Dist. Lect., Wolfson Coll., Cambridge, 2012. President: Dickens Soc. of America, 1973; Internat. Dickens Fellowship, 1988–90. Chm. Trustees, Dickens House Mus., 1996–99, 2000–02, now Hon. Academic Advr. Hon. Fellow, Birkbeck Coll., 2001; Sen. Res. Fellow, Inst. of English Studies, Univ. of London, 2002–. Editor, The Dickensian, 1968–77. *Publications:* The Catalogue of the Suzannet Charles Dickens Collection, 1975; (ed) Dickens 1970, 1970; Dickens on America and the Americans, 1978, repr. 2017; Dickens and Women, 1983, 2nd edn 1986, repr. 2017; (with N. Bentley and N. Burgis) The Dickens Index, 1988; (ed) The Dent Uniform Edition of Dickens's Journalism, Vol. 1 1994, Vol. 2 1996, Vol. 3 1998, (with J. Drew) Vol. 4 2000; The Intelligent Person's Guide to Dickens, 2000, reissued as The Genius of Dickens, 2011; Douglas Jerrold 1803–1857, 2002; Biographical Memoir of Kathleen Tillotson, 2006; Very Interesting People: Charles Dickens, 2007; Charles Dickens, 2009; The Great Charles Dickens Scandal, 2012; contrib. Oxford DNB. *Recreations:* theatre, visiting literary museums. *Address:* 8 Ridgmount Gardens, WC1E 7AP.

**SLATER, Michael Neal; His Honour Judge Slater**; a Circuit Judge, since 2016; *b* Rotherham, S Yorks; *s* of Sidney and Margaret Elizabeth Slater; partner, Sue Lister. *Educ:* Oakwood Comprehensive Sch.; Thomas Rotherham Coll.; Sheffield Univ. (LLB). Called to the Bar, Inner Temple, 1983; a Recorder, 2002–16. *Recreations:* music, reading, theatre, photography, aviation, football, cricket, golf. *Address:* Sheffield Combined Court Centre, The Law Courts, 50 West Bar, Sheffield S3 8PH.

**SLATER, Prof. Nigel Kenneth Harry**, PhD; FREng, CEng, FIChemE; 1999 Professor of Chemical Engineering, Cambridge University, since 2000 (Head, Department of Chemical Engineering and Biotechnology, 2010–15; Pro-Vice-Chancellor, 2016); Fellow, 1978–85 and since 2000, and President, 2009–13, Fitzwilliam College, Cambridge; *b* 22 March 1953; *s* of Arthur Geoffrey Slater; *m* 1976, Kay Bendle; one *s* two *d*. *Educ:* Bolton Sch.; Sidney Sussex Coll., Cambridge (MA; PhD). CEng 1990; FREng 2004; FIChemE 1997. Asst Lectr, 1979–82, Lectr, 1982–85, in Chemical Engrg, Cambridge Univ.; Bioprocessing Section Manager, Unilever Research NL, 1985–90; Head of Bioprocess Dept, Wellcome Foundation Ltd, 1990–95; Prof. and Head of Dept of Chem. Engrg and Applied Chemistry, Aston Univ., 1995–2000. Hon. Prof., Tianjin Univ. of Sci. and Technol., 2013–; Qiushi Prof. of Chem. Engrg, Univ. of Zhejiang, 2017–; Hon. Prof., Sichuan Univ., 2018–. Director: Birmingham Technology Ltd, 1995–2000; Cobra Bio-Manufacturing plc, 2002–10; Founder, Cobra Biosciences Ltd, 1997. Chm., Chemical and Pharmaceuticals Directorate, BBSRC, 1993–96; Mem. Governing Body, Silsoe Res. Inst., 1996–2000. Governor, King Edward VI Foundn, 1997–2000. *Publications:* numerous articles in learned science and engrg jls. *Recreation:* golf. *Address:* Shenstone House, 3 St Bernard's Road, Sutton Coldfield, W Midlands B72 1LE. *T:* (0121) 321 2349.

**SLATER, Rt Rev. Paul John;** *see* Kirkstall, Bishop Suffragan of.

**SLATER, Prof. Peter James Bramwell**, FRSE; Kennedy Professor of Natural History, University of St Andrews, 1984–2008, now Professor Emeritus; *b* 26 Dec. 1942; *s* of Dr James Kirkwood Slater, OBE and Margaret Claire Byrom Slater (*née* Bramwell); *m* 1968, Elisabeth Priscilla Vernon Smith; two *s*. *Educ:* Edinburgh Academy; Glenalmond; Univ. of Edinburgh (BSc 1964; PhD 1968; DSc 1983). FRSB (FIBiol 1986); FRSE 1991. Shaw Macfie Lang Fellow, 1964–66, Demonstrator in Zoology, 1966–68, Univ. of Edinburgh; Lectr in Biology, Univ. of Sussex, 1968–84; University of St Andrews: Head, Sch. of Biol and Med. Scis, 1992–97; Dean, Faculty of Sci., 1998–2002. Chm., Heads of Univ. Biol Scis, 1994–96. Association for Study of Animal Behaviour: Hon. Sec., 1973–78; Hon. Pres., 1986–89; Medallist, 1999. Chm., Orkney Univ. of Third Age, 2017–; Mem., Mgt Council, Orkney Coll., 2018–. Pres., Orkney Field Club, 2014–. European Editor, Animal Behaviour, 1979–82; Editor: Advances in the Study of Behavior, 1989–2005 (Associate Editor, 1982–88); Science Progress, 1983–89. *Publications:* Sex Hormones and Behaviour, 1978; (ed with T. R. Halliday) Animal Behaviour, 1983; An Introduction to Ethology, 1985; (ed) Collins Encyclopaedia of Animal Behaviour, 1986; (ed with T. R. Halliday) Evolution and Behaviour, 1994; (with C. K. Catchpole) Bird Song: biological themes and variations, 1995, 2nd edn 2008; Essentials of Animal Behaviour, 1999; numerous articles in learned jls. *Recreations:* ornithology, writing, listening to music. *Address:* Vagaland, Stromness, Orkney KW16 3AW. *T:* (01856) 850148.

*See also* Sir J. C. K. Slater.

**SLATER, Prof. Rebeccah Louise Elizabeth Ann**, PhD; Professor of Paediatric Neuroimaging, University of Oxford, since 2019; Fellow, St John's College, Oxford, since 2019; *b* Hammersmith, London, 1979; *d* of Harold and Josephine Slater; *m* 2012, Thomas Foulkes; two *s*. *Educ:* Imperial Coll. of Sci., Technol. and Medicine (BSc Physics 2001); University Coll. London (MSc Neurosci. 2002; PhD Neurosci. 2007); Univ. of Oxford (MA 2019). Wellcome Trust Res. Fellow, 2011–. *Recreations:* cycling, walking. *Address:* St John's College, St Giles, Oxford OX1 3JP. *T:* (01865) 234229. *E:* rebeccah.slater@paediatrics.ox.ac.uk.

**SLATKIN, Leonard**; conductor; music director; Music Director: Detroit Symphony Orchestra, 2008–18, now Music Director Laureate; Orchestre National de Lyon, 2010–18, now Hon. Music Director; National Symphony Orchestra, Washington, 1995–2008; Chief Conductor, BBC Symphony Orchestra, 2000–04; *b* Los Angeles, 1 Sept. 1944; *s* of Felix Slatkin and Eleanor Slatkin (*née* Aller); *m* 1986, Linda Hohenfeld; one *s*; *m* 2011, Cindy McTee. *Educ:* Indiana Univ.; LA City Coll.; Juilliard Sch. of Music. Conducting début as Asst Conductor, Youth Symphony Orch. of NY, Carnegie Hall, 1966; Asst Conductor, Juilliard Opera Theater and Dance Dept, 1967; St Louis Symphony Youth Orchestra: Founder, Music Dir and Conductor, 1969–75; Musical Advr, 1984–96; St Louis Symphony Orchestra: Asst Conductor, 1968–71; Associate Conductor, 1971–74; Music Dir and Conductor, 1979–95; Music Dir, New Orleans Philharmonic Symphony, 1977–78; débuts: with Chicago Symphony, NY Philharmonic, Philadelphia Orch., RPO, 1974; with USSR orchs, 1976–77; Tokyo, 1986; Metropolitan Opera, 1991. Guest conductor with orchs throughout world incl. Concertgebouw, English Chamber Orch., LPO, LSO, Vienna State Opera, Stuttgart Opera; Principal Guest Conductor: Minnesota Orch., 1974–79; Philharmonia, 1997–2000; RPO, 2005–; Los Angeles Philharmonic, 2005–07; Pittsburgh SO, 2008–; Music Advr, Nashville SO, 2006–09. Has made numerous recordings. Mem., Nat. Acad. Recording Arts and Scis, 1985. Holds hon. doctorates. Grammy Awards, 1984, 1991 and 1994. Declaration of Honor (Silver) (Austria), 1986; Nat. Medal of Arts, USA, 2003. *Compositions:* The Raven, 1971; Rhymes and Sonnets, 1974; Dialogue for Two Cellos and Orchestra, 1975; Absurd Alphabed-time Stories, 1976; Extensions, 1, 2, 3 and 4, 1973–75. *Publications:* Conducting Business: unveiling the mystery behind the maestro, 2012; Leading Tones: reflections on music, musicians and the music industry, 2018.

**SLATTERY, Dr David Antony Douglas**, MBE (mil.) 1958; Chief Medical Officer, Rolls-Royce plc, 1973–92; Dean, Faculty of Occupational Medicine, Royal College of Physicians, 1988–91 (Vice-Dean, 1986–88); *b* 28 Jan. 1930; *s* of Rear-Adm. Sir Matthew Slattery, KBE, CB and Mica Mary Slattery (*née* Swain); *m* 1st, 1954, Mary Winifred Miller; two *s* two *d*; 2nd, 1974, Claire Louise McGuinness; one *s*. *Educ:* Ampleforth Coll.; St Thomas' Hosp., London. MB BS; FFOM RCPI 1977; FFOM RCP 1981; FRCP 1986. Capt., RAMC, 1954–58. MO, E Midlands Gas Bd, 1959–69; Manager, Health and Safety, BSC, Rotherham, 1969–73. Special Lectr, Dept of Community Health, Nottingham Univ., 1978–93; Vis. Prof., Dept of Occupational Health, Univ. of Liverpool, 1992–97. Consultant Advr in occupational medicine, RAF, 1987–96; Advr on occupational health policy, Mersey RHA, 1992–94. Dir, Occupational Health Service, Aintree Hosps NHS Trust, 1993–94. Member: Standing Med. Adv. Cttee, DHSS, 1988–91; Adv. Bd, CS Occupational Health Service, 1988–91. Industrial Health Advr, Derbys Br., BRCS, 1976–93. *Publications:* The Pattens: the story of an Ulster-Scots family in Ireland, 2008; papers on occupational medicine and the employment of the disabled. *Recreations:* history, people. *Address:* 99 South Quay, Wapping Dock, Liverpool L3 4BW. *T:* (0151) 707 2022.

**SLAUGHTER, Andrew Francis**; MP (Lab) Hammersmith, since 2010 (Ealing, Acton and Shepherd's Bush, 2005–10); *b* 29 Sept. 1960; *s* of late Alfred Frederick Slaughter and Marie Frances Slaughter. *Educ:* Univ. of Exeter; Coll. of Law; Inns of Court Sch. of Law. Called to the Bar, Middle Temple, 1993; barrister, Bridewell Chambers, 1993–2006, Lamb Chambers, 2006–. Mem., Hammersmith and Fulham LBC, 1986–2006 (Dep. Leader, 1991–96; Leader, 1996–2005). *Address:* House of Commons, SW1A 0AA. *T:* (020) 7219 4990.

**SLAUGHTER, Audrey Cecelia, (Mrs Denis Lanigan)**; writer and freelance journalist; *d* of Frederick George Smith and Ethel Louise Smith; *m* 1st, 1949, W. A. Slaughter (marr. diss.); one *s* one *d*; 2nd, 1979, Charles Vere Wintour, CBE (*d* 1999); 3rd, 2002, Denis Lanigan, CBE (*d* 2009). *Educ:* Chislehurst High Sch.; Stand Grammar Sch., Manchester. Editor, Honey magazine, 1960; founded Petticoat magazine, 1964; columnist, Evening News, 1968; joined National Magazine Co., to edit Vanity Fair, 1969; founded and funded own magazine, Over 21, 1970; after sale to Morgan Grampian, 1972, remained as Dir and Editor until 1979; Associate Editor, Sunday Times, 1979; with husband founded Sunday Express colour magazine, 1981; Founder Editor, Working Woman magazine, 1984–86; Lifestyle Editor, The Independent, 1986–87; Editorial Consultant, Burda Publications, Germany, 1987–88. *Publications:* Every Man Should Have One (with Margaret Goodman), 1969; Getting Through…, 1981; Working Woman's Handbook, 1986; Your Brilliant Career, 1987; Private View (novel), 1990; Blooming (novel), 1992; Unknown Country (novel), 1994. *Recreations:* classical music, theatre, painting.

**SLAUGHTER, Giles David**, MA; Headmaster, University College School, 1983–96; *b* 11 July 1937; *s* of Gerald Slaughter and Enid Lillian Slaughter (*née* Crane); *m* 1965, Gillian Rothwell Shepherd; three *d*. *Educ:* Royal Masonic School; King's College, Cambridge. MA. Pierrepont School, Frensham, 1961–65; Campbell College, Belfast, 1965–68; Stockport Grammar School, 1968–70; Housemaster, Ormiston House, Campbell Coll., 1970–73; Headmaster, Solihull School, 1973–82. Non-exec. Dir, Heckett MultiServ plc, 1999–2002. Chm., London and SE, ISIS, 1995–98. Governor: Godolphin and Latymer Sch., 1988–99; Cobham Hall, 1989–2000; Aldwickbury Sch., 1974–2003; King's Coll. Sch., Wimbledon, 1995–2008; Woodbridge Sch., 1997–2007. JP Solihull, 1977–82. Church Warden, St Mary's, Ufford, 2007–12. *Recreations:* gardening, cricket, golf, theatre. *Address:* 6 Church Lane, Lower Ufford, Woodbridge, Suffolk IP13 6DS.

**SLAYMAKER, Christine Ann**, CBE 2014; Principal and Chief Executive, Farnborough College of Technology, 2001–16; *b* Emsworth, Hants, 7 May 1958; *d* of Mervyn Ronald and Lillian Ann Johnson; *m* 2010, James Henry Slaymaker; one *s* by a previous marriage. *Educ:* Purbrook Park Co. Grammar Sch.; Portsmouth Poly. (BA Hons Business Studies 1980; Cert Ed 1983). Dir of Mktg, Croydon Coll., 1985–87; Vice Principal, Salisbury Coll., 1987–98; Principal, Brinsbury Coll., 1998–2001. Mem., SE England Regl Assembly, 2007–09. Proto-Council Mem., Inst. of FE, 2014–. Board Member: Farnborough Aerospace Consortium, 2007–; Enterprise M3 LEP, 2014–. Advr, RE Educn Trust, 2007–. Governor: Frimley Park Hosp. NHS Trust, 2005–06; Talavera Infants Sch., Aldershot, 2012–; Treloar Sch. and Coll., 2014–. MCIM 1985. *Recreations:* friends and family, holidays and travelling, swimming to keep fit.

**SLEDGE, Ven. Richard Kitson**; Archdeacon of Huntingdon, 1978–96; *b* 13 April 1930; *s* of Sydney Kitson and Mary Sylvia Sledge; *m* 1958, Patricia Henley (*née* Sear); one *s* two *d* (and one *s* decd). *Educ:* Epsom College; Peterhouse, Cambridge (MA). Curate of Emmanuel, Plymouth, 1954–57; Curate-in-charge of St Stephen's, Exeter, 1957–63; Rector: Dronfield, 1963–78; Hemingford Abbots, 1978–89. *Address:* 7 Budge Close, Brampton, Huntingdon, Cambs PE28 4PL. *T:* (01480) 437789.

**SLEE, Prof. Peter Robert Horsman**, PhD; FRHistS; Vice-Chancellor, Leeds Beckett University, since 2015; *b* Chipping Norton, 27 Jan. 1958; *s* of George Horsman Slee and Phyllis Mary Slee (*née* Preston); *m* 1st, 1986, Corinne Lawes (marr. diss. 2015); two *d*; 2nd,

2016, Kathryn Elizabeth Smith; one step *s* one step *d*. *Educ*: Univ. of Reading (BA); Emmanuel Coll., Cambridge (PhD 1983; Hon. Fellow, 2015). ESRC and British Acad. Res. Fellow, Manchester Univ., 1983–86; Univ. Res. Fellow in Arts, Durham Univ., 1987–88; Hd, Educn Policy, CBI, 1988–89; Dir, Enterprise in HE, Durham Univ., 1989–90; Dir, Univ. Relns, Aston Univ., 1990–93; Dir, Corporate Affairs, Durham Univ., 1993–2002; Pro-Vice Chancellor, Northumbria Univ., 2002–10; Dep. Vice Chancellor, Univ. of Huddersfield, 2010–15. FRHistS 1987; FHEA 2013. *Publications:* Learning and Liberal Education, 1986. *Recreations:* cricket, ski-ing. *Address:* Leeds Beckett University, Old Broadcasting House, Woodhouse Lane, Leeds LS2 9EN. *E:* p.slee@leedsbeckett.ac.uk.

**SLEE, Prof. Richard;** artist; Professor, University of the Arts London (formerly The London Institute), 1992–2012, now Emeritus (Principal Lecturer, Camberwell College of Arts, 1998–2011); *b* 8 May 1946; *s* of Richard and Margaret Slee; *m* 1977, Diana Gill (marr. diss. 1987); one *d*. *Educ*: Carlisle Coll. of Art and Design; Central Sch. of Art and Design (BA 1st cl. Hons Ceramics 1970); Royal Coll. of Art (MA Design degree by project 1988). Full-time Lectr, Hastings Coll. of Further Educn, 1973–75; Vis. Lectr, Central Saint Martin's Coll. of Art and Design and Brighton Poly., and pt-time Sen. Lectr, Harrow Sch. of Art, 1975–90; Sen. Lectr, Camberwell Coll. of Arts, 1990–98. Theodore Randall Internat. Chair in Ceramic Art, Sch. of Art and Design, Alfred Univ., USA, 2011. External Examiner: Department of Ceramics: Camberwell Coll. of Arts, 1985–87; Loughborough Coll. of Art, 1987–90; Glasgow Sch. of Art, 1998–2002; Dept of Goldsmithing, Silversmithing, Metalwork and Jewellery (MA), RCA, 2007–10. Mem., Setting-up Grants Cttee, Crafts Council, 2000–04. Jerwood Prize, 2001. *Recreation:* pottery. *Address:* c/o Hales Gallery, Tea Building, 7 Bethnal Green Road, E1 6LA. *T:* (020) 7033 1938, *Fax:* (020) 7033 1939. *E:* info@halesgallery.com.

**SLEEMAN, His Honour Stuart Philip;** a Circuit Judge, 1993–2012; a Deputy Circuit Judge, 2012–14 and 2016–19; *b* 9 May 1947; *s* of His Honour (Stuart) Colin Sleeman; *m* 1973, Elisabeth Nina Brann; one *s* two *d*. *Educ*: Cranleigh Sch.; Merton Coll., Oxford (BA Jurisprudence 1969; MA 1972). Called to the Bar, Gray's Inn, 1970, Bencher, 2019; a Recorder, 1986–93. Tutor Judge, Civil and Family, Judicial Studies Bd, 2003–12; Designated Family Judge, Guildford Care Centre, 2003–11. Chm., Bar Tribunals and Adjudication Service, 2012–19. Chm., Old Cranleighan Soc., 1984–97; Gov., Cranleigh Sch., 1989–2005. Mem., Merton Deanery, 2014–18; Southwark Diocesan Synod, 2015–; Tooting Deanery, 2019–; Trustee, Southwark Diocesan Bd, 2016–18. Liveryman, Fruiterers' Co., 2009–. *Recreations:* music, history (in particular the Reformation), formerly hockey (Oxford Occasionals).

**SLEEP, Wayne Philip Colin,** OBE 1998; dancer, actor, choreographer; *b* Plymouth, 17 July 1948. *Educ*: Hartlepool; Royal Ballet Sch. (Leverhulme Scholar). Graduated into Royal Ballet, 1966; Soloist, 1970; Principal, 1973; roles in: Giselle; Dancers at a Gathering; The Nutcracker; Romeo and Juliet; The Grand Tour; Elite Syncopations; Swan Lake; The Four Seasons; Les Patineurs; Petroushka (title role); Cinderella; The Dream; Pineapple Poll; Mam'zelle Angot; 4th Symphony; La Fille mal gardée; A Month in the Country; A Good Night's Sleep (gala); Coppelia, English Nat. Ballet, 1994; chor., with Robert North, David & Goliath; also roles in operas, A Midsummer Night's Dream and Aida; roles created for him by Sir Frederick Ashton, Dame Ninette de Valois, Sir Kenneth MacMillan, Rudolf Nureyev, John Neumeier, Joe Layton and many others. *Theatre:* Ariel in The Tempest, New Shakespeare Co.; title role in Pinocchio, Birmingham Rep.; genie in Aladdin, Palladium; soldier in The Soldier's Tale, QEH, 1980 and 1981; Truffaldino in The Servant of Two Masters; chor. and played lead in The Point, Mermaid; Mr Mistoffelees in Cats, New London, 1981; co-starred in Song and Dance, Palace, 1982, Shaftesbury, 1990 (video, 1984); Cabaret, Strand, 1986; chor. Savoy Suite, 1993; The History of Dance, tour, 1995; Chitty Chitty Bang Bang, London Palladium, 2003; Into Thin Air!, New Players, 2005; High Society, tour, 2007; Cabaret, tour, 2008. Formed own company, DASH, 1980: Chichester Fest., 1980, national tour and Sadler's Wells, 1982, Apollo Victoria and national tour, Christmas season, Dominion, 1983; danced in and jtly choreographed Bits and Pieces, Dominion, 1989; Hollywood and Broadway tour, 1996–97; World of Classical Ballet tour, 1998; Precious Little Sleep tour, 2011; has directed several charity galas including 90 Years of Dance, 1995 and Stars of the Night, 1997. Teaches workshops around the world. *Films:* The Virgin Soldiers; The First Great Train Robbery; The Tales of Beatrix Potter, 1971. Chor. films and television, inc. Adam's Rib, Death on the Nile, and appeared in many television progs inc. Dizzy Feet and series, The Hot Shoe Show, 1983, 1984; Big Ballet, 2014; Tony Lumpkin in She Stoops to Conquer, radio. Patron: Wheelchair Dance Assoc.; Dance Teachers Benevolent Fund; Benesh Dance Inst. Hon. DLitt Exeter. Show Business Personality of the Year, 1983. *Publications:* Variations on Wayne Sleep, 1983; Precious Little Sleep (autobiog.), 1996. *Recreation:* entertaining.

**SLEIGH, Andrew Crofton,** FInstP; Director, Pinoak Innovation Consulting, since 2010; *b* 4 Nov. 1950; *s* of Arthur Ffennell Crofton Sleigh and Margaret Sleigh; *m* 1986, Christine Mattick; one *s* one *d*. *Educ*: Portsmouth Grammar Sch.; Maret Sch., Washington; Havant Grammar Sch.; St Catherine's Coll., Oxford (MA Physics). FInstP 2000. Superintendent, Pattern Processing and Machine Intelligence Div., RSRE, 1985–90; Director: of Science, Central Staff, MoD, 1990–93; Operation Studies Sector, DRA, 1993–94; Chief Exec., Defence Operational Analysis Centre, MoD, 1994–95; Man. Dir, Centre for Defence Analysis, DERA, 1995–98; Dir Gen. for Inf. and Communications Services, MoD, 1999–2001; UK Principal, NATO C4I Bd, 1998–2001; Capability Manager for Information Superiority, MoD Defence Equipment Capability Customer, 1999–2001; QinetiQ plc: Man. Dir, Defence Solutions, 2001–03; Man. Dir, Knowledge and Information Systems Div., 2003–05; Gp Man. Dir, Defence and Technol. Sector, 2005–07; Gp Chief Technol. Officer, 2007–09; Sen. Sci. Advr, 2009. Member: DTI Spectrum Mgt Adv. Gp, 1998–2002; OFCOM Spectrum Mgt Adv. Bd, 2003–; Res. and Develt Gp, NDIC, 2007–08; Hartwell Gp on Climate Change, 2011–14; Bd, Birmingham Science City, 2012– (Vice Chm., 2014–); Vice-Chm., Security Adv. Gp, Framework Prog. 7, EC, 2008–12. Council Mem., RUSI, 2002–06. Adjunct Prof., Imperial Coll. Business Sch. (formerly Tanaka Business Sch.), Imperial Coll. London, 2008–12. Chairman: GeoLang Hldgs Ltd, 2013–18; V-Auth Ltd, 2015–; Vice Chm., EU Horizon 2020 Secure Societies Adv. Gp, 2014–16; non-executive Director: Worcester Acute Hosps Trust, 2011–17; Alta Innovations Ltd, 2011– (Actg Chm., 2017–18); Vislink plc, 2011–14. Hon. Fellow, Worcester Univ., 2008. W Midlands Ambassador, 2005–07. Chairman: Malvern Fest. Fringe, 1977–82; Wyvern Trust Ltd, 1984–90. *Publications:* (with O. J. Braddick) The Physical and Biological Processing of Images, 1983. *Recreations:* ski-ing, windsurfing, helping my wife run the farm. *Club:* Savile.

**SLEIGHT, Prof. Peter,** MD (Cantab), DM (Oxon), FRCP; FACC; Field-Marshal Alexander Professor of Cardiovascular Medicine in the University of Oxford, and Fellow of Exeter College, Oxford, 1973–94, now Emeritus Professor and Fellow; Hon. Consultant Physician, Oxford Radcliffe Hospitals NHS Trust (formerly Oxford Health Authority), 1964–2011, Observer status, since 2012; *b* 27 June 1929; *s* of William and Mary Sleight, Boston Spa, Yorks; *m* 1953, Gillian France; two *s*. *Educ*: Leeds Grammar Sch.; Gonville and Caius Coll., Cambridge; St Bartholomew's Hosp., London. Ho. Phys. and Ho. Surg., Med. and Surg. Professorial Units, Bart's, 1953; Sen. Registrar, St George's Hosp., London, 1959–64; Bissinger Fellow, Cardiovascular Research Inst., Univ. of California, San Francisco, 1961–63; MRC Scientific Officer, Depts of Physiology and Medicine, Univ. of Oxford, 1964–66; Consultant Physician, Radcliffe Infirmary, Oxford, 1966–73. Visiting Prof., Univ. of Sydney (Warren McDonald Sen. Overseas Fellow of Aust. Heart Foundn), 1972–73; Hon. Prof. of Medicine, Federal Univ. of Pernambuco, 1975. Civil Consultant in Medicine, RAF, 1985–94. Co-Chairman: Heart Outcomes Prevention Evaluation Study Gp, 1995–2000; ON TARGET Study Gp, 2000–08; SEARCH, Heart Protection Study. Vice Pres., ASH, 1994– (Chm., 1982–93); President: British Hypertension Soc., 1993–95; World Hypertension League, 1995–2001; Member Council: Internat. Soc. of Hypertension, 1978–86; Eur. Soc. of Cardiology, 1983–88; Hon. Mem., Eur. Soc. of Hypertension, 2001. Mem. Editl Bd, British Heart Jl, 1976–83; Editor: Jl of Cardiovascular Res., 1983–92; Jl of Cardiovascular Risk, 1994–2001. Hon. MD Gdansk, 2000. Young Investigators Award, 1963, Bishop Lectr, 2004, Internat. Lecture, 2008, Amer. Coll. of Cardiology; Evian Prize, 1988; Merck Sharp and Dohme Award, Internat. Soc. of Hypertension, 1990; Galen Medal for Therapeutics, Soc. of Apothecaries, 2000; Sen. Internat. Award, Aspirin Foundn, 2000; MacKenzie Medal, British Cardiac Soc., 2003; Lifetime Achievement Award, Eur. Soc. Hypertension, 2005; Award for Lifetime Res., Russian Fedn Soc. of Cardiology, 2005; Gold Medal, Eur. Soc. of Cardiology, 2010; Jl of Physiol. Medal, 2011; Paton Lectr, Physiol Soc., 2014. *Films:* Control of Circulation; History of Hypertension (Medal, BMA Scientific Film Competition, 1981). *Publications:* Modern Trends in Cardiology, 1976; (ed) Arterial Baroreceptors and Hypertension, 1981; Hypertension, 1982; (ed) Scientific Foundations of Cardiology, 1983; (with D. Eckberg) Human arterial baroreflexes in Health and Disease, 1992; contribs on nervous control of the circulation, hypertension, treatment of myocardial infarction and Lipid res. in: Circulation Research; Jl Physiol; Lancet; clinical trials in: Lancet; New England Jl of Medicine; Circulation Research; Heart; Eur. Heart Jl; BMJ; Clinical Sci. *Address:* Wayside, 32 Crown Road, Wheatley, Oxon OX33 1UL.

**SLEIGHT, Sir Richard,** 4th Bt *cr* 1920, of Weelsby Hall, Clee; *b* 27 May 1946; *s* of Sir John Frederick Sleight, 3rd Bt and of Jacqueline Margaret, *o d* of late Maj. H. R. Carter, Brisbane, Queensland; *S* father, 1990; *m* 1978, Marie-Thérèse, *o d* of O. M. Stepan; two *s*. *Heir: s* James Alexander Sleight, *b* 5 Jan. 1981.

**SLEIMAN, Gen. Michel;** President of Lebanon, 2008–14; *b* Amchit-Jbeil, 21 Nov. 1948; *m* Wafaa; one *s* two *d*. *Educ*: Lebanese Univ. (BA Pol and Admin. Scis 1980). Graduated Mil. Acad., 2nd Lieut, 1970; Inf. Platoon Comdr; Co. Comdr; Bn Comdr; Trainer, Mil. Acad. and NCO Sch.; Chief, Mount Lebanon Intelligence Section, 1990–91; Staff Sec., 1991–93; Commander: 11th Inf. Bde, 1993–96; 6th Inf. Bde, 1996–98; C-in-C, Lebanese Army, 1998–2008. Dr *hc*: Moscow State Inst. for Internat. Relns, 2010; Nat. Univ. of Third of February, Buenos Aires, 2012. Holds numerous decorations and medals, including: OM, 1st Grade, 1998, Extraordinary Grade, 2008 (Lebanon); Military Medal (Lebanon), 2003; Medal of Honour (Arab Fedn), 2004; OM, Grade of Excellence (Syria), 2005; Grand Cross, Order of Merit (Italy), 2008; Grand Croix, Légion d'Honneur (France), 2009; Mil. Order (Oman), 2009; Collar: Order of Isabella la Catholique (Spain), 2009; Moubarak the Great (Kuwait), 2009; Order Pro Merito Melitensi (Malta), 2009; Grand Collar: Order of Makarios III (Cyprus), 2010; Nat. Order of Southern Cross (Brazil), 2010; Nat. Order of the Cedar, 2010; Necklace of Independence, Qatar, 2010; Kt Grand Cross, Order of St Charles (Monaco), 2011.

**SLESSOR, Catherine Helen,** MBE 2016; Contributing Editor, The Architectural Review (Editor, 2010–15); architecture critic, The Observer; *b* Aberdeen, 15 Nov. 1960; *d* of Donald Munro Slessor and Christina Catherine Slessor (*née* MacDonald). *Educ*: St Margaret's Sch. for Girls, Aberdeen; Univ. of Edinburgh (MA Architecture 1983; DipArch 1984); Bartlett Sch. of Architecture, University Coll. London (MA Architectural Hist. and Theory 2016). RIBA Pt 3 1986. Architectl Asst in private practice, 1984–87; Tech. Editor, The Architects' Jl, 1987–91; Asst Editor, 1992–93, Dep. Editor, 1993–2009, The Architectural Review. *Publications:* Eco-Tech, 1997; Concrete Regionalism, 1998. *Recreations:* art, architecture, gardening, opera, cinema, ice skating, swimming.

**SLEVIN, Maurice Louis,** MD; FRCP; Consultant Physician, Medical Oncology Department, St Bartholomew's and Homerton Hospitals, 1982–2008; Hon. Consultant, Barts Health NHS Trust (formerly Barts and the London NHS Trust); Founding Partner and Consultant Medical Oncologist, Leaders in Oncology Care (formerly London Oncology Clinic), since 2005; *b* 2 July 1949; *s* of David Slevin and Nita (*née* Rosenbaum); *m* 1st, 1975, Cherry Jacobsohn (marr. diss. 1987); two *d*; 2nd, 1993, Nicola Jane Harris (marr. diss. 2016); one *s* one *d*. *Educ*: Univ. of Cape Town (MB ChB 1973; MD 1984). MRCP 1978, FRCP 1989. Registrar in General Medicine, Groote Schuur Hosp., Cape Town, 1977–78; Registrar in Med. Oncology, St Bartholomew's Hosp., 1978–80, Sen. Registrar, 1980–82. Chm. and Trustee, Cancerbackup (formerly BACUP), 1987–2008; Trustee, Macmillan Cancer Support, 2008–09. *Publications:* Randomised Trials in Cancer, 1986; Metastases, 1988; Challenging Cancer: from chaos to control, 1991; Cancer: the facts, 1996; Cancer: how worthwhile is non-curative treatment?, 1998; numerous pubns on clinical oncology, clinical pharmacology and psychosocial oncology. *Address:* 95 Harley Street, W1G 6AF. *T:* (020) 7317 2525.

**SLIGO, 12th Marquess of,** *cr* 1800; **Sebastian Ulick Browne;** Baron Mount Eagle 1760; Viscount Westport 1768; Earl of Altamont 1771; Earl of Clanricarde 1543 and 1800; Baron Monteagle (UK) 1806; *b* 27 May 1964; *s* of Captain Lord Ulicke Browne, RA and his 2nd wife, Fiona Browne (*née* Glenn); *S* cousin, 2014; *m* 1st, 1984, Christina Maria Suaznabar (marr. diss. 1992); one *s* one *d*; 2nd, 2016, Claire Suzanne van Middelkoop. *Educ*: Rugby. Residential property consultant. *Heir: s* Lord Christopher Ulick Browne, Earl of Altamont, *b* 14 Nov. 1988.

**SLIM,** family name of **Viscount Slim**.

**SLIM, 3rd Viscount** *cr* 1960, of Yarralumla and Bishopston; **Mark William Rawdon Slim;** Executive Director, CBRE Ltd, since 2008; *b* Aldershot, 13 Feb. 1960; *s* of 2nd Viscount Slim, OBE and Elizabeth Joan Spinney; *S* father, 2019; *m* 1992, Harriet Laura Harrison; three *s*. *Educ*: Eton Coll.; Univ. of Bristol. Mktg Dir, Sterling Projects, Dallas, 1984–87; Partner: Jones Lang Wootton, 1988–96; BH2, 1996–2004; Mark Slim and Partners, 2004–08. Non-executive Director: Muntons plc, 2006–; Oakley Properties, 2006–. Chairman, Trustees: Burma Star Assoc., 2002–; Burma Star Meml Fund, 2006–. *Recreations:* military history, family life, country life. *Heir: s* Hon. Rufus William Rawdon Slim, *b* 15 April 1995. *Club:* White's.

**SLINGER, His Honour Edward;** a Circuit Judge, 1995–2010; *b* 2 Feb. 1938; *s* of Thomas Slinger and Rhoda (*née* Bradshaw); *m* 1965, Rosalind Margaret Jewitt; two *s* two *d*. *Educ*: Accrington Grammar Sch.; Balliol Coll., Oxford (Dist. Law Mods 1956; BA 1958). Admitted solicitor (with Hons), 1961; Partner, Ramsbottom & Co., Solicitors, Blackburn, 1964–95; Dep. Registrar, 1982–88; Asst Recorder, 1988–92; Recorder, 1992–95. Pres., Blackburn Incorporated Law Assoc., 1986; Member: Immigration Law Sub-cttee, Law Soc., 1990–95; Immigration Appeal Tribunal, 1997–2005; Chairperson List, Panel of Arbitrators, Sport Resolution Panel, 2007–14; Parole Bd, 2009–. Lancashire County Cricket Club: Captain, 2nd XI, 1967–75; Mem. Cttee, 1969–99; Trustee, 1978–96; Vice-Chm., 1985–98; Vice-Pres., 2000–. Mem., Discipline Cttee, TCCB (now ECB), 1990–;

Mem., Jury of Appeal, Horse of the Year Show, 2000–14. Governor: Samlesbury C of E Sch., Lancs, 1986–; Westholme Sch., Blackburn, 1985–2018 (Vice-Chm., 2002–12). *Recreations:* cricket, gardening. *Clubs:* MCC, Lansdowne.

**SLINGO, Dame Julia (Mary)**, DBE 2014 (OBE 2008); FRS 2015; PhD; Chief Scientist, Meteorological Office, 2009–16; *b* 13 Dec. 1950; *d* of late Herbert Walker and Lucy Mary Walker (*née* Hirons); *m* 1978, Anthony Slingo (*d* 2008); two *d*. *Educ:* King's High Sch. for Girls, Warwick; Univ. of Bristol (BSc Physics; PhD Atmospheric Physics). Scientist, Meteorol Office, 1972–80; Consultant, European Centre for Medium Range Weather Forecasts, 1981–85; Scientist, Nat. Center for Atmospheric Res., Boulder, Colo, 1986–90; University of Reading: Sen. Scientist, then Dep. Dir, NERC Centre for Global Atmospheric Modelling, 1990–2002; Dir, NERC Centre for Global Atmospheric Modelling, then Dir of Climate Res., Nat. Centre for Atmospheric Sci., 2002–08; Prof. of Meteorology, 2000–09; Founding Dir, Walker Inst. for Climate System Res., 2006–07. Hon. Professor: Univ. of Reading, 2009–; Univ. of Exeter, 2010–; Univ. of Bristol, 2017–. Mem., NERC, 2009–17, 2018–. Vice-Pres., 2003–05, 2007–08, Pres., 2008–10, RMetS. Member, Scientific Committees: of Met Office; of Eur. Centre for Medium-Range Weather Forecasts; of Centre for Ocean-Land-Atmosphere Studies; of Internat. Centre for Theoretical Physics; Member: Jt Sci. Cttee, World Climate Res. Prog., 2007–12; High Level Gp, EC Scientific Advice Mechanism, 2015–16; Chair, Ext. Adv. Bd, Cabot Inst., Univ. of Bristol, 2017–. Special Advr to Sec. Gen., WMO, 2016–. For. Mem., US NAE 2016. Hon. FRSC 2015; Hon. FInstP 2015; Hon. FRMetS 2017. Hon. DSc: Bristol, 2010; Reading, 2011; Exeter, 2014; Edinburgh, 2014; Harper Adams, 2015; S Wales, 2015; Leeds, 2016; Open, 2018. *Publications:* over 120 papers in leading jls. *Recreations:* music, walking, gardening. *Address:* Seafield House, Seafield Road, Sidmouth, Devon EX10 8HF.

**SLINN, David Arthur**, CMG 2008; OBE 2000; HM Diplomatic Service, retired; consultant on North Korea and Balkan affairs, since 2015; *b* 16 April 1959; *s* of Ronald Geoffrey Slinn and Christine Mary Slinn; *m* 2012, Heidi Alberta Hulan; one *d*. *Educ:* Univ. of Salford (BA Hons Mod Langs 1981). Joined FCO, 1981; Third Sec., UK Delegn to Conf. on Disarmament, Geneva, 1983–86; Second Secretary: Ulaanbaatar, 1987–89; Pretoria/Cape Town, 1990–93; FCO, 1993–95; Chargé d'Affaires, Tirana, 1995–96; First Sec. (Commercial), 1996–98, (Political), 1998–99, Belgrade; Head, British Liaison Office, Pristina, Kosovo, 1999–2000; HCSC 2001; seconded to EU/NATO, former Yugoslav Rep. of Macedonia, 2001–02; Ambassador, Democratic People's Republic of Korea, 2002–05; UK Regl Co-ordinator, Southern Afghanistan, 2007–08; Hd of Office Mitrovica, Internat. Civilian Office, Kosovo, 2008–09 (on secondment); Hd, Afghanistan Drugs and Justice Unit, FCO, 2009–11; Ambassador to Croatia, 2012–15. Sen. Associate, Centre for Internat. Policy Studies, Univ. of Ottawa, 2015–16. FRSA 2005. *Recreations:* sport (watching and participating), military history, malt whiskey. *E:* davidslinn@gmail.com.

**SLIPMAN, Sue**, OBE 1994; Director, Foundation Trust Network, NHS Confederation, 2004–12; *b* 3 Aug. 1949; *d* of Marks Slipman and Doris Barham; one *s*. *Educ:* Stockwell Manor Comprehensive School; Univ. of Wales (BA Hons 1st Class English; Post Graduate Cert Ed); Univs of Leeds and London. Sec. and Nat. Pres., Nat. Union of Students, 1975–78; Mem., Adv. Council for Adult and Continuing Educn, 1978–79; Area Officer, Nat. Union of Public Employees, 1979–85; Director: Nat. Council for One Parent Families, 1985–95; London TEC Council, 1995–96; Gas Consumers' Council, 1996–98; Dir for Social Responsibility, 1998–2001, for External Relns and Compliance, 2001–02, Camelot Gp plc; Chm., Financial Ombudsman Service Ltd, 2003–05. Mem. Exec., NCCL, 1974–75; Vice-Chair, British Youth Council, 1977–78; Chair: Women for Social Democracy, 1983–86; Advice Guidance and Counselling Lead Body, 1992–; Member: Exec. and Chair of Training, 300 Group, 1985–86; Exec., London Voluntary Service Council, 1986; Women's Issues Wkg Gp, Dept of Employment, 1990–94; Better Regulation Task Force, 1997–2001. Director: London East TEC, 1990; Social Market Foundn, 1992–93. Non-exec. Dir, King's Coll. Hosp. NHS Foundn Trust, 2012–. Trustee, NEST Corporation, 2010–15. *Publications:* chapter in The Re-Birth of Britain, 1983; Helping Ourselves to Power: a handbook for women on the skills of public life, 1986.

**SLOAN, Paul Kay**; QC 2001; **His Honour Judge Sloan**; a Circuit Judge, since 2011; a Senior Circuit Judge, since 2014; Honorary Recorder of Newcastle upon Tyne, since 2014; *b* Essex; *s* of late Stanley Buchanan Sloan and Susan Ann Sloan (*née* Usherwood). *Educ:* City of London Sch.; Queen Mary Coll., Univ. of London (LLB). Called to the Bar, Inner Temple, 1981, Bencher, 2016; Asst Recorder, 1998–2000; Recorder, 2000–11. Chm., Barmark, 2004–07; tutor judge, Judicial Coll., 2007–. *Address:* Newcastle upon Tyne Combined Court Centre, The Quayside, Newcastle Upon Tyne NE1 3LA.

**SLOANE, Ian Christopher**; HM Diplomatic Service, retired; *b* 28 Jan. 1938; *s* of Albert Henry Sloane and Ivy Rose (*née* Dennis); *m* 1968, June Barton; two *s*. *Educ:* Lewes Co. Grammar Sch. for Boys; DMS Poly. of Central London 1971. Joined FO, 1956; RAF, 1957–59; FO, 1959–60; MECAS, 1960–61; Vice-Consul: Khartoum, 1961–64; Algiers, 1964–66; Saigon, 1967; 2nd Secretary: Dacca, 1967; Lahore, 1967–70; FCO, 1970–73; UK Disarmament Delegn, Geneva, 1973–74; 1st Sec., Hd of Chancery and Consul, Seoul, 1974–77; 1st Sec. (Econ.), Bonn, 1978–82; W European Dept, FCO, 1983–85; Cultural Attaché, Moscow, 1985; 1st Sec. (Commercial), Ankara, 1986–88; Overseas Estate Dept, FCO, 1989–90; Counsellor and Dep. Consul-Gen., New York, 1990–93; Ambassador to Mongolia, 1994–96. Chm. Bd of Trustees, Electronic Aids for the Blind, 1997–2002; Exec. Dir, Prospect Burma, 1998–2007; Administrator, British-Egyptian Foundn for Children with Special Needs, 2000–08. *Recreations:* tennis, bridge, collecting antique maps, travelling. *Address:* 55 Maygar Avenue, Wodonga, Vic 3690, Australia.

**SLOANE, Prof. Peter James**, PhD; FRSE; Director, Welsh Economy Labour Market Evaluation and Research Centre, Swansea University (formerly University of Wales, Swansea), 2002–08, now Professor Emeritus; Research Fellow, Institute for the Study of Labour, Bonn, since 2001; *b* 6 Aug. 1942; *s* of John Joseph Sloane and Elizabeth (*née* Clarke); *m* 1969, Avril Mary Urquhart; one *s*. *Educ:* Cheadle Hulme Sch.; Univ. of Sheffield (BAEcon Hons 1964); Univ. of Strathclyde (PhD 1966). FRSE 1997. Asst Lectr in Pol Econ., Univ. of Aberdeen, 1966–67, Lectr in Pol Econ., Univ. of Nottingham, 1969–75; Economic Adviser, Unit for Manpower Studies, Dept of Employment (on secondment), 1973–74; Prof. of Econs and Management, Paisley Coll., 1975–84; Jaffrey Prof. of Political Econ., 1984–2002, now Emeritus, Vice Principal and Dean of Social Scis and Law, 1996–2002, Univ. of Aberdeen. Vis. Prof. (Commonwealth Fellow), Faculty of Business, McMaster Univ., Canada, 1978; Vis. Prof., Indiana Univ., 1996; Hon. Professorial Fellow, Univ. of Melbourne, 2007–10; Adjunct Professor: Nat. Inst. of Labour Studies, Flinders Univ., 2010–; Future of Employment and Skills Res. Centre, Univ. of Adelaide, 2018–. Member: ESRC (formerly SSRC), 1979–85 (Mem.), Peer Review Coll., 2010–); Mergers Cttee, SHEFC, 1994–97; Council, Scottish Economic Soc., 1983–2001. Sec., REconS Conf. of Heads of Univ. Depts of Econs, 1990–97. Vice-Pres., Internat. Assoc. of Sports Economists, 2000–10, now Hon. Vice Pres. FRSA 1997. *Publications:* (with B. Chiplin) Sex Discrimination in the Labour Market, 1976; (ed) Women and Low Pay, 1980; (with H. C. Jain) Equal Employment Issues, 1981; (with B. Chiplin) Tackling Discrimination, 1982; (with D. Carline *et al*) Labour Economics, 1985; (ed jtly) Low Pay and Earnings Mobility in Europe, 1998; (jtly) Employment Equity and Affirmative Action, 2003; (jtly) The Economics of Sport, 2004; (jtly) Modern Labour Economics, 2013; (ed jtly) Handbook on the Economics of Professional Football, 2014; monographs on changing patterns of working hours, discrimination and on sport in the market; articles in learned jls, incl. Econ. Jl, Economica, Econs Letters, Applied Econs, Bull. Econ. Res., Oxford Bull. of Econ. Stats, Scottish Jl of Pol Econ., British Jl of Indust. Relations, Managerial and Decision Econs, Lab., Lab. Econs, Ind. and Lab. Relns Review, Educn Econs, Nat. Inst. Econ. Review, Jl of Health Econs, Manchester School, Oxford Econs Papers, Regl Studies, Econ. Record, Econs of Educn Rev., Cambridge Jl Econs, Econ. Modelling. *Recreation:* sport. *Address:* 4 Shaw Park, Weston Lane, Oswestry, Shropshire SY11 2EQ. *T:* (01691) 680931. *Club:* Oswestry Golf.

**SLOBODA, Prof. John Anthony**, OBE 2018; PhD; FBA 2004; Professor of Psychology, Keele University, 1991–2008 (part-time, 2004–08), now Emeritus; Research Professor, Guildhall School of Music and Drama, since 2009; Co-Director, Every Casualty (formerly Every Casualty Programme, Oxford Research Group), since 2007 (Executive Director (part-time), Oxford Research Group, 2004–10); *b* 6 June 1950; *s* of late Mieczyslaw Herman Sloboda and Mary Edna Sloboda; *m* 1980, Judith Nussbaum (marr. diss. 1991); one *d*. *Educ:* St Benedict's Sch., Ealing; Queen's Coll., Oxford (MA 1st cl. (Psychol. and Philos.) 1971); UCL (PhD (Experimental Psychol.) 1974). Lectr, 1974–87, Sen. Lectr, 1987–91, in Psychol., Keele Univ. Mem. Exec. Council, European Soc. for the Cognitive Scis of Music, 1994–2009. Associate Researcher and Co-Founder, Iraq Body Count, 2003–. *Publications:* The Musical Mind: the cognitive psychology of music, 1985; Music and Emotion: theory and research, 2001; Exploring the Musical Mind, 2005; Psychology for Musicians, 2007; Beyond Terror, 2007; Handbook of Music and Emotion, 2010. *Recreation:* choral singing. *Address:* Every Casualty, 86–90 Paul Street, EC2A 4NE. *T:* (020) 7682 2684. *E:* john.sloboda@everycasualty.org.

**SLOCOCK, Caroline Ann, (Mrs C. A. Nightingale)**; Director, Civil Exchange, since 2011; *b* 30 Dec. 1956; *d* of Horace Slocock and Florence (Joyce) Slocock (*née* Wheelton); *m* 1990, John Nightingale; two *d*. *Educ:* Talbot Heath Sch., Bournemouth; University Coll. London (BA Hons English Lang. and Lit. 1978). Joined Dept of Employment, 1982; Private Sec. to Sec. of State for Employment, 1985–87; Mem., Next Steps Project Team, Cabinet Office, 1988–89; Private Sec. (Home Affairs) to Prime Minister, 1989–91; HM Treasury: Head: Spending Team Br. on Employment, 1991–92; Treasury Personnel, 1993–96; Sen. Policy Advr on Expenditure, 1997–2000; Jt Hd, Early Years and Childcare Unit, DfES, 2000–02; Chief Executive: Equal Opportunities Commn, 2002–07; Refugee and Migrant Justice (formerly Refugee Legal Centre), 2007–10. *Publications:* People Like Us: Margaret Thatcher and me, 2018. *Recreations:* gardening, photography, reading, swimming, walking. *E:* carolineslocock@civilexchange.org.uk.

**SLOCOMBE, Gillian Mary**, CBE 2015; Chief Guide, Girlguiding UK, 2011–16; *b* Exmouth, 25 Dec. 1955; *d* of Frederick and Beryl Bolt; *m* 1977, Nicholas Slocombe; two *s*. *Educ:* Bishop Blackall Grammar Sch., Exeter; Exeter Coll., Exeter (Inst. of Legal Execs 1976). Legal exec., 1975–84; youth justice worker (pt-time), 2000–10; Manager, The Buddy (formerly Teenage Parents' Buddy) Project, Som, 2010–16. Chair, Nat. Appropriate Adult Network, 2010–11. Mem., Duke of Edinburgh's Award Cttee, Somerset, 2016–. Parish Councillor, North Curry, 2002–08. *Recreations:* sport, gym, swimming, travelling, theatre, walking challenges, Girlguiding. *Club:* Camping and Caravanning (Hon. Vice-Pres., 2011–16).

**SLOGGETT, Jolyon Edward**, OBE 1995; CEng, Hon. FIMarEST, FRINA, FICS; Secretary, Institute of Marine Engineers, 1986–98; *b* 30 May 1933; *s* of Edward Cornelius Sloggett and Lena May (*née* Norton); *m* 1970, Patricia Marjorie Iverson Ward; two *d*. *Educ:* John Lyon Sch.; Univ. of Glasgow (BSc). CDipAF. William Denny & Brothers Ltd, Leven Shipyard, Dumbarton, 1951–57 and 1959–60. Served, Royal Navy, TA Sub Lieut (E), RNVR, 1957–58; Houlder Brothers & Co. Ltd, 1960–78, Director, 1972–78; Man. Dir, Offshore, British Shipbuilders Corp., 1978–81; Dir, Vickers Shipbuilding Group, 1979–80; Chm., Vickers Offshore (Projects & Development) Ltd, 1979–81; Consultant to Marine and Offshore Industries, 1981–86. *Publications:* Shipping Finance, 1984, 2nd edn 1998. *Recreations:* sailing, gardening, woodwork. *Address:* Corstone Farm, Broadwoodkelly, Winkleigh, Devon EX19 8EF. *T:* (01837) 851441. *E:* jsloggett5@gmail.com.

**SLOMAN, Anne**, OBE 2004; Chair, Church Buildings Council, 2009–14; Member, Archbishops' Council, 2003–09; *b* 24 April 1944; *d* of John Bibby and Kay Bibby (*née* Harvey); *m* 1st, 1966, Andrew Duncan-Jones (marr. diss. 1971); 2nd, 1972, Martyn George Morgan Sloman; two *s*. *Educ:* Farlington; St Hilda's Coll., Oxford (BA (Hons) PPE 1966). BBC journalist, programme maker and policy adviser, 1967–2003: Ed., Gen. Election Results Progs, 1974–92; Dep. Ed., Today Prog., 1981–82; Ed., Special Current Affairs (Radio), 1983–93; Dep. Hd, Weekly Progs (TV and Radio), 1993–96; Chief Political Advr, 1996–2003. Mem. Council, RIIA, 1992–2002. Guest Lectr, Berkeley, Southern Illinois and S Dakota Univs; Faculty, Salzburg Seminar, 2004. Vice Patron, Norfolk Community Foundn, 2011– (Trustee, 2005–10; Vice-Chm., 2006–10). Press Guild Award for Outstanding Prog., 1986 (The Thatcher Phenomenon), 1988 (My Country Right or Wrong). *Publications:* (with David Butler) British Political Facts, 2nd edn (1900–1968), 1968 to 5th edn (1900–1980), 1980; (with Hugo Young) No Minister, 1982; But Chancellor, 1984; The Thatcher Phenomenon, 1986; (with Simon Jenkins) With Respect Ambassador, 1985. *Recreations:* my garden, travel, looking at pictures, theatre, ballet. *Address:* All Saints Cottage, Bale Road, Sharrington, Norfolk NR24 2PF. *Club:* Fakenham Cricket.

**SLOMAN, Sir David (Morgan)**, Kt 2017; London Regional Director, NHS Executive Group, since 2019; *b* Cardiff, 13 April 1961; *s* of Vivian Jack Morgan Sloman and Enid Maude Sloman; *m* 2007, Catherine Sarah Martin; one *d*. *Educ:* Radyr Comprehensive Sch., Cardiff; Univ. of Kent at Canterbury (BA Hons); Birkbeck Coll., Univ. of London (MSc). Gen. Manager, HIV/Genitourinary Medicine Services, Bloomsbury Health Authy, 1990–92; Gen. Manager, Community Service, 1992–95, Dir, Primary and Community Care, 1995–2000, Camden and Islington NHS Trust; Chief Executive Officer: Marylebone Primary Care Gp, 1998–2000; Haringey Primary Care NHS Trust, 2000–05; Whittington Hosp. NHS Trust, 2005–09; Gp CEO, Royal Free London NHS Trust, later NHS Foundn Trust, 2009–19. Mem. Bd, UCL Partners, 2009–. *Recreations:* music, Rugby, poker, Tottenham Hotspur FC. *Clubs:* Reform; Royal Society of Medicine.

**SLOMAN, Prof. Morris Samuel**, PhD; FREng, FIEEE, FIET, FBCS; Professor of Distributed Systems Management, Imperial College London, since 1996; *b* Kwe Kwe, Southern Rhodesia, 5 Dec. 1947; *s* of Reuben Sloman and Hannah Sloman (*née* Rest); *m* 1975, Ruth Cass; two *d*. *Educ:* Univ. of Cape Town (BSc 1st Cl. Electrical Engrg 1970); Univ. of Essex (PhD 1974). CEng 1990; FBCS 2003; FIET 2004; FREng 2006; FIEEE 2011. Systems programmer, GEC Computers Ltd, 1974–75; Department of Computing, Imperial College London: Lectr, 1976–88; Sen. Lectr, 1988–92; Reader, 1992–96; Dep. Hd, 2004–14; Dean, 2010–13. Co-Ed., IEE/IOP/BCS Distributed Systems Engrg, 1993–99; Ed.-in-Chief, 2011–13, Mem., Adv. Bd, 2014–, IEEE Trans on Network and Service Mgt; Member: Adv. Bd, Jl Network and Systems Mgt, 1994–; Editl Adv. Bd, Internat. Jl Network Mgt, 2009–. Mem., Defence Security Adv. Cttee, Information Security Bd, MoD, 2006–08. Mem., Computing Panel, RAE 2001, 1998–2001; Deputy Chairman: Computing Panel, RAE 2008, 2005–08; Computing Sci. and Informatics Sub-panel, REF 2014, 2011–14. Member: Information and Communication Technologies Strategic Adv. Team, EPSRC, 2002–04; Exec. Cttee, UK Cttee for Res. on Computing, 2005–14. Member: Assessment Panel for Ireland Univs ICT Res., Forfás Ireland, 2002; Internat. Adv. Council, INESC ID-Lisboa, Portugal Res. Inst., 2005–. Dan Stokesberry Meml Award for dist. contribn to growth in field of network mgt, IEEE/IFIP. *Publications*: (with J. Kramer) Distributed Systems and Computer Networks, 1987; (ed) Network and Distributed Systems Management, 1994; contrib. jl and conf. papers on distributed computing systems, network security and mgt and policy based mgt. *Recreations*: theatre, classical music, going to the gym. *Address*: Department of Computing, Imperial College London, 180 Queen's Gate, SW7 2RH. *T*: (020) 7594 8279, *Fax*: (020) 7594 8282. *E*: m.sloman@imperial.ac.uk.

**SLOSS**; *see* Butler-Sloss.

**SLOT, His Honour Peter Maurice Joseph;** a Circuit Judge, 1980–97; *b* 3 Dec. 1932; *s* of Joseph and Marie Slot; *m* 1962, Mary Eiluned Lewis; two *s* three *d*. *Educ*: Bradfield Coll.; St John's Coll., Oxford (MA). Called to Bar, Inner Temple, 1957. A Recorder of the Crown Court, 1974–80. *Recreations*: golf, creating harmony. *Address*: The Red House, Betchworth, Surrey RH3 7DR. *T*: (01737) 842010. *Club*: Walton Heath Golf.

**SLUMBERS, Martin Richard;** Secretary, Royal and Ancient Golf Club of St Andrews, since 2015; *b* Brighton, 19 March 1960; *s* of George Denzil and Maureen Slumbers; *m* 1985, Jill Elizabeth Norman; two *s*. *Educ*: Lancing Coll.; Birmingham Univ. (BSc). ACA 1981. Chartered Accountant, Price Waterhouse, 1982–86; Salomon Brothers: financial mgt and control roles, 1986–94; Chief Financial Officer, Asia, 1994–97, Europe, 1997–98; Deutsche Bank: Global Business Area Controller, Sales and Trading, 1998–2001; Dep. Chief Operating Officer, Corporate and Investment Bank, 2001–03; Global Head and Chief Operating Officer, Orgn, 2004–13; CEO, Deutsche Bank Operation Internat. Global Services, 2005–13; Global Head, Investment Banking Ops, 2006–13, Global Business Services, 2007–13. *Address*: Royal and Ancient Golf Club, St Andrews, Fife KY16 9JD. *T*: (01334) 400000, *Fax*: (01334) 460001. *E*: TheSecretary@RandAgc.org. *Club*: Worplesdon Golf.

**SMALL, Annika**, OBE 2018; Founder and Chief Executive Officer, Centre for the Acceleration of Social Technology, since 2015; *b* London, 5 March 1966; *d* of Clive Small and Monica Small (*née* Wiechel). *Educ*: Holton Arms Sch., Washington, DC; St Paul's Girls' Sch.; Univ. of Warwick (BA Econ). Dir, Business Intelligence, 1995–98; Founder, Affiniti, 1999–2001; Chief Exec., Futurelab, 2001–08; Dir, Educn, Tony Blair Faith Foundn, 2008–10; Chief Exec., Nominet Trust, 2010–15. Non-exec. Dir, Lightful, 2016–19. Trustee: Access Foundn, 2014–; Design Council, 2014–; Founders4Schools, 2015–. Member: BAFTA; RSA. Bett Outstanding Contribution Award, 2010; First Women Award in Sci. and Technol., CBI, 2014. *Recreations*: film, photography, hiking, open swimming. *Address*: 57 Church Path, W4 5BL. *E*: annika.small@hotmail.co.uk.

**SMALL, Gareth**, FRAM; Principal Trumpet, Hallé Orchestra, since 2008; *b* Swansea, 14 Nov. 1970; *s* of Tony and Gillian Small; *m* 2005, Katherine Brown; two *s*. *Educ*: Gowerton Comprehensive Sch., Swansea; Royal Acad. of Music (GRSM Hons 1992). LTCL 1988; LRAM 1993, ARAM 1997, FRAM 2014. Co-Principal Trumpet: Hallé Orch., 1993–2008; London Brass, 2002–. *Recreations*: golf, Welsh Rugby, wine, family. *Address*: 80 Grove Park, Knutsford, Cheshire WA16 8QB. *T*: 07973 197148. *E*: garethsmall@yahoo.co.uk.

**SMALL, Prof. Helen Wenda**, PhD; FBA 2018; Merton Professor of English Language and Literature, University of Oxford, since 2018; Fellow, Merton College, Oxford, since 2018; *b* Wellington, NZ, 23 Oct. 1964; *d* of Colin McEwen Small and Wenda Mary Lavinia Heald; partner, Timothy David Gardam, *qv*; one *d*. *Educ*: Queen Margaret Coll., Wellington, NZ; Victoria Univ. of Wellington (BA 1985; BA Hons 1986); St Catharine's Coll., Cambridge (PhD 1991; Hon. Fellow 2018). Res. Fellow, St Catharine's Coll., Cambridge, 1990–93; Lectr in English, Univ. of Bristol, 1993–96; Lectr, then Prof. of English Lit., and Jonathan and Julia Aisbitt Fellow in English Lit., Pembroke Coll., Oxford, 1996–2018. *Publications*: Love's Madness: medicine, the novel and female insanity, 1800–1865, 1996; The Long Life, 2007; The Value of the Humanities, 2013. *Recreation*: cross-country running. *Address*: Merton College, Oxford OX1 4JD. *E*: helen.small@ell.ox.ac.uk.

**SMALL, Prof. John Rankin**, CBE 1991; Professor of Accountancy and Finance, Heriot-Watt University, 1967–98, now Emeritus; *b* 28 Feb. 1933; *s* of David and Annie Small; *m* 1957, Catherine Wood; one *s* two *d*. *Educ*: Harris Academy, Dundee; Dundee Sch. of Econs. BScEcon London; FCCA, FCMA, JDipMA. Dunlop Rubber Co., 1956–60; Lectr, Univ. of Edinburgh, 1960–64; Sen. Lectr, Univ. of Glasgow, 1964–67; Heriot-Watt University: Head, Dept of Accountancy and Finance, 1967–90; Dean of Faculty of Econ. and Social Studies, 1972–74; Vice-Principal, 1974–78, 1987–90; Dep. Principal, 1990–94. Director: Edinburgh Instruments Ltd, 1976–2003; Orkney Water Test Centre, Ltd, 1987–96; Environment and Resource Technology Ltd, 1991–99; Petroleum Science and Technology Ltd, 1992–97; Computer Application Services, 1997–2007; Mem. Bd, Scottish Homes, 1993–2002. Chm., Nat. Appeal Panel for Entry to Pharmaceutical Lists (Scotland), 1987–95. Trustee, Nat. Library of Scotland, 1991–99. Pres., Assoc. of Certified Accountants, 1982 (Mem. Council, 1971–99); Member: Educn Cttee, Internat. Fedn of Accountants, 1978–85 (Chm., 1978–82); Commn for Local Authority Accounts in Scotland, 1982–92 (Chm., 1983–92); Chm., Inst. of Offshore Engrg, 1988–90. Hon. DLitt Heriot-Watt, 1996. *Publications*: (jtly) Introduction to Managerial Economics, 1966; (contrib.) Business and Accounting in Europe, 1973; (jtly) Accounting, 1991; articles in accounting and financial jls on accounting and financial management. *Recreation*: golf. *Address*: 39 Caiystane Terrace, Edinburgh EH10 6ST. *T*: (0131) 445 2638. *Club*: New (Edinburgh).

**SMALL, Jonathan Edwin;** QC 2006; *b* 6 Aug. 1967; *s* of late Lensworth Small, E Grinstead, formerly Kingston, Jamaica, and of Marion Small (*née* Hickson); *m* Marcus Alfred Askew. *Educ*: Nottingham Univ. (BA Hist.); City Univ. (Dip. Law). Called to the Bar, Lincoln's Inn, 1990; joined Falcon Chambers, 1992; in practice, specialising in law of real property. Mem., Bar Council, 1994–97 and 2005–08. Trustee and Mem., Sing for Joy; Mem., London Internat. Gospel Choir. *Publications*: articles on history, human rights and the law. *Recreations*: singing, piano playing, painting. *Address*: Falcon Chambers, Falcon Court, Fleet Street, EC4Y 1AA. *T*: (020) 7353 2484.

**SMALL, Peter John**, CB 1999; Permanent Secretary, Department of Agriculture and Rural Development, Northern Ireland, 1996–2003; *b* 21 July 1946; *s* of John and Kathleen Small; *m* 1971, Pamela Hanna; two *s*. *Educ*: Univ. of London (LLB ext.). Northern Ireland Civil Service: Dept of Finance and Personnel, 1966–94: Treasury Officer of Accounts, 1986–88; Dir of Personnel, 1988–94; Finance Dir, Dept of Health and Social Services, 1994–96. *Recreations*: golf, gardening, reading, music, soccer.

**SMALLBONE, Graham**, MBE 2011; Headmaster, Oakham School, 1985–96; *b* 5 April 1934; *s* of Dr E. G. Smallbone and Jane Mann; *m* 1959, Dorothea Ruth Löw; two *s* two *d*. *Educ*: Uppingham School (music scholar); Worcester College, Oxford (Hadow Scholar; MA; Pres., Oxford Univ. Music Club, 1957). ARCO, ARCM. 2nd Lieut, RA, 1952–54. Asst Master, Oundle Sch., 1958–61; Director of Music: Dean Close Sch., 1961–66; Marlborough Coll., 1967–71; Precentor and Director of Music, Eton, 1971–85. Pres., Music Masters' Assoc., 1975; Warden, Music in Educn Section, ISM, 1977; Pres., International Cello Centre, 1985–2000. Conductor: Cheltenham Chamber Orch., 1963–66; N Wilts Orch., 1966–71; Windsor and Eton Choral Soc., 1971–85. Chm., Peterborough Cathedral Fabric Adv. Cttee, 1990–2018. Chm. of Govs, Purcell Sch., 1998–2010; Governor: Yehudi Menuhin Sch., 1989–2011; NYO, 1992–2012. FRSA. *Recreations*: music, golf, photography, reading. *Address*: The Old Manse, 56 High Street, Chinnor, Oxon OX39 4DH. *T*: (01844) 354572.

**SMALLDON, Ven. Keith;** Archdeacon of St Davids, 2011–13; *b* Newport, Monmouthshire, 14 Aug. 1948; *s* of Herbert and Edith Smalldon; *m* 1969, (Patricia) Anne McDonough; one *s* one *d*. *Educ*: Hartridge High Sch., St John's Coll., Ystrad Meurig; St Michael and All Angels Theol Coll., Llandaff (DipTh Univ. of Wales 1971); Open Univ. (BA 1976); Univ. of Newcastle upon Tyne (MA Applied Theol. 1994). Midland Bank Ltd, 1966–67; ordained deacon, 1971, priest, 1972; Curate: Cwmbran, 1971–73; Chepstow, 1973–75; Youth Advr, Dio. of Bradford, 1975–79; Sen. Youth and Community Officer (Trng), Bradford Metropolitan Council, 1979–82; Youth and Community Officer, Dio. of Manchester, 1982–90; Advr for Clergy Trng, Dio. of Carlisle, 1990–94; Team Rector, Daventry, 1994–98; Rector, Llantwit Major, 1998–2003; Dir of Ministry and Res. Canon, Dio. of Swansea and Brecon, 2003–11. Chaplain: Danetre Hosp., 1994–98; RBL Daventry, 1995–98, Llantwit Major, 1998–2003, Milford Haven, 2011–13. *Recreations*: photography, railways, film soundtracks, reading, Belgian ale, watching sport esp. speedway, soccer and Rugby League. *Address*: 41 Horsham Close, Banbury OX16 1XP. *T*: (01295) 269281. *E*: keithsmalldon@btinternet.com.

**SMALLER, Elizabeth Anne; Her Honour Judge Smaller;** a Circuit Judge, since 2015; *b* 31 Dec. 1971; *d* of Cyril and Pauline Smaller; *m* 2005, Craig Beevers; one *d*. *Educ*: Nottingham Univ. (BA Hons Hist.); City Univ. (CPE Law); Inns of Court Sch. of Law. Called to the Bar, Gray's Inn, 1995; in practice as barrister at Criminal Bar, 1995–2015; a Recorder, 2012–15. *Recreations*: going to the theatre, ski-ing, really good North Sea fish and chips. *Address*: Croydon Crown Court, The Law Courts, Altyre Road, Croydon CR9 5AB. *T*: (020) 8410 4700. *E*: croydoncrowncourt@justice.gov.uk.

**SMALLEY, Very Rev. Stephen Stewart;** Dean of Chester, 1987–2001; *b* 11 May 1931; *s* of Arthur Thomas Smalley and May Elizabeth Selina Smalley; *m* 1974, Susan Jane Paterson (*d* 1995); one *s* one *d*. *Educ*: Jesus Coll., Cambridge (MA, PhD); Eden Theological Seminary, USA (BD). Assistant Curate, St Paul's, Portman Square, London, 1958–60; Chaplain of Peterhouse, Cambridge, 1960–63; Lectr and Sen. Lectr in Religious Studies, Univ. of Ibadan, Nigeria, 1963–69; Lectr in New Testament, Univ. of Manchester, 1970–77, Sen. Lectr, 1977 (also Warden of St Anselm Hall, 1972–77); Canon Residentiary and Precentor of Coventry Cathedral, 1977–86, Vice-Provost, 1986. Vis. Prof., Univ. of Chester (formerly Chester Coll., then UC, Chester), 2001–. Mem., C of E Doctrine Commn, 1981–86. Mem., Studiorum Novi Testamenti Soc., 1965–. Manson Meml Lectr, Univ. of Manchester, 1986. Hon. LLD Liverpool, 2001. *Publications*: Building for Worship, 1967; Heaven and Hell (Ibadan), 1968; The Spirit's Power (Achimota), 1972; ed, Christ and Spirit in the New Testament, 1973; John: Evangelist and Interpreter, 1978, USA 1984, 2nd edn 1998, repr. 2012; 1, 2, 3 John, 1984, 2nd edn 2007; Thunder and Love, 1994, repr. 2013; The Revelation to John, 2005; Hope for Ever, 2005; numerous articles in learned jls, incl. New Testament Studies, Novum Testamentum, Jl of Biblical Lit. *Recreations*: literature, music, drama, travel. *Address*: 30 Orchard Park, Elton, Chester CH2 4NQ. *T*: 07950 118880. *E*: stephen.sssmalley@yahoo.co.uk. *Clubs*: City, Business (Chester), Pitt (Cheshire).

**SMALLMAN, David Leslie**, LVO 1990; HM Diplomatic Service, retired; Historical Records Adviser, Foreign and Commonwealth Office, 2000–05; *b* 29 April 1940; *s* of late Leslie Alfred Smallman and Millicent Jean (*née* Burton); *m* 1st, 1967 (marr. diss.); one *s*; 2nd, 1979, Sandra Jill (*née* Browne); one step *s* one step *d*. *Educ*: St Clement Danes; Kingston upon Hull Univ.; London Business Sch. RAFVR/RAF, 1958–60. Nat. Assistance Bd, 1961–66; Colonial, later Foreign and Commonwealth, Office, 1966–67; served Rawalpindi, Islamabad, Nicosia, 1967–72; attached DTI, 1973; Singapore, 1973–77; FCO, 1977; Consul, Aden, 1981–83; Head of Chancery, Rangoon, 1983–87; Head of Royal Matters, FCO, 1987–90; Dep. High Comr, Port of Spain, 1990–94; Gov. and C-in-C, St Helena and Dependencies, 1995–99 (first Gov. to visit Nightingale Is, Inaccessible Is and Gough Is.). Pres., 1995–98, Patron, 1998–99, St Helena Cricket Assoc. (played for Governor's XI, 1996–98); Founder, Governor's Cup internat. yacht race. Promoter, internat. sporting links, Louis Glanville Associates, 1999–. Trustee, Charles Wallace Burma Trust, 2005–10 (Chm., 2006–10). Mem., Towcester PROBUS, 2006–. MIEx; MCIM. *Publications*: Quincentenary, 2003; One of The Queen's Men, 2012; A View from the Castle, 2018; (as Louis Glanville) contrib. short stories to BEA Mag., Singapore; articles, incl. on travel. *Recreations*: novels, history and security, gardening, attending match days at Lord's Cricket Ground. *Address*: The Old School, Blakesley, Northamptonshire NN12 8RS. *Clubs*: MCC (Life Mem.); Royal Cornwall Yacht; Queen's Park Cricket (Trinidad); St Helena Yacht (Hon. Life Mem.); Royal Cape Yacht (Cape Town; Hon. Mem.).

**SMALLMAN, Ven. Wilhelmina T.;** Archdeacon of Southend, 2013–16; *b* Edgware, 29 Oct. 1956; *d* of Hector Abiodan Agbe and Catherine Watson Inglis Agbe; *m* 1992, Christopher Duncan Smallman; three *d*. *Educ*: Central Sch. of Speech and Drama (BEd Hons Drama, English and Voice 1988); Middlesex Univ. (BA Hons Contextual Theol. 2006); N Thames Ministerial Trng Course. Asst Principal, John Kelly Girls Tech. Coll., 2005; ordained deacon, 2006, priest, 2008; Assistant Curate: St Paul's, Harrow, 2006–07; St John the Evangelist, Stanmore, 2007–10; Team Vicar, St Margaret's, Barking, 2010–13. Chair of Govs, George Carey Sch., Barking, 2011. *Recreations*: theatre, travel, National Trust, family, film, singing. *Address*: 39 Liverpool Lawn, Ramsgate, Kent CT11 9HJ.

**SMALLRIDGE, Peter William**, CBE 1995; Chair, Avante Care and Support (formerly Partnership), 2012–17 (Trustee, since 2017); *b* 8 Aug. 1943; *s* of William Smallridge and Eileen (*née* Wilson); *m* 1965, Margaret Collis; two *s* one *d*. *Educ*: Sutton High Sch.; Chichester High Sch.; North-Western Polytechnic (CSW 1965); LSE (Dip. Mental Health 1970). Sen. Mental Health Social Worker, W Sussex CC, 1965–71; Area Officer, W Sussex Social Services, 1971–73; Sen. Lectr, Croydon Coll., 1973–75; Divl Manager, Social Services, Norfolk CC, 1975–82; Dep. Dir, 1982–83, Dir, 1983–91, Social Services, Warwicks CC; Dir of Social Services, Kent CC, 1991–98; Chairman: W Kent HA, 1998–2002; Ashford PCT, 2002–06; Kent and Medway NHS and Socialcare Partnership Trust, 2006–11. Dir, Initiatives in Care Ltd, 2002–12. Pres., Assoc. of Dirs of Social Services, 1992–93. Nat. Trustee, BRCS, 1997–2004; Trustee, Smith's Charity, 1999–2014. *Recreations*: reading, walking, golf, travel. *Address*: Maltmans Hill Barn, Maltmans Hill, Smarden, Kent TN27 8RD. *Club*: Tenterden Golf (Chm., 2018–).

**SMALLWOOD, Christopher Rafton;** Chairman, St George's University Hospitals NHS Foundation Trust (formerly Healthcare NHS Trust), 2011–16; *b* 13 Aug. 1947; *s* of James Rafton Smallwood and Josephine Smallwood (*née* Mortimer); *m* 1979, Ingeborg Hedwig Eva Wiesler; one *s* one *d*. *Educ*: Lancaster Royal Grammar Sch.; Exeter Coll., Oxford (MA

1st Cl. Hons PPE); Nuffield Coll., Oxford (MPhil Econs). Lecturer in Economics: Exeter Coll., Oxford, 1971–72; Edinburgh Univ., 1972–76; Special Advr, Constitution Unit, Cabinet Office, 1974–75; Econ. Advr, HM Treasury, 1976–81; Dir of Policy, SDP, 1981–83; Chief Economist, British Petroleum plc, 1983–86; Econs Ed., Sunday Times, 1986–89; Strategic Develt Dir, TSB Gp and Dir, TSB Bank, 1989–94; Partner: Makinson Cowell Ltd, 1994–98; Brunswick Gp Ltd, 1998–2001; Chief Economic Advr, Barclays plc, 2002–05. Member: Competition Commn, 2001–09; Sec. of State's Econ. Adv. Panel, BIS, 2013–15. Chairman: Hounslow PCT, 2007–09; Kingston Hosp. NHS Trust, 2009–11. Dir, Lombard Street Associates, 2005–15. *Recreations:* golf, opera, theatre. *Club:* Reform.
*See also* J. D. M. Smallwood.

**SMALLWOOD, (James) Douglas (Mortimer);** proprietor, Hertford Physiotherapy Ltd; Chair, Princess Alexandra Hospital NHS Trust, 2013–16; *b* 10 June 1955; *s of* James Rafton Smallwood and Josephine Smallwood (*née* Mortimer); *m* 1983, Sally Rayner; one *s* one *d*. *Educ:* Lancaster Royal Grammar Sch.; Exeter Coll., Oxford (MA). FCIH. CEO, Worcestershire Housing Assoc., 1983–87; Dir, Halifax Building Soc., 1987–2001; Man. Dir, HBOS plc, 2001–04; Chief Exec., Diabetes UK, 2004–10. Non-exec. Co-Chair, Long Term Conditions Prog. Bd, 2008–10, Consultant, 2010–13, E of England Strategic HA, later NHS Midlands and East; Mem., NHS Equality and Diversity Council, 2009–12. Non-exec. Dir, E and N Herts NHS Trust, 2011–13. Mem. Bd (non-exec.), Centrepoint, 2002–08. Chm., Headway Herts, 2013–17. Trustee, Herts and Middx Wildlife Trust, 2011–13. *Recreations:* running, gardening, birdwatching.
*See also* C. R. Smallwood.

**SMALLWOOD, Mark Stephen;** Headteacher, Sale Grammar School, since 2010; *b* Hertford, 27 Jan. 1961; *s of* Peter and Margery Smallwood; *m* 1984, Christine Ibberson; one *s* two *d*. *Educ:* Manchester Univ. (BEd); Lancaster Univ. (MA); Manchester Metropolitan Univ. (Postgrad. Dip Educn Mgt). NPQH 2001. Teacher of Science: Herries Sch., Sheffield, 1983–84; Bimini All Age Sch., Bimini, Bahamas, 1984–87; Alder Grange High Sch., Rossendale, 1987–90; Wardle High Sch., Rochdale, 1990–93; Hathershaw Sch., Oldham, 1993–97; Failsworth Sch., Oldham, 1997–2002; Headteacher, Fearns Community Sports College, 2002–10. *Recreation:* playing tuba. *Address:* Sale Grammar School, Marsland Road, Sale, Cheshire M33 3NH. *T:* (0161) 973 3217. *E:* office@salegrammar.co.uk.

**SMALLWOOD, Stuart David,** PhD; Headmaster, Bishop Wordsworth's School, Salisbury, since 2002 (Deputy Headmaster, 1998–2002); *b* 21 Feb. 1962; *s of* James Smallwood and Pamela Smallwood; *m* 1988, Charlotte Burlend; two *s* one *d*. *Educ:* Leeds Univ. (BSc Earth Scis 1982); Darwin Coll., Cambridge (PhD Geol 1986); Bristol Univ. (PGCE Geog 1989); NPQH 2002. Head of Geography, then of Humanities, Sir Thomas Rich's Sch., Gloucester, 1989–98. *Recreations:* ornithology, apiary, motorcycling, hill walking. *Address:* Bishop Wordsworth's School, 11 The Close, Salisbury SP1 2ED. *T:* (01722) 333851, *Fax:* (01722) 325899. *E:* sds@bws.wilts.sch.uk.

**SMALLWOOD, Trevor,** OBE 1995; DL; Chairman: Advanced Transport Systems, 2000–12; LDJ Design & Display Ltd, 2003–09; UKRD Group, 2006–19 (Director, 2001–06); Stage Electrics, since 2012; *b* 4 Nov. 1947; *s of* late Eric Smallwood and of Vera Smallwood; *m* 1986, Caroline Mary Ball; two *s* two *d*. *Educ:* Mexborough Grammar Sch. MILT. Mgt Trainee, Yorkshire Traction, 1966; National Bus Co., 1970–80; Traffic Manager, Potteries Motor Traction, 1980–82; Man. Dir, Bristol Country Bus, 1983; purchased Badgerline from Dept of Transport, 1986; developed and floated Badgerline, 1993; merged with GRT to become FirstBus, 1995, renamed FirstGroup, 1997, Exec. Chm., 1995–99; Chm., WestCom Media Ltd, 1999–2001. Director: Bristol Water plc, 1999–2008; Brandon Hire plc, 2004–06; Chairman: Catalist Ltd, 2002–06; Coull Ltd, 2005–06. Chm., Quartet Community Foundn (formerly Gtr Bristol Foundn), 2000–06. Pres., Confedn of Public Transport, 1994. Pres., St Monica Trust, 2009–16. Chairman: Colston's Girls' School Trust, Bristol, 2001–17; Venturers Trust, Bristol, 2017–19. DL Somerset, 2003. Master, Soc. of Merchant Venturers, 2009. *Recreations:* football, cricket, running.

**SMART;** *see* de Bernière-Smart.

**SMART, David Eynon;** Managing Director, 2002–16, and Head, Investment Solutions Europe, Middle East and Africa Region, 2014–16, Franklin Templeton Solutions; *b* Hampton Court, 4 July 1961; *s of* Donald Smart and Malvyn Smart; *m* 1989, Rona Shiach; two *s* two *d*. *Educ:* St Paul's Sch.; St John's Coll., Cambridge (BA Classics 1982). Fund Manager, Barings, 1982–85; Asst Dir, County Natwest Investment Mgt Ltd, 1985–88; Sen. Vice Pres., 1988–90, Man. Dir, 1990–2002, Fiduciary Trust Internat. Ltd; Co-CEO, Franklin Templeton Investment Mgt Ltd, 2006–12. National Trust: Chm., Investment Cttee, 2008–; Mem. Council, 2012–; Trustee, 2015–. *Publications:* contrib. article in Central Banking Qly Jl. *Recreations:* tennis, croquet, antiquarian books, piano, wine. *E:* d.smart421@btinternet.com. *Clubs:* Brooks's, Royal Automobile, MCC, Pilgrims.

**SMART, Ian Stewart;** Senior Partner, Cumbernauld Law Practice, since 2017; President, Law Society of Scotland, 2009–10; *b* Paisley. *Educ:* Univ. of Glasgow (LLB). Admitted Solicitor, 1980; with Pattison & Sim; Partner, Ross, Harper & Murray, 1988–91; Sole Principal, Ian S. Smart & Co., 1991–2017. Law Society of Scotland: Mem. Council, 1997–2008; Dep. Pres., 2007–09. *Address:* Cumbernauld Law Practice, 30 Ettrick Walk, Cumbernauld G67 1NE.

**SMART, Kenneth Peter Ross,** CBE 1996; Chief Inspector of Air Accidents, Department for Transport (formerly Department of Transport, then Department of Transport, Local Government and the Regions), 1990–2005; *b* 28 April 1946; *s of* Peter Smart and Evelyn Smart (*née* Ross); *m* 1st, 1969, Kathleen Rouse (marr. diss.); one *s* one *d*; 2nd, 1993, Christine Palmer. *Educ:* Coll. of Electronics, Malvern (FTC); Worcester Tech. Coll. (HNC Aero Engrg); Open Univ. (BA). Aircraft Engrg apprentice, Min. of Aviation, 1962–67; Technical Officer, RRE, 1967–75; Inspector of Accidents, Dept of Trade, 1975–82; Principal Inspector of Accidents, 1982–86, Dep. Chief Inspector of Accidents, 1986–90, Dept of Transport. Non-exec. Dir, British Airways, 2005–16. Mem. Council, The Air League, 2012–. Trustee, Vulcan to the Sky Trust, 2006–. *Recreations:* mountaineering, tennis, sailing, classic motorcycle restoration, walking, golf, Southampton FC. *Address:* 4 Clandon Drive, Boyatt Wood, Eastleigh, Hants SO50 4QQ.

**SMART, Air Vice-Marshal Michael David,** OBE 2017; DL; Director, Meer Consultants Ltd, 2000–10; *b* 18 March 1942; *s of* Gerald Sidney Smart and Keziah Smart (*née* Edwards); *m* 1964, Sheelagh Ann Gent (*d* 2018); one *d* (and one *d* decd). *Educ:* Trinity Sch. of John Whitgift, Croydon; BA Open Univ. Joined RAF Secretarial Branch, 1960; Air Sec.'s Branch, 1973–76 and 1983–85; ndc 1979; Comd, Admin Wing, RAF Coltishall, 1982–83; CO RAF Hereford, 1985–88; Sen. Personnel Staff Officer, HQ Strike Command, 1988–89; RCDS, 1990; Dir, Ground Training, 1991–92; Air Cdre, Training Support, 1993; Dir of Personnel, 1994–95; C of S to Air Mem. for Personnel, 1995–98. Dir, Govt Services, Arthur Andersen Business Consulting, 1998–2000. Vice Chairman (Air): W Midland Reserve Forces, 1998–; Council of Reserve Forces, 2004–15; Chm., Herefordshire, SSAFA, 2001–16; Council Mem., Forces Pension Soc., 1998–2010; Chm.,

Forces Pension Soc. Charitable Fund, 2010–18. Dep. Chm., Herefordshire Armed Forces Community Covenant Gp, 2012–. Chm., Herefordshire Poppies Weeping Window Cttee, 2017–18. Trustee, Regular Forces Employment Assoc., 1999–2009. Hon. Pres., W Mercian Wing, ATC, 2011–. DL Herefordshire, 2006. *Recreations:* track and field athletics and cross country, travelling, cooking, gardening. *Address:* c/o Drummonds Bank, 49 Charing Cross, SW1A 2DX. *Club:* Royal Air Force.

**SMART, Nick David;** professional jazz trumpeter, since 1997; Head of Jazz, Royal Academy of Music, since 2010; *b* Redhill, 6 June 1975; *s of* Richard and Anne Smart; *m* 2014, Helen Mayhew. *Educ:* Univ. of Salford (BA Band Musicianship 1st Cl. 1997); Guildhall Sch. of Music and Drama (Postgrad. Dip.; LGSM). Trumpet and Lectr, Jazz Course, Middx Univ., 2001–07; Dir, Jun. Jazz, 2003–10, Jazz Coordinator and BMus Tutor, 2004–10, RAM; Jazz Trumpet and Ensembles, GSMD, 2006–10. Teacher, Nat. Youth Jazz Collective, 2008–. Masterclasses: Grahamstown Fest., SA, 2014; Eur. Youth Big Band, 2015; Jazz Inst., Berlin, 2015; New England Conservatory, 2016. Recordings: Remembering Nick Drake, 2005; Remembering Louis Armstrong, 2008; Tower Casa, 2013. Hon. RAM 2015. *Recreations:* bird watching, photography. *Address:* Royal Academy of Music, Marylebone Road, NW1 5HT. *T:* (020) 7873 7438. *E:* n.smart@ram.ac.uk.

**SMART, Peter Geoffrey;** educational consultant, 2013–18; Headmaster, Wallington County Grammar School, 2010–13; *b* Streatham, London, 29 Jan. 1953; *s of* Geoffrey Reginald Ernest Smart and Doreen Ivy Smart (*née* Kipling); *m* 1st, 1984 (marr. diss. 2010); two *d*; 2nd, 2011, Chiquita Louise Hunt. *Educ:* Spencer Park Sch., Wandsworth; Chelsea Coll., Univ. of London (BSc Hons Maths 1975; PGCE Maths Educn 1976). NPQH 2003; Chartered London Teacher, 2007. Wallington County Grammar School: Teacher of Maths, 1976–2013; Hd of Maths, 1988–99; Asst Hd, 1993–2005; Dep. Hd, 2005–09; Actg Hd, 2009–10. Member: RHS; Nat. Trust; Hardy Plant Soc.; RSPB. Mem., Birdbrook Parish Council, 2015– (Chm., 2018–; Chm., Birdbrook Community Trust, 2018–). *Recreations:* cricket, tennis, opera, classical music, gardening, walking, nature, more recently bowls, family history. *E:* peter135smart@btinternet.com.

**SMART, Rosamund H.;** *see* Horwood-Smart.

**SMART, Timothy Spencer;** HM Diplomatic Service; Sahel Co-ordinator, Foreign and Commonwealth Office, since 2017; *b* Wimbledon, 17 Sept. 1974; *s of* Simon and Elizabeth Smart; *m* 2015, Dr Veronika Kanturovitch; one *d*. *Educ:* Taunton Sch., Som; Bristol Univ. (BA Hons Ancient Hist.); Peterhouse, Cambridge (MPhil Classics 1995). Business analyst, JP Morgan, 1997–98; entered FCO, 1999; OSCE Dept, FCO, 1999–2000; Second Sec., Tel Aviv, 2001–04; Hd of Chancery, Basra, 2004–05; Hd, EU, Middle E and N Africa Team, FCO, 2005–06; Press Sec. to Perm. Under Sec. of State, FCO, 2006–07; Hd, Strategic Communications Unit and Dep. Hd, Public Diplomacy Gp, FCO, 2007–08; High Comr to the Solomon Islands, 2008–11; Dean of Diplomatic Corps, 2010–11 and 2016; Chargé d'Affaires, Fiji, 2011–12; Ambassador to Republic of Madagascar, 2012–17; non-resident Ambassador to the Union of Comoros, 2017. *Publications:* (ed) Engagement: public diplomacy in a globalised world, 2018. *Recreations:* kite surfing, ski-ing, scuba diving, horse riding, reading history and archaeology. *Address:* c/o Foreign and Commonwealth Office, King Charles Street, SW1A 2AH. *E:* Timothy.Smart@fco.gov.uk.

**SMEATON, John Joseph;** Chief Executive (formerly National Director), Society for the Protection of Unborn Children, since 1996; *b* 20 Feb. 1951; *s of* John Henry Smeaton and Marguerite Amy Smeaton; *m* 1984, Josephine Ann Toner (*née* Clarke); one *s* one *d*, and two step *s*. *Educ:* Salesian Coll., Battersea; Greyfriars Hall, Oxford (MA Eng. Lang. and Lit.); London Univ. (Cert Ed). English Teacher, 1973–75 (full-time), 1975–78 (part-time), Salesian Coll., Battersea; Head of English, Whitefriars, Cheltenham, 1975–76; part-time volunteer worker, 1976–78, Gen. Sec., 1978–96, SPUC. Mem., Nat. Assoc. of Catholic Families, 2006. KSC 1984. *Recreations:* reading, enjoying company of my family. *Address:* Society for the Protection of Unborn Children, 3 Whitacre Mews, Stannary Street, SE11 4AB. *T:* (020) 7091 7091.

**SMEDLEY, Nicholas John;** educational consultant and film historian; *b* 23 Nov. 1959; *s of* Albert Glyn Smedley and Barbara Mary (*née* Sansom); partner, 1983, Kate Jennings. *Educ:* UCL (BA 1st cl. Hons (Hist.) 1981); Birkbeck Coll., London (PhD (Hist.) 1992). Lord Chancellor's Department: Admin. trainee, 1981–84; HEO, 1984–86; Grade 7, 1986–88; freelance advr to Dir, BFI, 1988–92; Dir, HR, PRO, 1992–94; Grade 7, Ct Service HQ, 1994–96; Grade 5, Dir Crown Ct Ops, 1996–99; Grade 3, Chief Exec., Public Trust Office, 1999–2001; Dir, Criminal Justice, LCD, then DCA, 2001–04; Dir, Asylum and Diversity, 2004–05, Diversity, 2005–06, DCA; on secondment as Res. Dir, Prince of Wales's Charities Office, 2006–08. Dir, Rosemary Works Sch., 2012–. *Publications:* The Dead Locust (novella), 2008; A Divided World: Hollywood cinema and émigré directors in the era of Roosevelt and Hitler, 1933–1948, 2011; The Roots of Modern Hollywood: the persistence of values in American cinema from the New Deal to the present day, 2014; (with Tom Sturges) Preston Sturges: the last years of Hollywood's first writer-director, 2019; articles on Hollywood film hist.; booklets on British film and TV. *Recreations:* opera, ballet, theatre, cinema, travel. *E:* nickandkate@yahoo.com. *Club:* Athenæum.

**SMEDLEY, Susan M.;** *see* Marsden, S.

**SMEE, Clive Harrod,** CB 1997; Visiting Professor of Economics, University of Surrey, since 1995; *b* 29 April 1942; *s of* Victor Woolley Smee and Leila Olive Smee (*née* Harrod); *m* 1975, Denise Eileen Sell; one *s* two *d*. *Educ:* Royal Grammar Sch., Guildford; LSE (BSc Econ); Indiana Univ. (MBA); Inst. of Commonwealth Studies, Oxford. British Council, Nigeria, 1966–68; Economic Advr, ODM, 1969–75; Sen. Economic Advr, DHSS, 1975–82; Nuffield and Leverhulme Travelling Fellow, USA and Canada, 1978–79; Advr, Central Policy Review Staff, 1982–83; Sen. Economic Advr, HM Treasury, 1983–84; Chief Economic Adviser: DHSS, 1984–88; DSS, 1988–89; DoH, 1988–2002; Sen. Policy Advr, NZ Treasury, 2002–04. Consultant: NZ Treasury, 1988; NZ Dept of Health, 1991. Chm., OECD Social Policy Working Party, 1987–90; Member: Internat. Co-ordinating Cttee, Commonwealth Fund, 1998–2004; Economics Adv. Panel, Home Office, 2006–08; Ind. Adv. Cttee on Develt Impact, DFID, 2007–10; Ref. Gps on Policy Evaluation of Pioneer and Vanguard Projects, DoH, subseq. DHSC, 2015–. Trustee, Medicines and People, 2006–12. Queen Mother Meml Fellow, Nuffield Trust, 2003–04. Horsley Neighbourhood Connector, 2017–. *Publications:* Speaking Truth to Power, 2005; articles on economics in learned jls. *Recreations:* painting, walking, gardening, cycling; Anna, David, Elizabeth, Andrew, Erin and Logan. *Address:* Appletree House, Ockham Road North, East Horsley, Surrey KT24 6PU.

**SMEE, John Charles O.;** *see* Odling-Smee.

**SMEE, Paul Howard;** Director General, Council of Mortgage Lenders, 2011–17; *b* Liverpool, 27 Dec. 1956; *s of* Mirek and Rene Smee; *m* 1983, Penny Fulbeck (*d* 2018); one *s* one *d*. *Educ:* Liverpool Coll.; Wadham Coll., Oxford (MA). DTI, 1978–88; Hd of Public Policy and Internat. Affairs, Stock Exchange, 1988–94; Hd, Life Insce, ABI, 1994–96; Dir, Public Affairs, ITC, 1996–99; Dir Gen., Assoc. of Ind. Financial Advrs, 1999–2004; Chief Exec., Payment Council/APACS, 2005–11. Mem., Social Housing Regulation Panel,

2018–. Chairman: Peer-to-Peer Finance Assoc., 2018–; Conveyancing Assoc., 2018–. Trustee, Money Advice Trust, 2017–. *Recreations:* reading, theatre, opera, family, watching cricket. *E:* smee.p@blueyonder.co.uk. *Club:* Surrey County Cricket.

**SMEETH, Prof. Liam,** PhD; FRCP, FRCGP, FFPH, FMedSci; Professor of Clinical Epidemiology, since 2009, and Dean, Faculty of Epidemiology and Population Health, London School of Hygiene and Tropical Medicine; NHS general practitioner, London, since 1996; *b* Hull, 26 Feb. 1965; *s* of Michael Smeeth and Angela Smeeth (*née* Nolan); *m* 1998, Ruth Hallgarten; one *s* two *d*. *Educ:* Univ. of Sheffield (MB ChB 1990); London Sch. of Hygiene and Tropical Medicine (MSc 1998; PhD 2002). MRCGP 1996, FRCGP 2010; FFPH 2008; FRCP 2013. NHS med. trng posts (medicine, surgery, paediatrics, A&E, obstetrics and gynaecol., psychiatry), Sheffield and London, 1990–96; Clin. Res. Fellow and Lectr, UCL, 1996–98; Lectr, Sen. Lectr, then Reader, LSHTM, 1999–2009. Trustee, BHF, 2015–. FMedSci 2016. *Publications:* over 450 articles. *Recreations:* anything involving mountains, walking by the sea, music, theatre, art. *Address:* London School of Hygiene and Tropical Medicine, Keppel Street, WC1E 7HT. *T:* (020) 7927 2296. *E:* liam.smeeth@lshtm.ac.uk.

**SMEETH, Ruth Lauren;** MP (Lab) Stoke-on-Trent North, since 2015; *b* Edinburgh, 29 June 1979; *d* of Lucille Kelly; *m* 2004, Michael Smeeth. *Educ:* Downend Comprehensive Sch.; Filton Sixth Form Coll.; Birmingham Univ. (BSocSc Hons; Postgrad. Dip. PR). Sen. researcher, Amicus/AEEU, 2000–04; Hd of Govt Relns, Sodexo, 2004–05; Dir, Public Affairs, Bicom, 2005–07; Public Affairs Manager, Nestlé UK, 2007; Campaign Co-ordinator, CST, 2008–10; Dep. Dir, Hope Not Hate, 2010–15. Mem., Defence Cttee, 2015–. *Recreations:* cinema, reading, travel. *Address:* House of Commons, SW1A 0AA. *T:* (020) 7219 4844. *E:* ruth.smeeth.mp@parliament.uk. *Club:* Royal Air Force.

**SMELLIE, David Craig Shaw;** Partner, Farrer & Co. LLP, since 1996; *b* Glasgow, 20 Oct. 1964; *s* of Prof. Martin Smellie and Dr Florence Smellie; *m* 1991, Lady Emma Caroline de Vere Beauclerk, *d* of Duke of St Albans, *qv;* one *s* two *d*. *Educ:* Glenalmond Coll.; St John's Coll., Cambridge (BA 1986); Coll. of Law, Guildford. Admitted solicitor, 1989; Solicitor, Farrer & Co., 1989–91 and 1993–96; served HM Diplomatic Service, FCO, 1992–93; Mem., Mgt Bd, Farrer & Co. LLP, 2007–13. Vis. Fellow, Eton Coll., 2013. Mem. Council, Radley Coll., 2003–. Governor: James Allen's Girls' Sch., 2002–12; Dulwich Prep. Sch., London and Cranbrook, 2011– (Chm., 2014–15). *Publications:* Common Employment Problems, 2000. *Recreations:* running, walking, opera, travel. *Address:* Farrer & Co. LLP, 66 Lincoln's Inn Fields, WC2A 3LH. *T:* (020) 7242 2022, *Fax:* (020) 7404 5127. *E:* dcs@farrer.co.uk. *Club:* New (Edinburgh).

**SMERDON, Matthew George;** Chief Executive, Legal Education Foundation, since 2013; *b* Basingstoke, 27 July 1972; *s* of George and Dee Smerdon; *m* 2000, Joanna Street; two *d*. *Educ:* St Ivo Comprehensive Sch., St Ives; Univ. of Birmingham (BA Special Hons Medieval and Modern Hist. 1994); Univ. of E Anglia (MA Develt Studies 1996). Res. Officer, CAF, 1996–99; Develt Worker, 1999–2002, Dir, Community Work, 2002–04, Advr (pt-time), 2004–12, Community Links; Dep. Dir, Baring Foundn, 2004–13. Lay Mem., Civil Justice Council, 2013–. Co-founder, Hackney Umpires Cricket Club, 2009–. Gov., Mossbourne Parkside Acad. (formerly Brook Community Primary Sch.), 2010–. Volunteer, Hackney Winter Night Shelter, 2017–. *Publications:* (ed jtly) Building Civil Society, West Malling: Charities Aid Foundation, 1998; Rights with Meaning, 2004; (jtly) Living Values, 2007; (with K. Bell) Deep Value, 2011; (with J. Randall) Future Advice, 2013. *Recreations:* pianist and double bassist (member, Norman Moy Trio, 2003–14, Normal Folk, 2014–16), cycling, snowboarding, water sports. *Address:* Legal Education Foundation, 1 Paper Buildings, Inner Temple, EC4Y 7EU. *T:* (020) 3005 5691. *E:* matthew.smerdon@thelef.org.

**SMETHAM, Andrew James,** MA; Headmaster, The Purbeck School, Wareham, Dorset, 1985–2002; *b* 22 Feb. 1937; *s* of Arthur James Smetham and Eunice (*née* Jones); *m* 1964, Sandra Mary Owen; two *s*. *Educ:* Vaynor and Penderyn Grammar Sch., Cefn Coed, Breconshire; King's Coll., Univ. of London (BA (Hons German) 1959, DipEd 1964, MA (Educn) 1968). Assistant Master: Wandsworth Sch., 1960–66; Sedgehill Sch., 1966–70; Dep. Headmaster, Holloway Sch., 1970–74; Headmaster, Wandsworth Sch., 1974–84. *Recreation:* music. *Address:* Catbells, Durfold Wood, Billingshurst RH14 0PN. *T:* (01483) 201076.

**SMETHURST, Richard Good,** MA; Provost, Worcester College, Oxford, 1991–2011; Pro Vice-Chancellor, University of Oxford, 1997–2011; *b* 17 Jan. 1941; *s* of Thomas Good Smethurst and Madeleine Nora Foulkes; *m* 1964, Dorothy Joan (*née* Mitchenall); two *s* two *d*; *m* 2000, Prof. Susan Edith Gillingham (*née* Mull); two step *d*. *Educ:* Liverpool Coll.; Worcester Coll., Oxford (Webb Medley Jun. Schol. 1962; BA 1st Cl. 1963; MA; Hon. Fellow, 2011); Nuffield Coll., Oxford. Research Fellow: St Edmund Hall, Oxford, 1964–65; Inst. for Commonwealth Studies, Oxford, 1965–66 (Consultant, UN/FAO World Food Program); University of Oxford: Fellow and Tutor in Economics, St Edmund Hall, 1966–67; Fellow and Tutor in Economics, Worcester Coll., and Univ. Lectr in Economics, 1967–76; Dir, Dept for External Studies, and Professorial Fellow, Worcester Coll., 1976–89; Supernumerary Fellow, Worcester Coll., and Chm., Gen. Bd of Faculties, 1989–91; non-exec. Dir, Nuffield Orthopaedic Centre, Oxford, 1992–2000. Economic Adviser, HM Treasury, 1969–71; Policy Adviser, Prime Minister's Policy Unit, 1975–76. Dir, IMRO, 1987–99. Member: Adv. Council for Adult and Continuing Educn, DES, 1977–83; Monopolies and Mergers Commn, 1978–89 (Dep. Chm., 1986–89); UGC/NAB Continuing Educn Standing Cttee, 1984–88; Acad. Consultative Cttee, Open Univ., 1986–92; Adv. Bd, Music at Oxford, 1988–94; Consumer Panel, FSA, 1998–2004. Chm., Unit for Develt of Adult Continuing Educn, 1991–92. Trustee: Eur. Community Baroque Orch., 1986–93; Oxford Philomusica, 2003–15. Mem. Council, Templeton Coll., Oxford (formerly Oxford Management Centre), 1982–95; Life Governor, Liverpool Coll., 1968. Foundn Hon. Fellow, Kellogg Coll., Oxford, 1990; Hon. Fellow: St Edmund Hall, Oxford, 1991; St Catharine's Coll., Cambridge, 2002. *Publications:* Impact of Food Aid on Donor Countries (with G. R. Allen), 1967; contribs to New Thinking About Welfare, 1969; Economic System in the UK, 1977, 2nd edn 1979; New Directions in Adult and Continuing Education, 1979; Continuing Education in Universities and Polytechnics, 1982; contrib. Jl of Development Studies, Oxford Rev. of Educn, Studies in Adult Education. *Recreations:* good food, travel. *Address:* 43 Cranham Street, Oxford OX2 6DD. *T:* (01865) 552837. *E:* richard.smethurst@worc.ox.ac.uk.

**SMILEY, Lt-Col Sir John (Philip),** 4th Bt *cr* 1903, of Drumalis, Larne, Co. Antrim and Gallowhill, Paisley, Co. Renfrew; *b* 24 Feb. 1934; *s* of Sir Hugh Houston Smiley, 3rd Bt and Nancy Elizabeth Louise Hardy (*née* Beaton) (*d* 1999); *S* father, 1990; *m* 1963, Davina Elizabeth, *e d* of late Denis Charles Griffiths; two *s* one *d*. *Educ:* Eton Coll.; RMA Sandhurst. Commnd Grenadier Guards, 1954; ADC to Governor of Bermuda, 1961–62; served in Cyprus, BAOR, Hong Kong; Lt-Col, 1981; retired 1986. Russell Reynolds Associates, 1986–89. Governor, Oundle Sch., 1987–99. Mem., Ct of Assts, Worshipful Co. of Grocers, 1987– (Master, 1992–93). *Recreations:* gardening, travel. *Heir: s* Christopher Hugh Charles Smiley [*b* 7 Feb. 1968; *m* 1998, Clare Annabel, *y d* of Maj. Henry Blosse-Lynch; three *s*]. *Address:* Cornerway House, Chobham, Woking, Surrey GU24 8SW. *T:* (01276) 858992. *Club:* Army and Navy.

**SMILEY, Miranda Caroline;** *see* Sawyer, M. C.

**SMILEY, Prof. Timothy John,** PhD; FBA 1984; Knightbridge Professor of Philosophy, University of Cambridge, 1980–98; Fellow of Clare College, Cambridge, since 1955; *b* 13 Nov. 1930; *s* of Prof. M. T. Smiley and Mrs T. M. Smiley (*née* Browne); *m* 1955, Benita Mary Bentley; four *d*. *Educ:* Ardwyn Grammar Sch., Aberystwyth; Ampleforth Coll.; Fribourg Univ.; Clare Coll., Cambridge (BA 1952, Math. Tripos; MA, PhD 1956). Holt Scholarship, Gray's Inn, 1954; called to the Bar, 1956. Pilot Officer, RAFVR, 1954. Scientific Officer, Air Min., 1955–56; Clare Coll., Cambridge: Res. Fellow, 1955–59; Asst Tutor, 1959–65; Sen. Tutor, 1966–69; Actg Master, 1984 and 1999–2000; Cambridge University: Asst Lectr in Phil., 1957–62; Lectr, 1962–79; Mem., Gen. Bd of Faculties, 1969–72; Chm., Bd of Scrutiny, 1995–96. Vis. Professor: Cornell Univ., 1964; Univ. of Virginia, 1972; Yale Univ., 1975; Univ. of Notre Dame, 1986; Yale Univ., 1990. Sec. for Postgrad. Studies, 1992–94, Mem., Humanities Res. Bd, 1994–96, British Acad. *Publications:* (with D. J. Shoesmith) Multiple-conclusion Logic, 1978; (with Alex Oliver) Plural Logic, 2013, 2nd enlarged edn 2016; articles in phil and math. jls. *Recreation:* orienteering. *Address:* Clare College, Cambridge CB2 1TL. *T:* (01223) 352152.

**SMILEY, Xan de Crespigny;** journalist; Editor at Large, The Economist, since 2014; *b* Hanover, 1 May 1949; *s* of Col David de Crespigny Smiley, LVO, OBE, MC and Bar and Moyra Eileen Smiley (*née* Montagu-Douglas-Scott); *m* 1983, Hon. Jane Acton; two *s* and two step *d*. *Educ:* Eton Coll.; New Coll., Oxford (MA Russian and Modern Hist.). Commentator, BBC Radio Ext. Service, 1974–75; corresp., Spectator and Observer, in Africa, 1975–77; Ed., 1977–81, co-owner, 1981–92, Africa Confidential; leader writer, The Times, 1981–83; foreign affairs writer, The Economist, 1983–86; Moscow corresp., Daily Telegraph, 1986–89; Washington corresp., Sunday Telegraph, 1989–92; Political Ed. and Bagehot columnist, 1992–94, Europe Ed., 1995–2003, Middle East and Africa Ed., 2003–14, The Economist. Sen. Mem., St Antony's Coll., Oxford, 2010–16. Mem. Council, Chatham House, 2010–16. *Recreations:* genealogy, shooting, food, sport (Mem., British Ski Team, 1969; winner, Oxford and Cambridge downhill race, 1969). *Address:* Lower Farm, Taston, Chipping Norton, Oxon OX7 3JL. *E:* xansmiley@economist.com. *Clubs:* Beefsteak, Grillions.

**SMIT, Sir Timothy (Bartel),** KBE 2012 (Hon. KBE 2011; Hon. CBE 2002); Executive Vice Chairman, Eden Project, since 2014 (Chief Executive, 1999–2013); Executive Co-Chair (formerly Executive Chairman), Eden International (formerly Regeneration) Ltd, since 2013; Director, Lost Gardens of Heligan, since 1990; *b* Scheveningen, The Hague, Holland, 25 Sept. 1954; *s* of Jan Adrianus Bartel Smit and late Anthea Margaret Smit (*née* Fairclough); adopted British citizenship, 2012; *m* 1978, Laura Candace Pinsent (marr. diss. 2013); three *s* one *d*. *Educ:* Cranbrook Sch.; Univ. of Durham (BA Hons Archaeol. and Anthropology). Archaeologist, 1977–78; record producer and composer, 1978–90; with John Nelson discovered, 1990, and restored Heligan estate, Cornwall, now open to visitors and known internationally as Lost Gardens of Heligan (Gardener of Year, Country Life, 1995; Garden of Year, Good Guide to Britain, 1999; Country File Garden of Year, 2018; Large Tourism Destination of Year, BTA, 2016, 2017, 2018); Co-Founder, Eden Project, 1994 (scientific instn featuring conservatories inside a 34 acre, 200ft deep clay pit near St Austell). Dir, Hurst Lodge Sch. Ltd Co. Vice-Pres., Garden History Soc.; Patron, Cornwall Garden Soc. Hon. Fellow, St Catherine's Coll., Oxford, 2003. Hon. MSc Gen. Sci. Plymouth, 1998; Hon. LLD Exeter, 2001; Warwick, 2002; Wolverhampton, 2003; Bradford, 2003; Reading, 2003; DUniv: UCE, 2005; Open, 2005; West of England, 2006; Oxford Brookes, 2006; Hon. DEd Bournemouth, 2016; Lincoln, 2018. Outstanding Contribution to Tourism, English Tourism Council, 2000; Alchemist Award, 2001; Social Entrepreneur of the Year, Southern Region, 2001; Lord Lloyd of Kilgerran Award, Foundn for Sci. & Tech., 2003; Albert Medal, Royal Soc. of Arts, 2003. *Publications:* The Lost Gardens of Heligan, 1997 (Illustrated Book of Year, BCA, 1998); The Complete Works: secrets locked in silence, 1999; (with Philip McMillan Browse) The Heligan Vegetable Bible, 2000; Eden, 2001, 10th Anniv. edn 2011. *Recreations:* music, reading, film, art, theatre. *Address:* Eden Project, Bodelva, Cornwall PL24 2SG.

**SMITH;** *see* Carleton-Smith.

**SMITH;** *see* Darwall Smith.

**SMITH;** *see* Dixon-Smith, family name of Baron Dixon-Smith.

**SMITH;** *see* Ferguson-Smith.

**SMITH;** *see* Hamilton-Smith, family name of Baron Colwyn.

**SMITH;** *see* Hastie-Smith.

**SMITH;** *see* Llewellyn Smith and Llewellyn-Smith.

**SMITH;** *see* McGregor-Smith.

**SMITH;** *see* Mackenzie Smith and McKenzie Smith.

**SMITH;** *see* Stewart-Smith.

**SMITH;** *see* Stuart-Smith.

**SMITH;** *see* Warnock-Smith.

**SMITH,** family name of **Viscount Hambleden, Barons Bicester, Kirkhill, Smith of Clifton, Smith of Kelvin** and **Smith of Leigh,** and **Baroness Smith of Gilmorehill.**

**SMITH OF BASILDON,** Baroness *cr* 2010 (Life Peer), of Basildon in the County of Essex; **Angela Evans Smith;** PC 2009; Vice President, Local Government Association, since 2010; *b* 7 Jan. 1959; *d* of Patrick Joseph Evans and Emily Meikle Evans (*née* Russell); *m* 1978, Nigel J. M. Smith. *Educ:* Chalvedon Comprehensive Sch., Basildon; Leicester Poly. (BA Hons Public Admin). Part-time shop asst, J Sainsbury, 1975–77; Trainee Accountant, Newham LBC, 1981–83; Head of Pol and Public Relations, League Against Cruel Sports, 1983–95; Researcher, Alun Michael, MP, 1995–97. Mem. (Lab) Essex CC, 1989–97. Contested (Lab) Southend W, 1987. MP (Lab and Co-op) Basildon, 1997–2010; contested (Lab and Co-op) S Basildon and E Thurrock, 2010. PPS to Minister of State, Home Office, 1999–2001; an Asst Govt Whip, 2001–02; Parliamentary Under-Secretary of State: NI Office, 2002–06; DCLG, 2006–07; PPS to Prime Minister, 2007–09; Minister of State (Minister for the Third Sector), Cabinet Office, 2009–10. Shadow Leader of H of L, 2015–. Chair: Resolving Chaos, 2012–15; Prodn Exchange, 2014–. Hon. President: St Clere's Co-operative Acad. Trust, 2012–; Airship Heritage Trust, 2014–; Patron: Basildon Women's Aid, 1998–2015; Sugarloaf Riding for the Disabled, 2012–15; Stanford and Corringham Sch. Trust, 2014–15. *Address:* House of Lords, SW1A 0PW.

**SMITH OF CLIFTON,** Baron *cr* 1997 (Life Peer), of Mountsandel, in the co. of Londonderry; **Trevor Arthur Smith,** Kt 1996; FRHistS, FAcSS; Vice-Chancellor, University of Ulster, 1991–99; *b* 14 June 1937; *e s* of late Arthur James Smith and Vera Gladys Smith (*née* Cross); *m* 1st, 1960, Brenda Susan (*née* Eustace) (marr. diss. 1973); two *s*; 2nd, 1979, Julia Donnithorne (*née* Bullock); one *d*. *Educ:* LSE (BSc Econ 1958).

Schoolteacher, LCC, 1958–59; temp. Asst Lectr, Exeter Univ., 1959–60; Research Officer, Acton Soc. Trust, 1960–62; Lectr in Politics, Hull Univ., 1962–67; Queen Mary College, later Queen Mary & Westfield College, London: Lectr, then Sen. Lectr, in Political Studies, 1967–83; Prof., Political Studies, 1983–91; Head of Dept, 1972–85; Dean of Social Studies, 1979–82; Pro-Principal, 1985–87; Sen. Pro-Principal, 1987–89; Sen. Vice-Prin., 1989–91; Hon. Fellow, 2003. Vis. Associate Prof., California State Univ., LA, 1969. Director: Job Ownership Ltd, 1978–85; New Society Ltd, 1986–88; Statesman & Nation Publishing Co. Ltd, 1988–90; G. Duckworth & Co., 1990–95. Mem., Tower Hamlets DHA, 1987–91 (Vice Chm., 1989–91); non-exec. Mem., N Yorks HA, 2000–02. Vice Pres., Patients' Assoc. of UK, 1988–97. Chm., Conf. of Rectors in Ireland, 1997. Vice-Pres., Political Studies Assoc. of UK, 1989– (Chm., 1988–89; Pres., 1991–93); Dep. Pres., Inst. of Citizenship Studies, 1991–2001; Member: Admin. Bd, Internat. Assoc. of Univs, 1995–96; Editl Bd, Government and Opposition, 1995–2013; UK Socrates Council, 1993–99 (Chm., 1996–99). Contested (L) Lewisham W, 1959. Mem., H of L, 1997–2019. House of Lords: Lib Dem Spokesman on NI, 2000–11; Chm., Select Cttee on Animals in Scientific Procedures, 2001–02; Member: Select Cttee on Communications, 2004–06; Select Cttee on Constitution, 2005–08; Select Sub-Cttee on Lords' Interests, 2006–08; Ad Hoc Select Cttee on Barnett Formula, 2008–09; Select Cttee on Works of Art, 2010, on Econ. Affairs, 2010–15; Sci. and Technol. Sub-Cttee on Complementary and Alternative Medicine, 1999–2000; EU Sub-Cttee E (Law and Instns), 2000–01. Trustee: Joseph Rowntree Reform (formerly Social Service) Trust, 1975–2006 (Chm., 1987–99); Stroke Assoc., 2002–05. Pres., Belfast Civic Trust, 1995–99; Member Board: Taste of Ulster, 1996–99; Opera NI, 1997–99. Governor: Sir John Cass and Redcoats Sch., 1979–84; Univ. of Haifa, 1985–92; Bell Educnl Trust, 1988–93. Hon. Mem. Senate, Fachhochschule Augsburg, 1994. FRHistS 1986; FICPD 1998. CCMI (CBIM 1992); FRSA 1994. FAcSS (AcSS 2000). Hon. LLD: Dublin, 1992; Hull, 1993; Belfast, 1995; NUI, 1996; Hon. DHL Alabama, 1998; Hon. DLitt Ulster, 2002; Hon. DSc Buckingham, 2019. *Publications*: (with M. Argyle) Training Managers, 1962; (with A. M. Rees) Town Councillors, 1964; Town and County Hall, 1966; Anti-Politics, 1972; (jtly) Direct Action and Democratic Politics, 1972; The Politics of the Corporate Economy, 1979; (with A. Young) The Fixers, 1996; numerous articles. *Club*: Reform.

**SMITH OF FINSBURY,** Baron *cr* 2005 (Life Peer), of Finsbury in the London Borough of Islington; **Christopher Robert Smith**; PC 1997; PhD; Master, Pembroke College, Cambridge, since 2015; *b* 24 July 1951; *s* of Colin Smith and Gladys (*née* Luscombe). *Educ:* Cassiobury Primary Sch., Watford; George Watson's Coll., Edinburgh; Pembroke Coll., Cambridge Univ. (BA 1st Cl. Hons 1972, PhD 1979; Hon. Fellow, 2005–15); Harvard Univ., Mass (Kennedy Scholar, 1975–76). Develt Sec., Shaftesbury Soc. Housing Assoc., 1977–80; Develt Co-ordinator, Soc. for Co-operative Dwellings, 1980–83. Dir, Clore Leadership Prog., 2003–08. Chm., London Cultural Consortium, 2005–08. Sen. Advr, Walt Disney Co., 2001–07; non-exec. Dir, PPL, 2006–. Councillor, London Bor. of Islington, 1978–83 (Chief Whip, 1978–79; Chm., Housing Cttee, 1981–83). MP (Lab) Islington South and Finsbury, 1983–2005. Opposition spokesman on treasury and economic affairs, 1987–92; principal opposition spokesman on environmental protection, 1992–94, on Nat. Heritage, 1994–95, on social security, 1995–96, on health, 1996–97; Sec. of State for Culture, Media and Sport, and Chm., Millennium Commn, 1997–2001. Chairman: Advertising Standards Authy, 2007–17; Environment Agency, 2008–14; Task Force on Shale Gas, 2015–16. Non-executive Director: Spencer Ogden, 2014–17; S Staffs Water, 2018–. Chairman: Tribune Gp of MPs, 1988–89 (Sec., 1985–88); Labour Campaign for Criminal Justice, 1985–88; Bd, Tribune Newspaper, 1990–93; Bd, New Century Magazine, 1993–96. Pres., Socialist Envmt and Resources Assoc., 1992–2007; Mem. Exec., Fabian Soc., 1990–97 (Chm., 1996–97). Mem., Cttee on Standards in Public Life, 2001–05. Pres., Cambridge Union, 1972; Vice-Chm., Young Fabian Gp, 1974–75; Chm., Charing Cross Br., ASTMS, 1980–83; Member: Exec., NCCL, 1986–88; Bd, Shelter, 1986–92; Exec. Cttee, Nat. Trust, 1995–97; Bd, RNT, 2001–09; Bd, Donmar Warehouse, 2001–03 (Chm., 2003–15); Film Policy Rev., DCMS, 2011–12. Chairman: Classic FM Consumer Panel, 2001–07; Man Booker Prize Judges, 2004; Art Fund, 2014– (Chm. Judges, ArtFund Prize for Museums, 2012); Intellectual Property Regulation Bd, 2018–. Vis. Prof. in Culture and the Creative Industries, Univ. of the Arts, London (formerly London Inst.), 2002–10; Vis. Fellow, Ashridge Business Sch., 2007–09. Founding Dir, Clore Leadership Prog., 2003–08. Governor: Sadler's Wells Theatre, 1987–91; Univ. of the Arts, 2005–08; Trustee: John Muir Trust, 1991–97; The Sixteen, 2013–; Chm., Wordsworth Trust, 2002–17 (Pres., 2018–). Pres., Ramblers' Assoc., 2004–08. Hon. FRIBA 2000; Hon. Sen. Fellow, RCA, 2007; Hon. FKC 2008; Hon. Fellow, Cumbria Univ., 2010. Hon. DArts City, 2003; DUniv: Lancaster, 2011; Westminster, 2015; Hon. PhD London Metropolitan, 2017. *Publications*: Creative Britain, 1998; (jtly) Suicide of the West, 2006. *Recreations*: mountaineering, literature, theatre, music. *Address*: House of Lords, SW1A 0PW.

**SMITH OF GILMOREHILL,** Baroness *cr* 1995 (Life Peer), of Gilmorehill in the City of Glasgow; **Elizabeth Margaret Smith**; DL; *b* 4 June 1940; *d* of Frederick William Moncrieff Bennett and Elizabeth Waters Irvine Shanks; *m* 1967, Rt Hon. John Smith, PC, QC (Scot.), MP (*d* 1994); three *d*. *Educ:* Hutchesons' Girls' Grammar Sch.; Univ. of Glasgow (MA, DipEd). Admin. Asst, 1962–64, Scottish Sec., 1982–88, Great Britain-USSR Assoc.; teacher of French, 1964–68. Mem., Press Complaints Commn, 1995–2001. Chm., Edinburgh Festival Fringe, 1995–2012; non-executive Director: Scottish Media Group plc (formerly Scottish Television), 1995–97; Deutsche Bank (formerly Deutsche Morgan Grenfell) (Scotland), 1996–2003; City Inn Ltd, 2001–10; Member: BP Adv. Bd, Scotland, 1996–2004; Adv. Bd, Know How Fund, 1998–99. Mem. Adv. Council, Russo-British Chamber of Commerce, 1996–; Mem. Bd, Covent Garden Fest., 1997–2001. Pres., Scottish Opera, 1997–2012. Trustee: John Smith Meml Trust, 1995– (Chair, 2018–); BHF, 1995–98; ESU, 1995–2001; Centre for European Reform, 1996–2003; World Monument Fund, 1996–2000; Hakluyt Foundn, 1998–2001; Mariinsky Theatre Trust, 2001–. Pres., Birkbeck Coll., London, 1998–2003. DL Edinburgh, 1996. Hon. LLD Glasgow, 1998. *Recreations*: family, cinema, music, theatre, travel. *Address*: House of Lords, SW1A 0PW.

**SMITH OF HINDHEAD,** Baron *cr* 2015 (Life Peer), of Hindhead in the County of Surrey; **Philip Roland Smith**, CBE 2013; Chief Executive (formerly National Secretary), Association of Conservative Clubs. *Address*: House of Lords, SW1A 0PW.

**SMITH OF KELVIN,** Baron *cr* 2008 (Life Peer), of Kelvin in the City of Glasgow; **Robert Haldane Smith**, KT 2013; CH 2016; Kt 1999; CA; FCIBS; Chairman: Green Investment Bank, 2012–17; Forth Ports, since 2015; IMI plc, since 2015; Clyde Gateway, since 2015; British Business Bank, since 2017; Scottish Enterprise, since 2019; *b* 8 Aug. 1944; *s* of Robert Haldane Smith and Jean Smith (*née* Adams); *m* 1969, Alison Marjorie Bell; two *d*. *Educ:* Allan Glen's Sch., Glasgow. CA 1968; FCIBS 1993. With ICFC, 1968–82; Royal Bank of Scotland plc, 1983–85; Man. Dir, Charterhouse Develt Capital Ltd, 1985–89; Chm., Morgan Grenfell Develt Capital Ltd, 1989–2001 (Chief Exec., 1989–96); Chief Exec., Morgan Grenfell Asset Mgt Ltd, 1996–2000; Vice Chm., Deutsche Asset Mgt, 2000–02. Chairman: The Weir Gp plc, 2002–13; SSE plc (formerly Scottish and Southern Energy plc), 2005–15; Alliance Trust, 2016–19. Director: MFI Furniture Gp plc, 1987–2000; Stakis plc, 1997–99 (Chm., 1998–99); Bank of Scotland, 1998–2000; Aegon UK, 2002–09; Standard Bank Gp Ltd, 2003–15; 3i plc, 2004–09. Vice-Pres., China-Britain Business Council, 2003–08. Dir, FSA, 1997–2000. Scottish Gov., BBC, 1999–2004; Bd Mem., British Council, 2002–05. Member: Financial Reporting Council, 2001–04 (Chm., FRC Gp on Guidance to Audit Cttees, 2003); Judicial Appts Bd, 2002–07; Scottish Council of Econ. Advrs, 2007–10. Chairman: Smith Gp Adv. Gp to Scottish Govt (formerly Scottish Exec.) on young people not in educn, employment or trng, 2006–12; Smith Commn on more powers for Holyrood Govt, 2014. Chairman: Commonwealth Games Organising Cttee, Glasgow 2014 Ltd, 2008–15; Commonwealth Games Fedn Partnership, 2017–. Pres., RHASS, 2010–11. Pres., ICA of Scotland, 1996–97. Chm., Bd of Trustees, Nat. Museums of Scotland, 1993–2002 (Trustee, 1985–2002); Mem., Museums and Galls Commn, 1988–98 (Vice Chm., 1996–98). Pres., British Assoc. of Friends of Museums, 1995–2005. Patron: Foundn Scotland (formerly Scottish Community Foundn), 2008–15; Capital Appeal, Prince and Princess of Wales Hospice, 2013–18. Chm., BBC Children in Need, 2003–04. Chancellor: UWS (formerly Paisley Univ.), 2003–13; Strathclyde Univ., 2013–. Dr *hc* Edinburgh, 1999; DUniv: Glasgow, 2001; Paisley, 2003. *Publications*: (jtly) Managing Your Company's Finances, 1981. *Recreation*: Inchmarnock Island. *Address*: House of Lords, SW1A 0PW.

**SMITH OF LEIGH,** Baron *cr* 1999 (Life Peer), of Wigan in the County of Greater Manchester; **Peter Richard Charles Smith**; Lecturer, Manchester College of Art and Technology, 1974–2001; Chairman, Greater Manchester Combined Authority, 2011–15; *b* 24 July 1945; *s* of Ronald Ernest Smith and Kathleen (*née* Hocken); *m* 1968, Joy Lesley (*née* Booth); one *d*. *Educ:* Bolton Sch.; LSE (BScEcon); Garnett Coll. of Educn (CertEd FE); Salford Univ. (MSc Urban Studies). Lectr, Walbrook Coll., 1969–74. Mem. (Lab) Wigan MBC, 1978– (Chm. Finance, 1982–91; Leader, 1991–2018). North West Regional Assembly: Vice Chm., 1998–99; Chm., 1999–2000; Chm. Exec. Bd, 2005–09. Board Member: Manchester Airport plc, 1986–2001 (Chm., 1989–90); Manchester Airports Gp plc, 2001. Chm., Assoc. of Gtr Manchester Authorities, 2000–. Hon. Freeman, Wigan, 2011. Hon DLaws Manchester Metropolitan, 2012. *Recreations*: gardening, reading political biographies, jazz. *Address*: Mysevin, Old Hall Mill Lane, Atherton, Manchester M46 0RG. *T*: (01942) 676127.

**SMITH OF NEWNHAM,** Baroness *cr* 2014 (Life Peer), of Crosby in the County of Merseyside; **Julie Elizabeth Smith**, DPhil; Fellow in Politics, Robinson College, Cambridge, since 1997; Reader in European Politics, since 2018, and Director, European Centre, Department of Politics and International Studies, since 2013, University of Cambridge (Senior Lecturer, 2004–18); *b* 1 June 1969; *d* of Hugh Francis Smith and Eileen Elizabeth Smith (*née* Murphy). *Educ:* Merchant Taylors' Sch. for Girls, Crosby; Brasenose Coll., Oxford (MA PPE); St Antony's Coll., Oxford (MPhil, DPhil Politics). Hd, 1999–2003, Assoc. Fellow, 2003–07, European Prog., RIIA (Chatham House). Hanseatic Scholar, Univ. of Hamburg, 1995–97; Vis. Prof., Internat. Relns and European Studies Prog., Central European Univ., Budapest, 1997. Mem., Internat. Relns Select Cttee, H of L, 2016–; Co-Sec., Armed Forces All Party Parly Gp, 2016–; Treas., Adult Educn All Party Parly Gp, 2017–; Vice-Chair, Polar Regions All Party Parly Gp, 2018–; Sec., Defence Gp, H of L, 2016–. Mem. (Lib Dem) Cambridge CC, 2003–15 (Exec. Cllr for Arts and Recreation, 2006–10, for Customer Services and Resources, 2012–14; Hon. Councillor, 2015–). Mem., Lib Dem Federal Policy Cttee, 2005–16, 2019– (Vice Chm., 2012–16). Mem. Council and Trustee, Cambridge Univ. Catholic Assoc., 2009–18; Trustee, Gladstone Library, 2014–. *Publications*: Voice of the People: the European Parliament in the 1990s, 1995; (ed jtly) Eminent Europeans: personalities who shaped contemporary Europe, 1996 (trans. Czech, 1998); A Sense of Liberty: a short history of the Liberal International 1947–97, 1997; (ed jtly) Democracy in the New Europe, 1999; Europe's Elected Parliament, 1999; (jtly) The New Bilateralism: the UK's bilateral relations within the EU, 2002; (ed jtly) Through the Paper Curtain: insiders and outsiders in the New Europe, 2003; Reinvigorating European Elections: the implications of electing the European Commission, 2005; (Series Ed.) New Horizons in European Politics, 2011–; (ed jtly and contrib.) Palgrave Handbook on National Parliaments and the European Union, 2015; The UK's Journeys Into and Out of The EU: destinations unknown, 2017. *Recreations*: theatre, ballet (watching), travel, spending time with family and friends. *Address*: Robinson College, Cambridge CB3 9AN. *T*: (01223) 766259, (020) 7219 3214. *E*: jes42@parliament.uk.

**SMITH, Rt Hon. Lady; Anne Smith;** PC 2013; a Senator of the College of Justice in Scotland, since 2001; President, Scottish Tribunals, since 2014; *b* 16 March 1955; *d* of John Mather and Jessica Douglas; *m* 1979, David Alexander Smith, WS; one *s* one *d*. *Educ:* Cheadle Girls' Grammar Sch.; Edinburgh Univ. (LLB Hons). Apprenticeship with Shepherd & Wedderburn WS, 1977–79; pupil of James McGhie, 1979–80; admitted Faculty of Advocates, 1980; QC (Scot.) 1993; Advocate Depute, 2000–01. Hon. Bencher, Gray's Inn, 2008. Chair, Scottish Child Abuse Inquiry, 2016–. Chm., Royal Scottish Nat. Orch. Foundn, 2008–16. *Recreations*: music, walking, gardening, cooking for friends and family. *Address*: Parliament House, Edinburgh EH1 1RF. *T*: (0131) 225 2595.

**SMITH, Adam de la Falaise Brett B.;** *see* Brett-Smith.

**SMITH, His Honour Adrian Charles;** a Circuit Judge, 1996–2014; First-tier Tribunal Judge (formerly Legal Member), Mental Health Review Tribunal (Restricted), 2002–19; *b* 25 Nov. 1950; *s* of late Fred Smith and Jenny Smith; *m* 1973, Sallie Ann Palmer (*d* 1994); two *d*. *Educ:* Blackpool Grammar Sch.; Queen Mary Coll., Univ. of London (LLB (Hons)). Called to the Bar, Lincoln's Inn, 1973; in practice on Northern Circuit, 1974–96; a Recorder, 1994–96. Mem., Liverpool Witness Support Mgt Cttee, 1990–93; Legal Mem., NW Mental Health Review Tribunal, 1994–96. *Recreations*: world travel, theatre, fell walking. *Club*: Waterloo Rugby Union.

**SMITH, Sir Adrian (Frederick Melhuish),** Kt 2011; PhD; FRS 2001; Director, Alan Turing Institute, since 2018; *b* 9 Sept. 1946; *s* of late Claude Herbert Melhuish Smith and Jean Margaret Eileen Smith (*née* Hunt); one *s*; partner, Lucy Lauris Heller, *qv*. *Educ:* Teignmouth Grammar Sch.; Selwyn Coll., Cambridge (MA 1968; Hon. Fellow, 2012); University Coll. London (MSc 1969; PhD 1971). Jun. Lectr, 1971–72, Univ. Lectr, 1972–74, in Maths, Univ. of Oxford; Tutorial Fellow in Maths, Keble Coll., Oxford, 1971–74; Lectr in Stats, UCL, 1974–77; Prof. of Mathematical Stats, Univ. of Nottingham, 1977–90; Prof. of Stats, Imperial Coll. of Sci., Technology and Medicine, 1990–98 (Vis. Prof., 1998–2008); Principal, QMW, subseq. Queen Mary, Univ. of London, 1998–2008; Dir Gen., Sci. and Res., DIUS, then BIS, 2008–10; Dir Gen., Knowledge and Innovation, BIS, 2010–12; Vice-Chancellor, Univ. of London, 2012–18. Dir, Imperial College Consultants, 1992–98 (Chm. of Bd, 1996–98). Member: Math. Cttee, SERC, 1985–91 (Chm., 1988–91); Sci. Bd, SERC, 1988–91; Technical Opportunities Panel, EPSRC, 1997–2000; Stats Adv. Cttee, ONS, 1997–99; Bd, UKAEA, 2018–; Chair: UK Inquiry into Post-14 Maths Educn, 2002–03; London Higher, 2004–06; Council for Mathematical Scis, 2013–; UK Inquiry into 16–18 Maths Educn, 2016–17; Dep. Chair, UK Statistics Authy, 2008, 2012–18 (Mem. Bd, 2019–). Chm. Bd, Diamond Synchrotron Ltd, Harwell, 2014–. Pres., Royal Statistical Soc., 1995–97 (Guy Medal in Bronze, 1977, in Silver, 1993). Member: Governing Body, London Business Sch., 1998–2008; Council, St George's Medical Sch., 2002–04; Dep. Vice-Chancellor, Univ. of London, 2006–08. FIS 1980; FCGI 2016. Hon. Fellow, Keble Coll., Oxford, 2014. Hon. DSc: City, 2003; Loughborough, 2006; Plymouth, 2011; Imperial Coll. London, 2013; State Univ. of Ohio,

2015; Hon. DLit QMUL, 2009. Guy Medal in Gold, Royal Statistical Soc., 2016. *Publications:* (jtly) The Statistical Analysis of Finite Mixture Models, 1985; (jtly) Bayesian Theory, 1994; (jtly) Bayesian Methods for Nonlinear Classification and Regression, 2002; (trans. jtly) Bruno de Finetti, Theory of Probability, vol. I, 1974, vol. II, 1975; papers in statistical jls. *Recreations:* edible gardening, cooking, internet chess. *Address:* Alan Turing Institute, British Library, 96 Euston Road, NW1 2DB. *Club:* Reform.

**SMITH, Prof. Alan,** DPhil; UNESCO Professor of Education, Ulster University (formerly University of Ulster), since 2000; *b* Belfast, 18 Jan. 1954; *s* of Walter Smith and Barbara Smith (*née* Stanex); *m* 1981, Elaine Steele; two *d*. *Educ:* Univ. of Ulster (BSc Hons; DPhil 1985). Teacher, NI and Zimbabwe, 1978–84; Research Fellow, Centre for Study of Conflict, Univ. of Ulster, 1985–96; Nuffield Foundn nominee to Integrated Educn Fund, 1992–99. Consultant to Dept of Education, NI, DFID, Council of Europe, UNICEF and World Bank, 1997–. Founding Chm., NI Council for Integrated Educn, 1987–89. Member: UNESCO Adv. Cttee on Peace, Human Rights and Democracy, Paris, 2000–04; Internat. Assessment Bd, Postgrad. Scholarship Scheme, Irish Res. Council, 2002–06 (Mem., Sen. Fellowships Bd, 2006–08); Civic Engagement Empowerment and Respect for Diversity External Adv. Cttee, World Bank, 2003–05; Global Monitoring Report Adv. Gp, Education for All, 2010–11. Vis. Prof., Hong Kong Inst. of Educn, 2006–07. Trustee, Speedwell Envmtl Centre, 1990–96. *Publications:* contribs to acad. jls on educn and conflict in NI, peace, human rights and democracy. *Address:* School of Education, Ulster University, Coleraine, Northern Ireland BT52 1SA. *T:* (028) 7032 4137.

**SMITH, Alan Christopher,** CBE 1996; Chief Executive, Test and County Cricket Board, 1987–96; *b* 25 Oct. 1936; *s* of Herbert Sidney and Elsie Smith; *m* 1963, Anne Elizabeth Boddy; one *s* one *d*. *Educ:* King Edward's Sch., Birmingham; Brasenose Coll., Oxford (BA). Played cricket: Oxford Univ. CC, 1958–60 (Captain, 1959 and 1960); Warwicks CCC, 1958–74 (Captain, 1968–74); rep. England in six Test Matches, Australia and NZ, 1962–63. Gen. Sec., Warwicks CCC, 1976–86; England overseas cricket tours: Asst Manager, Australia, 1974–75; Manager: West Indies, 1981; Fiji, NZ and Pakistan, 1984. Mem., England Cricket Selection Cttee, 1969–73, 1982–86; ICC Referee, 1998–2002. Director: Royds Advertising and Marketing, 1971–86; Aston Villa Football Club plc, 1972–78. President: Brasenose Soc., 1999–2000; OUCC, 2000–09. *Recreations:* both football codes, golf, bridge, motoring. *Address:* The Old Farmhouse, Wyck Rissington, Gloucestershire GL54 2PN. *T:* (01451) 820509. *Clubs:* MCC, I Zingari; Vincent's (Oxford); Warwickshire CC.

**SMITH, Alan Edward,** CBE 2005; PhD; FRS 2010; Senior Vice President, Research, 1989–2011 and Chief Scientific Officer, 1996–2011, Genzyme Corporation, Cambridge, Mass; Lady Margaret Beaufort Fellow, Christ's College, Cambridge, since 2012; *b* Fareham, Hants, 9 Oct. 1945; *s* of late William George Smith and Hilda Annie Smith; *m* 1st, 1979, Eva Paucha (*d* 1988); one *s* one *d*; 2nd, 1991, Mary Loeken (marr. diss. 2004); three *s*. *Educ:* Price's Sch., Fareham; Christ's Coll., Cambridge (BA Nat. Scis Tripos Biochem. 1967); MRC Lab. of Molecular Biol., Cambridge (PhD 1984). Scientific Staff, ICRF, 1972–80; Hd, Biochem. Div., NIMR, 1980–84; Scientific Dir and Vice Pres., Integrated Genetics, Inc., Framingham, Mass, 1984–89. Member, Board of Directors: Genzyme Transgenics Corp., 1993–2000; Cambridge in America, 2001–10, 2012– (Chm., 2014–); Genzyme Therapeutics Ltd, 2006–11; Arecor Ltd, 2008–; Advantagene, 2015–. Member, Scientific Advisory Board: Health Care Ventures, Princeton, NJ, 1999–2011; Massachusetts Life Scis Center, 2008–14; Pharnext, Paris, 2009–; ImmuneXcite, Lexington, Mass, 2014–17. Mem., Bd of Dirs, 1999–2000, Adv. Bd, 2002–07, Amer. Soc. of Gene Therapy. Mem., Bd of Trustees, New England Flower Soc., 2016– (Chm., 2017–). *Publications:* over 140 articles in learned jls incl. Cell, Nature, PNAS, Science; 38 reviews and chapters; 11 US patents. *Recreations:* Early English watercolours, mowing stripes, travelling hopefully, native plant gardening, New England wild flowers. *Address:* 111 Plain Road, Wayland, MA 01778, USA. *T:* (617) 2304572. *E:* alanesmith@me.com.

**SMITH, Alan Frederick;** Chairman, Acambis (formerly Peptide Therapeutics) plc, 1999–2006 (non-executive Director, 1995–2006); *b* 21 July 1944; *s* of Frederick Herbert Smith and Winifred Alice Bella (*née* Farthing); *m* 1966, Judith Mary Forshaw (marr. diss. 1991); one *s* one *d*. *Educ:* Gosfield Sch., Essex. CIPFA. Trainee, Colchester BC, 1961–66; Ipswich County Borough Council: Sen. Accountant, 1966–72; Asst Treas., 1972–74; Principal Accountant, Anglian Water Authy, 1974–75; Asst Dir of Finance, Southern Water Authy, 1975–80; Dir of Finance, Anglian Water Authy, 1980–89; Dep. Man. Dir and Dir of Finance, 1989–90, Gp Man. Dir, 1990–97, Anglian Water PLC. *Recreations:* walking, photography.

**SMITH, Rt Rev. Alan Gregory Clayton;** *see* St Albans, Bishop of.

**SMITH, Alan Keith Patrick;** non-executive Chairman, Space NK Ltd, since 1997; *b* 17 March 1941; *s* of Ernest and Mary Smith; *m* 1st, 1968, Veronica Soskin (marr. diss.); one *s* one *d*; 2nd, 1983, Joan Peregrine; two *s*. *Educ:* St Michael's Coll., Leeds; Edinburgh Univ. (MA). Marks & Spencer, 1964–93, Dir, 1978–93; Chief Exec., Kingfisher, 1993–95; Dir, Smith Peregrine Ltd, 1996–. Non-executive: Chm., Storehouse, then Mothercare, plc, 2000–02; Director: Colefax Gp, 1994–; Whitehead Mann Gp, 1997–2006; Planet Organic Ltd, 2000–; Tangent Communications, 2010–13. Governor: South Bank Bd, 1995–2008; Arts & Business, 1999–2007. *Recreations:* family, wine collecting, walking, cooking. *Clubs:* Brooks's, MCC.

**SMITH, Alasdair;** *see* Smith, M. A. M.

**SMITH, Alexander;** *b* Kilwinning, 2 Dec. 1943. *Educ:* Irvine Royal Acad. Former gardener. Chm., 1983–87, Trade Union Liaison Officer, 1986–88, Cunninghame S CLP; former Chm., Irvine and District Trades Council. MEP (Lab) Scotland S, 1989–99. Member: TGWU (Mem., Regl, Public Service and Political Cttees); Scottish CND; Anti-Apartheid Movement; Amnesty Internat.; Latin American Solidarity Campaign.

**SMITH, Rt Hon. Sir (Alexander) Lockwood,** KNZM 2013; High Commissioner for New Zealand in the United Kingdom, 2013–17; Speaker, House of Representatives, New Zealand, 2008–13; *b* Paparoa, NZ, 13 Nov. 1948; *s* of David and Heather Smith; *m* 2009, Alexandra Lang (*née* Morrison). *Educ:* Matakohe Primary Sch.; Ruawai Dist High Sch.; Auckland Grammar Sch.; Massey Univ. (BAgrSc; MAgrSc Hons); Univ. of Adelaide (PhD Animal Sci. 1980). Jun. Lectr, Massey Univ., 1971–72; Commonwealth Schol., 1973–76; Mktg Manager, NZ Dairy Bd, Central and SE Asia Area, 1981–83. MP (Nat.) Kaipara, 1984–96, Rodney, 1996–2011, NZ, 2011–13. Minister: responsible for Nat. Liby, and for Educn Rev. Office, 1990–95; of Educn, 1990–95; of Agric. and of Forestry, 1996; Dep. Minister of Finance, 1996; Minister: responsible for Contact Energy, 1996–99; for Internat. Trade, 1997–99; Associate Minister of Finance, 1998–99; Minister of Tourism, 1999. Dist. Alumni Award, Massey Univ., 2010. *Publications:* Maize Silage: a study of the nutritive value of ensiled zea mays, 1973; Ruminant Protein Metabolism: a study of the nitrogenous transactions of the small intestinal muscosa, 1979. *Recreations:* beef cattle farming, singing, weight training, rowing, surf lifesaving. *Club:* Lyall Bay Surf Lifesaving.

**SMITH, Alexander M.;** *see* McCall Smith.

**SMITH, Alfred Nicholas Hardstaff L.;** *see* Leigh–Smith.

**SMITH, Dr Alison;** Chief Curator, National Portrait Gallery, since 2017; *b* Brighton, 30 May 1962; *d* of Peter and Lyn Smith; *m* 1st, 1993, Donald Swann (*d* 1994); 2nd, 2004, Nicholas Tromans; two *d*. *Educ:* Nottingham Univ. (BA Hons 1984); Courtauld Inst. of Art (MA 1985; PhD 1990). Tutor Counsellor, Open Univ., 1991–93; Lectr in Hist. of Art, Barber Inst., Univ. of Birmingham, 1993–95; Sen. Lectr in Hist. of Art, Sotheby's Inst., London, 1995–99; Lead Curator, Nineteenth-Century British Art, Tate Britain, 2000–17. *Publications:* The Victorian Nude: sexuality, morality and art, 1996; John Petts and the Caseg Press, 2000; (jtly) Millais, 2007; (ed) Watercolour, 2011; (jtly) Pre-Raphaelites; Victorian avant garde, 2012; (jtly) Artist and Empire, 2015; Reflections: van Eyck and the Pre-Raphaelites, 2017; Burne-Jones, 2018. *Recreations:* listening to the radio, walking, film, drawing.

**SMITH, Alyn;** Member (SNP) Scotland, European Parliament, since 2004; *b* 15 Sept. 1973; *s* of Edward and Jane Smith. *Educ:* Univ. of Leeds (LLB Hons 1994); Univ. of Heidelberg; Coll. of Europe, Warsaw (MA European Studies 1995); Nottingham Law Sch. (Dip. Legal Practice 1996). Clifford Chance, Solicitors, 1997–99; Anderson Strathern, Solicitors, 2000–02; Gp Advr, Justice, Business and Europe, SNP Gp, Scottish Parlt, 2002–04. Dir, Turning Point Scotland, 2011–15. Trustee, LGBT Youth Scotland, 2012–17. Hon. Vice Pres., Scottish SPCA. *Address:* TechCube, 1 Summerhall, Edinburgh EH9 1PL. *E:* alyn.smith@europarl.europa.eu.

**SMITH, Andrea Catherine;** *see* Catherwood, A. C.

**SMITH, Sir Andreas W.;** *see* Whittam Smith.

**SMITH, Andrew;** QC 2016; QC (Scot.) 2002; advocate and barrister; *b* 22 Jan. 1963; *s* of David Abercrombie Smith and Margaret Smith; *m* 1st, Jane Russell (marr. diss. 2009); one *s* two *d*; 2nd, 2014, Jane Munro. *Educ:* Eastwood High Sch.; Dundee Univ. (LLB Hons 1985; DipLP 1986); Edinburgh Univ. (Dip. Advanced Legal Studies 1987); Aberdeen Univ. (Dip. Internat. Arbitration 2017); Southampton Univ. (Internat. Maritime Law Cert. 2018). MCIArb 2017. Admitted advocate, 1988; called to the Bar, Gray's Inn, 2006; ad hoc Advocate Depute, 1995–; Member: Compass Chambers, Edinburgh (Hd, 2006–09); Crown Office Chambers, London; Zenith Chambers, Leeds, 2018–. Former Assessor, Gen. Teaching Council of Scotland; apptd under Proceeds of Crime Act 2002 as Statutory Appointed Person. Mem., Supreme Court Users' Gp, 2015–. *Recreations:* running slowly, cooking badly, drinking enthusiastically, sailing into the wind, single malt whisky. *T:* (0131) 226 5071.

**SMITH, Dr Andrew Benjamin,** FRS 2002; FRSE; Senior Research Scientist, Natural History Museum, 1991; *b* 6 Feb. 1954; *s* of Benjamin Butler Smith and Elsie Marjory (*née* Fleming); *m* 1976, Mary Patricia Cumming Simpson; two *d*. *Educ:* Univ. of Edinburgh (BSc 1st Cl. Hons Geol. 1976; DSc 1993); Univ. of Exeter (PhD Biol Sci. 1979). Lectr, Dept of Geol., Univ. of Liverpool, 1981–82; Res. Scientist, Dept of Palaeontol., Natural History Mus., 1982–91. FRSE 1996. *Publications:* Echinoid Palaeobiology, 1984; Systematics and the Fossil Record, 1994; edited jointly: Echinoderm Phylogeny and Evolutionary Biology, 1988; Fossils of the Chalk, 1988, revd edn 2002; Echinoderm Research 1995, 1996; contrib. numerous scientific papers and monographs.

**SMITH, Hon. Sir Andrew (Charles),** Kt 2000; a Judge of the High Court of Justice, Queen's Bench Division, 2000–16; *b* 31 Dec. 1947; *s* of Charles George Smith and Winifrid Smith; *m* 1986, Indu Nathoo; one *s* two *d*. *Educ:* Wyggeston Grammar Sch. for Boys, Leicester; Wadham Coll., Oxford (BA). Called to Bar, Middle Temple, 1974, Bencher, 1999. QC 1990; a Recorder, 1996–2000; Presiding Judge, NE Circuit, 2003–06; Judge i/c, Commercial Court, 2008–09. *Address:* c/o Fountain Court, Temple, EC4Y 9DH. *Club:* Reform.

**SMITH, Rt Hon. Andrew (David);** *b* 1 Feb. 1951; *m*; one step *s*. *Educ:* Reading Grammar Sch.; St John's Coll., Oxford. Joined Labour Party, 1973. Mem., Oxford City Council, 1976–87 (Chairman: Recreation Cttee, 1980–83; Planning Cttee, 1984–87). Opposition spokesman on higher and continuing educn, 1988–92, on Treasury and Economic Affairs, 1992–94, on transport, 1996–97; Shadow Chief Sec. to HM Treasury, 1994–96; Minister of State, DFEE, 1997–99; Chief Sec. to HM Treasury, 1999–2002; Sec. of State for Work and Pensions, 2002–04. Contested (Lab) Oxford E, 1983; MP (Lab) Oxford E, 1987–2017. Chm., Bd, Oxford Brookes Univ. (formerly Oxford Poly.), 1987–93.

**SMITH, Andrew Duncan;** QC 2012; a Recorder, since 2009; *b* Grantham, Lincs, 14 Oct. 1974; *s* of Dr Duncan Smith and Patricia Smith; *m* 2006, Kate Hollingsworth; one *s* one *d*. *Educ:* St Hugh's Coll., Oxford (BA Juris. 1996; MA). Called to the Bar, Middle Temple, 1997; in practice as a barrister, specialising in criminal law, 1997–. *Address:* St Philips Chambers, 55 Temple Row, Birmingham B2 5LS. *T:* (0121) 246 0200. *Club:* Nottinghamshire County Cricket.

**SMITH, Andrew Mark;** Corporate Affairs Director, Pinewood Studios Ltd, since 2008; *b* Guildford, 5 July 1962; *s* of George Victor Smith and Margaret Beatrice Smith. *Educ:* St Columba RC Sch. Clerical Officer, MAFF, 1978–82; Gp Man. Dir, IGA, 1982–96; Man. Partner, Policy Partnership, 1996–2008. Member: Film Skills Council, 2009–18; Bd, Bucks Business First, 2011–; Nat. Adv. Bd, British Film Commn, 2011–; BAFTA, 2014–; British Screen Adv. Council, 2017–. Chm., Bucks LEP, 2015–. Gov., BFI, 2018–. *Recreations:* scuba diving, film/cinema, Egyptology. *E:* andrew.m.smith@hotmail.co.uk. *Club:* Soho House.

**SMITH, Andrew Paul H.;** *see* Hudson-Smith.

**SMITH, Sir Andrew (Thomas),** 5th Bt *cr* 1897, of Stratford Place, St Marylebone, London; Account Director, New Zealand Media and Entertainment (formerly The Radio Network), Wellington, 2012–18; *b* 17 Oct. 1965; *er s* of Sir Gilbert Smith, 4th Bt and of Patricia Christine Smith (*née* Cooper); *S* father, 2003; *m* 2007, Erin Katrina, *d* of Perry Aspros; three *s* one *d*. Account Dir, Mail Marketing Service, New Zealand Post, 2008–10. *Heir:* *s* Samuel James Thomas Smith, *b* 29 Aug. 2009.

**SMITH, Angela Christine;** MP for Penistone and Stocksbridge, since 2010 (Lab, 2010–19; Ind, 2019; Lib Dem, since 2019) (MP (Lab) Sheffield Hillsborough, 2005–10); *b* 16 Aug. 1961; *d* of Thomas Edward Smith and Patricia Ann Smith; *m* 2005, Steven Wilson; one step *s* one step *d*. *Educ:* Univ. of Nottingham (BA 1st cl. Hons (English studies) 1990); Newnham Coll., Cambridge. Lectr, Dearne Valley Coll., Wath on Dearne, 1994–2003. Mem., Sheffield CC, 1996–2005 (Chm., Finance, 1998–99; Cabinet Mem. for Educn and Trng, 2002–05). Opposition Whip, 2010–11; Shadow Dep. Leader of the House, 2011–14; Shadow Minister, DEFRA, 2014–15. Mem., Envmt, Food and Rural Affairs Select Cttee, 2015–. *Recreations:* hill-walking, bird watching, cooking. *Address:* 2 Maria House, 3 Fox Valley Way, Stocksbridge, Sheffield S36 2AA. *T:* (0114) 283 1855, *Fax:* (0114) 283 1850; House of Commons, SW1A 0AA. *T:* (020) 7219 6713. *E:* smithac@parliament.uk.

**SMITH, Anne;** *see* Smith, Rt Hon. Lady.

**SMITH, Anne;** Chief Executive, Primary Care Respiratory Society UK (formerly General Practice Airways Group), since 2004; *b* 6 May 1961; *d* of John and Gerry Bradley; *m* 2000, Amahl Smith. *Educ:* Christ's Coll., Cambridge (MA; tennis blue). Product Manager, then Gp Product Manager, Merck Sharp and Dohme Ltd, 1982–89; Allen & Hanburys: Mktg Manager, 1989–94; Business Zone Manager, 1994–96; Glaxo Wellcome UK Ltd, 1989–98: Regl Business Dir, 1994–96; Dir, Respiratory Mktg, 1996–98; Chief Exec., Nat. Asthma Campaign, 1998–2001; management consultant, 2001–04. Mem., Technol. Appraisal Cttee, NICE, 2002–04; Trustee, Long Term Med. Conditions Alliance, 2000–05. *Recreations:* travelling, hill walking, gardening, cycling, tennis. *E:* ce.pcrsuk@gmail.com.

**SMITH, Anne Margaret Brearley;** *see* Luther, A. M.

**SMITH, Lt-Gen. Sir Anthony Arthur D.;** *see* Denison-Smith.

**SMITH, Anthony David,** CBE 1987; President, 1988–2005, and Hon. Fellow, 2005, Magdalen College, Oxford; *b* 14 March 1938; *s* of Henry and Esther Smith. *Educ:* Brasenose Coll., Oxford (BA; Hon. Fellow, 1999). BBC TV Current Affairs Producer, 1960–71; Fellow, St Antony's Coll., Oxford, 1971–76; Director, BFI, 1979–88 (Fellow 1988). Bd Mem., Channel Four Television Co., 1980–84. Member: Arts Council, 1990–94; Bd of Dirs, The Sixteen, 2006–; Council, RADA, 2007–17. Member: Internat. Bd, Russia Mus., St Petersburg, 2009–; Internat. Adv. Bd, Tomsk State Univ., 2014–. Chairman: Writers and Scholars Educnl Trust, 1989–99 (Mem., 1982–); Jan Hus Educnl Foundn, 1989–2002; Chair: Hill Foundn, 1998–; Oxford-Russia Fund, 2004–; Trustee: Cambodia Trust, 1990–99; Med. Res. Foundn, 2005–14; Kidu Foundn of Bhutan, 2011–; Indian Nat. Trust for Art and Cultural Heritage UK, 2012–14. *Publications:* The Shadow in the Cave: the broadcaster, the audience and the state, 1973, 2nd edn 1976; British Broadcasting, 1974; The British Press since the War, 1976; Subsidies and the Press in Europe, 1977; The Politics of Information, 1978; Television and Political Life, 1979; The Newspaper: an international history, 1979; Newspapers and Democracy, 1980; Goodbye Gutenberg—the newspaper revolution of the 1980s, 1980; The Geopolitics of Information, 1980; The Age of the Behemoths, 1991; From Books to Bytes, 1993; The Oxford Illustrated History of Television, 1995; Software for the Self: culture and technology, 1996; (with F. Webster) The Postmodern University?, 1997. *Address:* Albany, Piccadilly, W1J 0AX. *Clubs:* Garrick, Grillions, Beefsteak.

**SMITH, Prof. (Anthony) David,** DPhil; FMedSci; Professor of Pharmacology, 1984–2005, now Emeritus, and Deputy Head, Division of Medical Sciences, 2000–05, University of Oxford; Director, Oxford Project to Investigate Memory and Ageing, 1988–2008, now Founding Director; Fellow, Lady Margaret Hall, Oxford, 1984–2005, now Emeritus Fellow; *b* 16 Sept. 1938; *s* of Rev. William Beddard Smith and Evelyn Smith; *m* 1st, 1962, Wendy Diana Lee (marr. diss. 1974); one *s* one *d*; 2nd, 1975, Dr Ingegerd Östman; one *s*. *Educ:* Kingswood Sch., Bath; Christ Church, Oxford (Bostock Exhibnr; BA 1963, MA 1966, DPhil 1966). Royal Soc. Stothert Res. Fellow, Oxford, 1966–70; Res. Lectr, Christ Church, Oxford, 1966–71; Wellcome Res. Fellow, Oxford, 1970–71; Univ. Lectr in Pharmacology and Student of Christ Church, 1971–84; Hd, Dept of Pharmacol., Univ. of Oxford, 1984–2000. Hon. Dir, MRC Anatomical Neuropharmacology Unit, Oxford, 1985–98, Hon. Assoc. Dir. 1998. Member: Gen. Bd of the Faculties, Oxford, 1980–84; Neurosciences Bd, MRC, 1983–88; Physiol Soc.; Pharmacol Soc.; Chm., Scientific Adv. Bd, Alzheimer's Res. Trust, 1998–2003. Dir of Pubns, IBRO, 1977–95; Editor: Methods in the Neurosciences (IBRO Handbook Series), 1981–; Neuroscience, 1976–2002; Mem., editorial bds of various scientific jls. FMedSci 2000; FBPhs 2017. Hon. Res. Fellow, Alzheimer's Res. Trust, 2007. Mem., Norwegian Acad. of Sci. and Letters, 1996; Hon. Mem., Hungarian Acad. of Sci., 1998. Dr *hc* Szeged Univ., 1993; MD *hc* Lund Univ., 1998. (Seventh) Gaddum Meml Prize, British Pharmacol Soc., 1979. *Publications:* (ed) Handbook of Physiology, Section 7 Vol. 6, 1974; (ed) Commentaries in the Neurosciences, 1980; articles on neuropharmacology and Alzheimer's disease in jls. *Recreations:* art, music, travel. *Address:* University Department of Pharmacology, Mansfield Road, Oxford OX1 3QT. *E:* david.smith@pharm.ox.ac.uk.

**SMITH, Anthony Donald Raymond,** CMG 2008; Chief Executive Officer, Westminster Foundation for Democracy, since 2014; *b* 8 Nov. 1958; *s* of Raymond and Flora Smith; *m* 1986, Kerry Rankine; one *s* one *d*. *Educ:* Univ. of Chicago High Sch.; Amherst Coll. (BA); Warwick Univ. (LLB). Joined FCO, 1986; Second, later First Sec., Madrid, 1988–91; First Sec., FCO, 1991–96; Head, EU Dept, then S Africa Dept, DFID, 1996–2006; Dir, Eur. Pol Affairs, FCO, 2006–08; Dir, Europe and Donor Relations, then Internat. Relations Div., DFID, 2008–14. *Recreations:* tennis, canoeing, pruning. *Address:* Westminster Foundation for Democracy, Artillery House, 11–19 Artillery Row, SW1P 1RT.

**SMITH, Anthony Glen;** independent consultant, since 2017; Managing Consultant, Cambridge Education, 2014–17; Lead for Local Authorities, Mott MacDonald Group (formerly Manager, Local Authority Division, then Director, Children's Services, then Director, Health and Education UK, Cambridge Education), 2005–14; *b* 29 July 1955; *s* of Bernard Neil Smith and Jean Margaret Smith; *m* 1978, Anne McLaren; one *s* one *d*. *Educ:* Price's Sch., Fareham; Christ's Coll., Cambridge (BA 1977; MA 1980); Open Univ. (MA 2015). Asst Teacher of Geog., Weston Favell Upper Sch., Northampton, 1977–81; Head of Geog., Sir Frank Markham Sch., Milton Keynes, 1981–84; Asst, later Sen. Educn Officer, Wilts CC, 1984–89; Devon County Council: Area Educn Officer, 1989–91; Sen. Educn Officer, 1991–94; Asst Chief Educn Officer, 1994–96; Dep. Chief Educn Officer, 1996–98; Dir of Educn, Arts and Libraries, 1998–2003; Dir of Learning and Culture, 2003, Dir for Children's Services, 2004–05, Torbay Council. Director: Leeds Local Educn Partnership, 2007–17; Sandwell Educn Futures, 2008–17; Victorious Multi-Acad. (formerly Carillion Academies) Trust, 2015–; Trustee, Viscount Nelson Educn Network, 2016–. *Recreations:* cricket, antique maps, watercolour painting, furniture restoration, gardening, family. *Address:* Trafalgar House, Dawlish Road, Teignmouth, Devon TQ14 8TQ. *T:* (01626) 774289. *Club:* Hawks (Cambridge).

**SMITH, Cdre Anthony Philip M.;** *see* Masterton-Smith.

**SMITH, Prof. Anthony Terry Hanmer,** LLD; Professor, Faculty of Law, Victoria University of Wellington, since 2015 (Pro Vice-Chancellor and Dean, 2007–15); Fellow, Gonville and Caius College, Cambridge, since 1973; *b* 12 Jan. 1947; *s* of William Duncan Hanmer Smith and Rima Patricia Smith (*née* Donnelly); *m* 1968, Gillian Innes (marr. diss. 1981); one *s*. *Educ:* St Bede's Coll., Christchurch, NZ; Univ. of Canterbury (LLB; LLM); PhD 1985, LLD 1999, Cantab. Barrister and solicitor, High Court of NZ, 1979; called to the Bar, Middle Temple, 1992 (Hon. Bencher, 2001). Asst Lectr, Univ. of Canterbury, 1970–72; Lectr in Law, 1973–81, and Tutor, 1974–81, Gonville and Caius Coll., Cambridge; Reader in Law, 1981–85, and Dean of Faculty, 1984, Univ. of Durham; Prof. of Law, 1986–90, and Head of Dept, 1988–90, Univ. of Reading; Prof. of Criminal and Public Laws, 1996–2006, and Chm., Faculty of Law, 1999–2001, Univ. of Cambridge. Visiting Professor: Univ. of Iowa, 1983; Northwestern Univ., Chicago, 1988; Otago Univ., 1991; Université de Panthéon Assas, Paris, 2001–06; City Univ., London, 2004–06; Auckland Univ., 2005; Arthur Goodhart Dist. Vis. Prof., Univ. of Cambridge, 2015–16. *Publications:* Offences Against Public Order, 1987; Property Offences, 1994; (ed jtly) Harm and Culpability, 1996; (with Sir David Eady) The Law of Contempt, 1998, 4th edn 2011;

(ed) Glanville Williams: Learning the Law, 15th edn, 2013, 16th edn, 2016. *Recreations:* cookery, travelling, architecture, wine, watching cricket and Rugby. *Address:* 86 Bolton Street, Kelburn, Wellington 6012, New Zealand. *Clubs:* Athenæum; Wellington (Wellington, NZ).

**SMITH, (Arthur) Jeffrey,** CEng, FREng; FIMMM; Senior Consultant, Wardell Armstrong (Mining, Minerals Engineering and Environmental Consultants), 2009–16 (Partner, 1983–2009, Managing Partner, 1994–2006; Chairman, 2006–09); *b* 1 Feb. 1947; *s* of Alfred and Doris Smith; *m* 1st (marr. diss. 2008); one *s* one *d*; 2nd, 2009, Fiona Mary Bazley. *Educ:* Univ. of Newcastle upon Tyne (BSc Engrg (Mech. and Mining) 1968; BSc Hons (Mining Engrg) 1969). CEng 1971; FIMMM 1988. Tech. asst to colliery manager, Golborne, NCB, 1971–73; Sen. Mining Engr, 1973–75, Associate, 1975–82, K. Wardell & Partners, subseq. Wardell Armstrong. Mem. Bd, British Geol Survey, 2000–08. Pres., IMMM, 2004–05. Mem. Council, Keele Univ., 2000–08. FREng 2001. Freeman, City of London, 1996; Mem., Co. of Engrs, 1999. *Recreations:* golf, boating, classic cars, music (playing guitar in private!)); opposing: the nanny state; political spin; Federalist Europe; social engineering; red tape. *E:* arthurjeffsmith@gmail.com.

**SMITH, Prof. Austin Gerard,** PhD; FRS 2006; FRSE; MRC Professor of Stem Cell Biology, University of Cambridge, since 2006 (Director, Wellcome Trust Centre for Stem Cell Research, 2006–16). *Educ:* Univ. of Oxford (BA). FRSE 2003. University of Edinburgh: Prof. of Stem Cell Biol.; Dir, BBSRC Centre for Genome Res., 1998; Dir, MRC Centre of Develt in Stem Cell Biol.; Chm., Inst. for Stem Cell Res., 2005–06. Louis-Jeantet Prize for Medicine, 2010. *Publications:* articles in learned jls. *Address:* Wellcome Centre for Stem Cell Research, University of Cambridge, Tennis Court Road, Cambridge CB2 1QR.

**SMITH, Barney;** *see* Smith, L. B.

**SMITH, Bartholomew Evan Eric,** OBE 2018; Chairman, Amber Foundation, since 1994; *b* 1 Feb. 1955; *s* of Sir John (Lindsay Eric) Smith, CH, CBE and of Christian Margaret Smith, OBE; *m* 1987, Catherine, *d* of Gavin and Mary Rowan Hamilton; three *s* one *d*. *Educ:* Eton Coll.; New Coll., Oxford. Littlemore Scientific Engrg Co., 1976–84; Dir, Lundy Co. Ltd, 1984–; Chairman: Smith Hamilton Ltd, 1989–; Coexis Ltd, 1990–2005 (Dir, 1985–2008); White Waltham Airfield Ltd, 1992–. Chm., Landmark Trust, 1995–2001. *Recreations:* flying, farming. *Address:* Garden House, Cornwall Gardens, SW7 4BQ; Shottesbrooke Farm, White Waltham, Berks SL6 3SD. *E:* b@rtysmith.com. *Clubs:* Pratt's, MCC; Swinley Forest Golf; West London Aero (White Waltham).

**SMITH, Beverley;** *see* Smith, Jenkyn B.

**SMITH, Bob and Roberta;** *see* Brill, P.

**SMITH, Sir Brian;** *see* Smith, Sir E. B.

**SMITH, Sir Brian;** *see* Smith, Sir N. B.

**SMITH, Brian,** CPFA; Chief Executive, Stoke on Trent City Council, 1992–2002; *b* 16 May 1947; *s* of Albert Frederick and Gladys Smith; *m* 1972, Susan Jane Lund; two *s*. *Educ:* Bristol Univ. (BA Hons). Graduate trainee accountant, Derbyshire CC, 1968; Accountancy Asst, Berkshire CC, 1972; Group Technical Officer, South Yorkshire CC, 1974; Asst County Treasurer, Dorset CC, 1976; Sen. Asst County Treasurer, Avon CC, 1979; Dep. County Treasurer, 1981, County Treasurer, 1983, Staffordshire CC. Chm., Surrey Ambulance NHS Trust, 2004–06 (non-exec. Dir, 2003–04); non-exec. Dir, Surrey PCT, 2006–11. Chm., Inst. of Public Finance Ltd, 2004–11. Public Mem., Network Rail, 2011–14. Hon. Sec., Soc. of County Treasurers, 1990–92; Hon. Treasurer: CIPFA, 2001–04 (Vice-Pres., 1998–99; Pres., 1999–2000); UNICEF UK, 2002–11. *Publications:* various articles in local govt finance jls. *Recreations:* music, gardening, travel.
*See also* T. J. *Smith.*

**SMITH, Ven. Brian;** Archdeacon of the Isle of Man, 2005–11, now Emeritus; *b* 15 July 1944; *s* of William Charles Freeman Smith and Frances Smith; *m* 1967, Christine Ann Masterman; one *s* one *d*. *Educ:* Preston Grammar Sch., Lancs; Barton Peveril Grammar Sch., Eastleigh, Hants; Salisbury and Wells Theol Coll.; Westminster Coll., Oxford (MTh 1995). In commerce and industry, 1960–71. Ordained deacon, 1974, priest, 1975; Curate, St Thomas, Pennywell with St Oswald, Grindon, Sunderland, 1974–77; Chaplain, RAF, 1977–95; Vicar, St John, Keswick, 1995–2005; RD, Derwent, 1998–2005; Priest-in-charge, St Bridget, Bridekirk, 2002–04; Vicar, St George, Douglas, 2005–11. Mem., Gen. Synod, C of E, 2005–11. Hon. Canon, Carlisle Cathedral, 1999–2005. *Recreations:* walking, golf, DIY. *Address:* 68 Greta Gardens, Crow Park Road, Keswick, Cumbria CA12 5EL.

**SMITH, Rt Rev. Brian Arthur;** Bishop of Edinburgh, 2001–11; *b* 15 Aug. 1943; *s* of late Arthur and Doris Marion Smith; *m* 1970, Elizabeth Berring (*née* Hutchinson); two *d*. *Educ:* George Heriot's School, Edinburgh; Edinburgh Univ. (MA Mental Philosophy 1966); Fitzwilliam Coll., Cambridge (BA Theology 1968; MA 1972); Westcott House, Cambridge; Jesus Coll., Cambridge (MLitt 1973). Curate of Cuddesdon, 1972–79; Tutor in Doctrine, Cuddesdon Coll., Oxford, 1972–75; Dir of Studies, Ripon Coll., Cuddesdon, 1975–78, Senior Tutor 1978–79; Diocese of Wakefield: Priest-in-charge of Cragg Vale, 1979–85; Dir of In-Service Training, 1979–81; Dir of Ministerial Trng, 1981–87; Warden of Readers, 1981–87; Sec. of Dio. Board of Ministry, 1979–87; Hon. Canon of Wakefield, 1981–87; Proctor in Convocation, 1985–87; Archdeacon of Craven, 1987–93; Bp Suffragan of Tonbridge, 1993–2001. Hon. Lectr, St Augustine's Theol Sch., Botswana, 2013, 2015. Vice-Chairman, Northern Ordination Course, 1985–93. Chm., Churches Together in Kent, 1999–2001; Vice-Pres., Modern Church (formerly Modern Churchpeople's Union), 2009–. Member: Scotland Cttee, UNESCO, 2008–15; Memory of the World Cttee, UNESCO, 2009–17. Dir, Waverley Care, 2002–11. Gov., Loretto Sch., 2012–17; Trustee, St Mary's Music Sch., 2009–17. A Director, Scottish Jl of Theology, 1977–81. DD Edinburgh, 2018. *Recreations:* browsing in junk shops, walking, reading, music, short-wave radio listening. *Address:* Flat E, 2A Dean Path, Edinburgh EH4 3BA. *T:* (0131) 220 6097. *E:* bishopsmith@btinternet.com. *Club:* New (Edinburgh).

**SMITH, Brian William,** AO 1988; PhD, FIEAust; Vice-Chancellor and Professor, University of Western Sydney, 1989–94; *b* 24 June 1938; *s* of William Lyle Smith and Grace Ellen Smith; *m* 1961, Josephine Peden; two *d* (one *s* decd). *Educ:* Univ. of Melbourne (BEng); Univ. of Cambridge (PhD). Australian Paper Manufacturers Ltd, 1964–70; Consolidated Electronic Industries Ltd, 1971–73; Head, School of Electrical Engineering, 1973–77, Dean, Faculty of Engineering, 1977–79, Dir, 1979–89, Royal Melbourne Inst. of Technology. Chairman of Board: UniSuper Ltd, 2004–2006; Cooperative Res. Centre for Intelligent Manufg Systems and Technologies, 1995–2006. Hon. LLD Hong Kong Baptist Univ., 1999. *Recreations:* music, golf, writing. *Address:* 60 Faraday Street, Carlton, Vic 3053, Australia. *Clubs:* Greenacres Golf, Melbourne Cricket.

**SMITH, Dr Bruce Gordon,** CBE 1999 (OBE 1992); FREng, FIET; President, Smith Institute for Industrial Mathematics and System Engineering, since 2018 (Chairman, 1993–2018); *b* 4 Oct. 1939; *s* of William Francis Smith and Georgina Lucy May Smith (*née* Tompkins); *m* 1964, Rosemary Jane Martineau (*d* 2007); two *s* two *d*. *Educ:* Dulwich Coll.;

Christ Church, Oxford (BA 1st cl. Hons Physics 1961; DPhil 1964; MA 1968). FIET (FIEE 1978; MIEE 1971); FREng (FEng 1998). Res. Associate, Univ. of Chicago, 1964–65; mem., tech. staff, Bellcomm Inc., 1965–68; Prin. Engr, Decca Radar Ltd, 1968–71; Man. Dir, 1971–87, Chm., 1987–97, Smith System Engineering Ltd; Chairman: Industrial Technology Securities Ltd, 1995–2019 (Dir, 1985–95); Univ. of Southampton Hldgs Ltd, 2001–06; Imagineer Systems Ltd, 2002–14; Director: Gordon and Co., 1996–; British Maritime Technology Ltd, 1996–99; Southampton Innovations Ltd, 1998–2003; Esys Ltd, 1999–2001; Innovision Res. and Technol. plc, 2001–04; Southampton Asset Mgt Ltd, 2002–03; IPGroup (formerly IP2IPO Gp) plc, 2002–15 (Chm., 2007–15); Orbital Optics Ltd, 2006–09; Mirriad Ltd, 2010–14; Oregan Networks Ltd, 2011–17. Domus Fellow, St Catherine's Coll., Oxford, 1991–. Chm., ESRC, 1994–2001; Member: Plenary Bd, RAE, 1987–91; BNSC Earth Observation Prog. Bd, 1986–2001 (Chm., 1998–2001); Exec. Cttee, Parly Space Cttee, 1989–97; Industrial R&D Adv. Cttee, EC, 1996–99; Chm., UK Industrial Space Cttee, 1992–94. Chm., Eur. Assoc. of Remote Sensing Cos, 1987–91 (Treas., British Assoc., 1985–95); Pres., Assoc. of Ind. Res. and Technol. Orgns, 1991–93; UK Deleg. and Pres., Eur. Assoc. of Contract Res. Orgns, 1995–97; Member: Council, SBAC, 1992–94; Bd, British Antarctic Survey, 2001–07. Chm., Nat. Space Sci. Centre, 1997–2005. Vice-Chm., Surrey Br., Business Div., Prince's Trust, 1991–2002; Chm., Rainbow Seed Fund, 2002–13; Trustee: Gordon Foundn, 1997–; Radio Communications Foundn, 2003–08. Vice-Chm. of Council, Southampton Univ., 2001–05 (Mem. Council, 2000–06); Gov., ICSTM, 1999–2005. Pres., Alleyn Club, 2011–12. Hon. Fellow, Inst. of Mathematics and its Applications, 2010. Hon. DSc Leicester, 2001. *Recreations:* mountain walking, dinghy sailing, cycling, music. *Address:* 11 Oxdowne Close, Cobham, Surrey KT11 2SZ.

**SMITH, Catherine;** MP (Lab) Lancaster and Fleetwood, since 2015; *b* Barrow-in-Furness, 16 June 1985; *d* of Alan and Joyce Smith; *m* 2016, Ben Soffa; one *s. Educ:* Lancaster Univ. (BA Hons Gender and Sociol. 2006). Campaigns and Policy Officer, British Assoc. of Social Workers, 2011–15. Shadow Minister for Voter Engagement and Youth Affairs, 2016–; Shadow Dep. Leader of H of C, 2016–. Contested (Lab) Wyre and Preston N, 2010. *Address:* House of Commons, SW1A 0AA. *T:* (020) 7219 6001. *E:* cat.smith.mp@parliament.uk.

**SMITH, Cecil Raymond Julian H.;** *see* Humphery-Smith.

**SMITH, Ceri Ivor Daniel;** Director, UK Government Investments Ltd, since 2016; *b* Greenwich, 23 April 1973; *s* of Lawrence F. T. Smith, OBE and Judith M. Smith; *m* 2002, Jessica Mary Lovell; two *s* one *d. Educ:* Emmanuel Coll., Cambridge (BA Soc. and Pol Scis 1995). Academic Affairs Officer, Students' Union, Univ. of Cambridge, 1995–96; HM Treasury, 1996–2003; DTI, 2003–04; HM Treasury, 2004–07; Dir, Business Envmt Unit, BERR, 2007–09; Department for Business, Innovation and Skills: Dir, New Industry, New Jobs, 2009–10; Dir, Business Envmt and Growth and Dir, Office of Life Scis, 2010–11; Dir, Labour Mkt, 2011–13; Dir, Shareholder Exec., 2013–16. Non-exec. Dir, British Business Bank plc, 2013–. Mem. Bd, Homes England, 2018–. Gov., Acland Burghley Sch., London, 2005–16. Trustee, MS Soc., 2017–. *Recreation:* my family. *E:* ceri.smith@ukgi.gov.uk.

**SMITH, Sir Charles B.;** *see* Bracewell-Smith.

**SMITH, Charles M.;** *see* Miller Smith.

**SMITH, Sir Charles Robert S.;** *see* Saumarez Smith.

**SMITH, Chloe;** MP (C) Norwich North, since July 2009; Parliamentary Secretary, Cabinet Office, since 2018; *b* May 1982; *d* of David and Claire Smith; *m* 2013, Sandy McFadzean; one *s* one *d. Educ:* Univ. of York (BA Hons 1st Class Eng. Lit.). Mgt Consultant, Deloitte, until 2009. An Asst Govt Whip, 2010–11; Economic Sec., HM Treasury, 2011–12; Parly Under-Sec. of State, Cabinet Office, 2012–13, NI Office, 2017–18; an Asst Govt Whip, 2017–18. *Address:* House of Commons, SW1A 0AA.

**SMITH, Dr Christopher,** FRCPath; science broadcaster and writer; Consultant Clinical Virologist, University of Cambridge, since 2011; Fellow Commoner, Queens' College, Cambridge, since 2006; *b* Chelmsford, 16 Jan. 1975; *s* of Geoffrey Smith and Jacqueline Smith; *m* 2003, Dr Sarah Urquhart; one *s* one *d. Educ:* Felsted Sch.; King Edward VI Grammar Sch., Chelmsford; London Hosp. Med. Coll.; University Coll. London (BSc Neurosci. 1996); Trinity Coll., Cambridge (MB BChir 2001; PhD 2001). FRCPath 2010. Surgical House Officer, Broomfield Hosp., 2001–02; Med. House Officer, Addenbrooke's Hosp., Cambridge, 2002; Med. SHO, Hammersmith Hosp., 2003; Registrar and Clinical Lectr in Virol., Univ. of Cambridge, 2003–11. Sir Walter Dist. Adjunct Prof., Murdoch Univ., WA, 2013–. Founder and Man. Editor, The Naked Scientist, 2001–; Man. Dir, Naked Science Ltd, 2008–. Weekly broadcasts on BBC Radio 5 Live and on Australian and S African radio. Vice Pres., Public Understanding of Sci., Genetics Soc., 2011–15. Hon. DSc QMUL, 2016. *Publications:* Naked Science, 2006; The Naked Scientist, 2006; Return of the Naked Scientists, 2008; (with Dave Ansell) Crisp Packet Fireworks, 2008; Stripping Down Science, 2010; Everyday Life Under the Microscope, 2012; The Naked Scientist, 2013; Boom!: 50 fantastic science experiments to try at home, 2016. *Recreations:* walking, four-wheel drive excursions, reading. *Address:* The Naked Scientists, Institute of Continuing Education, University of Cambridge, Madingley Hall, Cambridge CB23 8AQ. *T:* (01223) 761756, *Fax:* 07092 019697. *E:* chris@thenakedscientists.com.

**SMITH, Christopher Brian P.;** *see* Powell-Smith.

**SMITH, Christopher Frank;** QC 2009; *b* Leicester, 3 Dec. 1964; *s* of John Christopher Smith and Isabel Mary Smith; *m* 1995, Natalie Louise McGowan; one *d. Educ:* Oundle Sch.; Southampton Univ. (LLB 1st class Hons). Called to the Bar, Inner Temple, 1989; CEDR Accredited Mediator, 2007. *Publications:* (contrib.) Seafarer's Rights, 2005; (ed jtly) Scrutton on Charterparties and Bills of Lading, 21st edn 2008 to 23rd edn 2015. *Recreations:* carriage driving, riding, sailing. *Address:* Essex Court Chambers, 24 Lincoln's Inn Fields, WC2A 3EG. *T:* (020) 7813 8000, *Fax:* (020) 7813 8080. *E:* csmith@essexcourt.com.

**SMITH, Col Christopher Hugh S.;** *see* Sharwood-Smith.

**SMITH, Christopher John Addison,** CBE 2013; FCA; Chief of Staff to Archbishop of Canterbury, 2003–13; *b* 30 March 1949; *s* of Rev. Canon Anthony Cecil Addison Smith and Muriel Patricia Addison Smith; *m* 1973, Nina Jane Perry; two *d. Educ:* Univ. of East Anglia (BA Hons). FCA 1980. With Price Waterhouse, London, 1970–93, Human Resources Partner, 1989–93; Gen. Sec., Diocese of London, 1993–99; Gen. Manager, C. Hoare & Co. Bankers, 1999–2003. Mem., Gen. Synod, Church of England, 1995–2000. Vice Chm. Govs, Southwark Coll. of Further Educn, 1987–94; Dep. Chm. Govs, James Allen's Girls' Sch., 1994–2004. Hon. Treas., Holy Trinity Brompton, 1974–91. Chm. Council, St John's Sch. of Mission (formerly St John's Coll.), Nottingham, 2014–; Member: Council, Corp. of Church Hse, 2014–; Bd, Send A Cow UK, 2014–17; Bd, Abbeyfield Homes, 2015– (Chm., Audit Cttee, 2015–); Trustee: Gordon Russell Design Museum, 2014–; St Martin-in-the-Fields Charity, 2014–. Mediator, Lambeth Mediation Service, 2014– (Trustee, 2016–). *Recreations:* theatre, music, reading, railways, grandchildren. *Club:* Reform.

**SMITH, Rev. Canon Christopher Milne;** Vicar of the Minster Church of St George, Doncaster, 2002–10; Chaplain to the Queen, 2004–14; *b* 7 Sept. 1944; *s* of Alastair Gordon Smith and Marjorie Boulton Smith; *m* 1971, Christine Wright; three *s* one *d. Educ:* Selwyn Coll., Cambridge (BA (Theol.) 1966, MA 1970) Cuddesdon Theol Coll. Ordained deacon, 1969, priest, 1970; Curate, Our Lady and St Nicholas, Liverpool, 1969–74; Team Vicar, St Andrew's, Tower Hill, Kirkby, 1974–81; Rector, St Mary's, Walton-on-the-Hill, Liverpool, 1981–91; Canon Residentiary, Sheffield Cathedral, 1991–2002 (Hon. Canon, 2003–). Advr on the Paranormal to Bishop of Sheffield, 1997–2004. *Recreations:* contract bridge, gardening, philately. *Address:* 14 Ravensdowne, Berwick-upon-Tweed, Northumberland TD15 1HX. *T:* (01289) 330735, 07760 869785. *E:* smithrevcm@gmail.com.

**SMITH, Christopher Shaw G.;** *see* Gibson-Smith.

**SMITH, Claire Helen;** HM Diplomatic Service, retired; Director, CH Smith Consulting Ltd, since 2014; *b* 23 Dec. 1956; *d* of late Norman Eric Stubbs and Helen Evelyn Stubbs; *m* 1986, Michael Forbes Smith, *qv*; one *s* one *d. Educ:* Queen Mary Coll., London (BA Hons 1979); Open Univ. (Postgrad. Cert. Business Admin 2008); MSc Oxon 2017. FCO 1979; Second Sec., Peking, 1983; First Sec., FCO, 1985; Credit Suisse, Zurich, 1990–94; seconded to Auswärtiges Amt, Bonn, 1994–97; First Sec., Bonn, 1997–99; Counsellor, Islamabad, 1999–2001; on loan to Assessments Staff, Cabinet Office, 2001–04; Hd, Whitehall Liaison Dept, FCO, 2004–07. Non-exec. Dir, Mott Macdonald Gp Ltd, 2008–12. Vis. Prof., UEA London, 2011–13. Mem., Security Vetting Appeals Panel, 2009–17. Mem., St Laurence Educn Trust (formerly Abbot's Adv. Cttee), Ampleforth Coll., 2010– (Chm., 2017–19). Gov., Curwen Primary Sch., Plaistow, London E13, 2008–13 (Chair of Govs, 2009–11). *Recreations:* reading detective novels, travel. *Club:* Royal Over-Seas League.

**SMITH, Clive Adrian S.;** *see* Stafford Smith.

**SMITH, Colin Deverell,** OBE 2011; Chairman, Poundland Group Holdings (formerly Poundland Holdings), 2002–12 (non-executive Director, 2012–15); *b* 21 May 1947; *m* 1971, Kathy Morgan; two *s. Educ:* All Saints Sch., Bloxham, Banbury; Liverpool Univ. (BCom 1969). FCA 1973. Qualified with Arthur Andersen, Manchester; Argyll Foods: Gp Financial Controller and Co. Sec., 1979–83; Argyll Gp, subseq. Safeway plc: Gp Financial Controller and Co. Sec., 1983–84; Dir, 1984–99; Finance Dir, 1989–93; Gp Chief Exec., 1993–99. Chairman: Blueheath Hldgs (formerly Blue Heath Direct), 2000–06; Masstock Gp Hldgs, 2007–08; Assured Food Standards, 2003–09; Hilton Food Gp plc, 2016–18 (non-exec. Dir, 2010–18); non-executive Director: McBride plc, 2002–11; LXI REIT plc, 2017–. Trustee, SCF, 2001–05; Chair of Trustees, Challenge Network, 2012–18. *Recreations:* Rugby, travel, walking, military history, interesting vehicles.

**SMITH, His Honour Colin Milner;** QC 1985; a Circuit Judge, 1991–2009; *b* 2 Nov. 1936; *s* of late Alan Milner Smith and Vera Ivy Smith; *m* 1979, Moira Soraya, *d* of late Reginald Braybrooke; one *s* one *d. Educ:* Tonbridge; Brasenose College, Oxford (MA); Univ. of Chicago (JD). Called to the Bar, Gray's Inn, 1962; a Recorder, 1987–91. *Publications:* (jtly) The Law of Betting, Gaming and Lotteries, 1987. *Recreations:* cricket, skiing, reading. *Clubs:* MCC, Roehampton.

**SMITH, Colin Peter,** CBE 2012; DL; FRS 2014; FREng; FRAeS, FIMechE; Pro-Chancellor, University of Southampton, since 2017. *Educ:* Univ. of Southampton (BSc Hons Mech. Engrg). FREng 2003. Joined Rolls Royce, as undergrad. trainee, 1974; Chief Engineer: Small Engines, Rolls-Royce, Bristol; Anglo-French RTM322 helicopter engine; Trent 500 engine; Trent 700 engine; Hd, Compressor Engrg; Dir, Engrg and Technol., Civil Aerospace, 2001–04; Dir, Res. and Technol., 2004; Dir, Engrg and Technol., and Exec. Dir, 2005–17. DL Derbyshire, 2017. Silver Medal, RAEng, 2002. *Address:* University of Southampton, University Road, Southampton SO17 1BJ.

**SMITH, Colin Roderick,** CVO 1984; CBE 1995; QPM 1987; an appeals commissioner, 2001–11; HM Inspector of Constabulary, 1991–2000; *s* of Humphrey and Marie Smith; *m* 1961, Patricia Joan Coppin. *Educ:* Dorking County and Bexhill Grammar Schools; Univ. of Birmingham (BSocSc, Hons Social Admin.); rcds 1981. Royal Army Service Corps (Lieut), 18 Co. (Amph), 1959–62; East Sussex Constabulary, later Sussex Police, from Constable to Chief Supt, 1962–77; Asst Chief Constable, Thames Valley Police, 1977–82; Dep. Asst Comr, Metropolitan Police, 1982–85 (incl. founder, Royalty and Diplomatic Protection Dept); Chief Constable, Thames Valley Police, 1985–91. Mem., Police Authority, UKAEA Constabulary, 2000–05. With Sir John Chilcot, review of N Ireland nat. security, 2002–03; Mem., ACPO Wkg Gp, Providing the Future Chief Officers of Police, 1989. Dorset Vice-Pres., SSAFA, 2012– (Caseworker, 2001–11; Dorset Chm., 2005–11; Trustee, 2006–11; W of England Regl Rep., 2006–11; Chm., Nat. Br. Support Cttee, 2006–09; Hon. Life Mem., 2011; Special Advr to Chm. Council, 2011–17). Queen's Police Essay Gold Medal, 1968. *Publications:* contribs to Police Jl, Police Fedn Occasional Papers and RCDS Seaford Hse Paper. *Recreation:* walking.

**SMITH, Cyril Stanley,** CBE 1985; MSc, PhD; Secretary to Economic and Social Research Council (formerly Social Science Research Council), 1975–85; *b* 21 July 1925; *s* of Walter and Beatrice May Smith; *m* 1968, Eileen Cameron; two *d* (by first marr.). *Educ:* Plaistow Municipal Secondary Sch.; London Sch. of Economics. HM Forces, Dorset Regt, 1943–47. Univ. of Birmingham, 1950–51; Univ. of Sheffield, 1951–52; Dulwich Coll. Mission, 1952–56; Nat. Coal Board, 1956–61; Univ. of Manchester, 1961–71; Civil Service Coll., 1971–75. Man. Dir, ReStrat, 1985–90. Visiting Prof., Univ. of Virginia, 1965; Academic Visitor, Nuffield Coll., Oxford, 1980–81, 1985–86; Senior Res. Fellow, Wissenschaftszentrum Berlin für Sozialforschung, 1987. British Nat. Expert, European Poverty Prog., 1977–82. Mem., Sec. of State's Cttee on Inequalities in Health, DHSS, 1977–80. Chm., British Sociological Assoc., 1972–74; Pres., Sociol. Sect., British Assoc., 1979. *Publications:* Adolescence, 1968; (sen. author) The Wincroft Youth Project, 1972; (ed jtly) Society and Leisure in Britain, 1973; numerous articles on youth, leisure and developments in social science.

**SMITH, Prof. David;** *see* Smith, Anthony D.

**SMITH, Prof. David,** FRS 1988; CPhys, FInstP; Professor, Institute of Science and Technology in Medicine (formerly Department of Biomedical Engineering and Medical Physics), University of Keele, 1999–2016 (Visiting Professor, 1995–99); Director and Company Secretary, Trans Spectra Ltd, since 2001; *b* 26 Nov. 1935; *s* of J. and F. L. Smith. *Educ:* Keele Univ. (BA 1959); DSc 1975, PhD 1962, Birmingham Univ. FInstP 1973. Res. Fellow, 1962, Prof. of Chemical Physics, 1984–90, Birmingham Univ.; Prof. of Physics, Institut für Ionenphysik der Universität Innsbruck, Austria, 1991–95. Hon. DSc Keele, 1990. *Publications:* numerous res. pubns and review articles in physics, chemistry and astrophysics, for learned jls incl. British Inst. of Physics jls, Amer. Inst. of Physics jls, Breath Research, Analytical Chemistry. *Recreations:* classical music, sport. *Address:* 9 The Elms, Porthill, Newcastle-under-Lyme, Staffs ST5 8RP.

**SMITH, David Andrew;** Director, SonVida Wine, since 2014; Manager, SonVida Vineyard, since 2014; Correspondent on Argentina and Uruguay, The Economist, since 2019; *b* 5 March 1952; *s* of John and Patricia Smith; *m* 1996, Sonia Ruseler; one *s* one *d*, and two *s* from former marriage. *Educ:* Lincoln Coll., Oxford (BA Hons, MA Hons). Reuters Correspondent, Spain and Italy, 1975–78; Africa Correspondent, 1979–81, Middle East Correspondent, 1982–86, ITN; Channel 4 News: Diplomatic Correspondent, 1987–89; Moscow Correspondent, 1989–90; Washington Correspondent, 1991–2003. Dir, UN Office, Washington, 2004–06; Special Advr, UN, 2006–10; Dir, UN Office, Argentina, 2010–14. Vis. Prof., Univ. of Michigan, 1986–87. Member: Adv. Bd, OMFIF UK, 2014–; Bd, British Hospital, Argentina, 2014–; Bd, Conciencia NGO, Latin America, 2014–. Hon. Patron, VacProject, Lincoln Coll., Oxford, 2008–. RTS Award, 1983; NY TV Fest. Award, 2000. *Publications:* Mugabe: a biography, 1981; Prisoners of God: conflict of Arab and Israeli, 1987; Dream On: a memoir, 2010. *Recreations:* fatherhood, golf, study of wine. *Address:* Gelly y Obes 2299, 11A, 1425 Buenos Aires, Argentina. *E:* davidsmith.un@gmail.com. *Club:* Reform.

**SMITH, David Arthur George,** OBE 1996; Headmaster of Bradford Grammar School, 1974–96; *b* 17 Dec. 1934; *o s* of Stanley George and Winifred Smith, Bath, Somerset; *m* 1957, Jennifer, *o d* of John and Rhoda Anning, Launceston, Cornwall; one *s* two *d*. *Educ:* City of Bath Boys' Sch.; Balliol Coll., Oxford. MA, Dip. Ed (Oxon). Assistant Master, Manchester Grammar Sch., 1957–62; Head of History, Rossall School, 1963–70; Headmaster, The King's School, Peterborough, 1970–74. Chm., HMC, 1988. Mem., Parole Bd, 1995–2001. JP West Yorks, 1975–2003, Thames Valley, 2003–04. Chm., Woburn Parish Council, 2006–11. *Publications:* (with John Thorn and Roger Lockyer) A History of England, 1961; Left and Right in Twentieth Century Europe, 1970; Russia of the Tsars, 1971. *Recreations:* writing, walking. *Club:* East India.

**SMITH, Prof. David Burton,** CBE 2017; PhD; Raymond Williams Research Professor in Cultural History of Wales, Swansea University, 2005–16; Chair, Arts Council Wales, 2006–16; *b* Tonypandy, Rhondda, 11 Feb. 1945; *s* of Burton Smith and Enid Wyn Smith (*née* Owen); *m* 1969, Norette Ann Wyson; three *s*. *Educ:* Porth Co. Sch.; Barry Grammar Sch.; Balliol Coll., Oxford (BA 1st Cl. Hons Hist. 1966); Columbia Univ., NYC (MA Comparative Lit. 1967); University Coll. of Swansea; PhD Wales 1976. Lecturer in History: Univ. of Lancaster, 1969–71; Univ. Coll. of Swansea, 1971–76; Lectr in Hist. of Wales, Univ. Coll., Cardiff, 1976–85; Personal Chair, Univ. of Wales, 1986–93; Simon Senior Fellow, Manchester Univ., 1992–93; Ed., BBC Radio Wales, 1993; Hd of Progs, BBC Wales, 1994–2000; Pro-Vice-Chancellor, Univ. of Glamorgan, 2000–05. Presenter and writer, Wales! Wales?, BBC TV, 1984. Series Ed., Library of Wales, 2006–. *Publications:* (jtly) The Fed: history of South Wales miners in the 20th century, 1980; (jtly) Fields of Praise: official history of Welsh Rugby Union, 1980; Lewis Jones: writers of Wales, 1982; Wales! Wales?, 1984; Aneurin Bevan and the World of South Wales, 1993; Wales: a question for history, 1999; Raymond Williams: a warrior's tale, 2008; In the Frame: memory and society 1910–2010, 2010; Dream On, 2013; What I Know I Cannot Say/All That Lies Beneath, 2016. *Recreations:* watching Welsh club Rugby, collecting contemporary Welsh art, sea swimming, dog walking, drinking Languedoc wines. *Address:* Rockcliffe, 66 Redbrink Crescent, Barry Island, Vale of Glamorgan CF62 5TU. *T:* (01446) 721064. *E:* daibsmith@btinternet.com. *Club:* Pontypridd Rugby Football.
*See also* O. *Smith*.

**SMITH, Sir David C.;** *see* Calvert-Smith.

**SMITH, Air Marshal Sir David H.;** *see* Harcourt-Smith.

**SMITH, David Henry;** Economics Editor, since 1989, Policy Adviser, since 1995, Assistant Editor, since 1998, The Sunday Times; columnist, The Times, since 2016; *b* 3 April 1954; *s* of Charles Henry Smith and Elizabeth Mary Smith (*née* Williams), Walsall; *m* 1980, Jane Howells, Tenby; two *s* two *d*. *Educ:* West Bromwich Grammar Sch.; UC Cardiff (BSc Econ 1st cl. hons; Tassie Medallion, 1975); Worcester Coll., Oxford; Birkbeck Coll., London (MSc Econ). Economic report writer, Lloyds Bank, 1976–77; economist, Henley Centre for Forecasting, 1977–79; economics and business writer, Now! magazine, 1979–81; Asst Editor, Financial Weekly, 1981–84; Economics Corresp., The Times, 1984–89. Hon. Vis. Prof., Cardiff Univ., 2007–; Vis. Prof., Nottingham Univ., 2011–. Dir, UK Economics Ltd, 2011–. FRSA 1999. Wincott Sen. Financial Journalist of the Year, 2003; Econ. Commentator of Year, Editl Intelligence Comment Awards, 2013; Business Journalist of the Year, London Press Award, 2014. *Publications:* The Rise and Fall of Monetarism, 1987; Mrs Thatcher's Economics, 1988; North and South, 1989, 2nd edn 1994; From Boom to Bust, 1992, 2nd edn 1993; Mrs Thatcher's Economics: her legacy, 1992; UK Current Economic Policy, 1994, 2nd edn 1999; Job Insecurity *vs* Labour Market Flexibility, 1996; Eurofutures, 1997; Will Europe Work?, 1999; (ed) Welfare, Work and Poverty, 2000; Free Lunch, 2003, 2nd edn 2012; The Dragon and the Elephant: China, India and the new world order, 2007; The Age of Instability, 2010; Something Will Turn Up, 2015. *Recreations:* squash, golf, music, racketball, tennis. *Address:* 1 London Bridge Street, SE1 9GF. *T:* (020) 7782 5750. *E:* david@economicsuk.com. *Club:* Bexley Lawn Tennis and Squash.

**SMITH, Sir David (Iser),** KCVO 1990 (CVO 1977); AO 1986; BA; Director, Winston Churchill Memorial Trust, 1999–2013; Official Secretary to the Governor-General of Australia, 1973–90; Secretary of the Order of Australia, 1975–90; *b* 9 Aug. 1933; *s* of late W. M. Smith; *m* 1955, June F., *d* of late M. A. W. Forestier; three *s*. *Educ:* Scotch Coll., Melbourne; Melbourne Univ.; Australian National Univ., Canberra (BA). Commnd CMF, Melb. Univ. Regt, 1956. Entered Aust. Public Service, 1954; Dept of Customs and Excise, Melb., 1954–57; Trng Officer, Dept of the Interior, Canberra, 1957–58; Private Sec. to Minister for the Interior and Minister for Works, 1958–63; Exec. Asst to Sec., Dept of the Interior, 1963–66; Exec. Officer (Govt), Dept of the Interior, 1966–69; Sen. Adviser, Govt Br., Prime Minister's Dept, 1969–71; Sec., Federal Exec. Council, 1971–73; Asst Sec., Govt Br., Dept of the Prime Minister and Cabinet, 1972–73. Attached to The Queen's Household, Buckingham Palace, June–July 1975. Director: FAI Life Insurance Soc. Ltd, 1991–96; FAI Life Ltd, 1991–96. Australian National University: Vis. Fellow in Pol Sci., Res. Sch. of Social Scis, 1991–92; Vis. Fellow, 1998–99, Vis. Scholar, 2000–07, Faculty of Law. Dir, Canberra Symphony Orch., 1976–96 (Chm., 1991–93). Dir, Nat. Heart Foundn of Aust., 1991–97. Mem., Adv. Council, Old Parliament Hse, 2014–. Pres., Samuel Griffith Soc., 2006–10. Vice-Pres., Scout Assoc. of Australia, 1991–99 (Dist Comr, Capital Hill Dist, 1971–74). KStJ 1991 (CStJ 1974). *Publications:* Head of State: the Governor-General, the monarchy, the republic and the dismissal, 2005. *Recreations:* music, reading. *Address:* 1/36 Shackleton Circuit, Mawson, ACT 2607, Australia. *T:* (2) 62865094. *Club:* Commonwealth (Canberra).

**SMITH, Rt Rev. David James;** an Hon. Assistant Bishop, Diocese in Europe, and Diocese of York, since 2002; *b* 14 July 1935; *s* of Stanley James and Gwendolen Emie Smith; *m* 1961, Mary Hunter Moult; one *s* one *d*. *Educ:* Hertford Grammar School; King's College, London (AKC; FKC 1999). Assistant Curate: All Saints, Gosforth, 1959–62; St Francis, High Heaton, 1962–64; Long Benton, 1964–68; Vicar: Longhirst with Hebron, 1968–75; St Mary, Monkseaton, 1975–81; Felton, 1982–83; Archdeacon of Lindisfarne, 1981–87; Bishop Suffragan of Maidstone, 1987–92; Bishop to the Forces, 1990–92; Bishop of Bradford, 1992–2002. DUniv Bradford, 2001. *Recreations:* walking, reading novels. *Address:* 34 Cedar Glade, Dunnington, York YO19 5QZ. *T:* (01904) 481225. *E:* david@djmhs.force9.co.uk.

**SMITH, David James,** CB 2009; FCIPS; Managing Director, Procurement Direction Ltd, since 2014; *b* Leyton, 2 Oct. 1954; *s* of James William Smith and Marjorie Dorothy Jesse Smith; partner, Jane Nicolson; three *s*. *Educ:* Downsell Sch., Leyton; Leyton Co. High Sch. for Boys. Home Office, 1973–88; Sen. Procurement Advr, HM Treasury, 1988–91; Dep. Hd of Procurement, 1991–96, Hd of Procurement, 1996–2002, Inland Revenue; Commercial Dir, DWP, 2002–13; Govt Dep. Chief Procurement Officer and Crown Rep., 2011–13. Mem., Falkland Is Rev. Cttee, Cabinet Office, 1982–83. Gov., Saxon Sch., Shepperton, 2000–03. MCIPS 1998 (Mem., Bd of Mgt, 2005–08, 2010–; Vice Pres., 2010–11; Pres., 2011–12), FCIPS 2009. *Recreations:* music (popular), listening and playing guitar/keyboard/vocal (with 'The Front Covers', 'GlamSlam', 'Long Time Gone' and 'Gypsy's Kiss'), sport (Mem., Essex CCC; season ticket holder, West Ham United FC), football referee (FA qualified), golf, gardening, cooking. *Address:* Procurement Direction Ltd, 11 Whitehall Crescent, Chessington, Surrey KT9 1NF. *T:* 07771 591409. *E:* davidjamessmith@blueyonder.co.uk.

**SMITH, David James Benwell T.;** *see* Taylor-Smith.

**SMITH, David John;** *b* 4 Oct. 1949; *s* of Frederick and Olive Smith; *m* 2006, Julia Stanton; one *s*. *Educ:* Durham Univ. (Teaching Cert.). Wolters Kluwer, NV: Chief Executive Officer; Wayland Publishers, 1995–2001; Stanley Thornes, 1992–2001; Educn/Learning, 1999–2001; Legal, Tax and Business Europe, 2001–02; CEO, Taylor & Francis Gp plc, 2002–04; Chairman: T&F Informa plc, 2004–05; Sherston Publishing, 2006–09; Executive Chairman: Granada Learning, 2006–09; Critical Information Group plc, 2009–12. Non-exec. Dir, Vitesse Media plc, 2012–16 (non-exec. Chm., 2016–17). Mem., Adv. Bd, AZO Networks, 2016–. *Recreations:* horse-racing, gardening, tennis, golf.

**SMITH, David John Leslie,** PhD; CEng, FRAeS; Director of Group Services, Defence Research Agency, 1991–94; *b* 8 Oct. 1938; *s* of late Arthur George Smith and Gertrude Mary Smith; *m* 1962, Wendy Lavinia (*née* Smith); two *d*. *Educ:* Cinderford Tech. Coll.; N Glos Tech. Coll.; Coll. of Aeronautics (MSc); Univ. of London (PhD); rcds. Mech. Engrg Apprentice, Rotol Ltd, 1954–59; Nat. Gas Turbine Estabt, Min. of Aviation, 1961, Head of Turbomachinery Dept, 1973; RCDS 1979; Ministry of Defence (PE): Dir, Aircraft Mech. and Elect. Equipment, Controllerate of Aircraft, 1980–81; Head of Aero. Dept, RAE, 1981–84; Dep. Dir (Marine Technology), 1984–85, Dep. Dir (Planning), 1986–87, ARE; Hd, Defence Res. Study Team, MoD, 1988; Asst Under-Sec. of State (Civilian Management) (Specialists), MoD, 1988–91. *Publications:* contribs to learned jls on gas turbine technology and fluid mechanics. *Recreations:* garden (including exhibiting flowers), oil and watercolour painting. *Address:* Kyrle Grange, Peterstow, Ross-on-Wye, Herefordshire HR9 6JZ.

**SMITH, David Mark;** Chief Executive, Energy Networks Association, since 2007 (Deputy Chief Executive, 2003–07); *b* Middlesbrough, 17 April 1964; *s* of Derek and Beryl Smith. *Educ:* Teesside Poly. (BA Hons). PR Officer, Cleveland CC, 1983–89; Press and PR Officer, Assoc. of County Councils, 1989–91; Press and Public Affairs Manager, London Ambulance Service, 1991–94; Hd, Membership and Mktg, Finance and Leasing Assoc., 1994–2000; Dir, Corporate Affairs, British Retail Consortium, 2000–03. FEI; Fellow, Inst. of Association Mgt; FRSA. *Recreations:* cooking, reading, collecting vinyl records, local history. *Address:* Energy Networks Association, 4 More London Riverside, SE1 2AU. *T:* (020) 7706 5100. *E:* david.smith@energynetworks.org.

**SMITH, Prof. David Marshall,** PhD; FBA 2009; Professor of Geography, Queen Mary College, later Queen Mary, University of London, 1973–2001, now Emeritus; *b* Birmingham, 1936; *s* of late David Marshall Smith and Elizabeth Winifred Smith; *m* 1961, Margaret Harrup (*d* 2002); one *s* one *d*. *Educ:* Solihull Sch.; Univ. of Nottingham (BA 1958; PhD 1961). Lectr in Geog., Univ. of Manchester, 1963–66; Prof., Southern Illinois Univ., 1966–70; short-term posts at Univs of Florida, Natal, Witwatersrand and New England, 1970–73. *Publications:* The Industrial Archaeology of the East Midlands, 1965; Industrial Britain: the North West, 1969; Industrial Location: an economic geographical analysis, 1971; (with Margaret Smith) The United States: how they live and work, 1973; The Geography of Social Well-being in the United States: an introduction to territorial social indicators, 1973; Patterns in Human Geography: an introduction to numerical methods, 1975; Human Geography: a welfare approach, 1977; Where the Grass is Greener: living in an unequal world, 1979; (ed) Living under Apartheid: aspects of urbanization and social change in South Africa, 1982; Geography, Inequality and Society, 1987; (ed) The Apartheid City and Beyond: urbanization and social change in South Africa, 1992; Geography and Social Justice, 1994; Moral Geographies: ethics in a world of difference, 2000; *edited jointly:* Social Problems and the City: geographical perspectives, 1979; Qualitative Methods in Human Geography, 1988; Social Problems and the City: new perspectives, 1989; Shared Space, Divided Space: essays on conflict and territorial organization, 1990; Geography and Ethics: journeys in a moral terrain, 1999; Geographies and Moralities: international perspectives on development, justice and place, 2004; Society, Economy, Environment: towards the sustainable city, 2005. *Recreations:* reading, music. *Address:* 41 Traps Hill, Loughton, Essex IG10 1SZ.

**SMITH, David S.;** *see* Sands Smith.

**SMITH, Dame Dela,** DBE 2001; DL; Executive Director, Darlington Education Village, 2006–10 (Chief Executive, 2004–06); *b* Chester, 10 Oct. 1952; *d* of John Hethorne Wood and Norah Wood (*née* Read); *m* 1976, Colin Smith. *Educ:* schs in York, Bristol and Cambridge; Durham Univ. (AdvDip); Middleton St George Coll. (Cert Ed). Teacher, Dinsdale Park Residential Sch., nr Darlington, 1975–84; Dep. Head Teacher, 1984–85, Headteacher, 1985–92, Mayfair Special Sch. (Severe Learning Difficulties); Headteacher, Beaumont Hill Special Educnl Needs Centre, subseq. Beaumont Hill Technol. Coll., Primary Sch. and Information, Communication and Technol. Centre, 1992–2004. Member: various nat. wkg parties for SEN, 1998–2008; Adv. Panel, Nat. Forum for Neurosci. in Special Educn, 2011–. Dir, Ski Peisey, 2004–. Patron, Educn Centre for Children with Downs Syndrome, 2007–17 (Chair of Trustees, 2010–14; Vice Chair, 2014–17); Chm. Bd, Ascent Acad. Trust (formerly Ascent Trust), 2012–16 (Mem. and Dir, 2016–) (Gov., Barbara Priestman Special Sch., 2012–); Mem., Horizons (formerly Abbey Hill, then Horizons Multi) Acad. Trust, 2012–; Mem., Lingfield Acad. Trust (formerly Hurworth Primary Acad. Sch., then Hurworth Acad. Trust), 2013–; Trustee, Pioneering Care Centre, 2019–. DL Durham, 2001. *Recreations:* walking, travelling, reading, jewellery making, charity and voluntary work. *Address:* 20 West Green, Heighington, Co. Durham DL5 6RA. *T:* (01325) 314905.

**SMITH, Delia,** CH 2017; CBE 2009 (OBE 1995); cookery writer and broadcaster; *m* Michael Wynn Jones. Several BBC TV series; cookery writer: Mirror Mag., 1969; Evening Standard, later the Standard, 1972–85; columnist: Radio Times; Sainsbury's Mag., 1993–2005; launched: Delia Online, 2001; Delia Online Cookery Sch., 2013. Director: Norwich City FC, 1996–; Delia's Canary Catering, 1999–. FRTS 1996. Hon. Fellow,

Liverpool John Moores, 2000; Hon. DLitt: Nottingham, 1996; UEA, 1999. BAFTA Special Award, 2013. Is a Roman Catholic. *Publications:* How to Cheat at Cooking, 1971; Recipes from Country Inns and Restaurants, 1973; Family Fare, book 1, 1973; Family Fare 2 - Summer Cooking, 1974; Evening Standard Cook Book, 1974; Family Fare 3 - Spring into Summer, 1975; Country recipes from "Look East", 1975; More Country Recipes from "Look East", 1976; Frugal Food, 1976; Book of Cakes, 1977; Recipes from "Look East", 1977; Food for our Times, 1978; Cookery Course, part 1, 1978, part 2, 1979, part 3, 1981, The Complete Cookery Course, 1982; A Feast for Lent, 1983; A Feast for Advent, 1983; One is Fun, 1985; (ed) Food Aid Cookery Book, 1986; A Journey into God, 1988; Delia Smith's Christmas, 1990; Delia Smith's Summer Collection, 1993; Delia Smith's Winter Collection, 1995; Delia's Red Nose Collection (Comic Relief), 1997; Delia's How to Cook, Book One, 1998, Book Two, 1999, Book Three, 2001; Delia's Chocolate Collection (Comic Relief), 2001; Delia's Vegetarian Collection, 2002; The Delia Collection: Soup, Chicken, Chocolate, Fish, 2003; Italian, Pork, 2004; Delia's Kitchen Garden, 2004; Baking, 2005; Puddings, 2006; Delia's How to Cheat at Cooking, 2008; Delia's Frugal Food, 2008; Delia's Complete How to Cook, 2009; Delia's Happy Christmas, 2009; Delia's Cakes, 2013.

**SMITH, Derek;** management consultant; *b* 26 Sept. 1948; *s* of Arthur Edmund Smith and Hazel Smith (*née* Proudlove); *m* 1st, 1970, Carol Anne Susan Cunio (marr. diss. 2003); one *s* one *d*; 2nd, 2003, Ruth Patricia Harrison; one *s*. *Educ:* Univ. of Wales (BSc Hons Econs); Univ. of Strathclyde (Postgrad. Dip. in Russian Lang.). Gen. Manager, Frenchay Hosp., 1982–87; Dist Gen. Manager, S Beds HA, 1987–90; Chief Exec., King's Healthcare NHS Trust, 1990–99; Man. Dir, 1999–2001, Chm., 2000–01, London Underground Ltd; Chief Exec., Hammersmith Hosps NHS Trust, 2001–07. Chm., NHS Elect, 2004–06. *Recreations:* tennis, music, sailing, golf, walking.

**SMITH, Derek Frank;** Alternate Executive Director of the World Bank, and Counsellor (Overseas Develt), Washington, 1979–84; *b* 11 Feb. 1929; *s* of late Frank H. and Rose V. Smith; *m* 1954, Anne Carpenter (*d* 2007); one *s* one *d*. *Educ:* Chatham House Sch., Ramsgate. Served RAF, 1947–49. Colonial Office, 1949–66: Sec., Develt and Welfare Org. in WI, 1956–58; transf. to Min. of Overseas Develt, 1966; First Financial Adviser, British Develt Div. in the Caribbean, 1966–68; Principal, India Sect., ODA, 1968–72; Asst Sec., 1972; Founder Head of Southern African Develt Div., 1972–75; Establishment Officer, 1976–78, Head of UN Dept B, 1978–79, ODA. Consultant: ODA, 1985; World Bank, 1986–87. Chairman: Sevenoaks Area NT Association, 1992–96; Probus Club, Sevenoaks, 1997–98. *Address:* 9 Summerbank, Rockdale Road, Sevenoaks, Kent TN13 1BU. *T:* (01732) 452534.

**SMITH, Prof. Derek James,** PhD; Professor of Infectious Disease Informatics, since 2007, and Director, Centre for Pathogen Evolution, since 2010, University of Cambridge; *b* 27 Sept. 1959; *s* of Dorothy Mabel Smith. *Educ:* Pensby High Sch.; Univ. of Bradford (BSc); Univ. of New Mexico (MSc; PhD 1997). Software Engr, Texas Instruments, UK, 1982–83; Res. Scientist, Texas Instruments Res. Labs, USA, 1983–92; Graduate Fellow, Santa Fe Inst., 1992–97; Postdoctoral Fellow, Univ. of New Mexico, 1998–99; Res. Scientist, Dept of Virol., Erasmus Med. Centre, Rotterdam, 1999–; Chief Scientist, Popular Power Inc., San Francisco, 2000–01; Scientist, Eatoni Ergonomics, NY, 2001; Res. Associate, Dept of Zool., Univ. of Cambridge, 2003–07; Sen. Res. Fellow, Fogarty Internat. Center, NIH, 2008–12. Dir and Mem., Eur. Scientific Wkg Gp on Influenza, 2002–10 (Vice Pres., 2007–10; Mem., Exec. Cttee, 2007–10); Temp. Advr, WHO, 2005–; Mem., Sci. Bd, Santa Fe Inst., 2011–; Dir, WHO Collaborating Centre on Modeling, Evolution and Control of Emerging Infectious Diseases, Cambridge Univ., 2012–17. Dir's Pioneer Award, NIH, 2005. *Publications:* scientific papers in learned jls on evolution, immunol., virol., vaccination, computational biol., bioinformatics, epidemiology, public health, computer sci., computer design, integrated circuit design; patents on computer design and information encoding. *Address:* Department of Zoology, University of Cambridge, Downing Street, Cambridge CB2 3EJ.

**SMITH, Desmond;** *see* Smith, S. D.

**SMITH, Douglas Armitage,** CB 2005; Chief Executive, Child Support Agency, 2000–05; *b* 8 April 1947; *s* of James and Joan Smith; *m* 1968, Maureen Buckroyd; one *s* one *d*. *Educ:* Leeds Central High Sch.; Open Univ. (BA Hons). Board of Inland Revenue: Asst Dir, IT, 1989–93; Director: Change, 1993–95; Self Assessment, 1995–98; Business Ops, 1998–2000. Pres., Assoc. of Inspectors of Taxes, 1986–88. *Recreations:* smallholding/brewery in France, travelling, horse-racing, sport, reading. *Club:* Boxmoor Social.

**SMITH, Drew;** *see* Smith, F. D.

**SMITH, Drew;** Scotland Political and Policy Officer, GMB, since 2017; *b* Broxburn, 1982; *s* of Andrew and Mary Valentine Smith. *Educ:* St Kentigern's Acad., Blackburn; Aberdeen Univ. (MA Hons Politics and Internat. Relns 2004); Glasgow Univ. (Postgrad. Dip. Human Rights and Internat. Politics). Parly Asst to Pauline McNeill, MSP, 2005–08; PR and Social Mktg Manager, Paths for All Partnership, 2008–10; Officer Manager/Sen. Parly Asst to Ann McKechin, MP, 2010–11. Mem. (Lab) Glasgow, Scottish Parlt, 2011–16. Political Advr, GMB Scotland, 2016. *Recreations:* music, reading, walking, theatre, cinema.

**SMITH, Dugal N.;** *see* Nisbet-Smith.

**SMITH, Edward;** *see* Smith, J. E. K.

**SMITH, Edward Colin G.;** *see* Gordon-Smith.

**SMITH, Elaine Agnes;** Member (Lab) Scotland Central, Scottish Parliament, since 2016 (Coatbridge and Chryston, 1999–2016); *b* 7 May 1963; *m* 1996, James Vann Smith; one *s*. *Educ:* St Patrick's High Sch., Coatbridge; Glasgow Coll. (BA Hons Social Sci. (Econs and Politics)); St Andrews Teacher Trng Coll. (PGCE); DPSM 1995. Teacher, 1986; work in retail industry, Women's Aid Advice Worker and supply teacher, 1987; Local Authy Homeless Officer and Urban Prog. Asst Co-ordinator, 1988–90; posts in local authy depts, Monklands DC and W Highland Regl Council, 1990–97; Volunteers Manager, 1997–98; Supply Teacher, 1999. Dep. Presiding Officer, Scottish Parlt, 2011–16. *Recreations:* family life, reading, swimming, cinema, cooking, supporting local youth Rugby. *Address:* Scottish Parliament, Holyrood, Edinburgh EH99 1SP. *T:* (0131) 348 5824. *E:* Elaine.Smith.msp@parliament.scot.

**SMITH, Eleanor;** MP (Lab) Wolverhampton South West, since 2017; *m*; two *d*. *Educ:* Mount Pleasant Comprehensive Sch., Birmingham; Bournville Coll. (Foundn Nursing). Nurse trng for learning difficulties, N Warwickshire Hosp., 1976–79; RGN nurse trng, 1979–82, theatre nurse, 1982–83, George Eliot Hosp., Nuneaton; theatre nurse: Russell Hall Hosp., Dudley, 1983–84; Birmingham Women's Hosp., 1984–. Pres., UNISON, 2011–12. *Address:* House of Commons, SW1A 0AA.

**SMITH, Elizabeth H.;** *see* Hallam Smith.

**SMITH, Elizabeth Jane;** Member (C) Scotland Mid and Fife, Scottish Parliament, since 2007; *b* 27 Feb. 1960; *d* of late James Smith and (Margaret) Thelma Smith (*née* Moncrieff). *Educ:* George Watson's Coll., Edinburgh; Univ. of Edinburgh (MA Hons Econs and Politics 1982; DipEd 1983). Teacher, George Watson's Coll., 1983–98; Schoolteacher Fellow Commoner, Corpus Christi Coll., Cambridge, 1992; Political Advr to Sir Malcolm Rifkind, 1998–2001; Hd, Chairman's Office, Scottish Cons. and Unionist Party, 2001–03; self-employed political consultant, 2003–05; pt-time teacher, George Watson's Coll., 2005–06. *Publications:* Outdoor Adventures, 2003; An Illustrated History of George Watson's Ladies' College, 2006. *Recreations:* cricket, hill-walking, photography, travel. *Address:* Stables Cottage, Woodend, Madderty PH7 3PA. *E:* elizabeth.smith.msp@parliament.scot. *Club:* New (Edinburgh).

**SMITH, Elizabeth Jean,** OBE 2004; Consultant, Transforming Broadcasting, 2010–18; *b* 15 Aug. 1936; *d* of Lt-Gen. Sir Robert Hay, KCIE; *m* 1960, Geoffrey Smith; one *s* one *d*. *Educ:* St George's Sch., Edinburgh; Univ. of Edinburgh (MA Hons Hist. 1958). BBC Radio: Studio Manager, 1958–61; News Producer, 1961–70; Current Affairs Producer, 1970–78; Producer for BBC Current Affairs TV, 1978–79; Sen. Asst, BBC Secretariat, 1979–81; BBC World Service: Asst Head, Central Talks and Features, 1981–84; Head, Current Affairs, 1984–87; Controller, English Services, 1987–94; Sec.-Gen., Commonwealth Broadcasting Assoc., 1994–2010. Member: Council, RIIA, 1992–97; Speaker's Cttee, 1992–97; Bd, Population Communications Internat., 1994–2002; Bd, Internat. Trng and Res. Consultancies, 1994–98; Bd, Westminster Foundn for Democracy, 1998–2001; Communications and Inf. Cttee, UK Nat. Commn for UNESCO, 2006–11. Chair: Voice of the Listener and Viewer Trust, 2006–08; Commonwealth Media Gp, 2011–15. Trustee: Oneworld Broadcasting Trust, 1994–2000; Commonwealth Human Rights Initiative, 1998–2010; Television Trust for the Envmt, 2000–04. Consumer columnist, The Listener, 1978–80. Fellow, Radio Acad., 1996 (Mem. Bd, 1990–94). Trustee, Royal Commonwealth Soc., 2010–14. Hon. DLit Westminster, 2013. *Publications:* (jtly) Healing Herbs, 1974; (as Elizabeth Hay) Sambo Sahib: the story of Helen Bannerman, 1981; Sayonara Sanbo, 1993; A Road Map to Public Service Broadcasting, 2012. *Recreations:* gardening, walking, travelling in the developing world. *T:* (020) 7226 3519. *E:* elizabeth.smith226@gmail.com.

**SMITH, Emilie;** *see* Savage-Smith, E.

**SMITH, Prof. Emma Josephine;** Professor of Shakespeare Studies, University of Oxford, since 2015; Fellow, Hertford College, Oxford, since 1998; *b* Leeds, 15 May 1970; *d* of Vivien Smith; *m* 2012, Dr Elizabeth Macfarlane. *Educ:* Abbey Grange High Sch., Leeds; Somerville Coll., Oxford (BA). Prize Fellow, All Souls Coll., Oxford, 1991–98. Ed., Shakespeare Survey, 2018–. *Publications:* The Cambridge Shakespeare Guide, 2012; (ed) The Elizabethan Top Ten, 2013; Shakespeare's First Folio: four centuries of an iconic book, 2016, 2nd edn 2019; This is Shakespeare, 2019. *Recreations:* birdwatching, fast cars, silent films. *Address:* Hertford College, Oxford OX1 3BW. *T:* (01865) 279441. *E:* emma.smith@hertford.ox.ac.uk.

**SMITH, Sir (Eric) Brian,** Kt 1999; PhD, DSc; FRSC; Vice-Chancellor, Cardiff University (formerly Principal, University of Wales College of Cardiff), 1993–2001; *b* 10 Oct. 1933; *s* of Eric Smith and Dilys Olwen (*née* Hughes); *m* 1st, 1957, Margaret Barr (marr. diss. 1978); two *s* one *d*; 2nd, 1983, Regina Arvidson Ball; two step *d*. *Educ:* Alun Grammar Sch., Mold; Wirral Grammar Sch.; Univ. of Liverpool (BSc; PhD 1957); MA Oxon 1960, DSc Oxon 1988. FRSC 1981. Res. Associate, Univ. of Calif, Berkeley, 1957–59; Oxford University: ICI Fellow, 1959–60; Lectr in Physical Chemistry, 1960–88; Member: Gen. Bd of Faculties, 1980–87 (Chm., 1985–87); Hebdomadal Council, 1985–93; St Catherine's College: Fellow, 1960–88; Master, 1988–93; Hon. Fellow, 1993; Dir, Isis Innovation, 1988–97. Vis. Prof., Univ. of Calif, Riverside, 1967; Vis. Lectr, Stanford Univ., 1983, 1984 and 1985; Priestley Lectr, RSC, 1986. Chm., Thermodynamics and Statistical Mechanics Section, RSC, 1979–83; Member Board: WDA, 1998–2002; HEFCW, 2003–11; Dir, Higher Aims Ltd, 2002–. Vice-Chm., Oxford Soc. Cttee, 1988–2005; Trustee: Oxford Univ. Soc., 2005–06; Liverpool Sch. of Tropical Medicine, 2004–13. Pres., Assoc. of Oxford Univ. Pensioners, 2018–. Dir, Cardiff Internat. Fest. of Musical Theatre, 2001–07. Mem. Bd, Univ. of Glamorgan, 2002–06. Mem., Magic Circle, 2015–. FLSW 2012. Hon. Fellow, UWCM, 2003. Hon. DSc Glamorgan, 2000; Hon. LLD Wales, 2001. Pott's Medal, Univ. of Liverpool, 1969. *Publications:* (jtly) Virial Coefficients of Pure Gases and Mixtures, 1969, 2nd edn 1980; Basic Chemical Thermodynamics, 1973, 6th edn 2014; (jtly) Intermolecular Forces: origin and determination, 1981; (jtly) Forces between Molecules, 1986; Basic Physical Chemistry, 2012; The Boltzman Factor, 2016; papers in scientific jls. *Recreation:* mountaineering. *Address:* Appletree House, 2 Boults Lane, Old Marston, Oxford OX3 0PW. *Clubs:* Alpine; Gorphwysfa.

**SMITH, Ewen Dale,** FSAScot; Director, Hunterian Museum and Art Gallery, University of Glasgow, 2006–09; *b* 14 Sept. 1946; *s* of Norman Smith and Greta Smith (*née* Holton); *m* 1976, Kathleen Ann Kane; two *d*. *Educ:* George Heriot's Sch., Edinburgh; Univ. Nacional Autónoma de México; Univ. of Glasgow (MA, MLitt). MCIPD 1992. Cost clerk, Scottish & Newcastle Breweries Ltd, 1964–69; Investment Analyst, Ivory & Sime, 1969–74; fund-raiser, UNA, 1980–82; Adminr, Open Univ., 1982–85; University of Glasgow: Adminr, CPD Unit, 1985–89, Univ. Staff Develt Service, 1989–94; Planning Unit Adminr, Academic Services, 1994–99; Dep. Dir, Hunterian Mus. and Art Gall., 1999–2006. Member: Bd, Scottish Museums Council, 2007; Recognition Cttee, Mus and Galls Scotland, 2010–16. Mem. Council, Soc. of Antiquaries of Scotland, 2013–16 (Vice Pres., 2015–16). Trustee and Hon. Treas., Assoc. Certificated Field Archaeologists, 2010–15. FSAScot 1988. *Publications:* general articles. *Recreations:* archaeological field surveying, hill-walking, listing things alphabetically, reading, waiting for Aberdeen FC's next European Final.

**SMITH, Fiona Mary, (Lady Smith);** *see* Watt, F. M.

**SMITH, Sir Francis Graham-,** Kt 1986; FRS 1970; Langworthy Professor of Physics, Manchester University, 1987–90, now Emeritus (Professor of Radio Astronomy, 1964–74 and 1981–87); Director, Nuffield Radio Astronomy Laboratories, 1981–88; Astronomer Royal, 1982–90; *b* 25 April 1923; *s* of Claud Henry and Cicely Winifred Smith; *m* 1945, Dorothy Elizabeth (*née* Palmer); three *s* one *d*. *Educ:* Epsom Coll.; Rossall Sch.; Downing Coll., Cambridge. Nat. Sci. Tripos, Downing Coll., 1941–43 and 1946–47; PhD Cantab 1952. Telecommunications Research Estab., Malvern, 1943–46; Cavendish Lab., 1947–64; 1851 Exhibnr 1951–52; Warren Research Fellow of Royal Soc., 1959–64; Fellow of Downing Coll., 1953–64, Hon. Fellow 1970; Dir-Designate, 1974–75, Dir, 1976–81, Royal Greenwich Observatory. Vis. Prof. of Astronomy, Univ. of Sussex, 1975. Sec., Royal Astronomical Soc., 1964–71, Pres., 1975–77. Mem. Council and Physical Sec., 1988–94, Vice-Pres., 1990–94, Royal Soc.; For. Associate, RSSAf, 1988. Hon. DSc: QUB, 1986; Keele, 1987; Birmingham, 1989; TCD, 1990; Nottingham, 1990; Manchester, 1993; Liverpool, 2003; Salford, 2003. Royal Medal, Royal Soc., 1987; Glazebrook Medal, Inst. of Physics, 1991. *Publications:* Radio Astronomy, 1960; (with J. H. Thomson) Optics, 1971; Pulsars, 1977; (with Sir Bernard Lovell) Pathways to the Universe, 1988; (with A. G. Lyne) Pulsar Astronomy, 1990, 4th edn 2012; (with B. F. Burke) Introduction to Radio Astronomy, 1997, 4th edn (with B. F. Burke and P. N. Wilkinson) 2019; (with T. A. King) Optics and Photonics, 2000, 2nd edn (with T. A. King and Dan Wilkins) 2007; Unseen Cosmos, 2013; Eyes on the Sky, 2015; papers in Monthly Notices of RAS, Nature and other scientific jls. *Recreations:* beekeeping, walking. *Address:* Jodrell Bank Observatory, Macclesfield, Cheshire SK11 9DL; Old School House, Henbury, Macclesfield, Cheshire SK11 9PH.

**SMITH, Prof. Frank Thomas,** FRS 1984; Goldsmid Professor of Applied Mathematics in the University of London, at University College London, since 1984; *b* 24 Feb. 1948; *s* of Leslie Maxwell Smith and Catherine Matilda Smith; *m* 1972, Valerie Sheila (*née* Hearn); three *d*. *Educ:* Bournemouth Grammar Sch.; Jesus Coll., Oxford (BA; DPhil); University College London. Research Fellow in Theoretical Aerodynamics Unit, Southampton, 1972–73; Lectr in Maths Dept, Imperial Coll., London, 1973–78; Vis. Scientist, Applied Mathematics Dept, Univ. of Western Ontario, Canada, 1978–79; Reader in Maths Dept, 1979–83, Prof. in Maths, 1983–84, Imperial Coll., London. Director: Lighthill Inst., 2006–; London Taught Course Centre, 2007–. *Publications:* on applied mathematics, fluid mechanics, industrial modelling, biomedical modelling, societal models, computing and natural sciences, in jls. *Recreations:* the family, reading, music, sport. *Address:* Mathematics Department, University College London, Gower Street, WC1E 6BT. *T:* (020) 7679 2837.

**SMITH, (Fraser) Drew;** Director, Food By Design (formerly Food Factory), since 1991; senior adviser on food strategy, London Docklands Development Corporation, 1995–98; *b* 30 March 1950; *s* of Frank and Beatrice Smith; *m* 1988, Susan Maloney; one *s* one *d*. *Educ:* Westminster School. Worked on Student magazine, 1967; IPC magazines, 1969–72; Westminster Press Newspapers, 1972–81. Editor, Good Food Guide, 1982–89; launched: Good Food Directory, 1985; Budget Good Food Guide, 1986–88; Head of Media Develt, Dir's Office, Consumers' Assoc., 1988–90; Publishing Dir, Alfresco Leisure Publications, 1990–92. Director: Taste Publishing; West India Co. Columnist, Guardian, 1982–; creator, TV Food File, Channel 4. Chm., Guild of Food Writers, 1990. Trustee, Jane Grigson Liby. Chief Judge, British Cheese Awards, 1995, 1996. Restaurant Writer of the Year, 1981, 1988. *Publications:* Modern Cooking, 1990; Food Watch, 1994; Baby Food Watch, 1995; Good Food, 1995; The Circus (novel), 1997; Food Industry and the Internet, 2001; Oyster: a world history, 2010; (trans.) La Mère Brazier: the mother of modern French cooking, 2016; Broth to Bowl: mastering the art of great soup from six simple broths, 2017. *Recreations:* walking, music, cooking, people.

**SMITH, Geoffrey John;** writer and broadcaster; *b* Mich, USA, 23 Aug. 1943; *s* of Earl Willard Smith and Marian Kay Smith (*née* Eisele); dual UK/US citizenship, 2018; *m* 1968, Lenore Ketola (marr. diss. 1985; she *d* 2003); *m* 1995, Janette Grant; one *s*. *Educ:* Central High Sch., Bay City, Mich; Univ. of Michigan (BA English 1966); Univ. of Wisconsin (Woodrow Wilson Fellow; MA English 1967). Musician, 1959–69; Instr in English, Eastern Michigan Univ., 1967–68; NDEA Title IV Fellow, Univ. of Virginia, 1970–73; freelance writer and lectr, 1973–93; Lectr in English and American Lit., City Univ., 1979–91, City Lit., 1986–92. Music Critic and Consultant, Country Life, 1977–2017; Arts Corresp., The Economist, 1988–2016; columnist, BBC Music Mag., 2001–; Presenter, BBC Radio 3, 1988–: documentaries, interviews and concerts; series on Gilbert and Sullivan; CD Review; Jazz Record Requests, 1991–2012; Geoffrey Smith's Jazz, 2012–19. Mem., Critics' Circle. *Publications:* The Savoy Operas, 1983; Stéphane Grappelli, 1987; 100 Jazz Legends, 2011; contrib. poetry to Encounter, Mandeville Press, The Tablet. *Recreations:* playing the piano, jogging, family outings, 'gaping and dawdling' (Henry James). *Address:* BBC Radio 3, Broadcasting House, W1A 1AA. *T:* (020) 7580 4468, *Fax:* (020) 7765 5052.

**SMITH, Prof. Geoffrey Lilley,** PhD; FRS 2003; Wellcome Trust Principal Research Fellow, since 2000; Professor of Pathology, University of Cambridge, since 2011; Fellow, Emmanuel College, Cambridge, since 2011; *b* 23 July 1955; *s* of Irvine Battinson Smith and Kathleen Lilley Smith; *m* 1979, Tessa Marie Trico; two *s* two *d*. *Educ:* Bootham Sch., York; Univ. of Leeds (BSc Hons Microbiol./Biochem. 1977); Nat. Inst. for Med. Res., London (PhD 1981). Wellcome Trust Fellow, Div. of Virology, NIMR, London, 1980–81; Vis. Fellow, Lab. of Viral Diseases, Nat. Inst. of Allergy and Infectious Diseases, NIH, Bethesda, 1981–84; Lectr in Virology, Dept of Pathology, Univ. of Cambridge, 1985–89; Jenner Fellow, Lister Inst. of Preventive Medicine, 1988–92; Reader in Bacteriology, 1989–96, Prof. of Virology, 1996–2000, Sir William Dunn Sch. of Pathology, Univ. of Oxford; EPA Sen. Res. Fellow, Wadham Coll., Oxford, 1989–2000; Prof. of Virology, Imperial Coll. London, 2000–11. Chm., WHO Adv. Cttee for Variola Virus Res., 2004–07, 2009–; International Union of Microbiological Societies: Vice-Chm., 2002–05, Chm., 2005–08, Virology Div.; Pres., 2011–14; Member: MRC Infection and Immunity Bd, 2004–09; Royal Soc. Cttee on Scientific Aspects of Internat. Security, 2005–08 (Chm., 2009–12); New Agents Cttee, CRUK, 2008–10; Royal Soc. Adv. Gp to Sci. Policy Centre, 2009–12; Wellcome Trust Expert Review Gp, 2010–15; Scientific Adv. Bd, Bernard Nocht Inst., Hamburg, 2011–; Res. Grants Council, Hong Kong, 2015– (Mem., Biomedical Panel, 2012–17); Chm., Scientific Adv. Bd, Friedrich-Loeffler Inst., Germany, 2015– (Vice-Chm., 2011–15). Friedrich Loeffler Prize Lect., Greifswald, 2016; Marjory Stephenson Prize Lect., Microbiol. Soc., 2018. Gov., Lister Inst. of Preventive Medicine, 2003–13. FRSB (FIBiol 2000); FMedSci 2000. Mem., German National Acad. of Scis Leopoldina, 2011. GlaxoSmithKline Internat. Mem. of the Year Award, American Soc. for Microbiol., 2012. Ed.-in-Chief, Jl of Gen. Virology, 2003–07. *Publications:* editor of four books and author of 57 book chapters, 278 scientific papers, and several patents. *Recreations:* hockey, cricket, chess, bridge, gardening, carpentry, hill-walking, dry stone walling. *Address:* Department of Pathology, University of Cambridge, Tennis Court Road, Cambridge CB2 1QP. *T:* (01223) 333692. *E:* gls37@cam.ac.uk.

**SMITH, George D.;** *see* Davey Smith.

**SMITH, Prof. George David William,** DPhil; FRS 1996; FRSC; CEng, FIMMM; CPhys, FInstP; Professor of Materials Science, University of Oxford, 1996–2010, now Emeritus (Head of Department of Materials, 2000–05); Professorial Fellow, Trinity College, Oxford, 1992–2010, now Emeritus (Tutorial Fellow, 1991–92); *b* 28 March 1943; *s* of George Alfred William Smith and Grace Violet Hannah Dayton Smith; *m* 1968, Josephine Ann Halford (*d* 2014); two *s*. *Educ:* St Benedict's Sch., Aldershot; Salesian Coll., Farnborough; Corpus Christi Coll., Oxford (Scholar; BA Hons Metallurgy 1965; MA, DPhil 1968; Hon. Fellow, 2008). CEng 1978; CPhys, FInstP 1996; FIMMM (FIM 1996); FRSC 2003. SRC Res. Fellow, 1968–70; Jun. Res. Fellow, 1968–72, Res. Fellow, 1972–77, Wolfson Coll., Oxford; Oxford University: Res. Fellow, Dept of Metallurgy, 1970–75; Sen. Res. Fellow, 1975–77; Lectr in Metallurgy, 1977–92; George Kelley Reader in Metallurgy, 1992–96; Fellow, St Cross Coll., Oxford, 1977–91, Emeritus Fellow, 1991–. Adv. Prof., Chongqing Univ., China, 2005–; Hon. Prof., Univ. of Sci. and Technol., Beijing, 2005–. Man. Dir, Oxford Nanoscience Ltd (formerly Kindbrisk Ltd), 1987–2002 (Chm., 2002–04); Chm., Polaron plc, 2004–06; Scientific Advr, Tokamak Energy Ltd (formerly Tokamak Solutions UK Ltd), 2010–. Councillor (L), W Oxon DC, 1973–76. Co-Chm., UK Materials Congress, 1998. Mem., OST Foresight Panel for Materials, 1999–2003. Hatfield Meml Lect., Univ. of Sheffield, 2011; Hume Rothery Meml Lect., Univ. of Oxford, 2014. Pres., 1990–93, Inaugural Fellow, 2016, Internat. Field Emission Soc.; Member: Council, Inst. of Materials, Minerals and Mining (formerly of Materials), 1997–2004 (Vice-Pres., 2002–03); Council, Royal Soc., 2002–04; Oxfordshire Health and Social Care Panel, 2014–; Bd of Dirs, Healthwatch Oxfordshire, 2015– (Chair, 2017–). Associate MInstD, 2015–. Trustee and Mem. Bd, Sino-British Fellowship Trust, 2016– Fellow, Microscopy Soc. of Amer., 2016. Freeman, Armourers' and Brasiers' Co., 1998 (Liveryman, 2003). FRSA 1997. Sir George Beilby Medal and Prize, SCI, RSC, Inst. of Metals, 1985; (jtly) Vanadium Award, 1985, Rosenhain Medal and Prize, 1991, Inst. of Metals; Nat. Innovative Measurement Award, DTI, 2004; Gold Medal, Acta Materialia Inc., 2005; Platinum Medal, 2006, Material World Publication Prize, 2013, IMMM; Dist. Physical Scientist Award, Microscopy Soc. of America, 2016; William Hume Rothery Award, Minerals, Metals and Materials Soc., 2017. *Publications:* (with M. K. Miller) Atom Probe Microanalysis: principles and applications to materials problems, 1989 (trans. Russian 1993, Chinese 1994); (jtly) Atom Probe Field Ion Microscopy, 1996; over 400 scientific pubns and contribs to scientific jls. *Recreations:* walking, fishing, bird watching, travel, grandchildren. *Address:* Trinity College, Oxford OX1 3BH. *T:* (01865) 273777.

**SMITH, Dr George Elwood;** Head, Device Concepts Department, Bell Laboratories, Murray Hill, New Jersey, 1964–86; *b* White Plains, NY, 10 May 1930; *s* of George F. and Lillian Smith; partner, Janet Lee Murphy; one *s* two *d*. *Educ:* Univ. of Pennsylvania (BA Physics 1955); Univ. of Chicago (MS 1956; PhD Physics 1959). Mem., Tech. Staff, Res. Area, Bell Labs, Murray Hill, NJ, 1959–64. Founding Ed., IEEE pubn, Electron Device Letters, 1980–86. Member: US NAE, 1983–; Pi Mu Epsilon, 1985–; Phi Beta Kappa, 1985–; Sigma Xi, 1985–. Fellow, APS, 1963; FIEEE 1966. Ballantine Medal, Franklin Inst., 1973; Morris N. Liebmann Award, 1974, Electron Devices Soc. Dist. Service Award, 1997, Device Res. Conf. Breakthrough Award, 1999, IEEE; Progress Medal, Photographic Soc. of America, 1986; Prize for invention of Charge Coupled Device, Foundn for Computer and Communications Promotion, 1999; Edwin Land Medal, Optical Soc. of Amer., 2001; Charles Stark Draper Prize, NAE, 2006; (jtly) Nobel Prize in Physics, 2009. *Publications:* contrib. over 40 papers; 31 US patents. *Recreation:* sailing (started world cruise with Janet Murphy aboard 9.5 meter sailing vessel, Apogee, 1986; completed in 2003 after 55,000 miles of ocean sailing). *Address:* 221 Teaneck Road, PO Box 787, Barnegat, NJ 08005, USA. *T:* (609) 6983738. *E:* apogee2@comcast.net.

**SMITH, Rt Hon. (George) Iain D.;** *see* Duncan Smith.

**SMITH, (George) Neil,** CMG 1987; HM Diplomatic Service, retired; *b* 12 July 1936; *s* of George Smith and Ena (*née* Hill); *m* 1956, Elvi Vappu Hämäläinen (*d* 2013); one *s* one *d*. *Educ:* King Edward VII Sch., Sheffield. Joined HM Foreign (subseq. Diplomatic) Service, 1953; served RAF, 1954–56; Foreign Office, 1957; Rangoon, 1958–61; 2nd Sec., Berne, 1961–65; Diplomatic Service Administration, 1965–66; 1st Sec., CO, 1966–68; British Mil. Govt, Berlin, 1969–73; FCO, 1973–77; Counsellor (Commercial), Helsinki, 1977–80; Consul-Gen., Zürich and Principality of Liechtenstein, 1980–85; Head of Trade Relations and Exports Dept, FCO, 1985–87; RCDS, 1988; Ambassador to Finland, 1989–95. Sec. Gen., Soc. of London Art Dealers, 1996–2001; Sec., British Art Market Fedn, 1996–2001. *Recreations:* music, bowls. *Address:* 5 Linton Falls, Linton in Craven, N Yorks BD23 6BQ.

**SMITH, Prof. Gerald Stanton,** FBA 2001; Professor of Russian, 1986–2003, and Fellow of New College, 1986–2003, now Emeritus, University of Oxford; *b* 17 April 1938; *s* of Thomas Arthur Smith and Ruth Annie Stanton; *m* 1st, 1961, Frances Wetherill (marr. diss. 1981); one *s* one *d*; 2nd, 1982, Barbara Heldt; one step *s* (and one step *d* decd). *Educ:* Stretford Grammar Sch.; Sch. of Slavonic and E European Studies, Univ. of London (BA 1964 PhD 1977); DLitt Oxon 1996. Lectr in Russian, Univ. of Nottingham, 1964–71, Univ. of Birmingham, 1971–79; Univ. Research Fellow, Univ. of Liverpool, 1980–82. Visiting Professor: Indiana Univ., 1984; Univ. of California, Berkeley, 1984; Private Scholar, Social Scis and Humanities Res. Council, Canada, 1985; John Simon Guggenheim Meml Fellow, 1986. Pres., MHRA, 2000. *Publications:* (ed) Alexander Galich, Songs and Poems, 1983; Songs to Seven Strings, 1984; Russian Inside and Out, 1989; (ed) D. S. Mirsky, Uncollected Writings on Russian Literature, 1989; Contemporary Russian Poetry: a bilingual anthology, 1993; D. S. Mirsky: Letters to P. P. Suvchinskii, 1995; (co-ed and trans.) M. L. Gasparov, A History of European Versification, 1996; (ed and trans.) Boris Slutsky, Things That Happened, 1999; D. S. Mirsky: a Russian-English life, 2000; Vzgyad izvne: Izbrannye stat′i o russkoi poezii i poetike, 2002; (ed and trans.) Lev Loseff, As I Said, 2012; papers in learned jls. *Recreation:* jazz music. *Address:* 15 Dale Close, Oxford OX1 1TU.

**SMITH, Geraldine;** *see* Smith, Maria G.

**SMITH, Gilbert,** PhD; Member of Board, National Patient Safety Agency, 2001–05 (Acting Chairman, 2005); Vice Chairman, Northern Stage, 2004 (Board Member, 2002). *Educ:* Brentwood Sch., Essex; Univ. of Leeds (BA Hons 1966); Univ. of Essex (MA 1967); Univ. of Aberdeen (PhD 1973). Research Fellow and Attached Worker, MRC Medical Sociology Unit, Univ. of Aberdeen, 1969–73; Res. Advr, Central Research Unit, Scottish Office, Edinburgh, 1973–75; Sen. Lectr, then Reader, Dept of Social Admin and Social Work, Univ. of Glasgow, 1975–81; University of Hull: Prof. of Social Admin, 1981–96; Head, Dept of Social Admin, 1982–84; Foundn Head, Dept of Social Policy and Professional Studies, 1984–85; Dean, Faculty of Social Scis, 1985–87; Vice-Chancellor and Chief Exec., Univ. of Northumbria at Newcastle, 1996–2001. Sen. Travelling Scholar in Australia, ACU, 1988. Chm., E Yorks HA, then E Riding Health, 1990–93. Dep. Dir, R&D, DoH and NHS Exec., 1993–96. Foundn Trustee, Social Care Inst. for Excellence, 2001–02. Numerous board appts, directorships, commns and adv. posts with univs, res. councils, res. funding agencies, publishers, foundns, arts bodies, Govt depts, ACU, UUK and British Council. Mem., Res. Strategy Bd, Coeliac UK. Mem., Corbridge with Halton and Newton Hall PCC, 2002. Mem. Exec., Abbeyfield Atholl Soc. Elder, Church of Scotland. Mem., Amnesty Internat. Editor, Jl of Social Policy, 1991–93. DUniv Moscow State Univ. of Mgt, 1998. *Publications:* Social Work and the Sociology of Organisations, 1970, 2nd rev. edn 1979 (trans. Japanese and Korean); Social Need: policy practice and research, 1980 (trans. Japanese); (with C. Cantley) Assessing Health Care: a study in organisational evaluation, 1985; numerous book chapters; contrib. articles in professional and academic jls of social policy, sociology, social work and healthcare.

**SMITH, Godric William Naylor,** CBE 2004; Co-Founder, Inc. (Incorporated London Ltd), since 2013; *b* 29 March 1965; *s* of Eric and Phyl Smith; *m* 1991, Julia Barnes; two *s*. *Educ:* Perse Sch., Cambridge; Worcester Coll., Oxford (MA Lit Hum 1987). Appeals Manager, SANE, 1988–91; Sen. Inf. Officer, 1991–94, Chief Press Officer, 1995, DoH; Prime Minister's Office, 1996–2006: Dep. Press Sec., 1998–2001; Prime Minister's Official Spokesman, 2001–03; Hd of Strategic Communications, 2004–06; Dir of Communications, ODA, 2006–11; Dir of Govt Communications for London 2012 (on secondment from ODA), 2011–12; Interim Exec. Dir of Govt Communications, 2012. Trustee, Cambridge Junction, 2013–. Dir, Cambridge United FC, 2018–. *Recreations:* watching Cambridge United, cycling, family. *Address:* Inc., 4th Floor, The Stanley Building, N1C 4AG.

**SMITH, Prof. Gordon Campbell Sinclair,** MD, PhD, DSc; FRCOG; FMedSci; Professor of Obstetrics and Gynaecology, since 2001, and Head of Department of Obstetrics and Gynaecology, since 2004, University of Cambridge; Honorary Consultant in Maternal Fetal Medicine, Addenbrooke's Hospital, Cambridge, since 2001; Fellow, Hughes Hall, Cambridge, since 2014; *b* 11 May 1965; *s* of Robert (Roy) Smith and Peggy Smith; *m* 1986, Nicola Wilkinson; two *d*. *Educ:* Bankhead Primary Sch., Glasgow; Stonelaw High Sch.,

Glasgow; Univ. of Glasgow (BSc 1st Cl. Hons Physiol. 1986; MB ChB 1990; MD 1995; PhD 2001; DSc 2012). MRCOG 1996, FRCOG 2008. House officer and registrar appts, Glasgow, 1990–92 and 1993–96; Wellcome Trust Research Fellow: Dept of Physiol., Univ. of Glasgow, 1992–93; Dept of Physiol., Cornell Univ., Ithaca, NY, 1996–99; sub specialist trainee in Maternal-Fetal Medicine, Glasgow, 1999–2001. FMedSci 2010. *Publications:* contrib. numerous res. papers on physiol., pharmacol. and obstetrics to learned jls, incl. Lancet, BMJ, New England Jl of Medicine, Jl of Amer. Med. Assoc., Nature. *Recreations:* fly fishing, walking, reading. *Address:* Department of Obstetrics and Gynaecology, University of Cambridge, Box 223, The Rosie Hospital, Robinson Way, Cambridge CB2 0SW. *T:* (01223) 336871, *Fax:* (01223) 215327. *E:* paoandghod@medschl.cam.ac.uk.

**SMITH, Gordon James,** CBE 2004; Resident Director for Scotland, IBM, 1997–2007; *b* 17 Dec. 1947; *s* of Stanley and Agnes Smith; *m* 2001, Margaret McKenzie; two *s* two *d*. *Educ:* Univ. of Stirling (BA 2003). IBM: joined 1970; various appts, 1970–97. Chairman: Business Enterprise Trusts, 1996–99; CBI Scotland, 2003–05; Regl Chms Cttee, CBI, 2005–06. Dir, Dunfermline Bldg Soc., 2006–09. Board Member: Scottish Qualifications Authy, 2000–04; Young Enterprise Scotland, 2000–04; Trust Bd, Scottish Chamber Orch., 2000–04. *Recreations:* golf, travel, cooking.

**SMITH, Graeme David; His Honour Judge Graeme Smith;** a Circuit Judge, since 2015; *b* London, 16 Nov. 1963; *s* of David and Patricia Smith; *m* 1986, Helen Smith; two *s* one *d*. *Educ:* Archbishop Tenison's Grammar Sch.; Emmanuel Coll., Cambridge (BA 1985; MA); Coll. of Law, London. Admitted as solicitor, 1988; Solicitor, Pannone Blackburn, 1988–91; Partner, Pannone & Partners, Manchester, 1991–2003; Dep. Dist Judge, 1999–2003; Dist Judge, 2003–15; Recorder, 2008–15. Gen. Ed., Jordan's Civil Court Service, 2014–19. *Publications:* Was the Tomb Empty?, 2014. *Recreations:* reading, model making, spending time with family. *Address:* Bolton Combined Court, Blackhorse Street, Bolton BL1 1SU. *T:* (01204) 392881.

**SMITH, Very Rev. Graham Charles Morell;** Dean of Norwich, 2004–13, now Dean Emeritus; *b* 7 Nov. 1947; *s* of Philip and Helen Smith; *m* 1975, Carys Evans; one *s* two *d*. *Educ:* Whitgift Sch., Croydon; Univ. of Durham (BA Hons Theology 1974); Westcott House, Cambridge. Ordained deacon, 1976, priest, 1977; Asst Curate, All Saints, Tooting Graveney, 1976–80; Team Vicar, St Paul's, Thamesmead, 1980–87; Team Rector, Kidlington with Hampton Poyle, 1987–97; Rural Dean of Oxford, 1988–94; Rector of Leeds, 1997–2004; Hon. Canon, Ripon Cathedral, 1997–2004. *Recreations:* classic cars, theatre and cinema, biography, music, novels, hill walking. *Address:* Blacksmith's Cottage, Church Street, Ashreigney, nr Chulmleigh, Devon EX18 7LP. *T:* (01769) 520824.

**SMITH, Graham John Haley;** Of Counsel, Bird & Bird LLP, since 2019 (Partner, 1985–2019); *b* London, 27 Sept. 1953; *s* of Thomas Smith and Dr Sylvia Smith; *m* 1990, Penelope Jane Christie; one *s*. *Educ:* Uppingham Sch., Rutland; Bristol Univ. (LLB 1975). Admitted as solicitor, 1978; Res. Officer, Nat. Assoc. for Freedom, 1978–80; Solicitor, Penningtons Solicitors, 1981–83; Asst Solicitor, Bird & Bird LLP, 1983–85. *Publications:* Internet Law and Regulation, 1996, 4th edn 2007. *Recreations:* dancing, theatre, ballet. *Address:* Bird & Bird LLP, 12 New Fetter Lane, EC4A 1JP. *T:* (020) 7415 6000. *E:* graham.smith@twobirds.com.

**SMITH, Grahame;** General Secretary, Scottish Trades Union Congress, since 2006; *b* 8 Jan. 1959; *s* of Thomas Smith and Joyce Smith; partner, Liz Campbell; two *s*. *Educ:* Strathclyde Univ. (BA Hons). Asst Sec., 1986–96, Dep. Gen. Sec., 1996–2006, Scottish TUC. *Address:* Scottish Trades Union Congress, 333 Woodlands Road, Glasgow G3 6NG. *T:* (0141) 337 8100, *Fax:* (0141) 337 8101. *E:* gsmith@stuc.org.uk.

**SMITH, Maj. Gen. Gregory Stephen,** CB 2013; TD 1994; QVRM 2009; Chief Executive, Royal Norfolk Agricultural Association, since 2012; *b* Norwich, 18 May 1956; *s* of James Lee and Geraldine Mary Smith; *m* 1982, Rebecca Elizabeth Read; two *s* one *d*. *Educ:* Norwich Sch.; Univ. of Newcastle upon Tyne (BSc Hons Agricl and Food Mktg). Director: Taylor Nelson Sofres plc, 1992–2000; Ipsos MORI (formerly Market and Opinion Res. Internat. (MORI) Ltd, 2001–09; Founder, Read Smith Consulting, 2010. Chair, Internat. Adv. Bd, Newcastle Univ. Business Sch., 2009–14; Mem. Court, Newcastle Univ., 2011–. CO 5 (V) RGJ, 1996–99; Dir, Army Reserves, 2006–09; ACDS (Reserves and Cadets), MoD, 2010–13. Chair: East Anglia Reserves' and Cadets' Assoc., 2014–18; Council of Reserve Forces' and Cadets' Assocs, 2018–; Pres., UK Reserve Forces Assoc., 2014–. Director: Norfolk Showground Ltd, 2012–; Innovation for Agriculture, 2013–14; Norfolk Showground Develts Ltd, 2014–; Chair, Active Norfolk, 2015–. DL Bucks, 1998–2011. MInstD 2001. FRSA. Trustee, The Rifles, 2009–14. Hon. Col, Northumbrian Univs OTC, 2014–18; Dep. Hon. Col, F(Rifles) Co., London Regt, 2018–. Gov., Norwich Sch., 2018–. *Recreations:* sailing, walking, the Norfolk Broads, supporting the Canaries. *Address:* Norfolk Showground, Dereham Road, Costessey, Norwich, Norfolk NR5 0TT. *T:* (01603) 748931. *Clubs:* Army and Navy; Norfolk (Norwich); Horning Sailing.

**SMITH, Prof. Hamilton Othanel;** Scientific Director, Synthetic Biology and Bioenergy Groups, J. Craig Venter Institute, San Diego, since 2006 (Scientific Director, Institute for Biological Energy Alternatives, 2002–06); *b* 23 Aug. 1931; *s* of Bunnie Othanel Smith and Tommie Harkey Smith; *m* 1957, Elizabeth Anne Bolton; four *s* one *d*. *Educ:* Univ. of Illinois; Univ. of California (AB); Johns Hopkins Univ. Sch. of Medicine (MD). Research Associate, Dept of Human Genetics, Univ. of Michigan, 1964–67; Johns Hopkins University School of Medicine: Asst Prof. of Microbiology, 1967–69; Associate Prof. of Microbiology, 1969–73; Prof. of Microbiology, 1973–81; Prof. of Molecular Biology and Genetics, 1981–2002; Celera Genomics Corp., 1998–2002. During sabbatical leave in Zürich, worked in collaboration with Prof. Dr M. L. Birnstiel, Inst. für Molekularbiologie II der Univ. Zürich, 1975–76; Vis. Prof., Inst. of Molecular Pathol., Vienna, 1990–91. Nobel Prize in Medicine (jtly), 1978. *Publications:* A restriction enzyme from Hemophilus influenzae: I. Purification and general properties (with K. W. Wilcox), in Jl Mol. Biol. *51*, 379, 1970; A restriction enzyme from Hemophilus influenzae: II. Base sequence of the recognition site (with T. J. Kelly), in Jl Mol. Biol. *51*, 393, 1970. *Recreations:* piano, classical music. *Address:* J. Craig Venter Institute, 4120 Capricorn Lane, La Jolla, CA 92037, USA.

**SMITH, Harvey;** see Smith, Robert H.

**SMITH, Helen Sylvester,** MA; Headmistress, Perse School for Girls, Cambridge, 1989–2001; *b* 7 Jan. 1942; *d* of late S. J. Smith and K. R. Smith. *Educ:* King Edward VI High Sch. for Girls, Birmingham; St Hilda's College, Oxford (BA 1963, MA 1967 Maths); Hughes Hall, Cambridge (PGCE 1964). Cheltenham Ladies' College, 1964–69; International School of Brussels, 1969–71; Perse Sch. for Girls, 1971–2001 (Dep. Head, 1979–82, 1988–89). *Recreations:* music, gardening, painting in watercolour. *Address:* 6 Larch Court, Great Alne, Alcester B49 6FQ. *T:* 07711 845242.

**SMITH, Henry Edward Millar;** MP (C) Crawley, since 2010; *b* Epsom, 14 May 1969; *s* of late John Edwin Smith and Josephine Anne Smith (née Millar); *m* 1994, Jennifer Lois Ricks (marr. diss. 2015); one *s* one *d* (and one *s* decd). *Educ:* University Coll. London (BA Hons Philosophy 1991). Mem. (C) W Sussex CC, 1997–2010 (Leader, 2003–10).

Contested (C) Crawley, 2001, 2005. *Publications:* (jtly) Direct Democracy, 2005. *Recreations:* family, ski-ing, vexillology. *Address:* House of Commons, SW1A 0AA. *T:* (020) 7219 7043. *E:* henry.smith.mp@parliament.uk.

**SMITH, Prof. Henry Sidney,** FBA 1985; Edwards Professor of Egyptology, 1970–86, Head of Department of Egyptology, 1970–88, University College London, now Professor Emeritus; *b* 14 June 1928; *s* of Prof. Sidney Smith, FBA, and Mary, *d* of H. W. Parker; *m* 1961, Hazel Flory Leeper (*d* 1991). *Educ:* Merchant Taylors' Sch., Northwood; Christ's Coll., Cambridge (MA); DLit London, 1987. Lectr in Egyptology, Univ. of Cambridge, 1954–63; Budge Fellow in Egyptology, Christ's Coll., Cambridge, 1955–63; Reader in Egyptian Archaeology, University Coll. London, 1963–70. Field Dir for Egypt Exploration Soc. in Nubia, 1961, 1964–65, and at Saqqara and Memphis, Egypt, 1970–88. *Publications:* Preliminary Reports of the Egypt Exploration Society's Nubian Survey, 1962; A Visit to Ancient Egypt, 1974; The Fortress of Buhen: the inscriptions, 1976; The Fortress of Buhen: the archaeological report, 1979; (with W. J. Tait) Saqqara Demotic Papyri I, 1983; The Anubieion at Saqqara, Vol. I (with D. G. Jeffreys), 1988, Vol. II (with L. L. Giddy), 1992; (with Sue Davies): The Sacred Animal Necropolis at North Saqqara: the falcon complex and catacomb, the archaeological report, 2005; (with Sue Davis and K. J. Frazer) The Sacred Animal Necropolis at North Saqqara: the main temple complex, 2006; (with C. A. R. Andrews and Sue Davies) The Sacred Animal Necropolis at North Saqqara: the mother of Apis inscriptions, 2011; articles in Kush, Jl of Egyptian Arch., Orientalia, Rev. d'Egyptologie, Bull. Inst. Français d'Arch. Or., Z für Äg. Sprache und Altertumskunde, etc.

**SMITH, Iain-Mór L.;** see Lindsay-Smith.

**SMITH, Iain William;** senior consultant on Scottish public policy, since 2012; Policy and Public Affairs Officer, Inclusion Scotland, since 2017; *b* 1 May 1960; *s* of William Smith and Jane Allison Smith (née Farmer). *Educ:* Bell Baxter High Sch., Cupar; Newcastle upon Tyne Univ. (BA Hons Politics and Econs). Fife Regional Council: Mem. (Lib Dem), 1982–96; Sec., Alliance Gp, 1982–86; Leader of Opposition, 1986–96; Mem. (Lib Dem), and Leader of Opposition, Fife Council, 1995–99. MSP (Lib Dem) NE Fife, 1999–2011. Dep. Minister for Parlt, Scottish Exec., 1999–2000; spokesman on local govt and transport, 2003–05, on education, 2005–07, for Europe, external relns and culture, 2007–11. Scottish Parliament: Convener: Procedures Cttee, 2003–05; Educn Cttee, 2005–07; Economy, Energy and Tourism Cttee, 2008–11; Mem., Eur. and External Affairs Cttee, 2007–08. Convener, Lib Dems Scottish Parly Party, 2007–11; Policy and Information Officer, CHILDREN 1ST, 2012; Policy and Parly (formerly Engagement) Officer, Inclusion Scotland, 2013–17. Contested (Lib Dem) North East Fife, Scottish Parlt, 2011. *Recreations:* sport (mainly football and cricket), cinema, travel, reading, theatre. *Address:* Ambler Cottage, 14 Melville Road, Ladybank, Cupar, Fife KY15 7LU. *T:* (01337) 831115.

**SMITH, Prof. Ian Edward,** MD; FRCP, FRCPE; Professor of Cancer Medicine, Institute of Cancer Research, University of London, since 2000; Consultant Physician, since 1978, and Head of Breast Unit, since 2003, Royal Marsden Hospital, London; *b* 16 May 1946; *s* of late David Nicol Smith and Nettie, (Bunty), Thompson Smith (née Millar); *m* 1978, Suzanne Dorothy Mackey; three *d*. *Educ:* High Sch. of Dundee; Edinburgh Univ. (BSc Hons 1968; MB ChB 1971; MD 1978). FRCPE 1984; FRCP 1988. House Physician, SHO, then Registrar, Royal Infirmary, Edinburgh, 1971–73; Med. Registrar, Royal Marsden Hosp., London, 1973–75; Res. Fellow, Inst. of Cancer Res., London, 1975–76; UICC Travelling Fellow, Harvard Med. Sch., Boston, 1976–77; Lectr, Royal Marsden Hosp., 1977–78; Head of Section of Medicine, Inst. of Cancer Res., 1994–; Head of Lung Unit, 1994–2001, Med. Dir, 2000–03, Royal Marsden Hosp. Lectures worldwide on breast cancer and new cancer therapies. Chairman: Assoc. of Cancer Physicians, 1995–98; UKCCCR Lung Gp, 1999–; NCRI Lung Clinical Trials Gp, 2000–03; British Breast Gp, 2007–; UK Breast Intergroup, 2007–. Member: Amer. Soc. of Clin. Oncology, 1978; British Assoc. for Cancer Res., 1978; Eur. Soc. of Med. Oncology, 1991; William L. McGuire Meml Lect. Award, 2018. *Publications:* (jtly) Autologous Bone Marrow Transplantation, 1984; (jtly) Medical Management of Breast Cancer, 1991; multiple papers, articles and contribs to books on breast cancer. *Recreations:* ski-ing, supporting Chelsea, reading. *Address:* Royal Marsden Hospital, Fulham Road, SW3 6JJ. *T:* (020) 8661 3280, 3016; Royal Marsden Hospital, Downs Road, Sutton, Surrey SM2 5PT.

**SMITH, Ian Knight;** HM Diplomatic Service, retired; Counsellor and Deputy Head of Mission, Berne, 1993–97; *b* 18 June 1938; *m* 1st, 1964, Glenys Audrey Hayter (*d* 1981); one *s*; 2nd, 1989, Ellen Ragnhild Sweet-Escott; one *s* one *d*. FCO, 1962; Mexico City, 1964; Second Secretary: Calcutta, 1967; Caracas, 1969; First Secretary: FCO, 1972; UKREP Brussels, 1982; FCO, 1987; on secondment as Counsellor to EEC, 1989, to DSS, 1991.

**SMITH, Ian Richard;** Operating Partner, Trilantic Private Equity, since 2015; *b* 22 Jan. 1954; *s* of Albert and Drusilla Smith; *m* 1989, Caroline Firstbrook; three *c*. *Educ:* St Edmund Hall, Oxford (MA Hons); Univ. of Harvard (MBA high dist.). Gen. Manager, Jordan, Royal Dutch Shell, 1978–86; Chief Exec., Europe, Monitor (strategy consulting), 1986–98; Chief Exec., Europe, Exel (Transportation), 1998–2004; CEO, General Healthcare, 2004–06; Chief Exec., Taylor Woodrow plc, 2007; Mem., Govt Rev. of Royal Mail and UK Postal Sector (Hooper Rev.), 2008; Chm., Parly Rev. on Civil Service Reform (Smith Rev.), 2009; CEO, Reed Elsevier, 2009; Partner, Governance for Owners, 2011–12; Chm., Four Seasons Health Care, 2012–16. Interim Chm., King's Coll. Hosp. NHS Foundn Trust, 2017–19. Advr to Quartet Rep., 2009–12. *Publications:* Mosquito Pathfinder, 2002; Building a World Class NHS, 2007; (with S. K. Smith) Health and Social Care Reform in the UK, 2015. *Recreations:* sports, politics, history. *Club:* Royal Automobile.

See also Prof. S. K. Smith.

**SMITH, Prof. Ivor Ramsay,** FREng; Professor of Electrical Power Engineering, Loughborough University (formerly Loughborough University of Technology), 1974, now Emeritus; *b* 8 Oct. 1929; *s* of Howard Smith and Elsie Emily Smith; *m* 1962, Pamela Mary Voake; three *s*. *Educ:* Univ. of Bristol (BSc, PhD, DSc). CEng, FIET (FIEE 1974); FREng (FEng 1988). Sen. MIEEE 2011 (MIEEE 2010). Design and Develt Engr, GEC, Birmingham, 1956–59; Lectr, Sen. Lectr, Reader, Univ. of Birmingham, 1959–74; Loughborough University of Technology: Hd, Dept of Electronic and Electrical Engrg, 1980–90; Dean of Engrg, 1983–86; Pro-Vice-Chancellor, 1987–91. Director: Loughborough Consultants Ltd, 1980–; E Midlands Regl Technology Network, 1989–. Ind. Mem., Defence Scientific Adv. Council, 2003–. *Publications:* (jtly) Magnetocumulative Generators, 2000; Explosively Driven Pulsed Power, 2005; over 450 technical papers and articles on range of power engrg topics, incl. the efficient computation of power supply systems and the prodn, processing and application of very large pulses of electrical energy for various pulsed power applications. *Recreations:* gardening, walking, reading. *Address:* School of Electronic, Electrical and Systems Engineering, Loughborough University, Loughborough, Leics LE11 3TU. *T:* (01509) 227005.

**SMITH, Rt Hon. Jacqueline Jill, (Jacqui);** PC 2007; Chair: University Hospitals Birmingham NHS Foundation Trust, since 2013; Sandwell Children's Trust, since 2017; *b* 3 Nov. 1962; *d* of Michael and Jill Smith; *m* 1987, Richard James Timney; two *s*. *Educ:* Hertford Coll., Oxford (BA Hons PPE); Worcester Coll. of Higher Education (PGCE).

Res. Asst, Terry Davis, MP, 1984–85; Teacher: Arrow Vale High Sch., Redditch, 1986–88; Worcester Sixth Form Coll., 1988–90; Head of Econs, and GNVQ Co-ordinator, Haybridge High Sch., 1990–97. Mem. (Lab) Redditch BC, 1991–97. Contested (Lab) Mid Worcestershire, 1992. MP (Lab) Redditch, 1997–2010; contested (Lab) same seat, 2010. Parly Under-Sec. of State, DfEE, 1999–2001; Minister of State: DoH, 2001–03; DTI, 2003–05; Minister of State (Minister for Schs) DfES, 2005–06; Parly Sec. to HM Treasury (Govt Chief Whip), 2006–07; Sec. of State for the Home Dept, 2007–09. Chair, Public Affairs Practice, Westbourne Communications, 2015–17; Associate, Global Partners Governance, working in Jordan and Egypt, 2012–. Chair: Precious Trust, 2011–; Jo Cox Foundn, 2019–; Trustee, King's Fund, 2017–. *Recreations:* family, friends, football, theatre. *E:* smithjacqui@live.co.uk.

**SMITH, Sir James (Cuthbert)**, Kt 2017; PhD; FRS 1993; FMedSci; Director, Science Review, Wellcome Trust, since 2019 (Director of Science, 2016–19); Visiting Group Leader, Francis Crick Institute, since 2016 (Director of Research, 2015–16); *b* 31 Dec. 1954; *s* of late Leslie Cuthbert Smith and Freda Sarah (née Wragg); *m* 1979, Fiona Mary Watt, *qv*; two *s* one *d*. *Educ:* Latymer Upper Sch.; Christ's Coll., Cambridge (BA 1976; MA 1979; Hon. Fellow, 2009); London Univ. (PhD 1979). NATO Postdoctoral Fellow, Sidney Farber Cancer Inst. and Harvard Med. Sch., 1979–81; ICRF Postdoctoral Fellow, 1981–84; National Institute for Medical Research: Mem., Scientific Staff, 1984–2000; Head, Div. of Develtl Biol., 1991–2000; Head, Genes and Cellular Controls Gp, 1996–2000; John Humphrey Plummer Prof. of Develtl Biol., Univ. of Cambridge, 2001–08; Fellow of Christ's Coll., Cambridge, 2001–08; Chm., Wellcome Trust/CRUK Gurdon Inst. (formerly Wellcome Trust and CRUK Inst. of Cancer and Develtl Biol.), 2001–08; Dir, MRC Nat. Inst. for Med. Res., 2009–15; Dep. CEO and Chief of Strategy, MRC, 2014–16. Chm., British Soc. for Developmental Biol., 1994–99; Mem., EMBO, 1992. Howard Hughes Internat. Res. Scholar, 1993–97. Fellow, European Acad. of Cancer Scis, 2009. Founder FMedSci 1998. FRSA 2009. Scientific Medal, Zool Soc. of London, 1989; Otto Mangold Prize, Ges. für Entwicklungsbiologie, 1991; EMBO Medal, 1993; Feldberg Foundn Award, 2000; (jtly) William Bate Hardy Prize, Cambridge Phil Soc., 2001; Waddington Medal, British Soc. for Develtl Biology, 2013. *Publications:* (ed jtly) The Molecular Basis of Positional Signalling, 1989; (with L. Wolpert and others) Principles of Development, 2nd edn 2001, 3rd edn 2007; scientific articles in various jls. *Recreations:* cycling, running, music, reading. *Address:* Wellcome Trust, Gibbs Building, 215 Euston Road, NW1 2BE. *T:* (020) 7611 8232, 07802 745798. *E:* j.smith@wellcome.ac.uk.

**SMITH, Jane Caroline Rebecca P.**; see Parker-Smith.

**SMITH, Jane L.**; see Lewin Smith.

**SMITH, Rt Hon. Dame Janet (Hilary), (Dame Janet Mathieson)**, DBE 1992; PC 2002; a Lord Justice of Appeal, 2002–11; mediator and neutral evaluator; *b* 29 Nov. 1940; *d* of Alexander Roe and Margaret Holt; *m* 1st, 1959, Edward Stuart Smith; two *s* one *d*; 2nd, 1984, Robin Edward Alexander Mathieson. *Educ:* Bolton School. Called to the Bar, Lincoln's Inn, 1972, Bencher, 1992 (Treas., 2012); QC 1986; a Recorder, 1988–92; a Judge of the High Ct of Justice, QBD, 1992–2002; a Judge of the Employment Appeal Tribunal, 1994–2002; Presiding Judge, N Eastern Circuit, 1995–98. Pres., Council, Inns of Court, 2006–09. Chairman: Shipman Inquiry, 2001–05; BBC review into allegations of sexual abuse by Jimmy Savile, 2012–16. Member: Criminal Injuries Compensation Bd, 1988–92; QC Selection Panel, 2016–18; Court of Appeal of Gibraltar, 2016–; Chm., Security Vetting Appeals Panel, 2000–09; Ind. Assessor of Compensation for Miscarriages of Justice, 2011–16. Chm., Civil Cttee, Judicial Studies Bd, 2000–04. Chancellor, Manchester Metropolitan Univ., 2003–09. Pres., Personal Injuries Bar Assoc., 2009–11. Chm., Buxton Arts Festival, 2007–14. Hon. Fellow, Hughes Hall, Cambridge, 2012. Hon. LLD: Manchester Metropolitan, 2002; Lancaster, 2005; Manchester, 2015; Univ. of Law, 2015; Bolton, 2016. *Recreations:* gardening, music.

**SMITH, Jeff**; Head of Music, BBC Radio 2 and BBC Radio 6 Music, since 2007; *b* Fleetwood, Lancs, 24 Dec. 1960; *s* of William Henry Smith and Joyce Smith; *m* 2013, Deborah Stanley; one *s* one *d*. *Educ:* Baines' Sch., Poulton-le-Fylde; North Cheshire Coll., Warrington; Univ. of Manchester (BA Communication Studies). Producer, BBC World Service, 1984–87; Programme Manager, TFM Radio, 1987–90; BBC Radio 1: Producer and Creator, Evening Session, 1990–93; Editor, Mainstream Progs and Music Manager, 1993–95; Dir, Progs, Wise Buddah Independent Prodn, 1995–97; Hd, Music Policy, BBC Radio 1, 1997–2000 (created Live Lounge, Radio 1 Live); Prog. Controller, 95.8 Capital FM, 2000–03; Programming Dir, Napster UK and Internat., 2004–07. Commnd music drama for BBC Radio 2, Darkside, 2013; creator, music drama for BBC Radio, Queens of Noise: Shout to the Top, 2014. Chair, Mercury Music Prize. *Address:* BBC Radio 2, 99 Great Portland Street, W1A 1AA. *E:* jeff.smith@bbc.co.uk.

**SMITH, Jeffrey**; see Smith, A. J.

**SMITH, Jeffrey**; MP (Lab) Manchester Withington, since 2015; *b* Withington, 26 Jan. 1963; *s* of Alan Smith and Deidre Smith. *Educ:* Old Moat Primary Sch.; Manchester Grammar Sch.; Univ. of Manchester (BA(Econ) Hons 1984). Event manager, 1985–2010; DJ, 1992–2011. Mem. (Lab) Manchester CC, 1997–2015 (Executive Member: for Educn and Children's Services; for Finance; for Housing and Regeneration). An Opposition Whip, 2015–. *Address:* House of Commons, SW1A 0AA.

**SMITH, Prof. (Jenkyn) Beverley**, FRHistS; FLSW; Research Professor of Welsh History, University of Wales, Aberystwyth, 1995–98, now Emeritus Professor; Commissioner, 1984–99, Chairman, 1991–99, Royal Commission on Ancient and Historical Monuments for Wales; *b* 27 Sept. 1931; *s* of Cecil Nelson Smith and Hannah Jane (née Jenkins); *m* 1966, Llinos Olwen Wyn Vaughan, PhD, FRHistS, medieval historian; two *s*. *Educ:* Gowerton Grammar Sch.; UCW, Aberystwyth (BA, MA). FRHistS 1967. National Service, 1954–56. Researcher, Bd of Celtic Studies, Univ. of Wales, 1956–58; Asst Keeper, Dept of MSS and Records, Nat. Library of Wales, 1958–60; Lectr 1960–67, Sen. Lectr 1967–78, Reader 1978–86, Sir John Williams Prof. of Welsh History, 1986–95, Dept of Welsh History, UCW, Aberystwyth. Sir John Rhys Vis. Fellow, Univ. of Oxford, 1978–79. Member: Court and Council, Nat. Library of Wales, 1974–84; Bd of Celtic Studies, Univ. of Wales, 1965–2007 (Sec.), History and Law Cttee, 1979–85, Chm. 1985–91); Ancient Monuments Bd for Wales, 1992–98. FLSW 2013. Jt Editor, Bulletin of Bd of Celtic Studies, 1972–93; Editor, 1994–96, Chief Editor, 1996–2010, Studia Celtica. *Publications:* Llywelyn ap Gruffudd, Tywysog Cymru, 1986; Llywelyn ap Gruffudd, Prince of Wales, 1998, 2nd edn 2014; (ed) Medieval Welsh Society, Selected Essays by T. Jones Pierce, 1972; (ed with G. H. Jenkins) Politics and Society in Wales 1840–1922, 1988; (ed with Llinos Beverley Smith) History of Merioneth, vol. II, The Middle Ages, 2001; (ed with Ieuan M. Williams and Humphrey Llwyd) Cronica Walliae, 2002, 2nd edn 2016; Princes and Castles: the thirteenth-century legacy, 2010; articles in English Hist. Review, Welsh Hist. Review, Bulletin Bd of Celtic Studies, Studio Celtica and other jls. *Address:* 2 The Beeches Close, Sketty, Swansea SA2 7ND.

**SMITH, Hon. Dame Jennifer**, DBE 2005; JP; MP (Progressive Lab) St George's North, Bermuda, 1989–2012; Minister of Education, 2010–12; *d* of late Eugene Wilberforce Smith and Lillian Smith (née De Shields). *Educ:* Bermuda; Art Inst., Pittsburgh. Formerly newspaper and magazine editor, radio and TV promotions manager and choreographer. Mem., Senate of Bermuda, 1980–89; Premier of Bermuda, 1998–2003; Minister of Educn, 1998–99; Dep. Speaker, House of Assembly, 2003–10. Dep. Leader, 1994–96, Leader, 1996–2003, Progressive Labour Party. Exec. Mem., 2005–07, Vice-Chm., 2006–07, Commonwealth Parly Assoc. Election Observer, Bangladesh, Commonwealth Secretariat, 2008. Member: Bermuda Inst. of Ocean Scis; Bd of Trustees, Bermuda Nat. Gall.; Bermuda Heritage Assoc.; Bermuda Musical and Dramatic Soc.; Bermuda Dance Foundn; Masterworks of Bermuda. Hon. DHumLit: Mount St Vincent, Halifax, Canada, 2000; Morris Brown Coll., Atlanta, USA, 2000; Hon. DHum Art Inst. of Pittsburgh, 2003. *Publications:* Voice of Change, 2003.

**SMITH, Jennifer A.**; Principal, Harrogate Ladies' College, 1993–95; *b* 11 March 1950; *d* of Geoffrey and Elsie Bird; *m* 1974, Michael Smith; one *d*. *Educ:* Leeds Univ. (BSc Hons Physics, PGCE); Open Univ. (BA); Liverpool Univ. (MEd). Asst teacher, Physics, 1973–83, Head of Physics, 1983–85, St Richard Gwyn High Sch., Clwyd; Sen. Project Tutor, Science and Electronics, Bodelwyddan TVEI Centre, 1985–88; Dep. Head Teacher, West Kirby Grammar Sch. for Girls, 1988–93. Mem., Treuddyn Community Council, 2008– (Chair, 2010–11). Chair, Treuddyn Community Assoc., 2009–14. *Recreations:* skiing, climbing, music, theatre, computing.

**SMITH, Jeremy Fox Eric**; DL; Chairman, Smith St Aubyn (Holdings) plc, 1973–86, retired; *b* 17 Nov. 1928; *s* of late Captain E. C. E. Smith, MC, and B. H. Smith (née Williams); *m* 1st, 1953, Julia Mary Rona, DL (*d* 2004), *d* of Sir Walter Burrell, 8th Bt, CBE, TD; two *s* two *d*; 2nd, 2008, Lady Gillian Moyra Katherine Kertesz, *d* of 6th Marquess of Exeter, KCMG, DL. *Educ:* Eton; New College, Oxford. Chairman, Transparent Paper Ltd, 1965–76. Chairman, London Discount Market Assoc., 1978–80. Trustee, Henry Smith's Charity, 1971–97. DL 1988, High Sheriff, 1992–93, West Sussex. *Address:* The Old Rectory, Slaugham, Haywards Heath, W Sussex RH17 6AG. *T:* (01444) 400341. *Clubs:* Beefsteak, Cavalry and Guards.
*See also Fortune, Duchess of Grafton, Earl of Verulam, Countess of Verulam.*

**SMITH, Jeremy James Russell**; Director, Advocacy International Ltd, since 2010; Co-Director, PRIME Economics, since 2010; *b* 12 June 1947; *s* of Horace James Smith and Joan Alistair Russell. *Educ:* Peterhouse, Cambridge (BA Law 1968). Called to the Bar, Lincoln's Inn, 1969; Barrister, 1971–78; Sen. Legal Adviser, Brent Community Law Centre, 1978–83; Legal Services Liaison Officer, GLC, 1983–86; Clerk and Legal Advr, ILEA, 1986–89; Dir of Law and Admin, 1989–90, Chief Exec., 1990–95, London Borough of Camden; Dir, Local Govt Internat. Bureau, 1996–2002; Secretary General: IULA, 2002–04; CEMR, 2002–09. *Recreations:* history, current affairs, music, rambling. *Address:* Advocacy International Ltd, 51 Clarence Gate Gardens, Glentworth Street, NW1 6QS. *E:* jeremy.smith@advocacyinternational.co.uk.

**SMITH, Joan Alison**; journalist and novelist; *b* London, 27 Aug. 1953; *d* of Alan Smith and Ann Anita Smith (née Coltman); *m* 1985, Francis James Baird Wheen, *qv* (marr. diss. 1993); partner, 2003–10, Denis MacShane, *qv*. *Educ:* Girls' Grammar Sch., Stevenage; Basingstoke High Sch. for Girls; Univ. of Reading (BA Hons Latin). Reporter: Evening Gazette, Blackpool, 1976–78; Piccadilly Radio, Manchester, 1978–79; Sunday Times, 1979–84; freelance journalist, 1984–. Exec. Dir, Hacked Off, 2014–15. Non-exec. Dir, ALCS, 2010–15, 2017–. Chair: Writers in Prison Cttee, English PEN, 2000–04; Ending Violence Against Women Media Awards, 2016; Co-Chair, Mayor of London's Violence Against Women and Girls Panel, 2013–. Adjunct Associate Prof., Edith Cowan Univ., WA, 2002–05. Pres., Creators' Rights Alliance, 2011–13. Hon. Associate, Nat. Secular Soc., 2001; Patron (formerly Dist. Supporter), Humanists UK (formerly British Humanist Assoc.), 2013–; Chm., Labour Humanists, 2016–18. *Publications: non-fiction:* Clouds of Deceit, 1985; Misogynies, 1989; (ed) Femmes de Siècle, 1992; Hungry for You, 1996; Different for Girls, 1998; Moralities, 2001; The Public Woman, 2013; Down with the Royals, 2015; Home Grown, 2019; *novels:* A Masculine Ending, 1987; Why Aren't They Screaming?, 1988; Don't Leave Me This Way, 1990; What Men Say, 1993; Full Stop, 1995; What Will Survive, 2007. *Address:* c/o Peters Fraser & Dunlop, 55 New Oxford Street, WC1A 1BS. *T:* (020) 7344 1000. *E:* info@pfd.co.uk.

**SMITH, Joanna Angela**; QC 2009; a Deputy High Court Judge, since 2017; *b* London, 27 April 1968; *d* of Dr W. H. Smith and Pamela Smith (now Dickson); *m* 1994, Mark James Vanhegan, *qv*; two *d*. *Educ:* King's Sch., Ely; Christ Church, Oxford (MA 1st Cl. Juris.). Called to the Bar, Lincoln's Inn, 1990; in practice as barrister specialising in commercial litigation, professional negligence, construction and regulation. *Recreations:* wandering at a leisurely pace across Europe, laughing with my children, running. *Address:* Wilberforce Chambers, 8 New Square, Lincoln's Inn, WC2A 3QP. *T:* (020) 7306 0102, *Fax:* (020) 7306 0095. *E:* jsmith@wilberforce.co.uk.

**SMITH, Joe**; see Smith, Jonathan.

**SMITH, Sir John (Alfred)**, Kt 1994; QPM 1986; Deputy Commissioner of the Metropolitan Police, 1991–95; *b* 21 Sept. 1938; *s* of Ruth Alice and Alfred Joseph Smith; *m* 1960, Joan Maria Smith; one *s* one *d*. *Educ:* St Olave's and St Saviour's Grammar School. Irish Guards, 1959–62. Metropolitan Police, 1962; Head, Scotland Yard drugs squad, 1979; Commander 'P' (Bromley-Lewisham) Dist, 1980; Dep. Chief Constable, Surrey Constabulary, 1981; Metropolitan Police: Dep. Asst Comr, 1984; Inspectorate and Force Reorganisation Team, 1985; Asst Comr, 1987–90; Management Support Dept, 1987–89; Specialist Ops Dept, 1989–90; Inspector of Constabulary for SE England, 1990–91. Dir, Sabrewatch Ltd, 1995–2000. Mem., Ind. Commn on Policing for NI, 1998–99. Pres., ACPO, 1993–94. Consultant, Football Assoc., 1995–98; non-exec. Dir, Brighton and Hove Albion FC, 1997–2000, 2002–07; Member: Cttee, AA, 1996–99; Govt Football Task Force Wkg Gp, 1997–99; Trustee: Drinking Fountain Assoc., 1995–2013; English Nat. Stadium Trust, 1997–98. *Recreations:* gardening, sport spectating, walking. *Address:* 23 Winterbourne, Horsham, West Sussex RH12 5JW. *T:* (01403) 211076.

**SMITH, John Allan Raymond**, CBE 2008; PhD; FRCS, FRCSE; Consultant General Surgeon, Northern General Hospital NHS Trust (formerly Northern General Hospital, Sheffield), 1985–2007; President, Royal College of Surgeons of Edinburgh, 2003–06 (a Vice-President, 1997–2000); *b* 24 Nov. 1942; *s* of Alexander Macintyre Smith and Evelyn Joyce Smith; *m* 1979, Valerie Fullalove; two *s* three *d*. *Educ:* Boroughmuir Sch., Edinburgh; Edinburgh Univ. (MB ChB 1966); Aberdeen Univ. (PhD 1979). FRCS 1972; FRCSE 1972. House Officer, Royal Infirmary of Edinburgh, 1966–67; SSC, RAMC, 1967–72; Registrar, Dumfries and Galloway Royal Infirmary, and Royal Infirmary, Aberdeen, 1972–73; Res. Fellow, Lectr in Surgery and Sen. Surgical Registrar, Grampian Health Bd, 1972–78; Sen. Lectr in Surgery and Cons. Surgeon, Royal Hallamshire Hosp., Sheffield, 1978–85. Chm., Jt Cttee for Higher Surgical Trng, 2000–03; Med. Mem., 2006–10, Chair, Assessment Cttee, 2009–10, PMETB; Mem., Postgrad. Bd, GMC, 2010–11. Non-exec. Dir, Portsmouth Hosps NHS Trust, 2015–18. Editor, Complications in Surgery series, 1985. Trustee, Diverse Abilities Plus, Dorset, 2013–. Pres., Rotary Club of Ringwood,

2015–16. *Publications:* (jtly) Wounds and Wound Management, 1992; (ed jtly and contrib.) Pye's Surgical Handicraft. *Recreations:* family, sport, cooking, wine. *Address:* Hadley Wood, 2 Castlewood, Ringwood, Hants BH24 2AX. *T:* (01425) 291196.

**SMITH, John Barry,** FCCA; Chief Operating Officer, Burberry Group plc, 2013–17 (non-executive Director, 2009–13); *b* 16 Aug. 1957; *s* of Kenneth William Smith and Elsie Smith (*née* Jackson); *m* 1st, 1993, Catherine Hewetson (marr. diss. 2010); two *s* one *d*; 2nd, 2015, Carrie Beth Ferman; one *d*. *Educ:* South London Coll. (FCCA 1980); Harvard Business Sch. (AMP 1997). Chartered Certified Accountant: Bocock, Bew & Co., Chartered Accountants, 1973–75; BR Gp subsidiaries, 1975–83; BRB, 1983–90; BBC, 1990–2012: Dir of Finance, 1996–2004; Mem. Exec. Bd, 1996–2009; Chief Operating Officer, 2004–05; CEO, BBC Worldwide, 2004–12. Non-executive Director: Vickers PLC, 1999–2000; UK Enterprise Adv. Bd, Zurich Financial Services, 2000–01; Severn Trent PLC, 2003–08; Superdry, 2017–19; Travelport Worldwide Ltd, 2017–; Hilding Anders AV, 2018–; Chairman: Jungle Creations Ltd; On Purpose Gp. Member: 100 Gp of Finance Dirs, 2000–05; Public Services Productivity Panel, 2000–06; Accounting Standards Bd, 2001–04. Dir, Henley Festival, 2004–17. Vice Pres., RTS, 2010–15; Dir, BAFTA, 2015–. FRTS 2001; FRSA 2005. Hon. FRIBA 2004. *Address:* Inkerman House, Shogmoor Lane, Skirmett, Oxon RG9 6TB.

**SMITH, (John) Edward (Kitson),** CBE 2014; FCA; Chairman, NHS Improvement, 2015–17; *b* Calcutta, 24 Oct. 1954; *s* of late Jack Smith and Edith Smith; *m* 1981, Jennifer Linton; one *s* two *d*. *Educ:* St Dunstan's Coll., Catford; London Metropolitan Univ. (BA Hons). FCA 2000. CPFA 2013. Coopers & Lybrand, then PricewaterhouseCoopers, 1977–2007: Hd, Educn Practice, 1989–93; Exec. Partner, UK Audit, 1994–97; Global Leader, Learning and Develt, 1998–99; Mem., UK Bd, 2000–03; Sen. Partner and Global Assurance Chief Operating Officer and Strategy Chm., 2004–07. Financial Advr, DES, 1987–89; Lead non-exec. Dir, DfT, 2008–17; Chm., Crown Commercial Services, Cabinet Office, 2014–16. Member: Competition Commn, 2009–14; NHS England (formerly NHS Commissioning Bd), 2011–15; Competition and Markets Authy, 2014–17; Chairman: NHS Monitor, 2015; NHS Trust Develt Authy, 2015; Assura plc, 2018–; Adv. Bd, HCA Healthcare UK, 2018–; Adv. Bd, Pushdoctor, 2018–. Non-executive Director: NHS Property Service Ltd, 2016–17; HS2 Ltd, 2018–. Member: Adv. Bd, Opportunity Now, 2001–13; Bd, Demos, 2008–10. Mem. Bd, HEFCE, 2004–11; Chm., Student Loans Co., 2010–13. Mem., Commn on Future of Women's Sport, 2008–13. Chm., British Univs and Colls Sport, 2008–14. Mem. Bd, WWF Internat., 2008–14; Chm., WWF-UK, 2008–14. Trustee and Treas., Work Foundn, 2007–10; Mem. Council and Treas., Chatham House, 2008–17. Pro-Chancellor and Chm. Council, Univ. of Birmingham, 2010–; Gov., Univ. (formerly Poly.) of N London, 1991–95. Chm., Caterham Sch., 2016–. Liveryman, Educators' Co., 2014–. FRSA 2001. Hon. LLD: Bath, 2009; Roehampton, 2013; Aberdeen, 2014; DUniv Birmingham, 2015. *Publications:* Breakpoint/Breakthrough Strategies for Worklife Balance in the 21st Century, 1999; Accounting for People, 2003; Diversity Dimensions, 2004; (jtly) Papering Over the Cracks, 2006. *Recreations:* golf, cooking, wine collecting, travel, opera. *Address:* Old Mill Leat, Vicarage Hill, Westerham, Kent TN16 1TJ. *T:* 07711 793312. *E:* ed.smith@jeks.co.uk. *Clubs:* Athenaeum; Westerham Golf.

**SMITH, (John) Edward (McKenzie) L.;** *see* Lucie-Smith.

**SMITH, Sir John Hamilton S.;** *see* Spencer-Smith.

**SMITH, John Hilary,** CBE 1970 (OBE 1964); Secretary, Imperial College, London, and Clerk to the Governors, 1979–89 (Fellow, 1992); *b* 20 March 1928; 2nd *s* of late P. R. Smith, OBE and Edith Prince; *m* 1964, Mary Sylvester Head; two *s* one *d*. *Educ:* Cardinal Vaughan Sch., London; University Coll. London (Fellow, 1987); University Coll., Oxford. BA Hons London 1948; MA Oxon 1991. Mil. service, 1948–50, commnd Queen's Own Royal W Kent Regt. Cadet, Northern Nigerian Administration, 1951; Supervisor, Admin. Service Trng, 1960; Dep. Sec. to Premier, 1963; Dir Staff, Develt Centre, 1964; Perm. Sec., Min. of Finance, Benue Plateau State, 1968; Vis. Lectr, Duke Univ., 1970; Financial Sec., British Solomon Is, 1970; Governor of Gilbert and Ellice Islands, 1973–76, of Gilbert Islands, 1976–78. Procurator, 1990–94, and Fellow, 1991–94, University Coll., Oxford. Public Orator, Univ. of London, 1991–94. Director: Fleming Ventures, 1985–98; Empire Mus. Ltd, 2001–14. Mem. Council, Scout Assoc., 1980–98 (Chm., Cttee of Council, 1984–88); Pres., Pacific Is Soc. of UK and Ireland, 1981–85. Governor: St Mary's Coll., Strawberry Hill, 1980–88; Cardinal Vaughan School, 1982–88; Heythrop Coll., 1986–93 (Fellow, 2002); Member, Board of Management: LSHTM, 1989–98 (Treas., 1993–98; Fellow, 1999); St Mary's Sch., Shaftesbury, 1993–2001 (Chm. Govs, 1994–2001). Sir Arthur Keith Medal, RCS, 2008; Ana Tokabeti Kiribati (Kiribati), 2009. *Publications:* How to Write Letters that get Results, 1965; Colonial Cadet in Nigeria, 1968; (ed) Administering Empire, 1999; An Island in the Autumn, 2010; articles in S Atlantic Quarterly, Administration, Jl of Overseas Administration, Nigeria. *Recreations:* walking, writing, music. *Address:* 282 Old Bath Road, Cheltenham, Glos GL53 9AP.

**SMITH, Sir John Jonah W.;** *see* Walker-Smith.

**SMITH, Sir John Rathborne V.;** *see* Vassar-Smith.

**SMITH, (John) Stephen;** QC 2000; a Recorder, since 2004; a Deputy High Court Judge, since 2006; *b* 30 June 1960; *s* of John Slater Smith and Nancy Smith (*née* Clayton); *m* 1982, Lorraine Dunn; four *s* one *d*. *Educ:* Walton High Sch., Nelson; Nelson and Colne Coll. of FE; University Coll., Oxford (BA 1st Cl. Jurisprudence). Called to the Bar: Middle Temple, 1983; Eastern Caribbean (BVI), 1994; Bahamas, 2004, 2016 and 2018; Isle of Man, 2007; Cayman Islands, 2010. *Recreations:* family, alpaca farming, deer, gardening. *Address:* Erskine Chambers, 33 Chancery Lane, WC2A 1EN. *T:* (020) 7242 5532. *E:* ssmith@erskinechambers.com.

**SMITH, John William Patrick;** *b* 17 March 1951; *s* of John Henry Smith and Margaret Mary (*née* Collins); *m* 1971, Kathleen Mulvaney; two *s* one *d*. *Educ:* Penarth County Sch.; Gwent Coll. of Higher Educn (Dip. in Indust. Relations and Trade Union Studies); UCW Cardiff (BSc (Econ) Hons). Building worker, 1966–68; RAF, 1967–71; joiner, 1971–76; mature student, 1976–83; University Tutor, 1983–85; Sen. Lectr in Business Studies, 1985–89; Chief Exec., Gwent Image Partnership, 1992–97. MP (Lab) Vale of Glamorgan, May 1989–1992 and 1997–2010; contested (Lab) same seat, 1992. PPS to Dep. Leader of the Opposition, 1989–92, to Minister of State for the Armed Forces, 1997–98, to Minister of State (Minister of Transport), DETR, 1998–99. Mem., Select Cttee on Welsh Affairs, 1990–92; formerly Parly spokesperson for Vale of Glam. *Recreations:* reading, boating, walking. *Clubs:* West End Labour; Sea View Labour (Barry).

**SMITH, Jon;** Director, First Artist Company Ltd, since 2017 (Chief Executive Officer, 2011–17); Executive Director, Infinity Creative Media Ltd, since 2014; public speaker; media, sports, entertainment and political commentator; *b* London, 20 Sept. 1952; *s* of Mick and Rosemary Smith; *m* 1st, 1976, Lee M. (*d* 1981); 2nd, 1986, Janine; two *s*. *Educ:* Orange Hill Grammar Sch.; Kingsway Coll. of Further Educn. Chief Exec., London Monarchs, 1991; CEO, 2001–10, Exec. Vice Chm., 2011, First Artist Corp. plc. Mem., Govt Cttee on Replacement of Tobacco Sponsorship in Sport, 1998. Non-exec. Dir, British Taekwondo, 2013–18 (Chair, 2016–18). Non-executive Chair: Fans Agency, 2018–; Halfspace, 2019–. Mem. Bd, Inst. of Child Health, 1987. Trustee, Lee Smith Foundn, 1982–. Patron: British Stammering Assoc., 2004; Cancer Unit, Univ. of Middx. FInstD. *Publications:* The Deal: inside the world of a superagent, 2016. *Recreations:* running, swimming, erstwhile chef, family management. *Address:* First Artist Co. Ltd, 27 Old Gloucester Street, WC1N 3AX. *T:* 0333 305 5555. *E:* jon@firstartist.com.

**SMITH, Prof. Jonathan, (Joe),** PhD; FRGS; Director, Royal Geographical Society with Institute of British Geographers, since 2018; *b* Holbrook, Derbys, 7 March 1967; *s* of John Nicholas Wilkins Smith and Gretchen Margaret Smith (*née* Bradley); *m* 1991, Prof. Renata Anna Tyszczuk; three *s*. *Educ:* Ecclesbourne Comprehensive Sch., Derbys; Corpus Christi Coll., Cambridge (BA Social and Political Scis 1989; PhD Geography 1997). Dir of Progs, Cttee for Interdisciplinary Envmtl Studies, Univ. of Cambridge, 1995–99; Open University: Lectr, 1997–2007, Sen. Lectr, 2007–15, Dept of Geog. Discipline, Faculty of Social Scis; Prof. of Envmt and Society, 2015–18; Hd, Dept of Geog., 2017–18. Member: Empty Common Allotment Soc.; YHA. *Publications:* (ed) The Daily Globe: environmental change, the public and the media, 2000; (with S. Peake) Climate Change: from science to sustainability, 2003, repr. 2020; What Do Greens Believe?, 2006; (ed with A. Simms) Do Good Lives Have to Cost the Earth?, 2008; (ed jtly) Culture and Climate Change: recordings, 2011; (ed jtly) Atlas of Interdependence: architecture, geography and change in an interdependent world, 2012; (ed jtly) Culture and Climate Change: narratives, 2014; (with R. Tyszczuk) Energetic: the past, present and future of energy, 2018. *Recreations:* allotment gardening, preserving, cycling, walking. *Address:* Royal Geographical Society with IBG, 1 Kensington Gore, SW7 2AR. *T:* (020) 7591 3010. *E:* director@rgs.org.

**SMITH, Jonathan A.;** *see* Ashley-Smith.

**SMITH, Ven. Jonathan Peter;** Archdeacon of St Albans, since 2008; *b* Guildford, 10 Nov. 1955; *s* of John Smith and Dorothea Smith. *Educ:* Ipswich Sch.; King's Coll., London (BD, AKC 1977); Queens' Coll., Cambridge (PGCE 1978); Westcott House, Cambridge. Ordained deacon, 1980, priest, 1981; Assistant Curate: All Saints', Gosforth, 1980–82; Waltham Abbey, 1982–85; Chaplain, City Univ., 1985–88; Rector, Harrold and Carlton with Chellington, 1988–97; Vicar, St John's, Harpenden, 1997–2008. Rural Dean, Wheathampstead, 1999–2004. Chaplain, Bedfordshire Police, 1990–97. *Recreations:* Association Football, travel, opera, proroguing committees, the company of friends. *T:* (01727) 818121. *Clubs:* Farmers; Bridgman Bowls (Bedfordshire).

**SMITH, Dr Joseph,** FRHistS; Editor, History: Journal of the Historical Association, 2000–10; Reader in American Diplomatic History, University of Exeter, 1995–2010; *b* 2 May 1945; *m* 1971, Marjorie Rachael Eaves. *Educ:* Grey Coll., Univ. of Durham (BA 1966); UCL (PhD 1970). FRHistS 1979. Research Assistant: UCL, 1969–70; Inst. of Latin American Studies, Univ. of London, 1970–71; Lectr in History, Univ. of Exeter, 1971–95. Visiting Professor of History: Coll. of William and Mary, Va, 1976–77; Univ. of Colorado at Denver, 1990–91. Fulbright Schol., 1990–91. Historical Association: Mem. Council, 1985–2003; Chm. of Pubns, 1995–2000; Vice-Pres., 2002–03. FHA 2007. Ed., The Annual Bull. of Histl Literature, 1990–99. Rio Branco Prize, Casa do Brasil, London, 1971. *Publications:* Illusions of Conflict, 1979; The Cold War, 1989, 2nd edn 1998; Origins of NATO, 1990; Unequal Giants, 1991; The Spanish-American War, 1994; Historical Dictionary of the Cold War, 2000, 2nd edn (with S. Davis), 2017; History of Brazil, 2002; The United States and Latin America, 2005; Historical Dictionary of United States–Latin American Relations, 2007; Brazil and the United States, 2010. *Recreations:* travel, tennis. *Address:* 1 California Close, Exeter, Devon EX4 5ET.

**SMITH, Sir Joseph (William Grenville),** Kt 1991; MD; FRCP; FRCPath; FFPH; Director, Public Health Laboratory Service, 1985–92; *b* 14 Nov. 1930; *s* of Douglas Ralph and Hannah Letitia Margaret Smith; *m* 1954, Nira Jean (*née* Davies); one *s*. *Educ:* Cathays High School, Cardiff; Welsh Nat. Sch. of Medicine (MD 1966); Dip. Bact., London Univ., 1960; FRCPath 1975; FFPH (FFCM 1976); FRCP 1987. FRSB (FIBiol 1978). Lectr, 1960–63, Sen. Lectr, 1963–65, Dept of Bacteriology and Immunology, LSHTM; Consultant Clinical Bacteriologist, Radcliffe Infirmary, Oxford, 1965–69; Gen. Practitioner, Islington, 1970–71; Consultant Epidemiologist, Dep. Dir, Epidemiological Res. Lab., PHLS, 1971–76; Dir, Nat. Inst. for Biological Standards and Control, 1976–85. Consultant on immunisation to British Army, 1985–96. Special Prof., Nottingham Univ., 1989–94. Member: Cttee on Safety of Medicines, 1978–86 (Chm., Biol Sub-Cttee, 1981–86); Jt Cttee on Vaccination and Immunisation, 1976–93 (Chm., Influenza, Measles and Rubella Sub-Cttees, 1979–93); British Pharmacopoeia Commn, 1976–85 (Chm., Immunization Cttee, 1977–85); MRC, 1989–92; Council, RCPath, 1988–90; Adv. Gp on Rabies Quarantine, MAFF, 1997–98; Chairman: Cttee on Vaccination and Immunization Procedures, MRC, 1976–93; Simian Virus Cttee, MRC, 1982–93; Tropical Medicine Res. Bd, MRC, 1989–90; World Health Organisation: Chm., Expert Adv. Gp on Immunization, 1993–95, Chm., Poliomyelitis Commn, 1995–2006, Eur. Reg.; Chm., Global Polio Commn, 2001–03 (Co-Chm., 1998–2001). Mem., Ct of Govs and Bd of Management, LSHTM, 1994–97 (Chm. Bd of Mgt, 1995–97). Hon. DipHIC, LSHTM, 1999. *Publications:* (with E. B. Adams and D. R. Laurence) Tetanus, 1969; papers on tetanus, immunization, and epidemiology of infections in scientific and med. jls. *Recreation:* the arts.

**SMITH, Julia Clare;** *see* Buckingham, J. C.

**SMITH, Prof. Julia Mary Howard,** DPhil; FRSE; Chichele Professor of Medieval History, University of Oxford, since 2016; Fellow, All Souls College, Oxford, since 2016; *b* Cambridge, 29 May 1956; *d* of Geoffrey Howard Smith and Jane Katherine Smith (*née* Clausen); *m* 2005, Hamish Marshall Scott, *qv*. *Educ:* S Hampstead High Sch. GPDST; Newnham Coll., Cambridge (BA Hons 1978); Corpus Christi Coll., Oxford (DPhil 1985). Asst Prof., 1986–90, Associate Prof., 1990–95, Dept of Hist., Trinity Coll., Hartford, Conn; Reader in Medieval Hist., Univ. of St Andrews, 1995–2005; Edwards Prof. of Medieval Hist., Univ. of Glasgow, 2005–16. FRSE 2011. *Publications:* Province and Empire: Brittany and the Carolingians, 1992; Early Medieval Rome and the Christian West, 2000; (ed with L. Brubaker) Gender in the Early Medieval World: East and West, 300–900, 2004; Europe After Rome: a new cultural history 500–1000, 2005 (trans. Serbian, 2006, Italian, 2008, Polish, 2008, Greek, 2009, Turkish, 2014); (ed with T. F. X. Noble) Cambridge History of Christianity, vol. III: Early Medieval Christianities AD 600–1100, 2008; contribs to learned jls incl. Speculum, Trans RHistS, Past and Present, Early Medieval Europe. *Recreations:* classical music, hill-walking, gardening. *Address:* All Souls College, Oxford OX1 4AL.

**SMITH, Rt Hon. Julian,** CBE 2019; PC 2017; MP (C) Skipton and Ripon, since 2010; Secretary of State for Northern Ireland, since 2019; *b* Stirling, 30 Aug. 1971; *m* 2003, Amanda. *Educ:* Balfron Sch.; Millfield Sch.; Univ. of Birmingham (BA Hons English and Hist.). Founder and Man. Dir, Arq Internat., recruitment co., 1999–2010, non-exec. Dir, 2010–12. An Asst Govt Whip, 2015–16; Vice Chamberlain of HM Household (Govt Whip), 2016–17; Treasurer of HM Household (Dep. Chief Whip), 2017; Parly Sec. to the Treasury (Govt Chief Whip), 2017–19. Mem., Cttee of Selection, 2015–17. *Address:* House of Commons, SW1A 0AA.

**SMITH, Sir Julian (Stanley),** KNZM 2013; OBE 1994; Chairman and Managing Director, Allied Press Ltd, since 1986; *b* Dunedin, NZ, 29 Oct. 1943; *s* of Stanley David Smith and Mary Smith; *m* 1972, Beverley Anne Scott; two *s* one *d*. *Educ*: John McGlashan Coll.; Univ. of Otago. Co. Sec., Lovell Reilly Ltd, 1967–70; Gen. Manager and Dir, John M. Fraser and Co. Ltd, 1970–79; Man. Dir, Otago Press and Produce Ltd, 1979–86. Dir, NZ Press Assoc., 1983– (Chm., 1983–90, 2002–06); Mem., Newspaper Publishers' Assoc., 1983– (Pres., 2002–06). Pres., Otago Chamber of Commerce, 1993–94. Chm., Bd of Trustees, John McGlashan Coll., 1996–98. Hon. Col, 4th Otago Southland Bn Gp, 1998–2008. Patron, Otago Aero Club Inc., 2005–. FInstD 2009. *Recreations*: vintage cars, golf, boating. *Address*: Windover, 22 Belmont Lane, Dunedin 9013, New Zealand. *T*: (office) (3) 4793561, *Fax*: (3) 4747420. *E*: jcs@alliedpress.co.nz. *Clubs*: Dunedin, Commerce of Otago (Pres., 1992; Patron, 2010–) (Dunedin); Rolls-Royce Enthusiasts' (UK), Bentley Drivers (UK); Vintage Car of NZ; Waikouaiti Golf.

**SMITH, Julian William; His Honour Judge Julian Smith;** a Circuit Judge, since 2015; *b* Darlington, Co. Durham, 22 May 1968; *s* of Sir Graham William Smith, CBE and Jeanne Lilian Ann Smith; *m* 1995, Louise; two *s* two *d*. *Educ*: Dartford Grammar Sch. LLB. Called to the Bar, Inner Temple, 1991; in practice as barrister, 1991–2015; a Recorder, 2009–15. Hd of Chambers, New Park Court Chambers, Newcastle upon Tyne, 2010–15. *Recreations*: family, music, travel, early morning walks. *Address*: c/o The Law Courts, Barker Road, Maidstone, Kent ME16 8EQ. *T*: (01622) 202000.

**SMITH, Justin D.;** *see* Davis Smith.

**SMITH, Karen Ann;** *see* Mumford, K. A.

**SMITH, Karen Denise;** Managing Director, Tuesday's Child Television, since 2012; *b* 16 June 1970; *d* of Peter A. Smith and Janet E. Smith; partner, Paul R. Jacobs; one *s* one *d* (twins). *Educ*: Univ. of Liverpool (BA Hons English 1991). Producer, presenter, reporter, BBC Radio York, 1992–95; Producer, NMTV, 1996–97; Producer, 1998, Dep. Editor, 1999, Editor, 2000–01, This Morning, Granada Television; Series Producer, Endemol UK, 2002–04; Exec. Producer, Strictly Come Dancing, BBC, 2003–04 (Rose d'Or Award, 2005); Sen. Editor, BBC Entertainment, 2004–06; Creative Hd, BBC Format Entertainment, 2006; Creative Dir, BBC Entertainment, 2007; Jt Man. Dir, Shine TV, 2008–12.

**SMITH, Karen Jane;** *see* Holt, K. J.

**SMITH, Karen Jane W.;** *see* Walden-Smith.

**SMITH, Katherine Emma, (Kassie);** QC 2013; *b* Reading, 25 Nov. 1969; *d* of Keith Edward Smith and Marjorie Patricia, (Paddy), Smith; *m* 2007, Dominic Geer; one *s* one *d*. *Educ*: Sir William Perkins's Sch., Chertsey; Lincoln Coll., Oxford (MA 1991); Corpus Christi Coll., Oxford (BCL 1994). Called to the Bar, Inner Temple, 1995; in practice as a barrister, specialising in competition, regulation, public and EU law, Monckton Chambers, 1995–. *Publications*: (ed jtly) Competition Litigation in the UK, 2005. *Recreations*: family, good food and good wine. *Address*: Monckton Chambers, 1–2 Raymond Buildings, Gray's Inn, WC1R 5NR. *T*: (020) 7405 7211, *Fax*: (020) 7405 2084. *E*: ksmith@monckton.com.

**SMITH, Prof. Kenneth George Campbell,** PhD; FRCP, FRACP, FRCPA, FMedSci; Professor of Medicine and Head of Department of Medicine, University of Cambridge, since 2010 (Genzyme Professor of Experimental Medicine, 2006–10); Fellow, Pembroke College, Cambridge, since 1998 (Director of Studies in Clinical Medicine, 1998–2013); Senior Clinical Fellow, National Institute of Health Research, since 2015; *b* 18 April 1963; *s* of Trevor James Sylvester Smith and Margery Leonie Smith (*née* Campbell); two *s*; one *d*. *Educ*: Bell Post Hill Primary Sch.; Geelong Coll.; Univ. of Melbourne (BMedSc 1985; MB BS 1987; PhD 1996); Pembroke Coll., Cambridge (MA 2000). FRACP 1994; FRCPA 1999; FRCP 2002. Intern, RMO and Med. and Nephrology Registrar, 1988–94; Asst Nephrologist, 1995–96, Royal Melbourne Hosp.; Dir, Studies in Clinical Medicine, and J. Alexander Scott Fellow in Anatomy, Ormond Coll., Univ. of Melbourne, 1992–96; Univ. Lectr, 1996–2004, Reader, 2004–06, in Renal Medicine, Univ. of Cambridge. Hon. Consultant Physician, Addenbrooke's Hosp., Cambridge, 1996–. Khoo Oon Teik Prof. of Nephrology, Univ. of Singapore, 2007–. FHEA (ILTM 2003); FMedSci 2006. Lister Inst. Res. Prize, 2007. *Publications*: articles on immunology and medicine. *Recreations*: Real tennis, reading, natural history. *Address*: Cambridge Institute for Medical Research, Box 139, Addenbrooke's Hospital, Cambridge CB2 0XY. *T*: (01223) 762645, *Fax*: (01223) 762640. *E*: kgcs2@cam.ac.uk. *Clubs*: Melbourne Cricket; Cambridge Real Tennis.

**SMITH, Sir Kevin,** Kt 2007; CBE 1997; FRAeS; Partner, Unitas Capital Pte Ltd, Hong Kong, 2012–15; *b* 22 May 1954. *Educ*: Burnley Coll.; Lancashire Poly. (BA Hons). British Aerospace: Contract Officer, 1980–90; Commercial Dir, 1990–91; Dep. Man. Dir, 1991–93, Man. Dir, 1993–95, Mil. Aircraft Div.; British Aerospace plc: Man. Dir, Business Ops, 1995–98; Dep. Gp Man. Dir, New Business, 1998–99; Man. Dir, GKN Aerospace, 1999–2003; Chief Exec., GKN plc, 2003–11. Non-executive Director: Scottish and Southern Energy plc, 2004–08; Rolls-Royce, 2015– (Sen. Ind. Dir, 2016–). Dir, SBAC, 2003–07 (Pres., 2004–05; Dep. Pres., 2005–07). CCMI. FRAeS 1993.

**SMITH, Kingsley Ward,** OBE 2007; DL; non-executive Chairman, Newcastle Hospitals NHS Foundation Trust (formerly Newcastle Hospitals Foundation Trust), 2007–17; Adviser, NSK (Europe), since 2004; Clerk to the Lieutenancy, since 1990; *b* 24 Oct. 1946; *s* of Peter and Doris Evelyn Smith; *m* 1st, 1968, Kathy Rutherford (marr. diss. 1999); two *s*; 2nd, 2004, Sayoko Barbour. *Educ*: Blue Coat Secondary Sch., Walsall, Staffs; Dame Allan's Boys' Sch., Newcastle upon Tyne. CPFA (IPFA 1970). Trainee Accountant, Gateshead CBC, 1964–67; Durham County Council: Accountant, subseq. Sen. Accountant, 1967–76; Chief Internal Auditor, 1976–79; Sen. Asst County Treasurer, 1979–81; Dep. County Treasurer, 1981–84; County Treasurer, 1984–88; Chief Exec., 1988–2005; Exec. Chm., Co. Durham Develt Co., 2005–07; Interim Chief Exec., Teesdale DC, 2005–06. Non-exec. Dir, Durham Co. Waste Mgt Co., 2005–07; Chm., Time for Success, 2007–09. Mem., LSC, Co. Durham, 2001–05; Chm., Prince's Trust Regl Council, 1999–2005; formerly: founder Mem., Durham TEC; Chairman: ACCE; Fujtsu Response Gp; E Durham Task Force; Co. Durham Connexions Partnership; Co. Durham Youth Offending Service; Mem., Nat. Coalfields Task Force. DL Durham, 2011. *Recreations*: golfing, fishing, walking his labrador (Sam).

**SMITH, Kirstie Louise Stewart-;** *see* Hamilton, K. L.

**SMITH, Laura;** *see* Duncan, A. L. A.

**SMITH, Laura;** MP (Lab) Crewe and Nantwich, since 2017; *b* Crewe; one *s* one *d*. *Educ*: Brine Leas Sch., Nantwich; S Cheshire Coll.; Manchester Metropolitan Univ. Primary sch. teacher, until 2013. Founder, One to One Tutoring, 2013. Shadow Minister for the Cabinet Office, 2018. Mem., Transport Cttee, H of C, 2017–18. *Address*: House of Commons, SW1A 0AA.

**SMITH, Lauren Mary S.;** *see* Seager-Smith.

**SMITH, Lawrence Edward;** yachting consultant, since 1971; *b* 19 Feb. 1956; *s* of Harold and Jean Smith; *m* 1991, Penny Jane Smith (*née* Haydock); two *s* two *d* (of whom one *s* one *d* are twins). *Educ*: Bury Grammar Sch. America's Cup: Skipper, British challenger, Lionheart, 1980, Victory, 1983. Winning skipper: Fastnet Race, 1985; Admiral's Cup, 1989. Whitbread Round the World Race: Skipper, Rothmans, 1990 (4th), Intrum Justitia, 1994 (2nd), Silk Cut, 1997–98 (5th). Skipper, UK crew, Soling class, Olympic Games, 1988, 1992 (Bronze medal). Dragon Class World Champion, 2011. *Publications*: Dinghy Helming, 1985; Dinghy Tuning, 1986; Yacht Tuning, 1987; Science of Speed, 1994. *Recreations*: golf, tennis.

**SMITH, Lawrence Roger Hines,** FSA; Keeper of Japanese Antiquities, 1987–97, and Senior Keeper, 1995–97, British Museum, now Keeper Emeritus; *b* 19 Feb. 1941; *s* of Frank Ernest Smith and Eva Lilian Smith (*née* Hines); *m* 1st, 1965, Louise Geraldine Gallini (marr. diss. 1986); one *s* five *d*; 2nd, 1993, Louise Elaine Woodroff (*d* 2016); one *d*. *Educ*: Collyer's Grammar Sch., Horsham; Queens' Coll., Cambridge (Foundn Schol.; BA). British Museum: Asst Keeper, Dept of Manuscripts, 1962; Dept of Oriental Antiquities, 1965; Dep. Keeper, 1976; Keeper, 1977. British Acad. Exchange Fellow, Nihon Gakujutsu Shinkōkai, Kyoto, 1974–75. Academic adviser, Great Japan Exhibn, RA, 1981–82, and contrib. to catalogue. Mem. (Lib Dem), Broadland DC, 2003–07. Uchiyama Prize, Ukiyoe Soc. of Japan, 1986. *Publications*: Netsuke: the miniature sculpture of Japan (with R. Barker), 1976; Flowers in Art from East and West (with P. Hulton), 1979; Japanese Prints: 300 years of albums and books (with J. Hillier), 1980; Japanese Decorative Arts 1600–1900 (with V. Harris), 1982; The Japanese Print since 1900, 1983; Contemporary Japanese Prints, 1985; (ed) Ukiyoe: images of unknown Japan, 1988; (ed) Japanese Art: masterpieces in the British Museum, 1990; Nihonga: traditional Japanese painting, 1991; Japanese Prints 1912–1989: woodblocks and stencils, 1994; Japanese Prints during the Allied Occupation 1945–52, 2002; contribs to BM multi-cultural catalogues; articles and reviews in learned jls; conference and symposium papers. *Recreations*: walking, running, bellringing, music, wine. *Address*: 15 Repton Close, Aylsham, Norfolk NR11 6JE. *T*: (01263) 734499. *E*: lrhsumisu@paston.co.uk.

**SMITH, Leonard Wayne,** QC 2008; *b* Sydney, Australia, 21 July 1959; *s* of Leonard Bryan Smith and Beatrice Wendy Smith (*née* Bawden); *m* 1984, Anne Terese Walker; two *s* one *d*. *Educ*: Univ. of Sydney (BA, LLM). Called to the Bar: NSW, 1986; Australia, 1987; Gray's Inn, 1991; in practice as barrister specialising in corporate and regulatory crime, serious fraud and general criminal law. *Recreations*: golf, cricket, reading, travelling on Swiss railways. *Address*: Carmelite Chambers, 9 Carmelite Street, EC4Y 0DR. *Clubs*: Kibworth Golf (Kibworth Beauchamp); Luffenham Heath Golf.

**SMITH, Prof. Lewis Lauchlan,** PhD; FRCPath; FBTS; Interim Director, Centre for Translational Therapeutics, University of Leicester, 2009–12; *b* 21 Aug. 1947; *s* of Lewis Smith and Margaret (*née* Wilson); *m* 1972, Susan Lisbeth Baynes; one *s* one *d*. *Educ*: Hatfield Poly. (BSc, PhD). MRCPath 1990, FRCPath 1997. ICI Central Toxicology Laboratory: Res. Scientist, 1971–80; Sen. Scientist, 1980–85; Hd, Biochem. Toxicology Sect., 1985–91; Dir, Toxicology Unit, 1991–98, and Inst. for Envmt and Health, 1993–98, MRC; Dir, Syngenta (formerly Zeneca) Central Toxicology Lab., 1998–2002; Hd of Develt, Syngenta Crop Protection AG, Basel, Switzerland, 2002–09. *Publications*: numerous in res. jls on mechanisms of toxicity and cellular biochem. *Recreations*: golf, eating, dieting. *E*: lls10@leicester.ac.uk.

**SMITH, Lewis S.;** *see* Shand Smith.

**SMITH, Llewellyn Thomas;** *b* 16 April 1944; *m* 1969, Pamela Williams (*d* 2008); two *s* one *d*. *Educ*: Cardiff University. Formerly with Pilkington Glass, George Wimpey and Workers' Educational Assoc. MEP (Lab) SE Wales, 1984–94; MP (Lab) Blaenau Gwent, 1992–2005. Mem., CND. *Address*: The Mount, Uplands, Tynewydd, Newbridge NP11 3RH.

**SMITH, Lloyd Barnaby, (Barney),** CMG 2002; HM Diplomatic Service, retired; Director, Greenbarrel, since 2011; *b* 21 July 1945; *s* of Arthur and Zena Smith; *m* 1st, 1972, Nicola Mary Whitehead (marr. diss.); 2nd, 1983, Elizabeth Mary Sumner; one *s* one *d*. *Educ*: Merchant Taylors' Sch., Moor Park; Brasenose Coll., Oxford (MA). Joined Diplomatic Service, 1968; Third, later Second Sec., Bangkok, 1970–74; First Secretary: FCO, 1974–77; Paris, 1977–78; Head of Chancery, Dublin, 1978–81; Ecole Nat. d'Admin, Paris, 1981–82; First Sec., then Counsellor, UK Repn to EEC, Brussels, 1982–86; Counsellor, Bangkok, 1987–90; Dir, Know How Fund for Eastern Europe, 1990–92; Head, S Asia Dept, FCO, 1993–95; Ambassador: to Nepal, 1995–99; to Thailand, also accredited to Laos, 2000–03. Non-exec. Dir, 2006–14, Chm., 2011–14, Coastal Energy Co. Ltd. Editor, Asian Affairs, 2005–14. *Recreation*: sailing.

**SMITH, Rt Hon. Sir Lockwood;** *see* Smith, Rt Hon. Sir A. L.

**SMITH, Prof. Lorraine Nancy,** PhD; Professor of Nursing, University of Glasgow, 1990–2012, now Emeritus (Head, Nursing and Midwifery School, 1999–2001; Head of Department, 1990–99); *b* 29 June 1949; *d* of Geoffrey Leonard Millington and Ida May (*née* Attfield); *m* 1975, Christopher Murray Smith; one *s* one *d*. *Educ*: Univ. of Ottawa (BScN); Univ. of Manchester (MEd, PhD). Staff Nurse, Ottawa, 1971–73; Team Leader, Montreal, 1973–76; Sister, Withington Hosp., Manchester, 1976–77; Lectr, Dept of Nursing Studies, Univ. of Manchester, 1977–90. Member: Clin. Standards Adv. Gp (UK); Standards Cttee, Nat. Bd for Scotland, 1997–2000; RCN UK Rep., Work Gp, Eur. Nurse Researchers, 1999–2008 (Chm., 2005–08); Mem. Bd, RCN Scotland, 2009–10. Chair: RCN Res. Soc. Scotland, 1999–2005; Sign Guideline 120, 2008–10. *Publications*: articles in Advanced Jl of Nursing, Clinical Rehabilitation, BMJ, Cerebrovascular Diseases. *Recreations*: ski-ing, sailing, reading, bridge. *Address*: Nursing & Health Care School, University of Glasgow, 61 Oakfield Avenue, Glasgow G12 8LP. *T*: (0141) 330 5498. *Clubs*: S Caernarvonshire Yacht, Abersoch Golf (Abersoch, N Wales).

**SMITH, Dame Maggie, (Dame Margaret Natalie Cross),** CH 2014; DBE 1990 (CBE 1970); actress; *b* 28 Dec. 1934; *d* of Nathaniel Smith and Margaret Little (*née* Hutton); *m* 1st, 1967, Robert Graham Stephens (later Sir Robert Stephens) (marr. diss. 1975; he *d* 1995); two *s*; 2nd, 1975, Beverley Cross (*d* 1998). *Educ*: Oxford High School for Girls. Studied at Oxford Playhouse School under Isabel van Beers. First appearance, June 1952, as Viola in OUDS Twelfth Night; 1st New York appearance, Ethel Barrymore Theatre, June 1956, as comedienne in New Faces. Played in Share My Lettuce, Lyric, Hammersmith, 1957; The Stepmother, St Martin's, 1958. Old Vic Co., 1959–60 season: The Double Dealer; As You Like It; Richard II; The Merry Wives of Windsor; What Every Woman Knows; Rhinoceros, Strand, 1960; Strip the Willow, Cambridge, 1960; The Rehearsal, Globe, 1961; The Private Ear and The Public Eye (Evening Standard Drama Award, best actress of 1962), Globe, 1962; Mary, Mary, Queen's, 1963 (Variety Club of Gt Britain, best actress of the year); The Country Wife, Chichester, 1969; Design for Living, LA, 1971; Private Lives, Queen's, 1972, Globe, 1973, NY, 1975 (Variety Club of GB Stage Actress Award, 1972); Peter Pan, Coliseum, 1973; Snap, Vaudeville, 1974; Night and Day, Phoenix, 1979; Virginia, Haymarket, 1981 (Standard Best Actress Award, 1982); The Way of the World, Chichester and Haymarket, 1984 (Standard Best Actress Award, 1985);

Interpreters, Queen's, 1985; Lettice and Lovage, Globe, 1987, NY, 1990 (Tony Award, best leading actress, 1990); The Importance of Being Earnest, Aldwych, 1993; Three Tall Women, Wyndham's, 1994, 1995; Talking Heads, Chichester, 1996, Comedy Theatre, 1997, Australian tour, 2004; A Delicate Balance, Haymarket, 1997; Lady in the Van, Queen's, 1999; The Breath of Life, Haymarket, 2002; The Lady from Dubuque, Haymarket, 2007; A German Life, Bridge Th., 2019; *at National Theatre:* The Recruiting Officer, 1963; Othello, The Master Builder, Hay Fever, 1964; Much Ado About Nothing, Miss Julie, 1965; A Bond Honoured, 1966; The Beaux' Stratagem, 1970 (also USA); Hedda Gabler, 1970 (Evening Standard Best Actress award); War Plays, 1985; Coming in to Land, 1986; *at Festival Theatre, Stratford, Ontario:* 1976: Antony and Cleopatra, The Way of the World, Measure for Measure, The Three Sisters; 1977: Midsummer Night's Dream, Richard III, The Guardsman, As You Like It, Hay Fever; 1978: As You Like It, Macbeth, Private Lives; 1980: Virginia; Much Ado About Nothing. *Films:* The VIP's, 1963; The Pumpkin Eater, 1964; Young Cassidy, 1965; Othello, 1966; The Honey Pot, 1967; Hot Millions (Variety Club of GB Award), The Prime of Miss Jean Brodie (Oscar; SFTA award), Oh! What a Lovely War, 1968; Love and Pain (and the Whole Damned Thing), Travels with my Aunt, 1973; Murder by Death, 1976; California Suite, 1977 (Oscar); Death on the Nile, 1978; Quartet, Clash of the Titans, 1981; Evil Under the Sun, The Missionary, 1982; A Private Function, 1984 (BAFTA award, Best Actress, 1985); The Loves of Lily, 1985; A Room with a View, 1986 (Variety Club of GB Award; BAFTA award, Best Actress, 1986); The Lonely Passion of Judith Hearn, 1989 (Evening Standard British Films Award, 1988, and Best Film Actress BAFTA Award, 1988); Hook, Sister Act, 1992; The Secret Garden, 1993; Sister Act II, 1994; Richard III, The First Wives Club, 1996; Washington Square, 1998; Tea with Mussolini, 1999 (Best Supporting Actress, BAFTA, 2000); The Last September, 2000; Harry Potter and the Philosopher's Stone, 2001; Gosford Park, Divine Secrets of the Ya-Ya Sisterhood, Harry Potter and the Chamber of Secrets, 2002; Harry Potter and the Prisoner of Azkaban, Ladies in Lavender, 2004; Harry Potter and the Goblet of Fire, Keeping Mum, 2005; Becoming Jane, Harry Potter and the Order of the Phoenix, 2007; Harry Potter and the Half-Blood Prince, 2009; Nanny McPhee and the Big Bang, From Time to Time, Harry Potter and the Deathly Hallows, Part 1, 2010, Part 2, 2011; The Best Exotic Marigold Hotel, Quartet, 2012; My Old Lady, 2014; The Second Best Exotic Marigold Hotel, The Lady in the Van, 2015 (Evening Standard Best Actress Award, 2016); Nothing Like a Dame, 2018; Downton Abbey, 2019; *television:* Talking Heads: Bed Among the Lentils, 1989 (RTS Award); Memento Mori, 1992; Suddenly Last Summer, 1993; All The King's Men, 1999; David Copperfield, 1999; My House in Umbria, 2003 (Emmy Award for Best Actress); Capturing Mary, 2007; Downton Abbey, 2010, 2011, 2012, 2013, 2014, 2015 (Best Supporting Actress, Emmy Award, 2011 and 2012, Golden Globe Awards, 2012, Best Actress in a Drama Series, Screen Actors Guild Awards, 2014). Fellow: BFI; BAFTA. Hon. DLitt: St Andrews, 1971; Cambridge, 1995. Hanbury Shakespeare Prize, 1991. *Recreation:* reading. *Address:* c/o Independent Talent Agency Ltd, 40 Whitfield Street, W1T 2RH.
*See also* T. Stephens.

**SMITH, Hon. Sir Marcus (Alexander),** Kt 2017; **Hon. Mr Justice Marcus Smith;** a Judge of the High Court, Chancery Division, since 2017; *b* 1 July 1967; *s* of Ronald Smith and Hannelore Smith; *m* 1998, Louise Merrett; one *s* one *d*. *Educ:* Balliol Coll., Oxford (BA 1988; BCL 1990; MA 1992); Univ. of Munich. Called to the Bar, Lincoln's Inn, 1991; in practice as barrister, specialising in commercial and regulatory law, 1991–2017; QC 2010; pt-time Chm., Competition Appeal Tribunal, 2009. Chm., Appeals Cttee, HFEA, 2015–17. Lectr in Law, Balliol Coll., 1991–94. *Publications:* Private International Law of Reinsurance and Insurance, 2006; The Law of Assignment, 2007, 3rd edn 2018. *Recreations:* Norfolk, writing. *Address:* Royal Courts of Justice, Rolls Building, Fetter Lane, EC4A 1NL.

**SMITH, Margaret Elizabeth;** Lord Provost and Lord-Lieutenant of Aberdeen City, 1999–2003; *b* 10 Aug. 1931. *Educ:* Twickenham Grammar Sch.; Southport High Sch. for Girls; Lady Mabel Coll., Rotherham (DipPE 1953). Physical Education Teacher: Fleetwood Grammar Sch., 1953–58; Blairgowrie High Sch., 1958–67; Youth Officer, Chichester CC, 1967–73; Neighbourhood Worker, Easterhouse, Glasgow, 1973–78; Housing Worker, Scottish Special Housing Assoc., Glasgow, 1978–81; Community Educn Area Officer, Grampian Regl Council, 1981–91. Aberdeen District, now City, Council: Mem. (Lab), 1988–2003; Leader of Council, 1996–99; Mem., Drug Strategy Task Gp, 1996–99; Chair, Community Planning Core Gp; COSLA Rep., 1997–99; Convenor, Women's and Equal Opportunities Cttee, 1992–96. Lord High Adm., Northern Seas, 1999–2003; Vice Adm., Coast of GB and Ireland, 1999–2003. President: World Energy Cities Partnership, 2000–02; Voluntary Service, Aberdeen, 1999–2003; Aberdeen Br., RNLI, 1999–2003; Comr, Northern Lighthouse Bd, 1999–2003; Chair: Froghall Community Project, 1995–99; Aberdeen Alternative Fest. Trust, 1999–2001; Member: Sunnybank Community Educn Mgt Cttee, 1988–2003; NE Scotland Econ. Develt Partnership, 1997–99; Aberdeen Gomel Trust, 1999–2003; Aberdeen Safer Communities Trust, 1999–2003; Aberdeen Bulawayo Trust, 1999–2003; Patron: Mental Health, Aberdeen, 1999; Aberdeen Internat. Youth Fest., 1999. Hon. DL: Robert Gordon, Aberdeen, 1999; Aberdeen, 2004. *Recreations:* walking, theatre and concerts, family and friends, learning Russian, Aberdeen FC. *Address:* 49 Froghall Terrace, Aberdeen AB24 3JP.

**SMITH, Margaret Joy;** Director, Caledonia Public Affairs, since 2012; *b* 18 Feb. 1961; *d* of late John Murray and of Anna Murray; *m* 1983, Douglas Robert Smith (marr. diss. 2004); one *s* one *d*; civil partnership 2006, Suzanne Main; three step *s*. *Educ:* Edinburgh Univ. (MA Gen. Arts). Pensions Administrator, Guardian Royal Exchange Assurance, 1982–83; Civil Servant (EO), Registers of Scotland, 1983–88; tour guide and freelance journalist, 1988–90; Scottish Officer, UNA, 1990–96; Political Organiser, Edinburgh W Liberal Democrats, 1996–97. Mem. Edinburgh CC, 1995–99. Mem. (Lib Dem) Edinburgh W, Scottish Parlt, 1999–2011; contested (Lib Dem) same seat, 2011. Scottish Parliament: Convenor, Health and Community Care Cttee, 1999–2003; Lib Dem spokesperson on justice, 2003–05, on transport and local govt, 2005; Chief Whip (Lib Dem), 2005–07; Lib Dem Shadow Cabinet Sec. for Justice, 2007–11. *Recreations:* golf, reading. *Club:* Ravelston Golf (Edinburgh).

**SMITH, Margaret Osborne B.;** *see* Bickford Smith.

**SMITH, (Maria) Geraldine;** *b* 29 Aug. 1961; *d* of John and Ann Smith. *Educ:* Morecambe Bay Primary Sch.; Morecambe High Sch. Postal Administrator, Royal Mail, 1980–97. MP (Lab) Morecambe and Lunesdale, 1997–2010; contested (Lab) same seat, 2010. *Recreations:* chess, walking.

**SMITH, Marion Helen;** QC 2015; *b* Isleworth, 24 Dec. 1956; *d* of Arthur Owen Smith and Isabel Mary Smith (*née* Wiseman); *m* 1980, Alex Macgregor Mason; two *d*. *Educ:* Howell's Sch., Llandaff, Cardiff; Queen Mary Coll., Univ. of London (LLB); London Sch. of Econs and Pol Sci. (LLM). Called to the Bar, Gray's Inn, 1981; in practice as barrister, 1981–. Trustee, CIArb, 2017–. *Recreations:* theatre, travel, reading. *Address:* 39 Essex Chambers, 81 Chancery Lane, WC2A 1DD. *T:* (020) 7832 1111. *E:* marion.smithqc@39essex.com.

**SMITH, Marion Wallace,** RSA 2005; sculptor; Secretary, Royal Scottish Academy, 2012–18; *b* St Andrews, 14 Feb. 1969; *d* of Alistair Wallace Smith and Patricia Christian Hall Smith (*née* Bodie). *Educ:* Gray's Sch. of Art, Aberdeen (BA Hons Fine Art 1991). ARSA 1998. Artist/technician, Scottish Sculpture Workshop, Aberdeenshire, 1994–96; Workshop Manager, Glasgow Sculpture Studios, 1996–98; Gall. Manager, Crawford Arts Centre, St Andrews, 1998; fine art technician, Glasgow Sch. of Art, 1999–2004. Has exhibited in UK, Scandinavia, France and Japan; *solo exhibitions* include: Crawford Arts Centre, St Andrews, 1997; Bonhoga Gall., Shetland, 2004; Patriothall Gall., Edinburgh, 2005; Park Gall., Falkirk, 2009; *group exhibitions* include: Sculptors' Prints, 2013, Scottish Drawings, 2015, RSA; Ages of Wonder, 2017; *commissions:* first granite commn, Brittany, 2002; throughout UK, including: Fire Ball, Linlithgow, 2007; The Plough and the Reaper, Anstruther, 2009; Panmure Passage, Dundee, 2009; HMT Lancastria Meml, Clydebank, 2011; Loch Leven, Kinross-shire, 2014; Milestones, Irvine, 2016; Kirkintilloch Gateway Markers, 2017. *Recreations:* exploring landscapes, social history, cooking, gardening. *Address:* Royal Scottish Academy, The Mound, Edinburgh EH2 2EL. *T:* (0131) 225 6671. *E:* info@royalscottishacademy.org.

**SMITH, Prof. Mark Edmund,** CBE 2019; PhD; FInstP; President and Vice-Chancellor, University of Southampton, since 2019. *Educ:* Churchill Coll., Cambridge (BA Natural Scis 1984); Univ. of Warwick (PhD). Application scientist, Bruker Analytische Messtechnik, Germany, 1989–90; Res. Scientist, CSIRO, Australia, 1991–92; Lectr, then Reader, Univ. of Kent, 1992–98; University of Warwick: Reader, 1998–2002; Prof. of Physics, 2002–11; Chair, Faculty of Sci., 2005–07; Pro-Vice-Chancellor for Res., 2007–10; Dep. Vice-Chancellor, 2010–12; Vice-Chancellor, Lancaster Univ., 2012–19. Member: HEFCW, 2013–15; UKRI-EPSRC (formerly EPSRC), 2017–. Member, Board: UK Research Reserve; HESA, 2012–; Jisc, 2014–; Chair, UCEA, 2016–. Mem., Ampère Prize Cttee, French Acad. Scis. *Publications:* contribs to jls incl. Jl Amer. Chem. Soc., Applied Magnetic Resonance, Jl Magnetic Resonance, Jl Materials Chem., Chem. Materials, Jl Materials Res. *Address:* University of Southampton, Highfield Campus, University Road, Southampton SO17 1BJ.

**SMITH, Mark Gordon M.;** *see* Milliken-Smith.

**SMITH, Sir Martin (Gregory),** Kt 2013; entrepreneur and philanthropist; *b* 2 Feb. 1943; *s* of late Archibald Gregory Smith, OBE, and Mary Eleanor Smith (*née* Malone); *m* 1971, Elise Barr Becket (OBE 2015); one *s* one *d*. *Educ:* St Albans Sch.; St Edmund Hall, Oxford (BA, MA); Stanford Univ., Calif (MBA, AM Econ). Brewer, A. Guinness Son & Co. (Dublin) Ltd, 1964–69; McKinsey & Co. Inc., 1971–73; Dir, Citicorp Internat. Bank Ltd, 1974–80; Chm., Bankers Trust Internat., 1980–83; Co-founder, Phoenix Securities, 1983–97; Chairman: Phoenix Partnership, 1990–97; Phoenix Fund Managers, 1990–97; Eur. Investment Banking, Donaldson, Lufkin & Jenrette, 1997–2000; Amerindo Internet Fund PLC, 2000–06; GP Bullhound, 2005–; Worldwide Healthcare Trust PLC (formerly Finsbury Worldwide Pharmaceutical Ltd), 2008–; Founding Partner, Beaumont Partners LLP, 2009–16; Director: New Star Asset Management, 2000–09; Phoenix Equity Partners, 2000–06; Odgers, Ray & Berndtson, 2001–09; Oxford Capital Partners, 2010–; Energy Works plc, 2014–17; Sen. Advr, Bain Capital, 2001–09; Mem., Adv. Bd, IDDAS Ltd, 2005–08; Chm., Adv. Bd, Episode 1 LLP, 2013–15. Chairman: Bath Mozartfest, 2000–09; ENO, 2001–05; Orchestra of Age of Enlightenment, 2011– (Mem. Bd, 1985–). Deputy Chairman: South Bank Centre, 1992–97; Science Mus., 1999–2009; Trustee: IMS Prussia Cove, 1999–; Becket Collection, 1999–2014; Wigmore Hall, 2000–14; Tetbury Music Fest., 2006–; ClientEarth, 2016–; Dir, Glyndebourne Arts Trust, 2007–. Mem., Science Mus. Foundn, 2012–18. Visitor, Ashmolean Museum, 2006–14. Governor: RAM, 2006–16; Ditchley Foundn, 2013–. Mem., Prince's Council of Charities, 2009–10. Founder, Smith Sch. of Enterprise and the Envmt, Oxford Univ., 2007; Mem., Chancellor's Ct of Benefactors, Oxford Univ., 2009–. Liveryman, Co. of Musicians, 2000–. St Edmund Fellow, St Edmund Hall, Oxford, 2001. FRGS 2015. Hon. FRAM 2003; Hon. Fellow, Science Mus., 2009. Hon. DPhil Glos, 2017. *Recreations:* music, conducting, riding, ski-ing, golf, sailing, Real tennis. *Clubs:* Brooks's, Garrick, MCC; Eastward Ho! (USA); Huntercombe Golf; Minchinhampton Golf.

**SMITH, Maj. Gen. Martin Linn,** CB 2017; MBE 1998; Adviser to Ministry of the Interior, Afghanistan, 2016–17; Operations Director, Cyber Prism Maritime Ltd; *b* Pembury, Kent, 30 July 1962; *s* of Edward Linn Smith and Joanne Smith (*née* Liddell); *m* 1997, Susan Jane Robinson. *Educ:* Sevenoaks Sch., Univ. of Bristol (BSc Zoology). Joined Royal Marines, 1984; CO, 30 Cdo Information Exploitation Gp, 2003–05; Dep. Comdr, 2008–10, Comdr, 2011–13, 3 Cdo Bde; HCSC 2010; rcds 2013–14; Comdt Gen. RM and Comr UK Amphibious Forces, 2014–16. *Recreations:* mountaineering, sea kayaking, sailing.

**SMITH, Canon Maurice John,** CB 2007; Diocesan Director of Education, Church of England Manchester Diocese, since 2007; *b* 16 March 1955; *s* of George and Edna Smith; *m* 1980, Alison Mary Jones; two *s*. *Educ:* Quarry Bank Comp. Sch.; Univ. of Wales (BA Hons 1976); Univ. of Manchester (MA Econ 1983); Univ. of Central Lancashire (MBA Dist. 1991); Manchester Metropolitan Univ. (MRes (Educn and Soc.) 2007). Office for Standards in Education: HMI, 1996–2002; Dir, Early Years, 2002–06; HM Chief Inspector, 2006. Hon. Lay Canon, Manchester Cathedral, 2012. Pres., Bangor Old Stars on Merseyside, 1982–. *Recreation:* wandering around my garden in the evening, saying my prayers and contemplating the meaning of life. *Address:* Church of England Manchester Diocese, Church House, 90 Deansgate, Manchester M3 2GH.

**SMITH, Most Rev. Michael;** *see* Meath, Bishop of, (RC).

**SMITH, Michael A.;** *see* Acton Smith.

**SMITH, Michael Anthony;** Comment Editor, The Times, since 2014; *b* Bristol, 9 March 1968; *s* of Patrick and Frances Smith; *m* 2004, Charlotte Smith; one *s* one *d*. *Educ:* King Edward's Sch., Bath; Univ. of York (BA Hons). Reporter: Western Gazette, 1992–93; The People, 1993–95; Asst News Ed., 1995–97, Associate News Ed., 1997–99, Daily Mail; Asst Ed., 1999–2001, Dep. Ed., 2001–02, Metro; Exec. News Ed., Evening Standard, 2002–04; News Ed., 2005–06, Foreign Ed., 2006–08, Internat. Comment Ed., 2008, Daily Telegraph; Dep. Home Ed., 2009–11, Home Ed., 2011–12, Hd of News, 2012–14, The Times. *Recreation:* bagging Betty's in North Yorkshire. *Address:* The Times, 1 London Bridge Street, SE1 9GF. *T:* (020) 7782 5999. *E:* mike.smith@thetimes.co.uk. *Clubs:* Garrick; Lyke Wake Walk; Godfrey Evans Cricket.

**SMITH, Michael Forbes;** Director General, Chartered Institute of Arbitrators, 2006–12; Founding Director, The Tempered and True Consultancy (diplomacy skills, international briefing), 2004–06; *b* 4 June 1948; *s* of Forbes Weir Smith and Elizabeth Smith (*née* Mackie); *m* 1st, 1974, Christian Joanna Kersley (marr. diss. 1983, annulled 1986); one *d*; 2nd, 1986, Claire Helen Stubbs (*see* C. H. Smith); one *s* one *d*. *Educ:* Aberdeen Grammar Sch.; Southampton Univ. (BSc Hons Geog.); Heythrop Coll., London Univ. (MA Christianity and Interreligious Relns 2013). BoT, 1966–68; commnd Gordon Highlanders, 1971, retd as Captain, 1978. HM Diplomatic Service, 1978–2004: Second Sec., FCO, 1978–79; Second, later First, Sec. and Hd of Chancery, Addis Ababa, 1979–83; Pol Advr to Civil Comr, later Gov., Falkland Is, Port Stanley, 1983–85; First Sec., FCO (SE Asia Dept, later

FO Spokesman), 1985–89; Consul (Commercial), Zürich, 1990–94; Hd, Press and Public Affairs, Bonn, 1994–99; Dep. High Comr, Islamabad, 1999–2002; Ambassador to Republic of Tajikistan, 2002–04. Advr, Gulf Internat. Minerals Ltd, 2004–06. Non-exec. Dir, IDRS Ltd, 2007–11; Chm., City Disputes Panel Ltd, 2011–12 (non-exec. Dir, 2007–11). FRGS 1971; FRSA 1991; FSAScot 1995; MCIArb 2007; Accredited Mediator 2007; Dip. IoD, 2010. Mem., Appeal Cttee and Church Council, Farm St Ch, Mayfair, 1986–90; Vice-Pres., St Thomas More Parish Council, Bonn, 1996–99. Chm., Bonn Caledonian Soc., 1995–99; Mem., Northern Meeting, 2008–. Pres., St Francis Leprosy Guild, 2015– (Vice Pres., 2014–15). Mem., Highland Soc. of London, 2010–. *Publications:* contributor: Diplomacy in the 21st Century series, 2006, Diplomatic Acad. of London; Piping Times; Arbitration. *Recreations:* music, Scotland, Yachtmaster offshore, field and winter sports, entertaining and conviviality. *Clubs:* Army and Navy, Little Ship (Cdre, 2015–17); Itchenor Sailing.

**SMITH, Michael Gerard A.;** *see* Austin-Smith.

**SMITH, Michael John W.;** *see* Winkworth-Smith.

**SMITH, Michael Lynas,** OBE; Chief Executive, Livability, 2010–12; *b* Bolton, 22 April 1946; *s* of Alfred Smith and Ruby Smith; *m* 1970, Lynda Veronica; one *s* one *d*. *Educ:* Bedford Modern Sch.; Open Univ. (BA 1980); Camberley Staff Coll.; Royal Mil. Coll. of Sci. (MSc 1995); Exeter (Mktg 1996). MCIPD 1980. Served RAF; Chief Executive: St Loye's Foundn, 1994–96; Enham, 1996–2010. Non-executive Member of Board: Royal Devon and Exeter, 1995–96; North and Mid Hampshire HA, 1996–99; Hampshire and IoW Strategic HA, 1999–2006; Hampshire Partnership NHS Foundn Trust, 2007–10; R2M Ltd, 2006–10. *Recreations:* running, rugger, antique clocks. *Club:* Royal Air Force.

**SMITH, Prof. (Murdo) Alasdair (Macdonald);** DL; DPhil; Professor of Economics, 1981–2012, now Emeritus, and Vice-Chancellor, 1998–2007, University of Sussex; Member, Scottish Fiscal Commission, since 2017; *b* 9 Feb. 1949; *s* of late John Smith and Isabella Smith (*née* Mackenzie); *m* Sherry Ferdman; two *d*. *Educ:* Nicolson Inst., Stornoway; Univ. of Glasgow (MA 1969); London Sch. of Econs (MSc 1970); DPhil Oxford 1973. Lecturer: University Coll., Oxford, 1970–72; LSE, 1972–81. Vis. Prof. of Econs, Coll. of Europe, 1991–98. Chm., Armed Forces Pay Review Body, 2010–13; Dep. Chm., Competition Commn, 2012–14; Panel Dep. Chm., then Inquiry Chair, CMA, 2014–17. Sen. Advr, Payment Systems Regulator, 2018–. DL E Sussex, 2001. Hon. DSc(Econ) Warsaw, 2004; Hon. LLD Sussex, 2008. *Publications:* A Mathematical Introduction to Economics, 1982; (ed with P. Krugman) Empirical Studies of Strategic Trade Policy, 1994; articles on international economics in learned jls. *Recreations:* walking, gardening, cooking, twittering @AlasdairMSmith. *Address:* 11 Gundreda Road, Lewes BN7 1PT. *T:* (01273) 472940. *E:* alasdair@sussex.ac.uk.

**SMITH, Neil;** *see* Smith, G. N.

**SMITH, Prof. Neilson Voyne,** FBA 1999; Professor of Linguistics, University College London, 1982–2006, now Emeritus; *b* 23 June 1939; *s* of Voyne Smith and Lilian Freda Smith (*née* Rose); *m* 1966, Saraswati Keskar (*d* 2018); two *s*. *Educ:* Trinity College, Cambridge (BA 1961, MA 1964); UCL (PhD 1964). Lectr in W African Languages, SOAS, 1964–70; Harkness Fellow, MIT and UCLA, 1966–68; Lectr in Linguistics and W African Languages, SOAS, 1970–72; University College London: Reader in Linguistics, 1972–81; Hd, Dept of Phonetics and Linguistics, 1983–90; Vice-Dean, 1992–94. Pres., Assoc. of Heads and Profs of Linguistics, 1993–94. Chm., Linguistics Assoc., 1980–86. Hon. Mem., Linguistic Soc. of America, 1999. *Publications:* An Outline Grammar of Nupe, 1967; The Acquisition of Phonology, 1973; (with Deirdre Wilson) Modern Linguistics, 1979; (ed) Mutual Knowledge, 1982; Speculative Linguistics, 1983; The Twitter Machine, 1989; (with Ianthi Tsimpli) The Mind of a Savant, 1995; Chomsky: ideas and ideals, 1999, 3rd edn (with N. Allott) 2016; Language, Bananas and Bonobos, 2002; Language, Frogs and Savants, 2005; Acquiring Phonology: a cross-generational case-study, 2010; (jtly) The Signs of a Savant: language against the odds, 2011; (ed jtly) The Responsibility of Intellectuals: reflections by Noam Chomsky and others after 50 years, 2019; articles in learned jls. *Recreations:* music, travel, writing. *Address:* 32 Long Buftlers, Harpenden, Herts AL5 1JE; Department of Linguistics, University College London, Chandler House, Wakefield Street, WC1N 1PF. *T:* (020) 7580 5928. *E:* smithnv@gmail.com.

**SMITH, Nicholas Desmond John;** MP (Lab) Blaenau Gwent, since 2010; *b* Cardiff, 14 Jan. 1960; *s* of William Thomas Smith and Alma Anne Smith; *m* (marr. diss.); two *d*; *m* 2014, Jennifer Chapman, *qv*. *Educ:* Coventry Univ. (BA Hist., Pols and Internat. Relns 1981); Birkbeck Coll., London (MSc Econ. and Social Change 1991). Constituency Organiser to Frank Dobson, MP, 1989–91; Organiser, Wales Labour Party, 1991–93; Hd, Membership Develt, Labour Party, 1993–98; consultant on internat. campaigning, 1998–2000; Campaign Manager, Public Policy, NSPCC, 2000–04; Sec. Gen., Eur. Parly Labour Party, 2005–06; Dir, Policy and Partnerships, Royal Coll. of Speech and Lang. Therapists, 2006–10. PPS to Shadow Work and Pensions Sec., 2010–11, to Shadow Foreign Sec., 2011–15; Shadow Minister for Food, Farming and Rural Affairs, 2015–16; an Opposition Whip, 2016–. Mem., Public Accounts Cttee, 2010–15. Pres., Ebbw Valley Brass. Member: Aneurin Bevan Soc.; Fabian Soc. FRGS. *Recreations:* hiking, running (Mem., Parc Bryn Bach Running Club; completed London Marathon, 2018), reading, Scrabble. *Address:* House of Commons, SW1A 0AA. *T:* (020) 7219 7018. *E:* nick.smith.mp@parliament.uk.

**SMITH, Nicholas George Edward L.;** *see* Loraine-Smith.

**SMITH, Nicholas Paul;** Headteacher, Torquay Girls' Grammar School, since 2007; *b* Brighton, 9 Sept. 1964; *s* of C. and R. Smith; *m* 1993, Caroline Inglethorpe; one *s* one *d*. *Educ:* Cardinal Newman Sch., Hove; Royal Free Hosp. Sch. of Medicine, Univ. of London (MB BS 1987); Inst. of Educn, Univ. of London (PGCE Sci. 1993); Nat. Coll. of Sch. Leadership (NPQH 2005). Jun. Hse Officer, Royal E Sussex Hosp., Hastings and Fazakerley Hosp., Liverpool, 1988–89; Penguin Keeper, London Zoo, 1991; teaching in Cornwall, 1993–2002; Dir, Sixth Form, Liskeard Community Coll., 2002–04; Dep. Hd, Devonport High Sch. for Girls, 2004–07. *Recreations:* running, walking, fitness, annoying my family by being pedantic. *Address:* Torquay Girls' Grammar School, 30 Shiphay Lane, Torquay, Devon TQ2 7DY. *T:* (01803) 613215, *Fax:* (01803) 616724. *E:* admin@tggsacademy.org.

**SMITH, Nigel Christopher S.;** *see* Starmer-Smith.

**SMITH, Nigel Watkin Roberts,** CB 2011; Chairman, Spikes Cavell, 2011–16; *b* Newcastle upon Tyne, 9 June 1954; *s* of Captain Peter Watkin Roberts Smith and Brenda Smith; *m* 1982, Heather Scott; two *d*. *Educ:* Skinners' Grammar Sch., Tunbridge Wells; Bristol Poly. (BA Hons Business Studies 1976); Henley Mgt Coll. (GMC 1987). Dowty Group plc: grad. commercial apprentice, 1972–76; Personnel Exec./Manager, Dowty Rotol, 1976–86; Dir of Projects, Dowty Fuel Systems, 1986–88; Man. Dir, Dowty Aerospace Aviation Services, 1988–92; Commercial Dir, Dowty Landing Gear, 1993; Managing Director: GEC Marconi Ltd, 1993–95; Pandrol Internat., 1995; Charter plc: Chief Operating Officer, 1995–98; CEO, 1998–2001; on sabbatical and consulting, 2001–03; Pres., Invensys Rail Systems, 2003–06; Second Perm. Sec. and Chief Exec., Office of Govt Commerce, HM Treasury, 2007–10. Non-executive Director: Sellafield Ltd, 2012– (interim Chm., 2017–18); Sepura plc, 2013–17; Obillex Ltd, 2015–. Mem. Bd, BT Major Projects Centre, Saïd Business Sch., Oxford Univ., 2010–15. FCIPS 2007. *Recreations:* family, France, golf, walking, opera, Newcastle United FC. *E:* nigel@charleswood.me.uk.

**SMITH, Niove Rachel J., (Nia);** *see* Janis Smith.

**SMITH, Sir (Norman) Brian,** Kt 1998; CBE 1980; Chairman, Cable and Wireless HKT (formerly Hong Kong Telecommunications) Ltd, 1995–97 and 1998–2000 (non-executive Director, 1997–98); *b* 10 Sept. 1928; *s* of late Vincent and Louise Smith; *m* 1955, Phyllis Crossley; one *s* one *d* (and one *s* decd). *Educ:* Sir John Deane's Grammar Sch., Northwich; Manchester Univ. (PhD Phys. Chemistry, 1954). FTI 1981. Joined ICI Ltd, Terylene Council, 1954; Fibres Division: Textile Develt Dir, 1969; Dep. Chm., 1972; Chm., 1975–78; ICI Main Bd, 1978–85; Director: Fiber Industries Inc., 1972–83; Canadian Industries Ltd, 1981–85; Territorial Dir for the Americas, and Chm., ICI Americas Inc., 1981–85 (Dir, 1980–85); Non-exec. Dir, Carrington Viyella Ltd, 1979–81. Chairman: Metal Box plc, subseq. MB Group, 1986–89 (Dep. Chm., 1985–86); Lister & Co., 1991–94 (Dir, 1985–94; Dep. Chm., 1990–91); BAA plc, 1991–98; Cable and Wireless, 1995–98 (Dir, 1988–95); Hydron Ltd, 1994–2000; Director: Davy Corp., 1986–91; Yorkshire Chemicals, 1990–91; Mercury Communications, 1990–93; Berisford plc, 1990–96. Pres., British Textile Confedn, 1977–79; Chairman: Man-Made Fibres Producers Cttee, 1976–78; EDC for Wool Textile Industry, 1979–81; Priorities Bd for R&D in Agric. and Food, 1987–92; Heatherwood and Wexham Park Hosps Trust, 1991–97; Dir, John Cabot CTC Bristol Trust, 1997–98; Mem., BOTB, 1980–81, 1983–87 (Chm., N American Adv. Group, 1983–87). Chm., Standing Conf. on Schools' Sci. and Technology, 1992–96. Dir, Oxford Dio. Bd of Finance, 1990–2006. Freeman, City of London, 1986; Liveryman, Glovers' Co., 1986. Hon. DBA Buckingham, 1990. *Recreations:* sailing, tennis, gardening.

**SMITH, Norman Jack,** MA, MPhil, PhD; FEI; consultant and author; Chairman, Petroleum Venture Management Ltd, 2001–05; *b* 14 April 1936; *s* of late Maurice Leslie and Ellen Dorothy Smith; *m* 1967, Valerie Ann, *o d* of late Capt. A. E. Frost and Mrs M. Frost; one *s* one *d*. *Educ:* Grammar Sch., Henley-on-Thames; Oriel Coll., Oxford (MA); City Univ. (MPhil); Aberdeen Univ. (PhD); Harvard Univ. (Mgt Develt Prog.); CEDEP, France. Dexion Ltd, 1957; Vickers Ltd, 1960; Baring Brothers & Co. Ltd, 1969; seconded as Industrial Director, 1977, Dir-Gen., 1978–80, Offshore Supplies Office, Dept of Energy; Chairman: British Underwater Engineering Ltd, 1980–83; Mentor Engineering Consultants, 1987–92; Man. Dir, Smith Rea Energy Associates Ltd, 1981–2000; Director: Burntisland Engrs and Fabricators Ltd, 1974–76; Zenith Reed Ltd, 1975–76; Internat. Economic Services Ltd, 1975–76; SAI Tubular Services Ltd, 1983–88; Atkins Oil and Gas Engrg Ltd, 1984–86; Smith Rea Energy Analysts, 1985–2000; Smith Rea Energy Aberdeen, 1990–2000; Gas Transmission, 1989–95; Capcis, 1999–2000. Mem., Offshore Energy Technology Bd, 1978–80. Council Mem., Canterbury Archaeol Trust, 2003–07; Chm., Friends of Canterbury Archaeol Trust, 2003–07. Patron, Oriel Coll. Develt Trust, 2003–11. FEI (FInstPet 1978); FSPE. *Publications:* The Sea of Lost Opportunity: North Sea oil and gas, British industry and the Offshore Supplies Office, 2011; sundry articles in economic and oil industry jls, think-tank papers and family history pubns. *Recreations:* walking, swimming, history, writing, reading. *Club:* Oxford and Cambridge.

**SMITH, Olly;** wine columnist and TV presenter; wine expert, Saturday Kitchen, since 2007; *b* Darlington, 18 Sept. 1974; *s* of John and Mary Clare Smith; *m* 2002, Sophie; two *d*. *Educ:* Chorister, King's Coll., Cambridge; Charterhouse (Top Music Schol.); Edinburgh Univ. (MA English Lit.). Wine columnist, Mail on Sunday, 2009–; Food Hero wine expert, P&O Cruises, 2010–; Celebrity Drinks Ambassador, Ideal Home Show, 2013–; presenter: Secret Supper Club, Channel 4, 2013; Ale Trails (2 series), Travel Channel, 2016–17; A glass with… (podcast), 2017–; How Beer Changed the World, 2018; guest presenter, BBC Radio 2, 2014–15. Patron, Bumblebee Conservation Trust. Mem., BAFTA. *Publications:* Eat and Drink: good food that's great to drink with, 2010; Wine: both barrels, 2012; Behind Enemy Wines, 2017; Drinking for Chaps, 2018; Fizz, 2019. *Recreations:* bee keeping, gardening, music, walking, films, poetry, reading, art, writing. *Address:* c/o Curtis Brown Ltd, Haymarket House, 28–29 Haymarket, SW1Y 4SP. *E:* presenters@curtisbrown.co.uk. *Clubs:* Groucho, 67 Pall Mall.

**SMITH, Owen;** MP (Lab) Pontypridd, since 2010; *b* Morecambe, Lancs, 2 May 1970; *s* of Prof. David Burton Smith, *qv*; *m* 1995, Liz; two *s* one *d*. *Educ:* Sussex Univ. (BA Hist. and French). Producer, BBC Radio and TV, 1992–2002; Govt Special Advr to Wales Office, 2002, to NI Office, 2003–05; Hd, Govt Affairs, Pfizer Ltd, 2005–07; Dir, Corporate Affairs and Health Econs, Amgen Ltd, 2008–09. Shadow Minister, Wales Office, 2010–11; Mem., Shadow Health Team, 2010–11; Shadow Exchequer Sec. 2011–12; Shadow Sec. of State for Wales, 2012–15, for Work and Pensions, 2015–16, for NI, 2017–18. Contested (Lab) Blaenau Gwent, June 2006. *Recreations:* family, fishing, reading, Rugby. *Address:* House of Commons, SW1A 0AA. *T:* (020) 7219 1287, (constituency office) (01443) 401122. *E:* owen.smith.mp@parliament.uk. *Club:* Pontypridd Rugby Football.

**SMITH, Patrick J.;** *see* Janson-Smith.

**SMITH, Paul;** Principal, Swincliffe Consulting, since 2019; *b* Burnley, Lancs, 14 Nov. 1956; *s* of Fred Smith and Eileen Bartlett; *m* 1981, Carole; two *s* one *d*. *Educ:* Burnley Grammar Sch.; Univ. of Warwick (LLB). Articled clerk, then solicitor, Freshfields, 1980–84; Eversheds, subseq. Eversheds Sutherland LLP, 1984–2019: Partner, until 2019; Global Chm., 2014–18. *Publications:* (with S. Dyson) The Real Deal: law firm leadership that works, 2019. *Recreations:* puppetry, cooking, theatre, gardening. *Address:* Swincliffe Consulting, Compton Lodge, St Johns Park, Menston, Ilkley, W Yorks LS29 6ES.

**SMITH, Paul Adrian,** CBE 2012; Chairman: Celador Entertainment Ltd (formerly Complete Communications Corporation Ltd), since 1986; Celador Films Ltd, since 1999 (Joint Managing Director, 1999–2008); Celador Theatrical Productions Ltd, since 2009; *b* 16 Jan. 1947; *s* of Clifford Bryce Smith and Marjorie Doreen Smith (*née* Walker); *m* 1980, Sarah Anne King (marr. diss. 2015); one *s* one *d*. *Educ:* Royal Belfast Academical Instn. Joined BBC TV as trainee projectionist, 1966, various posts, incl. prodn manager and director, 1966–73; freelance television producer/dir, 1973–82; created It'll Be All Right on the Night, 1977; established: Complete Video Facilities, 1981; Celador Prodns, 1983 (Chm., 1983–2006); Complete Communications Corp., 1986; Celador Films, 1999; launched Who Wants to be a Millionaire? on UK TV, 1998, on US TV, 1999, sold worldwide rights, 2006. Chm., Celador Radio Broadcasting Ltd, 2004; estabd Celador radio stations: The Coast, 2008; The Breeze, 2010; Jack FM, 2011; Palm FM, later The Breeze, 2013; Fire Radio, 2014; Sam FM, 2015; acquired Anglian Radio Gp, 2017; owned and operated 27 UK commercial radio licences. Executive Producer (films): Dirty Pretty Things, 2002 (12 industry awards, inc. Best Film, British Ind. Film Awards, 2003, and Evening Standard Film Awards, 2003); The Descent, Separate Lies, 2005; Slumdog Millionaire, 2008 (awards incl. 8 Acad. Awards, 7 BAFTA Awards, 4 Golden Globe Awards); The Descent: Part 2, 2009; The Scouting Book for Boys, Centurion, 2010. BAFTA Award, 1999; Emmy Award, USA, 2000 and 2001. Hon. DSc Ulster, 2012; Hon. Dr Media Southampton Solent, 2014. *Recreations:* travelling, motor yachting, photography, cinema, collecting original sixties records, the countryside, family and home. *Address:* Celador Entertainment Ltd, Woodhill Manor, Shamley Green, Surrey GU5 0SP. *T:* (01483) 891000. *E:* psmith@celador.co.uk.

**SMITH, Sir Paul (Brierley),** Kt 2000; CBE 1994; RDI 1991; fashion designer; Chairman, Paul Smith Ltd; *b* 5 July 1946; *s* of late Harold and Marjorie Smith; *m* 2000, Pauline Denyer. *Educ:* Beeston Fields Grammar Sch. Opened own shop, 1970 (part-time), 1974 (full time); has shops in London, Nottingham, NY, LA, Paris, Milan, Moscow, Hong Kong, Singapore, San Francisco, Antwerp, Melbourne, Hamburg, Amsterdam and over 250 in Japan; exporter to numerous other countries; Nottingham and London-based design studios. Paul Smith True Brit exhibn, Design Mus., 1995; Hello, My Name is Paul Smith, Design Mus., 2013. Freeman, City of Nottingham, 1997. Hon. FRIBA 2007. Hon. MDes Nottingham Trent, 1991. Queen's Award for Export, 1995; Queen's Award for Enterprise, Internat. Trade, 2009; Outstanding Achievement in Fashion Award, British Fashion Awards, 2011. *Address:* Paul Smith Ltd, 20 Kean Street, WC2B 4AS. *T:* (020) 7836 7828.

**SMITH, Paul James;** Chief Executive, City and County of Swansea, 2006–11; *b* Colchester, 11 Nov. 1955; *s* of late Henry Joseph Smith and Jessie Elizabeth Mackenzie; *m* 1980, Keri Ann Jones; one *s*. *Educ:* Colchester Royal Grammar Sch.; Univ. of Wales Inst. of Science and Technol. (BSc Hons Town Planning; Postgrad. Dip. Town Planning). Asst Dir (Housing), Cardiff CC, 1988–91; Gloucester City Council: City Housing Officer, 1991–96; Dir, Community Services, 1996–2001; Chief Exec., 2001–06. Non-executive Director: Severnside Housing, 2013–16 (Chm.), 2013–15; Housing Plus Gp, 2016–17 (Chm., Homes Bd (Severnside Housing and S Staffs Housing), 2016–17). Trustee, Citizens Advice Shropshire, 2012–15; Dir, S Petherton Community Land Trust, 2019– . Mem., Munslow Parish Council, 2012–17 (Chm., 2014–17). *Recreations:* Colchester United FC, night sky, real ale and malt whisky. *E:* paulsmith.pjs@gmail.com.

**SMITH, Paul Jonathan,** OBE 1999; Director, Indonesia, British Council, since 2016; *b* 30 May 1956; *s* of late Arthur Godfrey Smith and Constance Mildred Smith (*née* Phelps); *m* 1999, Viveka Kumari; two *s* one *d*. *Educ:* King Edward's Sch., Birmingham; Queens' Coll., Cambridge (BA Hons double 1st 1978, MA 1982). Lectr in Lit., St Stephen's Coll., Univ. of Delhi, 1978–80; British Council: Asst Dir, Kano, 1983–85, Lagos, 1985–87; Dep. Dir, Drama and Dance Dept, 1987–89; Acting Director, Burma, Chile and Berlin, 1989–90; Dep. Dir, Dhaka, 1990–95; Director: NZ, 1995–99; Arts, 1999–2000; W India, 2000–05; Egypt, and Cultural Counsellor, British Embassy, Cairo, 2005–10; Afghanistan, and Cultural Counsellor, British Embassy, Kabul, 2010–12; USA, and Cultural Counsellor, British Embassy, Washington, 2012–16. Pres., EU Nat. Insts of Culture (Washington DC Cluster), 2013–14. Mem. Bd, British-Indonesia Chamber of Commerce, 2016– . Mem., Adv. Bd, Caravan, 2013– . Member, Board of Trustees: American Sch. of Bombay, 2003–05; Modern Sci. and Arts Univ., Cairo, 2008–10; Turquoise Mt Foundn, Afghanistan, 2010–12 (Mem., Bd of US Trustees, 2012– ); US Friends of British Council, 2012– ; Founder Mem., Bd of Trustees, British Univ. of Egypt, 2008–10. *Publications:* (contrib. sections on Shakespeare and Wordsworth) Reference Guide to English Literature, 2nd edn 1991; (contrib.) Colonial and Postcolonial Shakespeares, 2001; (contrib.) British-Egyptian Relations from Suez to the Present, 2007; Full Fathom Five: Shakespeare's old seas and new oceans, 2009; (contrib.) Vintage Shakespeare: new perspectives from India and Abroad, 2010. *Recreations:* directing Shakespeare, all arts, particularly literature, drama and film. *Address:* BFPO 5445, Hants HA4 6EP. *T:* (Indonesia) (811) 8715962. *E:* paul.smith@britishcouncil.or.id.

**SMITH, Prof. Paul Julian,** PhD; FBA 2008; Distinguished Professor of Hispanic and Luso-Brazilian Literatures and Languages, Graduate Center, City University of New York, since 2010; *b* 11 Nov. 1956; *s* of Albert Charles Smith and Margaret (*née* Tovey). *Educ:* Cambridge Univ. (BA 1980, MA 1982; PhD 1984). Res. Fellow, Trinity Hall, Cambridge, 1983–84; Lectr, QMC, London Univ., 1984–88; Reader, QMW, 1989–91; Prof. of Spanish, 1991–2010, Hd, Dept of Spanish and Portuguese, 1991–2001 and 2006–07, Cambridge Univ.; Fellow, Trinity Hall, Cambridge, 1991–2010. *Publications:* Quevedo on Parnassus, 1987; Writing in the Margin: Spanish literature of the Golden Age, 1988; The Body Hispanic: gender and sexuality in Spanish and Spanish American literature, 1989; A Critical Guide to El Buscón, 1991; Representing the Other: race, text and gender in Spanish and Spanish American narrative, 1992; Laws of Desire: questions of homosexuality in Spanish writing and film, 1992; Desire Unlimited: the cinema of Pedro Almodóvar, 1994; Vision Machines: cinema, literature and sexuality in Spain and Cuba, 1996; The Theatre of García Lorca: text, performance and psychoanalysis, 1998; The Moderns: time, space and subjectivity in contemporary Spanish culture, 2000; Contemporary Spanish Culture: television, fashion, art and film, 2003; Spanish Visual Culture: cinema, television, internet, 2007; Spanish Practices: literature, cinema, television, 2012; Mexican Screen Fiction: between cinema and television, 2014. *Address:* Hispanic and Luso-Brazilian Literatures, Graduate Center, City University of New York, 365 Fifth Avenue, New York, NY 10016, USA.

**SMITH, Dr Paul Philip;** Secretary General, Botanic Gardens Conservation International, since 2015; *b* Bexley, 8 Jan. 1964; *s* of Robert Langley Smith and Sheila Margaret Smith; *m* 1994, Deborah Ann Shah; one *d*. *Educ:* Univ. of Kent (BSc Hons Microbiol. 1986; PhD Ecol. 1991). Plant ecologist: N Luangwa Nat. Park, Zambia, 1993–96; Royal Botanic Gdns, Kew, 1997–2000; Internat. Co-ordinator, Millennium Seed Bank, 2000–05; Hd, Millennium Seed Bank, Royal Botanic Gdns, Kew, 2005–14. FLS 2012. Founders' Medal, New England Wildflower Soc., 2015; David Fairchild Medal for Plant Exploration, Nat. Tropical Botanical Garden, 2016. *Publications:* Common Trees, Shrubs and Grasses of the Luangwa Valley, 1995; The Ecological Survey of Zambia, 2001; Field Guide to the Trees and Shrubs of the Miombo Woodland, 2004; Vegetation Atlas of Madagascar, 2007; The Book of Seeds, 2018; contrib. papers to jls. *Recreations:* painting, walking, travel. *Address:* Botanic Gardens Conservation International, Descanso House, 199 Kew Road, Richmond, Surrey TW9 3BW. *T:* (020) 8332 5953. *E:* paul.smith@bgci.org.

**SMITH, Penelope R.;** *see* Russell-Smith.

**SMITH, Peter Alan,** FCA; Director, NM Rothschild & Sons Ltd, since 2001; Member, Supervisory Board, Rothschild & Co. SCA, since 2012; *b* 5 Aug. 1946; *s* of Dudley Vaughan Smith and Beatrice Ellen (*née* Sketcher); *m* 1971, Cherry Blandford; two *s*. *Educ:* Mill Hill Sch.; Univ. of Southampton (BSc); Wharton Sch., Univ. of Pennsylvania (AMP). FCA 1970. PricewaterhouseCoopers (formerly Coopers & Lybrand), 1967–2000: Partner, 1975–2000 (Senior Partner, 1998–2000); Chm., 1994–98. Mem., Global Leadership Team, 1998–2000. Dir and Dep. Chm., Equitable Life Assce Soc., 2001–10; Director: Safeway plc, 2002–04; Savills plc, 2004–16 (Chm., 2004–16); Templeton Emerging Markets Investment Trust plc, 2004–15 (Chm., 2007–15); Associated British Foods plc, 2007–16; Land Restoration Trust, 2009– (Chm., 2009– ); Chm., RAC plc, 2003–05. Hon. Treas., UK Housing Trust, 1979–83. Member: Finance Cttee, Nat. Trust, 1991–98, 2001–05; Cttee on Corporate Governance, 1996–97; Council, ICAEW, 1997–2003 (Treas., 2001–03); POW Business Leaders Forum, 1994–2000; President's Cttee, 1994–98, F and GP Cttee, 1999–2008, CBI. Liveryman, Chartered Accountants' Co., 1993– . FRSA 1993; CCMI 1994. *Publications:* Housing Association Accounts and Their Audit, 1980. *Recreations:* golf, gardens. *Address:* (office) New Court, St Swithin's Lane, EC4N 8AL. *Clubs:* Carlton, Walbrook; Beaconsfield Golf.

**SMITH, Peter Bruce,** MA; Head Master, Bradfield College, 1985–2003; *b* 18 March 1944; *s* of Alexander D. Smith and Grace Smith; *m* 1968, Diana Margaret Morgan; two *d*. *Educ:* Magdalen College School, Oxford; Lincoln College, Oxford (Old Members Scholar; MA). Asst Master, Rugby Sch., 1967–85 (Head of Hist. Dept, 1973–77, Housemaster of School Field, 1977–85). Mem. Governing Body, Downe House Sch., 1985–89; Gov., Abbey Sch., 2005 (Chm., 2007–13). Captain Oxfordshire County Cricket Club, 1971–77 (Minor Counties Champions, 1974). *Recreations:* antiquarian, sporting, literary. *Club:* Vincent's (Oxford).

**SMITH, Prof. Peter Charles;** Professor of Health Policy, Imperial College London, 2009–13, now Emeritus; Professor of Global Health Economics, University of York, since 2017; *b* 29 July 1952; *s* of Dennis John Smith and Evelyn Mary Smith (*née* Rush); *m* 1986, Sally Jane Stone; one *d*. *Educ:* Birkenhead Sch.; Oriel Coll., Oxford (MA Maths 1974). Res. Fellow, Univ. of Cambridge, 1977–82; University of York: Lectr, 1984–94; Reader, 1994–96; Prof. of Economics, 1996–2009; Dir, Centre for Health Economics, 2005–09. Sen. Res. Associate, WHO Eur. Observatory on Health Systems and Policy, 2007– ; Sen. Associate, Nuffield Trust, 2008– . Member: DoH Adv. Cttee on Resource Allocation, 1997–2002; Audit Commn, 2003–09; Co-operation and Competition Panel, NHS, 2009–14; Health England, DoH Adv. Gp to Minister for Public Health, 2007–10; Ind. Inquiry into Modernising Med. Careers, 2007–08; Wkg Party on Future Doctor and Patient, RCP, 2008–10; NHS Procurement and Efficiency Bd, 2014–16; Lancet Commn on Future of NHS, 2017– ; Chm., NHS Adv. Cttee on Resource Allocation, 2015– . Chm., UK Centre for Measurement of Govt Activity, 2005–08. Member: Scientific Peer Rev. Gp, WHO, 2001–02; Global Agenda Council on Healthcare Systems, WEF, 2008–10; OECD High-level Expert Gp on Access to Innovative Medicines, 2016–18; Tech. Adv. Gp, Financing Public Goods for Health, WHO, 2018– ; Global Fund Modelling Guidance Gp, 2018– ; Chair, Res. Adv. Panel, Macmillan Cancer Support, 2017– . Council Mem., Royal Statistical Soc., 2002–06. Vis. Prof., LSE, 2005– ; Hon. Professor: Univ. of St Andrews, 1997–2007; Monash Univ., 2006–11; Univ. of York, 2011–17. Hon. FRCP, 2010. Founding Editor-in-Chief, Health Care Mgt Science, 1997–2005; Ed., Health Policy, 2011–18. *Publications:* (ed) Outcome Measurement in the Public Sector, 1996; (ed) Reforming Markets in Health Care, 2000; (ed) Measuring Up: improving health system performance in OECD countries, 2002; Formula Funding of Public Services, 2006; (jtly) Measuring Efficiency in Health Care, 2006; (ed jtly) Performance Measurement for Health System Improvement: experiences, challenges and prospects, 2009; (ed with D. Pinto-Masís) Health Care Systems in Developing and Transition Economies: the role of research evidence, 2009; (ed with S. Glied) Oxford Handbook of Health Economics, 2011; (ed with I. Papanicolas) Health System Performance Comparison: an agenda for policy, information and research, 2013; (ed jtly) Paying for Performance in Healthcare: implications for health system performance and accountability, 2014; (ed jtly) Health System Efficiency: how to make measurement matter for policy and management, 2016; (ed jtly) What's In, What's Out: designing a health benefits plan for universal health coverage, 2017; over 150 papers in acad. jls. *Recreations:* bridge, allotment gardening, jazz, finding safe cycling routes. *Address:* Imperial College Business School, SW7 2AZ. *E:* peter.smith@imperial.ac.uk.

**SMITH, Most Rev. Peter David;** Archbishop of Southwark, (RC), 2010–19; *b* 21 Oct. 1943. *Educ:* Clapham Coll.; Univ. of Exeter (LLB 1966); St John's Seminary, Wonersh; Angelicum Univ., Rome (JCD *summa cum laude* 1977). Coutts Bank, London, 1962–63; ordained priest, 1972; Asst Priest, St Francis de Sales and St Gertrude, Stockwell, 1972–74; Prof. of Canon Law, St John's Seminary, Wonersh, 1977–84; Parish Priest, St Andrew's, Thornton Heath, 1984–85; Rector, St John's Seminary, Wonersh, 1985–95; Bishop of E Anglia, 1995–2001; Archbishop of Cardiff, (RC), 2001–10. Vice-Officialis and Judge, Diocesan Marriage Tribunal, 1977; Officialis, Metropolitan Tribunal, 1980–85. Bishops' Conference: Mem., Cttee for Ministerial Formation, 1989–95; Chairman: Cttee for Marriage and Family Life, 1995–2001; Dept for Christian Responsibility and Citizenship, 1998–2019; Central Religious Adv. Cttee, 2001–04; Vice Pres., 2009–19. Chairman: Catholic Truth Soc., 1993–2007; Catholic Assoc. Pilgrimage Trust, 1998–2001; Vice-Chm., Catholic Agency for Social Concern, 1996–2001. Mem. Mgt Cttee, Catholic Educn Service, 1998–2001. Hon. Fellow: Univ. of Wales, Lampeter, 2004; Cardiff Univ., 2006. Sub-Prelate and Chaplain, Order of St John of Jerusalem, 2002. KC★HS 2010. *Address:* c/o Archbishop's House, 150 St George's Road, Southwark, SE1 6HX.

**SMITH, Peter David V.;** *see* Vicary-Smith.

**SMITH, Sir Peter Frank Graham N.;** *see* Newson-Smith.

**SMITH, Prof. Peter George,** CBE 2001; Professor of Tropical Epidemiology, London School of Hygiene and Tropical Medicine, since 1989; *b* 3 May 1942; *s* of George Henry Smith and Lily Smith (*née* Phillips); *m* 1999, Jill Margaret Routledge; one *s*, and one step *s* one step *d*. *Educ:* City Univ. (BSc Applied Maths 1st Class 1963; DSc Med. Stats 1983). Statistical Res. Unit, MRC, 1965–67; Clinical and Population Cytogenetics Unit, MRC, 1967–69; Makerere Univ. Med. Sch., Uganda, 1970–71; WHO Internat. Agency for Res. on Cancer, Uganda, 1971–72; Cancer Epidemiology and Clinical Trials Unit, ICRF, Oxford, 1972–79; Dept of Epidemiology, Harvard Sch. of Public Health, 1975; Sen. Lectr, 1979–86, Reader, 1986–89, Hd, Dept of Epidemiol. and Population Scis, 1990–97, Hd, Dept of Infectious and Tropical Diseases, 1997–2002, LSHTM. WHO Tropical Diseases Res. Prog., Geneva, 1987–88. Chairman: Global Adv. Cttee on Vaccine Safety, WHO, 2009–11 (Mem., 2005–11; Dep. Chm., 2006–09); Prog. Bd for Global Health and Vaccination Res., Res. Council of Norway, 2011–19 (Mem., Portfolio Bd on Global Develt, 2019–); Member: WHO, MRC, and DoH Cttees, incl. Spongiform Encephalopathy Adv. Cttee, 1996–2004 (Chair, 2001–04); Nuffield Council on Bioethics, 2003–09 (Dep. Chm., 2006–09); Bd of Mgt, Medicines for Malaria Venture, 2009–12; Bd of Dirs, PATH, 2016; Scientific Advisory Committee: Coalition for Epidemic Preparedness, Innovations, 2016– ; Eur. and Developing Countries Clin. Trials Partnership, 2017– . Gov., Wellcome Trust, 2004–14. FMedSci 1999. Hon. MFPHM, then Hon. MFPH, 1991. Ronald Reid Medal, LSHTM, 2003; Ronald Ross Medal, LSHTM, 2016. *Publications:* (ed with R. H. Morrow) Field Trials of health interventions in developing countries, 1996, 3rd edn (ed with R. H. Morrow and D. A. Ross) as Field Trials of Health Interventions: a toolbox, 2015; numerous contribs to med. res. literature. *Recreations:* gardening, walking, cycling, swimming. *Address:* MRC Tropical Epidemiology Group, Department of Infectious Disease Epidemiology, London School of Hygiene and Tropical Medicine, Keppel Street, WC1E 7HT. *T:* (020) 7927 2246.

**SMITH, Peter John,** CPFA; Chairman, Gateshead Health NHS Foundation Trust (formerly NHS Trust), 1998–2012; *b* 31 Dec. 1936; *s* of Frank and Sarah Ann Smith; *m* 1st, Marie Louise Smith (marr. diss. 2001); one *s* one *d*; 2nd, 2001, Judith Anne Brown. *Educ:* Rastrick Grammar Sch., Brighouse, W Yorkshire. Trainee Accountant, Huddersfield CBC, 1953–59; Accountancy Asst, Bradford CBC, 1959–61; Asst Chief Accountant, Chester CBC, 1961–63; Computer Manager, Keighley BC, 1963–66; Asst City Treasurer, Gloucester CBC, 1966–69; Dep. Borough Treasurer, Gateshead CBC, 1969–73; Asst

County Treasurer, Tyne and Wear CC, 1973–74, Dep. County Treasurer, 1974–80, County Treasurer, 1980–86. Gen. Manager, Tyne and Wear Residuary Body, 1985–88. Treasurer: NE Regional Airport Jt Cttee, 1980–86; Northumbria Police Authority, 1980–86; Northumbria Probation and After Care Cttee, 1980–86; Mem., Tyne and Wear Passenger Transport Exec. Bd, 1981–86. Director: N American Property Unit Trust, 1982–93; Northern Investors Co., 1983–86; Westgate Trust, 1990–92; Chairman: Gateshead Healthcare and Community NHS Trusts, 1992–98; Northern Clinical Waste Consortium, 1994–2012. Mem. Bd, NHS Foundn Trust Network, 2006–10. *Recreations:* fell walking, bridge, county cricket supporter, cinema, travel. *Address:* Wheatsheaf House, 19 Station Road, Beamish, Co. Durham DH9 0QU. *T:* (0191) 370 0481.

**SMITH, Peter John,** CBE 1995; HM Diplomatic Service, retired; Governor, Cayman Islands, 1999–2002; *b* 15 May 1942; *s* of late John S. Smith and Irene (*née* Waple); *m* 1964, Suzanne Pauline Duffin; one *s* one *d*. *Educ:* St Dunstan's Coll., London. Joined FO, 1962; Vietnamese lang. student, then 3rd Sec., Saigon, 1964–67; Commercial Attaché, Paris, 1968–69; Commercial Publicity Officer, British Information Services, NY, 1970–73; FCO, 1973–76; 1st Sec., Commercial, Mexico City, 1976–80; Dep. High Comr, Port Louis, Mauritius, 1981–84; FCO, 1984–86; Deputy Consul General: Montreal, 1987–88; Toronto (also Dir, Trade and Investment), 1988–92; RCDS 1992; Ambassador to Madagascar and concurrently Ambassador (non-resident) to The Comoros, 1993–96; High Comr to Lesotho, 1996–99. *Recreations:* golf, cricket, chess, bridge. *Address:* 24 Barton Farm, Cerne Abbas, Dorset DT2 7LF. *Club:* MCC.

**SMITH, (Peter) Patrick J.;** *see* Janson-Smith.

**SMITH, His Honour Peter William;** a Circuit Judge, 1994–2009; *b* 31 Dec. 1945; *s* of late William and Bessie Smith; *m* 1970, Vanessa Mary (*née* Wildash); one *s*. *Educ:* Arnold Sch., Blackpool; Downing Coll., Cambridge (MA). Called to the Bar, Middle Temple, 1969. Practised (as William Smith) on Northern Circuit; a Dep. Judge Advocate, 1983–84; a Recorder, 1991–94. Mem., Mental Health Review Tribunal, 1993–2012. *Recreation:* weekends in the Lake District.

**SMITH, Prof. Peter William Frederick,** PhD; FBA 2019; Professor of Social Statistics, University of Southampton, since 2004; *b* Whitehaven, 28 Feb. 1965; *s* of William Bland Smith and Alison Grace Smith; *m* 1994, Wendy Suzanne Meaking. *Educ:* Wyndham Sch., Egremont; Lancaster Univ. (BSc 1st Cl. Maths 1986; PhD Stats 1990); Univ. of Sheffield (MSc Probability and Stats (Dist.) 1987). University of Southampton: Lectr in Social Stats, 1990–98; Sen. Lectr in Social Stats, 1998–2000; Reader in Social Stats, 2000–04. Vis. Schol., Center for Stats and Social Scis, Univ. of Washington, Seattle, 2003; Vis. Fellow, Sch. of Demography, ANU, 2018; Vis. Prof., Sch. of Math. and Phys. Scis, Univ. of Technol. Sydney, 2018. Guy Medal in Bronze, Royal Statistical Soc., 1999. *Publications:* contrib. papers to peer-reviewed jls incl. Jl Royal Statistical Soc., Series A, B and C, Biometrics, Biometrika, Jl Amer. Statistical Assoc. *Recreations:* orienteering, walking, theatre, gardening. *Address:* Department of Social Statistics and Demography, Southampton Statistical Sciences Research Institute, School of Economic, Social and Political Sciences, University of Southampton, Highfield, Southampton SO17 1BJ. *T:* (023) 8059 3191. *E:* P.W.Smith@soton.ac.uk.

**SMITH, Hon. Sir Peter (Winston),** Kt 2002; a Judge of the High Court of Justice, Chancery Division, 2002–17; *b* 1 May 1952; *s* of George Arthur Smith and Iris Muriel Smith; *m* 1980, Diane Dalgleish; one *s* two *d*. *Educ:* Selwyn Coll., Cambridge (BA 1974; MA 1976); Coll. of Law. Called to the Bar, Lincoln's Inn, 1975, Bencher, 2000. Lectr, Manchester Univ., 1977–83; practice on Northern Circuit, 1979–2002; QC 1992; Asst Recorder, 1994–97; Actg Deemster, IOM, 1994–2002; a Deputy High Court Judge, 1996–2002; a Recorder, 1997–2002. *Recreations:* Jackie Fisher fan, reading military history, football.

**SMITH, Philip Andrew B.;** *see* Brook Smith.

**SMITH, Philip Eric Main,** MD; FRCP; Consultant Neurologist, University Hospital of Wales, Cardiff, since 1996; *b* Northleach, Glos, 20 March 1957; *s* of Ian Smith and Betty Smith; *m* 1982, Ann Jean Clarke; two *s* two *d*. *Educ:* Rendcomb Coll., Cirencester; Univ. of Liverpool (MB ChB 1979; MD 1988). MRCP 1982, FRCP 1997; FAcadMed 2010. Lectr in Medicine, Univ. of Liverpool, 1985–87; Registrar in Neurol., Newcastle upon Tyne and Middlesbrough, 1987–90; Sen. Registrar in Neurol., University Hosp. of Wales, Cardiff, 1990–92; Consultant Neurologist, Royal Cornwall Hosps (Treliske), 1992–96. Cardiff University School of Medicine: Hon. Prof., 2007–; Sub-Dean for Assessments, Inst. of Med. Educn, 2011–. Chair, NICE guidelines cttee on heart valve disease in adults, 2019–. Member: Minister for Transport's Nat. Adv. Panel for Driving and Disorders of the Nervous System, 2009–14; Bd, UK Med. Schs Council Assessment Alliance, 2017–; Tests of Competence Panel, GMC, 2018–; Associate Med. Dir for Quality, Fedn of UK Colls of Physicians, 2015–19. President: Assoc. of British Neurologists, 2015–17; UK Jt Neuroscis Council, 2018–. Pres., UK Chapter, Internat. League Against Epilepsy, 2008–11. Co-Editor, Practical Neurology, 2011–. *Publications:* Key Topics in Neurology, 1998; (with S. Wallace) Clinicians' Guide to Epilepsy, 2001; (jtly) Specialist Training in Neurology, 2007; 130 scientific articles in jls incl. New England Jl of Medicine, Lancet, BMJ and Epilepsia. *Recreations:* running, cycling, tennis, yoga, reading. *Address:* Alan Richens Epilepsy Unit, Department of Neurology, University Hospital of Wales, Heath Park, Cardiff CF14 4XW. *T:* (029) 2074 2834. *E:* SmithPE@cf.ac.uk.

**SMITH, Philip Geoffrey;** Administration and Resources Manager, Information Services, Queen's University of Belfast, since 2017; *b* Belfast, 7 Nov. 1967; *s* of Derek and Lorna Smith; *m* 1997, Lindsay; one *s* one *d*. *Educ:* Royal Belfast Academical Instn; Lancaster Poly. (HND Business and Mktg 1988); Univ. of Ulster (MPA 2010). J. Sainsbury plc: grad. trainee, 1989–91; Mgt Services, 1991–94; Public Affairs Exec., 1994–95; HR Exec., 1995–96; Mgt Consultant, Industrial Soc., 1996–2001; Manager, Scotland and NI, Capital Learning and Develt, 2001–03; Nat. Business Develt Manager, Capita, 2003–04; Client Partner, Penna plc, 2004–06; Head, Learning Support, Police Service NI, 2007–16. Member: (Lib Dem) Wokingham Town Council, 1992–96; (UU) Ards BC, 2001–05 and 2010–14 (Mayor, 2013–14); Ards and N Down BC, 2019–. Mem. (UU) Strangford, NI Assembly, 2016–17; contested (UU) same seat, 2017. Party Officer, UUP, 2006– (Dir of Elections, 2017–). *Recreations:* family, watching Ulster Rugby, occasional running.

**SMITH, Rachel Catherine; Her Honour Judge Rachel Smith;** a Circuit Judge, since 2016; *b* London, 20 April 1966; *d* of James Smith and Mavourneen Smith; *m* 1993; one *s* one *d*. *Educ:* Parkstone Grammar Sch. for Girls, Poole; Leeds Univ. (BA Hons Internat. Hist. and Politics 1987); City Univ. (DipLaw 1989); Inns of Court Sch. of Law. Called to the Bar, Lincoln's Inn, 1990; a Recorder, 2008–16. *Address:* Liverpool Crown Court, The Queen Elizabeth II Law Courts, Derby Square, Liverpool L2 1XA.

**SMITH, Rain N.;** *see* Newton-Smith.

**SMITH, Ralph Andrew;** QC (Scot.) 1999; Legal Member, Lands Tribunal for Scotland, since 2014; *b* 22 March 1961; *s* of Rev. Ralph Colley Philip Smith and Florence Howat Smith; *m* 1989, Lucy Moore Inglis; one *s* one *d*. *Educ:* Edinburgh Acad.; Kelvinside Acad.; Aberdeen Univ. (LLB 1981; DLP 1982). Admitted to Faculty of Advocates, 1985; formerly in practice, specialising in commercial law and planning; Jun. Counsel to Lord Pres. of Court of Session, 1989–90; Standing Jun. Counsel to DoE (Scotland), 1992–99. *Publications:* contribs to Scots Law Times. *Recreations:* field sports, Scottish Jun. Foil Fencing Champion, 1982. *Address:* Castlemains, Gifford, E Lothian EH41 4PL. *Club:* New (Edinburgh).

**SMITH, Rt Rev. Raymond George;** Senior Associate Minister, Church Hill Parish, Diocese of Sydney, since 2014; *b* 7 March 1936; *s* of Gordon William Smith and Alice Mary (*née* Brett); *m* 1960, Shirley Jeanette Gilmore; three *s*. *Educ:* Australian Coll. of Theology (ThSchol); Univ. of New England (BA, Dip Cont. Ed, MEd). Parish priest, dio. of Armidale, 1959–76; Dir of Christian Educn and Archdeacon, Armidale, 1977–86; Dir of Extension Ministries, Trinity Episcopal Sch. for Ministry, Ambridge, Pa, USA, 1986–90; Rector of Wanniassa, 1990–93, and Archdeacon of S Canberra, 1991–93, dio. of Canberra and Goulburn; Bp of Liverpool, NSW, and an Asst Bp of Sydney, 1993–2001; Senior Associate Minister: St Clement, Mosman, NSW, 2002–04; St Philip's, York Street, Sydney, 2005–13. Chair, Next Phase Ministry Cttee, Anglican Deaconess Inst., dio. of Sydney, 2012–16. *Publications:* People Caring for People, 1990; (with John Rodgers) Confessing the Faith: Anglican doctrine, 2015. *Recreations:* swimming, cycling, photography, stamp collecting, Australian history. *Address:* 20/3A Blackwall Point Road, Abbotsford, NSW 2046, Australia.

**SMITH, Richard James Crosbie W.;** *see* Wilmot-Smith.

**SMITH, Prof. Richard John,** ScD; FBA 2007; Professor of Econometric Theory and Economic Statistics, University of Cambridge, 2006–16, now Emeritus; Lecturer in Economics and Fellow, Gonville and Caius College, Cambridge, 2005–16, now Emeritus; Academic Co-Director, Office for National Statistics Economic Statistics Centre of Excellence, since 2016; Professorial Fellow, Faculty of Business and Economics, University of Melbourne, since 2016; *b* Redhill, 14 May 1949; *s* of John Hayden Smith and Irene Smith (*née* Barlow); *m* 1975, Margaret Veronica Assumpta Breen. *Educ:* Bromley Grammar Sch.; Bournemouth Sch.; Churchill Coll., Cambridge (BA 1972); Univ. of Essex (MA 1976); PhD 1989, ScD 2010, Cantab. Res. Asst, SSRC Inflation Workshop, 1975–76, Lectr in Econometrics, 1976–89, Univ. of Manchester; Lectr in Econometrics, 1989–95, Reader in Theoretical Econometrics, 1995, Univ. of Cambridge; Coll. Lectr in Econs and Fellow, 1989–95, Dir of Studies in Econs, 1992–94, Gonville and Caius Coll., Cambridge; Professor: of Econs, Univ. of Bristol, 1995–2002; of Econometrics, Univ. of Warwick, 2002–05; Reader in Theoretical Econometrics, 2005–06, Dir, Centre for Res. in Microecons, 2005–13, Chair, Faculty of Econs, 2011–14, Univ. of Cambridge. Visiting Professor: Queen's Univ., Canada, 1983–84; Univ. of Montreal, 1994, 2001, 2006; CREST-INSEE, Paris, 1993, 1996, 2004; Univ. of Calif, Berkeley, 2006; UCL, 2016–; Vis. Fellow, 1997–2010, Fellow, 2016–, NIESR; Centre Fellow, Centre for Microdata Methods and Practice, UCL and IFS, 2001–; 2002 Leverhulme Maj. Res. Fellow, 2003–06. Mem., Academic Econometric Panel, ONS, 1997–2003. Mem., Eur. Standing Cttee, 2002–04, GB and Ireland Regl Consultant, 2003–08, Fellow, 2007, Econometric Soc. Mem., Exec. Cttee, 2007–, Mem. Council, 2007–, RÉconS. Gov., NIESR, 2004–. Mem., Editl Bd, Rev. of Econ. Studies, 1986–94; Associate Ed., Econometrica, 1995–2007; Co-Ed., Econometric Theory, 2000–08 (Mem., Adv. Bd, 2010–); Man. Ed., Econometrics Jl, 2007– (Founding Ed., 1997–2001). *Publications:* contribs to Biometrika, Econometrica, Econometric Theory, Jl Econometrics, Jl Amer. Statistical Assoc., Rev. Econ. Studies, Jl Business and Econ. Stats. *Recreations:* fell walking, Manchester United FC, FC United of Manchester, Manchester United Supporters Trust, modernist architecture, theatre, film, reading. *Address:* Faculty of Economics, University of Cambridge, Austin Robinson Building, Sidgwick Avenue, Cambridge CB3 9DD. *T:* (01223) 335230, *Fax:* (01223) 335475. *E:* rjs27@econ.cam.ac.uk.

**SMITH, Richard Lloyd,** QC 2001; a Recorder, since 2000; *b* 28 Jan. 1963; *s* of Lloyd and Dorothy Smith; *m* 1990, Anna Sara Webb; one *s* one *d*. *Educ:* King's Coll. London (LLB). Called to the Bar, Middle Temple, 1986. *Recreations:* Rugby, Leeds United Football Club. *Address:* Guildhall Chambers, 23 Broad Street, Bristol BS1 2HG. *T:* (0117) 930 9000.

**SMITH, Prof. Richard Lyttleton,** PhD; Mark L. Reed III Distinguished Professor of Statistics, since 2004, and Professor of Biostatistics, School of Public Health, since 2008, University of North Carolina (Professor of Statistics, 1991–2004 (on leave, 1994–96)); Director, Statistical and Applied Mathematical Sciences Institute, North Carolina, 2010–17 (Associate Director, 2017–18); *b* 31 March 1953; *s* of Stanley Lyttleton Smith and Hilary Margaret (*née* James); *m* 2002, Amy Grady; two *s*. *Educ:* Jesus Coll., Univ. of Oxford (BA Maths 1975; MA 1985); Cornell Univ., USA (PhD Ops Res. 1979). Lectr in Stats, Imperial Coll., London, 1979–85; Prof. of Statistics, Univ. of Surrey, 1985–90; Prof. of Statistical Sci., Univ. of Cambridge, 1994–96. Guy Medal in Silver, Royal Statistical Soc., 1991. *Publications:* (jtly) Statistical Analysis of Reliability Data, 1991; (with G. Alastair Young) Essentials of Statistical Inference, 2005; contrib. to Jl Roy. Statistical Soc., Proc. Royal Soc., Biometrika, Annals of Stats, etc. *Recreations:* cross-country and road running, chess, bridge, music. *Address:* 4314 Oak Hill Road, Chapel Hill, NC 27514–9731, USA.

**SMITH, Prof. Richard Michael,** PhD; FRHistS; FBA 1991; Professor of Historical Geography and Demography, 2003–11, now Emeritus, and Head, Department of Geography, 2007–10, University of Cambridge; Director, Cambridge Group for the History of Population and Social Structure, 1994–2012; Fellow, Downing College, Cambridge, 1994–2010, now Emeritus (Vice-Master, 2004–10); *b* 3 Jan. 1946; *s* of Louis Gordon Smith and Elsie Fanny (*née* Ward); *m* 1971, Margaret Anne McFadden. *Educ:* Earls Colne Grammar Sch.; University Coll. London (BA Hons); St Catharine's Coll., Cambridge (MA 1977; PhD 1974). Lectr in Population Studies, Plymouth Poly., 1973–74; Cambridge University: Asst Lectr in Histl Geography, 1974–76; Sen. Res. Officer, 1976–81, Asst Dir, 1981–83, Cambridge Gp for the Hist. of Population and Social Structure; Fellow, 1977–83, Tutor, 1979–83, Fitzwilliam Coll.; Oxford University: Univ. Lectr in Histl Demography, 1983–89; Fellow, All Souls Coll., 1983–94; Reader in Hist. of Medicine and Dir, Wellcome Unit for Hist. of Medicine, 1990–94; Reader in Historical Demography, Cambridge Univ., 1996–2003. Mem. Council, British Soc. for Population Studies, 1987–91; Pres., Economic History Soc., 2007–10. Sir John Neale Lectr, 1996. Editor: Social Hist. of Medicine, 1986–92; Economic History Review, 2001–07. *Publications:* (ed jtly) Bastardy and its Comparative History, 1980; (ed) Land, Kinship and Lifecycle, 1984; (ed jtly) The World We Have Gained: histories of population and social structure, 1986; (ed jtly) Life, Death and the Elderly: historical perspectives, 1991; (ed jtly) Medieval Society and the Manor Court, 1996; contribs to Annales ESC, Jl of Family Hist., Trans RHistS, Ageing and Society, Law and Hist. Rev., Population and Develt Rev. *Recreations:* listening to music, especially jazz and classical. *Address:* Cambridge Group for the History of Population and Social Structure, Sir William Hardy Building, Department of Geography, Downing Place, Cambridge CB2 3EN. *T:* (01223) 333182.

**SMITH, Richard Philip Morley R.;** *see* Reay-Smith.

**SMITH, Richard Sydney William,** CBE 2000; Chief Executive, UnitedHealth Europe, 2004; Visiting Professor, London School of Hygiene and Tropical Medicine, since 1996; *b* 11 March 1952; *s* of Sydney Smith and Hazel Smith (*née* Kirk); *m* 1977, Linda Jean Arnott;

two s one d. *Educ:* Roan Grammar Sch., London; Edinburgh Univ. (BSc 1973; MB ChB 1976); Stanford Univ. (MSc in Management 1990). MFPHM 1992, FFPH (FFPHM 1997); FRCPE 1992; MRCP 1993, FRCP 1995; FRCGP 1997; FRCSE 2000. Hosp. jobs in Scotland and New Zealand, 1976–79; British Medical Journal: Asst Editor, 1979; Sen. Asst Editor, 1984; Editor, and Chief Exec., BMJ Publishing Gp, 1991–2004. BBC Breakfast Time doctor, 1983–87. Founder, 1998, and Vice-Chm., 2001–04, Cttee on Publication Ethics; Member: Internat. Cttee of Med. Jl Editors, 1991–2004; Bd, World Assoc. of Med. Editors, 1994–2000; Editorial Boards: Nat. Med. Jl of India, 1992–2002; Ceylon Med. Jl, 1996–2002; Canadian Med. Assoc. Jl, 1997–2002; Hong Kong Jl of Family Practice, 1998–2002. Prof. of Med. Journalism, Univ. of Nottingham, 1993–2001. Chm., Foresight Wkg Pty on Inf. and Health, 2000; Member: UK Panel for Health and Biomed. Res. Integrity, 2006–; Medicines Partnership Taskforce, Nat. Prescribing Centre, 2006–. Member: Bd, Public Liby of Sci., 2004; Adv. Bd, Global Trial Bank, 2005–. Mem. Gov. Council, St George's Hosp. Med. Sch., 2004–. Patron: Contact a Family, 1985–; Project Hope UK, 2004– (Mem. Bd, 1996–2002). Founder FMedSci 1998; Fellow, Acad. of Gen. Educn, Karnataka, India, 1993. HealthWatch Award, 2004. *Publications:* Alcohol Problems, 1982; Prison Health Care, 1984; The Good Health Kit, 1987; Unemployment and Health, 1987; (ed) Health of the Nation, 1991; (ed) Rationing in Action, 1993; (ed jtly) Management for Doctors, 1995; (ed jtly) Scientific Basis of Health Services, 1996; The Trouble with Medical Journals, 2006; articles in learned jls; contrib. Guardian. *Recreations:* jazz, cycling, running, wine, talking first and thinking second.

**SMITH, Robert B.**; *see* Bettley-Smith.

**SMITH, Robert Carr,** CBE 1989; PhD; Vice-Chancellor, Kingston University, 1992–97 (Director, Kingston Polytechnic, 1982–92); *b* 19 Nov. 1935; *s* of late Edward Albert Smith and Olive Winifred Smith; *m* 1960, Rosalie Mary (*née* Spencer) (*d* 2004); one *s* one *d*. *Educ:* Queen Elizabeth's School, Barnet; Southampton Univ. (BSc); London Univ. (PhD). Research Asst, Guy's Hosp. Med. Sch., 1957–61; Lectr, Senior Lectr, Reader, Prof. of Electronics, Southampton Univ., 1961–82. Seconded to DoE, 1973–74. Chairman: Engineering Profs' Conf., 1980–82; Polytechnics and Colls Employers' Forum, 1988–90; Vice-Chm., Cttee of Dirs of Polytechnics, 1988–89; Member: Design Council, 1983–88; Council for Industry and Higher Educn, 1985–97; Council, Inst. for Manpower Studies, 1987–95; PCFC, 1988–93; TEC for Kingston, Merton and Wandsworth, 1989–97; Higher Educn Statistics Agency, 1993–97; Univs and Colls Employers' Assoc., 1994–97. Pt-time Chief Exec., SEARCH (careers service for Kingston, Merton and Wandsworth), 1998; Chm. Bd, Prospects Services Ltd, 2003–08. Chm., Bd of Govs, IoW Further Educn Coll., 1999–2003 and 2007–10; Gov. and Trustee, Dulwich Coll., 1998–2002; Governor: Treloars Sch. and Coll., 2008–13; Wolf Fields Primary Sch., 2015–19. Trustee, Prospects Acads Trust, 2013–15. Hon. Fellow, St George's Hosp. Med. Sch., 1998. Freeman, Royal Borough of Kingston upon Thames, 1997. *Publications:* research papers on radiation physics, laser physics, new technology, and stained glass artist, Keith New. *Recreations:* visual arts, classical music, local history. *Address:* 40 Oakbark House, High Street, Brentford, Middx TW8 8LF.

**SMITH, Sir Robert (Courtney),** Kt 1987; CBE 1980; FRSE; MA, CA; Chairman, Alliance and Second Alliance Trust, 1984–96; *b* 10 Sept. 1927; 4th *s* of late John Smith, DL, JP, and Agnes Smith, Glasgow and Symington; *m* 1954, Moira Rose, *d* of late Wilfred H. Macdougall, CA, Glasgow; one *s* two *d* (and one *s* decd). *Educ:* Kelvinside Academy, Glasgow; Sedbergh Sch.; Trinity Coll., Cambridge. BA 1950, MA 1957. Served, Royal Marines, 1945–47, and RMFVR, 1951–57; Hon. Col, RM Reserves Scotland, 1972–96. Partner, Arthur Young McClelland Moores & Co., Chartered Accountants, 1957–78. Director: Standard Life Assurance, 1975–94 (Chm., 1982–88); Sidlaw Gp, 1977–97 (Chm., 1980–88); Wm Collins, 1978–89 (Vice-Chm., 1979–89); Volvo Trucks (GB), later Volvo Truck and Bus, 1979–98; Edinburgh Investment Trust, 1983–98; British Alcan Aluminium, 1983–99; Bank of Scotland, 1985–97. Mem., Scottish Industrial Develt Adv. Bd, 1972–83 (Chm., 1981–88); Pres., Business Archives Council of Scotland, 1986–97; Chancellor's Assessor, Glasgow Univ., 1984–96. Mem., Horserace Betting Levy Bd, 1977–82; Deacon Convener, Trades House of Glasgow, 1976–78; Dir, Merchants House of Glasgow, 1991–96. Mem. Council, Inst. of Chartered Accountants of Scotland, 1974–79. Trustee, Carnegie Trust for Univs of Scotland, 1982–2002. FRSE 1988. Hon. LLD: Glasgow, 1978; Aberdeen, 1991. CStJ 2004. *Address:* The Old Rectory, Cathedral Street, Dunkeld, Perthshire PH8 0AW. *T:* (01350) 727574. *Clubs:* East India; Western (Glasgow); Hawks (Cambridge).

**SMITH, (Robert) Harvey;** show jumper, farmer; *b* 29 Dec. 1938; *m* 1st, Irene Shuttleworth (marr. diss. 1986); two *s*; 2nd, 1987, Susan Dye. First major win with Farmer's Boy. Leading Show Jumper of the Year; other major wins include: King George V Cup, Royal Internat. Horse Show, 1958; has won the John Player Trophy 7 times, King George V Gold Cup once, and the British Jumping Derby 4 times; Grand Prix and Prix des Nations wins in UK, Ireland, Europe and USA; took part in Olympic Games, 1968 and 1972; best-known mounts: Farmer's Boy, Mattie Brown, Olympic Star, O'Malley, Salvador, Harvester. BBC TV Commentator, Los Angeles Olympics, 1984. Assists wife in training of racehorses. *Publications:* Show Jumping with Harvey Smith, 1979; Bedside Jumping, 1985. *See also R. W. Smith.*

**SMITH, Prof. Robert Henry Tufrey,** AM 1998; PhD; Chancellor, University of Ballarat, Australia, 2005–12, now Emeritus Chancellor, Federation University Australia (formerly University of Ballarat); *b* 22 May 1935; *s* of late Robert Davidson Smith and Gladys Smith (*née* Tufrey); *m* 1959, Elisabeth Jones; one *s* one *d*. *Educ:* Farrer Memorial Agricultural High Sch., Tamworth, NSW; Univ. of New England, NSW (BA, 1st Cl. Hons Geography); Northwestern Univ. (MA); ANU (PhD). Lectr in Geography, Univ. of Melbourne, 1961–62; University of Wisconsin: Asst Prof. of Geography, 1962–64; Associate Prof., 1964–67; Prof., 1967–70; Chm., African Studies Programme, 1968–69 (on leave, 1964–66; Associate Res. Fellow, Nigerian Inst. for Social and Econ. Res., and Hon. Vis. Lectr in Geography, Univ. of Ibadan, 1964–65; Vis. Fellow, Dept of Geography, Univ. of Sydney, 1965–66); Prof. of Geography and Head of Dept, Queen's Univ., Kingston, Ontario, 1970–72; Prof. of Geography, Monash Univ., 1972–75 (Chm. of Dept, 1973–75; Associate Dean, Faculty of Arts, 1974–75); University of British Columbia: Prof. of Geography, 1975–85; Head of Dept, 1975–80; Associate Vice-Pres., Academic, 1979–83; Vice-Pres., Academic, 1983–85; Pres. *pro tem*, March–Nov. 1985; Vice-Chancellor, Univ. of WA, 1985–89; Chm., Nat. Bd of Employment, Educn and Trng, Aust., 1989–90; Vice-Chancellor, Univ. of New England, Australia, 1990–93; Exec. Dir and Pres., 1994–97, Sen. Consultant, 1997–99, Australian Educn Office, Washington; Dep. Chancellor, Southern Cross Univ., 1998–2002. Jubilee Fellow, Acad. Social Scis in Australia, 2015. DUniv: Southern Cross, 1995; Ballarat, 2012. *Address:* PO Box 5046, Victoria Point, Qld 4165, Australia.

**SMITH, Sir Robert Hill,** 3rd Bt *cr* 1945, of Crowmallie, Co. Aberdeen; *b* 15 April 1958; *s* of Sir (William) Gordon Smith, 2nd Bt, VRD, and of Diana (*née* Goodchild); *S* father, 1983; *m* 1993, Fiona Anne Cormack; three *d*. *Educ:* Merchant Taylors' School; King's Coll., Aberdeen Univ. Contested (SDP/Lib Alliance), Aberdeen North, 1987. MP (Lib Dem) W Aberdeenshire and Kincardine, 1997–2015; contested (Lib Dem) same seat, 2015. Mem. (Lib Dem) Aberdeenshire Unitary Council, 1995–97. Vice Chm., Grampian Jt Police Bd, 1995–97. Gen. Council Assessor, Aberdeen Univ. Court, 1994–98. *Heir:* b Charles Gordon Smith [*b* 21 April 1959; *m* 1990, Dr Ann Maria Kennedy; two *s* one *d*]. *Address:* Crowmallie House, Pitcaple, Inverurie, Aberdeenshire AB51 5HR. *E:* smithrh02@gmail.com.

**SMITH, Robert Lee,** CB 2004; Director General, Regional Development Group, Office of the Deputy Prime Minister, 2004–05. *Educ:* St Dunstan's Coll., Catford; Magdalene Coll., Cambridge (MA Eng. Lit.). Entered Civil Service as Administrative Trainee, 1974; DES, later DFE, then DFEE, subseq. DfES, 1981–2000: Principal Private Sec. to Sec. of State for Educn and Science, 1985–87; Under Sec., Pupils and Parents Br., 1994; Dir, Pupil Support and Inclusion Gp (formerly Pupils, Parents and Youth), 1995–2000; Dir Gen., Regional Co-ordination Unit, DETR, subseq. Cabinet Office, then ODPM, 2000–04. Public Sector Chm., Inst. of Mgt/CS Network, 1995–2000. Mem., Young People and Families Cttee, Joseph Rowntree Foundn, 1997–2000; Co-Chm., Social Policy Forum, 2003. *Recreation:* folk dancing and music.

**SMITH, Robert Walter;** show jumper; *b* 12 June 1961; *e s* of (Robert) Harvey Smith, *qv*, and Irene Smith; one *s* three *d*; *m* 2016, Raffaelle; one *s*. Member: GB junior and senior European events teams, 1977–; British Nations Cup Team, 1979–; World Class Performance Squad, 1999–2005; Gold team medal and Bronze individual medal, Jun. European Championships, 1977; Bronze team medal, European Championships, 1997; King George V Gold Cup winner, 1979, 1988, 1998. British Open Champion, 2005 and 2006; British Masters Champion, 2009. Top ranking rider and owner, BSJA, 2002. *Address:* Brook Furlong Farm, High Cross, Shrewley, Warwickshire CV35 7BD. *T:* (01926) 843886.

**SMITH, Robin Anthony,** MBE 2015; TD 1978; DL; Consultant, DLA Piper (formerly Dibb Lupton Alsop, then DLA), solicitors, 1999–2008; Chairman, Leeds Building Society, 2007–13; *b* 15 Feb. 1943; *s* of late Tom Sumerfield Smith and Mary Smith; *m* 1967, Jennifer Elizabeth Roslington; one *s* one *d*. *Educ:* St Michael's Coll.; Manchester Univ. (LLB). Solicitor, admitted 1966; joined Dibb Lupton & Co., 1966; Partner, 1966–99; Man. Partner, 1988–93; Sen. Partner, Dibb Lupton & Co., later Dibb Lupton Broomhead, then Dibb Lupton Alsop, 1993–98. Mem. Council, Law Society, 1982–91; Pres., Leeds Law Soc., 1993–94. Non-executive Director: Leeds (formerly Leeds & Holbeck) Bldg Soc., 1998–2013; Coutts & Co., 1999–2006; Town Centre Securities plc, 1999–2009; Bartlett Gp Hldgs Ltd, 2000–. Gov., Stonyhurst Coll., 1989–98. Commnd 5th Bn LI, TA, 1966; retired 1985, Lt-Col. DL W Yorks, 1991. KSG 2002. *Recreations:* golf, cricket. *Clubs:* Army and Navy, MCC; Alwoodley Golf; Yorkshire CC (Mem. Bd, 2000–; Pres., 2000–04; Chm., 2002–05 and 2018–; Vice Chm., 2005–18); Scarborough CC; Western Province Cricket (S Africa).

**SMITH, Robin F.;** *see* Field-Smith.

**SMITH, Robin Jeremy O.;** *see* Ord-Smith.

**SMITH, Rt Rev. Robin Jonathan Norman;** Suffragan Bishop of Hertford, 1990–2001; Hon. Assistant Bishop, diocese of St Albans, since 2001; *b* 14 Aug. 1936; *s* of Richard Norman and Blanche Spurling Smith; *m* 1961, Hon. Lois Jean, *d* of Baron Pearson, CBE, PC; three *s* one *d*. *Educ:* Bedford Sch.; Worcester Coll., Oxford (MA); Ridley Hall, Cambridge. RAF Regiment Commission, 1955–57. Curate, St Margaret's, Barking, 1962–67; Chaplain, Lee Abbey, 1967–72; Vicar, Chesham St Mary, 1972–80; Rector, Great Chesham, 1980–90. Hon. Canon, Christ Church, Oxford, 1988–90. *Recreations:* gardening, walking. *Address:* 7 Aysgarth Road, Redbourn, Herts AL3 7PJ.

**SMITH, Prof. Roderick Arthur,** PhD, ScD; FREng, FIMechE, FIMMM; Research Professor, Imperial College London, since 2011 (Professor and Head of Department of Mechanical Engineering, 2000–05; Royal Academy of Engineering Research Professor, 2006–11); Chief Scientific Adviser, Department for Transport, 2011–14; *b* 26 Dec. 1947; *s* of Eric and Gladys Mary Smith; *m* 1975, Yayoi Yamanoi. *Educ:* Hulme Grammar Sch., Oldham; St John's Coll., Oxford (BA, MA); Queens' Coll., Cambridge (MA; PhD 1975; ScD 1998; Hon. Fellow 2015). CEng 1976; FIMechE 1991; FIMMM (FIM 1992); FREng 1999. Queens' College, Cambridge: Godfrey Mitchell Res. Fellow, 1975–78; Official Fellow, College Lectr and Dir of Studies, 1978–88; Asst Lectr, Engrg Dept, Cambridge Univ., 1977–80; Lectr, 1980–88; Sheffield University: Prof. of Mech. and Process Engrg, 1988–2000; Hd, Dept of Mech. and Process Engrg, 1992–95; Royal Acad. of Engrg/BR Res. Prof., 1995–2000; Chm., Advanced Rly Res. Centre, 1993–2000; Warden, Stephenson Hall, 1992–2000. Sen. Vis. Res. Fellow, St John's Coll., Oxford, 2005–06; Vis. Prof., Oxford Univ., 2012–. Chm., Coll. of Rly Technol., Derby, 1996–97. Consultant to: British Steel plc, 1986–89; BR, 1992–96 (Mem. Bd, Res. and Tech. Cttee, 1992–96). Mem., Infrastructure Commn for Wales, 2018–. Mem., Res. and Tech. Cttee, AEA Technology, 1997–2006. Chm., Heathrow Airport Consultative Cttee, 2015–18. Institution of Mechanical Engineers: Mem. Council, 1999–; Trustee, 2006–; Dep. Pres., 2010–11; Pres., 2011–12. Trustee, Nat. Mus. of Science and Industry, 2002–10. FCGI 2000. Hon. DEng: Lincoln, 2012; Sheffield, 2015. *Publications:* Thirty Years of Fatigue Crack Growth, 1986; Innovative Teaching in Engineering, 1991; Engineering for Crowd Safety, 1993; ed books; papers and articles on mech. engrg, design, manufacture, engrg educn and crowd engrg. *Recreations:* mountaineering, reading, history, Japan: its people and technology; conversation, wine. *Address:* Department of Mechanical Engineering, Imperial College London, Exhibition Road, SW7 2AZ. *T:* (020) 7594 7007. *Clubs:* Oxford and Cambridge, Alpine; Fell and Rock (Lake District).

**SMITH, Rodger H.;** *see* Hayward Smith.

**SMITH, Roger Huntington,** FRCP, FRCPE; Joint Vice President, Royal College of Physicians of Edinburgh, 2005–06 (Vice President, 2003–05); *b* 9 April 1945; *s* of John Smith and Evelyn Smith; *m* 1971, Judith Elizabeth Martin; two *s*. *Educ:* Wallasey Grammar Sch.; Univ. of Edinburgh (BSc Hons (Physiol.) 1966; MB ChB 1969). FRCPE 1983; FRCP 1987. Consultant Physician and Cardiologist, Univ. Hosp. of N Tees, 1979–2007; Hon. Clinical Lectr, Univ. of Newcastle, 2000–. Associate Mem., 2001–08, Mem., Fitness to Practise Panel, 2001–13, GMC; Mem., Med. Panel, Nat. Patient Safety Authy, 2003–06; Public Interest Mem., Public Practice Cttee, ICAS, 2008–13. Royal College of Physicians of Edinburgh: Chm., Collegiate Mems Cttee, 1979; Mem. Council, 1992–93, 1996–2002; Sec., 2001–03. *Publications:* articles on early work in infective endocarditis, pioneering res. in acute thrombolysis (with H. A. Dewar), substantial trialling of thrombolytics in acute infarction. *Recreations:* serious singer (formerly Mem., Edinburgh Festival Chorus, and for 30 years of chamber choir, Michelmas Singers), village politics, gardening, classical music, art, walking in the Lake District, newly initiated golfer. *Address:* The Sheiling, High Street, Wolviston, Stockton on Tees TS22 5JS.

**SMITH, Roger John;** Chairman, Cotton Spring Farm Ltd (family holding company), since 1975; *b* 20 April 1939; *s* of Horace W. Smith and Marjorie E. Pummery; *m* 1962, Margaret R. Campbell; one *s* two *d*. *Educ:* Bedford School. Nat. Service, Subaltern, RCT, 1958–60. Dir, Family Group business, incl. Lea Heating Merchants (later part of Tricentrol), 1960–70; Man. Dir, Commercial Div., 1971–75, Dir, Special Projects, 1976–78, Tricentrol International; Dir, Group Co-ordination, Tricentrol, 1978–81; Man. Dir, Commercial

Div., 1981–83; Dep. Chm., Tricentrol plc, 1983–88; Chm. and Chief Exec., Trimoco plc, 1987–92. Dir, Close Brothers AIM (VCT) plc, and other cos. Chairman: European Motor Hldgs plc, 1994–2007; Harpenden Building Society, 1999–2009. President: Retail Motor Industry Fedn, 1991–93; Internat. Orgn for Motor Trade and Repair, 1998–2000. Sloan Fellow, Stanford Univ., 1976. Chm., Lord's Taverners, 2000–02. Board Mem., Univ. of Herts. Chm., Central Finance Bd, Methodist Church, 2000–17. Master, Coachmakers' and Coach Harnessmakers' Co., 2006. *Recreations:* sailing, shooting, tennis, reading. *Address:* Cotton Spring, Flamstead, Herts AL3 8AF. *Clubs:* Royal Automobile, Royal Thames Yacht.

**SMITH, Roger John Gladstone,** OBE 2008; legal researcher, consultant and journalist, since 2012; *b* 20 June 1948; *s* of late Kenneth Smith and Alice Smith; partner, Sue Berger; one *s* one *d*. *Educ:* York Univ. (BA 1970). Admitted solicitor, 1973; Solicitor, Camden Community Law Centre, 1973–75; Dir, W Hampstead Community Law Centre, 1975–79; Solicitor, Child Poverty Action Gp, 1980–86; Director: Legal Action Gp, 1986–98; Legal Educn and Training, Law Soc., 1998–2001; Justice, 2001–12. Hon. Prof., Kent Law Sch., 1998–; Vis. Prof., London South Bank Univ., 2008–. Author of blog on technol. and access to justice, www.law-tech-a2j.org, 2016–. Hon. LLD Westminster, 2007. *Publications:* Children and the Courts, 1981; A Strategy for Justice, 1992; Shaping the Future: new directions in legal services, 1995; Achieving Civil Justice, 1996; Justice: redressing the balance, 1997; Legal Aid Contracting: lessons from North America, 1998; (jtly) Effective Criminal Defence Rights in Europe, 2010; (jtly) Face to Face Legal Services and their Alternatives: global lessons from the digital revolution, 2013; Digital Delivery of Legal Services to People on Low Incomes, 2015; Law, Technology and Access to Justice, 2016. *Recreations:* sailing, reading, managing an allotment, struggling with classical guitar. *E:* rogerjgsmith@gmail.com.

**SMITH, Roger L.;** *see* Lane-Smith.

**SMITH, Roland Hedley,** CMG 1994; HM Diplomatic Service, retired; Clerk, Wakefield and Tetley Trust (formerly Wakefield Trust), 2004–18; *b* 11 April 1943; *s* of late Alan Hedley Smith and of Elizabeth Louise Smith; *m* 1971, Katherine Jane Lawrence; two *d*. *Educ:* King Edward VII School, Sheffield; Keble College, Oxford (BA 1st cl. hons 1965, MA 1981). Third Sec., Foreign Office, 1967; Second Sec., Moscow, 1969; Second, later First Sec., UK Delegn to NATO, Brussels, 1971; First Sec., FCO, 1974; First Sec. and Cultural Attaché, Moscow, 1978; FCO, 1980; attached to Internat. Inst. for Strategic Studies, 1983; Political Advr and Hd of Chancery, British Mil. Govt, Berlin, 1984–88; Dep. Hd, Sci., Energy and Nuclear Dept, FCO, 1988–90; Hd of Non-Proliferation and Defence Dept, FCO, 1990–92; Minister and Dep. Perm. Rep., UK Delegn to NATO, Brussels, 1992–95; Asst Under-Sec. of State, then Dir, (Internat. Security), FCO, 1995–98; Ambassador to Ukraine, 1999–2002. Dir, St Ethelburga's Centre for Reconciliation and Peace, 2002–04. *Publications:* Soviet Policy Towards West Germany, 1985. *Recreations:* music, esp. choral singing, football (Sheffield United), trams. *Address:* c/o Wakefield and Tetley Trust, Marshall House, 66 Newcomen Street, SE1 1YT.

**SMITH, Prof. Roland Ralph Redfern,** DPhil; FBA 2010; Lincoln Professor of Classical Archaeology and Art, University of Oxford, since 1995; *b* 30 Jan. 1954; *s* of Rupert and Elinor Smith; *m* 1988, Ingrid Gaitet. *Educ:* Fettes Coll., Edinburgh; Pembroke Coll., Oxford (BA 1977; MPhil 1979); Magdalen Coll., Oxford (DPhil 1983). Fellow, Magdalen Coll., Oxford, 1981–86; Asst Prof. of Classical Archaeology, 1986–90, Associate Prof., 1990–95, Inst. of Fine Arts, NY Univ. Harkness Fellow, Princeton, 1983–85; Alexander von Humboldt Fellow, Munich, 1991–92. Dir, Excavations at Aphrodisias, Caria, 1991–. *Publications:* Hellenistic Royal Portraits, 1988; Hellenistic Sculpture, 1991; The Monument of C. Julius Zoilos, 1993; Roman Portrait Statuary from Aphrodisias, 2006; (with B. Dignas) Historical and Religious Memory in the Ancient World, 2012; The Marble Reliefs from the Julio-Claudian Sebasteion at Aphrodisias, 2013; (with B. Ward-Perkins) The Last Statues of Antiquity, 2016; contrib. learned jls. *Address:* Ashmolean Museum, Oxford OX1 2PH.

**SMITH, Ronald Angus,** OBE 2009; General Secretary, Educational Institute of Scotland, 1995–2012; *b* 9 June 1951; *s* of William Angus and Daisy Smith; *m* 1976, Mary A. Lambie; one *s* one *d*. *Educ:* Anderson Educnl Inst., Lerwick; Univ. of Aberdeen (MA 1972); Aberdeen Coll. of Educn (PGCE 1973). Teacher, later Principal Teacher, Latin and Modern Studies, Broxburn Acad., W Lothian, 1973–88; Asst Sec., Educnl Inst. of Scotland, 1988–95. Hon. FEIS 2003. *Recreations:* Livingston FC, the Island of Foula.

**SMITH, Ronald George B.;** *see* Barclay-Smith, R. G.

**SMITH, Rosemary Ann;** Headmistress, Wimbledon High School, GPDST, 1982–92; *b* 10 Feb. 1932; *d* of late Harold Edward Wincott, CBE, editor of the Investors Chronicle, and Joyce Mary Wincott; *m* 1954, Rev. Canon Graham Francis Smith (*d* 2008); two *s* two *d*. *Educ:* Brighton and Hove High School, GPDST; Westfield College, Univ. of London (BA Hons); London Univ. Inst. of Education (post grad. Cert. in Education). Assistant Teacher: Central Foundation Girls' School, 1964–69; Rosa Bassett Girls' School, 1970–77; Furzedown Secondary School, 1977–80; Deputy Head, Rowan High School, 1980–82. Mem. Council, GDST (formerly GPDST), 1993–2005. *Recreations:* theatre, gardening, reading. *Address:* 1 Bentley Road, Chorlton-cum-Hardy, Manchester M21 9WD. *T:* (0161) 860 5594.

**SMITH, Air Marshal Sir Roy David A.;** *see* Austen-Smith.

**SMITH, Royston Matthew,** GM 2012; MP (C) Southampton, Itchen, since 2015; *b* Harefield, Southampton, 13 May 1964; *s* of Frank Wilmot Smith and Marie Cecilia Smith (*née* Page). RAF Kinloss (Nimrod), 1980–83; RAF St Mawgan (Nimrod), 1983–86; RAF Lyneham (Hercules C130), 1986–88; RAF Laarbruch, Germany (Tornado GR4), 1988–90; maintenance engr, BA, Heathrow, 1990–2006. Mem. (C), Southampton CC, 2000–16 (Leader of Council, 2010–12). Mem., Hants Fire and Rescue Authy, 2000–15 (Chm., 2009–15). Gov., Southampton Solent Univ. Contested (C) Southampton, Itchen, 2010. Mem., Foreign Affairs Select Cttee, 2017–. *Address:* House of Commons, SW1A 0AA.

**SMITH, Gen. Sir Rupert (Anthony),** KCB 1996; DSO 1991 (and Bar 1996); OBE 1982; QGM 1978; Deputy Supreme Allied Commander, Europe, 1998–2001; Aide-de-Camp General to the Queen, 2000–01; *b* 13 Dec. 1943; *s* of late Gp Captain Irving Smith, CBE, DFC (and Bar) and Joan Smith (*née* Debenham). Parachute Regt, 1964; Dep. Comdt, Staff Coll., Camberley, 1989–90; Comdr, 1st Armoured Div., BAOR, Gulf, 1990–92; ACDS (Ops), 1992–94; Comdr, UN Protection Force Bosnia-Herzegovina, 1995; GOC and Dir of Military Ops, NI, 1996–98. Lt Col, 1980; Col, 1985; Brig., 1986; Maj.-Gen., 1990; Lt-Gen., 1995. *Publications:* The Utility of Force: the art of war in the modern world, 2005. *Address:* c/o RHQ The Parachute Regiment, Merville Barracks, Colchester CO2 7UT.

**SMITH, Sandra Mary;** *see* Thomas, Sandra M.

**SMITH, Sandra Melanie, (Mrs K. M. Whittaker);** Head of Conservation and Technical Services (formerly of Conservation), Victoria and Albert Museum, 2002–19; *b* 28 Oct. 1962; *d* of Anthony Smith and Margaret Smith; *m* 1985, Kenneth Martin Whittaker; one *s* two *d*. *Educ:* Institute of Archaeology, London (BSc Hons Archaeol Conservation and Material Sci.). Accredited Mem. Icon (formerly UKIC) 2000; FIIC 2002; FSA 2012. British Museum: Hd of Ceramics and Glass Conservation, Dept of Conservation, 1992–97; Hd, Inorganic Materials Gp, 1997–2002; Actg Keeper, Conservation, 2002. Treas., Internat. Inst. for Conservation of Historic and Artistic Works, 2006–10. Trustee: Gabo Trust, 2011–; Inst. of Conservation, 2011–14. Advr on Conservation, Queen Elizabeth Scholarship Trust, 2010–. Chief Ed., V&A Conservation Jl, 2002–19. *Publications:* (contrib.) The Art of the Conservator, 1992; (ed jtly) Past Practice, Future Prospects, 2001. *Recreations:* walking, gardening, cycling.

**SMITH, Sarah Jane;** University Secretary, since 2013, and Vice-Principal, Strategic Change and Governance, University of Edinburgh; *b* Babraham, Cambs, 29 July 1962; *d* of Michael Waddington Smith and Frances Sheila Smith; *m* 2008, Norman McBeath. *Educ:* St Hugh's Coll., Oxford (BA Hons PPE 1984); Imperial Coll., London (MBA 1996); Harvard Business Sch. (AMP 2005); Acad. Exec. Coaching (Advanced Exec. Coach 2016). Department for Transport: Private Sec. to Minister for Aviation and Shipping, 1987–89; Hd, Internat. Shipping Br., 1989–93; Hd, Internat. Aviation Br., 1993–95; Department for International Development: Hd of Section, Latin Amer. and Caribbean Dept, 1996–98; Dep. Hd, Aid Policy and Resource Dept, 1998–99; Hd, Eastern Asia and Pacific Dept, 1999–2001; Scottish Executive, later Scottish Government: Hd, Children and Families Div., 2001–04; Hd, Strategy and Delivery Unit, 2004–06; Director: Strategy, 2006–07; Children, Young People and Social Care, 2008–11; Children and Families, 2011; Learning, 2011–12; Associate Vice-Principal, Univ. of Edinburgh, 2007–08 (on secondment). Non-exec. Dir, Bd, Archangels Informal Investment, 2004–07. Vis. Prof., Univ. of Edinburgh, 2008–13. *Recreations:* reading, theatre, art, fencing, creative writing. *Address:* University of Edinburgh, Old College, South Bridge, Edinburgh EH8 9YL.

**SMITH, Shaun Malden;** QC 2008; **His Honour Judge Shaun Smith;** a Circuit Judge, since 2018; *b* Sheffield, 3 March 1959; *s* of Jack and Jean Smith; *m* 1991, Janet Wilson. *Educ:* Grenoside Jun. Sch.; Ecclesfield Comp. Sch.; Sheffield Univ. (LLB Law 1980); Inns of Court Sch. of Law. Called to the Bar, Gray's Inn, 1981, Bencher, 2013; in practice as barrister specialising in crime; Figtree Chambers, Sheffield, 1982–90, King Street Chambers, Leicester, 1990–92, 1 High Pavement Chambers, Nottingham, 1992–17 (Jt Hd of Chambers, 2011–17); a Recorder, 2001–17. Sen. Barrister Mem., QC Appointments Panel, 2014–17. Bar Vocational Course Examiner: Nottingham, 2003–06; College of Law, 2006–10; External Examiner, Nottingham Trent LLM, 2012–16. Tutor Judge, Judicial Coll., 2012–; Vis. Prof. of Law, Univ. of Law, 2015–; Hon. Prof. of Law, Nottingham Trent Univ., 2016–. Gov., Coll. of Advocacy, 2016–18. *Recreations:* music (particularly Indie bands), reading, theatre, walking, supporting Sheffield Wednesday. *Address:* Derby Combined Court Centre, Morledge, Derby DE1 2XE.

**SMITH, Simon John Meredith,** CMG 2015; HM Diplomatic Service; Ambassador to Republic of Korea, since 2018; *b* 14 Jan. 1958; *s* of Philip and Mary Smith (*née* Williams); *m* 1984, Sian Rosemary Stickings, MBE; two *d*. *Educ:* Triple C Sch., Grand Cayman; Clifton Coll.; Wadham Coll., Oxford (BA Modern Langs 1980; MA 1984); SOAS, London (Japanese). Dept of Employment, 1981–86, Manager, Unemployment Benefit Office, Tottenham, 1983–84; joined FCO, 1986; Second, then First Sec. (Econ.), Tokyo, 1989–92; Dep. Hd, S European Dept, FCO, 1995–97; Counsellor (Econ./Commercial), Moscow, 1998–2002; Hd, NE Asia and Pacific Dept, 2002–04, Hd, Eastern Dept, 2004–05, Dir, Russia, South Caucasus and Central Asia, 2005–07, FCO; Ambassador to Austria, and UK Perm. Rep. to internat. orgns in Vienna, 2007–12; UK Gov., IAEA, 2007–12; Ambassador to Ukraine, 2012–15. Mem., Adv. Bd, UCL Sch. of Slavonic and E European Studies, 2006–07. Vice Chm., UN Commn on Crime Prevention and Criminal Justice, 2009. *Recreations:* reading in different languages, tromboning, Parkrun. *Address:* c/o Foreign and Commonwealth Office, King Charles Street, SW1A 2AH.

**SMITH, Prof. (Stanley) Desmond,** OBE 1998; FRS 1976; FRSE 1972; FInstP; Professor of Physics and Head of Department of Physics, Heriot-Watt University, Edinburgh, 1970–96, now Professor Emeritus (Dean of the Faculty of Science, 1981–84); Chairman and Founder, Edinburgh Instruments Ltd, 1971–2012; Founder and Director, since 2003 and Chief Scientific Officer, Edinburgh Biosciences Ltd (Chief Executive Officer, 2013–17); *b* 3 March 1931; *s* of Henry George Stanley Smith and Sarah Emily Ruth Smith; *m* 1956, Gillian Anne Parish; one *s* one *d*. *Educ:* Cotham Grammar Sch., Bristol; Bristol Univ. (BSc, DSc); Reading Univ. (PhD). FInstP 1965. SSO, RAE, Farnborough, 1956–58; Research Asst, Dept of Meteorology, Imperial Coll., London, 1958–59; Lectr, then Reader, Univ. of Reading, 1960–70. Member: ACARD, 1985–87; Defence Scientific Adv. Council, 1985–91; Astronomy, Space & Radio Bd, Engrg Bd, SERC, 1985–88; ACOST, Cabinet Office, 1987–88. Principal Investigator, Scottish Collaborative Initiative in Optoelectronics, 1991–97. Initiator and Tech. Co-ordinator, EU project CATACURE, 2014–17. Mem. Council, Inst. of Physics, 1984–87; Chm., Scottish Optoelectronics Assoc., 1996–98. Hon. DSc Heriot-Watt, 2003. C. V. Boys Prizeman, Inst. of Physics, 1976; Educn in Partnership with Industry or Commerce Prize, DTI, 1982; Technical or Business Innovation in Electronics Prize, Electronics Weekly, 1986; James Scott Prize, RSE, 1987; Royal Medal, RSE, 2011. *Publications:* (with J. T. Houghton) Infra-red Physics, 1966; Optoelectronic Devices, 1995; 230 papers on interference filters, semi-conductors, lasers, satellite meteorology, nonlinear optics, optical computing, application of fluorescence to cataract detection, lasers and LEDs to non-invasive treatment and instrumentation. *Recreations:* ski-ing, mountaineering, golf, interacting with seven grandchildren in France, Germany, Holland and USA. *Address:* Tree Tops, 29D Gillespie Road, Colinton, Edinburgh EH13 0NW. *T:* (0131) 441 7225, (office) (01506) 429274. *E:* desgillsmith@gmail.com; 106 Corniche du Pinateau, Chaillol 1600, 05260 St Michel de Chaillol, France. *T:* (4) 92500881. *E:* stanley-desmond.smith@orange.fr; Edinburgh Biosciences Ltd, Suite 1b, 3 Michaelson Square, Kirkton Campus, Livingston EH54 7DP. *T:* (01506) 429724. *E:* des@edinbio.com.

**SMITH, Stephen;** *see* Smith, J. S.

**SMITH, Stephen,** MA; educational consultant, since 2010; Headmaster, Bedford Modern School, 1996–2009; Secretary, Forum of Independent Day Schools Ltd, since 2011; *b* 8 Aug. 1948; *s* of late Joseph Leslie Smith and Audrey May Smith; *m* 1970, Janice Susan Allen; one *s* one *d*. *Educ:* Loughborough Grammar Sch.; Regent's Park Coll., Oxford (BA Modern History 1969; Cert. Ed. 1970; MA 1974). Loughborough Grammar School: Asst History Master, 1970–87; Junior Housemaster, 1976–79; Head of General Studies, 1983–87; Head of History, 1987–93; Dep. Headmaster, Birkenhead Sch., 1993–96. Mission Area Rep. and organist, St Bartholomew's Ch, Sealand, 2016–. Chm., HMC/GSA Sports Subcttee, 2001–09; Chm., Teaching and Learning Cttee, and Gov., Haberdashers' Aske's Boys Sch., 2007–14. Chm., Colmworth History Soc., 2000–15. *Recreations:* piano, organ, singing, oenology, Church and youth work, local history. *Address:* 115 Overlea Drive, Hawarden, Flintshire CH5 3HR.

**SMITH, Prof. Stephen Anthony,** PhD; FBA 2014; FRHistS; Professor of History, University of Oxford, since 2013; Senior Research Fellow, All Souls College, Oxford, since 2012; *b* 1952. *Educ:* Oriel Coll., Oxford (Open Schol.). BA Hons Modern Hist. 1973); Centre for Russian and E Eur. Studies, Univ. of Birmingham (MSocSci Soviet Studies 1974; PhD 1980); Beijing Langs Inst. and Peking Univ. (Cert. Advanced Studies in

Contemp. Chinese 1983). FRHistS 1995. British Council exchange student, Faculty of Hist., Univ. of Moscow, 1976-77; University of Essex: Department of History: Lectr, 1977-84; Sen. Lectr, 1984-91; Prof., 1991-2008; Hd of Dept, 1990-93; Dir, Russian and Soviet Studies Centre, 1985-88; Prof. of Comparative Hist., Eur. Univ. Inst., Florence, 2008-12. Social Sci. Res. Fellow, Nuffield Foundn, 1997-98; Fellow, Internat. Center for Advanced Studies New York Univ., 2004. Wiles Lectr, QUB, 1998. Member, Editorial Board: Jl Communist Studies, 1985-89; Revolutionary Russia, 1989-; Past and Present, 1995- (Ed., 2009-14); Cultural and Social Hist., 2004-; Antropologicheskii Forum, 2005-; Twentieth Century Communism, 2008-; Eurasian Rev. (Kookmin Univ., S Korea), 2008-; Ricerche Storiche, 2009-; Ethnography, 2009-; Jl Social Hist., 2011-. *Publications:* Red Petrograd: revolution in the factories, 1917-1918, 1983; (ed) Oktiabr skaia revoliutsiia i fabzavkomy, vols 1 and 2, 1993; (ed with D. Koenker) Notes of a Red Guard: the autobiography of Eduard Dune, 1993; A Road is Made: communism in Shanghai, 1920-27, 2000; Like Cattle and Horses: nationalism and labor in Shanghai, 1895-1927, 2002; The Russian Revolution: a very short introduction, 2002; (ed with A. Knight) The Religion of Fools? Superstition Past and Present, 2008; Revolution and the People in Russia and China: a comparative history, 2008; (ed) The Oxford Handbook of the History of Communism, 2014; (ed with Paul Betts) Science, Religion and Communism in Cold War Europe, 2016; Russia in Revolution: an empire in crisis, 1890 to 1928, 2017; contribs to jls incl. Past and Present, Revolutionary Russia, Cultural and Social Hist., Amer. Histl Rev., Hist. Today, Slavic Rev., Russian Rev. *Address:* All Souls College, 27 High Street, Oxford OX1 4AL.

**SMITH, Prof. Stephen Kevin,** DSc, MD; FRCOG; FMedSci; consultant, stephenksmith ltd, since 2015; Chairman, East Kent Hospitals University NHS Foundation Trust, since 2018; *b* 8 March 1951; *s* of Albert and Drusilla Smith; *m* 1978, Catriona Maclean Hobkirk Smith (marr. diss. 2017); one *s* two *d*. *Educ:* Birkenhead Sch.; Westminster Med. Sch., Univ. of London (MB BS 1974; MD 1982); MA Cantab 1993; DSc London 2002. FRCOG 1998 (MRCOG 1979); FRSB (FIBiol 1997). Lecturer: Univ. of Edinburgh, 1979-82; Univ. of Sheffield, 1982-85; Cons. Gynaecologist, MRC Reproductive Biology Unit, Edinburgh, 1985-88; Prof. of Obstetrics and Gynaecol., Univ. of Cambridge Clin. Sch., Rosie Maternity, subseq. Addenbrooke's, Hosp., Cambridge, 1988-2004; Fellow, Fitzwilliam Coll., Cambridge, 1991-2004; Principal, Faculty of Medicine, 2004-11, Pro-Rector, 2010-11, Imperial Coll. London; CEO, Imperial Coll. Healthcare NHS Trust, 2007-11; Founding Dean, Lee Kong Chian Sch. of Medicine, and Vice Pres. (Res.), Nanyang Technological Univ., Singapore, 2010-13; Dean, Medicine, Dentistry and Health Scis, Univ. of Melbourne, 2013-15. Non-executive Director: Gt Ormond St Hosp., 2016-18; Netscientific plc, 2016-; Cochrane Innovations, 2016-18. Trustee, Pancreatic Cancer UK, 2016- (Chm., Scientific Adv. Bd, 2017-). Founder FMedSci 1998; FAAHMS 2015. FRSA. *Publications:* pubns on Academic Health Science Centres and the NHS; contribs to sci. and med. pubns on the subject of Reproductive Medicine. *Recreations:* flying, football, music, natural history, politics. *Address:* 21 Holland Street, Cambridge CB4 3DL.
See also I. R. Smith.

**SMITH, Stephen Philip M.;** see Moverley Smith.

**SMITH, Prof. Stephen Robert,** PhD; Professor of Economics, University College London, since 1997 (Dean, Faculty of Social and Historical Sciences, 2008-13); *b* Durham, 25 Nov. 1955; *s* of Dr Russell Smith and Katherine Smith (née Truman); *m* 1987, Beverley Stanford. *Educ:* Durham Johnston Secondary Sch.; Wadham Coll., Oxford (BA Hons PPE); Manchester Univ. (MA (Econ)); University Coll. London (PhD Econs 1997). Econ. Asst, Dept of Industry, 1977-82; Econ. Advr, Dept of Trade, 1982-85; Institute for Fiscal Studies: Sen. Res. Officer, 1985-87; Programme Dir, 1987-90; Dep. Dir, 1990-97. Vis. Prof., Sciences Po, Paris, 2013-14. *Publications:* Britain's Shadow Economy, 1986; (jtly) Fiscal Harmonisation, 1988; Green Taxes and Charges: policy and practice in Britain and Germany, 1995; Environmental Economics: a very short introduction, 2011; Taxation: a very short introduction, 2015; monographs and acad. papers. *Recreations:* printmaking, railway journeys (real and imagined). *Address:* Department of Economics, University College London, WC1E 6BT. *T:* (020) 7679 5882. *E:* stephen.smith@ucl.ac.uk.

**SMITH, Maj.-Gen. Stephen Robert C.;** see Carr-Smith.

**SMITH, Stephen Wynn B.;** see Boys Smith.

**SMITH, Sir Steven Murray, (Sir Steve),** Kt 2011; PhD; FAcSS; Vice-Chancellor and Chief Executive, University of Exeter, since 2002; *b* 4 Feb. 1952; *s* of late William Smith and Doris Smith; *m* 2013, Dr Jeannie Forbes. *Educ:* Univ. of Southampton (BSc Soc. Scis 1973; MSc 1974; PhD 1978). Lectr in Politics, Huddersfield Poly., 1976-78; Lectr, 1979-85, Sen. Lectr, 1985-90, Prof., 1990-92, of Internat. Relns, UEA; Prof. of Internat. Politics, 1992-2002, Pro Vice Chancellor, 1999-2002, UCW, Aberystwyth, subseq. Univ. of Wales, Aberystwyth. Hon. Prof., Jilin Univ., China, 2007-. Member, Board: UUK, 2012-; Heart of SouthWest LEP, 2013-. President: Internat. Studies Assoc., 2003-04; UUK, 2009-11; Chm., Bd of Trustees, UCAS, 2012-. Hon. Fellow: Aberystwyth Univ., 2010; UWIC, 2011. FAcSS (AcSS 2000). Hon. DSc Southampton, 2004; Hon. DEd W of England, 2010. President's Global Leadership Award, Univ. of S Florida, 2012. *Publications:* Foreign Policy Adaptation, 1981; (ed with I. Forbes) Politics and Human Nature, 1983; (ed with M. Clarke) Foreign Policy Implementation, 1985; (ed) International Relations, 1985; (ed with R. Crockatt) The Cold War Past and Present, 1987; (ed jtly) British Foreign Policy, 1988; (ed with R. Little) Belief Systems and International Relations, 1988; (with M. Hollis) Explaining and Understanding International Relations, 1990; (jtly) Deciding Factors in British Politics, 1991; (ed with W. Carlsnaes) European Foreign Policy, 1994; (ed with K. Booth) International Relations Theory Today, 1995; (ed jtly) International Theory, 1995; (ed with J. Baylis) The Globalization of World Politics, 1997, 7th edn 2017; (ed jtly) International Relations Theory, 2007, 4th edn 2016; (ed jtly) Foreign Policy, 2008, 3rd edn 2016; (jtly) Introduction to Global Politics, 2011, 4th edn 2017. *Recreations:* Norwich City FC, theatre, music, firework displays, arctophile. *Address:* Vice-Chancellor's Office, University of Exeter, Northcote House, Queen's Drive, Exeter EX4 4QJ. *T:* (01392) 723000. *E:* vice-chancellor@exeter.ac.uk.

**SMITH, Stuart Graham,** OBE 2009; FRICS; Director: All England Lawn Tennis Ground plc, 1997-2013; International Tennis Federation, 2009-13 (Hon. Life Counsellor); *b* Paddington, 18 Feb. 1946; *s* of James Pettigrew and Ethel Mary Smith; *m* 1968, Marilyn Lesley; three *s*. *Educ:* John Ruskin Grammar Sch., Croydon; St Catharine's Coll., Cambridge (BA 1967; MA 1971). FRICS 1982. Partner, Collier & Madge, Chartered Surveyors, 1969-85; Dir, Lambert Smith Hampton, Chartered Surveyors, 1985-2002. Pres., LTA, 2006-09. *Recreations:* Association Football, gardening, family, tennis. *Address:* Upper Pryors, Cowden, Kent TN8 7HB. *T:* (01342) 850384. *E:* sgscowden@outlook.com. *Club:* All England Lawn Tennis.

**SMITH, Rt Rev. Stuart Meldrum;** Assistant Bishop, Diocese of Adelaide, 1992-98; *b* 8 June 1928; *s* of late F. R. and O. E. Smith; *m* 1st, 1957, Margaret (*d* 2006), *d* of J. L. F. and D. M. Sando; three *s* two *d*; 2nd, 2008, Judith Kay Nurton. *Educ:* Univ. of Adelaide (BA Hons English); St Michael's House, SSM (Scholar in Theol. (Hons), ACT). Ordained 1953; Asst Curate, Glenelg, 1954-56; Mission Chaplain, Meadows, 1956-57; Domestic Chaplain, Bishop of Adelaide, and Precentor, St Peter's Cathedral, 1957-58; Priest-in-charge, Kilburn, 1958-61; Editor, Adelaide Church Guardian, 1959-61 and 1965-76; Rector: Clare, 1961-65; Coromandel Valley (with Blackwood, Eden Hills and Belair), 1965-69; Belair, 1969-72; Unley, 1972-84; Canon of Adelaide, 1974-84; Archdeacon: of Sturt, 1976-84; of Adelaide, 1984-92; Dir of Home Mission and Evangelism, 1984-92. Acting Dean, St Peter's Cathedral, Adelaide, 1998-99; Associate in Ministry, St John's, Adelaide, 2000. Visiting Lecturer: St Barnabas Coll., 1966-81; St Michael's House, 1975-77. Hon. Chaplain, Walford C of E Girls' Grammar Sch., 1973-75. Mem., Gen. Synod and Gen. Synod Standing Cttee, 1979-98. Chm., Council of Govs, Pulteney Grammar Sch., 1973-97. *Recreations:* walking, reading, gardening. *Address:* 8 Fairway Avenue, Glenelg North, SA 5045, Australia. *T:* (8) 82952210.

**SMITH, Susan Gwynneth,** OBE 2009; Chair, Local Government Boundary Commission for Wales, 2001-08 (Member, 1996-2001); *b* 18 Dec. 1946; *d* of George Henry David Abbott and Victoria Gwynneth May Abbott; *m* 1969, David Charles Smith. *Educ:* Tiffin Sch. for Girls, Kingston-upon-Thames; University Coll. London (LLB ext. 1970). Admitted as solicitor, 1970; Asst Solicitor, Hammersmith and Fulham LBC, 1970-73; Sen. Solicitor, then Asst Borough Solicitor, 1973-78, Borough Solicitor, 1978-92, Wandsworth LBC; Dir, Admin. and Legal Services, Cardiff CC, 1992-96. Mem., Parly Boundary Commn for Wales, 1998-2008. Mem., Standing Orders Commn, Nat. Assembly for Wales, 1998-99. Chair, Standards Cttee, Pembrokeshire CC, 2001-10. Non-exec. Dir, Cardiff and Vale NHS Trust, 2000-02. Ind. Adjudicator for Local Authorities in Wales, 2003-08. *Recreations:* supporting Mothers' Union work, choral singing, visiting Venice. *E:* smith.sycamores@btinternet.com.

**SMITH, Prof. Susan Jane,** DPhil; FBA 2008; FRSE; FAcSS; Mistress of Girton College, Cambridge, since 2009. *Educ:* St Anne's Coll., Oxford (BA Geog. 1977; Hon. Fellow); Nuffield Coll., Oxford (DPhil 1982). Research Fellow: St Peter's Coll., Oxford, 1981-82; Dept of Govt, Brunel Univ., 1984-85; Dept of Social and Economic Res., Univ. of Glasgow, 1985-90; Ogilvie Prof. of Geog., Univ. of Edinburgh, 1990-2004; Prof. of Geog. and Dir, Inst. of Advanced Study, Durham Univ., 2004-09. Adjunct Prof., Sch. of Global Studies, RMIT Univ., Melbourne, 2008-; Hon. Prof. of Social and Econ. Geog., Univ. of Cambridge, 2011-; BCEC Professorial Fellow, Bankwest-Curtin Econs Centre, Curtin Business Sch., Curtin Univ., Perth, 2016-18. FAcSS (Founding AcSS 1999). FRSE 2000. *Publications:* (ed with P. Jackson) Social Interaction and Ethnic Segregation, 1981; (ed jtly) Ethnic Segregation in Cities, 1981; (with P. Jackson) Exploring Social Geography, 1984; Crime, Space and Society, 1986; (ed with J. Mercer) New Perspectives on 'Race' and Housing in Britain, 1987; The Politics of 'Race' and Residence, 1989; (jtly) Housing and Social Policy, 1990; (ed jtly) Housing for Health, 1991; (jtly) Children at Risk?, 1995; (jtly) A Review of Flexible Mortgages, 2002; (ed with R. Pain) Critical GeoPolitics of Fear, 2008; (ed with M. Munro) The Microstructures of Housing Markets, 2009; (ed jtly) Handbook of Social Geographies, 2010; (ed with B. A. Searle) The Blackwell Companion to the Economics of Housing: the housing wealth of nations, 2010; (Ed. in Chief) International Encyclopaedia of Housing and Home, 2012; contribs to books and academic jls. *Recreation:* brass band and early music enthusiast. *Address:* Girton College, Cambridge CB3 0JG.

**SMITH, Susan Louise;** Director, Accelerator Science and Technology Centre, since 2010, and Head, Daresbury Laboratory, since 2012, Science and Technology Facilities Council; *b* Paisley, 18 Nov. 1960; *d* of Thomas Prentice Thomson and Margaret Thomson (née McQue); *m* 1990, Robert James Smith; one *s* one *d*. *Educ:* West Primary Sch., Paisley; Castle Head Secondary Sch., Paisley; John Neilson Inst.; Glasgow Univ. (BSc Hons Natural Philosophy 1982). Postgrad. Physics, Glasgow Univ., 1982-85; Accelerator Physicist, SERC, Daresbury Lab., 1985-98; Gp Leader, Accelerator Physics, CCLRC, Daresbury Lab., 1998-2010. Vis. Prof., Liverpool Univ., 2008-. Gov., Riverside Sch., Widnes and Runcorn, 2015-. *Recreations:* table tennis, golf, keeping fit, family. *Address:* Daresbury Laboratory, SciTech Daresbury, Keckwick Lane, Warrington, Cheshire WA4 4AD. *E:* susan.smith@stfc.ac.uk.

**SMITH, Terence Charles,** MNZM 2012; Chief Executive, Fundsmith LLP, since 2010; *b* 15 May 1953; *s* of Ernest George and Eva Ada Smith; *m* 1974, Barbara Mary George; two *d*. *Educ:* Stratford Grammar Sch.; University Coll., Cardiff (BA); Management Coll., Henley (MBA). Mgt trainee, then Gp Finance Manager, Barclays Bank, 1974-83; Bank Analyst, W. Greenwell & Co., 1984-86; Hd, Financial Desk, BZW, 1986-88; Bank Analyst, James Capel, 1988-89; Hd of Res., UBS Phillips & Drew, 1990-92; Bank Analyst, 1992-96, Dir, 1996-2000, Chief Exec., 2000, Collins Stewart; Collins Stewart acquired Tullett, 2003 and Prebon, 2004; Collins Stewart Tullett Prebon demerged, 2006; Chm., 2006-10, Dep. Chm., 2010, Collins Stewart; Chief Exec., Tullett Prebon, 2006-14. ACIB 1976; Series 24, Nat. Assoc. of Securities Dealers. Hon. Fellow, Cardiff Univ., 2016. *Publications:* Accounting for Growth, 1992, 2nd edn 1996; Celebrating Five Years of Investing in Decades of Success: articles anthology 2010-2015, 2015. *Recreations:* kickboxing, Muay Thai, shooting. *Address:* Fundsmith LLP, 33 Cavendish Square, W1G 0PW. *T:* (020) 3551 6337, Mauritius.

**SMITH, Thomas C.;** see Cavalier-Smith.

**SMITH, Thomas Jonathan;** QC 2014; *b* Wakefield, 27 Jan. 1976; *s* of Brian Smith, *qv*; *m* 2008, Janice Wong; one *s* one *d* (and one *d* decd). *Educ:* Walton High Sch., Stafford; Clare Coll., Cambridge (BA 1997; MA; LLM 1998). Called to the Bar, Middle Temple, 1999; in practice as barrister, specialising in commercial and financial law, 1999-. *Recreations:* ski-ing, travel, family, Rugby League. *Address:* 3-4 South Square, Gray's Inn, WC1R 5HP. *T:* (020) 7696 9900, *Fax:* (020) 7696 9911. *E:* tomsmith@southsquare.com.

**SMITH, Thomas William McLardy;** Chairman: Nuclear Decommissioning Authority, 2017-Feb. 2020; Angel Trains Group Ltd, since 2015; *b* Perranporth, Cornwall, 15 May 1957; *s* of David Smith and Diana Mary Smith (née Drake); *m* 1984, Katherine Joanna Marles; one *s* one *d*. *Educ:* Hampton Grammar Sch.; Balliol Coll., Oxford (BA Chem. 1979). Joined FCO, 1979; Third Sec., FCO, 1979-83; Second Sec., Beijing, 1983-86; First Sec., FCO, 1986-90; Business Develt Exec., Trafalgar House plc, 1990-97; Man. Dir, Midland Expressway Ltd, 1997-2001; Develt Dir, 2001-07, Man. Dir Rail Develt, 2007-11, Go-Ahead Gp plc. Chm., Assoc. of Train Operating Cos, 2009-13; non-executive Director: Nuclear Decommissioning Authy, 2013-17; Highways England Co. Ltd, 2014-17. *Publications:* (contrib.) Balliol Studies, 1982. *Recreations:* rowing (a still competitive veteran), coastal walking, classical music, rivers. *Address:* Nuclear Decommissioning Authority, Herdus House, Westlakes Science and Technology Park, Moor Row, Cumbria CA24 3HU. *T:* (01925) 803020. *E:* tom.smith@nda.gov.uk. *Clubs:* Broxbourne Rowing, Lea Rowing.

**SMITH, Timothy;** see Smith, W. T. C.

**SMITH, Rt Rev. Timothy D.;** see Dudley-Smith.

**SMITH, Timothy John;** Principal, Nevill Hovey & Co. Chartered Accountants, since 2018 (Director, 2002-18); *b* 5 Oct. 1947; *s* of late Captain Norman Wesley Smith, CBE and Nancy Phyllis Smith; *m* 1980, Jennifer Jane Scott-Hopkins, *d* of Sir James Scott-Hopkins; two *s*. *Educ:* Harrow Sch.; St Peter's Coll., Oxford (MA). FCA; CTA. Articled with Gibson, Harris & Turnbull, 1969; Audit Sen., Peat, Marwick, Mitchell & Co., 1971; Company Sec., Coubro & Scrutton (Hldgs) Ltd, 1973. Sec., Parly and Law Cttee, ICA, 1979–82. Pres., Oxford Univ. Conservative Assoc., 1968; Chm., Coningsby Club, 1977–78. MP (C): Ashfield, April 1977–1979; Beaconsfield, May 1982–1997. PPS to Chief Sec. HM Treasury, 1983, to Sec. of State for Home Dept, 1983–85; a Vice Chm. and Treas., Conservative Party, 1992–94; Parly Under-Sec. of State, NI Office, 1994. Member: Public Accts Cttee, 1987–92, 1995–97; Select Cttee on NI, 1994–97; Vice-Chm., Cons. Finance Cttee, 1987–92. Partner, 2001–13, Consultant, 2013–15, H. M. Williams Chartered Accountants. Member: Truro Diocesan Synod, 2012–18; Bishop's Diocesan Council, Truro, 2015–16. Vice-Chm., Cornwall Area Conservatives, 2009–12. Director: Quality South West Ltd, 2003–07; Harbour Centre (Plymouth), 2004–08; W Country Renewables Ltd, 2011–13. Mem. Council, ICA, 1992–94. Chairman: Launceston Abbeyfield Soc., 2003–10; N Cornwall Cons. Assoc., 2016–19 (Treas., 2014–16); Treasurer: St Petroc's Soc., 2005–14; Cornwall Community Foundn, 2009–18 (Vice-Chm., 2018–); Cornwall and Devon Countryman's Fair, 2011–16; Trigg Major Deanery Synod, 2014–; Cornwall Garden Soc., 2018–. *Recreations:* theatre, gardening, tennis. *Address:* Queen's Acre, Boyton, Launceston, Cornwall PL15 9RJ.

**SMITH, Timothy John;** Technical Director, Tesco plc, 2012–17; *b* Sheffield, 15 Nov. 1955; *s* of John and Patricia Smith; *m* 1982, Sheila Truman; one *s* two *d*. *Educ:* Withernsea High Sch.; Leeds Univ. (BSc Microbiol. and Zool.). Unigate plc, 1978–80; gen. mgt, 1981–90, Divl Dir, 1990–94, Northern Foods; Pres. and CEO, Sara Lee UK, 1994–99; Dir, Express Dairies plc, 1999–2005; Chief Executive: Arla Foods UK plc, 2005–08; Food Standards Agency, 2008–12. Mem., Musicians' Union. *Recreations:* getting wet, guitar, cycling a long way. *Club:* Farmers.

**SMITH, Tobias Augustine William R.;** *see* Riley-Smith.

**SMITH, Vanessa Frances H.;** *see* Hall-Smith.

**SMITH, Prof. Vernon Lomax,** PhD; Professor of Economics and Law, Chapman University, Orange, California, since 2008; Professor of Economics and Law, George Mason University, 2001–08, now Emeritus; *b* 1 Jan. 1927; *s* of Vernon Chessman Smith and Lulu Belle Smith (*née* Lomax, then Bougher); *m* Candace C. Smith. *Educ:* North High Sch., Kansas; CIT (BS 1949); Univ. of Kansas (MA 1952); Harvard Univ. (PhD 1955). Purdue University, Indiana: Mem., Mgt Scis Res. Gp, 1955–56; Asst Prof., 1956–58, Associate Prof., 1958–61, Prof. of Econs, 1961–64, Krannert Prof., 1964–67; Professor of Economics: Brown Univ., Rhode Island, 1967–68; Univ. of Mass, Amherst, 1968–75; Prof. of Econs, 1975–88, Regents Prof., 1988–2001, Univ. of Arizona, Tucson. Vis. Associate Prof., Stanford Univ., 1961–62; Fellow, Center for Advanced Study in Behavioral Scis, Calif, 1972–73; Sherman Fairchild Dist. Scholar, CIT, 1973–74; Vis. Prof., USC and CIT, 1974–75; Adjunct Scholar, Cato Inst., Washington, 1983–. (Jtly) Nobel Prize for Econs, 2002. *Publications:* include: (jtly) Economics: an analytical approach, 1958; Investment and Production, 1961; Economics of Natural and Environmental Resources, 1977; (ed) Research in Experimental Economics, vol. 1, 1979, vol. 2, 1982, vol. 3, 1985; (ed) Schools of Economic Thought, 1990; Papers in Experimental Economics, 1991; Experiments in Decision, Organization and Exchange, 1993; Bargaining and Market Behavior: essays in experimental economics, 2000; Rationality in Economics, 2008; Discovery - A Memoir, 2008; (with S Gjerstad) Rethinking Housing Bubbles, 2014; articles in jls. *Address:* Dale E. Fowler School of Law, Chapman University, One University Drive, Orange, CA 92866, USA.

**SMITH, Vincent Neil;** solicitor; Visiting Fellow, British Institute of International and Comparative Law, since 2010; Assistant Professor, ESCP Europe Business School, since 2015 (Affiliate Professor in Law, 2014–15); *b* 11 Dec. 1962; *m* 1997, Barbara Cross; one *s*. *Educ:* Univ. of Surrey (BSc Hons); Univ. of Liège (licence spéciale en droit européen); King's Coll. London (PhD Law). Admitted solicitor, 1990; Simmons & Simmons, 1988–98; Partner, Pinsent Curtis, 1999–2000; Sen. Legal Advr, Office of Telecommunications, 2000–02; Office of Fair Trading: Dir, Competition Policy Co-ordination, and Dep. Divisional Dir, 2002–03; Dir, Competition Enforcement Div., 2003–06; Sen. Dir for Competition, 2006–07; Partner: Cohen, Milstein, Hausfeld & Toll, later Hausfeld & Co. LLP, 2007–10; Sheppard & Smith, 2011–13. *Address:* British Institute of International and Comparative Law, Charles Clore House, 17 Russell Square, WC1B 5JP. *E:* v.smith@biicl.org; ESCP Europe, London Campus, 527 Finchley Road, NW3 7BG. *E:* vsmith@escpeurope.eu.

**SMITH, Warren James;** Lord-Lieutenant of Greater Manchester, since 2007; *b* Manchester, 1 July 1948; *s* of William James Smith and Rowena Smith (*née* Gore). Various appts in banking and property development cos, 1965–2008. JP Manchester 1983–2003; DL 1995–2007, High Sheriff, 1997–98, Custos Rotulorum, 2007–, Gtr Manchester. High Steward, Manchester Cathedral, 2009–. President: Gtr Manchester W Co. Scout Council, 2007–; County Priory Gp, St John Gtr Manchester, 2007–. Hon. Col, Gtr Manchester ACF, 2007–18; Pres., ATC, 2008–. Chairman: Turning Point, 1995–98; Manchester Concert Hall Trust (Bridgewater Hall), 1995–2015; Trustee, Hallé Orch., 1989–2001; Life Mem., Hallé Concert Soc. Hon. DLitt: Salford 2011; Manchester Metropolitan, 2016; Hon. LLD Bolton, 2011. KStJ 2011 (CStJ 2008). Medal of Honour, Manchester Univ., 2011. *Recreations:* gardening, the arts. *Address:* Greater Manchester Lieutenancy Office, Parkway 5, Suite 6, Parkway Business Centre, Princess Road, Manchester M14 7HR. *T:* (0161) 834 0490. *E:* secretary@gmlo.org. *Club:* Salford Lads and Girls.

**SMITH, (Warwick) Timothy (Cresswell); His Honour Judge Timothy Smith;** a Circuit Judge, since 2014; *b* Liverpool, 16 June 1959; *s* of Peter and Prudence Smith; *m* 1986, Siân Layzell; two *s* one *d*. *Educ:* Birkenhead Sch.; Trinity Coll., Cambridge (BA 1981). FCIArb 1997. Called to the Bar, Middle Temple, 1982; in practice as barrister, 1982–2014; Asst Recorder, 2000, Recorder, 2000–14. *Recreations:* theatre, cinema, fair weather sailing.

**SMITH, Wendy Alison K.;** *see* Kenway-Smith.

**SMITH, Wilbur Addison;** author; *b* 9 Jan. 1933; *m* 1971, Danielle Antoinette Thomas (*d* 1999); *m* 2000, Mokhiniso Rakhimova; two *s* one *d* by former marriages. *Educ:* Michaelhouse, Natal; Rhodes Univ. (BCom). Business executive, 1954–58; factory owner, 1958–64; full-time author, 1964–. *Publications:* When the Lion Feeds, 1964; Dark of the Sun, 1965; Sound of Thunder, 1966; Shout at the Devil, 1968; Gold Mine, 1970; Diamond Hunters, 1971; The Sunbird, 1972; Eagle in the Sky, 1974; Eye of the Tiger, 1975; Cry Wolf, 1976; Sparrow Falls, 1977; Hungry as the Sea, 1978; Wild Justice, 1979; A Falcon Flies, 1980; Men of Men, 1981; The Angels Weep, 1982; The Leopard hunts in Darkness, 1984; The Burning Shore, 1985; Power of the Sword, 1986; Rage, 1987; A Time to Die, 1989; Golden Fox, 1990; Elephant Song, 1991; River God, 1993; The Seventh Scroll, 1995; Birds of Prey, 1997; Monsoon, 1999; Warlock, 2001; Blue Horizon, 2003; A Triumph of the Sun, 2005; The Quest, 2007; Assegai, 2009; Those in Peril, 2011; Vicious Circle, 2013; Desert God, 2014; (jtly) Golden Lion, 2015; (jtly) Predator, 2016; Pharaoh, 2016; (jtly) War Cry, 2017; (jtly) The Tiger's Prey, 2017; On Leopard Rock: a life of adventures (memoir), 2018; Courtney's War, 2018; (jtly) King of Kings, 2019. *Recreations:* fly fishing, big game angling, wing shooting, ski-ing, scuba diving.

**SMITH, Sir William Antony John R.;** *see* Reardon Smith.

**SMITH, William Austin N.;** *see* Nimmo Smith, Rt Hon. Lord.

**SMITH, William Francis W.;** *see* Wyldbore-Smith.

**SMITH, (William) Nigel W.;** *see* Wenban-Smith.

**SMITH, William Peter;** *see* Smith, His Honour P. W.

**SMITH, Her Honour Zoë Philippa;** DL; a Circuit Judge, 1999–2019; *b* 16 May 1949; *d* of late Basil Gerrard Smith and of Marjorie Elizabeth Smith (*née* Artz). *Educ:* Queenswood, Hatfield. Called to the Bar, Gray's Inn, 1970, Bencher, 2012; in practice at the Bar, 1970–99; a Recorder, 1991–99. DL Berks, 2011. *Recreation:* dining out.

**SMITH-BINGHAM, Col Jeremy David;** Director General, British Equestrian Federation, 1994–97; *b* 29 July 1939; *s* of Col Oswald Cyril Smith-Bingham and Vera Mabel Smith-Bingham (*née* Johnson); *m* 1969, Priscilla Mary Inceldon-Webber; three *s*. *Educ:* Cheam; Eton; RMA, Sandhurst. Commnd Royal Horse Guards (The Blues), 1959; Lt Col, 1981; jssc, 1982; CO, The Blues and Royals, 1982–85; CO, Tactical Sch., RAC, 1985–87; Col, 1987; Chief Exercise Planner, HQ N Army Gp, 1987–90; Comdr, Household Cavalry, and Silver Stick to the Queen, 1990–93; COS, HQ London Dist, 1993–94. Hon. Col, Royal Devon Yeomanry, 2013–. Chm., N Devon Cons. Assoc., 2010–15. *Recreations:* horses, tennis, rackets, ski-ing, water sports, fishing, shooting, golf, gardening. *Address:* St Brannocks House, Braunton, Devon EX33 1HN. *T:* (01271) 812270. *E:* mail@stbrannocks.com. *Clubs:* Cavalry and Guards, Queen's.

**SMITH-CAMERON, Rev. Canon Ivor Gill;** Chaplain to the Queen, 1995–99; *b* 12 Nov. 1929; *s* of James Smith-Cameron and Cynthia Smith-Cameron (*née* Fitzgerald). *Educ:* Madras Christian Coll., India (MA Eng. Lang. and Lit.); Coll. of the Resurrection, Mirfield, Yorks. Ordained deacon, 1954; priest, 1955; Curate, St George's, Rumboldswyke, Chichester, 1954–58; Chaplain, London Univ., 1958–72; Canon Residentiary and Diocesan Missioner, Dio. Southwark, 1972–92; Asst Curate, All Saints, Battersea, 1992–94; retd 1994; Canon Residentiary Emeritus, 1994. Hon. DD Serampore Coll., India, 2004. *Publications:* Pilgrimage: an exploration into God, 1982; The Church of Many Colours, 1998; New Lamps, 2000. *Recreations:* cooking, jam making, reading, walking. *Address:* 24 Holmewood Gardens, SW2 3RS. *T:* (020) 8678 8977. *E:* ivorsmithcameron@yahoo.co.uk.

**SMITH-DODSWORTH, Sir David (John),** 9th Bt *cr* 1784, of Newland Park and Thornton Watlass, Yorkshire; company director, since 1992; *b* Rotorua, NZ, 23 Oct. 1963; *s* of Sir John Christopher Smith-Dodsworth, 8th Bt and his 1st wife, Margaret Anne (*née* Jones); *S* father, 2012; *m* 1996, Elizabeth Anne Brady; one *s* one *d*. *Educ:* Ampleforth. Farming career. *Heir:* *s* Matthew David Smith-Dodsworth, *b* 26 May 2002. *Address:* Thornton Watlass Hall, Ripon, N Yorks HG4 4AS. *T:* (01677) 422803. *E:* sirdavid@twhall.co.uk.

**SMITH-GORDON, Sir (Lionel) Eldred (Peter),** 5th Bt *cr* 1838; engaged in book publishing, since 1960; *b* 7 May 1935; *s* of Sir Lionel Eldred Pottinger Smith-Gordon, 4th Bt, and Eileen Laura (*d* 1979), *d* of late Captain H. G. Adams-Connor, CVO; *S* father, 1976; *m* 1962, Sandra Rosamund Ann, *d* of late Wing Commander Walter Farley, DFC and Mrs Dennis Poore; one *s* one *d*. *Educ:* Eton College; Trinity College, Oxford. *Heir:* *s* Lionel George Eldred Smith-Gordon [*b* 1 July 1964; *m* 1993, Kumi, *d* of Masashi Suzuki, Japan; two *s* one *d*]. *Address:* 125 Rivermead Court, Ranelagh Gardens, SW6 3SD. *T:* (020) 7751 3134. *E:* publisher@smithgordon.com.

**SMITH-LAITTAN, James,** CMG 1995; HM Diplomatic Service, retired; *b* 13 May 1939; *s* of James Alexander and Etta Smith; *m* 1969, Mary Susan Messer; three *d*. *Educ:* Buckie High Sch.; North West London Poly. Nat. Service, 1st Queen's Dragoon Guards, 1958–60; Admiralty, 1961–62; joined CRO, 1963; Dacca, 1964–66; FCO, 1966–68; Brussels, 1968; Rabat, 1969–72; Accra, 1972–75; Rome, 1975–79; Asst Overseas Insp., FCO, 1979–82; Trade Comr, Hong Kong and concurrently Consul, Macao, 1982–86; Asst Head, Migration and Visa Dept, FCO, 1987–90; Commercial Mgt and Exports Dept, FCO, 1990–91; Trade Counsellor and Head of China Trade Unit, Hong Kong, 1991–95; Consul-Gen., Auckland, 1996–99. *Recreations:* hill-walking, family, travel. *Club:* Hong Kong (Hong Kong).

**SMITH-MARRIOTT, Sir Peter Francis,** 12th Bt *cr* 1774, of Sydling St Nicholas, Dorset; *b* 14 Feb. 1927; *yr* *s* of Sir Ralph George Cavendish Smith-Marriott, 10th Bt and Phyllis Elizabeth (*née* Kemp); *S* brother, 2013; *m* 1961, Jean Graham Martin (*née* Ritchie); five *s* (incl. twins). *Educ:* Bristol Cathedral Sch. *Heir:* *s* Martin Ralph Smith-Marriott, *b* 30 Dec. 1962.

**SMITHERS, Prof. Alan George,** PhD; CPsychol; author and commentator; Professor of Education and Director, Centre for Education and Employment Research, University of Buckingham, since 2004; *b* 20 May 1938; *s* of late Alfred Edward Smithers and Queenie Lilian Smithers; *m* 1962, Angela Grace Wykes (marr. diss. 2003); one *d* (and one *d* decd). *Educ:* Barking Abbey Grammar Sch.; King's Coll., Univ. of London (BSc, PhD 1966); Bradford Univ. (MSc, PhD 1974); Univ. of Manchester (MEd 1981). CPsychol 1988. Lecturer in: Biol., Coll. of St Mark and St John, Chelsea, 1962–64; Botany, Birkbeck Coll., Univ. of London, 1964–67; Research Fellow, then Sen. Lectr in Educn, Bradford Univ., 1967–76; Prof. of Educn, Univ. of Manchester, 1977–96; seconded to British Petroleum, 1991–92; Prof. of Educn (Policy Res.), Brunel Univ., 1996–98; Sydney Jones Prof. of Educn, Liverpool Univ., 1998–2004. Member: Nat. Curriculum Council, 1992–93; Beaumont Cttee on Vocational Qualifications, 1995–96; Special Advr, H of C Educn and Employment Cttee, 1997–2001, Educn and Skills Cttee, 2001–07, Children, Schs and Families Cttee, 2007–10, Educn Cttee, 2010–15. Fellow, Soc. for Res. into Higher Educn, 1986. *Publications:* Sandwich Courses: an integrated education?, 1976; The Progress of Mature Students, 1986; Graduates in the Police Service, 1990; The Vocational Route into Higher Education, 1991; Every Child in Britain, 1991; All Our Futures: Britain's education revolution, 1993; England's Education, 2004; Blair's Education: an international perspective, 2007; Confusion in the Ranks, 2013; Social Disadvantage and Widening Access to Universities, 2015; annual reviews of A-Levels, GCSEs and teacher trng; book chapters; contrib. papers to jls of biology, psychol. and educn; *with Dr Pamela Robinson:* The Growth of Mixed A-Levels, 1988; Increasing Participation in Higher Education, 1989; Teacher Provision: trends and perceptions, 1991; Beyond Compulsory Schooling, 1991; Technology in the National Curriculum, 1992; General Studies: breadth at A-Level?, 1993; Changing Colleges: further education in the market place, 1993; The Impact of Double Science, 1994; Post-18 Education: growth, change, prospect, 1995; Further Education Reformed, 2000; Coping with Teacher Shortages, 2000; Attracting Teachers, 2000; Five Years On, 2006; Patterns and Policies in Physics Education, 2006; The Paradox of Single Sex and Coeducation, 2006; Bucking the Trend, 2007; School Headships: present and future, 2007;

**SMITHERS**, Specialist Science Schools, 2009; Physics Participation and Policies, 2009; Worlds Apart, 2010; Choice and Selection in Education, 2010; Educating the Highly Able, 2012. *Recreations:* walking, theatre. *Address:* Centre for Education and Employment Research, University of Buckingham, Buckingham MK18 1EG. *T:* (01280) 820270, *Fax:* (01280) 820343. *E:* alan.smithers@buckingham.ac.uk. *W:* www.alansmithers.com.

**SMITHERS, Jonathan Robert Saville**; Chief Executive Officer, Law Council of Australia, since 2016; President, Law Society of England and Wales, 2015–16 (Vice President, 2014–15); Consultant, CooperBurnett Solicitors, since 2016; *b* Pembury, Kent, 3 May 1962; *s* of David and Margaret Smithers; *m* 1987, Mathea Blankers; two *d*. *Educ:* Beacon Sch., Crowborough, Sussex; Nottingham Trent Univ. (LLB). Admitted Solicitor, 1986; joined CooperBurnett, Solicitors, 1984, Partner 1989–2016, Sen. Partner, 2015–16. Mem. Council, Law Soc. of England and Wales, 2007–16. Mem., Rules Cttee, Land Registry, 2012–16. President: Tunbridge Wells, Tonbridge and Dist Law Soc., 2002; Kent Law Soc., 2007–08. Hon. DLaws Nottingham Trent, 2016. *Recreation:* Oriana Singers. *Address:* Law Council of Australia, 19 Torrens Street, Braddon, ACT 2612, Australia. *T:* (2) 6246 3788. *E:* jonathan.smithers@lawcouncil.asn.au.

**SMITHSON, Michael**; polling analyst, writer and blogger; Editor, politicalbetting.com, since 2004; *b* 11 May 1946; *s* of late Arthur Smithson and Doris Smithson (*née* Simpson); *m* 1969, Jacqueline Anne Cowan; one *s* two *d*. *Educ:* Burnage GS, Manchester; London Sch. of Econs (LLB). Thomson Orgn Grad. Trng Scheme, with Newcastle Jl and Evening Chronicle, 1968–71; BBC Radio News: Mem., Editl Staff, 1971–78; Duty Ed., 1978–80; Dep. Hd, BBC TV Licence Campaign, 1980–81; i/c Corporate Publicity Unit, BBC, 1982–84; Dir, Public Relns, RSPCA, 1984–88; Mgt Consultant, 1988–91, Dir, 1990–91, Finite Gp plc; Man. Dir, Pemberley Associates, 1991–94; Dir of Fundraising, LSE, 1994–96; Develt Dir, Univ. of Cambridge, and Fellow of Queens' Coll., Cambridge, 1996–99; Dir of Develt, Univ. of Oxford, 1999–2005; Fellow, Magdalen Coll., Oxford, 2000–05; Dir of Develt and Alumni Relns, Univ. of York, 2005–07. Councillor (Lib Dem): Beds CC, 1990–96; Bedford BC, 1996–2000. Contested (Lib Dem) N Beds, 1992. *Recreations:* talking politics, cycling, enjoying fine teas, my family. *Address:* 5 Devon Road, Bedford, Beds MK40 3DJ.

**SMITS, Simon Johannes Hendricus**; Ambassador of the Netherlands to the Court of St James's, since 2015; *b* Leiden, Netherlands, 13 Sept. 1955; *s* of Johannes Hendricus Smits and Aafje Eikelenboom; *m* 1982, Astrid M. H. J. Kleinen; four *s*. *Educ:* Amsterdam Free Univ. (MA English Lang. and Lit. with Internat. Law 1981); Manchester Coll., Oxford (Harting Fellow, 1977–78). English teacher, Dr de Bruyne Lyceum, Utrecht, 1981–82; Dep. Inspector for Staff Estabt, Min. of Interior and Kingdom Relns, 1982–83; diplomatic trng, Min. of Foreign Affairs (Netherlands Assoc. for Internat. Affairs), 1983; postings in Belgrade, Bangladesh, Geneva, Zagreb, The Hague, SA and Perm. Repn to EU, Brussels, 1984–2006; on secondment to Royal Dutch Shell as Sen. Govt Relns Advr, Shell HQ, The Hague, 2006–08; Dir, Econ. and Ecological Cooperation Dept, 2008–09; Dep. Dir-Gen. for Eur. Cooperation and Dir, Climate, Energy, Envmt and Water, 2009; Actg Dir-Gen. for Eur. Cooperation, 2009–10; Director-General: Internat. Relns, Min. of Econ. Affairs, Agric. and Innovation, 2011–12; for Foreign Econ. Relns, Min. of Foreign Affairs, 2012–15. Medal, Multinat. Peace Ops in former Yugoslavia, Netherlands, 1992; EC Monitor Mission Medal, EC, 1992. Kt Comdr and Cross, Order of Merit (Germany), 2011; Comdr, Most Dist. Order of Merit (Brunei Darussalam), 2013; Comdr's Cross and Star, Order of Merit (Poland), 2014; Order of Rising Sun with Gold Rays and Neck Ribbon 3rd Cl. (Japan), 2014; Comdr, 1st Cl., Order of Dannebrog (Denmark), 2015. *Recreations:* theatre, reading, running, tennis. *Address:* Embassy of the Netherlands, 38 Hyde Park Gate, SW7 5DP. *T:* (020) 7590 3299. *E:* LON@minbuza.nl. *Club:* Travellers.

**SMOL, Prof. John Paul**, OC 2013; PhD; FRS 2018; FRSC; Professor, Department of Biology, since 1991, and Canada Research Chair in Environmental Change, since 2000, Queen's University, Kingston, Ontario; *b* 10 Oct. 1955. *Educ:* McGill Univ. (BSc Marine Biol. 1977); Brock Univ. (MSc Limnology 1979); Queen's Univ., Kingston, Ont (PhD 1982). Postdoctoral work in High Arctic with Geol Survey of Canada, 1982–84; Faculty Mem., Queen's Univ., Kingston, Ont, 1984–; Co-Dir, Paleoecological Envmtl Assessment and Res. Lab., Queen's Univ., 1991–. Killam Fellow, Canada Council, 1995–97. Founding Ed., Jl Paleolimnology, 1982–2007; Ed., Envmtl Reviews, 2004–. FRSC 1996; Dist. Fellow, Geol Assoc. Canada, 1997; Fellow, Royal Canadian Geographical Soc. 2010. Steacie Prize, Nat. Res. Council, 1993; Rigler Prize, Soc. Canadian Limnologists, 1995; Miroslaw Romanowski Medal, 2001, Flavelle Medal, 2008, McNeil Medal for Public Awareness of Sci., 2015, RSC; Gerhard Herzberg Gold Medal, 2004, Brockhouse Canada Prize for Interdisciplinary Res. in Sci. and Engrg, 2014, NSERC; G. Evelyn Hutchinson Award, Amer. Soc. Limnology and Oceanography, 2007; Killam Prize, Canada Council, 2009; Erebus Medal, 2015, Martin Bergmann Medal for Excellence in Arctic Leadership and Sci., 2015, Royal Canadian Geographical Soc.; Naumann-Thienemann Medal, Internat. Soc. Limnology, 2018. Queen Elizabeth II Diamond Jubilee Medal, 2012. *Publications:* (ed jtly) Diatoms and Lake Acidity: reconstructing pH from siliceous algal-remains in lake sediments, 1986; (jtly) Atlas of Chrysophycean Cysts, vol. I, 1995, vol. II, 2001; (ed jtly) Chrysophyte Algae: ecology, phylogeny and development, 1995; (jtly) Diatoms from Lakes in British Columbia (Canada) and their Relationship to Lakewater Salinity, 1995; (with E. D. Reavie) Freshwater Diatoms from the St Lawrence River, 1998; (ed with E. F. Stoermer) The Diatoms: applications for the environmental and earth sciences, 1999, 2nd edn 2010; (ed with W. M. Last) Tracking Environmental Change Using Lake Sediments, vols 1 and 2, 2001, (ed jtly) vols 3 and 4, 2001, vol. 5, 2012; Pollution of Lakes and Rivers: a paleoenvironmental perspective, 2002, 2nd edn 2008; (jtly) The Ecology and Distribution of Diatoms in Wood Buffalo National Park, Northern Alberta and the North West Territories, Canada, 2004; (ed jtly) Long-Term Environmental Change in Arctic and Antarctic Lakes, 2004; (jtly) Diatoms of North America, 2008; (jtly) Ecology: a Canadian context, 2011, 2nd edn 2015; (ed jtly) Environmental Contaminants: using natural archives to track sources and long-term trends of pollution, 2015; contribs to scientific jls. *Address:* Department of Biology, Queen's University, Kingston, ON K7L 3N6, Canada. *T:* (613) 533 6147, *Fax:* (613) 533 6617. *E:* smolj@queensu.ca.

**SMOLIRA, Rev. David Richard**, SJ; Parish Priest, St Ignatius Catholic Parish, Stamford Hill, 2014; *b* 9 Sept. 1955; *s* of late Mieczysław Smolira and Eileen Smolira (*née* Taylor). *Educ:* Manchester Univ. (BSc); Heythrop Coll., London Univ. (BD); Liverpool Univ. (Advanced DipSocSc with CQSW); St Louis Univ., USA (MSocWork); Loyola Univ. Chicago, USA (MSc). UKCP Registered Psychotherapist, until 2006; organisational develt consultant. Entered Society of Jesus, 1978; ordained priest, 1988; Dir, Home & Away Project, Catholic Children's Soc., 1989–94; Provincial Asst for Formation, SJ, 1997–99; Provincial Superior of the British Province, SJ, 1999–2005; Founding Dir, 2006–10, Pres., 2010–14, Jesuit Inst. SA; Regl Superior, Jesuits, SA, 2008–14. *Recreations:* gardening, natural history, photography. *Address:* St Ignatius Jesuit Community, 27 High Road, Stamford Hill, N15 6ND.

**SMOOT, Prof. George F.**, PhD; Professor, Physics Department, 1994, now Emeritus, and Founding Director, Berkeley Center for Cosmological Physics, since 2007, University of California, Berkeley; *b* 1945; *s* of George and Talicia Smoot; *m* Maxine. *Educ:* Massachusetts Inst. of Technol. (BS 1966; PhD 1970). Research Physicist: Space Sciences Lab., Univ. of California, Berkeley, 1971–; Lawrence Berkeley National Lab., 1974–. (Jtly) Nobel Prize in Physics, 2006. *Publications:* (with K. Davidson) Wrinkles in Time, 1993; articles in jls. *Address:* Department of Physics, University of California, Berkeley, 366 LeConte Hall, Berkeley, CA 94720, USA.

**SMOUHA, Joseph**; QC 2003; *b* 20 Jan. 1963; *s* of Brian and Hana Smouha; *m* 1994, Lucy Howard; two *s*. *Educ:* Harrow Sch.; Magdalene Coll., Cambridge (MA); New York Univ. Sch. of Law (Kenneson Fellow; Fulbright Schol.). Called to the Bar, Middle Temple, 1986, Bencher, 2010; specializes in internat. commercial law. Chm., Commercial Bar Assoc., 2013–15. Dir, English Concert, 2003–. Trustee, British Friends of Hebrew Univ., Jerusalem, 2012–. *Recreations:* opera, ski-ing, walking, tennis, clarinet player. *Address:* Essex Court Chambers, 24 Lincoln's Inn Fields, WC2A 3EG. *T:* (020) 7813 8000, *Fax:* (020) 7813 8080.

**SMOUT, Prof. (Thomas) Christopher**, CBE 1994; PhD; FBA 1988; FRSE; FSAScot; Director, Institute for Environmental History, University of St Andrews, 1992–2001; Historiographer to the Queen in Scotland, since 1993; *b* 19 Dec. 1933; *s* of Sir Arthur and Lady (Hilda) Smout; *m* 1959, Anne-Marie Schøning; one *s* one *d*. *Educ:* The Leys Sch., Cambridge; Clare Coll., Cambridge (MA; PhD 1960). FRSE 1975; FSAScot 1991. Dept of Economic History, Edinburgh University: Asst Lectr, 1959; Lectr, 1962; Reader, 1964; Prof. of Econ. History, 1970; University of St Andrews: Prof. of Scottish History, 1980–91; Dir, St John's House Centre for Advanced Histl Studies, 1992–97. Visiting Professor: Strathclyde Univ., 1991–97; Dundee Univ., 1993–2005; York Univ., 1998–99; Hon. Prof., Stirling Univ., 2000–06. Member: Cttee for Scotland, Nature Conservancy Council, 1986–91; Bd, NCC (Scotland), 1991–92; Bd, Scottish Natural Heritage, 1992–98 (Dep. Chm., 1992–97); Royal Commn on Ancient and Historic Monuments of Scotland, 1987–2000 (Vice-Chm., 2000); Bd of Trustees, Nat. Museums of Scotland, 1991–95; Royal Commn on Historical Manuscripts, 1999–2003; Adv. Council on Public and Private Records, 2003–04. Chm., Scottish Coastal Archaeol. and the Problem of Erosion Trust, 2002–12; Chm., Strathmartine Trust, 2013–18; Trustee, Woodland Trust, 1998–2004. Patron, Scottish Native Woods, 2004–. Hon. Fellow, TCD, 1995. Hon. DSSc QUB, 1995; Hon. DSc (SocSci) Edinburgh, 1996; Hon. DLitt: St Andrews, 1999; Glasgow, 2001; DUniv Stirling, 2002. Patrick Geddes Medal, RSGS, 2014. *Publications:* Scottish Trade on the Eve of Union, 1963; A History of the Scottish People, 1969; (with I. Levitt) The State of the Scottish Working Class in 1843, 1979; A Century of the Scottish People, 1986; (with S. Wood) Scottish Voices, 1990; (with A. Gibson) Prices, Food and Wages in Scotland, 1995; Nature Contested, 2000; (jtly) A History of the Native Woodlands of Scotland 1500–1920, 2005; Exploring Environmental History: selected essays, 2009; (with M. Stewart) The Firth of Forth: an environmental history, 2012. *Recreations:* birdwatching, butterflies, bees. *Address:* Upper Flat, Chesterhill, Shore Road, Anstruther, Fife KY10 3DZ. *T:* (01333) 310330. *E:* christopher@smout.org.

**SMURFIT, Sir Michael (William Joseph)**, KBE 2005; Chairman, Smurfit Kappa Group, 2005–07; *b* 7 Aug. 1936; *s* of late Jefferson Smurfit; *m* 1st, Norma Treisman (marr. diss.); two *s* two *d*; 2nd, Birgitta Beimark; two *s*. Joined Jefferson Smurfit & Sons Ltd, Dublin, 1955; founded Jefferson Smurfit Packaging Ltd, Lancs, 1961; Jefferson Smurfit & Sons Ltd, subseq. Jefferson Smurfit Group: Dir, 1964; Jt Man. Dir, 1966–69; Dep. Chm., 1969–77; Chief Exec., 1977–2002; Chm., 1977–2005. Owner of K Club, host to Ryder Cup 2006. *Publications:* A Life Worth Living (autobiog.), 2014.

**SMYTH, Clare**, MBE 2013; Chef/Proprietor, Core, Notting Hill, since 2017; *b* Ballymoney, NI, 6 Sept. 1978; *d* of William Boyce Smyth and Doreen Brenda Margret Smyth. *Educ:* Dunluce High Sch.; Highbury Coll., Portsmouth. Commis chef, Bibendum, Chelsea; head chef, St Enodoc Hotel, Rock; chef de partie, later sen. sous chef, Restaurant Gordon Ramsay, 2002–05; worked as private chef, France, then at Louis XV, Monaco, 2005–07; Head Chef, 2007–13, Chef Patron, 2012–15, Restaurant Gordon Ramsay. Core achieved Two Stars, Michelin Guide 2019. World's Best Female Chef, The World's 50 Best Restaurants, 2018.

**SMYTH, David William**; QC (NI) 1989; **His Honour Judge Smyth**; a County Court Judge, Ards Division, Northern Ireland, 2011–13; a Deputy County Court Judge, since 2013; *b* 12 Nov. 1948; *s* of late William McKeag Smyth and Eva Maud Smyth (*née* Moran); *m* 1977, Anthea Linda Hall-Thompson, DL; one *s* two *d* (and one *d* decd). *Educ:* Methodist Coll., Belfast; Queen's Univ., Belfast (Porter Scholar, 1967; LLB 1971). Called to the NI Bar, 1972, Bencher, 1997, Treas., 2009–10; political res., London, 1972–74; called to the Bar, Gray's Inn, 1978, Ireland, 1989; a County Court Judge, Fermanagh and Tyrone Div., 1990–97, Antrim Div., 1997–2011, NI. Chairman: Legal Aid Adv. Bd, NI, 1994–2005; NI Council on Alcohol, 1996–98; Council of County Court Judges, 2005–; Member: Franco-British-Irish Judicial Co-operation Cttee, 1997–; Criminal Justice Wkg Gp on Drugs, 2002; Cttee, Anglo-French Judicial Gp, 2002; Youth Conferencing Adv. Gp, 2003; Lands Tribunal, 2014–; President: Addiction NI (formerly NI Community Addiction Service), 1998–; Methodist Coll. Belfast Former Pupils Assoc., 2012–14. Chm. Bd of Advrs, Inst. of Criminology, QUB, 2002–. Mem. Bd, Ulster Youth Orch., 2015– (Chm., 2017–). Trustee, N Belfast Wkg Men's Club, 1974–; Chm., Winston Churchill Meml Trust, NI, 2015–. Winston Churchill Scholar, 2002. FRSA 2009. *Publications:* contrib. to NI Legal Qly and Jl of Judicial Studies Bd (Ire.). *Recreations:* cycling, opera, history. *Address:* Royal Courts of Justice, Chichester Street, Belfast BT1 3JE. *E:* davidsmyth80@icloud.com.

**SMYTH, Desmond**; *see* Smyth, J. D.

**SMYTH, Joan Rutherford**, CBE 1998; Chairman, Progressive Building Society, 2005–12 (Director, 2001–12); Vice Chairman, Eirgrid, 2015–18 (Director, 2009–18); *b* 29 Dec. 1946; *d* of David James Hunter and Kathleen McRoberts (*née* Carson); *m* 1983, John Vernon Smyth (MBE 2016). *Educ:* Glenlola Collegiate Sch., Bangor; Dalriada Sch., Ballymoney; Queen's Univ., Belfast (BSc Econ.). Employee Relns Manager, Gallaher Ltd, 1969–89; Partner, Allen & Smyth, 1989–92; Chair and Chief Exec., EOC for NI, 1992–99. Chm., NI Transport Hldg Co., 1999–2005; Dir, Trinity Housing (formerly Choice Housing, then Sanctuary Housing Assoc.), 2002–12. Member: Bd, British Council, 1999–2002 (Chm., NI Cttee, 1999–2003); Steering Gp, Women's Nat. Commn, 1999–2002; NI QC Appts Panel, 2005–07; Ind. Assessor of Public Appts, 2005–12. Chm., Chief Executives Forum, NI, 2001–08; Mem., Women's Forum, NI, 2007–; Chair, Women's Fund for NI, 2012–. Pres., GB and Ireland Fedn, Soroptimist Internat., 2002–03; Vice-Chair, Soroptimist Internat. Convention Cttee, 2019–; President: British Red Cross, NI, 2005–12; Confedn of Ulster Socs, 2005–12; North Down Guides, 2007–12. Pres., Railway Preservation Soc. of Ireland, 2018– (Vice-Pres., 2012–18). Trustee, 2009–10, Mem., Adv. Bd, 2010–18, Gender Action for Peace and Security, UK. CIPD 1998. Trustee, Bangor Drama Club, 2013–16. Hon. LLD Ulster, 2000. *Recreations:* golf, drama. *Address:* 12 Shandon Park East, Bangor, Co. Down, Northern Ireland BT20 5HN. *T:* and *Fax:* (028) 9146 9889. *E:* joanrsmyth@btinternet.com.

**SMYTH, Prof. John Fletcher**, MD; FRCPE, FRCP, FRCSE, FRCR; FRSE; Professor of Medical Oncology, 1979–2008, Assistant Principal, since 2009, University of Edinburgh (Director of Cancer Research Centre, 2002–05); Hon. Director, Cancer Research UK (formerly Imperial Cancer Research Fund) Medical Oncology Unit, Edinburgh, 1980–2005; *b* 26 Oct. 1945; *s* of Henry James Robert Smyth and Doreen Stanger (*née* Fletcher); *m* 1st, 1973, Catherine Ellis; two *d* (marr. diss. 1992); 2nd, 1995, Ann Cull; two step *d*. *Educ:* Bryanston Sch.; Trinity Coll., Cambridge (choral exhibnr; BA 1967; MA 1971); St Bartholomew's Hosp. (MB BChir 1970); MD Cantab 1976; MSc London 1975. FRCPE 1981; MRCP 1973, FRCP 1983; FRCSE 1994; FRCR 1995; FRSE 1996. House Officer posts: St Bartholomew's Hosp. and RPMS, London, 1970–72; Asst Lectr, Dept of Med. Oncology, St Bartholomew's Hosp., 1972–73; CRC Res. Fellowship, Inst. Cancer Res., 1973–75; MRC Travelling Fellowship, Nat. Cancer Inst., USA, 1975–76; Sen. Lectr, Inst. Cancer Res., 1976–79. Honorary Consultant Physician: Royal Marsden Hosp. and Brompton Hosp., 1977–79; Lothian Health Bd, 1979–2008; Vis. Prof. of Medicine and Associate Dir for Med. Res., Univ. of Chicago, 1979. Chm., Expert Adv. Gp for Haematol. and Oncology for Commn on Human Medicines, 2006–13; Member: Cttee on Safety of Medicines, 1999–2005; Scientific Adv. Gp for Oncology, EMEA, 2005–07. Member: Council, 1990–94, Bd, 2001–10, EORTC; EORTC Charitable Trust, 1990–2016 (Vice Chm., 2014–16); Council, UICC, 1990–94; President: European Soc. of Med. Oncology, 1991–93; Fedn of European Cancer Socs, 2005–07 (Treas., 1992–97). Ed.-in-Chief, European Jl of Cancer, 2001–10. Founder Mem., Monteverdi Choir, 1967–2014 (Trustee, 2014–). Gov., Bryanston Sch., 1979–2014. *Publications:* Basic Principles of Cancer Chemotherapy, 1980; The Management of Lung Cancer, 1984; Communicating with Cancer Patients, 2013; more than 300 contribs to various med. and scientific jls on cancer medicine, pharmacology, clinical and exptl cancer therapeutics. *Recreations:* flying and singing (sometimes simultaneously). *Address:* 18 Inverleith Avenue South, Edinburgh EH3 5QA. *T:* (0131) 552 3775. *Club:* Athenæum.

**SMYTH, (Joseph) Desmond,** CBE 2000; FCA; Managing Director, Ulster Television, 1983–99; *b* 20 April 1950; *s* of Andrew and Annie Elizabeth Smyth; *m* 1975, Irene Janette (*née* Dale); one *s* one *d*. *Educ:* Limavady Grammar School; Queen's University, Belfast. BSc (Jt Hons Pure Maths and Statistics). Accountancy articles, Coopers and Lybrand, 1971–75; Ulster Television: Chief Accountant, 1975–76; Financial Controller and Company Secretary, 1976–83. Dir, Viridian (formerly NIE) plc, 1996–2005. Pres., NI Chamber of Commerce and Industry, 1991–92. FRTS 1993. *Recreations:* fishing, gardening. *E:* desmondsmyth@yahoo.co.uk.

**SMYTH, Karin;** MP (Lab) Bristol South, since 2015; *b* London, 8 Sept. 1964; *m*; three *s*. *Educ:* Bishopshalt Sch.; Uxbridge Tech. Coll.; Univ. of E Anglia (BA Econ. and Social Studies 1988); Univ. of Bath (MBA 1995). Joined NHS as Manager, 1988; Pol Asst to Valerie Davey, MP, 1997–2001; non-exec. Dir, Bristol N PCT, 2002–06; Ind. Project and Interim Manager, 2008–10; Locality Manager, South Bristol Consortium, 2010–. Mem., Public Accounts Select Cttee, 2015–17. Trustee, Bristol Deaf Centre, 2007–08. Governor: St Werburgh's Park Nursery Sch. and Children's Centre; St Thomas More Secondary Sch., 1996–2000. *Address:* House of Commons, SW1A 0AA.

**SMYTH, Liam Cledwyn L.;** *see* Laurence Smyth.

**SMYTH, Rev. Martin;** *see* Smyth, Rev. W. M.

**SMYTH, Michael Thomas,** CBE 2009; lawyer, senior advisor; *b* 3 March 1957; 2nd *s* of Rev. Kenneth Smyth and Freda Smyth; *m* 1983, Joyce Anne Young; one *s* one *d*. *Educ:* Royal Belfast Academical Instn; Clare Coll., Cambridge (MA). Admitted solicitor, 1982; Partner, 1990–2010, Head of Public Policy, 2003–10, Clifford Chance. Chairman: Public Concern at Work, 2001–11; Social Welfare Law Coalition, 2006–11. Mem., Press Complaints Commn, 2011–14. Visiting Professor: QMUL, 2011–17; Univ. of Essex, 2011–17. Associate Fellow, Centre for Public Law, Univ. of Cambridge, 2010–15. Chairman: Internat. Senior Lawyers' Project (UK), 2005–15; Law for Life: Foundn for Public Legal Educn, 2011–16; Community Links, 2012–17; Member: Lawyers Adv. Bd, Wesleyan Assurance Soc., 2011–; Adv. Council on Nat. Records and Archives, 2014–; Legal Services Bd, 2016–; Fundraising Regulator, 2016–. FRSA. Hon. QC 2014. Freeman, City of London, 2018. *Publications:* Business and the Human Rights Act, 2000; (jtly) The Law of Political Donations, 2012; (jtly) Sanctions Law, 2019. *Club:* Reform.

**SMYTH, Richard Ian;** Principal, Fulwood Academy, 2010–14; *b* 19 Nov. 1951; *s* of Ronald and Elsa Smyth; *m* 1983, Nicole Adrienne Ryser; one *s* two *d*. *Educ:* Sedbergh Sch.; Emmanuel Coll., Cambridge (BA 1974; PGCE). Asst Master, Christ's Hosp., 1975–77; worked in family baking and confectionery business, 1977–81; Lay Asst to Anglican Vicar of Berne, Switzerland, 1981–82; Asst Master, Gresham's Sch., 1982–85; Housemaster, Wellington Coll., 1985–92; Headmaster: King's Sch., Bruton, 1993–2004; St Peter's Sch., York, 2004–09. Gov., Terrington Hall Prep. Sch., 2007–. *Recreations:* cricket, golf, Rugby, ski-ing, alpine flowers, roses. *Clubs:* MCC; Easingwold Golf.

**SMYTH, Prof. Rosalind Louise,** CBE 2015; MD; FRCPCH, FMedSci, FERS; Professor of Child Health and Director, Great Ormond Street Institute of Child Health (formerly Institute of Child Health), University College London, since 2012; *b* 28 Sept. 1958; *d* of Robert Smyth and Louisa Smyth (*née* Noble); *m* 1986, Andrew Richard Bowhay; one *s* one *d*. *Educ:* Down High Sch., Downpatrick; Clare Coll., Cambridge (BA 1980; MA 1984); Westminster Med. Sch. (MB ChB 1983; MD 1993). DCH 1985; MRCP 1986; FRCPCH 1997. Jun. posts, Westminster and St Stephen's Hosps, Westminster Children's Hosp. and KCH, 1983–86; Registrar, Ipswich Hosp., 1987–88; Res. Registrar, Papworth Hosp., 1988–90; Sen. Registrar, 1990–93, Consultant Paediatrician, 1994–96, Alder Hey Children's Hosp.; University of Liverpool: Sen. Lectr, Dept of Child Health, 1996–99; Brough Prof. of Paediatric Medicine, 1999–2012; Hd, Div. of Child Health, 2001–12. Sen. Investigator, NIHR, 2008–. Dir, UK Medicines for Children Res. Network, 2005–12; Chm., Paediatric Expert Adv. Gp to Commn on Human Medicines, 2006–13. Non-exec. Dir, Gt Ormond St Hosp. NHS Foundn Trust, 2013–. FMedSci 2006; FERS 2014. *Publications:* (ed with J. V. Craig) The Evidence-based Manual for Nurses, 2002; (ed jtly) Forfar and Arneil's Textbook of Paediatrics, 6th edn 2003; numerous contribs to med. jls and books. *Recreations:* reading, ski-ing, running, gardening. *Address:* UCL Great Ormond Street Institute of Child Health, University College London, 30 Guilford Street, WC1N 1EH. *T:* (020) 7905 2189, *Fax:* (020) 7905 2820.

**SMYTH, Thomas Weyland B.;** *see* Bowyer, T. W.

**SMYTH, Dr Sir Timothy (John),** 2nd Bt *cr* 1956, of Teignmouth, Co. Devon; consultant and board director, since 2011; *b* 16 April 1953; *s* of Julian Smyth (*d* 1974) and late Phyllis, *d* of John Francis Cannon; S grandfather, Brig. Rt Hon. Sir John Smyth, 1st Bt, VC, MC, 1983; *m* 1981, Bernadette Mary, *d* of Leo Askew (marr. diss. 2005); two *s* two *d*. *Educ:* Univ. of New South Wales. MB, BS 1977; LLB 1987; MBA (AGSM) 1985; FRACMA 1985. Resident Medical Officer, 1977–79; Medical Administrator, Prince Henry Hosp., Prince of Wales Hosp. Gp, Sydney, 1980–86; Chief Exec. Officer, Sydney Health Service, 1986–88; Gen. Man., St George Hosp., Sydney, 1988–91; CEO, Hunter Area Health Service, 1992–97; Dep. Dir-Gen., Policy, DoH, NSW, 1997–2000; Health Partner, DLA Phillips Fox (formerly Phillips Fox) Lawyers, 2000–08; Dep. Dir-Gen., Health System Performance Div., DoH, NSW, 2008–11. *Heir:* *s* Dr Brendan Julian Smyth, FRACP, *b* 4 Oct. 1981. *Address:* PO Box 264, Enmore, NSW 2042, Australia.

**SMYTH, Rev. (William) Martin,** *b* 15 June 1931; *s* of James Smyth, JP, and Minnie Kane; *m* 1957, Kathleen Jean Johnston, BA; two *d* (and one *d* decd). *Educ:* Methodist Coll., Belfast; Magee University Coll., Londonderry; Trinity Coll., Dublin (BA 1953, BD 1961); Assembly's Coll., Belfast. Assistant Minister, Lowe Memorial, Finaghy, 1953–57; Raffrey Presbyterian Church, Crossgar, 1957–63; Alexandra Presbyterian Church, Belfast, 1963–82. Member, Northern Ireland Convention, 1975; Mem. (UU) Belfast S, NI Assembly, 1982–86 (Chm., Health and Social Services Cttee, 1983–84; Chm., Finance and Personnel Cttee, 1984–86). MP (UU) Belfast South, March 1982–2005 (resigned seat Dec. 1985 in protest against Anglo-Irish Agreement; re-elected Jan. 1986). Chief UU Whip, 1995–2000; Member, Select Committee: for Social Services, 1983–90; on Health, 1990–97; on NI Affairs, 2001–05. Member Executive: UK Branch, IPU, 1985–92, 1995–2005; CPA, 1986–2005. Ulster Unionist Council: Chm. Exec., 1974–76; Vice-Pres. 1974–2000; Hon. Sec., 2000–01; Pres., 2001–03. Dir, Ormeau Business Park, 1988–. Member, Council: Belfast Bible Coll., 1974–2013; Christian Witness to Israel, 1990–. Governor, Belfast City Mission. Grand Master, Grand Orange Lodge of Ireland, 1972–96; Grand Master of World Orange Council, 1974–82, Pres., 1985–88; Hon. Past Grand Master, Canada, and Hon. Deputy Grand Master, USA, NZ, NSW, of Orange Order. *Publications:* (ed) Faith for Today, 1961; pamphlets: Why Presbyterian?, 1963; Till Death Us Do Part, 1965; In Defence of Ulster, 1970; The Battle for Northern Ireland, 1972; A Federated People, 1988; (contrib.) Forbidden Faith, 2010; occasional papers, and articles in Christian Irishman, Evangelical Quarterly, Biblical Theology. *Recreations:* reading, photography; former Rugby player (capped for Magee University College). *Address:* 6 Mornington, Annadale Avenue, Belfast BT7 3JS. *T:* and *Fax:* (028) 90643816. *E:* wms1690@btinternet.com.

**SMYTH-OSBOURNE, Lt Gen. Sir Edward (Alexander),** KCVO 2016; CBE 2012; Commander, Allied Rapid Reaction Corps, since 2019; *b* Plymouth, 18 May 1964; *s* of late George William Smyth-Osbourne and Ann Katherine Louisa Smyth-Osbourne; *m* 1996, Lucy Helen Turner; one *s* one *d*. *Educ:* Eton; Univ. of St Andrews (MA). Joined Army, 1983; CO, Household Cavalry Regt, 2005–08; Comdr, 38 (Irish) Bde, 2010–11; Dir, Force Reintegration, HQ ISAF, Afghanistan, 2012–13; GOC London District and Maj. Gen. Household Div., 2013–16; Dep. Comdr NATO Rapid Deployable Corps, Italy, 2016–19. Lt Col, Comdg Household Cavalry and Silver Stick in Waiting, 2014–19; Col, Life Guards and Goldstick in Waiting, 2019–. *Recreations:* shooting, fishing, walking, ski-ing, sailing, gardening, rural life, collecting books. *Address:* 29 The Close, Salisbury, Wilts SP1 2EJ. *Club:* Endsleigh Fishing.

**SMYTHE, Brig. Michael,** OBE 1989; Clerk to the Vintners' Company, 1997–2012; *b* 30 April 1948; *s* of Peter and Kay Smythe; *m* 1st, 1976, Sally Paget-Cooke (marr. diss. 2001); one *s* one *d*; 2nd, 2004, Carole James. *Educ:* Ratcliffe Coll. Commnd RA, 1968: Adjt, King's Troop, RHA, 1975–78; psc 1980; CO 94th Regt, RA, 1986–88; MA to C-in-C UKLF, 1988–90; HCSC 1990; COS 2nd Inf. Div., 1990–91; Comdr, RA 1st Armd Div., 1991–93; rcds 1994; Brig., HQ Land, 1995–96. Chair, Trustees, Holly Lodge Centre, 2016–. *Recreations:* walking, wine.

**SNAPE,** Baron *cr* 2004 (Life Peer), of Wednesbury in the County of West Midlands; **Peter Charles Snape;** transport consultant; *b* 12 Feb. 1942; *s* of late Thomas and Kathleen Snape; *m* 1st, 1963 (marr. diss. 1980); two *d*; 2nd, 2004, Janet Manley. *Educ:* St Joseph's RC Sch., Stockport; St Winifred's Sch., Stockport; Dialstone Secondary Modern, Stockport. Railway signalman, 1957–61; regular soldier, RE and RCT, 1961–67; goods guard, 1967–70; clerical officer BR, 1970–74. Non-exec. Dir, W Midlands Travel, 1992–97; Chm., Travel W Midlands, 1997–2000. MP (Lab) West Bromwich East, Feb. 1974–2001. An Asst Govt Whip, 1975–77; a Lord Comr, HM Treasury, 1977–79; opposition spokesman for Defence, 1979–82, for Home Affairs, 1982–83, for Transport, 1983–92. Member: Council of Europe and WEU, May–Nov. 1975; N Atlantic Assembly, 1980–83. Consultant: National Express Gp, 2001–07; First Gp plc, 2007–09. Chm., Bus Appeals Body, 2009–13; Nat. Patron, Community Transport, 2008–13. Fellow, Inst. of Travel and Tourism, 2008–. Mem., Bredbury and Romiley UDC, 1971–74 (Chm., Finance Cttee). Chm., Stockport County AFC, 2011–13 (Dir, 2010–13). Hon. Freeman, Borough of Sandwell, 2010. *Address:* Hildercroft, 281 Highfield Road, Hall Green, Birmingham B28 0BU.

**SNAPE, Edward George Crighton;** theatre producer and impresario; Chief Executive, Fiery Angel Ltd, since 2001; *b* London, 7 Feb. 1966; *s* of John and Alison Snape; *m* 1999, Marilyn Eardley; one *s* one *d*. *Educ:* Taverham High Sch., Norwich; Norwich City Coll. Co-founder: The Ticketmachine Group, 1993; Fiery Dragons, 2011. Dir, Arts Th., London, 2000–05; Chair, League of Ind. Producers. Producer: The Complete Works of William Shakespeare: Abridged, Criterion, and UK tour, 1992; Salad Days, Vaudeville, 1996; Kindertransport, Vaudeville, 1997; Bugsy Malone, Queen's Th., 1998; Fascinating Aida, Vaudeville and Theatre Royal, Haymarket, 2003; Oleanna, Garrick, 2004; The 39 Steps, Criterion, 2006–15 (Olivier Award, 2007), UK tour and NY, 2008, 10th Anniv. tour, 2016; Swallows and Amazons, Vaudeville, 2011; Goodnight Mr Tom, nat. tour, 2011, Phoenix, 2013; The Ladykillers, Gielgud Th., 2012; Another Country, Trafalgar Studios, 2014; Ghost Stories, Arts, 2014–15; To Kill A Mockingbird, UK tour and Barbican, 2015; Kenneth Branagh Th. Co. prodns, Garrick, 2015–16; Goodnight Mr Tom, Duke of York's and UK tour, 2016; Young Frankenstein, Garrick, 2017; Long Day's Journey Into Night, Wyndham's, 2018; Mary Stuart, Duke of York's, 2018; Home I'm Darling, NT, transf. Duke of York's, 2019; Night of the Iguana, Noel Coward, 2019; The Son, Duke of York's, 2019. Mem. Exec. Bd, Soc. of London Theatre, 2011–. *Recreations:* anything apart from theatre. *Address:* Fiery Angel Ltd, 2nd Floor, National House, 60-66 Wardour Street, W1F 0TA. *T:* (020) 7292 8888. *E:* esnape@fiery-angel.com. *Clubs:* Garrick, Ivy.

**SNASHALL, Prof. David Charles,** FRCP; Professor of Occupational Medicine, King's College School of Medicine, University of London, 2011–15, now Emeritus (Senior Lecturer, 1982–2011); Honorary Consultant, Occupational Health and Safety Services, Guy's and St Thomas' NHS Foundation Trust (formerly Guy's and St Thomas' Hospitals), since 1982 (Clinical Director (formerly Head of Service), 1982–2015); *b* 3 Feb. 1943; *s* of Cyril Francis Snashall and Phyllis Mary Snashall; partner, Carolyn Graham; three *d*. *Educ:* Haberdashers' Aske's Sch., Hatcham; Edinburgh Univ. (MB ChB 1968); Univ. of Wales Coll. of Cardiff (LLM 1996); London Sch. of Hygiene and Tropical Medicine (MSc 1979). FFOM 1987; FRCP 1993; FFOMI 2004; FFTM (Glas) 2006. Jun. med. posts, Warwick, Edinburgh, Paris and Vancouver, 1968–73; Chief Medical Officer: Majes Project, Peru, 1975–77; Mufindi Project, Tanzania, 1981–82. Chief Medical Adviser: FCO, 1989–98; HSE, 1998–2003. Pres., Faculty of Occupational Medicine, 2002, 2004–08. Member: GMC, 1989–2003; Council, BMA, 2009–12; Ind. Medical Expert Gp, Armed Forces Compensation Scheme, 2009–. *Publications:* ABC of Work Related Disorders, 1997; (with D. Patel) ABC of Occupational and Environmental Medicine, 2003, 2nd edn 2012. *Recreations:* climbing, gardening, European languages, cycling, cooking, jazz. *Address:* 2 Charity Cottages, Petsoe End, Emberton, Bucks MK46 5JL. *E:* david.snashall1@btinternet.com.

**SNEADER, Kevin David;** Global Managing Partner, McKinsey & Co., since 2018; *b* Ottawa, Canada, 5 May 1966; *s* of Dr Walter Eric Sneader and Myrna Joan Sneader; *m* 1995, Amy Muntner; two *d*. *Educ:* Univ. of Glasgow (LLB 1st Cl. Hons 1988); Harvard

Univ. (MBA with Highest Dist. 1993). Joined McKinsey & Co., London, 1989; worked in Beijing, Paris and Hong Kong offices; Managing Partner: New Jersey, Philadelphia and Washington offices, 2007–10; UK and Ireland, 2010–14; Chm., Asian offices, 2014–18. *Publications*: contrib. reports on global econ. and business trends, productivity growth and innovation in China and Asia, and also gender and diversity. *Recreations*: Glasgow Celtic FC, fitness, Rugby, family. *Address*: McKinsey & Co., 40/F ICBC Tower, 3 Garden Road, Central, Hong Kong SAR. *T*: 28681188, *Fax*: 28459985. *E*: kevin_sneader@mckinsey.com. *Clubs*: Caledonian, Arts; Harvard (NYC).

**SNEATH, David Rupert,** TD 1991, and Bar 2000; DL; Fee-Paid Employment Judge, Nottingham, 2010–12 and 2014–15 (Sheffield, 2012–14); *b* 7 June 1948; *s* of John and Stella Doreen Sneath; *m* 1st, 1971, Anna Minding (marr. diss. 1984); two *d*; 2nd, 1986, Carol Parsons. *Educ*: Pembroke Coll., Cambridge (MA). Called to the Bar, Inner Temple, 1970; in practice at the Bar, Nottingham, 1971–92; pt-time Chm., 1983–92, full-time Chm., 1992–98, Industrial Tribunals; Regl Chm., Employment Tribunals, later Regl Employment Judge, Leeds, 1998–2010. Commnd TA, 1969; TA Comd and Staff Course, Camberley, 1989; Comd, 3rd Bn Worcestershire and Sherwood Foresters Regt (V), 1991; Col (TA) 1994; Dep. Hon. Col D (WFR) Co., E of England Regt, 1999–2007; Chief Mil. Ops, Office of Staff Judge Advocate, Multinat. Corps, Iraq, 2006. Pres., Territorial Commns Bd, 1997–99. Asst Sec. Gen., Interallied Confedn of Reserve Officers, 1996–98. County Pres., Notts, RBL, 2019– (Co. Vice Pres., 2004–19). Trustee: Worcs and Sherwood Foresters Regt, 1996–2007; Sherwood Foresters Mus., 1996–; Site of Sherwood Foresters Meml, Crich, Derbys, 2005–; Mercian Regt, 2009–18; Nottingham Community Foundn, 2015–. Gov., Portland Trng Coll., 2018–. Speaker at seminars for judiciary on discrimination, European Law Acad., 2008–16. DL 1998, High Sheriff, 2017–18, Notts. Bronze Star Medal (USA), 2006. *Publications*: Employment Tribunals, 2005; (jtly) booklet on pensions loss in employment tribunals; Jazz Music (novel), 2015. *Recreations*: flute playing, choral singing, opera, theatre, ski-ing, cycling for charity (coast to coast, 2014, 2015; Pedal to Paris (for RBL), 2016). *Address*: 7 Kirkby Road, Ravenshead, Nottingham NG15 9HD. *T*: (01623) 456310. *Clubs*: Army and Navy; Nottingham.

**SNELGROVE, Anne Christine;** *b* 7 Aug. 1957; *d* of Eric and Chris Stamper; *m* 1978, Michael H. Snelgrove. *Educ*: Ranelagh Sch., Bracknell; King Alfred's Coll., Winchester (BEd (Hons) 1979); City Univ. (MA 1986). Teacher of English and Drama, France Hill Sch., Camberley, 1979–86; vocational educn curriculum advr, Surrey CC, 1986–95; consultant, 1995–97; mgr, office of Barbara Follett, MP, 1997–99; community relns mgr, Magnox Ltd, 2001–04. MP (Lab) Swindon S, 2005–10; contested (Lab) same seat, 2010, 2015. PPS to the Prime Minister, 2009–10.

**SNELL, Arthur Gordon;** Managing Director, Actagon Ltd, since 2018; *b* Brighton, 30 Oct. 1975; *s* of Roderick Saxon Snell and Cecilia Mary Snell (*née* Gordon Clark); *m* 2006, Charlotte Bigland; one *s* one *d*. *Educ*: Bedales; Magdalen Coll., Oxford (BA 1st Cl. Hons Modern Hist.; MA 2003); Birkbeck Coll., Univ. of London (MSc (Dist.) Internat. Security and Global Governance). Entered FCO, 1998; Second Secretary: Harare, 2000–01; Abuja, 2001–03; First Secretary: Sana'a, 2003–05; Baghdad, 2005–06; Dep. Hd, Counter-Terrorism Dept, FCO, 2008–10; Dep. Hd of Mission, Helmand Provincial Reconstruction Team, Lashkar Gah, 2010; High Comr, Trinidad and Tobago, 2011–14. Dir, Aegis Defence Services Ltd, 2014–16; Man. Dir, PGI Intelligence, 2016–18. *Publications*: contribs to Asian Affairs, Alpine Jl, Caribbean Jl Internat. Relns and Diplomacy, London Rev. of Books, Prospect Mag. *Recreations*: mountaineering, ski-touring, rock-climbing, sailing. *Clubs*: Alpine, Savile.

**SNELL, Gareth Craig;** MP (Lab Co-op) Stoke-on-Trent Central, since Feb. 2017; *b* Suffolk, 1 Jan. 1986; *m* Sophia Baker; one *d*. *Educ*: Stowmarket High Sch.; Keele Univ. (BA Hist. and Politics 2008). Mem. (Lab), Newcastle-under-Lyme BC, 2010–14 and 2016–18 (Leader, 2012–14). Mem., Public Accounts Cttee, H of C, 2017–. *Address*: House of Commons, SW1A 0AA.

**SNELL, John Nicholas B.;** *see* Blashford-Snell.

**SNELL, Paul Stephen,** CBE 2009; independent consultant and executive coach, since 2009; Chief Inspector, Commission for Social Care Inspection, 2006–09; *b* 29 June 1955; *s* of Barnard Lionel Snell and Gabrielle Irene Snell (*née* Allman). *Educ*: Warwick Univ. (BA Hons Sociology 1976; MA, CQSW 1979). Social Worker, 1977–84, District Manager, 1984–88, Coventry CC; Area Manager, 1988–89, Asst Dir, Social Services, 1989–95, Birmingham CC; Chief Social Services Officer, Bexley LBC, 1995–97; Dir of Social Services, Nottingham CC, 1997–2004; Dir of Inspection, Regulation and Review, Commn for Social Care Inspection, 2004–06. Mem. Bd, Ofsted, 2011–18. Member, Board: Action for Children, 2009–17; Care Visions, 2012–. Non-executive Director: WDi Consulting, 2010–; Brighter Futures for Children, Reading, 2018–. *Recreations*: reading, theatre, French cinema, good food. *Address*: 3 Lindsay Square, SW1V 3SB.

**SNELSON, Rear Adm. David George,** CB 2004; RN retired; Chief Harbour Master, Port of London Authority, 2007–11; *b* 27 May 1951; *s* of W. M. Snelson; *m* 1973, Ruth Mary Clayton; two *s*. *Educ*: Alleyne's Grammar Sch., Uttoxeter, Staffs; BRNC, Dartmouth. Comdr, HMS Liverpool, 1987–88; Naval Asst to Controller of Navy, 1989–92; Staff Ops Officer, Comdr UK Task Gp, 1993–95; Comdr, HMS Liverpool, and Captain 3rd Destroyer Sqdn, 1996–98; Dir, Naval Ops, 1998–99, Naval Staff, 1999–2000, MoD; Captain, HMS Ark Royal, 2001–02; Comdr UK Maritime Force, 2002–04; COS (Warfare) to C-in-C Fleet, 2004–06. Chm., Thames Trng Alliance, 2011–13. Non-executive Director: Maritime and Coastguard Agency, 2012–16; Port of Milford Haven, 2012–18. Mem., Hon. Co. of Master Mariners, 2007. Elder Brother, Trinity House, 2013. FNI 2004. Officer, Operation Telic Legion of Merit (USA), 2003. *Recreations*: sailing, reading. *Address*: Trinity House, Tower Hill, EC3N 4DH.

**SNELSON, Rev. William Thomas;** Development Officer, Anglican Centre in Rome, 2008–14; General Secretary, Churches Together in England, 1997–2008; *b* 10 March 1945; *s* of Samuel and Dorothy Snelson; *m* 1968, Beryl Griffiths; one *s* one *d*. *Educ*: Exeter Coll., Oxford (BA 1967); Fitzwilliam Coll., Cambridge (BA 1969; MA 1975); Westcott House, Cambridge. Ordained deacon, 1969, priest, 1970; Curate: Godalming, 1969–72; Leeds Parish Church, 1972–75; Vicar: Chapel Allerton, Leeds, 1975–81; Bardsey, Leeds, 1981–93; W Yorks County Ecumenical Officer, 1993–97. *Publications*: Enriching Communion, 2006. *Recreations*: bridge, opera, continental holidays, choral singing. *E*: bill.snelson@btopenworld.com.

**SNIDAL, Prof. Duncan James,** PhD; FBA 2016; Professor of International Relations, University of Oxford, since 2010; Fellow of Nuffield College, Oxford, since 2010; *b* Winnipeg, Manitoba, 2 Sept. 1953; *s* of M. James Snidal and D. J. Snidal; *m* 1984, Joan E. Briller; two *s* one *d*. *Educ*: Univ. of Manitoba (BA Hons 1974); Yale Univ. (PhD 1981). University of Chicago, 1979–2010: Associate Prof., Dept of Political Sci. and Harris Sch.; Dir, Prog. on Internat. Politics, Econs and Security; Chm., Cttee on Internat. Relns. *Publications*: (ed jtly) The Rational Design of International Institutions, 2004; (ed jtly) The Oxford Handbook of International Relations, 2009; (jtly) Institutional Choice and Global Commerce, 2013; (ed jtly) International Organizations as Orchestrators, 2015. *Address*: Nuffield College, Oxford OX1 1NF. *E*: duncan.snidal@politics.ox.ac.uk.

**SNODDY, (Matthew) Raymond,** OBE 2000; freelance journalist; Presenter, Newswatch, BBC Television, 2005–12; *b* 31 Jan. 1946; *s* of Matthew and Mary Snoddy; *m* 1970, Diana Elizabeth Jaroszek; one *s* one *d*. *Educ*: Larne Grammar Sch., NI; Queen's Univ., Belfast; BA Hons Open Univ. Reporter: Middx Advertiser, 1966–68; Oxford Mail, 1968–71; Parly staff, The Times, 1971–72; Visnews, 1972–74; Dep. Eur. Editor, LA Times and Washington Post News Service, 1974–78; Financial Times, 1978–97; Media Ed., The Times, 1997–2004. Presenter, Hard News series, Channel 4, 1988–90. FRSA 2004. Chairman's Award, British Press Awards, 1992. *Publications*: The Good, the Bad and the Unacceptable, 1992; Green Finger: the rise of Michael Green and Carlton Communications, 1996; (with J. Ashworth) It Could be You: the untold story of the UK National Lottery, 2000; (ed jtly and contrib.) Trump, Brexit and the Media, 2017. *Recreations*: opera, tennis, chess, drinking and eating, supporting Queens Park Rangers. *Address*: 30 Bushey Road, Ickenham, Middx UB10 8JP. *T*: (01895) 639377. *E*: Raymond.Snoddy@gmail.com. *Club*: Wayfarers Tennis.

**SNODGRASS, Prof. Anthony McElrea,** FSA; FBA 1979; Laurence Professor of Classical Archaeology, University of Cambridge, 1976–2001; Fellow of Clare College, Cambridge, since 1977; *b* 7 July 1934; *s* of William McElrea Snodgrass, MC (Major, RAMC), and Kathleen Mabel (*née* Owen); *m* 1st, 1959, Ann Elizabeth Vaughan (marr. diss.); three *d*; 2nd, 1983, Annemarie Künzl; one *s*. *Educ*: Marlborough Coll.; Worcester Coll., Oxford (BA 1959; MA, DPhil 1963; Hon. Fellow, 1999). FSA 1978. Served with RAF in Iraq, 1953–55 (National Service). Student of the British School, Athens, 1959–60; University of Edinburgh: Lectr in Classical Archaeology, 1961; Reader, 1969; Prof., 1975. Sather Classical Vis. Prof., Univ. of California, Berkeley, 1984–85; Geddes-Harrower Vis. Prof., Aberdeen, 1995–96. Sen. Fellow, Harvard Univ. Center for Hellenic Studies, 2001–. Myres Meml Lectr, Oxford, 1981; Context and Human Society Lectr, Boston Univ., 2002. Chm., British Cttee for the Reunification of Parthenon Marbles, 2002–10. British Academy: Vice-Pres., 1990–92; Mem., Humanities Res. Bd, 1994–95. Corresponding Member: German Archaeol. Inst., 1977; Archaeol Inst. of America, 2009; Overseas Fellow, Russian Acad. of Scis, 2003. FRSA 2005. Hon. DLitt Edinburgh, 2008; DLitt Hum. Chicago, 2009. *Publications*: Early Greek Armour and Weapons, 1964; Arms and Armour of the Greeks, 1967; The Dark Age of Greece, 1971; Archaic Greece, 1980; Narration and Allusion in Early Greek Art, 1982; An Archaeology of Greece, 1987; Homer and the Artists, 1998; Archaeology and the Emergence of Greece (collected papers), 2006; contrib. Jl of Hellenic Studies, Proc. of Prehistoric Soc., Gnomon, etc. *Recreations*: mountaineering, ski-ing. *Address*: Clare College, Cambridge CB2 1TL. *Clubs*: Alpine, Alpine Ski.

**SNOW, Adrian John,** MA, MEd; construction and planning consultant; *b* 20 March 1939; *e s* of Edward Percy John Snow and Marjory Ellen Nicholls; *m* 1963 (marr. diss. 1994); one *s* one *d*. *Educ*: Hurstpierpoint Coll.; Trinity Coll., Dublin (BA, MA, HDipEd; Kt of the Campanile; Hon. Sec., Trinity Week); Reading Univ. (MEd). Asst Master, The New Beacon, Sevenoaks, 1958–59; RAF Pilot Officer, 1963; Assistant Master: King's Sch., Sherborne, 1964; High Sch., Dublin, 1964–65 (part-time); Brighton Coll., 1965–66; The Oratory School: Head of Econ. and Pol Studies, 1966–73; Head of Hist., 1967–73; Housemaster, 1967–73; acting Headmaster, Sept. 1972–Mar. 1973; Headmaster, 1973–88; farmer (part-time), Gellifelen, Gwyddgrug, 1975–94. Warden, Oratory Sch. Assoc., 1989–93; Managing Director: Oratory Construction Ltd, 1988–93; Oratory Trading Ltd, 1990–93. Governor: Prior Park Coll., 1981–87 (Mem., Action Cttee, 1980–81); Moreton Hall Prep. Sch., 1984–93; St Mary's Sch., Ascot, 1986–94; St Edward's Sch. and Highlands Sch., Reading, 1987–2001 (Chm., 1990–2001); Rendcomb Coll., 2004–11 (Chm., Academic and Personnel Cttee); St Edward's Sch., Cheltenham, 2004–06. Member: Berks Cttee, Prince's Trust, 1989–93 (Vice-Chm., 1990–91); Tennis Cttee, Tennis and Rackets Assoc., 1990–94 (Chm., Court Develt Cttee, 1992–2006; Develt Officer, 1990–2006); Hon. Court Develt Officer, Internat. Real Tennis Professionals Assoc., 2007–11. Pres., Old Oratorian CC, 1994–; Vice-Pres., Friends of Hardwick Tennis Court, 2009– (Hon. Treas., 1990–97; Chm., 1996–2009). Hon. Treas., Churches Together In Cirencester, 2011–. Mem., F and GP Cttee, St Peter's Catholic Ch, Cirencester, 2012– (Chm., 2013–17). *Recreations*: athletics (univ. colour), cricket, hockey (Jun. Internat. triallist), Real Tennis, Rugby (university colour and Combined Univs), bridge, croquet. *Address*: The Dormer House, Clarks Hay, South Cerney, Glos GL7 5UA.

**SNOW, Alexander Charles Wallace;** Chairman, Exscientia Ltd, since 2018 (Deputy Chairman, 2017–18); Chief Executive Officer, Lansdowne Partners Ltd, 2013–16; *b* London, 29 April 1969; *s* of late Peter Wallace Snow and of Sally Snow (*née* Hambro, now Sally, Viscountess Hampden); *m* 2009, Elizabeth; two *s* one *d*. *Educ*: Harrow Sch.; Univ. of St Andrews (MA Hons). Director: BZW; Credit Suisse First Boston; Chief Executive Officer: Evolution Gp plc; Williams de Broë Ltd; Evolution Securities Ltd, 2003–12; Dir, Investec Bank plc, 2012–13. Chm., IP2IPO plc, 2002–05; Sen. Ind. Dir, Amerisur Resources plc, 2017–. *Recreations*: walking, cricket. *Club*: White's.

**SNOW, Antony Edmund;** Chairman, Hill and Knowlton, Europe, Middle East and Africa, Ltd, 1990–98; *b* 5 Dec. 1932; 2nd *s* of Thomas Maitland Snow, CMG; *m* 1961, Caroline Wilson; one *s* two *d*. *Educ*: Sherborne Sch.; New College, Oxford. National Service, commnd in 10th Royal Hussars, 1952–53; Royal Wiltshire Yeomanry, TA, 1953–63. W. S. Crawford, 1958; joined Charles Barker & Sons, 1961, Dep. Chm., 1975, Chm. and Chief Exec., Charles Barker plc, 1983–88; Chm., 1992–98, non-exec. Dir, 1999–2008, Hill and Knowlton (UK). Non-exec. Dir, Hogg Gp plc (formerly Hogg Robinson & Gardner Mountain), 1989–94; Chm., Fraseer Trust, 1996–2002. Vice-Pres., Market Planning, Steuben Glass, 1976; Dep. Dir, Corning Museum of Glass, 1976 (Trustee, 1983–2012, now Trustee Emeritus); Director: Rockwell Museum, 1979; Heatherley Sch. of Fine Art, 2012–15. Member: Cttee of Management, Courtauld Institute of Art, 1984–89; Exec. Cttee, Nat. Art-Collections Fund, 1985–2008; Ancient Monuments Cttee, English Heritage, 1988–91; Design Council, 1989–94. Trustee: Monteverdi Choir, 1988–2001; V&A Mus., 1996–2002. Mem. Council, RCA, 1994–2002. *Recreations*: English watercolours, fishing. *Address*: Apartment 33, Battersea Place, 73 Albert Bridge Road, SW11 4DS. *Club*: Cavalry and Guards.
*See also* T. Snow.

**SNOW, Rear Adm. Christopher Allen,** CBE 2002; DL; Flag Officer Sea Training, 2009–11; Rear Admiral Surface Ships, 2009–11; director, mentor and advisor; *b* 16 April 1958; *s* of Rear Adm. Kenneth Arthur Snow, CB and of Pamela Elizabeth Snow; *m* 1983, Helen Maria Young; one *s* one *d*. *Educ*: Jun. King's Sch., Canterbury; Churcher's Coll., Petersfield; Durham Univ. (BA Hons Archaeol.). Joined RN 1976; 2nd Navigator, HM Yacht Britannia, 1982; i/c HM Prize Tiger Bay (ex-ARA Islas Malvinas), 1983; Navigator, HMS Birmingham, 1983–85; PWO(U), HMS Hermione and HMS Jupiter, 1985–87; Torpedo Officer, HMS Tireless, 1987–89; SWO(U) to FOST, 1990–92; i/c HMS Atherstone, 1993, Iron Duke, 1994–96; Mil. Asst to VCDS, 1996–98; i/c HMS Coventry, 1998–99; Asst Dir, Partnerships and Internat. Relns, Navy, MoD, 2002–01; Ops Team Leader, PJHQ Northwood, for UK Response Post 9/11 and for ops in Afghanistan,

2001–02; ACOS, Progs and Resources, Fleet HQ, 2002–04; Dir, Navy Resources and Plans, MoD, 2004–05; i/c HMS Ocean, 2005–06; Sen. Directing Staff (Navy), RCDS, 2007; Dep. Comdr, Naval Striking Forces NATO, and Comdr, Striking Forces NATO Maritime Force, 2008–09. Martitime Advr, H of C Defence Cttee, 2011–16; Sen. Jt Maritime Mentor to NATO, 2012–19; UK Sen. Mentor, JSCSC, 2012–. Strategic Leadership Consultation, Windsor Leadership Trust, 2007. Non-exec. Dir, Northern Devon Healthcare Trust, 2011–15; non-exec. Advr, Real Visual, 2012–14; Man. Dir, Chris Snow Consulting Ltd, 2014–. MInstD 2011. Gov., Kelly Coll. Sch., Tavistock, 2009–14 (Chair of Govs, 2013–14); Chair of Govs, Mount Kelly Foundn, 2014–18. DL Devon 2011. *Recreations:* sailing, walking Dartmoor and the coastal footpath.

**SNOW, Lady Edwina Louise;** *see* Grosvenor, Lady E. L.

**SNOW, John William,** PhD; Chairman, Cerberus Capital Management, LP, since 2006; Secretary of the Treasury, United States of America, 2003–06; *b* 2 Aug. 1939; *s of* William Dean Snow and Catharine Snow (*née* Howard); *m* 1st, 1964, Frederica Wheeler (marr. diss. 1973); two *s;* 2nd, 1973, Carolyn Kalk; one *s. Educ:* Univ. of Toledo (BA 1962); Univ. of Virginia (PhD 1965); George Washington Univ. (LLB 1967). Asst Prof. of Econs, Univ. of Maryland, 1965–67; Associate, Wheeler & Wheeler, law firm, 1967–72; US Department of Transportation: Asst Gen. Counsel, 1972–73; Dep. Asst Sec. for Policy, Plans and Internat. Affairs, 1973–74; Asst Sec. for Govtl Affairs, 1974–75; Dep. Under-Sec., 1975–76; Administrator, Nat. Highway Traffic Safety Admin, 1976–77; Vice-Pres., of Govt Affairs, Chessie Systems Inc., 1977–80; CSX Corporation: Sen. Vice-Pres., Corp. Services, 1980–84; Exec. Vice-Pres., 1984–85; Pres. and CEO, Chessie System Railroads, 1985–86, CSX Rail Transport, 1986–87, CSX Transport, 1987–88; Chief Operating Officer, 1988–89; Pres., 1988–2001; CEO, 1989–2003; Chm., 1991–2003. Co-Chm., Nat. Commn on Financial Instn Reform, Recovery and Enforcement, 1992–93; Chm., Business Roundtable, 1994–96. Adjunct Prof. of Law, George Washington Univ., 1972–75; Vis. Prof. of Econs, Univ. of Virginia, 1977. *Publications:* Perspectives in Economics, 1969. *Address:* Cerberus Capital Management, LP, 875 Third Avenue, New York, NY 10022, USA.

**SNOW, Jonathan George, (Jon);** television journalist; Presenter, Channel Four News, since 1989; *b* 28 Sept. 1947; *s of* late Rt Rev. George Snow and Joan Snow; two *d* with former partner, Madeleine Colvin; *m* 2010, Dr Precious Lunga. *Educ:* St Edward's School, Oxford; Liverpool Univ. (no degree; sent down following political disturbances, 1970). VSO, Uganda, 1967–68; Co-ordinator, New Horizon Youth Centre, Covent Garden, 1970–73 (Chm., 1986–2016; Patron, 2016–); Journalist, Independent Radio News, LBC, 1973–76; Independent Television News: Reporter, 1976–83; Washington Correspondent, 1983–86; Diplomatic Editor, 1986–89; main presenter, Election '92, ITV. Visiting Professor: Broadcast Journalism, Nottingham Trent Univ., 1992–2001; Media Studies, Univ. of Stirling, 2001–07; Univ. of Coventry, 2009–13. Chairman: Prison Reform Trust, 1992–97; On The Line Steering Gp, 1999–2003. Chm., Heart of England Forest Trust, 2014–; Trustee: Noel Buxton Trust, 1992–97; Chelsea Physic Garden, 1993–2003; Media Trust, 1995–2012 (Dep. Chm., 1995–2012); Nat. Gallery, 1999–2008; Stephen Lawrence Trust, 1999–2003; Tate Gall., 2000–08; Ashmolean Mus., Oxford, 2010–14; Mem. Council, Tate Modern, 2002–07; Chm., Tate Friends, 2010–. Chancellor, Oxford Brookes Univ., 2001–08. Mem., UK-India Round Table, 2008–. Pres., Cycle Touring Club GB, 2007–. Mem., RSA. Hon. FRIBA, 2005. Hon. DLitt: Nottingham Trent, 1994; Edinburgh, 2012; Sussex, 2015; DPhil Open, 2001; Hon. LLD Liverpool, 2011; Hon. Dr Media Studies Westminster, 2015. Monte Carlo Golden Nymph Award, for Eritrea Air Attack reporting, 1979; TV Reporter of the Year, for Afghanistan, Iran and Iraq reporting, RTS, 1980; Valiant for Truth Award, for El Salvador reporting, 1982; Internat. Award, for El Salvador reporting, RTS, 1982; Home News Award, for Kegworth Air Crash reporting, RTS, 1989; RTS Presenter of the Year, 1994, 2002, 2006, 2008, 2010, 2012; Richard Dimbleby Award, BAFTA, 2005; RTS Journalist of the Year, 2005; BAFTA Fellowship, 2015. *Publications:* Atlas of Today, 1987; (contrib.) Sons and Mothers, 1996; Shooting History, 2004. *Address:* Channel Four News, ITN, 200 Gray's Inn Road, WC1X 8HB. *T:* (020) 7430 4237. *E:* jon.snow@itn.co.uk. *W:* www.twitter.com/jonsnowc4.

**SNOW, Rt Rev. Martyn James;** *see* Leicester, Bishop of.

**SNOW, Peter John,** CBE 2006; television presenter, reporter and author; *b* Dublin, 20 April 1938; *s of* Brig. John F. Snow, CBE and Peggy Mary Pringle; *m* 1st, 1964, Alison Carter (marr. diss. 1975); one *s* one *d;* 2nd, 1976, Ann MacMillan; one *s* two *d. Educ:* Wellington College; Balliol College, Oxford (BA Hons Greats 1962). 2nd Lieut, Somerset Light Infantry, 1956–58, served Plymouth and Warminster. Independent Television News: newscaster and reporter, 1962–66; diplomatic and defence corresp., 1966–79; events covered include: Cyprus, 1964; Vietnam, Laos, Malaysia, 1968–70; China, 1972; Mideast war, 1973; Nigerian civil war, 1969; Oman, 1975; Rhodesia, 1965–79; Britain and EEC, 1970–73; co-presenter, Gen. Elections, Feb. and Oct. 1974, 1979; BBC: television: presenter, Newsnight, 1979–97; events covered or reported include: Zimbabwe independence, 1980; Falklands war, 1982; S Africa, 1986; co-presenter, Gen. Elections, 1983, 1987, 1992, 1997, 2001 and 2005, and US elections; presenter: Tomorrow's World, 1997–2001; (with Dan Snow): Battlefield Britain, 2004; Peter and Dan Snow: 20th Century Battlefields, 2007; Trainspotting Live, 2016; Great Rail Restorations with Peter Snow, 2018; Planespotting Live, 2019; radio: Random Edition, 1997–; Mastermind, 1998–2000; Masterteam, 2001–05. Vice-Patron, Jubilee Sailing Trust. Judges Award, RTS, 1998. *Publications:* (jtly) Leila's Hijack War, 1970; Hussein: a biography, 1972; (with Dan Snow) Battlefield Britain, 2004; (with Dan Snow) The World's Greatest Twentieth Century Battlefields, 2007; To War with Wellington, 2010; When Britain Burned the White House: the 1814 invasion of Washington, 2013; (with Dan Snow) The Waterloo Experience, 2015; (with Dan Snow) Treasures of British History, 2016; (with Ann MacMillan Snow) War Stories: tales of courage, cunning and compassion, 2017. *Recreations:* sailing (skipper Cerulean, Atlantic Rally crossing, 2001), ski-ing, model railways, photography. *E:* p.snow@athenaeumclub.co.uk. *Clubs:* Athenæum; Royal Cruising.
*See also* Lady E. L. Grosvenor, Prof. M. O. MacMillan.

**SNOW, Thomas;** Director, Oxford University Careers Service (formerly Secretary, Oxford University Appointments Committee), 1970–96; Fellow, New College, Oxford, 1973–96, then Emeritus; *b* 16 June 1929; *e s of* Thomas Maitland Snow, CMG; *m* 1961, Elena Tidmarsh; two *s* one *d. Educ:* Winchester Coll.; New Coll., Oxford. Joined Crittall Manufacturing Co. Ltd as Management Trainee, 1952; Dir 1966; Director: Crittall Hope Ltd, Darlington Simpson Rolling Mills, Minex Metals Ltd, 1968. Marriage Counsellor, 1964–70; Chm., Oxfordshire Relate (formerly Oxford Marriage Guidance Council), 1974–90; Member: Cttee of Management, Oxford Univ. Counselling Service, 1992–94 (Chm., 1994–96); Standing Cttee, Assoc. of Graduate Careers Adv. Services, 1973–77, 1985–89. Chm., Central and N Oxford Branch, Oxford Preservation Trust, 2008–10; Dir and Co-Sec., Murray Ct, Oxford, 2007–. Trustee: Thomas Wall Trust, 1980–99; Secure Retirement Assoc., 1996–2007 (Dep. Chm., 2002–07); Ethox, 1998–2002; Governor: Harpur Trust, 1996–2001; Bedford Sch., 1996–2001. Fellow, Winchester Coll., 1985–98. Mem. (Lab.), Witham UDC, Essex, 1957–61 (Mem., 1957–61, Chm., 1959–61, Finance Cttee); Mem. (Lib Dem), Oxfordshire CC, 1997–2001. JP Braintree, Essex, 1964–69. *Address:* Flat 9, Murray Court, 80 Banbury Road, Oxford OX2 6LQ.
*See also* A. E. Snow.

**SNOWBALL, Dame Priscilla Deborah, (Dame Cilla),** DBE 2017 (CBE 2009); Group Chairman and Group Chief Executive, Abbott Mead Vickers BBDO, 2006–18; *b* 1 Oct. 1958; *d of* late Rev. Frank Chadwick and Gwen Chadwick; *m* 1987, Geoff Snowball (marr. diss. 2007); two *s* one *d. Educ:* Sch. of St Mary and St Anne, Abbots Bromley; Birmingham Univ. (BA Hons French). Allen Brady and Marsh, 1981–83; Ogilvy and Mather, 1983–92; Abbott Mead Vickers.BBDO Ltd, 1992–2018: New Business Dir, 1992–94; Hd, Client Service, 1994–99; Man. Dir, 2000–02; Chief Exec., 2002–04; Chm., 2004–10. Non-executive Director: Fishburn Hedges, 1996–2016; Arcadia plc, 1999–2001; Derwent London plc, 2015–. Chm., Advertising Assoc., 2012–15; Mem., Women's Business Council, 2012– (Chm., 2016–). Chair, GREAT Private Sector Council, 2018–. Non-exec. Dir, Macmillan Cancer Support, 2004–08. Trustee, BITC, 2005–11. Trustee, Comic Relief, 2011–16. Lay Mem. Council, Univ. of Birmingham, 2010–13. Hon. Dr Birmingham, 2017. *Recreations:* travel, music, family. *Clubs:* Thirty (Pres., 2016–17), Women in Advertising and Communications London (Past Pres.), Marketing Gp of GB (Past Chm.).

**SNOWDEN, Prof. Sir Christopher (Maxwell),** Kt 2012; PhD; FRS 2005; FREng, FIEEE, FIET; consultant; President and Vice Chancellor, and Professor, University of Southampton, 2015–19, now Professor Emeritus; *b* 5 March 1956; *s of* William and Barbara Snowden; *m* 1993, Irena Lewandowska; two *s. Educ:* Univ. of Leeds (BSc Hons, MSc; PhD 1982). FIET (FIEE 1993); FIEEE 1996. Applications Engr, Mullard Applications Lab., Surrey, 1977–78; Lectr, Dept of Electronics, Univ. of York, 1982–83; University of Leeds, 1983–2005: Lectr, then Sen. Lectr, Dept of Electronic and Electrical Engrg, 1983–92; on secondment as Sen. Staff Scientist, M/A-COM Inc., Corporate R&D, Mass, 1990–91; Prof. of Microwave Engrg, 1992–2005; Hd, Sch. of Electronic and Electrical Engrg, 1995–98; Dir, Inst. of Microwaves and Photonics, 1997–98; Pres. (formerly Chief Exec.) and Vice Chancellor, and Univ. Prof., Univ. of Surrey, 2005–15. Filtronic plc: Exec. Dir of Technol., 1998–99; Jt CEO, 1999–2001; CEO, Compound Semiconductors, 2001–03; Chief Exec., Filtronic ICS, 2003–05. UK Govt Rep., Governance Bd, Jt Res. Centre, EC, 2011–13. Non-executive Director: Intense Ltd, 2004–09; Cenamps Ltd, 2003–06; SSTL Ltd, 2005–06; Res. Parks Develts Ltd, 2005–15; Univ. of Surrey Seed Fund Ltd, 2005–09; Engineering Technol. Bd Ltd, 2007–09; InnovateUK (formerly Technol. Strategy Bd), 2009–15; Solent LEP, 2015–18; non-exec. Chm., HERO Ltd, 2006–08. Mem. Bd, UUK, 2007–17 (Chm., Employment, Industry and Business Policy Cttee, 2007–11; Chm., England and NI Council, 2011–13; Vice-Pres., 2011–13; Pres., 2013–15). Distinguished Lectr, IEEE (Electron Devices Soc.), 1996–2006. Member: Electromagnetics Acad., MIT, 1990–; SE England Sci., Engrg and Technol. Adv. Council, 2005–11; Council, EPSRC, 2006–12; Nat. Centre for Univs and Business (formerly Council for Industry and Higher Educn), 2006–; PM's Adv. Council for Sci. and Technol., 2011–16; UK Govt Foresight Adv. Bd, 2011–16; Bd, Russell Gp, 2015–; Bd, Southampton Asset Mgt, 2015–. UK Rep., Governance Bd, Jt Res. Centre, EU Commn, 2011–12; Council, Royal Soc., 2011–12. Vice-Pres., Eur. Microwave Assoc., 2003–06 (Chm., Eur. Microwave Week, 2006); Vice-Pres., 2006–07, Dep. Pres., 2007–09, Pres., 2009–10, IET; Vice-Pres., RAEng, 2008–13 (Chair, Engrg Policy Cttee, 2008–13). FREng 2000; FRSA 2000; FCGI 2005. Mem., Council of Govs, Royal Surrey Co. Hosp. NHS Trust, 2009–10. Dir, ERA Foundn, 2010– (Chair, 2019–). Patron: Surrey Community Develt Trust, 2005–09; Surrey Youth Focus, 2009–15; Daphne Jackson Trust, 2009–15 (Chm., 2005–09). Chair, Judging Panel, Queen Elizabeth Prize for Engrg, 2016–. Hon. DSc: Strathclyde, 2015; Leeds, 2016; City, London, 2019; DUniv Surrey, 2016. Microwave Prize, 1999, Dist. Educator Award, 2009, IEEE; Eur. Microwave Assoc. Outstanding Career Award, 2012; Silver Medal, Royal Acad. of Engrg, 2004. *Publications:* Introduction to Semiconductor Device Modelling, 1986 (trans. Japanese 1988); (ed jtly and contrib.) Semiconductor Device Modelling, 1987; INCA Interactive Circuit Analysis, 1988; Semiconductor Device Modelling, 1988; (ed and contrib.) Semiconductor Device Modelling, 1989; (ed jtly and contrib.) Compound Semiconductor Device Modelling, 1993; (jtly) International Conference on Computational Electronics, 1993; contrib. numerous papers in IEEE, IEE and other learned jls. *Recreations:* photography, painting. *Address:* c/o Office of the President and Vice-Chancellor, Highfield Campus, University of Southampton, University Road, Southampton SO17 1BJ. *Club:* Athenæum.

**SNOWDEN, Ven. Elizabeth;** Archdeacon of Chelmsford, since 2016; *b* Leamington Spa, 3 Feb. 1958; *d of* Richard John Hall and Jean Valerie Hall; *m* 1983, Geoffrey William Snowden; two *s* two *d. Educ:* St Mary's Grammar Sch., Pinner; Plymouth Poly. (BSc Hons Geog. 1979); Inst. of Educn, Univ. of London (PGCE 1980); Queen's Foundn, Birmingham (Trng for Christian Ministry); Univ. of Birmingham (BA Applied Theol Studies 2002); Univ. of Stafford (Post-grad. Cert. in Theology, Culture and Imagination 2007); Sarum Coll., Univ. of Winchester (MA Theol., Imagination and Culture 2013). Asst Teacher, Edgbarrow Comprehensive, Crowthorne, Berks, 1980–85; Supply Teacher: Dudley LEA, 1993–95; Beauty Bank Primary Sch., Stourbridge, 1995–96; Belle Vue Primary Sch., 1995–96; home and hosp. tuition, Dudley Learning Support Services, 1997–2000; ordained deacon, 2001, priest, 2002; Curate, Christ Church, Burntwood, 2001–04; Resident Minister, Holy Trinity, Clayhanger, and Youth and Children's worker, Parish of St James, Brownhills, 2004–10; Asst Area Dean, Lichfield Deanery, 2007–10; Vicar, Bestwood Emmanuel with St Mark's, Southwell and Nottingham, 2010–16; Area Dean, Nottingham N Deanery, 2013–16. Part-time Chaplain, Brinsford Young Offenders, 2001–05; ATC Chaplain to 144 Squadron Brownhills, 2007–10; Chaplain, Nottingham Battalion Boys' Brigade, 2011–13. Member: Bd, S Staffs Youth for Christ, 2004–10; Standing Adv. Council on RE, Walsall, 2005–10. Governor: Holy Trinity C of E Primary Sch., Walsall, 2004–10; Hawthorne Primary Sch., Bestward Village, 2010–16. Volunteer local rep., Tearfund, 1987–97. *Publications:* contrib. Scripture Union Bible reading materials. *Recreations:* family, music, walking, bird watching, gardening, ski-ing. *Address:* Diocese of Chelmsford, 53 New Street, Chelmsford CM1 1AT.

**SNOWDEN, John Stevenson, (Steven);** QC 2017; *b* Lisburn, NI, 17 Sept. 1967; *s of* Brian and Ivy Snowden; *m* Joanna Whitehead. *Educ:* Boroughmuir High Sch., Edinburgh; Univ. of Nottingham (BA Law); Inns of Court Sch. of Law (BVC). Called to the Bar, Inner Temple, 1989; in practice as barrister, specialising in medical and personal injury law. *Publications:* (Ed.) Judicial College Guidelines for Assessment of General Damages in Personal Injury Cases, 11th edn 2012, 14th edn 2017. *Recreations:* opera, 1980s music, photography, travel, hill-walking. *Address:* 12 King's Bench Walk, Temple, EC4Y 7EL. *T:* (020) 7583 0811. *E:* chambers@12kbw.co.uk.

**SNOWDEN, Hon. Sir Richard Andrew,** Kt 2015; **Hon. Mr Justice Snowden;** a Judge of the High Court, Chancery Division, since 2015; Supervising Judge, Business and Property Courts for North and North-East Circuits, since 2019; Vice-Chancellor, County Palatine of Lancaster, since 2019; *b* 22 March 1962; *s of* late Dr Paul Snowden and of Patricia Snowden; *m* 1988, Kirsti Niinisalo; two *s. Educ:* Downing Coll., Cambridge (MA); Harvard Law Sch. (LLM). Called to the Bar, Lincoln's Inn, 1986, Bencher, 2010; Jun. Counsel to the Crown (A Panel), 1999–2003; QC 2003; a Recorder, 2006–15; a Dep. High

Court Judge, Chancery Div., 2008–15. Mem., Insolvency Rules Cttee, 2002–12. *Publications:* (ed jtly) Company Directors: law and liability, 1997; (ed jtly) Lightman and Moss, The Law of Receivers and Administrators of Companies, 3rd edn 2000, 6th edn as The Law of Administrators and Receivers of Companies, 2017; (contrib.) Commentary on the European Insolvency Regulation, 2016. *Recreations:* rowing, golf, cricket, Rugby refereeing, music. *Address:* Royal Courts of Justice, Rolls Building, Fetter Lane, EC4A 1NL.

**SNOWDEN, Steven;** *see* Snowden, J. S.

**SNOWDON, 2nd Earl of,** *cr* 1961; **David Albert Charles Armstrong-Jones;** Viscount Linley, 1961; *b* 3 Nov. 1961; *s* of 1st Earl of Snowdon, GCVO, RDI and HRH the Princess Margaret, CI, GCVO (*d* 2002); *S* father, 2017; *m* 1993, Hon. Serena Alleyne Stanhope, *o d* of Earl of Harrington, *qv*; one *s* one *d*. *Educ:* Bedales; Parnham School for Craftsmen in Wood. Designer and Cabinet maker; Chairman: Linley (formerly David Linley Furniture Ltd), 1985–; David Linley & Company Ltd, 1998–; Christie's UK, 2006– (Dir, Christie's International, 2005–). *Publications:* Classical Furniture, 1993, 2nd edn 1998; Extraordinary Furniture, 1996; Design and Detail in the Home, 2000; Star Pieces, 2010. *Heir:* s Viscount Linley, *qv*. *Address:* Linley, 60 Pimlico Road, SW1W 8LP.
*See under Royal Family.*

**SNOWDON, Leslie Colin;** Assistant Editor, The Sun, since 2016; *b* RAF Cosford, 23 June 1961; *s* of Alex and Jackie Snowdon; *m* 1984, Fiona Allison MacGregor; two *s* one *d*. *Educ:* Annan Acad.; Univ. of Edinburgh (MA Hons). Photographer, Dumfriesshire Newspapers, 1984–89; Photographer and Sub-editor, Dumfries and Galloway Standard, 1989–94; The Scotsman: Sub-ed., 1994–96; Chief Pol Sub-ed., 1996–97; Chief Sports Sub-ed., 1997–98; Dep. Sports Ed., 1998–99; Sports Ed., Sunday Times Scotland, 1999–2000; Dep. Sports Ed., The Sunday Times, 2000–03; Editor: Sunday Times Scotland, 2003–06; Scotland on Sunday, 2006–09; Sports Ed., Daily Mail, 2009–15; Scotland Ed., The Times, 2015–16. *Recreations:* walking accompanied by two dogs: Max and Cora, sport, exercise, music, cooking. *Address:* The Sun, 1 London Bridge Street, SE1 9GF.

**SNOWDON, Susan;** Lord-Lieutenant for Co. Durham, since 2013; *b* 1 April 1951; *d* of Leonard Hanselman; *m* 1977, Keith Snowdon. Primary sch. teacher, Chilton and Ferryhill, 1972–89; tutor for adult literacy and numeracy; Co-ordinator, Durham Writing Project. Fundraising Manager, Butterwick Hospice. Founder and Organiser, Bishop Auckland Food Festival, until 2011. Former Mem., Judicial Rev. Bd for England and Wales. Mem., Bishop Auckland Town Centre Forum (Chm., Mktg and Promotions Gp). JP Co. Durham and Darlington; DL Co. Durham, 2006. OStJ 2018. *Address:* c/o Clerk to the Lieutenancy, Rivergreen Centre, Aykley Heads, Durham DH1 5TS.

**SNOWLING, (George) Christopher (Edward);** Legal Member, Mental Health Review Tribunal, 1992–2007; *b* 12 Aug. 1934; *s* of George Edward Snowling and Winifred Beryl (*née* Cave); *m* 1961, Flora Skells; one *s* one *d*. *Educ:* The Mercers' Sch.; Fitzwilliam House, Cambridge (MA). Served RAF, 1953–55 (commnd in Fighter Control Br.). Admitted Solicitor, 1961; various local govt posts, Grantham Bor., Margate Bor., Eastbourne Co. Bor. and Assoc. of Municipal Corpns, 1958–71; Law Society: Legal Aid Admin, 1971–78; Secretary: Educn and Trng, 1978–85, Professional Purposes, 1985–86; Dir, Legal Aid, 1986–89; private practice, 1989–92. Mem., Cuckfield UDC, 1971–74; Mid Sussex District Council: Mem. (C), 1973–2015; Chm., 1981–82, 1986–87, 1987–88; Chm., Policy and Resources Cttee, 1988–91; Leader majority gp, 1991–95; Leader largest minority gp, 1995–99; Leader majority gp, Leader of Council, and Chm. Policy and Resources Cttee, 1999–2001; Chairman: Central Area Planning Cttee, 2001–03; Service Review and Performance Panel, 2001–03; Dep. Leader, 2003–06; Cabinet Mem. for Resources, subseq. Corporate Services, 2003–06, for Health and Community, 2006–15. Vice Chm., Brighton and Mid Sussex Res. Ethics Cttee, 2004–07; Alternate Vice Chm., Brighton and Sussex (formerly Brighton E) Res. Ethics Cttee, 2008–11; Mem., Crawley & Horsham Local Res. Ethics Cttee, 1994–2003 (Chm., 2003). Member: Council, Assoc. of Dist Councils, 1990–97; cttees, LGA, 1996–98; W Sussex (formerly Shadow W Sussex) Health and Wellbeing Bd, 2011–15; Affinity Sutton S and SW Regl Scrutiny Bd, 2012–15; Sussex (formerly Shadow Sussex) Police and Crime Panel, 2012–15. Legal Advr, Mid Sussex Older People's Council, 2016–. Member: Mid Downs CHC, 1988–96; Lindfield Parish Council, 1995–2019 (Vice Chm., 1999–2003; Chm., Planning and Traffic Cttee, 2003–11); Lindfield Rural Parish Council, 2003–15. Pres., Lindfield Br., Mid Sussex Cons. Assoc., 2010–. Pres., Old Mercers' Club, 1998–99 (Trustee, Old Mercers' Benevolent Fund, 2008–). *Recreations:* gentle bridge, gardening, enjoying retirement with the help of U3A. *Address:* Eldon Lodge, Pondcroft Road, Lindfield, West Sussex RH16 2HQ. T: (01444) 482172.

**SNOWLING, Prof. Margaret Jean,** CBE 2016; PhD; FBA 2009; FMedSci; Professor of Psychology, University of Oxford, since 2012; President, St John's College, Oxford, since 2012; *b* 15 July 1955; *d* of Walter and Jean Snowling; *m* 1st, 1986, Christopher Parker (marr. diss. 1992); one *s*; 2nd, 1995, Charles Hulme, *qv*; three step *d*. *Educ:* Univ. of Bristol (BSc Psychol. 1976); University Coll. London (PhD Psychol. 1979). Dip. Clin. Psychol., BPsS, 1988. National Hospital College of Speech Sciences, London: Lectr in Psychology, 1979–88; Sen. Lectr, 1988–89; Principal, 1989–92; Professor of Psychology: Univ. of Newcastle upon Tyne, 1992–94; Univ. of York, 1994–2012. Vice-Pres., British Dyslexia Assoc., 1997. FMedSci 2008. Hon. DSc: Goldsmiths, Univ. of London, 2007; UCL, 2014; Warwick, 2016; Bristol, 2019. *Publications:* (ed) Children's Written Language Difficulties, 1985; Dyslexia: a cognitive developmental perspective, 1987, 2nd edn 2000; (ed jtly) Dyslexia: integrating theory and practice, 1991; (ed jtly) Reading Development and Dyslexia, 1994; (ed jtly) Dyslexia, Speech and Language: a practitioner's handbook, 1996; (ed jtly) Dyslexia, Biology and Cognition, 1997; (ed jtly) The Science of Reading: a handbook, 2005; (ed jtly) Neurocognitive Approaches to Developmental Disorders, 2008; (jtly) Developmental Disorders of Language, Learning and Cognition, 2009; (jtly) Developing Language and Literacy, 2011; (jtly) Developing Reading Comprehension, 2013; A Very Short Introduction to Dyslexia, 2019. *Recreations:* walking, entertaining, music, yoga. *Address:* St John's College, St Giles, Oxford OX1 3JP. T: (01865) 277419.

**SNOWMAN, (Michael) Nicholas,** OBE 2014; General Director, Opéra National du Rhin, 2002–09; Chairman, Wartski, since 2002 (Co-Chairman, 1997–2002); Chargé de Mission, Maire de Strasbourg, 2009–12; *b* 18 March 1944; *s* of late Kenneth Snowman, CBE and Sallie Snowman (*née* Moghi-Levkine); *m* 1983, Margo Michelle Rouard; one *s*. *Educ:* Hall Sch., London; Highgate Sch., London; Magdalene Coll., Cambridge (BA Hons Eng. Lit.). Asst to Hd of Music Staff, Glyndebourne Fest., 1967–69; Co-Founder and Gen. Man., London Sinfonietta, 1968–72; Administrator, Music Th. Ensemble, 1968–71; Artistic Director: IRCAM, Centre d'Art et de Culture Georges Pompidou, 1972–86; Fest. de Lille, 1984; Gen. Dir (Arts), 1986–92, Chief Exec., 1992–98, South Bank Centre, London; Gen. Dir, Glyndebourne, 1998–2000. Co-Founder, 1975, Artistic Advr 1975–92, Bd Mem., 1992–, Vice-Chm., 1998–, Ensemble InterContemporain, Paris; Mem. Music Cttee, Venice Biennale, 1979–86; Artistic Dir, Projects in 1980 (Stravinsky), 1981 (Webern), 1983 (Boulez), Fest. d'Automne de Paris; Programme Consultant, Cité de la Musique, La Villette, Paris, 1991. Mem. Bd, Cultural Olympiad, 2012–13. Curator, Vienna Revisited, Kings Place, London, 2014. Mem. British Sect., 1995–2000, French Sect., 2009–, Franco-British Council. Mem. Bd, Music Restored, 2010–; Trustee: New Berlioz Edn, 1996–; Monteverdi Choir and Orchestra, 2012–18; Aurora Orchestra, 2016–; Berlioz Sesquicentenary Cttee, 2017–; V&A Mus. Foundn, 2017–. Mem., Develt Bd, Hampstead Th., 2014–. Gov., RAM, 1998–2006 (Hon. RAM 1999; Patron, 2011–). Hon. Fellow, Bangor Univ., 2015. Officier de l'Ordre des Arts et des Lettres (France), 1990 (Chevalier, 1985); Order of Cultural Merit (Poland), 1990; Chevalier: l'Ordre National du Mérite (France), 1995; Légion d'Honneur (France), 2008. *Publications:* (co-ed) The Best of Granta, 1967; (series ed.) The Contemporary Composers; papers and articles on music, architecture, cultural policy. *Recreations:* films, eating, spy novels, France, Arsenal. *Address:* Wartski, 60 St James's Street, SW1A 1LE.

**SNOXELL, David Raymond;** HM Diplomatic Service, retired; High Commissioner, Mauritius, 2000–04; *b* 18 Nov. 1944; *s* of late Gordon William Snoxell and of Norah Snoxell; *m* 1971, Anne Carter; two *s* one *d*. *Educ:* Bishop Vesey's Grammar Sch., Sutton Coldfield; Bristol Univ. (BA Hons Hist. 1966); Aston Univ. (Dip. Personnel Mgt 1967). MIPD. UNA Volunteer, Senegal, 1967–68; joined FCO, 1969; Islamabad, 1973–76; UK Mission to Geneva, 1976–81; FCO, 1981–86; Dir, British Information Services, NY, 1986–91; Dep. Head of Drugs and Internat. Crime Dept, FCO, 1991–94; Dep. Head of Southern Africa Dept, FCO, 1994–96; Ambassador to Senegal and concurrently to Mali, Guinea, Guinea Bissau and Cape Verde, 1997–2000. Co-ordinator, Chagos Islands All-Party Parly Gp, 2008–. Chm., Marine Educn Trust, 2009–. *Recreations:* choral singing, local history. *Address:* Old Mill Cottage, Bassetsbury Lane, High Wycombe, Bucks HP11 1QZ. T: (01494) 529318.

**SNYDER, Prof. Allan Whitenack,** FRS 1990; FAA; FTSE; 150th Anniversary Chair of Science and the Mind and University Professor, University of Sydney, 1999–2013, now Professor Emeritus; *s* of Edward H. Snyder, philanthropist, and Zelda (*née* Cotton), Broadway actress and psychodramatherapist; one *s* one *d*. *Educ:* Central High Sch., Phil. (AB); Pennsylvania State Univ. (BS); MIT (SM); Harvard Univ. (MS); University Coll. London (PhD); DSc London. Greenland Ice Cap Communications Project, 1961; Gen. Telecom. and Elec. Res. Lab., 1963–67; Cons. to Brit. PO and Standard Telecom. Lab., 1968–70; Nat. Sci. Foundn Fellow, Yale Univ., 1970–71; Professorial Fellow, IAS, ANU, 1971–77; John Simon Guggenheim Fellow, Yale Univ. Med. Sch., 1977–78; Institute for Advanced Studies, Australian National University: Prof. of Optical Physics and Visual Scis, 1978–98; Hd, Dept of Applied Maths, 1980–83; Hd, Optical Scis Centre, 1987–2003; Peter Karmel Chair and Dist. Prof., 1999–2006, now Prof. Emeritus; Dir, Centre for the Mind, ANU, 1997–2005, Univ. of Sydney, 1999–2012; Royal Soc. Guest Res. Fellow, Cambridge Univ., 1987. Foundn Dir, Aust. Photonics Cooperative Res. Centre, 1992–95. Associate Editor, Jl of Optical Soc. of America, 1981–83. Fellow, Optical Soc. of Amer., 1980; Foundn Fellow, Nat. Vision Res. Inst. of Aust., 1983. A. E. Mills Meml Orator, RACP, 1996; Harrie Massey Prize and Lect., Inst. of Phys, 1996; Inaug. Edwin Flack Lect., Australian Olympic Cttee, 1998; Clifford Paterson Prize and Lect., Royal Soc., 2001. Edgeworth David Medal, Royal Soc. NSW, 1974; Research Medal, Royal Soc. Vic, 1974; Thomas Rankin Lyle Medal, Aust. Acad. of Sci., 1985; Stuart Sutherland Meml Medal, Aust. Acad. of Technological Sci. and Engrg, 1991; CSIRO External Medal for Research, 1995; Australia Prize, 1997; Tall Poppy Prize, Australian Inst. of Political Sci., 2000; Marconi Internat. Prize, 2001; Australian Centenary Medal, 2003. *Publications:* Photoreceptor Optics, 1975; Optical Waveguide Theory, 1983; Optical Waveguide Sciences, 1983; What Makes a Champion, 2002; articles on the mind, the visual system of animals and on the physics of light propagation in internat. sci. jls. *Recreations:* art, culture, swimming, snorkelling. *Address:* Department of Physiology, University of Sydney Medical School, NSW 2006, Australia. T: (418) 633247, Fax: (2) 93518534. E: allan@centreforthemind.com.

**SNYDER, Sir Michael (John),** Kt 2008; Senior Partner: Kingston Smith LLP, Chartered Accountants, 1990–2016; Kingston Smith Consulting LLP, 2009–16; Bramdean Consultants LLP, since 2016; *b* 30 July 1950; *s* of Elsworth and Pauline Snyder; *m* 1974, Mary Dickinson; two *d*. *Educ:* Brentwood Sch.; City of London Coll. FCA 1973. Chairman: Cheviot Capital Ltd, 1983–2006; Kingston Sorel Internat. (KS Internat.), 1990–2016; Kingston Smith Services Ltd (formerly Kingston Smith Consultants Ltd), 1997–2016; Kingston Smith Financial Advisers Ltd, 1997–2016; Devonshire Corporate Finance Ltd, 2001–16; HR Insight Ltd, 2005–16; non-exec. Dir, Metro Bank plc, 2015– (Sen. Ind. Dir, 2019–). Mem., Lee Valley Regl Park Authy, 1993–2008. Member: Bd, Thames Gateway London Partnership, 2000–11; Gateway to London, 2001–11 (Chm., 2008–11). Chm., Assoc. of Practising Accountants, 1992–2016. Chm., London Business Loans, 2007–14; Dir, GLE Loan Finance Ltd, 2014– (Chm., 2014–17). Mem., Leaders Cttee, 2003–08, Vice Chm., London Councils (formerly Assoc. of London Govt), 2003–08. Chm., Nat. Business Angels Network, 1998–2004. Mem. Bd, Film London, 2004–08. Trustee, Academy Sponsor Trust, 2005–10. City of London Corporation: Dep., Ward of Cordwainer, 1993–; Member: Policy and Resources Cttee, 1994– (Chm., 2003–08); Chancellor's High Level Gp on Financial Services, 2008; Chairman: Professional Services Global Competitiveness Gp, 2008–09; Professional and Business Services Gp, 2010–12; Co-Chm., Professional and Business Services Council, 2012–15; Member: Ct of Common Council, 1986–; Finance Cttee, 1992– (Chm., 1998–2003); City Lands and Bridge House Estates Cttee, 1998–2003. Mem., Securities Inst., 1997–. Liveryman and Member of Court: Co. of Needlemakers, 1980– (Master, 2005–06); Tallow Chandlers' Co., 1990– (Master, 2012–13). Hon. Treas., Bow Bells Assoc. Governor: London Metropolitan Univ., 1999–2010; City of London Sch. for Girls, 1989– (Chm., 2013–16); Brentwood Sch., 1992– (Hon. Treas., 1992–2010; Vice Chm., 2005–16; Chm., 2016–). MCSI. FInstD 1986. FRSA 2008. Hon. FGS 2016. Hon. DSc City, 2001. Grand Cross, Order of Merit (FRG), 1998. *Recreations:* music, gardening, narrow boating. *Address:* Bramdean Manor, Church Lane, Bramdean, Alresford, Hants SO24 0JS. E: sirms@snyder.org.uk. *Clubs:* Athenæum, Ward of Cordwainer (Vice Pres.), City Pickwick.

**SOAME, Sir Richard (John) Buckworth-Herne-,** 13th Bt *cr* 1697, of Sheen, Surrey; *b* 17 Aug. 1970; *o s* of Sir Charles John Buckworth-Herne-Soame, 12th Bt and Eileen Margaret Mary Buckworth-Herne-Soame (*née* Minton); *S* father, 2013, but his name does not yet appear on the Official Roll of the Baronetage. *Heir:* none.

**SOAMES, Rt Hon. Sir (Arthur) Nicholas (Winston),** Kt 2014; PC 2011; MP for Mid Sussex, since 1997 (C, 1997–2019; Ind, since 2019) (MP (C) Crawley, 1983–97); *b* 12 Feb. 1948; *s* of Baron Soames, GCMG, GCVO, CH, CBE, PC and Lady Soames, LG, DBE; *m* 1st, 1981, Catherine Weatherall (marr. diss. 1990); one *s*; 2nd, 1993, Serena, *d* of Sir John L. E. Smith, CH, CBE; one *s* one *d*. *Educ:* Eton. Served 11th Hussars (PAO), 1967–72 (Lieut); Equerry to the Prince of Wales, 1970–72; Asst Dir, Sedgwick Group, 1976–82. PPS to Minister of State for Employment, 1984–85, to Sec. of State, DoE, 1987–89, to Sec. of State, DTI, 1989–90; Parly Sec., MAFF, 1992–94; Minister of State for the Armed Forces, MoD, 1994–97; Shadow Defence Sec., 2003–05. Pres., Conservative Middle East Council, 2010–. Mem., Commonwealth War Graves Commn, 2003–08. *Recreation:* country pursuits. *Address:* House of Commons, SW1A 0AA. T: (020) 7219 3000. *Clubs:* White's, Turf, Pratt's, Beefsteak.
*See also Hon. E. M. Soames, Hon. R. C. Soames.*

**SOAMES, Hon. Emma (Mary);** Editor at large, Saga Magazine, and Director, Saga Media, since 2008; *b* 6 Sept. 1949; *d* of Baron Soames, GCMG, GCVO, CH, CBE, PC and Lady Soames, LG, DBE; *m* 1981, James MacManus (marr. diss. 1989); one *d. Educ:* Hamilton House Sch. for Girls; Queen's Coll., London; Sorbonne, Univ. of Paris; Ecole des Sciences Politiques. Journalist, Evening Standard, 1974–81; Editor, Literary Review, 1984–86; Features Editor, Vogue, 1986–88; Editor: Tatler, 1988–90; Evening Standard mag., 1992–94; Telegraph mag., 1994–2002; Ed., Saga mag. and Editl Dir, Saga Publishing Ltd, 2002–08. Trustee: Turner Contemporary Art Trust, 2005–13; Fine Cell Work, 2012–; Swarovski Foundn, 2014–. Editor of Year Award for Gen. Interest and Current Affairs, BSME, 2003. *Recreations:* travel, gardening, self education.
See also Rt Hon. Sir A. N. W. Soames, Hon. R. C. Soames.

**SOAMES, Rt Hon. Sir Nicholas;** *see* Soames, Rt Hon. Sir A. N. W.

**SOAMES, Hon. Rupert Christopher,** OBE 2010; Chief Executive, Serco Group plc, since 2014; *b* 18 May 1959; *s* of Baron Soames, GCMG, GCVO, CH, CBE, PC and Lady Soames, LG, DBE; *m* 1988, Camilla Dunne; two *s* one *d. Educ:* Eton; Worcester Coll., Oxford (BA). Pres., Oxford Union, 1981. With GEC plc, 1982–96 (Man. Dir, Avery Berkel UK); Misys plc, 1996–2002 (Chief Exec., Banking and Securities Div., 2000–02); Chief Exec., Aggreko plc, 2003–14. *Recreations:* country sports, food and wine. *Address:* Serco Group plc, Serco House, 16 Bartley Wood Business Park, Bartley Way, Hook, Hants RG27 9UY. *Clubs:* White's, Turf, Pratt's.
See also Rt Hon. Sir A. N. W. Soames, Hon. E. M. Soames.

**SOANE, Tim;** Managing Partner, Persuasion Associates (formerly The Soanes) Ltd, 2010–16; *b* London, 9 May 1953; *s* of Morris Soane and Lore Soane (*née* Garratt); *m* 1975, Giorgina Perugini; one *s. Educ:* Dulwich Coll., London. BoT and Dept of Industry, 1974–92, incl. Private Sec. to Parly Under Sec. of State, DTI, 1985–86; Department of Trade and Industry: Director: Electrical Manufg, 1993–96; Competitiveness, 1996–99; Change and Knowledge Mgt, 2000–04; HR, 2001–03; Dir, Partnership, Employment Relns, DTI, later BERR, 2004–08; Dir, Regulatory Innovation, Better Regulation Exec., BIS, 2009–10. Dir, Rivermead Ct Ltd, 2017–. *Recreations:* web 2.0, genealogy, bridge. *Address:* Fulham, SW6 3RU. *T:* 07932 729134. *E:* mail@soane.net. *Club:* Hurlingham.

**SOANES, Zebedee;** broadcaster, BBC Radio and Television, since 1998; actor, since 1995; *b* Great Yarmouth, 24 June 1976; *s* of Rev. Robert Soanes and Jeanette Soanes. *Educ:* Univ. of E Anglia (BA Hons English and American Studies 1997). Teacher of speech and drama, Langley Sch., Norfolk, 1997–98; freelance broadcaster, BBC Radio Norfolk, 1997–98; Continuity Announcer, BBC Network TV, 1998–2002; newsreader, BBC Radio 4, 2001–; launched BBC Radio 4 Now, 2002; presenter, BBC Proms, BBC TV, 2006–17; reporter, From Our Own Correspondent, BBC Radio, 2008–; presenter, Saturday Classics, BBC Radio 3, 2012. Voice of God, Noye's Fludde by Benjamin Britten, Aldeburgh Music, 2013; recorded Walton's Façade, John Wilson (cond.), 2015; Derek Nimmo in All Mouth and Trousers, Radio 4, 2016; concert narrations include: Peter and the Wolf/Little Red Riding Hood; The Snowman; Paddington; The Story of Babar the Little Elephant. Patron: Awards for Young Musicians, 2013–; British Assoc. for Performing Arts Medicine, 2014–; first Patron, Mammal Soc., 2019–. Sunday Times Favourite UK Radio Voice, 2015. *Publications:* Gaspard the Fox, 2018; Gaspard Best in Show, 2019; contrib. The Observer, Country Life. *Recreations:* theatre, classical music, travel, Suffolk. *Address:* c/o BBC Radio 4, Broadcasting House, W1A 1AA. *W:* www.zebsoanes.com. *Clubs:* Garrick, Two Brydges.

**SOAR, Catherine;** *see* Wilson, C.

**SOAR, Adm. Sir Trevor (Alan),** KCB 2009; OBE 1994; DL; Commander-in-Chief Fleet and Commander Allied Maritime Command Northwood, 2009–12; Vice-Admiral of the United Kingdom, 2009–12; Director: Trevor Soar Strategic Consulting Ltd, since 2012; Trueleader Company, since 2014; *b* 21 March 1957; *s* of Colin and Hazel Soar; *m* 1978, Anne Matlock; two *s. Educ:* Loughborough Grammar Sch.; BRNC Dartmouth. Joined RN, 1975; qualified submariner, 1978; Captain: HMS Ocelot, 1987–90; HMS Talent, 1991–94; Navy Plans and Prog., MoD, 1996; Captain, HMS Chatham, 1997–98; Asst Dir Warfare, Navy Plans and Prog., then Captain Navy Plans, Navy Resources and Plans, MoD, 1998–2000; Dir Naval Staff responsible for pan-Navy policy across Defence, 2000–02; Captain, HMS Invincible, 2002–04; Rear Adm. 2004; Capability Manager (Precision Attack), 2004–06; Chief of Materiel (Fleet), Defence Equipment and Support, MoD, 2007–09. Chm., Clearwater Tracking, 2016–. President: Training Ship Wizard, 1990–; Training Ship Modwena, 2012–; Adm., City Livery Yacht Club, 2014–. Pres., The Leaders Club, 2016– (Chm., 2013–16); Chm., Historic Dockyard Chatham, 2016–. Mem., Rugby World Cup Legacy Bd, 2014–18. Gov., Loughborough Schs Foundn (formerly Loughborough Endowed Schs), 2015–; Chm. Govs, Loughborough Schs Foundn, 2019–. Younger Brother, Trinity House, 2002–. Freeman: City of London, 2004; Lightmongers' Co. DL Staffs, 2017. Hon. DEng Heriot-Watt, 2005. *Recreations:* Royal Navy Rugby Football Union (Past Pres.), supporter of Leicester Tigers. *Address:* c/o Naval Secretary, Leach Building, Whale Island, Portsmouth, Hants PO2 8BY. *E:* trevor.soar@me.com. *Clubs:* Army and Navy, Royal Navy of 1765 and 1785, Victory Services; Burton (Burton on Trent).

**SOBEL, Alexander David;** MP (Lab Co-op) Leeds North West, since 2017; *b* Leeds, April 1975; *s* of Leopold and Ruth Sobel; *m* Susan Docherty; two *s. Educ:* Univ. of Leeds (BSc Information Systems 1997). Finance Officer, Leeds Univ. Union, 1997–98; Call Centre Operative, Romec, 1998–99; Convenor, W Yorks Area NUS, 1999–2000; Community Relns Officer, Univ. of Leeds, 2000–01; Community Participation Co-ordinator, Leeds Voice, 2001–03; Sen. Develt Officer, Univ. of Bradford, 2004–06; Develt Manager, UnLtd, 2006–08; Centre Manager, Urban Biz, 2008–09; Gen. Manager, Social Enterprise Yorks and Humber, 2009–17. Mem. (Lab), Leeds CC, 2012–18. Mem., Envmtl Audit Cttee, H of C, 2017–. Contested (Lab Co-op) Leeds NW, 2015. *Recreations:* attending Indie gigs, basketball, cycling, video games, going to the gym. *Address:* House of Commons, SW1A 0AA.

**SOBER, Phillip,** FCA; consultant; non-executive Director: Liberty International (formerly Transatlantic Holdings, then Liberty International Holdings), 1983–2002; Capital and Counties, 1993–2002; Capital Shopping Centres, 1994–2002; *b* 1 April 1931; *s* of Abraham and Sandra Sober; *m* 1957, Vivien Louise Oppenheimer; two *d* (and one *d* decd). *Educ:* Haberdashers' Aske's. Qual. as Chartered Accountant, 1953; FCA 1963. Stoy Hayward, Chartered Accountants: Partner, 1958; Internat. Partner, 1975–90; Sen. Partner, 1985–90. Eur. Regl Dir, Horwath Internat., 1990–94. Crown Estate Comr, 1983–94. Mem. Council, UK Central Council for Nursing, Midwifery and Health Visiting, 1980–83. Pres., Norwood Child Care, 1974–. Trustee, Royal Opera House Trust, 1985–91. Gov., London Inst. Higher Educn Corp., 1994–2003; Mem. Council, London Univ., 1999–2008. *Publications:* articles in prof. press on various subjects but primarily on property co. accounting. *Recreations:* interested in all the arts, partic. music; golf main sporting activity. *Address:* Flat 1, 5 Sheffield Terrace, W8 7NG. *T:* (020) 3220 0165. *Clubs:* Savile, Royal Automobile, Hurlingham.

**SOBERS, Sir Garfield St Auburn, (Sir Garry),** Kt 1975; AO 2003; OCC; former cricketer; Consultant, Barbados Tourism Authority, since 1980; *b* Bridgetown, Barbados, 28 July 1936; *m* 1969, Prudence Kirby (marr. diss.); two *s* one *d. Educ:* Bay Street Sch., Barbados. First major match, 1953, for Barbados; played in 93 Test Matches for West Indies, 39 as Captain, 1953–74 (made world record Test Match score, Kingston, 1958); captained West Indies and Barbados teams, 1965–74; Captain of Nottinghamshire CCC, 1968–74. On retirement from Test cricket held the following world records in Test Matches: 365 not out; 26 centuries; 235 wickets; 110 catches. *Publications:* Cricket Advance, 1965; Cricket Crusader, 1966; King Cricket, 1967; (with J. S. Barker) Cricket in the Sun, 1967; Bonaventure and the Flashing Blade, 1967; (with Brian Scovell) Sobers: Twenty Years At The Top (autobiog.), 1988; (jtly) The Changing Face of Cricket, 1995; (with Bob Harris) Garry Sobers: my autobiography, 2002. *Address:* Barbados Tourism Authority, PO Box 242, Harbour Road, Bridgetown, Barbados, West Indies. *Fax:* 4264080.

**SOCKETT, Prof. Renée Elizabeth, (Liz),** PhD; FRS 2019; Professor of Bacterial Genetics, University of Nottingham, since 2006; *b* Newcastle-upon-Tyne, 1962; *d* of Ernest Wrightson Sockett and Renée Sockett (*née* Lambert); *m* Andrew William Fielding. *Educ:* Westerhope Infants Sch.; Chapel Hse Middle Sch.; Dame Allan's Girls' Sch., Newcastle-upon-Tyne; Univ. of Leeds (BSc Hons 1983); University Coll. London (PhD 1986). Researcher: Univ. of Illinois at Urbana-Champaign, 1986–88; Univ. of Oxford, 1988–91; Lectr, 1991–2000, Associate Prof., 2000–05, Univ. of Nottingham. *Publications:* contribs to learned scientific jls. *Recreations:* art and architecture of Charles Rennie Mackintosh and Margaret Macdonald Mackintosh, Frank Lloyd Wright and of arts and crafts and art deco periods, aeroplanes - vintage and modern, archaeology, visiting Italy. *Address:* School of Life Sciences, University of Nottingham, QMC Medical School, Derby Road, Nottingham NG7 2UH. *T:* (0115) 823 0325. *E:* liz.sockett@nottingham.ac.uk.

**SODANO, His Eminence Cardinal Angelo,** STD, JCD; Secretary of State to His Holiness the Pope, 1990–2006, now Emeritus; Dean, Sacred College of Cardinals, since 2005; *b* Asti, Italy, 23 Nov. 1927; *s* of Giovanni Sodano and Delfina (*née* Brignolo). *Educ:* Seminario di Asti; Pontifical Università Gregoriana (STD); Pontifical Università Lateranense (JCD). Ordained priest, 1950; Titular Archbishop, 1978; Apostolic Nuncio, Chile, 1978–88; Sec., Council for Public Affairs of Church, later Section for Relns of Holy See with States, 1988–90. Several hon. distinctions. *Address:* c/o Secretariat of State, 00120 Vatican City State.

**SODOR AND MAN, Bishop of,** since 2017; **Rt Rev. Peter Andrew Eagles;** *b* 6 July 1959; *s* of Peter Frank Eagles and Elizabeth Howie Eagles; *m* 1992, Gail Seager; one *s. Educ:* Royal Grammar Sch., Guildford; King's Coll., London (BA 1st cl. Hons German and Russian 1982); Univ. of Heidelberg (Deutsche Akademische Austauschdienst Scholarship); St Stephen's House, Oxford (BA Hons Theol. 1988; MTh Theol. 2004). Asst Master, Tonbridge Sch., 1982–86; freelance translator, 1982–86; ordained deacon, 1989, priest, 1990; Asst Priest, St Martin's, Ruislip, 1989–92; Chaplain to the Forces, Royal Army Chaplains' Dept, 1992–2017; Asst Chaplain-Gen., 2008–14; Archdeacon for the Army, 2011–17; Dep. Chaplain-Gen., HM Land Forces, 2014–17. QHC 2013–17. Mem., RCDS, 2013–14. Mem., Gen. Synod, 2011–. Hon. Canon, Salisbury Cathedral, 2015–17. *Recreations:* hills and mountains, languages and literature, European history, piano and oboe. *Address:* Thie yn Aspick, 4 The Falls, Douglas, Isle of Man IM4 4PZ. *T:* (01624) 622108. *E:* bishop@sodorandman.im.

**SODOR AND MAN, Dean of;** *see* Godfrey, Very Rev. N. P.

**SOFAT, Janardan,** FCA; Director, Addidi Wealth (formerly AJS Wealth Management) Ltd, since 2006; *b* 11 May 1958; *s* of Didar Chand Sofat and Ved Kumari Sofat; *m* 1981, Anna Mathur; two *d. Educ:* Univ. of Hull (BSc Econ). FCA 1992. Finance Dir, J. S. Hamilton Ltd, 1983–90; Chief Exec., AJS Financial Consultants Ltd, 1990–97; Ops Dir, Business Link London E, 1997–2000; Regional Dir, Small Business Service, 2000–04; Regl Comr for SE, NHS Appts Commn, subseq. Appts Commn, 2004–07; Chm., Kent Probation Area, Nat. Probation Services, 2007–14. Non-exec. Dir, W Kent HA, 1994–2000; Chairman: Medway NHS Trust, 2000–04; Dartford and Gravesham NHS Trust, 2014–17. Chm., Medway Racial Equality Council, 2001–11; Chief Operating Officer, Business Link for London, 2004–05. Trustee, Mencap, 2005–09. *Recreations:* family, good food, travel. *Address:* 47 Pilgrims Road, Halling, Kent ME2 1HN. *E:* janardan@addidi.com.

**SOFER, Anne Hallowell;** Chief Education Officer, London Borough of Tower Hamlets, 1989–97; *b* 19 April 1937; *d* of Geoffrey Crowther (later Baron Crowther) and Margaret Worth; *m* 1958, Jonathan Sofer (*d* 2003); two *s* one *d. Educ:* St Paul's Sch.; Swarthmore Coll., USA; Somerville Coll., Oxford (MA); DipEd London. Secretary, National Assoc. of Governors and Managers, 1972–75; Additional Member, ILEA Education Cttee, 1974–77; Chairman, ILEA Schools Sub-Cttee, 1978–81; Mem. (SDP), GLC/ILEA for St Pancras N, Oct. 1981–86 (by-election) (Labour, 1977–81). Dir, Channel Four Television Co. Ltd, 1981–83; Columnist, The Times, 1983–87. Mem., SDP Nat. Cttee, 1982–87. Contested Hampstead and Highgate (SDP) 1983, (SDP/Alliance) 1987. Trustee, Nuffield Foundn, 1990–2005. Chm., Nat. Children's Bureau, 2000–06. *Publications:* (with Tyrrell Burgess) The School Governors and Managers Handbook and Training Guide, 1978; The London Left Takeover, 1987. *Address:* 46 Regent's Park Road, NW1 7SX. *T:* (020) 7722 8970.

**SOFTLEY, Prof. Timothy Peter,** PhD; FRS 2018; FRSC; FInstP; Pro-Vice-Chancellor (Research and Knowledge Transfer), University of Birmingham, since 2015; *b* Norwich, 16 Nov. 1958; *s* of Peter and Joyce Softley; *m* 1987, Tertia Belt; one *s* one *d. Educ:* Hewett Sch., Norwich; Wadham Coll., Oxford (BA 1981; MA 1984); Southampton Univ. (PhD 1985). FInstP 2009; FRSC 2012. Harkness Fellow, Stanford Univ., 1984–86; Royal Soc. Univ. Res. Fellow, Cambridge Univ., 1987–90; Charles and Katharine Darwin Fellow, Darwin Coll., Cambridge, 1988–90; University of Oxford: Lectr, 1990–2002; Prof. of Chem. Physics, 2002–15; Hd, Dept of Chem., 2011–15; Sen. Proctor, 2002–03; Tutorial Fellow, 1990–2015, Sub-Warden, 2005–08, Merton Coll., Oxford. *Publications:* Atomic Spectra, 1994; contribs to scientific jls. *Recreations:* tennis, cycling, walking, choral singing, oboe playing. *Address:* University of Birmingham, Edgbaston, Birmingham B15 2TT. *T:* (0121) 414 8986, *Fax:* (0121) 414 4534. *E:* t.p.softley@bham.ac.uk.

**SOGA, Prof. Kenichi,** PhD; FREng, FICE; Chancellor's Professor, Department of Civil and Environmental Engineering, University of California at Berkeley, since 2016; *b* New York, 5 Nov. 1964; *s* of Naohiro and Kuniko Soga; *m* 1999, Mikiko Ashikari; one *d. Educ:* Kyoto Univ. (BSc 1987; MEng 1989); Univ. of Calif, Berkeley (PhD 1994). FICE 2007; FREng 2013. Res. Asst, Univ. of Calif, Berkeley, 1991–94; University of Cambridge: Lectr, 1994–2000, Sen. Lectr, 2000–03, Geotechnic Gp; Reader, 2003–07; Prof. of Civil Engrg, 2007–16; Fellow, Churchill Coll., Cambridge, 1995–2016. George Stephenson Medal, 2006, Crampton Prize, 2007, Telford Gold Medal, 2010, ICE. *Publications:* (with J. K. Mitchell) Fundamentals of Soil Behavior, 3rd edn 2005. *Address:* Department of Civil and Environmental Engineering, University of California, 760 Davis Hall, Berkeley, CA 94720–1710, USA.

**SOHLMAN, (Per) Michael (Sverre Rolfsson);** Executive Director, Nobel Foundation, 1992–2011; *b* 24 May 1944; *s* of Rolf Rolfsson Sohlman and Zinaida Sohlman (*née* Yarotskaya); *m* 1965, Margareta Borg-Sohlman (marr. diss. 1980); one *s* two *d*. *Educ:* Univ. of Uppsala (BA 1964). Asst Sec., Commn on Environmental Problems, 1969–70; Min. of Industry, 1972–74; Internat. Div., 1974–76, Budget Dept, 1976, Min. of Finance; Financial Counsellor, Permt Swedish Delegn to OECD, Paris, 1977–80; Res. Dept, Social-Democratic Parly Gp, 1981–82; Head of Planning, Econ. Dept, 1982–84, Dir of Budget, 1985–87, Min. of Finance; Under-Sec. of State, Min. of Agriculture, 1987–89; Under-Sec. of State for Foreign Trade, Min. for Foreign Affairs, 1989–91. Chm. Bd, Swedish Inst. of Internat. Affairs. Member: Stockholm Inst. of Transition Econs, 1990–2011; Swedish Internat. Develt Agency, 1995–98; Chm., Bd of Dirs, Royal Dramatic Theatre, Stockholm, 1993–96. Member: Royal Swedish Acad. of Scis, 1996; Acad. of Engineering Scis, 1995. Hon. DHL Gustavus Adolphus Coll., 1992.

**SOKOL, Christopher John Francis;** QC 2006; *b* 22 April 1953; *s* of Emil Sokol and Madge Sokol (*née* Woolley); four *d*. *Educ:* Brighton Coll.; Trinity Coll., Cambridge (BA 1974, MA 1977). Called to the Bar, Lincoln's Inn, 1976, Bencher, 2002; in practice, specialising in tax law. *Publications:* contribs to professional jls. *Recreations:* travel, country sports, old books, fencing, wine. *Clubs:* Lansdowne, Buck's, Oxford and Cambridge.

**SOKOLOV, Dr Avril,** FBA 1996; Reader in Russian, University of Durham, 1989–96, Emeritus since 1996; *b* 4 May 1930; *d* of Frederick Cresswell Pyman and Frances Gwenneth Pyman (*née* Holman), MBE; *m* 1963, Kirill Konstantinovich Sokolov (*d* 2004); one *d*. *Educ:* Newnham Coll., Cambridge (BA Mod. Langs 1951; PhD 1958). FCIL (FIL 1949). British Council post-grad. scholarship to Leningrad, 1959–61; freelance writer on and translator of Russian lit., 1962–75; lived in Moscow, 1963–74; University of Durham: part-time Lectr in Russian Lit., 1975–77; Lectr, 1977–86; Sen. Lectr, 1986–89. Mem., Soc. of Authors (Translators' Section), 1974–. Hon. Mem., Blok Gp, Russian Acad. of Scis, 2002–; Mem. Hon. Cttee, Fondn Centre d'Etudes Vjatcheslav Ivanov, Rome, 2005. Hon. Fellow, St Chad's Coll., Durham, 2019. Cert. of Merit, Moscow Patriarchate, 1973. *Publications:* as Avril Pyman: The Distant Thunder: a life of Aleksandr Blok, Vol. I, 1979 (trans. Russian 2005); The Release of Harmony: a life of Aleksandr Blok, Vol. II, 1980 (trans. Russian 2006); Aleksandr Blok's The Twelve, 1989; A History of Russian Symbolism, 1994 (trans. Russian 1998); (contrib.) Mapping Lives: the uses of biography, 2002; (trans.) Requiem, by Anna Akhmatova, 2002; Pavel Florensky: a quiet genius, 2010 (trans. Italian 2010); Metropolitan Anthony of Sourozh: a life, 2016; ed and trans. works by Blok, Bulgakov, Shvarts; trans. poetry, prose, art books; numerous articles on Russian Symbolism and later 20th century literature. *Recreations:* travelling, art, theatre, cinema. *Address:* 213 Gilesgate, Durham DH1 1QN. *T:* (0191) 384 2482.

**SOLA, Maggie;** *see* Koumi, M.

**SOLANA MADARIAGA, Javier,** Hon. KCMG 1999; Secretary-General, and High Representative for Common Foreign and Security Policy, European Union, 1999–2009; Secretary-General, Western European Union, 1999–2009; Head, European Defence Agency, 2004–09; *b* 14 July 1942; *s* of Luis Solana and Obulia Madariaga; *m* 1972, Concepción Giménez; two *c*. *Educ:* Colegio del Pilar; Univ. Complutense de Madrid (PhD Physics). Fulbright Schol., USA, 1968. Asst to Prof., Univ. of Valencia, 1968–71, then Univ. Autónoma de Madrid; Mem. Exec., Federación Socialista Madrileña and Federación de Trabajadores de la Enseñanza, Unión General de Trabajadores; Prof. of Physical Scis, Univ. Complutense de Madrid. Mem., Congress of Deputies for Madrid; Mem., Fed. Exec. Cttee, PSOE (Press Sec. and Sec. for Res. and Programmes); Minister of: Culture, and Govt Spokesman, 1982–88; Educn and Sci., 1988–92; Foreign Affairs, 1992–95; Sec.-Gen., NATO, 1995–99. Pres., ESADE Centre for Global Economy and Geopolitics, 2010–. *Publications:* several on physics and solid state physics. *Recreations:* swimming, jogging, tennis, paddle tennis.

**SOLANDT, Jean Bernard;** Chairman: Schroder France SA, 1992–97; J. Henry Schroder & Co. Ltd, 1994–97; Director, Woolwich Building Society, 1993–98; *b* 23 Dec. 1936; *s* of Alfred Solandt and Mathilde Braun Solandt; *m* 1966, Sheila Hammill; one *s* one *d*. *Educ:* Lycée Pasteur, Strasbourg; Collège Technique Commercial, Strasbourg. Société Générale, Strasbourg, Paris, London, 1954–68; Schroder Gp, 1968–97: Director: J. Henry Schroder & Co., 1973; Schroders plc, 1982; IBJ Schroder Bank & Trust Co. Inc., 1984–86; Schroders Japan Ltd, 1984–95; Schroder & Co. Inc., 1986–96; Schroder Wertheim Hldgs Inc., 1986–97; Schroder Wertheim & Co. Inc., 1986–97; Schroders Asia, 1991; Schroders AG, 1992; Chairman: Schroder Securities Ltd, 1985–89; Schroder Structured Investments Inc., 1995–97. Director: Royal Trust Co. of Canada (London) Ltd, 1978–82; Banca Woolwich SpA, 1996–98; Banque Woolwich SA, 1996–98. Mem. Exec. Cttee, BBA, 1990–94. Advr, Royal Trustees Investment Cttee, 1991–96. Hon. FCIB. *Recreations:* walking, driving, music. *Address:* 27 Heathgate, NW11 7AP. *T:* (020) 8458 2950.

**SOLANKI, Ramniklal Chhaganlal,** CBE 2007 (OBE 1999); author; Editor-in-Chief: Garavi Gujarat, newsweekly, since 1968 (US edition, since 1992); Asian Trader, business journal, with controlled circulation in English, Gujarati and Urdu, since 1985; GG2, since 1990; Pharmacy Business, since 1998; Asian Hospitality, since 2002; Eastern Eye Newspaper, since 2009; Asian Rich List, since 2010; GG2 Power List, since 2011; Asian Rich List Midlands, since 2013; Correspondent, Janmabhoomi Group, Bombay, since 1968; *b* 12 July 1931; *s* of Chhaganlal Kalidas and Mrs Ichchhaben Solanki, Surat, Gujarat, India; *m* 1955, Mrs Parvatiben, *d* of Makanji Dullabhji Chavda, Nani Pethan, India; two *s* two *d*. *Educ:* Irish Presbyterian Mission Sch., Surat (Matriculation Gold Medal, 1949); MTB Coll., Gujarat Univ. (BA(Econ)); Sarvajanik Law Coll., Surat, Gujarat (LLB). Pres., Rander Student Union, 1950–54; Sec., Surat Dist Students' Assoc., 1954–55. Sub-Editor, Nutan Bharat and Lok Vani, Surat, 1954–56; freelance columnist for several newspapers, while serving State Govt in India, 1956–63; London correspondent, Gujarat Mitra Surat, 1964–68; European Correspondent, Janmabhoomi Gp of Newspapers, 1968–; Managing Director: Garavi Gujarat Publications Ltd, Garavi Gujarat Property Ltd and Asian Media Marketing Gp (USA) Inc.; Asian Trade Publications Ltd (columnist of thought of the week on Indian philosophy, Garavi Gujarat, newsweekly). Member: Soc. of Editors (formerly Guild of British Newspaper Editors), 1976–; Asian Adv. Cttee, BBC, 1976–80; Nat. Centre for Ind. Language Trng Steering Gp, 1976–; Exec. Cttee, Gujarati Arya Kshtriya Maha Sabha UK, 1979–84; Exec. Cttee, Gujarati Arya Assoc., 1974–84 (Vice-Pres., 1980–81, 1982–83); CPU, 1964–; Foreign Press Assoc., 1984–; Parly Press Gallery, House of Commons; Sec., Indian Journalists Assoc. of Europe, 1978–79. Founder: Asian Trader Awards for Retail Excellence, 1989; (and Mem. Judging Panel), annual GG2 Leadership and Diversity Awards, 1999; Pharmacy Business Awards, 2001; (and Mem., Judging Panel) Asian Business Awards, 2010; Eastern Eye Arts, Culture of Th. Awards, 2016. Trustee, Gandhi Bapu Meml Trust, 1993–. Best Reporter of the Year in Gujarati, 1970. *Publications:* contrib. many articles. *Recreations:* reading, writing. *Address:* (office) Garavi Gujarat House, 1/2 Silex Street, SE1 0DW. *T:* (020) 7928 1234, *Fax:* (020) 7261 0055. *E:* ram@gujarat.co.uk; (office) 2020 Beaver Ruin Road, Norcross, Atlanta, GA 30071, USA. *T:* (770) 2637728, *Fax:* (770) 2638617; (office) AMG Business Solutions Pvt Ltd, Commerce House II, Satya Marg, Bodakdev, Ahmedabad, 380054, Gujarat, India. *T:* (79) 40005000.

**SOLARI TUDELA, Luis;** Ambassador of Peru to the Court of St James's, and concurrently to Ireland, 2004–06; *b* 5 Dec. 1935; *s* of Luis Solari Saco and Rosa Tudela Salmón; *m* 1961, Martha Reinoso Castañeda; one *s* one *d*. *Educ:* Catholic Univ., Lima (graduate in law); Diplomatic Acad., Peru (postgrad. dip.); Institut des Hautes Etudes Internationales, Geneva (postgrad. dip.). Third Sec., 1961; Second Sec., 1966; Ambassador to Panama, 1977–82; Prof. of Internat. Law, Central Univ., Panama, 1978–82; Ambassador to Italy, 1986–88; Vice Minister of Foreign Affairs and Sec. Gen. *ad interim*, 1990; Ambassador to the Holy See, and concurrently to Croatia, Cyprus and Malta, 1992–95; Juridical Advr to Min. of Foreign Affairs, 2002; Sec. of Foreign Policy, 2002–03; Vice Minister and Sec. Gen. of Foreign Affairs, 2003–04. Prof. in Public Internat. Law, Univ. of Lima, Villarreal Univ., San Martin de Porres Univ. and Diplomatic Acad. of Peru, 1986–2004. Mem., Internat. Law Commn, 1987–91. Grand Cross: Order of Peruvian Sun, 1985; Order of Merit for Dist. Services (Peru), 2000. Knight, Order of Condor of Andes (Bolivia), 1955; Grand Cross: Order of Vasco Núñez de Balboa (Panama), 1982; Ordo Pianus (Holy See), 1995; SMO Malta, 1995; Order of Rio Branco (Brazil), 2003; Order of Bernardo O'Higgins (Chile), 2004. *Publications:* Derecho Internacional Público, 1982, 10th edn 2011. *E:* solaritudela@hotmail.com. *Clubs:* Nacional, Regatas (Lima); Jockey Club del Perú.

**SOLBES MIRA, Pedro;** Second Deputy Vice President and Minister of Economy and Finance, Spain, 2004–09; Chairman, Supervisory Board, European Financial Reporting Advisory Group, 2009; *b* 31 Aug. 1942; *m* 1973, Pilar Castro; one *s* two *d*. *Educ:* Univ. of Madrid (BL, Dr Pol Scis); Univ. Libre de Bruxelles (Dip. in European Econs). Entered Min. of Foreign Trade, Spain, 1968; Commercial Counsellor, Spanish Mission to EC, 1973–78; Special Advr to Minister for Relns with EC, 1978–79; Dir Gen. of Commercial Policy, Min. of Econs and Trade, 1979–82; Gen. Sec., Min. of Econs and Finance, 1982–85; Sec. of State for Relns with EC, 1985–91; Minister of Agriculture, Food and Fisheries, 1991–93; Minister of Econs and Finance, 1993–96; Deputy (Socialist Party), Cortes, 1996–99; European Comr for Econs and Monetary Affairs, 1999–2004. Chm., EBRD, 1994.

**SOLCAN, Natalia;** Ambassador of Moldova to the Court of St James's, 2008–10; *b* Floresti, Moldova. Lectr, Acad. of Econ. Studies of Moldova, 1995–97; Sen. Consultant, Foreign Relns Service and Protocol, Presidency of Moldova, 1997–2001; linguistic studies, Princes Coll., London, 2001–03; Counsellor: Directorate for Europe and N America, Min. of Foreign Affairs, 2003–04; Mission to EC, 2004–06; Control and Internal Audit Div., Cabinet of Dep. Prime Minister and Minister, Min. of Foreign Affairs and Eur. Integration, 2006–07; Hd, Political Cooperation with EU Div., Dept of Eur. Integration, Min. of Foreign Affairs and Eur. Integration, 2007–08. *Address:* c/o Embassy of the Republic of Moldova, 5 Dolphin Square, Edensor Road, W4 2ST.

**SOLESBURY, William Booth;** researcher and writer, since 2010; *b* 10 April 1940; *s* of William and Hannah Solesbury; *m* 1966, Felicity Andrew; one *s* two *d*. *Educ:* Hertford Grammar Sch.; Univ. of Cambridge (BA Hons Geography); Univ. of Liverpool (MCD Town Planning). London County Council, 1961–65; London Borough of Camden, 1965–66; City of Munich, 1966–67; Min. of Housing, 1967–72; NATO Res. Fellow, Univ. of California, Berkeley, 1973; Dept of Environment, 1974–89; Gwilym Gibbon Res. Fellow, Nuffield Coll., Oxford, 1989–90; Sec., ESRC, 1990–95; res. mgt consultant, 1995–2010. Senior Visiting Research Fellow: Queen Mary, Univ. of London, 2000–05; KCL, 2005–18. *Publications:* Policy in Urban Planning, 1974; World Cities, City Worlds, 2013; Modern Cities: ten variations, 2019; articles in Public Administration, Policy and Politics, Public Money and Management, Research Fortnight, London Liby Mag., Town and Country Planning. *Recreations:* home life, films, reading, travel. *Address:* 1 Dolby Road, SW6 3NE. *T:* (020) 7736 2155.

**SOLEY,** Baron *cr* 2005 (Life Peer), of Hammersmith in the London Borough of Hammersmith and Fulham; **Clive Stafford Soley;** *b* 7 May 1939; *s* of Joseph Soley and Doris Soley (*née* Despard); *m* Roslyn Brown (separated); one *s* one *d*. *Educ:* Downshal Sec. Modern School, Ilford; Newbattle Abbey Coll., Dalkeith; Strathclyde Univ. (BA Hons Politics and Psychol.); Southampton Univ. (Dip. in Applied Social Studies). Various unskilled jobs to 1959; RAF Air Traffic Control and Air Defence, 1959–61; British Council officer, 1968–69; Probation Officer, 1970–75, Senior Probation Officer, 1975–79, Inner London Probation Service. Chairman: Alcohol Educn Centre, 1974–84; Mary Seacole Meml Statue Appeal, 2004–16 (Life Patron, Mary Seacole Trust, 2016–); Arab-Jewish Forum, 2005–14. Mem., Hammersmith and Fulham Council, 1974–78; MP (Lab): Hammersmith N, 1979–83; Hammersmith, 1983–97; Ealing, Acton and Shepherd's Bush, 1997–2005. Opposition front bench spokesman on N Ireland, 1982–85, on Home Affairs, 1985–87, on Housing and Local Govt, 1987–89, on Housing and Planning, 1989–92. Chairman: Select Cttee on NI, 1995–97; All Party Parly Gp on Parenting, 1994–96; Jt Cttee, Draft Children (Contact) and Adoption Bill, 2005; Intergovtl Orgns Select Cttee, H of L, 2007–08; Member: Jt Cttee on H of L Reform, 2002–05; Constitutional Affairs Cttee, 2003–05; Delegated Powers and Regulatory Reform Cttee, 2009–13; Inquiries Act 2005 Cttee, 2013–14; Arctic Cttee, 2014–15; EU Sub-Cttee on Home Affairs, 2015–; promoted Home Educn (Duty of Local Authorities) Bill, H of L, 2017–. Chair: Labour Campaign for Criminal Justice, 1974–78; PLP, 1997–2001; Mem., NEC, Lab. Pty, 1998–2001. Fellow, Industry and Parlt Trust, 1984. Campaign Dir, Future Heathrow, 2005–10; Chm. and Dir, Good Governance Foundn, 2010–15. *Publications:* (jtly) Regulating the Press, 2000; (jtly) A Statue for Mary: the Seacole legacy, 2016. *Recreations:* walking, photography, scuba diving, metal detecting, writing articles for publication and book reviews. *Address:* House of Lords, SW1A 0PW.

**SOLICARI, Sonia Natasha Clara;** Director, Geffrye Museum of the Home, since 2017; *b* London, 5 July 1978; *d* of Bruno and Linda Solicari; *m* 2007, Tim Killick; two *d*. *Educ:* Bishop Stopford's Sch., Enfield; Royal Holloway, Univ. of London (BA English Lit.); King's Coll. London (MA Victorian Studies); University Coll. London (MA Mus. Studies). Asst Curator, Paintings, 2002–06, Curator, Ceramics and Glass, 2006–10, V&A Mus.; Principal Curator, 2010–13, Hd, 2013–17, Guildhall Art Gall. and London's Roman Amphitheatre. *Publications:* (ed) Victoriana: a miscellany, 2013. *Recreation:* collecting vintage brooches and strange Victorian things. *Address:* Geffrye Museum of the Home, 136 Kingsland Road, E2 8EA. *T:* (020) 7739 9893. *E:* ssolicari@geffrye-museum.org.uk. *Clubs:* Two Brydges, Shoreditch House.

**SOLKIN, Prof. David Hersh,** PhD; FBA 2012; Walter H. Annenberg Professor of the History of Art, Courtauld Institute of Art, 2010–16, Emeritus Professor of the History of Art, 2017; *b* Montreal, 16 March 1951; *s* of Wolf William Solkin and Elaine Waddington (*née* Robinson); *m* 1st, 1979, Sally Marie Kolker (*d* 1999); one *s* one *d*; 2nd, 2011, Gillian Archer; one step *d*. *Educ:* Harvard Coll. (AB *magna cum laude* Fine Arts); Courtauld Inst. of Art (MA with Dist.); Yale Univ. (PhD Hist. of Art 1978). Asst Prof., Dept of Fine Arts, Univ. of BC, 1978–85; Courtauld Institute of Art: Lectr in Hist. of Art, 1986–93; Reader, 1993–2002; Dep. Dir, 1994–96; Prof. of Social Hist. of Art, 2002–10; Dean and Dep. Dir, 2007–16. Paul Mellon Lectr, 2004–05. Guest Curator, Turner and the Masters exhibn, Tate Britain, London, Grand Palais, Paris and Museo del Prado, Madrid, 2009–10; Sen. Res. Fellow, Paul Mellon Centre, 2010–11; Guest Curator, Gainsborough's Family Album exhibn, NPG, London and Princeton Art Mus., 2018–19. *Publications:* Richard Wilson: the landscape of reaction, 1982; Painting for Money: the visual arts and the public sphere in eighteenth-century England, 1993; (ed and jt author) Art on the Line: the Royal Academy exhibitions at Somerset House 1780–1836, 2001; Painting out of the Ordinary: modernity and the art of everyday life in early nineteenth-century Britain, 2008; (ed and jt author) Turner and the Masters, 2009; Art in Britain 1660–1815, 2015; Gainsborough's Family Album, 2018. *Recreations:* collecting art, swimming, supporting Tottenham Hotspur. *Address:* 117 Crouch Hill, N8 9QN. *T:* (020) 8340 6919. *E:* david.solkin@courtauld.ac.uk.

**SOLLEY, Stephen Malcolm;** QC 1989; a Recorder, 1989–2017; *b* 5 Nov. 1946; *s* of late Leslie Solley, sometime MP, and José Solley; *m* 1971, Helen Olivia Cox; four *s. Educ:* University College London (LLB 1968). Called to the Bar, Inner Temple, 1969, Bencher, 1998 (Master of the Cellar, 2000–). The Recorder, South Eastern Circuit, 1984–87. Chm., Bar Human Rights Cttee, 1999–2003. Trustee, Reprieve, 2008–15. Dir, Hackney Empire Theatre, 1994–2013. *Recreations:* jazz, opera, wine, football. *Address:* 67a Endell Street, WC2H 9AJ. *Club:* Les Six.

**SOLLOWAY, Amanda Jane;** *b* 6 June 1961. *Educ:* Bramcote Hills Grammar Sch. Tennis player; Hd of Trng and Develt, Baird Clothing, 1998–2009; mgt consultant, 2009–. MP (C) Derby N, 2015–17; contested (C) same seat, 2017. Mem., Business, Innovation and Skills Select Cttee, 2015–17. Associate, 3aaa. Chair, Cons. Friends of Internat. Develt. Mem., Ockbrook and Borrowash Parish Council, 2011. FCIPD. *Publications:* (with A. Cartwright) Emotional Intelligence: activities for developing you and your business, 2009.

**SOLOMON, Adam Jonathan;** QC 2018; *b* Watford, 16 Feb. 1971; *s* of David and Helen Solomon; *m* 2000, Dani Harrison; one *s* two *d. Educ:* Haberdashers' Aske's Sch., Elstree; Exeter Coll., Oxford (BA); Sussex Univ. (MA); City Univ. (CPD). Sch. Master, Worksop Coll., 1992–93; Research Assistant: Houses of Parliament, 1992; Eur. Commn, 1994–96; called to the Bar, Gray's Inn, 1998; in practice as barrister, 1998–. Mem., Bar Standards Bd, 2014–. *Publications:* (contrib.) Employee Competition, 2018. *Recreations:* boxing, wood turning. *Address:* Littleton Chambers, 3 King's Bench Walk, Temple, EC4Y 7HR. *T:* (020) 7797 8600. *E:* adamqc@littletonchambers.com.

**SOLOMON, Ashley Darren;** musician; Professor, since 1994, and Head, Historical Performance, since 2006, Royal College of Music; Director, Florilegium, since 1991; *b* Hove, 15 March 1968; *s* of Henry Solomon and Meta Solomon; *m* 1998, Dr Sarah Tunkel; four *d. Educ:* Haberdashers' Aske's Sch. for Boys; Royal Acad. of Music (BMus; LRAM; ARAM). Dir, Arakaendar Bolivia Choir, 2005–. Hon. RCM 2000. *Recreations:* family, sport. *Address:* 21 Village Road, N3 1TL. *T:* (020) 8346 2896. *E:* asolomon@rcm.ac.uk, ashleysolomon@florilegium.org.uk.

**SOLOMON, Prof. David Henry,** AC 2016 (AM 1990); PhD, DSc; FRS 2004; FAA, FRACI, FTSE, FIChemE; Professorial Fellow, Department of Chemical and Biomolecular Engineering, University of Melbourne, 1996–2015, now Emeritus Professor; *b* 19 Nov. 1929; *s* of H. J. Solomon and Mary Solomon; *m* 1954, Harriet Valerie Dawn Newport; three *d. Educ:* Sydney Technical Coll.; NSW Univ. of Technol. (BSc Hons 1952; MSc 1954; PhD 1959); Univ. of NSW (DSc 1968). ASTC; FRACI 1966; Foundation FTSE 1975; FAA 1975; FIChemE 2007. Joined, 1946, Leader, 1955–63, Resin and Polymer Resin BALM Paints Ltd; Demonstrator and Teaching Fellow, Univ. of NSW, 1953–55; Commonwealth Scientific and Industrial Research Organization (Australia): Div. of Applied Mineralogy, 1963–70; Chief Res. Scientist, Div. of Applied Chemistry, 1970–74; Chief, Div. of Chemicals and Polymers, 1974–89; Dep. Dir, Inst. of Industrial Technol., 1989–90; Hd of Sch. and ICI Aust.–Masson Prof. of Chemistry, Sch. of Chemistry, Univ. of Melbourne, 1990–94. Pres., RACI, 1979–80. Hon. DAppSc Melbourne, 2005. Victoria Prize, Govt of Vic, Australia, 2006; (jtly) Australian Prime Minister's Sci. Prize, 2011. *Publications:* Chemistry of Organic Film Formers, 1967, 2nd edn 1977; (ed) Step-Growth Polymerizations: kinetics and mechanisms, 1972; The Catalytic Properties of Pigments, 1977; Chemistry of Pigments and Fillers, 1983; The Chemistry of Free Radical Polymerization, 1995, 2nd edn 2006; Australia's Plastic Banknotes: from concept to reality, 2014. *Recreation:* fishing. *Address:* Department of Chemical and Biomolecular Engineering, University of Melbourne, Vic 3010, Australia. *T:* (3) 8344 8200. *E:* davids@unimelb.edu.au.

**SOLOMON, David Joseph;** Senior Partner, D. J. Freeman, solicitors, 1992–96; *b* 31 Dec. 1930; *s* of Sydney and Rosie Harriet Solomon; *m* 1959, Hazel Boam; one *s* two *d. Educ:* Torquay Grammar Sch.; Univ. of Manchester (LLB). Admitted as solicitor, 1955. Partner, Nabarro Nathanson, 1961–68; Head of Property Dept, 1976–90, Chief Exec., 1990–93, D. J. Freeman. Trustee: Highgate Literary and Scientific Instn, 1999–2006 (Pres., 1993–98); Public Art Develt Trust, 1996–2002 (Chm., Public Art Develt Trust, 1998–2001). Mem. Council, Oriental Ceramic Soc., 1988–91, 1994–97, 1998–2001, 2003–06. *Recreations:* Chinese ceramics, music, poetry, art, wine, the championing of unjustly neglected writers. *Address:* Russell House, 9 South Grove, N6 6BS. *T:* (020) 8341 6454; 6 Rue de Cussy, Longecourt les Culetre, 21230 Arnay le Duc, France. *T:* 380900555. *Club:* Athenæum.

**SOLOMON, Sir Harry,** Kt 1991; Deputy Chairman, Portland Trust, since 2003; Director, Q Tec Analytics Ltd (formerly Monitor/Quest Ltd), since 2008; *b* 20 March 1937; *s* of Jacob and Belle Solomon; *m* 1962, Judith Diana Manuel; one *s* two *d. Educ:* St Albans School; Law Society School of Law. Qualified solicitor, 1960; in private practice, 1960–75; Hillsdown Holdings: Man. Dir, 1975–84; Jt Chm., 1984–87; Chm., 1987–93; Dir, 1993–97; Chm., Harvey Hldgs, 1994–2000; Director: West City (QEC) Ltd, 2003–06; Falkland Islands Hldgs plc, 1999–2009. Pres., Help Medicine, RCP, 1990–97. Trustee, Nat. Life Story Collection, 2005–14. Hon. FRCP 1992. *Recreations:* jogging, tennis, theatre, collector of historical autographed letters. *Address:* Hillsdown House, 32 Hampstead High Street, NW3 1QD.

**SOLOMON, Kate Victoria;** see Branigan, K. V.

**SOLOMON, Nicola;** Chief Executive (formerly General Secretary), Society of Authors, since 2011; *b* Pembury, 1 May 1960; *d* of Aaron Kenneth Solomon and Rosalie Ursula Solomon; *m* 1991, Rabbi Jonathan Wittenberg; one *s* two *d. Educ:* Paddock Wood County Primary Sch.; Tonbridge Grammar Sch. for Girls; Univ. of Warwick (LLB Hons 1981). Admitted solicitor, 1984; trainee solicitor, Taylor, Tyrell, Lewis and Craig, 1982–84; solicitor, Norton Rose, 1985; Stephen Innocent, later Finers Stephens Innocent: solicitor, 1985–88; Partner, 1988–2007; Hd, IP and Media Dept, 2002–07; Consultant, 2007–11. A Dep. District Judge, 1998–. Freeman, City of London, 2008; Freeman, Stationers' and Newspaper Makers' Co., 2008. *Publications:* (jtly) Personal Injury Litigation, 7th edn 1992 to 10th edn 2002; articles on IP law, publishing, fashion. *Recreations:* family, reading, gardening, people, laughter, nature. *Address:* Society of Authors, 24 Bedford Row, WC1R 4EH. *T:* (020) 7373 6642. *E:* nsolomon@societyofauthors.org.

**SOLOMON, Rabbi Dr Norman;** Fellow, Oxford Centre for Hebrew and Jewish Studies, 1995–2000; Lecturer, Faculty of Theology, University of Oxford, 1995–2001; *b* Cardiff, 31 May 1933; *s* of late Phillip Solomon and Esther Solomon (*née* Lewis); *m* 1st, 1955, Devora, (Doris), Strauss (*d* 1998); three *s* one *d;* 2nd, 2000, Dr Hilary Nissenbaum. *Educ:* Cardiff High Sch.; St John's Coll., Cambridge (BA 1954); Univ. of Manchester (PhD 1966). London Univ. (BMus 1958); ARCM 1956. Rabbi: Whitefield Synagogue, Manchester, 1961–66; Greenbank Drive Synagogue, Liverpool, 1966–74; Hampstead Synagogue, 1974–83; Central Synagogue, Birmingham, 1994; Lectr in Judaism, 1983–89, Dir, Centre for Study of Judaism and Jewish/Christian Relations, 1989–94, Selly Oak Colls, Birmingham. Vis. Lectr, Oxford Centre for Postgraduate Hebrew Studies, 1985–94; Koerner Vis. Fellow, Oxford Centre for Hebrew and Jewish Studies, 1994–95; Scholar-in-Residence, Mandelbaum House, Univ. of Sydney, 2004. Mem., Commn on Religion and Belief in British Public Life, 2013–15. Editor, Jewish Christian Relations, 1985–91. Adviser, Internat. CCJ, 1988–; Specialist Adviser, CNAA, 1989–92. Vice-Pres., World Congress of Faiths, 1998– (Vice-Chm., 1992–98); President: Birmingham Inter-Faiths Council, 1984–85; British Assoc. for Jewish Studies, 1994; Soc. for Jewish Studies, 2006–. FBIS 1986. 15th Annual Sir Sigmund Sternberg Award, CCJ, 1993; Distinguished Service Medal, Univ. of San Francisco, 2001. *Publications:* Judaism and World Religion, 1991; The Analytic Movement, 1993; Judaism: a very short introduction, 1996; Historical Dictionary of the Jewish Religion, 1998; (ed) Abraham's Children, 2006; The Talmud: selections, 2009; Torah from Heaven, 2012; (ed) Ernest Bloch Studies, 2016; articles in learned jls. *Recreations:* hiking, chamber music. *Address:* Oxford Centre for Hebrew and Jewish Studies, Clarendon Institute, Walton Street, Oxford OX1 4QG. *T:* (01865) 610422. *W:* www.normansolomon.info.

**SOLOMONS, Anthony Nathan,** FCA; Chairman: Singer & Friedlander Ltd, 1976–99 (Chief Executive, 1973–90); Singer & Friedlander Group plc, 1987–99; *b* 26 Jan. 1930; *s* of Leslie Emanuel Solomons and Susie Schneiders; *m* 1957, Jean Golding; two *d.* Qual. as chartered accountant, 1953; FCA 1963. National Service, 1953–54: commnd Dorset Regt. Articled 1952; Accountant, Kennedy, Fox & Oldfield, 1955; Asst Accountant, then Chief Accountant, Lobitos Oilfields Ltd, 1955–58; Singer & Friedlander, 1958–99: successively Exec. Dir, Man. Dir, and Jt Chief Exec.

**SOLOW, Prof. Robert Merton;** Professor of Economics, Massachusetts Institute of Technology, 1949–95, now Emeritus; *b* 23 Aug. 1924; *s* of Milton H. Solow and Hannah Solow (*née* Sarney); *m* 1945, Barbara Lewis (*d* 2014); two *s* one *d. Educ:* New York City schools; Harvard College (BA 1947); Harvard University (MA 1949, PhD 1951). Served US forces, 1942–45 (Bronze Star, 1944). Joined MIT Faculty as Asst Prof. of Statistics, 1949, Inst. Prof. of Economics, 1974–95. Senior Economist, Council of Economic Advisers, 1961–62. Eastman Prof. and Fellow of Balliol Coll., Oxford, 1968–69; Overseas Fellow, Churchill Coll., Cambridge, 1984, 1991; Robert K. Merton Foundn Fellow, Russell Sage Foundn, 2007–. President: Econometric Soc., 1965; Amer. Econ. Assoc., 1976; Member: Amer. Acad. of Arts and Scis, 1963; Nat. Acad. of Sciences, USA, 1972; Accademia dei Lincei, 1984; Corresp. Mem., British Acad., 1975; Mem., Amer. Philosophical Soc., 1974–. Hon. degrees: Chicago, 1967; Brown, 1972; Williams, 1974; Paris I, 1975; Warwick, 1976; Lehigh, 1977; Geneva, Wesleyan, 1982; Tulane, 1983; Yale, 1986; Bryant, 1987; Massachusetts at Boston, Boston Coll., 1989; Colgate, Dartmouth, Helsinki, 1990; New York at Albany, 1991; Harvard, Glasgow, Chile, 1992; Conservatoire Nat. des Arts et Métiers, Paris, 1995; Colorado Sch. of Mines, 1996; New York, 2000; Rensselaer Poly. Inst., 2003; New Sch. Univ., NY, 2006; Rochester, 2007; Iowa, 2008. Nobel Prize for Economics, 1987; Nat. Medal of Sci., USA, 1996. Order of Merit (Germany), 1995. *Publications:* Linear Programming and Economic Analysis (with P. Samuelson and R. Dorfman), 1958; Capital Theory and the Rate of Return, 1964; The Sources of Unemployment in the US, 1964; Growth Theory: an exposition, 1970, 2nd edn 1999; The Labor Market as a Social Institution, 1990; (with F. Hahn) A Critical Essay on Modern Macroeconomic Theory, 1995; Learning from Learning by Doing, 1996; (with J. Taylor) Inflation, Unemployment and Monetary Policy, 1998; Monopolistic Competition and Macroeconomic Theory, 1998; Work and Welfare, 1998; articles in learned jls. *Address:* 1010 Waltham Street, Apt 328, Lexington, MA 02421–8057, USA. *T:* (781) 5385412.

**SOLTI, (Anne) Valerie, (Lady Solti);** Chairman, Solti Foundation to assist young musicians, since 1998; President, Sadler's Wells Theatre, since 2002 (Trustee and Governor, since 1995); Hungarian Government Global Ambassador for Culture, since 2007; *b* Leeds, 19 Aug. 1937; *d* of William Pitts and Nancy Pitts; *m* 1st, 1960, James Sargant; 2nd, 1967, Sir Georg Solti, KBE; two *d. Educ:* Leeds Girls High Sch.; Royal Acad. of Dramatic Art (Licentiate). (As Valerie Pitts) TV and radio announcer, 1960–70, interviewer, 1960–67, BBC; freelance writer and broadcaster, 1967–97; programmes include: Face the Music, 1971–81, Town and Around, South at Six, BBC; North East Roundabout, Tyne Tees TV; for children: Playschool, BBC, 1967–70; Extraordinary, Gammon and Spinach, Yorkshire TV, 1978–81; contrib. to radio progs in UK and US. Appeared in play, Roseland's Variation on a Theme, W End, 1958–59. Dir, 1998, Trustee, 1999–, Chm., 1999–2006, Mariinsky Th. Trust; Chm., Develt Campaign for rebuilding Sadler's Wells Th., 1990–98. Mem., BBC Adv. Bd (SE), 1975–80. Adviser: Hungarian Cultural Centre; Liszt Acad., Budapest. Jt Pres., Jewish Music Inst., 2000. Trustee: Hampstead Old People's Housing Trust, 1975–83; LPO, 1980–86 (Chm., Friends); Voice of the Listener; Eur. Orgn for Res. Treatment of Cancer. Hon. Trustee, Chicago SO, 1997–. Gov., Brit Sch. for Performing Arts and Technol., 1997–2006. Patron: Longborough Fest. Opera, 2007. Patron, Frankfurt Internat. Conducting Comp., 2000–; Geneva Internat. Comp.; Jeunesse Musicale Suisse; Mem. Jury, Whittaker Prize for Trios. Comdr, Hungarian Cross with Star, 2002; Pro Cultura Hungarica, 2006; Hungarian Order of Merit, 2012. *Recreations:* swimming, sailing, walking, travelling by steam train, music and theatre. *Address:* c/o Solti Foundation, PO Box 67, 1410 Waterloo, Belgium. *E:* Soltioffice51@googlemail.com. *Club:* Athenæum.
*See also* G. T. *Solti-Dupas*.

**SOLTI-DUPAS, Gabrielle Teresa;** Vice Principal and Head of Primary, The Grammar School at Leeds, since 2019; *b* London, 25 April 1970; *d* of Sir Georg Solti, KBE and Anne Valerie Solti, *qv;* *m* 1998, Frederic Dupas; one *s* one *d. Educ:* Francis Holland Sch.; King's Sch., Canterbury; Jesus Coll., Oxford (BA Hons Mod. Hist. 1991); Inst. of Educn, London (PGCE 1997). Intern, EC, 1991–92; Mktg Exec., Nestlé, 1992–94; Teacher, Trevor Roberts Prep. Sch., 1994–96; Teacher, then Dep. Headteacher, Primrose Hill Prim. Sch., 1997–2003; Head, Junior School: Notting Hill and Ealing High Sch., 2003–13; S Hampstead High Sch., 2013–19. Trustee, Solti Foundn for Young Musicians, 1999–. *Recreations:* classical music, travel, cooking. *Address:* The Grammar School at Leeds, Alwoodley Gates, Harrogate Road, Leeds LS17 8GS.

**SOLYMAR, Prof. Laszlo,** FRS 1995; PhD; Professor of Applied Electromagnetism, University of Oxford, 1992–97, now Emeritus Professor; Professorial Fellow of Hertford College, Oxford, 1986–97, now Emeritus Fellow; Consultant, Metaboards Ltd, since 2017; *b* 24 Jan. 1930; *s* of Pál and Aranka Solymar; *m* 1955, Marianne Klopfer; two *d. Educ:* Technical University, Budapest (Hungarian equivalents of BSc and PhD in Engineering). Lectr, Technical Univ., Budapest, 1952–53; Research Engineer, Res. Inst. for Telecommunications, Budapest, 1953–56; Res. Engineer, Standard Telecom Labs, Harlow, 1956–65; Fellow in Engineering, Brasenose Coll., Oxford, 1966–86 (Emeritus Fellow, 2011); Lectr, 1971–86, Donald Pollock Reader in Engrg Sci., 1986–92, Univ. of Oxford. Visiting Professor: Ecole Normale Supérieure, Paris, 1965–66; Tech. Univ. of Denmark, 1972–73; Univ. Osnabrück, 1987; Tech. Univ., Berlin, 1990; Univ. Autónoma, Madrid, 1993, 1995; Tech. Univ., Budapest, 1994; ICSTM, 2000–. Consultant: Tech. Univ. of Denmark, 1973–76; Thomson-CSF, Orsay, 1984; British Telecom, 1986–88; GEC Wembley, 1986–88; Pilkington Technol. Centre, 1989–90. Faraday Medal, IEE, 1992. Anaxagoras, Archimedes, Hypatia (radio plays with John

Wain), 1991. *Publications:* Lectures on the Electrical Properties of Materials (with D. Walsh), 1970, 10th edn 2018; Superconductive Tunnelling and Applications, 1972; (ed) A Review of the Principles of Electrical and Electronic Engineering, 1974; Lectures on Electromagnetic Theory, 1976, 2nd edn 1984; (with D. J. Cooke) Volume Holography and Volume Gratings, 1981; Lectures on Fourier Series, 1988; (jtly) The Physics and Applications of Photorefractive Materials, 1996; Getting the Message: a history of communications, 1999; (with E. Shamonina) Waves in Metamaterials, 2008; The Rhineland War: 1936, 2012; The Portrait of a Genius, 2013; (with J. Wain) Three Scientists of the Ancient World, 2013; Anatomy of Assassinations, 2013; Past, Present and Future, 2014; The Passenger Plane Shot Down by the Russians, 2016; Soviet Potpourri, 2017; articles. *Recreations:* history, languages, chess, swimming. *Address:* Hertford College, Cattle Street, Oxford OX1 3BW. *E:* laszlo.solymar@hertford.ox.ac.uk.

**SÓLYOM, László;** Professor, Faculty of Law, Péter Pázmány Catholic University, Budapest, 1995–2012; President, Republic of Hungary, 2005–10; *b* Pécs, 3 Jan. 1942; *m* Erzsébet Nagy; one *s* one *d*. *Educ:* Univ. of Pécs (grad 1965); Univ. of Jena (Dr 1969); Dr Pol and Legal Scis, Hungarian Acad. Scis, 1981. Asst Lectr, Inst. Civil Law, Friedrich Schiller Univ. of Jena, 1966–69; Fellow, Inst. Political and Legal Scis, Hungarian Acad. Scis, 1969–78; Librarian, Liby of Parlt, 1975; Associate Prof., 1978–83, Prof., 1983–98, Dept of Civil Law, Eötvös Loránd Univ., Budapest. Justice, 1989, Dep. Pres., 1990, Pres., three times, 1990–98, Constitutional Court, Hungary. Vis. Prof., Univ. of Cologne, 1999–2000. Mem., Hungarian Acad. Scis, 2013 (Corresp. Mem., 2001). Hon. Dr: Cologne, 1999; Johann Wolfgang Goethe, 2006; Yonsei, 2009. Humboldt Prize to foreign social scientists, 1998. *Publications:* A polgári jogi felelősség hanyatlása (The Decline of Civil Law Liability), 1977, 1980; Környezetvédelem és polgári jog (Environmental Protection and Civil Law), 1980; A személyiségi jogok elmélete (The Theory of Personality Rights), 1983; Die Persönlichkeitsrechte, 1984; (ed with M. Szabó) A Zöld Hullám: Olvasókönyv a környezetvédelmi társadalmi mozgalmakról (The Green Wave: a reader on environmental social movements), 1988; (with Georg Brunner) Versassungsgerichtsbarkeit in Ungarn, 1995; (with Georg Brunner) Constitutional Judiciary in a New Democracy: the Hungarian Constitutional Court, 2000; Az alkotmánybíráskodás kezdetei Magyarországon (The Beginnings of Constitutional Jurisdiction in Hungary), 2001; Pártok és érdekszervezetek az Alkotmányban (Parties and Interest Organisations in the Constitution), 2004; Egy elnökség lenyomata (Imprints of a Presidency), 2010; Das Gewand des Grundgesetres, 2017. *Address:* Kelenhegyi ut 32, 1118 Budapest, Hungary.

**SOMARE, Rt Hon. Sir Michael (Thomas),** GCMG 1990; CH 1978; PC 1977; Prime Minister of Papua New Guinea, 1975–80, 1982–85 and 2002–11; *b* 9 April 1936; *m* 1965, Veronica Bula Kaiap; three *s* two *d*. *Educ:* Sogeri Secondary Sch. Admin. Coll. Teaching, 1956–62; Asst Area Educn Officer, Madang, 1962–63; Broadcasts Officer, Dept of Information and Extension Services, Wewack, 1963–66; Journalism, 1966–68. Member for E Sepik Region (Nat. Parlt), PNG House of Assembly, 1968–2017; Parly Leader, Pangu Pati, 1968–93; First Chief Minister, 1972–75; first Prime Minister, 1975; Leader of Opposition in House of Assembly, 1980–82; Minister for Foreign Affairs, 1988–94; National Alliance Leader. Gov., E Sepik Province, PNG, 1995–2002. Dep. Chm., Exec. Council, 1972–73, Chm., 1973–75. Mem., Second Select Cttee on Constitutional Develt, 1968–72; Mem. Adv. Cttee, Australian Broadcasting Commission. *Publications:* Sana: an autobiography. *Recreations:* golf, fishing, reading. *Address:* Karan, Murik Lakes, East Sepik, Papua New Guinea.

**SOMAVIA, Juan O.;** Co-Chair, Independent Team of Advisors, United Nations Economic and Social Council, since 2016; *m*; two *c*. *Educ:* Catholic Univ. of Chile; Univ. of Paris. Joined Min. of Foreign Relations, Chile; Mem. Bd of Dirs and Vice Pres. for Latin America, Inter-Press Service, 1976–87; Sec. Gen., S American Peace Commn, 1987; Perm. Rep. of Chile to UN, NY, 1990–99; Dir Gen., Internat. Labour Orgn, 1999–2012; former consultant to GATT and UNDP; Special Advr on Inter-regl Policy Cooperation, UN, 2013. Founder and Dir, Latin American Inst. for Transnational Studies. Dr *hc* Univ. Central, Chile, 2012. Leonidas Proaño Prize, Latin American Human Rights Assoc.

**SOMERLEYTON,** 4th Baron *cr* 1916; **Hugh Francis Savile Crossley;** Bt 1863; DL; *b* Norwich, 27 Sept. 1971; *s* of 3rd Baron Somerleyton, GCVO, and Belinda Maris, OBE (*née* Loyd); *S* father, 2012; *m* 2009, Lara Kate Bailey; one *s* two *d*. *Educ:* Eton; Anglia Polytechnic Univ. (BA Hist. 1st cl.). Entrepreneur: developed Dish Dash Middle-Eastern restaurant chain, 2000–04, Hot Chip kiosks chain, 2012. Estate manager, Somerleyton Estate, 2005– (Duke's Head pub, 2005–; Fritton Hse Hotel, 2006–). Chm., Waveney Tourism, 2008–11. DL Suffolk, 2019. *Recreations:* Middle East and Islam, tennis, running, forestry, history. *Heir: s* Hon. John de Bathe Savile Turner Crossley, *b* 9 Feb. 2010. *Address:* Somerleyton Hall, Lovingland, Suffolk NR32 5QQ. *T:* (01502) 734901. *Club:* Soho House.

**SOMERS,** 9th Baron *cr* 1784; **Philip Sebastian Somers Cocks;** Bt 1772; *b* 4 Jan. 1948; *o s* of John Sebastian Somers Cocks, CVO, CBE (*d* 1964), and late Marjorie Olive (*née* Weller); *S* cousin, 1995. *Educ:* abroad; Elston Hall, Newark; Craig-y-Parc, Cardiff. *Recreations:* opera, music generally, foreign travel. *Heir: cousin* Jonathan Bromley Cocks [*b* 18 Aug. 1985; *m* 2009, Kerry-Lee Ann, *d* of R. Thysse; three *d*].
*See also Hon. A. G. Somers Cocks.*

**SOMERS, Shaw Stefano,** MD; FRCS; Specialist Upper Gastrointestinal and Bariatric Surgeon; Consultant Surgeon: Portsmouth Hospitals NHS Trust, since 1998; The London Clinic, since 2007; Director, Streamline Surgical Group, since 2008; *b* London, 7 Aug. 1962; *s* of Derek and Edelweiss Somers; *m* 1991, Joanne Ward; two *s*. *Educ:* Latymer Sch., Edmonton; Univ. of Leeds (BSc Hons Pathol. 1983; MB ChB Medicine 1986; MD Surgery 1992). FRCS 1992. Lectr in Surgery, Univ. of Leeds, 1994–95; Associate Prof. of Surgery, Prince of Wales Hosp., Hong Kong, 1995–97; Sen. Lectr in Surgery, Univ. of Leeds, 1997–98. Presenter, TV series: Fat Doctor, 2006–; Food Hospital, 2011–12. Pres., British Obesity and Metabolic Surgery Soc., 2017–19. *Recreations:* off-road cycling, ski-ing, travel, wild mushrooms, Italian wine, collecting fountain pens. *Address:* The Sudbury Clinic, Harrow, Middx HA1 3RX; Department of Upper Gastrointestinal Surgery, Portsmouth Hospitals NHS Trust, Portsmouth PO6 3LY. *T:* 0845 643 1400, *E:* info@shawsomers.com.

**SOMERS COCKS, Hon. Anna Gwenllian, (Hon. Mrs Allemandi),** OBE 2011; FSA; Group Editorial Director, Giornale dell' Arte and The Art Newspaper, since 2003; Hon. Chairman, U. Allemandi & Co. Publishing Ltd, since 2018 (Chief Executive Officer, 2012; Chairman, 2016); *b* 18 April 1950; *d* of late John Sebastian Somers Cocks, CVO, CBE and Marjorie Olive Weller; *m* 1st, 1971, Martin Walker (marr. diss.); 2nd, 1978, John Hardy (marr. diss.); one *s* one *d*; 3rd, 1991, Umberto Allemandi. *Educ:* abroad; Convent of the Sacred Heart, Woldingham; St Anne's College, Oxford (MA); Courtauld Inst., Univ. of London (MA). Asst Keeper, Dept of Metalwork, 1973–85, Dept of Ceramics, 1985–87, Victoria and Albert Museum; Editor: Apollo Magazine, 1987–90; The Art Newspaper, 1990–94, 1996–2003. Chm., Umberto Allemandi Publishing, 1995–96. Member: Mus., New Buildings and Refurbishment Panel, Heritage Lottery Fund, 1996–97; Adv. Council, Sotheby's Inst. of Art, 2002–; Trustee: Gilbert Collection, 1998–; Cass Sculpture Foundn, 2004–13; Fondo Ambiente Italiano UK, 2016–. Gov., Courtauld Inst., 2010–. Chairman: Venice in Peril, 1999–2012; Bd of Trustees, Antarctic Biennale, 2016–17. Mem., Ateneo Veneto, 2007. Foreign Fellow, Istituto Veneto di Scienze, Lettere e Arti, 2019. Annual Prize, Nat. Art Collections Fund, 1992; European Women of Achievement Award (Arts and Media), 2006; Advocate Award, Internat. Inst. of Conservation, 2011; Istituto Veneto Prize for journalism about Venice, 2013. Commendatore, Ordine della Stella della Solidarietà Italiana (Italy), 2003. *Publications:* The Victoria and Albert Museum: the making of the collection, 1980; (ed and jt author) Princely Magnificence: court jewels of the Renaissance, 1980; (with C. Truman) Renaissance Jewels, Gold Boxes and Objets de Vertu in the Thyssen Collection, 1985; journalism in The Daily Telegraph etc, articles in magazines, incl. NY Rev. of Books. *Recreations:* learning Arabic, travelling in the Middle and Far East. *Address:* via Giulio 6, Turin 10122, Italy.
*See also Baron Somers.*

**SOMERSET,** family name of **Duke of Beaufort** and **Baron Raglan**.

**SOMERSET,** 19th Duke of, *cr* 1547; **John Michael Edward Seymour;** DL; FRICS; Baron Seymour 1547; Bt 1611; *b* 30 Dec. 1952; *s* of 18th Duke of Somerset and Gwendoline Collette (Jane) (*d* 2005), 2nd *d* of Major J. C. C. Thomas; *S* father, 1984; *m* 1978, Judith-Rose, *d* of J. F. C. Hull, *qv*; two *s* two *d*. *Educ:* Eton; Univ. of Neuchatel; Royal Agricl Univ. Elected Mem., H of L, 2014. DL: Wilts, 1993, Devon, 2003. *Heir: s* Lord Seymour, *qv*. *Address:* Bradley House, Maiden Bradley, Wilts BA12 7HL.

**SOMERTON, Viscount; Arthur Alexander Christian Welbore Ellis Agar;** *b* 14 Feb. 2016; *s* and *heir* of 7th Earl of Normanton, *qv*.

**SOMERVILLE, Prof. Christopher Roland,** PhD; FRS 1991; Scientific Advisor, Open Philanthropy Project, San Francisco, since 2017; *b* 11 Oct. 1947; *s* of Hubert Roland Somerville and Teresa Marie (*née* Bond); *m* 1976, Shauna Christine Phimester. *Educ:* Univ. of Alberta, Canada (PhD, BS). Asst Prof. of Genetics, Univ. of Alberta, Canada, 1980–82; Associate Prof. of Botany and Genetics, Michigan State Univ., Mich, 1982–86; Prof. of Botany and Genetics, Michigan State Univ., 1982–93; Dir, Carnegie Instn for Science and Prof. of Biology, Stanford Univ., 1994–2007; Dir, Energy Bioscis Inst., 2007–16, Prof. of Plant and Microbial Biology, 2007–17, now Emeritus, Univ. of Calif, Berkeley. (Jtly) Balzan Prize in Plant Molecular Genetics, Internat. Balzan Foundn, Italy, 2006. *Publications:* numerous research articles on genetics, physiology and biochemistry of plants. *Recreation:* sailing. *Address:* PO Box 225, 182 Howard Street, San Francisco, CA 94105, USA.

**SOMERVILLE, Sir James Lockett Charles A.;** *see* Agnew-Somerville.

**SOMERVILLE, Prof. Jane,** MD; FRCP; Consultant Cardiologist, Grown-Up Congenital Heart Disease Clinic: Middlesex Hospital, University College London, 1997–2003; Mater Die Hospital, Malta, since 2006; Emeritus Professor of Cardiology, Imperial College School of Medicine, 1999; *b* 24 Jan. 1933; *d* of Joseph Bertram Platnauer and Pearl Ashton; *m* 1957, Dr Walter Somerville, CBE, FRCP (*d* 2005); three *s* one *d*. *Educ:* Queen's Coll., London; Guy's Hosp., London Univ. MB, BS (Treasurer's Gold Medal for Clin. Surg.) 1955; MD 1966. MRCS 1955; FRCP 1973 (LRCP 1955, MRCP 1957). FACC 1972. Med. Registrar, Guy's Hosp., 1956–58; Registrar, Nat. Heart Hosp., 1958–59; First Asst to Dr Paul Wood, 1959–63, Sen. Lectr 1964–74, Inst. of Cardiol.; Hon. Cons. Phys., Nat. Heart Hosp., 1967–74, Hosp. for Sick Children, Gt Ormond St, 1968–88; Consultant Physician: Nat. Heart Hosp., then Royal Brompton & Nat. Heart Hosp., 1974–99; Cardiac Dept, Grown-Up Congenital Heart Disease Clinic, St Bartholomew's Hosp., 1988–92. Lectr in Cardiovascular Disease, Turin Univ., 1973. Vis. Prof. and Guest Lectr, Europe, ME, USA, Mexico, S America, USSR, China; Lectures: St Cyres, Imperial Coll., London, 1976; 6th Mahboubian, NY, 1981; World Congress Gold Medal, Bombay, 1982; Edgar Mannheimer, Hamburg, 1987; John Keith, Montreal, 1988; Tudor Edwards, RCP, 1991; Paul Wood, British Cardiac Soc., 1995; McCue, Washington, 1997; Henry Neufeld, Israel, 1999; Dan G. McNamara, American Coll. of Cardiol., Chicago, 2012. Chm., Staff Cttee, 1988–89, Jt Adv. Cttee, 1989–90, Nat. Heart Hosp.; Chm., Cardiol. Cttee, Royal Brompton & Nat. Heart Hosp., 1990–99. Sci. Sec., World Congress, Paed. Cardiol., 1980; Advr on congenital heart disease, Sec. of State's Hon. Med. Adv. Panel on driving and disorders of cardiovascular system, 1986–96; Advr to Florence, Trieste and Baltic States on setting up Grown-up Congenital Heart Disease Services. Founder, 1993, Pres., 2004–, Somerville Foundn (formerly Grown-Up Congenital Heart Patient Assoc.) (Chm., 1993–2003); Member: Assoc. Eur. Pæd. Cardiol.; British Cardiac Soc. (Mem., Paediatric Cardiol. Services Sub-cttee, 1987–94; Chm., Wkg Pty on Grown-up Congenital Heart Disease, 2002); RSocMed; Harveian Soc.; 300 Gp; Sci. Council, Monaco Cardiothoracic Centre, 1986 (Pres., 2016–18). Hon. Member: Argentine Pæd. Soc.; Chilean Cardiac Soc.; Argentine Soc. of Cardiol.; Brazilian Cardiac Soc.; Argentine Cardiac Soc.; French Cardiac Soc.; Italian Cardiac Soc.; Spanish Cardiac Soc. Founding Fellow, Eur. Soc. of Cardiol. Member: Council, Stonham Housing Assoc.; Governing Council, Beaconhouse Educn Gp, 2009–. Gov., Nat. Heart and Chest Hosps, 1977–82, 1988–90; Chm. Council, Queen's Coll., London, 2000–07. Woman of the Year, 1968. Gold Medal, Eur. Soc. of Cardiol., 2008; Dist. Service Award, Amer. Coll. of Cardiol., 2009. *Publications:* numerous contribs to med. lit. on heart disease in children, adolescents and adults, congenital heart disease and results of cardiac surgery; chapters in Paul Wood's Diseases of Heart and Circulation (3rd edn), Oxford Textbook of Medicine, and Perspectives in Pediatric Cardiology, Vols I and II. *Recreations:* collecting, roof gardening, travel, opera, 7 grandchildren. *Address:* 30 York House, 39 Upper Montagu Street, W1H 1FR. *T:* (020) 7262 2144, *Fax:* (020) 7724 2238; 81 Harley Street, W1G 8PP.

**SOMERVILLE, Julia Mary Fownes,** OBE 2013; broadcaster and journalist; *b* 14 July 1947; *d* of late John Arthur Fownes Somerville, CB, CBE, and Julia Elizabeth (*née* Payne); *m* 1st, 1970, Stephen Band (marr. diss. 1975); 2nd, 1984, Ray Gowdridge (separated, 1992); one *s* one *d*; partner, Sir Jeremy Dixon, *qv*. *Educ:* Headington Sch., Oxford; Sussex Univ. (BA Hons English 1969). IPC Magazines, 1969–70; ed., company newspaper, ITT Creed, 1970–72; BBC Radio News: journalist, 1972–79; news reporter, 1979–81; labour/industrial correspondent, 1981–84; Newscaster: Nine o'clock News, BBC TV, 1984–87; ITN, 1987–2001; presenter, Rip Off Britain, BBC TV, 2011–. Mem., Marshall Aid Commn, 1998–2000. Chm., Adv. Cttee, Govt Art Collection, 2003–13. Supporter, Advance Housing & Support Ltd, 1995–; Patron: British Brain and Spine Foundn, 1993; Children of Chernobyl Fund, 1993; Friends United Network, 1993; Samantha Dickson Res. Trust, 1997; Barnet Cancer Care, 1998; Vice Patron, Apex Trust, 1995; Companion, Headway. *Recreations:* music, reading, wining, dining, walking.

**SOMERVILLE, Sir Lockett;** *see* Agnew-Somerville.

**SOMERVILLE, Shirley-Anne;** Member (SNP) Dunfermline, Scottish Parliament, since 2016; Cabinet Secretary for Social Security and Older People, since 2018; *b* 2 Sept. 1974. *Educ:* Kirkcaldy High Sch.; Univ. of Strathclyde (BA Hons Econs and Pol. 1996); Univ. of Stirling (Dip. Housing Studies 1999); Queen Margaret Univ. Coll. (Dip. Public Relns). Policy and Public Affairs Officer, Chartered Inst. of Housing, 2001–04; Media and Campaigns Officer, Royal Coll. of Nursing, 2004–07; public affairs consultant, 2011; Campaign Strategist, SNP, 2012; Dir of Communities, Yes Scotland, 2012–13; Dep. Chief Exec., SNP, 2013–16. MSP (SNP) Lothians, Sept. 2007–2011; contested (SNP) Edinburgh

Northern and Leith, Scottish Parlt, 2011. Minister for Further Educn, Higher Educn and Sci., Scottish Parlt, 2016–18. Trustee, Shelter UK, 2011–. *Recreations:* hill-walking, golf. *Address:* Scottish Parliament, Edinburgh EH99 1SP.

**SOMMARUGA, Cornelio;** President, International Committee of the Red Cross, 1987–99 (Hon. Member, 2000); *b* 29 Dec. 1932; *s* of Carlo Sommaruga and Anna-Maria Valagussa; *m* 1957, Ornella Marzorati; two *s* four *d*. *Educ:* schs in Rome and Lugano; Univs of Zürich (LLD 1957), Paris and Rome. Bank trainee, Zürich, 1957–59; joined Swiss Diplomatic Service, 1960: Attaché, Swiss Embassy, The Hague, 1961; Sec., Bonn, 1962–64; Rome, 1965–68; Dep. Hd of Delegn to EFTA, GATT, UNCTAD and ECE/UN, Geneva, 1969–73; Dep. Sec. Gen., EFTA, 1973–75; Minister plenipotentiary, Div. of Commerce, Fed. Dept of Public Economy, Berne, 1976; Amb., 1977; Delegate, Fed. Council for Trade Agreements, 1980–83; State Sec. for External Econ. Affairs, 1984–86. Pres., Initiatives of Change Internat. (formerly Moral Rearmament) Assoc., 2002–06, now Hon.; Chm., Geneva Internat. Centre for Humanitarian De-mining, 2000–08, now Hon. Chm; Chm., Internat. Cancer Foundn, Geneva, 2006–09. Member: Panel on UN Peace Operations, 2000; Internat. Commn on Intervention and State Sovereignty, 2001. Hon. Dr: (Political Affairs) Fribourg, 1985; (Internat. Relns) Minho, Braga, 1990; (Medicine) Bologna, 1991; (Internat. Law) Nice-Sophia Antipolis, 1992; (Law) Seoul Nat. Univ., 1992; (Law) Geneva, 1997; (Internat. Relns) Webster Univ., 1998; (Law) Insubria, Como, 2008. Presidential Award, Tel Aviv Univ., 1995; Dr Jean Mayer Global Citizens Award, Tufts Univ., 2003; Presidential Award, Peace Univ., San José de Costa Rica, 2009. *Publications:* La posizione costituzionale del Capo dello Stato nelle Costituzioni francese ed italiana del dopoguerra, 1957; numerous articles in jls and periodicals; *relevant publication:* Cornelio Sommaruga: diplomatie im Dienste der Menschlichkeit, by Jürg Bischoff, 2004; Im weltweiten Einsatz für Humanität: Cornelio Sommaruga—Präsident des IKRK 1987–1999, by Joseph Jung, 2016; Cornelio Sommaruga: l'humanité en mission, by Virginie Poyetton, 2018. *Address:* 16 chemin des Crêts-de-Champel, 1206 Geneva, Switzerland. *T:* (22) 3474552. *E:* cornelio.sommaruga@bluewin.ch.

**SOMMER, Peter Michael;** Managing Director, Virtual City Associates, since 1981; expert witness and author, since 1985; Professor of Digital Forensics, Birmingham City University, since 2015; *b* 21 April 1943; *s* of Fritz and Beate Sommer. *Educ:* King Edward VI Five Ways Sch., Birmingham; St Catherine's Coll., Oxford (BA 1965, MA Hons Juris. 1967). Editor: Harrap Books, 1966–73; Paladin Books, 1973–77; Dep. Editl Dir, Granada Paperbacks, 1977–81; Tech. Dir, Data Integrity, 1987–98; Sen. Res. Fellow, Inf. Systems and Innovation (formerly Inf. Systems Integrity) Gp, Dept of Mgt (formerly Inf. Systems Dept), LSE, 1994–2008; Vis. Prof., Inf. Systems and Innovation Gp, Dept of Mgt, LSE, 2008–11. Specialist Advisor: H of C Trade and Industry Select Cttee, 1998–2001; Jt Parly Cttee on Draft Investigatory Powers Bill, 2015–16. Vis. Sen. Res. Fellow, Faculty of Maths, Computing and Technology (formerly Maths and Computing), 2006–08, Vis. Reader, 2008–13, Open Univ.; Vis. Prof., De Montfort Univ., 2011–. Jt Lead Assessor, Computing, Council for Registration of Forensic Practitioners, 2005–09. Ext. Exmr, Defence Acad. of UK (Cranfield Univ.), 2002–06. Member: Adv. Council, Foundn for Information Policy Res., 2001–; Scientific Adv. Panel for Emergency Response, 2003–09; Digital Evidence Specialist Gp, Forensic Sci. Regulator, 2008–16; Digital Forensics Adv. Cttee for Standards, Nederlands Register Gerechtelijk Desindien, 2014–; Specialist Advr, Jt Select Cttee, Draft Investigatory Powers Bill, 2015–16; Mem., Hotline Audit Team, Internet Watch Foundn, 2009 and 2017. Self-employed expert in digital forensics: major instructions include: Rome Labs hack, 1997; Wonderland Club of internet paedophiles (Op. Cathedral), 2001; DrinkorDie software piracy conspiracy (Op. Blossom), 2005; State of SA *v* Zuma and Thales, 2005–09; Op. Crevice terrorism, 2006–07; Sorrell *v* FullSix defamation, 2007; PharmaCare Labs Pty *v* Commonwealth of Australia, 2010; Operation Alpine (Child Exploitation and Online Protection Centre), 2010–11; UN Special Tribunal on Lebanon, 2011–15; Al-Sweady Public Inquiry, 2012–14; Internat. Criminal Court (Uhuru Kenyatta), 2012–14; R *v* Moazzem Begg, 2014–15; Privacy Internat. and others *v* GCHQ (IPT), 2015; AY *v* Facebook, 2017–18; R *v* Daniel Kaye, 2017–. FBCS 2014. FRSA 2013. *Publications:* Guide to Electronic Publishing, 1982; The PC Security Guide, 1993, 2nd edn 1994; (contrib.) Fraud: law, procedure and practice, 2004; Digital Evidence: a guide for directors and corporate advisors, 2005, 2nd edn 2009; Digital Evidence, Digital Investigations and E-Disclosure, 2005, 4th edn 2013; (jtly) Reducing Systematic Cybersecurity Risk, 2011; Digital Evidence Handbook, 2017; *as Hugo Cornwall:* The Hacker's Handbook, 1985; Data Theft, 1987; The Industrial Espionage Handbook, 1991; articles in learned jls incl. Criminal Law Rev., Telecommunications Law Rev., IEEE Security and Privacy, Digital Investigation. *Recreations:* reading, book collecting, gardening, jazz, amateur radio, the ethical abuse of technology. *Address:* PO Box 6447, N4 4RX. *E:* peter@pmsommer.com.

**SOMMERLAD, Brian Clive,** FRCS, FRCPCH; Consultant Plastic Surgeon: Great Ormond Street Hospital for Children, 1995–2010, now Hon. Consultant; St Andrew's Centre, Broomfield Hospital, Chelmsford (formerly St Andrew's Hospital, Billericay), 1978–2010, now Hon. Consultant; *b* 1 Feb. 1942; *s* of Verdun and Winsome Sommerlad; *m* 1971, Gwyneth Watkins; four *s* one *d*. *Educ:* Newington Coll., Sydney; Sydney Univ. (MB BS 1966). FRCS 1971. Jun. and Sen. MO, Sydney Hosp., 1966–67; Surgical Registrar, UCH, 1969–73; Surgeon, Australian Surgical Team, Bien Hoa, Vietnam, 1971; Sen. Registrar in Plastic Surgery, London, Billericay and Glasgow, 1974–78. Hunterian Prof., RCS, 1999. President: Plastic Surgery Section, RSocMed, 1985–86; Craniofacial Soc. of GB, 1997–98; British Assoc. of Plastic Surgeons, 1998. Chm., CLEFT, 2011–. Hon. FRCSLT 1998; Hon. FRCSE 2001. Hon. DSc(Med) UCL, 2017. Active Service Medal (Australia), 1994; Vietnam Logistic and Support Medal (Australia), 1994. *Publications:* co-editor: Recent Advances in Plastic Surgery 3, 1985; Recent Advances in Plastic Surgery 4, 1992; Recent Advances in Plastic Surgery 5, 1996; book chapters; contrib. papers to several jls on many subjects, but especially cleft lip and palate. *Recreations:* sailing, running (including occasional half marathons), ski-ing, theatre, supporting cleft lip and palate services in the developing world. *Address:* 25 Doughty Mews, WC1N 2PF. *E:* brian@sommerlad.co.uk.

**SOMOGYI, Prof. Peter,** PhD, DSc; FRS 2000; Professor of Neurobiology, University of Oxford, since 1996; Nicholas Kurti Senior Research Fellow, Brasenose College, Oxford, since 2004. *Educ:* Loránd Eötvös Univ., Budapest (PhD); Semmelweis Med. Sch., Budapest; Univ. of Oxford; Flinders Med. Centre, SA, Australia. Associate, later Co-Dir, 1985–98, Dir, 1998–2015, MRC Anatomical Neuropharmacology Unit, Oxford. Adjunct Prof., Med. Univ., Vienna, 2016. FMedSci 2006; Fellow, Hungarian Acad. Scis, 2013. Dr and Prof. *hc:* Eötvös Loránd Univ., Budapest, 2013; Zurich, 2014. Brain Prize, Lundbeck Foundn, 2011; Semmelweis Budapest Award, 2012. Commander's Cross, Order of Merit (Hungary), 2012. *Address:* Department of Pharmacology, University of Oxford, Mansfield Road, Oxford OX1 3QT; 129 Staunton Road, Oxford OX3 7TN.

**SØNDERGÅRD, Thomas;** Music Director, Royal Scottish National Orchestra, since 2018 (Principal Guest Conductor, 2012–18); *b* Holstebro, Denmark, 4 Oct. 1969. *Educ:* Royal Danish Acad. of Music. Mem., EU Youth Orch., 1989–92; teacher, Royal Danish Acad. of Music, Copenhagen, 2001–02; Principal Conductor: Norwegian Radio Orch., 2009–12; BBC Nat. Orch. of Wales, 2012–18. Guest conductor appearances worldwide. Queen Ingrid Prize for services to music (Denmark), 2011. *Address:* c/o Askonas Holt Ltd, 15 Fetter Lane, EC4A 1BW. *T:* (020) 7400 1700. *E:* info@askonasholt.co.uk.

**SONDHEIM, Stephen Joshua;** composer-lyricist; *b* 22 March 1930; *s* of Herbert Sondheim and Janet (*née* Fox). *Educ:* Williams Coll. (BA 1950). Lyrics: West Side Story, 1957; Gypsy, 1959; Do I Hear a Waltz?, 1965; (additional lyrics) Candide, 1973; music and lyrics: A Funny Thing Happened on the Way to the Forum, 1962; Anyone Can Whistle, 1964; Company, 1970; Follies, 1971; A Little Night Music, 1973 (filmed, 1976); The Frogs, 1974; Pacific Overtures, 1976; Sweeney Todd, 1979; Merrily We Roll Along, 1981; Sunday in the Park with George, 1984 (Pulitzer Prize, 1985); Into The Woods, 1987 (filmed, 2015); Assassins, 1991; Passion, 1994; Bounce, 2003; Road Show, 2011; incidental music: The Girls of Summer, 1956; Invitation to a March, 1961; Twigs, 1971; film scores: Stavisky, 1974; Reds, 1981; Dick Tracy, 1990; Sweeney Todd: The Demon Barber of Fleet Street, 2008; co-author, The Last of Sheila (film), 1973; songs for Evening Primrose (TV), 1966; *play:* co-author, Getting Away with Murder, 1996; anthologies: Side By Side By Sondheim, 1976; Marry Me A Little, 1981; You're Gonna Love Tomorrow, 1983; Putting It Together, 1992. Vis. Prof. of Drama, and Fellow of St Catherine's Coll., Oxford, Jan.–June 1990. Mem. Council, Dramatists Guild, 1963 (Pres., 1973–81); Mem., AAIL, 1983. Hon. Doctorate, Williams Coll., 1971. Freedom, City of London, 2018. Tony Awards and New York Drama Critics' Circle Award for Company, Follies, A Little Night Music, Sweeney Todd, Into the Woods, and Passion; London Evening Standard Best Musical Award for Into the Woods; New York Drama Critics' Circle Award for Pacific Overtures and Sunday in the Park with George; London Evening Standard Best Musical Award, 1987, and SWET Laurence Olivier Award, 1988, for Follies; Ivor Novello Internat. Award, 2011; Critics' Circle Award for Services to the Arts, 2011. *Publications:* (book and vocal score): West Side Story, 1958; Gypsy, 1960; A Funny Thing Happened on the Way to the Forum, 1963; Anyone Can Whistle, 1965; Do I Hear a Waltz?, 1966; Company, 1971; Follies, 1972; A Little Night Music, 1974; Pacific Overtures, 1977; Sweeney Todd, 1979; Sunday in the Park with George, 1986; Into the Woods, 1989; Assassins, 1991; Passion, 1996; Finishing the Hat: collected lyrics 1954–1981, 2010; Look, I Made a Hat, 2011. *Address:* c/o John Breglio, Paul, Weiss, Rifkind, Wharton & Garrison, 1285 Avenue of the Americas, New York, NY 10019–6064, USA.

**SONDHI, Ranjit,** CBE 1999; a Civil Service Commissioner, 2007–12; *b* 22 Oct. 1950; *s* of Prem Lal Sondhi and Kanta Sondhi; *m* 1979, Anita Bhalla; one *s* one *d*. *Educ:* Bedford Sch.; Univ. of Birmingham (BSc Hons Physics). Handsworth Action Centre, Birmingham, 1972–76; Dir, Asian Resource Centre, Birmingham, 1976–85; Sen. Lectr, Westhill Coll., Birmingham, 1985–2007. Freelance lectr and researcher, 1975–2003. A Gov., BBC, 1998–2006; Member: IBA, 1987–90; Radio Authority, 1991–94; Chairman: Jt Council of Welfare for Immigrants, West Midlands, 1987–90; Refugee Employment, Trng and Educn Forum, 1990–93; Home Sec.'s Race Equality Adv. Panel, 2003–; Dep. Chm., CRE, 1993–95 (Mem., 1991–93); Member: Digbeth Trust, 1986–90; Prince's Youth Business Trust, Birmingham, 1986–91; Royal Jubilee and Prince's Trust, Birmingham, 1986–88; Admin. Council, Prince's Trust, 1986–88; Council for Educn and Trng in Youth and Community Work, 1987–90; Ethnic Minorities Adv. Cttee, Judicial Studies Bd, 1991–95; John Feeney Charitable Trust, 1991–2003; Glidewell Panel of Enquiry into Immigration and Asylum Bill, 1996; Lord Chancellor's Adv. Cttee on Legal Educn and Conduct, 1997–99; DFEE Task Force on Disability Rights, 1997–99; Tenant Services Authy, 2009–12; Judicial Appts Commn, 2012–14; Criminal Cases Rev. Commn, 2012–. Trustee: Nat. Primary Centre, 1993–2007 (Chm., 2003–07); Nat. Gall., 2000–08. Director: Birmingham TEC, 1990–93; Birmingham HA, 1998–2002; Chm., Heart of Birmingham Primary Care Trust, 2002–11; Vice-Chm., Sandwell and W Birmingham CCG, 2011. Vis. Prof., Diversity Cohesion and Intercultural Relns, Coventry Univ., 2010. FRSA 1988. DUniv: UCE, 2003; Birmingham, 2010; Hon. DLitt Wolverhampton. *Publications:* (jtly) Race in the Provincial Press, 1977; Divided Families, 1987; contribs to: Ethnicity and Social Work, 1982; Community Work and Racism, 1982; Minorities: community and identity, 1983; Analysing Inter-cultural Communication, 1987; Community Work in the Nineties, 1994; (ed jtly) 20 Years After the RRA76, 1999. (contrib.) Intercultural Europe, 2000; Equality and Diversity in Birmingham, 2005; Navigating Difference, 2006. *Recreations:* Indian classical music, yoga, travel, antiquarian books. *Address:* 89 Hamstead Hall Avenue, Handsworth Wood, Birmingham B20 1JU.

**SONENBERG, Prof. Nahum,** OC 2010; PhD; FRS 2006; FRSC; Gilman Cheney Professor, Department of Biochemistry, McGill University, since 2017 (James McGill Professor, 2002–16); *b* Wetzlar, Germany, 29 Dec. 1946; *s* of Meyer Sonenberg and Fradl Sonenberg (*née* Kutchinsky); *m* 1972, Yocheved Shrot; two *d*. *Educ:* Tel-Aviv Univ. (BSc, MSc); Weizmann Inst. of Sci. (PhD 1976). Chaim Weizmann Fellow, Roche Inst. of Molecular Biol., NJ, 1976–79; Asst Prof., 1979–82, Associate Prof., 1983–86, Prof., 1987–, Dept of Biochem., McGill Univ. Internat. Res. Scholar, Howard Hughes Med. Inst.; Dist. Scientist, CIHR. FRSC 1992. For. Associate, US NAS, 2015; Mem., Nat. Acad. Medicine, USA, 2015. Robert L. Noble Prize, Nat. Cancer Inst. of Canada, 2002; Killam Prize for Health Scis, 2005; Gairdner Award, 2008; Rosenstiel Award, Brandeis Univ., 2012; Wolf Prize, Wolf Foundn, 2014. *Publications:* articles in jls. *Address:* Department of Biochemistry, McGill University, McIntyre Medical Building, 3655 Promenade Sir William Osler, Montreal, QC H3G 1Y6, Canada.

**SONUGA-BARKE, Prof. Edmund James Stephen;** *see* Barke.

**SOOD, Prof. Ajay Kumar,** Padma Shri, 2013; PhD; FRS 2015; Professor, Department of Physics, Indian Institute of Science, Bangalore, India, 1994–2016, now Hon. Professor; *b* Gwalior, India, 26 June 1951; *s* of Ishwar Singh and Bimla Devi; *m* 1980, Anita Sood; one *s* one *d*. *Educ:* Punjab Univ., Chandigarh (BSc Physics 1971; MS Physics 1972); Indian Inst. of Sci., Bangalore (PhD Physics 1982). Scientist, Indira Gandhi Centre for Atomic Res., Kalpakkam, India, 1973–88; postdoctoral res., Max Planck Inst. für Festkörperforschung, Stuttgart, 1983–85; Associate Prof., Dept of Physics, 1988–94, Divl Chm., Div. of Physical and Math. Scis, 1998–2008, Indian Inst. of Sci., Bangalore. Hon. Prof., Jawaharlal Nehru Centre for Advanced Scientific Res., Bangalore, 1993–. Exec. Ed., Solid State Communications; Co-Ed., Europhysics Letters, 2012–; Member: Internat. Editl Adv. Bd, Particle, 2012–; Editl Bd, Scientific Reports, 2013–. Mem., Scientific Adv. Council to Prime Minister of India, 2009–14. Chm., Res. Council, Nat. Physical Lab., New Delhi. Sec. Gen., World Acad. of Scis, 2013–18. Vice Pres., 2008–10, Pres., 2017–19, Indian Nat. Sci. Acad.; Pres., Indian Acad. of Scis, 2010–12. FASc 1991; Fellow, Nat. Acad. of Scis, India 1995; FNA 1996; Fellow, World Acad. of Sci., 2002. Mem., Asia-Pacific Acad. of Materials, 2008. Awards include: Award in Physics, Third World Acad. of Scis, 2000; Homi Jehangir Bhabha Medal, Indian Nat. Sci. Acad., 2002; Millennium Gold Medal, 2000, M. N. Saha Birth Centenary Award, 2003–04, Award for outstanding contribs to Sci., 2014, Indian Sci. Congress; Goyal Prize in Physics, Kurukshatra Univ., 2003; Nat. Award in Nanosci. and Nanotechnol., Dept of Sci. and Technol., Govt of India, 2006; Lifetime Achievement Award, 2006, Vigyan Ratan Award, 2010, Punjab Univ.; Bangalore Nano Award, Govt of Karnataka, 2010; G. M. Modi Award for Sci., 2012; R. D. Birla Award for Excellence in Physics, Indian Physics Assoc., 2014. *Publications:* contribs to scientific jls incl. Nature Physics, Procs NAS, Nature Communications, Physical Rev. Letters, Soft Matter,

Science, Nature Nanotechnol., Clin. Chem. *Recreations:* classical music, sports. *Address:* Department of Physics, Indian Institute of Science, Bangalore 560012, India. *T:* 8023602238, *Fax:* 823602602. *E:* asood@physics.iisc.ernet.in.

**SOOLE, Hon. Sir Michael (Alexander),** Kt 2015; **Hon. Mr Justice Soole;** a Judge of the High Court, Queen's Bench Division, since 2015; *b* 18 July 1954; *yr s* of late Brian Alfred Seymour Soole and Rosemary Una Soole (*née* Salt); *m* 2002, Catherine Gavine Marshall (*née* Gardiner); three step *s* two step *d*. *Educ:* Berkhamsted Sch. (schol.); University Coll., Oxford (schol.; MA). Pres., Oxford Union, 1974. Called to the Bar, Inner Temple, 1977, Bencher, 2008; practising barrister, 1978–2015; a Recorder, 2000–15; QC 2002. Chm., Technol. and Construction Bar Assoc., 2013–15. Contested (SDP), Aylesbury, 1983, 1987. Mem. Bd, Christian Aid, 1991–2002. Trustee, Oxford Literary and Debating Union Trust, 2005–16 (Chm., 2013–16). *Recreations:* conversation, long rail journeys, brisk walks, live classical music. *Address:* Royal Courts of Justice, Strand, WC2A 2LL. *Clubs:* Beefsteak, Buck's.

**SOPEL, Jon(athan);** North America Editor, BBC, since 2014; *b* 22 May 1959; *s* of late Myer Sopel and Miriam Sopel; *m* 1988, Linda Twissell; one *s* one *d*. *Educ:* Christ's Coll. Finchley; Univ. of Southampton (BA Politics 1981). BBC: Radio Solent, 1983–87; reporter, World at One, Radio 4, 1987–89; Political Correspondent, 1989–98; Chief Political Correspondent, 1998–99; Paris Correspondent, 1999–2003; Presenter: News Channel (formerly BBC News 24), 2003; reported on war in Afghanistan, 2001, on war in Iraq, 2003, on tsunami, from Sri Lanka, 2004–05; Presenter, The Politics Show, BBC One, 2005–11; Global with Sopel, World News, 2013–14; has presented PM and Today progs, Radio 4. Political Journalist of the Year, 2007. *Publications:* Tony Blair: the moderniser, 1994; If Only They Didn't Speak English, 2017; A Year at the Circus, 2019; contrib. widely to newspapers and mags. *Recreations:* travel, tennis, golf, running, cinema, watching football. *Address:* BBC News Centre, Broadcasting House, Portland Place, W1A 1AA. *E:* jon.sopel@bbc.co.uk.

**SOPER, Dr Alan Kenneth,** FRS 2014; STFC Senior Fellow, STFC Rutherford Appleton Laboratory, 2009–17 (Consultant, since 2017); *b* Romford, Essex, 16 June 1951; *s* of Stanley John Soper and Joan Jessamine Soper (*née* Ayling); *m* 1981, Krista Ann McAuley; two *d*. *Educ:* Campion Sch., Hornchurch, Essex; Univ. of Leicester (BSc Hons; PhD 1977). Postdoctoral Fellow, Physics Dept, Univ. of Guelph, Canada, 1977–79; staff mem., Los Alamos Nat. Lab., USA, 1979–82; Asst Prof., Dept of Physics, Univ. of Guelph, 1982–86; Instrument Scientist, 1986–97; Gp Leader, 1997–2009, STFC Rutherford Appleton Lab. *Publications:* contribs to jls incl. Jl Chem. Physics, Jl Physical Chem., Physical Rev. Letters, Chem. Physics. *Recreations:* cycling, gardening, classical music. *Address:* Slate House, Upper Common, Faringdon, Berks SN7 7RU.

**SOPER, Andrew Keith;** HM Diplomatic Service; Ambassador to Venezuela, since 2017; *b* 6 July 1960; *s* of late Rev. Brian Soper and Doreen Soper; *m* 1987, Kathryn Garrett Stevens; one *s* one *d*. *Educ:* Cranbrook Sch., Kent; Sidney Sussex Coll., Cambridge (MA, PGCE). Student helper, Flying Angel Club, Fremantle, Australia, 1978–79; Teacher, Woodstock Sch., Uttar Pradesh, India, 1983–84; Admin. Trainee, DES, 1984–85; entered FCO, 1985; Second, later First, Sec. (Chancery), Mexico City, 1987–90; First Secretary: FCO, 1990–95; Washington, 1995–99; FCO, 1999–2001; Counsellor and Dep. Hd of Mission, Brasilia, 2001–04; Hd, Sustainable Develt and Commonwealth Gp, FCO, 2004–07; High Comr, Republic of Mozambique, 2007–10; Ambassador to Latvia, 2010–13; Minister Counsellor (Pol and Press), New Delhi, 2013–17. *Recreations:* travelling, music, golf, bridge, reading. *Address:* c/o Foreign and Commonwealth Office, King Charles Street, SW1A 2AH. *Club:* Royal Over-Seas League.

**SOPER, Rt Rev. (Andrew) Laurence,** OSB; STD; General Treasurer, Benedictine Confederation, 2002–11; Titular Abbot of St Alban's, 2000–11; *b* 17 Sept. 1943; *s* of late Alan and Anne Soper. *Educ:* St Benedict's Sch., Ealing; Blackfriars, Oxford; Sant Anselmo, Rome (STD); Strawberry Hill (PGCE; Hon. Fellow, 1996). Banking until 1964; entered Novitiate at Ealing, 1964; St Benedict's School: Master, 1973–83; Bursar, 1975–91; Prior, 1984–91; Asst Chaplain, Harrow Sch., 1981–91; Abbot of Ealing, 1991–2000. Mem. Council, Union of Monastic Superiors, 1994–99 (Chm., 1995–99). Episcopal Vicar for Religious for Westminster (Western Area), 1995–2001. FRSA. *Publications:* (ed with Rev. Peter Elliott) Thoughts of Jesus Christ, 1970; articles and thesis on T. H. Green and 19th century English theology. *Recreations:* reading, hill walking.

**SOPER, Tony;** freelance writer, since 1963; *b* Southampton, 10 Jan. 1929; *s* of Albert Ernest Soper and Ellaline May Soper; *m* 1971, Hilary Claire Brooke; two *s*. *Educ:* Devonport High Sch. Joined BBC as youth-in-training, 1947; Technical Asst, 1947–49; Studio Manager, 1949–55; Features Producer, BBC Bristol, 1955–57; Film Producer, BBC Natural Hist. Unit, 1957–63; various LOOK progs, incl. Faraway Look-Galapagos; writer and presenter, BBC wildlife series incl. Wildtrack, Beside the Sea, Animal Design, Discovering Birds, Soper at Large, Nature, Birdwatch, 1990–2010; expedition leader for Noble Caledonia, Lindblad Expeditions and Quark Expeditions; lecturer for P&O, Holland America and Crystal Cruises. *Publications:* The Bird Table Book, 1965, 7th edn 2006; Penguins, 1967, 2nd edn 1987; Owls, 1970, 2nd edn 1989; Oceans of Birds, 1989; The Shell Book of the Shore, 1991; Antarctica, 1995, 7th edn 2018; The Arctic, 2001, 4th edn 2019; Wildlife of the North Atlantic, 2008; The Northwest Passage, 2012, 2nd edn 2019; The Northeast Passage, 2016, 2nd edn 2018. *Recreations:* beachcombing, seagoing, watching the garden pond. *E:* tonysoper@icloud.com.

**SORABJI, Sir Richard (Rustom Kharsedji),** Kt 2014; CBE 1999; FBA 1989; Professor of Ancient Philosophy, King's College London, 1981–2000, now Emeritus; Supernumerary Fellow, Wolfson College, Oxford, 1996–2002, now Hon. Fellow; *b* 8 Nov. 1934; *s* of Richard Kaikushru Sorabji and late Mary Katherine (*née* Monkhouse); *m* 1958, Margaret Anne Catherine Taster; one *s* two *d*. *Educ:* Dragon Sch.; Charterhouse; Pembroke Coll., Oxford (BA Greats; MA; BPhil). CS Commn in Russian Lang. Cornell University: joined Sage Sch. of Philosophy, 1962; Associate Prof., 1968; Sen. Res. Fellow, Soc. of Humanities, 1979; King's College, London, 1970–: Designer and Dir, King's Coll. Centre for Philosophical Studies, 1989–91; FKC 1990; British Acad./Wolfson Res. Prof., 1996–99; Chm., Bd of Philosophical Studies, London Univ., 1979–82; Dir, Inst. of Classical Studies, London, 1991–96. Sen. Fellow, Council of Humanities, Princeton Univ., 1985; Vis. Prof., Indian Council of Philos. Res., 1989, 2004 and 2015; Adjunct Prof., Philosophy Dept, Univ. of Texas at Austin, 2000–; Ranieri Vis. Scholar, New York Univ., 2000–03; Vis. Prof., CUNY Graduate Center, 2004–07 and 2010–13; Cyprus Global Distinguished Prof., New York Univ., 2007–09. Member: Common Room, Wolfson Coll., Oxford, 1991–95; Sen. Common Room, Pembroke Coll., Oxford, 1992–. Gresham Prof. of Rhetoric, 2000–03. Lectures: Read-Tuckwell, Bristol, 1985; Simon, Toronto, 1990; Gray, Cambridge, 1991; Townsend, Cornell, 1991–92; Gaisford, Oxford, 1993; Webster, Stanford, 1994; Donnellan, Dublin, 1995; Radhakrishnan Meml, Indian Inst. of Advanced Study, Simla, 1996; Gifford, St Andrews, 1997; Edinburgh, 1997; Prentice, Princeton, 1998. Pres., Aristotelian Soc., 1985–86. Founder and dir of internat. project for translating the Ancient Commentators on Aristotle (106 vols of trans., 6 vols of exposition), 1985–. Foreign Honorary Member: Amer. Acad. of Arts and Scis, 1997; Royal Flemish Acad. of Arts and Scis, Belgium, 2008. MAE 2014. Hon. DLitt: Union Coll., Schenectady, 2007; McGill Univ., 2009. *Publications:* Aristotle on Memory, 1973, 2nd edn 2004; (ed jtly) Articles on Aristotle, 4 vols, 1975–79; Necessity, Cause and Blame, 1980; Time, Creation and the Continuum, 1983; (ed) Philoponus and the Rejection of Aristotelian Science, 1987, 2nd edn 2010; (ed) The Ancient Commentators on Aristotle, 106 vols, 1987–; Matter, Space and Motion, 1988 (Choice Award for Outstanding Academic Book, 1989–90); (ed) Aristotle Transformed, 1990, 2nd edn 2016; Animal Minds and Human Morals: the origins of the western debate, 1993; (ed) Aristotle and After, Supplement 68 to the Bulletin of Inst. of Classical Studies, 1997; Emotion and Peace of Mind: from Stoic agitation to Christian temptation, 2000; Philosophy of the Commentators 200–600 AD, 3 vols, 2004; (contrib.) Metaphysics, Soul and Ethics in Ancient Thought: themes from the work of Richard Sorabji, 2005; (ed jtly) The Ethics of War: shared problems in different traditions, 2005; Self: ancient and modern insights about individuality, life and death, 2006; (ed jtly) Greek and Roman Philosophy 100 BC–200 AD, 2 vols, 2007; Opening Doors: the untold story of Cornelia Sorabji, reformer, lawyer and champion of women's rights in India, 2010; Gandhi and the Stoics: modern experiments on ancient values, 2012; Perception, Conscience and Will, 2013; Electrifying New Zealand, Russia and India: the three lives of Engineer Allan Monkhouse, 2014; Moral Conscience through the Ages: fifth century BCE to the present, 2015; (ed) Aristotle Re-Interpreted: new findings on seven hundred years of the ancient commentators with introduction on diffusion to Persian, Syriac, Arabic, 2016. *Recreations:* architecture, archaeology, occasional verses and songs. *Address:* Wolfson College, Oxford OX2 6UD.

**SORBIE, Prof. Kenneth Stuart,** DPhil; FRSE; Professor of Petroleum Engineering, Heriot-Watt University, since 1992; *b* Prestwick, 15 Jan. 1950; *s* of late Kenneth Sorbie and of Lucy (*née* Ferguson); *m* 1976, Prof. Sheila Riddell; two *d*. *Educ:* Strathclyde Univ. (BSc 1st cl. Hons, 1972); Sussex Univ. (DPhil 1975). Res. Fellow, Cambridge Univ., 1975–76; teaching and lecturing, 1976–80; Group leader, oil res. and enhanced oil recovery, AEE Winfrith, 1980–88; Lectr, 1988–90, Reader, 1990–92, Heriot-Watt Univ. Vis. Prof., China Univ. of Petroleum, Qingdao, 2010. Mem., Soc. of Petroleum Engrs, 1985. FRSE 2001. Tech. Achievement Award, Soc. of Core Analysts, 2004; Improved Oil Recovery Pioneer Award, Soc. Petroleum Engrs, 2008; Lifetime Achievement Award, RSC, 2013; Prodn and Ops Award, Soc. Petroleum Engrs, 2017. *Publications:* Polymer Improved Oil Recovery, 1991; over 450 technical papers on petroleum-related research. *Recreations:* collecting and listening to classical, rock and contemporary music, reading, science, politics, long-distance walking. *Address:* Institute of Petroleum Engineering, Heriot-Watt University, Edinburgh EH14 4AS. *T:* (0131) 451 3139, *Fax:* (0131) 451 3127. *E:* k.sorbie@hw.ac.uk.

**SORENSEN, (Kenneth) Eric (Correll);** Chief Executive, Thames Gateway London Partnership, 2003–08; *b* 15 Oct. 1942; *m* Susan; two *s* one *d*. *Educ:* Bedford Sch.; Keele Univ. (BA (Hons) Econs and History). Voluntary work, India; joined DoE, 1967; Private Sec. to Sec. of State for Envmt, 1977; NW Regl Dir, Depts of the Envmt and Transport, 1980–81; Dir, Merseyside Task Force, DoE, 1981–84; Dir, Inner Cities Directorate, DoE, 1984–87; Head of Urban Policy Unit, Cabinet Office, 1987–88; Dir of Personnel Management and Trng, Depts of Envmt and Transport, 1988–90; Dep. Sec., Housing and Construction Comd, DoE, 1990–91; Chief Executive: LDDC, 1991–97; Millennium Commn, 1997–98; London Develt Partnership, 1998. Civil Service Comr (part-time), 1992–95. Chm., Royal Docks Trust (London); Dep. Chm., St Katharine and Shadwell Trust. Non-exec. Dir, Homerton Univ. Hosp. NHS Foundn Trust, 2005. Gov., Museum of London, 2008.

**SØRENSEN, Vagn Ove Brondholt;** Chairman, SSP Group plc, since 2006; *b* Randbol, Denmark, 12 Dec. 1959; *s* of Karl and Anna Sørensen; *m* 1998, Annette Brondholt; one *s* two *d*. *Educ:* Aarhus Business Sch., Denmark (MSc Econs and Business Admin 1984). Scandinavian Airlines System: mktg roles, 1984–90; Vice Pres., Internat., 1990–93; Sen. Vice Pres., Business Systems Div., 1993–99; Exec. Vice Pres. and Dep. CEO, 1999–2001; CEO, Austrian Airlines Gp, 2001–06. Chairman of Board: Codan, 2004–07; BTX Gp, 2005–09; TDC A/S, 2006–17; Scandic Hotels, 2007–18; Air Canada, 2007– (Dir, 2006–); KMD, 2012–; FLSmidth, 2011– (Dir, 2009–); Automic Software, 2012–17; Bureau van Dijk, 2014–16; TIA Technol., 2014–; Zebra A/S, 2015–; Center Parcs, 2015; Board Member: Royal Caribbean Cruises, 2011–; Nordic Aviation Capital, 2013–; Unilode, 2016–; VFS Global, 2016–; Rock 'n' Roll Forever Foundn, 2016–; Global Fund for Children UK Trust, 2016–18. *Recreations:* running, music, travel, family. *Address:* 5 Chester Place, NW1 4NB. *T:* (020) 7487 5001, 07718 481848. *E:* vagn@vagnsoerensen.com. *Club:* George.

**SORIANO, Kathleen;** Director of Exhibitions, Royal Academy of Arts, 2009–14; Director, Kathleen Soriano Ltd, since 2014; curator, broadcaster and strategic advisor in the arts; *b* London, 18 July 1963; *d* of Salvador Soriano and Kathleen Soriano; *m* 1995, Peter Greenhough; one *d*. *Educ:* Putney High Sch.; Univ. of Louisville; Univ. of Leicester (BA Hons Combined Arts). RA, 1986–89; Hd, Exhibns and Collections, NPG, 1989–2006; Dir, Compton Verney, Warwicks, 2006–09; Interim Dir, Firstsite, Colchester, 2015–16. Sen. Associate, AEA Consulting, 2017–. Member: Bd, Tourism W Midlands, 2006–09; Women Leaders in Mus Steering Gp, 2008–11; Bd, Sainsbury Centre, UEA, 2008–10; Contemp. Art Panel, Nat. Trust, 2009–12; Contemp. Art Panel, English Heritage, 2011–12; Comité d'orientation stratégique, Réunion des Musées Nationaux, Grand Palais, Paris, 2014–16; Arts Adv. Cttee, Art UK, 2018–; Adv. Cttee, Two Temple Place, London, 2018–; Chair: Arts Adv. Cttee, Churches Conservation Trust, 2015–16; Exhibns and Collections Cttee, House of Illustration, 2014–16; Liverpool Biennial of Contemp. Art, 2016–. Mem. Faculty, Oxford Univ. Cultural Leaders Prog., 2018–. Specialist Advr, Nat. Trust, 2016–. Judge: Sky Arts Portrait Artist of Year, 2013–20; Sky Arts Landscape Artist of the Year, 2015–19. Trustee: MLA W Midlands, 2007–09; Student Hubs Oxford, 2012–14; House of Illustration, 2012–16; Patron: Crisis Charity Art Commn, 2011–14; Stroke Assoc., 2014–16; volunteer, Oxford Foodbank, 2014–16. Clore Leadership Fellow, 2004; Grad., Salzburg Global Seminar, 2007. Hon. Kentucky Col, 1982. *Publications:* Compton Verney, 2009; Australia, 2013; Anselm Kiefer, 2014; A Little Book of Portraits, 2014; Merry Art, 2015; Eileen Cooper, RA, 2015; Stephen Chambers, RA, 2017; (with L. Rideal) Madam and Eve: women portraying women, 2018; Every Landscape is a State of Mind, 2019. *E:* kathleen.soriano@outlook.com. *Clubs:* Arts, Soho House.

**SORKIN, (Alexander) Michael;** Senior Adviser, N M Rothschild & Sons, since 2015 (Vice-Chairman, 2001–15); *b* 2 March 1943; *s* of Jose Sorkin and Hildegard Ruth Sorkin; *m* 1977, Angela Lucille Berman; one *s* two *d*. *Educ:* St Paul's Sch.; Manchester Univ. (BA (Hons) Econs). Chartered accountant. Joined Hambros, 1968; Dir, 1973–2001, Vice Chm., 1987–2001, SG Hambros (formerly Hambros Bank Ltd); Dep. Chm., Hambros Bank Ltd, 1995–98; Dir, Hambros plc, 1986–98; Man. Dir, SG Hambros, 1998–2001. *Recreations:* golf, tennis, football, opera. *Address:* N M Rothschild & Sons Ltd, New Court, St Swithin's Lane, EC4N 8AL.

**SOROS, Flora;** *see* Fraser, F.

**SOROS, George;** Chairman, Soros Fund Management (President, 1973); Founder and Chairman, Open Society Foundations; *b* Budapest, 12 Aug. 1930; *s* of Tivadar Soros and Elisabeth Soros (*née* Szucs); *m* 1960, Annaliese Witschak (marr. diss. 1983); two *s* one *d*; *m* 1983, Susan Weber (marr. diss. 2005); two *s*; *m* 2013, Tamiko Bolton. *Educ:* LSE, London

Univ. (BS 1952). Arbitrage trader, F. M. Mayer, NYC, 1956–59; Economic Analyst, Wertheim & Co., NYC, 1959–63; Vice Pres., Arnhold and S. Bleichroeder, NYC, 1963–73. Member: Exec. Cttee, Helsinki Watch, 1982–; Cttee, Americas Watch, 1982–; Council on Foreign Relations, 1988–. Chm. and Founding Pres., Central European Univ., Prague, Budapest, 1991. Mem., RIIA, 1990. Hon. FBA 2017. Hon. DCL Oxford, 1990; Hon. DHL Yale, 1991. *Publications:* The Alchemy of Finance, 1987, 2nd edn 1994; Opening the Soviet System, 1990; Underwriting Democracy, 1991; (jtly) Soros on Soros: staying ahead of the curve, 1995; The Crisis of Global Capitalism (Open Society Endangered), 1998; Open Society: reforming global capitalism, 2000; George Soros on Globalisation, 2002; The Bubble of American Supremacy, 2004; The Age of Fallibility: consequences of the war on terror, 2006; The New Paradigm for Financial Markets: the credit crisis of 2008 and what it means, 2008; (with G. P. Schmitz) The Tragedy of the European Union: disintegration or revival?, 2014. *Address:* Soros Fund Management LLC, 250 West 55th Street, Floor 27, New York, NY 10019, USA. *Clubs:* Brooks's; Queen's; NY Athletic, Town Tennis.

**SORRELL, Frances Mary, (Lady Sorrell),** OBE 2016; Co-Chair, Sorrell Foundation, since 1999; Chancellor, University of Westminster, since 2015; *d* of late Alexander Crawford Newell and Julia Susanne Newell (*née* Clayton); *m* 1974, Sir John William Sorrell, *qv*; two *s* one *d*. *Educ:* Epsom Sch. of Art. Designer and illustrator, 1968–76; Founder and Co-Chm., Newell and Sorrell, 1976–97, subseq. Interbrand Newell & Sorrell, 1997–2000; Chair, Interbrand Foundn, 1997–2000. Vis. Prof., UAL, 2006–15. Member: Bd, Royal Acad. Enterprises, 1996–99; Adv. Bd, Nat. Mus. of Photography, Film and TV, 1997–2003; Bd, Inst. for Employment Studies, 2000–02; Arts Adv. Gp, QCA, 2000–03; NHS Design Adv. Gp, 2001–03; Design Adv. Gp, British Council, 2004–08. Mem., Nat. Adv. Cttee for Craft Design and Art, 1994–96, Affairs and Awards Cttee, 1999–2001, C&G. Judge: BBC Design Awards, 1990–; D&AD Awards, 1995–; RIBA Awards, 2007–. Trustee, Mencap, 1999–2005; Founder and Trustee, Saturday Club Trust, 2016–. Hon. Mem., C&G. FCSD; FRSA. Hon. Fellow: University Coll., Falmouth, 2006; Hereford Coll. of Arts, 2011; Liverpool John Moores Univ., 2018. Hon. FRIBA 2002. DUniv Open, 2010; Hon. DA: Coventry, 2013; Nottingham Trent, 2017; Lincoln, 2018; Hon. MA Creative Arts Epsom, 2015. D&AD President's Award, 2008; Mont Blanc de la Culture Arts Patronage Award, 2016. *Publications:* Joinedupdesignforschools, 2005. *Recreations:* art, crafts, design, architecture, gardens. *Address:* Sorrell Foundation, Somerset House, Strand, WC2R 1LA.

**SORRELL, Sir John (William),** Kt 2008; CBE 1996; Co-Chairman, Sorrell Foundation, since 1999; Founder and Chairman, London Design Festival, since 2002; *b* 28 Feb. 1945; *s* of late John William Sorrell and Elizabeth Jane Sorrell (*née* Taylor); *m* 1974, Frances Mary Newell (*see* F. M. Sorrell); two *s* one *d*. *Educ:* Hornsey Coll. of Art (NDD 1964). Designer, Main Wolff & Partners, 1964; Partner, Goodwin Sorrell, 1964–71; Design Manager, Wolff Olins, 1971–76; Newell & Sorrell, subseq. Interbrand Newell & Sorrell: Founder, 1976; Partner, 1976–83; Chm., 1983–2000. Chairman: Design Council, 1994–2000; CABE, 2004–09; Founder and Chm., Creative Industries Fedn, 2014–17. A Vice-Pres., CSD, 1989–92; Chm., Design Business Assoc., 1990–92. Chairman: NHS London Design Adv. Gp, 2001–03; UK Trade & Investment Creative Industries Adv. Bd, 2007–12; Member: BR Architecture and Design Panel, 1991–93; RSA Design Adv. Gp, 1991–93; Panel 2000, FCO, 1998–2000; Culture and Creativity Adv. Gp, DCMS, 2002–03; Adv. Gp on Sch. Bldgs Design, 2002–04, London Challenge Ministerial Adv. Gp, 2002–06, DfES; Public Diplomacy Strategy Bd, FCO, 2002–06; Design and Technol. Alliance, Home Office, 2007–12; Creative Economy Prog. Ministerial Steering Bd, DCMS, 2008–09. UK Business Ambassador, 2009–19. Chm., Univ. of the Arts London, 2013–18. Gov., Design Dimension, 1991–93. Chm., Victory Ceremonies Medal Panel, 2012 Olympics, 2010–12. Founder and Pres., London Design Biennale, 2016–. Trustee: RIBA Trust, 2004–05; V&A Mus., 2011–19; Founder and Trustee, Saturday Club Trust, 2016–. Hon. Mem., Romanian Design Foundn, 1996. Hon. FRIBA 2002; Hon. FREng 2009; Hon. Fellow: UC Falmouth, 2006; Plymouth Coll. of Art, 2016–; Shenkar Coll. of Engrg, Design and Art, 2017; Liverpool John Moores Univ., 2018. CCMI 2006. Hon. DDes: De Montfort, 1997; Greenwich, 2007; Hon. Dr: London Inst., 1999; Middlesex, 2006; Huddersfield, 2014; Hon. PhD London Metropolitan, 2006; Hon DLit Hull, 2017; Hon. DA Lincoln, 2018; Hon. DEd Bolton, 2019. Bicentenary Medal, RSA, 1998; D&AD President's Award, 2008; Mont Blanc de la Culture Arts Patronage Award, 2016. *Publications:* Creative Island, 2002; Joined up Design for Schools, 2005; Creative Island II, 2009; The Virtuous Circle, 2014. *Recreations:* architecture, Arsenal, art, film. *Clubs:* Chelsea Arts, Groucho.

**SORRELL, Sir Martin (Stuart),** Kt 2000; Group Chief Executive, WPP Group, 1986–2018; Chairman, S4 Capital, since 2018; *b* 14 Feb. 1945; *s* of late Jack and Sally Sorrell; *m* 1971, Sandra Carol Ann Finestone (marr. diss. 2005); three *s*; *m* 2008, Cristiana Falcone; one *d*. *Educ:* Haberdashers' Aske's School; Christ's College, Cambridge (MA); Harvard Graduate School of Business (MBA 1968). Consultant, Glendinning Associates, Conn, 1968–69; Vice-Pres., Mark McCormack Orgn, London, 1970–74; Dir, James Gulliver Associates, 1975–77; Gp Financial Dir, Saatchi & Saatchi, 1977–86. Non-executive Director: Colefax & Fowler Gp plc, 1997–2003; Alpha Topco Ltd, until 2017; Alcoa; Bloomberg Family Foundn. Mem. Bd, NASDAQ, 2001–04. Chm., Adv. Gp, KPMG, 2002–07; Member, Advisory Board: Bowmark Capital Gp, 2009–; Stanhope Capital, 2011–; Mem., ATP Mktg Adv. Bd, 2001–; Internat. Adv. Bd, CBI, 2002–. Modern Apprenticeship Taskforce, DfES, 2003–. Mem., Engrg and Technol. Bd, 2002. Mem., Business Council, US, 2009–. Chairman: Mayor of London Internat. Business Adv. Council, 2008–; Internat. Business Council, WEF, 2010–; Mayor of Rome Internat. Business Adv. Council, 2010–; Internat. Business Adv. Council, Jerusalem, 2012–; Vice-Chm., Shanghai Internat. Business Leaders Adv. Council, 2010–. Member: Adv. Bd, Internat. Graduate Sch. of Mgt, Univ. of Navarra, Spain, 1989–; Deans Adv. Council, Boston Univ. Sch. of Mgt, 1998–; Bd of Dirs of Associates, Harvard Business Sch., 1998–2005 (Mem., Adv. Bd, 1998–); Bd, Indian Sch. of Business, 1998–; Internat. Adv. Bd, Russian Mus., St Petersburg, 2009–; Internat. Adv. Bd, China Europe Internat. Business Sch., 2012–. Mem., Council for Excellence in Mgt and Leadership, 1999–. Ambassador for British Business, 1997–2010. Member: Bd and Cttee, Special Olympics, 2000–05; Corporate Adv. Gp, Tate Gall., 2000–; Bd, Paley Center for Media, NY, 2002–; Adv. Gp, England 2018 FIFA World Cup Bid, 2009–. Gov., London Business Sch., 1990–2012 (Dep. Chm., 1998–). Trustee, Cambridge Foundn, 1990–; Patron: Christ's Coll., Cambridge; British Mus., 2011–; Hon. Patron, Cambridge. *Recreations:* ski-ing, cricket. *Clubs:* Reform, MCC; Harvard (New York).

**SORRELL, Robert Michael,** PhD; Vice President, Research and Innovation, Formulated Products Technology, BP, since 2017; *b* London, 3 Oct. 1959; *s* of Robert Arthur Sorrell and Shirley Peggy Sorrell; *m* 1988, Karen Chapman; three *d*. *Educ:* Queen Elizabeth Coll., Univ. of London (BSc Chem. 1st Cl. Hons 1982); St John's Coll., Cambridge (PhD 1985). Royal Soc. Fellow, Univ. of Wurzburg, 1985; Sen. Demonstrator, St Aidan's Coll., Univ. of Durham, 1986; BP: joined, 1987; Res. and Develt Team Leader, 1987–91; Mkt Develt Manager, 1991–93; Customer Service Gp Manager, 1993–98; Mktg Manager, 1998–2001; Mktg Dir, Europe and Asia, 2001–03; Technol. Strategy Manager, Downstream, 2003–05; Technol. Vice Pres., Business Mktg, 2005–06; Vice Pres., Technol. Strategy, Downstream, 2006–08; Vice Pres., Public Partnerships, 2008–16. Non-exec. Dir, Breathing Buildings Ltd, 2010–16. Member: Strategic Adv. Cttee (Energy), EPSRC, 2010–16 (Chm., 2014–16); UK Technol. Strategy Bd, 2011–15; Main Panel B, UK REF, 2011–14; UK Energy Res. Partnership, 2014–17; Energy Catalyst Adv. Bd, 2014–17; Sci. and Technol. Adv. Council, Nat. Physical Lab., 2015–. Chair, Audit and Risk Cttee, Innovate UK, 2014–16. Fellow, Centre for Sci. and Policy, Univ. of Cambridge, 2010–13. Member: Governing and Prog. Mgt Bd, BP Internat. Centre for Advanced Materials, 2013–16; Bd of Trustees, Campaign for Sci. and Engrg, 2015–; Advanced Materials Leadership Council, 2014–. FRSC 2012; FInstD 2014. *Recreations:* family, gardening, music, theatre, cycling. *Address:* BP Technology Centre, Whitchurch Hill, Pangbourne, Berks RG8 7QR. *T:* 07769 881350. *E:* robertsorrell@btinternet.com.

**SOSA, Hon. Sir Manuel,** Kt 2014; OB 2012; CBE 1998; **Hon. Mr Justice Sosa;** a Judge, since 1999, and President, since 2011, Court of Appeal of Belize; *b* Corozal Town, British Honduras, 24 Dec. 1950; *s* of Marcelino and Agustina Sosa; *m* 1981, Elba Rosado; one *s* two *d*. *Educ:* Univ. of W Indies (LLB Hons 1974); Norman Manley Law Sch., Jamaica (Cert. Legal Ed. 1976). Admitted as Attorney-at-Law, Belize, 1976; licensed to practice as NP, 1981; Sen. Counsel, Belize, 1986; Temp. Justice, 1993, Justice, 1998–99, Supreme Court of Belize. Mem., Bd of Dirs, Central Bank of Belize, 1993–97. Mem., Belize Adv. Council, 1987–97. Pres., Bar Assoc. of Belize, 1988–89. Cert. of Recognition for Outstanding Leadership and Public Service, Univ. of W Indies, 2018. *Publications:* (contrib.) The Caribbean Court of Justice: the first ten years, 2016; contrib. W Indian Law Jl. *Recreations:* walking, jogging, reading, listening to music. *Address:* Court of Appeal, 1 Treasury Lane, Belize City, Belize.

**SOSKICE, Prof. David William,** FBA 2013; School Professor of Political Science and Economics, since 2012, Research Director, International Inequalities Institute, since 2016, and Co-Director, Leverhulme Doctoral Programme, since 2016, London School of Economics and Political Science; *b* London, 6 July 1942; *s* of Rt Hon. Baron Stow Hill, QC; *m* 1st, 1966, Alison Black (marr. diss.); one *s* one *d*; 2nd, 1991, Nicola Mary Lacey, *qv*. *Educ:* Winchester Coll.; Trinity Coll., Oxford (Hon. Fellow, 2015); Nuffield Coll., Oxford (MA). Economics Fellow, University Coll., Oxford, 1967–90; Res. Dir, Wissenschaft Zentrum, Berlin, 1990–2005; Res. Prof., Pol Sci. Dept, Duke Univ., 2005–12; Res. Prof. of Comparative Pol Economy, Univ. of Oxford, 2007–12. Vis. Prof., Scuola Superiore St Anna, Pisa, 2000–02; Semans Distinguished Vis. Prof., Dept of Pol Sci., Duke Univ., 2001; Mars Vis. Prof., Dept of Pol Sci., Yale Univ., 2004; Vis. Prof., Dept of Govt, Harvard Univ., 2007. Chair, British Acad. Wkg Gp on Interdisciplinarity, 2015–16. Pres., Eur. Pol Sci. Assoc., 2011–13. *Publications:* (with R. Flanagan and L. Ulman) Unionism, Economic Stabilization, and Incomes Policies: European experiences, 1983; (with W. Carlin) Macroeconomics and the Wage Bargain, 1992; (ed with P. A. Hall) Varieties of Capitalism, 2001; (with W. Carlin) Macroeconomics: institutions, instability and financial institutions, 2015; (with T. Iversen) Democracy and Prosperity: reinventing capitalism through a turbulent century, 2019. *Address:* 19 Church Row, Hampstead, NW3 6UP. *E:* d.w.soskice@lse.ac.uk.

**SOSKICE, Prof. Janet Martin,** DPhil; Professor of Philosophical Theology, University of Cambridge, 2009–18, now Emeritus; Fellow, Jesus College, Cambridge, 1988–2018, now Emeritus (President, 2014); *b* 16 May 1951; *d* of Alison M. Martin and F. Claire Jamieson; *m* 1982, Oliver C. H. Soskice; two *d*. *Educ:* Cornell Univ. (BA); Sheffield Univ. (MA); Oxford Univ. (DPhil 1982). Gordon Milburn Jun. Res. Fellow, Oxford Univ. and Somerville Coll., 1980–83; Lectr, Ripon Coll., Cuddesdon, 1983–88; University of Cambridge: Lectr, 1988–2001; Reader in Philos. Theol., 2001–09; Chm. Bd, Faculty of Divinity, 2014–. Canada Commonwealth Fellow, 1996; British Acad. Sen. Res. Fellow, 2000–01. Visiting Professor: Univ. of Uppsala, 1992; Univ. of Calgary, 1996; Univ. of Virginia, 2006; Eugene McCarthy Vis. Prof., Gregorian Univ., 1997. Lectures: Stanton, Univ. of Cambridge, 1997–99; Richards, Univ. of Virginia, 2006. Ecumenical Advr to Archbp of Canterbury, 1990–96. Chm. Bd, Margaret Beaufort Inst. of Theol., 1998–2005. Mem., Bd of Dirs, Concilium, 1998–2006 (Ed., some issues of Concilium). President: Catholic Theol Assoc. of GB, 1992–94; Soc. for Study of Theol., 2008–11. Trustee, The Tablet, 2013–. Hon. DD Heythrop Coll., Univ. of London. *Publications:* Metaphor and Religious Language, 1985, Japanese edn 1992; (ed) After Eve, 1990; (ed jtly) Medicine and Moral Reasoning, 1994; (ed with Diana Lipton) Feminism and Theology, 2003; (ed jtly) Fields of Faith, 2005; The Kindness of God, 2007; Sisters of Sinai: how two lady adventurers found the hidden Gospels, 2009. *Recreations:* ski-ing, travel. *Address:* Jesus College, Cambridge CB5 8BL. *T:* (01223) 339606, *Fax:* (01223) 339313.

**SOSKICE, Nicola Mary;** *see* Lacey, N. M.

**SOUBRY, Rt Hon. Anna (Mary);** PC 2015; MP for Broxtowe, since 2010 (C, 2010–19; Ind Gp for Change (formerly Change UK), since 2019); *b* Lincoln, 7 Dec. 1956; *d* of David and Frances Soubry; two *d*; partner, Neil Davidson, CBE. *Educ:* Hartland Comprehensive Sch., Worksop; Univ. of Birmingham (LLB). Presenter and reporter, Central Television, 1984–92; called to the Bar, Inner Temple, 1995; in practice as barrister, 1995–2010. Parly Under-Sec. of State, DoH, 2012–13; Parly Under-Sec. of State, 2013–14, Minister of State, 2014–15, MoD; Minister of State, BIS, 2015–16. Leader, Ind. Gp for Change (formerly Change UK), 2019–. Contested (C) Gedling, 2005. *Recreations:* gardening, cooking, ski-ing, watching football, cricket and Rugby. *Address:* House of Commons, SW1A 0AA. *T:* (020) 7219 7211. *E:* anna.soubry.mp@parliament.uk.

**SOUEIF, Ahdaf;** writer; *b* 23 March 1950; *d* of Mustapha Soueif and Fatma Moussa; *m* 1st, 1972, Sherif Hosni (marr. diss. 1977); 2nd, 1981, Ian Hamilton (*d* 2001); two *s*. *Educ:* schs in Cairo and London; Cairo Univ. (BA English Lit. 1971); American Univ. in Cairo (MA English Lit. 1973); Univ. of Lancaster (PhD Linguistics 1978). Cairo University: Associate Lectr, 1971–79; Lectr, 1979–84; Project Leader and Arabic Ed., Cassel Ltd (Macmillan Inc.), London and Cairo, 1978–84; Associate Prof. of Linguistics, King Saud Univ., Riyadh, 1987–89; Exec. Officer, Al-Furqan Islamic Heritage Foundn, London, 1989–2008. Columnist, al-Shorouk News, Cairo, 2011–15. Member: Amnesty Internat., 1990–; Cttee for Advancement of Arab-British Understanding, 1995–; Bd, Egyptian Initiative for Personal Rights, 2011–; Bd, Arab Culture Resource, 2018–. Member: Egyptian-British Soc., 1990–; Egyptian Writers' Union, Egypt, 1999–; PEN, Egypt, 1999–; PEN, UK, 1999–. Patron: Palestine Solidarity Campaign, 2000–; Caine Prize for African Lit., 2010– (Mem. Bd, 2010–); Trustee: Internat. Prize for Arab Fiction, 2011–; BM, 2012–19. Founding Chm., Engaged Events (charity), 2007–. Fellow: Lannan Foundn, USA, 2002; Bogliasco Foundn, Italy, 2002; FRSL 2003. Hon. DLitt: Lancaster, 2004; London Metropolitan, 2004; Exeter, 2008; Hon. PhD Amer. Univ. of Beirut, 2017. Mahmoud Darwish Award, 2010. *Publications: fiction:* Aisha: a collection of short stories, 1983; In the Eye of the Sun, 1992; Sandpiper and Other Stories, 1996; Zīnat al-Ḥayāh wa Qiṣas Ukhrā (collection of stories in Arabic), 1996 (Best Short Stories of the Year Award, Cairo Book Fair); Ahdāf Suwayf: Mukhtārāt min A'māliha (collection of Arabic writings), 1998; The Map of Love, 1999; I Think of You (short stories), 2007; *non-fiction:* Mezzaterra: fragments from the common ground (essays), 2004; (ed) Reflections on Islamic Art (essays), 2011; Cairo: my city, our revolution, 2012, new edn as Cairo: memoir of a city transformed, 2013; (ed) This is not a Border: reportage and reflections from the Palestinian Festival of Literature (essays), 2017; *translation:* In Deepest Night (play), 1998; I Saw Ramallah, memoir by Mourid al-Barghouti, 2000. *Recreations:* friends, film, music, cooking. *Address:* c/o Wylie Agency, 17 Bedford Square, WC1B 3JA. *T:* (020) 7908 5900, *Fax:* (020) 7908 5901. *E:* cbuchan@wylieagency.co.uk. *W:* www.ahdafsoueif.com. *Clubs:* Frontline; Gezira (Cairo).

**SOUHAMI, Prof. Robert Leon,** CBE 2004; MD, DSc; FRCP, FRCR, FMedSci; Professor of Medicine, University College London, 1997–2001, now Emeritus; *b* 26 April 1938; *s* of John Souhami and Freda Harris; *m* 1966. *Educ:* St Marylebone Grammar Sch.; University Coll. Hosp. Med. Sch. (BSc, MB BS). MD 1975; FRCP 1979; FRCR 1992. Hon. Lectr, St Mary's Hosp. Med. Sch., 1969–71; Sen. Registrar, UCH, 1971–73; Consultant Physician, Poole Gen. Hosp., 1973–75; Consultant Physician and Sen. Lectr, UCH, 1975–87; Kathleen Ferrier Prof. of Clinical Oncology, later Cancer Medicine, UCMSM, subseq. UCL Med. Sch., 1987–97; Dean, Faculty of Clinical Scis, 1997–99, Principal, 1999–2001, UCL Med. Sch., subseq. Royal Free and UC Med. Sch., UCL; Exec. Dir of Policy and Communications, 2003–05, Dir of Clinical Res. and Trng, 2001–05, Cancer Research UK. Hon. Consultant Physician, Whittington Hosp. and Royal Nat. Orthopaedic Hosp., 1976–2001. Chairman: Cancer Therapy Cttee, MRC, 1987–93; Protocol Review Cttee, EORTC, 1994–97; Sci. Adv. Bd, London Res. Inst., 2006–12; Mem., Sci. Adv. Bd, MRC Clinical Scis Centre, 2008–16; Member, Science Council: Institut Curie, 1999–2010; Centre Leon Bérard, 2001–08; Institut Bergonié, 2003–08. Fellow: UCL, 1990; Faculty of Medicine, Imperial Coll. London, 2012. FMedSci 1998. Foreign Sec., Acad. of Med. Scis, 2008–13. Hon. DSc Inst. Cancer Res., 2009. *Publications:* Tutorials in Differential Diagnosis, 1974, 4th edn 2003; Cancer and its Management, 1986, 5th edn 2005; Textbook of Medicine, 1990, 4th edn 2002; (ed) Oxford Textbook of Oncology, 2001; clinical and scientific articles on aspects of cancer research.

**SOULBURY,** 4th Viscount; *see* Ramsbotham, O. P.

**SOULSBY, Sir Peter (Alfred),** Kt 1999; Mayor of Leicester (Lab), since 2011; *b* 27 Dec. 1948; *s* of late Robert and Mary Soulsby; *m* 1969, Alison Prime (*d* 2011); three *d. Educ:* Minchenden Sch., Southgate; City of Leicester Coll. (BEd Leicester Univ.). Teacher of children with special educational needs, 1973–90. Mem. (Lab), Leicester City Council, 1973–2003 (Leader, 1981–94 and 1995–99). MP (Lab) Leicester S, 2005–April 2011. Mem., Audit Commission, 1994–2000. Vice-Chairman: Waterways Trust, 1999–2003; British Waterways Bd, 2000–04 (Mem., 1998–2004). *Address:* City Mayor's Office, Leicester City Council, City Hall, 115 Charles Street, Leicester LE1 1FZ.

**SOUNDY, Andrew John;** Senior Partner, Ashurst Morris Crisp (Solicitors), 1992–98; *b* 29 March 1940; *s* of Harold Cecil Soundy and Adele Monica Templeton (*née* Westley); *m* 1963, Jill Marion Steiner; one *s* two *d. Educ:* Boxgrove Sch.; Shrewsbury Sch.; Trinity Coll., Cambridge (BA, MA). Ashurst Morris Crisp: articled clerk, 1963–66; qualified as solicitor, 1966; Partner, 1969. Non-exec. Dir, EWFact plc, 1994–98 (Chm., 1997–98). Vice Pres., 1998–2009, Trustee (Dir), 2003–10, The Lord Slynn of Hadley Eur. Law Foundn. Director: St Michael's Hospice, Basingstoke, 1996–2017 (Chm., 2007–11; Pres., 2011–); Anglo-Russian Opera and Ballet Trust, 2001–. Mem. Bd Govs, De Montfort Univ., 2001–05. Churchwarden, Parish of Mattingley, 2002–10, now Emeritus. FRSA 1993. *Recreations:* countryside, shooting, opera, maintenance of historic buildings. *Address:* Gainsborough House, 69 High Street, Odiham, Hants RG29 1LB. *T:* (01256) 704290. *Clubs:* Cavalry and Guards, City Law, Bishopsgate Ward.

**SOUNESS, Graeme James;** Manager, Newcastle United Football Club, 2004–06; Commentator, Sky TV, since 2006; *b* 6 May 1953; *s* of James and Elizabeth Souness; *m* 1994, Karen; one *s*, and two *s* one *d* from previous marriage. *Educ:* Carrickvale Sch., Edinburgh. Professional football player: Tottenham Hotspur, 1969–73; Middlesbrough FC, 1973–78 (Old 2nd Div. Champions, 1974); Liverpool FC, 1978–84 (3 European Cups, 1978, 1981 and 1984; 5 League Championships, 1979–84 and 4 League Cups, 1981–84); Sampdoria, Italy, 1984–86 (Italian Cup, 1982); played for Scotland, 1975–86 (54 full caps); Manager: Glasgow Rangers, 1986–91 (also player, 1986–90; 4 Scottish League Championships, 1987, 1989, 1990, 1991; 4 Scottish League Cups, 1987–90); Liverpool FC, 1991–94 (FA Cup, 1992); Galatasaray, Turkey, 1995–96 (Turkish Cup, 1996); Southampton FC, 1996–97; Torino, Italy, 1997–98; Benfica, Portugal, 1998–99; Blackburn Rovers, 2000–04 (Worthington Cup, 2002). *Publications:* (with B. Harris) No Half Measures, 1984; A Manager's Diary, 1990; Football: my life, my passion, 2017. *Recreations:* golf, gardening, walking.

**SOUROZH, Archbishop of, (Russian Orthodox),** since 2017; **Rt Rev. Matthew, (Gennady Andreev);** Bishop of Sourozh, since 2017; *b* Tambov, Russia, 18 May 1971; *s* of Lev Andreev and Lidia Andreeva. *Educ:* Tambov Univ.; Theol Sch., Moscow; Theol Acad., Moscow; Postgraduate Theol Sch. Dean of Northern England, 2009; Bishop of Skopin and Shatsk, 2015; Bishop of Bogorodsk, 2017; Interim Bishop for USA and Canada, 2018. Medal, Order of St Innocent, Orthodox Church in America, 2012. *Recreations:* art, history. *Address:* London Russian Orthodox Cathedral, 67 Ennismore Gardens, SW7 1NH. *T:* (020) 7584 0056. *E:* sourozhdiocese@me.com.

**SOUTAR, David Strang;** Consultant Plastic Surgeon, Nuffield Health Glasgow Hospital, 2008–12; *b* 19 Dec. 1947; *s* of Alexander Anderson Soutar and Lizbeth Agnes Bailey Soutar; *m* 1972, Myra (*née* Banks); two *s* one *d. Educ:* Univ. of Aberdeen (MB ChB 1972; ChM 1987). Registrar, Gen. Surgery, Grampian Health Bd, 1975–78; Registrar, then Sen. Registrar, Plastic Surgery, 1978–81, Consultant Plastic Surgeon, 1981–2008, W of Scotland Regional Plastic Surgery Unit, Canniesburn Hosp., Bearsden, Glasgow. Hon. Clinical Sen. Lectr, Univ. of Glasgow, 1981–2009. Chm., Div. of Trauma and Related Services, N Glasgow Univ. Hosps NHS Div., 2002–06. *Publications:* Practical Guide to Free Tissue Transfer, 1986; Microvascular Surgery and Free Tissue Transfer, 1993; Excision and Reconstruction in Head and Neck Cancer, 1994; contrib. 30 chapters in books and over 80 papers in peer-reviewed jls. *Recreations:* music, travel, golf.

**SOUTAR, Michael James;** Chairman, ShortList Media Ltd, 2016–18 (Chief Executive, 2007–16); *b* Dundee, 8 Nov. 1966; *s* of David Bruce Soutar and Patricia Grace Anne Buik; *m* 1994, Beverly; one *s* and one step *s. Educ:* Glenrothes High Sch., Fife; Univ. of Michigan (Exec. MBA 2004). Editor: Smash Hits, 1990–94; FHM, 1994–97; Man. Dir, Kiss FM, 1997–99; Ed. in Chief, Maxim USA, 1999–2000; Man. Dir, IPC Ignite, 2000–03; Editl Dir, IPC Media, 2003–06; Founder, Crash Test Media Ltd, 2006–. Chm., Wallpaper Media, 2001–03. Trustee, Comic Relief, 2003–10. Mem. Bd, IPSO, 2016–. *Recreations:* running, cooking, reading, travelling, Arsenal FC. *Clubs:* Soho House, Ivy, h, Paramount.

**SOUTER, Sir Brian,** Kt 2011; Chairman, Stagecoach Group plc, 1980–2002 and since 2013 (Chief Executive, 2002–13); *b* 1954; *s* of late Iain and Catherine Souter; *m* 1988, Elizabeth McGoldrick; three *s* one *d. Educ:* Dundee Univ.; Univ. of Strathclyde (BA Accountancy). CA; MCIT. Dep. Pres., 2016–17, Pres., 2017–18, ICAS. *Address:* Stagecoach Group plc, 10 Dunkeld Road, Perth PH1 5TW.

*See also* Dame A. H. Gloag.

**SOUTER, Carole Lesley,** CBE 2011; FSA; Master, St Cross College, Oxford, since 2016; *b* 2 May 1957; *d* of late Richard Teague and June Teague; *m* 1979, David Norman Souter; one *s* one *d. Educ:* Truro High Sch. for Girls; St Austell 6th Form Coll.; Jesus Coll., Oxford (BA Hons PPE); Birkbeck Coll., London (MA Victorian Studies). Various posts, DHSS, later DSS, 1978–2000; Dir, Planning and Develt, English Heritage, 2000–03; Dir, later Chief Exec., Heritage Lottery Fund, 2003–16. Dir, Nat. Communities Resource Centre, 2013–17. Trustee: London (formerly SE London, then Capital) Community Foundn, 1996–2013 (Chm., 2004–07); London Bombings Relief Charitable Fund, 2005–08; Creativity, Culture and Education, 2008–17; Kent Wildlife Trust, 2012–16; Historic Royal Palaces, 2016–; Horniman Mus., 2016–; Oxford Preservation Trust, 2016–; London Emergencies Trust, 2016–; Hung Cheng and Baroness Olga Knoop Trust for Ophthalmic Res., 2019–. Lay Canon, Salisbury Cathedral, 2016–. FRSA 2003; FSA 2014. *Recreations:* gardening, visiting historic sites, museums and galleries, theatre. *Address:* St Cross College, 61 St Giles, Oxford OX1 3LZ. *T:* (01865) 278493.

**SOUTER, David Hackett;** Associate Justice of the Supreme Court of the United States, 1990–2009; *b* 17 Sept. 1939. *Educ:* Harvard Univ. (LLB); Oxford Univ. (Rhodes Scholar; MA). Admitted to NH Bar; Associate, Orr & Reno, Concord, NH, 1966–68; Asst Attorney-Gen., 1968–71, Dep. Attorney-Gen., 1976, Attorney-Gen., 1976–78, New Hampshire; Associate Justice: NH Superior Court, 1978–83; NH Supreme Court, 1983–90. *Address:* c/o Supreme Court Building, 1 First Street NE, Washington, DC 20543, USA.

**SOUTH, Martin Christopher;** President, USA and Canada Division, Marsh, since 2016; *b* Kenya, 4 Jan. 1965; *s* of Anthony and Adelheid South; *m* 2010, Traci Alford; one *d*, and one *s* three *d* by a previous marriage. *Educ:* Charterhouse Sch. Minet Gp, 1983–85; C T Bowring, later Marsh Ltd, 1985–96; Zurich Re, 1996–2000; Chief Executive Officer: Zurich London, 2000–04; Zurich Specialities, 2003; Internat. Business Div., Zurich Financial Services, 2003–07; Marsh UK Ltd, 2007–12; Marsh Europe, 2012; CEO, Marsh Asia-Pacific, 2013–16. Dep. Pres., Insce Inst. of London, 2010–11. *Recreations:* ski-ing, tennis, family, epicurean activities. *Address:* Marsh, 1166 Avenue of the Americas, New York, NY 10036, USA. *T:* (212) 3456410. *E:* martin.south@marsh.com.

**SOUTHALL, Anna Catherine,** OBE 2013; Vice Chairman: Big Lottery Fund, 2006–14 (Member Board, 2004–06); Wales Millennium Centre, 2011–17; *b* 9 June 1948; *d* of Stephen Readhead Southall and Philippa (Cadbury) Southall; *m* 1st, 1975, Neil Burton (marr. diss. 1978); 2nd, 1983, Christopher Serle (marr. diss. 2003); two *s. Educ:* Univ. of E Anglia (BA Hons 1970); Gateshead Tech. Coll. (Post Grad. Dip. 1974). Ecclesiastical Insce Office, 1970; Adv. Bd for Redundant Churches, Church Comrs, 1970–71; teacher, Shoreditch Secondary Sch., ILEA (full and part-time), 1971–74; Conservator, Polychrome Monuments (freelance), 1974–75; Senior Conservator: S Eastern Museums' Service, 1975–81; Tate Gall. London, 1981–96; Asst Dir, 1996–98, Dir, 1998–2002, Nat. Museums and Galls of Wales; Chief Exec., Resource: The Council for Museums, Archives and Libraries, 2002–03. Mem., Govt's Spoliation Adv. Panel, 2000–. Chm., Council of Mgt, Arnolfini, 2014–. Trustee: Barrow Cadbury Trust, 1975– (Chm., 1996–2006); Clore Social Leadership, 2010–; Tobacco Factory Arts Trust, 2012–. *Publications:* numerous contribs on 18th and 19th century British artists' materials and techniques in conf. papers, exhibn catalogues and professional jls. *Recreations:* my small-holding in Wales, family and friends, and sharing their sporting and cultural interests.

**SOUTHAMPTON,** 7th Baron *cr* 1780; **Edward Charles FitzRoy;** *b* Norwich, 8 July 1955; *s* of 6th Baron Southampton and Pamela Anne FitzRoy (*née* Henniker); *S* father, 2015; *m* 1978, Rachel Caroline Vincent Millett; one *s* three *d. Educ:* Gresham's Sch., Holt; Royal Agricl Coll., Cirencester. *Heir: s* Hon. Charles Edward Millett FitzRoy, *b* 18 Jan. 1983. *Address:* Venn Farm, Morchard Bishop, Crediton, Devon EX17 6SQ. *E:* esouthampton@yahoo.com.

**SOUTHAN, Elizabeth Andreas;** *see* Evatt, Hon. E. A.

**SOUTHBY, Sir John (Richard Bilbe),** 3rd Bt *cr* 1937, of Burford, Co. Oxford; *b* 2 April 1948; *s* of Sir Archibald Richard Charles Southby, 2nd Bt, OBE and Olive Marion (*d* 1991), *d* of late Sir Thomas Bilbe-Robinson; *S* father, 1988; *m* 1971, Victoria Jane, *d* of John Wilfred Sturrock; two *s* one *d. Educ:* Peterhouse, Marandellas, Rhodesia; Loughborough Univ. of Technology (BSc Elec. Eng). CEng, MIET. East Midlands Electricity: Graduate Trainee, 1971; Asst Engineer 1973, O & M Engineer 1976, Shepshed, Leics; Senior Asst Engineer 1979, O & M Engineer 1981, Boston, Lincs; District Engineer, Grantham, 1986; Dist Manager, then Gen. Manager, Milton Keynes, 1991; Network Gen. Manager Northampton, 1996–99. Pres., Milton Keynes Business Leaders (formerly Milton Keynes Large Employers Assoc.), 1998– (Chm., 1994–98); Chm., Milton Keynes Police Area Adv. Cttee, 1995–99; Mem. Bd, Milton Keynes Economic Partnership, 1994–99; Dir, Milton Keynes Theatre and Gallery Mgt Co., 1996–2000; non-exec. Dir, Milton Keynes Gen. NHS Trust, 2001–08. Pres., Milton Keynes Rotary Club, 1997–98 (Sen. Vice Pres., 1996–97; Sec., 1999–2004, 2006–12); Asst Sec., 1998–99, 2012–14, Sec., 1999–2004, 2014–17, Asst Gov., 2006–09, Rotary Dist 1260. FCMI. *Recreations:* ski-ing, gardening, music, DIY, photography. *Heir: s* Peter John Southby [*b* 20 Aug. 1973; *m* 1995, Katherine Margaret, *d* of Dr R. N. Priestland; three *d*]. *Address:* Lomagundi, High Street, Nash, Bucks MK17 0EP.

**SOUTHEND,** Archdeacon of; *see* Lodge, Ven. M. J.

**SOUTHERN, Dr David Boardman;** QC 2014; barrister; Director and Visiting Professor, School of Tax Law, Queen Mary, University of London, since 1998; *b* Bexhill-on-Sea, 12 May 1946; *s* of Leslie Southern and Emily Southern (*née* Boardman); *m* 1975, Jane Heslop; one *s* one *d. Educ:* Christ Church, Oxford (Open, Dixon and Sen. Scholar; BA, MPhil; DPhil 1976); Bonn Univ. CTA (Fellow) 1998 (FIIT 2009). Lectr, Univ. of Kent at Canterbury, 1973–82; called to the Bar, Lincoln's Inn, 1982, Bencher, 2010; Legal Advr, Bd of Inland Revenue, 1983–90; Tax Advr, Lloyds Bank, 1990–97; in practice as a barrister, 1997–; Mem., Attorney Gen.'s Panel, 2012–14. Treas., Bar Council, 2004–07; Trustee, Council of Inns of Court, 2012–19. *Publications:* Governing Germany, 1990; Taxation of Corporate Debt and Financial Instruments, 1997, 10th edn as Taxation of Loan Relationships and Derivative Contracts, 2016; articles in legal and tax jls. *Recreations:* Germany, opera, theatre. *Address:* Temple Tax Chambers, 3 Temple Gardens, Temple, EC4Y 9AU. *T:* (020) 7353 7884. *E:* David.SouthernQC@templetax.com. *Club:* Athenæum.

**SOUTHERN, Graham;** Director, Blain|Southern Gallery, since 2010; *b* Cornwall, 21 Sept. 1960; *s* of John and Barbara Southern; *m* 1995, Antje Schmitt; two *d.* Christie's London: Specialist, Modern and Impressionist Dept, 1985–88, Modern British Dept, 1988–94; Founding Dir, Post War and Contemporary British Art Dept, 1994–97; Dir, Contemporary Art Dept, 1997–2001; Director: Christie Manson & Wood, 1990–2001; Anthony d'Offay Gall., London, 2001; Founding Dir, Haunch of Venison Gall., 2002–10. Trustee, Art UK (formerly Public Catalogue Foundn), 2008–. Chm., Ind. Assessment Bd, Royal Drawing Sch. (formerly Adjudicator, Prince's Drawing Sch.), 2011–19; Dep. Chm., Soc. of London Art Dealers. Mem., Art World Professional Adv. Gp, Christie's Educn. *Club:* Chelsea Arts.

**SOUTHERN, Rt Rev. Humphrey Ivo John**; Principal, Ripon College, Cuddesdon, since 2015; an Honorary Assistant Bishop, Diocese of Oxford, since 2015; Suffragan Bishop of Repton, 2007–15; *b* 17 Sept. 1960; *s* of late Guy Hugo Southern and of Rosamund Antonia Southern; *m* 1996, Emma Jane, *o d* of Robin and Brenda Lush; two *d*. *Educ*: Harrow Sch.; Westminster Tutors; Christ Church, Oxford (MA 1986); Ripon Coll., Cuddesdon. Ordained deacon, 1986, priest, 1987; Assistant Curate: St Margaret's, Rainham, Kent, 1986–89; Walton-on-the-Hill, Liverpool, 1989–92; Vicar and Team Rector, Hale with Badshot Lea, Farnham, Surrey, 1992–99; Ecumenical Officer, Dio. of Guildford, 1992–99; Team Rector, Tisbury and Nadder Valley, Wilts, 1999–2007. Chm., House of Clergy, Dio. of Salisbury, 2004–07; Non-res. Canon and Prebendary, Salisbury Cathedral, 2006–07; Warden of Readers, Dio. of Derby, 2009–10; Chair: Derbyshire Churches and Church of N India Partnership, 2009–15; Derby Diocesan Bd of Educn, 2013–15. Occasional contrib., Pause for Thought, BBC Radio 2, 2009–11. *Publications*: contrib. to Theology. *Recreations*: conversation, cooking, horse racing, English Bull Terriers, bonfires, reading widely and walking gently. *Address*: Ripon College, Cuddesdon, Oxford OX44 9EX. *T*: (01865) 877400. *E*: Principal@rcc.ac.uk. *Club*: Brooks's.

**SOUTHERN, Paul David; His Honour Judge Southern**; a Circuit Judge, since 2018; *b* 3 Feb. 1954; *m* 1987, Anne Prosser; three *s* one *d*. *Educ*: Tetherdown Primary Sch.; William Ellis Grammar Sch.; Lanchester Poly. (BA Hons Business Law 1976). Admitted as solicitor, 1979; Dep. Dist Judge, 2000–18; Immigration Adjudicator, 2002–05; Immigration Judge, 2005–06; a Sen. Immigration Judge, Asylum and Immigration Tribunal, then a Judge of the Upper Tribunal (Immigration and Asylum Chamber), 2006–18; Principal Resident Judge of the Upper Tribunal (Immigration and Asylum Chamber), 2011–14. *Recreation*: motorcycling. *Address*: Snaresbrook Crown Court, 75 Hollybush Hill, Snaresbrook, E11 1QW.

**SOUTHERN, Penny Ann**; Corporate Director, Adult Social Care and Health, Kent County Council, since 2018; *b* Ripley, Derbys, 25 June 1962; *d* of Kennarth George Southern and Margaret Southern; *m* 2012, Russell Thwaites. *Educ*: Swanwick Hall Sch.; Central Council for Educn and Trng in Social Work (Cert. Social Service); Univ. of Kent at Canterbury (Dip. Mgt Studies); Practice Teaching Award, CCETSW. Asst and instructor, Special Care Units, Derbys CC, 1981–87; Kent County Council: Community Care Organiser, 1987–97; Team Leader and Dist Manager, Social Work, 1997–2008; Hd, Strategic Commng, Learning Disabilities, 2008–11; Dir, Disabled Children's, Adult Learning Disabilities, and Mental Health, 2011–18. *Recreations*: running, netball, long distance walking (Mem., Long Distance Walkers Assoc.). *Address*: Lisheen, Sandgate, Kent. *T*: 07887 742746. *E*: penny.southern@btinternet.com. *Club*: South Kent Harriers.

**SOUTHERN, Dr Peter Campbell David**; Director, International College Spain, 2009–13; *b* 28 Feb. 1947; *s* of Sir Richard Southern, FBA; *m* 1972, Dinah Mitchell; two *s*. *Educ*: Dragon Sch., Oxford; Magdalen College Sch., Oxford; Merton Coll., Oxford (MA); Edinburgh Univ. (PhD). Malosa Secondary Sch., Malawi, 1964–65; Tutorial Asst, Edinburgh Univ., 1970–71; Asst Master, Dulwich Coll., 1973–78; Head of History Dept, Westminster Sch., 1978–85; Head Master: Bancroft's Sch., 1985–96; Christ's Hospital, 1996–2007. Governor: Dulwich Coll., 2007–12; Bancroft's Sch., 2008–. History Awarder and Reviser, Oxford and Cambridge Examn Bd, 1980–90; Sec., Nat. Centre for Cued Speech, 1990–92. Vice-Chm., Redbridge and Waltham Forest Dist HA, 1993–96. Trustee, Lumos, 2007–12. *Publications*: articles on P. G. Wodehouse. *Recreations*: sailing, golf.

**SOUTHERN, Richard Michael**; QC 2006; *b* Yorks, 1964; *s* of Michael and Merle Southern; *m* 2001, Yvette Austin; two *d*. *Educ*: St Catharine's Coll., Cambridge (BA 1986). Called to the Bar, Middle Temple, 1987; in practice as barrister specialising in commercial litigation. Mem., Oxford & Cambridge Sailing Soc. *Recreation*: sailing. *Address*: 7 King's Bench Walk, Temple, EC4Y 7DS. *T*: (020) 7910 8300. *E*: rsouthern@7kbw.co.uk. *Clubs*: Bar Yacht, Royal Corinthian Yacht (Cowes).

**SOUTHESK, Earl of; Charles Duff Carnegie**; *b* 1 July 1989; *s* and *heir* of Duke of Fife, *qv*. *Educ*: Eton.

**SOUTHEY, (David) Hugh**; QC 2010; a Recorder of the Crown Court, since 2009; *b* Redhill, 29 Feb. 1964; *s* of David Southey and Mary Southey; *m* 1989, Jacqueline Margaret Peirce. *Educ*: Salvatorian Coll.; Harrow Weald 6th Form Coll.; Imperial Coll., London (MEng); City of London Poly. Trainee solicitor, Lewis Silkin, 1989–91; admitted solicitor, 1991; solicitor, Glazer Delmar, 1991–96; called to the Bar, Inner Temple, 1996; barrister, Tooks Chambers, 1997–2013, Matrix Chambers, 2013–; Acting Justice, Grand Court of Cayman Is, 2018–. *Publications*: (jtly) A Criminal Practitioner's Guide to Judicial Review and Case Stated, 1999; (jtly) United Kingdom Human Rights Reports, 2000–; (jtly) Judicial Review: a practical guide, 2004, 3rd edn 2017. *Recreations*: cricket, running, ski-ing, theatre, contemporary music, Marco and Maggie. *Address*: Matrix Chambers, Griffin Building, Gray's Inn, WC1R 5LN. *E*: hughsouthey@matrixlaw.co.uk.

**SOUTHGATE, Sir Colin (Grieve)**, Kt 1992; Chairman, Whitehead Mann Group plc, 2003–06 (non-executive Director, 1997–2006); *b* 24 July 1938; *s* of Cyril Alfred and Edith Isabelle Southgate; *m* 1962, Sally Patricia Mead; two *s* two *d*. *Educ*: City of London Sch. ICT, later ICL, 1960–70; formed Software Sciences, 1970; apptd Chief Exec., BOC Computer Services Div. on sale of Software Sciences to BOC, 1980–82; Chief Executive: THORN EMI Information Technology, 1983; THORN EMI, subseq. EMI Gp plc, 1989–99 (Dir, 1984–99); Dir, 1990–96, Chm., 1993–96, PowerGen; Dir, Bank of England, 1991–99; Chm., Terence Chapman Gp plc, 1999–2003 (non-exec. Dir, 1997–99). Chm., Royal Opera House, Covent Gdn, 1998–2003; Trustee: Nat. Gall., 1998–2005; Music Sound Foundn, 1998–2002. Vice Patron, Home Farm Develt Trust, 1991 (Trustee, 1988–91). *Recreation*: gardening.

**SOUTHGATE, Gareth**, OBE 2019; Manager, England Football Team, since 2016; *b* Watford, 3 Sept. 1970; *m* 1997, Alison Bird; one *s* one *d*. Football player: Crystal Palace Under 18 team, 1989–90; Crystal Palace, 1990–95; Aston Villa, 1995–2001 (winner, League Cup Final, 1996); Middlesbrough, 2001–06 (Captain, 2002–06) (winner, League Cup Final, 2004; Mem., UEFA Cup Final team, 2006); internat. appearances for England (57 caps), 1995–2004; Member: European Championship team, 1996, 2000; World Cup team, 1998, 2002; Manager, Middlesbrough FC, 2006–09; Hd, Elite Develt, FA, 2011–12; Head Coach, England Under 21 team, 2013–16. Coach of the Year, BBC, 2018. *Publications*: (with A. Woodman) Woody and Nord: a football friendship, 2003. *Address*: c/o The Football Association, Wembley Stadium, PO Box 1966, London, SW1P 9EQ.

**SOUTHGATE, Joanna Mary**; *see* Donaldson, J. M.

**SOUTHGATE, Dame Lesley (Jill)**, DBE 1999; DSc; FRCP, FRCGP; Professor of Medical Education, St George's, University of London, 2004; *b* 25 Sept. 1943; *m* Richard Boyd Bennet, GP (*d* 2007); three *c*. *Educ*: Liverpool Univ. (MB ChB 1967); Univ. of Western Ontario (MClinSci 1980). MRCGP 1974, FRCGP 1985; FRCP 1997. House surgeon and phys., St Helen's Hosp.; W. K. Kellogg Fellow, Univ. of Western Ontario; former GP, Hoddesdon; Sen. Lectr, then Prof. of Gen. Practice, 1992–95, St Bartholomew's Hosp. Med. Coll.; Prof. of Primary Care and Medical Educn, Royal Free and University College Med. Sch. (formerly at UCL), 1995–2004; founder Mem., Centre for Health Informatics and Multiprofessional Educn, UCL. Convenor, Panel of MRCGP Examnrs, 1994–99; Chm., Perf. Assessment Implementation Gp, GMC, 1994–2004; Mem., Postgrad. Med. Educn and Trng Bd, 2003–06. President: RCGP, 2000–03; ASME, 2006–09; Eur. Bd of Med. Assessors, 2008–. Mem. Bd, Royal Vet. Sch. Mem. at Large, Nat. Bd Med. Examnrs, Philadelphia. Trustee, Thalidomide Trust, 2010–15. Founder FMedSci 1998. Hon. FAcadMed. *Publications*: (contrib.) The Certification and Recertification of Doctors, 1993; (jtly) Infection, 1997; (contrib.) Teaching Medicine in the Community, 1997; contrib. to learned jls.

**SOUTHGATE, Robert**; Chairman, Birmingham Royal Ballet, 2000–04 (Vice-Chairman, 1994–99); *b* 20 Jan. 1934; *s* of Robert Bevis Southgate and Ann Southgate (*née* Boyes); *m* 1st, 1957, Elizabeth Benson; four *s*; 2nd, 2002, Ann Yeandle (*d* 2015), *d* of Edward Yeandle and Kate (*née* Walker). *Educ*: Morecambe Grammar Sch. Work on national newspapers, 1954–64; Dep. Northern Editor, The Sun, 1964–68; Reporter and Presenter, ITN, 1969–78; Presenter, Thames TV, 1978–80; Controller, News and Current Affairs: TVS, 1980–84; Central TV, 1984–92; non-executive Director: Meridian TV, 1995–97; Central Broadcasting, 1994–97 (former Dep. Man. Dir and Man. Dir). Mem., Arts Council, 1993–97; Chairman: W Midlands Regl Arts Bd, 1992–97; City of Birmingham Touring Opera, 1992–97; Dir, Birmingham Rep. Th., 1996–2002. *Recreations*: Lyric Theatre, travel, food, wine.

**SOUTHGATE, Dr Vaughan Robert**; DL; FZS, FRSB; President, Linnean Society of London, 2009–12; *b* Kempston, 13 May 1944; *s* of Stanley Robert Double and Hilda Louisa Peggy Southgate (*née* Dean); *m* 1966, Marilyn Kuhn; one *s* one *d*. *Educ*: Bedford Modern Sch.; University Coll. of Wales, Aberystwyth (BSc); Christ's Coll., Cambridge (PhD 1969). FZS 1970; MInstBiol 1980, FRSB (FInstBiol 1988). Natural History Museum: Jun. Res. Fellow, 1968–71; SSO, 1971–76; PSO, 1976–92; SPSO (Individual Merit), 1992–2004. Hd, Biomed. Parasitol. Div. and Dir, WHO Collaborating Centre for Identification of schistosomes and their snail intermediate hosts, 1983–2004; Mem., Expert Cttee on parasitic diseases (schistosomiasis), WHO, 1986–2011. Ed., Jl Natural Hist., 1972–83. Royal Society of Tropical Medicine and Hygiene: Fellow, 1970; Mem. Council, 1979–82; Hon. Sec., 1986–91; Vice Pres., 1993–95. FRSocMed 2006. Linnean Society of London: Fellow, 1988 (Hon. Fellow, 2019); Zool Sec., 1997–2009; Vice Pres., 1998–2008; Pres. Elect, 2008–09. Hon. Fellow, Dept of Biol., UCL, 2002–12. British Society for Parasitology: Mem., 1965–; Mem. Council, 1975–77; Chm., Autumn Symposium Cttee, 1984–88. Mem., Bedford Cttee, Forum 71, 2016– (Vice Chm., 2018–19). Trustee: John Spedan Lewis Foundn, 2001–18; Beds and Luton Crimebeat, 2006–15; Bedford Hosps Charity, 2008–; Chm., Trustees, Friends of Cople Ch, 2003–15. Patron, The Higgins, Bedford (formerly Cecil Higgins Art Gall. and Bedford Mus.), 2009–. Vice Patron: Almshouse Assoc., 2018–; Families United Network, 2018–. Mem., Bedford Camera Club (Pres., 2008–10); President: London Soc. of Old Aberystwythians, 2012–14; Old Bedford Modernians, 2013–14 (Vice-Pres., 2012–13); Bedford Millennium Probus Club, 2014–15 (Vice-Pres., 2013–14); Mem., Biggleswade Ivel Rotary Club, 2000–11 (Paul Harris Fellow, 2009; Hon. Mem., 2014). Mem., Beds High Sheriff's Panel, 2008–12. High Sheriff, 2007–08, DL 2009–, Beds. C. A. Wright Meml Medal, British Soc. of Parasitol., 1990. *Publications*: contrib. chapters in books; contrib. articles to learned jls specialising in parasitol. and tropical medicine. *Recreations*: fly fishing, shooting, photography, natural history, family. *Address*: The Coach House, Woodlands Close, Cople, Bedford MK44 3UE. *T*: (01234) 838714. *E*: V.Southgate714@btinternet.com. *Clubs*: Royal Society of Medicine; Sheerhatch Shoot; Roxton Park Trout Fishery.

**SOUTHGATE, Sir William (David)**, Kt 1995; conductor and composer; *b* Waipukurau, NZ, 4 Aug. 1941; *s* of Alfred John Southgate and Phyllis (*née* Maden); *m* 1967, (Alison) Rosemary Martin, *d* of (Alexander James) Lloyd Martin and (Gwendolene) Noel (*née* McGeorge). *Educ*: Otago Boys' High Sch.; Otago Univ. (MA Hons First Cl.; BMus Hons First Cl.); Guildhall Sch. of Music and Drama (Ricordi Conducting Prize). Worked in UK with variety of musical orgns incl. Phoenix Opera Co., RSC and BBC TV, 1969–74; worked in NZ, 1974–; Musical Dir, then Principal Guest Conductor, Christchurch Symphony Orch., 1986–97, Conductor Laureate, 1997–; Guest Conductor, NZ Symphony Orch., 1975–, and all main NZ orchs and opera cos; Musical Director: Royal NZ Ballet, 1976–93; Wellington Youth Orch., 1978–90; Wellington Regional Orch.; Conductor, Wellington City Opera Co. Has conducted orchs in Europe, NZ and Australia, incl. Hallé, Royal Philharmonic, Berlin Radio Symphony, and Sydney Symphony. Own arts and music progs on TV and radio in NZ. Patron: Wellington Audio Club; Performing Arts Comp. Assoc. of NZ; New Plymouth Orch. Hon. DMus Otago, 1994. Queen's Sesquicentennial Medal, NZ, 1990; Kirk-Burnand and Brown Citation, Composers' Assoc. of NZ, 1993; NZ Music Award, 2003. Internationally accredited as major interpreter of classic/romantic symphonic repertoire in Wand to Furtwangler/German tradition. *Compositions include*: Capital Variations, 1983; Symphony No 1, 1984; Symphony No 2, 1988; Erewhon (for wind quintet), 1989; Cello Concerto, 1991; Psalmody, 1992; Hamlet (ballet), 1992, Hamlet Suite, 1993; Overture: Réjouissance, 1994; Symphony No 3, 1997; In Emmanuel's Land (piano quartet), 2003. *Recreations*: golf, billiards, snooker, sports of all kinds (Otago Univ. soccer blue), dining with friends, gardening. *Address*: PO Box 25 261, Featherston Street, Wellington 6146, New Zealand.

**SOUTHWARD, Eileen**; *see* Cooper, Eileen.

**SOUTHWARD, Sir Nigel (Ralph)**, KCVO 2003 (CVO 1995; LVO 1985); Apothecary to the Queen, Apothecary to the Household and to the Households of Princess Alice Duchess of Gloucester and the Duke and Duchess of Gloucester, 1975–2003; *b* 8 Feb. 1941; *s* of Sir Ralph Southward, KCVO; *m* 1965, Annette, *d* of J. H. Hoffmann; one *s* two *d*. *Educ*: Rugby Sch.; Trinity Hall, Cambridge; Middlesex Hosp. Med. Sch. MA, MB, BChir, 1965; MRCP 1969. Ho. Surg., Middx Hosp., 1965; Ho. Phys., Royal Berkshire Hosp., Reading, 1966; Ho. Phys., Central Middx Hosp., 1966; Casualty MO, Middx Hosp., 1967; Vis. MO, King Edward VII Hosp. for Officers, 1972–2003. Apothecary to the Households of Princess Margaret Countess of Snowdon, 1975–2002, and of Queen Elizabeth the Queen Mother, 1986–2002. *Recreations*: sailing, golf, ski-ing. *Address*: Drokesfield, Bucklers Hard, Beaulieu, Hants SO42 7XE. *T*: (01590) 616252. *Clubs*: Royal Yacht Squadron, Royal Cruising.

**SOUTHWARK, Archbishop of, (RC)**, since 2019; **Most Rev. John Wilson**; *b* Sheffield, 4 July 1968; *s* of Victor Wilson and of Patricia Wilson. *Educ*: Univ. of Leeds (BA Theol. and Religious Studies 1989); Pontifical Gregorian Univ., Rome (STB 1993); Pontifical Lateran Univ., Rome (STL 1995); Durham Univ. (PhD 2003). Ordained priest, Archdio. of Leeds, 1995; Assistant Priest: St Joseph's, Pontefract, 1995–98; St Joseph's, Bradford, 1998–99; Lectr in Moral Theol. and Vice Rector, Ushaw Coll., Durham, 1999–2005; Episcopal Vicar, Leeds, 2005–12; Apostolic Administrator, Leeds, 2012–14; Parish Priest, St Martin de Porres, Wakefield, 2015–16; an Aux. Bishop of Westminster, (RC), and Titular Bishop of Lindisfarne, 2016–19. Chair, Educn Commn, 2015. Sessional Chaplain, HMP Leeds, 2008–14. *Recreations*: reading, swimming, travel, theatre. *Address*: Archbishop's House, 150 St George's Road, SE1 6HX. *T*: (020) 7928 5592. *E*: archbishop@rcaos.org.uk.

**SOUTHWARK, Bishop of,** since 2011; **Rt Rev. Christopher Thomas James Chessun;** *b* 5 Aug. 1956; twin *s* of late Thomas Frederick Chessun and Joyce Rosemary Chessun. *Educ:* Hampton Grammar Sch.; University Coll., Oxford (BA Hons Modern Hist. 1978; MA 1982); Trinity Hall, Cambridge (BA Hons Pt II Theol. Tripos 1982); Westcott House Theol Coll., Cambridge. Ordained deacon, 1983, priest, 1984; Asst Curate, St Michael and All Angels, Sandhurst, 1983–87; Sen. Curate, St Mary, Portsea, 1987–89; Chaplain and Minor Canon, St Paul's Cathedral, 1989–93; Vocations Advr, Dio. London, 1991–93; Rector of St Dunstan and All Saints', Stepney, 1993–2001; Area Dean, Tower Hamlets, 1997–2001; Archdeacon of Northolt, 2001–05; Area Bishop of Woolwich, 2005–11. Bishop for Urban Life and Faith, 2010–13. Took seat, H of L, 2014. Freeman, City of London, 1993; Hon. Chaplain, 1992–, Freeman and Hon. Liveryman, 2001, Needlemakers' Co. *Recreations:* music, history, travel, overseas church links. *Address:* Bishop's House, 38 Tooting Bec Gardens, SW16 1QZ. *T:* (020) 8769 3256, *Fax:* 0843 290 6894; Trinity House, 4 Chapel Court, Borough High Street, SE1 1HW. *T:* (020) 7939 9420. *E:* bishop.christopher@southwark.anglican.org.

**SOUTHWARK, Auxiliary Bishop of, (RC);** *see* Hendricks, Rt Rev. P. J.

**SOUTHWARK, Dean of;** *see* Nunn, Very Rev. A. P.

**SOUTHWARK, Archdeacon of;** *see* Steen, Ven. J. E.

**SOUTHWELL,** family name of **Viscount Southwell**.

**SOUTHWELL,** 7th Viscount *cr* 1776; **Pyers Anthony Joseph Southwell;** Bt 1662; Baron Southwell, 1717; International Management and Marketing Consultant, now retired; *b* 14 Sept. 1930; *s* of Hon. Francis Joseph Southwell (2nd *s* of 5th Viscount) and Agnes Mary Annette Southwell (*née* Clifford); *S* uncle, 1960; *m* 1955, Barbara Jacqueline Raynes; two *s*. *Educ:* Beaumont Coll., Old Windsor, Berks; Royal Military Academy, Sandhurst. Commissioned into 8th King's Royal Irish Hussars, 1951; resigned commission, 1955. *Recreation:* golf. *Heir: s* Hon. Richard Andrew Pyers Southwell [*b* 15 June 1956; *m* 1985, Alison Margaret Huntington; one *d* (one *s* decd)]. *Clubs:* Army and Navy, MCC.

**SOUTHWELL AND NOTTINGHAM, Bishop of,** since 2015; **Rt Rev. Paul Gavin Williams;** *b* Weston-Super-Mare, 16 Jan. 1968; *s* of Bryan Williams and Heather Williams; *m* 1997, Sarah Cossham; three *s*. *Educ:* Court Fields Comp. Sch., Wellington, Som; Richard Huish Coll., Taunton; Grey Coll., Univ. of Durham (BA Hons Theology 1989); Wycliffe Hall, Oxford. Youth Pastor, St Andrew's Church, Oxford, 1989–90; ordained deacon, 1992, priest, 1993; Curate, St James's Church, Muswell Hill, 1992–95; Associate Vicar, Christ Church, Clifton, Bristol, 1995–99; Rector, St James, Gerrards Cross with Fulmer, 1999–2009; Area Bishop of Kensington, 2009–15. Hon. Canon, Christ Church, Oxford, 2007–09. *Recreations:* fell-walking, football, choral music, family. *Address:* Jubilee House, 8 Westgate, Southwell, Notts NG25 0JH.

**SOUTHWELL, Dean of;** *see* Sullivan, Very Rev. N. A.

**SOUTHWELL, His Honour Edward;** *see* Southwell, His Honour R. C. E.

**SOUTHWELL, Richard Charles;** QC 1977; *s* of late Sir Philip Southwell, CBE, MC and Mary Burnett (*née* Scarratt); *m* Belinda Mary, *d* of late Col F. H. Pownall, MC; two *s* one *d*. Former Judge of the Courts of Appeal of Jersey and Guernsey. Commercial Arbitrator. Treasurer, Inner Temple, 2002. Pres., Lloyd's Appeal Tribunal, 1997–2010. Lt Bailiff, Guernsey Royal Ct, 2005–14. Lay Canon, Salisbury Cathedral, 2007–12, now Lay Canon Emeritus; Chm., House of Laity, Salisbury Diocesan Synod, 2006–10; former Lay Co-Chm., Heytesbury Deanery Synod. Chm. Trustees, Wessex MS Therapy Centre; Vice Chm. Trustees, Hosp. of St John and St Katherine, Heytesbury; Former Founding Trustee, Tropical Health and Educn Trust. Former Chm. of Govs: St Mary's Sch., Calne (now Patron); Warminster Sch. (now Patron). *Address:* Serle Court, 6 New Square, Lincoln's Inn, WC2A 3QS. *T:* (020) 7242 6105, *Fax:* (020) 7405 4004. *E:* clerks@serlecourt.co.uk.

**SOUTHWELL, His Honour (Richard Charles) Edward;** a Circuit Judge, 2000–13; *b* 31 March 1946; *s* of Dr Neville Southwell and Elizabeth Southwell; *m* 1974, Judith Mary Bowdage; one *s* two *d* (and one *s* decd). *Educ:* Charterhouse Sch. Called to the Bar, Inner Temple, 1970. *Recreations:* golf, sailing, ski-ing, motoring. *Clubs:* MCC; West Surrey Golf; Royal London Yacht; Bar Yacht; Old Carthusian Yacht; Austin 7 Owners'; MG Owners'.

**SOUTHWELL, Robin,** OBE 1999; FRAeS; Chief Executive Officer, Airbus Group UK (formerly EADS UK) Ltd, 2005–14; *b* 10 April 1960; *s* of Peter and Susan Southwell; *m* 1988, Sally Deakin (*d* 2010); one *s* one *d*. *Educ:* Univ. of Hull (BA Hons). FRAeS 1998. With British Aerospace, then BAE Systems, 1981–2000 (Gp Man. Dir, Customer Solutions and Support, 1998–2000); Chief Executive Officer: W. S. Atkins plc, 2001–02; AirTanker Ltd, 2002–05. Non-executive Director: Chloride Gp Plc, 2002–08; Aurum Mining, then Shearwater Gp plc, 2016–; Dir, David Linley Hldgs, 2014–. Pres., UK Aerospace, Defence and Security Orgn, 2012–14. *Recreations:* family, football.

**SOUTHWOOD, Prof. David John,** CBE 2019; PhD; Professor of Physics, 1986–2008, Senior Research Investigator, since 2011, Imperial College London; *b* 30 June 1945; *s* of H. H. J. Southwood and H. M. Southwood; *m* 1967, Susan Elizabeth Fricker; two *s* one *d*. *Educ:* Torquay Boys' Grammar Sch.; Queen Mary Coll., London (BA; Hon: Fellow 2003); Imperial Coll., London (PhD, DIC). UCLA 1970; Lectr, 1971–86, Head of Physics Dept, 1994–97, Imperial Coll., London; on leave of absence as Hd, Earth Observation Strategy, ESA, Paris, 1997–2000; Dir of Sci., 2001–08, Dir of Sci. and Robotic Exploration, 2008–11, ESA. Vis. Prof., 1976, Regents' Prof., 2000, UCLA; Vis. Prof., Plymouth Univ., 2011–; Dist. Vis. Scholar, Jet Propulsion Lab., Calif Inst. of Technol., Pasadena, 2011– (Mem. Adv. Council, 2011–); Hon. Prof., Univ. of Lancaster, 2013–. Mem., SERC Boards, 1989–94; Chairman: Commn D, COSPAR, 1986–92; Space Sci. Adv. Cttee, ESA, 1990–93; Sci. Prog. Cttee, ESA, 1993–96; Sci. Adv. Cttee, Internat. Space Sci. Inst., 1995–2001; Trustees, Inst. for Space Policy and Law, Univ. of London, 2013–; Mem. Steering Bd, UK Space Agency, 2011–19 (Chair, 2016–19). Pres., RAS, 2012–14 (Vice-Pres., 1989–91; Trustee, 2010–11). Trustee: Nat. Space Centre, 2001–19; Sir Alister Hardy Foundn for Ocean Sci., 2016–18. Fellow, Amer. Geophys. Union (James B. Macelwane Award, 1981); Mem., Internat. Acad. of Astronautics, 1999; For. Mem., Nat. Acad. of Air and Space, France, 2005. FRAeS 2011. Hon. DSc Plymouth, 2011; Hon. Dr Bern, 2012. Silver Medal, Royal Aerospace Soc., 2005; Gold Medal, Eur. Aerospace Socs, 2007; Sir Arthur Clarke Award for exceptional space achievement, Space Educnl Trust, 2011; Public Service Award, NASA, 2011. *Publications:* numerous contribs in solar terrestrial physics and planetary science to learned jls. *Recreations:* reading, theatre, cinema. *Address:* Space and Atmospheric Physics Group, Physics Department, Imperial College London, South Kensington Campus, SW7 2BZ. *T:* (020) 7594 7679. *E:* d.southwood@imperial.ac.uk.

**SOUTHWOOD, Sara Michel;** *see* Selwood, S. M.

**SOUTHWORTH, Benedict;** Chief Executive, Ramblers, 2012–16; strategist to non profits and philanthropy, since 2017; *b* Preston, Lancs, 28 Aug. 1965; *s* of Edmund Campion Southworth and Kathleen Southworth; *m* 1997, Michaela Claire O'Brien; two *d*. *Educ:* Preston Catholic Coll.; Newman Coll., Preston; Univ. of Liverpool (BA Hons Pol Theory and Instns 1987); Univ. of East London (MSc Architecture: Advanced Envmtl and Energy Studies (distance learning) 2011). Campaigner, Friends of the Earth, England, Wales and NI, 1990–95; Campaign Manager, Newbury Bypass Campaign, 1995–96; Coordinator, Mgt Support Proj., NSW Community Legal Centres Secretariat, 1996–98; Campaigns Manager, Greenpeace Australia-Pacific, 1998–2001; Dir, Internat. Climate Campaign, Greenpeace Internat., 2001–03; Campaigns Prog. Dir, Internat. Secretariat, Amnesty Internat., 2003–05; Dir, World Develt Movement, 2005–09; charity consultant, 2009–12. Member, Board: 38 Degrees Ltd, 2009–; 38 Degrees Trust, 2010–; Friends of the Earth Charitable Trust, 2019–; Mem., Mgt Cttee, People and Planet Student Activities Ltd, 2009–10. Gov., Oxted Sch., 2013–14. *Recreations:* walking, archery, democracy, family history, British post-apocalyptic TV, growing fruit and herbs. *E:* benedict.southworth@ntlworld.com.

**SOUTHWORTH, Helen Mary;** Chief Executive, Age Concern (formerly Age) Isle of Man, since 2014; *b* 13 Nov. 1956; *m* Edmund Southworth; one *s*. *Educ:* Larkhill Convent Sch., Preston; Univ. of Lancaster (BA Hons). Director: Age Concern, St Helens; Grosvenor Housing Assoc.; St Helens and Knowsley HA. Mem. (Lab) St Helens MBC, 1994–98 (Chm., Leisure Cttee, 1994–96). Contested (Lab) Wirral S, 1992. MP (Lab) Warrington S, 1997–2010.

**SOWARD, Prof. Andrew Michael,** FRS 1991; Professor of Applied Mathematics, University of Exeter, 1996–2009, now Emeritus; Strategic Research Adviser, School of Mathematics, Statistics and Physics, Newcastle University, since 2011; *b* 20 Oct. 1943; *s* of Arthur Layton Soward and Sybil Jessica Lilian Soward (*née* Greathurst); *m* 1968, Elaine Celia McCaully; one *s* one *d*. *Educ:* St Edward's Sch., Oxford; Queens' College, Cambridge (BA 1st cl. Hons Maths 1965; PhD 1969; ScD 1984). University of Newcastle upon Tyne: Lectr, 1971, Reader, 1981–86, Dept of Maths and Stats; Head, Div. of Applied Maths, 1985–95; Prof. of Fluid Dynamics, 1986–95. Visiting appointments: Courant Inst. of Mathematical Scis, NY, 1969–70; CIRES, Boulder, Colorado, 1970–71; IGPP, UCLA, 1977–78. Editor, Jl of Geophysical and Astrophysical Fluid Dynamics, 1991–. *Publications:* (ed jtly) Rotating Fluids in Geophysics, 1978; (ed) Stellar and Planetary Magnetism, vol. 2, 1983; (ed jtly) Geomagnetism and Palaeomagnetism, 1989; (ed jtly) Dynamics and Magnetic Fields of the Earth's and Planetary Interior, 2001; (ed jtly) Magnetohydrodynamics and the Earth's Core, 2003; (ed jtly) Earth's Core and Lower Mantle, 2003; (ed jtly) Fluid Dynamics and Dynamos in Astrophysics and Geophysics, 2005; (ed jtly) Mathematical Aspects of Natural Dynamos, 2007; over 120 published res. papers. *Address:* 1 Stephenson Terrace, Wylam, Northumberland NE41 8DZ. *Clubs:* Fell and Rock Climbing; Tyne Amateur Rowing.

**SOWDEN, Susan, (Mrs Philip Sowden);** Registrar, Headington School, Oxford, 2007–15; *b* 10 June 1951; *d* of Albert Henry Letley and Ethel May Letley; *m* 1st, 1973, Michael Geoffrey Bodinham (marr. diss. 1990); one *s* two *d*; 2nd, 2000, Philip Sowden. *Educ:* Clarendon House Grammar Sch. for Girls, Ramsgate; King's Coll., London (BSc 2nd Cl. Hons; AKC; PGCE); Open Univ. (Adv. Dip Ed Man). Geography teacher, Peers Upper Comprehensive, Oxford, 1973–77 and 1984–85; Headington School, Oxford: Geog. teacher, 1985–87; Head of Dept, 1987; Housemistress, 1988; Head of Lower Sixth, 1991–93; Dep. Head, 1993–94; Headmistress, St Mary's Sch., Wantage, 1994–2006. Sen. examng posts with EMREB, Southern Examng Gp and Northern Exams and Assessment Bd. Gov., Twyford Sch., 2003–10; Foundation Governor: Radley C of E Primary Sch., 2016–; Manor Prep. Sch., Abingdon, 2016–. Lay Minister (formerly Reader), Church of England, 1993–. *Publications:* articles in Britain and the British (pubd in Poland). *Recreations:* walking, reading, theatre, canoeing, camping, music.

**SOWERBY, Rt Rev. Mark Crispin Rake;** Principal, College of the Resurrection, Mirfield, since 2019; *b* Ripon, 28 Oct. 1963; *s* of Rev. Geoffrey Sowerby and Hilary Sowerby (*née* Evans); *m* 1989, Ruth Mary Jones; three *d*. *Educ:* Barnard Castle Sch.; St Aidan and St John Fisher's Sixth Form, Harrogate; King's Coll., London (BD 1985; AKC 1985); Univ. of Lancaster (MA 1994); Coll. of the Resurrection, Mirfield. Ordained deacon, 1987, priest, 1988; Curate: Knaresborough, 1987–90; Darwen St Cuthbert with Tockholes, 1990–92; Vicar, St Mary Magdalen, Accrington, 1992–97; Selection Sec./Vocations Officer, Ministry Div. of Archbishop's Council, 1997–2001; Vicar, St Wilfrid's, Harrogate, 2001–09 (Team Rector, 2004–09); Bishop Suffragan of Horsham, 2009–19. Assistant Director of Ordinands: Dio. of Blackburn, 1993–96; Dio. of Ripon and Leeds, 2005–09. Chaplain: St Christopher's C of E Sch., Accrington, 1992–97; Victoria Hosp., Accrington, 1992–97. *Recreations:* cooking, sea fishing, opera. *Address:* College of the Resurrection, Stocks Bank Road, Mirfield, W Yorks WF14 0BN.

**SOYINKA, Wole;** Nigerian writer; *b* 13 July 1934; *s* of Ayo and Eniola Soyinka; *m*; *c*. *Educ:* Univ. of Ibadan, Nigeria; Univ. of Leeds. Res. Fellow in Drama, Univ. of Ibadan, 1960–61; Lectr in English, Univ. of Ife, 1962–63; Sen. Lectr in English, Univ. of Lagos, 1965–67; political prisoner, 1967–69; Artistic Dir and Head of Dept of Theatre Arts, Univ. of Ibadan, 1969–72; Res. Prof. in Dramatic Literature, 1972, Prof. of Comparative Literature, 1976–85, Emeritus Prof., 2004, Univ. of Ife (later Obafemi Awolowo Univ., Iwe-Ife); Goldwin Smith Prof. of Africana Studies and Theatre, Cornell Univ., 1988–92; Elias Ghanem Chair of Creative Writing, Univ. of Nevada, until 2005; President's Marymount Inst. Prof. in Residence, Loyola Marymount Univ., 2007; Distinguished Vis. Prof., Univ. of Johannesburg, 2017–. Fellow: Churchill Coll., Cambridge, 1973–74; Dubois Inst., Harvard Univ., 2004. Reith Lectr, BBC Radio 4, 2004. Hon. DLitt: Leeds, 1973; Yale, 1981; Paul Valéry, 1984; Morehouse Coll., 1988. Nobel Prize for Literature, 1986; AGIP/Enrico Mattei Award for the Humanities, 1986; Benson Medal, RSL, 1990. Comdr, Légion d'Honneur (France). *Publications:* plays: The Lion and the Jewel, 1959; The Swamp Dwellers, 1959; A Dance of the Forests, 1960; The Trials of Brother Jero, 1961; The Strong Breed, 1962; The Road, 1964; Kongi's Harvest, 1965; Madmen and Specialists, 1971; Before the Blackout, 1971; Jero's Metamorphosis, 1973; Camwood on the Leaves, 1973; The Bacchae of Euripides, 1974; Death and the King's Horsemen, 1975; Opera Wonyosi, 1978; A Play of Giants, 1984; From Zia with Love, 1992; A Scourge of Hyacinths, 1992; The Beatification of Area Boy, 1995; *novels:* The Interpreters, 1964; The Forest of a Thousand Daemons (trans.), Season of Anomy, 1973; *poetry:* Idanre and other poems, 1967; A Shuttle in the Crypt, 1972; (ed) Poems of Black Africa, 1975; Ogun Abibman, 1977; Mandela's Earth and other Poems, 1989; Selected Poems, 2002; Samarkand And Other Markets I Have Known, 2002; *non-fiction:* The Man Died (prison memoirs), 1972; Myth, Literature and the African World (lectures), 1972; Ake, the Years of Childhood (autobiog.), 1982; Art, Dialogue and Outrage (essays), 1988; Isara: a voyage around "Essay" (biog.), 1989; Ibadan (memoir), 1995; The Open Sore of a Continent, 1996; The Burden of Memory, the Muse of Forgiveness (essays), 1999; Climate of Fear: the quest for dignity in a dehumanized world (essays), 2005; You Must Set Forth At Dawn (memoirs), 2006.

**SOYOYE, Babatunde Temitope;** Co-Founder and Managing Partner, Helios Investment Partners, since 2005; *b* Lagos, Nigeria, 26 Nov. 1968; *s* of Gabriel Abolade Soyoye and Esther Sijuola Soyoye (*née* Akinosi); *m* 1999, Claudia; one *s* two *d*. *Educ:* Allhallows Sch., Dorset; King's Coll. London (BEng Hons 1991); Imperial Coll. London (MBA 1995). Manager: BT, 1996–98; Business Develt, Singapore Telecom Internat.; Principal, TPG Capital. Dir, Commonwealth Enterprise and Investment Council, 2016–. Mem., LSE-Univ. of Oxford Commn on State Fragility, Growth and Develt, 2017–18.

Trustee, Save the Children UK, 2017–. *Address:* Helios Investment Partners, 12 Charles II Street, SW1Y 4QU. *T:* (020) 7484 7705. *E:* bsoyoye@helioslip.com. *Clubs:* Reform, Lansdowne, 5 Hertford Street.

SPACEY, Kevin, Hon. KBE 2015 (Hon. CBE 2010); actor, director and producer; Artistic Director, Old Vic, 2004–15 (Trustee, 2000–04); *b* 26 July 1959; *né* Kevin Spacey Fowler; *s* of Thomas and Kathleen Fowler. *Educ:* Chatsworth High Sch., LA; Juilliard Drama Sch., NY. Cameron Mackintosh Vis. Prof. of Contemporary Th., St Catherine's Coll., Oxford, 2008–09. MacTaggart Lectr, Edinburgh Internat. TV Fest., 2013. *Theatre includes:* Ghosts, NY, 1982; Hurlyburly, 1985; Long Day's Journey into Night, 1986; National Anthems, Long Wharf Th., New Haven, CT, 1988, Old Vic, 2005; Lost in Yonkers, NY (Tony Award), 1991; The Iceman Cometh, Almeida, 1998, NY 1999; The Philadelphia Story, Richard II (Critics' Circle Award), Old Vic, 2005; A Moon for the Misbegotten, Old Vic, 2006, NY 2007; Speed-the-Plow, Old Vic, 2008; Inherit the Wind, Old Vic, 2009; Richard III, Old Vic, 2011; Clarence Darrow, Old Vic, 2014. *Television includes:* Wiseguy (series), 1988; The Murder of Mary Phagan, 1988; Fall from Grace, 1990; When You Remember Me, 1990; Darrow, 1991; House of Cards, 2013–17 (Golden Globe Award, 2015). *Films include:* Working Girl, 1988; See No Evil, Hear No Evil, Dad, 1989; A Show of Force, Henry and June, 1990; Glengarry Glen Ross, Consenting Adults, 1992; The Ref, Swimming with Sharks (also co-prod.), 1994; Outbreak, The Usual Suspects (Acad. Award for Best Supporting Actor), Se7en, 1995; Looking for Richard, A Time to Kill, 1996; L. A. Confidential, Midnight in the Garden of Good and Evil, 1997; The Negotiator, 1998; The Big Kahuna (also prod.), 1999; American Beauty (Academy, BAFTA and London Film Critics' Circle Awards for Best Actor), Hurlyburly, Ordinary Decent Criminal, 2000; Pay it Forward, 2001; K-PAX, The Shipping News, 2002; The Life of David Gale, 2003; Beyond the Sea (also dir and prod.), 2004; The United States of Leland (also prod.), 2005; Superman, 2006; Fred Claus, 2007; 21, 2008; The Men Who Stare At Goats, 2009; Shrink, 2010; Horrible Bosses, 2011; Margin Call, 2012; Elvis and Nixon, Nine Lives, 2016; Baby Driver, 2017; Dir, Albino Alligator, 1996; Producer: Interstate 84, 2000; Uncle Frank, 2002; Triggerstreet.com, 2004.

SPACIE, Maj.-Gen. Keith, CB 1987; OBE 1974; Chairman, Sudbury Consultants Ltd, 1989–2000; *b* 21 June 1935; *s* of Frederick and Kathleen Spacie; *m* 1st, 1961, Valerie Rich (*d* 2008); one *s*; 2nd, 2015, Clare Annette Sylvester. Commnd Royal Lincolns, 1955; transf. Parachute Regt, 1959; Staff Coll., Camberley, 1966; DAA&QMG 16 Parachute Bde, 1968–70; Staff, RMA, Sandhurst, 1970–72; Comd, 3rd Bn Parachute Regt, 1973–75; SHAPE, 1976–78; Comdr 7 Field Force, 1979–81; RCDS, 1982; Mil. Comr and Comdr, British Forces Falkland Is, 1983–84; Dir of Army Training, 1984–87 Pres., Arnhem 1944 Fellowship, 2013–17. Pres., Milocarian Athletic Club, 2012–. *Recreations:* cross-country running, athletics, walking, battlefield touring. *Clubs:* Army and Navy; Thames Hare and Hounds.

SPACKMAN, Brig. John William Charles, PhD; Director, KC3 NET Ltd, 2007–09; *b* 12 May 1932; *s* of Lt-Col Robert Thomas Spackman, MBE and Ann (*née* Rees); *m* 1955, Jeanette Vera; two *s* one *d*. *Educ:* Cyfarthfa Castle Grammar School, Merthyr Tydfil; Wellington Grammar School; RMCS. BSc 1st cl. Hons London (external) 1960, PhD 1964; MSc (Management Sci.) UMIST, 1968; Open Univ. (BA Humanities with Eng. Lit. 2015). Nat. Service, 1950–52; Regular Commission, RAOC, 1952; Regtl appts, 1952–72; Project Wavell, 1969–72; RARDE, 1972–75; Senior Mil. Officer, Chem. Defence and Microbiological Defence Estab., Porton Down, 1975–78; Branch Chief, Inf. Systems Div., SHAPE, 1978–80; Dir, Supply Computer Services, 1980–83; retired from Army, 1983 (Brig.); Under Sec., and Dir, Social Security Operational Strategy, DHSS, 1983–87; Director: Computing and Information Services, BT, 1987–90; Eur. Telecommunications Informatics Services, 1991–93; Management Systems Unit, Govt of Malta, 1993–96; KFKI (CSC), Hungary, 1993–2004; Logan Orviss Internat., 1993–2009; Intelligent Networks Ltd, 1997–98. FBCS 1987 (MBCS 1970); CITP 2007; CEng 1990; MCMI (MBIM 1970); MInstD 1983. Liveryman, Information Technologists' Co., 1989 (Mem., 1987). Freeman, City of London, 1987. *Recreations:* gardening, opera. *Address:* The Hermitage, Snow Street, Roydon, Diss, Norfolk IP22 5RZ. *T:* (01379) 651650.

SPACKMAN, Michael John; affiliated consultant, NERA Economic Consulting (formerly National Economic Research Associates), since 2007 (special adviser, 1996–2007); Visiting Senior Fellow, Department of Geography and Environment, London School of Economics and Political Science, since 2019 (Visiting Fellow, Centre for Analysis of Risk and Regulation, 2001–10; Visiting Senior Fellow, Grantham Institute for Climate Change and the Environment, 2010–18); *b* 8 Oct. 1936; *s* of late Geoffrey Spackman and Audrey (*née* Morecombe); *m* 1965, Judith Ann Leathem; two *s* two *d*. *Educ:* Malvern Coll.; Clare Coll., Cambridge (MA); Queen Mary Coll., London (MScEcon). Served RA (2nd Lieut), 1955–57; Physicist, UKAEA, Capenhurst, 1960–69; Sen. Physicist/Engr, Nuclear Power Gp Ltd, 1969–71; PSO, then Economic Advr, Dept of Energy, 1971–77; Economic Advr, HM Treasury, 1977–79; Dir of Econs and Accountancy, CS Coll., 1979–80; Hd of Public Services Econs Div., HM Treasury, 1980–85; Under Sec., 1985; Hd of Public Expenditure Econs Gp, HM Treasury, 1985–91 and 1993–95; Chief Economic Advr, Dept of Transport, 1991–93. Gwilym Gibbon Res. Fellow, Nuffield Coll., Oxford, 1995–96. *Recreations:* walking, climbing. *Address:* 44 Gibson Square, N1 0RA. *T:* (020) 7359 1053.

SPALDING, Alistair William, CBE 2012; Chief Executive and Artistic Director, Sadler's Wells, since 2004 (Director of Programming, 2000–04); *b* 25 Aug. 1957; *s* of Robert and Pauline Spalding; *m* 2000, Katy McPhee; one *s*. *Educ:* Hatfield Poly. (BA Hons Combined Studies in Humanities); Edge Hill Coll. (PGCE). Arts Programmer, Hawth Th., Crawley, 1988–94; Hd of Dance and Performance, South Bank Centre, London, 1994–2000. Chm., Dance UK, 2004–09. Mem. Council, Arts Council England, 2009–17. Hon. Dr: Middlesex, 2012; Herts, 2014; Roehampton, 2015. Lifetime Achievement Award, Internat. Soc. for the Performing Arts, 2019. Chevalier des Arts et des Lettres (France), 2005. *Recreations:* swimming, hill walking. *E:* artisticdirector@sadlerswells.com. *Club:* 2 Brydges.

SPALDING, Prof. Frances, CBE 2005; PhD; art historian, biographer and critic; Fellow, Clare Hall, Cambridge, 2016, now Emeritus; *b* 16 July 1950; *d* of Hedley Stinston Crabtree and Margaret (*née* Holiday); *m* 1974, Julian Spalding, *qv* (marr. diss. 1991); one *s*. *Educ:* Farringtons Sch.; Univ. of Nottingham (BA Hons 1972); PhD CNAA 1988. Lectr in Art Hist., Sheffield City Poly., 1978–88; ind. scholar, 1989–99; Lectr in Art Hist., 2000–02, Reader in 20th Century British Art, 2002–07, Prof. of Art History, 2007–15, Univ. of Newcastle upon Tyne. Ed., The Burlington Mag., 2015–16. Res. co-ordinator, Writers-in-Prison Cttee, 1991–93, Mem. Exec. Cttee, English Centre of Internat. PEN, 1997–2004 (Vice-Chm., 2000). Member, Council: Charleston Trust, 1990–2011 (Emeritus Trustee, 2011); RSL, 2005–09; Editor, Charleston Mag., 1992–2000. Ashby Lectr, 1997, Vis. Fellow, 1998, Clare Hall, Cambridge; Assoc. Vis. Mem., Darwin Coll., Cambridge, 2002; Paul Mellon Sen. Res. Fellow and Vis. Fellow, Newnham Coll. Cambridge, 2005–06. Chair of Trustees, Art and Christianity, 2017–; Trustee: Hampstead Church Music Trust, 1999–; NW Essex Art Collection, 2014–; Artworkers' Guild, 2019–. FRSL 1984; Hon. FRCA 1998. *Publications:* Magnificent Dreams: Burne-Jones and the late Victorians, 1978; Whistler, 1979, rev. edn 1994; Roger Fry: art and life, 1980, rev. edn 1999; Vanessa Bell, 1983; British Art since 1900, 1986; Stevie Smith: a critical biography, 1988, rev. edn 2002; A Dictionary of 20th Century British Painters and Sculptors, 1990; Paper Darts: selected letters of Virginia Woolf, 1991, rev. as The Illustrated Letters of Virginia Woolf, 2017; Dance Till the Stars Come Down: a biography of John Minton, 1991, rev. edn 2005; Duncan Grant, 1997; The Tate: a history, 1998; The Bloomsbury Group, 1998, rev. edn 2005; Gwen Raverat: friends, family and affections, 2001; Ravilious in Public, 2003, rev. edn 2019; (with David Fraser Jenkins) John Piper in the 1930s: abstraction on the beach, 2003; John Piper, Myfanwy Piper: lives in art, 2009; Prunella Clough: regions unmapped, 2012; Virginia Woolf: art, life and vision, 2014; (with Simon Martin) John Minton: a centenary, 2017; contrib. TLS, Guardian, Burlington Mag., etc. *Recreation:* music. *Address:* c/o Coleridge & Rogers, 20 Powis Mews, W11 1JN. *T:* (020) 7221 3717; The Flat, 70 Gloucester Crescent, NW1 7EG. *Clubs:* Athenæum, PEN.

SPALDING, Julian, FMA; writer and broadcaster; Master, Guild of St George (John Ruskin's Guild), 1996–2005 (Director, 1983–2005; Companion, 1978); *b* 15 June 1947; *s* of Eric Peter Spalding and Margaret Grace Savager; *m* 1st, 1974, Frances (*née* Crabtree) (*see* F. Spalding) (marr. diss. 1991); one *s*; 2nd, 1991, Gillian (*née* Tait), conservation advisor. *Educ:* Chislehurst and Sidcup Grammar Sch. for Boys; Univ. of Nottingham (BA Hons Fine Art). Dip. Museums Assoc., 1973; FMA 1983. Art Assistant: Leicester Museum and Art Gall., 1970; Durham Light Infantry Mus. and Arts Centre, 1971; Sheffield City Art Galleries: Keeper, Mappin Art Gall., 1972–76; Dep. Dir, 1976–82; Dir of Arts, Sheffield City Council, 1982–85; Dir, Manchester City Art Galls, 1985–89; Acting Dir, Nat. Mus. of Labour History, 1987–88; Dir, Glasgow Museums and Art Galls, 1989–98. Res. Fellow, Nat. Mus. of Denmark, Copenhagen, 1999–2000. Art Panel Mem., Arts Council of GB, 1978–82 (Chm., Exhibns Sub-Cttee, 1981–82 and 1986–); Founder: Art Galleries Assoc., 1976 (Mem. Cttee, 1976–89, Chm., 1987–89); Campaign for Drawing, 2000. Member: Crafts Council, 1986–90 (Member: Projects and Orgn Cttee, 1985–87; Purchasing Cttee, 1986–90; Exhibns Cttee, 1986–90); British Council, 1987–96 (Mem., Fine Arts Adv. Cttee, 1987–96). Dir, Niki de Saint Phalle Foundn, 1994. BBC broadcaster (talks and reviews); Third Ear, BBC Radio Three, 1988. *Publications:* L. S. Lowry, 1979; Three Little Books on Painting, 1984; Is There Life in Museums?, 1990; Glasgow Gallery of Modern Art, 1996; The Poetic Museum: reviving historic collections, 2002; The Eclipse of Art: tackling the crisis in art today, 2003; The Art of Wonder: a history of seeing, 2005 (Sir Banister Fletcher Award, Authors' Club, 2006); Peter Angermann: art and life, 2009; The Best Art You've Never Seen: 101 hidden treasures from around the world, 2010; Con Art: why you should sell your Damien Hirsts while you can, 2012; Nothing On: a satirical novel about contemporary art, 2012; The Art of Peter Angermann, 2012; (contrib.) Summers of Discontent: the purpose of the arts today, 2014; Realisation: from seeing to understanding, 2015; pamphlets and exhibition catalogues, including: Modern British Painting 1900–1960, 1975; Fragments against Ruin, 1981; Francis Davison, 1983; George Fullard Drawings, 1984; The Forgotten Fifties, 1984; Modern Art in Manchester, 1986; The Art of Watercolour, 1987; L. S. Lowry, 1987; Ken Currie, 1988; Funfair or Church?, RSA, 1989; Glasgow's Great British Art Exhibition, 1990; Clouds and Tigers: the art of Hock Aun Teh, 1996; Elisabeth Frink Catalogue Raisonné, 2012; contrib. Art Newspaper, Museums Jl, Jackdaw. *Recreations:* drawing, gardening. *Address:* The Stables, Torsonce, Stow, Galashiels TD1 2SN. *E:* julianspalding@me.com.

SPALL, Timothy Leonard, OBE 2000; actor, since 1978; *b* 27 Feb. 1957; *s* of Joseph and Sylvia Spall; *m* 1981, Shane Baker; one *s* two *d*. *Educ:* Battersea Co. Comprehensive Sch.; Kingsway and Princeton Coll.; RADA. Birmingham Rep., 1978–79; *theatre* includes: Royal Shakespeare Co., 1978–80: Merry Wives of Windsor, Nicholas Nickleby; The Three Sisters; National Theatre: Saint Joan, 1985; Mandragola, 1985; Le Bourgeois Gentilhomme, 1993; A Midsummer Night's Dream, 1994; This is a Chair, Royal Court, 1996; The Caretaker, Old Vic, 2016; *television* includes: The Brylcreem Boys, 1978; Auf Wiedersehen Pet, 4 series, 1983–84, 2002–04; Christmas Special, 2004; Roots, 1993; Frank Stubbs Promotes, 1994–95; Outside Edge, 1994–96; Neville's Island, 1997; Our Mutual Friend, 1997; Shooting the Past, 1999; The Thing About Vince, 2000; Vacuuming Completely Nude in Paradise, 2001; Perfect Strangers, 2001; Bodily Harm, 2002; Cherished, 2005; Mr Harvey Lights a Candle, 2005; The Street, 2006, 2007; Mysterious Creatures, 2006; A Room with a View, 2007; Oliver Twist, 2007; The Street, 2008–09; Gunrush, 2009; The Fattest Man in Britain, 2009; The Syndicate, 2012; Blandings, 2013–14; The Enfield Haunting, 2015; Fungus the Bogeyman, 2015; Hatton Garden, 2019; Summer of Rockets, 2019; documentaries: Timothy Spall: Somewhere at Sea, 2010; Timothy Spall: Back at Sea, 2011; Timothy Spall: All at Sea, 2013; *films* include: Quadrophenia, 1978; Gothic, 1986; The Sheltering Sky, 1989; Life is Sweet, 1990; Secrets and Lies, Hamlet, 1996; The Wisdom of Crocodiles, Still Crazy, 1998; Topsy Turvy, Clandestine Marriage, 1999; Love's Labours Lost, Vatel, 2000; Lucky Break, Intimacy, 2001; Rock Star, Vanilla Sky, All or Nothing, 2002; Nicholas Nickleby, My House in Umbria, Gettin' Square, The Last Samurai, 2003; Harry Potter and the Prisoner of Azkaban, Lemony Snicket's A Series of Unfortunate Events, 2004; Harry Potter and the Goblet of Fire, 2005; Pierrepoint, 2006; Enchanted, Death Defying Acts, 2007; Sweeney Todd: The Demon Barber of Fleet Street, Appaloosa, 2008; The Damned United, Harry Potter and the Half-Blood Prince, From Time to Time, Desert Flower, 2009; Heartless, Harry Potter and the Deathly Hallows, Pt 1, 2010; The King's Speech, Wake Wood, Harry Potter and the Deathly Hallows, Pt 2, Reuniting the Rubins, 2011; Comes a Bright Day, Ginger & Rosa, Love Bite, 2012; Love Punch, Mr Turner, 2014; Stanley a Man of Variety, 2016; Denial, The Journey, Away, The Party, 2017; Finding Your Feet, 2018; Mrs Lowry and Son, 2019. Patron: Horniman Mus., 1999–; ChildHope, 2002–. Fellow, Goldsmiths, Univ. of London, 2011; FRSA 2000. *Recreations:* boating, strolling. *Address:* c/o Markham, Froggatt & Irwin, 4 Windmill Street, W1T 2HZ. *T:* (020) 7636 4412. *Club:* Colony.

SPALTON, Prof. David John, FRCS, FRCP, FRCOphth; Consultant Ophthalmic Surgeon, St Thomas' Hospital, London, 1983–2012, now Emeritus; Professor of Ophthalmology, King's College, London, since 2010; *s* of John and Babs Spalton; *m* 1979, Catherine Bompas; three *s*. *Educ:* Buxton Coll., Buxton, Derbys; Westminster Med. Sch., London (MB BS 1970). FRCS 1976; FRCOphth 1989; FRCP 1992. RSO, Moorfields Eye Hosp., 1973–77; Consultant Ophthalmic Surgeon, Charing Cross Hosp., 1980–83. Hon. Consultant Ophthalmic Surgeon: Royal Hosp., Chelsea, 1989–2012; King Edward VII's Hosp. (Sister Agnes), London, 1998–2018; Hon. Civilian Advr in Ophthalmology, Metropolitan Police, 1999–. Pres., UK and Ireland Soc. of Cataract & Refractive Surgeons, 2007–09 (Choyce Medal Lectr, 2001; Lifetime Achievement Award, 2013; Rayner Medal Lectr, 2018). Member: Amer. Soc. of Cataract and Refractive Surgeons, 1992–; Board, Eur. Soc. of Cataract and Refractive Surgeons, 2006–13 (Ridley Medal Lectr, 2011; Pres., 2016–18; Chairman: Exec. Cttee, 2016–18; Program Cttee, 2016–18 (Mem., 2018–); Res. Cttee, 2016–18; Educn Cttee, 2018–). Ophthalmic Advr, Motor Sports Assoc., 2013–. Consultant to ophthalmic device companies. Trustee: Elizabeth Frankland Moore and Star Foundn, 1997–; Fight for Sight, 2012–. *Publications:* (ed jtly) Atlas of Clinical Ophthalmology, 1985 (Best Med. Textbook of Year, Abbott Prize for Med. Writing), 3rd edn 2004 (BMA prize for Best Med. Textbook of Year); over 170 peer-reviewed scientific papers. *Recreations:* my family and other animals, fly fishing, gardening, ophthalmology. *Address:* The Spalton LLP, 3 Highdown Road, SW15 5BU. *T:* (020) 8789 8309. *E:* profspalton@gmail.com. *W:* www.davidspalton.com. *Club:* Garrick.

**SPALVINS, Janis Gunars, (John)**; Chairman: Galufo Pty Ltd, since 1991; Westall Pty Ltd, since 1981; *b* 26 May 1936; *s* of Peter Spalvins and Hilda Blumentals; *m* 1961, Cecily Westall Rymill (*d* 1991); two *s*. *Educ*: Concordia College, Adelaide; Univ. of Adelaide (BEc). FCIS 1961; FASA 1967. Camelec Group of Cos, 1955–73 (Group Sec./Dir, subsidiary cos); Adelaide Steamship Co.: Asst Gen. Manager, 1973; Gen. Manager, 1977; Chief Gen. Manager and Dir, 1979; Man. Dir, 1981–91. Dir and Chief Exec., David Jones Ltd, 1980–91. Mem., Business Council of Australia, 1986–91. FAIM; MInstD Australia, 1981. *Recreations*: snow ski-ing, water ski-ing, tennis, sailing. *Address*: Galufo Pty, 2 Brookside Road, Springfield, SA 5062, Australia. *T*: (8) 83792965.

**SPANIER, Suzy Peta, (Mrs D. G. Spanier)**; *see* Menkes, S. P.

**SPARKE, Andrew Philip**; Director, Andrew Sparke Consulting, since 2009; Owner and Managing Director, APS Publications, since 2014; *b* 22 July 1956; *s* of Philip Aubrey Sparke and Sheila Myrtle Sparke; *m* 1980, Laura Emma Simmons; one *s* one *d*; partner, Elizabeth Mary Bennett; one *s* (and one *s* decd). *Educ*: Manchester Univ. (LLB Hons 1977). Technician and Surveying Asst, S Hams DC, 1974; admitted Solicitor, 1980. Articled Clerk, Derby CC, 1978–80; Printing Asst, BP, 1981; Solicitor, Kingston upon Hull CC, 1981–85; Asst Town Clerk, 1985–90, Dep. Dir of Corporate Services, 1990–94, Enfield LBC; Chief Exec., Lincoln CC, 1994–99; Clerk to W Midlands Police Authy, 1999–2005; Chief Exec., Dudley MBC, 1999–2008. Adviser: Public Sector plc, 2008–19; Leaps & Bounds (Inspiring Change) Trust Ltd, 2008–18. *Publications*: The Compulsory Competitive Tendering Guide, 1993, rev. edn 1995; The Practical Guide to Externalising Local Authority Services, 1994; The Butterworths Best Value Manual, 1999; Broken English (verse), 2013; Indie Publishing: the journey made easy, 2013; Abuse Cocaine & Soft Furnishings (novel), 2013; Copper Trance & Motorways (novel), 2014; Bella in the Wych Elm, 2014, 3rd edn 2018; Rear Gunner, 2014; Fractured Time (verse), 2015; Refracted Light (verse), 2015; Silent Melodies (verse), 2015; Stutthof, 2015; Piggery Jokery in Tonga, 2015; Istanbul: the essential guide, 2015; Istanbul in Pictures, 2015; War Shadows, 2016; Gutter Verse & The Baboon Concerto (verse), 2016; Vital Nonsense (verse), 2016; Wicked Virtue (verse), 2016; Aramoana, 2017; Love & Levity (verse), 2017; Tequila & Me (verse), 2017; Mother Lode (verse), 2017; Tea Among Kiwis, 2017; The Magna Carta Wars of Lincoln Cathedral, 2018; Istanbul: The Essential Visitor Guide, 2019. *Recreations*: writing fiction, travel, ski-ing, badminton, Chelsea FC, creating writing circles. *Address*: 4 Oakleigh Road, Old Swinford, Stourbridge DY8 2JX. *T*: (01384) 390401. *W*: www.andrewsparke.com.

**SPARKE, Prof. Penelope Anne**, PhD; Professor of Design History, Kingston University, since 1999; *b* London, 6 Nov. 1948; *d* of Kenneth Stanley Sparke and Jacqueline Anne Sparke; *m* 1987, John William Small (marr. diss. 2014); three *d*. *Educ*: Green Sch. for Girls, Isleworth; Sussex Univ. (BA 1971; PGCE 1972); Brighton Poly. (PhD 1975). Lectr in Design History, Brighton Poly., 1972–82; Lectr in Design History, RCA, 1982–99; Dean, Faculty of Art, Design and Music, 1999–2005, Pro-Vice Chancellor, Res. and Enterprise, 2005–14, Kingston Univ. *Publications*: (ed) Design by Choice, 1981; Ettore Sottsass Jnr, 1982; Consultant Design: the history and practice of the designer in industry, 1983; Modern Furniture, 1986; Electrical Appliances, 1986; Japanese Design, 1986; (ed) Did Britain Make It?, 1986; An Introduction to Design and Culture, 1900 to the present, 1986, 3rd edn 2012; Design in Context, 1987; Italian Design, 1988; (ed) The Plastics Age: from modernity to postmodernity, 1990; As Long as It's Pink, 1995, rev. edn 2010; A Century of Design: design pioneers of the twentieth-century, 1998; Design Directory: Great Britain, 2001; A Century of Car Design, 2002; (ed jtly) Women's Places: architecture and design 1860–1960, 2003; (ed jtly) Interior Design and Identity, 2004; Elsie de Wolfe: the birth of modern decoration, 2005; (ed jtly) The Modern Period Room: the construction of the exhibited interior 1870–1950, 2005; The Modern Interior, 2008; The Genius of Design, 2009; Japanese Design, 2009; (ed jtly) European Design Since 1985: shaping the new century, 2009; (ed jtly) Designing the Modern Interior: from the Victorians to today, 2009; (ed jtly) Biography and the Interior, 2013. *Recreations*: swimming, historic houses. *Address*: Galveston Lodge, Galveston Road, Putney, SW15 2SA. *T*: (020) 8870 9115, 07799 348650. *E*: penny.sparke@btinternet.com.

**SPARKES, Andrew James**, CMG 2007; HM Diplomatic Service, retired; Ambassador to Nepal, 2013–15; Senior Fellow, Winchester College, since 2016; *b* 4 July 1959; *s* of Rev. James Reginald Sparkes and Brenda Mary Sparkes (*née* Brown); *m* 1985, Jean Mary Meakin (marr. diss. 2003); one *s* one *d*. *Educ*: King Edward's Sch., Edgbaston; Manchester Grammar Sch.; Trinity Hall, Cambridge (MA Hons). MCIPD 1999. English teacher, Japan, 1981–82; joined HM Diplomatic Service, 1983; Second Sec., Political, Ankara, 1985–88; Hd, Political Section, Bangkok, 1992–95; Asst Dir, Personnel Mgt, FCO, 1996–97; on secondment as Dir, Service Exports, DTI, 1997–99; Dep. Hd of Mission, Jakarta, 1999–2001; Dep. High Comr, S Africa, 2001–04; Ambassador: Congo, 2004–07; Kosovo, 2008–10; Dep. Hd, EU Rule of Law Mission, Kosovo, 2010–12 (Acting Hd, 2012). Mem. Council, Royal Soc. for Asian Affairs, 2016–. Chm., Britain-Nepal Soc., 2018–. *Recreations*: music, writing poetry, sailing, golf. *Address*: c/o Winchester College, College Street, Winchester, Hants SO23 9NA. *Clubs*: Oakland Park Golf (Chalfont St Giles); Tanjung Lesung Sailing (W Java, Indonesia).

**SPARKES, Fiona Jane**; *see* Stafford, F. J.

**SPARKES, Jonathan Winston**; Chief Executive, Crisis, since 2014; *b* Elston, Notts, 3 March 1968; *s* of late Donald and Mary Sparkes. *Educ*: Loughborough Univ. (BSc Hons Mgt Sci. 1990). FCIPD 2008. Gp HR Dir, Generics Gp, 1995–2002; Hd of HR, Cambridgeshire CC, 2002–04; HR Dir, 2004–06, Chief Exec., 2006–09, Scope; Director: Workforce Develt, Cornwall and Isles of Scilly PCT, 2010; HR and Orgnl Develt, Royal Cornwall Hosps NHS Trust, 2010–11; Chief Operating Officer, UNICEF UK, 2012–14. *Publications*: (jtly) Leading HR, 2001. *Recreations*: reading, films, travel. *Address*: Crisis, 66 Commercial Street, E1 6LT.

**SPARKS, Leslie Thomas**, OBE 1997; RIBA; consultant architect/planner, specialising in conservation and urban design, since 1999; *b* 3 March 1943; *s* of Eric and Dorothy Leonie Sparks; *m* 1967, Yvonne Ann Sawyer; one *s* one *d*. *Educ*: Kingston Coll. of Art (DipArch); Central London Poly. (DipTP). RIBA 1971; MRTPI 1973. Severn Gorge Projects Manager, Telford Develt Corp., 1977–80; Dir, Envmtl Services, Bath CC, 1980–90; Dir, Planning and Architecture, Birmingham CC, 1991–99; Planning Inspector (pt-time), 1999–2002. Vis. Prof., UWE, 1998–2007. Chm., Expert Panel on Historic Buildings and Land, Heritage Lottery Fund, 1999–2001. Commissioner: CABE, 1999–2006; English Heritage, 2001–08 (Chm., Adv. Cttee, Historic Built Envmt, 2002–03); Chairman: English Heritage/CABE Urban Panel, 2003–10; West Midlands Design Rev. Panel, 2007–16; CABE/Crossrail Design Rev. Panel, 2009–13; West Midlands Cttee, Heritage Lottery Fund, 2010–16; Steering Gp, Ironbridge World Heritage Site, 2011–18; Member: HS2 Design Panel, 2015–; Worcester Cathedral Fabric Adv. Cttee, 2017–18. Hon. Life Mem., English Historic Towns Forum, 1992. Patron, Urban Design Gp, 1997–2010; Chm., Chamberlain Highbury Trust, 2016–; Trustee, Birmingham Conservation Trust, 1999–2012. FRSA 1981. Hon. DDes UWE, 2000. *Recreations*: painting, music, Rugby, cricket, architecture, historic towns.

**SPARKS, Sir (Robert) Stephen (John)**, Kt 2018; CBE 2010; FRS 1988; Chaning Wills Professor of Geology, Bristol University, since 1990 (Professor of Geology, since 1989); Natural Environment Research Council Professor of Earth Sciences, 1998–2003; *b* 15 May 1949; *s* of Kenneth Grenfell Sparks and Ruth Joan Rugman; *m* 1971, Ann Elizabeth Talbot; two *s*. *Educ*: Imperial College London (BSc Hons 1971, PhD 1974). Postdoctoral fellowships, Lancaster Univ., 1974–76, Univ. of Rhode Island, 1976–78, studying physics of volcanic eruptions; Cambridge University: Demonstrator, 1978–82; Lectr in Geology, 1982–89; Fellow, Trinity Hall, 1981–89; Chief Scientist, Montserrat Volcano Observatory, 1997–99. Sherman Fairchild Dist. Scholar, Calif Inst. of Technology, 1987; Hon. Res. Fellow, Nat. History Mus., 2002–05. Studies of volcanic eruptions: Heimaey, Iceland, 1973; Etna, 1975; Soufrière, St Vincent, WI, 1979; Mount St Helens, 1980; Soufrière Hills, Montserrat, WI, 1996–. Chm., Adv. Cttee for Maths Educn, 2012–15; Mem. Council, Royal Soc., 2015–17. Trustee, Natural Hist. Mus., 2015–. President: Geol Soc. of London, 1994–96; Internat. Assoc. of Volcanology and Chemistry of Earth's Interior, 1999–2003. Bakerian Lectr, Royal Soc., 2000. Fellow, Amer. Geophys. Union, 1999. Hon. DSc: Université Blaise Pascal, Clermont-Ferrand, 1999; Lancaster Univ., 2000; Inst. de Physique du Globe, Paris, 2005. Wager Prize for Volcanology, Internat. Assoc. of Volcanology and Chemistry of Earth's Interior, 1983; Bigsby Medal, 1985, Murchison Medal, 1998, Geol Soc.; Arthur L. Day Medal, Geol Soc. of America, 2000; Arthur Holmes Medal, European Geosciences Union, 2004; Thorarinsson Medal, IAVCEI, 2008; Vetlesen Prize, 2015. *Publications*: Volcanic Plumes, 1997; over 460 papers on physics of volcanic eruptions, geology of young volcanoes and origins of volcanism. *Recreations*: music, cricket, travel, cooking, grandchildren. *Address*: Walnut Cottage, 19 Brinsea Road, Congresbury, Bristol BS49 5JF.

**SPARROW, Bryan**, CMG 1992; HM Diplomatic Service, retired; Ambassador to Croatia, 1992–94; *b* 8 June 1933; *m* 1958, Fiona Mary Mylechreest; one *s* one *d*. *Educ*: Hemel Hempstead Grammar Sch.; Pembroke Coll., Oxford (BA Hons; MA). Served Army, 1951–53. Belgrade, 1958–61; FO, 1961–64; Moscow, 1964–66; Tunis, 1967–68; Casablanca, 1968–70; FO, 1970–72; Kinshasa, 1972–76; Prague, 1976–78; Counsellor (Commercial), Belgrade, 1978–81; Ambassador, United Republic of Cameroon, 1981–84, and concurrently to Republic of Equatorial Guinea and Central African Republic, 1982–84; Canadian Nat. Defence Coll., 1984–85; Consul-General: Toronto, 1985–89; Lyon, 1989–92. *Recreations*: gardening, travel. *Address*: The Haven, The Green Avenue, Ambleside, Cumbria LA22 9AU.

**SPARROW, Sir John**, Kt 1984; Chairman, Horserace Betting Levy Board, 1991–98; *b* 4 June 1933; *s* of Richard A. and Winifred R. Sparrow; *m* 1967, Cynthia Whitehouse. *Educ*: Coldfall Primary Sch.; Stationers' Company's School; London School of Economics (BSc Econ 1954; Hon. Fellow, 1994). FCA 1957–77. With Rawlinson & Hunter, Chartered Accountants, 1954–59; Ford Motor Co. Ltd, 1960; AEI-Hotpoint Ltd, 1960–63; United Leasing Corporation, 1963–64; Morgan Grenfell Group (formerly Morgan Grenfell & Co.), 1964–88; Dir, Morgan Grenfell Gp (formerly Morgan Grenfell Hldgs), 1971–88; Chairman: Morgan Grenfell Asset Management, 1985–88; Morgan Grenfell Laurie Hldgs, 1985–88. National & Provincial Building Society: Mem., London Adv. Bd, 1986–89; Dir, 1989–96; Dep. Chm., 1994–96; Chm., Universities Superannuation Scheme Ltd, 1988–96. Chm., Mather & Platt, 1979–81; Director: Federated Chemicals, 1969–78 (Chm., 1974–78); Harris Lebus, 1973–79; United Gas Industries, 1974–82 (Dep. Chm., 1981–82); Coalite Group plc, 1974–82, 1984–89; Gas and Oil Acreage, 1975–78; Tioxide Gp, 1977–78; Peterborough Develt Corp., 1981–88; Short Brothers plc, 1984–89 (Dep. Chm., 1985–89); ASW Holdings Plc, 1987–93; Regalian Properties PLC, 1990–93. Seconded as Head of Central Policy Review Staff, Cabinet Office, 1982–83. Chm., EDC for Process Plant Industry, 1984–85; Chairman: National Stud, 1988–91; Horseracing Forensic Lab., 1991–98. Gov., LSE, 1984–2003 (Vice-Chm. Govs, 1984–93; Actg Chm., 1987–88); Pres., Old Stationers' Assoc., 1995–96. Hon. Fellow, Wolfson Coll., Cambridge, 1987. *Recreations*: cricket, crosswords, horse-racing, reading, lunching. *Address*: Padbury Lodge, Padbury, Buckingham MK18 2AJ. *Club*: MCC.

**SPARROW, Timothy Charles**; Finance and Commercial Director, Department for Digital, Culture, Media and Sport (formerly for Culture, Media and Sport), since 2016; *b* Chelmsford, 7 Oct. 1972; *s* of Alan Sparrow and Christine Sparrow (*née* Mudd); *m* 2001, Lynn Green; one *s* one *d* and one step *s*. *Educ*: Univ. of Luton (HND Land Mgt 1993); Univ. of Greenwich (Postgrad. Cert. Mgt 2004); Anglia Ruskin Univ. (Postgrad. Dip. Mgt 2007). CIPFA 2000. Finance roles, Barking, Havering and Brentwood Community Healthcare NHS Trust, 1994–2000; Corporate Finance Manager, Haringey Council, 2000–01; Finance Manager, Essex CC, 2001–07; Department for Culture, Media and Sport: Hd, Financial Mgt and Accounting, 2007–09; Dep. Hd of Finance, 2009–12; Dep. Dir, Finance, 2012–16. *Recreations*: family, walking, climbing, canoeing, art, conservation. *Address*: Department for Digital, Culture, Media and Sport, 100 Parliament Street, SW1A 2BQ.

**SPAWFORTH, David Meredith**, MA; Headmaster, Merchiston Castle School, Edinburgh, 1981–98; *b* 2 Jan. 1938; *s* of Lawrence and Gwen Spawforth, Wakefield, Yorks; *m* 1963, Yvonne Mary Gude; one *s* one *d*. *Educ*: Silcoates School; Hertford Coll., Oxford (Heath Harrison Travelling Schol.; MA Mod. Langs). Assistant Master: Winchester Coll., 1961–64; Wellington Coll., 1964–80; Housemaster, Wellington Coll., 1968–80. British Petroleum Education Fellow, Keble Coll., Oxford, 1977. FRSA 1994. *Recreations*: gardening, France, history, theatre, walking, sailing, model railways. *Address*: Kimberley, Netherbarns, Galashiels, Selkirkshire TD1 3NW.

**SPEAIGHT, Anthony Hugh**; QC 1995; *b* 31 July 1948; *s* of late George Victor Speaight and Mary Olive Speaight (*née* Mudd); *m* 1991, Gabrielle Anne Kooy-Lister; two *s* one *d*. *Educ*: St Benedict's Sch., Ealing; Lincoln Coll., Oxford (MA; Sec., Oxford Union Soc., 1970). Called to the Bar, Middle Temple, 1973 (Bencher, 2004). Member: Bar Council, 1986–92, 1998–2000; Bar Working Party on Televising Courts, 1990; Chm., Bar Council Access to the Bar Cttee, 2004–06. Mem., Govt Commn on UK Bill of Rights, 2011–12. Chm. of Res., Soc. of Conservative Lawyers, 2016–19. Chm., Editl Bd, Counsel, jl of Bar of England and Wales, 1990–94. Schuman Silver Medal, FVS Foundn, Germany, 1976. *Publications*: (with G. Stone) The Law of Defective Premises, 1982; Architects Legal Handbook, (ed jtly) 3rd edn 1982 to (ed) 9th edn 2010; (ed jtly) Butterworths Professional Negligence Service, 2 vols, 2000. *Recreations*: theatre, cricket. *Address*: 4 Pump Court, Temple, EC4Y 7AN. *T*: (020) 7842 5555. *Clubs*: Garrick, Carlton (Chm., Political Cttee, 2009–13), Hurlingham.

**SPEAKMAN, Prof. John Roger**, FRS 2018; Professor of Zoology, University of Aberdeen, since 1997; 1000 Talents A Professor, Institute of Genetics and Developmental Biology, Chinese Academy of Sciences, since 2011; *b* Leigh, Lancs, 29 Nov. 1958; *s* of Ernest Wilcock Speakman and Mirian Freda Speakman (*née* Holtom); *m* 1980, Mary Strachan; one *s* one *d*. *Educ*: Leigh Grammar Sch.; Univ. of Stirling (BSc Jt Hons Biol. and Psychol. 1980; PhD 1984; DSc 2011); Univ. of Aberdeen (DSc 1997); Open Univ. (BSc Jt Hons Maths and Stats). University of Aberdeen: Postdoctoral Res. Fellow, 1985–91; Lectr, 1991–93; Sen. Lectr, 1993–95; Reader, 1995–97; Royal Soc. Leverhulme Res. Fellow, 1999; Hd of Div., Rowett Inst., 2000–05; Dir, Inst. of Biol and Envmtl Scis, 2006–11; RSE

Lloyds TSB Fellow, 2007; Wolfson Royal Soc. Merit Award Prof., 2016–. Chinese Academy of Sciences: Bing zhi Forum Prof., 2010; Chinese Acad. of Scis-Novonordisk Great Wall Prof., 2012. Hon. Professor: Univ. of Wenzhou, 2014; Univ. of Dali, 2014. FRSE 2004; FMedSci 2008; MAE 2011; FAAAS 2017; FSS 2017; Fellow, Obesity Soc., USA, 2016. Life Mem., Soc. for Experimental Biol., 1991; Member: Amer. Physiol. Soc.; UK Nutrition Soc.; Amer. Soc. of Nutrition; Mammal Soc.; Soc. for Study of Animal Behaviour; Soc. for Study of Ingestive Behaviour; Assoc. Mem., IMA, 2017. FRSA 2009. *Publications:* Doubly-labelled Water: theory and practice, 1997; Body Composition Analysis in Animals: a handbook of non-destructive methods, 2001; Pandas - Dead end or Dead wrong?: and eleven other short stories from the frontiers of bioscience, 2014; How Dogs Make Us Fall in Love with Them: and eleven other short stories from the frontiers of bioscience, 2015; Shrinking Birds: and eleven other short stories from the frontiers of bioscience, 2016; (jtly) Animal Physiology: an environmental perspective, 2018; over 500 articles in peer-reviewed jls. *Recreations:* photography, travel. *Address:* Institute of Biological and Environmental Sciences, Zoology Building, Tillydrone Avenue, Aberdeen AB24 2TZ. *T:* (01224) 272879, *Fax:* (01224) 272396. *E:* j.speakman@abdn.ac.uk; Institute of Genetics and Developmental Biology, Chinese Academy of Sciences, Olympic Science Park, 1 Beichen xilu, Chaoyang, Beijing 100101, People's Republic of China. *E:* j.speakman@genetics.ac.cn.

**SPEARING, Prof. Anthony Colin,** LittD; William R. Kenan Professor of English, University of Virginia, 1989–2016, now Emeritus (Professor of English, 1987–89); *b* 31 Jan. 1936; *s* of Frederick Spearing and Gertrude Spearing (*née* Calnin); *m* 1961, Elizabeth; one *s* one *d. Educ:* Alleyn's Sch., Dulwich; Jesus Coll., Cambridge (BA 1957; MA 1960); Cambridge Univ. (LittD 2014). University of Cambridge: W. M. Tapp Res. Fellow, Gonville and Caius Coll., 1959–60; Univ. Asst Lectr in English, 1960–64; Supernumerary Fellow, Gonville and Caius Coll., 1960; Official Fellow, Queens' Coll., 1960–87; Univ. Lectr in English, 1964–85; Dir of Studies in English, Queens' Coll., 1967–85; Reader in Medieval English Literature, 1985–87; Life Fellow, Queens' Coll., 1987. Vis. Prof. of English, Univ. of Virginia, 1979–80, 1984. Hon. PhD Lund, 2011. *Publications:* Criticism and Medieval Poetry, 1964, 2nd edn 1972; The Gawain-Poet: a critical study, 1970; Chaucer: Troilus and Criseyde, 1976; Medieval Dream-Poetry, 1976; Medieval to Renaissance in English Poetry, 1985; Readings in Medieval Poetry, 1987; The Medieval Poet as Voyeur, 1993; (trans.) The Cloud of Unknowing, 2001; Textual Subjectivity, 2005; Medieval Autographies, 2012; texts, articles in learned jls.

**SPEARMAN, Sir Alexander Young Richard Mainwaring,** 5th Bt *cr* 1840; *b* 3 Feb. 1969; *s* of Sir Alexander Bowyer Spearman, 4th Bt, and Martha, *d* of John Green, Naauwpoort, S Africa; *S* father, 1977; *m* 1st, 1994, Anne Stine (marr. diss. 1997), *d* of K. Munch; 2nd, 1997, Theresa Jean, *d* of Dr Thomas Sutcliffe; one *s. Heir: s* Alexander Axel Spearman, *b* 9 March 1999.

**SPEARMAN, John;** Chairman: Playback Ltd, 1987–2011; Scholz & Friends, 2002–10; FrameStore Group, since 2001; *b* 25 Nov. 1941; *s* of Thomas Spearman and Elizabeth Alexandra Spearman (*née* Leadbeater); *m* 1st, 1966, Susan Elizabeth Henderson Elms (marr. diss. 1986); one *s* one *d*; 2nd, 1988, Angela Josephine van Praag; one *d. Educ:* Trinity Coll., Dublin (MA). Unilever Grad. Trng Scheme; Lintas Ltd; London Press Exchange; Collett Dickenson Pearce, 1972–89: Man. Dir, 1982–83; Chm. and Chief Exec., 1983–89; Chief Exec., 1992–97, Dep. Chm., 1996–97, Classic FM; Operating Partner, Cognetas LLP, 1995–2008. Chm., Laser Sales (LWT), 1990–93. Member: Government Lead Body for Design, 1991–94; Arts Council of England, 1996–98. Patron Dir, RIBA. Trustee, World Monuments Fund. FRSA 1996. *Recreations:* music, sailing, ski-ing, walking, gardening. *Address:* c/o FrameStore Ltd, 28 Chancery Lane, WC2A 1LB. *Clubs:* Athenæum, Hurlingham; Royal Irish Yacht (Dublin).
*See also T. D. Spearman.*

**SPEARMAN, Richard;** QC 1996; a Recorder, since 2000; a Deputy High Court Judge: Chancery Division, since 2013; Queen's Bench Division, since 2019; *b* 19 Jan. 1953; *s* of late Clement Spearman, CBE and Olwen Regina Spearman (*née* Morgan); *m* 1983, Sandra Elizabeth Harris; three *d. Educ:* Bedales; King's Coll., Cambridge. Called to the Bar, Middle Temple, 1977, Bencher, 2006. An Asst Recorder, 1998–2000; Hd of Chambers, 4–5 Gray's Inn Square, 2012. *Publications:* (with F. A. Philpott) Sale of Goods Litigation, 1983, 2nd edn 1994; (contrib.) Information Rights, Coppel, 2004, 3rd edn 2017; (contrib.) UK Supreme Court Yearbook, vol. 9, 2019. *Recreations:* racquet sports, ski-ing, family. *Address:* 39 Essex Chambers, 81 Chancery Lane, WC2A 1DD. *T:* (020) 7832 1111. *Clubs:* Brooks's, Hurlingham, MCC.

**SPEARMAN, Prof. Thomas David,** PhD; President, Royal Irish Academy, 1999–2002; Pro-Chancellor, University of Dublin, 2009–12; *b* 25 March 1937; *s* of Thomas Spearman and Elizabeth Alexandra Spearman (*née* Leadbeater); *m* 1961, Juanita Smale; one *s* two *d. Educ:* Greenlanes Sch., Dublin; Mountjoy Sch., Dublin; Trinity Coll., Dublin (BA, MA); St John's Coll., Cambridge (PhD 1961). Res. Fellow, UCL and CERN, Geneva, 1961–62; Res. Associate, Univ. of Ill, 1962–64; Lectr in Theoretical Physics, Univ. of Durham, 1964–66; Univ. Prof. of Natural Philosophy, Univ. of Dublin, 1966–97; Trinity College, Dublin: Fellow, 1969, Sen. Fellow, 1994–97, Fellow Emeritus, 1997; Vice-Provost, 1991–97. Chm., Trustee Savings Bank, Dublin, 1989–92. Mem. Council, Dublin Inst. for Advanced Studies, 1999–2002. MAE 1988 (Treas., 1989–2000); Chm., Eur. Acads' Sci. Adv. Council, 2004–08; Vice-Pres., 1983–89, Mem., Governing Council, 1999–2002, ESF; Mem., ESTA, 1994–98. Mem., Rep. Body, C of I; 1968–2001. Gov. and Guardian, Nat. Gall. of Ireland, 1999–2002. *Publications:* (with A. D. Martin) Elementary Particle Theory, 1970; contrib. papers in elementary particle theory, inverse problems and history of science. *Recreations:* walking, reading, gardening, looking at pictures, listening to music. *Address:* St Elmo, Marlborough Road, Glenageary, Co. Dublin, Ireland; Trinity College, Dublin 2, Ireland. *Clubs:* Kildare Street and University, Royal Dublin Soc. (Dublin).
*See also J. Spearman.*

**SPECK, Adrian;** QC 2012; *b* Brighton, 15 Jan. 1969; *s* of Neil Speck and Doreen Hobden; *m* 1995, Kathryn Anne Wilson; one *s* one *d. Educ:* Seaford Head Comprehensive Sch.; King's Coll., Cambridge (BA 1991). Called to the Bar, Gray's Inn, 1993; in practice as a barrister, specialising in intellectual property law, 1994–. *Publications:* (jtly) The Modern Law of Copyright and Designs, 3rd edn 2000 to 5th edn 2018. *Recreation:* long distance gardening, especially vegetables and soft fruit. *Address:* 8 New Square, Lincoln's Inn, WC2A 3QP. *T:* (020) 7405 4321.

**SPECTOR, Prof. Roy Geoffrey,** MD, PhD; FRCP, FRCPath; Professor of Applied Pharmacology, Guy's Hospital Medical School, 1972–89, now Emeritus; Hon. Physician, Guy's Hospital, since 1967; *b* 27 Aug. 1931; *s* of Paul Spector and Esther Cohen; *m* 1st, 1960, Evie Joan Freeman (marr. diss. 1979); two *s* one *d*; 2nd, 1986, Dr Annette Skinner, botanist. *Educ:* Roundhay Sch., Leeds; Sch. of Medicine, Leeds Univ. (MB, ChB, MD); Guy's Hosp. Med. Sch., Univ. of London (PhD 1964; Dip. in Biochem. 1966). FRCP 1971; FRCPath 1976. Lectr in Paediatric Res. Unit, Guy's Hosp., 1961–67; Guy's Hosp. Medical School, subseq. United Medical and Dental Schools of Guy's and St Thomas's Hosps: Reader in Pharmacology, 1968–71; Sub Dean for Admissions, 1975–89; Chm., Div. of Pharmacology, 1985–88. Vis. Prof. in Clin. Pharmacology, West China Med. Univ., Chengdu, 1986–87. External Examiner, Hong Kong Univ., 1994–95 and 1996–97. Vice Chm., British Univs' Film Council, 1976–87. FRSocMed. *Publications:* (jtly) The Nerve Cell, 1964, 2nd edn 1986; (jtly) Clinical Pharmacology in Dentistry, 1975, 6th edn 1995; (jtly) Mechanisms in Pharmacology and Therapeutics, 1976; (jtly) Aids to Pharmacology, 1980, 3rd edn 1993; (jtly) Textbook of Clinical Pharmacology, 1981, 2nd edn 1986, (contrib.) 3rd edn, 1994; (jtly) Aids to Clinical Pharmacology and Therapeutics, 1984, 3rd edn 1993; (jtly) Common Drug Treatments in Psychiatry, 1984; Catechism in Clinical Pharmacology Therapeutics, 1986; (jtly) Drugs and Medicines, 1989; (contrib.) Handbook of Clinical Research, 1994; contribs to jls on pathology, medicine, gen. science, and applied pharmacology. *Recreations:* cookery, music. *Address:* 3 St Kilda Road, Orpington, Kent BR6 0ES. *T:* (01689) 810069. *E:* r.spector@ntlworld.com.

**SPECTOR, Prof. Timothy David,** MD; FRCP; Professor of Genetic Epidemiology, and Director, Department of Twin Research and Genetic Epidemiology (formerly Twin Research Unit), King's College London, since 1993; Consultant Rheumatologist, St Thomas' Hospital, since 1993; *b* 14 July 1958; *s* of Walter and June Spector; *m* 1988, Veronique Bataille; one *s* one *d. Educ:* St Bartholomew's Hosp. Med. Sch. (MB BS 1982); London Sch. of Hygiene and Tropical Medicine (MSc 1986); MD London 1989. FRCP 1995. SHO in Medicine, 2-year Eur. rotation, St Bartholomew's Hosp., UCL and Brussels, 1983–85; Wellcome Res. Fellow in Clin. Epidemiol., London Hosp. Med. Coll., 1985–88; Sen. Registrar in Rheumatol., St Bartholomew's Hosp., 1988–93. FMedSci 2016. *Publications:* An Introduction to General Pathology, 1999; Your Genes Unzipped, 2003; Identically Different, 2012; The Diet Myth, 2015; over 800 res. medical articles. *Recreations:* ski-ing, sailing, wine. *Address:* Department of Twin Research and Genetic Epidemiology, King's College London, St Thomas' Campus, Lambeth Palace Road, SE1 7EH. *E:* tim.spector@kcl.ac.uk.

**SPEDDING, John Henry Fryer F.;** *see* Fryer-Spedding.

**SPEED, Jeffery John,** CBE 1991; Director of Fundraising and Treasurer's Department, Conservative Central Office, 1995–96; *b* 3 Oct. 1936; *s* of late Herbert Victor Speed and Dorothy Barbara Speed (*née* Mumford); *m* 1985, Hilary Anne Busfield, *d* of late Haley Busfield, Mayfield, Sussex. *Educ:* Bedford Modern Sch. General Motors (Vauxhall), 1955–58; Sales Manager, later Sales Dir, Tompkins Moss Gp, 1959–65; Conservative Party Agent, 1965–78; Dep. Central Office Agent, S Eastern Area, 1978–82; Central Office Agent: E Midlands Area, 1982–88; Greater London Area, 1988–93; Dir, Constituency Services, Cons. Central Office, 1993–95. Election Agent for: Rt Hon. Iain MacLeod, 1970; Cecil Parkinson, Nov. 1970; Rt Hon. Edward Heath, Feb. and Oct. 1974. FInstLM (FISM 1995; MISM 1993). FRSA 1993; FRGS 2003. *Publications:* Tudor Townscapes, 2000; articles in Internat. Map Collectors' Jl. *Recreations:* antique maps (especially those by John Speed, 1552–1629), oenology, travel (particularly in Spain), musical theatre and film.

**SPEED, Malcolm Walter;** Chairman: Brian Ward & Partners, 2009; Cycling Australia, 2014–17; *b* 14 Sept. 1948; *s* of Walter and Audrey Speed; *m* 1971, Allison Cutter; three *d. Educ:* Melbourne Univ. (LLB). Admitted barrister and solicitor, Melbourne, 1971; called to Victorian Bar, 1981; Solicitor, 1971–81, Barrister, 1981–94, Melbourne; sports consultant, and Exec. Chm., Basketball Australia, 1994–97; Chief Executive: Australian Cricket Bd, 1997–2001; ICC, 2001–08. Sen. Fellow, Melbourne Law Sch., Univ. of Melbourne. *Recreations:* golf, cricket, walking, reading, Australian history. *Clubs:* Wentworth Golf; Australian, Melbourne Cricket.

**SPEED, Stephen John Charles,** CB 2018; Director, Nuclear (formerly Civil Nuclear), Department for Business, Energy and Industrial Strategy, since 2016; *b* Liverpool, 28 May 1962; *s* of John Raymond Speed and Sheila Veronica Speed (*née* Kelly); *m* 1992, Louise Elizabeth Nash; one *d. Educ:* St Edward's Coll., Liverpool; Univ. of Sheffield (BSc Hons Physics 1983); Imperial Coll. London (MBA 1998). Researcher, nano-metrology and X-ray optics, Nat. Physical Lab., 1983–89; Department of Trade and Industry: Eur. Policy, 1989–90; Post Office Sponsorship, 1990–91; Private Secretary: to Sec. of State for Trade and Industry, 1991–92; to Parly Under Sec. of State, 1992; Service Mgt Directorate, 1992–94; Prog. Finance Coordinator, 1994–97; Dep. Dir, Sci. Res. Policy and Funding, OST, 1999–2003; Dep. Dir, Broadband and Telecoms, DTI, 2003–05; Dir, Regl Econ. Develt, DTI, subseq. BERR, 2005–07; Inspector Gen. and Chief Exec., Insolvency Service, 2007–12; Dir, Energy Develt, DECC, subseq. BEIS, 2012–16; Acting Dir Gen., Internat. Climate Change and Energy Efficiency, DECC, 2013–14. Chm., ACE (formerly Assoc. of Chief Execs of Govt Bodies), 2011–12; Vice-Chm., Internat. Assoc. of Insolvency Regulators, 2011–12. *Recreations:* cycling, ski-ing, walking, music. *Address:* Department for Business, Energy and Industrial Strategy, 1 Victoria Street, SW1H 0ET.

**SPEED, Prof. Terence Paul,** PhD; FRS 2013; Honorary Research Associate and Laboratory Head, Walter and Eliza Hall Institute of Medical Research, since 2015 (Senior Principal Research Scientist, 1997–2015); *b* Victor Harbor, SA, 14 March 1943; *s* of Harold Hector Speed and Jeanette Elizabeth Speed (*née* Hacklin); *m* 1964, Freda Elizabeth Pollard. *Educ:* University High Sch., Melbourne; Univ. of Melbourne (BSc Hons 1965); Monash Univ. (PhD 1969; DipEd 1969). Tutor, 1965–66, Sen. Tutor, 1966–67, Lectr, 1967–69, Dept of Maths, Monash Univ.; Lectr, Dept of Probability and Stats, Univ. of Sheffield, 1969–73; Associate Prof., 1974–75, Prof., 1975–82, Dept of Maths, Univ. of WA; Chief, Div. of Maths and Stats, CSIRO, 1983–87; Prof. of Statistics, 1987–2009, Prof. Emeritus, 2009–18, Univ. of Calif, Berkeley. Walter and Eliza Hall Institute of Medical Research: Jt Hd, Genetics and Bioinformatics Div., 1997–2005; Hd, Bioinformatics Div., 2005–14. Hon. DSc: WA, 2005; Chicago, 2014. *Publications:* (trans.) J. Neveu, Discrete Parameter Martingales, 1974; (trans. with T. Hida) T. Hida, Brownian Motion, 1980; (ed with L. Rade) Teaching Statistics in the Computer Age: proceedings of the Round Table Conference on the impact of calculators and computers on teaching statistics, 1985; (ed with M. S. Waterman) Genetic Mapping and DNA Sequencing, 1996; (with D. Nolan) Stat Labs: mathematical statistics through applications, 2000; (ed) Statistical Analysis of Gene Expression Microarray Data, 2003; (ed jtly) Research in Computational Molecular Biology: proceedings of the 11th Annual International Conference RECOMB, 2007; (with Deborah Nolan) Probability and Statistics: essays in honor of David A. Freedman, 2008; approx. 300 articles on maths, statistics, genetics and genomics in jls. *Recreations:* running, reading, opera, movies. *Address:* Walter and Eliza Hall Institute of Medical Research, 1G Royal Parade, Parkville, Vic 3052, Australia. *T:* (3) 93452697, *Fax:* (3) 93470852. *E:* terry@wehi.edu.au.

**SPEIGHT, Prof. Paul Michael,** PhD; FDSRCPSGlas, FDSRCS, FRCPath; Professor of Oral and Maxillofacial Pathology and Consultant Histopathologist, University of Sheffield, 2003–17, now Emeritus (Dean, School of Clinical Dentistry, 2007–15); *b* Harrogate, Yorks, 25 Oct. 1954; *s* of John Maurice Speight and Beryl Estelle Speight (*née* Somerwell); *m* 1989, Prof. Paula Farthing; two *s* two *d. Educ:* Harrogate Grammar Sch.; Univ. of Manchester (BDS 1978); Univ. of Dundee (PhD 1984). FDSRCPSGlas 1982, Hon. FDSRCPSGlas 2017; FRCPath 1989; FDSRCS *ad eundem* 1998; FDSRCSEd *ad hominem* 2003. House Surgeon, Dundee Dental Hosp., 1979–80; MRC Res. Trng Fellow, Univ. of Dundee, 1980–83; Postgrad. Tutor, Riyadh, Saudi Arabia, 1984–85; Sen. Lectr in Oral Pathol., Med. Coll., 1985–89; University College London: Hd, Oral Pathol., Eastman Dental Inst., 1990–2003; Prof. of Oral Pathol., 1997–2003; Hd, Cellular Pathol., UCL Hosps NHS Trust, 2002–03. President: British Soc. for Oral and Maxillofacial Pathol.,

2000–03 (Mem., 1985–; Mem. Council, 1989–2010; Treas., 1989–2000); Internat. Assoc. of Oral Pathologists, 2006–08 (Mem., 1994–; Sec. and Treas., 1996–2004; Hon. Life Mem., 2016); British Soc. for Oral and Dental Res., 2009–11 (Mem., 1988–; Mem., Mgt Cttee, 1998–2002, 2007–15; Chair, Awards Cttee, 2007–09; Graham Embery Meml Lectr, 2012). Chm., Scottish Bd for Academic Dentistry, 2014–. Member: Panel C10, RAE 2008, 2005–08; Panel A3, REF 2014, 2011–14; Adv. Gp, NIHR Dean for Acad. Trng, 2007–17; Bd, Faculty of Dental Surgery, RCS, 2011–17 (Chm., Res. Cttee, 2011–17; Awards Cttee, 2015–17; Vice Dean, 2015–16); Dental Prog. Bd, Health Educn England, 2012–14; Internat. Assoc. for Dental Res., 1988– (Mem., Hatton Awards Cttee, 1998–2000, 2008–10; Dist. Scientist Award, 2008). Lecturer: TC White Prize, RCPSGlas, 1986; Charles Tomes, RCS, 2003; William Guy, RCSEd, 2008. Editor-in-Chief, Archives of Oral Biol., 2002–07. Senate Award for Excellence, Univ. of Sheffield, 2012; John Tomes Medal, British Dental Assoc., 2019. *Publications:* Cysts of the Oral and Maxillofacial Regions (with M. Shear), 4th edn 2007; 250 papers in learned jls; 35 book chapters; over 180 research presentations. *Recreations:* ski-ing, hill walking, travel, family, cafés, vintage cameras, photography, reading (novels and biographies). *Address:* School of Clinical Dentistry, University of Sheffield, Claremont Crescent, Sheffield S10 2TA. *T:* 07774 704869. *E:* p.speight@sheffield.ac.uk.

**SPEIGHT, Rebecca;** Chief Executive Officer, Royal Society for the Protection of Birds, since 2019; *b* Dorchester, 20 June 1967; *d* of Richard and Elizabeth Speight. *Educ:* St Genevieve's Convent, Dorchester; Canford Sch., Wimborne; Durham Univ. (BA English Lang. and Lit.); Heriot-Watt Univ. (MBA). Local Govt Officer, Lothian Regl Council, 1990–95; Sen. Consultant, 1995–99, Dir, 1999–2000, Smythe Dorward Lambert; Gen. Manager, 2000–05, Midlands Dir, 2005–14, National Trust; CEO, Woodland Trust, 2014–19. *Recreations:* walking, cinema, singing, arts. *Address:* Royal Society for the Protection of Birds, The Lodge, Potton Road, Sandy, Beds SG19 2DL.

**SPEIRS, Robert;** Chairman, Stagecoach Group plc, 2002–10 (Director, 1996–2010); *b* 23 Oct. 1936; *s* of John and Isabella Speirs; *m* 1958, Patricia Holt; two *s*. *Educ:* Alleyne's Grammar Sch., Uttoxeter. Cooper Bros, London, 1964–68; Tax Administrator, Texaco Ltd, 1968–77; Tax/Finance Dir, BNOC, subseq. Britoil plc, 1977–88; Finance Director: Olympia and York Canary Wharf Ltd, 1988–93; Royal Bank of Scotland Gp plc, 1993–98; Chairman: Miller Gp Ltd, 1999–2008; Bell Gp plc, 1999–2004; Dir, Canary Wharf Gp plc, 1999–2004. *Recreations:* hill-walking, gardening, military history. *Address:* Arden, Pitts Lane, Pitts Haven, Binstead, Isle of Wight PO33 3AX. *T:* (01983) 568708. *E:* bob.speirs@btopenworld.com.

**SPELLAR, Rt Hon. John (Francis);** PC 2001; MP (Lab) Warley, since 1997 (Warley West, 1992–97); *b* 5 Aug. 1947; *s* of William David and Phyllis Kathleen Spellar; *m* 1981, Anne Rosalind Wilmot (*d* 2003); one *d*. *Educ:* Bromley Parish Primary Sch.; Dulwich Coll.; St Edmund Hall, Oxford (BA PPE). Electrical, Electronic, Telecommunication and Plumbing Union: Res. Officer, 1969–76; Nat. Officer, 1976–92. Contested (Lab) Bromley, 1970. MP (Lab) Birmingham Northfield, 1982–83; contested (Lab) same seat, 1983, 1987. Parly Under-Sec. of State, 1997–99, Minister of State, 1999–2001, MoD; Minister of State (Minister for Transport), DTLR, then DFT, 2001–03; Minister of State, NI Office, 2003–05; Comptroller of HM Household, 2008–10; Opposition Dep. Chief Whip, 2010; Opposition Dep. Spokesman on Foreign Affairs, 2010–15. Mem., Defence Select Cttee, 2015–. *Recreation:* gardening. *Address:* House of Commons, SW1A 0AA. *T:* (020) 7219 0674. *Clubs:* Bromley Labour; Brandhall Labour.

**SPELLER, John Christopher,** MA (Ed); JP; Headteacher, Norton Knatchbull School, 1997–2010; *b* 10 May 1949; *s* of Sydney and Doris Speller, Woodford Green, Essex; *m* 1981, Jennifer Edgar; twin *s* one *d*. *Educ:* Forest Sch., London; Hatfield Coll.; Univ. of Durham (BA Hons French; PGCE); Open Univ. (MA Educn). Asst Teacher, Davenant Foundn Sch., Essex, 1972–76; Head of Languages, Grahame Park Comp. Sch., Barnet, 1977–80; Head of Upper Sch., Nicholas Comp. Sch., Basildon, 1981–83; Dep. Head, Ilford County High Sch. for Boys, 1983–89; Headteacher, Liverpool Blue Coat Sch., 1989–97. PGCE Tutor, Open Univ., 2011–15. JP E Kent, 2011. *Recreations:* cricket, walking, travel (UK and abroad), voluntary education advisory and regulatory work, incl. school governor, independent appeals panel membership. *Address:* 45 Joyce Close, Cranbrook, Kent TN17 3LZ. *E:* johncspeller@hotmail.co.uk.

**SPELLER, Marcelle Elizabeth,** OBE 2011; Founder and Executive Chairman, Localgiving.com, 2008–16; Founder and Chairman, Brevio, since 2018; *b* Manchester, 6 March 1950; *d* of Vernor Speller and Antonia Speller-Kuijpers. *Educ:* Gumley House Grammar Sch.; Univ. of East Anglia (BSc); INSEAD (MBA 1982). Grad. Trainee, British Railways Bd, 1971–74; Account Manager, Lintas, then Benton & Bowles, London, 1974–77; Account Dir, Young & Rubicam, then Doyle Dane Bernbach, Amsterdam, 1977–81; Sen. Manager, European Projects, Heineken BV, Amsterdam, 1982–84; Sen. Mktg Manager, Europe, Avis Car Rental, 1985–86; Vice-Pres., Mktg, EMEA, Inter-Continental Hotels, 1987–88; Vice-Pres., UK Strategic Planning and Irish Ops, American Express, 1988–89; ind. mktg consultant, 1989–92; Bd Dir, Mktg and Sales, Air UK Ltd, 1992–93; Speller Coundley Associates, 1993–96; Co-Founder and Jt Man. Dir, Holiday-Rentals.com, 1996–2005. Dir and Trustee, New Philanthropy Capital, 2016–. Hon. DCL UEA, 2014. Beacon Fellow for Pioneering Philanthropy, 2013; Philanthropist of the Year, Spears Wealth Mgt, 2013. *Recreations:* hill-walking, horse riding, classical music.

**SPELLER, Paul Anthony;** HM Diplomatic Service, retired; Chairman, New Forest Hospital Radio, 2015–18; *b* 21 Jan. 1954; *s* of Cecil Edmund Kirby Speller and Shelagh Maureen Clifford Speller; *m* 1998, Jane Hennessy. *Educ:* Wellington Coll.; University Coll. London (BSc Econ 1976). Joined FCO, 1979; Soviet Dept, 1979–83; Nuclear Energy Dept, 1983–86; Second, later First, Sec., Bonn, 1986–89; EU Dept, 1989–91; Private Sec. to Parly Under-Sec. of State, 1991–93; First Sec., UK Repn to EU, Brussels, 1993–96; Southern Eur. Dept, 1996–98; Dep. Governor, Gibraltar, 1998–2002; Consul Gen. and Dep. Hd of Mission, Jakarta, 2002–05; Hd, SE Asia and Pacific Dept (formerly Gp), FCO, 2005–08. Dir, Internat. Office, Lib Dem Party, 2008–12; Sec. Gen., Lib Dems Abroad, 2010–12. *Recreations:* cricket, tennis, theatre, guitars.

**SPELLMAN, (Irene) Ruth, (Lady Melville-Ross),** OBE 2007; General Secretary and Chief Executive Officer, Workers' Educational Association, since 2012; *b* 14 Aug. 1951; *d* of Vernon A. Hewlett and Jean Hewlett (*née* Weir); *m* 1st, 1979, Dr William Spellman (*d* 2009); one *s* two *d*; 2nd, 2014, Sir Timothy David Melville-Ross, *qv*. *Educ:* Girton Coll., Cambridge (BA Hons Econs and Pol Sci. 1972). FCIPD 1992; CMgr 2010. National Coal Board: Investment Analyst, Pension Fund, 1972–73; Industrial Relns Asst, Manpower and Industrial Res., 1973–76; Educn and Trng Advr, NEDO, 1976–86 (pt-time, 1978–86); Consultant in HR and Managing Change, then Managing Consultant, Coopers & Lybrand, 1986–91; Dir, HR, NSPCC, 1991–98; Chief Exec., Investors in People UK, 1998–2006; CEO, IMechE, 2007–09; Chief Exec., Chartered Mgt Inst., 2009–12. Non-executive Director: Centre for Talent Innovation, 2008–18; Cooperative Gp, 2015–17; Educn and Trng Foundn, 2019–. Member: Council, Open Univ., 2010–15; Bd, NIACE, 2012–15. Trustee: Adviza, 2015–; Learning and Work Inst., 2019–. FRSA 2003. Hon. DSc Cranfield, 2010; Hon. DEd Wolverhampton, 2018. *Publications:* Economic Consequences of New Technology, 1981; Perspectives in Managing Change, 1990; Management and Leaders Who Can, 2011. *Recreations:* music (singing), literature, politics, walking. *Address:* 9 Maybury Mews, Highgate, N6 5YT. *T:* 07824 865389.

**SPELMAN, Rt Hon. Dame Caroline (Alice),** DBE 2016; PC 2010; MP (C) Meriden, since 1997; Second Church Estates Commissioner, since 2015; *b* 4 May 1958; *d* of Marshall Cormack and Helen Margaret Greenfield; *m* 1987, Mark Gerald Spelman; two *s* one *d*. *Educ:* Herts and Essex Grammar Sch. for Girls; Queen Mary Coll., London (BA 1st cl. Hons European Studies). Sugar Beet Advr, NFU, 1981–84; Dep. Dir, European Confedn of Sugar Beet Growers, Paris, 1984–89; Dir, Spelman, Cormack and Associates (food and biotechnology consultancy), 1989–2009. Contested (C) Bassetlaw, 1992. Shadow Secretary of State: for internat. develt, 2001–03; for envmt, 2003–04; for local and devolved govt affairs, 2004–05; DCLG, 2006–07; Shadow Minister: for women, 2001–04; ODPM, 2005–06; Chm., Cons. Party, 2007–09; Shadow Sec. of State for Communities and Local Govt, 2009–10; Sec. of State for Envmt, Food and Rural Affairs, 2010–12. Member: Envmtl Audit Cttee, 2013–15; Jt Cttee on Modern Slavery Bill, 2014; Chair, All Party Parly Gp for the Horse, 2016–. Chm., Parliament Choir, 2013–15. Vice-Pres., Tearfund, 2013–16 (Ambassador, 2017–). *Publications:* The Non-Food Uses of Agricultural Raw Materials, 1994. *Recreations:* tennis, riding, singing. *Address:* House of Commons, SW1A 0AA. *T:* (020) 7219 4189.

**SPENCE, Prof. (Andrew) Michael,** PhD; Philip H. Knight Professor of Management, and Dean, Graduate School of Business, Stanford University, 1990–99, now Professor Emeritus; William R. Berkley Professor in Economics and Business, Stern Business School, New York University, since 2010; *b* 7 Nov. 1943; *s* of Ernest John Hamilton Spence and Mary Jane Spence (*née* Gotschal); *m* 1st, Ann Bennett (marr. diss.); one *s* two *d*; 2nd, 1997, Monica Cappuccini (marr. diss.); 3rd, 2006, Giuliana Ferraino; one *s*. *Educ:* Princeton Univ. (BA Philosophy 1966); Oxford Univ. (Rhodes Schol.; MA Maths 1968); Harvard Univ. (PhD Econs 1972). Asst Prof. of Pol Econ., Kennedy Sch. of Govt, Harvard Univ., 1971–75; Associate Prof. of Econs, Stanford Univ., 1973–75; Harvard University: Hon. Res. Fellow, 1975–76, Vis. Prof., 1977–79, Econs Dept; Prof. of Econs, 1977–83, and Prof. of Business Admin, 1979–83; George Gund Prof. of Econs and Business Admin, 1983–86; Chm., Econs Dept, 1983–84; Dean, Faculty of Arts and Scis, 1984–90. Mem., Econs Adv. Cttee, Sloan Foundn, 1979–. Chm., Commn on Growth and Develt, 2006–09; Mem., Global Commn on Internet Governance. Affiliate, 1999–2009, Sen. Advr, 2009–, Oak Hill Investment Mgt (formerly Oak Hill Venture Partners). Mem. Bd, Stanford Mgt Co., 2008–. Consulting Advr, PIMCO, 2009–. Mem., editl bds of jls incl. Amer. Econs Rev., Bell Jl Econs, Jl of Econ. Theory and Public Policy, at various times. Fellow: Econometric Soc., 1975; Amer. Acad. Arts and Scis, 1983. John Bates Clark Medal, Amer. Econ. Assoc., 1981; (jtly) Nobel Prize for Econs, 2001. *Publications:* Market Signaling: informational transfer in hiring and related processes, 1974; (jtly) Industrial Organization in an Open Economy, 1980; (jtly) Competitive Structure in Investment Banking, 1983; contrib. numerous articles to professional jls incl. Bell Jl Econs, Qly Jl Econs, Econometrica. *Recreations:* windsurfing, motorcycle riding, golf. *Address:* Ohana Investors, 899 Northgate Drive, Suite 301, San Rafael, CA 94903, USA. *E:* mspence98@gmail.com.

**SPENCE, Bill;** *see* Spence, J. W.

**SPENCE, Prof. Charles Jason,** PhD; Professor of Experimental Psychology, University of Oxford, since 1997; Fellow, Somerville College, Oxford, since 1997; *b* Leeds, 18 June 1969; *s* of Allan Wright Spence and Norah Spence; *m* 2008, Barbara Maria Vargas-Escobar. *Educ:* Balliol Coll., Oxford (BA 1991); Corpus Christi Coll., Cambridge (PhD 1995). Jun. Res. Fellow, St John's Coll., Cambridge, 1994–97. Presidential Vis. Prof., Temple Univ., Philadelphia, 2015. Eur. Psychologist of Year, European Soc. for Cognitive Psychol., 2003; 10th Exptl Psychol. Prize, EPsS, 2003; Friedrich Wilhelm Bessel Res. Award, Alexander von Humboldt Foundn, Germany, 2005; IG Nobel Prize for Nutrition, Annals of Improbable Res. mag., 2008. *Publications:* The Secrets of the Senses, 2002; (with J. Driver) Crossmodal Space and Crossmodal Attention, 2004; (jtly) The Handbook of Multisensory Processing, 2004; (with C. Ho) The Multisensory Driver, 2008; (with A. Gallace) In Touch with the Future: the sense of touch from cognitive neuroscience to virtual reality, 2014; (with B. Piqueras-Fiszman) The Perfect Meal: the multisensory science of food and dining, 2014 (Prose Prize for Popular Science, 2015); Gastrophysics: the new science of eating, 2017. *Recreation:* neurogastronomy. *Address:* Department of Experimental Psychology, University of Oxford, Anna Watts Building, Radcliffe Observatory Quarter, Woodstock Road, Oxford OX2 6GG. *T:* (01865) 271364, *Fax:* (01865) 310447. *E:* charles.spence@psy.ox.ac.uk.

**SPENCE, Christopher Alexander,** CBE 2006 (MBE 1992); Chief Executive: National Centre for Volunteering, since 1998; Volunteering England, 2004–07; Hon. President, London Lighthouse, 1996–2000; *b* 24 April 1944; *s* of late Robert Donald Spence and Margaret Summerford Spence; *m* 1990, Nancy Corbin Meadors Kline. *Educ:* Bromsgrove Sch.; South West London Coll. (Dip. in Counselling Skills). Dir, Task Force, 1968–70; Private Sec. to Speaker of House of Commons, 1970–76; freelance organisational develt consultant, 1976–86; Founder and Dir, London Lighthouse, 1986–96. Dir, Oxfordshire Learning Disability NHS Trust, 1996–2002 (Vice-Chm., 1998–2002). Founding Chair, Pan London HIV/AIDS Providers Consortium, 1992–96; Chair, HIV Project, 1997– (Dir, 1995–97). Chm., Diana, Princess of Wales Meml Fund, 1999–2006 (Trustee, 1998–2006; Chair, Grants Cttee, 1998–2006). Pres., Eur. Volunteer Centre, 2002–07. FRSA 1998. Hon. Fellow, Univ. of Wales, Lampeter, 1999. *Publications:* (with Nancy Kline) At Least a Hundred Principles of Love, 1985, revd edn 1994; AIDS: time to reclaim our power, 1986; On Watch: views from the Lighthouse, 1996. *Recreations:* gardening, reading, writing, walking, vegetarian cooking. *Address:* Lower Farm Orchard, Preston Crowmarsh, Wallingford, Oxon OX10 6SL. *T:* (01491) 835266.

**SPENCE, Christopher John;** Chairman, English Trust Co. Ltd, 1991–2002 (Managing Director, 1978–91); *b* 4 June 1937; *s* of late Brig. Ian Fleming Morris Spence, OBE, MC, TD, ADC and Ruth Spence (*née* Peacock); *m* 1st, 1960, Merle Aurelia (marr. diss. 1968), *er d* of Sir Leonard Ropner, Bt; one *d* (one *s* decd); 2nd, 1970, Susan, *d* of late Brig. Michael Morley, MBE; one *s* one *d*. *Educ:* Marlborough. 2nd Lieut, 10 Royal Hussars (PWO), 1955–57; Royal Wilts Yeomanry, 1957–66. Mem., London Stock Exchange, 1959–78. Sen. Steward, Jockey Club, 1998–2003. Chairman: Nat. Stud Ltd, 2007–11; Newbury Racecourse plc, 2010–11 (Dir, 2003–15). High Sheriff, Berks, 1996–97. *Recreations:* racing, shooting, golf. *Address:* Chieveley Manor, Chieveley, Newbury, Berks RG20 8UT. *T:* (01635) 248208. *Club:* Jockey.

**SPENCE, David Lane,** CA; London Senior Partner, Grant Thornton, 1998–2006; *b* 5 Oct. 1943; *s* of Dr Alex S. Spence and Edith F. Spence; *m* 1966, Beverley Esther Cardale; one *s* two *d*. *Educ:* Fettes Coll., Edinburgh; Univ. of Surrey (BA 2012); Univ. of Buckingham (MA 2018). CA 1967. C. F. Middleton & Co., 1962–67; Grant Thornton (formerly Thornton Baker), 1967–2006: Partner, 1970; Eur. Practice Partner, 1974–80; Exec. Partner, 1983–89. DTI Inspector, 1989 and 1992. Chm., Chartered Accountants Jt Ethics Cttee, 1995–97. Pres., Inst. Chartered Accountants of Scotland, 1998–99 (Vice-Pres., 1996–98). Mem. Council, Royal Holloway, Univ. of London, 2010–19. Trustee, DEBRA, 2009–18 (Chm., 2015–18). *Recreations:* golf, occasional cycling, tinkering with old MGs.

*Address:* Hendred, Hatton Hill, Windlesham, Surrey GU20 6AB. *Clubs:* Caledonian; Sunningdale Golf (Captain, 2006–07), Royal and Ancient Golf (Mem., Rules Cttee, 2009–13).

**SPENCE, Rt Rev. (David) Ralph;** Bishop of Niagara, 1997–2008; *b* 10 March 1942; *m* Carol Anne Beatty (*d* 2016); one *s* two *d*. *Educ:* Univ. of Guelph (BA 1964); Wycliffe Coll. (LTh 1968). Ordained priest, 1968; Asst Curate, St George's, Guelph, 1968–70; Rector: St Bartholomew, Hamilton, 1970–74; St John, Thorold, 1974–82; St Luke's, Burlington, 1982–97; Archdeacon of Trafalgar, 1992–97. Chancellor, Renison University Coll., Univ. of Waterloo, 2008–16. Hon. DD: Wycliffe Coll., 1999; Trinity Coll., Toronto, 2000; Huron Coll., 2004. Albion Herald Extraordinary, 2006.

**SPENCE, Dr Isabel Rebecca;** Director, STEMgagement Consulting, since 2018; *b* Chester, 9 March 1979; *d* of Keith Lee and Susan Rothwell (*née* McDonald); *m* 2008, Euan Spence; one *s* one *d*. *Educ:* Birkenhead High Sch. GPDST; Univ. of Warwick (MChem 1st Cl. Chem. and Medicinal Chem.; PhD Chem. 2005). Res. Liaison Officer, Stroke Assoc., 2006–08; Physical Scis Manager, Royal Soc. of Chem., 2008–09; Sen. Policy Advr, BIS, 2009–14; Hd, Public Affairs, Microbiol. Soc., 2014–18. Exec. Sec., Parly and Scientific Cttee, 2017–18. *Recreations:* dog walking, yoga. *Address:* 11 Kingsway, Chalfont St Peter, Gerrards Cross, Bucks SL9 8NS. *E:* isabel.spence@outlook.com.

**SPENCE, James William, (Bill);** Lord-Lieutenant, Orkney, since 2014 (Vice Lord-Lieutenant, 2011–14); *b* St Ola, Orkney, 19 Jan. 1945; *s* of late James William Spence and Margaret Duncan Spence (*née* Peace); *m* 1st, 1971, Margaret Paplay Stevenson (*d* 2000); two *s* (and one *s* decd); 2nd, 2003, Susan Mary Price. *Educ:* Stenness Public Sch.; Firth Jun. Secondary Sch.; Leith Nautical Coll.; Robert Gordon's Inst. of Technol., Aberdeen (Master Mariner 1971); Univ. of Wales, Cardiff (BSc Maritime Law and Maritime Econs 1974). Served Merchant Navy, 1961–74: apprentice deck officer, Watts Watts & Co. Ltd, 1961–65; certificated deck officer, NZ Shipping Co. (P&O Steam Navigation Co. Ltd), 1965–74. Temp. asst site co-ordinator, Scapa Flow Project, Micoperi SpA, 1974–75; John Jolly, Shipbrokers and Stevedores, Kirkwall: Manager, 1975; Jun. Partner, 1976–77; Sen. Partner, 1978–; Man. Dir and Proprietor, 1978–; Chm. Bd, 2003–. MRIN 1971; MNI 1972; MICS 1979. Mem., Kirkwall Community Council, 1978–82. Member: Kirkwall Port Employers' Assoc., 1975– (Chm., 1979–87); Orkney Pilotage Cttee, 1979–88. Kirkwall Station, RNLI: Dep. Launching Authy, 1976–87; Stn Hon. Sec., 1987–96; Chm., Br. Cttee, 1997–2004. Vice Consul for Norway, 1976–77, Actg Consul, 1977–78, Consul, 1978–2015; Vice Consul for Netherlands, 1978–94. Chm., Assoc. of Hon. Norwegian Consuls in UK and Ireland, 1993–95 (Vice Chm., 1991–93). Chm., Orkney Riding Club, BHS, 1985–92 (Mem., 1984–). Trustee, Pier Arts Centre Trust, Orkney, 1980–91 (Chm., 1989–91). DL Orkney, 1988. Hon. Sheriff, Grampian, Highland and Islands in Kirkwall, 2000–. RNLI Gold Badge, 2005. Comdr, Royal Norwegian Order of Merit, 1987; Chevalier, Order of Orange-Nassau (Netherlands), 1994. *Recreations:* oenophilist, equestrian matters, Orcadian history, vintage motoring. *Address:* Alton House, Kirkwall, Orkney KW15 1NA. *T:* (01856) 872268. *E:* bs3920@yahoo.com.

**SPENCE, Canon John Andrew,** CBE 2013 (OBE 2006; MBE 1999); DL; Governor, Church Commissioners, 2005–13; *b* Edinburgh, 30 Jan. 1951; *s* of Henry John Spence and Thelma Spence; *m* 1974, Yvonne May Cameron; one *s* two *d*. *Educ:* George Watson's Coll., Edinburgh; Trinity Coll., Dublin (BA Hons Econs); Harvard Business Sch. (PMD Exec. Educn). Lloyds Banking Group, 1973–2005: posts include: Man. Dir, Business Banking, 1994–98; Chief Exec., Lloyds TSB Scotland, 1998–2000; Managing Director: Branch Networks, 2000–01; Retail Distribn, 2001–03; Dir, Policy and Risk, 2003–05. Non-executive Director: HMRC, 2005–12; Capital for Enterprise Ltd, 2005–13; Skipton Gp Hldgs Ltd, 2009–10; Chairman: Spicer Haart Gp, 2010–; Callcredit Information Gp Ltd, 2014–18 (non-exec. Dir, 2006–09). Dep. Chm., BITC, 2000–16. President: Enable, 1999–2010; Royal Zool Soc. of Scotland, 2007–16; Chairman: Vitalise, 2005–10; Action for Blind People, 2007–10; Essex Community Foundn, 2009–14; SE LEP, 2011–13; Finance Cttee, Archbishops' Council, 2013–; Treas., Queen Elizabeth Diamond Jubilee Trust, 2013–. Lay Canon, Chelmsford Cathedral, 2006–. Member, Board: Anglia Ruskin Univ., 2010–19; Money Advice Service, 2012–14. Mem. (C), Essex CC, 2013– (Cabinet Mem. for Finance, 2014–17, for Health and Adult Social Care, 2017–). DL Essex, 2008. Hon. DEd Anglia Ruskin, 2009. *Recreations:* cooking, eating, drinking, listening to sport and arts, motorcycling, swimming. *Address:* Cuton Hall, Chelmer Village Way, Chelmsford, Essex CM2 6TD. *T:* (01245) 465108. *E:* john.spence@hotmail.co.uk.

**SPENCE, Prof. Jonathan Dermot,** CMG 2001; PhD; Sterling Professor of History, Yale University, 1993–2008, now Emeritus; *b* 11 Aug. 1936; *s* of Dermot Gordon Chesson Spence and Muriel Evelyn Crailsham; *m* 1st, 1962, Helen Alexander (marr. diss. 1993); two *s*; 2nd, 1993, Annping Chin; one step *s* one step *d*. *Educ:* Winchester Coll.; Clare Coll., Cambridge (BA 1959; Hon. Fellow, 2006); Yale Univ. (MA 1961; PhD 1965). Yale University: Asst Prof., then Prof., 1966–, Chm., 1984–86, History Dept; George Burton Prof., 1976; Dir, Div. of Humanities, 1981–83; Mem. Bd of Govs, Yale Univ. Press, 1994–. Hon. Prof., Univ. of Nanjing, 1994–2008; Guggenheim Fellow, 1979–80; MacArthur Fellow, 1988–92. Council of Scholars, Library of Congress, 1988–96. Fellow: Amer. Acad. of Arts and Scis, 1985; Amer. Philosophical Soc., 1993; Corresp. FBA 1997. Hon. degrees from 8 American colls, and Chinese Univ. of Hong Kong, 1996; Hon. DLitt: Oxon, 2003; Cambridge, 2013. *Publications:* Ts'ao Yin and the K'ang-hsi Emperor: bondservant and master, 1966, 2nd edn 1988; To Change China: Western advisers in China 1620–1960, 1969, 2nd edn 1980; Emperor of China: self-portrait of K'ang-hsi, 1974; The Death of Woman Wang, 1978; (ed with John E. Wills) From Ming to Ch'ing: conquest, region and continuity in seventeenth-century China, 1979; The Gate of Heavenly Peace: the Chinese and their revolution 1895–1980, 1981; The Memory Palace of Matteo Ricci, 1984; The Question of Hu, 1988; The Search for Modern China, 1990, 2nd edn 1999; Chinese Roundabout: essays in history and culture, 1992; God's Chinese Son: the Taiping heavenly kingdom of Hong Xiuquan, 1996; (with Annping Chin) The Chinese Century: a photographic history of the last hundred years, 1996; The Chan's Great Continent: China in Western minds, 1998; Mao Zedong, 1999; Treason by the Book, 2001; Return to Dragon Mountain: memories of a late Ming man, 2007. *Recreation:* gardening. *Address:* 691 Forest Road, West Haven, CT 06516, USA. *Clubs:* Athenæum; Yale (New York City).

**SPENCE, Dr Joseph Arthur Francis;** Master, Dulwich College, since 2009; *b* 18 Dec. 1959; *s* of Joseph Arthur Spence and Lenice Mary Spence (*née* Woolley); *m* 1985, Angela Margaret Alexander Fiddes; two *s* one *d*. *Educ:* St Philip's Grammar Sch., Edgbaston; Salesian Coll., Battersea; Univ. of Reading (BA Hons Modern History and Politics); Birkbeck Coll., London (PhD 1991). Master in College, Eton Coll., 1992–2002; Headmaster, Oakham Sch., 2002–09. Governor: St John's Sch., Cambridge, 2005–14; Dragon Sch., Oxford, 2007–15; Windlesham House, 2011–. Trustee: Demarco Archive Trust, 2007–16; Dulwich Picture Gall., 2011–14; Inspiring Futures Foundn, 2011–; Blackbird Acad. Trust, Oxford, 2015–; The Art Fund, 2017–; Place2Be, 2018–. *Publications:* (ed) The Sayings of W. B. Yeats, 1993; (ed) The Sayings of G. B. Shaw, 1993; (ed) The Sayings of Jonathan Swift, 1994; contrib. to Oxford DNB, TLS, Irish Historical Studies, Sunday Times. *Address:* Dulwich College, Dulwich, SE21 7LD. *T:* (020) 8693 3601. *E:* spencejaf@dulwich.org.uk. *Club:* Athenæum.

**SPENCE, Julie Anne,** OBE 2006; QPM 2010; Lord-Lieutenant for Cambridgeshire, since 2017; Chair, Cambridgeshire and Peterborough NHS Foundation Trust, since 2014 (non-executive Director, since 2012); *b* Framlingham, 7 Aug. 1955; *d* of late Alan Edwin Thomas Miller and of Rita Margaret Miller; *m* 1987, (Alfred) John Spence. *Educ:* Colchester Co. High Sch. for Girls; I. M. Marsh Coll. of Educn (BEd Hons Univ. of Liverpool); Univ. of West of England (LLB); Univ. of Exeter (MA); Henley Mgt Coll. and Brunel Univ. (MBA). Teacher, Sidcot Sch., Winscombe, Som, 1977–78; constable to superintendent, Avon and Somerset Constabulary, 1978–99; Asst Chief Constable, Thames Valley Police, 1999–2004; Cambridgeshire Constabulary: Dep. Chief Constable, 2004–05; Chief Constable, 2005–10. Chm., Police Mutual Assce Soc., 2011–. Mem., Press Complaints Commn, 2010–14. *Recreations:* keeping fit, photography, travelling to and walking in beautiful places near and far, wildlife conservation. *Address:* Lieutenancy Office, Shire Hall, Castle Street, Cambridge CB3 0AP. *T:* (01223) 699189. *E:* lord.lieutenant@cambslieutenancy.uk, lieutenancy@cambridgeshire.gov.uk.

**SPENCE, Malcolm Hugh;** QC 1979; a Recorder, 1985–99; a Deputy High Court Judge, 1988–99; barrister-at-law, 1958–2012; *b* 23 March 1934; *s* of late Dr Allan William and Martha Lena Spence; *m* 1967, Jennifer Jane, *d* of Lt-Gen. Sir George Cole, KCB, CBE; one *s* one *d*. *Educ:* Summer Fields, Oxford; Stowe Sch.; Gonville and Caius Coll., Cambridge (MA, LLM). Gray's Inn: James Mould Schol., Holker Sen. Exhibnr, Lee Prizeman; called to the Bar, 1958; Bencher, 1988. Worcester Regt, First Lieut. 1954. Marshal to Mr Justice McNair, 1957; Pupil to Mr Nigel Bridge (later Lord Bridge of Harwich), 1958; entered chambers of Mr John Widgery, QC, 1958; practised mainly in Town and Country Planning and Compensation for Compulsory Purchase; Asst Recorder, 1982–85. Chm., Planning and Envmt (formerly Local Govt Planning and Envmtl) Bar Assoc., 1994–98. Chartered Arbitrator, 2003; Accredited Mediator, 2006; FCIArb 1999. Freeman, City of London, 2001; Liveryman, Arbitrators' Co., 2001. Chm., Wagner Soc., 2002–08. *Publications:* (jtly) Rating Law and Valuation, 1961; The Chambers of Marshall Hall: 125 years, 2005. *Recreations:* trout and salmon fishing, forestry, golf (Captain: Cambridge University Stymies, 1957; Old Stoic Golfing Soc., 1972; Semi-finalist, Scandinavian Amateur Championship, 1964), opera. *Address:* 1 Gray's Inn Square, WC1R 5AA. *T:* (020) 7405 4379, *T:* (01687) 450698. *Club:* Hawks (Cambridge).

**SPENCE, Michael;** *see* Spence, A. M.

**SPENCE, Michael James,** AC 2017; DPhil; Vice-Chancellor and Principal, University of Sydney, since 2008; *b* Sydney, 10 Jan. 1962; *s* of James Spence and Judith Fay Spence; *m* 1st, 1990, Beth Ann Peterson (*d* 2012); two *s* three *d*; 2nd, 2015, Jenny Seon-Young Ihn; two *s* one *d*. *Educ:* Univ. of Sydney (BA Hons 1985; LLB Hons 1987); St Catherine's Coll., Oxford (DPhil 1996); St Stephen's House, Oxford (Post Grad. Dip. Theol. 2005). Fellow and Tutor in Law, 1992–2008, Dean, 1993 and 1995–2000, St Catherine's Coll., Oxford; University of Oxford: Chairman: Law Faculty, 2001–02; Law Bd, 2002–04; Hd, Social Scis Div., 2005–08. Consultant, Olswang Solicitors, 1997–2008. Curate, Cowley Parish, Oxford, 2006–08. Member: Bd, NSW Bd of Studies, Teaching and Educnl Standards, 2014–; Hong Kong Quality Assurance Council, 2015–. *Publications:* Protecting Reliance: the emergent doctrine of equitable estoppel, 1999; (with A. Ohly) The Law of Comparative Advertising, 1999; (ed jtly) The Modern Law of Patents, 2005; Intellectual Property, 2007; contribs to jls incl. Current Legal Problems, Law Qly Rev. *Recreations:* oboe, piano, Chinese, Korean, walking, cycling. *Address:* Office of the Vice-Chancellor and Principal, F23 Administration Building, University of Sydney, NSW 2006, Australia. *T:* (2) 93516980. *E:* vice.chancellor@sydney.edu.au. *Clubs:* Oxford and Cambridge; Australian (Melbourne).

**SPENCE, Prof. Nicola Jane,** PhD; Chief Plant Health Officer, Department for Environment, Food and Rural Affairs, since 2014; *b* W Runton, Norfolk, 22 Feb. 1961; *d* of Sqdn Leader John Spence and Leoné Spence; *m* 1993, Julian Horsley; one *s* one *d*. *Educ:* Mount Sch., York; Bridlington High Sch.; Univ. of Durham (BSc Botany 1982); Birkbeck Coll., Univ. of London (MSc Microbiol. 1986); Univ. of Birmingham (PhD Plant Virology 1992). Res. Scientist, Horticulture Res. Internat., Wellesbourne, 1987–2003; Team Leader, Internat. Plant Health, 2003–06, Hd of Plant Health, 2006–09, Central Sci. Lab., York; Chief Scientist, Food and Envmt Res. Agency, York, 2009–10; Chief Exec., Science City York, 2010–14. Special Prof. in Plant Patholi., Univ. of Nottingham, 2007–; Vis. Prof., Harper Adams Univ., 2017–; Hon. Prof., Univ. of Birmingham, 2019–. Trustee, Royal Botanic Gdns, Kew, 2009–16. *Publications:* The Distribution, Identification, Ecology and Control of Bean Common Mosaic Virus in Africa, 1992; (contrib.) The Gene-for-Gene Relationship in Host-Parasite Interactions, 1997; (contrib.) Biotic Interactions in Plant-Pathogen Associations, 2001; (contrib. with A. J. Murant) Compendium of Umbelliferous Crop Diseases, 2002; (contrib. with S. L. Hughes) Handbook of Plant Virology, 2005; contrib. papers to learned jls, incl. Plant Pathol., Outlook in Agriculture, Plant Disease, Jl Virological Methods, Annals Applied Biol., Jl Phytopathol., Eur. Jl Plant Pathol., Bulgarian Jl Agricl Sci., Archives of Virol., Jl Applied Econs. *Recreations:* walking, cycling, surfing, skiing. *Address:* Department for Environment, Food and Rural Affairs, 2 Marsham Street, SW1P 4DF. *Club:* Farmers.

**SPENCE, Rt Rev. Ralph;** *see* Spence, Rt Rev. D. R.

**SPENCE, Prof. Robert,** FREng; Professor of Information Engineering, Imperial College of Science, Technology and Medicine, 1984–2000, now Emeritus; *b* 11 July 1933; *s* of Robert Whitehair Spence and Minnie Grace Spence (*née* Wood); *m* 1960, Kathleen Potts (*d* 2003); one *s* one *d*. *Educ:* Hymers Coll., Hull; Hull Coll. of Technology (BScEng Hons London External 1954); Imperial College, London (DIC 1955; PhDEng 1959; DScEng 1983; DSc 2018); Dr RCA 1997. FCGI; FREng (FEng 1990). Hull Corp. Telephones, 1950–51; General Dynamics/Electronics, Rochester, NY, 1959–62; Department of Electrical Engineering, Imperial College: Lectr, 1962–68; Reader, 1968–84. Vis. Erskine Fellow, Univ. of Canterbury, NZ, 2002. Hon. Prof., Univ. of Waikato, 2007–. Chm. and Founding Dir, Interactive Solutions Ltd, 1985–90. Officier de l'Ordre des Palmes Académiques (France), 1995 (Chevalier, 1985). *Publications:* Linear Active Networks, 1970; Tellegen's Theorem and Electrical Networks, 1970 (trans. Russian and Chinese); Resistive Circuit Theory, 1974; Modern Network Theory, 1978; Sensitivity and Optimization, 1980; Circuit Analysis by Computer, 1986; Tolerance Design of Electronic Circuits, 1988 (trans. Japanese); Information Visualization, 2001; Information Visualization: design for interaction, 2007 (trans. Chinese); Introductory Circuits, 2008; Rapid Serial Visual Presentation, 2013; Information Visualization: an introduction, 2014; numerous papers in learned jls. *Recreation:* mosaic sculpture. *Address:* 1 Regent's Close, Whyteleafe, Surrey CR3 0AH. *T:* (020) 8668 3649.

**SPENCE, Roger Norman Abbot;** freelance theatre consultant; project director and adviser on arts building projects, since 1984; *b* Lincoln, 28 Sept. 1947; *s* of John, (Jack), H. Spence and Norah M. Spence (*née* Harrison); *m* 1st, 1968, Carmen A. Siedschlag (marr. diss.); one *s* one *d*; 2nd, 1984, Judith Marie Mohekey; one *s* one *d*. *Educ:* Lincoln Grammar Sch.; Lincoln Coll. of Art. Lighting Designer and Chief Electrician: Lincoln Th. Co., 1965–67; Perth Th. Co., 1967–68; Tyneside Th. Co., 1968–72; Prodn Manager, Tyneside Th. Co., 1972–74; Gen. Manager, Scottish Ballet, Glasgow, 1974–80; Admin. Dir, Tynewear Th. Co., 1980–83; Man. Dir, Royal Lyceum Th. Co., Edinburgh, 1983–94;

Associate Producer, Boxcar Films, Edinburgh, 1994–95; Project Director: Sadler's Wells Th., 1995–2000; Wales Millennium Centre, Cardiff, 2000–07; Principal Project Advr, Northern Ballet, Dance Hse, Leeds, 2005–10; Principal Consultant, Nat. Concert Hall, Dublin, 2007–10; Principal Advr, Birmingham Royal Ballet, 2011–14; Project Dir, Sadler's Wells Th., 2012–16; Project Adviser: Dance Hub, Birmingham Royal Ballet, 2016–; Royal Irish Acad. of Music, Dublin, 2016–; Univ. Concert Hall, Limerick, 2017–18. Mem., Dance Cttee, Scottish Arts Council, 1984–91. Director: Edinburgh Capital Gp, 1989–95; Fedn of Scottish Th., 1989–95; SALVO Arts Ltd, 1991–95. Mem. Council, Theatrical Mgt Assoc., 1985–98 (Vice-Pres., 1989–92 and 1995–98; Pres., 1992–95). Director: Th. Investment Fund Ltd, 1992–95; Nat. Ballet of Ireland, Dublin, 2009–16; Sadler's Wells Foundn Ltd, 2016– (Trustee, 2000–08). Member: Assoc. of British Th. Technicians, 1971; UK Theatre (formerly TMA), 1980; Theatre Trust, 2007. FRSA. *Publications:* contributor: Association of British Theatre Technicians Theatre Planning, 1972; Theatre Buildings: a design guide, 2010. *Recreations:* art, heritage, European travel and culture, fine food and wine, gardening, genealogy. *Address:* Rose Bank, 33 Ulundi Road, Blackheath, SE3 7UQ. *T:* (020) 8305 2606, 07885 536072. *E:* roger@abbotspence.com.

**SPENCE, Ronald Blackwood,** CB 1997; Chairman: Probation Board for Northern Ireland, 2004–12; Northern Ireland Legal Services Commission, 2010–15 (Member, 2003–15); Deputy Chairman, National Heritage Memorial Fund and Heritage Lottery Fund, 2006–13; *b* 13 July 1941; *s* of Harold Spence and Margaret Spence (*née* McClure); *m* 1st, 1964, Julia Fitton (marr. diss. 1989); one *s* one *d*; 2nd, 1989, Sarah McKnight. *Educ:* Methodist Coll., Belfast; Queen's Univ., Belfast (BA Hons). Entered NICS as Asst Principal, 1963; Principal, Min. of Develt, 1967–74; Asst Sec., DoE, 1974–80; Head, Econ. and Social Div., NI Office, 1980–82; Under Sec., Dept of Finance and Personnel, 1982–85; Head, Central Secretariat, 1985–90; Under Sec., Dept of Econ. Develt, 1990–94; Permanent Secretary: DoE (NI), 1994–99; Dept for Regl Develt (NI), 1999–2001. Chairman: NI Partnership Bd, 1996–2001; NI Events Co., 1997–2002; The Change Alliance, 2001–09; Blackwood Enterprises Ltd, 2001–09; Ulster Sports Mus. Assoc., 2008–. Mem. Council, Univ. of Ulster, 2007–08. Hon. Sen. Res. Fellow, Inst. of Governance, QUB, 2001–07. *Recreation:* golf.

**SPENCE, Simon Peter;** QC 2009; barrister, since 1985; a Recorder, since 2007; *b* York, 29 June 1963; *s* of Arthur John Spence and Nora Emily Spence (*née* Mills); *m* 1990, Diane Mavis Horsey (marr. diss. 2008); two *s* two *d*. *Educ:* Pocklington Sch.; De Montfort Univ. (LLB Hons 1984); Inns of Court Sch. of Law. Called to the Bar, Inner Temple, 1985; in practice as barrister specialising in criminal law. Mem., Bd of Dirs, Th. Royal, Bury St Edmunds, 2000–07; Chm., Bd of Trustees, Co-Opera Co., 2012–15. FRSA 2006. *Recreations:* walking, reading, opera, theatre, classical music (listening and singing), jazz, cooking, history. *Address:* 18 Red Lion Court, EC4A 3EB. *T:* (020) 7520 6000, *Fax:* (020) 7520 6248. *E:* Simon.Spence@18rlc.co.uk; Dere Street Chambers, 14 Toft Green, York YO1 6JT. *Club:* Farmers (Bury St Edmunds) (Vice-Chm., 2016–18; Chm., 2018–).

**SPENCE, His Honour Stanley Brian;** a Circuit Judge, 1991–2006; Resident Judge, Reading Crown Court, 1999–2006; *b* 3 May 1937; *s* of George Henry Spence and Sarah Spence (*née* Hoad); *m* 1961, Victoria Rosaleen Tapper; one *s* one *d*. *Educ:* Portsmouth Grammar Sch.; Britannia Royal Naval College, Dartmouth. Commissioned Supply and Secretariat Specialisation, RN, 1958; served: HMS Eagle; Staff of FO2 FEF; Portsmouth; 3rd Frigate Sqdn; HMS St Vincent; legal training, 1966–68; called to the Bar, Middle Temple, 1968; served: HMS Terror, Singapore; Staff of Commander FEF; 8th Frigate Sqdn; Legal Advr to C-in-C Naval Home Command and Flag Officer Spithead; retired from RN, 1975; Office of Judge Advocate General of the Forces (Army and RAF), 1975–90; Recorder of the Crown Court, 1987–91. *Recreations:* maintaining a cottage in France, wine.

**SPENCER,** family name of **Earl Spencer,** and **Baron Churchill.**

**SPENCER, 9th Earl** *cr* 1765; **Charles Edward Maurice Spencer;** DL; Baron and Viscount Spencer 1761; Viscount Althorp 1765; Viscount Althorp (UK) 1905; writer; *b* 20 May 1964; *s* of 8th Earl Spencer, LVO and Hon. Frances Ruth Burke Roche, *yr d* of 4th Baron Fermoy; *S* father, 1992; *m* 1st, 1989, Victoria (marr. diss. 1997), *d* of John Lockwood; one *s* three *d* (incl. twin *d*); 2nd, 2001, Caroline Freud (*née* Hutton) (marr. diss. 2009); one *s* one *d*; 3rd, 2011, Karen Gordon (*née* Villeneuve); one *d*. *Educ:* Maidwell Hall; Eton College; Magdalen Coll., Oxford. Page of Honour to HM the Queen, 1977–79; contributing correspondent, NBC News, 1987–91 and 1993–95; reporter, Granada Television, 1991–93; presenter, NBC Super Channel, 1995–96; writer, Planet Wild, 1998–2000; freelance writer, 2001–. Mem. Bd, Whole Child Internat., 2011–. Trustee, Nelson Mandela's Children's Fund, 1997–2001. Patron: Friends of Cynthia Spencer Hospice, 1989–; Royal and Derngate Th., 1999–; Naseby Battlefield Project, 2010–; Northampton Hope Centre, 2011–; Thomas's Fund, 2011–; Brain Tumour Charity, 2012–; Northants Heritage Forum, 2018–. Pres., 1999–2001, Patron, 2002–, Northants CCC. DL Northants, 2005. *Publications:* Althorp: the story of an English home, 1998; The Spencer Family, 1999; Blenheim: battle for Europe, 2004; Prince Rupert: the last cavalier, 2007; Killers of the King, 2014; To Catch a King, 2017; The White Ship, 2020. *Heir: s* Viscount Althorp, *qv*. *Address:* Althorp, Northampton NN7 4HG.

**SPENCER, Charles Easdale;** theatre critic, Daily Telegraph, 1991–2014; *b* 4 March 1955; *s* of Graham Easdale Spencer and Dorothy Aileen Spencer (*née* Brundan); *m* 1983, Nicola Katrak; one *s*. *Educ:* Charterhouse; Balliol Coll., Oxford (BA Hons Eng. Lang. and Lit.). Surrey Daily Advertiser, 1976–79; Arts Reporter, Evening Standard, 1979–84; Chief Sub-editor, The Stage, 1984–86; Dep. Theatre Critic, London Daily News, 1986–87; Asst Arts Editor and Dep. Theatre Critic, Daily Telegraph, 1987–91. Pres., Critics' Circle, 2008–10. Critic of the Year, British Press Awards, 1999, 2008. *Publications:* I Nearly Died, 1994; Full Personal Service, 1996; Under the Influence, 2000. *Recreations:* food, music, staring into space. *Address:* 16 Derwent Close, Claygate, Esher, Surrey KT10 0RF. *T:* (01372) 465591.

**SPENCER, Sir Derek (Harold),** Kt 1992; QC 1980; QC (NI) 1992; a Recorder, 1979–92 and 1998–2001; *b* 31 March 1936; *s* of Thomas Harold Spencer and Gladys Spencer (*née* Heslop); *m* 1st, 1960, Joan (*née* Nutter) (marr. diss.; she *d* 2012); two *s* one *d*; 2nd, 1988, Caroline Alexandra (*d* 2003), *yr d* of Dr Franziskus Pärn, Hamburg; one *s*. *Educ:* Clitheroe Royal Grammar Sch.; Keble Coll., Oxford (MA, BCL). 2nd Lieut, King's Own Royal Regt, 1954–56; served in Nigeria. Part-time Law Tutor, Keble Coll., Oxford, 1960–64; called to the Bar, Gray's Inn, 1961 (Holt Scholar; Arden Scholar; Bencher, 1991–2012); in practice as barrister, SE Circuit, 1961–2013. Councillor, London Borough of Camden, 1978–83; Dep. Leader, Conservative Gp, London Borough of Camden, 1979–81. Contested (C) Leicester South, 1987. MP (C): Leicester South, 1983–87; Brighton Pavilion, 1992–97; contested (C) same seat, 1997. PPS: to Home Office Ministers, 1986; to the Attorney General, 1986–87; Solicitor-Gen., 1992–97. Joint Sec. Cons. Parly Legal Affairs Cttee, 1985–87. Vice-Chm., St Pancras North Cons. Assoc., 1977–78; Treas., City of London and Westminster Cons. Assoc., 1990–91. *Recreations:* reading, swimming, walking.

**SPENCER, Isobel;** *see* Johnstone, I. T.

**SPENCER, His Honour James;** QC 1991; a Circuit Judge, 2001–17; *b* 27 May 1947; *s* of James Henry Spencer and Irene Dulcie (*née* Wilson). *Educ:* The King's Sch., Pontefract; Univ. of Newcastle upon Tyne (LLB). Admitted solicitor, 1971; called to the Bar, Gray's Inn, 1975. A Recorder, 1990–2001. A Pres., Mental Health Review Tribunal, 1999–2017. Mem., Parole Bd, 2002–09. *Recreations:* reading history, cooking and the occasional light exercise.

**SPENCER, Janet;** *see* Carsten, J.

**SPENCER, Prof. John Rason,** CBE 2017; Professor of Law, University of Cambridge, 1995–2013, now Emeritus; Fellow, Selwyn College, Cambridge, 1970–2013, now Emeritus; Bye Fellow, Murray Edwards College, since 2014; *b* 19 March 1946; *s* of Donald Edward Spencer and Catherine Mary Spencer (*née* Cozens); *m* 1972, Rosemary Stewartson; one *s* two *d*. *Educ:* Blandford Grammar Sch.; Selwyn Coll., Cambridge (MA; LLB; LLD 2007). Cambridge University: Asst Lectr, Law Faculty, 1973–76; Lectr, 1976–91; Reader, 1991–95; Chm., Law Faculty, 1995–97; Dep. Vice Chancellor, 2014–16. Ganshof van der Meersch Vis. Prof., Université Libre de Bruxelles, 2015. Mem., Calcutt Cttee on Privacy and Related Matters, 1990; Consultant, Criminal Courts Review, 2000. Hon. QC 2003; Academic Bencher, Inner Temple, 2003; Hon. Member of Chambers: Hardwicke Bldg, 2003; 15 New Bridge St, 2014. DenD *hc* Poitiers, 2004. Chevalier, Ordre des Palmes Académiques (France), 2000. *Publications:* Jackson's Machinery of Justice, 8th edn 1989; (with Rhona Flin) The Evidence of Children: the law and the psychology, 1990, 2nd edn 1993; La procédure pénale anglaise (Que sais-je?), 1998; (jtly) European Criminal Procedures, 2002; Evidence of Bad Character, 2006, 3rd edn 2016; Hearsay Evidence in Criminal Proceedings, 2008, 2nd edn 2014; (jtly) Children and Cross-examination: time to change the rules?, 2012; Noted, But Not Invariably Approved, 2014. *Address:* Murray Edwards College, Cambridge CB3 0DF.

**SPENCER, Dr Jonathan Page,** CB 2002; Chairman, Church of England Pensions Board, 2009–19; Chair, Gibraltar Financial Services Commission, since 2016 (Member, since 2011); *b* 24 April 1949; *s* of John Spencer and Doreen (*née* Page); *m* 1976, Caroline Sarah Armitage; one *s* two *d*. *Educ:* Bournemouth Sch.; Downing Coll., Cambridge (BA); Oxford Univ. (DPhil). ICI Res. Fellow, Oxford, 1973–74; joined Department of Trade and Industry, 1974: Principal, 1977; Principal Private Sec. to successive Secs of State, 1982–83; Asst Sec., 1983; Cabinet Office, 1987–89; Under Sec., 1991; Dir, Insurance Div., then Directorate, 1991–97; Director General: Resources and Services, 1997–2000; Business Competitiveness, 2000–02; Dir Gen., Policy, then Clients and Policy, LCD, later DCA, 2002–05. Member: Admin. Justice & Tribunals Council (formerly Council on Tribunals), 2005–13; SRA (formerly Law Soc. Regulation Bd), 2006–09. Co. dir and public policy consultant, 2006–14. Non-exec. Dir, East Kent Hosps Univ. NHS Foundn Trust, 2007–15 (Dep. Chair, 2010–15). *Recreations:* music, keeping the house up and the garden down. *Address:* Little Eggarton, Godmersham, Canterbury, Kent CT4 7DY.

**SPENCER, Prof. Jonathan Robert,** DPhil; FBA 2018; FRSE; FAcSS; Regius Professor of South Asian Language, Culture and Society, University of Edinburgh, since 2014 (Professor of Anthropology of South Asia, 1999–2014); *b* Dorking, 23 Dec. 1954; *s* of George Spencer and Maisie Spencer; *m* 1st, 1986, Julia Swannell (*d* 1992); 2nd, 1994, Prof. Janet Carsten, *qv*; one *d*. *Educ:* Univ. of Edinburgh (MA Hons Social Anthropol. 1977); Univ. of Chicago (AM 1981); Univ. of Oxford (DPhil 1986). Lecturer: Univ. of Sussex, 1987; LSE, 1989–90; Univ. of Edinburgh, 1990–99. FRSE 2011; FAcSS 2017. *Publications:* A Sinhala Village in a Time of Trouble, 1990, 2nd edn 2000; Anthropology, Politics and the State, 2007; Checkpoint, Temple, Church and Mosque, 2014. *Recreations:* books, jazz, family. *Address:* School of Social and Political Science, University of Edinburgh, Edinburgh EH8 9LD. *T:* (0131) 650 3944. *E:* jonathan.spencer@ed.ac.uk.

**SPENCER, Rt Hon. Mark (Steven);** PC 2019; MP (C) Sherwood, since 2010; Parliamentary Secretary to the Treasury (Government Chief Whip), since 2019; *b* 20 Jan. 1970; *s* of Cyril and Dorothy Spencer; *m* Claire; one *s* one *d*. *Educ:* Colonel Frank Seely Sch., Calverton; Shuttleworth Agricl Coll. (Nat. Cert. Agric.). Farmer, Spring Lane Farm, Nottingham; Proprietor, Floralands Garden Village, Lambley. Member (C): Gedling BC, 2003–11; Notts CC, 2005–13. An Asst Govt Whip, 2016–17; a Lord Comr of HM Treasury (Govt Whip), 2017–18; Vice Chamberlain of HM Household (Govt Whip), 2018; Comptroller of HM Household (Govt Whip), 2018–19. *Address:* House of Commons, SW1A 0AA.

**SPENCER, Hon. Sir Martin (Benedict),** Kt 2017; **Hon. Mr Justice Martin Spencer;** a Judge of the High Court, Queen's Bench Division, since 2017; *b* 19 June 1956; *s* of late Dr Seymour Spencer and Margaret Spencer; *m* 1977, Lisbet Steengaard Jensen; two *s* one *d*. *Educ:* Hertford Coll., Oxford (MA, BCL). Called to the Bar, Inner Temple, 1979, Bencher, 2011; in practice, Hailsham Chambers, 1981–2017 (Hd of Chambers, 2009–16); QC 2003; a Recorder, 2011–17. Chm., Expert Witness Inst., 2017–. *Publications:* (jtly) The Danish Criminal Code, 1999; (jtly) The Civil Procedure Rules in Action, 2000; (contrib.) Risk Management and Litigation in Obstetrics and Gynaecology, ed by R. V. Clements, 2001; (contrib.) McGregor on Damages, 19th edn 2014. *Recreation:* music (Member: St Albans Bach Choir; Carillon Chamber Choir). *Address:* Royal Courts of Justice, Strand, WC2A 2DL. *Club:* Danish.
*See also* M. G. Spencer.

**SPENCER, Matthew Dominic;** Director of Campaigns, Policy and Influencing, Oxfam, since 2016; *b* London, 1964; *s* of Brian Spencer and Ann Spencer; *m* 1999, Eleanor Knight; two *d*. *Educ:* Whitehaven Grammar Sch.; Heaton Comp.; Univ. of Liverpool (BSc Hons Envmtl Biol. 1987). Internat. Coordinator, Rio Mazan Project, Ecuador, 1989–92; Campaigner, then Campaign Manager, subseq. Campaign Dir, Greenpeace UK, 1994–2003; Founder Chief Exec., Regen SW, 2003–08; Hd, Govt Affairs, Carbon Trust, 2008–10; Dir, Green Alliance, 2010–16. Mem., Renewables Adv. Bd, 2005–10, CCS Develt Forum, 2010–12, DECC. Trustee, Oxfam GB, 2016–. *Recreations:* mountains, family, cycling, wildlife. *Address:* Oxfam International, Oxfam House, John Smith Drive, Oxford OX4 2JY.

**SPENCER, Michael Alan;** Group Chief Executive, NEX Group (formerly ICAP) plc, 1999–2018; Treasurer, Conservative Party, 2007–10; *b* 30 May 1955; *s* of Oscar and Diana Spencer; *m* 1st, 1983, Lorraine Geraldine Murphy (marr. diss. 2011); two *s* one *d*; 2nd, 2016, Sarah Georgina Milford Haven. *Educ:* Worth Abbey; Corpus Christi Coll., Oxford (MA). Analyst, Simon & Coates, 1976–80; Vice Pres., Drexel Burnham Lambert, 1981–83; Dir, Charles Fulton, 1983–86; Chairman: Intercapital, 1986–99; Numis plc, 2003–09; FCFM Gp Ltd, 2018–; IPGL Ltd; Dir, CME Gp. *Recreations:* running, riding, shooting, wine, art, politics. *Clubs:* White's, 5 Hertford Street, 67 Pall Mall, Oswald's.

**SPENCER, Michael Gerald;** QC 1989; a Recorder, 1987–2005; *b* 1 Dec. 1947; *s* of Dr Seymour J. G. Spencer and late Margaret (*née* Behn); *m* 1969, Catherine Helen (*née* Dickinson); three *s*. *Educ:* Ampleforth Coll.; Hertford Coll., Oxford (MA Hons). Called to the Bar, Inner Temple, 1970, Bencher, 1996; Mem., Oxford Circuit, 1971, Midland and Oxford, then Midland, Circuit, 1972–. Dir, Yattendon Gp (formerly Yattendon Investment Trust), 1992–. Member: Hertford Coll. Boat Club Soc.; Ampleforth Soc. Chm. and

Trustee, Ampleforth Beagles, 1995–. *Publications:* (contrib.) Medical Negligence, 1990; (contrib.) Doctors, Patients and the Law, 1992. *Recreations:* golf, reading, classical music, beagling, paragliding, ski-ing. *Address:* Crown Office Chambers, 2 Crown Office Row, Temple, EC4Y 7HJ. *T:* (020) 7797 8100. *Clubs:* Pegasus, Bar Yacht, Chiltern Rugby Football; Beaconsfield Golf, Inner Temple Golf, Bar Golf.
*See also Hon. Sir M. B. Spencer.*

**SPENCER, Dr Neal Andrew;** Keeper, Department of Ancient Egypt and Sudan, British Museum, since 2012; *b* Brussels, 18 Dec. 1974; *s* of Edward John Spencer and Catherine Spencer (*née* Hunt). *Educ:* Downing Coll., Cambridge (BA Egyptol. 1996; PhD 2001). British Museum: Asst Keeper, Dept of Ancient Egypt and Sudan, 2000–11; Manager, Internat. Trng Prog., 2006–11. *Publications:* A Naos of Nekhthorheb from Bubastis, 2006; The Gayer Anderson Cat, 2007; Kom Firin I: the Ramesside Temple and the site survey, 2008; (jtly) The International Training Programme: towards a global network, 2011; Kom Firin II: the urban fabric and landscape, 2014. *Recreations:* music, food and wine, history of London. *Address:* British Museum, Great Russell Street, WC1B 3DG. *T:* (020) 7323 8311. *E:* nspencer@britishmuseum.org.

**SPENCER, Hon. Sir Robin (Godfrey),** Kt 2010; **Hon. Mr Justice Spencer;** a Judge of the High Court, Queen's Bench Division, since 2010; *b* 8 July 1955; *s* of late Eric Spencer and of Audrey Elaine Spencer (*née* Brown); *m* 1978, Julia Margaret Eileen Burley; three *d*. *Educ:* King's Sch., Chester; Emmanuel Coll., Cambridge (MA). Called to the Bar, Gray's Inn, 1978 (Holker Sen. Award; Colyer Prize), Bencher, 2005; in practice, Wales and Chester Circuit, 1978–2010, Leader, 2004–06; an Asst Recorder, 1993–98; a Recorder, 1998–2010; QC 1999; a Dep. High Ct Judge, 2001–10; a Presiding Judge, South Eastern Circuit, 2013–17. *Recreations:* music, cricket, football, Methodist history. *Address:* Royal Courts of Justice, WC2A 2LL.

**SPENCER, Dame Rosemary (Jane),** DCMG 1999 (CMG 1991); HM Diplomatic Service, retired; Ambassador to the Netherlands, 1996–2001; *b* 1 April 1941; *d* of Air Vice-Marshal Geoffrey Roger Cole Spencer, CB, CBE, and Juliet Mary Spencer (*née* Warwick). *Educ:* Upper Chine Sch., Shanklin, IoW; St Hilda's Coll., Oxford (BA Hons Modern Langs). Joined Foreign Office, 1962; FO, 1962–65; Third Secretary, Nairobi, 1965–67; Second Sec., FCO, 1967–70; Second Sec., UK Delegn to EEC, and Private Sec. to Hon. Sir Con O'Neill, Official Leader of UK negotiating team, 1970–71; First Sec., Office of UK Permanent Representative to EEC, Brussels, 1972–73; First Sec. (Economic), Lagos, 1974–77; First Sec., Asst Head of Rhodesia Dept, FCO, 1977–80; RCDS 1980; Counsellor (Agric. and Economic Affairs), Paris, 1980–84; Counsellor (External Relations), Office of UK Perm. Rep. to EEC, 1984–87; Hd of European Community Dept (External), FCO, 1987–89; Asst Under-Sec. of State, FCO, 1989–92; Minister and Hd of British Embassy Berlin Office, 1993–96. Member: Salisbury Cathedral Chapter, 2001–07; Salisbury Cathedral Council, 2007–17; Bd, Salisbury Festival, 2003–12; Council, Wyndham Place Charlemagne Trust, 2009–18 (Trustee, 2013–18); Pres., Salisbury Civic Soc., 2007–. Lay Canon, Salisbury Cathedral, 2007–17, now Emeritus. Trustee: Heinz Koeppler Trust, 2001–09 (Chm., 2005–09); Magna Carta Trust, 2002–; World Faiths Develt Dialogue, 2002–05. Chm., Nikaean Club, 2002–12. Member: Council and Court, Imperial Coll., London Univ., 2001–05; Council, St Swithun's Sch., 2001–04; Gov., Internat. Coll., Sherborne Sch., 2001–11; Hon. Pres., Berlin British Sch., 2002–19. *Recreations:* country walking, travel, the arts. *Address:* c/o FCO Association, Room K G/117 King Charles Street, SW1A 2AH. *Clubs:* Oxford and Cambridge; International (Berlin).

**SPENCER, Sarah Ann,** CBE 2007; PhD; Director, Global Exchange on Migration and Diversity, Centre on Migration, Policy and Society, University of Oxford, since 2014 (Open Society Fellow (formerly Director of Policy Research, then Associate Director, later Deputy Director), 2003–14); Chair, Equality and Diversity Forum, 2002–12; *b* 11 Dec. 1952; *d* of late Dr I. O. B. Spencer and of Dr Elspeth Wilkinson; *m* 1978, Brian Anthony Hackland, *qv*; two *s*. *Educ:* Nottingham Univ. (BA Hons); University Coll. London (MPhil); Erasmus Univ. (PhD 2012). Researcher, Law Faculty, UCL, 1977–79; Res. Officer, Cobden Trust (Civil Liberties Charity), 1979–84, Dir 1984–85; Gen. Sec., NCCL, 1985–89; Res. Fellow, 1990–2003, Dir Citizenship and Governance (formerly Human Rights) Prog., 1994–2003, IPPR. Member: Home Office Task Force on Implementation of the Human Rights Act, 1998–2001; Commn on Future of Multi-Ethnic Britain, 1999–2000; CRE, 2002–06 (Dep. Chm., 2003–05); Chm., Inquiry into site provision for Gypsies and Travellers, 2004–06); DTI Task Force Commn on Equality and Human Rights, 2003–05; Task Gp on Gypsies and Travellers, DCLG, 2006–07; Sen. Stakeholder Gp, Govt Equality Office, 2008–. Advr, Cabinet Office, 2000 and 2002–03. Vis. Prof., Human Rights Centre, Univ. of Essex, 2002–. Associate Mem., Nuffield Coll., Oxford, 2004–08. Trustee, National Flood Forum, 2011–14. Gov., British Inst. of Human Rights, 2002–. Advr, Atlantic Philanthropies (Ireland), 2006–. Editor, Rights JI, 1979–84. FRSA. *Publications:* Called to Account: police accountability in England and Wales, 1985; (jtly) The New Prevention of Terrorism Act, 1985; The Role of Police Authorities during the Miners' Strike, 1985; (jtly) A British Bill of Rights, 1990; (jtly) Accountable Policing: effectiveness, empowerment and equity, 1993; (ed) Strangers and Citizens: a positive approach to migrants and refugees, 1994; (ed) Immigration as an Economic Asset: the German experience, 1994; Migrants, Refugees and the Boundaries of Citizenship, 1995; (jtly) A UK Human Rights Commission, 1998; (jtly) Mainstreaming Human Rights in Whitehall and Westminster, 1999; (jtly) Migration: an economic and social analysis, 2001; (jtly) Reluctant Witness, 2001; (jtly) Them and Us? The Public, Offenders and the Criminal Justice System, 2002; (ed) The Politics of Migration: managing opportunity, conflict and change, 2003; (jtly) Age as an Equality Issue: legal and policy perspectives, 2003; (jtly) Age Equality Comes of Age, 2003; (jtly) Fair Enough: Central and East European migrants in low wage employment in the UK, 2006; (contrib.) Blair's Britain, 1997–2007, 2007; (jtly) Migrant Care Workers in Ageing Societies, 2009; The Migration Debate, 2011. *Address:* (office) 58 Banbury Road, Oxford OX2 6QS.

**SPENCER, His Honour Shaun Michael;** QC 1988; a Circuit Judge, 2002–14; a Deputy High Court Judge, 1999–2014; Designated Civil Judge, Bradford Group of County Courts, 2008–12; *b* 4 Feb. 1944; *s* of late Edward Michael Spencer, Leeds and Barbara Spencer (*née* Williams); *m* 1971, Nicola, *e d* of late F. G. Greenwood, Tockwith, York; three *s* two *d*. *Educ:* Middleton Boys' Sch., Leeds; Cockburn High Sch., Leeds; King's Coll., Newcastle (Univ. of Durham); Open Univ. (Dip. Classical Studies 2010). LLB 1st cl. Hons 1965. Asst Lectr and Lectr in Law, Univ. of Sheffield, 1965–68; called to the Bar, Lincoln's Inn, 1968, Bencher, 1997; a Recorder, 1985–2002. *Recreations:* singing, classical guitar, the literature and history of Spain. *Address:* 10 Park View, Harrogate, N Yorks HG1 5LZ.

**SPENCER, Thomas Newnham Bayley, (Tom);** Executive Director, European Centre for Public Affairs, Templeton College, Oxford, 1987–89, then at University of Surrey, then at Brunel University, 1999–2011; Vice-Chairman, Institute for Environmental Security, The Hague, since 2002 (Vice Chairman, Global Military Advisory Council, since 2012); Visiting Professor of Public Affairs: Brunel University, since 2003; University of Chester, since 2010; *b* 10 April 1948; *s* of Thomas Henry Newnham Spencer and Anne Hester (*née* Readett-Bayley); *m* 1979, Elizabeth Nan Maltby, *er d* of late Captain Ronald Edgar Bath and of Doreen Lester (*née* Bush); two *d* and one step *d*. *Educ:* Nautical Coll., Pangbourne; Southampton Univ. (BSc Social Sciences). Peat, Marwick, Mitchell & Co., 1972–75; Asst to Dir, Britain-in-Europe Campaign, 1975; J. Walter Thompson & Co., 1975–79. Associate Dean, Templeton Coll., Oxford, 1984–89. MEP (C) Derbyshire, 1979–84, contested same seat, 1984; MEP (C) Surrey West, 1989–94, Surrey, 1994–99. European Democratic Group: Dep. Chief Whip, 1989–91; spokesman on: Social Affairs and Employment, 1979–81; External Econ. Relations, 1982–84; Social Affairs, 1993–94; Chm., British Section, EPP Gp, 1994–95; European Parliament: Member: Envmtl, Public Health and Consumer Affairs Cttee, 1991–99; Institutional Affairs Cttee, 1991–94; Foreign Affairs Cttee, 1993–99; Chairman: Cttee on Foreign Affairs, Security and Defence Policy, 1997–99; delegn to Czech, Slovene and Slovak Republics, 1993–99; Jt Parly Cttee with Czech Republic, 1995–97. Chm., European Union Cons. and Christian-Democratic Students, 1971–73; Mem. Council, Cons. Gp for Europe, 1999–. Member: Global Legislators for a Balanced Environment, 1989–99; Commn on Globalisation, 2000–03; Professional Practice Panel, European Public Affairs Consultants' Assoc. Convenor, Global Public Affairs Network, 2011–. Chm., Counterpart Europe, 2000–02. Vis. Prof., Global Governance, Univ. of Surrey, 2000–04. Sen. Advr, Inst. for Global Envmtl Strategies, Japan, 1997–2001. Pres., Globe Internat., 1995–99; Patron, Global Commons Inst. Trust, 1997–. Member: Bd of Trustees, Friends of Europe, 2000; Council, Federal Trust, 2003–. Mem. Court, Univ. of Surrey, 1992–; Member, Advisory Board: Centre for Corporate and Public Affairs, Manchester Metropolitan Univ., 2000–; Centre for Res. on the European Matrix, Univ. of Surrey, 2012–. Member Editorial Board: Eur. Business Jl, 1991–2003; Jl of Public Affairs, 2000–. Robert Schuman Silver Medal, 1974; Green Ribbon Award for most envmtl MEP, Forum for the Future, 1999. Great Golden Medal for Merit (Republic of Austria), 1995. *Publications:* Public Affairs and Power: essays in a time of fear, 2003; Everything Flows: essays on public affairs and change, 2005; Challenge and Response: essays on public affairs and transparency, 2006; The Future of Public Trust: public affairs in a time of crisis, 2009. *Recreations:* gardening, opera, Conservative Party. *Clubs:* Carlton, Brass Monkey.

**SPENCER, Timothy John;** QC 2001; **His Honour Judge Timothy Spencer;** a Circuit Judge, since 2015; *b* 6 Nov. 1958; *s* of John Spencer and Muriel Spencer (*née* Rowe); *m* 1983, Ann Fiona Rigg; two *s* one *d* (of whom one *s* one *d* are twins). *Educ:* Baines Grammar Sch.; Downing Coll., Cambridge (MA Hons Law). 1st Lieut, 1st RTR, 1978. Called to the Bar, Middle Temple, 1982; Asst Recorder, 1998–2000; Recorder, 2000–15. *Recreations:* Preston North End, Lancashire County Cricket Club, gardening. *Address:* Nottingham Crown Court, 60 Canal Street, Nottingham NG1 7EL. *Clubs:* MCC; Hawks (Cambridge).

**SPENCER-CHURCHILL,** family name of **Duke of Marlborough.**

**SPENCER-NAIRN, Sir Robert (Arnold),** 3rd Bt *cr* 1933; Vice Lord-Lieutenant of Fife, 1996–2008; *b* 11 Oct. 1933; *s* of Sir Douglas Spencer-Nairn, 2nd Bt, TD, and Elizabeth Livingston (*d* 1985), *d* of late Arnold J. Henderson; *S* father, 1970; *m* 1963, Joanna Elizabeth, *d* of late Lt-Comdr G. S. Salt, RN; two *s* one *d*. *Educ:* Eton College; Trinity Hall, Cambridge (MA). Fellow, Game Conservancy, 1993. Mem. Council, Macmillan Cancer Support (formerly Macmillan Cancer Relief), 1997–2008. DL Fife, 1995. *Heir:* *s* James Robert Spencer-Nairn [*b* 7 Dec. 1966; *m* 1994, Dominique Jane, *o d* of Michael Williamson and Mrs Charles Newman; two *s*]. *Address:* Barham, Cupar, Fife KY15 5RG. *Clubs:* Farmers; Royal and Ancient Golf (St Andrews); Falkland Palace Royal Tennis.

**SPENCER-SMITH, Sir John Hamilton,** 7th Bt *cr* 1804; *b* 18 March 1947; *s* of Sir Thomas Cospatric Hamilton-Spencer-Smith, 6th Bt, and Lucy Ashton, *o d* of late Thomas Ashton Ingram, Hopes, Norton-sub-Hamdon, Somerset; *S* father, 1959; *m* 1st, 1980, Christine (marr. diss. 1990), *d* of late John Theodore Charles Osborne, Durrington, Worthing, Sussex; one *d*; 2nd, 2017, Peta, *d* of late Arthur Charles Bellringer, Andover, Hants. *Educ:* Milton Abbey; Lackham College of Agriculture, Wilts. *Heir:* cousin Michael Philip Spencer-Smith, *b* 2 April 1952.

**SPENCER WILLS;** *see* Wills.

**SPENS,** family name of **Baron Spens.**

**SPENS, 4th Baron** *cr* 1959, of Blairsanquar, Fife; **Patrick Nathaniel George Spens;** Director, Transformation and Assurance, PwC UK, since 2016; *b* 14 Oct. 1968; *s* of 3rd Baron Spens and of Barbara Janet Lindsay Spens; *S* father, 2001; *m* 1998, Hon. Philippa Patricia Lennox-Boyd (marr. diss. 2008), *yr d* of Viscount Boyd of Merton, *qv*; one *s* two *d*. *Educ:* Rugby. Strauss Turnbull, 1987–93; Merrill Lynch International, 1993–99; Dir, 1999–2005, Man. Dir, 2001–05, Schroder Salomon Smith Barney, subseq. Citigroup; Partner, Copenhagen Capital LLP, 2005–09; Head, Market Monitoring: FSA, 2009–13; Financial Conduct Authy, 2013–16. Ind. Mem., Whitechapel Think Tank, 2014–. Hon. Adjunct Prof., Macquarie Univ., NSW, 2015–. Exec. Fellow, Henley Business Sch., 2016–. *Recreations:* racing, claret. *Heir:* *s* Hon. Peter Lathallan Spens, *b* 3 March 2000. *Address:* Top Floor, 23 Earls Court Square, SW5 9BY. *Clubs:* Bluebird; Cercle de Deauville.

**SPENS, David Patrick;** QC 1995; a Recorder of the Crown Court, since 1991; *b* 2 May 1950; *s* of late Hugh Stuart Spens and Mary Jean Drake (*née* Reinhold); *m* 1st, 1979, Danièle Irving (marr. diss. 2003); two *d*; 2nd, 2010, Robbin Leak-Piccioni. *Educ:* Rugby Sch.; Univ. of Kent at Canterbury (BA). Called to the Bar, Inner Temple, 1973, Bencher, 2005; Junior Treasury Counsel, CCC, 1988–95; Leader, S Eastern Circuit, 2007–08. Chm., Criminal Bar Assoc., 2004–05. *Address:* QEB Hollis Whiteman, 1–2 Laurence Pountney Hill, EC4R 0EU. *T:* (020) 7933 8855.

**SPENS, John Alexander,** RD 1970; WS; Partner, Maclay, Murray & Spens, Solicitors, Glasgow and Edinburgh, 1960–91, later Consultant; *b* 7 June 1933; *s* of Thomas Patrick Spens and Nancy F. Spens (*née* Anderson); *m* 1961, Finella Jane, *d* of Donald Duff Gilroy; two *s* one *d* (and one *s* decd). *Educ:* Cargilfield; Rugby School; Corpus Christi College, Cambridge (BA); Glasgow Univ. (LLB). WS 1977. Director: Scottish Amicable Life Assurance Soc., 1963–97 (Chairman, 1978–81); Standard Property Investment PLC, 1977–87. Carrick Pursuivant, 1974–85; Albany Herald, 1985–2011. *Recreations:* sailing, countryside and opera. *Address:* The Old Manse, Gartocharn, Dunbartonshire G83 8RX. *T:* (01389) 830456. *Clubs:* Naval; Western (Glasgow).

**SPENS, Michael Colin Barkley,** MA; education consultant; Headmaster, Fettes College, 1998–2017; *b* 22 Sept. 1950; *s* of Richard Vernon Spens and (Theodora) Margaret Yuille Spens (*née* Barkley); *m* 1989, Deborah Susan Lane; one *s* two *d*. *Educ:* Marlborough Coll.; Selwyn Coll., Cambridge (BA 1972; MA Natural Scis 1976). Asst Master, Rathkeale Coll., NZ, 1968–69; Mktg Dept, United Biscuits plc, 1973–74; Asst Master, 1974–93, Housemaster, 1984–93, Radley Coll.; Headmaster, Caldicott Sch., 1993–98. Liveryman, Grocers' Co., 1981–. *Recreations:* mountaineering, golf, bridge, crosswords, geology, electronics, wood turning, gardening. *Clubs:* Hawks (Cambridge); New (Edinburgh); Denham Golf; Royal and Ancient Golf (St Andrews); Hon. Company of Edinburgh Golfers (Muirfield).

**SPERRYN, Simon George;** consultant, interim manager and chief executive officer mentor, since 2010; Chief Executive, Chartered Institute of Purchasing and Supply, 2008–09; *b* 7 April 1946; *s* of George Roland Neville Sperryn and Wendy Sperryn (*née*

King); *m* 1993, Jessica Alice Hayes (marr. diss. 2008); two *s* one *d*. *Educ:* Rydal School; Pembroke College, Cambridge (MA); Cranfield School of Management (MBA). Birmingham Chamber of Commerce and Industry, 1967–77; Chief Executive: Northants Chamber of Commerce and Industry, 1979–85; Manchester Chamber of Commerce and Industry, 1986–92; London Chamber of Commerce and Industry, 1992–2000; Chief Exec., Lloyd's Market Assoc., 2001–06. Director: Manchester TEC, 1989–92; Manchester Camerata, 1989–92 (Chm.); Business Link London, 1995–2000. British Chambers of Commerce: Mem. Nat. Council, 1986–97; Dir, 1998–2000; Pres., British Chambers of Commerce Executives, 1994, 1995; Administrator, London Chamber of Commerce and Industry Commercial Educn Trust, 1992–2000; Mem. UK Council, ICC, 2000–06. Ind. Assessor for Nat. Accreditation by British Chambers of Commerce, 2013–16. Vice Pres., World Chambers Fedn, 2000; Dir, Internat. Fedn of Purchasing and Supply Mgt, 2008–09. Mem. Council, Chartered Insurance Inst., 2003–06. Chm., City of London Early Years Develt and Childcare Partnership, 1998–2000. Mem., London Regl Cttee, FEFC, 1996–2000. Trustee, UNIAID, 2002–10 (Dep. Chm., 2006–10). Gov., UC Salford, 1988–92. Freeman, City of London, 1998. CCMI; FRSA; MIEx. *Address:* 33 Halifax Road, Cambridge CB4 3QB.

**SPICE, Chris;** National Performance Director, British Swimming, since 2013; *b* Brisbane, Australia, 25 Dec. 1959; *s* of Henry Albert Edward Spice and June Spice (*née* Siggs); partner, Yodrak Janthai. *Educ:* Edith Cowan Univ., Perth (BA 1991). Grade 1 Hockey Coach, Internat. Hockey Fedn, 1997. Coach, Women's Hockey Australia, 1993–96; Performance Director: GB Hockey, 1997–2000; England Rugby, 2001–06; British Basketball, 2007–12. Mem., Strategic GB, Performance Dirs Forum, 2007– (Chair, 2018–); Team Leader, Wkg Gp, British Olympic Assoc., 2007–14. *Recreations:* travel, theatre, dog walking, eating Thai. *Address:* British Swimming, Sportpark, 3 Oakwood Drive, Loughborough LE11 3QF. *T:* (01509) 618700. *E:* chris.spice@swimming.org.

**SPICELEY, Peter Joseph,** MBE 1976; HM Diplomatic Service, retired; Ambassador to Costa Rica, 1999–2002; *b* 5 March 1942; *s* of late Robert Joseph Spiceley and Lucy Violet Spiceley; *m* 1965, Cecilia Orozco-Lemus; two *d*. *Educ:* Trinity Sch. of John Whitgift, Croydon. Entered Diplomatic Service, 1961; FCO, 1961–64; Bogotá, 1964–66; DSAO, 1966–69; Lima, 1969–72; Second Sec., Yaoundé, 1972–74; Consul, Douala, 1974–76; Second, later First, Sec., Quito, 1976–81; FCO, 1982–86; Consul, Miami, 1986–90; Asst Head of Aviation Dept, FCO, 1991–94; Dep. Consul-Gen. and Dir of Trade Promotion, Sydney, 1994–98. *Recreations:* travel, reading. *Address:* Flat 41, 2 Tavistock Road, Croydon, Surrey CR0 2AS.

**SPICER, Gail Scott S.;** *see* Scott-Spicer.

**SPICER, Harriet Greville;** coach and mentor, since 2007; Partner, Working Edge Coaching and Mentoring, since 2007; *b* 24 April 1950; *d* of James Spicer and Patricia Spicer (*née* Palmer); one *s* one *d*. *Educ:* St Anne's Coll., Oxford (BA Hons English Lit.). Virago Press Ltd, 1973–96, Man. Dir, 1990–96. Mem., 1999–2005, Chair, 2001–02, Nat. Lottery Commn. Chm., The Friendly Almshouses, 2002–05. Mentor and Trainer, UpRising Foundn and Young Foundn Accelerator Prog., 2010–16. Adviser: Talk for Health, 2014–; Carers Trust Advance Prog., 2015–18. Mem., Judicial Appts Commn, 2006–12. Govt Equalities Office, 2009–11; Croydon Social Work Acad., 2011–13. Advr, Piccadilly Dance Orch., 2007–12. Gov., LSE, 2009–18, now Emeritus (Mem. Council, 2011–17; Mem., Audit Cttee, 2017–18). *Recreations:* friends, reading, music, theatre.

**SPICER, Ina;** *see* De, I.

**SPICER, Sir Nicholas (Adrian Albert),** 5th Bt *cr* 1906, of Lancaster Gate, Paddington; General Medical Practitioner, 1982–2007; *b* 28 Oct. 1953; *o s* of (Sir) Peter James Spicer (4th Bt, but did not use the title) and Margaret (*née* Wilson); *S* father, 1993; *m* 1st, 1992, Patricia Carol Dye (marr. diss. 2008); two *s*; 2nd, 2012, Priscilla Anne Davey (*née* Kennedy). *Educ:* Eton; Birmingham Univ. (MB ChB 1977). *Recreations:* amateur singing, mowing. *Heir: s* James Peter Warwick Spicer, *b* 12 June 1993. *Address:* Tower House, Burley, Craven Arms, Shropshire SY7 9LN.

**ŠPIDLA, Dr Vladimír;** Member, European Commission, 2004–10; Director, Department of Advisers and Adviser to Prime Minister of Czech Republic, 2014–17; *b* Prague, 22 April 1951; *s* of Václav and Dagmar Špidla; *m* 1st; two *s*; 2nd, Viktorie; one *s* one *d*. *Educ:* Charles Univ., Prague (PhD Hist. and Prehist.). Formerly archaeologist, worker at historical monuments, sawmill worker and worker in dairy and livestock industry. Jindřichův Hradec: Vice-Pres. for Educn, Health Service, Social Affairs and Culture, Dist Cttee, 1990–91; Dir, Labour Office, 1991–96; Mem. (CSSD) Chamber of Deps, Czech Republic, 1996–2004; Dep. Prime Minister and Minister of Labour and Social Affairs, 1998–2002; Prime Minister, 2002–04. Czech Social Democratic Party: Founding Mem., S Bohemian Br., 1989; joined party leadership, 1992; Vice-Chm., 1997–2001; Chm., 2001–04. *Recreations:* care of historical monuments, books, cross-country running, other outdoor sports.

**SPIEGELHALTER, Sir David (John),** Kt 2014; OBE 2006; FRS 2005; Chair, Winton Centre for Risk and Evidence Communication, University of Cambridge, since 2019 (Winton Professor for the Public Understanding of Risk, 2007–18); *b* 16 Aug. 1953; *s* of Edmund Spiegelhalter and late Faith Spiegelhalter (*née* Baker); *m* 1978, Eva Sommerschield (marr. diss. 1987); one *d*; partner, 1988, Kate Bull; one *d* (and one *s* decd). *Educ:* Barnstaple Grammar Sch.; Keble Coll., Oxford (BA); University Coll. London (PhD 1978). Lectr, Univ. of Calif, Berkeley, 1977–78; Res. Asst, Univ. of Nottingham, 1978–81; MRC Biostatistics Unit, Cambridge, 1981–2012 (Sen. Scientist, 1986–2012; Hon. Prof., 1996–). Hon. FIRM, 2011; Hon. FRCP 2013. Hon. DSc: Aalborg, Denmark, 1994; Plymouth, 2010; Heriot-Watt, 2013; Bath, 2013. Weldon Meml Prize, Univ. of Oxford, 2010; Science Communication Award, Soc. of Biol., 2011. *Publications:* (jtly) Leucocyte Typing III: White Cell Differentiation Antigens, 1987; (jtly) Machine Learning, Neural and Statistical Classification, 1994; (jtly) Markov Chain Monte Carlo Methods in Practice, 1996; (jtly) Bayesian Analysis in Probabilistic Networks, 1999; (jtly) Bayesian Approaches to Clinical Trials and Health Care Evaluation, 2004; (jtly) The Norm Chronicles: stories and numbers about danger, 2013; Sex By Numbers: what statistics can tell us about sexual behaviour, 2015; The Art of Statistics: learning from data, 2019; papers in Jl Royal Statistical Soc., etc. *Recreations:* trekking, samba drumming, making stained-glass panels, watching old films with family, talking to Michael Traynor. *Address:* Department of Pure Mathematics and Mathematical Statistics, Centre for Mathematical Sciences, University of Cambridge, Wilberforce Road, Cambridge CB3 0WB.

**SPIELBERG, Steven,** Hon. KBE 2001; American film director and producer; Chairman and Chief Executive Officer, Amblin Partners, since 2015; *b* 18 Dec. 1947; *s* of Arnold Spielberg and Leah (*née* Posner); *m* 1985, Amy Irving (marr. diss. 1989); one *s*; *m* Kate Capshaw; one *s* two *d*, and one adopted *s* one adopted *d*. *Educ:* Calif State Coll. TV Director, Universal Pictures, 1968. Founder: Amblin Entertainment, 1981; DreamWorks SKG, 1994. Fellow, BAFTA, 1986. *Films include: directed:* Sugarland Express, 1974; Jaws, 1975; Close Encounters of the Third Kind, 1977; 1941, 1979; Raiders of the Lost Ark, 1981; (also produced) E.T., 1982; (also produced) Twilight Zone—the movie, 1983; Indiana Jones and the Temple of Doom, 1984; The Color Purple, 1985; Empire of the Sun, 1988; Indiana Jones and the Last Crusade, 1989; Hook, 1991; Jurassic Park, 1992; Schindler's List (Academy Award for Best Dir), 1994; The Lost World: Jurassic Park, 1997; Amistad, 1998; Saving Private Ryan (Academy Award for Best Dir), 1998; A. I. Artificial Intelligence, 2001; Minority Report, 2002; Catch Me If You Can, 2003; The Terminal, 2004; War of the Worlds, 2005; Munich, 2006; Indiana Jones and the Kingdom of the Crystal Skull, 2008; The Adventures of Tintin: The Secret of the Unicorn, 2011; War Horse, 2012; Lincoln, 2013; Bridge of Spies, 2015; The BFG, 2016; The Post, Ready Player One, 2018; *produced:* I Wanna Hold Your Hand, 1978; (also co-wrote) Poltergeist, 1982; Gremlins, 1984; The Goonies, 1985; Young Sherlock Holmes, 1985; Back to the Future, 1986; Who Framed Roger Rabbit, 1988; Always, 1990; The Flintstones, 1994; Casper, 1995; Men in Black, 1997; The Last Days, 1999; Jurassic Park III, 2001; Men in Black 2, 2002; The Legend of Zorro, 2005; Memoirs of a Geisha, Monster House, Flags of Our Fathers, 2006; Letters from Iwo Jima, Transformers, 2007; Eagle Eye, 2008; Transformers: Revenge of the Fallen, 2009; The Lovely Bones, 2010; Hereafter, True Grit, Super 8, Transformers: Dark of the Moon, Cowboys & Aliens, Real Steel, 2011; Men in Black 3, 2012; Transformers: Age of Extinction, The Hundred-Foot Journey, 2014; Jurassic World, 2015. *Television series:* co-prod., Band of Brothers, 2001; executive producer: Into the West, 2006; United States of Tara, 2009–11; The Pacific, 2010; Falling Skies, 2011–15; Terra Nova, 2011; The River, 2012; Smash, 2012–13; Under the Dome, 2013–15; Extant, 2014–15; The Whispers, 2015; Minority Report, 2015; Public Morals, 2015; Bull, 2016–18. *Publications:* (jtly) Close Encounters of the Third Kind. *Address:* Amblin Partners, 100 Universal City Plaza, Universal City, CA 91608, USA.

**SPIELMAN, Amanda Mary Victoria;** HM Chief Inspector of Education, Children's Services and Skills, since 2017; *b* London, 22 May 1961; *d* of Sebastian Robinson and Prof. Olivia Robinson; *m* 1996, Adam Spielman; two *d*. *Educ:* Clare Coll., Cambridge (BA Hons Maths and Law 1982); Inst. of Educn, Univ. of London (MA Comparative Educn 2002). ACA 1985. KMG Thomson McLintock, 1982–86; Kleinwort Benson, 1986–92; Director: Newstead Capital, 1992–94; Bridgewater Business Analysis, 1994–95; Principal, Mercer Mgt Consulting, Boston, 1995–97; Nomura Principal Finance, USA and UK, 1997–2001; educn consultancy, 2002–04; Res. and Develt Dir, ARK Schools, 2005–13; Educn Advr, ARK, 2013–16; Chm., Ofqual, 2011–16. Member, Council: Inst. of Educn, Univ. of London, 2011–15; Brunel Univ., 2016–. Trustee: Pilotlight, 2001–04; New Schools Network, 2009–11; Mem. Bd, Wales Millennium Centre, 2004–11; Governor: Evelyn Grace Acad., 2008–15; Bolingbroke Acad., 2012–15. *Address:* Ofsted, Clive House, 70 Petty France, SW1H 9EX.

**SPIELMANN, Dean Frank;** Judge, General Court of the European Union, since 2016; *b* Luxembourg, 26 Oct. 1962; *s* of Alphonse Spielmann and Catherine Spielmann (*née* Hildgen); partner, Veerle Willems. *Educ:* Univ. Catholique de Louvain (Licence en droit 1988); Fitzwilliam Coll., Cambridge (Foreign and Commonwealth Schol.; LLM Internat. Law 1990; Hon. Fellow 2013). Asst Lectr and Res. Asst, Univ. of Louvain, 1991–97; Lecturer: Univ. of Luxembourg, 1996–2006; Univ. of Nancy, 1997–2009; barrister, Luxembourg Bar: Avocat, 1989–92; Avocat à la Cour, 1992–2004; European Court of Human Rights: Judge, 2004–15; Section Pres., 2011–12; Vice-Pres., 2012; Pres., 2012–15. Hon. Prof., UCL, 2014–. Mem., Inst. Grand-Ducal, Luxembourg, 2005–. Co-founder and Co-dir, Annales du droit luxembourgeois, 28 vols, 1990–. Member: Adv. Commn of Human Rights, Luxembourg, 2000–04; EU Network of Ind. Experts in Fundamental Rights, 2002–04. Hon. Bencher, Gray's Inn, 2013–. Dr *hc*: Yerevan, 2013; Cluj-Napoca, 2015; Bucharest, 2015; Hon. LLD UCL, 2016. Kt Grand Cross, Equestrian Order of St Agatha (San Marino), 2014; Commandeur: Order of Merit (Luxembourg), 2015; Légion d'honneur (France), 2015. *Publications:* (jtly) La Convention européenne des droits de l'homme et le droit luxembourgeois, 1991; L'effet potentiel de la Convention européenne des droits de l'homme entre personnes privées, 1995; (with Nathalie Hustin-Denies) L'infraction inachevée en droit pénal comparé, 1997; Le Luxembourg devant la Cour européenne des droits de l'homme (Recueil de jurisprudence 1995–2003), 2003; (with Alphonse Spielmann) Droit pénal général luxembourgeois, 2002, 2nd edn 2004; (jtly) La Convention européenne des droits de l'homme, un instrument vivant, Mélanges offerts à Christos Rozakis, 2011; contrib. articles to legal periodicals. *Recreations:* music, organ playing, history, gardening. *Address:* General Court of the European Union, Rue du Fort Niedergrünewald, 2925 Luxembourg. *T:* 43034984, *Fax:* 43038669. *E:* dean.spielmann@curia.europa.eu. *Club:* Oxford and Cambridge.

**SPIER, Prof. Steven;** Vice-Chancellor, Kingston University, since 2016; *b* Montreal, 16 April 1959; *s* of Ira and Anja Spier; *m* Natalie Littleson; one *d*. *Educ:* Haverford Coll., Philadelphia (BA 1981); Southern Calif Inst. of Architecture (MArch). Hd, Dept of Architecture, Univ. of Strathclyde, 2000–06; Founding Pres., HafenCity Univ., Hamburg, 2006–10; Prof. and Hd, Sch. of Architecture and Design, Univ. of Ulster, 2010–12; Dean, Sch. of Art, Kingston Univ., 2012–16. *Publications:* Swiss Made, 2003; William Forsythe and the Practice of Choreography, 2011; contribs to AA Files, Jl Architecture, Arq, Dance Res. Jl. *Address:* Kingston University, Penrhyn Road, Kingston upon Thames KT1 2EE. *E:* s.spier@mac.com. *Clubs:* Groucho, House of St Barnabas.

**SPIERS, Sir Donald (Maurice),** Kt 1997; CB 1987; TD 1966; FREng; Chairman, Farnborough Aerospace Consortium, since 2003; *b* 27 Jan. 1934; *s* of Harold Herbert Spiers and Emma (*née* Foster); *m* 1958, Sylvia Mary Lowman (*d* 2014); two *s*. *Educ:* Raynes Park County Grammar Sch.; Trinity Coll., Cambridge (MA). CEng. Commnd RE, 1952–54. de Havilland Engine Co., Hatfield, 1957–60; joined Air Min. as SSO, 1960; operational res. on deterrence, 1960–63; trials and analysis, Aden and Radfan, 1964; Kestrel evaluation trial, 1965; Scientific Adviser to FEAF, Singapore, 1967–70; Asst Chief Scientist (RAF), MoD, 1972–77; Asst Dir, Mil. Aircraft Projs, MoD (PE), 1978; Dir of Aircraft Post Design Services, MoD (PE), 1979–81; Dir Gen. Aircraft 1, MoD (PE), 1981–84; Dep. Controller Aircraft, MoD (PE), 1984–86; Controller of R&D Estabts, later of Estabts, Res. and Nuclear Programmes, and Hd of Profession Defence Engrg Service, MoD, 1986–89; Controller Aircraft, and Head of Profession Defence Sci. and Engrg, MoD, 1989–94. Chairman: European Helicopter Industries Ltd, 1998–2004; Farnborough Enterprise Hub, 2004–08; AgustaWestland International, 2004–09. Director: Computing Devices Co. Ltd, 1994–2001 (Chm., 1997–2001); Meggitt plc, 1995–2003 (Chm., 1998–2001); Messier-Dowty Internat. Ltd, 1998–2004; TAG Aviation (UK) Ltd, 1999–2005; General Dynamics UK Ltd, 2001–10. Hon. FRAeS (Vice Pres., 1993–95; Pres., 1995–96). Pres., Popular Flying Assoc., 1997–2000. Gold Medal, RAeS, 1989. *Recreations:* mending cars, mowing lawns. *Address:* 20 Paddock Close, Camberley, Surrey GU15 2BN. *Club:* Royal Air Force.

**SPIERS, Prof. Edward Michael,** PhD; FRHistS; Professor of Strategic Studies, University of Leeds, since 1993; *b* 18 Oct. 1947; *s* of Ronald Arthur Spiers, DSC and Margaret Carlisle Laing Spiers (*née* Manson); *m* 1971, Fiona Elizabeth McLeod; one *s* one *d*. *Educ:* Royal High Sch., Edinburgh; Edinburgh Univ. (MA, PhD). FRHistS 1980. University of Leeds: Defence Lectr, 1975–85; Lectr in History, 1985–87; Reader in Strategic Studies, 1987–93; Chm., School of History, 1994–97; Dean, 1999–2002, Pro-Dean, 2006–11, of Res. (Arts), of Res. and Evaluation, 2011–; Actg Pro-Vice Chancellor for Res. and Innovation, 2011. Vis. Lectr, Univ. of Alberta, 1987; Leverhulme Res. Fellow, 1991–92. Chief Examiner, Army, 1992–2002; Peer Reviewer, AHRC, 2004–14. Mem. (C), Edinburgh DC, 1974. *Publications:* Haldane: an army reformer, 1980; The Army and Society 1815–1914, 1980;

Radical General: Sir George de Lacy Evans 1787–1870, 1983; Chemical Warfare, 1986; Chemical Weaponry: a continuing challenge, 1989; The Late Victorian Army 1868–1902, 1992; Chemical and Biological Weapons: a study of proliferation, 1994; (ed) Sudan: the reconquest reappraised, 1998; Weapons of Mass Destruction, 2000; The Victorian Soldier in Africa, 2004; The Scottish Soldier and Empire 1854–1902, 2006; A History of Chemical and Biological Weapons, 2010; (ed) Letters from Ladysmith: eyewitness accounts from the South African War, 2010; (co-ed) A Military History of Scotland, 2012 (Scottish History Book of the Year, Saltire Soc., 2012; Templer Medal, Soc. for Army Histl Res., 2012); (ed) Letters from Kimberley: eyewitness accounts from the South African war, 2013; Engines for Empire: the Victorian military and its use of railways, 2015; Letters from Mafeking: eyewitness accounts from the longest siege of the South African war, 2019. *Recreation:* supporting the Green Bay Packers. *Address:* 170 Alwoodley Lane, Leeds LS17 7PF. *T:* (0113) 268 5493. *Club:* Army and Navy.

**SPIERS, John Raymond;** Chairman: John Spiers Publishing Ltd, since 1988; Edward Everett Root Publishers Ltd, since 2015; Senior Research Fellow, Institute of English Studies, School of Advanced Study, University of London, since 2003; Professorial Research Fellow, Global Policy Institute, London Metropolitan University, since 2013; *b* 30 Sept. 1941; *s* of Horace Henry Spiers and Kate Dawson (*née* Root); *m* 1967, Prof. Margaret Ann Boden, *qv* (marr. diss. 1981); one *s* one *d*; *m* 2003, Leigh Richardson, MBE (*née* Radford); one step *s* one step *d*. *Educ:* Redhill Sch., E Sutton, Kent; Catford Coll. of Commerce; Univ. of Sussex (BA 1st Cl. Hons Hist. 1968). Writer and publisher, 1960–; Founder: Harvester Press Ltd (Chm., 1969–88); Harvester Press Microform Pubns Ltd (Chm., 1973–87) (Queen's Award for Export Achievement, 1986); Wheatsheaf Books Ltd (Chm., 1980–88). Special Advr to Dep. Chm., Cons. Party, 1989–90; Consultant Dir, Special Services Dept, Cons. Central Office, 1990–94; Mem., Citizens' Charter Adv. Panel to PM, 1994; Dep. Treas., Cons. Party SE England Area, 1990–92 (Mem., SE Area Council, 1990–92); Pres., Brighton Kemp Town Cons. Assoc., 1991–95. Founder and Chm., Brighton Business Gp, 1989–95. Health Policy Advr, Social Market Foundn, 1994–99; Chairman: Brighton HA, 1991–92; Brighton Health Care NHS Trust, 1992–94; National Association of Health Authorities and Trusts: Mem., Nat. Council and Exec. Cttee, 1993–94; Chm., Nat. Conf. Cttee, 1993–94; Co-Chm., S Thames Network, 1994; Vice-Chm., Provider Cttee, 1993–94; Member: NHS Mgt Exec. Adv. Gps, 1991–98; Bd, Nat. Care Standards Commn, 2001–04. Chairman: Patients Assoc., 1995–97 (Actg Chief Exec., 1995–96); Health Policy Cttee, Centre for Policy Studies, 1997–99; Founding Chm., Civitas: Inst. for Study of Civil Soc., 1999–2000; Member: Exec. Bd, Internat. Health Policy and Management Inst., 1994–98; Adv. Council, Health and Welfare Unit, IEA, 1989–92, 1997–99; (co-opted), Nat. Exec., Voluntary Euthanasia Soc., 1997–99. Co-Chm., The Radical Soc., 1991–2001; Mem., Adv. Council, Reform, 2001–10. Vice-Chm., Grant Maintained Schools Foundn, 1992–98 (Trustee, 1992–98). Trustee: Choice in Educn, 1990–92; Trident Trust, 1992–99 (Vice Chm., 1993–94; Chm., 1994–97); Brighton Internat. Arts Fest., 1989–96; English Nat. Schs Orch., 1998–2004; League of Mercy, 1999–2004 (Companion, 2002); Shakespeare Authorship Trust, 2002–05 (Associate, 2005–); Ruskin Foundn, 2002–08; Pres., Gissing Foundn, 2005–. Chm., Alumni Soc., 1983–2004 (Hon. Fellow, 1998; Vice-Pres., 2002), and Mem. Court, 1989–, Univ. of Sussex. Visiting Fellow: NHS Staff Coll., Wales, 1995–2010; King's Fund Mgt Coll., 1996–2010; IEA, 2003–10; Ruskin Prog., Univ. of Lancaster, 2005–; Res. Fellow, 1997–2011, Sen. Res. Fellow, Health and Welfare Unit, 1998–99, Head of Health Care Studies, 1999–2000, IEA; Ext. Prof., Business Sch., 1998–2001, Ext. Prof., then Vis. Prof., Sch. of Humanities and Social Studies, 2001–12, Univ. of Glamorgan; Adjunct Schol., Cascade Policy Inst., Portland, Oregon, 1999. Mem., Ext. Adv. Bd, Centre for Book Hist., Univ. of Bangor, 2015–. Librarian and Mem. Nat. Council, Francis Bacon Soc., 1998–2005, 2019– (Vice-Chm., 2003–05). Founding Chm., E. W. Cole Meml Assoc., 2018–. Pres., Hoxton Hawks Vintage Cycling Club, 2006–. Fellow, Progressive Vision, 2007–10. Companion, Guild of St George, 1971 (Founding Editor, The Companion, 2000–04; Dir, 2001–04). Freeman, City of London, 2000. FRSA 1994. DUniv Sussex, 1994. JP E Sussex, 1988–90. Companion's Cross, League of Mercy, 2002. Kt Grand Cross, Order of St Stanislaus (Poland), 1998. *Publications:* (with P. Coustillas) The Re-discovery of George Gissing, Novelist, 1971; The Invisible Hospital and the Secret Garden: an insider's commentary on the NHS reforms, 1995; Who Owns Our Bodies?: making moral choices in health care, 1997; (ed) Dilemmas in Modern Health Care, 1997; The Realities of Rationing: priority setting in the National Health Service, 1999; Coming, Ready or Not: the present, future and politics of the NHS, 2003; Patients, Power and Responsibility in British Health Care, 2003; (ed) George Gissing and the City: cultural crisis and the making of books in late-Victorian England, 2005; Serious About Series, 2007, 2nd edn 2015; Who Decides Who Decides?, 2008; (ed) The Culture of the Publisher's Series (2 vols), 2011; Just the Ticket!: railway library fiction of the 19th century, 2015; (jtly) The Secret Trollope, 2019; contrib. Health Service Jl, British Jl of Health Management, Health Summary, Healthcare Today, Health Director, Sunday Telegraph, Guardian, Daily Express, Independent, English Literature in Transition, Jl of Printing Historical Soc., Sunday Times, Gissing Jl, Publishing History, The Sun. *Recreations:* collecting 19th century novels (and reading them), writing, walking, supporting The Arsenal, exploring inland waterways. *E:* jr.spiers@btinternet.com.

**SPIERS, Ven. Peter Hendry;** Archdeacon of Knowsley and Sefton, since 2015; *b* Liverpool, 13 Aug. 1961; *s* of Graeme Spiers and Ann Spiers (*née* Chadwick); *m* 1988, Annie Bush; two *s* two *d*. *Educ:* Liverpool Coll.; Durham Univ. (BA Hons 1982); Ridley Hall, Cambridge (CTh 1986). Deputy Pres., Educn and Welfare, Durham Students' Union, 1982–83; ordained deacon, 1986, priest, 1987; Curate, St Luke's, W Derby, 1986–90; Team Vicar, St Peter's, Everton, 1990–95; Vicar: St George's, Everton, 1995–2005; St Luke's, Crosby, 2005–15; Area Dean, Sefton, 2008–15. Member: Gen. Synod, 2000–; Crown Nominations Commn, 2007–12; Chair of Clergy, Dio. of Liverpool, 2003–08. Canon, Liverpool Cathedral, 2006–. *Recreations:* theatre, cinema, Liverpool FC, travel, U2, real ale. *Address:* 2A Monfa Road, Bootle, Liverpool L20 6BQ. *T:* (0151) 284 2289. *E:* pete.spiers@liverpool.anglican.org.

**SPIERS, Ronald Ian;** consultant on international affairs, since 1992; Under-Secretary-General, Department of Political and General Assembly Affairs and Secretariat Services, United Nations, 1989–92; *b* 9 July 1925; *s* of Tomas H. and Blanca De P. Spiers; *m* 1949, Patience Baker; one *s* three *d*. *Educ:* Dartmouth Coll., New Hampshire (BA); Princeton Univ. (Master in Public Affairs, PhD). Mem., US Delegn to UN, 1956–60; US Department of State: Dir, Office of Disarmament and Arms Control, 1960–62; Dir, Office of NATO Affairs, 1962–66; Political Counsellor, London, 1966–69; Asst Sec. of State, Politico-Military Affairs, 1969–73; Ambassador to the Bahamas, 1973–74; Minister, London, 1974–77; Ambassador to Turkey, 1977–80; Asst Sec. of State, Bureau of Intelligence and Research, Dept of State, 1980–81; Ambassador to Pakistan, 1981–83; Under Sec. of State for Management, 1983–89. *Recreations:* swimming, music, theatre-going, gardening, adult education. *Address:* 5 Timber Lane, Apt K312, Exeter, NH 03833, USA.

**SPIERS, Shaun Mark;** Executive Director, Green Alliance, since 2017; *b* 23 April 1962; *s* of Charles Gordon Spiers and Ann Kathleen Spiers (*née* Hutton); *m* 2006, Louise Humphrey; one *s* two *d*. *Educ:* St John's Coll., Oxford (BA Hons PPE); King's Coll. London (MA War Studies). Political Officer, SE Co-op., 1987–94. MEP (Lab Co-op) London SE, 1994–99; contested (Lab) London Region, 1999. Chief Executive: Assoc. of British Credit Unions, 1999–2004; Campaign to Protect Rural England, 2004–17. Chm., Greener UK, 2017–; Trustee, Sustain, 2012–. *Publications:* How to Build Houses and Save the Countryside, 2018. *Recreation:* cooking. *Address:* (office) 11 Belgrave Road, SW1V 1RB. *E:* sspiers@green-alliance.org.uk.

**SPIGELMAN, James Jacob,** AC 2000; international commercial arbitrator; *b* 1 Jan. 1946; *s* of Majloch and Gucia Spigelman; *m* 1979, Alice Kalmar; one *s* two *d*. *Educ:* Maroubra Bay Public Sch.; Sydney Boys' High Sch.; Univ. of Sydney (BA, LLB). Sen. Advr and Principal Private Sec. to Prime Minister, 1972–75; Sec., Dept of Media, 1975; called to the Bar, NSW, 1976; in practice at NSW Bar, 1980–98; QC (NSW) 1986; Actg Solicitor Gen., NSW, 1997; Lieut-Gov. and Chief Justice, NSW, 1998–2011. Arbitrator, One Essex Ct, London, 2011–; Non-Permanent Judge, HK Ct of Final Appeal, 2013–. Chairman: Nat. Liby of Australia, 2010–12; Australian Broadcasting Corporation, 2012–17; Judith Neilson Inst. of Journalism, 2019–. *Publications:* Secrecy: political censorship in Australia, 1972; (jtly) The Nuclear Barons, 1981; Becket and Henry, 2004; Statutory Interpretation and Human Rights, 2008; Speeches of a Chief Justice, 2008; Opening Law Term, 2010; Transitions in the Court: ceremonial speeches of Chief Justice Spigelman, 1998–2011, 2012. *Recreations:* swimming, recumbency, walking.

**SPIKINGS, Barry Peter;** Partner, Spikings Entertainment (formerly Pleskow/Spikings Partnership), international production and distribution of feature films, since 1992; *b* Boston, Lincs, 23 Nov. 1939; *m* 1st, 1962, Judith Anne; one *s* one *d*; 2nd, 1978, Dorothy; two step *d*. *Educ:* Boston Grammar School. Joint Managing Director: British Lion Films Ltd, 1973–75; EMI Films Ltd, 1975–78; Director, EMI Films Inc., 1975–78; Chm. and Chief Exec. Officer, EMI Film and Theatre Corp., 1978–80; Chm., Elstree Studios, 1978–82; Chm. and Chief Exec., Thorn EMI Films Worldwide, 1980–82; Pres. and Chief Operating Officer, Nelson Entertainment Inc., 1986–91. Member: Acad. of Motion Picture Arts and Scis; BAFTA. Oscar award as Producer of Best Picture of the Year, for The Deer Hunter, 1979; elected one of America's Greatest Hundred Movies by Amer. Film Inst., 1999; other films include: as producer: Conduct Unbecoming; The Man Who Fell to Earth; Convoy; Texasville; Beyond Rangoon; Lone Survivor; as distributor: Close Encounters of the Third Kind; The Deep; City Slickers; When Harry Met Sally; The Last Emperor. Hon. DArts Lincoln, 2006. *Recreation:* making films.

**SPILLANTINI, Prof. Maria Grazia,** PhD; FRS 2013; FMedSci; William Scholl Professor of Molecular Neurology, Department of Clinical Neurosciences, University of Cambridge, since 2007; Fellow of Clare Hall, Cambridge, since 1994; *b* Arezzo, Italy, 10 Nov. 1957; *d* of late Otello Spillantini and Leonide Spillantini (*née* Mazzoni); partner, Michel Goedert, *qv*; one *s*. *Educ:* Liceo Scientifico Piero della Francesca, Sansepolcro; Univ. of Florence (Laurea Biol Scis 1981); Peterhouse, Cambridge and MRC Lab. of Molecular Biol. (PhD Molecular Biol. 1993). Mem., Scientific Staff, Nat. Res. Council Inst. of Cell Biol., Rome, 1992–93, 1995–96; Res. Scientist, MRC Lab. of Molecular Biol., 1993–95; Cambridge Centre for Brain Repair, University of Cambridge: Sen. Res. Associate, 1996–97; William Scholl Lectr in Neurol. (non clinical), 1997–2002; William Scholl Reader in Molecular Neurol., 2002–07. Mem. Council, Royal Soc., 2019–. FMedSci 2010. Citizen, Caprese Michelangelo, 2002. Potamkin Prize, Amer. Acad. of Neurol., 2000; Alessandro Agnoli Prize, Italian League Against Movement Disorders and Dementia, 2003; Fair Play Prize for Scientific Res., Semplicemente Donna, 2013; Cotzias Prize, Spanish Soc. of Neurol., 2014; Career Achievements Award, Italian Assoc. Frontotemporal Degeneration Patients, 2015; Jay Van Andel Award, Van Andel Inst., 2015; Camillo Golgi Medal, Golgi Foundn, 2017; Knight, Order of the Star of Italy, 2018; Thudicum Medal, Biochem. Soc., 2020. *Publications:* contrib. res. papers and reviews in scientific jls. *Recreations:* walking, travelling, watching old movies. *Address:* Clifford Allbutt Building, Department of Clinical Neurosciences, University of Cambridge, Hills Road, Cambridge CB2 0AH. *T:* (01223) 331160, *Fax:* (01223) 331174. *E:* mgs11@cam.ac.uk.

**SPILLER, John Anthony Walsh,** MBE 1979; Technical Adviser to Organisation for Security and Co-operation in Europe/Office for Democratic Institutions and Human Rights Mission, Montenegro, on secondment to Foreign and Commonwealth Office, 1998; *b* 29 Dec. 1942; *s* of C. H. Spiller and Sarah (*née* Walsh), Moycullen, Co. Galway, Eire; *m* 1972, Angela, *d* of Surtees Gleghorn; one *s* one *d*. *Educ:* County Secondary Sch., Bideford; North Devon College. Member Executive, Nat. League of Young Liberals, 1960–61; Organiser, Torrington Constituency Liberal Assoc., 1962–64; Divl Liberal Agent, Cornwall (Northern) Parly Constituency, 1965–71; Northern Regional Organiser (Election Agent, Rochdale By-elecn 1972 and Berwick-upon-Tweed By-elecn 1973), 1972–74; Nat. Agent, Liberal Central Assoc., 1974–76; Mem., Liberal Party Gen. Elecn Campaign Cttee, and Press Officer, Gen. Elections Feb. and Oct. 1974; Western Area Agent, 1977–80; Advisor, African Peoples Union, Independence Elections, Zimbabwe, 1980; By-elecn and Marginal Seats Agent, Liberal Party Org. Headquarters, 1981–82; Sec. Gen., Liberal Party, 1983–85; Co. Liaison Officer, Devonshire PHAB Organisation UK, 1990–92; Sen. Consultant, Western Approaches PR Ltd, 1993–96. Chm., Lib Dem Campaign, Cornwall (Northern), Gen. Elecn 1992; Advr, Electoral Reform Soc., Democracy Conf., Lithuania, 1992, Estonia, 1995, Croatia, 1997. Conf. Deleg., Moscow, 1995, Armenia, 1996, Estonia, 1999, on behalf of OSCE. Mem. Bd of Management, Gladstone Benevolent Fund, 1980–98 (Sec. 1980, Hon. Sec., 1993). *Recreations:* golf, walking in Connemara. *Address:* 34 Fore Street, Northam, Bideford, Devon EX39 1AW.

**SPILLER, Prof. Robin Charles,** MD; FRCP; Professor of Gastroenterology, Nottingham University, since 2000; *b* Limpsfield, 3 April 1950; *s* of Reginald Harvey Spiller and Margaret Spiller; *m* 1978, Susan Angela Smith; one *s* two *d*. *Educ:* Whitgift Sch., Croydon; Magdalene Coll., Cambridge (BA 1971; BChir 1975; MB 1976; MD 1986); London Sch. of Econs and Pol Sci. (MSc). MRCP 1977, FRCP 1993. Trng in London, incl. Registrar posts at Charing Cross, W Middx and Central Middx Hosps, 1975–84; MRC Travelling Fellow, Mayo Clinic, Minn, 1984–85; Sen. Registrar, Central Middx Hosp., 1985–88; Consultant Physician, Nottingham Univ. Hosps, 1988–2000; Dir, Biomed. Res. Unit, Nottingham Digestive Diseases Centre, 2009–15. Ed., GUT: Internat. Jl Gastroenterol. and Hepatol., 2003–09. *Publications:* (ed jtly) Irritable Bowel Syndrome: a clinician's guide, 2002; (ed with D. Grundy) Pathophysiology of the enteric nervous system: a basis for understanding functional diseases, 2004. *Recreations:* hill walking, sailing, gardening, stone carving. *Address:* Nottingham Digestive Diseases Centre, Nottingham University Hospitals NHS Trust, Queen's Medical Centre Campus, Clifton Boulevard, Nottingham NG7 2UH. *T:* (0115) 823 1090, *Fax:* (0115) 823 1409. *E:* robin.spiller@nottingham.ac.uk.

**SPINDLER, Susan Mary;** consultant and writer, since 2008; Deputy Director, Drama, Entertainment and Children's, BBC, 2005–07; *b* 1 March 1955; *d* of Kenneth Spindler and Elsie Spindler (*née* Knapper); *m* 1980, Peter Guy Brown, two *s* one *d*. *Educ:* Wycombe High Sch.; Newnham Coll., Cambridge (BA Hons English 1977). Grad. trainee, Thomson Newspapers, 1978–80; BBC, 1980–2007: prodn trainee, 1980–82; Asst Producer and Producer, 1983–88; Producer, Doctors to Be, 1988–92; Ed., QED, 1992–94; Dep. Hd, Sci. Dept, 1994–96; Chief Advr, Editl Policy, 1997; Hd of Strategy, Drama, 1998–99;

Controller, Drama Production, 1999–2000; Controller, Factual Drama and New Media, 2000–01; Project Dir, Making It Happen, 2002–04. *Publications:* The Tomorrow's World Book of Food, 1984; Doctors to Be, 1992. *E:* susanspindler@gmail.com

**SPINK, Andrew John Murray;** QC 2003; a Recorder, since 2005; a Deputy High Court Judge, since 2008; *b* 21 April 1962; *s* of Nigel Spink and Penny Spink; *m* 1994, Susan Katherine Vivien Taylor; one *s* two *d*. *Educ:* Sherborne Sch.; Queens' Coll., Cambridge (MA). Called to the Bar, Middle Temple, 1985, Bencher, 2010. *Address:* Outer Temple Chambers, Outer Temple, 222 Strand, WC2R 1BA. *T:* (020) 7353 6381, *Fax:* (020) 7583 1786.

**SPINK, Air Marshal Clifford Rodney,** CB 2002; CBE 1992 (OBE 1989); FRAeS; Managing Director, Clifford Spink Associates Ltd, since 2003; Chairman, Spitfire Ltd, since 2005; *b* 17 May 1946; *s* of Ronald Charles Spink and Beryl Spink (*née* Phillips); *m* 1977, Caroline Anne Smith; one *s* one *d*. *Educ:* Sheerness Sch.; Halton Apprentice, RAF Coll., Cranwell. FRAeS 1997. Commissioned RAF 1968; Sqn Pilot, 111/56 Sqn, 1970–76; Instructor, RMA Sandhurst, 1976–78; Flight Comdr, 111 Sqn, 1979–82; NDC, 1982–83; HQ RAF Germany, 1983–86; OC No 74 (Fighter) Sqn, 1986–89; Stn Comdr and Dep. Comdr British Forces, Falkland Islands, 1989–90; Detachment Comdr, Dhahran, Gulf conflict, 1990–91; Stn Comdr, RAF Coningsby, 1990–93; rcds, 1993; SASO, No 11 Group, 1993–95; COS No 18 Group, 1995–96; AOC No 11/18 Gp, 1996–98; DG, Saudi Armed Forces Project, 1998–2002; retired RAF, 2003. Director: Contingency Planning Associates Ltd, 2004–14; Eastern Airways Ltd, 2019–. Chairman: Atlantic Reconnaissance, 2003–06; London Ashford Airport Ltd, 2004–10; Trustees, Battle of Britain Mus., Bentley Priory, 2016–. President: ROC Assoc., 1996–; Battle of Britain Meml Flight Assoc., 2007. FCMI (FIMgt 1992). Liveryman, Hon. Co. of Air Pilots, (formerly GAPAN), 2004– (Master, 2012–13). *Recreations:* vintage aircraft flying, winter sports, golf. *Club:* Royal Air Force.

**SPINK, Dr Robert Michael;** *b* 1 Aug. 1948; *s* of George and Brenda Spink; *m* 1968, Janet Mary Barham (marr. diss. 2002); three *s* one *d*. *Educ:* Manchester Univ. (research and academic prizes; BSc 1st Cl. Hons Eng 1971); Cranfield Inst. of Technology (MSc Indust Eng 1974; PhD, Sch. of Management, 1989). CEng, MIProdE, MIIM, MIMC, CDipAF. Mill labourer, 1962–64; RAF, 1964–66; EMI Electronics, 1966–77 (Engrg Apprentice; EMI Graduate Apprentice of the Year, 1971); Management consultant, 1977–; Dir and Co-Owner, Seafarer Navigation International, 1980–84; industrial engr, 1984–; Dir, Bournemouth Internat. Airport, 1989–93. Dorset County Councillor, 1985–93 (Chm., Educn Policy Cttee, 1989–91); Mem., Dorset Police Authy, 1985–93. Contested (C) Castle Point, 1997. MP Castle Point, 1992–97 and 2001–10 (C, 1992–97 and 2001–08, UK Ind, 2008, Ind 2008–10); contested (Ind) same seat, 2010. PPS to Minister of State, Dept of Employment, then Home Office, 1994–97. Mem., Educn Select Cttee, 1992–97; Vice Chm., Backbench Employment Cttee, 1993–94; Chm., All Party Parly Gp for Prisoners Abroad, 1995–97. Founder Mem., Better Off Out Campaign, 2006; Chairman: Pro-Referendum Alliance, 2007; Campaign for Ind. Britain, 2008–10. Dep. Chm., Poole Cons. Assoc., 1984–92; Mem. Nat. Exec., Baby Life Support Systems Charity, 1985–92. MCMI. *Recreations:* occasional marathons, gardening, potter.

**SPINKS, Mary Cecilia,** CBE 2010; RGN; health services consultant, specialising in risk management, audit and expert opinion on malpractice, 1993–2010; *b* 20 Sept. 1940; *d* of Francis and Mary Clark; *m* 1st, 1961, Robert Donn (marr. diss. 1975); 2nd, 1992, Leslie Oswald Spinks (*d* 2014). *Educ:* St Vincent's Convent, Cork; Student Nurse, Whipps Cross Hosp. (RGN 1962); DipN London; William Rathbone Coll.; Thames Polytechnic (DMS). Post-graduate Staff Nurse, Charing Cross Hosp., 1962; Theatre Sister, St Mary's Hosp., Paddington, 1963–64; Theatre Sister, Nursing Officer, Sen. Nursing Officer, Bromley AHA, 1964–83; Dir, Nursing Services, Lewisham and N Southwark HA, 1983–84; Chief Nursing Officer and Dir, Consumer Affairs, Brighton HA, 1984–90; Regl Nursing Officer, NE Thames RHA, 1990–93. Former chm. and mem., nursing, health, editorial and advisory cttees; Chm., Nat. Assoc. of Theatre Nurses, 1975–78; Member: Maidstone HA, 1985–90; NHS Training Authy, 1988–91. Chm., E Berks Community Trust, 1998–2002 (Life Vice Pres., Windsor League of Friends). Dir, Florence Nightingale Foundn, 1996–2010 (Vice Pres., 2010–). Vis. Prof., Univ. of Ulster, 2007–11. MRSM 1992. *Publications:* From SRN to CBE: celebrating 50 remarkable years in nursing, 2014; numerous contribs to professional jls. *Recreations:* horse-racing, cricket, gardening. *Address:* 2 Somerford Close, Maidenhead, Berks SL6 8EJ. *T:* (01628) 675526.

**SPIRA, Catherine Ruth, (Kate);** *see* Pakenham, C. R.

**SPIRO, Dafna Miriam; Her Honour Judge Spiro;** a Circuit Judge, since 2018; *b* Oxford, 2 Aug. 1969; *d* of Robin and Nitza Spiro; *m* 2003, William Evans; one *s* one *d* and two step *s* one step *d*. *Educ:* South Hampstead High Sch.; Univ. of Sussex (BA Hons); Thames Valley Univ. (CPE); Inns of Court Sch. of Law (BVC). Called to the Bar, Inner Temple, 1994; a Recorder, 2009–18. *Recreations:* family, cinema, reading, TV dramas, dog walks, food/cooking. *Address:* Harrow Crown Court, Hailsham Drive, Harrow HA1 4TU.

**SPIRO, Prof. Stephen George,** MD; FRCP; Professor of Respiratory Medicine, University College London, 1997–2009; Consultant Physician, University College London Hospitals NHS Trust, 1997–2009, now Hon. Consultant, Royal Brompton Hospital and University College London Hospitals; *b* 24 Aug. 1942; *s* of late Ludwig Spiro and Anna Spiro (*née* Freidmann); *m* 1971, Alison Mary Brown; three *s*. *Educ:* Manchester Univ. (BSc Anatomy 1964; MB ChB 1967; MD 1975). FRCP 1981. Consultant Physician, Royal Brompton Hosp., 1977–93. Res. Fellow, Hammersmith Hosp., 1971–73; Sen. Registrar, Royal Brompton Hosp., 1973–77; Clin. Dir of Med. Services, 1994–2000, Med. Dir, 2001–03, UCL Hosps NHS Trust. Fulbright-Hayes Travelling Scholarship, Seattle, 1975–76. Visiting Professor: South African Respiratory Soc., 1993; Univ. of Queensland, Australia, 1994. Chairman: London Lung Cancer Clinical Trials Gp, 1997–2008; N London Cancer Network for Lung Cancer, 1997–2008; Trustees, Rennie Grove Hospice Care, 2013–; Vice-Chairman: NE London Adv. Cttee for Clinical Excellence, 2003–08; British Lung Foundn, 2008–13, 2015–. President: European Respiratory Soc., 1996–97; British Thoracic Soc., 2004; Section of Respiratory Medicine, RSocMed, 2014–17. Trustee, Chai Cancer Care, 1994–2017. Chief Investigator, CRUK nat. trial of screening for lung cancer in high risk populations, 2006–17. British Thoracic Soc. Medal, 2013. Exec. Ed., Thorax, 1991–95. *Publications:* Drug Treatment of Respiratory Disease, 1994; (jtly) New Perspectives on Lung Cancer, 1994; Carcinoma of the Lung, 1995, 2nd edn 2001; (ed) Self-Assessment Colour Review of Respiratory Medicine, 1997, 3rd edn 2012; The Lung in Auto-Immune Disease, 1997; (ed) Comprehensive Respiratory Medicine, 1999, 4th edn as Clinical Respiratory Medicine, 2012; Sarcoidosis, 2012; over 300 articles and chapters in textbooks. *Recreations:* tennis, flyfishing, worrying about Arsenal, home handyman. *Address:* 66 Grange Gardens, Pinner, Middx HA5 5QF. *Clubs:* Croxley Hall Fly Fishery; Eastcote Tennis.

**SPITTLE, Graham Nigel,** CBE 2008; Dean of Innovation, University of Edinburgh, since 2017; Chairman, Health Data Research UK, since 2017; *b* Lewisham, 2 Nov. 1955; *s* of Richard and Ruby Spittle; *m* 1983, Julie Ann Wooldridge; two *s*. *Educ:* Edinburgh Univ. (MA Hons). FBCS 2001. Ford Motor Co., 1978–85; joined IBM, 1985: Internat. Assignment, IBM NY, 1995–97; Dir, MQSeries Develt, 2000–01; Vice-Pres., Develt, IBM UK and Dir, IBM Hursley Lab., 2001–07; Vice-Pres., Software, IBM UK and Ireland, 2007–10; Chief Technol. Officer, Europe, and Vice-Pres., Software Gp, IBM, 2010–17. Chm., Technol. Strategy Bd, 2002–11. Mem., UKRI-MRC, 2018–. Visiting Professor: Edinburgh Univ., 2002–; Southampton Univ., 2002–; Bristol Univ., 2007–. Member: Ct of Benefactors, Oxford Univ., 2001–; Council, Southampton Univ., 2008–. FRSA 2018. Hon. DSc Southampton, 2005. *Recreations:* music, sailing, motor racing, astronomy.

**SPITTLE, His Honour Leslie;** a Circuit Judge, 1996–2010; a Deputy Circuit Judge, 2010–15; *b* 14 Nov. 1940; *s* of Samuel and Irene Spittle; *m* 1963, Brenda Clayton; three *s*. *Educ:* Teesside Poly. (ACIS); Hull Univ. (LLB). Mgt trainee, Head Wrightson & Co., 1956–62; Lectr in Law, Econs and Accountancy, Bradford Tech. Coll., 1965–66; Sen. Lectr in Law, Teesside Poly., 1966–70. Called to the Bar, Gray's Inn, 1970; in private practice, 1970–96. Member: Parole Bd, 2010–; Judicial Rep., Standards Cttee, 2016–. Mem., Eyam Parish Council, 2018–. Paul Harris Fellow, Teesside West Rotary Club. Visitor, Teesside Univ. *Recreations:* family, National Trust volunteer, beekeeping, trying to play ukelele.

**SPITTLE, Dr Margaret Flora, (Mrs David Hare),** OBE 2004; FRCP, FRCR; Consultant Clinical Oncologist: University College Hospital (formerly at Middlesex Hospital), 1971–2008; St John's Centre for Diseases of the Skin, St Thomas' Hospital, 1971–2008; *b* 10 Nov. 1939; *d* of Edwin William Spittle and Ada Florence Spittle (*née* Axam); *m* 1st, 1965, Dr Clive Lucas Harmer (marr. diss. 1977); two *d*; 2nd, 1986, David John Hare. *Educ:* King's Coll., London (AKC 1963; MSc 1969); Westminster Hosp. Med. Sch. (MB BS 1963). MRCS 1963; LRCP 1963, MRCP 1993, FRCP 1995; DMRT 1966; FRCR (Rohan Williams Gold Medal) 1968. Sen. Registrar, Radiotherapy Dept, Westminster Hosp., 1969; Instr, Radiation Div., Stanford Univ. Med. Centre, 1970; Hon. Consultant Clinical Oncologist: W Middx Univ. Hosp., 1971–2002; Royal Nat. Throat, Nose and Ear Hosp., 1986–2008; St Luke's Hosp. for the Clergy, 1993–2006. Civilian Consultant Advr in Radiation Medicine, RN, 2000–. Member: Nat. Radiation Protection Bd, 1991–98; Govt Adv. Cttee on Breast Screening, 1986–96; Govt Cttee on Medicine and Radiation in the Envmt, 1993–; Govt Adv. Gp on Ionizing Radiation, 1995–; DoH Commng Gp for Health of the Nation Projects, 1996; Defence Nuclear Safety Cttee, 2002–14; Depleted Uranium Oversight Bd, 2002–10. Chairman: Multicentre Cancer Chemotherapy Gp, 1985–; UK AIDS Oncology Gp, 1988–. Vice-President: RSocMed, 1994–96 (Sen. Hon. Treas., 1988–94; Pres., Oncology Sect., 1987, Radiology Sect., 1989); Royal Coll. of Radiologists, 1995–96 (Dean, Faculty of Clin. Oncology, 1994–96); Pres., Assoc. of Head and Neck Oncologists of GB, 1990–92. *Publications:* chapters and articles on cancer of breast, head and neck, skin, and AIDS-related malignancy. *Recreations:* family, flying, golf, ski-ing, gardening. *Address:* The Manor House, 20 Beaconsfield Road, Claygate, Surrey KT10 0PW. *T:* (01372) 465540. *Clubs:* Royal Automobile, Royal Society of Medicine.

**SPITZ, Prof. Lewis,** PhD; FRCS, FRCSE, FRCPCH; Nuffield Professor of Paediatric Surgery, and Head of Surgical Unit, Institute of Child Health, London, 1979–2004, now Emeritus Nuffield Professor; Consultant Surgeon, Great Ormond Street Hospital for Children Trust (formerly Hospital for Sick Children, Great Ormond Street), 1979–2006, now Hon. Consultant Surgeon; *b* 25 Aug. 1939; *s* of Woolf and Selma Spitz; *m* 1972, Louise Ruth Dyzenhaus; one *s* one *d*. *Educ:* Univ. of Pretoria (MB, ChB); Univ. of the Witwatersrand (PhD). FRCS (*ad eundem*) 1980; FRCSE 1969; FRCPCH 1997, Hon. FRCPCH 2004. Smith and Nephew Fellow, Liverpool and London, 1971; Paediatric Surgeon, Johannesburg, 1971–74; Consultant Paediatric Surgeon, Sheffield Children's Hosp., 1974–79. Hon. Consultant in Paediatric Surgery to the Army, 1983–2006. Windermere Vis. Prof., Univ. of Melbourne, 1988; Chafin-Snyder Vis. Prof., Children's Hosp., UCLA, 1992; Santuli Vis. Prof., Babies Hosp., Columbia Univ., NY, 1992; Penman Vis. Prof., Red Cross Meml Hosp. and Univ. of Cape Town, 2000; Guttman Vis. Prof., Montreal, 2000; Jewitt Vis. Prof., Children's Hosp. of Buffalo, 2001–; Visiting Professor: Toronto, 1991; Seattle, 1992; Univ. of Hong Kong, 1993; Indianapolis, Pittsburgh, Washington, 1995; Royal Coll. of Surgeons, Thailand, 1995; Ann Arbor, 1997; Royal Coll. of Surgeons, Korea, 1997; Japanese Surgical Soc., 1998; Albert Einstein Coll. of Medicine, NY, 1999; Univ. of Alabama, 2003; Kansas, 2005; Adelaide, 2005; Chile, 2005. Hunterian Prof., RCS, 2001–02; Lectures: Sulamaa, Children's Hosp., Univ. of Helsinki, 1993 (Sulamaa Medal, 1990); Amer. Pediatric Surgical Assoc., 1995; P. Rickham Meml, Liverpool, 2004; J. Grosfeld, Indianapolis, 2005; Jl of Pediatric Surgery, Amer. Pediatric Surgical Assoc., 2011; Stephen Gans Meml, Amer. Acad. of Pediatrics, 2013. Member: British Assoc. of Paediatric Surgeons (Pres., 1996–98); Assoc. of Surgeons of GB and Ireland; BPA (Mem. Acad. Bd, 1991–93); British Soc. of Gastroenterology; Med. Bd, Tracheo-oesophageal Support Soc., 1982–; Central London Res. Ethics Cttee, 2008– (Dep. Vice-Chm., 2017–); Invited Mem., RCS, 1997–2000; Chm., Specialist Adv. Cttee in Paediatric Surgery, 1994–2004 (RCS Rep., 1991–96); RCS Rep on Intercollegiate Bd of Paediatric Surgery, 1994–97. Trustee, Hunterian Mus., RCS, 2011–. Television: Your Life in their Hands, BBC TV: The baby who could not swallow, 1984; Siamese Twins, 1986; Separating Twins, BBC TV, 2005. Exec. Editor, Progress in Paediatric Surgery, 1982; Member, Editorial Board: Jl of Paediatric Surgery, 1980–; Archives of Diseases in Childhood, 1984–89; Turkish Jl of Paediatric Surgery, 1987–; Jl of RCSE, 1992–97; Associate Editor, Pediatric Surgery International, 1986–2004; Editorial Consultant: Surgery in Childhood International, 1996–; Annals of College of Surgery of Hong Kong, 1996–. Patron, Children's Wish, 1998. MRSocMed. Hon. FAAP 1987; Hon. FRCSI 2005; Hon. Fellow, Inst. of Child Health, UCL, 2011; Hon. FACS 2012; Hon. FCSSA; Hon. FCMSA. Hon. Mem., Paediatric Surgical Assocs of Switzerland, Austria, Greece, Germany, Asia, America and S Africa. Hon. MD: Sheffield, 2002; Witwatersrand, 2008. Bronze Medal, Nordik Soc. of Paediatric Surgeons, 1990; James Spence Medal, RCPCH, 2004; Denis Browne Gold Medal, Brit. Assoc. of Paediatric Surgeons, 2004; Clement-Price Thomas Award, RCS, 2004; Rehbein Medal, German Assoc. of Paediatric Surgeons, 2008; Rehbein Medal, Eur. Pediatric Surgical Assoc., 2010; Ladd Medal, Amer. Assoc. of Pediatrics (Surgical Section), 2012; P. P. Rickham Medal, Alder Hey Children's Hosp., 2015. *Publications:* A Colour Atlas of Paediatric Surgical Diagnosis, 1981; A Colour Atlas of Surgery for Undescended Testes, 1984; Paediatric Surgery, 4th edn (with H. H. Nixon) 1988 (Rob and Smith Operative Surgery series), 7th edn as Operative Paediatric Surgery (with A. G. Coran) 2013; (ed jtly) The Great Ormond Street Colour Handbook of Paediatrics & Child Health, 2007, 2nd edn as Great Ormond Street Handbook of Paediatrics, 2016; Visual Handbook of Paediatrics and Child Health: the core, 2008; chapters in books on paediatrics and surgery; articles on oesophageal atresia, oesophageal replacement, gastro-oesophageal reflux, neonatal surgical conditions, paediatric oncology, and conjoined twins; contribs to Seminars in Pediatric Surgery. *Recreations:* sport, reading, food and wine. *Address:* Flat 2, Roseneath Mansions, 59 Woodside Avenue, N10 3JA.

**SPOFFORTH, (David) Mark,** OBE 2014; FCA; Partner, Kreston Reeves LLP (formerly Spofforths), Chartered Accountants, since 1982 (Managing Partner, 1997–2000, 2010–12); President, Institute of Chartered Accountants in England and Wales, 2012–13 (Deputy President, 2011–12); *b* Worthing, Sussex, 26 July 1956; *s* of Michael Gordon Spofforth and Joan Mary Spofforth (*née* Marsh); *m* 1st, 1983, Dorothy Lesley (*d* 2007); one *s* one *d*; 2nd, 2015, Veronica Anne. *Educ:* Durham Univ. (BSc). FCA 1982; CTA 2005. Coopers and

Lybrand, 1979–82. Institute of Chartered Accountants in England and Wales: Member: Council, 1993– (Chm., 2003–05); Main Bd (formerly Exec.), 1998–2007, 2009–; Tech. Adv. Cttee, 1985–94; Gen. Practitioner Bd, 1993–99 (Chm., 1995–98); Remuneration Cttee, 2010–13; Chm., Educn and Trng Bd, 2000–03, 2005–07. Mem., Internat. Accounting Educn Standards Bd, 2005–10 (Dep. Chm., 2009–10). Bd Observer, IFAC, 2014–. Broadcaster, BBC Southern Counties Radio, 1996–2006. Gov., Sion Sch., Worthing, 1987–. Trustee, Thalidomide Trust 2013–. Liveryman: Horners' Co., 1979– (Master, 2009); Chartered Accountants' Co., 2005– (Master, 2016–17). High Sheriff, W Sussex, 2016–. *Recreations:* watching Rugby, watching international swimming (daughter, Gemma, is a 2008 and 2012 Olympian and world record holder in 100m backstroke event), scuba diving. *Address:* Kreston Reeves LLP, 9 Donnington Park, 85 Birdham Road, Chichester, Sussex PO20 7AJ. *T:* (01243) 787627. *E:* mark.spofforth@krestonreeves.com. *Clubs:* City Livery, Carlton.

**SPOKES, Ann;** *see* Spokes Symonds, A. H.

**SPOKES, John Arthur Clayton;** QC 1973; *b* 6 Feb. 1931; 2nd *s* of late Peter Spencer Spokes and Lilla Jane Spokes (*née* Clayton), Oxford; *m* 1961, Jean, *yr d* of late Dr Robert McLean and Jean Symington McLean (*née* Barr), Carluke; one *s* one *d*. *Educ:* Westminster Sch.; Brasenose Coll., Oxford (BA 1954; MA 1959); King Alfred's Coll., Winchester (MA Southampton Univ. 2000). Nat. Service, Royal Artillery, 1949–51 (commnd 1950). Called to Bar, Gray's Inn, 1955, Bencher, 1985; a Recorder, 1972–93. Chm., Data Protection, subseq. Inf., Tribunal, 1985–2001. Chancellor, Dio. of Winchester, 1985–93. *Recreation:* local history. *Address:* 31 Southgate Street, Winchester, Hants SO23 9EB. *Club:* Leander (Henley-on-Thames).
*See also* A. H. Spokes Symonds.

**SPOKES SYMONDS, Ann (Hazel);** Chairman, Age Concern England, 1983–86 (Vice-President, 1987–94; Patron, 1994–2010); *b* 10 Nov. 1925; *d* of Peter Spencer Spokes and Lilla Jane Spokes (*née* Clayton); *m* 1980, (John) Richard (Charters) Symonds (*d* 2006). *Educ:* Wychwood Sch., Oxford; Masters Sch., Dobbs Ferry, NY, USA; St Anne's Coll., Oxford (BA 1947; MA). Organising Secretary: Oxford Council of Social Service, 1959–74; Age Concern Oxford, 1958–80. Dir, ATV, 1978–81; Mem. W Midlands Bd, Central Ind. Television plc, 1981–92. Mem., Thames Valley Police Authy, 1973–85; Chm., No 5 Police Dist Authy Cttee, 1982–85; Vice-Chm., Personal Social Services Council, 1978–80; Chm., Social Services Cttee, ACC, 1978–82; Mem. Bd, Anchor Housing Assoc., 1976–83, 1985–94; Member: Prince of Wales' Adv. Gp on Disability, 1983–90; Oftel Adv. Cttee for Disabled and Elderly People, 1985–91; Hearing Aid Council, 1986–89; Trustee, CERT, 1986–89. Member: Oxford City Council, 1957–95 (Lord Mayor, 1976–77; Hon. Alderman, 1995–); Oxfordshire CC, 1974–85 (Chm., 1981–83). Contested (C) NE Leicester, 1959, Brigg, 1966 and 1970. Mem., Soc. of Authors, 1992–. FRSA 1991. *Publications:* Celebrating Age: an anthology, 1987; Havens Across the Sea, 1990, rev. edn 2015; The Great Grosvenor Hotel Scandal, 1993; Storks, Black Bags and Gooseberry Bushes, 1993; The Changing Faces of Wolvercote, Wytham and Godstow, 1997, 2nd edn 2011; The Changing Faces of North Oxford, Books One and Two, 1998; The Changing Faces of Iffley, 1999; The Changing Faces of Rose Hill, 2000; Oxfordshire People and the Forgotten War: the Anglo-Boer conflict 1899–1902, 2002; (with Richard Symonds) Follow Me: a dog's view of the gospel story, 2006; (with Chris Nichols) The Changing Faces of Summertown and Cutteslowe, Book Two, 2009; (with Nigel Morgan) The Origins of Oxford Street Names, 2010, 2nd edn 2011; Also-Rans: the injustice of history, 2014. *Recreations:* lawn tennis, golf, photography, enjoying cats. *Address:* 43 Davenant Road, Oxford OX2 8BU. *T:* (01865) 515661.
*See also* J. A. C. Spokes.

**SPOTTISWOODE, Clare Mary Joan,** CBE 1999; Chairman: Gas Strategies Ltd, since 2000; Xoserve Ltd, since 2019; *b* 20 March 1953; *d* of late Charlotte and of Tony Spottiswoode; *m* 1977, Oliver Richards; one *s* three *d*. *Educ:* Cheltenham Ladies' Coll.; Clare Coll., Cambridge (MA Maths Pt 1, Economics Pt 2); Yale Univ. (MPhil). HM Treasury, 1977–80; Spottiswoode Trading, 1980–84 (wholesale importing business); Chm. and Chief Exec., Spottiswoode and Spottiswoode (micro computer software), 1984–90; Dir Gen. of Gas Supply, 1993–98; Sen. Vice Pres. of Regulatory Affairs, Europe, Azurix, Enron, 1998–99; Mem., Mgt Gp, PA Consulting Gp, 1999–2000; Dep. Chm., British Energy, 2001–07; Policyholder Advocate, Aviva, 2006–09. Dir, BioFuels, 2003–07; Chairman: Flow Energy, 2011–17; Magnox, 2011–14; Supervisory Bd, Naftogaz, 2017–; non-executive Director: Tullow Oil plc, 2002–11; Energy Solutions, 2009–13; Ilika, 2010–; G4S, 2010–; EnQuest plc, 2011–; RBC Europe Ltd, 2012–14; Ind. Dir, Payments Council, 2012–; BW Offshore, 2013–; Just Gp plc, 2016–. Hon. DSc Brunel, 1997. *Publications:* Quill, 1984; Abacus, 1984. *Recreations:* children, gardening, theatre.

**SPRACKLING, David Martin;** Parliamentary Counsel, since 2009; *b* Nottingham, 3 April 1963; *s* of Dr Peter Sprackling and Dr Margaret Sprackling (*née* Hughes). *Educ:* Nottingham High Sch.; Jesus Coll., Cambridge (BA Hons 1985); Worcester Coll., Oxford (MLitt Theol. 1995). Admitted as solicitor, 1988; Solicitor, Martineau Johnson, 1988–90; joined Parly Counsel Office, 1995; Asst Parly Counsel, 1995–99; Sen. Asst Parly Counsel, 1999–2003; on secondment to Law Commn, 1999–2001; Dep. Parly Counsel, 2003–09. *Recreations:* travel, books, languages, singing. *Address:* Office of the Parliamentary Counsel, 1 Horse Guards Road, SW1A 2HQ. *T:* (020) 7276 6561. *E:* david.sprackling@cabinetoffice.gov.uk.

**SPRAGG, Robert Forrester; His Honour Judge Spragg;** a Circuit Judge, since 2016; *b* Welwyn Garden City, 1 Feb. 1968; *s* of late John Spragg and of Vanessa Spragg; *m* 1997, Jennifer Sinclair; one *s* two *d*. *Educ:* Oundle Sch.; Newcastle Univ. (LLB Hons). Admitted solicitor, 1995; called to the Bar, Middle Temple, 2003; a Recorder, 2012–16. *Recreations:* family, walking, founder and coach of Wylam Rockettes. *Address:* Sheffield Crown Court, 50 West Bar, Sheffield S3 8PH. *T:* (0114) 281 2415; Newcastle Crown Court, Quayside, Newcastle upon Tyne NE1 3LA. *T:* (0191) 201 2000.

**SPRAGUE, David Keith,** MVO 1972; HM Diplomatic Service, retired; High Commissioner, Sierra Leone, 1991–93; *b* 20 Feb. 1935; *m* 1958, Audrey Mellon; two *s* one *d*. *Educ:* King Edward VI Grammar Sch., Camp Hill, Birmingham. Foreign Office, 1953; Nat. Service, 1953–55; FO, 1955, served Addis Ababa, Paris, Belgrade, Budapest, Kuala Lumpur, Abidjan, Sofia, and FCO; Dep. High Comr, Madras, 1986–89; Ambassador to Mongolia, 1989–91. *Recreations:* bridge, heathers. *Address:* 18 Springfield Road, Exmouth EX8 3JX.

**SPRAKE, Anthony Douglas;** HM Diplomatic Service, retired; Consul-General, Melbourne, 2001–03; *b* 16 July 1944; *s* of Douglas Alfred Sprake and Doris Elizabeth Sprake (*née* Grindley); *m* 1977, Jane Bonner McNeill; one *s* (and one *s* decd). *Educ:* City of Bath Boys' Sch.; Univ. of Keele (BA Hons Maths and Physics). Asst Principal, Min. of Labour, 1968–72; Private Sec. to Parly Under-Sec. of State for Employment, 1972–73; Principal, Dept of Employment, 1973–77; Labour Attaché, British Embassy, Brussels, 1977–79; joined Diplomatic Service, 1980: FCO, 1980–82; Dep. High Comr, Freetown, Sierra Leone, 1982–85; Defence Dept, FCO, 1986–88; MoD (on secondment), 1989; Counsellor (Commercial), The Hague, 1990–94; Head, Cultural Relns Dept, FCO, 1994–96; Minister and Consul Gen., Peking, 1996–2000; Hd, China and Hong Kong Dept, FCO, 2000. *Recreations:* sailing, theatre, bridge. *Address:* 1 Loggetts, 65 Alleyn Park, SE21 8AS.

**SPRANGE, Thomas Kimpton;** QC 2015; Partner, King & Spalding International LLP, since 2011; *b* Sydney, Australia, 21 Feb. 1972; *s* of Michael Sprange and Rosemary Sprange; two *s* one *d*. *Educ:* Cranbrook Sch.; Univ. of Sydney (DipLaw); Univ. of New South Wales (LLM). Admitted Solicitor, 2001; Associate, Vandervords, 1998–2000; Barlow Lyde & Gilbert, 2000–02; Steptoe & Johnson, 2002–11 (Partner, 2004–11). *Recreations:* swimming (Red Top Swim), martial arts (KO Muay Thai), reading, cinema, travel. *Address:* c/o King & Spalding International LLP, 125 Old Broad Street, EC2N 1AR. *T:* (020) 7551 7529. *E:* tsprange@kslaw.com.

**SPRATT, Prof. Brian Geoffrey,** CBE 2008; PhD; FMedSci; FRS 1993; Professor of Molecular Microbiology, Imperial College Faculty of Medicine, 2001–18, now Emeritus (Head of Department of Infectious Disease Epidemiology, 2004–12); *b* 21 March 1947; *s* of Clarence Albert Spratt and Marjory Alice (*née* Jeffreys); *m* 1st, 1986, Dr Jennifer Broome-Smith (marr. diss. 1995); one *s*; 2nd, 1995, Dr Jiaji Zhou (*d* 2017); one *s*. *Educ:* Tonbridge Sch.; University Coll. London (BSc, PhD). Research Fellow: Princeton Univ., 1973–75; Leicester Univ., 1975–80; Sussex University: Lectr in Biochem., 1980–87; Reader in Molecular Genetics, 1987–89; Prof., 1989–98; Prof. of Biology, Oxford Univ., 1998–2001; Wellcome Trust Principal Res. Fellow, 1989–2014. Founder FMedSci 1998. Fellow, Amer. Acad. of Microbiol., 2003. Fleming Award, Soc. for Gen. Microbiol., 1982; Pfizer Award, 1983; Hoechst-Roussel Award, Amer. Soc. for Microbiol., 1993; Kitasato Medal for Microbial Chemistry, Kitasato Inst., Japan, 1995; Leeuwenhoek Lect. and Medal, Royal Soc., 2003; Garrod Medal, British Soc. for Antimicrobial Chemotherapy, 2011; GlaxoSmithKline Internat. Award, Amer. Soc. for Microbiol., 2011. *Publications:* numerous pubns on microbiol. and genetics in learned jls. *Address:* Department of Infectious Disease Epidemiology, Imperial College Faculty of Medicine, St Mary's Hospital, W2 1PG. *T:* (020) 7594 3625.

**SPRAY, Martin Coulson,** CBE 2013; Chief Executive, Wildfowl and Wetlands Trust, since 2004; *b* London, 16 June 1951; *s* of Lionel Spray and Constance Spray; *m* 1977, Marian Madden; one *s* one *d*. *Educ:* Tiffin Boys' Sch., Kingston upon Thames; University Coll. of Swansea (BSc Hons). Mgt positions, SRC, subseq. SERC, 1974–88; Area Manager, WWF, 1988–91; Chief Exec., Berks, Bucks and Oxfordshire Wildlife Trust, 1991–2004; Actg Chief Exec., RSNC, 2003–04. Chm., North Wessex Downs Area of Outstanding Natural Beauty, 2001–03. Chm., Marine Conservation Soc., 2010–15. MInstD 2006; FInstD 2015. Hon. DSc Roehampton, 2013. *Recreations:* countryside, travel, family, friends. *Address:* Wildfowl and Wetlands Trust, Slimbridge, Glos GL2 7BT. *T:* (01453) 891131, *Fax:* (01453) 890827. *E:* Martin.Spray@wwt.org.uk. *Clubs:* Athenæum, Farmers.

**SPRENT, Prof. Janet Irene,** OBE 1996; DSc; FRSE; Professor of Plant Biology, University of Dundee, 1989–98, now Emeritus (Deputy Principal, 1995–98); *b* 10 Jan. 1934; *d* of James William and Dorothy May Findlater; *m* 1955, Peter Sprent (*d* 2016). *Educ:* Slough High Sch. for Girls; Imperial Coll. of Science and Technol., London (BSc; ARCS 1954); Univ. of Tasmania (PhD 1958); Univ. of London (DSc 1988). FRSE 1990. Scientific Officer, Rothamsted Exptl Stn, 1954–55; ICIANZ Res. Fellow, Univ. of Tasmania, 1955–58; Botany Mistress, Rochester Girls' Grammar Sch., 1959–61; Lectr, subseq. Sen. Lectr, Goldsmiths' Coll., London, 1960–67; University of Dundee: successively Res. Fellow, Lectr, Sen. Lectr and Reader, 1967–89; Dean, Faculty of Science and Engrg, 1987–89; Hd, Dept of Biol Scis, 1992–95. Hon. Res. Fellow, 1991, then Res. Associate, James Hutton (formerly Scottish Crop Res.) Inst. Extensive overseas collaboration, e.g. Australia, Brazil, Kenya, in nitrogen fixing crop and tree research. Member: Council, NERC, 1991–95; SHEFC, 1992–96; (ind.) JNCC, 1994–2000; Bd, Scottish Natural Heritage, 2001–07; Royal Commn on Envmtl Pollution, 2002–08. Trustee, 2007–15, Res. Associate, 2015–, Royal Botanic Gardens, Edinburgh. Mem. Governing Body and Trustee, MacAulay Land Use Res. Inst., 1990–2001 (Chm., 1995–2001). Hon. DAgrSc Uppsala, 2010. *Publications:* The Biology of Nitrogen Fixing Organisms, 1979; The Ecology of the Nitrogen Cycle, 1987; (with P. Sprent) Nitrogen Fixing Organisms: pure and applied aspects, 1990; (with P. Sprent) Suilven's World, 1995; Nodulation in Legumes, 2001; Legume Nodulation: a global perspective, 2009; papers in scientific jls and chapters in books and symposium vols. *Recreations:* walking, gardening, music. *Address:* 32 Birkhill Avenue, Wormit, Newport on Tay, Fife DD6 8PW. *T:* (01382) 541706. *Club:* Farmers.

**SPRIDDELL, Peter Henry;** Director: Capital & Counties plc, 1988–94; Capital Shopping Centres plc, 1994–2000; Royal Artillery Museums Ltd, 1990–94; *b* 18 Aug. 1928; *s* of Thomas Henry Spriddell and Eva Florence Spriddell; *m* 1952, Joyce Patricia (*née* Haycock); two *s* one *d*. *Educ:* Plymouth Coll.; Exeter Coll., Oxford (MA); Harvard Business Sch. Marks & Spencer: store management, 1951–68; Sen. Exec. Store Operations, 1968–70; Dir, 1970–88; Alternate Exec. Dir, 1970–72; Exec. Dir Personnel, 1972–75; Exec. Dir Store Operations, Transport, Building and Store Develt, Real Estate, 1975–88; Dir, NFC, 1978–82; non-exec. Mem., British Rail Property Bd, 1986–2001. Mem. Bd, British Council of Shopping Centres, 1983–95 (Pres., 1988–89; Hon. Life Mem., 1998). Mem. Council, 1978–94, Barclay Fellow, 1994–2003, Hon. Life Fellow, 2003, Templeton Coll., Oxford (formerly Oxford Centre for Management Studies). Mem. Cttee, Wine Soc., 1998–2000. FRSA. Freeman, City of London; Liveryman, Worshipful Co. of Paviors, 1984. *Recreations:* music, golf. *Club:* Moor Park Golf.

**SPRING,** family name of **Baron Risby**.

**SPRING, Sir Dryden (Thomas),** Kt 1994; dairy farmer; Director, 1983–98, Chairman, 1989–98, New Zealand Dairy Board; *b* 6 Oct. 1939; *s* of Maurice Spring and Violet Grace Spring; *m* 1st, 1960, Christine Margaret McCarthy (marr. diss. 2002); three *s* three *d*; 2nd, 2003, Margaret Skews. *Educ:* Walton Primary Sch.; Matamata Coll. NZ Co-operative Dairy Co. Ltd: Dir, 1973–98; Dep. Chm., 1979–82; Chm., 1982–89. Director: Rural Banking and Finance Corp., 1974–88; Maramarua Coalfields Ltd, 1978–84; Nufarm (formerly Fernz Corp.) Ltd, 1982–2004; Goodman Fielder Ltd, 1989–2003 (Dep. Chm., 2000–03); Nat. Bank of NZ, 1994–2003; Maersk New Zealand Ltd, 1999–2004; Fletcher Building Ltd, 2001–11; Sky City Entertainment Group Ltd, 2003–11; Port of Tauranga Ltd, 2004–14, and other cos; Chairman: WEL Networks Ltd, 1999–2005; Ericsson Communications NZ Ltd, 1999–2003; Tenon (formerly Fletcher Challenge Forests) Ltd, 2001–04; ANZ Nat. Bank, 2006–12 (Dir, 2003–12); Coda Gp LP, 2015–; Dep. Chm., Ports of Auckland Ltd, 1988–94. Member: Prime Minister's Enterprise Council, 1991–94; Asian Pacific Econ. Co-operation Eminent Persons Gp, 1994–96; Internat. Adv. Bd, Chile Pacific Foundn, 2005–; Chm., Asia 2000 Foundn of NZ, 2001–06. Hon. Chm., NZ/Philippines Business Council, 1992–98. Chm., ASEAN/NZ Combined Business Council, 1998–99; NZ Chm., Business Adv. Council, Asia Pacific Econ. Co-operation, 2000–06; Patron, NZ/Thailand Business Council, 1995–98. Fellow, 1993, Dist. Fellow, 2000, Inst. of Dirs in NZ; Paul Harris Fellow, 2010. Life Mem., Federated Farmers of NZ (Waikato), 1987. Dist. Fellow, Massey Univ. of Agric., 1999. Hon. DSc Massey, 2000; Hon. Dr Waikato, 2014. NZ Commemoration Medal, 1990; NZ Bus. Hall of Fame, 2013. *Recreations:* sport, reading. *Address:* 52 St Michaels Avenue, Bethlehem, Tauranga 3110, New Zealand. *Club:* Wellington.

**SPRING, Richard, (Dick);** non-executive Deputy Chairman, Financial Exchange Co. of Ireland, since 2008 (Executive Vice Chairman, 1997–2008); Chairman, Industrial Development Ireland, since 1998; *b* 29 Aug. 1950; *s* of late Daniel and Anne Spring; *m* 1977, Kristi Lee Hutcheson; two *s* one *d*. *Educ*: Mt St Joseph Coll., Roscrea; Trinity Coll., Dublin (BA 1972). Called to the Bar, King's Inns, Dublin, 1975; in practice on Munster Circuit, 1977–81. Mem. Dáil (TD) (Lab), N Kerry, 1981–2002. Minister of State, Dept of Justice, 1981–82; Dep. Prime Minister of Ireland, 1982–87 and 1993–97; Minister for the Environment, 1982–83; Minister for Energy, 1983–87; Minister for Foreign Affairs, 1993–97. Leader of Irish Labour Party, 1982–97. Director: Repak Ltd, 2006–13; Allied Irish Banks, 2009–14; Goodbody Stockbroking Ltd, 2012–; Chairman: Fexco Stockbroking Ltd, 2002–12; Alder Capital, 2004– (Dir, 2000–). Chm., Réalta HIV Global Foundn, 2005–17. Associate Fellow, Kennedy Sch. of Govt, Harvard, 1998–; Fellow, Salzburg Seminar, 1998–. *Recreations*: reading, golf, walking, grandkids. *Address*: Ridge Lodge, The Spa, Tralee, Co. Kerry, Ireland. *T*: (87) 2391200. *E*: dspring@fexco.com.

**SPRING, Stephanie, (Stevie),** CBE 2017; FIPA, FMS; Chairman, Mind, since 2018; *b* 10 June 1957; *d* of William Harold Spring and Marlene Maud Spring (*née* Coleman, now Green). *Educ*: Eggars Grammar Sch., Alton; Univ. of Kent, Canterbury (LLB Hons 1978). FIPA 1990; FMS 2004. Mktg Manager, Alpine Hldgs, 1978–82; Business Develt, TV-am, 1982–84; Business Dir, Grey Advertising, 1984–88; Dep. Man. Dir, Gold Greenlees Trott, 1988–92; Managing Director: Woollams Moira Gaskin O'Malley, 1992–94; Young & Rubicam, 1994–2000; Chief Executive: Clear Channel UK, 2000–06; Future plc, 2006–12; Luxup, 2013. Sen. Ind. Dir, Engine Gp, 2012–14; Chairman: ITG Gp, 2014–; Kino-Mo, 2014–. Non-executive Director: Co-operative Gp, 2015– (Chm., Remuneration Cttee, 2015–); Ladbroke Coral Gp plc, 2016– (Chm., Remuneration Cttee, 2016–); Sen. Ind. Dir, ALCS, 2014–17. Chair, BBC Children in Need, 2008–18. Mem. Council, Univ. of Kent, 2014–17. Chm., Fedn of Groundwork Trusts, 2001–08. Trustee, Arts & Business, 2006–09. Hon. PhD Kent, 2011. *Recreations*: travel, socialising, swimming, running. *Address*: 34 Courtnell Street, W2 5BX. *E*: stevie@steviespring.com. *Clubs*: Soho House, Thirty, WACL.

**SPRING RICE,** family name of **Baron Monteagle of Brandon**.

**SPRINGALL, Diana;** artist; *b* 16 Sept. 1938; *d* of William Gordon Alexander and Stella Alice Fuller; *m* 1960, Ernest Thomas Springall (marr. diss. 1975); two *s*. *Educ*: Goldsmiths' Coll. Sch. of Art (NDD Painting 1960; ATC 1961); City and Guilds of London Inst. (Embroidery 1963); Univ. of London (Dip. Hist. of Art 1968). Hd, Art Dept, West Heath Sch., Sevenoaks, 1961–63; Lectr, Fashion Dept, Maidstone Coll. of Art, 1963–68; Principal Lectr and Hd, Dept of Fashion and Textiles, Stockwell Coll. of Educn, Bromley, 1968–80; Panel Lectr, V&A Mus., 1980–. Chm. and Emeritus Mem., Embroiderers' Guild, 1978–85; Chm. and Fellow, Soc. of Designer-Craftsmen, 1987–90. Design consultant, Embroidery (TV series), BBC TV, 1980; Twelve British Embroiderers (exhibn), Tokyo, 1985; retrospective exhibn, Knitting and Stitching Show, London, Dublin and Harrogate, 2011. FRSA. Freeman, City of London, 2018; Liveryman, Broderers' Co., 2019– (Broderers' Prize, 2011). *Publications*: Canvas Embroidery, 1969; Embroidery, 1980; Twelve British Embroiderers, 1985; Design for Embroidery, 1988; Inspired to Stitch, 2005; An Embroiderer's Eye, 2009; *relevant publication*: Diana Springall A Brave Eye, by June Hill, 2011. *Recreations*: gardening, cooking, travel. *Address*: Oast Cottage, 2 Park Lane, Kemsing, Sevenoaks, Kent TN15 6NU. *T*: and *Fax*: (01732) 761501. *E*: dianaspringall@btinternet.com. *W*: www.dianaspringallcollection.co.uk.

**SPRINGETT, Rt Rev. Robert Wilfred;** *see* Tewkesbury, Bishop Suffragan of.

**SPRINGFORD, Prof. Michael,** PhD; FInstP; H. O. Wills Professor of Physics, 1996–2001, and Director, Physics Laboratory, 1994–2001, University of Bristol, now Emeritus Professor of Physics; *b* 10 Jan. 1936; *s* of Stanley Walter Springford and Lilian Springford (*née* Tyler); *m* 1st, 1958, Kathleen Elizabeth Wyatt (marr. diss. 1983); two *s* one *d*; 2nd, 1991, Maria Sergeyevna (*née* Morosova). *Educ*: Durham Univ. (BSc); Hull Univ. (PhD). Nat. Res. Council of Canada, 1962–64; Univ. of Sussex, 1964–89; Prof. of Experimental Physics, Univ. of Bristol, 1989–2001. Mott Prize Lectr, and Charles Vernon Boys Medal and Prize, 1995, Guthrie Medal and Prize, 2003, Inst. of Physics. *Publications*: (ed) Electrons at the Fermi Surface, 1980; (ed) Electron: a centenary volume, 1997; papers on the quantum properties of condensed matter in learned jls. *Recreations*: writing, piano, hill walking, cooking, pursuit of quietness. *Address*: 12A Royal York Crescent, Bristol BS8 4JY. *E*: m.springford@bristol.ac.uk.

**SPRINGMAN, Prof. Sarah Marcella,** CBE 2012 (OBE 1997); PhD; CEng, FREng, FICE; Professor of Geotechnical Engineering, Department of Civil, Environmental and Geomatic Engineering, since 1997, and Rector, since 2015, ETH Zürich (Swiss Federal Institute of Technology, Zurich) (Deputy Head of Department, 2013–14); *b* 26 Dec. 1956; *d* of late (Paul) Michael Eyre Springman and Dame Ann Marcella Springman, DBE. *Educ*: Wycombe Abbey Sch.; Girton Coll., Cambridge (MA; Roscoe Meml Prize 1978; Hon. Fellow, 2015); St Catharine's Coll., Cambridge (MPhil; Hon. Fellow, 2015); Magdalene Coll., Cambridge (PhD 1989; Hon. Fellow, 2014). 11 blues/half blues in lacrosse, tennis, squash, cross country, swimming, athletics. CEng 1993; FICE 2005; FREng 2009. Engr, Sir Alexander Gibb & Partners, UK, Australia and Fiji, 1979–83; Cambridge University: Soil Mechanics Group, Engineering Department: Res. Asst, 1984–88; Res. Associate, 1989–90; Asst Lectr, 1990–93; Lectr, 1993–96; Res. Fellow, 1988–90, Lectr and Fellow, 1991–96, Magdalene Coll.; Chm. and Initiator, Lang. Prog. for Engrs, 1992–96. Lectures: Cross Canada, Canadian Geotech. Soc., 2010; Suklje, Slovenian Geotech. Soc., 2011; Croce, Italian Geotech. Soc., 2015. Member: Swisscode Commn Geodesign, 1998–2003; Swiss Natural Hazards Competence Centre, 1998–2011; Swiss Council for Sci. and Technol., 2000–07; Peer Review Coll., EPSRC, 2005–09, 2013–14; Swiss Platform for Natural Hazards, PLANAT, 2008–15; Bd, Implenia AG, 2013–14. MInstRE 1990; Member: Women's Engrg Soc., 1983– (Fellow, 2015); Swiss Soc. of Engrs and Architects, 1999–; Swiss Acad. of Engrg Scis, 2015–; Res. Cttee, RAEng, 2011–13; Search Cttee, Queen Elizabeth Prize for Engrg, 2012; Swiss Geotech. Soc., 2013–14; Bd, Swiss Study Foundn, 2015–; Chm., Tech. Cttee on Physical Modelling in Geotechnics, Internat. Soc. for Soil Mechanics and Geotech. Engrg, 2005–10. Regl Ed., Internat. Jl of Physical Modelling in Geotechnics, 2007–14; Associate Ed., Permafrost and Periglacial Processes, 2013–14. Pres., Stiftung für Studentisches Wohnen Zürich, 2015–; Vice Pres., Kinderbetreuung im Hochschulraum Zürich, 2015–. Mem., British Triathlon Team, 1984–93 (Nat. Champion 11 times, European Champion 3 times, European Team Champion 5 times); Mem., GB World Cup Rowing team, 1997; Vice Pres., Internat. Triathlon Union, 1992–96, 2008–16 (Hon. Mem., 2001); Gov., World Masters Games, 1993–2002; Member: UK (formerly GB) Sports Council, 1993–2001; Exec. Bd, British Triathlon, 2005–12 (Pres., 2007–12); Nat. Olympic Cttee, British Olympic Assoc., 2008–12; Bd, UK Sport, 2013–19; Bd, English Inst. of Sport, 2014; Swiss Univs Sports Foundn, 2015–. Governor: Marlborough Coll., 1991–94; Wycombe Abbey Sch., 1993–96. FRSA 1993 (Life Fellow 2005). Hon. DSc Bath, 2013; Hon. DPhil Bern, 2016. Lifetime Achievement Award, Sunday Times and Sky Sportswoman of Year Awards, 2013. *Publications*: (ed) Constitutive and Centrifuge Modelling: two extremes, 2002; (ed jtly) Permafrost, 2003; (ed jtly) Physical Modelling in Geotechnics (2 vols), 2010; contrib. geotechnical jls. *Recreations*: sculling/rowing, triathlon, cross-country ski-ing (multiple world and European masters titles in rowing, sculling, ergometer and winter triathlon since 1997); opera. *Address*: ETH Zürich, Rectorate, HG F61, Rämistrasse 101, 8092 Zürich, Switzerland; Institute for Geotechnical Engineering, Stefano Franscini Platz 5, Hönggerberg, 8093 Zürich, Switzerland. *T*: (44) 6333805, *Fax*: (44) 6331079. *Clubs*: Cambridge Triathlon (Cambridge) (Hon. Pres., 1996–); Leander (Henley); Belvoir (Zurich).

**SPROT, Lt-Col Aidan Mark,** MC 1944; JP; landed proprietor and farmer (Haystoun Estate); Lord-Lieutenant of Tweeddale, 1980–94; *b* 17 June 1919; *s* of Major Mark Sprot of Riddell. *Educ*: Stowe. Commissioned Royal Scots Greys, 1940; served: Middle East, 1941–43; Italy, 1943–44; NW Europe, 1944–45, and after the war in Germany, Libya, Egypt, Jordan and UK; Adjt 1945–46; CO, 1959–62, retired. Councillor, Peeblesshire CC, 1963–75; JP 1966, DL 1966–80, Peeblesshire. Member, Royal Company of Archers (Queen's Body Guard for Scotland), 1950–; Pres., Lowlands of Scotland, TAVRA, 1986–89. Vice-Pres., RHASS, 1986; Trustee, Royal Scottish Agricl Benevolent Instn, 1989–98. British Red Cross Society: County Dir, 1966–74, Patron, 1983–98, Tweeddale Br.; Patron, Borders Br., 1998–; County Comr, 1968–73, Chm., 1975–80, Pres., 1980–94, Tweeddale Scout Assoc.; President: Borders Area Scout Assoc., 1994–99; Lothian Fedn of Boys' Clubs, 1988–96. Hon. President: Tweeddale Soc., 1995–; Peebles Br., RBL, Scotland, 1990–; Hon. Mem., Rotary Club, Peebles, 1986–. Hon. Sec., Royal Caledonian Hunt, 1964–74 (Hon. Mem., 2007). Mem., Service Chaplains Cttee, Church of Scotland, 1974–82 and 1985–92. Freeman, Tweeddale Dist, 1994. Scout Medal of Merit, 1994; Badge of Honour, BRCS, 1998. *Publications*: Swifter than Eagles—War Memoirs 1939–1945, 1998. *Recreations*: country pursuits, motor cycle touring. *Address*: Crookston, Peebles EH45 9JQ. *T*: (01721) 740209. *Club*: New (Edinburgh).

**SPRUCE, John Charles;** Vice Lord-Lieutenant for Clackmannanshire, since 2017; *b* Altrincham, Cheshire, 17 Dec. 1954; *s* of Thomas William and Doreen Spruce; *m* 1978, Elizabeth Anne Winder; two *s*. *Educ*: William Hulme's Grammar Sch., Manchester; Univ. of Manchester Inst. of Sci. and Technol. (BSc 1st Cl. Hons Mech. Engrg 1976). FIMechE 1997. ICI: plant engr, Northwich, 1979–84; project engr/Manager, Grangemouth, 1984–90; Site Maintenance Manager, Astra Zeneca, Grangemouth, 1990–95; Site Engr, Avecia Grangemouth, 1995–2000; Hd, Engrg, Avecia, 2000–05. DL Clackmannanshire, 2015. Dir, Dalgety Bay Sailing Club, 2015–. Depute Session Clerk, Alva Parish Church, 2018–. *Recreations*: sailing, walking, ski-ing, gardening, Scouting (Mem., Scout Assoc. for 44 years). *Address*: Alva, Clackmannanshire, Scotland.

**SPRÜTH, Monika Ilse Gabriele;** Co-owner, Sprüth Magers, contemporary art gallery, since 1998; *b* Memmingen, Germany, 18 May 1949; *d* of Gerhard Merfort and Hannelore Sprüth; one *s* one *d*. *Educ*: Rheinisch-Westfälische Technische Hochschule, Aachen (Dip Ing Architecture 1975). Diplom Ingenieur, Stadtplanungsamt Oberhausen, 1975–79; Teacher of construction, maths and art, Fachhochschule für Bauwesen, Cologne, 1981–83; Founder, Monika Sprüth Gallery, 1983; merged with Galerie Philomene Magers as Sprüth Magers, Cologne, 1998; Sprüth Magers, Munich, opened 2000; addnl project space for young and emerging art in Munich, opened 2002; Sprüth Magers, London, opened 2003, Berlin, 2008, LA, 2016, Hong Kong, 2016. *Recreation*: soccer. *Address*: Sprüth Magers, Oranienburger Strasse 18, 10178 Berlin, Germany. *E*: info@spruethmagers.com.

**SPRY, Christopher John,** CBE 2002; self-employed healthcare management consultant, since 2006; Director, OD Partnerships Network, 2001–11; *b* 29 Aug. 1946; *s* of late Reginald Charles Spry and Kathleen Edith Spry (*née* Hobart); *m* 1st, Jean Banks (marr. diss. 1989); two *s*; 2nd, 1989, Judith Christina (*née* Ryder). *Educ*: Sir Roger Manwood's Sch., Sandwich; Exeter Univ. (BA 1967). AHSM. Dep. Hosp. Sec., Lewisham Hosp., 1970; Hosp. Sec., Nottingham Gen. Hosp., 1973; Asst Dist Administrator, S Nottingham, 1975, Dist Administrator, 1978; Dist Administrator, 1981, Dist Gen. Manager, 1984, Newcastle HA; Regl Gen. Manager, SW Thames RHA, 1989–94; Regl Dir, NHS Exec., S Thames, 1994–96; Chief Exec., Gtr Glasgow Health Bd, 1996–2001. Non-exec. Dir, Dorset County Hosp. NHS Federation Trust (formerly W Dorset Gen. Hosps NHS Trust), 2005–10. Dir, Redwood House Mgt Co., 2010–14. Vis. Prof., Glasgow Univ., 2001. *Recreations*: the Arts, enjoying townscapes, travel, biographies, history, modern novels, keeping fit. *Address*: 31 Redwood House, Charlton Down, Dorchester, Dorset DT2 9UH.

**SPUFFORD, Francis Peter;** writer, since 1990; *b* Cambridge, 22 April 1964; *s* of Prof. Peter Spufford, FBA and Prof. (Honor) Margaret Spufford, OBE, FBA; *m* 1994, Jessica Martin; two *d*. *Educ*: Trinity Hall, Cambridge (BA English Lit. 1985). Publisher's reader, Chatto & Windus Ltd, 1986–90; freelance writer and journalist, 1990–2004; Royal Literary Fund Writing Fellow, Anglia Ruskin Univ., 2005–07; Sen. Lectr in Creative Writing, 2007–17, Prof. of Creative Writing, 2018–, Goldsmiths, Univ. of London. *Publications*: I May Be Some Time, 1996; The Child That Books Built, 2002; Backroom Boys, 2003; Red Plenty, 2010; Unapologetic, 2012; Golden Hill, 2016 (Ondaatje Prize, RSL; Costa First Novel Award; Desmond Elliott Prize); True Stories and Other Essays, 2017. *Recreations*: cooking, playing with words, caffeine. *Address*: c/o Faber & Faber, Bloomsbury House, 74–77 Great Russell Street, WC1B 3DA. *E*: f.spufford@gold.ac.uk.

**SPUNNER, Lt Gen. Sir Barnabas William Benjamin W.;** *see* White-Spunner.

**SPURGEON, Prof. Sarah Katherine,** OBE 2015; DPhil; CEng, FREng; CMath; FIET; Professor of Control Engineering, and Head, Department of Electronic and Electrical Engineering, University College London, since 2016; *b* Wolverhampton, 4 Dec. 1963; *d* of Michael and Sheila Mudge; *m* 1986, Dr Christopher Thomas Spurgeon; two *s* one *d*. *Educ*: Ounsdale High Sch., Wombourne; Univ. of York (BSc Hons Maths; DPhil Electronics 1988). CEng 1996; CMath 1996; FIET 2006; FREng 2008. Department of Engineering, University of Leicester: Lectr, 1991–95; Sen. Lectr, 1995–2000; Reader, 2000–02; Prof. of Engrg, 2002–08; Hd, Dept of Engrg, 2005–08; Prof. of Control Engrg, and Head, Sch. of Engrg and Digital Arts, Univ. of Kent, 2008–16. Chm., UK Automatic Control Council, 2008–11. Mem. Bd, DSTL, 2018–. President: Inst. of Measurement and Control, 2014–17; Engineering Professors' Council, 2017–19 (Vice-Pres., 2019–). FInstMC 2004; FIMA; SMIEE 2004. *Publications*: Sliding Mode Control, Theory and Applications, 1998; (ed) Variable Structure Systems: from principles to implementation, 2004. *Recreation*: gardening. *Address*: Department of Electronic and Electrical Engineering, University College London, WC1E 7JE. *T*: (020) 3108 7871. *E*: s.spurgeon@ucl.ac.uk.

**SPURLING, Hilary;** *see* Spurling, S. H.

**SPURLING, Sir John (Damian),** KCVO 2012; OBE 1999; Chairman, PetPartners Inc., USA, since 2004; *b* Ilford, 11 July 1939; *s* of William Edgar Spurling and Winnefred Spurling; *m* 1989, Gwyneth Wycherley. *Educ*: St David's Coll., Johannesburg; St Ignatius Coll., London. Dir, Kenya Advertising Corp., 1963–70; Chairman and Chief Executive Officer: Advertising Associates, Kenya, 1970–82; Pet Protect Ltd, 1984–2001; PetPartners Ltd, 2002–09. Chm., Bryanston Freehold Ltd, 2014–. Trustee, Hon. Treas. and Fellow, Animal Health Trust, 1999–; Chm., London Marathon, 2008– (Trustee, London Marathon Charitable Trust, 2008–); Vice-Pres., Kennel Club, 2011– (Trustee, Kennel Club Charitable Trust, 2009–15); Trustee, Foundn of Coll. of St George, Windsor Castle, 2011–

Chm., Bray Fellowship. Mem., Lord's Taverners. *Recreations:* golf playing, watching all sport except football, travelling. *T:* 07974 735819. *E:* john@spurls.co.uk. *Clubs:* Oriental, Caledonian, Buck's; Sunningdale Golf; Muthaiga Country (Nairobi).

**SPURLING, (Susan) Hilary,** CBE 2007; biographer; *b* 25 Dec. 1940; *d* of Gilbert Alexander Forrest and Emily Maureen Forrest; *m* 1961, John Spurling; two *s* one *d*. *Educ:* Somerville Coll., Oxford (BA; Hon. Fellow, 2006). FRSL 2005. Theatre Critic of the Spectator, 1964–70, Literary Editor, 1966–70. Founding Chair, Writers' Fellowship Scheme, 1999, Hon. Mem., 2008, Royal Literary Fund. Hon. Dr Anglia Ruskin, 2007. (Jtly) Heywood Hill Lit. Prize, 2003. *Publications:* Ivy When Young: the early life of I. Compton-Burnett 1884–1919, 1974; Handbook to Anthony Powell's Music of Time, 1977; Secrets of a Woman's Heart: the later life of I. Compton-Burnett 1920–1969, 1984 (Duff Cooper Meml Prize, 1984; Heinemann Literary Award (jtly), 1985); Elinor Fettiplace's Receipt Book, 1986; Paul Scott, A Life, 1990; Paper Spirits, 1992; The Unknown Matisse 1869–1908, vol. i, 1998; La Grande Thérèse, 1999; The Girl from the Fiction Department: a portrait of Sonia Orwell, 2002; Matisse the Master, A Life of Henry Matisse: the conquest of colour 1909–1954 (Whitbread Book of the Year, Los Angeles Times Biography Prize), 2005; Burying the Bones: Pearl Buck in China, 2010 (James Tait Black Prize); Anthony Powell: dancing to the music of time, 2017. *Recreations:* reading, ratting, country walks. *Address:* c/o David Higham Associates, 7th Floor, Waverley House, 7–12 Noel Street, W1F 8GQ.

**SPURR, Margaret Anne,** OBE 1994; DL; Headmistress, Bolton School, Girls' Division, 1979–94; Governor, BBC, 1993–98; *b* 7 Oct. 1933; *m* 1st, 1953, John Spurr (*d* 2003); one *s* one *d*; 2nd, 2009, Prof. Peter Young (*d* 2011). *Educ:* Abbeydale Girls' Grammar Sch., Sheffield; Univ. of Keele. BA (Hons); PGCE. Tutor: Eng. Lit., Univ. of Glasgow, 1971; Eng. Lit. Dept, Adult Educn, Univ. of Keele, 1972–73. Chm., Scholaservices, 1990–94. Sen. Examiner, Univ. of London, 1971–80. Pres., GSA, 1985–86. Chairman: Nat. ISIS Cttee, 1987–90; BBC English Nat. Forum, 1994–98; Member: Adv. Cttee, American Studies Resources Centre, Polytechnic of Central London, 1977–90; Scholarship Selection Cttee, ESU, 1983–94; CBI Schools Panel, 1985–89; Exec. Cttee, GBGSA, 1994–99. Vice-Provost, Woodard Corp., 1994–98. Governor: Kent Coll., Tunbridge Wells, 1993–99; John Moores Univ., Liverpool, 1994–98; Colfe's Sch., 1995–2009; Stafford Coll. of Further Educn, 1996–2000; Newton Prep. Sch., Battersea, 1999–2006; Univ. of Lincoln, 2008–; Life Gov., Liverpool Coll., 2001; Mem. Governing Council, Keele Univ., 1996–2007. Trustee: School Fees Trust Fund, 1994–2000; Raven Mason Collection, Univ. of Keele, 2001–07; Westminster Abbey Article 26 Fund, 2009–14. Dir, SFS Gp, 1999–2005; Mid-Atlantic Club, 2000–05. Pres., Staffs Soc., 1999–2001. Chm., Croxden Parochial Charities Trusts, 2001. Mem., Exec. Cttee, Lichfield Br., Prayer Book Soc., 2002–04. Dir, Helena Kennedy Scholarship Fund, 2008–14. FRSA 1991. Freeman, City of London, 2006. DL Staffs, 1998. Hon. DLitt Keele, 1995. *Publications:* (ed) A Curriculum for Capability, 1986; (ed) Girls First, 1987. *Recreations:* gardening, poetry, music. *Address:* Sherborne, Mottingham Lane, SE9 4RW. *Club:* Reform.

**SPURR, Dr (Michael) Stephen,** DPhil; Group Education Director, Inspired, since 2014; *b* 9 Oct. 1953; *s* of late (Arthur) Michael (Marshall) Spurr and of Patricia (Ann) Spurr (*née* Newell); *m* 1982, Susanna Armani; one *s* one *d*. *Educ:* King's Sch., Canterbury; Sydney Grammar Sch.; Univ. of Sydney (BA 1st cl. Hons Classics 1975); Corpus Christi Coll., Univ. of Oxford (Oxford Ancient History Prize, 1981; DPhil 1984). Rome Scholar, British Sch. at Rome, 1981–82; Lectr in Classics and Ancient History, ANU, 1982–83; Eton College, 1984–2000: Curator, Myers Mus. of Egyptian Art, 1989–2000; Hd of Classics, 1992–96; House Master, 1996–2000; Hd of College and Headmaster, Upper Sch., Clifton Coll., Bristol, 2000–05; Head Master, Westminster Sch., 2005–14. Chm. Govs, Reddam Hse, Berks, 2014–. *Publications:* Arable Cultivation in Roman Italy, 1986; Egyptian Art at Eton College, 1995; (trans.) Another Sea by Claudio Magris, 1993; (contrib.) The Oxford Classical Dictionary, 1996; various articles and reviews. *Recreations:* Roman archaeology, Egyptology, mountaineering, Mediterranean agriculture.

**SPURRIER, Martha;** Director, Liberty, since 2016; *b* London, 2 Feb. 1986; *d* of Barnaby Spurrier and Jill Spurrier (*née* Meager); *m* 2016, Jesse Nicholls. *Educ:* Godolphin and Latymer Sch.; Emmanuel Coll., Cambridge (BA Hons 1st Cl. Hist.); City Univ., London (Grad. Dip. Law (distinction)); BPP Univ. (BVC (outstanding)). Called to the Bar, Middle Temple, 2010; barrister, 2013–16, associate tenant, 2016–, Doughty Street Chambers. *Publications:* (contrib. ed) Halsbury's Laws of England, Rights and Freedoms, 5th edn 2013, 2018; (contrib.) Disabled Children: a legal handbook, 2nd edn 2016. *Recreations:* theatre, novels, cooking. *Address:* Liberty House, 26–30 Strutton Ground, SW1P 2HR. *T:* (020) 7378 3679. *E:* director@liberty-human-rights.org.uk.

**SPY, James;** Sheriff of North Strathclyde at Paisley, since 1988; *b* 1 Dec. 1952; *s* of James Spy and Jean Learmond; *m* 1980, Jennifer Margaret Malcolm; three *d*. *Educ:* Hermitage Acad., Helensburgh; Glasgow Univ. (LLB Hons). Admitted Solicitor, 1976; passed Advocate, 1979. *Recreations:* music, clocks, model ships, model trains. *Address:* St Ann's, 171 Nithsdale Road, Glasgow G41 5QS.

**SPYER, Prof. (Kenneth) Michael,** PhD, DSc; FMedSci; Sophia Jex-Blake Professor of Physiology, UCL Medical School (formerly Royal Free and University College Medical School), University College London, 1980–2010, now Emeritus; Chairman, Brunel University London, since 2017; *b* 15 Sept. 1943; *s* of late Harris Spyer and Rebecca Spyer (*née* Jacobs); *m* 1971, Christine Spalton; two *s*. *Educ:* Coopers' Co. Sch.; Univ. of Sheffield (BSc); Univ. of Birmingham (PhD 1969; DSc 1979). Res. Fellow, Univ. of Birmingham Med. Sch., 1969–72; Royal Soc. European Prog. Fellow, Instituto de Fisologia, Pisa, 1972–73; Res. Fellow, 1973–78, Sen. Res. Fellow, 1978–80, Dept of Physiology, Univ. of Birmingham; joined Royal Free Hosp. Sch. of Medicine, 1980; Dir, Neural Control Gp, BHF, 1985–2000; Head, Jt Depts of Physiology, UCL and Royal Free Hosp. Sch. of Medicine, 1994–99; Dir, Autonomic Neurosci. Inst., 1997–2010; Dean, Royal Free and UC Med. Sch., UCL, 2001–06 (Dean, Royal Free Campus, 1998–2001); Vice-Provost (Biomedicine), 2002–06 (Enterprise), 2006–10, UCL. Chm., NHS London, 2010–13. Chm., St George's, Univ. of London, 2013–17; Dep. Chair, Cttee of Univ. Chairs, 2017–. Fellow, Physiological Soc., 2017 (Pres., 2010–12). Founder FMedSci 1998. Hon. FRCP 2002. Hon. MD Lisbon, 1991; Hon. DSc Middlesex, 2005. *Publications:* (ed jtly) Central Regulation of Autonomic Functions, 1990; papers in Jl of Physiology, Neurosci., Brain Res., Amer. Jl of Physiology, Jl of Autonomic Nervous System, Exptl Physiology, Science, Nature. *Recreations:* fly fishing, travelling (particularly in Italy), gardening, books, fine arts, bookbinding. *Address:* University College London, Gower Street, WC1E 6BT.

**SPYROPOULOS, Andrea;** healthcare management consultant, since 2016; Project Manager, Alder Hey Children's NHS Foundation Trust, 2012–15; President, Royal College of Nursing, 2010–14; *b* Liverpool, 1954; *d* of Albert and Margaret Styles; *m* 1985, Sotiris Spyropoulos; one *s*. *Educ:* John Moores Univ. (BA Hons Health Studies 1995; LLB Hons 2000); Univ. of Wales, Cardiff (Cert Ed 1992; LLM 2004). RGN 1976; SCM 1979; DPSN; RNT 1992; English Nat. Bd No 7 1995. Staff nurse, sister, stomacare specialist, Sefton Gen. Hosp., 1976–78; pupil, then staff midwife, Countess of Chester Hosp., 1978–79; Nursing Officer, Chandris Cruise Line, 1979–80; Sister, Occupational Health, Darjerba, Evia, Greece, 1980–81; various posts, incl. mgt, sister, tutor, Royal Liverpool and Broadgreen Univ. Hosps, 1981–90; Sen. Lectr in law professional issues, John Moores Univ., 1991–2000. Bid Manager, Health Care Projects, 2001–06; Clin. Strategist, UK and Canada, Health Care Projects Social Infrastructure, 2006–12. Non-exec. Dir, Clatterbridge Centre for Oncol., 1998–2007. Pres., Liverpool and Knowsley Br., RCN, 2015–. Mem., Honour Soc. of Nursing, Sigma Theta Tau Internat., 2011. Trustee, BUPA Foundn, 2015–. Hon. DSc: Lincoln, 2014; Liverpool, 2015. *Recreations:* family, community activity, Life President of Riverside Residents' Association. *T:* 07780 977111. *E:* andrea.spyropoulos@hotmail.com.

**SQUAIR, George Alexander;** non-executive Chairman, British Approvals Service for Cables, 1993–2002; *b* 26 July 1929; *s* of Alexander Squair and Elizabeth (*née* Macdonald); *m* 1953, Joy Honeybone (*d* 2013); two *s* one *d*. *Educ:* Woolwich Polytechnic; Oxford Technical Coll.; Southampton Univ. CEng, FIET (FIEE 1986); CIMgt (CBIM 1984). Gen. distribution engrg posts, 1950–68; Southern, later South Eastern, Electricity Board, subseq. SEEBOARD: 1st Asst Dist Engr, 1968–69; Dist Engr, Swindon, 1969–70; Area Engr, Newbury, 1970–73; Dist Manager, Oxford, 1973–74; Area Manager, Newbury, 1974–78; Mem., Exec. Bd, 1976–78; Dep. Chm., 1978–83; Chm. and Chief Exec., 1983–92. *Recreations:* reading, golf. *Address:* Mews Cottage, Swallow Grove Farmhouse, Mangrove Lane, Hertford SG13 8QG.

**SQUIRE, Dr (Clifford) William,** CMG 1978; LVO 1972; HM Diplomatic Service, retired; Chairman, Grenzebach Glier Europe, 1996–2008; *b* 7 Oct. 1928; *s* of Clifford John Squire and Eleanor Eliza Harpley; *m* 1st, 1959, Marie José Carlier (*d* 1973); one *s* two *d* (and one *s* decd); 2nd, 1976, Sarah Laetitia Hutchison (see S. L. Squire); one *s* one *d*. *Educ:* Royal Masonic Sch., Bushey; St John's Coll., Oxford; Coll. of Europe, Bruges. PhD London 1979. British Army, 1947–49. Nigerian Admin. Service, 1953–59; FO, 1959–60; British Legation, Bucharest, 1961–63; FO, 1963–65; UK Mission to UN, New York, 1965–69; Head of Chancery, Bangkok, 1969–72; Head of SE Asian Dept, FCO, 1972–75; Extramural Fellow, Sch. of Oriental and African Studies, London Univ., 1975–76; Counsellor, later Head of Chancery, Washington, 1976–79; Ambassador to Senegal, 1979–82, concurrently to Cape Verde Is, Guinea (Bissau), Guinea (Conakry), Mali and Mauritania; Asst Under-Sec. of State, FCO, 1982–84; Ambassador to Israel, 1984–88. Develt Dir, Univ. of Cambridge, 1988–96; Fellow of Wolfson Coll., Cambridge, 1988–96. *Publications:* University Fundraising in Britain, 2014. *Address:* 11A Chaucer Road, Cambridge CB2 7EB. *Club:* Travellers.
See also E. L. Squire.

**SQUIRE, Emma Laetitia, (Mrs C. J. Pell);** Director, Arts, Heritage and Tourism, Department for Digital, Culture, Media and Sport, since 2018; *b* Washington, DC, 10 April 1979; *d* of Dr (Clifford) William Squire, *qv*, and Sara Laetitia, (Sarah), Squire, *qv*; *m* 2007, Christopher Jon Pell; two *s* one *d*. *Educ:* Mansfield Coll., Oxford (BA Hons PPE); Coll. d'Europe (MA Eur. Politics and Admin). Sen. Policy Advr, New Nuclear Policy, DTI, 2008; Hd, Energy Br., HM Treasury, 2008–09; Department for Business, Innovation and Skills: Dep. Dir, Access to Finance for SMEs, 2009–11; Deputy Director: Local Growth Policy, 2012–13; Strategy, 2014–15; Principal Private Sec. to Sec. of State for Business, Innovation and Skills, 2015–16; Dir, Ministerial and Strategy, DIT, 2016–18. *Address:* Department for Digital, Culture, Media and Sport, 100 Parliament Street, SW1A 2BQ.

**SQUIRE, Peter John;** Headmaster, Bedford Modern School, 1977–96; *b* 15 Feb. 1937; *s* of Leslie Ernest Squire and Doris Eileen Squire; *m* 1965, Susan Elizabeth (*née* Edwards); one *s* one *d*. *Educ:* King Edward's Sch., Birmingham; Jesus Coll., Oxford (BA 1960, MA 1964); Pembroke Coll. and Dept of Educn, Cambridge (Cert. in Educn 1961). Asst Master, Monkton Combe Sch., Bath, 1961–65; Haberdashers' Aske's Sch., Elstree, 1965–77: Sen. Boarding Housemaster, 1968–77; Sen. History Master, 1970–77. Reporting Inspector, HMC/ISI Inspections, 1994–2004. Chm., Bedfordshire Victim Support, 1997–2001. Mem., Whitgift Council, 1997–2014. *Recreations:* foreign travel, gardening, antique collecting. *Address:* 98A Bromham Road, Biddenham, Bedford MK40 4AH. *T:* (01234) 342373.

**SQUIRE, Robin Clifford;** Trust Secretary: Veolia Havering Riverside Maintenance (formerly ES Cleanaway Havering Riverside) Trust and Veolia Pitsea Marshes Maintenance (formerly ES Cleanaway Pitsea Marshes) Trust, 2002–18 (Trustee, since 2002); Veolia North Thames Trust, 2013–17 (Trustee, since 2002); *b* 12 July 1944; *s* of late Sidney John Squire and Mabel Alice Squire (*née* Gilmore); *m* 1981, Susan Margaret Fey, OBE (marr. diss. 2007), *d* of late Arthur Frederick Branch and Mahala Branch (*née* Parker); one step *s* one step *d*. *Educ:* Tiffin School, Kingston-upon-Thames. FCA. Qualified as Chartered Accountant, 1966; joined Lombard Banking Ltd (subsequently Lombard North Central Ltd) as Accountant, 1968, becoming Dep. Chief Accountant, 1972–79. Dir Advocacy Ltd, 1997–2000. Councillor, London Borough of Sutton, 1968–82; Chm., Finance Cttee, 1972–76; Leader of Council, 1976–79. Chm., Greater London Young Conservatives, 1973; Vice-Chm., Nat. Young Conservatives, 1974–75. Personal Asst to Rt Hon. Robert Carr, Gen. Election, Feb. 1974; contested (C) Havering, Hornchurch, Oct. 1974. MP (C) Hornchurch, 1979–97; contested (C) same seat, 1997, 2001. PPS to Minister of State for Transport, 1983–85, to Rt Hon. Chris Patten, Chm. of Cons. Party, 1991–92; Parliamentary Under-Secretary of State: DoE, 1992–93; DFE, later DFEE, 1993–97. Mem., Commons Select Cttee on Environment, 1979–83 and 1987–91, on European Legislation, 1985–88; Sec., Cons. Parly European Affairs Cttee, 1979–80; Vice-Chm., Cons. Parly Trade Cttee, 1980–83; Chm., Cons. Parly Environment Cttee, 1990–91 (Jt Vice-Chm., 1985–89); Originator of Local Govt (Access to Information) Act, 1985. Chm., Cons. Action for Electoral Reform, 1988 (Vice-Chm., 1982–83); Dep. Chm., Anglo-Asian Cons. Soc., 1982–83. Comr, Nat. Lottery Commn, 1999; Adjudicator for Schs Orgns and Admissions, 1999. Mem. Bd, Shelter, 1982–91; Dir, Link Assured Homes series of cos, 1988–92. Chm., Assoc. of Distributive Envmtl Bodies, 2005–07. Freeman, City of London, 2003; Liveryman, Co. of Makers of Playing Cards, 2003–. *Publications:* (jtly) Set the Party Free, 1969. *Recreations:* films, ballroom dancing, duplicate bridge, classical music, meditation, gnosticism, reiki healing, learning Spanish. *Address:* Flat 3, 63 Millbank, SW1P 4RW.

**SQUIRE, Dame Rosemary (Anne), (Lady Panter),** DBE 2018 (OBE 2008); Joint Chief Executive Officer, Trafalgar Entertainment Group, since 2017; *b* 27 May 1956; *d* of late Donald Squire and of Mary Squire (*née* Sykes); *m* 1st, 1982, Alan Brodie (marr. diss. 1994); one *s* one *d*; 2nd, 1994, Howard Hugh Panter (*see* Sir Howard Panter); one *d*. *Educ:* Nottingham High Sch. for Girls; Southampton Univ. (BA 1st Cl. Hons Spanish with Catalan and French 1979); Brown Univ. (Postgrad. Schol. 1979). Gen. Manager, Maybox Gp plc, 1984–88; Gen. Manager, 1988–90, Exec. Dir, 1990–97, Turnstyle Gp Ltd; Exec. Dir, then Jt Chief Exec., 1997–2016, Dep. Chm., 2016–17, Ambassador Theatre Group Ltd. Mem., Arts Council England, 2009–18. Pres., SOLT, 2005–08. Hon. DLitt Southampton, 2009. EY UK Entrepreneur of the Year, 2014. *Recreations:* gardens, walking, reading. *Address:* Trafalgar Entertainment Group, 55 Strand, WC2N 5LR. *T:* (020) 7451 1700. *E:* rsquire@trafalgarentertainment.com. *Club:* Ivy.

**SQUIRE, Sara Laetitia, (Sarah);** HM Diplomatic Service, retired; President, Hughes Hall, Cambridge, 2006–14; *b* 18 July 1949; *d* of Michael Duncan Hutchison and Margery Betty Hutchison (*née* Martin); *m* 1976, (Clifford) William Squire, *qv*; one *s* one *d*. *Educ:* St Paul's

Girls' Sch.; Newnham Coll., Cambridge (BA Hons Hist., MA). Entered HM Diplomatic Service, 1971: FCO, 1971–72; Tel Aviv, 1972–75; SE Asian Dept, FCO, 1975–76; Washington, 1977–79; Falkland Is Dept, FCO, 1982–84; Tel Aviv, 1986–88; Policy Officer, Cambridge CC, 1989–90; Sen. Inf. Officer, COI, 1990–95; Dep. Dir, Know How Fund, FCO, 1995–96; Dep. Hd, Central Eur. Dept, FCO, 1996–99; Ambassador to Estonia, 2000–03; Gp Dir, FCO Services, FCO, 2004–06. Adv. Bd, SSEES, UCL, 2006–12. Dep. Vice Chancellor, Cambridge Univ., 2008–14; Syndic, Fitzwilliam Mus., 2007–12. Deputy Chairman: Cambridge Commonwealth and Overseas Trusts, 2009–15; Cambridge Alumni Adv. Bd, 2010–14. Trustee: PHG Foundn, 2008–10; Bell Foundn, 2016–; Trustee, United Learning, and Mem. Gp Bd, United Church Schs Trust, 2013–. Gov., St Mary's Sch., Cambridge, 2016–. Canon and Mem. Chapter, Ely Cath., 2013–17. *Address:* 11a Chaucer Road, Cambridge CB2 7EB. *T:* (01223) 329547. *Club:* Oxford and Cambridge.
*See also* E. L. Squire.

**SQUIRE, William;** *see* Squire, C. W.

**SQUIRES, (Charles) Ian;** broadcast and media consultant, since 2018; Director, Media and Broadcasting, IRC UK, 2015–17; *b* 22 April 1951; *s* of Charles Ian Squires and Mary Squires; *m* 1993, Vanessa Marie Sweet; two *d*. *Educ:* Bede Grammar Sch., Sunderland; University Coll. London (BA Hons English). Westminster Press, 1973–75; Current Affairs and Editor, Omnibus, BBC TV, 1975–86; freelance producer, 1986–88; Head of Network TV, North West, BBC, 1988–90; Managing Director: Zenith North, 1990–94; Carlton Studios, 1994–2004; ITV Central (formerly Central Broadcasting), 1996–2008; Director of Regional Production: ITV News Gp, 2004–08; ITV plc, 2008–09; Controller: ITV Regions and Current Affairs, 2009–11; ITV News Ops and Current Affairs, 2011–15. Chm., EMMedia, 2001–05; Director: West Midlands Life, 1999–2003; NEC, 2005–10; Birmingham City Univ. (formerly Univ. of Central England), 2005–09; Fair Cities (Birmingham), 2005–07; Midland Heart Housing Assoc., 2007–09. Chairman: Birmingham City Pride, 2001–04; Marketing Birmingham, 2004–09; Birmingham Repertory Theatre, 2005–13; Curve Theatre, Leicester, 2016–; Dir, Birmingham Hippodrome Theatre, 2005–09; Mem. Bd and Gov., Royal Shakespeare Co., 2014–; Member, Board: Birmingham Royal Ballet, 2015–; Belarus Free Th., 2015–17. Pres., Birmingham Chamber of Commerce and Industry, 2004–05 (Vice-Pres., 2002–04). FRSA 2015. BAFTA Award, Best Arts Prog., for A Simple Man (TV ballet on life of L. S. Lowry), 1987. *Recreations:* theatre, ballet, piano, music, writing. *Address:* Manor Cottage, Bottom Lane, Bisbrooke, Rutland LE15 9EJ. *T:* (01572) 821340. *Club:* Royal Automobile.

**SRINIVASAN, Krishnan;** Deputy Secretary-General, Commonwealth Secretariat, 1995–2002; *b* 15 Feb. 1937; *s* of late Captain C. Srinivasan, Indian Navy, and Rukmani Chari; *m* 1975, Brinda Mukerjea; one *s*. *Educ:* Bedford Sch.; Christ Church, Oxford (MA). Joined Indian Foreign Service, 1959; Chargé d'Affaires, Tripoli, 1968–71; High Comr to Zambia and Botswana, 1974–77; Consul-Gen., NY, 1977–80; High Comr to Nigeria, and Ambassador to Benin and Cameroon, 1980–83; Ambassador, Netherlands, 1986–89; High Comr, Bangladesh, 1989–92; Perm. Sec., Min. of External Affairs, 1992–94; Foreign Secretary, 1994–95. Visiting Fellow: Wolfson Coll., Cambridge, 2002–05; Centre of Internat. Studies, Cambridge, 2002–05; Sen. Res. Fellow, Inst. of Commonwealth Studies, Univ. of London, 2002–08; Fellow: Azad Inst. of Asian Studies, Calcutta, 2006–15; Swedish Collegium, 2008, 2012–13. Dist. Vis. Schol., Netherlands Inst. for Advanced Study, 2003–04; Vis. Prof., Indian Admin. Staff Coll., 2004–. Ramsden Sermon, Oxford, 2002. Hind Ratna, 2001; Chevalier de l'Ordre de la Valeur (Cameroon), 2007. *Publications:* Selections in Two Keys, 1974; The Water's Edge, 1975; The Eccentricity Factor, 1980; The Fourth Profile, 1991; A Fizzle Yield, 1992; Tricks of the Trade, 2000; The Eccentric Effect, 2001; The Ugly Ambassador, 2003; Guesswork, 2005; The Rise, Decline and Future of the British Commonwealth, 2005; The Jamdani Revolution, 2008; (with Prof. J. B. L. Mayall) Towards the New Horizon: world order in the 21st century, 2009; The Invisible African, 2012; Diplomatic Channels, 2012; Europe in Emerging Asia, 2015; Old Europe, New Asia: strategies, challenges, responses, 2015; Ambassador Marco's Indian Instincts, 2017; Values in Foreign Policy: investigating ideals and interests, 2019; book reviews and articles on internat. relns in Indian and foreign newspapers and jls. *Recreations:* music, watching sports. *Address:* Flat 8, Courtleigh, 126 Earls Court Road, W8 6QL. *Clubs:* Royal Over-Seas League; Vincent's (Oxford); Bengal (Calcutta); International Centre, Habitat Centre, Gymkhana (New Delhi).

**SRINIVASAN, Prof. Mandyam Veerambudi,** AM 2012; PhD; FRS 2001; FAA; Professor of Visual Neuroscience, Queensland Brain Institute, University of Queensland, 2007, now Emeritus; *b* 15 Sept. 1948; *s* of Mandyam Veerambudi Sundararajan and Mandyam Veerambudi Vedavalli Ammal; *m* Jaishree Srinivasan. *Educ:* Bangalore Univ. (BE 1st Cl. Electrical Engrg 1968); Indian Inst. of Sci., Bangalore (Masters in Applied Electronics and Servomechanisms 1970); Yale Univ. (MPhil 1973, PhD 1976, Engrg and Applied Sci.). Res. Scientist, Dept of Ophthalmol. and Visual Sci., Yale Univ. Sch. of Medicine, 1977–78; Res. Fellow, Depts of Neurobiol. and Applied Maths, ANU, 1978–82; Asst Prof. of Biophysics, Dept of Neurobiol., Univ. of Zurich, 1982–85; Australian National University: Fellow, Visual Sciences, 1985–91, Sen. Fellow, 1992–93, Prof. of Visual Sci., 1994–2006, Res. Sch. of Biol Scis; Dir, Centre for Visual Sci., 1994–96 and 2000–06. Daimler-Benz Fellow, Inst. Advanced Studies, Berlin, 1996–97. FAA 1995; Fellow, Acad. of Scis of Developing World, 2006. Hon. DSc Neuroethol., ANU, 1994; Dr *hc* Zurich, 2002. Australian Prime Minister's Sci. Prize, 2006; UK Rank Prize in Optoelectronics, 2008; Dist. Alumni Award, Indian Inst. Sci., 2009. *Publications:* (ed with S. Venkatesh) From Living Eyes to Seeing Machines, 1997; (jtly) Flying Insects and Robots, 2009; contrib. numerous res. articles and rev. chapters, one internat. patent. *Address:* Queensland Brain Institute, University of Queensland, St Lucia, Qld 4072, Australia.

**SRISKANDARAJAH, Dr Dhananjayan;** Chief Executive, Oxfam GB, since 2018; *b* Jaffna, Sri Lanka, 31 Dec. 1975; *s* of Prof. N. Sriskandarajah and Dr Sridevy Sriskandarajah; *m* 2003, Suzanne Lambert; two *s* one *d*. *Educ:* James Ruse Agricl High Sch., Sydney, NSW; Univ. of Sydney (BEc (Social Scis) Hons 1997); Magdalen Coll., Oxford (MPhil Develt Studies 2000; DPhil 2005). Institute for Public Policy Research: researcher, 2004–06; Associate Dir, 2006–08; Dep. Dir, 2008; Dir, Royal Commonwealth Soc., 2009–12; Interim Dir, Commonwealth Foundn, 2011–12 (on secondment); Sec. Gen., CIVICUS, 2013–18. Member: UN High Level Panel on humanitarian finance, 2015–16; UN Sec. Gen.'s High Level Panel on digital co-operation, 2018–19. Non-exec. Dir, Equality Works Ltd, 2007–08. Member: Lead Gp, Scaling Up Nutrition, 2016–; Bd, Disasters Emergency Cttee, 2019–. Trustee: Ockenden Internat., 2004–15; Praxis Community Projects, 2006–12; Baring Foundn, 2009–17; Internat. Alert, 2012–18; Comic Relief, 2016–. Vice Pres. and Dir, Univ. of Sydney Union, 1995–97; Fellow, Univ. of Sydney Senate, 1996–97. Young Global Leader, WEF, 2012. *Publications:* (jtly) Brits Abroad: mapping the scale and nature of British emigration, 2006; (jtly) Development on the Move: measuring and optimising migration's social and economic impacts, 2010; (ed and contrib.) Queen and the Commonwealth, 2012; contrib. articles to learned jls incl. Contemp. S Asia, Geog., Health, Internat. Migration, Oxford Develt Studies, Social Policy Rev., Studies in Christian Ethics, Third World Qly and World Econs. *Recreations:* travel, family, planespotting. *Address:* Oxfam GB, Oxfam House, John Smith Drive, Oxford OX4 2JY.

**STABLE, His Honour (Rondle) Owen (Charles);** QC 1963; a Circuit Judge, 1979–95; Senior Circuit Judge, Snaresbrook Crown Court, 1982–95; *b* 28 Jan. 1923; *yr s* of late Rt Hon. Sir Wintringham Norton Stable, MC, and Lucie Haden (*née* Freeman); *m* 1949, Yvonne Brook (*d* 2010), *y d* of late Maj. L. B. Holliday, OBE; two *d*. *Educ:* Winchester. Served with Rifle Bde, 1940–46 (Captain). Barrister, Middle Temple, 1948; Bencher, 1969. Dep. Chm., QS, Herts, 1963–71; a Recorder of the Crown Court, 1972–79. Board of Trade Inspector: Cadco Group of Cos, 1963–64; H. S. Whiteside & Co. Ltd, 1965–67; International Learning Systems Corp. Ltd, 1969–71; Pergamon Press, 1969–73. Sec. National Reference Tribunal for the Coal Mining Industry, 1953–64; Chancellor of Diocese of Bangor, 1959–88; Member, Governing Body of the Church in Wales, 1960–88; Licensed Parochial Lay Reader, Diocese of St Albans, 1961–2003; Member: General Council of the Bar, 1962–66; Senate of 4 Inns of Court, 1971–74; Senate of the Inns of Court and the Bar, 1974–75. Chm., Horserace Betting Levy Appeal Tribunal, 1969–74. Mem. Council, Benslow Music Trust, 1995–2001; Chm., Benslow Develt Appeal, 1995–2000. JP Hertfordshire, 1963–71. *Publications:* (with R. M. Stuttard) A Review of Coursing, 1971. *Recreations:* listening to music, playing the flute. *Address:* Buckler's Hall, Much Hadham, Herts SG10 6EB. *T:* (01279) 842604. *Club:* Boodle's.

**STACE, Prof. Anthony John,** PhD; FRS 2002; FRSC; Professor of Physical Chemistry, University of Nottingham, 2004–19, now Emeritus. *Educ:* Univ. of Essex (BA, PhD). Univ. of Sussex, 1974–77; Advanced Res. Fellow, SERC, Univ. of Southampton, 1977–83; Lectr, 1984–93, Prof. of Chemistry, 1993–2004, Univ. of Sussex. Leverhulme Emeritus Fellow, 2016–. Tilden Medal and Lectr, RSC, 1995; Aston Medal, British Mass Spectrometry Soc., 2013. *Address:* School of Chemistry, University of Nottingham, University Park, Nottingham NG7 2RD.

**STACE, Nicholas Charles;** Chief Executive Officer, Prince's Trust, since 2017; *b* Brighton, 11 July 1971; *s* of Timothy and Irene Stace; *m* 2007, Emma Chittenden; two *s* one *d*. *Educ:* Patcham Fawcett High Sch., Brighton; Brighton, Hove and Sussex Sixth Form Coll.; Univ. of Hull (BA Politics and Legislative Studies 1993). Account exec., Keene Public Affairs, 1994–95; Public Affairs, Age UK, 1995–98; Hd, Public Affairs, then Sen. Public Affairs Officer, Which?, 1998–2001; Dir, Citigate Communications, 2001–03; Dep. CEO, Which?, 2003–08; Strategic Communications Dir, Prime Minister's Office, 2008; CEO, CHOICE (Australian Consumers' Assoc.), 2009–12; CEO and Sec., RCVS, 2012–17. Director: BEUC (Eur. Consumer Orgn), 2003–08; Consumers Internat., 2004–13. Member: Bd and Council, NT, 2015–; Bd, Financial Conduct Authy, 2017–. Founding Chair: Sheila McKechnie Foundn, 2005–08; Wild Network, 2014–17. Gov. and Chm. Govs, Royal Agricl Univ., 2015–18. Hon. DLitt Hull, 2019. *Address:* Prince's Trust, Prince's Trust House, 9 Eldon Street, EC2M 7LS. *T:* (020) 7543 1202. *E:* nick.stace@princes-trust.org.uk. *Club:* House of St Barnabas.

**STACEY, Hon. Lady; Valerie Elizabeth Stacey;** a Senator of the College of Justice in Scotland, since 2009; a Judge of the Employment Appeal Tribunal, 2013–15; *b* 25 May 1954; *d* of James and Helen Thom; *m* 1981, Andrew Stacey; two *s*. *Educ:* Elgin Acad.; Edinburgh Univ. (LLB Hons). Solicitor, 1978–86; admitted to Faculty of Advocates, 1987 (Vice Dean, 2004–07); Advocate Depute, 1993–96; Standing Jun. Counsel to Home Office in Scotland, 1996–99; Temp. Sheriff, 1997–99; QC (Scot.) 1999. Member: Sentencing Commn for Scotland, 2003–06; Judicial Appts Bd for Scotland, 2005–07. *Recreation:* listening to music. *Address:* Parliament House, Parliament Square, Edinburgh EH1 1RQ.

**STACEY, Dame Glenys (Jean),** DBE 2016; HM Chief Inspector of Probation, 2016–19; *b* Walsall, Staffs, 25 March 1954; *d* of Robert Main and Dorothy McBride; *m* 2007, David William Kyle, *qv*; two *c*. *Educ:* Shire Oak, Grammar Sch., Walsall Wood; Univ. of Kent at Canterbury (BA Hons Law); Open Univ. (MBA). First Chief Exec., Criminal Cases Rev. Commn, 1997–2000; Chief Executive: Gtr Manchester Magistrates' Courts Cttee, 2000–04; Animal Health, 2004–08; Chief Regulator and CEO, Ofqual, 2011–15. Chair, ind. review of farm inspection and regulation, DEFRA, 2018. Mem. Bd, Assoc. of Chief Execs, 2016–. Mem. Bd, Centre for Data Ethics and Innovation, 2019–. *Recreations:* walking, theatre.

**STACEY, Air Marshal Sir Graham (Edward),** KBE 2017 (MBE 1988); CB 2011; Chief of Staff to Supreme Allied Commander Transformation, 2015–18; *b* London, 1 Sept. 1959; *s* of Kenneth and Kay Stacey; *m* 2007, Maria Stuttaford; one *s* one *d*. *Educ:* Epsom Coll.; Leeds Univ. (BSc Hons); King's Coll. London (M). Joined RAF, 1980; in comd RAF Honington, 2001–03; Dep. Head. British Mil. Advr, Iraq, 2003; rcds 2004; Asst COS J7 UK PJHQ, 2005–07; Dir, J3 Ops, NATO Jt Forces Comd Brunssum, 2007–09; Sen. British Mil. Advr, US Central Comd, 2009–10; Comdr British Forces Cyprus and Adminr Sovereign Base Areas, 2010–12; Dep. Comdr Jt Force Comd Brunssum, 2013–15. Chm., RAF Rugby Union, 2001–06. *Recreations:* travel, cycling, squash, amateur chef.

**STACEY, Mary Elizabeth; Her Honour Judge Stacey;** a Circuit Judge, since 2014; a Deputy High Court Judge, since 2018; *b* 15 May 1961; *d* of late Rev. Nicolas David Stacey; *m* 2004, Stuart Bell; two *s*. *Educ:* Keble Coll., Oxford (BA Hons English 1982; MA). Admitted solicitor, 1987; solicitor in private practice, 1987–98; Partner and Hd of Equality, 1993–98, Consultant, 1999–2003, Thompsons, Solicitors; Chm., Industrial Tribunal, then Employment Tribunals, later Employment Judge, 2003–14 (part-time Chm., 1997–2003); a Recorder, 2007–14; Diversity and Community Relations Judge, 2011–; Probation Liaison Judge, 2016–; a Visiting Judge, Employment Appeal Tribunal, 2017–. Ind. Chair, Jt Negotiating Cttee for Higher Educn Staff, 2001–07. Dep. Chm., Central Arbitration Cttee, 2000–; Asst Certification Officer for Trade Unions and Employers' Assocs, 2017–. Mem., Gtr London Magistrates' Courts Authy, 1999–2003 (Chm., Audit Cttee). Mem., CIPD (Law Faculty), 1995–2014. Chm., Industrial Law Soc., 2006–10 (Hon. Vice-Pres., 2011–). Chm., Visitatorial Bd, Oxford Univ., 2009–14; Ind. Mem. Council, Goldsmiths, Univ. of London, 2008–14; Mem., Equal Treatment Adv. Cttee, Judicial Coll., 2011–14. Trustee, Midlands Legal Support Trust, 2014–. *Publications:* Part-time Workers and the Law, 1995; Challenging Disability Discrimination at Work, 2001; Discrimination Law Handbook, 2002, 2nd edn 2006. *Address:* Birmingham Crown Court, Queen Elizabeth ll Law Courts, 1 Newton Street, Birmingham B4 7NA.

**STACEY, Morna Dorothy, (Mrs W. D. Stacey);** *see* Hooker, M. D.

**STACEY, Paul Howard;** Executive Partner, Slaughter and May, since 2017 (Partner, since 1990); *b* Redhill, 9 May 1959; *s* of Colin Stacey and Maré Stacey; *m* 1985, Marie Morris; two *s*. *Educ:* Dulwich Coll.; Trinity Coll., Cambridge (BA Law 1980); Coll. of Law. Admitted solicitor, 1983; Slaughter and May, 1981–. *Address:* Slaughter and May, One Bunhill Row, EC1Y 8YY. *T:* (020) 7600 1200. *E:* paul.stacey@slaughterandmay.com. *Club:* Royal Automobile.

**STACEY, Valerie Elizabeth;** *see* Stacey, Hon. Lady.

**STACEY, Very Rev. Victor George;** Dean, St Patrick's Cathedral, Dublin, 2012–16; *b* Newtownbarry, Co. Wexford, 19 March 1944; *s* of George William Stacey and Norah Eleanor Stacey (*née* Young). *Educ:* Kilkenny Coll.; Mountjoy Sch.; University Coll., Dublin (BA Hons; Dip. Applied Psychol.); Trinity Coll., Dublin; Queen's Univ., Belfast (MTh). Yorks Insurance Co. Ltd, 1960–66. Ordained deacon, 1972, priest, 1973; Assistant Curate:

Derriaghy, 1972–76; Knock, 1976–79; Hd, Southern Church Mission, Down, 1979–86; Rector: Santry and Glasnevin, Dublin, 1986–95; Dun Laoghaire, Dublin, 1995–2012. *Recreations:* music, travel, theatre, walking, dining. *Address:* 27 The Poplars, Monkstown Valley, Monkstown, Co. Dublin, Ireland. *Clubs:* University (Dublin); Royal Irish Yacht; National Yacht.

**STACK, Most Rev. George;** *see* Cardiff, Archbishop of, (RC).

**STACY, Graham Henry,** CBE 1993; FCA; Chairman, Sanctuary Housing Association, 2004–09 (Treasurer, 1995–2004); *b* 23 May 1933; *s* of Norman Winny Stacy and Winifred Frances Stacy (*née* Wood); *m* 1958, Mary Fereday; one *s* three *d*. *Educ:* Stationers' Co.'s Sch. FCA 1955. Articled to Walter Smee Will & Co., 1950–55; Nat. Service, RN (Sub-Lieut), 1955–57; joined Price Waterhouse, 1957: Partner, 1968–93; Dir of Technical Services, 1976–88; Dir of Professional Standards (UK and Europe), 1988–93; Mem., Policy Cttee, 1987–93. Member: Auditing Practices Cttee, 1976–84; Accounting Standards Cttee, 1986–90; Accounting Standards Bd, 1990–94. Mem., Monopolies and Mergers, subseq. Competition, Commn, 1995–2001. Hon. Treas.: URC in UK, 1995–2002. *Recreations:* bridge, reading, painting watercolours, DIY.

**STADLEN, Hon. Sir Nicholas Felix,** Kt 2007; a Judge of the High Court of Justice, Queen's Bench Division, 2007–13; *b* 3 May 1950; *s* of late Peter Stadlen and Hedi (*née* Simon); *m* 1972, Frances Edith Howarth, *d* of T. E. B. and Margaret Howarth; three *s*. *Educ:* St Paul's School (Scholar); Trinity Coll., Cambridge (Open Scholarship and McGill Exhibition; BA Hons Classics Part 1, History Part 2). Pres., Cambridge Union Soc., 1970. First in order of merit, Part 1 Bar Exams, 1975; called to the Bar, Inner Temple, 1976. QC 1991; Asst Recorder, 1997–2000; Recorder, 2000–07. Mem., Bar Council Public Affairs Cttee, 1987; Chm., Bar Caribbean pro bono Cttee, 1999–2007. Chm. of Trustees, Volunteer Reading Help, 2005–08. First Sec., British-Irish Assoc., 1972–74. *Publications:* (with Michael Barnes) Gulbenkian Foundation Reports on National Music and Drama Education, 1974–75; (contrib.) Convention: an account of the 1976 US Democratic Party Presidential Nominating Convention, 1976. *Recreation:* listening to classical music.

**STAFFORD,** 15th Baron *cr* 1640; **Francis Melfort William Fitzherbert;** DL; Chancellor, Staffordshire University, since 2014; *b* 13 March 1954; *s* of 14th Baron Stafford and of Morag Nada, *yr d* of late Lt-Col Alastair Campbell; *S* father, 1986; *m* 1980, Katharine Mary Codrington; two *s* two *d*. *Educ:* Ampleforth College; Reading Univ.; RAC, Cirencester. Director (non-executive): Tarmac Industrial Products Div., 1987–93; Mid Staffs Mental Health Foundn, 1990–99; Hanley Economic BS, 1992–2014 (Vice Chm., 2005–14). Pro-Chancellor, Keele Univ., 1993–2004. Pres., Staffs CCC, 1999–2008; Pres. and Patron various orgns in North Staffs. Chm., Countryside Learning, 2010–. Governor, Harper Adams University (formerly Agricl) Coll., 1990–2007 (Chm. Govs, 2004–07). DL Stafford, 1994; High Sheriff, Staffs, 2005. DUniv: Keele, 2005; Staffs, 2006; Hon. DLitt Harper Adams, 2009; Hon. DSc Aston, 2014. *Recreations:* shooting, cricket, golf. *Heir: s* Hon. Benjamin John Basil Fitzherbert [*b* 8 Nov. 1983; *m* 2011, Georgina, *d* of Hon. Thomas Anthony Hewlett]. *Address:* Swynnerton Park, Stone, Staffordshire ST15 0QE. *T:* (01782) 796228. *Club:* Lord's Taverners.

**STAFFORD, Marquis of; James Granville Egerton;** *b* 12 Aug. 1975; *s* and *heir* of Duke of Sutherland, *qv; m* 2007, Barbara Ruth, *d* of Dr Graham Schneider, Vienna; four *d*. *Educ:* Eton Coll., Windsor; Univ. of Edinburgh; Cass Business Sch. *Address:* Ley Farm, Stetchworth, Newmarket, Suffolk CB8 9TX.

**STAFFORD, Area Bishop of;** *no new appointment at time of going to press.*

**STAFFORD, Andrew Bruce;** QC 2000; *b* 30 March 1957; *s* of Cyril Henry Stafford and Audrey Estelle Stafford; *m* 1982, Catherine Anne, *d* of Derek and Kathleen Johnson; one *s* four *d*. *Educ:* Royal Grammar Sch., Newcastle upon Tyne; Trinity Hall, Cambridge (BA Law, MA). Called to the Bar, Middle Temple, 1980, Bencher 2008. Part-time Chm., Employment Tribunals, 2000–08. Jt Editor, Transfer of Undertakings, 2006–; Mem., Adv. Bd, Gore-Browne on Companies, 2007–. *Publications:* (with Stuart Ritchie) Fiduciary Duties: directors and employees, 2008, 2nd edn 2015. *Recreations:* art, theatre, Newcastle United, Apostrophe Chambers. *Address:* Kobre & Kim LLP, Tower 42, 25 Old Broad Street, EC2N 1HQ. *Club:* Athenæum.

**STAFFORD, Christopher James;** Chief Executive Officer, Curve Theatre, since 2015; *b* Southport, 18 Nov. 1980; *s* of James and Margaret Stafford; partner, Michael Pearce. *Educ:* King George V Coll., Southport; Royal Central Sch. of Speech and Drama (BA Hons Drama and Educn; Postgrad. Dip. Teaching and Learning in Higher Educn). Practitioner in Residence, 2002–06, Projects and Develt Manager, 2006–09, Shakespeare's Globe; Clore Fellow, Clore Leadership Prog., 2009–10; Actg Hd of Develt, Bristol Old Vic, 2010–11; Exec. Dir, Dreamthinkspeak, 2011–13; Exec. Producer, Curve Th., 2013–15. *Recreations:* theatre, music, travel. *Address:* Curve Theatre, Rutland Street, Leicester LE1 1SB. *T:* (0116) 242 3579. *E:* c.stafford@curvetheatre.co.uk.

**STAFFORD, Prof. Fiona Jane,** DPhil; FBA 2018; FRSE; Professor of English Language and Literature, University of Oxford, since 2008; Fellow, Somerville College, Oxford, since 1992; *b* RAF Scampton, Lincs, 27 July 1960; *s* of Gp Captain Tom Stafford, OBE and Gillian Stafford; *m* 1988, Malcolm Sparkes; one *s* one *d*. *Educ:* De Aston Sch., Market Rasen; Univ. of Leicester (BA English); Lincoln Coll., Oxford (MA, MPhil; DPhil 1986). Lectr, Univ. of Evansville, 1985–87; British Acad. Post-doctoral Fellow, Lincoln Coll., Oxford, 1987–90; Lecturer: Nene Coll., 1990–91; St Anne's Coll., Oxford, 1991–92. FRSE 2006. *Publications:* The Sublime Savage, 1988; The Last of the Race, 1994; Starting Lines in Scottish, Irish and English Poetry, 2000; Local Attachments, 2010; Reading Romantic Poetry, 2012; The Long, Long Life of Trees, 2016; Jane Austen: a brief life, 2017; The Brief Life of Flowers, 2018. *Recreations:* family, travel, walking, art, theatre, gardens. *Address:* Somerville College, Oxford OX2 6HD. *T:* (01865) 270600. *E:* fiona.stafford@some.ox.ac.uk.

**STAFFORD, Prof. Nicholas David,** OBE 2018; FRCS; Professor of Head and Neck Surgery and Otolaryngology, University of Hull, 1995–2015, now Emeritus (Director, Postgraduate Medical Institute (formerly Head, Postgraduate School of Medicine), 1997–2012); Director, Research and Development, Hull and East Yorkshire Hospitals NHS Trust, 2013–17; *b* 13 Aug. 1954; *s* of late David Valentine Stafford; *m* 1977, Heather Gay Sims; four *d*. *Educ:* Farnborough Grammar Sch.; Univ. of Leeds (MB ChB 1977). FRCS 1983. Various SHO posts, 1978–82; Registrar in ENT Surgery, RNTNEH, 1982–84; Sen. Registrar in ENT/Head and Neck Surgery, Royal Marsden Hosp. and St Mary's Hosp., London, 1985–89; Consultant Head and Neck/ENT Surgeon, St Mary's, Ealing and Charing Cross Hosps, 1989–95. Résident Etranger, Inst. Gustave-Roussy, Paris, 1987–88. Chm. Trustees, Hull and E Yorks Med. Res. Centre Appeal, 2002–; Trustee, Hull and E Yorks Cardiac Trust Fund, 2006–. *Publications:* (with R. Youngs) Colour Aids: ENT, 1988, 3rd edn 2006; (ed with J. Waldron) Management of Oral Cancer, 1989; (contrib.) Treatment of Cancer, 2014; contribs mainly in field of head and neck oncology. *Recreation:* classic cars. *Address:* 29 Eastgate, Beverley HU17 0DR. *T:* (01482) 871541. *Club:* BMW Owners.

**STAFFORD, Peter Moore,** FCA; Director and Trustee, Rathbone Training Ltd, 2002–11; Member, Board of Partners, Deloitte & Touche (formerly Touche Ross & Co.), 1990–2000 (Chairman, 1992–95); *b* 24 April 1942; *s* of late Harry Shaw Stafford and May Alexandra (*née* Moore); *m* 1973, Elspeth Anne, *d* of James Steel Harvey; one *s* one *d*. *Educ:* Charterhouse. FCA 1976 (ACA 1965). Articled Clerk, Garnett Crewdson & Co., Manchester, 1960–64; Arthur Andersen, 1966–68; Partner, 1968–71, Garnett Crewdson & Co., merged with Spicer & Oppenheim: Partner, 1971–90; Managing Partner, 1990; merged with Touche Ross & Co. Member: Council for Industry and Higher Educn, 1993–97; Professional Standards Dept, ICAEW, 1998–2002. Trustee: Rathbone Trng, 2002–11; CRH Charitable Trust, 2015– (Chm., 2019–). Governor, Terra Nova Sch., 1976–2004. *Recreations:* travel, gardening. *Address:* Goostrey, Cheshire. *T:* (01477) 533339. *Club:* St James's (Manchester) (Hon. Treas., 2002–04).

**STAFFORD-CLARK, Maxwell Robert Guthrie Stewart, (Max);** artistic director and founder, Out of Joint Theatre Company, 1993–2017; *b* 17 March 1941; *s* of late Dr David Stafford-Clark, FRCP, FRCPsych and Dorothy Stewart (*née* Oldfield); *m* 1st, 1971, Carole Hayman; 2nd, 1981, Ann Pennington; one *d*; 3rd, 2010, Stella Feehily. *Educ:* Felsted School; Riverdale Country Day School, NY; Trinity College, Dublin. Associate dir, Traverse, 1966, artistic dir, 1968–70; dir, Traverse Workshop Co., 1970–74; founder, Joint Stock Theatre Group, 1974; Artistic Dir, English Stage Company at Royal Court Theatre, 1979–93. Productions include: Cloud 9, 1980; Top Girls, 1982; Falkland Sound, 1983; Tom and Viv, Rat in the Skull, 1984; Serious Money, 1987; Our Country's Good, 1988; King Lear, 1993; The Steward of Christendom, 1995; Shopping and Fucking, 1996; Blue Heart, 1997; Feelgood, 2001; Duck, The Permanent Way, 2003, Macbeth, Talking to Terrorists, 2004; O Go My Man, The Overwhelming, 2006; The Convict's Opera, 2008; Dreams of Violence, Mixed Up North, 2009; Andersen's English, The Big Fellah, 2010; A Dish of Tea with Dr Johnson, Bang Bang Bang, 2011; This May Hurt a Bit, Pitcairn, 2014; Crouch, Touch, Pause, Engage, All That Fall, 2015; A View From Islington North, 2016. *Publications:* Letters to George, 1989; Taking Stock, 2006; Our Country's Good: page to stage, 2010; Journal of the Plague Year, 2014. *Address:* 7 Thane Works, Thane Villas, N7 7NU.

**STAFFORD SMITH, Clive Adrian,** OBE 2000; Founder and Counsel, Reprieve; *b* 9 July 1959; *s* of Richard Stafford Smith and Jean Stafford Smith; *m* 1998, Emily MacSween Bolton; one *s*. *Educ:* Radley Coll., Abingdon; Univ. of North Carolina, Chapel Hill (John Motley Morehead Scholar; BA Pol Sci. 1981); Columbia Law Sch., NY (Harlan Fiske Stone Merit Scholar 1982, 1983, 1984; JD 1984). Staff attorney, Southern Prisoners' Defense Cttee, subseq. Southern Center for Human Rights, Atlanta, Ga, 1984–93; Dir, Louisiana Capital Assistance Center, New Orleans, 1993–2004. Patron, Lifelines. Documentaries: Fourteen Days in May, 1987; The Journey, 1988; Murder in Room 1215, 1997; The Death Belt, 2003; Torture (presenter), 2005. Hon. LLM Wolverhampton, 2001; Hon. DCL City, 2006; Hon. DLaws: Staffs, 2006; Oxford Brookes, 2008; Exeter, 2009; Bath, 2011; Bournemouth, 2011. Lifetime Achievement Award, Law Soc., 2003; Benjamin Smith Award, ACLU, La, 2004; Gandhi Peace Award, 2005; Contrarian Prize, 2014. *Publications:* (contrib.) A Punishment in Search of a Crime, 1989; Bad Men: Guantanamo and the secret prisons, 2007; Injustice, 2012. *Address:* Reprieve, PO Box 72054, London, EC3P 3BZ. *T:* (020) 7553 8140, *Fax:* (020) 7553 8189. *E:* clive@reprieve.org.uk. *Club:* Chelsea Arts.

**STAGG, Sir (Charles) Richard (Vernon),** KCMG 2008 (CMG 2001); HM Diplomatic Service, retired; Chairman, Rothschild (India), since 2015; Warden, Winchester College, since 2019; *b* 27 Sept. 1955; *s* of Walter and Elise Patricia Stagg; *m* 1982, Arabella Clare Faber; three *s* two *d*. *Educ:* Winchester; Oriel Coll., Oxford. Joined Diplomatic Service, 1977; FCO, 1977–79; Sofia, 1979–82; The Hague, 1982–85; FCO, 1985–86; UK Repn to EC, Brussels, 1987–88; FCO, 1988–91; UK Repn to EC, Brussels, 1991–93; Private Sec. to Foreign Sec., 1993–96; Head, EU (Ext.) Dept, FCO, 1996–98; Ambassador to Bulgaria, 1998–2001; Dir of Information, 2001–03; Dir Gen. (Corporate Affairs), 2003–07, FCO; High Comr to India, 2007–11; Ambassador to Afghanistan, 2012–15. *Recreations:* racing, gardening. *Clubs:* Turf, Beefsteak; Millennium.

**STAHEL, Rolf;** Chairman, Chesyl Pharma Ltd, since 2003; non-executive Chairman: Midatech Pharma plc (formerly Midatech Ltd), since 2014; Ampha Ltd, since 2016; *b* 21 April 1944; *s* of Hermann Stahel and Bluette Maillard; *m* 1970, Ewa Stachurska; two *s*. *Educ:* Kantonsschule, Lucerne (Dip. Kfm (CH) Business Studies, 1962; Handels Matura, 1963); 97th AMP, Harvard. Sales Administration, Rhône Poulenc, Switzerland, 1963–67; Wellcome: Rep., UK, 1967; Asst Manager, Switzerland, 1968; Gen. Manager, Italy, 1969–74; Man. Dir, Wellcome Thailand, 1974–79; Regl Dir, Wellcome Singapore, 1979–90; Dir of Marketing, Wellcome plc, UK, 1990–94; Chief Exec., Shire Pharmaceuticals Gp plc, 1994–2003. Non-executive Chairman: Newron Pharmaceuticals SPA, 2004–14; PowderMed Ltd, 2005–06; Cosmo SPA, 2006–12 (Dep. Chm., 2004–06); EUSA Pharma Inc., 2007–12; Connexios Life Sciences Pvt Ltd, 2009–16; Ergomed plc, 2014–17. Mem., Adv. Bd, Imperial Coll. Business Sch., 2007–. FRSA 1996; MInstD 1997. CEO of Year, Global Pharmaceutical Award, Informa, 2001; Techmark award, 2003; UK Lifetime Achievement Award, Bioindustry Assoc., 2009; Scrip's Lifetime Achievement Award, Informa, 2017. *Recreations:* golf, opera, musicals. *Address:* Neatham, Sleepers Hill, Winchester, Hants SO22 4NB. *T:* (01962) 868224. *E:* rstahel@chesyl.com. *Clubs:* Royal Automobile, Harvard Business School.

**STAINES, Paul De Laire;** Director and Chief Investment Officer, Global & General Nominees Ltd (Hong Kong), since 2009; Founder and Editor, Guido Fawkes, since 2004; *b* London, 11 Feb. 1967; *s* of Terril De Laire Staines and Mary De Laire Staines; *m* 2003, Orla Murphy; two *d*. *Educ:* Salvatorian Coll., Harrow. ADC to David Hart, Cttee for a Free Britain, 1988–89; Sunrise rave promoter, 1989–90; futures clerk, Cargill Investor Services, 1993; derivatives broker, Yasuda Trust Europe, 1993–96; Broker, Capital Mkts, Yamaichi Europe, London, 1996–97; Fund Manager, Mondial Global Investors LLC, 1997–2001; Trader, Westminster Investors (Bahamas) Ltd, 2002–03; Investment Advisor: United Growth Opportunities LLC, 2004–05; Global & Gen. Nominees Ltd, St Kitts and Nevis, 2007–11; Co-Founder and Man. Dir, MessageSpace Ltd, 2011–13; Dir, Campaign Action Ltd. Mem. Bd, Centre for Medical Cannabis. *Publications:* In the Grip of the Sandinistas: human rights in Nicaragua, 1979–89, 1989; The Big Red Book of New Labour Sleaze, 2007. *T:* 07092 840531, *Fax:* 07092 012337. *E:* paul.staines@order-order.com.

**STAIR,** 14th Earl of, *cr* 1703; **John David James Dalrymple;** Bt 1664 and 1698 (Scot); Viscount Stair, Lord Glenluce and Stranraer, 1690; Viscount Dalrymple, Lord Newliston, 1703; Baron Oxenfoord (UK), 1841; Vice Lord-Lieutenant of Wigtown, since 2017; *b* 4 Sept. 1961; *s* of 13th Earl of Stair, KCVO, MBE and Davina Katharine, *d* of late Hon. Sir David Bowes-Lyon, KCVO; *S* father, 1996; *m* 2006, Hon. Emily Mary Julia Stonor, 2nd *d* of Baron Camoys, *qv*; one *s* one *d*. Commnd Scots Guards, 1982. Elected Mem., H of L, 2008. *Heir: s* Viscount Dalrymple, *qv*.

**STAIR, Claire;** *see* Wilcox, C.

**STAIR, Julian Francis,** PhD; potter, since 1981; *b* 9 March 1955; *s* of Derek Anthony Guthrie (*né* Plank) and Christine Marie Stair (*née* Kelly); *m* 1992, Claire Wilcox, *qv*; two *d* (one *s* decd). *Educ:* Camberwell Sch. of Art (BA Hons 1978); Royal Coll. of Art (MA 1981;

PhD 2003). Sen. Lectr, Univ. of Surrey, 1983–98. Fellow in Craft and Criticism, Univ. of Newcastle, 1997–99; Vis. Lectr, Brighton Univ., Westminster Univ. and Cardiff Univ., 1998–2006; Vis. Prof. of Ceramics and Theory, Camberwell Coll. of Art, Univ. of London, 2003–; Vis. Prof., Muthesius Kunsthochschule, Kiel, 2009; Sen. Res. Fellow, Camberwell Coll., UAL, 2002–11; Res. Fellow, RCA, 2004; Principal Res. Fellow, Univ. of Westminster, 2012–14. Crafts Council: Trustee, 2000–06; Interim Chm., 2005–06; Dep. Chm., 2006–08. Trustee, Contemporary Applied Arts, 1997–2003. FRSA. *Solo exhibitions* include: Anatol Orient, London, 1985, 1987; Paul Rice Gall., London, 1995; Contemp. Applied Arts, London, 1997, 2001; V&A Mus., 2004; Scottish Gall., Edinburgh, 2010; Quietus: death, the vessel and the human body, Middlesbrough Inst. of Modern Art, 2012, Nat. Mus. of Wales, Cardiff, Winchester Cathedral, 2013, Somerset Hse, 2013–14; Quotidian, Corvi-Mora Gall., London, 2014–15; Quietus Revisited, Manchester Cathedral, 2016; *selected exhibitions* incl. (with Simone ten Hompel) Re-naturing the Vessel, Rosemarie Jaeger Gall., Frankfurt, Wolverhampton Art Gall., Nat. Centre for Craft and Design, Sleaford, 2016, Exempla Fair, Munich, Material: Earth, Messums Wiltshire, 2017; *work in public collections* incl. V&A Mus., BM, Amer. Mus. of Art and Design, NY, Mashiko Mus. of Ceramic Art, Japan, and Mus. Boijmans van Beuningen, Rotterdam. *Publications:* (ed) The Body Politic: the role of the body and contemporary craft, 2000; (contrib.) The Persistence of Craft, ed by Paul Greenhalgh, 2002; (contrib.) Ceramics, Art and Cultural Production in Modern Japan, 2017; (contrib.) Things of Beauty Growing: British studio pottery, 2017; contribs to The Times, Art in America, Crafts, Ceramic Review, American Craft and New Art Examiner. *Recreations:* croquet, bird watching, walking, cinema. *Address:* 52a Hindmans Road, SE22 9NG. *T:* (020) 8693 4877. *E:* studio@julianstair.com.

**STAITE, Sara Elizabeth, (Mrs John Peet); Her Honour Judge Staite;** a Circuit Judge, since 2010; *b* Sussex, 17 Aug. 1957; *d* of Anthony Staite; *m* 1990, John Peet; two *s* one *d*. *Educ:* Cheltenham Ladies' Coll.; Leeds Univ. (LLB). Called to the Bar, Inner Temple, 1979; in practice as a barrister specialising in ancillary relief, 1980–2010. *Recreations:* walking, gardening, theatre. *Address:* Chelmsford County Court, Priory Place, New London Road, Chelmsford CM2 0PP.

**STALFORD, Christopher David Matthew;** Member (DemU) Belfast South, Northern Ireland Assembly, since 2016; *b* Belfast, 17 Jan. 1983; *s* of Clifford and Karen Stalford; *m* 2004, Laura Getty; two *s* one *d*. *Educ:* Wellington Coll., Belfast; Queen's Univ. Belfast (BA Hons Pol. and Modern Hist.). Policy Officer, Democratic Unionist Party, 2007–16. Mem. (DemU) Belfast CC, 2005–16 (Dep. Lord Mayor of Belfast, 2013). High Sheriff, Belfast, 2010. *Recreations:* reading, classical music, cooking. *Address:* Northern Ireland Assembly, Parliament Buildings, Stormont, Belfast BT4 3XX. *E:* christopher_stalford1912@outlook.com.

**STAMER, Sir Peter (Tomlinson),** 6th Bt *cr* 1809, of Beauchamp, Dublin; *b* 19 Nov. 1951; *o s* of Sir (Lovelace) Anthony Stamer, 5th Bt and Stella Huguette (*née* Binnie); *S* father, 2012; *m* 1st, 1979, Dinah Louise Berry (marr. diss. 1989); one *s* one *d*; 2nd, 1999, Vera Řeháková (marr. diss. 2002). *Educ:* Malvern; Southampton Univ. RAF 1972–89 (Sqdn Ldr 1988). *Heir: s* William Peter Alexander Stamer, *b* 20 Sept. 1983.

**STAMP,** family name of **Baron Stamp**.

**STAMP,** 4th Baron *cr* 1938, of Shortlands, **Trevor Charles Bosworth Stamp,** MD; FRCP; Hon. Consultant Physician, Royal National Orthopaedic Hospital, since 1999; Consultant Physician and Director, Department of Bone and Mineral Metabolism, Institute of Orthopaedics, Royal National Orthopaedic Hospital, 1974–99; *b* 18 Sept. 1935; *s* of 3rd Baron Stamp, MD, FRCPath and Frances Hammond (*d* 1998), *d* of late Charles Henry Bosworth, Evanston, Illinois, USA; *S* father, 1987; *m* 1st, 1963, Anne Carolynn Churchill (marr. diss. 1971); two *d*; 2nd, 1975, Carol Anne (marr. diss. 1997), *d* of late Robert Keith Russell; one *s* one *d*. *Educ:* The Leys School; Gonville and Caius Coll., Cambridge; Yale Univ.; St Mary's Hosp. Medical School. MSc (Yale) 1957; MD (Cantab) 1972; FRCP 1978. Qualified in medicine, 1960; Med. Registrar, Professorial Medical Unit, St Mary's Hosp., 1964–66; Hon. Senior Registrar 1968–73, and Hon. Sen. Lecturer 1972–73, Dept of Human Metabolism, University College Hosp. and Medical School; Hon. Consultant Physician and Sen. Lectr, Middlesex Hosp. and UCL School of Medicine, 1974–99, now Emeritus Consultant, UCL Hosps. Mem., Scientific Adv. Bd, Nat. Osteoporosis Soc. Patron, Nat. Assoc. for Relief of Paget's Disease; Vice-Patron, British Sch. of Osteopathy. Hon. Life Member: Bone and Tooth Soc.; Internat. Skeletal Soc. Prix André Lichtwitz, France, 1973. *Publications:* numerous papers on disorders of mineral metabolism. *Recreations:* music, golf, contract bridge. *Heir: s* Hon. Nicholas Charles Trevor Stamp, *b* 27 Feb. 1978.

**STAMP, Francesca Isabella;** *see* Simon, F. I.

**STAMP, Malcolm Frederick,** CBE 2002; Chief Executive, Metro North Hospital and Health Service, Brisbane, Queensland, 2013–14; *b* 29 Dec. 1952; *s* of Frederick and Elizabeth Stamp; *m* Linda (marr. diss.); two *d*. *Educ:* Stand Grammar Sch. Unit Gen. Manager, N Manchester HA, 1982–86; District General Manager: Crewe HA, 1986–88; Liverpool HA, 1988–90; Chief Executive: Royal Liverpool Univ. Hosps NHS Trust, 1990–94; Norfolk and Norwich Univ. Hosp. NHS Trust, 1994–2002; Addenbrooke's NHS Trust, then Cambridge Univ. Hosps NHS Foundn Trust, 2002–06; Waikato Dist Health Bd, 2006–07; Provider Agency, NHS London, 2007–09; University Hosps Coventry and Warwickshire NHS Trust, 2009–11; Mid Essex Hosp. Service NHS Trust, 2011–13. Mem., IMS, 1975; MIHM 1978. Hon. DCL UEA, 2000. *Publications:* Appraisal for Consultants in the NHS, 2000. *Recreations:* football, gardening, family.

**STAMP, Terence Henry;** actor and author; *b* 22 July 1938; *s* of Thomas Stamp and Ethel Esther Perrott. *Educ:* Plaistow County Grammar School; Webber-Douglas Dramatic Acad. (Amhurst Webber Meml Schol., 1958). *Films include:* Billy Budd, 1962; The Collector, 1964; Far from the Madding Crowd, 1966; Blue, 1967; Spirits of the Dead (Fellini sect.), 1967; Theorem, 1968; Superman, 1977; Meetings with Remarkable Men, 1977; Superman 2, 1978; The Hit, 1984; Legal Eagles, 1985; Wall Street, 1987; Young Guns, 1988; The Sicilian, 1988; Prince of Shadows, or Beltenebros, 1993; The Real McCoy, 1994; The Adventures of Priscilla the Queen of the Desert, 1994; Bliss, 1995; Limited Edition, 1995; Kiss the Sky, 1998; Love Walked In, 1998; The Limey, 1999; Red Planet, 2000; My Wife is an Actress, 2002; My Boss's Daughter, 2003; The Haunted Mansion, 2003; These Foolish Things, 2006; Valkyrie, 2009; Song for Marion, 2013; Miss Peregrine's Home for Peculiar Children, 2016; Bitter Harvest, 2017; Crooked House, 2017; Viking Destiny, 2018; *stage:* Alfie, Morosco, NY, 1965; Dracula, Shaftesbury, 1978; Lady from the Sea, Roundhouse, 1979. Launched, with Elizabeth Buxton, Stamp Collection range of organic food, 1994. Hon. DArts East London, 1993. *Publications:* autobiography: Stamp Album, 1987; Coming Attractions, 1988; Double Feature, 1989; The Night (novel), 1992; (with Elizabeth Buxton) The Stamp Collection Cookbook, 1997; Rare Stamps: reflections on living, breathing, and acting, 2012; The Ocean Fell Into the Drop, 2017. *Club:* New York Athletic (New York).

**STANAGE, Rt Rev. Thomas Shaun;** Bishop of Bloemfontein, 1982–97; *b* 6 April 1932; *s* of late Robert and Edith Clarice Stanage. *Educ:* King James I Grammar Sch., Bishop Auckland; Univ. of Oxford (MA, Hons Theology, 1956). Curate, St Faith, Great Crosby, 1958–61; Minister of Conventional District of St Andrews, Orford, 1961–63; Vicar, St Andrew, Orford, 1963–70; Rector, All Saints, Somerset West, 1970–75; Dean of Kimberley, 1975–78; Bishop Suffragan of Johannesburg, 1978–82. Liaison Bishop to Missions to Seafarers, Southern Africa. Lectr in Systematic Theol., Biblical Studies and Religious Educn, Univ. of Orange Free State, 1998–2001. Hon. DD Nashotah Theol Sem., Wisconsin, 1986. *Recreation:* music (organ, violin and piano). *Address:* Walden, 42a Union Avenue, Waverley, Bloemfontein 9301, S Africa. *Clubs:* Bloemfontein; Good Hope Flying, Cape Aero (Cape Town).

**STANBRIDGE, Roger Andrew;** Headteacher, Stratford-upon-Avon Grammar School for Girls, 1991–2005; *b* 22 June 1948; *s* of Bert and Kit Stanbridge; *m* 1972, Sandy Black; three *d*. *Educ:* Varndean Boys' Grammar Sch., Brighton; Hull Univ. (BSc 1969); Univ. of Newcastle upon Tyne. Hd of Sci., Moulton Sch., Northampton, 1980–87; Dep. Headteacher, Stratford-upon-Avon Grammar Sch. for Girls, 1987–91. Principal Examiner: for Cambridge Assessment (formerly Univ. of Cambridge Local Exams Syndicate), 1988–; for Edexcel, 2005–09. *Recreations:* overseas travel, supporter of Brighton and Hove Albion FC, seven grandchildren. *E:* zen79983@zen.co.uk.

**STANCIOFF, Ivan;** Ambassador-at-Large for Bulgaria, since 1994; *b* 1 April 1929; *s* of late Ivan Robert Stancioff and Marion (*née* Mitchell); *m* 1st, 1957, Deirdre O'Donnell (marr. diss.); two *s* two *d*; 2nd, Alexandra Lawrence. *Educ:* Georgetown Univ., Washington (BA); New York Univ. Sch. of Business. Economist, Amer. and Foreign Power Corp., 1957–60; Dir Marketing, IBM World Trade Corp., São Paulo, 1961–63; Rio, 1963–65; Paris, 1965–70; Manager, ITT, Athens, 1970; Vice-Pres., ITEL Corp., London, 1971–74; Dir, Safestore Ltd, London, 1975–77; Vice-Pres., Storage Technol. Corp., London, 1977–81; Dir, Cresta Marketing SA, Geneva, 1981–90; Advr to UDF, Sofia, 1990–91; Ambassador to UK, 1991–94; Minister of Foreign Affairs, Bulgaria, 1994–95. Dir, Inst. for Intercultural Relations, Sofia, 1992; Chm., Karin Dom Foundn, 1995–. FLS. Good Conduct Medal, US Army, 1956; Commander, Legion of Honour (France), 1994; Grand Cross, Rio Branco (Brazil), 2002; Star of Solidarity, Italy, 2006; Stara Planina 1st cl., Bulgaria, 2010. *Recreations:* history, gardening, travel, painting.

**STANCLIFFE, Rt Rev. David Staffurth,** FRSCM; Bishop of Salisbury, 1993–2010; an Honorary Assistant Bishop: Diocese of Europe, since 2011; Diocese of Durham, since 2013; *b* 1 Oct. 1942; *s* of late Very Rev. Michael Staffurth Stancliffe; *m* 1965, Sarah Loveday Smith; one *s* two *d*. *Educ:* Westminster School; Trinity College, Oxford (MA; Hon. Fellow 2003); Cuddesdon Theological College. Assistant Curate, St Bartholomew's, Armley, Leeds, 1967–70; Chaplain to Clifton Coll., Bristol, 1970–77; Canon Residentiary of Portsmouth Cathedral, Diocesan Director of Ordinands and Lay Ministry Adviser, 1977–82; Provost of Portsmouth, 1982–93. Hon. Fellow, 1999–2010, Fellow, 2010–, St Chad's Coll., Durham. Dir, The Bishop's Consort, 1993–. Member: Gen. Synod, 1985–2010; Liturgical Commn, 1986–2005 (Chm., 1993–2005); Cathedrals' Fabric Commn, 1991–2001. Pres., Council, Marlborough Coll., 1994–2010. Vice-Pres., RSCM, 2005–. FRSCM 2001; Hon. FGCM 2005. Hon. DLitt Portsmouth, 1993; DD Lambeth, 2004. *Publications:* God's Pattern: shaping our worship, ministry and life, 2003; The Pilgrim Prayer Book, 2003; Celebrating Daily Prayer, 2005; The Lion Companion to Church Architecture, 2008; The Gospels in Art, Music and Literature: the story of salvation in three media, 2014. *Recreations:* old music, Italy. *Address:* Butts House, 15 The Butts, Stanhope, Bishop Auckland, Co. Durham DL13 2UQ. *T:* (01388) 526912. *E:* d.s.stancliffe@durham.ac.uk.
*See also* M. J. Stancliffe.

**STANCLIFFE, Martin John,** FSA; RIBA; Surveyor to the Fabric, St Paul's Cathedral, 1990–2011, Surveyor Emeritus, 2013; *b* 28 Dec. 1944; *s* of Very Rev. Michael Staffurth Stancliffe and Barbara Elizabeth Tatlow; *m* 1979, Sara Judith Sanders (*d* 2017); two *d*. *Educ:* Westminster Sch.; Magdalene Coll., Cambridge (MA, DipArch). AABC. Dir, Martin Stancliffe Architects, 1975–2004; Partner (formerly Strategy Partner, then Sen. Principal), 2004–15, Consultant, 2015–17, Purcell (formerly Purcell Miller Tritton). Architect to: Lichfield Cath., 1983–2003; Southwell Minster, 1989–2009; Christ Church Cath., Oxford, 1990–95; Consultant Architect to Canterbury Cath., 2014–16. Member: Exec. Cttee, Council for the Care of Churches, 1980–91; Cathedrals' Fabric Commn for England, 1991–2001; Archbishops' Commn on Cathedrals, 1992–94; Historic Bldgs and Areas Adv. Cttee, English Heritage, 1995–2001; Expert Adv. Panel on Bldgs and Land, Heritage Lottery Fund, 1997–99; Cultural Tourism Cttee, ICOMOS UK, 1997–; Fabric Adv. Cttee, York Minster, 2007–; Fabric Adv. Cttee, Canterbury Cath., 2016–. Chairman: Cathedral Architects Assoc., 1999–2005; York Consortium for Conservation and Craftsmanship, 2005–. Trustee: York Civic Trust, 2008–; Landmark Trust, 2011–; Nat. Centre for Early Music, 2017–. Marvin Breckinridge Patterson Lectr, Univ. of Maryland, 2000. Hon. Vis. Fellow, Dept of Archaeol., Univ. of York, 2002–. Pres., Surveyors' Club, 1998–99, 2010–11. FSA 1995. *Publications:* (contrib.) St Paul's: the Cathedral Church of London 604–2004, 2004. *Recreations:* the baroque oboe, old buildings, sailing. *Address:* 16 Bootham Terrace, York YO30 7DH. *T:* (01904) 630105.
*See also* Rt Rev. D. S. Stancliffe.

**STANDAGE, Simon Andrew Thomas;** violinist; *b* 8 Nov. 1941; *s* of Thomas Ralph Standage and Henrietta Florence Sugg; *m* 1964, Jennifer Ward; three *s*. *Educ:* Bryanston Sch.; King's Coll., Cambridge (MA). Harkness Fellow, 1967–69; Sub-leader, English Chamber Orch., 1974–78; leader and soloist, English Concert, 1973–91; Founder and Leader, Salomon String Quartet, 1981–; founded Collegium Musicum 90, 1990; Associate Dir, Acad. of Ancient Music, 1991–95. Professor of Baroque Violin: Royal Acad. of Music, 1983–; Dresdner Akademie für Alte Musik, 1993–2004; Franz Liszt Acad. of Music, 2010–. Has made numerous recordings. Hon. RAM 2009. Georg Philipp Telemann Prize, City of Magdeburg, 2010; Medal of Honour, Polish Min. of Culture and Nat. Heritage, 2008. *Recreation:* crosswords. *Address:* 106 Hervey Road, Blackheath, SE3 8BX. *T:* (020) 8319 3372.
*See also* T. W. Standage.

**STANDAGE, Thomas William;** Deputy Editor and Head of Digital Strategy, The Economist, since 2015; *b* London, 1969; *s* of Simon Andrew Thomas Standage, *qv*; *m* 1996, Kirstin McKee; one *s* one *d*. *Educ:* Dulwich Coll.; Worcester Coll., Oxford (BEng Engrg and Computer Sci.). Freelance journalist and photographer, 1992–96; Dep. Ed., Technol., Daily Telegraph, 1996–98; The Economist: Sci. and Technol. Corresp., 1998–2003; Technol. Ed., 2003–06; Business Ed., 2006–09; Business Affairs Ed., 2009–10; Digital Ed., 2010–15. *Publications:* The Victorian Internet, 1998, 3rd edn 2014; The Neptune File, 2000; The Mechanical Turk, 2002; A History of the World in Six Glasses, 2005; An Edible History of Humanity, 2009; Writing on the Wall, 2013. *Recreations:* playing the drums, food and wine, video games. *Address:* The Economist, The Adelphi Building, 1–11 John Adam Street, WC2N 6HT. *T:* (020) 7830 7131. *E:* tws@economist.com.

**STANDEN, Iain Gordon;** Chief Executive Officer, Bletchley Park Trust, since 2012; *b* Lincoln, 2 April 1963; *s* of Kenneth Standen and Janet Standen; *m* 1989, Anna Robertson; two *s* one *d*. *Educ:* Christ's Hospital; King's Coll. London (BA Geog. 1985); Royal Mil. Acad. Sandhurst; Cranfield Univ. (MA Mil. Studies 1996). Royal Corps of Signals, British Army: Univ. Cadet, 1982–85; Regtl Duty, GB, Cyprus, NI and Germany, 1986–95; psc 1996; D Army Plans, MoD, 1996–99; OC 20 Armoured Bde HQ and Signal Sqdn,

1999–2001; COS 1 Signal Bde, 2001–02; SO1 Orgn & Deployment HQ Signal Officer in Chief (Army), 2002–03; CO Jt Service Signal Unit, Cyprus, 2003–05; COS HQ Signal Officer in Chief (Army), 2005–08; Chief Campaign Plans HQ Multinat. Force-Iraq, Baghdad, 2008; Dep. Hd NEC Prog. Office, MoD, 2009–10; Comd Jt Service Signals Orgn, 2010–11. Pt-time battlefield tour guide, 2000–. FRSA. *Recreations:* studying history, travel, listening to live music, long-distance running. *Address:* Bletchley Park Trust, The Mansion, Bletchley Park, Milton Keynes, Bucks MK3 6EB. *T:* (01908) 272682. *Club:* Army and Navy.

**STANDING, John;** *see* Leon, Sir J. R.

**STANDING, Rev. Dr Roger;** Senior Research Fellow, Spurgeon's College, since 2017 (Principal, 2013–17); *b* Downham Market, Norfolk, 19 April 1959; *s* of John and Margaret Standing; *m* 1978, Marion Neale; one *s* two *d. Educ:* Downham Market Secondary Modern Sch.; Norfolk Coll. of Arts and Technol.; Univ. of Manchester (BA 1984; MPhil 1992); Denver Seminary, Colo (DMin. 2000). Evangelist, Liverpool Central Hall, 1978–81; Methodist Minister, Horsforth, 1984–90; Baptist Minister, W Croydon, 1990–2001; Regl Minister, Southern Counties Baptist Assoc., 2001–07; Spurgeon's College, London: Tutor, 2007–09; Dir of Trng, 2009–11; Dep. Principal, 2011–13. FRSA. *Publications:* Preaching for the Unchurched, 2002; Finding the Plot, 2004, 2nd edn 2012; Re-emerging Church, 2008; As a Fire by Burning, 2013; Mosaic Evangelism, 2013; The Forward Movement, 2015; Called and Equipped, 2017; Getting the Word Out, 2017. *Recreations:* Norwich City Football Club, writing, music, sport.

**STANDRING, Prof. Susan Margaret,** MBE 2015; PhD, DSc; Professor of Anatomy, 2007–09, now Emeritus, and Head, Department of Anatomy and Human Sciences (formerly Division of Anatomy, Cell and Human Biology), 2000–09, School of Biomedical and Health Sciences (formerly Guy's, King's and St Thomas' School of Biomedical Sciences), King's College London; *b* 22 Feb. 1947; *d* of William and Margaret Hall; *m* 1970, Guy Lewis Standring (*d* 2014); two *d. Educ:* Sch. of St Clare, Penzance; Guy's Hosp. Medical Sch., Univ. of London (BSc, PhD; DSc); King's Coll. London (Postgrad. Dip. in Teacher Educn Medicine and Dentistry). FRSB (FSB 2010). Reader in Experimental Neurobiology, UMDS of Guy's and St Thomas' Hosps, 1989–98; Admissions Dean for Medicine, UMDS, subseq. GKT, KCL, 1996–2002; Prof. of Experimental Neurobiol., Sch. of Biomed. and Health Scis (formerly GKT Sch. of Biomed. Scis), KCL, 1998–2007. President: Peripheral Nerve Soc., 2001–03; Anatomical Soc. (formerly Anatomical Soc. of GB and Ireland), 2008–10; Hunterian Soc., 2019–20; Mem., Court of Examiners, 2002–15, Anatomy Develt Tutor, 2008–13, RCS. Trustee: Damilola Taylor Trust, 2005–07; Changing Faces, 2008–10; Hunterian Collection, RCS, 2012–. FKC 2008. Hon. FRCS 2009; Hon. FAS 2015. *Publications:* Gray's Anatomy, (section ed.) 37th edn 1989, 38th edn 1995, (ed.-in-chief) 39th edn 2005 to 41st edn 2015; (as Susan Hall) over 200 papers in peer-reviewed scientific jls. *Recreations:* walking, reading, gardening, anatomical history. *Address:* c/o School of Biomedical and Health Sciences, King's College London, Hodgkin Building, Guy's Campus, SE1 1UL. *E:* susan.standring@kcl.ac.uk.

**STANES, Ven. Ian Thomas;** Archdeacon of Loughborough, 1992–2005, now Archdeacon Emeritus; *b* 29 Jan. 1939; *s* of Sydney Stanes and Iris Stanes (*née* Hulme); *m* 1962, Sylvia Alice (*née* Drew); one *d* (one *s* decd). *Educ:* Sheffield Univ. (BSc 1962); Linacre Coll., Oxford (BA 1965; MA 1969); Wycliffe Hall, Oxford. Ordained: deacon, 1965; priest, 1966; Curate, Holy Apostles, Leicester, 1965–69; Vicar, Broom Leys, Coalville, Leicester, 1969–76; Priest Warden, Marrick Priory, Ripon, 1976–82; Willesden Area Officer for Mission, Ministry and Evangelism, London, 1982–92. Prebendary, St Paul's Cathedral, 1989–92. *Recreations:* walking, photography, theatre, singing, music, art appreciation, model and stamp collecting, reading. *Address:* 192 Bath Road, Bradford on Avon, Wilts BA15 1SP. *T:* (01225) 309036. *E:* istanes@btinternet.com.

**STANESBY, Rev. Canon Derek Malcolm,** PhD; Canon of St George's Chapel, Windsor, 1985–97 (Steward, 1987–94; Treasurer, 1994–97); *b* 28 March 1931; *s* of late Laurence J. C. Stanesby and Elsie L. Stanesby (*née* Stean); *m* 1958, Christine A. Payne; three *s* one *d. Educ:* Orange Hill Central School, London; Northampton Polytechnic, London; Leeds Univ. (BA Hons); Manchester Univ. (MEd, PhD); College of the Resurrection, Mirfield. GPO Radio Research Station, Dollis Hill, 1947–51; RAF (Navigator), 1951–53. Ordained, 1958; Curate: Old Lakenham, Norwich, 1958–61; St Mary, Welling, Dio. Southwark, 1961–63; Vicar, St Mark, Bury, Dio. Manchester, 1963–67; Rector, St Chad, Ladybarn, Manchester, 1967–85. Mem., Archbishop's Commn on Christian Doctrine, 1986–91. *Publications:* Science, Reason and Religion, 1985; (contrib.) Theology, Evolution and the Mind, 2009; various articles and papers. *Recreations:* hill walking, sailing, woodwork, idling. *Address:* 32 Elizabeth Way, Uppingham, Rutland LE15 9PQ. *T:* (01572) 821298. *Club:* Royal Air Force.

**STANFORD, Rear Adm. Christopher David,** CB 2002; Partner, 2002–15, part-time adviser, since 2015, Odgers Berndtson (formerly Odgers Ray and Berndtson), Executive Search (Head of Global Healthcare Practice (formerly Head of Practice (Healthcare and Life Sciences), 2002–15); *b* 15 Feb. 1950; *s* of late Joseph Gerald Stanford and Dr Elspeth Stanford (*née* Harrison); *m* 1972, Angela Mary, (Annie), *d* of late Commander Derek G. M. Gardner, VRD, RSMA; one *s* three *d. Educ:* St Paul's Sch.; Britannia RN Coll., Dartmouth; Merton Coll., Oxford (MA History and French). Joined RN 1967; served HM Ships Puma, Jupiter, Hubberston, Exmouth, Newcastle, Antrim, Brilliant, Fife; commanded: HMS Boxer, 1988–89; HMS Coventry and First Frigate Sqdn, 1993–94; Asst Dir (Ships), Directorate of Operational Requirements, 1990–93; rcds 1995; Dir, Naval Staff Duties, 1995–97; Dir, Operational Capability, 1997–98; COS to Surgeon Gen., MoD, 1999–2002. FNI (Vice Pres., 1999–2007). Gov., King Edward VII's Hosp., 2008–. Lay Chm., St Lawrence, Cucklington PCC, 2002–. Freeman: City of London, 2000; Master Mariners' Co., 2000; Younger Brother, Trinity House, 2006. Chm., Combined Services Rugby Union, 2001–02; Vice President: RN Rugby Union, 1996–2002; N Dorset RFC, 1999–; Chairman: Royal Naval Lay Readers Soc., 1999–2002; Somerset and Dorset Sea Cadet Assoc., 2002–12. Mem. Council, White Ensign Assoc., 2009–. DUniv UCE, 2002. OStJ 2001. *Publications:* contribs to learned and professional jls on maritime, health and leadership issues. *Recreations:* art, maritime affairs, industrial archaeology (especially railways), healthcare. *Address:* Odgers Berndtson, 20 Cannon Street, EC4M 6XD. *Clubs:* Royal Naval of 1765 and 1785, Hon. Society of Anchorites (Pres., 2003), Chelsea Arts.

**STANFORD, Geoffrey;** Headmaster, Fettes College, since 2017; *b* UK, 1971; *s* of late Julian Stanford and Elizabeth Stanford (*née* Aglionby); *m* 2003, Susanna Hall; two *s. Educ:* Dragon Sch., Oxford; Eton Coll.; St Hugh's Coll., Oxford (MA Classics 1994); RMA, Sandhurst; INSEAD (MBA 2001). Captain, Grenadier Guards, 1994–98. Consultant, Boston Consulting Gp, 1998–2000; Associate and Vice Pres., Citigroup, 2002–06; Teacher, Millfield Sch., 2006–08; Housemaster and Hd of Econs and Business, Pangbourne Coll., 2008–14; Dep. Hd, Co-Curriculum, Sevenoaks Sch., 2014–17. Governor: Downs Sch., Newbury, 2010–14; Dragon Sch., Oxford, 2012–17. Adult volunteer, CCF, 2009–. Mem., Stewards at Henley Royal Regatta. FRGS 2000. *Recreations:* spending time in mountains, running with my dogs, playing the French horn, travel. *Address:* Fettes College, Carrington Road, Edinburgh EH4 1QX. *Clubs:* Alpine, Lansdowne.

**STANFORD, Martin;** Presenter, Sky News, 1991–2016; *b* Didcot, 2 May 1958; *s* of Rev. P. Guy Stanford and Barbara Alice Stanford; *m* Sarah Strike; three *s.* BBC Transcription Recording Unit, 1977–79; BBC Radio Oxford, 1979–81; BBC Trng Dept, 1981; BBC Radio Northampton, 1982–86; BBC TV South, 1986–89; British Satellite Broadcasting TV, 1989–90; freelance producer and reporter, 1991. Lay Steward, St George's Chapel, Windsor Castle, 2012–; Gov., St George's Sch., Windsor Castle, 2012–. *Recreations:* technology, theatre, family, boating.

**STANFORD, Peter James;** writer, journalist and broadcaster; *b* 23 Nov. 1961; *s* of late Reginald James Hughes Stanford and Mary Catherine (*née* Fleming); *m* 1995, Siobhan, *d* of James Cross and late Celine Cross; one *s* one *d. Educ:* St Anselm's Coll., Birkenhead; Merton Coll., Oxford (BA Hons 1983). Reporter, The Tablet, 1983–84; News Editor, 1984–88, Editor, 1988–92, The Catholic Herald. Feature writer: for various titles incl. Guardian, Independent; for Daily Telegraph, 2007–; Columnist, The Tablet, 2003–. Mem. Panel, Coates Rev. of Prison Educn, 2015–16. Chm., ASPIRE (Assoc. for Spinal Res., Reintegration and Rehabilitation), 1992–2001 and 2005–11. Dir, Candoco Dance Co., 1994–98 (Patron, 1998–). Dir, Frank Longford Charitable Trust, 2002–. Panellist: FutureWatch, TV, 1996; radio: The Moral Maze, 1996; Vice or Virtue, 1997; Presenter: The Mission, TV, 1997; various Radio 2, Radio 4 and BBC World Service documentaries, 1999–. Trustee: Circles UK, 2015–16; Chance UK, 2017–18. *Publications:* (ed) Hidden Hands: child workers around the world, 1988; (with Simon Lee) Believing Bishops, 1990; (ed) The Seven Deadly Sins, 1990; (with Kate Saunders) Catholics and Sex, 1992 (televised, 1992; Bronze Medal, NY TV Fest., 1993); Cardinal Hume and the changing face of English Catholicism, 1993; Lord Longford: an authorised life, 1994; revd edn as The Outcasts' Outcast, 2003; (with Gerard Noel) The Anatomy of the Catholic Church, 1994; (with Leanda de Lisle) The Catholics and their Houses, 1995; The Devil: a biography, 1996 (televised 1998); The She-Pope: a quest for the truth behind the mystery of Pope Joan, 1998 (televised 1998); Bronwen Astor: her life and times, 2000; Heaven: a travellers' guide, 2002; Being a Dad, 2004; (ed) Why I'm Still a Catholic, 2005; (ed with Julian Filochowski) Opening Up, 2005; C. Day-Lewis: a biography, 2007; Teach Yourself Catholicism, 2008; A Life of Christ, 2009; The Extra Mile: a 21st century pilgrimage, 2010; (ed) The Death of a Child, 2011; How to Read a Graveyard: journeys in the company of the dead, 2013; Judas Iscariot: the troubling history of the renegade apostle, 2015; Martin Luther: Catholic dissident, 2017; What We Talk About When We Talk About Faith, 2018; Angels: a visible and invisible history, 2019. *Recreations:* old cars, old churches, north Norfolk. *Address:* c/o Sheil Land Associates, 52 Doughty Street, WC1N 2LS. *W:* www.peterstanford.co.uk.

**STANFORD, Maj. Gen. Richard James Æthelstan,** MBE 1993; Senior British Loan Service Officer, Oman, since 2017; *b* Luton, 10 Aug. 1966; *s* of John Rodney Stanford and Jane Stanford (*née* Oliver-Bellasis); *m* 1995, Fiona Mary Dear; one *s* one *d. Educ:* RMA Sandhurst; CGLI (Grad. Military Technol., 1998); Cranfield Univ. (MA 1999); Open Univ. (MBA 2003). FCMI 2011. Welsh Guards: 2nd Lt, 1987; psc 1999; CO 1st Bn, 2006–08; COS Theatre Troops, 2009–12; Chief Jt Fire and Influence, HQ ARRC, 2012–14; ACOS Land Forces, 2014–15; GOC Regl Comd, 2015–17. Regtl Lt Col, Welsh Guards, 2015–. Freeman, Merchant Taylors' Co., 1999. FRGS 1991. *Recreations:* conservation (deer management), travel. *Address:* c/o Regimental Headquarters Welsh Guards, Wellington Barracks, Birdcage Walk, SW1E 6HQ. *Club:* Boodle's.

**STANGER, David Harry,** OBE 1987; FCQI; CQP; Partner, Al Hoty-Stanger Ltd, Saudi Arabia/United Arab Emirates, 1975–2017; Chairman and Managing Director, David H. Stanger sprl, 1997–2000; *b* 14 Feb. 1939; *s* of Charles Harry Stanger, CBE and Florence Bessie Hepworth Stanger; *m* 1963, Jill Patricia (*née* Barnes); one *s* two *d. Educ:* Oundle Sch.; Millfield Sch. FCQI (FIQA 1982); MSocIS 1982; CQP 2007; MInstRE. Served Corps of RE, 1960–66; joined R. H. Harry Stanger, 1966; Chm. and Man. Dir, Harry Stanger Ltd, 1975–90 (Sen. Partner, 1972–90); non-exec. Chm., Stanger Consultants Ltd, 1990–93. Chm., Adv. Cttee, NAMAS, 1985–87. Secretary General: Union Internationale des Laboratoires Indépendants, 1983–93 and 2001–03 (Mem. Governing Bd, 1997–2010; Hon. Mem., 1993–); Eur. Orgn for Testing and Certification, 1993–97. Member: Steering Cttee, NATLAS, 1981–87; Adv. Council for Calibration and Measurement, 1982–87; Council, EUROLAB, 1990–93; Adv. and Technical Cttee, Dubai Accreditation Centre, 2008–10; CQI Adv. Council, 2007–10; Chairman: Standards, Quality and Measurement Adv. Cttee, 1988–92; British Measurement and Testing Assoc., 1990–93 (Associate Mem., 2009–); Inst. of Quality Assurance, 1990–93 (a Vice-Pres., 1986–2010); Adv. Bd, Brunel Centre for Manufacturing Metrology, 1991–93; ILAC Lab. Cttee, 1998–2002 (Mem., 1998–). FInstD 1982; FRSA 1989. Pingat Peringatan, Malaysia, 1966; Pingat Jasa Malaysia, 2009. *Recreation:* collecting vintage wines. *Address:* 7C Forth Mansions, Ta'Xbiex Seafront, Ta'Xbiex, XBX 1027, Malta.

**STANHOPE,** family name of **Earl of Harrington**.

**STANHOPE, Janet Anne, (Lady Stanhope);** Special Adviser to Devon and Cornwall Police and Crime Commissioner, 2012–16; *b* 3 Oct. 1952; *d* of late Thomas Flynn and Anne Flynn (*née* Atkinson); *m* 1975, Adm. Sir Mark Stanhope, *qv*; one *d. Educ:* Nottingham High Sch. for Girls; Somerville Coll., Oxford (MA Hons Physics). CIPFA 1978. Trainee stockbroker, Montagu, Loebl, Stanley & Co., 1974–75; trainee accountant, W Sussex CC, 1975–77; Devon County Council: various accountancy posts, 1977–93; Dep. Co. Treas., 1993–98; Dep. Dir of Resources, 1998–2000; Dir of Resources, 2000–04. Ind. Mem., Devon and Cornwall Police Authy, 2009–12. Mem., Exeter Southernhay Rotary Club, 1994– (Pres., 2011–12). Lady Sponsor, RFA Cardigan Bay, 2005–; Pres., Central London Cttee, RNLI, 2009–13; Trustee, RN and RM Charity, 2008–14. Chm. Govs, Maynard Sch., 2013– (Gov., 2008–13). *Recreations:* reading, spending time with the family, playing bridge, golf. *Address:* Following Seas, 6 Barton Close, Exton, Exeter, Devon EX3 0PE.

**STANHOPE, Adm. Sir Mark,** GCB 2010 (KCB 2004); OBE 1988; FNI; DL; First Sea Lord and Chief of the Naval Staff, 2009–13; First and Principal Naval Aide-de-Camp to the Queen, 2009–13; *b* 26 March 1952; *s* of late Frederick William Stanhope and Sheila Mary Hattemore (*née* Cutler); *m* 1975, Janet Anne Flynn (*see* J. A. Stanhope); one *d. Educ:* London Nautical Sch.; Worthing High Sch.; St Peter's Coll., Oxford (MA Hons Physics; Hon. Fellow 2009). FNI 2008. Joined Royal Navy, 1970: Commanding Officer: HMS Orpheus, 1982–84; HMS Splendid, 1987–88; Submarine Comd Course (Teacher), 1989–90; HMS London, 1991–92; Capt., Submarine Sea Trng, 1993–94; Dep. Principal Staff Officer to CDS, MoD, 1994–96; rcds 1997; CO and ADC, HMS Illustrious, 1998–2000; Dir, Operational Mgt, NATO Regl Comd N, 2000–01; on secondment to Cabinet Office, 2002; Dep. C-in-C Fleet, 2002–04; Dep. Supreme Allied Comdr (Transformation), 2004–07; C-in-C Fleet and Comdr Allied Maritime Component Comd Northwood, 2007–09; Vice-Adm. of the UK, 2007–09. Dir, White Ensign Assoc., 2013– (Life Mem., 2007). President: Marine Soc. and Sea Cadets, 2014–; Britannia Assoc., 2014–; Assoc. of RN Officers, 2015–; Chm., Naval Review, 2014–. Trustee, Royal Museums Greenwich, 2015–. Member: RNSA; RUSI, 2003–. Life Mem., Guild of Freemen of London, 1993. Freeman, City of London, 1993; Liveryman, Upholders' Co., 1996–2019; Hon. Member: Co. of Master Mariners, 2009–13; Co. of Shipwrights, 2010–. Younger Brother, Trinity House, 2003. DL Devon, 2013. Hon. DSc Plymouth, 2012. Meritorious Service Medal, NATO, 2007; Prince Hendrik Medal, Netherlands Navy, 2010. Legion of Merit (USA),

2007; Commemorative Medal (Slovak Republic), 2007; Order of Adm. Padilla (Colombia), 2008; Tong-il Medal, Order of Nat. Security Merit (S Korea), 2011; Norwegian Defence Medal with Laurel, 2011. *Publications:* contribs to Naval Rev., RUSI, military pubns. *Recreations:* family life, reading, sailing, golf. *E:* stanhopemark@hotmail.com. *Clubs:* Army and Navy, Royal Navy of 1765 and 1785 (Chm., 2016–).

**STANIER, Sir Beville (Douglas),** 3rd Bt *cr* 1917, of Peplow Hall, Market Drayton, Shropshire; Chairman of Trustees, Shotover Estate, Oxon, since 2006 (Trustee, since 1973); Member (C), Aylesbury Vale District Council, since 1999 (Cabinet Member: Environment and Health, 2003–18; Waste and Licensing, since 2018); *b* 20 April 1934; *o s* of Brig. Sir Alexander Stanier, 2nd Bt, DSO, MC and Dorothy Gladys Miller (*d* 1973); *S* father, 1995; *m* 1st, 1963, Shelagh Sinnott (*d* 2007); one *s* two *d*; 2nd, 2010, Nerena Stephenson (*née* Villiers) (*d* 2015). *Educ:* Eton Coll. Joined Welsh Guards, 1952; commnd 2nd Lieut, 1953; Lieut, 1955; Captain, 1958; ADC to Governor-General of Australia, 1959–60. Stockbroker with Kitcat & Aitken, 1960–76 (Partner, 1968–76). Chairman: Buckingham Constituency Cons. Assoc., 1999–2003 (Pres., 2015–); Oxon and Bucks Area Cons. Party, 2003–04. *Recreations:* shooting, cricket. *Heir: s* Alexander James Sinnott Stanier, *b* 10 April 1970. *Address:* Kings Close House, Whaddon, Buckinghamshire MK17 0NG. *T:* (01908) 501738, 07778 305419. *Club:* MCC.

**STANIFORTH, Martin John;** non-executive Director, Local Care Direct, 2005–13; *b* 11 Feb. 1953; *s* of late Trevor Staniforth and Doris Nellie Staniforth (*née* Quaife). *Educ:* Kingston Grammar Sch., Kingston upon Thames; Univ. of Newcastle upon Tyne (BA Hons Eng. Lang. and Lit.); Open Univ. (MA 2008); Univ. of Leeds (PhD 2015). Joined DHSS as Admin. Trainee, 1975, Principal, 1985–91; Department of Health: Asst Sec., 1991–96; Hd of Corp. Affairs, NHS Exec., 1996–99; Dep. Dir of Human Resources, subseq. Workforce, 1999–2005. Mem., Registration and Conduct Cttees, Gen. Social Care Council, 2007–12. Mem. Council, Leeds Civic Trust, 2006–14. Chm., Leeds Mencap, 2010–. Trustee, Leeds Library, 2013– (Chm., 2015–). *Recreations:* hill walking, opera going, cricket watching. *Address:* 2 Ashwood Terrace, Leeds LS6 2EH. *Club:* New Headingley (Leeds).

**STANIFORTH, Sarah Elizabeth, (Hon. Lady Porritt),** CBE 2015; President, International Institute for Conservation of Historic and Artistic Works, 2013–19 (Vice-President, 1998–2005); *b* 14 Jan. 1953; *d* of Malcolm Arthur Staniforth and Bridget Christian Salkeld Hall; *m* 1986, Hon. Sir Jonathon Porritt, *qv*; two *d*. *Educ:* St Hilda's Coll., Oxford (BA Hons); Courtauld Inst. of Art, London Univ. (Dip Conservation of Easel Paintings). Higher Scientific Officer, Scientific Dept, Nat. Gall., 1980–85; National Trust: Advr on Paintings Conservation and Envmtl Control, 1985–2002; Head Conservator, 2002–04; Historic Properties Dir, 2005–11; Museums and Collections Dir, 2011–14. Trustee: Hunterian Collection, RCS, 1997–2008 and 2011–; Sci. Mus. Gp, 2018–; Westminster Abbey Fabric Comr, 1998–. Chair, Nat. Heritage Sci. Forum, 2013–14. Chm., Accreditation Cttee, UKIC, 2002–05; Ind. Museums Councillor, Museums Assoc., 2005–11; Mem. Council, Assoc. of Ind. Museums, 2011–14. Member: SW Cttee, HLF, then NLHF, 2015–19; Gloucester DAC, 2016–. Trustee: Pilgrim Trust, 2011–; Landmark Trust, 2014–; English Heritage, 2015–. FIIC 1989; FSA 2010; FRSA 2010. *Publications:* (ed jtly) Durability and Change, 1994; (ed with C. Sitwell) Studies in the History of Painting Restoration, 1998; (ed jtly) National Trust Manual of Housekeeping, 2005; (ed jtly) Historical Perspectives on Preventive Conservation, 2013; papers in mus. and conservation jls and conf. procs. *Recreation:* swimming. *Address:* 9 Lypiatt Terrace, Lypiatt Road, Cheltenham, Glos GL50 2SX.

**STANLEY,** family name of **Earl of Derby** and **Baron Stanley of Alderley**.

**STANLEY, Lord; Edward John Robin Stanley;** *b* 21 April 1998; *s* and *heir* of Earl of Derby, *qv*. *Educ:* Ludgrove; Eton Coll.; St Hilda's Coll., Oxford. A Page of Honour to the Queen, 2008–12. Patron, Big Help Project, 2016–. *Address:* Knowsley, Prescot, Merseyside L34 4AF. *T:* (0151) 489 6148. *E:* stanley@knowsley.com.

**STANLEY OF ALDERLEY,** 9th Baron *cr* 1839; **Richard Oliver Stanley;** Bt 1660; Baron Sheffield (Ire.) 1783; Baron Eddisbury 1848; *b* 24 April 1956; *e s* of 8th Baron Stanley of Alderley and Jane Barrett Stanley (*née* Hartley); *S* father, 2013; *m* 1983, Carla Mary Angela McKenzie; three *d* (one *s* decd). *Educ:* St Edward's Sch., Oxford; University Coll., London (BSc). *Heir: b* Hon. Charles Ernest Stanley [*b* 30 June1960; *m* 1989, Beverley Ann Emmitt; three *d*].

**STANLEY, Alison;** Partner, Bindmans LLP, since 1995 (Managing Partner, 2014–18); *b* UK. *Educ:* Univ. of Sussex (BA Hons English 1979); Coll. of Law. Admitted solicitor, 1984; Winstanley-Burgess, 1983–86; Evans Butler Smith, 1986–87; Jt Council for the Welfare of Immigrants, 1988–92; Racial Discrimination Legal Defence Fund, 1992–93; Deighton Guedalla, 1993–94; Bindmans LLP, 1994–. *Publications:* The Rights of Third Country Nationals in the New European Order, 1994; (jtly) Putting Children First: a guide for immigration practitioners, 2002; Asylum Seekers: a guide to current legislation, 2001; (jtly) Asylum: a guide to recent legislation, 2004; The Asylum and Immigration Tribunal: practice and procedure, 2005; (jtly) Representation at Immigration Appeals, 2006. *Address:* Bindmans LLP, 236 Gray's Inn Road, WC1X 8HB. *T:* (020) 7833 4433, *Fax:* (020) 7837 9792. *E:* a.stanley@bindmans.com.

**STANLEY, Barbara Elizabeth;** Independent Schools Specialist, Association of School and College Leaders, since 2015; GSA Education Consultant, since 2016; *b* Belfast, 2 July 1950; *d* of John Morrison Hunter, CBE and I. Elizabeth Hunter; *m* 1978, Graham Stanley; two *d*. *Educ:* Glenlola Collegiate Sch., Bangor, Co. Down; Queen's Univ., Belfast (BA Hons 1972); Leicester Univ. (PGCE 1973). Teacher: Devizes Sch., 1973–75; Glenlola Collegiate Sch., 1975–78; Hd of House, Forest Sch., Snaresbrook, 1986–90; Hd of Geog., St Bernard's Convent, 1990–92; Dep. Headmistress, Channing Sch., 1992–95; Headmistress, Bedford High Sch., 1995–2000; Principal, Alexandra Coll., Dublin, 2000–02; Headmistress, The Abbey School, Reading, 2002–14. FRGS 2001. Mem. and speaker, Corrymeela Community (NI reconciliation community), 1970–. *Recreations:* church and community involvement, geographical interests, amateur dramatics, travel, hill walking. *Address:* Northcote, Swallowfield Street, Swallowfield, Reading RG7 1QX. *T:* 07793 249385. *E:* Barbara.Stanley@ascl.org.uk.

**STANLEY, Clare Fiona Louise;** QC 2015; *b* Adelaide, Australia, 25 Jan. 1967; *d* of Dr Philip Edward Stanley and Prof. Margaret Anne Stanley, *qv*; *m* 1998, Geoffrey Charles Chapman; one *s* one *d*. *Educ:* King's Sch., Ely; Univ. of Adelaide (BEc); Downing Coll., Cambridge (BA Law 1993). Called to the Bar, 1994; in practice as barrister, 1994–. *Recreations:* swimming, music, cooking, travelling. *Address:* Wilberforce Chambers, 8 New Square, Lincoln's Inn, WC2A 3QP. *T:* (020) 7306 0102, *Fax:* (020) 7306 0095. *E:* cstanley@wilberforce.co.uk.

**STANLEY, David Raymond;** sustainability and environmental management adviser, since 1998; speaker on sustainability, climate change, food, farming and mitigation; Director: E3 Ltd, environmental consultancy, since 1998; Fellow, Institute of Environmental Management Assessment, 2013–16 (Member, Strategic Advisory Council, since 2016); Pasture-Fed Livestock Association, since 2013; *b* Bristol, 18 April 1946; *s* of Raymond Frank Stanley and Gwyneth Kate Stanley; *m* 1973, Patricia Jane Cross; one *s* one *d*. *Educ:* Cotham Grammar Sch.; RAF Coll.; Open Univ. (BA Envmtl Studies and Econs 1983). Dip. Internat. Envmtl Mgt 2003; CEnv 2004. Dock worker, Avonmouth Docks, 1964–65. Served RAF, 1965–84: Air Liaison Officer, 16 Parachute Bde, 1973–75; Flt Comdr, Hunters, Tactical Weapons Unit, 1976–78; 1 (F) Sqdn Harriers, 1979–81; Lectr in Defence Strategy, Dept of Air Warfare, 1982–84; retired in rank of Sqdn Leader, 1984. Regl Trng Manager, Anglian Water, 1984–89; Regl Admin Manager, NRA, 1989–92; Hd, Envmtl Mgt, Environment Agency, 1993–97. Envmtl Auditor, 1998. Vis. Lectr and envmtl advr, Nat. Sch. of Govt, 1998–2012; Visiting Lecturer: in Sustainable Estate Mgt, Reading Univ., 2002–10; in Sustainable Agric., Centre for Alternative Technol., 2007–10. Sustainability Advr, Jersey Govt, 2015. Mem., UK Wkg Party, ISO14000 Internat. Envmtl Mgt Standard, 1994–96. Guest Speaker: Greener World Conf., San Francisco, 2015; EU Conf., Eur. Envmt Bureau, 2016. Farmer; zero carbon Pedigree Lincoln Red Beef producer, 1998–. MIEMA (MIEMgt 1998), FIEMA 2005. Parish Councillor, Grimley, 2015–. Diocesan Gov., Hallow C of E Sch., 2015–. Lincolnshire Envmtl Award for Farming, Lincolnshire Wildlife Trust, 2012. *Publications:* Achieving the UK GHG Reduction Commitments Through Food, 2001. *Recreations:* pedigree herd of Lincoln Red cattle sequestrating carbon through grassland, shooting and stalking, gardening, producing sustainability videos. *Address:* Holly House, Camp Lane, Grimley, Worcs WR2 6LX. *T:* (01905) 641529. *E:* dave@sustainability.works.

**STANLEY, Prof. Fiona Juliet,** AC 1996; MD; Patron, Telethon Kids Institute (formerly Telethon Institute for Child Health Research), since 2012 (Director, 1990–2012); Professor, 1990–2012, Distinguished Research Professor, since 2012, School of Paediatrics and Child Health, University of Western Australia; Chair, Australian Research Alliance for Children and Youth, 2007–11 (Chief Executive Officer, 2001–04; Executive Director, 2004–07); *b* 1 Aug. 1946; *d* of Prof. Neville Stanley and Muriel MacDonald Stanley; *m* 1973, Prof. Geoffrey Shellam; two *d*. *Educ:* Univ. of Western Australia (MB BS 1970; MD 1986); LSHTM, Univ. of London (MSc 1976). FFPH (FFPHM 1989); FAFPHM 1991; FRACP 1994; FRANZCOG 1995; FASSA 1996; FAA 2002. Doctor, Princess Margaret Hosp. Aboriginal Clinic, Perth, 1972; Scientific Staff, MRC Social Medicine Unit, 1972–73, NH & MRC Fellow in Clin. Scis, 1974–75, LSHTM; vis. appt, Nat. Inst. Child Health and Human Develt, NIH, 1976; University of Western Australia: NH & MRC Clin. Scis Res. Fellow, Unit of Clin. Epidemiology, Dept of Medicine, 1977; SMO (Child Health), Community and Child Health Services, Public Health Dept, 1978–79; Dep. Dir, 1980–88, Dir, 1988–90, NH & MRC Res. Unit in Epidemiology and Preventive Medicine. Dir, 2013 Fest. of Ideas, Univ. of Melbourne, 2012–. Vice Chancellor's Fellow, Univ. of Melbourne, 2012–. Hon. FRACGP 2004; Hon. FRCPCH 2006. Hon. DSc Murdoch, 1998; DUniv Queensland Univ. of Tech., 2001; Hon. MD: Sydney, 2005; Melbourne, 2008. Australian of the Year, Nat. Australia Day Council, 2003. *Publications:* (ed jtly) The Epidemiology of Prematurity, 1977; (ed jtly) The Epidemiology of the Cerebral Palsies, 1984; (ed) The Role of Epidemiology and Perinatal Databases for both Research and Care, 1997; (jtly) The Cerebral Palsies: epidemiology and causal pathways, 2000; (jtly) Children of the Lucky Country?: how Australian society has turned its back on children and why children matter, 2005; papers in learned jls, reports, and chapters in books. *Recreations:* bushwalking, swimming. *Address:* Telethon Kids Institute, PO Box 855, West Perth, WA 6872, Australia. *T:* (8) 9489 7968.

**STANLEY, Rev. John Alexander,** OBE 1999; Vicar of Huyton, 1974–2018; Chaplain to the Queen, 1993–2001; *b* 20 May 1931; *s* of Edward Alexander Stanley and Lucy Vida Stanley; *m* 1956, (Flora) Elaine Wilkes; three *s* two *d*. *Educ:* Birkenhead Sch.; Tyndale Hall Theol Coll., Bristol. Assistant Curate: All Saints', Preston, 1956; St Mark's, St Helens, 1960; Vicar, St Cuthbert's, Everton, Liverpool, 1963; Priest in Charge, St Saviour, Everton, 1969; Vicar, St Saviour with St Cuthbert, Everton, 1970; Area Dean of Huyton, 1989–2003; Hon. Canon of Liverpool Cathedral, 1987–2018, now Emeritus. Mem., Gen. Synod, and Proctor in Convocation, 1973–2000; Chm., Diocesan House of Clergy, 1979–85; Prolocutor, York Convocation, 1990–2000. A Church Comr, 1983–99 (Mem., Bd of Govs, 1989–99); Member: Crown Appointments Commn, 1992–2000; Archbishops' Council, 1999–2000. Mem., BCC, 1984–87; Trustee, Church Urban Fund, 1987–2003. *Recreations:* golf, photography. *Address:* 14 Meadowfield Road, Westminster Park, Chester CH4 7QJ. *T:* (01244) 678903. *E:* John.Stanley@btinternet.com.

**STANLEY, Prof. John Knowles,** FRCSE, FRCS; Professor of Hand Surgery, Manchester University, 1996–2009, now Emeritus; Consultant Hand Surgeon, Wrightington Hospital, Wigan, 1979–2011; Vice President, Royal College of Surgeons, 2010–12; *b* Cardiff, 30 March 1944; *s* of Frederick John and Mary Thelma Stanley; *m* 1964, Gail Simpson; one *s* one *d*. *Educ:* Oswestry Boys' High Sch.; Liverpool Univ. (MB ChB 1968; MChOrth 1975). FRCSE 1973; FRCS 1974. Senior Registrar in Orthopaedics: Broadgreen Hosp., 1974; Royal Southern Hosp., 1974; Royal Liverpool Hosp., 1975; Wrightington Hosp., 1975; Broadgreen Hosp., 1976; rotation, Royal Southern Hosp. and Broadgreen Hosp., 1977–79. Robert Jones' Lect., British Orthopaedic Assoc., 2004; Hunterian Prof., RCS, 2010; Visiting Professor: Yoshiba Univ., NY, 1988; Dept of Orthopaedics and Plastic and Reconstructive Surgery, Univ. of Marseille, 1989; Pellenburg Hosp. Leuven Univ., Belgium, 1991; St Joseph's Hosp., Univ. of London, Ontario, 1991; Univ. of Otago Med. Sch., NZ, 1997; Royal Coll. of Surgeons, Australasia, 1998; Mayo Clinic, Rochester, USA, 2001; Univ. of Cape Town, 2001; Univ. of Bloemfontein, 2001; Univ. of Durban, 2001; Univ. of Pretoria, 2001; Univ. of Stellenbosch, 2001; NZ Soc. of Surgery of the Hand, Napier NZ Orthopaedic Soc., 2002; Aust. Orthopaedic and Hand Soc., 2003; Asia/Pacific Orthopaedic Soc., 2004; Mgt of Complex Elbow Problems, Hand Rehabilitation Foundn, Philadelphia, 2005. Pioneer of Hand Surgery, Internat. Fedn of Socs for Surgery of the Hand, 2016. *Publications:* Wrist Arthroscopy, 1994; contrib. articles to learned jls. *Recreations:* golf, military aircraft, gliding, travelling, volunteer and friend, Manchester Mus. of Sci. and Industry. *Address:* 20 Derby Street West, Ormskirk, Lancs L39 3NH. *T:* and *Fax:* (01695) 575210. *E:* profstanley@btinternet.com. *Club:* Ormskirk Golf.

**STANLEY, John Mallalieu;** Director of Legal Services A, Department of Trade and Industry, 1996–2001; *b* 30 Sept. 1941; *s* of William and Rose Margaret Stanley; *m* 1968, Christine Mary Cunningham; two *s* one *d*. *Educ:* Welwyn Garden City Grammar Sch.; Clare College, Cambridge (MA). Solicitor. Church, Adams, Tatham & Co., 1965–68; Jaques & Co., 1968–75; Department of Industry, later of Trade and Industry, 1975–2001: Under Sec. (Legal), 1989–96. *Recreation:* charitable work as Trustee of Greenwich Charity and Meridian Money Advice. *Address:* 12 Westcombe Park Road, SE3 7RB.

**STANLEY, Rt Hon. Sir John (Paul),** Kt 1988; PC 1984; *b* 19 Jan. 1942; *s* of late Mr and Mrs H. Stanley; *m* 1st, 1968, Susan Elizabeth Giles (marr. diss. 2005); one *s* one *d* (and one *s* decd); 2nd, 2006, Elizabeth Roselle Willett Brooks (*née* Tait). *Educ:* Repton Sch.; Lincoln Coll., Oxford (MA). Conservative Research Dept with responsibility for Housing, 1967–68; Research Associate, Internat. Inst. for Strategic Studies, 1968–69; Rio Tinto-Zinc Corp. Ltd, 1969–79. MP (C) Tonbridge and Malling, Feb. 1974–2015. PPS to Rt Hon. Margaret Thatcher, 1976–79; Minister of State (Minister for Housing and Construction), DoE, 1979–83; Minister of State: for the Armed Forces, MoD, 1983–87; Northern Ireland Office, 1987–88. Mem., Parly Select Cttee on Nationalised Industries, 1974, on Foreign Affairs, 1992–2015; Mem., 1999–2010, Chm., 2010–15, Parly Select Cttee on Arms Export

Controls, 1999–2010. Mem., NATO Parly Assembly, 2001–15. Director: Fidelity Japanese Values plc, 1994–2005; Henderson High Income Trust plc, 1997–2007. Trustee, ActionAid, 1989–99. *Publications:* (jtly) The International Trade in Arms, 1972. *Recreations:* music, sailing.

**STANLEY, Khatun;** *see* Sapnara, K.

**STANLEY, Prof. Margaret Anne,** OBE 2004; PhD; Professor of Epithelial Biology, University of Cambridge, 2001–09, now Emeritus; Fellow, Christ's College, Cambridge, 1990–2014, now Hon. Fellow; *b* 19 July 1939; *d* of Colin Campbell Coutts and Clara Coutts; *m* 1964, Philip Edward Stanley; one *s* one *d*. *Educ:* Bedford Coll., London (BSc); Univ. of Bristol (PhD 1964). Sen. Lectr in Pathol., Univ. of Adelaide, S Australia, 1974–80; Lectr in Pathol., 1980–96, Reader in Epithelial Biol., 1996–2001, Univ. of Cambridge. FMedSci 2004; Hon. FRCOG 2008. *Publications:* numerous articles in peer-reviewed jls. *Recreation:* cooking. *Address:* Department of Pathology, University of Cambridge, Tennis Court Road, Cambridge CB2 1QP. *T:* (01223) 333690, *Fax:* (01223) 333346. *E:* mas1001@cam.ac.uk.
*See also* C. F. L. Stanley.

**STANLEY, Martin Edward;** writer and adviser on government and regulation, since 2010; *b* 1 Nov. 1948; *s* of Edward Alan and Dorothy Stanley; *m* 1971, Marilyn Joan Lewis (marr. diss. 1992); one *s*; *m* 1996, Janice Margaret Munday, *qv*; one *s* (and one *s* decd). *Educ:* Royal GS, Newcastle upon Tyne; Magdalen Coll., Oxford (BA Hons). Inland Revenue, 1971–80; Department of Trade and Industry, 1980–98: various posts, 1980–87; Head, Industry/Educn Unit, 1987–90; Principal Private Sec., 1990–92; Hd of Vehicles, Metals and Minerals Div., later Engrg Automotive and Metals Div., 1992–96; Chief Exec., Oil and Gas Projects and Supplies Office, then Infrastructure and Energy Projects Directorate, 1996–98; Dir, Better Regulation, then Regulatory Impact, Unit, Cabinet Office, 1998–2000; Chief Executive: Postal Services Commn, 2000–04; Competition Commn, 2004–09; Turks and Caicos Islands Govt, 2009, 2011. Hon. Fellow, Manchester Univ., 2013–. Editor of websites: Understanding the Civil Service, 2000–; Understanding Regulation, 2010–; Understanding Policy Making. *Publications:* How to be a Civil Servant, 2000, 3rd edn 2016. *Recreations:* walking, fostering homeless dogs. *Address:* 68 Richborne Terrace, SW8 1AX. *E:* 68rtsw8@gmail.com.

**STANLEY, Oliver Duncan;** Chairman, 1972–97 and Director, 1972–2000, Rathbone Brothers (formerly Comprehensive Financial Services) PLC; *b* 5 June 1925; *s* of Bernard Stanley and Mabel Best; *m* 1954, Ruth Brenner, JP, BA (*d* 2002); one *s* three *d*. *Educ:* Christ Church, Oxford (MA); Harvard Univ., USA. Called to the Bar, Middle Temple, 1963. Served War, 8 Hussars, 1943–47. HM Inspector of Taxes, 1952–65; Dir, Gray Dawes Bank, 1966–72; founded Comprehensive Financial Services Gp of Cos, 1971. Chief Taxation Adviser, CLA, 1975–83 (Mem., Tax Cttee, 1983–2002). Chairman: Profile Books Ltd, 1996–2005; Esterel Ltd, 2003–15; Dir, Axa Equity and Law, 1992–97. Member: Soc. of Authors, 1967–; Council of Legal Educn, 1992–96. Gov., Inns of Court Sch. of Law, 1996–99. Trustee: Age Concern Barnet, 2003–12; Barnet Carers, 2015–18 (Trustee and Chm., 2007–13). Hon. Fellow, Liverpool John Moores Univ., 2011. *Publications:* A Guide to Taxation, 1967; Taxology, 1971; Creation and Protection of Capital, 1974; Taxation of Farmers and Landowners, 1981; Offshore Tax Planning, 1986; Hotel Victoire (novel), 2007; 1941 (novel), 2008; contrib. The Times and The Sunday Times, 1966–83; numerous articles in legal and agricultural periodicals. *Recreations:* music, French language and literature. *Club:* Travellers.

**STANLEY, Hon. Peter Hugh Charles;** Manager: New England Stud, since 1990; Stanley House Stud, since 1993; *b* London, 4 March 1964; *s* of late Hon. Hugh Henry Montagu Stanley and of Mary Rose Stanley (née Birch, now Spiegelberg); *m* 1990, Hon. Frances Caroline Burke Roche, *d* of 5th Baron Fermoy; two *s* one *d*. *Educ:* Ludgrove; Eton Coll. Chairman: New Astley Club, 2009–; Jockey Club Estates, 2018– (non-exec. Dir, 2010–); Steward, Jockey Club, 2014–. *Recreations:* shooting, horseracing. *Address:* New England Stud, Newmarket, Suffolk CB8 0XA. *T:* (01223) 811249, *Fax:* (01223) 812723. *E:* stanley@newenglandstud.com.
*See also* Earl of Derby, Baron Fermoy.

**STANNARD, Ven. Colin Percy,** TD 1966; Archdeacon of Carlisle and Residentiary Canon of Carlisle Cathedral, 1984–93, now Archdeacon and Canon Emeritus; *b* 8 Feb. 1924; *s* of Percy and Grace Adelaide Stannard; *m* 1950, Joan Callow; one *s* two *d*. *Educ:* Woodbridge School; Selwyn Coll., Cambridge (BA 1947, MA 1949); Lincoln Theological Coll. Deacon 1949, priest 1950; Curate, St James Cathedral, Bury St Edmunds, 1949–52; Priest-in-charge, St Martin's, Grimsby, 1952–55; CF (TA), 1953–67; Vicar: St James's, Barrow-in-Furness, 1955–64; St John the Baptist's, Upperby, 1964–70; Rector of Gosforth, 1970–75; RD of Calder, 1970–75; Hon. Canon of Carlisle, 1975–84; Priest-in-charge of Natland, 1975–76, Vicar, 1976–84; RD of Kendal, 1975–84. *Recreations:* walking, bringing order out of chaos—especially in gardens. *Address:* Flat 4, Manormead Supported Housing, Tilford Road, Hindhead, Surrey GU26 6RA. *T:* (01428) 601504.

**STANNARD, Prof. (Frank) Russell,** OBE 1998; PhD; Professor of Physics, Open University, 1971–98, now Emeritus; *b* 24 Dec. 1931; *s* of Frank and Lillie Stannard; *m* 1984, Glenys Margaret Hawkins; two *s* two *d*, and two step *s* (and one step *s* decd). *Educ:* University Coll. London (BSc 1953; PhD 1956; Fellow, 2000). FInstP 1973. Res. Asst, UCL, 1956–59; Res. Physicist, Radiation Lab., Berkeley, 1959–60; Lectr, UCL, 1960–69; Open University: Reader, 1968–71; Hd, Physics Dept, 1971–75 and 1977–92; Pro Vice Chancellor, 1975–77. Mem., Center of Theological Inquiry, Princeton, 1988–89. Trustee, John Templeton Foundn, 1993–99 and 2000–06. Bragg Medal, Inst. of Physics, 2000. *Publications: for adults:* Science and the Renewal of Belief, 1982; Grounds for Reasonable Belief, 1989; Doing Away with God?, 1993; Science and Wonders, 1996; The God Experiment, 1999; The New World of Mr Tompkins, 1999; God for the 21st Century, 2000; Why?, 2003; Relativity, 2008; The End of Discovery, 2010; Science and Belief, 2012; The Divine Imprint, 2017; *for children:* The Time and Space of Uncle Albert, 1989; Black Holes and Uncle Albert, 1991; Here I Am!, 1992; World of 1001 Mysteries, 1993; Uncle Albert and the Quantum Quest, 1994; Our Universe, 1995; A Short History of God, Me and the Universe, 1995; Letters to Uncle Albert, 1996; More Letters to Uncle Albert, 1997; Ask Uncle Albert: 100½ tricky science questions answered, 1998; The Curious History of God, 1998; Space, Time, Rhythm and Rhyme, 1999; Lab Cats on the Move, Lab Cats Get up Steam, Lab Cats Switch On, and Lab Cats See the Light, 2001; Dr Dyer's Academy, 2002; Virtutopia, 2003; over 60 articles in jls incl. Physical Rev., Physical Rev. Letters, Nature, Physics Letters, Procs of Physical Soc., etc. *Recreations:* sculpture, attending opera, ballet and concerts, enjoying 16 grandchildren and five great grandchildren. *Address:* 21 Alwins Field, Leighton Buzzard, Beds LU7 2UF. *T:* (01525) 371106.

**STANSFIELD, Jill Veronica;** Executive Director for Communities, London Borough of Barnet, 2006–09 (Director of Children's Services, 2002–06); *b* 18 Sept. 1951; *d* of Richard and Ivy Stansfield; *m* 1977, Paul Temple. *Educ:* Royal Holloway Coll., London (BA Hons Hist. 1973); Warwick Business Sch. (MPA 2005). Administrative officer, GLC and ILEA, 1973–89; Asst Dir, 1989–95, Actg Dir, 1995–96, of Educn, Lambeth BC; Strategic Dir of Learning and Develt, Milton Keynes Council, 1996–2002. Chair, Milton Keynes Cultural Educn Partnership, 2016–. Member: Barnet Coll. Corp., 2003–11; Bd, Milton Keynes Gall., 2003–18 (Vice Chair, 2013–18); Barnet and Southgate Coll. Corp., 2011– (Chair, 2012–13). *Recreations:* gardening, playing the piano, art.

**STANSFIELD, Piers Alistair;** QC 2012; *b* Welwyn Garden City, 16 Aug. 1970; *s* of Jeffrey Stansfield and Alison Buchanan; *m* 2000, Rachel Claire Murdoch; two *s* one *d*. *Educ:* Loretto Sch., E Lothian; Bristol Univ. (LLB 1992); Inns of Court Sch. of Law. Called to the Bar, Inner Temple, 1993; in practice as barrister, specialising in construction, professional negligence and energy, 1993–. *Publications:* (contrib.) Keating on Construction Contracts, 9th edn 2012; (contrib.) Keating on NEC 3, 2012. *Recreations:* cycling, art, family. *Address:* Keating Chambers, 15 Essex Street, WC2R 3AA. *T:* (020) 7544 2600. *E:* pstansfield@keatingchambers.com.

**STANSGATE,** 3rd Viscount *cr* 1942, of Stansgate, co. Essex; **Stephen Michael Wedgwood Benn;** Director of Parliamentary Affairs, Royal Society of Biology (formerly Society of Biology); *b* 21 Aug. 1951; *e s* of Rt Hon. Tony Benn, PC (who disclaimed his peerage for life, 1963); *S* father, 2014; *m* 1988, Ishika Nita, *d* of Stuart Ashley Bowes; one *s* one *d*. *Educ:* Holland Park Sch.; Keele Univ. *Heir: s* Hon. Daniel John Wedgwood Benn, *b* 10 Dec. 1991.
*See also* Rt Hon. H. J. W. Benn.

**STANSTED, Archdeacon of;** *see* King, Ven. R. L. C.

**STANTON, Alan William,** OBE 2014; RA 2009; RDI 2005; RIBA; Director, Stanton Williams Architects, since 1985; *b* 19 April 1944; *s* of William and Irene Stanton; *m* 1st, 1967, Marilyn Tindall (marr. diss. 1983); one *d*; *m* 2nd, 1985, Wendy Robin; one *d*. *Educ:* Architectural Assoc., London (AA Dip. Hons); Univ. of California, Los Angeles (MArch). RIBA 1979. Architect: with Norman Foster, 1967–68; Centre Pompidou, Paris (Piano & Rogers), 1970–77; in private practice, 1978–85 (projects in Paris, Italy and London); in partnership with Paul Williams, 1985–: award-winning projects in UK, Switzerland and Italy include: Casa Fontana, Lugano, 2000; Wellcome Trust Millennium Seed Bank, Sussex, 2000; Whitby Abbey Mus. and Visitor Centre, 2002; Tower Hill Environs, London, 2004; Compton Verney Art Gall., 2004; Belgrade Theatre extension, Coventry, 2007; House of Fraser, Bristol, 2008; Bourne Hill Offices, Salisbury, 2010; Sainsbury Lab., Cambridge, 2011. Lectr, AA, 1978–81. Chm., Architecture Cttee, AA, 2014–; Mem., Design Rev. Panel, CABE, 2001–05. Mem. Council and Vice Pres., AA, 2000–04. Trustee, Open-City, 2013–. Has lectured in Europe and USA. FRSA 1993. SADG Medal 1967. *Publications:* numerous contribs to architectural books and jls. *Address:* Stanton Williams, 36 Graham Street, N1 8GJ. *T:* (020) 7880 6400, *Fax:* (020) 7880 6401. *E:* info@stantonwilliams.com.

**STANTON, David,** CB 2000; Director (Grade 3), Analytical Services Division, Department for Work and Pensions (formerly Department of Social Security), 1992–2002; *b* 5 Nov. 1942; *s* of Frederick Charles Patrick Stanton and Ethel (née Cout); *m* 1967, Isobel Joan Blair; one *s* one *d*. *Educ:* Bishop's Stortford Coll.; Worcester Coll., Oxford (BA PPE 1965); LSE (MSc(Econ) 1970). ODI/Nuffield Fellow, Govt of Uganda, 1965–67; Lectr, Brunel Univ., 1967–70; Economic Adviser: Min. of Transport, 1970; Min. of Housing, then DoE, 1971–74; HM Treasury, 1974–75; Senior Economic Adviser: seconded to Hong Kong Govt, 1975–77; also Head of Unit for Manpower Studies, Dept of Employment, 1977–81; Econs Br., Dept of Employment, 1981–83; also Dir, Employment Market Res. Unit, 1983–87; Chief Economist (Grade 3), Dept of Employment, 1988–92. Econ. Advr, Turner Pensions Commn, 2003–04. Chm., Indicators Sub Gp, Social Protection Cttee, EC, 2001–09. *Recreations:* people, dogs and other animals, singing, playing the flute.

**STANTON, Ven. Canon David John;** Canon Treasurer, since 2013, and Sub-Dean and Archdeacon, since 2018, Westminster Abbey; *b* London, 10 Oct. 1960; *s* of Peter Frederick Stanton and Frances Margaret Stanton (née Grumitt); *m* 1990, Sarah Jane Norris; two *d*. *Educ:* Exeter Cathedral Sch.; Blundell's Sch.; St Andrews Univ. (MTh); Exeter Univ. (MA); Cuddesdon Theol Coll., Oxford. Ordained deacon, 1985, priest, 1986; Curate, Beckenham Parish Ch, 1985–88; Asst Chaplain and Tutor, Shrewsbury Sch., 1988–90; Priest in Charge: St Mary Abbotskerswell, 1990–94; St John Bovey Tracey, 1994–2005; Chaplain, Plymouth Univ., 1992–97; Rural Dean, Moreton, 1998–2005; Diocese of Exeter: Vocations Chaplain, 1995–2005; Warden of Readers, 1996–2005; Mem., Bishop's Council and Bd of Educn, 2000–03; Diocesan Moderator and Chair, SW Dioceses, 2002–05; Diocesan Dir of Ordinands, 2003–05; Residentiary Canon (Precentor and Pastor), Worcester, 2005–13; Diocese of Worcester: Member: Diocesan Adv. Cttee for Care of Churches, 2005–13; Bishops' Selection Advr for Ordained Ministry, 2006–18; Ind. Mem., Worcester Cathedral Council, 2005–13; Almoner, Westminster Abbey, 2013–18. A Church Comr, 2010–14 (Mem., Assets Cttee, 2011–14). Chair, Central London Council for Christians and Jews, 2013–16. Ind. Mem., Standards Cttee, Worcester CC, 2008–13; Mem., Lord Chancellor's Adv. Cttee (W Mercia) on Justices of the Peace, 2010–13; non-exec. Mem., Wales Audit Office, 2011–14; Ind. Mem., Public Service Honours Cttee, 2019–. Sec. of State Mem., Dartmoor Nat. Park Authy, 2002–05. Vice Chair, Inter-Divl Res. Ethics Cttee, Oxford Univ., 2010–18. Trustee, C of E Pensions Bd, 2016–; Mem., Westminster Abbey Trust, 2013– (Trustee, Pensions Bd, 2013–). Governor: Heathfield C of E Sch., 1994–2005; Stover Sch., 2003–07; Westminster Sch., 2013–; Westminster Abbey Choir Sch., 2013–; Sutton Valence Sch., 2016–19; Westminster Univ., 2017–. FSA(Scot) 1989. FRSA 1998. Distinguished Friend, Oxford Univ., 2015. *Publications:* contribs to theol jls. *Recreations:* sport, the arts, the countryside. *Address:* 1 Little Cloister, Westminster Abbey, SW1P 3PL. *T:* (020) 7654 4804. *E:* david.stanton@westminster-abbey.org. *Club:* Travellers (Chm., 2018–).

**STANTON, David Leslie,** CMG 2014; Chairman of Trustees, UNICEF UK, 2004–13; Director, Friends Trusts Ltd, 2009–15; *b* 29 April 1943; *s* of Leslie Stanton and C. Mary Stanton (née Staynes); *m* 1989, Rosemary Jane Brown; one *d*. *Educ:* Bootham Sch., York; Balliol Coll., Oxford (BA Hons). Asst Principal, ODM, 1965–69; SSRC Sen. Scholarship, Oxford Univ., 1969–71; Principal, ODA, 1971–75; First Sec., Office of UK Permanent Rep. to EC, 1975–77; Mem., Bd of Dirs, Asian Develt Bank, 1979–82; Head of Dept, ODA, 1982–92; Advr, Finance and Admin, EBRD, 1990–91 (on secondment); Mem. Bd of Dirs, World Bank Gp, 1992–97; UK Ambassador and Perm. Delegate to UNESCO, 1997–2003. Mem., Exec. Bd, 1997–2003, Chm., Finance and Admin. Commn, 2000–01, UNESCO. Chm., Campaign for Nubia and Cairo Museums, 2002–03. Mem., Quaker Peace and Social Witness Central Cttee, 2014–16. Vice Chair of Govs, Canonbury Sch., 2003–06; Gov., Bootham Sch., York, 2016–. *Recreations:* mountaineering, ski-ing, painting, gardening. *Address:* 11 Canonbury Park South, N1 2JR. *E:* davidstanton@canonburypark.plus.com.

**STANTON, Jonathan Adam;** Chief Executive, Weir Group plc, since 2016; *b* Nottingham, 1 March 1967; *s* of John Rodney Stanton and Lucy Helen Stanton; *m* 1994, Rachel Jones; four *d*. *Educ:* King Edward's Sch., Bath; Univ. of Warwick (BSc Accounting and Finance 1988). Chartered Accountant; Mem., ICAEW 1991. Ernst & Young: graduate trainee to Sen. Manager, Birmingham, 1988–97; Sen. Manager, Detroit, 1997–99; Sen. Manager, 1999–2001, Partner, 2001–10, London; Gp Finance Dir, Weir Gp plc, 2010–16. *Address:* Weir Group plc, 1 West Regent Street, Glasgow G2 1RW. *T:* (0141) 308 3701. *E:* jon.stanton@mail.weir.

**STANTON, Louise Jane,** OBE 2012; HM Diplomatic Service; Consul-General, Kabul, since 2017; *b* Bedfordshire, 14 Aug. 1968; *d* of Robert Charles Stanton and Jane Rosannah Sinclair (*née* Baker). *Educ:* Dominican Convent Benoni, S Africa; Dame Alice Harpur Sch., Bedford; Queen Mary and Westfield Coll., Univ. of London (BA Hons German and Linguistics 1990); Univ. of Sussex (Dip. Human Resource Mgt 2003); King's Coll. London (MA Internat. Security and Strategic Studies, 2013). Entered FCO, 1990; Desk Officer for Brunei, SE Asia Dept, FCO, 1990–91; Japanese lang. trng, 1991–93; Third Sec. (Commercial), Tokyo, 1993–96; Worldwide Floater, 1997–98 (incl. British Liaison Officer, Nagano Winter Olympics, Japan, 1998); Dep. Hd of Peacekeeping, UN Dept, FCO, 1999–2001; Hd, Personnel Unit, HR Gp, FCO Services, 2001–03; HR Manager for Consular Directorate, UK Visas and Protocol Div., FCO, 2004; HR Manager and Team Leader for Directorate Gen., Economic, FCO, 2004–06; Dep. Hd of Mission, Slovenia, 2006–08; High Comr, Malta, 2009–12; rcds, 2012–13; Dep. Hd, Counter Proliferation Dept, FCO, 2013–16; Dep. Hd of Mission, Brazil, 2016–17. MCIPD 2004. *Recreations:* slow food, wine, cooking, dancing, travel. *Address:* c/o Foreign and Commonwealth Office, King Charles Street, SW1A 2AH.

**STANTON, Lyndon,** PhD; non-executive Director: Environment Agency, 2002–09; Nuclear Decommissioning Authority, 2004–08; *b* 22 Dec. 1942; *s* of late Joseph Reginald Stanton and of Violet Hazel Stanton (*née* Sears); *m* 1964, Carol Ann Smith; two *d. Educ:* Newport High Sch. for Boys; Univ. of Wales (BSc 1st cl. Hons; PhD); Emmanuel Coll., Cambridge (Salters' Res. Fellowship). Various tech. and commercial appts, ICI Ltd, UK and Brussels, 1969–79; Arco Chemical Europe: Gen. Manager, Sales and Mktg, 1979–81; Manager, Mergers and Acquisitions, 1981–83; Business Manager, Urethanes, 1983–88; Dir of Business Develt, 1988–91; Vice Pres., Business Mgt, 1991–94; Pres. and Chief Exec., Arco Chemical Europe, 1994–98, subseq. Lyondell Chemical Europe, 1998–2000. Chm., Industry Cttee, and Southern Reg. Adv. Panel, EA, 2002–09. Trustee: Prince of Wales's Phoenix Trust, 1996–2004 (Chm., 2003–04); Earthwatch Europe, 1997–2002; Churches Conservation Trust, 1999–2005 (Dep. Chm., 2001–05); Norden Farm Centre for Arts, 2002–12. Liveryman, Horners' Co., 2000– (Mem., Ct of Assts, 2004–16; Hon. Asst, 2016–). *Publications:* scientific papers on nonlinear optics, scattering and atomic and molecular physics in learned jls, various business pubns and speeches in conf. procs. *Recreations:* water sports (esp. scuba diving), collecting antique furniture and antiquarian scientific books, photography, music. *E:* lyndon.stanton@btinternet.com. *Club:* Athenæum.

**STANTON, Prof. Stuart Lawrence Richard,** FRCS, FRCSE, FRCOG; Professor of Pelvic Surgery and Urogynaecology, St George's Hospital Medical School, 1997–2003, now Emeritus Professor; Consultant Gynaecologist and Director of Urogynaecology Unit, St George's Hospital, 1984–2003; in practice as private gynaecologist, urogynaecologist and medico-legal consultant, 1974–2012; *b* 24 Oct. 1938; *s* of Michael Arthur Stanton and Sarah (*née* Joseph); *m* 1965, Anne Frances Goldsmith (marr. diss. 1991); three *d*; *m* 1991, Julia Heller; one *s* one *d. Educ:* City of London Sch.; London Hosp. Med. Sch. (MB BS 1961). FRCS 1966; FRCSE 1966; FRCOG 1987. Surgical Registrar, Royal Masonic Hosp., 1964–65; SHO, Queen Charlotte's Hosp., 1967; Res. Registrar, Inst. of Urology, London, 1971–72; Sen. Registrar, Dept of Obstetrics and Gynaecology, St George's Hosp., London, 1972–74; Consultant Obstetrician and Gynaecologist, St Helier Hosp., 1974–84. Lectures: William Blair Bell Meml, 1974, William Meredith Fletcher Shaw, 1996, RCOG; Victor Bonney, RCS, 1984; J. Marion Sims, Amer. Urogynecologic Soc., 1995. Pres., British Soc. of Urogynaecology, 2003–. Vice Chm., Hadassah UK, 2011– (Chm., 2010–11); Chair: Medical Friends, British Friends of Hebrew Univ., Jerusalem, 2014–; British Friends of Boys Town Sch., Jerusalem, 2017–; Trustee, Jewish Music Inst., 2013–. FRSocMed 1975. Hon. FRANZCOG 2000. Cert. of Recognition for Lifetime Achievement, Israel, 2016. *Publications:* (ed jtly) Surgery of Female Incontinence, 1980, 2nd edn 1986; Clinical Gynaecologic Urology, 1984; (ed) The Principles of Gynaecological Surgery, 1987; Gynaecology in the Elderly, 1988; (ed jtly) Gynaecology, 1992, 3rd edn 2003; (ed jtly) Pelvic Floor Re-education, 1994, 2nd edn 2008; (ed jtly) Clinical Urogynaecology, 1999; (ed jtly) Urinary Tract Infections in the Female, 2000. *Recreations:* family, photography, modern ceramics, biographies, music. *Address:* 20 Yehoshua Bin Nun, Jerusalem 9314540, Israel. *E:* stuartstanton@hotmail.co.uk.

**STAPELY, Sue;** solicitor; independent reputation management consultant with Sue Stapely Consulting, since 2001; *b* 11 July 1946; *d* of Stanley Sly and Kathleen MacIvor; *m* 1968, Simon Stapely; two *s*; *m* 2012, David Fitt. *Educ:* Kingston Univ. (LLB Hons); Coll. of Law (Solicitors Final Exam.). Production posts, BBC TV, 1966–73; Manager, various CABx, 1973–83; Partner, Heald Nickinson (solicitors), 1985–89; Hd of PR, Law Soc., 1989–96 (Mem., 1989–); Dir, Fishburn Hedges, 1996–2001. Contested (SDP) Chertsey and Walton, 1987. Mem., Nat. Exec. Cttee, SDP, 1986–88; Chm., Women for Social Democracy, 1987–88; Founding Nat. Chm., 300 Group, 1986–88. Member Board: SW Thames RHA, 1993–94; London Ambulance Service, 1993–94; Countryside Agency, 2000–03; LAMDA, 1998–2016; Spare Tyre Theatre Co., 1999–2012; Brighton Fest., 2006–16; Media Standards Trust, 2007–; Mem. Develt Council, Royal Court Theatre, 1998–2006; Gov., RSC, 2016–. Mem. Bd, Dignity in Dying (formerly Voluntary Euthanasia Soc.), 2004–06. Trustee, Solicitors' Pro Bono Gp. FRSA 1994; FCIPR (FIPR 2002). *Publications:* Media Relations for Lawyers, 1994, 2nd edn 2003. *Recreations:* conversation, travel, theatre, fast cars. *Address:* Wood Lane House, Cherington, Warwicks CV36 5HY; Star Cottage, Little Compton, Glos GL56 0RY.

**STAPLE, George Warren,** CB 1996; Partner, Clifford Chance, 1987–92 and 1997–2001, Consultant, 2001–12; Director, Serious Fraud Office, 1992–97; *b* 13 Sept. 1940; *s* of late Kenneth Harry Staple and Betty Mary Staple; *m* 1968, Olivia Deirdre Lowry; two *s* two *d. Educ:* Haileybury. Articled to Walker Charlesworth and Jefferson, Westminster, and Coll. of Law, 1958–62; Associate with Condon and Forsyth, NY, 1963; admitted Solicitor, 1964; Asst Solicitor, 1964–67, Partner, 1967–87, Clifford-Turner & Co. Legal Assessor, Disciplinary Cttee, Stock Exchange, 1978–92; DTI Inspector, Consolidated Gold Fields, 1986, Aldermanbury Trust, 1988; a Chairman, Authorisation and Disciplinary Tribunals: of The Securities Assoc., 1987–91; of Securities and Futures Authy, 1991–92; Member: Commercial Court Cttee, 1977–92; Law Adv. Cttee, British Council, 1998–2001; Sen. Salaries Review Body, 2000–04; Tribunal Panel, Accountancy and Actuarial Discipline Bd, 2005–13; Chairman: Fraud Adv. Panel, 1998–2003; Review Bd for Govt Contracts, 2002–09. Mem. Council, Law Soc., 1986–2000 (Treas., 1989–92). Trustee: Romney Marsh Historic Churches Trust, 2002–; Royal Humane Soc., 2007–18. Gov., City of London Polytechnic, subseq. London Guildhall Univ., 1982–94; Chm. Govs, Haileybury, 2001–08. Hon. QC 1997; Hon. Bencher, Inner Temple, 2000. *Recreations:* cricket, walking, gardening. *Address:* Clifford Chance, 10 Upper Bank Street, E14 5JJ. *Clubs:* Brooks's, City of London, MCC.
*See also* W. P. Staple.

**STAPLE, William Philip;** non-executive Deputy Chairman, Westhouse Holdings plc, 2011–14 (Managing Partner, Westhouse Securities LLP, then Chief Executive, Hanson Westhouse Ltd, later Chief Executive, Westhouse Holdings plc, 2005–11); *b* 28 Sept. 1947; *s* of late Kenneth Harry Staple and Betty Mary Staple (*née* Lemon); *m* 1977, Jennifer Frances Walker (marr. diss. 1986); one *s* one *d. Educ:* Haileybury; Coll. of Law. Called to the Bar, Inner Temple, 1971; Executive at Cazenove & Co., 1972–81; N. M. Rothschild and Sons Ltd: Asst Dir, 1981–86; Dir, 1986–94 and 1996–99; Dir Gen., Takeover Panel, 1994–96; Man. Dir, Benfield Advisory, 1999–2001; Dir, Corporate Finance, Brown, Shipley & Co. Ltd, 2001–04. *Recreations:* golf, theatre, reading. *Address:* Bartlemas, Dover Road, Sandwich, Kent CT13 0BH. *E:* billstaple@hotmail.co.uk. *Clubs:* White's, Royal St George.
*See also* G. W. Staple.

**STAPLEFORD, Sally Anne,** OBE 1999; President, National Ice Skating Association of UK Ltd, 1995–2006; *b* 7 July 1945; *d* of Richard Harvey Stapleford and Alice Elizabeth Stapleford. *Educ:* Streatham Hill High Sch.; Clapham High Sch.; private tutor. British Jun. Ice Skating Champion, 1961; Southern Regl Sen. Ice Skating Champion, 1961–63; Gold Medal: Britain, and Canada, 1961; America, 1962; British Sen. Ice Skating Champion, 1963–68; competed in: European Championships, 1963–68 (Silver Medal, 1965); World Championships, 1964–68; Winter Olympics, 1964, 1968; won Edinburgh Internat. Trophy, 1968. Nat. judge and referee, 1968–2006; internat. judge and referee, 1972–2003; National Ice Skating Association (formerly National Skating Association): Mem., Governing Body, 1970–; Chm., Ice Figure Cttee, 1989–94; Vice-Chm., Fedn of Ice Skating, 1990; Technical Orgnr, internat. figure skating events in UK; Mem., 1988–92, Chm., 1992–2002, Figure Skating Technical Cttee, Internat. Skating Union; Mem., Nat. Olympic Cttee, 1994–99. *Address:* Flat 3, St Valery, 54 Beulah Hill, Upper Norwood, SE19 3ER. *T:* (020) 8771 0778.

**STAPLES, Brian Lynn;** Chairman: Pendle (UK) Ltd, since 2003; Effective Waste Solutions Ltd, 2003–09; European Scanning Centre, since 2008; St Joseph's Hospital Ltd, since 2014; *b* 6 April 1945; *s* of Stanley Holt Staples and Catherine Emma Annie Staples (*née* Walding); *m* 1st, 1965; one *d*; 2nd, 1973; one *s* two *d*; 3rd, 1999, Anne-Marie Smith; two *s. Educ:* Sweyne Grammar Sch., Rayleigh. Joined Tarmac Group, 1964; Chief Executive: Tarmac Construction, 1991–94; United Utilities Plc (formerly North West Water Gp), 1994–97; Amey PLC, 1997–2003; Dir and Chief Exec., Scottish BioPower Ltd, 2003–07. Chm., Scottish Resources Gp, 2005–11 (non-exec. Dir, Mining Scotland Gp, 2004; Dep. Chm., Mining (Scotland) Ltd, 2006). *Recreations:* Rugby, music, theatre, outdoor pursuits. *Address:* Pendle House, Castle Hill, Prestbury, Cheshire SK10 4AR.

**STAPLES, (Hubert Anthony) Justin,** CMG 1981; HM Diplomatic Service, retired; Ambassador to Finland, 1986–89; *b* 14 Nov. 1929; *s* of late Francis Hammond Staples, formerly ICS, and Catherine Margaret Mary Pownall; *m* 1962, Susan Angela Collingwood Carter; one *s* one *d. Educ:* Downside; Oriel Coll., Oxford. Served in RAF 1952–54 (Pilot Officer). Entered Foreign (later Diplomatic) Service, 1954; 3rd Sec., Bangkok, 1955; Foreign Office, 1959; 1st Sec., Berlin (Dep. Political Adviser), 1962; Vientiane, 1965 (acted as Chargé d'Affaires in 1966 and 1967); transf. to FO and seconded to Cabinet Office, 1968; Counsellor, UK Delegn to NATO, Brussels, 1971; Counsellor and Consul-General, Bangkok, 1974 (acted as Chargé d'affaires, 1975 and 1977); Counsellor, Dublin, 1978–81; Ambassador to Thailand, 1981–86 and concurrently to Laos, 1985–86. Pres., Anglo-Finnish Soc., 1993–2014. Order of the Lion (Finland), 2003. *Recreation:* golf. *Address:* 48 Crescent Road, Kingston, Surrey KT2 7RF. *Clubs:* Travellers (Chm., 2003–06); Roehampton; Royal Bangkok Sports (Bangkok).

**STAPLETON, Annamarie;** *see* Phelps, A.

**STAPLETON, Prof. (Barbara) Jane,** DPhil, DCL; Master, Christ's College, Cambridge, since 2016; *b* Sydney, Australia, 26 March 1952; *d* of Colin Arthur Stapleton and Olga Jean Stapleton (*née* Perry); *m* 1st, 1976, Ross Frederick Cranston (*see* Hon. Sir R. F. Cranston) (marr. diss. 1985); 2nd, 1985, Prof. Peter Cane; one *s* one *d. Educ:* Univ. of NSW (BSc 1974); Univ. of Adelaide (PhD Chem. 1977); Australian Nat. Univ. (LLB 1981); Balliol Coll., Oxford (DPhil 1984; DCL 2008). Postdoctoral Researcher (Dudley Williams' Gp), Univ. of Cambridge, 1977; called to the Bar: NSW, 1981; High Court of Australia, 1984; Legal, then Sen. Legal Officer, Australian Attorney Gen.'s Dept, 1981–84; Lecturer: Univ. of Sydney Law Sch., 1985; Trinity Coll., Oxford, 1985–86; CUF Lectr, 1987–97, Reader in Law, 1996–97, Univ. of Oxford; Fellow and Tutor in Law, 1987–97, Estates Bursar, 1996–97, Emeritus Fellow, 1998, Balliol Coll., Oxford; Res. Prof. of Law, 1997–2016, now Emeritus, Dist. Prof., 2016, ANU; Ernest E. Smith Prof. of Law, Sch. of Law, Univ. of Texas, 2002–16. Visiting Professor: in Law, Univ. of Oxford, 2000–14; Columbia Law Sch., 2007; Harvard Law Sch., 2012; Prof. of Comparative Private Law, Eur. Univ. Inst., 2001; Arthur Goodhart Vis. Prof. of Legal Sci., Univ. of Cambridge, 2011–12. Mem., Amer. Law Inst., 2000– (Mem. Council, 2004–). FASSA, 2007–15; Fellow, Australian Acad. Law, 2010; Hon. Fellow, St John's Coll., Cambridge, 2012. Corresp. FBA 2015. Hon. Bencher, Gray's Inn, 2009. *Publications:* Disease and the Compensation Debate, 1986; Product Liability, 1994; contrib. articles to sci. and law jls. *Recreations:* theatre, cinema. *Address:* Christ's College, Cambridge CB2 3BU. *T:* (01223) 334900. *E:* masters-assistant@christs.cam.ac.uk. *Club:* Oxford and Cambridge.

**STAPLETON, Graham Barry;** Chief Executive Officer, Halfords Group plc, since 2018; *b* Portsmouth, 29 Jan. 1968; *s* of Barry and Alexandra Stapleton; *m* 2001, Joanna; two *s. Educ:* Highbury Coll., Portsmouth (BTEC Nat. Dip. Business Studies). Chief Executive Officer: Carphone Warehouse UK and Ireland, 2012–14; Dixons Carphone Connected World Services, 2014–15; Dixons Carphone Honeybee, 2015–18. *Address:* Halfords Ltd, Icknield Street Drive, Washford West, Redditch B98 0DE. *T:* (01527) 513276. *E:* graham.stapleton@halfords.co.uk.

**STAPLETON, Very Rev. Henry Edward Champneys,** MBE 2009; Dean of Carlisle, 1988–98; *b* 17 June 1932; *s* of Edward Parker Stapleton and Frances Mary Champneys; *m* 1964, Mary Deborah Sapwell; two *d. Educ:* Lancing College; Pembroke Coll., Cambridge (BA 1954, MA 1958); Ely Theological Coll. Deacon 1956; priest 1957, York; Assistant Curate: St Olave with St Giles, 1956–59; Pocklington, 1959–61; Vicar of Seaton Ross with Everingham, Harswell and Bielby, 1961–67; RD of Weighton, 1966–67; Rector of Skelton, 1967–75; Vicar of Wroxham with Hoveton, 1975–81; Priest in Charge of Belaugh, 1976–81, with Hoveton St Peter, 1979–81; Canon Residentiary and Precentor of Rochester Cathedral, 1981–88; Warden of Readers, 1981–88. Sec., York Diocesan Adv. Cttee, 1959–75; Church Comr, 1993–98; Member: Council for the Care of Churches, 1965–91; Churches Conservation Trust (formerly Redundant Churches Fund), 1976–98; Royal Commn on Historical Manuscripts, 1992–2002. Chm., Incorp. Church Building Soc., 2002–13. Trustee, Nat. Churches Trust (formerly Historic Churches Preservation Trust), 1983–2008. Chm., Cathedral Libraries and Archives Assoc., 1988–97; Member: Liby Cttee, Lambeth Palace, 1999–2006; Archbishops' Adv. Panel for Archives and Libraries, 2006–12. Fellow, Woodard Corp., 1990–2002. FSA 1974. Editor, Cathedral, 1976–82. Hon. Fellow, Univ. of Northumbria, Newcastle, 1995. *Publications:* Skelton Village, 1971; Heirs without Title, 1974; The Skilful Master Builder, 1975; The Model Working Parson, 1976; (ed and contrib.) Churchyards Handbook, 2nd edn 1976, 3rd edn 1988; articles in Churchscape and other ecclesiastical jls. *Recreations:* the writings of R. H. Benson, genealogy, visiting churches, second-hand bookshops. *Address:* Rockland House, 20 Marsh Gardens, Honley, Holmfirth, W Yorks HD9 6AF. *T:* (01484) 666629. *E:* hec.stapleton@talktalk.net.

**STAPLETON, Jane;** see Stapleton, B. J.

**STAPLETON, Nigel John;** Chairman, Postal Services Commission, 2004–10; Chairman of Trustees: Mineworkers Pension Scheme, 2009–17; National Grid UK Pension Scheme, since 2015 (Independent Trustee, 2012–14); *b* 1 Nov. 1946; *s* of Frederick Ernest John Stapleton and Katie Margaret Stapleton (*née* Tyson); *m* 1982, Johanna Augusta Molhoek; one *s* one *d*. *Educ:* City of London Sch.; Fitzwilliam Coll., Cambridge (MA; Hon. Fellow 1998). Planning, finance and gen. mgt positions, incl. Vice Pres., Finance, Unilever United States Inc., Unilever plc, 1968–86; Reed International plc: Dir, 1986–99; Finance Dir, 1986–96; Dep. Chm., 1994–97; Chm., 1997–99; Co-Chm., 1996–98, Co-Chief Exec., 1998–99, Reed Elsevier plc; Chairman: Veronis, Suhler Internat. Ltd, 1999–2002; Uniq plc, 2001–06. Dir, London Stock Exchange, 2001–10. Non-executive Director: Allied Domecq plc, 1992–99; Marconi plc (formerly GEC), 1997–2002; Axa UK (formerly Sun Life and Provincial Hldgs) plc, 1999–2002; Reliance Security Gp Ltd, 2002–11; Independent Director: Kazpost, 2008–13; Real Estate Fund Samruk Kazyna, 2011–13; Sovereign Wealth Fund Samruk Kazyna, 2013–15. Trustee, Royal Opera House Trust, 1999–2001. *Recreations:* theatre, opera, travel, tennis. *Club:* Oxford and Cambridge.

**STAPLETON, Prof. Richard Christopher,** PhD; Professor of Finance (part-time), University of Manchester, 2003–14; *b* 11 Oct. 1942; *s* of Leonard Stapleton and Rosamund Kathleen May Stapleton; *m* 1968, Linda Cairns; one *s* one *d*. *Educ:* Univ. of Sheffield (BAEcon, PhD Business Studies); Open Univ. (BA Maths). Lectr in Business Finance, Sheffield Univ., 1965–73; Asst Prof. of Finance, New York Univ., 1973–76; Sen. Res. Fellow, 1976–77, Nat. West. Bank Prof. of Business Finance, 1977–86, Manchester Business Sch., Univ. of Manchester; Fellow, Churchill Coll., Cambridge, 1986–89; Wolfson Prof. of Finance, Lancaster Univ., 1989–98; Prof. of Finance, Strathclyde Univ., 1998–2003. Hon. MBA Manchester, 1980. *Publications:* The Theory of Corporate Finance, 1970; International Tax Systems and Financing Policy, 1978; Capital Markets and Corporate Financial Decisions, 1980; contrib. Econ. Jl, Jl of Finance, Jl of Financial Econs, Qly Jl of Econs. *Recreations:* running, golf, reading, travel.

**STAPLETON, Victoria Lucy Annabel, (Mrs Jonathan Pilkington);** Founder and Creative Director, Brora Ltd, since 1993; *b* Chelmsford, 5 April 1967; *d* of David Stapleton and Annabel Stapleton; *m* 1999, Jonathan Pilkington; three *d*. *Educ:* St Mary's Sch., Ascot; Univ. of East Anglia (BA). Film prodn asst, 1988–89; Founder, Pyjamarama, 1989–91; Account Manager, Lindsay Hiscox Designs, 1991–92; Retail Manager, Hunters of Brora, 1992–93. *Recreations:* art exhibitions, theatre, adventures, fishing, ski-ing, golf. *Address:* Brora Ltd, 5–6 The Orbital Centre, Gunnels Wood Road, Stevenage, Herts SG1 2NB. *T:* (01438) 744300.

**STAPLETON-COTTON,** family name of **Viscount Combermere**.

**STARGARDT, Lyndal Anne;** see Roper, L. A.

**STARK, Christopher;** Chief Executive, UK Committee on Climate Change, since 2018; *b* Glasgow, 11 Aug. 1978; *s* of Alan and Elizabeth Stark; *m* 2010, Marianne Clavé; one *s* one *d*. *Educ:* Jordanhill Sch., Glasgow; Univ. of Glasgow (BA Hons Law and Financial Studies 2002). HM Treasury, 2003–08; Dep. Dir, BIS, 2008–09; Scottish Government: Head: Strategy Unit, 2009–12; Energy Div., 2013–16; Dir, Energy and Climate Change, 2016–18. *Recreations:* music collecting, concert going. *Address:* 92 Dowanhill Street, Glasgow G12 9EG.

**STARK, David;** see Stark, J. D. S.

**STARK, George Robert,** PhD; FRS 1990; Distinguished Scientist, Lerner Research Institute, Cleveland Clinic Foundation, since 2002 (Chairman, 1992–2002); *b* 4 July 1933; *s* of Jack and Florence Stark; *m* 1956, Mary Beck; one *s* one *d*. *Educ:* Columbia College, NY (BA 1955); Columbia Univ., NY (Chemistry; PhD 1959). Asst Prof., Rockefeller Univ., 1961; Stanford University: Asst Prof., 1963; Associate Prof., 1966; Prof. of Biochemistry, 1971; ICRF, 1983–92 (Associate Dir of Res., 1989–92). Member: European Molecular Biol. Orgn, 1985; NAS, USA, 1987; Inst. of Medicine, USA, 2002. *Publications:* contribs to scientific jls. *Recreations:* sports, stamps, books, records. *Address:* Cleveland Clinic Foundation, 9500 Euclid Avenue, Cleveland, OH 44195, USA. *T:* (216) 4443900, *Fax:* (216) 4443279.

**STARK, (John) David (Sinclair),** CEng; Chairman, Norcros Group (Trustee) Ltd, 2005–09 (Director, 1999–2009); *b* 16 April 1939; *s* of John and Bertha Stark; *m* 1964, Pamela Margaret Reed; one *s* one *d*. *Educ:* St Bees Sch., Cumberland; Leeds Univ. (BSc). CEng, MIET (MIEE 1966). GEC plc, 1960–62; Morgan Crucible plc, 1962–76; Bestobell plc, 1976–81; Man. Dir, Bestobell Australia Ltd, 1981–84; Divl Chief Exec., Unitech plc, 1984–85; Divl Dir 1985–86, Dir, 1986–97, Tomkins plc; Chm., Glentay, subseq. Brauer Technologies, Ltd, 1997–2004; Dir, Norcros plc, 1997–99. Non-exec. Dir, Royal Mint, 2000–04 (Chm., 2002–04). Mem., Monopolies and Mergers, subseq. Competition, Commn, 1998–2005. Gov., Esher Church Sch., 1998–2006. *Recreations:* inland waterways, opera, amateur dramatics. *Address:* Tara, 15 Copsem Drive, Esher, Surrey KT10 9HD. *T:* (01372) 466781.

**STARK, Jürgen;** independent economist, since 2012; Member, Executive Board, European Central Bank, 2006–11; *b* 31 May 1948. *Educ:* Univ. of Hohenheim (first degree in econs 1973; DEc 1975); Eberhard Karls Univ., Tübingen. Res. Asst, Univ. of Hohenheim, 1973–78; Official, Econ. Policy Dept, Min. of Econs, Germany, 1978–88; First Sec., Perm. Repn of Fed. Rep. of Germany to GATT, Geneva, 1982–83; Hd of Div., For. Trade and Payments, Money and For. Currency, Financial Mkts, Federal Chancellery, 1988–92; Ministry of Finance: Dep. Hd of Dept, Nat. Monetary Policy, Capital Mkt Policy, Germany as Financial Centre, Borrowing, 1992; Hd of Dept, Internat. Monetary and Financial Relns, Financial Relns in EC, 1993–94; State Sec. and Personal Rep. of Federal Chancellor in preps for G7/G8 Econ. Summits, 1995–98; Vice Pres., Deutsche Bundesbank, 1998–2006. Hon. Prof., Faculty of Econs, Eberhard Karls Univ., Tübingen, 2005–. Alternate Gov. and Delegate for Germany to IMF, 1995–2006; Member: Monetary Cttee, 1995–98, Econ. and Financial Cttee, 1999–2011, EU; G7 and G10 Deputies, 1995–2006, G20 Deputies, 1999–2006; Internat. Relns Cttee, ESCB, 1998–2006; Cttee on Global Financial System (G10, BIS), 1998–2006; Financial Stability Forum, 1999–2006. Member Supervisory Board: Deutsche Telekom AG, 1995–98; Deutsche Bahn AG, 1995–98; German Investment and Develt Corp., 1997–98; Dep. Mem., Bd of Dirs, BIS, 1998–2006. Dep. Chm., Ifo Inst., Munich, 1999–; Chm., Univ. of Hildesheim Foundn, 2003–15. Trustee, Bertelsmann Foundn, 2012–.

**STARKEY, Amy;** Regional Director, East, Jockey Club Racecourses, since 2012; *b* York, 27 April 1981; *d* of Steven and Deborah Starkey. *Educ:* All Saints RC Sch., York; Trinity and All Saints Coll., Leeds Univ. (BA Business Mgt). Commercial Exec., Northern Racing, Sedgefield and Newcastle Racecourses, 2002–05; Jockey Club: Managing Director: Huntingdon Racecourse, 2005–08; Kempton Park Racecourse, 2008–12. *Recreations:* horseracing, reading, snowboarding. *Address:* 4 The Gallops, Old Station Road, Newmarket CB8 8LA. *E:* amy.starkey@thejockeyclub.co.uk.

**STARKEY, Dr David Robert,** CBE 2007; FSA; FRHistS; historian and broadcaster; *b* 3 Jan. 1945; *s* of Robert Starkey and Elsie Starkey (*née* Lyon). *Educ:* Kendal GS; Fitzwilliam Coll., Cambridge (Open Schol.; Hon. Fellow, 2006). FRHistS 1984; FSA 1994. Fitzwilliam College, Cambridge: Res. Fellow, 1970–72; Vis. Fellow, 1998–2001; Bye-Fellow, 2001–06; Pres., Fitzwilliam Soc., 2003–04. Lectr in History, Dept of Internat. History, LSE, 1972–98. Vis. Vernon Prof. of Biography, Dartmouth Coll., New Hampshire, 1987, 1989; British Council Specialist Visitor, Australia, 1989; Hon. Vis. Prof. of History, Univ. of Kent, 2007–; Vis. Prof. of History, Canterbury Christ Church Univ., 2018; Hon. Prof. of History, Univ. of Buckingham, 2019. Lectr, Goldsmiths' Co., 2017; Monckton Copeman Lect., RCP and Apothecaries' Co., 2017. Guest Curator: Henry VIII: a European court in England, Nat. Maritime Mus., 1991; Elizabeth, Nat. Maritime Mus., 2003; Making History, RA, 2007; Lost Faces, Philip Mould Ltd, 2007; Henry VIII: man and monarch, British Library, 2009; Royal River: power, pageantry and the Thames, Nat. Maritime Mus., 2012. Presenter and writer of television series: This Land of England, 1985; Henry VIII, 1998 (Indie Award, 2002); Elizabeth I, 2000; Six Wives of Henry VIII, 2001 (Silver Medal, NY Festivals World, 2004; Cine Golden Eagle, Thirteen/WNET, NY, 2006); The Unknown Tudors, 2002; Monarchy, 2004–07; Starkey's Last Word, 2006; Henry VIII: Mind of a Tyrant, 2009; The Churchills, 2012; Music and Monarchy, 2013; David Starkey's Magna Carta, 2015; presenter and writer: TV prog., Kate and William: Romance and the Royals, 2011; (with Lucy Worsley), A Night at Hampton Court Palace, 2015; Reformation: Europe's Holy War, 2017; contributor, TV series: The Genius of British Art, 2010; Jamie's Dream School, 2011; panellist, Moral Maze, BBC Radio 4, 1992–2001; Presenter, Starkey on Saturday, then Starkey on Sunday, Talk Radio, 1995–98. Mem., Commemorative Plaques Wkg Gp, English Heritage, 1993–2006; Pres., Soc. for Court Studies, 1996–2005. Vice-Pres., Tory Campaign for Homosexual Equality, 1994–; Liveryman, Co. of Barbers, 1999– (Freeman, 1992). Mem. Editl Bd, History Today, 1980–; Hon. Associate: Rationalist Press Assoc., 1995–; Nat. Secular Soc., 1999–. Hon. Commodore, Nat. Maritime Mus., 2005; Trustee and Hon. Commodore, Mary Rose Trust. Hon. DLitt: Lancaster, 2004; Kent, 2006; Buckingham, 2019. Norton Medlicott Medal, for services to history, Historical Assoc., 2001. *Publications:* (jtly) This Land of England, 1985; The Reign of Henry VIII: personalities and politics, 1985, 3rd edn 2002; (ed jtly) Revolution Reassessed: revisions in the history of Tudor government and administration, 1986; (ed) The English Court from the Wars of the Roses to the Civil War, 1987; (ed) Rivals in Power: the lives and letters of the great Tudor dynasties, 1990; Henry VIII: a European court in England, 1991; (ed jtly) The Inventory of Henry VIII, vol. I, 1998; Elizabeth: apprenticeship, 2000 (W H Smith Award for Biog./Autobiog., 2001); Six Wives: the Queens of Henry VIII, 2003; The Monarchy of England, vol. 1: the beginnings, 2004; Monarchy: from the Middle Ages to Modernity, 2006; Henry: virtuous prince, 2008; Crown and Country: a history of England through the monarchy, 2010; (with K. Greening) Music and Monarchy, 2013; Magna Carta: the true story behind the charter, 2015; contribs to newspapers, numerous articles in learned jls. *Recreations:* decorating, gardening, treading on toes. *Address:* Fitzwilliam College, Cambridge CB3 0DG.

**STARKEY, Sir John (Philip),** 3rd Bt *cr* 1935; DL; *b* 8 May 1938; *s* of Sir William Randle Starkey, 2nd Bt, and Irene Myrtle Starkey (*née* Francklin) (*d* 1965); *S* father, 1977; *m* 1966, Victoria Henrietta Fleetwood (marr. diss. 2014), *y d* of Lt-Col Christopher Fuller, TD; one *s* three *d*. *Educ:* Eton College; Christ Church, Oxford. A Church Comr and Mem., Comrs' Assets Cttee, 1985–91; Mem., Archbp's Commn on Rural Areas, 1988–90. Chairman: Notts Br., CLA, 1977–80; E Midlands Regl Cttee, Nat. Trust, 1986–97. UK Vice Pres., Confedn of Eur. Agric., 1989–2000; Pres., Newark Chamber of Commerce, 1980–82. Sloan Fellow, London Business School. JP Newark, 1981–88; Notts: DL, 1981; High Sheriff, 1987–88. *Recreations:* cricket, painting, golf. *Heir: s* Henry John Starkey [*b* 13 Oct. 1973; *m* 2002, Georgina Gemma, *y d* of Richard Whittington; two *s*]. *Address:* Ossington House, Ossington, Newark, Notts NG23 6LD. *Club:* MCC.

**STARKEY, Dr Phyllis Margaret;** *b* 4 Jan. 1947; *d* of Dr John Williams and Catherine Hooson Williams (*née* Owen); *m* 1969, Hugh Walton Starkey; two *d*. *Educ:* Perse Sch. for Girls, Cambridge; Lady Margaret Hall, Oxford (BA Biochem.); Clare Hall, Cambridge (PhD). Research posts: Strangeways Lab., Cambridge, 1970–81; Sir Wm Dunn Sch. of Pathology, Oxford, 1981–84; Lectr in Obstetrics and Gynaecology, 1984–93, and Fellow of Somerville Coll., 1987–93, Univ. of Oxford; Head of Assessment, BBSRC, 1993–97. Sen. Associate Mem., St Antony's Coll., Oxford, 2011–18. Mem. (Lab) Oxford City Council, 1983–97 (Leader, 1990–93); Chm., Local Govt Inf. Unit, 1996–97. MP (Lab) Milton Keynes SW, 1997–2010; contested (Lab) Milton Keynes S, 2010. PPS to FCO Ministers, 2001–02, to Minister of State (Minister for Europe), FCO, 2002–05. Mem., Foreign Affairs Select Cttee, 1999–2001; Chm., Select Cttee for DCLG (formerly ODPM), 2005–10. Chm., POST, 2002–05. Mem. Bd St Martin of Tours Housing Assoc., 2011–; Ind. Mem. Bd, Landscape Inst., 2013–; Mem. Bd, Greensquare Housing Assoc., 2015–; Chm., Jericho Wharf Trust, 2012–. Trustee, Med. Aid for Palestinians, 2011–. *Publications:* numerous scientific articles in learned jls. *Recreations:* gardening, cinema, walking. *Address:* 8 Walton Crescent, Oxford OX1 2JG.

**STARLING, Keith Andrew;** Headmaster, The Judd School, 1986–2004; *b* 12 June 1944; *s* of Stanley Ernest Starling and Gladys Joyce Starling; *m* 1968, Jacqueline Eagers; two *s*. *Educ:* The Perse Sch.; Fitzwilliam Coll., Cambridge (MA, CertEd). Asst Master, Lancaster Royal Grammar Sch., 1968–71; Head of Geography, Sedbergh Sch., 1971–80; Dep. Headmaster, Portsmouth Grammar Sch., 1980–86. Gov., Stamford Endowed Schs, 2005–15. Treas., Percy Whitlock Trust, 2012–16; Trustee, Hosp. of St John and St Anne, Oakham, 2014–. Liveryman, Skinners' Co., 2004–. *Recreations:* music, walking, gardening. *Address:* Elderberry Cottage, Orchard Close, Egleton, Rutland LE15 8AG.

**STARLING, Nicholas James;** Director, Nick Starling Consultancy, since 2014; Director of General Insurance (formerly Director of General Insurance and Health), Association of British Insurers, 2005–13; *b* 16 March 1956; *s* of late Richard James Starling and Helen Mary Starling; *m* 1984, Catherine Susannah Thompson; two *d*. *Educ:* George Watson's Coll., Edinburgh; St John's Coll., Cambridge (BA Archaeol. and Anthropology 1977); St John's Coll., Oxford (DPhil 1983). Theodor Heuss Fellow, Univ. of Cologne, 1981–82; Randall Maciver Student in Archaeol., Queen's Coll., Oxford, 1982–83; Department of Transport: joined, 1984; Pvte Sec. to Minister for Roads and Traffic, 1986–88; Principal, 1988–94; Asst Sec., 1994–98; Dep. Dir, Internat. Aviation, 1994–98; Hd, Nuclear and Hazardous Installations Policy, 1998–2000, Dir, Safety Policy, 2000–03, Policy Dir, 2003–05, HSE. *Publications:* various articles in archaeol. jls. *Recreations:* family, music, especially Schubert, singing, cooking, Guardian crossword. *E:* nick_starling@hotmail.com.

**STARMER, Rt Hon. Sir Keir,** KCB 2014; PC 2017; QC 2002; MP (Lab) Holborn and St Pancras, since 2015; *b* 2 Sept. 1962; *s* of Rod and late Jo Starmer; *m* 2007, Victoria Alexander; one *s* one *d*. *Educ:* Reigate Grammar Sch.; Leeds Univ. (LLB 1st Cl. Hons 1985); St Edmund Hall, Oxford (BCL 1986; Hon. Fellow, 2012). Called to the Bar: Middle Temple, 1987, Bencher, 2009; St Lucia, 1997; St Vincent, 1997; Belize, 2002. Dir of Public Prosecutions, 2008–13. Human Rights Centre, Essex Univ., 1998–. Human Rights Advr to NI Policing Bd, 2003–08; Mem., Foreign Sec.'s Adv. Panel on the Death Penalty, 2002–08. Shadow Sec. of State for Exiting the EU, 2016–. Mem., Governance Adv. Bd, British Council, 2002–07. Mem. Council, Justice, 1999–2008. DUniv Essex, 2011; Hon.

DLaws Leeds, 2012. Human Rights Lawyer of the Year Award, Justice/Liberty, 2001. *Publications:* (ed) Justice in Error, 1995; Three Pillars of Liberty: political rights and freedom in the UK, 1996; Signing up for Human Rights: the UK and international standards, 1998; (ed) Miscarriages of Justice, 1999; European Human Rights Law, 1999; Blackstone's Human Rights Digest, 2001; Criminal Justice, Police Powers and Human Rights, 2001; (contrib.) Human Rights Principles, 2001; (contrib.) Mithani's Directors' Disqualification, 2001; (contrib.) Human Rights and Civil Practice, 2001; contribs to Public Law. *Recreations:* football, classical music. *Address:* House of Commons, SW1A 0AA.

**STARMER-SMITH, Nigel Christopher;** International Rugby Board consultant and TV commentator, since 2002; *b* 25 Dec. 1944; *s* of late Harry Starmer-Smith and Joan Mary Starmer-Smith (*née* Keep); *m* 1973, Rosamund Mary Bartlett; one *s* (and one *s* one *d* decd). *Educ:* Magdalen Coll. Sch., Oxford; University Coll., Oxford (MA). Schoolmaster, Epsom Coll., 1967; Producer and Reporter, BBC Radio Outside Broadcasts, 1971; Sports Commentator, BBC TV, 1973–2002; Commentator, ITV Rugby World Cup, 2003; Presenter and Commentator, Rugby Special; commentator, hockey and other sports. Publisher and Editor, Rugby World and Post magazine, 1984–93. Former Rugby Union international: Harlequins, Oxford Univ., Barbarians, England. Gov., Shiplake Coll., 2003–09. Trustee, Reading and Dist Hospitals Charity, 1991–. *Publications:* include: The Barbarians, 1977; Rugby: a way of life, 1986. *Recreations:* family, tennis, piano playing, horse racing, gardening. *Address:* Cobblers Cottage, Skirmett, Henley-on-Thames RG9 6TD. *T:* (01491) 639422. *Clubs:* Vincent's (Oxford); Leander (Henley); Harlequins FC.

**STARR, Lesley Ann;** *see* Page, L. A.

**STARR, Nicholas Frederick,** CBE 2013; Co-founder and Director, London Theatre Company, since 2014; *b* Swanley, Kent, 23 Oct. 1957; *s* of Anthony and Marian Starr. *Educ:* Chislehurst and Sidcup Grammar Sch.; Merton Coll., Oxford (BA Hons English Lang. and Lit.). Lectr, Oxford Coll. of Further Educn, 1980–83; Mktg Officer, Cambridge Th. Co., 1983–84; Mktg Manager, Half Moon Th., 1984–86; Mktg Manager, Paton Walker Associates, 1986–87; Press Officer, 1987–91, Hd of Planning, 1991–96, RNT; Dir, Warwick Arts Centre, 1996–97; Exec. Dir, Almeida Th., 1997–2001; Dir, US Prodns, 2001–02; Exec. Dir, NT, 2002–14. Chm., Battersea Arts Centre, 2001–09; Bd Dir, Soc. of London Theatre, 2003–12. Chm. Trustees, Bush Th., 2009–16; Chm., Yard Th., 2018–; Trustee: NESTA, 2007–13; Young Vic Th., 2007–12. Trailblazer in Theatre and Dance Award, Internat. Inst. of Dance and Theatre, 2018. *Recreations:* piano-playing, gardening. *Address:* Abbey Farmhouse, Abbey Road, Faversham ME13 7BL.

**STATMAN, Philip Richard; His Honour Judge Statman;** a Circuit Judge, since 2002; *b* 28 March 1953; *s* of Martin and Evelyn Statman; *m* 1997, Mary Louise Cameron (*d* 2006); two *s. Educ:* Mid Essex Tech. Coll. (LLB Hons London (ext.)); Inns of Court Sch. of Law. Called to the Bar, Middle Temple, 1975; specialised in criminal law; Asst Recorder, 1997–2000; a Recorder, 2000–02. *Recreations:* travel, Association Football, cinema, literature, antiques. *Address:* Maidstone Combined Court Centre, Barker Road, Maidstone ME16 8EQ. *T:* (01622) 202000.

**STAUNTON, Imelda Mary Philomena Bernadette,** CBE 2016 (OBE 2006); actress, since 1976; *b* 9 Jan. 1956; *d* of Joseph Staunton and Bridie McNicholas; *m* 1983, Jim Carter, actor; one *d. Educ:* La Sainte Union Convent, Highgate; RADA. *Theatre* includes: rep., 1976–81; The Corn is Green, Old Vic, 1985; Calico, Duke of York's, 2004; There Came a Gypsy Riding, Almeida, 2007; Entertaining Mr Sloane, Trafalgar Studios, 2009; A Delicate Balance, Almeida, 2011; Sweeney Todd, Chichester, 2011 (Olivier Award for Best Actress in a Musical, 2013); Adelphi, 2012; Circle Mirror Transformation, Rose Lipman Building, 2013; Good People, Hampstead, transf. Noël Coward Th., 2014; Gypsy, Chichester, 2014, Savoy, 2015 (Olivier Award for Best Actress in a Musical, 2016); Who's Afraid of Virginia Woolf?, Harold Pinter Th., 2017; *National Theatre:* Guys and Dolls, 1982, 1996; Beggar's Opera, Chorus of Disapproval (Olivier Award, best supporting actress), 1985; Life × 3, 2000, transf. Old Vic; Follies, 2017; *Royal Shakespeare Company:* Fair Maid of the West, Wizard of Oz, 1986; Uncle Vanya, Vaudeville, 1988; Into the Woods, Phoenix, 1990 (Olivier Award, best actress in a musical, 1991); *television* includes: The Singing Detective, 1986; Yellowbacks, 1990; Sleeping Life; Roots; Up the Garden Path, 1990; Antonia & Jane; Is it Legal?; Murder, 2002; Cambridge Spies, 2003; Fingersmith, 2005; Cranford, 2007, 2009; Psychoville, 2010–11; The Girl, 2012; That Day We Sang, 2014; A Confession, 2019; *films* include: Peter's Friends, 1992; Much Ado About Nothing, 1993; Deadly Advice, 1994; Sense and Sensibility, Twelfth Night, Remember Me, 1996; Shakespeare in Love, 1999; Rat, 2001; Crush, 2002; Blackball, Virgin of Liverpool, Bright Young Things, 2003; Vera Drake, 2004 (BAFTA Award, best actress, 2005); Nanny McPhee, 2005; Freedom Writers, 2006; Harry Potter and the Order of the Phoenix, 2007; Three and Out, A Bunch of Amateurs, 2008; Another Year, Harry Potter and the Deathly Hallows, Pt 1, 2010; The Awakening, 2011; Pride, Maleficent, 2014; Finding Your Feet, 2018; Downton Abbey, 2019. *Address:* c/o ARG, 4A Exmoor Street, W10 6BD.

**STAUNTON, Prof. James,** PhD; FRS 1998; Professor of Chemical Biology, University of Cambridge, 1999–2002, now Emeritus; Fellow of St John's College, Cambridge, since 1969; *b* 18 March 1935; *s* of James and Elizabeth Staunton; *m* 1961, Dr Ruth Mary Berry, MB, ChB. *Educ:* St Edward's Coll., Liverpool; Univ. of Liverpool (BSc 1956; PhD 1959); MA Cantab 1969. Postdoctoral Fellow, Stanford Univ., 1959–60; Fellow, 1960–62, Lectr in Organic Chemistry, 1962–69, Liverpool Univ.; Lectr in Organic Chemistry, 1969–78, Reader, 1978–99, Cambridge Univ. Natural Products Award, 1987, Tilden Medal, 1989, Robert Robinson Award, 2001, RSC. *Publications:* Primary Metabolism: a mechanistic approach, 1978; articles in chemical and biochemical jls. *Recreations:* walking, cycling, gardening, travel, DIY. *Address:* St John's College, Cambridge CB2 1TP.

**STAUNTON, Marie,** CBE 2013; Chair, Crown Agents, since 2015 (non-executive Director, since 2013); *b* 28 May 1952; *d* of Ann and Austin Staunton; *m* 1986, James Albert Provan; two *d. Educ:* Lancaster Univ.; College of Law (BA). Solicitor. Head of casework for Simon Community Hostels for Addicts, Alcoholics and Homeless Families (England, NI and Eire), 1970–72; Articled Clerk and Solicitor in private practice and Law Centres, 1976–83; Legal Officer, NCCL, 1983–87; Dir, British Section, Amnesty Internat., 1987–90 (Vice-Chm., Internat. Exec. Cttee, 1993–95); Publishing Dir, Longman Law Tax & Finance, then Financial Times Law & Tax, 1990–96; Ed., Solicitors' Jl, 1990–95; Dep. Dir, UK Cttee for UNICEF, 1997–2000; Chief Executive: Plan Internat. UK, 2000–12; Interact Worldwide, 2009–12; Interim Chief Exec., Plan Canada, 2015–16; Interim CEO, Internat. Fedn of Anti Leprosy Orgns, 2014–15. UK Ind. Mem., Mgt Bd, EU Fundamental Rights Agency, 2007–12. Trustee: Disasters Emergency Cttee, 2011–13; Baring Foundn, 2013–; Chairman, Trustees: Equality and Diversity Forum, 2012–16; Raleigh Internat., 2013–17; Internat. Broadcasting Trust, 2013–; SOAS, Univ. of London, 2016–. *Publications:* Data Protection: putting the record straight, 1987; Because I am a Girl, 2010; contribs to NCCL works; chapters in books on allied subjects.

**STAVERT, Most Rev. Alexander Bruce;** Metropolitan of the Ecclesiastical Province of Canada, and Archbishop of Quebec, 2004–09; *b* 1 April 1940; *s* of Ewart and Kathleen Stavert; *m* 1982, Diana Greig; one *s* two *d. Educ:* Lower Canada Coll., Montreal; Bishop's Univ., Lennoxville, PQ (BA 1961); Trinity Coll., Univ. of Toronto (STB 1964; MTh, 1976). Incumbent of Schefferville, Quebec, 1964–69; Fellow, 1969–70, Chaplain, 1970–76, Trinity Coll., Univ. of Toronto; Incumbent, St Clement's Mission East, St Paul's River, PQ, 1976–81; Chaplain, Bishop's Univ., Lennoxville, 1981–84; Dean and Rector, St Alban's Cathedral, Prince Albert, Sask., 1984–91; Bishop of Quebec, 1991–2009. Hon. DD Toronto, 1986; Hon. DCL Bishop's Univ., 2007. *Recreations:* swimming, ski-ing. *Address:* 149 Charleswood, Hudson, Québec, QC J0P 1H0, Canada. *T:* (418) 6923858. *Club:* Garrison (Québec).

**STEAD, Prof. Christian Karlson,** ONZ 2007; CBE 1985; PhD, DLitt; FRSL; FEA; writer; Professor of English, University of Auckland, 1968–86, now Emeritus; Poet Laureate, New Zealand, 2015–17; *b* 17 Oct. 1932; *s* of James Walter Ambrose Stead and Olive Ethel Stead; *m* 1955, Kathleen Elizabeth Roberts; one *s* two *d. Educ:* Mt Albert Grammar Sch.; Univ. of NZ (MA 1955); Univ. of Bristol (PhD 1962); Univ. of Auckland (DLitt 1981). Lectr in English, Univ. of New England, NSW, 1956–57; Michael Hiatt Baker Schol., Univ. of Bristol, 1957–59; Lectr, then Sen. Lectr in English, 1960–64, Associate Prof., 1964–68, Univ. of Auckland. Nuffield Fellow, London, 1965; Hon. Vis. Fellow, UCL, 1977; Fulbright Travelling Fellow, UCLA, 1987; Sen. Vis. Fellow, St John's Coll., Oxford, 1996–97. Katherine Mansfield Menton Fellow, 1972; Arts Laureate, Waitakere City, 2006; Bogliasco Foundn Fellow in Arts, 2007, 2011. FRSL 1995; FEA 2003. Hon. DLitt Bristol, 2001. Jessie McKay Award for Poetry, PEN NZ, 1972; NZ Book Award, for Poetry, 1976, for Fiction, 1985, 1995; King's Lynn Award for Merit in Poetry, 2001; Distinguished Citizen Award, Auckland, 2007; Distinguished Alumni Award, Univ. of Auckland, 2008; Prime Minister's Award for Fiction, NZ, 2009; Sunday Times EFG Private Bank Short Story Award, 2010; Open Internat. Award, Hippocrates Prize for Poetry and Medicine, 2010; Sarah Broom Poetry Prize, 2014; Honoured NZ Writer, Auckland Writers Fest., 2015. *Publications:* South-West of Eden: a memoir, 1932–56, 2010; *poetry:* Whether the Will is Free, 1964; Crossing the Bar, 1972; Quesada, 1975; Walking Westward, 1978; Geographies, 1981; Paris, 1984; Poems of a Decade, 1985; Between, 1987; Voices, 1990; Straw into Gold: poems new and selected, 1997; The Right Thing, 2000; Dog, 2002; The Red Tram, 2004; The Black River, 2007; Collected Poems, 1951–2006, 2008 (Montana Book Award, Creative NZ, 2009); The Yellow Buoy, 2013; In the Mirror and Dancing, 2017; That Derrida Whom I Derided Died, 2018; *fiction:* Smith's Dream, 1971; Five for the Symbol (stories), 1981; All Visitors Ashore, 1984; The Death of the Body, 1986; Sister Hollywood, 1988; The End of the Century at the End of the World, 1991; The Singing Whakapapa, 1994; Villa Vittoria, 1996; The Blind Blonde with Candles in her Hair (stories), 1998; Talking about O'Dwyer, 1999; The Secret History of Modernism, 2002; Mansfield: a novel, 2004; My Name Was Judas, 2006; Risk, 2012; The Name On The Door Is Not Mine: stories new and selected, 2016; The Necessary Angel, 2018; *literary criticism:* The New Poetic, 1964; In the Glass Case: essays on New Zealand literature, 1981; Pound, Yeats, Eliot and the Modernist Movement, 1986; Answering to the Language, 1989; The Writer at Work, 2000; Kin of Place: essays on twenty New Zealand writers, 2002; Book Self: the reader as writer and the writer as critic, 2008; Shelf Life: review, replies and reminiscences, 2016; *edited:* New Zealand Short Stories, 2nd series, 1966; Measure for Measure: a casebook, 1971; Letters and Journals of Katherine Mansfield, 1977; Collected Stories of Maurice Duggan, 1981; Faber Book of Contemporary South Pacific Stories, 1993; Werner Forman's New Zealand (photographs with commentary), 1995. *Recreations:* swimming, music, walking. *Address:* 37 Tohunga Crescent, Auckland 1052, New Zealand.

**STEAD, Ian Mathieson,** PhD; FSA; FBA 1991; Deputy Keeper, Department of Prehistoric and Romano-British Antiquities, British Museum, 1977–96 (Assistant Keeper, 1974–77); *b* 9 Jan. 1936; *er s* of Sidney William Stead and Edith Johann (*née* Mathieson); *m* 1962, Sheelagh Mary Johnson; one *s* one *d. Educ:* Nunthorpe Grammar Sch., York; Fitzwilliam House, Cambridge Univ. (MA; PhD 1965). FSA 1966. Asst Inspector of Ancient Monuments, 1962, Inspector, 1964–74, Min. of Works. Chairman: Herts Archaeol Council, 1970–75; Humberside Jt Archaeol Cttee, 1974–81; Sec., Prehistoric Soc., 1974–76. Hon. Life Mem., Yorks Philosophical Soc., 1982; Corresp. Mem., Deutsches Archäologisches Institut, 1976. Silver Medal, Yorks Archaeol Soc. 2005. *Publications:* La Tène Cultures of Eastern Yorkshire, 1965; Winterton Roman Villa, 1976; Arras Culture, 1979; (with J.-L. Flouest) Iron Age Cemeteries in Champagne, 1979; Rudston Roman Villa, 1980; The Gauls, 1981; Celtic Art in Britain, 1985, 2nd edn 1996; Battersea Shield, 1985; (with J. B. Bourke and D. Brothwell) Lindow Man, the Body in the Bog, 1986; (with V. Rigby) Baldock, 1986; (with V. Rigby) Verulamium, the King Harry Lane Site, 1989; Iron Age Cemeteries in East Yorkshire, 1991; (with Karen Hughes) Early Celtic Designs, 1997; The Salisbury Hoard, 1998 (British Archaeol Awards Book Award, 2000); (with V. Rigby) The Morel Collection, 1999; British Iron Age Swords and Scabbards, 2006; (with J.-L. Flouest and V. Rigby) Iron Age and Roman Burials in Champagne, 2006; papers in learned jls. *Address:* Adam House, 11 Ogleforth, York YO1 7JG.

**STEAD, Rt Rev. John;** *see* Willochra, Bishop of.

**STEAD, Rt Rev. Dr Michael Rennie;** Bishop of South Sydney and an Assistant Bishop, Diocese of Sydney, since 2016; *b* Sydney, 25 Feb. 1969; *s* of John Stead and Wendy Stead; *m* 1991, Felicity Cooper; two *s* one *d. Educ:* Univ. of New South Wales (BComm Accounting 1990); Moore Theol Coll. (BD Hons 2001); Univ. of Gloucestershire (PhD 2007). IT Consultant, PricewaterhouseCoopers, 1990–96; ordained deacon, 2001, priest, 2002; Minister, 2001–07, Sen. Minister, 2008–15, St James, Turamurra. Vis. Lectr in Old Testament, Moore Theol Coll., 2007–. *Publications:* Zechariah and the 'former prophets', 2007; The Intertextuality of Zechariah 1–8, 2009; Christ Died for our Sins, 2013; Zechariah: the Lord returns, 2015. *Recreations:* woodworking, sailing. *Address:* Diocese of Sydney, PO Box Q190, QVB Post Office, NSW 1230, Australia. *T:* (2) 92651598. *E:* mstead@sydney.anglican.asn.au.

**STEADMAN, Alison,** OBE 2000; actress; *b* Liverpool, 26 Aug. 1946; *d* of late George Percival Steadman and Marjorie Steadman; *m* 1973, Mike Leigh, *qv* (marr. diss. 2001); two *s. Theatre* includes: Abigail's Party, Hampstead (Best Actress, Evening Standard Awards), 1977; Joking Apart, Globe, 1979; Uncle Vanya, Hampstead, 1979; Cinderella and her Naughty Sisters, Lyric, Hammersmith, 1980; A Handful of Dust, Lyric, Hammersmith, 1982; Tartuffe, Maydays, RSC, 1985; Kafka's Dick, Royal Court, 1986; Cat on a Hot Tin Roof, NT, 1988; The Rise and Fall of Little Voice, Aldwych (Olivier Best Actress Award), 1992; Marvin's Room, Hampstead, transf. Comedy, 1993; When We Are Married, Chichester, transf. Savoy, 1996; The Provok'd Wife, Old Vic, 1997; The Memory of Water, Vaudeville, 1999; Entertaining Mr Sloane, Arts, 2001; The Woman Who Cooked Her Husband, New Ambassadors, 2002; Losing Louis, Hampstead, transf. Trafalgar Studios, Whitehall, 2005, nat. tour, 2006; Enjoy, Th. Royal, Bath, 2008, transf. Gielgud, 2009; Blithe Spirit, Th Royal, Bath, transf. Apollo, 2011; Here, Rose Th., Kingston, 2012; Thérèse Raquin, Th. Royal, Bath, 2014; *television* includes: Nuts in May, 1976; Through the Night, 1976; Abigail's Party, 1977; Our Flesh and Blood, 1978; Pasmore, 1980; P'tang Yang Kipperbang, 1982; The Singing Detective, 1986; Virtuoso, 1989; A Small Mourning, 1989; News Hounds, Gone to the Dogs, 1990; Gone to Seed, 1991; Selling Hitler, 1992; Pride and Prejudice, 1995; Wimbledon Poisoner, 1995; Karaoke, 1996; No Bananas, 1996; The Missing Postman, 1997; Let Them Eat Cake, 1999; Fat Friends, 2000, 2002, 2004, 2005; Adrian Mole: The Cappuccino Years, 2001; The Worst Week of my Life, 2004; The

Worst Christmas of My Life, 2006; The Last Detective, 2006; The Dinner Party, 2007; Fanny Hill, 2007; Gavin and Stacey, 2007–09; King of the Teds, 2012; Civil Arrangement, 2012; The Syndicate, 2013; Love and Marriage, 2013; Alison Steadman's Shetland, 2014; Boomers, 2014–16; The Secrets, 2014; Orphan Black, 2015–16; Broken Biscuits, 2016 (Best Perf. in Comedy, RTS NW); Little British Isles, 2016; Hold the Sunset, 2018, 2019; Butterfly, 2018; Care, 2018; *radio includes*: Beyond Black, 2010; Clarissa, 2010; A Tale of Two Cities, 2012; Bird Island, 2012; Gloomsbury, 2012, 2014, 2017, 2018; Wysinnwyg, 2015; The Break, 2016, 2018; Blood, Sex and Money by Emile Zola, 2016; Woof, 2017; Relativity, 2017, 2019; Sick, 2019; *films include*: Champions, 1983; A Private Function, 1984; Number One, 1985; Clockwise, 1986; The Adventures of Baron Münchhausen, Shirley Valentine, Wilt, 1989; Life is Sweet, Blame it on the Bellboy, 1991; Topsy-Turvy, 1999; DIY Hard, 2002; Chunky Monkey, The Life and Death of Peter Sellers, 2004; Peterman, 2014; Burn Burn Burn, 2015; Dad's Army, 2016. Hon. MA Univ. of East London, 1996; DU Essex, 2003. BIFA Richard Harris Award, 2016. *Address*: c/o ARG, 4A Exmoor Street, W10 6BD.

**STEADMAN, Dr John Hubert;** consultant in regulatory and environmental toxicology and environmental health, 1996–2013; *b* 10 Aug. 1938; *s* of late Dr Harry Hubert Steadman and Janet Gilchrist Steadman (*née* MacDonald); *m* 1972, Dr Anthea Howell; one *s* one *d*. *Educ*: Wimbledon Coll.; Guy's Hosp. (MB, BS); University Coll. London (MSc). University College Hospital, London: Beit Meml Fellowship, 1968–72; Sen. Registrar, Dept of Haematology, 1972–78, with secondments to Ahmadu Bello Univ. Hosp., Nigeria, 1973, and Royal Perth Hosp., WA, 1974; Cons. Haematologist, King George Hosp., Ilford, 1978–81; MO 1981, SMO 1982, PMO 1984, DHSS; SPMO, Head of Div. of Toxicology and Envmtl Health, subseq. Health Aspects of Envmt and Food, DoH, 1988–93; Hd of Consumer and Envmtl Safety, Unilever, 1993–96. Expert Advr on food safety, WHO, 1988–93. *Publications*: articles in learned jls on regulatory toxicology, haematology and biochemistry. *Recreations*: cooking, languages, cosmology. *Address*: 38 Kingswood Avenue, NW6 6LS.
See also J. M. M. Curtis-Raleigh.

**STEADMAN, Ven. Mark John;** Archdeacon of Stow and Lindsey, since 2015; *b* 20 May 1974; *s* of John Edward Steadman and Gloria Ann Steadman (*née* Williams). *Educ*: Southampton Univ. (LLB 1995); Westcott House, Cambridge; Christ's Coll., Cambridge (MA 2005). Called to the Bar, Inner Temple, 1996; ordained deacon, 2002, priest, 2003; Curate, St Mary's, Portsea, 2002–05; Priest-in-charge, St Philip's, Camberwell, 2005–12; Area Dean, Bermondsey, 2008–11; Chaplain to the Bishop of Southwark, 2011–15. *Recreations*: opera, travel, cooking. *Address*: Edward King House, Minster Yard, Lincoln LN2 1PU. *T*: (01522) 504050.

**STEADMAN, Ralph Idris;** freelance cartoonist, artist and writer; *b* 15 May 1936; *s* of Lionel Raphael Steadman (English), and Gwendoline (Welsh); *m* 1st, 1959, Sheila Thwaite (marr. diss. 1971); two *s* two *d*; 2nd, 1972, Anna Deverson; one *d*. *Educ*: Abergele Grammar Sch.; London Coll. of Printing and Graphic Arts. Apprentice, de Havilland Aircraft Co., 1952; Cartoonist, Kemsley (Thomson) Newspapers, 1956–59; freelance for Punch, Private Eye, Telegraph, during 1960s; Political Cartoonist, New Statesman, 1978–80; retired to work on book about Leonardo da Vinci; as a positive political statement, refuses to draw another politician; 15 Save the Children originals auctioned in aid of Ethiopia Fund, 1990. Retrospective exhibitions: Nat. Theatre, 1977; Royal Festival Hall, 1984; Cartoon Mus., 2013; exhibitions: Wilhelm Busch Mus., Hannover, 1988; October Gall. (sculptures and silk screen prints), 1990, Gulf war collages, 1991; Peacock Gall., Aberdeen, 1993; Aberdeen City Art Gall., 1994; The Lord is an Animal, One on One Gall., Denver, USA, 1997; Contemporary Satirists, RA, 1997; Les Sixties, Les Invalides, Paris, transf. Brighton, 1997; centenary Lewis Carroll exhibn, Warrington Mus., 1998; Making a Mark, William Havu Gall., Denver, 2000; Who? Me! No!! Why?? (pictures and artefacts from book Doodaaa), NY, 2003. Designed set of stamps of Halley's Comet, 1986; opera libretto and concept, Plague and the Moonflower, Exeter Cathedral and Festival, 1989 (artist-in-residence), St Paul's Cathedral, 1989, Canterbury Cathedral and Festival, 1990, performed as Hearts Betrayed, St Martin-in-the-Fields, 1993, televised 1995, recorded 1999; libretto and concept, Love Underground, Norwich Fest., 1997; artist-in-residence, Cheltenham Fest., 1994; designer, Gulliver's Travels, Theatr Clwyd, 1995; artist-in-residence, Leviathan series of films, BBC2, 1999; designer of set and costumes, The Crucible, Royal Ballet, 2000. Writer, dir and performer, TV film, Hanging Garden Centres of Kent, 1992; artist, film, For No Good Reason, 2014. Hon. Fellow, Kent Inst. of Art and Design, 1993. Hon. DLitt Kent, 1995. D & AD Gold Award (for outstanding contribution to illustration), 1977, and Silver Award (for outstanding editorial illustration), 1977; Black Humour Award, France, 1986; W. H. Smith Illustration Award for best illustrated book for last five years, 1987; BBC Design Award for postage stamps, 1987; Empire Award (for involvement with film Withnail and I), Empire Magazine, 1996; Milton Caniff Award, Nat. Cartoonists Soc. of America, 2005; Star of Saatchi and Saatchi Clio Creative Hero Show, 2008. *Publications*: Jelly Book, 1968; Still Life with Raspberry: collected drawings, 1969; The Little Red Computer, 1970; Dogs Bodies, 1971; Bumper to Bumper Book, 1973; Two Donkeys and the Bridge, 1974; Flowers for the Moon, 1974; America: drawings, 1975; America: collected drawings, 1977 (rev. edn, Scar Strangled Banger, 1987); Between the Eyes, 1984; Paranoids, 1986; The Grapes of Ralph, 1992; Teddy! Where are you?, 1994; Untrodden Grapes, 2005; The Joke's Over: memories of Hunter S. Thompson, 2006; *written and illustrated*: Sigmund Freud, 1979 (as The Penguin Sigmund Freud, 1982); A Leg in the Wind and other Canine Curses, 1982; I, Leonardo, 1983; That's My Dad, 1986 (Critici in Erba Prize, 1987); The Big I Am, 1988; No Room to Swing a Cat, 1989; Near the Bone, 1990; Tales of the Weirrd, 1990; Still Life with Bottle, Whisky According to Ralph Steadman, 1994; Jones of Colorado, 1995; Gonzo: the art, 1998; little.com, 2000; Garibaldi's Biscuits, 2008; designed and printed, Steam Press Broadsheets; Proud Too Be Weirrd, 2013; *illustrated*: Frank Dickens, Fly Away Peter, 1961, 2008; Mischa Damjan: The Big Squirrel and the Little Rhinoceros, 1962; The False Flamingoes, 1963; The Little Prince and the Tiger Cat, 1964; Two Cats in America, 1968; Richard Ingrams, The Tale of Driver Grope, 1964; Love and Marriage, 1964; Daisy Ashford, Where Love Lies Deepest, 1964; Fiona Saint, The Yellow Flowers, 1965; Alice in Wonderland, 1967; Midnight, 1967; Tariq Ali, The Thoughts of Chairman Harold, 1968; Dr Hunter S. Thompson: Fear and Loathing in Las Vegas, 1972, 25th anniv. edn, 1997; The Curse of Lono, 1984, 2nd (limited) edn 2004; Kurt Baumann, The Watchdog and the Lazy Dog, 1974; Contemporary Poets set to Music series, 1972; Through the Looking Glass, 1972; Night Edge: poems, 1973; The Poor Mouth, 1973; John Letts Limericks, 1974; The Hunting of the Snark, 1975; Dmitri Sidjanski, Cherrywood Cannon, 1978; Bernard Stone: Emergency Mouse, 1978; Inspector Mouse, 1980; Quasimodo Mouse, 1984; Ted Hughes, The Threshold (limited edn), 1979; Adrian Mitchell, For Beauty Douglas, 1982; Flann O'Brien, More of Myles, 1982; Wolf Mankowitz, The Devil in Texas, 1984; Treasure Island, 1985; The Complete Alice and The Hunting of the Snark, 1986; Friendship (short stories), 1990 (in aid of John McCarthy); Animal Farm, 50th anniv. edn, 1995; Adrian Mitchell, Heart on the Left, Poems 1953–1984, 1997; Roald Dahl, The Mildenhall Treasure, 1999; Doodaaa: the balletic art of Gavin Twinge (novel), 2002; Ambrose Bierce, The Devil's Dictionary, 2003; Fahrenheit 451, 50th anniv. limited edn, 2003; Hunter S. Thompson, Fire in the Nuts, 2004; Will Self, PsychoGeography, 2007; Will Self, Psycho Too, 2009; Ralph Steadman's Extinct Boids, 2012; Nextinction, 2015; Critical Critters, 2017. *Recreations*: gardening (planted vineyard), collecting, writing, sheep husbandry, fishing, guitar, trumpet. *W*: www.ralphsteadman.com. *Club*: Chelsea Arts.

**STEAR, Air Chief Marshal Sir Michael (James Douglas),** KCB 1990; CBE 1982; QCVSA 1969; DL; Deputy Commander-in-Chief, Allied Forces Central Europe, 1992–96; *b* 11 Oct. 1938; *s* of late Melbourne Douglas Stear and Barbara Jane Stear (*née* Fletcher); *m* 1966, Elizabeth Jane (*d* 2015), *d* of late Donald Edward Macrae, FRCS and Janet Wallace Macpherson Macrae (*née* Simpson); two *s* one *d*. *Educ*: Monkton Combe Sch.; Emmanuel Coll., Cambridge (MA; CU Air Sqn (RAFVR), 1959–62). Nat. Service, RAF, 1957–59. Joined RAF, 1962; served on 1 Sqn, Hunters, 1964–67, on 208 Sqn, Hunters, Persian Gulf, 1967–69; exchange tour with USAF, F4 Phantom, 1969–71; RAF Staff Coll., 1972; Air Sec.'s Br., MoD, 1972–74; OC 17 Sqn, Phantom, Germany, 1974–76; OC 56 Sqn, Phantom, RAF Wattisham, 1976; PSO to CAS, MoD, 1976–79; OC RAF Gutersloh and Harrier Force Comdr, RAF Germany, 1980–82; Asst C of S (Ops), HQ 2 ATAF, 1982; Air Cdre Plans, HQ Strike Command, 1982–85; AOC No 11 Gp, UK Air Defence, 1985–87; ACDS (Nato/UK), MoD, 1987–89; AOC No 18 Gp, Maritime, and Comdr Maritime Air Eastern Atlantic and Channel, 1989–92. Mem., Commonwealth War Graves Commn, 1998–2003. Member: RUSI, 1989–99; Council, Malcolm Clubs, 1988–2003; RFU Cttee, 1987–98 (Mgt Bd Jt Vice-Chm. (admin), 1997–98); Air League, 1999–; Pres., RAF RU, 1992–97 (Chm., 1983–86). Nat. Pres., RAFA, 1998–2002 (Vice-Pres., 1997–98; Life Vice-Pres., 2002–; Service Vice-Pres., Europe Area, 1992–96); Pres., RAF and Allied Air Forces Monument Service Cttee, 2010–; Hon. Pres., Devon & Som Wing, ATC, 2000–11. Pres., Exeter and District Br. Cttee, ESU, 2013– (Mem., 2009–; Progs Sec., 2009–12; Vice Chm., 2010–12; Chm., 2012–13). FRAeS 1997–2011. DL Devon, 2000. *Recreations*: Rugby football, gardening, fishing, shooting, music – jazz to grand opera, history – ancient and modern. *Club*: Royal Air Force (Vice-Pres., 1990–98).

**STEAR, Roderick Morton, (Rory);** Executive Chairman, Flambard Capital Ltd, since 2007; non-executive Chairman, Lifeline Energy Ltd, since 2011; Chief Executive, Blackwood Power, since 2014; *b* 17 March 1959; *s* of Robert and Natalie Stear; *m* 1995, Kristine Joy Pearson. *Educ*: Grey High Sch., Port Elizabeth, SA; Rhodes Univ., SA; Sloan Sch. of Mgt, Mass Inst. of Technol. Founder and Man. Dir, Seeff Corporate Finance, 1990–94; Founder and Exec. Chm., Freeplay Energy Gp, 1994–2008; Exec. Chm., MobileWave Gp (formerly Fieldbury) plc, 1995–2013. Chm., Minlam Asset Mgt LLP, 2009–11. Member, President Nelson Mandela's business delegation: to UK, 1996; to USA, 1998. Student, Birthing of Grants prog., MIT, 2000. Member: Dean's Council, John F. Kennedy Sch. of Govt, Harvard Univ., 2005–14; Adv. Bd, Business Sch., Nelson Mandela Univ., Port Elizabeth, SA, 2005– (Chm., 2005–); Adv. Bd, Melton Foundn, 2014–. Dep. Chm., Isuzu Southern Kings, 2019–. Mem., African Business Roundtable, 1995. Member: Global Agenda Council on Renewable Energies, World Economic Forum, 2008–11; Pres. of S Africa's Business Delegn to UK and to India, 2010. Founder, Lifeline Energy (formerly Freeplay Foundn), 1998. CNN Principal Voice, 2007; Hero of the Envmt, Time, 2007. *Recreations*: golf, gym, music, reading. *Address*: Flambard Capital Ltd, Suite 153, 8 Shepherd Market, W1J 7JY. *E*: rory@flambardcapital.com. *Clubs*: Royal Automobile; Steenberg Golf.

**STEARNS, Elizabeth Jane Elford,** FFFLM; HM Coroner, Eastern District, Greater London, 1998–2011; *b* 20 Nov. 1946; *d* of Cecil Smith and Audrey Quelch; *m* 1972, Michael Patrick Stearns; three *s*. *Educ*: Wycombe Abbey Sch.; Guy's Hosp. Dental and Med. Schs, London (BDS Hons, LDS RCS 1970; MB BS 1974). FFFLM 2006. Assistant Deputy Coroner: City of London, 1993; N London, 1994–95; Dep. Coroner, N London, 1995–98. Called to the Bar, 1997. Examr for Dips in Forensic Med. Scis. Pres., SE Coroners' Soc., 2005–06; Vice-Pres., Faculty of Forensic and Legal Medicine, RCP, 2006–10.

**STEBBING, Nowell,** PhD; Chairman, Pharmagene plc (formerly Pharmagene Laboratories Ltd), 1996–2003; *b* 5 Sept. 1941; *s* of Lionel Charles Stebbing and Margarita (*née* Behrenz); *m* 1st, 1963, Nancy Lynah (marr. diss.); two *d* (one *s* decd); 2nd, 1973, Birgit Griffiths (*née* Evjen); one *s*. *Educ*: Michael Hall Sch., Sussex; Univ. of Edinburgh (BSc Hons 1964; PhD 1968). Demonstrator, Univ. of Edinburgh, 1967–69; Director of Biology: G. D. Searle & Co., 1969–79; Genentech Inc., San Francisco, 1979–82; Vice-Pres., Scientific Affairs, Amgen Inc., Thousand Oaks, Calif, 1982–86; Gen. Manager, Res., ICI Pharmaceuticals, UK, 1986–93; Chief Exec. and Dep. Chm., Chiroscience Gp PLC, 1993–95. Chm., Axis Genetics, 1995–99. *Publications*: numerous papers and articles in scientific and med. jls and books. *Recreations*: theatre, old cars, gardens, wine making in Italy.

**STEDMAN JONES, Prof. Gareth,** DPhil; FBA 2013; Professor of the History of Ideas, Queen Mary University of London, since 2010; Co-Director, Centre for History and Economics, Cambridge, since 1991; Fellow of King's College, Cambridge, since 1974; *b* 17 Dec. 1942; *s* of Lewis and Joan Olive Stedman Jones; one *s* by Prof. Sally Alexander; one *s* by Prof. Miri Rubin. *Educ*: St Paul's Sch.; Lincoln Coll., Oxford (BA 1964); Nuffield Coll., Oxford (DPhil 1970). Res. Fellow, Nuffield Coll., Oxford, 1967–70; Sen. Associate Mem., St Antony's Coll., Oxford, 1971–72; Humboldt Stiftung Fellow, Dept of Philosophy, Goethe Univ., Frankfurt, 1973–74; University of Cambridge: Lectr in History, 1979–86; Reader in History of Social Thought, 1986–97; Prof. of Political Thought (formerly Political Sci.), 1997–2010. Mem., CNRS, 2005–10. Mem., Editl Bd, New Left Review, 1964–81; Jt Founder and Jt Ed., History Workshop Jl, 1976–. *Publications*: Outcast London, 1971, 3rd edn 2013; Languages of Class, 1983; Klassen, Politik, Sprache, 1988; (ed) Charles Fourier, The Theory of the Four Movements, trans. I. Patterson, 1994; (ed) Karl Marx and Friedrich Engels, The Communist Manifesto, 2002 (trans. German 2013); An End to Poverty?, 2004 (trans. French 2007); Columbia, 2005; (ed) Religion and the Political Imagination, 2010; (ed jtly) Cambridge History of Nineteenth-Century Political Thought, 2011; Karl Marx: greatness and illusion, 2016 (trans. German, Dutch and Portuguese 2017; Spanish, Brazilian Portuguese and Korean 2018); (ed jtly) The 1848 Revolutions and European Political Thought, 2018. *Recreations*: country walks, collecting old books, cricket. *Address*: King's College, Cambridge CB2 1ST. *T*: (01223) 331120.

**STEDMAN-SCOTT, Baroness** *cr* 2010 (Life Peer), of Rolvenden in the County of Kent; **Deborah Stedman-Scott,** OBE 2008; DL; Parliamentary Under-Secretary of State, Department for Work and Pensions, since 2019; *b* Paddington, London, 23 Nov. 1955; *d* of Jack and Doreen Margaret Scott; civil partnership 2006, Gabrielle Joy Stedman-Scott. *Educ*: Ensham Secondary Sch. for Girls; Southwark Tech. Coll.; Salvation Army Trng Coll. Nat. Westminster Bank, 1972–76; The Salvation Army, 1978–83; Royal Tunbridge Wells Chamber of Commerce, 1983–84; Tomorrow's People Trust: Develt Manager, Hastings, 1984–86; Manager, Kent and Sussex Area, 1986–88, SE Region, 1988–93; Nat. Ops Dir, 1993–95; Trust Dir, 1995–2005; Chief Exec., 2005–15. A Baroness in Waiting (Govt Whip), 2017–19. DL E Sussex, 2007. Charity Principal of the Year, UK Charity Awards, 2005. *Recreations*: reading, art – particularly Lowry, travelling, opera. *Address*: House of Lords, SW1A 0PW. *T*: (020) 7219 8919. *E*: stedmanscottd@parliament.uk.

**STEEDEN, Dr Michael Frank,** FRAeS; Corporate Adviser, Defence Science and Technology Laboratory, 2012–14; *b* London, 23 March 1952; *s* of Frank and late Joyce Steeden; *m* 1975, Hilary Bridget Alison Ambrose; one *s* one *d*. *Educ*: Judd Sch., Tonbridge;

Kent; King's Coll. London (BSc Hons Physics; PhD Nuclear Structure Physics 1981); Open Univ. (MBA). CDipAF 1996. FInstP 1995–2012; FRAeS 1995. PSO, AWRE, 1983–87; Hd, Atomic Co-ordinating Office, UK Embassy, Washington, 1987–89; Asst Dir, Guided Weapons Air, 1989–91, Dir, Mil. Aircraft Procurement, 1991–94, MoD Procurement Exec.; rcds 1995; Dir, Air Systems Sector, 1996–98, Aircraft Test and Evaluation, 1998–2000, DERA; Pres. and Man. Dir, Computing Devices Co. Ltd, 2000–02; Dir, Civil Air Transport, Soc. of British Aerospace Cos, 2002–06; Tech. Dir, 2006–09, Dir, Strategic Relns, 2009–12, Defence Sci. and Technol. Lab. Non-executive Director: Ploughshare Innovations Ltd, 2007–; Tetricus Ltd, 2007–10. Pres., RAeS, 2009–10 (Chm., Medals and Awards Cttee, 2011–17). FInstD 2008–13. Liveryman, Engrs' Co., 2005–12. *Publications*: contribs to Jl Physics G, World Defence Systems. *Recreations*: grandchildren Colette, Benedict, Gus, Emmeline and Louis, guitar and harmonica, family history, modern jive and Argentinian tango.

**STEEDMAN, Prof. Carolyn Kay**, PhD; FBA 2011; Professor of History, University of Warwick, 1999–2013, now Emeritus; *b* 20 March 1947. *Educ*: Rosa Bassett Grammar Sch. for Girls, London; Univ. of Sussex (BA Hons English and Amer. Studies 1968); Newnham Coll., Cambridge (MLitt 1974; PhD 1989). Teacher, E Sussex and Warwicks, 1974–81; Institute of Education, University of London: project asst to Lang. in the Multicultural Primary Classroom Project, 1982–83; Fellow, Sociol. Dept, 1983–84; University of Warwick: Lectr, 1984–88, Sen. Lectr, 1988–91, Reader, 1991–93, Dept of Arts Educn; Reader, 1993–95, Prof. of Social Hist., 1995–98, Dir, 1998–99, Centre for Study of Social Hist. ESRC Res. Prof., 2004–07. Vis. Prof., Univ. of Michigan, Ann Arbor, 1992. Sen. Simon Res. Fellow, Univ. of Manchester, 1990–91. *Publications*: The Tidy House, 1982 (Fawcett Soc. Book Prize, 1983); Policing the Victorian Community, 1984; (ed jtly) Language, Gender and Childhood, 1984; Landscape for a Good Woman, 1986; The Radical Soldier's Tale: John Pearman, 1819–1908, 1988; Childhood, Culture and Class in Britain: Margaret McMillan, 1860–1931, 1990; Past Tenses: essays on writing, history and autobiography, 1980–1990, 1992; Strange Dislocations: childhood and the idea of human interiority, 1780–1930, 1995; Dust, 2001; Master and Servant: love and labour in the English industrial age, 2007; Labours Lost: domestic service and the making of modern England, 2009; An Everyday Life of the English Working Class: work self, and sociability in the early nineteenth century, 2013; Poetry for Historians: or, W. H. Auden and history, 2018. *Address*: Department of History, University of Warwick, Humanities Building, University Road, Coventry CV4 7AL.

**STEEDMAN, Deborah Jane**; *see* Keith, Hon. D. J.

**STEEDMAN, Prof. Mark**, PhD; FRSE; FBA 2002; Professor of Cognitive Science, University of Edinburgh, since 1998; *b* 18 Sept. 1946; *s* of George and Nan Steedman; *m* 1987, Prof. Bonnie Lynn Webber. *Educ*: Univ. of Sussex (BSc); Univ. of Edinburgh (PhD 1973). Res. Fellow, Univ. of Sussex, 1973–76; Lectr in Psychology, Univ. of Warwick, 1976–83; Lectr, 1983–86, Reader, 1986–88, in Computational Linguistics, Univ. of Edinburgh; Associate Prof. of Computer and Inf. Sci., 1988–92, Prof., 1992–98, Adjunct Prof., 1998–, Univ. of Pennsylvania. FAAAI 1993; FRSE 2002; MAE 2006; Fellow, Assoc. of Computational Linguistics, 2012. *Publications*: Surface Structure and Interpretation, 1996; The Syntactic Process, 2000; Taking Scope, 2012; articles in Linguistics & Philosophy, Cognition, Cognitive Science, Linguistic Inquiry, Computational Linguistics, etc. *Recreations*: jazz, hill-climbing. *Address*: School of Informatics, University of Edinburgh, 10 Crichton Street, Edinburgh EH8 9AB. *T*: (0131) 650 4631, *Fax*: (0131) 650 6626.

**STEEDMAN, Dr Robert Russell**, OBE 1997; RSA 1979 (ARSA 1973); RIBA; FRIAS; MLI; Partner, Morris and Steedman, Architects and Landscape Architects, Edinburgh, 1959–2002; *b* 3 Jan. 1929; *s* of late Robert Smith Steedman and Helen Hope Brazier; *m* 1st, 1956, Susan Elizabeth (marr. diss. 1974), *d* of Sir Robert Scott, GCMG, CBE; one *s* two *d*; 2nd, 1977, Martha Hamilton, OBE (*d* 2015). *Educ*: Loretto Sch.; School of Architecture, Edinburgh College of Art (DA); Univ. of Pennsylvania (MLA). RIBA 1955; ALI 1979. Lieut, RWAFF, 1947–48. Worked in office, Alfred Roth, Zürich, 1953. Architectural works include: Principal's House, Univ. of Stirling; Head Offices for Christian Salvesen, Edinburgh; Administration Building for Shell UK Exploration and Production; Moss Morran Fife; Restoration of Old Waterworks, Perth, to form Tourist Information Centre and Offices; Nat. Lighthouse Mus., Fraserburgh. Ten Civic Trust Awards, 1963–88; British Steel Award, 1971; Saltire Award, 1971, 1999; RIBA Award for Scotland, 1974 and 1989; European Architectural Heritage Medal, 1975; Assoc. for Preservation of Rural Scotland Award, 1977 and 1989. Chm., Central Scotland Woodlands Project, 1984–87; Member: Countryside Commn for Scotland, 1980–88; Adv. Panel on Management of Popular Mountain Areas in Scotland, 1989; Royal Fine Art Commn for Scotland, 1984–96 (Dep. Chm., 1994–96); Council, Nat. Trust for Scotland, 1999–2005; Sec., Royal Scottish Acad., 1983–90 (Mem. Council 1981–, Dep. Pres. 1982–83, 2000–01); Mem. Bd, Friends of Royal Scottish Acad., 1984–92; Governor, Edinburgh College of Art, 1974–88; Mem., Edinburgh Festival Soc., 1978–; past Mem. Council, RIAS and Soc. of Scottish Artists. Trustee: House of Falkland, 1999–; St Andrews Preservation Trust, 2002–10 (Hon. Pres., 2014–); Royal Scottish Acad. Foundn, 2012–. Member Panel: Saltire Patrick Geddes Award, 1995–; Assoc. for Protection of Rural Scotland Annual Awards, 1995–99. Hon. Senior, St Leonards Sch., 1987–. FRSA 1995. Hon. DLitt St Andrews, 2006; DUniv Stirling, 2011. Gold Medal for Lifetime Achievement in Architecture, RIAS, 2009; Architecture Lifetime Achievement Award, Scottish Design Awards, 2009. *Recreations*: hill-walking, photography, redesigning other people's houses. *Address*: Muir of Blebo, Blebocraigs, by Cupar, Fife KY15 5UG. *T*: (01334) 850781. *Clubs*: New (Edinburgh); Royal & Ancient Golf (St Andrews).
*See also* R. S. Steedman.

**STEEDMAN, (Robert) Scott**, CBE 2010; PhD; FREng; Director of Standards, British Standards Institution, since 2012; *b* Edinburgh, 10 Sept. 1958; *s* of Dr Robert Russell Steedman, *qv*; *m* 1st, 1981, Zoreh Kazemzadeh (marr. diss. 2002); one *s* one *d*; 2nd, 2005, Hon. Deborah Jane Keith, *qv*. *Educ*: Edinburgh Acad.; Univ. of Manchester Inst. of Sci. and Technol. (BSc 1980); Queens' Coll., Cambridge (MPhil 1983); St Catharine's College, Cambridge (PhD 1985). CEng 1989; FICE 1994; FREng 2001; FInstRE 2009. University of Cambridge: Fellow, St Catharine's Coll., 1983–93; Lectr, Dept of Engrg, 1983–90; Director: Gibb Ltd, 1993–2000; Whitbybird & Partners Ltd, 2000–03; ind. consultant, 2003–06; Director: Strategy, High-Point Rendel Ltd, 2006–09; Engrg, Foster Wheeler Energy, 2009–10; BRE Global Ltd, 2010–11. Non-exec. Dir, Port of London Authy, 2009–15. Ind. Mem., Defence Scientific Adv. Council, 2005–11. Vice President: Royal Acad. of Engrg, 2003–09; ICE, 2005–09; CEN, 2013–17; ISO, 2017–. *Recreations*: family, North-West Scotland, Bhutan, ski-ing, sailing. *Address*: 42 Hillgate Place, W8 7ST. *T*: (020) 7727 9663. *Club*: New (Edinburgh).
*See also* Hon. H. G. Keith.

**STEEDS, Prof. John Wickham**, FRS 1988; FInstP; Professor of Physics, 1985–2008, now Emeritus, Henry Overton Wills Professor, 2002–06, and Leverhulme Emeritus Research Fellow, 2008–11, Bristol University; *b* 9 Feb. 1940; *s* of John Henry William Steeds and Ethel Amelia Tyler; *m* 1969, Diana Mary Kettlewell; two *d*. *Educ*: University College London (BSc 1961); PhD Cantab 1965. FInstP 1991. Research Fellow, Selwyn Coll., Cambridge, 1964–67; IBM Res. Fellow, 1966–67; Fellow, Selwyn Coll., Cambridge, 1967; Bristol University: Lectr in Physics, 1967–77; Reader, 1977–85; Hd of Microstructural Gp, 1985–2001; Dir, Interface Analysis Centre, 1990–2001; Hd of Physics Dept, 2001–05. Visiting Professor: Univ. of Santiago, Chile, 1971; Univ. of California, Berkeley, 1981. Chairman: Science Res. Foundn, Emersons Green, 1989–99; Commn on Electron Diffraction, Internat. Union of Crystallography, 1993–99; Emersons Innovations Ltd, 1999–2006; Mem., Council, European Pole Univ., Lille, 1993–97. Pres., W of England Metals and Materials Assoc., 2003–04. Patient Gov., Univ. Hosps Bristol Foundn Trust, 2010–16 (Lead Gov., 2010–11). Holweck Medal and Prize, French Physical Soc., 1996; Gjønnes Medal, Internat. Union of Crystallography, 2014. *Publications*: Introduction to Anisotropic Elasticity Theory of Dislocations, 1973; (with J. F. Mansfield) Electron Diffraction of Phases in Alloys, 1984; (ed jtly) Thin Film Diamond, 1994; papers on electron diffraction, materials science and solid state physics. *Recreations*: tennis, overseas travel. *Address*: Hall Floor Flat 4, Codrington Place, Clifton, Bristol BS8 3DE. *T*: (0117) 973 2183.

**STEEL**, family name of **Baron Steel of Aikwood**.

**STEEL OF AIKWOOD**, Baron *cr* 1997 (Life Peer), of Ettrick Forest in the Scottish Borders; **David Martin Scott Steel**, KT 2004; KBE 1990; PC 1977; DL; journalist and broadcaster; Member (Lib Dem) Lothians, and Presiding Officer, Scottish Parliament, 1999–2003; Lord High Commissioner, General Assembly, Church of Scotland, 2003 and 2004; *b* Scotland, 31 March 1938; *s* of late Very Rev. Dr David Steel; *m* 1962, Judith Mary, *d* of W. D. MacGregor, CBE, Dunblane; two *s* one *d*. *Educ*: Prince of Wales School, Nairobi, Kenya; George Watson's Coll.; Edinburgh Univ. (MA 1960; LLB 1962). President: Edinburgh University Liberals, 1959; Students' Representative Council, 1960. Asst Secretary, Scottish Liberal Party, 1962–64. MP (L 1965–88, Lib Dem 1988–97) Roxburgh, Selkirk and Peebles, 1965–83, Tweeddale, Ettrick and Lauderdale, 1983–97; youngest member of 1964–66 Parliament. Liberal Chief Whip, 1970–75; Mem. Parly Delegn to UN Gen. Assembly, 1967; Sponsor, Private Member's Bill to reform law on abortion, 1966–67. Pres., Africa All Party Parly Gp, 2011–. Leader of Liberal Party, 1976–88; Co-Founder, Social and Liberal Democrats, 1988. Pres., Liberal International, 1994–96. President: Anti-Apartheid Movement of GB, 1966–70; Med. Aid for Palestinians, 1996–2004; Scottish Castles Assoc., 2002–10; Chairman: Shelter, Scotland, 1969–73; Countryside Movement, 1995–96; Patron, Prostate Cancer Scotland (formerly Scottish Assoc. of Prostate Cancer Support Gps), 2002–. Mem., British Council of Churches, 1971–75. Chubb Fellow, Yale Univ., 1987; Vis. Fellow, St Antony's Coll., Oxford, 2013. BBC television interviewer in Scotland, 1964–65; Presenter of STV weekly religious programme, 1966–67, and for Granada, 1969, and BBC, 1971–76. Pres., Jaguar Drivers' Club, 2007–. Rector, Edinburgh Univ., 1982–85. DL Roxburgh, Ettrick and Lauderdale, 1990–2013. Awarded Freedom of Tweeddale, 1988, of Ettrick and Lauderdale, 1990. Hon. FRCOG 2013; Hon. FRZSScot 2016. DUniv: Stirling, 1991; Heriot-Watt, 1996; Open, 2001; Hon. DLitt Buckingham; Hon. LLD: Edinburgh, 1997; Strathclyde, 2000; Aberdeen, 2001; St Andrews, 2003; Glasgow Caledonian, 2004; Brunel, 2010. Kt, Habsburg-Lothringen Order of St George, 2016. Commander's Cross, Order of Merit (Germany), 1992; Chevalier, Légion d'Honneur (France), 2003; Order of Brilliant Star (Taiwan), 2004. *Publications*: Boost for the Borders, 1964; Out of Control, 1968; No Entry, 1969; The Liberal Way Forward, 1975; A New Political Agenda, 1976; Militant for the Reasonable Man, 1977; New Majority for a New Parliament, 1978; High Ground of Politics, 1979; A House Divided, 1980; (with Judy Steel) Border Country, 1985; (presenter) Partners in One Nation: a new vision of Britain 2000, 1985; (with Judy Steel) Mary Stuart's Scotland, 1987; Against Goliath: David Steel's autobiography, 1989; contrib. to The Times, The Guardian, The Scotsman, other newspapers and political weeklies. *Recreations*: angling, classic car rallying (bronze medallion in London - Cape Town, 1998). *Address*: House of Lords, SW1A 0PW; Ettrick Lodge, Selkirk TD7 4LE. *Clubs*: National Liberal, Royal Over-Seas League.
*See also* C. M. Steel.

**STEEL, Dame (Anne) Heather, (Dame Heather Beattie)**, DBE 1993; a Judge of the High Court of Justice, Queen's Bench Division, 1993–2001; Judge of the Courts of Appeal of Jersey and Guernsey, 2004–12; *b* 3 July 1940; *d* of late His Honour Edward Steel and Mary Evelyn Griffith Steel; *m* 1967, David Kerr-Muir Beattie; one *s* one *d*. *Educ*: Howell's School, Denbigh; Liverpool University (LLB). Called to the Bar, Gray's Inn, 1963, Bencher, 1993; practice on N Circuit; Prosecuting Counsel to DHSS on N Circuit, 1984–86; a Recorder, 1984–86; a Circuit Judge, 1986–93. Mem., Criminal Cttee, Judicial Studies Bd, 1992–95. President: Merseyside Medico Legal Soc., 1992–94; Law Faculty Assoc., Liverpool Univ., 1994–. Member: Council, Rossall Sch., 1990–2002; Adv. Council, Soc. for Advanced Legal Studies, 2001–. Mem., Guild of Freemen, City of London, 1996–. Freeman, City of London, 1993; Liveryman: Pattenmakers' Co., 1993 (Master, 2003–04); Fan Makers' Co., 2005. *Recreations*: theatre, gardening, art, antiques.
*See also* E. M. Steel.

**STEEL, Prof. (Christopher) Michael**, PhD, DSc; Professor in Medical Science, University of St Andrews, 1994–2005, now Emeritus; *b* 25 Jan. 1940; *s* of late Very Rev. David Steel; *m* 1962, Dr Judith Margaret Spratt, MBE; two *s* one *d*. *Educ*: Prince of Wales Sch., Nairobi; George Watson's Coll., Edinburgh; Univ. of Edinburgh (BSc Hons, MB, ChB Hons, PhD, DSc). FRCPE; FRCSE (*ad hominem*) 1994; FRCPath; FRSE. Jun. hosp. posts in Edinburgh teaching hosps, 1965–68; Graduate Res. Fellow, Univ. of Edinburgh Faculty of Medicine, 1968–71; Mem. of Clin. Sci. Staff, MRC Human Genetics Unit, Edinburgh, 1971–93 (Asst Dir, 1979–93); MRC Travelling Res. Fellow, Univ. of Nairobi Med. Sch., 1972–73. Hon. Cons., Lothian Health Bd, 1976–. Member: Adv. Cttee, UK Gene Therapy, 1995–2000; MRC Adv. Bd, 2000–05; Bd, Worldwide Cancer Res. (formerly Assoc. for Internat. Cancer Res.), 2003–; Bd, Med. Res. Scotland, 2005–10. Founder FMedSci 1998. *Publications*: (with D. K. Apps and B. B. Cohen) Biochemistry: a concise text for medical students, 1992; papers on molecular biology of cancer in learned jls. *Recreations*: golf, theatre, DIY. *Address*: 89 South Oswald Road, Edinburgh EH9 2HH. *T*: (0131) 281 9049.
*See also* Baron Steel of Aikwood.

**STEEL, Danielle**; *see* Schüelein-Steel, D. F.

**STEEL, Vice Adm. Sir David (George)**, KBE 2015 (CBE 2009); DL; Second Sea Lord and Chief of Naval Personnel, Training and Infrastructure, 2012–15; *b* Walthamstow, 6 April 1961; *s* of late George Malcolm Steel and Doreen Steel. *Educ*: Rossall Sch., Fleetwood; Britannia Royal Naval Coll.; Durham Univ. (BA Hons Law 1983); Inns of Court Sch. of Law. Joined Royal Navy, 1979. Called to the Bar, Middle Temple, 1987, Bencher, 2014; in practice as barrister, 1987–. Comdr (Supply) HMS Invincible, 1998–2000; CSO (Personnel and Logistics) C-in-C Fleet, 2000–02; Sec. to First Sea Lord and Chief of Naval Staff, 2002–05; Naval Base Comdr, Portsmouth, 2005–09; Chief Naval Logistics Officer, 2008–15; Naval Sec. and COS (Personnel), 2010–12. QCVS 1999. Freeman, City of London, 2010. Yr Brother, Trinity House, 2014. DL Hants, 2014. *Recreations*: theatre and opera, history, gardening, cycling and travel. *Club*: Union Jack (Pres. and Chm., 2019–).

**STEEL, Sir David (William)**, Kt 1998; commercial arbitrator and mediator, since 2011; a Judge of the High Court of Justice, Queen's Bench Division, 1998–2011; a Judge of the Commercial Court, 1998–2011 (Judge in charge, 2006–07); Deputy Chief Justice, Court of Dubai International Financial Centre, 2016–18; *b* 7 May 1943; *s* of Sir Lincoln Steel and late Barbara (*née* Goldschmidt); *m* 1970, Charlotte Elizabeth Ramsay; two *s*. *Educ*: Eton Coll.; Keble Coll., Oxford (MA Hons Jurisprudence). Called to the Bar, Inner Temple, 1966, Bencher, 1991; with Coudert Bros (Attorneys), New York, 1967–68; commenced practice in England, 1969; Junior Counsel to the Treasury (Common Law) 1978–81; Junior Counsel to the Treasury (Admiralty), 1978–81; QC 1981; a Recorder, 1991–98; a Dep. High Court Judge, 1993–98, 2011–; Judge, Admiralty Ct, 1998–2011; Presiding Judge, Western Circuit, 2002–06; Justice, Ct of Dubai Internat. Financial Centre, 2011–16. Wreck Commissioner for England and Wales, 1982–98; Mem., panel of Lloyd's Salvage Arbitrators, 1982–98. Chm., Commercial Bar Assoc., 1990–91; Mem., Lord Chancellor's Adv. Cttee on Legal Educn and Conduct, 1994–98. Chm., OUBC Trust Fund Cttee, 1990–93. Mem., Dubai World Tribunal, 2012–. Younger Brother, Trinity House, 2012–. *Publications*: Editor: Temperley: Merchant Shipping Acts, 1976–98; Forms and Precedents: British Shipping Laws, 1977–98; Kennedy: Salvage, 1981–98. *Recreations*: golf, reading, fishing, theatre. *Address*: 10 Fleet Street, EC4Y 1AU. *Club*: Garrick.

**STEEL, Donald MacLennan Arklay**; golf correspondent and golf course architect; *b* 23 Aug. 1937; *s* of William Arklay Steel and Catherine Fanny (*née* Jacobs), internat. golfer; *m* 1988, Rachel Ellen. *Educ*: Fettes Coll.; Christ's Coll., Cambridge (MA). Golf correspondent: Sunday Telegraph, 1961–90; Country Life, 1983–93; golf course architect, 1965–: with C. K. Cotton, Pennink, Lawrie and Partners; with C. K. Cotton, Pennink, Steel & Co.; with Donald Steel & Co. President: British Inst. of Golf Course Architects, 1989–91 (Hon. Sec., 1971–83); Chm., 1983–86); Assoc. of Golf Writers, 1993–98 (Treas., 1977–90); English Golf Union, 2006. *Publications*: (ed jtly) Shell World Encyclopaedia of Golf, 1975; (ed) Guinness Book of Golf Facts and Feats, 1980; Bedside Books of Golf, 1965, 1971; The Classic Links, 1992; (ed) 14 edns, The Golf Course Guide of the British Isles (Sunday Telegraph), 1968–96; (jtly) Traditions and Change: the Royal and Ancient Golf Club 1939–2004, 2004; The Open: golf's oldest Major, 2010; Thin End of the Wedge (autobiog.), 2017; Par Excellence: the biography of Sir Michael Bonallack, OBE, 2018. *Recreations*: cricket, wine. *Address*: 1 March Square, Chichester, West Sussex PO19 5AN. *T*: (01243) 528506. *Clubs*: MCC; Hawks (Cambridge); Royal and Ancient Golf.

**STEEL, Her Honour Elizabeth Mary, (Mrs Stuart Christie)**; DL; a Circuit Judge, 1991–2007; *b* 28 Nov. 1936; *d* of His Honour Edward Steel and Mary Evelyn Griffith Steel (*née* Roberts); *m* 1972, Stuart Christie (*d* 2011); one *s* one *d*. *Educ*: Howell's Sch., Denbigh; Liverpool Univ. (LLB Hons). Articled clerk and Asst Solicitor, Percy Hughes and Roberts, 1955–60; admitted solicitor, 1960; Partner, John A. Behn Twyford & Co., 1968–80; Partner, Cuff Roberts, 1980–91; a Recorder, 1989. Member: Cripps Cttee, 1967–69; Race Relations Bd, 1970–78; Council, Radio Merseyside, 1974–78; Gen. Adv. Council, BBC, 1979–82 (Chm., NW Adv. Council). Member: Law Soc., 1960; Liverpool Law Soc., 1960 (Pres., 1989–90); Chm., Steering Cttee, Hillsborough Solicitors' Gp, 1989–91. Member: Royal Liverpool Univ. Hosp. NHS Trust, 1991; Liverpool Playhouse Bd, 1968–95 (Vice-Pres., 1995–99). Nat. Vice-Chm., YCs, 1965–67. Pres., Merseyside Br., ESU, 2006–. Chm., Royal Court Liverpool Trust Ltd, 2008–13; Trustee, Liverpool Cathedral Centenary Trust, 2003–10. Gov., Liverpool John Moores Univ., 2001–12 (Hon. Fellow, 2013). DL Merseyside, 1991. Hon. LLD Liverpool, 2007. *Recreations*: theatre (amateur and professional), music, needlework, cooking, entertaining, being entertained. *Address*: 70 Knowsley Road, Cressington Park, Liverpool L19 0PG. *E*: elizabeth_christie@hotmail.com. *Club*: Athenæum (Pres., 2002–03) (Liverpool).
*See also Dame A. H. Steel.*

**STEEL, Dame Heather;** *see* Steel, Dame A. H.

**STEEL, John Brychan**; QC 1993; a Recorder, Midland Circuit, since 2000; *m* 1981, Susan Rebecca Fraser; two *s* one *d*. *Educ*: Harrow Sch.; Durham Univ. (BSc Hons Chem.; Hon. Fellow, Durham Law Sch., 2010). Pres., Durham Univ. Athletic Union, 1975–76; Capt., Durham Univ. Ski Club, 1975. Lieut, Inns of Court and City Yeomanry, 1977–81; called to the Bar, Gray's Inn, 1978 (Gray's Inn Moots Prize, 1979), Bencher, 2006 (Mem., Mgt Cttee, 2011–13, 2018– (Chm., 2012–13); Master of Estate, 2011–12, 2019–20); Attorney-General's Suppl. Panel (Common Law), 1989–93; an Asst Recorder, 1998–2000. Mem. Cttee, Planning and Envmtl Bar Assoc., 2008–12. Chm., Air League, 2018– (Hon. Legal Advr and Trustee, 2002–17); Mem., Royal Air Squadron, 2002–; Hon. Legal Advr and Trustee, Bentley Priory Battle of Britain Trust, 2006–17; Trustee: Mission Aviation Fellowship, 2008–12; Blenheim Palace, 2009–. Chm., Strategic Develt Bd, 2009–11, Mem. Bd, Durham Global Securities Inst., 2011–, Durham Univ.; Chm., Oxford Airport Gen. Aviation Gp, 2009–. Jt Founder, Busoga Trust, 1982–. Dep. Chm., Ski Club of GB, 1980–82; Chm., Kandahar Racing, 1998–2000. FRGS 2002; FRAeS 2003; FRSA 2006; FCIArb 2014. *Recreations*: ski-ing, flying, walking. *Address*: 39 Essex Chambers, 81 Chancery Lane, WC2A 1DD. *T*: (020) 7832 1111. *Clubs*: Boodle's; Kandahar (Chm., 1992–97).

**STEEL, Prof. Karen**, PhD; FRS 2009; Professor of Sensory Function, Wolfson Centre for Age-Related Diseases, King's College London, since 2012. *Educ*: Univ. of Leeds (BSc Genetics and Zool. 1974); University Coll. London (PhD 1978). Postdoctoral Fellow, MRC Inst. of Hearing Res., Nottingham, then postdoctoral role at Inst. für Zoologie, Munich, 1978–83; res. role, MRC Inst. of Hearing Res., Nottingham, 1983–2003; Principal Investigator for the Genetics of Deafness and Founder, Mouse Genetics Prog., Wellcome Trust Sanger Inst., 2003–12. Hon. Prof. of Genetics, Univ. of Nottingham, 1995. Mem., Scientific Adv. Bd, Mouse Genome Database. Scientific Adviser: Deafness Res. UK; SENSE. Mem. Council, Royal Soc., 2017–. FMedSci 2004. Brain Prize, Grete Lundbeck Eur. Brain Res. Foundn, 2012. *Publications*: contribs to jls incl. Nature Genetics, Neurosci., Human Molecular Genetics, Molecular and Cell. Biol. *Address*: Wolfson Centre for Age-Related Diseases, King's College London, Wolfson Wing, Hodgkin Building, Guy's Campus, SE1 1UL.

**STEEL, Michael;** *see* Steel, C. M.

**STEEL, Patricia Ann**, OBE 1990; Secretary, Institution of Highways and Transportation, 1973–90; *b* 30 Oct. 1941; *d* of Thomas Norman Steel and Winifred Steel. *Educ*: Hunmanby Hall, near Filey, Yorks; Exeter Univ. (BA). Parly Liaison, Chamber of Shipping of UK and British Shipping Fedn, 1968–71; Sec., Highway and Traffic Technicians Assoc., 1972–73. Director: LRT, 1984–91; Docklands Light Railway, 1984–91 (Chm., 1988–89); Victoria Coach Station Ltd, 1988–91. Non-executive Director: TRL, 1992–96; Richmond, Twickenham and Roehampton Healthcare NHS Trust, 1992–99; NHS Litigation Authy, 2002–08. Mem., Occupational Pensions Bd, 1979–84; Non-legal (formerly Lay) Mem., Transport Tribunal, 1999–2012. Dir, Avonreach Academy Trust. *Recreations*: music, travel, politics.

**STEEL, Robert**, CBE 1979; Secretary-General, Royal Institution of Chartered Surveyors, 1968–85 (Fellow, 1961; Hon. Member, 1985); *b* 7 April 1920; *e s* of late John Thomas Steel and Jane (*née* Gordon), Wooler, Northumberland; *m* 1943, Averal Frances (*d* 2007), *d* of Arthur Pettitt; one *s* one *d*. *Educ*: Duke's Sch., Alnwick, Northumb.; Univ. of London (BSc 1945); Gray's Inn (Barrister, 1956). Surveyor, 1937–46; Asst Sec., Under Sec., RICS, 1946–61; Dir of Town Development, Basingstoke, 1962–67. Hon. Sec.-Gen., Internat. Fedn of Surveyors, 1967–69, Vice-Pres., 1970–72, Hon. Mem., 1983; Hon. Sec., Commonwealth Assoc. of Surveying and Land Economy, 1969–90; Sec., Aubrey Barker Trust, 1970–96; Member: South East Economic Planning Council, 1974–76; Council, British Consultants Bureau, 1977–85. Chm., Geometers Liaison Cttee, EEC, 1972–86. Hon. Editor, Commonwealth Surveying and Land Economy, 1975–90. Founder Mem., 1977, Mem. Ct of Assts, 1977–94, Master, 1988–89, Worshipful Co. of Chartered Surveyors. Organised national networks of beacons for Queen's Silver Jubilee celebrations, 1977, and for the Wedding of Prince Charles and Lady Diana Spencer, 1981. Raised: £71,210 for RICS Benev. Fund by sponsored walk of 1000 miles, John O'Groats to Land's End, 1979; £66,333 for RICS Benev. Fund and The Prince's Trust by walk of 1100 miles, Cape Wrath to Dover and London, 1985; £113,739 for Lord Mayor of London's Charity Appeal for Children, 1988, by walk of 1,200 miles from Strathy Point, Sutherland, to Portland Bill, Dorset, and London; £133,500 for National Trust Enterprise Neptune, 1990, by walk of 2,000 miles around the perimeter of England; £116,820 for Nat. Trust Centenary 1995 by walk of 4,444 miles around the perimeter of mainland Britain; £80,015 for RICS Benev. Fund and Marie Curie Cancer Care, by walk of 2,000 kms, Iona to Canterbury, 2000; £75,000 for RICS Benev. Fund, Macmillan Cancer Support and Treloar Trust, by walk of 650 miles, Balmoral to Snowdon, 2007. Hon. Member: Bulgarian Mountain Rescue Service, 1964; Union Belge des Géomètres Experts, 1976; Hon. Fellow, Inst. of Surveyors, Malaysia, 1983. Hon. LLD Aberdeen, 1985. Distinguished Service Award, Surveyors Inst. of Sri Lanka, 1986; Help the Aged Tunstall Golden Award for Outstanding Achievement, 1995. Silver Jubilee Medal, 1977. *Publications*: The Housing Repairs and Rent Act, 1954; The Rent Act, 1957; Steel Nuggets: a personal chronicle, 2002; Walking Wonderlands: an account of eight long walks, 2009; contrib. professional jls and internat. conferences. *Recreations*: mountain walking, travel, music, family genealogy.

**STEELE, Prof. Fiona Alison**, OBE 2011; FBA 2009; Professor of Statistics, London School of Economics and Political Science, since 2013. *Educ*: Univ. of Edinburgh (BSc 1st Cl. Hons Maths and Stats 1992); Univ. of Southampton (MSc Social Stats with Dist. 1993; PhD Stats 1996). Lectr in Stats and Res. Methodology, LSE, 1996–2001; Res. Lectr in Stats, Inst. of Educn, Univ. of London, 2001–05; Reader in Social Stats, 2005–08, Prof. of Social Stats, 2008–13, Dir, Centre for Multilevel Modelling, 2010–13, Univ. of Bristol. Vis. Fellow, Centre for Advanced Study, Norwegian Acad. Sci. and Letters, 2007. *Publications*: (jtly) Analysis of Multivariate Science Data, 2nd edn 2008; (jtly) A User's Guide to MLwiN, Version 2.10, 2009; contribs to Public Opinion Qly, Jl Royal Statistical Soc., Demography, Jl American Statistical Assoc. *Address*: Department of Statistics, London School of Economics and Political Science, Houghton Street, WC2A 2AE.

**STEELE, Ven. Gordon John**; Archdeacon of Oakham, since 2012; *b* Stoke Newington, 6 April 1955; *s* of Henry John Steele and Jeanie MacKechnie Steele; *m* 1991, Helen Beverley Maria Rixon; one *s* one *d*. *Educ*: Owen's Grammar Sch., London; Univ. of Kent (BA 1976); Worcester Coll., Oxford (BA 1982; MA 1987). Diocesan Treas., Tanzania, 1977–80; ordained deacon, 1984, priest, 1985; Curate, St John the Baptist, Greenhill, Harrow, 1984–88; pt-time Chaplain to the Bishop of Willesden, 1987–92; Team Vicar, St Andrew's, Uxbridge, 1988–94; Vicar: St Alban's, Northampton, 1994–2001; St John the Baptist, Peterborough, 2001–12; Rural Dean of Peterborough, 2004–10. Hon. Canon, Peterborough Cath., 2004–. *Recreations*: travel, music, family. *Address*: The Diocesan Office, The Palace, Peterborough PE1 1YB. *T*: (01733) 887017, *Fax*: (01733) 555271. *E*: archdeacon.oakham@peterborough-diocese.org.uk.

**STEELE, John Charles**; Chair, Armed Forces Pay Review Body, 2013–18 (Member, 2009–18); *b* Essex, 10 Aug. 1942; *s* of Charles and Florence Steele; *m* 1965, Jennifer Knopp; two *s*. *Educ*: Royal Liberty Grammar Sch.; SE Essex Tech. Coll. (HND Business Studies 1963; Dip. Personnel Mgt 1968). Ford Motor Company: Mgt trainee, 1961–63; Personnel Officer, 1963–67; IBM UK Ltd: Job Evaluation Officer, 1967–69; Personnel Manager, 1969–74; assignment, IBM Europe as Personnel Ops Manager, 1974–76; Personnel and Communications Dir, Gen. Business Gp, 1976–81; Personnel Dir, Data Processing Gp, 1981–83; assignment, IBM Corp. as Internat. Compensation Dir, 1983–84; Internat. Employee Relns Dir, 1984–85; UK Personnel Dir, 1985–89; British Telecommunications plc: Personnel Dir, BT UK, 1989–90; Gp Personnel Dir and Mem., Exec. Cttee, 1990–2002; Chm., Adv. Council, Accenture HR Services, 2002–03. Mem. Bd, Orgn Resources Counsellors Inc. (NY), 2005–12. Member: Teacher Trng Authy, 1995–98; Council, ACAS, 1997–2003. Mem., Court of Govs, Henley Mgt Coll., 1996–2007 (Hon. Fellow 2008). Trustee, Industrial Relns Counsellors Inc. (NY), 2013–. FIPD (FIPM 1981); FCIPD 2003; FRSA. *Recreations*: opera, ballet, golf, theatre, family. *Address*: Frith Cottage, Bowlhead Green, Godalming, Surrey GU8 6NW. *T*: 07802 798324. *E*: john.c.steele@btopenworld.com. *Clubs*: Athenæum, Royal Air Force.

**STEELE, John Ernest**, FCIPS; consultant to shipbuilding and allied industries, 1989–94; Director, Morganite Special Carbons Ltd, 1990–97; *b* 4 June 1935; *s* of William Steele and Amelia Steele (*née* Graham); *m* 1958, Lucy Wilkinson; one *s* three *d*. *Educ*: Rutherford College of Technology, Newcastle upon Tyne. MNECInst. Swan Hunter and Wigham Richardson Ltd: apprentice shipbuilder, 1951–56; Management Progression, 1956–68; Swan Hunter Shipbuilders Ltd: Local Dir, 1968–71; Purchasing Dir, 1971–74; Dep. Chm. and Dep. Chief Exec., 1974–78; Chief Exec., 1977–82; Chm. and Chief Exec., 1978–82; British Shipbuilders: Div. Man. Dir, Composite Yards, 1981–83; part time Bd Mem., 1979–82; Exec. Bd Mem., Offshore, 1982–84; a Corp. Man. Dir, Offshore, 1982–84; Exec. Bd Mem., Procurement, 1984–85; Corporate Man. Dir, Procurement and Special Projects, 1985–89; North East Shipbuilders Ltd: Commercial Dir, 1986–88; Man. Dir, 1988–89. Chairman: Cammell Laird Shipbuilders Ltd, 1981–84; V. O. Offshore Ltd, 1982–84; Scott Lithgow Ltd, 1983–84; Lyon Street Railway Ltd, 1977–84; Vosper Thorneycroft (UK) Ltd, 1984–86; Sunderland Forge Services, 1987–89; Exec. Cttee, Rigby Metal Components Ltd, 1990–91. British Cttee Mem., Det Norske Veritas, 1981–91. Director: Euroroute Construction Ltd, 1985–89; Sunderland Shipbuilders Ltd, 1988–89; non-exec. Dir, Gibraltar Shiprepair Ltd, 1987–90. Freeman, Shipwrights' Co. *Recreations*: Rugby football, golf, reading.

**STEELE, John Martin**, CB 1995; OBE 1986 (MBE 1979); TD 1970; DL; a Civil Service Commissioner for Northern Ireland, 1999–2006; *b* 20 May 1938; *s* of John and Margaret Steele; *m* 1st, 1961, Molly Fulton (*d* 1988); one *s* two *d*; 2nd, 1992, Margaret Norma Armstrong, ISO. *Educ*: Belfast High Sch.; Queen's Univ., Belfast. Various posts, NI Civil Service, 1962–66; staff of NI Parlt, 1966–72; Dept of Community Relations, 1972–73; Second Clerk Asst, NI Assembly, 1973–74; Co-Sec., Gardiner Cttee on measures to deal with terrorism in NI, 1974; Second Clerk Asst, NI Constitutional Convention, 1975–76; DoE, NI, 1976–78; DHSS, NI, 1978–82; Dir, NI Court Service, 1982–87; Northern Ireland Office: Controller of Prisons, 1987–92; Dir, Security, 1992–96; Sen. Dir (Belfast), and Dir, Policing and Security, 1996–98. Mem., TA, 1958–85; formerly Dep. Comd 23 Artillery Bde and CO 102 Air Defence Regt, RA(V); Hon. Colonel: 102 AD Regt, 1987–93; 105 AD Regt, 1998–2004; Pres., NI Area, RAA; Vice-Chm., Council of NI War Meml Bldg, 2008–. Director: Multi-Cultural Resource Centre, Belfast, 2008–12; North

City Training, Belfast, 2008–13. Chm., Bryson Charitable Gp (formerly Bryson House), Belfast, 2001–08. DL Belfast, 1992. FRSA 2009. *Recreations:* gardening, fly-fishing, reading, cooking. *Clubs:* Army and Navy; Ulster Reform (Belfast).

**STEELE, Jonathan Peter**; journalist and author; Chief Reporter, Middle East Eye, 2014–19; Senior Foreign Correspondent and Assistant Editor, The Guardian, 1994–2009; *b* Oxford, 15 Feb. 1941; *s* of Paul Herbert Steele and Gabriele Steele (*née* Wiegand); *m* 1967, Ruth Gordin; two *s*. *Educ*: Eton Coll.; King's Coll., Cambridge (BA 1963); Yale Univ. (MA 1965). The Guardian: reporter, 1965–67; leader-writer, 1967–71; E Eur. corresp., 1971–75; Washington corresp., 1975–79; Foreign News Ed., 1979–82; Chief Foreign Corresp., 1982–88; Moscow corresp., 1988–94. Member: Exec. Cttee of Council, Chatham Hse, 2005–10; Adv. Bd, SSEES, 2006–. Hon. DLitt Herts, 2009. Internat. Reporter of Year, British Press Awards, 1981, 1991; James Cameron Award, 1998; Media Award, Amnesty Internat., 1999; Martha Gellhorn Special Award, 2006; Press Award, One World Media, 2011. *Publications*: (with Ruth First and Christabel Gurney) The South African Connection, 1972; Eastern Europe since Stalin, 1974; Socialism with a German Face, 1977; (with Noam Chomsky and John Gittings) Superpowers in Collision, 1982; (with Eric Abraham) Andropov in Power, 1984; The Limits of Soviet Power, 1985; Eternal Russia, 1994; Defeat: why they lost Iraq, 2008; Ghosts of Afghanistan, 2011. *Recreations:* tennis, yoga, reading, walking. *Club:* Athenæum.

**STEELE, Prof. Robert James Campbell**, CBE 2018; MD; FRCSE, FRCS, FCSHK, FRCPE; FRSE; FMedSci; Senior Research Professor, Prevention, Early Detection and Treatment of Colorectal Cancer, University of Dundee, since 2018 (Professor of Surgery (formerly Surgical Oncology), 1996–2018); Director, Scottish Bowel Cancer Screening Programme, since 2009; *b* 5 March 1952; *s* of Robert Steele and Elizabeth (*née* Sheridan); *m* 1st, 1981, Susan Cachia (marr. diss. 2007); one *s* two *d*; 2nd, 2008, Prof. Annie Anderson. *Educ*: Univ. of Edinburgh (BSc; MB ChB; MD). FRCSE 1984; FRCS 1995; FCSHK 1995; FRCPE 2012. Lecturer in Surgery: Univ. of Edinburgh, 1980–85; Chinese Univ. of Hong Kong, 1985–86; Univ. of Aberdeen, 1986–90; Sen. Lectr and Reader in Surgery, Univ. of Nottingham, 1990–95. Chm., UK Nat. Screening Cttee, 2016–. Chm., Scottish Cancer Foundn, 2010–. Mem. Council, RCSE, 2005–15. Pres., Assoc. Coloproctology of GB and Ireland, 2015–16. FRSE 2017; FMedSci 2018. *Publications:* Practical Management of Acute Gastrointestinal Bleeding, 1993; Gastrin Receptors in Gastrointestinal Tumours, 1993; Essential Surgical Practice, 2002; many articles in learned jls. *Recreations:* music, Scottish country dancing, country sports. *Address:* Medical Research Institute, Mailbox 4, Ninewells Hospital and Medical School, Dundee DD1 9SY. *T:* (01382) 383542, *Fax:* (01382) 383615. *E:* r.j.c.steele@dundee.ac.uk.

**STEELE, Tommy, (Thomas Hicks)**, OBE 1979; actor; *b* Bermondsey, London, 17 Dec. 1936; *s* of late Thomas Walter Hicks and Elizabeth Ellen (*née* Bennett); *m* 1960, Ann Donoghue; one *d*. *Educ*: Bacon's Sch. for Boys, Bermondsey. First appearance on stage in variety, Empire Theatre, Sunderland, Nov. 1956; first London appearance, variety, Dominion Theatre, 1957; Buttons in Rodgers and Hammerstein's Cinderella, Coliseum, 1958; Tony Lumpkin in She Stoops to Conquer, Old Vic, 1960; Arthur Kipps in Half a Sixpence, Cambridge Theatre, London, 1963–64 and Broadhurst Theatre (first NY appearance), 1965; Truffaldino in The Servant of Two Masters, Queen's, 1969; Dick Whittington, London Palladium, 1969; Meet Me In London, Adelphi, 1971; Jack Point, in The Yeomen of the Guard, City of London Fest., 1978; London Palladium: The Tommy Steele Show, 1973; Hans Andersen, 1974 and 1977; one-man show, Prince of Wales, 1979; Singin' in the Rain (also dir.), 1983; Some Like It Hot, Prince Edward, (also dir.), 1992; What a Show!, Prince of Wales, 1995; Scrooge (title rôle), UK tour, 2003, London Palladium, 2005, 2012, UK and Dublin tour, 2010; Dr Doolittle, UK tour, 2008; The Glenn Miller Story, UK tour, 2015–16, London Coliseum, 2018; *films:* Kill Me Tomorrow, 1956; The Tommy Steele Story, 1957; The Duke Wore Jeans; Tommy the Toreador; Touch It Light; It's All Happening; The Happiest Millionaire; Half a Sixpence; Finian's Rainbow; Where's Jack?; *television:* wrote and acted in Quincy's Quest, 1979. Composed and recorded, My Life, My Song, 1974; composed: A Portrait of Pablo, 1985; Rock Suite— an Elderly Person's Guide to Rock, 1987. Hon. DLitt South Bank, 1998. *Publications:* Quincy, 1981; The Final Run, 1983; Bermondsey Boy, 2007. *Recreations:* tennis, squash, sculpture, painting.

**STEELE-PERKINS, Crispian G.**; trumpet soloist; *b* 18 Dec. 1944; *s* of Dr Guy Steele-Perkins and Sylvia de Courcey Steele-Perkins; *m* 1st, 1967, Angela Helen Hall (*d* 1991); one *s* two *d*; 2nd, 1995, Jane Elizabeth Mary (*née* Steele-Perkins). *Educ*: Marlborough Coll.; Guildhall Sch. of Music (LGSM, AGSM; Alumni 1995). Has performed with: Sadler's Wells (later ENO), 1966–73; London Gabrieli Brass Ensemble, 1974–84; RPO, 1976–80; English Baroque Soloists, 1980–91; The King's Consort, 1985–2015. *Address:* Dormy Cottage, 204 Cooden Sea Road, Bexhill-on-Sea, E Sussex TN39 4TR. *T:* (01424) 842401, (01306) 885339. *E:* crispiansp@trumpet1.co.uk. *W:* www.crispiansteeleperkins.com.

**STEEMERS, Prof. Koen Alexander**, PhD; RIBA; Professor of Sustainable Design, University of Cambridge, since 2005 (Head of Department of Architecture, 2008–14); Fellow, Jesus College, Cambridge, since 2014; *b* 21 Nov. 1961; *s* of Theo and Greetje Steemers; *m* 1992, Jeanette Peasey; two *s*. *Educ*: European Sch., Karlsruhe; Springdale First Sch., Dorset; Queen Elizabeth's Sch., Dorset; European Sch., Brussels; Univ. of Bath (BSc, BArch); Darwin Coll., Cambridge (MPhil 1988; PhD 1992). RIBA 1991; ARB. Architect: ECD, London, 1984 and 1988–91; Borchers Metzner Kramar, Darmstadt, 1986–87; Cambridge University: Res. Associate, then Sen. Res. Associate, 1992–95; Lectr, 1995–2000; Sen. Lectr, 2000–03; Reader in Envmtl Design, 2003–05; Dir, Martin Centre for Architectural and Urban Studies, 2002–08; Fellow, Wolfson Coll., Cambridge, 1998–2014. Dir, Cambridge Architectural Res. Ltd, 1991–. Guest Prof., Chongqing Univ., China, 2002–; Vis. Prof., Kyung Hee Univ., Republic of Korea, 2010–12. Pres., Passive and Low Energy Architecture Internat., 2005–11. Hon. LLD Bath, 2017. *Publications:* (jtly) Daylighting in Architecture, 1993; (with N. V. Baker) Energy and Environment in Architecture, 2000; (with N. V. Baker) Daylight Design in Architecture, 2002; (jtly) The Selective Environment, 2002; (with M. A. Steane) Environmental Diversity in Architecture, 2004. *Recreation:* red wine and Roquefort. *Address:* Department of Architecture, University of Cambridge, 1 Scroope Terrace, Cambridge CB2 1PX.

**STEEN, Anthony David**, CBE 2015; barrister; youth leader; social worker; underwriter; *b* 22 July 1939; *s* of late Stephen Nicholas Steen; *m* 1965, Carolyn Padfield, educational psychologist; one *s* one *d*. *Educ*: Westminster Sch.; occasional student University Coll., London. Called to Bar, Gray's Inn, 1962; practising Barrister, 1962–74; Defence Counsel, MoD (Court Martials), 1964–68. Lectr in Law, Council of Legal Educn, 1964–67; Adv. Tutor, Sch. of Environment, Central London Poly., 1982–83. Youth Club Leader, E London Settlement, 1959–64; Founder, 1964, and First Director, 1964–68, Task Force recruiting young people to help London's old and lonely, with Govt support; Govt Foundn YVFF, tackling urban deprivation, 1968–74; Consultant to Canadian Govt on student and employment matters, 1970–71; Special Envoy to Home Sec. on tackling human trafficking, 2013–14. MP (C) Liverpool Wavertree, Feb. 1974–1983, S Hams, 1983–97, Totnes, 1997–2010. PPS to Sec. of State for Nat. Heritage, 1992–94. Member, Select Committee: on Race Relations, 1975–79; on the Envmt, 1991–94; on European Scrutiny, 1997–2010. Chairman: Backbench gps on Youth and Young Children, 1976–79; Cons. Cttee on Cities, Urban and New Town Affairs, 1979–83; Parly Urban and Inner City Cttee, 1987–90; Parly Cttee on Deregulation, 1993–97; All-Party Gp on Trafficking of Women and Children, 2006–10; Vice-Chairman: Health and Social Services Cttee, 1979–80; All-Party Fisheries Cttee, 1997–2010; Secretary: Parly Caribbean Gp, 1979–2010 (Vice-Chm.); Cons. back bench Trade and Industry Cttee, 1997–99; 1922 Cttee, 2001–10; Founder Mem., All Party Friends of Cycling, 1975–88. Chm., Chm.'s Unit Marginal Seats, 1982–84, Minority Parties Unit, 1999–2000, Cons. Central Office. Vice-Chm., Envmt Cttee, 1983–85; Chairman: Prime Minister's Cons. Deregulation Cttee, 1993–97; Sane Planning Gp, 1989–96; West Country Mems, 1992–94; Member: Parly Population and Develt Gp; Commons and Lord's Cycle Gp; Services Cttee; Chm., Cons. Friends of English Wine; Jt Nat. Chm., Impact 80's Campaign. Chm., Human Trafficking Foundn, 2010–; Special Advr, All-Party Gp on Human Trafficking, 2010–. Member: Exec. Council, NPFA; Board, Community Transport; Council of Reference, Internat. Christian Relief; Council Mem., Anglo-Jewish Assoc.; Founder Mem., CSA Monitoring Gp; Chm., Outlandos Charitable Trust, 1980–97; Vice-Chm., Task Force Trust, 1964–; Vice-President: Ecology Bldg Soc.; Internat. Centre for Child Studies; Bentley Operatic Soc.; S Hams Young Farmers; Assoc. of District Councils; Marlborough with S Huish Horticultural Soc.; Devon CPRE; Dartmoor Preservation Assoc.; Trustee: Educn Extra; Dartington Summer Arts Foundn; Patron: Liverpool's Open Circle for Detached Youth Work; St Luke's Hospice, Plymouth; Kidscape; Sustrans. Pres., Devon Youth Assoc. *Publications:* New Life for Old Cities, 1981; Tested Ideas for Political Success, 1983, 7th edn 1991; Public Land Utilisation Management Schemes (Plums), 1988. *Recreations:* Dartmoor, piano playing, chess. *Clubs:* Royal Automobile; Churchill (Liverpool); Totnes Conservative (South Hams).

**STEEN, Ven. Dr Jane Elizabeth**; Archdeacon of Southwark, since 2013; *b* Thornton Heath, 1964; *m* 1990, Pip Steen. *Educ*: Newnham Coll., Cambridge (BA 1987; PhD 1992); Trinity Coll., Cambridge; Westcott House, Cambridge. Ordained deacon, 1996, priest, 1997; Curate, Chipping Barnet with Arkley, 1996–99; Chaplain to Bishop of Southwark, 1999–2005; Canon Chancellor, Southwark Cath., 2005–13; Dir of Ministerial Educn, Dio. of Southwark, 2005–13. *Publications:* (contrib.) Samuel Johnson's Pendulum, 2012; contribs to jls incl. New Rambler, Theology. *Recreations:* walking, reading, gardening, cooking. *Address:* Trinity House, 4 Chapel Court, Borough High Street, SE1 1HW. *T:* (020) 7939 9409. *E:* jane.steen@southwark.anglican.org.

**STEER, Sir Alan (William)**, Kt 2004; Headmaster, Seven Kings High School, Redbridge, 1985–2008; *b* 30 Jan. 1948; *s* of Jack and Esther Steer; *m* 1970, Julie Hodgkin. *Educ*: Magdalen Coll. Sch., Oxford; Univ. of Warwick (BA Hons 1970). Teacher: West Leeds Boys' High Sch., Leeds, 1971–76; Weavers Sch., Wellingborough, 1976–82; Dep. Hd, then Actg Hd, Grange Park Sch., Herts, 1982–85. FRSA. *Recreations:* political cartoons, Fulham Football Club, ancient history, gardening.

**STEER, David**; QC 1993; DL; a Recorder, 1991–2005; *b* 15 June 1951; *s* of Alcombe Steer and Nancy Steer; *m* 1974, Elizabeth May Hide; one *s*. *Educ*: Rainford High Sch.; Manchester Poly. (BA Hons Law). Called to the Bar, Middle Temple, 1974, Bencher, 2001; Hd of Chambers, 1992–2012; in practice as barrister, 1974–2012; Leader, Northern Circuit, 2002–04. Mem., Bar Council, 1995–97, 2002–04. Chm. of Trustees, Merseyside Scouts, 2018–. DL, 2016, High Sheriff, 2019–20, Merseyside. *Recreations:* Rugby League, gardening, horse-riding.

**STEER, Deirdre V.**; *see* Clancy, D. V.

**STEER, James Kelly**, CEng, FICE, FCILT; transport consultant; Founder, 1978, and Director, since 2005, Steer (formerly Steer Davies Gleave) (Managing Director, 1978–2002); Director and Founder, Greengauge 21, since 2005; *b* 7 Dec. 1948; *s* of Desmond and Josephine Steer; *m* 1973, Adrianne Jenifer Harris (*d* 1979); two *s*; partner, Mary Anderson Wright; one *d*. *Educ*: Somers Park Primary Sch., Malvern; Worcester Royal Grammar Sch.; University of Wales Swansea (BSc Hons Civil Engrg); Imperial Coll., London (MSc Transport; DIC). CEng 1975; MICE 1975; MCIHT (MIHT 1975); FCILT (MCIT 1976, FCIT 1999); FICE 2016. Asst Engr, Freeman Fox Wilbur Smith Associates, 1969–71; Consultant, Alan M. Voorhees Associates, then Associate, MVA, 1972–78; on secondment to Strategic Rail Authy as Mem., Exec. and Man. Dir, Strategic Planning, 2002–05. Mem., West End Commn, 2012–13. Non-exec. Dir, GCR Develt Ltd, 2011–14. Dir, High Speed Rail Industry Leaders Gp, 2014–. Pres., CILT, 2013–14 (Vice-Pres., 2009–). Columnist, Transport Times, 2005–. Pres., Railway Study Assoc., 2008–09. *Publications:* contrib. jl articles on rail, LRT, economic appraisal, research, finance and planning. *Recreations:* boating, exploring world and English history. *Address:* Steer, 28–32 Upper Ground, SE1 9PD.

**STEER, Dr Peter Anthony**; Chief Executive Officer, Mater Group, since 2019; *b* Australia, 15 Feb. 1959; *m* 1983, Glenys. *Educ*: Univ. of Queensland (MB BS 1981). FRACP (Paediatrics) 1989; FRCPC (Paediatrics) 2003; FAAP 2005. Mater Adult Hospital, Brisbane: Intern, 1982; Jun. Resident MO, 1983; Sen. MO/Med. Registrar, 1984; Sen. Registrar/Neonatology, 1988, Actg Staff Neonatologist, 1988–89, Nat. Women's Hosp., Auckland; Neonatal Fellowship, McMaster Univ., Hamilton, 1989–91; Staff Neonatologist and Dir, Post-Grad. Educn, Mater Mother's Hosp. and Mater Children's Hosp., Brisbane, 1991–94; Actg Med. Superintendent, Mater Children's Hosp., Brisbane, 1995; Neonatologist, Mater Mother's Hosp., Brisbane, 1995–2000; Exec. Dir, Mater Children's Public and Private Hosps, Brisbane, 1995–2000; Neonatologist and Dir, Centre for Clin. Studies - Women's and Children's Health (formerly Mater Perinatal Epidemiol. Unit), Mater Hosp., Brisbane, 2001; Div. Chief, Clin. Dir and Academic Hd, Div. of Neonatol., McMaster Univ., Hamilton, 2001; Neonatologist and Dir, Centre for Clin. Studies - Women's and Children's Health, Mater Hosp., Brisbane, 2002–03; Chief of Paediatrics, St Joseph's Healthcare, Hamilton, 2003–08; Chief, Dept of Paediatrics, Pres., McMaster Children's Hosp., Hamilton, 2003–08; Prof. and Chair, Dept for Paediatrics, McMaster Univ., Hamilton, 2003–08; Exec. Lead, McMaster Univ. Med. Centre, Hamilton Health Services, Hamilton, 2005–08; Chief Executive: Children's Health Queensland Hosp. and Health Services, Queensland Health, Brisbane, 2009–14; Gt Ormond St Hosp. for Children NHS Foundn Trust, 2015–18. University of Queensland: Adjunct Associate Prof., Dept for Paediatrics and Child Health, 1995–2000; Associate Prof., Central Clin. Sch., Fac. of Health Scis, 2002–03; Adjunct Prof., Sch. of Public Health, Queensland Univ. of Technol., Brisbane, 2003–08. GAICD 2011. *Address:* Mater Group, Raymond Terrace, South Brisbane, Qld 4101, Australia.

**STEER, Richard**; Chairman, Gleeds, since 1999; *b* London, 9 Sept. 1955; *s* of Peter Leslie Steer and Patricia Alice Steer; *m* Elizabeth Ann Tyszkiewicz; two *d*. *Educ*: Leighton Park Sch., Reading; Univ. of Reading (BSc Hons 1976). FRICS. Gleeds, 1981–. Columnist: Building Mag., 2006–; Property Week Mag., 2012–. Advr, Inquiry into Restoration and Renewal of Palace of Westminster, 2017–. Non-exec. Dir, This Land, 2019–. FCIOB; FAPM. Hon. FRIBA 2016. *Publications:* reports on construction. *Recreations:* sailing, ski-ing. *Address:* 1 Althorp Road, SW17 7ED. *T:* (020) 8767 2902. *E:* richard.steer@gleeds.co.uk. *Clubs:* Royal Automobile, City Livery; Royal Southern Yacht; Leander.

**STEERE, Gordon Ernest L.**; *see* Lee-Steere.

**STEFF-LANGSTON, Group Captain John Antony**, MBE 1959; Executive Secretary, Royal Astronomical Society, 1980–91; *b* 5 Nov. 1926; *s* of William Austen Paul Steff-Langston, organist and composer, and Ethel Maude (*née* Fletcher); *m* 1959, Joyce Marian Brown. *Educ*: Cathedral Choir Sch., Canterbury; King's Sch., Canterbury; Pembroke Coll., Cambridge. RAF Coll., 1945–46; 45 Sqn, Ceylon, 1948; 61 Gp, Kenley, 1949; 34 Sqn, 1950–51; 80 Sqn, Hong Kong, 1951–54; 540, 58 and 82 Sqns, Wyton and Singapore, 1955–57; HQ 3 Gp, 1957–59; 80 Sqn, Germany, 1959–62; Staff Coll., Andover, 1962–63; Air Sec.'s Dept, 1963–65; OC 114 Sqn, Benson, 1966–68; aws 1968; CO Northolt, 1969–71; Defence Advr to High Comrs to NZ and Fiji, 1971–74; sowc Greenwich, 1974–75; AMPs Dept, 1975–78; retd 1978. FCMI (FBIM 1978); FRAS 1992. Affiliate, RAeS 1987. Freeman, City of London, 1994; Liveryman, Fletchers' Co., 1994–. *Recreations*: ornithology, photography, travel, music, cricket. *Address*: 6 Beech Wood, Church Hill, Caterham, Surrey CR3 6SB. *T*: (01883) 344348. *Club*: Royal Air Force.

**STEFFENSEN, Anne Hedensted**; Director General and Chief Executive Officer, Danish Shipping (formerly Danish Shipowners' Association), since 2013; *b* Aalborg, 14 Nov. 1963; *d* of Palle H. Steffensen and Tove Steffensen; *m* 1989, Lars Lundorf Nielsen; three *d*. *Educ*: Univ. of Aarhus (Cand. Scient. Pol.); London Sch. of Econs and Pol Sci. (MSc); Univ. of Oslo (Exam. Philasoficum). Ministry of Foreign Affairs, Denmark: Hd of Section, 1990–92, 1996–98; Dep. Hd, Commercial Dept, London, 1992–95; Dep. Consul Gen., New York, 1998–2000; Chief Consultant, Financial Dept, 2000–01; Hd of Dept, Bilateral Relns, 2001–03, Hd of Dept, Secretariat, 2003–04, Trade Council; Under Sec. of State for Trade, 2004–06; State Sec. for Trade and Corporate Resources, 2006–11; Ambassador of Denmark to the Court of St James's, 2011–13. Knight, Order of Dannebrog, 1 Degree (Denmark), 2008. *Recreations*: contemporary literature, walking, cycling, good food (fish). *Address*: Danish Shipping, Amaliegade 33, 1256 Copenhagen K, Denmark. *Club*: Danish Shipowners.

**STEGMANN, Graham Murray**, CBE 2006; independent development consultant, since 2011; Member of Board, Africa Capacity Building Foundation, since 2017; *b* 1 Nov. 1948; *s* of Andrew Murray Stegmann and Mary Isobel Stegmann; *m* 1979, Carol Anne Mayle; one *s* two *d*. *Educ*: University Coll., Rhodesia (BA Hons London); Fitzwilliam Coll., Cambridge (Commonwealth Schol.; MLitt 1979). Posts with DFID and FCO in London and abroad, 1975–96: Hd of Div., N, Central and Southern Africa, Malaŵi, 1986–89; Hd of Estabts, 1989–93; Hd, Develt Div., Southern Africa, Pretoria, 1993–95; Department for International Development: Hd, Aid Policy Resources, then Principal Finance Officer, 1996–2000; Africa Dir, 2000–04; Strategic Advr, 2004–06 and Dir, 2005; Special Advr to Pres. of African Develt Bank, 2006–11. Chm., SciDev.Net, 2014–17. Internat. Trustee, British Red Cross, 2007–12. *Recreations*: tennis, cricket, squash, travel. *Address*: London. *T*: 07742 103136. *E*: graham.stegmann@btinternet.com.

**STEICHEN, René**; Chairman of Board, Société Européene des Satellites, 1996–2014; *b* Luxembourg, 27 Nov. 1942; *s* of Félix Steichen and Hélène Rausch; *m* 1975, Marianne Belche; two *s* one *d*. *Educ*: Lycée Classique, Diekirch; Cours Supérieurs, Luxembourg; Univ. of Aix-en-Provence; Univ. of Paris (LLD); Institut d'Etudes Politiques, Paris (Dip. Econs and Finance 1966). Qualified as notary, then solicitor, 1969; practised in Diekirch, 1969–84. Mem., Diekirch DC, 1969–84, Mayor, 1974–84. MP (Social Christian) North constituency, Luxembourg, 1979–93; Sec. of State for Agric. and Viticulture, 1984–89; Minister for Agric., Viticulture and Rural Develt and Minister for Cultural Affairs and Scientific Res., 1989–93; Mem., Commn of the European Communities, 1993–95; Sen. Partner, Arendt & Medernach, Luxembourg and Brussels, 1995–2010. *Address*: 36 rue Clairefontaine, 9201 Diekirch, Luxembourg.

**STEIN, Christopher Richard, (Rick)**, CBE 2018 (OBE 2003); broadcaster; Chef, The Seafood Restaurant, Padstow, since 1975; *b* 4 Jan. 1947; *s* of late Eric and Dorothy Stein; *m* 1st, 1975, Jill Newstead (OBE 2013) (marr. diss. 2007); three *s*; 2nd, 2011, Sarah Burns. *Educ*: Uppingham; New Coll., Oxford (BA English Lit. 1971). Proprietor: St Petroc's Hotel, Rick Stein's Café, Stein's Gift Shop, Stein's Patisserie, Stein's Deli, Stein's Fish & Chips, Padstow Seafood School, Stein's Fisheries, Ruby's Bar (all in Padstow); Rick Stein's Fish, Falmouth; Rick Stein at Bannisters, Mollymook, Australia; Rick Stein Winchester; Rick Stein Porthleven; Rick Stein Fistral; Rick Stein Sandbanks; Rick Stein, Marlborough; Rick Stein, Barnes; Tenant, Cornish Arms, St Merryn. Presenter, BBC TV series: Rick Stein's Taste of the Sea, 1995; Rick Stein's Fruits of the Sea, 1997; Rick Stein's Seafood Odyssey, 1999; Fresh Food, 1999; Rick Stein's Seafood Lovers' Guide, 2000 (Glenfiddich Food and Drink Award, for best TV prog., 2001; Glenfiddich Trophy, 2001); Rick Stein's Food Heroes, 2002; Rick Stein's Food Heroes: another helping, 2004; Rick Stein's French Odyssey, 2005; Rick Stein in Du Maurier Country, 2006; Rick Stein and the Japanese Ambassador, Escapes, 2007; Betjeman and Me - Rick Stein's Story, 2006; Rick Stein's Mediterranean Escapes, 2007; Rick Stein's Far Eastern Odyssey, 2009; Rick Stein's Spain, 2011; Rick Stein Tastes the Blues, 2011; Rick Stein's Indian Odyssey, 2013; Rick Stein: From Venice to Istanbul, 2015; Rick Stein's Taste of Shanghai, 2016; Rick Stein's Long Weekends, 2016; Rick Stein's Road to Mexico, 2017. *Publications*: English Seafood Cookery, 1988 (Glenfiddich Cook Book of the Year, 1989); Taste of the Sea, 1995 (André Simon Cook Book of the Year, 1996); Fish, 1996; Fruits of the Sea, 1997; Rick Stein's Seafood Odyssey, 1999; Rick Stein's Seafood Lovers' Guide, 2000 (Glenfiddich Food Hero Award, 2001 (James Beard Award, 2005); Rick Stein's Food Heroes, 2002; Rick Stein's Guide to the Food Heroes of Britain, 2003; Rick Stein's Food Heroes: another helping, 2004; Rick Stein's French Odyssey, 2005; Rick Stein's Mediterranean Escapes, 2007; Coast to Coast, 2008; Rick Stein's Far Eastern Odyssey, 2009; Rick Stein's Spain, 2011; Rick Stein's India, 2013; Under a Mackerel Sky: a memoir, 2013; Fish and Shellfish, 2014; Rick Stein: From Venice to Istanbul, 2015; Rick Stein's Long Weekends, 2016; Rick Stein's Road to Mexico, 2017. *Address*: The Seafood Restaurant, Riverside, Padstow, Cornwall PL28 8BY. *T*: (01841) 532700. *Clubs*: Groucho, Chelsea Arts, Ivy.

**STEIN, Colin Norman Ralph**; Sheriff of Tayside Central and Fife at Arbroath, 1991–2011; *b* 14 June 1948; *s* of late Colin Hunter Stein and of Margaret Lindsay Stein; *m* 1979, Dr Linda McNaught; one *s*. *Educ*: Glenalmond Coll.; Durham Univ. (BA Hons Modern History); Edinburgh Univ. (LLB). Admitted Member of Faculty of Advocates, 1975. Standing Jun. Counsel to MoD (RAF), Scotland, 1983–91; Temp. Sheriff, 1987–91. *Recreations*: angling, gardening.

**STEIN, Paul Jonathan**, CEng, FREng, FIET, FRAeS; Chief Technology Officer, Rolls-Royce plc, since 2017; *b* London, 26 July 1957; *s* of late Philip Stein and of Greta Stein (now Bennett); *m* 2007, Juliet Esther Goodden; two step *s*; two *d* from a previous marriage. *Educ*: Beverley Boys' Sch., New Malden; King's Coll., London (BScEng Electronic Engrg). CEng 1995; FIET 2003; FREng 2006; FRAeS 2009. Electronic Engr, Philips Research Labs, 1978–84; Advanced Develt Manager, MEL, 1984–91; Business Sector Manager, Thomson UK, 1991–93; Roke Manor Research: Business Unit Dir, Radio Communications Dept, 1993–96; Man. Dir, 1996–2006; Sci. and Technol. Dir, MoD, 2006–09; Chief Scientific Officer, 2010–16, Dir, Res. and Technol., 2016–17, Rolls-Royce plc. Mem., Siemens UK Exec. Mgt Bd, 2000–06. DUniv Derby 2017; Hon. Dr Cranfield, 2018. *Recreations*: electronics, computing, guitar, motorcycling. *Address*: Rolls-Royce plc, 65 Buckingham Gate, SW1E 6AT. *T*: (01332) 249575, *Fax*: (01332) 249408.

**STEIN, Richard Stenton**; Partner, Leigh Day, 2001–17; *b* Geneva, Switzerland, 15 Dec. 1954; *s* of late Gunther Stein and of Zabelle Stein (*née* Yardumian, now Stenton); *m* 1993, Maria Duggan (marr. diss. 2011); one *s* one *d*; partner, Sally Lovell. *Educ*: William Ellis Sch., Highgate; Leeds Univ. (BA Hons Pol Studies); Manchester Univ. (PGCE); Poly. of Central London (DipLaw); Inns of Court Sch. of Law; University Coll. London (LLM). Lecturer: Trowbridge Coll., 1978–79; Hackney Coll., 1979–81; called to the Bar, Inner Temple, 1982; Campaigns Co-ordinator, Camden Tribunal and Rights Unit, 1982–88; Solicitor, 1988–90, Principal Solicitor, 1990–93, London Bor. of Lewisham; admitted Solicitor, 1994; joined Leigh Day, 1993, Solicitor, 1994–2017. Mem. (Lab) Camden LBC, 1983–86. Trustee, Public Law Project, 2000–17. Treas., N Knapdale Community Council, 2018–. *Publications*: (with W. Birtles) Planning and Environmental Law, 1994. *Recreations*: fell walking, gardening, DIY, Labour Party, Chelsea FC, badminton, running (slowly). *Address*: Eilean da Mheinn, Crinan, Lochgilphead, Argyll PA31 8SW. *T*: (01546) 830233, 07976 780305; Brook Cottage, Llanveynoe, Longtown, Herefordshire HR2 0NE. *E*: Richard@homestein.co.uk.

**STEIN, Rick**; *see* Stein, C. R.

**STEIN, Samuel**; QC 2009; *b* Canterbury, 5 March 1964; *s* of Maurice and Gillian Stein; *m* 1997, Karen Stubbs. *Educ*: South Bank Poly. (LLB). Called to the Bar, Inner Temple, 1988, Bencher, 2011; in practice as barrister, specialising in crime, 1988–. Mem., Bar Standards Bd, 2010– (Chm., Pupillage Cttee, 2009–; Chm., Quality Assce Cttee, 2010–). *Recreation*: trying to sail. *Address*: Nexus Chambers, 7 New Square, Lincoln's Inn, WC2A 3QS. *Club*: Herne Bay Sailing.

**STEIN, Thea Suzanna Ruth**; Chief Executive, Leeds Community Healthcare NHS Trust, since 2014; *b* London, 1964; *d* of Clive and June Stein. *Educ*: Haberdashers' Aske's Sch. for Girls; St Anne's Coll., Oxford (BA Psychol. and Physiol.; MA); Univ. of London (MBA). Clinical Psychol. trng, London Regl Health Service; clinical psychologist and family therapist, Barnet, Camden and Islington, 1986–93; Public Health Lead on Mental Health, then Dep. Dir, Commissioning, Hillingdon HA, 1993–97; Dep. Chief Exec., Dumfries and Galloway Health Bd; on secondment, working on Health Plan, Scottish Parliament; Chief Exec., Leeds NE PCT, 2002–06; Exec. Dir, 2006–10, Chief Exec., 2010–12, Yorkshire and Humber Regl Develt Agency; Chief Exec., Carers Trust, 2012–14. Non-exec. Dir, St Annes Housing Assoc., 2005–09. Gov., Leeds Beckett (formerly Leeds Metropolitan) Univ., 2011–. *Recreations*: astanga yoga, collecting cookery books, enthusiastic novice beekeeper, reading (anything from the cereal box onwards). *Address*: Stockport, Manchester. *E*: theasrstein@gmail.com. *W*: www.twitter.com/thea_stein.

**STEINBERG, Prof. Hannah**; Professor Emerita of Psychopharmacology, University of London, since 1989; Hon. Research Professor in Psychology, School of Social Science, Middlesex University, 1992–2001; *b* 16 March; *d* of late Michael Steinberg, doctor of law, and Marie (*née* Wein). *Educ*: Schwarzwaldschule, Vienna; Putney High School; Queen Anne's School, Caversham; Univ. of Reading (Cert. Comm.); Denton Secretarial Coll., London; University College London (BA 1st cl. Hons Psychology, PhD; Troughton Schol., 1948–50); DSc Psychopharmacol., London, 2002. FBPsS 1959 (Hon. Fellow, 2007), CPsychol 1990. Pres., Univ. of London Union, 1947–48; Univ. of London Postgrad. Studentship in Psychol., 1948–50. Sec. to Man. Dir, Omes Ltd, 1943–44. Part-time Lectr, LSE, 1951; University College London: Asst Lectr in Pharmacology, 1954–55; Lectr, 1955–62; Reader in Psychopharmacology, 1962–70; Prof. of Psychopharmacology (first in W Europe and USA), 1970–92; Head of Psychopharmacology Gp, Dept of Psychology, 1979–92; Hon. Res. Fellow, Dept of Psychol., 1992–. Hon. Consulting Clinical Psychologist, Dept of Psychological Medicine, Royal Free Hosp., 1970. Member MRC working parties on: Biochemistry and Pharmacology of Drug Dependence, 1968–73; Biological Aspects of Drug Dependence, 1971–75. Vice-President: Collegium Internationale Neuro-Psychopharmacologicum (CINP), 1968–74 (Emeritus Fellow, 1996; Pioneer Award, 2008); Brit. Assoc. for Psychopharmacology, 1974–76 (Mem., 1st Council, 1974; Hon. Mem., 1989; launched Hannah Steinberg-Wolfson Foundn annual bursary, 2011); Mem., Biological Council, 1977–80. Distinguished Affiliate of Amer. Psychol. Assoc., Psychopharmacology Div., 1978–; Founder Member: European Coll. of Neuropsychopharmacology; European Behavioural Pharmacol Soc.; British Psychological Society: Mem., 1954; Ed., Bulletin, 1955–62; First Hon. Sec., Psychology of Sport and Exercise Section, 1995–2000. Member: British Pharmacol Soc. (Mem., Editl Bd, 1965–72); Experimental Psychol. Soc.; Soc. for Study of Addiction; European Health Psychol Soc.; Soc. for Medicines Res. Convener, Academic Women's Achievement Gp, 1979–92. Accredited Sport Psychologist, British Assoc. of Sport and Exercise Scis, 1992. Special Trustee, Middx Hosp., 1989–92. Discovered (with E. A. Sykes) mutual potentiation of amphetamine and barbiturate drugs ('purple hearts'), 1963; Initiator (with E. A. Sykes), Steinberg Principle on new develts in conservation areas, Steinberg v Sec. of State for the Envmt, Planning Law Reports, vol. 2, 1989. British Assoc. for Psychopharmacology/AstraZeneca Lifetime Achievement Award, 2001. Past ed. of scientific jls. *Publications*: (trans. and ed jtly) Animals and Men, 1951; organiser of symposia, workshops and editor: (jtly) Animal Behaviour and Drug Action, 1963; Scientific Basis of Drug Dependence, 1968; (jtly) Psychopharmacology, Sexual Disorders and Drug Abuse, 1972; Joint Editor, Occasional Publications of British Psychological Society: Exercise Addiction, 1995; Quality and Quantity, 1996; Teams and Teamwork, 1996; Cognitive Enhancement, 1997; What Sport Psychologists Do, 1998; Sport Psychology in Practice: the early stages, 2000; chapters and reviews on psychopharmacology, drug addiction, drug combinations, psychological benefits and hazards of physical exercise, exercise addiction, creativity and writer's block.

**STEINBERG, Max Laurence**, CBE 2013 (OBE 1998); Chief Executive, Liverpool Vision, 2010–18; *b* Liverpool, 22 Jan. 1952; *s* of Ronald Steinberg and Golda Steinberg; *m* 1975, Sharon Abisgold; one *s* one *d*. *Educ*: King David High Sch., Liverpool. Regl Dir, Merseyside Housing Corp., 1987–95; Housing Corporation, Liverpool: Dir, NW and Merseyside, 1995–2001; Dir, Investment and Regeneration - North, 2001–03; Chief Executive: Elevate East Lancashire, 2003–08; Regenerate Pennine Lancashire Ltd, 2009–10. Mem., Social Exclusion Unit's Policy Action Team 7, 1997; Member, Board: Nat. Housing and Planning Advice Unit, 2006–10; Liverpool and Sefton Chamber of Commerce, 2012–18; Internat. Business and Diplomatic Exchange, 2016–. Chairman: Riverside Housing Gp, 2014–; Internat. Fest. for Business, 2014, 2016, 2018; Liverpool Arena and Convention Centre, 2019–. Trust Mem., Royal Court Theatre Liverpool, 2014–18; Trustee, Nat. Museums Liverpool, 2019–; Shakespeare in the North (Chm., Develt Cttee). Chm., European Inst. for Urban Affairs, Liverpool John Moores Univ., 2001–12. Chm., Bd of Trustees, Roy Castle Lung Cancer Foundn, 2016–. Chm. Govs, King David High Sch., 1999–2013. FRSA. *Recreations*: theatre, cinema, family, reading, travel. *E*: msteinberg@liverpoolvision.co.uk.

**STEINBERGER, Prof. Jack**; Physicist, European Center for Particle Physics, CERN, Geneva, 1968–86; *b* 25 May 1921; *s* of Ludwig and Bertha Steinberger; *m* 1st, 1943, Joan Beauregard; two *s*; 2nd, 1962, Cynthia Eve Alff; one *s* one *d*. *Educ*: New Trier Township High Sch.; Armour Inst. of Technology; Univ. of Chicago (BS Chem. 1942; PhD Phys 1948). Mem., Inst. of Advanced Study, Princeton, 1948–49; Asst, Univ. of California, Berkeley, 1949–50; Prof., Columbia Univ., 1950–68 (Higgins Prof., 1965–68). Vis. Prof.

of Physics, Scuola Normale Superiore, Pisa, 1986. Member: Nat. Acad. of Sciences; Amer. Acad. of Arts and Sciences; Heidelberg Acad. of Science; Accad. Nationale dei Lincei. Hon. Dr: Autònoma, Barcelona; Dortmund; Würzburg; Glasgow; Clermont-Ferrand. (Jtly) President's Science Award, USA, 1988; (jtly) Nobel Prize for Physics, 1988; Mateuzzi Medal, Soc. Italiana della Scienze, 1991. *Publications:* papers in learned jls on discoveries leading to better understanding of elementary particles. *Recreations:* flute; formerly mountaineering, tennis, yachting. *Address:* CERN, 1211 Geneva 23, Switzerland; 25 Ch. des Merles, 1213 Onex, Switzerland.

**STEINBRÜCK, Peer;** Member (SPD), Bundestag, Germany, 2009–16; Minister of Finance, Germany, 2005–09; *b* Hamburg, 10 Jan. 1947; *m* 1976, Gertrud Isbary; one *s* two *d*. *Educ:* Christian-Albrechts Univ., Kiel (degree in econs 1974). Military service, 1968–70; Federal Government of Germany: Construction Ministry (Regl Planning), 1974–76; Planning Gp, Min. of Res. and Technol., 1976–77; Personal Sec. to Ministers Matthöfer and Hauff, 1977–78; div. responsible for Ministry of Res. and Technol., Federal Chancellery, 1978–81; Econs Directorate, Perm. Mission of Federal Rep. of Germany, E Berlin, 1981; Personal Sec. to Minister of Res. and Technol., 1981–82; Co-ordinating Desk Officer, envmtl protection, SPD Parly Gp, Bundestag, 1983–85; North Rhine-Westphalia: Desk Officer for nat. econ. policy, Planning Gp, Min. of Envmt and Agric., 1985–86; Hd, Office of the Premier, 1986–90; Schleswig-Holstein: State Secretary: Min. of Nature, Envmt and Land Develt, 1990–92; Min. of Econs, Technol. and Transportation, 1992–93; Minister of Econs, Technol. and Transportation, 1993–98; North Rhine-Westphalia: Minister of Econs and Small Business, Technol. and Transportation, 1998–2000; Finance Minister, 2000–02; Mem., State Assembly, 2002; Premier, 2002–05. Chm., USA Parly Gp, 2014–16. Joined SPD, 1969 (a Dep. Chm., 2005–16). *Publications:* Unterm Strich, 2010; (with Helmut Schmidt) Zug um Zug, 2011; Vertagte Zukunft, 2015; Das Elend der Sozialdemokratie, 2018.

**STEINBY, Prof. Eva Margareta,** FSA; Professor of Archaeology of the Roman Empire, University of Oxford, 1994–2004; Fellow of All Souls College, Oxford, 1994–2004, now Emeritus; *b* 21 Nov. 1938; *d* of Kaarlo Erkki Wilén and Doris Margareta Steinby. *Educ:* Univ. of Helsinki (Hum. Kand. 1963; Fil. Kand. 1964; Fil. Lic. 1970; Fil. Dr 1976); MA Oxon 1995. FSA 1997. Institutum Romanum Finlandiae, Rome: Asst, 1973–77; Dir, 1979–82 and 1992–94; Sen. Res. Fellow, Finnish Acad., Helsinki, 1985–92. Docent in History, Univ. of Helsinki, 1977–; Vis. Fellow, All Souls Coll., Oxford, 1990–91. Fellow, Suomen Historiallinen Seura, 1978; Corresp. Fellow, Pontificia Accademia Romana di Archeologia, 1982, Fellow, 1993; Fellow: Societas Scientiarum Fennica, 1983; Academia Scientiarum Fennica, 2000; Corresp. Fellow, Deutsches Archäologisches Institut, 1984; For. Hon. Mem., Archaeol Inst. of America, 1998. Ed., I bolli doliari romani dell'Italia centro-occidentale, 2014–. Medaglia d'Oro per Benemeriti Culturali (Italy), 1983; Finnish Cultural Foundn Prize, 2003. Officer, 1st Cl., Order of White Rose (Finland), 1991. *Publications:* La cronologia delle figlinae doliari urbane, 1976; Lateres signati Ostienses, Vol. I 1977, Vol. II 1978; Indici complementari ai bolli doliari urbani (CIL, XV, 1), 1987; (ed) Lacus Iuturnae I, 1989; (ed) Lexicon Topographicum Urbis Romae, 6 vols, 1993–2000; (ed) Ianiculum-Gianicolo, 1997; La necropoli della Via Triumphalis: il tratto sotto l'Autoparco vaticano, 2003; Edilizia pubblica e potere politico nella Roma repubblicana, 2012; Lacus Iuturnae II, Saggi degli anni 1982–85, (ed and contrib.) 1. Saggi e conclusioni, (ed) 2. Materiali, 2012; articles in Italian, German and Finnish learned jls. *Address:* Kalevank 61 A 13, 00180 Helsinki, Finland. *T:* (50) 4924522.

**STEINER, Achim;** Administrator, United Nations Development Programme, since 2017; *b* Carazinho, Brazil, 17 May 1961; *s* of Roland Steiner and Helga Steiner; *m* 2001, Elizabeth Clare Rihoy; two *s*. *Educ:* Worcester Coll., Oxford (BA 1983); Sch. of Oriental and African Studies, Univ. of London (MA 1985); German Development Inst.; Harvard Business Sch. Tech. Advr, Masaara Shams Omania, Sultanate of Oman, 1979–80; community develt worker, Anthyodhaya Sangh, 1983–84; GTZ: Tech. Advr, 1986–88; Desk Officer, Asia/Middle East, 1988–89; Policy Advr, 1989–91; International Union for Conservation of Nature: Prog. Coordinator, Regl Office for S Africa, 1991–94; Sen. Policy Advr, Global Policy Unit, 1994–97; Chief Tech. Advr, Mekong River Commn, 1997–98; Sec. Gen., World Commn on Dams, 1998–2001; Dir Gen., IUCN, 2001–05; Exec. Dir, UNEP, 2006–16; Dir-Gen., UN Office, Nairobi, 2009–11; Dir, Oxford Martin Sch., Univ. of Oxford, 2016–17. *Address:* United Nations Development Programme, One United Nations Plaza, New York, NY 10017, USA. *E:* achim.steiner@undp.org.

**STEINER, Prof. (Francis) George,** MA, DPhil; FBA 1998; FRSL; Fellow, Churchill College, Cambridge, since 1961; Weidenfeld Professor of Comparative Literature, and Fellow of St Anne's College, Oxford, 1994–95; *b* 23 April 1929; *s* of Dr F. G. and Mrs E. Steiner; *m* 1955, Zara Shakow (*see* Z. Steiner); one *s* one *d*. *Educ:* Paris (BèsL); Univ. of Chicago (BA); Harvard (MA); Oxford (DPhil). Member, staff of the Economist, in London, 1952–56; Inst. for Advanced Study, Princeton, 1956–58; Gauss Lectr, Princeton Univ., 1959–60; Prof. of English and Comparative Literature, Univ. of Geneva, 1974–94, Prof. Emeritus, 1994–. Lectures: Massey, 1974; Leslie Stephen, Cambridge, 1986; W. P. Ker, 1986, Gifford, 1990, Univ. of Glasgow; Page-Barbour, Univ. of Virginia, 1987; Paul Tillich, Harvard, 1999. Fulbright Professorship, 1958–69; Vis. Prof., Collège de France, 1992; Charles Eliot Norton Prof., Harvard, 2001–02. Pres., English Assoc., 1975; Corresp. Mem., (Federal) German Acad. of Literature, 1981; Hon. Mem., Amer. Acad. of Arts and Scis, 1989; Hon. RA 2000. FRSL 1964. Hon. Fellow: Balliol Coll., Oxford, 1995; St Anne's Coll., Oxford, 1998. Hon. DLitt: East Anglia, 1976; Louvain, 1980; Mount Holyoke Coll., USA, 1983; Bristol, 1989; Glasgow, 1990; Liège, 1990; Ulster, 1993; Durham, 1995; Kenyan Coll., USA, 1996; Trinity Coll., Dublin, 1996; Rome, 1998; Sorbonne, 1998; Salamanca, 2002; Athens, 2004; Bologna, 2006; London, 2006; Lisbon, 2009; Dr *hc* École Normale Supérieure, Paris, 2014. O. Henry Short Story Award, 1958; Guggenheim Fellowship, 1971–72; Zabel Award of Nat. Inst. of Arts and Letters of the US, 1970; Faulkner Stipend for Fiction, PEN, 1983; PEN Macmillan Fiction Prize, 1993; Truman Capote Lifetime Award for Lit., 1999; Prince of Asturias Prize, Spain, 2001; Ludwig Börne Prize, Germany, 2003; Mondello Prize, Italy, 2004; Redonda Prize, Spain, 2007; Eureka Prize, Italy, 2016. Chevalier de la Légion d'Honneur (France), 1984; Comdr, Ordre des Arts et des Lettres (France), 2001. *Publications:* Tolstoy or Dostoevsky, 1958; The Death of Tragedy, 1960; Anno Domini, 1964; Language and Silence, 1967; Extraterritorial, 1971; In Bluebeard's Castle, 1971; The Sporting Scene: White Knights in Reykjavik, 1973; After Babel, 1975 (adapted for TV as The Tongues of Men, 1977); Heidegger, 1978; On Difficulty and Other Essays, 1978; The Portage to San Cristobal of A. H., 1981; Antigones, 1984; George Steiner: a reader, 1984; Real Presences: is there anything in what we say?, 1989; Proofs and Three Parables, 1992; The Deeps of the Sea (fiction), 1996; No Passion Spent, 1996; Errata: an examined life, 1997; Grammars of Creation, 2001; Lessons of the Masters, 2003; My Unwritten Books, 2008; George Steiner at the 'New Yorker', 2009; The Poetry of Thought, 2012; Un long samedi, 2014 (trans. English 2017). *Recreations:* music, chess, mountain walking. *Address:* 32 Barrow Road, Cambridge CB2 2AS. *Clubs:* Athenæum; Harvard (New York).

**STEINER, Prof. Hillel Isaac,** PhD; FBA 1999; Professor of Political Philosophy, University of Manchester, 1995–2009, now Emeritus; *b* 1942; *m* (marr. diss.); three *s*. *Educ:* Univ. of Toronto (BA); Carleton Univ. (MA); Univ. of Manchester (PhD). Lectr in Politics and Public Admin, Univ. of Saskatchewan, 1966–67; Res. Associate, 1967–71, Lectr, then Sen. Lectr, 1971–95, Reader, 1995, in Pol Philosophy, Univ. of Manchester. *Publications:* Essay on Rights, 1994; A Debate Over Rights, 1998; Left-Libertarianism and its Critics, 2000; Freedom: a philosophical anthology, 2007; contrib. to learned jls.

**STEINER, Prof. Ullrich;** Professor of Soft Matter Physics, Adolphe Merkle Institute, University of Fribourg, since 2014; *b* 27 March 1963; *s* of Richard Steiner and Elisabeth Steiner (*née* Konrad); *m* 1995, Barbara Gorodecki; one *d*. *Educ:* Dip. Physics; Dr rer. nat.; Habilitation. Prof. of Polymer Science, Univ. of Groningen, 1999–2004; John Humphrey Plummer Prof. of Physics of Materials, Univ. of Cambridge, 2004–14. (Jtly) Raymond and Beverley Sackler Prize for Physical Scis, Tel Aviv Univ., 2002. *Publications:* 60 articles in scientific jls; 3 patents. *Recreations:* ski-ing, sailing, cycling. *Address:* Adolphe Merkle Institute, Chemin des Verdiers, 1700 Fribourg, Switzerland.

**STEINER, Dr Zara,** FBA 2007; Fellow, New Hall, Cambridge, 1965–96, Fellow Emeritus, 1997; *b* 6 Nov. 1928; *d* of Joseph and Frances Shakow; *m* 1955, Prof. (Francis) George Steiner, *qv*; one *s* one *d*. *Educ:* Swarthmore Coll. (BA 1948); St Anne's Coll., Oxford (BA 1950); Radcliffe Coll., Harvard Univ. (PhD 1962). Lectr, Center of Internat. Studies, Princeton Univ., 1957–58 and 1960–61. Visiting Professor: Stanford Univ., Calif, 1979–80; Inst. des Hautes Études Internationales, Geneva, 1980–81; Univ. of N Carolina, 1985. Hon. DLitt: S, Sewanee, Tennessee, 1997; E Anglia, 2011. *Publications:* The State Department and the Foreign Service, 1958; Present Problems of the Foreign Service, 1961; The Foreign Office and Foreign Policy 1898–1914, 1969, rev. edn 1986; Britain and the Origins of the First World War, 1977, 2nd edn (with K. Neilson), 2005; (ed) The Times Survey of Foreign Ministries of the World, 1982; The Lights that Failed: European international history 1919–1933, 2005; (ed jtly) History and Neorealism, 2010; The Triumph of the Dark: European international history, 1933–39, 2011; articles in jls incl. Jl Modern Hist., Historical Jl, Relns Internationales, Diplomacy and Statecraft. *Recreation:* dog walking. *Address:* 32 Barrow Road, Cambridge CB2 8AS. *T:* (01223) 461043. *E:* zs202@hermes.cam.ac.uk. *Club:* Lansdowne.

**STEINFELD, Alan Geoffrey;** QC 1987; *b* 13 July 1946; *s* of Henry Chaim Steinfeld and Deborah Steinfeld; *m* 1976, Josephine Nicole (*née* Gros); two *s*. *Educ:* City of London Sch.; Downing Coll., Cambridge (BA Hons, LLB). Arnold McNair Schol. in Internat. Law, 1967; Whewell Schol. in Internat. Law, 1968. Called to the Bar, Lincoln's Inn, 1968, Bencher, 1996; commenced pupillage at the Bar, 1968, practice at the Bar, 1969; a Dep. High Court Judge, 1995–2016. *Recreations:* tennis, sailing, opera. *Address:* (chambers) 24 Old Buildings, Lincoln's Inn, WC2A 3UP. *T:* (020) 7691 2424. *Club:* Royal Automobile.

**STEINMEIER, Frank-Walter;** President, Federal Republic of Germany, since 2017; *b* 5 Jan. 1956; *s* of Walter Steinmeier and Ursula Steinmeier (*née* Broy); *m* 1995, Elke Büdenbender; one *d*. *Educ:* Blomberg Grammar Sch.; Justus Liebig Univ., Giessen (1st State Law Exam 1982, 2nd State Law Exam 1986; Doctorate 1991). State Chancellery of Lower Saxony: Hd, Dept, 1994–96, responsible for policy guidelines and interministerial co-ordination and planning; State Sec. and Head, 1996–98; State Sec., Federal Chancellery and Comr for Federal Intelligence Services, 1998–99; Hd, Federal Chancellery, 1999–2005; Minister for Foreign Affairs, 2005–09, Vice-Chancellor, 2007–09; Germany; Mem. (SPD), Bundestag, Germany, 2009–17; Leader of the Opposition, 2009–13; Minister for Foreign Affairs, 2013–17. Hon. Dr: Ural Federal Univ., 2010; Hebrew Univ. Jerusalem, 2015; Piraeus, 2015; Paderborn, 2016; Lebanese Univ. Beirut, 2018. Cavaliere di Gran Croce, 2006. *Publications:* Made in Germany; Sicherheit im Wandel (The Changing Face of Security); Bürger ohne Obdach (Citizens without Shelter). *Address:* Bundespräsidialamt, Spreeweg 1, 10557 Berlin, Germany.

**STELL, Edward Jedidiah;** Parliamentary Counsel, 2005–18; *b* 8 June 1962; *s* of late Christopher Fyson Stell, OBE and of Dorothy Jean Stell (*née* Mackay); *m* 1991, Jocelyn Helen Whyte; two *s* one *d*. *Educ:* Merchant Taylors' Sch., Northwood; Corpus Christi Coll., Oxford (BA 1985, MA 1988); Warburg Inst., Univ. of London. Articled clerk, 1988–90, asst solicitor, 1990–93, Ashurst Morris Crisp; Office of the Parly Counsel, 1993–2018. *Recreations:* cycling, books.

**STELMACH, Hon. Edward Michael;** MLA (Progressive C) Fort Saskatchewan-Vegreville, Canada, 2004–12 (Vegreville-Viking, 1993–2004); Premier of Alberta and Minister for Public Affairs Bureau, 2006–11; Leader, Progressive Conservative Party, 2006–11; *b* 11 May 1951; *s* of Michael Stelmach and Nancy Stelmach; *m* Marie Warshawski; four *c*. *Educ:* Univ. of Alberta. Mixed farm business, 1973–. Minister: of Agriculture, Food and Rural Develt, 1997–99; of Infrastructure, 1999–2001; of Transportation, 2001–04; of Internat. and Intergovtl Relns, 2004–06. Vice Chm., Genalta Power, 2012–. Chm. Bd, Vegreville Health Unit; Member Board: Archer Meml Hosp.; Lamont Auxiliary Hosp. and Nursing Home; Covenant Health, 2012– (Chm., 2016–). Member: Andrew Co-op. Assoc.; Lamont 4-H Dist Council; Andrew 4-H Beef Club. Hon. LLD Alberta, 2013. *Recreations:* golf, reading.

**STELZER, Irwin Mark,** PhD; Director, Economic Policy Studies, and Senior Fellow, Hudson Institute, since 1998; President, Irwin M. Stelzer Associates, since 1981; Columnist, Sunday Times, since 1985; *b* 22 May 1932; *s* of Abraham Stelzer and Fanny Dolgins Stelzer; *m* 1981, Marian Faris Stuntz; one *s*. *Educ:* New York Univ. (BA 1951; MA 1952); Cornell Univ. (PhD 1954). Researcher and consultant, 1951–61; Lectr, New York Univ., and City Coll., NY, 1951–61; Teaching Asst, Cornell Univ., 1953–54; Instr, Univ. of Connecticut, 1954–55; Pres., Nat. Economic Res. Associates, 1961–81; Dir, Energy and Envmtl Policy Center, Harvard Univ., 1985–88; Resident School, American Enterprise Inst., 1990–98. Vis. Fellow, Nuffield Coll., Oxford, 2004–; Sen. Res. Fellow, Smith Inst., 2005–10. Mem., Pres., Adv. Cttee to US Trade Rep. Mem. Bd of Dirs, Regulatory Policy Inst., Oxford, 2000–08; Dir, Centre for Policy Studies, 2010–. Mem., Vis. Cttee, Harris Sch., Univ. of Chicago, 2007–13. Mem., Editl Bd, Public Interest. *Publications:* Selected Antitrust Cases: landmark decisions, 1955; The Antitrust Laws: a primer, 1996, 4th edn 2001; Neoconservatism, 2004; The Murdoch Method: notes on running a media empire, 2018; contrib. to Public Interest, Commentary and other jls. *Recreation:* photography. *Clubs:* Cosmos, Metropolitan (Washington).

**STEMBRIDGE, David Harry;** QC 1990; a Recorder of the Crown Court, 1977–97; *b* 23 Dec. 1932; *s* of Percy G. Stembridge and Emily W. Stembridge; *m* 1956, Therese C. Furer; three *s* one *d*. *Educ:* St Chad's Cathedral Choir Sch., Lichfield; Bromsgrove Sch.; Birmingham Univ. (LLB Hons). Called to the Bar, Gray's Inn, 1955; practising barrister, 1956–2003. *Recreations:* music, sailing. *Address:* Omega, 101 Court Road, Newton Ferrers, Plymouth PL8 1DE. *Club:* Bar Yacht.

**STEMPLOWSKI, Prof. Ryszard;** Professor of Human Sciences (History), Akademia Ignatianum, Cracow, 2010–16; *b* 25 March 1939; *s* of Kazimierz Stemplowski and Eugenia Białecka; *m* 1975, Irena Zasłona; two *d*. *Educ:* Tech. Lycée (Civil Build.), Bydgoszcz; Tech. Univ., Wrocław; Univ. of Wrocław (MJur 1968); Inst. of History, Polish Acad. of Scis (PhD 1973); Dr Habilitatus (Hist.) Warsaw Univ., 1999. Res. Fellow, Inst. of History, Polish Acad. of Scis, 1973–90; Chief of Chancellery of Sejm (Chamber of Deputies), Poland, 1990–93; Polish Ambassador to UK, 1994–99; Dir, Polish Inst. of Internat. Affairs,

Warsaw, 1999–2004; Prof. of Political Theory, Warsaw Sch. of Econs, 2001–05; Prof. of History and Internat. Relns, Jagiellonian Univ., Cracow, 2005–10. Ed., Polish Diplomatic Rev., 2000–04. Vis. Fellow, St Antony's Coll., Oxford, 1974; Vis. Scholar and Alexander von Humboldt Fellow, Univ. of Cologne, 1981–82. Interfaith Golden Medallion, Peace Through Dialogue, UK, 1999. Kt Cross, Order of Polonia Restituta (Poland), 2000; Grand Cross of Merit, Constantinian Order of St George (House of Bourbon Two Sicilies), 1996. *Publications*: Dependence and Defiance: Argentina and rivalries among USA, UK and Germany 1930–46, 1975, 2nd edn 2014; (jtly) History of Latin America 1850–1980, 3 vols, 1978–80; (jtly) Economic Nationalism in East Central Europe and South America 1918–39, 1990; (jtly) The Slavic Settlers in Misiones 1897–1947, 1992; State-Socialism in the Actually Existing Capitalism: Chile 1932, 1996, 2nd edn 2013; Development of Polish Foreign Policy, 2004; An Introduction to Polish Foreign Policy Analysis, 2006, 3rd edn 2015; Government Projects and Theoretical Concepts of European Integration, 2007, 2nd edn 2012; (ed) On the State of Latin American States: approaching the bicentenary, 2009; Political Philosophy of the Integration of States in Europe (20th-21st centuries), 2010, 2nd edn 2012; (ed) Europe—Latin America: looking at each other?, 2010; (ed) The Poles, Ruthenians and Ukrainians, Argentines: the agricultural colonization of Misiones, 1892–2009, 2011, 2nd edn 2013; On Policy-Making and Policy-Analysing, 2013; Political Cultures of Our Times: a European-Latin-Americanist sketch, 2016; (ed) Contemporary Diplomatic Culture: the first approximation, 2017; The Polish Students' Association under State-Socialism 1950–1973, 2018; other works and translations in Polish, German, Spanish, English, Russian. *Recreations*: music, cosmology, reading bilingual editions of poems. *E*: ryszard@stemplowski.pl. *W*: www.stemplowski.pl.

**STENNETT, Sarah Jane;** Co-Founder and Chief Executive Officer, First Access Entertainment, since 2015; *b* Ormskirk, Lancs; *d* of Frank Harold and Rosemarie Stennett; *m* 2008, George Astasio; one *s* two *d*. *Educ*: Nottingham Trent Univ. (LLB). Co-Founder, SSB Solicitors, 1996–; Founder, Turn First Artists. Vis. Fellow, Univ. of Westminster, 2015. Internat. Award, Marché Internat. du Disque et de l'Edition Musicale, 2017; Strat Award, Music Week Awards, 2017. *Address*: (office) Grove Studios, Adie Road, W6 0PW. *T*: (020) 8742 6700, *Fax*: (020) 8563 7570. *E*: Georgia.dixon@firstaccessent.com.

**STENNING, Emma;** Executive Director, Soulpepper Theatre Company, Toronto, since 2018; *b* Frimley, 19 April 1975; *d* of Vic and Sheila Stenning. *Educ*: Yateley Sch.; Gonville and Caius Coll., Cambridge (BA Hist. 1997; MA). Exec. Dir, Battersea Arts Centre, 2002–05; Clore Fellow, 2005–06; Cultural Prog. Advr, LOCOG, 2006; Head: of Theatre, Arts Council England, 2007–08; of Producing, Manchester Internat. Fest., 2008–09; Chief Exec., Bristol Old Vic, 2009–18. Dep. Chm., Shakespeare's Globe, 2012–18. Hon. DLitt Bristol, 2017. *Address*: Soulpepper Theatre Company, 50 Tank House Lane, Toronto, ON M5A 3C4, Canada.

**STEPHAN, Prof. Douglas W.,** PhD; FRS 2013; FRS(Can) 2005; FRSC; Professor of Chemistry, University of Toronto, since 2008. *Educ*: McMaster Univ. (BSc 1976); Univ. of Western Ontario (NSERC Schol.; PhD 1980); FRSC 2010. NATO Postdoctoral Fellow, Harvard Univ., 1980–82; University of Windsor: Asst Prof., 1982–85; Associate Prof., 1985–92; Prof., 1992–2002; University Prof., 2002–07; Hd of Dept, 2003–06. Corresp. Mem., N-Rhein Westfalia Acad. of Scis and Arts, 2014; Hon. Mem., Israeli Chem. Soc., 2013. Fellow, Chem. Inst. of Canada, 1994. Ludwig Mond Award, 2012, Applied Catalysis Award, 2014, Royal Soc. of Chem.; Henry Marshall Tory Medal, Royal Soc. of Canada, 2013; Canadian Green Chemistry and Engrg Award, GreenCentre Canada, 2014; CIC Medal, Chem. Inst. of Canada, 2014. *Publications*: contribs to learned jls, incl. Dalton Trans, Chem. Eur. Jl, Jl Amer. Chem. Soc., Israel Jl Chem., Proc. NAS, Organometallics, Angewandte Chemie Internat. Edn, Science; 75 patents. *Address*: Department of Chemistry, University of Toronto, 80 St George Street, Toronto, ON M5S 3H6, Canada.

**STEPHEN,** family name of **Baron Stephen**.

**STEPHEN,** Baron *cr* 2011 (Life Peer), of Lower Deeside in the City of Aberdeen; **Nicol Ross Stephen;** *b* 23 March 1960; *s* of R. A. Nicol Stephen and Sheila G. Stephen; *m* Caris Doig; two *s* two *d*. *Educ*: Robert Gordon's Coll., Aberdeen; Aberdeen Univ. (LLB 1980); Edinburgh Univ. (DipLP 1981). Admitted Solicitor, 1983; C&PH Chalmers, 1981–83; Milne & Mackinnon, 1983–88; Sen. Corporate Finance Manager, Touche Ross & Co., 1988–90. Director: Glassbox Ltd, 1992–99; Renewable Energy Ventures Ltd, 2009–. Mem. (Lib Dem) Grampian Regl Council, 1982–92 (Chm., Econ. Develt and Planning Cttee, 1986–91). MP (Lib Dem) Kincardine and Deeside, Nov. 1991–1992. MSP (Lib Dem) Aberdeen S, 1999–2011. Scottish Executive: Dep. Minister for Enterprise and Lifelong Learning, 1999–2000, for Educn, Europe and Ext. Affairs, 2000–01, for Educn and Young People, 2001–03; Minister for Transport, 2003–05; Dep. First Minister, and Minister for Enterprise and Lifelong Learning, 2005–07. Leader, Scottish Lib Dems, 2005–08. Lib Dem spokesperson on Scotland, H of L, 2015–16. Contested: Kincardine and Deeside, (L/All) 1987, (Lib Dem) 1992; (Lib Dem) Aberdeen S, 1997. *Recreations*: golf, swimming. *Address*: House of Lords, SW1A 0PW.

**STEPHEN, Alexander,** OBE 2009; FCCA; Chief Executive, Dundee City Council, 1995–2009; *b* 17 Sept. 1948; *m* Joyce Robertson; one *s* one *d*. FCCA 1977. Local govt posts, 1970–2009; Chief Exec., Dundee City DC, 1991–95. Treas., Revival, 1991–. *Address*: 1 Golspie Terrace, Dundee DD5 2PW. *T*: (01382) 776895.

**STEPHEN, Barrie Michael Lace;** *see* Stephen, Michael.

**STEPHEN, David;** *see* Stephen, J. D.

**STEPHEN, Dr (George) Martin;** Chairman, since 2015, and President, since 2018, National Mathematics and Science College (Principal, 2017); *b* 18 July 1949; *s* of Sir Andrew Stephen, MB, ChB and late Lady Stephen (*née* Frances Barker); *m* 1971, Jennifer Elaine Fisher, JP; three *s*. *Educ*: Uppingham Sch.; Univ. of Leeds (BA); Univ. of Sheffield (Dip Ed, Dist., PhD; Hallam Prize for Educn, 1971). Child supervisor, Leeds and Oxford Remand Homes, 1966–67; Teacher of English, Uppingham, 1971–72, Haileybury, 1972–83 (and Housemaster); Second Master, Sedbergh, 1983–87; Headmaster, Perse Sch. for Boys, Cambridge, 1987–94; High Master: Manchester Grammar Sch., 1994–2004; St Paul's Sch., 2004–11; Dir of Educn, GEMS (UK), 2012–14; Interim Headmaster, Portland Place Sch., 2017. Vis. Lectr, Manchester Univ., 2001–04. Dir, Gifted and Talented Prog. and Gov., Hartland Internat. Sch., 2015–16. Member: ESRC, 1990–2000; Naval Review, 1992–; Community Service Volunteers' Educnl Adv. Council, 1994–; HMC/GSA Univ. Admissions Working Gp, 1994–2004; British Assoc. for Sport and Law, 1995–98; Chm., HMC, 2004 (Chm., Community Service Cttee, 1992–95); non-exec. Chm., Clarendon Academies, 2011–. Associate Mem., Combination Room, GCCC, 1988–94. Member: Portico Library, Manchester, 1995–2000; Bd, Royal Exchange Theatre, Manchester, 1999–2004; Bd, LAMDA, 2004–10. Trustee: Project Trust, 1994–; Nat. Youth Advocacy Service, 2010–14; Gold Standard Trust, 2014–; Member, Board: Never Such Innocence, 2013– (Trustee, 2014–); Educate a Child, 2015– (Trustee, 2014–); Mem., Adv. Bd, Concept Education, 2018–; Advr, BECSLink, 2018–. Mem. Court, Univ. of Salford, 2000–04; Governor: Withington Sch., Manchester, 1994–2002; Pownall Hall Sch., Wilmslow, 1994–2004; Ducie High Sch., Moss Side, 1995–2004; Orley Farm Sch., 2004–11; Manchester City Acad., 1998–2004; The Hall Sch., Hampstead, 2004–11; Durston House Sch., 2005–11; London Acad. of Excellence, 2012; Sidra School, 2014–; Mem. Council, United World Schools, 2014–. FRSA 1996. Hon. DEd De Montfort, 1997. *Publications*: An Introductory Guide to English Literature, 1984; Studying Shakespeare, 1984; British Warship Designs since 1906, 1985; English Literature, 1986, 4th edn 1999; (ed) Never Such Innocence, 1988, 3rd edn 1993; Sea Battles in Close Up, 1988, 2nd edn 1996; The Fighting Admirals, 1991; (ed) The Best of Saki, 1993, 2nd edn 1996; The Price of Pity: poetry, history and myth in the Great War, 1996; (contrib.) Machiavelli, Marketing and Management, 2000; The Desperate Remedy, 2002; The Conscience of the King, 2004; The Galleons' Grave, 2005; The Rebel Heart, 2007; (contrib.) Sea Stories, 2007; The Diary of a Stroke, 2008; (contrib.) The School of Freedom: a liberal education reader from Plato to the present day, 2009; The Coming of the King, 2011; Scapegoat: the death of 'Prince of Wales' and 'Repulse', 2014; Poetry and Myths of the Great War: how poets altered our perception of history, 2014; Never Such Innocence (play), 2014; Educating the More Able Student: what works and why, 2015; The English Public School: a personal and irreverent history, 2018; The Mephistopheles Letters: letters on education to people in Hell, 2020; In Defence of Elitism, 2020; contrib. York Notes series; articles and reviews for various jls. *Recreations*: writing, drama, pen and ink drawing, field and water sports, music, creating schemes for education of more able children. *Address*: 23 Merthyr Terrace, SW13 8DL; Thornage Watermill, Holt Road, Thornage, Norfolk NR25 7QN. *Clubs*: Athenæum, East India (Hon. Mem.), Garrick.

**STEPHEN, Henrietta Hamilton, (Rita),** MBE 1973; National Officer, GMB, 1989–91; *b* 9 Dec. 1925; *d* of late James Pithie Stephen, engine driver, Montrose and late Mary Hamilton Morton, South Queensferry. *Educ*: Wolseley Street and King's Park Elem. Schs, Glasgow; Queen's Park Sen. Secondary, Glasgow; Glasgow Univ. (extra-mural); LSE (TUC Schol.). McGill Univ. and Canada/US Travel, 1958–59. Law office junior, 1941; Clerk, Labour Exchange (Mem. MLSA), 1941–42; Post Office Telephonist, 1942–60; Officer, Union of Post Office Workers, Glasgow Br., 1942–60; Member: UPW Parly Panel, 1957; London and Home Counties Area Organiser, CAWU, 1960–65; Nat. Sec., CAWU, subseq. APEX, 1965–89. Editor, The Clerk, 1965–71; Union Educn Officer, 1965–72; Delegate: TUC; Labour Party Annual Confs; Member: EDC for Food and Drink Manufacturing, 1976–90; Food Standards Cttee, 1968–80; Mary Macarthur Educnl Trust, 1965–2010; Distributive Industry Trng Bd, 1968–73; Monopolies and Mergers Commn, 1973–83; British Wool Marketing Bd, 1973–88; Trustee: Duke of Edinburgh's Commonwealth Study Conferences, 1968–91; Mary Macarthur Holiday Trust, 1993– (Vice Chair, 2009–). Mem., TUC Women's Adv. Cttee, 1983; Chair, Nat. Jt Cttee of Working Women's Organisations, 1983–84. Mem., Adv. Council, Canadian Caribbean Emerging Leaders Conference, 2011. Life Mem., Work Foundn (formerly Industrial Soc.), 1992–. Member: Gen. Cttee, Greenwich and Woolwich Labour Party, 1995–; Exec. Cttee, Greenwich Link, 2008–. Mem., Court of Govs, LSE, 1976–2005 (Gov. Emeritus, 2005). *Publications*: (jtly) Training Shop Stewards, 1968; (with Roy Moore) Statistics for Negotiators, 1973; contrib. Clerk, Industrial Soc. Jl, Target, etc. *Recreations*: food, walking, conversation, travel, theatre, reading. *Address*: 3 Pond Road, SE3 9JL. *T*: and *Fax*: (020) 8852 7797.

**STEPHEN, (John) David;** Director, European Movement, 2004–06; *b* 3 April 1942; *s* of late John Stephen and Anne Eileen Stephen; *m* 1968, Susan Dorothy (*née* Harris); three *s* one *d*. *Educ*: Denbigh Road Primary Sch., Luton; Luton Grammar Sch.; King's Coll., Cambridge (BA Mod. Langs, 1964); Univ. of San Marcos, Lima, Peru; Univ. of Essex (MA Govt, 1968). Educn Officer, CRC, 1969–70; with Runnymede Trust, 1970–75 (Dir, 1973–75); Latin American Regional Rep., Internat. Univ. Exchange Fund, 1975–77; Special Adviser to Sec. of State for Foreign and Commonwealth Affairs, 1977–79; Editor, International Affairs, 1979–83; Dir, UK Immigrants Advisory Service, 1983–84; Commonwealth Development Corporation: Mem., Management Bd, 1984–92; Head of External Relations, 1985–89; Dir of Corporate Relns, 1989–92; Principal Officer, Exec. Office of Sec.-Gen., UN, 1992–96 and March–Sept. 1997; Dir, UN Verification Mission, Guatemala, June 1996–Feb. 1997; Rep. of UN Sec.-Gen., and Dir, UN Office for Somalia, 1997–2001; Rep. of UN Sec.-Gen., and Hd, UN Peace-building Support Office for Guinea-Bissau, 2002–04. Chm., Action for a Global Climate Community, 2009–13; Bd Mem., Internat. Action Network on Small Arms, 2009–13. EU Election Observer, Madagascar, 2013; Advr and Election Observer, All-Party Parly Gp on Guinea-Bissau, 2014. Trustee, Action Aid, 1981–92. Contested: (SDP-Liberal Alliance) N Luton, 1983, 1987; (Lib Dem) Norwich N, 2010. *Address*: Cobble Cottage, School Road, Brisley, Dereham, Norfolk NR20 5LH. *Club*: Royal Automobile.

**STEPHEN, Martin;** *see* Stephen, George M.

**STEPHEN, Mhairi Margaret;** QC (Scot.) 2015; Sheriff Principal of Lothian and Borders, since 2011; President, Sheriff Appeal Court, since 2015; *b* 22 Jan. 1954; *d* of William Strachan Stephen and Alexandrina Wood Stephen (*née* Grassam). *Educ*: George Watson's Ladies' Coll.; Univ. of Edinburgh (BA 1974; LLB 1976). With Allan McDougall & Co., SSC, Edinburgh, 1976–97, Partner, 1981–97; Sheriff of Lothian and Borders at Edinburgh, 1997–2011. Gov., Dean Orphanage and Cauvin's Trust, 2004–14. *Recreations*: curling, hillwalking, golf, music. *Address*: Sheriff Principal's Chambers, Edinburgh Sheriff Court, 27 Chambers Street, Edinburgh EH1 1LB. *T*: (0131) 225 2525. *Clubs*: New (Edinburgh); Murrayfield Golf, Murrayfield Curling.

**STEPHEN, Michael;** Group Deputy Chairman, Symphony Environmental Technologies plc, since 2007; *b* 25 Sept. 1942; *s* of late Harry Lace Stephen and Edna Florence Stephen; *m* 1989, Virginia Mary (*née* de Trensé). *Educ*: Stanford Univ. (LLM 1971); Harvard Univ. Admitted Solicitor, 1964 (DistCompany Law); called to the Bar, Inner Temple, 1966 (Hons); commissioned, The Life Guards, 1966–70; Harkness Fellowship in Internat. Law, 1970–72; Asst Legal Adviser, UK Delegn to UN, 1971; London Bar practice, 1972–87. Chm., Severnside Internat. Airport Consortium, 2000–05. County Councillor, Essex, 1985–91; contested (C) Doncaster North, 1983. MP (C) Shoreham, 1992–97. Member: Select Cttee on the Environment, 1994–97; Trade and Industry Select Cttee, 1996–97; European Standing Cttee, 1994–97. Vice Chm., Cons. Parly Home Affairs and Legal Cttees, 1994–97. Chm., Planning Cttee, Chelsea Soc., 2015–. Author: S. 36 Criminal Justice Act, 1988; Bail (Amendment) Act, 1993. *Publications*: numerous political pamphlets. *Recreations*: golf, history, theatre. *E*: kkrkyz@gmail.com.

**STEPHEN, Peter James;** Lord Lieutenant and Lord Provost, City of Aberdeen, 2007–12; *b* 24 April 1937; *m* 1960, Sandra McDonald; one *s* one *d*. *Educ*: Robert Gordon's Coll., Aberdeen. Nat. Service, RAF, 1955–57. Union Bank of Scotland Ltd, subseq. Bank of Scotland: mgt apprentice, 1953; Accountant, 1969, Asst Manager, 1973, Stirling Br.; Manager, Strathaven, Lanarkshire, 1977; Senior Manager: Fraserburgh, 1982; Kirkcaldy, 1989–91; self-employed business consultant, 1992–96; Inland Revenue Tax Comr, 1999–2007. Mem. (Scottish Lib Dem) Aberdeen CC, 2002–12. Mem., Chartered Inst. of Banking in Scotland, 1961. Dhc Aberdeen, 2012. OStJ 2009. *Recreation*: outdoor mostly. *Clubs*: Rotary, Probus (Aberdeen).

**STEPHEN, Rita;** *see* Stephen, H. H.

**STEPHENS, Barbara Marion, (Mrs T. J. Stephens)**, OBE 2002; Director, Student Casework, Open University, 2014–16; *b* 25 Aug. 1951; *d* of late Sydney and Edna Webb; *m* 1970, Trevor James Stephens. *Educ:* Mid-Essex Technical Coll. (HNC Engrg); NE London Poly. (DMS); City Univ. (MBA Engrg Mgt). IEng; MIET (MIProdE 1976); MIIE (MIET 1992). Mechanical technician apprentice, Marconi Co., 1969–73; various technical and managerial posts, Marconi Communication Systems Ltd, 1973–88; Industrial Advr, Electronic Applications, NEDO, 1988–92; Dir of Ops, then Chief Exec., W Cumbria Develt Agency, 1993–98; Chief Exec., Local Govt Commn for England, 1998–2002; Hd of Public Sector, subseq. Higher Educn, Practice, kmc internat., 2002–07; Principal, Carbon Leadership, 2007–09; Regl Dir, Open Univ. in London, 2009–11; Dir, Student Coursework and Special Projects, Open Univ., 2011–14. Co. Sec., Carbon-NfP Ltd, 2008–14. Member: Engineering Council, 1990–96; HEFCE, 1995–2002; Adv. Forum (formerly Council) for Develt of RN Personnel, 1995–2002 (Chm., 2001–02); a Dir, Assoc. of MBAs, 2001–06 (Chm., 2005–06). Chm., NHSU, 2003–05; Chair, Governing Body, Energy Coast Univ. Tech. Coll., 2016–. Non-executive Director: Cumbria Ambulance Service NHS Trust, 1996–98; EBS Trust, 2001–08. Board Member: New Opportunities Fund, 2001–04; Univ. of Cumbria, 2007–12; Equality Challenge Unit, 2008–14; London Higher, 2009–14. Lay Mem., Professional Conduct and Complaints Cttee, Gen. Council of Bar, 2000–09 (Lay Vice Chm., 2006–09). Ext. Trustee, Univ. of Cumbria Student Union, 2016–; Trustee: SafetyNet (UK), 2016–19; Hospice at Home, W Cumbria, 2019–. Gov., Carlisle Central Acad., 2016–. Hon. Fellow, Univ. of Cumbria, 2015–. FCMI (FIMgt 1994; MBIM 1978); FRSA 1992. DUniv Bradford, 2005. *Address:* Edgefield, 120A Stainburn Road, Workington, Cumbria CA14 1ST. *T:* (01900) 871095.

**STEPHENS, Sir Barrie;** *see* Stephens, Sir E. B.

**STEPHENS, Rt Hon. Sir Ben;** *see* Stephens, Rt Hon. Sir W. B. S.

**STEPHENS, Catherine Anne, (Mrs C. P. G. Qadir)**, OBE 1996; Acting Director, Education and Society, until 2011, and Member of Executive Board, 2007–11, British Council (Director, Innovation, 2007); *b* 24 Feb. 1951; *d* of Geoffrey Francis Stephens and Jeannine Christianne Langer Stephens; *m* 1998, Cecil Parvaiz Ghulam Qadir; one *d*, and one step *s*. *Educ:* Univ. of Hull (BA 1st Cl. American Studies 1978). Sec., George G. Harrap, 1970; Personal Asst, Penguin Books, 1970–71; Sec., UNESCO, Paris, 1972–73; Admin. Asst, US Peace Corps, Kabul, 1973–74; joined British Council, 1978: Asst, Educnl Contracts Dept, 1978–81; Zimbabwe, 1981–82; Asst Rep., Cameroon, 1982–85; Regl Officer, Central and E Africa S of Sahara Dept, 1985–88; First Sec., Develt, New Delhi, 1988–93; Deputy Director: Indonesia, 1993–96; India, 1996–2000; Regl Dir, W Africa, 2001–03; Dir, Africa and Asia, 2003–07. *Recreations:* travel, reading.

**STEPHENS, Christopher;** MP (SNP) Glasgow South West, since 2015; *b* Glasgow, 20 March 1973; *m*. *Educ:* Trinity High Sch., Renfrew. With Glasgow CC. Lead negotiator, UNISON, Glasgow. SNP spokesperson on Trade Unions and Workers' Rights, 2017–. Mem., Work and Pensions Select Cttee, 2017–. Mem., Nat. Exec. Cttee, SNP. Contested (SNP) Glasgow Pollock, Scottish Parlt, 2007, 2011. *Address:* House of Commons, SW1A 0AA.

**STEPHENS, Christopher Berkeley**, CBE 2016; Chairman, Judicial Appointments Commission, 2011–16; Senior Independent Director, since 2017, and Chairman, since 2018, OCS Group Ltd; *b* London, 28 April 1948; *s* of Sir David Stephens, KCB, CVO and (Mary) Clemency Stephens (*née* Gore Browne); *m* 1976, Anne Justine Margaret Lloyd Morgan; two *s* one *d*. *Educ:* Christ Church, Oxford (MA PPE 1970); St John's Coll., Nottingham (BA Theol. 1973). Prodn Trainee, United Biscuits, 1973–75; Human Resources Manager: Unilever plc, 1975–76; Nestlé SA, 1976–84; Unisys, 1984–88; Human Resources Director: Bet plc (Rentokil), 1988–93; Gen. Utilities (Vivendi), 1994–96; Gp HR Dir, Exel plc (DHL), 1996–2004. Member: CS Commn, 2005–09; Sen. Salaries Rev. Bd, 2009–11. Sen. Ind. Dir, WSP plc, 2003–12; Chm., Traidcraft plc, 2006–11; non-exec. Dir, Holidaybreak plc, 2008–11. Chm., DHL UK Foundn, 2015–18. Gov., Gordonstoun Sch., 2012–18. Trustee, Power to Change, 2016–. *Recreations:* allotment gardening, walking. *E:* chris.b.stephens@gmail.com.

**STEPHENS, Prof. Christopher David**, OBE 1999; FDSRCS, FDSRCSE; Professor of Child Dental Health, University of Bristol, 1984–2002, now Emeritus; *b* 29 May 1942; *s* of late Wilfred Ernest Donnington Stephens, OBE, PhD, and of Phyllis Margaret Stephens (*née* Lecroissette); *m* 1966, Marion Kay Prest; two *s*. *Educ:* Dulwich Coll.; Guy's Hosp. Dental Sch. (BDS); MDS Bristol. DOrthRCS 1968, MOrthRCS 1988; FDSRCSE 1970; FDSRCS 1986. Hse Surgeon, 1965, Registrar in Children's Dentistry, 1966–69, Guy's Hosp. Dental Sch.; Registrar in Orthodontics, Royal Dental Hosp., 1969–71; Lectr in Orthodontics, 1971–76, Consultant Sen. Lectr in Orthodontics, 1976–84, Univ. of Bristol. Civil Consultant in Orthodontics to RAF, 1988–2005. Mem., Standing Dental Adv. Cttee, 1992–98. Pres., British Orthodontic Soc., 2001–02. Hon. Life Mem., European Orthodontic Soc., 2003. Fellow, BDA, 2004. Ballard Medal, Consultant Orthodontists Gp, 2003. Trustee, Dry Stone Walling Assoc. of GB, 2002–08 (Vice Pres., 2018–). *Publications:* (jtly) Functional Orthodontic Appliances, 1990; (with K. G. Isaacson) Practical Orthodontic Assessment, 1990; (jtly) A Textbook of Orthodontics, 2nd edn 1992; A History of the University of Bristol Dental School, 2012; The Rev. Dr Thomas Sedgwick Whalley and the Queen of Bath, 2014; Bristol's Australian Pioneer: Robert Edwin Bush and the Bishop's Knoll WW1 Hospital, 2016; contrib. numerous papers to refereed jls. *Recreations:* amateur radio, dry stone-walling, woodland management, walking. *Address:* 12 Berkshire Road, Bristol BS7 8EX. *T:* (0117) 942 9944.

**STEPHENS, Prof. David John**, PhD; Professor of Cell Biology, since 2010, and Faculty Research Director, Life Sciences, since 2018, University of Bristol; *b* Torquay, 8 Nov. 1971; *m* 2014; two *s*. *Educ:* N Devon Coll.; Royal Holloway and Bedford New Coll., Univ. of London (BSc Hons); St George's Hosp. Med. Sch., Univ. of London (PhD 1996). Res. Asst, Univ. of Bristol, 1996–99; EMBO Fellow, EMBL Heidelberg, 1999–2001; MRC Fellow, Univ. of Bristol, 2001–10. Mem., UKRI-BBSRC, 2018–20. Ed., Jl Cell Sci., 2015–. *Publications:* contribs to scholarly jls. *Address:* School of Biochemistry, Biomedical Sciences Building, University of Bristol, University Walk, Bristol BS8 1TD.

**STEPHENS, Sir (Edwin) Barrie**, Kt 1998; CEng; Chairman, 1990–98, Hon. President, since 1998, Siebe plc. *Educ:* Christ Coll., Brecon; Manchester Univ. CEng 1962. Industrial Engr, General Dynamics, USA, 1954; Production Manager, Barden Corp., Conn, USA, 1962; Dir of Manufg, Barden Corp. Ltd, UK, 1962–63; Man. Dir, Siebe Gorman and Co. Ltd, 1963–75; Gp Man. Dir and CEO, Siebe Gorman Hldgs Ltd, 1975–86; Vice-Chm., 1987–90, CEO, 1987–93, Siebe plc. Hon. DSc Plymouth, 1993. *Club:* Carlton.

**STEPHENS, Dame Elan Closs**, DBE 2019 (CBE 2001); non-executive Director, Welsh Government Board, and Chairman, Corporate Governance, 2009–18; Chairman, Wales Public Leaders Forum, since 2018; *b* 16 June 1948; *d* of William Jones and Mair Closs Roberts (*née* Williams); *m* 1972, Roy Stephens (*d* 1989); one *s* one *d*. *Educ:* Ysgol Dyffryn Nantlle, Penygroes; Somerville Coll., Oxford (Open Schol.); BA 1969). Aberystwyth University (formerly University of Wales, Aberystwyth): Lectr, 1976–84; Hd of Dept, 1984–91; Sen. Lectr, 1994–2001; Prof. of Communications and Creative Industries, 2001–11, now Emeritus. Member: Broadcasting Council for Wales, 1984–89; S4C Authy, 1990–95; Council, Nat. Liby of Wales, 1995–2005; Wales Adv. Cttee, CRE, 2003–; Vice-Chm., Welsh Language Bd, 1994–98; Chairman: Welsh Fourth Channel Authy, 1998–2006; Chwarae Teg, 2002–04; Wales Adv. Cttee, British Council, 2005–10 (Global Trustee, 2006–08). Author, report on funding and governance model for Wales Arts Council, 2006. Governor: BFI, 2001–07 (Dir, Big Screen Ltd, 2006–); Univ. of Glamorgan. 2002. Mem., Electoral Commn, 2017–; Trustee (for Wales), BBC Trust, 2010–17; non-exec. Dir, BBC Bd, 2017– (Chm., Wales Cttee, 2018–); Mem. Bd and Chm., BBC Commercial Holdings, 2019–. FRSA 2002; FLSW 2019. Hon. Fellow: Trinity Coll., Carmarthen, 2004; Coleg Cymraeg Cenedlaethol, 2014; Bangor Univ. 2019. Hon. Dr: Glamorgan, 2010; Wales, 2017. Cyfrwng Award, 2007. High Sheriff, Dyfed, 2012–13. *Publications:* chapters and articles on Welsh theatre and media policy. *Recreations:* reading, theatre, television, film, cookery and eating out with friends. *Address:* Fronhyfryd, Ffordd Llanbadarn, Aberystwyth SY23 1EY. *T:* (01970) 625653.

**STEPHENS, Eldridge**, OBE 2009; High Commissioner for St Lucia in the United Kingdom, 2008–12; *b* St Lucia, 19 Oct. 1946; *s* of Emmanuel Octave and Mary Anna Stephens; *m* 1972, Peternise Peter; one *s*. *Educ:* Vieux Fort Boys Primary Sch.; St Mary's Coll.; Sir Arthur Lewis Community Coll. Primary sch. teacher, 1962–71; St Lucia Civil Service, 1971; Traffic Superintendent, LIAT (1974) Ltd, 1971–94; Man. Dir, Phoenix Services Ltd and Hewanorra Air Cargo Services, 1994–2008. Mem., Vieux Fort Town Council, 1974–79 (Chm., 1989–91). MP and Dep. Speaker, House of Assembly, 1982–87. Dep. Chm., Nat. Develt Corp., 1987–95; Dir, Windward & Leeward Brewery, 1987–95; Dir, Housing and Urban Develt Corp., 1996–97; Dep. Chm., Develt Control Authy, 2007–08; Dir, St Lucia Bureau of Standards, 2007–08. Founder and Pres., Sports and Cultural Orgn, 1969; Manager/Sec., Goodwill Fishermen Co-op., 1972–74; Chm., Develt Cttee, Southern Carnival, 1980–81; Pres., Parents and Teachers Assoc. Vieux Fort Comp. Sec. Sch., 1989–91; Dist Gov. and Chm. Council of Govs, Lions Club Internat., 1999–2001; Chm. Council, St John's, St Lucia, 2002–08. JP 1987. OStJ 2004. *Recreations:* sports (football, cricket and athletics), travelling, volunteering. *Address:* Moule a Chique, Vieux Fort, St Lucia. *T:* 4546268. *E:* eldridges@candw.lc. *Club:* Lions Club International (Vieux Fort).

**STEPHENS, Jean Marie;** Chief Executive Officer, RSM International Ltd, since 2006; *b* Calif, USA, 1959. *Educ:* Univ. of Redlands, Calif (BSc Accounting 1981); California State Univ., San Bernardino (MS Finance 1990). Partner and Hd, Audit Practice, Fleming Reiss & Co., 1990–94; Sen. Manager, 1994–2001, Partner, 2001–11, RSM McGladrey; Chief Operating Officer, RSM Internat. Ltd, 2003–06. Pres., Inland Empire Chapter, YWCA, 1992–96; Vice Pres., Finance, Inland Empire Symphony, 1995; Treas., United Way, 1995. MInstD. Hon. Dr Humane Letters Redlands, 2009. Athena Award for Outstanding Business Woman of the Year, San Bernardino Chamber of Commerce, 1993. *Address:* RSM International Ltd, 50 Cannon Street, EC4N 6JJ. *T:* (020) 7601 1080, *Fax:* (020) 7601 1090. *E:* jean.stephens@rsmi.com.

**STEPHENS, Sir Jonathan (Andrew de Sievrac)**, KCB 2013; Permanent Under-Secretary, Northern Ireland Office, since 2014; *b* 8 Feb. 1960; *s* of Prescot and Peggy Stephens; *m* 1983, Rev. Penny; one *s* one *d*. *Educ:* Sevenoaks Sch.; Christ Church, Oxford (MA). NI Office, 1983–89; HM Treasury, 1989–92; Northern Ireland Office, 1992–2000: Principal Private Sec., 1993–94; Associate Pol Dir, 1996–2000; Dir, Modernising Public Services, Cabinet Office, 2000–01; Dir, Public Services, 2001–03, Public Spending, 2003–04, Man. Dir, Public Services, 2004–06, HM Treasury; Permanent Secretary: DCMS, 2006–13; HM Treasury, 2013–14. *Address:* Northern Ireland Office, 1 Horse Guards Road, SW1A 2HQ.

**STEPHENS, Malcolm George**, CB 1991; Group Chairman, International Financial Consulting, since 1998; Chairman, IFC Training, 2001–11; *b* 14 July 1937; *s* of Frank Ernest Stephens and Janet (*née* McQueen); *m* 1975, Lynette Marie Caffery, Brisbane, Australia. *Educ:* St Michael's and All Angels; Shooters Hill Grammar Sch.; St John's Coll., Oxford (Casberd Scholar; BA 1st Cl. Hons PPE; MA 1995). National Service, RAOC, 1956–58. CRO, 1953; British High Commission: Ghana, 1959–62; Kenya, 1963–65; Export Credits Guarantee Dept, 1965–82: Principal, 1970; seconded to Civil Service Coll., 1971–72; Asst Sec., 1974; Estab. Officer, 1977; Under Sec., 1978; Head of Proj. Gp B, 1978–79; Principal Finance Officer, 1979–82; Internat. Finance Dir, Barclays Bank Internat. Ltd, 1982–84; Dir, Barclays Export Services, 1984–87; Export Finance Dir, Barclays Bank PLC, 1985–87; Chief Executive: ECGD, 1987–91; London Chamber of Commerce and Industry, 1991–92; Pres., 1989–91, Sec.-Gen., 1992–98, Internat. Union of Credit and Investment Insurers (Berne Union); Man. Dir and Dep. Chm., Commonwealth Investment Guarantee Agency, 1998–99; Exec. Dir, IPCIS, 1999–2001. Chm., Del Credere Insurance Services Ltd, 1999–2001; Director: European Capital, 1992–2000; Arab-British Chamber of Commerce, 1992–95; Major Projects Assoc., 1995–99; Berry, Palmer & Lyle, 1997–2001; EULER Internat., 1998–2000. Mem. Adv. Council, Zurich Emerging Markets, 2001–14; Advr to Sinosure, China, 2000–; Consultant: to EU PHARE Prog., 1997–99; to World Bank, 1997–2001; Eur. Commn, 1999–2000, 2011; OECD (Russia), 2001; APEC, 2002, 2003; Asian Develt Bank, 2005; Govt of Chile, 1999, of Bangladesh, 1999, of Iran, 2000, of Sri Lanka, 2000, of S Africa, 2000, 2002, of Australia, 2000, 2001, 2002, 2003, of NZ, 2001, of Turkey, 2001, of Canada, 2001, 2003, 2007, 2008, 2009, of Fiji, 2003, of Romania, 2007, of Singapore, 2011–12. Advr, CDR Internat., 1998–2000; Exec. Vice-Pres., SGA Internat., Florida, 1998–2000. Member: Overseas Projects Bd, 1985–87; BOTB, 1987–91. Vis. Schol., IMF, 1998–99. Member: Cook Soc., 2002–; Australia Britain Soc., 2002. Order of Australia Assoc., 2004– (Treas., Southern Highlands Gp, 2005–). Nat. Hon. Sec., Assoc. of Australian Decorative and Fine Arts Socs, 2012–14 (Nat. Vice Chm., 2010–11); Chm., Southern Highlands Australia Britain Soc., 2012– (Treas., 2006–12); Pres., Southern Highlands Opera Appreciation Gp, 2013–19 (Dep. Pres., 2012). FCIB (FIB 1984); FIEx 1987; MCICM (MICM 1990). *Publications:* The Changing Role of Export Credit Agencies, 1999. *Recreations:* gardening, reading, tapestry, watching cricket and football (Charlton Athletic). *Address:* 38 Argyle Street, Bong Bong Hill, Moss Vale, NSW 2577, Australia. *Clubs:* Union, University and Schools (Sydney).

**STEPHENS, Mark Howard**, CBE 2011; lawyer; broadcaster; writer; lecturer; Senior Member, Howard Kennedy (formerly Finers Stephens Innocent, later HowardKennedyFSI) LLP, since 1999; Mediator, since 2007; *b* Old Windsor, Berks, 7 April 1957; *s* of Howard Stephens and Evelyn Phyllis Stephens (*née* Banks); *m* 1982, Donna Michelle Coote; three *d*. *Educ:* St Paul's Secondary Modern Sch.; Cambridge Manor Acad. for Dramatic Arts; Strode's Grammar Sch.; North East London Poly. (BA Hons Law); Coll. of Law. Legal Dir, Art Law, 1982–84; Founder and Sen. Partner, Stephens Innocent, solicitors, 1983–99. Member: British Copyright Council, 1986–98; Bd, ICSTIS, 1990–96; Founder Chm., Policy Bd, 1996–99, Vice Chm., 1999–2003, Internet Watch Foundn. Chm., Mgt Cttee, Prog. in Comparative Media Law and Policy, Wolfson Coll., Centre for Socio-Legal Studies, Univ. of Oxford, 1997–. Trustee: Index on Censorship, 2002–12 (Hon. Solicitor, 2012–); Bianca Jagger Human Rights Foundn, 2007– (Chm.); Bd, Internat. Law Book Trust; Founding Trustee, Solicitors' Pro Bono Gp, 1997–2004; Chairman: Solicitors' Law Fest., 1998–2001; Greenwich and Docklands Internat. Fests, 1999–2004;

Contemp. Art Soc., 2010–14 (Trustee, 1987–2009; Hon. Solicitor, 2002–09); Design Artists Copyright Soc., 2011–; Media Law Defence Initiative, 2011–; Global Network Initiative, 2014–. Mem., FCO Free Expression Adv. Bd, 2002–. Mem. Exec. Cttee and Dir, Commonwealth Lawyers Assoc., 2007– (Vice Pres., 2011–13; Pres., 2013–15); Mem. Human Rights Council, IBA, 2009– (Trial Observer, 2005). Patron, Internat. Alert, 2011–. Ind. Dir, ISI, 2011–. Chm. Govs, Univ. of E London, 2009–; Gov., Rose Bruford Coll. of Theatre and Performance, 2003–07. Gov., Wanstead C of E Primary Sch., 1996–2002. Freeman, City of London, 1989; Liveryman, Stationers' Co., 2004; Freeman, Solicitors' Co., 2005. Hon. DLaws East London, 2001. *Publications:* (contrib.) Miscarriages of Justice: a review of justice in error, 1999; (contrib.) International Libel and Privacy Handbook, 2005, 4th edn 2016; (contrib.) This is Not a Book about Gavin Turk, 2012; (contrib) La Presunción de Inocencia Y Los Juicios Paralelos, 2013; (contrib.) Media Law and Ethics in the 21st Century, 2014; (contrib.) Media Law International: specialist guide to media law practice; (contrib.) Media Law and Policy in the Internet Age. *Recreations:* bees, badinage and anglophism. *Address:* Howard Kennedy LLP, No 1, London Bridge, SE1 9BG. *T:* (020) 3755 5725, *Fax:* (020) 3650 7075. *E:* mark.stephens@howardkennedy.com. *Clubs:* Chelsea Football; Aston Martin Owners.

**STEPHENS, His Honour Martin;** *see* Stephens, His Honour S. M.

**STEPHENS, Philip Francis Christopher;** Associate Editor, since 2003, Chief Political Commentator, since 2004, and Director, Editorial Board, since 2018, Financial Times; *b* 2 June 1953; *s* of Haydn Stephens and Theresa (*née* Martin); partner, Patty Hemingway; one *s* one d. *Educ:* Wimbledon Coll.; Worcester Coll., Oxford (BA Hons Mod. Hist.). Correspondent London and Brussels, Reuters, 1979–83; Financial Times: Econs Correspondent, 1983–88; Political Ed., 1988–94; Political Commentator, 1994–99; Ed., UK Edn, 1999–2003. Fulbright Fellow, LA Times, 1988. Gov., 2006–, Mem. Council, 2008–, Vice-Chm., 2013–, The Ditchley Foundn; Member: Steering Gp, Anglo-French Colloque, 2006–; Adv. Council, IPPR, 2010–. David Watt Meml Prize for Outstanding Political Journalism, RTZ, 2002; Political Journalist of the Year, Political Studies Assoc., 2004; Political Journalist of the Year, British Press Awards, 2008. *Publications:* Politics and the Pound, 1996; Tony Blair: the price of leadership, 2004. *Recreations:* trying to understand history, talking to my adult children, rediscovering good books. *Address:* c/o Financial Times, Bracken House, 1 Friday Street, EC4M 9BT. *E:* stephenspfc@hotmail.com. *Club:* Chelsea Football.

**STEPHENS, Simon William;** playwright; Artistic Associate, Lyric Theatre, Hammersmith, since 2009; Professor of Scriptwriting, Manchester Metropolitan University, since 2018; Associate Professor, Royal Danish School of Music and Drama; *b* Manchester, 6 Feb. 1971; *s* of Graham Stephens and Carole Stephens; *m* 2005, Polly Heath; two *s* one d. *Educ:* Stockport Sch.; Univ. of York (BA Hons Hist. 1992); London Inst. of Educn (PGCE 1998). Resident Dramatist: Royal Court Th., 2000; Royal Exchange, 2000; NT, 2007. *Plays include:* Bluebird, 1998; Herons, 2001; Port, 2002; Christmas, 2003; One Minute, 2003; Country Music, 2004; On the Shore of the Wide World, 2005; Motortown, 2006; Pornography, 2007; Harper Regan, 2008; Punk Rock, 2009; Sea Wall, 2009; Marine Parade, 2010; The Trial of Ubu, 2010; (jtly) A Thousand Stars Explode in the Sky, 2010; T5, 2010; Wastwater, 2011; Three Kingdoms, 2011–12; (adaptation) The Curious Incident of the Dog in the Night-Time, 2012; (adaptation) A Doll's House, 2012; Morning, 2012; Blindsided, 2014; Birdland, 2014; (trans.) The Cherry Orchard, 2014; Carmen Disruption, 2015; The Funfair, 2015; Song from Far Away, 2015; (adaptation) The Threepenny Opera, 2016; Nuclear War, 2017; Fatherland, 2017; Heisenberg: The Uncertainty Principle, 2017; Maria, 2019; Light Falls, 2019; Fortune, 2019. *Publications:* plays: Bluebird, 1998; Herons, 2001; Port, 2002; Christmas, 2003; One Minute, 2003; Country Music, 2004; On the Shore of the Wide World, 2005; Motortown, 2006; Pornography, 2007; Harper Regan, 2008; Punk Rock, 2009; (jtly) Marine Parade, 2010; The Trial of Ubu, 2010; (jtly) A Thousand Stars Explode in the Sky, 2010; Wastwater and T5, 2011; Three Kingdoms, 2012. *Recreations:* drinking wine, listening to dissonant music, playing with my children, irresponsible evils of Tweeting. *Address:* Lyric Theatre, Lyric Square, Hammersmith, W6 0QL. *E:* simonwstephens@mac.com. *W:* www.twitter.com/StephensSimon

**STEPHENS, His Honour (Stephen) Martin;** QC 1982; a Circuit Judge 1986–2012; a Judge of the Central Criminal Court, 1999–2012; *b* 26 June 1939; *s* of late Abraham Stephens and Freda Stephens, Swansea; *m* 1965, Patricia Alison, *d* of late Joseph and Anne Morris, Mapperley, Nottingham; one *s* one *d* (and one *s* decd). *Educ:* Swansea Grammar Sch.; Wadham Coll., Oxford (MA). Called to the Bar, Middle Temple, 1963, Bencher, 2004; Wales and Chester Circuit; a Recorder, 1979–86. Mem., Parole Bd, 1995–2001, 2010–18. Mem., Criminal Cttee, 1995–2000, Main Bd, 1997–2000, Judicial Studies Bd. *Recreations:* cricket, theatre.

**STEPHENS, Toby;** actor; *b* 21 April 1969; *s* of Sir Robert Graham Stephens and of Dame Maggie Smith, *qv*; *m* 2001, Anna-Louise Plowman; one *s* one d. *Educ:* Aldro Sch.; Seaford Coll.; LAMDA. Crewed, Chichester Festival Th., 1986 and 1987; *theatre* includes: Tartuffe, Playhouse, 1991; Royal Shakespeare Company: All's Well That Ends Well, Antony and Cleopatra, Tamburlaine, Unfinished Business, Wallenstein, 1992; Coriolanus, A Midsummer Night's Dream, Measure for Measure, 1994; Hamlet, The Pilate Workshop, 2004; A Streetcar Named Desire, Haymarket, 1996; Phèdre, Britannicus, Almeida, 1998, transf. NY, 1999; Ring Round the Moon, NY, 1999; Japes, The Royal Family, Haymarket, 2001; Betrayal, Donmar Warehouse, The Country Wife, Haymarket, 2007; A Doll's House, Donmar Warehouse, 2009; The Real Thing, Old Vic, 2010; Danton's Death, NT, 2010; Private Lives, Chichester Festival Th., 2012, Gielgud, 2013; Oslo, NT, 2017; A Day in the Death of Joe Egg, Trafalgar Studios, 2019; *films* include: Photographing Fairies, 1997; Cousin Bette, 1998; Onegin, 1999; Space Cowboys, 2000; Possession, Die Another Day, 2002; Severance, 2006; All Things to All Men, 2013; The Journey, 2017; Hunter Killer, 2018; *television* includes: The Camomile Lawn, 1992; The Tenant of Wildfell Hall, 1996; The Great Gatsby, 2000; Perfect Strangers, 2001; Cambridge Spies, Poirot - Five Little Pigs, 2003; The Queen's Sister, 2005; The Best Man, Sharpe's Challenge, Jane Eyre, 2006; Wired, 2008; Vexed, 2010, 2012; Black Sails, 2015; And Then There Were None, 2015; Summer of Rockets, 2019. *Address:* c/o United Agents, 12–26 Lexington Street, W1F 0LE.

**STEPHENS, Rt Hon. Sir (William) Ben(jamin Synge),** Kt 2007; PC 2017; **Rt Hon. Lord Justice Stephens;** a Lord Justice of Appeal, Northern Ireland, since 2017; *b* 28 Dec. 1954; *s* of Denis Synge Stephens and Gladys Joyce Stephens (*née* Clarke); *m* 1982, Nicola Gladys Skrine; one *s* one d. *Educ:* Swanbourne House Sch., Swanbourne, Bucks; Campbell Coll., Belfast; Manchester Univ. (LLB 1st cl. Hons). Called to the Bar: NI, 1977; Lincoln's Inn, 1978; Ireland, 1996; QC (NI) 1996; a Judge of the High Court of Justice, NI, 2007–17. Vice-Chm., Gen. Council of the Bar of NI, 2006–07. *Address:* Royal Courts of Justice, Belfast BT1 3JF.

**STEPHENSON, Andrew George;** MP (C) Pendle, since 2010; Minister of State, Department for International Development and Foreign and Commonwealth Office, since 2019; *b* 17 Feb. 1981; *s* of Malcolm and Ann Stephenson. *Educ:* Poynton Co. High Sch.; Royal Holloway, Univ. of London (BSc Business Mgt 2002). Partner, Stephenson and Threader, 2002–10. Mem. (C), Macclesfield BC, 2003–07. Vice Chm., (Youth) Conservative Party, 2010–13. PPS to Minister without Portfolio and Dep. Chm. Cons. Party, 2015–16; PPS, Home Office, 2015–16; PPS to Foreign Sec., 2016–17; an Asst Govt Whip, 2017–18; a Lord Comr of HM Treasury (Govt Whip), 2018; Vice Chamberlain of HM Household (Govt Whip), 2018–19; Parly Under-Sec. of State, BEIS, 2019. *Address:* House of Commons, SW1A 0AA.

**STEPHENSON, Ashley;** *see* Stephenson, R. A. S.

**STEPHENSON, Charles Lyon,** TD 1972; Vice Lord-Lieutenant of Derbyshire, 2004–10; *b* 15 Aug. 1935; *s* of Col C. E. K. Stephenson and Nancy Stephenson; *m* 1st, 1960, Jane Tinker (marr. diss. 1972); two *s* one d; 2nd, 1974, Hon. Sarah Norrie. *Educ:* Eton Coll. Employed in family engrg business Stephenson Blake (Holdings) Ltd, 1956–2000, Gp Man. Dir, 1985–2000. Non-executive Director: Bramber Engrg Co. Ltd, 1980–87; Lyon and Lyon plc, 1982–90; Director: Carlton Main Brickworks Ltd, 1977–2017; Kestrel Travel Consultancy Ltd, 1998–; Hotel and Catering Staff Supplies Ltd, 1998–. Chairman: Derbys Br., Rural Devolt Commn, 1987–93; Wynkin de Worde Soc., 1990; Derbys Br., SSAFA Forces Help, 2001–13. High Sheriff, 1984–85, DL, 2004, Derbys. *Recreations:* gardening, shooting, fishing, theatre, travel. *Address:* The Cottage, Great Longstone, Bakewell, Derbyshire DE45 1UA. *T:* (01629) 640213, *Fax:* (01629) 640135. *E:* Charles@kestreltravel.com. *Clubs:* Cavalry and Guards; MCC.

**STEPHENSON, Darryl Leslie;** DL; Managing Director, Hardmoor Associates Ltd, since 2005; Chief Executive, Hull City Council, 2012–15; *b* 4 Sept. 1950; *s* of late Lawrence Stephenson and of Olga Mary Stephenson; *m* 1984, Susan Marialuisa Lockwood; one *s* one d. *Educ:* Warwick Sch.; Trent Poly. (BA Hons); Coll. of Law, Chester; Univ. of Birmingham (Advanced Mgt Develt Prog., 1986). Admitted Solicitor, 1980. Articled Clerk, W Bromwich CBC, 1972–74; Solicitor, Warwick DC, 1974–80; Principal Asst Chief Exec., Leicester CC, 1980–89; Dep. Town Clerk, subseq. Town Clerk and Chief Exec., Hull CC, 1989–95; Chief Exec., ER of Yorks Unitary Council, 1995–2005; Interim Chief Exec., NE Lincs Council, March–Nov. 2004; Strategic Advr, Deloitte, 2005–12. Vis. Prof., Univ. of Hull, 2005–. Co. Sec., Humber Forum Ltd, 1992–2005. Clerk to: Humber Bridge Bd, 1993–96, 2010–17; Humberside Police Authy, 1996–97; Lord Lieut, E Riding of Yorks, 1996–2005; Sec., N Eastern Sea Fisheries Cttee, 1996–2005; Humberside Police Appts Cttee, 2004–. Chm., E Riding Drug Action Team, 1995–2002; Mem. Council, Hull and E Riding Chamber of Commerce, Industry and Shipping, 1995–. Member: First-tier Tribunal (Local Govt Standards) (formerly Adjudication Panel for England), 2002–; Bd, Hull Pathfinders, 2004–11. Mem. of Court, Univ. of Hull, 1993; Gov., Beverley Coll., 1998. Chm., AgeUK E Riding, 2007–18; Trustee: Age Concern E Yorks, 2005; Beverley Meml Hall, 2006–. DL ER of Yorks, 2005. Hon. LLD Hull, 2006. *Recreations:* motor boating, music, painting, food and wine. *Address:* Hardmoor Grange, Hardmoor Lane, Hotham, ER Yorks YO43 4UJ. *Club:* Portcullis (Warwick).

**STEPHENSON, David Arnold;** QC (Scot.) 2009; *b* Dumfries, 6 June 1959; *s* of Arnold Stephenson and Sylvia Walker Stephenson; *m* Catherine Johan Paterson; three d. *Educ:* Royal High Sch. of Edinburgh; Univ. of Aberdeen (LLB Hons, DipLP). Admitted as solicitor, 1983; solicitor in private practice, 1982–90; Advocate at Scottish Bar, specialising in professional negligence, personal injury, insce and medical law, 1991–; Westwater Advocates, 1991–2013; Ampersand Advocates, 2013–. Mem., Mason Inst. for Medicine, Life Scis and the Law, Univ. of Edinburgh, 2013–. *Recreations:* cycling, walking, arts, music and literature, travel, family. *Address:* Advocates' Library, Parliament House, Edinburgh EH1 1RF.

**STEPHENSON, Rev. Canon Eric George;** Vicar, St George's Church, East Boldon, 1985–2008; Chaplain to the Queen, 2002–11; *b* 26 April 1941; *s* of Albert and Nora Stephenson. *Educ:* Bede Coll., Durham (Teaching Cert., 1963); Birmingham Univ. (DipTh 1965; Dip. Liturgy and Architecture 1968). Ordained deacon, 1966, priest, 1967; Curate: St John the Baptist, Wakefield, 1966–69; Seaham with Seaham Harbour, Durham, 1969–73; Cockerton, Darlington, 1973–75; Licence to officiate, 1975–85; Teacher, Haughton Comp. Sch., Darlington, 1975–85. Area Dean of Jarrow, 1992–2001; Non-residentiary Canon, 1993–2008, Canon Emeritus, 2008, Durham Cathedral. *Recreations:* current affairs, history, archaeology, music appreciation.

**STEPHENSON, George Anthony C.;** *see* Carter-Stephenson.

**STEPHENSON, Dr Helen Mary,** CBE 2014; Chief Executive, Charity Commission for England and Wales, since 2017; *b* Rochford, 16 Dec. 1960; *d* of Gordon, (Bill), Cartwright and Rhoda Mary Cartwright; *m* 2004, Roger Stephenson; one d. *Educ:* Dover Grammar Sch.; Westcliff High Sch. for Girls; Goldsmiths' Coll., London (BA Hons Drama and English); Surrey Univ. (MSc Social Res.); Bristol Univ. (PhD 1999). Researcher, Consumer Involvement Project, 1991–94; Dir, Outlook Associates, 1994–96; Develt Manager, Shaftesbury Soc., 1999–2001; Hd of Policy, Big Lottery Fund, 2001–07; Dep. Dir, Office for Civil Society, 2007–11, Dir, Govt Innovation Unit, 2012–14, Cabinet Office; Dir, Early Years and Childcare, DFE, 2014–17. *Recreations:* theatre, reading, gym, family. *Address:* Charity Commission for England and Wales, 102 Petty France, SW1H 9AJ. *T:* 0300 065 2140. *E:* helen.stephenson@charitycommission.gsi.gov.uk.

**STEPHENSON, Sir Hugh Upton,** 3rd Bt *cr* 1936; TD; Director: Stephenson Blake & Co. Ltd, 1952–75; Stephenson, Blake (Holdings) Ltd, 1972–99; *b* 26 Nov. 1926; *s* of Lt-Col Sir Henry Francis Blake Stephenson, 2nd Bt, OBE, TD, and Joan, *d* of Major John Herbert Upton (formerly Upton Cottrell-Dormer); *S* father, 1982, but his name does not appear on the Official Roll of the Baronetage; *m* 1962, Susan, *o d* of Major J. E. Clowes, Ashbourne, Derbyshire; four d. *Educ:* Eton. Formerly Major, QO Yorkshire Dragoons. High Sheriff of Derbyshire, 1975. *Heir:* cousin Matthew Francis Timothy Stephenson [*b* 24 Aug. 1960; *m* 1984, Philippa Delphine Lincoln; one *s* two d]. *Address:* Tissington Cottage, Rowland, Bakewell, Derbyshire DE45 1NR.

**STEPHENSON, Prof. Hugh;** writer and journalist; Professor of Journalism, City University, 1986–2003, now Emeritus; *b* 18 July 1938; *s* of late Sir Hugh Stephenson; *m* 1st, 1962, Auriol Stevens, *qv* (marr. diss. 1987); two *s* one d; 2nd, 1990, Diana Eden. *Educ:* Winchester Coll.; New Coll., Oxford (BA); Univ. of Calif, Berkeley. Pres., Oxford Union, 1962. HM Diplomatic Service, 1964–68; joined The Times, 1968; Editor, The Times Business News, 1972–81; Editor, The New Statesman, 1982–86. Dir, Eur. Journalism Centre, Maastricht, 1993–2008 (Chm., 1995–2002). Mem., Cttee to Review Functioning of Financial Instns, 1977–80. Councillor, London Bor. of Wandsworth, 1971–78. Dir, History Today Ltd, 1981–2014 (Chm., 2011–14). FRSA 1987. *Publications:* The Coming Clash, 1972; Mrs Thatcher's First Year, 1980; Claret and Chips, 1982; (jtly) Libel and the Media, 1997; Secrets of the Setters, 2005. *Address:* 7 Clifton Terrace, Brighton, E Sussex BN1 3HA.

**STEPHENSON, Lynne, (Mrs Chaim Stephenson);** *see* Banks, L. R.

**STEPHENSON, Paul,** OBE 2009; Regional Director, Wales and the West, Focus Consultancy Ltd, 1992–2000; *b* 6 May 1937; *s* of Olive Stephenson; *m* 1965, Joyce Annikie; one *s* one d. *Educ:* Westhill Coll. of Educn, Selly Oak, Birmingham. MCIPR (MIPR 1978). Youth Tutor, St Paul's, Bristol, 1962–68; Sen. Community Relations Officer, Coventry,

1968–72; National Youth Trng Officer, Community Relations Commn, 1972–77; Sen. Liaison Officer, CRE, 1980–92. Chm., Muhammad Ali Sports Develt Assoc., Brixton and Lambeth, 1974–; Member: British Sports Council, 1976–82; Press Council, 1984–90. Chm., Bristol Legacy Commn, 2008–. Freeman, City of Bristol, 2007. *Recreations:* travel, cinema, reading, international politics. *Address:* 12 Downs Park East, Westbury Park, Bristol BS6 7QD. *T:* (0117) 962 3638.

**STEPHENSON, Sir Paul (Robert),** Kt 2008; QPM 2000; Commissioner, Metropolitan Police, 2009–11 (Deputy Commissioner, 2005–09); *b* 26 Sept. 1953; *s* of late Jack Stephenson and of Rose Cathryne (*née* Sullivan); *m* 1974, Lynda, *d* of late James Alexander Parker; three *d*. *Educ:* Bacup and Rawtenstall Grammar Sch. Mgt trainee, E. Sutton & Son, 1973–75; with Lancashire Constabulary, 1975–94: Chief Inspector, 1986; Supt, 1988; Asst Chief Constable, Merseyside, 1994–99; Dep. Chief Constable, 1999–2001, Chief Constable, 2002–05, Lancs Constabulary. Company dir, 2012–. Ind. Regulatory Dir, British Horse Racing Authy, 2015–. Trustee, Crimestoppers, 2012–. Hon. Fellow, Univ. of Central Lancs, 2007. *Recreations:* country sports, reading.

**STEPHENSON, (Robert) Ashley (Shute),** LVO 1990 (MVO 1979); FCIHort; Bailiff of the Royal Parks, 1980–90; *b* 1 Sept. 1927; *s* of late James Stephenson and Agnes Maud Stephenson; *m* 1955, Isabel Dunn, BEM; one *s* one *d*. *Educ:* Walbottle Secondary Sch. Diploma in Horticulture, RHS, Wisley, 1954; MIHort 1987, FCIHort (FIHort 1998). Apprenticeship, Newcastle upon Tyne Parks Dept, 1942; served RASC, Palestine and Cyprus, 1946; Landscape Gardener, Donald Ireland Ltd, 1949; Student, RHS's gardens, Wisley, 1952; Royal Parks, 1954–90: Supt, Regent's Park, 1969; Supt, Central Royal Parks, 1972. Gardening Correspondent, The Times, 1982–87. President: British Pelargonium and Geranium Soc., 1983–95; South East in Bloom, 2001 (Chm., 1990–2001); Member: Cttee, RHS, 1981–; London in Bloom Cttee, English Tourism Council (formerly English Tourist Bd), 1980–91 (Vice-Chm., 1983); Chm., Floral Jersey, 1990–2001; Nat. Chm., Britain in Bloom, 1991–2001; Mem., The Queen's Anniversary Cttee 1952–92, 1992– (Chm., Horticl Cttee, 1992–). Contributor to television and radio programmes; regularly on BBC Radio Sussex gardening programmes; gardening correspondent to professional and amateur papers. *Publications:* The Garden Planner, 1981; contribs to nat. press. *Recreations:* sport, judging horticultural shows, natural history, walking, golf. *Address:* 17 Sandore Road, Seaford, E Sussex BN25 3PZ.

**STEPHENSON, Sir Terence (John),** Kt 2018; DM; FRCP, FRCPCH; Nuffield Professor of Child Health, University College London, since 2009; Honorary Consultant Paediatrician, University College Hospital and Great Ormond Street Hospital, since 2009; Co-Director, Policy Research Unit for Children, Young People and Families for England, since 2011; *b* 6 Dec. 1957; *s* of late James Ewing Stephenson and Cora Bell Stephenson (*née* Elliott); *m* 1st, 1987, Amanda Jane Lilley (marr. diss. 2011); one *s* one *d*; 2nd, 2016, Alison Johns. *Educ:* Larne Grammar Sch.; Bristol Univ. (BSc 1st Cl. Hons); Imperial Coll. London; New Coll., Oxford (BM BCh); DM Nottingham 1992. MRCP 1986, FRCP 1995; FRCPCH 1997. Jun. hosp. appts at John Radcliffe Hosp., Oxford, Royal United Hosp., Bath, St Thomas' Hosp., London, Nat. Hosp. for Nervous Diseases, Queen Sq. and UCH, London, 1983–86; University of Nottingham: Lectr in Child Health, 1986–90; Sen. Lectr, 1990–96; Prof. of Child Health, 1996–2009; Dean, Faculty of Medicine and Health Scis, 2003–09, Nottingham Univ. Sometime advisor: Official Solicitor to Supreme Court, 1997; DoH, 1999–2006; Eur. Agency for Evaluation of Med. Products, 2001–05. External Examiner: UCL; TCD; UC, Galway; Univs of Hong Kong, Leicester, Birmingham and Putra. Vice Chm., Adv. Gp for Nat. Specialised Services, 2011–13; Chm., Ext. Reviewer Panel, Expert Clinical Advice - Medicines and Healthcare products Regulatory Agency Medical Devices, 2014; Mem., Ind. Panel Inquiry into Child Sexual Abuse, 2014–15. Treas., Council of Heads of Med. Schs, 2005–09. Vice-Pres. for Res. and Sci., 2007–09, Pres., 2009–12, RCPCH; Chairman: Acad. of Medical Royal Colls, 2012–15; GMC, 2015–18. Pres., Trent Paediatric Soc., 1999–2005; Sec., Neonatal Soc., 2001–03; Treas., Paediatric Res. Soc., 2001–03. Trustee, NSPCC, 2011–14. Hon. Sec., Assoc. of Clinical Profs of Paediatrics, 2003–05. Hon. FRACP 2010; Hon. FRCPI 2013; Hon. Fellow, HK Acad. of Pharmacy 2013; Hon. FRCS 2014; Hon. FRCGP 2014; Hon. FRCA 2015; Hon. FCAI 2015; Hon. FRCSE 2015; Hon. FRCOG 2015; Hon. FRCPE 2015; Hon. FAcadMed 2015. James Spence Medal, RCPCH, 2016. *Publications:* (with H. Wallace) Clinical Paediatrics for Post Graduate Examinations, 1991, 2nd edn 1995; (with C. O'Callaghan) Pocket Paediatrics, 1992, 2nd edn 2003; (with C. O'Callaghan) Data Interpretation for the MRCP, 1994; (jtly) Pocket Neonatology, 2000; (jtly) Short Cases for the MRCPCH, 2004; (jtly) How to Write a Guideline, 2008; Swine Flu: the facts, 2009; over 275 peer-reviewed papers, editorials and chapters in various fields of medicine, child health and physiology. *Recreations:* golf (badly), football and Rugby (former competitor, now spectator), ski-ing, ecclesiastical architecture, piano, guitar. *Address:* Institute of Child Health, University College London, 30 Guilford Street, WC1N 1EH. *T:* (020) 7092 6000. *Clubs:* Athenæum, 1942; Paediatric Visiting, Medical Pilgrims.

**STEPHENSON, Prof. Thomas,** PhD; CEng, FREng; FIChemE; Professor, since 1994, and Pro-Vice-Chancellor Research, since 2014, Cranfield University; *b* Cambridge, 26 Nov. 1957; *s* of Andrew and Viiu Stephenson; *m* 1985, Gillian Horrell; two *d*. *Educ:* Newport Grammar Sch., Essex; York Univ. (BSc Biochem. 1979); Imperial Coll. London (PhD Civil Engrg 1983). FCIWEM 1994; CEng 1999; FIChemE 2001; FREng 2010. Sen. Lectr in Biochem. Engrg, Teesside Poly., 1986–90; Cranfield Institute of Technology, subseq. Cranfield University: Dep. Dir of Water Scis, 1990–92; Dir of Water Scis, 1992–2004; Hd, Sch. of Applied Scis, 2004–14. Man. Dir, 2004–16, Chm., 2016–, Cranfield Innovative Manufg Ltd; Tech. Dir, 2005–10, Chm., 2010–, Water Innovate Ltd; Chm., British Water, 2010–12; Dir, Selgus Ltd, 2018–. FHEA 2007. *Recreations:* cycling, pubs, reading, collecting sewage treatment textbooks. *Address:* Cranfield University, Cranfield MK43 0BD. *T:* (01234) 754054. *E:* t.stephenson@cranfield.ac.uk.

**STEPNEY, Area Bishop of,** since 2019; **Rt Rev. Dr Joanne Woolway Grenfell;** *b* Enfield, 27 May 1972; *d* of John Woolway and Christine Woolway; *m* 1998, Rev. Dr James Grenfell; two *s* one *d*. *Educ:* Oriel Coll., Oxford (BA 1993; DPhil 1997); Univ. of British Columbia (MA English Lit. 1994); Anglia Ruskin Univ. (PGDPT). Advr to Women Students, 1995–98, Lectr, 1997–98, Oriel Coll., Oxford; ordained deacon, 2000, priest, 2001; Curate, Kirkby Team Ministry, 2000–03; Priest-in-charge, Manor Ecumenical Parish, 2003–06; Diocese of Sheffield: Dir of Ordinands and Res. Canon, 2006–13; Dean of Women's Ministry, 2008–13; Archdeacon of Portsdown, 2013–19. *Publications:* (contrib.) Literature, Mapping and the Politics of Space in Early Modern Britain, 2001; (contrib.) Women and Men in Scripture and the Church, 2013; (contrib.) Reflections for Daily Prayer, 2014; (jtly) Pilgrim: The Commandments, 2014; articles in Early Modern Literary Studies. *Recreations:* poetry, swimming, running. *Address:* 63 Coborn Road, E3 2DB. *T:* 07936 043945.

**STEPTOE, Prof. Andrew Patrick Arthur,** DPhil; FMedSci, FBPsS, FAcSS; Professor of Psychology, since 2000 and Head, Department of Behavioural Science and Health, since 2017, University College London; *b* 24 April 1951; *s* of Patrick Christopher Steptoe, CBE, FRS, and Sheena Macleod Steptoe; *m* 1st, 1980, Jane Horncastle (marr. diss. 1984); one *s*; 2nd, 1991, (Frances) Jane Wardle, FBA (*d* 2015); one *s*. *Educ:* Gonville and Caius Coll., Cambridge (BA 1972; MA 1976); Magdalen Coll., Oxford (DPhil 1976); DSc London, 1995. FBPsS 1988. Res. Lectr, Christ Church Coll., Oxford, 1975–77; St George's Hospital Medical School: Lectr in Psychology, 1977–81; Sen. Lectr, 1981–87; Reader, 1987–88; Prof. of Psychology, 1988–2000; Chm. Acad. Bd, 1997–99; University College London: Dep. Hd, 2005–11, Hd, 2011, Dept of Epidemiol. and Public Health; BHF Prof. of Psychology, 2000–16; Dir, Inst. of Epidemiology and Health Care, 2011–17. Principal Investigator, English Longitudinal Study of Ageing, 2008–. President: Soc. of Psychosomatic Res., 1983–85; Internat. Soc. of Behavioral Medicine, 1994–96. Editor, British Jl of Health Psychology, 1995–2001; Associate Editor: Psychophysiology, 1982–86; Jl of Psychosomatic Res., 1989–97; British Jl of Clinical Psychology, 1992–95; Annals of Behavioral Medicine, 1992–97. FAcSS (AcSS 2001); MAE 2003. FMedSci 2008; FRSB 2018. *Publications:* Psychological Factors in Cardiovascular Disorders, 1981; Problems of Pain and Stress, 1982; Health Care and Human Behaviour, 1984; Clinical and Methodological Issues in Cardiovascular Psychophysiology, 1985; The Mozart-Da Ponte Operas, 1988; Behavioural Medicine in Cardiovascular Disorders, 1988; Stress, Personal Control and Health, 1989; Psychosocial Processes and Health, 1994; Mozart, 1996; Genius and the Mind: studies of creativity and temperament, 1998; Depression and Physical Illness, 2006; Handbook of Behavioral Medicine, 2010; Stress and Cardiovascular Disease, 2012; Routledge International Handbook of Psychosocial Epidemiology, 2018. *Recreations:* music, theatre, reading, family, running. *Address:* Department of Behavioural Science and Health, University College London, 1–19 Torrington Place, WC1E 6BT. *T:* (020) 7679 1804, *Fax:* (020) 7916 8542. *E:* a.steptoe@ucl.ac.uk.

**STERCKX, Prof. Roel,** PhD; FBA 2013; Joseph Needham Professor of Chinese History, Science and Civilisation, University of Cambridge, since 2008 (Professor of Chinese, 2007–08); Fellow of Clare College, Cambridge, since 2006; *b* 13 May 1969; *s* of Herman Sterckx and Angèle Sterckx (*née* Vos); *m* 2003, Dr Ang Cheng Eng; one *s*. *Educ:* Gemeentelijke Basisschool Retie, Belgium; St Jan Berchmans Coll., Mol; Katholieke Universiteit Leuven (BA, MA Sinology and Hist. 1991; PGCE 1991); National Taiwan Univ., Taipei (studied philosophy 1992); Univ. of Cambridge (MPhil 1993; PhD Oriental Studies 1997); DPhil Oxon 1998. Jun. Res. Fellow, Wolfson Coll., Oxford, 1997–2000; Asst Prof. of E Asian Studies, Univ. of Arizona, 2000–02; University of Cambridge: Univ. Lectr, then Sen. Lectr, in Chinese Studies, 2002–07; Head, Dept of E Asian Studies, 2007–10, 2014–17; Chm., Faculty of Asian and Middle Eastern Studies, 2013, 2016–17; Race and Equality Champion, 2013–17. Vis. Fellow, Academia Sinica, Taipei, Republic of China, 2011–12. Guanghua Lectr, Fudan Univ., 2014; Chen Yinke Lectr, Sun Yat-sen Univ., 2018. Sec.-Gen., Eur. Assoc. for Chinese Studies, 2006–12; Member: Conseil d'Admin, Ecole Française d'Extrême-Orient, Paris, 2009–11; Eur. Fellowship Panel, Chiang Ching-kuo Foundn, 2011–. Trustee: Needham Res. Inst., 2007–; Percival David Foundn of Chinese Art, 2011–15. FRAS 2006; FRHistS 2006. *Publications:* The Animal and the Daemon in Early China, 2002; Of Tripod and Palate: food, politics and religion in traditional China, 2005; Of Self and Spirits: exploring 'shen' in China, 2007; Food, Sacrifice and Sagehood in Early China, 2011; Energia Vitale: il cosmo nel pensiero cinese antico, 2012; Animals through Chinese History: earliest times to 1911, 2018; Chinese Thought, 2019; various scholarly articles. *Recreations:* music, gardening, fishing. *Address:* Clare College, Trinity Lane, Cambridge CB2 1TL.

**STERLING,** family name of **Baron Sterling of Plaistow**.

**STERLING OF PLAISTOW,** Baron *cr* 1991 (Life Peer), of Pall Mall in the City of Westminster; **Jeffrey Maurice Sterling,** GCVO 2002; Kt 1985; CBE 1977; Executive Chairman, The Peninsular and Oriental Steam Navigation Company, 1983–2005, now Life President; Chairman: Sterling Guarantee Trust, since 2005; P&O Princess Cruises, 2000–03; Swan Hellenic, 2007–15, now Hon. President; Hebridean Island Cruises, 2009–15, now Hon. President; Chairman and Joint Founder, Motability, since 1994 (Chairman of Executive, since 1977); Chairman of Trustees, National Maritime Museum, 2005–13; *b* 27 Dec. 1934; *s* of late Harry and of Alice Sterling; *m* 1985, Dorothy Ann Smith; one *d*. *Educ:* Reigate Grammar Sch.; Preston Manor County Sch.; Guildhall School of Music. Paul Schweder & Co. (Stock Exchange), 1955–57; G. Eberstadt & Co., 1957–62; Fin. Dir, General Guarantee Corp., 1962–64; Man. Dir, Gula Investments Ltd, 1964–69; Chm., Sterling Guarantee Trust plc, 1969–85, when it merged with P&O Steam Navigation Co. Mem., British Airways Bd, 1979–82. Special Advr to Sec. of State for Industry, later for Trade and Industry, 1982–90. Mem. Exec., 1966–, Chm. Organisation Cttee, 1969–73, World ORT Union; Chm., ORT Technical Services, 1974–; Vice-Pres., British ORT, 1978–; President: Gen. Council of British Shipping, 1990–91; EC Shipowners' Assocs, 1992–94. Dep. Chm. and Hon. Treasurer, London Celebrations Cttee, Queen's Silver Jubilee, 1975–83; Chm., Queen's Golden Jubilee Weekend Trust, 2002. Chm., Young Vic Co., 1975–83; Chm., of the Governors, Royal Ballet Sch., 1983–99; Gov., Royal Ballet, 1986–99. Pres., AJEX, 2012–. Freeman, City of London. Hon. Captain, 1991, Hon. Cdre, 2005, Hon. Rear Adm., 2010, Hon. Vice Adm., 2015, RNR. Elder Brother, Trinity House, 1991. Hon. FIMarEST (Hon. FIMarE 1991); Hon. FICS 1992; Hon. MRICS 1993; FSVA 1995; Hon. FRINA 1997. Hon. DBA Nottingham Trent, 1995; Hon. DCL Durham, 1996; Hon. DSc City, 2006. Interfaith Medallion, Internat. CCJ, 2003. KStJ 1998. Grand Officer, Order of May (Argentina), 2002; Officer's Cross, Order of Merit (Germany), 2004; Officier, Légion d'Honneur (France), 2005. *Recreations:* music, the arts. *Clubs:* Garrick, Hurlingham.

**STERLING, David Robert;** Head of Northern Ireland Civil Service, Permanent Secretary, Executive Office and Secretary to Northern Ireland Executive, since 2017; *b* 7 March 1958; *s* of Ronald and Kathleen Sterling; *m* 1987, Lynda Elaine Robinson; one *s* one *d*. *Educ:* Royal Belfast Academical Instn; Univ. of Ulster (MSc). Northern Ireland Civil Service, 1978–: Police Authority; NI Office; Dept of Finance and Personnel; Dep. Sec., Dept for Regl Develt, 2003–08; Dep. Sec., 2008–09, Perm. Sec., 2009–14, Dept of Enterprise, Trade and Investment; Perm. Sec., Dept of Finance and Personnel, then Dept of Finance, 2014–17. *Recreations:* golf, cycling, walking. *E:* hocs@executiveoffice-ni.gov.uk.

**STERLING, Dr (Isobel Jane) Nuala,** CBE 1993; FRCP; Consultant Physician in Geriatric Medicine, Southampton University Hospitals NHS Trust (formerly Royal South Hants Hospital), 1979–2002, now Emeritus; *b* 12 Feb. 1937; *d* of Prof. F. Bradbury and Mrs J. Bradbury; *m* 1961, Dr G. M. Sterling; five *s* (one *d* decd). *Educ:* Friends' Sch., Saffron Walden; King's Coll. and St George's Hosp., London (MB BS 1960). MRCS LRCP 1960; MRCP 1971, FRCP 1982. House Officer and Registrar posts, St George's Hosp., 1960–67; in general practice: London, 1963–64; Oxford, 1968; Lectr in Medicine, Univ. of Calif., San Francisco, 1969–70; Sen. House Officer then Registrar, Oxford, 1970–71; Sen. Registrar and Lectr in Geriatric Medicine, Southampton Univ. Hosps, 1972–79. Member: Standing Med. Adv. Cttee to Sec. of State for Health, 1986–96 (Chm., 1990–94); Clinical Standards Adv. Gp, 1990–94; Ind. Review Panel on Advertising of Medicines, 2000–; Vice-Chairman: Wessex Regl Adv. Cttee on Distinction Awards, 1998–99; Southern Regl Adv. Cttee on Distinction Awards, 2000–03. Royal College of Physicians: Chm., Standing Cttee of Mems, 1978–79; Mem., Jt Consultants Cttee, 1986–92; Pres., Medical Women's Fedn, 1989–90. Trustee: Wessex Medical Trust, 1999–2004; King Edward VII Hosp., Midhurst, 2000–06. *Publications:* research publications on immunology and cancer, endocrine and respiratory disorders in the elderly, provision of medical services and training;

contribs to Lilies and Related Plants. *Recreations:* music, modern art, growing orchids and lilies (Mem. Cttee, 2006–, Chm., 2012–18, Vice Chm., 2019–, RHS Lily Gp; Lyttel Lily Cup, RHS, 2016), gardening (Mem., 2013–, Vice Chm., 2014–20, RHS Bulb Cttee), watching cricket. *Address:* Vermont House, East Boldre, Hants SO42 7WX.

**STERLING, Prof. Sir Michael (John Howard),** Kt 2012; FREng, FIET; FInstMC; Chairman: Science and Technology Facilities Council, 2009–18; OCEPS Ltd, 1990–2015; *b* 9 Feb. 1946; *s* of Richard Howard Sterling and Joan Valeria Sterling (*née* Skinner); *m* 1969, Wendy Karla Anstead; two *s*. *Educ:* Hampton Grammar Sch., Middx; Univ. of Sheffield (BEng 1968; PhD 1971; DEng 1988). CEng 1975. Student apprentice, AEI, 1964–68; research engineer, GEC-Elliott Process Automation, 1968–71; Sheffield University: Lectr in Control Engineering, 1971–78; Industrial Liaison Officer, 1976–80; Sen. Lectr in Control Engineering, 1978–80; Prof. of Engineering, Univ. of Durham, 1980–90 (Dir, Microprocessor Centre, 1980–85); Vice-Chancellor and Principal: Brunel Univ., 1990–2001 (Emeritus Prof., 2001); Birmingham Univ., 2001–09 (Emeritus Prof., 2009). Chairman: WASMACS Ltd, 1994–2002; MidMAN, 2001. Director: UCAS, 2001–06; COBUILD Ltd, 2001–09; Universitas 21, 2001–09. Member: UUK (formerly CVCP), 1990–2009 (Mem. Council, 1994–95); Cttee for Internat. Co-op. in Higher Educn, British Council, 1991–96. Chairman: Univs Statistical Record, 1992–95; Higher Educn Stats Agency, 1992–2003; Jt Performance Indicators Wkg Gp, Higher Educn Councils for England, Scotland and Wales, 1992–95; Russell Gp, 2003–06; STEMNET, 2006–11; Member: Quality Assessment Cttee, 1992–95, Additional Student Numbers and Funds Adv. Gp, 1997–99, HEFCE; Mech. Aeronautical and Prodn Engrg Assessment Panel, RAE, 1992, 1996; Bd, W Midlands Higher Educn Assoc., 2001–09; Bd, AWM, 2003–09; Science Review Gp, DECC, 2011–12; Lead Expert Gp on Manufg, BIS, 2012–14; Chairman: AWM ITC Steering Gp, 2002–09; IET/DECC Transmission Costing Gp, 2011–12. Member: Electricity Supply Res. Council, 1987–89; Engrg Bd, SERC, 1989–92; Engrg Council, 1994–96; Prime Minister's Council for Sci. and Technol., 2004–14. Academic Grand Master, Energy Systems, Chinese Govt, 2014–; Consultant, Global Energy Interconnection Develt and Cooperation Orgn, Beijing, 2017–. Guest Prof., South Eastern Univ., China, 2014–. FREng (FEng 1991); Member: Standing Cttee for Educn, Trng and Competence to Practise, 1993–97; Membership Panel, 2000–02 (Chm., 2002–05); Membership Cttee, 2002–05 (Chm., 2005–08)); FInstMC 1983 (Mem. Cttee, 1975–80, Chm., 1979–80, S Yorks Sect.; Mem. Council, 1983–91; Vice Pres., 1985–88; Nat. Pres., 1988); FIEE 1985 (Mem. Council, 1991–93 and 1997–2002; Chm., Qualifications Bd, 1997–2002; Vice-Pres., 1997–2000; Dep. Pres., 2000–02; Pres., 2002–03). FRSA 1984. CCMI 2002. Dir, W London TEC, 1999–2001 (Dir, Charitable Trust, 1999–2001). Governor: Hampton Sch., 1991–2001 (Chm., 1997–2001); Burnham Grammar Sch., 1991–2001; Pres., Elmhurst Sch. for Dance, 2002–09. Trustee: Hillingdon Partnership Trust, 1993–98; Barber Inst. of Fine Art, 2001–09. Freeman, City of London, 1996; Liveryman, Engineers' Co., 1998–. Fellow, Engrg Acad. of the Czech Republic, 2008; Foreign Fellow, Chinese Soc. for Electrical Engrg, 2019. Hon. Fellow, Inst. of Measurement and Control, 2003; Hon. FIET, 2006. Hon. DEng: Sheffield, 1995; Brunel, 2008; Hon. Dr: Tashkent, Uzbekistan, 1999; West Bohemia, Czech Republic, 2001; Medal of Honour, Univ. of Bohemia, Czech Republic, 2000. *Publications:* Power Systems Control, 1978; contribs to: Large Scale Systems Engineering Applications, 1980; Computer Control of Industrial Processes, 1982; Real Time Computer Control, 1984; Comparative Models for Electrical Load Forecasting, 1985; over 120 papers in learned jls. *Recreations:* gardening, DIY, computers, model engineering.

**STERLING, Nuala;** *see* Sterling, I. J. N.

**STERN,** family name of **Baron Stern of Brentford**.

**STERN,** Baroness *cr* 1999 (Life Peer), of Vauxhall, in the London Borough of Lambeth; **Vivien Helen Stern,** CBE 1992; Secretary-General, Penal Reform International, 1989–2006; Senior Research Fellow, International Centre for Prison Studies, King's College, London, 1997–2010; *b* 25 Sept. 1941; *d* of Frederick Stern and Renate Mills; *m* Andrew Gerard Coyle, *qv*. *Educ:* Kent Coll., Pembury, Kent; Bristol Univ. (BA, MLitt, CertEd). Lectr in Further Educn until 1970; Community Relations Commn, 1970–77; Dir, NACRO, 1977–96. Vis. Fellow, Nuffield Coll., Oxford, 1984–91; Vis. Prof., Essex Univ., 2011–14. Member: Special Programmes Bd, Manpower Services Commn, 1980–82; Youth Training Bd, 1982–88; Gen. Adv. Council, IBA, 1982–87; Cttee on the Prison Disciplinary System, 1984–85; Adv. Council, PSI, 1993–96; Bd, Assoc. for Prevention of Torture, Geneva, 1993–99; Bd, Eisenhower Foundn, Washington, 1993–2007; Law Adv. Council, 1995–2001, Governance Adv. Cttee, 2002–06, British Council; Adv. Council, ILANUD (UN Latin Amer. Inst. for Prevention of Crime and Treatment of Offenders), 2001–12; Council, Français Incarcérés au Loin, 2001–07; Co-Chm., Know Violence in Childhood, 2014–18; Bd, Internat. Legal Foundn, NY, 2014–. Convener, Scottish Consortium on Crime and Criminal Justice, 2003–09. Member: Select Cttee on EU, H of L, 1999–2003; Jt Cttee on Human Rights, 2004–08; Jt Cttee on Statutory Instruments, H of L, 2010–15; Select Cttee on Inquiries Act 2005, H of L, 2013–14; Secondary Legislation Cttee, H of L, 2014–17. Chm., Govt Rev. on how rape complaints are handled by public authorities, 2009–10 (report pub. 2010). Pres., New Bridge, 2001–05. Pres., Assoc. of Members of Ind. Monitoring Bds, 2004–. Trustee: Civil Liberties Trust, 2009–18; Redress Trust, 2015–. Hon. Fellow, LSE, 1997. Hon. LLD: Bristol, 1990; Oxford Brookes, 1996; Glasgow, 2012; DUniv Stirling, 2008; Hon. DLaws Edinburgh, 2010; Hon. DCL Kent, 2014; Hon. Dr Sheffield Hallam, 2016. Margaret Mead Award for contribution to social justice, Internat. Assoc. for Residential & Community Alternatives, 1995. *Publications:* Bricks of Shame, 1987; Imprisoned by Our Prisons, 1989; Deprived of their Liberty, a report for Caribbean Rights, 1990; A Sin Against the Future: imprisonment in the world, 1998; Alternatives to Prison in Developing Countries, 1999; (ed) Sentenced to Die?: the problem of TB in prisons in Eastern Europe and Central Asia, 1999; Developing Alternatives to Prison in East and Central Europe and Central Asia: a guidance handbook, 2002; Creating Criminals: prisons and people in a market society, 2006. *Address:* House of Lords, SW1A 0PW.

**STERN OF BRENTFORD,** Baron *cr* 2007 (Life Peer), of Elsted in the County of West Sussex and of Wimbledon in the London Borough of Merton; **Nicholas Herbert Stern,** CH 2017; Kt 2004; FBA 1993; FRS 2014; I. G. Patel Professor of Economics and Government, Chairman, Grantham Institute on Climate Change and the Environment, and Director, India Observatory, London School of Economics, since 2007; President: British Academy, 2013–17; Royal Economic Society, 2018–19; *b* 22 April 1946; *s* of Adalbert Stern and Marion Fatima Stern; *m* 1968, Susan Ruth (*née* Chesterton); two *s* one *d*. *Educ:* Peterhouse, Cambridge (BA Mathematics; Hon. Fellow, 2006); Nuffield Coll., Oxford (DPhilEcon). Jun. Res. Fellow, The Queen's Coll., Oxford, 1969–70; Fellow/Tutor in Econs St Catherine's Coll., and Univ. Lectr, Oxford, 1970–77; Prof. of Econs, Univ. of Warwick, 1978–85; Sir John Hicks Prof. of Econs, LSE, 1986–97; Chief Economist, 1994–99, and Special Counsellor to Pres., 1997–99, EBRD; School Prof. of Econs, LSE, 1999–2003 (on leave of absence); Chief Economist and Sen. Vice-Pres., World Bank, 2000–03); HM Treasury: Second Perm. Sec., Hd of Govt Econ. Service and Hd Review on Econs of Climate Change, 2003–05 (report published 2006); Man. Dir, Budget and Public Finance, 2003–04. Dir of Policy and Res., Prime Minister's Commn for Africa, 2004–05. Trustee, BM, 2008–16 (Vice-Chm., 2012–16). Research Associate/Visiting Professor: MIT, 1972; Ecole Polytech., 1977; Indian Statistical Inst. (Overseas Vis. Fellow of British Acad., 1974–75, and Ford Foundn Vis. Prof., 1981–82); People's Univ. of China, Beijing, 1988, Hon. Prof., 2001; Prof., Collège de France, 2009–10. Mem., American Philosophical Soc., 2015. For. Hon. Mem., Amer. Acad. of Arts and Scis, 1998. Fellow, Econometric Soc., 1978. Hon. Fellow: St Catherine's Coll., Oxford, 2003; Queen's Coll., Oxford, 2007. Hon. DSc Warwick, 2006; Hon. Dr: Cambridge, Nottingham, Exeter, Sussex, Roehampton, Geneva Sch. of Diplomacy and Internat. Relns, 2007; Sheffield, York, E Anglia, 2008; Brighton, Paris-Dauphine, Technische Berlin, 2009; Oxford, 2018; Ghent, 2019. Prizes include: Blue Planet, 2009; Leontief, 2010; BBVA Foundn Frontiers of Knowledge Award, 2011; Schumpeter Award, 2015. Editor, Journal of Public Economics, 1980–98. *Publications:* An Appraisal of Tea Production on Smallholdings in Kenya, 1972; (ed jtly) Theories of Economic Growth, 1973; (jtly) Crime, the Police and Criminal Statistics, 1979; (jtly) Palanpur: the economy of an Indian village, 1982; (jtly) The Theory of Taxation for Developing Countries, 1987; (jtly) Economic Development in Palanpur over Five Decades, 1998; (jtly) Growth and Empowerment: making development happen, 2005; Economics of Climate Change, 2007; A Blueprint for a Safer Planet: how to manage climate change and create a new era of progress and prosperity, 2009; Why Are We Waiting? The logic, urgency, and promise of tackling climate change, 2015; (jtly) How Lives Change: Palanpur, India and development economics, 2018; articles in American Econ. Rev., Econ. Jl, Rev. of Econ. Studies, Jl of Public Econs, Jl of Develt Econs, Jl of Econ. Theory, Econs and Phil., and others. *Recreations:* reading novels, walking, watching sport, food. *Address:* London School of Economics, Houghton Street, WC2A 2AE.

**STERN, Prof. Claudio Daniel,** DPhil, DSc; FRS 2008; J. Z. Young Professor, since 2001, and Head, 2001–11, Department of Cell and Developmental Biology (formerly Department of Anatomy and Developmental Biology), Vice-Dean (International), Faculty of Life Sciences, since 2015, and Pro-Vice-Provost (South East Asia and Australasia), since 2018, University College London; *b* 9 Feb. 1954; *s* of Erico and Trude Stern; *m* 2000, Andrea Streit. *Educ:* Univ. of Sussex (BSc Hons Biol Scis 1975; DPhil Develt Biol. 1978); Univ. of Oxford (DSc Physiol Scis 1994). FRSB (FIBiol 2008). Res. Fellow, UCL, 1978–84; Univ. Demonstrator, Univ. of Cambridge, 1984–85; Univ. Lectr, Univ. of Oxford, and Fellow, Christ Church, Oxford, 1985–94; Prof. and Chm. of Genetics and Develt, Columbia Univ., NY, 1994–2001. Pres., Internat. Soc. for Develtl Biol., 2010–14. Member: Ibero-Amer. Molecular Biol. Orgn, 1998; EMBO, 2002; MAE 2013. Foreign Hon. Mem., Amer. Acad. of Arts and Scis, 2014. FMedSci 2001. Foreign Fellow, Latin-Amer. Acad. of Scis, 2001. Waddington Medal, British Soc. for Develtl Biol., 2006; Ross G Harrison Medal, Internat. Soc. for Develtl Biol., 2017. *Publications:* (jtly) The Making of the Nervous System, 1988; (with P. W. Ingham) Gastrulation (Development 1992 supplement), 1992; (with P. W. H. Holland) Essential Developmental Biology: a practical approach, 1993 (trans. Japanese); (jtly) Cellular and Molecular Procedures in Developmental Biology, 1998; Gastrulation: from cells to embryo, 2004; more than 200 articles in internat. learned jls inc. Nature, Science, Cell, Neuron, Developmental Cell, Development and others. *Recreations:* playing Baroque and Renaissance woodwind musical instruments, gastronomy. *Address:* Department of Cell and Developmental Biology, Anatomy Building, University College London, Gower Street, WC1E 6BT.

**STERN, Ian Michael;** QC 2006; a Recorder, since 2000; *b* 26 Jan. 1957; *s* of late Harold and of Laura Stern; *m* 1987, Helen Appleton; three *d*. *Educ:* Queen Elizabeth's Grammar Sch. for Boys, Barnet; Univ. of Warwick (BA Hons Pol Sci 1979); City Univ., London (Dip. Law 1982). Called to the Bar, Inner Temple, 1983, Bencher, 2011; in practice as a barrister; Asst Recorder, 1998–2000. *Recreations:* running, travel, family. *Address:* 2 Bedford Row, WC1R 4BU. *T:* (020) 7440 8888. *E:* istern@2bedfordrow.co.uk.

**STERN, John Andrew;** freelance writer; Editor at Large, Wisden Cricket Monthly, since 2017; *b* 12 March 1970; *s* of Peter and Gill Stern; *m* 2004, Clare Alison Henderson (marr. diss.); two step *d*. *Educ:* Arnold House; King's Sch., Canterbury; Univ. of Manchester (BA Hons Classics). Hayters Sports Agency, 1992–97; freelance sports writer, 1997–2001 (mostly cricket reporting for The Times and Sunday Times); cricket columnist, Sunday Times, 1998–; Dep. Ed., Wisden Cricket Monthly, 2001–03; Ed., The Wisden Cricketer, 2003–11; Ed. at Large, All Out Cricket, 2012–17; Ed., England and Wales Cricket Bd match programmes, 2014–. *Publications:* Cricket: the definitive guide to the international game, 2012; (with Marcus Williams) The Essential Wisden: an anthology of 150 years of Wisden Cricketers' Almanack, 2013; (with Rob Maier) Youth Cricket Coaching, 2013; The Periodic Table of Cricket, 2016; (contrib.) Wisden Cricketers' Almanack, annually 1999–. *Recreations:* cricket, golf, travel, wine.

**STERN, Michael Charles,** FCA; Proprietor and Partner, Michael Stern & Co., 1998–2012, now consultant; Company Secretary, since 2005, and Director, since 2014, Lafferty Gp companies; Director, Shalimar Accountancy Ltd, since 2012; Company Secretary, Gandlake Ltd, since 2012; *b* 3 Aug. 1942; *s* of late Maurice Leonard Stern and Rose Stern; *m* 1976, Dr Jillian Denise Aldridge; one *d*. *Educ:* Christ's College Grammar School, Finchley. Mem. ICA 1964; FCA 1969. Partner, Percy Phillips & Co., Accountants, 1964–80; Partner, Halpern & Woolf, Chartered Accountants, 1980–92; Consultant, Cohen Arnold & Co., 1992–98. Chm., The Bow Group, 1977–78; co-opted Mem., Educn Cttee, Borough of Ealing, 1980–83. Contested (C) Derby S, 1979. MP (C) Bristol NW, 1983–97; contested (C) same seat, 1997. PPS to Minister of State, HM Treasury, 1986–87, to Paymaster General, 1987–89, to Minister for Corporate Affairs, DTI, 1991. Chief Finance Officer, 1988–91, Vice-Chm., 1991–92, Cons. party. *Publications:* papers for The Bow Group. *Recreation:* chess. *Address:* 61 Shalimar Gardens, Acton, W3 9JG. *Clubs:* Royal Automobile, United and Cecil.

**STERN, Prof. Robert Arthur,** PhD; FBA 2019; Professor of Philosophy, University of Sheffield, since 2000; *b* Norwich, 28 Feb. 1962; *s* of Jacob Stern and Isabella Stern (*née* Cohen); *m* 1988, Crosby Stevens; one *s* one *d*. *Educ:* Gresham's Sch.; St John's Coll., Cambridge (BA 1983; PhD 1986). Jun. Res. Fellow, St John's Coll., Cambridge, 1987–89; Lectr, 1989–98, Reader, 1998–2000, Univ. of Sheffield. *Publications:* Hegel, Kant and the Structure of the Object, 1990; Transcendental Arguments and Scepticism: answering the question of justification, 2000; Hegel and the 'Phenomenology of Spirit', 2002, 2nd edn 2013; Hegelian Metaphysics, 2009; Understanding Moral Obligation: Kant, Hegel, Kierkegaard, 2012; Kantian Ethics: value, agency and obligation, 2015; The Radical Demand in Løgstrup's Ethics, 2019. *Recreations:* running and walking in the Peak District, gardening. *Address:* Department of Philosophy, University of Sheffield, 45 Victoria Street, Sheffield S3 7QB. *T:* (0114) 222 0582. *E:* r.stern@sheffield.ac.uk.

**STERNBERG, Prof. Michael Joseph Ezra,** DPhil; FRSB; Professor of Structural Bioinformatics, since 2001, and Director, Centre for Integrative Systems Biology and Bioinformatics, since 2011, Imperial College London; *b* London, 24 June 1951; *s* of Charles Sternberg and Klara Sternberg; *m* 1984, Michelle Bernice Wolfson; one *s* one *d*. *Educ:* Hendon Co. Grammar Sch.; Gonville and Caius Coll., Cambridge (BA 1st Cl. Nat. Scis Theoretical Physics 1972); Imperial Coll. London (MSc Computing); Wolfson Coll., Oxford (DPhil Molecular Biophysics 1978). Postdoctoral Res., Lab. of Molecular Biophysics, Oxford, 1977–83; Royal Soc. Univ. Res. Fellow and Lectr, Crystallography Dept, Birkbeck Coll., Univ. of London, 1983–88; Hd, Biomolecular Modelling Lab.,

Imperial Cancer Res. Fund, 1988–2001. Founder and Dir, Equinox Pharma Ltd, 2001–. Member: Strategy Bd, BBSRC, 2003–04; Scientific Adv. Bd, Inst. of Food Res., 2007–15. Co-developer, Phyre2 protein structure prediction web server, 2000. FRSB (FIBiol 2001). Lectures to schs and teachers. Mem. Editl Bd, Jl of Molecular Biol., 2005–. *Publications:* (with A. R. Rees) From Cells to Atoms: an illustrated introduction to molecular biology, 1984; (jtly) Protein Engineering: a practical approach, 1992; Protein Structure Prediction: a practical approach, 1996; contrib. articles to jls incl. Nature, Proc. NAS, Jl of Molecular Biol., Proteins, Human Mutation, Bioinformatics. *Recreations:* swimming, family. *Address:* Sir Ernst Chain Building, Imperial College London, SW7 2AZ.

**STERNBERG, Michael Vivian;** QC 2008; barrister; *b* Belsize Park, London, 12 Sept. 1951; *s* of Sir Sigmund Sternberg and Ruth Sternberg; *m* 1975, Dr Janine Levinson; one *s* two *d*. *Educ:* Carmel Coll., Wallingford; Queens' Coll., Cambridge (BA 1973, LLB 1975). Called to the Bar, Gray's Inn, 1975, Bencher, 2014; Mem., Inner Temple, 2006; in practice as barrister, 1975–, specialising in all aspects of family law, esp. allocation of resources on divorce; 4 Paper Buildings, 1994–. Asst Sec., Family Law Bar Assoc., 1986–88. Qualified collaborative lawyer, 2010; qualified mediator, 2011. Trustee, Sternberg Charitable Foundn, 1983– (Chm., 2016–); Chm., Trustees, Faith and Belief Forum (formerly Three Faiths Forum), 2009–. Gov., NLCS, 1994–2009. Freeman, City of London, 1983; Liveryman, Horners' Co., 1986–. MCIArb 2012. FRSA 2007. Silver Benemerenza Medal, Sacred Mil. Constantinian Order of St George, 1990; Knight Comdr, Royal Order of Francis I, 2018; Cross, Order of Merit (Germany), 2019. *Publications:* (contrib.) Pension and Marriage Breakdown, 2005, 2nd edn as Pensions and Family Breakdown, 2008. *Recreations:* walking, Mozart, family law. *Address:* 4 Paper Buildings, Temple, EC4Y 7EX. *T:* (020) 7583 0816, *Fax:* (020) 7353 4979. *E:* clerks@4pb.com. *Club:* Reform.

**STEVELY, Prof. William Stewart,** CBE 2004; DPhil; FRSB; Principal and Vice-Chancellor, Robert Gordon University, 1997–2005; Chairman, NHS Ayrshire and Arran, 2006–11; *b* 6 April 1943; *s* of Robert Reid Stevely and Catherine Callow Stevely; *m* 1968, Sheila Anne Stalker; three *s* two *d*. *Educ:* Ardrossan Acad.; Glasgow Univ. (BSc 1965; DipEd 1973); St Catherine's Coll., Oxford (DPhil 1968). FRSB (FIBiol 1988). Asst Lectr, 1968–70, Lectr, 1970–83, Sen. Lectr, 1983–88, in Biochemistry, Univ. of Glasgow; Prof. and Head of Dept of Biology, 1988–92, Vice Principal, 1992–97, Paisley Coll. of Tech., then Univ. of Paisley. Chm., Scottish Council, Inst. of Biology, 1993–95. Chm., UCAS, 2001–05; Member: Nat. Bd for Nursing, Midwifery and Health Visiting for Scotland, 1992–2002; SHEFC, 1993–96; Bd, QAA, 1998–2002; Bd, Scottish Enterprise Grampian (formerly Grampian Enterprise) Ltd, 1998–2006, Bd, Scottish Univs for Industry, 2004–08; Bd, Skills Development Scotland, 2008–11. Member: Council, Inst. for Learning and Teaching in Higher Educn, 1998–2000; Bd, SRUC (formerly Scottish Agricl Coll.), 2005–13 (Vice Chm., 2007–13); Council, Open Univ., 2009–17 (Vice Chm., 2011–17). Convener, Universities Scotland, 2002–04. Fellow, SCDI, 2006. Hon. LLD Aberdeen, 2004; Hon. DEd Robert Gordon, 2005; DUniv Paisley, 2007. *Publications:* papers on herpes viruses. *Address:* 10 Evergreen Estate, Coalhall, Ayr KA6 6PQ.

**STEVEN, Dr Andrew John Maclean;** Member, Scottish Law Commission, since 2011; *b* Banff, 8 Nov. 1972; *s* of Rev. Harold Andrew Maclean Steven and Mary Allison Steven (*née* Little). *Educ:* Banff Acad.; Univ. of Edinburgh (LLB Hons 1994; PhD 1998; DipLP 1998). Admitted soliciting, 1999; NP 1999; WS 2009. University of Edinburgh: Lectr in Law, 2000–10; Sen. Lectr in Law, 2010–. *Publications:* Pledge and Lien, 2008; (with G. L. Gretton) Property, Trusts and Succession, 2009, 3rd edn 2017; papers in learned jls. *Address:* Scottish Law Commission, 140 Causewayside, Edinburgh EH9 1PR. *T:* (0131) 668 2131.

**STEVEN, Rosemary Margaret;** Chief Executive, Warrington Hospital NHS Trust, 1993–98; *b* 2 Nov. 1945; *d* of Donald and Margaret Robson; *m* 1983, Michael A. Knights (*d* 2005); *m* 2008, Angus C. Steven. *Educ:* Houghton-le-Spring Grammar School; Coll. of Nursing, Sunderland AHA. RGN, OND. Clinical nursing career, 1962–75 (Ward Sister posts, Sunderland and Harrogate); Nursing Officer, Harrogate, 1975–78; Sen. Nursing Officer, North Tees, Stockton, 1978–80; Dir of Nursing, Central Manchester HA, 1981–85; Unit Gen. Manager and Dist Nursing Officer, Manchester Royal Eye Hosp., 1985–88; Regl Nursing Officer, 1988–90, Dep. Chief Exec., 1989–91, Mersey RHA; Exec. Dir, NHS Mgt Exec. Trust Monitoring Unit (NW), 1991–93. Mem., S Manchester HA, 1983–88; Sec. and Chief Exec., Ophthalmic Nursing Bd, 1983–88. Lead Gov., Salford Royal NHS Foundn Trust, 2007–11. *Publications:* articles in nursing and health service papers. *Recreations:* music (piano); Friends of Hallé, fashion. *Address:* 21 Crossfield Drive, Worsley, Manchester M28 1GP. *Club:* Soroptomist International (Manchester).

**STEVENS,** family name of **Barons Stevens of Kirkwhelpington** and **Stevens of Ludgate.**

**STEVENS OF KIRKWHELPINGTON,** Baron *cr* 2005 (Life Peer), of Kirkwhelpington in the county of Northumberland; **John Arthur Stevens,** Kt 2000; QPM 1992; DL; Commissioner, Metropolitan Police, 2000–05; Senior Adviser to the Prime Minister on International Security Issues, since 2007; *b* 21 Oct. 1942; *s* of C. J. and S. Stevens; *m*; two *s* one *d*. *Educ:* St Lawrence Coll., Ramsgate; Leicester Univ. (LLB Hons; LLD 2000); Southampton Univ. (MPhil). Joined Metropolitan Police, 1963; DS, Police Staff Coll., 1983–84; Asst Chief Constable, Hampshire Constabulary, 1986–89; Dep. Chief Constable, Cambridgeshire Constabulary, 1989–91; Chief Constable, Northumbria, 1991–96; HM Inspector of Constabulary, 1996–98; Dep. Comr, Metropolitan Police, 1998–99. Chairman: Jt Cttee on Offender Profiling, 1991; ACPO Crime Prevention Sub-Cttee, 1994. Chm., NI Enquiry into alleged collusion between paraml. and security forces (Stevens Enquiry), 1989–92; headed Enquiry into alleged malpractice at Nat. Criminal Intelligence Service, 1994–96; 'Stevens 3' NI Enquiry into Collusion, 1999–2003; inquiry into the deaths of Diana, Princess of Wales and Dodi Al-Fayed, 2003–06. Advr, Forensic Sci. Service; Advr to Govts of S Africa, Jamaica and Romania on police matters and anti corruption, 2002–; Chairman: Strategic Adv. Panel, Interpol, 2005; Monitor Quest (formerly Quest) Ltd, 2005–; Skills for Security, 2005–; Protector Gp, 2008–. Vis. Prof., City Univ., NY, 1984–85; Vis. Lectr, Internat. Crime Prevention Centre, Canada, 1998–; Sen. Mem., 1996, Hon. Fellow, 2000, Wolfson Coll., Cambridge. Chancellor, Northumbria Univ., 2005–15. Pres., Aircraft Owners and Pilots Assoc., 2005–. Patron, Northumbria Youth Action, 2000–; Patron of charities, Brixton and Romania. Hon. Col, Northumbria Cadet Force, 2006–. Freeman, City of London, 2002. DL: Greater London, 2001; Northumberland, 2007. FRSA 2002. Hon. DCL Northumbria, 2001; Hon. LLD Newcastle, 2006; Hon. PhD London Metropolitan, 2008; Hon. DLitt Newcastle, 2008. KStJ 2002. Hon. Air Cdre, RAAF, 2008–. *Publications:* Not for the Faint-hearted (autobiog.), 2005. *Recreations:* walking, cricket, squash, Rugby, flying (qualified pilot). *Address:* House of Lords, SW1A 0PW. *Clubs:* East India, Royal Air Force; Northern Counties, Durham County Cricket (Pres., 2004–06; Dir, 2006–).

**STEVENS OF LUDGATE,** Baron *cr* 1987 (Life Peer), of Ludgate in the City of London; **David Robert Stevens;** Chairman: United News & Media (formerly United Newspapers plc), 1981–99 (Director, 1974–99); Express Newspapers, 1985–99 (Deputy Chairman, 2014–18); *b* 26 May 1936; *s* of late (Arthur) Edwin Stevens, CBE; *m* 1st Patricia Rose (marr. diss. 1971); one *s* one *d*; 2nd, 1977, Melissa Milicevich (*d* 1989); 3rd, 1990, Meriza Giori. *Educ:* Stowe Sch.; Sidney Sussex Coll., Cambridge (MA Hons Econ; Hon. Fellow, 1991).

2nd Lieut, Royal Artillery, 1955–56. Management Trainee, Elliott Automation, 1959; Director: Hill Samuel Securities, 1959–68; Drayton Group, 1968–74; Man. Dir. 1974–80, Chm., 1985–86, Drayton Montagu Investment Mgt. Chairman: Alexander Proudfoot Hldgs (formerly City & Foreign), 1976–95; Drayton Far East, 1976–93; English & International, 1976–79; Consolidated Venture (formerly Montagu Boston), 1979–93; Drayton Consolidated, 1980–92; Drayton Japan, 1980–88; Oak Industries, 1989–96; Mid States, 1989–95; Premier Asset Mgt plc, 1997–2001; PNC Tele.Com (formerly Personal Number Co.), 1998–2002; Chief Exec., 1980–87, Chm., 1980–93, Montagu Investment Management, subseq. INVESCO MIM Management; Dep. Chm., 1987–89, Chm., 1989–93, Britannia Arrow Hldgs, subseq. INVESCO MIM. Chm., EDC for Civil Engrg, 1984–86. Dir, ENO, 1980–87. Founder Dir, Helicopter Emergency Rescue Service, London Hosp., 1988. Patron, RCS, 1998. Grand Order of Southern Cross (Brazil), 1993. *Recreations:* golf, gardening. *Address:* House of Lords, SW1A 0PW. *Clubs:* White's; Sunningdale Golf, Swinley Golf.

**STEVENS, Andrew John;** Chief Executive Officer, Cobham plc, 2010–12; *b* Sedgley, W Midlands, 30 Aug. 1956; *s* of Alfred Stevens and Margaret Stevens; *m* 1980, Elizabeth Crabb; two *d*. *Educ:* Aston Univ. (BSc Hons 1st cl. 1978). CEng 1982; FIET 2001; FRAeS 2001. Provident Gp Trng Scheme, 1972–76; Dowty Group plc, subseq. TI Group plc, 1976–94: student apprentice, 1976–78; Dowty Rotol Ltd: machinist, 1978; Proj. Engr, Propellers and Gearboxes, 1978–80; Landing Gear Controller, 1980–82; Dep. Prodn Engrg Manager, 1982–86; Exec. Dir, Works, 1986–89; Prodn Dir and Mem. Bd, 1989–90; Mem. Bd, Dowty Aerospace IOM, 1989–92; Designate Dir and Gen. Manager, 1990–92, Dir and Gen. Manager, 1992–94, Landing Gear UK; Sector Exec., Cable Mgt, Bowthorpe plc, 1994–96; Messier Dowty International: Man. Dir UK, 1996–97; Man. Dir Europe, 1997–99; Man. Dir, Defence Aerospace, Bristol, Rolls-Royce plc, 2001–03; Cobham plc: Gp Pres., Aerospace Systems, 2003–05; Chief Operating Officer, 2005–09. Non-executive Director: De La Rue plc, 2013–19; CAE Inc., 2013–; Héroux-Devtek Inc., 2014–. Ext. Examr, Brunel Univ., 1992–94. *Recreations:* walking, gardening, cars and driving.

**STEVENS, Prof. Anne Frances,** PhD; Professor of European Studies, Aston University, 1998–2008, now Emeritus (Head, School of Languages and European Studies, 1998–2003); *b* 28 Dec. 1942; *d* of late Robert Ross, FLS and Margaret Helen Ross (*née* Steadman); *m* 1966, Handley Michael Gambrell Stevens, *qv*; two *d* (and one *d* decd). *Educ:* Blackheath High Sch. for Girls; Newnham Coll., Cambridge (BA 1964; MA 1975); LSE, Univ. of London (MSc Econ (with distinction) 1975; PhD 1980). Asst Principal, Dept of Technical Co-operation, ODM, 1964–66; part-time Lectr, Univ. of Malaya, 1966–68; HEO, British High Commn, Kuala Lumpur, 1968–69; School of European Studies, University of Sussex: Lectr in Politics, 1978–90; Dean, 1988–90; Prof. of European Studies, Univ. of Kent at Canterbury, 1991–98. *Publications:* (jtly) Hostile Brothers: competition and closure in the European electronics industry, 1990; The Government and Politics of France, 1992, 3rd edn 2003; Brussels Bureaucrats: the administration of the European Union, 2000; Women, Power and Politics, 2007; articles on comparative admin. *Recreations:* walking, watching opera, needlework. *Address:* Flat 1, 20 Netherhall Gardens, NW3 5TH. *T:* (020) 7794 0874.

**STEVENS, Annette;** *see* King, Annette.

**STEVENS, Auriol, (Lady Ashworth);** journalist, retired; Editor, Times Higher Education Supplement, 1992–2002; *d* of Capt. Barry Stevens and Ruth M. Stevens Howard; *m* 1st, 1962, Prof. Hugh Stephenson, *qv* (marr. diss. 1987); 2nd, 1988, Dr J. M. Ashworth (*see* Sir J. M. Ashworth). *Educ:* Somerville Coll., Oxford (BA Hons); London Univ. (Dip. (Ext.)). Freelance journalist, 1962–72; TES, 1972–78; educn corresp., Observer, 1978–83; reporter, A Week in Politics, TV, 1983–86; Dir, Univs Inf. Unit, Cttee of Vice-Chancellors, 1986–92. Chm. Govs, Elliot Sch., Putney, 1981–85; Council Member: PSI, 1985–91; RCA, 1998–2006 (Vice-Chm., 2004–06); Essex Univ., 2002–12 (Pro-Chancellor, 2005–12; Hon. Fellow, 2013); Educn Review Gp, 2008–; Governor: UEL, 2002–05; St Helena Sch., Colchester, 2009–17. Member: Exec. Cttee, Forum UK, 1999–2003; Inst. of Cancer Res., 2000–; Exec. Cttee, Wivenhoe Soc., 2003–06. Hon. FRCA 2007. Hon. DLitt Nottingham Trent, 2003. *Publications:* Clever Children in Comprehensive Schools, 1978; The State of the Universities, 1991; Women in the Media, 1998. *Recreations:* history, textiles, grandchildren. *Address:* Garden House, Wivenhoe, Essex CO7 9BD; 307 Gilbert House, Barbican, EC2Y 8BD. *Clubs:* Royal Over-Seas League; Wivenhoe Sailing.

**STEVENS, Christopher Paul C.;** *see* Claxton Stevens, C. P.

**STEVENS, Claire Lamorna,** CBE 2018; FDSRCSE; Consultant in Paediatric Dentistry, Manchester University NHS Foundation Trust, since 2009; *b* Chelmsford, 5 July 1977; *d* of Charles and Jane Patchett; one *s* one *d*. *Educ:* Perse Sch. for Girls; Univ. of Bristol (BDS 2000); Newcastle Univ. (MPhil 2009). FDS (Paediatric Dentistry) RCSE 2009. Advr, Brush DJ Ltd, 2018–. Pres., British Soc. of Paediatric Dentistry, 2017–18. *Recreations:* spending time with my children Ava and Archie, surfing, good food with great company, feeling sand between my toes, Tynemouth life, gardening, afternoon naps, dismantling the patriarchy. *Address:* Department of Child Dental Health, University Dental Hospital of Manchester, Higher Cambridge Street, Manchester M15 6FH. *T:* (0161) 275 6614. *E:* claire.stevens@mft.nhs.uk.

**STEVENS, Darren James;** Director, Corporate Resources, East Riding of Yorkshire Council, since 2017; *b* Guildford, Surrey, 24 Nov. 1970; *s* of Geoffrey and Veronica Stevens; civil partnership, 2017, Jose Osuna Osuna. *Educ:* Univ. of Chichester (BA Hons Sports Studies 1992); Birkbeck Coll., Univ. of London (MSc Social and Political Theory 2000); Univ. of Leicester (MSc Sociol. of Sport (Sports Mgt) 2007). Lectr in Leisure Mgt (pt-time), Univ. of Chichester, 1996–2001; Principal Leisure and Tourism Policy Officer, E Riding of Yorks Council, 2001–04; Cultural Services Manager, 2004–07, Hd, Chief Exec.'s Office, 2007–09, London Bor. of Sutton; Hd, Culture and Information, E Riding of Yorks Council, 2009–17. *Recreations:* travel, walking, history, football (grounds and spectating). *Address:* East Riding of Yorkshire Council, County Hall, Beverley HU17 9BA. *T:* (01482) 393000. *E:* darren.stevens@eastriding.gov.uk.

**STEVENS, Rt Rev. Dr Douglas;** Bishop of Riverina, 2005–12; Rector, Parish of Mt Gravatt, since 2012; *b* 19 May 1952; *s* of Robert Henry Stevens and Dorothy Phyllis Cooper; *m* 1979, Denise Karen; two *d*. *Educ:* Newcastle Univ., NSW (BA); Aust. Coll. of Theol. (BTh Hons); Univ. of Dublin (MPhil); Melbourne Coll. of Divinity (Dr of Ministry Studies). Rector: Merriwa, 1981–84; Botton Point, 1986–90; Wingham, 1990–94; Nambucca Heads, 1994–99; Tweed Heads, 1999–2005. *Address:* St Bartholomew's Anglican Church, PO Box 275, Mt Gravatt, Qld 4122, Australia.

**STEVENS, Glenn Robert,** AC 2016; Chairman and Governor, Reserve Bank of Australia, 2006–16; *b* 23 Jan. 1958; *s* of Robert Frank Hollis Stevens and Audrey Grace Stevens; *m* 1983, Susan Elizabeth Dunbar; two *d*. *Educ:* Univ. of Sydney (BEc Hons 1979); Univ. of Western Ontario (MA Econ 1985). Reserve Bank of Australia: joined, 1980; Head: Econ. Analysis Dept, 1992–95; Internat. Dept, 1995–96; Asst Gov. (Econ.), 1996–2001; Dep. Gov., 2001–06. Vis. Scholar, Fed. Reserve Bank of San Francisco, 1990. Non-exec. Dir, Macquarie Gp. Dep. Chm., Temora Aviation Mus.; Dir, Lowy Inst. Dir, Anika Foundn. *Recreation:* flying.

**STEVENS, Handley Michael Gambrell,** PhD; Under Secretary, Department of Transport, 1983–94; *b* 29 June 1941; *s* of Ernest Norman Stevens and Kathleen Emily Gambrell; *m* 1966, Anne Frances Ross (*see* A. F. Stevens); two *d* (and one *d* decd). *Educ:* The Leys Sch., Cambridge; Phillips Acad., Andover, Mass (E-SU schol.); King's Coll., Cambridge (BA 1963; MA 1971; PhD 2007). Joined Foreign Office, 1964; Third, later Second, Sec., Kuala Lumpur, 1966; Asst Private Sec. to the Lord Privy Seal, 1970; Principal: CSD, 1971; DTI, 1973; Asst Sec., Dept of Trade, 1976. Vis. Res. Associate, Eur. Inst., LSE, 1994–2007. *Publications:* Transport Policy in Britain, 1998; Brussels Bureaucrats?, 2000; Transport Policy in the European Union, 2003; Air Transport and the European Union, 2010; The Life and Death of a Treaty: Bermuda 2, 2018. *Recreations:* music, hill walking, travel. *Address:* 20 Netherhall Gardens, NW3 5TH.

**STEVENS, Howard Linton;** QC 2012; *b* Kent, 6 March 1965; *s* of Donald John Stevens and Shirley Marion Stevens; *m* 1995, Anthea Lucy Michaelson-Yeates; two *d*. *Educ:* Tonbridge Sch.; Univ. of Durham (BA Jt Hons); City Univ. (DipLaw). Called to the Bar, Middle Temple, 1990; barrister in independent practice, 1990–. *Recreations:* family, travel, ski-ing, restoring Grade II listed home. *Address:* 3 Hare Court, Temple, EC4Y 7BJ. *T:* (020) 7415 7800. *E:* howardstevens@3harecourt.com.

**STEVENS, Jo;** MP (Lab) Cardiff Central, since 2015; *b* Swansea, 6 Sept. 1966. *Educ:* Ysgol Uwchradd Argoed; Elfed High Sch.; Univ. of Manchester (LLB Hons 1988); Manchester Poly. (CPE 1989). Admitted Solicitor, 1991; Solicitor and Dir, Thompsons Solicitors, 1989–2015. Shadow Justice Minister and Shadow Solicitor Gen., 2016; Shadow Sec. of State for Wales, 2016–17. Mem., Digital, Culture, Media and Sport Select Cttee, 2017–. *Recreations:* football, cricket, Rugby, darts. *Address:* House of Commons, SW1A 0AA. *E:* jo.stevens.mp@parliament.uk; (office) 116 Albany Road, Roath, Cardiff CF24 3RU. *T:* (029) 2132 9736. *W:* www.jostevens.co.uk. *Clubs:* Cardiff City Football, Glamorgan County Cricket.

**STEVENS, John Christopher Courtenay;** Adviser, Partners Investment Co. LLP, since 2017; *b* 23 May 1955; *s* of Sir John Melior Stevens, KCMG, DSO, OBE. *Educ:* Winchester Coll.; Magdalen Coll., Oxford (BA Jurisprudence). Foreign exchange and Bond trader, Banque Indosuez, Paris, 1976–77; Bayerische Hypotheken und Wechselbank, Munich, 1977–78; Morgan Grenfell, London, 1979–89, Internat. Dir, 1986–89; Advr, St James's Place Capital plc, 1989. MEP (C) Thames Valley, 1989–99. Advr, THS Capital Fund, later THS Partners LLP, 1999–2016. Contested (Ind) Buckingham, 2010. Vis. Sen. Hon. Fellow, LSE IDEAS, 2011–. *Recreations:* riding, ski-ing. *Address:* Flat 19, Cleland House, 32 John Islip Street, SW1P 4FF.

**STEVENS, Sir Kenneth (Allen),** KNZM 2009 (DCNZM 2007); Owner and Manager, Glidepath Ltd, 1972–2008; Chairman, Glidepath Group, since 1997; *b* Christchurch, NZ, 1 Feb. 1944; *s* of Arthur Edward Stevens and Marion Glover Cotter; *m* Glenice Jean McKenzie; one *s* one *d*. *Educ:* Seddon Memorial Tech. Coll., Auckland. Chm., NZ Aviation Jt Action Gp, 1994–97. Chairman: Export New Zealand, 2008– (Mem. Bd, NZ Export Inst., 1980–83); Howick Ltd, 2008–; Member: Bd of Trustees, Asia NZ Foundn, 2007–; Bd, Icehouse, 2008–. Business Champion, Export Year 2007, 2006–07. Mem., Experimental Aircraft Assoc., Milwaukee, 2003–12. Trustee: Vex Robotics, NZ, 2010–; NZ Business Mentors, 2010–. *Recreations:* Rugby, boating, cricket, mentoring exporters. *Address:* Glidepath Group, 17–19 Patiki Road, PO Box 71115, Avondale, Auckland 1026, New Zealand. *T:* (9) 8183354, *Fax:* (9) 8189994. *E:* ken.stevens@glidepathgroup.com. *Club:* Royal New Zealand Yacht Squadron.

**STEVENS, Lewis David,** MBE 1982; management and industrial engineering consultant (self-employed), since 1979; *b* 13 April 1936; *s* of Richard and Winnifred Stevens; *m* 1959, Margaret Eileen Gibson; two *s* one *d*. *Educ:* Oldbury Grammar Sch.; Liverpool Univ.; Lanchester Coll. RAF 1956–58. Various engrg cos, mainly in industrial engrg and production management positions, 1958–79. Mem., Nuneaton Borough Council, 1966–72. MP (C) Nuneaton, 1983–92; contested (C) Nuneaton, 1992. *Address:* 151 Sherbourne Avenue, Nuneaton, Warwicks CV10 9JN. *T:* (024) 7674 4541.

**STEVENS, Marie Adelaide Grizella;** regulatory consultant to gaming industry, since 2004; Director: Prometheus Bound Ltd, since 2010; BooksbyMetre Ltd, since 2015; *b* London, 5 July 1950; *d* of David Henry John Griffiths Powell and Judith Amy Powell (*née* Lennard); *m* 1st, 1973, David John Stevens (marr. diss. 1988); one *s* two *d*; 2nd, 1988, David Cooper; one *s* one *d*, and one step *s* one step *d*. *Educ:* Wadhurst Coll.; London Sch. of Econs and Pol Sci. (LLB Hons); Coll. of Law. Admitted solicitor, 1974; Slaughter and May, 1972–77; Gp Solicitor, Ladbrokes, 1987–97. Chm., 888 Hldgs plc, 2005–06. Mem., Gaming Bd for GB, 1999–2004; Chm., Adv. Bd, Global Leaders in Law, 2010–. Trustee, Royal Armouries, 2008–12. *Recreations:* children and grandchildren, dollhouses, vintage fairs, 20th century English women's literature, making lists. *Address:* 3 Wilton Crescent, SW1X 8RN. *T:* (020) 7245 0005. *E:* mariestevens@btconnect.com.

**STEVENS, Michael Doherty,** CB 2017; Head, Chief Scientist Office, 2011–16; *b* Greenock, 20 June 1956; *s* of Joseph and Jessie Stevens; partner, 1981, Anne McCool; two *d*. *Educ:* St Mirin's Acad., Paisley; Strathclyde Univ. Asst Manager, DHSS, 1972–89; Hd, Children's Br., Social Work Services Gp, 1989–94; Manager and Implementation Team Leader, Children (Scotland) Act 1995 Parly Bill, 1994–99; Dep. Dir, Chief Scientist Office, 1999–2011. Member, Committee: Donaldson Area Amenity Assoc., 2009–16 (Chm., 2016–); Murrayfield Community Council, 2016–. *Recreations:* history, driving, walking, reading. *Address:* 7 Pembroke Place, Edinburgh EH12 5HX. *T:* (0131) 337 8529. *E:* mikestevens7@icloud.com.

**STEVENS, Sir Michael (John),** KCVO 2017 (CVO 2009; LVO 2002); Keeper of the Privy Purse, Treasurer to the Queen, and Receiver-General of the Duchy of Lancaster, since 2018; *b* Southampton, 1 May 1958; *s* of John and Jean Stevens; *m* 1984, Jane Catherine Cockshaw; three *d*. *Educ:* King Edward VI Sch., Southampton; Birmingham Univ. (BCom Hons). FCA 1992. KPMG, 1979–95. Sen. Manager, 1989–95; Finance Dir, 1995–2002, Man. Dir, 2002–07, Royal Collection Trust; Dep. Treas. to the Queen, 2007–17; Dep. Keeper of the Privy Purse, 2011–17. Trustee: King Edward VII Sister Agnes Hosp., 2010–19; Historic Royal Palaces Trust, 2015–; Royal Collection Trust, 2018–. *Recreations:* tennis, walking, family, Southampton FC, Rugby. *Address:* Buckingham Palace, SW1A 1AA.

**STEVENS, Philip Simeon St J.;** *see* St John-Stevens.

**STEVENS, Dr Robert Bocking;** Of Counsel, Covington & Burling, Washington and London, since 1992; Senior Research Fellow, Constitution Unit, University College London, since 2001; *b* 8 June 1933; *s* of John Skevington Stevens and Enid Dorothy Stevens; *m* 1st, 1961, Rosemary Anne Wallace (marr. diss. 1982); one *s* one *d*; 2nd, 1985, Katherine Booth; one *d*. *Educ:* Oakham Sch.; Keble Coll., Oxford (BA 1956; BCL 1956; MA 1959; DCL 1984; Hon. Fellow, 1983); Yale Univ. (LLM 1958). Called to the Bar, Gray's Inn, 1956, Bencher, 1999. Yale University: Asst Prof. of Law, 1959–61; Associate Prof., 1961–65; Prof., 1965–76 (Hon. Fellow, 2001); Provost, Tulane Univ., 1976–78; Pres., Haverford Coll. 1978–87; Chancellor, Univ. of Calif., Santa Cruz, 1987–91; Master, Pembroke Coll., Oxford, 1993–2001 (Hon. Fellow, 2001). Mem., Nat. Council of the Humanities, 1982–88. Chairman: Marshall Aid Commemoration Commn, 1995–2000; Sulgrave Manor Trust, 2002–06. Gov., Abingdon Sch., 1993–2000. Hon. LLD: NY Law Sch., 1984; Villanova, 1985; Pennsylvania, 1987; Hon. DLitt Haverford Coll., 1991. *Publications:* (with B. S. Yamey) The Restrictive Practices Court, 1965; (with B. Abel-Smith) Lawyers and the Courts, 1967; (with B. Abel-Smith) In Search of Justice, 1968; Income Security, 1970; (with R. A. Stevens) Welfare Medicine in America, 1974; Law and Politics, 1978; The American Law School, 1983; The Independence of the Judiciary, 1993; The English Judges, 2002, 2nd edn 2005; From University to Uni, 2004, rev. edn 2015. *Recreations:* history, politics, scepticism. *Address:* 19 Burgess Mead, Oxford OX2 6XP. *T:* (01865) 558420; Covington & Burling, 265 Strand, WC2R 1BH. *T:* (020) 7067 2000. *Clubs:* Reform; Elizabethan (New Haven, Conn).

**STEVENS, Rear Adm. Robert Patrick,** CB 2000; Managing Director, Stevens Marine Ltd, since 2013; *b* 14 March 1948; *s* of late Major Philip Joseph Stevens, RMP and Peggy Stevens (*née* Marshall); *m* 1973, Vivien Roberts; one *s* one *d*. *Educ:* Prince Rupert Sch., Wilhelmshaven; BRNC, Dartmouth. Commanding Officer: HMS Odin, 1979–81; comdg officers qualifying course, HMS Dolphin, 1983–85; HMS Torbay, 1985–88; USN War Coll., 1988–89; Asst Dir, Strategic Systems, MoD, 1989–91; Captain: 7th Frigate Sqdn and CO, HMS Argonaut, 1992–93; Navy Presentation team, 1993–94; Dir, Jt Warfare, MoD, 1994–98; FO, Submarines, Comdr Submarines (NATO), Eastern Atlantic and NW, and COS (Ops) to C-in-C Fleet, 1998–2001; COS to Comdr Allied Naval Forces Southern Europe, and Sen. British Officer Southern Reg., 2002–05. Chm. and non-exec. Dir, Perpetuus Tidal Energy Centre, 2016–. CEO, British Marine Fedn, 2006–12. Chm., Solent Marine Forum, 2013–14. Adjunct Prof., Univ. of Southampton, 2015–. Pres., RN Football Assoc., 1998–2005; Trustee, 1851 Trust (Americas Cup), 2014–. Liveryman, Shipwrights' Co., 2006–. *Recreations:* tennis, ski-ing, sailing. *Address:* Long Reach, Hensting Lane, Fishers Pond, Hants SO50 7HH. *Clubs:* Royal Navy of 1765 and 1785; South West Shingles Yacht; Hockley Golf.

**STEVENS, Simon Laurence;** Chief Executive, NHS England, since 2014; *b* Birmingham, 4 Aug. 1966; *s* of Laurence and Vivien Stevens; *m* 1998, Maggie Thurer; one *s* one *d*. *Educ:* St Bartholomew's Comprehensive Sch., Newbury; Balliol Coll., Oxford (BA Hons PPE 1987; MA); Strathclyde Univ. (MBA 1996). Econ. devel analyst, Guyana, 1987–88; NHS Mgt Trng Scheme, Newcastle upon Tyne and Asst Gen. Manager, NW Durham Hosps, 1988–90; Gen. Manager, Psychiatric Hosps, Northumberland and N Tyneside, 1990–92; Gp Manager, Guy's and St Thomas' Hosps, 1992–94; Harkness Fellow, Columbia Univ./NYC Health Dept, 1994–95; Exec. Dir, E Sussex, Brighton and Hove HA, 1995–97; Policy Advr to Sec. of State for Health, DoH, 1997–2001; Prime Minister's Health Advr, 10 Downing St Policy Unit, 2001–04; Pres., United Health Europe, 2004–06; CEO, United Healthcare Medicare, USA, 2006–09; Pres., Global Health and Exec. Vice Pres., United Health Gp, USA, 2009–14. Vis. Prof., LSE, 2004–08. Mem. (Lab), Lambeth LBC, 1998–2002. Director: Medicare Rights Center, NY, 2009–13; Amil, Brazil, 2012–13; Commonwealth Fund, NY, 2013–. Director: Minnesota Histl Soc., 2008–13; Minnesota Opera, 2008–13. Trustee: King's Fund, 2007–11; Nuffield Trust, 2012–14. Hon. FRCGP 2017. DUniv Birmingham, 2015. *Recreations:* family, books, boats, cooking without recipes. *Address:* c/o NHS England, 80 London Road, SE1 6LH. *E:* england.ce@nhs.net.

**STEVENS, Rt Rev. Timothy John,** CBE 2016; Bishop of Leicester, 1999–2015; *b* 31 Dec. 1946; *s* of late Ralph and Jean Ursula Stevens; *m* 1973, Wendi Kathleen; one *s* one *d*. *Educ:* Chigwell Sch.; Selwyn Coll., Cambridge (BA 1968; MA 1972); Ripon Hall, Oxford (Dip Th). BOAC, 1968–72; FCO, 1972–73. Ordained priest, 1976; Curate, East Ham, 1976–79; Team Vicar, Upton Park, 1979–80; Team Rector, Canvey Island, 1980–88; Bp of Chelmsford's Urban Officer, 1988–91; Archdeacon of West Ham, 1991–95; Bishop Suffragan of Dunwich, 1995–99. Hon. Canon of Chelmsford, 1987–95. Chm., Urban Bishops' Panel, Gen. Synod of C of E, 2001–06; Member: Archbps' Council, 2005–15; Standing Cttee, House of Bishops, 2006–10; Convenor of the Lords Spiritual, H of L, 2009–15. Non-exec. Dir, Norfolk and Suffolk NHS Trust, 2015–. Chm., Council, Children's Soc., 2004–10. Mem. Bd of Govs, De Montfort Univ., 2006–13; Chm. Bd of Govs, Westcott House Theol Coll., 2006–12. Took seat in H of L, 2004. Trustee, Woolf Inst., 2017–. Hon. DCL De Montfort, 2002; Hon. DLitt Leicester, 2003. GCStJ 2016 (Prelate of Ven. Order of St John of Jerusalem, 2016–). *Recreations:* golf, cricket. *Address:* 62 Horringer Road, Bury St Edmunds, Suffolk IP33 2DR. *Club:* Royal Over-Seas League.

**STEVENS, Timothy John,** OBE 2000; FSA; Director, Gilbert Collection, Somerset House, 2002–08 (Executive Director, Hermitage Rooms, 2001–03); *b* 17 Jan. 1940; *s* of Seymour Stevens and Joan Rudgard; *m* 1969, Caroline Sankey; twin *s*. *Educ:* King's Sch., Canterbury; Hertford Coll., Oxford (MA); Courtauld Inst., Univ. of London (Academic Diploma, History of Art). Walker Art Gallery: Asst Keeper of British Art, 1964–65; Keeper of Foreign Art, 1965–67; Dep. Dir, 1967–70; Dir, 1971–74; Dir, Merseyside CC Art Galls, 1974–86; Dep. Dir, Nat. Museums and Galleries on Merseyside, 1986–87; Keeper of Art, Nat. Mus. of Wales, 1987–94; Asst Dir (Collections), V&A Mus., 1994–2000. Trustee: NACF, 2000–11; Leeds Castle Foundn, 2008–. Hon. LittD Liverpool, 1985. Chevalier de l'Ordre des Arts et des Lettres (France), 1988. *Recreation:* gardening. *Address:* Luddenham Court, Faversham, Kent ME13 0TH.

**STEVENS-HOARE, Michelle, (Brie);** QC 2013; *b* Wokingham, 21 Oct. 1963; *d* of Edward John Stevens-Hoare and Jacqueline Stevens-Hoare; civil partnership 2006, Paula Louise Ives. *Educ:* Kendrick Girls' Grammar Sch., Reading; London Sch. of Econs and Pol Sci. (LLB, LLM); Inns of Court Sch. of Law. Called to the Bar, Middle Temple, 1986; Bencher, Lincoln's Inn, 2017; in practice as a barrister specialising in property law, 1986–. First-tier Tribunal Judge, Property Chamber (Land Registration) (pt-time), 2005–. Chm., London Common Law and Commercial Bar Assoc., 2015–18. Comr, Judicial Appts Commn, 2018–. Ambassador, Stonewall, 2013–; Mem. Bd, Freehold, 2012–; Founding Mem., FreeBar. *Publications:* (contrib.) The Law and Practice of Compromise, 5th edn 2002 to 8th edn 2015; (contrib.) Cousins: the law of mortgages, 2nd edn 2001 to 3rd edn 2010. *Recreations:* roller coasters, motorbikes, international travel, good food. *Address:* Hardwicke, New Square, Lincoln's Inn, WC2A 3SB. *T:* (020) 7242 2523, *Fax:* (020) 7691 1234. *E:* brie@hardwicke.co.uk.

**STEVENSON,** family name of **Barons Stevenson of Balmacara** and **Stevenson of Coddenham**.

**STEVENSON OF BALMACARA,** Baron *cr* 2010 (Life Peer), of Little Missenden in the County of Buckinghamshire; **Robert Wilfrid, (Wilf), Stevenson;** Senior Policy Adviser, Prime Minister's Office, 2008–10; *b* 19 April 1947; *s* of James Alexander Stevenson and Elizabeth Anne Stevenson (*née* Macrae); *m* 1st, 1972, Jennifer Grace Antonio (marr. diss. 1979); 2nd, 1991, (Elizabeth) Ann Minogue, *qv*; one *s* two *d*. *Educ:* Edinburgh Academy; University College, Oxford (MA Natural Sciences, Chemistry); Napier Polytechnic (ACCA). Research Officer, Edinburgh Univ. Students' Assoc., 1970–74; Sec., Napier Coll., Edinburgh, 1974–87; Dep. Dir, 1987–88, Dir, 1988–97, BFI; Dir, Smith Inst., 1997–2008. Chm., Foundn for Credit Counselling, 2010–15. Governor: Prestwood Lodge Sch., 2008–10; Chiltern Way Fedn Sch., 2010–14. Hon. DArts Napier, 2008. *Publications:* (ed) Gordon Brown Speeches, 2006; (ed) Moving Britain Forward, 2006; (ed) The Change

We Choose: speeches 2007–2009, 2010. *Recreations:* cinema, bee keeping, bridge. *Address:* Missenden House, Little Missenden, Amersham, Bucks HP7 0RD. *T:* (01494) 890689. *E:* wilf@wilfstevenson.co.uk.

**STEVENSON OF BALMACARA, Lady;** *see* Minogue, E. A.

**STEVENSON OF CODDENHAM,** Baron *cr* 1999 (Life Peer), of Coddenham, in the county of Suffolk; **Henry Dennistoun Stevenson, (Dennis),** Kt 1998; CBE 1981; DL; *b* 19 July 1945; *s* of Alexander James Stevenson and Sylvia Florence Stevenson (*née* Ingleby); *m* 1972, Charlotte Susan, *d* of Hon. Sir Peter Vanneck, GBE, CB, AFC, AE; four *s. Educ:* Glenalmond; King's Coll., Cambridge (MA). Chairman: SRU Gp of cos, 1972–96; GPA, then AerFi, Gp, 1993–2000; Pearson plc, 1997–2005 (Dir, 1986–97); HBOS plc, 2001–09; Director: British Technology Gp, 1979–89; Tyne Tees Television, 1982–87; Manpower Inc. (formerly Blue Arrow), 1988–2006; Thames Television plc, 1991–93; J. Rothschild Assurance plc, 1991–97; J. Rothschild Assurance Hldgs plc, 1991–99; English Partnerships, 1993–99; Bd, BSkyB Gp plc, 1994–2000; Lazard Bros, 1997–2000; Whitehall Trust Ltd, 1997–2004; St James's Place Capital, 1997–2002 (Hon. Pres., 2002–04); Economist Newspapers, 1998–2011; Western Union Co., 2006–12; Loudwater Investment Partners Ltd, 2007–12; Culture and Sport Glasgow, 2007–09; Cloaca Maxima Ltd, 2010–13; Waterstones Hldgs Ltd, 2011–16; Inter Mediate, 2011–19. Chm., Trustees, Tate Gall., 1989–98. Chairman: Newton Aycliffe and Peterlee New Town Develt Corp., 1971–80; Intermediate Technology Develt Gp, 1983–90; Director: Nat. Building Agency, 1977–81; LDDC, 1981–88. Chairman: govt working party on role of voluntary movements and youth in the envmt, 1971, '50 Million Volunteers' (HMSO); Ind. Adv. Cttee on Pop Fests, 1972–76, 'Pop Festivals, Report and Code of Practice' (HMSO); Advr on Agricl Marketing to Minister of Agric., 1979–83; Special Advr to PM and Sec. of State for Educn on use of IT in Educn, 1997–2000; Chairman: H of L Appts Commn, 2000–09; Arts and Media Honours Cttee, 2008–12; Member: Panel on Takeovers and Mergers, 1992–2000; Bd, British Council, 1996–2003; Standards Cttee, Westminster CC, 2008–12; H of L Works of Art Cttee, 2009–14. Chairman: NAYC, 1973–81; Sinfonia 21 (formerly Docklands Sinfonietta), 1989–99; Aldeburgh Music (formerly Aldeburgh Prodns), 2000–12; MQ: Transforming Mental Health, 2010–15; Director: Glyndebourne Prodns, 1998–2016; London Music Masters, 2011–17; Inst. for Govt, 2008–13; Think Ahead, 2016–. Pres., Aldeburgh Music, 2012–. Trustee: Tate Gall. Foundn, 1998–; Horse's Mouth, 2006–15. Mem. Admin. Council, Royal Jubilee Trusts, 1978–80. Chancellor, Univ. of the Arts London (formerly London Institute), 2000–10. Governor: LSE, 1995–99; London Business Sch., 1999–2002. DL Suffolk, 2008. *Recreation:* home. *Clubs:* Brooks's, Garrick, MCC.

**STEVENSON, (Andrew) John;** MP (C) Carlisle, since 2010; *b* Aberdeen, 4 July 1963; *s* of late Andrew Lochart Stevenson and of Jane Wilson Stevenson. *Educ:* Aberdeen Grammar Sch.; Dundee Univ. (MA Hons Hist. and Pols); Chester Law Coll. Admitted solicitor, 1990; Partner, Bendles Solicitors, Carlisle, 1994–. Mem. (C) Carlisle CC, 1999–2010. *Recreation:* sport. *Address:* Wood Villa, Great Corby, Carlisle CA4 8LL. *E:* john.stevenson.mp@parliament.uk.

**STEVENSON, Anne Katharine, (Mrs Peter Lucas);** poet; *b* Cambridge, England, 3 Jan. 1933; *d* of Charles Leslie Stevenson, philosopher, and Louise Destler Stevenson; *m* 1987, Peter David Lucas; two *s* one *d* by previous marriages. *Educ:* Univ. of Michigan, Ann Arbor (BA 1954, Major Hopwood Award 1954; MA 1961; Athena Award for dist. alumni 1990). School teacher, 1955–61; Advertising Manager (as Mrs A. Hitchcock), A&C Black Publishers Ltd, 1956–57; Fellow: Radcliff Inst., Harvard, 1970–71; in Writing, Univ. of Dundee, 1973–75; Lady Margaret Hall, Oxford, 1975–77; Bulmershe Coll., Reading, 1977–78; Northern Arts Fellow, Newcastle and Durham, 1982–86; Fellow in Writing, Edinburgh Univ., 1987–89. FEA 2002. Hon. Fellow, St Chad's Coll., Durham Univ., 2010. Hon. DLitt: Loughborough, 1997; Durham, 2005; Hull, 2006; Michigan, 2008; Newcastle, 2010; London, 2010. Poetry Award, Scottish Arts Council, 1974; Cholmondeley Award, Soc. of Authors, 1997; Writer's Award, Northern Rock Foundn, 2002; Neglected Masters Award, Poetry Foundn, USA, 2007; Lannan Literary Award for Lifetime Achievement for Poetry, 2007; Aiken-Taylor Award, Sewanee Rev., 2007. *Publications: poetry:* Living in America, 1965; Reversals, 1967; Correspondences, 1974; Travelling Behind Glass, 1974; Enough of Green, 1977; Minute by Glass Minute, 1982; The Fiction Makers, 1985; Winter Time (pamphlet), 1986; Selected Poems, 1987; The Other House, 1990; Four and a Half Dancing Men, 1993; Collected Poems, 1996; Granny Scarecrow, 2000; Hearing with my Fingers (pamphlet), 2001; A Report from the Border, 2003; Poems 1955–2005, 2006; A Lament for the Makers, 2006; Stone Milk, 2007; Selected Poems, 2008; Astonishment, 2012; In the Orchard, 2016; Le Vie delle Parole (anthology in Italian, trans. by C. Buranello), 2018; Completing the Circle, 2020; *criticism and biography:* Elizabeth Bishop, 1966; Bitter Fame: a life of Sylvia Plath, 1989; Five Looks at Elizabeth Bishop, 1998, 2nd edn 2006; Between the Iceberg and the Ship (essays in criticism), 1998; trans., Eugene Dubnov, The Thousand-Year Minutes, 2013; contrib. articles and revs to TLS, Poetry Nation Rev., Poetry Rev., Hudson Rev., Michigan Qly Rev., and to many other poetry pubns in UK and USA; About Poems and how poems are not about, 2017; trans., Dubnov, Beyond the Boundaries, 2017; *festschrift:* The Way You Say the World, 2003; (ed Angela Leighton) Voyages over Voices: critical essays on Anne Stevenson, 2010; Ian Gordon, The Poetry of Anne Stevenson, 2016. *Recreations:* good music, good company, laughter. *Address:* 38 Albert Street, Western Hill, Durham DH1 4RJ. *T:* (0191) 386 2115; Pwllymarch, Llanbedr, Gwynedd, N Wales LL45 2PL. *T:* (01341) 241208.

**STEVENSON, Christopher Terence S.;** *see* Sinclair-Stevenson.

**STEVENSON, Prof. David John,** PhD; FRS 1993; Marvin L. Goldberger (formerly George Van Osdol) Professor of Planetary Science, California Institute of Technology, since 1995; *b* 2 Sept. 1948; *s* of Ian McIvor Stevenson and Gwenyth (*née* Carroll). *Educ:* Rongotai Coll.; Victoria Univ., Wellington, NZ (BSc, BSc Hons, MSc); Cornell Univ., NY (PhD). Res. Fellow, ANU, 1976–78; Asst Prof., UCLA, 1978–80; California Institute of Technology: Associate Prof., 1980–84; Prof. of Planetary Science, 1984–95; Chm., Div. of Geol and Planetary Scis, 1989–94. Fellow, Amer. Geophysical Union, 1986 (Whipple Award, 1994; Hess Medal, 1998). Hon. DSc Victoria Univ. of Wellington, 2002. Urey Prize, Amer. Astronomical Soc., 1984. *Publications:* numerous papers in learned jls, principally in earth and planetary scis. *Recreations:* hiking, biking. *Address:* Division of Geological and Planetary Sciences, California Institute of Technology, Pasadena, CA 91125, USA. *T:* (626) 3956534.

**STEVENSON, Prof. Freda Kathryn,** DPhil; FRCPath, FMedSci; Professor of Immunology, and Consultant (non-clinical) Immunologist, University of Southampton, since 1997; *b* 27 April 1939; *d* of Richard Pollard Hartley and Joyce Elizabeth Hartley; *m* 1963, George Telford Stevenson, *qv;* three *s. Educ:* Univ. of Manchester (BSc 1960, MSc 1961); St Hugh's Coll., Oxford (DPhil 1964). FRCPath 1995. Lectr in Biochem., Univ. of Sydney, 1965–67; Post-doctoral Fellow, Univ. of Oxford, and Lectr in Biochem., Oriel Coll., Oxford, 1967–70; Southampton General Hospital: MRC Staff (external), 1970–73, Tenovus Post-doctoral Fellow, 1973–81, Tenovus Lab.; PSO, Regl Immunology Service, 1981–86; Top Grade SO, 1986–97; Reader in Immunology, Southampton Univ., 1986–97. Mem., Assoc. of Sen. Mems, St Hugh's Coll., Oxford. FMedSci 2000. Henry M. Stratton Medal, American Soc. of Hematology, 2018. *Publications:* over 200 peer-reviewed articles, mainly in internat. jls, in field of immunology with focus on strategies to vaccinate against cancer using genetic technology and on the nature and behaviour of human B-cell malignancies. *Recreations:* music, literature, walking. *Address:* University of Southampton, Cancer Sciences Division, Somers Cancer Research Building, Mailpoint 891, Southampton General Hospital, Tremona Road, Southampton SO16 6YD. *T:* (023) 8079 6923, *Fax:* (023) 8070 1385. *E:* fs@soton.ac.uk; Sudbury House, Sudbury Lane, Longworth, Abingdon OX13 5EL. *T:* (01865) 820646.

**STEVENSON, Prof. George Telford;** Professor of Immunochemistry, Faculty of Medicine, University of Southampton, 1974–97, now Emeritus; *b* 18 April 1932; *s* of Ernest George Stevenson and Mary Josephine Madden; *m* 1963, Freda Kathryn Hartley (*see* F. K. Stevenson); three *s. Educ:* North Sydney High Sch.; Univ. of Sydney (MB, BS; MD); Univ. of Oxford (DPhil). Resident MO, 1955–56, Resident Pathologist, 1957, Sydney Hosp.; Research Fellow, Dept of Medicine, Univ. of Sydney, 1958–61; Nuffield Dominions Demonstrator, Dept of Biochemistry, Univ. of Oxford, 1962–64; Sen. Research Fellow, Dept of Biochemistry, Univ. of Sydney, 1965–66; Scientific Staff, MRC Immunochemistry Unit, Univ. of Oxford, 1967–70; Dir, Tenovus Research Lab., Southampton Gen. Hosp., 1970–97; Consultant Immunologist, Southampton Univ. Hosps, 1976–97, now Hon. Consultant Immunologist. Hon. DSc Southampton, 2016. Hammer Prize for Cancer Research (jtly) (Armand Hammer Foundn, LA), 1982. *Publications:* Immunological Investigation of Lymphoid Neoplasms (with J. L. Smith and T. J. Hamblin), 1983; research papers on immunology and cancer, considered mainly at molecular level. *Address:* Sudbury House, Sudbury Lane, Longworth, Abingdon OX13 5EL. *T:* (01865) 820646.

**STEVENSON, George William;** *b* 30 Aug. 1938; *s* of Harold and Elsie May Stevenson; *m* 1st, 1958, Doreen June (decd); two *s* one *d;* 2nd, 1991, Pauline Brookes (*d* 2018). *Educ:* Uttoxeter Road Primary School; Queensberry Road Secondary School, Stoke-on-Trent. Pottery caster, 1953–57; coal miner, 1957–66; transport driver, 1966–84; shop steward, TGWU 5/24 Branch, 1968–84 (Mem., 1964–; Chm., 1975–81). Deputy Leader: Stoke-on-Trent City Council, 1972–83; Staffs County Council, 1981–85. MEP (Lab) Staffs East, 1984–94; Pres., Eur. Parlt Delegn for Relations with S Asia, 1989–92 (Vice-Pres., 1984–89). MP (Lab) Stoke on Trent South, 1992–2005. Member, Select Committee: on European Legislation, 1995–2005; on Environment, Transport and the Regions, 1997–2005; Mem., Speaker's Panel of Chairmen. Chairman: All-Party Tibet Gp, 1995–2005; PLP Agric. Cttee, 1993–2001. *Recreations:* walking, cinema, travel, reading.

**STEVENSON, Sir Hugh (Alexander),** Kt 2010; Chairman, Equitas Ltd, 1998–2009; *b* 7 Sept. 1942; *s* of William Hugh Stevenson and Elizabeth Margaret (*née* Wallace); *m* 1965, Catherine May Peacock; two *s* two *d. Educ:* Harrow Sch.; University Coll., Oxford (BA 1964; Hon. Fellow 1999); Harvard Business School (AMP 103). Admitted as solicitor, 1967; with Linklaters & Paines, 1964–70; with S. G. Warburg & Co., 1970–92; Dir, S. G. Warburg Gp plc, 1986–95; Chairman: Mercury Asset Management Gp plc, 1992–98 (Dir, 1986–98); The Merchants Trust plc, 2000–10 (Dir, 1999–2010); Standard Life Investments, 2004–08 (Dir, 2000–04); Dir, Standard Life plc (formerly Standard Life Assurance), 1999–2008. Director: British Museum Co., 1984–2006; Securities Inst., 1994–98 (Hon. FSI 1998); IMRO, 1995–2000; FSA, 2004–10 (Dep. Chm., 2009–10). Mem., Adv. Cttee on Business Appts, 2010–15 (Interim Chm., 2014). Chm., Instnl Fund Managers Assoc., 1998–99. Hon. Treas., Inst. of Child Health, 1991–96 (Hon. Fellow 1996); Chairman: The Sick Children's Trust, 1982–99; Gt Ormond St Hosp. Redevelt Adv. Bd (formerly Gt Ormond St Hosp. Develt Trust), 1999–2006; Special Trustee, Gt Ormond St Hosp., 1996–2007. Hon. Treas., Millennium Bridge Trust, 1998–2002. Chm., Swinley Forest Golf Club, 2007–. Hon. Fellow, UCL, 2000.
*See also* R. W. Ellis.

**STEVENSON, (James Alexander) Stewart;** Member (SNP) Banffshire and Buchan Coast, Scottish Parliament, since 2011 (Banff and Buchan, June 2001–2011); *b* 15 Oct. 1946; *s* of late James Thomas Middleton Stevenson, MB ChB and Helen Mary Berry MacGregor, MA; *m* 1969, Sandra Isabel Pirie, MA. *Educ:* Bell Baxter Sch., Cupar; Univ. of Aberdeen (MA 1969). Various technology posts, later Dir of Technology Innovation, Bank of Scotland, 1969–99; pt-time Lectr, Sch. of Mgt, Heriot-Watt Univ., 2001–. Scottish Parliament: contested (SNP) Linlithgow, 1999; Shadow Dep. Minister for Health and Social Justice, 2003–07; Minister for Transport, Infrastructure and Climate Change, 2007–10, for Envmt and Climate Change, 2011–12. Member: Rural Develt Cttee, 2001–03; Justice Cttee, 2001–03; Rural Economy and Connectivity Cttee, 2016–; Envmt, Climate Change and Land Reform Cttee, 2017–. Mem., SNP, 1961–. *Recreations:* computing, travel, public speaking. *Address:* Scottish Parliament, Edinburgh EH99 1SP; (constituency) Unit 8, Burnside Business Centre, Burnside Road, Peterhead, Aberdeenshire AB42 3AW.

**STEVENSON, Prof. Jane Barbara, (Mrs P. R. K. A. Davidson),** PhD; Senior Research Fellow, Campion Hall, Oxford, since 2017; *b* 12 Feb. 1959; *d* of John Lynn Stevenson and Winifred Mary Stevenson (*née* Temple); *m* 1989, Prof. Peter Robert Keith Andrew Davidson, *qv. Educ:* Haberdashers' Aske's Sch. for Girls, Elstree; Newnham Coll., Cambridge (BA 1981; PhD 1986). Drapers' Res. Fellow, Pembroke Coll., Cambridge, 1985–88; Lectr in Late Antique and Early Medieval Hist., Univ. of Sheffield, 1988–95; Sen. Res. Fellow, Univ. of Warwick, 1995–2000; University of Aberdeen: Reader in English, 2000–02; Reader in Postclassical Latin and Renaissance Studies, Sch. of Divinity, Hist. and Philosophy, 2002–05; Prof. of Latin, 2005–07; Regius Professor of Humanity, 2007–17. *Publications:* Women Writers in English Literature, 1992; The Laterculus Malalianus and the School of Archbishop Theodore, 1995; Several Deceptions, 1999; London Bridges, 2000; Astraea, 2001; The Pretender, 2002; The Empress of the Last Days, 2003; Good Women, 2005; Women Latin Poets: language, gender and authority from antiquity to the Eighteenth Century, 2005; Edward Burra: Twentieth Century eye, 2007; Baroque Between the Wars, 2018; edited with Peter Davidson: Walter Scott, Old Mortality, 1993; The Closet of Sir Kenelm Digby, Kt, Opened, 1997; Early Modern Women Poets, 2001. *Recreations:* sleeping, being nice to cats. *Address:* 21 Cobden Crescent, Oxford OX1 4LJ. *T:* (01865) 721335. *E:* janebstevenson@yahoo.com.

**STEVENSON, Dr John,** FRHistS; Reader in History, University of Oxford, 1994–2006; President, William Cobbett Society, since 2013; *b* 26 Sept. 1946; *s* of John Stevenson and Bridget Stevenson; *m* 1971, Jacqueline Patricia Johns. *Educ:* Boteler GS, Warrington; Worcester Coll., Oxford (MA 1968; DPhil 1975). Lectr in Hist., Oriel Coll., Oxford, 1971–76; Lectr, 1976, Sen. Lectr, 1979, Reader in History, 1986–90, Univ. of Sheffield; Fellow and Tutor, Worcester Coll., Oxford, 1990–2006; Fellow, Greyfriars Hall, Oxford, 2006–08; Vis. Fellow, Oriel Coll., Oxford, 2007–09. Editor, English Historical Rev., 1996–2000. *Publications:* (with R. E. Quinault) Popular Protest and Public Order, 1974; Social Conditions in Britain between the Wars, 1977; London in the Age of Reform, 1977; (jtly) Crime and Law in Nineteenth Century Britain, 1978; Popular Disturbances in England, 1700–1870, 1979, 2nd edn 1992; (with M. Bentley) High and Low Politics in Modern Britain, 1983; British Society 1914–45, 1984; (with A. J. Fletcher) Order and Disorder in early modern England, 1985; (with S. Salter), The Working Class and Politics in Europe and America 1929–1945, 1990; The Macmillan Dictionary of British and European History since 1914, 1991; (with A. O'Day) Irish Historical Documents since 1800, 1992; Third Party Politics since 1945, 1993; (with J. C. Binfield) Sport, Culture and

Politics, 1993; (with J. Gregory) The Longman Companion to the Eighteenth Century, 1999; (jtly) Advancing with the Army 1790–1850, 2006; with C. P. Cook: The Slump: society and politics during the Depression, 1977, new edn 2009; The Longman Atlas of Modern British History, 1978; British Historical Facts 1760–1830, 1980; The Longman Handbook of Modern British History 1714–1980, 1983, 4th edn 2001; The Longman Handbook to Modern European History 1760–1985, 1987, 2nd edn 1998; British Historical Facts 1688–1760, 1988; The Longman Handbook of World History since 1914, 1991; The Longman Companion to Britain since 1945, 1996, 2nd edn 2000; The Longman Handbook of the Modern World, 1998; The History of Europe, 2002; The Longman Handbook of Twentieth Century Europe, 2003; The Routledge Companion to European History since 1763, 2005; The Routledge Companion to World History since 1914, 2005; (jtly) Advancing with the Army, 2006; (with J. Grande and R. Thomas) The Opinions of William Cobbett, 2013; (with C. P. Cook) The History of British Elections since 1689, 2014; (ed with J. Grande) William Cobbett, Romanticism and the Enlightenment: contexts and legacy, 2015; (ed with C. P. Cook) The Cambridge Dictionary of Modern World History, 2017; (ed with R. Petre) A Provost's War: the Great War correspondence of Lancelot Ridley Phelps, 2018. *Recreations:* book-collecting, gardening. *Address:* Merrifield, Down St Mary, Crediton, Devon EX17 6ED.

**STEVENSON, John**; *see* Stevenson, A. J.

**STEVENSON, Julia Charlotte**; *see* Palca, J. C.

**STEVENSON, Juliet Anne Virginia**, CBE 1999; actress; Associate Artist, Royal Shakespeare Company; *b* 30 Oct. 1956; partner, Hugh Brody; one *s* one *d. Educ:* RADA (Bancroft Gold Medal). With Royal Shakespeare Company, 1978–86: Les Liaisons Dangereuses; As You Like It; Troilus and Cressida; Measure for Measure; A Midsummer Night's Dream; The Witch of Edmonton; Money; Henry IV parts I and II; Once in a Lifetime; The White Guard; Hippolytus; Antony and Cleopatra; The Churchill Play; Breaking the Silence; *other plays* include: Yerma, NT, 1987; Hedda Gabler, NT, 1989; Burn This, Hampstead, transf. Lyric, 1990; Death and the Maiden, Royal Court, transf. Duke of York's, 1991; The Duchess of Malfi, Greenwich, transf. Wyndham's, 1995; Caucasian Chalk Circle, RNT, 1997; Not I, and Footfalls, RSC and European tour, 1998; Private Lives, RNT, 1999; The Country, 2000, Alice Trilogy, 2005, Royal Court; The Seagull, NT, 2006; Duet for One, Almeida, transf. Gielgud, 2009; The Heretic, Royal Court, 2011; Happy Days, Young Vic, 2014, 2015; Mary Stuart, Almeida, 2016, transf. Duke of York's, 2018; Wings, Young Vic, 2017; Hamlet, Almeida, 2017, transf. Harold Pinter Th., 2017; The Doctor, Almeida, 2019; *films* include: Drowning by Numbers, 1988; Ladder of Swords, 1990; Truly, Madly, Deeply, 1991; The Trial, 1993; The Secret Rapture, 1994; Emma, 1996; Bend It Like Beckham, 2002; Food of Love, 2002; Nicholas Nickleby, 2003; Mona Lisa Smile, 2004; Being Julia, 2004; Pierrepoint, 2006; Breaking and Entering, 2006; Infamous, 2007; And When Did You Last See Your Father?, 2007; The Secret of Moonacre, 2008; Desert Flower, 2009; The Letters, 2013; Diana, 2013; Departure, 2015; Love is Thicker Than Water, 2016; several television rôles. *Publications:* (jtly) Clamorous Voices, 1988; (jtly) Fifty Shades of Feminism, 2013.

**STEVENSON, Katharine Jane**; *see* Marshall, K. J.

**STEVENSON, Michael Charles**; global education consultant, since 2013; Vice President of Global Public Sector: Strategy, Education and Healthcare, Cisco Systems, 2012–13 (Vice President of Global Education, 2007–12); Senior Adviser, OECD Education and Skills Directorate, since 2016; *b* 14 Aug. 1960; *s* of Michael Anthony and Ena Elizabeth Stevenson; *m* 1987, Deborah Frances Taylor; one *s* two *d. Educ:* Doncaster Grammar Sch.; Christ Church, Oxford (LitHum). British Broadcasting Corporation, 1983–2003: trainee, 1983; Producer, Talks and Documentaries, Radio, 1984; Producer, News and Current Affairs, TV, 1988; Chief Assistant, Policy and Planning Unit, 1990; Dep. Editor, On The Record, 1991; Secretary, 1992–96; Dep. Dir, Regl Broadcasting, 1996–99; Dir of Educn, 1999–2000; Jt Dir, Factual and Learning, 2000–03; Department for Education and Skills: Dir of Strategy and Communications, 2003–05; Dir of Technology and Chief Information Officer, 2005–06. Non-executive Director: Granada Learning, 2007–10; Surrey and Borders Partnership NHS Foundn Trust, 2011–. Sen. Associate, NESTA, 2014–. Expert Advr, 2014–, Sen. Advr, Prog. for Internat. Student Assessment, OECD, 2016–. Mem. Bd, Re:source, then MLA, 2000–06. Mem. Council, Nat. Coll. for Sch. Leadership, 2000–03. Sir Huw Wheldon Fellow, Univ. of Wales, 1989; Sen. Res. Fellow, Nat. Centre for Univs and Businesses, 2013–. Hon. Prof., Glasgow Caledonian Univ., 2013–. Hon. Bencher, Inner Temple, 2018. *Recreation:* sport. *Address:* 49 Thurleigh Road, SW12 8TZ.

**STEVENSON, Maj.-Gen. Paul Timothy**, OBE 1985 (MBE 1975); Clerk to Carpenters' Co., 1992–2007; *b* 9 March 1940; *s* of Ernest Stevenson and Dorothy Stevenson (*née* Trehearn); *m* 1965, Ann Douglas Drysdale; one *s* one *d. Educ:* Bloxham Sch. Commissioned Royal Marines 1958; 41 Commando, 1960; 45 Commando, Aden, 1962; HMS Mohawk, Gulf and W Indies, 1965–68; Army Staff Coll., 1972; 45 Commando, 1973–75; HMS Bulwark, 1975; Instructor, RN Staff Coll., 1978; SO Plans, HQ Land Forces, Falklands Campaign, 1982; CO 42 Commando, 1983; NATO Defence Coll., 1986; Dir, RM Personnel, 1987–88; RCDS 1989; Comdr, British Forces, Falkland Is, 1989–90. Pres., RMA, 1997–2002. Pres., Glos Co., RBL, 2011–14. Modern Pentathlon British Team, 1962–69 (Olympic Team Manager, 1964); Biathlon British Team, 1965. *Recreations:* field sports, golf, gardening, ski-ing. *Address:* Lacys, Wortley, Wotton-under-Edge, Glos GL12 7QP.

**STEVENSON, Robert Lindsay, (Robert Lindsay)**; actor; *b* 13 Dec. 1949; *s* of late Norman Stevenson and Joyce Stevenson; one *d* by Diana Weston; *m* 2006, Rosemarie Ford; two *s. Educ:* Gladstone Boys' Sch., Ilkeston; Clarendon Coll.; RADA. *Theatre:* The Roses of Eyam, 1970, Guys and Dolls, 1972, Northcott, Exeter; Godspell, Wyndham's, 1973; The Changeling, Riverside Studios, 1978; Trelawny of the Wells, Old Vic, 1980; How I Got That Story, Hampstead, 1981; Me and My Girl, Adelphi, 1985, NY, 1986 (Laurence Olivier Award, 1985; Tony Award, 1987); Becket, 1991, Cyrano de Bergerac, 1992, Th. Royal, Haymarket; Oliver!, Palladium, 1996 (Laurence Olivier Award, 1997); Richard III, RSC, 1998, Savoy, 1999; Power, RNT, 2003; The Entertainer, Old Vic, 2007; Aristo, Chichester, 2008; Onassis, Novello Th., 2010; The Lion in Winter, Th. Royal, Haymarket, 2011; Dirty Rotten Scoundrels, Savoy, 2014; Prism, Hampstead, 2017; In Praise of Love, Ustinov Th., Bath, 2018; Peter Pan, Richmond Th., 2018; Royal Exchange, Manchester: The Cherry Orchard; Lower Depths; Hamlet, 1983 (and UK tour); Beaux Stratagem; Philoctetes; Julius Caesar; Leaping Ginger; Three Musketeers. *Films:* That'll Be the Day, 1973; Three for All, 1974; Strike It Rich, 1990; Fierce Creatures, 1997; Remember Me?, 1997; Divorcing Jack, 1998; Wimbledon, 2004; Grace of Monaco, 2014. *Television:* Get Some In, 1975–77; Citizen Smith, 1977; Twelfth Night, 1980; Seconds Out, 1981; All's Well That Ends Well, 1981; A Midsummer Night's Dream, 1981; Cymbeline, 1982; Give Us a Break, 1983; King Lear, 1984; Much Ado About Nothing, 1984; Confessional, 1989; Bert Rigby, You're a Fool, 1989; Nightingales, 1990; GBH, 1991 (BAFTA Award, RTS Award, 1992); Genghis Cohn, 1993; The Wimbledon Poisoner, 1994; Jake's Progress, 1995; The Office, 1996; Brazen Hussies, 1996; Goodbye My Love, 1997; Hornblower, 1998, 1999, 2001, 2003; Oliver Twist, 1999; My Family (11 series), 2000–11; Hawk, 2001; Don't Eat the Neighbours, 2001; Friends and Crocodiles, 2005, 2006; A Very Social Secretary, 2005; Jericho, 2005; Gideon's Daughter, 2006; The Trial of Tony Blair, 2007; Spy, 2011; Bull, 2015; Galavant, 2016; Genius, 2017; Bounty Hunters, 2017. *Publications:* Letting Go (autobiog.), 2009. *Address:* c/o Hamilton Hodell Ltd, 20 Golden Square, W1F 9JL.

**STEVENSON, Stewart**; *see* Stevenson, J. A. S.

**STEVENSON, Struan John Stirton**; author and international lecturer; Chief Executive Officer, Scottish Business UK; *b* 4 April 1948; *s* of late Robert Harvey Ure Stevenson and Elizabeth Robertson (*née* Stirton); *m* 1974, Patricia Anne Taylor; two *s. Educ:* Strathallan Sch.; West of Scotland Agricl Coll. (DipAgr 1970). Member (C): Girvan DC, 1970–74; Kyle and Carrick DC, 1974–92 (Leader, 1986–88); Conservative Gp Leader, COSLA, 1986–88; Scottish agriculture spokesman, 1992–97, Scottish spokesman on envmt, transport, media, arts, heritage and tourism, 1997–98, Conservative Party. MEP (C) Scotland, 1999–2014. European Parliament: UK spokesman on fisheries, and dep. UK spokesman on agric., 1999–2002, 2004–14; Chm., 2002–04, Sen. Vice Pres., 2009–14, Fisheries Cttee; Vice-Pres., EPP-ED Gp, 2005–09; President: Climate Change, Biodiversity and Sustainable Devlt Intergroup, 2009–14; Delegn for Relations with Iraq, 2009–14. Personal Rep. of Chm.-in-Office Responsible for Envmt, OSCE, 2010. Sen. Policy Advr on EU and Brexit, Indigo PR Ltd, Edinburgh, 2016–. Internat. lectr, Globe Events Consulting Ltd, 2016–. Contested (C): Carrick, Cumnock and Doon Valley, 1987; Edinburgh S, 1992; Dumfries, 1997; NE Scotland, EP, Nov. 1998. Chm., Tuesday Club, 1998–2001 (Hon. Pres., 2001–). Pres., European Iraqi Freedom Assoc., 2014–. Hon. Prof., Semey State Shakarim Univ., Kazakhstan, 2007. Hon. DSc State Med. Acad. of Semipalatinsk, Kazakhstan, 2000. Hon. Citizen, Semipalatinsk, Kazakhstan, 2003. Shapagat Medal, Kazakhstan, 2007. *Publications:* Crying Forever, 2006; The Refugee Crisis in Iraq, 2009; Green Biotechnology: sowing the seeds for a better future, 2010; Stalin's Legacy: the Soviet war on nature, 2012; So Much Wind: the myth of green energy, 2013; Self Sacrifice: life with the Iranian Mojahedin, 2015 (Aufopferung, 2016; Le Prix De La Liberté, 2016); The Course of History: ten meals that changed the world, 2017. *Recreations:* contemporary art, music, opera, poetry, theatre, cinema, photography. *Club:* New (Edinburgh).

**STEVENSON, Timothy Edwin Paul**, OBE 2004; Lord-Lieutenant of Oxfordshire, since 2008; Chairman, Johnson Matthey plc, 2011–18; *b* 14 May 1948; *s* of late Derek Paul Stevenson, CBE; *m* 1973, Marion Emma Lander Johnston; three *d. Educ:* Canford Sch., Dorset; Worcester Coll., Oxford (BA Jurisp.). Called to the Bar, Inner Temple, 1971. Burmah Castrol: Asst Gp Legal Advr, 1975–77; Gp Planning Manager, 1977–81; Chief Exec., Castrol España, 1981–85; Marketing Manager, Devlt, 1985–86; Manager, Corporate Devlt, 1986–88; Chief Exec., Expandite Gp, 1988–90; Chief Exec., Fuels Gp, 1990–93; Dir, Lubricants, 1993–98; Chief Exec., 1998–2000; Chairman: Travis Perkins plc, 2001–10; Morgan Crucible Co. plc, 2006–12. Non-executive Director: DfES, 1997–2004; Partnerships UK Ltd, 2000–04; Tribal Gp plc, 2004–08; Sen. Ind. Dir, and Chm. Audit Cttee, National Express, 2001–05. Mem. Council, Modern Art Oxford (formerly MOMA, Oxford), 1998–2004. Chm. Govs, Oxford Brookes Univ., 2004–08 (Gov., 2002–). Sloan Fellow, London Business Sch., 1988. DL Oxon, 2006. DUniv Oxford Brookes, 2009. *Recreations:* hill walking, reading, music. *Address:* 263 Woodstock Road, Oxford OX2 7AE. *T:* (01865) 515477.

**STEW, Timothy David**, MBE 1996; HM Diplomatic Service; High Commissioner, Trinidad and Tobago, since 2015; *b* Oxford, 8 Oct. 1966; *s* of David John Stew and Gillian Primrose Stew; one *s* two *d. Educ:* Magdalen Coll. Sch., Oxford; Liverpool Univ. (BA Jt Hons English and Latin 1988). Entered FCO, 1988; Arabic lang. trng, Cairo, 1990; Press Officer, Riyadh, 1991–95; Political Officer, Sarajevo, 1995–96; Dep. High Comr, Belize, 1996–99; Head: Iraq Humanitarian and Sanctions Gp, FCO, 2000–03; Pol/Econ. Teams, Cairo, 2003–06; Dep. Ambassador, Kuwait, 2007–10; Sen. Finance Strategist, FCO, 2010; Hd, Arab Partnership Dept, FCO, 2010–15. *Recreations:* family, music, dog walking. *Address:* BFPO 5565, FCO, West End Road, Ruislip HA4 6EP. *T:* (Trinidad and Tobago) 3746194. *E:* tim.stew@fco.gov.uk.

**STEWARD, Rear Adm. Cedric John**, CB 1984; Chief of Naval Staff, New Zealand, 1983–86, retired; *b* 31 Jan. 1931; *s* of Ethelbert Harold Steward and Anne Isabelle Steward; *m* 1952, Marie Antoinette Gurr; three *s. Educ:* Northcote College, Auckland, NZ; RNC Dartmouth; RNC Greenwich. Served: HMS Devonshire, 1950; HMS Illustrious, 1950; HMS Glory, 1951 (Korean Campaign and UN Medals, 1951); HMAS Australia, HMAS Barcoo, 1952; HM NZ Ships Hawea, 1953, Kaniere, 1954 (NZ GSM Korea 2002), Tamaki, 1955–58, Stawell, 1958–59; HMAS Creswell (RAN College), 1959–62; HM NZ Ships Rotoiti, 1962–63 (Antarctic support, Operation Deep Freeze), Tamaki, 1963–64, Royalist, 1965–66 (Confrontation; Naval GSM Malaya 2002), Philomel, 1966, Inverell (in Command), 1966–67; JSSC Latimer, 1968; RNZN Liaison Officer Australia and Dep. Head, NZ Defence Liaison Staff, Canberra, 1969–73; in Command, HMNZS Otago, NZ Force SE Asia, 1973–74; in Command and Captain F11, HMNZS Canterbury, 1974–75; Defence HQ, 1976–77; RCDS, 1978; Dep. Chief of Naval Staff, NZ, 1979–81; Commodore, Auckland, and NZ Maritime Comdr, 1981–83. Life Mem., US Naval Inst., 1983; Mem., Australian Naval Inst., 1993. NZ Armed Forces Medal and Clasp, 1984; NZ Operational Service Medal, 2002; NZ Defence Service Medal, 2011. Pingat Jasa Malaysia, 2006.

**STEWARD, Dr Katherine Mary**; Director, Board Leadership Programme, and Assistant Director, Leadership, King's Fund, 2006–15; Founder, Humanising Healthcare, since 2015; *b* Malaysia, 18 April 1964; *d* of Robert Edward Alan Steward and Rosemary Steward (*née* Mather); *m* 1994, (Achilles) James Daunt, *s* of Sir Timothy Lewis Achilles Daunt, *qv*; two *d. Educ:* Presdales Sch.; Haileybury; Girton Coll., Cambridge (BA Hons 1986); Imperial Coll. of Sci., Technol. and Medicine, London (MBA 1990; PhD 1994). Overseas Devlt Consultant, Cambridge Educn Consultants, 1986–89; Co-owner, Daunt Books, 1989–; Orgn Devlt Consultant, OASiS, 1994–97; Sen. Consultant, KPMG, 1997; Vice Pres., Emerging Local Corporates, Citigroup, 1997–2000; freelance, 2001; business transformation at H of C Liby, 2002; Associate, Judge Business Sch., 2002; Hd, Governance Policy, Monitor, 2005–06. Trustee: Kaloko Trust, 2010–15; Amref Health Africa, 2012–15; Oxfam, 2013– (Chair, Recruitment and Devlt Gp, 2013–; Mem., Remuneration Cttee, 2013–). *Recreations:* travelling, books, living well. *Address:* 39 Downshire Hill, NW3 1NU. *T:* 07774 221780. *E:* katysteward@stewardod.co.uk.

**STEWART**; *see* Vane-Tempest-Stewart, family name of Marquess of Londonderry.

**STEWART**, family name of **Earl of Galloway**.

**STEWART, Hon. Lord; Angus Stewart**; a Senator of the College of Justice in Scotland, 2010–17; *b* 14 Dec. 1946; *s* of late Archibald Ian Balfour Stewart, CBE, BL, FSAScot and of Ailsa Rosamund Mary Massey; *m* 1975, Jennifer Margaret Stewart; one *d. Educ:* Edinburgh Acad.; Balliol Coll., Oxford (BA); Edinburgh Univ. (LLB). Called to the Scottish Bar, 1975; QC (Scot.) 1988. Keeper, Advocates' Liby, 1994–2002. Sen. Advocate Depute, 2005–08; Leading Counsel, Billy Wright Inquiry, NI, 2008–10. Hon. Sheriff at Campbeltown, 2014–. Chm., Scottish Council of Law Reporting, 1997–2001. Trustee: Nat. Liby of Scotland, 1994–2005; Stewart Heritage Trust, 1994–2001; Internat. E Boat

Class Assoc., 1993–. Chm., Abbotsford Liby Project, 1996–2002. President: Stewart Soc., 2001–04; Stair Soc., 2013–. *Address:* c/o Court of Session, Parliament House, Edinburgh EH1 1RQ. *T:* (0131) 225 2595.

See also P. L. McI. Stewart.

**STEWART, Dame Adrienne;** *see* Stewart, Dame E. A.

**STEWART, Sir Alan (d'Arcy),** 13th Bt *cr* 1623; yachtbuilder; *b* 29 Nov. 1932; *s* of Sir Jocelyn Harry Stewart, 12th Bt, and Constance Mary (*d* 1940), *d* of D'Arcy Shillaber; *S* father, 1982; *m* 1952, Patricia, *d* of Lawrence Turner; two *s* two *d*. *Educ:* All Saints College, Bathurst, NSW. *Heir: s* Nicholas Courtney d'Arcy Stewart, BSc, HDipEd, *b* 4 Aug. 1953. *Address:* One Acre, Ramelton, Co. Donegal, Ireland.

**STEWART, Alastair James,** OBE 2006; ITV News presenter; *b* 22 June 1952; *s* of late Group Captain James F. Stewart and Joan Mary Stewart (*née* Lord); *m* 1978, Sally Ann Jung; three *s* one *d*. *Educ:* St Augustine's Abbey Sch., Ramsgate; Univ. of Bristol. Dep. Pres., Nat. Union of Students, 1974–76. Reporter and presenter, Southern ITV, 1976–80; industrial corresp., ITN, 1980; presenter, ITN: News at Ten, 1981; Channel 4 News, 1983; News at One, 1985; News at 5.45, 1986; Parliament Programme, 1988; News at Ten, 1989, 1991–92; Washington corresp., 1990–91; London Tonight, 1993–2009; Live with Alastair Stewart, ITV News Channel, 2003–05; ITV News at 10.30, 2006–09; ITV Lunchtime News, 2007–; ITV News at 10, 2009–15; ITV News at 6.30, 2009–; presenter: BBC Radio, 1994; Missing, LWT, 1992–96; The Carlton Debates, 1993–2006; The Sunday Prog. with Alastair Stewart, GMTV, 1994–2001; Police, Camera, Action, Carlton TV, 1994–2003, ITV, 2007–09; Ask Ken, 2001–08; Moral of the Story, ITV, 2006–07; Unbelievable Moments Caught on Camera, 2016–. Commentator and presenter, numerous parly programmes and State occasions, UK and overseas, incl. first live transmission from House of Lords, 1985, House of Commons, 1989; ITV General Election, 1987, 1992, 1997, 2005, 2010, 2015; Gulf War and liberation of Kuwait, 1991; Who Wants to be a London Mayor?, 2000; King of the Castle, 2001; Funeral of Pope John Paul II, 2005; London's Mayor - You Decide, 2008; moderator: Party Leader's Debate, ITV, 2010; Brexit Debate, Channel 5, 2016; Knife Crime Debate, Channel 5, 2018. Trustee, Just a Drop, 2004–08. Vice President: Homestart UK, 1997–; Action for Children (formerly NCH Action for Children), 1998–. Patron: Lord Mayor Treloar Coll.; Scope, 2006–16; Naomi House Hospice, 2014–; Brooke, 2016–; Mark Davies Injured Riders Fund, 2018–; Vice Patron: Missing Person's Helpline, 1993–; SANE, 1999–. Ambassador: Crisis, 2007–; CARE Internat. UK, 2006–. Governor, Ravensbourne Coll., 2006–14. Hon. LLD Bristol, 2007; Hon. DLitt: Plymouth, 2010; Winchester, 2011; Hon. DArt Sunderland, 2012. Annual Award, RBL 1996; Face of London, RTS, 2002; Presenter of the Year, RTS, 2004. *Recreations:* travel, cartography, a catholic taste in music. *Address:* ITN, 200 Gray's Inn Road, WC1X 8XZ. *T:* (020) 7833 3000.

**STEWART, Alastair Lindsay;** QC (Scot.) 1995; Sheriff of Tayside, Central and Fife at Dundee, 1990–2004; Temporary Judge in Supreme Courts, Scotland, 1996–2013; *b* 28 Nov. 1938; *s* of Alexander Lindsay Stewart and Anna Stewart; *m* 1st, 1968, Annabel Claire Stewart (marr. diss. 1991), *yr d* of late Prof. W. McC. Stewart; two *s*; 2nd, 1991, Sheila Anne Mackinnon (*née* Flockhart), *o d* of late David H. Flockhart. *Educ:* Edinburgh Academy; St Edmund Hall, Oxford (BA); Univ. of Edinburgh (LLB). Admitted to Faculty of Advocates, 1963; Tutor, Faculty of Law, Univ. of Edinburgh, 1963–73; Standing Junior Counsel to Registrar of Restrictive Trading Agreements, 1968–70; Advocate Depute, 1970–73; Sheriff of South Strathclyde, Dumfries and Galloway, at Airdrie, 1973–79, of Grampian, Highland and Islands, at Aberdeen and Stonehaven, 1979–90; Interim Sheriff Principal, Lothian and Borders, Glasgow and Strathkelvin, 2005. Chairman: Grampian Family Conciliation Service, 1984–87 (Hon. Pres., 1987–90); Scottish Assoc. of Family Conciliation Services, 1986–89. Mem., Judicial Studies Cttee, 2000–04. Governor, Robert Gordon's Inst. of Technology, 1982–90 (Vice-Chm. of Governors, 1985–90). Hon. Prof., Sch. of Law (formerly Faculty of Law and Accountancy), Univ. of Dundee, 2001–13. Editor, Scottish Civil Law Reports, 1992–95. *Publications:* (contrib.) Sheriff Court Practice, by I. D. Macphail, 1988, jt gen. editor, 2nd edn, vol. 1 1998, vol. 2 2002; The Scottish Criminal Courts in Action, 1990, 2nd edn 1997; Evidence reissue, Stair Memorial Encyclopædia of the Laws of Scotland, 2006; various articles in legal jls. *Recreations:* reading, music, walking. *Address:* 86 Albany Road, Broughty Ferry, Dundee DD5 1JQ. *T:* (01382) 477580. *Club:* Western (Glasgow).

**STEWART, Sir Alastair (Robin),** 3rd Bt *cr* 1960, of Strathgarry, Perth; *b* 26 Sept. 1925; 2nd *s* of Sir Kenneth Dugald Stewart, 1st Bt, GBE and Noel (*d* 1946), *yr d* of Kenric Brodribb, Melbourne; *S* brother, 1992; *m* 1953, Patricia Helen, MBE, ARIBA, *d* of late J. A. Merrett; three *d* (one *s* decd). *Educ:* Marlborough Coll. Lieut, 1st Royal Gloucestershire Hussars, 1945–47. Dir, Neale & Wilkinson Ltd, 1947–71; Man. Dir, Stewart & Harvey Ltd, 1971–90. *Recreation:* gardening. *Heir:* none. *Address:* Walters Cottage, North Hill, Little Baddow, Chelmsford, Essex CM3 4TQ. *T:* (01245) 222445.

**STEWART, Alec James,** OBE 2003 (MBE 1998); cricketer; Director of Cricket, Surrey County Cricket Club, since 2014; *b* 8 April 1963; *s* of Michael James, (Micky), Stewart and Sheila Marie Macdonald Stewart; *m* 1991, Lynn Blades; one *s* one *d*. *Educ:* Tiffin Boys' Sch. Joined Surrey County Cricket Club, 1981, capped 1985, Captain, 1992–97, retired from County team, 2003; Test début, 1989; Mem., 1989–2003, Captain, 1998–99, England Test team; played 133 Test Matches, scored 15 centuries, took 263 catches, 14 stumpings; overseas tours with England team: W Indies, 1989–90, 1993–94 (Vice Capt.), 1997–98; Australia and NZ, 1990–91; India and Sri Lanka, 1992–93; Australia, 1994–95, 1998–99, 2002–03; S Africa, 1995–96, 1999–2000; Zimbabwe and NZ, 1996–97. *Publications:* (with Brian Murgatroyd) Alec Stewart: a Captain's Diary, 1999; Playing for Keeps (autobiog.), 2003. *Address:* c/o Surrey County Cricket Club, The Oval, Kennington, SE11 5SS.

**STEWART, Alexander James,** MBE 2016; Member (C) Scotland Mid and Fife, Scottish Parliament, since 2016; *b* Perth, 29 Nov. 1962; *s* of James Stewart and Sarah McDonald Stewart (*née* Duncan); *m* 2006, Shiona Hodge. *Educ:* Craigclowan Prep. Sch.; Morrisons Acad., Crieff; Glasgow Caledonian Univ. (HNC Mgt Studies); Cert. Creative Communications); Open Univ. (Dip. Govt and Politics); BA Hons Politics and Social Sci.). Mgt trainee, House of Fraser plc, 1986–87; exec. trainee, Harrods Ltd, 1987–89; Sen. Retail Manager, Naff Naff Ltd, London, 1989–91; proprietor, Zanders, Crieff, 1992–93; Sen. Manager, Central Reservations, Toby Hotels, 1993–2001; Lectr (pt-time) in Business Mgt, 2001–03; Sen. Support Worker (pt-time), Ark Housing, 2003–10. Mem. (C), Perth and Kinross Council, 1999–2017. Freeman, City of London, 1993. MStJ. *Address:* Scottish Parliament, Edinburgh EH99 1SP. *E:* alexander.stewart.msp@parliament.scot.

**STEWART, Alexandra Joy;** Recruitment Consultant, 2003–16, Head of Global Higher Education Practice, 2004–16, and Equity Partner, 2010–16, Saxton Bampfylde Ltd (formerly Saxton Bampfylde Hever Ltd); *b* 11 April 1953; *d* of Charles Stewart and Myrtle Stewart (*née* Sheppard); *m* 1st, 1976, Andrew Smyth (marr. diss. 1990); one *d*; 2nd, 1991, Michael McBride (*d* 2014). *Educ:* Bexhill Grammar Sch. for Girls; Durham Univ. (BA Hons). Joined DES, 1975; admin trainee, 1975–79; Private Sec. to Minister for Educn, 1979–81; Principal, 1981–88; Assistant Secretary: Hd of City Technol. Unit, 1988–92; with DNH, subseq. DCMS, 1992–2003; Hd of Sports Div., then Finance Dir, 1992–99; Dir, Museums, Galleries, Libraries and Heritage, subseq. Art and Culture, 1999–2003. *Recreations:* my family, gardening, the South Downs, poultry.

**STEWART, Andrew Fleming;** *see* Ericht, Hon. Lord.

**STEWART, Angus;** *see* Stewart, Hon. Lord.

**STEWART, Brian Edward;** HM Diplomatic Service, retired; Ambassador to Algeria, 2004–05; *b* 4 Feb. 1950; *s* of late Edward Stewart and of Carrol Stewart (*née* Medcalf); *m* 1975, Anne Cockerill. *Educ:* Melsetter Sch., Southern Rhodesia; Keith Grammar Sch., Scotland; Keele Univ. (BA Hons). Entered FCO, 1972; MECAS, Lebanon, 1973–75; 3rd, later 2nd Sec., Amman, 1975–78; on loan to Cabinet Office, 1978–80; First Sec., FCO, 1980–82; First Secretary and Head of Chancery: Singapore, 1982–85; Tunis, 1986–89; First Sec., FCO, 1989–93; Dep. Hd of Mission, Damascus, 1993–96; Counsellor, FCO, 1996–98; Dep. Hd of Mission and Counsellor, Kuwait, 1998–2001; FCO, 2002; rcds 2003. *Publications:* (contrib.) The Arabists of Shemlan, 2006. *Recreations:* restoring and maintaining potential classic cars, tackling essential household DIY, playing tennis and cricket with more enthusiasm than skill. *Address:* 33 Albert Street, Nairn IV12 4HF.

**STEWART, Sir Brian (John),** Kt 2002; CBE 1996; Chairman: Miller Group Ltd, 2009–12; C&C, 2010–18; *b* 9 April 1945; *m* 1971, Seonaid Duncan; two *s* one *d*. *Educ:* Edinburgh Univ. (MSc). Mem., Scottish Inst. of Chartered Accountants. Scottish and Newcastle Breweries, subseq. Scottish and Newcastle plc: joined 1976; Finance Dir, 1988–91; Gp Chief Exec., 1991–2000; Dep. Chm., 1997–2000; Chm., 2000–03; non-exec. Chm., 2003–08. Dir, Booker, 1993–99; Chm., Standard Life Assurance Co., 2003–07 (Dir, 1993–2007). *Recreations:* golf, ski-ing.

**STEWART, Rev. Dr Charles Edward;** Chaplain, Royal Hospital School, 2000–10; *b* 10 June 1946; *s* of Charles Stewart and Mary Stewart (*née* McDougall); *m* 1970, Margaret Marion Smith; two *s* one *d*. *Educ:* Strathclyde Univ. (BSc; PhD); Glasgow Univ. (BD); Edinburgh Univ. (MTh). Ordained, C of S, 1976; Chaplain: HMS Sea Hawk, RNAS Culdrose, 1976–78; Clyde Submarine Base, 1978–80; Staff of Flag Officer 3rd Flotilla, 1980; Chaplain: HMS Hermes, Falklands Conflict, 1981; HMS Neptune, 1982–85; HMS Drake and Staff of Flag Officer Plymouth, 1985–87; HMS Raleigh, 1987–90; BRNC, Dartmouth, 1990–93; Asst Dir Naval Chaplaincy Service, 1992–94; HMS Invincible, Bosnia, 1994–96; Dir Naval Chaplaincy Service, 1996–97; Dir Gen. Naval Chaplaincy Service, 1997–2000; Chaplain of the Fleet, 1998–2000. QHC 1996–2000. South Atlantic Medal, 1982; NATO Medal, 1995. *Recreations:* gardening, water colours (painting), music, hill walking, photography.

**STEWART, Sir David James H.;** *see* Henderson-Stewart.

**STEWART, David John;** Member (Lab) Highlands and Islands, Scottish Parliament, since 2007; *b* 5 May 1956; *s* of John and Alice Stewart; *m* 1982, Linda MacDonald; one *s* one *d*. *Educ:* Paisley Coll. (BA Hons); Stirling Univ. (Dip. Social Wk, CQSW); Open Univ. (Professional Dip. Mgt). Social work manager, 1980–97; Asst Dir for Rural Affairs, SCVO, 2005–07. Member (Lab): Nithsdale DC, 1984–86; Inverness DC, 1988–96 (Dep. Leader, Labour Gp). Contested (Lab): Inverness, Nairn and Lochaber, 1987 and 1992; Inverness, Nairn, Badenoch and Strathspey, 2005. MP (Lab) Inverness E, Nairn and Lochaber, 1997–2005. Scottish Parliament: a Labour Whip, 2007–11 (Chief Whip, 2008–11); Shadow Envmt Minister, 2007–08; Shadow Minister: for Transport and Islands, 2015–16; for Envmtl Justice, 2015–16; for Envmt, Climate Change and Land Reform, 2016–18; for Health, 2018–; Convener, Petitions Cttee, 2011–15; Mem., Scottish Parly Corporate Body, 2011–15 and 2016–. Contested (Lab) Inverness and Nairn, Scottish Parlt, 2016. *Address:* Scottish Parliament, Edinburgh EH99 1SP.

**STEWART, Captain Sir David (John Christopher),** 7th Bt *cr* 1803, of Athenree, Tyrone; *b* 19 June 1935; *s* of Sir Hugh Charlie Godfray Stewart, 6th Bt and his 1st wife, Rosemary Elinor Dorothy, *d* of Maj. George Peacocke; *S* father, 1994; *m* 1959, Bridget Anne, *er d* of late Patrick W. Sim; three *d*. *Educ:* Bradfield Coll.; RMA Sandhurst. Commnd Royal Inniskilling Fusiliers, 1956; seconded to Trucial Oman Scouts, 1957–58 (Jebel Akhdar Campaign, 1957); Adjt 1958; served in Trucial States, Oman and Muscat, 1957–58, Germany, 1958–59, Kenya, 1960–62 (Kuwait Operation, 1961), UN Peacekeeping Force, Cyprus, 1964; retd as Captain, 1965. Representative for E. S. & A. Robinson, Bristol, 1965–69; Director: Maurice James Holdings, Coventry, 1969–77; Papropak UK, 1977–79; self-employed, 1979–; owner, George Inn, Middlezoy, Somerset, 1982–85. Hon. Organiser, RBL Poppy Appeal, Wiveliscombe, 1996–2002; Hon. Treas., Friends of Somerset SSAFA-Forces Help, 1998–2006; Hon. Pres., Trucial Oman Scouts Assoc., 2014–. Medal, Order of the Tower of Al Qassimi (UAE), 2003. *Recreations:* golf, cricket. *Heir: half b* Hugh Nicholas Stewart [*b* 20 April 1955; *m* 1976, Anna Leeke; one *s* three *d*]. *Address:* 16 Blackdown View, Curry Rivel, Langport, Somerset TA10 0ER.

**STEWART, Dawn Jacquelyn;** *see* Austwick, D. J.

**STEWART, Dame (Ellen) Adrienne, (Lady Stewart),** DNZM 2015 (ONZM 2006); Director, PDL Holdings Ltd, 1982–2001; *b* Melbourne, 6 Feb. 1936; *d* of Joseph Peake and Ellen Mabel Peake (*née* Parker); *m* 1970, Sir Robertson Huntly Stewart, CBE (*d* 2007); two *s*. *Educ:* Presbyterian Ladies' Coll., Melbourne. Dir, Trustbank Canterbury, 1980–85. Chair, Christchurch Symphony Orch. Foundn, 2002–; Governing Patron, Art and Industry Biennial Trust, 1998–2016; Trustee, Christchurch Cathedral Foundn, and Canon Almoner; Patron: Univ. of Canterbury Foundn; Court Theatre Supporters; Woolston Brass Band. FNZIM; Dist. Fellow, NZ Inst. of Dirs. Hon. DLitt Canterbury, 2011. QSM 1995; Patron of the Year, Arts Foundn of NZ, 2009. *Recreations:* arts, music. *Address:* PO Box 2043, Christchurch, New Zealand. *T:* (3) 3485040. *E:* adrienne.stewart@masthead.co.nz. *Clubs:* Zonta (Past Pres.), Christchurch (Christchurch).

**STEWART, George Girdwood,** CB 1979; MC 1945; TD 1954; Cairngorm Estate Adviser, Highlands and Islands Enterprise, 1988–98; *b* 12 Dec. 1919; *o s* of late Herbert A. Stewart, BSc, and of Janetta Dunlop Girdwood; *m* 1950, Shelagh Jean Morven Murray (*d* 2004); one *s* one *d*. *Educ:* Kelvinside Academy, Glasgow; Glasgow Univ.; Edinburgh Univ. (BSc). Served RA, 1940–46 (MC, despatches); CO 278 (Lowland) Field Regt RA (TA), 1957–60. Dist Officer, Forestry Commn, 1949–61; Asst Conservator, 1961–67; Conservator, West Scotland, 1967–69; Comr for Forest and Estate Management, 1969–79; National Trust for Scotland: Mem., Council, 1975–79; Rep., Branklyn Garden, Perth, 1980–84; Regional Rep., Central and Tayside, 1984–88; Forestry Consultant, 1989–93. Specialist advr, Select Cttee on EEC Forestry Policy, 1986; Associate Dir, Oakwood Envmtl, 1990–2003. Member: BR Bd Envmt Panel, 1980–90; Countryside Commn for Scotland, 1981–88; Chm., Scottish Wildlife Trust, 1981–87; Cairngorm Mountain Trust (formerly Cairngorm Recreation Trust), 1986–; Hon. Vice-Pres., Royal Scottish Forestry Soc., 2019. Pres., Scottish Nat. Ski Council, 1988–94 (Hon. Vice-Pres., 1998–2014). Pres., Scottish Ski Club, 1971–75; Vice-Pres., Nat. Ski Fedn of GB; Chm., Alpine Racing Cttee, 1975–78. Mem., British Team, ITF Veterans World Team Tennis Championships, 1999, 2001, 2002; Winner of Doubles, ITF Super-Seniors World Individual Championships, 2006, 2007. FRSA; FICFor; Hon. FLI. Nat. Service to Sport Award, Scottish Sports

Council, 1995. Olympic torch bearer, Newburgh, Fife, 2012. *Recreations:* ski-ing, tennis, studying Scottish painting, gardening. *Address:* 11 Mansfield Road, Scone, Perth PH2 6SA. *T:* (01738) 551815. *Club:* Ski Club of Great Britain.

**STEWART, Prof. George Russell,** PhD, DSc; Dean, Faculty of Life and Physical Sciences, University of Western Australia, 2002–10 (Executive Dean, Faculty of Science, 1998–2001); *b* 25 Feb. 1944; *s* of George and Isobella Stewart; *m* 1978, Janice Anne Grimes; three *d*. *Educ:* Pinner County Grammar Sch.; Univ. of Bristol (BSc 1965; PhD 1968); DSc London 1991. Lectr in Botany, Univ. of Manchester, 1968–81; London University: Prof. of Botany and Head of Dept, Birkbeck Coll., 1981–85; Quain Prof. of Botany, 1985–91 and Head of Dept of Biology, 1987–91, UCL; Dean of Faculty of Sci., 1990–91; Prof. of Botany, Univ. of Queensland, 1992–98. Vis. Lectr, Dept of Biology, Univ. of Lagos, Nigeria; Visiting Professor: Dept of Botany, Univ. of Queensland, Aust.; Dept of Biology, Univ. of Campinas, Brazil; Dept of Biology, Univ. of WA. Member: Plants and Envmt Cttee, AFRC, 1989–91; Plants and Envmt Res. Bd, AFRC (Chm., 1989–91); Agriculture Cttee, Long Ashton Res. Station, 1990–91; Inter-Agency Cttee on Res. into Global Envmtl Change (Working Gp 2), 1990–91; Zool Parks Authy, WA, 2006–08. Mem., Bd of Dirs, SciTech Discovery Centre, 1999–2008. Dep. Pres., WA Br., Australia-China Business Council, 2005–07. Foreign expert consultant, Beijing Assoc. for Sci., 2008–. Hon. Mem., Shanghai Assoc. for Sci. and Tech., 2006. *Publications:* (ed jtly) The Genetic Manipulation of Plants and its Application to Agriculture, 1984; numerous scientific papers on plant physiology and metabolism and chapters in books and conf. proc. *Recreations:* cycling, cooking.

**STEWART, Iain Aitken;** MP (C) Milton Keynes South, since 2010; an Assistant Government Whip, since 2018; *b* 18 Sept. 1972; *s* of James Stewart and Leila Stewart. *Educ:* Hutchesons' Grammar Sch., Glasgow; Univ. of Exeter (BA Pols 1993); Chartered Mgt Inst. (Dip. Mgt 2006). Trainee chartered accountant, Coopers & Lybrand, 1993–94; Hd, Research, Scottish Cons. Party, 1994–98; Dep. Dir, 1998–2001, Dir, 2001–06, Parly Resources Unit, H of C; Associate, Odgers Berndtson (formerly Odgers, Ray & Berndtson), 2006–10. Contested (C) Glasgow Rutherglen, Scottish Parlt, 1999; contested (C) Milton Keynes SW, 2001, 2005. PPS to Sec. of State for Transport, 2013–15, to Sec. of State for Scotland, 2015–16, to Sec. of State for Internat. Trade, 2016–17. Mem., Transport Select Cttee, 2010–13 and 2015–18. Mem. (C), Shenley Brook End and Tattenhoe Parish Council, 2005–11. *Address:* House of Commons, SW1A 0AA.

**STEWART, Prof. Iain Alastair,** PhD; FBCS; Professor of Computer Science, Durham University, since 2002; *b* Durham, 16 March 1961; *s* of Allan and Dorothy Stewart; *m* 1988, Sheila; two *s* one *d*. *Educ:* Royal Grammar Sch., Newcastle upon Tyne; Christ Church, Oxford (MA Maths); Queen Mary Coll., London (PhD Maths 1986). FBCS 1997. Lectr, Computer Lab., Univ. of Newcastle upon Tyne, 1986–92; Lectr, 1992–94, Sen. Lectr, 1994–95, Reader, 1995–96, University Coll. of Swansea; Prof. of Computer Sci., Leicester Univ., 1996–2002. *Publications:* contribs to learned jls on maths and computer sci. *Recreations:* supporting Newcastle United, cinema, fly fishing, rambling. *Address:* School of Engineering and Computing Sciences, Durham University, South Road, Durham DH1 3LE. *T:* (0191) 334 1720. *E:* i.a.stewart@durham.ac.uk.

**STEWART, Prof. Ian;** Professor of Government, Industry, Voluntary and Education Sector Relations, and Special Advisor on Greater Manchester City Region Projects, University of Bolton, since 2017 (Visiting Professor and Special Advisor to President and Vice Chancellor, 2010–16); City Mayor of Salford, 2012–16; *b* 28 Aug. 1950; *s* of John and Helen Stewart; *m* 1969, Merilyn Holding; two *s* one *d*. *Educ:* Auchinraith Road Primary Sch., Blantyre; David Livingstone Primary Meml Sch., Blantyre; Calder Street Secondary, Blantyre; Alfred Turner Secondary Modern Sch., Salford; Stretford Technical Coll.; Bolton Art Coll.; Univ. of Salford (MSc 1988); Manchester Metropolitan Univ. (PhD 1997); Univ. of Manchester (PhD 2010). Regl Trade Gp Sec., TGWU, 1978–97. MP (Lab) Eccles, 1997–2010. PPS to Minister of State for Industry and Energy, subseq. for Energy and Construction, 2001–03, to Minister of State (Minister for Energy, the Post Office, E-Govt and Corporate Social Responsibility), 2003–04, DTI; PPS to Financial Sec. to HM Treasury, 2004–05; PPS to Sec. of State, DTI, 2005–07. Member: Deregulation Select Cttee, 1997–2001; Information Select Cttee, 1998–2001; Innovation, Sci. and Skills Select Cttee, 2007–10; PLP Employment and Trng Cttee, 1997–2010; PLP Trade and Industry Cttee, 1997–2010; PLP Foreign Affairs Cttee, 1997–2010; Exec., PITCOM, 1998–2010; Founder and Chm., All Party Community Media Gp, 1997–2010; Founder and Vice Chm., All Party China Gp, 1997–2010 (Mem., GB China Centre Exec., 1997–2010); Founder and Chair: Parly Gp for Vaccine Damaged Children, 1998–2010; All Party Parly Gp for Prevention of Violence at Work, 1998–2010; All Party Parly Gp for Prevention of Bullying, 1998–2010; Chair, Parly Boxing Gp, 2000–10. Defence Sports Advr to Minister of State (Minister for Sport), DCMS, 2002–10; former Govt Rep. for Defence Sports incl. boxing, wrestling and martial arts. Mem. Bd, GB China Gp, 1998–2010. Founder, owner and Man. Dir, Education Matters Ltd, 2010–12. Founder and Chm., Eur. Foundn for Social Partnership and Continuing Trng Initiatives, 1993–94; Co-Founder and Chm., Centre for Employment Initiatives, 1994–. Member: Bd, Atlantic Gateway, 2012–16; Bd, Gtr Manchester Combined Authy, 2012–16; Bd, Manchester Sci. Partnership (formerly Manchester Sci. Parks), 2012–16; Bd, CityCo, Manchester, 2012–16; Dir, Manchester Growth Co., 2012–16. Hon. Vis. Fellow, 1993–2014, Hon. Vis. Prof., 2014–17, Univ. of Salford. Member: Unite (formerly TGWU), 1965–; Soc. for Educn and Trng (formerly UK Soc. of Industrial Tutors), 1980–; Manchester Industrial Relations Soc., 1994–; Internat. Soc. of Industrial Relations, 1996–. Fellow, Industry and Parlt Trust, 1977–2010; Council, Eur. Informatics Market, 1997–2010. Mem., Editl Bd, Internat. Labour Reports Mag., 1980–97.

**STEWART, Prof. Ian George;** Professor of Economics, University of Edinburgh, 1967–84; *b* 24 June 1923; *s* of David Tweedie Stewart, MA and Ada Doris Montgomery Haldane; *m* 1949, Mary Katharine Oddie; one *s* two *d*. *Educ:* Fettes Coll.; Univ. of St Andrews (MA 1st Class Hons); MA Cantab 1954. Pilot, RAF, 1942–46. Commonwealth Fund Fellow, 1948–50. Research Officer, Dept of Applied Economics, Univ. of Cambridge, 1950–57; University of Edinburgh: Lectr in Economics, 1957–58; Sen. Lectr, 1958–61; Reader, 1961–67; Curator of Patronage, 1979–84. Vis. Associate Prof., Univ. of Michigan, 1962; Vis. Prof., Univ. of S Carolina, 1975. Dir, Scottish Provident Instn, 1980–90, Dep. Chm., 1983–85. Mem., British Library Bd, 1980–87. Governor, Fettes Coll., 1976–89. *Publications:* National Income of Nigeria (with A. R. Prest), 1953; (ed) Economic Development and Structural Change, 1969; articles in jls and bank reviews. *Recreations:* golf, fishing, gardening. *Club:* New (Edinburgh).

**STEWART, Rev. Canon Ian Guild;** Priest-in-charge, St David, Inverbervie, 1992–2008; Rector, St Mary and St Peter, Montrose, 2002–2008; Dean of Brechin, 2007–08; *b* 1943. *Educ:* Edinburgh Theol Coll. Ordained deacon, 1984, priest, 1985; Non-Stipendiary Minister, St Mary Magdalene, Dundee, 1984–87; Non-Stipendiary Minister, 1987–90, Asst Curate, 1990–92, St Martin, Dundee; Non-Stipendiary Minister, 1987–90, Asst Curate, 1990–92, St John the Baptist, Dundee. Canon, St Paul's Cathedral, Dundee, 2001–12, now Canon Emeritus. *Address:* 36 Forbes Road, Edinburgh EH10 4ED.

**STEWART, Ian James,** CB 1997; Director, Cambridge Concepts Ltd, since 2007; *b* 30 Aug. 1946; *m* 1967, Morag Gardiner Duncan; two *d*. *Educ:* Perth Acad. Area Dir, Newcastle Benefits Directorate, 1990–92; Mem. Bd of Mgt and Dir, Benefits Agency, DSS, 1993–95; Project Dir, Jobseeker's Allowance, DfEE, 1995–97; Dir Gen., Benefit Fraud Inspectorate, DSS, 1997–99; Chief Executive: Bradford CC, 1999–2003; Cambs CC, 2003–07.

**STEWART, Ian James;** journalist and author; *b* Kingston-upon-Thames, 4 Aug. 1960; *s* of William Stewart and Colina Stewart; *m* 1988, Lesley Innes; one *s* one *d*. *Educ:* Royal High Sch., Edinburgh; Napier Coll. (HND Journalism Studies 1986). Royal Marines, 1979–82; reporter, Nottingham Evening Post, 1986–91; News Editor, The Scotsman, 1991–98; Assistant Editor: Daily Mail, 1998–99; Scotland on Sunday, 1999–2001; Editor, Edinburgh Evening News, 2001–04; Dep. Editor, The Scotsman, 2004–12; Editor: Scotland on Sunday, 2009–17; The Scotsman, 2012–17. Trustee, Sadaya and Veterans Community Cafe. *Publications:* Telling Scotland's Story, 2017. *Recreations:* sailing, mountain biking, shooting, walking, not attending meetings.

**STEWART, Prof. Ian Nicholas,** PhD; FRS 2001; CMath, FIMA; Professor of Mathematics, University of Warwick, 1990–2009, now Emeritus Professor; *b* 24 Sept. 1945; *s* of Arthur Reginald Stewart and Marjorie Kathleen Stewart (née Diwell); *m* 1970, Avril Bernice Montgomery; two *s*. *Educ:* Cambridge Univ. (MA); Univ. of Warwick (PhD). FIMA 1993; CMath 1993; CBiol 2003–07, FIBiol 2003–07. University of Warwick: Lectr, 1969–84; Reader, 1984–90. Humboldt Fellow, Tübingen, 1974; Vis. Fellow, Auckland, 1976; Associate Prof., Storrs, Conn, 1977–78; Professor: Carbondale, Ill, 1978; Houston, Texas, 1983–84; Gresham Prof. of Geometry, 1994; Adjunct Prof., Houston Univ., 2001–. Author, Incredible Numbers iPad app, 2014. Hon. DSc: Westminster, 1999; Louvain, 2000; Kingston, 2003; Brighton, 2014; DUniv Open, 2005. Michael Faraday Medal, Royal Soc., 1995; IMA Gold Medal, 2000; Ferran Sunyer i Balaguer Prize, 2001; Public Understanding of Sci. and Tech. Award, AAAS, 2002; Zeeman Medal, London Math. Soc., 2009; (jtly) Lewis Thomas Prize, Rockefeller Univ., 2015; Euler Book Prize, Math. Assoc. of America, 2017; Pythagorean Universe Award, Warsaw Univ. of Technol., 2018. *Publications* include: Galois Theory, 1973; Concepts of Modern Mathematics, 1975; Catastrophe Theory and its Applications, 1978; The Problems of Mathematics, 1987; Does God Play Dice?, 1989; Game Set & Math, 1991; Another Fine Math You've Got Me Into, 1992; Fearful Symmetry, 1992; The Collapse of Chaos, 1994; Nature's Numbers, 1995; From Here to Infinity, 1996; Figments of Reality, 1997; The Magical Maze, 1997; Life's Other Secret, 1998; (jtly) The Science of Discworld, 1999; (jtly) Wheelers, 2000; Flatterland, 2001; What Shape is a Snowflake?, 2001; The Annotated Flatland, 2001; (jtly) The Science of Discworld II: the globe, 2002; (jtly) Evolving the Alien, 2002; (jtly) What Does a Martian Look Like?, 2004; Math Hysteria, 2004; (jtly) Heaven, 2004; (jtly) The Science of Discworld III: Darwin's watch, 2005; The Mayor of Uglyville's Dilemma, 2005; Letters to a Young Mathematician, 2006; How to Cut a Cake, 2006; Why Beauty is Truth: the history of symmetry, 2007; Professor Stewart's Cabinet of Mathematical Curiosities, 2008; Professor Stewart's Hoard of Mathematical Treasures, 2009; Cows in the Maze, 2010; Mathematics of Life, 2011; Seventeen Equations that Changed the World, 2012; Great Mathematical Problems, 2013; (jtly) The Science of Discworld IV: Judgement Day, 2013; Symmetry: a very short introduction, 2013; Professor Stewart's Casebook of Mathematical Mysteries, 2014; Professor Stewart's Incredible Numbers, 2015; Calculating the Cosmos, 2016; (jtly) The Living Labyrinth, 2016; Infinity: a very short introduction, 2017; Significant Figures, 2017; (jtly) Rock Star, 2017; The Beauty of Numbers in Nature, 2018. *Recreations:* science fiction, painting, guitar, geology, Egyptology, snorkelling. *Address:* Mathematics Institute, University of Warwick, Coventry CV4 7AL.

**STEWART, Sir Jackie;** *see* Stewart, Sir John Young.

**STEWART, James Alexander Gustave Harold,** OBE 2007; FICE; Vice Chair, since 2017, and Head of Brexit, since 2018, KPMG (Chairman, Global Infrastructure, 2011–17); *b* London, 29 April 1962; *s* of H. Ivan Stewart; *m* 1988, Gill; two *s* two *d*. *Educ:* Harrow Sch.; Pembroke Coll., Oxford (BA Chem.). Dir, Hambros Bank, 1984–98; Chief Executive: Partnerships UK, 2000–09; Infrastructure UK, 2009–11. Non-exec. Dir, Sport England, 2006–13. *Recreations:* golf, photography, walking. *Address:* Goddards Green House, Goddards Green Road, Benenden, Kent TN17 4AR. *Clubs:* Leander; Rye Golf.

**STEWART, James Harvey;** former consultant in healthcare management; Chief Executive (formerly District General Manager), Barking and Havering (formerly Barking, Havering and Brentwood) Health Authority, 1985–95; *b* 15 Aug. 1939; *s* of Harvey Stewart and Annie (née Gray); *m* 1st, 1965, Fiona Maria Maclay Reid (*d* 2004); three *s* one *d*; 2nd, 2015, Sally Ann Marsh (née Childerley). *Educ:* Peterhead Acad.; Aberdeen Univ. (MA 1962); Manchester Univ. (DSA 1964). Hosp. Sec., Princess Margaret Rose Orthopaedic Hosp., Edinburgh, 1965–67; Principal Admin. Asst, 1967–68, and Dep. Gp Sec. and sometime Acting Gp Sec., 1968–73, York A HMC; Area Administrator, 1973–82, and Dist Administrator, 1982–83, Northumberland AHA; Regional Administrator, East Anglian RHA, 1983–85. Mem., Cambridge CHC, 1999–2002; Bd Mem., S Cambs PCT, 2002–05. Hon. Treasurer, Assoc. of Chief Administrators of Health Authorities in England and Wales, 1982–85 (Mem. Council, 1975–82). Member: (Lib Dem) S Cambs DC, 1998–2015 (Chm., 2007–09); Hardwick Parish Council, 1999–2016. Mem., Cambridge Rotary Club, 1983– (Pres., 1998–99). Hon. Pres., Cambs Rehab. Club for Visually Handicapped, 1999–2010; Trustee, Cambridgeshire Soc. for Blind (Camsight), 2005–. Chm., Cambridge Friends of Nat. Trust for Scotland, 2014–. *Recreations:* music, reading, walking, sport. *Club:* National Liberal.

**STEWART, Sir (James) Moray,** KCB 1995 (CB 1990); Chairman, Board of Management, North Glasgow College, 2005–08 (Member, since 1996); President, SSAFA (formerly SSAFA-Forces Help), Fife, 2003–15; *b* 21 June 1938; third *s* of James and Evelyn Stewart; *m* 1963, Dorothy May Batey, *o d* of Alan and Maud Batey; three *s*. *Educ:* Marlborough Coll.; Univ. of Keele (BA First Cl. Hons History and Econs). Sec., Univ. of Keele Union, 1960–61. Breakdown and Information Service Operator, AA, 1956–57; Asst Master, Northcliffe Sch., Bognor Regis, 1957–58; Asst Principal, Air Min., 1962–65; Private Sec. to 2nd Permanent Under Sec. of State (RAF), MoD, 1965–66; Principal, MoD, 1966–70; First Sec. (Defence), UK Delegn to NATO, 1970–73; Asst Sec., MoD, 1974–75; Private Sec. to successive Secs of State for NI, 1975–77; Dir, Naval Manpower Requirements, MoD, 1977; Dir, Defence Policy Staff, MoD, 1978–80; Asst Under Sec. of State, MoD, 1980–84; Asst Sec. Gen. for Defence Planning and Policy, NATO, 1984–86; Dep. Under Sec. of State, Personnel and Logistics, 1986–88, Defence Procurement, 1988–90, MoD; Second Permanent Under Sec. of State, MoD, 1990–96. Chm., CS Healthcare, 1993–2000. Commissioner: Royal Hosp. Chelsea, 1986–88; Queen Victoria Sch., Dunblane, 1996–2006; Trustee, Imperial War Museum, 1986–88; Mem. Council, RUSI, 1988–92. Vice Pres., Eurodefense UK, 2002–09. Vice Pres., Civil Service RFU, 1993–. Chairman: Arvon Foundn in Scotland, 1998–2003; Elie Harbour Trust, 1999–2007; Member: Bd, Assoc. of Scotland's Colls, 2005–08; Cttee, Elie and Earlsferry Hist. Soc., 2009–. Trustee, Pegasus Trust, 1993–. Hon. DLitt Keele, 1995. *Recreations:* reading, listening to music. *Address:* c/o Drummonds, Royal Bank of Scotland, 49 Charing Cross, SW1A 2DX. *Clubs:* Farmers; New (Edinburgh).

**STEWART, His Honour James Simeon Hamilton**; QC 1982; a Circuit Judge, 2002–12; Resident Judge, Bradford Crown Court, 2009–12; *b* 2 May 1943; *s* of late Henry Hamilton Stewart, MD, FRCS and Edna Mary Hamilton Stewart, JP; *m* 1st, 1972, Helen Margaret Whiteley (*d* 1998); one *d* (and one *d* decd); 2nd, 2006, Deborah Marion Rakusen (*née* Rose). *Educ*: Cheltenham Coll.; Univ. of Leeds (LLB Hons). Called to the Bar, Inner Temple, 1966, Bencher, 1992. A Recorder, 1982–2002; a Dep. High Court Judge, 1993–2002. Hon. Recorder of Bradford, 2009–12. *Recreations*: cricket, golf, British Heart Foundation. *Club*: Yorkshire Taverners (Leeds).

**STEWART, Lt Col John Cochrane**; farmer, since 1999; Lord-Lieutenant of Clackmannanshire, since 2014; *b* Edinburgh, 21 Aug. 1957; *s* of Lt-Col Sir Robert (Christie) Stewart, *qv*, *m* 1999, Katie Dook; one *s* two *d*. *Educ*: Aysgarth Sch.; Eton Coll. Served Scots Guards, 1977–99: Platoon Comdr, 1977–81; Adjt, Cyprus, 1984–86; Co. Comd, 1986–90, 1992–94; MoD, 1990–92, 1996–97; 2 i/c, 1994–96, CO, 1997–99, 1st Bn. Equerry, 1981–84, Extra Equerry, 1999–, to the Duke of Kent. Golf tour operator, JCS Golf, 2002–. Adjt, Royal Co. of Archers, 2010–. Chm., Scots Guards Assoc., 2004–15. *Recreations*: golf, shooting, ski-ing, tennis. *Address*: Arndean, Dollar, Clackmannanshire FK14 7NH. *T*: (01259) 743525, 07940 530499. *E*: johnny@arndean.co.uk. *Clubs*: Muirfield Golf; Royal & Ancient Golf (St Andrews).

**STEWART, Rt Rev. John Craig**; Episcopal Chaplain, Diocese of Ballarat, Victoria, since 2010; *b* 10 Aug. 1940; *s* of J. J. Stewart; *m* 1967, Janine (*née* Schahinger); two *s*. *Educ*: Newington Coll., Sydney; Wesley Coll., Melbourne; Ridley Theol Coll., Melbourne. Ordained: deacon, 1965; priest, 1966; Curate, S Australia, 1965–68; Associate Priest, St John's, Crawley, 1968–70; Vicar: St Aidan's, Parkdale, 1970–74; St Luke's, Frankston, 1974–79; Gen. Sec., Church Missionary Soc., Victoria, 1979–84; Asst Bishop, Dio. Melbourne, 1984–2001; Rector, Parish of Woodend, Vic, 2001–04; Associate Priest, Parish of Holy Trinity, Bacchus Marsh, Vic, 2005–10. *Publications*: From London to Dartmoor, 1996; From Bolton to Ballarat, 1996; From Peebles to Port Phillip, 2006; From Penicuik to Penola, 2009. *Recreations*: family history, geology, music. *Address*: PO Box 928, Bacchus Marsh, Vic 3340, Australia.

**STEWART, Prof. John David**, DPhil; Professor of Local Government and Administration, Birmingham University, 1971–96, Hon. Professor, 1996–99, Emeritus Professor, since 1999; *b* 19 March 1929; *s* of Dr David Stewart and Phyllis Stewart (*née* Crossley); *m* 1953, Theresa Stewart, *qv*; two *s* two *d*. *Educ*: Stockport Grammar Sch.; Balliol Coll., Oxford (MA 1966); Nuffield Coll., Oxford (DPhil 1966). Industrial Relns Dept, NCB, 1954–66; Birmingham University: Sen. Lectr, 1966–71, Dir, 1976–83, Inst. of Local Govt Studies; Hd of Sch. of Public Policy, 1990–93. Member: Layfield Cttee on Local Govt Finance, 1974–76; Acad. Adv. Panel on local govt, DETR, 1997–98. President's Award for Outstanding Contribn to Local Govt, SOLACE, 2007; Local Govt Chronicle Lifetime Achievement Award, 2013. *Publications*: British Pressure Groups, 1958; Management in Local Government, 1971; The Responsive Local Authority, 1974; (jtly) Corporate Management in English Local Government, 1974; Local Government: the conditions of local choice, 1983; (jtly) The Case for Local Government, 1983; Understanding the Management of Local Government, 1988; (jtly) The Politics of Hung Authorities, 1992; Management for the Public Domain, 1994; (jtly) The Changing Organisation and Management of Local Government, 1994; (ed jtly) Local Government in the 1990s, 1995; The Nature of British Local Government, 2000; Modernising British Local Government, 2003; (with S. Leach and G. Jones) Centralisation, Devolution and the Future of Local Government, 2017. *Recreation*: gardening. *Address*: 15 Selly Wick Road, Birmingham B29 7JJ. *T*: (0121) 472 1512. *E*: johnstewart@tinyonline.co.uk.

**STEWART, John Duncan Maclean**; Chairman, Heathrow Association for the Control of Air Noise, since 1998; *b* Bulawayo, 17 June 1949; *s* of James and Mary Stewart. *Educ*: Bristol Poly. (Dip. Social Policy). Co-ordinator, Lambeth Public Transport Gp, 1981–90; Hon. Chm., 1987–90, Chm., 1990–97, Alarm UK. Hon. Chair: Road Peace, 1994–2000; Slower Speeds Initiative, 1996–2005; UK Noise Assoc., 2000–; Transport 2000, 2001–08. *Publications*: Roadblock, 1995; Rough Crossing, 1998; Roads for People: policies for liveable streets, 2001; The Night Flight Question, 2005; Location, Location, Location, 2006; Victory Against All the Odds: the story of how the campaign to stop a third runway was won, 2010; Why Noise Matters, 2011. *Address*: 13 Stockwell Road, SW9 9AU. *E*: johnstewart2@btconnect.com.

**STEWART, John Morrison**, FCIB; Chairman, Legal & General Group plc, 2010–16; Group Chief Executive, National Australia Bank, 2004–08 (Executive Director, Principal Board, and Chief Executive of European Operations, 2003–04); Chairman, Guide Dogs for the Blind Association, 2012–15; *b* 31 May 1949; *s* of Peter and Jane Stewart; *m* 1971, Sylvia Jameson; one *s* one *d*. *Educ*: Boroughmuir Sch., Edinburgh; Open Univ. (BA 1975). ACII 1979; FCIB 1989. Posts with Legal & General; Woolwich Building Society: joined 1977, as Br. Manager; Asst Gen. Manager, Insurance Services, 1988–91; General Manager: Financial Services, 1991–92; Retail Ops, 1992–95; Group Ops Dir, 1995–96; Gp Chief Exec., Woolwich Bldg Soc., subseq. Woolwich plc, 1996–2000; Dep. Gp Chief Exec., Barclays Bank, 2000–03. Chm., Woolwich Ind. Financial Adv. Services (Dir, 1989–95); Director: Banca Woolwich, Italy, 1996–2000; Banque Woolwich, France, 1996–2000. Non-executive Director: Business Council, Australia, 2006–08; Telstra Corp. Ltd, 2008–11; Bank of England, 2009–15; Financial Reporting Council, 2014–15. Pres., CIB, 2002–03 (Dep. Pres., 2001–02); Chm., Australian Bankers' Assoc., 2007–08. Member: Business–Govt Adv. Gp on nat. security, 2004–08; Prime Minister's task gp on emissions trading, 2007. Chm., Southern Cross Stud, 2009–. CCMI (CIMgt 1996). Hon. DLitt Heriot-Watt, 1997. *Recreation*: sailing.

**STEWART, Sir (John) Simon (Watson)**, 6th Bt *cr* 1920, of Balgownie; MD, FRCP, FRCR; Consultant in Clinical Oncology at St Mary's Hospital and Imperial College School of Medicine (formerly Royal Postgraduate Medical School), 1989–2017; *b* 5 July 1955; *s* of Sir John Keith Watson Stewart, 5th Bt and of Mary Elizabeth, *d* of John Francis Moxon; *S* father, 1990; *m* 1978, Dr Catherine Stewart, *d* of H. Gordon Bond; one *s* one *d*. *Educ*: Uppingham Sch.; Charing Cross Hosp. Med. Sch. BSc (1st cl. Hons) 1977; MB BS Lond. 1980; MRCP 1983, FRCP 1994; FRCR 1986; MD 1989. *Heir*: *s* John Hamish Watson Stewart, *b* 12 Dec. 1983. *Address*: 8 Chiswick Wharf, Chiswick, W4 2SR. *T*: (020) 8995 2213. *Club*: Oriental.

**STEWART, Sir John Young, (Sir Jackie)**, Kt 2001; OBE 1972; racing driver, retired 1973; developed Gleneagles Jackie Stewart Shooting School; Chairman, Stewart Grand Prix Ltd, 1996–2000; *b* 11 June 1939; *s* of late Robert Paul Stewart and of Jean Clark Young; *m* 1962, Helen McGregor; two *s*. *Educ*: Dumbarton Academy. First raced, 1961; competed in 4 meetings, 1961–62, driving for Barry Filer, Glasgow; drove for Ecurie Ecosse and other private entrants, winning 14 out of 23 starts, 1963; 28 wins out of 53 starts, 1964; drove Formula 1 for BRM, 1965–67 and for Ken Tyrrell, 1968–73; has won Australian, New Zealand, Swedish, Mediterranean, Japanese and many other non-championship major internat. Grands Prix; set up new world record by winning his 26th World Championship Grand Prix (Zandvoort), July 1973, and 27th (Nurburgring), Aug. 1973; 3rd in World Championship, 1965; 2nd in 1968 and 1972; World Champion, 1969, 1971, 1973. Global Ambassador, Royal Bank of Scotland, 2004–12; Strategic Advr, Genii Business Exchange, 2011–13. Chm., Motorsport Steering Cttee, Cranfield Univ., 2000–07. President: Dyslexia Scotland, 2004–; Springfield Club, 1976–; Vice President: British Dyslexia Assoc., 1998–; Vice-Chm. and Founding Trustee, Scottish Internat. Educn Trust, 1970– (Mem., Internat. Adv. Bd to the Scottish Parlt, 2002–10). Founder, Trustee and Chm., Grand Prix Mechanics Charitable Trust, 1987–; Founding Trustee and Chm., Race Against Dementia, 2016–. Hon. Prof., Stirling, 2001–. Hon. Dr Automotive Engrg, Lawrence Inst. of Technology, Mich, USA, 1973; Hon. DEng: Glasgow Caledonian, 1986; Heriot-Watt, 1996; Glasgow, 2001; Hon. Dr: Cranfield, 1998; Stirling, 1998; Edinburgh, 2006; Edinburgh Napier, 2013; Hon. DSc St Andrews, 2008. BARC Gold Medal, 1971, 1973. Daily Express Sportsman of the Year, 1971, 1973; World Sportsman of the Year, 1973; BBC Sports Personality of the Year, 1973; Scottish Sportsman of the Year, 1973; Sports Illustrated American Sportsman of the Year, 1973; ABC Sports Personality of the Year, 1973; Seagrove Trophy, 1973, 1999. *Film*: Weekend of a Champion, 1972. *Publications*: World Champion, 1970 (with Eric Dymock); Faster!, 1972 (with Peter Manso); On the Road, 1983; (with Alan Henry) Jackie Stewart's Principles of Performance Driving, 1986; The Jackie Stewart Book of Shooting, 1991; Winning is Not Enough: the autobiography, 2007; Collage: Jackie Stewart's Grand Prix album, 2010. *Recreations*: golf, fishing, tennis, shooting (Mem. Scottish and British Teams for Clay Pigeon shooting; former Scottish, English, Irish, Welsh and British Champion; won Coupe des Nations, 1959 and 1960; reserve for two-man team, 1960 Olympics). *Clubs*: (Hon.) Royal Automobile, British Racing Drivers' (Pres., 2000–06; Vice Pres., 2006–); Royal and Ancient (St Andrews); (Hon.) Gleneagles; Sunningdale; Loch Lomond Golf; Geneva Golf; Domaine Imperial, Club De Bonmont (Switzerland).

**STEWART, Joseph Martin**, OBE 1994; JP; Director of Human Resources, Police Service of Northern Ireland, 2001; *b* 5 Nov. 1955; *s* of late Joseph Aloysius Stewart and of Annie Margaret Mary Stewart (*née* Friel); *m* 1978, Deirdre Ann Ritchie. *Educ*: Queen's Univ., Belfast (LLB Hons 1978); Univ. of Ulster (Post Grad. Dip. in Mgt Studies 1980). Engineering Employers Federation (NI) Association: Asst Indust. Relns Officer, 1978–80; Indust. Relns Officer, 1980–85; Dir, 1985–90; Personnel Dir, Harland & Wolff Shipbuilding and Heavy Industries Ltd, 1990–95; Sec. and Chief Exec., Police Authy for NI, 1995–2001. Non-exec. Dir, Public Health Agency, NI, 2018–. JP Ards Circuit, 1990. *Recreations*: game shooting, pedigree sheep breeding, motorcycle touring. *Club*: Ulster Reform (Belfast).

**STEWART, Karen Ann Elizabeth**; *see* Shuman, K. A. E.

**STEWART, Kevin Morrice**; Member (SNP) Aberdeen Central, Scottish Parliament, since 2011; Minister for Local Government, Housing and Planning (formerly Minister for Local Government and Housing), since 2016; *b* Aberdeen, 3 June 1968; *s* of Michael Stewart and Sandra Stewart. *Educ*: Summerhill Acad., Aberdeen; Univ. of Aberdeen (degree unfinished due to lack of finances). Worked at ASDA, then in family retail business. Mem. (SNP), Aberdeen CC, 1999– (Leader, SNP Gp, 1999–2011; Dep. Leader of Council, 2007–11). Mem., ACC, 1999–2012. Convener, Local Govt and Regeneration Cttee, Scottish Parlt, 2012–16. Chm., Nestrans, 2007–11. Burgess, Guild of Burgh of Aberdeen, 2008–. *Recreation*: reading. *Address*: Scottish Parliament, Edinburgh EH99 1SP. *T*: (0131) 348 6382; (office) Third Floor, 27 John Street, Aberdeen AB25 1BT. *T*: (01224) 624719. *E*: Kevin.Stewart.msp@parliament.scot. *W*: www.twitter.com/KevinStewartMSP.

**STEWART, Sir Ludovic Houston S.**; *see* Shaw Stewart.

**STEWART, Marjorie Sally, (Susie)**; Vice Lord-Lieutenant of Renfrewshire, 2007–16; *b* Glasgow, 13 Aug. 1941; *d* of Colin W. H. Gourlay and Aileen M. Gourlay (*née* Millen); *m* 1973, (John) Allan Stewart (*d* 2016); one *s* one *d*. *Educ*: St Leonards Sch., St Andrews; St Andrews Univ. (MA Spanish and French 1962); Edinburgh Univ. (Postgrad. Dip. Social Studies 1963). FFPH 2001. Ed., Dept of Community Medicine, St Thomas' Hosp. Med. Sch., 1966–76; Technical Editor: BMA Special Jls, 1977–84; Panel of Social Medicine and Epidemiol., Eur. Communities, 1984–90; Exec. Sec., Scottish Forum for Public Health Medicine, 1990–95; Res. Manager, Dept of Public Health, Univ. of Glasgow, 1995–98. DL Renfrewshire, 1996. *Publications*: (with Walter W. Holland): Screening in Health Care, 1990; Public Health: the vision and the challenge, 1997; Screening in Disease Prevention: what works?, 2005. *Recreations*: creative writing, reading, gardening, dogs and cats, wildlife, tapestry, Menorca, beekeeping. *Address*: Broadlie View, 8 Holehouse Brae, Neilston, E Renfrewshire G78 3LU. *T*: (0141) 881 2698. *E*: susiestewart113@btopenworld.com. *Club*: Western (Glasgow).

**STEWART, Michael James**; Reader in Political Economy, University College, London University, 1969–94, now Emeritus; *b* 6 Feb. 1933; *s* of late John Innes Mackintosh Stewart; *m* 1962, Frances Kaldor, *d* of Baron Kaldor, FBA; one *s* two *d* (and one *d* decd). *Educ*: Campbell Coll., Belfast; St Edward's Sch., Oxford; Magdalen Coll., Oxford (1st cl. PPE 1955). Asst Res. Officer, Oxford Univ. Inst. of Statistics, 1955–56; Barnett Fellow, Cornell Univ., 1956–57; Econ. Asst, HM Treasury, 1957–60; Sec. to Council on Prices, Productivity and Incomes, 1960–61; Econ. Adviser, HM Treasury, 1961–62, Cabinet Office, 1964–67 (Senior Econ. Advr, 1967), Kenya Treasury, 1967–69; Special Adviser to Sec. of State for Trade, Apr.–Oct. 1974; Economic Adviser to Malta Labour Party, 1970–73; Special Econ. Advr to Foreign Sec., 1977–78. Guest Scholar, Brookings Instn, Washington, DC, 1978–79. Mem., Acad. Adv. Panel, Bank of England, 1977–83. Contested (Lab): Folkestone and Hythe, 1964; Croydon North-West, 1966. Asst Editor, Nat. Inst. Econ. Review, 1962–64. Consultant to various UN agencies, 1971–. *Publications*: Keynes and After, 1967; The Jekyll and Hyde Years: politics and economic policy since 1964, 1977; Controlling the Economic Future: policy dilemmas in a shrinking world, 1983; (with Peter Jay) Apocalypse 2000: economic breakdown and the suicide of democracy 1989–2000, 1987; Keynes in the 1990s: a return to economic sanity, 1993. *Recreations*: looking at paintings, eating at restaurants in France. *Address*: 79 South Hill Park, NW3 2SS. *T*: (020) 7435 3686. *Club*: Oxford and Cambridge.

**STEWART, Sir Moray**; *see* Stewart, Sir J. M.

**STEWART, His Honour Neill Alastair**; a Circuit Judge, 1999–2017; *b* 8 June 1947; *yr s* of James Robertson Stewart, CBE; *m* 2000, Tiffany, *d* of His Honour William Llewellyn Monro Davies, *qv*; one *s* one *d*. *Educ*: Whitgift Sch.; Clare Coll., Cambridge (BA Mech. Scis Tripos). Engr, Sir Alexander Gibb & Partners, 1968–70; called to the Bar, Middle Temple, 1973; in practice at the Bar, 1975–99.

**STEWART, Nicholas John Cameron**, QC 1987; *b* 16 April 1947; *s* of John Cameron Stewart and Margaret Mary (*née* Botsford); *m* 1974, Pamela Jean Windham (marr. diss. 2000); one *s* two *d*, one *d* by Dr Tabea Lauktien. *Educ*: Bedford Modern Sch.; Worcester Coll., Oxford (Open Exhibnr; BA 1968); Birkbeck, Univ. of London (BA 1st Cl. Hons German and Spanish 2015). Called to the Bar, Inner Temple, 1971, Bencher, 1999; Dep. High Ct Judge, Chancery Div., 1991–. CEDR Accredited Mediator, 1996–. Chm., Bar Human Rights Cttee, 1994–98. Chairman: Dialogue Adv. Gp, Amsterdam, 2008–15; Democratic Progress Inst., London, 2012–. Pres., Union Internationale des Avocats, 2001–02. Narrator, No Further Questions, BBC Radio series, 1993 and 1995. FCIArb 2000. *Recreations*: mountain walking, ski-ing, languages.

STEWART, Nikola Caroline, (Mrs A. R. Milne); Sheriff of South Strathclyde, Dumfries and Galloway at Lanark, since 2000; Appeal Sheriff, Sheriff Appeal Court, since 2015; *b* 29 July 1956; *d* of James Lumsden Stewart and Joyce Elizabeth Stewart (*née* Urquhart); *m* 1989, Alastair Robert Milne; two *d*. *Educ*: Harris Acad., Dundee; Dundee Univ. (MA, LLB, DipLP). Admitted Advocate, 1987; called to the Scottish Bar, 1987; in practice as advocate, 1987–2000; Temp. Sheriff, 1997–99. Chm., Child Support Appeal Tribunals, 1990–97. *Address*: Medwynbrae, Carlops Road, West Linton EH46 7DS.

STEWART, Norman MacLeod; Senior Partner, 1984–97, Consultant, 1997–99, Allan, Black & McCaskie; President, The Law Society of Scotland, 1985–86; *b* 2 Dec. 1934; *s* of George and Elspeth Stewart; *m* 1959, Mary Slater Campbell; four *d*. *Educ*: Elgin Acad.; Univ. of Edinburgh (BL); SSC. Alex. Morison & Co., WS, Edinburgh, 1954–58; Allan, Black & McCaskie, Solicitors, Elgin, 1959–99, Partner, 1961–97. Law Society of Scotland: Mem. Council, 1976–87; Convener: Public Relations Cttee, 1979–81; Professional Practice Cttee, 1981–84; Vice-Pres., 1984–85. Chm., Elgin and Lossiemouth Harbour Bd, 1993–2009. Hon. Mem., American Bar Assoc., 1985–. *Recreations*: walking, golf, music, Spanish culture. *Address*: 25 Saltcoats Gardens, Bellsquarry South, Livingston, W Lothian EH54 9JD. *T*: (01506) 419439. *E*: norman666@btinternet.com.

STEWART, Patricia Ann; Deputy Chief Executive, Food Standards Agency, 2003–07; *b* 22 March 1949; *d* of late Walter William Stewart and Freda Dorothy Stewart (*née* Rolfe); *m* 1st, 1978, Jeremy Gye Colman, *qv* (marr. diss.); 2nd, 1996, Lt Comdr Nicholas Austen Bates, RN. *Educ*: Palmer's Grammar Sch. for Girls, Grays; Univ. of Sussex (BSc (Maths with Electronic Engrg) 1970). FSS 1975. Statistician: Civil Service Dept, 1970–79; Local Govt Finance, DoE, 1979–83, seconded to EC, Luxembourg, 1983; Department of Health: Chief Statistician, 1984–86; Assistant Secretary: NHS Finance, 1986–89; NHS Liaison, 1989–91; Facilities and Corporate Mgt, 1991–95; Public Health Div., 1996–97; Food Standards Agency: Implementation Div., 1997–2000; Dir, Corporate Resources and Strategy, 2000–07. *Recreations*: music (singing, playing the viol; Chair, Southern Early Music Forum, 2010–), computers and gadgets, contributing to village life, reading. *E*: pas.whwh@gmail.com.

STEWART, Sir Patrick, Kt 2010; OBE 2001; actor; *b* 13 July 1940; *s* of late Alfred Stewart and Gladys Stewart (*née* Barrowclough); *m* 1st, 1966, Sheila Falconer (marr. diss. 1990); one *s* one *d*; 2nd, 2002, Wendy Neuss (marr. diss.); 3rd, 2013, Sunny Ozell. *Educ*: Mirfield Secondary Modern Sch.; Bristol Old Vic Theatre Sch. Joined RSC, 1966, Associate Artist, 1967–87; CEO, Flying Freehold Prodns, 1998–. *Theatre includes*: Antony and Cleopatra, 1979; Henry IV, RSC, 1984; Yonadab, NT, 1986; Who's Afraid of Virginia Woolf?, Young Vic, 1987; A Christmas Carol (one-man show), NY, 1991, 1992, Albery, 2005; The Tempest, NY, 1995; Othello, Washington, 1997; The Ride Down Mount Morgan, NY, 1998, 2000; The Master Builder, Albery, 2003; A Life in the Theatre, Apollo, 2005; Antony and Cleopatra, RSC, 2006; The Tempest, RSC, 2006, transf. Novello, 2007; Twelfth Night, Chichester, 2007; Macbeth, Chichester, transf. Gielgud, 2007; Hamlet, RSC, 2008; Waiting for Godot, UK tour then Th. Royal, Haymarket, 2009, NY 2013; Bingo, Chichester, 2010, transf. Young Vic, 2012; The Merchant of Venice, RSC, 2011; No Man's Land, NY, 2013, UK tour then Wyndham's, 2016; *television includes*: Hedda, 1975; I Claudius, 1976; Oedipus Rex, 1976; Tinker Tailor Soldier Spy, 1979; Hamlet, Prince of Denmark, 1980; Smiley's People, 1982; Maybury, 1980; The Mozart Inquest, 1985; The Devil's Disciple, 1987; Star Trek: The Next Generation (series), 1987–94; Death Train, 1993; The Canterville Ghost (also co-prod), 1996; Moby Dick, 1998; A Christmas Carol (also prod), 1999; King of Texas (also prod), 2002; The Lion in Winter (also prod), 2003; Eleventh Hour, 2006; Hamlet, 2009; Richard II, 2012; Blunt Talk (US), 2015; *films include*: Excalibur, 1981; Dune, 1984; Lady Jane, 1986; LA Story, 1991; Robin Hood: Men in Tights, 1993; Gunmen, 1994; Star Trek: Generations, 1994; Jeffrey, 1996; Star Trek: First Contact, 1996; Conspiracy Theory, 1997; Masterminds, 1997; Dad Savage, 1998; Star Trek: Insurrection, 1998; X Men, 2000; Star Trek: Nemesis, 2002; X2, 2003; Steamboy, 2005; X-Men: The Last Stand, 2006; X Men: Days of Future Past, 2014; Green Room, 2015; Logan, 2017; The Kid Who Would Be King, 2019. Cameron Mackintosh Vis. Prof. of Contemporary Th., Univ. of Oxford, 2007. Chancellor, 2004–15; Prof. of Performing Arts, 2008, Univ. of Huddersfield. Emeritus Fellow, St Catherine's Coll., Oxford, 2010–. *Address*: c/o Independent Talent Group Ltd, 40 Whitfield Street, W1T 2RH.

STEWART, Patrick Loudon McIain, MBE 2000; Consultant, Messrs Stewart Balfour & Sutherland, Solicitors, Campbeltown, Argyll, 2000–13; Lord-Lieutenant, Argyll and Bute, since 2011 (Vice Lord-Lieutenant, 2003–11); *b* 25 July 1945; *s* of late Archibald Ian Balfour Stewart, CBE and of Ailsa Rosamund Mary Stewart (*née* Massey); *m* 1969, Mary Anne McLellan; one *s* one *d*. *Educ*: Dalintober Primary Sch.; Edinburgh Acad.; Edinburgh Univ. (LLB). WS 1968. Partner, 1970–82, Sen. Partner, 1982–2000, Stewart Balfour & Sutherland, Solicitors. Asst Sec., 1970–74, Sec., 1974–2009, Adminr, 2009–14, Clyde Fishermen's Assoc.; Marine Envmt, then Marine Legislation Consultant, Scottish Fishermen's Fedn, 2009–12. Clerk to Comrs of Income Tax, Argyll-Islay, 1972–2009. DL Argyll and Bute, 1987. Hon. Sheriff at Campbeltown, 1997–. CO, Campbeltown Unit, Sea Cadet Corps, 1972–88; Mem., Sea Cadet Council, 1983–93; Trustee, Sea Cadet Assoc., 2000–04; Life Vice Pres., Marine Soc. and Sea Cadets, 2005. Chm., Argyll and Bute World War I Steering Gp, 2014–19. Patron: Clyde Fishermen's Trust, 2016–; Campbeltown Heritage Centre, 2018–; Hon. Pres., Clyde Fishermen's Assoc. Cadet Forces Medal, 1984. *Recreations*: sailing, walking, reading. *Address*: Craigadam, Campbeltown, Argyll PA28 6EP. *T*: (01586) 552161. *E*: plms1914@gmail.com.

*See also Hon. Lord Stewart.*

STEWART, Dame Pieter (Ane), DNZM 2012; Founder and Managing Director, New Zealand Fashion Week, 1999–2015, now Strategic Director; *b* Christchurch, NZ; *d* of Reginald George McKenzie and Joan McKenzie; *m* 1968, Peter Maxwell Stewart; one *s* three *d*. *Educ*: St Margaret's Coll., Christchurch. Anaesthetic and Operating Theatre Sec., North Canterbury Hosp. Bd, 1965–68; Founder, Pieters Model Agency and Sch., 1981; Associate Editor, Fashion Quarterly mag., 1985–87; Founder, Pieter Stewart Promotions, public relns and promotions co., 1988; coordinated Corbans Fashion Collections, annual TV special, 1990–95; produced and coordinated Wella Fashion Collections and Wella Fashion Report, TV specials, 1996–99; launched NZ Fashion Festival, 2010. Member: Bd, St Margaret's Coll. Trust, 1992–2003 (Chm., 1994–2003); Bd, Ind. Schs Assoc., 1996–2003 (Dep. Chm., 1999–2003); Trust Bd, Sir George Seymour Coll. of Travel and Tourism, 1997–2004. Former Mem., Exec. Cttee, Child Cancer Soc.; former Coordinator, Child Cancer Foundn House. MInstD. *Recreations*: family activities, sailing, reading, cooking. *Address*: Heatherlea Homestead, Darfield 7572, New Zealand. *T*: (9) 3778033, *Fax*: (3) 3180891. *E*: pieter@pieterstewart.com. *Clubs*: Global Women; Windwhistle Winter Sports.

STEWART, Col Robert Alexander, (Bob), DSO 1993; MP (C) Beckenham, since 2010; *b* 7 July 1949; *s* of late A. A. Stewart, MC and Marguerita Joan Stewart; *m* 1st (marr. diss. 1993); one *s* one *d*; 2nd, 1994, Claire Podbielski; one *s* three *d*. *Educ*: Chigwell Sch.; RMA Sandhurst; Univ. of Wales, Aberystwyth (BSc 1st Cl. Hons Internat. Politics). Commnd, Cheshire Regt, 1969; Instructor, RMA, 1979–80; Army Staff Coll., Camberley, 1981; Company Comdr, N Ireland, 1982–83; Staff Officer, MoD, 1984–85; 2 i/c 1st Bn Cheshire Regt, 1986–87; JSSC 1988; MA to Chm., NATO Mil. Cttee, HQ NATO, Brussels, 1989–91; CO, 1st Bn Cheshire Regt, 1991–93; Chief of Policy, SHAPE, 1994–95; resigned Regular Army, 1996. Sen. Consultant, Public Affairs, Hill & Knowlton (UK) Ltd, 1996–98; Sen. Vice Pres., WorldSpace UK, 1998–2001; Dir, Action Leadership, 2001–10. Member: Defence Select Cttee, 2010–17; NI Select Cttee, 2017–; Chm., All-Party Parly Gp for Army, 2010, for Defence and Security Issues, 2018–. Non-exec. Chm., Premier Gold Resources, 2012–15. Chm., Ind. Defence Media Assoc., 2003–10. Patron: Elifar Foundn, 2007–; Bede Griffiths Charitable Trust (UK), 2014–. Companion, RAF Regt Officers' Dinner Club, 2012. *Publications*: Broken Lives, 1993; Thoughts on Leadership, 2004; Leadership under Pressure, 2009. *Recreations*: writing, history. *Address*: House of Commons, SW1A 0AA. *T*: 07771 863894. *Clubs*: Army and Navy, Royal Air Force.

STEWART, Lt-Col Sir Robert (Christie), KCVO 2002; CBE 1983; TD 1962; Lord-Lieutenant of Clackmannan, 1994–2001; *b* 3 Aug. 1926; *m* 1953, Ann Grizel Cochrane; three *s* two *d*. *Educ*: Eton; University College, Oxford. Lt Scots Guards, 1945–49. Oxford Univ., 1949–51 (BA Agric.). TA, 7 Argyll and Sutherland Highlanders, 1948–66; Lt-Col Comdg 7 A & SH, 1963–66. Hon. Col, 1/51 Highland Volunteers, 1972–75. Chm. and Pres., Bd of Governors, E of Scotland Coll. of Agric., 1970–83. Chm., Kinross CC, 1963–73. DL Kinross, 1956, Vice Lieut, 1958; Lord-Lieutenant, Kinross-shire, 1966–74. Mem., Queen's Bodyguard for Scotland, 1961–. *Address*: Mains of Arndean, by Dollar, Clackmannanshire FK14 7NT. *T*: (01259) 742527.

*See also Countess of Romney, Lt-Col J. C. Stewart.*

STEWART, Sir Roderick David, Kt 2016; CBE 2007; singer and songwriter; *b* 10 Jan. 1945; *s* of Robert Joseph Stewart and Elsie Stewart; *m* 1st, 1979, Alana Collins (marr. diss. 1984); one *s* one *d*; 2nd, 1990, Rachel Hunter (marr. diss.); one *s* one *d*; one *d* by Kelly Emberg; 3rd, 2007, Penny Lancaster; two *s*. *Educ*: William Grimshaw Secondary Modern Sch., Hornsey. Singer with Jeff Beck Group, 1968–69, with The Faces, 1969–75. Albums include: with Jeff Beck Group: Truth, 1968; Cosa Nostra Beck Ola, 1969; with The Faces: First Step, 1970; Long Player, 1971; A Nod's as Good as a Wink…To a Blind Horse, 1971; Ooh La La, 1973; Coast to Coast, 1974; solo: An Old Raincoat Won't Ever Let You Down, 1969; Gasoline Alley, 1970; Every Picture Tells a Story, 1971; Never a Dull Moment, 1972; Smiler, 1974; Atlantic Crossing, 1975; A Night on the Town, 1976; Foot Loose and Fancy Free, 1977; Blondes Have More Fun, 1978; Foolish Behaviour, 1980; Tonight I'm Yours, 1981; Body Wishes, 1983; Camouflage, 1984; Every Beat of My Heart, 1986; Out of Order, 1988; Vagabond Heart, 1991; A Spanner in the Works, 1995; When We Were the New Boys, 1998; Human, 2001; It Had To Be You—The Great American Songbook, 2002; Sweet Little Rock N Roller, 2002; As Time Goes By—The Great American Songbook, Vol. II, 2003; Stardust—The Great American Songbook, Vol. III, 2004; Thanks For The Memory—The Great American Songbook, Vol. IV, 2005; Still the Same, 2006; Soulbook, 2009; Fly Me To The Moon—The Great American Songbook, Vol. V, 2010; Merry Christmas, Baby, 2012; Time 2013; Another Country, 2015; Blood Red Roses, 2018. *Publications*: Rod: the autobiography, 2012.

STEWART, Rt Hon. Roderick James Nugent, (Rt Hon. Rory), OBE 2004; PC 2019; MP for Penrith and The Border, since 2010 (C, 2010–19; Ind, since 2019); *b* 3 Jan. 1973; *s* of Brian Thomas Webster Stewart, CMG; *m* 2012, Shoshana Clark; two *s*. *Educ*: Eton; Balliol Coll., Oxford (MA). Served Black Watch (RHR), 1991–92. Entered FCO, 1995; Second Secretary: Jakarta, 1997–99; Montenegro, 1999–2000; crossed Iran, Afghanistan, Pakistan, India and Nepal on foot, 2000–02; Dep. Governorate Co-ordinator, Al Amarah, Coalition Provisional Authy, 2003–04; Sen. Advr, Nasiriyah, 2004; Fellow, Carr Center, Harvard Univ., 2004–05; Chief Exec., Turquoise Mt Foundn, Afghanistan, 2005–08; Ryan Family Prof. of Human Rights and Dir, Carr Center for Human Rights Policy, Harvard Univ., 2008–10. Parly under-Sec. of State, DEFRA, 2015–16; Minister of State: DFID, 2016–18; FCO, 2017–18; MoJ, 2018–19; Sec. of State for Internat. Develt, 2019. Member: Foreign Affairs Select Cttee, 2010–14; Defence Select Cttee, 2014–15 (Chm., 2014–15); Envmtl Audit Cttee, 2015–16. Gov., Internat. Res. Develt Council, 2008–10. Presenter, The Legacy of Lawrence of Arabia, 2010, Afghanistan: the Great Game, 2012, BBC TV. FRSL 2008. DUniv Stirling, 2009; Hon. Dr American Univ. Paris, 2011. Livingston Medal, RSGS, 2010. *Publications*: The Places in Between, 2004 (Ondaatje Prize, RSL, 2005); Occupational Hazards, 2006 (adapted for stage, 2017); (jtly) Can Intervention Work?, 2011; The Marches, 2014. *Recreations*: walking, history, trees. *Address*: House of Commons, SW1A 0AA. *Clubs*: Athenæum, Travellers, Beefsteak.

STEWART, Roger Paul Davidson; QC 2001; a Recorder, since 2002; *b* 17 Aug. 1963; *s* of late Martin Neil Davidson Stewart and of Elizabeth Janet Stewart (*née* Porter); *m* 1st, 1988, Georgina Louise Smith (marr. diss. 2011); two *s* one *d*; 2nd, 2011, Elizabeth Jane Wiseman; one *d* and two step *s* two step *d*. *Educ*: Oundle Sch.; Jesus Coll., Cambridge (MA, LLM). Called to the Bar, Inner Temple, 1986, Bencher, 2002; Barrister, Lincoln's Inn, 2000–; Hd of Chambers, 2006–10. *Publications*: (ed) Jackson and Powell on Professional Negligence, 3rd edn 1992, 4th edn 1997, (gen. ed.) 5th edn 2002, 7th edn 2012. *Recreations*: sailing, ski-ing, reading military history. *Address*: 4 New Square, Lincoln's Inn, WC2A 3RJ. *Clubs*: National Liberal; Lost Valley Mountaineering (Glencoe).

STEWART, Rt Hon. Rory; *see* Stewart, Rt Hon. R. J. N.

STEWART, Sir Simon; *see* Stewart, Sir J. S. W.

STEWART, Hon. Sir Stephen (Paul), Kt 2013; Hon. Mr Justice Stewart; a Judge of the High Court of Justice, Queen's Bench Division, since 2013; Judge in Charge of Queen's Bench Division Civil List, since 2019; *b* 9 Oct. 1953; *s* of Cyril Stewart and Phyllis Mary Stewart; *m* 1980, Prof. (Mary) Felicity Dyer; one *s* one *d*. *Educ*: Stand GS, Whitefield, Manchester; St Peter's Coll., Oxford (MA; half blue for badminton; Hon. Fellow, 2015); Open Univ. (BA 1st cl. Hons Mod. Langs (French and Spanish), 2012). Called to the Bar, Middle Temple, 1975 (Harmsworth Major Exhibnr, 1973; Harmsworth Schol., 1975), Bencher, 2013; in practice on Northern Circuit; QC 1996; Asst Recorder, 1995–99; a Recorder, 1999–2003; Dep. Judge, Technol. and Construction Court, 2000–03; a Circuit Judge, 2003–13; Senior Circuit Judge and Designated Civil Judge: Liverpool, 2003–11; Gtr Manchester, 2011–13; Queen's Bench Admin. Court Judge, N and NE Circuits, 2014–16. Hon. Lectr, Univ. of Manchester, 2012–. Pres., Thomas More Soc., 2018–. *Recreations*: running, music, foreign languages, writing poetry. *Address*: Royal Courts of Justice, Strand, WC2A 2LL.

STEWART, Susie; *see* Stewart, M. S.

STEWART, Suzanne Freda; *see* Norwood, Her Honour S. F.

STEWART, Theresa; Member (Lab), Birmingham City Council, 1970–2002 (Leader, 1993–99); Lord Mayor of Birmingham, 2000–01; *b* 24 Aug. 1930; *d* of John Raisman and Ray Raisman (*née* Baker); *m* 1953, John David Stewart, *qv*; two *s* two *d*. *Educ*: Cowper Street Sch., Leeds; Allerton High Sch., Leeds; Somerville Coll., Oxford (MA; Hon. Fellow, 2001). Member: Birmingham Regl Hosp. Bd, 1968–71; W Midland CC, 1974–77; Birmingham City Council: Chair: Birmingham Community Develt Project, 1973–76; Social Services Cttee, 1981–82 and 1984–87; Direct Labour Contract Services Cttee, 1989–93; Policy and Resources Cttee, 1997–99; W Midlands Jt Cttee, 1998–2001. Vice-

Chm., AMA Social Services Cttee, 1985–87; Chair, W Midlands LGA, 1999–2000 (Sen. Vice Chair, 1998–99). Chm., Assoc. of Direct Labour Orgns, 1994–95. Hon. LLD Birmingham, 2000. *Recreations:* relaxing in a hot bath with a good book, walking, cooking. *Address:* 15 Selly Wick Road, Birmingham B29 7JJ. *T:* (0121) 472 1512.

**STEWART, Sir William (Duncan Paterson),** Kt 1994; PhD, DSc; FRS 1977; FRSE; Chief Scientific Adviser, Cabinet Office, 1990–95; President, Royal Society of Edinburgh, 1999–2002; *b* 7 June 1935; *s* of John and Margaret Stewart; *m* 1st, 1958, Catherine MacLeod (*d* 1998); one *s* decd; 2nd, 2000, Elizabeth Smales. *Educ:* Bowmore Junior Secondary Sch., Isle-of-Islay; Dunoon Grammar Sch.; Glasgow Univ. (BSc, PhD, DSc). FRSE 1973. Asst Lectr, Univ. of Nottingham, 1961–63; Lectr, Westfield Coll., Univ. of London, 1963–68; Boyd Baxter Prof. of Biology, 1968–95, Vice-Principal, 1985–87, Univ. of Dundee; Sec. and Chief Exec., AFRC, 1988–90. Head, UK Office of Sci. and Technol., 1992–95. Chairman: Microbiol Res. Authy, Porton Down, 1999–2002; HPA, 2003–09. Chairman: Internat. Cttee on Microbial Ecology, 1983–86; Royal Soc. Biotechnology and Educn Wkg Gp, 1980–81; Independent Adv. Gp on Gruinard Is., 1985–87; President: British Phycological Soc., 1975–77; Council, Scottish Marine Biol. Assoc., 1985–87; Bioindustry Assoc., 1995–99; BAAS, 2000–01; Member: Council, Marine Biol. Assoc., 1973–76, 1977–80, 1981–84; British Nat. Cttee for problems of environment, 1979–85; UNESCO Panel on Microbiology, 1975–81; Council, NERC, 1979–85; Internat. Cell Res. Org., 1979–84; Royal Soc. Study Gp on Science Educn, 1981–82; Council, Royal Soc., 1984–86 (Vice-Pres., 1995–97); Royal Commn on Environmental Pollution, 1986–88; DSAC, 1990–95. Chairman: Govt Technol. Foresight Steering Gp, 1993–95; Govt Sci. and Engrg Base Co-ordinating Cttee, 1993–95; Ind. Expert Gp on Mobile Phones and Health, 1999–2000; Nat. Radiological Protection Bd, 2003–05; Mem., DTI Link Steering Gp, 1990–94. Dir (non-exec.), Water Research Centre plc, 1995–2002; Chm., Cyclacel Ltd, 1998–2002. Member, Governing Body: Scottish Hort. Res. Inst., 1971–80; Scottish Crop Res. Inst., 1980–88; Macaulay Land Use Res. Inst., 1987–88; Trustee, Royal Botanic Gardens, Kew, 2006–11. Chairman: Dundee Teaching Hosps NHS Trust, 1997–99; Tayside Univ. Hosps NHS Trust, 1999–2000. 25 hon. degrees and fellowships. President's Medal, Royal Acad. Engrg, 1995. *Publications:* Nitrogen Fixation in Plants, 1966; (jtly) The Blue-Green Algae, 1973; Algal Physiology and Biochemistry, 1974; (ed) Nitrogen Fixation by Free-living Organisms, 1975; (ed jtly) Nitrogen Fixation, 1980; (ed jtly) The Nitrogen Cycle of the United Kingdom, 1984; Mobile Phones and Health, 2000; over 250 papers in learned jls of repute. *Recreations:* watching soccer, watching people. *Address:* 1 Clarendon Drive, Perth Road, Dundee DD2 1JU. *Club:* Dundee United.

**STEWART-CLARK, Sir John, (Sir Jack),** 3rd Bt *cr* 1918; Chairman, Dundas Castle Ltd, since 1999; Member (C) European Parliament, East Sussex and Kent South, 1994–99 (Sussex East, 1979–94); a Vice-President, 1992–97; *b* 17 Sept. 1929; *e s* of Sir Stewart Stewart-Clark, 2nd Bt, and Jane Pamela (*d* 1993), *d* of late Major Arundell Clarke; *S* father, 1971; *m* 1958, Lydia Frederike, *d* of J. W. Loudon, Holland; one *s* four *d*. *Educ:* Eton; Balliol College, Oxford; Harvard Business School. Commissioned with HM Coldstream Guards, 1948–49. Oxford, 1949–52. With J. & P. Coats Ltd, 1952–69; Managing Director: J. & P. Coats, Pakistan, Ltd, 1961–67; J. A. Carp's Garenfabrieken, Holland, 1967–69; Philips Industries, 1971–79: Managing Director: Philips Electrical Ltd, London, 1971–75; Pye of Cambridge Ltd, 1975–79. Director: A. T. Kearney Ltd, 1979–92; Low and Bonar plc, 1980–95; Pioneer Concrete plc, 1986–99; TSB Scotland, 1986–89. Pres. Supervisory Bd, Eur. Inst. for Security, 1984–86; Mem. Council, RUSI, 1979–83. Dir and Trustee, Eur. Centre for Work and Society, 1982–2005; Mem., Bd of Govs, Eur. Inst. for Media, 1995–2000; Chairman: Conf. of Regions of North Western Europe, 1986–92; Eur. Parliamentarians and Industrialists Council, 1990–99. European Drugs Monitoring Centre: Mem., Mgt Bd, 1999–2006; Mem., Policy Bureau, 2001–06; Trustee, Mentor UK Foundn, 1999–2014. Chm., EP delegn to Canada, 1979–84; Mem., EP delegn to Japan, 1984–94. Treas., Eur. Democratic Group, 1979–92. Member Royal Company of Archers, Queen's Body Guard for Scotland. Contested (U) North Aberdeen, Gen. Election, 1959. *Publications:* Competition Law in the European Community, 1990; It's My Problem As Well: drugs prevention and education, 1993. *Recreations:* golf, tennis, photography, vintage cars. *Heir:* s Alexander Dudley Stewart-Clark, *b* 21 Nov. 1960. *Address:* Dundas Castle, South Queensferry, near Edinburgh EH30 9SP. *T:* (0131) 331 1114. *Club:* Sloane.

**STEWART-RICHARDSON, Sir Simon (Alaisdair),** 17th Bt *cr* 1630; *b* 9 June 1947; *er s* of Sir Ian Rorie Hay Stewart-Richardson, 16th Bt, and Audrey Meryl (who *m* 1975, Patrick Allan Pearson Robertson, CMG and *d* 2018), *e d* of late Claude Odlum; *S* father, 1969; *m* 1990, Marilene Cabal do Nascimento (marr. diss.); one *s* one *d*. *Educ:* Trinity College, Glenalmond. *Heir:* s Jason Rorie Stewart-Richardson, *b* 5 Oct. 1990.

**STEWART-SMITH, Christopher Dudley,** CBE 1995; DL; Chairman, Cautley Ltd, 1997–2019; Producer, Stanley Hall Opera, 2001–19; Partner, Stanley Hall Farm, since 2014; *b* 21 Jan. 1941; *s* of late Ean Stewart-Smith and Edmee von Wallerstain und Marnegg; *m* 1964, Olivia Barstow (marr. diss. 1989); one *s* two *d*. *Educ:* Winchester; King's Coll., Cambridge (MA Mod Langs); MIT (SM Management). Courtaulds, 1962–65; McKinsey & Co. Management Consultants, 1966–71; joined Sterling Guarantee Trust, 1971, Dir, 1973; served on main bd after merger with Town & City Properties and later with P&OSNCo., until 1986; Chairman: Earls Court and Olympia Exhibns Gp, 1974–85; Sutcliffe Catering Gp, 1975–85; Butlers Warehousing & Distribution, 1971–85; Sterling Guards, 1974–85; P&O Cruises, Swan Hellenic, and Princess Cruises, 1985–86; Conder Group plc, 1987–92; Collett Dickenson Pearce Internat., 1990–91; Producer Responsibility Gp and V-Wrag, 1994–96; London & Henley Ltd, 1995–98; Healthcall Gp plc, 1991–98; Leighton & Henley PLC, 2007–14. Director: Outer London Reg. Bd, 1984–88, Southern Adv. Bd, 1988–92, Nat. Westminster Bank; Williamson Tea Holdings, 1986–94; Life Sciences Internat., 1987–97; Erith plc, 1992–95; Strategic Partnership, 1997–2000; Gartmore SNT plc, 1998–2005; Brompton Bicycle Ltd, 2000–15. Chm., London Chamber of Commerce and Industry, 1988–90; Pres., British Chambers of Commerce, 1992–94; Vice-Pres. and Hd of UK Delegn, Eurochambres SA, Brussels, 1994–2002. Member: Council, Worldaware, 1988–2000 (Trustee, 2000–02); Council of Management, Acad. of St Martin-in-the-Fields, 1990–93; Cttee, Royal Tournament, 1976–85; Vice-Pres., Olympia Internat. Showjumping, 1977–85; Hon. Mem., Royal Smithfield Club, 1985–. Trustee, Personal Support Unit, Royal Courts of Justice, 2001–12. Chm. of Govs, Oundle Sch., 2001–04. Mem. Ct of Assts, Grocers' Co., 1990– (Master, 1996). Pres., Essex Club, 2010–11. High Sheriff, Essex, 2006–07; DL Essex, 2008. *Recreations:* organic farming, design of gardens and buildings, tennis, shooting, ski-ing. *Address:* 52 Westbourne Terrace, W2 3UJ. *T:* (020) 7262 0514. *Club:* Travellers.

**STEWART-SMITH, Kirstie Louise;** *see* Hamilton, K. L.

**STEYN, Hon. Dame Karen (Margaret),** DBE 2019; Hon. Mrs Justice Steyn; a Judge of the High Court, Queen's Bench Division, since 2019; *b* Cape Town, 20 Oct. 1970; *d* of Baron Steyn, PC and of Jean Steyn; *m* 1997, Alexander Glassbrook; two *s*. *Educ:* Tonbridge Grammar Sch.; Univ. of Liverpool (BA Hons Hist.); City Univ. (CPE). Called to the Bar, Middle Temple, 1995; in practice as a barrister, specialising in public law, human rights, information law and public internat. law, 4–5 Gray's Inn Square, 1996–2000, 11 King's Bench Walk, 2000–19; QC 2014; a Dep. High Court Judge, 2016–19. *Recreations:* family, friends, forests and oceans. *Address:* Royal Courts of Justice, Strand, WC2A 2LL.

**STHEEMAN, Sir Robert (Alexander Talma),** Kt 2016; CB 2008; Chief Executive, United Kingdom Debt Management Office, since 2003; *b* 7 June 1959; *s* of Sape Talma Stheeman and Cécile Talma Stheeman (*née* Mendelssohn Bartholdy); *m* 1989, Elisabeth Haas; four *s*. *Educ:* Stowe Sch.; Chamber of Commerce, Hamburg (Bank Business Degree 1982). Vereins-und Westbank AG, Hamburg, 1979–85; Deutsche Bank AG, Frankfurt and London, 1986–2002 (Dir, 1991–2002). *Recreations:* family, music, walking. *Address:* United Kingdom Debt Management Office, Eastcheap Court, 11 Philpot Lane, EC3M 8UD. *T:* (020) 7862 6500, *Fax:* (020) 7862 6509. *E:* robert.stheeman@dmo.gov.uk.

**STIBBARD, Peter Jack,** CStat; Head, Labour Market Statistics Group, Central Statistical Office, 1995–96; international consultancies, 1996–99; *b* 15 May 1936; *s* of late Frederick Stibbard and Gladys Stibbard (*née* Daines); *m* 1964, Christine Fuller; two *d*. *Educ:* City of Norwich Grammar School; Hull Univ. (BSc Econ). Served RAF, 1954–56. Kodak Ltd, 1959–64; Thos Potterton Ltd, 1964–66; Greater London Council, 1966–68; Central Statistical Office, 1968–82; HM Treasury, 1982–85; Under Sec., Statistics Div. 2, DTI, 1985–89; Dir of Statistics, Dept of Employment, 1989–95. *Publications:* articles in official and trade jls. *Address:* 62 Allington Drive, Tonbridge, Kent TN10 4HH.

**STIBBON, Emma Louise,** RA 2013; artist; *b* Münster, Germany, 1 March 1962; *d* of Gen. Sir John James Stibbon, KCB, OBE and of Jean Ferguson Stibbon. *Educ:* Goldsmiths, Univ. of London (BA Fine Art 1984); Univ. of West of England (MA Res. Fine Art 2005). Sen. Lectr in Fine Art (pt-time), Univ. of Brighton, 2008–. Artist residencies include: Derek Hill Schol., British Sch. at Rome, 2010; Arctic Circle Expedn to Svalbard, 2013; Friends of Scott Polar Res. Inst./HMS Protector Artist Placement in Antarctica, 2013; Volcanoes National Park, Hawaii, 2016. Solo exhibitions include: Glacial Shift, Scott Polar Res. Inst., 2008; Stadtlandschaften, Stadtmuseum, Berlin, 2009; Now's the Time, upstairs berlin, 2010; Falls the Shadow, ROOM, London, 2011; Terra Infirma, Rabley Contemporary Drawing Centre, 2013; Ice Mirage, Galerie Bastian, Berlin, 2015; Ice Limit, Polar Mus., Cambridge, 2015; Volcano, 2017, Fire and Ice, 2019, Alan Cristea Gall., London. *Publications:* Fire and Ice, 2019. *Recreations:* walking, mountains, ruins.

**STICKLAND, Maj. Gen. Charles Richard,** CB 2019; OBE 2009; Assistant Chief of Defence Staff (Commitments), Ministry of Defence, since 2019; *b* Pembury, 16 May 1968; *s* of Michael John Stickland and Janet Catherine Stickland (*née* Allen); *m* 1993, Marysia Powys Maurice; three *s*. *Educ:* Sevenoaks Sch.; City Univ. (BSc Hons Systems and Mgt Sci.; MA Defence Studies). Joined RM, 1987; CO, 42 Commando, RM, 2008–09; Fleet Operational Policy, 2009–11; Chief Jt Force HQ, 2011–13; hcsc 2014; Comdr 3 Commando Bde, RM, 2014–15; Chief, Jt Force Ops, 2015–17; Comdt Gen., RM, 2018–19. *Recreations:* family, ski-ing, walking, dangerous DIY. *Club:* Naval and Military. *See also* V. L. Wallace.

**STIGLITZ, Prof. Joseph Eugene,** PhD; Professor of Economics, Columbia Business School, Columbia University, since 2001; Chief Economist and Senior Fellow, Roosevelt Institute; *b* 9 Feb. 1943; *m*; two *s* two *d*. *Educ:* Amherst Coll. (BA 1964); MIT (PhD 1967); Fitzwilliam Coll., Cambridge Univ. (MA 1970; Hon. Fellow, 2006). Professor of Economics: Yale Univ. 1970–74; Stanford Univ., 1974–76; Drummond Prof. of Political Economy, Oxford Univ. and All Souls Coll., 1976–79; Prof. of Economics, Princeton Univ., 1979–88; Prof. of Econs, Stanford Univ., 1992–2001. Mem., 1993–97, Chm., 1995–97, Council of Econ. Advrs to Pres. of USA; Chief Economist, World Bank, 1997–2000. Fellowships: Nat. Sci. Foundn, 1964–65; Fulbright, 1965–66; SSRC Faculty, 1969–70; Guggenheim, 1969–70; Oskar Morgenstern Distinguished Fellowship, Mathematica and Inst. for Advanced Study, Princeton, 1978–79. Consultant: Nat. Sci. Foundn, 1972–75; Ford Foundn Energy Policy Study, 1973; Dept of Labor (Pensions and Labor Turnover), 1974; Dept of Interior (Offshore Oil Leasing Programs), 1975; Federal Energy Admin (Intertemporal Biases in Market Allocation of Natural Resources), 1975–79; World Bank (Cost Benefit Analysis; Urban Rural Migration; Natural Resources, 1975–; Electric Power Res. Inst., 1976–; OECD; Office of Fair Trading; Treasury (Office of Tax Analysis), 1980; US AID (commodity price stabilization), 1977; Inter-American Development Bank; Bell Laboratories; Bell Communications Research; State of Alaska; Seneca Indian Nation. Chm., Brooks World Poverty Inst., Univ. of Manchester, 2006. Internat. Prize, Academia Lincei, 1988; Union des Assurances de Paris Scientific Prize, 1989; Rechtenwald Prize, 1999. Gen. Editor, Econometric Soc. Reprint Series; Associate Editor: Jl of Economic Theory, 1968–73; American Economic Rev., 1972–75; Jl of Economic Perspectives, 1988–93; Co-editor, Jl of Public Economics, 1968–83; American Editor, Rev. of Economic Studies, 1968–76; Editorial Bd, World Bank Economic Review, The Geneva Papers, Revista de Econometrica, Assicurazioni. Vice-Pres., American Econ. Assoc., 1985. Fellow: Econometric Soc., 1972 (Sec./Treasurer, 1972–75); Amer. Acad. of Arts and Scis; Inst. for Policy Reform, 1990–; American Philosophical Assoc.; NAS; Senior Fellow: Hoover Instn, 1988–93; Brookings Instn, Washington, 2000–01. Corresp. FBA 1993; Foreign Mem., Royal Soc., 2009. Hon. MA Yale, 1970; Hon. DHL Amherst, 1974; Hon. Dr: Pomona Coll.; New Sch.; Northwestern; Bard Coll.; Toronto; Naumur; Leuven; Ben Gurion; Barcelona; Bucharest; Lisbon Tech.; Charles Univ., Prague. John Bates Clark Medal, Amer. Econ. Assoc.; (jtly) Nobel Prize for Economics, 2001; Sydney Peace Prize, 2018. *Publications:* (ed) Collected Scientific Papers of P. A. Samuelson, 1965; (ed with H. Uzawa) Readings in Modern Theory of Economic Growth, 1969; (with A. B. Atkinson) Lectures in Public Finance, 1980; (with D. Newbery) The Economic Impact of Price Stabilization, 1980; Economics of the Public Sector, 1986; Globalization and its Discontents, 2002, new edn as Globalization and its Discontents Revisited: anti-globalization in the era of Trump, 2017; Making Globalization Work, 2006; (with L. Bilmes) The Three Trillion Dollar War: the true cost of the Iraq conflict, 2008; Freefall: free markets and the sinking of the global economy, 2010; Creating a Learning Society: a new approach to growth, development and social progress, 2014; The Great Divide: unequal societies and what we can do about them, 2015; The Euro: and its threat to the future of Europe, 2016; People, Power and Profits: progressive capitalism for an age of discontent, 2019; contribs to economics of growth, development, natural resources, information, uncertainty, imperfect competition, corporate finance and public finance in Amer. Econ. Rev., Qly Jl of Econs, Jl of Pol Econ., Econometrica, Internat. Econ. Rev., Econ. Jl, Rev. of Econ. Studies, Jl of Public Econs, Jl of Econ. Theory, Oxford Econ. Papers. *Address:* Room 814, Uris Hall, Columbia Business School, New York, NY 10027, USA. *T:* (212) 8540671.

**STIHLER, Catherine Dalling,** OBE 2019; Chief Executive Officer, Open Knowledge Foundation (formerly Open Knowledge International), since 2019; *b* 30 July 1973; *d* of Gordon McLeish Taylor and Catherine Doreen Taylor; *m* 2000, David Stihler; two *s*. *Educ:* Coltness High Sch., Wishaw; Univ. of St Andrews (MA Hons Geography and Internat. Relns 1996; MLitt Internat. Security Studies 1998). Pres., Univ. of St Andrews Students' Assoc., 1994–95; Open Univ. (MBA with Merit 2013). Young Labour Representative: Exec. Cttee, SLP, 1993–95; Lab Party NEC, 1995–97; Women's Rep. and Local Orgns Rep., SLP Exec., 1997–99. Researcher and facilitator to Anne Begg, MP, 1997–99.

Contested (Lab) Angus, 1997. MEP (Lab) Scotland, 1999–Jan. 2019. European Parliament Parliamentary Labour Group: health spokesperson, 1999–2004; spokesperson on fisheries and regl develt; Dep. Leader, 2004–06; Whip, 2014–18. European Parliament: Pres., Health Intergroup, 2000–02; Mem., Internal Market and Consumer Protection Cttee, 2009–19 (Vice-Chm., 2014–19); Substitute, Econ. and Monetary Affairs Cttee, 2009–19; Founder and Chm., All Party Library Gp, 2014–19; MEP Ed., Parliament mag., 2002–11. Rector, Univ. of St Andrews, 2014–17. Hon. DLitt St Andrews, 2018. *Publications:* (contrib.) Women and the Military, 2000. *Recreations:* running marathons, yoga, swimming, music, film, studying languages. *Address:* Open Knowledge Foundation, 86–90 Paul Street, EC2A 4NE.

**STILGOE, Sir Richard (Henry Simpson),** Kt 2012; OBE 1998; DL; songwriter, lyricist, entertainer and broadcaster, since 1962; *b* 28 March 1943; *s* of late John Henry Tweedie Stilgoe and Joan Lucy Strutt Stilgoe; *m* 1st, 1964, Elizabeth Caroline Gross; one *s* one *d*; 2nd, 1975, Annabel Margaret Hunt (OBE 2016); two *s* one *d*. *Educ:* Liverpool Coll.; Monkton Combe Sch.; Clare Coll., Cambridge (choral exhibnr). One-man show worldwide, incl. Windsor Castle, 1982 and British Embassy, Washington, 1986; Two-man show with Peter Skellern, 1985–2002. Author and composer: Bodywork, 1987; Brilliant the Dinosaur, 1991; Orpheus the Mythical, 2010, new version 2018; librettist: Road Rage, Garsington Opera, 2013; The Freedom Game, 2015. Word-processor for Andrew Lloyd Webber on Cats, Starlight Express and Phantom of the Opera. Stilgoe Saturday Concerts, RFH, 1999–2005. Founder and Trustee, Orpheus Centre (music and disabled people), 1985–; Founder and Chm., Alchemy Foundn, 1985–; Pres., Surrey Care Trust, 1986–2000; Trustee, Nat. Foundn for Youth Music, 1999–2012 (Chm., 2007–12). FRSA 1992. Hon. ARAM 2003; Hon. RCM 2012. Hon. Fellow, Liverpool John Moores Univ., 2008. Hon. DLitt: Greenwich, 1999; Southampton, 2005; DUniv Surrey, 2014. Monaco Radio Prize, 1984, 1991, 1996; NY Radio Fest. Gold Award, 1989; Prix Italia, 1991. DL, 1996, High Sheriff, 1998, Surrey. *Publications:* The Richard Stilgoe Letters, 1981; Brilliant The Dinosaur, 1994. *Recreations:* sailing, cricket, architecture, building, music, demolition, family. *Address:* c/o The Orpheus Centre, Trevereux Manor, Limpsfield Chart, Oxted, Surrey RH8 0TL. *Clubs:* MCC, Lord's Taverners (Pres., 2003); Surrey CC (Pres., 2005).

**STILITZ, Daniel Malachi;** QC 2010; barrister; *b* London, 1 Aug. 1968; *s* of Ivor Bernard Stilitz and Linda Stilitz; *m* 1996, Ruth Walker (marr. diss. 2017); two *s* one *d*; *m* 2019, Emma Terry. *Educ:* William Ellis Sch.; New Coll., Oxford (BA Hons PPE 1990); City Univ. (DipLaw 1991; MA 1992). Called to the Bar, Lincoln's Inn, 1992; in practice as barrister, specialising in employment, commercial and public law. Mediator, CEDR, 1997. *Recreations:* photography, music, reading. *Address:* 11KBW, 11 King's Bench Walk, Temple, EC4Y 7EQ. *T:* (020) 7632 8500, *Fax:* (020) 7583 9123. *E:* daniel.stilitz@11kbw.com.

**STILLMAN, Dr Bruce William,** AO 1999; FRS 1993; Chief Executive Officer, since 2000, President, since 2003, Cold Spring Harbor Laboratory, New York (Director, 1994–2003); *b* Melbourne, Australia, 16 Oct. 1953; *s* of Graham Leslie Stillman and Jessie May (*née* England); *m* 1981, Grace Angela Begley; one *s* one *d*. *Educ:* Glen Waverley High Sch.; Sydney Boys' High Sch.; Univ. of Sydney (BSc Hons); ANU (PhD). Cold Spring Harbor Laboratory, New York: Damon Runyon-Walter Winchell Postdoctoral Res. Fellow, 1979–80; Staff Investigator, 1981–82; Sen. Staff Investigator, 1983–85; Sen. Scientist, 1985–90; Asst Dir, 1990–93; Adjunct Prof. of Microbiology, SUNY, 1982–. Damon Runyon-Walter Winchell Cancer Fund Fellow, 1979–80; Rita Allen Foundn Scholar, 1982–87; Charter Fellow, Molecular Medicine Soc., 1995. Lectures: Harvey Soc., 1993; Nieuwland, Univ. of Notre Dame, 1993; Doty, Harvard Univ., 1998. For. Associate, NAS, USA, 2000; Fellow, Amer. Acad. of Microbiol., 2000. Hon. DHL Hofstra, 2001; Hon. DSc NY Inst. Tech. Commonwealth Postgrad. Award, 1976–80; Merit Award, NIH, 1986; (jtly) Canada Gairdner Internat. Award, 2019. *Publications:* numerous scientific pubns. *Address:* Cold Spring Harbor Laboratory, One Bungtown Road, Cold Spring Harbor, NY 11724, USA. *T:* (516) 3678383.

**STIMSON, Prof. Gerald Vivian,** PhD; Director, Knowledge-Action-Change, since 2010; *b* 10 April 1945; *s* of late Geoffrey Edward Vivian Stimson and Maud Ellen Stimson; *m* 1st, 1971, Carol Anne Fowler (marr. diss. 1992, she *d* 1997); two *s*; 2nd, 1993, Elizabeth Louise Vivian Tacey; one *s*. *Educ:* City of London Sch.; London Sch. of Econs (BSc 1966; MSc 1967); Inst. of Psychiatry, Univ. of London (PhD 1971). Res. worker, Addiction Res. Unit, Inst. of Psychiatry, Univ. of London, 1967–71; Res. Fellow, Med. Sociology Res. Centre, UC of Swansea, 1971–75; London University: Lectr, then Sen. Lectr, Addiction Res. Unit, Inst. Psychiatry, 1975–78; Goldsmiths' College: Sen. Lectr in Sociology, 1978–89; Head, Sociology Dept, 1980–83; Dir, Monitoring Res. Gp, Sociology Dept, 1987–89; Imperial College: Dir, Centre for Res. on Drugs and Health Behaviour, 1990–2004; Prof. of Sociology of Health Behaviour, 1991–2004, now Emeritus; Hd, Dept of Social Science and Medicine, 1997–2004. Exec. Dir, Internat. Harm Reduction Assoc., 2004–10; Founder and Prog. Dir, Global Forum on Nicotine, 2014– (Organiser, City Health Internat. confs 2012–). Fulbright Schol., NY Univ., 1983; Vis. Prof., Univ. of W London (formerly Thames Valley Univ.), 1995–2000; Hon. Prof., LSHTM, 2006–. Advisory Council on Misuse of Drugs: Mem., 1984–99; Mem., Wkg Gp on AIDS and Drug Misuse, 1987–92; Chm., Stats Inf. and Res. Cttee, 1990–99; Member: Council, Inst. for Study of Drug Dependence, 1985–90 (Vice-Chm., 1987); Scientific Cttee, Eur. Monitoring Centre for Drugs and Drug Addiction, 1994–97; Founder Mem., UK Harm Reduction Alliance, 2001 (Chm., 2001–02). Chm., New Nicotine Alliance UK, 2015–18. Pres., Action on Hepatitis C, 2000–04. Member, Editorial Board: Addiction, 1982–2006; Addiction Res., 1991–2000; AIDS, 1993–96; Ed., Internat. Jl Drug Policy, 2000–16; Founder, Sociology of Health and Illness. Trustee, AIDS Educnl and Res. Trust, 1995–2003. Internat. Rolleston Award, Harm Reduction Internat., 2010. *Publications:* Heroin and Behaviour: diversity among addicts attending London clinics, 1973; (with B. Webb) Going to See the Doctor: the consultation process in general practice, 1975; (with E. Oppenheimer) Heroin Addiction: treatment and control in Britain, 1982; (ed jtly) AIDS and Drug Misuse: the challenge for policy and practice in the 1990s, 1990; (ed jtly) Drug Injecting and HIV Infection: global issues and local responses, 1998; (ed jtly) Drug Use in London, 1998; (ed jtly) Drugs and the Future: brain science, addiction and society, 2006; (ed) Drinking in Context: patterns, interventions and partnerships, 2006; over 250 academic pubns. *Recreations:* walking, the countryside, travel, putting the 'public' and 'health' back into Public Health. *Club:* Athenæum.

**STIMSON, Robert Frederick,** CBE 1992; Governor and Commander-in-Chief of St Helena and its Dependencies, 1988–91; *b* 16 May 1939; *s* of Frederick Henry Stimson and Gladys Alma Stimson (*née* Joel); *m* 1st, 1961, Margaret Faith Kerry (*d* 2004); two *s* one *d*; 2nd, 2012, Penn Pusao; one *s*. *Educ:* Rendcomb Coll.; Queen Mary Coll., London (BSc First Cl. Hons; MSc (by thesis) mathematical physics). HM Diplomatic Service: FO, 1966–67; Saigon, 1967–68; Singapore, 1968–70; Cabinet Office, 1970–73; Mexico City, 1973–75; FCO, 1975–80; Counsellor, East Berlin, 1980–81; Head of Home Inspectorate, 1982–83; Counsellor and Hd of Chancery, Dublin, 1984–87. Order of Aztec Eagle, Mexico, 1975. *Publications:* contrib. Jl Physics and Chemistry of Solids.

**STINCHCOMBE, Paul David;** QC 2011; barrister; *b* 25 April 1962; *s* of Lionel Walter Stinchcombe and Pauline Sylvia Ann (*née* Hawkins); *m* 1990, Suzanne Jean Gardiner; two *s* one *d*. *Educ:* Royal Grammar Sch., High Wycombe; Trinity Coll., Cambridge (Sen. Schol.; BA Law double 1st cl. Hons 1983); Harvard Law Sch. (Frank Knox Fellow; LLM 1984). Called to the Bar, Lincoln's Inn, 1985; in practice at the Bar, 1985–97 and 2005–. Vis. Fellow, Centre of Public Law, Cambridge Univ., 2005–06. Mem. (Lab), Camden Council, 1990–94 (Chm., Labour Gp, 1992–94). MP (Lab) Wellingborough, 1997–2005; contested (Lab) same seat, 2005. *Recreations:* football, cricket, golf. *Address:* 39 Essex Chambers, 81 Chancery Lane, WC2A 1DD.

**STING;** *see* Sumner, G. M.

**STIPRAIS, Eduards;** Head, European Union Delegation to Republic of Uzbekistan, since 2016; *b* Riga, 19 Feb. 1969; *s* of Andreas Stiprais and Ludmila Stipra; *m* 2004, Zanda Grauze. *Educ:* Univ. of Latvia (Dip. Econs 1993). Desk Officer, Min. of Foreign Trade, Latvia, 1992–93; Ministry of Foreign Affairs: Sen. Desk Officer, 1993; Hd, EC/EFTA Relns Div., 1993–94; Dep. Dir, Dept of Internat. Econ. Relns, 1994–95; Second Sec., 1995, First Sec., 1995–98, Mission of Latvia to EU, Brussels; Hd, Task Force for preparations of EU accession negotiations, 1998–99, Secretariat of Delegn for EU accession negotiations, 1999–2003; Ambassador: and Dep. Hd of Mission of Latvia to EU, Brussels, 2003–04; and Dep. Perm. Rep. of Latvia to EU, 2004; and Perm. Rep. of Latvia to EU, 2004–07; Hd, State President's Chancellery, 2007–08; Ambassador and Hd of Directorate for Bilateral Relns, 2009; Ambassador to Court of St James's, 2009–13; Under-Sec. of State - Pol Dir, Min. of Foreign Affairs, Latvia, 2013–16. Officer, Order of Three Stars (Latvia), 2004; Chevalier, Order of Merit (Ukraine), 2009. *Recreations:* travelling, walking, basketball, reading. *E:* eduards.stiprais@mfa.gov.lv. *Clubs:* Travellers; Circle Royal Gaulois (Brussels).

**STIRLING, Alison Nancy;** Sheriff of Lothian and Borders at Edinburgh, since 2017; *b* Stirling, 14 May 1965; *d* of Robert Louis Stirling and Dorothy Jean Stirling; *m* (marr. diss.); one *s*. *Educ:* Dollar Acad.; Univ. of Edinburgh (MA Hons 1987; LLB 1992). Admitted to Faculty of Advocates, 1997; Sheriff (pt-time), 2011–14; Sheriff of Grampian, Highlands and Islands at Aberdeen, 2014–17. Founding Sheriff, Aberdeen Problem Solving Court, 2015–. Dep. Ed., Session Cases, 2001–15. *Publications:* (contrib.) Green's Litigation Styles, 2001–; (contrib.) Litigation Styles: family actions and adoption, 2010. *Recreations:* foreign travel, Turkish speaker, swimming, cycling. *Address:* Sheriff Court House, 27 Chambers Street, Edinburgh EH1 1LB.

**STIRLING, Prof. Andrew Charles,** DPhil; FAcSS; Professor of Science and Technology Policy, since 2006, and Co-Director, ESRC Centre on Social, Technological and Environmental Pathways to Sustainability, since 2006, University of Sussex; *b* Portsmouth, 3 March 1961; *s* of Charles and Rosemary Stirling; partner, Vanessa Topsy Jewell; one *s* one *d*. *Educ:* Westfield Comprehensive Sch., Yeovil; Yeovil Tertiary Coll.; Univ. of Edinburgh (MA Hons Archaeol. and Social Anthropol. 1984); Univ. of Sussex (DPhil Sci. and Technol. Policy 1995). Field archaeologist, Univ. of Edinburgh, 1984; Greenpeace International: campaigner, 1985–87; Campaign Dir, 1987–90; Mem. Bd, 1994–98; University of Sussex: Res. Fellow, 1993–2000; Sen. Lectr and Sen. Fellow, 2000–06; Res. Dir, SPRU - sci. and technol. policy res., 2007–13. Mem., Energy Policy Consultative Cttee, 1998–2001, Expert Gp on Sci. and Governance, 2005–08, EU Commn; Member: UK Adv. Cttee on Toxic Substances, 1999–2004; UK Genetic Modification Sci. Rev. Panel, 2002–04; Sci. Adv. Council, DEFRA, 2004–11; Sciencewise Steering Cttee, DIUS, later BIS, then BEIS, 2008–; Steering Gp on Neurosci. and Policy, Royal Soc., 2010–; Working Gp on Emerging Biotechnologies, Nuffield Council on Bioethics, 2010–; Res. Cttee, ESRC, 2010–. Mem. Bd, Greenpeace UK Ltd, 2010–. Member, Editorial Board: Jl Risk Res., 1999–; Technol. Analysis and Strategic Mgt, 2007–; Minerva, 2007–; Nature EMBO Reports, 2009–; Jl Envmtl and Societal Transitions, 2010–. *Publications:* On Science and Precaution in the Management of Technological Risk, 1999; (ed jtly) The Precautionary Principle in the Twentieth Century: late lessons from early warnings, 2002; (ed jtly) Precautionary Risk Appraisal and Management: an orientation for meeting the precautionary principle in the European Union, 2009; (jtly) Dynamic Sustainabilities: technology, environment, social justice, 2010; contribs to jls incl. Energy Policy, Envmt and Planning C, Nature EMBO Reports, Futures, Ecol. and Society, Global Envmtl Change, Annals of NY Acad. Scis, Res. Policy, Royal Soc. Interface, Sci., Technol. and Human Values, Sustainable Develt, Yearbook of Eur. Envmtl Law. *Recreations:* backpacking/ cycling, field archaeology, history, mythology, music, politics. *Address:* SPRU - science and technology policy research, Jubilee Building, University of Sussex, Brighton, E Sussex BN1 9SL. *T:* (01273) 877118, *Fax:* (01273) 685865. *E:* a.c.stirling@sussex.ac.uk.

**STIRLING, Sir Angus (Duncan Æneas),** Kt 1994; Director-General, National Trust, 1983–95 (Deputy Director-General, 1979–83); *b* 10 Dec. 1933; *s* of late Duncan Alexander Stirling and Lady Marjorie Murray, *e d* of 8th Earl of Dunmore, VC, DSO, MVO; *m* 1959, Armyne Morar Helen Schofield, *e d* of late W. G. B. Schofield and Hon. Armyne Astley, *d* of 21st Baron Hastings; one *s* two *d*. *Educ:* Eton Coll.; Trinity Coll., Cambridge; London Univ. (Extra Mural) (Dip. History of Art). Christie, Manson and Woods Ltd, 1954–57; Lazard Bros and Co. Ltd, 1957–66; Asst Dir, Paul Mellon Foundn for British Art, 1966–69 (Jt Dir, 1969–70); Dep. Sec.-General, Arts Council of GB, 1971–79. Sen. Policy Advr, Nat. Heritage Meml Fund, 1996–97; Chairman: Greenwich Foundn for RNC, 1996–2003; JNCC, 1997–2002. Mem., Govt Task Force on Tourism and the Envmt, 1991. Mem. Bd, Royal Opera House, Covent Garden, 1979–96 (Chm., 1991–96); Mem., Council, Friends of Covent Garden, 1981–2011 (Chm., 1981–91); Dep. Chm., Royal Ballet Bd, 1988–91; a Gov., Royal Ballet, 1988–96; Member: Crafts Council, 1980–85; Council of Management, Byam Shaw Sch. of Art, 1965–89; Bd of Trustees, Courtauld Inst. of Art, 1981–83, 2002–14; Adv. Council, London Symphony Orchestra, 1979–; Bd of Governors, Live Music Now, 1982–89; Bd of Trustees, The Theatres Trust, 1983–91; Bd of Trustees, Heritage of London Trust, 1983–95; Tourism Cttee, ICOMOS UK, 1993–2003; Council, RSCM, 1996–98; Fabric Adv. Cttee, Wells Cathedral, 2001–15. Chm., Adv. Panel for Local Heritage Initiative, Countryside Commn, 1998–99; Chm., Policy Cttee, 1996–2001, Pres., Som Br., 2002–07, CPRE; Mem. Adv. Cttee, Stowe Landscape Gardens, 1996–2018; Trustee: Stowe House Preservation Trust, 1998–2012; Samuel Courtauld Trust (formerly Home House (Courtauld Collection)), 1983–2012; World Monuments Fund in Britain, 1996–2008. President: Friends of Holland Park, 2003–; NADFAS Kensington and Chelsea, 2008–15. Vice Patron, Almshouses Assoc., 2000–09 (Chm., Adv. Panel, Patron's Award, 2001–03). Member, Board of Governors: Gresham Sch., 1999–2007; City and Guilds Art Sch., 2003–11. CCMI. Hon. FTCL 2004. Mem., Court, Fishmongers' Co., 1991– (Prime Warden, 2004–05). Chm., Fisheries Cttee, 2007–14). Hon. Fellow, Courtauld Inst. of Art, 2015. Hon. DLitt: Leicester, 1995; Greenwich, 2002. *Recreations:* painting, music, travel, walking. *Address:* 30 Upper Addison Gardens, W14 8AJ. *Clubs:* Garrick, Brooks's, Beefsteak, Grillions.

**STIRLING, Prof. Charles James Matthew,** FRS 1986; CChem, FRSC; Professor of Organic Chemistry, University of Sheffield, 1990–98, now Emeritus; *b* 8 Dec. 1930; *s* of Brig. Alexander Dickson Stirling, DSO, MB, ChB, DPH, RAMC, and Isobel Millicent Stirling, MA, DipPsych; *m* 1956, Eileen Gibson Powell, BA, MEd (*d* 2012), *yr d* of William

Leslie and Elsie May Powell; two d (and one d decd). *Educ:* Edinburgh Acad.; Univ. of St Andrews (Harkness Exhibn; BSc; Biochem. Medal 1951); Univ. of London (PhD, DSc). FRSC, CChem 1967. Civil Service Jun. Res. Fellowship, Porton, 1955, Sen. Fellowship, 1956; ICI Fellowship, Univ. of Edinburgh, 1957; Lectr, QUB, 1959; Reader in Org. Chem., KCL, 1965; University of Wales, Bangor: Prof. of Organic Chemistry, 1969–81; Dean of Faculty of Science, 1977–79; Hd of Dept of Chemistry, 1981–90; Sheffield University: Hd, Dept of Chemistry, 1991–94; Dir, Engrg and Physical Scis Div., Grad. Sch., 1994–97; Public Orator, 1995–. Visiting Professor: Hebrew Univ. of Jerusalem, 1981; ANU, Canberra, 1999; Akademia Jan Dlugosz, Czestochowa, 2013. Royal Instn Christmas Lects, BBC TV, 1992. Mem., IUPAC Commn on Physical Organic Chemistry, 1992–95. Mem., Perkin Council, RSC, 1971–93 (Vice-Pres., 1985–88 and 1991–93, Pres., 1989–91); Pres., Section B (Chemistry), BAAS, 1990; Pres., Yorks and Humberside Sect., ASE, 1993–95. Founding FLSW 2010. Hon. Mem., Società Chimica Italiana, 2002. Hon. Fellow, Univ. of Wales, Bangor, 2004. Hon. DSc: St Andrews, 1994; Aix-Marseille, 1999; Sheffield, 2007. Award for Organic Reaction Mechanisms, RSC, 1988; Millennium Commn Award, 1999. *Publications:* Radicals in Organic Chemistry, 1965; (ed) Organic Sulphur Chemistry, 1975; (ed) The Chemistry of the Sulphonium Group, 1981; (ed) The Chemistry of Sulphones and Sulphoxides, 1988; numerous res. papers mainly in Jls of RSC. *Recreations:* choral music, the collection of chiral objects, the avoidance of expense. *Address:* Department of Chemistry, University of Sheffield, Sheffield S3 7HF. *T:* (0114) 222 9453; 114 Westbourne Road, Sheffield S10 2QT.

**STIRLING of Garden, Col Sir James,** KCVO 2006; CBE 1987; TD; FRICS; Lord-Lieutenant of Stirling and Falkirk, 1983–2005; *b* 8 Sept. 1930; *s* of Col Archibald Stirling of Garden, OBE; *m* 1958, Fiona Janetta Sophia Wood Parker; two *s* two *d*. *Educ:* Rugby; Trinity Coll., Cambridge (BA; Dip. Estate Mgt). FRICS 1966. Commnd Argyll and Sutherland Highlanders, 1950; served in Korea, wounded; transf. 7th Bn TA, comd 1965–67, 3rd Bn, 1967–68. Chartered Surveyor in private practice. Partner, K. Ryden and Partners, Chartered Surveyors, 1962–89. Director: Local Bd, Scotland and N Ireland, Woolwich Building Soc., 1973–97; Scottish Widows and Life Insurance Fund, 1975–96. Hon. Sheriff, Stirling, 1998. DL 1970, Vice-Lieutenant 1979–83, Stirling. Hon. Guild Brother, Stirling Guildry, 1996. Chm., Highland TAVR Assoc., 1982–87 (Pres., 1992–97). Hon. Col, 3/51st Highland Volunteers, TA, 1979–86. DUniv Stirling, 2004. GCStJ 2005 (KStJ 1987; Prior, Order of St John, Scotland, 1995–2009). *Address:* Dambrae, Buchlyvie, Stirlingshire FK8 3NR. *T:* (01360) 850225. *Club:* New (Edinburgh).

**STIRLING, John Fullarton;** JP; Librarian, University of Exeter, 1972–94; *b* 12 April 1931; *s* of Reginald Stirling and Jeanette Sybil (*née* Fullarton); *m* 1960, Sheila Mary Fane; two *d*. *Educ:* Waterloo Grammar Sch.; Univ. of Liverpool (BA 1st Cl. Hons 1953; MA 1962). Asst, Liverpool Public Libraries, 1953–56; Asst Librarian, UCL, 1956–62; Sub-librarian, 1962–64, Dep. Librarian, 1964–66, Univ. of York; Librarian, Univ. of Stirling, 1966–71; Librarian designate, Univ. of Exeter, 1971–72. Member: various cttees, SCONUL, 1977–; UGC Working Gp on Liby Automation, 1986; British Liby Cttee for Bibliographic Services, 1987. JP Exeter, 1976. *Publications:* (ed) University Librarianship, 1981; contrib. various professional jls. *Recreations:* woodcarving, puppetry. *Address:* c/o Devon and Exeter Institution, 7 Cathedral Close EX1 1EZ. *T:* (01392) 274727. *Club:* Devon and Exeter Institution (Chm., 2001–04) (Exeter).

**STIRLING-HAMILTON, Sir Malcolm William Bruce,** 14th Bt *cr* 1673 (NS), of Preston, Haddingtonshire; *b* 6 Aug. 1979; *s* of Sir Bruce Stirling-Hamilton, 13th Bt and of Stephanie (who *m* 1990, Anthony Tinsley), *d* of Dr William Campbell, LRCP, LRCS; *S* father, 1989. *Educ:* Stowe. *Heir: cousin* Rev. Andrew Robert Hamilton [*b* 5 Sept. 1937; *m* 1972, Josephine Mary, *d* of Reginald Sargant].

**STIRRAT, Canon Prof. Gordon Macmillan,** MA, MD; FRCOG; Research Fellow, Centre for Ethics in Medicine, 2011–14 (Senior Research Fellow, 2000–10); Professor of Obstetrics and Gynaecology, University of Bristol, 1982–2000, now Emeritus; *b* 12 March 1940; *s* of Alexander and Caroline Mary Stirrat; *m* 1965, Janeen Mary (*née* Brown); three *d*. *Educ:* Hutchesons' Boys' Grammar Sch., Glasgow; Glasgow Univ. (MB, ChB); MA Oxon, MD London. FRCOG 1981. Jun. hosp. doctor appts, Glasgow and environs, and London, 1964–71; Lectr, St Mary's Hosp. Med. Sch., London, 1971–75; Clinical Reader, Univ. of Oxford, 1975–81; Dean, Faculty of Medicine, 1990–93, Pro-Vice-Chancellor, 1993–97, Univ. of Bristol. Dep. Chm., Bristol and Dist HA, 1991–96. Member: Acad. of Experts, 1996–2004 (Fellow, 2004–09); Expert Witness Inst., 1997–2006. Chm., House of Laity, Bristol Dio., 2003–12. Lay Canon, Bristol Cathedral, 2008–10, now Emeritus. Hon. Vice-Pres., IME, 2012–. *Publications:* Legalised Abortion: the continuing dilemma, 1979; Obstetrics Pocket Consultant, 1981, 2nd edn 1986; Aids to Reproductive Biology, 1982; (jtly) You and Your Baby—a Mother's Guide to Health, 1982; Aids to Obstetrics and Gynaecology, 1983, 4th edn 1996; (jtly) The Immune System in Disease, 1992; (jtly) Handbook of Obstetric Management, 1996; (jtly) Notes on Obstetrics and Gynaecology, 2002; (jtly) Medical Ethics and Law for Doctors of Tomorrow, 2010. *Recreations:* photography, walking. *Address:* Malpas Lodge, 24 Henbury Road, Westbury-on-Trym, Bristol BS9 3HJ. *T:* (0117) 950 5310.

**STIRRUP,** family name of **Baron Stirrup**.

**STIRRUP, Baron** *cr* 2011 (Life Peer), of Marylebone in the City of Westminster; **Marshal of the Royal Air Force Graham Eric, (Jock), Stirrup,** KG 2013; GCB 2005 (KCB 2002; CB 2000); AFC 1983; FRAeS; Chief of the Defence Staff, 2006–10; Air Aide-de-Camp to the Queen, since 2003; *b* 4 Dec. 1949; *s* of William Hamilton Stirrup and Jacqueline Brenda Stirrup (*née* Coulson); *m* 1976, Mary Alexandra Elliott; one *s*. *Educ:* Merchant Taylors' Sch., Northwood; Royal Air Force Coll., Cranwell. Qualified Flying Instr, 1971–73; Loan Service, Sultan of Oman's Air Force, 1973–75; Fighter Reconnaissance Pilot, 1976–78; Exchange Pilot, USAF, 1978–81; Flt Comdr, 1982–84; OC No II (Army Co-operation) Sqn, 1985–87; PSO to CAS, 1987–90; OC RAF Marham, 1990–92; rcds, 1993; Dir, Air Force Plans and Progs, MoD, 1994–97; AOC No 1 Gp, 1997–98; ACAS, 1998–2000; Dep. C-in-C, Strike Comd, Comdr NATO Combined Air Ops Centre 9, and Dir European Air Gp, 2000–02; Dep. Chief of Defence Staff (Equipment Capability), MoD, 2002–03; Chief of Air Staff, MoD, 2003–06. FCMI (FIMgt 1983); FRAeS 1991. Hon. DSc Cranfield, 2005. *Recreations:* golf, music, theatre, history. *Address:* House of Lords, SW1A 0PW. *Clubs:* Royal Air Force, Beefsteak.

**STIRTON, Prof. Charles Howard,** PhD; FLS; botanist, mentor, writer; *b* 25 Nov. 1946; *s* of late Charles Aubrey and Elizabeth Maud Stirton; *m* 1979, Jana Žantovská (*d* 2015); one *d*. *Educ:* Univ. of Natal (BSc, BSc Hons, MSc); Univ. of Cape Town (PhD 1989). Botanist, Botanical Res. Inst., Pretoria, 1975–82; S African Liaison Botanist, 1979–82, B. A. Krukoff Botanist for Neotropical Legumes, 1982–87, Royal Botanic Gardens, Kew; Associate Prof., Univ. of Natal, Pietermaritzburg, 1988–90; self-employed, 1990; economic botanist, 1990–92, Dep. Dir, and Dir, Sci. and Horticulture, 1992–96, Royal Botanic Gardens, Kew; Founding Dir, Nat. Botanic Gdn of Wales, 1996–2002. Chm., Contexua, 2002–05. Dir, St Vincent Capital Ltd, 2010–; Founding Dir, Matara Gdns of Wellbeing, 2012–17. Vis. Prof., Univ. of Reading, 1993–96; Hon. Prof., Univ. of Wales, 1997–2002; Hon. Res. Associate, Univ. of Cape Town, 2008–. Trustee, Gateway Gardens Trust, 2003–10. Mentor, Mellon Foundn, 2007–09. Founding Trustee, Ourobos Res. and Educn Trust;

Special Advr, Overberg Lowlands Conservation Trust, 2013– (Founding Trustee, 2012–13). FLS 1975. Hon. DSc Glamorgan, 2001. *Publications:* (ed) Plant Invaders: beautiful but dangerous, 1978; (ed with J. Zarucchi) Advances in Legume Biology, 1990; (ed) Advances in Legume Systematics 3, 1987; (ed) The Changing World of Weeds, 1995; contrib. numerous scientific papers. *Recreations:* gardening, postcards, photography, philately, postal history, writing, books, travelling, cinema. *E:* chstirton@gmail.com. *W:* http://chstirton.wordpress.com.

**STOATE, Dr Howard Geoffrey Alvan,** FRCGP; general medical practitioner, since 1982, and Senior Partner, since 2014, Albion Surgery, Bexleyheath; *b* 14 April 1954; *s* of Alvan Stoate and Maisie Stoate (*née* Russell); *m* 1979, Deborah Jane Dunkerley; two *s*. *Educ:* Kingston Grammar Sch.; King's Coll., London (MB BS 1977; MSc 1989). DRCOG 1981; FRCGP 1994. GP training, Joyce Green Hosp., Dartford, 1978–81; GP Tutor, Queen Mary's Hosp., Sidcup, 1989–2006; Chm., Local Res. Ethics Cttee, Bexley HA, 1995–97; Vice-Chm., Regl Graduate Educn Bd, South Thames, 1997–99; Chm., Clinical Cabinet, Bexley PCT, then NHS Bexley CCG, 2011–15. Mem. (Lab) Dartford BC, 1990–99 (Chm., Finance and Corporate Business Cttee, 1996–99); Vice Pres., Dartford Racial Equality Council. MP (Lab) Dartford, 1997–2010. PPS to Minister of State for Crime Reduction, Policy and Community Safety, Home Office, 2001–03; PPS to Minister for the Arts, 2003–05. Mem., Health Select Cttee, 1997–2001 and 2005–10; Co-Chairman: All Party Parly Gp on Primary Care and Public Health, 1998–2010; All Party Parly Gp on Obesity, 2002–10; Chairman: All Party Pharmacy Gp, 2000–10; All Party Gp on Men's Health, 2001–10. Mem. Assembly, Univ. of Greenwich, 1997–. *Recreations:* running, sailing, travelling, reading, car building.

**STOATE, Jane Elizabeth;** *see* Davidson, J. E.

**STOBART, John;** a District Judge (Magistrates' Courts), 2004–15; *b* 6 May 1948; *s* of Joe and Jean Stobart; *m* 2001, Tracey Kirwin. *Educ:* Birmingham Univ. (LLB Hons 1971); Inns of Court Sch. of Law. Called to the Bar, Gray's Inn, 1974; in practice as barrister, specialising in crime, 1974–2004; a Dep. Dist Judge, 1999–2004. *Recreations:* golf, ski-ing, sailing, drinking and eating.

**STOCK, Francine Elizabeth;** writer and broadcaster; *b* 14 March 1958; *d* of John Hubert Stock and Jean Anne Stock (*née* Mallet); *m* 1987, Robert Lance Hughes; two *d*. *Educ:* St Catherine's, Bramley; Jesus Coll., Oxford (MA Hons Modern Langs; Hon. Fellow, 2007). Journalist, Petroleum Economist, 1980–82; joined BBC, 1983: Producer, The World at One, 1983–85; reporter: Money Prog., 1986–87; and Presenter, Newsnight, 1988–93; Presenter: Europe on the Brink series, 1993; Money Prog., 1995–96; Antiques Show, 1997–98; Front Row, 1998–2004; The Film Programme, 2004–. Film Critic, The Tablet, 2008–. Chair, Tate Members' Council, 2005–10; a Judge, Man Booker Prize, 2003; Mem. Cttee, Kim Scott Walwyn Prize 2003–; Chair of Judges, Gulbenkian Prize for Mus and Galls, 2007; Vice Pres., Hay Fest., 2009–. Guest Curator, From Page to Screen Fest., 2012. Patron, Borderlines Film Fest., 2012–. Trustee, Sidney Nolan Trust, 2011–. Hon. MA Worcester, 2006. *Publications:* A Foreign Country, 1999; Man-Made Fibre, 2002; In Glorious Technicolor: a century of film and how it has shaped us, 2011. *Address:* c/o Aitken Alexander Associates, 291 Gray's Inn Road, WC1X 8EB.

**STOCK, Rt Rev. Marcus Nigel Ralph Peter;** *see* Leeds, Bishop of, (Catholic).

**STOCK, Very Rev. Victor Andrew,** OAM 2002; Dean of Guildford, 2002–12, now Dean Emeritus; Priest Vicar, Westminster Abbey, since 2012; Hon. Assistant Priest: St Paul's Knightsbridge, since 2018; St Mary's Bourne Street, since 2018; *b* 24 Dec. 1944; *s* of Arthur and Violet Stock. *Educ:* Christopher Wren Sch.; King's Coll., London (AKC 1968); St Boniface Coll., Warminster. Ordained deacon, 1969, priest, 1970; Curate, Pinner, 1969–73; Resident Chaplain, London Univ. Church of Christ the King, Gordon Sq., 1973–79; Rector: Friern Barnet, 1979–86; St Mary le Bow, City of London, 1986–2002. Mem., Gen. Synod, 1980–86. Chaplain, UK/Europe Gp, Order of Australia Assoc., 1988–. Pres., Sion Coll., 1994–95. Gov., Emmanuel Sch., 2013–. FRSA 1995. DUniv Surrey, 2012. *Publications:* Taking Stock: confessions of a city priest (autobiog.), 2001. *Recreations:* gardening, London, travel, politics, broadcasting. *Address:* 62 Bramwell House, Churchill Gardens, SW1V 3DS. *Clubs:* Reform; Guildford County.

**STOCK, Rt Rev. (William) Nigel;** Bishop at Lambeth, 2013–17; Bishop for the Falkland Islands, 2014–17; Bishop to the Forces, 2014–17; an Honorary Assistant Bishop: Diocese of London, 2013–18; Diocese of Southwark, since 2013; Diocese of Bath and Wells, since 2016; *b* 29 Jan. 1950; *s* of Ian Heath Stock, MC, and Elizabeth Mary Stock; *m* 1973, Carolyne Grace (*née* Greswell); three *s*. *Educ:* Durham Sch.; Durham Univ. (BA Hons Law and Politics); Ripon Coll., Cuddesdon (Oxford Univ. DipTh). Ordained deacon, 1976, priest, 1977; Asst Curate, Stockton St Peter, Durham, 1976–79; Priest-in-charge, Taraka St Peter, Aipo Rongo, PNG, 1979–84; Vicar, St Mark, Shiremoor, Newcastle, 1985–91; Team Rector, North Shields Team Ministry, 1991–98; RD, Tynemouth, 1992–98; Hon. Canon, Newcastle Cathedral, 1997–98; Residentiary Canon, Durham Cathedral, 1998–2000; Bishop Suffragan of Stockport, 2000–07; Bishop of St Edmundsbury and Ipswich, 2007–13. Commissary for Archbp of PNG, 1986–2015. Entered House of Lords, 2011. *Recreations:* walking, photography, travel. *Address:* 18 Trendle Lane, Bicknoller, Taunton, Somerset TA4 4EG.

**STOCKDALE, David Andrew;** QC 1995; **His Honour Judge Stockdale;** a Circuit Judge, since 2010; Senior Circuit Judge and Honorary Recorder of Manchester, since 2013; a Deputy High Court Judge, Queen's Bench Division, since 2008; *b* 9 May 1951; 2nd *s* of late John Ramsden Stockdale and Jean Stewart Stockdale (*née* Shelley); *m* 1985, Melanie Jane, *e d* of late Anthony Benson and Barbara Benson; one *s* three *d*. *Educ:* Giggleswick Sch.; Pembroke Coll., Oxford (MA Lit.Hum.). Called to the Bar, Middle Temple, 1975, Bencher, 2003; in practice on Northern Circuit, 1976–2010 (Jun., 1978; Treas., 2008–10); Asst Recorder, 1990–93; Recorder, 1993–2010. Governor: Giggleswick Sch., 1982–2016 (Chm. of Govs, 1997–2007); Terra Nova Sch., 2000–08. *Recreations:* the outdoors, motorcycling, remote Scotland. *Address:* Courts of Justice, Crown Square, Manchester M3 3FL. *T:* (0161) 954 1800. *Club:* Sloane.

**STOCKDALE, His Honour Eric;** a Circuit Judge, 1972–94; *b* 8 Feb. 1929; *m* 1952, Joan (*née* Berry); two *s*. *Educ:* Collyer's Sch., Horsham; London Sch. of Economics; LLB, BScEcon, LLM, PhD (Lond.); MSc (Cranfield). 2nd Lieut, RA, 1947–49; Lieut, RARO, 1952–84. Called to the Bar, Middle Temple, 1950, Bencher, 2004; practised in London and on Midland Circuit until 1972; admitted to State Bar, Calif, 1983. Mem., Supreme Court Procedure Cttee, 1982–94. Tech. Advr, Central Council of Probation Cttees, 1979–84; Vice-Pres., NACRO, 1980–94 (Mem. Council, 1970–80); President: British Soc. of Criminology, 1978–81; Soc. of English and Amer. Lawyers, 1986–89 (Chm., 1984–86). Member: Central Council for Educn and Trng in Social Work, 1984–89; Parole Board, 1985–89; Criminal Injuries Compensation Bd, 1995–2000; Criminal Injuries Compensation Appeals Panel, 1997–2005. Vis. Prof., Queen Mary and Westfield Coll., London Univ., 1989–93. Governor, 1977–89, Vis. Fellow, 1986–94, Vis. Prof., 1994–2009, Univ. of Hertfordshire (formerly Hatfield Poly.). Consultant Ed., Blackstone's Criminal Practice, first 16 edns, 1991–2006. Hon. LLD Hertfordshire, 1995. *Publications:*

The Court and the Offender, 1967; A Study of Bedford Prison 1660–1877, 1977; Law and Order in Georgian Bedfordshire, 1982; The Probation Volunteer, 1985; (with Keith Devlin) Sentencing, 1987; (ed with Silvia Casale) Criminal Justice Under Stress, 1992; 'Tis Treason, My Good Man!, 2005; (with Randy J. Holland) Middle Temple Lawyers and the American Revolution, 2007; From Wig and Pen to Computer, 2008; The Man Who Shot the President - and other lawyers, 2008; Further and Worse Particulars, 2009; (contrib.) History of the Middle Temple, 2011; Send for Benson!, 2015. *Address:* 20 Lyonsdown Road, New Barnet, Herts EN5 1JE. *T:* (020) 8449 7181. *Club:* Athenæum.

**STOCKDALE, Sir Thomas (Minshull),** 2nd Bt *cr* 1960, of Hoddington, Co. Southampton; *b* 7 Jan. 1940; *s* of Sir Edmund Villiers Minshull Stockdale, 1st Bt and Hon. Louise Fermor-Hesketh (*d* 1994), *er d* of 1st Lord Hesketh; *S* father, 1989; *m* 1965, Jacqueline Ha-Van-Vuong (*d* 2010); one *s* one *d*. *Educ:* Eton; Worcester Coll., Oxford (MA). Called to Bar, Inner Temple, 1966; Bencher, Lincoln's Inn, 1994. Prime Warden, Fishmongers' Co., 2001–02. *Recreations:* shooting, travel. *Heir:* s John Minshull Stockdale, *b* 13 Dec. 1967. *Address:* Manor Farm, Weston Patrick, Basingstoke, Hants RG25 2NT. *Clubs:* Turf, MCC.

**STOCKEN, Oliver Henry James,** CBE 2013; Chairman, Stanhope plc, since 2000; *b* 22 Dec. 1941; *s* of late Henry Edmund West Stocken and Sheila Guiscard Stocken (*née* Steele); *m* 1967, Sally Forbes Dishon (*d* 2019); two *s* one *d*. *Educ:* Felsted Sch.; University Coll., Oxford (BA). FCA 1978. Director: N M Rothschild & Sons Limited, 1968–77; Esperanza Trade & Transport, 1977–79; Barclays Merchant Bank, 1979–81; Man. Dir, Barclays Australia, 1982–84; Finance Director: BZW, 1985–93; Barclays plc, 1993–99. Non-executive Director: Steel Burrill Jones Group plc, 1992–96; MEPC plc, 1995–2000; Pilkington plc, 1998–2006; Rank plc, 1998–2006; Bunzl plc, 1998–2000; 3i Group plc, 1999–2009 (Dep. Chm., 2002–09); Novar plc, 2000–05; GUS plc, 2000–06; Standard Chartered Bank plc, 2004–14. Chairman: Rutland Trust, 1999–2007; Lupus Capital plc, 1999–2002; Oval Insurance Gp, 2006–11; Home Retail Gp, 2006–12; Starling Bank, 2015–. Trustee: Natural Hist. Mus., 1999–2013 (Chm., 2006–13); Henley River and Rowing Mus., 2002–09; Chichester Fest. Th., 2010–15; Care (UK), 2012–18 (Chm., 2012–18). Mem. Council, RCA, 1998–2007 (Treas., 2002–07). Chairman, Trustees: Children's Leukaemia Trust, 1993–2002; Devas Club, 1997–2004. Gov., Felsted Sch., 2008–. *Recreations:* golf, running, Rugby, cricket. *Address:* 25c Marryat Road, Wimbledon, SW19 5BB. *Clubs:* Brooks's, Garrick, MCC (Mem. Cttee, 1998–2015, Treas., 2000–06, Trustee, 2007–09, Chm., 2009–15), Chelsea Arts; Royal Wimbledon Golf, West Sussex Golf.

**STOCKER, Diane Louise;** *see* Corner, D. L.

**STOCKER, John Wilcox,** AO 1999; PhD; FRACP; Principal, Foursight Associates Pty Ltd, since 1996; *b* 23 April 1945; *s* of W. R. Stocker and Gladys Noelle Davies; *m* 1973, Joanne Elizabeth Gross; two *d*. *Educ:* Wesley Coll., Univ. of Melbourne (MB BS BMedSc; PhD). FTSE (FTS). RMO, Royal Melbourne Hosp., 1970–72; Res. Scientist, Walter & Eliza Hall Inst. of Med. Res., 1974–76; Mem., Basel Inst. of Immunology, 1976–78; Central Res. Unit, 1979–84; Dir, Pharm. Res., Hoffman-La Roche & Co., Basel, 1986–87; Dir, Vic. Govt Strategic Res. Foundn, 1988–93; Chief Exec., CSIRO, 1990–95; Govt Chief Scientist, Australia, 1996–99. Founding Man. Dir, AMRAD, 1987–90; Director: Gene Shears Pty, 1992–96; Cambridge Antibody Technology Ltd, 1995–2006; Telstra Corp., 1996–2012; Circadian Technologies Pty Ltd, 1996–2009; Rothschild Bioscience Managers Ltd, 1996–98; Nufarm Ltd, 1998–; Chairman: Sigma Co. Ltd, 1999–2005; Sigma Pharmaceuticals Ltd, 2005–09. Chairman: Australian Sci. Technol. and Engrg Council, 1997–98; Grape and Wine R&D Corp., 1997–2004; CSIRO, 2007–10; Dir, Victorian Envmt Protection Authy, 2017–19; Mem., numerous Industry and Govt sci. orgns. Dep. Chm., R. G. Menzies Foundn, 2017–. Hon. DMedSc Melbourne; Hon. DSc: Wollongong; Central Qld. Centenary Medal, Australia, 2003. *Publications:* scientific papers, contribs to learned jls. *Recreations:* tennis, tiling, viticulture, reading. *Address:* 27 Gouldian Court, Peregian Beach, Qld 4573, Australia. *Club:* Winzergemeinschaft zur Landskron Flueh (Switzerland).

**STOCKING, Dame Barbara (Mary), (Dame Barbara MacInnes),** DBE 2008 (CBE 2000); President, Murray Edwards College, Cambridge, since 2013; *b* 28 July 1951; *d* of Percy Frederick Stocking and Mary Stocking; *m* 1981, Dr R. John MacInnes; two *s*. *Educ:* New Hall, Cambridge (BA); Univ. of Wisconsin (MS). Teaching Asst, Dept of Physiology and Biophysics, Univ. of Illinois, 1972–73; Staff Associate, Nat. Acad. of Scis, Washington, 1974–76; Jt Research Fellow, Nuffield Provincial Hosps Trust and Centre for Med. Res., Univ. of Sussex, 1977–79; Sec., WHO Independent Commn on Long Term Prospects of Onchocerciasis Control Programme, LSHTM, 1979–81; Fellow in Health Policy, Innovation and Evaluation, King's Fund Coll., 1983–86; Dir, King's Fund Centre for Health Services Develt, 1987–93; Chief Executive: Oxford RHA, 1993–94; Anglia and Oxford RHA, 1994–96; Regl Dir, Anglia and Oxford, 1994–98, South East, 1999–2000, NHS Exec., DoH; Dir, NHS Modernisation Agency, 2000–01 (on secondment); Chief Exec., Oxfam GB, 2001–13. Chair: NHS Patient Partnership Steering Gp, 1993–98; NHS Resource Allocation Gp, 1995–97. Chm., Ebola Interim Assessment Panel, WHO, 2015. Member: UK Harkness Fellowships Adv. and Selection Cttee, 1989–95; NHS Central R&D Cttee, 1992–96. Member: UN Inter Agency Standing Cttee for Humanitarian Response, 2005–10; High Level Panel on delivering Millennium Develt Goals, FAO, 2006–11; Founder Bd Mem., Global Humanitarian Forum, 2007–12; Mem. Bd, Cabinet Office, 2010–15. Hon. DSc: Luton, 1998; Oxford Brookes, 1999; Loughborough, 2003. *Publications:* (jtly) The Image and the Reality: a case study of the impacts of medical technology, 1978; Initiative and Inertia: case studies in the health services, 1985; (ed) Expensive Medical Technologies, 1988; (Series Editor) A Study of the Diffusion of Medical Technology in Europe, 3 vols, 1991; (jtly) Criteria for Change, 1991; Medical Advances: the future shape of acute services, 1991. *Recreations:* music, family.

**STOCKINGER, Dr Brigitta,** FRS 2013; FMedSci; Researcher, Francis Crick Institute, since 2015. *Educ:* Univ. of Mainz (PhD Biol. 1978). Postdoctoral researcher: Clinical Res. Centre, Harrow, 1980–82; Babraham Inst., Cambridge, 1982–83; Cancer Res. Inst., Heidelberg, 1983–85; Mem., Basel Inst. for Immunol., Switzerland, 1985–91; Hd, Div. of Molecular Immunology, MRC NIMR, 1991–2015. Hon. Prof., Div. of Infection and Immunity, UCL. Mem., EMBO, 2008. FMedSci 2005. *Publications:* contribs to learned jls incl. Nature Immunol., Nature, Immunity. *Address:* Francis Crick Institute, 1 Midland Road, NW1 1AT.

**STOCKMANN, Caroline Anne;** Chief Executive, Association of Corporate Treasurers, since 2017; *b* Leeds, 26 Oct. 1961; *d* of John Anthony Stockmann and Anita Edith Elizabeth Stockmann; *m* 1996, Michael John Thurlow Stuttard; one *s* one *d*. *Educ:* Durham Univ. (BA Hons); Guildhall Sch. of Music and Drama (LGSM). ACA 1994, FCA 2006; DChA 2008. Freelance musician and teacher, 1986–88; course leader, Lancaster Dio., 1988–90; trainee accountant, KPMG, 1990–94; Sen. Internal Auditor, Cadbury Schweppes, 1994–95; Financial Controller, Granada plc, 1995–96; Financial Accountant/Controller, 1996–99, Finance Dir, Benelux, 2000–01, Bestfoods; Vice Pres. Finance, Unilever Foods Europe, 2001–04; Chief Financial Officer/Chief Inf. Officer, Unilever Thailand, 2004–06; Hd, Business Planning, Novartis, 2006–07; Finance and Commercial Dir, Southbank Centre, 2007–09; Dir, Internat. Progs, Sue Ryder Care, 2010; Chief Financial Officer, Save the Children Internat., 2010–14; Chief Financial Officer, British Council, 2014–16. Judge, Investor Relations Soc. Awards, 2017–. Mem., Finance and Investment Cttee, Elton John AIDS Foundn, 2016–. Trustee: Sue Ryder Care, 2008–10; The Brooke, 2011–14; Lay Trustee, Archdio. of Southwark (RC), 2017–. Mem., Adv. Bd, Rehearsal Orch., 2008–12; Treas., Epsom Symphony Orch., 2010–14; PR Officer, Kent County Assoc. of Change Ringers, 2016–; Ind. Examiner, Central Council of Church Bell Ringers, 2019– (PR Officer, 2016–18). Member: Adv. Bd, Faculty of Arts and Humanities, 2012–, Adv. Bd, Law School, 2017–, Durham Univ.; Audit Cttee, Univ. of Cambridge, 2014–15; Treas., Open Univ., 2018. Foundn Gov., St Gregory's Comp. Sch., 2013–17. *Recreations:* bell ringing, musician, reading, DJ, fell walking, family, cooking, travel, languages. *Address:* Association of Corporate Treasurers, 69 Leadenhall Street, EC3A 2BG. *T:* (020) 7847 2542. *E:* cstockmann@treasurers.org.

**STOCKPORT, Bishop Suffragan of;** *no new appointment at time of going to press.*

**STOCKTON, 2nd Earl of,** *cr* 1984; **Alexander Daniel Alan Macmillan;** Viscount Macmillan of Ovenden, 1984; *b* Oswestry, Shropshire, 10 Oct. 1943; *s* of Viscount Macmillan of Ovenden, PC, MP (*d* 1984) and Katharine, Viscountess Macmillan of Ovenden, DBE (*d* 2017); *S* grandfather, 1986; *m* 1st, 1970, Hélène Birgitte Hamilton (marr. diss. 1991); one *s* two *d*; 2nd, 1995, Miranda Elizabeth Louise, Lady Nuttall (marr. diss. 2010), *d* of Richard Quarry and Diana, Lady Mancroft; 3rd, 2012, Linda Shirley Rimington. *Educ:* Eton; Université de Paris; Strathclyde Univ. FRICS 1999. Sub Ed., Glasgow Herald, 1964–66; Reporter, Daily Telegraph, 1966–68; Foreign Corresp., Daily Telegraph and Sunday Telegraph, 1968–74; Corresp., BBC TV and Radio, Toronto Star, San Francisco Examiner, 1969–74; Macmillan Publishers: Dir, 1974–80; Man. Dir, 1980–86; Chm. 1986–2000; Pres., Internat. Gp, 2000–06. Mem. Council, Publishers Assoc., 1980–88. Contested (C) Bristol, EP elecns, 1994; MEP (C) SW Region, England, 1999–2004. Mem. (C), S Bucks DC, 2011–. FRSA 1987. Liveryman: Worshipful Co. of Merchant Taylors, 1972 (Mem., Ct of Assts, 1987–; Master, 1992–93); Worshipful Co. of Stationers and Newspaper Makers, 1973 (Mem., Ct of Assts, 1996–2008). DUniv Strathclyde, 1993; Hon. DLitt: De Montfort, 1993; Westminster, 1995; London Inst., 2003. *Heir:* s Viscount Macmillan of Ovenden, *qv*. *Address:* The Priory, Old Mill Road, Denham Village, Bucks UB9 5AS. *T:* (01895) 834181, 07860 461497. *E:* thepriory@dbac.co.uk. *Clubs:* Beefsteak, Pratt's.

**STOCKWELL, (Graham) Clive;** QC 2018; *b* Fulham, 15 Feb. 1965; *s* of Graham and Reidun Stockwell; *m* 1991, Jane Rimmington; two *s*. *Educ:* St Dunstan's Coll., S London; Leicester Poly. (LLB). Called to the Bar, Inner Temple, 1988; in practice as barrister specialising in crime, 1988–; Hd of Chambers, One High Pavement, 2016–. *Recreations:* I enjoy spending time with my friends, family and reflecting on issues such as: when will my level of maturing match my age?; why does my wife still tolerate me?; how are my sons so gifted?; I also enjoy all that outdoor life has to offer! *Address:* One High Pavement Chambers, 1 High Pavement, Nottingham NG1 1HF. *T:* (0115) 941 8218. *E:* clivestockwellqc@1highpavement.co.uk.

**STOCKWIN, Prof. (James) Arthur (Ainscow),** OBE 2009; Nissan Professor of Modern Japanese Studies, and Director of Nissan Institute of Japanese Studies, University of Oxford, 1982–2003; Fellow, St Antony's College, Oxford, 1982–2003, now Emeritus (Sub-Warden, 1999–2001); *b* 28 Nov. 1935; *s* of Wilfred Arthur Stockwin and Edith Mary Stockwin; *m* 1960, Audrey Lucretia Hobson Stockwin (*née* Wood) (*d* 2018); one *s* two *d* (and one *s* decd). *Educ:* Exeter Coll., Oxford Univ. (MA); Australian Nat. Univ. (PhD). Australian National University: Lectr, Dept of Political Science, 1964–66; Sen. Lectr, 1966–72; Reader, 1972–81. Pres., British Assoc. of Japanese Studies, 1994–95. Gen. Ed., then Jt Gen. Ed., Nissan Inst./Routledge Japanese Studies Series, 1988– (Hd, Editl Bd, Nissan Inst./Croom Helm, Japanese Studies Series, 1986–88). Japan Foundn Prize, 2009. Order of the Rising Sun (Japan), 2004. *Publications:* The Japanese Socialist Party and Neutralism, 1968; (ed) Japan and Australia in the Seventies, 1972; Japan, Divided Politics in a Growth Economy, 1975, 2nd edn 1982; Why Japan Matters, 1983; (jtly, also ed) Dynamic and Immobilist Politics in Japan, 1988; (trans.) Junji Banno, The Establishment of the Japanese Constitutional System, 1992; The Story of Tim, 1993; (ed jtly) The Vitality of Japan: sources of national strength and weakness, 1997; Governing Japan, 1999, new edn 2008; Dictionary of the Modern Politics of Japan, 2003; Collected Writings of J. A. A. Stockwin, Part I, 2004; Thirty-Odd Feet Below Belgium: an affair of letters in the Great War 1915–1916, 2005, 2nd edn 2016; (trans.) Michael Lucken et al., Japan's Postwar, 2011; The Writings of J. A. A. Stockwin: Japanese foreign policy and understanding Japanese politics, 2 vols, 2012; (trans.) Sébastien Lechevalier, The Great Transformation of Japanese Capitalism, 2014; (trans.) Junji Banno, Japan's Modern History, 1857–1937: a new political narrative, 2014; (trans.) Junji Banno and Jirō Yamaguchi, The Abe Experiment and the Future of Japan: don't repeat history, 2016; (with Keiko Tamura) Bridging Australia and Japan: the writings of David Sissons, historian and political scientist, vol. 1, 2016; (with Kweku Ampiah) Rethinking Japan: the politics of contested nationalism, 2017; articles, largely on Japanese politics and foreign policy, in Pacific Affairs, Japanese Studies, Asia-Pacific Review, Japan Forum, etc. *Recreations:* languages, admiring pottery. *Address:* Glym Cottage, Glympton Road, Wootton, Woodstock, Oxon OX20 1EL. *T:* (01993) 811449.

**STODDART,** family name of **Baron Stoddart of Swindon**.

**STODDART OF SWINDON,** Baron *cr* 1983 (Life Peer), of Reading in the Royal County of Berkshire; **David Leonard Stoddart;** *b* 4 May 1926; *s* of Arthur Leonard Stoddart, coal miner, and Queenie Victoria Stoddart (*née* Price); *m* 1961, Jennifer Percival-Alwyn; one *s* (and one *s* decd) one *d* by previous marr.). *Educ:* elementary; St Clement Danes and Henley Grammar Schools. Youth in training, PO Telephones, 1942–44; business on own account, 1944–46; Railway Clerk, 1947–49; Hospital Clerk, 1949–51; Power Station Clerical Worker, 1951–70. Joined Labour Party, 1947; Reading County Borough Council: Member, 1954–72; served at various times as Chairman of Housing, Transport and Finance Cttees; Leader, Labour Group of Councillors, 1962–72; Leader of Council, 1967–72. Contested (Lab) Newbury, 1959 and 1964, Swindon, 1969, 1983. MP (Lab) Swindon, 1970–83; PPS to Minister for Housing and Construction, 1974–75; an Asst Govt Whip, 1975; a Lord Comr, HM Treasury, 1976–77; an opposition whip, and opposition spokesman on energy, House of Lords, 1983–88. Chairman: Alliance Against the European Constitution (formerly Anti-Maastricht Alliance), 1992–2007; Global Britain, 1998–; Jt Pres., Campaign for an Ind. Britain, 2007–11 (Chm., 1985–2007); Mem. Council, Freedom Assoc., 2006–13. *Recreations:* gardening, music. *Address:* Sintra, 37A Bath Road, Reading, Berks RG1 6HL. *T:* (0118) 957 6726.

**STODDART, Caroline Ann Tuke;** *see* Malone, C. A. T.

**STODDART, Charles Norman,** PhD; Sheriff of Lothian and Borders at Edinburgh, 1995–2009; *b* 4 April 1948; *s* of Robert Stoddart and Margaret (*née* Allenby); *m* 1981, Anne Lees; one *d*. *Educ:* Edinburgh Univ. (LLB, PhD); McGill Univ. (LLM). Admitted Solicitor, 1972, practised, 1972–73, 1980–88; Lectr in Scots Law, Edinburgh Univ., 1973–80; Sheriff of N Strathclyde at Paisley, 1988–95. Dir, Judicial Studies in Scotland, 1997–2000. Member: Maclean Cttee on Serious, Violent and Sexual Offenders, 1999–2000; Sentencing

**STODDART**, Commn for Scotland, 2003–06; Civil Courts Rev. Policy Gp, 2007–09; Post-corroboration Safeguards Rev., 2014–15. Mem., Parole Bd for Scotland, 2011–14. Editor, Green's Criminal Law Bulletin, 1992–2008. *Publications*: (with H. Neilson) The Law and Practice of Legal Aid in Scotland, 1979, 4th edn 1994; (with C. H. W. Gane and J. Chalmers) A Casebook on Scottish Criminal Law, 1980, 4th edn 2009; Bible John (crime documentary), 1980; (with C. H. W. Gane) Cases and Materials on Scottish Criminal Procedure, 1983, 2nd edn 1994; Criminal Warrants, 1991, 2nd edn 1999; contribs to professional jls. *Recreations*: music, foreign travel.

**STODDART, Christopher West**; Chief Executive Officer, ATR plc (formerly Go Racing), 2001–03; *b* 10 April 1950; *s* of Sir Ian West Stoddart and Bridget Stoddart (*née* Pilditch); *m* 1st, 1972, Deborah Ounsted (marr. diss. 1984); 2nd, 1985, Dr Hazel Grasmere, *d* of Hon. Robert and Evelyn Grasmere, USA. *Educ*: Winchester Coll.; Churchill Coll., Cambridge (BA Hons 1971). Joined CS, 1971; DoE, 1971–75; Research Sec., Centre for Envmtl Studies, 1976–80; Regl Companies Sec., 1980–81, Sec. 1981–82, ITCA; Tyne Tees Television: Gen. Manager, 1982–83; Dir of Resources, 1983–88; Man. Dir and Chief Exec., Satellite Information Services Ltd, 1988–92; Man. Dir, GMTV, 1992–2001. Non-exec. Dir, Sterling Publishing Gp, 1999–2001. Chm., Trustees, Changing Faces, 1999–2002. *Publications*: The Inner City as Testing Ground for Government-funded Research, 1980. *Recreations*: mountaineering, photography, travel.

**STODDART, Sir (James) Fraser**, Kt 2007; FRS 1994; CChem, FRSC; FRSE; Board of Trustees Professor of Chemistry, and Director, Center for Chemistry of Integrated Systems, Northwestern University, since 2008; Kavli Professor of NanoSystems Science, University of California at Los Angeles, 2003–07, Emeritus Professor of Chemistry, 2008; *b* 24 May 1942; *s* of Thomas Fraser Stoddart and Jane Spalding Hislop Stoddart; *m* 1968, Norma Agnes Scholan (*d* 2004); two *d*. *Educ*: Melville Coll., Edinburgh; Univ. of Edinburgh (BSc 1964; PhD 1966; DSc 1980). CChem, FRSC 1978 (Hon. FRSC). Nat. Res. Council of Canada Post-doctoral Fellow, Queen's Univ., Canada, 1967–69; University of Sheffield: ICI Res. Fellow, subseq. Lectr in Chemistry, 1970–82; seconded to Catalysis Gp, ICI Corporate Lab., Runcorn, 1978–81; Reader in Chemistry, 1982–91; Prof. of Organic Chem., 1990–97, Hd, Sch. of Chem., 1993–97, Univ. of Birmingham; Winstein Prof. of Organic Chemistry, 1997–2003, Dir, California NanoSystems Inst., 2003–07, UCLA. Vis. Lectr, Univ. of Parana, Brazil, 1972; SRC Sen. Vis. Fellow, UCLA, 1978; Visiting Professor: Texas A&M Univ., 1980; Univ. of Messina, Italy, 1986–88; Mulhouse, France, 1987; Tianjin Univ., 2014; Univ. of Nottingham, 2015; Univ. of NSW, 2018. FRSE 2008 (Hon. FRSE); Fellow, American Acad. of Arts and Scis, 2012. Mem., NAS, 2014; Foreign Mem., Chinese Acad. of Sci., 2017. Hon. DSc: Birmingham, 2005; Twente, 2006; Sheffield, 2008; Trinity Coll. Dublin, 2009; St Andrews, 2010; Nottingham, 2017; Autonoma Univ., Madrid, 2018; Univ. of Southern Denmark, 2018. Awards include: Internat. Izatt-Christensen in macrocyclic chem., 1993; Arthur C. Cope Schol. Award, 1999, Arthur C. Cope Award, 2008, ACS; Nagoya Gold Medal in Organic Chemistry, Nagoya Univ., Japan, 2004; Alumnus of the Year Award, Univ. of Edinburgh, 2005; Fusion Award, Univ. of Nevada, 2006; King Faisal Internat. Award in Sci. (Chemistry), King Faisal Foundn, 2007; Tetrahedron Prize, 2007; Albert Einstein World Award of Sci., World Cultural Council, 2007; Davy Medal, Royal Soc., 2008; Royal Medal, RSE, 2010; Centenary Prize, RSC, 2014; (jtly) Nobel Prize in Chemistry, 2016. Mem., various editl bds in Europe and USA. *Publications*: The Stereochemistry of Carbohydrates, 1971; The Nature of the Mechanical Bond, 2016; over 1150 papers, reviews and monographs in Angewandte Chemie, Chemical Science, Chemistry—A Europ. Jl, Jl of the American Chemical Soc., Proc. Nat. Acad. Scis, Science, Nature, Nature Chem., Nature Nanotechnol., Natural Energy on nanoscale science, templated synthesis, mechanical bonds, rotaxanes, catenanes, self-assembly processes, topology, molecular switches and machines. *Address*: Department of Chemistry, Northwestern University, 2145 Sheridan Road, Evanston, IL 60208-3113, USA.

**STODDART, John Maurice**, CBE 1995; Principal and Vice-Chancellor, Sheffield Hallam University, 1992–98 (Principal, Sheffield City Polytechnic, 1983–92); *b* 18 Sept. 1938; *s* of Gordon Stoddart and May (*née* Ledger). *Educ*: Wallasey Grammar Sch.; Univ. of Reading (BA Pol Econ.). Teacher, Wallasey GS, 1960–62; Lectr, Mid Cheshire Coll. of Further Educn, 1962–64; Lectr, Enfield Coll., 1964–70; Head, Dept of Econs and Business Studies, Sheffield Polytechnic, 1970–72; Asst Dir, NE London Polytechnic, 1972–76; Dir, Hull Coll. of Higher Educn, 1976–83. Dir, Sheffield Science Park Co. Ltd, 1988–96; Deputy Chairman: Northern Gen. Hosp. NHS Trust, 1999–2001; Sheffield Teaching Hosps NHS Trust, 2001–06. Chm., CNAA Cttee for Business and Management, 1985–88 (Chm., Undergrad. Courses Bd, 1976–83); Mem., CNAA, 1982–88, 1991–93; Chm., Cttee of Dirs of Polys, 1990–93 (Vice-Chm., 1988–90). Member: Sea Fisheries Trng Council, 1976–80; Architects Registration Council, UK, 1979–85; Council for Industry and Educn, 1989–94; Council for Educn and Trng in Social Work, 1989–94; BTEC, 1991–95; Chm., Higher Educn Quality Council, 1992–97. Member: Court, Univ. of Hull, 1976–83; Council, Univ. of Sheffield, 1983–92. Companion, British Business Graduates Soc., 1983; Hon. Fellow: Humberside Coll., 1983; Univ. of Bolton, 2005. FRSA 1977. CCMI (FBIM 1977; CBIM 1990). Hon. DEd CNAA, 1992; Hon. DLitt Coventry, 1993; DUniv: Middlesex, 1993; Sheffield Hallam, 1998; Hon. LLD Sheffield, 1998. *Publications*: articles on business and management educn. *Address*: 6 Tapton Park Gardens, Sheffield S10 3FP. *T*: (0114) 230 5467. *Club*: Reform.

**STODDART, Dr Simon Kenneth Fladgate**, FSA; Fellow, Magdalene College, Cambridge, since 1998; Reader in Prehistory, University of Cambridge, since 2013; *b* 8 Nov. 1958; *s* of Kenneth Bowring Stoddart and Daphne Elizabeth Fladgate (*née* Hughes); *m* 1983, Prof. Caroline Ann Tuke Malone, *qv*; two *d*. *Educ*: Winchester Coll.; Magdalene Coll., Cambridge (BA 1980; PhD 1987); Univ. of Michigan (MA 1983). FSA 1994. Rome Schol. in Archaeol., British Sch. at Rome, 1980–81; Power Schol., Univ. of Michigan, 1981–83; Res. Fellow, Magdalene Coll., Cambridge, 1986–89; Lecturer: Univ. of York, 1988–90; Univ. of Bristol, 1990–94 (Sen. Lectr, 1994–96); University of Cambridge: Lectr, 1996–2000; Sen. Lectr, 2000–14; Actg Dep. Dir, McDonald Inst. for Archaeol Res., Univ. of Cambridge, 2014–17. Ed., Antiquity, 2001–02. Charter Fellow, Wolfson Coll., Oxford, 1992–93; Balsdon Fellow, British Sch. at Rome, 2004; Res. Associate Prof., State Univ. of NY, 2004–06. MCIfA (MIFA 1987). *Publications*: (ed with C. Malone) Papers in Italian Archaeology, Vols 1–4, 1985; (with N. Spivey) Etruscan Italy, 1990; (ed with C. Mathers) Development and Decline in the Mediterranean Bronze Age, 1994; (ed with C. Malone) Territory, Time and State: the archaeological development of the Gubbio Basin, 1994; (ed) Landscapes from Antiquity, 2000; (ed with G. Carr) Celts from Antiquity, 2002; (ed with C. Malone) Mortuary Ritual in Prehistoric Malta, 2009; Historical Dictionary of the Etruscans, 2009; (ed with G. Cifani and S. Neil) Landscape, Ethnicity and Identity in the Archaic Mediterranean, 2012; (ed with C. Popa) Fingerprinting the Iron Age, 2014; (ed) Pre-Roman German Urbanism, 2017; (ed with E. Aines) Gardening Time, 2017; (ed) Delicate Urbanism in Context: pre-Roman German urbanism, 2017; (ed with E. Aines) Gardening Time, 2019; Power and Place in Etruria, 2020; contrib. acad. articles. *Recreations*: walking, travel, cycling, recycling. *Address*: Magdalene College, Cambridge CB3 0AG. *T*: (01223) 332168.

**STODDART, Thomas**; photo-journalist; *b* 28 Nov. 1953; *s* of Tommy and Kathleen Stoddart. *Educ*: Seahouses Secondary Sch., Northumberland. Freelance photographer working on humanitarian issues, such as the siege of Sarajevo, 1992–97, Sudan famine, and AIDS catastrophe in Sub-Saharan Africa, for internat. magazines, incl. Time, Newsweek, Stern, and Sunday Times Mag. Member: RPS; RGS. *Publications*: Sarajevo, 1998; A Day in the Life of Africa, 2002. *Recreations*: lifelong fan of Newcastle United, watching sport, photography, enjoying good food, friends and wine. *Address*: 13 Tradewinds Court, Asher Way, E1W 2JB. *E*: tom@tomstoddart.com.

**STOER, John Edmund**; Head Master, St Aloysius' College, Glasgow, 2004–13; *b* Point Fortin, Trinidad, 7 May 1954; *s* of Edmund Stoer and Lilly Stoer; *m* 1983, Janet Lewis; one *s* one *d*. *Educ*: Douai Sch.; Bristol Univ. (BA Theol. and Sociol.); Inst. of Educn, Univ. of London (PGCE). Teacher, St Thomas More Sch., Chelsea, 1978–81; Hd of Religious Educn, St Philip Howard Sch., 1981–84; Dir, Sixth Form, Gunnersbury Catholic Sch., 1984–89; Dep. Hd, Campion Sch., 1989–94; Headmaster, St Joseph's Coll., Stoke-on-Trent, 1994–2004. *Recreation*: researching inter-religious dialogue.

**STOKE-UPON-TRENT, Archdeacon of**; *see* Parker, Ven. M. J.

**STOKER, John Francis**; *b* 11 Sept. 1950; *s* of Francis Charles Stoker and Joyce Stoker (*née* Barnwell); *m* 1982, Julie Puddicombe. *Educ*: King Edward's Sch., Birmingham; Brasenose Coll., Oxford (BA Lit.Hum.; MA). Department of the Environment: Admin. Trainee, 1973–78; Principal, 1978; Tenant's Right to Buy, 1979–81; Alternatives to Rates, 1981–83; Cabinet Office, 1983–85; Grade 5, 1985; Envmt White Paper Div., 1990–92; Grade 3, 1992; Regl Dir, Govt Office for Merseyside, 1992–96; Dep. Dir Gen., 1997–98, Dir Gen., 1998–99, Nat. Lottery; Chief Charity Comr, 1999–2004. Chief Exec., London Bombings Relief Charitable Fund, 2005. Comr for the Compact (between Govt and voluntary/ community sector), 2006–07. Mem., SRA (formerly Law Soc. Regulation Bd), 2006–09. Mem. Ct, Univ. of Greenwich, 2010–15 (Mem., Audit Cttee, 2010–15; Chair, Staffing Cttee, 2014–15). FRSA. *Recreations*: books, music, ski-ing. *Club*: Travellers.

**STOKES, Dr Adrian Victor**, OBE 1983; CChem; CEng; FBCS; Chief Executive, CAT Ltd, 2000–19; *b* 25 June 1945; *s* of Alfred Samuel and Edna Stokes; *m* (marr. diss.). *Educ*: Orange Hill Grammar School, Edgware; University College London (BSc (1st cl. Hons) 1966; PhD 1970); Univ. of Hertfordshire (LLB 1st cl. Hons 2014); Postgrad. Cert. Commercial Mediation 2014. CChem 1976; MRSC 1976; FBCS 1978; CEng 1990; CSci 2004; CITP 2004. Research Programmer, GEC-Computers Ltd, 1969–71; Research Asst, Inst. of Computer Science, 1971–73; Research Fellow, UCL, 1973–77; Sen. Research Fellow and Sen. Lectr, Hatfield Polytechnic, 1977–81; Dir of Computing, St Thomas' Hosp., 1981–89 (King's Fund Fellow, 1981–84); Consultant, 1986–88 (on secondment), Principal Consultant, 1989–97, NHS Centre for IT, then Inf. Mgt Centre; Asst Dir, NHS Inf. Mgt Centre, 1997–99; Jt Dir, NHS Inf. Authy (Standards), 1999–2000. Man. Dir, Elvis Memories (UK) Ltd, 2001–15. Chairman: European Workshop for Open Systems Expert Gp on Healthcare, 1991–97; BSI Inf. Communications and Technol. Sector (formerly Systems Assembly) and Exec. Cttee, 2000–18. Vis. Prof., Nene Coll., 1994–96 (Hon. Vis. Prof., 1996–99); Hon. Research Fellow, King Alfred's Coll., Winchester, 2001–04. Non-executive Director: NHS Barnet (formerly Barnet Primary Care Trust), 2001–11; Nat. Clinical Assessment Authy, 2001–05; Special Trustee, RNOH Charity (formerly Royal Nat. Orthopaedic Hosp. NHS Trust), 2003–13. Mem., Administrative Justice & Tribunals Council (formerly Council on Tribunals), 2003–11. Member: Silver Jubilee Cttee on Improving Access for Disabled People, 1977–78; Cttee on Restrictions Against Disabled People, 1979–81; Social Security Adv. Cttee, 1980–2001; Dept of Transport Panel of Advisers on Disability, 1983–85; Disabled Persons' Transport Adv. Cttee, 1986–89; First-tier Tribunal (Social Entitlement Chamber) (formerly Disability Appeal Tribunal), 1992–. Chm., Disabled Drivers' Motor Club, 1972–82, 1991–94, 1997–2000, Vice-Pres., 1982–2005; Chm., Exec. Cttee, RADAR, 1985–92 (Vice-Pres., 1999–). Founder Governor, Motability, 1978–; Trustee: PHAB, 1982–90; Independent Living (1993) Fund, 1993–2002; Independent Living (Extension) Fund, 1993–2002; Mobility Choice, 1998–2013; Disabled Motoring UK (formerly Mobilise Orgn), 2005–18 (Life Vice-Pres., 2005–18; Jt Pres., 2018–), Vice-Chm., 2007–09 and 2012–13, Chm., 2009–12 and 2015–18, Treas., 2013–15. Freeman, City of London, 1988; Freeman, Co. of Information Technologists, 1988. Gov., Univ. of Hertfordshire, 2005–11. MCMI (MBIM 1986); FInstD 1986; FRSA 1997. Hon. DSc Hertfordshire, 1994. Mem., Editl Bd, Tribunals jl, 2015–. *Publications*: An Introduction to Data Processing Networks, 1978; Viewdata: a public information utility, 1979, 2nd edn 1980; The Concise Encyclopaedia of Computer Terminology, 1981; Networks, 1981; (with C. Saiady) What to Read in Microcomputing, 1982; Concise Encyclopaedia of Information Technology, 1982, 3rd edn 1986, USA edn 1983; Integrated Office Systems, 1982; (with M. D. Bacon and J. M. Bacon) Computer Networks: fundamentals and practice, 1984; Overview of Data Communications, 1985; The A to Z of Business Computing, 1986; Communications Standards, 1986; OSI Standards and Acronyms, 1987, 3rd edn 1991; (with H. de Glanville) The BJHC Abbreviary, 1995; numerous papers and articles, mainly concerned with computer technology. *Recreations*: philately, science fiction, collecting Elvis Presley records, computer programming. *Address*: 97 Millway, Mill Hill, NW7 3JL. *T*: (020) 8959 6665.

**STOKES, Dr Alistair Michael**; Chairman, Solent NHS Trust (formerly Solent Healthcare), 2010–19; *b* 22 July 1948; *s* of Alan Philip and Janet Ross Stokes; *m* 1st, 1970, Stephanie Mary Garland (marr. diss. 2015); two *d*; 2nd, 2016, Alexandra Muriel Paton. *Educ*: University College, Cardiff (BSc, PhD). With Pharmacia AB (Sweden), 1974–76; Monsanto Co., St Louis, USA, 1976–82; Glaxo Pharmaceuticals, 1982–85; Regional Gen. Manager, Yorkshire RHA, 1985–87; Dir Glaxo Pharmaceuticals, 1987–90; Dir and Chief Operating Officer, Porton Internat., 1990–95; CEO, Speywood Pharmaceuticals, then Ipsen Ltd, 1995–2007. Chairman: Stowic PLC, 1998–99; Quadrant Healthcare PLC, 1999–2000; Ipsen Ltd, 2007–10; Ipsen Biopharm Ltd, 2007–10. Director: Octagen Corp., 1999–2008; Spirogen Ltd, 2003–10. Chm., E Berks Community Health NHS Trust, 1993–98. Gov., Univ. of W London (formerly Thames Valley Univ.), 2007–15. FInstD 2009. *Publications*: Plasma Proteins, 1977; biochemical and scientific papers. *Recreations*: music, cricket, travel. *Clubs*: Naval and Military; Royal Southampton Yacht.

**STOKES, Antony**; *see* Stokes, N. A. D.

**STOKES, Prof. Martin**, DPhil; FBA 2012; King Edward Professor of Music, King's College London, since 2012. *Educ*: Univ. of Oxford (BA 1984; DPhil Social Anthropol. 1989). Lectr, Dept of Social Anthropol., QUB, 1989–97; Associate Prof. of Music, Univ. of Chicago, 1997–2007; Lectr in Ethnomusicol., then Prof. of Music, Univ. of Oxford, 2007–12; Fellow, St John's Coll., Oxford, 2007–12. Vis. Prof., Bogazici Univ., Istanbul, 1996, 2006; Hon. Prof., Univ. of Copenhagen, 2012–17; Vis. Bloch Prof., Univ. of Calif, Berkeley, 2013. Dent Medal, Royal Musical Assoc., 2010. *Publications*: The Arabesk Debate: music and musicians in modern Turkey, 1992, 2nd edn 2016; (ed) Ethnicity, Identity and Music: the musical construction of place, 1994, 2nd edn 1997; (ed jtly) Nationalism, Minorities and Diasporas: identities and rights in the Middle East, 1996; (ed jtly) Celtic Modern: music on the global fringe, 2004; The Republic of Love: cultural intimacy in Turkish popular music, 2010; (ed jtly) Islam and Popular Culture, 2016; (ed jtly) Theory and Practice in the Music of the Islamic World: essays in honour of Owen Wright, 2017. *Address*: Music Department, King's College London, Strand Campus, WC2R 2LS.

**STOKES, His Honour Michael George Thomas**; QC 1994; DL; a Senior Circuit Judge, 2006–16 (a Circuit Judge, 2001–16); Resident Judge, Nottingham Crown Court, 2006–16; Hon. Recorder of Nottingham, 2007–16; a Deputy High Court Judge, 2010–16; a Judge of the First-tier Tribunal (Health Education and Social Care Chamber), 2013–16; Deputy Judge of the Upper Tribunal, since 2016; a Deputy Circuit Judge, 2017–19; *b* 30 May 1948; *e s* of late M. P. Stokes and E. Stokes, Leyland, Lancs; *m* 1994, Alison Hamilton Pollock; one *s* one *d*. *Educ*: Preston Catholic Coll.; Univ. of Leeds (LLB Hons 1970); Univ. of Buckingham (MA with Merit 2019). Asst Lectr, Univ. of Nottingham, 1970–72; called to the Bar, Gray's Inn, 1971, Bencher, 2013; in practice on Midland and Oxford Circuit, 1973–2001; Asst Recorder, 1986–90, Recorder, 1990–2001; Res. Judge, Leicester Crown Ct, 2002–06. Pres., Mental Health Review Tribunals, 1999–2007. Circuit Rep., Remuneration and Terms of Work (formerly Fees & Legal Aid) Cttee, Bar Council, 1996–2000; Mem., Northants Criminal Justice Strategy Cttee, 2000–01. Vis. Prof. of Law, Nottingham Trent Univ., 2013–. Governor: Haddon Park High Sch., Nottingham, 2007–09; Sycamore Primary Sch., Nottingham, 2010–13; Ratcliffe Coll., Leics, 2012–. DL Notts, 2016. *Publications*: Blackmail (novel), 2016; A Private and Convenient Place (novel), 2018; The Tinkerman (novel), 2020. *Recreations*: racing, France, gardening, writing.

**STOKES, Dr (Nigel) Antony (David)**, LVO 1996; HM Diplomatic Service; Ambassador to the Republic of Cuba, since 2016; *b* 21 Jan. 1965. *Educ*: Queens' Coll., Cambridge (BA 1986); University Coll., London (PhD 1990). With Schlumberger Ltd, 1989–90; Mars GB, 1990–94; Centre for Exploitation of Sci. and Technol., 1994; entered FCO, 1994; Security Policy Dept, FCO, 1994–96; First Sec. (Pol), Bangkok, 1996–99; Pol Counsellor, Seoul, 2000–04; Hd, Tsunami Response Team, Bangkok, 2005; Hd, S Asia, FCO, 2005–08; Hd of Mission, Riga, 2009–10; Ambassador to the Socialist Republic of Vietnam, 2010–14. *Address*: c/o Foreign and Commonwealth Office, King Charles Street, SW1A 2AH.

**STOKES, Rear Adm. Richard**, CBE 2018; CEng; FIET; Director, RCS Associates Ltd, since 2018; *b* Cannock, Staffs, 9 May 1963; *s* of Maurice Richard Stokes and Denise Stokes; *m* 2011, Claire Hall; two *s*. *Educ*: Royal Naval Engrg Coll. (BScEng); Royal Mil. Coll. of Sci. (MDA); ACCA DipFM. Tactical Weapons Engr Officer, HMS Resolution, 1987–89; Weapon Engr Officer, HMS Ocelot, 1989–90; Mgt Planner, Flag Officer Submarines, 1992–95; Weapon Engr Officer, HMS Torbay, 1995–97; Weapon Engrg Instructor, Submarine Sea Trng, 1998; Sqdn Weapon Engrg Officer, First Submarine Sqdn, 1999–2001; Logistics, Infrastructure and Engrg Support SO, Directorate of Naval Resources and Plans, MoD, 2001–03; Engr Officers Appointer, Directorate of Naval Officer Appts, 2003–05; Asst Dir, Capability Strategy, Directorate of Equipt Planning, MoD, 2005–08; Asst Dir, Career Mgt (Engrs), 2008–10; rcds 2011; Dir, RN Defence Reform Implementation Prog., 2011–12; Hd, Nuclear Capabilities, MoD, 2012–15; ACNS (Support), 2015–18. MInstD 2018. *Recreations*: ski-ing, sailing, mountain walking, music.

**STOKES, Simon George Garbutt**; theatre director; Artistic Director, Theatre Royal Plymouth, 1998–2018; *b* Llansantffraid, Wales, 22 Oct. 1950; *s* of late Rev. George Smithson Garbutt Stokes and Betty Stokes; *m* (marr. diss.). *Educ*: Barnard Castle Sch., Co. Durham; Bristol Old Vic Th. Sch. Follow-spot operator, Liby Th., Manchester, 1974; Assistant Stage Manager: 69 Th. Co., Manchester, 1974–75; Liverpool Playhouse, 1975; Stage Manager, 1975, Artistic Dir, 1976–87, Bush Th., London; Artistic Associate and Dir of Develt, Turnstyle Gp, 1988–95; freelance directing internationally, 1988–98. Director: Sputnik Th. Co., 2009–; Dance Consortium, 2011–18; Told by an Idiot, 2019–. Gov., British American Drama Acad., 2000–18. DArts Plymouth, 2014. *Recreation*: glass of wine with convivial company speaking wise words or chatting the breeze…. *E*: simonstokes536@gmail.com.

**STOKES-LAMPARD, Prof. Helen Jayne**, PhD; FRCGP; Professor of General Practice, University of Birmingham, since 2016; GP Principal, The Cloisters Medical Practice, Lichfield, since 2002; *b* Carmarthen, S Wales, 14 Oct. 1970; *d* of Dr David Howard Stokes and Valerie Stokes; *m* 1994, Paul Adrian Lampard. *Educ*: Penyrheol Comprehensive Sch., Swansea; Gorseinor Tertiary Coll., Swansea; St George's Hosp. Med. Sch., London Univ. (MB BS); Univ. of Birmingham (MSc 2003; PhD 2010). MRCGP 2002, FRCGP 2010. Clin. Dir, Primary Care Trials Unit, 2010–12, Clin. Sen. Lectr, 2011–16, Univ. of Birmingham. Hon. Prof. of General Practice, St George's Hosp. Med. Sch., 2016–. Hon. Treas., 2012–16, Chair, 2016–19, RCGP. Gov., Birmingham Women's Hosp., 2014–16.

**STOKOE, Maj. Gen. John Douglas**, CB 1999; CBE 1991 (MBE 1981); Director, Dassault Systèmes EuroNorth, 2015–18; *b* 30 Dec. 1947; *s* of late Major John Alexander Gordon Stokoe and Elsie Mary Stokoe; *m* 1972, Jenny (*née* Beach); one *s* two *d*. *Educ*: Richmond Grammar Sch.; Army Apprentices Coll., Harrogate; RMA, Sandhurst. Commnd Royal Signals, 1968; served Far East, UK and BAOR; Comdr Communications, Germany, 1991–93; Higher Comd and Staff Course, 1992; DCS, Germany, 1993–94; rcds 1994; Dir, Army Staff Duties, 1994–97; DCS, HQ Land Comd, 1997–98; Dep. C-in-C, HQ Land Comd and Insp. Gen., TA, 1998–99. Defence Business Develt Dir, Amey Gp, 1999–2001; Man. Dir, Amey Defence, 2001–03; Director: Defence, Lend Lease, 2003–04; Corporate Affairs, Lend Lease Europe, 2004–06; Dir, Central Govt, Defence and Nat. Security (formerly Defence), 2006–09, Man. Dir, UK Nat. Govt Div., 2009–11, BT. Chm., Debut Services Ltd, 2006–14. Non-exec. Dir, Salisbury NHS Foundn Trust, 2008–12. Chairman: Regular Forces Employment Assoc., 2008–13; Defence Med. Welfare Service, 2013–17. Chm., Dorset Historic Churches Trust, 2019–. Col Comdt, RCS, 1998–2004; Hon. Col, 31 (City of London) Signal Regt (Vols), 2002–07; Hon. Col, FANY, 2006–08. *Recreations*: fell walking, sailing, water colour artist.

**STOLLER, Dr Anthony David**, CBE 2004; Visiting Professor, Faculty of Media and Communications, Bournemouth University, since 2015; *b* 14 May 1947; *s* of Louis and Pearl Stoller; *m* 1969, Andrea Lewisohn; one *s* one *d*. *Educ*: Hendon County Grammar Sch.; Gonville and Caius Coll., Cambridge (MA, LLB); Bournemouth Univ. (PhD 2015). Head of Radio Programming, IBA, 1974–79; Dir, Assoc. of Ind. Radio Contractors, 1979–81; Man. Dir, Thames Valley Broadcasting, 1981–85; John Lewis Partnership, 1985–95: Man. Dir, Tyrrell and Green, 1987–95; Chief Exec., Radio Authy, 1995–2003; External Relations Dir, Ofcom, 2003–06. Member: Administrative Appeals Chamber, Upper Tribunal; Gen. Regulatory Chamber, First-tier Tribunal, 2010–11. Dep. Chair, 2005–11, Chair, 2011–17, Joseph Rowntree Foundn; Dep. Chair, 2005–11, Chair, 2011–17, Joseph Rowntree Housing Trust. Mem., Competition Commn, 2009–14. Chairman: Winchester Action on Climate Change, 2014–18; Orchestras Live, 2018–. Ed., The Friends Quarterly, 2008–. *Publications*: Wrestling with The Angel, 2001; Sounds of Your Life: the history of independent radio in the UK, 2010; Classical Music Radio in the United Kingdom 1945–1995, 2017. *Recreations*: cricket, sailing, music. *Address*: 16 Denham Close, Hyde, Winchester SO23 7BL.

**STOLLER, Sir Norman (Kelvin)**, Kt 2016; CBE 2010 (MBE 1976; OBE 1999); President, SSL International plc (formerly Seton Healthcare Group plc, then Seton Scholl plc), 1999–2004 (non-executive Chairman, Seton Healthcare Group plc, 1995–99); *b* London, 6 Sept. 1934; *s* of Ivor and Sally Stoller; *m* 1st, 1960, Diane Morris (marr. diss. 1998); one *s* one *d*; 2nd, 2003, Sheila Ashton. *Educ*: Eccles High Sch., Gtr Manchester. Served RAF, 1952–55. Joined Seton Products Ltd, 1955: Dir, 1958–62; Man. Dir, 1962–80; Gp Man. Dir, 1980–85, Chm., 1985–95, Seton Healthcare Gp. Non-executive Chairman: LakeInvest Ltd; Mountain Goat Ltd; non-exec. Dir, AO World (formerly Appliances on Line) plc, 2000–14. Co. Pres., Gtr Manchester, St John Ambulance. Founding Chairman: Oldham TEC; Oldham Export Club. Founding Chm., Stoller Charitable Trust. Founding Chairman: Pennine Chapter, Young Presidents' Orgn; Pennine Chapter, World Presidents' Orgn. Pres., Mahdlo Youth Zone, Oldham. Hon. Life Mem., Macmillan Fund, 1997. Hon. RNCM 1999. Hon. Fellow, Bolton Inst. of Higher Educn, 2002. Hon. MSc Salford, 1993; Hon. DBA Bolton, 2010; Hon. DSc Manchester, 2016. DL 1995, High Sheriff, 1999–2000, Gtr Manchester. Freeman, Oldham, 2008. KStJ 2014 (CStJ 1995). Businessman of Year, CBI/Daily Telegraph, 1991. *Recreations*: golf, sailing, wines of Bordeaux, whisky of Scotland. *Address*: The Orchard, Newby Bridge Road, Bowness, Windermere, Cumbria LA23 3LL. *T*: (01539) 442077. *E*: norman@nkstoller.co.uk. *Club*: Army and Navy.

**STOLLIDAY, Deborah Mary**; *see* Jenkins, D. M.

**STOLTENBERG, Jens**; Secretary General, NATO, since 2014; *b* Oslo, 16 March 1959; *m* Ingrid Schulerud; two *c*. *Educ*: Univ. of Oslo (postgrad. degree Econs 1987). Statistics Norway; State Sec., Min. of Envmt, 1990–91. MP Norway, 1991–2014; Minister of Industry and Energy, 1993–96, of Finance, 1996–97; Prime Minister of Norway, 2000–01 and 2005–13. Leader, Norwegian Labour Party, 2002–14. *Address*: NATO, Boulevard Leopold III, 1110 Brussels, Belgium.

**STOMBERG, Dr Rolf Wilhelm Heinrich**; non-executive Chairman, Management Consulting Group (formerly Proudfoot Consulting), 2000–08; *b* Emden, Germany, 10 April 1940; *s* of Friedrich Stomberg and Johanna (*née* Meiners). *Educ*: Univ. of Hamburg (Dipl. Kfm. 1966; Dr rer. pol. 1969). Apprenticeship in shipping; Asst Prof., Univ. of Hamburg, 1966–69; joined BP Group, 1970; Finance Dir and Mem., Bd of Mgt, Deutsche BP, 1981–83; Oilstream Dir, 1983–86; Dep. Chm., Deutsche BP, 1986–89; Chm., Europe-Continental Div., BP Oil Internat., 1988; Chm., Bd of Mgt, Deutsche BP, 1989–91; CEO, BP Oil Europe, 1990; Chm., BP Europe, 1994; Man. Dir, BP plc and CEO, BP Oil Internat., 1995–97. Non-executive Chairman: John Mowlem & Co. PLC, 1999–2001; Unipoly SA, Luxembourg, 1999–2002; non-executive Director: Smith & Nephew, 1998–2009; Cordiant Communications plc, 1998–2003; Scania AB, 1998–2004; Stinnes AG, 1998–2003; TPG Gp, 1998–2008; Reed Elsevier plc, 1999–2007. Mem. Adv. Bd, Dresdner Bank AG, 1991–2003; Chm., Supervisory Bd, Lanxess AG, 2005–18, now Hon. Chm. Hon. Vis. Prof., Imperial Coll., London, 1997–2004.

**STONE**, family name of **Baron Stone of Blackheath**.

**STONE OF BLACKHEATH**, Baron *cr* 1997 (Life Peer), of Blackheath in the London Borough of Greenwich; **Andrew Zelig Stone**; *b* 7 Sept. 1942; *s* of Sydney Stone and Louise Sophia Stone (*née* Gould); *m* 1973, Vivienne Wendy Lee; one *s* two *d*. *Educ*: Cardiff High School. Joined Marks & Spencer, 1966: Dir, 1990–99; Jt Man. Dir, 1994–99. Chairman, Falcon Power, 2012–14; Deputy Chairman: Deal Gp Media plc, 2005–08; Sindicatum Carbon Capital Hldgs Ltd, 2007–09; non-executive Director: Thorn plc, 1996–98; Design Ville Ltd, 2001–03; N. Brown Gp, 2002–14; Ted Baker plc, 2002–05; Moon Valley Enterprises, 2009–14; Mem., Adv. Bd, McDonald's Restaurants, 2005–07. Chm., Dipex, 2004–. Mem., Nat. Adv. Cttee on Culture and Creativity in Educn, 1998–2001. Non-executive Director: Science Media Centre, 2001–07; ODI, 2002–05. Governor: Weizmann Inst. of Sci., 1996–07 (Life Mem., 2009); Tel Aviv Univ., 2000–05; British Univ. of Egypt, 2006–; Mem., European Council, Ben Gurion Univ., 2002–08. Trustee, The Olive Tree Project, 2003–09; Dir, Sindicatum Climate Change Foundn, 2009–12. Hon. Vice Pres., Reform Synagogues of GB, 2000–. Patron, The Forgiveness Project, 2004–. Risk Comr, RCA, 2007–09. Hon. Dr Law Oxford Brookes, 1998; Hon. DDes Kingston, 1999. *Recreations*: reading, walking, thinking. *Address*: House of Lords, SW1A 0PW.

**STONE, Maj.-Gen. Anthony Charles Peter**, CB 1994; independent defence policy and security analyst, writer and commentator, 2009–18; *b* 25 March 1939; *s* of late Major Charles C. Stone and Kathleen M. Stone (*née* Grogan); *m* 1967, (Elizabeth) Mary, *d* of Rev. Canon Gideon Davies; two *s*. *Educ*: St Joseph's Coll.; RMA, Sandhurst; Staff Coll., Camberley. Commnd RA, 1960; served in light, field, medium, heavy, locating and air defence artillery in BAOR, FE and ME and in various general and weapons staff appts in MoD; commanded 5th Regt, RA, 1980–83; founded Special OP Troop, 1982; Col, Defence Progs Staff, MoD, 1983–84; Mil. Dir of Studies, RMCS, 1985–86; Ministry of Defence: Dir of Operational Requirements (Land), 1986–89; Dir of Light Weapons Projects, 1989–90; Dir Gen. Policy and Special Projects (VMGO), 1990–92; Dir Gen. Land Fighting Systems, MoD (PE), 1992–95. Chm. and Man. Dir, The Nash Partnership Ltd, internat. defence advrs, 1996–2005; Defence Advr, Gracemoor Consultants (UK) Ltd, 1997–2006; Military Advr, PricewaterhouseCoopers, 2006–08; Military Advr to Bd, Simrad Optronics, Norway, 2007–10. Internat. Conference Chm., IQPC Defence, 2004–10. Hon. Col, 5th Regt, RA, 1990–2008; Col Comdt, 1993–2001, Rep. Col Comdt, 1998, Royal Regt of Artillery. Vis. Res. Fellow, Dept of Defence Studies, Univ. of York, 1996. Army Mem., Steering Cttee, UK Defence Forum, 1997–2007; Member: European-Atlantic Gp, 1999–2007; Military Commentators' Circle, 2013–. Patron, Lateo Assoc. (Special Observers), 2011–. Pres., Friends of Royal Artillery Mus., 2019–. FRUSI 1997. *Publications*: papers, commentaries and briefings on defence, security, counter-terrorism, defence policy and acquisition. *Recreations*: family, sudoku, writing, tennis. *Club*: Army and Navy.

**STONE, Sir Christopher**, Kt 2013; Chief Education Officer, GEMS MENASA, since 2015; Deputy Chairman, Global Academic Council, GEMS, since 2015; *b* Liverpool, 7 April 1958; *m* 1981, Kathryn Turvey; two *s*. *Educ*: Caereinion High Sch.; St Katharine's Coll. (BEd 1980 (Hons 1981)); Univ. of Leicester (MA 1989). Teacher of Physical Educn, Hist. and Life Skills, John Hanson Sch., Andover, Hants 1981–86; Hd of Performing and Creative Arts and Sixth Form, Ousedale Sch., Newport Pagnell, Bucks, 1986–92; Dep. Headteacher, Byng Kenrick Central Sch., Birmingham, 1992–95; Headteacher: Perry Beeches Sch., Birmingham, 1995–2000; Arthur Terry Sch., Birmingham, 2000–08; Exec. Headteacher, 2008–12, Chief Exec., 2012–15, Arthur Terry Learning Partnership. Nat. Leader in Educn, 2008–. Chm., Birmingham Sch. Improvement Gp, 2010–12. Hon. Dr Birmingham City, 2012; Hon. DEd Liverpool Hope, 2018. *Recreations*: all sport, walking, travelling, family. *Address*: PO Box 8607, Dubai, United Arab Emirates. *T*: 3477770, ext. 439. *E*: christopher.stone@gemseducation.com.

**STONE, David Lewis**, MD; FRCP; Consultant Cardiologist, 1988–2010, and Medical Director, 2002–09, Papworth Hospital; *b* 31 May 1948; *s* of Sidney David Stone and Dorothy Stone; *m* 1972, Helen Sharman; one *s* one *d*. *Educ*: Bancroft's Sch.; Charing Cross

Hosp. Med. Sch., London (BSc 1968; BBS 1971; MD 1985); MA Cantab 2001; King's Coll. London (MA 2010). MRCP 1974, FRCP 1992. Associate Lectr, Faculty of Clinical Medicine, Univ. of Cambridge, 1997–2009. Consultant Cardiologist, W Suffolk Hosps, 1988–2007. *Publications:* (contrib.) The Future of the NHS, 2006; articles in field of cardiac imaging. *Recreations:* music, travel, literature. *Address:* 18 Bigwood Road, NW11 7BD. *T:* (020) 8728 0438. *E:* stonedavid1@mac.com.

STONE, David Radcliffe, CBE 2010 (OBE 1997); CEng, FIMMM; Chairman, Sheffield Teaching Hospitals NHS Foundation Trust (formerly Sheffield Teaching Hospitals NHS Trust), 2001–11; Interim Chairman, Mid Yorkshire NHS Trust, 2012; *b* 19 Sept. 1935; *s* of Arthur Thomas Stone and Esther Stone; *m* 1st, 1959, Janet Clarke (*d* 1996); two *d*; 2nd, 2010, Jean Amy Day (*née* Broddley). *Educ:* Barking Abbey Sch., Essex; Univ. of Manchester (BSc Hons 1957). CEng 1983; FIMMM (FIM 1994). Manager, United Steel Cos Ltd, 1957–68; Consultant, PA Mgt Consultants, 1968–73; Works Dir, Firth Brown Ltd, 1973–78; Managing Director: Doncaster Sheffield Ltd, 1978–85; Stocksbridge Engrg Steels Ltd, 1985–89; UES Steels 1989–94; United Engrg Steels Ltd, 1994–96. Pres., British Iron and Steel Producers Assoc., 1993–94. Chairman: Weston Park Hosp. NHS Trust, 1997–99; Central Sheffield Univ. Hosps NHS Trust, 1999–2001; S Yorks Forum, 1997–2001; Convenor, UK Univ. Hosps Chairs Gp, 2004–08; Interim Chm., Mid Staffs NHS Foundn Trust, 2009. Trustee: Weston Park Cancer Care Appeal, 1996–2010; Freshgate Foundn, 1996–; Sheffield Botanical Gardens, 1997–2011. Pres., Longshaw Sheepdog Trials Assoc., 2012–13. Guardian, Sheffield Assay Office, 1998–2010. Freeman, City of London, 1995; Liveryman, Co. of Blacksmiths, 1997–; Master Cutler, Co. of Cutlers in Hallamshire, 1995–96 (Freeman, 1979–). Hon. LittD Sheffield, 2010. Hon. Consul, Finland, 1996–2014. Knight (1st Class), Order of the Lion of Finland. *Recreations:* golf, gardening, fishing, music. *Address:* Broadlea, North Green, East Drayton, near Retford, Notts DN22 0LF. *T:* (01777) 248315. *E:* davidr.stone@btinternet.com. *Club:* Hallamshire and Lindrick Golf.

STONE, Prof. Diane Lesley, PhD; Professor of Politics and International Studies, University of Warwick, since 2007; Centenary Professor of Governance, University of Canberra, 2015–20; *b* Collie, WA, 22 April 1964; *d* of Roy John and Pauline Hilda Stone; *m* 1990, Richard Higgott. *Educ:* Murdoch Univ. (BA Hons Asian Studies and Pol and Social Theory); Australian Nat. Univ. (MA; PhD Pol Sci. and Internat. Relns 1993). Tutor, Murdoch Univ., 1990; Fulbright Schol., Public Policy Prog., Georgetown Univ., 1991; Lectr, Manchester Metropolitan Univ., 1993–95; Lectr, then Reader, Univ. of Warwick, 1996–2006; Marie Curie Chair and Foundn Prof. of Public Policy, Central Eur. Univ., 2004–08; Winthrop Prof. in Politics and Internat. Relations, Univ. of Western Australia, 2010–13; Prof. of Governance, Murdoch Univ., 2013–15. Mem., Steering Cttee, 2004–10, Chm. 2006–08, Researchers Alliance for Develt. Mem., Governing Body, Global Develt Network, 2001–04. Trustee and Mem. Council, ODI, 2000–12. Fellow, Acad. of Soc. Scis in Aust., 2012. *Publications:* Capturing the Political Imagination: think tanks and the policy process, 1996; (ed with S. Maxwell) Global Knowledge Networks and Development, 2005; (ed with C. Wright) The World Bank and Governance, 2006; contrib. articles to jls. *Recreations:* swimming, travel. *Address:* Department of Politics and International Studies, University of Warwick, Coventry CV4 7AL. *T:* 07968 19177. *E:* diane.stone@warwick.ac.uk.

STONE, Emma Ace; *see* Gladstone, E. A.

STONE, Gerald Charles, PhD; FBA 1992; University Lecturer in non-Russian Slavonic Languages, Oxford University, and Fellow of Hertford College, Oxford, 1972–99; *b* 22 Aug. 1932; *s* of Albert Leslie Stone and Grace Madeline Stone (*née* Varndell); *m* 1st, 1953, Charlotte Johanna Steinbach (marr. diss. 1973); two *s* one *d*; 2nd, 1974, Vera Fedorovna Konnova; one *d*. *Educ:* Windsor Grammar Sch.; School of Slavonic Studies, London Univ. (BA 1964; PhD 1969). Nat. service, Army, Trieste, 1951–53. Metropolitan Police, 1953–64; Asst Master, Bexhill Grammar Sch., 1964–65; Asst Lectr, 1966–67, Lectr, 1967–71, Nottingham Univ.; Asst Dir of Res., Cambridge Univ., 1971–72. General Editor, Oxford Slavonic Papers, 1983–94. *Publications:* The Smallest Slavonic Nation: the Sorbs of Lusatia, 1972; (with B. Comrie) The Russian Language since the Revolution, 1978; An Introduction to Polish, 1980, 2nd edn 1992; (ed with D. Worth) The Formation of the Slavonic Literary Languages, 1985; (ed) Kěrluše, 1995; (with B. Comrie and M. Polinsky) The Russian Language in the Twentieth Century, 1996; (ed) Kjarliže, 1996; (ed) A Dictionarie of the Vulgar Russe Tongue Attributed to Mark Ridley, 1996; Upper Sorbian-English Dictionary, 2002; Der erste Beitrag zur sorbischen Sprachgeographie, 2003; The Göda Manuscript 1701, 2009; Slav Outposts in Central European History: the Wends, Sorbs and Kashubs, 2016. *Recreations:* gardening, walking, visiting pubs. *Address:* 6 Lathbury Road, Oxford OX2 7AU. *T:* (01865) 558227.

STONE, Ven. Godfrey Owen; Archdeacon of Stoke-upon-Trent, 2002–13; *b* 15 Dec. 1949; *s* of Guy and Shirley Stone; *m* 1977, Dot Caswell; one *s* one *d*. *Educ:* Exeter Coll., Oxford (BA Geog. 1971, Theol. 1978); W Midlands Coll. of Educn (PGCE 1972); Sheffield Univ. (Dip. Leadership, Renewal and Mission Studies, 1997). Ordained deacon, 1981, priest, 1982; Asst Curate, Rushden-with-Newton Bromswold, 1981–87; Dir, Pastoral Studies, Wycliffe Hall, Oxford, 1987–92; Team Rector, Bucknall Team Ministry, 1992–2002; RD, Stoke-upon-Trent, 1998–2002. Associate, Church Mission Soc., 2014–. Chm., Friends of the Church in China, 2017–. FRGS 2009. *Recreations:* walking, gardening, travel, meteorology, music. *Address:* 12 William Lucy Way, Jericho, Oxford OX2 6EQ.

STONE, His Honour Gregory; QC 1994; a Circuit Judge, 2001–12; a Deputy High Court Judge, 2008–12; *b* 12 Dec. 1946; *s* of Frederick Albert Leslie Stone and Marion Gerda Stone (*née* Heller); *m* 1974 (separated; she *d* 2018); three *d*. *Educ:* Chislehurst and Sidcup Grammar Sch.; St Joseph's Coll., London; Université de Rennes; Queen's Coll., Oxford (MA); Univ. of Manchester (Dip. Econ. Develt (distinction) 1971; MA (Econ.) 1972). Sen. Economist, Morgan Grenfell, 1974–76; called to the Bar, Inner Temple, 1976, Bencher, 2008; Standing Counsel to DTI for Criminal Matters on South Eastern Circuit, 1989–90; a Recorder, 2000–01. *Publications:* The Law of Defective Premises, 1982; The Architect's Legal Handbook, 2nd edn 1978, to 8th edn 2009. *Recreations:* travel, walking, cinema, theatre, opera, architecture, landscape. *Club:* Athenæum.

STONE, James Hume Walter Miéville; MP (Lib Dem) Caithness, Sutherland and Easter Ross, since 2017; *b* 16 June 1954; *s* of Edward Reginald Stone and Susannah Gladys Hume (*née* Waddell-Dudley); *m* 1981, Flora Kathleen Margaret Armstrong; one *s* two *d*. *Educ:* Tain Royal Acad.; Gordonstoun Sch.; St Andrews Univ. (MA 1977). Cleaner, Loch Kishorn, fish-gutter, Faroe Is, English teacher, Sicily, 1977–79; stores clerk, Wimpey Internat., 1979–81; Asst Site Administrator, then Site Administrator, subseq. Project Co-ordinator, Bechtel GB Ltd, 1981–84; Admin. Manager, Odfjell Drilling and Consulting Co. Ltd, 1984–86; Dir, Highland Fine Cheeses Ltd, 1986–94; Mem., Cromarty Firth Port Authy, 1998–2000; freelance newspaper columnist and broadcaster, 1990–. Chm., Tain Community Council, 1984; Member: (Ind, 1986–88, Lib Dem, 1988–96) Ross and Cromarty DC, 1986–96 (Vice Chm., Policy and Resources); (Lib Dem) Highland Council, 1995–99 (Vice-Chm., Finance) and 2012–17; Scottish Constitutional Convention, 1988–96; Scottish Lib Dem agriculture spokesman, 1998–99. MSP (Lib Dem) Caithness, Sutherland and Easter Ross, 1999–2011; contested (Lib Dem) same seat, 2016. Scottish Parliament: Lib Dem spokesman on educn and children, 1999–2000, on Highlands and Fisheries, 2000–01, on equal opportunities, 2001–03, on finance, 2002–03, on enterprise, lifelong learning and tourism, 2003–07; on housing, 2008; dep. spokesman on health, 2008; Mem., Holyrood Progress Gp, 2000–04; Co-Convener: Cross Pty Gp on tackling debt, 2004; Cross Pty Gp on Scottish economy, 2005; Cross Pty Gp on oil and gas, 2007 (Vice-Convener, 2003–07); Convener: Subordinate Legislation Cttee, 2007; Cross Pty Gp on Russia, 2008; Dep. Convener, Communities Cttee, 2006–07; Chm., Scottish Parlt Business Exchange, 2004–06 (Dir, 2003). Lib Dem Spokesman on Scotland, 2017, on Defence, 2017–. Mem., Exec. Cttee (Scotland), CPA, 2005. Chm., Dornoch Firth Fest., 1990–92; Director: Highland Fest., 1994–2000; Grey Coast Theatre, 2000–. Trustee: Tain Guildry Trust, 1987–; Tain Mus. Trust, 1992–; Highland Building Preservation Trust, 1995–2002. Gov., Eden Court Th., Inverness, 1995–99. FRSA. *Recreations:* shooting, reading, music, gardening, funghi, steam engines, the identification of butterflies. *Address:* Knockbreck, Tain IV19 1LZ; House of Commons, SW1A 0AA. *T:* (020) 7219 1654; (office) Hill View, Market Street, Tain, Ross-shire IV19 1AR. *T:* (01862) 892726. *Clubs:* New (Edinburgh); Armagh (N Ireland).

STONE, Prof. James McLellan, PhD; Professor, 2003–19, now Emeritus, Lyman Spitzer Jr Professor of Theoretical Astrophysics. 2016–19, now Emeritus, and Chairman, Department of Astrophysical Sciences, 2016, Princeton University; Professor, Institute for Advanced Study, Princeton, since 2019; *b* 29 Nov. 1962; *s* of William and Helen Stone; *m* 1984, Penelope Janet (*née* Rose); two *d*. *Educ:* Queen's Univ., Kingston, Ont. (BS Hons, MS); Univ. of Illinois, Champaign-Urbana (PhD 1990). Postdoctoral Fellow, Univ. of Illinois, 1990–92; Prof., Dept of Astronomy, Univ. of Maryland, College Park, 1992–2002; Prof. of Mathematical Physics, Cambridge Univ., 2002–03. *Publications:* contrib. numerous papers to refereed jls. *Recreations:* hiking, ski-ing. *Address:* School of Natural Sciences, Institute for Advanced Study, 1 Einstein Drive, Princeton, NJ 08540, USA.

STONE, Joseph; QC 2013; *b* 28 Jan. 1964; *s* of Nicholas Stone and Lorraine Stone; *m* 2001, Keir Posner; one *d*. *Educ:* Brighton Coll.; Hammersmith and West London Coll.; Manchester Univ. (BA 1st Cl. Hons Pols and Phil. 1985). Called to the Bar, Inner Temple, 1989; in practice specialising in criminal defence, homicide. *Recreations:* swimming, sailing, windsurfing. *Address:* 53–54 Doughty Street, WC1N 2LS. *T:* (020) 7404 1313.

STONE, Kathryn, OBE 2007; Parliamentary Commissioner for Standards, since 2018; *b* Derby, 8 Aug. 1963; one *s* two *d*. *Educ:* Univ. of E London (BA Hons Sociol. 1985); CQSW 1985; Loughborough Univ. (MA Women's Studies 1990); Inst. of Dirs (Cert. and Dip. in Co. Direction 2007); Internat. Truth and Justice Inst., NY (Dip. Truth Commns 2013). Family Social Worker, Family Welfare Assoc., 1985–87; Derbyshire County Council: Sen. Practitioner, Social Work, 1987–89; Asst Women's Officer (Trng), 1989–91; Sen. Practice Teacher, 1991–94; Ind. Inspector, Barking and Dagenham LBC, Cambs CC, Hackney LBC, Hammersmith and Fulham LBC, Bucks CC, Kirklees MBC, 1994–98; Head of Inspection: Barking and Dagenham LBC 1999; Hammersmith and Fulham LBC, 1999–2000; Principal Inspector, Milton Keynes Council, 2000–01; CEO, Voice UK, 2001–12; Commissioner: Commn for Victims and Survivors, NI, 2012–14; Ind. Police Complaints Commn, 2014–16; Chief Legal Ombudsman, 2016–17. FInstD 2009. Hon. LLD Derby, 2018. *Recreations:* gardening, spending time with family and fantastic friends. *Address:* Office of the Parliamentary Commissioner for Standards, House of Commons, SW1A 0AA.

STONE, Lucy Madeline, (Mrs C. Coleman); QC 2001; *b* 16 Oct. 1959; *d* of late Alexander Stone and of Rene Stone; *m* 1994, Charles Coleman; one *s*. *Educ:* Newnham Coll., Cambridge (MA 1984); Inns of Court Sch. of Law. Called to the Bar, Middle Temple, 1983, Bencher, 2010; specialist in divorce law. *Recreations:* family, entertaining, reading. *Address:* Queen Elizabeth Building, Temple, EC4Y 9BS. *T:* (020) 7797 7837.

STONE, Oliver William; actor, screenwriter and director; *b* NYC, 15 Sept. 1946; *s* of Louis Stone and Jacqueline Stone (*née* Goddet). *Educ:* Yale Univ.; NY Univ. (BFA). Film Sch. Teacher, Cholon, Vietnam, 1965–66; wiper, US Merchant Marine, 1966; served US Army, Vietnam, 1967–68 (Purple Heart with oak leaf cluster, Bronze Star); taxi driver, NYC, 1971. *Screenwriter:* Seizure, 1974; Midnight Express, 1978 (Acad. Award, Writers' Guild of Amer. Award); The Hand, 1981; (with J. Milius) Conan the Barbarian, 1982; Scarface, 1983; (with M. Cimino) Year of the Dragon, 1985; (with D. L. Henry) 8 Million Ways to Die, 1986; (with R. Boyle) Salvador, 1986; (also Dir) Platoon, 1986 (Acad. Award, Dirs Guild of Amer. Award, BAFTA Award); *co-writer:* Evita, 1996; *co-writer and director:* Wall Street, 1987; Talk Radio, 1988; The Doors, 1991; *screenwriter, producer and director:* Born on the Fourth of July, 1989 (Acad. Award, 1990); JFK, 1991; Heaven & Earth, 1993; Natural Born Killers, 1994; Nixon, 1995; Any Given Sunday, 1999; Commandante, 2003; Persona Non Grata, 2003, Looking for Fidel, 2004; Alexander, 2005; Wall Street: Money Never Sleeps, 2010; Savages, 2012; *co-writer, producer and director:* Oliver Stone's Untold History of the United States (TV series), 2013; *producer and director:* World Trade Center, 2006; The Putin Interviews (TV series), 2017; *director:* U-Turn, 1997; W., 2008; South of the Border, 2010; Snowden, 2016; *producer:* Reversal of Fortune, 1990; Blue Steel, 1990; South Central, 1992; Zebrahead, 1992; The Joy Luck Club, 1993; New Age, 1994; Wild Palms (TV mini-series), 1993; Freeway, 1996; The People vs Larry Flynt, 1996; Saviour, 1998; *executive producer:* Iron Maze, 1991; Killer: A Journal of Murder, 1996; (HBO) Indictment: The McMartin Preschool, 1995; The Last Day of Kennedy and King, 1998; The Corrupter, 1999; The Day Reagan Was Shot, 2001. Member: Writers' Guild of America; Directors' Guild of America; Acad. of Motion Picture Arts and Scis. *Publications:* A Child's Night Dream, 1997; The Untold History of the United States, 2013.

STONE, Maj.-Gen. Patrick Philip Dennant, CB 1992; CBE 1984 (OBE 1981 MBE 1975); Director General, Personal Services (Army), 1988–91; *b* 7 Feb. 1939; *s* of Philip Hartley Stone and Elsie Maude Stone (*née* Dennant); *m* 1967, Christine Iredale Trent; two *s* one *d*. *Educ:* Christ's Hospital; psc 1972. Nat. Service, 1959; commissioned East Anglian Regt, 1959; seconded 6 KAR, 1960–62 (Tanganyika); served British Guyana and Aden, 1962–65; ADC to Governor of W Australia, 1965–67; RAF Staff Coll., 1972; Comd 2nd Bn, Royal Anglian Regt, 1977–80 (UK and Berlin); Chief of Staff, 1st Armoured Div., 1981–84; Comdr, Berlin Inf. Bde, 1985–86; Dep. Mil. Sec. (B), 1987. Dep. Col, Royal Anglian Regt, 1986–91, Col, 1991–97; Col Comdt, Mil. Provost Staff Corps, 1988–92; Dep. Col Comdt, AGC, 1992–93. *Recreations:* country interests, travel, conservation, veteran and classic cars. *Address:* c/o Lloyds Bank, 90A Mill Road, Cambridge CB1 2BE. *Club:* Army and Navy.

STONE, Prof. Richard Thomas Horner; Professor of Law, University of Lincoln, 2003–14, now Emeritus; *b* 7 March 1951; *s* of late Rev. Ross Stone and Bettine Stone (*née* Horner); *m* 1973, Margaret Peerman; one *s* three *d*. *Educ:* Reading Sch.; Southampton Univ. (LLB); Hull Univ. (LLM 1978). Called to the Bar, Gray's Inn, 1998. Leicester University: Lectr in Law, 1975–89; Sen. Lectr in Law, 1989–93; Dean, Faculty of Law, 1987–90; Resident Dir, Sunway Coll., Malaysia, 1989; Prof., 1993–97, Dean, 1996–97, Nottingham Law Sch., Nottingham Trent Univ.; Principal, Inns of Court Sch. of Law, 1997–2001. Vis. Lectr, Loughborough Univ., 1978–91; Visiting Professor: City Univ., 1997–2002; UC, Northampton, 2002–04. FRSA 1998. *Publications:* Entry, Search and Seizure, 1985, 5th edn 2013; Textbook on Civil Liberties, 1994, 11th edn (with Ruth

Costigan), 2017; Principles of Contract Law, 1994, 13th edn, as Modern Law of Contract (with James Devenney), 2019; Law of Agency, 1996; Offences Against the Person, 1999; (with Ralph Cunnington) Text, Cases and Materials on Contract Law, 2007, 4th edn (with James Devenney), 2017; articles in legal jls. *Recreations:* singing, walking, books. *Address:* Lincoln Law School, University of Lincoln, Brayford Pool, Lincoln LN6 7TS. *E:* rstone@lincoln.ac.uk.

**STONE, Rt Rev. Ronald Francis,** AM 2008; Ministry Development Officer, 2004–08, Vicar General, 2008, and Archdeacon, 2009, Diocese of Bendigo; Executive Assistant to Bishop of Bendigo, 2007–15; *b* Armadale, Vic, 10 Sept. 1938; *s* of late Allan Francis Stone and Beatrice Rose Stone (*née* Hubber); *m* 1964, Lisbeth Joan Williams; two *s* one *d*. *Educ:* Caulfield South High Sch.; Caulfield Tech. Coll.; Taylors' Coll., Melbourne; St John's Coll., Morpeth, NSW (ThL 1963). Rector of Kerang, 1969–83; Canon, All Saints Cathedral, Bendigo, 1979–82; Archdeacon of Bendigo, 1983–92; VG, Diocese of Bendigo, 1983–92; Provincial Officer, Province of Victoria, 1988–92; Asst Bishop of Tasmania, 1992–96; Bishop of Rockhampton, 1996–2003. Convener, Gen. Synod Rural Ministry Task Gp, 1991–98; Member: Gen. Synod Ministry and Trng Commn, 1991–98; Episcopal Standards Commn, 2004–11. Chairman: Bd of Dirs, Anglican Superannuation Australia, 1999–2003; Nat. Home Mission Fund—Anglican Outback Fund, 2007–11. Editor, The Anglican Gazette, 1997–2003. *Publications:* A Kangaroo is Designed to Move Forward…But Which Direction for the Rural and Remote Area Church?, 1998 (Felix Arnott Meml Lect.); paper on rural ministry in Bush Telegraph. *Recreations:* gardening, philately, furniture restoration, golf, music, radio broadcasting. *Address:* 55 Barnett Drive, Kangaroo Flat, Vic 3555, Australia. *E:* stonebgo@bigpond.net.au. *Club:* Barham.

**STONE, Sir Roy (Alexander),** Kt 2019; CBE 2014; Principal Private Secretary to Government Chief Whip, since 1998; *b* Hornchurch, Essex, 19 June 1961; *s* of Stanley and Doris Stone; *m* 1996, Dawn Smailes; one *s* one *d*. Project mgt, Supply, 1977–83, Logistics, Procurement Exec., 1983–88, MoD; Duty Clerk, 1988–89, Parly Clerk, 1989–98, 10 Downing St. *Recreations:* swimming, walking, family. *Address:* 9 Downing Street, SW1A 2AG. *T:* (020) 7276 2020. *E:* roy.stone@cabinetoffice.gov.uk.

**STONE, Dr Timothy John,** CBE 2010; CEng, FICE; Chairman: Nuclear Risk Insurers, since 2015; Nuclear Industry Association, since 2018; *b* Rotherham, 11 May 1951; *s* of Jack and Kathleen Elsa Stone; *m* 1977, Joanne Mary Egan Lee; one *s* one *d*. *Educ:* Maltby Grammar Sch.; St Catherine's Coll., Oxford (MA; DPhil 1976). MBCS 1982; CEng 1985; FICE 2010. Sen. Manager, Arthur Andersen, 1976–83; Man. Dir, Chase Manhattan Bank, NY, 1983–89; Dir, S. G. Warburg & Co., 1989–95; Partner, and Chm., Global Infrastructure and Projects, KPMG, 1995–2011. Sen. Advr to Sec. of State for Energy and Climate Change, 2007–13; Expert Chair, Office for Nuclear Develt, DECC, 2008–13. Non-executive Director: Anglian Water Gp, 2011–15; Horizon Nuclear Power, 2014–19; Arup Gp, 2015–. Expert, Bd, EIB, 2003–18. Hon. FNucI 2012. *Recreations:* double bass playing (classical), classical music, computing, AI/machine learning. *Club:* Reform.

**STONE, Prof. Trevor William,** PhD, DSc; FBPhS; Professor of Pharmacology, University of Glasgow, 1989–2017; Hon. Senior Research Fellow, University of Oxford, since 2017; *b* 7 Oct. 1947; *s* of late Thomas William Stone and Alice Stone (*née* Reynolds); *m* 1st, 1971, Anne Corina (marr. diss. 2003); 2nd, 2005, Dr Lynda Gail Ramsey (*née* Darlington). *Educ:* Sch. of Pharmacy, London Univ. (BPharm 1969; DSc 1983); Aberdeen Univ. (PhD 1972). Lectr in Physiology, Univ. of Aberdeen, 1970–77; Sen. Lectr, 1977–83, Reader, 1983–86, Prof., 1986–88, in Neurosci., St George's Hosp. Sch. of Medicine, Univ. of London. Res. Fellow, Nat. Inst. of Mental Health, Washington, 1974, 1977; Vis. Prof. of Pharmacology, Univ. of Auckland, 1988. Man. Dir, Imagery, 1984–89; Dir of Res., Shinkanco, 2001–; Dir, PharmaLinks, 2002–10. Mem., Inst. of Neuroscis and Psychol., 2010–. FRSocMed; FBPhS (FBPharmacolS 2005). Hon. FRCP 2011. Hon. Mem., Portuguese Pharmacol Soc., 1989. *Publications:* Microiontophoresis and Pressure Ejection, 1985; Purines: basic and clinical aspects, 1989; Quinolinic Acid and Kynurenines, 1989; Adenosine in the Nervous System, 1991; CNS Transmitters and Neuromodulators, I 1994, II and III 1995, IV 1996; Neuropharmacology, 1995; Pills, Potions & Poisons, 2000; over 400 sci. papers. *Recreations:* piano, photography, snooker, music, work. *Address:* Nuffield Department of Orthopaedics, Rheumatology and Musculoskeletal Sciences, University of Oxford OX3 7FY.

**STONE-FEWINGS, Nancy;** *see* Carroll, N.

**STONEHAM,** family name of **Baron Stoneham of Droxford**.

**STONEHAM OF DROXFORD,** Baron *cr* 2011 (Life Peer), of the Meon Valley in the County of Hampshire; **Benjamin Russell Mackintosh Stoneham;** *b* Tunbridge Wells, 24 Aug. 1948; *m* 1975, Anne Kristine MacKintosh (MBE 2012); two *s* one *d*. *Educ:* Harrow Sch.; Christ's Coll., Cambridge (BA Econs 1970); Warwick Univ. (MA Industrial Relns 1971); London Business Sch. (Advanced Sen. Mgt Prog. 1990). Res. Officer, Dept of Social and Admin. Studies, Univ. of Oxford, 1971–74; trainee, 1974–76, staff officer to Chm., 1976–78, Hd, Wages Planning Unit 1978–79, NCB; Nat. Officer, NUR, 1979–82; Portsmouth and Sunderland Newspapers plc, 1982–99; Man. Dir, Portsmouth Publishing and Printing Ltd, 1989–99; Gp Prodn Dir and Personnel Dir, News Internat., 2000–03; Ops Dir, Liberal Democrat HQ, 2003–10. Mem. (SDP) Herts CC, 1985–89. Chief Whip, Lib Dem Gp, H of L, 2016–. Contested: (Lab) Saffron Walden, 1977, 1979; (SDP/Alliance) Stevenage, 1983, 1987. Founder Member: SDP, 1981 (Mem., Federal Exec., 1986–88); Lib Dem, 1988. Chairman and Director: Portsmouth Harbour Renaissance Ltd, 1996–2005; First Wessex Housing Gp, 2007–12; Housing and Care 21, 2011–18; Dir, Thames Gateway-Thurrock Urban Develt Corp., 2004–11. *Address:* House of Lords, SW1A 0PW.

**STONER, Christopher Paul;** QC 2010; *b* Shoreham by Sea, W Sussex, 29 April 1967; *s* of Gordon and Marie Stoner; *m* 2005, Lydia Simpson. *Educ:* Shoreham Coll.; Univ. of East Anglia (LLB 1st Cl.). Called to the Bar, Lincoln's Inn, 1991; in practice as barrister, specialising in property litigation, sports, regulatory and disciplinary law. *Recreations:* Bath Rugby, motor racing. *Address:* Serle Court, 6 New Square, Lincoln's Inn, WC2A 3QS. *T:* (020) 7242 6105. *E:* cstoner@serlecourt.co.uk.

**STONHAM, Rt Rev. Dom Paul,** OSB; Abbot of Belmont, since 2000; *b* 22 Feb. 1947; *s* of Robert Stonham and Anna Maria (*née* Frezzini). *Educ:* Univ. of Birmingham (BA (Hons) Mod. Langs 1969); Coll. Sant'Anselmo, Rome (STB 1975). Housemaster, Belmont Abbey Sch., 1975–81; Parish Priest, Tambogrande, Peru, 1981–86; Superior, Monasterio de la Encarnación, Peru, 1986–2000; Prof., Seminario Arquidiocesano, Piura, Peru, 1988–2000; Parish Priest, San Lorenzo, Peru, 1994–98. Dean, Herefordshire, 2001–11. Mem., Equipe Internat. Alliance Inter Monastères, 2001–. *Recreations:* reading, walking, music, travel, animal life. *Address:* Belmont Abbey, Hereford HR2 9RZ. *T:* (01432) 374718. *E:* abbot@belmontabbey.org.uk.

**STONHOUSE, Ven. Sir Michael Philip,** 19th Bt *cr* 1628 and 15th Bt *cr* 1670, of Radley, Berkshire; Archdeacon of the Battlefords, 2015–16, now Emeritus; *b* 4 Sept. 1948; *er s* of Sir Philip Allan Stonhouse, 18th Bt and 14th Bt, and Winnifred Emily (*d* 1989), *e d* of J. M. Shield; *S* father, 1993; *m* 1977, Colleen Coucill (marr. diss. 2006); three *s*. *Educ:* Medicine Hat Coll., Univ. of Alberta (BA); Wycliffe Coll. (MDiv). Ordained deacon, 1977, priest, 1978, Dio. of Calgary, Canada. Asst Curate, St Peter's, Calgary, 1977–80; Rector and Incumbent: Parkland Parish, Alberta, 1980–87; St Mark's Innisfail and St Matthew's Bowden, Alberta, 1987–92; St James, Saskatoon, Saskatchewan, 1992–2007; St John's Minster and Associated Churches, Lloydminster, Saskatchewan, 2007–16; Canon, Dio. of Saskatoon, 2006. Prolocutor, Provincial Synod of Rupert's Land, 2009–12. *Heir: s* Allan James Stonhouse, *b* 20 March 1981. *Address:* 4809–47 Street, Lloydminster, Saskatchewan, SK S9V 0K2, Canada.

**STONIER, Prof. Peter David,** PhD; consultant in pharmaceutical medicine, since 2000; Director of Education and Training, Faculty of Pharmaceutical Medicine, Royal Colleges of Physicians of the UK, since 2003; *b* 29 April 1945; *s* of Frederick Stonier and Phyllis Maud Stonier; *m* 1989, Elizabeth Margaret Thomas; one *s* one *d*. *Educ:* Cheadle Hulme Sch.; Univ. of Birmingham (BSc 1st cl. Hons 1966); Univ. of Sheffield (PhD 1969); Univ. of Manchester (MB ChB Hons 1974); Open Univ. (BA 1990). FFPM 1989; FRCPE 1993; MRCPsych 1994; FRCP 1998. House Officer, Manchester Royal Infirmary, 1974–75; Senior House Officer: Univ. Hosp. S Manchester, 1975–76; Leicester Royal Infirmary, 1976–77; Med. Advr, 1977–80, Head of Med. Services, 1980–81, Med. Dir, 1982–2000, and Bd Mem., 1994–2000, Hoechst UK Ltd, later Hoechst Roussel Ltd, then Hoechst Marion Roussel Ltd. Gp Med. Dir, Amdipharm plc, 2004–13; Med. Dir, Axess Ltd, 2005–. Visiting Professor: Univ. of Surrey, 1992–2010 (Course Dir, MSc in Pharmaceutical Medicine, 1993–2001); KCL, 1998–. Member: Pharm. Industry Trng Council, 1998–2002; Appeal Panel, NICE, 2000–; Bd, PharmaTrain, 2009–14; Bd, PharmaTrain Fedn, 2014–. Chm., British Assoc. of Pharmaceut. Physicians, 1988–90; Mem. Council, British Assoc. of Psychopharmacology, 1993–97; Council, RCP, 1997–2001; Faculty of Pharmaceutical Medicine, Royal Colleges of Physicians of UK: Vice Pres., 1992–96, Pres., 1997–2001; Mem., Bd of Examrs, 1994–97; Chm., Fellowship Cttee, 1997–2001; Convenor and Chair, Task Force for Specialist Trng in Pharmaceut. Medicine, 1995–99. Pres., Internat. Fedn of Assocs of Pharmaceut. Physicians, 1996–98. FRSocMed 1982 (Pres., Sect. of Pharmaceut. Medicine and Res., 1994–96); FMS 1999; FRSA 2000. Founder Ed., Pharmaceutical Physician, 1989–98; Associate Ed., Human Psychopharmacology, 1990–2007; Mem., Editl Adv. Panel, Internat. Jl of Pharmaceut. Medicine, 1997–. Lifetime Achievement Award, Acad. of Pharmaceutical Physicians & Investigators, 2006. *Publications:* (ed jtly) Perspectives in Psychiatry, 1988; (ed with I. Hindmarch) Human Psychopharmacology: methods and measures, vol. 1 1988, vol. 2 1989, vol. 3 1991, vol. 4 1993, vol. 5 1996, vol. 6 1997; (ed) Discovering New Medicines: careers in pharmaceutical research and development, 1994, 2nd edn as Careers with the Pharmaceutical Industry, 2003; (ed jtly) Clinical Research Manual, 1994–; (ed jtly) Medical Marketing Manual, 2001; (ed jtly) Principles and Practice of Pharmaceutical Medicine, 2002, 3rd edn 2010; (ed jtly) Paediatric Clinical Research Manual, 2005; articles on psychopharmacology and pharmaceut. medicine. *Recreations:* opera, gardening, travel. *Address:* 5 Branstone Road, Kew, Richmond-on-Thames, Surrey TW9 3LB. *T:* (020) 8948 5069.

**STONOR,** family name of **Baron Camoys**.

**STONOR, Sara Jane;** Vice Lord-Lieutenant of East Sussex, since 2008; professional embroiderer and cushion maker; *b* Portsmouth, 22 June 1948; *d* of Rt Rev. Gerald Alexander Ellison, KCVO and of Jane Elizabeth Ellison; *m* 1969, Desmond Michael Stonor; one *s* one *d*. *Educ:* Moreton Hall; Château Brillantmont, Lausanne. Chm., Chichester Cathedral Restoration Trust, 2003–08; Member: Chichester Cathedral Council, 2001–17; Chichester Cathedral Chapter, 2002–17; Provincial Panel, Clergy Discipline Measure, 2003–12; Exec., Assoc. of English Cathedrals, 2010–15; Council, St John, Sussex, 2011–12; Centenary Appeals Cttee, Charleston Manor Farmhouse, 2014–; Sussex St John County Priory Gp, 2018–; Chichester Bishop's Council, 2018–. Trustee, Sussex Historic Churches Trust, 2011– (Vice-Chm., 2015–). Vice-Chm., Trustees, De La Warr Pavilion, Bexhill-on-Sea, 2008–14. Patron: Friends of Crowborough Meml Hosp., 2013–; Girl Guiding E Sussex, 2016–; Fellowship of St Nicholas, St Leonards on Sea, 2018–; Vice-Patron, Mothers' Union, Chichester Dio., 2015–; Vice-Chm., Conquest £1m Scanner Appeal, 2016–. Vice Pres., E Sussex Magistrates Assoc., 2014–. DL E Sussex, 2001–08. Churchwarden, St Bartholomew's, Burwash, 1996–2003. Chm., Order of St Richard, 2018–. *Recreations:* walking, needlework, art, music, theatre, cooking. *Address:* Pound Platt, Northbridge Street, Robertsbridge, E Sussex TN32 5NY. *T:* (01580) 880569. *E:* sara@stonor.org.uk.

**STONOR, Air Marshal Sir Thomas (Henry),** KCB 1989; Group Director and Controller, National Air Traffic Services, 1988–91; *b* 5 March 1936; *s* of Alphonsus and Ann Stonor; *m* 1964, Robin Antoinette, *er d* of Wilfrid and Rita Budd; two *s* one *d*. *Educ:* St Cuthbert's High Sch., Newcastle upon Tyne; King's Coll., Univ. of Durham (BSc (Mech Eng) 1957). Commissioned, RAF, 1959; served No 3 Sqn, 2ATAF, 1961–64; CFS, 6 FTS and RAF Coll., Cranwell, 1964–67; No 231 Operational Conversion Unit, 1967–69; RAF Staff Coll., Bracknell, 1970; HQ, RAF Germany, 1971–73; OC 31 Sqn, 1974–76; Mil. Asst to VCDS, MoD, 1976–78; OC RAF Coltishall, 1978–80; RCDS, 1981; Inspector of Flight Safety, RAF, 1982–84; Dir of Control (Airspace Policy), NATS, 1985–86; Dep. Controller, NATS, 1986–88. Sen. Consultant, Siemens Plessey Systems, 1991–98; Defence Advr, BT Defence Sales Sector, 1991–2003; non-exec. Dir, Parity PLC (formerly COMAC Gp), 1994–2001. *Recreations:* gardening, music. *Address:* 20 Sunderland Avenue, Oxford OX2 8DX. *Club:* Royal Air Force.

**STONOR, Timothy Dominic,** RIBA; Managing Director, Space Syntax, since 1995; Director, Morrison Brink Stonor Architects, since 1996; *b* Newcastle upon Tyne, 13 Feb. 1968; *s* of William Stonor and Eleanor Stonor (*née* Pattinson); *m* 1996, Joanna, *er d* of Robin and late Hazel Grimble; one *s* one *d*. *Educ:* St Cuthbert's High Sch., Newcastle upon Tyne; University Coll. London (BSc Hons Arch. 1989; MSc Arch. (Dist.) 1991; Part 3 Professional Exam in Arch., 1995); Oxford Brookes Univ. (Grad. DipArch (Dist.) 1994). RIBA 1995; MRTPI 2005. Loeb Fellow, 2011, Lincoln Loeb Fellow, 2011, Harvard Univ. Vis. Prof., UCL, 2011–. Major projects: Trafalgar Sq. redesign, 2003; Waterloo and South Bank masterplan, 2005; Colchester, St Botolph's Quarter masterplan, 2005; Jeddah Central Urban Area masterplan, 2006; Beijing, Chaoyang Central Business Dist masterplan, 2009; Darwin, City Centre masterplan, 2014. Member: SE of England Design Panel, 2002–04; NHS Nat. Design Rev. Panel, 2003–11; Nat. Design Rev. Panel, CABE, 2004–07; Health and the Built Envmt Steering Gp, NICE, 2005–08; CABE Crossrail Design Panel, 2008–10; Lead Expert Gp on Future of Cities, Govt Office for Sci., 2013–15. Advocate, EPSRC, 2009–. Sen. Internat. Advr, China Urban and Rural Construction Industry Union, 2017–. Kevin Lynch Meml Lect., Urban Design Gp, 2017. Dir, London Promenade Co., 2008–. Dir, Acad. of Urbanism, 2008–10 and 2011– (Founder Academician, 2006). Trustee: Design Council, 2015– (Dep. Chm., 2018–); Faversham Soc., 2016–. Freeman, City of London, 2016; Liveryman, Chartered Architects' Co., 2016. Changchun Friendship Award, 2017. *Recreations:* swimming, drawing, urban living. *Address:* 46 Tanners Street, Faversham, Kent ME13 7JL. *E:* t.stonor@spacesyntax.com. *Clubs:* Harvard Faculty; Faversham.

**STOPFORD,** family name of **Earl of Courtown**.

**STOPFORD, Viscount; James Richard Ian Montagu Stopford**; *b* 30 March 1988; *s* and *heir* of Earl of Courtown, *qv*. *Educ*: Eton; Univ. of Durham; BPP Law Sch. (Grad. Dip. Law; Legal Practice Course). Researcher, Office of Mark Menzies, MP, 2011–12. Admitted solicitor, 2015. Trainee Solicitor, 2013, Associate, 2015–, Mishcon de Reya, LLP. *Recreations*: ski-ing, Rugby.

**STOPPARD, Miriam, (Lady Hogg)**, OBE 2010; MD; FRCP; writer and broadcaster; Founder and Executive Chairman, Miriam Stoppard Lifetime Ltd, since 2001; *b* 12 May 1937; *d* of Sydney and Jenny Stern; *m* 1st, 1972, Sir Tom Stoppard, *qv* (marr. diss. 1992); two *s* and two step *s*; 2nd, 1997, Sir Christopher Hogg, *qv*. *Educ*: Newcastle upon Tyne Central High Sch. (State Scholar, 1955); Royal Free Hosp. Sch. of Medicine, Univ. of London (Prize for Experimental Physiol., 1958); King's Coll. Med. Sch. (Univ. of Durham), Newcastle upon Tyne (MB, BS Durham, 1961; MD Newcastle, 1966). FRCP 1998 (MRCP 1964). Royal Victoria Infirmary, King's Coll. Hosp., Newcastle upon Tyne: House Surg., 1961; House Phys., 1962; Sen. House Officer in Medicine, 1962–63; Univ. of Bristol: Res. Fellow, Dept of Chem. Pathol., 1963–65 (MRC Scholar in Chem. Pathol.); Registrar in Dermatol., 1965–66 (MRC Scholar in Dermatol.); Sen. Registrar in Dermatol., 1966–68; Syntex Pharmaceuticals Ltd: Associate Med. Dir, 1968; Dep. Med. Dir, 1971; Med. Dir, 1974; Dep. Man. Dir, 1976; Man. Dir, 1977–81. TV series: Where There's Life (5 series), 1981; Baby & Co. (2 series), 1984; Woman to Woman, 1985; Miriam Stoppard's Health and Beauty Show, 1988; Dear Miriam, 1989; The Real Marigold Hotel, 2017. MRSocMed (Mem. Dermatol. Sect., Endocrinol. Sect.); Member: Heberden Soc.; Brit. Assoc. of Rheumatology and Rehabilitation. Hon. DSc Durham, 2000; Hon. DCL Newcastle, 2004. *Publications*: Miriam Stoppard's Book of Baby Care, 1977; (contrib.) My Medical School, 1978; Miriam Stoppard's Book of Health Care, 1979; The Face and Body Book, 1980; Everywoman's Lifeguide, 1982; Your Baby, 1982; Fifty Plus Lifeguide, 1982; Your Growing Child, 1983; Baby Care Book, 1983; Pregnancy and Birth Book, 1984; Baby and Child Medical Handbook, 1986; Everygirl's Lifeguide, 1987; Feeding Your Family, 1987; Miriam Stoppard's Health and Beauty Book, 1988; Every Woman's Medical Handbook, 1988; Lose 7 lb in 7 Days, 1990; Test Your Child, 1991; The Magic of Sex, 1991; Conception, Pregnancy and Birth, 1993; The Menopause, 1994; Questions Children Ask and How to Answer Them, 1997; Sex Ed—Growing up, Relationships and Sex, 1997; The New Parent, 1998; Healthcare series (15 titles), 1998–2002; Drugs Info File, 1999; Baby's Play and Learn Pack, 2000; Women's Health Handbook, 2001; Teach Your Child, 2001; Family Health Guide, 2002; Baby First Aid, 2003; Defying Age, 2003; The Grandparent's Book: making the most of a very special relationship, 2006; My Pregnancy Planner, 2007; Bonding with Your Bump, 2008; Grandparents: enjoying and caring for your grandchild, 2011; Trusted Advice series (6 titles), 2011–12; over 40 pubns in med. jls. *Recreations*: my family, gardening. *Address*: Miriam Stoppard Lifetime Ltd, Bentinck House, 3–8 Bolsover Street, W1W 6AB.

**STOPPARD, Sir Tom**, OM 2000; Kt 1997; CBE 1978; FRSL; playwright and novelist; *b* 3 July 1937; *yr s* of late Eugene Straussler and of Mrs Martha Stoppard; *m* 1st, 1965, Jose (marr. diss. 1972), *yr d* of John and Alice Ingle; two *s*; 2nd, 1972, Dr Miriam Moore-Robinson (*see* Miriam Stoppard) (marr. diss. 1992); two *s*; 3rd, 2014, Sabrina Guinness. *Educ*: abroad; Dolphin Sch., Notts; Pocklington, Yorks. Journalist: Western Daily Press, Bristol, 1954–58; Bristol Evening World, 1958–60; freelance, 1960–63. *Plays*: Enter a Free Man, London, 1968 (TV play, A Walk on the Water, 1963); Rosencrantz and Guildenstern are Dead, Nat. Theatre, 1967, subseq. NY, etc (Tony Award, NY, 1968; NY Drama Critics Circle Award, 1968), Old Vic, 2017; The Real Inspector Hound, London, 1968; After Magritte, Ambiance Theatre, 1970; Dogg's Our Pet, Ambiance Theatre, 1972; Jumpers, National Theatre, 1972 (Evening Standard Award); Travesties, Aldwych, 1974 (Evening Standard Award; Tony Award, NY, 1976); Dirty Linen, Newfoundland, Ambiance Theatre, 1976; Every Good Boy Deserves Favour (music-theatre), 1977; Night and Day, Phoenix, 1978 (Evening Standard Award); Dogg's Hamlet and Cahoot's Macbeth, Collegiate, 1979; Undiscovered Country (adaptation), NT, 1979; On the Razzle, NT, 1981; The Real Thing, Strand, 1982 (Standard Award), subseq. NY (Tony Award, 1984); Rough Crossing (adaptation), NT, 1984; Dalliance (adaptation), NT, 1986; Hapgood, Aldwych, 1988; Arcadia, NT, 1993 (Evening Standard Award; Olivier Award); Indian Ink, Aldwych, 1995; The Seagull (trans.), Old Vic, 1997; The Invention of Love, NT, 1997 (Evening Standard Award); The Coast of Utopia (trilogy), NT, 2002, NY (Tony Award), 2007; Henry IV (adaptation), Donmar Warehouse, 2004; Heroes (trans.), Wyndham's, 2005; Rock 'n' Roll, Royal Court, transf. Duke of York's (Best Play, London Evening Standard Theatre Awards, and Critics' Circle Theatre Awards), 2006; Ivanov (adaptation), Wyndham's, 2008; The Cherry Orchard (adaptation), Harvey Th., NY, 2009; The Hard Problem, NT, 2015; *radio*: The Dissolution of Dominic Boot, 1964; M is for Moon Among Other Things, 1964; If You're Glad I'll Be Frank, 1965; Albert's Bridge, 1967 (Prix Italia); Where Are They Now?, 1970; Artist Descending a Staircase, 1972; The Dog it was That Died, 1982 (Giles Cooper Award; televised 1988); In the Native State, 1991; Dark Side, 2013; *television*: A Separate Peace, 1966; Teeth, 1967; Another Moon Called Earth, 1967; Neutral Ground, 1968; (with Clive Exton) Boundaries, 1975; (adapted) Three Men in a Boat, 1976; Professional Foul, 1977; Squaring the Circle, 1984; (adapted) Parade's End, 2012; *screenplays*: (with T. Wiseman) The Romantic Englishwoman, 1975; Despair, 1978; The Human Factor, 1979; (with Terry Gilliam and Charles McKeown) Brazil, 1985; Empire of the Sun, 1987; Rosencrantz and Guildenstern are Dead, 1990 (also dir); The Russian House, 1991; Billy Bathgate, 1991; (with Marc Norman) Shakespeare in Love (Oscar Award for Best Screenplay), 1999; Enigma, 2001; Anna Karenina, 2012; (with D. Moggach) Tulip Fever, 2018. Mem. Bd, RNT, 1982–2003. Pres., London Library, 2004–. Hon. FBA 2017. Hon. degrees: Bristol, 1976; Brunel, 1979; Leeds, 1980; Sussex, 1980; London, 1982; Kenyon Coll., 1984; York, 1984. John Whiting Award, Arts Council, 1967; Evening Standard Award for Most Promising Playwright, 1968; Shakespeare Prize, 1979; Praemium Imperiale, Japan Art Soc., 2009; (jtly) PEN Pinter Prize, 2013; David Cohen Prize for Literature, John S. Cohen Foundn, 2017. *Publications*: (short stories) Introduction 2, 1964; (novel) Lord Malquist and Mr Moon, 1965; *plays*: Rosencrantz and Guildenstern are Dead, 1967; The Real Inspector Hound, 1968; Albert's Bridge, 1968; Enter a Free Man, 1968; After Magritte, 1971; Jumpers, 1972; Artists Descending a Staircase, and, Where Are They Now?, 1973; Travesties, 1975; Dirty Linen, and New-Found-Land, 1976; Every Good Boy Deserves Favour, 1978; Professional Foul, 1978; Night and Day, 1978; Undiscovered Country, 1980; Dogg's Hamlet, Cahoot's Macbeth, 1980; On the Razzle, 1982; The Real Thing, 1983; The Dog it was that Died, 1983; Squaring the Circle, 1984; Four plays for radio, 1984; Rough Crossing, 1985; Dalliance and Undiscovered Country, 1986; (trans.) Largo Desolato, by Vaclav Havel, 1987; Hapgood, 1988; In the Native State, 1991; Arcadia, 1993; The Television Plays 1965–1984, 1993; The Invention of Love, 1997; The Coast of Utopia, 2002; Henry IV, 2004; Heroes, 2005; Rock 'n' Roll, 2006. *Address*: c/o United Agents, 12–26 Lexington Street, W1F 0LE.

**STOPPS, Ian Robert**, CBE 2003; FRAeS; Senior Board Advisor, McLean Group, since 2016; Chairman and Founder, McLean Partnership, 2007–16; Chairman, Raytheon UK, 2012–16; *b* 7 Oct. 1946; *s* of late Rowland Arthur Stopps and Megan Maynard Stopps; *m* 1969, Alexandra Margaret Gebbie; two *d*. *Educ*: Loughborough Univ. of Technol. (BSc 1st cl. Hons (Mech. Engrg) 1969). MIMechE 1969; MASME 1970; FRAeS 2005. Various posts with GE Co. (USA), 1971–87; General Manager: Dynamic Products, BF Goodrich, 1987–90; GE-Aerospace-Europe, 1990–93; Pres., European Region, Martin Marietta, London, 1993–95; merged with Lockheed, 1995 to form Lockheed Martin; Pres., Western Europe Region, Lockheed Martin Corp., 1995–99. Chief Exec., Lockheed Martin UK Ltd, 1999–2009; Chm., Arundel Aerospace and Defence Systems Ltd, 2010–12; Chm., 2003–05, Mem. Adv. Bd, 2005–, British American Business Inc. (BABi). Chm. Adv. Bd, Sch. of Business and Econs, Loughborough Univ., 2011–; Mem. Adv. Bd, Centre for Blast Injury Studies, Imperial Coll. London, 2011–; Member Council: SBAC, 1996–2009; RUSI, 2002–04; UK Council for Electronic Business, 2006–09; Mem. of Ct, Cranfield Univ., 2002–09. Hon. DTech Loughborough, 2014. *Publications*: contribs to ASME, IMechE and RUSI jls. *Recreations*: county and national squash and lawn tennis, Real tennis, golf, travel. *Clubs*: Foxhills; Queen's.

**STOPS, Timothy William Ashcroft J.**; *see* Jackson-Stops.

**STORER, David George**; Under Secretary, Department of Social Security (formerly of Health and Social Security), 1984–89; *b* 27 June 1929; *s* of Herbert Edwards Storer; *m* 1960, Jean Mary Isobel Jenkin; one *s* two *d*. *Educ*: Monmouth School; St John's Coll., Cambridge (MA). Assistant Principal, Min. of Labour, 1952; Principal, 1957; Cabinet Office, 1963–66; Asst Secretary, Dept of Employment, 1966–73; Director, Training Opportunities Scheme, 1973–77; Dir of Corporate Services, MSC, 1977–84. *Recreations*: reading history, still walking. *Address*: 5a Carlton Road, Redhill, Surrey RH1 2BY.

**STORER, Robert Andrew**; Consultant, Harbottle & Lewis LLP, since 2007; *b* Burton-on-Trent, 29 April 1947; *s* of Horace and Nancy Storer; *m* 1982, Linda Pritchard; one *s* two *d*. *Educ*: Buxton Coll., Derbys; London Sch. of Econs and Pol Sci. (LLB 1968). Admitted as solicitor, 1971; joined Harbottle & Lewis, 1969; Partner, 1975–2007; Hd, Film and TV Dept, 1980–2007; Sen. Partner, 2000–09. Mem., BAFTA, 1998–. *Recreations*: golf, tennis, watching Fulham FC and Middlesex Cricket, film, theatre, bridge. *Address*: 35 Gerard Road, Barnes, SW13 9QH. *T*: (020) 8748 1898. *E*: bobstorer@hotmail.com. *Club*: Roehampton.

**STOREY, Baron** *cr* 2011 (Life Peer), of Childwall in the City of Liverpool; **Michael John Storey**, CBE 2002 (OBE 1994); Headteacher, Plantation County Primary School, Halewood, Knowsley, 1986–2012; Member (Lib Dem), Liverpool City Council, 1973–2011 (Leader, 1998–2005); Lord Mayor, City of Liverpool, 2009–10; *b* 25 May 1949; *m* Carole; one *d*. *Educ*: Liverpool Univ. (BEd). Teacher: Prescot C of E Primary Sch.; New Hutte Primary Sch., Halewood; Deputy Headteacher, Halsnead Primary Sch., Whiston; Headteacher, St Gabriel's C of E Primary Sch., Huyton. Liverpool City Council: Chm., Educn Cttee, and Dep. Leader, 1980–83; Leader, Lib Dem Opposition, 1991–98. Member, Board: Mersey Partnership, 1993–2008; Liverpool Vision (Dep. Chm.); North West Develt Agency; Speke Garston Develt Co. *Address*: 36 Countisbury Drive, Liverpool L16 0JJ; House of Lords, SW1A 0PW. *W*: www.twitter.com/LordStorey.

**STOREY, Alastair Dunbar**, OBE 2017; Founder Chairman and Chief Executive Officer, WSH Ltd (owner of hospitality businesses BaxterStorey, benugo, Searcys, Holroyd Howe, Caterlink, Portico and WSH Restaurants), since 2000; *b* Fyvie, Aberdeenshire, 22 Jan. 1953; *s* of Robert Storey and May Storey; *m* 1977, Elizabeth Linden; one *s* four *d*. *Educ*: Robert Gordon's Coll., Aberdeen; Strathclyde Univ. (BA); Harvard Business Sch. (PMD). Mgt trainee, later Man. Dir, Sutcliffe Catering, 1975–96; Gp Man. Dir, Granada Food Services, 1996–99. Vice Pres., Food Service Europe, 2012–; Dir, British Hospitality Assoc., 2013–18; Pres., Inst. of Hospitality, 2016–. Chairman: Trustees, Gold Service Scholarship, 2012–; Springboard Charity, 2019–. Gov., Royal Acad. of Culinary Arts, 2012–. Trustee, Nicholls Spinal Injury Foundn, 2014–. Hon. DLitt West London, 2013. *Recreations*: food and wine, art, reading, family, cycling, ski-ing and other sports, guitar. *Address*: WSH Ltd, TVP 2, 300 Thames Valley Park Drive, Reading, Berks RG6 1PT. *T*: (0118) 935 6700, *Fax*: (0118) 935 6701. *E*: astorey@baxterstorey.com.

**STOREY, Christopher Thomas**; QC 1995; a Recorder, 2000–15; *b* 13 Feb. 1945; *s* of Leslie Hall Storey and Joan Storey; *m* 1968, Hilary Johnston; two *s*. *Educ*: Rugby Sch. Chartered Accountant, 1967; Glass & Edwards, Liverpool, 1964–68; Price Waterhouse & Co., 1968–70; A. E. Smith Coggins Group, 1970–72; Stacey's, 1972–74; private practice as Chartered Accountant, 1974–82; called to the Bar, Lincoln's Inn, 1979; practising Barrister, NE Circuit, 1982–2007; an Asst Recorder, 1996–2000. *Recreations*: music, cricket, classic cars, flying light aircraft (instructor), undergardening. *Address*: Park Lane Plowden, 19 Westgate, Leeds LS1 2RD. *T*: (0113) 228 5000.

**STOREY, Dr Hugo Henry**; a Judge of the Upper Tribunal (Immigration and Asylum Chamber) (formerly a Vice President, Immigration Appeal Tribunal, later a Senior Immigration Judge, Asylum and Immigration Tribunal), 2000–15; *b* 30 Sept. 1945; *s* of Harry MacIntosh Storey and Barbara Storey; *m* 1983, Sehba Haroon; three *s*. *Educ*: N Sydney Boys' High Sch.; Univ. of Sydney (BA Hons 1967; Medal in Govt); Balliol Coll., Oxford (BPhil Politics); Nuffield Coll., Oxford; Univ. of Leeds (PhD 1988). Adult educn teaching, legal res., and journalism, 1971–76; Organiser, Tribunal Assistance Unit, Chapeltown CAB, 1976–78; Sen. Legal Worker, Chapeltown and Harehills Law Centre, 1978–88; Human Rights Fellow, Council of Europe, 1983–88; legal worker, John Howell & Co., 1989–90; Sen. Lectr, Law Dept, Leeds Poly., 1990–91; Lectr and Dep. Dir for Study of Law in Europe, Law Dept, 1991–95, Hon. Res. Fellow, 1995–98, Univ. of Leeds. Adjudicator, Immigration Appellate Authy, 1995–2000. Mem. Council, Internat. Assoc. Refugee Law Judges, 1998–. *Publications*: (jtly) I Want to Appeal: a guide to Supplementary Benefit Appeal Tribunals, 1978; (jtly) Social Security Appeals: a guide to National Insurance Local Tribunals and Medical Appeal Tribunals, 1980; (with G. Crawford) Sacked? Made Redundant? Your Rights if You Lose Your Job: a guide to Industrial Tribunals and the Employment Appeal Tribunal, 1981; (with W. Collins) Immigrants and the Welfare State, 1985; (ed jtly) Asylum Law, 1995; (ed jtly) Butterworth's Immigration Law Handbook, 2001; contribs to various legal jls in UK, Europe and internat. *Recreations*: family, travel, golf, writing poetry (esp. haiku), music, chess.

**STOREY, Jeremy Brian**; QC 1994; a Recorder, since 1995; Judge of Appeal, Isle of Man, since 2017 (Acting Deemster, 1999–2009; Deemster, 2009–17); *b* 21 Oct. 1952; *s* of late Captain James Mackie Storey and Veronica Walmsley; *m* 1981, Carolyn Margaret Ansell; two *d*. *Educ*: Uppingham Sch.; Downing Coll., Cambridge (Scholar; BA Law 1st Cl. Hons, MA). MCIArb 1999 (ACIArb 1997). Called to the Bar, Inner Temple, 1974, Bencher, 2006; Asst Recorder, 1991–95; Head of Chambers, 2008–17; Dep. Judge of the Technol. and Construction Ct (formerly Official Referee), 1996–; a Dep. High Ct Judge, 2008–. *Recreations*: travel, cricket, theatre. *Address*: Isle of Man Courts of Justice, Deemsters Walk, Bucks Road, Douglas, Isle of Man IM1 3AR. *T*: (01624) 687576. *Clubs*: MCC; Glamorgan CC.

**STOREY, Prof. Kate Gillian**, PhD; FRSB, FRSE; FMedSci; Professor of Neural Development, since 2007, and Head, Division of Cell and Developmental Biology, since 2010, University of Dundee; *b* London, 27 Nov. 1960; *d* of late David Malcolm Storey (writer and artist) and Barbara Rudd Storey (née Hamilton); *m* 2010, Jonathan Gordon; one *s* one *d*. *Educ*: Parliament Hill Sch.; Camden Sch., London; Univ. of Sussex (BSc 1st Cl. Hons 1980); King's Coll., Cambridge (PhD Zool. 1983). FRSB (FSB 2011). Harkness

Fellow, Univ. of Calif., Berkeley, 1987; postdoctoral research: Univ. of Calif, Berkeley, 1987; Dept of Human Anatomy, Univ. of Oxford, 1989; Lectr, Dept of Human Genetics and Anatomy, Univ. of Oxford, 1994–2000; Fellow, Christ Church Coll., Oxford, 1995–2000; School of Life Sciences, University of Dundee: Hon. Sen. Lectr, 2000–04; Reader, 2004–07; Associate Dean of Res., 2008–10. Science/Art Exhibn, in collaboration with fashion designer, Helen Storey, 1997–. Member: Lister Inst. of Preventive Medicine, 2014; EMBO, 2016. FRSE 2012; FMedSci 2017. FRSA 2011. MRC Suffrage Sci. Heirloom Award, 2014; Royal Soc. Wolfson Res. Merit Award, 2015; Waddington Medal, 2019. *Recreations:* long distance running, beach combing. *Address:* School of Life Sciences, Division of Cell and Developmental Biology, University of Dundee, Dow Street, Dundee DD1 5EH. *T:* (01382) 385691. *E:* k.g.storey@dundee.ac.uk.

**STOREY, Maurice,** CB 2003; CEng, FIMarEST; FRINA; Chief Executive, Maritime and Coastguard Agency, 1998–2003; Hon. Chairman, Evergreen-Marine UK Ltd (formerly Hatsu Marine Ltd), since 2007 (Chairman, 2003–06, Hon. Chairman, 2006–07, Hatsu Marine Ltd); *b* 14 June 1943; *s* of Albert Henry Storey and Violet Esther Storey; *m* 1987, Linda Mears; two *s* one *d. Educ:* HNC Naval Architecture 1963. CEng 1969; FRINA 1969; FIMarEST 1972. Apprentice, Swan Hunter Shipbuilders, 1958–62; Ship Repair Manager, Swan Hunter Ship Repairers, 1962–67; Asst to Marine Superintendent, then Tech. Superintendent, Shaw Savill Line, 1967–72; Hd, Tech. Dept, Kuwait Oil Tanker Co., 1972–76; Director: Sea Containers Ltd, 1976–90; Hoverspeed Ltd, 1986–90; Ship and Port Mgt, Stena Line Ltd, 1990–98; non-exec. Dir, James Fisher plc, 2003–13. Chm. and Dir, Fishguard and Rosslare Rlys and Harbours Co., 1992–98; Dir, Soc. du Terminal Transmanche de Dieppe, 1992–98. Chamber of Shipping UK: Vice-Chm., Cruise Ship and Ferry Section, 1991–96; Chm., Marine Policy Cttee, 1996–98; Vice-Pres., 2005–06; Pres., 2006–07. Pres., Inst. of Marine Engrg, Sci. and Tech., 2005–06. RNLI: Mem. Council, 2002–14; Mem. Technical Cttee, 2003–14; Vice Pres., 2014–. Trustee, Historic Dockyard Chatham, 2007–17; Dir, Master Ropemakers Chatham, 2007–. Hon. MBA Nottingham Trent, 2000. *Recreations:* walking, golf. *Address:* 69 Greenhill, Staplehurst, Tonbridge, Kent TN12 0SU. *T:* and *Fax:* (01580) 890530.

**STOREY, Mervyn;** Member (DemU) North Antrim, Northern Ireland Assembly, since 2003; *b* Armoy, Co. Antrim, 4 Sept. 1964; *m* Christine; two *s* one *d. Educ:* Armoy Primary Sch.; Ballmoney Secondary Sch. Posts with Lovell & Christmas (Ulster Ltd), incl. Prodn Manager, until 2000; Campaign Manager for DUP: S Antrim, 2000; E Londonderry, 2001; N Antrim, 2010. Minister for Social Develt, 2014–16, for Finance and Personnel, 2016, NI. Mem. (DemU) Ballymoney BC, 2001–14. Mem., NI Policing Bd, 2018–. *Address:* Northern Ireland Assembly, Parliament Buildings, Belfast BT4 3XX.

**STOREY, Most Rev. Patricia;** see Meath and Kildare, Bishop of.

**STOREY, Paul Mark;** QC 2001; a Recorder, since 2000; a Deputy High Court Judge, since 2004; *b* 12 March 1957; *s* of late George Daniel Storey and Denise Edna Storey (*née* Baker); *m* 1st, 1977, Margaret Jane Aucott (marr. diss. 1994); two *d;* 2nd, 1994, Alexa Roseann Rea; three *s* one *d. Educ:* Notre Dame Sch., Lingfield; John Fisher Sch., Purley; N London Poly.; Newcastle Poly.; UCL; Inns of Court Law Sch.; BA Hons; CPE. Called to the Bar, Lincoln's Inn, 1982; in practice as barrister, 1983–; Asst Recorder, 1999–2000. *Publications:* contrib. various articles to Family Law. *Recreations:* football (Fulham FC), cycling, Rugby (Harlequins RFC), cricket, my family. *Address:* (chambers) 29 Bedford Row, WC1R 4HE.

**STOREY, Hon. Sir Richard,** 2nd Bt *cr* 1960; CBE 1996; DL; Chairman of Portsmouth and Sunderland Newspapers plc, 1973–98 (Director, 1962–99); *b* 23 Jan. 1937; *s* of Baron Buckton (Life Peer) and Elisabeth (*d* 1951), *d* of late Brig.-Gen. W. J. Woodcock, DSO; *S* to baronetcy of father, 1978; *m* 1961, Virginia Anne, 3rd *d* of Sir Kenelm Cayley, 10th Bt; one *s* two *d. Educ:* Winchester; Trinity Coll., Cambridge (BA, LLB). National service commission, RNVR, 1956. Called to the Bar, Inner Temple, 1962. Administers agricultural land and woodland in Yorkshire. Director: One Stop Community Stores Ltd, 1971–98; Croydon Cable, 1983–89; Reuters Hldgs PLC, 1986–92; Press Association Ltd, 1986–95 (Chm., 1991–95); Fleming Enterprise Investment Trust PLC, 1989–2002 (Chm., 1996–2002); Foreign & Colonial Smaller Cos PLC, 1993–2002; Sunderland PLC, 1996–2004; eFinancialNews Ltd, 2000–06. Chm., York Health Services Trust, 1991–97. Member: Nat. Council and Exec., CLA, 1980–84, Yorks Exec., CLA (Chm., 1974–76); Employment Policy Cttee, CBI, 1984–88, CBI Regl Council, Yorks and Humberside, 1974–76; Press Council, 1980–86; Pres., Newspaper Soc., 1990–91 (Mem. Council, 1980–98). Chairman: Sir Harold Hillier Arboretum Management Cttee, 1989–2005; Internat. Dendrology Soc., 2007–12; Trustee: Royal Botanic Gardens Kew Foundn, 1990–2004; Castle Howard Arboretum Trust, 1997–2013. Mem. Council: INCA-FIEJ Res. Assoc., 1983–88; European Newspaper Publishers' Assoc., 1991–96. Contested (C): Don Valley, 1966; Huddersfield W, 1970. High Sheriff, 1992–93, DL 1998, N Yorks. Trustee, Hope and Homes for Children, 2002–09. Hon. Fellow, Univ. of Portsmouth, 1989. Hon. DLitt Sunderland Poly., 1992. Veitch Meml Medal, RHS, 2005. *Recreations:* architecture, silviculture, dendrology. *Heir: s* Kenelm Storey [*b* 4 Jan. 1963; *m* 2001, Karen, *d* of Keith Prothero; one *s* two *d.*]. *Address:* Settrington Grange, Malton, Yorks YO17 8NU. *T:* (01944) 768200; 11 Zetland House, Marloes Road, W8 5LB. *T:* (020) 7937 8823. *E:* storey.london@btinternet.com.

**STOREY, Dame Sarah (Joanne),** DBE 2013 (OBE 2009; MBE 1998); athlete, since 1992; *b* Manchester, Oct. 1977; *née* Bailey; *m* 2007, Barney Storey, MBE; one *s* one *d. Educ:* Leeds Metropolitan Univ. (BSc (Hons) Sport and Exercise Sci. 1999). GB internat. swimmer, 1992–2005; GB internat. cyclist, 2005–; Paralympic Games Barcelona 1992, Atlanta 1996, Sydney 2000, Athens 2004, Beijing 2008, London 2012, Rio 2016 (14 Gold Medals (5 swimming, 9 cycling), 8 Silver Medals (swimming), 3 Bronze Medals (swimming)); Team England, Commonwealth Games, Delhi, 2010; GB Team Pursuit Squad, Track World Cup, Manchester, 2011 (Gold Medal), Cali, Colombia, 2011 (Gold Medal); winner: 33 World Championship titles (6 swimming, 27 cycling); 21 Europ. titles (18 swimming, 3 cycling); 7 World Cup titles (5 paracycling, 2 able-bodied cycling). Dir, Team Storey Sport Ltd, 2009–. Co-founder, Storey Racing, 2017–. Member: Escentual For VioRed Racing Team, 2012; Breast Cancer Care Cycling Team, 2013; Pearl Izumi Sports Tours Internat. Women's Cycling Team, 2014–15; Podium Ambition Pro Cycling Powered by Club La Santa, 2016. Active Travel Comr, Sheffield City Region, 2019–. *Address:* Team Storey Sport Ltd, PO Box 80, Disley, Cheshire SK12 2WF.

**STOREY, Susannah Jemima;** Director General, Department for Exiting the European Union, since 2018 (Director, Planning and Analysis, 2016–17; Acting Director General, 2017–18); *b* London, 7 March 1973; *d* of Tom Storey and Victoria Storey; *m* 2003, Robin Hooper; three *c. Educ:* Benenden Sch.; St John's Coll., Cambridge (BA Hist. 1995). SFA Rep. 1996. UK Corporate Finance, Schroders, 1996–2000; UK M&A, Citigroup Global Markets, 2000–07; Shareholder Executive, BIS (formerly BERR), 2007–13, incl. Dir, Royal Mail and Postal Services, 2010–12; Dir, Corp. Strategy and Change, DECC, 2013–16. Non-exec. Dir, Post Office Ltd, 2012–14. *Recreations:* family, art. *Address:* Department for Exiting the European Union, 9 Downing Street, SW1A 2AS.

**STORKEY, Elaine;** President, Tear Fund, 1997–2013; *b* 1 Oct. 1943; *d* of James and Anne Lively; *m* 1968, Alan James Storkey; three *s. Educ:* UCW, Aberystwyth (BA); McMaster Univ., Ontario (MA); York Univ. Tutor, Manchester Coll., Oxford, 1967–8; Res. Fellow, Univ. of Stirling, 1968–69; Tutor, then Lectr, Open Univ., 1976–90; Exec. Dir, Inst. for Contemporary Christianity, 1990–98. Dir of Training, Church Army, 2009–12. Visiting Professor: Calvin Coll., USA, 1980–81; Covenant Coll., Chattanooga, USA, 1981–82; Vis. Scholar, KCL, 1996–; New Coll. Schol., Univ. of NSW, 1997; Sen. Res. Fellow, Wycliffe Hall, Univ. of Oxford, 2003–07; Micah Lectr, Port au Prince, Haiti, 2008; Templeton-Cambridge Journalism Fellow, 2009; Frumentius Vis. Scholar, Graduate Sch. of Theology, Addis Ababa, Ethiopia, 2010. Associate Ed., Third Way, 1988–2016. Member: Cathedrals Commn, 1992–96; Crown Nominations (formerly Crown Appts) Commn, 2002–08; Gen. Synod of C of E, 1987–2015; Gen. Assembly of C of S, 2014; Forum for the Future, 1994–2001; Emerging Mkts Symposium, 2013–; Power Shift Forum for Women in World Economy, 2016–; founding Mem., Restored, 2010–. Pres., Fulcrum, 2011–. Reviewer, Free Thinking, BBC Radio 3, 2013–. Vice-Pres., Gloucestershire Univ. (formerly Cheltenham & Gloucester Coll.), 1995–. Mem., High Table, Newnham Coll., Cambridge, 2008–. Mem., RSA, 2012. Hon. Fellow, Aberystwyth Univ., 2013. DD Lambeth 1998; Hon. PhD Gloucester, 2000. Kuyper Prize, Princeton Theol Seminary, 2016. *Publications:* What's Right with Feminism, 1986, 2nd edn 2013; Mary's Story, Mary's Song, 1993; The Search for Intimacy, 1995; Magnify the Lord, 1998; (with Margaret Hebblethwaite) Conversations on Christian Feminism, 1999; Men and Women: created or constructed, 2000; Origins of Difference, 2002; Word on the Street, 2003; Scars Across Humanity, 2015; contrib. to Scottish Jl Theol., Gospel and Culture, The Independent, Church Times, Encounter With God, Dagen (Sweden). *Recreations:* broadcasting, making film documentaries. *Address:* (home) The Old School, Coton, Cambs CB23 7PL. *T:* (01954) 212381.

**STORMER, Prof. Horst Ludwig,** PhD; physicist; Professor of Physics and Applied Physics, Columbia University, 1998, now Emeritus; Adjunct Physics Director, Lucent Technologies (formerly AT&T Bell Laboratories), 1997–2006; *b* Frankfurt am Main, 6 April 1949; *s* of Karl Ludwig Stormer and Marie Stormer (*née* Ihrig); *m* 1982, Dominique A. Parchet. *Educ:* Univ. of Stuttgart (PhD 1977). AT&T Bell Laboratories: Mem., Technical Staff, 1978–83; Dept Head, 1983–92; Dir, Physical Res. Lab., 1992–97. Bell Labs Fellow, 1983. Mem., US Nat. Acad. of Scis, 1999. Buckley Prize, 1984; Otto Klung Prize, Free Univ., Berlin, 1985; Benjamin Franklin Medal, 1998; (jtly) Nobel Prize for Physics, 1998; NYC Mayor's Award for Excellence in Sci. and Technol., 2000. Officier de la Légion d'Honneur (France), 1999; Grosse Verdienstkreuz mit Stern (Germany), 1999. *Address:* Department of Physics, Columbia University, 704 Pupin Hall, New York, NY 10027, USA.

**STORMONT, Viscount; William Philip David Mungo Murray;** *b* 1 Nov. 1988; *s* and heir of Earl of Mansfield and Mansfield, *qv. Educ:* Eton Coll.; Durham Univ. (BA); Univ. of Oxford (MBA 2018). ADC to Grand Master of Order of Malta, 2011–14. Family Business Lead, Cathedral Consulting Gp, NY, 2014–16; Associate: Kulczyk Investments, 2017; inCredibles Accelerator, 2017; Kluz Ventures, 2018. Co-Chm., Oxford Business Network for Entrepreneurship, 2017–. Non-exec. Dir, Scone Estates, 2011–; Founder, Scone Project, 2016–; Founder and Co-Chair, White Cross Ball of New York, 2015–; Co-Founder and Chief Security Officer, Fettl Ltd, 2018–; Co-Founder and Man. Partner, SFXY, 2018–.

**STORMONTH DARLING, Peter;** Director, Soditic Limited, since 2007; *b* 29 Sept. 1932; *s* of Patrick Stormonth Darling and Edith Mary Ormston Lamb; *m* 1st, 1958, Candis Hitzig; three *d;* 2nd, 1971, Maureen O'Leary (*d* 2015). *Educ:* Winchester; New Coll., Oxford (MA). 2nd Lieut, Black Watch, 1950–53, served Korean War; RAFVR, 1953–56. Dir, 1967–2001, Chm., 1995–2001, Deltec Panamerica, then Deltec Internat., SA. Chairman: Mercury Asset Mgt Gp, 1979–92 (Dir, 1969–98); Mercury International Investment Trust, 1990–98; Mercury European Investment (formerly Mercury Europe Privatisation) Trust, 1994–2004; Atlas Capital Gp (incorporating Deltec Internat. Gp), 2001–06; Alta Advisers Ltd, 2004–07. Director: S. G. Warburg & Co. Ltd, 1967–85 (Vice-Chm., 1977–85); S. G. Warburg Group plc, 1974–94; Europe Fund, 1990–2000; Scottish Equitable plc, 1992–99; Merrill Lynch UK (formerly Mercury Keystone) Investment Co., 1992–2002; Greenwich Associates, 1993–2006; Scottish and Southern Energy (formerly Scottish Hydro-Electric) plc, 1994–2000; Sagitta Asset Mgt Ltd, 1996–2003; Guardian Capital Gp Ltd (Canada), 1998–2013; Aegon (UK) plc, 1999–2003; Invesco Perpetual Select Trust plc, 2001–08; Howard de Walden Estates Ltd, 2001–14; Galahad Gold plc, 2005–08. Director: The UK Fund Inc., 1994–2000; Advent Capital Hldgs, 2006–09; Genagro Services Ltd, 2008–14. Member: UN Pension Fund Investments Cttee, 1990–2005; Exec. (formerly Finance and Investments) Cttee, IISS, 1994–2007; Finance Cttee, World Monuments Fund, 2002–11. Chm. Council, Winchester Coll. Soc., 2007–09. *Publications:* City Cinderella, 1999. *Address:* Soditic Limited, 12 Charles II Street, SW1Y 4QU.

**STORR, Farrah;** Editor-in-Chief, Elle, since 2019; *b* Manchester, 8 Nov. 1978; *d* of Jerry and Linda Butt; *m* 2011, William D. Storr. *Educ:* Bury Grammar Sch. for Girls; Bury Coll.; King's Coll. London (BA English and French Lit.). Features Dir, Marie Claire, 2008; Associate Ed., Madison Mag., 2008–11; Acting Ed./Dep. Ed., Top Sante Mag., 2011; Ed.-in-Chief and Founder, Women's Health Mag., 2011–15; Ed.-in-Chief, Cosmopolitan, 2015–19. New Ed. of Year, BSME, 2013. *Publications:* The Discomfort Zone, 2018. *Address:* Manor Cottage, Church Lane, Hothfield, Kent TN26 1EL. *E:* Farrahstorr@gmail.com. *Club:* AllBright.

**STOTHARD, Sir Peter (Michael),** Kt 2003; author; Editor, The Times Literary Supplement, 2002–16; *b* 28 Feb. 1951; *s* of late Wilfred Max Stothard and of Patricia J. Stothard (*née* Savage); *m* 1980, Sally Ceris Emerson; one *s* one *d. Educ:* Brentwood Sch., Essex; Trinity Coll., Oxford (BA Lit Hum.; MA; Hon. Fellow, 2000). BBC journalist, 1974–77; with Shell Internat. Petroleum, 1977–79; business and political writer, Sunday Times, 1979–80; The Times: Features Ed. and Leader writer, 1980–86; Dep. Ed., 1986–92; US Ed., 1989–92; Editor, 1992–2002. Chairman of Judges: Forward Poetry Prize, 2003; Hessell Tiltman Prize for History, 2004; Man Booker Prize, 2012. Mem. Adv. Bd, Bodleian Liby, 2011–. Pres., Classical Assoc., 2011–12. Dir, Roundhouse Trust, 2004–10. Trustee, NPG, 2017– (Chair, Adv. Ethics Cttee, 2018–). President's Medal, British Acad., 2013; Criticos Prize, 2013. *Publications:* Thirty Days: a month at the heart of Blair's war, 2003; On the Spartacus Road: a spectacular journey through ancient Italy, 2010; Alexandria: the last nights of Cleopatra, 2013; The Senecans: four men and Margaret Thatcher, 2016. *Recreation:* ancient and modern literature. *Club:* Garrick.

**STOTT, Sir Adrian,** 4th Bt *cr* 1920; management consultant, since 1989; *b* 7 Oct. 1948; *s* of Sir Philip Sidney Stott, 3rd Bt, and Cicely Florence (*d* 1996), *o d* of Bertram Ellingham; *S* father, 1986. *Educ:* Univ. of British Columbia (BSc (Maths) 1968, MSc (Town Planning) 1974); Univ. of Waterloo, Ont (MMaths (Computer Science) 1971). Dir of Planning for a rural region of BC, 1974; formed own consulting practice, 1977; property develt, gen. management and town planning consultant, 1977–85; Manager: BC Govt Real Estate

Portfolio, 1980; Islands Trust (coastal conservation and property develt control agency), 1985; Man. Dir, direct sales marketing company, 1986–88. Mem., Assoc. for Computing Machinery. *Recreations:* music, inland waterways, politics. *Heir:* b Vyvyan Philip Stott, b 5 Aug. 1952.

**STOTT, Andrew Charles,** CBE 2011; Director of Digital Engagement, Government Communications, Cabinet Office, 2009–10; b 11 Sept. 1955; s of Prof. Peter Frank Stott and Vera Stott (*née* Watkins). *Educ:* Westminster Sch.; Clare Coll., Cambridge (BA 1976). Civil Service Dept, 1976; Prime Minister's Efficiency Unit, 1983–85; HM Prison Service, 1985–87; DSS, 1987–2001; Dir, Digital Infrastructure and e-Champion, DWP, 2001–03; Modernisation Dir, DfT, 2003–04; Hd, Service Transformation, e-Govt Unit, later Dep. Govt Chief Information Officer and Dir, Service Transformation, Cabinet Office, 2004–08. Mem., Public Sector Transparency Bd, Cabinet Office, 2011–15. Sen. Consultant, World Bank, 2012–. *Recreation:* walking. *Address:* PO Box 191, Sevenoaks, Kent TN13 2AW. *E:* andrew.stott@dirdigeng.com.

**STOTT, Kathryn Linda;** pianist; b 10 Dec. 1958; d of Desmond Stott and Elsie Stott (*née* Cheetham); m 1st, 1979, Michael Ardron (marr. diss. 1983); 2nd, 1983, John Elliott (marr. diss. 1997); one d. *Educ:* Yehudi Menuhin Sch.; Royal Coll. of Music, London (ARCM). Regular duo partner of Yo-Yo Ma, Isabelle van Keulen, Christian Poltera; has worked with all major British orchs; recitals throughout UK; tours of Europe, USA and Far East; world premières of concertos by Graham Fitkin, George Lloyd, Michael Nyman and Sir Peter Maxwell Davies. Artistic Director: Fauré and the French Connection, 1995; Piano 2000, Piano 2003; Incontri in terra de Siena; Artistic Dir, Australian Fest. of Chamber Music, 2018–. Internat. Chair of Piano Studies, RNCM, 2015–; Vis. Prof. of Piano, Norwegian Acad. of Music, 2016–. Mem., Nordoff Robbins Music Therapy. Numerous recordings. Hon. RAM, 2013. Chevalier de l'Ordre des Arts et des Lettres (France), 1996. *Recreations:* food, travel, Italian language. *Address:* c/o Jane Ward, 60 Shrewsbury Road, Oxton, Wirral CH43 2HY.

**STOTT, Kenneth Campbell;** actor; b Edinburgh, 19 Oct. 1954; s of David and Antonia Stott; one s; m 2016, Nina Gehl. *Educ:* George Heriot's Sch., Edinburgh; Mountview Th. Sch., London. *Theatre* includes: appearances with RSC; The Sea, RNT, 1992; Art, Wyndham's, 1996; Faith Healer, Almeida, 2001; God of Carnage, Gielgud, 2008, NY 2009; A View From the Bridge, Duke of York's, 2009; Uncle Vanya, Vaudeville Th., 2012; The Entertainer, The Dresser, Duke of York's, 2016; *films* include: Shallow Grave, 1994; Franz Kafka's It's a Wonderful Life, 1995; Fever Pitch, 1997; The Debt Collectors, 1999; Charlie Wilson's War, 2007; One Day, 2011; The Hobbit: An Unexpected Journey, 2012; The Hobbit: The Desolation of Smaug, 2013; The Hobbit: The Battle of the Five Armies, 2014; Café Society, 2016; 100 Streets, 2016; The Mercy, 2018; *television* includes: The Singing Detective, 1986; Your Cheatin' Heart, 1990; Takin' Over the Asylum, 1994; Silent Witness, 1996; The Vice, 1999–2003; Messiah, 2001–05; The Key, 2003; Rebus, 2006–07; Hancock and Joan, 2008; Toast, 2010; The Runaway (series), 2011; The Missing, 2014; An Inspector Calls, 2015; War and Peace, 2016; Fortitude (series), 2017. *Recreations:* watching Heart of Midlothian FC, dining out, visiting galleries. *Club:* Chelsea Arts.

**STOUGHTON-HARRIS, Anthony Geoffrey,** CBE 1989; DL; FCA; Deputy Chairman, Nationwide Building Society, 1990–95; b 5 June 1932; s of Geoffrey Stoughton-Harris and Kathleen Mary (*née* Baker Brown); m 1959, Elizabeth Thackery (*née* White); one s two d. *Educ:* Sherborne Sch., Dorset. FCA 1956. Partner, Norton Keen & Co., chartered accountants, 1958–74; Maidenhead & Berkshire Building Society, subseq. South of England, London & South of England, Anglia, Nationwide Anglia, then Nationwide Building Society: Dir, 1967–95; Man. Dir, 1975; Chief Gen. Manager, 1983–87; Vice-Chm., 1987–90. Chm., Electronic Funds Transfer Ltd, 1984–89; Director: Southern Electric, 1981–98 (Dep. Chm., 1993–98); Guardian Royal Exchange, 1990–95. Gen. Comr, Inland Revenue, 1982–2000. Part-time Treasurer, W Herts Main Drainage Authority, 1964–70. Chairman: BSA, 1987–89; Northants TEC, 1990–95; Northants Chamber of Commerce, Trng and Enterprise, 1995–96. FCBSI. DL 1994, High Sheriff, 2000, Northants. *Recreations:* sport, gardening, DIY. *Address:* The Beeches, 26 Granville Road, Limpsfield, Oxted, Surrey RH8 0DA. *T:* (01883) 717026.

**STOURTON,** family name of **Baron Mowbray, Segrave and Stourton.**

**STOURTON, Edward John Ivo;** Presenter, BBC News and Current Affairs programmes, since 1993; b 24 Nov. 1957; s of Nigel John Ivo Stourton, CBE, and Rosemary Jennifer Rushworth Stourton (*née* Abbott), JP; m 1st, 1980, Margaret (marr. diss. 2001), e d of Sir James Napier Finnie McEwen, 2nd Bt; two s one d; 2nd, 2002, Fiona Murch, d of late John Edward King. *Educ:* Ampleforth; Trinity Coll., Cambridge (MA; Pres., Cambridge Union, Lent, 1979). Joined ITN, 1979; founder mem., Channel 4 News, 1982, Washington Corresp., 1986–88; Paris Corresp., BBC TV, 1988–90; Diplomatic Ed., ITN, 1990–93; BBC Television: Presenter: One O'Clock News, 1993–99; Call Ed Stourton, 1997–98; Reporter: Correspondent, 1996–2001; Panorama, 1998; Presenter, Today, 1999–2009, Sunday, 2001–; Main Presenter, 2010–), Radio 4; has written and presented series for BBC2 and Radio 4, incl. Asia Gold (Sony Gold Award for Current Affairs, 1997), and Israel Accused (Amnesty Award for best television current affairs prog., 2001). *Publications:* Absolute Truth: the Catholic Church in the world today, 1998; In the Footsteps of St Paul, 2004; Paul of Tarsus: a visionary life, 2005; John Paul II: man of history, 2006; It's a PC World: what it means to live in a land gone politically correct, 2008; Diary of a Dog Walker, 2011; (ed) Trinity: a portrait, 2011; Cruel Crossing: escaping Hitler across the Pyrenees, 2013; Auntie's War: the BBC during the Second World War, 2017; The Publishing Game: adventures in books - 150 years of Hodder & Stoughton, 2019. *Recreations:* conversation, buying books, croquet, racing demon. *Address:* c/o Curtis Brown, 5th Floor Haymarket House, 28–29 Haymarket, SW1Y 4SP. *T:* (020) 7393 4400. *Clubs:* Hurlingham, Travellers.

**STOUT, Andrea Mary;** see Sutcliffe, A. M.

**STOUT, Prof. Robert William,** MD, DSc; FRCP, FMedSci; Professor of Geriatric Medicine, Queen's University, Belfast, 1976–2007, now Emeritus; Director of Research and Development, Northern Ireland Health and Personal Social Services, 2001–08; b 6 March 1942; s of William Ferguson Stout, CB and Muriel Stout (*née* Kilner); m 1969, Helena Patricia Willis (d 2015); two s one d. *Educ:* Campbell Coll., Belfast (schol.); Queen's Univ., Belfast (MD, DSc). FRCP 1979; FRCPE 1988–2014; FRCPI 1989–2014; FRCPGlas 1994. MRC Eli Lilly Foreign Educnl Fellow, Univ. of Washington Sch. of Medicine, Seattle, 1971–73; Queen's University, Belfast: BHF Sen. Res. Fellow, 1974; Sen. Lectr in Medicine, 1975; Dean, Faculty of Medicine, 1991–96; Provost for Medicine and Health Scis, 1993–98; Dean, Faculty of Medicine and Health Scis, 1998–2001. Mem., GMC, 1991–2003 (Member: Standards Cttee, 1993–94; Educn Cttee, 1992–93, 1995–98, 1999–2002). Chairman: Specialty Adv. Cttee on Geriatric Medicine, Jt Cttee on Higher Med. Trng, 1986–92; Benchmark Cttee for Medicine, QAA, 2000–02; Main Panel B (Clinical Medicine), 2008 RAE; Member, Health & Social Services Boards: Southern, 1982–91; Eastern, 1993–2002; Member: Royal Commn on Long-Term Care for the Elderly, 1997–99; Distinction and Meritorious Awards Cttee for NI, 2001–04; Health Res. Bd, Dublin, 2002–07; Public Inquiry into C.diff outbreak, Northern HSC Trust, NI, 2009–10; Dep. Chm. and Med. Dir, NI Clinical Excellence Awards Cttee, 2005–14. Vice-Pres., Age Concern Northern Ireland, 1988–2001 (Chm., 1985–88). NI Regl Advr, RCP, 1984–90; British Geriatrics Society: Mem., Council, 1984–90; Chm., NI Reg., 1984–90; Mem., Exec., 1987–90; Chm., Editl Bd, Age and Ageing, 1999–2002; Pres.-elect, 2000–02; Pres., 2002–04. Jt Chm., Centre for Ageing Res. and Develt in Ireland, 2005–15; Mem., NI Cttee, 2007–15 (Chm., 2009–15), Mem. Council, 2009–15, Stroke Assoc.; Mem., Bd of Dirs, Extra Care NI, 2008–13; NI Chair, Abbeyfield Soc., 2015–. Mem., Bd of Govs, Methodist Coll., Belfast, 1983–2002 (Chm., 1994–97); Chm. Bd of Govs, Edgehill Theol Coll., Belfast, 2005–11; Governor, Research in Ageing, 1989–2001 (Mem., Med. Adv. Cttee, 1982–89). Visiting Professor: Univ. of Auckland, NZ, 1990; Hong Kong Geriatric Soc., 1993. Founder FMedSci 1998. *Publications:* Hormones and Atherosclerosis, 1982; Arterial Disease in the Elderly, 1984; Diabetes and Atherosclerosis, 1992; articles in scientific jls on geriatric medicine and related topics. *Recreations:* golf, gardening, reading. *Address:* 9 Carolsteen Avenue, Helen's Bay, Co. Down BT19 1LJ. *T:* (028) 9185 3830. *Club:* Royal Belfast Golf.

**STOUTE, Sir Michael (Ronald),** Kt 1998; race horse trainer, since 1972; b 22 Oct. 1945; m; one s one d. *Educ:* Harrison College, Barbados. Leading flat racing trainer, 1981, 1986, 1989, 1994, 1997, 2000, 2003, 2005, 2006 and 2009; trained: Derby winners, Shergar, 1981, Shahrastani, 1986, Kris Kin, 2003, North Light, 2004; Workforce, 2010; Irish Derby winners, Shergar, 1981, Shareef Dancer, 1983, Shahrastani, 1986; 1000 Guineas winners, Musical Bliss, 1989, Russian Rhythm, 2003; Irish 1000 Guineas winner, Sonic Lady, 1986; 2000 Guineas Winners, Shadeed, 1985, Doyoun, 1988, Entrepreneur, 1997, King's Best, 2000, Golan, 2001; Irish 2000 Guineas winner, Shaadi, 1989; Oaks winners, Fair Salinia, 1978, Unite, 1987; Irish Oaks winners, Fair Salinia, 1978, Colorspin, 1986, Unite, 1987, Melodist, 1988, Pure Grain, 1995, Petrushka, 2000; St Leger winner, Conduit, 2008; Breeders' Cup Turf winners, Pilsudski, 1996, Kalanisi, 2000, Conduit, 2008, 2009; Breeders' Cup Filly and Mare Turf winner: Islington, 2003; Dank, 2013; Queen's Trust, 2016; Breeders' Cup Mile winner, Expert Eye, 2018; Japan Cup winner, Singspiel, 1996, Pilsudski, 1997; Dubai World Cup winner, Singspiel, 1997. *Recreations:* golf, deep sea fishing. *Address:* Freemason Lodge, Bury Road, Newmarket, Suffolk CB8 7BY. *T:* (01638) 663801.

**STOUTZKER, Sir Ian,** Kt 2019; CBE 2012 (OBE 1993); FRCM; Chairman: London Interstate Bank, 1971–75; Dawnay Day International, 1985–2000; b 21 Jan. 1929; s of late Aron Stoutzker and Doris Stoutzker; m 1968, Mercedes; one s one d. *Educ:* Berkhamsted Sch.; Royal Coll. of Music (ARCM); London Sch. of Econs and Pol Sci. (BSc). Chm., 1972–76, Pres., 1976–79, Philharmonia Orch.; Founder Chm., Live Music Now, 1977–2019 (Pres., 2019–); Chm., Adv. Cttee, LSO, 1992–2007; Co-Chair, EU Youth Orch., 2015–. Mem. Council, Musicians Benevolent Fund, 2004–12. Co-Chair, Voices Foundn, 1994–2003. Vice President: RCM, 1999–; RWCMD, 2019. Hon. FRAM; Hon. FRWMCD. Prince of Wales Medal for Arts Philanthropy, 2013. *Recreation:* countryside hiking. *Address:* Barengesschen 6, Salzburg 5020, Austria.

**STOW AND LINDSEY, Archdeacon of;** see Steadman, Ven. M. J.

**STOW, Graham Harold,** CBE 2004; DL; Executive Vice Chairman, Britannia Building Society, 2002–03 (Group Chief Executive, 1999–2002); Chairman, Home and Legacy Insurance Services, 2003–06 Vice-Lord Lieutenant, Staffordshire, 2016–19; b 29 April 1944; s of Joseph Stow and Carrie Stow (*née* Meakin); m 1st, 1966, Susan Goldingay (marr. diss. 1983); two s (and one s decd); 2nd, 1984, Christine Probert. *Educ:* Liverpool Collegiate Sch. Captain, Royal Signals (TA), 1976–82. Retail Ops, then Divl Dir, Personnel, Littlewoods Orgn, 1962–82; Dir, Marlar Internat., 1982–84; ASDA Group plc: Personnel Dir, ASDA Stores, 1984–87; Gp Human Resources Dir, 1987–88; Man. Dir, 1988–89, Chief Exec., 1989–91, ASDA Stores; Director: George Davies Corp., 1991–92; Sandpiper Consultants, 1992; Exec. Vice Pres., Minet Gp, 1992–96; Retail Ops Dir, 1996–98, Dep. Gp Chief Exec., 1998–99, Britannia Building Soc. Non-executive Director: Northern Racing, 2001–07 (Chm., 2004–07); Uttoxeter Leisure & Develt Co., 2003–04; Co-op. Financial Services, 2003–09; Co-op. Bank, 2003–09; CIS, 2003–09; Co-op. Gen. Insce, 2006–09; Co-op. Food Div., 2007–09; non-exec. Chm., Iprism Underwriting Agency Ltd, 2006–15; Mem., Adv. Bd, Kiddy & Partners, 2004–11. Chm., Building Socs Assoc., 2002–03 (Dep. Chm., 2001–02). Chm., Staffordshire Moorlands Local Agenda 21 Cttee, 1999–2001; Ind. Bd Mem., DSS, 2000–01; Mem. Bd, Lichfield City Centre Develt Partnership, 2017–; non-executive Director: DWP, 2001–05; Jobcentre Plus, 2003–05. Chm., InStaffs, 2007–09. Trustee: Second World War Experience Centre, 2003–07 (Chm. of Trustees, 1998–2002); Staffordshire Yeomanry Mus., 2007–12 (Chm. of Trustees, 2008–11); Lichfield Cathedral, 2007–11 (Dep. Chm. of Trustees, 2009–11). Chm. of Trustees, Staffs Community Foundn, 2008–11. Member: Regl Council, Nat. Meml Arboretum, 2008–16 (Trustee, 2010–11); Council, St John Ambulance, Staffs, 2009–11. Pres., Inst. of Home Econs, 1990–91; Mem., Council and Court, Leeds Univ., 1991–94; Vice Chm. of Govs, Harrogate GS, 1989–91; Governor: Leeds GS, 1989–94; Staffordshire Univ., 1999–2009 (Dep. Chm., 2002–04, Chm., 2004–09); Denstone Coll., 1999–2001. Mem., HAC. Hon. Col, Staffs and W Midland Army Cadet Force, 2008–15; Chm., 2008–13, Trustee, 2015–17, Hon. Pres., 2017–, Friends of Staffs and W Midlands (N) Army Cadet Force Trust; Hon. Pres., Leek Squadron RAF Air Cadets, 2019–. FCIPD (FIPD 1986); FRSA 1990; FCIB 2002. Freeman, City of London, 1994; Liveryman, Co. of Curriers, 1994– (Master, 2013–14); Liveryman, Co. of Cordwainers of York, 2017–. High Sheriff, 2007–08, DL 2009, Staffs. DUniv Staffordshire, 2009. *Recreations:* military history, collecting Irish stamps 1922 to 1939. *Clubs:* Special Forces, Victory Services; Potters' (Stoke-on-Trent); Burton (Burton upon Trent).

**STOW, Sir Matthew P.;** see Philipson-Stow.

**STOW, His Honour Timothy Montague Fenwick;** QC 1989; a Circuit Judge, 2000–13; b 31 Jan. 1943; s of late Geoffrey Montague Fenwick Stow and Joan Fortescue Stow (*née* Flannery); m 1965, Alisoun Mary Francis Homberger; one s one d. *Educ:* Eton Coll. Called to the Bar, Gray's Inn, 1965, Bencher, 1998; became a tenant in common law chambers of David Croom-Johnson, QC (later Lord Justice Croom-Johnson), 1966; Hd of Chambers, 1998; a Recorder, 1989–2000. *Recreations:* swimming, chain sawing, tennis, foreign travel, music, looking after their country property. *E:* tmfstow@gmail.com.

**STOW, William Llewelyn,** CMG 2002; Director General and Head of Policy and Support Career Home, Department for Environment, Food and Rural Affairs, 2009–12; b 11 Jan. 1948; s of Alfred Frank and Elizabeth Mary Stow; m 1976, Rosemary Ellen Burrows; two s. *Educ:* Eastbourne Grammar Sch.; Churchill Coll., Cambridge (MA). Joined DTI, 1971; seconded to FCO, 1980–83 (UK Delegn to OECD) and 1985–88 (UK Perm. Repn to EC, Brussels); Internal European Policy, 1988–91; Financial and Resource Management, 1991–94; Hd, EC and Trade Policy Div., 1994–96; Dep. Dir-Gen., Trade Policy and Europe, 1996–98; Dir, Employment Relns, 1998; UK Dep. Perm. Rep. to EU, 1999–2003; Dir Gen., Envmt, 2003–07, Strategy and Evidence Gp, 2007–09, DEFRA. Mem. Bd, Sustrans Ltd, 2011–17 (Chm., 2015–17). Chm., Steering Gp on Meat Charging, Food Standards Agency, 2013–17. Chairman: Radnorshire Wildlife Trust, 2012–15; Wildlife Trusts Wales, 2013–17; Rhayader 2000, 2018–; Bd Mem., Council, Wildlife Trusts UK, 2012–18 (Vice-Chair, 2017–18). *Recreations:* hill and coastal walking, bird-watching, cricket, reading, cycling.

**STOWELL OF BEESTON,** Baroness *cr* 2011 (Life Peer), of Beeston in the County of Nottinghamshire; **Tina Wendy Stowell,** MBE 1996; PC 2014; Chairman, Charity Commission, since 2018; *b* Nottingham, 2 July 1967; *d* of David and Margaret Stowell. *Educ:* Chilwell Comprehensive; Broxtowe Coll. of Further Educn. PA to Dir, RAF Regt, MoD, 1986–88; PA to Counsellor (Defence Supply), Defence Section, British Embassy, Washington, 1988–91; PA to Chief Press Sec., Press Office, Prime Minister's Office, 1991–96; various posts, private sector cos, 1996–98; Dep. Chief of Staff to Leader of Cons. Party and Leader of the Opposition, 1998–2001; BBC: Dep. Sec., 2001–03; Hd of Communications to Chm. and Governing Body, 2003–08; Hd of Corporate Affairs, 2008–10; independent strategic communications consultant, 2010–11; Dir, Tina Stowell Associates, 2010–11. A Baroness in Waiting (Govt Whip), 2011–13; Parly Under-Sec. of State, DCLG, 2013–14; Leader of the H of L and Lord Privy Seal, 2014–16. Non-executive Director: Impellam Gp plc, 2017–; ABTA Ltd, 2017–. *Address:* House of Lords, SW1A 0PW. *T:* (020) 7219 5353. *E:* stowellt@parliament.uk. *W:* www.tinastowell.co.uk, www.twitter.com/tinastowell.

**STOWELL, Dr Michael James,** FRS 1984; Research Director, Alcan International Ltd, 1990–94; *b* 10 July 1935; *s* of Albert James Stowell and Kathleen Maud (*née* Poole); *m* 1st, 1962, Rosemary Allen (marr. diss. 1990; she *d* 2007); one *s* one *d*; 2nd, 1995, Kerry June Brice (*née* Kern) (*d* 1998). *Educ:* St Julian's High Sch., Newport; Bristol Univ. (BSc 1957, PhD 1961). Res. Scientist and Gp Leader, Tube Investments Research Labs, 1960–78; Research Manager, Materials Dept, TI Research, 1978–88; Prin. Consulting Scientist, Alcan Internat. Ltd, 1989–90. Post-doctoral Res. Fellow, Ohio State Univ., 1962–63; Res. Fellow, Univ. of Minnesota, 1970; Dist. Res. Fellow, Dept of Materials Sci. and Metallurgy, Univ. of Cambridge, 1999–2013. L. B. Pfeil Medal, Metals Soc., 1976; Sir Robert Hadfield Medal, Metals Soc., 1981. *Publications:* papers on electron microscopy, epitaxy, nucleation theory, superplasticity and physical metallurgy, in various jls. *Recreation:* music. *Address:* 7 Marking's Field, Saffron Walden, Essex CB10 2BB. *T:* (01799) 500112. *E:* stowell290@virginmedia.com.

**STOYE, Dr Jonathan Paul,** FRS 2017; Senior Group Leader, Francis Crick Institute, since 2015; *b* Oxford, 25 Feb. 1952; *s* of John Walter Stoye and Catherine Stoye; *m* 1982, Susan Joan Nimmo-Smith; two *s*. *Educ:* Magdalen Coll. Sch., Oxford; Magdalene Coll., Cambridge (BA 1973); Basel Univ., Switzerland (PhD 1981). Res. Asst, Friedrich Miescher Inst., Basel, 1973–81; Res. Associate, Tufts Univ. Sch. of Medicine, Boston, Mass, 1982–89; Gp Leader, MRC-NIMR, 1989–2015 (Hd, Div. of Virol., 2001–15; Jt Hd, Infectious and Immunity Gp, 2006–15). Adjunct Prof., Imperial Coll. London, 2013–. *Publications:* contribs to scientific jls. *Recreations:* travelling, supporting Saracens. *Address:* Francis Crick Institute, 1 Midland Road, NW1 1AT. *T:* (020) 3796 2439. *E:* jonathan.stoye@crick.ac.uk.

**STRABANE, Viscount; James Alfred Nicholas Hamilton;** *b* 30 Oct. 2005; *s* and heir of Marquess of Hamilton, *qv*.

**STRABOLGI,** 12th Baron *cr* 1318, of England; **Andrew David Whitley Kenworthy;** Data Engineer/Data Scientist, inovex GmbH, Stuttgart, Germany; *b* London, 25 Jan. 1967; *s* of late Rev. Hon. Jonathan Malcolm Atholl Kenworthy and of Victoria Kenworthy (*née* Hewitt); *S* uncle, 2010; *m* 1998; one *s* one *d*. *Educ:* Pembroke Coll., Cambridge (BA Engrg Tripos 1989; MA 1993). *Heir: s* Hon. Joel Brendan Kenworthy, *b* 3 Sept. 2004.

**STRACEY, Sir John (Simon),** 9th Bt *cr* 1818; *b* 30 Nov. 1938; *s* of Captain Algernon Augustus Henry Stracey (2nd *s* of 6th Bt) (*d* 1940) and Olive Beryl (*d* 1972), *d* of late Major Charles Robert Eustace Radclyffe; *S* cousin, 1971; *m* 1968, Martha Maria, *d* of late Johann Egger; two *d*. *Heir:* cousin Rupert Stracey, *b* 28 May 1951. *Address:* Dunedin, Beaconsfield Road, Chelwood Gate, Haywards Heath RH17 7JU. *T:* (01825) 740551.

**STRACHAN, Alan Lockhart Thomson;** theatre director, writer and broadcaster; *b* 3 Sept. 1946; *s* of Roualeyn Robert Scott Strachan and Ellen Strachan (*née* Graham); *m* 1977, Jennifer Piercey-Thompson. *Educ:* Morgan Acad., Dundee; St Andrews Univ. (MA); Merton Coll. Oxford (BLitt). Associate Dir, Mermaid Theatre, 1970–75; Artistic Director: Greenwich Th., 1978–88; Theatre of Comedy Co., 1991–97; Churchill Theatre, Bromley, 1995–97. *Productions directed include:* Mermaid: The Watched Pot, 1970; John Bull's Other Island, The Old Boys, 1971; (co-deviser) Cowardy Custard, 1972; Misalliance, 1973; Children, (co-deviser and dir) Cole, 1974; *Greenwich:* An Audience Called Edouard, 1978; The Play's the Thing, I Sent a Letter to my Love, 1979; Private Lives (transf. Duchess), Time and the Conways, 1980; Present Laughter (transf. Vaudeville), The Golden Age, The Doctor's Dilemma, 1981; Design for Living (transf. Globe), The Paranormalist, French Without Tears, 1982; The Dining Room, An Inspector Calls, A Streetcar Named Desire, 1983 (transf. Mermaid, 1984); The Glass Menagerie, Biography, 1985; One of Us, Relatively Speaking, For King and Country, 1986; The Viewing, The Perfect Party, 1987; How the Other Half Loves (transf. Duke of York's), 1988; *freelance:* Family and a Fortune, Apollo, 1975; (deviser and dir) Shakespeare's People, world tours, 1975–78; Confusions, Apollo, 1976; (also jt author) Yahoo, Queen's, 1976; Just Between Ourselves, Queen's, 1977; The Immortal Haydon, Mermaid, 1977 (transf. Greenwich, 1978); Bedroom Farce, Amsterdam, 1978; Noël and Gertie, King's Head, 1983, Comedy, 1989; (replacement cast) Woman in Mind, Vaudeville, 1987; The Deep Blue Sea, Haymarket, 1988; Re: Joyce!, Fortune, 1988 (transf. Vaudeville, 1989; USA, 1990), Vaudeville, 1991; (replacement cast) Henceforward…, Vaudeville, 1989; June Moon, Scarborough, 1989, Hampstead, transf. Vaudeville, 1992; Toekomstmuziek, Amsterdam, 1989; Alphabetical Order, Scarborough, 1990; (replacement cast) Man of the Moment, Globe, 1990; Other People's Money, Lyric, 1990; Taking Steps, NY, 1991; London Assurance, Dublin, 1993; Make Way for Lucia, Bromley and tour, 1995; Switchback, Bromley and tour, 1996; Høfeber, Copenhagen, 1996; All Things Considered, Scarborough, 1996, Hampstead, 1997; Loot, W Yorks Playhouse, 1996; Live and Kidding, Duchess, 1997; Mrs Warren's Profession, Guildford and tour, 1997; Hooikoorts, Amsterdam, 1997; New Edna—The Spectacle!, Haymarket, 1998; Troilus and Cressida, Regent's Park, 1998; How the Other Half Loves, Oxford Playhouse and tour, 1998; The Merry Wives of Windsor, Regent's Park, 1999; Private Lives, Far East tour, 1999; Hobson's Choice, Scarborough, 1999; Larkin with Women, Scarborough, 1999, Orange Tree Th., Richmond, 2006; A Midsummer Night's Dream, Regent's Park, 2000, 2001; Harvey, Singapore, 2000; The Real Thing, Bristol Old Vic and tour, 2001, Plymouth and tour, 2002; Henry IV, Pt One, Regent's Park, 2004; Going Straight, Windsor and tour, 2004; Glorious!, Birmingham Rep., transf. Duchess, 2005; Entertaining Angels, Chichester, 2006, revised version, Bath and tour, 2009; The Letter, Wyndham's, 2007; How the Other Half Loves, Bath and tour, 2007, Th. Royal Haymarket, 2016, Windsor and tour, 2017; Absurd Person Singular, Garrick, 2007, tour, 2009; Year of the Rat, W Yorks Playhouse, 2008; Relatively Speaking, Bath and tour, 2008; Balmoral, Bath and tour, 2009; The Promise, Orange Tree Th., Richmond, 2010; (revised) Cowardy Custard, Guildford and tour, 2011; Three Days in May, Trafalgar Studios, 2011; Storm in a Flower Vase, Arts Th., 2013; Mrs Pat, Chichester, 2015; The Chalk Garden, Chichester, 2018. *Producer/co-Producer:* Out of Order, tour, 1991; The Pocket Dream, Albery, 1992; Six Degrees of Separation, Royal Court, transf. Comedy, 1992; Hay Fever (also dir), Albery, 1992; Happy Families, tour, 1993; Hysteria, Royal Court, 1993; Under Their Hats (also devised), King's Head, 1994; The Prime of Miss Jean Brodie (also dir.), Strand, 1994; (exec. prod.) Love on a Branch Line, BBC1, 1994. *Publications:* Secret Dreams: a biography of Michael Redgrave, 2004; Putting It On: the West End Theatre of Michael Codron, 2010; Dark Star: a biography of Vivien Leigh, 2018; contribs to periodicals and newspapers. *Recreations:* music, tennis, travelling. *Address:* c/o MLR Ltd, 3 The Glass House, Royal Oak Yard, SE1 3GE.

**STRACHAN, Crispian;** *see* Strachan, J. C.

**STRACHAN, (Douglas) Mark (Arthur);** QC 1987; SC (Hong Kong) 2013; a Recorder, 1990–2002; a Deputy High Court Judge, Queen's Bench Division, 1993–2002; *b* 25 Sept. 1946; *s* of late William Arthur Watkin Strachan and Joyce Olive Strachan; *m* 1995, Elizabeth Vickery; one *s*. *Educ:* Orange Hill Grammar Sch., Edgware, Middx; St Catherine's Coll., Oxford (Open Exhibnr in Eng. Lit.; BCL, MA); Nancy Univ. (French Govt Schol.). Called to the Bar, Inner Temple, 1969 (Major Schol. 1969–71), Hong Kong, 2002; Asst Recorder, 1987–90. Lifetime Achievement Award, Asialaw, 2017. *Publications:* contributor to Modern Law Rev. *Recreations:* son Charlie, France, Far East, antiques, paintings, food.

**STRACHAN, Sir Hew (Francis Anthony),** Kt 2013; PhD; FBA 2017; FRSE; Wardlaw Professor of International Relations, University of St Andrews, since 2017 (Professor of International Relations, 2015–17); Chichele Professor of The History of War, University of Oxford, 2002–15; Fellow of All Souls College, Oxford, 2002–15, now Emeritus; Lord Lieutenant of Tweeddale, since 2014; *b* 1 Sept. 1949; *s* of late Michael Francis Strachan, CBE and Iris Strachan; *m* 1st, 1971, Catherine Margaret Blackburn (marr. diss. 1980); two *d*; 2nd, 1982, Pamela Dorothy Tennant (*née* Symes); one *s*, and one step *s* one step *d*. *Educ:* Rugby; Corpus Christi Coll., Cambridge (MA, PhD 1977). FRSE 2003. Res. Fellow, Corpus Christi Coll., Cambridge, 1975–78; Sen. Lectr in War Studies, RMA, Sandhurst, 1978–79; Corpus Christi College, Cambridge: Fellow, 1979–92, Life Fellow, 1992; Admissions Tutor, 1981–88, Sen. Tutor, 1989–92; Dean of Coll., 1981–86; Prof. of Modern Hist., 1992–2001, and Dir, Scottish Centre for War Studies, 1996–2001, Glasgow Univ.; Dir, Oxford Prog. (formerly Leverhulme Prog.) on the Changing Character of War, Univ. of Oxford, 2004–12. Vis. Prof., Royal Norwegian Air Force Acad., 2000–; Sir Howard Kippenberger Vis. Prof., Victoria Univ. of Wellington, NZ, 2009; Major Res. Fellow, Leverhulme Trust, 2008–11; Inaugural Humanitas Vis. Prof. in War Studies, Univ. of Cambridge, 2011. Lees Knowles Lectr, Cambridge, 1995; Thank Offering to Britain Fellow, British Acad., 1998–99. Comr, Commonwealth War Graves Commn, 2006–18; Mem., Chief of the Defence Staff's Strategic Adv. Panel, 2010–; Advr, Jt Parly Cttee, Nat. Security Strategy, 2011–; Chm., Prime Minister's Taskforce on the Military Covenant, 2010. Member: First World War Centenary Adv. Gp, 2012–; Scottish Cttee for Centenary of First World War, 2013–; Comité Scientifique du Mission du Centenaire, France, 2013–. Trustee, Imperial War Mus., 2010–18. Member of Council: Lancing Coll., 1982–90; Nat. Army Mus., 1994–2003; IISS, 2012–18; Governor: Rugby Sch., 1985–2007; Stowe Sch., 1990–2002. Mem., Royal Co. of Archers, Queen's Bodyguard for Scotland, 1996– (Mem., Council, 2003–12; Brigadier, 2008–19; Ensign, 2019–). Award for Lifetime Achievement in Military Writing, Pritzker Mil. Mus. and Liby, 2016; Samuel Eliot Morison Prize, Soc. for Military History, 2018. DUniv Paisley, 2005. DL Tweeddale, 2006. *Publications:* British Military Uniforms 1768–1796, 1975; History of Cambridge University Officers' Training Corps, 1976; European Armies and the Conduct of War, 1983; Wellington's Legacy: the reform of the British Army, 1984; From Waterloo to Balaclava: tactics, technology and the British Army 1815–1854, 1985 (Templer Medal, Soc. for Army Histl Res.); The Politics of the British Army, 1997 (Westminster Medal, RUSI); (ed) Oxford Illustrated History of the First World War, 1998, 2nd edn 2014; (ed) The British Army, Manpower and Society, 2000; The First World War: vol. 1, To Arms, 2001; The First World War: a new illustrated history, 2003; (ed) Big Wars and Small Wars, 2006; Clausewitz's On War: a biography, 2007; (ed jtly) Clausewitz in the 21st Century, 2007; (ed jtly) The Changing Character of War, 2011; (ed jtly) La guerre irrégulière, 2011; (ed jtly) How Fighting Ends, 2012; (ed jtly) British Generals in Blair's Wars, 2013; The Direction of War: contemporary strategy in historical perspective, 2013. *Recreations:* shooting, Rugby football (now spectating). *Address:* Glenhighton, Broughton, by Biggar ML12 6JF. *Clubs:* Hawks (Cambridge); New (Edinburgh).

**STRACHAN, James Murray;** photographer; *b* 10 Nov. 1953; *s* of Eric Alexander Howison Strachan and Jacqueline Georgina Strachan. *Educ:* King's Sch., Canterbury; Christ's Coll., Cambridge (exhibnr, BA); London Coll. of Printing. Chase Manhattan Bank, 1976–77; joined Merrill Lynch, 1977, Exec. Dir, 1982–86, Man. Dir, 1986–89; writer and photographer, 1989–97; Associate Photographer, Getty Images (formerly Tony Stone), 1990–; Chief Exec., 1997–2002, Chm., 2002–07, Vice Pres., 2008–, RNID (Mem., Finance Cttee and Trustee, 1994–96); Chm., Audit Commn, 2002–06. Mem. Court, Bank of England, 2006–09 (Mem., Audit Cttee, 2006–09). Vis. Fellow, 2005–11, Sen. Vis. Fellow, 2011–13, LSE. Rotating Chair, Disability Charities Consortium, 1997–2002; Co-Chair: Task Force on Social Services Provision for Deaf and Hard of Hearing People, 1998–2002; NHS Modernising Hearing Aid Services Gp, 1999–2002; Chm., Task Force on Audiology Services, 2000–02; Member: Ministerial Disability Rights Task Force, 1997–99; Ministerial Disability Benefits Forum, 1998–99; Bd and Audit Cttee, Ofgem, 2000–04; Bd, Community Fund, 2001–03; Comr for Communications, Disability Rights Commn, 1999–2002. Non-executive Director: Legal and General Gp plc, 2003–11 (Mem., Remuneration Cttee, 2003–10, Risk Cttee, 2010–11); Welsh Water Ltd, 2007–15 (Mem., Audit Cttee; Chm., Remuneration Cttee, 2010–15); JP Morgan Asian Investment Trust plc, 2009–17 (Mem., Audit Cttee); Sarasin and Partners LLP, 2008–16 (Chm., Remuneration Cttee, 2008–16); Care UK plc, 2006–10 (Chm. Remuneration Cttee); Social Finance Ltd, 2007–12; FSA, 2009–13 (Mem., Audit and Remuneration Cttees, 2009–13); Towergate Insurance, 2011–14 (Chm., Risk Cttee, 2012–14). Ext. Mem., DTI Transition Gp (Energy), 2001–02; Ind. Mem., DTI Business Bd, 2002–04. Mem., Adv. Gp on Diversity, NCVO, 2001–03; Pres., Midland Regl Assoc. for Deaf, 2001–07. Trustee: Save the Children, 1999–2002; Somerset House Trust, 2003–08 (Chm., Audit and Finance Cttee, 2006–08). Leadership Patron, Nat. Coll. of School Leadership, 2003–10. Hon. Fellow, Univ. of the Arts, London (formerly London Inst.), 2002. *Publications:* Madrid, 1991; numerous illustrated travel books as photographer; contrib. The Times, Financial Times and Sunday Times. *Recreations:* film, reading, swimming, tennis. *Address:* 10B Wedderburn Road, NW3 5QG. *E:* james.strachan@mac.com.

**STRACHAN, James Oliver John;** QC 2013; a Deputy High Court Judge, since 2018; *b* London, 17 May 1971; *s* of John Strachan and Caroline Strachan; *m* 2000, Imogen; two *s* one *d*. *Educ:* Winchester Coll.; St Peter's Coll., Oxford (BA Hons). Called to the Bar, Middle Temple, 1996; Attorney Gen.'s Counsel to Crown 'A' Panel, 2008–13. *Recreations:* theatre, opera, tennis, Real tennis, sailing, fishing. *Address:* 39 Essex Chambers, 81 Chancery Lane, WC2A 1DD. *T:* (020) 7832 1111, *Fax:* (020) 7353 3978. *E:* james.strachan@39essex.com. *Club:* Garrick.

**STRACHAN, Jeremy Alan Watkin;** Secretary, British Medical Association, 2001–04; *b* 14 Dec. 1944; *s* of William Arthur Watkin Strachan and Joyce Olive Strachan; *m* 1976, Margaret Elizabeth McVay; two step *d*. *Educ:* Haberdashers' Aske's Sch., Elstree; St Catharine's Coll., Cambridge (MA, LLM). Called to the Bar, Inner Temple, 1969 (Paul

Methven Entrance Schol.); Legal Asst, Law Commn, 1967–72; Legal Advr, BSC, 1972–78; Principal Legal Advr and Hd, Legal and Patent Services, ICL, 1978–84; Gp Legal Advr, Standard Telephones and Cables, 1984–85; Dir, Gp Legal Services, and Corporate Affairs, Glaxo Hldgs, 1986–91; Exec. Dir, responsible for legal services, corporate policy and public affairs, and business develt, Glaxo Wellcome, 1992–2000. Co. Sec., Forensic Science Service Ltd, 2005–12. Non-exec. Dir, NHS Business Services Authy, 2005–13. Vice-Chm., Disciplinary Appeals Cttee, CIMA, 2005–12. *Recreations:* France, Victoria & Albert Museum, controversy.

**STRACHAN, John Andrew;** Chairman, Intu Properties plc, since 2017 (non-executive Director, 2016–17); *b* Reading, 1 Feb. 1951; *s* of Alan Leslie Strachan and Kathleen Strachan; *m* Magdeleine Anne Wrenn; three *s*. *Educ:* Brentwood Sch.; Reading Univ. Joined Healey & Baker, 1972, Partner, 1981, Man. Partner, 1993–2002; Global Hd of Retail, Cushman & Wakefield, 2003–16. Mem., Adv. Bd, True Capital, 2013–. Pres., British Council of Shopping Centres, 2006; Mem. Bd, Internat. Council of Shopping Centres, 2007–. Governor: Heath Mount Prep. Sch., 1997–2004; Dulwich Coll., 1998–2003; Harrow Sch., 1999–2014. *Recreations:* theatre, rugby, cricket, racing, loves an old Jag. *Address:* Intu Properties plc, 40 Broadway, SW1H 0BT. *T:* (020) 7960 1201. *E:* john.strachan@intu.co.uk. *Clubs:* Oriental, MCC.

**STRACHAN, (John) Crispian,** CBE 2003; QPM 1996; DL; Director, Holyoake CIR Ltd, since 2011; *b* 5 July 1949; *s* of late Dr (Mark) Noel Strachan and Barbara Joan Strachan; *m* 1974, Denise Anne Farmer; one *s* three *d*. *Educ:* Jesus Coll., Oxford (BA Jurisp 1971; MA 1989); Sheffield Univ. (MA Criminology 1972). Joined Metropolitan Police, 1972; Inspector, 1977–83; Chief Inspector, 1983–87; Superintendent, 1987–90; Chief Superintendent, 1990–93; Asst Chief Constable, Strathclyde Police, 1993–98; Chief Constable, Northumbria Police, 1998–2005. Vis. Schol. in Applied Criminol. and Police Mgt, Cambridge Inst. of Criminology, 2011–. Non-exec. Dir, Restorative Solutions CIC, 2016–. Dep. County Pres., St John Ambulance Northumbria, 2006–14. Trustee: Royal Grammar Sch. (Newcastle upon Tyne) Educnl Trust, 2006–16; St Mary the Virgin Estate Mgt Charity, 2010–16. DL Tyne and Wear, 2002. OStJ 2005. *Publications:* (with A. Comben) A Short Guide to Policing in the UK, 1992; (contrib.) Clinical Forensic Medicine, 3rd edn 2009. *Recreations:* woodworking, photography, the countryside, family above all. *Address:* 4 Rectory Close, High Wycombe, Bucks HP13 6HF. *E:* crispianstrachan@gmail.com.

**STRACHAN, Mark;** see Strachan, D. M. A.

**STRACHAN, Peter;** Chairman: UK Rail, Serco, since 2017 (Managing Director, Serco Caledonian Sleeper, 2014–17); North East Ambulance Service NHS Foundation Trust, since 2018; *b* Aberdeen, 29 Aug. 1959; *s* of Alexander Strachan and Ina Strachan (*née* Mitchell); *m* 1981, Fiona Jill Colgate; two *s*. *Educ:* Kirkcudbright Acad.; Univ. of Durham (BA Hons). MIRO 2005. British Rail: graduate trainee, 1980–82; local and line mgt posts, 1982–90; Intercity Manager, Birmingham, 1990–93; Dir, Midlands, Railtrack, 1993–97; Man. Dir, North Western Trains, 1997–98; Chief Exec. (Rail), National Express Australia, 1999–2003; Man. Dir, Arriva Trains Wales, 2003–05; Route Dir, London North Western, Network Rail, 2005–09; Chief Exec., TransLink Transit Authy, Brisbane, 2009–11; Dir Gen., Major Projects and London, DfT, 2011–13; Bid Dir, Serco Gp Pty Ltd, Sydney, 2013–14. *Recreations:* football, golf, opera.

**STRACHAN, Dame Valerie (Patricia Marie),** DCB 1998 (CB 1991); Chairman, HM Customs and Excise, 1993–2000; *b* 10 Jan. 1940; *d* of John Jonas Nicholls and Louise Nicholls; *m* 1965, John Strachan; one *s* one *d*. *Educ:* Newland High Sch., Hull; Manchester Univ. (BA). Joined HM Customs and Excise, 1961; Dept of Economic Affairs, 1964; Home Office, 1966; Principal, HM Customs and Excise, 1966; Treasury, 1972; Asst Secretary, HM Customs and Excise, 1974, Comr, 1980; Head, Joint Management Unit, HM Treasury/Cabinet Office, 1985–87; a Dep. Chm., Bd of Customs and Excise, 1987–93. External Mem., H of L Audit Cttee, 2002–08. Mem. Panel, Rosemary Nelson Inquiry, 2005–11; Mem., Judicial Appts Commn, 2012–19. Chm., Communications and Public Service (formerly CS, PO and BT) Lifeboat Fund, 1998–2004; Dep. Chair, Community Fund (formerly Nat. Lottery Charities Bd), 2000–04; Vice Chm., Big Lottery Fund, 2004–06. Pres., British Internat. Freight Assoc., 2002–04. Chairman: Govs, James Allen's Girls' Sch., 2004–09; Council, Univ. of Southampton, 2006–12. CCMI. Hon. LLD: Manchester, 1995; Southampton, 2013.

**STRACHEY,** family name of **Baron O'Hagan**.

**STRACHEY, Sir Henry Leofric Benvenuto,** 7th Bt *cr* 1801, of Sutton Court, Somerset; *b* 17 April 1947; *o s* of John Ralph Severs Strachey and Rosemary Strachey (*née* Mavor); *S* kinsman (Charles Strachey, who did not use the title) 2014, but his name does not yet appear on the Official Roll of the Baronetage; *m* 1st, 1971, Julie Margaret Hutchens (marr. diss. 1982); 2nd, 1983, Susan Christine Skinner. *Heir:* none.

**STRADBROKE, 6th Earl of,** *cr* 1821; **Robert Keith Rous;** Bt 1660; Baron Rous 1796; Viscount Dunwich 1821; grazier, Mount Fyans Station, Darlington, Victoria; *b* 25 March 1937; *s* of 5th Earl of Stradbroke and Pamela Catherine Mabell (*d* 1972), *d* of Captain Hon. Edward James Kay-Shuttleworth; *S* father, 1983, but does not use the title; *m* 1960, Dawn Antoinette (marr. diss. 1977), *d* of Thomas Edward Beverley, Brisbane; two *s* five *d*; 2nd, 1977, Roseanna Mary Blanche, *d* of late Francis Reitman, MD; six *s* two *d*. *Educ:* Harrow. *Recreation:* making babies. *Heir:* s Viscount Dunwich, qv. *Address:* Box 383, Richmond, Vic 3121, Australia. *T:* (4) 27901294, *Fax:* (3) 98152668.

**STRADLING, Donald George;** Group Personnel Director, John Laing & Son Ltd, then John Laing plc, 1969–89; Director, Quantum Care, 2000–04; *b* 7 Sept. 1929; *s* of George Frederic and Olive Emily Stradling; *m* 1st, 1955, Mary Anne Hartridge (*d* 2000); two *d*; 2nd, 2004, Elizabeth Lilian Jane Dennis (*née* Hewitt). *Educ:* Clifton Coll.; Magdalen Coll., Oxford (Open Exhibnr; MA). CIPM. School Master, St Albans Sch., 1954–55; Group Trng and Educn Officer, John Laing & Son Ltd, Building and Civil Engrg Contractors, 1955. Vis. Prof., Univ. of Salford, 1989–94. Comr, Manpower Services Commn, 1980–82; Mem. Council, Inst. of Manpower Studies, 1975–81; Member: Employment Policy Cttee, CBI, 1978–84, 1986–91; Council, CBI, 1982–86; FCEC Wages and Industrial Cttee, 1978–95; Council, FCEC, 1985–95; National Steering Gp, New Technical and Vocational Educn Initiative, 1983–88; NHS Trng Authy, 1985–89. Director: Building and Civil Engrg Benefits Scheme (Trustee, 1984–2004); Building and Civil Engrg Holidays Scheme Management, 1984–2004; Construction ITB, 1985–90. Vice-Pres., Inst. of Personnel Management, 1974–76. Vice-Chm. of Governors, St Albans High Sch., 1977–95; Mem. Council, Tyndale House, 1977–96. Liveryman, Glaziers' and Painters of Glass Co., 1983–95, 2003–. Hon. PhD Internat. Management Centre, Buckingham, 1987; Hon. DSc Salford, 1995. *Publications:* contribs on music and musical instruments, et al. to New Bible Dictionary, 1962. *Recreations:* listening to music (espec. opera), walking. *Address:* Courts Edge, 12 The Warren, Harpenden, Herts AL5 2NH.

**STRAFFORD, 9th Earl of,** *cr* 1847; **William Robert Byng;** Baron Strafford, 1835; Viscount Enfield, 1847; computer systems developer, Vimysoft Ltd, since 2007; *b* 10 May 1964; *s* of 8th Earl of Strafford and Jennifer Mary Byng (*née* May); *S* father, 2016; *m* 1994, Karen Elizabeth, *d* of S. Graham Lord, Leyland, Preston; twin *s* four *d*. *Educ:* Winchester Coll.; Durham Univ. Computer systems developer, CCP York, 2002. *Heir:* s Viscount Enfield, *qv. Address:* 1 Lowes Court, Durham DH1 4NR.

*See also* Hon. J. E. Byng.

**STRAKER, Anita,** CB 2001; OBE 1990; *b* 22 June 1938; *d* of David William Barham and Laura Barham; *m* 1961, Patrick Vincent Straker; four *s*. *Educ:* Weston-super-Mare Grammar Sch. for Girls; University Coll. London (BSc Hons); Royal Holloway Coll., Univ. of London (MSc); Univ. of Cambridge Inst. of Educn (PGCE). Teacher, 1961–62 and 1968–74; Inspector for maths, Surrey LEA, 1974–78; Gen. Advr, Wilts LEA, 1978–83; Dir, Microelectronics Educn Prog. Primary Project, DES, 1983–86; Dist Inspector, ILEA, 1986–89; Principal Advr, Berks LEA, 1989–93; Dep. Dir of Educn, Camden LEA, 1993–96; Dir, Nat. Numeracy Strategy, DFE, then DfEE, 1996–2000; Dir, Key Stage 3 Nat. Strategy, DfEE, then DfES, 2000–02. Hon. LLD UEA, 2002. *Publications:* Mathematics for Gifted Pupils, 1980; Children Using Computers, 1988; Mathematics from China, 1990; Primary Maths Extension Activities, 1991; Talking Points in Mathematics, 1993; Mental Maths (series), 1994; Home Maths (series), 1998; Exploring Maths (series), 2008. *Recreations:* holidays abroad, cooking, reading, swimming. *Address:* Mundays, St Mary Bourne, Andover, Hants SP11 6AY. *T:* (01264) 738474.

**STRAKER, Timothy Derrick;** QC 1996; a Recorder, since 2000; a Deputy High Court Judge, since 2010; Justice of Appeal, Court of Appeal of the Falklands, since 2011; *b* 25 May 1955; *s* of late Derrick Straker, solicitor, and Dorothy Elizabeth, *o d* of late Brig. T. L. Rogers, CBE; *m* 1982, Ann Horton Baylis (marr. diss. 2007); two *d*. *Educ:* Malvern Coll.; Downing Coll., Cambridge (BA 1st Cl. Hons Law, MA). Called to the Bar: Gray's Inn, 1977 (Holt Schol.), Bencher, 2004; Lincoln's Inn, *ad eundem*, 1979; NI, 2001; Trinidad and Tobago, 2001; in practice at the Bar, 1977–; an Asst Recorder, 1998–2000. Jt Hd of Chambers, 2002–12, 2013–15, 2017–; Hd of Chambers, 2015–17. Election Comr for various petitions, 2007–; Advr to Home Sec. under Animals (Scientific Procedures) Act, 2011–. Member: Admin. Law Bar Assoc., 1986–; Local Govt, Planning and Envmtl Bar Assoc., 1986–; Crown Office Users' Cttee, 1993–2000; Administrative Court Users' Assoc., 2000–; Parly Bar Mess, 2011–. Gov. and Mem. Council, Malvern Coll., 2011–. Contrib. Ed., Civil Court Practice, 1999–2008. *Publications:* Annotated Current Law Statutes, 1994; (Consultant Ed.) Registration of Political Parties: a guide to Returning Officers, 1999; (with Iain Goldrein) Human Rights and Judicial Review: case studies in context, 2000; Information Rights, 2004; Electoral Administration Act, 2006; contrib. Halsbury's Laws of England (Public Health and Environmental Protection, 2000; Local Government, 2001; Markets, 2002); contrib. Rights of Way Law Review, Judicial Review. *Recreations:* theatre, history, rackets (with Steve Tulley, finalists, Winchester Invitation Doubles, 2011 and 2013, winners, Tonbridge Tournament, 2013, finalists, 2014). *Address:* 4–5 Gray's Inn Square, Gray's Inn, WC1R 5AH. *T:* (020) 7404 5252. *Clubs:* Lansdowne, Oxford and Cambridge, MCC; Manchester Tennis and Racquet; St Paul's Rackets.

**STRAND, Prof. Kenneth T.;** Professor, Department of Economics, Simon Fraser University, 1968–86, now Emeritus; *b* Yakima, Wash, 30 June 1931; Canadian citizen since 1974; *m* 1960, Elna K. Tomaske; no *c*. *Educ:* Washington State Coll. (BA); Univ. of Wisconsin (PhD, MS). Woodrow Wilson Fellow, 1955–56; Ford Foundn Fellow, 1957–58; Herfurth Award, Univ. of Wisconsin, 1961 (for PhD thesis). Asst Exec. Sec., Hanford Contractors Negotiation Cttee, Richland, Wash, 1953–55; Asst Prof., Washington State Univ., 1959–60; Asst Prof., Oberlin Coll., 1960–65 (on leave, 1963–65); Economist, Manpower and Social Affairs Div., OECD, Paris, 1964–66; Assoc. Prof., Dept of Econs, Simon Fraser Univ., 1966–68; Pres., Simon Fraser Univ., 1969–74 (Acting Pres., 1968–69). Mem., Canadian Industrial Relations Assoc. (Pres., 1983). Hon. LLD Simon Fraser Univ., 1983. FRSA 1972. *Publications:* Jurisdictional Disputes in Construction: The Causes, The Joint Board and the NLRB, 1961; contribs to Review of Econs and Statistics, Amer. Econ. Review, Industrial Relations, Sociaal Mannblad Arbeid. *Recreations:* fishing, ski-ing. *Address:* PO Box 5009, Lac Le Jeune, BC V1S 1Y8, Canada.

**STRANG, David James Reid,** CBE 2019; QPM 2002; Chief Inspector of Prisons for Scotland, 2013–18; *b* Glasgow, 9 April 1958; *s* of William Guthrie Strang and Morag Langlands Strang; *m* 1981, Alison; one *s* two *d*. *Educ:* Glasgow Acad.; Loretto Sch.; Univ. of Durham (BSc 1980); Birkbeck Coll., London (MSc 1989). Metropolitan Police, 1980–98; Asst Chief Constable, Lothian and Borders Police, 1998–2001; Chief Constable: Dumfries and Galloway Constabulary, 2001–07; Lothian and Borders Police, 2007–13.

**STRANG, Rt Hon. Gavin (Steel);** PC 1997; *b* 10 July 1943; *s* of James Steel Strang and Marie Strang (*née* Finkle); *m* 1973, Bettina Smith (*d* 2016). *Educ:* Univs of Edinburgh and Cambridge. BSc Hons Edinburgh, 1964; DipAgricSci Cambridge, 1965; PhD Edinburgh, 1968. Mem., Tayside Econ. Planning Consultative Group, 1966–68; Scientist with ARC, 1968–70. MP (Lab) Edinburgh E, 1970–97 and 2005–10, Edinburgh E and Musselburgh, 1997–2005. Opposition front bench spokesman on Scottish affairs, 1972–73, on energy, 1973–74; Parly Under-Sec. of State, Dept of Energy, March–Oct. 1974; Parly Sec., MAFF, 1974–79; Opposition front bench spokesman on agriculture, 1979–82, on employment, 1987–89, on food, agriculture and rural affairs, 1992–97; Mem., Shadow Cabinet, 1994–97; Minister for Transport, 1997–98. Chm., PLP Defence Group, 1984–87. *Publications:* articles in Animal Production. *Recreations:* golf, swimming, watching football. *E:* gavin.s.strang@gmail.com.

**STRANG, Sir John (Stanley),** Kt 2016; MD; FRCPsych; FRCP; FMedSci; Professor of the Addictions, Institute of Psychiatry and Director, National Addiction Centre, since 1995, and Head, Addictions Department, since 2009, King's College, London; Director, Addictions Clinical Academic Group, King's Health Partners, since 2010; *b* 12 May 1950; *s* of late William John Strang, CBE, FRS, and of Margaret Nicholas Strang (*née* Howells); *m* 1984, Jennifer Abbey; two *s* (one *d* decd). *Educ:* Bryanston Sch., Dorset; Guy's Hosp. Med. Sch. (MB BS 1973; MD 1995). FRCPsych 1994; FRCP 2006. Consultant psychiatrist in drug dependence: Manchester, 1982–86; Maudsley Hosp., London, 1986–; Getty Sen. Lectr in the Addictions, Nat. Addiction Centre, Inst. of Psychiatry, 1991–95. Consultant Advr (drugs), DoH, 1990–2003. Mem., Adv. Council on Misuse of Drugs, 1989–2001. FMedSci 2015. Hon. FAChAM 2005. *Publications:* (with G. Stimson) AIDS and Drug Misuse: the challenge for policy and practice in the 1990s, 1990; (jtly) Drugs, Alcohol and Tobacco: making the science and policy connections, 1993; (with M. Gossop) Heroin Addiction and Drug Policy: the British system, 1994; (with J. Sheridan) Drug Misuse and Community Pharmacy, 2002; (with G. Tober) Methadone Matters, 2003; (with M. Gossop) Heroin Addiction and the British System, 2 vols, 2005; (with T. Babor *et al*) Drug Policy and the Public Good, 2010; (with P. Miller *et al*) Addiction Research Methods, 2010; (jtly) New Heroin-Assisted Treatment: recent evidence and current practices of supervised injectable heroin treatment in Europe and beyond, 2012. *Address:* National Addiction Centre, Addiction Sciences Building, 4 Windsor Walk, SE5 8AF. *T:* (020) 7848 0438. *Club:* Athenæum.

**STRANG STEEL, Major Sir (Fiennes) Michael,** 3rd Bt *cr* 1938, of Philiphaugh, Selkirk; CBE 1999; Vice Lord-Lieutenant, Borders Region (Roxburgh, Ettrick and Lauderdale), 2008–19; *b* 22 Feb. 1943; *s* of Sir (Fiennes) William Strang Steel, 2nd Bt and Joan Strang Steel (*d* 1982), *d* of Brig.-Gen. Sir Brodie Haldane Henderson, KCMG, CB; *S* father, 1992;

*m* 1977, Sarah Jane Russell; two *s* one *d. Educ*: Eton. Major, 17/21 Lancers, 1962–80, retd. Forestry Comr, 1988–99. Captain, Royal Co. of Archers, Queen's Body Guard for Scotland, 2016–19 (Ensign, 2007–10; Lieut, 2010–16). DL Borders Region (Districts of Roxburgh, Ettrick & Lauderdale), 1990. *Heir*: *s* (Fiennes) Edward Strang Steel, *b* 8 Nov. 1978. *Address*: Philiphaugh, Selkirk TD7 5LX. *Club*: Cavalry and Guards.

**STRANGE**, 17th Baron *cr* 1628; **Adam Humphrey Drummond**; *b* 20 April 1953; *s* of Captain Humphrey ap Evans, MC, who assumed name of Drummond of Megginch by decree of Lord Lyon, 1965, and Baroness Strange (16th in line); *S* mother, 2005; *m* 1988, Hon. Mary Emma Jeronima Dewar, *d* of Baron Fortevoit, *qv*; one *s* one *d. Educ*: Eton; RMA Sandhurst; Heriot-Watt Univ. (MSc (Housing)). MCIH 2007. Major, Grenadier Guards, retd. Farmer. Mem., Queen's Body Guard for Scotland (Royal Co. of Archers). *Heir*: *s* Hon. John Adam Humphrey Drummond, *b* 3 Nov. 1992. *Club*: Perth.

**STRANGE, Most Rev. Mark Jeremy**; *see* Moray, Ross and Caithness, Bishop of.

**STRANGWAYS**; *see* Fox-Strangways, family name of Earl of Ilchester.

**STRANRAER-MULL, Very Rev. Gerald**; Dean of Aberdeen and Orkney, 1988–2008, now Emeritus; Rector of Ellon and Cruden Bay, 1972–2008; *b* 24 Nov. 1942; *s* of Gerald and Lena Stranraer-Mull; *m* 1967, Glynis Mary Kempe (*d* 2015); one *s* one *d* (and one *s* decd). *Educ*: Woodhouse Grove School, Apperley Bridge; King's College, London (AKC 1969); Saint Augustine's College, Canterbury. Journalist, 1960–66. Curate: Hexham Abbey, 1970–72; Corbridge, 1972; Priest-in-Charge of St Peter's, Peterhead, 2001–04. Editor of Aberdeen and Buchan Churchman, 1976–84, 1991–94; Director of Training for Ministry, Diocese of Aberdeen and Orkney, 1982–90; Canon of Saint Andrew's Cathedral, Aberdeen, 1981–2008. Dir of Ordinands, Dio. of Moray, Ross and Caithness, 2014–16. Director: Oil Chaplaincy Trust, 1993–2008; Duncraig, Iona (formerly Iona Cornerstone Foundn), 1995–2009. Warden, Soc. of Our Lady of the Isles, Isle of Fetlar, then Isle of Unst, Shetland, 2006–19, now Warden Emeritus. Hon. Priest-in-Charge, St Paul's, Strathnairn, 2009–12; Hon. Priest, St Michael and All Angels, Inverness, 2011–. FSAScot 2011. *Publications*: A Turbulent House: the Augustinians at Hexham, 1970; View of the Diocese, 1977; A Church for Scotland: the story of the Scottish Episcopal Church, 2000, 3rd edn 2012; Steps on the Way: the history of the Scottish Episcopal Church 1513–2013, 2013, rev. edn 2019. *Address*: 4 Lochlann Avenue, Culloden, Inverness-shire IV2 7LT. *T*: (01463) 793943.

**STRASBURGER**, Baron *cr* 2011 (Life Peer), of Langridge in the County of Somerset; **Paul Cline Strasburger**; businessman and philanthropist; *b* 31 July 1946. *Address*: House of Lords, SW1A 0PW.

**STRATFORD, Ian Dodd**; Managing Director, Bodis Associates, since 2009; *b* 26 June 1954; *s* of John and Elsie Stratford; *m* 1994, Debra Jean Wolstenholme; one *s* one *d. Educ*: Univ. of Salford (BSc Hons Geog. 1977); Newcastle Business Sch., Northumbria Univ. (Postgrad. Cert. in Coaching 2010). MCIH 1982. Area Housing Manager, Middlesbrough, 1983–88; Dep. Dir, 1987–90, Dir, 1990–97, of Housing, Enfield LBC; Exec. Dir, Personal Services, 1997–2000, Dep. Chief Exec., 2000–02, Thurrock Council; Chief Exec., Newcastle CC, 2002–08. Chm., London Business Innovation Centre, 1995–97; Clerk, Tyne and Wear PTA, 2002–08; non-exec. Dir, Nexus Transport Exec., 2002–08; Director: NewcastleGateshead Initiative, 2002–08; Tyne and Wear Develt Co., 2002–08; My Life Plus CIC, 2013–18. Company Sec., Newcastle Th. Royal, 2002–08; Member of Board: Newcastle Science City, 2005–08; NewcastleGateshead City Develt Co., 2008; Lay Mem., Court, Univ. of Newcastle upon Tyne, 2005–10. *Recreations*: live music, sailing, walking in Northumberland, advisor to Trustees of Tyne Amateur Rowing Club. *E*: ianstratford@talktalk.net.

**STRATFORD, Jemima Lucy**; QC 2010; *b* London, 23 July 1968. *Educ*: S Hampstead High Sch.; New Coll., Oxford (BA Modern Hist.); City Univ. (Dip. Law). Called to the Bar, Middle Temple, 1993; tenant at Brick Court Chambers, specialising in EU, public law and human rights, 1995–. *Address*: Brick Court Chambers, 7–8 Essex Street, WC2R 3LD.

**STRATFORD, Neil Martin**; Keeper of Medieval and Later Antiquities, 1975–98, Keeper Emeritus, 1998–2001, British Museum; *b* 26 April 1938; *s* of late Dr Martin Gould Stratford and Dr Mavis Stratford (*née* Beddall); *m* 1966, Anita Jennifer Lewis; two *d. Educ*: Marlborough Coll.; Magdalene Coll., Cambridge (BA Hons English 1961, MA); Courtauld Inst., London Univ. (BA Hons History of Art 1966). 2nd Lieut Coldstream Guards, 1956–58; Trainee Kleinwort, Benson, Lonsdale Ltd, 1961–63; Lecturer, Westfield Coll., London Univ., 1969–75; Prof. of Hist. of Medieval Art, Ecole Nationale des Chartes, Paris, 2000–03. British Academy/Leverhulme Sen. Res. Fellow, 1991; Mem., Inst. for Advanced Study, Princeton, 1998–99; Appleton Vis. Prof., Florida State Univ., 2000; Vis. Sen. Lecturing Fellow, Duke Univ., 2006. Chm., St Albans Cathedral Fabric Cttee, 1995–; Chm. Trustees, Corpus of Romanesque Sculpture in Britain and Ireland, 2017–; Member: Conseil Scientifique, Société Française d'Archéologie, 1994– (Gold Medal, 2011); Comité d'orientation scientifique et culturelle, Centre des monuments nationaux, 2011–; Pres., Comité scientifique pour la restauration et mise en valeur de l'ancienne abbaye de Cluny, 2005–. Liveryman, Haberdashers' Co., 1959–. Hon. Mem., Académie de Dijon, 1975; For. Mem., 1985, Mem. Honoraire, 2018, Société Nationale des Antiquaires de France; Associate Mem., Acad. des Inscriptions et Belles-Lettres, 2012 (For. Corresp. Mem., 2002). FSA 1976. Comdr, Ordre des Arts et des Lettres (France), 2013 (Officier, 2006). *Publications*: La Sculpture Oubliée de Vézelay, 1984; Catalogue of Medieval Enamels in the British Museum, vol. II, Northern Romanesque Enamel, 1993; Westminster Kings and the medieval Palace of Westminster, 1995; The Lewis Chessmen and the enigma of the hoard, 1997; Studies in Burgundian Romanesque Sculpture, 1998; La Frise romane monumentale de Souvigny, 2002; Chronos et Cosmos: le pilier roman de Souvigny, 2005; (ed and principal contrib.) Cluny 910–2010: onze siècles de rayonnement, 2010; (ed and principal contrib.) Corpus de la sculpture de Cluny: les parties orientales de la Grande Eglise Cluny III, 2011; articles in French and English periodicals. *Recreations*: opera, food and wine, cricket and football. *Address*: 17 Church Row, NW3 6UP. *T*: (020) 7794 5688. *Clubs*: Beefsteak, Garrick, MCC, I Zingari; University Pitt, Hawks (Cambridge).

**STRATFORD, Stuart**; Music Director, Scottish Opera, since 2015; *b* Preston, Lancs, 28 Feb. 1973; *s* of Kenneth Parnell Stratford and Janette Mulholland O'Brien Stratford; *m* 2002, Tatyana Kochanova; one *s. Educ*: Broughton High Sch., Preston; Preston Coll.; Trinity Coll., Cambridge (BA 1995); St Petersburg State Conservatoire. Jun. Fellow, RNCM, 1999–2000. Guest Conductor appointments include: Opera Holland Park; ENO; Opera North; WNO; Birmingham Opera Co.; Finnish Nat. Opera; Theater St Gallen; LPO; BBC Philharmonic Orch.; RPO; Philharmonia; LSO; City of London Sinfonia; Manchester Camerata. *Recreations*: history, drama, art, cricket.

**STRATFORD, Very Rev. Dr Timothy Richard**; Dean of Chester, since 2018; *b* Liverpool, 26 Feb. 1961; *s* of George Alexander Stratford and Vera June Stratford; *m* 1986, Jennifer Anne Stratford; three *s. Educ*: Knowsley Hey Comprehensive; Univ. of York (BSc Hons 1982); Wycliffe Hall, Oxford (CTh); Sheffield Univ. (PhD 2008). Ordained deacon, 1986, priest, 1987; Assistant Curate: Mossley Hill Parish Church, 1986–89; St Helens Parish Church, 1989–91; Chaplain to Bishop of Liverpool, 1991–94; Vicar, Good Shepherd, W Derby, 1994–2003; Team Rector, Kirkby, 2003–12; Archdeacon of Leicester, 2012–18. *Publications*: Interactive Preaching, 1998; Liturgy and Technology, 1999; Liturgy and Urban Mission, 2002; Using Common Worship: a service of the word, 2002; (ed) Worship Window of the Urban Church, 2006; (jtly) Introducing Times and Seasons: 1: the Christmas cycle, 2016; (jtly) The Richard III Reinterment Liturgies; (jtly) Reimagining Worship, 2017. *Recreations*: photography, mountain biking, music. *Address*: The Deanery, 7 Abbey Street, Chester CH1 2JF. *T*: (01244) 324756.

**STRATHALLAN, Viscount; James David Drummond**; Director, End of the Road Festival Ltd, 2014–17 and since 2018; *b* 24 Oct. 1965; *s* and *heir* of Earl of Perth, *qv*.

**STRATHALMOND**, 3rd Baron *cr* 1955; **William Roberton Fraser**, CA; Finance Director, Gerling at Lloyd's (formerly Owen & Wilby Underwriting Agency) Ltd, 1995–2000; *b* 22 July 1947; *s* of 2nd Baron Strathalmond, CMG, OBE, TD, and of Letitia, *d* of late Walter Krementz, New Jersey, USA; *S* father, 1976; *m* 1973, Amanda Rose, *yr d* of Rev. Gordon Clifford Taylor; two *s* one *d. Educ*: Loretto. Man. Dir, London Wall Members Agency Ltd, 1986–91 (Dir, 1985–91); Dir, London Wall Hldgs plc, 1986–91; Chm., R. W. Sturge Ltd, 1991–94. Dir, N Atlantic Salmon Fund (UK), 2003–08. Pres., RSAS AgeCare, 2008– (Chm. Trustees, 1984–2001; Vice-Pres., 2001–08); Trustee, Medusa Trust, 2013–. Liveryman, Girdlers' Co., 1979– (Master, 2010–11). *Heir*: *s* Hon. William Gordon Fraser [*b* 24 Sept. 1976; *m* 2011, Charlotte, *d* of Dr Ralph Stephenson; two *s* one *d*]. *Address*: Holt House, Elstead, Surrey GU8 6LF.

**STRATHAVON, Lord; Cosmo Alistair Gordon**; *b* 27 July 2009; *s* and *heir* of Earl of Aboyne, *qv*.

**STRATHCARRON**, 3rd Baron *cr* 1936; **Ian David Patrick Macpherson**; Bt 1933; Chairman, Unicorn Publishing Group LLP (formerly Managing Director, Unicorn Press Ltd), since 2010; Partner, Art Resolve (formerly Senior Partner, Mediation Process) LLP, since 2012; *b* 31 March 1949; *er s* of 2nd Baron Strathcarron and Diana Hawtrey Curle (*née* Deane); *S* father, 2006; *m* 1974, Gillian Rosamund Allison; one *s* one *d. Educ*: Hill House Sch.; Horris Hill; Eton; Hollingbourne Manor; Grenoble Univ. Proprietor and Ed., Japan Europa Press Agency, 1970–2005; Partner, Strathcarron & Co., 1974. Trustee, Nat. Motor Museum, Beaulieu. *Publications*: Invisibility, 2004; Black Beach, 2007; Joy Unconfined! Lord Byron's Grand Tour Re-toured, 2010; Innocence & War, Mark Twain's Holy Land Tour Re-toured, 2011; Living with Life, 2012; The Indian Equator: Mark Twain's India revisited, 2013; Never Fear: reliving the life of Sir Francis Chichester, 2016; Mysticism and Bliss, 2017; Painting with Both Hands, 2017; Crikey! How Did That Happen?: the refreshingly unauthorised biography of Sir Bertram Wooster, KG, 2018. *Heir*: *s* Hon. Rory David Alasdair Macpherson, *b* 15 April 1982. *W*: www.istrath.com.

**STRATHCLYDE**, 2nd Baron *cr* 1955, of Barskimming; **Thomas Galloway Dunlop du Roy de Blicquy Galbraith**, CH 2013; PC 1995; Leader of the House of Lords and Chancellor of the Duchy of Lancaster, 2010–13; *b* 22 Feb. 1960; *s* of Hon. Sir Thomas Galloway Dunlop Galbraith, KBE, MP (*d* 1982) (*e s* of 1st Baron) and Simone Clothilde Fernande Marie Ghislaine (*d* 1991), *e d* of late Jean du Roy de Blicquy; *S* grandfather, 1985; *m* 1992, Jane, *er d* of John Skinner; three *d. Educ*: Wellington College; Univ. of East Anglia (BA 1982); Université d'Aix-en-Provence. Insurance Broker, Bain Dawes, subseq. Bain Clarkson Ltd, 1982–88. Contested (C) Merseyside East, European Parly Election, 1984. Spokesman for DTI, Treasury and Scotland, H of L, 1988–89; Govt Whip, 1988–89; Parly Under-Sec. of State, Dept of Employment, 1989–90, DoE, 1990, 1992–93; Scottish Office (Minister for Agric. and Fisheries), 1990–92, DTI, 1993–94; Minister of State, DTI, 1994; Captain of the Hon. Corps of Gentlemen at Arms (Govt Chief Whip in H of L), 1994–97; Opposition Chief Whip, House of Lords, 1997–98; elected Mem., H of L, 1999; Leader of the Opposition, H of L, 1998–2010. Director: Trafalgar Capital Management Ltd, 2001–10 (Chm., 2001–10); Scottish Mortgage Investment Trust plc, 2004–10; Galena Asset Management Ltd, 2004–10; Marketform Group Ltd, 2004–10; Hampden Agencies Ltd, 2008–10; non-exec. Dir, Trafigura, 2013–16; Chairman: Adv. Bd, Battersea Power Station, 2013–; Bd, CPS, 2013–; Bank and Clients plc, 2016–; Raytheon UK, 2018–. Chm., Battersea Power Station Foundn, 2015–. Gov., Wellington Coll., 2010–. *Heir*: *b* Hon. Charles William du Roy de Blicquy Galbraith [*b* 20 May 1962; *m* 1992, Bridget, *d* of Brian Reeve; three *s* one *d*]. *Address*: House of Lords, SW1A 0PW. *T*: (020) 7219 5353.

**STRATHCONA AND MOUNT ROYAL**, 5th Baron *cr* 1900; **Donald Alexander Smith Howard**; *b* 24 June 1961; *s* of 4th Baron Strathcona and Mount Royal and Lady Jane Mary Waldegrave; *S* father, 2018; *m* 1992, Jane Maree, *d* of Shaun Gibb; one *s* one *d. Educ*: Gordonstoun Sch.; London Business Sch. (MBA). *Heir*: *s* Hon. Donald Angus Ruaridh Howard, *b* 29 Sept. 1994.

**STRATHEDEN**, 7th Baron *cr* 1836, **AND CAMPBELL**, 7th Baron *cr* 1841; **David Anthony Campbell**; *b* 13 Feb. 1963; *o s* of 6th Baron Stratheden and Campbell and Hilary Ann Holland (*née* Turner); *S* father, 2011; *m* 1993, Jennifer Margaret Owens; two *d. Educ*: Qld, Australia. *Heir*: none. *Address*: 71 Magpie Lane, Cooroy, Qld 4563, Australia.

**STRATHERN, Prof. Andrew Jamieson**, PhD; Andrew Mellon Professor of Anthropology, University of Pittsburgh, since 1987; Emeritus Professor of Anthropology, University of London; Hon. Research Fellow, Institute of Papua New Guinea Studies, Port Moresby, since 1977 (Director, 1981–86); *b* 19 Jan. 1939; *s* of Robert Strathern and Mary Strathern (*née* Sharp); *m* 1963, Ann Marilyn Evans (marr. diss. 1986); two *s* one *d*; *m* 1997, Pamela J. Stewart. *Educ*: Colchester Royal Grammar Sch.; Trinity Coll., Cambridge (BA, PhD). Research Fellow, Trinity Coll., Cambridge, 1965–68; Research Fellow, then Fellow, Australian National Univ., 1969–72; Professor, later Vis. Professor, Dept of Anthropology and Sociology, Univ. of Papua New Guinea, 1973–77; Prof. of Anthropology and Hd of Dept of Anthropology, UCL, 1976–83. Hon. Mem., Phi Beta Kappa, 1993. Rivers Memorial Medal, RAI, 1976. 10th Independence Anniv. Medal (PNG), 1987. *Publications*: The Rope of Moka, 1971; One Father, One Blood, 1972; (with M. Strathern) Self-decoration in Mount Hagen, 1972; Melpa Amb Kenan, 1974; Myths and Legends from Mt Hagen, 1977; Beneath the Andaiya Tree, 1977; Ongka, 1979; (with Malcolm Kirk) Man as Art, 1981; Inequality in New Guinea Highlands Societies, 1982; Wiru Laa, 1983; A line of power, 1984; (ed jtly) Strauss, The Mi Culture of the Mount Hagen People, 1990; (with P. Birnbaum) Faces of Papua New Guinea, 1991; Landmarks: reflections on anthropology, 1993; Voices of Conflict, 1993; Ru, 1993; Body Thoughts, 1996; (ed jtly) Millennial Markers, 1997; (ed jtly) Bodies and Persons, 1998; (ed jtly) Identity Work, 2000; (jtly) Oceania: an introduction to the cultures and identities of Pacific Islanders, 2002, 2nd edn 2017; with P. J. Stewart: A Death to Pay For: individual voices, 1998; Curing and Healing, 1999; Collaborations and Conflicts: a leader through time, 1999; Arrow Talk, 2000; The Python's Back: pathways of comparison between Indonesia and Melanesia, 2000; Minorities and Memories: survivals and extinctions in Scotland and western Europe, 2001; Humors and Substances: ideas of the body in New Guinea, 2001; Gender, Song and Sensibility: folktales and folksongs in the Highlands New Guinea, 2002; Remaking the World: myth, mining and ritual change among the Duna of Papua New Guinea, 2002; Violence: theory and ethnography, 2002; (ed) Landscape, Memory and History, 2003; Witchcraft, Sorcery, Rumors and Gossip, 2004; Empowering the Past, Confronting the Future, 2004; (ed) Terror and Violence: imagination and the unimaginable, 2006; (ed) Asian Ritual Systems: syncretisms and ruptures, 2007; (ed) Exchange and Sacrifice, 2008; (ed) Religious and Ritual Change, 2009 (Chinese edn 2010); (ed) Ritual, 2010; Kinship in Action: self and group, 2011; Peace-making and the Imagination: Papua New Guinea perspectives, 2011; Ritual: key concepts in religion, 2014; Working in the Field: anthropological experiences across the world, 2014; (ed) Ashgate Research Companion to Anthropology, 2015; Breaking the Frames: anthropological conundrums, 2017; Story of the Kuk UNESCO World Heritage Prehistoric Site and The Melpa, Western Highlands Province, Papua New Guinea: pride in place, 2018; Diaspora, Disasters and the Cosmos: rituals and images, 2018; Language and Culture in Dialogue, 2019; articles in Man, Oceania, Ethnology, Jl Polyn Soc., Amer. Anthropology, Amer. Ethnology, Mankind, Bijdragen, Jl de la Soc. des Océanistes, Oral History, Bikmaus, Pacific Studies, Ethos, Jl of Ethnomusicology, Canberra Anthropology, Historische Anthropologie, Aust. Jl of Anthropology, Ethnohistory. *Address:* Department of Anthropology, University of Pittsburgh, Pittsburgh, PA 15260, USA. *T:* (office) (412) 6487519.

**STRATHERN, Dame (Ann) Marilyn,** DBE 2001; FBA 1987; Mistress of Girton College, Cambridge, 1998–2009; William Wyse Professor of Social Anthropology, University of Cambridge, 1993–2008; *b* 6 March 1941; *d* of Eric Charles Evans and Joyce Florence Evans; *m* 1963, Andrew Jamieson Strathern, *qv* (marr. diss. 1986); twin *s* one *d*. *Educ:* Bromley High Sch. (GPDST); Girton Coll., Cambridge (MA, PhD). Asst Curator, Mus. of Ethnology, Cambridge, 1966–68; Res. Fellow, ANU, 1970–72 and 1974–75; Bye-Fellow, Sen. Res. Fellow, then Official Fellow, Girton Coll., 1976–83; Fellow and Lectr, Trinity Coll., Cambridge, 1984–85 (Hon. Fellow, 1999); Prof. and Hd of Dept of Social Anthropology, Manchester Univ., 1985–93; Professorial Fellow, Girton Coll., Cambridge, 1993–98 (Life Fellow, 2009). Sen. Res. Fellow, ANU, 1983–84; Vis. Prof., Univ. of California, Berkeley, 1984. Mem., APS, 2018–. Hon. Foreign Mem., Amer. Acad. Arts and Scis, 1996; Hon. Life Pres., Assoc. of Social Anthropologists, 2008. Hon. FLSW 2018. Hon. DSc (Soc Sci): Edinburgh, 1993; Copenhagen, 1994; Hon. DLitt: Oxford, 2004; ANU, 2015; Hon. DSc: Helsinki, 2006; Panteion, Athens, 2006; Durham, 2007; St Andrews, 2013; Hon. PhD Papua New Guinea, 2009; Hon. DSocSc: QUB 2009; Yale, 2010; Universidad del País Vasco, 2011; KCL, 2011. Rivers Meml Medal, 1976, Huxley Meml Medal, 2004, RAI; Viking Fund Medal, Wenner-Gren Foundn for Anthropol Res., NY, 2003; Leverhulme Medal, British Acad., 2012; Internat. Balzan Prize for Social Anthropology, 2018. *Publications:* Self-Decoration in Mt Hagen (jtly), 1971; Women In Between, 1972; (co-ed) Nature, Culture and Gender, 1980; Kinship at the Core: an anthropology of Elmdon, Essex, 1981; (ed) Dealing with Inequality, 1987; The Gender of the Gift, 1988; Partial Connections, 1991; (ed) Big Men and Great Men in Melanesia, 1991; After Nature, 1992; Reproducing the Future, 1992; (jtly) Technologies of Procreation, 1993; (ed) Shifting Contexts, 1995; Property, Substance and Effect, 1999; (ed) Audit Cultures, 2000; (ed) Transactions and Creations, 2004; Kinship, Law and the Unexpected, 2005; Before and After Gender, 2016. *Address:* c/o Girton College, Cambridge CB3 0JG.

**STRATHMORE AND KINGHORNE,** 19th Earl of, *cr* 1677 (Scot.); Earl (UK) *cr* 1937; **Simon Patrick Bowes Lyon;** Lord Glamis, 1445; Earl of Kinghorne, Lord Lyon and Glamis, 1606; Viscount Lyon, Lord Glamis, Tannadyce, Sidlaw and Strathdichtie, 1677; Baron Bowes (UK), 1887; *b* 18 June 1986; *e s* of 18th Earl of Strathmore and Kinghorne and of Isobel Charlotte Bowes Lyon (*née* Weatherall); *S* father, 2016. *Heir: b* Hon. John Fergus Bowes Lyon, *b* 22 Aug. 1988. *Clubs:* Beefsteak, Pratt's.

**STRATHNAVER, Lord; Alistair Charles St Clair Sutherland;** Master of Sutherland; with Sutherland Estates, since 1978; Vice Lord-Lieutenant of Sutherland, 1993–2017; *b* 7 Jan. 1947; *e s* of Charles Noel Janson, and the Countess of Sutherland, *qv*; heir to mother's titles; *m* 1st, 1968, Eileen Elizabeth, *o d* of Richard Wheeler Baker, Jr, Princeton, NJ; two *d*; 2nd, 1980, Gillian, *er d* of Robert Murray, Gourock, Renfrewshire; one *s* one *d*. *Educ:* Eton; Christ Church, Oxford. BA. Metropolitan Police, 1969–74; with IBM UK Ltd, 1975–78. DL Sutherland, 1991. *Heir: s* Hon. Alexander Charles Robert Sutherland, *b* 1 Oct. 1981. *Address:* Sutherland Estates Office, Duke Street, Golspie, Sutherland KW10 6RP. *T:* (01408) 633268.

**STRATHSPEY,** 6th Baron *cr* 1884; **James Patrick Trevor Grant of Grant;** Bt (NS) 1625; Chief of Clan Grant; *b* 9 Sept. 1943; *s* of 5th Baron and his 1st wife, Alice, *oc* of late Francis Bowe; *S* father, 1992; *m* 1st, 1966, Linda (marr. diss. 1984), *d* of David Piggott; three *d*; 2nd, 1985, Margaret (marr. diss. 1993), *d* of Robert Drummond. *Heir:* half *b* Hon. Michael Patrick Francis Grant of Grant, *b* 22 April 1953.

**STRATTON, Allegra Elizabeth Jane;** National Editor, ITV News, since 2016; *b* Nottingham, 10 April 1980; *d* of Neil Stratton and Mary Addison; *m* 2011, James Forsyth; one *s* one *d*. *Educ:* Chiswick Community Sch.; Latymer Upper Sch.; Emmanuel Coll., Cambridge. Researcher, Foreign Desk, The Times, 2001; producer, This Week, BBC One, 2002–05; Political Producer, Newsnight, BBC, 2005–07; Political Corresp., The Guardian, 2007–12; Political Editor, Newsnight, BBC, 2012–15; presenter, Peston on Sunday, ITV, 2016–18. *Publications:* Muhajababes, 2006. *Recreations:* watching and playing tennis, bad surfing, hiking, memorising poetry, 20 minute meals, reading. *Address:* 8 St Paul's Place, N1 2QE. *T:* 07824 408473. *E:* allegra.stratton@itn.co.uk.

**STRATTON, Sir Michael (Rudolf),** Kt 2013; PhD; FRCPath, FMedSci; FRS 2008; Director, since 2010, and Head, Cancer Genome Project, since 2000, Wellcome Sanger Institute (formerly Sanger Centre, then Wellcome Trust Sanger Institute) (Deputy Director, 2006–10); Professor of Cancer Genetics, Institute of Cancer Research, since 1997; *b* 22 June 1957; *s* of Henry Stratton and Nita Stratton; *m* 1981, Dr Judith Breuer; one *s* one *d*. *Educ:* Brasenose Coll., Oxford (BA Physiol Scis); Guy's Hosp. Med. Sch., London (MB BS 1982); Inst. Cancer Res., London (PhD 1989). MRCPath 1991, FRCPath 2008. House and res. posts at Guy's Hosp., Beckenham Hosp., Inst. Psychiatry and Westminster Hosp., 1982–84; Registrar in Histopathol., RPMS, Hammersmith Hosp., 1984–86; MRC Trng Fellow, Inst. Cancer Res., 1986–89; Sen. Registrar, Dept Neuropathol., Inst. Psychiatry, 1989–91; Institute of Cancer Research: Team Leader, 1991–; Reader in Molecular Genetics of Cancer, 1996–97. Hon. Consultant, Royal Marsden Hosp., 1992–. FMedSci 1999. *Publications:* contrib. papers on genetic basis of cancer. *Address:* Wellcome Sanger Institute, Genome Campus, Hinxton, Cambridge CB10 1SA.

**STRAUSFELD, Prof. Nicholas James,** PhD; FRS 2002; Regents' Professor of Neurobiology, since 1987, MacArthur Fellow, since 1995, and Director, Center for Insect Science, since 2005, University of Arizona, Tucson (Guggenheim Fellow, 1994); *b* 22 Oct. 1942. *Educ:* University Coll. London (BSc 1965; PhD 1968). Scientist, Max Planck Inst. for Biol Cybernetics, Tübingen, Germany, 1970–75; Gp Leader, Neurobiol., EMBL, 1975–86. *Publications:* Atlas of an Insect Brain, 1976; (jtly) Neuroanatomical Techniques: insect nervous system, 1981; Functional Neuroanatomy, 1984; Arthropod Brains: evolution, functional elegance, and historical significance, 2012; contrib. learned jls. *Address:* Division of Neurobiology, University of Arizona, Arizona Research Laboratories, 611 Gould-Simpson Building, Tucson, AZ 85721, USA.

**STRAUSS, Nicholas Albert;** QC 1984; *b* 29 July 1942; *s* of late Walter Strauss and Ilse Strauss (*née* Leon); *m* 1972, Christine M. MacColl; two *d*. *Educ:* Highgate School; Jesus College, Cambridge (BA 1964; LLB 1965). Called to the Bar, Middle Temple, 1965 (Harmsworth Scholar); a Dep. High Court Judge, 1994–2015; a Recorder, 2000–15. *Address:* 1 Essex Court, Temple, EC4Y 9AR. *T:* (020) 7583 2000.

**STRAUSS, Toby;** Group Director, Insurance, Lloyds Banking Group, and Chief Executive, Scottish Widows, 2011–15; *b* London, 4 Oct. 1959; *m* 1995, Cressida; one *s* one *d*. *Educ:* St Paul's Sch., London; Loughborough Univ. (BTech Mech. Engrg). Account Manager, IBM, 1984–88; Founder, Psiax, 1988–92; Associate Partner, McKinsey & Co., 1993–99; Man. Dir, Charcol, 1999–2003; Chief Exec., John Scott & Partners, 2003–05; Chm., OrderWork, 2005–08; Chief Exec., Chief Operating Officer and Man. Dir, Aviva Life UK, 2008–11. Ind. non-exec. Dir, Legal & General Gp plc, 2017–. Trustee, Macmillan Cancer Support, 2013–. *Recreations:* sailing, cycling.

**STRAUSS-KAHN, Dominique Gaston André;** Managing Director, International Monetary Fund, 2007–11; *b* 25 April 1949; *s* of Gilbert Strauss-Kahn and Jacqueline (*née* Fellus); *m* 1991, Anne Sinclair (marr. diss. 2013); four *c* from previous marriages. *Educ:* Lycée de Monaco; Lycée Carnot à Paris; Univ. de Paris X-Nanterre (DEconSc). Lectr, Univ. de Nantes II, 1977–80; Scientific Advr, l'Institut national de la statistique et des études économiques, 1978–80; Dir, Cerepi, CNRS, 1980–; Prof., Univ. de Paris X-Nanterre, 1981; Hd, Dept of Planning, Gen. Commn of the Nat. Plan, 1982–84, Asst Comr, 1984–86. Mem., Exec. Cttee, Socialist Party, 1983– (Nat. Sec., 1984–89). National Assembly, France: Deputy (Soc.) from Haute-Savoie, 1986–88, from Val-d'Oise, 1988–91, 2001–07; Pres., Commn of Finance, 1988–91; Minister: in Dept of Finance, 1991–92; for Industry and Foreign Trade, 1992–93; of the Econ. and of Finance, 1997–99. Mayor, 1995–97, Dep. Mayor, 1997–2001, Sarcelles. *Publications:* Economie de la famille et Accumulation patrimoniale, 1977; (jtly) La Richesse des Français, 1977; (jtly) L'Epargne et la Retraite, 1982.

**STRAW, Alice Elizabeth, (Mrs J. W. Straw);** *see* Perkins, A. E.

**STRAW, Edward, (Ed);** writer and campaigner on systems of government; Chairman of Trustees, Demos, 2007–08; *b* Buckhurst Hill, Essex, 16 Jan. 1949; *s* of Walter Arthur Whitaker Straw and Joan Sylvia Straw; *m* 2008, Lindsey Colbourne; three *s* two *d* from previous marriages. *Educ:* Staples Rd Prim. Sch., Loughton; Brentwood Sch.; Univ. of Manchester (BSc Engrg 1971); Manchester Business Sch. (MBA 1973). Coopers & Lybrand, subseq. PricewaterhouseCoopers: Local Govt Consultant, 1982–88; Partner, Govt Services, and Dir of Quality, 1988–94; Hd, Entertainment and Media Consulting, EMEA, 1994–2002; Partner, Central Govt, 2002–08; Bd Dir, 1996–98; Global Bd Dir, 1997–2002. Chm., 1994–2000, Vice-Pres., 2000–15, Relate. Founder Trustee, Family and Parenting Inst., 1999–2007; Trustee, Stroud Valley Arts, 2003–. Vis. Fellow, Applied Systems Thinking in Practice, Open Univ., 2015–. Orgnl Architect, New Labour, 1992–95. FCMI. *Publications:* Relative Values, 1998; The Dead Generalist, 2004; Stand and Deliver: a design for successful government, 2014; numerous articles on government, politics, electoral system, schools, health service, relationships, public engagement, and media industries. *Recreations:* thinking, camping, entertaining with words, electronic music composition. *Address:* 17 Blue Lion Place, SE1 4PU. *W:* www.edstraw.com.

**STRAW, Rt Hon. John Whitaker, (Rt Hon. Jack);** PC 1997; *b* 3 Aug. 1946; *s* of Walter Arthur Whitaker Straw and Joan Sylvia Straw; *m* 1st, 1968, Anthea Lilian Weston (marr. diss. 1978); (one *d* decd); 2nd, 1978, Alice Elizabeth Perkins, *qv*; one *s* one *d*. *Educ:* Brentwood Sch., Essex; Univ. of Leeds (LLB 1967); Inns of Court Sch. of Law. Called to Bar, Inner Temple, 1972, Bencher, 1997. Political Advr to Sec. of State for Social Services, 1974–76; Special Advr to Sec. of State for Environment, 1976–77; on staff of Granada TV (World in Action), 1977–79. Pres., Leeds Univ. Union, 1967–68; Pres., Nat. Union of Students, 1969–71; Mem., Islington Borough Council, 1971–78; Dep. Leader, Inner London Educn Authority, 1973–74; Chm., Jt Adv. Cttee on Polytechnic of N London, 1973–75. Contested (Lab) Tonbridge and Malling, Feb. 1974. MP (Lab) Blackburn, 1979–2015. Opposition spokesman on the Treasury, 1980–83, on the environment, 1983–87; Principal Opposition Spokesman on educn, 1987–92, on the envmt (local govt), 1992–94, on home affairs, 1994–97; Sec. of State for the Home Office, 1997–2001; Sec. of State for Foreign and Commonwealth Affairs, 2001–06; Lord Privy Seal and Leader of H of C, 2006–07; Lord Chancellor and Sec. of State for Justice, 2007–10; Shadow Lord Chancellor and Sec. of State for Justice, 2010. Mem., Shadow Cabinet, 1987–97 and 2010. Mem., NEC, Labour Pty, 1994–95. Mem., Commn on Freedom of Information, 2015–16. Vis. Fellow, Nuffield Coll., Oxford, 1990–98; Vis. Prof., UCL, 2011–; Sen. Associate Fellow, RUSI, 2018–. Member Council: Inst. for Fiscal Studies, 1983–96; Lancaster Univ., 1988–91; Mem., Adv. Council, Oxford Centre for Islamic Studies, 2007–; Governor: Blackburn Coll., 1990–2016; Pimlico Sch., 1994–2000 (Chm., 1995–98). Co-Chm., British-Turkish Forum., 2011–; Chm., Appts Cttee, Dean of Blackburn Cathedral, 2016–17; Mem., Archbishops' Working Gp on Cathedrals, 2017–; Trustee: Global Strategy Forum, 2011–; Atlantic Partnership, 2015–; Tauheedul Educn Trust, 2017–. Chm., Blackburn Youth Zone, 2015–. Hon. Vice-Pres., Blackburn Rovers FC, 1998–. Fellow, Royal Statistical Soc., 1995. Hon. LLD: Leeds, 1999; Brunel, 2007. Order of the Republic Medal (Turkey), 2012. *Publications:* Granada Guildhall Lecture, 1969; University of Leeds Convocation Lecture, 1978; Policy and Ideology, 1993; Last Man Standing, 2012; Hamlyn Lectures, 2013; The English Job: understanding Iran and why it distrusts Britain, 2019; contrib. pamphlets, articles. *Recreations:* walking, cycling, cooking puddings, music. *Address:* 46 Hanover Gardens, SE11 5TN.
*See also* E. Straw.

**STREAMS, Peter John,** CMG 1986; HM Diplomatic Service, retired; Ambassador to Sudan, 1991–94; *b* 8 March 1935; *s* of Horace Stanley Streams and Isabel Esther (*née* Ellaway); *m* 1956, Margareta Decker (*d* 2012); two *s* one *d*. *Educ:* Wallington County Grammar Sch. BoT, 1953; Bombay, 1960, Calcutta, 1962, Oslo, 1966; FCO, 1970; Mexico, 1973; FCO, 1977, Counsellor, 1979; Consul-Gen., Karachi, 1982; Counsellor, Stockholm, 1985; Ambassador to Honduras and concurrently to El Salvador, 1989. Head, EU Monitoring Mission to former Yugoslavia, 1998. *Address:* c/o Foreign and Commonwealth Office, SW1A 2AH.

**STREATFEILD-JAMES, David Stewart;** QC 2001; a Recorder, since 2010; *b* 22 Oct. 1963; *e s* of Capt. John Jocelyn Streatfeild-James, *qv*; *m* 1991, Alison; two *s* two *d*. *Educ:* Charterhouse; University Coll., Oxford. Called to the Bar, Inner Temple, 1986. *Recreations:* family, sport, gardening, cookery. *Address:* The Manor, Queen Charlton Lane, Queen Charlton, Bristol BS31 2SH. *T:* (0117) 986 2025.

**STREATFEILD-JAMES, Captain John Jocelyn;** RN retired; *b* 14 April 1929; *s* of late Comdr Rev. Eric Cardew Streatfeild-James, OBE, and Elizabeth Ann (*née* Kirby); *m* 1962, Sally Madeline (*née* Stewart); three *s* (one *d* decd). *Educ:* RNC, Dartmouth. Specialist in Undersea Warfare. Naval Cadet, 1943–47; Midshipman, 1947–49; Sub-Lt, 1949–51; Lieutenant: Minesweeping, Diving and Anti-Bandit Ops, Far East Stn, 1951; Officer and Rating Trng, Home Stn, 1952–53; specialised in Undersea Warfare, 1954–55; Ship and Staff Duties, Far East Stn, 1955–57; Exchange Service, RAN, 1957–59; Lieutenant-

Commander: instructed Officers specialising in Undersea Warfare, 1960–61; Sea Duty, Staff of Flag Officer Flotillas, Home Stn, 1962–63; Sen. Instr, Jt Anti-Submarine Sch., HMS Sea Eagle, 1964–65; Commander: Staff of C-in-C Western Fleet and C-in-C Eastern Atlantic Area, 1965–67; Jt Services Staff Coll., 1968; Staff of Comdr Allied Naval Forces, Southern Europe, Malta, 1968–71; HMS Dryad, 1971–73; Captain: Sen. Officers' War Course, RNC, Greenwich, 1974; Dir, OPCON Proj., 1974–77; HMS Howard (i/c), Head of British Defence Liaison Staff, Ottawa, and Defence Advr to British High Comr in Canada, 1978–80 (as Cdre); HMS Excellent (i/c), 1981–82; ADC to the Queen, 1982–83. *Recreations:* sailing, carpentry, painting. *Address:* South Lodge, Tower Road, Hindhead, Surrey GU26 6SP. *T:* (01428) 606064.
*See also* D. S. Streatfeild-James.

**STREEP, Mary Louise, (Meryl);** American actress; *b* 22 June 1949; *d* of Harry and Mary Streep; *m* 1978, Donald Gummer; one *s* three *d*. *Educ:* Vassar Coll. (BA 1971); Yale (MA 1975). *Stage appearances include:* New York Shakespeare Fest., 1976; Alice in Concert, NY Public Theater, 1981; The Seagull, NY, 2001; Mother Courage and Her Children, NY, 2006; *television appearances include:* The Deadliest Season (film), 1977; Holocaust, 1978; Angels in America (film), 2004; Big Little Lies, 2019; *films include:* The Deer Hunter, 1978; Manhattan, The Seduction of Joe Tynan, Kramer versus Kramer, 1979 (Academy Award, 1980); The French Lieutenant's Woman (BAFTA Award), 1981; Sophie's Choice (Academy Award), Still of the Night, 1982; Silkwood, 1983; Falling in Love, 1984; Plenty, Out of Africa, 1985; Heartburn, 1986; Ironweed, 1987; A Cry in the Dark, 1989; She-Devil, 1990; Postcards from the Edge, Defending your Life, 1991; Death Becomes Her, 1992; The House of the Spirits, 1994; The River Wild, The Bridges of Madison County, 1995; Before and After, 1996; Marvin's Room, 1997; Dancing at Lughnasa, 1998; One True Thing, 1999; Music of the Heart, 2000; The Hours, Adaptation, 2003; Stuck on You, The Manchurian Candidate, Lemony Snicket's A Series of Unfortunate Events, 2004; Prime, The Devil Wears Prada, 2006; A Prairie Home Companion, Evening, Rendition, Lions for Lambs, 2007; Mamma Mia!, 2008; Doubt, Julie and Julia, 2009; It's Complicated, 2010; The Iron Lady (Best Actress, BAFTA and Academy Awards), 2012; Hope Springs, 2012; August: Osage County, The Giver, The Homesman, 2014; Into The Woods, Ricki and the Flash, Suffragette, 2015; Florence Foster Jenkins, 2016; The Post, Mamma Mia! Here We Go Again, Mary Poppins Returns, 2018; Little Women, 2019. Hon. DFA: Dartmouth Coll., 1981; Yale, 1983. Cecil B. DeMille Award, Golden Globe Awards, 2017. *Address:* c/o Creative Artists Agency, 2000 Avenue of the Stars, Los Angeles, CA 90067, USA.

**STREET, Hon. Anthony Austin;** *b* 8 Feb. 1926; *s* of late Brig. the Hon. G. A. Street, MC, MHR; *m* 1951, Valerie Erica, *d* of J. A. Rickard; three *s*. *Educ:* Melbourne C of E Grammar Sch. RAN, 1945–46. MP (L) Corangamite, Vic, 1966–84 (resigned); Mem., various Govt Mems Cttees, 1967–71; Mem., Fed. Exec. Council, 1971–; Asst Minister for Labour and Nat. Service, 1971–72; Mem., Opposition Exec., 1973–75 (Special Asst to Leader of Opposition and Shadow Minister for Labour and Immigration, March–Nov. 1975); Minister for Labour and Immigration, Caretaker Ministry after dissolution of Parliament, Nov. 1975; Minister for Employment and Industrial Relations and Minister Assisting Prime Minister in Public Service Matters, 1975–78; Minister for: Industrial Relations, 1978–80; Foreign Affairs, 1980–83. Chm., Fed. Rural Cttee, Liberal Party, 1970–74. *Recreations:* cricket, golf, tennis, flying. *Address:* 153 The Terrace, Ocean Grove, Vic 3226, Australia. *Clubs:* MCC; Melbourne; Barwon Heads Golf.

**STREET, Prof. Peter Ronald,** PhD; Development Director, Genus International Consultancy, 1999; Director, Produce Studies Ltd, 1992; *b* 4 May 1944; *s* of Leslie Arthur John and Winifred Marjorie Street; *m* 1969, Christine Hill; two *d*. *Educ:* Univ. of Reading (BScAgr, PhD Management and Econs). Lectr in Management and Econs, Faculty of Agricl Sci., Univ. of Nottingham, 1971–74; Tropical Products Institute: Principal Res. Officer, 1974–82; Sen. Principal Res. Officer and Head, Mkting and Industrial Econs Dept, 1982–85; Mem., Directorate Bd, 1982–85; Dir and Chief Economist, Produce Studies Ltd, 1985–89; Prof. of Agricl Systems and Head, Dept of Agriculture, Univ. of Reading, 1989–92. Visiting Professor: Imperial Coll., London, 1998–; RAU (formerly RAC), 2000–. Chm., Selskya Zhign Consultants, Moscow, 1994–; Mem. Bd, British Consultants Bureau, 1999; Man. Dir, GFA-RACE Partners Ltd, 2000; Vice Pres., Online Global Commodities Exchange, 2000–. Numerous internat. consultancy assignments. MCMI (MBIM 1972). *Publications:* (ed with J. G. W. Jones) Systems Theory Applied to Agriculture and the Food Chain, 1990. *Recreations:* gardening, fly fishing. *Address:* Brooklyn, Crow, Ringwood, Hants BH24 3EA. *T:* (01425) 475222.

**STREET, Sarah Elizabeth;** *see* Brown, Sarah Elizabeth.

**STREET, Dame Susan (Ruth),** DCB 2005; strategic advisor, Deloitte LLP, 2006–13; Chair, Ballet Rambert, since 2019; *b* 11 Aug. 1949; *d* of late Dr Stefan Galeski and of Anna Galeski; *m* 1972, Richard Street; one *s* one *d*. *Educ:* St Andrews Univ. (MA Philosophy). Home Office, 1974–2001: Course Dir, Top Mgt Prog., Cabinet Office, 1989–91 (on secondment); Supervising Consultant, Price Waterhouse, 1991–94; Director: Central Drugs Co-ordination Unit, Cabinet Office, 1994–96 (on secondment); Fire and Emergency Planning, 1996–99; Sentencing and Correctional Policy, 1999–2000; Criminal Policy, 2000–01; Permanent Sec., DCMS, 2001–06. Non-executive Director: MoJ, 2009–15; Adlens plc, 2014–. Executive Coach: Praesta, 2014–16; Korn Ferry Hay Gp, 2016–. Associate Mem., BUPA, 2007–17; Associate Fellow, Inst. for Govt, 2010–17. Trustee, Royal Opera House, 2007–15; Dir and Trustee, Thistle Trust, 2017–; Gov., Royal Ballet, 2007–17. FRSA 1992; CCMI 2007. Mem., Firefighters' Co., 2014–17. *Recreations:* family, ballet, theatre. *Address:* 85 South Lodge, Circus Road, NW8 9EU.

**STREET-PORTER, Janet,** CBE 2016; journalist and broadcaster, since 1967; columnist: The Independent and i, since 1999 (Editor, 1999–2001, Editor-at-large, 2001, The Independent on Sunday); MailOnline; *b* 27 Dec. 1946; *m* 1st, 1967, Tim Street-Porter (marr. diss. 1975); 2nd, 1976, A. M. M. Elliott, *qv* (marr. diss. 1978); 3rd, 1978, Frank Cvitanovich (marr. diss. 1988; he *d* 1995). *Educ:* Lady Margaret Grammar Sch., Fulham; Architectural Assoc. TV presenter, 1975–; TV producer, 1981–; Exec., BBC TV, 1988–94; Man. Dir, Live TV, 1994–95. Pres., Ramblers Assoc., 1994–97. Trustee, Sci. Mus. Gp (formerly NMSI), 2008–14. FRTS 1994. Hon. FRIBA 2001. Award for originality, BAFTA, 1988; Prix Italia, 1993. *Publications:* The British Teapot, 1977; Scandal, 1981; Coast to Coast, 1998; As the Crow Flies, 1999; Baggage: my childhood, 2004; Fallout, 2006; Life's Too F***ing Short, 2008; Don't Let the B*****ds Get You Down, 2009. *Recreations:* walking, talking, modern art. *T:* (c/o Rosie Money-Coutts) 07979 157873. *E:* rosie@paprlondon.com.

**STREETER, Sir Gary (Nicholas),** Kt 2019; MP (C) South West Devon, since 1997 (Plymouth Sutton, 1992–97); *b* 2 Oct. 1955; *s* of Kenneth Victor Streeter and Shirley Nellie (*née* Keable); *m* 1978, Janet Stevens; one *s* one *d*. *Educ:* Tiverton Grammar Sch.; King's Coll., London (LLB 1st cl. Hons). Articled at Coward Chance, London, 1978–80; admitted solicitor, 1980; joined Foot & Bowden, solicitors, Plymouth, 1980, Partner, 1984–99. Plymouth City Council: Mem., 1986–92; Chm., Housing Cttee, 1989–91. PPS to Solicitor-General, 1993–95, and to Attorney-General, 1994–95; an Asst Govt Whip, 1995–96; Parly Sec., Lord Chancellor's Dept, 1996–97; Opposition front bench spokesman on European affairs, 1997–98; Shadow Sec. of State for Internat. Develt, 1998–2001; Shadow Minister of State for Foreign Affairs, 2003–04. Member: Panel of Chairs (formerly Chairmen's Panel), 2008–; Speaker's Cttee overseeing Electoral Commn, 2008–15; Ecclesiastical Cttee, 2010–15; Cttee on Standards, 2017–; Cttee on Privileges, 2017–; Chairman: Christians in Parliament, 2010–; Westminster Foundn for Democracy, 2010–14. A Vice Chm., Cons. Party, 2001–02; Chm., Cons. Party Internat. Office, 2005–08. *Publications:* (ed) There is Such a Thing as Society, 2002. *Recreation:* lover of cricket and Rugby. *Address:* House of Commons, SW1A 0AA. *T:* (020) 7219 4070.

**STREETING, Wesley Paul William;** MP (Lab) Ilford North, since 2015; *b* London, 21 Jan. 1983. *Educ:* Westminster City Sch.; Selwyn Coll., Cambridge (BA Hist.). Pres., Cambridge Univ. Students' Union, 2004–05; Vice Pres. (Educn), 2006–10, Pres., 2008–10, NUS; Chief Exec., Helena Kennedy Foundn, 2010–12; Hd of Educn, Stonewall, 2012–13; Associate, Magic Breakfast, 2015. Mem. (Lab) Redbridge LBC, 2010–18 (Dep. Leader, 2014–15). Mem., Treasury Cttee, H of C, 2015–. *Recreations:* theatre, cinema, walking, travelling. *Address:* House of Commons, SW1A 0AA. *T:* (020) 7219 6132. *E:* wes.streeting.mp@parliament.uk.

**STREISAND, Barbra Joan;** singer, actress, director, producer, writer, composer, philanthropist; *b* Brooklyn, NY, 24 April 1942; *d* of Emanuel and Diana Streisand; *m* 1963, Elliott Gould (marr. diss. 1971); one *s*; *m* 1998, James Brolin. *Educ:* Erasmus Hall High Sch. Nightclub début, Bon Soir, Greenwich Village, 1961; NY theatre début, Another Evening with Harry Stoones, 1961; musical comedy, I Can Get It For You Wholesale, 1962 (NY Critics' Best Supporting Actress Award, 1962); musical, Funny Girl, NY, 1964, London, 1966 (Best Foreign Actress, Variety Poll Award, 1966). Special Tony Award, 1970. *Films:* Funny Girl, 1968 (Golden Globe Award, Acad. Award, 1968); Hello Dolly, 1969; On a Clear Day You Can See Forever, 1970; The Owl and the Pussycat, 1971; What's Up Doc?, 1972; Up the Sandbox, 1972; The Way We Were, 1973; For Pete's Sake, 1974; Funny Lady, 1975; A Star is Born (also prod), 1976; The Main Event (also prod), 1979; All Night Long, 1981; Yentl (also co-wrote, dir. and prod), 1984 (Golden Globe Award for Best Picture and Best Dir); Nuts (also prod), 1987; The Prince of Tides (also dir. and prod), 1990; The Mirror Has Two Faces (also dir. and co-prod), 1997; Meet the Fockers, 2005; Little Fockers, 2010. *Television specials:* My Name is Barbra, 1965 (5 Emmy Awards, Peabody Award); Color Me Barbra, 1966; Belle of 14th Street, 1967; A Happening in Central Park, 1968; Musical Instrument, 1973; One Voice, 1986; Barbra Streisand, the Concert (also prod and co-dir.), 1994 (Peabody Award, 3 Cable Ace Awards, 5 Emmy Awards); Serving in Silence: the Margarethe Cammermeyer story (exec. prod.), 1995. Began recording career, 1962; Grammy Awards for best female pop vocalist, 1963, 1964, 1965, 1977, 1986, for best songwriter (with Paul Williams), 1977; (jtly) Acad. Award for composing best song (Evergreen), 1976; awarded: 52 Gold Albums (exceeded only by Elvis Presley); 31 Platinum Albums; 13 Multi-Platinum Albums (most for any female artist). *Albums include:* People, 1965; My Name is Barbra, 1965; The Way We Were, 1974; Guilty, 1980; The Broadway Album, 1986; Just for the Record (retrospective album), 1991; Back to Broadway, 1993; Barbra Streisand, the Concert (double album and video), 1994; The Mirror Has Two Faces (soundtrack), 1996; Higher Ground, 1997; A Love Like Ours, 1999; Christmas Memories, 2001; Guilty Pleasures, 2005; Love Is The Answer, 2009; What Matters Most, 2011; Release Me, 2012; Partners, 2014; Encore, 2016; Walls, 2018. Presidential Medal of Freedom (USA), 2015. *Address:* Barwood Films, 330 West 58th Street, Suite 301, New York, NY 10019, USA.

**STRETTON, James,** MBE 2017; Chairman, Trustees, Lloyd's Pension Scheme, 2010–14; *b* 16 Dec. 1943; *s* of Donald and Muriel Stretton; *m* 1968, Isobel Robertson; two *d*. *Educ:* Laxton Grammar Sch., Oundle; Worcester Coll., Oxford (BA Maths). FFA 1970–2008. Standard Life Assurance Company, 1965–2001: Asst Pensions Manager, 1974–77; Asst Investment Manager, 1977–84; General Manager (Ops), 1984–88; Dep. Man. Dir, 1988–94; Chief Exec., UK Ops, 1994–2001. Chm., Wise Gp, 2002–09. Dir, Bank of England, 1998–2003; Chm., Bank of England Pension Fund Trustee Co., 2001–05; Member: Franchise Bd, Lloyd's of London, 2003–09; Disciplinary Bd of Actuarial profession, 2004–06. Member: Scottish New Deal Adv. Task Force, 1997–99; Scottish Business Forum, 1998–99. Pres., YouthLink Scotland, 1994–2000. Director: PIA, 1992–94; Scottish Community Educn Council, 1996–99. Chm., Foresight Ageing Population Panel, 1999–2000. Dir, Edinburgh Internat. Fest. Ltd, 1997–2008; Chm., Lammermuir Fest., 2010–17. Mem. Court, 1996–2002, Rector's Assessor, 2003–06, Univ. of Edinburgh. *Recreations:* music, reading, gardening.

**STRETTON, His Honour Peter John;** a Circuit Judge, 1986–2002; *b* 14 June 1938; *s* of Frank and Ella Stretton; *m* 1973, Eleanor Anne Wait; three *s* one *d*. *Educ:* Bedford Modern Sch. Called to the Bar, Middle Temple, 1962; Head of Chambers, 1985. A Recorder, 1982–86. *Recreations:* squash, gardening, golf.

**STREVENS, Bonnie Jean Holford;** *see* Blackburn, B. J.

**STRICK, Robert Charles Gordon;** Clerk to the Drapers' Company, 1980–93 (Liveryman, Court of Assistants, 1994); *b* 23 March 1931; *m* 1st, 1960, Jennifer Mary Hathway (*d* 2013); one *s* one *d*; 2nd, 2015, Talei Ann Irwin (*née* Pocock). *Educ:* Royal Grammar Sch., Guildford; Sidney Sussex Coll., Cambridge (MA). Served RA, 1949–51; TA, 1951–55. Spicers Ltd, 1954–55; joined HMOCS, 1955; Dist Officer, Fiji, 1955–59; Sec., Burns Commn into Natural Resources and Population Trends, 1959–60; Asst Sec., Suva, 1960–61; Sec. to Govt, Tonga, 1961–63; Develt Officer and Divl Comr, 1963–67, Sec. for Natural Resources, 1967–71, Fiji; retired 1971; Under Sec., ICA, 1971–72; Asst Sec.-Gen., RICS, 1972–80; Clerk, Chartered Surveyors' Co., 1977–80. Hon. Member: CGLI, 1991; Shrewsbury Co. of Drapers, 1992. Hon. Old Student, Aberystwyth, 1993. Hon. Fellow, Queen Mary, London Univ. (formerly QMW), 1993. Hon. DLitt Coll. of William and Mary, Virginia, USA, 1993. Grand Cross, Order of Crown (Tonga), 2010. *Recreations:* the countryside, walking, golf, gardening. *Address:* Lane End, Sheep Lane, Midhurst GU29 9NT. *T:* (01730) 813151.

**STRICKLAND, Benjamin Vincent Michael,** FCA; Group Managing Director (Group Strategy, Finances and Operations), and Director, Schroders PLC, 1983–91; *b* 20 Sept. 1939; *s* of Maj.-Gen. Eugene Vincent Michael Strickland, CMG, DSO, OBE, MM, and of Barbara Mary Farquharson Meares Lamb, *d* of Major Benjamin Lamb, RFA; *m* 1965, Tessa Mary Edwina, *d* of Rear-Adm. John Grant, CB, DSO; one *s* one *d*. *Educ:* Mayfield Coll.; University Coll., Oxford, 1960–63 (MA PPE); Harvard Business Sch. (AMPDip 1978). FCA 1967. Lieutenant: 17/21 Lancers, BAOR, 1959–60; Inns of Court and City Yeomanry, 1963–67. Joined Price Waterhouse & Co., 1963, Manager, 1967–68; joined J. Henry Schroder Wagg & Co. in Corp. Finance, 1968: Director: Schroder Wagg, 1974–91; Schroders Internat., 1975–85; Chm., G. D. Peters Engineering, 1972–74; Dir, Property Hldgs Internat. (USA), 1974–75; Chm. and Chief Exec., Schroders Australia, 1978–82. Adviser: *inter alia*, on strategy to City law firm, to media gp, on mission and finances to Westminster Cathedral (Chm., Planning and Finance Cttee, 1991–96); mentor to chief execs, 2005–12. Mem. steering gp, Vision for London, 1991–2001. Chm., Chester Street Insce Assoc. (formerly Iron Trades Insce Gp), 1996–. Voluntary reading help and leader of hist. club and book club in Falconbrook Primary Sch., 2004–15, Westbridge Primary Sch., 2015–17; Kenmont Primary Sch., 2017–. Mem. Council, St George's Med. Sch., 1984–87.

FRSA. *Publications:* Bow Group pamphlet on Resources of the Sea (with Laurance Reed), 1965. *Recreations:* travel, reading, family, military and general history, theatre, film. *Address:* 23 Juer Street, SW11 4RE. *T:* (020) 7585 2970. *Clubs:* Boodle's, Hurlingham.

**STRICKLAND-CONSTABLE, Sir Frederic,** 12th Bt *cr* 1641, of Boynton, Yorkshire; *b* 21 Oct. 1944; *er s* of Sir Robert Frederick Strickland-Constable, 11th Bt and Lettice, *yr d* of Major Frederick Strickland; *S* father, 1994; *m* 1981, Pauline Margaret Harding (*d* 2009), one *s* one *d*. *Educ:* Westminster; Corpus Christi Coll., Cambridge (BA); London Business Sch. (MSc). *Heir: s* Charles Strickland-Constable, *b* 10 Oct. 1985. *Address:* c/o Strickland Estate, Pear Tree Farm, Harton, York YO60 7NP.

**STRIDE, Rt Hon. Melvyn (John),** PC 2017; MP (C) Central Devon, since 2010; *b* 30 Sept. 1961; *m* 2005, Michelle King Hughes; three *d*. *Educ:* Portsmouth Grammar Sch.; St Edmund Hall, Oxford (BA PPE 1984). President: Oxford Univ. Cons. Assoc., 1981; Oxford Union, 1984. Founder and Owner, Venture Mktg Gp, 1987–2007. An Asst Govt Whip, 2014–15; a Lord Comr of HM Treasury (Govt Whip) 2015–16; Comptroller of HM Household (Govt Whip), 2016–17; Financial Sec. to HM Treasury and Paymaster Gen., 2017–19; Leader of H of C and Lord Pres. of the Council, 2019. *Address:* House of Commons, SW1A 0AA.

**STRIKE, Prof. Peter,** PhD; FRSB; Professor of Genetics, and Vice Chancellor and Chief Executive, University of Cumbria, 2011–16; *b* Barrow in Furness, 26 Nov. 1948; *s* of Fred and Kathleen Rose Strike; *m* 1st, 1970, Christine M. Pratt (marr. diss. 2001); one *s* one *d*; 2nd, 2004, Jill Hughes (*d* 2004); 3rd, 2011, Victoria Geraldine Bruce (*see* Dame V. G. Bruce); one step *s* three step *d*. *Educ:* Barrow in Furness Grammar Sch. for Boys; Univ. of Sussex (BSc Hons Biochem. 1970); Univ. of Newcastle upon Tyne (PhD Biochem. 1974). University of Liverpool: Lectr, 1974–84; Sen. Lectr, 1984–88; Reader, 1988–93; Prof. of Genetics and Microbiol., 1993–2002; Dir of Teaching (Life Scis), 1999–2002; Prof. of Genetics and Vice Principal, Res. and Knowledge Transfer, Napier Univ., Edinburgh, 2002–07; Prof. of Genetics and Dep. Vice Chancellor, Res. and Innovation, Northumbria Univ., 2007–09; Prof. of Genetics and Dep. Vice Chancellor (Res., Knowledge Transfer and Business Engagement), Univ. of Sunderland, 2009–11. Vis. Res. Fellow, Yale Univ., 1983. Sen. Trng Officer, RNR (Liverpool Univs RN Unit), 1984–2002 (Lt Comdr, RNR). FRSB 2015; FRSA 2015. *Publications:* articles on molecular biol. and genetics. *Recreations:* sailing, hill-walking. *Address:* 15 Cade Hill Road, Stocksfield, Northumberland NE43 7PB. *T:* (01661) 842325, 07747 760915.

**STRIKER, Prof. Gisela,** DPhil; Walter C. Klein Professor of Philosophy and of the Classics, Harvard University, 2002–11, now Emerita (Professor of Classical Philosophy, 2000–02); *b* 26 Nov. 1943. *Educ:* Univ. of Göttingen (DPhil 1969). Asst Prof., 1970–83, Prof., 1983–86, Univ. of Göttingen; Prof., Dept of Philosophy, Columbia Univ., NY, 1986–89; Prof. of Classical Philosophy, 1989–90, George Martin Lane Prof. of Philosophy and Classics, 1990–97, Harvard Univ.; Laurence Prof. of Ancient Philosophy, Univ. of Cambridge, and Fellow, Trinity Coll., Cambridge, 1997–2000. *Publications:* Essays on Hellenistic Epistemology and Ethics, 1996; (trans. and commentary) Aristotle, Prior Analytics book I, 2009; articles in learned jls. *Address:* Langenfelder Strasse 71, 22769 Hamburg, Germany.

**STRINGER, Prof. Christopher Brian,** PhD, DSc; FRS 2004; Research Leader in Human Origins, Natural History Museum, London, since 2006 (Head, Human Origins Programme, 1990–93 and 1999–2006); *b* 31 Dec. 1947; *s* of late George Albert Stringer and Evelyn Beatrice Stringer, and foster *s* of late Harry Kennett and Lilian Kennett; *m* 1977, Rosemary Susan Margaret (marr. diss. 2004); two *s* one *d*. *Educ:* UCL (BSc Hons (Anthropol.) 1969); Univ. of Bristol (PhD 1974; DSc 1990). Natural History Museum, London, 1973–: Sen. Res. Fellow, 1973–77; SSO, 1977–87; PSO, 1987–94; Hd, Anthropology, 1989–90; Individual Merit Promotion Band 2, 1994. Vis. Prof., Royal Holloway, London, 1998–; Res. Associate, Centre for Ecology and Evolution, UCL, 1999–; Dir, Ancient Human Occupation of Britain project, 2001–. Vis. Lectr, Dept of Anthropol., Harvard Univ., 1979. Lectures: Lyell, BAAS, 1988; Radcliffe, Green Coll., Oxford, 1996; Dalrymple, Univ. of Glasgow, 2001; Mulvaney, ANU, 2001; Darwin, Centre for Ecology and Evolution, London, 2003; Annual Science, Natural History Mus., London, 2011; Galton, Galton Inst., 2011; Millennium Distinguished Lectr, Amer. Anthropol Assoc., 2000. FAAAS 2012. Hon. FSA 2010. Hon. Dr of Laws Bristol, 2000; Hon. DSc Kent, 2009. Osman Hill Medal, Primate Soc. of GB, 1998; Henry Stopes Medal, Geologists' Assoc., 2000; Rivers Meml Medal, RAI, 2004; Frink Medal, Zool Soc. of London, 2009; Coke Medal, Geol Soc., 2011; James Croll Medal, Quaternary Res. Assoc., 2012. *Publications:* (ed) Aspects of Human Evolution, 1981; (with A. Gray) Our Fossil Relatives, 1983; (ed with P. Mellars) The Human Revolution: behavioural and biological perspectives in the origins of modern humans, 1989; (with P. Andrews) Human Evolution: an illustrated guide, 1989; (ed jtly) The Origin of Modern Humans and the Impact of Chronometric Dating, 1993; (with C. Gamble) In Search of the Neanderthals: solving the puzzle of human origins, 1993 (Archaeol. Bk of the Year, 1994); (with R. McKie) African Exodus, 1996, 2nd edn 1997; (jtly) Westbury Cave: the Natural History Museum excavations 1976–1984, 1999; (ed jtly) Neanderthals on the Edge: 150th anniversary conference of the Forbes' Quarry discovery, Gibraltar, 2000; (with J. Weiner) The Piltdown Forgery, 2003; (with P. Andrews) The Complete World of Human Evolution, 2005, 2nd edn 2011; Homo britannicus, 2006 (Kistler Book Award, 2008; British Archaeological Book Award, 2008); The Origin of Our Species, 2011; (ed jtly) The Ancient Human Occupation of Britain, 2011; Lone Survivors, 2012; (jtly) Neanderthals in Context: a report of the 1995–1998 excavations at Gorham's and Vanguard Caves, Gibraltar, 2012; (ed jtly) Culture Evolves, 2012; (with R. Dinnis) Britain: one million years of the human story, 2014; (with L. Humphrey) Our Human Story, 2018; articles in learned jls. *Recreations:* music, current affairs, travel, watching soccer, astronomy. *Address:* Department of Earth Sciences, Natural History Museum, Cromwell Road, SW7 5BD. *Clubs:* Tetrapods; West Ham United Football.

**STRINGER, Graham Eric;** MP (Lab) Blackley and Broughton, since 2010 (Manchester Blackley, 1997–2010); *b* 17 Feb. 1950; *s* of late Albert Stringer and Brenda Stringer; *m* 1999, Kathryn Carr; one *s*, and one step *s* one step *d*. *Educ:* Moston Brook High Sch.; Sheffield Univ. (BSc Hons Chemistry). Analytical chemist. Mem. (Lab), Manchester City Council, 1979–98 (Leader, 1984–96; Chm., Policy and Resources Cttee); Chm., Manchester Airport, 1996–97. Parly Sec., Cabinet Office, 1999–2001; a Lord Comr of HM Treasury (Govt Whip), 2001–02. *Address:* House of Commons, SW1A 0AA.

**STRINGER, Sir Howard,** Kt 2000; Chairman, Sony Corporation, 2005–13 (Board Member, 1999–2013; Vice Chairman, 2003–05; Group Chief Executive Officer and Representative Corporate Executive Officer, 2005–12; President, 2009–12); Chairman, Sony Corporation of America, 1998–2013 (Chief Executive Officer, 1998–2012); *b* Cardiff, 19 Feb. 1942; naturalised US citizen, 1985 (dual nationality); *s* of late Harry Stringer, MBE and Marjorie Mary Stringer; *m* 1978, Jennifer Kinmond Patterson; one *s* one *d*. *Educ:* Oundle Sch.; Merton Coll., Oxford (BA Modern History 1964; MA; Hon. Fellow, 2000). Served US Army, Vietnam, 1965–67 (Commendation Medal). Joined CBS Inc., 1965; Executive Producer: CBS Reports, 1976–81; CBS Evening News, 1981–84; Exec. Vice Pres., 1984–86, Pres., 1986–88, CBS News; Pres., CBS Broadcast Gp, 1988–95; Chm. and CEO, Tele-TV, 1995–97. Joined Sony Corp. of America, 1997; Corp. Hd, Sony Corp. Entertainment Business Gp, 2003–13; Board Member: Sony BMG, 2004–13; Sony Ericsson, 2006–13. Non-executive Director: TalkTalk, 2012–; BBC, 2013–17; non-exec. Chm., Atrium TV, 2017–. Board Member: Amer. Theater Wing; Amer. Friends of BM; NY Presbyterian Hosp. Chm., Bd of Trustees, Amer. Film Inst., 1999– (Mem., 1989–); Trustee, Paley Center for Media (Visionary award, 2007). Chm. Bd, Saïd Business Sch., Oxford Univ., 2013–. Pres., Merton Soc., 2014–. Hon. FRWCMD 2001. Hon. PhD London Inst., 2003; Hon. Dr Glamorgan, 2005; Hon. DLitt: Oxford, 2012; Swansea, 2013. Foundn Award, Internat. Radio and TV Soc., 1994; Steven J. Ross Humanitarian Award, UJA-Fedn of NY, 1999; Internat. Emmy (Founders) Award, 2002; Phoenix House Award for Public Service, 2002; Medal of Honor, St George Soc., 2004; Dist. Service Award, Lincoln Center for the Performing Arts, 2006.

**STRINGER, Prof. Dame Joan (Kathleen),** DBE 2009 (CBE 2001); PhD; FRSE; Principal and Vice-Chancellor, Edinburgh Napier (formerly Napier) University, 2003–13; *b* 12 May 1948; *d* of Francis James and Doris Joan Bourne; *m* 1993, Roelof Marinus Mali. *Educ:* Portland House High Sch., Stoke-on-Trent; Stoke-on-Trent Coll. of Art; Keele Univ. (BA, CertEd, PhD Politics 1986). Graphic designer, ICL, 1966–70; Local Govt Officer, Staffs, 1970–74; teacher, Sudbury Open Prison, Derbys, 1978–80; Robert Gordon University: Lectr, 1980–88; Head, Sch. of Public Admin and Law, 1988–91; Asst Principal, 1991–96; Queen Margaret College, subseq. Queen Margaret University College, Edinburgh: Principal and Vice Patron, 1996–2002. Comr (Scotland), EOC, 1995–2001; Chm. Wkg Gp, NI Equality Commn, 1999. Mem., Scottish Parlt Consultative Steering Gp and Financial Issues Adv. Gp, 1998–99; Comr, Scottish Election Commn, 1999–2000; Chm., Scottish Exec. Strategic Gp on Women, 2003. Mem., HFEA, 1996–99. Vice-Convener, Univs Scotland (formerly Cttee of Scottish Higher Educn Prins), 1998–2002; Chair, Education UK Scotland, 2006–12. Member: CVCP Commn on Univ. Career Opportunities, 1996–2001; Scottish Cttee, Cttee of Inquiry into Higher Educn (Dearing Cttee), 1996–97; Scottish Council for Postgrad. Med. and Dental Educn, 1999–2002; Scottish Health Minister's Learning Together Strategy Implementation Gp, 2000–01; Exec. Cttee, Scottish Council Develt and Industry, 1998–2013; Scottish Cttee, British Council, 2000–12; Bd, Higher Educn Careers Services Unit, 2000–05; DoH Wkg Gp on modernisation of SHO, 2001–02; Adv. Gp, Scottish Nursing and Midwifery Educn Council, 2001–02; UUK Equality Challenge Steering Gp, 2001–03; Bd, UCEA, 2001–10; Judicial Appts Bd for Scotland, 2002–08; Bd, QAA, 2002–06; Bd, Higher Educn Statistics Agency, 2003–13; Bd, Leadership Foundn for Higher Educn, 2005–10; Bd, UCAS, 2009–13. Sen. HE Advr, British Council, 2013–15. Convener, SCVO, 2001–07. Non-exec. Dir, Grampian Health Bd, 1994–96. Convenor, Product Standards Cttee, Scottish Quality Salmon, 2001–03. Non-executive Director: City Refrigeration Holdings Ltd, 2013–; Grant Property Investment, 2013– (Chm., 2015–). Member: Develt Adv. Bd, Scottish Opera and Ballet, 2000–02; Bd, National Theatre of Scotland, 2009–16; Bd, Scottish Improvement Sci. Collaborating Centre, 2014–17. Mem., Bd of Mgt, Aberdeen Coll., 1992–96. Member Council: World Assoc. for Co-op. Educn, 1998–2003; Edinburgh Internat. Festival Soc., 1999–2005; IoD, 2013– (Sen. Ind. Council Mem., 2015–); RSE, 2014–; Chair: Capital Theatres (formerly Festival City Theatres Trust), 2013–; Scotch Whisky Action Fund, 2014–. Trustee: David Hume Inst., 2004–17; Community Integrated Care, 2013–19 (Chm., 2014–19); Freedom from Fistula Foundn, 2015–; Entrepreneurial Scotland Foundn, 2015–; IMPACT Scotland, 2016–17; Fellow, 48 Group Club, 2006. CCMI (CIMgt 1999; MIMgt 1990); FRSA 1994; FRSE 2001. Hon. DLitt Keele; Hon. Dr: Edinburgh, 2011; Open Univ., 2014; Hon. Citizen, Shandong Province, China, 2007. Yellow River Friendship Award, Henan Province, 2008. *Publications:* contrib. articles in field of politics with particular ref. to British Public Admin and employment and trng policy. *Recreations:* music (especially opera), gardening, travelling.

**STROHM, Prof. Paul Holzworth,** PhD; Anna S. Garbedian Professor of the Humanities and Professor of Medieval Literature, Columbia University, 2003–11, now Emeritus; Emeritus Fellow, St Anne's College, University of Oxford, since 2003; *b* 30 July 1938; *s* of Paul H. Strohm and Catherine Poole Strohm; *m* 1st, 1960, Jean Sprowl (marr. diss. 1977); two *s*; 2nd, 2008, Claire P. Harman. *Educ:* Amherst Coll. (BA 1960); Univ. of California, Berkeley (PhD 1965); Univ. of Oxford (MPhil 1998). Indiana University: Asst Prof., 1965–68; Associate Prof., 1968–73; Full Prof. of English, 1973–98; J. R. R. Tolkien Prof. of Medieval Lang. and Lit., and Fellow, St Anne's Coll., Oxford Univ., 1998–2003. Guggenheim Fellow, 1994–95; Vis. Fellow, Clare Hall, Cambridge, 1994–95; Henry R. Luce Fellow, Nat. Humanities Center, 1996–97; Leverhulme Vis. Prof., 2012–13, Hon. Professorial Fellow, 2013–, QMUL. First Vice Pres., Amer. Assoc. of Univ. Profs, 1985–86, Ed., Academe: Bull. of AAUP, 1986–92; Pres., New Chaucer Soc., 1998–2000. *Publications:* Social Chaucer, 1989; Hochon's Arrow: the social imagination of medieval texts, 1992; England's Empty Throne: usurpation and the language of legitimation, 1998; Theory and the Premodern Text, 2000; Politique, 2005; Middle English, 2008; Conscience: a very short introduction, 2011; The Poet's Tale: Chaucer and the year that made The Canterbury Tales, 2015. *Address:* 560 Carroll Street, Apt 12A, Brooklyn, New York, NY 11215, USA; 76 Southfield Road, Oxford OX4 1PA.

**STROHM, Prof. Reinhard,** PhD; FBA 1993; Professor of Music, Oxford University, 2007–10, now Emeritus; Fellow, Wadham College, Oxford, 1996–2007, now Emeritus; *b* 4 Aug. 1942. *Educ:* Tech. Univ., Berlin (PhD 1971). Lectr, then Reader, in Music, KCL, 1975–83; Prof. of Music Hist., Yale Univ., 1983–89; Reader, 1990–91, Prof. of Histl Musicology, 1991–96, KCL; Heather Prof. of Music, Univ. of Oxford, 1996–2007. Edward J. Dent Medal, Royal Musical Assoc., 1977. *Publications:* Italienische Opernarien des frühen Settecento, 1976; Die italienische Oper im 18 Jahrhundert, 1979, 2nd edn 1991; Music in Late Medieval Bruges, 1985, 2nd edn 1990; Essays on Handel and Italian Opera, 1985; The Rise of European Music 1380–1500, 1993; Dramma per Musica: Italian opera seria of the 18th century, 1997; (ed) The Eighteenth-century Diaspora of Italian Music and Musicians, 2001; (ed with B. J. Blackburn) Music as Concept and Practice in the Late Middle Ages, 2001; The Operas of Antonio Vivaldi, 2008; many contribs to books and learned jls. *Recreations:* travel, mountaineering. *Address:* Faculty of Music, St Aldate's, Oxford OX1 1DB; 19 Hunt Close, Bicester, Oxon OX26 6HX.

**STRONACH, David Brian,** OBE 1975; FSA; Professor of Near Eastern Studies, University of California, Berkeley, 1981–2004, now Emeritus (Chair of Department, 1994–97); *b* 10 June 1931; *s* of Ian David Stronach, MB, FRCSE, and Marjorie Jessie Duncan (*née* Minto); *m* 1966, Ruth Vaadia; two *d*. *Educ:* Gordonstoun; St John's Coll., Cambridge (MA). Pres., Cambridge Univ. Archaeological Field Club, 1954. British Inst. of Archaeology at Ankara: Scholar, 1955–56; Fellow, 1957–58; Fellow, British Sch. of Archaeology in Iraq, 1957–60; Brit. Acad. Archaeological Attaché in Iran, 1960–61; Dir, British Inst. of Persian Studies, 1961–80, Hon. Vice Pres., 1981–; Curator of Near Eastern Archaeol., Hearst (formerly Lowie) Mus. of Anthropol., Berkeley, 1982–2001. Asst on excavations at: Istanbul, 1954; Tell Rifa'at, 1956; Beycesultan, 1956–58; Hacilar, 1957–59; Nimrud, 1957–60; Charsada, 1958. Director, excavations at: Ras al'Amiya, 1960; Yarim Tepe, 1960–62; Pasargadae, 1961–63; Tepe Nush-i Jan, 1967–77; Nineveh, 1987–90; Co-director, excavations at: Shahr-i Qumis, 1967–78; Horom, 1992–93; Velikent, 1994–97; Erebuni, 2007–10. Mem., Internat. Cttee of Internat. Congresses of Iranian Art and

Archaeology, 1968–80. Hagop Kevorkian Visiting Lectr in Iranian Art and Archaeology, Univ. of Pennsylvania, 1967; Lectures: Rhind, Edin., 1973; Norton, Amer. Inst. of Archaeology, 1980; Columbia in Iranian Studies, Columbia Univ., 1986; Leventritt, Harvard Univ., 1991; Cohodas, Hebrew Union Coll. Jerusalem, 1992; McNicoll, Univ. of Sydney, 1994. Vis. Prof. of Archaeology, Hebrew Univ., Jerusalem, 1977; Vis. Prof. of Archaeology and Iranian Studies, Univ. of Arizona, Tucson, 1980–81; Vis. Prof., Collège de France, Paris, 1999; Walker Ames Prof., Univ. of Washington, 2002. Mem., German Archaeological Inst., 1973 (Corresp. Mem., 1966); Associate Mem., Royal Belgian Acad., 1988–; Ghirshman Prize, Académie des Inscriptions et Belles-Lettres, Paris, 1979; Sir Percy Sykes Meml Medal, Royal Soc. for Asian Affairs, 1980; Gold Medal, Archaeol Inst. of America, 2004. Adv. Editor: Jl of Mithraic Studies, 1976–79; Iran, 1981–96; Iranica Antiqua, 1984–; Bulletin of Asia Inst., 1986–; Amer. Jl of Archaeol., 1989–96; Ancient West and East, 2002–. *Publications*: Pasargadae, a Report on the Excavations conducted by the British Institute of Persian Studies, 1978; (with M. Roaf) Nush-i Jan I, The Major Buildings of the Median Settlement, 2007; (ed with A. Mousavi) Irans Erbe in Flugbildern von Georg Gerster, 2009; (ed with A. Mousavi) Ancient Iran from the Air, 2012; archaeological articles in: Jl of Near Eastern Studies; Iran; Iraq; Anatolian Studies, etc. *Recreations*: fly fishing, mediaeval architecture, tribal carpets; repr. Cambridge in athletics, 1953. *Address*: 815 Shattuck Avenue, Berkeley, CA 94707, USA. *Clubs*: Achilles; Hawks (Cambridge); Explorers (New York).

**STRONG, Benjamin James Quentin**; QC 2014; *b* 6 Aug. 1968; *s* of Harry and Mary Strong; *m* 2002, Anita Drew; one *s*. *Educ*: Nottingham High Sch.; Jesus Coll., Cambridge (BA 1991). Admitted as solicitor, 1994; Solicitor, Slaughter and May, 1994–2001; called to the Bar, Middle Temple, 2001; in practice as a barrister, specialising in commercial litigation, 2002–. *Address*: One Essex Court, Temple, EC4Y 9AR. *T*: (020) 7583 2000. *E*: bstrong@oeclaw.co.uk.

**STRONG, Hilary Jane Veronica**; Director, Making Theatre Gaining Skills CIC, since 2014; *b* 3 June 1957; *d* of late Robert Hedley Strong and Estelle Flora Strong (*née* Morris). *Educ*: Chichester High Sch. for Girls; Lombard Sch. of Dancing. Freelance stage-manager and actress, 1979–83; Administrator: Merlin Theatre, Frome, 1986–88; Natural Theatre Co., Bath, 1989–94; Dir, Edinburgh Festival Fringe, 1994–99; Exec. Dir, Greenwich Theatre, 1999–2007; estabd Greenwich Musical Theatre Acad., 2003; Dir, Nat. Council for Drama Trng, 2007–10; Dir and Consultant, Strong Ideas Ltd, 2011–16. Member Board: Nat. Campaign for Arts, 1990–92; Dance Base, Edinburgh, 1995–99; Mem., Arts Council of England, 1998–2002. *Recreation*: travelling on buses abroad. *E*: hilary@makingtheatre.co.uk.

**STRONG, James Christian Burrell**; television and film director and writer; *b* Bristol, 1973; *s* of Arnold Strong and Sally Burrell; partner, Antonia Lowe; two *s* one *d*. *Educ*: Univ. of Sussex (BA Geog.; MA Internat. Relns). Trainee dir, Granada TV, 1992–96; credits include: World in Action, 1995; The Clothes Show, 1997; Doctors, 2000; Holby City, 2002–05; Lady Jane, 2003; Sold, 2003; Torchwood, 2006; Rocket Man, 2006; Hustle, 2006; Doctor Who, 2006–08 (Best Dir, BAFTA Cymru, 2009); United, 2011; Downton Abbey, 2011; Best Possible Taste, 2012; The Great Train Robbery, 2013; Broadchurch, 2013–15; Code of a Killer, 2015; 11-22-63, 2016; Liar, 2017–19; Vanity Fair, 2018. *Recreations*: Tottenham Hotspur FC, walking, travel, reading. *Address*: c/o United Agents, 12–26 Lexington Street, W1F 0LE. *Club*: Soho House.

**STRONG, Jaqueline Ann Mary**; education consultant, 2004–10; *b* 2 Oct. 1944; *d* of Donald Cameron McKeand and Gwendoline Mary Ann McKeand (*née* Graham); *m* 1966, Roger Francis Strong (*d* 2014). *Educ*: Sexey's Grammar Sch.; Chipping Sodbury Grammar Sch.; Univ. of Wales (BSc, DipEd 1st cl.); Univ. of Bristol (MEd). Teacher, St Julian's Jun. High Sch., Newport, 1966–69; Lectr, Rhydyfelin Coll. of FE, 1967–70; teacher: Belfast, 1970–73; St Peter's Comp. Sch., Huntingdon, 1974, Dep. Head Teacher, 1974–81; Warden, The Village Coll., Bassingbourn, 1981–88; Asst Dir of Educn, Cambs CC, 1988–93; Director of Education: Leeds MDC, 1993–95; Leics CC, 1995–2004. Mem., Exec. Bd, Encounter, 1984–2008. Mem. Council, Univ. of Loughborough, 1995–2012. Voluntary worker for animal charities, Blue Cross and Pets as Therapy, 2004–. *Publications*: articles in educational magazines. *Recreations*: singing, exotic foreign travel, photography, walking, reading, concert and theatre going, taking in unwanted Great Danes.

**STRONG, Liam**; Partner, since 2007 and Chief Executive Officer, since 2009, Cerberus European Capital Advisers LLP; Chairman, Cerberus European Operations, since 2017; Chairman, Virtual IT, since 2002; *b* 6 Jan. 1945; *s* of Gerald Strong and Geraldine Strong (*née* Crozier); *m* 1970, Jacqueline Gray; one *s* one *d*. *Educ*: Trinity Coll., Dublin. Procter & Gamble, 1967–71; Reckitt & Colman, 1971–88; Dir of Mktg and Ops, British Airways, 1988–91; Chief Executive: Sears plc, 1991–97; MCI (formerly WorldCom) Internat., 1997–2001; Teleglobe Inc., 2003–06. Chairman: Torex, 2009–12; Greenstar, 2014–17; WFS, 2018–; Director: Aercap Holdings NV, 2006–13 (Vice-Chm., 2011–13); Admiral, 2013–17. Chm., UK Govt Telecoms Adv. Bd, 2005–. Gov., Ashridge Management Coll., 1996–2015. *Recreations*: sailing, history, writing.

**STRONG, Liza**; *see* Marshall, L.

**STRONG, Sir Roy (Colin)**; CH 2016; Kt 1982; PhD; FSA; FRSL; writer and historian, diarist, lecturer, critic, columnist, contributor to radio and television and organiser of exhibitions, gardener; Director, Oman Productions Ltd; *b* 23 Aug. 1935; *s* of G. E. C. Strong; *m* 1971, Julia Trevelyan Oman, CBE, RDI (*d* 2003). *Educ*: Edmonton Co. Grammar Sch.; Queen Mary Coll., London (Fellow, 1976); Warburg Inst., London. Asst Keeper, 1959, Director, Keeper and Secretary 1967–73, Nat. Portrait Gallery; Dir, Victoria and Albert Museum, 1974–87. Ferens Prof. of Fine Art, Univ. of Hull, 1972. Walls Lectures, Pierpont Morgan Library, 1974; Andrew Carnduff Ritchie Lectr, Yale Univ., 1999. Member: Fine Arts Adv. Cttee, British Council, 1974–87; Westminster Abbey Architectl Panel, 1975–89; Council, RCA, 1979–87; Arts Council of GB, 1983–87 (Chm., Arts Panel, 1983–87); Vice-Chm., South Bank Centre (formerly South Bank Bd), 1985–90. High Bailiff and Searcher of the Sanctuary, Westminster Abbey, 2000–19. Pres., 2001–02, 2004–, Vice-Pres., 2002–04, Garden History Soc.; Vice-Pres., RSPCA, 2000–05. Trustee: Arundel Castle, 1974–86; Chevening, 1974–87; Sutton Place, 1982–84; Patron, Pallant House, Chichester, 1986– (Trustee, 1980–86). Writer and presenter, TV series incl. Royal Gardens 1992; The Diets That Time Forgot, 2008; (contrib.) The Genius of British Art, 2010. Sen. Fellow, RCA, 1983; FRSL. Hon. DLitt: Leeds, 1983; Keele, 1984; London, 2018; Hon. MA Worcester, 2005. Shakespeare Prize, FVS Foundn, Hamburg, 1980. *Publications*: Portraits of Queen Elizabeth I, 1963; (with J. A. van Dorsten) Leicester's Triumph, 1964; Holbein and Henry VIII, 1967; Tudor and Jacobean Portraits, 1969; The English Icon: Elizabethan and Jacobean Portraiture, 1969; (with Julia Trevelyan Oman) Elizabeth R, 1971; Van Dyck: Charles I on Horseback, 1972; (with Julia Trevelyan Oman) Mary Queen of Scots, 1972; (with Stephen Orgel) Inigo Jones: the theatre of the Stuart court, 1973; contrib. Burke's Guide to the Royal Family, 1973; Splendour at Court: Renaissance Spectacle and the Theatre of Power, 1973; (with Colin Ford) An Early Victorian Album: the Hill-Adamson collection, 1974; Nicholas Hilliard, 1975; (contrib.) Spirit of the Age, 1975; The Cult of Elizabeth: Elizabethan Portraiture and Pageantry, 1977; And When Did You Last See Your Father?, 1978; The Renaissance Garden in England, 1979; (contrib.) The Garden, 1979; Britannia Triumphans: Inigo Jones, Rubens and Whitehall Palace, 1980; (introd.) Holbein, 1980; (contrib.) Designing for the Dancer, 1981; (jtly) The English Miniature, 1981; (with Julia Trevelyan Oman) The English Year, 1982; (contrib.) Pelican Guide to English Literature vol. 3, 1982; (with J. Murrell) Artists of the Tudor Court, 1983; The English Renaissance Miniature, 1983; (contrib.) Glyndebourne: a celebration, 1984; Art & Power, 1984; Strong Points, 1985; Henry, Prince of Wales and England's Lost Renaissance, 1986; (contrib.) For Veronica Wedgwood These, 1986; Creating Small Gardens, 1986; Gloriana, Portraits of Queen Elizabeth I, 1987; A Small Garden Designer's Handbook, 1987; Cecil Beaton: the Royal Portraits, 1988; Creating Small Formal Gardens, 1989; (contrib.) British Theatre Design, 1989; Lost Treasures of Britain, 1990; (contrib.) Sir Philip Sidney's Achievements, 1990; (contrib.) England and the Continental Renaissance, 1990; (ed) A Celebration of Gardens, 1991; The Garden Trellis, 1991; Small Period Gardens, 1992; Royal Gardens, 1992; A Country Life, 1994; Successful Small Gardens, 1994; William Larkin, 1995; The Tudor and Stuart Monarchy, vol. I, Tudor, 1995, vol. II, Elizabethan, 1996, vol. III, Jacobean and Caroline, 1998; The Story of Britain, 1996, rev. edn 2019; Country Life 1897–1997: the English Arcadia, 1996; The Roy Strong Diaries 1967–1987, 1997; (with Julia Trevelyan Oman) On Happiness, 1998; The Spirit of Britain, 1999, 2nd edn as The Arts in Britain: a history, 2004; Garden Party, 2000; The Artist and the Garden, 2000; Ornament in the Small Garden, 2001; Feast: a history of grand eating, 2002; The Laskett: the story of a garden, 2003; Passions Past and Present, 2005; Coronation: a history of kingship and the British monarchy, 2005; A Little History of the English Country Church, 2007; Visions of England, 2011; Self-Portrait as a Young Man, 2013; Remaking a Garden: the Laskett transformed, 2014; (with John Swannell) Sir Portrait, 2015; Scenes and Apparitions: the Roy Strong diaries 1988–2003, 2016; The Elizabethan Image: an introduction to English portraiture 1558–1603, 2019. *Recreations*: gardening, keeping fit, cycling. *Address*: The Laskett, Much Birch, Herefords HR2 8HZ. *Club*: Garrick.

**STRONG, Prof. Russell Walker**, AC 2001; CMG 1987; RFD 1995; FRCS, FRACS, FACS; FRACDS; Professor of Surgery, University of Queensland, 1992–2004, now Emeritus; Director of Surgery, Princess Alexandra Hospital, Brisbane, 1981–2004; *b* 4 April 1938; *s* of Aubrey and Anne Strong; *m* 1960, Judith Bardsley; two *d*. *Educ*: Lismore High Sch.; Univ. of Sydney (BDS); Charing Cross Hosp. Med. Sch., Univ. of London (MB BS). LRCP 1965; MRCS 1965, FRCS 1970; FRACDS 1966; FRACS 1974; FACS 1984, Hon. FACS 2008. Intern, Bromley Hosp., Kent, 1965–66; Tutor in Anatomy, Charing Cross Hosp. Med. Sch., 1966–67; SHO, Birmingham Accident Hosp., 1968; Surgical Registrar: Charing Cross Hosp., 1969; St Helier Hosp., 1970–71; Sen. Surgical Registrar, Whittington Hosp., 1972–73; Surgical Supervisor, Princess Alexandra Hosp., Brisbane, 1973–80. Vis. Prof. and Guest Lectr on numerous occasions worldwide. James IV Surgical Traveller, 1987; Vis. Schol., Pembroke Coll., Cambridge, 2001. Hon. Fellow: Assoc. of Surgeons of GB and Ireland, 1996; Surgical Res. Soc. of SA, 1996; Hon. FRCSE 2001; Distinguished Academician, Acad. of Medicine, Singapore, 1998; Hon. Mem., Internat. Coll. of Surgeons, 1989; Hon. Fellow, American Surgical Assoc., 2003. Inaugural Award for Excellence in Surgery, RACS, 1993; Prize, Internat. Soc. of Surgeons, 2001; Brand Laureate Award, Malaysia, 2012. Knight Comdr, Distinguished Order of Malaysia, 2010. *Publications*: contrib. book chapters and numerous articles in scientific jls. *Recreations*: golf, tennis. *Address*: U5313 Farringford, 197 King Arthur TCE, Tennyson, Brisbane, Qld 4105, Australia. *T*: (7) 38481130.

**STRONGE, Christopher James**; Partner, Coopers & Lybrand Deloitte, 1967–92; *b* 16 Aug. 1933; *s* of Reginald Herbert James Stronge and Doreen Marjorie Stronge; *m* 1964, Gabrielle; one *s* one *d*. *Educ*: Chigwell Sch.; Magdalene Coll., Cambridge (MA Math.). FCA. Deloitte Haskins & Sells: joined 1957; Partner 1967; Dep. Sen. Partner, 1985. Member: Accounting Standards Cttee, 1980–83; Internat. Accounting Standards Cttee, 1985–90; Treasurer, RIIA, 1981–91. *Recreations*: opera, golf, sailing.

**STRONGE, Sir James Anselan Maxwell**, 10th Bt *cr* 1803; *b* 17 July 1946; *s* of Maxwell Du Pré James Stronge (*d* 1973) (ggs of 2nd Bt) and Eileen Mary (*d* 1976), *d* of Rt Hon. Maurice Marcus McCausland, PC, Drenagh, Limavady, Co. Londonderry; *S* cousin, 1981, but his name does not appear on the Official Roll of the Baronetage. *Heir*: none. *Address*: Camphill Community Clanabogan, 15 Drudgeon Road, Clanabogan, Omagh, Co. Tyrone BT78 1TJ.

**STRONGMAN, Ian Melville**, TD 1993; a District Judge (Magistrates' Courts), since 2011; *b* St Dennis, Cornwall, 1958; *s* of Ronald Strongman and Lilian Strongman; *m* 1984, Carol Gray; two *s*. *Educ*: Univ. of Leeds (LLB 1980). Called to the Bar, Lincoln's Inn, 1981; in practice as a barrister, 8 Fountain Court, Birmingham, 1986–2011, Hd of Chambers, 1997–2011; a Dep. Dist Judge, 1999–2011. Served TA, Staffs Regt (rank of Major). *Recreations*: walking, water colour painting. *Address*: Victoria Law Courts, Corporation Street, Birmingham B4 6QA.

**STROUD**, family name of **Baroness Stroud**.

**STROUD**, Baroness *cr* 2015 (Life Peer), of Fulham in the London Borough of Hammersmith and Fulham; **Philippa Claire Stroud**; Chief Executive Officer, Legatum Institute, since 2016; *b* Whitestone, Devon, 2 April 1965; *d* of Peter and Wendy Duffy; *m* 1989, David Stroud; one *s* two *d*. *Educ*: St Catherine's Sch., Bramley; Univ. of Birmingham (BA Hons). Work in Hong Kong and Macau amongst addict community, 1987–89; Founder, King's Arms Project (night shelter and hostel), Bedford, 1989–98; Exec. Dir, Bridge Project, Birmingham, 1998; Centre for Social Justice: Co-founder, 2004; Exec. Dir, 2004–10; Chm., Implementation Strategy Bd, 2008–10; Dir, Policy, 2008–10; Special Advr, DWP, 2010–15; Chief Exec., Centre for Social Justice, 2015–16. Contested (C): Birmingham Ladywood, 2005; Sutton and Cheam, 2010. *Address*: House of Lords, SW1A 0PW.

**STROUD, Prof. Michael Adrian**, OBE 1993; MD; FRCP, FRCPE; Professor of Clinical Nutrition, University of Southampton, since 2017 (Senior Lecturer, 1998–2017); Consultant in Medicine, Gastroenterology and Nutrition, University Hospital Southampton NHS Foundation Trust, since 1998 (Research Fellow in Nutrition and Gastroenterology, 1995–98); *b* 17 April 1955; *s* of Victor and Vivienne Stroud; *m* 1987, Thea de Moel (*d* 2018); one *s* one *d*. *Educ*: University Coll. London (BSc; Fellow 2005); St George's Hosp. Med. Sch. (MB, BS, MD); FRCP 1994; FRCPE 1994. Med. trng, St George's Hosp., London, 1973–79; postgrad. trng and work in various NHS hosps, 1979–89; govt res. in survival and endurance physiology, 1989–95. Has taken part in many expeditions to Polar regions, incl. the first unassisted crossing of Antarctica on foot, with Sir Ranulph Fiennes, 1992–93; Land Rover 7x7x7 Challenge (7 marathons in 7 days on 7 continents), with Sir Ranulph, 2003. Hon. DSc Robert Gordon, 2006. Polar Medal, 1995. *Publications*: Shadows on the Wasteland: crossing Antarctica with Ranulph Fiennes, 1993; Survival of the Fittest, 1998; articles on thermal and survival physiology, endurance exercise, and nutrition in med. jls. *Recreations*: climbing, multi-sport endurance events. *Address*: Gastroenterology Department, Southampton General Hospital, Tremona Road, Southampton SO16 6YD. *T*: (023) 8079 6317.

**STROYAN, Rt Rev. John Ronald Angus**; *see* Warwick, Bishop Suffragan of.

**STRUDWICK, Maj. Gen. Mark Jeremy,** CBE 1990; Chief Executive, The Prince's Scottish Youth Business Trust, 2000–12; *b* 19 April 1945; *s* of late Ronald Strudwick and Mary Strudwick (*née* Beresford); *m* 1st, 1970, Janet Elizabeth Coleridge Vivers (*d* 2013); one *s* one *d*; 2nd, 2015, Sue Garrett-Cox (*née* Guest); two step *s* one step *d*. *Educ*: St Edmund's Sch., Canterbury; RMA Sandhurst. Commnd Royal Scots (The Royal Regt), 1966; served UK, BAOR, Cyprus, Canada, India, NI (despatches twice); Comd, 1st Bn Royal Scots, 1984–87; Instr, Staff Coll., 1987–88; ACOS HQ NI, 1988–90; Higher Comd and Staff Course, 1989; Comd 3 Inf. Bde, 1990–91; NDC New Delhi, 1992; Dep. Mil. Sec., MoD, 1993–95; Dir of Infantry, 1996–97; ADC to the Queen, 1996–97; GOC Scotland and Gov. of Edinburgh Castle, 1997–2000. Col, Royal Scots, 1995–2005; Col Comdt, Scottish Div., 1997–2000. Mem., Queen's Body Guard for Scotland, Royal Company of Archers, 1994 (Ensign, 2016; Lieutenant, 2018). Dir, Royal Edinburgh Military Tattoo, 2007–15; Chairman: Scottish Veterans' Residences, 2001–16; Scottish Nat. War Meml, 2009–. Trustee, Historic Scotland Foundn, 2001–15; President: Highland and Lowland Brigades Club, 2007–; Soc. of Friends of St Andrew's, Jerusalem, 2011–15. Cdre, Infantry Sailing Assoc., 1997–2000. Governor: Royal Sch., Bath, 1993–2000; Gordonstoun Sch., 1999–2007; Excelsior Acad., Newcastle, 2009–15. KStJ 2015; Prior, Order of St John, Scotland, 2015–. *Recreations*: fishing, golf, shooting, sailing. *Club*: Royal Scots (Trustee, 1995–; Chm., 2014–) (Edinburgh).

**STRUNIN, Prof. Leo,** MD; FRCA; BOC Professor of Anaesthesia, Bart's and The London School of Medicine and Dentistry, Queen Mary (formerly London Hospital Medical College, then St Bartholomew's and Royal London School of Medicine and Dentistry, Queen Mary and Westfield College), University of London, 1990–2003, now Emeritus Professor; *b* 19 Nov. 1937; *m* 1968, Jane Smith. *Educ*: Univ. of Durham (MB BS 1960); Univ. of Newcastle upon Tyne (MD 1974). FRCA (FFARCS 1964); FRCP(C) 1980. Training posts, Newcastle upon Tyne, Sunderland, Manchester and London, 1960–67; Lectr, 1967–69, Sen. Lectr, 1969–72, Anaesthetics Unit, London Hosp. Med. Coll.; Sen. Lectr, 1972–74, Prof., 1975–79, Anaesthetic Dept, King's Coll. Hosp. and Med. Sch.; Prof. and Head, Dept of Anaesthesia, Univ. of Calgary, Canada, 1980–90. President: RCAnaes, 1997–2000; Assoc. of Anaesthetists of GB and Ire., 2000–02. *Publications*: Anaesthesia and the Liver, 1977; (with S. Thomson) Anaesthesia and the Liver, 1992; (with J. A. Stamford) Neuroprotection, 1996. *Recreation*: whippet and greyhound racing. *Address*: The Grange, Firsby, Spilsby, Lincs PE23 5QL. *T*: (01754) 830585. *Club*: Athenæum.

**STRUTHERS, Alastair James,** OBE 1995; *b* 25 July 1929; *s* of Alexander Struthers and Elizabeth Struthers (*née* Hutchison); *m* 1967, Elizabeth Henderson (*d* 2014); three *d*. *Educ*: Stowe; Trinity Coll., Cambridge (MA). Chairman: J. & A. Gardner & Co. Ltd, 1962–; Scottish National Trust plc, 1983–98; Caledonian MacBrayne Ltd, 1990–94. Chairman: Steamship Mutual Underwriting Assoc., 1988–95; Steamship Mutual Trustees (Bermuda) Ltd, 2000–. Dir, Hamilton Park Racecourse, 1973–. Chm., Racing and Thoroughbred Breeding Trng Bd, 1992–98. Comr, Northern Lighthouse Bd, 1980–99. Dep. Sen. Steward, Jockey Club, 1990–94. *Recreations*: racing, shooting, golf. *Address*: Garden Cottage, Craigmaddie, Milngavie, by Glasgow G62 8LB. *T*: (0141) 956 1262. *Club*: Western (Glasgow).

**STRUTHERS, Prof. Allan David,** MD; FRCP, FESC; FRSE; FMedSci; Professor of Cardiovascular Medicine, since 1992, and Head, Division of Molecular and Clinical Medicine (formerly Medicine and Therapeutics), since 2002, University of Dundee; *b* Glasgow, 14 Aug. 1952; *s* of Dr David Struthers and Margaret Struthers; *m* 1979, Julia Elizabeth Anne Diggens; one *s* one *d*. *Educ*: Hutcheson's Boys' Grammar Sch., Glasgow; Univ. of Glasgow (BSc Hons Biochem. 1973; MB ChB Hons 1977; MD 1984). FRCPE 1990; FRCP 1992; FESC 1994; FRSE 2010; FMedSci 2011. Sen. Med. Registrar, RPMS and Hammersmith Hosp., London, 1982–85; Wellcome Sen. Lectr, Univ. of Dundee, 1985–89. Chairman: SIGN Guidelines on Heart Failure, 2003–07 and 2013–16; Nat. Scientific Adv. Cttee, TENOVUS charity, 2004–18; Heart Failure Clinical Standards, NHS Quality Improvement Scotland, 2008–10; SIGN/RCPSG CPD Cttee, 2009–10. SmithKline Beecham Prize, Brit. Pharmacol Soc., 1990. *Publications*: Atrial Natriuretic Peptide, 1993; papers on B-type natriuretic peptide (BNP), aldosterone antagonists and xanthine oxidase inhibitors in cardiovascular jls. *Recreations*: cycling, walking, travel, opera. *Address*: Division of Molecular and Clinical Medicine, Ninewells Hospital and Medical School, Dundee DD1 9SY. *T*: (01382) 383013. *E*: a.d.struthers@dundee.ac.uk.

**STRUTT,** family name of **Barons Belper** and **Rayleigh**.

**STUART;** *see* Moody-Stuart.

**STUART;** *see* Crichton-Stuart, family name of Marquess of Bute.

**STUART,** family name of **Earl Castle Stewart, Earl of Moray** and **Viscount Stuart of Findhorn**.

**STUART, Viscount; Andrew Richard Charles Stuart;** lecturer, now retired; *b* 7 Oct. 1953; *s* and *heir* of 8th Earl Castle Stewart, *qv*; *m* 1st, 1973, Annie Le Poulain (marr. diss. 2003), St Malo, France; one *d*; 2nd, 2009, Carol Ann Reid. *Educ*: Wynstones, Glos; Millfield, Som.; Univ. of Exeter. *Recreations*: running, hiking, bellringing, cycling, sailing. *Address*: The Old Barn, Stone Lane, E Pennard, Shepton Mallet, Somerset BA4 6RZ.

**STUART OF FINDHORN,** 3rd Viscount *cr* 1959, of Findhorn co. Moray; **Dominic Stuart;** *b* 25 March 1948; *s* of 2nd Viscount Stuart of Findhorn and his 1st wife, Grizel Mary Wilfreda, *d* of D. T. Fyfe and *widow* of Michael Gillilan; *S* father, 1999, but does not use the title; *m* 1979, Yvonne Lucienne (marr. diss. 2002), *d* of Edgar Després. *Educ*: Eton. *Heir*: *half-b* Hon. Andrew Moray Stuart, *b* 20 Oct. 1957.

**STUART, Hon. Sir Antony James Cobham E.;** *see* Edwards-Stuart.

**STUART, Caroline Jean;** Director, Scotland, Oracle Corporation Ltd, 2009–16; *b* Glasgow, 16 May 1965; *d* of John and Margaret Stuart; one *d*. *Educ*: Craigholme Sch.; Univ. of Strathclyde (BSc Hons Technol. and Business Studies 1986). Manager, Portfolio Performance Measurement, Crown Agents Asset Mgt, 1986–88; Investment Analyst, Charterhouse Tilney, 1988–89; Dir, Blendwell Ltd, 1990–92; Gen. Manager, Reid Furniture Recovery Services, and Ops Manager, Reid Furniture Gp, 1992–94; Gen. Manager, Database Direct Ltd, 1994–95; Sen. Business Consultant, Clydesdale Business Devel Ltd, 1995–97; Branch Manager, Office Angels, 1997–98; Sen. Business Consultant, Lomond Enterprise Partners, 1998–2000; Oracle Corporation Ltd: E-Advr, 2000–03; Dir, Public Sector Industries EMEA, 2003–08. Member: Tech. Partnership Scotland, 2009– (Chm., 2013–); Bd, Scotland IS, 2010–16; Women at Work Cttee, Scottish Govt, 2013–; Digital Scotland Econ. Bd, 2014–; Widening Access Commn, 2015–16. Member, Board: Skills Develt Scotland, 2013–; SFC, 2015–. Mem. Court, Glasgow Caledonian Univ., 2015–. Trustee, Common Purpose, 2010–15. *Recreations*: swimming, pilates, golf, Rugby, basketball. *E*: carolinejstuart@hotmail.com.

**STUART, (Charles) Murray,** CBE 1995; Chairman, Scottish Power, 1992–2000 (Director, 1990–2000); *b* 28 July 1933; *s* of Charles Maitland Stuart and Grace Forrester Stuart (*née* Kerr); *m* 1963, Netta Caroline; one *s* one *d*. *Educ*: Glasgow Acad.; Glasgow Univ. (MA, LLB). Scottish Chartered Accountant; CA. With P. & W. McLellan, Ford Motor Co., Sheffield Twist Drill & Steel Co., and Unicorn Industries, 1961–73; Finance Dir, Hepworths, 1973–74; Finance Dir and Dep. Man. Dir, ICL, 1974–81; Metal Box, subseq. MB Group: Finance Dir, Dir—Finance, Planning and Admin, 1981–86; Man. Dir, Dec. 1986–Dec. 1987; Gp Chief Exec., 1988–89; Chm., 1989–90; Finance Dir, 1990–91, Chief Exec., 1991, Berisford International. Vice Chm., CMB Packaging SA, 1989–90; Vice-Chm. and Dir, Hill Samuel, 1992–93; Chairman: Hill Samuel Scotland, 1993–94; Intermediate Capital Group PLC, 1993–2001; Hammersmith Hospitals NHS Trust, 1996–2000; non-executive Director: Save & Prosper Insurance, 1987–91; Save & Prosper Securities, 1988–91; Hunter Saphir, 1991–92; Clerical Medical & General Life Assurance Soc., 1993–96; Royal Bank of Scotland Gp, 1996–2002; Royal Bank of Scotland, 1996–2002; Willis Corroon Gp plc, 1996–97; CMG plc, 1998–2002; Old Mutual PLC, 1999–2003; Nat. Westminster Bank, 2000–02; Administrateur, 2000–09, and Prés., Comité des comptes et de l'audit, 2004–09, Veolia Environnement SA; Mem., European Adv. Bd, Credit Lyonnais, 2000–04. Dep. Chm., Audit Commn, 1991–95 (Mem., 1986–95); Mem., Private Finance Initiative Panel, 1995–97. Mem., W Surrey and NE Hants HA, 1990–93. Mem., Meteorological Office, 1994–98. Non-exec. Dir, Royal Scottish Nat. Orch., 1998–2000. DUniv: Paisley, 1999; Glasgow, 2001. *Recreations*: theatre, gardening, travel. *Address*: Longacre, Guildford Road, Chobham, Woking, Surrey GU24 8EA. *T*: (01276) 857144. *Club*: Caledonian.

**STUART, Christopher Charles;** HM Diplomatic Service, retired; Ambassador to Mongolia, 2012–15; *m* 1986, Isabelle Julie Louise Brown; one *s*. Develt chemist, 1982–86; Inspector of Health and Safety, HSE, 1986–96; Lectr (pt-time), Basford Hall Coll., 1993–97; entered FCO, 1997; First Sec., Sci. and Technol., Tokyo, 1997–2001; Hd, Near East and N Africa Unit, UK Trade and Investment, 2001–02; Japanese lang. trng, 2003–04; Hd, Investment and Dep. Consul Gen., W Japan, 2004–07; Consul Gen., and Hd, UK Trade and Investment, Osaka, 2007–09; Dir, Corporate Develt, Energy Technologies Inst. (on secondment), 2009–12.

**STUART, Prof. David Ian,** PhD; FMedSci; FRS 1996; MRC Professor of Structural Biology, since 1996, and Joint Head of Division of Structural Biology, Wellcome (formerly Wellcome Trust) Centre for Human Genetics, University of Oxford; Fellow of Hertford College, Oxford, since 1985. *Educ*: London Univ. (BSc); PhD Bristol; MA Oxon. Lectr in Structural Molecular Biology, Univ. of Oxford, 1985–96. Life Sci. Dir, Diamond Light Source, 2008–. FMedSci 2006. Hon. DSc Leeds, 2011; Hon. Dr: Helsinki; Bristol. *Address*: Wellcome Centre for Human Genetics, Roosevelt Drive, Headington, Oxford OX3 7BN.

**STUART, Duncan,** CMG 1989; HM Diplomatic Service, retired; *b* 1 July 1934; *s* of late Ian Cameron Stuart and Patricia Forbes; *m* 1961, Leonore Luise Liederwald; one *s* one *d*. *Educ*: Rugby Sch.; Brasenose Coll., Oxford (MA). Served 1st Bn Oxfordshire and Bucks LI, 1955–57 (2nd Lieut). Joined Foreign, later Diplomatic, Service, 1959; Office of Political Advr, Berlin, 1960–61; FO, 1961–64; Helsinki, 1964–66; Head of Chancery, Dar-es-Salaam, 1966–69; FCO, 1969–70; Helsinki, 1970–74; FCO, 1974–80; Counsellor, Bonn, 1980–83; FCO, 1983–86; Counsellor, Washington, 1986–89; FCO, 1988–92; Advr, MoD, 1992–94; Special Ops Exec. Advr, FCO, 1996–2002. Chm. and Chief Exec., Cyrus Internat., 1994–95. Gov., St Clare's, Oxford, 1991–2008. *Address*: c/o C. Hoare & Co., 37 Fleet Street, EC4P 4DQ. *Clubs*: Oxford and Cambridge, Special Forces.

**STUART, Sir Geoffrey Phillip,** 10th Bt *cr* 1660, of Hartley Mauduit, Hampshire; Air Canada mechanic, since 2007; *b* Winnipeg, Manitoba, 5 July 1973; *o s* of Sir Phillip Luttrell Stuart, 9th Bt and of Beverley Claire Stuart (*née* Pieri); *S* father, 2016, but his name does not appear on the Official Roll of the Baronetage; *m* 1999, Ashley Shannon Glen; one *s* one *d*. *Heir*: *s* Alexander David Stuart, *b* 21 Dec. 2004. *Address*: 533 Charleswood Road, Winnipeg, MB R3R 1K5, Canada.

**STUART, Rt Hon. Gisela (Gschaider);** PC 2015; Chair: Change Britain, since 2016; Wilton Park, since 2018; *b* 26 Nov. 1955; *d* of late Martin and of Liane Gschaider; *m* 1st, 1980, Robert Scott Stuart (marr. diss. 2000); two *s*; 2nd, 2010, Derek John Scott (*d* 2012). *Educ*: Staatliche Realschule, Vilsburg; Manchester Poly.; London Univ. (LLB 1991). Dep. Dir, London Book Fair, 1982; Law Lectr, Worcester Coll. of Technol., 1992–97; res. in pension law, Birmingham Univ., 1995–97. MP (Lab) Birmingham Edgbaston, 1997–2017. PPS to Minister of State, Home Office, 1998–99; Parly Under-Sec. of State, DoH, 1999–2001. Member: Social Security Select Cttee, 1997–98; Foreign Affairs Select Cttee, 2001–10; Defence Select Cttee, 2010–15; Intelligence and Security Cttee, 2015–17; Chair, All Party Parly Gp on Kazakhstan, 2015–17. Chm., Vote Leave, 2016. Mem. Presidium, Convention on Future of Europe. Associate Ed., 2001–05, Ed., 2006–, The House mag. Member: Ext. Bd, Birmingham Business Sch., 2007–; London Univ. Ext. Prog., 2008–15; Bd, Birmingham City Univ., 2019–. Pres., Birmingham Bach Choir, 2015–. Trustee: Henry Jackson Soc., 2006–; Reading Force, 2014–; Armed Forces Parly Scheme, 2014–. Hon. Dr Aston, 2008; DUniv Birmingham City, 2015. Bundesverdienstkreuz (Germany), 2008. *Publications*: The Making of Europe's Constitution, 2003.

**STUART, Graham Charles;** MP (C) Beverley and Holderness, since 2005; Parliamentary Under-Secretary of State, Department for International Trade, since 2018; *b* 12 March 1962; *s* of late Dr Peter Stuart and Joan Stuart; *m* 1989, Anne Crawshaw; two *d*. *Educ*: Glenalmond Coll.; Selwyn Coll., Cambridge. Dir, CSL Publishing Ltd, 1987–. Mem. (C) Cambridge CC, 1998–2004 (Leader, Cons. Gp, 2000–04). An Asst Govt Whip, 2016–18. Chm., Educn Select Cttee, 2010–15. Chm., Cambridge Univ. Cons. Assoc., 1985. *Recreations*: cricket, cycling, motorcycling. *Address*: House of Commons, SW1A 0AA. *T*: (020) 7219 4340. *E*: grahamstuartmp@parliament.uk.

**STUART, Ian;** Group Managing Director and Chief Executive Officer, HSBC UK, since 2017; *b* Aberfeldy, 21 Sept. 1963. *Educ*: Univ. of Reading (Mgt Dip.). Bank of Scotland, 1979–85; Nat. Westminster Bank, then RBS, 1985–2007; Barclays Bank Ltd, 2007–13; Gp Gen. Manager and Hd, Commercial Banking Europe, HSBC, 2014–17. *Recreations*: keen golfer and sports fan.

**STUART, Rt Rev. Ian Campbell;** an Hon. Assistant Bishop, Diocese of Liverpool, 1999–2011; Pro Vice-Chancellor (formerly Assistant Vice-Chancellor), Liverpool Hope University, 2005–11, now Pro Vice-Chancellor Emeritus; *b* 17 Nov. 1942; *s* of Campbell Stuart and Ruth Estelle Stuart (*née* Butcher); *m* 1976, Megan Helen Williams; one *s* two *d*. *Educ*: Univ. of New England (BA, Cert Ed); Univ. of Melbourne (MA, DipEdAdmin). Headmaster, Christchurch Grammar Sch., Melbourne, 1977–84; ordained deacon and priest, 1985; Principal, Trinity Anglican Sch., Queensland, 1984–93; Warden, St Mark's Coll., James Cook Univ., 1993–96; Principal, All Souls' and St Gabriel's Sch., 1993–98; Diocese of North Queensland: Archdeacon, 1989–92; Asst Bishop, and Bishop Administrator, 1992–98; Chaplain, 1999–2001, Provost and Dir, Student Services, 2001–05, Liverpool Hope Univ. *Recreations*: reading, travel.

**STUART, Sir (James) Keith,** Kt 1986; Chairman, Associated British Ports Holdings PLC, 1983–2002; *b* 4 March 1940; *s* of James and Marjorie Stuart; *m* 1966, Kathleen Anne Pinder (*née* Woodman); three *s* one *d*. *Educ*: King George V School, Southport; Gonville and Caius College, Cambridge (MA). FCILT. District Manager, South Western Electricity Bd, 1970–72; British Transport Docks Board: Sec., 1972–75; Gen. Manager, 1976–77; Man.

Dir, 1977–82; Dep. Chm., 1980–82; Chm., 1982–83. Dir, Internat. Assoc. of Ports and Harbors, 1983–2000 (Vice-Pres., 1985–87); Pres., Inst. of Freight Forwarders, 1983–84. Director: Royal Ordnance Factories, 1983–85; BAA Plc, 1986–92; Seeboard plc, 1989–96 (Chm., 1992–96); City of London Investment Trust plc, 1999–2011; RMC Group plc, 1999–2005; Mallett plc, 2005–06. Consultant, Gas and Electricity Markets Authy, 2007– (Mem., 2000–06). Chm., UK-S Africa Trade Assoc., 1988–93; Vice-Chairman: UK-Southern Africa Business Assoc., 1994–95; Southern Africa Business Assoc., 1995–2002. Chartered Inst. of Transport: Mem. Council, 1979–88; Vice-Pres., 1982–83; Pres., 1985–86. Pres. and Chm. Bd, British Quality Foundn, 1997–2001. Freeman, City of London, 1985; Liveryman, Clockmakers' Co., 1987 (Mem. Ct of Assts, 1998–). Vice-Chm., Mgt Bd, London Mozart Players, 2002–09. Governor: Trinity Coll. of Music, 1991–2003; NYO of GB, 1997–2004; Chm., Trinity Coll. London, 2009–15, now Pres. Emeritus (Dir, 1992–2009); Trustee: Trinity Coll. of Music Trust, 2001–17 (Chm., 2008–17); Cambridge Univ. Musical Soc., 2012–15 (Chm., 2012–15). FRSA. Hon. FTCL 1998. *Recreation:* music. *Clubs:* Brooks's, Oxford and Cambridge (Trustee, 1989–94).

**STUART, Prof. (John) Trevor,** FRS 1974; Professor of Theoretical Fluid Mechanics, Imperial College of Science, Technology and Medicine, University of London, 1966–94, now Emeritus; Dean, Royal College of Science, 1990–93; *b* 28 Jan. 1929; *s* of Horace Stuart and Phyllis Emily Stuart (*née* Potter); *m* 1957, Christine Mary (*née* Tracy); two *s* one *d*. *Educ:* Gateway Sch., Leicester; Imperial Coll., London. BSc 1949, PhD 1951; FIC 1998. Aerodynamics Div., Nat. Physical Lab., Teddington, 1951–66; Sen. Principal Scientific Officer (Special Merit), 1961; Hd, Maths Dept, Imperial Coll., London, 1974–79, 1983–86. Vis. Lectr, Dept of Maths, MIT, 1956–57; Vis. Prof. of Maths, MIT, 1965–66; Vis. Prof. of Theoretical Fluid Mechanics, Brown Univ., 1978–; Hon. Prof., Tianjin Univ., China, 1983–. Member: Council, Royal Soc., 1982–84; SERC, 1989–94 (Chm., Mathematics Cttee, 1985–88). Pres., London Mathematical Soc., 2000–02 (Vice-Pres., 1999–2000). Editor, Biographical Memoirs of the Royal Soc., 2012–16. 1st Stewartson Meml Lectr, Long Beach, Calif., 1985; 1st DiPrima Meml Lectr, Troy, NY, 1985; Ludwig Prandtl Meml Lectr, Dortmund, 1986. Hon. ScD: Brown Univ., 1986; East Anglia, 1988. Senior Whitehead Prize, London Mathematical Soc., 1984; Otto Laporte Award, Amer. Physical Soc., 1987. *Publications:* (contrib.) Laminar Boundary Layers, ed L. Rosenhead, 1963; articles in Proc. Royal Soc., Phil. Trans Royal Soc., Jl Fluid Mech., Proc. 10th Internat. Cong. Appl. Mech., Jl Lub. Tech. (ASME). *Recreations:* theatre, music, gardening, reading, ornithology. *Address:* Mathematics Department, Imperial College, SW7 2AZ. *T:* (020) 7594 1033. *E:* t.stuart@imperial.ac.uk; 3 Steeple Close, Wimbledon, SW19 5AD. *T:* (020) 8946 7019. *E:* trevorstuart29@gmail.com.

**STUART, Sir Keith;** *see* Stuart, Sir J. K.

**STUART, Marian Elizabeth;** consultant on social issues, particularly child care projects, Department of Health, 1993–99; *b* 17 July 1944; *d* of William and Greta Stuart; one *s* one *d*. *Educ:* Eye Grammar School, Suffolk; Mount Grace Comprehensive School, Potters Bar; Leicester Univ. (MA). Joined Min. of Health as Asst Principal, 1967; Principal, DHSS, 1971; Asst Sec., 1979; Dep. Chief Inspector of Social Services, 1988; Under Sec., Finance Div., DoH, 1989–93; Resident Chm., CSSB, 1993–99 (on secondment). *Publications:* (jtly) Progress on Safeguards for Children Living Away from Home: a review of action since the People Like Us report, 2004; (jtly) Safeguards for Vulnerable Children, 2004. *Recreations:* golf, reading, bridge. *Address:* 18 Tower Rise, Richmond, Surrey TW9 2TS. *T:* (020) 8404 9709.

**STUART, Prof. Mary,** Hon. CBE 2017; DPhil; Vice Chancellor, University of Lincoln, since 2009; *b* Cape Town, SA, 4 March 1957; *d* of Thomas Cleary and Isobel Cleary (now Thompson); *m* 1978, Douglas Ian Stuart; two *d*. *Educ:* Chisipite Sen. Sch., Salisbury, Rhodesia; Univ. of Cape Town (BA Hist. and Drama 1979); Open Univ. (BA Hons Social Scis 1990; DPhil Social Policy 1998). Community Th. Coordinator and People's Educn Worker, People's Space Th., Cape Town, 1979–81; drama teacher, Westminster Play Assoc., 1981–82; Dir, Cast Underground Community Th., London, 1984–87; Lectr in Women's Educn, Streatham and Tooting Adult Educn Inst., 1987–89; Sen. Lectr in Special Educn, Lambeth Community Coll., 1990–91; University of Sussex: Lectr in Continuing Educn, 1991–95; Asst Dir, Centre for Continuing Educn, 1995–2000; Dir, Inst. of Educn, 2000–01; Pro Vice Chancellor, 2000–05; Dep. Vice Chancellor, Kingston Univ., 2006–09. Associate Res. Dir, Nat. Co-ordinating Team for HEFCE, DfES and LSC, 2001–05; Mem. Bd, HEFCE, 2015–18. Inspiring Leader Award, Guardian Higher Educn Network, 2018. *Publications:* Engaging with Difference: the 'other' in adult education (with A. Thomson), 1995; Collaborating for Change: managing widening participation in further and higher education, 2002; Not Quite Sisters: women with learning difficulties and social policy, 2002; Social Mobility and Higher Education: the life experiences of first generation entrants in higher education, 2012; contrib. chapters in books; contribs to Oral Hist., Jl Access Studies, Jl Access and Credit Studies, Adults Learning, Jl Access Policy and Practice, Internat. Jl of Lifelong Educn and Active Learning. *Recreations:* modern art, travel, jazz, theatre, film. *Address:* Vice Chancellor's Office, University of Lincoln, Brayford Pool, Lincoln LN6 7TS. *T:* (01522) 886100, *Fax:* (01522) 886200. *E:* mstuart@lincoln.ac.uk.

**STUART, Michael Albert;** QC (Scot.) 2017; *b* Leicester, 24 April 1966; *s* of Jonathan Balfour Stuart, TD and Gloria Josephine Stuart (*née* Della Porta); *m* 1998, Susan Kilgore; one *s* one *d*. *Educ:* BA Econs 1989; Univ. of Edinburgh (LLB 1999); DipLP 2000. Company director, 1994–97; Maclay Morley & Spens, LLP, 2000–02; admitted to Faculty of Advocates, 2003; Advocate Depute, 2009–13; Standing Jun. Counsel to Scottish Govt, 2016–17. Mem., Queen's Body Guard for Scotland, Royal Co. of Archers. *Recreations:* longbow archery, karate, scuba diving. *Address:* 16 Findhorn Place, Edinburgh EH9 2JP. *E:* msqc@advocates.org.uk. *Club:* New (Edinburgh).

**STUART, Moira,** OBE 2001; Presenter, Classic FM, since 2019; *b* 2 Sept. 1949; *d* of Harold and Marjorie Stuart. Joined BBC Radio as prodn asst, Talks and Documentaries Dept, 1981; newsreader, Radio 4; presenter of news progs incl. News After Noon, 5.40 News, Nine O'Clock News, Six O'Clock News; Presenter, Breakfast News, 2000–06. Presenter of radio and TV progs incl.: The Quincy Jones Story, Best of Jazz, Open Forum, Holiday Programme, Cashing In, Moira Stuart in Search of Wilberforce; BBC Radio 2 Breakfast News, 2010–19; Strong and Sassy: inspiring women of jazz, Radio 4, 2011; Kings of Cool, Radio 2, 2012; Music until Midnight, Radio 2, 2014–19; The Big Spell, Sky, 2016. Mem., Human Genetics Adv. Commn, 1996–99. Dr hc Edinburgh, 2006; Hon. Dr Canterbury Christ Church, 2013. *Address:* c/o Knight Ayton Management, 29 Gloucester Place, W1U 8HX.

**STUART, Murray;** *see* Stuart, C. M.

**STUART, Nicholas Willoughby,** CB 1990; Director General for Lifelong Learning, Department for Education and Skills (formerly Department for Education and Employment), 2000–01; *b* 2 Oct. 1942; *s* of late Douglas Willoughby Stuart and Margaret Eileen Stuart; *m* 1st, 1963, Sarah Mustard (marr. diss. 1974); one *d* (one *s* decd); 2nd, 1975, Susan Jane Fletcher; one *s* one *d*. *Educ:* Harrow Sch.; Christ Church Coll., Oxford (MA). Asst Principal, DES, 1964–68; Private Sec. to Minister for the Arts, 1968–69; Principal, DES, 1969–73; Private Secretary to: Head of the Civil Service, 1973; Prime Minister, 1973–76; Asst Sec., DES, 1976–78; Advr, Cabinet of Pres. of EEC, 1978–80; Under Sec., 1981–87, Dep. Sec., 1987–92, DES; Dir of Resources and Strategy, Dept of Employment, 1992–95; Dir Gen. for Employment and Lifelong Learning, later for Employment, Lifelong Learning and Internat. Directorate, DFEE, 1995–2000. Bd Mem., Investors in People (UK), 1995–2001; Dir, UFI Ltd, 2001–07. Pres., Nat. Learning and Work Inst. (formerly Nat. Inst. of Adult Contg Educn), 2012– (Vice-Pres., 2001–03; Chm., 2003–12); Council Member: Univ. of London Inst. of Educn, 2001–10; C&G, 2001–02; GDST, 2002–13; Member: QCA, 2002–10; Bd, CAFCASS, 2003–12. Trustee: Harrow Mission, 2001–18; PSI, 2002–09; Specialist Schs and Acads Trust, 2003–12 (Chm., 2009–12); Primary Shakespeare Co., 2014–; Mem., Grants Cttee, John Lyon's Charity, 1996–2018 (Chm., 2002–10); Hon. Treas., British Assoc. for Adoption and Fostering, 2015. Governor: John Lyon's Sch., 1996–2005; Harrow Sch., 1996–2009; South Hampstead High Sch., 1997–2002; Edward Wilson Sch., 2001–12 (Chm.). *Recreations:* collecting Tunbridgeware, cruising the canals.

**STUART, Rt Rev. Peter Derrick James;** *see* Newcastle, (NSW), Bishop of.

**STUART, Steven Lawrence;** QC (Scot.) 2008; *b* Dundee, 12 April 1954; *s* of Lawrence and Helen Stuart; *m* 1994, Elizabeth Hayter; one *d*. *Educ:* High Sch. of Dundee; Aberdeen Univ. (LLB Hons). Admitted as Advocate, 1979; Lectr in Scots Private Law, Univ. of Dundee, 1979–86; in practice as Advocate, specialising in valuation for rating, land law, planning law, licensing law, 1986–2019. *Publications:* (with A. Hajducki) Scottish Civic Government Licensing Law, 1994, 4th edn 2016. *Recreations:* gardening, walking, film noir.

**STUART, Trevor;** *see* Stuart, J. T.

**STUART-GRUMBAR, Jocelyn Atholl;** Clerk to the Clothworkers' Company and Chief Executive, Clothworkers' Foundation, since 2015; *b* London, 12 Dec. 1957; *s* of Raymond George Julian Grumbar and Shaen Grumbar; *m* 1987, Catherine Ponting; one *s* two *d*. *Educ:* Harrow Sch. With Grand Metropolitan, subseq. Diageo, incl. Internat. Brand Dir and Regl Dir, N Asia, 1983–96; Dyson: Dir, Internat. Business Develt, 1998–2002; Customer Services Dir, 2002–07; Man. Dir, Dyson China, 2007–09; Internat. Customer Dir, 2009–12; Internat. Develt Dir, Xerox Technol. Gp plc, 2013–15. *Address:* Clothworkers' Company, Clothworkers' Hall, Dunster Court, Mincing Lane, EC3R 7AH. *T:* (020) 7397 0100. *E:* jocelynstuartgrumbar@clothworkers.co.uk.

**STUART-MENTETH, Sir Charles (Greaves),** 7th Bt *cr* 1838, of Closeburn, Dumfriesshire; non-executive director and business angel, since 2000; *b* Cheshire, 25 Nov. 1950; *er s* of Sir James Wallace Stuart-Menteth, 6th Bt, and (Dorothy) Patricia, *d* of late Frank Greaves Warburton; *S* father, 2008; *m* 1976, Nicola St Lawrence; four *d* (one *s* decd). *Educ:* Radley Coll.; Trinity Coll., Oxford (BA Jurisprudence 1972); INSEAD, France (MBA 1977). Worked in banking, 1972–76; venture capital, 1977–85; Founder and CEO, Datavault Ltd, 1985–2000. *Recreations:* classic cars, grouse moors, farming. *Heir: b* (William) Jeremy Stuart-Menteth [*b* 31 Jan. 1952; *m* 1983, Rosalind Ann, *e d* of John Stephen Lane; one *s* one *d*]. *Address:* Monkcastle, Kilwinning, Ayrshire KA13 6PN. *T:* 07976 248563. *E:* csmmonkcastle@gmail.com.

**STUART-MOORE, Michael;** QC 1990; Vice-President of the Court of Appeal of Hong Kong, 1999–2009; a Deputy High Court Judge, since 2009; *b* 7 July 1944; *s* of (Kenneth) Basil Moore and Marjorie (Elizabeth) Moore; *m* 1973, Katherine Ann, *d* of William and Ruth Scott; one *s* one *d*. *Educ:* Cranleigh School. VSO, The Lawrence School, Sanawar, India, 1962–63. Called to the Bar, Middle Temple, 1966. A Deputy Circuit Judge, 1981–85; a Recorder of the Crown Court, 1985–2010; a Judge of the High Court, later of the Court of First Instance of the High Court, Hong Kong, 1993–98; a Judge of the Court of Appeal of the High Court, Hong Kong, 1998–99. Chairman: Hong Kong Market Misconduct Tribunal, 2011–15; Hong Kong Securities and Futures Appeals Tribunal, 2011–14; Hong Kong Deposit Protection Appeals Tribunal, 2011–14; Mandatory Provident Fund Schemes Appeal Bd, 2011–14. GBS (Hong Kong), 2009. *Recreations:* photography, travel, music, tennis. *Address:* 2 Hare Court, Temple, EC4Y 7BH. *T:* (020) 7353 5324. *Club:* Hong Kong.

**STUART-PAUL, Air Marshal Sir Ronald (Ian),** KBE 1990 (MBE 1967); RAF, retired; Chief Executive, British Aerospace, Saudi Arabia, 1997–2001; *b* 7 Nov. 1934; *s* of Dr J. G. Stuart-Paul and Mary (*née* McDonald); *m* 1963, Priscilla Frances (*née* Kay); one *s* one *d*. *Educ:* Dollar Acad.; RAF Coll., Cranwell. Served 14, 19, 56 and 92 Sqns and 11 and 12 Groups, 1957–73; Defence Attaché, Saudi Arabia, 1974–75; Stn Comdr, RAF Lossiemouth, 1976–78; RCDS, 1979; Dep. Comdr, NAEW Force, SHAPE, 1980–82; Dir of Ops Air Defence, RAF, 1982–83; AO Training, RAF Support Command, 1984–85; Dir Gen., Saudi Air Force Project, 1985–92. Freemason (Jun. Grand Warden, 2010–11; Asst Provincial Grand Master, Wilts, 2007–11). Pres., E Dorset Scouts, 2004–. *Recreation:* dog training. *Address:* Sycamore House, Gaunts Common, Wimborne, Dorset BH21 4JP. *T:* (01258) 840430. *Club:* Royal Air Force.

**STUART-SMITH, Rt Hon. Sir Murray,** KCMG 2012; Kt 1981; PC 1988; a Lord Justice of Appeal, 1988–2000; *b* 18 Nov. 1927; *s* of Edward Stuart-Smith and Doris Mary Laughland; *m* 1953, Joan Elizabeth Mary Motion, BA, JP, DL (High Sheriff of Herts, 1983) (*d* 2015); three *s* three *d*. *Educ:* Radley; Corpus Christi Coll., Cambridge (Foundn Scholar; 1st Cl. Hons Law Tripos, Pts I and II; 1st Cl. Hons LLM; MA; Hon. Fellow 1994). 2nd Lieut, 5th Royal Inniskilling Dragoon Guards, 1947. Called to the Bar, Gray's Inn, 1952 (Atkin Scholar), Bencher 1977; Vice-Treas., 1997; Treas., 1998; QC 1970; a Recorder of the Crown Court, 1972–81; a Judge of the High Court of Justice, QBD, 1981–88; Presiding Judge, Western Circuit, 1983–87. Judge of Court of Appeal: Gibraltar, 2001–11 (Pres., 2007–11); Bermuda, 2004. Jt Inspector into Grays Bldg Soc., 1979. Mem., Criminal Injuries Compensation Bd, 1980–81. Commissioner: for the Security Service, 1989–2000; for the Intelligence Services, 1994–2000. Chairman: Proscribed Orgns Appeal Commn, 2001–02; Pathogens Access Appeal Commn, 2002. Pres., Dacorum SO, 1994–. *Recreations:* playing 'cello, shooting, building, playing bridge. *Address:* Serge Hill, Abbots Langley, Herts WD5 0RY.

See also D. Docherty, T. R. S. P. Stuart-Smith.

**STUART-SMITH, Thomas Richard Stephen Peregrine;** landscape architect; Director, Tom Stuart-Smith Ltd, since 1998; *b* Watford, 14 Feb. 1960; *s* of Rt Hon. Sir Murray Stuart-Smith, *qv*; *m* 1986, Susan Jane Evans; two *s* one *d*. *Educ:* Radley Coll.; Corpus Christi Coll., Cambridge (BA 1981); Manchester Univ. (MLA 1984). Chartered Landscape Architect 1986. Landscape Architect: Colvin and Moggridge, 1985–87; Elizabeth Banks Associates, 1989–98; Chatsworth, 2018–. Major projects include: Broughton Grange, 2001; Queen's Jubilee Gdn, Windsor Castle, 2002; Trentham Gdns, 2004; Bicentenary Glasshouse Gdn, RHS Wisley, 2007; Le Jardin Secret, Marrakech, 2016; RHS Bridgewater, 2017. Chelsea Flower Show: Gold Medals 1998, 2000, 2001, 2003, 2005, 2006, 2008, 2010; Best in Show 2005, 2006, 2008. Trustee, Garden Mus., 2009–. Vice Pres., RHS, 2016–. Hon. Fellow, RIBA, 2017. *Publications:* The Barn Garden, 2011. *Recreations:* music, gardening. *Address:* Tom Stuart-Smith Ltd, 90–93 Cowcross Street, EC1M 6BF. *T:* (020) 7253 2100. *E:* info@tomstuartsmith.co.uk.

**STUART TAYLOR, Sir Nicholas (Richard),** 4th Bt cr 1917; b 14 Jan. 1952; s of Sir Richard Laurence Stuart Taylor, 3rd Bt, and of Iris Mary, d of Rev. Edwin John Gargery; S father, 1978; m 1984, Dr Malvena Elizabeth Sullivan, (marr. diss. 1999); two d. Educ: Bradfield. Admitted Solicitor, 1977. Recreation: ski-ing and other sports. Heir: none. Address: 30 Siskin Close, Bishop's Waltham, Hants SO32 1RQ. Club: Ski Club of Great Britain.

**STUART-WHITE, Ven. William Robert;** Archdeacon of Cornwall, 2012–18; Priest-in-charge, All Saints', Falmouth, since 2018; Team Leader, Transforming Mission in Falmouth, since 2018; b Bromsgrove, 21 Jan. 1959; s of Sir Christopher Stuart Stuart-White and of Pamela Stuart-White (née Grant); m 2012, Brenda Susan Venning (née Kendall); one s two d by a previous marriage. Educ: Winchester Coll.; Merton Coll., Oxford (BA Lit.Hum.; MA); Trinity Coll., Bristol (BA Theol.). Ordained deacon, 1986, priest, 1987; Asst Curate, Upper Armley, Leeds, 1986–91; Vicar, Austrey and Warton, Birmingham, 1991–98; Rector, Camborne, 1998–2006; Priest-in-charge: Stoke Climsland and Linkinhorne, 2006–09; Wadebridge, 2009–12; Rural Officer, Dio. of Truro, 2006–12. Hon. Canon, Truro Cath., 2009–. Recreations: rambling, photography. E: wstuartwhite@gmail.com.

**STUBBINGS, Paul John;** Headmaster, Cardinal Vaughan Memorial School, since 2011; b London, 13 Feb. 1966; s of John Stubbings and Moira Hamilton; m 1995, Anna Swaebe; one s one d. Educ: Royal Grammar Sch., Worcester; Univ. of Durham (BA Hons Classics); King's Coll. London (PGCE); Inst. of Education, Univ. of London (MA Dist.). Cardinal Vaughan Memorial School: Teacher of Classics, 1989–97; Asst Headmaster, 1997–2004; Dep. Headmaster, 2004–11. Recreations: Byzantine Empire, birdwatching. Address: Cardinal Vaughan Memorial School, 89 Addison Road, W14 8BZ. T: (020) 7603 8478, Fax: (020) 7602 3124. E: mail@cvms.co.uk. Club: National Liberal.

**STUBBS, Andrew James;** QC 2008; His Honour Judge Stubbs; a Circuit Judge, since 2016; b York, 16 April 1965; s of William Charles Stubbs and Janice Pickles; m 1998, Jane Louise; two s. Educ: St Peter's Sch., York; Nottingham Univ.; Inns of Court Sch. of Law. Called to the Bar, Lincoln's Inn, 1988; a Recorder, 2003–16; Hd of Chambers, 2012–16; Mem., QC Panel of Prosecution Counsel for Serious Fraud Office, 2013–16. Recreations: golf, theatre, cycling, wine. Address: York Crown Court, The Castle, York YO1 9WZ.

**STUBBS, Imogen Mary, (Lady Nunn);** actress; b 20 Feb. 1961; d of late Robin Desmond Scrivener Stubbs and Heather Mary Stubbs (née McCracken); m 1994, Trevor Robert Nunn (see Sir T. R. Nunn) (marr. diss. 2011); one s one d. Educ: St Paul's Girls' Sch.; Westminster Sch.; Exeter Coll., Oxford (BA 1st cl. Hons); RADA. Theatre: Cabaret, Ipswich, 1985; The Rover, 1986, The Two Noble Kinsmen, 1987, Desdemona in Othello, 1989, RSC; Heartbreak House, Theatre Royal, Haymarket, 1992; title rôle, St Joan, Strand, 1994; Uncle Vanya, Chichester Fest., then Albery, 1996; A Streetcar Named Desire, Theatre Royal, Haymarket, 1996; Closer, Lyric, 1998; Betrayal, RNT, 1998; The Relapse, RNT, 2001; Three Sisters, Bath Royal and tour, 2002; Mum's The Word, Albery and tour, 2003; Hamlet, Old Vic, 2004; title rôle, The Duchess of Malfi, W Yorks Playhouse, 2006; Alphabetical Order, Hampstead Th., 2009; The Glass Menagerie, Salisbury Playhouse and tour, 2010; Private Lives, Royal Exchange, Manchester, 2011; Little Eyolf, Jermyn St Th., 2011; Salt, Root and Roe, Trafalgar Studios, 2011; A Marvellous Year for Plums, Chichester Fest., 2012; Orpheus Descending, Royal Exchange, Manchester, 2012; Third Finger, Left Hand, Trafalgar Studios, 2013; Strangers on a Train, Gielgud, 2013; Little Revolution, Almeida, 2014; Communicating Doors, Menier Chocolate Factory, 2015; The Long Road South, King's Head Th., 2016; Things I Know to be True, Lyric Hammersmith, 2016; The Be All and End All, York Th. Royal, 2018; Honour, Park Th., 2018; play written: We Happy Few, Gielgud, 2004; television: The Rainbow, 1988; Othello, 1990; After the Dance, 1992; Anna Lee, 1994; Big Kids; films: Nanou, 1985; Erik the Viking, 1988; Fellow Traveller, 1990; True Colors, 1990; Sandra, c'est la vie; Lucy in Sense and Sensibility, 1995; Viola in Twelfth Night, 1996; Three Guesses; dir, Snow on Saturday (Kino Best British Short Award). Publications: (jtly) Amazonians, 1998; regular contribs to Daily Telegraph and Harpers & Queen.

**STUBBS, Prof. Michael Wesley,** PhD; Professor of English Linguistics, University of Trier, Germany, 1990–2013; b 23 Dec. 1947; s of late Leonard Garforth Stubbs and Isabella Wardrop (née McGavin). Educ: Glasgow High Sch. for Boys; King's Coll., Cambridge (MA); Univ. of Edinburgh (PhD 1975). Res. Associate, Univ. of Birmingham, 1973–74; Lectr in Linguistics, Univ. of Nottingham, 1974–85; Prof. of English in Educn, Inst. of Educn, Univ. of London, 1985–90. Vis. Prof. of Linguistics, Univ. of Tübingen, Germany, 1985; Hon. Sen. Res. Fellow, Univ. of Birmingham, 1994–99. Chm., BAAL, 1988–91. Mem., Nat. Curriculum English Working Gp (Cox Cttee), 1988–89. Publications: Language, Schools and Classrooms, 1976, 2nd edn 1983; Language and Literacy, 1980; Discourse Analysis, 1983; Educational Linguistics, 1986; Text and Corpus Analysis, 1996; Words and Phrases, 2001; (jtly) Text, Discourse and Corpora, 2007; articles in Lang. and Educn, Applied Linguistics, Jl of Pragmatics, Functions of Lang., Text, Internat. Jl of Corpus Linguistics, Lang. and Lit. Recreation: walking. Address: FB2 Anglistik, University of Trier, 54286 Trier, Germany.

**STUBBS, Rebecca;** QC 2012; b Barnsley, S Yorks, 1971; d of James Stuart Stubbs and Diane Stubbs; m 2007, Sharif Asim Shivji; two s. Educ: Darton High Sch.; Downing Coll., Cambridge (BA Hons Law 1993). Called to the Bar, Middle Temple, 1994 (Harmsworth Entrance Exhibnr, Queen Mother Scholar), Bencher, 2013; called to Supreme Court of Grenada and WI Associated States, 2005; Jun. Counsel to the Crown, 2000–07. Vice Chm., Access to the Bar Cttee, 2007, Mem., One Case One Fee Wkg Gp, 2008, Bar Council; Mem., Wkg Gp on Alternative Business Structures, Bar Standards Bd, 2008–09. Barrister Rep., Bankruptcy and Companies Court Users' Cttee, 2007–15. Member: Chancery Bar Assoc., 1995– (Mem., Cttee, 2013–); Commercial Bar Assoc., 1995–; Advocates for Internat. Develt, 2009–. Registered to appear in DIFC Court, 2012. FRSA 2004. Publications: (contrib.) Butterworths Practical Insolvency, 1999; (contrib.) Mithani on Directors' Disqualification, 2002; (Consultant Ed.) French on Applications to Wind Up Companies, 2007; (contrib.) Butterworths Guide to the Legal Services Act, 2009. Address: Maitland Chambers, 7 Stone Buildings, Lincoln's Inn, WC2A 3SZ. T: (020) 7406 1200, Fax: (020) 7406 1300. E: rstubbs@maitlandchambers.com. Clubs: Kandahar; Spinnaker Sailing.

**STUBBS, Sukhvinder K.;** see Kaur-Stubbs, S.

**STUBBS, Thomas,** OBE 1980; HM Diplomatic Service, retired; b 12 July 1926; s of Thomas Stubbs and Lillian Marguerite (née Rumball, formerly Bell); m 1951, Dorothy Miller (d 1997); one s one d. Educ: Heaton Tech. Sch., Newcastle upon Tyne. Served in Army, 1944–48. Joined Min. of Nat. Insce, later Min. of Pensions and Nat. Insce, 1948; transf. to CRO, 1960; New Delhi, 1962; CRO, 1964; Wellington, NZ, 1965; Vice-Consul, Düsseldorf, 1970; seconded to BOTB, 1974; First Sec. (Commercial) and Consul, Addis Ababa, 1977; Consul, Hannover, 1980; Dep. High Comr, Madras, 1983–86. Mayor, Borough of Spelthorne, 1992–93 (Mem. (C) Council, 1987–2003; Vice-Chairman: Leisure and Amenities Cttee, 1987–89; Planning Cttee, 1999–2002; Chairman: Personnel Cttee, 1989–91; Resources Cttee, 1995–96; Finance Sub-Cttee, 1996–98; Dep. Mayor, 1991–92). Chm., SE Employers, 2000–03. Pres., Spelthorne Cons. Constituency Assoc., 2002–05. Hon. Pres., County of Middlesex Trust, 1992–. Recreation: reading. Address: 17 Chester Close, Ashford, Middx TW15 1PH. Club: Sunbury-on-Thames Conservative.

**STUBBS, Sir William (Hamilton),** Kt 1994; Chairman, Oxford Radcliffe Hospitals NHS Trust, 2003–08; b 5 Nov. 1937; s of Joseph Stubbs and Mary Stubbs (née McNicol); m 1963, Marie Margaret Pierce; three d. Educ: Workington Grammar Sch.; St Aloysius Coll., Glasgow; Glasgow Univ. (BSc, PhD). Res. Associate, Univ. of Arizona, 1963–64; with Shell Oil Co., San Francisco, 1964–67; teaching, 1967–72; Asst Dir of Educn, Carlisle, 1972–74; Asst Dir of Educn, 1974–76, Second Dep. Dir of Educn, 1976–77, Cumbria; Second Dep. Educn Officer, 1977–79, Dir of Educn (Schools), 1979–82, Educn Officer and Chief Exec., 1982–88, ILEA; Chief Exec., PCFC, 1988–93; Chief Exec., FEFC, 1992–96; Rector, The London Inst., 1996–2001. Member: Council, CRAC, 1993–2004; Nat. Cttee of Inquiry into Higher Educn, 1996–97; Bd, NACETT, 1997–2002; Council, Inst. of Employment Studies, 1997–2005; Design Council, 1999–2004; Chairman: CBI Educn Foundn, 1996–99; Qualifications and Curriculum Authority, 1997–2002. Hon. Prof., Dept of Continuing Educn, Univ. of Warwick, 1993. Trustee, Geffrye Mus., 1999–2007; Pres., Assoc. of Colls Trust, 2001–03; Mem., Awards Council, Royal Anniversary Trust, 2002–12. Chancellor, Thames Valley Univ., 2001–04. Chm. Govs, Capel Manor Coll., 2014–17 (Hon. Fellow, 2017); Gov., Birkbeck Coll., London, 1998–2004. CCMI; FRSA. DUniv: Open, 1995; Sheffield Hallam, 1996; Strathclyde, 2004; Hon. DLitt: Exeter, 1996; Bath Spa, 2010; Hon. DSc UWE, 1997; Hon. DEd Greenwich, 2007; Hon. LLD Brighton, 2007. Address: Churchill House, 4 Oxford Street, Woodstock, Oxon OX20 1TR.

**STUCKEY, Rev. Thomas James;** lecturer, preacher and teacher; President of the Methodist Conference, 2005–06; b 10 May 1940; s of Howard and Pat Stuckey; m 1966, Christine Plympton; two s one d. Educ: Yeovil Grammar Sch.; City Univ. (BScEng 1964); Richmond Coll. (BD London Univ. 1967); Edinburgh Univ. (MTh 1972). Engrg appts with Westland Aircraft and Fairey Aviation, 1956–63; theol trng, Richmond Coll., 1964–67; Methodist Circuit appts, Coatbridge, Airdrie and Armadale, Bristol Mission, Exeter, 1967–76; Tutor in Applied Theol., Hartley Victoria Coll., 1982–90; Supt, Reading and Silchester Methodist Circuit, 1990–98; Chair, Southampton Methodist District, 1998–2006; Canon, Salisbury Cathedral, 2002–06. Vis. Scholar, Sarum Coll., 2000–19. Publications: Into the Far Country, 2003; Beyond the Box, 2005; The Edge of Pentecost, 2007; The Wrath of God Satisfied?, 2012; (contrib.) As a Fire By Burning, 2013; Singing the Lord's Song in a Strange Land, 2017; Methodism Unfinished, 2019; articles in Worship and Preaching, Epworth Review, etc. Recreations: music, theology, theatre, films, watercolour painting, MG club, enjoying the company of my wife. Address: 11 The Meadway, Christchurch BH23 4NT.

**STUCLEY, Sir Hugh (George Coplestone Bampfylde),** 6th Bt cr 1859; DL; Lieut Royal Horse Guards, retired; b 8 Jan. 1945; s of Major Sir Dennis Frederic Bankes Stucley, 5th Bt, and Hon. Sheila Bampfylde (d 1996), o d of 4th Baron Poltimore; S father, 1983; m 1969, Angela Caroline, e d of Richard Charles Robertson Toller, MC, Theale, Berks; two s two d. Educ: Milton Abbey School; Royal Agricultural College, Cirencester. Chm., Badgworthy Land Co., 1999–2004. Chm., Devon Br., CLA, 1995–97; Pres., Devonshire Assoc., 1997–98. Chm., Wessex Br., Historic Houses Assoc., 2007–12. DL 1998, High Sheriff, 2006–07, Devon. Heir: s George Dennis Bampfylde Stucley [b 26 Dec. 1970; m 1997, Amber (marr. diss. 2013), yr d of Thomas Gage; two s]. Address: Affeton Castle, Worlington, Crediton, Devon EX17 4TU. Club: Sloane.

**STUDD, Anne Elizabeth;** QC 2012; a Recorder, since 2007; b London, 1 July 1964; y d of Sir (Robert) Kynaston Studd, 3rd Bt and late Anastasia Studd (née Leveson-Gower); m 2000, Simon Dennis Marsden Freeland, qv; one s one d. Educ: Southover Manor Sch., Lewes; Westfield Coll., Univ. of London (BA Hons Hist.); Poly. of Central London (DipLaw). Called to the Bar, Gray's Inn, 1988, Bencher, 2017. Recreations: gardening, cooking, family. Address: 5 Essex Court, Temple, EC4Y 9AH. T: (020) 7410 2000. E: studd@5essexcourt.co.uk.
See also Sir E. F. Studd, Bt.

**STUDD, Sir Edward (Fairfax),** 4th Bt cr 1929; b 3 May 1929; s of Sir Eric Studd, 2nd Bt, OBE, and Stephana (d 1976), o d of L. J. Langmead; S brother, 1977; m 1960, Prudence Janet, o d of Alastair Douglas Fyfe, OBE, Riding Mill, Northumberland; two s one d. Educ: Winchester College. Lieutenant Coldstream Guards, London and Malaya, 1947–49; Macneill & Barry Ltd, Calcutta, 1951–62; Inchcape & Co. Ltd, London, 1962–86 (Dir, 1974–86). Master, Merchant Taylor's Co., 1987–88 and 1993–94. Recreation: rural activities. Heir: s Philip Alastair Fairfax Studd [b 27 Oct. 1961; m 1987, Georgina (marr. diss. 1999), d of Sir Roger Neville, VRD; one s one d].

**STUDD, Prof. John William Winston,** MD, DSc; FRCOG; Professor of Gynaecology, Imperial College London, 1998–2005, now Emeritus; Consultant Gynaecologist, Chelsea and Westminster Hospital, 1994–2005; b 4 March 1940; s of late Eric Dacombe Studd and Elsie Elizabeth (née Kirby); m 1980, Margaret Anne Johnson, qv; one s two d. Educ: Royal Hosp. Sch., Holbrook; Univ. of Birmingham (MB ChB 1962; MD 1969; DSc 1995). MRCOG 1967, FRCOG 1982. Res. Fellow, Queen Elizabeth Hosp., Birmingham, 1967–70; Lectr in Obstetrics and Gynaecol., UC of Rhodesia, 1970–71; Consultant and Sen. Lectr, Univ. of Nottingham, 1974–75; Consultant Obstetrician and Gynaecologist, KCH, 1975–94; Dir, Fertility and Endocrine Centre, Lister Hosp., Chelsea, 1987–95. Visiting Professor: Yale Univ. 1982; Duke Univ. 1984; Univ. of Singapore, 1989; Harvard Univ., 1995; Cornell Univ., 2008. Mem. Council, 1980–97, and Pres., Sect. of Obstetrics and Gynaecol., 1994–95, RSocMed. Vice Pres., Nat. Osteoporosis Soc., 1995– (Chm., 1992–95); Pres., Internat. Soc Reproductive Medicine. Chm., PMS and Menopause Trust. Ed., Yearbook, 1993–97, Publications Officer, 1994–97, RCOG. Editor: Menopause Digest, 1994–; Obstetric and Gynaecol Reviews, 1994–; The Diplomate, 1995–; Member Editorial Board: Brit. Jl Obstetrics and Gynaecol.; Jl RSocMed; N American Jl of Menopause; Eur. Menopause Jl; Brit. Jl Hosp. Medicine; Osteoporosis Internat.; Ed.-in-Chief, Menopause Internat., 2009–. Blair Bell Gold Medal, RSM, 2009. Publications: Management of Labour, 1985; Self Assessment in Obstetrics and Gynaecology, 1985; Management of the Menopause, 1988, 4th edn 2003; (ed) Progress in Obstetrics and Gynaecology, Vols 1–18, 1982–2008; Multiple Choice Questions in Obstetrics and Gynaecology, 1993; The Menopause and Osteoporosis, 1993; Annual Progress in Reproductive Medicine, Vols 1 and 2, 1993–94; (with S. S. Sheth) Vaginal Hysterectomy, 2001; contrib. numerous articles on the menopause, osteoporosis, pre-menstrual syndrome, post-natal depression, labour, sickle cell disease and HIV infection in women. Recreations: theatre, opera, history of medicine, collecting antiquarian medical books. Address: 27 Blomfield Road, W9 1AA. T: (020) 7266 0101; London PMS & Menopause Centre, 46 Wimpole Street, W1G 8SD.

**STUDD, Margaret Anne;** see Johnson, Margaret A.

**STUDER, Cheryl Lynn;** opera singer, freelance since 1986; Professor of Voice, University of Music, Wuerzburg, since 2003; b Midland, USA, 24 Oct. 1955; m 1982, G. Marmarides; one d; m 1992, E. Schwarz; one d; m 2008, Michalis Doukakis. Educ: Interlochen Arts Acad.; Oberlin Coll. Conservatory, Ohio; Univ. of Tennessee; Tanglewood Berkshire

Music Center; Hochschule für Musik und darstellende Kunst, Vienna (Masters Degree). First professional recital, Virginia Highlands Fest., 1977; operatic début, Bavarian State Opera, 1980; débuts: Lyric Opera, Chicago, 1984; Bayreuth Fest., 1985; La Scala, Milan, 1987; Royal Opera House, Covent Garden, 1987; NY Met, 1988; Vienna State Opera, 1989; has sung at all major opera houses and festivals in the world; regular appearances at Bayreuth and Salzburg Fests; extensive concert tours with all major orchestras and conductors; world-wide recitals. Many recordings, incl. La Traviata, Faust, Salomé, Lohengrin, Figaro, Strauss' Four Last Songs. Franz Schubert Inst. Award, 1979; Grammy Award, 1991, 1994; Internat. Classical Music Award for best female singer, 1992; Furtwängler Preis, 1992; Vocalist of the Year Award, Musical America Directory of Performing Arts, 1994; Terras Sem Sombre, 2011; Ovation Award, 2012.

**STUDHOLME, Sir Henry (William),** 3rd Bt *cr* 1956, of Perridge, Co. Devon; DL; *b* 31 Jan. 1958; *s* of Sir Paul Henry William Studholme, 2nd Bt and Virginia (*d* 1990), *yr d* of Sir (Herbert) Richmond Palmer, KCMG, CBE; *S* father, 1990; *m* 1988, Sarah Lucy Rosita (*née* Deans); two *s* one *d. Educ*: Eton; Trinity Hall, Cambridge (MA). FCA, CTA. Man. Dir, Wood & Wood Internat. Signs Ltd, 1990–92; Chm., Integer plc, 2002–07. Chairman: SW Woodland Show, 1995–2004; SW Regl Adv. Cttee on Forestry, 2000–07; SW Cttee Country Land and Business Assoc., 2001–03; SW Chamber of Rural Enterprise, 2003–09; SW Food and Drink, 2004–08; Member: England Forestry Forum, 2002–07; Bd, SW RDA, 2002–12 (Chm., Rural Adv. Gp and Audit Cttee, 2003–08; Chm., 2009–12). A Forestry Comr, 2007– (Chm., 2013–). Dir, Phaunos Timber Fund Ltd, 2011–17 (Chm., 2012–17). Dir, Assoc. of Lloyd's Members, 2009–. Chm., William Robinson Gravetye Charity, 2009–. Hon. Prof., Univ. of Exeter, 2017–. Pres., Devon County Agricultural Show, 2019–20. Hon. FICFor. DL Devon, 2006. Peter Savill Award, 2019. *Heir: s* Joshua Henry Paul Studholme, *b* 2 Feb. 1992. *Address*: Forestry Commission, 620 Bristol Business Park, Bristol BS16 1EJ. *Clubs*: Brooks's; MCC.

*See also* J. G. Studholme.

**STUDHOLME, Joseph Gilfred,** MBE 2015; Chairman and Co-founder, Getmapping (formerly Getmapping.com) plc, 1998–2002; *b* 14 Jan. 1936; *s* of Sir Henry Gray Studholme, 1st Bt, CVO and Judith Joan Mary (*née* Whitbread); *m* 1959, Rachel Fellowes, *d* of Sir William Albemarle Fellowes, KCVO; three *s. Educ*: Eton; Magdalen Coll., Oxford (MA). Nat. Service, 2nd Lieut, KRRC (60th Rifles), 1954–56. Man. Dir, King & Shaxson Ltd (Billbrokers), 1961–63; Co-founder, Chm. and Man. Dir, Editions Alecto Gp, 1963–2002. Chm., Byam Shaw Sch. of Art, 1988–94 (Mem. Council, 1963–94). Chm., Wessex Regl Cttee, NT, 1996–2006 (Mem., 1993–2006). Chm., Salisbury and South Wiltshire Mus., 2007–14. Sen. Fellow, RCA, 1999. *Address*: The Court House, Lower Woodford, Salisbury, Wilts SP4 6NQ. *T*: (01722) 782237. *Clubs*: Garrick, Double Crown, MCC.

**STUDZINSKI, John Joseph,** CBE 2008; Managing Director and Vice Chairman, PIMCO, since 2018; *b* 19 March 1956; *s* of Alfred Edward Studzinski and Jennie Mary Studzinski (*née* Gaieski). *Educ*: Bowdoin Coll., Maine (AB Biol. and Sociol. 1978); Univ. of Chicago (MBA Finance and Marketing 1980). Morgan Stanley International Ltd: Head: Corporate Finance, Europe, 1989–92; M&A, Europe, 1992–97; Investment Banking, Europe, 1997–2001; Dep. Chm., 2001–03; Chief Exec., Corporate, Investment Banking and Markets, and Mem., Gp Mgt Bd, HSBC, 2003–06; Vice Chm., Investor Relations and Business Develt, and Sen. Man. Dir, Blackstone Gp Internat. Ltd, 2006–18. Trustee: Royal Parks Foundn, 1996; Bowdoin College, 1998–; Tate Foundn, 2006–; Internat. Youth Foundn, 2012–; Getty Foundn, 2015–. Founder and Chm., Genesis Foundn, 2000–. Member: Bd of Dirs, Human Rights Watch, 1999– (Vice-Chm., 2005–); Trustees, Passage Day Centre for Homeless, 2000–; Council, Royal Coll. of Art, 2004–. Chairman: Emmaus Revives Lives Campaign, 2006–; Benjamin Franklin House, 2007–. Vice Chair, Atlantic Council. Prince of Wales's Ambassador's Award, 2000; Pres., American Friends of Royal Foundn of Duke and Duchess of Cambridge (formerly of Duke and Duchess of Cambridge and Prince Harry, then the Duke and Duchess of Sussex), 2013–. KSS, KSG 2001. Prince of Wales Medal for Arts Philanthropy, 2014. *Recreations*: voluntary work with homeless, human rights, nurturing young artists. *Address*: PIMCO, 1633 Broadway, New York, NY 10019, USA.

**STUNELL,** family name of **Baron Stunell**.

**STUNELL,** Baron *cr* 2015 (Life Peer), of Hazel Grove in the County of Greater Manchester; **Robert Andrew Stunell,** Kt 2013; OBE 1995; PC 2012; *b* 24 Nov. 1942; *s* of late Robert George and Trixie Stunell; *m* 1967, Gillian (*née* Chorley); two *s* three *d. Educ*: Surbiton Grammar Sch.; Manchester Univ.; Liverpool Poly. Architectural asst, CWS Manchester, 1965–67, Runcorn New Town, 1967–81, freelance, 1981–85; various posts incl. Political Sec., Assoc. of Liberal Democrat Councillors, 1985–97. Member: Chester City Council, 1979–90; Cheshire CC, 1981–91 (Leader, Lib Dem Gp); Stockport MBC, 1994–2002. Vice-Chm., ACC, 1985–90. Contested: (L) 1979, (Lib/Alliance), 1983 and 1987, City of Chester; (Lib Dem) Hazel Grove, 1992. MP (Lib Dem) Hazel Grove, 1997–2015. Lib Dem Chief Whip, 2001–06; Lib Dem front bench spokesman on communities and local govt, 2006–08; Parly Under-Sec. of State, DCLG, 2010–12. Chair, Local Election Campaign Team, 2008–10. Mem., Cttee on Standards in Public Life, 2016–. *Address*: 84 Lyme Grove, Romiley, Stockport SK6 4DJ; House of Lords, SW1A 0PW.

**STURDY, Julian Charles;** MP (C) York Outer, since 2010; *b* Yorks, 1971; *s* of Robert William Sturdy, *qv; m* Victoria; one *s* one *d. Educ*: Harper Adams Univ. Farming and property business. Mem., Harrogate BC, 2002–07. Member: Transport Select Cttee, 2010–12; Energy and Climate Change Cttee, 2015–16; Envmt, Food and Rural Affairs Cttee, 2017–. Contested (C) Scunthorpe, 2005. *Address*: House of Commons, SW1A 0AA.

**STURDY, Robert William;** Member (C) Eastern Region, England, European Parliament, 1999–2014 (Cambridgeshire, 1994–99); *b* 22 June 1944; *s* of late Gordon Sturdy and of Kathleen Sturdy (*née* Wells); *m* 1969, Elizabeth Hommes; one *s* one *d. Educ*: Ashville Coll., Harrogate. Partner, G. E. Sturdy & Son. European Parliament: Cons. spokesman on agriculture, 1994–2001, on rural affairs, 2001–04, on internat. trade, 2004–06; Vice-Pres., Canadian Interparly Delegn, 1999–2002; Chm., Aust. and NZ Interparly Delegn, 2002–04; Mem., ACP-EU Delegn, 2004–14; Mem., Agriculture Cttee, 1994–2004; Substitute Mem., Cttee on Envmt, 1999–2009, on Agriculture, 2004–14; EPP-ED Co-ordinator for Internat. Trade, 2004–09; ECR Co-ordinator for Internat. Trade, 2009–14; Co-Chair, WTO Steering Gp of Parly Assembly, 2004–14; Vice Chm., Internat. Trade Cttee, 2009–14. *Recreations*: fishing, ski-ing, cricket, golf.

*See also* J. C. Sturdy.

**STURGEON, Rt Hon. Nicola;** PC 2014; Member (SNP) Glasgow Southside, Scottish Parliament, since 2011 (Glasgow, 1999–2007, Glasgow Govan, 2007–11); First Minister, since 2014 (Deputy First Minister, 2007–14); Leader, Scottish National Party, since 2014; *b* 19 July 1970; *d* of Robert and Joan Sturgeon; *m* 2010, Peter Murrell. *Educ*: Univ. of Glasgow (LLB Hons; Dip. Legal Practice). Trainee Solicitor, McClure Naismith, Glasgow, 1993–95; Asst Solicitor, Bell & Craig, Stirling, 1995–97; Associate Solicitor, Drumchapel Law Centre, Glasgow, 1997–99. Dep. Leader, SNP, 2004–14. Cabinet Sec., for Health and Wellbeing, 2007–12, for Cities Strategy, 2011–12, for Infrastructure, Investment and Cities, 2012–14, Scottish Parlt. *Recreations*: theatre, reading. *Address*: Scottish Government, St Andrew's House, Edinburgh EH1 3DG. *T*: (0300) 244 4000.

**STURGIS, Dr Alexander John;** Director, Ashmolean Museum, since 2014; Fellow, Worcester College, Oxford, since 2014; *b* London, 6 Nov. 1963; *s* of Tim and Jean Sturgis; *m* 1994, Anna Benn; two *s* one *d. Educ*: Marlborough Coll.; University Coll., Oxford (BA Hons Hist.); Courtauld Inst. (PhD Hist. of Art 1990). Educn Officer, 1991–99, Curator, Exhibns and Progs, 1999–2005, National Gall.; Dir, Holburne Mus., Bath, 2005–14. *Publications*: Faces, 1998; Telling the Time, 2000; Understanding Paintings, 2000; Dan's Angel, 2002; Rebels and Martyrs, 2006; Presence: the art of portrait sculpture, 2012. *Recreations*: magic, Arsenal FC. *Address*: Ashmolean Museum, Beaumont Street, Oxford OX1 2PH.

**STURKEY, (Robert) Douglas,** CVO 1995; AM 1999; PhD; Official Secretary to the Governor-General of Australia, 1990–98; Secretary of the Order of Australia, 1990–98; *b* 7 Sept. 1935; *s* of late James Robert Sturkey and Jessie Grace (*née* Meares). *Educ*: Wesley Coll., S Perth; Univ. of WA (BA Hons); ANU (MA 2000; PhD 2004). Mem., Australian Diplomatic Service, 1957–90: service abroad at Wellington, Lagos, Suva, Malta, Calcutta; Counsellor, later Dep. Perm. Rep., UN, New York, 1974–77; Ambassador to Saudi Arabia (also concurrently to countries of Arabian peninsula), 1979–84; Head, S Asia, Africa and ME Br., Dept of Foreign Affairs, Canberra, 1984–87; Principal Advr, Asia Div., Dept of Foreign Affairs and Trade, Canberra, 1987–90. Dir, ACT Bd, St John Ambulance (Australia), 2005–14. Priory Officer, Australian Priory of the Order of St John, 1999–2011. KStJ 2008 (CStJ 1992). *Publications*: The Limits of American Power: prosecuting a Middle East peace, 2007. *Recreations*: opera, music, theatre.

**STURLEY, Air Marshal Philip Oliver,** CB 2000; MBE 1985; FRAeS; defence adviser and mentor; *b* 9 July 1950; *s* of William Percival Sturley and Delia Agnes Sturley (*née* Grogan); *m* 1972, Micheline Leetch; one *d. Educ*: St Ignatius Coll., London; Southampton Univ. (BSc 1971). FRAeS 1993. Pilot trng, RAF Coll., Cranwell, 1971–72; 41 Sqn Coningsby, 1973–76; II (Army Co-operation) Sqn Laarbruch, 1977–80, 1982–84, OC, 1987–89; HQ 1 (British) Corps Bielefeld, 1980–82; jsdc, 1984; Comd Briefing Team, 1984–85, Plans, 1985–86, HQ Strike Comd; Air Plans, 1989–90, Dir of Air Staff Briefing and Co-ordination, 1990–92, MoD; OC RAF Cottesmore, 1992–94; Sec. IMS, HQ NATO, 1994–98; SASO HQ Strike Comd and AOC No 38 Gp, 1998–2000; ACAS, MoD, 2000–03; COS AirNorth Comd, Ramstein, 2003–05; Sen. Mentor, HCSC, Shrivenham, 2006–. Specialist Advr to H of C Defence Cttee, 2006–14. Sen. Military Advr, Shephard Gp, 2006–12; Mil. Advr, Tangent Link, 2012–. Manager, British Gliding Team, 2008–12. Pres., 2005–11, Life Vice Pres., 2011, Pres., European Area, 2012–18, RAFA. Hon. Air Cdre 4624 Sqdn, RAuxAF, 2012–. CCMI 2010–15. QCVSA 1980. *Recreations*: gliding, golf. *Address*: c/o RAFA HQ, Atlas House, Wembley Road, Leicester LE3 1UT. *Club*: Royal Air Force.

**STURMAN, James Anthony;** QC 2002; *b* 19 July 1958; *s* of Gp Capt. Roger Sturman, RAF (retd) and Anne Sturman; *m* 1986, Marcella Mineo; three *s. Educ*: Bembridge Sch., Isle of Wight; Reading Univ. (LLB). Called to the Bar, Gray's Inn, 1982, Bencher, 2005; criminal defence, regulatory and sports law barrister. *Recreations*: soccer, cricket, punk rock music, my three children. *Address*: 2 Bedford Row, WC1R 4BU. *T*: (020) 7440 8888, *Fax*: (020) 7242 1738. *E*: jsturman@2bedfordrow.co.uk.

**STURRIDGE, Charles;** writer and director; *b* 24 June 1951; *s* of Jerome Francis Sturridge and Alyson Sturridge (*née* Burke); *m* 1985, Phoebe Nicholls; two *s* one *d. Educ*: Beaumont Coll.; Stonyhurst Coll.; University Coll., Oxford (BA). Mem., NYT, 1967–70; film début as actor, If..., 1968; director: theatre includes: The Seagull, Queen's, 1985; Endgame, Gate, Dublin, transf. Barbican, 2006; films include: Runners, 1982; (co-writer) A Handful of Dust, 1988; (co-writer) Where Angels Fear to Tread, 1991; (screenplay) Fairytale—A True Story, 1997 (Best Children's Film, British Acad., 1998); Ohio Impromptu, 2001 (Best TV Drama, LWT Awards); (writer and producer) Lassie, 2005; television includes: 16 episodes of Coronation Street; 4 documentary films for World in Action, 1976; Brideshead Revisited, 1981 (Best Series, BAFTA); A Foreign Field, 1993; Gulliver's Travels, 1996 (Best Series, Emmy Awards); (also writer) Longitude, 2000 (Best Series, BAFTA); (also writer) Shackleton, 2002; The No 1 Ladies Detective Agency, 2009; The Road to Coronation Street, 2010; (also writer) The Scapegoat, 2012; Dates, 2013; Churchill's Secret, 2016; Marcella, 2018; MotherFatherSon, 2019. Chair, Dirs UK (formerly DPRS), 2007–15. *Address*: c/o Independent Talent Group, 40 Whitfield Street, W1T 2RH.

**STURRIDGE, Sir Nicholas (Antony),** KCVO 2007 (CVO 1986); Surgeon-Dentist to the Queen, 1975–2007; *s* of Frank Sturridge. *Educ*: Royal Dental Hosp., Univ. of London (BDS 1961); Northwestern Univ., Chicago (DDS 1963). LDSRCS. Pt-time clin. teaching post, UCH Dental Sch., 1964–74; in practice with Drs Sturridge & Barrett, later Drs Sturridge, Capp & Barrett, 1964. Hon. Consultant, King Edward VII Hosp., Sister Agnes. Past President: Amer. Dental Soc. of Europe; Amer. Dental Soc. of London. *Address*: c/o 152 Harley Street, W1G 7LH.

**STURROCK, John Garrow;** QC (Scot.) 1999; Chief Executive, Core Solutions Group, since 2004; *b* 15 April 1958; *s* of John Chesser Sturrock and Lilian Sturrock; *m* 1984, Fiona Swanson; two *s* one *d. Educ*: Univ. of Edinburgh (LLB 1st Cl. Hons 1980); Univ. of Pennsylvania (LLM 1985). MCIArb 2001. Solicitor, 1983–84; Harkness Fellow, 1984–85; admitted Faculty of Advocates, 1986; in practice as advocate, 1986–2002; Dir, Trng and Educn, Faculty of Advocates, 1994–2002. Door Tenant, Brick Court Chambers, 2013–. Standing Jun. Counsel to Dept of Transport in Scotland, 1991–94; Accredited Mediator, CEDR, 1996. Visiting Professor: of Advocacy Skills and Conflict Resolution, Univ. of Strathclyde, 1999–2009; Sch. of Social and Political Sci., Univ. of Edinburgh, 2016–. Member: Jt Standing Cttee on Legal Educn, Scotland, 1988–2005; Judicial Studies Cttee, Scotland, 1997–2005. Assessor, SHEFC, 1995–96. FRSA 2001. Dist. Fellow, Internat. Acad. of Mediators, 2009–. Hon. LLD Edinburgh Napier, 2010. *Recreations*: family, church, golf, music. *Address*: Core Solutions Group, 10 York Place, Edinburgh EH1 3EP. *E*: John.Sturrock@core-solutions.com.

**STURROCK, Philip James,** MBE 2014; Chairman, PanCathay Consulting Ltd, since 2004; *b* 5 Oct. 1947; *s* of James Cars Sturrock and Joyce Sturrock (*née* Knowles); *m* 1st, 1972, Susan Haycock (marr. diss. 1995); one *s* two *d*; 2nd, 2000, Madeleine Frances Robinson. *Educ*: Queen Mary's School, Walsall; Trinity College, Oxford (MA); Manchester Business School (MBA). Managing Director: IBIS Information Services, 1972–80; Pitman Books, 1980–83; Group Man. Dir, Routledge & Kegan Paul, 1983–85; Chm., Redwood Publishing Ltd, 1985–86; Chm. and Man. Dir, Cassell, 1986–99; Chm. and Gp Chief Exec., Continuum Internat. Publishing Gp, 1999–2006; Chm., Osprey Publishing, 2007–08. Chm., Wandle Housing Assoc., 2010–13; Dir, The Publishing Partnership, 2010–16. Mem., Industrial Develt Adv. Bd, 2009–15. Chm., Soc. of Bookmen, 2001–02. Governor, Pusey House, Oxford, 1975–95. Trustee: St Albans Cathedral Educn Trust, 1988–2003; United St Saviour's Charity, 2008–14 (Treas., 2008–10; Chm., Trustees, 2010–14); Southwark Cathedral Develt Trust, 2012–; Mem., Southwark Cathedral Fundraising Council, 2012–16; Mem., Salisbury Diocese Investment

**STUTTARD**, Panel, 2016–. Gov., Queen Mary's Grammar Sch., Walsall, 2008–17 (Chm., Finance, 2009–11; Chm., Govs, 2011–17); Mem. Council and Chm., Finance and Gen. Purposes Cttee, Inst. of Educn, Univ. of London, 2012–15; Mem. Council, UCL, 2015– (Treas., 2017–19); Chm., Mercian Multi-Acad. Trust, 2018–. Chairman: St Albans Internat. Organ Fest., 1983–84; Hatfield Philharmonic Orch., 1988–92; S Wessex Organ Soc., 2016–. Hon. Vis. Prof., Beijing Normal Univ., 2005–10. FRSA 1992. Liveryman, Glaziers' Co., 1983– (Master's Steward, 2010–11). *Recreations:* reading, walking, music, food and wine. *Address:* Allington Lodge, 52 West Allington, Bridport, Dorset DT6 5BH. *T:* (01308) 420304. *Club:* Athenæum.

**STUTTARD, Caroline Anne**; *see* Stockmann, C. A.

**STUTTARD, David Ashton**; freelance writer, lecturer and dramaturg, since 2004; *b* Perth, Scotland, 1959; *s* of Philip Stuttard and Isobel Stuttard; *m* 2010, Emily Jane Birtwell. *Educ:* Morrison's Acad., Crieff; Univ. of St Andrews (MA Hons Classics); Dundee Coll. of Educn (PGCE). Teacher of Classics, Edinburgh Acad., 1985–87; Curriculum Coordinator, St Leonards Sch., St Andrews, 1987–94; Hd of Classics, Queen Margaret's Sch., Escrick, York, 1994–96; Founder and Jt Artistic Dir, Actors of Dionysus, 1993–2004. Course tutor, Madingley Hall, Univ. of Cambridge, 2015. Fellow, Goodenough Coll., London, 2018. *Publications:* An Introduction to Trojan Women, 2005; (with Sam Moorhead) AD410: the year that shook Rome, 2010; (ed) Looking at Lysistrata, 2010; Power Games, 2012; (with Sam Moorhead) The Romans Who Shaped Britain, 2012; (with Sam Moorhead) 31BC: Antony, Cleopatra and the fall of Egypt, 2012; Parthenon: power and politics on the Acropolis, 2013; A History of Ancient Greece in 50 Lives, 2014; (ed) Looking at Medea, 2014; (ed) Looking at Bacchae, 2016; Greek Mythology, A Traveller's Guide, 2016; Nemesis: Alcibiades and the fall of Athens, 2018; (ed) Looking at Antigone, 2017; Roman Mythology, A Traveller's Guide, 2019; Looking at Ajax, 2019; Phoenix: Cimon and the rise of Athens, 2020; articles in Wall Street Jl, Minerva, British Mus. Magazine and All About History. *Recreations:* baroque music, spending time in Graeco-Roman theatres, opera, reading detective fiction, gardening, making and eating ice cream. *Address:* c/o A. M. Heath & Company Ltd, 6 Warwick Court, Holborn, WC1R 5DJ. *E:* david@davidstuttard.com.

**STUTTARD, Sir John (Boothman)**, Kt 2008; JP; Lord Mayor of London, 2006–07; *b* 6 Feb. 1945; *s* of Thomas Boothman Stuttard and Helena Stuttard (*née* Teasdale); *m* 1970, Lesley Sylvia Daish; two *s. Educ:* Shrewsbury Sch.; Churchill Coll., Cambridge (BA 1966, MA 1970). FCA 1979. Teacher with VSO, SOAS Coll., Brunei, 1966–67; Coopers & Lybrand, then PricewaterhouseCoopers: articled clerk, then Chartered Accountant, 1970–75; Partner, 1975–2005; Chm., Coopers & Lybrand China, subseq. PricewaterhouseCoopers China, 1994–99; Advr, 2005; Dep. Chm., Adv. Panel, PricewaterhouseCoopers LLP, 2008–12; Consultant, 2012–18. Advr, Central Policy Rev. Staff, Cabinet Office, 1981–83. Director: China-Britain Business Council, 2000–06; Finnish-British Chamber of Commerce, 2001–10 (Chm., 2002–06; Life Pres., 2007); Co-Chm., Kazakh-British Trade and Industry Council, 2009–13. Fellow, 48 Gp, 2008. Mem., Fund Raising Adv. Bd, 2000–05, Council, 2006–13, VSO. University of Cambridge: Mem., Appts Bd, 1977–81; Mem. Adv. Cttee, East Asia Inst., Faculty of Oriental Studies, 2001–; By-Fellow, Møller Centre, Churchill Coll., Cambridge, 2008–14. Chancellor, City Univ., 2006–07. Mem. Court and Fellow, Bridewell Royal Hosp. and Gov., King Edward VII Sch., Witley, 2002–13. President: London and Gtr London Merchant Navy Assoc., 2007–; City of London Sheriffs' Soc., 2010–; Shaftesbury Civic Soc., 2013–; Shaftesbury and Dist Histl Soc., 2018–. Trustee: Lord Mayor of London's Disaster Relief Appeal, 2002–12; Charities Aid Foundn, 2003–09 (Chm., Audit, Risk and Compliance Cttee, 2003–06); Lord Mayor's 800th Anniv. Appeal, 2005–12; Morden Coll., 2005–; St Paul's Cathedral Foundation: Advr, 2005–11; Chm., 2011–13; Fellow, 2013–. Patron: Three Faiths Forum, 2007–; Churchill Archives Centre, 2015–. Hon. Treas., New Horizon Youth Centre, 1972–77; Dir, Totteridge Manor Assoc., 1980–2005 (Chm., 2002–05); Hon. Vice-President: Totteridge Residents Assoc., 2006–13; Cambridge Univ. Land Soc., 2008. Hon. ACCA 2007; Hon. FCSI 2007; Hon. FGS (Hon. FGSM 2007). Hon. Fellow, Foreign Policy Assoc., USA, 2000; Hon. Mem., Maritime London, 2007. Alderman, City of London, Lime Street, 2001–13; Sheriff, City of London, 2005–06; Liveryman: Glaziers' and Painters of Glass Co., 2000– (Ct Asst, 2003–; Master, 2009–10); Chartered Accountants' Co., 2002– (Ct Asst, 2004–17; Master, 2011–12); Plumbers' Co., 2005– (Hon. Ct Asst, 2005–); Hon. Liveryman, Educators' Co., 2014– (Hon. Freeman, 2002–14, Ct Asst, 2002–14, Master, 2013–14, Guild, later Co. of Educators). JP City of London, 2001. Freedom, City of Lahore, 2007. Hon. DLitt City, 2006. KStJ 2006. Knight 1st Cl., 1995, Comdr, 2004, Order of the Lion (Finland); Companion, League of Mercy, 2007; Silver Medal, City of Helsinki, 2007; 20th Anniversary Jubilee Medal (Kazakhstan), 2011. *Publications:* The New Silk Road—Secrets of Business Success in China Today, 2000; Whittington to World Financial Centre: the City of London and its Lord Mayor, 2008; Travels in a Lifetime, 2015; A History of British McCalls, 2016; The Worshipful Company of Chartered Accountants in England and Wales, The First Forty Years, 2017; The Turbulent Quaker of Shaftesbury, 2018. *Recreations:* travelling, rallying old cars, theatre, opera, tennis. *Clubs:* Travellers, East India, Walbrook; Rolls-Royce Enthusiasts of Great Britain, 20-Ghost (Chm., 2010–18); China (Beijing and Hong Kong).

**STUTTLE, Barbara Charmaine**, CBE 2004; independent healthcare consultant, specialising in transformation and turn-around, since 2011; Deputy Chief Executive Officer, Chief Nurse and Director of Quality and Nursing, South West Essex Primary Care Trust, 2008–11; *b* 4 May 1952; *d* of Philip George Albert Coote and Edith Marion Coote; two *s. Educ:* Hurlingham Sch. for Girls, Fulham; Sweyne Sch., Rayleigh; Southend Hosp.; City Univ., London (MSc Health Mgt 1996). SRN, 1971–73; Staff Nurse, Southend Hosp., 1974–75; Dist Nurse, Southend, 1975–79; Southend Community Care Trust: Dist Nurse, 1981–89; Nursing Officer, 1989–90; Asst Dir of Nursing, 1990–93; Sen. Manager, Thameside Community Care Trust, 1993–99; Dir of Integrated Care and Exec. Nurse, Castle Point and Rochford PCT, 1999–2005; Dir, Primary Care and Modernisation, Thurrock PCT, 2005–06; Exec. Nurse, SW Essex PCT, 2006–08. Nurse Prescribing Proj. Lead, London and SE Reg., DoH, 1998–2002; Nat. Clinical Lead Nursing and Midwifery, Connecting for Health, NHS, 2005–09. Fellow, Queen's Nursing Inst., 2007. Hon. Dr Health Scis Anglia Ruskin, 2009. *Publications:* Independent and Supplementary Prescribing: an essential guide, 2004, 2nd edn 2009. *Recreations:* going to the gym - reluctantly, reading, eating out, drinking wine, spending time with grandchildren.

**STYBELSKI, Peter Stefan**; Chief Executive, Cumbria County Council, 2004–09; *b* 26 Oct. 1952; *s* of Czeslaw and Mary Stybelski; *m* 1980, Lorna Bell; one *s. Educ:* Plymouth; Univ. of London (BSc Hons Geog. 1972); Wye Coll., Univ. of London (MSc Landscape, Ecol., Design and Maintenance 1976). Dist Grounds Superintendent, Bucks AHA, 1976–78; Parks Superintendent, Oxford CC, 1978–80; Asst Dir (Ops), Blackpool BC, 1980–83; Chief Amenities Officer, RBK&C, 1983–89; Dir, Leisure Services, Bolton MBC, 1989–2000; Town Clerk and Chief Exec., Carlisle CC, 2000–04. Vice Chm., Carlisle Youth Zone Ltd, 2010–12; non-executive Director: Story Homes Ltd, 2012–15; Story Contracting Ltd, 2012–15; Land and Lakes (Anglesey) Ltd, 2014–16. Mem. Bd, Sport England, 2010–13. Trustee, Churches Trust for Cumbria, 2010–16. *E:* peter@stybelski.com.

**STYLE, Vice-Adm. Charles Rodney**, CBE 2002; Commandant, Royal College of Defence Studies, 2008–12; Director, White Water Wave Ltd, since 2011; *b* 15 Jan. 1954; *s* of Lt-Comdr Sir Godfrey William Style, CBE, DSC, RN, and Sigrid Elisabeth Julin (*née* Carlberg); *m* 1981, Charlotte Amanda Woodford; three *d. Educ:* Eton; St Catharine's Coll., Cambridge (Exhibnr; BA Geog. 1975; MA); BRNC Dartmouth (Queen's Sword, 1976); Pinnacle course, USA. Served: HMS Endurance, 1977–78; Navigating Officer, HMS Bacchante, 1978–79; Royal Yacht Britannia, 1980–81; Commanding Officer: HMS Sandpiper, 1981–82; HMS Wotton, 1982–83; Ops Officer, HMS Arethusa, 1984–85; Naval Assistant to C-in-C Fleet, 1985–87; CO, HMS Andromeda, 1988–89; Naval Planner, MoD, 1989–92; COS to Comdr UK Task Gp, 1992–93; CO, HMS Campbeltown, 1993–95 (Task Gp Comd, Gulf, 1993–94); Dep. Flag Officer Sea Trng, 1995–96; hcsc 1997; Prin. SO to CDS, 1997–98; rcds 1999; CO, HMS Illustrious, 2000–01 (Task Gp Comd, Arabian Sea, 2001); Capability Manager (Strategic Deployment and Precision Attack), MoD, 2002–04; Comdr UK Maritime Force, 2004–05; DCDS (Commitments) and Dir of Ops, MoD, 2006–07. US Mil. Pinnacle course, 2006. Exec.-in-Residence, Manchester Business Sch., 2009–. Vis. Res. Fellow, Dept of War Studies, KCL, 2012–. Mem. Adv. Gp, Eur. Mentoring and Coaching Council, 2010–12. Mem., Adv. Panel, Concordis Internat., 2012–; Consultant, Veritas Internat., 2012–13. Trustee: Britannia Assoc., 2000–09; Kids4Kids, 2012–15; Queen Elizabeth Foundn, 2013–18 (Dep. Chm., 2016–); Advr, St Martin-in-the-Fields Renewal Proj., 2005–09; Mem. Cttee, Never Such Innocence, 2014–. Maritime Advr, Confidential Hazardous Incident Reporting Prog., 2015–16. Mem., Master Mariners' Co., 2003–14. Younger Brother, Trinity House, 1991–. *Publications:* (jtly) In Business and Battle, 2012. *Recreations:* sailing, fishing, reading, music, paramotoring. *E:* charlesstyle.cs@gmail.com. *Club:* Royal Yacht Squadron (Cowes).

**STYLE, Christopher John David**; QC 2006; *b* 13 April 1955; *s* of David and Anne Style; *m* 1990, Victoria Miles; three *s* one *d. Educ:* St Bees Sch.; Trinity Hall, Cambridge (BA Law 1976). Admitted solicitor, 1979; called to the Bar, Lincoln's Inn, 2012. Solicitor with Linklaters, 1977–2012. *Publications:* (with Charles Hollander) Documentary Evidence, 1984, 6th edn 1997. *Recreations:* my family, the country, high mountains. *Address:* One Essex Court, Temple, EC4Y 9AR. *T:* (020) 7583 2000, *Fax:* (020) 7583 0118. *E:* cstyle@oeclaw.co.uk.

**STYLE, Sir William Frederick**, 13th Bt *cr* 1627, of Wateringbury, Kent; *b* 13 May 1945; *s* of Sir William Montague Style, 12th Bt, and La Verne, *d* of late T. M. Comstock; *S* father, 1981, but his name does not appear on the Official Roll of the Baronetage; *m* 1st, 1968, Wendy Gay (marr. diss. 1971), *d* of Gene Wittenberger, Hartford, Wisconsin, USA; two *d*; 2nd, 1986, Linnea Lorna (*d* 2015), *d* of Donn Erickson, Sussex, Wisconsin, USA; one *s* two *d. Heir: s* William Colin Style, *b* 1 Sept. 1995.

**STYLER, His Honour Granville Charles**; a Circuit Judge, 1992–2013; *b* 9 Jan. 1947; *s* of Samuel Charles Styler and Frances Joan Styler (*née* Clifford); *m* 1971, Penelope Darbyshire; three *d. Educ:* King Edward VI Sch., Stratford-upon-Avon. Called to the Bar, Gray's Inn, 1970; a Recorder, 1988–92; Resident Judge and Designated Family Judge, Stoke on Trent Combined Court Centre, 1995–2007. *Recreations:* carriage driving, tennis, gardening, horse racing, golf. *Club:* Outer Hebrides Tennis.

**STYLES, Amanda Jane**; *see* Vickery, A. J.

**STYLES, Graham Charles Trayton**; HM Diplomatic Service, retired; Head, Kosovo, Albania and Macedonia Team, Foreign and Commonwealth Office, 2015–16; *b* Farnborough, 16 April 1958; *s* of late Roy Trayton Styles and of Audrey Jean Breething (*née* Kelynack); *m* 1984, Rachael Jane Hopkins; two *d. Educ:* Sevenoaks Sch.; Orpington Coll. of Further Educn; Birmingham Univ. (BA Hons English 1981). Entered FCO, 1977; Registry Officer, Central and Southern African Dept, FCO, 1977–78; on sabbatical, 1978–81; Registry Officer, Eastern Eur. Soviet Dept, FCO, 1981–85; Registry/Communications Officer, Mauritius, 1985–88; Entry Clearance Officer, Paris, 1989–92; Postings Officer, FCO, 1992–95; Third Sec., UK Delegn to OSCE, Vienna, 1995–98; Desk Officer Sierra Leone, Africa Dept, FCO, 1998–2001; Nat. Contact Point, EU Twinning Prog., EU Dept, FCO, 2001–02; Deptl Report Writer, Directorate for Strategy and Innovation, FCO, 2002–04; Hd, Mekong and Burma Team, SE Asia Dept, FCO, 2004–06; First Sec., UK Mission to UN, Vienna, 2006–11; Ambassador to Rep. of Guinea, 2011–14. *Recreations:* reading, running, disused railways, Arsenal FC, eating rice pudding. *E:* rachaelstyles@ymail.com.

**STYLES, Prof. Morag Chrystine Campbell**; Professor of Children's Poetry, University of Cambridge, 2011–14; Fellow, Homerton College, Cambridge, until 2014, now Emeritus; *b* Dundee, 19 Sept. 1947; *d* of Ruairidh Ross and Bette McRobb Ross; *m* 1968, Jon Styles (marr. diss. 1983); one *s. Educ:* Edinburgh Univ. (BSc Social Sci. 1970); Homerton Coll., Cambridge (PGCE 1971). Primary sch. teacher, Cambridge, 1971–74; Homerton College, Cambridge: Lectr (pt-time) in English and Maths Educn, 1974–84; Dep. Co-ordinator of Curriculum Studies; Homerton College, then Faculty of Education, 1984–2014: Lang. Co-ordinator; Sen. Lectr; Reader. *Publications:* From the Garden to the Street: 300 years of poetry for children, 1998; (with E. Arlzpe) Children Reading Pictures, 2003; (with E. Arlzpe) Reading Lessons from the 18th Century: mothers, children and text, 2006; (ed jtly) Acts of Reading, 2009; (ed jtly) Poetry and Childhood, 2010; (with M. Salisbury) Children's Picturebooks: the art of visual storytelling, 2012; (ed jtly) Teaching Caribbean Poetry, 2013. *Recreations:* theatre, music, opera, art, reading, bird-watching, nature, socialising with friends, travelling, miniature glamorous shoe collecting.

**STYLES, Prof. Peter**, PhD; CGeol, FGS; FRAS; CSci; FIMMM; geophysicist; Professor of Applied and Environmental Geophysics, 2000–15, now Emeritus Professor, Head of Energy and Sustainability Strategy, 2009–10, and Professorial Research Fellow in Applied and Environmental Geophysics, since 2010, Keele University; *b* 4 Sept. 1950; *s* of Daniel and Alice Styles; *m* 1975, Roslyn Schmeisser; two *s* two *d. Educ:* Dukes Grammar Sch., Alnwick; Wadham Coll., Oxford (BA Hons Physics 1972); Univ. of Newcastle upon Tyne (PhD Geophysics 1977). Lectr, 1977–87, Sen. Lectr, 1987–88, in Geophysics, Univ. of Wales, Swansea; Sen. Lectr, 1988–98, Reader, 1998–99, in Geophysics, Univ. of Liverpool; Hd, Sch. of Earth Sci. and Geog., 2001–03, Dir, Envmt, Phys. Scis and Applied Maths Res. Inst., 2005–09, Keele Univ. Chair, Criteria Proposals Gp: Managing Radioactive Waste Safely, DEFRA, 2007–; Member: Geosphere Characterisation Panel, Nuclear Decommissioning Agency, 2009–; Royal Soc. Working Party on Nuclear Non-Proliferation, 2009–11. Pres., Internat. Commn on Hydrocarbon Exploration and Seismicity, 2013–. Mem. Bd, British Geol. Survey, 2001–09. Dist. Vis. Lectr in Near-Surface Geophysics, European Assoc. of Geoscientists and Engrs, 2012. Professional Sec., 1996–99, Pres., 2004–06, Geol. Soc. of London; Pres., BAAS (Geol. Section), 2007. Trustee, Underground Coal Gasification Assoc., 2009–. Jt author, report for DECC, Preese Hall Shale Gas Fracturing: review and recommendations for induced seismic mitigation, 2012. FRSA. William Smith Medal, Geol Soc., 2014; Medal of Merit, Eur. Fedn of Geologists, 2014; Service Award for Geophysics, RAS, 2016. *Recreations:* guitar, singing British folk music, photography, travelling. *Address:* 6 Swan Lane, Bunbury, Cheshire CW6 9RA.

**STYLIANIDES, Christos;** Member, European Commission, 2014–19; European Union Ebola Coordinator, 2014–19; *b* Nicosia, Cyprus, 26 June 1958; *m*; one *s. Educ:* Aristoteleion Univ., Thessaloniki (Dental Surgeon 1984); JFK Sch. of Govt, Harvard Univ. Govt spokesperson, Cyprus, 1998–99; MHR, Cyprus, 2006–13; Govt spokesperson, 2013–14. Mem., OSCE Parly Assembly, 2006–11.

**SUÁREZ, Michael Angel;** management consultant, since 2018; Chief Executive, Cheshire East Council, 2013–18; *b* 1 Nov. 1967; *s* of Antonio Suárez and Mary Theresa Suárez; *m* 1996, Jacqueline Elizabeth Bates; two *s* one *d. Educ:* Keele Univ. (BSc Jt Hons Biol. and Mgt Sci.). CPFA 1995. Southwark LBC, 1989–98; Asst Dir Finance for Educn, Soc. Services and Housing, Westminster CC, 1998–2002; Strategic Dir of Finance and Property, Slough BC, 2002–05; Exec. Dir of Finance, subseq. Finance and Resources, Lambeth LBC, 2005–13. Non-exec. Dir, London Authorities' Mutual Ltd (Dep. Chm., 2009–); Mem., London Finance Adv. Cttee, 2006–. Member: Soc. of London Treasurers, 2005; Soc. of Municipal Treasurers, 2005. Mem. Bd, CIPFA, 2011–13 (Member: Internat. Strategy Bd; Remuneration Cttee; Chm., Local Govt Policy Panel, 2011–). Treas., Squirrels Day Nursery, 2003–05; non-exec. Dir, Lambeth Coll., 2012–13. Columnist, MJ, 2008–. Public Sector Finance Dir of Yr, Accountancy Age Awards, 2008. *Recreations:* squash, swimming and when I can, scuba diving, five-a-side football.

**SUBAK-SHARPE, Prof. John Herbert,** CBE 1991; FRSE 1970; Professor of Virology, University of Glasgow, 1968–94, now Emeritus; Hon. Director, Medical Research Council Virology Unit, 1968–94; *b* 14 Feb. 1924; *s* of late Robert Subak and late Nelly (*née* Bruell), Vienna, Austria; *m* 1953, Barbara Naomi Morris (*d* 2018); two *s* one *d. Educ:* Humanistic Gymnasium, Vienna; Univ. of Birmingham. BSc (Genetics) (1st Cl. Hons) 1952; PhD 1956. Refugee by Kindertransport from Nazi oppression, 1939; farm pupil, 1939–44; HM Forces (Parachute Regt), 1944–47. Asst Lectr in Genetics, Glasgow Univ., 1954–56; Mem. scientific staff, ARC Animal Virus Research Inst., Pirbright, 1956–60; Nat. Foundn Fellow, California Inst. of Technology, 1961; Mem. Scientific staff of MRC, in Experimental Virus Research Unit, Glasgow, 1961–68. Visiting Professor: US Nat. Insts of Health, Bethesda, Md, 1967; US Univ. of Health Services, Bethesda, Md, 1985; Vis. Fellow, Clare Hall, Cambridge, 1986–87. Sec., Genetical Soc., 1966–72, Vice-Pres. 1972–75, Trustee 1971–99. Member: European Molecular Biology Orgn, 1969– (Chm., Course and Workshops Cttee, 1976–78); Genetic Manipulation Adv. Gp, 1976–80; Biomed. Res. Cttee, SHHD Chief Scientist Orgn, 1979–84; British Nat. Cttee of Biophysics, 1970–76; Governing Body, W of Scotland Oncological Orgn, 1974–; Scientific Adv. Body, W German Cancer Res. Centre, 1977–82; Governing Body, Animal Virus Res. Inst., Pirbright, 1986–87; MRC Training Awards Panel, 1985–89 (Chm., 1986–89); Scientific Adv. Gp of Equine Virology Res. Foundn, 1987–98; MRC Cell and Disorders Bd, 1988–92. CIBA Medal, Biochem. Soc., 1993. *Publications:* articles in scientific jls on genetic studies with viruses and cells. *Recreations:* travel, hill walking, bridge. *Address:* 63 Kelvin Court, Glasgow G12 0AG. *T:* (0141) 334 1863. *Club:* Athenæum.

**SUBBA ROW, Raman,** CBE 1991; Chairman, Test and County Cricket Board, 1985–90; *b* 29 Jan. 1932; *s* of Panguluri Venkata Subba Row and Doris Mildred Subba Row; *m* 1960, Anne Dorothy (*née* Harrison); two *s* one *d. Educ:* Whitgift Sch., Croydon; Trinity Hall, Cambridge (MA Hons). Associate Dir, W. S. Crawford Ltd, 1963–69; Man. Dir, Management Public Relations Ltd, 1969–92; internat. cricket match referee, 1993–2002. *Recreations:* sport, bridge. *Address:* Leeward, Manor Way, South Croydon, Surrey CR2 7BT. *T:* (020) 8688 2991. *Clubs:* Royal Air Force, Institute of Directors, MCC, Surrey County Cricket (former Chm.); Bloemfontein (South Africa); Cricket of India (Bombay); Kingston Cricket (Jamaica).

**SUBEDI, Dr Durga Bahadur;** Ambassador of Nepal to the Court of St James's, since 2016, and to Ireland, since 2017; *b* Jhapa, Nepal, 5 Aug. 1966; *s* of Man Bahadur Subedi and Basundhara Devi Subedi; *m* Poonam Rajyalaxmi Karki. *Educ:* Univ. of Leeds (MA Internat. Relns); Tribhuvan Univ., Nepal (MPA; PhD Foreign Policy and Diplomacy of Modern Nepal 2008); Lumbini Buddhist Univ., Nepal (PhD Buddhism in Modern Japan 2017). Desk Officer, Ministry of Foreign Affairs, Nepal, 1990–93; Second Sec., Embassy of Nepal, Yangon, 1994–99; Official Sec. to Minister of Foreign Affairs, 1999–2002; First Sec., Permanent Mission of Nepal to UN, NY and Consul, Consulate Gen. of Nepal, NY, 2002–05; Dep. Chief of Protocol, 2005–07; Minister-Counsellor and Dep. Chief of Mission, Tokyo, 2007–11; Dir, Dept of Hospitality, 2011–13; Jt Sec., Min. of Foreign Affairs, 2013–15. Vis. Prof., Ehime Univ., Matsuyama, Japan, 2010–15. Mem., Internat. Relns Cttee, Nepal Acad., 2009–12. Nepal Acad. Gold Medal, 1988; Nat. Talent Award, 2000; Civil Service Medal, 2001; Civic Gold Medal, 2003; Tribhuvan Univ. Gold Medal, 2011; Govt Literary Gold Medal, 2014. *Publications: in Nepali:* Selected Poems of DuBaSu Chhetri, 1990; Primary Poems of DuBaSu Chhetri, 1990; Contemporary Nepali Ghazal, 1993; Contemporary Nepali Poems, 1996; Timile Chhodeka Yadharu, 1997; Jyoti Jyoti Jiban-Jyoti, 1998; Mutu Chorne Aakhaharu, 2003; Primary Ghazals of DuBaSu Chhetri, 2009; Kolaz Man, 2010; Nepali Language, Literature and Culture in Myanmar, 2010; Ashwamedh Yagyaka Ghodahan, 2010; Nepali Language and Literature in Japan, 2011; Chupchap-Chupchap, 2013; Nepalese Poetry on Human Rights, 2015; Nepalese Poets and Poetry in Britain, 2016; Man Bhitra Pani Akash Hunchha, 2016; Ardhamudit Adharharu, 2016; Pagliyou Poonam Palpal, 2016; Nirbandha Man, 2017; Amalekh Man, 2017; Atirikta Man, 2017; New Poems of DuBaSu Chhetri, 2017; *in English:* New Nepal, 2010; Digital Freedom of Expression, 2016; All in One, 2017; 200 Years of Nepal-Britain Relations, 2017. *Recreations:* badminton, yoga, music. *Address:* Embassy of Nepal, 12A Kensington Palace Gardens, W8 4QU. *T:* (020) 7229 1594. *E:* ambassador@nepembassy.org.uk, dubasuchhetri@gmail.com.

**SUBRAMANIAN, Lilian Rachel;** see Greenwood, L. R.

**SUCH, Frederick Rudolph Charles;** Immigration Adjudicator, later Immigration Judge, London Region, 2000–06; *b* 19 June 1936; *s* of Frederick Sidney Such and Anne Marie Louise (*née* Martin); *m* 1961, Elizabeth, *d* of late Judge Norman and Mrs Harper, Cloughton, Yorkshire; one *s* one *d. Educ:* Mbeya Sch., Tanganyika Territory, E Africa (Tanzania); Taunton Sch.; Keble Coll., Oxford (MA). Called to the Bar, Gray's Inn, 1960; practised: London, 1960–69, then North Eastern Circuit, 1969–2000; a Recorder, 1979–2001. FCIArb 1995. *Recreations:* theatre, opera, Real tennis. *Address:* 38 Church Road, Barnes, SW13 9HN. *Clubs:* Jesters, Queen's; Jesmond Dene Real Tennis.

**SUCHET, David,** CBE 2011 (OBE 2002); actor; associate artiste, Royal Shakespeare Co., since 1970 (Governor, since 2005); *b* 2 May 1946; *s* of late Jack Suchet and Joan Suchet (*née* Jarché); *m* 1976, Sheila Ferris, actress; one *s* one *d. Educ:* Wellington Sch.; LAMDA (Best Drama Student, 1968). *Stage:* repertory theatres, incl. Chester, Birmingham, Exeter, Worthing, Coventry, 1969–73; for Royal Shakespeare Co.: Romeo and Juliet (Mercutio and Tybalt), As You Like It (Orlando), Once in a Lifetime (Glogauer), Measure for Measure (Angelo), The Tempest (Caliban), King Lear (The Fool), King John (Hubert), Merchant of Venice (Shylock), Troilus and Cressida (Achilles), Richard II (Bolingbroke), Every Good Boy Deserves Favour, 1983, Othello (Iago), 1986, Timon of Athens (title rôle), 1991; Separation, Comedy, 1988; Oleanna, Royal Court, 1993 (Variety Club Award for Best Actor, 1994); Who's Afraid of Virginia Woolf?, Aldwych, 1996 (Best Actor Award, Critics' Circle and South Bank Awards); Saturday, Sunday, Monday, Chichester, 1998; Amadeus, Old Vic, 1998 (Variety Club Award for Best Actor, 1999), Los Angeles and NY, 1999–2000 (Drama League Award); Man and Boy, Duchess, 2005; Once in a Lifetime, NT, 2006; The Last Confession, Chichester, transf. Th. Royal, Haymarket, 2007; Complicit, Old Vic, 2009; All My Sons, Apollo, 2010; Long Day's Journey into Night, Apollo and tour, 2012; The Last Confession, world tour, Toronto, LA, Perth, Brisbane, Sydney, Melbourne, 2014; The Importance of Being Earnest (Lady Bracknell), Vaudeville, 2015; The Price, Th. Royal, Bath, 2018, transf. Wyndham's, 2019; The Lover/The Collection, Harold Pinter Th., 2018; *films include:* Tale of Two Cities, 1978; The Missionary, 1982; Red Monarch (Best Actor award, Marseilles Film Fest.), 1983; Falcon and the Snowman, 1985; Thirteen at Dinner, 1985; Song for Europe, 1985; Harry and the Hendersons, 1986; When the Whales came, 1990; Deadly Voyage, 1995; Executive Decision, 1996; Sunday, 1996 (winner, Sundance Film Festival); Wing Commander, 1998; A Perfect Murder, 1998; RKO, 2000; Sabotage, 2000; The In-Laws, 2003; Live from Baghdad, 2003; Fool Proof, 2003; The Bank Job, 2007; Diverted, 2008; Effie Gray, 2014; *television includes:* Oppenheimer, 1978; Reilly, 1981; Saigon, 1982; Freud, 1983; Blott on the Landscape, 1984; Oxbridge Blues, 1984; Playing Shakespeare, 1985; Great Writers, 1988; Agatha Christie's Hercule Poirot, 1989–94, 2000–03, 2005, 2007–10, 2013; The Secret Agent, 1992; Solomon, 1997; Seesaw, 1998; National Crime Squad, 2001; Murder in Mind, 2001; Victoria and Albert, 2001; The Way We Live Now, 2001; Henry VIII, 2003; Get Carman, 2003; The Flood, 2006; Dracula, 2006; Maxwell, 2007; Great Expectations, 2011; Richard II, 2012; People I Have Shot, 2012; In the Footsteps of St Paul, 2012; In the Footsteps of St Peter, 2014; Decline and Fall, 2017; Dr Who, 2017; The Dali & The Cooper, 2017; Press, 2018; *radio:* one-man show, Kreutzer Sonata (Best Radio Actor, Pye Radio Awards, 1979); The Gorey Details, 2003; Einstein in Crome, 2004; Dracula, 2006; The Last Confession, 2008; The Willows in Winter, David Golder, 2010; numerous other parts; audio: entire Bible, 2014. Mem. Council, LAMDA, 1985–. Lectr, US univs; Vis. Prof., Univ. of Nebraska, 1975. FRSA 2005. Freeman, City of London, 2008. Hon. Fellow, Chichester Univ., 2008. Hon. DArts Kent, 2010. Numerous awards, incl. Best Actor, RTS, 1986; Best Actor, Critics' Circle Award, 2010. *Publications:* (contrib.) Players of Shakespeare, 2 vols, 1985 and 1988; Poirot and Me, 2013; essays on interpretation of roles. *Recreations:* clarinet, photography, reading, ornithology, theology, narrow boating. *Address:* c/o Roger Charteris, The Artists Partnership, 21–22 Warwick Street, W1B 5NE. *Clubs:* Garrick, St James's.
*See also* J. A. Suchet.

**SUCHET, John Aleck;** television and radio broadcaster; author; *b* 29 March 1944; *s* of late Jack and Joan Suchet; *m* 1st, 1968, Moya Hankinson (marr. diss. 1985); three *s*; 2nd, 1985, Bonnie Simonson (*d* 2015); 3rd, 2016, Nula Black. *Educ:* Uppingham; Univ. of St Andrews (MA Hons). Reuters News Agency, 1967–71; BBC TV News, 1971–72; Independent Television News, 1972–2004: reporter, 1976–86; Washington corresp., 1981–83; newscaster, 1986–2004; newscaster, Channel Five, 2006–07; Morning prog. presenter, Classic FM, 2011–. Gov., RAM, 2003–07; Pres., Friends of RAM, 1998–2006; Hon. Pres., Dementia UK, 2010–11. Hon. FRAM 2001. Hon. LLD Dundee, 2000; Hon MA Worcester, 2010. TV Journalist of the Year, RTS, 1986; Newscaster of the Year, TRIC, 1996; Lifetime Achievement Award, RTS, 2008; Radio Personality of Year, Assoc. for Internat. Broadcasting, 2013; Gold Award for Best Personality, NY Internat. Radio Awards, 2014. *Publications:* TV News: the inside story, 1989; The Last Master (fictional biography of Ludwig van Beethoven): vol. 1, Passion and Anger, 1996; vol. 2, Passion and Pain, 1997; vol. 3, Passion and Glory, 1998; (with Darren Henley) The Classic FM Friendly Guide to Beethoven, 2006; The Treasures of Beethoven, 2008; My Bonnie, 2010; Beethoven: the man revealed, 2012, 250th anniv. edn 2020; The Strauss Dynasty and Vienna, 2015; Mozart: the man revealed, 2016; Verdi: the man revealed, 2017; Tchaikovsky: the man revealed, 2018. *Recreations:* classical music, exploring the life, times and music of Beethoven. *Address:* c/o David Foster Management, PO Box 1805, Andover, Hants SP10 3ZN.
*See also* D. Suchet.

**SUCKLING, Prof. Colin James,** OBE 2006; PhD, DSc; FRSC, FRSE; Freeland Professor of Chemistry, 1989–2012, Research Professor, since 2012, University of Strathclyde; *b* 24 March 1947; *s* of Dr Charles Walter Suckling, CBE, FRS; *m* 1972, Catherine Mary Faulkner; two *s* one *d. Educ:* Univ. of Liverpool (BSc 1967; PhD 1970; DSc 1989). CChem 1977; FRSC 1980. University of Strathclyde: Lectr, 1972–84; Prof. of Organic Chemistry, 1984–89; Dean, Faculty of Sci., 1992–94; Dep. Principal, 1995–98; Vice Principal, 1998–2002. Chairman: West of Scotland Schs Orch. Trust, 1995–2016; Harmony Music Scotland Trust, 2011–17; Scottish Adv. Cttee for Distinction Awards, NHS Scotland, 2002–10; Mem., Jt Cttee on Higher Surgical Trng and Senate of Surgery, 2002–05; Public Partner, Scottish Medicines Consortium, 2011–14 (Chm., Patient and Public Interest Gp, 2012–14). Member: Bd of Govs, Bell Coll. of Technol., 1999–2007; Court, Univ. of Paisley, 2007–08; Court, Univ. of West of Scotland, 2008–13. B. D. Tilak Vis. Fellow, Indian Inst. of Chemical Technol., Mumbai, 2019. FRSE 1987; FRSA 1991; FRCSGlas 2004. Hon. FRCSEd 2005; Hon. Life Fellow, Indian Soc. of Chemists and Biologists, 2015. Gold Medal, Lord Provost of Glasgow, 2000; Adrien Albert Medal, RSC, 2009; Gold Medal, Indian Soc. of Chemists and Biologists, 2011; Nexxus Lifetime Career Award, 2011. *Publications:* (with C. W. Suckling and K. E. Suckling) Chemistry through Models, 1978; Biological Chemistry, 1980; Enzyme Chemistry Impact and Applications, 1984, 3rd edn 1998; approx. 250 papers and patents on medicinal and biol chemistry. *Recreations:* horn playing, composing and conducting. *Address:* Department of Pure and Applied Chemistry, University of Strathclyde, 295 Cathedral Street, Glasgow G1 1XL. *T:* (0141) 548 2271, *Fax:* (0141) 548 5473. *E:* c.j.suckling@strath.ac.uk.

**SUDBOROUGH, Air Vice-Marshal Nigel John,** CB 2002; OBE 1989; JP; DL; Director, Sudborough Investments Ltd, since 2003; non-executive Director, 2007–13 and Deputy Chairman, 2009–13, Leicester Partnership NHS Trust; *b* 23 March 1948; *s* of late Alexander Sudborough and Beryl Sudborough; *m* 1971, Anne Brown (*d* 2015); one *s* one *d. Educ:* Oundle Sch. Commnd as navigator, Royal Air Force, 1967; various flying tours, incl. Vulcan, Phantom and Tornado; PSO to Vice-Chief of Air Staff, MoD, 1983–85; i/c 29 (F) sqdn, 1985–87; RAF Mt Pleasant, Falkland Is, 1987–88; DS, RAF Staff Coll., 1988–90; HQ RAF Germany, 1990–93; i/c RAF Leuchars, 1993–95; rcds 1996; AO Plans, HQ Strike Comd, 1997–2000; DCS Ops, Strike Comd, 2000–02. Dir Gen., Winston Churchill Meml Trust, 2002–07. FCIPD 2000; FRAeS 2001. Freeman, City of London, 1985. JP Leicester, 2004; DL Rutland, 2018. *Recreations:* fly-fishing, philately. *Address:* Knoll House, 5 London Road, Uppingham, Rutland LE15 9TJ. *Club:* Royal Air Force.

**SUDBURY, Archdeacon of;** see Jenkins, Ven. D. H.

**SUDBURY, Dr Wendy Elizabeth, (Mrs A. J. Bates);** Director: Cambridge Management Group, since 1994; HF Holidays Ltd, 2012–16 and since 2017; *b* 14 June 1946; *d* of Clifford Frank Edwards and Betty Edwards (*née* Foster); one *d*; *m* 1st, 1973, R. M. Sudbury (marr. diss. 1980); 2nd, 1993, Alexander John Bates; one step *s* two step *d. Educ:* Finchley Co. Grammar Sch.; Lucy Cavendish Coll., Cambridge (MA); Christ Church, Oxford; Cranfield Sch. of Mgt (PhD 1992). Chief Exec., Mus. Documentation Assoc., 1989–97; Dir, Records Centre, C of E, 2001–03. Expert Advr, EC, 1996–. Mem., RCHME, 1997–99. Mem. Adv. Bd, Judge Inst. of Mgt Studies, Cambridge Univ.,

1992–94. FRSA 2002. *Publications:* (with A. Fahy) Information: the Hidden Resource, Museums & the Internet, 1995; contrib. to learned jls. *Recreations:* humanities, travel, gardening, hiking, family life.

**SUDELEY**, 7th Baron *cr* 1838; **Merlin Charles Sainthill Hanbury-Tracy**, FSA; *b* 17 June 1939; *oc* of late Captain Michael David Charles Hanbury-Tracy, Scots Guards, and Colline Ammabel (*d* 1985), *d* of late Lt-Col C. G. H. St Hill and *widow* of Lt-Col Frank King, DSO, OBE; *S* cousin, 1941; *m* 1st, 1980, Hon. Mrs Elizabeth Villiers (marr. diss. 1988; she *d* 2014), *d* of late Viscount Bury (*s* of 9th Earl of Albemarle); 2nd, 1999, Mrs Margarita Kellett (marr. diss. 2006); 3rd, 2010, Dr Tatiana Dudina. *Educ:* Eton; Worcester Coll., Oxford; in the ranks of the Scots Guards. Former Chairman: Monday Club; Constitutional Monarchy Assoc.; Vice-Chancellor, Monarchist League. Pres., Traditional Britain; Vice-Pres., Soc. of Genealogists. Lay Patron, Prayer Book Soc. *Publications:* Guide to Hailes Church, 1981, 3rd edn 2013; (jtly) The Sudeleys—Lords of Toddington, 1987; (contrib.) The House of Lords: a thousand years of British tradition, 1994; Peers Through the Mists of Time: observations on the origin and evolution of the old House of Lords, 2018; contribs to Quarterly Review, Contemporary Review, Family History, Trans of Bristol and Gloucestershire Archaeol. Soc., Trans of Cymmrodorion Soc., Montgomeryshire Collections, Bull. of Manorial Soc., Die Waage (Zeitschrift der Chemie Grünenthal), Monday Club Jl, London Miscellany, Faith and Worship. *Recreations:* ancestor worship; cultivating his sensibility. *Heir:* kinsman Nicholas Edward John Hanbury-Tracy, *b* 13 Jan. 1959. *Address:* 25 Melcombe Court, Dorset Square, NW1 6EP. *Club:* Brooks's.

**SUDJIC, Deyan,** OBE 2000; Co-Director, Design Museum, since 2016 (Director, 2006–16); *b* 6 Sept. 1952; *s* of Milivoj Jovo Sudjic and Miroslava Pavlovic; *m* 2002, Sarah Isabel Miller; one *d*. *Educ:* Latymer Upper Sch.; Edinburgh Univ. (BSc Soc. Sci.; DipArch). Founding Ed., Blueprint mag., 1983–94; Architecture Critic: Guardian, 1991–97; Observer, 2000–06; Ed., Domus mag., 2000–04; Dean, Faculty of Art and Design, Kingston Univ., 2005–06; Director: Glasgow 1999 UK City of Architecture and Design, 1996–2000; Venice Architecture Biennale, 2002. Visiting Professor: Acad. for Applied Arts, Vienna, 1993–98; RCA, 2002–11. Exhibition Curator: *exhibitions:* Royal Acad., 1986; ICA, 1988; Louisiana Mus., Copenhagen, 1996; McLennan Galls, Glasgow, 1999; BM, 2001. Fellow, Glasgow Sch. of Art, 1999; Sen. FRCA 2007. Hon. FRIAS 2000; Hon. FRIBA 2003. Hon. DArts Lincoln, 2008; Hon. Dr London Metropolitan; Hon. DLitt Brighton, 2012; Hon. MA Univ. of Creative Arts, 2012; Hon. LLD Dundee, 2013. Bicentennial Medal, RSA, 2005. *Publications:* Cult Objects, 1983; Foster, Rogers, Stirling: new British architecture, 1986; Rei Kawskubo and Comme des Garçons, 1991; The Hundred Mile City, 1992; The Architecture Pack, 1996; Ron Arad, 1999; John Pawson: Works, 2000; The Edifice Complex, 2005; The Language of Things, 2009; (ed) Design in Britain: big ideas (small island), 2010; Norman Foster: a life in architecture, 2010; B is for Bauhaus: an A–Z of the modern world, 2014; The Language of Cities, 2016. *Recreation:* looking at buildings. *Address:* Design Museum, 224–238 Kensington High Street, W8 6AG.

**SUE-LING, Henry Michael,** MD; FRCS, FRCSGlas; Consultant Gastrointestinal Surgeon and Senior Clinical Lecturer, Leeds General Infirmary, later at St James' University Hospital, since 1995; *b* 3 Feb. 1956; *s* of James and Sheila Sue-Ling; *m* 1979, Susan Marie Lewis; two *s* one *d*. *Educ:* Univ. of Leeds (MB ChB 1980; MD 1986). FRCSGlas 1986; FRCS 1988. Registrar, University Hosp. Wales, Cardiff, 1985–88; Leeds General Infirmary: Lectr in Surgery and Hon. Sen. Registrar, 1988–92; Sen. Lectr in Surgery and Hon. Consultant Surgeon, 1992–95; Lead Clinician in upper gastrointestinal cancer services. Chm., Yorks Cancer Network, 2000–. Silver Scalpel Award for UK Surgical Trainer of the Year, Smith & Nephew Foundn, 2001. *Publications:* contribs to learned jls incl. Lancet, BMJ, Gut and Jl Nat. Cancer Inst. *Recreations:* walking, swimming, tennis, travel. *Address:* St James' University Hospital, Beckett Street, Leeds LS9 7TF. *T:* (0113) 206 8521. *E:* henry.sue-ling@nhs.net.

**SUENSON-TAYLOR,** family name of **Baron Grantchester**.

**SUFFIELD,** 13th Baron *cr* 1786; **John Edward Richard Harbord-Hammond;** Bt 1745; *b* London, 10 July 1956; 2nd *s* of 11th Baron Suffield, MC and Elizabeth Eve (*née* Edgedale); *S* brother, 2016; *m* 1983, Katharine Margaret Lucy Seymour; three *s* one *d*. *Educ:* Eton Coll.; Coll. of Law; Univ. of Glasgow (MLitt History of Art 2007). Called to the Bar, 1978. FCSI 1979. *Heir:* s Hon. Sam Charles Anthony Harbord-Hammond, *b* 4 Feb. 1989.

**SUFFOLK AND BERKSHIRE,** 21st Earl of, *cr* 1603; **Michael John James George Robert Howard;** Viscount Andover and Baron Howard, 1622; Earl of Berkshire, 1626; *b* 27 March 1935; *s* of 20th Earl of Suffolk and Berkshire, GC (killed by enemy action, 1941) and Mimi (*d* 1966), *yr d* of late A. G. Forde Pigott; *S* father, 1941; *m* 1st, 1960, Mme Simone Paulmier (marr. diss. 1967), *d* of late Georges Litman, Paris; (one *d* decd); 2nd, 1973, Anita (marr. diss. 1980), *d* of R. R. Fuglesang, Haywards Heath, Sussex; one *s* one *d*; 3rd, 1983, Linda Viscountess Bridport; two *d*. Owns 5,000 acres. *Heir: s* Viscount Andover, qv. *Address:* Charlton Park, Malmesbury, Wilts SN16 9DG.

**SUFFOLK, Archdeacon of;** *see* Morgan, Ven. I. D. J.

**SUFFOLK, John;** a Senior Vice President, and Global Cyber Security and Privacy Officer, Huawei Technologies Co. Ltd, since 2015 (Global Head of Cyber Security, 2011–15); *b* 25 Feb. 1958; *s* of Thomas and Elspeth Suffolk; *m* 1989, Julie Davies. *Educ:* Wolverhampton Business Sch. (MBA; DMS). Various tech. roles, Freight Computer Services, 1975–79; Sen. Programmer, TRW Valves, 1979–80; Midshires Building Society: Sen. Designer, 1980–81; Chief Programmer/Programming Manager, 1981–85; Systems Develt Manager, 1985–86; Technical Services Manager, 1986–87; Birmingham Midshires: Planning and Develt Manager, 1987–89; Asst Gen. Manager, Business Systems, 1989–91; Inf. Services Dir, 1991–95; Hd, Customer Services, 1995–98; Britannia Building Society: Dir of Ops, 1998–2001; Ops Dir, 2001–02; Man. Dir, 2002–03; Dir Gen., Criminal Justice IT, Home Office, 2004–06; Govt Chief Information Officer and Sen. Information Risk Officer (formerly Govt Chief Information Officer and Head of e-Govt Unit, then Dir Gen., Transformational Govt), Cabinet Office, 2006–11. Chm., MutualPlus, 2001. Non-exec. Dir, PITO, 2004. *Recreations:* farming, raising money for charity through challenges. *Address:* Back Forest Farm, Swythamley, Rushton Spencer, Macclesfield, Cheshire SK11 0RF. *T:* (01260) 227643.

**SUGAR,** family name of **Baron Sugar**.

**SUGAR,** Baron *cr* 2009 (Life Peer), of Clapton in the London Borough of Hackney; **Alan Michael Sugar,** Kt 2000; Executive Chairman: Amstrad (formerly Betacom) Plc, 1997–2008; Viglen, 1997–2014; Amshold Group; *b* 24 March 1947; *s* of Nathan and Fay Sugar; *m* 1968, Ann Simons; two *s* one *d*. *Educ:* Brooke House School, London. Founder Chm., Amstrad, 1968–97; co. divided into Betacom and Viglen, 1997. Chm., 1991–2001, Chief Exec., 1998–2000, Tottenham Hotspur plc. Non-exec. Chm., YouView Ltd, 2011–13. Presenter: The Apprentice (15 series), BBC TV, 2005–; Junior Apprentice, BBC TV, 2010; Young Apprentice, BBC TV, 2011. Govt Enterprise Champion, 2009–10, 2016–. Hon. DSc City, 1988. *Publications:* The Apprentice: how to get hired not fired, 2005; What You See is What You Get: my autobiography, 2010; The Way I See It: rants, revelations and rules for life, 2011; Unscripted: my ten years in telly, 2015. *Recreations:* tennis, flying (Private Pilot).

**SUGAR, Vivienne,** FCIH; local government consultant; Member, Board, Consumer Futures, 2013–14 (Chair, Consumer Focus Wales (formerly Welsh Consumer Council), 2003–13); *b* Gorseinon, 23 Feb. 1947; *d* of Jack Hopkins and Phyllis Hopkins (*née* Suter); *m* 1972, Adrian Sugar. *Educ:* Mynydd Cynnfig Comprehensive Sch.; Leeds Univ. (BA). Area Improvement Officer, 1979–88, Dir of Housing, 1988–90, Newport BC; Dir of Housing, Cardiff CC, 1990–95; Chief Exec., City and County of Swansea, 1995–2002. Wales Advr to Joseph Rowntree Foundn, 2005–09. Pro Chancellor, Swansea Univ. (formerly Vice Pres., Univ. of Wales, Swansea), 2005–12. Chair, Bd of Trustees, Bevan Foundn, 2014–. *Publications:* various articles in Municipal Jl, Local Govt Chronicle and Inside Housing. *Recreations:* politics and current affairs, walking, birdwatching, cooking.

**SUGARMAN, Jason Ashley;** QC 2017; *b* Brighton, 1969; *s* of Cyril and Edna Sugarman; *m* 2000, Katherine Harding; two *d*. *Educ:* Brighton Coll.; Durham Univ. (BA Hons); Westminster Univ. (DipLaw). Called to the Bar, Inner Temple, 1995; in practice as a barrister, specialising in business crime, 1995–. *Recreations:* riding, history, classic cars. *Address:* Foundry Chambers, London. *Clubs:* Carlton, Mark's.

**SUGDEN, Prof. David Edward,** DPhil; FRSE; Professor of Geography, since 1987, and Head, School of GeoSciences, 2003–06, University of Edinburgh; *b* 5 March 1941; *s* of late John Cyril Gouldie Sugden and of Patricia Sugden (*née* Backhouse); *m* 1966, Britta Valborg, *d* of Harald Stridsberg, Sweden; two *s* one *d*. *Educ:* Warwick Sch.; Jesus Coll., Oxford (BA; DPhil 1965). Scientific officer, British Antarctic Survey, 1965–66; Lectr, then Reader, Univ. of Aberdeen, 1966–87. Vis. Prof., Arctic and Alpine Inst., Boulder, Colo, 1975–76. Pres., IBG, 1995. Member: RSGS; RGS; FRSE 1990. Hon. Dr Stockholm, 1998; Hon. LLB Dundee, 1999. Cuthbert Peek Award, RGS, 1980; Vega Medal, Stockholm, 1993; Polar Medal, 2003; Linton Award, BSG, 2004; Seligman Crystal, Internat. Geological Soc., 2012; Coppock Res. Medal, RSGS, 2012. *Publications:* Glaciers and Landscape, 1976 (with B. S. John); Arctic and Antarctic: a modern geographical synthesis, 1982; (with R. J. Chorley and S. A. Schumm) Geomorphology, 1984. *Recreations:* hill-walking, gardening, ski-ing. *Address:* Geography, School of GeoSciences, University of Edinburgh, Drummond Street, Edinburgh EH8 9XP. *E:* david.sugden@ed.ac.uk.

**SUGDEN, Prof. Robert,** DLitt; FBA 1996; Professor of Economics, University of East Anglia, since 1985; *b* 26 Aug. 1949; *s* of late Frank Gerald Sugden and Kathleen Sugden (*née* Buckley); *m* 1982, Christine Margaret Upton; one *s* one *d*. *Educ:* Eston GS, Cleveland; Univ. of York (BA; DLitt 1988); UC, Cardiff (MSc). Lectr in Econs, Univ. of York, 1971–78; Reader in Econs, Univ. of Newcastle upon Tyne, 1978–85. *Publications:* (with A. Williams) The Principles of Practical Cost-Benefit Analysis, 1978; The Political Economy of Public Choice, 1981; The Economics of Rights, Co-operation and Welfare, 1986; (jtly) The Theory of Choice: a critical guide, 1992; (ed with D. Gauthier) Rationality, Justice and the Social Contract, 1993; (ed with Benedetto Gui) Economics and Social Interaction, 2005; (jtly) Experimental Economics: rethinking the rules, 2009; The Community of Advantage: a behavioural economist's defence of the market, 2018. *Recreations:* family, walking, gardening. *Address:* School of Economics, University of East Anglia, Norwich NR4 7TJ. *T:* (01603) 593423.

**SUGG,** Baroness *cr* 2016 (Life Peer), of Coldharbour in the London Borough of Lambeth; **Elizabeth Grace Sugg,** CBE 2015; Parliamentary Under-Secretary of State, Department for International Development, since 2019; *b* Surrey, 2 May 1977; *d* of Paul and Deborah Sugg. *Educ:* Newcastle Univ. (BA Hons Politics and Econs). Cons. Party Campaign HQ, 2004–10; Dir of Ops and Campaigns, No 10 Downing St, 2010–16. A Baroness in Waiting (Govt Whip), 2017; Parly Under-Sec. of State, DfT, 2017–19. *Address:* House of Lords, SW1A 0PW.

**SUGHRUE, Dr Cynthia Marie, (Cindy),** OBE 2013; Director, Charles Dickens Museum, London, since 2015; *b* Boston, Mass, 30 March 1963; *d* of Robert Emmett Sughrue and Catharine Isabel Sughrue (*née* Guthrie). *Educ:* Boston Univ. (BA *summa cum laude*); Univ. of Sheffield (PhD 1992). Marshall Schol., 1985–88; Dir, Collective Gall., 1990–94; Gen. Manager, Dance Base, 1994–97; Sen. Officer, Performing Arts, 1997–2001, Hd of Dance, 2001–04, Scottish Arts Council; Chief Exec. and Exec. Producer, Scottish Ballet, 2004–15; freelance theatre producer and consultant, 2015–16. Member, Board of Directors: Benchtours Prodns, 1993–96 (Chm., 1995–96); Dance Base, 2006–08; New Moves Internat., 2006–11; Nat. Youth Jazz Orch., 2015–; Alexander Whitely Dance Co., 2017–. Trustee, Dame Margot Fonteyn Scholarship Fund, 2007–; Chm., Culture Sparks, 2010–14; Mem., Bd of Dirs, Culture Republic, 2013–15. Mem., Bd of Govs, Royal Conservatoire of Scotland, 2012–16. Mem., Scotland Adv. Cttee, British Council, 2015–. Fellow, Goodenough Coll., London, 2019. FRSA 2008; FRCS 2016. *Recreations:* arts, culture, heritage, hill walking, cooking, travel. *Address:* c/o Charles Dickens Museum, 48 Doughty Street, Bloomsbury, WC1N 2LX.

**SUIRDALE, Viscount; John Michael James Hely Hutchinson;** management consultant, since 2007; *b* 7 Aug. 1952; *s* and *heir* of 8th Earl of Donoughmore, qv; *m* 1st, 1976, Marie-Claire Carola Etienne van den Driessche (marr. diss. 2006); one *s* two *d*; 2nd, 2008, Nutjarin Photiruk. *Educ:* Harrow. Dep. Man. Dir, Bagajavion, Paris, 1978–89; Purchasing Manager, Alfred Dunhill Ltd, 1989–92; Royalties Dir, Burberry Ltd, 1993–2003; Rep. Dir, Burberry Japan KK, Tokyo, 2003–06; Gp Supply Chain Dir, Lambert Howarth Gp plc, 2007; Man. Dir, DAKS Simpson Gp plc, 2009; Gp CEO, Integrix Sports Gp Ltd, 2011. *Recreations:* golf, ski-ing, fishing, keeping fit, etc. *Heir: s* Hon. Richard Gregory Hely Hutchinson, *b* 3 July 1980. *Address:* 40 Guildford Road, Fleet, Hants GU51 3EY.

*See also* Hon. T. M. Hely Hutchinson.

**SULEYMAN, Touker;** entrepreneur; Chairman, Low Profile Holdings Ltd, since 1989; *b* Famagusta, Cyprus, 1953; *s* of Mustafa and Meyrem Suleyman; marr. diss.; two *d*. *Educ:* Peckham Manor Sch. Estabd Kingsland Models, clothing manufr, 1971, Low Profile Fashions, 1978; owner: Hawes & Curtis, 2001–; Ghost, 2008–; Chm. and mentor to start-up businesses. *Recreation:* business. *Address:* c/o Hawes & Curtis Ltd, 85 Frampton Street, NW8 8NQ. *T:* (020) 7402 8600. *Clubs:* Harry's Bar, Arts, George.

**SULIVAN, Maj.-Gen. Timothy John,** CB 2001; CBE 1991; DL; Vice-President, Customer Relations, General Dynamics (formerly CDC Systems) UK Ltd, 2001–13; *b* 19 Feb. 1946; *s* of late Col John Anthony Sulivan, OBE and Elizabeth Joyce Sulivan; *m* 1977, Jane Annette Ellwood; one *s* one *d*. *Educ:* Wellington Coll.; RMCS (BSc). Commnd RA, 1966; psa 1978; transf. Blues and Royals, 1980; CO, Blues and Royals, 1987–89; HCSC, 1990; attached US Special Plans Team, C-in-C US CENTCOM, 1990–91; Comd 7 Armd Bde, 1991–93; PSO to CDS, 1993–94; Dir-Gen., Develt and Doctrine, MoD, 1994–96 (deployed as Jt Force Comd Op. Driver, Kuwait/Saudi Arabia, 1994); COS, HQ ARRC, Bosnia and BAOR, 1996–98; GOC Fourth Div., 1998–2001; Chief Operating Officer, RICS, 2002–05. Dir, Screen plc, 2002–06; Dir, Customer Relations, Land Securities

Trillium, 2006–07. Mem., Ind. Assessment Panel, Army Trng Centre, Pirbright, 2013– (Chm., 2015–). Chm., Surrey Br., ABF, 2014–. DL Surrey, 2015. Bronze Star, USA, 1991. *Recreations:* shooting, ski-ing, squash, cabinet making. *Club:* Army and Navy.

**SULKIN, David Charles Chester,** OBE 2014; Director of Artist Development, National Opera Studio, since 2017; *b* Worthing, W Sussex, 1 Jan. 1949; *s of* Emmanuel Sulkin and Dorothy May Sulkin (*née* Chester); partner, 1993, civil partnership, 2010, Geoffrey Milton. *Educ:* St Andrew's High Sch., Worthing; Guildhall Sch. of Music and Drama; Rose Bruford Coll., Sidcup. Partner, Hoxton Th. Trust, 1975–78; Lectr, Rose Bruford Coll., 1978–80; Dir, Royal Court Young People's Th., 1980–85; Co-Dir, Baylis Prog., ENO, 1985–95; Associate Dir, Janáčkovy Hukvaldy, Czech Republic, 1993–97 (Mem., Exec. Cttee, 2016–); Lectr, RADA, 1997–2004; Dir of Policy and Progs, Nat. Foundn for Youth Music, 1999–2008; Exec. Dir, Help Musicians UK, 2009–15. Finzi Scholarship to study the work of Leoš Janáček in Brno, 2016–17. Gov., Cripplegate Foundn, 2004–14; Chair of Govs, Clerkenwell Parochial Sch., 2007–17. Chair of Trustees, New London Children's Choir, 2012–17; Chair, Sing Up Foundn, 2016–. Mem. Cttee, Amwell Soc., 1993– (Chair, 1995–2015). Liveryman, Musicians' Co. *Publications:* (with A. Roth) Gretel and Hansel, 1987; (with K. Duncan) New Old - Thirty Thousand Years of Experience, 1999; Rough Stuff, 2000; (ed) A Village in London, 2005; (ed) The New River Head, 2012. *Recreations:* motorcycles and motorcyclists, early recording and gramophones, Czech and Russian language and culture, 20th century architecture. *Address:* National Opera Studio, The Clore Building, 2 Chapel Yard, Wandsworth, SW18 4HZ.

**SULLIVAN, Edmund Wendell,** FRCVS; Chief Veterinary Officer, Department of Agriculture for Northern Ireland, 1983–90; *b* 21 March 1925; *s of* Thomas Llewellyn Sullivan and Letitia Sullivan; *m* 1957, Elinor Wilson Melville; two *s* one *d*. *Educ:* Portadown College; Queen's University, Belfast; Royal (Dick) Veterinary College. MRCVS 1947, FRCVS 1991. General Veterinary Practice, Appleby, Westmoreland, 1947; joined staff of State Veterinary Service, Dept of Agriculture for N Ireland, 1948; Headquarters staff, 1966–90. *Recreations:* hill walking, wood craft, following rugby and cricket. *Address:* Kinfauns, 26 Dillon's Avenue, Newtownabbey, Co. Antrim BT37 0SX. *T:* (028) 9086 2323.

**SULLIVAN, Francis John;** Adviser on the Environment, since 2004, and Acting Head, Sustainability, HSBC Holdings plc (Deputy Head, Global Corporate Sustainability and Head of Europe, 2012); *b* London, 6 March 1963; *s of* Vernon and Shirley Sullivan; *m* 1994, Jackie Nickson; two *d*. *Educ:* Marlborough Coll.; St John's Coll., Oxford (MA Hons Agriculture and Forest Scis; MSc forestry and its reln to land use 1986). Forest officer, WWF-UK, 1987–95; Dir, Forests for Life Campaign, WWF-Internat., 1995–99; Dir of Progs, WWF-UK, 1999–2004. Mem., Adv. Bd, Envmt Change Inst., Univ. of Oxford, 2006–. Member: Internat. Bd, Forest Stewardship Council, 1996–98; Ind. Adv. Gp on Sustainability, Inter-American Develt Bank, 2007–; Corporate Responsibility Expert Adv. Panel, Vodafone, 2007–12; Corporate Responsibility Adv. Gp, Centrica, 2011–15. Trustee Dir, HSBC Pension Trust (UK), 2009–. Trustee: Baynards Zambia Trust, 2012–; Whitley Fund for Nature, 2012– (Judge, Whitley Awards for Nature Conservation, 2000–12). Gov., St Hilary's Sch., Godalming, 2012–. Freeman, City of London, 2001; Liveryman, Co. of Stationers and Newspaper Makers, 2001. *Recreations:* allotment, sailing, family, running half-marathons. *Address:* HSBC Holdings plc, 8 Canada Square, E14 5HQ. *T:* (020) 7992 3771. *E:* francissullivan@hsbc.com.

**SULLIVAN, Hannah Beatrice;** *see* Brown, H. B.

**SULLIVAN, Jane Teresa; Her Honour Judge Jane Sullivan;** a Circuit Judge, since 2009; *b* Bristol, 21 April 1956; *d of* late Timothy Gerard Sullivan and Margaret Sullivan; *m* 1990, Duncan Macleod. *Educ:* La Retraite High Sch.; University Coll. London (LLB Hons 1977); Univ. of London ext. (BA Hons Eng. 1981). Admitted solicitor, 1980; in practice as a solicitor, 1980–84; called to the Bar, Inner Temple, 1984; in practice as a barrister, 1984–2009; Recorder, 1998–2009. Legal Chm. of Appeals, Postgrad. Med. Educn and Trng Bd, 2005–09; Legal Advr, Royal Pharmaceutical Soc., 2006–09. *Recreations:* travel, arts, reading, swimming. *Address:* Blackfriars Crown Court, 1–15 Pocock Street, SE1 0BJ. *T:* (020) 7922 5800.

**SULLIVAN, Rt Hon. Sir Jeremy (Mirth),** Kt 1997; PC 2009; a Lord Justice of Appeal, 2009–15; Senior President of Tribunals, 2012–15; *b* 17 Sept. 1945; *s of* late Arthur Brian and Pamela Jean Sullivan; *m* 1st, 1970, Ursula Klara Marie Hildenbrock (marr. diss. 1993); two *s*; 2nd, 1993, Dr Sandra Jean Farmer; two step *s*. *Educ:* Framlingham Coll.; King's Coll., London. LLB 1967, LLM 1968; LAMTPI 1970, LMRTPI 1976. 2nd Lieut, Suffolk & Cambs Regt (TA), 1963–65. Called to the Bar, Inner Temple, 1968, Bencher, 1993; Lectr in Law, City of London Polytechnic, 1968–71; in practice, Planning and Local Govt Bar, Parly Bar, 1971–97; QC 1982; a Recorder, 1989–97; a Dep. High Court Judge, 1993–97; Attorney Gen. to the Prince of Wales, 1994–97; a Judge of the High Court, QBD, 1997–2009. Hon. Standing Counsel to CPRE, 1994–97. Chm., Tribunals Cttee, Judicial Studies Bd, 1999–2007; Dep. Chm., Parly Boundary Commn for England, 2004–09. Ind. Consultation Advr on Draft Airports Nat. Policy Statement to Sec. of State for Transport, 2017. Mem. Council, RTPI, 1984–87. Gov., Highgate Sch., 1991–2003. *Recreation:* the Wotton Light Railway. *Address:* 50A Montpellier Spa Road, Cheltenham, Glos GL50 1UL. *Clubs:* Athenæum; New (Cheltenham).

**SULLIVAN, Her Honour Linda Elizabeth, (Mrs J. W. Blake-James);** QC 1994; a Circuit Judge, 2009–18; *b* 1 Jan. 1948; *d of* Donal Sullivan and Esmé Beryl Sullivan (*née* McKenzie); *m* 1972, Dr Justin Wynne Blake-James (marr. diss. 1994); one *s* twin *d*. *Educ:* St Leonards-Mayfield Sch.; Univ. of Kent (BA Hons Phil. and English 1969); St Hilda's Coll., Oxford (Cert Ed 1970). Called to the Bar, Middle Temple, 1973, Bencher, 1993; Mem., Western Circuit; Recorder, 1990–2009. Acting Deemster, Isle of Man, 1994. Legal Mem., Mental Health Review Tribunal, 2002–09.

**SULLIVAN, Michael Frederick,** MBE 1981; HM Diplomatic Service, retired; Consul-General, Hamburg, 1994–99; *b* 22 June 1940; *s of* late Frederick Franklin Sullivan and Leonora Mary Sullivan; *m* 1967, Jennifer Enid Saunders. *Educ:* King's Sch., Canterbury; Jesus Coll., Oxford (BA). CRO 1962–66; Moscow, 1967; Ulan Bator, Mongolia, 1967–69; Sydney, 1970–74; FCO, 1975–77; First Sec., W Indian and Atlantic Dept, FCO, 1977–79; Consul (Industrial Develt), British Trade Develt Office, NY, 1979–81; Cultural Attaché, Moscow, 1981–85; Assistant Head: Personnel Services Dept, FCO, 1985–86; Energy, Sci. and Space Dept, FCO, 1986–88; Counsellor (Cultural Affairs), Moscow, 1988–89; Counsellor, Export Promotion Policy Unit, DTI, 1989–90; Hd of Nationality, Treaty and Claims Dept, FCO, 1990–93. Res. analyst, FCO, 2000 and 2003. Mem., Panel of Inquiry Secs, Competition Commn, 2004–14. Mem., FCO Assoc., 2007–. *Recreations:* piano playing, music and the arts, tennis, jogging, swimming. *Club:* Übersee.

**SULLIVAN, Very Rev. Nicola Ann, (Mrs T. J. Westwood);** Dean of Southwell, since 2016; *b* 15 Aug. 1958; *d of* late Peter John Sullivan and Margaret Irene Sullivan (*née* Hancock); *m* 2014, Terence John Westwood. *Educ:* Convent of Jesus and Mary, Ipswich; Mills GS, Framlingham, Suffolk; St Bartholomew's Hosp. (SRN 1981) Bristol Maternity Hosp. (RM 1984); Wycliffe Hall, Oxford (BTh 1995). Various NHS nursing and midwifery posts, 1981–92; Tear Fund UK, in Ethiopia, 1984, Swaziland, 1988. Ordained deacon, 1995, priest, 1996; Asst Curate, St Anne's, Earlham, Norwich, 1995–99; Associate Vicar, Bath Abbey with St James, 1999–2002; Chaplain, Royal Nat. Hosp. for Rheumatic Diseases NHS Trust, 1999–2002; Bishop's Chaplain and Pastoral Asst to Bishop of Bath and Wells, 2002–07; Sub-Dean and Preb., Wells Cathedral, 2003–07; Archdeacon of Wells, and Canon Res., Wells Cathedral, 2007–16; Participating Observer, House of Bishops, 2013–16. *Recreations:* reading, theatre (professional and amateur), current affairs, music, walking, relaxing in Suffolk, Bob Dylan. *Address:* The Residence, 1 Vicars' Court, Southwell, Notts NG25 0HP. *T:* (01636) 817282. *E:* dean@southwellminster.org.uk.

**SULLIVAN, Prof. Richard,** PhD; FRCS; Professor of Cancer and Global Health, Director, Institute of Cancer Policy and Co-Director, Centre for Study of Conflict and Health, King's College London, since 2013; *b* Aden, 24 Aug. 1968; *s of* Victor and Audrey Sullivan; *m* 1st, 1999, Samantha Tarbuck (marr. diss.); one *d*; 2nd, 2010, Isabel Behncke (marr. diss.). *Educ:* Lord Wandsworth Coll.; St Mary's Hosp. Med. Sch. (BSc Hons 1990; MB BS 1993); University Coll. London (PhD Biochem. 1999). FRCS 1996. Acad. surgical rotations, NHS, 1993–99; Clin. Dir, CRUK, 2000–08; LSE, 2009–10. Noncommunicable Diseases Expert, WHO, 2016–. Visiting Professor: Pontificia Univ. Católica, Santiago, 2013; Tata Meml Centre, Mumbai, 2014. Hon. FFPM 2017. *Publications:* (jtly) Medicinal Mushrooms: their therapeutic properties and current medical usage with special emphasis on cancer treatments, 2002. *Recreations:* sky-diving, ski-ing, Egyptology, rock climbing. *Address:* Institute of Cancer Policy, King's College London, Guy's Hospital Campus, Bermondsey Wing (Research Oncology), Great Maze Pond, SE1 9RT. *E:* sulliv01@mac.com.

**SULLIVAN, Richard Arthur,** (9th Bt *cr* 1804, but does not use the title); retired geotechnical engineer; *b* 9 Aug. 1931; *s of* Sir Richard Benjamin Magniac Sullivan, 8th Bt, and Muriel Mary Paget (*d* 1988), *d of* late Francis Charles Trayler Pineo; *S* father, 1977; *m* 1962, Elenor Mary, *e d of* late K. M. Thorpe; one *s* three *d*. *Educ:* Univ. of Cape Town (BSc); Massachusetts Inst. of Technology (SM). Chartered Engineer, UK; Professional Engineer, Ontario, Texas and Louisiana. FASCE 2013. *Publications:* papers and articles to international conferences and technical journals. *Recreation:* tennis. *Heir: s* Charles Merson Sullivan, MA, VetMB Cantab, MRCVS [*b* 15 Dec. 1962; *m* 1993, Helen Mary Alexander; one *s* one *d*]. *Address:* 1 Sea Watch Place, Florence, OR 97439–8967, USA.

**SULLIVAN, Susan Elizabeth; Her Honour Judge Susan Sullivan;** a Circuit Judge, since 2018; *b* Pontypool, Gwent, 1 April 1957; *d of* Walter and Joan Sullivan; *m* 1980, Timothy Bacon; two *s*. *Educ:* Monmouth Sch. for Girls; Liverpool Univ. (LLB). Admitted as solicitor, 1982; Solicitor: Brabler Son & Holden, 1982–83; Levett Son & Baldwin, 1983–91; Partner: Hill Bailey, 1991–95; Thomson Snell-Passmore, 1998–2010; a Dep. Dist Judge, 2002–10; Dist Judge, 2010–18. *Recreations:* opera, Rugby, reading, quizzes. *Address:* Maidstone County Court, Barker Road, Maidstone ME16 8EQ.

**SULONG, Datuk Zakaria,** PSD 2007; JSM 2005; DIMP 2005; SSA 1998; High Commissioner of Malaysia in the United Kingdom, 2010–13; *b* Kuala Lumpur, 23 Dec. 1952; *s of* Sulong Bin Jawi and Suma Binti Mahatam; *m* 1978, Hazizah Zakaria; two *s* one *d*. *Educ:* Univ. of Malaya (BA Hons). Entered Malaysian Diplomatic Service, 1975; Consul Gen., Hong Kong, 1996–98; Under Sec., Multilateral Dept, 1998–2000; Ambassador to Bosnia and Herzegovina, 2000–04; Chief of Protocol, Min. of Foreign Affairs, 2004–07; Ambassador to Germany, 2007–10. *Recreations:* golf, badminton, reading, music, photography. *Clubs:* Travellers; Brocket Hall Golf; Morib Golf, Kelab Golf (Malaysia).

**SUMBERG, David Anthony Gerald;** *b* 2 June 1941; *s of* Joshua and Lorna Sumberg; *m* 1972, Carolyn Ann Rae Franks; one *s* one *d*. *Educ:* Tettenhall Coll., Staffs; Coll. of Law, London. Qualified as a Solicitor, 1964. Mem. (C) Manchester City Council, 1982–84. Contested (C) Manchester, Wythenshawe, 1979. MP (C) Bury South, 1983–97; contested (C) same seat, 1997. PPS to: Solicitor-General, 1986–87; Attorney-General, 1987–90. Member: Home Affairs Select Cttee, 1991–92; Foreign Affairs Select Cttee, 1992–97. MEP (C) NW Region, 1999–2009. European Parliament: Member: Cttee on Internat. Trade, 2008–09; Delegn to USA. Mem., Adv. Council on Public Records, 1993–97. *Recreations:* travel, reading, enjoying grandparenthood. *E:* sumberg.david@gmail.com.

**SUMMERFIELD, Prof. (Arthur) Quentin,** MBE 2019; PhD; Anniversary Professor of Psychology, University of York, 2004–18, now Emeritus (Head, Department of Psychology, 2011–17); *b* 18 Sept. 1948; *s of* Arthur Summerfield and Aline Summerfield (*née* Whalley); *m* 1989, Diana Lyn Field; two *d*. *Educ:* Tetherdown Primary Sch., Muswell Hill; University Coll. Sch., Hampstead (ILEA Schol.); Corpus Christi Coll., Cambridge (BA 1971, MA Natural Scis); Queen's Univ., Belfast (PhD Psychol. 1975). NATO Postdoctoral Res. Fellow, Haskins Labs, Yale Univ., 1975–77; Speech and Hearing Scientist, 1977–2004, Dep. Dir, 1993–2004, MRC Inst. of Hearing Res.; Special Prof. of Speech and Hearing, Univ. of Nottingham, 1991–2004. Chair: Med. Res. Adv. Panel, RNID, 2003–05; NHS Rev. of cochlear implantation in Scotland, 2005–06. Chief Res. Advr, Deafness Res. UK, 2007–11. Mem. Council, Univ. of York, 2015–18. Fellow, Acoustical Soc. of America, 1988. Trustee, Action on Hearing Loss, 2013–19. FASA. *Publications:* (with Dr D. H. Marshall) Cochlear Implantation in the UK 1990–1994, 1995. *Recreation:* repairing and riding bicycles. *Address:* Department of Psychology, University of York, Heslington, York YO10 5DD. *T:* (01904) 322913. *E:* quentin.summerfield@york.ac.uk. *Clubs:* British Cycling; York Cycleworks.

**SUMMERFIELD, Lesley;** *see* Regan, L.

**SUMMERFIELD, Quentin;** *see* Summerfield, A. Q.

**SUMMERFIELD, Prof. Rodney John,** DSc; JP; Professor of Crop Production, 1995–2001, now Emeritus, and Dean, Faculty of Agriculture and Food, 1998–2001, University of Reading; *b* 15 Nov. 1946; *s of* Ronald John Summerfield and Doris Emily Summerfield (*née* Ellis); *m* 1969, Kathryn Dorothy Olive; one *s* one *d*. *Educ:* Hinckley GS; Univ. of Nottingham (BSc 1st cl. Hons Botany 1968; PhD Eco-Physiol. 1971); Univ. of Reading (DSc 1987); FIBiol 1982–2001. Univ. Demonstr, Univ. of Nottingham, 1969–71; (part-time) Lectr, Trent Poly., 1970–71; University of Reading: Res. Fellow, 1971–73, Lectr in Crop and Plant Physiology, 1973–83, Dept of Agriculture and Horticulture; Dep. Dir, 1979–94, Dir, 1994–99, Plant Envmt Lab.; Reader in Crop Physiology, 1983–90, Prof. of Crop Physiology, 1990–95, Dept of Agriculture; Hd, Dept of Agric., 1992–98. Pres., Eur. Assoc. for Res. in Grain Legumes, 1995–99. EurBiol 1995. JP: Devon and Cornwall, 2004; S and W Devon, 2012. Dr *hc* Debrecen Univ., Hungary, 1999. *Publications:* (ed jtly) Advances in Legume Science, 1980; (ed jtly) Grain Legume Crops, 1985; (ed) World Crops: cool season food legumes, 1988; articles in learned jls. *Recreations:* walking, angling.

**SUMMERHAYES, Dr Colin Peter;** Emeritus Associate, Scott Polar Research Institute, University of Cambridge, since 2010; *b* 7 March 1942; *s of* late Leonard Percy Summerhayes and Jessica Adelaide (*née* Crump); *m* 1st, 1966 (marr. diss. 1977); one *s* one *d*; 2nd, 1978 (marr. diss. 1979); 3rd, 1981, Diana Ridley (*née* Perry); one step *s* one step *d*. *Educ:* Slough Grammar Sch.; UCL (BSc 1963); Keble Coll., Oxford; Victoria Univ., Wellington, NZ (MSc 1967; DSc 1986); Imperial Coll., London (DIC; PhD 1970). CGeol; FGS; CMarSci, FIMarEST, 2005–16. Scientific Officer, DSIR, NZ Oceanographic Inst.,

1964–67; Res. Asst, Geol. Dept, Imperial Coll., London, 1967–70; Sen. Scientific Officer, CSIR, Marine Geosci. Unit, Univ. of Cape Town, 1970–72; Asst Scientist, Geol. and Geophys Dept, Woods Hole Oceanographic Instn, 1972–76; Research Associate/Project Leader: Geochem. Br., Exxon Prodn Res. Centre, Houston, 1976–82; Global Paleoreconstruction Sect., Stratigraphy Br., BP Res. Centre, 1982–85; Manager and Sen. Res. Associate, Stratigraphy Br., BP Res. Centre, 1985–88; Dir, NERC Inst. of Oceanographic Scis Deacon Lab., 1988–95; Dep. Dir, and Hd of Seafloor Processes Div., Southampton Oceanography Centre, 1995–97; Dir, Global Ocean Observing System Project Office, Intergovernmental Oceanographic Commn, Unesco, 1997–2004; Exec. Dir, Scientific Cttee on Antarctic Res., 2004–10; Mem., UK Cttee, Scientific Cttee on Oceanic Res., 2012–15. Chairman: Internat. Adv. Bd, Korea Polar Res. Inst., 2011–12; Internat. Adv. Cttee, IASC, 2015–16; Mem., Internat. Anthropocene Wkg Gp, 2014–19. Vis. Prof., UCL, 1987–95; Erskine Fellow, Univ. of Canterbury, Christchurch, 2015–16. Member: Challenger Soc. for Marine Sci.; RSPB; WWF; American Geophysical Union; Pres., Soc. for Underwater Technol., 2010–11; Vice Pres., Geological Soc., 2010–14. *Publications:* (ed with N. J. Shackleton) North Atlantic Palaeoceanography, 1986; (ed jtly) Upwelling Systems: evolution since the Early Miocene, 1992; (ed jtly) Sequence Stratigraphy and Facies Association, 1993; (ed jtly) Upwelling in the Oceans: Dahlem Conference Report, 1995; (with S. A. Thorpe) Oceanography: an illustrated guide, 1996; (ed jtly) Understanding the Oceans, 2001; (ed jtly) Oceans 2020: science, trends and the challenge of sustainability, 2002; (jtly) Antarctic Climate Change and the Environment, 2009; (ed jtly) Understanding Earth's Polar Challenges: International Polar Year 2007–2008, 2011; (ed jtly) Science in the Snow, 2011, 2nd edn 2018; (with C. Luedecke) Third Reich in Antarctica, 2012; Earth's Climate Evolution, 2015; The Anthropocene as a Geological Time Unit: an analysis, 2019; 240 papers and abstracts. *Recreations:* birdwatching, jogging, reading, lawn bowls, films and theatre. *Address:* Scott Polar Research Institute, Lensfield Road, Cambridge CB2 1ER.

**SUMMERHAYES, Gerald Victor,** CMG 1979; OBE 1969; *b* 28 Jan. 1928; *s* of Victor Samuel and Florence A. V. Summerhayes. Administrative Service, Nigeria, 1952–81; Permanent Secretary: Local Govt, North Western State, 1975–76, Sokoto State, 1976–77; Cabinet Office (Political and Trng), 1977–79; Dir of Trng, Cabinet Office, Sokoto, 1979–81. *Address:* Bridge Cottage, Bridge Street, Sidbury, Devon EX10 0RU.

**SUMMERS, Hon. Lord; Alan Andrew Summers;** QC (Scot.) 2008; a Senator of the College of Justice in Scotland, since 2017; *b* Bridge of Allan, 27 Aug. 1964; *s* of Andrew and Helen Summers; *m* 1990, Rosemary Craig; one *s* four *d. Educ:* Dundee Univ. (LLB); Oxford Univ. (BCL); Edinburgh Univ. (DipLP). Admitted as Advocate, 1994; in practice as an Advocate, 1994–; Standing Jun. Counsel to Scottish Exec., 2000–07; Special Counsel to UK Govt, 2008–17. Chm., Faculty Services Ltd, 2008–12. Treas., Faculty of Advocates, 2012–17. *Recreation:* reading. *Address:* Craigelm, 19 Park Road, Dalkeith EH22 3DH. *T:* (0131) 226 5071.

**SUMMERS, Andrew William Graham,** CMG 2001; Chief Executive, Design Council, 1995–2003; *b* 19 June 1946; *s* of Basil Summers and Margaret (*née* Hunt); *m* 1971, Frances Halestrap; one *s* two *d. Educ:* Mill Hill Sch. (Exhibnr); Fitzwilliam Coll., Cambridge (MA Natural Scis and Econs); Harvard Business Sch. (Internat. SMP). Various mgt rôles, Ranks Hovis McDougall plc, 1968–75; J. A. Sharwood & Co.: Mkting Manager, 1975–78; Mkting Dir, 1978–80; Man. Dir, 1980–85; RHM Foods Ltd: Commercial Dir, 1986; Man. Dir, 1987–90; Chief Exec., Management Charter Initiative, 1991–94; non-executive Director: S. Daniels plc, 1991–2002; Ramboll UK (formerly Whitbybird Ltd), 2005–12. Chairman: Brandsmiths, 2003–06; Creative Connexions, 2007–09. Chm., Companies House, 2007–12. Adjunct Prof., Hong Kong Polytechnic Univ., 2004–. Policy Advr, DTI, later BERR, then BIS, 2003–10. Member: Food from Britain Export Council, 1982–86; DTI European Trade Cttee, 1986–2000 (Chm., 1998–2000); BOTB, 1998–99; British Trade Internat., 1999–2003; Creative Industries Export Promotion Adv. Gp, 1998–2002; Adv. Council, Design Mgt Inst. USA, 1998–2006; Small Business Service Strategy Bd, 2000–07; Bd, QAA, 2005–11; Bd, CRAC, 2008–10; Council, KCL, 2010– (Chm., Audit and Risk Cttee, 2011–; Dep. Chm., 2016–); Bd, UKTI Olympic Task Force, 2010–12; Bd, Public Data Gp, 2011–12; Chairman: Internat. Adv. Bd, Hong Kong Design Centre, 2004–07; Cala Social Capital, 2011; Adv. Bd, Westminster Business Sch., 2010–17; Design Effectiveness Awards, 2010–; Design Jury, Expo 2015 UK Pavilion, 2014–15; Design Partners, 2004–; Dir, Partners in Quality, 2011–12. Trustee, RSA, 2004–10 (Chm., Migration Commn, 2004–06). Mem., VSO Adv. Bd, 2004–06. Gov., Conservatoire for Dance and Drama, 2005–13. Chairman: Friends of St Mary's, Barnes, 2000–; Barnes Music Fest., 2011–. Stockton Lectr, London Bus. Sch., 2000. Mem., Bd of Companions, Chartered Mgt Inst., 2007–13 (Chm., 2010–13). CCMI (CIMgt 1997). FRSA 1991 (Dep. Pres., 2003–10); Sen. Fellow, Design Mgt Inst., 2003. Hon. DLitt Westminster, 2003. *Publications:* (contrib.) Future Present, 2000; contribs on design to Design Mgt Jl and Sunday Times. *Recreations:* fives (Pres., OM Eton Fives Club, 2004–), theatre, cooking, music, cycling. *Address:* 114 Station Road, SW13 0NB. *E:* andrew@andrewsummers.co.uk.

**SUMMERS, Janet Margaret, (Mrs L. J. Summers);** *see* Bately, J. M.

**SUMMERS, Jonathan;** baritone; *b* 2 Oct. 1946; *s* of Andrew James Summers and Joyce Isabel Smith; *m* 1969, Lesley Murphy; three *c. Educ:* Macleod High Sch., Melbourne; Prahran Tech. Coll., Melbourne. Professional début, Rigoletto (title rôle), Kent Opera, 1975; performances include: Royal Opera, Covent Garden: début, Der Freischütz, 1977; Samson et Dalila, Don Pasquale, Werther, 1983; Andrea Chénier, A Midsummer Night's Dream, Der Rosenkavalier, 1984; Die Zauberflöte, Le Nozze di Figaro, 1985; Simon Boccanegra, 1986; Falstaff, 1987; Madama Butterfly, 1988; La Bohème, 1990; Fedora, 1994; Nabucco, 1996; The Tempest, 2007; Peter Grimes, 2011; English National Opera: début, I Pagliacci, 1976; Rigoletto, 1982; Don Carlos, 1985; La Bohème, 1986; Simon Boccanegra, 1987; Eugene Onegin, 1989; Macbeth, 1990; Peter Grimes, 1991; The Force of Destiny, 1992; The Pearl Fishers, 1994; Tristan and Isolde, 1996; Figaro's Wedding, 1997; Parsifal, 1999; Billy Budd, 2012; Opera Australia, Sydney: début, La Traviata, 1981; Il Trovatore, 1983; Otello, 1991; Un Ballo in Maschera, 1993; Il Tabarro, 1995; Nabucco, Falstaff, 1996; Wozzeck, 1999; Simon Boccanegra, 2000; Peter Grimes, 2001; Tosca, 2002; Otello, 2003; Der fliegende Holländer, 2004; Rigoletto, 2006; La Traviata, 2012; Metropolitan Opera, NY: début, La Bohème, 1988; has also appeared at Glyndebourne, with Opera North, Welsh National Opera, in Toulouse, Chicago, Lausanne, Paris, Hamburg, Munich etc, and as concert soloist. Numerous recordings. *Address:* c/o Patricia Greenan, 7 White Horse Close, 27 Canongate, Edinburgh EH8 8BU. *T:* (0131) 557 5872.

**SUMMERS, Hon. Lawrence H.;** Charles W. Eliot University Professor, Harvard University, 2006–09 and since 2010; *b* 30 Nov. 1954; *s* of Robert and Anita Summers; *m* (marr. diss.); one *s* twin *d; m* 2005, Prof. Elisa New, PhD. *Educ:* MIT (BS 1975); Harvard Univ. (PhD 1982). Economics Prof., MIT, 1979–82; Domestic Policy Economist, President's Council of Economic Advrs, 1982–83; Prof. of Economics, 1983–93, Nathaniel Ropes Prof., 1987, Harvard Univ.; Vice-Pres., Develt Economics and Chief Economist, World Bank, 1991–93; Under Sec. for Internat. Affairs, 1993–95, Dep. Sec., 1995–99, Sec., 1999–2001, US Treasury; Arthur Okun Dist. Fellow, Brookings Instn, 2001; Pres., Harvard Univ., 2001–06, now Pres. Emeritus; Dir, Nat. Economic Council and Asst to Pres. of USA for Economic Policy, 2008–10. Alan Waterman Award, 1987; John Bates Clark Medal, 1993. *Publications:* Understanding Unemployment, 1990; (jtly) Reform in Eastern Europe, 1991. *Recreations:* tennis, ski-ing. *Address:* Harvard University, Massachusetts Hall, Cambridge, MA 02138, USA.

**SUMMERS, Mark John;** QC 2014; *b* Colchester, 17 Dec. 1973; *s* of John and Elspeth Summers; partner, Lindsay Ruth Busfield Lane, *qv;* one *s* one *d. Educ:* Chantry Sixth Form Coll.; Exeter Univ. (LLB Hons). Called to the Bar, Inner Temple, 1996; in practice as barrister, 1996–. *Publications:* Abuse of Process in Criminal Proceedings, 2000, 4th edn 2014; Human Rights and Criminal Justice, 2001, 3rd edn 2012; The Law of Extradition and Mutual Legal Assistance, 2003, 3rd edn 2013. *Recreations:* travel, American football. *Address:* Matrix Chambers, Griffin Building, Gray's Inn, WC1R 5LN. *T:* (020) 7404 3447, *Fax:* (020) 7404 3448. *E:* marksummers@matrixlaw.co.uk.

**SUMMERS, Nicholas;** Under Secretary, Department for Education and Employment (formerly of Education and Science, then for Education), 1981–96; *b* 11 July 1939; *s* of Henry Forbes Summers, CB; *m* 1965, Marian Elizabeth Ottley (*d* 2019); four *s. Educ:* Tonbridge Sch.; Corpus Christi Coll., Oxford. Min. of Educn, 1961–64; DES, 1964–74; Private Sec. to Minister for the Arts, 1965–66; Cabinet Office, 1974–76; DES, subseq. Dept for Educn, 1976–96. Mem., Stevenson Commn on Information and Communications Technol. in Schs, 1996–97. Trustee, Inclusion Trust (formerly TheCademy), 2005–16. *Recreations:* family, music.

**SUMMERS, William Hay;** Sheriff of Grampian, Highland and Islands at Aberdeen, since 2011; *b* Ellon, 18 Dec. 1960; *s* of Joseph B. Summers and Helen B. Summers (*née* Thain); *m* 1990, Gillian E. Craig; two *s* two *d. Educ:* Peterhead Acad.; Aberdeen Univ. (LLB, DipLP). Admitted solicitor, 1983; Milne & MacKinnon, 1982–87; Partner: MMP, 1987–94; Davies Wood Summers, 1994–2010; pt-time Sheriff, 2008–10; All-Scotland Floating Sheriff, 2010–11. *Recreations:* golf, ski-ing, walking, reading. *Clubs:* Royal Northern and University (Aberdeen); Royal Aberdeen Golf.

**SUMMERSCALE, David Michael,** MA; Head Master of Westminster School, 1986–98; *b* 22 April 1937; *s* of late Noel Tynwald Summerscale and Beatrice (*née* Wilson); *m* 1975, Pauline, *d* of late Prof. Michel Fleury, formerly Président de l'Ecole des Hautes Etudes, Paris, and Directeur des Antiquités Historiques de l'Ile-de-France; one *s* one *d. Educ:* Northaw; Sherborne Sch.; Trinity Hall, Cambridge. Lectr in English Literature and Tutor, St Stephen's Coll., Univ. of Delhi, 1959–63; Charterhouse, 1963–75 (Head of English, Housemaster); Master of Haileybury, 1976–86. Director: Namdang Tea Co. (India) Ltd, 1991–95; The Education Group Ltd, 1996–98. Oxford and Cambridge Schs Examination Bd Awarder and Reviser in English. Vice-Chm., E-SU Scholarship Cttee, 1982–93; Member: Managing Cttee of Cambridge Mission to Delhi, 1965; C. F. Andrews Centenary Appeal Cttee, 1970; HMC Academic Policy Sub-Cttee, 1982–86; Council, Charing Cross and Westminster Med. Sch., 1986–97. Governor: The Hall Sch., Hampstead, 1986–98; Arnold House Sch., St John's Wood, 1988–98; King's House Sch., Richmond, 1991–98; Hellenic Coll., London, 1996–2006; Shri Ram Sch., Delhi, 1996–2006; Gayhurst Sch., Gerrards Cross, 1998–2002; Solihull Sch., 1998–2006; Step by Step Sch., Noida, India, 2008–; Future Hope Acad., Kolkata, 2009–; Barrett Hodgson Internat. Sch., Karachi, 2010–11. Staff Advisor, Governing Body, Westminster Abbey Choir Sch., 1989–98; Member, Governing Body: Merchant Taylors' Sch., 1996–2001 (Nominated Mem., Sch. Cttee, Merchant Taylors' Co., 1988–96); Haberdashers' Aske's Schs, 2001–06; Advr and Gov., Assam Valley Sch., India, 1989– (Chm. Govs, 2015–); Consultant and Gov., Sagar Sch., India, 2001–11; Exec. Advr, British Sch., Colombo, Sri Lanka, 1999–2011; Adviser: Amman Baccalaureate Sch., Jordan, 2002–04; Al Ain English Speaking Sch., 2006–08; Scholars Internat. Acad., Dubai, 2006–11; Anglo-Chinese Sch., London, 2010– (Chm. Govs, 2017–). Member Council: Queen's Coll., London, 1991–2006 (Vice-Chm., 2000–06); Book Aid Internat. (formerly Ranfurly Library Service), 1992–98. Trustee, Criterion Theatre Trust, 1992–2002. Adviser: Rajiv Gandhi (UK) Foundn, 1999–2002; Pahamune Rehab. Centre, Sri Lanka, 2005–; Ext. Advr, Hong Kong Mgt Assoc. Coll., 1999–2002. Patron, Multi Lang. Acad., Yangon, Myanmar, 1999–2004. FRSA 1984. *Publications:* articles on English and Indian literature; dramatisations of novels and verse. *Recreations:* music, reading, mountaineering, games (squash (Mem. SRA and GB Veterans), cricket, tennis, rackets (Mem. Tennis and Rackets Assoc.), golf), grandchildren. *Address:* 4 Ashley Gardens, Ambrosden Avenue, SW1P 1QD. *Clubs:* Athenæum, I Zingari, Free Foresters, Jesters; New Zealand Golf; Club Alpin Suisse.

**SUMMERSCALE, Katharine Lucy Claire, (Kate);** writer; *b* London, 2 Sept. 1965; *d* of late Peter Wayne Summerscale and Valerie Summerscale; one *s* by Robert Randall. *Educ:* Bedales Sch.; St John's Coll., Oxford (BA Hons English Lang. and Lit.); Stanford Univ., Calif (MA Hons Communication Studies). Sub-Ed. and Commissioning Ed., The Independent Mag., 1989–93; Obituaries Writer, 1993–95, Obituaries Ed., 1995–96, Daily Telegraph; Ed., Sunday Rev., Independent on Sunday, 1998–99; Literary Ed., Daily Telegraph, 1999–2005. *Publications:* The Queen of Whale Cay, 1997 (Somerset Maugham Award, 1998); The Suspicions of Mr Whicher: or, the murder at Road Hill House, 2008 (Samuel Johnson Prize for Non-fiction, BBC Four, 2008; Galaxy Book of Year, 2009; televised, 2011); Mrs Robinson's Disgrace: the private diary of a Victorian lady, 2012; The Wicked Boy: the mystery of a Victorian child murderer, 2016. *Address:* c/o Georgia Garrett, Rogers, Coleridge & White, 20 Powis Mews, W11 1JN. *T:* (020) 7221 3717.

**SUMMERSKILL, Ben Jeffrey Peter,** OBE 2009; Director, Criminal Justice Alliance, 2015–18; *b* 6 Oct. 1961; *s* of late Hon. Michael Brynmôr Summerskill and Florence Marion Johnston Summerskill (*née* Elliott). *Educ:* Sevenoaks Sch.; Merton Coll., Oxford (Exhibnr). Dep. Gen. Manager, Mario & Franco Restaurants, 1983–85; Gen. Manager, Lennoxcourt Ltd, 1985–86; Operations Dir, Kennedy Brookes plc, 1986–90; freelance journalist, Time Out, The Face, etc., 1990; Ed., The Pink Paper, 1992; Deputy Editor: Roof, 1993–96; Londoner's Diary, Evening Standard, 1996–98; Media Ed., Daily Express and Sunday Express, 1998–2000; Society and Policy Ed., 2000, Asst Ed., 2001–03, The Observer; Chief Exec., Stonewall, 2003–14. Mem., Equality and Human Rights Commn, 2006–09 (Mem., Govt Steering Cttee, 2004–06). Mem., Westminster CC, 1994–98. Mem., Parkside CHC, 1993–95; Vice Chm., Kensington Chelsea & Westminster CHC, 1995–96. Mem., Bd, ACAS, 2017–. Trustee: Covent Garden Area Trust, 1995–99; The Silver Line, 2017–18 (Chair, 2018). Mem. of Cttee, Queen's Award for Voluntary Service, 2009–. Mem. Exec. Cttee, Fabian Soc., 2004–07. Lifetime Achievement Award, British LGBT Awards, 2015. *Publications:* (ed) The Way We Are Now: gay and lesbian lives in the 21st century, 2006.

**SUMMERSKILL, Dr the Hon. Shirley Catherine Wynne;** Medical Practitioner; Medical Officer in Blood Transfusion Service, 1983–91; *b* London, 9 Sept. 1931; *d* of late Dr E. J. Samuel and Baroness Summerskill, CH, PC. *Educ:* St Paul's Girls' Sch.; Somerville Coll., Oxford; St Thomas' Hospital. MA, BM, BCh, 1958. Treas., Oxford Univ. Labour Club, 1952. Resident House Surgeon, later House Physician, St Helier Hosp., Carshalton, 1959; Partner in Gen. Practice, 1960–68. Contested (Lab): Blackpool North by-election, 1962; Halifax, 1983. MP (Lab) Halifax, 1964–83; opposition spokesman on health, 1970–74; Parly Under-Sec. of State, Home Office, 1974–79; opposition spokesman on home affairs, 1979–83. Vice-Chm., PLP Health Gp, 1964–69, Chm., 1969–70; Mem., Labour Party NEC, 1981–83. UK delegate, UN Status of Women Commn, 1968 and 1969;

Mem. British delegn, Council of Europe and WEU, 1968, 1969. Mem., BMA. *Publications:* A Surgical Affair (novel), 1963; Destined to Love (novel), 1986. *Recreations:* music, reading, attending literature classes.

**SUMMERSON, Hugo Hawksley Fitzthomas;** Director, Palatine Properties Ltd, since 1983; Director (formerly Principal), Speaker Skills Training, since 1994; *b* 21 July 1950; *s* of late Thomas Summerson, OBE and Joan Florence Summerson; *m* 2nd, 1995, Diana, *d* of late Lt-Col T. J. C. Washington, MC; one *s. Educ:* Harrow School; Royal Agricultural College. FRICS; MRAC. Land Agent with Knight, Frank and Rutley, 1973–76; travel in S America, 1977; self-employment, 1978–83. Consultant: Amhurst Properties Ltd, 1992–94; Grandfield Public Affairs Ltd, 1996–98; Butler Kelly Ltd, 2001–13; Dir, Meridian Clocks Ltd, 1999–2003. Clerk, Chartered Secretaries' and Administrators' Co., 2011–14. Contested (C): Barking, 1983; Walthamstow, 1992. MP (C) Walthamstow, 1987–92. Mem., Select Cttee on Envmt, 1991–92; Treas., British Latin-American Parly Gp, 1990; Vice-Chm., All-Party Parly Gp on Child Abduction, 1991–92; Sec., Cons. Back Bench Agriculture Cttee, 1991–92. Chm., Greater London Area Adopted Parly Candidates Assoc., 1986; Vice-Pres., Greater London Area, Nat. Soc. of Cons. and Unionist Agents, 1989; Mem. Council, British Atlantic Gp of Young Politicians, 1989; Parly Advr to Drinking Fountain Assoc., 1989; Treas., Assoc. of Cons. Parly Candidates (formerly Westminster Candidates' Assoc.), 1998–2001. Fellow, Industry and Parlt Trust, 1991. Member: Professional Speakers Assoc., 2001–05; Assoc. of Former MPs, 2004–; UK Speechwriters' Guild, 2010–13. Mem., Internat. Bruckner Soc., 2007–. Trustee: Trinity Chapel Site Charity, 1998–2002; Hyde Park Place Estate Charity, 1998–2002; St George's Hanover Sq. Sch., 1998–2002; Hon. Treas., Parents in Need, 2014–17 (Mem. Cttee, 2017–). Churchwarden, St George's, Hanover Sq., 1998–2002; Rep. for St George's, Westminster (St Margaret) Deanery Synod, 2004–07; Mem. Council, Emmanuel Church, Wimbledon, 2019–. Sir Anthony Berry Meml Scholar, 1985. Freedom, Musicians' Co., 2018–. Composer, March of the Master Mercer, for piano and two trumpets, dedicated to Mercers' Co., 2013, perf. at Mansion House, 2014. *Recreations:* music, fishing, watching cricket. *Club:* Royal Over-Seas League.

**SUMMERTON, Dr Neil William,** CB 1997; Secretary, Partnership (UK) Ltd, since 2014 (Chairman and Executive Secretary, 1997–2002, Chairman and Executive Director, 2002–05; Executive Chairman, 2005–07; Chairman, 2007–14); *b* 5 April 1942; *s* of H. E. W. Summerton and Nancy Summerton; *m* 1965, Pauline Webb; two *s. Educ:* Wellington Grammar Sch., Shropshire; King's Coll., London (BA History 1963; PhD War Studies 1970). Min. of Transport, 1966–69; PA to Principal, 1969–71, Asst Sec. (Co-ordination), 1971–74, KCL; DoE, 1974–97; Asst Sec., heading various housing Divs, 1978–85; Under Sec., Planning Land-Use Policy Directorate, 1985–87; Under Sec., Planning and Develt Control Directorate, 1987–88; Under Sec., Local Govt Finance Policy Directorate, 1988–91; Under Sec., Water, 1991–95; Dir, Water and Land, 1996–97; Director: Oxford Centre for the Envmt, Ethics and Society, 1997–2002; Oxford Centre for Water Res., 1998–2002; Supernumerary Fellow, Mansfield Coll., Oxford, 1997–2003, now Emeritus Fellow. Attended HM Treasury Centre for Admin. Studies, 1968–69; Civil Service Top Management Programme, 1985. Non-executive Director: Redland Bricks Ltd, 1988–91; Veolia Water Southeast (formerly Folkestone and Dover Water Services Ltd, 1998–2012); North Surrey Water Co. Ltd, 1998–2000; Veolia Water Central plc (formerly Three Valleys Water), 2000–12; Director and Trustee: Partnership (UK) Ltd, 1994–; Christian Impact Ltd, 1989–98; London Christian Housing plc, 1990–98; Christian Research Assoc., 1992–98; George Müller Charitable Trust, 1998–2015; Church Planting Initiative, 2005–. Member: Cttee of Management, Council on Christian Approaches to Defence and Disarmament, 1983–2014 (Hon. Sec., 1984–91); Evangelical Alliance Council, 1989–2014 (Trustee, 1990–96 and 1997–2000). *Publications:* A Noble Task: eldership and ministry in the local church, 1987, 2nd edn 1994; Learning from the Past, Facing the Future: essays for 'Brethren', 2011; articles and essays on historical, envmtl, theological and ethical matters. *Address:* Mansfield College, Oxford OX1 3TF.

**SUMMONS, Roger Everett,** PhD; FRS 2008; Schlumberger Professor of Geobiology, Massachusetts Institute of Technology, since 2001; *b* Sydney, NSW, 11 June 1946; *s* of Neil James Summons and Jean Catherine Summons; *m* 1970, Elizabeth Kristine Diment; three *d. Educ:* Univ. of New South Wales (BSc Cl. 1 Hons Chem. 1969; PhD Chem. 1972). Fellow in Genetics, Stanford Univ., 1972–73; Australian National University: Postdoctoral Fellow in Chem., 1973–75; Res. Fellow in Chem., 1975–77; Res. Officer in Biol., 1977–83; Sen. Res. Scientist, Baas Becking Geobiological Lab., 1983–87; Principal to Chief Res. Scientist, Geoscience Australia, 1987–2001. Australian Lectr, Petroleum Explorationists Soc. of Australia, 1998. FAA 1998; Fellow: Amer. Geophysical Union, 2006; Hanse-Wissenschaftskolleg, Delmenhorst, 2008. Hon. DSc Wollongong, 2009. Treibs Award, Geochem. Soc., 2003; Halpern Medal, Univ. of Wollongong, 2005. *Publications:* over 390 articles in jls and books. *Recreations:* music, fishing, oenology, gardening. *Address:* Department of Earth, Atmospheric and Planetary Sciences, Massachusetts Institute of Technology, E25–633, 45 Carleton Street, Cambridge, MA 02139, USA. *T:* (617) 4522791, *Fax:* (617) 2538630. *E:* rsummons@mit.edu.

**SUMNER, Prof. Ann Beatrice,** PhD; Public Art Project Officer, since 2015, and Head of Cultural Engagement, since 2016, University of Leeds; *b* Bath, 1960; *d* of late Tim Sumner and of Rita Sumner; *m* 2009, Martin Johnson; two *d* by a previous marriage. *Educ:* Royal Sch., Bath; Kingswood Sch., Bath; Courtauld Inst. of Fine Art, Univ. of London (BA Hons); Newnham Coll., Cambridge (PhD 1985). Archive asst, NPG, 1981–83; Asst Curator, Holburne Mus., Bath, 1983–88; Res. Asst, Whitworth Art Gall., Manchester, 1988–90; Curator (pt-time), Wilmer Hse, Farnham, 1990–91; Keeper, Dulwich Picture Gall., 1991–95; Keeper, Holburne Mus., Bath, 1996–2000; Hd of Fine Art, Nat. Mus. of Wales, Cardiff, 2000–07; Dir, Barber Inst. of Fine Arts and Prof. of Fine Art and Curatorial Practice, 2007–12, Vis. Prof., 2012–, Univ. of Birmingham; Dir, Birmingham Mus Trust, 2012; Exec. Dir, Brontë Soc., 2012–14. Vis. Prof., Univ. of Leeds, 2015–. Mem., Steering Cttee, Nat. Inventory of Eur. Paintings, Nat. Gall., 1997. Member: Methodist Histl Adv. Gp, Oxford Brookes Univ., 2008; Curatorial and Academic Adv. Bd, Ironbridge Mus. Trust; Adv. Bd, School of Art Mus., Univ. of Aberystwyth. Historic Collections Advr, Harewood House Trust, 2015–. Pres., Bath Evening NADFAS. Trustee: Methodist Collection of Modern Art, 2004–; Mus. of Bath at Work, 2017–. *Publications:* Death, Passion and Politics: Van Dyck and the Digbys, 1995; (with Greg Smith) Thomas Jones: an artist rediscovered, 2003; Colour and Light: 50 Impressionist paintings, 2004; Gwen John and the Catholic Church, 2008; Court on Canvas: tennis in art, 2011; In Front of Nature: landscapes by Thomas Fearnley, 2012; Mitzi Cunliffe's Man-Made Fibres Commission in Context: the American sculptor's work in 1950s Britain, 2016; (jtly) Connecting Threads: Yorkshire year of the textile 2016–17, 2017; exhibn catalogues; contrib. articles to jls. *Recreations:* tennis, walking, cinema, theatre, reading, history, family. *Clubs:* Lansdown Tennis; Ilkley Lawn Tennis.

**SUMNER, Gordon Matthew, (Sting),** CBE 2003; musician, songwriter and actor; *b* Northumberland, 2 Oct. 1951; *s* of late Ernest and Audrey Sumner; *m* 1st, 1976, Frances Tomelty (marr. diss. 1984); one *s* one *d*; 2nd, 1992, Trudie Styler; two *s* two *d. Educ:* St Cuthbert's Grammar Sch., Newcastle; Warwick Coll., Newcastle (BEd 1973). Teacher, St Paul's Primary Sch., Cramlington, Newcastle, 1971–74. Singer, bass-player and songwriter, The Police, 1977–86; tours in UK, Europe and USA; reformed and toured worldwide, 2007–08. Theatre début in The Threepenny Opera, Washington, 1989. *Records include: with The Police: albums:* Outlandos d'Amour, 1978; Regatta de Blanc, 1979; Zenyatta Mondatta, 1980; Ghost in the Machine, 1981; Synchronicity, 1983; *singles:* Roxanne, 1978; Message in a Bottle, 1979; Walking on the Moon, 1979; Every Breath You Take, 1983; *solo: albums:* Dream of the Blue Turtles, 1985; Bring on the Night, 1986 (Grammy Award for Best Male Pop Vocal Perf., 1988); Nothing Like the Sun, 1987; The Soul Cages, 1991; Ten Summoner's Tales, 1993; Mercury Falling, 1996; Brand New Day, 1999 (Grammy Awards for Best Pop Album and Best Male Pop Vocal Perf., 1999); All This Time, 2001; Sacred Love, 2003; Songs from the Labyrinth, 2006; If On A Winter's Night, 2009; Symphonicities, 2010; 57th & 9th, 2016; (with Shaggy) 44/876, 2018; My Songs, 2019; *singles:* Nothing Like the Sun, 1987; The Soul Cages, 1991 (Grammy Award for Best Rock Song, 1992); Englishman in New York; After the Rain has Gone, 2000. *Film appearances include:* Quadrophenia, 1979; Radio On, 1980; Brimstone and Treacle, 1982; Dune, 1984; The Bride, 1985; Plenty, 1985; Julia and Julia, 1987; Stormy Monday, 1988; The Adventures of Baron von Munchausen, 1989; The Grotesque, 1995; Lock, Stock and Two Smoking Barrels, 1998. Composer and lyricist, musical, The Last Ship, NY, 2014, UK, 2018, Toronto, 2019. Co-founder, Rainforest Foundn, 1989. Hon. DMus: Northumbria, 1992; Newcastle, 2006. *Publications:* Jungle Stories: the fight for the Amazon, 1989; Broken Music: a memoir, 2003.

**SUMPTION, Rt Hon. Lord; Jonathan Philip Chadwick Sumption,** OBE 2003; PC 2012; FRHistS, FSA; a Justice of the Supreme Court of the United Kingdom, 2012–18; *b* 9 Dec. 1948; *s* of late Anthony James Chadwick Sumption, DSC; *m* 1971, Teresa Mary (*née* Whelan); one *s* two *d. Educ:* Eton; Magdalen College, Oxford (MA). Fellow (in History) of Magdalen College, Oxford, 1971–75; called to the Bar, Inner Temple, 1975, Bencher, 1990; QC 1986; Recorder, 1993–2001; a Judge of the Courts of Appeal of Jersey and Guernsey, 1995–2011. Mem., Judicial Appts Commn, 2006–11. Trustee: RAM, 2002–; Holburne Mus. of Art, Bath, 2008–11; London Library, 2008–12; Dir, ENO, 2015–. Sen. Res. Fellow, Inst. of Historical Res., 2009; Vis. Fellow, All Souls Coll., Oxford, 2019–20. BBC Reith Lectr, 2019. FRHistS 2006; FSA 2009. Hon. FRAM 2004. *Publications:* Pilgrimage: an image of medieval religion, 1975; The Albigensian Crusade, 1978; The Hundred Years' War, vol. 1, 1990, vol. 2, 1999, vol. 3, 2009 (Wolfson History Prize, 2009), vol. 4, 2015; Trials of the State: law and the decline of politics, 2019. *Recreations:* music, history.

**SUNAK, Rt Hon. Rishi;** PC 2019; MP (C) Richmond, Yorks, since 2015; Chief Secretary to the Treasury, since 2019; *b* 12 May 1980; *m* 2009, Akshatha, *d* of N. R. Narayana Murthy; two *d. Educ:* Winchester Coll.; Oxford Univ. (BA 1st Cl. Hons PPE 2001); Stanford Univ. (Fulbright Schol.; MBA 2006). Analyst, Principal Investment Area, Goldman Sachs, 2001–04; Partner, TCI, London, 2006; Co-Founder, investment firm; Hd, Black and Minority Ethnic Res. Unit, Policy Exchange. Dir, Catamaran Ventures. Parly Under-Sec. of State, MHCLG, 2018–19. Mem., Envmt, Food and Rural Affairs Select Cttee, 2015–17. *Address:* House of Commons, SW1A 0AA.

**SUNDERLAND, Archdeacon of;** *see* Cooper, Ven. R. G.

**SUNDERLAND, (Godfrey) Russell,** CB 1991; FCILT; Deputy Secretary, Aviation, Shipping and International, Department of Transport, 1988–94; *b* 28 July 1936; *s* of Allan and Laura Sunderland; *m* 1965, Greta Jones; one *s* one *d. Educ:* Heath Grammar Sch., Halifax; The Queen's College, Oxford (MA). Ministry of Aviation: Asst Principal, 1962; Asst Private Sec. to Minister, 1964; Principal, 1965; HM Diplomatic Service: First Sec. (Civil Air), Beirut, and other Middle East posts, 1969; Principal, Board of Trade, 1971; Asst Sec., DTI, 1973; Under Sec., DTI, 1979; Dir of Shipping Policy and Emergency Planning, Dept of Transport, 1984. Chairman: Consultative Shipping Group, 1984–88; Maritime Transport Cttee, OECD, 1992–94. Non-exec. Dir, Air Miles Travel Promotions Ltd, 1995–2001. Advr, Maersk Co. Ltd, 1994–2001. FCILT (FCIT 1995; Vice Pres., CIT, 1997–2001; Chm., Transport Faculty, CILT(UK), 2004–07). FRSA 1991. *Recreations:* garden, piano.

**SUNDERLAND, Sir John (Michael),** Kt 2006; Chairman, Cadbury Schweppes plc, 2003–08 (Chief Executive, 1996–2003); *b* 24 Aug. 1945; *s* of Harry Sunderland and Joyce Eileen Sunderland (*née* Farnish); *m* 1966, Jean Margaret Grieve; three *s* one *d. Educ:* St Andrews Univ. (MA Hons). Joined Cadbury, 1968. Non-executive Director: Rank Gp plc, 1998–2006; Barclays plc, 2005–15; AFC Energy plc, 2012–15; Member, Advisory Board: CVC Capital Partners, 2004–; Ian Jones & Partners, 2007–. Chairman: Merlin Entertainments, 2009–; Cambridge Educn Gp Ltd, 2014–17. Dir, Financial Reporting Council, 2004–11 (Chm., Corporate Governance Cttee, 2010); Trinsum (formerly Marakon Associates), 2006–09. President: ISBA, 2002–05; UK Food and Drink Fedn, 2002–04; CBI, 2004–06 (Dep. Pres., 2003–04, 2007–08). Pres., 2006–07, Dep. Pres., 2007–09, Chartered Management Inst. Gov., Council, 2008–11, Chancellor, 2011–, Aston Univ.; Gov., Council, Reading Univ., 2008–15. Associate Mem., BUPA, 2005–. *Address:* Three Barrows, Seale Road, Elstead, Surrey GU8 6LF.

**SUNDERLAND, Russell;** *see* Sunderland, G. R.

**SUNNUCKS, Stephen Richard;** Chairman, Helly Hansen, since 2016; *b* 30 Sept. 1957; *s* of late Richard George Drummond Clitherow Sunnucks and of Hilary Mary Sunnucks; *m* 1993, Louise Anita Marston; three *s. Educ:* Dr Challoner's Grammar Sch., Amersham; Sheffield Univ. (BA Hons Econs). Various posts with Marks & Spencer plc, 1979–89 (retail mgt, 1979–84; buying depts, 1984–89); J. Sainsbury plc, 1989–94 (Dir, Non-food, Savacentre, 1989–92; Deptl Dir, J. Sainsbury, 1992–94); Burton Gp plc, subsequently Arcadia Gp plc, 1994–98: Man. Dir, Dorothy Perkins Ltd, 1994–97; Man. Dir, Mergers, Acquisitions and New Business Develt, 1997–98; Man. Dir, Retail, New Look plc, 1998–2000; Chief Exec., New Look Gp plc, 2000–04; Pres., Europe and Strategic Alliances, 2005–11, Internat. Div., 2011–12, Global Pres., 2012–14, Gap Inc. Chm., Turner Contemporary Gall., 2015–16. *Recreations:* golf, photography, ski-ing. *E:* stephen.sunnucks@btinternet.com.

**SUPACHAI PANITCHPAKDI,** PhD; Secretary-General, UN Conference on Trade and Development, 2005–13; Member, Secretariat, and President, Program on Global Economy, Institute for Cultural Diplomacy; *b* Bangkok, 30 May 1946; *m* Mrs Sasai; one *s* one *d. Educ:* Netherlands Sch. of Econs, Rotterdam (Bank of Thailand Schol.; BA, MA, PhD 1973). Vis. Fellow, Dept of Applied Econs, Univ. of Cambridge, 1973; Bank of Thailand, 1974–86, latterly Dir of Financial Instns Supervision Dept; Pres., Thai Military Bank, 1988–92. MP (Democrat Party) Bangkok, 1986–88, 1992–2002; Dep. Minister of Finance, 1986–88; Mem., Nat. Assembly, 1991; Senator, 1992; Dep. Prime Minister, 1992–95; Dep. Prime Minister and Minister of Commerce, Thailand, 1997–2002; Dir Gen., WTO, 2002–05. Kt Grand Cordon (Special Class), Order of White Elephant (Thailand). *Publications:* Globalization and Trade in the New Millennium, 2001; (with Mark Clifford) China and WTO: changing China changing WTO, 2002.

**SUPPERSTONE, Hon. Sir Michael (Alan)**, Kt 2010; **Hon. Mr Justice Supperstone**; a Judge of the High Court, Queen's Bench Division, since 2010; a Judge of the Employment Appeal Tribunal, since 2011; Judge in Charge of the Administrative Court, since 2017; *b* 30 March 1950; *s* of late Harold Bernard Supperstone and Muriel Supperstone; *m* 1985, Dianne Jaffe; one *s* one *d*. *Educ*: St Paul's School; Lincoln College, Oxford (MA, BCL). Called to the Bar, Middle Temple, 1973, Bencher, 1999; in practice, 1974; QC 1991; Asst Recorder, 1992–96; Recorder, 1996–2010; a Dep. High Ct Judge, 1998–2010; Liaison Judge (with resp. for Admin. Ct) for N and NE, QBD, 2013–14. Vis. Scholar, Harvard Law Sch., 1979–80; Vis. Lectr, Nat. Univ. of Singapore, 1981, 1982. Chm., Administrative Law Bar Assoc., 1997–99 (Sec., 1986–91; Treas., 1991–94; Vice-Chm. 1995–96). Consulting Ed., Butterworths Local Government Reports, 1999–2010. *Publications*: Brownlie's Law of Public Order and National Security, 2nd edn 1981; Immigration: the law and practice, 1983, 3rd edn 1994, cons. ed., 4th edn, as Immigration and Asylum, 1996; (contrib.) Halsbury's Laws of England, 4th edn reissue, Administrative Law, 1989, 2001 (Gen. Ed.), Extradition Law, 2000; (ed jtly and contrib.) Judicial Review, 1992, 4th edn 2010; (contrib.) Butterworths Local Government Law, 1998; (jtly) Local Authorities and the Human Rights Act 1998, 1999; (jtly) The Freedom of Information Act 2000, 2001; (Jt Gen. Ed.) Administrative Court Practice, 2002, 2nd edn 2008; (ed) Judicial Review, Halsbury's Laws of England, 5th edn, 2010; articles on public law. *Recreations*: playing tennis, watching cricket, reading history. *Address*: High Court of Justice, Royal Courts of Justice, WC2A 2LL. *Clubs*: MCC, Garrick, Royal Automobile.

**SUPPLE, Prof. Barry Emanuel**, CBE 2000; FRHistS; FBA 1987; Director, Leverhulme Trust, 1993–2001; Professor of Economic History, University of Cambridge, 1981–93, now Professor Emeritus; *b* 27 Oct. 1930; *s* of Solomon and Rose Supple; *m* 1st, 1958, Sonia (*née* Caller) (*d* 2002); two *s* one *d*; 2nd, 2003, Virginia (*née* Tincher) (*d* 2016). *Educ*: Hackney Downs Grammar Sch.; London Sch. of Econs and Pol Science (BScEcon 1952; Hon. Fellow, 2001); Christ's Coll., Cambridge (PhD 1955); LittD Cantab 1993. FRHistS 1972. Asst Prof. of Business History, Grad. Sch. of Business Admin, Harvard Univ., 1955–60; Associate Prof. of Econ. Hist., McGill Univ., 1960–62; University of Sussex: Lectr, Reader, then Prof. of Econ. and Social Hist., 1962–78; Dean, Sch. of Social Sciences, 1965–68; Pro-Vice-Chancellor (Arts and Social Studies), 1968–72; Pro-Vice-Chancellor, 1978; University of Oxford: Reader in Recent Social and Econ. Hist., 1978–81; Professorial Fellow, Nuffield Coll., 1978–81; Professorial Fellow, 1981–83, Hon. Fellow, 1984, Christ's Coll., Cambridge; Master of St Catharine's Coll., Cambridge, 1984–93 (Hon. Fellow, 1993). Hon. Fellow, Worcester Coll., 1986; Associate Fellow, Trumbull Coll., Yale, 1986. Chm., Consultative Cttee of Assessment of Performance Unit, DES, 1975–80; Member: Council, SSRC, 1972–77; Social Science Fellowship Cttee, Nuffield Foundn, 1974–97. Pres., Econ. Hist. Soc., 1992–95. Foreign Sec., British Acad., 1995–99. Co-editor, Econ. Hist. Rev., 1973–82. Hon. Fellow, Inst. of Historical Res., 2001. Hon. FRAM 2001. Hon. DLitt: London Guildhall, 1993; Sussex, 1998; Leicester, 1999; Warwick, 2000; Bristol, 2001. *Publications*: Commercial Crisis and Change in England, 1600–42, 1959; (ed) The Experience of Economic Growth, 1963; Boston Capitalists and Western Railroads, 1967; The Royal Exchange Assurance: a history of British insurance, 1720–1970, 1970; (ed) Essays in Business History, 1977; History of the British Coal Industry: vol. 4, 1914–46, The Political Economy of Decline, 1987; (ed) The State and Economic Knowledge: the American and British experience, 1990; (ed) The Rise of Big Business, 1992; Doors Open, 2008; Ten Days in Poland, 2010; It Will Go Away: a memoir of the Solovitch family, 1911–2013, 2013; Hoops of Steel: letters to departed friends, 2015; articles and revs in learned jls. *Recreations*: reading, writing. *Address*: 3 Scotts Gardens, Whittlesford, Cambridge CB22 4NR. *T*: (01223) 830606.
*See also* T. A. Supple.

**SUPPLE, Timothy Adam**; stage director; *b* 24 Sept. 1962; *s* of Prof. Barry Emanuel Supple, *qv* and late Sonia Caller; one *s* two *d* by Melly Still; *m* 2009, Archana Ramaswamy; one *d*. *Educ*: Lewes Priory Comprehensive Sch.; Gosford Hill Sch.; Gonville and Caius Coll. and Churchill Coll., Cambridge (BA Hist./English). Assistant Director: York Th. Royal, 1985–87; Royal Court Th., 1987; RNT, 1988–89; Associate Dir, Leicester Haymarket, 1989–90; Artistic Dir, Young Vic Th., 1993–2000; Jt Founder and Artistic Dir, Dash Arts, 2005–. *Productions include*: *theatre*: Accidental Death of an Anarchist, NT, 1990; Grimm Tales, Young Vic, 1994, 1998; Spring Awakening, 1995; Comedy of Errors, RSC, 1996; Haroun and the Sea of Stories, NT, 1998; Tales from Ovid, RSC, 1999; A Servant to Two Masters, RSC, Young Vic, 1999; Midnight's Children, RSC, NY, 2003; Cosmonaut's Last Message, Donmar Warehouse, 2005; A Midsummer Night's Dream, Dash Arts/British Council, India, 2005–06, Verona, 2006, Stratford upon Avon, 2006, 2007, London, 2007, UK Tour, 2007, Australia, USA and Canada, 2008; As You Like It, Curve, Leicester, 2009; One Thousand and One Nights, Dash Arts/Luminato, Toronto, Chicago and Edinburgh Internat. Fest., 2011; Freedom on the Tyne, Tyne Bridge, Newcastle upon Tyne, 2017; Tempest, Nat. Centre for Performing Arts, Beijing, 2018; prodns at Chichester Fest. Th.; Nat. Th. of Norway; Maxim Gorki Th., Berlin; Tel Aviv Opera House; Sheffield Crucible Th.; BBT Istanbul; also tours, British Isles, Europe, USA, Far East, S America, Australia and India; *opera*: Hansel and Gretel, Opera North, 2001; Babette's Feast, Royal Opera, 2002, 2004; The Magic Flute, Opera North, 2003, 2007; Il Ritorno d'Ulisse in Patria, Grange Fest., 2017; *films*: Twelfth Night, 2002; Rockabye, 2004. *Publications*: co-adaptor, theatre adaptations: Dario Fo, Accidental Death of an Anarchist, 1990; Carol Ann Duffy: Grimm Tales, 1994; More Grimm Tales, 1997; Beasts and Beauties, 2004; Salman Rushdie: Haroun and the Sea of Stories, 1998; Midnight's Children, 2003; Ted Hughes, Tales from Ovid, 1999; Hanan al Shaykh, One Thousand and One Nights, 2011. *Recreations*: reading, walking, music, politics, history, philosophy, yoga, cooking, travel, children. *E*: timsupple@gmail.com.

**SUR, Prof. Mriganka**, PhD; FRS 2006; Newton Professor of Neuroscience, Department of Brain and Cognitive Sciences, since 1997, and Director, Simons Center for the Social Brain, since 2012, Massachusetts Institute of Technology; *b* Fatehgarh, India, 1953. *Educ*: Indian Inst. of Technol. (BTech 1974); Vanderbilt Univ. (MS 1975; PhD 1978). Postdoctoral res., SUNY Stony Brook; Sch. of Medicine, Yale Univ., 1983–86; joined Dept of Brain and Cognitive Scis, MIT, 1986, Prof., 1993–; Hd of Dept, 1997–2012; Sherman Fairchild Prof. of Neurosci., 1998. *Publications*: articles in jls. *Address*: Mriganka Sur Laboratory, Massachusetts Institute of Technology, 43 Vassar Street, 46–6227, Cambridge, MA 02139, USA.

**SURANI, Prof. Azim**, PhD; CBE 2007; FRS 1990; Mary Marshall and Arthur Walton Professor of Physiology and Reproduction, 1991–2013, now Emeritus, and Director, Germline and Epigenomics Research, Gurdon Institute, University of Cambridge; Fellow, King's College, Cambridge, since 1994. *Educ*: Univ. of Cambridge (PhD 1976). Sen. Principal Investigator, AFRC Inst. of Animal Physiol., later Inst. of Animal Physiol. and Genetics Res., 1979–91. FMedSci 2001. Canada Gairdner Internat. Award, 2018. *Publications*: articles in jls. *Address*: Gurdon Institute, Henry Wellcome Building of Cancer and Developmental Biology, University of Cambridge, Tennis Court Road, Cambridge CB2 1QN.

**SURBER, Elizabeth**; Headmistress, King's High School for Girls, Warwick, 2001–15; *b* Kingston upon Thames; *d* of George Morphett and Olive Morphett; *m* 1976, Thomas Gordon Surber. *Educ*: Tiffin Girls' Sch., Kingston upon Thames; Univ. of Exeter (BA, MA Hons); Jesus Coll., Oxford (PGCE Dist.). Teacher of French: Tiffin Girls' Sch., Kingston upon Thames, 1979–82; Cheltenham Ladies' Coll., 1982–88; Second Dep. Headmistress, Bedford High Sch., 1988–94; Headmistress, Laurel Park Sch., Glasgow, 1995–2001. *Recreations*: ballet, walking, travel.

**SURFACE, Richard Charles**; Partner, Oliver Wyman (formerly Oliver, Wyman & Co., then Mercer Oliver Wyman) (Director, 2000–05; Managing Director, 2005). *Educ*: Univ. of Minnesota; Univ. of Kansas (BA Maths); Harvard Grad. Sch. of Business Admin (MBA). Actuarial Asst, Nat. Life & Accident Insce Co., Nashville, Tenn, 1970–72; Corporate Treasury Analyst, Mobil Corp., NY, 1974–77; Dir, Corporate Planning, Northwest Industries Inc., Chicago, 1977–81; American Express Co., London and Frankfurt, 1981–89: Regl Vice-Pres. (Card Strategic Planning), 1981–82; Divisional Vice-President: Business Develt, 1982–86; Card Mkting, 1986–87; and Gen. Manager, Personal Financial Services, 1987–89; Gen. Manager, Corporate Develt, Sun Life, 1989–91; Managing Director: Sun Life Internat., 1991–95; Pearl Group PLC, 1995–99; AMP (UK) PLC, 1995–99. *Publications*: Das Vermächtnis (The Legacy), 2014.

**SURI, Baron** *cr* 2014 (Life Peer), of Ealing in the London Borough of Ealing; **Ranbir Singh Suri**; Chairman, Oceanic Jewellers Ltd, since 1991; *b* 1935. Pres., British Asian Conservative Link, 2011– (founding Chm., 1997–2011).

**SURREY, Archdeacon of**; *see* Davies, Ven. R. P.

**SUSMAN, Hon. Louis B.**; Ambassador of the United States of America to the Court of St James's, 2009–13; Senior Adviser, Perella Weinberg Partners, since 2018; *b* St Louis, Missouri; *m* Marjorie Sachs; one *s* one *d*. *Educ*: Univ. of Michigan (BA 1959); Washington Univ. (LLB 1962). In practice as lawyer, Thompson & Mitchell, St Louis, 1962–89, Sen. Partner, 1981–89; with Salomon Brothers Inc., 1989–98, Vice Chm., Investment Banking, 1996; Chm., N Amer. Customer Cttee, Citibank and Citigroup Inc., 1998–2000; Vice Chm., Citigroup Corporate and Investment Banking, 2000–09; former Mem., Internat. Adv. Bd, Citigroup; non-exec. Chm., DJE Hldgs, 2013. Mem., Bd of Dirs and Mgt Cttee, St Louis Cardinals, 1975–89. Mem., Adv. Commn on Public Diplomacy, 1988; Dir, Center for Nat. Policy, Washington, DC. Member: Chm.'s Circle, Chicago Council on Global Affairs; Bd, Art Inst. of Chicago; Bd, Northwestern Children's Meml Hosp.

**SUSMAN, Peter Joseph**; QC 1997; a Recorder, 1993–2016; *b* 20 Feb. 1943; *s* of Albert Leonard Susman and Sybil Rebecca Susman (*née* Joseph); *m* 1st, 1966, Peggy Judith Stone (marr. diss. 1996); one *s* one *d*; 2nd, 2006, Belinda Zoe Schwehr (separated 2013); one *s*. *Educ*: Dulwich Coll.; Lincoln Coll., Oxford (Oldfield Open Law Schol.; BA 1964; MA 1970); Law Sch., Univ. of Chicago (British Commonwealth Fellow; Fulbright Schol.; JD 1965). Called to the Bar, Middle Temple, 1966, Bencher, 2005; in practice as a barrister, 1966–70 and 1972–; Associate, Debevoise, Plimpton, Lyons & Gates, NYC, 1970–71; Asst Recorder, 1989–93. Ind. Standing Counsel to Ofcom, 2003–05. *Recreations*: playing the clarinet, windsurfing, ski-ing. *Address*: Henderson Chambers, 2 Harcourt Buildings, Temple, EC4Y 9DB. *T*: (020) 7583 9020.

**SUSSEX, Paula Elizabeth**; Chief Executive, Student Loans Company, since 2018; *b* Horsham, 19 Dec. 1964; *d* of Albert and Giuliana Sussex. *Educ*: King's Coll. London (LLB 1987); Inns of Court Sch. of Law; London Business Sch. (MSc 1996). Consultant, Coopers & Lybrand, 1988–95; analyst, TXU Energy, 1996–99; Dir, KPMG, 1999–2002; Senior Vice President: Atos Origin, 2002–12; CGI, 2012–14; Chief Exec., Charity Commn, 2014–17. FRSA. *Recreations*: art, walking, music. *Address*: 6a Denbigh Street, SW1V 2ER. *T*: (020) 7630 8739. *E*: paulasussex@gmail.com.

**SUSSKIND, Janis Elizabeth**, OBE 2014; Managing Director, Boosey & Hawkes Music Publishers Ltd, London, since 2012; *b* 27 Nov. 1952; *d* of John H. Tomfohrde, Jr, and Ruth Elizabeth Robbins Tomfohrde; *m* 1st, 1973, Walter Susskind (*d* 1980); 2nd, 1993, Antony Fell (*d* 2011). *Educ*: Princeton Univ. (BA *cum laude*). Boosey & Hawkes Music Publishers Ltd: Hd of Promotion, 1984–96; Dir, Composers and Repertoire, 1997–2004; Publishing Dir, 2005–12; Dir, Boosey & Hawkes Hldgs Ltd, 2008–. Director: NMC Record Co., 1991–92; Classic Copyright (Hldgs) Ltd, 2004–08. Chm., SPNM, 1983–88. Arts Council of England, subseq. Arts Council England: Mem., Music Panel, 1993–2001; Mem. and Dep. Chm., Stabilization Adv. Panel, 1996–2006. Mem. Council, RCM, 1996–2005. Member Board: Birmingham Contemporary Music Gp, 1991–2000; English National Opera, 2004–12; Internat. Artist Managers' Assoc., 2012–14; LSO, 2020–; Mem. Council, Royal Philharmonic Soc., 2016–. Trustee, Britten-Pears Foundn, 2001–10, 2011–. Hon. RCM 2007. *Recreations*: reading, theatre, contemporary art, ski-ing, tennis, playing chamber music. *Address*: c/o Boosey & Hawkes Music Publishers Ltd, Aldwych House, 71–91 Aldwych, WC2B 4HN.

**SUSSKIND, Prof. Richard Eric**, OBE 2000; DPhil; FRSE; author and independent consultant, since 1997; Strategy and Technology (formerly Information and Technology) Adviser to Lord Chief Justice of England, since 1998; *b* 28 March 1961; *s* of Dr Werner and late Shirley Susskind; *m* 1985, Michelle Latter; two *s* one *d*. *Educ*: Hutchesons' Grammar Sch., Glasgow; Univ. of Glasgow (LLB Hons 1st class; Dip. Legal Practice); Balliol Coll., Oxford (Snell Exhibnr; DPhil 1986). FRSE 1997. CITP 2004. Tutor in Law, Univ. of Oxford, 1984–86; Head of Expert Systems, Ernst & Young, 1986–89; Special Advr, 1989–94, Mem. of Mgt Bd, 1994–97, Masons. Vis. Prof., 1990–2001, Prof., 2001–, Law Sch., Univ. of Strathclyde; Gresham Prof. of Law, 2000–04; Hon. Prof., 2005, Emeritus Prof. of Law, 2007, Gresham Coll.; Founder Mem., Adv. Bd, 2002–, Vis. Prof. of Internet Studies, 2009–, Oxford Internet Inst., Univ. of Oxford (Chm., Adv. Bd, 2011–); Larry J. Hoffman, Greenberg Traurig Dist. Vis. Prof. in Business of Law, Univ. of Miami Sch. of Law, 2013–14. IT Advr, Lord Woolf's Access to Justice Inquiry, 1995–96. Pres., Soc. for Computers and Law, 2011– (Chm., 1990–92; Hon. Mem., 1992–). Member: Inf. Technol. and the Courts Cttee, 1990– (Co-Chair, 2006–); Court of Appeal (Civil Div.) Review Team, 1996–97; Modernising Govt Project Bd, 1999–2001; Freedom of Inf. Project Bd, 2003–05; Public Legal Educn Strategy Gp, 2008–; Inf. System Improvement Strategy Prog. Bd, Nat. Policing Improvement Agency, 2008–09; Prog. Bd, Making Justice Work, Scottish Govt, 2010–13; Pres. of QBD's Rev. of Efficiency of Criminal Proceedings, 2014–15; Chairman: Adv. Panel on Crown Copyright, subseq. Public Sector Inf., 2003–08; Online Dispute Resolution Adv. Gp, Civil Justice Council, 2014–; Lord Chief Justice's Artificial Intelligence Adv. Gp, 2019–. IT Advr, Jersey Legal Inf. Bd, 1998–. Mem., Adv. Bd, Lyceum Capital, 2008–; Chm., Client Adv. Bd, Integreon, 2011–12. Expert Consultee: Criminal Courts Rev., 2000–01; Tribunals Rev., 2000–01. Special Advr, Canadian Bar Assoc., 2009–. Mem., Adv. Bd, UCL Judicial Inst., 2011–; Hon. Prof., Faculty of Laws, UCL, 2011–. Gen. Editor, 1992–2014, Founding Ed., 2014–, Internat. Jl of Law and Information Technology; Law columnist, The Times, 1999–2008. Trustee, Lokahi Foundn, 2005–. Freeman, City of London, 1992; Freeman, 1992, Liveryman, 1993, Mem. Court, 1994–2003, Co. of Information Technologists. Member: Council, Gresham Coll., 2002–04; External Adv. Bd, AHRC Res. Centre for Studies in Intellectual Property and Technol. Law, Univ. of Edinburgh, 2002–. Gov., Haberdashers' Aske's Schs, Elstree,

1998–2013; Mem., Balliol Coll. Campaign Bd, 2000–07. FRSA 1992; FBCS 1997. Hon. Fellow, Centre for Law and Computing, Durham Univ., 2001–. Hon. Bencher, Gray's Inn, 2015. George & Thomas Hutcheson Award, 2001. *Publications:* Expert Systems in Law, 1987; (with P. Capper) Latent Damage Law: the expert system, 1988; Essays on Law and Artificial Intelligence, 1993; The Future of Law, 1996; Transforming the Law, 2000; (ed jtly) Essays in Honour of Sir Brian Neill, 2003; (ed) The Susskind Interviews: legal experts in changing times, 2005; The End of Lawyers?, 2008; Tomorrow's Lawyers, 2013, 2nd edn 2017; (with D. Susskind) The Future of the Professions, 2015; Online Courts and the Future of Justice, 2019. *Recreations:* running, reading, golf, cinema, ski-ing. *Address:* 67 Aldenham Avenue, Radlett, Herts WD7 8JA. *T:* (01923) 469655. *E:* richard@susskind.com.

**SUTCH, Rev. Dom Antony;** see Sutch, C. T.

**SUTCH, Ven. (Christopher) David,** TD 1992; Chaplain, St Andrew's, Costa del Sol, 2007–13; Archdeacon of Gibraltar, 2008–13; *b* Oxford, 27 Aug. 1947; *s* of Christopher Lang Sutch and Gladys Ethelwyn Sutch; *m* 1969, Margaret Anne, (Megan); three *s*. *Educ:* King's Coll., London (AKC 1969); DipHE 2000. Ordained deacon, 1970, priest, 1971; Curate, St Andrew's, Hartcliffe, Bristol, 1970–75; Team Vicar, Dorcan, Swindon, 1975–79; Vicar, St Helen's, Alveston, Bristol, 1979–89; Rector, St Mary's, Yate New Town, 1989–99; Vicar, St Matthew's, Cainscross with Selsey, Glos, 1999–2007. Area Dean: Westbury, 1988–89; Stapleton, 1996–99; Stonehouse, 2005–07. Royal Army Chaplains Dept (Volunteers), 1980–2003; Chaplain, RBL, Glos, 2005–07; Hon. Col, N Somerset Yeomanry Sqdn, 2003–09. *Recreations:* digital photography, grandchildren.

**SUTCH, Christopher Timothy, (Rev. Dom Antony Sutch);** Parish Priest, St Benet, Beccles, 2003–12; *b* 19 June 1950; *s* of late Ronald Antony Sutch and of Kathleen Sutch (*née* Roden). *Educ:* Downside Sch.; Exeter Univ.; St Benet's Hall, Oxford. Chartered Accountant, 1971–75; postulant, 1975, novice, 1977, professed Benedictine monk, 1981; priest, 1981; Housemaster, Caverel House, 1985–95, Headmaster, 1995–2003, Downside Sch. Member: BBC Ind. Assessment Bd on Religious Broadcasting, 1998; Cttee, Catholic Ind. Schs Conf., 2000–03. Mem. (Ind), Beccles Town Council, 2007–10. Mem., Governing Body, Bath Univ., 1995–2002; Governor: All Hallows Prep. Sch., 1996–2004; Sacred Heart Primary, Chew Magna, 1996–2004 (Chm., 1997–99); St Mary's Sch., Woldingham, 2001–04; Moor Park Sch., 2002–09; St Benet's Primary Sch., Beccles (Vice-Chm.), 2003–10; Moreton Hall Prep. Sch., 2004–10; St Felix Sch., Southwold, 2006–11; Downside Sch., 2006–10; Guardian, St Mary's Sch., Shaftesbury, 1999–2003; Trustee, St Edward's Sch., Cheltenham, 2004–08. Trustee: Jackdaws Educnl Trust, 2003–06; Theodore Trust, 2006–11. Mem. Strategy Bd, Hobsons Guide, 2003–10. Dir, Catholic Herald Ltd, 2003–08. Chair, Adv. Bd, AEGIS, 2008–10. Patron: Dementia UK, 2010–11; Kairos, 2011–14. Presenter and contributor, Thought for the Day, BBC Radio 4, 2003–10; TV and radio progs. Co-ordinator, Janet Seymour Wedderburn Painting Exhibition, Lindores Abbey Distillery, 2019. Silver Medal, 2018, Bronze Medal 2019, Dalemain Internat. Marmalade Competition; Winner, Man-made Category, Mackays Dundee Marmalade Competition, 2019. Canonical Dispensation Procedures, 2019–. *Publications:* articles in newspapers, magazines and jls. *Recreations:* gardening, cricket, horse racing. *Address:* c/o PO Box 95, 87 Tay Street, Newport on Tay, Dundee DD6 8AR. *Clubs:* East India, Naval and Military, Lord's Taverners; Emeriti, Stratton Cricket (Pres., 1995–2003).

**SUTCH, Ven. David;** see Sutch, Ven. C. D.

**SUTCLIFFE, Allan;** a Director, British Gas plc, 1986–91; *b* 30 Jan. 1936; *s* of Bertie and May Sutcliffe; *m* 1983, Pauline (*d* 2018), *d* of Mark and Lilian Abrahams; one *s* one *d* by a previous marr. *Educ:* Neath Grammar Sch.; University Coll. London (LLB). FCMA. Graduate trainee, BR, 1957–60; various positions in Finance in Western, Eastern and Southern Regions and at HQ, BR, 1960–70; Wales Gas Board: Chief Accountant, 1970; Dir of Finance, 1972; Deputy Chairman: British Gas W Midlands, 1980; British Gas N Thames, 1983; Man. Dir, Finance, British Gas plc, 1986. Freeman, City of London, 1985. *Publications:* articles on Pepper's Ghost and the Birmingham stage and Dickens in the music hall. *Recreations:* music, pre-1940 entertainment based on Dickens's writings. *Address:* Southview, Town Mill Road, Cowbridge, Vale of Glamorgan CF71 7BE. *T:* (01446) 774165. *Club:* Royal Automobile.

**SUTCLIFFE, Andrea Mary,** CBE 2018; Chief Executive and Registrar, Nursing and Midwifery Council, since 2019; *b* Bradford, 22 March 1964; *d* of David and Rita Sutcliffe; *m* 2008, David Stout. *Educ:* Longfield Sch., Darlington; Queen Elizabeth Sixth Form Coll., Darlington; London Sch. of Econs (BA Hons Medieval and Modern Hist. 1985). Finance Manager, Tower Hamlets HA, 1986–89; Contracting and Policy Manager, Bloomsbury and Islington HA, 1989–92; General Manager: Camden and Islington Community Health Services NHS Trust, 1992–95; St George's Healthcare NHS Trust, 1995–99; Asst Dir, Social Services, London Bor. of Camden, 1999–2000; Planning and Resources Dir, 2000–04, Dep. Chief Exec., 2004–07, NICE; Chief Exec., Appointments Commn, 2007–12; Chief Exec., Social Care Inst. for Excellence, 2012–13; Chief Inspector of Adult Social Care, Care Quality Commn, 2013–19. Mem., Audit Commn, 2013–15. Hon DSc Leeds, 2016. *Recreations:* friends and family, quirky films, reading, hiking, Sunderland FC. *Address:* Nursing and Midwifery Council, 23 Portland Place, W1B 1PZ.

**SUTCLIFFE, Andrew Harold Wentworth;** QC 2001; a Recorder, since 2000; a Deputy High Court Judge, since 2004; *b* 7 Sept. 1960; *s* of John Harold Vick Sutcliffe, *qv*; *m* 1988, Emma Elisabeth Stirling; three *d* (one *s* decd). *Educ:* Winchester Coll.; Worcester Coll., Oxford (MA). Pres., Oxford Union Soc., 1981. 2nd Lieut, Royal Scots Dragoon Guards, 1978–79. Called to the Bar, Inner Temple, 1983; in practice as barrister, 1983–, specialising in commercial law, esp. banking and entertainment. Chm., Great Fosters (1931) Ltd, 2009–. Mem., Special Project Gp, Duke of Edinburgh's Award, 1986–96. Mem., Cttee, Moorland Assoc., 1996–; Chm., Kildale Agricl and Horticultural Show Cttee, 1988–; Vice Pres., Black Face Sheep Breeders' Assoc., 1989–. Liveryman, Co. of Fishmongers, 1996–. Gov., Fox Primary Sch., Kensington, 1993–. Trustee, Zebra Housing Assoc., 1988–. *Recreations:* walking, bees, listening to music. *Address:* Kildale Hall, Whitby, Yorks YO21 2RQ; 3 Verulam Buildings, Gray's Inn, WC1R 5NT. *T:* (020) 7831 8441. *Clubs:* MCC; Kildale Cricket (Pres.).

**SUTCLIFFE, Anne-Marie Christine Elizabeth;** Headmistress, Thorpe House School, 2008–10; *b* 24 Jan. 1949; *d* of late Dr Norman Mutton and Mary Mutton (*née* Dobson); *m* 1970, Victor Herbert Sutcliffe; one *s* one *d*. *Educ:* convent schs; Girton Coll., Cambridge (BA 1st cl. Hons History tripos). Teacher, Stroud Girls' High Sch., 1975–79; Head of History Department: Bishop Thomas Grant Sch., 1979–81; Ursuline Convent High Sch., 1981–86; organising confs, servicing cttees, etc, CAFOD, Council on Christian Approaches to Defence and Disarmament, 1986–88; Teacher, 1988–95, Head of History, 1991–95, St Paul's Girls' Sch.; Dep. Head, Channing Sch., 1995–98; Headmistress, Emanuel Sch., 1998–2004. Mem. Cttee, HMC, 2002–03. Ind. Chm., Cranial Forum, 2004–07. Governor: King's Hse Sch., Richmond, 1999–2004; Hampton Sch., Middx, 2004–10. *Recreations:* theatre, opera, travel, history. *Address:* 15 Fort Picklecombe, Maker, Torpoint, Cornwall PL10 1JF. *T:* (01752) 829214.

**SUTCLIFFE, Gerard;** *b* 13 May 1953; *s* of Henry and Margaret Sutcliffe; *m* 1972, Maria Holgate; three *s*. *Educ:* Cardinal Hinsley Grammar Sch.; Bradford Coll. Salesperson, Brown Muff dept store, 1969–71; display advertising clerk, Bradford Telegraph and Argus, 1971–75; Field Printers, 1975–80; Dep. Sec., SOGAT, subseq. GPMU, 1980–94. Bradford Metropolitan District Council: Councillor, 1982–88 and 1990–94; Leader, 1992–94. MP (Lab) Bradford S, June 1994–2015. PPS to Chief Sec., HM Treasury, 1998, to Sec. of State for Trade and Industry, 1998–99; an Asst Govt Whip, 1999–2001; Vice Chamberlain, HM Household, 2001–03; Parly Under-Sec. of State, DTI, 2003–06, Home Office, 2006–07, Ministry of Justice, 2007, DCMS, 2007–10. Chm., Parly Football Team. *Recreations:* sport, music, politics.

**SUTCLIFFE, James Harry,** FIA; Chairman, Arboretum Partners LLP, since 2013; *b* 20 April 1956; *s* of Robert William Sutcliffe and Margaret Sutcliffe; *m* 1977, Esther Sharon Pincus; two *s*. *Educ:* Univ. of Cape Town (BSc). FIA 1979. Chief Operating Officer, Jackson Nat. Life, 1989–92; Chief Exec., Prudential UK plc, 1995–97; Dep. Chm., Liberty Internat., 1998–99; Chief Exec., Life, 2000–01; Gp Chief Exec., Old Mutual plc, 2001–08. Non-executive Director: Lonmin plc, 2007–17 (Sen. Ind. Dir, 2012–17); Liberty Life (S Africa), 2009–; Chairman: Sun Life Financial (Canada), 2011–; Cover Genius, 2018–; Certua, 2018–; Vice Chm., Gunn Agri Partners, 2014–. Dir, Financial Reporting Council, 2009–15; Chm., Codes and Standards Cttee, 2009–15. Sen. Advr, CVC Capital Partners, 2009–15. *Recreations:* golf, bridge. *E:* Jim.Sutcliffe1@gmail.com. *Club:* Pinner Hill Golf.

**SUTCLIFFE, James Thomas, (Tom);** opera critic and author; *b* 4 June 1943; *s* of Lt-Comdr James Denis Sutcliffe, OBE, RN and Rosamund Frances Sutcliffe, *d* of Major T. E. G. Swayne; *m* 1973, Meredith Frances Oakes, playwright, librettist, music critic, translator; one *s* one *d*. *Educ:* Prebendal Sch., Chichester; Hurstpierpoint Coll.; Magdalen Coll., Oxford (MA English 1967). English Teacher, Central Tutorial Sch. for Young Musicians, 1964–65; Manager, Musica Reservata, 1965–69; concert perfs with Musica Reservata, Schola Polyphonica, Pro Cantione Antiqua, Concentus Musicus, Vienna, 1965–70; opera début, Ottone in L'incoronazione di Poppea, Landestheater, Darmstadt, 1970; Countertenor Lay Clerk, Westminster Cathedral, 1966–70; Editor, Music and Musicians, 1970–73; Sub-Editor, Features, Dep. Arts Editor, opera & music critic, and feature writer, Dep. Obituaries Editor, The Guardian, 1973–96; opera, theatre and music critic, Vogue, 1975–87; Opera Critic, Evening Standard, 1996–2002; dramaturg on productions: Turn of the Screw, Brussels, 1998; Macbeth, Brussels, 2001; Ernest Bloch's Macbeth, Vienna, 2003; Don Giovanni, Flammen, Vienna, 2006. Chm., music sect., 1999–2009, Pres., 2010–12, Critics' Circle. Mem., Gen. Synod, C of E, 1990–2015; Member: Exec. Cttee, Affirming Catholicism, 1996–2002; Cathedrals Fabric Commn for England, 2002–11. Leverhulme Fellow, 1991, 2005; Fellow, Rose Bruford Coll., 2006. *Publications:* (contrib.) Theatre 71, 1972, Theatre 72, 1973, and Theatre 74, 1975; (ed) Tracts for our Times, 1983; (ed) In Vitro Veritas, 1984; Believing in Opera, 1996; (ed) The Faber Book of Opera, 2000; (contrib.) The Cambridge Companion to Twentieth-Century Opera, 2005; contrib. San Francisco Opera, Glyndebourne, Brussels, Naples and Vienna opera progs, and in Music and Musicians, Opera News, Musical Times, Opera Now, The Spectator, New Statesman, Prospect, The Times, The Guardian, Wall Street Journal, Financial Times, Opern Welt, New Directions, Le Monde, The London Mag., Jl British Cinema and TV. *Address:* 67 Stanthorpe Road, Streatham, SW16 2EA. *T:* (020) 8677 5849. *E:* tomsutcliffe@email.msn.com.

**SUTCLIFFE, John Harold Vick,** CBE 1994; DL; Chairman, Great Fosters (1931) Ltd, 1958–2009; *b* 30 April 1931; *o s* of late Sir Harold Sutcliffe and Emily Theodora Cochrane; *m* 1st, 1959, Cecilia Mary (*d* 1998), *e d* of Ralph Meredyth Turton; three *s* one *d*; 2nd, 2001, Katherine Fox. *Educ:* Winchester Coll.; New Coll., Oxford (MA). 2nd Lieut RA, 1950–51. Called to Bar, Inner Temple, 1956; practised until 1960, Midland Circuit. Chm., North Housing Association Ltd, 1985–94 (Dir, 1977–86); Director: Allied Investors Trusts Ltd, 1958–69; Norton Junction Sand & Gravel Ltd, 1958–64; Tyne Tees Waste Disposal Ltd, 1964–71. Estate management, Kildale, 1965–95. Member: Housing Corp., 1982–88; Bd, Teesside Develt Corp., 1987–98. Mem. Bd, Civic Trust, 1989–93; Chairman: Northern Heritage Trust, 1981–89; NE Civic Trust, 1989–93 (Vice-Chm., 1977–89). Contested (C): Oldham West, 1959; Chorley, Lancs, 1964; Middlesbrough West, 1966. MP (C) Middlesbrough W, 1970–Feb. 1974. Contested (C) Teesside Thornaby, Oct. 1974. Chairman: Country Endeavour, 1983–88; Bow Street Project, Guisborough, 1988–2008; Pres., N Yorks Youth Clubs, 1984–93 (Chm., 1966–70); Mem., N Yorks Moors Nat. Park Cttee, 1982–88. DL Cleveland, 1983–96, N Yorks, 1996–; High Sheriff, N Yorks, 1987–88. *Recreations:* woodlands, gardening, travel. *Address:* 8 Meadow Road, SW8 1QB. *T:* (020) 7582 9806.
*See also* A. H. W. *Sutcliffe.*

**SUTCLIFFE, Kevin Anthony;** Managing Director, Vice Studios UK, 2017–18; *b* Blackpool, 6 Sept. 1960; *s* of Donald and June Sutcliffe; one *s* one *d*. *Educ:* Arnold Sch., Blackpool; Blackpool Technical Coll.; Hornsey Coll. of Art, London (BA Hons Fine Art). Freelance journalist, 1983–86; Researcher, Watchdog, Asst Prod., Breakfast Time, Prod., Newsnight, BBC TV, 1986–89; Producer: Hard News, Channel 4 TV, 1990; The Late Show, BBC Music and Arts, 1991; Taking Liberties, BBC Documentaries, 1992–94; Public Eye, 1994, Panorama, 1995–99, BBC News and Current Affairs; Exec. Prod., Louis Theroux, MacIntyre Investigates, Anna in Wonderland, BBC Documentaries, 1999–2001; Channel 4 Television: Ed., Dispatches, 2002–12; Commissioning Ed., 2004–06, Dep. Head, 2006–12, News and Current Affairs; Hd, News Programming (EMEA), Vice Media Gp, 2013–15; Sen. Vice Pres., TV and Video Programming, Viceland Internat., 2015–17. *T:* 07789 205930. *E:* sutcliffe.kevin@gmail.com.

**SUTCLIFFE, Her Honour Linda, (Mrs P. B. Walker);** a Circuit Judge, 1993–2006; *b* 2 Dec. 1946; *d* of James Loftus Woodward and Florence Woodward; *m* 1st, 1968 (marr. diss. 1979); 2nd, 1987, Peter Brian Walker. *Educ:* Eccles Grammar Sch.; LSE (LLB Hons 1968); Open Univ. (Dip. French 2007). Called to the Bar, Gray's Inn, 1975; Lectr in Law, Univ. of Sheffield, 1968–76, part-time 1976–81; in practice at the Bar, 1976–93; an Asst Recorder, 1987–91; a Recorder, 1991–93. Part-time Chm., Industrial Tribunals, 1983–92. *Recreations:* music, gardening.

**SUTCLIFFE, Margaret Helen;** see O'Farrell, M. H.

**SUTCLIFFE, Tom;** see Sutcliffe, J. T.

**SUTER, Michael;** solicitor in private practice, 1992–2002; Chief Executive, Shropshire County Council, 1987–92; *b* 21 Jan. 1944; *s* of Robert and Rose Suter; *m* 1963, Sandra Harrison; two *s*. *Educ:* Liverpool Collegiate Sch.; Liverpool Univ. (LLB). Solicitor. Dep. Chief Exec., Notts CC, 1980–87. *Recreations:* music, gardening, watching old Hollywood films, visiting Spain.

**SUTHERELL, Maj.-Gen. John Christopher Blake,** CB 2002; CBE 1993 (OBE 1990; MBE 1982); DL; General Secretary (Chief Executive), Officers' Association, 2003–13; *b* 23 Oct. 1947; *s* of Ernest John and Vera Louise Sutherell; *m* 1st, 1979, Stephanie Glover (*d* 1983); 2nd, 1987, Amanda Maxwell-Hudson; one *d*. *Educ:* Christ's Hosp., Horsham; Durham Univ. (BA Hons Geog. 1968); Staff Coll., Camberley. Commnd Royal Anglian

Regt, 1968; SO1 DS Staff Coll., 1984–87; CO, 1st Bn, Royal Anglian Regt, 1987–90; Divl Col, Staff Coll., 1990; Comdr, 8th Inf. Bde, 1990–92; Mem., RCDS, 1993; Dep. Mil. Sec. (A), 1994–96; DSF, 1996–99; Comdt, RMCS, 1999–2002. Col Comdt, Queen's Div., 1999–2002; Col, Royal Anglian Regt, 2002–07 (Dep. Col, 1997–2002). Pres., Royal Norfolk Regt Assoc., 2000–12. Mem. Council, Army Records Soc., 2001–05, 2006–10, 2011–15, 2016–. Member: Exec. Cttee, COBSEO, 2006–13; British Commn for Mil. Hist., 2014–. Governor: Heathfield Sch., Ascot, 2004–06; Heathfield St Mary's Sch., Ascot, 2006–09. Church Warden, St Peter's, Yoxford, 2009–. Mem., Yoxford Parish Council, 2015–. DL Suffolk, 2006. *Recreations:* family, military history, gardening.

**SUTHERLAND**, family name of **Countess of Sutherland**.

**SUTHERLAND**, 7th Duke of, *cr* 1833; **Francis Ronald Egerton**; Bt 1620; Baron Gower 1703; Earl Gower, Viscount Trentham 1746; Marquis of Stafford 1786; Viscount Brackley and Earl of Ellesmere 1846; *b* 18 Feb. 1940; *o s* of Cyril Reginald Egerton and Mary, *d* of Rt Hon. Sir Ronald Hugh Campbell, GCMG; *S* cousin, 2000; *m* 1974, Victoria Mary, twin *d* of Maj.-Gen. Edward Alexander Wilmot Williams, CB, CBE, MC; two *s*. *Educ:* Eton; RAC Cirencester. *Heir: s* Marquis of Stafford, *qv*. *Address:* Mertoun, St Boswells, Melrose, Roxburghshire TD6 0EA.

**SUTHERLAND**, Countess of (24th in line), *cr* (*c*) 1235; **Elizabeth Millicent Sutherland**; Lady Strathnaver (*c*) 1235; Chief of Clan Sutherland; *b* 30 March 1921; *oc* of Lord Alistair St Clair Sutherland-Leveson-Gower, MC (*d* 1921; 2nd *s* of 4th Duke), and Hélène Elizabeth (*née* Demarest, later Baroness Osten Driesen) (*d* 1931); *niece* of 5th Duke of Sutherland, KT, PC; *S* (to uncle's Earldom of Sutherland and Lordship of Strathnaver), 1963; *m* 1946, Charles Noel Janson (DL, 1959–93), late Welsh Guards (*d* 2006); two *s* one *d* (and one *s* decd). *Educ:* Queen's College, Harley Street, W1, and abroad. Land Army, 1939–41; Laboratory Technician: Raigmore Hospital, Inverness, 1941–43; St Thomas' Hospital, SE1, 1943–45. Chm., Dunrobin Castle Ltd. *Recreations:* reading, swimming. *Heir: e s* Lord Strathnaver, *qv*. *Address:* Dunrobin Castle, Golspie, Sutherland KW10 6SF; House of Tongue, by Lairg, Sutherland IV27 4XH; 39 Edwardes Square, W8 6HH.

**SUTHERLAND, Rt Hon. Lord; Ranald Iain Sutherland;** PC 2000; a Senator of the College of Justice in Scotland, 1985–2001; *b* 23 Jan. 1932; *s* of J. W. and A. K. Sutherland, Edinburgh; *m* 1964, Janice Mary, *d* of W. S. Miller, Edinburgh; two *s*. *Educ:* Edinburgh Academy; Edinburgh University (MA 1951, LLB 1953). Admitted to Faculty of Advocates, 1956; QC (Scot.) 1969. Advocate Depute, 1962–64, 1971–77; Standing Junior Counsel to Min. of Defence (Army Dept), 1964–69. Mem., Criminal Injuries Compensation Bd, 1977–85. Surveillance Comr, 2001–10. Justice of Appeal, Botswana, 2002–05. *Recreations:* sailing, shooting. *Address:* 1/5 The Cedars, Edinburgh EH13 0PL. *T:* (0131) 667 5280. *Club:* New (Edinburgh).

**SUTHERLAND, Alan David Alexander;** Chief Executive, Water Industry Commission for Scotland, since 2005 (Water Industry Commissioner for Scotland, 1999–2005); *b* Glasgow, 8 April 1962; *s* of George and Kathleen Sutherland; *m* 1994, Olga Krasnorylkina; one *s* one *d*. *Educ:* Univ. of St Andrews (MA Hons Mod. Russian Studies 1984); Univ. of Pennsylvania (MBA 1993; MA 1993). Mgt trainee, Lloyds Bank, London, 1984; Analyst, Savory Milln & Co., London, 1985; Analyst, 1986–88, Manager, 1988–92, Robert Fleming and Co., London; Consultant, 1992–95, Team Leader, 1995–97, Bain & Co., Moscow, London and Kiev; Man. Dir, Wolverine Russia Ltd, and Gen. Dir, Wolverine CIS, Moscow and Grand Rapids, Mich, 1997–99. Mem., NI Govt Panel of Experts providing advice on reform of water industry in NI, 2001; Advr to EU and to Special Secretariat for Water, Greece, under auspices of EU Task Force for Greece, then EU Structural Reform Support Service, 2014–15; Advr to Romanian National Regulatory Authy for Public Utilities Services, 2016–; Mem. Bureau, Network of Econ. Regulators, OECD, 2018–. Mem., Governing Cttee, UNESCO Centre for Water Law and Policy, Univ. of Dundee, 2008–. Beesley Lect., RA, 2006. *Recreations:* theatre, fine restaurants, family trips to Walt Disney World in Florida. *Address:* 2 Northbank Farm Steadings, Strathkinness High Road, St Andrews, Fife KY16 9TZ. *T:* (01334) 473535, *Fax:* (office) (01786) 462018. *E:* alan.sutherland@watercommission.co.uk, adas62@hotmail.co.uk.

**SUTHERLAND, Catherine Elizabeth;** *see* West, C. E.

**SUTHERLAND, Colin John MacLean;** *see* Carloway, Rt Hon. Lord.

**SUTHERLAND, Duncan;** Chairman, Sigma InPartnership Ltd, since 2011; *b* Glasgow, 2 Dec. 1951; *s* of Robert MacKay Sutherland and Margaret Sutherland. *Educ:* Glasgow Sch. of Art (Dip. Town and Country Planning 1976). Planner, Lobban and Mollineux Partnership, Dingwall, 1976–78; Planning Officer, Borders Regl Council, 1978–79; Sen. Planning Officer, 1979–84, Hd of Tourism, 1984–86, Lancs CC; Hd, Implementation, English Tourist Bd, 1986–89; Dir, Inner City Enterprises plc, 1989–92; Dir, City Develt, Coventry CC, 1992–97; Chief Exec., EDI Gp, Edinburgh, 1997–2000; Founder Dir, InPartnership Ltd, 2000–11; Dir, Regeneration, Sigma Capital Gp, 2012–. Non-executive Director: British Waterways Bd, 2006–12; Scottish Canals Bd, 2012–14; HS2 Ltd, 2012–; First Choice Homes, Oldham, 2013–; Mem. Bd, Homes England, 2018–. Dir, Assoc. of Town Centre Mgt, 1995–2002. Director: Cockburn Conservation Trust, 1998–2003; South Bank Sinfonia, 2013–. *Recreations:* music, walking, travel, France, historic cars, buildings and architecture. *Address:* Sigma Inpartnership Ltd, Floor 3, 1 St Ann Street, Manchester M2 7LR. *E:* duncanws@me.com.

**SUTHERLAND, Euan Ross,** CB 1993; Parliamentary Counsel, 1989–2003; *b* 24 Nov. 1943; *s* of Dr Alister Sutherland and Margaret Sutherland; *m* 1st, 1967, Katharine Mary Jenkins, *qv* (marr. diss. 1995); one *s* one *d*; 2nd, 2002, Mary Anne Kenyon. *Educ:* Kingswood Sch., Bath; Balliol Coll., Oxford (BA Hist.). Called to the Bar, Inner Temple, 1969; Office of the Parliamentary Counsel, 1974–2003; seconded to: Govt of Solomon Is, 1979–81; Law Commn, 1986–88. Director: InSpire, St Peter's, Walworth, 2003–15; Walter Carrington Educnl Trust, 2010–12. Mem., Ind. Monitoring Bd, HM Prison, Norwich, 2008–09. Trustee, Burgate Singers, 2010–. *Recreations:* choral music, hill-walking, gardening, wildlife, photography, built environment. *Address:* 57 Sutherland Square, SE17 3EL.

**SUTHERLAND, Prof. Grant Robert,** AC 1998; FRS 1996; FAA; Emeritus Geneticist, Women's and Children's Hospital, Adelaide, since 2007 (WCH Foundation Research Fellow, 2002–07); Affiliate Professor, Department of Paediatrics, University of Adelaide, 1991–2017, now Emeritus; *b* 2 June 1945; *s* of John Sutherland and Hazel Wilson Mason McClelland; *m* 1979, Elizabeth Dougan; one *s* one *d*. *Educ:* Numurkah High Sch.; Univ. of Melbourne (BSc 1967; MSc 1971); Univ. of Edinburgh (PhD 1974; DSc 1984). FAA 1997. Cytogeneticist, Mental Health Authy, Melbourne, 1967; Cytogeneticist i/c, Royal Hosp. for Sick Children, Edinburgh, 1971; Dir, Dept of Cytogenetics and Molecular Genetics, Women's and Children's Hosp., Adelaide, 1975–2002. Internat. Res. Scholar, Howard Hughes Med. Inst., Maryland, 1993–97. President: Human Genetics Soc. of Australasia, 1989–91; Human Genome Orgn, 1996–97. Hon. FRCPA 1994; Hon. Mem., Eur. Cytogeneticists Assoc., 2005. Hon. MD Adelaide, 2013. Australia Prize in Molecular Genetics (jtly), 1998; Thomson ISI Aust. Citation Laureate, 2004; High Achiever in Health and Med. Res., National Health and Med. Res. Council, 2013. *Publications:* (with F. Hecht) Fragile Sites on Human Chromosomes, 1985; (with R. J. M. Gardner) Chromosome Abnormalities and Genetic Counselling, 1989, 4th edn 2011; over 480 papers in sci. and med. jls. *Recreations:* reading, gardening. *Address:* Women's and Children's Hospital, Adelaide, SA 5006, Australia. *T:* (8) 81617284. *E:* grant.sutherland@adelaide.edu.au; PO Box 1635, Victor Harbor, SA 5211, Australia. *T:* (4) 18548022.

**SUTHERLAND, John Alexander Muir;** Chairman, Celtic Films Entertainment Ltd, since 2017 (Chief Executive, 1986–2017); *b* 5 April 1933; *m* 1970, Mercedes Gonzalez; two *s*. *Educ:* India; Trinity Coll., Glenalmond; Hertford Coll., Oxford (MA). 2nd Lieut, HLI, 1952–53. Economist, Fed. Govt of Nigeria, 1957–58; film production, Spain and Portugal, 1958–62; Head of Presentation and Programme Planning, Border TV, 1963–66; Programme Co-Ordinator: ABC TV, 1966–68; Thames TV, 1968–72; Controller of Programme Sales, Thames TV, 1973–74; Man. Dir, 1975–82, Dep. Chm., 1982–86, Thames TV Internat.; Dir of Programmes, Thames TV, 1982–86. Dir, Border TV, 1986–. *Productions include:* The Saint (TV), 1989; The Monk (film), 1990; Red Fox (TV), 1991; Sharpe (TV films), 1992–96; Kiszko (TV film), 1998; Girl from Rio (film), 2000; Sharpe's Challenge (TV film), 2005; Sharpe's Peril, 2008. *Address:* Celtic Films Entertainment Ltd, 9 Orme Court, W2 4RL.

**SUTHERLAND, Prof. John Andrew,** PhD; FRSL; Lord Northcliffe Professor of Modern English Literature, University College London, 1992–2004, now Emeritus; *b* 9 Oct. 1938; *s* of Jack Sutherland and Elizabeth (*née* Salter); *m* 1st, 1967, Guilland Watt (marr. diss. 2005); one *s*; 2nd, 2005, Sarah Lee. *Educ:* Colchester Royal Grammar Sch.; Leicester Univ. (BA 1964; MA 1966); Edinburgh Univ. (PhD 1973). FRSL 1991. Nat. Service, 2nd Lieut, Suffolk Regt, 1958–60. Lectr in English, Univ. of Edinburgh, 1965–72; Lectr, then Reader in English, UCL, 1972–84, Fellow, 2004; Prof. of English, CIT, 1984–92. Hon. DLitt: Leicester, 1998; Surrey, 2002. *Publications:* Thackeray at Work, 1974; Victorian Novelists and Publishers, 1976; Fiction and the Fiction Industry, 1978; Bestsellers, 1980; Offensive Literature, 1982; The Longman Companion to Victorian Fiction, 1989; Mrs Humphry Ward, 1992; The Life of Walter Scott: a critical biography, 1995; Victorian Fiction: writers, publishers, readers, 1995; (ed) The Oxford Book of English Love Stories, 1996; Is Heathcliff a Murderer?, 1996; Can Jane Eyre Be Happy?, 1997; Who Betrays Elizabeth Bennet?, 1999; Last Drink to LA, 2001; Reading the Decades, 2002 (televised, 2002); Stephen Spender, 2004; How to Read a Novel: a user's guide, 2006; The Boy Who Loved Books: a memoir, 2007; Bestsellers: a very short introduction, 2007; Curiosities of Literature: a book-lover's anthology of literary erudition, 2008; Magic Moments: life-changing encounters with books, film, music (memoir), 2008; (with Stephen Fender) Love, Death, Sex and Words, 2010; Fifty Literature Ideas, 2010; Lives of the Novelists, 2011; A Little History of Literature, 2013; Jumbo: the unauthorised biography of a Victorian sensation, 2014; (with Jack Sutherland) Stars, Cars and Crystal Meth, 2016; Brontësaurus, 2016; Who is Dracula's Father?, 2017; The War on the Old, 2017; The War on the Young, 2018; (with V. Melnyk) Rogue Publisher, 2018; Frankenstein's Brain, 2018; The Good Brexiteer's Guide to English Lit, 2018. *Recreation:* walking. *Address:* Department of English, University College London, Gower Street, WC1E 6BT. *T:* (020) 7387 1839, 07792 587695.

**SUTHERLAND, John Brewer;** (3rd Bt *cr* 1921, but does not use the title); *b* 19 Oct. 1931; *s* of Sir (Benjamin) Ivan Sutherland, 2nd Bt, and Marjorie Constance Daniel (*d* 1980), *yr d* of Frederic William Brewer, OBE; *S* father, 1980; *m* 1st, 1958, Alice Muireall (*d* 1984), *d* of late W. Stamford Henderson, Kelso; three *s* one *d*; 2nd, 1988, Heather, *d* of late David A. Gray, Chester-le-Street. *Educ:* Sedbergh; St Catharine's Coll., Cambridge. *Heir: s* Peter William Sutherland [*b* 18 May 1963; *m* 1988, Suzanna Mary, *d* of R. M. Gledson; one *s* two *d*].

**SUTHERLAND, Prof. Kathryn,** DPhil; Professor of Bibliography and Textual Criticism, University of Oxford, 2002–17, now Emeritus; Professorial Fellow, 1996–2017, now Emeritus, and Senior Research Fellow, since 2017, St Anne's College, Oxford; *b* 7 July 1950; *d* of Ian Donald Sutherland and Joyce Sutherland (*née* Bartaby). *Educ:* Bedford Coll., Univ. of London (BA 1971); Somerville Coll., Oxford (DPhil 1978; MA 1996). Lectr in English Literature, Univ. of Manchester, 1975–93; Prof. of Modern English Literature, Univ. of Nottingham, 1993–96; Reader in Bibliography and Textual Criticism, 1996–2002. Project Dir and Principal Investigator, Jane Austen's Fiction Manuscripts, 2006–10 (digital edition, 2010). Trustee, Jane Austen's House Mus. and Meml Trust, Chawton, Hampshire, 2013–. *Publications:* Adam Smith: interdisciplinary essays, 1995; Electronic Text: method and theory, 1997; Women Prose Writers 1780–1830, 1998; Jane Austen's Textual Lives: from Aeschylus to Bollywood, 2005; Transferred Illusions: digital technology and the forms of print, 2009; Jane Austen's Fiction Manuscripts, 5 vols, 2018; critical edns; contrib. books and learned jls. *Recreation:* gardening. *Address:* St Anne's College, Oxford OX2 6HS.

**SUTHERLAND, Lorraine,** OBE 2016; Editor, Official Report (Hansard), 2005–15; *b* 11 Jan. 1958; *d* of Bunty Sutherland (now Potts); *m* 1982, Robert Kremer. *Educ:* Lybster Primary Sch.; Wick High Sch.; Aberdeen Coll. of Commerce. Official Report (Hansard): Principal Asst Editor, 1994–97; Dep. Editor, 1997–2005. *Recreations:* travelling, planning travel, tennis, cinema, theatre, dreaming on trains.

**SUTHERLAND, Martin Conrad;** Chief Executive Officer, De La Rue plc, 2014–19; *b* Aylesbury, 8 Dec. 1968; *s* of Edmond Mackintosh Sutherland and Margaret Hilary Sutherland; *m* Sally Jennifer; two *c*. *Educ:* N Bromsgrove High Sch.; New Coll., Oxford (MA Physics); University Coll. London (MSc Remote Sensing). Andersen Consulting, 1990–92; British Telecom, 1995–96; Detica Ltd, 1996–2008; BAE Systems plc, 2008–14. *Recreations:* cycling, running, golf.

**SUTHERLAND, Muir;** *see* Sutherland, J. A. M.

**SUTHERLAND, Ranald Iain;** *see* Sutherland, Rt Hon. Lord.

**SUTHERLAND, Roderick Henry, (Rory);** Vice Chairman, Ogilvy London (formerly Ogilvy Group, later Ogilvy & Mather Group UK), since 2005; Founder and Creative Director, Ogilvy Behavioural Science Practice (formerly Ogilvy Change), since 2012; *b* Llanbadoc, near Usk, Monmouthshire, 12 Nov. 1965; *s* of James Alan Sutherland and late Florence Mary Sutherland (*née* Townsend); *m* 1989, Sophie Louisa Whitmore; two *d*. *Educ:* Haberdashers' Monmouth Sch.; Christ's Coll., Cambridge (BA 1987; MA). Joined Ogilvy & Mather Direct Ltd, subseq. OgilvyOne Worldwide Ltd, as grad. trainee, 1988; Copywriter, 1990–94; Head of Copy, 1994–97; Exec. Creative Dir, 1997–2004. Columnist, Spectator (Wiki Man), 2008–. Hon. Prof., Warwick Business Sch., 2012–. Pres., Inst. of Practitioners in Advertising, 2009–11. Trustee, Benjamin Franklin House, 2012–; Patron, Rochester Cathedral Trust, 2018–. FIPA 2008; FRSA. Hon. DLitt Brunel, 2012. *Publications:* The Wiki Man, 2011; Alchemy: the surprising power of ideas that don't make sense, 2019. *Recreations:* reading, behavioural science, crosswords. *Address:* Ogilvy & Mather, Sea Containers, 18 Upper Ground, SE1 9RQ. *T:* (020) 7345 3000. *E:* rory.sutherland@ogilvy.com. *Clubs:* Walbrook, Ivy, Arts.

**SUTHERLAND, Dame Veronica (Evelyn),** DBE 1998; CMG 1988; HM Diplomatic Service, retired; President, Lucy Cavendish College, Cambridge University, 2001–08; *b* 25 April 1939; *d* of late Lt-Col Maurice George Beckett, KOYLI, and Constance Mary

Cavenagh-Mainwaring; *m* 1981, Alex James Sutherland. *Educ:* Royal Sch., Bath; London Univ. (BA); Southampton Univ. (MA); MA Cantab 2001. Joined HM Diplomatic Service, 1965; Second, later First Sec., Copenhagen, 1967–70; FCO, 1970–75; First Sec., New Delhi, 1975–78; FCO, 1978–80; Counsellor, 1981; Perm. UK Deleg. to UNESCO, 1981–84; Counsellor, FCO, 1984–87; Ambassador to Côte d'Ivoire, 1987–90; Asst Under-Sec. of State (Personnel), FCO, 1990–95; Ambassador to Republic of Ireland, 1995–99; Dep. Sec. Gen. (Econ. and Social Affairs), Commonwealth Secretariat, 1999–2001. Chm., Airey Neave Trust, 2000–11; Member: Exec. Cttee, British/Irish Assoc., 2002–13; Cttee, Elizabeth Nuffield Educnl Fund, 2005–08; Trustee, Cambridge Relate, 2015–19. Pro-Chancellor, Univ. of Southampton, 2019–. Hon. LLD TCD, 1998. *Recreations:* theatre, painting (diploma, Society of Botanical Artists, 2010). *Address:* Summer Hill, Robin's Lane, Lolworth, Cambridge CB23 8HH. *Club:* Athenæum.

**SUTHERLAND, Sir William (George MacKenzie),** Kt 1988; QPM 1981; HM Chief Inspector of Constabulary for Scotland, 1996–98; *b* 12 Nov. 1933; *m* 1957, Jennie Abbott; two *d. Educ:* Inverness Technical High Sch. Cheshire Police, 1954–73; Surrey Police, 1973–75; Hertfordshire Police, 1975–79; Chief Constable: Bedfordshire, 1979–83; Lothian and Borders Police, 1983–96. Hon. Sec., ACPO in Scotland, 1985–96; Chm., British Police Athletic Assoc., 1991–96 (Chm., Squash Section, 1984–96; Chm., Ski Section, 1992–96). *Recreations:* golf, ski-ing, hill walking.

**SUTHERLAND, Prof. William James,** PhD; Miriam Rothschild Professor of Conservation Biology, University of Cambridge, since 2006; Fellow, St Catharine's College, Cambridge, since 2008; *b* 27 April 1956; *s* of late Alasdair Cameron Sutherland and Gwyneth Audrey Sutherland; *m* 1996, Nicola Jane Crockford; two *d. Educ:* Univ. of East Anglia (BSc); Liverpool Poly. (PhD). NERC Postdoctoral Fellow, Wolfson Coll., Oxford, 1980–82; Lectr, Zoology Dept, Liverpool Univ., 1982–83; University of East Anglia: Demonstrator, Sch. of Envmtl Scis, 1983–85; Lectr, 1985–93, Reader, 1993–96, Prof. of Biology, 1996–2006, Sch. of Biol Scis; Nuffield Fellow, 1992–93; Associate Fellow, Centre for Sci. and Policy, Univ. of Cambridge, 2011–. Trustee, FFI, 1998–. Scientific Medal, Zool Soc., 1997; Marsh Award for Ecology, British Ecol Soc., 2001; Marsh Award for Conservation Biol., Zool Soc., 2005; Ecological Engagement Award, British Ecol Soc., 2012; Dist. Service Award, Soc. for Conservation Biol., 2013; Sir John Burnett Meml Lect. Medal, Nat. Biodiversity Network, 2013. *Publications:* (ed with D. A. Hill) Habitat Management, 1995; From Individual Behaviour to Population Ecology, 1996; (ed) Ecological Census Techniques: a handbook, 1996, 2nd edn 2006; (ed) Conservation Science and Action, 1998; The Conservation Handbook: research, management and policy techniques, 2000; (ed with L. M. Gosling) Behaviour and Conservation, 2000; (ed jtly) Bird Ecology and Conservation: a handbook of techniques, 2004; (jtly) Bee Conservation: evidence for the effects of interventions, 2010; (jtly) Bird Conservation: global evidence for the effects of interventions, 2013; (jtly) Amphibian Conservation: evidence for effectiveness of interventions, 2014; (jtly) Farmland Conservation: evidence for effectiveness of conservation, 2014; (jtly) What Works in Conservation, 2015, 3rd edn 2018; articles on ecology, behaviour and conservation in scientific jls. *Recreations:* natural history, prehistory, photography, painting, cooking. *Address:* Department of Zoology, Cambridge University, Downing Street, Cambridge CB2 3EJ. *E:* w.sutherland@zoo.cam.ac.uk.

**SUTHERLAND-ARDEN, Sian, (Sian Sutherland);** Co-Founder, A Plastic Planet, since 2016; Founder and Chief, Insider Consultancy, since 2016; *b* Windsor, 29 Jan. 1961; *d* of Hugh Sutherland-Dodd and Molly Sutherland; *m* 1991, Christian Arden; two *s. Educ:* Garth Hill Comp. Sch., Bracknell; Reading Tech. Coll. Founder and Gen. Manager, Sutherlands Restaurant, Soho, London, 1985–91 (Michelin star, 1988); Co-Founding Partner, Miller Sutherland, design and brand creation agency, 1991–2011; Co-Founder and Partner, Arden Sutherland-Dodd, later ASD Lionheart, commercials prodn co., 1994–2014; Founding Partner and CEO, Mio and Mama Mio Ltd, 2005–16. Then, FilmAid UK, 2012–18. *Recreations:* basketball (founded Badabings women's basketball team, 1997, still playing!), sailing, regular mini-breaks in Greek Isles, boxing, mixology. *T:* 07768 385383. *E:* sian@siansutherland.com.

**SUTHIWART-NARUEPUT, Dr Owart,** Kt Grand Cordon: Order of Crown of Thailand, 1981; Order of White Elephant, 1985; Hon. CMG 1972; Permanent Secretary for Foreign Affairs, Thailand, 1979–80; *b* 19 Sept. 1926; *s* of Luang Suthiwart-Narueput and Mrs Khae; *m* 1959, Angkana (*née* Sthapitanond); one *s* one *d. Educ:* Thammasat Univ., Thailand (BA Law); Fletcher Sch. of Law and Diplomacy, Tufts Univ., USA (MA, PhD); Nat. Defence Coll. Joined Min. of For. Affairs, 1945; Asst Sec. to Minister, 1958; SEATO Res. Officer, 1959; Protocol Dept, 1963; Econ. Dept, 1964; Counsellor, Thai Embassy, Canberra, 1965; Dir-Gen. of Inf. Dept, 1969; Ambassador to India, Nepal, Sri Lanka, and Minister to Afghanistan, 1972; Ambassador to Poland, E Germany and Bulgaria, 1976; Dir-Gen. of Political Dept, 1977; Ambassador to France and Perm. Representative to UNESCO, 1980; Ambassador: to Switzerland and to Holy See, 1983; to UK, 1984–86, concurrently to Ireland, 1985–86. Mem., Civil Service Bd, Min. of Foreign Affairs, 1994–2006. Commander: Order of Phoenix, Greece, 1963; Order of Orange-Nassau, Netherlands, 1963; Bintang Djasa (1st Cl.), Indonesia, 1970; Order of Merit, Poland, 1979; Grand Officier, l'Ordre Nat. du Mérite, France, 1983. *Publications:* The Evolution of Thailand's Foreign Relations since 1855: from extraterritoriality to equality, 1955. *Recreations:* reading, music. *Address:* 193 Lane 4 Navathanee, Serithai Road, Kannayao, Bangkok 10230, Thailand. *Clubs:* Old England Students' Association, American University Alumni Association (Bangkok).

**SUTLIEFF, Barry John;** communications consultant, Poland, Macedonia, Kosovo, Georgia, Tanzania and China, 2000–12; Director, Communications and Learning, Civil Contingencies Secretariat, Cabinet Office, 2001–02; *b* 26 Dec. 1942; *s* of Basil Eric and Ruby Ellen Sutlieff; *m* 1967, Linda Valerie Hook; one *s* one *d. Educ:* Brooklands Coll., Weybridge; Coll. for Distributive Trades, London (CAM Dip. PR). Trainee advertising exec., 1961–66; gen. publicity roles, Depts of Trade, Transport and the Envmt, and Price Commn, 1966–75; Chief Press Officer: DoE, 1975–79; Dept of Trade, 1979–83; Dep. Hd of Inf., Home Office, Feb.–July 1985; Dir, Inf. Services, MSC, 1985–87; Director: of Inf. Dept of Employment, 1987–94; of Communication, Cabinet Office, 1994–2000; Fellow, Centre for Management and Policy Studies, Cabinet Office, 2000–01. Non-exec. Dir, Lewis Live Ltd, 2004–06. *Recreations:* travel, reading modern history, lifelong Dickens fanatic, sport, notably football and cricket. *Address:* The Hollies, 26 Hutton Road, Ash Vale, Aldershot, Hants GU12 5HA. *T:* (01252) 654727.

**SUTTIE,** Baroness *cr* 2013 (Life Peer), of Hawick in the Scottish Borders; **Alison Mary Suttie;** political consultant, since 2012; Associate, Global Partners Governance, since 2015; *b* Hawick, Scotland, 27 Aug. 1968; *d* of late Dr Alastair Suttie and of Gillian Suttie. *Educ:* Hawick High Sch.; Heriot-Watt Univ. (BA Hons Interpreting and Translating (French and Russian)); Univ. of Voronezh, Russia. Teacher of English, St Petersburg, USSR, 1990–91; res. asst to Sir Russell Johnston, MP, 1991–93; Chief Whip's Asst, Lib Dem Whip's Office, H of C, 1993–96; Policy Advr, Eur. Parlt, 1996–99; Press Sec. and Policy Advr to Patrick Cox, MEP as Pres., ELDR, 1999–2002, as Pres. of Eur. Parlt, 2002–04; Hd of Office of Lib Dem Leader, H of C, 2006–10; Dep. COS, Office of the Dep. Prime Minister, 2010–11. House of Lords: Member: Select Cttee on the EU, 2015–; EU Sub-Cttee on Ext. Relns, 2015–; Vice-Chair, All-Party Parly Gp on Global Tuberculosis, 2014–; Lib Dem Party Whip, 2013–; Lib Dem Spokesperson on NI, 2016–. Trustee, IPPR, 2015–. *Recreations:* trekking, particularly in the Himalayas, outdoor swimming. *Address:* House of Lords, SW1A 0PW.

**SUTTIE, Sir James (Edward) Grant,** 9th Bt *cr* 1702, of Balgone, Haddingtonshire; farmer; *b* 29 May 1965; *o s* of Sir Philip Grant-Suttie, 8th Bt and of Elspeth Mary Grant-Suttie (*née* Urquhart); *S* father, 1997; *m* 1st, 1989, Emma Jane Craig (marr. diss. 1996); one *s*; 2nd, 1997, Sarah Jane Smale; two *s. Educ:* Fettes Coll., Edinburgh; Aberdeen Coll. of Agric. *Recreations:* golf, shooting. *Heir: s* Gregor Grant-Suttie, *b* 29 Oct. 1991.

**SUTTLE, Stephen John;** QC 2003; *b* 28 Sept. 1949; *s* of Ernest Suttle, DMus and Judith Suttle (*née* Gummer); *m* 1984, Rosemary Ann Warren (marr. diss. 2005; remarried 2014); two *s* two *d. Educ:* Westminster Sch.; Christ Church, Oxford (MA Lit.Hum.). Asst classics master, Stowe Sch., 1973–78; called to the Bar, Gray's Inn, 1980; in practice, specialising in defamation, confidence, privacy and media law, 1981–2010. Pt-time classics teacher: Classics Acad., 2011–13; Gumley House Sch., Isleworth, 2014–. *Recreations:* music, cricket, running.

**SUTTON, Prof. Adrian Peter,** PhD; FRS 2003; Professor of Nanotechnology, Department of Physics, Imperial College London, 2005–18, now Emeritus; *b* 1 July 1955; *s* of Peter Michael Sutton and Beryl Margaret Sutton; partner, 1985, *m* 2003, Patricia Joan White. *Educ:* St Catherine's Coll., Oxford (BA 1st cl. (Metallurgy and Sci. of Materials) 1977; MSc by res. 1978); Univ. of Pennsylvania (PhD 1980). CPhys, FInstP 2000; CEng 2001; CChem, FRSC 2003. Oxford University: SRC postdoctoral researcher, 1981–83; Royal Soc. Res. Fellow, 1983–91; Lectr, 1991–97; Prof. of Materials Science, 1997–2004; Fellow, Linacre Coll., Oxford, 1991–2004; Prof. of Computational Engrg, Helsinki Univ. of Technol., 2002–04; Imperial College London: Head of Condensed Matter Theory, 2005–11; Chm., EPSRC Centre for Doctoral Trng on theory and simulation of materials, 2011–18 (Dir, 2009–11). *Publications:* Electronic Structure of Materials, 1993 (trans. German 1996); (with R. W. Balluffi) Interfaces in Crystalline Materials, 1995, reissued 2006 (trans. Chinese 2016); numerous scientific papers in physics, materials science, engrg and chemistry jls. *Recreations:* cycling, walking, travelling, enthusing children about science. *Address:* 516 Banbury Road, Oxford OX2 8LG.

**SUTTON, Alan John;** Founder Chairman and Chief Executive, Anglolink Ltd, since 1985; *b* 16 March 1936; *s* of William Clifford Sutton and Emily Sutton (*née* Batten); *m* 1957, Glenis (*née* Henry); one *s* one *d. Educ:* Bristol Univ. BSc (Hons) Elec. Engrg; MIET. Design, Production and Trials Evaluation of Guided Missiles, English Electric Aviation Ltd, 1957–63; Design, Production, Sales and General Management of Scientific Digital, Analogue and Hybrid Computers, Solartron Electronic Group Ltd, 1963–69; International Sales Manager, Sales Director, of A. B. Electronic Components Ltd, 1969–73; Managing Director, A. B. Connectors, 1973–76; Industrial Dir, Welsh Office, 1976–79; Welsh Development Agency: Exec. Dir (Industry and Investment), 1979–83; Exec. Dir (Marketing), 1983–85; Sen. Vice-Pres., USA W Coast Div., WINvest, 1985–88. CEO, DigiTec Direct Ltd, subseq. Chm., A NOVO Digitec Ltd, 1998–2004; Dir, A NOVO UK Ltd, 2001–05; non-exec. Dir, A NOVO SA, 2003–09; Chm., 2007–09, non-exec. Dir, 2009–10, Conforto Financial Management Ltd. *Recreations:* golf, travel. *Address:* 56 Heol-y-Delyn, Lisvane, Cardiff CF14 0SR. *T:* (029) 2075 3194.

**SUTTON, David Christopher,** PhD; Director, Research Projects, University of Reading Library, since 1982; *b* 18 Oct. 1950; *e s* of late Derek John Sutton and Sheila Sutton; *m* 1973, Dr Deborah Jenkins. *Educ:* Leicester Univ. (BA; MA 1973); Sheffield Univ. (MA 1975); Université de Paris VIII; Polytechnic of Central London (PhD 1979). Librarian: Trinity Coll., Dublin, 1973–74; Polytechnic of Central London, 1975–76; BL, 1976–78; Warwick Univ. Library, 1980–82. Mem. (Lab) Reading BC, 1988–2008 (Leader of the Council, 1995–2008); Chm., Reading Miners' Support Cttee, 1984–85; Trustee, Earley Charity, 1987–. Chm. Bd, Reading Buses, 2010–. Chairman: Gp for Literary Archives and Manuscripts, 2010–18; Literary Archives Section, Internat. Council of Archives, 2010–. UK Editor, Writers, Artists and Their Copyright Holders, 1994–. FRSA; FRSL 2012. Archivist of Year, Scone Foundn, 2006. Benson Medal for services to literature, RSL, 2002. *Publications:* Points of View in the Writing of History, 1981; (ed) Location Register of Twentieth-Century English Literary Manuscripts and Letters, 1988; (ed) Location Register of English Literary Manuscripts and Letters: eighteenth and nineteenth centuries, 1995; Figs: a global history, 2014; Rich Food Poor Food, 2017; (ed) The Future of Literary Archives, 2018; numerous articles on copyright, literary manuscripts, politics and food history. *Recreations:* football, badminton, walking in Dorset, sitting by the Mediterranean. *Address:* The Coach House, 22 Eldon Place, Reading RG1 4ED. *E:* D.C.Sutton@reading.ac.uk.

**SUTTON, Dr (Howard) Michael;** Principal Research Fellow, University of Warwick, 1999–2003; *b* 12 Nov. 1942; *s* of Albert Sutton and Constance Olive Sutton (*née* Topham); *m* 1967, Diane Cash; one *s* one *d. Educ:* Univ. of Edinburgh (BSc 1965; PhD 1968). CChem, FRSC 1977–2008. Res. Fellow, Univ. of Kent at Canterbury, 1968–70; Warren Spring Laboratory: Materials Handling Div., 1970–78; Head, Planning and Marketing, 1978–85; Dep. Dir, 1985–88; Department of Trade and Industry: Head, Shipbuilding and Marine Engineering, 1988–91; Head, Single Market Unit, 1991–93; Head, Mech. Engrg Sponsorship, 1993–94; Dir, Trade and Industry, W Midlands, 1994–98; Hd of Secretariat, W Midlands Regl Develt Agency (in preparation), 1998–99; Advr, Advantage W Midlands—the Develt Agency, 1999–2000. Non-exec. Dir, Manufg Foundn Ltd, 2001–03. *Publications:* contribs to learned jls. *Recreations:* philosophy, music, walking. *E:* mikesutton161@gmail.com. *W:* www.mikesutton.academia.edu, www.twitter.com/mikesutton161.

**SUTTON, Prof. John,** PhD; FBA 1996; Sir John Hicks Professor of Economics, London School of Economics and Political Science, since 1998 (Professor of Economics, 1988–98); *b* 10 Aug. 1948; *s* of John Sutton and Marie (*née* Hammond); *m* 1974, Jean Drechsler; one *s* two *d. Educ:* University Coll., Dublin (BSc Physics 1969); Trinity Coll., Dublin (MSc Econ. 1973); PhD Sheffield 1978. Voluntary service, UNA, Turkey, 1969–70; Mgt Services, Herbert-BSA, Coventry, 1970–72; Lectr, Sheffield Univ., 1973–77; Lectr, 1977–84, Reader, 1984–88, LSE. Visiting Professor: Tokyo Univ., 1981; Univ. of Calif, San Diego, 1986; Marvin Bower Fellow, Harvard Business Sch., 1990–91; Gaston Eyskens Prof., Leuven Univ., 1996–97; Vis. Prof. of Econs, Harvard Univ., 1998; William Davidson Vis. Prof., Michigan Univ., 2003; Vis. Prof., Graduate Sch. of Business, Univ. of Chicago, 2006. Member: Adv. Council, Japan External Trade Orgn, Tokyo, 1995–2002; Council for Econ. Analysis, EU, 2002–04; Enterprise Policy Gp, Ireland, 2003–04. Pres., REconS, 2004–07. Fellow, Econometric Soc., 1991; European Econ. Assoc., 2004; Dist. Fellow, Industrial Orgn Soc., 2012. Foreign Hon. Mem., AEA, 2007. Hon. DSc(Econ) NUI 2003; Hon. DSciEcon Dublin, 2004. Hon. LLD Dublin, 2004. Medal of Franqui Foundn, Belgium, 1992. *Publications:* (jtly) Protection and Industrial Policy in Europe, 1986; Sunk Costs and Market Structure, 1991; Technology and Market Structure: theory and history, 1998; Marshall's Tendencies: what can economists know?, 2000; (jtly) An Enterprise Map of Ethiopia, 2010; (jtly) An Enterprise Map of Ghana, 2012; (jtly) An Enterprise Map of Tanzania, 2012; Competing in Capabilities: the globalization process, 2012. *Address:* London School of Economics, Houghton Street, WC2A 2AE. *T:* (020) 7955 7716.

**SUTTON, Kenneth David,** CB 2008; Director for Learning from Experience and for Hillsborough, Home Office, since 2013 (Director, Hillsborough Independent Panel, 2010–12); *b* 17 May 1958; *s* of David Vivien Sutton and Audrey Sutton; *m* 1982, Ruth Hopkin; two *s* one *d*. *Educ*: Cefn Hengoed Comprehensive Sch., Swansea; University Coll., Oxford (BA 1st Cl. Hons PPE 1979). Joined Home Office, 1979; Private Sec. to Parly Under Sec. of State, 1983–85; Private Sec. to Permanent Under Sec. of State, 1991–92; Asst Sec., Immigration and Nationality Dept, 1992–95; Principal Private Sec. to Home Secretary, 1995–99; Dir of Regimes, subseq. of Resettlement, HM Prison Service, 1999–2002; Dir, Street Crime Action Team, 2002; Sen. Dir for Asylum Support, Casework and Appeals, 2003–06; Dep. Chief Exec., Border and Immigration Agency (formerly Dep. Dir Gen., Immigration and Nationality), 2006–08; Dir for Policy, Marie Curie Cancer Care, 2008–09. *Recreations:* cycling, walking, holidays in Europe and Wales. *Address:* c/o Home Office, 2 Marsham Street, SW1P 4DF.

**SUTTON, Michael;** *see* Sutton, H. M.

**SUTTON, Ven. Peter Allerton;** Priest-in-charge, Greatham, Empshott and Hawkley with Priors Dean, since 2018; *b* Liss, Hants, 18 July 1959; *s* of John and Jean Sutton; *m* 2007, Pippa Dice; two *d*. *Educ*: Warblington Sch.; Exeter Univ. (BA Theol. 1985); Lincoln Theol Coll. Ordained deacon, 1987, priest, 1988; Curate: Holy Trinity and St Columba, Fareham, 1987–90; St Mary, Alverstoke, 1990–93; Chaplain, HM Prison Haslar, 1990–93; Vicar, St Faith, Lee-on-the-Solent, 1993–2012; Archdeacon of the Isle of Wight, 2012–18. *Recreations:* music, reading, walking, kayaking, time with family.

**SUTTON, Philip,** CBE 2012; PhD; FREng, FInstP, CPhys, CEng; Director (formerly Director General), Science and Technology Strategy (formerly Research and Technology), Ministry of Defence, 2004–11; Director, SSES Ltd, since 2011; *b* 28 Nov. 1953; *s* of Percy Ronald and Ivy Nora Sutton; *m* 1974, Kim Cummins; one *s* one *d*. *Educ*: Southampton Univ. (BSc Hons Physics; PhD Electronics 1982). CEng 1990, FIET (FIEE 1996); CPhys 1998; FInstP 1998; FREng 2006. Ministry of Defence: ASWE, Portsdown 1975–83; BAe Dynamics, Bristol, 1983–85; Above Water Sector, ARE, then DRA, Portsdown, 1985–92, Chief Scientist, 1992–94; Hd, Battlefield and Vehicle Systems Dept, DERA, 1994–98; Director: of Corporate Res., 1998–2001; of Technol. Develt, 2001–04. Visiting Professor: Cranfield Univ., 1990–; Loughborough Univ., 1992–2012; Imperial Coll. London, 2006–; UCL, 2011–; Chm., Industrial Adv. Bd, Centre for Secure Information Technols, QUB, 2010–. Dir, Cancer Care Soc., 2000–. Gov., Welbeck Coll., 2005–11; Community Gov., Ampfield Sch., 2013–15. Member: Whiteley Ch Council, 1998–2012; Ampfield Ch Council, 2012–. Member: NT; RNLI (Mem. Council, 2014–). *Publications:* numerous tech. reports and papers; named inventor on 17 patents and patent applications. *Recreations:* sailing, sub-aqua diving, snow-boarding, cycling.

**SUTTON, Philip John,** RA 1989 (ARA 1977); *b* 20 Oct. 1928; *m* 1954; one *s* three *d*. *Educ:* Slade Sch. of Fine Art, UCL. One-man exhibitions: Roland Browse and Delbanco (now Browse and Darby) Gallery, London, 1958–81; Leeds City Art Gallery, 1960; Newcastle-on-Tyne, 1962; Bradford, 1962; Edinburgh, 1962; Sydney, 1963, 1966, 1970, 1973; Perth, 1963, 1972; Royal Acad. (Diploma Gall.), London, 1977; David Jones Gall., Sydney, 1980; Bonython Art Gall., Adelaide, 1981; Norwich, Bath and New York, 1983; Lichfield Fest., 1985; Beaux Arts Gall., Bath, 1985; Galerie Joël Salaün, Paris, 1988; Gallery 27, and Cork St, London, 2004, 2019; Richmond Hill Art Gall., 2006; Sladers Yard, Bridport, 2015, 2017; Bridport Arts Centre, 2018; Red House, Britten-Pears Foundn, 2018; Russell-Cotes Gall., Bournemouth, 2018; exhibn of ceramics, Oditte Gilbert Gall., London, 1987; Agnews, London, 1992; touring exhibn, Wales, 1993–94; Shakespeare exhibn, RA, Internat. Shakespeare Globe Centre, RSC Stratford, Royal Armouries Mus., Leeds, Berkeley Square Gall., 1997; Piano Nobile, London 2001; Hay-on-Wye Fest., 2001; exhibn of woodcuts 1962–1976, RA, 2005. Designed Post Office 'Greetings' stamps, 1989. *Recreations:* swimming, running. *Address:* Harbour Cottage, Harbour House, George Street, West Bay, Bridport, Dorset DT6 4EY.

**SUTTON, Prof. Richard,** DSc (Med); FRCP, FACC, FESC, FAHA; FHRS; Consultant Cardiologist, Imperial College Healthcare NHS Trust (formerly St Mary's Hospital NHS Trust), 2007–11, now Hon. Consultant; Professor of Clinical Cardiology, Imperial College London, 2003–11, now Emeritus; Hon. Consultant Cardiologist, Hammersmith Hospital, since 2014; *b* 1 Sept. 1940; *s* of late Dick Brasnett Sutton and Greta Mary (*née* Leadbeater); *m* 1st, 1964, Anna Gunilla (*née* Cassö) (marr. diss. 1998); one *s*; 2nd, 2014, Jeanne-Marie Arrighi. *Educ:* Gresham's Sch.; King's Coll., London; King's Coll. Hosp. (MB, BS 1964); DSc (Med) London 1988. FRCP 1983 (MRCP 1967); FACC 1975; FESC 1990; FAHA 2001; FHRS 2006. Gen. medical trng followed graduation; career in cardiology began at St George's Hosp., London, 1967; Fellow in Cardiol., Univ. of NC, 1968–69; Registrar, Sen. Registrar, then Temp. Consultant, National Heart Hosp., London, 1970–76. Consultant Cardiologist: St Stephen's Hosp., 1976–89; Chelsea and Westminster Hosp. (formerly Westminster Hosp.), 1976–2007; Royal Brompton Nat. Heart and Lung Hosp., subseq. Royal Brompton and Harefield Trust, 1993–2007; Hon. Consultant Cardiologist: Italian Hosp., London, 1977–89; St Luke's Hosp., London, 1980–2011. Guest Prof. of Cardiology, Univ. of Lund. Chm., Eur. Wkg Gp on Cardiac Pacing, 1998–2000. Exec. Bd Mem., Eur. Heart Rhythm Assoc., 2004–06. Member: British Cardiovascular Soc. (formerly British Cardiac Soc.); Heart Rhythm Soc.; British Heart Rhythm Soc. (formerly British Pacing and Electrophysiology Gp, then Heart Rhythm UK) (Co-Founder, Past Pres. and Hon. Sec.). Fellow: European Heart Rhythm Assoc., 2017; British Heart Rhythm Soc., 2018. Governors' Award, Amer. Coll. of Cardiol., 1979 (Scientific Exhibit, Physiol Cardiac Pacing), and 1982 (1st Prize; Scientific Exhibit, 5 yrs of Physiol Cardiac Pacing). Editor in Chief: European Jl of Cardiac Pacing and Electrophysiology, 1991–97; Europace, 1998–2006 (Founding Ed., 2007–). Lifetime Achievement Award, Heart Rhythm UK, 2007; Pioneer in Cardiac Pacing and Electrophysiology, Heart Rhythm Soc., 2016. *Publications:* Foundations of Cardiac Pacing, pt 1, 1991, pt 2, 1999; European Soc. of Cardiology textbook of Cardiology, 2019; articles on many aspects of cardiology incl. cardiac pacing, syncope, coronary artery disease, left ventricular function, and assessment of pharm. agents, in Nature Cardiol., Circulation, Jl of Amer. Coll. of Cardiol., Amer. Jl of Cardiol., Amer. Heart Jl, Brit. Heart Jl, Heart, Pace, Lancet, BMJ, Europace, and Oxford Textbook of Medicine, 1967–; over 312 peer-reviewed papers. *Recreations:* opera, foreign travel, walking. *Address:* 9 avenue d'Ostende, Monte Carlo, Monaco, MC 98000.

**SUTTON, Richard Lewis;** Regional Director, Northern Region, Department of Industry, 1974–81; *b* 3 Feb. 1923; *s* of William Richard Sutton and Marina Susan Sutton (*née* Chudleigh); *m* 1944, Jean Muriel (*née* Turner) (*d* 2014). *Educ:* Ealing County Grammar Sch. Board of Trade, 1939. Served War: HM Forces (Lieut RA), 1942–47. Asst Trade Comr, Port of Spain, 1950–52; BoT, 1952–62; Trade Comr, Kuala Lumpur, 1962–66; Monopolies Commn, 1966; BoT, 1967–68; Dir, British Industrial Develt Office, New York, 1968–71; Regional Dir, West Midland Region, Dept of Trade and Industry, 1971–74. *Recreations:* music, walking, bridge. *Address:* Barton Toft, Dowlish Wake, Ilminster, Somerset TA19 0QG. *T:* (01460) 57127.

**SUTTON, Sir Richard (Lexington),** 9th Bt *cr* 1772; Director, Sir Richard Sutton Ltd; *b* 27 April 1937; *s* of Sir Robert Lexington Sutton, 8th Bt, and Gwynneth Gwladys, *o d* of Major Arnold Charles Gover, MC; *S* father, 1981; *m* 1959, Fiamma (separated 2000), *o d* of G. M. Ferrari, Rome; one *s* one *d*; partner, 2002, Mrs Anne Schreiber. *Educ:* Stowe. *Recreations:* ski-ing, sailing, swimming, gym. *Heir: s* David Robert Sutton [*b* 26 Feb. 1960; *m* 1st, 1992, Annette (marr. diss. 2003), *o d* of B. David; three *d*; 2nd, 2007, Mrs Gay Mary van der Meulen (*née* Luscombe)]. *Address:* Moorhill, Higher Langham, Gillingham, Dorset SP8 5NY. *T:* (01747) 822665.

**SUTTON, Richard Patrick;** QC 1993; a Recorder, 1994–2017 (Assistant Recorder, 1991–94); *b* 13 Nov. 1944; *s* of Jack Doherty Sutton and Beryl Clarisse Scholes Sutton (*née* Folkard); *m* 1978, Jean Folley; one *s* one *d*. *Educ:* Culford Sch.; Wadham Coll., Oxford (BA Hons Jurisprudence). Called to the Bar, Middle Temple, 1969, Bencher, 2002. *Recreations:* playing guitar, meeting people.

**SUTTON, Robert Hiles;** Chairman, Tulchan Communications Group, since 2009; *b* 19 Jan. 1954; *s* of late John Ormerod Sutton and (Margaret) Patricia Sutton; *m* 1981, Carola, (Tiggy), Dewey; one *s* one *d* (and one *s* decd). *Educ:* Winchester Coll.; Magdalen Coll., Oxford (BA 1st Cl. Hons Modern Hist.). Admitted solicitor, 1979; joined Macfarlanes, Solicitors, 1976: Partner, 1983–2009; Sen. Partner, 1999–2008; Sen. Advr, 2009–13. Chm., OMC Partners, 2009–13; non-exec. Dir, Numis Corp. plc, 2014–. Fellow, Winchester Coll., 2003–18. *Recreations:* golf, tennis, wine, family. *Address:* c/o Tulchan Communications, 85 Fleet Street, EC4Y 1AE. *T:* (020) 7353 4200. *E:* rhsutton@outlook.com. *Club:* Boodle's.

**SUTTON, Prof. Stephen Robert,** PhD; Professor of Behavioural Science, University of Cambridge, since 2001; *b* 24 Feb. 1952; *s* of Robert Frank Sutton and Marjorie Sutton (*née* Hook); *m* 1985, Pamela Anne (*née* Stevens). *Educ:* Univ. of Leicester (BA 1973); LSE (MSc 1975); Inst. of Psychiatry, Univ. of London (PhD 1981); City Univ. (MSc 1991). Institute of Psychiatry, University of London: Res. Worker, 1975–90, Lectr, 1980–88, Sen. Lectr, 1988–90, Addiction Res. Unit; Sen. Lectr in Social Psychology, Health Behaviour Unit, 1990–96; Reader in Social/Health Psychology, 1996–2000, Prof. in Social/Health Psychology, 2000–01, Health Behaviour Unit, Dept of Epidemiology and Public Health, UCL. Vis. Prof. of Psychology, Univ. of Bergen, 1996–; Vis. Prof. of Social/Health Psychology, Dept of Psychiatry and Behavioural Scis, UCL, 2000–. *Publications:* numerous papers in learned jls. *Recreations:* walking, bird-watching. *Address:* University of Cambridge, Institute of Public Health, Forvie Site, Robinson Way, Cambridge CB2 0SR. *T:* (01223) 330594, *Fax:* (01223) 762515. *E:* srs34@medschl.cam.ac.uk.

**SUVANAJATA, Pisanu;** Ambassador of Thailand to the Court of St James's, since 2017; *b* 7 Dec. 1961; *m* Thipayasuda. *Educ:* Thammasat Univ., Thailand (Master of Internat. Relns and Diplomacy); Northern Illinois Univ. (Master of Political Sci.). Press Officer, Prime Minister's Office, 1984; transf. to Diplomatic Service, 1986; served Min. of Foreign Affairs to rank of Dep. Dir-Gen.; First Sec., Phnom Penh; served in Australia; Consul-Gen., Guangzhou, China, 2009; Ambassador to Myanmar, until 2017. *Recreation:* sports. *Address:* Royal Thai Embassy, 30 Queen's Gate, SW7 5JB. *T:* (020) 7225 5509, *Fax:* (020) 78213 9695.

**SUZMAN, Dame Janet,** DBE 2011; actress and director; *b* 9 Feb. 1939; *d* of Saul Suzman; *m* 1969, Trevor Robert Nunn (*see* Sir T. R. Nunn) (marr. diss. 1986); one *s*. *Educ:* Kingsmead Coll., Johannesburg; Univ. of the Witwatersrand (BA); London Acad. of Music and Dramatic Art. Hon. Associate Artist, RSC, 1980. Vis. Prof. of Drama Studies, Westfield Coll., London, 1983–84; Hon. Lectr, Shakespeare Inst., Univ. of Birmingham, 2011–12. Lectures: Spencer, Harvard Univ., 1988; Tanner, Brasenose Coll., Oxford, 1995; Sixth World Shakespeare Congress, LA, 1996; Judith Wilson, Trinity Coll., Cambridge, 1996; Drapers', QMW, 1997; Morrell Meml Address on Toleration, Univ. of York, 1999. Vice-Pres., LAMDA Council, 2002– (Mem., 1978–2002, Vice-Chm., 1992–2002); Pres., Shakespeare Birthday Celebrations, 2010–11. Trustee: The Theatres Trust, 1977–83; Rose of Kingston Th. Trust, 2007–. Chair, British Cttee for the reunification of the Parthenon Marbles. Hon. Fellow, Shakespeare Birthplace Trust, 2012; Life Fellow, British Shakespeare Assoc., 2015. Freeman, City of London, 2015. Rôles played for *Royal Shakespeare Co.* incl.: Joan La Pucelle in The Wars of the Roses, 1963–64; Lulu in The Birthday Party, Rosaline, Portia, 1965; Ophelia, 1965–66; Katharina, Celia, and Berinthia in The Relapse, 1967; Beatrice, Rosalind, 1968–69; Cleopatra and Lavinia, 1972–73; Clytemnestra and Helen of Troy in The Greeks, 1980; The Hollow Crown, 2002, tour of Australia, 2003; Volumnia in Coriolanus, 2007; *other rôles* incl.: Kate Hardcastle, and Carmen in The Balcony, Oxford Playhouse, 1966; Hester in Hello and Goodbye, King's Head Theatre, 1973; Masha in Three Sisters, Cambridge, 1976; Good Woman of Setzuan, Newcastle, 1976, Royal Court, 1977; Hedda Gabler, Duke of York's, 1977; Boo-hoo, Open Space, 1978; The Duchess of Malfi, Birmingham, 1979; Cowardice, Ambassadors, 1983; Boesman and Lena, Hampstead, 1984; Vassa, Greenwich, 1985; Andromache, Old Vic, 1988; Another Time, Wyndham's, 1989; Hippolytus, Almeida, 1991; The Sisters Rosensweig, Greenwich, 1994, Old Vic, 1994–95; The Retreat from Moscow, Chichester, 1999; Cherished Disappointments in Love, Soho, 2001; Whose Life is it Anyway?, Comedy, 2005; Dream of the Dog, Finborough Th., 2010, Trafalgar Studios, 2010; Solomon and Marion, Baxter Th., Cape Town, 2011, Edinburgh Fest., 2013, Kennedy Center, Washington, 2014, Birmingham Rep., 2014; Rose, Home Th., Manchester, 2017 (Best Actress in a Leading Rôle, Manchester Th. Awards, 2017); *director:* Othello, Market Theatre, Johannesburg, 1987 (Best Prodn, Vita Awards, 1988); A Dream of People, The Pit, 1990; The Cruel Grasp, Edinburgh Fest., 1991; No Flies on Mr Hunter, Chelsea Centre, 1992; Death of a Salesman, 1993 (Liverpool Echo and Daily Post Arts Awards, Best Production, 1994); The Deep Blue Sea, 1996, Theatr Clywd; The Good Woman of Sharkville, Market Theatre, Johannesburg, 1996, UK tour, 1998; The Free State, Birmingham, 1999, UK tour, 2000 (Barclays Theatrical Managers' Assoc. Award, Best Dir, 1997); The Snow Palace, tour and Tricycle Theatre, 1998, Warsaw Fest., 1999; The Guardsman, Albery, 2000; Measure For Measure, Guildhall Sch., 2004; Hamlet, Cape Town, 2005, Stratford, 2006; Master Harold And the Boys, LAMDA, 2010; Antony and Cleopatra, Liverpool Playhouse, 2010 (Best Prodn, Liverpool Daily Post Awards), Chichester Fest., 2012; Le Nozze di Figaro, RAM, Hackney Empire, 2015; A Lesson from Aloes, Finborough Th., 2019; The Cherry Orchard, Royal Central Sch. of Speech and Drama, 2019. *Films:* A Day in the Death of Joe Egg, 1970; Nicholas and Alexandra, 1971; The Priest of Love, 1980; The Draughtsman's Contract, 1981; E la Nave Va, 1983; A Dry White Season, 1990; Nuns on the Run, 1990; Leon the Pig Farmer, 1993; Max 2001; *television:* plays for BBC and ITV incl.: St Joan, 1968; Three Sisters, 1969; Macbeth, 1970; Hedda Gabler, 1972; Twelfth Night, 1973; Three Men in a Boat, 1973; Antony and Cleopatra, 1974; Miss Nightingale, 1974; Clayhanger, serial, 1975–76; Mountbatten—The Last Viceroy, 1986; The Singing Detective, 1986, The Miser, 1987; dir., Othello, 1988; Cripples, 1989; The Amazon, 1989; master class on Shakespearean comedy, BBC, 1990; White Clouds, 2002; Sinbad, 2012; Labyrinth, 2013. Evening Standard Drama Awards, Best Actress, 1973, 1976; Plays and Players Award, Best Actress, 1976; Pragnell Shakespeare Award, 2012. Hon. Fellow: Sch. of Arts, Liverpool Univ., 2010–16; Liverpool John Moores Univ., 2011. Hon. MA Open, 1984; Hon. DLitt: Warwick, 1990; Leicester, 1992; QMW, 1997; Southampton, 2002; Middx, 2003; Kingston, 2006; Cape Town, 2010; Buckingham, 2014; Edge Hill, 2015. *Publications:* Acting with Shakespeare: the comedies, 1996; The Free State: a South African response to

Chekhov's Cherry Orchard, 2000; (textual commentary) Antony and Cleopatra, 2001; Not Hamlet: meditations on the frail position of women in drama, 2012. *T:* (020) 7434 9055. *E:* sk@sknco.com.

**SUZUKI, Prof. Akira,** PhD; Professor, Hokkaido University, 1973–94, now Emeritus; *b* Mukawa, Japan, 12 Sept. 1930; *m* Yoko; two *d. Educ:* Hokkaido Univ. (PhD 1959). Hokkaido University: Res. Asst, Chem. Dept, 1959–61; Asst Prof., Synthetic Chemical Engrg Dept, 1961; Postdoctoral Res. Associate, Purdue Univ., 1963–65. Professor: Okayama Univ. of Sci., 1994; Kurashiki Univ. of Sci. and the Arts, 1995–2002. Chemical Soc. of Japan Award, 1989; Japan Acad. Prize, 2004; (jtly) Nobel Prize in Chemistry, 2010; H. C. Brown Award, Amer. Chemical Soc., 2011. Order of Culture (Japan), 2010. *Address:* c/o Faculty of Engineering, Hokkaido University, N13, W8, Kita-ku, Sapporo 060–8628, Japan.

**SVANBERG, Carl-Henric;** Chairman: BP, 2010–18 (non-executive Director, 2009–18); Volvo, since 2012; *b* Porjus, Sweden; *m* Agneta (marr. diss. 2009); three *c*; *m* 2013, Louise Julian. *Educ:* Linköping Inst. of Technol. (MSc Applied Physics); Univ. of Uppsala (BA Business Admin). With Asea, later Asea Brown Boveri, 1977–86; Securitas, 1986–94, Exec. Vice-Pres., 1990–94; President and Chief Executive Officer: Assa Abloy, 1994–2003; Ericsson, 2003–09 (non-exec. Dir, 2003–12); Chm., Sony Ericsson Mobile Communications AB, 2003–09. King of Sweden's Medal for contrib. to Swedish industry.

**SVEJSTRUP, Dr Jesper Qualmann,** FRS 2009; FMedSci; Senior Scientist, Francis Crick Institute, since 2015 (Principal Scientist, 2005–15, and Head, Mechanisms of Gene Transcription Laboratory, 1996–2015, London Research Institute, Cancer Research UK (formerly Imperial Cancer Research Fund)); *b* 28 March 1963; *s* of Regner and Inga Svejstrup; *m* 1990, A. Barbara Dirac; two *s. Educ:* Aarhus Univ. (PhD 1993). Postdoctoral Fellow, Dept of Structural Biology, Stanford Univ. Sch. of Medicine, 1993–96; Res. Scientist, 1996–2000, Sen. Scientist, 2000–05, Imperial Cancer Research Fund, later Cancer Research UK. University College London: Hon. Sen. Res. Fellow, 1996–2000; Hon. Reader, 2000–05; Hon. Prof., 2005–; Adjunct Prof., Novo Nordisk Foundn Center for Protein Res. and Dept of Cellular and Molecular Medicine, Univ. of Copenhagen, 2011–; Hon. Prof., Imperial Coll. London, 2015–. Member: EMBO, 2003; Royal Danish Acad. of Scis and Letters, 2016. FMedSci 2018. *Publications:* articles in jls. *Address:* Mechanisms of Transcription Laboratory, Francis Crick Institute, 1 Midland Road, NW1 1AT.

**SVENSON, Dame Beryl;** *see* Grey, Dame Beryl.

**SVENSSON, Lars;** author, since 1989; editor; ornithologist; *b* 30 March 1941; *s* of Georg Svensson and Cecilia Svensson (*née* Lovén); *m* 2003, Lena Rahoult; one *s* one *d. Educ:* Univ. of Graphic Arts, Stockholm. Graphic designer and publishing editor, 1965–; ornithologist. Swedish Ornithological Society: Mem. Bd, 1971–77; Ed., jl, Vår Fågelvärld, 1971–74; Founder, Swedish Rarities Cttee (Chm., 1971–86); Member: Nomenclature Cttee, 1971–84; Taxonomic Cttee, 2000–14. Mem., BOU Taxonomic Sub-cttee, 2005–11. Hon. Ringer, British Trust for Ornithology, 1985–; Hon. Mem., Spanish Ornithol Soc., 2004–. PhD *hc* Uppsala, 2014. *Publications:* Identification Guide to European Passerines, 1970, 4th edn 1992; (with H. Delin) Birds of Britain and Europe, 1986, 3rd edn 1992; Fågelsång i Sverige (Birdsong in Sweden), 1990; Collins Bird Guide, 1999; (with J. Pedersen and J. Elphick) Birdsong, 2012; (with H. Shirihai) Handbook of Western Palearctic Birds: Passerines, 2018. *Address:* S:ta Toras väg 28, 269 77 Torekov, Sweden. *T:* 86632655, 708152122. *E:* lars@lullula.se.

**SWABY, Peter;** County Treasurer, 1991–2006, Strategic Director, 2006–07, Derbyshire County Council; *b* 8 Oct. 1947; *s* of late Arthur Swaby and Mona Swaby; *m* 1974, Yvette Shann; one *s* one *d. Educ:* Longcroft Sch., Beverley; Univ. of Sheffield (BMus (Hons) 2011). CPFA (CIPFA 1973). E Riding CC, 1967; Humberside CC, 1974, Chief Internal Auditor, 1983; Asst County Treasurer, S Glam CC, 1985. Hon. Sec., 2001–04, Vice Pres., 2004–05, Pres., 2005–06, Soc. of Co. Treasurers; Pres., Police Authy Treasurers' Soc., 2003–04. *Recreation:* classical guitarist (ALCM, ALCM(TD)).

**SWADE, Doron David,** MBE 2009; PhD; FBCS; independent researcher, history of computing; Honorary Research Fellow, Department of Computer Science, Royal Holloway, University of London, 2006–14 (Research Associate, History of Computing, 2014–17; Honorary Fellow, 2018); *b* 14 Oct. 1946; *s* of Max Jack Swade and Ruth Leah Swade (*née* Rosenberg). *Educ:* Univ. of Cape Town (BSc Hons 1969; MSc 1971); UCL (PhD 2003). CEng 1994; FBCS 2000 (Hon. Fellow, 2019). Consultant to computer industry, 1972–96; consultant electronics design engr, UK and USA, 1975–82; Science Museum: Electronics Design Engr, 1982–83; Section Head, audiovisual, electronics and computer-based displays, 1983–85; Sen. Curator, Computing and IT, 1985–99; Asst Dir and Hd of Collections, 1999–2002. Dir, Babbage Proj. and Guest Curator, Computer Hist. Mus., Mountain View, Calif, 2006–08. Mus. Mentor, Nat. Mus. of Computing, Bletchley, 2017–. Visiting Professor: (Interaction Design), RCA, 2004–06; Hist. of Computing, Univ. of Portsmouth, 2005–10. Mem., Scientific Cttee, Musée Nat. de la Voiture et du Tourisme, Compiègne, 2002–09. Trustee, Plan 28, 2012–. Lifetime Achievement Award, Computer Conservation Soc., 2017. *Publications:* Charles Babbage and his Calculating Engines, 1991; (jtly) The Dream Machine: exploring the computer age, 1991; The Cogwheel Brain: Charles Babbage and the quest to build the first computer, 2000; popular and scholarly articles. *Recreations:* writing, restoring woodworking machinery, making things. *Address:* 54 Park Road, Kingston upon Thames, Surrey KT2 6AU. *T:* (020) 8392 0072.

**SWAIN, Emma;** independent creative consultant, publishing, digital and agencies; Founder and Creative Director, On Purpose Group, since 2018; *b* Fakenham, Norfolk, 10 June 1963; *d* of Anthony Swain and Diana Nurse; partner, Laurence Jack Fitzgerald Martin Bowen; one *s* one *d. Educ:* St Martin's Coll. of Art. BBC: Researcher, Dir and Exec. Producer, 1996–2000; Commng Ed., Specialist Factual, 2001–07; Hd, In-house Commng, 2008–09; Hd, Knowledge TV Commng, 2009–11; Controller, Factual Commng, 2011–15; Mem. Bd, BBC TV, 2013–16; Dir, Digital Transformation, 2016. *Recreations:* cycling, wild swimming, non-fiction.

**SWAINSON, Charles Patrick,** FRCPE, FRCSE; FFPH; consultant, coach and mentor; Consultant Renal Physician, 1986–2010, and Medical Director, 1999–2010, NHS Lothian (formerly Royal Infirmary of Edinburgh); Director, CSwainson Consulting, since 2011; *b* Gloucester, 18 May 1948; *s* of John Edwin Swainson and Mary Diana Swainson (*née* O'Rourke); *m* 1981, Marie Adele Irwin; one *s. Educ:* St Edward's Sch., Cheltenham; Univ. of Edinburgh (MB ChB 1971). FRCPE 1986; FFPH 2004; FRCSE 2007. Sen. Lectr, Univ. of Otago, NZ, 1982–86. Ehealth Advr, Scottish Govt, 2011–. Med. Dir, Edinburgh Internat. Investments Ltd, 2018–. Hon. Prof., Univ. of Edinburgh, 2009– (Hon. Sen. Lectr, 2004–09). Convenor, Business Cttee, Gen. Council, Univ. of Edinburgh, 2012–16. Treas., RCPE, 2011–16. *Publications:* contrib. articles to gen. and med. specialist jls. *Recreations:* skiing, golf, wine appreciation. *Address:* 33 Granby Road, Edinburgh EH16 5NP. *T:* (0131) 667 6700. *E:* cpswainson@gmail.com. *Clubs:* New (Edinburgh); Luffness New Golf.

**SWAINSON, Roy;** Executive Director, Merseyside Special Investment Fund, since 1998; *b* 15 April 1947; *s* of William Swainson and Florence Swainson (*née* Moss); *m* 1973, Irene Ann Shearson; one *s* one *d. Educ:* Merchant Taylors' Sch., Crosby; Univ. of Manchester (LLB). Southport County Borough Council: Asst Solicitor, 1969–71; Sen. Asst Solicitor, 1971–74; Asst Borough Solicitor and Sec., Sefton MBC, 1974–82; Dep. City Solicitor and Sec., Liverpool CC, 1982–90; Chief Exec. and Dir Gen., Merseytravel, 1990–98. Non-exec. Chm., Air Safety Support Internat. Ltd, 2003–06; non-exec. Dir, St Helens and Knowsley Hosps NHS Trust, 2006–14 (Chm.). *Recreations:* reading, theatre, travel. *Address:* Merseyside Special Investment Fund, Exchange Court, 1 Dale Street, Liverpool L2 2PP. *T:* (0151) 236 4040.

**SWAINSTON, Michael George;** QC 2002; barrister; *b* 30 Jan. 1961; *s* of George and Ruth Swainston; *m* 1993, Carmita Ferreira Guerreiro; two *s. Educ:* Sir William Turner's Grammar Sch.; Downing Coll., Cambridge (MA); University Coll., Oxford (BCL). Called to the Bar: Lincoln's Inn, 1985, Bencher, 2008; California (inactive), 1988. *Address:* Brick Court Chambers, 7-8 Essex Street, WC2R 3LD.

**SWALES, Ian Cameron;** *b* Leeds, 5 April 1953; *s* of Harry Swales and Elizabeth Adamson Swales (*née* Doig); *m* 1972, Patricia; two *s* one *d. Educ:* Manchester Univ. (BSc Chemical Engrg). FCCA 1977. Yorkshire Electricity, 1973–78; ICI, 1978–99: various financial and business mgt roles, then Global Hd, Leadership Develt, 1997–99; trng and consultancy business, 1999–2008. Contested (Lib Dem) Redcar, 2005. MP (Lib Dem) Redcar, 2010–15. Mem., Public Accounts Cttee, H of C, 2010–14; Lib Dem Treasury spokesman, 2013–15; PPS to Sec. of State for Business, 2014–15. Chair, NE Process Industries Cluster, 2015–18. Chair, The Link Tees Valley Ltd, 2015–. Dir, Sirius Minerals Foundn Ltd, 2018–. Mem. Bd, Redcar Racecourse, 2019–. Hon. Life Mem., Humanists UK (formerly British Humanist Assoc.), 2015. Hon. FIChemE 2015. *Address:* 39 Coast Road, Redcar, N Yorks TS10 3NN.

**SWALES, Prof. Martin William,** PhD; FBA 1999; Professor of German, University College London, 1976–2003, now Emeritus; *b* 3 Nov. 1940; *s* of Percy Johns Swales and Doris (*née* Davies); *m* 1966, Erika Marta Meier; one *s* one *d. Educ:* King Edward's Sch., Birmingham; Christ's Coll., Cambridge (BA 1961); Univ. of Birmingham (PhD 1963). Lectr in German, Univ. of Birmingham, 1964–70; Associate Prof. of German, Univ. of Toronto, 1970–72; Reader in German, KCL, 1972–75; Prof. of German, Univ. of Toronto, 1975–76. Hon. Fellow, UCL, 1996; Hon. Sen. Fellow, Inst. of Modern Languages Res., Univ. of London, 2013–. Verdienstkreuz (Germany), 1994. Hon. DLitt Birmingham, 2003. *Publications:* Arthur Schnitzler, 1971; The German Novelle, 1977; The German Bildungsroman, 1978; Thomas Mann, 1980; (with E. M. Swales) Adalbert Stifter, 1984; Goethe's Werther, 1987; Thomas Mann's Buddenbrooks, 1991; Epochenbuch Realismus, 1997; (with E. M. Swales) Reading Goethe, 2007. *Recreations:* music, theatre (incl. amateur dramatics), incompetent house and car maintenance. *Address:* Department of German, University College London, Gower Street, WC1E 6BT. *T:* (020) 7380 7120.

**SWALLOW, Prof. Deborah Anne,** PhD; Märit Rausing Director, since 2004, and Professor, since 2008, Courtauld Institute of Art; *b* 27 Aug. 1948; *d* of Arnold Birkett Swallow and Denise Vivienne Swallow (*née* Leighton). *Educ:* Perse Sch. for Girls; New Hall, Cambridge (MA); Darwin Coll., Cambridge (PhD). Cambridge University: Asst Curator, Mus. of Archaeology and Anthropology, 1974–83; Lectr, Girton Coll., 1975–80; Fellow, Darwin Coll., 1975–83; Victoria and Albert Museum: Asst Keeper, Indian Dept, 1983–89; Chief Curator, Indian and SE Asian Dept, 1989–2001; Dir of Collections, and Keeper, Asian Dept, 2001–04. *Address:* Courtauld Institute of Art, Somerset House, Strand, WC2R 0RN. *T:* (020) 3947 7575. *E:* Deborah.Swallow@courtauld.ac.uk.

**SWAMINATHAN, Dr Monkombu Sambasivan,** FRS 1973; Founder Chairman and Chief Mentor, M. S. Swaminathan Research Foundation, since 2012 (Chairman, 1990–2012, now Emeritus Chairman); Hon. Director, since 1990, and UNESCO Professor in Ecotechnology, since 1996, Centre for Research on Sustainable Agricultural and Rural Development, Madras; Member, Rajya Sabha, India, since 2007; *b* 7 Aug. 1925; *m* Mina Swaminathan; three *d. Educ:* Univs of Kerala, Madras and Cambridge. BSc Kerala, 1944; BSc (Agric.) Madras, 1947; Assoc. IARI 1949; PhD Cantab. 1952. Responsible for developing Nat. Demonstration Project, 1964, and for evolving Seed Village concept; actively involved in develt of High Yielding Varieties, Dryland Farming and Multiple Cropping Programmes. Dir, Indian Agricultural Res. Inst., 1961–72; Sec., Dept of Agricultural Res. and Educn, India, 1972–79; Principal Sec., Min. of Agriculture, 1979–80; Acting Dep. Chm. and Mem. (Sci. and Agriculture), Planning Commn, 1980–82; Dir-Gen., Internat. Rice Res. Inst., Manila, 1982–88. Vice-Pres., Internat. Congress of Genetics, The Hague, 1963; Gen. Pres., Indian Science Congress, 1976. President: IUCN, 1984–90; WWF (India), 1989–96; Nat. Acad. of Agricultural Scis, 1991–96, 2005–07; Pugwash Confs on Science and World Affairs, 2002–07. Chairman: UN Science Adv. Cttee, 1980; Nat. Commn on Farmers, 2004–06; Ind. Chm., FAO Council, 1981–85. First Zakir Hussain Meml Lectr, 1970; UGC Nat. Lectr, 1971; lectures at many internat. scientific symposia. Foreign Associate, US Nat. Acad. of Scis; For. Mem., All Union Acad. of Agricl Scis, USSR; Hon. Mem., Swedish Seed Assoc.; Hon. Fellow, Indian Nat. Acad. of Sciences. FNA; Fellow, Italian Nat. Sci. Acad. Hon. DSc from 60 univs. Shanti Swarup Bhatnagar Award for contribs in Biological Scis, 1961; Mendel Centenary Award, Czechoslovak Acad. of Scis, 1965; Birbal Sahni Award, Indian Bot. Soc., 1965; Ramon Magsaysay Award for Community Leadership, 1971; Silver Jubilee Award, 1973, Meghnath Saha Medal, 1981, Indian Nat. Science Acad.; R. B. Bennett Commonwealth Prize, RSA, 1984; Albert Einstein World Science Award, 1986; World Food Prize, 1987; Tyler Prize for Envmtl Achievement, 1991; Honda Prize for Eco-technology, 1991; Jawaharlal Nehru Centenary Award, 1991; Sasakawa Envmt Prize, UN, 1994; Volvo Internat. Envmt Prize, 1999; Indira Gandhi Prize for Peace, Disarmament and Development, 2000; Franklin D. Roosevelt Four Freedoms Medal, 2000; UNESCO Mahatma Gandhi Prize, 2000; Lal Bahadur Sastri Nat. Award, 2007. Padma Shri, 1967; Padma Bhushan, 1972; Padma Vibhushan, 1989. *Publications:* numerous scientific papers. *Address:* 21 Rathna Nagar, Teynampet, Madras 600018, India; M. S. Swaminathan Research Foundation, Third Cross Street, Taramani Institutional Area, Chennai (Madras) 600113, India.

**SWAN, Jeanna Catherine;** Lord Lieutenant for Berwickshire, since 2014; *b* Aldershot, 11 Aug. 1953; *d* of late Lt Col John Nevin Agnew and Margaret Scott Agnew (*née* Thomson); *m* 1979, Richard Gilroy Swan; one *s* two *d. Educ:* Elmhurst, Camberley, Surrey; St Leonards, St Andrews; Royal Dick Sch. of Vet. Studies, Univ. of Edinburgh (BVMS). MRCVS 1976. Vet. Asst, Rogerson Baird and Wain, 1976–78; Vet. Partner, Renton Swan and Partners, 1978–2013. Trustee, MacRobert Trust, 2001–17. DL Berwickshire, 2014. *Recreations:* socialising, farming, horse riding. *Address:* Blackhouse Farm, Eyemouth, Berwickshire TD14 5LR. *T:* (01361) 882802, 07557 675342. *E:* jeanna.swan@gmail.com.

**SWAN, Sir John (William David),** KBE 1990; JP; Founder, Chairman, Swan Group of Companies, since 1999; Premier of Bermuda, 1982–95; *b* 3 July 1935; *s* of late John N. Swan and of Margaret E. Swan; *m* 1965, Jacqueline A. D. Roberts (*d* 2016); one *s* one *d. Educ:* West Virginia Wesleyan Coll. (BA). Salesman, Real Estate, Rego Ltd, 1960–62; Founder, John W. Swan Ltd, 1962 (Chm. and Chief Exec., 1962–2008). MP (United Bermuda Party) Paget E, 1972–95; Minister for: Marine and Air Services; Labour and

Immigration, 1977–78; Home Affairs, 1978–82; formerly: Parly Sec. for Finance; Chairman: Bermuda Hosps Bd; Dept of Civil Aviation; Young Presidents' Organization, 1974–86. Member: Chief Execs Orgn; World Business Council, 1986. Mem. and Fellow, Senate, Jun. Chamber Internat., 1992. Hon. Freeman of London, 1985. Hon. LLD: Univ. of Tampa, Fla, 1985; W Virginia Wesleyan Coll., 1987; Atlantic Union Coll., Mass, 1991. Internat. Medal of Excellence (1st recipient), Poor Richard Club of Philadelphia, 1987; Outstanding Learning Disabled Achiever Award, Lab Sch. of Washington, 1992; Eminent Professional Mem., RICS, 2005. *Recreations*: sailing, tennis. *Address*: 11 Grape Bay Drive, Paget PG 06, Bermuda. *T*: 2361303; Challenger Banks Ltd, PO Box HM 2413, Hamilton HM JX, Bermuda. *T*: 2951785, *Fax*: 2991789. *E*: sirjohn@challengerbanks.bm. *Clubs*: Sandys Rotary, Royal Bermuda Yacht (Bermuda); Bohemian (San Francisco); Chevy Chase (Maryland).

**SWAN, Robert Charles,** OBE 1995; FRGS; polar explorer, since 1980; *b* 28 July 1956; *s* of late Robert Douglas Swan and of Margaret Swan; *m*; one *s*; *m* 2003, Nicole Beyers. *Educ*: Aysgarth Sch.; Sedbergh Sch.; Durham Univ. (BA). With British Antarctic Survey, 1980–81; planning and fund raising, In the Footsteps of Scott, Antarctic Expedn, 1979–84; arrived at South Pole with R. Mear and G. Wood, 11 Jan. 1986; planning and fund raising, Icewalk, North Pole Expedn, 1988–89; Icewalk Internat. Student Expedn (22 participants from 15 nations), 1989; reached North Pole with 8 walkers from 7 nations (first person to have walked to both Poles), 14 May 1989; One Step Beyond (35 young explorers from 25 nations), 1996–97; started Mission Antarctica, ten year challenge dedicated to preservation of Antarctic wilderness, 1997; Internat. Antarctic Expedns, annually, 2003–. Vis. Prof., Sch. of Envmt, Leeds Beckett (formerly Leeds Metropolitan) Univ., 1992–. Founded 2041.com, for promotion of renewable energy and youth and scientific endeavour, 2003; started Voyage for Cleaner Energy with yacht '2041', 2005–; South Polar Energy Challenge (first expedn to South Pole only surviving on renewable energy, 600 miles on foot, with son), 2017–18. Keynote speaker at first Earth Summit, Rio de Janeiro, 1992. Mem. Council, WWF (UK), 1987; Vice-Pres., Countryside Mgt Assoc., 1995; Pres., Scott Soc., 2000. UN Goodwill Ambassador with special resp. for youth, 1989; Special Envoy to Dir Gen., UNESCO, 1994; EC Goodwill Ambassador for Envmt, 2003. Liveryman, Wheelwright's Co., 2002. FRGS 1987. Hon. LittD Robert Gordon, 1993; Hon. DSc Durham, 2010. Polar Medal, 1988; Global 500 Award, UN, 1989; Paul Harris Fellow, Rotary Internat., 1991; Smithsonian Award, 1998. *Publications*: In the Footsteps of Scott, 1987; A Walk to the Pole, 1987; Antarctic Survival, 1989; Destination South, 1990; Icewalk, 1990; Antarctica 2041, 2009. *Recreations*: yachting, running, tree surgery, road cycling. *Address*: 130 Westcott Court, Auburn, CA 95603, USA. *T*: 07767 780135, (808) 2189396. *E*: Robert@RobertSwan.com. *W*: www.2041.com, www.facebook.com/2041ClimateForce. *Clubs*: Special Forces; Amstel (Netherlands); Explorers (New York).

**SWAN, Hon. Wayne Maxwell;** National President, Australian Labor Party, since 2018; *b* Nambour, Qld, 30 June 1954; *s* of Maurice Roy Swan and Maida Joy Swan; *m* 1984, Kim Williamson; one *s* two *d*. *Educ*: Nambour High Sch.; Queensland Univ. Lectr in Public Admin, Qld Inst. of Technol., 1976–77, 1981–82 and 1985–88; policy analyst, Office of Youth Affairs, 1978; Advr to Leader of Opposition and Opposition spokesperson on industrial affairs and employment, 1978–80; Private Sec. to Minister of State, 1983, to Minister of Foreign Affairs, 1984; Campaign Dir and Asst State Sec., 1988–91, State Sec., 1991–93, ALP, Qld; Advr to Leader of Opposition, 1996–98. MHR (ALP) for Lilley, Queensland, 1993–96 and 1998–2019. Shadow Minister for Family and Community Services, 1998–2000 and 2001–04; Manager of Opposition Business, House of Reps, 2001–03; Shadow Treas., 2004–07; Treas., 2007–13; Dep. Prime Minister, 2010–13.

**SWANN, Julian Dana Nimmo H.;** *see* Hartland-Swann.

**SWANN, Kathryn, (Kate);** Chief Executive, SSP, 2013–19; *b* 1964; *d* of Ian and Sheila Prior; *m* 1987; two *d*. *Educ*: Bradford Univ. (BSc Hons Business Mgt). Grad. trainee, Tesco, 1986–88; Brand Manager, Homepride Foods, 1988–91; Mktg Controller, Coca Cola Schweppes, 1991; Mktg Dir, Currys, 1992–96; Homebase: Mktg Dir, 1996–99; Man. Dir, 1999; Man. Dir, Argos, 2000–03; CEO, WH Smith, 2003–13. Chancellor, Bradford Univ., 2016–.

**SWANN, Sir Michael (Christopher),** 4th Bt *cr* 1906, of Prince's Gardens, Royal Borough of Kensington; TD 1979; Partner: Smith Swann & Co., 1992–99; Payman's, 1999–2006; *b* 23 Sept. 1941; *s* of Sir Anthony Swann, 3rd Bt, CMG, OBE and Jean Margaret, *d* of late John Herbert Niblock-Stuart; *S* father, 1991; 1st, 1965, Hon. Lydia Hewitt (marr. diss. 1985), *e d* of 8th Viscount Lifford; two *s* one *d*; 2nd, 1988, Marilyn Ann Morse (*née* Tobitt). *Educ*: Eton Coll. APMI 1978. Lt KRRC (The Royal Green Jackets), 1960–63; T&AVR 4th Bn The Royal Green Jackets, 1964–79 (Brevet Lt-Col 1979). Director: Wright Deen (Life and Estate Duty), 1964–74; Richards Longstaff (Holdings) Ltd, 1974–86; Richards Longstaff Ltd, 1974–88; Gerrard Vivian Gray (Life & Pensions), 1988–92 (Man. Dir). Trustee, Gabbitas Truman and Thring, 1978–2008 (Chm., 1998–2008). General Comr of Income Tax, 1988–2008. *Recreations*: bridge, golf, ski-ing, gardening, racing. *Heir*: *s* Jonathan Christopher Swann [*b* 17 Nov. 1966; *m* 1994, Polly, *d* of Comdr David Baston; twin *s*]. *Address*: 38 Hurlingham Road, SW6 3RQ. *Clubs*: Turf, Hurlingham, IZ, MCC; New Zealand Golf.

**SWANN, Paul Phillip;** Regional Employment Judge, East Midlands Region, since 2012; *b* Birmingham, 24 July 1956.

**SWANN, Robert Samuel, (Robin);** Member (UU) North Antrim, Northern Ireland Assembly, since 2011; Leader, Ulster Unionist Party, since 2017; *b* Kells, Co. Antrim, 24 Sept. 1971; *s* of Robert Swann and Ida Swann; *m* 2008, Jennifer McIlroy; one *s* one *d*. *Educ*: Open Univ. (BSc; Professional Cert. Mgt). NI Manager, SGS, 2005–11. Chief Whip (UU), 2012–17. Northern Ireland Assembly: Chairman: Employment and Learning Cttee, 2013–16; Public Accounts Cttee, 2016–17; Chm., All Party Gp on Congenital Heart Disease, 2013–. Trustee, Commonwealth Parly Assoc., 2016–. Contested (UU) N Antrim, 2015. Pres., Young Farmers' Clubs, 2005–07; Chm., Rural Youth Europe, 2008–10. Governor: Cambridge House Grammar Sch., 2010–15; Ballee Community High Sch., 2010–15. *Recreation*: Ulster Scots culture and traditions. *Address*: (office) 13–15 Queen Street, Harryville, Ballymena BT42 2BB. *T*: (028) 2565 9595. *E*: robin.swannmla@gmail.com.

**SWANNELL, John,** FRPS; professional photographer specialising in fashion and portraits; *b* 27 Dec. 1946; *s* of Ted and Lily Swannell; *m* 1982, Marianne Lah; one *s* three *d*. *Educ*: Bishopswood's, Highgate. FRPS 1993. Left sch. at 16; Vogue Studios, 1966–69; asst to David Bailey, 1969–74; founded own studio, 1975; worked for Vogue, Harpers & Queen, Sunday Times, Tatler. Exhibitions: show, Royal Acad., Edinburgh, 1989; NPG, Edinburgh, 1990; retrospective of fashion work, RPS, 1990; exhibn of nudes, Hamilton Gall., 1991; exhibn of portraits, NPG, 1996–97, 2011; photographs in permanent collections: V&A; NPG, London and Scotland; RPS. Royal portraits: the Princess Royal, 40th birthday 1992, 50th birthday 2002, 60th birthday, 2010; Diana, Princess of Wales with Princes William and Harry, 1994; the Queen, Queen Mother, Prince of Wales and Prince William, 2001; the Queen and Duke of Edinburgh for Golden Jubilee, 2002; Prince Charles for rainforest project, 2008; the Queen and Duke of Edinburgh for Diamond Jubilee, 2012; Royal Mail stamps: wedding of Duke and Duchess of Wessex, 1999; Queen Mother's 100th birthday; other portraits include: King Hussein of Jordan, King Abdullah and Queen Rania of Jordan, Rowan Atkinson, Helena Bonham Carter, Michael Caine, Joan Collins, Billy Connolly, Dame Judi Dench, Bryan Ferry, Sir Norman Foster, Sir John Gielgud, Gilbert and George, John Hurt, Elton John, Joanna Lumley, Spike Milligan, Roger Moore, Peter O'Toole, Michael Palin, Michael Parkinson, Margaret Thatcher, Tony Blair, Susan Boyle, Rod Stewart, Pete Townshend. *Publications*: Fine Lines, 1982; Naked Landscape, 1986; Twenty Years On, 1996; Ten Out of Ten, 2001; I'm Still Standing, 2002; Nudes 1978–2006, 2007; Landscapes, 2009; Highgate Cemetery, 2010; Foxgloves, 2011; Snowdrops, 2012; Daffodils, 2012; Bluebells, 2012; (with Sir Roy Strong) Sir Portrait, 2015. *Recreation*: landscape photography. *Address*: 62 North Road, Highgate, N6 4AA. *T*: (020) 8348 5965. *E*: info@johnswannell.com.

**SWANNELL, Nicola Mary, (Mrs Graham Swannell);** *see* Pagett, N. M.

**SWANNELL, Robert William Ashburnham,** CBE 2018; Chairman: Marks and Spencer plc, 2011–17; UK Government Investments (formerly Shareholder Executive, Department for Business, Innovation and Skills), since 2014; *b* Nanyuki, Kenya, 18 Nov. 1950; *s* of David William Ashburnham Swannell and Pamela Mary Swannell; *m* 1982, Patricia Ann Ward; one *s* one *d*. *Educ*: Rugby Sch.; Inns of Court Sch. of Law. FCA 1973. Called to the Bar, Lincoln's Inn, 1976. Peat Marwick Mitchell, 1969–73; Investment Banking, Schroders, later Citigroup, 1977–2010: Co-Chm., Citigroup European Investment Bank, 2003–06; Vice Chm., Citigroup Europe, 2006–10. Chm., HMV Gp plc, 2009–11; non-executive Director: British Land Co. plc, 1999–2010; 3i Gp plc, 2006–10; Investor Forum, 2015–. Member: Industrial Adv. Bd, DTI, later BERR, 1999–2008; Regulatory Decisions Cttee, FSA, 2001–05; Takeover Appeal Bd, 2007–. Trustee: Royal Nat. Children's SpringBoard Foundn, 2014– (Chm., 2019–); Teach First, 2015–. Chm., Governing Body, Rugby Sch., 2009–14. *Recreations*: golf, opera, ballet, theatre. *Club*: Turf.

**SWANNEY, Rajni;** Sheriff of North Strathclyde at Greenock, 2012–14 (Floating Sheriff, 1999–2012); *b* 27 Aug. 1954; *d* of Sat Dev Dhir and Swarn Lata Dhir; *m* 1981, Robert Todd Swanney; two *s*. *Educ*: Glasgow Univ. (LLB). Court Assistant: MacRoberts, Glasgow, 1978–80; various Glasgow firms, 1982–88; Chm. (pt-time), Child Support Tribunal, 1993–96; Immigration Adjudicator (pt-time), 1995–99. *Recreations*: cooking, reading, gardening, sewing, painting, jewellery making.

**SWANSEA,** 5th Baron *cr* 1893, of Singleton, co. Glamorgan; **Richard Anthony Hussey Vivian;** Bt 1882; *b* 24 Jan. 1957; *s* of 4th Baron Swansea and Miriam Antoinette Vivian (*née* Caccia-Birch); *S* father, 2005; *m* 1996, Anna Clementine Brooking (*née* Austin); one *s* one *d*. *Educ*: Eton Coll.; Univ. of Durham (BA Hons); City Univ. Business Sch. (MBA). Financial journalist, 1979–97; res. ed., various investment banks, 1998–2006; Supervisory Analyst: WestLB AG, 2006–10; Nomura International plc, 2010–11; Franchise Partner, Rosemary Bookkeeping, 2013–16. Mem. (C) Wandsworth BC, 1994–2006 (Dep. Mayor, 2000–01); Hon. Alderman, 2006). Mem. Sch. Council, Newton Prep. Sch., Battersea, 2001–12. Vice Pres., Morriston RFC Male Choir, 2007–. *Publications*: China's Metals and World Markets, 1992. *Recreations*: racing, Su Doku puzzles, croquet. *Heir*: *s* Hon. James Henry Hussey Vivian, *b* 25 June 1999. *Address*: 3 Court Cottages, Cold Ashby Road, Guilsborough, Northampton, Northants NN6 8QW.

**SWANSEA AND BRECON, Bishop of;** *see* Wales, Archbishop of.

**SWANSON, Alayne Elizabeth;** Sheriff of Glasgow and Strathkelvin at Glasgow, since 2010; *b* Elgin, 16 April 1959; *d* of David Alan Lawrie and Ethel Lawrie; *m* 1984, Magnus Swanson; three *s*. *Educ*: Elgin Acad.; Univ. of Edinburgh (LLB Hons, DipLP). Trainee, Shepherd & Wedderburn, 1982–84; Asst, McLure Naismith, 1984–86; Foreign Associate, Hughes Hubbard & Reed, 1986–87; Asst and Partner, Bird Semple Fyfe, Ireland, 1987–94; Partner, Dundas & Wilson, 1994–98; Solicitor Advocate, 1996; Partner, Maclay Murray & Spens, 1998–2010. *Recreations*: golf, ski-ing, walking, music. *Address*: Glasgow Sheriff Court, Sheriff's Chambers, 1 Carlton Place, Glasgow G5 9DA. *T*: (0141) 429 8888, *Fax*: (0141) 429 2217. *E*: sheriffaswanson@scotcourts.gov.uk.

**SWANSON, His Honour John Alexander;** a Circuit Judge, 1996–2012; *b* 31 May 1944; *s* of Sidney Alexander Swanson and Joan Swanson; *m* 1981, Pauline Ann Hearn (*née* Woodmansey) (marr. diss.); two *d*. *Educ*: Giggleswick Sch., Settle; Univ. of Newcastle upon Tyne (LLB 1966). Solicitor, 1970–75; called to the Bar, Inner Temple, 1975; a Recorder, 1994–96. Asst Comr, Boundary Commn for England, 1992–95. *Recreations*: remembering hill-walking, history of the American West, 19th and 20th century music, steam locomotives and the history of railways, malt whisky. *Clubs*: Bridlington Rugby Union Football; Bridlington Yacht.

**SWANSON, Prof. Sydney Alan Vasey,** FREng; Professor of Biomechanics, Imperial College, University of London, 1974–97; *b* 31 Oct. 1931; *s* of Charles Henry William Swanson and Hannah Elizabeth Swanson (*née* Vasey); *m* 1956, Mary Howarth; one *s* one *d*. *Educ*: Scarborough Boys' High Sch.; Imperial Coll., London. DSc (Eng), PhD, DIC, FCGI, FIMechE; FREng (FEng 1987). Engineering Laboratories, Bristol Aircraft Ltd, 1955–58; Imperial College, London: Lectr, Mechanical Engineering, 1958–69; Reader in Biomechanics, 1969–74; Dean, City and Guilds Coll., 1976–79; Head of Mechanical Engineering Dept, 1978–83; Pro Rector, 1983–86; Pro Rector (Educnl Quality), 1994–97; Dep. Rector, 1997. *Publications*: Engineering Dynamics, 1963; Engineering in Medicine (with B. M. Sayers and B. Watson), 1975; (with M. A. R. Freeman) The Scientific Basis of Joint Replacement, 1977; papers on bone, cartilage and joints in learned jls. *Recreations*: photography, cycling, fell-walking. *Address*: 12 Holmwood Gardens, Wallington, Surrey SM6 0HN. *Club*: Lyke Wake (Northallerton).

**SWANSTON, Roy;** Chairman, Shaftesbury Housing Group, 2005–07; *b* 31 Oct. 1940; *s* of Robert Trotter Swanston and Margaret Ann Swanston (*née* Paxton); *m* 1963, Doreen Edmundson; one *s* one *d*. *Educ*: Berwick-upon-Tweed Grammar Sch. FRICS. County Borough of Sunderland, 1958–67; Clasp Develt Gp, Nottingham, 1967–71; Notts CC, 1971–74; Durham CC, 1974–75; Dir of Building Economics, 1975–82, of Dept of Architecture, 1982–87, Cheshire CC; Sen. Management Consultant, Peat Marwick McLintock, 1987–88; Dir of Develt, Bucknall Austin, 1988–90; Dir, Properties in Care, 1990–93, Res. and Professional Services, 1993–95, English Heritage; Chm., Local Govt Residuary Bd (England), 1995–99. Chairman: W Herts HA, 1996–2001; E and N Herts NHS Trust, 2001–02. Chairman: Jones Lang Wootton Educn Trust, 1995–2000; Jt Contracts Tribunal for Standard Form of Building Contract, 1995–2002. Mem., E of England Heritage Lottery Cttee, 2006–12. Pres., RICS, 1994–95 (Pres., QS Div., 1982–83); Hon. Treas., 1987–90; Chm., Bldg Conservation Diploma Adv. Bd, 2000–09); Sec. Gen., Internat. Fedn of Surveyors, 1995–99. Visiting Professor: Liverpool John Moores Univ., 1995–2005; Bedfordshire (formerly Luton) Univ., 1996– (Mem. Court, 1999–); Salford Univ., 1999–2005 (Vis. Fellow, 1986–99). Mem., Yorks Dales Nat. Park Authy, 2001–04. Trustee, NE Civic Trust, 1998–2010 (Chm., 2006–08). Mem., Barnardo's Council, 1989–2005; Chm., Barnardo's Pension Fund, 2003–05 (Trustee, 1998–2002). Governor: Culford Methodist Ind. Sch., 1999–2015 (Chm., 2008–14); Springhill Special Sch.,

2001–04 (Chm., 2001–04). Methodist Local Preacher; Chair, Methodist Ch House Mgt Cttee, 2014–; Mem., Methodist Property Develt Cttee, 2016–. Hon. DSc Salford, 1994. *Recreations:* supporter of Sunderland AFC, fell walking.

**SWANTEE, Olaf;** Chief Executive, Sunrise Communications AG, since 2016; *b* Netherlands; *m. Educ:* BA Econs; European Sch. of Mgt, Paris (MBA 1989). IT industry, Europe and USA, latterly EMEA Sen. Vice Pres. for enterprise sales and software, Hewlett-Packard; former Mem., Exec. Bd, Orange France-Telecom; CEO, EE (formerly Everything Everywhere) Ltd, 2011–16. Ind. non-exec. Dir, Legal and General Gp plc, 2014–16; Mem. Bd, Telia Co. (formerly Telia Sonera), 2016–. *Address:* Sunrise Communications AG, Binzmühlestrasse 130, 8050 Zürich, Switzerland.

**SWANTON, Prof. (Robert) Charles,** PhD; FRCP; FMedSci; FRS 2018; Professor of Personalised Medicine, University College London, since 2011; Senior Group Leader, Francis Crick Institute, since 2013; *b* Poole, Dorset, 24 Feb. 1972; *s* of Robert Howard Swanton, *qv*; *m* 1997, Brianna Cloke; two *d. Educ:* St Paul's Sch.; University Coll. London (BSc; PhD 1997; MB BS 1999). MRCP 2003, FRCP 2011. Dir, CRUK/UCL/Manchester Lung Cancer Centre of Excellence, 2013–; Chief Clinician, CRUK, 2017–. FMedSci 2015. *Publications:* contrib. articles to learned jls incl. Nature, Cancer Cell, New England Jl Medicine, Nature Genetics, Science. *Recreations:* photography, cycling, hill-walking. *Address:* Francis Crick Institute, Midland Road, NW1 1AT. *E:* charles.swanton@crick.ac.uk.

**SWANTON, Robert Howard,** MD; FRCP; Consultant Cardiologist, University College London Hospitals, since 1979; *b* 30 Sept. 1944; *s* of Robert Neil and Sue Swanton; *m* 1969, Lindsay Ann (*née* Jepson); one *s* one *d. Educ:* Monkton Combe Sch.; Queens' Coll., Cambridge (MB BChir 1969; MA; MD 1980); St Thomas's Hosp. Med. Sch. FRCP 1984. Senior Registrar: St Thomas' Hosp., 1975–77; Nat. Heart Hosp., 1977–79; Consultant Cardiologist: Middlesex Hosp., 1979–2005; King Edward VII Hosp. for Officers, 1984–; The Heart Hosp., 2005–15; University Coll. Hosp., 2015–. Mem. Med. Adv. Panel on Cardiology, CAA, 1998–; Chm. Adv. Panel on Cardiology, DVLA, 2002–09. Hon. Sec., 1988–90, Pres., 1998–2001, British Cardiac Soc. FESC 1994; FACC 2005. Mem. Editorial Bd, Hospital Medicine, 1986–2016. *Publications:* Cardiology, 1984, 6th edn 2008; Essential Angioplasty, 2012; articles in med. literature incl. Heart, American Jl Cardiology, Hospital Medicine, European Heart Jl, etc. *Recreations:* music, photography. *Address:* (home) Kent Lodge, 10 Dover Park Drive, Roehampton, SW15 5BG. *T:* (020) 8788 6920. *E:* howard.swanton@nhs.net; (office) 22 Upper Wimpole Street, W1G 6NB. *T:* (020) 7034 4030, *Fax:* (020) 7224 1486. *Clubs:* Arts; St Albans Medical; Chelsea Clinical.

*See also R. C. Swanton.*

**SWARBRICK, Catherine Marie;** Director of Administration, University of London, 2004–11; *b* 25 Nov. 1950; *d* of Hubert Joseph Swarbrick and Margaret Swarbrick. *Educ:* Goldsmiths' Coll., Univ. of London (BA Hons, PGCE). Secondary sch. teacher, 1973–79; Sec., Law Dept, LSE, 1980–82; Exams Officer, British Computer Soc., 1982–85; Sen. Manager, RCGP, 1985–95; Dir, Nat. Childbirth Trust, 1995–99; School Sec., St George's Hosp. Med. Sch., 1999–2004. *Recreations:* reading, art history.

**SWARBRICK, Prof. James,** PhD, DSc; FRSC, CChem; FRPharmS; President, PharmaceuTech Inc., 2001–17; *b* 8 May 1934; *s* of George Winston Swarbrick and Edith M. C. Cooper; *m* 1960, Pamela Margaret Oliver. *Educ:* Sloane Grammar Sch.; Chelsea Coll., Univ. of London (BPharm Hons 1960; PhD 1964; DSc 1972). FRSC (FRIC 1970); FRPharmS (FPS 1978; MPS 1961). Asst Lectr, 1962, Lectr, 1964, Chelsea Coll.; Vis. Asst Prof., Purdue Univ., 1964; Associate Prof., 1966, Prof. and Chm. of Dept of Pharmaceutics, 1969, Asst Dean, 1970, Univ. of Conn; Dir of Product Develt, Sterling-Winthrop Res. Inst., NY, 1972; first Prof. of Pharmaceutics, Univ. of Sydney, 1975–76; Dean, Sch. of Pharmacy, Univ. of London, 1976–78; Prof. of Pharmacy and Chm., Res. Council, Univ. of S California, Los Angeles, 1978–81; Prof. of Pharmaceutics and Chm., Div. of Pharmaceutics, Univ. of N Carolina, 1981–93; Vice-Pres., R&D, 1993–99, Scientific Affairs, 1999–2006, Applied Analytical Industries Inc., subseq. aaiPharma Inc. Vis. Scientist, Astra Labs, Sweden, 1971; Vis. Prof., Shanghai Med. Univ., 1991–92. Indust. Cons., 1965–72, 1975–; Cons., Aust. Dept of Health, 1975–76; Mem., Cttee on Specifications, National Formulary, 1970–75; Chm., Jt US Pharmacopoeia-Nat. Formulary Panel on Disintegration and Dissolution Testing, 1971–75. Member: Cttee on Grad. Programs, Amer. Assoc. of Colls of Pharmacy, 1969–71; Practice Trng Cttee, Pharm. Soc. of NSW, 1975–76; Academic Bd, Univ. of Sydney, 1975–76; Collegiate Council, 1976–78; Educn Cttee, Pharmaceutical Soc. of GB, 1976–78; Working Party on Pre-Registration Training, 1977–78. Pharmaceutical Manufacturers Assoc. Foundation: Mem., Basic Pharmacology Adv. Cttee, 1982–91; Chm., Pharmaceutics Adv. Cttee, 1986–2007; Mem., Scientific Adv. Cttee, 1986–2007; Mem., Generic Drugs Adv. Cttee, Food and Drug Admin, 1992–96 (Chm., 1994–96). FAAAS 1966; Fellow: Acad. of Pharm. Sciences, 1973; Amer. Assoc. of Pharmaceutical Scientists, 1987. Kenan Res. Study Award, 1988. Mem. Editorial Board: Jl of Biopharmaceutics and Pharmacokinetics, 1973–79; Drug Development Communications, 1974–82; Pharmaceutical Technology, 1978–; Biopharmaceutics and Drug Disposition, 1979–; series Editor: Current Concepts in the Pharmaceutical Sciences, Drugs and the Pharmaceutical Sciences. *Publications:* (with A. N. Martin and A. Cammarata) Physical Pharmacy, 2nd edn 1969, 3rd edn 1983; (ed) Encyclopedia of Pharmaceutical Technology, 1988–2010, 4th edn as Encyclopedia of Pharmaceutical Science and Technology, 2013; (ed jtly) Drug Delivery and Targeting, 2001; contributed: American Pharmacy, 6th edn 1966 and 7th edn 1974; Remington's Pharmaceutical Sciences, 14th edn 1970 to 22nd edn 2012; contrib. Current Concepts in the Pharmaceutical Sciences: Biopharmaceutics, 1970; res. contribs to internat. sci. jls. *Recreations:* woodworking, listening to music, golf. *Address:* 180 Doral Drive, Pinehurst, NC 28374–8682, USA. *T:* (910) 2553015. *E:* jswar180@gmail.com.

**SWARBRICK, Rt Rev. Paul;** *see* Lancaster, Bishop of, (RC).

**SWAROOP, Sudhanshu,** QC 2016; *b* New Delhi, 20 April 1973; *s* of Dr Mukul Swaroop and Dr Deepshikha Swaroop; *m* 2014, Raageshwari Loomba; one *d. Educ:* Wellingborough Sch.; Magdalene Coll., Cambridge (BA 1994); Exeter Coll., Oxford (BCL). Pres., Cambridge Union Soc., Lent 1994. Called to the Bar, Inner Temple, 1997; in practice as barrister, specialising in internat., commercial and human rights law. *Recreations:* cricket, tennis, art. *Address:* 20 Essex Street, WC2R 3AL. *T:* (020) 7842 6713. *E:* sswaroop@20essexst.com.

**SWARUP, Prof. Govind,** PhD; FRS 1991; Professor of Eminence, Physics and Radio Astronomy, 1990–94, Professor Emeritus, 1994–99, Homi Bhabha Senior Fellow, 1999–2001, Tata Institute of Fundamental Research, Bombay; *b* 29 March 1929; *m* Bina Jain; one *s* one *d. Educ:* Allahabad Univ. (BSc 1948; MSc 1950); Stanford Univ., USA (PhD 1961). Sec., Radio Res. Cttee, CSIR, Nat. Physical Lab., New Delhi, 1950–53; Colombo-Plan Fellowship, CSIRO, Sydney, 1953–55; Res. Associate, Harvard Univ., 1956–57; Grad. Student, Stanford Univ., USA, 1957–60, Asst Prof. 1961–63; Tata Institute of Fundamental Research, Bombay: Reader, 1963–65; Associate Prof., 1965–70; Prof., 1970–79; Sen. Prof., 1979–90; Dir, Giant Metrewave Radio Telescope Project, 1987–96. INSA Hon. Scientist, 2001–05. Visiting Professor: Univ. of Md, USA, 1980; Univ. of Groningen, Netherlands, 1980–81; Univ. of Leiden, Netherlands, 1981. Chm., Indian Nat. Cttee, URSI, 1986–88, 1994–97. Fellow: Indian Nat. Sci. Acad.; Indian Acad. Scis; Nat. Acad. Scis, India; Indian Geophysical Union; Third World Acad. of Scis; Academician: Internat. Acad. of Astronautics; Pontifical Acad. of Scis. Associate, RAS; Member: Astronomical Soc. India (Pres., 1975–77); IAU (Pres., Radio Astronomy Commn, 1979–82); Indian Physics Assoc.; Indian Physical Soc. Member Editorial Board: Indian Jl Radio and Space Physics; Nat. Acad. of Science, India. Numerous awards, incl. Delinger Award, URSI; S. S. Bhatnager Award, India, 1972; Tsiolkovsky medal, Fedn of Cosmonautics, USSR, 1987; Third World Acad. of Scis Award, Trieste, 1988; R. D. Birla Award, India, 1990; Khwarizmi Award, Iran, 1999; Herschel Medal, RAS, 2006; Grote Reber Medal, Tasmania, 2007. Holder of 2 patents. *Publications:* (ed jtly) Quasars, 1986; (ed jtly) History of Oriental Astronomy, 1987; (ed jtly) Universe at Low Frequency, 2003. *Address:* 10 Cozy Retreat, Road No 3, Sindh Society, Aundh, Pune 411007, India. *T:* (office) (20) 25719000, (home) (20) 25851630.

**SWASH, Prof. Michael,** MD; FRCP, FRCPath; Consultant Neurologist: Royal London Hospitals, 1972–2006; London Independent Hospital, 1980; Professor of Neurology, Bart's and the London School of Medicine and Dentistry, Queen Mary (formerly St Bartholomew's and the Royal London School of Medicine and Dentistry, Queen Mary and Westfield College), University of London, 1993–2006, now Emeritus; *b* 29 Jan. 1939; *s* of Edwin Frank Swash and Kathleen Swash; *m* 1966, Caroline Mary Payne; three *s. Educ:* Forest Sch., London; London Hosp. Med. Coll., Univ. of London (MB BS 1962; MD 1973); Univ. of Virginia, USA. FRCP 1977; FRCPath 1991. House appts, London and Bath, 1962–63; GP, Westbury, Wilts and Tottenham, 1965; postgrad. trng in neurol. and neurophysiol., Case-Western Reserve Univ., Cleveland, Ohio and Washington Univ., St Louis, Mo, 1965–68; MRC Res. Fellow in Neuropathol., then Sen. Registrar in Neurol., Royal London Hosp., 1968–72; Consultant Neurologist, Newham HA, 1972–91; Sen. Lectr in Neuropathol., London Hosp. Med. Coll., 1976–90; Med. Dir, Royal London NHS Trust, 1990–93. CMO, Swiss Re (formerly Swiss Reinsce) Ltd, 1985–2012. Mem., Med. Adv. Bd, Best Doctors Inc., 2013–19. Dir, Medhand Internat. AB, 2002–19. Vis. lectr or vis. prof., various univs in Europe, Asia, Australia and N America; Spinoza Vis. Prof., Univ. of Amsterdam, 1999–2000. Hon. Prof. of Neurology, Univ. of Lisbon, 2006–. Ed., Associate Ed. and mem. editl bds, various neurol and other scientific jls. Mem., Neurosci. Bd, MRC, 1987–91. Hon. Secretary: Sect. Neurol., RSocMed, 1977–79; Assoc. of British Neurologists, 1981–87; Motor Neurone Disease Association: Chm., Annual Symposium Cttee, 1991–99; Member: Trustees, 1998–2001; Chm., World Fedn of Neurol. Res. Gp on MNDs, 1997–2005. Medals and prizes include: Forbes H. Norris Internat. Prize for res. and care in MND/ALS; Medallist, Assoc. of British Neurologists, 2010. *Publications:* (jtly) Colour Guide to Neurology, 1972, 3rd edn 2005; (ed) Hutchison's Clinical Methods, 16th edn, 1975 to 22nd edn, 2007; (jtly) Neuromuscular Disorders: a practical approach to diagnosis and management, 1981, 3rd edn 1999; (jtly) Clinical Neuropathology, 1983; (jtly) Biopsy Pathology of Muscle, 1984, 2nd edn 1991; (jtly) Scientific Basis of Neurology, 1985; (jtly) Coloproctology and the Pelvic Floor, 1985, 2nd edn 1992; (jtly) Neurology: a concise clinical text, 1989; (jtly) Hierarchies in Neurology, 1989; (jtly) Clinical Neurology, 2 vols, 1989; (jtly) Motor Neuron Disease, 1994; Outcomes in Neurology and Neurosurgery, 1998; (jtly) Amyotrophic Lateral Sclerosis, 2000, 2nd edn 2006; (jtly) ALSAQ User Manual, 2001; (jtly) The Pelvic Floor, 2002; (jtly) Neurology in Focus, 2009; The Neurological Tradition at the London Hospital, 2020; contrib. numerous papers to med. and scientific jls. *Recreations:* pianoforte, chamber music and opera, hill walking, Morgan Plus 8, poetry, stained glass. *T:* (020) 7638 4043, *Fax:* (020) 7638 4043. *E:* mswash@btinternet.com. *Clubs:* Athenæum; London Rowing; Rowfant (Cleveland, Ohio).

**SWAYNE, Rt Hon. Sir Desmond (Angus),** Kt 2016; TD 2000; PC 2011; MP (C) New Forest West, since 1997; *b* 20 Aug. 1956; *s* of George Joseph Swayne and Elizabeth McAlister Swayne (*née* Gibson); *m* 1987, Moira Cecily Teek; one *s* two *d. Educ:* Bedford Sch.; Univ. of St Andrews (MTh). Schoolmaster: Charterhouse, 1980–81; Wrekin Coll., 1982–87; Systems Manager, Royal Bank of Scotland, 1988–96. Opposition front bench spokesman on health, Jan.–Sept. 2001, on defence, 2001–02, on NI, 2003–04; Opposition Whip, 2002–03; PPS to Leader of the Opposition, 2004–10, to Prime Minister, 2010–12; a Lord Comr of HM Treasury (Govt Whip), 2012–13; Vice Chamberlain of HM Household (Dep. Chief Whip), 2013–14; Minister of State, DFID, 2014–16. TA Officer, 1987–. Prison visitor, 1989–. *Address:* House of Commons, SW1A 0AA. *Club:* Serpentine Swimming.

**SWAYNE, Giles Oliver Cairnes;** composer; *b* 30 June 1946; *s* of Sir Ronald Oliver Carless Swayne, MC and Charmian (*née* Cairnes); *m* 1st, 1972, Camilla Rumbold (marr. diss. 1983); one *s*; 2nd, 1984, Naa Otua Codjoe (marr. diss. 2001); 3rd, 2002, Malu Lin. *Educ:* Ampleforth; Trinity Coll., Cambridge; Royal Acad. of Music. Dir, Gonzaga Music Ltd, 2002–. Composer in Residence, Clare Coll., Cambridge, 2006–14. *Compositions:* Six early songs, La rivière, 1966; The kiss, 1967; Sonata for string quartet, 1968; Three Shakespeare songs, 1969; Chamber music for strings, Four lyrical pieces, 1970; The good-morrow, String quartet no 1, Paraphrase, 1971; Trio, Canto for guitar, 1972; Canto for piano, Canto for violin, 1973; Orlando's music, Synthesis, Scrapbook, 1974; Canto for clarinet, Charades, Duo, 1975; Suite for Guitar, Pentecost-music, Alleluia!, 1976; String quartet no 2, 1977; A world within, 1978; Phoenix variations, CRY, 1979; The three Rs, Freewheeling, 1980; Count-down, Canto for cello, 1981; Rhythm-studies 1 and 2, Magnificat I, 1982; Riff-raff, A song for Haddi, 1983; Symphony for small orchestra, Le nozze di Cherubino, NaaOtwa Lala, 1984; Missa Tiburtina, 1985; Into the light, Solo, godsong, Nunc dimittis I, O magnum mysterium, 1986; PP, Tonos, Veni creator I and II, Songlines, The coming of Saskia Hawkins, 1987; The song of Leviathan, Harmonies of Hell, 1988; A memory of sky, 1989; No quiet place, No man's land, 1990; Circle of silence, 1991; Zebra music, The song of the Tortoise, 1992; The Owl and the Pussycat I, String quartet no 3, 1993; Fiddlesticks, Goodnight sweet ladies, Squeezy, 1994; All about Henry, The tiger, Communion service in D, A convocation of worms, 1995; Two romantic songs, The silent land, Ophelia drowning, 1996; Tombeau, Beatus vir, Mr Leary's mechanical maggot, Chinese whispers, Petite messe solitaire, Missa brevissima, Echo, 1997; Winter Solstice carol, Groundwork, Merlis Lied, 1998; The flight of the Swan, HAVOC, 1999; Perturbèd spirit, Canto for flute, The Akond of Swat, 2000; Mancanza, The murder of Gonzago, 2001; Bits and Bobs, Epitaph and refrain, 2002; The Owl and the Pussycat II, Midwinter, Sangre viva, 2003; Stabat Mater, Four Passiontide motets, Ave verum corpus, Stations of the Cross I, Mr Bach's Bottle-bank, Magnificat II, 2004; Four Christmas Carols, Nunc dimittis II, Lonely hearts, Stations of the Cross II, Bits of Mrs Bach, Epithalamium, Elegy for a wicked world, 2005; Sonata for cello and piano, Sinfonietta concertante, Ten Terrible Tunes, A Clare Eucharist, Creepy-crawlies, Two little motets, There is no rose, 2006; Suite for solo cello, Symphony no 1, Threnody, 2007; Leonardo's Dream, Agnes Wisley's Chillout Fantasy, Magnificat III, 2008; The human heart, Bagatelles (Book I) for piano, Toil and trouble, Zig-zag, String quartet No 4, The Joys of Travel, Adam lay ibounden, O mysteria, 2009; Der Wandersmann, Hubbub, The Word, Complaintes, 2010; Dolorosa, Laulu Laululle, Bagatelles for piano (Book 2), 2011; Clare Canticles, Uncommon Prayers, 2012; Strumming, Two Little Prayers, I Do Not Sleep, Double Act, 2013; The Yonghy-Bonghy-Bo, God is gone up, Chansons dévotes et poissonneuses, Our orphan souls, 2014; Golgotha,

Kaleidoscope, Sommertage, 2015; Everybloom, Bloomfantasy, Benedicta filia, 2016; Leapfrog, 2017; Endellionigma, 2018; The Ribs and Terrors, 2019. *Recreations:* walking, talking and listening. *E:* gs@gonzagamusic.co.uk. *W:* www.gilesswayne.com.

**SWAYTHLING,** 5th Baron *cr* 1907, of Swaythling, co. Southampton; **Charles Edgar Samuel Montagu;** Bt 1894; Director, The Health Partnership; *b* 20 Feb. 1954; *o s* of 4th Baron Swaythling and of Christine Françoise (*née* Dreyfus); *S* father, 1998; *m* 1996, Hon. Angela, *d* of Baron Rawlinson of Ewell, PC, QC; one *d.* Member: Amer. Council of Hypnotist Examiners (Mem. Adv. Bd); British Council of Hypnotist Examiners; Scientific and Medical Network; Adv. Bd, British Council for Complementary Medicine. Trustee, Crossroads Foundn, Antigua. *Heir: cousin* Rupert Anthony Samuel Montagu [*b* 5 Aug. 1965; *m* 2007, Nancy Bondshu, *d* of Donald Wilson; three *s*]. *Address:* c/o The Health Partnership, 12A Thurloe Street, SW7 2ST.

**SWEASEY, Peter Duncan;** freelance television producer and director, since 1999; *b* Chertsey, Surrey, 14 July 1970; *s* of Denis Sweasey, OBE, JP, DL and of Diana Sweasey. *Educ:* Fullbrook Secondary Sch., Surrey; St Catherine's Coll., Oxford (BA 1st Cl. English Lang. and Lit. 1993). Television productions include: Petworth House, 2011; Imagine: Dancing with Titian, 2012; David Starkey's Music and Monarchy, 2013; The Brits who Built the Modern World, 2014; How to be Bohemian, 2015; Victorian Bakers, 2016. Hon. FRIBA 2015. *Publications:* From Queer to Eternity: spirituality in the lives of lesbian, gay and bisexual people, 1997. *Recreations:* music, meditation, architecture, pilates, swimming, eating (ideally cake). *E:* peters@afterglowtv.co.uk.

**SWEENEY, Brendan,** MBE 2003; FRCGP; Principal in general practice, Govan, 1975–2010; *b* 11 July 1946; *s* of James and Angela Sweeney; *m* 1973, Dr Rosalie T. Dunn; two *s* three *d. Educ:* Univ. of Glasgow (MA 1965; MB ChB 1971). DObstRCOG 1973; MRCGP 1975, FRCGP 1985. McKenzie Lectr, RCGP, 1997. Hon. Sen. Lectr, Dept of Postgrad. Med. Educn, Univ. of Glasgow. Medical Mem., Appeal Tribunal Service, 1995–. Royal College of General Practitioners: Vice-Chm., Council, 1994–97; Chairman: Cttee of Med. Ethics, 1992–98; W of Scotland Cttee on Postgrad. Med. Educn, 1996; Medical and Dental Defence Union of Scotland, 2012–18 (Treas., 2005–12). *Recreations:* squash, golf, opera, theatre, books. *Address:* 25 Stewarton Drive, Cambuslang, Glasgow G72 8DF. *T:* (0141) 583 1513. *Clubs:* Turnberry Golf, Cathkin Braes Golf, Pollok Golf; Newlands Squash and Tennis.

**SWEENEY, Brian Philip,** QFSM 2005; Chief Officer/Chief Executive, Strathclyde Fire & Rescue (formerly Strathclyde Fire Brigade), 2004–13; *b* 14 July 1961; *s* of Philip and Mary Sweeney; *m* 1995, Pamela Barratt; three *s. Educ:* Holyrood; Coventry Univ. (MA Mgt 2000). Strathclyde Fire Brigade: Firefighter, 1981, Leading Firefighter, 1983; Station Officer, Bde Trng Centre, 1990; Asst Divl Officer, N Glasgow, 1993; Hd of Ops, E Command HQ, Motherwell, 1996; Hd of Personnel and Trng, Central Command, 1997; Dep. Comdr, Central Command, 1998–2000; Dir of Ops, 2000–03; Dep. Chief Officer, 2003; Temp. Firemaster, 2004. MIFireE 1996; Mem., Chief Fire Officers' Assoc., 2000–. Freeman, City of Glasgow, 2004. DUniv Glasgow Caledonian, 2005. *Recreations:* reading, music, accumulating stress.

**SWEENEY, Edward,** CBE 2014; Chairman, Advisory, Conciliation and Arbitration Service, 2007–14; *b* 6 Aug. 1954; *s* of William Sweeney and Louise Sweeney; *m* 1987, Janet Roydhouse. *Educ:* Warwick Univ. (BA Hons); London Sch. of Economics (MSc Econ.). Banking, Insurance and Finance Union: Research Officer, 1976–79; Negotiating Officer (TSB), 1979–86; National Officer: Scotland, 1986–89; Insurance, 1989–91; Dep. Gen. Sec., 1991–96; Gen. Sec., 1996–99, when BIFU amalgamated with UNIFI; UNIFI: Jt Gen. Sec., 1999–2000; Gen. Sec., 2000–04, when UNIFI merged with Amicus; Dep. Gen. Sec., Amicus, 2004–07. *Recreations:* sport, reading, Egyptology.

**SWEENEY, Sir George,** Kt 2000; Principal, Knowsley Community College, 1990–2007; *b* 26 Jan. 1946; *s* of George Sweeney and Margaret, (Peggy), Sweeney (née Carlin); *m* 1968, Susan Anne Wilson; two *d. Educ:* Prescot Boys' GS; Hull Univ. (BA Hons Hist. and Pols 1967; MA 1973). Teacher: Hull Coll. of Technol., 1967–70; Kirby Coll., Teesside, 1970–73; S Trafford Coll., 1973–75 and 1977–83; S Cheshire Coll., 1975–77; Vice Principal, Grimsby Coll. of Technol., 1983–90; Actg Principal, Sheffield Coll., Jan.–Aug. 2000. Hon. DEd Chester, 2008. *Recreations:* painting, drawing, gardening, political biography. *Address:* 12 Red Lane, Appleton, Cheshire WA4 5AD. *T:* (01925) 265113.

**SWEENEY, Mark Darren;** Director General, Policy, Communications and Analysis, Ministry of Justice, since 2019; *b* London, 4 June 1974; *s* of Terry Sweeney and Marie Sweeney; *m* 2002, Cheryl Louise Robinson; one *s* one *d. Educ:* St Edward's Sch., Oxford; Selwyn Coll., Cambridge (BA Hons Hist. 1995). Cabinet Office: graduate fast stream prog., 1995–99; Govt IT prog. review team, 1999–2000; Desk Officer, Eur. Secretariat, 2000–02; Northern Ireland Office: Hd, Political Develt Unit, 2002–04; Dep. Dir, Rights and Internat. Relns, 2004–07; Dep. Dir, Elections and Democracy, MoJ, 2007–10, Cabinet Office, 2010–11; Principal Private Sec. to the Lord Chancellor and Sec. of State for Justice, 2011–12; Dir, Law, Rights and Internat., MoJ, 2012–14; Constitution Dir, Cabinet Office, 2014–15; Dir, Government and Parliament, Ofcom, 2015–17; Dir Gen., Justice Policy, Strategy and Communications, MoJ, 2017–19. *Recreations:* family, music, reading, socialising, sport. *Address:* Ministry of Justice, 102 Petty France, SW1P 3AL. *E:* Mark.sweeney@justice.gov.uk.

**SWEENEY, Hon. Sir Nigel Hamilton,** Kt 2008; **Hon. Mr Justice Sweeney;** a Judge of the High Court of Justice, Queen's Bench Division, since 2008; *b* 18 March 1954; *s* of Alan Vincent Sweeney and Dorothy Sweeney; *m* 1st, 1985, Joanna Clair Slater (marr. diss.); one *s* one *d*; 2nd, 2002, Dr Sheila Theresa Diamond. *Educ:* Wellington Sch., Som; Nottingham Univ. (LLB 1975). Called to the Bar, Middle Temple, 1976 (Harmsworth Schol. 1976), Bencher, 1997. Central Criminal Court: Jun. Prosecuting Counsel to the Crown, 1987–91; First Jun. Prosecuting Counsel, 1991–92; Sen. Prosecuting Counsel, 1992–97; First Sen. Prosecuting Counsel, 1997–2000; Recorder, 1997–2008; QC 2000. Mem., Investigatory Powers Tribunal, 2016–19. Hon. LLD Nottingham, 2015. *Recreations:* golf, tennis, the arts. *Address:* Royal Courts of Justice, Strand, WC2A 2LL. *Clubs:* Garrick; Wisley Golf, Merion Golf.

**SWEENEY, Paul John;** MP (Lab Co-op) Glasgow North East, since 2017; *b* 16 Jan. 1989; *s* of John Gordon Sweeney and Anne Sweeney (née Doherty). *Educ:* Turnbull High Sch.; Univ. of Stirling (Cert. Higher Educn 2008); Univ. of Glasgow (MA 1st Cl. Hons Econ. Hist. and Politics 2011). Manufg and Prodn Ops graduate, 2011–13, Ops Strategy Co-ordinator, 2013–15, BAE Systems; Sen. Exec. Account Manager, Scottish Enterprise, 2015–17. Shadow Minister for Scotland, 2017–. Mem. Council, Instn Engrs and Shipbuilders in Scotland, 2016–. Served TA, 52nd Lowland, 6th Bn, Royal Regt of Scotland, 2006–. *Address:* House of Commons, SW1A 0AA.

**SWEENEY, Timothy Patrick;** Director: Waste Resources Action Programme plc, 2001–11; Cafbank, 2008–10 (Interim Chairman, 2008–09); *b* 2 June 1944; *s* of John Sylvester Sweeney and Olive Bridget (née Montgomery-Cunningham); *m* 1965, Carol Ann Wardle; one *s* one *d. Educ:* Pierrepont School; Sussex Univ. (MA Philosophy); Surrey Univ. (MSc Econs). With Bank of England, 1967–94; Dir Gen., BBA, 1994–2001. Chm., Amicus Vision, 2001–05. Director: Money Advice Trust, 2000–04; AIB Gp UK, 2001–13. Mem., Better Regulation Commn (formerly Task Force), 2002–06. *Recreations:* music, archery, walking. *Address:* Hollowell Hill House, W Chinnock, Crewkerne, Som TA18 7PS.

**SWEENEY, Walter Edward;** Solicitor, Yorkshire Law (formerly Walter Sweeney & Co.), 1997–2010; Consultant, Ingrams Solicitors, Hessle, 2010–12; Head of Probate, Williamsons Solicitors, Hull, 2013–14; locum solicitor, since 2014; *b* Dublin, 23 April 1949; *s* of late Patrick Anthony Sweeney, veterinary surgeon and Jane Yerbury Sweeney, head teacher; *m* 1992, Dr Nuala Maire Kennan; three *d. Educ:* Church Lawford Primary Sch.; Lawrence Sheriff Sch., Rugby; Univ. of Aix-Marseille; Univ. of Hull (BA Hons; MA); Darwin Coll., Cambridge (MPhil); Cert. Ed. TEFL. Admitted Solicitor, 1976. Mem., Vale of Glam CHC, 1991–92. Joined Cons. Party, 1964; Chairman: Rugby Div. YCs, 1965; Church Lawford Cons. Br., 1969; Rugby Cons. Political Centre, 1970. Member: Church Lawford Parish Council, 1971–74; Rugby BC, 1974–77; Beds CC, 1981–89 (Vice-Chm. and Gp spokesman on Police Cttee). Contested (C) Stretford, 1983. MP (C) Vale of Glamorgan, 1992–97; contested (C) same seat, 1997. Member, Select Committee: on Welsh Affairs, 1992–97; on Home Affairs, 1995–97; on Channel Tunnel Rail Link, 1995–96; Vice Chairman: All-Party Penal Affairs Cttee, 1993–97 (Sec., 1992–93); Cons. back bench Legal Affairs Cttee, 1995–97 (Sec., 1994–95); Sec., Cons. back bench Home Affairs Cttee, 1994–97. Contested (Ind): Haltemprice and Howden, July 2008; Humberside Police and Crime Comr, 2012; contested (UK Ind) St Mary's Ward, Beverley, 2015. Rejoined Cons. Party, 2016. Pres., Hull Incorp. Law Soc., 2004–05 (Vice-Pres., 2003–04). Mem., N Cave Parish Council, 2003–07 (Vice-Chm., 2005–07). Owner and proprietor, Newbegin House B&B, 2008– (Visit Hull and E Yorks Award, 2012). Gov., N Cave C of E Primary Sch., 2003–10. *Recreations:* walking, theatre, reading, renovating Georgian house. *Address:* (home) Newbegin House, 10 Newbegin, Beverley HU17 8EG.

**SWEENEY, William Martin;** Chief Executive, Rugby Football Union, since 2019; *b* Calcutta, 10 Oct. 1957; *s* of James Sweeney and Rose Catherine Sweeney; *m* 1984, Elizabeth Anne Smith; one *s* one *d. Educ:* Birkenhead Sch. for Boys; Woking Co. Grammar Sch.; Univ. of Salford (BSc Hons). Shell Internat.; Unilever; Mars; BAT; Reebok International: Pres. and Gen. Manager, Reebok Japan/Asia Pacific; Sen. Vice Pres. and Gen. Manager, N America; Sen. Vice Pres., adidas Reebok Gp, 2003–10; Global Hd, Business Develt, PUMA AG, 2010–13; CEO, British Olympic Assoc., 2013–19. Mem., Exec. Bd, European Olympic Cttee, 2017–19. *Recreations:* golf, ski-ing, fitness, roses, red wine. *E:* billsweeney@rfu.com. *Clubs:* East India; Singapore Cricket.

**SWEET, Andrew Francis;** a District Judge (Magistrates' Courts), since 2004; *b* 12 Nov. 1954; *s* of Rev. Mervyn Thomas Sweet and Joan Myra Dorothy Sweet (née Reece); *m* 1980, Fiona (née McMurdy); two *d. Educ:* Cordwalles Prep. Sch., SA; Northbrook Secondary Sch., London; South Bank Polytech. (BA Hons Law); Coll. of Law, Guildford. Admitted solicitor of Supreme Court, 1984; solicitor in private practice: Surrey, 1980–90; London, 1992–2004; Crown Prosecutor, 1990–92. Administrator to Richmond Court Duty Solicitor Scheme and Police Station Duty Solicitor Administrator, 1995–2004. Dep. Dist Judge, 1997–2004. LEA Sch. Gov., Grand Avenue Primary Sch., 1994–2004. *Recreations:* reading, motorcycles, mountain trekking. *Address:* Westminster Magistrates' Court, 181 Marylebone, NW1 5BR.

**SWEET, Anna Isabel;** *see* Poole, A. I.

**SWEET, Louise June;** QC 2016; *b* Sutton Coldfield, 6 Dec. 1970; *d* of Michael and Elizabeth Sweet; *m* 2001, Adrian Macho; two *d. Educ:* John Wilmott Sch.; Univ. of Hull (LLB Hons). Called to the Bar, Gray's Inn, 1994. *Recreations:* walking, cinema, gym, family, school governor (primary). *Address:* 2 Bedford Row, WC1R 4BU.

**SWEETBAUM, Henry Alan;** Managing Director, PS Capital LLC, since 1997; *b* 22 Nov. 1937; *s* of late Irving and Bertha Sweetbaum; *m* 1st, 1960, Suzanne Milberg (decd); three *s*; 2nd, 1971, Anne Betty Leonie de Vigier; one *s. Educ:* Wharton School, Univ. of Pennsylvania (BS Econ 1959). Underwood Corp., 1960; Exec. Vice-Pres. and Dir, Reliance Corp., 1962–70; Exec. Dir, Plessey Corp., 1970; Chm., Huntingdon Securities, 1973–2006; Data Recording Instrument Co.: non-exec. Dir, 1973–76; Chm., 1976–82; Chm. and Chief Exec., Wickes plc, 1982–96. Non-executive Director: Law Finance Gp Hldgs Ltd, 2009–; Silicon Badia Global, 2017–. Founder and Chm., Internat. Centre for the Study of Radicalisation and Political Violence, 2007–. University of Pennsylvania, Wharton School, Board Member: Bd of Overseers, 1994–2005; European Adv. Bd, 1988–2006; SEI Center for Advanced Management Studies, 1989–2017. Mem., American Bankruptcy Inst. CCMI (CIMgt 1993). Hon. FKC 2013. *Publications:* Restructuring the Management Challenge, 1990; Best Practice, or Just Best People, 1995; (contrib.) Society and Business Review, vol. 3, 2008. *Recreations:* swimming, wine. *Clubs:* Reform; University, Penn (New York).

**SWEETING, Col John William Frederick,** CBE 2004; Chief Executive, Treloar Trust, 1997–2005; *b* 16 Feb. 1946; *s* of late Quilter William Victor Sweeting and Mary Edith Violet Sweeting (née Dewey); *m* 1976, Mary Clark (née Millington); two *s* one *d. Educ:* Tonbridge Sch.; Univ. of Bristol (LLB 1967). Commnd RE 1967; Staff Coll., Camberley, 1978; SO1 Defence Commitments (Rest of World), 1985–86; CO 28 Amph. Engr Regt, 1987–89; COS Engr in Chief (Army), 1990–91. Bursar, Lord Mayor Treloar Coll., 1991–97. Founder Mem. and Treas., Nat. Assoc. of Ind. and Non-maintained Special Schs (NASS), 1998–2001; Chm., Assoc. of Nat. Specialist Colls (NATSPEC), 1999–2004; Founder Trustee and Chm., RECOM (nat. org. for recycling computers to disabled), 2000–04; Trustee, Fortune Centre of Riding Therapy, 2005–10. Licensed Lay Minister (formerly Reader), C of E, 1968–; Chaplain to High Sheriff of Hampshire, 2008–09. *Recreations:* choral singing, travel, gardening, golf. *Address:* 17 Lynn Way, Kings Worthy, Winchester, Hants SO23 7TG. *T:* (01962) 884325. *E:* johnwfsweeting@gmail.com.

**SWEETING, Malcolm;** Partner, Clifford Chance LLP, since 1990 (Senior Partner, 2011–18). *Address:* Clifford Chance LLP, 10 Upper Bank Street, Canary Wharf, E14 5JJ. *T:* (020) 7006 2028, *Fax:* (020) 7006 5555. *E:* malcolm.sweeting@cliffordchance.com.

**SWEETING, Prof. Sir Martin (Nicholas),** Kt 2002; OBE 1996; FRS 2000; FREng, FIET, FRAeS, FInstP; Professor of Satellite Engineering, since 1990, Distinguished Professor, since 2006, and Chairman, Surrey Space Centre (formerly Centre for Satellite Engineering Research), since 2015 (Director, 1996–2014), University of Surrey; Founder and Executive Chairman, Surrey Satellite Technology Ltd, since 2008; *b* 12 March 1951; *s* of Frank Morris Sweeting and Dorothy May Sweeting; *m* 1975, Christine Ruth Taplin. *Educ:* Aldenham School, Elstree; University of Surrey (BSc Hons 1974; PhD 1979). Marconi Space & Defence Systems, 1972–73; University of Surrey: Research Fellow, 1978–81; Lectr, 1981–86; Univ. Research Fellow in Satellite Engrg, 1984–87; Dir, Satellite Engrg, 1986–90; Dep. Dir, Centre for Satellite Engrg Res., 1990–96. Res. Dir, Satellites Internat., 1983–84; Surrey Satellite Technology: Technical Dir, 1985–94; Acting Man. Dir, 1989–94; CEO, 1995–2008. Member: Internat. Acad. of Astronautics, 1999–; Defence and Aerospace Panel, UK Technology Foresight Cttee, 2003–05; EU Framework Prog. 6 Space Adv. Panel, 2003–06; Aurora Adv. Cttee, 2003–06, Human Spaceflight Microgravity and Exploration Adv. Cttee, 2006–08, ESA; UK Space Leadership Council, 2010–; a Vice-

Pres., Internat. Astronautics Fedn, 2000–05. FREng (FEng 1996); FInstP 2001. Hon. Fellow, IED, 2012; Hon. FRAeS 2016. Silver Medal, Royal Acad. Engrg, 1995; Gold Medal, UK Engrg Council, 1998; Space Achievement Medal, British Interplanetary Soc., 1998; Mullard Prize, Royal Soc., 2000; Frank Malina Medal, Internat. Acad. of Astronautics, 2003; Gold Medal, Royal Inst. Navigation, 2006; Sir Arthur Clarke Lifetime Achievement Award, UK Space Council, 2008; Faraday Medal, IET, 2010; Elektra Lifetime Achievement Award, Eur. Electronics Industry, 2010; Guildford Roll of Honour, 2011; Internat. von Karman Wings Award, CIT, 2012; Jeoujang Jaw Award, Chinese Acad. of Scis/COSPAR, 2014. *Publications:* over 250 professional papers and pubns. *Recreations:* amateur radio, photography, travelling, languages, table tennis, cycling. *Address:* Surrey Satellite Technology Ltd, Tycho House, 20 Stephenson Road, Surrey Research Park, Guildford, Surrey GU2 7YE.

**SWEETMAN, Jennifer Joan, (Mrs Ronald Andrew);** *see* Dickson, J. J.

**SWEETMAN, Stuart John,** FCA; Group Managing Director, Royal Mail Group plc (formerly Post Office, then Consignia plc), 1999–2002; *b* 6 Aug. 1948; *s* of Arthur John Sweetman and Joan Sweetman; *m* 1977, Patricia Dean; two *s* one *d. Educ:* University Coll. London (BSc Geog.). FCA 1979. Joined Touche Ross & Co., Chartered Accountants, 1969; held various posts from Articled Clerk to Sen. Manager; Dir, Financial Accounts, PO, 1982–86; Royal Mail: Finance Dir, 1986–92; Business Centres Dir, 1992–94; Service Delivery Dir, 1994–95; Asst Man. Dir, 1995–96; Man. Dir, PO Counters Ltd, 1996–99. Chm. and Dir, Consignia (Customer Mgt) Ltd (formerly Subscription Services Ltd), 1999–2001. Dir, British Quality Foundn, 1998–2002; Mem. Bd, Inst. of Customer Services, 1998–2001. Mem. Adv. Cttee for Business in the Envmt, DTI/DETR, 1997–2001. Pres., Banstead Neville Bowling Club Ltd, 2011–13 (Dir, 2013–; Capt., 2009–10); Chairman: Banstead History Centre, 2010–; Banstead History Research Gp, 2012–; Probus Club of Banstead, 2015–16. *Recreations:* family, walking, archaeology, golf, bowls, watercolour painting, cooking and eating. *Address:* 1 Chalmers Road, Banstead, Surrey SM7 3HF.

**SWENARTON, Prof. Mark Creighton,** PhD; FRHistS; James Stirling Professor of Architecture, University of Liverpool, 2011–15, now Professor Emeritus; *b* India, 1952; *s* of Joseph Swenarton and Mavis Swenarton. *Educ:* Magdalen Coll., Oxford (BA 1973); Univ. of Sussex (MA 1974); University Coll. London (PhD 1979). FRHistS 1987. Lecturer in History of Architecture: Middx Univ., 1975–77; UCL, 1977–89; Founding and Publishing Ed., Architecture Today, 1989–2005; Prof. and Hd, Sch. of Architecture, Oxford Brookes Univ., 2005–10. Special Prof. of Architecture, Univ. of Nottingham, 2003–05; Thank-Offering to Britain Fellow, Royal Acad., 2013–14. Founding Ed., Construction Hist., 1985. Design Review Chair, Cabe at Design Council (formerly CABE), 2008–15; Oxford Design Review Panel, 2014–. Non-exec. Dir, Timber R&D Assoc., 2006–09. FRSA 2004. Hon. FRIBA 2014. *Publications:* Homes fit for Heroes: the politics and design of early state housing in Britain, 1981, 2nd edn 2018; Artisans and Architects: the Ruskinian tradition in architectural thought, 1989; Dixon Jones: buildings and projects, 2002; Feilden Clegg Bradley: the environmental handbook, 2007; Building the New Jerusalem: architecture, politics and housing 1900–1930, 2008; Architecture and the Welfare State, 2014; Cook's Camden: the making of modern housing, 2017; contrib. articles to AA Files, Architectural Hist., Econ. Hist. Rev., Histl Res., Jl Architecture, Planning Perspectives, Town Planning Rev. *Recreations:* tennis, classical music, opera, theatre, visual arts, travel. *Address:* School of Architecture, University of Liverpool, Leverhulme Building, Abercromby Square, Liverpool L69 7ZN. *E:* m.swenarton@liv.ac.uk.

**SWIFT, Rt Rev. Andrew Christopher;** *see* Brechin, Bishop of.

**SWIFT, Anita;** *see* Klein, A.

**SWIFT, Dame Caroline Jane, (Lady Openshaw),** DBE 2005; a Judge of the High Court of Justice, Queen's Bench Division, 2005–15; Chair, Medical Practitioners Tribunal Service, since 2017; *b* 30 May 1955; *d* of late Vincent Seymour Swift and Amy Ruth Swift; *m* 1999, Charles Peter Lawford Openshaw (*see* Hon. Sir C. P. L. Openshaw); one *s* one *d. Educ:* Lancaster Girls' Grammar Sch.; Univ. of Durham (BA Hons Law). Pres., Durham Union Soc., 1975. Called to the Bar, Inner Temple, 1977, Bencher, 1997; practised on Northern Circuit, 1978–2005; Asst Recorder, 1992–95; QC 1993; a Recorder, 1995–2005; a Dep. High Court Judge, 2000–05. Leading counsel, Shipman Inquiry, 2001–05. Patron, Lancashire Wildlife Trust, 2017–. *Publications:* (jtly) Ribchester: 100 years in photographs, 1994; Ribchester: a millennium record, 2001. *Recreations:* home and family, cooking, theatre, walking, wildlife.

**SWIFT, His Honour David Rowland;** a Circuit Judge, 1997–2012; *b* 21 April 1946; *s* of James Rowland Swift and Iris Julia Swift; *m* 1974, Josephine Elizabeth Williamson; two *s* two *d. Educ:* Kingsmead Sch., Hoylake; Ruthin Sch.; Liverpool Coll. of Commerce. Admitted Solicitor, 1970; Partner, Percy Hughes and Roberts, Birkenhead, 1971–97; a Recorder, 1993–97. Pres., Liverpool Law Soc., 1995–96. Chairman: Wirral Adult Literacy Project, 1978–84; Liverpool Bd of Legal Studies, 1985–88. Gov., Ruthin Sch., 1988–2005 (Chm. Govs, 1993–99). *Publications:* Proceedings Before the Solicitors Disciplinary Tribunal, 1996; articles in legal jls. *Recreations:* sailing, walking, history, photography. *Club:* Athenæum (Pres., 2013–14).

**SWIFT, Graham Colin,** FRSL; author; *b* 4 May 1949; *s* of Sheila Irene Swift and Lionel Allan Stanley Swift. *Educ:* Dulwich Coll.; Queens' Coll., Cambridge (MA; Hon. Fellow, 2005); Univ. of York. Hon. LittD: UEA, 1998; London, 2003; Sussex 2015; DUniv York, 1998. *Publications:* novels: The Sweet Shop Owner, 1980; Shuttlecock, 1981 (Geoffrey Faber Meml Prize, 1983); Waterland, 1983 (Winifred Holtby Award, RSL, 1983; Guardian Fiction Prize, 1983; Premio Grinzane Cavour, 1987); Out of This World, 1988; Ever After, 1992 (Prix du Meilleur Livre Etranger, 1994); Last Orders (Booker Prize, James Tait Black Meml Prize), 1996; The Light of Day, 2003; Tomorrow, 2007; Wish You Were Here, 2011; Mothering Sunday, 2016 (Hawthornden Prize, 2017); Here We Are, 2020; *short stories:* Learning to swim and other stories, 1982; England and Other Stories, 2014; *non-fiction:* (ed with David Profumo) The Magic Wheel (anthology), 1985; Making an Elephant, 2009. *Recreation:* fishing. *Address:* c/o A. P. Watt, United Agents, 12–26 Lexington Street, W1F 0LE.

**SWIFT, Maj. Gen. James Francis Pardoe,** OBE 2008 (MBE 2006); General Officer Commanding 3rd (UK) Division, since 2018; *b* Bottisham, 6 Oct. 1967; *s* of Philip Lionel Swift and Perdita le Marchant Swift (*née* Hutchesson); *m* 1998, Petra Christina Gudgin; two *s. Educ:* Netherhall Sch., Cambridge; Hills Rd Sixth Form Coll.; Christ Church, Oxford (BA Chem. 1989; MA 1992); Cranfield Univ. (MSc Defence Technol. 2000). Commnd Army, 1990; CO, 2 Royal Welsh, 2007–09; Col Army Strategy, 2009–12; Comdr, 20 Armd Bde, 2012–14; Hd Capability Strategy, MoD, 2014–16; Dir Strategy, Army HQ, 2016–18; Asst Chief of Gen. Staff, 2018. Col, Royal Welsh, 2016–. Cdre, ASA, 2016–. *Recreations:* sailing, ski-ing, bridge.

**SWIFT, John Anthony;** QC 1981; Head of Monckton Chambers, 1999–2001; *b* 11 July 1940; *s* of late Jack Swift and Clare Medcalf; *m* 1972, Jane Carol Sharples; one *s* one *d. Educ:* Birkenhead Sch.; University Coll., Oxford (MA); Johns Hopkins Univ.; Bologna. Called to the Bar, Inner Temple, 1965, Bencher, 1992. Rail Regulator, 1993–98. Member: NHS Cooperation and Competition Panel, 2009–14; Determinations Panel, Pensions Regulator, 2017–; Chm., Ofgem Enforcement Decision Panel, 2014–19; Ind. Mem., Ofwat Casework Cttee, 2014–19; Advr, Monitor, later NHS Improvement, 2014–16. FCILT (FCIT 1994). *Recreations:* theatre, walking, gardening, golf. *Address:* Monckton Chambers, Gray's Inn, WC1R 5NR. *Clubs:* Reform; Huntercombe Golf.

**SWIFT, Hon. Sir Jonathan (Mark),** Kt 2018; **Hon. Mr Justice Swift;** a Judge of the High Court, Queen's Bench Division, since 2018; *b* Rochford, Essex, 11 Sept. 1964; *s* of John Christopher Swift and Margaret Fanny Swift (*née* Shead); *m* 2008, Helen Mary Evans; one *s* one *d. Educ:* Southend on Sea High Sch. for Boys; New Coll., Oxford (BA 1987); Emmanuel Coll., Cambridge (LLM 1988). Called to the Bar, Inner Temple, 1989, Bencher, 2007; First Treasury Counsel, 2007–14; QC 2010; a Recorder, 2010–18; a Dep. High Court Judge, 2016–18. *Publications:* (contrib.) Judicial Review, 1992, 6th edn 2017; (ed jtly) Employment Court Practice, 2007, 2nd edn 2008; (contrib.) Administrative Court Practice, 2008; (contrib.) The UK Supreme Court Yearbook, 2016–; (contrib.) Conduct and Pay in the Financial Services Industry, 2017. *Recreations:* football (Southend United), playing the ukelele, waiting. *Address:* Royal Courts of Justice, Strand, WC2A 2LL.

**SWIFT, Malcolm Robin Farquhar;** QC 1988; Acting Judge, Grand Court of Cayman Islands, 2013–17; *b* 19 Jan. 1948; *s* of late Willie Swift and Heather May Farquhar Swift, OBE (*née* Nield); *m* 1st, 1969, Anne Rachael (marr. diss. 1993), *d* of Ernest Rothery Ayre; one *s* two *d;* 2nd, 2003, Angela, *d* of Reuben Walters. *Educ:* Colne Valley High Sch., Yorks; King's Coll. London (LLB, AKC). Called to the Bar, Gray's Inn, 1970, Bencher, 1998; barrister, 1970–2015; a Recorder, 1987–2007. Co-opted Mem., Remuneration Cttee of Bar Council, 1978–89 (rep. NE Circuit); Mem., Bar Council, 1995–2001; Leader, NE Circuit, 1998–2001.

**SWINBURNE, Dr Kay;** Vice-Chair of Financial Services, KPMG, since 2019; *b* Aberystwyth, 8 June 1967; *m;* one *c. Educ:* Llandysul Grammar Sch.; King's Coll. London (BSc Biochem. and Microbiol.; PhD); Univ. of Surrey (MBA). Work in internat. healthcare and finance; with Deutsche Bank until 1999. Mem. (C) Herefordshire CC, 2007–10. MEP (C) Wales, 2009–19.

**SWINBURNE, Prof. Richard Granville,** FBA 1992; Nolloth Professor of Philosophy of Christian Religion, University of Oxford, 1985–2002, now Emeritus; Fellow, Oriel College, Oxford, 1985–2002, now Emeritus; *b* 26 Dec. 1934; *s* of William Henry Swinburne and Gladys Edith Swinburne (*née* Parker); *m* 1960, Monica Holmstrom (separated 1985); two *d. Educ:* Exeter College, Oxford (Scholar). BPhil 1959, MA 1961, DipTheol 1960. Fereday Fellow, St John's Coll., Oxford, 1958–61; Leverhulme Res. Fellow in Hist. and Phil. of Science, Univ. of Leeds, 1961–63; Lectr in Philosophy, then Sen. Lectr, Univ. of Hull, 1963–72; Prof. of Philosophy, Univ. of Keele, 1972–84. Vis. Associate Prof. of Philosophy, Univ. of Maryland, 1969–70; Dist. Vis. Schol., Univ. of Adelaide, 1982; Vis. Prof. of Philosophy, Syracuse Univ., 1987; Vis. Lectr, Indian Council for Philosophical Res., 1992; Visiting Professor: Univ. of Rome, 2002; Catholic Univ. of Lublin, 2002; Yale Univ., 2003; St Louis Univ., 2003; Lectures: Wilde, Oxford Univ., 1975–78; Forwood, Liverpool Univ., 1977, 2009; Marrett Meml, Exeter Coll., Oxford, 1980; Gifford, Univ. of Aberdeen, 1982–84; Edward Cadbury, Univ. of Birmingham, 1987; Wade, St Louis Univ., 1990; Dotterer, Pennsylvania State Univ., 1992; Aquinas, Marquette Univ., 1997; Paul Holmer, Univ. of Minnesota, 2006; Sophia Forum, Azusa Pacific Univ., 2013; Gilbert Ryle, Trent Univ., 2014; Gunning, Edinburgh Univ., 2016; Edith Stein, Franciscan Univ., Ohio, 2016. Hon. Dr: Catholic Univ. of Lublin, 2015; Dimitrie Casimir Christian Univ., 2016; Internat. Acad. of Philosophy, Liechtenstein, 2017. *Publications:* Space and Time, 1968, 2nd edn 1981; The Concept of Miracle, 1971; An Introduction to Confirmation Theory, 1973; The Coherence of Theism, 1977, 2nd edn 2016; The Existence of God, 1979, 2nd edn 2004; Faith and Reason, 1981, 2nd edn 2005; (with S. Shoemaker) Personal Identity, 1984; The Evolution of the Soul, 1986, rev. edn 1997; Responsibility and Atonement, 1989; Revelation, 1992, 2nd edn 2007; The Christian God, 1994; Is There a God?, 1996, rev. edn 2010; Providence and the Problem of Evil, 1998; Epistemic Justification, 2001; The Resurrection of God Incarnate, 2003; Was Jesus God?, 2008; Mind, Brain, and Free Will, 2013; Are We Bodies or Souls?, 2019; articles and reviews in learned jls. *Address:* 50 Butler Close, Oxford OX2 6JG. *T:* (01865) 514406. *See also* D. R. Cope.

**SWINBURNE, Prof. Terence Reginald;** Professor of Horticultural Development, Wye College, London University, 1994–98, now Emeritus; *b* 17 July 1936; *s* of Reginald and Gladys Swinburne; *m* 1958, Valerie Parkes; two *s. Educ:* Imperial Coll., Univ. of London (DSc, ARCS, DIC, PhD); FCIHort. Plant Pathology Res. Div., Min., later Dept, of Agriculture for NI, 1960–80; Scientific Officer, 1960–62; Sen. Scientific Officer, 1962–71; PSO, 1971–79; SPSO, 1979–80; Queen's University, Belfast: Asst Lectr, Faculty of Agriculture, 1961–64; Lectr, 1965–77; Reader, 1977–80; Head of Crop Protection Div., E Malling Res. Stn, 1980–85; Dir, Inst. of Horticl Res., AFRC, 1985–90; Sen. Res. Fellow, Wye Coll., London Univ., 1990–94. Kellogg Fellow, Oregon State Univ., 1964–65; Vis. Prof., Dept of Pure and Applied Biology, Imperial Coll., London, 1986–91. Gov., Hadlow Coll., 2000–06 (Chm., 2003–06). *Publications:* Iron Siderophores and Plant Diseases, 1986. *Recreation:* sailing. *Address:* The Orchard, St Andrews Road, Bridport, Dorset DT6 3BB. *E:* trswinburne@msn.com.

**SWINDELLS, Her Honour Heather Hughson, (Mrs R. Inglis);** QC 1995; a Circuit Judge, 2005–14; a Deputy High Court Judge, 2000–14; *d* of late Mrs Debra Hughson Swindells; *m* 1976, Richard Inglis, *qv;* one *s. Educ:* Nottingham High Sch. for Girls; St Anne's Coll., Oxford (MA Lit.Hum.). Called to the Bar, Middle Temple, 1974, Bencher, 2005; a Recorder, 1994–2005. *Publications:* Family Law and the Human Rights Act 1998, 1999; (contrib.) Family Law: essays for the new millennium, 2000; Adoption: the modern law, 2003; (jtly) Adoption: the modern procedure, 2006. *Recreations:* books, music, art, archaeology.

**SWINDELLS, Matthew James;** Founder, MJS Healthcare Consulting, since 2019; *b* Brighton, 31 Dec. 1964; *s* of Derek and Jacqueline Swindells; *m* 1995, Victoria Rae; two *d. Educ:* Blatchington Mill Comp. Sch.; Brighton, Hove and Sussex 6th Form Coll.; Univ. of Hull (BSc Hons Econs); Brunel Univ. (MBA). NHS graduate supplies trainee, NW RHA, 1987–89; IT Purchasing Manager, SE Thames RHA, 1989–91; IT Strategy Prog. Manager, St Thomas' Hosp., London, 1991–93; IT Manager, 1993–94, Clin. Ops Manager, 1994–99, Guy's and St Thomas' Hosp., London; Dir of Clin. Services, Heatherwood and Wexham Park Hosp., Slough, 1999–2002; Principal Advr, Prime Minister's Office of Public Service Reform, 2002–03; Chief Exec., Royal Surrey County Hosp., Guildford, 2003–05; Policy Advr to Sec. of State for Health, 2005–07, Dir Gen. for Inf. and Prog. Integration and Chief Inf. Officer, 2007–08, DoH; Gp Man. Dir for Health, Tribal Gp, 2008–10; Vice Pres., 2010–11, Sen. Vice Pres. and Man. Dir. later Sen. Vice Pres. for Population Health and Global Strategy, 2011–16, Cerner Ltd; Nat. Dir for Ops and Inf. (formerly Commissioning Ops and Inf.), 2016–19, Dep. Chief Exec., 2019, NHS England. Chm., BCS, Health,

2009–12. Chm., Charity Trustees, Imperial Coll. Healthcare NHS Trust, 2008–13. Vis. Prof., Sch. of Clinical and Experimental Medicine (formerly Sch. of Mgt), Univ. of Surrey, 2005–. MinstD 2016. *Recreations:* playing football, listening to the poetry of Bob Dylan, supporting Everton, travel, spending time with my wife, enjoying the company of my children. *Address:* MJS Healthcare Consulting, Preston Park House, South Road, Brighton BN1 6SB. *E:* matthew@mjs-hc.com.

**SWINDELLS, Robert Edward;** children's author, 1973–2014, full-time author, 1980–2014; *b* 20 March 1939; *s* of Albert Henry Hugh and Alice Alberta Swindells; *m* 1st, 1962, Catherine Hough (marr. diss. 1976); two *d*; 2nd, 1982, Brenda Blamires. *Educ:* Huddersfield Poly. (Teacher's Cert.); Univ. of Bradford (MA Peace Studies). Copyholder, local newspaper, 1954–57; RAF, 1957–60; clerk, local newspaper, 1960–66; engineering inspector, 1966–69; student teacher, 1969–72; teacher, 1972–80. Hon. Fellow, Bradford Coll., 2017. *Publications:* When Darkness Comes, 1973; The Very Special Baby, 1977; Dragons Live Forever, 1978; Moonpath and other stories, 1979; Norah's Ark, 1979; Norah's Shark, 1979; Ghostship to Ganymede, 1980; Norah to the Rescue, 1981; Norah and the Whale, 1981; Science Fiction Stories, 1982; Candle in the Dark, 1983; Weather Clerk, 1983; World Eater, 1983; Brother in the Land, 1984 (Children's Book Award, 1985); Ghost Messengers, 1988; Mavis Davis, 1988; Night School, 1989; A Serpent's Tooth, 1989; Room 13 (Children's Book Award), 1990; Staying Up, 1990; Tim Kipper, 1990; Daz 4 Zoe, 1991; Dracula's Castle, 1991; Follow a Shadow, 1991, 2nd edn 2010; Hydra, 1991; Postbox Mystery, 1991; Go-Ahead Gang, 1992; Ice Palace, 1992; Rolf and Rosie, 1992; You Can't Say I'm Crazy, 1992; Inside the Worm, 1993; Sam and Sue and Lavatory Lou, 1993; Secret of Weeping Wood, 1993, repubd 2014; Siege of Frimly Prim, 1993; Stone Cold (Carnegie Medal), 1993; Thousand Eyes of Night, 1993; We Didn't Mean To, Honest, 1993, repubd 2014; Kidnap at Denton Farm, 1994, repubd 2014; Timesnatch, 1994; Voyage to Valhalla, 1994; Ghosts of Givenham Keep, 1995, repubd 2014; The Muckitups, 1995; Unbeliever, 1995; Jacqueline Hyde, 1996; Last Bus, 1996; Hurricane Summer, 1997, repubd 2015; Nightmare Stairs, 1997; Smash, 1997; Abomination, 1998; Peril in the Mist, 1998, repubd 2014; Strange Tale of Ragger Bill, 1998, repubd 2014; Invisible, 1999; Orchard Book of Vikings, 1999; Roger's War, 1999, repubd 2015; Doodlebug Alley, 2000, repubd 2015; Orchard Book of Egyptian Gods and Pharaohs, 2000; A Wish For Wings, 2001; Wrecked!, 2001; Blitzed, 2002; No Angels, 2003; Ruby Tanya, 2004; Branded, 2005; Snapshot, 2005; Snakebite, 2006; In the Nick of Time, 2007; Burnout, 2007; The Shade of Hettie Daynes, 2008; Knife Edge, 2008; Shrapnel, 2009; A Midsummer Night's Dream (retelling), 2009; The First Hunter, 2009; Just a Bit of Fun, 2009; Henry V (retelling), 2010; Blackout, 2011; Dan's War, 2012; A Skull in Shadow's Lane, 2012; The Deep End, 2013. *Recreations:* walking, reading, theatre, painting, travel. *Address:* Reservoir Cats, 4 Spring Row, Denholme Road, Oxenhope, Keighley, W Yorks BD22 9NR.

**SWINDON, Bishop Suffragan of,** since 2005; **Rt Rev. Lee Stephen Rayfield,** PhD; *b* 30 Sept. 1955; *s* of Ronald Reginald Rayfield and Doris Lilian Rayfield; *m* 1978, Elizabeth Vivienne Rundle; two *s* one *d*. *Educ:* Univ. of Southampton (BSc Hons (Biology) 1978); St Mary's Hosp. Med. Sch., Univ. of London (PhD 1981); Ridley Hall, Cambridge. Post-doctoral Res. Fellow, St Mary's Hosp. Med. Sch., Univ. of London, 1981–84; Lectr in Immunology, UMDS, Guy's and St Thomas' Hosps, Univ. of London, 1984–91. Ordained deacon, 1993, priest, 1994; Asst Curate, Woodford Wells, dio. Chelmsford, 1993–97; Priest-in-charge, 1997–2004, Vicar, 2004–05, Furze Platt, dio. Oxford; part-time Chaplain, St Mark's Hosp., Maidenhead, 1997–2005; Area Dean: Maidenhead, 2000–03; Maidenhead and Windsor, 2003–05. Member: UK Gene Therapy Adv. Cttee, 2000–09; HFEA, 2012–18. Mem., SOSc, 1995–. *Publications:* contrib. chapters in med. and dental textbks; many scientific papers in immunol jls, incl. Nature, Transplantation, European Jl of Immunology; two papers in theol jls. *Recreations:* cycling, watching athletics and Rugby Union, motor mechanics. *Address:* Mark House, Field Rise, Swindon, Wilts SN1 4HP. *T:* (01793) 538654. *E:* bishop.swindon@bristoldiocese.org. *Club:* Swindon Road.

**SWINFEN, 3rd Baron** *cr* 1919; **Roger Mynors Swinfen Eady,** MBE 2016; *b* 14 Dec. 1938; *s* of 2nd Baron Swinfen and Mary Aline (*née* Farmar, later Siepmann); writer, as Mary Wesley, CBE) (*d* 2002); *S* father, 1977; *m* 1962, Patricia Anne (MBE 2006), *o d* of late F. D. Blackmore, Dundrum, Dublin; one *s* three *d*. *Educ:* Westminster; RMA, Sandhurst. ARICS 1970–99. Mem., Direct Mail Services Standards Bd, 1983–97. Mem., Select Cttee on EC Sub-Cttee C (Envmtl and Social Affairs), 1991–94; elected Mem., H of L, 1999; Member: Select Cttee on Draft Disability Bill, 2004–; Select Cttee on EU Sub-Cttee B, 2004–06; Select Cttee on EU Sub-Cttee C, 2006–10; Hybrid Bill Cttee, 2010–; Jt Cttee on Consolidation Bills, 2010–13; Select Cttee on Mental Capacity Act 2005, 2013–14; Select Cttee on Artificial Intelligence, 2017–19. Chm., Parly Gp, Video Enquiry Working Party, 1983–85. Dir, Swinfen Charitable Trust, 1998–; Patron: Disablement Income Gp, 1995–; 1 in 8 Gp, 1996–2004; Labrador Rescue SE, 1996–; World Orthopaedic Concern, 2002–; KunDe Foundn, 2007–; Dir, American Telemedicine Assoc., 2009–13; Hon. Res. Fellow, Centre for Online Health, Univ. of Queensland, 2001–10; Hon. Pres., Britain Bangladesh Friendship Soc., 1996–2004. Fellow, Industry and Parlt Trust. Liveryman, Drapers' Co. JP Kent, 1983–85. *Publications:* reports in med. jls. *Heir: s* Hon. Charles Roger Peregrine Swinfen Eady, *b* 8 March 1971. *Address:* House of Lords, SW1A 0PW.

**SWINGLAND, Prof. Ian Richard;** Founder and Director, Durrell Institute of Conservation and Ecology, 1989–99 and Professor of Conservation Biology, University of Kent, 1994–99, now Emeritus; *b* 2 Nov. 1946; *s* of late Hugh Maurice Webb Swingland and of Flora Mary Swingland (*née* Fernie); *m* 1985, Fiona Mairi Lawson (marr. diss. 2014); one *s* one *d*. *Educ:* Haberdashers' Aske's Sch.; QMC, Univ. of London (BSc 1969); Univ. of Edinburgh (Throgmorton Trotman Sen. Exhibn; FCO Schol.; PhD 1974). FZS 1974; FRSB (FIBiol 1993). Res. Scientist, Shell Research, 1969; Wildlife Mgt Biologist, Kafue Nat. Park, Zambia, 1973–74; Vis. Scientist, Royal Soc. Res. Station, Aldabra Atoll, Seychelles, 1974–79; Post-doctoral Fellow and Tutor, St Peter's Hall, St Catherine's Coll., Magdalen Coll., Lady Margaret Hall, Oxford, 1974–79; Lectr, then Sen. Lectr in Natural Scis, Univ. of Kent, 1979–94. Res. Associate, Smithsonian Instn, 1987–2010; Visiting Professor: of Biology, Univ. of Michigan, 1986–87 (Sen. Res. Fellow, Mus. of Zoology, 1986–87); of Conservation, Univ. of Florence, 1996–2000; of Conservation Biology, Univ. of Auckland, 1996–2001; of Conservation Biology, Manchester Metropolitan Univ., 1998–2001; Ext. Examiner in Biodiversity and Conservation, Univ. of Leeds, 1998–2002. Founding Editor, Biodiversity and Conservation, 1989–99. Member: IUCN Species Survival Commn, 1979–; Council, RURAL, 1980– (Founding Mem.); Council, Fauna and Flora Preservation Soc., 1985–91; Council, RSPCA, 1990–96 (150th Anniv. Lecture, 1990); Darwin Initiative, 2000–09; IUCN Nat. Parks Commn, 2000–03; Director: First World Congress of Herpetology, 1984–89; Sustainable Forestry Mgt LLC, 1998–2005. Founder and Vice Pres., Herpetological Conservation Trust, 1989–2009; Pres., British Chelonia Gp, 1989–2005 (Hon. Life Member, 1989–); Chairman: Apple and Pear Res. Council, 1997–2003; Internat. Bd of Trustees, Iwokrama Internat. Centre for Rain Forest Conservation and Develt, 2002–03; Rural Regeneration Unit, 2009–11; Advisor: Swedish Res. Council (Vetenskapsrådet), 2010–12; Swedish Res. Council for Envmt, Agricl Scis and Spatial Planning (Formas), 2010–12; Governor, Powell Cotton Mus., 1984–2006; Trustee: Biodiversity Foundn for Africa, 1992–; Earthwatch, 1999–2009; Operation Wallacea Trust, 1999– (Chm., 2010–14; Patron, 2014–); Durrell Trust for Conservation Biology, 1999– (Chm., 1999–2014; Patron, 2014–); Durrell Wildlife Conservation Trust, 2005–07 (Hon. Life Mem., 2000); Fauna and Flora Internat., 2005–08; Dir, Derwent Forest, 2004–07. Staff Consultant, Asian Devlt Bank, 1996–2007; Chief Policy Advr, Countryside Alliance, 1999–2003; Scientific Advr, FCO, 1999–2002; Panel of Experts, World Bank, 1999–2002; Mem. Adv. Bd, Centre for Biodiversity and Restoration Ecology, Victoria Univ. of Wellington, 2006–12. Ambassador, Galapagos Conservation Trust, 2008–; Patron, Hadlow Coll., Kent, 2013–. Bioscience Fellow, Commonwealth Agricl Bureau Internat., 2002. Freedom of the City of London, 2001. DSc Kent 2005. *Publications: edited jointly:* The Ecology of Animal Movement, 1983; Living in a Patchy Environment, 1990; New Techniques in Integrated Protected Area Management, 1998; Carbon, biodiversity, conservation and income: an analysis of a free-market approach to land-use changes and forestry in developing and developed countries, 2002; Capturing Biodiversity and Conserving Biodiversity: a market approach, 2003; Integrated Wetlands Management, 2012; contrib. books and jls incl. Nature, Phil Trans Royal Soc., Jl Theor. Biology, Jl Zoology, London Jl Animal Ecology, Biodiversity and Conservation, Proc. Biol. Soc. Washington, Applied Animal Behaviour Sci., Animal Behaviour, Can. Jl Zool., Proc. Royal Soc. of London, etc. *Recreations:* growing trees, cooking, being alone in remote wild places, being iconoclastic, losing things. *Address:* 9 Alexander Close, Sandwich, Kent CT13 0EY. *T:* 07971 669915.

**SWINLEY, Margaret Albinia Joanna,** OBE 1980; British Council Service, retired; *b* 30 Sept. 1935; *er* twin *d* of late Captain Casper Silas Balfour Swinley, DSO, DSC, RN and Sylvia Jocosa Swinley, 4th *d* of late Canon W. H. Carnegie. *Educ:* Southover Manor Sch., Lewes; Edinburgh Univ. (MA Hons Hist.). English Teacher/Sec., United Paper Mills, Jämsänkoski, Finland, 1958–60; joined British Council, 1960; Birmingham Area Office, 1960–63; Tel Aviv, 1963; Lagos, 1963–66; seconded to London HQ of VSO, 1966–67; New Delhi, 1967–70; Dep. Rep., Lagos, 1970–73; Dir, Tech. Assistance Trng Dept, 1973–76; Rep., Israel, 1976–80; Asst, then Dep., Controller, Educn, Medicine and Science Div., 1980–82; Controller, Africa and Middle East Div., 1982–86; Controller, Home Div., 1986–89. Mem., S Wales Shire Horse Soc., 1993– (Pres., 1998, 2005). Pres., Flaxley WI, 2002–05. Lay Mem., Local Ministry Team, benefice of Westbury-on-Severn with Flaxley and Blaisdon, 1998–. *Recreations:* theatre-going, country life, keeping dogs and Shire horses.

**SWINNEY, John Ramsay;** Member (SNP) Perthshire North, Scottish Parliament, since 2011 (North Tayside, 1999–2011); Deputy First Minister, since 2014; *b* 13 April 1964; *s* of Kenneth Swinney and Nancy Swinney (*née* Hunter); *m* 1st, 1991, Lorna Ann King (marr. diss. 2000); one *s* one *d*; 2nd, 2003, Elizabeth Quigley; one *s*. *Educ:* Univ. of Edinburgh (MA Hons Politics). Sen. Managing Consultant, Developments Options Ltd, 1988–92; Strategic Planning Principal, Scottish Amicable, 1992–97. MP (SNP) North Tayside, 1997–2001. Scottish Parliament: Dep. Leader of the Opposition, 1999–2000, Leader, 2000–04; SNP spokesman for finance and public service reform, 2005–07; Cabinet Sec. for Finance and Sustainable Growth, 2007–14, for Finance, Constitution and Economy, 2014–16; Convener: Enterprise and Lifelong Learning Cttee, 1999–2000; European Cttee, 2004–05. Scottish National Party: Nat. Sec., 1986–92; Vice Convener for Publicity, 1992–97; Treasury Spokesman, 1995–2000; Dep. Leader, 1998–2000; Leader, 2000–04. *Recreations:* cycling, hill walking. *Address:* 17–19 Leslie Street, Blairgowrie, Perthshire PH10 6AH. *T:* (01250) 876576.

**SWINSON, Dr Christopher,** OBE 2006; FCA; Comptroller and Auditor General, Jersey, 2005–12; Senior Partner, BDO Stoy Hayward, 1997–2004 (Partner, 1993–97); *b* 27 Jan. 1948; *s* of Arthur Montagu Swinson and Jean Swinson; *m* 1972, Christine Margaret Hallam; one *s*. *Educ:* Wadham Coll., Oxford (MA); Durham Univ. (PhD 2016). FCA 1979 (ACA 1974). Price Waterhouse, 1970–77; Hacker Young, 1977–79; with Binder Hamlyn, 1979–92 (Nat. Man. Partner, 1989–92). Institute of Chartered Accountants in England and Wales: Mem. Council, 1985–2001; Vice-Pres., 1996–97; Dep. Pres., 1997–98; Pres., 1998–99; Chm., Regulation Review Working Party, 1995–2001. Mem., Audit Commn, 2000–03; Chm., Audit Cttee, HM Treasury, 2001–05; Bd Mem., Pensions Regulator, 2005–13. Vis. Prof., Bournemouth Univ., 2006–; Vis. Fellow, Durham Univ. Business Sch. Treasurer: Navy Records Soc., 1987–94; Soc. for Nautical Res., 1991–95; NCVO, 1993–97. Trustee: NMSI, 1987–; Greenwich Foundn, RNC, 1997–2002. FRSA 1992. *Publications:* Companies Act 1989, 1990; Regulation of Auditors, 1990; Delivering a Quality Service, 1992; Group Accounts, 1993; Regulation of the London Stock Exchange 1914–1945, 2017; Share Trading, Fraud and the Crash of 1929: a biography of Clarence Hatry, 2019. *Recreation:* model railway construction. *Address:* No Ways, Frithsden, Hemel Hempstead, Herts HP1 3DD. *T:* (01442) 864640. *E:* chris@swinson.co.uk. *Club:* Athenæum.

**SWINSON, Joanna Kate, (Jo),** CBE 2018; MP (Lib Dem) Dunbartonshire East, 2005–15 and since 2017; Leader, Liberal Democrats, since 2019 (Deputy Leader, 2017–19); *b* 5 Feb. 1980; *d* of Peter and Annette Swinson; *m* 2011, Duncan John Hames, *qv*; two *s*. *Educ:* London Sch. of Econs (BSc 1st Cl. Hons Mgt 2000). Mktg Exec. then Manager, Viking FM, 2000–02; Mktg Manager, SpaceandPeople Ltd, 2003–04; Scottish Develt Officer, UK Public Health Assoc., 2004–05. Vice Chm., Lib Dem Youth and Students, 1999–2001; Chm., Lib Dem Campaign for Gender Balance (formerly Gender Balance Task Force), 2006–08 (Vice Chm., 2003–06). Contested (Lib Dem): Hull East, 2001; Strathkelvin and Bearsden, Scottish Parlt, 2003. Lib Dem Shadow posts: Minister for Culture, Media and Sport, 2005–06; Sec. of State for Scotland, 2006–07; Minister for Women and Equality, 2007; Minister for Foreign Affairs, 2008–10; PPS to Sec. of State, BIS, 2010–12, to Dep. Prime Minister, 2012; Parliamentary Under-Secretary of State: BIS, 2012–15; Women and Equalities, 2012–15. Contested (Lib Dem) Dunbartonshire E, 2015. Chair, Maternity Action, 2015–17. Gov., Ditchley Foundn, 2014–. *Recreations:* reading, running. *Address:* House of Commons, SW1A 0AA. *E:* jo.swinson.mp@parliament.uk.

**SWINTON, 3rd Earl of,** *cr* 1955; **Nicholas John Cunliffe-Lister;** Viscount Swinton, 1935; Baron Masham, 1955; *b* 4 Sept. 1939; *s* of Major Hon. John Yarburgh Cunliffe-Lister (*d* of wounds received in action, 1943) and Anne Irvine (*m* 2nd, 1944, Donald Chapple-Gill; she *d* 1961), *yr d* of late Rev. Canon R. S. Medlicott; *S* brother, 2006; *m* 1st, 1966, Hon. Elizabeth Susan (*see* Hon. Dame E. S. Cunliffe-Lister) (marr. diss. 1996), *e d* of 1st Viscount Whitelaw, KT, CH, MC, PC; two *s* one *d*; 2nd, 1996, Pamela June Sykes (*née* Wood). *Educ:* Winchester; Worcester Coll., Oxford. *Heir: s* Lord Masham, *qv*.

**SWINTON, Susan, Countess of;** *see* Masham of Ilton, Baroness.

**SWIRE, Barnaby Nicholas;** Chairman, John Swire & Sons Ltd, since 2015; *b* London, 10 Jan. 1964; *s* of Sir John Anthony Swire, CBE; *m* 1991, Camilla Husband; two *s* two *d*. *Educ:* Eton Coll.; University Coll., Oxford (BA); INSEAD. John Swire & Sons Ltd, 1985–. *Address:* John Swire & Sons Ltd, Swire House, 59 Buckingham Gate, SW1E 6AJ. *T:* (020) 7834 7717.

**SWIRE, Rt Hon. Sir Hugo (George William),** KCMG 2016; PC 2011; MP (C) East Devon, since 2001; *b* 30 Nov. 1959; *s* of late Humphrey Roger Swire and of Philippa Sophia Montgomerie (she *m* 2004, 7th Marquess Townshend); *m* 1996, Alexandra, (Sasha), Petruška Mina, *d* of Rt Hon. Sir John William Frederic Nott, *qv*; two *d*. *Educ:* Eton; Univ.

of St Andrews; RMA Sandhurst. Lieut, 1 Bn Grenadier Guards, 1980–83; Head, Develt Office, Nat. Gall., 1988–92; Sotheby's, 1992–2001: Dep. Dir, 1996–97; Dir, 1997–2001. Contested (Scottish C and Unionist) Greenock and Inverclyde, 1997. Shadow Minister for the Arts, 2004–05, for Culture, 2005; Shadow Sec. of State for Culture, Media and Sport, 2005–07; Minister of State, NI Office, 2010–12, FCO, 2012–16. Chm., Cons. Middle East Council, 2016–. Dep. Chm., Commonwealth Enterprise and Investment Council, 2016–. FRSA 1993. *Address*: House of Commons, SW1A 0AA. *Clubs*: White's, Pratt's, Beefsteak.

**SWIRE, Merlin Bingham;** Chairman, Swire Pacific Ltd, since 2018 (Director, since 2009); *b* London, 4 Dec. 1973; *s* of Sir Adrian Christopher Swire; *m* 2014, Laura Carlyn Chisholm; two *d*. *Educ*: Eton Coll.; University Coll., Oxford (MA Lit.Hum.). Joined John Swire & Sons (Hong Kong) Ltd, 1997; seconded to Cathay Pacific Airways, 1997–98 and 2002–04, to China Navigation Co. Ltd, 1998–2002, to Coca-Cola (China) Ltd, 2004–06; Chief Exec., Taikoo (Xiamen) Aircraft Engrg Co. Ltd, 2006–08; Finance Dir, 2009–12, Chief Exec., 2015–18, John Swire & Sons Ltd; Chm., James Finlay Ltd, 2009–17; Director: Swire Properties Ltd, 2009– (Chm.); Hong Kong Aircraft Engrg Co. Ltd, 2009– (Chm., 2018–). Dir, United States Cold Storage Inc., 2003–13. *Recreations*: Greece, walking, cricket. *Address*: John Swire & Sons Ltd, Swire House, 59 Buckingham Gate, SW1E 6AJ.

**SWITZER, Barbara;** Assistant General Secretary, Manufacturing Science Finance, 1988–97; *b* 26 Nov. 1940; *d* of late Albert and Edith McMinn; *m* 1973, John Michael Switzer. *Educ*: Chorlton Central Sch., Manchester; Stretford Technical Coll. City & Guilds Final Cert. for Electrical Technician. Engrg apprentice, Metropolitan Vickers, 1957–62; Draughtswoman: GEC, Trafford Park, 1962–70; Cableform, Romiley, 1970–71; Mather & Platt, 1972–76; Divisional Organiser 1976–79, National Organiser 1979–83, AUEW (TASS); Dep. Gen. Sec., TASS—The Manufacturing Union, 1983–87. President: CSEU, 1995–97; Nat. Assembly of Women, 1998–2010; Mem., TUC Gen. Council, 1993–97. Mem., Employment Appeal Tribunal, 1996–2010. Mem. Council, Women of the Year Lunch and Assembly, 1996–2011. TUC Women's Gold Badge for services to Trade Unionism, 1976. *Address*: 16 Follett Drive, Abbots Langley, Herts WD5 0LP.

**SWORD, Dr Ian Pollock,** CBE 2002; FRCPE; FRSC; FRSE; Chairman, Inveresk Research Group Inc. (formerly Inveresk Research International Ltd), 1989–2004; *b* 6 March 1942; *s* of John Pollock Sword and Agnes Fyfe; *m* 1967, Flora Collins; two *s* one *d*. *Educ*: Univ. of Glasgow (BSc; PhD). FRSC 1975; FRSE 1996; FRCPE 1997. Univ. of Princeton, 1967–69; Res. Associate, Univ. of Oxford, 1969–70; Hd of Metabolism, then Chemistry Dept, Huntington Res. Centre, 1970–73; Inveresk Research International Ltd: Dep. Man. Dir, 1973–78; Man. Dir, 1978–89. Sen. Exec. Vice-Pres., Société Générale de Surveillance, 1993–2002. Mem., MRC, 1995–98. Chm., Scottish Stem Cell Network, 2006–08. Dir, Archangel Informal Investment Ltd, 2003–08. Trustee: Carnegie Trust for Univs of Scotland, 2005–17; Royal Botanic Garden Edinburgh, 2007–14. Hon. DSc Glasgow, 2008. *Publications*: (ed) Standard Operating Procedures, vol. 3, 1980, vol. 4, 1981. *Recreations*: music, gardening. *Club*: New (Edinburgh).

**SYAL, Meera,** CBE 2015 (MBE 1998); FRSL; actress and writer; *b* 27 June 1964; *d* of Surendra Kumar Syal and Surrinder Syal; *m* 2005, Sanjeev Bhaskar, *qv*; one *s*; one *d* from previous marriage. *Educ*: Manchester Univ. (BA Hons English and Drama, double 1st). Various regular appearances on national television and theatre, 1992–; *actress*: television: Goodness Gracious Me, 1998–2001; The Kumars at No. 42, 2001–06, The Kumars, 2014; All About Me, 2002; Life Isn't All Ha Ha Hee Hee (also co-writer), 2005; Murder Investigation Team, 2005; Broadchurch, 2015; The Split, 2018; theatre: Rafta, Rafta, Nat. Th., 2007; Shirley Valentine, Trafalgar Studios, 2010; The Killing of Sister George, Arts Th., 2011; Much Ado About Nothing, Courtyard Th., Stratford, 2012, transf. Noël Coward Th., 2012; If You Don't Let Us Dream, We Won't Let You Sleep, Royal Court, 2013; Behind the Beautiful Forevers, NT, 2014; Romeo and Juliet, Garrick, 2016; a profoundly affectionate, passionate devotion to someone (-noun), Royal Court, 2017; Annie, Piccadilly Th., 2017; Pinter Three, Harold Pinter Th., 2018; Peter Pan, Birmingham Hippodrome, 2018; Noises Off, Lyric Hammersmith, 2019; film: Dr Strange, 2016; The Nutcracker and the Four Realms, 2018; Yesterday, 2019; *writer*: My Sister Wife (film), 1992; Bhaji on the Beach (film), 1993; Anita and Me (film), 2002; co-writer, Bombay Dreams (musical), Apollo, 2002, transf. Broadway Th., NY, 2004. Cameron Mackintosh Vis. Prof. of Contemporary Th., Oxford Univ., 2011–. Hon. PhD: Wolverhampton, 2000; Leeds, 2002; Birmingham, 2003. FRSL 2016. *Publications*: novels: Anita and Me, 1997; Life Isn't All Ha Ha Hee Hee, 1999; The House of Hidden Mothers, 2015. *Recreations*: netball, jazz singer. *Address*: c/o Rochelle Stevens, 2 Terretts Place, Islington, N1 1QZ.

**SYCAMORE, Phillip; His Honour Judge Sycamore;** a Circuit Judge, since 2001; a President, First Tier Tribunal, and a Judge of the Upper Tribunal, since 2008; a Deputy High Court Judge, since 2010; *b* 9 March 1951; *s* of late Frank and Evelyn Martin Sycamore; *m* 1974, Sandra, JP, *d* of late Peter Frederick Cooper and of Marjorie Cooper; two *s* one *d*. *Educ*: Lancaster Royal Grammar Sch.; Holborn Coll. of Law (LLB London (ext.) 1972). Admitted Solicitor, 1975; in private practice, 1975–2001; Asst Recorder, 1994–99; a Recorder, 1999–2001; Liaison Judge, Mental Health Review Tribunal, 2002–08. Law Society: Mem. Council, 1991–99; Vice-Pres., 1996–97; Pres., 1997–98. Member: Woolf Civil Justice Review (Access to Justice), 1994–96; Criminal Injuries Compensation Panel, 2000–01; Sen. Judicial Appts Comr, 2014–. Gov., Lancaster Royal Grammar Sch., 2001–. Hon. Recorder of Lancaster, 2008–. Hon. LLD: Westminster, 1998; Lancaster, 1999. *Recreations*: family, golf, theatre, travel, ski-ing. *Address*: The Civil Justice Centre, 1 Bridge Street West, Manchester M60 9DJ. *Clubs*: Athenæum; Royal Lytham and St Anne's Golf.

**SYDNEY, Archbishop of,** and Metropolitan of the Province of New South Wales; since 2013; **Most Rev. Dr Glenn Naunton Davies;** *b* 26 Sept. 1950; *s* of Rodger Naunton Davies and Dorothy Joan Davies; *m* 1979, Dianne Frances Carlisle; two *d*. *Educ*: Univ. of Sydney (BSc 1972); Westminster Theol Seminary, Philadelphia (MDiv, ThM 1979); DD 2016); Moore Theol Coll. (DipA 1981); Sheffield Univ. (PhD 1988). Ordained deacon, priest, 1981; Asst Minister, St Stephen's, Willoughby, 1981–82; Lectr, Moore Theol Coll., 1983–95; Rector, St Luke's, Miranda, 1995–2001; Asst Bishop, Dio. of Sydney, and Bishop of N Sydney, 2002–13; Archdeacon of N Sydney, 2009–13. Canon Theologian, Dio. of Ballarat, 2000–13. Centenary Medal, Australia, 2003. *Publications*: Job, 1989; Faith and Obedience: studies in Romans 1–4, 1990. *Address*: PO Box Q190, QVB Post Office, NSW 1230, Australia.

**SYDNEY, Archbishop of, (RC),** since 2014; **Most Rev. Anthony Colin Joseph Fisher,** OP; *b* Sydney, 10 March 1960; *s* of Colin George Fisher and Maria Gloria Fisher (*née* Maguregui). *Educ*: St Ignatius Coll., Riverview; Univ. of Sydney (BA; LLB); Melbourne Coll. of Divinity (BTh); Univ. of Oxford (DPhil 1995). Lawyer, Clayton Utz, Sydney, 1984; Dominican Friar, 1985–; ordained priest, 1991; Parish Priest, Our Lady Star of the Sea, Watsons Bay, 2003–10; Aux. Bishop of Sydney, (RC), 2003–10; Bishop of Parramatta, (RC), 2010–14. Episcopal Vicar for Healthcare, Archdio. of Melbourne, 1997–2002, Archdio. of Sydney, 2003–10. Lectr, Ethics and Moral Theology, Aust. Catholic Univ., Melbourne, 1995–2000; Adjunct Prof. of Bioethics, Univ. of Notre Dame, Sydney, 2007–. Dir, John Paul II Inst., 2000–03; Dep. Chancellor, Catholic Inst., Sydney, 2004–; Chair: Catholic Educn Commn, NSW, 2004–06, 2009–; Sydney Archdio. Catholic Schs Bd, 2009–; Bishops Commn for Family, Youth and Life, 2015–; Member: Pontifical Acad. for Life, 2001–; Congregation for the Doctrine of Faith, 2015–. Co-ord., World Youth Day, 2008. Hon. LLD Notre Dame, Sydney, 2011. *Publications*: (jtly) A History of Solicitors in New South Wales, 1984; Abortion in Australia, 1985, 2nd edn, 1991; IVF: the critical issues, 1989; I Am a Stranger: will you welcome me? The Immigration Debate, 1991; (jtly) Relevant Ethical Issues in Healthcare, 1996; (jtly) Healthcare Allocation: an ethical framework for public policy, 2001; (jtly) Faith and Reason, 2004; Catholic Bioethics for a New Millennium, 2012; The Healing Peace of Chirst: reflections on illness and recovery, 2017; War and Terror, Peace and Hope, 2018; My Dear Young Friend: forty letters on youth, faith and future, 2018; over 100 academic articles on ethical, legal and theological subjects. *Recreations*: prayer, cooking, reading, tennis. *Address*: Polding Centre, 133 Liverpool Street, Sydney, NSW 2000, Australia. *E*: archbishop@sydneycatholic.org.

**SYDNEY, SOUTH, Bishop of;** *see* Stead, Rt Rev. M. R.

**SYDNEY, Assistant Bishop of;** *see* Stead, Rt Rev. M. R.

**SYED, Matthew Philip;** table tennis player; writer and sports journalist; *b* 2 Nov. 1970; *s* of Abbas Syed and Dilys Syed. *Educ*: Maiden Erleigh Comprehensive Sch.; Balliol Coll., Oxford (MA). Represented GB, Olympic Games, Barcelona, 1992 and Sydney, 2000; British No. 1, 1995–2004; English Men's Singles Champion, 1997, 1998, 2000, 2001; Commonwealth Men's Singles Champion, 1997, 1999, 2001. Sports columnist, The Times, 1999–. Co-founder, TTK Greenhouse (sports charity), 2002–; Trustee, Greenhouse Charity, 2012–. Feature Writer of the Year, Sports Journalists' Assoc., 2007, 2010, 2011; Sports Journalist of the Year, British Press Awards, 2009. *Publications*: Bounce: how champions are made, 2010 (Best New Writer, British Sports Book Awards, 2011); Black Box Thinking, 2015; You Are Awesome, 2018; Rebel Ideas: the power of diverse thinking, 2019. *Recreations*: walking in Richmond Park, looking at London architecture. *Address*: Dolphin House, Ormond Road, Richmond, Surrey TW10 6TH. *T*: (020) 8948 6050. *E*: matthew@matthewsyed.co.uk.

**SYFRET, Nicholas;** QC 2008; a Recorder, since 2001; *b* Windlesham, Surrey, 25 Oct. 1954; *s* of Edward Herbert Vyvyan Syfret and Anne Syfret; *m* 1980, Katharine Frances, *d* of Sir (Walter) Leonard Allinson, *qv*; two *s* one *d*. *Educ*: Winchester Coll.; Emmanuel Coll., Cambridge (BA 1976). Called to the Bar, Middle Temple, 1979; in practice as barrister specialising in criminal law; 6 King's Bench Walk, 1980–93, 13 King's Bench Walk, 1993–2014; Cornwall Street Chambers, Birmingham, 2014–. *Recreations*: countryside, messing about in boats, painting, chess. *Address*: St Margaret's Cottage, 15 The Moors, Pangbourne, Reading RG8 7LP. *T*: (0118) 984 3690. *E*: NSyfret@aol.com.

**SYKES, Alastair John,** CBE 2011; Chief Executive, 2001–08, and Chairman, 2001–09, Nestlé UK; *b* 25 Jan. 1953; *s* of John and Jackie Sykes; *m* 1982, Kate Rutter; one *s*. *Educ*: UMIST (BSc Hons Mgt Sci. 1978). Joined Gillette, 1978; held various commercial roles, 1978–89; Eur. Sales and Mktg Dir, 1989–91; Managing Director: McCormick Foods, 1991–95; Spillers UK, 1995–98; Nestlé Rowntree, 1998–2001. Pres., Inst. of Grocery Distribution, 2007–08. *Recreations*: golf, Rugby.

**SYKES, Prof. Brian Douglas,** PhD; FRS 2000; FRSC 1986; Distinguished University Professor, Department of Biochemistry, University of Alberta, since 1997; *b* Montreal, 30 Aug. 1943; *s* of Douglas Lehman Sykes and Mary Anber Sykes; *m* 1st, 1968, Nancy Sengelaub (*d* 2009); two *s*; 2nd, 2015, Wendy Richards. *Educ*: Univ. of Alberta (BSc 1965); Stanford Univ. (PhD 1969). Asst Prof. of Chemistry, 1969–74, Associate Prof., 1974–75, Harvard Univ.; University of Alberta: Associate Prof., 1975–80, Prof., 1980–97; Mem., 1975–, Dir, 1995–, MRC Gp in Protein Structure and Function; Leader, Alberta Node, 1990–, Dep. Scientific Leader, 1995–98, Protein Engrg Network of Centres of Excellence; Actg Chair, 1998–99, Chair, 1999–2004, Dept of Biochem.; Canada Res. Chair, 2001–08. Pres., Canadian Biochem. Soc., 1989–90. *Publications*: over 510 scientific papers. *Address*: Department of Biochemistry, University of Alberta, Edmonton, AB T6G 2H7, Canada; 11312–37 Avenue, Edmonton, AB T6J 0H5, Canada.

**SYKES, Prof. Bryan Clifford,** PhD, DSc; Professor of Human Genetics, University of Oxford, 1997–2016, now Emeritus; Fellow, Wolfson College, Oxford, now Emeritus; *b* London, 9 Sept. 1947; *s* of Frank and Irene Sykes; *m* Ulla Plougmand; one *s*. *Educ*: Eltham Coll., London; Univ. of Liverpool (BSc); Univ. of Bristol (PhD); Univ. of Oxford (MA, DSc). Res. Fellow, Dept of Orthopaedic Surgery, 1973–87, Lectr in Molecular Pathol., 1987–97, Univ. of Oxford. Founder and Chm., Oxford Ancestors Ltd, 2001–18. Mem., Portree Angling Soc. *Publications*: The Seven Daughters of Eve, 2001; Adam's Curse, 2003; Blood of the Isles, 2006; DNA USA: a genetic portrait of America, 2012; The Nature of the Beast, 2015; The Wolf Within, 2018; contrib. papers on human genetics and evolution. *Recreations*: natural history, museums, fishing, croquet, travel, mountains. *Address*: Wolfson College, Oxford OX2 6UD. *E*: bryan.sykes@wolfson.ox.ac.uk. *Club*: Athenæum.

**SYKES, Sir David Michael,** 4th Bt *cr* 1921, of Kingsknowes, Galashiels, co. Selkirk; Chairman, Bennett Sykes Group (formerly Libra Office Equipment) Ltd, 2000–09; *b* 10 June 1954; *s* of Michael le Gallais Sykes and Joan Sykes (*née* Groome); *S* uncle, 2001; *m* 1st, 1974, Susan Elizabeth Hall (marr. diss. 1987); one *s*; 2nd, 1987, Margaret Lynne McGreavy; one *d*. *Educ*: Purbrook Park Grammar Sch. Sales Dir, Frank Groome (Nottingham) Ltd, 1974–85; Sen. Partner, Sykes Office Supplies, 1985–2007. *Recreations*: travel, food and wine, tennis. *Heir*: *s* Stephen David Sykes, *b* 14 Dec. 1978.

**SYKES, Dr Donald Armstrong;** Principal of Mansfield College, Oxford, 1977–86, now Hon. Fellow; *b* 13 Feb. 1930; *s* of late Rev. Leonard Sykes and Edith Mary Sykes (*née* Armstrong); *m* 1st, 1962, Marta Sproul Whitehouse (*d* 2000); two *s*; 2nd, 2002, Sarah Yates. *Educ*: The High Sch. of Dundee; Univ. of St Andrews (MA 2nd cl. Classics 1952; Guthrie Scholar); RAEC, 1952–54; Mansfield Coll., Oxford (BA 1st cl. Theol. 1958; MA 1961; DPhil 1967); Univ. of Glasgow (DipEd). Fellow in Theology, 1959–77, Senior Tutor, 1970–77, and Sen. Res. Fellow, 1986–89, Mansfield Coll., Oxford; retired from tutoring, 2000. Vis. Prof. in Classics and Religion, St Olaf Coll., Northfield, Minn, 1969–70, 1987. Hon. DD St Olaf, 1979. *Publications*: (contrib.) Studies of the Church in History: essays honoring Robert S. Paul, ed Horton Davies, 1983; (introd., trans. and commentary) Gregory of Nazianzus, Poemata Arcana, 1997; articles and reviews in Jl Theological Studies, Studia Patristica, Byzantinische Zeitschrift. *Recreations*: miscellaneous reading, recorded music, walking, gardening. *Address*: Mulberry House, Brimley Lane, Bovey Tracey, Newton Abbot, Devon TQ13 9JS. *Club*: Oxford and Cambridge.

**SYKES, Sir (Francis) John (Badcock),** 10th Bt *cr* 1781, of Basildon, Berkshire; Partner, Thring Townsend (formerly Townsends), solicitors, Bath, Swindon and Newbury, 1972–2002, Consultant, 2002–05; *b* 7 June 1942; *s* of Sir Francis Godfrey Sykes, 9th Bt and Lady Eira Betty Sykes (*née* Badcock), (*d* 1970); *S* father, 1990; *m* 1966, Susan Alexandra, *e d* of Admiral of the Fleet Sir Edward Beckwith Ashmore, GCB, DSC; three *s*. *Educ*: Shrewsbury; Worcester Coll., Oxford (MA). Admitted solicitor, 1968; Assistant Solicitor: Gamlens, Lincoln's Inn, 1968–69; Townsends, 1969–71. Hon. Solicitor, 1973–98, Pres., 1981, Swindon Chamber of Commerce. Governor: Swindon Coll., 1982–90; Swindon Enterprise Trust, 1982–89. Trustee: Roman Research Trust, 1990–2002; Wilts

Community Foundn, 1993–2000; Duchess of Somerset's Hosp., 2003–09; Marlborough Literature Fest., 2010–. President: Nat. Trust Reading Centre, 2008–; Merchant's House (Marlborough) Trust, 2016– (Trustee, 1991–2016). Member: HAC; City Barge Club, Oxford. *Recreations:* local, family and Anglo-Indian history, Venetian rowing. *Heir: s* Col Francis Charles Sykes [*b* 18 June 1968; Princess of Wales's Royal Regt]. *Address:* Kingsbury Croft, 13 Kingsbury Street, Marlborough, Wilts SN8 1HU.

**SYKES, Sir Hugh (Ridley),** Kt 1997; DL; Chairman, Bamford Group Ltd (formerly Bamford Hall Holdings Ltd, then BHH (Brookfield) Ltd), since 1972; *b* 12 Sept. 1932; *m* 1st, 1957, Norah Rosemary Dougan; two *s*; 2nd, 1978, Ruby Anderson; two *s*. *Educ:* Bristol Grammar Sch.; Clare Coll., Cambridge (MA, LLB). CA 1960. Articled with Thomson McLintock, Chartered Accountants, 1956–61; Treas., 1961–69, Asst Man. Dir, 1969–72, Man. Dir (Finance), 1972–73, Steetley & Co.; Chm. and Chief Exec., Thermal Scientific plc, 1977–88. Non-exec. Dep. Chm., Harris Queensway plc, 1978–83; non-executive Chairman: TCI plc, 1985–88; Harveys Furnishings, 1988–94; Yorkshire Bank plc, 1999–2004 (Dir, 1990–2004); Nat. Australia Gp (Europe) Ltd, 2002–04 (Dir, 1997–2004); non-executive Director: Clydesdale Bank plc, 1999–2004; A4e Ltd, 2005–14. Consultant, Bd, Nat. Australia Bank, 2002–04. Chairman: Sheffield Develt Corp., 1988–97; Renaissance S Yorks, 2004–09; Mid Yorks NHS Trust, 2005–08; SheffCare, 2009–11 (Patron, 2012–16); non-exec. Chm., 2000–05, Dir, 2005–07, Sheffield One; Dir, Creative Sheffield, 2007–11; Member of Board: Sheffield TEC, 1990–95; 1NG, 2009–11. Dir, Inst. of Dirs, 2003–09. Chairman: Sir Hugh and Lady Sykes (formerly Hugh and Ruby Sykes) Charitable Trust, 1988–; Sheffield Galleries and Museums Trust, 1998–2008; Industrial Trust, 2001–11 (Trustee, 1998–2011); Adv. Bd, One Powerhouse, 2017–; Mem. Bd, TCV—The Conservation Volunteers, 2008–14 (Mem., Audit Cttee, 2008–16); Trustee, Engineering Develt Trust, 2011–12. Life Patron, Royal Humane Soc., 2015. Mem. Council, Univ. of Sheffield, 1997–2002 (Treas., 1998–2002). DL S Yorks, 1996. Freeman, City of London, 1990. FCIB 2001. Hon. FInstD 2009. Hon. Fellow, Sheffield Hallam Univ., 1991. Hon. LLD Sheffield, 1996. *Publications:* Working for Benefit, 1997; Welfare to Work: the new deal—maximising the benefits, 1998; (ed with Peter Roberts) Urban Regeneration: a handbook, 2000, 2nd edn 2016; Lighting the Furnace (autobiog.), 2017. *Recreations:* walking, travel, golf, Victorian paintings, helping to find a solution to the problems of the North/South Divide. *Address:* Brookfield Manor, Hathersage, Hope Valley S32 1BB. *T:* (01433) 651190. *Clubs:* Carlton; Sickleholme Golf.

**SYKES, Jean Margaret,** MBE 2010; Chief Information Officer, London School of Economics and Political Science, 2009–12 (Librarian and Director of IT Services, 1998–2009); *b* 11 April 1947; *d* of David Thomson and Doreen Thomson (*née* Rose). *Educ:* Univ. of Glasgow (MA Hons, MLitt); Liverpool Poly. (DipLib). Actg Hd, Library Services, Middlesex Poly., 1985–87; Dep. Dir, Information Resource Services, Poly. of Central London, subseq. Univ. of Westminster, 1987–97. Chairman: M25 Consortium of Higher Educn Libraries, 1994–96; Soc. of College, Univ. and Nat. Libraries, 2000–02; Nereus Consortium of Eur. Econs Libraries, 2003–12. Mem., various nat. and internat. rev. panels, 2012–. FRSA 2002. *Publications:* contrib. librarianship and IT jls. *Recreations:* theatre, travel, French language and literature, wine.

**SYKES, Sir John;** *see* Sykes, Sir F. J. B.

**SYKES, Rev. Canon John;** Vicar, St Mary with St Peter, Oldham and Team Rector, Parish of Oldham, 1987–2004; Chaplain to the Queen, 1995–2009; *b* 20 March 1939; *s* of George Reginald Sykes and Doris Sykes (*née* Briggs); *m* 1967, Anne Shufflebotham; one *s* one *d*. *Educ:* St James C of E Sch., Slaithwaite; Royds Hall Grammar Sch., Huddersfield; W Bridgford Grammar Sch., Nottingham; Manchester Univ. (BA); Ripon Hall, Oxford. Ordained deacon, 1963, priest, 1964; Curate: St Luke's, Heywood, 1963–67; i/c Holy Trinity, Bolton, 1967–71; Lectr, Bolton Inst. of Technol., 1967–71; Chaplain to Bolton Colls of Further Educn, 1967–71; Rector, St Elisabeth, Reddish, 1971–78; Vicar, Saddleworth, 1978–87. Proctor in Convocation and Mem., Gen. Synod of C of E, 1980–90. Council for the Care of Churches: Mem., 1986–90; Vice-Chm., Art and Design Sub-cttee, 1988–90. Mem., various Manchester Diocesan Cttees and Councils, 1968–93. Chaplain to: Coliseum Theatre, Oldham, 1987–2006; eight Mayors of Oldham, 1989–99 and 2011–14; High Sheriff of Gtr Manchester, 1993–94, 1996–97; Gtr Manchester Police, Q Div., 1995–99; Royal Soc. of St George, Gtr Manchester br., 2015–. Hon. Canon, Manchester Cathedral, 1991–2004, now Canon Emeritus. *Recreations:* architecture, fine arts, music, walking. *Address:* 53 Ivy Green Drive, Springhead, Oldham OL4 4PR. *T:* (0161) 678 6767. *E:* sykesjohn76@gmail.com. *Club:* Manchester Pedestrians.

**SYKES, John David;** Chairman, Shawspetroleum Ltd, 2008–12 (Director, 1986–2012); Director, Farnley Tyas Estates Ltd, since 1986; *b* 24 Aug. 1956; *m* 1st, 1981, Jane Aspinall (marr. diss. 2003); one *s* two *d*; 2nd, 2006, Vivien Broadbent. *Educ:* St David's Prep. Sch., Huddersfield; Giggleswick Sch., W Riding; Univ. of Sheffield (BA Hons Hist. 2008). Joined Shaws Fuels Ltd (family company), 1974: graduated through every company dept, specialising in sales and transport; Dir, 1978–84; also Dir, subsid. cos. MP (C) Scarborough, 1992–97; contested (C) Scarborough and Whitby, 1997, 2001. PPS to Lord Privy Seal and Leader of H of L, 1995–97. Mem., Select Cttee on Culture and Heritage, 1993–95, on Deregulation, 1995–97; Vice Chm., Backbench Deregulation Cttee, 1995–97 (Sec., 1993–95). *Recreations:* walking, reading, Rugby Union, playing piano, history.

**SYKES, Prof. Katharine Ellen,** OBE 2009; PhD; CPhys, FInstP; Professor of Sciences and Society, University of Bristol, 2006, now Honorary Professor (Collier Professor of Public Engagement in Science and Engineering, 2002–06); *b* 20 Dec. 1966; *d* of Dr John Sykes and Pauline Sykes. *Educ:* Univ. of Bristol (BSc Hons (Physics) 1989; PhD (Physics) 1996). VSO as Hd, Maths Dept and physics teacher, Zhombe High Sch., Zimbabwe, 1989–92; researcher; Hd of Sci., Explore@Bristol, 1996–2001. Dir, Cheltenham Fest. of Sci., 2001–09. Mem., Council for Science and Technology, 2004–11; Trustee, NESTA, 2007–12. Presenter, TV series, incl. Genius of Britain, Hot Planet, Alternative Therapies, Rough Science, Ever Wondered and Mindgames. *Publications:* papers in scientific jls on biodegradable plastic poly hydroxybutyrate; numerous conf. procs on science engagement; contrib. Science. *Recreations:* scuba-diving, mountain-climbing, dancing, singing, good food. *Address:* Royal Fort House, University of Bristol, Bristol BS8 1UJ. *E:* kathy.sykes@bristol.ac.uk.

**SYKES, Laurent Charles;** QC 2016; *b* Wimbledon, London; *s* of Jeremy Sykes and Micheline Sykes; *m* 2004, Simona Foglia; one *s*. *Educ:* St Paul's Sch., London; Corpus Christi Coll., Oxford (BA Mod. Langs). ACA. Ernst & Young, 1996–99; Freshfields, 2001–07; called to the Bar, Gray's Inn, 2007; in practice as a barrister, Gray's Inn Tax Chambers, 2007–. *Recreations:* Italian culture—food, film and tourism. *Address:* Gray's Inn Tax Chambers, 36 Queen Street, EC4R 1BN. *T:* (020) 7242 2642. *E:* ls@taxbar.com.

**SYKES, Lynda Glenis; Her Honour Judge Sykes;** a Circuit Judge, since 2018; *b* Birkenhead; *d* of John Joseph Croft and Jean Adelaide Croft; *m* 1986, Mark Delavis Sykes; one *s* one *d*. *Educ:* Birkenhead High Sch.; Durham Univ. (BA). Admitted solicitor, 1983; Norton Rose Botterell and Roche, 1981–85, Solicitor, 1983–85; Solicitor, Berkson, 1985–99; Dep. Dist Judge, 1996–2000; Dist Judge, 2000–18. *Recreations:* tennis, choral singing, theatre, jazz, walking. *Address:* Chester Civil and Family Justice Centre, Little St John Street, Chester CH1 1SN.

**SYKES, Sir (Malcolm) Keith,** Kt 1991; Nuffield Professor of Anaesthetics, University of Oxford, 1980–91, Emeritus Professor since 1991; Hon. Fellow of Pembroke College, Oxford, since 1996 (Fellow, 1980–91, Supernumerary Fellow, 1991–96); *b* 13 Sept. 1925; *s* of Joseph and Phyllis Mary Sykes; *m* 1956, Michelle June (*née* Ratcliffe) (*d* 2017); two *d* (and one *s* one *d* decd). *Educ:* Magdalene Coll., Cambridge (MA, MB, BChir); University Coll. Hosp., London (DA; FFARCS). RAMC, 1950–52. House appointments, University Coll. and Norfolk and Norwich Hosps, 1949–50; Sen. House Officer, Registrar and Sen. Registrar in anaesthetics, UCH, 1952–54 and 1955–58; Rickman Godlee Travelling Scholar and Fellow in Anesthesia, Mass. General Hosp., Boston, USA, 1954–55; RPMS and Hammersmith Hosp., 1958–80: Lectr and Sen. Lectr, 1958–67; Reader, 1967–70; Prof. of Clinical Anaesthesia, 1970–80. Vis. Prof., univs in Canada, USA, Australia, NZ, Malaysia, Europe. Eponymous lectures: Holme, 1970; Clover, 1976; Weinbren, 1976; Rowbottom, 1978; Gillespie, 1979; Gillies, 1985; Wesley Bourne, 1986; Husfeldt, 1986; Della Briggs, 1988; E. M. Papper, 1991; BOC Healthcare, 1992; Harold Griffith, 1992; Sir Robert Macintosh, 1992. Mem. Bd, Fac. of Anaesthetists, 1969–85; Pres., Section of Anaesthetics, RSM, 1989–90; Vice Pres., Assoc. of Anaesthetists, 1990–92 (Mem. Council, 1967–70); Senator and Vice Pres., European Acad. of Anaesthesiology, 1978–85. Hon. FANZCA (Hon. FFARACS 1979); Hon. FCA(SA) (Hon. FFA(SA) 1989). Dudley Buxton Prize, Fac. of Anaesthetists, 1980; Fac. of Anaesthetists Medal, 1987; John Snow Medal, Assoc. of Anaesthetists, 1992; Hickman Medal, RSocMed, 2008. *Publications:* Respiratory Failure, 1969, 2nd edn 1976; Principles of Measurement for Anaesthetists, 1970; Principles of Clinical Measurement, 1980; Principles of Measurement and Monitoring in Anaesthesia and Intensive Care, 1991; Respiratory Support, 1995; Respiratory Support in Intensive Care, 1999; Anaesthesia and the Practice of Medicine: historical perspectives, 2007; chapters and papers on respiratory failure, intensive care, respiratory and cardiovascular physiology applied to anaesthesia, etc. *Recreations:* walking, birdwatching, gardening, music. *Address:* Treyarnon, Cricket Field Lane, Budleigh Salterton, Devon EX9 6PB. *T:* (01395) 445884.

**SYKES, Sir Richard (Brook),** Kt 1994; FRS 1997; Chairman: Royal Institution, since 2010; Imperial College Healthcare NHS Trust, since 2012; *b* 7 Aug. 1942; *s* of late Eric Sykes and of Muriel Mary Sykes; *m* 1969, Janet Mary Norman; one *s* one *d*. *Educ:* Queen Elizabeth Coll., London (1st Cl. Hons Microbiol.); Bristol Univ. (PhD Microbial Biochem.); DSc London, 1993. Glaxo Res. UK (Head of Antibiotic Res. Unit), 1972–77; Squibb Inst. for Med. Res., USA, 1977–86 (Vice-Pres., Infectious and Metabolic Diseases, 1983–86); Glaxo Group Research: Dep. Chief Exec., 1986; Chm. and Chief Exec., 1987–93; Glaxo plc: Group R&D Dir, 1987–93; Dep. Chm. and Chief Exec., 1993–97; Dep. Chm. and Chief Exec., 1993–97, Chm., 1997–2000, Glaxo Wellcome; Chm., GlaxoSmithKline, 2000–02. Dir, British Pharma Gp, 1998–2001. Rector, Imperial Coll. of Sci., Technol. and Med., Univ. of London, 2001–08; Chm., NHS London, 2008–10. Chm., PDS Biotechnol. Corp., 2014–; non-executive Chairman: Merlion Pharmaceuticals Pte Ltd, 2005–09; Circassia Ltd, 2007–13; NetScientific, 2010–; non-executive Director: Rio Tinto plc, 1997–2008; Rio Tinto Ltd, 1997–2008; Lonza, 2003–13; Eurasian Nat. Resources Corp., 2007–11; ContraFect, USA, 2012–14; Mem., Adv. Bd, Virgin Gp, 2010–12. Chairman: Adv. Council, Life Scis Exec. Cttee, EDB, Singapore, 2000–; Healthcare Adv. Gp (Apax Partners Ltd), 2002–; Bioscience Leadership Council, 2004–07; WHO Internat. Adv. Bd overseeing Internat. Clinical Trials Registry Platform, 2005–; CATALYST, 2005–08. Member: Council for Sci. and Technol., 1993–2003; Adv. Council, Save British Science, subseq. Campaign for Sci. and Engrg, 1993–; Foundn for Sci. and Technol. Council, 1994–2000; Trade Policy Forum, 1995–2000; Internat. Adv. Council, Economic Develt Bd, 1995–; Council for Industry and Higher Educn, 1995–2008; Bd, Eur. Fedn of Pharm. Industries and Assocs, 1997–2000; Council, Internat. Fedn of Pharm. Manufrs Assocs, 1998–2001; HEFCE, 2002–08; Engrg & Tech. Bd, 2002–05; DTI Strategy Bd, 2002–04; Temasek Internat. Adv. Panel, Singapore, 2004–. President: BAAS, 1998–99; Res. and Develt Soc., 2002–. Hon. Vice-Pres., Res. Defence Soc., 2004–; Hon. Mem., British Soc. for Antimicrobial Chemotherapy, 2006. Chairman: Business Leader Gp, British Lung Foundn, 1993–2013; Global Business Council on HIV/AIDS, 1997–2000; UK Stem Cell Foundn, 2005–. Vice-Pres., Nat. Soc. for Epilepsy, 1995–. Mem. Council, St George's House, Windsor Castle, 2004–10. Patron, Huddersfield Enterprise Foundn, 2005–. Mem. Bd Trustees, Natural Hist. Mus., 1996–2005; Trustee, Royal Botanic Gardens Kew, 2003–05. Member: Bd of Mgt, LSHTM, 1994–2003; Council, RCM, 2001–; Internat. Adv. Council, King Abdullah Univ. of Sci. and Technol., 2007–; Bd of Trustees, Masdar Inst. of Sci. and Technol., 2008–, Nanyang Technol Univ., Singapore, 2008–; Chancellor, Brunel Univ., 2013–. MInstD 1995. Fleming Fellow, Lincoln Coll., Oxford, 1992; FKC 1997; FIC 1999. Founder FMedSci 1998. Hon. FRCP 1995; Hon. FRSC 1999; Hon. FRPharmS 2001; Hon. FRCPath 2003; Hon. FREng 2004. Hon. Fellow, Univ. of Wales, 1997; Hon. FCGI 2002. Hon. DPharm Madrid, 1993; Hon. DSc: Brunel, Hull, Hertfordshire, 1994; Bristol, Newcastle, 1995; Huddersfield, Westminster, 1996; Leeds, 1997; Edinburgh, Strathclyde, 1998; London, Cranfield, Leicester, Sheffield, Warwick, 1999; Hon. MD Birmingham, 1995; Hon. LLD Nottingham, 1997. *Recreations:* opera, tennis, swimming. *Address:* Flat 11, Hale House, 34 De Vere Gardens, W8 5AQ. *T:* (020) 7937 0742. *Club:* Athenæum.

**SYKES, Robert Hedley,** OBE 2008; Chief Executive, Worcestershire County Council, 1997–2007; *b* 21 Aug. 1952; *s* of Hedley Sykes and Edith (*née* Oliver); two *d*; *m* 2013, Maureen Gamble. *Educ:* Danum Grammar Sch.; Leeds Univ. (BSc, CQSW); Sheffield Poly. (DMS). Social worker, later Principal Officer (Children's Services), Doncaster MBC, 1975–86; Dep. Divl Dir, Social Services, N Yorks CC, 1986–89; Dep. Dir, Social Services, Oxfordshire CC, 1989–95; Dir, Social Services, Hereford and Worcester CC, 1995–97; non-executive Director: Crown Prosecution Service, 2007–12; Core Assets, 2008–16; Nat. Audit Office, 2015–. Sen. Fellow, Univ. of Worcester, 2008–15. CInstLM 2007. FRSA 1999–2016. *Recreations:* family, golf, theatre.

**SYKES, Roger Michael Spencer,** OBE 2002; HM Diplomatic Service, retired; High Commissioner to Fiji, and concurrently to Tonga, Vanuatu, Tuvalu, Kiribati and Nauru, 2006–09; *b* 22 Oct. 1948; *s* of Kenneth and Joan Sykes; *m* 1976, Anne Lesley Groves Gidney; three *s*. *Educ:* Wintringham Grammar Sch.; John Wilmott Grammar Sch.; Newport Grammar Sch. Entered FCO, 1969; served: Caracas, 1971–72; Freetown, 1972–75; Karachi, 1976–78; Cultural Attaché, Valetta, 1978–81; Press Officer, FCO, 1981–82; Attaché, Lagos, 1982–86; Dep. High Comr, Vila, 1986–90; S Asia Dept, FCO, 1990–93; Political and Econ. Sec., Amman, 1993–97; Hd of Post, Alkhobar, 1997–2001; Dep. Hd of Mission, Karachi, 2002–05. Privy Council Rep., Univ. of S Pacific, 2006–. *Recreations:* golf, game fishing, cricket, social history, National Trust research volunteer, comparing the different attributes of old and new world red wines. *Clubs:* Weston Park Golf, Ryston Park Golf.

**SYKES, Sir Tatton (Christopher Mark),** 8th Bt *cr* 1783; landowner; *b* 24 Dec. 1943; *s* of Sir (Mark Tatton) Richard Tatton-Sykes, 7th Bt and Virginia (*d* 1970), *d* of late John Francis Grey Gilliat; *S* father, 1978; granted use of additional arms of Tatton, 1980. *Educ:* Eton; Univ. d'Aix-Marseille; Royal Agricl Coll., Cirencester. *Heir: b* Jeremy John Sykes [*b* 8

March 1946; *m* 1st, 1982, Pamela June (marr. diss. 1995; she *m* 2nd, Earl of Swinton, *qv*), *o d* of Thomas Wood; 2nd, 2008, Annabel Celia Dorothy Evans (*d* 2012), *yr d* of Sir Somerled Bosville Macdonald of Sleat, 16th Bt, MC]. *Address:* Sledmere, Driffield, East Yorkshire YO25 3XG.

**SYLVA, Prof. Kathleen D.,** Hon. OBE 2007; PhD; Professor of Educational Psychology, University of Oxford, since 1998; Fellow of Jesus College, Oxford, 1997, now Emeritus. *Educ:* Harvard Univ. (MA 1972; PhD 1974). Lectr in Applied Social Studies, Univ. of Oxford, 1977–88; Fellow of Jesus Coll., Oxford, 1977–88; Prof. of Primary Educn, Univ. of Warwick, 1988–90; Prof. of Child Develt and Primary Educn, Inst. of Educn, Univ. of London, 1990–97; Reader in Educnl Studies, Univ. of Oxford, 1997–98. *Publications:* (ed jtly) Play: its role in development and evolution, 1976; (jtly) Childwatching at Playgroup and Nursery School, 1980; (with I. Lunt) Child Development: a first course, 1982; (ed jtly) Assessing Children's Social Behaviour and Competence, 1997; (jtly) Assessing Quality in the Early Years, 2003; (ed jtly) Early Childhood Matters, 2010; articles in learned jls. *Address:* Department of Education, University of Oxford, 15 Norham Gardens, Oxford OX2 6PY.

**SYLVESTER, Rachel Mynfreda;** Columnist, The Times, since 2008; *b* London, 13 Nov. 1969; *d* of Nigel Sylvester and Mary Sylvester (*née* Cawston); *m* 2002, Patrick Wintour, *qv*; two *s* and one step *s* one step *d*. *Educ:* S Hampstead High Sch.; Somerville Coll., Oxford (BA English). Reporter, Sunday Telegraph, 1992–96; political corresp., Daily Telegraph, 1996–98; Political Ed., Independent on Sunday, 1998–99; political writer, Daily Telegraph, 1999–2008. *Recreations:* family, theatre, gardening. *E:* rachel.sylvester@thetimes.co.uk.

**SYLVESTER JOHNSON, Anna;** Headmistress, Ibstock Place School, since 2000; *m* 1976, Dr Ian Johnson; one *s* one *d*. *Educ:* Pate's Grammar Sch.; Kent Univ. (BA Hons); King's Coll. London (PGCE). Teacher of English: Elliott Sch., Putney, 1972–74; Lycée, London, 1974–76; Bermuda Coll., Bermuda, 1976–78; Head of English: Green Sch. for Girls, Isleworth, 1978–87; Lycée Français, Charles de Gaulle, 1987–97; Headmistress, Arts Educnl Schs, 1997–2000. FRSA. *Recreations:* theatre, opera, art, cinema, antiques (especially 20th century). *Address:* Ibstock Place School, Clarence Lane, Roehampton, SW15 5PY. *E:* head@ibstockplaceschool.co.uk. *Club:* Roehampton.

**SYMES, Susie;** economist; Chairman, Museum of Immigration and Diversity, since 1998; *b* 24 April 1954; *d* of late Oliver Symes and Judith Symes (*née* Blumberg); *m* 1972, Ian Paul Abson (marr. diss. 1977); partner, Philip Jonathan Black; (one *d* decd). *Educ:* Withington Girls' Sch.; Anglo-American Coll.; City Univ., London (Adam Smith Prize 1974); St Antony's Coll., Oxford (Pres., JCR); London Sch. of Econs. Vis. Lectr, Univ. of Buckingham, 1975–77; Lectr and Sen. Res. Officer, Civil Service Coll., 1977–84; Econ. Advr, HM Treasury, 1985–90; Sen. Official, EC, 1990–92; Dir, European Prog., RIIA, 1992–95. Vis. Prof., Nat. Inst. of Defence Studies, Tokyo, 1994. Dir, Charter for Europe, 1997. Fellow, British American Proj., 1993–; Conseiller, Federal Trust, 1996–97; Trustee: Foundn for English Coll. in Prague, 1996–2011; Alzheimer's Soc., 2000–03; Mem. Adv. Council, London East Res. Inst., 2004. Founding Pres., La Légion des Femmes Efficaces, 1998–; Co-Founder, Probo, 2006–. Mem. Adv. Bd, Prospect magazine, 1995; exec. co-producer, Voices (audio anthol.), 1998 (prize for special achievement, Talking Newspaper Assoc. of UK). *Publications:* (jtly) Economics Workbook, 1989; (jtly) European Futures: alternative scenarios, 1998; occasional articles in learned and light jls. *Recreations:* making connections, marmalade and papier mâché. *Address:* The Museum of Immigration and Diversity, c/o 19 Princelet Street, E1 6QH. *T:* (020) 7247 5352. *E:* office@19princeletstreet.org.uk. *Clubs:* Reform, Serpentine.

**SYMMONDS, Dame (Olga) Patricia,** DBE 2000; GCM 1985; Senator, Parliament of Barbados, 1994–2007; Deputy President of the Senate, 2003–07; *b* 18 Oct. 1925; *d* of late Algernon French Symmonds and Olga Ianthe Symmonds (*née* Harper). *Educ:* Queen's Coll., Barbados; Univ. of Reading (BA 2nd Cl. Hons); Inst. of Educn, Univ. of London (PGCE). Teacher, 1945–85, Dep. Principal, 1963–76, Principal, 1976–85, St Michael Sch., Barbados; pt-time Lectr and Tutor, Cave Hill Campus, Univ. of WI, 1963–65. PC (Barbados), 1997–2000. *Publications:* On Language and Life Styles, 1989; (jtly) Caribbean Basic English, 1993; Longer Lasting than Bronze, 1993; Recalling These Things, 2009; contrib. to educnl jls. *Recreations:* reading, music. *Address:* Bank Hall Main Road, St Michael BB11078, Barbados. *T:* 4266470. *Clubs:* Barbados Cricket, Barbados Tennis Association Inc.

**SYMMONS ROBERTS, Michael;** see Roberts, M. S.

**SYMON, Prof. Lindsay,** CBE 1994; TD 1967; FRCS, FRCSE; Professor of Neurological Surgery, Institute of Neurology, London University and the National Hospital, Queen Square, 1978–95, now Emeritus; *b* 4 Nov. 1929; *s* of William Lindsay Symon and Isabel Symon; *m* 1954, Pauline Barbara Rowland; one *s* two *d*. *Educ:* Aberdeen Grammar Sch.; Aberdeen Univ. (MB, ChB Hons). FRCSE 1957; FRCS 1959. House Physician and Surgeon, Aberdeen Royal Infirmary, 1952–53; Jun. Specialist in Surgery, RAMC, 1953–55; Surgical Registrar, Aberdeen Royal Infirmary, 1956–58; Neurosurgical Registrar, Middlesex and Maida Vale Hosps, 1958–61, Sen. Neurosurgical Registrar, 1962–65; Mem., External Scientific Staff, MRC, 1965–78; Consultant Neurosurgeon: Nat. Hosp. for Nervous Diseases, Queen Square and Maida Vale, 1965–78; St Thomas' Hosp., 1970–78. Hon. Consultant Neurological Surgeon, St Thomas' Hosp., Hammersmith Hosp., Royal Nose, Throat and Ear Hosp., 1978–95; Hon. Consultant Neurosurgeon, Nat. Hosp. for Neurology and Neurosurgery, 1978–95; Civilian Advr in Neurological Surgery to RN, 1979–95. Hunterian Prof., 1982, Arnott Demonstrator, 1989, RCS. Adjunct Prof., Dept of Surgery, Southwestern Med. Sch., Dallas, 1982–95. Rockefeller Travelling Fellow in Medicine, Wayne State Univ., Detroit, 1961–62. Lectures: Herbert Olivecrona, Karolinska Inst., Sweden, 1980; Mayfield/Aring, Univ. of Cincinnati, 1990; Sir Thomas Willis, Stroke Council of America, 1994. Pres., Harveian Soc., of London, 1998. Hon. Pres., World Fedn Neurosurgical Socs, 1993– (Pres., 1989–93). Mem., Acad. of Scis, Ukraine, 1992. TA, 1955–68, Major i/c Mobile Neurosurgical Team, 1961–68. Freeman, City of London, 1982. Hon. Sen. Fellow, Amer. Neurological Assoc., 1982; Hon. FACS 1994; Hon. FRSocMed 1997. Jamieson Medal, Australasian Neurosurgical Soc., 1982; John Hunter Medal, RCS, 1985; K. J. Zulch Medal, Max Planck Ges., 1993; Otfrid Förster Medal, Deutsche Ges. für Neurochirurgie, 1998; Medal of Honour, Soc. of British Neurol Surgeons, 2008; Samii Medal, WFNS, 2013. *Publications:* Operative Surgery/Neurosurgery, 1976, 2nd edn 1986; Advances and Technical Standards in Neurosurgery, 1972, 18th edn 1991; numerous papers on cerebral circulation and metabolism, brain tumours, general neurosurgical topics, etc. *Recreation:* golf. *Address:* Maple Lodge, Rivar Road, Shalbourne, near Marlborough, Wilts SN8 3QE. *T:* and *Fax:* (01672) 870501. *Clubs:* Caledonian; Royal & Ancient (St Andrews).

**SYMON, Rev. Canon Roger Hugh Crispin;** Canon Residentiary, Canterbury Cathedral, 1994–2002, now Canon Emeritus; *b* 25 Oct. 1934; *s* of Rev. Alan Symon and Margaret Sarah Symon (*née* Sharp); *m* 1963, Daphne Mary Roberts; two *d*. *Educ:* King's Sch., Canterbury; St John's Coll., Cambridge (MA); Coll. of the Resurrection, Mirfield. Curate, St Stephen's, Westminster, 1961–66; Priest-in-Charge, St Peter's, Hascombe, 1966–68; Chaplain, Univ. of Surrey, Guildford, 1966–74; Vicar, Christ Church, Lancaster Gate, 1974–79, with St James, Sussex Gardens, 1977–79; Home Staff, USPG, 1980–86; Actg Sec. for Anglican Communion Affairs to Archbp of Canterbury, 1987–91, Sec., 1991–94. *Address:* 5 Bath Parade, Cheltenham, Glos GL53 7HL.

**SYMONDS, Ann Hazel S.;** *see* Spokes Symonds.

**SYMONDS, Matthew John;** Executive Director, Larry Ellison Foundation, since 2018; *b* 20 Dec. 1953; *s* of Lord Ardwick and late Anne Symonds; *m* 1981, Alison Mary Brown; one *s* two *d*; one *d*. *Educ:* Holland Park, London; Balliol College, Oxford (MA). Graduate trainee, Daily Mirror, 1976–78; Financial Times, 1978–81; economics and defence leader writer, economics columnist, Daily Telegraph, 1981–86; Founding Director, Newspaper Publishing plc, 1986–94; The Independent: Dep. Editor, 1986–94; Exec. Editor, 1989–94; columnist, Sunday Express, 1995; Dir of Strategy, BBC Worldwide Television, 1995–97; The Economist: Technol. and Communications Ed., 1997–2000; Associate Ed., 2001; Political Ed., 2002–07; Industry Ed., 2007–10; Defence and Diplomatic Ed., 2010–18. Dir, Reach to Teach, 2007–. Trustee, IISS, 2019–. Sen. Financial Journalist, Wincott Awards, 1999. *Publications:* Softwar, 2003. *Recreations:* walking dog, history, churches, novels, theatre, boating, tennis, Chelsea FC. *Address:* Twickenham, Middx.

**SYMONDS, Nicklaus T.;** *see* Thomas-Symonds.

**SYMONS OF VERNHAM DEAN,** Baroness *cr* 1996 (Life Peer), of Vernham Dean in the county of Hampshire; **Elizabeth Conway Symons;** PC 2001; *b* 14 April 1951; *d* of Ernest Vize Symons, CB and Elizabeth Megan Symons (*née* Jenkins); *m* 2001, Philip Alan Bassett (*d* 2018); one *s*. *Educ:* Putney High Sch. for Girls; Girton Coll., Cambridge (MA; Hon. Fellow, 2001). Research, Girton Coll., Cambridge, 1972–74; Administration Trainee, DoE, 1974–77; Asst Sec. 1977–88, Dep. Gen. Sec., 1988–89, Inland Revenue Staff Fedn; Gen. Sec., Assoc. of First Div. Civil Servants, 1989–96. Parly Under-Sec. of State, FCO, 1997–99; Minister of State, MoD, 1999–2001; Minister of State (Minister for Trade), FCO and DTI, 2001–03; Minister of State (Minister for ME), FCO, 2003–05. Mem., Employment Appeal Tribunal, 1995. Mem., EOC, 1995–97. Member: Gen. Council, TUC, 1989–96; Council, RIPA, 1989–97; Exec. Council, Campaign for Freedom of Information, 1989–97; Hansard Soc. Council, 1992–97; Council, Industrial Soc., 1994–97; Trustee, IPPR, 1993; Exec. Mem., Involvement and Participation Assoc., 1992. Member: Council, Open Univ., 1994–97; Adv. Council, Civil Service Coll., 1992–97; Governor: Polytechnic of North London, 1989–94; London Business Sch., 1993–97. FRSA. Hon. Associate, Nat. Council of Women, 1989. *Recreations:* reading, gardening, friends.

**SYMONS, Christopher John Maurice;** QC 1989; international commercial arbitrator; a Deputy High Court Judge, 1998–2015; *b* 5 Feb. 1949; *s* of late Clifford Louis Symons and Pamela Constance Symons; *m* 1974, Susan Mary Teichmann; one *s* one *d*. *Educ:* Sherborne Prep. Sch.; Clifton Coll.; Kent Univ. (BA Hons (Law)). Called to the Bar, Middle Temple, 1972, Bencher, 1998 (Treas., 2013); called to the Bar of Gibraltar, 1985, to the Irish Bar, 1988, to the NI Bar, 1990, to the Brunei Bar, 1999. Jun. Crown Counsel (Common Law), 1985–89; an Asst Recorder, 1990–93; a Recorder, 1993–2004. Pres., Lloyd's Appeal Tribunal, 2010–; Mem., Investigatory Powers Tribunal, 2018–. *Recreation:* hitting balls. *Address:* 3 Verulam Buildings, Gray's Inn, WC1R 5NT. *T:* (020) 7831 8441. *Clubs:* Boodle's; All England Lawn Tennis; Berkshire Golf, Jesters; Royal Sotogrande Golf, Royal Valderrama Golf (Spain).

**SYMONS, Sir Patrick (Jeremy),** KBE 1986; Chairman, Sussex Weald and Downs (formerly Chichester Priority Care Services) NHS Trust, 1994–98; *b* 9 June 1933; *s* of Ronald and Joanne Symons; *m* 1961, Elizabeth Lawrence; one *s* one *d*. *Educ:* Dartmouth Royal Naval College. Commissioned 1951; in command, HMS Torquay, 1968–70, HMS Birmingham, 1976–77, HMS Bulwark, 1980–81; Naval Attaché, Washington, 1982–84; C of S to Comdr, Allied Naval Forces Southern Europe, 1985–88; SACLANT's Rep. in Europe, 1988–92; retired in rank of Vice-Adm. *Recreation:* swimming.

**SYMS, Sir Robert (Andrew Raymond);** Kt 2017; MP (C) Poole, since 1997; *b* 15 Aug. 1956; *s* of Raymond Syms and Mary Syms (*née* Brain); *m* 1st, 1991, Nicola Guy (marr. diss. 1999); 2nd, 2000, Fiona Mellersh (marr. diss. 2016); one *s* one *d*. *Educ:* Colston's Sch., Bristol. Dir, C. Syms & Sons Ltd, family building and plant hire gp, 1975–. Mem., Wessex RHA, 1988–90. Member (C): N Wilts DC, 1983–87 (Vice Chm., 1984–87; Leader, Cons. Gp, 1984–87); Wilts CC, 1985–97. Contested (C) Walsall N, 1992. PPS to Chm., Conservative Party, 1999; opposition front bench spokesman on the envmt, 1999–2001; an Opposition Whip, 2003; opposition spokesman, DCLG (formerly ODPM), 2003–07; an Asst Govt Whip, 2012–13; a Lord Comr of HM Treasury (Govt Whip), 2016–17. Chairman: Regulatory Reform Select Cttee, 2010–12; HS2 (formerly High Speed Rail) Select Cttee, 2014–16; Member: Health Select Cttee, 1997–2000 and 2007–10; Procedure Select Cttee, 1998–99; Transport Select Cttee, 2001–03; Liaison Cttee, 2010–12; Vice-Chm., Cons. back bench Constitutional Cttee, 1997–2001. A Vice-Chm., Cons. Party, 2001–03. N Wiltshire Conservative Association: Treas., 1982–83; Dep. Chm., 1983–84; Chm., 1984–96; Vice Pres., 1986–88. *Recreations:* reading, travel, cycling. *Address:* House of Commons, SW1A 0AA; c/o Poole Conservative Association, 38 Sandbanks Road, Poole BH14 8BX. *T:* (01202) 739922.

**SYNGE, Sir Allen James Edward,** 9th Bt *cr* 1801, of Kiltrough; *b* 15 Jan. 1942; *s* of Neale Francis Synge (*d* 1998), *gs* of Sir Francis Robert Millington Synge, 6th Bt, and Katherine Caroline Bowes; S cousin, 2011, but his name does not appear on the Official Roll of the Baronetage.

**SZÉLL, Patrick John,** CMG 2001; Head, International and EC Environmental Law Division, 1985–2002, and Director (Legal), Department for Environment, Food and Rural Affairs (formerly Department of the Environment, then Department of the Environment, Transport and the Regions), 1992–2002; *b* Budapest, Hungary, 10 Feb. 1942; *s* of Dr János Széll and Vera Széll (*née* Beckett); *m* 1967, Olivia (*née* Brain), JP (*d* 2010); two *s* one *d*. *Educ:* Reading Sch.; Trinity Coll., Dublin (MA, LLB; Julian Prize 1964). Called to the Bar, Inner Temple, 1966. Joined Min. of Housing and Local Govt as Legal Asst, 1969; Department of the Environment: Sen. Legal Asst, 1973–85; Asst Solicitor, 1985–92. Legal Advr to UK Delegns at internat. envmtl negotiations, 1974–2002, including: UN/ECE Convention on Long-Range Transboundary Air Pollution and its protocols, 1979–2002; Vienna Convention for Protection of Ozone Layer and Montreal Protocol, 1982–2002; Basle Convention on Transboundary Movements of Hazardous Wastes, 1988–93; Climate Change Convention and Kyoto Protocol, 1990–2002; Biodiversity Convention and Biosafety Protocol, 1990–2000. Member: Internat. Council of Envmtl Law, Bonn, 1982–; IUCN Commn on Envmtl Law, 1994–2005. Clerk, Lurgashall Parish Council, 2005–11. Global Ozone Award, UNEP, 1995; Elizabeth Haub Prize, Free Univ. of Brussels, 1995; Stratospheric Ozone Protection Award, US Envmtl Protection Agency, 2002; Montreal Protocol Visionaries Award, UNEP, 2007. *Recreations:* travel, hockey, ancient churches. *Address:* Croft's Folly, Windfallwood Common, Haslemere, Surrey GU27 3BX.

**SZENTIVÁNYI, Gábor,** Hon. GCVO 1999; Ambassador, Ministry of Foreign Affairs, Hungary, 2013–15; *b* 9 Oct. 1952; *s* of József Szentiványi and Ilona Fejes; *m* 1976, Gabriella Gönczi; one *s* one *d*. *Educ:* Budapest Univ. of Economic Scis. Min. of Foreign Affairs, Hungary, 1975; Sec. for Press, Cultural and Educnl Affairs, Baghdad, 1976–81; Protocol

Dept, Min. of Foreign Affairs, 1981–86; Counsellor for Press and Media Relations, Washington, 1986–91; Man. Dir, Burson-Marsteller Budapest, 1991–94; Spokesman and Dir Gen., Press and Internat. Information Dept, Min. of Foreign Affairs, 1994–97; Ambassador to UK, 1997–2002; Dep. State Sec., Min. of Foreign Affairs, 2002–04; Ambassador to the Netherlands and to OPCW, 2004–07; State Sec. and Political Dir, Min. of Foreign Affairs, 2007–09; Ambassador to Sweden, 2009–13. Member: Foreign Affairs Soc., Hungary, 1993–; Atlantic Council, Hungary, 1997–. Officer, Order of Prince Henry the Navigator (Portugal), 1983; Grand Cross of Merit (Chile), 2002; Middle Cross, Order of Merit (Hungary), 2004; Knight Grand Cross, Order of Orange-Nassau (Netherlands), 2007; Grand Officer's Cross of Merit, SMO (Malta), 2009. *Recreation:* boating.

**SZIRTES, George Gábor Nicholas,** PhD; FRSL; FEA; freelance writer; Reader in Creative Writing, University of East Anglia, 2006–13; *b* Budapest, 29 Nov. 1948; *s* of László Szirtes and Magdalena Szirtes (*née* Nussbacher); *m* 1970, Clarissa Upchurch; one *s* one *d*. *Educ:* Leeds Coll. of Art (BA 1st cl. Hons (Fine Art) 1972); Goldsmiths Coll., London (ATC 1973); Anglia Polytechnic Univ. (PhD by published work 2002). Teacher, Art, Hist. of Art and English, various schs and colls, 1973–91; Dir, Art, St Christopher Sch., Letchworth, 1982–89; Norwich School of Art and Design: Vis. Lectr, 1989–91; estabd Creative Writing course, 1991–94; Co-ordinator of Creative Writing, Norwich Sch. of Art and Design, later Norwich Univ. Coll. of the Arts, 1994–2006. Mem., Hungarian Széchenyi Acad. of Arts and Letters, 2014–. FRSL 1982; FEA 2006. Gold Star, Hungarian Republic, 1991. *Publications: poetry:* Poetry Introduction 4, 1978 (jtly); The Slant Door, 1979 (Faber Meml Prize, 1980); November and May, 1981; Short Wave, 1984; The Photographer in Winter, 1986; Metro, 1988; Bridge Passages, 1991; Blind Field, 1994; Selected Poems, 1996; The Red-All-Over Riddle Book (for children), 1997; Portrait of my Father in an English Landscape, 1998; The Budapest File, 2000; An English Apocalypse, 2001; (with Ana Maria Pacheco) A Modern Bestiary, 2004; Reel, 2004 (T. S. Eliot Prize, 2005); Collected and New Poems, 2008; The Burning of Books, 2009; The Burning of Books and Other Poems, 2009; Shuck, Hick, Tiffey, 2009; Bad Machine, 2013; In the Land of Giants (for children), 2012; Wordless, 2014; Langoustine, 2014; Notes on the Inner City, 2015; Mapping the Delta, 2016; How to be a Tiger, 2017; Thirty Poets Go to the Gym, 2018; The Children, 2018; Thirty Clouds, 2018; *translations:* Madách, The Tragedy of Man, 1989 (Déry Prize for Translation, 1990); (pt translator) Csoóri, Barbarian Prayer, 1989; (ed and pt translator) Vas, Through the Smoke, 1989; Kosztolányi, Anna Édes, 1991; (ed and translator) Orbán, The Blood of the Walsungs, 1993; (ed and translator) Rakovszky, New Life, 1994 (European Poetry Translation Prize, 1995); (ed jtly and translator) The Colonnade of Teeth: twentieth century Hungarian poetry, 1996; (ed and translator) The Lost Rider: Hungarian poetry 16th–20th century, 1998; Krúdy, The Adventures of Sindbad, 1999; Krasznahorkai, The Melancholy of Resistance, 1999; (ed and translator) The Night of Akhenaton: selected poems of Ágnes Nemes Nagy, 2004; Márai, Casanova in Bolzano, 2004; Krasznahorkai, War and War, 2005; Márai, The Rebels, 2007; Márai, Esther's Inheritance, 2009; Karinthy, Metropole, 2008; Márai, Portraits of a Marriage, 2010; Krasznahorkai, Satantango, 2012; Kiss: the summer my father died, 2012; Szabó, Iza's Ballad, 2014; *other works:* (ed) Birdsuit (nine anthologies), 1991–99; (ed) The Collected Poems of Freda Downie, 1995; (ed with Penelope Lively) New Writing 10, 2001; Exercise of Power: the art of Ana Maria Pacheco, 2001; (ed jtly) An Island of Sound: Hungarian fiction and poetry at the point of change, 2004; Fortinbras at the Fishhouses: responsibility, the Iron Curtain and the sense of history as knowledge (criticism), 2010; (ed) New Order: Hungarian poets of the post-1989 generation, 2010; (ed) In Their Own Words: contemporary poets on poetry, 2012; Uncle Zoltán, 2014; Germania, 2014; Child Helga, 2014; The Photographer at Sixteen, 2019. *Recreations:* music, art, some sports, blogging at georgeszirtes.blogspot.com. *Address:* 16 Damgate Street, Wymondham, Norfolk NR18 0BQ. *T:* (01953) 603533, 07752 713533. *E:* georgeszirtes@gmail.com.

**SZMUKLER, Prof. George Isaac,** MD; FRCPsych, FRANZCP; Professor of Psychiatry and Society, Institute of Psychiatry, Psychology and Neuroscience (formerly Institute of Psychiatry), King's College, London, 2007–14, now Emeritus; *b* 23 April 1947; *s* of Judel Szmukler and Leja Soyka; *m* 1983, Linnet Michele Lee; one *d*. *Educ:* Univ. of Melbourne (MB BS 1970; MD 1984); DPM 1974. MRCPsych 1977, FRCPsych 1989; FRANZCP 1985. Jun. RMO, Royal Melbourne Hosp., 1971–72; SHO, then Registrar in Psychiatry, Royal Free Hosp., 1972–75; Lectr in Psychiatry, Royal Free Hosp. Sch. of Medicine, Univ. of London, 1975–79; Lectr in Psychiatry, Inst. of Psychiatry, Univ. of London, 1980–82; Sen. Lectr, Inst. of Psychiatry, and Hon. Consultant Psychiatrist, Maudsley and Bethlem Royal Hosp., 1982–85; Consultant Psychiatrist, Royal Melbourne Hosp., and Sen. Associate, Univ. of Melbourne, 1985–92; Consultant Psychiatrist, 1993–2010, Jt Med. Dir, 1999–2001 (Med. Dir, Bethlem and Maudsley NHS Trust, 1997–99), Hon. Consultant Psychiatrist, 2010–14, Maudsley Hosp., S London and Maudsley NHS Trust, later S London and the Maudsley NHS Trust; Dean and Hd of Sch., Inst. of Psychiatry, 2001–06, Co-Dir (formerly Chm.), King's Health and Society Centre (formerly Network), 2007–13, KCL. Associate Dir, NIHR-Mental Health Res. Network, 2007–15. Vis. Prof., BIOS, LSE, 2007–13. Chair, Special Cttee on Human Rights, RCPsych, 2016–. FKC 2008. *Publications:* (jtly) Making Sense of Psychiatric Cases, 1986; (jtly) The Family in the Practice of Psychiatry, 1994; (ed) Eating Disorders: a handbook of theory, practice and research, 1994; (ed) A handbook on Mental Illness for Carers, 2001; (ed with G. Thornicroft) Textbook of Community Psychiatry, 2001; (ed jtly) Oxford Textbook of Community Mental Health, 2010; Men in White Coats: treatment under coercion, 2018; papers on eating disorders, families, health services res., mental health law and ethics. *Recreations:* music (especially Baroque and opera), art, cinema. *Address:* Institute of Psychiatry, Psychology and Neuroscience, King's College London, De Crespigny Park, Denmark Hill, SE5 8AF. *T:* (020) 7848 0002. *E:* george.szmukler@kcl.ac.uk.

**SZOMBATI, Béla;** Head of Section, Human Rights, Delegation of the European Union to the United Nations, Geneva, since 2016; *b* 16 July 1955; *s* of Béla Szombati and Éva Szombati (*née* Herbály); *m* 1978, Zsuzsa Mihályi; two *s*. *Educ:* Eötvös Loránd Univ., Budapest (MA Hist. and French Lang. and Lit.). Joined Hungarian Diplomatic Service, 1980; Dept of Internat. Security, Min. of Foreign Affairs, 1980–82; Third Sec., Hanoi, 1982–85; Dept of W Europe and N America, Min. of Foreign Affairs, 1986–88; Second Sec., Washington, 1988–91; Foreign Policy Advr, Office of Pres. of the Republic, 1991–94; Ambassador, Paris, 1994–99; Dep. Hd, State Secretariat for European Integration, Min. of Foreign Affairs, 1999–2002; Ambassador to UK, 2002–06; Hd, Dept for Strategic Planning and Inf. Mgt, Min. of Foreign Affairs, Hungary, 2006–09; Ambassador to USA, 2009–10; Dep. Hd, Delegn of EU to Turkey, 2012–16. Commander's Cross, Order of Merit (Poland), 2001; Officier, Légion d'Honneur (France), 2002. *Recreations:* music, walking, football. *Address:* Delegation of the European Union to the United Nations, Rue du Grande-Pré 64, 1211 Geneva, Switzerland.

**SZOSTAK, Prof. Jack William,** PhD; FRS 2019; Professor of Genetics, Harvard Medical School, since 1988; Investigator, Howard Hughes Medical Institute, since 1998; Alex Rich Distinguished Investigator, Department of Molecular Biology, Massachusetts General Hospital, since 2000 (Molecular Biologist, since 1988); *b* London, 9 Nov. 1952; *s* of Bill and Vi Szostak. *Educ:* McGill Univ. (BS Cell Biol. 1972); Cornell Univ. (PhD 1977). Res. Associate in Biochem., Cornell Univ., 1977–79; Harvard Medical School: Asst Prof., 1979–83, Associate Prof., 1983–84, Sidney Farber Cancer Inst., subseq. Dana Farber Cancer Inst. and Dept of Biol Chem.; Associate Prof., Dept of Genetics, 1984–87. Co-Chm., Nat. Res. Council Cttee on Origin and Evolution of Life, 2003–. MNAS 1998; Fellow, NY Acad. of Scis, 1999. Medal, Genetics Soc. of America, 2000; (jtly) Nobel Prize in Physiology or Medicine, 2009. *Address:* Department of Genetics, Massachusetts General Hospital, Simches Research Center CPZN# 7215, 185 Cambridge Street, Boston, MA 02114, USA.

# T

**TAAFFE, Jonathan Paul**; a District Judge (Magistrates' Courts), since 2010; *b* Sheffield, 11 June 1961; *s* of Dr John Hilary and Dinah Taaffe; *m* 1989, Louise Frederick; one *s*. *Educ*: Stonyhurst Coll.; Southampton Univ. (LLB Hons Law 1982); Guildford Law Sch. Admitted as solicitor, 1985; Hd of Criminal Defence, Banner Jones Solicitors, 1985–2011; a Dep. Dist Judge, 2006–10. *Recreations*: keen golfer and footballer, avid follower of Chesterfield FC, keen runner. *Address*: c/o Derby Magistrates' Court, St Mary's Gate, Derby DE1 3JR. *E*: DJMC.Jonathan.Taaffe@ejudiciary.net. *Club*: Chesterfield Golf.

**TABACHNIK, Andrew Daniel**; QC 2017; *b* London, 18 Dec. 1968; *s* of Eldred Tabachnik, *qv*; *m* 1998, Margo Miller; two *d*. *Educ*: King's Coll. Sch., Wimbledon; Pembroke Coll., Cambridge (MA 1st Cl.); Columbia Univ. Law Sch. (LLM). Called to the Bar, Inner Temple, 1991; in practice as barrister, specialising in planning and regulatory law, 1995–; Mem., NY Bar, 1993. *Recreations*: cricket, cooking, over-working, opera. *Address*: 39 Essex Chambers, 81 Chancery Lane, WC2A 1DD. *T*: (020) 7832 1111. *E*: andrew.tabachnik@39essex.com.

**TABACHNIK, Eldred**; QC 1982; a Recorder, 2000–08; *b* 5 Nov. 1943; *s* of Solomon Joseph Tabachnik and Esther Tabachnik; *m* 1966, Jennifer Kay Lawson; two *s* one *d*. *Educ*: Univ. of Cape Town (BA, LLB); Univ. of London (LLM). Called to the Bar, Inner Temple, 1970, Bencher, 1988. Lectr, UCL, 1969–72. Pres., Bd of Deputies of British Jews, 1994–2000. *Recreation*: reading. *Club*: Reform.
See also A. D. Tabachnik.

**TABBERER, Ralph Edwin**, CB 2009; Owner and Chief Executive, BBD Education, since 2012; *b* 5 Aug. 1954; *s* of James William Waring Tabberer and Joyce (*née* Eldered); *m* 1996, Helen Margaret White (*d* 2008); one *s* one *d* (and one *d* decd), and three step *s* two step *d*. *Educ*: Gonville and Caius Coll., Cambridge (BA 1976; MA); Brunel Univ. (PGCE 1977). Sen. Advr, W Sussex LEA, 1989–94; Asst Dir, NFER, 1994–97; Department for Education and Employment: Sen. Educn Advr, Standards and Effectiveness Unit, 1997–99; Hd, Nat. Grid for Learning, 1999–2000; Chief Exec., TTA, subseq. TDA, 2000–06; Dir Gen., Schs, DFES, later DCSF, 2006–09; Chief of School, GEMS, Dubai, 2009–12; consultant-at-large, Dubai, 2012. FRSA 2001.

**TABRIZI, Prof. Sarah Joanna, (Mrs M. J. Nath)**, PhD; FRCP, FMedSci; Professor of Clinical Neurology, since 2009, Joint Head, Department of Neurodegenerative Disease, Institute of Neurology, since 2017, and Founder and Director, Huntington's Disease Centre, since 2016, University College London; Hon. Consultant Neurologist, National Hospital for Neurology and Neurosurgery, since 2003; *b* London, 26 Sept. 1965; *d* of Gholam-Reza Sabri-Tabrizi and Jacqueline Sabri-Tabrizi; *m* 2011, Michael John Nath. *Educ*: Heriot-Watt Univ. (BSc 1st Cl. Hons Biochem. 1986); Edinburgh Univ. (MB ChB Hons 1992; Gold Medal); University Coll. London (PhD 2000). MRCP 1995, FRCP 2007; Cert. Completion of Specialist Trng in Neurol. 2003. Jun. Hse Officer, Royal Infirmary Edinburgh, 1992–93; SHO, Hammersmith Hosp. and Nat. Hosp. for Neurol. and Neurosurgery, 1993–94; SHO St Bartholomew's Hosp., London, 1994–95; Medical Registrar, St Thomas' Hosp., London, 1995–96; MRC Clinical Trng Fellow, UCL, 1996–99; Neurol. Specialist Registrar, Nat. Hosp. for Neurol. and Neurosurgery, 1999–2002; Nat. Clinician Scientist, DoH, 2002–07; Department of Neurodegenerative Disease, UCL Institute of Neurology: Clin. Lectr, 2002; Clin. Sen. Lectr, 2003–07; Reader in Neurol. and Neurogenetics, 2007–09. FMedSci 2014. *Publications*: (ed jtly) Huntington's Disease, 4th edn 2014; contrib. articles to jls incl. New England Jl of Medicine, Lancet, Nature, Cell and specialist neurol. jls. *Recreations*: working my way through all the classics in literature, walking and swimming in Gower and Mallorca, boxing, attending the theatre, ballet, opera, cinema and musicals, and, above all, spending as much time as I can with my family. *Address*: Department of Neurodegenerative Disease, UCL Institute of Neurology, Box 104, National Hospital for Neurology and Neurosurgery, Queen Square, WC1N 3BG. *T*: (020) 3108 7473, *Fax*: (020) 7676 2180. *E*: s.tabrizi@ucl.ac.uk.

**TACK, Dame Louise Agnetha L.**; *see* Lake-Tack.

**TACKABERRY, John Antony**; QC 1982; FCIArb; a Recorder, 1988–2005; Commissioner, UN Compensation Commission, 1998–2003; *b* 13 Nov. 1939; *s* of late Thomas Raphael Tackaberry and Mary Catherine (*née* Geoghegan); *m* 1st, 1966, Penelope Holt (*d* 1994); two *s*; 2nd, 1996, Kate Jones (*d* 2008); one *d*. *Educ*: Downside; Trinity Coll., Dublin; Downing Coll., Cambridge (MA, LLM); Mountview Theatre Sch. Called to the Bar, Gray's Inn, 1967, Ireland, 1987, California, 1988. FCIArb 1973; FFB 1979. Teacher in China, 1964–65; Lectr, Poly. of Central London, 1965–67. Adjunct Prof. of Law, Qld Univ. of Technology, 1989. Chm., CIArb, 1990–91 (Mem. Council, 1985–94; Vice-Pres., 1988); President: Soc. of Construction Law, 1983–85; Eur. Soc. of Construction Law, 1985–87; Soc. of Construction Arbitrators, 2007–10; Mem., Dispute Bd Register, RICS, 2014–. Registered Arbitrator, 1993; Mem., many panels of internat. arbitrators. Chm., Street UK, 2004–. *Publications*: (contrib.) Bernstein's Handbook of Arbitration and Dispute Resolution, 1st edn 1987, 2nd edn 1993, (Principal Ed.) 3rd edn 1998, 4th edn 2003; (ed jtly) International Dispute Resolution, vol. I, Materials, 2004, (ed) vol. II, Cases, 2004; contrib. numerous articles. *Recreations*: good food, good wine, good company, photography. *Address*: 39 Essex Chambers, 81 Chancery Lane, WC2A 1DD. *T*: (020) 7832 1111, *Fax*: (020) 7353 3978; Arbitration Chambers, 22 Willes Road, NW5 3DS. *T*: (020) 7267 2137, *Fax*: (020) 7482 1018. *E*: john.tackaberry@39essex.com, john.tackaberry@arbitration-chambers.com. *Club*: Athenæum.

**TACON, Christine Mary, (Mrs William Thomas-Davies)**, CBE 2004; FIMechE; Groceries Code Adjudicator, Department for Business, Energy and Industrial Strategy (formerly Department for Business, Innovation and Skills), since 2013; *b* Eye, Suffolk, 1959; *s* of Peter and Beryl Tacon; *m* 1992, William Thomas-Davies; one *s* one *d*. *Educ*: Wycombe Abbey Sch.; Girton Coll., Cambridge (BA 1981; MEng 1992); Cranfield Univ. (MBA 1986). CEnv 2010; FIMechE 2012; FRAgS 2013. Engrg graduate trainee, then Quality Manager, Coats Viyella, 1982–85; Prodn Planner, then Brand Manager, Mars Confectionery, 1985–92; Mktg Consultant, Vodafone, 1993–94; Mktg Dir, Redland plc, 1994–96; Mktg and Sales Dir, Fonterra, 1996–2000; Man. Dir, Co-operative Farms, 2000–12. Chair, Management and Development Services Ltd, 2016–; non-executive Director: AF Gp (formerly Anglia Farmers), 2012–; Met Office, 2013–16. Mem., NERC, 2013–17. Gov., Harper Adams Univ., 2012–16. Hon. DSc Cranfield, 2014. Mem., Farmers' Co., 2009–. *Recreations*: narrow-boating, veteran cars, walking, gardening (vegetables) and cooking them. *Address*: (office) Victoria House, Southampton Row, Holborn, WC1B 4DA. *E*: christine.tacon@groceriescode.gov.uk. *Club*: Farmers.

**TADIÉ, Prof. Jean-Yves**; Chevalier de la Légion d'honneur, 2002; Chevalier de l'Ordre National du Mérite, 1974; Officier des Palmes académiques, 1988; Commandeur de l'Ordre des Arts et des Lettres, 2011; Professor of French Literature, Université de Paris-Sorbonne, 1991–2005, now Emeritus; Editor, Gallimard, since 1991; *b* 7 Sept. 1936; *s* of Henri Tadié and Marie (*née* Férester); *m* 1962, Arlette Khoury; three *s*. *Educ*: St Louis de Gonzague, Paris; Lycée Louis-le-Grand; Ecole Normale Supérieure (Agrégé de lettres); DèsL Sorbonne 1970; MA Oxford 1988. Lectr, Univ. of Alexandria, 1960–62; Asst Prof., Faculté des Lettres de Paris, 1964; Professor: Univ. de Caen, 1968–69; Univ. de Tours, 1969–70; Univ. de la Sorbonne nouvelle, Paris III, 1970; Hd of French Dept, Cairo Univ., 1972–76; Dir, French Inst., London, 1976–81; Marshal Foch Prof. of French Literature, and Fellow, All Souls Coll., Oxford Univ., 1988–91. Corresp. FBA, 1991; Corresp. Mem., Académie des Beaux-Arts, France, 2019. Grand Prix de l'Acad. française, 1988. Officier de l'Ordre de la Couronne de Belgique, 1979. *Publications*: Introduction à la vie littéraire du XIX$^e$ Siècle, 1970; Lectures de Proust, 1971; Proust et le Roman, 1971; Le Récit poétique, 1978; Le Roman d'aventures, 1982, 2nd edn 2013; Proust, 1983; La Critique littéraire au XX$^e$ Siècle, 1987; (ed) M. Proust, A la Recherche du Temps perdu, 1987–89; Portrait de l'Artiste, 1990; Le Roman au XX$^e$ Siècle, 1990; Marcel Proust (biography), 1996, Eng. edn 2000; (ed) N. Sarraute, Oeuvres Complètes, 1996; Le Sens de la Mémoire, 1999; (ed) W. Scott, Romans, 2003; (ed) A. Malraux, Ecrits sur l'art, 2004; Regarde de tous tes yeux - regarde!: Jules Verne, 2005; De Proust à Dumas, 2006; (ed) W. Scott, Romans II, 2007; Le Songe musical: Debussy, 2008; (ed) Proust et ses amis, 2010; (ed) A. Malraux, Essais, 2010; La Création littéraire au XIXe siècle, 2011; Le Lac inconnu: entre Proust et Freud, 2012; Le Roman d'hier à demain, 2012; (ed) Le Cercle de Proust, 2013, vol. II 2015; Marcel Proust: croquis de l'épopée, 2019. *Recreations*: opera, cinema. *Address*: 15 rue Raynouard, 75016 Paris, France. *Club*: Athenæum.

**TADROS, Prof. Victor**, PhD; FBA 2018; Professor of Law, University of Warwick, since 2006; *b* Reading, 27 Oct. 1972; *s* of Tharwat Fouad Tadros and Wikie Butler-Tadros; *m* 2012, Emily Phillips; two *s* one *d*. *Educ*: Emmbrook Sch., Wokingham; Trinity Coll., Oxford (BA 1994); King's Coll. London (PhD 1998). Lecturer in Law: Aberdeen Univ., 1998–2000; Edinburgh Univ., 2000–06. *Publications*: Criminal Responsibility, 2005; The Ends of Harm, 2011; Wrongs and Crimes, 2016. *Recreations*: playing guitar, reading, music, visiting art galleries. *Address*: School of Law, University of Warwick, Coventry CV4 7AL. *T*: (024) 7615 0409. *E*: v.tadros@warwick.ac.uk.

**TAEL, Dr Kaja**; Ambassador, and Permanent Representative of Estonia to the European Union, since 2016; *b* 24 July 1960. *Educ*: Tartu Univ., Estonia; Estonian Acad. Scis (PhD 1985). Researcher, 1984–90, Dir, 1991–95, Estonian Inst. for Lang. and Lit.; foreign policy advr to Pres. of Estonia, 1995–98; Ministry of Foreign Affairs, Estonia: Exec. Sec., Estonian-Russian Inter-govtl Commn, 1998–99; Dir Gen., Dept of Policy Planning, 1995–2001; Estonian Ambassador to UK, 2001–05; Under Sec. of EU Affairs, 2006–12; Ambassador to Germany, 2012–16. Order of White Star (Estonia), 2000. Order of: Polar Star (Sweden), 1995; Lion (Finland), 1995; Aztec Eagle (Mexico), 1996; Cejalvo Cruz (Spain), 2007; Leopold (Belgium), 2008. *Publications*: translated into Estonian: John Stuart Mills, On Liberty, 1996; Henry Kissinger, Diplomacy, 2002; Eric Hobsbawm, The Age of Extremes, 2002; articles and abstracts for internat. confs. *Address*: Rue Guimard 11–13, 1040 Brussels, Belgium.

**TAFAZOLLI, Prof. Rahim**, PhD; FIET; Professor of Mobile and Satellite Communications, since 2000, Regius Professor of Electrical Engineering, since 2018, Director, Institute of Communication Systems (formerly Centre for Communication Systems Research), since 2010, and Founder Director, 5G Innovation Centre, since 2012, University of Surrey; *b* Abadan, Iran, 24 Jan. 1958; *s* of Nabiolah and Khavar Tafazolli; *m* 1989, Joan O'Regan; two *s* one *d*. *Educ*: Bath Univ. (BSc 1984); King's Coll. London (MSc 1987); Univ. of Surrey (PhD 1995). University of Surrey: Hd, Mobile Communications Rcs. Gp, 1989–2010; Lectr, 1991–98; Reader, 1998–2000. Fellow, Wireless World Res. Forum, 2011. Khwarizmi Internat. Laureate Award, Iran, 2015. *Publications*: (ed) Technologies for the Wireless Future, vol. 1, 2004, vol. 2, 2006. *Recreations*: football, reading. *Address*: 184 Mulgrave Road, Sutton, Surrey SM2 6JT. *E*: r.tafazolli@surrey.ac.uk. *Club*: Arsenal Football.

**TAFFIN de GIVENCHY, Olivier Jean**; Managing Director, and Head, United States West Region, JP Morgan Private Bank; *b* Beauvais, France, 27 Aug. 1963; *s* of Jean-Claude Taffin de Givenchy and Patricia Taffin de Givenchy (*née* Myrick); *m* (marr. diss.); one *s* one *d*. *Educ*: Manhattanville Coll., Purchase, NY (BA Internat. Studies 1985). Citibank, 1985–89; Bankers Trust, 1989–93; JP Morgan, 1993–: Dir, 1999, Chm., 2010, JP Morgan Internat. Bank Ltd; Man. Dir, UK, JP Morgan Private Bank, 2005. Trustee, JP Morgan UK Foundn, 2005; Supervisory Cttee, JP Morgan Chase Foundn, 2006. Chm., Children in Crisis, 2006–12. *Recreations*: tennis, fishing, shooting. *Address*: JP Morgan Private Bank, 2029 Century Park East, Los Angeles, CA 90067, USA. *Club*: Racquet and Tennis (New York).

**TAFIDA, Dr Dalhatu Sarki**, CFR 2011 (OFR 1983); FNMCP; FWACP; High Commissioner of Nigeria to the United Kingdom, 2008–15; *b* Zaria, Kaduna State, 24 Nov. 1940; *s* of Garba Tafida and Badariyyatu Tafida; *m* Salamatu Ndana Mohammed; six *s* three *d*. *Educ*: Coll. of Medicine, Univ. of Lagos (MB BS 1967); Univ. of Liverpool (Postgrad. Dip. Public Health 1972). MRCP 1971; FNMCP 1975; FWACP 1975. Ahmadu Bello University: House Officer, 1967–68; Sen. House Officer, 1968–69; Registrar, 1969–70; Clin. Asst in Medicine, Royal Victoria Infirmary, Newcastle upon Tyne, 1970–71; Sen. Registrar in Medicine, Katsina Specialist Hosp., 1972–73; Consultant Physician, 1973–76, Perm. Sec., 1976–80, Min. of Health, Kaduna; Chief Physician to Pres. of Nigeria, 1980–83; Comr for Health, Agric. and Educn, Kaduna State,

1984–87; Mem., Constituent Assembly to review Nigerian Constitution, 1988–89; Chm. and Pro Chancellor, Univ. of Agric., Makurdi; Federal Minister of Health, 1993–95. Mem. Kaduna North, Senate, 1999–2003 (Senate Majority Leader, 2003–07). Tafidan Zazzau, 1995. *Publications*: Purple Parliament, 2007. *Recreations*: Scrabble, table tennis.

**TAFROV, Stefan Lubomirov;** Permanent Representative of Bulgaria to the United Nations, 2001–06 and 2012–16; *b* Sofia, 11 Feb. 1958; *s* of Lubomir Tafrov and Nadezhda Tafrova. *Educ*: Sofia Univ. (MA in Journalism). Foreign News Editor, Democratzia, newspaper, Jan. 1990; Chief, Foreign Affairs Dept, Union of Democratic Forces, Feb.–Aug. 1990; Foreign Affairs Advr to Pres. of Bulgaria, 1990–92; First Dep. Minister of Foreign Affairs, 1992–93; Ambassador to Italy, 1993–95, to UK, 1995–98; Ambassador to France, and Perm. Deleg. to UNESCO, 1998–2001. *Recreation*: music.

**TAFT, William Howard,** IV; Of Counsel, Fried, Frank, Harris, Shriver & Jacobson, since 2005 (Partner, 1992–2001); *b* 13 Sept. 1945; *s* of William Howard Taft, III and Barbara Bradfield Taft; *m* 1974, Julia Ann Vadala; one *s* two *d*. *Educ*: St Paul's Sch., Concord, NH; Yale Coll. (BA 1966); Harvard Univ. (JD 1969). Attorney, Winthrop, Stimson, Putnam & Roberts, NY, 1969–70; Attorney Advr to Chm., Federal Trade Commn, 1970; Principal Asst to Dep. Dir., Office of Management and Budget, 1970–72, Exec. Asst to Dir, 1972–73; Exec. Asst to Sec., Health, Educn and Welfare, 1973–76; Gen. Counsel, Dept of Health, Educn and Welfare, 1976–77; Partner, Leva, Hawes, Symington, Martin & Oppenheimer, 1977–81; General Counsel, 1981–84, Dep. Sec. of Defense, 1984–89, US Dept of Defense; US Perm. Rep. on N Atlantic Council, 1989–92; Legal Advr, US Dept of State, 2001–05. Mem., DC Bar Assoc., Washington. Bd Mem., Washington Opera, 1977–81, 1992–2001. Woodrow Wilson Vis. Teaching Fellow, Woodrow Wilson Foundn, 1977–81. Dir, Atlantic Council, 1993–2001. *Publications*: contrib. Indiana Law Jl. *Recreation*: tennis. *Address*: Fried, Frank, Harris, Shriver & Jacobson, 801 17th Street, NW, Washington, DC 20006, USA. *Clubs*: Cosmos, Leo, Literary Society (Washington, DC).

**TAGER, Romie;** QC 1995; *b* 19 July 1947; *s* of Osias Tager and Minnie Tager (*née* Mett); *m* 1971, Esther Marianne Sichel; twin *s*. *Educ*: Hasmonean Grammar Sch., Hendon; University Coll. London (Hurst prize; LLB 1st Cl. Hons 1969). Called to the Bar, Middle Temple, 1970; Head of Chambers, Selborne Chambers, 2002–15. Chm., Greenquest Gp, 1998–. Trustee, Jewish Book Council, 2007–. PhD *hc* Bar Ilan, Israel, 2010. *Recreations*: grandchildren, opera, theatre, travel. *Address*: Selborne Chambers, 10 Essex Street, WC2R 3AA. *T*: (020) 7420 9500.

**TAIN, Paul Christopher; His Honour Judge Tain;** a Circuit Judge, since 2005; *b* 18 Feb. 1950; *s* of Reginald Tain and Kathleen (*née* Hoffland); *m* 1971, Angela Margaret Kirkup (marr. diss. 2011); four *s*. *Educ*: London Univ. (BA Hist.); Inst. of Judicial Admin, Birmingham Univ. (MJur). Admitted solicitor, 1975; solicitor, Wolverhampton MBC and N Yorks County Council, 1976–80; private practitioner, 1980–92; Dep. Stipendiary Magistrate, 1989–92; Stipendiary Magistrate, subseq. District Judge (Magistrates' Courts), 1992–2005; Asst Recorder, 1996–2000, Recorder, 2000–05. Columnist, Solicitors' Jl, 1998. *Publications*: Local Authority Lawyers and Childcare, 1980; Childcare Law, 1993; Criminal Justice Act, 1994; Public Order Law, 1996; Public Order: the criminal law, 2001. *Recreations*: sailing, sailing and sailing. *Address*: Lewes Crown Court, Lewes, East Sussex BN7 1YB.

**TAIPALE, Prof. (Anssi) Jussi (Nikolai),** PhD; Herchel Smith Professor of Biochemistry, University of Cambridge, since 2017; *b* Helsinki, Finland, 20 Oct. 1968; *s* of Vappu and Ilkka Taipale; *m* 1998, Minna Tsubari; two *s* one *d*. *Educ*: Helsingin Yhtenäiskoulu; Univ. of Helsinki (BSc 1991; PhD 1996). Postdoctoral Fellow, Johns Hopkins Univ. Sch. of Medicine, 1998–2003; Principal Investigator, 2003–06, Prof. of Med. Systems Biol., 2006–10, Univ. of Helsinki; Prof. of Med. Systems Biol., Karolinska Inst., Stockholm, 2009–. *Publications*: contrib. jl articles. *Recreations*: boating, random statements (in lieu of humour). *Address*: Department of Biochemistry, University of Cambridge, 80 Tennis Court Road, Cambridge CB2 1GA. *E*: ajt208@cam.ac.uk.

**TAIT, Andrew Charles Gordon;** QC 2003; *b* 18 May 1957; *s* of Adm. Sir (Allan) Gordon Tait, KCB, DSC and of Philippa, *d* of Sir Bryan Todd; *m* 1990, Francesca Sulivan; one *s* three *d*. *Educ*: Scots Coll., NZ; St Peter's Sch., Seaford; Eton; Hertford Coll., Oxford (Open Exhibnr; MA Modern History); City Univ. (DipLaw). Called to the Bar, Inner Temple, 1981, Bencher, 2011; in practice as barrister, 1982–; Head of Chambers, Francis Taylor Building, 2012–. Asst Comr, Parly Boundary Commn for England (Fifth Review). Chm., Planning and Envmt Bar Assoc., 2016–. Liveryman, Gardeners' Co., 2011–. *Address*: Francis Taylor Building, Temple, EC4Y 7BY. *T*: (020) 7353 8415. *Clubs*: White's, Hurlingham, Northern (Auckland).

**TAIT, Arthur Gordon;** Secretary-General, Institute of Actuaries, 1991–97; *b* 28 July 1934; *s* of George Aidan Drury Tait and Margaret Evelyn Tait (*née* Gray); *m* 1958, Ann Sutcliffe Gilbert; two *s* two *d* (and one *s* decd). *Educ*: Eton Coll.; St John's Coll., Cambridge (BA Hist., MA). FCIPD. Commnd KRRC, 1953–54. Imperial Chemical Industries, 1957–91: Personnel Dir, Mond Div., 1976–82; Internat. Personnel Manager, 1983–91. Chairman: Friends of Brompton Cemetery, 1998–; Nat. Fedn of Cemetery Friends, 2003–15. Church Warden, St Mary, The Boltons, 2005–09. FRSA. *Publications*: A Story of Staple Inn on Holborn Hill, 2001; St Mary, The Boltons: the country church in Kensington and Chelsea, 2004. *Recreations*: family, travel, friends who visit, following most sports, concerts, theatre, opera, reading. *Address*: 65 Cheyne Court, SW3 5TT. *T*: (020) 7352 5127.

**TAIT, Blyth;** *see* Tait, R. B.

**TAIT, Eric,** MBE 1980; Director of European Operations, 1989–2010, and International Executive Director, 1992–2010, PKF International Ltd (formerly Pannell Kerr Forster, Chartered Accountants); *b* 10 Jan. 1945; *s* of William Johnston Tait and Sarah Tait (*née* Jones); *m* 1st, 1967, Agnes Jean Boag (*née* Anderson) (marr. diss. 1998); one *s* one *d*; 2nd, 1998, Stacey Jane (*née* Todd). *Educ*: George Heriot's Sch., Edinburgh; RMA Sandhurst; Univ. of London (BSc Eng); Churchill Coll., Cambridge (MPhil). 2nd Lieut, Royal Engineers, 1965; despatches 1976; 68 advanced staff course, RAF Staff Coll., Bracknell, 1977; OC 7 Field Sqn, RE, 1979–81; Lt-Col 1982; Directing Staff, Staff Coll., Camberley, 1982–83, retired, at own request, 1983; Sec., Inst. of Chartered Accountants of Scotland, 1984–89. Mem. of Exec., Scottish Council (Develt and Industry), 1984–89. Editor in Chief, The Accountant's Magazine, 1984–89. Chm., European Forum, Nottingham Trent Univ., 1993–98. FRSA 1997. *Recreations*: swimming, hill walking, reading. *Address*: c/o Bank of Scotland, PO Box 17235, Edinburgh EH11 1YH.

**TAIT, Fiona;** Sheriff of Lothian and Borders at Edinburgh, since 2016; *b* Bridge of Allan, 9 Jan. 1966; *d* of John Paterson and Isabella Wyllie Paterson (*née* Fyfe); *m* 1996, Brian John Tait; two *s*. *Educ*: Lornshill Acad., Alloa; Univ. of Edinburgh (LLB 1st Cl. Hons; DipLP). Admitted as solicitor, 1991. Tutor (pt-time), Univ. of Edinburgh, 1990–97; Sheriff (pt-time), 2006–10; All Scotland Floating Sheriff, 2011–13; Sheriff of Tayside, Central and Fife at Perth, 2013–16. *Recreations*: walking, tennis, Duning. *Address*: Sheriff Court House, 27 Chamber Street, Edinburgh EH1 1LB. *E*: sheriff.ftait@scotcourts.gov.uk. *Club*: Dunning Tennis.

**TAIT, Michael Logan,** CMG 1987; LVO 1972; HM Diplomatic Service, retired; Chairman, Oxford and Hertfordshire Consultants, 1995–2014; *b* 27 Sept. 1936; *s* of William and Dorothea Tait; *m* 1st, 1968, Margaret Kirsteen Stewart (marr. diss. 1990); two *s* one *d*; 2nd, 1999, Amel Boureghda (marr. diss., 2015); one *d*. *Educ*: Calday Grange Grammar Sch.; New College, Oxford. Nat. service, 2nd Lieut Royal Signals, 1955–57. Foreign Office, 1961; served MECAS, 1961; Bahrain, 1963; Asst Political Agent, Dubai, Trucial States, 1963; FO, 1966; Private Sec. to Minister of State, FO, later FCO, 1968; First Sec. and Hd of Chancery, Belgrade, 1970; First Sec. (Political), Hd of Chancery and Consul, Amman, 1972; FCO, 1975; Counsellor and Hd of Chancery, Baghdad, 1977; Counsellor, FCO, 1978; Dep. Hd of Delegn, CSCE, Madrid, 1980; Dep. Hd of Delegn and Counsellor (Econ. and Finance), OECD, Paris, 1982; Hd of Economic Relns Dept, FCO, 1984; Ambassador to UAE, 1986–89; Asst Under-Sec. of State with responsibility for Soviet Union and Eastern Europe, 1990–92; Ambassador to Tunisia, 1992–95. *Recreations*: languages, mountains, sailing. *Club*: Garrick.

**TAIT, Prof. Richard Graham,** CBE 2003; DPhil; Professor, School of Journalism, Media and Cultures (formerly Journalism, Media and Cultural Studies), Cardiff University, since 2003 (Director, Centre for Journalism (formerly Centre for Journalism Studies), 2003–12); *b* 22 May 1947; *s* of Dr William Graham Tait and Isabella Dempster Tait (*née* Cumiskey); *m* 1st, 1980, Sandra Janine McKenzie McIntosh (marr. diss. 1984); 2nd, 1995, Kathryn Jane Ellison; one *d*. *Educ*: Bradfield Coll.; New Coll., Oxford (BA Mod. Hist.; MA; DPhil 1978). St Edmund Jun. Res. Fellow, St Edmund Hall, Oxford, 1972–74; BBC Television: Researcher, Money Prog., 1974–75; Producer, Nationwide, 1976–82; Editor: People and Power, 1982; Money Prog., 1983–85; Newsnight, 1985–87; General Election Results Prog., 1987; Independent Television News: Editor: Channel Four News, 1987–90; Channel Four progs, 1990–95; Editor-in-Chief, 1995–2002. A Governor, BBC, 2004–06; a Trustee, BBC Trust, 2007–10; Ind. Trustee, Disasters Emergency Cttee, 2014–. Chm., INSIUK, 2012–13 (Treas., 2013–17). Member: Internat. Bd, IPI, 1998–2004 (Vice-Chm. 2000–06); Adv. Bd, Internat. News Safety Inst., 2003–. Gov., Kensington Prep. Sch., 2013–. FRTS 1996; Fellow, Soc. of Editors, 2002. Lifetime Achievement Award, RTS, 2013. *Recreations*: history, ballet, opera, tennis, ski-ing. *Address*: 2 Central Square, Cardiff University, Cardiff CF10 1PN.

**TAIT, (Robert) Blyth,** MBE 1992; three-day event rider; *b* 10 May 1961; *s* of Robert and Glenise Tait. *Educ*: Whangarei Boys' High Sch., NZ. Individual World Champion: Stockholm, 1990, Rome, 1998; Olympic Games: Individual Bronze, Barcelona, 1992; Individual Gold, Atlanta, 1996; ranked World No 1, 1992, 1994, 1995, 1996, 1998; winner: Burghley Horse Trials, 1998, 2001; Kentucky Horse Trials, 2000. Hon. Dr Essex. *Publications*: Eventing Insights, 1991; Blyth Tait's Cross Country Clinic, 1998; Six of the Best, 1999. *Recreations*: water ski-ing, snow ski-ing, tennis. *E*: blythtait@hotmail.com.

**TAJ, Mohammad,** OBE 2017; President, Trades Union Congress, 2013–14 (Vice-President, 2014–16); *b* Mirpur Azad Kashmir, 7 July 1952; *s* of Mohammed Shaffi and Fazal Begum; *m* Naseem; one *s* one *d*. *Educ*: Bradford Coll. Worker Dir, Yorkshire Rider Ltd, 1993–96. Branch Sec., 1981–2015, Mem., Exec. Council, 1999–2017, TGWU, later Unite the Union. Mem., Gen. Council, TUC, 2001–17. Hon. Fellow, Bradford Coll., 2015. Hon. Dr Bradford, 2014. *Recreations*: politics, mountain walking. *Address*: 6 Ederoyd Drive, Pudsey, Leeds LS28 7RB. *T*: 07929 004831. *E*: mohammad.taj@gmail.com.

**TAK;** *see* Drummond, T. A. K.

**TAKOLIA, Museji Ahmed,** CBE 2011; Executive Chairman, Intellicomm Solutions Ltd, 2009–17; *b* Coventry, 10 Dec. 1960; *s* of Ahmed Suleman Takolia and Momin Takolia (*née* Bhunger); *m* 1987, Noorjehan Ebrahim (marr. diss. 2006); one *s* two *d*. *Educ*: John Gulson Jun. Sch., Coventry; Sidney Stringer Sch. and Community Coll., Coventry; Homerton Coll., Cambridge (BEd Hons 1984); Bristol Univ. (MSc Social Scis 1987). Commonwealth Fund Harkness (Exec. Educn) Fellow, Woodrow Wilson Sch. of Public and Internat. Affairs, Princeton Univ., 1993–94; Social Policy Officer, Hackney CRE; sen. rôles with Bristol CC and Gloucester CC; Advr, Coopers & Lybrand, then PricewaterhouseCoopers; Sen. Civil Servant, Cabinet Office. Mem., Commn for Health Improvement; Mem. Bd, OFSTED, 2006–12. Gp Chm., Metropolitan Housing Partnership, 2003–09. Chm., Members' Panel, NEST Corp., 2011–16. Non-exec. Dir, Glos Hosps NHS Foundn Trust, 2007–10; Chm., Wye Valley NHS Trust, 2014–16. Mem. Bd, Ruskin Coll., Oxford. Chm., CEED Charity, St Paul's Bristol. *Recreations*: public policy and current affairs, avid follower of international cricket and football.

**TALBOT;** *see* Chetwynd-Talbot, family name of Earl of Shrewsbury and Waterford.

**TALBOT OF MALAHIDE,** 11th Baron *cr* 1831 (Ire.); **Richard John Tennant Arundell;** Hereditary Lord Admiral Malahide and Adjacent Seas; JP, DL; farmer and landowner; *b* Salisbury, Wilts, 28 March 1957; *s* of 10th Baron Talbot of Malahide and Laura Tennant; *S* father, 2016; *m* 1984, Jane Catherine Rose Unwin; one *s* four *d*. *Educ*: Stonyhurst Coll.; RAC, Cirencester. JP 1991, DL 2016, Wilts. *Heir*: *s* Hon. John Richard Arundell, *b* 25 June 1998. *Clubs*: Farmers, MCC.

**TALBOT, John Andrew,** DPhil; Executive Chairman, Johnson Service Group plc, 2008–14 (Chief Executive, 2007–08); *b* 2 Aug. 1949; *s* of Robert Talbot and Lucy E. Talbot (*née* Jarvis); *m* 1st, 1969, Susan Hollingbery (marr. diss.); one *s* one *d*; 2nd, 1983, Jennifer Anne Houghton; one *s* two *d*. *Educ*: Queen's Boys Sch., Wisbech; Wolfson Coll., Oxford (DPhil Archaeol. 2016). CA 1971; accountant in manufacturing, 1972–73; Bernard Phillips & Co., Accountants, 1973–75; Spicer & Pegler, 1975–83, Partner, 1979; Partner, Arthur Andersen, 1983–99: Hd, UK Insolvency Practice, 1988; Man. Partner, Worldwide Global Corporate Finance Practice, 1995–99; Administrator, Maxwell Private Cos, 1991; Receiver: Leyland DAF, 1993; Transtec plc, 2000; Sen. Partner, Talbot Hughes, then Talbot Hughes McKillop, LLP, 2001–05; European Chm., Kroll Talbot Hughes, 2005–08; Chief restructuring officer, Marconi PLC, 2002–03. Chm., English Nat. Ballet, 2004–12; Member: Bd, Conservatoire for Dance and Drama, 2001–07; Cttee, Kettles Yard Art Gall., Cambridge, 2003–13. Dir, Plas Ynyshir Hall Hotel, 2016–. *Publications*: Made for Trade: a new view of Icenian coinage, 2017. *Recreations*: contemporary art, iron age history, modern and classical dance. *E*: john@jtalbot.com. *Club*: St Moritz Tobogganing.

**TALBOT, Prof. Michael Owen,** FBA 1990; James and Constance Alsop Professor of Music, University of Liverpool, 1986–2003, Emeritus Professor, 2004; *b* 4 Jan. 1943; *s* of Alan and Annelise Talbot; *m* 1970, Shirley Ellen Mashiane; one *s* one *d*. *Educ*: Welwyn Garden City Grammar Sch.; Royal Coll. of Music (ARCM); Clare Coll., Cambridge (Open, later Meml Scholar; MusB Hons 1963; MA; PhD 1968). Lectr in Music, 1968, Sen. Lectr, 1979, Reader, 1983–86, Univ. of Liverpool. Corresp. Mem., Ateneo Veneto, Venice, 1986. Mem., Slovenian Acad. of Arts and Scis, 2018. Order of Merit (Italy), 1990. *Publications*: Vivaldi, 1978 (Italian, German and Polish edns); Vivaldi, 1979 (Japanese, Brazilian and Spanish edns); Albinoni: Leben und Werk, 1980; Antonio Vivaldi: a guide to research, 1988 (Italian edn); Tomaso Albinoni: the Venetian composer and his world, 1990; Benedetto Vinaccesi: a musician in Brescia and Venice in the age of Corelli, 1994; The sacred vocal music of Antonio Vivaldi, 1995; Venetian Music in the Age of Vivaldi, 1999;

The Finale in Western Instrumental Music, 2001; The Chamber Cantatas of Antonio Vivaldi, 2006; Vivaldi and Fugue, 2009; The Vivaldi Compendium, 2011. *Recreations:* chess, reading novels, travel. *Address:* 36 Montclair Drive, Liverpool L18 0HA. *T:* (0151) 722 3328.

**TALBOT, Prof. Nicholas José,** PhD; FRS 2014; Executive Director, Sainsbury Laboratory, since 2018; *b* Haslemere, Surrey, 5 Sept. 1965; *s* of late Ivan Talbot and of Rosita Talbot; *m* 1989, Catherine Ann Walsh; two *s* one *d.* *Educ:* Midhurst Grammar Sch.; Univ. of Wales, Swansea (BSc Hons Microbiol.); Univ. of East Anglia (PhD Molecular Genetics 1990). Res. Fellow, Purdue Univ., 1990–93; School of Biosciences, University of Exeter: Lectr, 1993–97; Reader, 1997–99; Prof. of Molecular Genetics, 1999–2018; Hd, 2005–10; Dep. Vice Chancellor, 2010–18. Gatsby Plant Sci. Advr, 2009–. Chm., Bd of Govs, Rothamsted Res., 2009–14 (Trustee/Dir, 2006–); Dir/Trustee, 2007–13, Chm., 2013–18, Sainsbury Lab., Norwich. Mem., EMBO 2013–; Mem. Council, John Innes Centre, 2018–. MAE 2014. Ed., The Plant Cell, 2004–10. *Publications:* (ed) Molecular and Cellular Biology of Filamentous Fungi, 2001; (ed) Plant-Pathogen Interactions, 2001; more than 150 scientific articles in learned jls. *Recreations:* walking by the sea, being with my children, looking at the stars. *Address:* Sainsbury Laboratory, Norwich Research Park, Norwich NR4 7UH. *E:* Nick.Talbot@sainsbury-laboratory.ac.uk. *W:* www.twitter.com/talbotlabTSL.

**TALBOT, Patrick John;** QC 1990; a Recorder, 1997–2019; *b* 28 July 1946; *s* of late John Bentley Talbot, MC and Marguerite Maxwell Talbot (née Townley); *m* 1st, 1976, Judith Anne Urwin (marr. diss. 1999); one *s* two *d;* 2nd, 2000, Elizabeth, (Beth), Evans; two *s*. *Educ:* Charterhouse (Foundn Schol.); University Coll., Oxford (MA). Called to Bar, Lincoln's Inn, 1969, Bencher, 1996; in practice at Chancery Bar, 1970–. Member: Senate of Inns of Court and the Bar, 1976–78; Council of Legal Educn, 1977–95 (Vice-Chm., 1992–95). A Judicial Chm., City Disputes Panel, 1997–2000; CEDR Accredited Mediator, 2005–. A Lieut Bailiff of Guernsey, 2000–; a Lieut Seneschal of Sark, 2008–. Mem., Ripieno Choir, 2001– (Chm., 2003–07). Hon. Life Mem., Nat. Union of Students, 1982. *Recreations:* watching cricket, singing, researching family history. *Address:* 9 Grove Road, East Molesey, Surrey KT8 9JS. *Clubs:* MCC, Wimbledon Wanderers Cricket, East Molesey Cricket (Chm., 2009–12).

**TALBOT, Dame Sarah Patricia;** see Connolly, Dame S. P.

**TALBOT RICE, (Alice) Elspeth (Middleton);** QC 2008; barrister; *b* Newcastle upon Tyne, 5 May 1967; *d* of David Middleton Lindsley and Elizabeth Anne Dickinson Lindsley; *m* 1991, Maj. Gen. Robert Harry Talbot Rice, *qv;* three *d*. *Educ:* Queen Mary's Sch., Duncombe Park; Roedean Sch.; Univ. of Durham (BA Hons Law). Called to the Bar, Lincoln's Inn, 1990, Bencher, 2012; in practice as barrister specialising in commercial chancery litigation. *Recreations:* playing polo enthusiastically but badly, playing lacrosse increasingly slowly, playing the French horn occasionally, cooking and eating. *Address:* 24 Old Buildings, Lincoln's Inn, WC2A 3UP. *T:* (020) 7691 2424. *E:* etr@xxiv.co.uk.

**TALBOT RICE, Maj. Gen. Robert Harry,** CBE 2016; FIET; Director Land Equipment, Defence Equipment and Support, Ministry of Defence, 2016–17; *b* London, 19 Aug. 1963; *s* of David Arthur Talbot Rice and Sylvia Dorothea Talbot Rice; *m* 1991, (Alice) Elspeth (Middleton) Lindsley (see A. E. M. Talbot Rice); three *d*. *Educ:* Eton Coll.; RMA, Sandhurst; Durham Univ. (BA Hons 1990); Army Staff Coll. and Cranfield Univ. (MA 1995); Saïd Business Sch., Oxford Univ. (Major Projects' Leadership Acad. course); Inst. of Dirs (Cert. 2013, Dip. 2014, in Co. Direction). FIET 2014. Commnd Welsh Guards, 1983; 1st Battalion: Platoon Comdr, 1983–85; Trng Officer, 1986–87; Adjutant, 1990–91; SO3, G3 Ops, HQ 24 Airmobile Bde, 1992–93; sc 1994–95; i/c Prince of Wales's Co., 1st Bn, 1996–98; Military Asst to ACDS OR Land, MoD, 1998–2000; SO1, J5 Plans, HQ KFOR, Kosovo, 2000; Directing Staff, RMCS Shrivenham, 2001–02; i/c 1st Bn, 2002–04; SO1, Plans, Army Resources and Plans, 2004–05; Asst Dir, Equipment Prog., MoD, 2005–08; Chief Liaison Officer to Iraqi MoD, HQ Multi-Nat. Force, Iraq, 2008; rcds 2009; Dir Equipment, Army HQ, 2009–11; Hd, Armoured Vehicles, Defence Equipment and Support, 2011–16. Regtl Lt Col, Welsh Guards, 2010–15 (Chm., Trustees, 2010–15). Non-exec. Dir, SC Gp Ltd, 2018–. FInstD 2018; CDir 2018. *Recreations:* choral singing, game shooting, polo (Chm., 2016–18, Pres., 2018–, Army Polo). *Address:* c/o Regimental Headquarters Welsh Guards, Wellington Barracks, SW1E 6HQ. *T:* (020) 7414 3291. *Clubs:* Cavalry and Guards; Tidworth Polo.

**TALIJANCICH, Sir Peter Ivan, (Sir Peter Talley),** KNZM 2015 (ONZM 2002); Joint Managing Director, Talley's Group Ltd (formerly Talley's Fisheries), since 1964; *b* Motueka, Nelson, NZ, 11 July 1945; *s* of Ivan and Margaret Talijancich (Talley); *m* 1968, Judith Drummond; one *s* two *d*. *Educ:* Motueka High Sch. Dir, Sunderland Marine Insce Co., UK. Chm., NZ Seafood Industry Policy Council. Founding Trustee and Mem. Bd, Seafarers Trust. Past Pres., NZ Fishing Industry Assoc. *Recreations:* Rugby, recreational fishing, hunting, motor racing. *Address:* Talley's Group Ltd, PO Box 5, Motueka, New Zealand. *T:* (3) 5282800. *E:* peter.talley@talleys.co.nz.

**TALINTYRE, Douglas George;** Director, Office of Manpower Economics, 1989–92; *b* 26 July 1932; *o s* of late Henry Matthew Talintyre and Gladys Talintyre; *m* 1st, 1956, Maureen Diana Lyons (*d* 2004); one *s* one *d;* 2nd, 2010, Mrs Audrey Cruse. *Educ:* Harrow County Grammar School; London School of Economics. BSc (Econ.) 1956; MSc (Industrial Relns and Personnel Management) 1983. Joined National Coal Board, 1956: Administrative Assistant, 1956–59; Marketing Officer, Durham Div., 1959–61; Head of Manpower Planning and Intelligence, HQ, 1961–62; Dep. Head of Manpower, HQ, 1962–64; Head of Wages and Control, NW Div., 1964–66. Entered Civil Service, 1966: Principal, Naval Personnel (Pay) Div., MoD, 1966–69; Senior Industrial Relations Officer, CIR, 1969–71; Director of Industrial Relations, CIR, 1971–74; Asst Secretary, Training Services Agency, 1974–75; Counsellor (Labour), HM Embassy, Washington DC, 1975–77; Head of Policy and Planning, Manpower Services Commn, 1977–80; Department of Employment: Hd of Health and Safety Liaison, 1980–83; Asst Sec., Industrial Relations Div., 1983–86; Under Sec., 1986; Dir of Finance and Resource Management, and Principal Finance Officer, 1986–89. Freeman, Co. of Cordwainers, Newcastle upon Tyne, 1952. *Recreations:* travel, wine, walking, short tennis, jazz. *Address:* 4 Foxborough Court, Maidenhead SL6 2PX. *Club:* Reform.
See also P. A. Rowan.

**TALL, Stephen Joseph Fairweather;** Director, Development and Communications (formerly Development Director), Education Endowment Foundation, since 2012; *b* Epsom, 19 March 1977; *s* of late John Fairweather Tall and of Christine Fairweather Tall; partner, Noa Vázquez Barreiro; two *s*. *Educ:* St Margaret's C of E High Sch., Aigburth, Liverpool; Mansfield Coll., Oxford (BA Mod. Hist. 1998). University of Oxford: Develt Officer, Mansfield Coll., 1999–2002; Dir, Strategy and Develt, St Anne's Coll., 2002–08; Dir, Develt, Bodleian Libraries, 2008–10; Associate Dir, Develt, 2010–12; Actg Dir, Develt, 2011. Mem. (Lib Dem), Oxford CC, 2000–08 (Dep. Lord Mayor, 2007–08). Res. Associate, CentreForum, 2012–15. Liberal Democrat Voice: Ed., 2007–09; Co-Ed., 2009–15; Contrib. Ed., 2015–18. Columnist, ConservativeHome, 2013–15. *Publications:* (contrib.) Politico's Guide to Political Blogging, 2007, 2008; (contrib.) Total Politics Guide to Political Blogging, 2010; (ed) Coalition and Beyond: Liberal reforms for the decade ahead, 2013; (contrib.) One Hundred Days for Early Action, 2015. *Recreations:* family, failing to keep fit, occasional writing. *Address:* c/o Education Endowment Foundation, Millbank Tower, 21–24 Millbank, SW1P 4QP. *E:* sjftall@gmail.com. *Club:* Everton Football.

**TALLEY, Sir Peter (Ivan);** see Talijancich, Sir P. I.

**TALLIS, Prof. Raymond Courteney,** FRCP; Professor of Geriatric Medicine, University of Manchester, 1987–2006; Hon. Consultant Physician in Health Care of the Elderly, Salford Royal Hospitals NHS Trust, 1987–2006; *b* 10 Oct. 1946; *s* of Edward Ernest Tallis and Mary Tallis (née Burke); *m* 1972, Theresa Bonneywell; two *s*. *Educ:* Liverpool Coll.; Keble Coll., Oxford (Open schol., 1964; BA 1967; BM BCh 1970); St Thomas' Hosp. Med. Sch. FRCP 1989. Clinical Res. Fellow, Wessex Neurological Centre, 1977–80; Sen. Lectr in Geriatric Medicine, Univ. of Liverpool, 1982–87. Chairman: Cttee on Ethical Issues in Medicine, RCP, 2003–05; Healthcare Professionals for Assisted Dying, 2011–15. Numerous vis. professorships, named lectures, etc. Mem., various med. socs. Mem. Bd, Compassion in Dying, 2008–11; Patron, Dignity in Dying. FMedSci 2000. Hon. Vis. Prof. in English Literature, Univ. of Liverpool, 2008–13. Hon. DLitt Hull, 1997; Hon. LittD Manchester, 2002; Hon. DSc: St George's, Univ. of London, 2015; UEA, 2017. *Publications:* Not Saussure, 1988, 2nd edn 1995; In Defence of Realism, 1988, 2nd edn 1998; Clinical Neurology of Old Age, 1988; The Explicit Animal, 1991, 2nd edn 1999; (ed jtly) Brocklehurst's Textbook of Geriatric Medicine and Gerontology, 4th edn 1992, 6th edn 2003; Newton's Sleep, 1995; Epilepsy in Elderly People, 1996; Enemies of Hope, 1997, 2nd edn 1999; Theorrhoea and After, 1998; Increasing Longevity: medical, social and political implications, 1998; On the Edge of Certainty: philosophical explorations, 1999; A Raymond Tallis Reader, 2000; A Conversation with Martin Heidegger, 2002; The Hand: a philosophical inquiry into human being, 2003; I Am: a philosophical inquiry into first-person being, 2004; Hippocratic Oaths: medicine and its discontents, 2004; Why the Mind is Not a Computer: a pocket lexicon of neuromythology, 2004; The Knowing Animal: a philosophical inquiry into knowledge and truth, 2005; The Enduring Significance of Parmenides: unthinkable thought, 2008; The Kingdom of Infinite Space: a fantastical journey around your head, 2008; Hunger: the art of living, 2008; Michelangelo's Finger: an inquiry into everyday transcendence, 2009; Aping Mankind: neuromania, Darwinitis and the misrepresentation of humanity, 2011; In Defence of Wonder and Other Philosophical Reflections, 2012; Reflections of a Metaphysical Flaneur and Other Essays, 2013; (ed jtly) NHS SOS: how the NHS was betrayed and how we can save it, 2013; Epimethean Imaginings, 2014; (with Julian Spalding) Summers of Discontent: the purpose of the arts today, 2014; The Black Mirror: fragments of an obituary for life, 2015; The Mystery of Being Human: God, free will and the NHS, 2016; Of Time and Lamentation: reflections on transience, 2017; Logos: the mystery of how we make sense of the world, 2018; Seeing Ourselves: reclaiming humanity from God and science, 2019; *fiction:* Absence (novel), 1999; short stories; *poetry:* Between the Zones, 1985; Glints of Darkness, 1989; Fathers and Sons, 1993; Sunburst, 2019; over 200 scientific papers and articles mainly in the fields of neurology and neurological rehabilitation of older people; numerous pubns in literary criticism, theory and philosophy, especially philosophy of the mind and time. *Recreations:* thinking, my family, walking, music. *Address:* 5 Valley Road, Bramhall, Stockport, Cheshire SK7 2NH. *T:* (0161) 439 2548. *Club:* Athenæum.

**TALLON, John Mark;** QC 2000; FCA; *b* 19 March 1948; *s* of late Claude Reginald Tallon and Blanche Mary Tallon; *m* 1st, 1974, Josephine Rowntree (marr. diss.); one *s* one *d;* 2nd, 1988, Patricia Steel. *Educ:* Rugby Sch. FCA 1970. Called to the Bar, Middle Temple, 1975; Mem., Pump Court Tax Chambers, 1976–. *Recreations:* golf, tennis, reading. *Address:* 16 Bedford Row, WC1R 4EF. *T:* (020) 7414 8080. *Club:* Berkshire.

**TALMA STHEEMAN, Sir Robert Alexander;** see Stheeman, Sir R. A. T.

**TALMON, Prof. Stefan Alexander Gustav,** DPhil; barrister and arbitrator; Supernumerary Fellow, St Anne's College, Oxford, since 2011; Professor of Public Law, Public International Law and European Law, and Co-Director of the Institute of Public International Law, University of Bonn, since 2011; *b* Pforzheim, Germany, 22 Jan. 1965; *s* of Roland and Sigrid Talmon; *m* 2008, Bettina Hahn; two *d*. *Educ:* Neuenbürg Grammar Sch.; Wolfson Coll., Cambridge (LLM 1989); Univ. of Munich; Univ. of Tübingen (First State Exam in Law 1992; Habilitation 2002); Univ. of Oxford (DPhil 1996; MA 2003); Second State Exam in Law, Stuttgart, 1997. Admitted Rechtsanwalt, Germany, 2003; Associate Prof., Univ. of Tübingen, 2002–03; Lectr in Public Internat. Law, 2003–06, Reader, 2006–08, Prof. of Public Internat. Law, Univ. of Oxford, 2008–11; Tutorial Fellow in Law, St Anne's Coll., Oxford, 2003–11; called to the Bar, Lincoln's Inn, 2007; in practice as barrister, 2008–. Visiting Professor: Univ. Aix-Marseille III, 2002, 2003; Yeditepe Univ., Istanbul, 2003; Univ. Panthéon-Assas (Paris II), 2006; Moritz Coll. of Law, Ohio State Univ., 2008; Univ. of Leuven, Belgium, 2010; Xiamen Acad. of Internat. Law, 2012; Centro di Direito Internacional, Belo Horizonte, Brazil, 2013; European University Inst., Florence, 2016. Dir of Studies, Hague Acad. of Internat. Law, 2011. Erskine Fellow, Univ. of Canterbury, NZ, 2006. *Publications:* (jtly) Alles fließt. Kulturgüterschutz und innere Gewässer im Neuen Seerecht, 1998; (ed jtly) The Reality of International Law, 1998; Recognition of Governments in International Law, 1998; (ed) Recognition in International Law, 2000; Kollektive Nichtanerkennung illegaler Staaten, 2006; La non reconnaissance collective des Etats illégaux, 2007; (ed jtly) The Legal Order of the Oceans, 2009; (ed) The Occupation of Iraq, 2012; (ed) Über Grenzen. Colloquium zum 70 Geburtstag von Wolfgang Graf Vitzthum, 2012; (ed jtly) The South China Sea Arbitration: a Chinese perspective, 2014; (ed) Essential Texts in International Law, 2016; contrib. chapters in books; contrib. articles to learned jls, incl. Amer. Jl Internat. Law, British Year Book of Internat. Law, Chinese Jl Internat. Law, Eur. Jl Internat. Law. *Recreation:* walking. *Address:* 20 Essex Street, WC2R 3AL. *T:* (020) 7842 1200, *Fax:* (020) 7842 1270. *E:* stalmon@20essexst.com; Institute for International Law, University of Bonn, Adenauerallee 24–42, 53113 Bonn, Germany. *E:* talmon@jura.uni-bonn.de.

**TALWAR, Rana Gurvirendra Singh;** Co-founder and Chairman, Sabre Capital Worldwide, since 2003; *b* 22 March 1948; *s* of R. S. and Veera Talwar; *m* 1st, 1970, Roop Som Dutt (marr. diss.); one *s* one *d;* 2nd, 1995, Renuka Singh; one *s*. *Educ:* Lawrence Sch., Sanawar, India; St Stephen's Coll., Delhi (BA Hons Econs). Citibank, 1969–97: exec. trainee for internat. banking, 1969–70; various operational, corporate and institutional banking assignments, India, 1970–76; Gp Hd for Treasury and Financial Instns, 1976; Regl Manager for Eastern India, 1977; Gp Hd, Treasury and Financial Instns Gp, Saudi American Bank (Citibank affiliate), Jeddah, 1978–80; COS, Asia Pacific Div., 1981; Regl Consumer Business Manager, Singapore, Malaysia, Indonesia, Thailand and India, 1982–88; Div. Exec., Asia Pacific, 1988–91; Exec. Vice Pres. and Gp Exec. responsible for Consumer Bank in Asia Pacific, ME and Eastern Europe, 1991–95; Exec. Vice Pres., Citicorp and principal subsid., Citibank, resp. for US and Europe, 1996–97; Standard Chartered Plc: Gp Exec. Dir, 1997–98; CEO, 1997–2002. Non-executive Director: Pearson plc, 2000–07;

Fortis SA, 2004–09; Schlumberger Ltd, 2005–08; Chm., Centurion Bank of Punjab, 2004–08. Governor: Indian Business Sch., 1998–; London Business Sch., 1999. *Recreations:* golf, tennis, bridge, travel. *Clubs:* Tanglin (Singapore); Bengal (Calcutta); Delhi Golf (New Delhi).

**TAM, Prof. Patrick Ping Leung,** FRS 2011; FRSB; FAA; Head, Embryology Research Unit, since 1990, NHMRC Senior Principal Research Fellow, since 2000, and Deputy Director, since 2008, Children's Medical Research Institute; Professor, School of Medical Sciences (formerly Discipline of Medicine), Sydney Medical School, University of Sydney, since 2008; *b* 27 Nov. 1952. *Educ:* Univ. of Hong Kong (BSc Hons; MPhil); University Coll. London (PhD 1980). Lectr, 1981–87, Sen. Lectr, 1987–90, Dept of Anatomy, Chinese Univ. of Hong Kong. Croucher Foundn Fellow, Univ. of Oxford, 1986; joined Children's Med. Res. Inst., NSW, 1991. Mok Hing-Yiu Dist. Vis. Prof., Univ. of Hong Kong, 2012–16. FRSB (FInstBiol 1989); FAA 2008; FAHMS 2015. Editor, Development, 2007–. Symington Meml Prize, Anatomical Soc. of GB, 1987; President's Medal, Australia and NZ Soc. of Cell and Develtl Biol., 2007. *Publications:* (ed with J. Rossant) Mouse Development, 2002; contribs to scientific jls incl. Nature, Nature Rev. Genetics, Develtl Biol., Human Genetics, Develt, Develtl Cell, Internat. Jl Develtl Biol., Eur. Jl Cell Biol. *Address:* Children's Medical Research Institute, Locked Bag 23, Wentworthville, NSW 2145, Australia.

**TAM, Robin Bing-Kuen;** QC 2006; *b* 1 June 1964; *s* of Sheung Wai Tam and Arleta Yau Ling Tam (*née* Chang); *m* 2007, Rosemary Jane Anger. *Educ:* Leys Sch., Cambridge; St John's Coll., Cambridge (BA 1985); Inns of Court Sch. of Law. Called to the Bar, Middle Temple, 1986; in practice as barrister, 1987–, specialising in admin. and public law, immigration and asylum work; Standing Prosecuting Jun. Counsel to Inland Revenue, 1993; Jun. Counsel to the Crown, 1994–2006 (A Panel, 1999–2006). *Publications:* (jtly) Asylum and Human Rights Appeals Handbook, 2008. *Address:* Temple Garden Chambers, 1 Harcourt Buildings, Temple, EC4Y 9DA. *T:* (020) 7583 1315.

**TAMARÓN,** 9th Marqués de; **Santiago de Mora-Figueroa;** Spanish Ambassador for Cultural Diplomacy, 2012–17; *b* 18 Oct. 1941; *s* of José de Mora-Figueroa, 8th Marqués de Tamarón, and Dagmar Williams; *m* 1966, Isabelle de Yturbe; one *s* one *d*. *Educ:* Univ. of Madrid; Escuela Diplomática. Lieut, Spanish Marine Corps, 1967; joined Spanish Diplomatic Service, 1968; Secretary: Mauritania, 1968–70; Paris, 1970–73; Banco del Noroeste (on voluntary leave), 1974; Counsellor, Denmark, 1975–80; Minister Counsellor, Ottawa, 1980–81; Private Sec. to Minister of Foreign Affairs, 1981–82; Head of Studies and Dep. Dir, Escuela Diplomática, 1982–88; Dir, Inst. de Cuestiones Internacionales y Política Exterior, 1988–96; Dir, Inst. Cervantes, 1996–99; Spanish Ambassador to the Court of St James's, 1999–2004. Comdr, Orden de Carlos III (Spain), 1982; Gran Cruz, Orden del Mérito Naval (Spain), 1999; Commander: Order of Dannebrog (Denmark), 1980; Order of Merit (Germany), 1981; Officier, Ordre Nat. du Mérite (France), 1974. *Publications:* Pólvora con Aguardiente, 1983; El Guirigay Nacional, 1988, rev. edn 2006; Trampantojos, 1990; El Siglo XX y otras Calamidades, 1993; (jtly) El Peso de la Lengua Española en el Mundo, 1995; El Rompimiento de Gloria, 2003; El Avestruz, Tótem Utópico, 2012; Entre líneas y a contracorriente: Bitácora 2008–2010, 3 vols, 2018. *Recreations:* mountain walking, gardening, philology. *Address:* Castillo de Arcos, 11630 Arcos de la Frontera, Spain.

**TAMBINI, Helen;** *see* Mountfield, H.

**TAMBLING, Pauline Ann,** CBE 2014; arts and education writer and consultant; Managing Director, National Skills Academy for Creative and Cultural Skills, since 2009; *b* 23 April 1955; *d* of James William and Anne Dorling; *m* 1976, Jeremy Tambling; one *s* one *d*. *Educ:* Ely High Sch. for Girls; Stockwell Coll., Bromley (Cert Ed London); Univ. of Leeds (MA). Teacher, 1976–83; Head of Educn, Royal Opera House, 1983–97; Arts Council of England, subseq. Arts Council England: Dir, Educn and Trng, 1997–99; Exec. Dir, Res. and Develt, 1999–2001; Change Prog. Dir, 2001–03; Exec. Dir, Develt, 2003–07; arts consultant, 2007; Exec. Dir, Progs and Industry, 2007–08; Chief Operating Officer, 2008–09, Jt CEO, 2011–13, CEO, 2013–18, Creative and Cultural Skills. Chair: Shape, 2007–16; Da Vinci Studio Sch. for Creative Enterprise, Letchworth, 2013–16. Mem., Strategy Cttee, Clore Leadership Prog., 2003–17. Trustee: Shakespeare Schs Fest., 2007–10; Drama UK, 2013–17; High House Prodn Park, 2014–18; Roundhouse Trust, 2016–. Mem. Bd, Univ. (formerly UC) of the Creative Arts, 2007–13, Deviser/writer, Top Score, TV series, 1996–97; co-dir/researcher, orchestral educn programmes, NFER, 1997–98. FRSA 1990. *Publications:* Performing Arts in the Primary School, 1990; Lessons in Partnership, 1996; articles in Cultural Trends, British Jl Music Educn. *Recreations:* arts, cinema, travel, current affairs. *Address:* 402 Mountjoy House, EC2Y 8BP. *T:* 07983 526830. *E:* paulinetambling@me.com.

**TAMEN, (Maria) Isabel (Bénard da Costa);** Executive Director, Richard Alston Dance Company, 2009–March 2020; *b* Lisbon, 8 July 1963; *d* of Dr Pedro Mário Alles Tamen and Dr Maria Isabel Bénard da Costa Tamen; *m* 1999, Henri Oguike (marr. diss. 2013); one *s* one *d*. *Educ:* Univ. Nova de Lisboa, Lisbon (Modern Langs and Lit. 1982); London Contemp. Dance Sch. (Dip. Contemp. Dance and Choreography 1986). Dancer: Images Dance Co., 1986–88; London Contemp. Dance Th., 1988–94; Richard Alston Dance Co., 1994–99; trainee manager, Independance, 1999–2000; Educn Officer, Sakoba, 2000–02; Gen. Manager, Henri Oguike Dance Co., 1998–2009. *Recreations:* literature, languages, music and dance.

**TAMI, Rt Hon. Mark (Richard);** PC 2018; MP (Lab) Alyn and Deeside, since 2001; *b* 3 Oct. 1962; *s* of Michael John Tami and Patricia Tami; *m* 1992, Sally Daniels; two *s*. *Educ:* Enfield Grammar Sch.; UCW, Swansea (BA Hons). Head of Res. and Communications, 1992–99, Head of Policy, 1999–2001, AEEU. An Asst Govt Whip, 2007–10; an Opposition Whip, 2010–11; Opposition Asst Chief Whip, 2011–. Chm., Welsh PLP, 2006–07. *Publications:* Votes for All: compulsory voting in elections, 2000. *Recreations:* football, cricket, antiques. *Address:* House of Commons, SW1A 0AA.

**TAMWORTH, Viscount; William Robert Charles Shirley;** *b* 10 Dec. 1984; *s* and *heir* of Earl Ferrers, *qv*; *m* 2010, Camilla, *d* of late Richard Lutyens; two *d*. *Educ:* Eton; Christ Church, Oxford (BA 1st cl. Econs and Mgt). Equity research analyst: Citigroup, 2006–09; Liberum, 2009–15; Fund Manager, Artemis, 2015–.

**TAN, Melvyn,** FRCM; pianist; *b* 13 Oct. 1956; *s* of Keng Hian Tan and Sov Yuen Wong. *Educ:* Anglo-Chinese Sch.; Yehudi Menuhin Sch.; Royal Coll. of Music. FRCM 2000. Performer of classical piano repertoire on period instruments, 1983–; solo career, 1985–; extended repertoire to include modern piano, 1996–; performs in internat. music festivals, incl. Austria, Germany, Holland, France, Scandinavia, UK, USA, Japan, Australia, in major venues and with leading orchestras worldwide; pioneered interest in keyboard music of 18/19th centuries, incl. tour with Beethoven's own Broadwood piano, 1992; cycle of complete Beethoven sonatas, Japan, 1994–97. Numerous recordings incl. piano sonatas and complete piano concertos of Beethoven and Debussy Preludes Books 1 and 2, Beethoven and Mozart piano concertos with London Chamber Orch., bagatelles of Beethoven, Czerny variations and Liszt sonata, Ravel's Valses Nobles et Sentimentales, and pieces by Liszt, Weber and Scarlatti. *Recreations:* swimming, wine, travelling to places where free of performing. *Address:* c/o Ching Lee Goh, Culturelink, Singapore. *W:* www.melvyntan.com.

**TAN, Prof. Tian Yuan,** PhD; Shaw Professor of Chinese, University of Oxford, since 2019; Fellow of University College, Oxford, since 2019; *b* Singapore, 24 April 1972; *s* of Kong Urn Tan and Kim Kee Seah; *m* 1999, Puay Li Tay. *Educ:* National Univ. of Singapore (BA, MA); Harvard Univ. (PhD 2006). Teaching Fellow, 2003, Asst Hd Tutor, 2003–06, Harvard Univ.; School of Oriental and African Studies, University of London: Lectr, 2006–11; Sen. Lectr, 2011–13; Reader, 2013–16; Prof. of Chinese Studies, 2016–19; Associate Dean (Res.), Faculty of Languages and Cultures, 2015–18. Sec.-Gen., Eur. Assoc. for Chinese Studies, 2012–18. *Publications:* (ed jtly) Text, Performance and Gender in Chinese Literature and Music: essays in honor of Wilt Idema, 2009; Songs of Contentment and Transgression: discharged officials and literati communities in sixteenth-century North China, 2010; Kang Hai sanqu ji jiaojian (A Critical Edition of Kang Hai's Songs with Introduction, Notes and Two Essays), 2011; (ed jtly) Yingyu shijie de Tang Xianzu yanjiu lunzhu xuanyi (An Anthology of Critical Studies on Tang Xianzu in Western Scholarship), 2013; (jtly) Passion, Romance and Qing: the world of emotions and states of mind in Peony Pavilion, 3 vols, 2014; (ed jtly) 1616: Shakespeare and Tang Xianzu's China, 2016. *Recreations:* books, travel, global gastronomy, jogging, follower of sports, gardening novice. *Address:* University of Oxford China Centre, Dickson Poon Building, Canterbury Road, Oxford OX2 6LU.

**TANAKA, Koichi;** General Manager, Koichi Tanaka Laboratory of Advanced Science and Technology (formerly Mass Spectrometry Laboratory), Shimadzu Corporation, Japan, since 2003 (Assistant Manager, Life Science Laboratory, 2002); *b* 3 Aug. 1959; *m* 1995, Yuko Ikegami. *Educ:* Toyama Chubu High Sch.; Tohoku Univ. (BEng). Shimadzu Corporation: joined Central Res. Lab., 1983; Kratos Analytical Ltd, UK, 1992; R&D Dept, Analytical Instruments Div., Japan, 1992–97; Shimadzu Res. Lab. (Europe) Ltd, 1997–99; Kratos Analytical Ltd, UK, 1999–2002. (Jtly) Nobel Prize in Chemistry, 2002. *Address:* Shimadzu Corporation, 1 Nishinokyo-Kuwabara-cho, Nakagyo-ku, Kyoto 604–8511, Japan.

**TANBURN, Jennifer Jephcott;** research consultant, 1984–94; *b* 6 Oct. 1929; *d* of late Harold Jephcott Tanburn and Elise Noel Tanburn (*née* Armour). *Educ:* St Joseph's Priory, Dorking; Settrington Sch., Hampstead; University Coll. of the South West, Exeter (BSc Econ). Market Research Dept, Unilever Ltd, 1951–52; Research and Information, Lintas Ltd, 1952–66, Head of Div., 1962–66, Head of Special Projects, 1966–74; British Airways Board, 1974–76; Head of Res. and Consumer Affairs, 1975–76, a Dir, 1976–83, Booker McConnell Food Distribn Div. Member: Marketing Policy Cttee, 1977–80, and Potato Product Gp, 1980–82, Central Council for Agricl and Horticl Co-operation; Packaging Council, 1978–82; Chm., Consumers' Cttees for GB and England and Wales under Agricl Marketing Act of 1958, 1982–91; Hon. Mem., Marketing Gp of GB, 2000–. Hon. Vis. Academic, Middlesex Univ., 1997–2003. Hon. Fellow, Durham Univ. (Business Sch.), 1991–94. *Publications:* Food, Women and Shops, 1968; People, Shops and the '70s, 1970; Superstores in the '70s, 1972; Retailing and the Competitive Challenge: a study of retail trends in the Common Market, Sweden and the USA, 1974; Food Distribution: its impact on marketing in the '80s, 1981; (with Judy Slinn) The Booker Story, 2004; articles on retailing and marketing subjects. *Recreations:* television viewing, reading. *Address:* 5 Finch Green, Cedars Village, Dog Kennel Lane, Chorleywood, Herts WD3 5GE. *T:* (01923) 497422.

**TANCRED, Sir Andrew Peter L.;** *see* Lawson-Tancred.

**TANDY, Virginia Ann,** OBE 2009; arts and heritage consultant, since 2011; Director of Culture, Manchester City Council, 2008–11; *b* 29 Feb. 1956; *d* of William Arthur Francis Tandy and Lucy Tandy (*née* Saunders); *m* 1984, Brian Stephen Fell; one *s*. *Educ:* Newcastle upon Tyne Poly. (BA Hons); Manchester Univ. (Post-grad. Dip. Mus. Studies; PhD 2009). Museums Officer, Tameside MBC, 1980–84; Exhibns Officer, Cornerhouse Arts Centre, 1985–87; Visual Arts Officer and Hd, Visual Arts, NW Arts Bd, 1988–94; Dir, Cornerhouse Arts Centre, 1994–98; Dir, Manchester City Galls, 1998–2008. Member: Arts Council Capital Services Adv. Panel, 1998–2001; Creative Industries Develt Service, 2001–09; Commns in the Envmt, 2002–04; Bd, Museums, Libraries and Archives Council, 2004–06 (Mem., Bd of Mgt, NW, 2003–09); Fabric Adv. Cttee, St Paul's Cathedral, 2015–. Museums Association: Mem. Council and Public Affairs Cttee, 2001–10; Professional Vice Pres., 2004–06; Pres., 2006–08. Chair, Curious Minds, 2014–; Trustee: Campaign for Museums, 2005–06; Nat. Heritage Meml Fund, 2009–15 (Mem., NW Cttee, 2009–15); Volunteer Centre Glossop, 2013–14; Nat. Museums of Liverpool, 2016–; Granada Foundn, 2017–(Mem., Adv. Council, 2012–17). FRSA 2006. *Recreations:* family, gardening, singing.

**TANFIELD, Dr Amanda Susannah;** Ambassador to Eritrea, 2012–14; *b* Sutton, Surrey, 12 Dec. 1961; *d* of Maurice and Gillian Pagella; *m* 2003, Matthew Vernon Connolly. *Educ:* Univ. of London (BSc 1st Cl. Genetics 1984; PhD Cytogenetics 1987). Ministry of Defence: various posts, 1988–92; Principal: Directorate of Defence Policy, 1992–95; Resources and Progs (Air), 1995–98; Head: Regl Proliferation, Non Proliferation Dept, FCO, 1998–2001; Iraq Policy, FCO, 2001–03; Pol Counsellor and Dep. Hd of Mission, UK Delegn to OSCE, Vienna, 2003–07; Head: Drugs and Internat. Crime Dept, FCO, 2008–11; Libya Ops, FCO, 2011. *Recreations:* birdwatching and nature, reading, computer games and puzzles, classical music, Daleks.

**TANFIELD, Jennifer Bridget, (Mrs J. B. Bannenberg);** Librarian, House of Commons, 1993–99; *b* 19 July 1941; *d* of Doylah and Phyllis Tanfield; *m* 2002, Nick Bannenberg, Australia. *Educ:* Abbots Bromley; LSE (BSc Econ 1962). House of Commons: Library Clerk, 1963–72; Head, Econ. Affairs Section, later Statistical Section, 1972–87; Head, Parly Div., 1987–91; Dep. Librarian, 1991–93. Mem., IFLA Sect. on Liby and Res. Services for Parlts (Chm., 1997–99). *Publications:* In Parliament 1939–1951, 1991; (ed) Parliamentary Library, Research and Information Services of Western Europe, 2000. *Recreations:* opera, theatre, travel.

**TANKERVILLE,** 10th Earl of, *cr* 1714; **Peter Grey Bennet;** Baron Ossulston, 1682; *b* 18 Oct. 1956; *s* of 9th Earl of Tankerville, and Georgiana Lilian Maude (*d* 1998), *d* of late Gilbert Wilson, MA, DD, PhD; *S* father, 1980. *Educ:* Oberlin Conservatory, Ohio (Bachelor of Music); San Francisco State Univ. (Master of Music). Working as musician, San Francisco. *Heir:* cousin Adrian George Bennet [*b* 5 July 1958; *m* 1st, 1984, Lucinda Mary Bell (marr. diss. 1991); 2nd, 1991, Karel Ingrid Juliet Wensby-Scott]. *Address:* 139 Olympia Way, San Francisco, CA 94131, USA.

**TANLAW,** Baron *cr* 1971 (Life Peer), of Tanlawhill, Dumfries; **Hon. Simon Brooke Mackay;** Chairman, Fandstan Electric Group Ltd (formerly Fandstan Ltd), 1973–2014; *b* 30 March 1934; *s* of 2nd Earl of Inchcape; *m* 1st, 1959, Joanna Susan, *d* of Major J. S. Hirsch; one *s* two *d* (and one *s* decd); 2nd, 1976, Rina Siew Yong Tan, *d* of late Tiong Cha Tan and Mrs Tan; one *s* one *d*. *Educ:* Eton College; Trinity College, Cambridge (MA 1966). Served as 2nd Lt XII Royal Lancers, Malaya. Inchcape Group of Companies, India and Far East, 1960–66; Managing Director, Inchcape & Co., 1967–71, Dir 1971–92; Chm.,

Thwaites & Reed Ltd, 1971–74; Chm. and Man. Dir, Fandstan Electric Group of private cos, 1973–2014. University of Buckingham (formerly University College at Buckingham): Chm., Building Cttee, 1973–78; Mem. Council of Mgt, 1973–2000; Hon. Fellow, 1981; DUniv 1983; Chancellor, 2010–14; Mem. Ct of Governors, LSE, 1980–96. Mem., Lord Chancellor's Inner London Adv. Cttee on Justices of the Peace, 1972–83. Contested (L) Galloway, by-election and gen. election, 1959, and gen. election, 1964. Mem., H of L, 1971–2017. Mem., EC Cttee Sub-Cttee F (Energy, Transport Technology and Research), H of L, 1980–83; Chairman: Parly Liaison Gp for Alternative Energy Strategies, 1981–83; Parly Astronomy and Space Envmt Gp, 1999–2007 (Pres., 2007); Lighter Evenings All-Party Gp, 2007–17. Joint Treasurer, 1971–72, Dep. Chm., 1972, Scottish Liberal Party. Pres., Sarawak Assoc., 1973–75, 1999–2001. Chm., Tanlaw Foundn, 1996–. FBHI 1996; FRAS 2003. *Publications:* Haiku: moments of perception, 2014; articles and papers on horology in learned jls. *Recreations:* horology, astronomy, piscatorial pursuits. *Address:* Tanlawhill, By Langholm, Dumfriesshire DG13 0PQ; 21 Provenance House, 8 Kew Bridge Road, Brentford, Middx TW8 0HS. *Clubs:* White's, Oriental; Puffin's (Edinburgh).

**TANNER, Brian Michael,** CBE 1997; DL; Chairman, Taunton and Somerset NHS Trust, 1998–2006; *b* 15 Feb. 1941; *s* of Gerald Evelyn Tanner and Mary Tanner; *m* 1963, June Ann Walker; one *s* one *d*. *Educ:* Acklam Hall Grammar Sch., Middlesbrough; Bishop Vesey's Grammar Sch., Sutton Coldfield; Bristol Univ. (BA 1st class Hons). CIPFA. Trainee Accountant, Birmingham CBC, 1962–66; Economist, Coventry CBC, 1966–69; Chief Accountant, Teesside CBC, 1969–71; Warwickshire County Council: Asst County Treasurer, 1971–73; Asst Chief Exec., 1973–75; Somerset County Council: County Treasurer, 1975–90; Chief Exec., 1990–97; Treasurer, Avon and Somerset Police Authy, 1975–91. Advr, ACC Cttees on agric., educn, nat. parks, finance, policy, police, 1976–92; Mem., Accounting Standards Cttee, 1982–85; Chief Negotiator with Central Govt on Rate Support Grant, 1985–88; Mem., Investment Cttee, Nat. Assoc. of Pension Funds, 1988–91. Director: Avon Enterprise Fund, 1988–97; Somerset TEC, 1990–97; Jupiter Internat. Green Investment Trust, 1997–2001; Somerset Community Foundn, 2002–07; Redstone Trust, 2007–11. Chairman: SW Reg., Nat. Lottery Charities Bd, 1997–2002; Taunton Town Centre Partnership, 1998–2002; Taunton Vision Commn, 2002; Council, Wells Cath., 2007–12; a Comr, Public Works Loan Bd, 1997–2009; Member: SW Regl FEFC, 1997–99; Wessex Ofwat, 1998–99. Trustee: Central Bureau for Educnl Visits and Exchanges, 1981–92; Avon and Somerset Police Trust, 1999–2009; Somerset Crimebeat, 2000–06; St Margaret's Hospice, Somerset, 2005–13. Governor: Millfield Sch., 1989–99; Bridgwater Coll., 1994–2002; Somerset Coll. of Arts and Technol., 2004–12; Queen's Coll., Taunton, 2009–17. Pres., Wyvern Sports and Social Club, 2011–17. Freeman, City of London, 1990. DL 1998, High Sheriff, 2003–04, Somerset. *Publications:* Financial Management in the 1990s, 1989. *Recreations:* gardening, golf, Rugby, cricket. *Address:* 8 Broadlands Road, Taunton, Somerset TA1 4HQ. *T:* (01823) 337826.

**TANNER, Lt-Col Cecil Eustace;** Vice Lord-Lieutenant of Bedfordshire, 1998–2005; *b* 14 Oct. 1934. Commnd 2nd Lieut, RASC, 1955; GSO 2, MoD, 1969–71; DAQMG (Logistics), HQ Land SE, 1973–75; Lt-Col 1976; CO 156 Regt, RCT(V), 1977; retd 1987. Formerly Cadet EO for Beds, ACF, TA. *Address:* c/o Lieutenancy Office, Central Bedfordshire Council, Chicksands, Shefford SG17 5TQ.

**TANNER, Sir David (Whitlock),** Kt 2013; CBE 2009 (OBE 2003); Performance Director, British Rowing (formerly Amateur Rowing Association), 1996–2018; *b* 29 Dec. 1947; *s* of late Douglas and Connie Tanner. *Educ:* Univ. of Bristol (BA Hons Hist.); Univ. of London (PGCE). Dep. Head, Greenford High Sch., 1985–87; Headmaster, Longford Community Sch., 1987–96. Olympic Rowing Coach, GB Team, Olympic Games: Moscow, 1980; Seoul, 1988; Team Leader, Rowing, Team GB, Olympic Games: Barcelona, 1992; Atlanta, 1996; Sydney, 2000; Athens, 2004; Beijing, 2008; London, 2012; Rio de Janeiro, 2016. Non-executive Director: English Inst. of Sport, 2015–; LTA, 2018–. Gov., Shiplake Coll., Henley-on-Thames, 2003–; Chm., Bd of Govs, Orleans Park Acad., Twickenham, 2018–. FRSA 1992. Freeman: City of London, 2012; Watermen and Lightermen's Co., 2012. DUniv Oxford Brookes, 2013; Hon. LLD Bristol, 2017. *Recreations:* theatre, classical music, sport, travel, history. *Address:* 22 Cumberland Close, St Margarets, Twickenham, Middx TW1 1RS. *T:* (020) 8892 4452. *Clubs:* Leander, London Rowing, Molesey Boat, Remenham.

**TANNER, Elizabeth;** see Tanner, K. E.

**TANNER, James Jonathan;** Managing Director, since 1999, and Chairman, since 2014, Tanners Wines Ltd (Director, since 1993); *b* Shrewsbury, 5 Jan. 1968; *s* of late Richard Tanner and Susan Tanner (née Mowat); *m* 1994, Katherine Barrett, DL; one *s* two *d*. *Educ:* Radley Coll., Abingdon; Univ. of Bristol (BSc Hons Geog.); Imperial Coll. Business Sch. (MBA, DIC). Dir, 1993–, Man. Dir, 1999–, Tanners Shrewsbury Ltd. Dir, 1999–, Chm., 2015–, Merchant Vintners Co. Ltd. *Recreations:* hunting, fishing, gardening, travel. *Address:* Tanners Wines Ltd, 26 Wyle Cop, Shrewsbury, Shropshire SY1 1XD. *T:* (01743) 234500, *Fax:* (01743) 234501. *E:* secretarial@tanners-wines.co.uk. *Club:* Flyfishers'.

**TANNER, Prof. (Kathleen) Elizabeth,** OBE 2016; DPhil; CEng, FREng, FRSE; FIMechE, FIMMM; FIPEM; Bonfield Professor of Biomedical Materials, Queen Mary, University of London, since 2018; *b* 20 March 1957; *d* of late John Darley Tanner and Elizabeth Gordon Tanner (née Holmes). *Educ:* Wycombe Abbey Sch.; Lady Margaret Hall, Oxford (MA; DPhil 1985). CEng 1989; FIMechE 1994; FIMMM (FIM 1997); FBSE 2004; CSci 2004; FREng 2006; FIPEM 2013. Queen Mary and Westfield College, subsequently Queen Mary, University of London: Res. Asst, 1983–88; EPSRC Advanced Res. Fellow, 1988–93; Lectr, 1993–95; Reader, 1995–98; Prof. of Biomedical Materials, 1998–2007; Associate Dir of IRC in Biomed. Materials, 1998–2001; Dean of Engrg, 1999–2000; Prof. of Biomed. Materials, Univ. of Glasgow, 2007–18. Adjunct Prof., Dept of Orthopaedics, Lund Univ., Sweden, 1998–. Pres., UK Soc. for Biomaterials, 2000. Sec., Eur. Soc. for Biomaterials, 2005–09. Fellow, Eur. Alliance for Med. and Biol Engrg and Sci., 2015; FRSE 2015. Hon. PhD Lund, 2017. Gisela Sturm Prize, Eur. Fedn of Nat. Assocs in Orthopaedics and Traumatol., 1996; Göran Selvik Prize, Eur. Orthopaedics Res. Soc., 1999; President's Prize, UK Soc. for Biomaterials, 2009. *Publications:* (ed jtly) Bioceramics 4, 1991; (ed jtly) Strain Measurement in Biomechanics, 1992; (ed jtly) Biomaterials for Spinal Applications, 2012; res. papers on biomaterials and biomechanics in learned jls. *Recreations:* riding, tennis, cookery, dress-making. *Address:* School of Engineering and Materials Science, Queen Mary, University of London, Mile End Road, E1 4NS. *T:* (020) 7882 6785. *E:* k.e.tanner@qmul.ac.uk.

**TANNER, Rt Rev. Mark Simon Austin;** see Berwick, Bishop Suffragan of.

**TANNER, Dame Mary (Elizabeth),** DBE 2008 (OBE 1999); European President, World Council of Churches, 2006–13; *b* 23 July 1938; *d* of Harold Fussell and Marjorie (née Teucher); *m* 1961, John Bryan Tanner; one *s* one *d*. *Educ:* Colston's Girls' Sch., Bristol; Birmingham Univ. (BA Hons). Lecturer in: OT and Hebrew, Hull Univ., 1960–67; OT and Hebrew, Bristol Univ., 1972–75; OT, Westcott House, Cambridge, 1978–82; Theol Sec., Bd for Mission and Unity, C of E, 1982–91; Sec., Council for Christian Unity, General Synod of C of E, 1991–98. Lay Canon, Guildford Cathedral, 2002. Visiting Professor: Gen. Seminary, NY, 1988, 1998; Pontifical Univ. of St Thomas Aquinas, Rome, 2000. Chm., Gov. Council, Cambridge Fedn of Theol Colls, 2015–18. DD Lambeth, 1988; Hon. DD: General Seminary, NY, 1991; Birmingham, 1997; Virginia Seminary, 1999; Hull, 2010; Liverpool Hope, 2012. Plaque of St Erik, Ch of Sweden, 1997. Officer's Cross, Order of Merit (Germany), 1991; Comdr, Royal Order of the Polar Star (Sweden), 2000. *Publications:* essays in: Feminine in the Church, 1984; The Study of Anglicanism, 1988; Runcie by His Friends, 1989; Women and Church, 1991; Encounters for Living, 1995; Living Evangelism, 1996; Festschrift for Jean Tillard, 1996; The Vision of Christian Unity, 1997; A Church for the 21st Century, 1998; Ecumenical Theology in Worship, Doctrine and Life, 1999; Runcie on Reflection, 2002; The Unity we have and the Unity we seek, 2003; Apostolicity and Unity, 2003; Seeking the Truth of Change in the Church, 2004; Cracks in the Wall, 2005; The Holy Spirit, the Church and Christian Unity, 2005; A Theology for Europe, 2005; One Lord, One Faith, One Baptism, 2006; Who is That Man?: Christ in the renewal of the Church, 2006; BEM at 25: essays in honour of Lukas Vischer, 2007; Inter-Church Relations, Developments and Perspectives: a tribute to Bishop Anthony Farquhar, 2008; Receptive Ecumenism and the Call to Catholic Learning, 2008; Some Implications for a Common Martyrology, 2010; The Ecumenical Patriarch Bartholomew, 2012; Celebrating a Century of Ecumenism, 2012; Unity in Process, 2012; Theological Studies and Ecumene, 2013; Hope of Unity: living ecumenism today, 2013; More Than I Can Say, 2015; Towards Unity: ecumenical dialogue 500 years after the Reformation, 2017; articles in One in Christ, Ecclesiology. *Recreations:* music, gardening. *Address:* Bainton Farmhouse, Bainton, Stamford, Lincs PE9 3AF. *T:* (01780) 740216.

**TANNER, Matthew Richard,** MBE 2007; Director and Chief Executive, SS Great Britain Trust, since 2000; *b* Tynemouth, 3 April 1966; *s* of John and Valerie Tanner; *m* 1st, 2000, Rebecca Stevens (marr. diss. 2012); one *s* two *d*; 2nd, 2013, Rhian Tritton. *Educ:* Sevenoaks Sch., Kent; St Andrews Univ. (MA Hons Classics; MPhil Maritime Archaeol.). Curator, Scottish Fisheries Mus., 1990–93; Maritime Curator, Merseyside Maritime Mus., 1993–97; Curator, SS Great Britain Project, 1997–2000. Member: Adv. Cttee on Historic Ships, DCMS, 2006–10; Arts Council SW Area Cttee, 2013–18. Chm., Assoc. of Ind. Museums, 2011–16 (Vice Chm., 2008–11). Pres., Internat. Congress of Maritime Museums, 2019–. Trustee: Underfall Restoration Trust, 2007–13 (Hon. Vice Pres., 2013–); Bristol Ensemble (formerly Emerald Ensemble) Ltd, 2008–11; St George's Trust, 2009–15; Black Country Living Mus., 2013–17. FRSA. Hon. LLD Bristol 2015. *Publications:* Scottish Fishing Boats, 1995; The Ship and Boat Collection of Merseyside Maritime Museum, 1995; (ed) Manual of Maritime Curatorship, 2003; Royal Yacht Mary: the discovery of the first royal yacht, 2008. *Recreations:* classical music (listening and playing), sailing, popular science writings. *Address:* c/o SS Great Britain Trust, Great Western Dock, Bristol BS1 6TY. *T:* (0117) 926 0680, *Fax:* (0117) 925 5788. *E:* matthewt@ssgreatbritain.org.

**TANNER, Meg;** see Beresford, M.

**TANNER, Prof. Roger Ian,** PhD; FRS 2001; FAA, FTSE; P. N. Russell Professor of Mechanical Engineering, University of Sydney, since 1975; *b* 25 July 1933; *s* of Reginald Jack Tanner and Ena Maud Tanner (née Horsington); *m* 1957, Elizabeth Bogen; two *s*, three *d*. *Educ:* Univ. of Bristol (BSc 1956); Univ. of California (MS 1958): Manchester Univ. (PhD 1961). FAA 1979; FTSE 1977. Lectr, Manchester Univ., 1958–61; Reader, Univ. of Sydney, 1961–66; Prof. Brown Univ., Providence, USA, 1966–75. *Publications:* Engineering Rheology, 1985, 2nd edn 2000; (with K. Walters) Rheology: an historical perspective, 1998; several hundred jl papers. *Recreations:* tennis, golf. *Address:* School of Aerospace, Mechanical and Mechatronic Engineering, University of Sydney, Sydney, NSW 2006, Australia. *T:* (2) 9351 7153.

**TANNER, Simon John,** FFPH; Regional Director of Public Health for London, Director of Public Health, Strategic Health Authority for London, and Health Adviser to Greater London Authority, 2007–13; *b* 2 Sept. 1957; *s* of John George Tanner and Marianne Tanner; *m* 1982, Katrina Anne Morris; two *d*. *Educ:* St Olave's and St Saviour's Grammar Sch., Orpington; Univ. of Southampton (BM 1981); London Univ. (MSc 1993); DCH 1983; DRCOG 1984; MRCGP 1985; MFPHM 1997, FFPH 2003. Principal in gen. practice, Alresford, 1986–93; Specialist Registrar in Public Health, 1993–97; Consultant in Public Health Medicine, 1997–99; Director of Public Health: N and Mid Hampshire HA, 1999–2002; Hampshire and IoW Strategic HA, 2002–06; Regl Dir of Public Health, NHS S Central, 2006–07. Sen. Mgt Advr to PHE, 2013–14; Strategic Advr to LSHTM, 2013–15. Member: Responsible Gambling Strategy Bd, 2013–; Treatment Expert Panel, Responsible Gambling Trust, 2014–17. *Recreations:* cycle touring, piano playing, my family.

**TANNOCK, Dr (Timothy) Charles Ayrton;** Member (C) London, European Parliament, 1999–2019; *b* 25 Sept. 1957; *s* of Robert Cochrane William Tannock and Anne (née England); *m* 1st, 1984, Rosa Maria Vega Pizarro (marr. diss. 1988); one *s*; 2nd, 2007, Dr Silvia Janicinova; one *s* twin *d*. *Educ:* St George's Sch., Rome; St Julian's Sch., Lisbon; Bradfield Coll.; Balliol Coll., Oxford (BA Hons Natural Scis; MA); Middlesex Hosp. Med. Sch. (MB BS). MRCPsych 1988. House surgeon, Middx Hosp., and house physician, Harefield Hosp., 1984–85; W London Psychiatric Registrar Rotation, Charing Cross and Westminster Hosps, 1985–90; Res. Fellow, Charing Cross and Westminster Hosp. Med. Sch., 1988–90; N London Psychiatric Sen. Registrar Rotation, UCH and Middx Hosp., 1990–95; Consultant Psychiatrist and Hon. Sen. Lectr, Camden and Islington NHS Community Trust at UCH and UCL Med. Sch., 1995–99. European Parliament: Member: Economic and Monetary Affairs Cttee, 1999–2001; Foreign Affairs, Human Rights, Common Security and Defence Policy Cttee, 2002–19 (Vice-Pres., EP-Human Rights Sub-Cttee, 2004–07); Cons. Party Human Rights Commn, 2011–19; substitute Member: Envmt, Public Health and Consumer Affairs Cttee, 1999–2004; Develt Cttee, 2000–01; Economic and Monetary Affairs, 2002–08; Conservative delegation: financial services spokesman, 1999–2001, Asst Whip, 2000–03, Dep. Chief Whip, 2003–05; foreign affairs spokesman, 2002–19; Foreign Affairs and Human Rights Co-ordinator, ECR Gp, 2009–; Member: EP-Slovakia Jt Parly Cttee, 1999–2004; EP-Ukraine, Belarus and Moldova Delegn, 2002–04 (Vice-Pres., Ukraine Delegn, 2004–09); Vice-Pres., EP Delegn to NATO Parly Assembly, 2009–14. Contested (C) London, EP, 2019. Mem. (C), RBK&C, 1998–2000. Freeman: City of London, 2000; City of Cartagena, Colombia, 2006. Commendatore, Order of St Maurice and St Lazarus, 2000; Order of Merit (Ukraine), 2006; Presidential Medal of Mkhitar Gosh (Armenia), 2009; Gran Official, Order of San Carlos (Colombia), 2010; Medal of Honour, Legislative Yuan of Taiwan, Republic of China, 2011; Presidential Order of Excellence (Georgia), 2013; Order of Brilliant Star (Taiwan), 2014; Presidential Order of Gratitude (Armenia), 2016; Special Dip. of Appreciation (Slovakia), 2018. *Publications:* political: Community Care: the need for action, 1989; A Marriage of Convenience - or reform of the Community Charge, 1991; medical: numerous contribs to med. jls in areas of mood disorders and chronic fatigue syndrome; numerous articles in internat. press and for Project Syndicate. *Recreations:* travel, family. *E:* charles@charlestannock.com. *W:* www.charlestannock.com.

**TANNOUDJI, Claude C.;** see Cohen-Tannoudji, C.

**TANSEY, Geoffrey William;** freelance writer and consultant, since 1981; *b* 3 June 1950; *s* of William Tansey and Lucy Tansey (née Dando); *m* 1973, Kathleen Allan Christie; two *d*. *Educ:* Prescot Grammar Sch.; Univ. of Aberdeen (BSc Hons Soil Sci); Sussex Univ. (MSc Hist. and Social Studies of Sci.); Case Western Reserve Univ.

(Rotary Foundn Grad. Fellow in Hist. of Sci. and Technol.). Editl asst, Energy Policy, 1974–75; Asst Ed., Food Policy, 1975–77; freelance writer, 1977–78; Tech. Co-operation Officer, Ege Univ., Izmir, ODA, 1978–81. Consultant on develt work in Turkey, Albania, Kazakhstan, Mongolia; contributor to BBC, Financial Times and specialist media; advisor on food biodiversity and intellectual property: to Quaker UN Office, Geneva, 2000–07; Quaker Internat. Affairs Prog., Ottawa, 2003–07. Chm., Fabian Commn on Food and Poverty, 2014–15; Curator, Food Systems Acad., 2014–; Mem., Food Ethics Council, 2000– (Trustee, 2003–16). Hon. Vis. Prof. in Food Policy, Leeds Metropolitan Univ., 1996–99; Hon. Visiting Fellow: Food Policy Res. Unit, Univ. of Bradford, 1990–97; Centre for Rural Econ., Univ. of Newcastle upon Tyne, 2005–; Hon. Vis. Res. Fellow, Dept of Peace Studies, Univ. of Bradford, 2000–15; Hon. Teaching Fellow, Lancaster Envmt Centre, Univ. of Lancaster, 2016–; Hon. Res. Fellow, Geog. and Planning Sch., Cardiff Univ., 2017–. Joseph Rowntree Charitable Trust funded Visionary, working for a fair and sustainable food system, 2006–10. Hon. Campaigns Consultant, World Develt Movt, 1989–94. Derek Cooper Award for best food campaigner/educator, BBC Radio Food and Farming Awards, 2008. *Publications:* (ed jtly) A World Divided: militarism and development after the Cold War, 1994; (with A. Worsley) The Food System: a guide, 1995; (ed with J. D'Silva) The Meat Business: devouring a hungry planet, 1999; (ed jtly) Negotiating Health: intellectual property and access to medicines, 2006; (ed with T. Rajotte) The Future Control of Food: a guide to international negotiations and rules on intellectual property, biodiversity and food security, 2008 (Derek Cooper Award for Campaigning and Investigative Food Writing, Guild of Food Writers, 2009); contrib. various monographs, book chapters and jl articles on food, agriculture, develt and intellectual property. *Recreations:* reading, cinema. *E:* geoff@tansey.org.uk. *W:* www.tansey.org.uk. *Club:* Penn.

**TANSEY, Rock Benedict;** QC 1990; a Recorder, 1995–2014; *m* 1964, Wendy Carver; one *s* two *d*. *Educ:* Bristol Univ. (LLB Hons; Dip. Social Studies). Called to the Bar, Lincoln's Inn, 1966, Bencher, 2004. Chm., European Criminal Bar Assoc. of Defence Advocates, 1996–2003. *Recreations:* politics, theatre, opera, football, tennis, golf.

**TANSLEY, (Anthony) James (Nicholas);** Manager (formerly Lead Associate), International Banks Division, Prudential Regulatory Authority, Bank of England, since 2014 (Senior Associate, 2013–14); *b* 19 July 1962; *er s* of late Thomas Anthony Tansley and Marian Tansley; *m* 1998, Bláithín Mary Curran; two *s* one *d* (of whom one *s* one *d* are twins). *Educ:* Tonbridge Sch.; St John's Coll., Oxford (MA); Sch. of Oriental and African Studies, Univ. of London (MSc); London Business Sch. (MSc). Joined FCO, 1984: lang. trng, 1986; Second Secretary (Chancery): Riyadh, 1988–89; Baghdad, 1989–91; First Secretary: FCO, 1991–94; Dublin, 1994–98; Counsellor and Dep. Hd of Mission, Muscat, 1998–2001; Sloan Masters Prog., London Business Sch., 2002–03; Hd, Strategic Planning Team, FCO, 2003–05; Hd, British Office, and Consul-Gen., Basra, 2005–06; Dep. High Comr, Abuja, 2006–08; Hd of Africa Dept (Equatorial), FCO, 2008–09. Associate, Building Societies Div., later UK Banks and Mutuals Dept, FSA, 2010–13. Mem. (C), Kent CC, 2012–. *Recreations:* Islamic architecture, history, cricket, wine. *Address:* c/o Bank of England, 20 Moorgate, EC2R 6DA.

**TANSLEY, Mridul;** *see* Hegde, M.

**TANTER, Katharine Mary;** *see* Braddick, K. M.

**TANTUM, Sir Geoffrey Alan,** Kt 2018; CMG 1995; OBE 1981; Middle East consultant; HM Diplomatic Service, retired; *b* 12 Nov. 1940; *s* of George Frederick Tantum and Margaret Amelia Tantum (*née* Goozée); *m* 1st, 1977, Caroline Kent (marr. diss. 2005); three *d*; 2nd, 2007 (marr. diss., 2014), partner, 2015, Carin Lake (*née* Wood); two step *d*. *Educ:* Hampton Grammar Sch.; RMA Sandhurst; St John's Coll., Oxford (MA 1st Class Hons Oriental Studies (Arabic)). MCIL. HM Forces, 1959–66; joined Diplomatic Service, 1969; Kuwait, 1970–72; Aden, 1972–73; FCO, 1973–76; Amman, 1977–80; FCO, 1980–85; Counsellor, Rome, 1985–88; FCO, 1988–95. Mem. Sen. Adv. Bd, Good Governance Gp, 2008–14. Order of the Star of Jordan, 1995. *Publications:* Muslim Warfare: Islamic arms and armour, 1979. *Recreations:* sailing, oriental studies. *Club:* Travellers.

**TANZER, His Honour John Brian Camille;** a Circuit Judge, 2001–16; *b* 27 Dec. 1949; *s* of late William and Edith Tanzer; *m* 1980, Suzanne Coates, *qv*; two *s*. *Educ:* Town Sch., NY; St Faith's Sch., Cambridge; The Leys, Cambridge; Keble Coll., Oxford; Sussex Univ. (BA); Inns of Court Sch. of Law. Teacher, Japan, 1968; engr, Southampton, 1973; called to the Bar, Gray's Inn, 1975; in practice, specialising in criminal and common law, Brighton, 1975–91, London, 1991–2001; involved with estabt of eJudiciary and Criminal Justice Efficiency Prog., 2013–16, full-time in judicial IT, 2016. Dir, Legal IT Strategies Ltd, 2016–. *Recreations:* sailing, ski-ing, photography, computing. *Address:* Woodfield House, Isaacs Lane, Burgess Hill, W Sussex RH15 8RA. *E:* john@tanzer.co.uk. *Clubs:* Travellers, Bar Yacht; Royal Gibraltar Yacht.

**TAO, Prof. Terence Chi-Shen,** PhD; FRS 2007; James and Carol Collins Professor of Mathematics, University of California, Los Angeles, since 2007; *b* Adelaide, 17 July 1975; *s* of Dr Billy Tao and Grace Tao; *m*; one *s*. *Educ:* Flinders Univ., S Australia (BSc Maths 1991; MSc Maths 1992); Princeton Univ. (PhD Maths 1996). Assistant researcher: Flinders Med. Centre, 1992–94; Princeton Univ., 1993–94; University of California, Los Angeles: Hedrick Asst Prof., 1996–98; Actg Asst Prof., 1999; Asst Prof., 2000; Prof., 2000–. Fulbright Postgrad. Schol., 1992–95. Vis. Fellow, 1999, Vis. Prof., 2000, Univ. of NSW; Hon. Prof., ANU, 2001–03; CMI Long-term Prize Fellow, Clay Mathematical Inst., 2001–03; MacArthur Fellow, MacArthur Foundn, 2007–11. Corresp. Mem., Australian Acad. Scis, 2006; For. Mem., NAS, 2008. Salem Prize, 2000; Bôcher Meml Prize, 2002, (jtly) Levi L. Conant Award, 2004, Amer. Math. Soc.; Clay Res. Award, Clay Mathematical Inst., 2003; Australian Mathematical Soc. Medal, 2005; Fields Medal, IMU, 2006; Ramanujan Prize, Shanmugha Arts, Sci., Technol. and Res. Acad., India, 2006; Ostrowski Prize, Ostrowski Foundn, 2007. *Publications:* Solving Mathematical Problems: a personal perspective, 1992; Analysis (2 vols), 2006; (with Van Vu) Additive Combinatorics, 2006; Nonlinear Dispersive Equations: local and global analysis, 2006; contribs to jls incl. Annals Maths, Acta Mathematica, Amer. Jl Maths. *Address:* Department of Mathematics, University of California, Los Angeles, Box 951555, Los Angeles, CA 90095–1555, USA.

**TAPLIN, Prof. Oliver Paul,** DPhil; FBA 1995; Professor of Classical Languages and Literature, University of Oxford, 1996–2008; Tutorial Fellow in Classics, Magdalen College, Oxford, 1973–2008, now Emeritus; *b* 2 Aug. 1943; *s* of Walter Taplin and Susan (*née* Rosenberg); *m* 1st, 1964, Kim Stampfer (marr. diss. 1996); one *s* one *d*; 2nd, 1998, Beaty Rubens; one *d*. *Educ:* Sevenoaks Sch.; Corpus Christi Coll., Oxford (MA; DPhil 1974; Hon. Fellow 2015). Fellow by Examination, Magdalen Coll., Oxford, 1968–72; Fellow, Center for Hellenic Studies, Washington, 1970–71; Lectr, Bristol Univ., 1972–73; Reader in Greek Lit., Oxford Univ., 1994–96. Visiting Professor: Dartmouth Coll., 1981; UCLA, 1987, 1990. Pres., Classical Assoc., 1999. Dr *hc* Athens, 2013. *Publications:* The Stagecraft of Aeschylus, 1977; Greek Tragedy in Action, 1978; Greek Fire, 1989; (jtly) An Odyssey Round Odysseys, 1990; Homeric Soundings, 1992; Comic Angels, 1993; (ed) Literature in the Greek and Roman Worlds, 2000; Pots and Plays, 2007; (ed jtly) The Pronomos Vase and its Context, 2010; Sophocles, Four Tragedies: a new verse translation, 2015; (trans.) The Oresteia, 2018. *Recreations:* theatre, swimming in the Aegean. *Address:* Magdalen College, Oxford OX1 4AU. *T:* (01865) 276000.

**TAPOLCZAY, Dr David Joszef,** CChem, FRSC; CSci; Chairman, Nuformix plc, since 2017; *b* Oldham, Lancs; *s* of Joseph and Mavis Tapolczay. *Educ:* Wallington High Sch. for Boys; Univ. of Southampton (BSc Hons; PhD). Postdoctoral Res. Fellow, Univ. of Oxford; Sen. Vice Pres., Millennium Pharmaceuticals Inc., 2000–03; CSO, Sigma Aldrich Fine Chemicals, 2003–05; Vice Pres., GlaxoSmithKline Pharmaceuticals, 2005–08; CEO, Med. Res. Council Technol., 2008–18. Trustee, St George Street Capital Ltd, 2018–. FInstD. *Recreations:* sport, weight training. *Address:* Nuformix plc, 6th Floor, 60 Gracechurch Street, EC3V 0HR. *Club:* Royal Over-Seas League.

**TAPPER, Prof. Colin Frederick Herbert;** Professor of Law, Oxford University, 1992–2002; Fellow, Magdalen College, Oxford, 1965–2002, now Emeritus; *b* 13 Oct. 1934; *s* of Herbert Frederick Tapper and Florence Gertrude Tapper; *m* 1961, Margaret White; one *d*. *Educ:* Bishopshalt Grammar Sch.; Magdalen Coll., Oxford. Lectr, LSE, 1959–65; All Souls Reader in Law, Oxford Univ., 1979–92. Special Consultant on Computer Law to Masons (Solicitors), 1990–2002. Visiting Professor, Universities of: Alabama, 1970; NY, 1970; Stanford, 1975; Monash, 1984; Northern Kentucky, 1986; Sydney, 1989; Western Australia, 1991. *Publications:* Computers and the Law, 1973; Computer Law, 1978, 4th edn 1990; (ed) Crime Proof and Punishment, 1981; (ed) Cross on Evidence, 6th edn 1985 to 12th edn (as Cross and Tapper on Evidence) 2010; (ed) Cross and Wilkins Introduction to Evidence, 6th edn 1986; (ed) Handbook of European Software Law, 1993. *Recreations:* reading, computing, writing. *Address:* Corner Cottage, Stonesfield, Oxon OX29 8QA. *T:* (01993) 891284.

**TAPPIN, Michael;** Lecturer in Politics, School of Politics and the Environment (formerly Department of American Studies), 1974–2010, Fellow, since 2010, University of Keele; Chief Executive, Hartsluz Ltd, since 2009; *b* 22 Dec. 1946; *s* of Thomas and Eileen Tappin; *m* 1971, Angela Florence (*née* Reed); one *s* one *d*. *Educ:* Univ. of Essex; LSE; Strathclyde Univ. Mem. (Lab), Newcastle-under-Lyme BC, 1980–84; Staffordshire County Council: Mem. (Lab), 1981–97; Chairman: Planning Cttee, 1985–89; Enterprise and Econ. Develt Cttee, 1989–94; European Cttee, 1990–94; Mem. (Lab), Stoke-on-Trent CC, 2004–08 (Cabinet Mem. for Resources, 2006–08; Leader, Labour Gp, 2007–08). MEP (Lab) Staffordshire West and Congleton, 1994–99; contested (Lab) W Midlands Reg., 1999. European Parliament: Member: Budget Cttee, 1994–99; Budget Control Cttee, 1994–99; Substitute Mem., Econ. and Monetary Affairs Cttee, 1994–99; Mem., Delegn for relations with USA, 1994–99. Dep. Chm., Staffs Develt Assoc., 1985–94; Chm., N Staffs Steel Partnership Trng, 2000–04; Member: Stoke-on-Trent Local Strategic Partnership, 2000–08 (Chair: Health & Social Care Cttee, 2002–04); Econ. Develt and Enterprise Cttee, 2004–07); Bd, N Staffs Regeneration, 2006–08 (Chm., Employment and Enterprise Sub-Cttee, 2006–08); Stoke-on-Trent Transition Bd, 2008–10. Chm., W Midlands Regl Forum of Local Authorities, 1993–94. Chm., S Stoke Primary Care Trust, 2001–06. Pres., Staffs Ramblers' Assoc., 1998–2000. *Publications:* (jtly) American Politics Today, 1980, 3rd edn 1993. *Recreations:* walking, reading, cinema, theatre. *Address:* 63 Moorcroft Avenue, Westbury Park, Newcastle-under-Lyme, Staffs ST5 4HQ. *T:* (01782) 946117. *E:* michaeltappin@yahoo.com. *Club:* Potters' (Stoke-on-Trent).

**TAPPIN, Michael John;** QC 2009; DPhil; *b* Cheltenham, 11 Nov. 1964; *s* of Christopher John Tappin and Jean Lee, (Pip), Tappin; *m* 1991, Mary Ruth Clarkson; one *s* three *d*. *Educ:* Cheltenham Grammar Sch.; St John's Coll., Oxford (BA Chem. 1986); Merton Coll., Oxford (DPhil Biochem. 1990). Called to the Bar, Middle Temple, 1991; in practice at the Bar specialising in intellectual property, 1992–; Standing Counsel to Comptroller-Gen. of Patents, Designs and Trade Marks, 2003–08. *Publications:* papers in scientific jls, 1987–91. *Recreations:* family, hockey, cycling, theatre, reading. *Address:* 8 New Square, Lincoln's Inn, WC2A 3QP. *T:* (020) 7405 4321. *E:* michael.tappin@8newsquare.co.uk.

**TAPPING, Her Honour Susan Amanda Mary;** a Circuit Judge, 2001–19; *b* 3 Nov. 1953; *d* of Tony and Frankie Tapping; *m* 1988, Michael; one *s* one *d*. *Educ:* Bristol Univ. (LLB). Called to the Bar, Middle Temple, 1975, Bencher, 2010; specialised in criminal law; Asst Recorder, 1995–99; Recorder, 1999–2001.

**TAPPS GERVIS MEYRICK;** *see* Meyrick.

**TAPSTER, Caroline Marion,** CBE 2013; Chief Executive, Hertfordshire County Council, 2003–12; *b* 9 April 1957. *Educ:* Weymouth Grammar Sch.; Goldsmiths' Coll., London. Social work services: Dorset, 1978–82; E Sussex, 1982–89; NHS, 1989–90; Kent CC, 1990–95; Hertfordshire County Council, 1995–: Asst Dir (Commng) for Social Services, 1995–2000; Dir, Social Services, 2000–01; Dir, Adult Care Services, 2001–03. Non-exec. Dir, Poole NHS Foundn Trust, 2015–.

**TARAR, Muhammad Rafiq;** President of Pakistan, 1998–2001; *b* 2 Nov. 1929; *s* of Chaudhry Sardar Tarar; *m* Razia Tarar; three *s* one *d*. *Educ:* Univ. of the Punjab, Lahore (BA, LLB). Pleader, 1951–53; Advocate of the High Court, 1953–66; Additional Dist and Sessions Judge, 1966; Dist and Sessions Judge, 1967–74; Judge, High Court Bench, 1974–89; Chief Justice, Lahore High Court, 1989–91; Judge, Supreme Court of Pakistan, 1991–94. Mem., Senate, 1997–98. *Recreations:* reading, walking. *Club:* Islamabad (Islamabad).

**TARASSENKO, Prof. Lionel,** CBE 2012; DPhil; FREng; FMedSci; FIET; Professor of Electrical and Electronic Engineering, since 1997, and Head, Department of Engineering Science, since 2014, University of Oxford; Fellow of St John's College, Oxford, since 1997 (Vice-President, 2011–12); *b* 17 April 1957; *s* of Sergei and late Rachel Tarassenko; *m* 1st, 1978, Lady Ann Mary Elizabeth (marr. diss. 2001), *d* of 6th Earl of Craven; two *s* one *d*; 2nd, 2001, Anne Elizabeth Le Grice (*née* Moss); two step *s* one step *d*. *Educ:* Keble Coll., Oxford (BA 1978; Edgell Shepee Prize, 1978; MA; DPhil 1985; Hon. Fellow, 2015). FIET (FIEE 1996). Electronics Engr, Racal Research Ltd, 1978–81; University of Oxford: Lectr in Engrg Science, 1988–97; Dir, Inst. of Biomed. Engrg, 2008–12; Dir, Centre of Excellence in Med. Engrg, 2008–14; Mem. Council, 2013–17; Fellow of St Hugh's Coll., Oxford, 1988–97. Founder Director: Third Phase Ltd, 2000–02; Oxford BioSignals Ltd, 2000–11; t+ Medical (formerly e-San) Ltd, 2002–11; Oxehealth, 2012–; non-exec. Dir, Isis Innovation, 2012–. Scientific co-ordinator, Foresight Project on Cognitive Systems, OST, DTI, 2002–04; Mem. Sub-Panel 13, REF, 2011–13. Chm., Biomedical Engr Panel, RAEng, 2010–14. Chm., Oxford Pastorate Trust, 2006–; Lay Canon, Christ Church Cathedral, Oxford, 2012–. Centenary Lectr, Indian Inst. of Sci., 2010. FREng 2000; FMedSci 2013. Fellow, St Hugh's Coll., Oxford, 2016. BCS Medal, 1996; Rolls-Royce Chairman's Award, 2001; Silver Medal, Royal Acad. of Engrg, 2006; Innovation in Engrg IT Award, IET, 2006; Sir Henry Royce Award for High Value Patent, IET, 2008; EPSRC RISE Fellow, 2014. *Publications:* (with A. F. Murray) Analogue Neural VLSI, 1994;

A Guide to Neural Computing Applications, 1998; (ed jtly) Cognitive Systems: information processing meets brain science, 2005; contribs to jls on signal processing and biomed. engrg. *Recreations:* Oxford United, cinema. *Address:* Department of Engineering Science, University of Oxford, Parks Road, Oxford OX1 3PJ. *T:* (01865) 273002.

**TARBAT, Viscount; Colin Ruaridh Mackenzie;** *b* 7 Sept. 1987; *s* and *heir* of Earl of Cromartie, *qv*.

**TARGETT, Prof. Geoffrey Arthur Trevor,** PhD, DSc; Professor of Immunology of Protozoal Diseases, London School of Hygiene and Tropical Medicine, 1983–2006, now Emeritus; *b* 10 Dec. 1935; *s* of Trevor and Phyllis Targett; *m* 1st, 1958, Sheila Margaret Gibson (*d* 1988); two *s* three *d*; 2nd, 1997, Julie Ann Thompson. *Educ:* Nottingham Univ. (BSc Hons Zool. 1957); London Univ. (PhD 1961; DSc 1982). Research Scientist: MRC Bilharzia Res. Gp, 1957–62; Nat. Inst. for Med. Res., 1962–64; Lectr, Dept of Natural History, St Andrews Univ., 1964–70; London School of Hygiene and Tropical Medicine: Sen. Lectr, 1970–76; Reader, 1976–83; Hd of Dept of Med. Parasitology, 1988–97; Acting Dean, 2000. Develt Ambassador, Gates Malaria Partnership, 2001–08 (Dep. Dir, 2000–07). Ronald Ross Medal, LSHTM, 2010. *Publications:* (ed) Malaria: waiting for the vaccine, 1991; (ed jtly) Prospectus on Malaria Elimination; Shrinking the Malaria Map: a prospectus on malaria elimination, 2009; numerous papers in internat. med. and scientific jls. *Recreations:* golf, music, travel. *Address:* London School of Hygiene and Tropical Medicine, Keppel Street, WC1E 7HT. *T:* (01438) 812577, 07483 231066.

**TARIN, Shaukat Fayaz Ahmed,** Quaid-e-Azam Gold Medal 2005; Sitara-e-Imtiaz 2007; Adviser to Prime Minister on Finance, Revenue, Economic Affairs and Statistics, then Minister for Finance, Government of Pakistan, 2008–10; Adviser to Chairman, Silkbank Ltd, since 2010; *b* Multan, Pakistan, 1 Oct. 1953; *s* of Jamshed Ahmed Tarin and Mumtaz Tarin; *m* 1980, Razalia; one *s* two *d*. *Educ:* Punjab Univ., Lahore (MBA Major Finance). Citibank Pakistan: Country Manager, UAE and Oman and Regl Manager, Consumer Business in Gulf and Pakistan, 1985–91; Country Manager, Pakistan, 1991–96, Thailand, 1996–97; Chm. and Pres., Habib Bank, 1997–2000; Chm., 2000–03, Pres. and CEO, 2003–06, Union Bank; Chairman: Karachi Stock Exchange Ltd, 2007–08; Nat. Commodity Exchange Ltd, 2007; Pres. and CEO, Saudi Pak Commercial Bank Ltd, 2008. *Recreations:* golf, sightseeing. *Address:* Silkbank Ltd, 22nd Floor, Centrepoint Building, off Shaheed-e-Millat Expressway, near KPT Interchange, Korangi, Karachi 74900, Pakistan. *Clubs:* Golf, Sind, Boat (Karachi); Punjab, Gymkhana (Lahore).

**TARLO, Christine;** *see* McCafferty, C.

**TARN, Prof. John Nelson,** OBE 1992; DL; Professor of Architecture, 1995–99 (Roscoe Professor, 1974–95), and Pro-Vice-Chancellor, 1988–91 and 1994–99, University of Liverpool; *b* 23 Nov. 1934; *s* of Percival Nelson Tarn and Mary I. Tarn (*née* Purvis); unmarried. *Educ:* Royal Grammar Sch., Newcastle upon Tyne; Univ. of Durham (1st cl. hons BArch); Univ. of Cambridge (PhD). FRIBA, FRSA, FRHistS, FSA. Lectr in Architecture, Univ. of Sheffield, 1963–70; Prof. of Architecture, Univ. of Nottingham, 1970–73; Actg Vice-Chancellor, 1991–92, Public Orator, 1994–2002, Liverpool Univ. Member: Professional Literature Cttee, RIBA, 1968–77; RIBA Educn Cttee, 1978–97 (Vice-Chm., 1983–95; Chm., Moderators and Examiners Cttee, 1975–97); Council, RIBA, 1987–93; Council, ARCUK, 1980–90 (Vice-Chm., 1986–87; Chm., 1987–90; Vice-Chm., Bd of Educn, 1981–83, Chm., 1983–86); Technology Sub-Cttee, UGC, 1974–84; Adv. Cttee on Architectural Educn to EEC, Brussels, 1987–90; CNAA Built Environment Bd, 1987–90; Ministerial nominee, Peak Park Jt Planning Bd, 1973–82, a rep. of Greater Manchester Council, PPJPB, 1982–86 (Vice-Chm. of Bd, 1981–86; co-opted Mem., Planning Control Cttee and Park Management Cttee, 1986–97; Chm., Planning Control Cttee, 1979–97); Mem., National Parks Review Cttee, 1990. Trustee, Museums and Art Galls in Merseyside, 1996–2006 (Chm., Building and Design Cttee, 1996–2006). Chm., Art and Architecture Dept, Liturgy Commn, Archdio. of Liverpool, 1978–; Member: Design and Planning Cttee, Central Council for Care of Churches, 1981–86; Historic Churches Cttee for the NW, 1994– (Vice-Chm., 2009–); DAC for Derby, 1979–93; Liverpool Cathedral Adv. Cttee, 1992–2015; Sub-cttee for Patrimony, Catholic Bishops' Conf. for England and Wales, 1995–2001. Chm., Riverside Gp (formerly Riverside Housing Assoc.), 1998–2010 (Dep. Chm., 1997–98). Pres., Wirral Soc., 2001–; Vice-President: Peak Dist and S Yorks CPRE, 2002–; Merseyside Civic Soc., 2007–. DL Merseyside, 1999. Hon. Fellow, Chinese Univ. of HK, 2004. DUniv Sheffield Hallam, 1997; Hon. LLD Liverpool, 1999. KSG 2016. *Publications:* Working Class Housing in Nineteenth Century Britain, 1971; The Peak District National Park: its architecture, 1971; Five Per Cent Philanthropy, 1974; (adv. ed.) Sir Banister Fletcher's History of Architecture, 19th edn, 1987. *Recreations:* music, cooking. *Address:* 2 Ashmore Close, Barton Hey Drive, Caldy, Wirral CH48 2JX. *Club:* Athenæum.

**TARR, Robert;** Principal, The OakVine Consultancy, since 1997; Director, OakVine.net, since 1999; *b* 1944; *s* of Jack William Tarr; *m* 1966, Linda Andrews. *Educ:* Whytemead and Downsbrook Schools, Worthing; Worthing High Sch. for Boys; BScEcon Hons London, 1977; BA Open Univ., 1979. CPFA (IPFA 1967); FCILT (FCIT 1989). W Sussex CC, Worthing BC, Denbighshire CC, Sunderland Met. BC to 1975; Corporate Planning Co-ordinator and Head of Policy Unit, Bradford Met. Council, 1975–81; Chief Exec., Royal Borough of Kingston upon Thames, 1981–83; Chief Exec. and Town Clerk, Coventry City Council, 1983–87; Dir Gen., Centro (W Midlands PTE), 1987–95; Sec. Gen., Light Rail Transit Assoc., 1997–99. *Publications:* contribs to jls and conf. papers; articles on public transport and light rail transit. *Recreations:* viticulture and wine-making, gardening, art, architecture and history (especially Victorian and industrialisation), soaking up sun and scenery, naturism, running, photography, the internet (blogs and editorial comment on several websites), amateur radio (call sign G3PUR).

**TARRANT, Christopher John,** OBE 2004; radio and television presenter, producer and writer; *b* 10 Oct. 1946; *s* of late Major Basil Tarrant, MC, and Joan Ellen Tarrant (*née* Cox); *m* 1st, 1977, Sheila Roberton (marr. diss.); two *d*; 2nd, 1991, Ingrid Dupré (marr. diss. 2008); one *s* one *d*. *Educ:* King's Sch., Worcester; Univ. of Birmingham (BA Hons). *Television* includes: presenter and writer, ATV Today, 1972–74; presenter, writer and producer: Tiswas, 1974–82; OTT, 1981–83; presenter: Everybody's Equal, 1989–91; Tarrant on Television, 1989–; Lose a Million, 1993; Pop Quiz, 1994–95; Man o Man, 1996–98; Who Wants to be a Millionaire?, 1998–2014; The Colour of Money, 2009; Chris Tarrant: Extreme Railways, 2012–; The Railways That Built Britain, 2017; *radio:* presenter, Breakfast Show, Capital Radio, 1987–2004. Sony Radio Awards: Radio Personality of the Year, 1990; Best Use of Comedy, 1990; Silver Medal, 1992, 1993; Best Breakfast Show, 1995; Gold Award, 2001; Best On-Air Personality, Internat. Radio Fest. of NY, 1987; Radio Personality of the Year, TRIC, 1989; Ind. Radio Personality, Variety Club of GB, 1991; Best Breakfast Show, NY World Awards, 1997; ITV Personality of the Year, Variety Club of GB, 1998; GQ Radio Man of the Year, 1999; Best TV Performer in non-acting role, BPG TV Awards, 1999; Nat. TV Awards Special Recognition, 2000; Lifetime Achievement Award, ITV, 2000; Lifetime Achievement Award, Radio Acad., 2002; Lifetime Achievement Award, British Comedy Awards, 2006. Pres., Anglers' Conservation Assoc., 2002–04. *Publications:* Ken's Furry Friends, 1986; Fishfriar's Hall Revisited, 1987; Ready Steady Go, 1990; Rebel Rebel, 1991; Tarrant off the Record, 1997; The Ultimate Book of Netty Nutters, 1998; Tarrant on Millionaires, 1999; Millionaire Moments, 2002; Tarrant on Top of the World: in search of the polar bear, 2005; Dad's War: father, soldier, hero, 2014. *Recreations:* fishing, cricket. *Clubs:* Lord's Taverners (Pres., 2009–11), White Swan Piscatorials, Red Spinners Fishing, Variety Club of Great Britain.

**TARRANT, Prof. John Rex;** DL; PhD; Secretary General, Association of Commonwealth Universities, 2007–10; *b* 12 Nov. 1941; *s* of Arthur Rex Tarrant and Joan Mary (*née* Brookes); *m* 1991, Biddy Fisher (OBE 2012). *Educ:* Marling Grammar Sch., Stroud; Univ. of Hull (BSc; PhD 1966). Asst Lectr, UC, Dublin, 1966–68; University of East Anglia: Lectr, 1968–74; Sen. Lectr, 1974–82; Dean, Sch. of Envmtl Scis, 1974–77 and 1981–84; Reader, 1982–94; Pro Vice-Chancellor, 1985–88; Dep. Vice-Chancellor, 1989–95; Prof., 1994–95; Hon. Fellow, 1996; Vice-Chancellor and Principal, Univ. of Huddersfield, 1995–2006. Vis. Prof., Dept of Geog., Univ. of Nebraska, 1970; Vis. Lectr, Dept of Geog., Univ. of Canterbury, NZ, 1973; Vis. Res. Associate, Internat. Food Policy Res. Inst., Washington, 1977–78; Vis. Schol., Food Res. Inst., Stanford Univ., USA, 1978; Harris Vis. Prof., Coll. of Geoscis, Texas A&M Univ., 1989. Chm., MLA Yorkshire, 2007–09. DL W Yorks, 2007. Hon. Fellow, Commonwealth of Learning, 2010. Hon. DSc: Hull, 2000; Huddersfield, 2007. *Publications:* Agricultural Geography, 1974; Food Policies, 1980; Food and Farming, 1991; contrib. chapters in books; numerous articles in professional jls. *Recreations:* gliding, motor-cycling. *Address:* Spring Cottage, Leak Hall Lane, Denby Dale, W Yorks HD8 8QU. *T:* (01484) 866697.

**TARRIER, Prof. Nicholas,** PhD; FBA 2015; FBPsS; Professor of Clinical Psychology, University of Manchester, 1991–2011, Professor Emeritus, 2015; *b* Bushey, Herts, 1 May 1951; *s* of late Frederick Tarrier and Lillian Tarrier; *m* 1988, Christine Barrowclough; one *s* two *d*. *Educ:* Headstone Sec. Mod. Sch.; Pinner Co. Grammar Sch.; Univ. of Nottingham (BSc Hons 1st Cl. Zoology 1972); Univ. of Sussex (MSc Experimental Psychol. 1973); Inst. of Psychiatry, Univ. of London (PhD Psychol. 1977); Univ. of Manchester (MSc Clin. Psychol. 1981). FBPsS 1989. Prof. of Psychol., Federal Univ. of Paraíba, Brazil, 1977–79; Trainee Clin. Psychologist, Manchester AHA and Univ. of Manchester, 1979–81; Clin. Psychologist, Salford HA, 1981–89; Lectr in Clin. Psychol., Univ. of Sydney, 1989–91; Hon. Consultant Clin. Psychologist, NHS, 1991–2011; Consultant Clin. Psychologist (pt-time), medico-legal practice, 1994–; Prof. of Clin. Psychol. and eHealth Studies (pt-time), Inst. of Psychiatry, KCL, 2011–14. NIHR Sen. Investigator, 2008–13. Hon. Fellow, British Assoc. for Behavioural and Cognitive Psychotherapy, 1988. M. B. Shapiro Lect., BPsS, 2007. Univ. Gold (Sports-Karate), Univ. of Nottingham, 1971; 1st dan black belt, Karate Union of GB, 1975. *Publications:* Living with Breast Cancer and Mastectomy, 1987 (trans. Turkish 1997); (with C. Barrowclough) Families of Schizophrenic Patients: a cognitive-behavioural intervention, 1992; (ed with M. Birchwood) Psychological Approaches to Schizophrenia: innovations in assessment, treatment and services, 1992; (ed with M. Birchwood) Psychological Management of Schizophrenia, 1994; (ed with K. Mueser) Handbook of Social Functioning in Schizophrenia, 1998; (ed jtly) Outcomes and Innovation in the Psychological Treatment of Schizophrenia, 1998; (ed jtly) Cognitive Behaviour Therapy for Complex Cases: an advanced guidebook for the practitioner, 1998; (ed) Case Formulation in Cognitive Behaviour Therapy: the treatment of challenging and complex clinical cases, 2006, 2nd edn (ed with J. Johnson) 2015; (jtly) Cognitive Behavioural Therapy in the Treatment of Addictions, 2007; (jtly) Cognitive Behavioural Prevention of Suicide in Psychosis, 2013; over 300 articles in learned jls. *Recreations:* attempting to slow the steep trajectory of age by swimming, yoga, weight training, hiking, playing bridge and taking foreign holidays; unsuccessfully entering photographic competitions; writing unpublishable novels very slowly. *E:* nicholas.tarrier@manchester.ac.uk.

**TARRY, Jason Mark;** Chief Executive Officer, UK and Republic of Ireland, Tesco plc, since 2018; *b* Pembury, Kent, 6 May 1967; *s* of Gordon and Gillian Tarry; *m* 1999, Cathryn Walker; two *s* one *d*. *Educ:* Maidstone Grammar Sch. for Boys; Staffordshire Poly. (BA Hons Business Studies). Tesco plc: grad. trainee, Finance, 1990–93; Category Dir, Grocery, 1999–2005; Commercial Dir, Gen. Merchandise, 2005–07; CEO, F&F Clothing, 2012–15; Chief Commercial Officer, 2015–18. *Recreations:* fishing, cycling, family, sports follower. *Address:* Tesco plc Head Office, Kestral Way, Shire Park, Welwyn Garden City AL7 1GA. *T:* 07740 844196. *E:* jason.tarry@tesco.com.

**TARTAGLIA, Most Rev. Philip;** *see* Glasgow, Archbishop of, (RC).

**TARUSCHIO, Franco Vittorio,** Hon. OBE 2003; chef and restaurateur, Walnut Tree Inn, Abergavenny, 1963–2001; *b* 29 March 1938; *s* of Giuseppe Taruschio and Apina (*née* Cecati); *m* 1963, Ann Forester; one adopted *d* (and one *d* decd). *Educ:* Hotel Sch., Bellagio, Italy. Trainee Chef: Hotel Splendide, Lugano, 1958; Restaurant La Belle Meunière, Clermont-Ferrand, 1959–60; Head Waiter, Three Horseshoes Hotel, Rugby, 1961–63. Pres., St Anne's Hospice, Malpas, Gwent, 2001–13. Patron, Abergavenny Food Fest., 2009–. *Publications:* Leaves from the Walnut Tree: recipes of a lifetime, 1993; Bruschetta, Crostoni and Crostini, 1995; Franco and Friends: Food from the Walnut Tree, 1997; Ice Creams and Semi Freddi, 1997; 100 Great Pasta Dishes, 2002. *Recreations:* funghi and wild food foraging, swimming, walking, teaching cookery, having fun with my grandchildren. *Address:* The Willows, 26 Pen-y-Pound, Abergavenny, Monmouthshire NP7 7RN. *T:* (01873) 859026.

**TARVER, Clive Duncan;** General Manager, Secure Information Systems, Thales Australia, since 2017; *b* Bromsgrove, Worcs, 30 Nov. 1969; *s* of David Tarver and Diane Tarver; *m* 2004, Dr Kate Rebecca Clemons; one *s* two *d*. *Educ:* Alvechurch Primary and Middle Schs; Abbey High Sch.; Jesus Coll., Cambridge (BA Hons Engrg 1992); Warwick Business Sch. (MBA 2002). CEng 1997; MAPM 1998, FAPM 2015; ACCA CDipAF 2000; FIMechE 2011; FIET 2014. Ministry of Defence, 1992–2017: Proj. Manager, Special Projects, 1996–98; Business Manager, Ships Support Agency, 1998–2000; Team Leader, Special Communications, 2000–01; Private Sec. to Chief Defence Procurement, 2003; Team Leader, Marine Electrical Systems, 2004–07; Sen. Civil Service, 2007; Director: Information, Defence Equipment and Support, 2007–08; Infrastructure, 2008–09; Hd, Air Comd and Control Prog. Delivery Gp, 2009–11; Dir, Intelligence, Surveillance, Target Acquisition and Reconnaissance, Defence Equipment and Support, 2011–17. *Recreations:* family and outdoor activities, ski-ing, mountain biking, cycling, distance running, cricket, watching Rugby Union and now Aussie Rules Football. *Address:* Thales Australia, Equinox 3, 70 Kent Street, Deakin, ACT 2600, Australia.

**TAS, Jacob;** Chief Executive, Koninklijke Nederlandse Redding Maatschappij, since 2019; *b* The Hague, 23 June 1965; *s* of Jan Jacob Tas and late Eva Tas-Hueting; *m* 2019, Sallyanne Marsh; one *s* three *d*. *Educ:* Haags Montessori Lyceum; Univ. of Amsterdam (MSc Applied Econometrics); Univ. of Oxford (AMP); Regent's Coll. (Accredited Mediator). Royal Nedlloyd, subseq. Royal P&O Nedlloyd: Country/Business Manager, Taiwan, 1995–96; Manager, Merger Office, 1997; Gen. Manager, 1998–2001, Equipment Europe; Global HR & Develt Dir, 2001–05; Ops Dir, 2005–06; Dir England and Hd of Volunteering, The Prince's Trust, 2007–11; Dep. CEO, 2011–13, Interim CEO, 2013–14, Action for Children; Chief Exec., Nacro, 2014–19. Chm. Trustees and Co. Sec., St Paul's Steiner

Sch., 2005–13; Trustee, Rudolf Steiner Sch., Kings Langley, 2017–18. Trustee: Nedlloyd Pension Fund, 2004–16; War Child, 2012–18; Dutch Centre, 2014–19. Founding Mem., Centre for Narrative Leadership. *Address*: Koninklijke Nederlandse Redding Maatschappij, Haringkade 2, 1970 AK IJmuiden, Netherlands. *E*: j.tas@knrm.nl.

**TASKER, Prof. Philip Westerby**, PhD; FRSC, FInstP; Vice Chancellor, De Montfort University, 1999–2010; Chairman, Leicester Theatre Trust, 2010–16; *b* 6 July 1950; *s* of John Westerby Tasker and Alianore Doris Tasker (*née* Whytlaw-Gray); *m* 1974, Alison Helen Davis; one *s* one *d*. *Educ*: King Alfred's Grammar Sch., Wantage; Univ. of Birmingham (BSc Chem. 1971; PhD 1974). CPhys 1989; FInstP 1989; FRSC 1990. Research Fellow: Univ. of Bristol, 1974–75; Theoretical Physics Div., Harwell Lab., UKAEA, 1975–90; Divl Manager, AEA Technol., 1990–93; Chief Exec., Safeguard Internat., 1993–96; Pro-Vice Chancellor, De Montfort Univ., 1996–99. Member: Bd, E Midlands Develt Agency, 2004–12; Midlands Regl Adv. Bd, Nat. Trust, 2012–18. Hon. DSc St Petersburg Univ. of Technol. and Design, 2007; DUniv De Montfort, 2011. *Publications*: contribs to Philosophical Mag., Jl Physics, Faraday Trans, Physical Rev., etc.

**TATA, Dr Jamshed Rustom**, FRS 1973; Head, Division of Developmental Biochemistry, National Institute for Medical Research, 1973–96; Emeritus Scientist, Francis Crick Institute; *b* 13 April 1930; *s* of Rustom and Gool Tata; *m* 1954, Renée Suzanne Zanetto; two *s* one *d*. *Educ*: Univ. of Bombay (BSc); Univ. of Paris, Sorbonne (DèsSc). Post-doctoral Fellow, Sloan-Kettering Inst., New York, 1954–56; Beit Memorial Fellow, Nat. Inst. for Med. Research, 1956–60; Vis. Scientist, Wenner-Gren Inst., Stockholm, 1960–62; Mem., Scientific Staff, MRC, Nat. Inst. for Med. Research, 1962–96. Visiting Professor: King's Coll., London, 1968–69, and 1970–77; Univ. of California, Berkeley, 1969–70; Vis. Senior Scientist, Nat. Institutes of Health, USA, 1977, 1997; Fogarty Scholar, NIH, USA, 1983, 1986, 1989. The Wellcome Trust: Chm., Cell and Molecular Panel, 1990–92; Mem., Basic Sci. Gp, 1992–93; Mem., Internat. Interest Gp, 1997–2002. Chm., Bd of Trustees, Oxford Internat. Biomed. Centre, 1999–2007 (Trustee, 1996–2008). Non-exec. Dir, Biotech Analytics, 2000–05. Chm., Elections and Awards, Third World Acad. of Sci., 2000–08; Mem., Grants Cttee, 2005–08, Mem., Internat. Exchanges Cttee, 2012–18, Royal Soc. Sci. Advr, EU Nuclear Receptor Consortium, 2006–11. Fellow: Indian Nat. Science Acad., 1978; Third World Acad. of Sci., 1986. Dr *hc* École Normale Supérieure, France, 2009. Van Meter Award, 1954; Colworth Medal, 1966; Medal of Soc. for Endocrinology, 1973; Jubilee Medal, Indian Inst. of Sci., 1985. *Publications*: (jtly): The Thyroid Hormones, 1959; The Chemistry of Thyroid Diseases, 1960; Metamorphosis, 1996; Hormonal Signalling and Postembryonic Development, 1998; papers in jls of: Biochemistry; Developmental Biology; Endocrinology. *Address*: 15 Bittacy Park Avenue, Mill Hill, NW7 2HA. *T*: (020) 8346 6291.

**TATA, Ratan Naval**, Hon. GBE 2014 (Hon. KBE 2009); Chairman, Tata Sons Ltd, 1991–2012, now Chairman Emeritus; *b* Bombay, 28 Dec. 1937; *s* of Naval H. Tata. *Educ*: Cornell Univ. (BSc Arch. with Structl Engrg, 1962); Harvard Business Sch. (AMP 1975). Joined Tata Steel Ltd, 1962; Dir, National Radio & Electronics Co. Ltd, 1971; Chm., Tata Industries Ltd, 1981–2012; Tata cos incl. Tata Motors, Tata Steel, Tata Consultancy Services, Tata Power, Tata Tea, Tata Chemicals, Indian Hotels, Tata Teleservices. Pres. Court, Indian Inst. of Sci.; Chm. Council, Tata Inst. of Fundamental Res. Former Chm. Trustees, Sir Dorabji Tata Trust. Hon. FREng 2012. Padma Bhushan, 2000; Padma Vibhushan, 2008. *Address*: c/o Tata Group, Bombay House, 24 Homi Mody Street, Mumbai 400 001, India.

**TATAM, Fiona Mary**; *see* Ross, F. M.

**TATCHELL, Peter Gary**; human rights and lesbian, gay, bisexual and transgender rights campaigner; journalist and author; *b* Melbourne, 25 Jan. 1952; *s* of Gordon Basil Tatchell and Mardi Aileen Tatchell (*née* Rhodes, now Nitscke). *Educ*: Mount Waverley High Sch., Melbourne; Polytech. of N London (BSc Hons (Sociol.) 1977). Sec., Christians for Peace, 1970–71; Exec., Vietnam Moratorium Campaign, 1971; Chm., Rockingham Estate Tenants' Assoc., 1980–81; Sec., Southwark and Bermondsey, Labour Party, 1980–85; activist/organiser: Gay Liberation Front London, 1971–73; UK AIDS Vigil Orgn, 1987–89; Green and Socialist Confs, 1987–89; ACT UP London, 1989–91; co-organiser, OutRage!, 1990–2012; spokesperson on human rights, Green Party of England and Wales, 2007–15. Dir, Peter Tatchell Foundn, 2011–. Contested (Lab) Bermondsey by-election, 1983; candidate (ind. green left) London Assembly, 2000; Prospective Parly Cand. (Green), Oxford East, 2007–09. Member: NUJ, 1986–; Republic, 2002–; Green Party, 2004–. Ambassador, Make Justice Work, 2010–; Distinguished Supporter, Humanists UK (formerly British Humanist Assoc.), 2013–; Patron: Pride London, 2010–; Animal Aid, 2011–; Tell Mama, 2014–. Hon. Fellow, Goldsmiths, Univ. of London, 2014. FRSA 2016. Hon. DLitt Sussex, 2010; Hon. LLD London South Bank, 2011; Hon. DLaw De Montfort, 2014; Hon. Dr Liberal Arts Abertay, 2018. Blue Plaque erected at residence, Southwark, 2010. Campaigner of the Year, *Observer* Ethical Awards, 2009; Irwin Prize, Nat. Secular Soc., 2012; Lifetime Achiever Award, Nat. Diversity Awards, 2012; Icon Award for Outstanding Achievement, Attitude Awards, 2012; Lifetime Achievement Award, Out in the City and G3 Awards, 2013; Politics Award, Winq Mag. Men of the Year, 2015; James Joyce Award, Lit. and Histl Soc., UCD, 2016; Gandhi Internat. Peace Award, Gandhi Foundn, 2016; Albert Medal, RSA, 2016; Outstanding Contrib. to LGBT Life, British LGBT Awards, 2019. *Publications*: The Battle for Bermondsey, 1983; Democratic Defence: a non-nuclear alternative, 1985; AIDS: a guide to survival, 1986, 3rd edn 1990; Europe in the Pink: lesbian and gay equality in the New Europe, 1992; Safer Sexy: the guide to gay sex safely, 1994; We Don't Want to March Straight: masculinity, queers and the military, 1995; *contributor*: Nuclear-Free Defence, 1983; Into the Twenty-First Century, 1988; Getting There: steps to a green society, 1990; Anti-Gay, 1996; The Penguin Book of Twentieth Century Protest, 1998; Teenage Sex: what should schools teach children?, 2002; The Hate Debate: should hate be punished as a crime?, 2002; Sex and Politics in South Africa, 2005; Good Company: ideas on modern republicanism, 2009; 50 Voices of Disbelief, 2009; The Meaning of Matrimony: debating same-sex marriage, 2013; The Alphabet Anthology Book, 2016. *Recreations*: mountain hiking, surfing, art and design, ambushing tyrants and torturers. *Address*: Peter Tatchell Foundation, Studio 5, Disney Place House, 14 Marshalsea Road, SE1 1HL. *E*: Peter@PeterTatchellFoundation.org. *W*: www.PeterTatchell.net, www.twitter.com/PeterTatchell. *Club*: Heaven.

**TATE, Ann**, CBE 2011; Vice Chancellor, University of Northampton, 2005–10; Chairman, Ipswich Hospital NHS Trust, 2012–16; *b* 27 May 1949; *d* of Norman Cooper and Sybil (*née* Judson); *m* 1975, Rodney Tate; one *d*. *Educ*: Queen Elizabeth's Grammar Sch., Middleton; Univ. of London ext. (BSc Hons Sociol. 1970); Bedford Coll., Univ. of London (MSc Sociol. Applied to Medicine 1984). Asst Teacher, Lancs LEA, 1970–71; Lecturer: Belfast Coll. of Business Studies, 1972–74; Ulster Poly., 1974–84; University of Ulster: Sen. Lectr, 1984–95; Pro-Vice-Chancellor, 1995–2002; Rector, UC Northampton, 2002–05. Board Member: HEFCE, 2003–09; W Northants Develt Corp., 2005–10; Mem., Northants LSC, 2003–08. Non-exec. Dir, Thedwastre Educnl Trust, 2016–. Mem. Bd, Arden Univ. Ltd, 2017. FRSA 1999. DUniv Ulster, 2007. *Recreations*: cooking, walking, gardening. *Address*: Two Chimneys, 5 Spencer's Piece, Rattlesden, Suffolk IP30 0SA. *Club*: Reform.

**TATE, Prof. Austin**, PhD; FREng; FRSE; Professor of Knowledge-Based Systems, since 1995, and Director, Artificial Intelligence Applications Institute, since 1985, University of Edinburgh; *b* Knottingley, W Yorks, 12 May 1951; *s* of Charles Tate and Irene Tate; *m* 1975, Margaret Mowbray. *Educ*: King's Sch., Pontefract; Lancaster Univ. (BA Hons Computer Studies 1972); Univ. of Edinburgh (PhD Machine Intelligence 1975; MSc E-Learning 2012). CEng 1993; FBCS 2000; FREng 2012. University of Edinburgh: Res. Fellow, Dept of Artificial Intelligence, 1975–76; Software Engineer, Data Base Gp, Computer Support Officer and Manager, Microcomputer Support Unit, Edinburgh Regl Computing Centre, 1976–83; Information Technol. Fellow, 1983–84; Asst Dir, Artificial Intelligence Applications Inst., Leader, Knowledge Based Planning Gp and Systems Designers Fellow, 1984–85; Professorial Fellow, 1989–95; Coordinator, Virtual Univ. of Edinburgh, 2005–; Coordinator, Distance Educn, 2012–17, Sch. of Informatics. Sen. Res. Scientist, Inst. for Human and Machine Cognition, Florida, 2010–. FRSE 1999. FAAAI 1993; Fellow; Workflow Mgt Coalition, 1998; Soc. for Study of Artificial Intelligence and Simulation of Behaviour, 1999; Eur. Assoc. for (formerly Coordinating Cttee on) Artificial Intelligence, 1999. *Recreations*: travel, walking, photography, graphic art, space. *Address*: School of Informatics, University of Edinburgh, Crichton Street, Edinburgh EH8 9AB. *T*: (0131) 651 3222. *E*: a.tate@ed.ac.uk.

**TATE, Dr (Edward) Nicholas**, CBE 2001; Director-General, International School of Geneva, 2003–11; Chairman, International Education Systems, 2011–13; *b* 18 Dec. 1943; *s* of Joseph Edwin Tate and Eva Elsie Tate; *m* 1973, Nadya Grove; one *s* two *d*. *Educ*: Huddersfield New Coll.; Balliol Coll., Oxford (Scholar; MA); Univ. of Bristol (PGCE); Univ. of Liverpool (MA; PhD 1985). Teacher, De La Salle Coll., Sheffield, 1966–71; Lectr, City of Birmingham Coll. of Educn, 1972–74; Lectr, then Sen. Lectr, Moray House Coll. of Educn, Edinburgh, 1974–88; Professional Officer, Nat. Curriculum Council, 1989–91; Asst Chief Exec., Sch. Exams and Assessment Council, 1991–93; Asst Chief Exec., 1993–94, Chief Exec., 1994–97, SCAA; Chief Exec., QCA, 1997–2000; Headmaster, Winchester Coll., 2000–03. Pres., Earth Focus Foundn, 2005–10. Chair, Aiglon Coll. Assoc., 2019–. Member, Board of Governors: Internat. Schs Assoc., 2005–10; Internat. Baccalaureate, 2009–15. Trustee: Nat. Trust, 1996–99; Richmond, The American Internat. Univ. in London, 2008– (Vice-Pres., 2013–17; Chm., 2017–19). Hon. DCL Huddersfield, 1998. *Publications*: What Is Education For?, 2015; The Conservative Case for Education, 2017; various history books for schools; articles on history and education. *Recreation*: reading. *E*: nick@nicholastate.com.

**TATE, Sir Edward Nicolas**, 6th Bt *cr* 1898, of Park Hill, Streatham; *b* 2 July 1966; *e s* of Sir (Henry) Saxon Tate, 5th Bt, CBE and Sheila Ann (*née* Robertson); *S* father, 2012, but his name does not appear on the Official Roll of the Baronetage; *m* 1996, Rosalind Susan (*née* Coward); two *d*. *Heir*: *b* Duncan Saxon Tate [*b* 30 April 1968; *m* 2006, Nicola Stockwell; two *s* one *d* (and one *s* decd)]. *Address*: The Isle, Isle Lane, Bicton, Shrewsbury SY3 8EE.

**TATE, John Richard**; Chief Executive Officer, Tamkeen LLC, Abu Dhabi, since 2015; *b* British Forces, Hanover, 3 Jan. 1975; *s* of Anthony James Tate and Patricia Mary Skipper (*née* McKay); *m* 2003, Fatiha Selmi; one *s* one *d*. *Educ*: Queen's Coll., Oxford (MPhil 1999). Sen. Associate, McKinsey & Co., 2000–03; Hd, Cons. Party Policy Unit, 2003–05; Mgt Consultant, PA Consulting, 2005–07; Dir, Policy and Strategy, BBC, 2007–14; Chm., BBC Studios, 2011–14. Founding Ambassador, TeachFirst, 2002–; Sen. Advr, Medopad, 2010–. *Publications*: What's Right Now?, 2006. *Address*: Tamkeen LLC, 409 Muraigeb Tower, Hamdan Street, Abu Dhabi, UAE.

**TATE, Nicholas**; *see* Tate, E. N.

**TATE, William John**; non-executive Chairman, Your Healthcare CIC, 2010–14; *b* 12 June 1951; *s* of William Kenneth Tate and Dorothy Tate; *m* 1976, Helen Elizabeth Quick; one *s* one *d*. *Educ*: Eastcliffe Grammar Sch., Newcastle upon Tyne; King's Coll., London (LLB 1973). Called to the Bar, Gray's Inn, 1974; Flt Lieut, RAF Directorate of Legal Services, 1976–78; Solicitor's Office, HM Customs and Excise: Legal Asst, 1978–80; Sen. Legal Asst, 1980–86; Sen. Prin. Legal Officer, 1986–88; Asst Dir, Serious Fraud Office, 1988–96; Dep. Parly Comr for Admin, 1996–99; Solicitor to Bloody Sunday Inquiry, 1999–2003; Dir of Legal Services, Ind. Police Complaints Commn, 2004–09. Non-executive Director: Kingston NHS PCT, 2007–10; First Community Health and Care CIC, 2011–12. Lay Mem., Gen. Social Care Council, 2009–12; Chair of Specialist Schs, NHS London Deanery, 2010–14. *Publications*: (Delegated Legislation Ed.) Current Law, annually 1975–95. *Recreations*: reading, music, gardening. *Club*: Royal Air Force.

**TATHAM, David Everard**, CMG 1991; HM Diplomatic Service, retired; consultant; *b* 28 June 1939; *s* of late Lt-Col Francis Everard Tatham and Eileen Mary Wilson; *m* 1963, Valerie Ann Mylechreest; three *s*. *Educ*: St Lawrence Coll., Ramsgate; Wadham Coll., Oxford (BA History). Entered HM Diplomatic Service, 1960; New York, 1962–63; Milan, 1963–67; ME Centre for Arabic Studies, 1967–69; Jeddah, 1969–70; FCO, 1971–74; Muscat, 1974–77; Asst Head of ME Dept, FCO, 1977–80; Counsellor, Dublin, 1981–84; Ambassador to Yemen Arab Republic, also accredited to Republic of Djibouti, 1984–87; Hd of Falkland Is Dept, FCO, 1987–90; Ambassador to Lebanese Republic, 1990–92; Governor, Falkland Is, and Comr for S Georgia and S Sandwich Is, 1992–96; High Comr, Sri Lanka, also accred to Republic of Maldives, 1996–99. Adviser to Palestinian Authy on Diplomatic Trng, 2000; Census Dist Manager, Ledbury/Ross, 2000–01. Chm., Shackleton Scholarship Fund, 1999–2019; Vice Pres., Falkland Islands Assoc., 2012– (Chm., 2004–11); President: S Georgia Assoc., 2012–; Friends of Falklands Mus. and Archives, 2013–. Ed., Dictionary of Falklands Biography Project, 2002–08. *Publications*: (ed) The Dictionary of Falklands Biography, 2008; (ed) A Book of Boltown, 2015; contrib. Oxford DNB. *Recreations*: walking uphill, fishing, historical research. *Address*: South Parade, Ledbury, Hereford HR8 2HA. *T*: (01531) 579090. *E*: d_tatham@hotmail.com. *Clubs*: Athenæum, Geographical.

*See also* M. H. Tatham.

**TATHAM, Michael Harry**; HM Diplomatic Service; Deputy Head of Mission, Washington, since 2018; *b* 2 July 1965; *s* of David Everard Tatham, *qv*; *m* 1998, Belinda Cherrington. *Educ*: Oundle Sch.; Merton Coll., Oxford (BA Hons). Entered FCO, 1987; Third, later Second, Sec., Prague, 1989–93; FCO, 1993–95; Private Sec. to Minister of State, 1995–96; Dep. Hd of Mission, Sofia, 1997–99; on secondment as Private Sec. to Prime Minister, 1999–2002; Dep. Hd of Mission, Prague, 2002–05; Balkans Co-ordinator and Hd, Western Balkans Gp, 2006–08; Ambassador to Bosnia and Herzegovina, 2008–11; Political Counsellor, UK Mission to UN, NY, 2011–15; Dir, Eastern Europe and Central Asia, FCO, 2015–17. *Recreations*: mountain hiking, the music of Bob Dylan, cookery. *Address*: c/o Foreign and Commonwealth Office, SW1A 2AH.

**TATTEN, Jonathan Altenburger**; Consultant, Dentons (formerly Denton Hall, then Denton Wilde Sapte, then SNR Denton), Solicitors, since 2008 (Partner, 1983–2008; Managing Partner, 1993–99; Head of European and Competition Law Department, 2003–07); *b* 17 March 1952; *s* of John Stephenson Tatten and Anna Tatten. *Educ*: Duke of

York Sch., Nairobi; Exeter Univ. (LLB); Harvard Business Sch. (AMP). Trainee solicitor, Trower Still & Keeling, 1973–76; solicitor, Holman Fenwick & Willan, Solicitors, 1976–83. *Recreations:* opera, pugs, eating, walking, gardening. *Address:* 4 Coutts Crescent, St Albans Road, NW5 1RF.

**TATTERSALL, Geoffrey Frank;** QC 1992; a Recorder, since 1989; a Deputy High Court Judge, since 2003; Judge of Appeal, Isle of Man, 1997–2017; *b* 22 Sept. 1947; *s* of late Frank Tattersall and of Margaret (*née* Hassall); *m* 1971, Hazel Shaw; one *s* two *d*. *Educ:* Manchester Grammar Sch.; Christ Church, Oxford (MA Jurisprudence). Called to the Bar, Lincoln's Inn, 1970 (Tancred Studentship in Common Law), Bencher, 1997; in practice, Northern Circuit, 1970–; called to the Bar, NSW, 1992; SC 1995. External Reviewer of Decisions of Dir of Fair Access, 2005–13. Lay Chm., Bolton Deanery Synod, 1993–2002; Chm., House of Laity and Vice Pres., Manchester Diocesan Synod, 1994–2003; Mem., Gen. Synod, 1995– (Chm., Standing Orders Cttee, 1999–; Mem., Legislative Cttee, 2010– (Vice-Chm., 2017–); Panel of Chairmen, 2011–16); Diocesan Chancellor: Carlisle, 2003–; Manchester, 2004–; Dep. Diocesan Chancellor, Durham, 2003–05; Vicar-Gen., Dio. of Sodor and Man, 2015– (Dep. Vicar-Gen., 2004–08, 2014–15); Chairman: Disciplinary Tribunals under Clergy Discipline Measure, 2006–15; Revision Cttees for draft C of E Marriage Measure, 2006–07, draft Ecclesiastical Offices Measure, 2007–08, draft C of E Safeguarding and Clergy Discipline Measure, 2015, and draft Mission and Pastoral (Amendment) Measure, 2016; Synodical Govt Amendment Measure, 2014; Mem., Steering Cttee, Draft Bishops and Priests (Consecration and Ordination of Women) Measure, 2009–. Hon. Lay Canon, Manchester Cathedral, 2003–; Parish Clerk, St George-in-the-East, London, 2008–. Mem., Parish Clerks' Co., 2009–. *Recreations:* family, music, travel. *Address:* 12 Byrom Street, Manchester M3 4PP. *T:* (0161) 829 2100.

**TATTERSALL, Jane Patricia;** *see* Griffiths, Jane P.

**TATTERSFIELD, Prof. Anne Elizabeth,** OBE 2005; MD; FRCP, FMedSci; Professor of Respiratory Medicine, University of Nottingham, 1984–2005, now Emeritus; Hon. Consultant Physician, City Hospital, Nottingham, 1984–2005; *b* 13 June 1940; *d* of Charles Percival Tattersfield and Bessie Wharton Tattersfield (*née* Walker). *Educ:* Fairfield High Sch., Manchester; Durham Univ. (MB BS 1963); MD Newcastle 1970. MRCP 1966, FRCP 1979. Jun. hosp. posts, Royal Victoria Infirmary, Newcastle, Leicester Royal Infirmary, Central Middx Hosp. and Brompton Hosp., 1963–66; Medical and Research Registrar posts: Central Middx Hosp., 1966–69; Hammersmith Hosp., 1969–71; Sen. Registrar, London Hosp., 1971–74; Sen. Lectr and Reader in Medicine, Southampton Univ., 1974–83. Sir James Wattie Meml Vis. Prof., NZ, 1987. Altounyan Lectr, British Thoracic Soc., 1995; Philip Ellman Lectr, RCP, 1999. Pres., British Thoracic Soc., 2000 (Gold Medal, 2004). FMedSci 1998. *Publications:* (with M. W. McNicol) Respiratory Disease, 1987; contribs to scientific pubns on asthma, airway pharmacol. and lymphangioleiomyomatosis. *Recreations:* travel, opera, gardening. *Address:* 4 Wharfedale Grange, Ben Rhydding Drive, Ilkley LS29 8AR.

**TATTERSFIELD, Christian Alexander;** Founder and Director, Good Soldier Songs and Good Soldier Records; *b* London; *s* of Margaret van der Poest Clement; *m*, Eleanor Lewis-Bale; two *s*. *Educ:* King Alfred Sch.; Selwyn Coll., Cambridge (BA Hons Eng. Lit. 1989; MA). London Records, 1990–97 (est. Systematic and Internal labels; signed Orbital, Whigfield, Baby D, Cappella); BMG, 1997 (Founder, NorthWestSide; signed Jay-Z, Another Level, N Sync); Man. Dir, Eastwest Records (signed David Gray), 2000–03; Founder, 14th Floor, 2003 (signed Birdy, Biffy Clyro, The 1975, The Wombats, Damian Rice, Ray Lamontagne); CEO, Warner Music UK and Chm., Warner Bros Records UK, 2009–14. *Recreation:* cricket. *Address:* Good Soldier, Top Floor, Unit 16, Tileyard Studios, N7 9AH. *T:* (020) 3728 9100. *E:* christian@goodsoldiersongs.com.

**TATTON-BROWN, Timothy William Trelawny,** OBE 2018; architectural historian; freelance archaeologist; *b* 3 Feb. 1947; *s* of Robert and Daphne Tatton-Brown; *m* 1979, Veronica Wilson (*d* 2012); two *s* two *d*. *Educ:* Tonbridge Sch., Kent; Inst. of Archaeol. University Coll. London (BA Hons Roman Archaeol.). Dir, Canterbury Archaeological Trust, 1975–85; consultant archaeologist: to Canterbury Cathedral, 1976–87; Rochester Cathedral, 1987–2006; Chichester Cathedral, 1988–93; Salisbury Cathedral, 1990–2011; St George's Chapel, Windsor Castle, 1991–2013; Westminster Abbey, 1998–2004; Lambeth Palace, 1998–2001; Westminster Sch., 2002–. Mem., Adv. Cttee, Historic England (formerly English Heritage), 2012–17. Chairman: British Brick Soc., 1981–86; Rescue – British Archaeol Trust, 1983–86. Vice Pres., Royal Archaeol Inst., 2008–14. *Publications:* Great Cathedrals of Britain, 1989; (ed jtly) St Dunstan: his life, times and cult, 1992; Canterbury: history and guide, 1994; Lambeth Palace: a history of the Archbishops of Canterbury and their houses, 2000; The English Cathedral, 2002; (ed with R. Mortimer) Westminster Abbey: the Lady Chapel of Henry VII, 2003; The English Church, 2005; The Abbeys and Priories of England, 2006; (ed with T. Ayers) Medieval Art, Architecture and Archaeology at Rochester, 2006; Salisbury Cathedral: the making of a medieval masterpiece, 2009; (ed with N. Saul) St George's Chapel, Windsor: history and heritage, 2011. *Recreations:* choral singing, canal boating, book collecting, walking and landscape study, church crawling. *Address:* Fisherton Mill House, Mill Road, Salisbury, Wilts SP2 7RZ.

**TAUB, Prof. Liba,** PhD; FSA; FRHistS; Director and Curator, Whipple Museum of the History of Science, since 1995, Professor of History and Philosophy of Science, since 2010, and Head, Department of History and Philosophy of Science, since 2015, University of Cambridge; Fellow, Newnham College, Cambridge, since 1996; *b* NY, 15 Nov. 1954; *d* of Ronald Herbert Taub and Ethel Betty Flecker Taub; *m* 1988, Niall Caldwell. *Educ:* Newcomb Coll., Tulane Univ. (BA 1975); Univ. of Chicago (MA 1978); Univ. of Oklahoma (MA 1981; PhD 1987); Univ. of Texas. Vis. Instructor, Univ. of Kentucky, 1985–87; Mary Isabel Sibley Fellow in Greek Studies, United Chapters of Phi Beta Kappa, 1987–88; Res. Fellow, Amer. Council of Learned Socs, 1988–89; Curator and Hd of Hist. of Astronomy Dept, Adler Planetarium, Chicago, 1991–94; Reader in Hist. and Philosophy of Sci., Univ. of Cambridge, 2003–10. Visiting Scholar: Univ. of Leiden, 2000; Deutsches Mus., 2005; Karman Centre for Advanced Studies in Humanities, Univ. of Bern, 2006; Horning Vis. Schol., Oregon State Univ., 2007; Einstein Foundn Vis. Fellow, TOPOI Excellence Cluster, Berlin, 2010–14. Member: UK Spoliation Adv. Panel, 2000–; Mgt Bd, Cambridge Inst. for Sustainability Leadership, 2009–14; Evaluation Panel, Res. in Museums, VolkswagenStiftung, 2013. Mem., Wissenschaftliche Beirat, Deutsches Mus., 2002–14; Corresp. Mem., Acad. Internat. d'Histoire des Scis, 2012–. Trustee, Freud Mus., 2007–13. Mem., Heritage Cttee, RAS, 2010–14. FSA 2007; FRHistS 2014. *Publications:* Ptolemy's Universe: the natural, philosophical and ethical foundations of Ptolemy's astronomy, 1993; Ancient Meteorology, 2003 (trans Greek, 2008); (ed with Frances Willmoth) The Whipple Museum of the History of Science: instruments and interpretations, 2006; Aetna and the Moon: explaining nature in ancient Greece and Rome, 2008; (ed with Aude Doody) Authorial Voices in Greco-Roman Technical Writing, 2009; Science Writing in Greco-Roman Antiquity, 2017; contrib. articles to books and jls. *Recreations:* opera, the outdoors, cake. *Address:* Whipple Museum of the History of Science, Free School Lane, Cambridge CB2 3RH. *T:* (01223) 334500. *Club:* Athenæum.

**TAUBE, Prof. (Hirsch) David,** FRCP; Professor of Transplant Medicine, Imperial College London, since 2006; Consultant Nephrologist, St Mary's Hospital, London and Royal Brompton Hospital, London, since 1990, and Hammersmith Hospital, London, since 2004; *b* 4 Oct. 1948; *s* of Ernest and Hilary Taube; *m* 1990, Dr Clare Allen; one *s* one *d*. *Educ:* St Catharine's Coll., Cambridge (BA 1970); Magdalen Coll., Oxford (BM BCh 1970). FRCP 1987. Consultant Nephrologist, King's Coll. Hosp., 1985–90. Chief of Service, W London Renal and Transplant Medicine, St Mary's NHS Trust and Hammersmith Hosps NHS Trust, 1990–2004; Hammersmith Hospitals NHS Trust, later Imperial College Healthcare NHS Trust: Clinical Dir, W London Renal and Transplant Centre, 2004–07; Medical Dir, 2007–12; Dir, Imperial Coll. Academic Health Science Centre, 2012–14. Non-exec. Dir, Northwest London Hosps., 2013–. *Publications:* over 160 articles in learned jls, mainly on transplantation and renal medicine. *Recreations:* swimming, digital photography, work. *Address:* Imperial College Renal and Transplant Centre, Imperial College Healthcare NHS Trust, Hammersmith Hospital, Du Cane Road, W12 0HS. *T:* (020) 8383 4355, *Fax:* (020) 3313 3100; 66 Harley Street, W1G 7HD. *T:* (020) 7636 6628, *Fax:* (020) 7631 5341. *E:* davidtaube@msn.com.

**TAUBE, Simon Axel Robin;** QC 2000; *b* 16 June 1957; *s* of late Nils Taube and of Idonea Taube; *m* 1984, Karen Pilkington; three *d*. *Educ:* Merton Coll., Oxford (BA Hist.). Called to the Bar, Middle Temple, 1980; in practice at Chancery Bar, 1980–. Bencher, Lincoln's Inn, 2008. *Recreations:* singing, tennis, hill-walking. *Address:* 10 Old Square, Lincoln's Inn, WC2A 3SU. *T:* (020) 7405 0758.

**TAUNTON, Bishop Suffragan of,** since 2015; **Rt Rev. Ruth Elizabeth Worsley;** *b* 1962; *m* Rev. Dr Howard Worsley; three *s*. *Educ:* Univ. of Manchester; St John's Coll., Nottingham. Ordained deacon, 1996, priest, 1997; Curate, Basford with Hyson Green, 1996–98; Asst Curate, 1998–2001, Priest-in-charge, 2001–08, Hyson Green and Forest Fields; Area Dean, Nottingham N, 2006–08; Dean of Women's Ministry, Dio. of Southwell and Nottingham, 2007–10; Area Dean, Nottingham S, 2008–10; Priest-in-charge, St Christopher with St Philip, Sneinton, 2008–10; Parish Develt Officer, Dio. of Southwark, 2010–13; Archdeacon of Wilts, 2013–15. A Chaplain to the Queen, 2009–15. Hon. Canon, Southwell Minster, 2007–10. *Address:* c/o Diocese of Bath and Wells, The Old Deanery, St Andrew's Street, Wells, Som BA5 2UG.

**TAUNTON, Archdeacon of;** *see* Hill, Ven. S. J.

**TAUSSIG, Andrew John,** PhD; Director of Foreign Language Services, BBC World Service, 1996–2000; *b* 30 March 1944; *s* of Leo Charles Taussig and Magdalene Taussig (*née* Szücs); *m* 1971, Margaret Celia Whines; one *s* two *d*. *Educ:* Bramcote Sch., Scarborough; Winchester Coll. (Schol.); Magdalen Coll., Oxford (MA Hons Modern History 1962); Harvard Univ. (PhD Pol Sci. 1970). British Broadcasting Corporation, 1971–2000: Gen. Trainee, World Service Talks Dept, BBC North Leeds, and Radio Current Affairs, 1971–72; TV Current Affairs, 1973–80; Special Asst to Dir, News and Current Affairs, 1979–80; Dep. Editor, Nationwide, 1980–81; Chief Asst, TV Current Affairs, 1982–86; Head of Central European Service, 1986–88; Controller, European Services, 1988–94; Regl Head, Europe, 1994–96. Res. Associate (Media Prog.), Centre for Socio-Legal Studies, Univ. of Oxford, 2001–11; Consultant, British Council, World Summit on Inf. Soc., Geneva, 2003; Moderator, Asia-Europe Foundn Colloquium, Larnaca, 2006, Nanjing, 2007; Consultant to UNESCO, New Delhi Internat. Conf. on Disability, 2014–15. Lectr, Cardiff Univ. Sch. of Journalism, Media and Cultural Studies, 2002–03; Consultant, Faculty of Social Scis, Open Univ., 2009–11. Dir, CPTM Ltd (Commonwealth Partners for Technol. Management), 2012– (Mem., 2001–); Member: Council, RIIA (Chatham Hse), 2002–05; Internat. Adv. Council, Asia Media Inf. and Communication Centre, Singapore, 2004–11; Bd, Assoc. for Internet Accountability and Democracy, 2016–; Trustee, Internat. Inst. of Communications, 2005–14. Trustee, Voice of the Listener & Viewer, 2004–13. MInstD 2002. *Recreations:* photography, travelling. *Address:* 115 Rosebery Road, Langley Vale, Epsom Downs, Surrey KT18 6AB. *T:* (01372) 276257. *Club:* Le Beaujolais.

**TAUWHARE, Richard David,** MVO 1983; Senior Director, Dechert LLP, 2015–19; independent consultant on international trade regulations, since 2019; *b* 1 Nov. 1959; *s* of Albert and Ann Tauwhare; *m* 1985, Amanda; one *s* two *d*. *Educ:* Abingdon Sch.; Jesus Coll., Cambridge (BA Hist. 1980); Sch. of Oriental and African Studies, London. Joined FCO, 1980; Swahili lang. trng, 1982; Third, then Second Sec., Nairobi, 1982–86; Second, then First Sec., UK Delegn to OECD, 1986–89; FCO, 1989–94; First Sec., then Dep. Perm. Rep., UK Disarmament Delegn, Geneva, 1994–99; FCO, 1999–2005; Gov., Turks and Caicos Islands, 2005–08; FCO, 2008–14; Dir, Green Light Exports Consulting, 2014–15. *Recreations:* tennis, golf, reading, travel.

**TAVARÉ, Prof. Simon,** PhD; FMedSci; FRS 2011; Professor of Statistics and Biological Sciences, Herbert and Florence Irving Professor of Cancer Research, and Founding Director, Herbert and Florence Irving Institute of Cancer Dynamics, Columbia University, since 2018; *b* 13 May 1952; *s* of Sir John Tavaré, CBE; *m* 1973, Caroline Jane Page; one *s* one *d*. *Educ:* Oundle Sch.; Univ. of Sheffield (BSc 1974, MSc 1975; PhD 1979). CStat 1993; CSci 2009. Lectr, Univ. of Sheffield, 1977–78; Res. Fellow, 1978–79, Instructor, 1978–81, Univ. of Utah; Asst and Associate Prof., Colorado State Univ., 1981–85; Associate Prof., Univ. of Utah, 1985–89; Prof., 1989–2014, George and Louise Kawamoto Chair of Biol Scis, 1998–2014, USC; University of Cambridge: Prof. of Cancer Res. (Bioinformatics), Dept of Oncology and Prof., Dept of Applied Maths and Theoretical Phys, 2003–19; Dir, Cancer Res. UK Cambridge Inst., 2013–18; Fellow, Christ's Coll., Cambridge, 2004–19. Vis. posts at univs in USA, Australia, England, Sweden, Switzerland and France. Medallion Lectr, Inst. Mathematical Stats, 1993, 2001; Invited Lectr, 8th Internat. Congress on Industrial and Applied Maths, 2015; Einstein Public Lectr in Maths, Amer. Math. Soc., 2015. Pres., LMS, 2015–17. FIMS 1992; FAAAS 1998; FASA 2004; FMedSci 2009; FRSB (FSB 2009); FIMA 2010; Mem., EMBO, 2015; FAMS 2018; MNAS 2018. Hon. DTech Chalmers Univ. of Technol., 2014; Hon. DSc Sheffield, 2017. *Publications:* (ed with P. J. Donnelly) Progress in Population Genetics and Human Evolution, 1997; (jtly) Logarithmic Combinatorial Structures: a probabilistic approach, 2003; (with O. Zeitouni) Lectures on Probability and Statistics, Ecole d'Eté de Probabilité de Saint-Flour XXXI, 2004; (jtly) Computational Genome Analysis: an introduction, 2005; numerous articles in learned jls. *Address:* Department of Statistics, Columbia University, 1255 Amsterdam Avenue, New York, NY 10027, USA. *T:* (917) 6909364. *E:* st3193@columbia.edu.

**TAVARES, Nathan Warren;** QC 2018; *b* Surrey, 2 Aug. 1967; *s* of John and Janet Tavares. *Educ:* BSc Aeronautical Engrg; CPE. Called to the Bar, Middle Temple, 1992; in practice as barrister, specialising in clinical negligence, product liability and personal injury, 1992–; Judge (part-time): Mental Health Tribunal, 2004–; Court of Protection, 2018–. *Address:* Outer Temple Chambers, 222 Strand, WC2R 1BA.

**TAVERNE,** family name of **Baron Taverne**.

**TAVERNE, Baron** *cr* 1996 (Life Peer), of Pimlico in the City of Westminster; **Dick Taverne**; QC 1965; *b* 18 Oct. 1928; *s* of Dr N. J. M. and Mrs L. V. Taverne; *m* 1955, Janice Hennessey; two *d*. *Educ*: Charterhouse School; Balliol College, Oxford (First in Greats). Oxford Union Debating tour of USA, 1951. Called to Bar, 1954. MP (Lab) Lincoln, March 1962–Oct. 1972, resigned; MP (Democratic Lab) Lincoln, March 1973–Sept. 1974; Parliamentary Under-Secretary of State, Home Office, 1966–68; Minister of State, Treasury, 1968–69; Financial Secretary to the Treasury, 1969–70. Chm., Public Expenditure (General) Sub-Cttee, 1971–72. Institute for Fiscal Studies: First Dir, 1970; Dir-Gen., 1979–81; Chm., 1981–82; Chm., Public Policy Centre, 1984–87. Dir, 1972–97, Chm., 1997–2001, AXA Equity & Law Life Assurance Society plc; Chm., Monitoring Bd, AXA Sun Life plc, 2001–11, Non-exec. Dir, BOC Gp, 1975–95; Dir, PRIMA Europe Ltd, 1987–98 (Chm., 1991–93; Pres., 1993–98). Mem., Internat. Ind. Review Body to review workings of European Commn, 1979. Chairman: Alcohol and Drug Prevention and Treatment Ltd, 1996–2008; (and Founder) Sense About Science, 2002–12. Member: Nat. Cttee, SDP, 1981–87; Federal Policy Cttee, Liberal Democrats, 1989–90. Contested (SDP): Southwark, Peckham, Oct. 1982; Dulwich, 1983. Parly Sci. Communicator of the Year, Assoc. of British Sci. Writers, 2006. *Publications*: The Future of the Left: Lincoln and after, 1973; The March of Unreason - Science, Democracy and the New Fundamentalism, 2005; Against the Tide: politics and beyond: a memoir, 2014. *Recreation*: sailing. *Address*: 25 Tufton Court, Tufton Street, SW1P 3QH.
*See also M. F. Jermey, S. Taverne.*

**TAVERNE, Suzanna;** Chair, Marie Stopes International, since 2018; *b* 3 Feb. 1960; *d* of Baron Taverne, *qv* and Janice Taverne (née Hennessey); *m* 1993, Marc Vlessing; one *s* one *d*. *Educ*: Balliol Coll., Oxford (BA Hons 1982). S. G. Warburg and Co. Ltd, 1982–90; Head, Strategic Planning, 1990–92, Finance Dir, 1992–94, Newspaper Publishing plc; Consultant, Saatchi and Saatchi, 1994–95; Dir, Strategy and Develt, then Man. Dir FT Finance, Pearson plc, 1995–98; Man. Dir, British Museum, 1999–2002; Dir of Ops, Imperial Coll. London, 2003–05; Chm., Gingerbread (formerly NCOPF, then One Parent Families|Gingerbread), 2002–11 (Trustee, 1996–2011). Non-executive Director: Nationwide Building Soc., 2005–12; Ford Credit Europe Bank (formerly Ford Financial Europe), 2008–. Trustee: Design Museum, 2007–12; StepChange Debt Charity (formerly Consumer Credit Counselling Service), 2009–17; Shakespeare Schools Festival, 2010–15; BBC Trust, 2012–17; Age UK, 2017–. *Address*: 35 Camden Square, NW1 9XA.

**TAVERNER, Marcus Louis;** QC 2000; *b* 24 April 1958; *s* of late Geoffrey Clifford Taverner, DFC, Légion d'Honneur and of Mildred Taverner (née Thomas); *m* 1983, Dr Deborah Mary Hall; one *s* three *d*. *Educ*: Monmouth Sch.; Leicester Univ. (LLB Hons); King's Coll. London (LLM). Called to the Bar, Gray's Inn, 1981, Bencher, 2007; Hd, Keating Chambers, 2015. Dir, Taverner Develts Ltd, 1996. *Recreations*: 4 children, opera, guitar, dramatics, theatre, Stevenage FC (Dir, 2008–).

**TAVERNOR, Prof. Robert William,** PhD; RIBA; Professor of Architecture and Urban Design, London School of Economics, 2005–10, now Emeritus; Founding Director: Professor Robert Tavernor Consultancy Ltd, London and Bath, since 2001; Tavernor Consultancy Ltd, London, since 2017; *b* 19 Dec. 1954; *s* of late Michael Frederic Tavernor and of Elisabeth Veronica Tavernor (née Hooker); *m* 1976, Denise Alexandra Mackie; one *s* two *d*. *Educ*: Poly. of Central London (BA 1976; DipArch with Dist. 1979); British Sch. at Rome (Scholar in Arch. 1980); St John's Coll., Cambridge (PhD 1985). RIBA 1985. Lectr in Arch., Univ. of Bath, 1987–92; Forbes Prof. of Arch., Univ. of Edinburgh, 1992–95; University of Bath: Prof. of Arch., 1995–2005; Hd, Dept of Arch. and Civil Engrg, 2003–05; Dir, Cities Prog., LSE, 2005–08. Visiting Professor: UCLA, 1998; Univ. of São Paulo, 2004; Univ. of Bath, 2009–; EU Vis. Scholar, Texas A&M Univ., 2002. *Publications*: Palladio and Palladianism, 1991; (ed) Edinburgh, 1996; On Alberti and the Art of Building, 1998; (ed jtly) Body and Building: essays on the changing relation of body and architecture, 2002; Smoot's Ear: the measure of humanity, 2007; (ed) The London Plan 2000–2010: a decade of transformation, 2010; *translations*: (jtly) Alberti, On the Art of Building in Ten Books, 1988; (jtly) Palladio, The Four Books on Architecture, 1997; (jtly) Vitruvius, On Architecture, 2009. *Recreations*: Bath Rugby, walking and sailing. *Address*: Southcot House, 37 Lyncombe Hill, Bath BA2 4PQ. *E*: robert@tavernorconsultancy.co.uk.

**TAVINOR, Very Rev. Michael Edward;** Dean of Hereford, since 2002; *b* 11 Sept. 1953; *s* of Harold and Elsie Tavinor. *Educ*: Durham Univ. (BA Music 1975); Emmanuel Coll., Cambridge (PGCE 1976); King's Coll., London (AKC, MMus 1977); Ripon Coll., Cuddesdon (BA 1981, MA 1986, Oxon); Univ. of Wales, Lampeter (MTh 2010). ARCO 1977; ARSCM 2015. Ordained deacon, 1982, priest, 1983; Curate, St Peter, Ealing, 1982–85; Precentor, Sacrist and Minor Canon, Ely Cathedral, 1985–90; Priest i/c, Stuntney, 1987–90; Vicar, Tewkesbury Abbey with Walton Cardiff, 1990–2002, also Twyning, 1999–2002. Hon. Canon, Gloucester Cathedral, 1997–2002. Pres., Ch Music Soc., 2003–. Hon. FGCM, 2006. *Publications*: Pilgrim Guide to Tewkesbury Abbey, 1998; Pilgrim Guide to Hereford Cathedral, 2003; (contrib.) Sacred Space: House of God, Gate of Heaven, 2007; Saints and Sinners of the Marches, 2012; Shrines of the Saints in England and Wales, 2016. *Recreations*: walking, music, gardening, coin collecting. *Address*: The Deanery, College Cloisters, Cathedral Close, Hereford HR1 2NG. *T*: (01432) 374203. *E*: Dean@herefordcathedral.org.

**TAVISTOCK, Marquess of; Henry Robin Charles Russell;** *b* 7 June 2005; *s* and *heir* of Duke of Bedford, *qv*.

**TAVNER, Teresa, (Terry);** freelance consultant editor, since 2017; Consultant Editor, Essentials, 2014–16; Director, Headztrong Ltd, since 2009; Editor: Chat magazine, 1989–96; Woman's Own, 1998–2002 (Editor at large, 2012–14); She magazine, 2003–05; *b* 18 Jan. 1952; *d* of Bernard Joseph Hayes and Hanorah Hayes; *m* 1972, Barry Tavner (decd); one *s* one *d*. *Educ*: Notre Dame Grammar Sch., Battersea. Sub Ed. and Fiction Ed., Honey mag., 1981–84; Dep. Chief Sub-Ed., then Chief Sub-Ed., then Asst Ed., She mag., 1984–88; Ed., Eva mag., 1997–98. Editors' Editor, BSME, 1990. *Recreations*: ski-ing, travelling, cinema, reading, socialising. *E*: ttavner@aol.com.

**TAYLOR;** *see* Suenson-Taylor, family name of Baron Grantchester.

**TAYLOR,** family name of **Barons Kilclooney, Taylor of Goss Moor, Taylor of Holbeach** and **Taylor of Warwick,** and **Baroness Taylor of Bolton.**

**TAYLOR OF BOLTON,** Baroness *cr* 2005 (Life Peer), of Bolton in the county of Greater Manchester; **Winifred Ann Taylor;** PC 1997; *b* Motherwell, 2 July 1947; *m* 1966, David Taylor; one *s* one *d*. *Educ*: Bolton Sch.; Bradford Univ.; Sheffield Univ. Formerly teaching. Past part-time Tutor, Open Univ.; interested in intelligence and security matters, and education. Monitoring Officer, Housing Corp., 1985–87. Member: Association of Univ. Teachers; APEX; Holmfirth Urban District Council, 1972–74. Contested (Lab): Bolton W, Feb. 1974; Bolton NE, 1983. MP (Lab): Bolton W, Oct. 1974–1983; Dewsbury, 1987–2005. PPS to Sec. of State for Educn and Science, 1975–76; PPS to Sec. of State for Defence, 1976–77; an Asst Govt Whip, 1977–79; Opposition front bench spokesman on education, 1979–81, on housing, 1981–83, on home affairs, 1987–90 (Shadow Water Minister, 1988), on environment, 1990–92, on education, 1992–94; Shadow Chancellor of Duchy of Lancaster, 1994–95; Shadow Leader of H of C, 1994–97; Pres. of Council and Leader of H of C, 1997–98; Parly Sec. to HM Treasury (Govt Chief Whip), 1998–2001; Parly Under-Sec. of State, MoD, 2007–10, FCO, 2009–10. Member: Select Cttee on Standards and Privileges, 1995–97; Jt Cttee on Nat. Security Strategy, 2010–14; Chairman: Select Committee: on modernisation, 1997–98; on intelligence and security, 2001–05. Mem. Adv. Bd, Thales Holdings UK plc, 2010–. Chair, Council and Pro-Chancellor, Univ. of Bradford, 2015–. Hon. Fellow: Birkbeck Coll., 1995; St Antony's Coll., Oxford, 2004. *Address*: House of Lords, SW1A 0PW.

**TAYLOR OF GOSS MOOR,** Baron *cr* 2010 (Life Peer), of Truro in the County of Cornwall; **Matthew Owen John Taylor;** *b* 3 Jan. 1963; *s* of late Kenneth Heywood Taylor and of Gillian Dorothea Taylor (née Black); *m* 2007, Victoria Sophie Garner (marr. diss. 2017); three *s*. *Educ*: Treliske School, Truro; University College School; Lady Margaret Hall, Oxford (Scholar; BA Hons; MA). Pres., Oxford Univ. Student Union, 1985–86. Economic policy researcher to Parly Liberal Party (attached to David Penhaligon, MP), 1986–87. MP Truro, March 1987–1997 (L, 1987–88, Lib Dem, 1988–97); MP (Lib Dem) Truro and St Austell, 1997–2010. Parly spokesman on energy, 1987–88, on local govt, 1988–89, on trade and industry, 1989–90, on educn, 1990–92, on citizen's charter, 1992–94, on environment, 1994–99, and transport, 1997–99, on the economy, 1999–2003, on social exclusion, 2006–10; Special Advr to Govt on sustainable rural communities, 2007–08 (report, Living, Working, Countryside, 2008); Chm., DCLG Planning Practice Guidance Rev., 2013–14. Liberal Democrats: Communications Chm., 1989–92; Chm. of Campaigns and Communications, 1992–94; Chm., Parly Party, 2003–05. Director: South West Water Ltd, 2010–; Taylor & Garner Ltd, 2010–; Mayfield Market Towns Ltd, 2013–; Kensa Gp Ltd, 2013–. Chairman: Nat. Housing Fedn, 2009–15; Rural Coalition, 2009–12; Carclaze Garden Village Strategic Partnership Bd (formerly St Austell Eco-town Strategic Partnership Bd), 2010–; Bridgehall Real Estate Ltd, 2013–. Vis. Prof. of Planning, Plymouth Univ., 2016–; Sen. Vis. Fellow, Planning Sch., Univ. of Cambridge, 2016–. Hon. MRTPI 2016. *Address*: House of Lords, SW1A 0PW.
*See also V. M. T. Heywood.*

**TAYLOR OF HOLBEACH,** Baron *cr* 2006 (Life Peer), of South Holland in the County of Lincolnshire; **John Derek Taylor,** CBE 1992; PC 2014; Captain of the Honourable Corps of Gentlemen at Arms (Government Chief Whip in House of Lords), 2014–19; Deputy Chairman, Conservative Party, and Chairman, National Conservative Convention, 2000–03; *b* 12 Nov. 1943; *s* of late Percy Otto Taylor and Ethel Taylor (née Brocklehurst); *m* 1968, Julia Aileen Cunnington, *d* of late Leslie and Evelyn Cunnington, Bedford; two *s*. *Educ*: Holbeach Primary Sch.; St Felix Sch., Felixstowe; Bedford Sch. Dir, family horticultural and farming businesses, 1968–2010. Dir, 1990–2009, Chm., 2000–09, Springfields Horticl Soc. Ltd, and associated cos. Chairman: EC Working Party on European Bulb Industry, 1982; NFU Bulb Sub-cttee, 1982–87. Governor: Glasshouse Crops Res. Inst., 1984–88; Inst. of Horticl Res., 1987–90; Mem., Horticl Develt Council, 1986–91. Member, Minister of Agriculture's Regional Panel: Eastern Reg., 1990–92; E Midlands Reg., 1992–96. Chm., Holbeach and E Elloe Hosp. Charitable Trust, 1989–2006, now Patron; Trustee, Brogdale Horticl Trust, 1998–2005. Mem., Lincoln Diocesan Bd of Finance, 1995–2001 (Mem., Assets Cttee, 1995–2001, 2003–12). East Midlands Conservative Council: Mem., Exec. Cttee, 1966–98; Hon. Treas., 1984–89; Chm., 1989–94; Mem., Cons. Bd of Finance, 1985–89; Mem., Cons. Bd of Mgt, 1996–98; National Union of Conservative Associations: Member: Exec. Cttee, 1966–68 and 1984–98; Gen. Purposes Cttee, 1988–98; Standing Rev. Cttee, 1988–98; Agents Employment Adv. Cttee, 1988–94; Agents Exam Bd, 1994–98; Vice Pres., 1994–97; Pres. and Cons. Conf. Chm., 1997–98; Chairman: Candidates Cttee, Cons. Party, 1997–98, 2002–05; Cons. Party Constitutional Review, 1998–2000; Cons. Agents' Superannuation Fund, 2006–10; Conservatives Abroad, 2001–08. House of Lords: Opposition Whip, 2006–10; Opposition Spokesman: on Envmt, and on Wales, 2006–07; on Work and Pensions, 2006–10; Shadow Minister, Environment, Food and Rural Affairs, 2007–10; govt spokesman for Cabinet Office, for work and pensions and for energy and climate change, 2010–11; a Lord in Waiting (Govt Whip), 2010–11; Parliamentary Under-Secretary of State: DEFRA, 2011–12; Home Office, 2012–14. Chm., Taylor Rev., Sci., Agriculture and Horticulture, 2010. Founder Chm., local Young Cons. Br., 1964; Mem., Holland with Boston Cons. Assoc., 1964–95 (formerly Treas., Vice Chm., Chm. and Pres.); Pres., S Holland and The Deepings Cons. Assoc., 1995–2001, now Patron; Contested (C): Chesterfield, Feb. and Oct. 1974; Nottingham, EP elections, 1979. President: Lincs Agricl Soc., 2012; E of England Agricl Soc., 2014. FRSA 1994; ARAgS 2012, FRAgS 2018; MIHort 2013, FCIHort 2014, CHort 2015. Liveryman: Farmers' Co., 2009–; Gardeners' Co., 2010–. Peer of the Year, House Magazine Awards, 2011; Farm Business Personality of the Year, Business Mag., 2012. *Publications*: (ed) Taylor's Bulb Book, 1994. *Recreations*: English landscape and vernacular buildings, France, literature, arts, music. *Address*: House of Lords, SW1A 0PW. *Clubs*: Farmers, Carlton.

**TAYLOR OF WARWICK,** Baron *cr* 1996 (Life Peer), of Warwick in the county of Warwickshire; **John David Beckett Taylor;** barrister-at-law; author; journalist; international keynote speaker; radio and television presenter; *b* 21 Sept. 1952; *s* of late Derief David Samuel Taylor and Enid Maud Taylor; *m* 1981 (marr. diss. 2005); one *s* two *d*; *m* 2015, Laura Colleen Taylor; one *s* four *d*. *Educ*: Univ. of Keele (BA Hons Law 1977). Called to the Bar, Gray's Inn, 1978, Gray's Inn Advocacy Prize 1978; practised on Midland and Oxford Circuit, 1978–90; District Judge, 2001–06. Special Advr to Home Sec. and Home Office Ministers, 1990–91. Member: IPU; CPA; Industry and Parlt Trust. Consultant, Lowe Bell Communications Ltd, 1991–92; Producer/Presenter, BBC Radio and Television, 1994–; Chairman: Warwick Consulting Internat. Ltd, 1997–2000; Warwick Leadership Acad., 1997–. Bank consultant. Member: Solihull FPC, 1986–90; Greater London FEFC, 1992–95. Non-executive Director: NW Thames RHA, 1992–93; Currencies Direct Ltd, 2010; Internat. Small Business Congress, 2015–; Asia Now Resources Inc., Canada. Vice-President: Nat. Small Business Bureau, 1997–2000; BBFC, 1998–2008. Pres., African Caribbean Westminster Business Initiative. Dir, City Technology Colls Trust, 1994–95. Chancellor, Bournemouth Univ., 2002–07. Member: NUJ; RTS; Radio Acad.; Indep. Football Commn, 2002–03; Internat. Trade Council, 2014–. Mem. (C), Solihull DC, 1986–91. Contested (C): Birmingham, Perry Barr, 1987; Cheltenham, 1992. MInstD 1997. Barker, Variety Club Children's Charity; Patron: Parents for Children, adoption charity; Kidscape, 1997; West Indian Sen. Citizens Assoc.; Mem. Exec. Cttee, Sickle Cell Anaemia Relief. Pres., Ilford Town FC, 1998–; Mem., Aston Villa FC. Freeman: City of London, 1998; Lexington, Ky, USA, 2004; Las Vegas, USA, 2007. Hon. LLD: Warwick, 1999; Asbury Coll., Ky, USA, 2004. *Publications*: The System on Trial, 1996; No Blacks, No Irish, No Dogs (audiobook), 2004. *Recreations*: music, spending time with my wife and family, sport, travel. *Address*: House of Lords, SW1A 0PW. *T*: (020) 7219 5604, *Fax*: (020) 7219 5979. *E*: taylorjdb@parliament.uk. *W*: www.lordtaylor.org, www.twitter.com/lordjohntaylor.

**TAYLOR, Alan;** *see* Taylor, Robert A.

**TAYLOR, His Honour Alan Broughton;** a Circuit Judge, 1991–2005; *b* 23 Jan. 1939; *yr s* of Valentine James Broughton Taylor and Gladys Maud Taylor; *m* 1964, Diana Hindmarsh; two *s*. *Educ:* Malvern Coll.; Geneva Univ.; Birmingham Univ. (LLB); Brasenose Coll., Oxford (BLitt, re-designated MLitt 1979). Called to the Bar, Gray's Inn, 1961; barrister on Oxford Circuit, subseq. Midland and Oxford Circuits, 1963–91; a Recorder, 1979–91. A Pres., Mental Health Rev. Tribunal, 2001–09. Gov., St Matthew's Sch., Sandwell, 1988–92. FCIArb 1994; Chartered status, 2005. Lay-reader, Dio. of Carlisle, 2009–13, Reader Emeritus, 2014; Permission to Officiate, Dio. of Exeter, 2016. *Publications:* (contrib.) A Practical Guide to the Care of the Injured, ed P. S. London, 1967; (contrib.) Crime and Civil Society, ed Green, Grove and Martin, 2005. *Recreations:* philately, country and coastal walking. *Address:* 10 Wellswood Park, Torquay, Devon TQ1 2QB.

**TAYLOR, Andrew David;** Partner, Reed Smith (formerly Richards Butler, then Reed Smith Richards Butler), Solicitors, since 1983; *b* 6 March 1952; *s* of Vernon Stephen Taylor and Elizabeth Taylor; *m* 1977, Alison Jane Wright; one *s* two *d*. *Educ:* Magdalen Coll. Sch., Oxford; Lincoln Coll., Oxford (MA). Joined Richards Butler, Solicitors, 1977, Chm., 2000–05; specialises in shipping law. Treas./Sec., British Maritime Law Assoc., 2005–. *Publications:* Voyage Charters, 1993, 4th edn 2014. *Recreations:* ski-ing, walking, opera, wine. *Address:* Reed Smith, The Broadgate Tower, 20 Primrose Street, EC2A 2RS. *Clubs:* Travellers, City Law; Vincent's (Oxford).

**TAYLOR, Andrew Dawson,** OBE 1999; DPhil; FRS 2019; FRSE; FInstP; Executive Director, National Laboratories, Science and Technology Facilities Council, 2012–19 (Director, Facility Operations and Development, 2007–12); Head, Rutherford Appleton Laboratory, 2007–19; *b* Falkirk, 1 March 1950; *s* of Millar Taylor and Jean Taylor (*née* Dawson); *m* 1973, Elizabeth Slimming; two *s* two *d*. *Educ:* Denny High Sch., Stirlingshire; Univ. of Glasgow (Joseph Black Medal 1969; BSc 1st Cl. Hons 1972); St John's Coll., Oxford (DPhil 1976). FRSE 2006; FInstP 2007. SSO, Rutherford Lab., 1975–80; Vis. Scientist, Los Alamos Nat. Lab., New Mexico, 1980–83; SSO, 1983–85, Excitations Gp Leader, 1985–93, Director, 1993–2012, ISIS Facility, Rutherford Appleton Lab. Dep. Chief Exec., 2000–04, Exec. Dir, CCLRC Facilities, 2005–07, Mem., 2007–, CCLRC. European Spallation Source: Sec., Council, 1992–2000; Mem., Scandinavia Round Table, Sweden, 2007–09; Mem., Steering Cttee, Sweden, 2012–. Member: Steering Cttee, Institut Laue Langevin, 1993–2012; Adv. Bd, Los Alamos Neutron Sci. Center, 1994–2004; Neutron Rev. Panel, Univ. of Chicago, 1996–2004; Spallation Neutron Source Adv. Bd, USA, 1998–2008; Internat. Adv. Cttee, Japan Proton Accelerator Res. Complex, 2002–; Chairman: Canadian Foundn for Innovation Spallation Neutron Source Review, 2004; RIKEN Muon Review, 2007–16. Hon. Fellow, Mansfield Coll., 2011. Hon. DSc: Glasgow, 2010; London, 2012. Glazebrook Medal, Inst. of Physics, 2006. *Publications:* articles on develt and exploitation of pulsed neutron sources for condensed matter research. *Recreations:* family, hill walking, ski-ing, gastronomy. *Address:* Rutherford Appleton Laboratory, Harwell Science and Innovation Campus, Chilton, Oxon OX11 0QX. *T:* (01235) 446681. *E:* andrew.taylor@stfc.ac.uk.

**TAYLOR, Andrew John,** FCA; Chairman: Phantom Music Management Ltd, since 2006; Concept Venues Ltd, since 2006; *b* 23 Feb. 1950; *s* of Thomas Sowler Taylor and Sarah Taylor; *m* 1985, Elizabeth (*née* Robertson); two *d*. *Educ:* Trinity Coll., Cambridge (MA). FCA 1982. Sanctuary Group plc: Founder, 1976; CEO and Chm., 1976–98; CEO, 1998–2002; Chm. and Chief Exec., 2002–06. FRSA. *Recreations:* wine, cinema, books, fell walking, horse racing. *Address:* Bridle House, 36 Bridle Lane, W1F 9BZ. *E:* andy.taylor@phantom-music.com.

**TAYLOR, Andrew John Robert;** author, since 1982; *b* 14 Oct. 1951; *s* of Rev. Arthur Taylor and Hilda Taylor (*née* Haines); *m* 1979, Caroline Jane Silverwood; one *s* one *d*. *Educ:* King's Sch., Ely; Woodbridge Sch.; Emmanuel Coll., Cambridge (BA 1973); University Coll. London (MA). Boatbuilder, wages clerk, labourer, teacher; Librarian, London Bor. of Brent, 1976–81. Ed., The Author, jl of Soc. of Authors, 2004–06. Freelance ed. and book reviewer. Cartier Diamond Dagger for Sustained Excellence in Crime Writing, CWA, 2008. *Publications:* The Second Midnight, 1988; Blacklist, 1988; Toyshop, 1990; The Raven on the Water, 1991; The Barred Window, 1993; The American Boy, 2003 (CWA Histl Dagger); A Stain on the Silence, 2006; Bleeding Heart Square, 2008 (Martin Beck Award, Sweden); The Anatomy of Ghosts, 2010; The Scent of Death, 2013 (CWA Histl Dagger); The Silent Boy, 2014; Fireside Gothic (3 novellas), 2016; *Dougal series:* Caroline Minuscule, 1982 (CWA John Creasey Meml Award); Waiting for the End of the World, 1984; Our Fathers' Lies, 1985; An Old School Tie, 1986; Freelance Death, 1987; Blood Relation, 1990; The Sleeping Policeman, 1992; Odd Man Out, 1993; *Lydmouth series:* An Air That Kills, 1994; The Mortal Sickness, 1995; The Lover of the Grave, 1997; The Suffocating Night, 1998; Where Roses Fade, 2000; Death's Own Door, 2001; Call the Dying, 2004; Naked to the Hangman, 2006; *Roth Trilogy:* The Four Last Things, 1997; The Judgement of Strangers, 1998; The Office of the Dead, 2000 (CWA Histl Dagger) (trilogy televised as Fallen Angel, 2007); *Marwood and Lovett series:* The Ashes of London, 2016; The Fire Court, 2018; The King's Evil, 2019; The Last Protector, 2020; *for children:* Hairline Cracks, 1988; Private Nose, 1989; Snapshot, 1989; Double Exposure, 1990; Negative Image, 1992; The Invader, 1994. *Recreation:* making it up as I go. *Address:* c/o Greene & Heaton, 37 Goldhawk Road, W12 8QQ. *Club:* Detection.

**TAYLOR, Sir Anthony John N.;** *see* Newman Taylor.

**TAYLOR, Bernard David,** CBE 1993; Director, Cambridge Laboratories Ltd, 2006–11 (Chairman, 1997–2007); *b* 17 Oct. 1935; *s* of Thomas Taylor and Winifred (*née* Smith); *m* 1959, Nadine Barbara; two *s* two *d*. *Educ:* Univ. of Wales, Bangor (BSc Zoology). Science Teacher, Coventry Educn Authority, 1958; Sales and Marketing, SK&F, 1960; Sales and Marketing Manager, Glaxo NZ, 1964; New Products Manager, Glaxo UK, 1967; Man. Dir, Glaxo Australia, 1972; Dir, Glaxo Holdings plc, and Man. Dir, Glaxo Pharmaceuticals UK, 1984; Man. Dir, Glaxo Holdings, 1986–89; Chm., Medeva plc, 1990–96. Councillor and Vice-Pres., Aust. Pharm. Manufrs' Assoc., 1974–79; Councillor, Victorian Coll. of Pharmacy, 1976–82. Member: CBI Europe Cttee, 1987–89; BOTB, 1987–96. Trustee, WWF (UK), 1990–96. CCMI (CBIM 1986). Fellow, London Business Sch., 1988. Hon. Fellow, Bangor Univ., 2015.

**TAYLOR, Bernard John,** CBE 2017; DL; CChem, FRSC; CSci; Vice-Chairman, Evercore Partners Inc., since 2007; non-executive Chairman, Evercore Partners International LLP, since 2012; Chairman and Chief Executive, Evercore Partners Ltd (formerly Braveheart Financial Services Ltd), 2006–12; *b* 2 Nov. 1956; *s* of late John Taylor and Evelyn Frances Taylor; *m* 1984, Sarah Jane, *d* of John Paskin Taylor, Paris; one *s*. *Educ:* Cheltenham Coll.; St John's Coll., Oxford (Schol.; MA; Hon. Fellow 2008). LRPS 1974; CChem, FRSC 1991; CSci 2004. Business Planning and Acquisitions, 1979–82, Dir, Med. Div., 1983–85, Smiths Industries plc; Exec. Dir, Baring Bros & Co. Ltd, 1985–94; Chm. and Chief Exec., Robert Fleming & Co. Ltd, 1994–2001; Dir, Robert Fleming Hldgs Ltd, 1995–2001 (Jt Chief Exec., Investment Banking, 1998–2000); Vice Chm., EMEA, Chase Manhattan, 2000; Vice-Chm., JP Morgan, 2001–06. Non-executive Director: New Focus Healthcare Ltd, 1986–89; Isis Innovation Ltd, 1997–2013 (Chm., 2001–13); Ti Automotive Ltd, 2001–07 (Dep. Chm.); Oxford Instruments plc, 2002–12; Texture Restaurants Ltd, 2007–; Oxford Sciences Innovation plc, 2015–; Chm., Rycote Park Farms, 2000–. Chm., Bd of Mgt, Royal Commn for Exhibn of 1851, 2012– (Mem., 2005–; Chm., Finance Cttee, 2006–12). University of Oxford: Mem. Council, 2003–12; Chairman: Audit and Scrutiny Cttee, 2006–12; Remuneration Cttee, 2007–12; Member: Nominations Cttee, 2007–10; Finance Cttee, 2011–; Bd, Med. Scis Div., 2012–; Math., Physical and Life Scis Bd, 2014–; Endowment Mgt Bd, 2016– (Mem., Remuneration Cttee, 2007–); Dep. Steward, 2012–; Chairman: Remuneration Cttee, St John's Coll., Oxford, 2010–14; Trustees, Ashmolean Mus., 2011–. Mem., Court, Imperial Coll. London, 2015–. ERA Foundn Dir, 2010–; Mem., Investment Cttee, 2010–13, Audit Cttee, 2013–16 (Chm., 2013–16), Adv. Bd, 2012– (Chm.), Royal Soc.; Mem., Develt Cttee, Royal Opera House, 2003–11; Chm., Garsington Opera, 2012– (Mem., Adv. Bd, 2005–07; Trustee, 2007–; Chm., Relocation Cttee, 2010–11). Dir, Oxon County Agricl Assoc., 2000–09 (Pres., Thame Show, 2003). Patron, Oxon Churches Historic Trust (Chm., Jubilee Appeal, 2014); Chm., English Churches and Cathedrals Sustainability Review, HM Treasury and DCMS, 2016–17; Churches Sustainability Review Pilots Review Cttee, 2018–. DL Oxon, 2011. *Publications:* Photosensitive Film Formation on Copper, I, 1974, II, 1976; Synthesis and Mesomorphic Properties of a Liquid Crystal, 1977; Oxidation of Alcohols to Carbonyl Compounds, Synthesis, 1979; Selective Organic Reactions, 1979. *Recreations:* gardening, photography, wine, opera. *Address:* Evercore Partners LLP, 15 Stanhope Gate, W1K 1LN. *Clubs:* Brooks's, Oxford and Cambridge, White's, No 5 Hertford Street.

**TAYLOR, Sir Bill;** *see* Taylor, Sir W. G.

**TAYLOR, Prof. Brent William,** PhD; FRACP, FRCPCH; Professor of Community Child Health, University College London Institute of Child Health (formerly at Royal Free Hospital School of Medicine, then Royal Free and University College Medical School), 1988–2008, now Emeritus; *b* 21 Nov. 1941; *s* of Robert Ernest Taylor and Norma Gertrude Taylor; *m* 1970, Moira Elizabeth Hall; one *s* one *d*. *Educ:* Christchurch Boys' High Sch.; Otago Univ. (MB ChB 1966); Bristol Univ. (PhD 1986). FRACP 1977; FRCPCH 1997. Jun. hosp. posts, Christchurch, NZ, 1967–71; Res. Fellow and Sen. Registrar, Great Ormond Street Hosp. for Sick Children and Inst. of Child Health, 1971–74; Senior Lecturer: in Paediatrics, Christchurch Clin. Sch. of Medicine, 1975–81; in Social Paediatrics and Epidemiology, Bristol Univ., 1981–84; in Child Health, St Mary's Hosp. Med. Sch., 1985–88. Vis. Prof., Tongji Med. Univ., Wuhan, China, 1995–2008. Chm., Nat. Child Health Informatics Consortium, 1995–2008. *Publications:* chapters and papers on child health, social influences, vaccine safety, respiratory problems and informatics. *Recreations:* family, music (Handel), walking. *Address:* General and Adolescent Paediatric Unit, University College London Institute of Child Health, 30 Guilford Street, WC1N 3EH. *E:* brent.taylor@mac.com.

**TAYLOR, Brian Arthur Edward,** CB 2002; Director General, Civilian Personnel (formerly Assistant Under-Secretary of State, Civilian Management), Ministry of Defence, 1996–2001; *b* 10 Jan. 1942; *s* of Arthur Frederick Taylor and Gertrude Maclean Taylor (*née* Campbell); *m* 1967, Carole Ann Smith; three *s* one *d*. *Educ:* St Benedict's Sch., Ealing; Corpus Christi Coll., Oxford (MA Lit.Hum.). Ministry of Defence, 1965–2001: Asst Private Sec. to Sec. of State, 1969–70; Private Sec. to Chief of Air Staff, 1973–75; Head, Management Services Div., 1977–79; Head, Naval Personnel Div., 1979–81; RCDS 1982; Central Policy Review Staff, Cabinet Office, 1983; Head, Civilian Management Div., MoD, 1984–86; Asst Under-Sec. of State (Quartermaster), 1986–88, Air (PE), 1988–91; Head of Personnel Policy Gp (Under Sec.), HM Treasury, 1992–94; Asst Under-Sec. of State (Civilian Mgt (Policy)), MoD, 1994–96. Assessor, Fast Stream Assessment Centre, 2005–11. *Recreations:* sport, music, reading, family. *Club:* Richmond Rugby.

**TAYLOR, (Bryan) Hugo M.;** *see* Mascie-Taylor.

**TAYLOR, Carol Edwina;** Regional Employment Judge, London East, since 2011; *b* London, 5 July 1957. Admitted Solicitor, 1985; fee-paid Employment Judge, 1992; full-time Employment Judge, 1996; fee-paid Legal Chm., Reserve Forces Appeal Tribunal, 2003. *Address:* East London Tribunal Service, Anchorage House, 2 Clove Crescent, E14 2BE.

**TAYLOR, Caroline Bayantai;** *see* Plumb, C. B.

**TAYLOR, Catherine Dalling;** *see* Stihler, C. D.

**TAYLOR, Cavan;** Senior Partner, Lovell White Durrant, 1991–96; *b* 23 Feb. 1935; *s* of late Albert William Taylor and Constance Muriel (*née* Horncastle); *m* 1962, Helen Tinling; one *s* two *d*. *Educ:* King's Coll. Sch., Wimbledon; Emmanuel Coll., Cambridge (BA 1958; LLM 1959). 2nd Lieut, RASC, 1953–55. Articled with Herbert Smith & Co., 1958–61; qualified as solicitor, 1961; Legal Dept, Distillers' Co. Ltd, 1962–65; Asst Solicitor, Piesse & Sons, 1965–66, Partner, 1966; by amalgamation, Partner, Durrant Piesse and Lovell White Durrant; Dep. Sen. Partner, Lovell White Durrant, 1990–91. Director: Hampton Gold Mining Areas plc, 1979–86; Ludorum Management Ltd, 1996–2000; Link Plus Corp., 1999–2003. Adjudicator for Investment Ombudsman, 1996–2001. Gov., King's Coll. Sch., Wimbledon, 1970–2004 (Chm., 1973–90, 2000–04; Hon. Fellow, 2004). Vice-Pres., Surrey Co. RFU, 2006–. Trustee, School Fees Charitable Trust, 2000–10. Pres., Old Boys RFC, King's Coll. Sch., Wimbledon, 1997–2002. Pres., Le Cercle Français d'Esher, 2010–. Liveryman, Solicitors' Co., 1983–. *Publications:* articles in legal jls. *Recreations:* reading, gardening, conversation with my children, Rugby football. *Address:* Covenham House, 10 Broad High Way, Cobham, Surrey KT11 2RP. *T:* (01932) 864258. *Club:* Travellers.

**TAYLOR, (Charles) Jeremy (Bingham);** Chief Executive, Cheshire County Council, 2002–09; *b* 28 Oct. 1947; *s* of Dr Charles Bingham Taylor and Sydna Mary Taylor (*née* Howell); *m* 1972, Rachel Suzanne Hampson; one *d*. *Educ:* Selwyn Coll., Cambridge (BA, MA 1968). FCIPD 1987. Personnel Manager, ICI Ltd, 1968–72; Sen. Lectr, Univ. of Huddersfield, 1972–79; Cheshire County Council: Director: of Personnel, 1987–91; of Policy, 1991–97; of Community Develt, 1997–2002; Clerk, Cheshire Lieutenancy, 2002–09. Sen. Vice Chm., ACCE, 2008–09 (Hon. Sec., 2006–08). Gov. and Trustee, Brathay Hall Trust, 1987–91; Trustee: Keep Britain Tidy, 2010–11; Ormiston Children and Families, 2010–11. Mem. (C) E Northamptonshire DC, 2011–15. Churchwarden, Nassington, 2011–12. FCMI 1989; FRSA 1990. Hon. MBA Chester, 2009. *Recreations:* gardening, film, theatre, the Greek Islands, opera, cats. *Address:* Coppers, 28 Woodnewton Road, Nassington, Peterborough PE8 6QQ. *T:* (01780) 781220. *E:* cjbtaylor@btinternet.com. *Club:* Royal Over-Seas League.

**TAYLOR, Prof. Charles Margrave,** CC 1996; GOQ 2000; DPhil; FBA 1979; Professor of Political Science, McGill University, 1982–98, now Professor Emeritus of Philosophy; *b* 5 Nov. 1931; *s* of Walter Margrave Taylor and Simone Beaubien; *m* 1st, 1956, Alba Romer (*d* 1990); five *d*; 2nd, 1995, Aube Billard. *Educ:* McGill Univ. (BA History); Oxford Univ. (BA PPE, MA, DPhil). Fellow, All Souls Coll., Oxford, 1956–61; McGill University: Asst Prof., later Associate Prof., then Prof. of Pol Science, Dept of Pol Science, 1961–76; Prof. of Philosophy, Dept of Philos., 1973–76; Chichele Prof. of Social and Political Theory, and Fellow of All Souls Coll., Oxford Univ., 1976–81; Mem., Sch. of Social Science, Inst. for Advanced Study, Princeton, 1981–82. Prof. asst, later Prof. agrégé, later Prof. titulaire, Ecole Normale Supérieure, 1962–64, Dept de Philos., 1963–71, Univ. de Montréal. Vis.

Prof. in Philos., Princeton Univ., 1965; Mills Vis. Prof. in Philos., Univ. of Calif, Berkeley, 1974. For. Hon. Mem., Amer. Acad. of Arts and Scis, 1986. *Publications:* The Explanation of Behavior, 1964; Pattern of Politics, 1970; Hegel, 1975; Erklärung und Interpretation in den Wissenschaften vom Menschen, 1975; Social Theory as Practice, 1983; Philosophical Papers, 1985; Negative Freiheit, 1988; Sources of the Self, 1989; The Ethics of Authenticity, 1992; Philosophical Arguments, 1995; Varieties of Religion Today, 2002; Modern Social Imaginaries, 2004; A Secular Age, 2007; The Language Animal, 2016. *Recreations:* ski-ing, swimming. *Address:* 6603 Rue Jeanne Mance, Montréal, QC H2V 4L1, Canada.

**TAYLOR, Very Rev. Charles William;** Dean of Peterborough, 2007–16, now Dean Emeritus; *b* 16 March 1953; *s* of Rev. Preb. Richard John Taylor and Marjorie Taylor; *m* 1983, Catherine Margaret, *d* of Very Rev. Trevor Randall Beeson, *qv*; one *s* one *d. Educ:* Chorister, St Paul's Cathedral Choir Sch.; Marlborough Coll.; Selwyn Coll., Cambridge (BA Hons Theology; MA 1977); Cuddesdon Coll., Oxford; Church Divinity Sch. of the Pacific, Berkeley, Calif, USA. Ordained deacon, 1976, priest, 1977; Curate, Collegiate Church of St Peter, Wolverhampton, 1976–79; Chaplain, Westminster Abbey, 1979–84; Vicar, Stanmore with Oliver's Battery, Winchester, 1984–90; Rector, N Stoneham and Bassett, Southampton, 1990–95; Tutor in Liturgy, Salisbury and Wells Theol Coll., 1992–94; Canon Residentiary and Precentor, Lichfield Cathedral, 1995–2007; Associate Canon, Salisbury Cathedral, 2017–18. Chm., Cathedrals Plus, 2011–17. Hon. Chaplain, Plaisterers' Co., 2017–. Permission to officiate, Dio. of Newcastle, 2018–. Hon. FGCM 2007. *Publications:* The Word Revealed (with Peter Moger), 2011; numerous papers for Cathedrals' Liturgy and Music Gp. *Recreations:* music, food and wine, hospitality, Black Country humour, classic cars, following sport from a sedentary position, family holidays. *Address:* 38 Rochester Drive, Felton, Northumberland NE65 9DS.

**TAYLOR, Christopher Charles,** FSA; FBA 1995; Head, Archaeological Survey, Royal Commission on Historical Monuments, 1985–93, retired; *b* 7 Nov. 1935; *s* of Richard Hugh Taylor and Alice Mary Taylor (*née* Davies); *m* 1st, 1961, Angela Ballard (*d* 1983); one *s* one *d*; 2nd, 1985, Stephanie, *d* of Wing Comdr R. J. S. Spooner; one step *d. Educ:* King Edward VI Sch., Lichfield; Univ. of Keele (BA 1958); Inst. of Archaeol., Univ. of London (Dip. Archaeol.). FSA 1966; MCIfA (MIFA 1987). Investigator, Sen. Investigator and Principal Investigator, RCHM, 1960–93. Member: Historic Parks and Gardens Adv. Cttee, 1987–2001, Historic Settlement and Landscape Adv. Cttee, 2001–03, English Heritage. Pres., Cambridge Antiquarian Soc., 1994–96. Hon. DLitt Keele, 1997. John Coles Medal for Landscape Archaeology, British Acad., 2013. *Publications:* Dorset, 1970, 2nd edn 2004; The Making of the Cambridgeshire Landscape, 1973; Fieldwork in Medieval Archaeology, 1974; Fields in the English Landscape, 1975, 3rd edn 1987; Roads and Tracks in Britain, 1979, 2nd edn 1982; The Archaeology of Gardens, 1983; Village and Farmstead, 1983; (ed) W. G. Hoskins, The Making of the English Landscape, rev. edn 1988; Parks and Gardens of Britain, 1998; contrib. to various pubns of RCHM; papers in learned jls on archaeol. and landscape hist. *Recreations:* gardening, garden history. *Address:* 11 High Street, Pampisford, Cambridge CB22 3ES.

**TAYLOR, Prof. Christopher John,** OBE 2001; PhD; FREng; Professor of Medical Biophysics, since 1990, and Associate Vice President for Digital Strategy and Business Engagement, since 2018, University of Manchester; *b* Coventry, 25 Dec. 1945; *s* of Harold Herbert and Gwendoline May Taylor; *m* 1968, Jill Andrea Neal; one *s* one *d. Educ:* Gt Yarmouth Grammar Sch.; Univ. of Manchester (BSc Hons Physics; PhD 1972). FREng 2006. University of Manchester: Lectr in Biophysics, 1974–80; Sen. Lectr, 1980–90; Dir, Wolfson Image Analysis Unit, 1980–93; Head: Sch. of Diagnostic and Investigational Sci., 1993–96; Sch. of Computer Sci., 2003–08; Dir of Manchester Informatics, 2006; Associate Vice Pres. for Res., 2009. Chair: UK Foresight Health Informatics Wkg Party, 1996–98; UK Inst. for Health Informatics, 1998–2004; Vice Pres., UK Council for Health Informatics Professions, 2002–05. Chm., 1988–91, Dist. Fellow, 2003, British Machine Vision Assoc. (formerly British Pattern Recognition Assoc.). Dist. Fellow, Internat. Assoc. for Pattern Recognition, 2004; Fellow, Med. Image Computing and Computer-Aided Intervention Soc., 2009 (Enduring Impact Award, 2011). *Publications:* (jtly) Statistical Models of Shape: optimisation and evaluation, 2008; contribs to scientific pubns. *Recreations:* mountain biking, running, playing guitar, sky-diving (lapsed). *Address:* Imaging Science, Stopford Building, University of Manchester, Oxford Road, Manchester M13 9PT. *T:* (0161) 275 5403, *Fax:* (0161) 275 5145. *E:* chris.taylor@manchester.ac.uk. *W:* www.manchester.ac.uk/research/chris.taylor.

**TAYLOR, Prof. Christopher Malcolm,** FREng, FIMechE, FCGI; Vice-Chancellor and Principal, University of Bradford, 2001–07, now Emeritus Professor; *b* 15 Jan. 1943; *s* of William Taylor and Esther Hopkinson; *m* 1st, 1968, Gillian Walton (marr. diss. 1986); one *d*; 2nd, 1994, Diane Shorrocks (marr. diss. 2017). *Educ:* King's College London (BScEng); Univ. of Leeds (MSc, PhD, DEng). FIMechE 1986. Research Engineer, English Electric Co.; Sen. Engr, Industrial Unit of Tribology, Leeds, 1968–71; University of Leeds: Lectr, 1971–80; Sen. Lectr, 1980–86; Reader, 1986–90; Prof. of Tribology, 1990–2001; Head of Dept of Mechanical Engrg, 1992–96; Dean of Faculty of Engrg, 1996–97; Pro-Vice-Chancellor, 1997–2001. Vice-Pres., 1997–2001, Dep. Pres., 2001–03, Pres., 2003–04, IMechE. Editor, Part J, Procs IMechE, 1993–2011. FREng (FEng 1995); FCGI 1999. Tribology Trust Silver Medal, 1992; Donald Julius Groen Prize, IMechE, 1993; Jacob Wallenberg Foundn Prize, 1994. *Publications:* numerous contribs to learned jls. *Recreations:* walking, cycling. *Address:* Low Fold Cottage, Adel Mill, Eccup Lane, Leeds LS16 8BF. *T:* (0113) 267 2628. *E:* cmtchris@btinternet.com.

**TAYLOR, Claire;** *see* Taylor, S. C.

**TAYLOR, Clifford;** Director, Resources Television, BBC, 1988–93 (Deputy Director, 1987–88); *b* 6 March 1941; *s* of Fred Taylor and Annie Elisabeth (*née* Hudson); *m* 1962, Catherine Helen (*née* Green); two *d. Educ:* Barnsley and District Holgate Grammar Sch.; Barnsley College of Mining and Technology. ACMA. NCB, 1957–65; Midlands Counties Dairies, 1965–68; BBC: Radio Cost Accountant, 1968–71; Television Hd of Costing, 1971–76; Chief Accountant, Corporate Finance, 1976–77 and 1982–84; Chief Accountant, Engineering, 1977–82; Dep. Dir, Finance, 1984–86. *Recreations:* sport - plays golf, enjoys horse racing. *Address:* 8 Regency Drive, West Byfleet, Surrey KT14 6EN. *Clubs:* MCC, BBC.

**TAYLOR, Daria Jean, (Dari);** *b* 13 Dec. 1944; *d* of Daniel and Phyllis Jones; *m* 1970, David Taylor; one *d. Educ:* Nottingham Univ. (BA Hons 1970); Durham Univ. (MA 1990). Lectr in Further Educn, Nottingham, 1970–80; part-time Lectr in Sociology and Social Policy, N Tyneside, 1986–90; Regl Educn Officer, GMB, 1990–97. Mem. (Lab) Sunderland CC, 1986–97. MP (Lab) Stockton S, 1997–2010; contested (Lab) same seat, 2010. PPS to Parly Under Sec. of State, MoD, 2001–03, to Minister of State, Home Office, 2003–05. Member: Defence Select Cttee, 1997–99; Intelligence and Security Select Cttee, 2005–10. Member: All Party Cancer Gp, 1998–2010; All Party Parly Gp on Pakistan and Kashmir, 2007–10; Chairman: All Party Gp on Adoption, 2001–10; All Party Parly Gp on Infertility, 2005–08 (Mem., 2008–10); Treasurer: All Party Chemical Industries Gp, 1997–2010; All Party Opera Gp, 1998–2010; Secretary: All Party Parly Gp on Child Abduction; All Party Parly Gp on Cardiac Risk in the Young. Vice Chm., Westbridgford Br., NATFHE, 1970–80. *Recreations:* opera, walking, classical music, travelling.

**TAYLOR, Hon. (David) Louis;** Chief Executive, UK Export Finance, since 2015; *b* Newcastle upon Tyne, 7 Dec. 1966; *s* of Baron Taylor of Gosforth, PC and Irene Shirley Taylor (*née* Harris); *m* 1996, Kate Riddell; one *s* two *d. Educ:* Royal Grammar Sch., Newcastle upon Tyne; Pembroke Coll., Cambridge (BA Law 1989). Vice Pres., J. P. Morgan & Co., 1990–98; Dir, Strategy and Develt, BTR plc, 1998–99; Dir, Corporate Finance and Strategy, Cookson Gp plc, 1999–2004; Standard Chartered Bank: Man. Dir, Gp Corporate Develt, 2004–10; CEO, Vietnam, Cambodia and Laos, 2010–13; Chief Operating Officer, Gp Treasury, 2013–15. Vice-Chm., Eur. Chamber of Commerce, Vietnam, 2011–13. Chm. Trustees, Music in Prisons, 1996–2010. Gov., Royal GS, Newcastle upon Tyne, 1998–2010 (Chm., 2005–10). *Recreations:* wine, cycling, theatre, Northumberland, rowing (watching…). *Address:* UK Export Finance, 1 Horse Guards Road, SW1A 2HQ. *T:* (020) 7271 8268. *E:* louis.taylor@ukexportfinance.gov.uk. *Clubs:* Garrick; Hawks (Cambridge), Leander (Henley on Thames).

**TAYLOR, Prof. David Samuel Irving,** FRCP, FRCS, FRCOphth, FRCPCH; Consultant Ophthalmologist, Great Ormond Street Hospital, London, 1976–2007; Professor, Institute of Child Health, London, University College London, 2003–07, now Emeritus (Senior Lecturer, 1976–2003); Chairman, Examinations Committee, International Council of Ophthalmology, 2007–14; *b* 6 June 1942; *s* of Samuel Donald Taylor and Winifred Alice May Marker; *m* 1976, Anna (*née* Rhys Jones); two *s. Educ:* Dauntsey's Sch.; Liverpool Univ. (MB ChB 1967); DSc (Med) London 2001. FRCS 1973; FRCP 1984; FRCOphth 1990; FRCPCH 1998. House Surgeon and Physician, Liverpool Royal Infirmary, 1967–68; Registrar, then Sen. Registrar, Moorfields Eye Hosp., 1972–75; Research Fellow: Great Ormond Street Hosp., London, 1975–76; Neuro-ophthalmology Dept, Univ. of California, San Francisco, 1976–77; Consultant Neuro-ophthalmologist, National Hosps, London, 1976–89. Medico-legal expert in med. negligence and child abuse, 2006–16. Hon. Mem. Council, Royal London Soc. for the Blind, 1988. Hon. FRSocMed 2005; Hon. FRCOphth 2006. Member, Editorial Board: Brit. Jl of Ophthalmology, 1977–90, 2000–07; European Jl of Ophthalmology, 1998–2007. *Publications:* (ed) Paediatric Ophthalmology, 1990, (author) 5th edn as Taylor and Hoyt's Pediatric Ophthalmology and Strabismus 2017; (with C. S. Hoyt) Practical Paediatric Ophthalmology, 1997 (trans. Japanese, Portuguese, Spanish, Russian); 260 other publications as book chapters or in learned jls. *Recreations:* tennis, sailing, forestry, growing vegetables. *Address:* 23 Church Road, Barnes, SW13 9HE. *T:* (020) 8878 0305, 07836 344028. *E:* dsit@btinternet.com.

**TAYLOR, David William;** educational consultant, since 2004; Director of Inspection, Office for Standards in Education, 1999–2004; *b* 10 July 1945; *s* of Harry William Taylor and Eva Wade Taylor (*née* Day); *m* 1972, Pamela Linda (*née* Taylor); one *s* one *d. Educ:* Bancroft's Sch.; Worcester Coll., Oxford (BA Hons 1967; MA 1972); Inst. of Education, Univ. of London (PGCE, Distinction; Story-Miller Prize, 1968). Watford Grammar School: Classics Teacher, 1968–73; Head of Classics, 1973–78; HM Inspector of Schools, 1978–86; Staff Inspector, 1986–92; seconded to Touche Ross Management Consultants, 1991; Office for Standards in Education: Manager, Work Prog., 1992–93; Head, Strategic Planning, 1993–96; Head, Teacher Educn and Training, 1996–99. Exec. Sec., JACT, 1976–78. Schoolteacher Fellowship, Merton Coll., Oxford, 1978. Mem. Bd, Assoc. of Governing Bodies of Ind. Schs, 2013– (Dep. Chair). Chair of Govs, St Lawrence Coll., Ramsgate, 2011–. FRSA. Ed., Classical Literature and Society series, Bloomsbury Publishing (formerly Duckworth), 2006–. *Publications:* Cicero and Rome, 1973; Work in Ancient Greece and Rome, 1975; Acting and the Stage, 1978; Roman Society, 1980; The Greek and Roman Stage, 1999; numerous articles in professional jls. *Recreations:* chess, classical (esp. choral) music, cricket, classical literature, theatre, poetry, travel, gardening. *Address:* Firgrove, Seal Hollow Road, Sevenoaks, Kent TN13 3SF. *T:* (01732) 455410. *Club:* Athenæum.

**TAYLOR, David William;** a District Judge (Magistrates' Courts), since 2009; *b* 1 March 1957. *Educ:* St Chad's Coll., Wolverhampton; Univ. of Southampton (LLB Hons). Admitted as solicitor, 1982. Recorder, 2002–14. Mem., Mental Health Rev. Tribunal, later Tribunal Judge, Mental Health (pt-time), 1999–. *Address:* Taunton Deane Magistrates' Court, St John's Road, Taunton, Somerset TA1 4AX.

**TAYLOR, David William;** Senior Vice President, Ingram Content Group, since 2009; Group Managing Director, Lightning Source UK, since 2009; *b* Wolverhampton, 18 July 1960; *s* of William and Lillian Joyce Taylor; *m* 1988, Clare Caroline Grace Tate; two *s. Educ:* Municipal Grammar Sch., Wolverhampton; Colton Hills Comprehensive Sch., Wolverhampton; Univ. of Reading (BA English Lit.; MA English Lit.); Univ. of Westminster (DMS); Oxford Brookes Univ. (MBA). Blackwell: bookseller, 1984–89; Mktg Manager, 1989–94; Regl Manager, 1994–96; Dir, Liby Services, 1996–2000; Founder and Chm., swotbooks.com, 2000–04; Man. Dir, Lightning Source UK, 2004–06; Sen. Vice Pres., 2006–08, Pres., 2008–09, Lighting Source Inc. Mem., Book Soc., 2006–. *Publications:* (contrib.) Writers' and Artists' Yearbook, 2009–17; contrib. articles to Bookseller, Publishing News, Assoc. Learned Professional Publishers, Logos, Congressional Qly, Bookbrunch. *Recreations:* cycling, drinking single malt whisky, supporting Wolverhampton Wanderers, collecting Biggles books. *Address:* Old Upper Farm, 154 Wroslyn Road, Freeland, Oxon OX29 8AQ. *T:* (01993) 882209. *E:* david.taylor@ingramcontent.com. *Club:* Wolverhampton Wanderers.

**TAYLOR, David Wilson,** CBE 2007; DL; Chairman, David Taylor Partnerships Ltd, since 2000; *b* 9 May 1950; *s* of Eric and Sybil Taylor; *m* 1980, Brenda Elizabeth Birchall; two *s. Educ:* Galashiels Acad.; Dundee Univ. Sch. of Architecture; Architectural Assoc. (DipArch, Dip. Urban and Regl Planning). Research and journalism, 1979–81; Advisor on regl policy to John Prescott, MP, 1981–83; Lancashire Enterprises Ltd: Dep. Man. Dir, 1983–85; Man. Dir, 1985–89; AMEC plc: Man. Dir, AMEC Regeneration, 1989–92; Man. Dir, AMEC Develts, 1992–93; Chief Exec., English Partnerships, 1993–96; Gp Chief Exec., Lancs Enterprises, subseq. Enterprise plc, 1996–2000. Director: INWARD, 1996–99; Preston North End plc, 1996– (Dep. Chm.); non-executive Chairman: Vektor Ltd, 1996–2004; Angela Campbell Gp, 1996–98; Era Ltd, 1997–2005; Hull Citybuild Ltd, 2003–09; Elevate East Lancs, 2003–09; Silvertown Quays Ltd, 2003–10; BL-Canada Quays Ltd, 2005–; Parking Eye Ltd, 2005–13; Professional Development TV Ltd, 2005–09; Venture Extreme Ltd, 2006–; Rockpools Resourcing & Consulting Ltd, 2010–; Energy 10 Ltd, 2012–; Allied Lighting Ltd, 2012–; Endo Enterprises (UK) Ltd, 2012–; Momentum + Ltd, 2012–; non-executive Director: John Maunders Gp plc, 1996–98; Central Lancs Develt Agency, 1997–2001; United Waste Services, 1997–2000; Manchester Commonwealth Games Ltd, 1999–2003; London and Southern Ltd, 2000–05; UK Regeneration Ltd, 2004–06. Special Advr to Dep. Prime Minister, 1997–98. Chm., NW Film Commn, 1996–2001; Dir, Olympic Delivery Authy, 2006–14. Chm., Phoenix Trust, 1997–2001; Trustee, Prince's

Foundn, 2000–03. Pro-Chancellor and Chm., Univ. of Central Lancashire, 2014–. FRSA 2006. Hon. Fellow, Univ. of Central Lancashire, 1996. DL Lancs, 2014. *Recreations:* football (British and American), Rugby (Union and League). *Address:* (office) 4 Riversway Business Village, Navigation Way, Preston PR2 2YP. *T:* (01772) 883888. *Club:* Royal Automobile.

**TAYLOR, Deborah Elizabeth;** a Judge of the Upper Tribunal (Immigration and Asylum Chamber) (formerly a Senior Immigration Judge, Asylum and Immigration Tribunal), 2005–16; *b* Bolton, Lancs, 14 March 1953; *d* of Bernard and Barbara Crossley; *m* 1976, Christopher Marc Taylor; four *s*. *Educ:* Bolton Sch.; York Univ. (BA Hons Hist. 1974); Hughes Hall, Cambridge (Cert Ed 1975). Solicitor, Mary Ward Legal Settlement, 1981–85; teacher, British Sch., New Delhi, 1987–89; solicitor, Stockwell and Clapham Law Centre, 1990–92; Immigration Adjudicator, 1992–97; Centre Adjudicator, Manchester, 1997–2002; Regl Adjudicator, 2002–05. Under Sheriff of York, 2016–17. *Recreations:* fell-walking, music, travel, caring for three granddaughters, spending time with friends.

**TAYLOR, Desmond Philip S.;** *see* Shawe-Taylor.

**TAYLOR, Duncan John Rushworth,** CBE 2002; HM Diplomatic Service, retired; Ambassador to Mexico, 2013–18; *b* 17 Oct. 1958; *s* of Sir John Lang, (Jock), Taylor, KCMG and of Molly Taylor; *m* 1981, Marie-Béatrice Terpougoff; two *s* three *d*. *Educ:* Trinity Coll., Cambridge (MA Hons Modern Langs 1980). Retail analyst, Gulf Oil GB, 1980–82; entered FCO, 1982; Third Sec., FCO, 1982–83; Third, later Second, Sec., Havana, 1983–87; First Sec., FCO, 1987–92; Hd, Commercial Section, Budapest, 1992–96; on secondment to Rolls Royce plc as Dir, Latin American Affairs, 1996–97; Counsellor, FCO, 1997–2000; Dep. Consul Gen. and Dep. Hd of Mission, New York, 2000–05; High Comr, Barbados and Eastern Caribbean States, 2005–09; Gov., Grand Cayman, 2010–13. *Recreations:* sports, travel, theatre, films, books, food. *Address:* Bredeweg 127, 8420 De Haan, Belgium.

**TAYLOR, Prof. Edwin William,** FRS 1978; Louis Block Professor of Molecular Genetics and Cell Biology, University of Chicago, 1984–99, half-time, 1999, now Emeritus (Professor, Department of Biophysics, 1975–99); part-time Research Professor, Department of Cell and Molecular Biology, Northwestern University Medical School, since 2000; *b* Toronto, 8 June 1929; *s* of William Taylor and Jean Taylor (*née* Christie); *m* 1956, Jean Heather Logan; two *s* one *d*. *Educ:* Univ. of Toronto (BA 1952); McMaster Univ. (MSc 1955); Univ. of Chicago (PhD 1957). Asst Prof., 1959–63, Associate Prof., 1963–67, Prof., 1967–72, Univ. of Chicago; Prof. of Biology, King's College and MRC Unit, London, 1972–74; Associate Dean, Div. of Biol Sci. and Medicine, 1977–79, Prof. and Chm., Dept of Biology, 1979–84, Univ. of Chicago. Rockefeller Foundn Fellow, 1957–58; Nat. Insts of Health Fellow, 1958–59, cons. to NIH, 1970–72, 1976–80. Instructor in Physiology, Marine Biol Lab. summer program, Woods Hole, Ma, 1991–98. Member: Amer. Biochem. Soc.; Biophysical Soc.; Fellow, Amer. Acad. of Arts and Scis, 1991; NAS, USA, 2001. E. B. Wilson Medal, Amer. Soc. for Cell Biology, 1999. *Address:* Cummings Life Sciences Center, University of Chicago, 920 East 58th Street, Chicago, IL 60637, USA. *T:* (773) 7021660; 5805 South Dorchester Avenue, Apt 11C, Chicago, IL 60637, USA. *T:* (773) 9552441.

**TAYLOR, Enid,** FRCS, FRCOphth; Consultant Ophthalmic Surgeon, North Middlesex Hospital, 1974–98; *b* 18 June 1933; *d* of Joseph William Wheldon and Jane Wheldon; *m* 1959, Thomas Henry Taylor; two *s*. *Educ:* Girton Coll., Cambridge (MA); London Hosp. Med. Coll. (MB BChir; DO 1963). FRCS 1965; FRCOphth 1988. Consultant Ophthalmic Surgeon, Elizabeth Garrett Anderson Hosp., 1966–73. Chm., NE Thames Ophthalmic Adv. Cttee, DHSS, 1979–86. Member Council: Faculty of Ophthalmologists, 1980–88; Coll. of Ophthalmologists, 1988–90; Sect. Ophthalmol, RSocMed, 1981–85 (Vice-Pres., 1985–88); Mem., Ophthalmic Cttees, BMA, 1982–2000. Liveryman, 1973, Asst, 1989–2008, Master, 2002–03, Soc. of Apothecaries. *Publications:* contrib. papers and presentations on diabetic retinal disease. *Recreations:* cooking, needlework. *Address:* 60 Wood Vale, N10 3DN. *T:* (020) 8883 6146.

*See also* S. W. Taylor.

**TAYLOR, Prof. Eric Andrew,** FRCP, FRCPsych, FMedSci; Professor of Child and Adolescent Psychiatry, Institute of Psychiatry, King's College London, 1999–2009, now Emeritus; Hon. Consultant, Maudsley Hospital, since 1978; *b* 22 Dec. 1944; *s* of Dr Jack Andrew Taylor and Grace Taylor; *m* 1969, Anne Patricia Roberts (*d* 2000); two *s*. *Educ:* Trinity Hall, Cambridge (MA); Harvard Univ.; Middx Hosp. Med. Sch. (MB). FRCP 1986; FRCPsych 1988. SHO, Middx Hosp., 1969–71; Res. Fellow, Harvard Univ., 1971; Registrar, then Sen. Registrar, Maudsley Hosp., 1973–76; Institute of Psychiatry: Lectr, then Sen. Lectr, 1976–86; Reader, 1986–93; Prof. of Developmental Neuropsychiatry, 1993–99; Clinical Scientist, MRC, 1990–99. Cantwell Lectr, UCLA, 2004; Emanuel Miller Lectr, Assoc. for Child Psychol. and Psychiatry, 2004. Non-exec. Dir, S London and Maudsley NHS, 2008–10. Trustee: Nat. Acad. of Parenting Practitioners, 2008–10; Place2Be, 2010–; Autistica, 2015–. Corresp. Mem., Argentina Acad. of Sci., 2009–. Editor: Jl Child Psychol. and Psychiatry, 1984–95; Eur. Child and Adolescent Psychiatry, 2003–13. FMedSci 2000. Hon. FRCPsych 2012. Hon. Mem., child psychiatry assocs in Germany, Chile and UK. Ruane Prize, Nat. Assoc. for Res. in Schizophrenia and Affective Disorders, 2009; Heinrich Hoffman Medal, World Fedn of Attention Deficit Hyperactivity Disorder, 2011; President's Medal, Assoc. for Child and Adolescent Mental Health, 2018. *Publications:* The Hyperactive Child: a parents' guide, 1985, 3rd edn 1997; The Overactive Child, 1986 (Spanish and Japanese edns 1991); The Epidemiology of Childhood Hyperactivity, 1991; (ed jtly) Child and Adolescent Psychiatry: modern approaches, 3rd edn 1994 to 6th edn (as Rutter's Child and Adolescent Psychiatry) 2015; People with Hyperactivity: understanding and managing their problems, 2009; (with A. Stringaris) Disruptive Mood: irritability in children and adolescents, 2015; contrib. numerous papers to scientific jls on child neuropsychiatry. *Address:* Department of Child and Adolescent Psychiatry, Institute of Psychiatry, Psychology and Neuroscience, King's College London, De Crespigny Park, SE5 8AF. *T:* (020) 7848 0489. *Clubs:* Athenæum, Royal Society of Medicine.

**TAYLOR, Errol Christopher Loth;** Chief Executive, Royal Society for the Prevention of Accidents, since 2017; *b* Glasgow, 1962; three *c*. *Educ:* Univ. of Southampton (BSc Hons Mech. Engrg); Warwick Business Sch. (MBA); Inst. of Dirs (Dip. Co. Direction). Hd, Global Mktg, BSI, 2001–04; Business Develt Dir, 2004–08, Dep. Chief Exec., 2006–17, ROSPA. Mem. Council, NHBC, 2016–; Mem. Adv. Bd, Office of Product Safety and Standards, 2019–. Chm., Eurosafe, 2014–. Patron, Lifeskills, 2016–. CDir 2012; FInstD 2012. FRSPH 2014. *Recreations:* scuba diving, cycling, hiking. *Address:* Royal Society for the Prevention of Accidents, ROSPA House, 28 Calthorpe Road, Edgbaston, W Midlands B15 1RP. *T:* (0121) 248 2000.

**TAYLOR, Dr Frank Henry,** CBE 2003; Secretary, Charles Wallace India Trust, 1992–2004; *b* 20 Jan. 1932; *s* of Frank Taylor and Norah (*née* Dunn). *Educ:* Frimley and Camberley Co. Grammar Sch.; King's Coll., London (BSc 1953; PhD 1957). Beit Meml Fellow for Med. Res., Imperial Coll., London and Pasteur Inst., Paris, 1957–60; British Council, 1960–92: Science Officer, 1960–61; Asst Cultural Attaché, Cairo, 1961–64; Asst Regl Rep., Calcutta, 1965–69; Science Officer, Rio de Janeiro, 1970–74; Dir, Science and Technology Dept, 1974–78; Rep., Saudi Arabia, 1978–81; Head Operations, Technical Educn and Trng in Overseas Countries, and Dep. Controller, Science, Technology and Education Div., 1981–84; Counsellor, British Council and Cultural Affairs, Ankara, 1984–87; Dep. Controller, Asia and Pacific Div., then S and W Asia Div., 1987–88; Controller, Africa and ME Div., 1989–90; Dir, Libraries, Books and Inf. Div., 1990–92. *Publications:* articles on surface chemistry and reviews in Proc. Royal Soc., etc. *Recreations:* music, bridge, bookbinding, Middle East. *Address:* 9 Shaftesbury Road, Richmond, Surrey TW9 2TD.

**TAYLOR, Prof. Fredric William,** DPhil; Halley Professor of Physics, Oxford University, 2000–11, now Emeritus (Head of Department of Atmospheric, Oceanic and Planetary Physics, 1979–2000); Fellow, Jesus College, Oxford, 1979–2011, now Emeritus; *b* 24 Sept. 1944; *s* of William Taylor and Ena Lloyd (*née* Burns); *m* 1969, Doris Jean Buer. *Educ:* Duke of Northumberland's Sch.; Univ. of Liverpool (BSc 1966); Univ. of Oxford (DPhil 1970; MA 1983). Resident Res. Associate, US Nat. Res. Council, 1970–72; Sen. Scientist, 1972–79, Dist. Vis. Scientist, 1996–, Jet Propulsion Lab., CIT; Oxford University: Reader in Atmospheric Physics, 1983–89; Prof. of Atmospheric Physics, 1990–99. *Publications:* Cambridge Atlas of the Planets, 1982, 2nd edn 1986 (trans. German 1984, Italian 1988); Remote Sounding of Atmospheres, 1984, 2nd edn 1987; (with A. Coustenis) Titan, 1999, 2nd edn 2008; (with M. Lopez-Puertas) Non-LTE Radiative Transfer in the Atmosphere, 2001; The Cambridge Guide to the Planets, 2002; Elementary Climate Physics, 2005; (with I. Vardavas) Radiation and Climate, 2007, 2nd edn 2011; The Scientific Exploration of Mars, 2009; Planetary Atmospheres, 2010; The Scientific Exploration of Venus, 2014; Exploring the Planets: a memoir, 2016; contrib. to learned jls. *Recreations:* exploring the planets, understanding climate change, railways, classic cars, H. G. Wells, pottering in garden, Newcastle United, England cricket, fine wine, real ale. *Address:* Clarendon Laboratory, Oxford OX1 3PU. *T:* (01865) 272903; Jesus College, Oxford OX1 3DW.

**TAYLOR, Gemma Mary;** QC 2018; *b* London, 13 July 1964; *d* of Dr Gordon William Taylor, *qv*; *m* 1998, Dr Adam Robinson; one *s* one *d*. *Educ:* St Paul's Girls' Sch., Hammersmith; Queen Mary. Coll., Univ. of London (LLB 1986). Called to the Bar, Inner Temple, 1988; in practice as barrister, specialising in family law. Member: Family Law Bar Assoc.; Assoc. of Lawyers for Children. *Recreations:* books, ballroom dancing, all things Italian. *Address:* 42 Bedford Row, WC1R 4LL. *T:* (020) 7831 0222. *E:* clerks@42br.com.

**TAYLOR, Geoffrey Keith,** CB 2007; PhD; Director, External Relations, Government Communications Headquarters, 2001–16; *b* 1 March 1948; *s* of Wilfred Taylor and Irene Isobel Taylor (*née* Smith); *m* 1969, Patricia Anne Angell; two *s*. *Educ:* Nottingham High Sch.; Queens' Coll., Cambridge (BA 1970); Univ. of Leicester (PhD 1973). Res. Demonstrator, Univ. of Leicester, 1970; Government Communications Headquarters: joined, 1973, Asst Deptl Specialist; Principal, 1978; Sen. Civil Service, 1987; Dir, Special Progs, 1999–2001. Bd Advr, ARQIT Ltd (formerly OMEGA QKD Ltd), 2017–. Mem., Croquet Assoc. *Publications:* papers on quantum molecular dynamics in Physical Rev., etc. *Recreations:* croquet, buying, selling and mending anything, foreign travel, playing 1930s popular piano music poorly, mooching. *Clubs:* Nottingham Croquet, Cheltenham Croquet.

**TAYLOR, Gordon,** OBE 2008; Chief Executive, Professional Footballers' Association, 1981–2019; *b* 28 Dec. 1944; *s* of Alec and Mary Taylor; *m* 1968, Catharine Margaret Johnston; two *s*. *Educ:* Ashton-under-Lyne Grammar Sch.; Bolton Technical Coll.; Univ. of London (BScEcon Hons (ext.)). Professional footballer with: Bolton Wanderers, 1960–70; Birmingham City, 1970–76; Blackburn Rovers, 1976–78; Vancouver Whitecaps (N American Soccer League), 1977; Bury, 1978–80, retd. Professional Footballers Association: Mem., Management Cttee, 1971; Chm., 1978–80; (full-time) Asst Sec., 1980; Sec./Treasurer, 1981; Pres., Internat. Assoc. of Professional Footballers Unions, 1994–2005 (Hon. Pres., 2005–). Hon. MA Loughborough Univ. of Technol., 1986 (for services to football); Hon. DArts De Montfort, 1998 (for services to football and res.). Lifetime Contribution to League Football Award, Football League Awards, 2010. *Recreations:* theatre, dining-out, watching football, reading, doing crosswords.

**TAYLOR, Dr Gordon William;** Managing Director, Firemarket Ltd, since 1988; *b* 26 June 1928; *s* of William and Elizabeth Taylor; *m* 1954, Audrey Catherine Bull; three *s* one *d*. *Educ:* J. H. Burrows Sch., Grays, Essex; Army Technical Sch.; London Univ. (BScEng Hons, PhDEng). MICE, MIMechE, MIET. Kellogg Internat. Corp., 1954–59; W. R. Grace, 1960–62; Gen. Man., Nalco Ltd, 1962–66; BTR Industries, 1966–68; Managing Director: Kestrel Chemicals, 1968–69; Astral Marketing, 1969–70; Robson Refractories, 1970–87. Greater London Council: Alderman, 1972–77; Mem. for Croydon Central, 1977–80; Chairman: Public Services Cttee, 1977–78; London Transp. Cttee, 1978–79. Chm., W London Residents' Assoc., 2003–. *Recreations:* theatre, reading, tennis, croquet. *Club:* Holland Park Lawn Tennis.

*See also* G. M. Taylor.

**TAYLOR, Hamish Wilson;** Chief Executive, Hamish Taylor Skills Exchange Network, since 2004; *b* Kitwe, N Rhodesia, 18 June 1960; *s* of late Dr Douglas James Wilson Taylor and of Mairi Helen Taylor (*née* Pitt); *m* 1984, Fiona Marion Darroch; three *s*. *Educ:* Skinners' Sch., Tunbridge Wells; Univ. of St Andrews (Pres., Athletic Union, 1981–82; MA Hons Econs 1982); Emory Univ., Atlanta (Robert T. Jones Schol., 1983; Business Sch. Fellow; St Andrews Soc. of Washington Schol., 1983–84; MBA 1984). FCILT (FCIT 1999); FCIB 2001. Brand Manager, Procter and Gamble Ltd, 1984–90; Mgt Consultant, Price Waterhouse, 1990–93; Gen. Manager, Brands, British Airways, 1993–97; Man. Dir, Eurostar (UK) Ltd, 1997–99; Chief Exec., Eurostar Gp, 1999; Chief Executive: Sainsbury's Bank, 2000–02; Vision UK, 2002–04. Non-exec. Dir, Chartered Brands, 2003–08; Mem., Adv. Panel, Bright Grey, 2003–08. Chm., Europe, Middle East and Africa Adv. Bd, Emory Univ., 2006–08. Trustee, Robert T. Jones Meml Trust, 2005–. Mem. Bd, Edinburgh Rugby, 2010–14. Mentor, BBC TV series, Teen Canteen, 2013. FRSA 1999. Freeman, City of Glasgow, 1979. Rail Professional Business Manager of the Year, Rail Professional Magazine, 1998; Sheth Dist. Internat. Alumni Award, Emory Univ., 2004. *Recreations:* athletics (Scottish Junior international, 1979), football, Rugby, piano. *E:* hamish@hamishtaylor.com.

**TAYLOR, Dr Hilary Anne, (Mrs Peter Vickers);** Director, Hilary Taylor Landscape Associates Ltd, 1998–2017; Partner, Howgill Tattershall Fine Art, since 2012; *b* Spital, Cheshire, 16 March 1948; *d* of Derek George Dawson Taylor and Dorothy Taylor (*née* Fullerton); *m* 1992, Peter Vickers; one *s*. *Educ:* Wycombe High Sch. for Girls, High Wycombe; Univ. of E Anglia (BA Hons Art/Architecture Hist. 1969); Univ. of Nottingham (PhD 1974). Hd, Art and Design Hist., Trent Poly., 1974–88; freelance lectr, researcher and campaigner, historic public parks and gardens, 1988–94; Dir, Dawson Taylor Landscapes, 1990–96. England-wide survey of public parks, English Heritage, 1994–95. Churchill Fellow, 1994. Member: Expert Panel on Historic Bldgs and Land, Heritage Lottery Fund, 2001–08; Church Bldgs Council and Statutory Adv. Cttee, 2008– (Chair, Bells Conservation Cttee, 2016–19). Lead design for several major contracts for restoration and renewal of public parks incl. Grade II* Battersea Park, Grade I Birkenhead Park, and Roberts Park (part of WHS, Saltaire); Jury Mem., internat. competition for reordering and redevelt of Grade I St Mary's Redcliffe, Bristol, 2015–16. Work on conservation mgt plans for English landscapes for Nat. Trust incl. Studley Royal and Fountains Abbey, Calke

Abbey, Kedleston and Lyveden New Bield. Trustee, Horniman Mus. and Gardens, 2009–14. Res. and lectr on significance of historic trees in churchyards; presentations to confs, Conservation Foundn, London and Liverpool, 2006. FRSA. *Publications:* James McNeill Whistler, 1976; British Impressionism, 1989; (contrib.) The Regeneration of Public Parks, 2000; (contrib.) Encyclopedia of Gardens: history and design, 2001; contrib. articles to Art Hist., Garden Hist. *Recreations:* Pembrokeshire coast, churches, gardening, reading, art galleries, sharing my husband's and my son's love of cricket. *Address:* 1 Scotsmansfield, Burway Road, Church Stretton, Shropshire SY6 6DP. *T:* (01694) 723273. *E:* hilary-taylor@htla.co.uk.

TAYLOR, Sir Hugh (Henderson), KCB 2009 (CB 2000); Permanent Secretary, Department of Health, 2006–10; Chairman, Guy's and St Thomas' NHS Foundation Trust, since 2011; Interim Chair, King's College Hospital NHS Foundation Trust, since 2019; *b* 22 March 1950; *s* of late Leslie Henderson Taylor and Alison Taylor; *m* 1989, Diane Bacon; two *d*. *Educ:* Brentwood Sch.; Emmanuel Coll., Cambridge (BA). Joined Home Office, 1972; Private Sec. to Minister of State, 1976–77; Principal Private Sec. to Home Sec., 1983–85; Asst Sec., 1984; Prison Service, 1985–88 and 1992–93; seconded to Cabinet Office, 1988–91; Under Sec., 1993–96, and Dir, Top Mgt Prog., 1994–96, Cabinet Office; Dir of Services, Prison Service, 1996–97; Dir of Human Resources, NHS Exec., 1998–2001; Dir Gen. of Ext. and Corporate Affairs, then Corporate Affairs, subseq. of Deptl Mgt, DoH, 2001–06. Chairman: Nat. Skills Acad. for Health, 2013–17; Health Foundn, 2017–. Trustee: Macmillan Cancer Support, 2011–17; Nuffield Trust, 2011–17; RCP, 2011–14; Cicely Saunders Inst., 2011–. Trustee, James Allen's Girls Sch., 2008–16 (Chm., 2014–16). *Recreations:* arts, sport. *Clubs:* MCC, Athenæum.

TAYLOR, Hugo M.; *see* Mascie-Taylor.

TAYLOR, Rt Rev. Humphrey Vincent; Bishop Suffragan of Selby, 1991–2003; an Hon. Assistant Bishop, Diocese of Worcester, since 2004; *b* 5 March 1938; *s* of late Maurice Humphrey Taylor and Mary Patricia Stuart Taylor (*née* Wood, later Pearson); *m* 1965, Anne Katharine Dart; two *d*. *Educ:* Harrow School; Pembroke College, Cambridge (MA); London University (MA). Nat. Service Officer, RAF, 1956–58; Cambridge 1958–61; College of the Resurrection, Mirfield, 1961–63; Curate in London, 1963–66; Rector of Lilongwe, Malaŵi, 1967–71; Chaplain, Bishop Grosseteste Coll., Lincoln, 1971–74; Sec. for Chaplaincies in Higher Education, Gen. Synod Bd of Education, 1974–80; Mission Programmes Sec., USPG, 1980–84; Sec., USPG, 1984–91. Hon. Canon of Bristol Cathedral, 1986–91; Provincial Canon of Southern Africa, 1989. Moderator, Conf. for World Mission, BCC, 1987–90; Chairman: Internat. and Develt Affairs Cttee, Archbps' Council, 1996–2003; Northern and Yorkshire Adv. Cttee on Spiritual Care and Chaplaincy, 1997–2003. *Recreations:* music, gardening. *Address:* 10 High Street, Honeybourne, Worcs WR11 7PQ.

*See also* R. M. Thornely-Taylor.

TAYLOR, Ian Colin, MBE 1974; Managing Director, Fentiman Consultants Ltd, since 1997; *b* 18 April 1945; *s* of late Horace Stanley Taylor and Beryl Taylor (*née* Harper); *m* 1974, Hon. Carole Alport, *d* of Baron Alport, PC, TD; two *s*. *Educ:* Whitley Abbey Sch., Coventry; Keele Univ. (BA); London School of Economics (Res. Schol.). Corporate financial adviser. Mem. Council, STFC, 2011–18. Nat. Chm., Fedn of Cons. Students, 1968–69; Chm., Eur. Union of Christian Democratic and Cons. Students, 1969–70; Hon. Sec., Brit. Cons. Assoc. in France, 1976–78; Chairman: Commonwealth Youth Exchange Council, 1980–84; Cons. Foreign and Commonwealth Council, 1990–96; Nat. Chm., Cons. Gp for Europe, 1985–88 and 2007–10. Contested (C) Coventry SE, Feb. 1974. MP (C) Esher, 1987–97, Esher and Walton, 1997–2010. Parliamentary Private Secretary: FCO, 1990; to Sec. of State for Health, 1990–92; to Chancellor of Duchy of Lancaster, 1992–94; Parly Under-Sec. of State, DTI (Minister for Sci. and Technol.), 1994–97; opposition front bench spokesman on NI, 1997. Member, Select Committee on: Foreign Affairs, 1987–90; Science and Technol., 1998–2001. Chm., Parly and Scientific Cttee, 2009–10; Vice Chm., Parly Information Technol. Cttee. Chairman: Cons. Parly European Affairs Cttee, 1988–89; Cons. Policy Taskforce on Sci., 2006–10. Chairman: European Movement, 2000–04; Cuba Initiative, 2008–11; Mem., IPPR Commn on Nat. Security, 2006–09. Chm., Tory Europe Network, 2002–10. Vice-Chm., Assoc. of Cons. Clubs, 1988–92. Gov., Research into Ageing, 1997–2001; Centre of Cell, 2004–14. Chair: Living Planet SA, 2009–; Adv. Bd, Rainbow Seed Fund, 2010–; League of Remembrance, 2015–; Liveryman, Co. of Information Technologists, 1998–. *Publications:* various pamphlets; contrib. to various jls, etc, on politics and business. *Recreations:* opera, cigars. *Club:* Savile.

TAYLOR, Ian Roper; Chairman, Vitol Group, since 2018 (Chief Executive, 1995–2018); *b* Croydon, 7 Feb. 1956; *s* of John and Margaret Taylor; *m* 1982, Cristina Hare; two *s* two *d*. *Educ:* King's Sch., Macclesfield; Merton Coll., Oxford (BA 1978| MA). Shell: Supply Trading Asst, Shell UK, 1978–79; Supply Trading Manager, Shell Venezuela, 1979–82; Shell Singapore, 1982–85; Hd, Crude Oil, Vitol Gp, 1985–95. Dir, Harris Tweed Hebrides. Chm. Trustees, Royal Opera Hse, 2016–. *Recreations:* arts, especially the performing arts, golf. *Clubs:* Arts, Royal Automobile, Mark's, Annabel's, George, 5 Hertford Street, Harry's Bar; Royal Wimbledon Golf; Queenwood Golf.

TAYLOR, Prof. Irving, MD; FRCS; Professor of Surgery, 1993–2016, now Emeritus Professor, and Vice Dean, UCL Medical School (formerly University College London Medical School, then Royal Free and University College Medical School), 2002–16, University College London (Chairman, Academic Division of Surgical Specialties and Head of Department, 1993–2004); *b* 7 Jan. 1945; *s* of Sam and Fay Taylor; *m* 1969, Berenice Penelope Brunner; three *d*. *Educ:* Roundhay Sch., Leeds; Sheffield Univ. Med. Sch. (MB ChB 1968; MD 1973; ChM 1978). FRCS 1972. Royal Infirmary, then Royal Hospital, Sheffield: House Officer, 1968; SHO, 1969–70; Surg. Registrar, 1971–73; Sen. Registrar in Surgery, 1973–77; Sen. Lectr and Consultant Surgeon, Liverpool Univ., 1977–81; Prof. of Surgery, Univ. of Southampton, 1981–93. Hunterian Prof., RCS, 1981 (Jacksonian Award, 1986; Stanford Cade Medal, 2000; Bradshaw Medal, 2012); Bennett Lectr, TCD, 1990; Gordon Bell Lectr, RACS, 1996. Mem. Council, RCS, 2004–13 (Examr, 2000–01; Chair, Sen. Fellows Soc.); Chm., MRC Colorectal Cancer Cttee, 1990–95; President: British Assoc. of Surgical Oncology, 1995–98; Soc. of Academic and Res. Surgery, 2005–06; Eur. Soc. of Surgical Oncology, 2006–08 (Vice-Pres., 2004–06); Sec., Surgical Res. Soc., 1988–90; Editorial Sec., Assoc. of Surgeons, 1988–91. Case Examiner, Fitness to Practise Directorate, GMC, 2003–16. Editor-in-Chief: Eur. Jl of Surgical Oncology, 1995–2003; Annals of RCS, 2004–09; Lives of Fellows of RCS, 2017–. FRSocMed 1983; FMedSci 2000; FRCPSGlas 2001. *Publications:* Progress in Surgery, 1985, 3rd edn 1989; Complications of Surgery of the Gastrointestinal Tract, 1985; Benign Breast Disease, 1990; Essential General Surgical Oncology, 1995; Surgical Principles, 1996; Recent Advances in Surgery, annually, 1991–; Fast Facts: colorectal cancer, 1999, 3rd edn 2010; Mind Maps in Surgery, 2008; articles and papers on gen. surgery, surgical educn, surgical oncology, breast, colorectal and liver cancer in med. jls. *Recreations:* bridge, swimming, rambling, watching cricket, golf, travel, supporting Leeds United. *Address:* 43 Francklyn Gardens, Edgware HA8 8RU. *T:* (020) 8958 8364.

TAYLOR, Isabel Amelia Mason; Partner, Slaughter and May, since 2008; *b* Wandsworth, 2 Aug. 1974; *d* of Rodney Mason Taylor and Margaret Taylor; *m* 2014, David Perkins; one *s* one *d* (twins). *Educ:* Tiffin Girls' Sch., Kingston upon Thames; Peterhouse, Cambridge (BA Law 1995). Res. Asst, Law Commn, 1995–96; trainee solicitor, Slaughter and May, 1997–99; admitted as solicitor, 1999; Associate, Slaughter and May, 1999–2008. *Recreations:* theatre, parkrun, walking. *Address:* Slaughter and May, One Bunhill Row, EC1Y 8YY. *T:* (020) 7090 4316. *E:* isabel.taylor@slaughterandmay.com.

TAYLOR, Jacqueline, FRCP; Consultant Physician in Medicine for the Elderly, Glasgow Royal Infirmary, since 1997; President, Royal College of Physicians and Surgeons of Glasgow, since 2018; *b* Usk, S Wales, 30 July 1961; *d* of Raymond and Elsie Taylor; *m* 1991, Colin Thomson; one *s* one *d*. *Educ:* Hamilton Grammar Sch.; Univ. of Glasgow (MB ChB). Consultant, Falkirk Royal Infirmary, 1991–97; Hon. Sen. Clin. Lectr, Univ. of Glasgow, 1992–. Hon. Sec., 2006–12, Vice-Pres., Medical, 2013–16, RCPSG. *Publications:* contribs to peer-reviewed jls. *Recreations:* ski-ing, ballet, all forms of dance, music. *Address:* Royal College of Physicians and Surgeons of Glasgow, 232 St Vincent Street, Glasgow G2 5RJ. *T:* (0141) 221 6072. *E:* jackie.taylor@rcpsg.ac.uk.

TAYLOR, Dr James; Geographical Director, Africa, Middle East and South Asia, British Council, 2000–03; *b* 22 April 1951; *s* of George Thomson Taylor and Elizabeth Gibson Taylor (*née* Dunsmore); *m* 1986, Dianne Carol Cawthorne; one *s*. *Educ:* Cumnock Acad.; Strathclyde Univ. (BSc 1973; PhD 1977). ACS Petroleum Res. Fellow, Bristol Univ., 1977–78; von Humboldt Fellow, Univ. des Saarlandes, Germany, 1978–79; Res. Chemist, Procter & Gamble, 1979–80; SSO, Scottish Marine Biol Assoc., 1980–84; British Council: Asst Dir, Kuwait, 1984–86; First Sec. (Sci. and Develt), British High Commn, Calcutta, 1986–88; Head, Tech. Adv. Service, Sci. and Technol. Dept, 1988–90; Asst Registrar, Res. Support Unit, Leeds Univ., 1990–92; Development and Training Services, British Council: Contract Dir, Central and Eastern Europe, 1992–93; Head, Europe Gp, 1993–95; Head, Africa and ME Gp, 1995–97; Dir, Zimbabwe and Head, Africa Gp, 1997–2000. *Publications:* contribs on marine sediment chem. to sci. jls. *Recreations:* gardening, TV soaps, walking.

TAYLOR, James Alastair; Sheriff Principal of Glasgow and Strathkelvin, 2005–11; *b* 21 Feb. 1951; *s* of Alastair and Margaret Taylor; *m* 1980, Lesley Doig Macleod; two *s*. *Educ:* Nairn Acad.; Univ. of Aberdeen (BSc; LLB). Partner, A. C. Morrison & Richards, Solicitors, Aberdeen, 1980–87; Partner, 1988–98, Hd of Litigation Dept, 1992–98, McGrigor Donald, Solicitors, Glasgow; Sheriff: of Lothian and Borders, 1998–99; of Glasgow and Strathkelvin, 1999–2005. Chm., Disciplinary Tribunal, ICAS, 2000–16. Mem. Bd, Civil Justice Review, 2007–09; Chm., Review into the Expenses and Funding of Civil Litigation in Scotland, 2011–13. Dir, Lodging House Mission, 2002–12. Sec., Nairn URC, 2015–. Hon. LLD Glasgow, 2013. *Publications:* (contrib.) International Intellectual Property Litigation, 1998; (contrib.) Sentencing Practice, 2000; (contrib.) Macphail Sheriff Court Practice, 3rd edn, 2006. *Recreations:* golf, wine, good food, jazz. *Address:* Tyninghame, Albert Street, Nairn IV12 4HQ. *Clubs:* Nairn Golf, Royal Aberdeen Golf.

TAYLOR, Prof. (James) Roy, PhD; FRS 2017; Professor of Ultrafast Physics and Technology, Imperial College London, since 2002; *b* Carrickfergus, NI, 29 April 1949; *s* of James Wylie Taylor and Helena Muriel Taylor (*née* Lockhart); *m* 1979, Silvie Jennifer Logan; three *s*. *Educ:* Central Primary Sch., Carrickfergus; Larne Grammar Sch.; Queen's Univ. Belfast (BSc 1st Cl. Hons Physics 1971; PhD 1974). Res. Fellow, Technical Univ. of Munich, 1975–77; Imperial College London: Res. Asst, Optics Section, Physics Dept, 1977–87; Acad. Related Staff Grade III, 1987–90; Professorial Res. Fellow, 1990–2002. *Publications:* (with P. French) How it is Made – Lasers, 1988; Optical Solitons: theory and experiment, 1992; (ed with J. Dudley) Supercontinuum Generation in Optical Fibres, 2011; contribs to learned jls. *Recreations:* music, record collector, walking. *Address:* Lynton Road, Queen's Park, NW6 6BD. *T:* (020) 7594 7786. *E:* jr.taylor@ic.ac.uk.

TAYLOR, James S.; *see* Sinclair Taylor, R. J.

TAYLOR, Jason; QC 2018; His Honour Judge Jason Taylor; a Circuit Judge, since 2018; *b* Newport, Gwent, 27 Aug. 1972; *s* of Glynne and Judith Taylor; *m* 1996, Lorraine Edge; one *s* one *d*. *Educ:* Bassaleg Comprehensive Sch.; Crosskeys Tertiary Coll.; Univ. de Grenoble (Dip. de Français 1991); University Coll. of Wales, Aberystwyth (LLB Hons 1994). Called to the Bar, Gray's Inn, 1995; a Recorder, 2016–18. *Recreations:* ski-ing, walking, family, travelling, Church, golf, reading, cycling.

TAYLOR, Jeremy; *see* Taylor, C. J. B.

TAYLOR, Jeremy Paul, OBE 2019; Chief Executive, National Voices, 2009–19; *b* Leeds, 30 Dec. 1962; *s* of David Taylor and late Rosalind Taylor (*née* Sacks); *m* 1999, Meriel Schindler; one *s* two *d*. *Educ:* Gonville and Caius Coll., Cambridge (BA Social and Pol Scis 1985; MA). Res. Asst, Univ. of Glasgow, 1985–87; Res. Officer, Scottish Consumer Council, 1987–89; civil servant, Scottish Office, incl. Hd, Perm. Sec.'s Office, and Hd, London Office, Locate in Scotland, 1989–97; civil servant, then sen. civil servant, HM Treasury, incl. Sec., Lyons relocation review, and Hd, Performance and Efficiency Team, 1997–2007; Exec. Dir, Groundwork E London, 2007–09. *Recreations:* running, walking, ski-ing, theatre, family. *E:* jeremyatwapping@msn.com.

TAYLOR, Rev. John Brian, PhD; President, Methodist Conference, 1997–98; Chairman, Liverpool District, Methodist Church, 1995–2003; *b* 3 July 1937; *s* of Frank and Alice Taylor; *m* 1959, Patricia Margaret Lord; two *s*. *Educ:* Buxton Coll.; Durham Univ. (BA, DipEd); Hartley Victoria Coll. and Manchester Univ. (BD); PhD Open Univ. 1992. Headmaster, Cours Secondaire Protestant de Dabou, Côte d'Ivoire, 1961–64; Methodist Minister, 1964–; Chaplain, Univ. of Sheffield, 1976–79; Tutor, Queen's Coll., Birmingham, 1979–88 (Hon. Fellow, 2001); Gen. Sec., Methodist Church Div. of Ministries, 1988–95. Commandeur: l'Ordre National (Côte d'Ivoire), 1997; l'Ordre du Mono (Togo), 2000. *Publications:* Preaching as Doctrine, 2001; Commonsense: the musings of a cloth-cap theologian, 2019; various articles in learned jls. *Recreations:* genealogy, gardening, music, cooking. *Address:* 7 Mordaunt Drive, Four Oaks, Sutton Coldfield B75 5PT.

TAYLOR, Prof. John Bryan, FRS 1970; Fondren Professor of Plasma Theory, University of Texas at Austin, 1989–94; Chief Physicist, 1981–89, Consultant, 1994–2008, UKAEA Culham Laboratory; *b* 26 Dec. 1928; *s* of Frank and Ada Taylor, Birmingham; *m* 1951, Joan M. Hargest; one *s* one *d*. *Educ:* Oldbury Grammar Sch.; Birmingham Univ., 1947–50 and 1952–55. RAF, 1950–52. Atomic Weapons Research Establishment, Aldermaston, 1955–59 and 1960–62; Harkness Fellow, Commonwealth Fund, Univ. of California (Berkeley), 1959–60; Culham Laboratory (UKAEA), 1962–69 and 1970–89 (Head of Theoretical Physics Div., 1963–81); Inst. for Advanced Study, Princeton, 1969. FInstP 1969. Fellow, Amer. Phys. Soc., 1984. Maxwell Medal, IPPS, 1971; Max Born Medal, German Phys. Soc., 1979; Award for Excellence in Plasma Physics Res., 1986, James Clerk Maxwell Prize, 1999, Amer. Phys. Soc.; Dist. Career Award, Fusion Power Associates, 1999; Hannes Alfven Prize, Eur. Phys. Soc., 2004. *Publications:* contribs to scientific learned jls. *Address:* 2 The Paddock, The Street, Bishops Cannings, Wilts SN10 2LD. *T:* (01380) 860502.

**TAYLOR, John Clayton,** PhD; FRS 1981; FInstP; Professor of Mathematical Physics, Cambridge University, and Fellow of Robinson College, Cambridge, 1980–95, now Professor and Fellow Emeritus; *b* 4 Aug. 1930; *s* of Leonard Taylor and Edith (*née* Tytherleigh); *m* 1959, Gillian Mary (*née* Schofield); two *s*. *Educ:* Selhurst Grammar Sch., Croydon; Peterhouse, Cambridge (MA). Lectr, Imperial Coll., London, 1956–60; Lectr, Cambridge Univ., and Fellow of Peterhouse, 1960–64; Reader in Theoretical Physics, Oxford Univ., and Fellow of University Coll., Oxford, 1964–80 (Hon. Fellow, 1989). *Publications:* Gauge Theories of Weak Interactions, 1976; Hidden Unity in Nature's Laws, 2001; Gauge Theories in the Twentieth Century, 2001. *Address:* 9 Bowers Croft, Cambridge CB1 8RP.

**TAYLOR, John Crawshaw,** OBE 2011; FREng; inventor, entrepreneur and philanthropist; Chairman: Sterna Aviation, since 1993; John C Taylor Ltd, since 1997; Auctor Ltd, since 2000; Fromanteel Ltd, since 2003; Arragon Mooar Estate Ltd, since 2004; John C. Taylor Collection Ltd, since 2018; *b* Buxton, Derbys, 25 Nov. 1936; *s* of Eric Hardman Taylor and Gwendolen Majorie Taylor (*née* Jones); *m* 1964, Heather Patricia Anderson (marr. diss. 1979); one *s* one *d*; partner, 1989, Valerie Whiteway (separated 1991); one *d*; *m* 1993, Jean Kathleen Turley (marr. diss. 2018); two step *c* (and one step *c* decd). *Educ:* King William's Coll., I of M; Corpus Christi Coll., Cambridge (BA Nat. Sci. Tripos 1959; MA 1963; Hon. Fellow 2002). Mem., Cambridge expeditions to Spitsbergen, 1958, 1961; Otter Controls Ltd: graduate trainee, 1959; Develt Manager, 1961; Dir, 1962; Chm., 1971–76; Dir, 1976–99, Chm., 1980–99, Castletown Thermostats, later Strix Ltd. Mem. Bd, Manx Electricity Authy, 2000–05. Visiting Professor: Manchester Sci. Enterprise Centre, UMIST, 2001; Physics Dept, Durham Univ., 2006–. Fellow, Inst. of Patentees and Inventors, 1965; FREng 2011; Fellow, I of M Coll., 2018. Companion, Guild of Cambridge Benefactors, 2006. Mem., RYA. Hon. DEng UMIST, 2001; Hon. DSc Durham, 2017. Percy Dawson Medal, Antiquarian Horol Soc., 2004; Master's Medal, Clockmakers' Co., 2009; Chancellor's 800th Anniversary Medal for Outstanding Philanthropy, Univ. of Cambridge, 2009; Harrison Medal, Clockmakers' Co., 2015. *Publications:* (contrib.) Horological Masterworks, 2003; (contrib.) Huygen's Legacy, 2004; (jtly) The Excitement of Time, 2006; Innovation and Collaboration, 2018; over 400 patents. *Recreations:* flying (TBM 910 and LS8-t glider), rock climbing and mountaineering, ski-ing, photography, RYA yachtmaster ocean instructor. *E:* john@johnctaylor.com. *Clubs:* Royal Air Squadron; Scottish Gliding; Isle of Man Yacht.

**TAYLOR, John Edward,** CBE 2013; Chief Executive, Advisory, Conciliation and Arbitration Service, 2001–13; Independent Member, Joint Industry Board, since 2015 (Chairman, Major Contractors' Committee, since 2016); *b* 14 Nov. 1949; *s* of Thomas Taylor and Margaret Jane Taylor (*née* Renwick). *Educ:* Chester-le-Street Grammar Sch.; Durham Univ. (BA Gen. Arts). Grad. Trainee, Littlewoods Orgn, 1971–72; Department of Employment: various posts as Exec. Officer, 1972–79; Private Sec. to Minister of State, 1979–80; Head: of Personnel, 1980–83; of Res. Br., 1983–84; Regl Employment Manager, Midlands, 1984–86; Hd, Overseas Labour Div., 1986–88; Dep. Chief Exec., Rural Develt Commn, 1988–95; Chief Executive: Develt Bd for Rural Wales, 1995–98; SE Wales TEC, 1998–2001. German Marshall Fellowship Schol., USA, 1986. Vis. Prof. for Employment Relns, Glamorgan Univ., 2001–10. Public Sector examiner, Inst. of Dirs, 2006–10. UK Advr to Botswana on public sector unionisation, 2011; Expert Advr to Internat. Labour Orgn, 2012–; Olympic Legacy Advr to Rio, 2012–16. Member: UK Delegn to USSR on SME Develt, 1991; NHS Partnership Forum (formerly NHS Partnership Bd), 2001–13; Employment Tribunal System Taskforce, 2003–06; Learning and Skills Develt Agency, 2004–06; Central Govt Sector Skills Council, 2005–10; Employment Tribunal System Steering Bd, 2006–10; Quality Improvement Agency, 2006–08; Adv. Bd, unionlearn, 2006–; UK Delegn to Colombia on industrial relns, 2008; Skills Strategy Delivery Bd, 2009–10; Chartered Mgt Inst. Skills Acad., 2010–13; Skill Exchange UK (formerly Skill Exchange Partnership), 2010–16; Lay Council, Reading Univ., 2019–; Chm., Careers Services Wales, 2013–16. Non-exec. Dir, Employee Relations Inst., 2012–15. Chm. Trustees, WEA, 2012–16. Governor: Univ. of W London (formerly Thames Valley Univ.), 2005– (Dep. Chm., 2010–14); Reading Further Educn Coll., 2007–10. CCMI 2003. Fellow, Inst. of Assoc. Mgt, 2010. Hon. DLitt W London, 2014. *Recreations:* Sunderland AFC, all sport, CAMRA, travel, conservation. *Address:* Joint Industry Board, Swanley, Kent BR8 9BH. *Club:* Durham County Cricket.

**TAYLOR, John H.;** *see* Hermon-Taylor.

**TAYLOR, (John) Martin,** CBE 2019; Chairman, RTL Group SA, since 2019 (Director, since 2000; Vice-Chairman, 2004–19); *b* 8 June 1952; *m* 1st, 1976, Janet Davey (marr. diss. 2002); two *d*; 2nd, 2008, Pippa Wicks; one *s*. *Educ:* Eton; Balliol Coll., Oxford. Reuters, 1974–78; Financial Times, 1978–82; Courtaulds plc, 1982–90 (Dir, 1987–90); Courtaulds Textiles plc, 1990–93 (Chief Exec., 1990–93, Chm., 1993); Chief Exec., Barclays plc, 1994–98; Chairman: W. H. Smith Gp plc, 1999–2003; Syngenta AG, 2005–13 (Dir, 2000–13; Vice-Chm., 2004–05). Director: Antigenics Inc., 1999–2003; CiBO Technologies, 2015–; advr, Goldman Sachs Internat., 1999–2005. Govt advr on tax and welfare issues. Mem., Ind. Commn on Banking, 2010–11; Ext. Mem., Bank of England Financial Policy Cttee, 2013–April 2020. Sec.-Gen., Bilderberg Gp, 1999–2005.

**TAYLOR, (John) Maxwell (Percy);** Chairman, Mitsui Sumitomo (London) Ltd, 2008–17 (non-executive Director, 2006–17); *b* 17 March 1948; *s* of Harold Guy Percy Taylor and Anne Katherine Taylor (*née* Stafford); *m* 1970, Dawn Susan Harling; one *s* one *d*. *Educ:* Haileybury; ISC. Joined Willis Faber & Dumas, 1970; Dir, Willis Faber, then Willis Corroon Gp plc, 1990–97; Chm., Lloyd's, 1998–2000. Chm., Lloyd's Insce Brokers Cttee, 1997. Dep. Chm., Aon Ltd, 2001–08; Director: Henderson Smaller Companies Investment Trust plc, 1997–2008; Qatar Insce Services, 2009–13. Dir, Financial Services Compensation Scheme, 2007–13. Chairman: BIIBA, 2004–07; BIPAR, 2004; ANV Syndicates (formerly Jubilee Managing Agency) Ltd, 2011–16; Pioneer Underwriters, 2013–19; Cobalt Insurance Hldgs, 2015–. Pres., Insurance Inst. of London, 2001. Pro-Chancellor, Univ. of Surrey, 2015– (Chm. Council, 2007–13). *Recreations:* music, travel, classic cars. *Clubs:* Royal Automobile, City.

**TAYLOR, Sir John (Michael),** Kt 2004; OBE 1994; PhD; FRS 1998; FREng; Director General of Research Councils, Office of Science and Technology, Department of Trade and Industry, 1999–2003; *b* 15 Feb. 1943; *s* of Eric and Dorothy Taylor; *m* 1965, Judith Moyle; two *s* two *d*. *Educ:* Emmanuel Coll., Cambridge (MA; PhD 1969; Hon. Fellow, 2000). FIET (FIEE 1985); FBCS 1986; FREng (FEng 1986). Supt, Communication Systems Div., 1977–79, Computer Applications Div., 1979–81, RSRE; Head, Command, Control and Communications Dept, ARE, 1981–84; Dir, Hewlett-Packard Labs, Europe, 1984–98. Chm., Roke Manor Research Ltd, 2004–10. Non-exec. Dir, Rolls Royce, 2004–07. Chm., Web Science Trust, 2009–14 (Hon. Fellow, 2014). Pres., IEE, 1998–99; Mem. Council, Royal Acad. Engrg, 2004–07. Vis. Prof., Univ. of Oxford, 2003–09. FInstP. Hon. Fellow, Cardiff Univ., 2002. Hon. DEng: Bristol, 1998; UWE, 1999; Surrey, 1999; Exeter, 2000; Brunel, 2000; Birmingham, 2002. *Recreations:* family, grandchildren, sailing and boating, photography, music. *E:* john@taylorfamily.tv.

**TAYLOR, Rt Rev. John Mitchell;** Bishop of Glasgow and Galloway, 1991–98; Assistant Bishop of Glasgow and Galloway, 2000–09; *b* 23 May 1932; *m* 1959, Edna Elizabeth (*née* Maitland); one *s* (one *d* decd). *Educ:* Banff Acad.; Aberdeen Univ. (MA 1954); Edinburgh Theol Coll. Ordained deacon, 1956, priest, 1957; Asst Curate, St Margaret, Aberdeen, 1956–58; Rector: Holy Cross, Glasgow, 1958–64; St Ninian, Glasgow, 1964–73; St John the Evangelist, Dumfries, 1973–91; Chaplain: Crichton Royal Hospital; Dumfries and Galloway Royal Infirmary, 1973–91; Canon, St Mary's Cathedral, 1979–91, Hon. Canon, 1999–. *Recreations:* angling, hill walking, music, ornithology. *Address:* 85 Lord Lyell Drive, Kinnordy View, Kirriemuir DD8 4LF. *T:* (01575) 573132. *E:* j.taylor897@btinternet.com.

**TAYLOR, John Russell;** Art Critic, The Times, 1978–2005; *b* 19 June 1935; *s* of Arthur Russell and Kathleen Mary Taylor (*née* Picker); civil partnership 2006, Ying Yeung Li. *Educ:* Dover Grammar Sch.; Jesus Coll., Cambridge (MA); Courtauld Inst. of Art, London. Sub-Editor, Times Educational Supplement, 1959; Editorial Asst, Times Literary Supplement, 1960; Film Critic, 1962–73, Amer. Cultural Correspondent, 1972–78, The Times. Dir of Film Studies, Tufts Univ. in London, 1970–71; Prof., Div. of Cinema, Univ. of Southern California, 1972–78. Editor, Films and Filming, 1983–90. *Publications:* Anger and After, 1962; Anatomy of a Television Play, 1962; Cinema Eye, Cinema Ear, 1964; Penguin Dictionary of the Theatre, 1966; The Art Nouveau Book in Britain, 1966; The Rise and Fall of the Well-Made Play, 1967; The Art Dealers, 1969; Harold Pinter, 1969; Look Back in Anger: a casebook, 1969; The Hollywood Musical, 1971; The Second Wave, 1971; David Storey, 1974; Directors and Directions, 1975; Peter Shaffer, 1975; Hitch, 1978, rev. edn 2016; (contrib.) The Revels History of Drama in English, vol. VII, 1978; Impressionism, 1981; Strangers in Paradise, 1983; Ingrid Bergman, 1983; Alec Guinness, 1984; Vivien Leigh, 1984; Portraits of the British Cinema, 1985; Hollywood 1940s, 1985; Orson Welles, 1986; Edward Wolfe, 1986; Great Movie Moments, 1987; Post-war Friends, 1987; Robin Tanner, 1989; Bernard Meninsky, 1990; John Copley 1875–1950, 1990; Impressionist Dreams, 1990; Liz Taylor, 1991; Ricardo Cinalli, 1993; Igor Mitoraj, 1993; Muriel Pemberton, 1993; Claude Monet, 1995; Michael Parkes: the stone lithographs, 1996; Bill Jacklin, 1997; Antonio Saliola, 1998; The Sun is God, 1999; Roberto Bernardi, 2001; (contrib.) The Ben Uri Story, 2001; Peter Coker, 2002; Philip Sutton Printmaker, 2005; Roboz, 2005; (contrib.) Skrebneski: moving pictures!, 2005; Adrian George, 2005; Donald McGill, 2006; The Art of Michael Parkes, 2006; (contrib.) La Risurrezione di Ricardo Cinalli, 2006; (contrib.) The Painter's Quarry, 2006; (with David Watkin) Carl Laubin, 2007; The Art of Jeremy Ramsay, 2007; (with Simon Tate) Philip Sutton, 2008; Glamour of the Gods, 2008; Exactitude, 2009; (contrib.) Kurt Jackson, 2010; Face to Face, 2011; (contrib.) David Breuer-Weil: radical visionary, 2011; Philip Hicks, 2013; High Relief: Paul Day, 2017; T. Allen Lawson, 2018; Derek Stafford, 2019. *Address:* c/o The Times, 1 London Bridge Street, SE1 9GF.

**TAYLOR, Jonathan Francis,** CBE 2005; President, Booker Prize Foundation, since 2015 (Chairman, 2001–15); Chairman, Booker plc, 1993–98 (Chief Executive, 1984–93); *b* 12 Aug. 1935; *s* of Sir Reginald Taylor, CMG and Lady Taylor; *m* 1965, Anthea Gail Proctor; three *s*. *Educ:* Winchester College; Corpus Christi College, Oxford (Schol.; BA Mod. Hist.; MA; Hon. Fellow 1996). Joined Booker, 1959; Chm., Agricultural Div., 1976–80; Dir, Booker plc, 1980; Pres., Ibec Inc. (USA), 1980–84; Dir, Arbor Acres Farm Inc., 1980–98 (Dep. Chm., 1985–90; Chm., 1990–95). Director: Sifida Investment Bank, Geneva, 1978–90; Tate & Lyle, 1988–99; MEPC, 1992–2000; Equitable Life Assurance Soc., 1995–2001; Chm., Ellis & Everard, 1993–99. Mem., Adv. Council, UNIDO, 1986–93; Director: Foundn for Develt of Polish Agric., 1991–99 (Chm., 1992–99); Internat. Agribusiness Management Assoc., 1991– (Pres., 1993–94); Winrock Internat. Inst. for Agricl Develt (US), 1991–2001. Chm., Marshall Aid Commemoration Commn, 2000–07. Chm., Governing Body, SOAS, London Univ., 1999–2005 (Gov., 1988–2005; Hon. Fellow, 2010); Governor: RAC, Cirencester, 1995–2010; Commonwealth Inst., 1998–2005. Co-opted Curator, Bodleian Library, 1989–97; Chairman: Bodleian Liby Develt Bd, 1989–2000; Paintings in Hosps, 1996–2006. Chairman: Council, Caine Prize for African Writing, 1999–2016; Trustees, Internat. Prize for Arabic Fiction, 2006–; Chair, David Vaisey Trust, 2016–. *Recreations:* collecting water colours, travel, reading, grandchildren. *Address:* 48 Edwardes Square, W8 6HH. *Club:* Brooks's.

**TAYLOR, Sir Jonathan (McLeod Grigor),** KCMG 2019; Vice-President and Member, Management Committee, European Investment Bank, 2013–18; *b* 5 March 1955; *s* of late John Grigor Taylor and Dorothy Jean Taylor (*née* McLeod); *m* 1984, Stella Schimmel; one *s* one *d*. *Educ:* Bedales Sch.; New Coll., Oxford (MA PPE). HM Treasury, 1977–2002: Admin. trainee, 1977–79; Private Sec. to Perm. Sec., 1979–81; Principal, 1981; First Sec. (Budget), UK Perm. Rep., Brussels, 1982–84 (on secondment); Private Sec. to Chancellor of Exchequer, 1987–89; Asst Sec., 1990; Counsellor (Econ. and Financial), UK Perm. Rep., Brussels, 1994–98 (on secondment); Dir, Macroeconomic Policy and Internat. Finance Directorate, 1998–2002; Man. Dir and Hd of Public Policy, Internat., UBS AG, 2002–05; Dir Gen., London Investment Banking Assoc., 2005–09; CEO, Assoc. for Financial Markets in Europe, 2009; Man. Dir, Internat. and Finance Directorate, then Dir Gen., Financial Services, HM Treasury, 2010–12.

**TAYLOR, Jonathan Peter;** QC 2017; Partner, Bird & Bird Solicitors, since 2007; *b* Bristol, 6 Nov. 1967; *s* of Gavin and Louise Taylor; *m* 1994, Kate Thefaut; two *d*. *Educ:* University Coll., Oxford (BA 1st Cl. Hons Juris. 1989); Univ. of Virginia (LLM 1990). Called to the Bar, NY, 1991; admitted solicitor, England and Wales, 1997; Associate, Schulte Roth & Zabel, NYC, 1990–97; Solicitor, Townleys, 1997–2001; Partner, Hammonds, 2001–07. Stipendiary Lectr in Law, University Coll., Oxford, 1992–93; Dir of Studies in Sports Law, KCL, 2000–08. Member: Anti-Doping Panel, Internat. Baseball Fedn, 2008–18; Ethics Cttee, British Horseracing Authy, 2009–18; Panel of Arbitrators, Sports Resolutions, 2012–; World Anti-Doping Agency: Mem., Ind. Observer Mission, Asian Games, 2014; Chair: Ind. Observer Mission, Olympic Games, Rio de Janeiro, 2016; Compliance Rev. Cttee, 2016–. *Publications:* (ed jtly) Sport: law & practice, 2003, 3rd edn 2014; (contrib.) The New Oxford Companion to Law, 2008; (ed jtly) Challenging Sports Governing Bodies, 2016. *Recreations:* family, Fulham FC. *Address:* c/o Bird & Bird LLP, 12 New Fetter Lane, EC4A 1JP. *E:* jonathan.taylor@twobirds.com.

**TAYLOR, Prof. Joseph Hooton, Jr,** PhD; James S. McDonnell Distinguished University Professor of Physics, Princeton University, 1986–2006, now Emeritus (Professor of Physics, 1980–86; Dean of the Faculty, 1997–2003); *b* 29 March 1941; *s* of Joseph Taylor and Sylvia Taylor (*née* Evans); *m* 1st, 1963, Alexandra Utgoff (marr. diss. 1975); one *s* one *d*; 2nd, 1976, Marietta Bisson; one *d*. *Educ:* Haverford Coll. (BA Physics 1963); Harvard Univ. (PhD Astronomy 1968). Res. Fellow and Lectr, Harvard Univ., 1968–69; University of Massachusetts, Amherst: Asst Prof. of Astronomy, 1969–72; Associate Prof., 1973–77; Prof., 1977–81. World Prize in Physics, Wolf Foundn, 1982; Einstein Prize, Albert Einstein Soc., 1991; (jtly) Nobel Prize in Physics, 1993. *Publications:* (with R. N. Manchester) Pulsars, 1977; over 200 articles in jls. *Recreations:* sailing, ham radio, golf. *Address:* Department of Physics, Princeton University, PO Box 708, Princeton, NJ 08544, USA.

**TAYLOR, Judy, (Julia Marie), (Judy Hough)**, MBE 1971; writer and publisher; *b* 12 Aug. 1932; adopted *d* of Gladys Spicer Taylor; *m* 1980, Richard Hough, writer (*d* 1999). *Educ:* St Paul's Girls' Sch. Joined The Bodley Head, 1951, specialising in children's books; Director: The Bodley Head Ltd, 1967–84 (Dep. Man. Dir, 1971–80); Chatto, Bodley Head & Jonathan Cape Ltd, 1973–80; Chatto, Bodley Head & Jonathan Cape Australia Pty Ltd, 1977–80. Publishers Association: Chm., Children's Book Gp, 1969–72; Mem. Council, 1972–78; Member: Book Develt Council, 1973–76; Unicef Internat. Art Cttee, 1968–70, 1976, 1982–83; UK Unicef Greeting Card Cttee, 1982–85. Consultant to Penguin (formerly to Frederick Warne) on Beatrix Potter, 1981–87, 1989–92; Associate Dir, Weston Woods Inst., USA, 1984–2003; Consulting Ed., Reinhardt Books, 1988–93. Chm., Beatrix Potter Soc., 1990–97, 2000–03, 2006–09 (Vice-Pres., 2012); Volunteer Reading Help: Mem., 1993–99, Chm., 1989–99, London, subseq. Inner London, Cttee; Trustee, 2000–05. *Publications: children's:* Sophie and Jack, 1982; Sophie and Jack Help Out, 1983; Sophie and Jack in the Snow, 1984; Dudley and the Monster, 1986; Dudley Goes Flying, 1986; Dudley in a Jam, 1986; Dudley and the Strawberry Shake, 1986; My Dog, 1987; My Cat, 1987; Dudley Bakes a Cake, 1988; Sophie and Jack in the Rain, 1989; *non-fiction:* My First Year: a Beatrix Potter baby book, 1983; Beatrix Potter: artist, storyteller and countrywoman, 1986, 3rd edn 2002; That Naughty Rabbit: Beatrix Potter and Peter Rabbit, 1987, 2nd edn 2002; Beatrix Potter and Hawksheads, 1988; Beatrix Potter and Hill Top, 1989; (ed) Beatrix Potter's Letters: a selection, 1989; (ed) Letters to Children from Beatrix Potter, 1992; (ed) So I Shall Tell You a Story: encounters with Beatrix Potter, 1993; (ed) The Choyce Letters: Beatrix Potter to Louie Choyce 1916–1943, 1994; (ed) Beatrix Potter: a holiday diary, 1996; (ed) Beatrix Potter's Farming Friendship, 1998; (ed) Sketches for Friends, by Edward Ardizzone, 2000; *play:* (with Patrick Garland) Beatrix, 1996; numerous professional articles. *Recreations:* collecting early children's books, growing things.

**TAYLOR, Julie;** Director General, Head Office and Commissioning Services, Ministry of Defence, since 2016; *b* London, 26 March 1968; *d* of Robert John Taylor and Virginia Taylor; *m* 1999, David Lawrence. *Educ:* Forest Sch., London; Lady Margaret Hall, Oxford (BA Hons Maths 1989). Qualified Accountant 1992; Qualified Psychotherapist, Human Givens Inst., 2011. Dir, Service Develt, E London and City HA, 1998–2000; Department of Health: Hd, Planning and Progs, 2000–02; Director: Corp. Services, 2002–04; System Reform, 2005–06; Dir, Offender Mgt Strategy, Home Office, subseq. MoJ, 2006–11; Dep. Chief Exec., London Bor. of Barnet, 2011–13; Dir, Strategy and Change, UK Border Force, 2013–15, Dir Gen., Transformation, 2015–16, Home Office. *Recreations:* ski-ing, sailing, walking, bridge. *Address:* Ministry of Defence, 3rd Floor, Main Building, Whitehall, SW1A 2HB.

**TAYLOR, Keith;** Member (Green) South East Region, European Parliament, May 2010–2019; *b* Rochford, Essex, 1 Aug. 1953. Mem. (Green); Brighton and Hove CC, 1999–2010 (Leader, Green Gp, 2001–10). Principal Speaker for Green Party of England and Wales, 2004–06; Regl Liaison Officer for Leader of Green Party. Contested (Green) Brighton Pavilion, 2001, 2005.

**TAYLOR, Kenneth John,** PhD; Headteacher, St Mary's Music School, Edinburgh, since 2013; *b* Croydon, 7 June 1965; *s* of John Taylor and Daphne Taylor; *m* 1993, Katherine Mathieson; two *s* one *d*. *Educ:* Dulwich Coll.; Univ. of Edinburgh (BSc Hons Chem. 1987; PhD Chem. 1991); Moray House Coll. of Educn (PGCE (Secondary) 1995); Univ. of Strathclyde (Post Grad. Cert. Educnl Leadership and Mgt 2011). Lectr in Inorganic Chem., Univ. of Edinburgh, 1995–97; Teacher of Physics and Chemistry, Firrhill High Sch., 1997–2001; Asst Principal Teacher of Sci., Liberton High Sch., 2001–02; Principal Teacher of Sci., Holy Rood RC High Sch., 2002–04; Principal Teacher of Sci., Peebles High Sch., 2004–10; Depute Head Teacher, Biggar High Sch., 2010–13. *Recreations:* music (viola, piano, singing), running, golf. *Address:* St Mary's Music School, Coates Hall, 25 Grosvenor Crescent, Edinburgh EH12 5EL. *T:* (0131) 538 7766. *E:* ktaylor@st-marys-music-school.co.uk.

**TAYLOR, Prof. Kenneth MacDonald,** MD; FRCSE, FRCSGlas; FSAScot; Professor and Chief of Cardiac Surgery, Imperial College School of Medicine (formerly Royal Postgraduate Medical School), Hammersmith Hospital, 1983–2007, now Emeritus; British Heart Foundation Professor of Cardiac Surgery, University of London, 1983–2007; Deputy Head, National Heart & Lung Institute (formerly Division of Heart, Lung and Circulation), Imperial College Faculty of Medicine, 1997–2007; Clinical Director of Cardiac Sciences, Imperial College Healthcare NHS Trust (formerly Hammersmith Hospitals NHS Trust), 2003–07; *b* 20 Oct. 1947; *s* of late Hugh Baird Taylor and Mary Taylor; *m* 1971, Christine Elizabeth (*née* Buchanan) (*d* 2010); one *s* one *d*. *Educ:* Jordanhill College School; Univ. of Glasgow (MB ChB, MD; Cullen Medal, 1968; Gairdner Medal, 1969; Allan Hird Prize, 1969). Univ. of Glasgow: Hall Fellow in Surgery, 1971–72, Lectr and Sen. Lectr in Cardiac Surgery, 1975–83; Consultant Cardiac Surgeon, Royal Infirmary and Western Infirmaries, Glasgow, 1979–83. Vis. Prof., Dept of Bio-engineering, Univ. of Strathclyde, 1997–2007. Chm., Specialist Adv. Cttee in Cardiothoracic Surgery, 1992–95 (Mem., 1986–92); Dir, UK Heart Valve Registry, 1986–2007; Clin. Dir, UK Sch. of Perfusion Science, 1987–97. Member: Exec. Cttee, Soc. of Cardiothoracic Surgeons of GB and Ire., 1992–95; Wkg Gp on Cardiac Waiting Times, DoH, 1994–95; Central R & D Cttee, Acute Sector Panel, DoH, 1996–2007; Reference Gp, Nat. Service Framework, Coronary Heart Disease, DoH, 1999–2002; Chairman: Database Cttee, European Assoc. for Cardiothoracic Surgery, 1994–2000; UK Cardiac Audit Steering Gp, 1994–2001. FESC 1995; FECTS 1998 (Mem., 1988); Member: British Cardiac Soc., 1983–; Amer. Soc. of Thoracic Surgeons, 1984–; Council and Exec. Cttee, BHF, 2001–10 (Trustee, 2006–10); Hon. Member: Amer. Acad. of Cardiovascular Perfusion, 1993; Amer. Assoc. for Thoracic Surgery, 1998 (Mem., 1988–98; Honoured Guest, 1998); Soc. of Perfusionists of GB and Ire., 1998 (Pres., 1989–93; Hon. Life Mem., 1999). Trustee: Garfield Weston Trust, 1998–; European Soc. of Perfusion, 2002–. Hon. Alumnus, Cleveland Clinic, USA, 2000. Governor, Drayton Manor High Sch., London, 1989–96. Pres., Friends of Hammersmith Hosp., 2007–. Church Warden, St Stephen's C of E, Ealing, 2010. Editor, Perfusion, 1986–2008; Member, Advisory Editorial Board: Annals of Thoracic Surgery, 1990–2000; Jl of Cardiovascular Anaesthesia, 1993–2000; Jl of Heart Valve Disease, 1993–2000. Peter Allen Prize, Soc. of Thoracic and Cardiovascular Surgeons, 1975; Patey Prize, Surgical Res. Soc., 1977; Fletcher Prize, RCSG, 1977; Watson Prize, RCSG, 1982. *Publications:* Pulsatile Perfusion, 1979, 2nd edn 1982; Handbook of Intensive Care, 1984; Cardiopulmonary Bypass, 1986; Cardiac Surgery, 1987; Principles of Surgical Research, 1989, 2nd edn 1995; The Brain and Cardiac Surgery, 1992; numerous articles on cardiac surgery. *Recreations:* family, church, music.

**TAYLOR, Prof. Kevin Michael Geoffrey,** PhD; FRPharmS; Professor of Clinical Pharmaceutics, UCL School of Pharmacy, University College London (formerly School of Pharmacy, University of London), since 2006; Chair, British Pharmacopoeia Commission, since 2013; *b* Dartford, 8 June 1961; *s* of Geoffrey and Janet Taylor; *m* 1984, Pauline McBride; one *s* one *d*. *Educ:* Chislehurst and Sidcup Grammar Sch.; Welsh Sch. of Pharmacy, Univ. of Wales Inst. of Sci. and Technol. (BPharm 1982; PhD 1987). MRPharmS 1983, FRPharmS 2013. Pre-registration pharmacist, Boots the Chemist, Lewisham, 1982–83; School of Pharmacy, University of London: Teaching and Res. Fellow, 1986–88; Lectr, 1988–94; Sen. Lectr, 1994–2002; Reader, 2002–04; Prof. of Clin. Pharmaceutics, UCL Hosps and Sch. of Pharmacy, 2004–06; Hd, Dept of Pharmaceutics, Sch. of Pharmacy, Univ. of London, later UCL Sch. of Pharmacy, University Coll. London, 2006–13. Hon. Prof., Inst. of Nanotechnol. and Bioengrg, Univ. of Central Lancs, 2012–. Member: Commn on Human Medicines, 2012– (Mem., 2006–, Chm., 2013–, Chem., Pharmacy and Standards Expert Adv. Gp); UK Delegn to Eur. Pharmacopoeia Commn, 2014–; Inhalanda Wkg Party, Eur. Pharmacopoeia, 2014–; Pharmacy Expert Adv. Gp, British Pharmacopoeia Commn, 2015–. Mem., Chem., Pharmacy and Standards Sub-cttee, Cttee on Safety of Medicines, 2002–06. Freeman, City of London, 1987. *Publications:* (jtly) Sociology for Pharmacists: an introduction, 1990, 2nd edn 2003; (ed jtly) Social Pharmacy: innovation and development, 1994; (ed jtly) Pharmacy Practice, 2001, 2nd edn 2016; (jtly) Nanocarrier Systems for Drug Delivery for the Treatment of Asthma, 2011; (ed jtly) Aulton's Pharmaceutics: the design and manufacture of medicines, 4th edn 2013, 5th edn 2018; (ed jtly) Integrated Pharmacy Case Studies, 2015; contrib. articles to scientific jls on pharmaceutical formulation and drug delivery. *Recreations:* travel, vegetable growing, humming. *Address:* UCL School of Pharmacy, 29–39 Brunswick Square, WC1N 1AX. *T:* (020) 7753 5853. *E:* kevin.taylor@ucl.ac.uk.

**TAYLOR, Prof. Laurence John, (Laurie);** Professor of Sociology, University of York, 1974–93; *s* of Stanley Douglas Taylor and Winifred Agnes (*née* Cooper); marr. diss.; one *s*; *m* 2010, Sally Joy Feldman, *qv*. *Educ:* St Mary's Coll., Liverpool; Rose Bruford College of Drama, Kent; Birkbeck Coll., Univ. of London (BA); Univ. of Leicester (MA). Librarian, 1952–54; Sales Asst, 1954–56; Professional Actor, 1960–61; English Teacher, 1961–64; Lectr in Sociology, 1965–73, Reader in Sociology, 1973–74, Univ. of York. Vis. Prof., 1994–, Fellow, 1996–, Birkbeck Coll., Univ. of London. *Publications:* Deviance and Society, 1971; (jtly) Psychological Survival, 1972; (jtly) Crime, Deviance and Socio-Legal Control, 1972; (ed jtly) Politics and Deviance, 1973; Man's Experience of the World, 1976; (jtly) Escape Attempts, 1976, 2nd edn 1992; (jtly) Prison Secrets, 1978; (jtly) In Whose Best Interests?, 1980; In the Underworld, 1984; (jtly) Uninvited Guests, 1986; Professor Lapping Sends His Apologies, 1987; The Tuesday Afternoon Time Immemorial Committee, 1989; Laurie Taylor's Guide to Higher Education, 1994; (jtly) What Are Children For?, 2003; In Confidence: talking frankly about fame and fortune, 2014; articles, reviews, broadcasts, TV series. *E:* lolsoc@dircon.co.uk.

*See also* Matthew Taylor.

**TAYLOR, Louis;** *see* Taylor, D. L.

**TAYLOR, Louise Méarie;** Relationship Partner, Rockpool Investments, since 2016 (freelance Relationship Partner, 2013–16); writer and curator; *b* 8 Sept. 1967; *d* of Prof. A. Taylor and J. M. Taylor; *m* 2000, Jason Brooks (marr. diss.); one *d*. *Educ:* Univ. of Warwick (BA Hons (Hist. of Art) 1988); Staffordshire Univ. (PhD (Design Hist.) 1995). Craftspace Touring: Exhibns Dir, 1991–95; Actg Dir, 1995–96; Crafts Council: Hd, Exhibns and Collection, 1996–99; Dir, Artistic Programming and Information, 1999–2002; Dir, 2002–05; arts consultant, writer and mentor, 2006–14; Associate, Modus Operandi, 2012–15. Trustee, Craft Pottery Charitable Trust, 2003–17. Hon. FRCA 2004. *Publications:* editor and joint author: Recycling: forms for the next century, 1996; Handmade in India, 1998; Satellites of Fashion, 1998; No Picnic, 1998; (ed and introd.) Contemporary International Basketmaking, 1999; (ed and introd.) Contemporary Japanese Jewellery, 2000; (ed jtly and introd.) Wendy Ramshaw: rooms of dreams, 2012; (ed jtly and introd.) Necklace for an Elephant and Other Stories: the working lives of David Poston, 2014; Shelved, 2018. *Recreations:* tennis, yoga, pilates, art exhibitions. *Address:* 40 Eardley Road, Sevenoaks, Kent TN13 1XT. *E:* louisembtaylor@yahoo.co.uk.

**TAYLOR, Malcolm;** *see* McDowell, M.

**TAYLOR, Mark Christopher;** Chief Executive, Society of Homeopaths, since 2015; *b* 24 Nov. 1958; *s* of Norman and June Taylor; *m* (marr. diss.); two *s* one *d*; *m* Carol Newberry. *Educ:* Loughborough Grammar Sch.; Birmingham Univ. (BA Medieval and Modern Hist.); Leeds Poly. (postgrad. Hotel Management qualification). Hotel Management, Norfolk Capital Hotels, 1981–84; Conf. Manager, 1984–89, Dir, 1989–2014, Museums Assoc.; Chief Exec., VocalEyes, 2014–15. Chairman: Network of Eur. Museum Orgns, 1998–2001; Campaign for Learning through Museums, 1998–2003; Cultural Tourism and Heritage Export Cttee, 2003–05; HeritageMK, 2017–; Board Member: Nat. Campaign for Arts, 1999–2008; Bedfordshire Music Trust, 2003–15; Creative and Cultural Industries Sector Skills Council, 2004–05. Trustee: Museum Prize Trust, 2002–14; Campaign for Museums, 2004–09; Culture Unlimited, 2008–12; Harpur Trust, 2016–. *Recreations:* sport, films, food. *E:* taylors.bedford@ntlworld.com.

**TAYLOR, Prof. Mark Peter,** PhD, DSc; FCIPD; FAcSS; Professor of Finance and Dean, John M. Olin School of Business, Washington University in St Louis, since 2016; *b* 17 May 1958; *s* of Arthur Leslie Taylor and Lorna Kathleen Taylor; *m* 1980, Anita Margaret Phillips (marr. diss. 2015); two *s* one *d*. *Educ:* St John's Coll., Oxford (BA (PPE) 1980; MA 1984); Birkbeck Coll., London (MSc (Econs) 1982; PhD (Econs) 1984); Liverpool Univ. (MA (Eng. Lit.) 2001); Inst. of Educn, Univ. of London (MBA (HE Mgt) 2010); Warwick Univ. (DSc (Finance) 2012). Foreign exchange dealer, Citibank, London, 1980–82; Lectr in Econs, Univ. of Newcastle upon Tyne, 1984–86; Res. Economist, Bank of England, 1986–87; Professor of Economics: Dundee Univ., 1987–88; City Univ. Business Sch., 1988–90; Sen. Econ. Advr, IMF, Washington, 1990–94; Prof. of Econs, Univ. of Liverpool, 1994–97; Fellow in Econs, University Coll., Oxford, 1997–99; Prof. of Macroecons, later Internat. Finance and Macroecons, 1999–2016, Dean, Warwick Business Sch., 2010–16, Univ. of Warwick. Consultant, IMF, 1999–2005; Managing Director: Barclays Global Investors Ltd, 2006–09; BlackRock, 2009–10. Res. Fellow, Centre for Econ. Policy Res., 1987–. Councillor, REconS, 2002–09. FRSA 1995; FAcSS (AcSS 2009); FCIPD 2013. *Publications:* Macroeconomic Systems, 1987; The Balance of Payments: new perspectives on open economy macroeconomics, 1990; Money and Financial Markets, 1991; Applied Econometric Techniques, 1992; Policy Issues in the Operation of Currency Unions, 1993; Modern Perspectives on the Gold Standard, 1996; Speculation and Financial Markets, 2001; The Economics of Exchange Rates, 2002; Economics, 2006, 4th edn 2016; Macroeconomics, 2007, 3rd edn 2016; numerous articles in learned jls. *Recreations:* horology, antique clocks, languages, literature, wine. *Address:* Dean's Office, John M. Olin School of Business, Washington University, One Brookings Drive, St Louis, MO 63130–4899, USA. *T:* (314) 9356344, *Fax:* (314) 9354074. *E:* mark.p.taylor@wustl.edu. *Club:* Reform.

**TAYLOR, Martin;** *see* Taylor, John M.

**TAYLOR, Sir Martin (John),** Kt 2009; PhD; FRS 1996; Warden, Merton College, Oxford, 2010–18 (Hon. Fellow, 2019); *b* 18 Feb. 1952; *s* of John Maurice Taylor and Sheila Mary Barbara Taylor (*née* Camacho); *m* 1973, Sharon Lynn Marlow; two *s* two *d*. *Educ:* St Clare's Prep. Sch., Leicester; Wyggeston Boys' Sch., Leicester; Pembroke Coll., Oxford (BA 1st Class; Hon. Fellow, 2012); King's College, London (PhD). Res. Assistant, KCL, 1976–77; Jun. Lectr, Oxford Univ., 1977–78; Lectr, QMC, 1978–81; Fellow, Trinity Coll., Cambridge, 1981–85; Univ. Asst Lectr, Cambridge, 1984–85; Prof. of Pure Maths, UMIST, later Univ. of Manchester, 1986–2010. Associate Researcher, CNRS, Besançon, 1979–80; NSF Researcher, Univ. of Illinois, Urbana, 1981; Royal Soc. Leverhulme Sen.

Res. Fellowship, 1991–92; CNRS Poste Rouge, Bordeaux, 1996; EPSRC Sen. Res. Fellow, 1999–2004; Royal Soc. Wolfson Res. Fellow, 2002–07. Pres., London Mathematical Soc., 1998–2000; Mem. Council, 2000–01, Vice-Pres. and Physical Sec., 2004–09, Royal Soc. (Chairman: The Scientific Century Cttee (reported 2010); Vision for Science and Maths Educn Cttee (reported 2014); Mem. Council, EPSRC, 2004–09. Trustee: Mitsubishi UFJ Trust Oxford Foundn, 2014–; Dame Kathleen Ollerenshaw Trust, 2015–. Freeman, City of London, 2016. Citizen of Grenada, WI, 2019. Hon. DSc: Leicester, 2006; Bordeaux, 2009; UEA, 2012. *Publications:* Class Groups of Group Rings, 1984; (with Ph. Cassou-Noguès) Elliptic Functions and Rings of Integers, 1987; (with J. Coates) L-functions and Arithmetic, 1991; (with A. Fröhlich) Algebraic Number Theory, 1991; (with K. Roggenkamp) Group Rings and Class Groups, 1992. *Recreations:* fly fishing, hill walking. *Address:* c/o Merton College, Oxford OX1 4JD.

**TAYLOR, Matthew,** CBE 2019; Chief Executive, Royal Society for the Encouragement of Arts, Manufactures and Commerce, since 2006; *b* 5 Dec. 1960; *s of* Prof. Laurence John Taylor, *qv* and Jennifer Howells; two *s* one *d*. *Educ:* Southampton Univ. (BA Sociol.); Warwick Univ. (MA Industrial Relns). Set up Res. Unit, NAS/UWT, 1985–88; Dir, W Midlands Health Service Monitoring Unit, 1988–90; Sen. Res. Fellow, Univ. of Warwick, 1990–93; Asst Gen. Sec., Labour Party, 1994–98; Dir, IPPR, 1998–2003; Chief Advr on Political Strategy to Prime Minister, 2003–06. Chairman: Social Integration Commn, 2014–; Ind. Rev. of Employment Practices in the Modern Economy, 2016–17. Regular contributor on public service reform, political strategy and communities to newspapers and jls. *Publications:* (with L. J. Taylor) What Are Children For?, 2003. *Recreations:* running, learning the guitar, West Bromwich Albion. *Address:* Royal Society for the Encouragement of Arts, Manufactures and Commerce, 8 John Adam Street, WC2N 6EZ. *T:* (020) 7451 6883.

**TAYLOR, Rt Rev. Maurice,** DD; Bishop of Galloway, (RC), 1981–2004, now Emeritus; *b* 5 May 1926; *s of* Maurice Taylor and Lucy Taylor (*née* McLaughlin). *Educ:* St Aloysius Coll., Glasgow; Our Lady's High School, Motherwell; Pontifical Gregorian Univ., Rome (DD). Served RAMC in UK, India, Egypt, 1944–47. Ordained to priesthood, Rome, 1950; lectured in Philosophy, 1955–60, in Theology 1960–65, St Peter's Coll., Cardross; Rector, Royal Scots Coll., Valladolid, Spain, 1965–74; Parish Priest, Our Lady of Lourdes, East Kilbride, 1974–81. Vice-Pres., Progressio (formerly Catholic Inst. for Internat. Relations), 1985–2017; Episcopal Sec., Bishops' Conf. of Scotland, 1987–2004; Chm., Internat. Commn on English in the Liturgy, 1997–2002. *Publications:* The Scots College in Spain, 1971; Guatemala: a bishop's journey, 1991; El Salvador: portrait of a parish, 1992; (with Ellen Hawkes) Opening Our Lives to the Saviour, 1995; (with Ellen Hawkes) Listening at the Foot of the Cross, 1996; (compiled) Surveying Today's World, 2003; Being a Bishop in Scotland, 2006; It's the Eucharist, Thank God, 2009; Life's Flavour: a variety of experiences, 2014; What Are They Talking About?: background notes for the readings and collects at Sunday Mass, 2015; Weekday Thoughts on the Sunday Gospels, 2017. *Address:* 41 Overmills Road, Ayr KA7 3LH. *T:* (01292) 285865. *W:* www.bishopmauricetaylor.org.uk.

**TAYLOR, Maxwell;** *see* Taylor, J. M. P.

**TAYLOR, Rev. Prof. Michael Hugh,** OBE 1998; Professor of Social Theology, University of Birmingham, 1999–2004, now Emeritus; Director, World Faiths Development Dialogue, 2002–04; *b* 8 Sept. 1936; *s of* Albert Ernest and Gwendoline Louisa Taylor; *m* 1960, Adèle May Dixon (*d* 2015); one *s* one *d* (and one *s* decd). *Educ:* Northampton Grammar School; Univ. of Manchester (BA, BD, MA); Union Theological Seminary, NY (STM). Baptist Minister, N Shields, 1961–66, Birmingham Hall Green, 1966–69; Principal, Northern Baptist Coll., Manchester, 1970–85; Lectr, Univ. of Manchester, 1970–85; Dir, Christian Aid, 1985–97; Pres. and Chief Exec., Selly Oak Colls, 1998–99. Mem. Council, ODI, 1989–2000; Chairman: Assoc. of Protestant Develt Agencies in Europe, 1991–94; The Burma Campaign UK, 2000–10; Health Unlimited, 2002–10; Oxford Mencap, 2018–; Member: WCC Commn on Sharing and Service, 1991–98; Adv. Bd, High Pay Commn, 2012– (Comr, 2010–11). Trustee: Mines Adv. Gp, 1998– (Chm., 2000–13); Responding to Conflict, 2004–09 (Chm., 2007–09); St Philip's Centre, Leicester, 2006–19; Getting Heard, 2017–; Refugee Resource, 2018–; The Mint House, 2018–19. Gov., Fircroft Coll., Birmingham, 1998–2016 (Chm., 2006–16). Vis. Res. Fellow, Regents Park Coll., Oxford, 2016–. Hon. Canon, Worcester Cathedral, 2002–07. JP Manchester, 1980–85. DLitt Lambeth, 1997. *Publications:* Variations on a Theme, 1973; Sermon on the Mount, 1982; (ed) Christians and the Future of Social Democracy, 1982; Learning to Care, 1988; Good for the Poor, 1990; Christianity and the Persistence of Poverty, 1991; Not Angels But Agencies, 1996; NGOs and their Future in Development, 1997; Poverty and Christianity, 2000; Christianity, Poverty and Wealth, 2003; Eat, Drink and Be Merry for Tomorrow We Live, 2005; Border Crossings: social theology in Christianity and Islam, 2006; Sorting out Believing, 2011; Christ and Capital, 2015; contribs to books and jls. *Recreations:* walking, cooking, music, cinema, theatre. *Address:* 4 Harpes Road, Oxford OX2 7QL.

**TAYLOR, His Honour Michael John;** a Circuit Judge, 1996–2016; *b* 28 Feb. 1951; *m* 1973, Pamela Ann Taylor. *Educ:* Hull Univ. (LLB). Called to the Bar, Inner Temple, 1974; in practice, 1974–96; Asst Recorder, 1990–94; Recorder, 1994–96.

**TAYLOR, Michael John Ellerington,** CBE 1992; TD 1972; DL; Chair, Action for Health, Cumbria, since 2017; *b* 15 Sept. 1937; *s of* Leonard George Taylor and Marjorie Ellerington Taylor. *Educ:* Harrow Sch.; Emmanuel Coll., Cambridge (BA Hons 1962; LLB Hons 1963; MA 1967). Shell UK and Shell Internat., 1969–91; Chief Exec., Mgt Charter Initiative, 1990–91; Investors in People: Nat. Assessor, 1991–96; Chief External Verifier, 1996–2001; Regl Comr, NW, 2001–06, NW and W Mids, 2006–10, Appts Commn (formerly NHS Appts Commn); Chm., NHS Cumbria, 2010–11. Chairman: NW TAVRA, 1995–2000; Council, RFCA, 2000–04; Nat. Artillery Assoc., 1988–2003 (Vice Pres., 2004–); W Chester Regeneration Bd, 2000–05; Chester Aid to the Homeless, 2001–09; Cumbria Partnership NHS Foundn Trust, 2011–17; Council, Cumbria, St John Ambulance, 2009–12 (Co. Pres., 2018–); Royal Artillery Officers' Assoc. (NW), 2015–; Bolton Volunteer Artillery Assoc. Ltd, 2015–; Pres., Nat. Home Service Force Assoc., 2004–12 (Patron, 2012–). Trustee: Cumbria CVS, 2017–; Citizens Advice, 2017–. Vice-Chm., W. Cheshire Coll., 2001–04. Col, TA, 1982–93; ADC to the Queen, 1988–92; Hon. Col Comdt, RA, 1994–2005. DL Cheshire, 1998. *Recreations:* Territorial Army, walking the dogs, running small Cumbrian hospitality business. *Address:* Lowther House, Clifton, Penrith, Cumbria CA10 2EG. *Club:* Army and Navy.

**TAYLOR, Prof. Miles,** PhD; FRHistS; Professor of Modern History, University of York, since 2004; *b* Farnham Common, Bucks, 19 Sept. 1961; *s of* late Geoffrey Peter Taylor and of Dorothy Pearl Taylor (*née* Weaver, later Irish); *m* 2012, Dr Shalini Sharma; one *s*, one *s* two *d* by a previous marriage. *Educ:* Tapton Sch., Sheffield; Queen Mary Coll., Univ. of London (BA 1st Cl. Hist. and Politics 1983); Harvard Univ. (Kennedy Scholar); St John's Coll., Cambridge (PhD 1989). FRHistS 1997. Eugenie Strong Res. Fellow in Hist., Girton Coll., Cambridge, 1988–91; Fellow and Dir of Studies in Hist., Christ's Coll., Cambridge, 1991–95; Lectr in Mod. Hist., KCL, 1995–2001; Prof. of Mod. British Hist., Univ. of Southampton, 2001–04; Prof. of Hist. and Dir, Inst. of Historical Res., Univ. of London, 2008–14; Leverhulme Major Res. Fellow, 2014–16. *Publications:* (ed) The European Diaries of Richard Cobden, 1846–1849, 1994; The Decline of British Radicalism, 1847–1860, 1995; (ed jtly) Party, State and Society: electoral behaviour in Britain since 1820, 1997; (ed) Bagehot's The English Constitution, 2001; Ernest Jones, Chartism and the Romance of Politics, 1819–69, 2003; (ed jtly) The Victorians since 1901: histories, representations and revisions, 2004; (ed jtly) Palmerston Studies, 2 vols, 2007; (ed) Southampton: gateway to the British Empire, 2007; (ed) The Victorian Empire and Britain's Maritime World, 1837–1901: the sea and global history, 2013; (ed) The Age of Asa: Lord Briggs, history and public life in Britain since 1945, 2015; Empress: Queen Victoria and India, 2018; articles in Past and Present, Histl Jl, Hist. Workshop Jl, Jl of Imperial and Commonwealth Hist., Social Hist., etc. *Recreations:* tennis, long-distance running, crosswords. *Address:* Department of History, University of York, Vanbrugh College, Heslington, York YO10 5DD.

**TAYLOR, Miranda,** *see* Haines, M.

**TAYLOR, Neil;** *see* Taylor, Richard N.

**TAYLOR, Neville,** CB 1989; Director-General, Central Office of Information and Head of Government Information Service, 1985–88; *b* 17 Nov. 1930; *y s of* late Frederick Taylor and Lottie Taylor (*née* London); *m* 1954, Margaret Ann (*d* 2014), *y d of* late Thomas Bainbridge Vickers and Gladys Vickers; two *s*. *Educ:* Sir Joseph Williamson's Mathematical Sch., Rochester; Coll. of Commerce, Gillingham, Kent. Junior Reporter, Chatham News Group, 1947; Royal Signals, 1948–50; Journalism, 1950–58; Asst Information Officer, Admiralty, 1958; Information Officer (Press), Admiralty, 1960; Fleet Information Officer, Singapore, 1963; Chief Press Officer, MoD, 1966; Information Adviser to Nat. Economic Develt Office, 1968; Dep. Dir, Public Relns (Royal Navy), 1970; Head of Information, Min. of Agriculture, Fisheries and Food, 1971; Dep. Dir of Information, DoE, 1973–74, Dir of Information, 1974–79; Dir of Information, DHSS, 1979–82; Chief of Public Relations, MOD, 1982–85. Hon. Vice Pres., Pen and Sword Club, 2011–. *Recreation:* fishing. *Address:* 16 Seaford Court, The Esplanade, Rochester, Kent ME1 1QA. *T:* (01634) 842990.

**TAYLOR, Sir Nicholas Richard S.;** *see* Stuart Taylor.

**TAYLOR, Nicola Jane N.;** *see* Nelson-Taylor.

**TAYLOR, Prof. Pamela Jane, (Mrs J. C. Gunn),** CBE 2017; FRCPsych; FMedSci; Professor of Forensic Psychiatry, Cardiff University (formerly University of Wales College of Medicine), since 2004; Hon. Consultant Psychiatrist, Bro Morgannwg NHS Trust, since 2004; *b* 23 April 1948; *d of* Philip Geoffrey Taylor and Joan Taylor (*née* Alport); *m* 1989, John Charles Gunn, *qv*. *Educ:* Merchant Taylors' Girls' Sch., Liverpool; Guy's Hosp. Med. Sch. and King's Coll. Hosp. Med. Sch. (MB BS 1971). MRCP 1974; MRCPsych 1976, FRCPsych 1989, Hon. FRCPsych, 2016. Gen. prof. trng in psychiatry, Guy's Hosp., 1972–74; Teaching Fellow in Psychiatry, Univ. of Vermont, 1975; clin. res., Guy's Hosp. Trustees, 1976–79; MRC res. scientist, Inst. of Psychiatry, 1979–81; Sen. Lectr in Forensic Psychiatry, and Hon. Cons. Psychiatrist, 1982–89, Dir of Medium Secure Service, 1988–89, Inst. of Psychiatry and Bethlem Royal and Maudsley Hosp.; Hd of Med. Services, Special Hosps' Service Authy, 1990–95; Prof. of Special Hosp. Psychiatry, Inst. of Psychiatry, KCL, 1995–2004; Hon. Consultant Psychiatrist: Broadmoor Hosp., 1995–2005; Bethlem Royal and Maudsley Hosp., 1995–2005. Vis. Prof., Inst. of Psychiatry, KCL, 2004–. Advr on Forensic Psychiatry to CMO, Welsh Assembly Govt, 2004–. Member: Inner London Probation Bd, 1990–2001; DoH and Home Office Steering Gp, Review of Health and Social Services for Mentally Disordered Offenders and other requiring similar services, 1990–94; Wkg Party on Genetics of Mental Disorders, Nuffield Council on Bio-Ethics, 1996–99. Member: RSocMed, 1972–; British Soc. of Criminology, 1980–; Mental Health Foundn, 1990–94; Howard League for Penal Reform, 1990– (Trustee); Council, RCPsych, 2003– (Mem., various cttees and wkg parties, 1982–). Chair, Forensic Psychiatry Faculty, 2016–20. Jt Founder and Lead Editor, Criminal Behaviour and Mental Health, 1991–; Internat. Ed., Behavioral Scis and the Law, 2003–. FMedSci 2004. Gaskell Gold Medal and Prize, RCPsych, 1978. *Publications:* (ed with J. C. Gunn) Forensic Psychiatry: clinical, legal and ethical issues, 1993, 2nd edn 2014; (ed) Violence in Society, 1993; (ed with T. Swann) Couples in Care and Custody, 1999; (ed jtly) Personality Disorder and Serious Offending, 2006; numerous sci. papers, editorials, reviews and contribs to books. *Recreations:* family, friends, an acre of previously neglected garden and, in every spare moment, a book. *Address:* Institute of Psychological Medicine and Clinical Neurosciences, Cardiff University, Hadyn Ellis Building, Maindy Road, Cathays, Cardiff CF24 4HQ.

**TAYLOR, Pamela Margaret,** OBE 2004; Chief Executive, Water UK, 1998–2015; *b* 25 March 1949; *d of* late Geoffrey Higgins and Elena Higgins; *m* 1972, John Marc Taylor. Hd of Public Affairs, BMA, 1977–92; Dir, Corporate Affairs, BBC, 1992–94; mgt consultant, 1994–95; Chief Exec., Water Companies Assoc., 1995–98. President: IPR, 1993; Eur. Union of Nat. Assocs of Water Suppliers and Waste Water Services, 2002. Member Board: PHLS, 1998–2003; Health Protection Agency, 2002–13. Trustee, Wateraid, 2003–11 (Vice Chm., 2008–11). Trustee and Treas., RSA, 2000–09; Mem. Council, RSPH (formerly Trustee, RIPH). MInstD. *Publications:* (ed) Smoking Out the Barons, 1986; articles in BMJ and Jl of American Med. Assoc. *Recreations:* running, working out, wines, ballet, football, cricket. *Clubs:* Mosimann's, Annabel's.

**TAYLOR, Paul Richard;** QC 2018; a Recorder, since 2019; *b* London, 25 Aug. 1966; *s of* late Ivor Taylor and Anita Taylor (*née* Bluestone); *m* 1990, Samantha Moss; one *s* three *d*. *Educ:* Orange Hill Comprehensive Sch.; Poly. of South Bank (LLB Hons); Downing Coll., Cambridge (LLM); Inns of Court Sch. of Law. Called to the Bar, Middle Temple, 1989; in practice as barrister, 1990–, specialising in criminal appeals, 2000–. Mem., Bar of NI, 2012–. Door Tenant, Allum Chambers, Trinidad and Tobago, 2018–; Consultant, PST Law, BVI, 2019–. *Publications:* Taylor on Appeals, 2000; (ed and contrib.) Taylor on Criminal Appeals, 2012; contrib. case commentaries to Criminal Law Rev. *Recreations:* family, studying Jewish religious texts, gardening. *Address:* Doughty Street Chambers, 53 Doughty Street, WC1N 2LS. *T:* (020) 7404 1313. *E:* p.taylor@doughtystreet.co.uk.

**TAYLOR, Ven. Paul Stanley;** Archdeacon of Sherborne, and Canon and Prebendary of Salisbury Cathedral, from now Archdeacon Emeritus; *b* 28 March 1953; *s of* Stanley and Beryl Taylor; *m* 1984, Janet Wendy Taylor (*née* Harris); three *s*. *Educ:* Westminster Coll., Oxford (BEd 1975; MTh 1998); Westcott House, Cambridge. Ordained deacon, 1984, priest, 1985; Curate, St Stephen, Bush Hill Park, 1984–88; Asst Dir, 1987–94, Dir, 1994–2000 and 2002–04, Post Ordination Trng, Dio. London; Vicar: St Andrew, Southgate, 1988–97; St Mary, Hendon, 1997–2001; Priest-in-charge, Christ Ch, Hendon, 1997–2001; Vicar, St Mary and Christ Ch, Hendon, 2001–04; Area Dean, W Barnet, 2000–04. *Recreations:* golf, fell walking, running, Rugby Union, sailing, football. *Address:* 2 Blackwell Lane, Redditch, Worcs B97 6SS. *T:* 07796 691203, (01527) 591699. *E:* pstaylor53@gmail.com. *Club:* Redditch Golf.

**TAYLOR, Ven. Peter Flint;** Archdeacon of Harlow, 1996–2009; *b* 7 March 1944; *s of* late Alan Flint Taylor and Josephine Overbury Taylor (*née* Dix); *m* 1971, Joy M. Sampson; one *d*. *Educ:* Clifton Coll., Bristol; Queens' Coll., Cambridge (MA); London Coll. of Divinity (BD ext. London Univ.). Ordained deacon, 1970, priest, 1971; Assistant Curate: St

Augustine's, Highbury, 1970–73; St Andrew's, Plymouth, 1973–77; Vicar, Christ Church, Ironville, Derbys, 1977–83; Priest-in-charge, St James, Riddings, 1982–83; Rector, Holy Trinity, Rayleigh, Chelmsford, 1983–96. Part-time Chaplain, Bullwood Hall Prison and Youth Custody Centre, 1986–90; Rural Dean of Rochford, 1989–96. *Recreations:* walking, electronics and computing, astronomy, archaeology of Jerusalem, Dartmoor and its history. *Address:* 5 Springfield Terrace, Springfield Road, South Brent, Devon TQ10 9AP. *T:* (01364) 73427. *E:* peterftaylor@lineone.net.

**TAYLOR, Prof. Peter James**, PhD; FBA 2004; Professor of Geography, Loughborough University, 1995–2010, now Emeritus, and founding Director, Globalization and World Cities Research Network; Professor of Human Geography, Northumbria University, 2010; *b* 21 Nov. 1944; *s* of Peter Taylor and Margaret Alice Taylor; *m* 1965, Enid; one *s* one *d. Educ:* Univ. of Liverpool (BA Hons; PhD). Lectr, Sen. Lectr, Reader, then Prof., Univ. of Newcastle upon Tyne, 1971–95. Visiting positions: Univ. of Iowa, 1970–71; Univ. of Alberta, 1976; Clark Univ., 1978–79; Univ. of Illinois, 1985; Binghamton Univ., 1990; Univ. of Amsterdam, 1991; Virginia Tech, 1992–93, 2002, 2003; Univ. of Paris, 1995; Ghent Univ., 2004–05. Francqui Medal, Francqui Foundn, Brussels, 2005; Ghent Univ. Medal, 2005. *Publications:* (with Colin Flint) Political Geography: world-economy, nation-state, locality, 1985, 6th edn 2011; Britain and the Cold War: 1945 as geopolitical transition, 1990; The Way the Modern World Works, 1996; Modernities: a geohistorical introduction, 1999; World City Network, 2004; (ed jtly) Cities in Globalization, 2006; (ed jtly) Global Urban Analysis: a survey of cities in globalization, 2010; (ed jtly) The Globalization of Advertising: agencies, cities and spaces of creativity, 2010; (ed jtly) International Handbook of Globalization and World Cities, 2011; (with G. Gudgin) Seats, Votes and the Spatial Organisation of Elections, 2012. *Recreations:* watching sport, collecting postcards, playing with grandchildren. *Address:* 33 Percy Park, Tynemouth NE30 4JZ. *T:* (0191) 259 1113, *Fax:* (01509) 223930.

**TAYLOR, Peter William Edward**; QC 1981; *b* 27 July 1917; *s* of late Peter and Julia A. Taylor; *m* 1948, Julia Mary Brown (*d* 1997), *d* of Air Cdre Sir Vernon Brown, CB, OBE; two *s. Educ:* Peter Symonds' Sch., Winchester; Christ's Coll., Cambridge (MA; Wrangler, Math. Tripos, Part II; 1st Class, Law Tripos, Part II). Served RA, 1939–46: France and Belgium, 1939–40; N Africa, 1942–43; NW Europe, 1944–45 (mentioned in dispatches); Actg Lt-Col 1945; transferred to TARO as Hon. Major, 1946. Called to the Bar, Inner Temple, 1946; Lincoln's Inn, *ad eundem*, 1953 (Bencher, 1976); practice at the Bar, 1947–94; Occasional Lectr, LSE, 1946–56; Lectr in Construction of Documents, Council of Legal Educn, 1952–70; Conveyancing Counsel of the Court, 1974–81. Member: General Council of the Bar, 1971–74; Senate of Inns of Court and the Bar, 1974–75; Inter-Professional Cttee on Retirement Provision, 1974–92; Land Registration Rule Cttee, 1976–81; Standing Cttee on Conveyancing, 1985–87; Incorporated Council of Law Reporting, 1977–91 (Vice-Chm., 1987–91); Council, Selden Soc., 1977–. Bar Musical Society: Hon. Sec., 1952–61; Treas. and External Sec., 1961–80; Chm., 1980–86; Vice-Pres., 1986–. *Recreation:* music. *Address:* 46 Onslow Square, SW7 3NX. *T:* (020) 7589 1301.

**TAYLOR, Philippe Arthur**; Managing Director, SeaTrain Sailing, 1993–99; *b* 9 Feb. 1937; *s* of Arthur Peach Taylor and Simone Vacquin; *m* 1973, Margaret Nancy Wilkins; two *s. Educ:* Trinity College, Glenalmond; St Andrews University. Procter & Gamble, 1963; Masius International, 1967; British Tourist Authority, 1970; Chief Executive, Scottish Tourist Board, 1975–80; Man. Dir, Taylor and Partners, 1980–92; Chief Exec., Birmingham Convention and Visitor Bureau Ltd, 1982–94. Vice-Chm., Ikon Gall., 1982–92; Chm., British Assoc. of Conf. Towns, 1987–90. *Publications:* children's books; various papers and articles on tourism. *Recreations:* sailing, making things, tourism, reading. *Address:* The Granary, Theberton, Suffolk IP16 4RR. *Clubs:* Royal Northumberland Yacht (Blyth); Orford Sailing.

**TAYLOR, Rebecca**; Account Director, JPA Health Communications London, since 2018; *b* Todmorden, W Yorks, 10 Aug. 1975. *Educ:* Univ. of Leeds (BA Japanese and Mgt Studies 1997); Univ. of Kent (MA Internat. Relns 2001); Open Univ. (Human Biol. 2010); King's Coll. London (Master in Public Health 2014). Public affairs asst, Plasma Protein Therapeutics Assoc. Europe, 1998–2000; web ed. and journalist, IMS Health, Brussels, 2000–01; Information and Communications Officer, Pharmaceutical Gp of EU, Brussels, 2002–05; Ext. Communications Manager, Internat. Fedn of Animal Health, Brussels, 2005–06; consultant, Food, Health and Retail team, Fleishman-Hillard, Brussels, 2006–09; Stakeholder Relns Manager, NHS Commng Support for London, 2009–10; Sen. Researcher, Internat. Longevity Centre-UK, 2010–11; Account Dir, Healthcare team, Hanover Communications, 2011–12; Project Manager, Macmillan Cancer Support, 2014–16; Coordinator, Grand Challenges Global Health, UCL, 2016–17. Mem. (Lib Dem) Yorks and the Humber, Eur. Parlt, 2012–14. Contested (Lib Dem): Rotherham, 2010; Morley and Outwood, 2015. *W:* www.twitter.com/RTaylor_LibDem.

**TAYLOR, Prof. Richard Kenneth Stanley**, PhD; Professor and Director of Continuing Education and Lifelong Learning, University of Cambridge, 2004–09; Fellow, Wolfson College, Cambridge, 2004–09, now Emeritus Professorial Fellow; *b* 18 Nov. 1945; *s* of Jeanne Ann Taylor and Kenneth Charles Taylor; *m* 1967, Jennifer Teresa Frost (marr. diss. 2004); one *s* two *d. Educ:* Merchant Taylors' Sch., Northwood; Exeter Coll., Oxford (MA 1967); PhD Leeds 1983. Admin. Asst, Univ. of Lancaster, 1967–70; University of Leeds: Admin. Asst, Dept of Adult and Continuing Educn, 1970–73; Warden, Non-Residential Centre for Adult Educn, Bradford, 1973–83; Dir of Extramural Studies, 1985–88; Head, Dept of Adult and Continuing Educn, 1988–91; Prof. and Dir of Continuing Educn, 1991–2004. Sec., Univs Assoc. for Continuing Educn, 1994–98, 2002–03; Chairman: Nat. Inst. for Adult Continuing Educn, 1999–2006 (Vice Chm., 1996–99); Trustees, WEA, 2006–13. *Publications:* (with Colin Pritchard) Social Work: reform or revolution?, 1978; (with Colin Pritchard) The Protest Makers, 1980; (jtly) Adult Education in England and the USA, 1985; (with Kevin Ward) Adult Education and the Working Class, 1986, 2nd edn 2012; (with Nigel Young) Campaigns for Peace, 1987; Against the Bomb: the British peace movement 1958–65, 1988; (with Tom Steele) Learning Independence, 1995; Beyond the Walls, 1996; (with David Watson) Lifelong Learning and the University: a post-Dearing agenda, 1998; (with Tom Steele and Jean Barr) For a Radical Higher Education: after postmodernism, 2002; (with Tom Steele) British Labour and Higher Education, 1945–2000: ideologies, policies and practice, 2011; (with Roger Fieldhouse) E. P. Thompson and English Radicalism, 2013; English Radicalism in the Twentieth Century: a distinctive politics?, 2020. *Recreations:* mountain walking and climbing, cricket, politics, pubs. *Address:* Bowerbank Cottage, Pooley Bridge, Penrith, Cumbria CA10 2NG. *Club:* Yorkshire County Cricket.

**TAYLOR, Prof. Richard Lawrence**, PhD; FRS 1995; Barbara Kimball Browning Professor of Mathematics, Stanford University, since 2018; *b* 19 May 1962; *s* of John Clayton Taylor and Gillian Mary Taylor (*née* Schofield); *m* 1995, Christine Jiayou Chang; one *s* one *d. Educ:* Magdalen Coll. Sch., Oxford; Clare Coll., Cambridge (BA); Princeton Univ. (PhD). Fellow, Clare Coll., Cambridge, 1988–95; Asst Lectr, 1989–92, Lectr, 1992–94, Reader, 1994–95, Cambridge Univ.; Savilian Prof. of Geometry, and Fellow of New Coll., Oxford Univ., 1995–96; Prof. of Mathematics, 1996–2002, Herchel Smith Prof. of Maths, 2002–12, Harvard Univ.; Prof. of Mathematics, 2012–13, Robert and Luisa Fernholz Prof., Inst. for Advanced Study, 2013–19, Princeton. *Publications:* (with M. Harris) The Geometry and Cohomology of Some Simple Shimura Varieties, 2001. *Recreation:* hill walking. *Address:* Department of Mathematics, Stanford University, 450 Serra Mall, Stanford, CA 94305, USA. *T:* (650) 4970640.

**TAYLOR, Sir Richard (Leslie)**, KNZM 2010 (ONZM 2003); Managing Director, Weta Workshop, since 1994; *b* Cheadle, Staffs, UK, 8 Feb. 1965; *s* of Norman Taylor and Jean Taylor; *m* 2010, Tania Rodger; one *s* one *d. Educ:* Wesley Coll., Auckland; Wellington Poly. (Dip. Visual Communication and Design 1987). Design and Effect Supervisor, RT Effects Ltd, 1987–94. Films contributed to include: The Fellowship of the Ring, 2001 (jtly) Best Special Visual Effects, and Best Make up and Hair, BAFTA, 2002; (jtly) Best Visual Effects and Make up, Academy Awards, 2002); The Two Towers, 2002 (jtly) Best Costume Design, BAFTA, 2003); The Return of the King, 2003 (jtly) Best Costume Design, and Best Make up, Academy Awards, 2004); King Kong, 2005 (jtly) Best Special Visual Effects, BAFTA, 2006; (jtly) Best Visual Effects, Academy Awards, 2006). New Zealander of the Year Award, 2012. *Recreations:* sculpting, 7¼ inch trains, family, art, sculpture. *Address:* PO Box 15208, Miramar, Wellington 6243, New Zealand. *T:* (4) 9094000, *Fax:* (4) 3889722.

**TAYLOR, Prof. R(ichard) Neil**, PhD; Professor of Geotechnical Engineering, City, University of London (formerly City University London), since 1996; *b* 14 May 1955; *s* of Charles L. Taylor and Mary Taylor. *Educ:* Emmanuel Coll., Cambridge (BA 1976; MPhil 1979; MA 1980; PhD 1984). MICE 1990. Lectr in Geotechnical Engrg, 1984–91, Sen. Lectr, 1991–96, City Univ. London. Associate, Geotechnical Consulting Gp, 1990–. Sec. Gen., Internat. Soc. for Soil Mechanics and Geotechnical Engrg, 1999–. *Publications:* (ed) Geotechnical Centrifuge Technology, 1995; contrib. papers to jls and confs mainly associated with ground movements caused by tunnels and excavations incl. geotechnical centrifuge modelling and analysis. *Recreations:* running (5km+), walking. *Address:* Research Centre for Multi-scale Geotechnical Engineering, City, University of London, Northampton Square, EC1V 0HB. *T:* (020) 7040 8157.

**TAYLOR, Richard Thomas**, MBE 2014; FRCP; *b* 7 July 1934; *s* of Thomas Taylor and Mabel (*née* Hickley); *m* 1st, 1962, Ann Brett (marr. diss.); one *s* two *d*; 2nd, 1990, Christine Miller; one *d. Educ:* Leys Sch.; Clare Coll., Cambridge (BA); Westminster Med. Sch. (MB, BChir). FRCP 1979. Jun. hosp. doctor trng posts, Westminster Hosp. and other London hosps, 1959–72; MO, RAF, 1961–64; Consultant Physician, Kidderminster Gen. Hosp., 1972–95 (Chm., Hosp. Med. Staff Cttee, 1975–77 and 1986–90). Consultant Rep., Kidderminster DHA, 1982–86. MP (Ind) Wyre Forest, 2001–10; contested (Ind) same seat, 2010; contested (Nat. Health Action) same seat, 2015. Mem., Select Cttee on Health, 2001–10. Chairman: Kidderminster Hosp. League of Friends, 1996–2001; Save Kidderminster Hosp. Campaign Cttee, 1997–2001. President: Kidderminster Civic Soc., 2010–; Leukaemia CARE, 2010–; Nat. Health Action, 2011–; Life Pres., Ind. Community and Health Concern, 2011–. Patron, Kemp Hospice, 2011–. *Publications:* articles on drug treatment and rheumatic diseases in med. jls. *Recreations:* family, ornithology, gardening, classic cars. *Address:* 11 Church Walk, Kidderminster, Worcs DY11 6XY. *Club:* Royal Society of Medicine.

**TAYLOR, (Robert) Alan**; Chief Executive and Town Clerk, Royal Borough of Kensington and Chelsea, 1990–2000; *b* 13 Sept. 1944; *s* of Alfred Taylor and Hilda Mary (*née* Weekley); *m* 1st, 1965, Dorothy Joan Walker (*d* 1986); two *s*; 2nd, 1987, Margaret Susanne Barnes. *Educ:* Thornbury Grammar Sch., Thornbury, Glos; King's Coll., Univ. of London (LLB). Solicitor. Asst Solicitor, Plymouth CBC, 1970–74; Plymouth City Council: Dep. City Solicitor and Sec., 1974–76; Asst Town Clerk, 1976–81; Chief Exec., London Borough of Sutton, 1981–90. Lay Mem., Investigation Cttee, CIMA, 2002–05. Pres., SOLACE, 1998–99 (Hon. Sec., 1992–95; Sen. Vice-Pres., 1997–98); Trustee, Voluntary Reading Help, 2001–07. Chm., Dartmoor Local Access Forum, 2003–06; Mem., Devon and Cornwall Regl Cttee, NT, 2004–13. *Recreations:* theatre, books, walking, choral singing. *Address:* Catkins, Green Lane, Exton, Devon EX3 0PW. *T:* (01392) 873850.

**TAYLOR, Robert Bruce**; Head of Global Asset Management Regulatory Strategy, Financial Conduct Authority, since 2017 (Head of Wealth Management and Private Banking, 2014–17); *b* London, 4 Jan. 1960; *s* of Robert Wilson Taylor and Joy Rosina Taylor; partner, Michael David Julius Kallenbach. *Educ:* Sam Barlow High Sch.; Lewis & Clark Coll. (BA Internat. Affairs 1982); Columbia Univ. (MS Journalism 1986). Congressional Aide to Congressman Les AuCoin, 1982–85; Editor, Bond Buyer, 1987–90; Vice Pres., Merrill Lynch, 1990–98; Man. Dir, SG Hambros Bank & Trust, 1998–2000; Hd, Private Banking, Coutts & Co., 2000–04; CEO, Kleinwort Benson, 2004–11. Mem., Jury, Turner Prize, Tate Britain, 2004; Chm., Trustees, Whitechapel Gall., 2005–14. Gov., Charlotte Sharman Sch., 2001–08; Chm., Bd of Govs, Univ. for Creative Arts, 2012–. *Recreations:* reading, theatre, Rugby, tennis, music, opera. *Club:* Royal Automobile.

**TAYLOR, His Honour Robert Carruthers**; a Circuit Judge, 1984–2004; *b* 6 Jan. 1939; *o s* of late John Taylor, CBE and Barbara Taylor; *m* 1968, Jacqueline Marjorie, *er d* of Nigel and Marjorie Chambers; one *s* one *d. Educ:* Wycliffe Coll.; St John's Coll., Oxford. MA 1967; Open Univ. (BA 2011). Called to Bar, Middle Temple, 1961; practised NE Circuit, 1961–84; a Recorder, 1976–84. Chm., Agricl Land Tribunal, Yorks and Humberside Areas, 1979–2013; Mem., Mental Health Tribunal, 2001–12. *Recreations:* reading, music, gardening, walking, family. *Address:* Abbotsview, 59 King's Road, Ilkley, W Yorks LS29 9BZ. *T:* (01943) 607672.

**TAYLOR, Prof. Robert Henry**, PhD; Vice-Chancellor, University of Buckingham, 1997–2001; *b* 15 March 1943; *s* of Robert E. Taylor and Mabelle L. Taylor (*née* Warren), Greenville, Ohio; *m* 1st (marr. diss.); one *s* one *d*; 2nd, 2000, Ingrid Porteous. *Educ:* Ohio Univ. (BA 1965); Antioch Coll. (MA 1967); Cornell Univ. (PhD 1974). Social Studies Teacher, Cardozo High Sch., Washington DC, 1965–67; Instructor in Pol Sci., Wilberforce Univ., Ohio, 1967–69; Lectr in Govt, Univ. of Sydney, 1974–98; School of Oriental and African Studies, University of London: Lectr, 1980–88, Sen. Lectr, 1988–89, in Politics (with ref. to SE Asia); Prof. of Politics, 1989–96. Associate Sen. Fellow, 2003–12, Vis. Professorial Res. Fellow, 2012–14, Vis. Sen. Res. Fellow, 2014–, Inst. of Southeast Asian Studies, Yusof Ishak Inst., Singapore; Visiting Professor: Univ. of Buckingham, 2007–; City Univ. of Kong Kong, 2010–12; Vis. Res. Fellow, Inst. for Southeast Asian Studies, Kyoto Univ., 2017. Lay Mem., Asylum and Immigration Tribunal, 2002–11. *Publications:* Marxism and Resistance in Burma, 1985; The State in Burma, 1987; (contrib.) In Search of Southeast Asia: a modern history, 1987; (ed) Handbooks of the Modern World: Asia and the Pacific, 2 vols, 1991; (ed) The Politics of Elections in Southeast Asia, 1996; (ed) Burma: political economy under military rule, 2001; (ed) The Idea of Freedom in Asia and Africa, 2002; (contrib.) The Emergence of Southeast Asia, 2005; (ed jtly) Myanmar: beyond politics to societal imperatives, 2005; (ed) Dr Maung Maung: gentleman, scholar and patriot, 2008; The State in Myanmar, 2009; General Ne Win: a political biography, 2015; numerous articles in books and learned jls. *T:* (020) 8361 4002. *E:* dr.tinhla@gmail.com. *Club:* Travellers.

**TAYLOR, Dr Robert Thomas,** CBE 1990; Chairman, Management Interviewing and Research Institute, 1993–2004; *b* 21 March 1933; *s* of George Taylor and Marie Louise Fidler; *m* 1st, 1954, Ina Wilson (marr. diss. 1965); one *s*; 2nd, 1965, Rosemary Janet Boileau; two *s* one *d*. *Educ*: Boteler Grammar Sch., Warrington; University Coll., Oxford (Open Exhibnr; BA 1954, MA 1957; DPhil 1957). Fulbright Scholar. Research Associate, Randall Lab. of Physics, Univ. of Michigan, USA, 1957–58; ICI Research Fellow, 1958–59, Lectr, Physics Dept, 1959–61, Univ. of Liverpool; Chief Examr for NUJMB, GCE Physics (Scholarship Level), 1961; British Council: Asst Regional Rep., Madras, 1961–64; Science Officer, Madrid, 1964–69; Dir, Staff Recruitment Dept, 1969–73; Regional Educn Advr, Bombay, 1973–77; Rep., Mexico, 1977–81; Controller, Personnel, 1981–86; Rep., Greece, 1986–90; Asst Dir-Gen., British Council, 1990–93. Mem. (C), Weald Central Ward, Ashford BC, 2003–15. Vis. Sen. Fellow, Manchester Business Sch., 1993–99. *Publications*: contrib. to Chambers Encyclopaedia, 1967 edn; papers in scientific jls. *Recreations*: computers, war and war gaming. *Address*: Mark Haven, Ashford Road, High Halden, Kent TN26 3LJ. *T*: (01233) 850994.

**TAYLOR, (Robin) James S.;** *see* Sinclair Taylor, R. J.

**TAYLOR, Roger Miles Whitworth;** Director, London's Growth Boroughs Unit (formerly Olympic Host Boroughs Unit), 2008–13; *b* 18 May 1944; *s* of Richard and Joan Taylor; *m* 1969, Georgina Lucy Tonks (marr. diss. 2002); two *s* two *d*; *m* 2003, Gabriele Eva Bock. *Educ*: Repton School; Birmingham University (LLB). Solicitor, admitted 1968; Asst Solicitor, Cheshire CC, 1969–71; Asst County Clerk, Lincs parts of Lindsey, 1971–73; Dep. County Secretary, Northants CC, 1973–79; Dep. Town Clerk, 1979–85, Town Clerk and Chief Exec., 1985–88, City of Manchester; Chief Exec., Birmingham CC, 1988–94; Dir, 1994–2000, Chm., 1997–2000, Newchurch and Co.; Man. Dir, Pinnacle Consulting, 2000–06; Dir, Pinnacle Public Services Gp (formerly Pinnacle PSG), 2000–10; Chief Exec., Waltham Forest LBC, 2007–08. Dir, Fermosa Consulting Ltd, 2011–15. Mem., Farrand Cttee on Conveyancing, 1983–84; Clerk, Greater Manchester Passenger Transport Authy, 1986–88. Sec., W Midlands Jt Cttee, 1988–94. Chairman: Birmingham Marketing Partnership, 1993–94; Birmingham Common Purpose, 1994; Local Govt Television Adv. Bd, 1994–95; Dir, Birmingham TEC, 1990–93. Mem., Standards Bd for England, 2001–07. Dir, Ex Cathedra Chamber Choir, 1996–98. Mancunian of the Year, Manchester Jun. Chamber of Commerce, 1988; SOLACE Interim Manager of the Year, 2009. *Publications*: contribs to Local Govt Chronicle, Municipal Review, Municipal Jl. *Recreations*: sailing, walking, organic olive farming and olive oil making. *Address*: Codigo Postal SP 10170, Montanchez, Caceres, Extremadura, Spain. *T*: 07967 057054. *E*: rogermwt@gmail.com.

**TAYLOR, Roger William;** Chair, Ofqual, since 2017 (Member of Board, since 2012); *b* Liverpool, 1965; *s* of Daniel and Mathilda Taylor; *m* 1992, Elizabeth Stubbs; one *s* one *d*. *Educ*: Univ. of Oxford (BA PPE 1987); Birkbeck, Univ. of London (MA Econs 1992). Correspondent, FT, 1995–2000; Co-founder and Dir of Res., Dr Foster, 2000–15. *Publications*: God Bless the NHS, 2014; Transparency and the Open Society, 2016. *Recreations*: music, piano. *Address*: Sidbury, Devon.

**TAYLOR, Roy;** *see* Taylor, J. R.

**TAYLOR, Rufus Alexander Ottley; His Honour Judge Rufus Taylor;** a Circuit Judge, since 2019; *b* Wegberg, W Germany, 7 Feb. 1973; *s* of Sqdn Leader Roland Taylor and Jill Taylor (*née* Ottley); *m* 2003, Joanna Morrissey; two *s* three *d*. *Educ*: The Leys, Cambridge; Edinburgh Univ. (LLB Hons); Univ. des Saarlandes, Saarbrücken; City Univ., London (DipLaw). Called to the Bar, Middle Temple, 1998; in practice as barrister, 2000–19; a Dep. Dist Judge (Magistrates' Cts), 2009–19; a Recorder, 2012–19. *Recreations*: fly fishing, sea swimming. *Address*: Guildford Crown Court, Bedford Road, Guildford, Surrey GU1 4ST. *Clubs*: Pegasus; Castle Cove Sailing (Weymouth).

**TAYLOR, Rupert Maurice T.;** *see* Thornely-Taylor.

**TAYLOR, Russell Philip,** MBE 2003; writer, cartoonist and composer; *b* 8 July 1960; *s* of Captain Hal Taylor and Iona Taylor (*née* Mackenzie); *m* 1990, Anne-Frederique Dujon (marr. diss. 2007). *Educ*: St Anne's Coll., Oxford (BA Russian and Philosophy). Freelance writer and journalist, 1984–87; writer of Alex cartoon (with Charles Peattie) in: London Daily News, 1987; The Independent, 1987–91; Daily Telegraph, 1992–; writer of Celeb cartoon (with Charles Peattie and Mark Warren), Private Eye, 1987–90; Alex (stage play), Arts Th., 2007; composer of film and TV music, 1991–. *Publications*: The Looniness of the Long Distance Runner, 2001; (with Marc Polonsky) USSR from an original idea by Karl Marx, 1986; with Charles Peattie: Alex, 1987; The Unabashed Alex, 1988; Alex II: Magnum Force, 1989; Alex III: Son of Alex, 1990; Alex IV: The Man with the Golden Handshake, 1991; Celeb, 1991; Alex V: For the Love of Alex, 1992; Alex Calls the Shots, 1993; Alex Plays the Game, 1994; Alex Knows the Score, 1995; Alex Sweeps the Board, 1996; Alex Feels the Pinch, 1997; The Full Alex, 1998; The Alex Technique, 1999; The Best of Alex, 1998–2001, 2001; The Best of Alex, annually 2002–. *Recreations*: playing piano, running, perudo, time-wasting. *E*: alex@alexcartoon.com. *Clubs*: Groucho, Soho House.

**TAYLOR, (Samantha) Claire,** MBE 2010; international cricketer; Member, England Women's cricket team, 1998–2011; *b* Amersham, 25 Sept. 1975; *d* of Frederick Roger Taylor and Barbara Taylor (*née* MacDonald). *Educ*: Kendrick Sch., Reading; Queen's Coll., Oxford (BA Maths 1997); Henley Business Sch. (MA Applied Mgt 2016). Procter and Gamble, 1998–2001; semi-professional cricketer, 2002–05; Mgt Consultant, Sums Consulting, 2006–. One-day internat. début, Australia, 1998; England Women's Test cricket début, India, 1999; Mem., winning team: Ashes, 2005 and 2008; Women's World Cup, 2009; Women's ICC World Twenty20, 2009; Member of team: Reading CC, 1989–2011 (Club Capt., 2007–12); Berks Cricket, 1992–2011. Chair, Women's Cricket Subcttee, 2012–18, Member: Cricket Cttee, 2012–; MMC Cttee, 2018–, MCC. Trustee, Berks Community Cricket Foundn, 2012– (Vice Chair, 2017–). (Jtly) Wisden Cricketer of the Year, 2009; Women's Cricketer of the Year, ICC, 2009. *Recreations*: reading, playing the violin for Aldworth Philharmonic and Reading Symphony Orchestras, dog walking, cooking. *Address*: c/o Sums Consulting, University of Reading, Reading Enterprise Centre, Earley Gate, Whiteknights Road, Reading RG6 6BU.

**TAYLOR, Sandra Anne;** independent consultant, writer; Chief Executive, Barnsley Hospital NHS Foundation Trust, 2007–10; *b* 5 Sept. 1953; *d* of Harold E. Taylor and May Taylor (*née* Draper). *Educ*: Portsmouth Poly. (BA Hons); Essex Univ. (MA). Lectr and Tutor, Hull Univ., 1977–80; Res. Fellow and Lectr, UCL, 1981–82; Nottinghamshire County Council: Community Develt Officer, 1982–86; Principal Officer, 1986–88, Principal Asst, 1988–89, Asst Dir, 1990–96, Social Services Dept; Dir, Social Services, Leics City Council, 1996–99; Dir of Social Services, Birmingham CC, 1999–2002. Social Services expert consultant, Capita Business Services, 2003; Advr, Vertex Customer Services, 2003; interim Dir of Policy, 2003–04, interim Exec. Dir of Develt, 2004–05, Surrey and Sussex Strategic HA; Project Dir, Health Reconfiguration, E Berks Health Economy/Slough BC, 2006–07. *Publications*: (ed) Nottinghamshire Labour Movement, 1986; (jtly) Housing Futures: housing policy, management and practice, 1992; (ed) Managing Housing in a larger authority, 1993. *Recreations*: swimming, gardening, walking.

**TAYLOR, Simon Wheldon;** QC 2003; a Recorder, since 2002; *b* 4 July 1962; *s* of Thomas Henry Taylor and Enid Taylor, *qv*; *m* 1990, Elizabeth Lawes Paine; one *s* two *d*. *Educ*: Trinity Coll., Cambridge (BA Hons); London Hosp. Med. Coll. (MB BChir); Inns of Court Sch. of Law. Called to the Bar, Middle Temple, 1984; qualified doctor, 1987; pupillage, 1988; tenancy, 1989; in practice as barrister, 1989–. Ordained deacon, 2012, priest, 2013; Curate (pt-time), St Philip's, Tunbridge Wells, 2013–15; Associate Priest (part-time), St Andrew's, Stapleford, Cambridge, 2015–. *Address*: Cloisters, 1 Pump Court, Temple, EC4Y 7AA. *T*: (020) 7827 4000. *E*: st@cloisters.com.

**TAYLOR, Ven. Stephen Ronald,** MBE 2009; Archdeacon of Maidstone, since 2011; *b* Bradford, 2 May 1955; *s* of Ronald Taylor and Joyce Taylor; *m* 1981, Julie Anderson; three *d* (one *s* decd). *Educ*: Durham Univ. (MA 1999). Community Recreation Officer, Bradford, 1978; ordained deacon, 1983, priest, 1984; Curate, Chester le Street, 1983; Vicar: Newbottle, 1988–93; Stranton, Hartlepool, 1993–2000; Canon Provost, Sunderland, 2000–11. Hon. Chaplain, Frankland Prison, 1989–93; Hon. Canon, dio. of Rift Valley, Tanzania, 1999–. Chm., Sunderland Partnership, 2007–11. Founder, Kilimatinde Trust, Tanzania, 1997. Hon. Fellow, Univ. of Sunderland, 2009. *Recreations*: Isles of Scilly holidays, supports Maidstone FC, walking, bird photography; Chair of Arts Group, Lansdowne Club. *Address*: The Archdeaconry, 4 Redcliffe Lane, Penenden Heath, Maidstone ME14 2AG. *T*: 07944 680855. *E*: Stephen.Taylor@archdeacmaid.org.

**TAYLOR, Thomas William;** Director, Finance and Portfolio, Department for Business, Energy and Industrial Strategy, since 2017; *b* London, 19 Oct. 1971; *s* of Sidney Taylor and Catherine Taylor (*née* Hewitt); *m* 2000, Jayne Marie Priddin (marr. diss. 2019); one *s*. *Educ*: Highbury Grove Sch., Islington; Girton Coll., Cambridge (BA 1993); Sch. of Oriental and African Studies, Univ. of London (MSc Econs); Univ. of Warwick (Post Grad. Dip. Finance). CPFA 2011. Department of Social Security, then Department for Work and Pensions: Econ. Advr, Welfare Benefits, 1994–2001; Deputy Director: Child Poverty, 2001–04; Housing Benefits, 2004–06; on loan as Dep. Dir, Analytical Audit, Office of Climate Change, 2006–07; Dep. Dir, Corporate Performance, 2007–09, Dir, Finance and Performance, 2009–13, DEFRA; Dir, Corporate Ops and Orgnl Develt, Office of Rail Regulation, later Rail and Road, 2013–17. *Recreations*: motorcycling, cabinet making. *Address*: Department for Business, Energy and Industrial Strategy, 1 Victoria Street, SW1H 0ET.

**TAYLOR, Timothy Hugh Christian;** QC 2011; Partner, King & Wood Mallesons (formerly SJ Berwin) LLP, since 1988; *b* Barton, 22 June 1956; *s* of Hugh Garner Taylor and Doreen May Taylor; *m* 2010, Jessica Yao Affi; four *s* one *d*, and one step *d*. *Educ*: King's Sch., Canterbury; St John's Coll., Oxford (BA Juris.). Solicitor Advocate. Solicitor, Herbert Smith, 1980–87. Founder Dir, Internat. Lawyers for Africa, 2007–. *Recreations*: carousing, laughter and reflection. *Address*: King & Wood Mallesons Dubai, Office 401, Level 4, Gate Village 6, Dubai International Financial Centre, PO Box 24482, Dubai, UAE. *T*: 07775 681391, (50) 2485354. *E*: tim.taylor@me.kwm.com.

**TAYLOR, Victoria Mary;** *see* Edwards, V. M.

**TAYLOR, Wendy Ann,** CBE 1988; FRSS; sculptor; Member, Royal Fine Art Commission, 1981–99; *b* 29 July 1945; *d* of late Edward Philip Taylor and Lilian Maude Wright; *m* 1982, Bruce Robertson; one *s*. *Educ*: St Martin's School of Art. LDAD (Hons). FRSS (FRBS 1995). One-man exhibitions: Axiom Gall., London, 1970; Angela Flowers Gall., London, 1972; 24th King's Lynn Fest., Norfolk, and World Trade Centre, London, 1974; Annely Juda Fine Art, London, 1975; Oxford Gall., Oxford, 1976; Oliver Dowling Gall., Dublin, 1976 and 1979; Building Art—the process, Building Centre Gall., 1986; Austin, Desmond and Phipps, 1992; Nature and Engineering, Osborne Gp, London, 1998; Cass Gall., London, 2005; Seed Series, Canary Wharf, London, 2009. Shown in over 100 group exhibitions, 1964–82. Represented in collections around the world. Major commissions: The Travellers 1970, London; Gazebo (edn of 4) 1970–71, London, New York, Suffolk, Oxford; Triad 1971, Oxford; Timepiece 1973, London (Grade II listed, 2004); Calthae 1978, Leicestershire; Octo 1980, Milton Keynes; Counterpoise 1980, Birmingham; Compass Bowl 1980, Basildon; Sentinel 1981, Reigate; Bronze Relief 1981, Canterbury; Equatorial Sundial 1982, Bletchley; Essence 1982, Milton Keynes; Opus 1983, Morley Coll., London; Gazebo 1983, Golder's Hill Park, London; Network, 1985, London; Roundacre Improvement Scheme Phase I, 1985–88, Phase II, 1989–90, Basildon; Geo I & Geo II 1986, Stratford-Upon-Avon; Landscape, and Tree of the Wood 1986, Fernhurst, Surrey; Pharos 1986, Peel Park, E Kilbride; Ceres 1986, Fernhurst, Surrey; Nexus 1986, Corby, Northants; Globe Sundial 1987, Swansea Maritime Quarter; Spirit of Enterprise 1987, Isle of Dogs, London; Silver Fountain 1988, Continuum 1990, Guildford, Surrey; The Whirlies 1988, Pharos II 1989, Phoenix 1989–90, E Kilbride; Pilot Kites 1988, Norwich Airport; Fireflow 1988, Strathclyde Fire Brigade HQ, Hamilton; Armillary Sundial 1989, The New Towns, Essex; Globe Sundial II 1990, London Zool Gdns; Butterfly Mosaic 1990, Barking and Dagenham Council; Square Piece 1991, Plano, Ill; Sundial Meml 1991, Sheffield; Anchorage 1991, Salford Quays, Manchester; Wyvern 1992, Leics; stained glass window, St George's Church, Sheffield Univ., 1994; The Jester, Emmanuel Coll., Cambridge, 1994; Challenge, Stockley Park, Middx, 1995; Equilibrium, Coopers & Lybrand, London, 1995; Spirit, Vann, Guildford, 1996; Rope Circle, Hermitage Waterside, London, 1997; Waves, Berners Mews, London, 1998; Dancer, Chelsea and Westminster Hosp., 1998; Dung Beetles, Millennium Conservation Bldg, Zool Soc., Regent's Park, 1999; Mariner's Astrolabe, Virginia Settlers Meml, Brunswick Quay, 1999; Globe View, Blackfriars, 2000; Millennium Fountain, Chase Gardens, Enfield, 2000 (Civic Trust Award, 2002); Voyager, Cinnabar Wharf, London, 2001; Three Reclining Rope Figures, and Conqueror, GlaxoSmithKline, Middx, 2001; Through the Loop, and Around the Square, Pacific Place, HK, 2002; Hunters Square, Chain Piece, Warren, Ohio, 2002; Knowledge, Library Sq., Queen Mary, Univ. of London, 2003; Acorn Wall Relief, Switch House, Brunswick Wharf, London, 2003; Anchor Iron, Anchor Iron Wharf, Greenwich, 2004; Feather Piece, Capital East, Royal Victoria Docks, 2005; Gravesend Heritage, Gravesham, 2005; Silver Fountain II, Bryn Mawr, Penn, 2006; Square Chain Piece, Bartlesville, Oklahoma, 2007; WW II Meml to civilians of E London, Hermitage Meml Gdn, Wapping, 2007; Spirit I, Royal Docks, London, 2008; Running Hares, Gravesend, 2009; Unity, Unison Centre, Euston, 2011; Swirl, Park Rd, London, 2013. Mem., CNAA, 1980–85 (Specialist Advr, 1985–93; Mem., Cttee for Art and Design, 1987–91); Consultant, New Town Commn (Basildon) (formerly Basildon Develt Corp.), 1985–88; Design Consultant, London Borough of Barking and Dagenham, 1989–93 and 1997–2003; LDDC Mem., Design Adv. Panel, 1989–98; Mem., Design Panel, Kent N, 2005–09. Mem., Adv. Gp, PCFC, 1989–90. Examiner, Univ. of London, 1982–83; Mem. Court, RCA, 1982–; Mem. Council, Morley Coll., 1984–88. Trustee, Leicestershire's Appeal for Music and the Arts, 1993–2010. FZS 1989; Fellow, QMW, 1993; FRSA 2004. Awards:

Walter Neurath, 1964; Pratt, 1965; Sainsbury, 1966; Arts Council, 1977; Duais na Ríochta (Kingdom Prize), 1977; Gold Medal, Eire, 1977; 1st Prize Silk Screen, Barcham Green Print Comp., 1978. *Recreation:* gardening. *Address:* 73 Bow Road, Bow, E3 2AN. *T:* (020) 8981 2037. *W:* www.wendytaylorsculpture.co.uk.

**TAYLOR, Sir William,** Kt 1990; CBE 1982; *b* 31 May 1930; *s* of Herbert and Maud E. Taylor, Crayford, Kent; *m* 1954, Rita, *d* of Ronald and Marjorie Hague, Sheffield; one *s* two *d*. *Educ:* Erith Grammar Sch.; London Sch. of Economics (BSc Econ 1952); Westminster Coll., Oxford (Hon. Fellow, 1990); Univ. of London Inst. of Educn (PhD 1960). Teaching in Kent, 1953–56; Deputy Head, Slade Green Secondary Sch., 1956–59; Sen. Lectr, St Luke's Coll., Exeter, 1959–61; Head of Educn Dept, Bede Coll., Durham, 1961–64; Tutor and Lectr in Educn, Univ. of Oxford, 1964–66; Prof. of Educn and Dir of Sch. of Educn, Univ. of Bristol, 1966–73; Dir, Univ. of London Inst. of Educn, 1973–83; Principal, Univ. of London, 1983–85; Vice-Chancellor: Univ. of Hull, 1985–91; Univ. of Huddersfield, 1994–95; Thames Valley Univ., 1998–99. Hd, Winchester Sch. of Art, Univ. of Southampton, 2004. Visiting Professor of Education: Oxford Univ., 1991–97; Southampton Univ., 1998–2012; Commonwealth Vis. Fellow, Australian States, 1975; NZ UGC Prestige Fellowship, 1977; Hon. Vis. Fellow, Green Coll., Oxford, 1991–97; Hon. Prof., Univ. of Winchester, 2010–16. Academic Adviser: States of Jersey Educn Cttee, 2000–05; SE Essex Coll., 2001–03; Special Advr, H of C Cttee on Educn and Skills, 2000–07. Research Consultant, Dept of Educn and Science (part-time), 1968–73; Chairman: European Cttee for Educnl Research, 1969–71; UK Nat. Commn for UNESCO Educn Cttee, 1975–83 (Mem., 1973–83); Educnl Adv. Council, IBA, 1974–82; UCET, 1976–79; Cttee on Training of Univ. Teachers, 1981–88; NFER, 1983–88; CATE, 1984–93; Univs Council for Adult and Continuing Educn, 1986–90; N of England Univs Management and Leadership Prog., 1987–91; Studies in Education, 1991–95; Convocation of Univ. of London, 1994–97; UUK Higher Educn Funding Review Gp, 2000–01; IoW Tertiary Strategy Gp, 2002–03; Southampton Travel-to-learn Review, 2002–04; Strategic Area Rev. of 16+ educn and trng, Hants and IoW, 2002–05; Skills Commn Inquiry into Apprenticeship, 2008–09. Member: UGC Educn Cttee, 1971–80; British Library Res. and Develt Cttee, 1975–79; Open Univ. Academic Adv. Cttee, 1975–82; SSRC Educnl Research Board, 1976–80 (Vice-Chm., 1978–80); Adv. Cttee on Supply and Training of Teachers, 1976–79; Working Gp on Management of Higher Educn, 1977–78; Steering Cttee on Future of Examinations at 16+, 1977–78; Cttee of Vice-Chancellors and Principals, 1980–91; Adv. Cttee on Supply and Educn of Teachers (Sec. of State's nominee), 1980–83. UK Rep., Permanent Educn Steering Cttee, Council of Europe, 1971–73; Rapporteur, OECD Review of Educn in NZ, 1982–83. Member: Senate, Univ. of London, 1977–85; Cttee of Management, Inst. of Advanced Legal Studies, 1980–83; Council, Open Univ., 1984–88; Council, Coll. of Preceptors, 1987–89; Editl Adv. Bd, World Book Internat., 1989–2007; CBI Educn Foundn, 1993–98. President: Council for Educn in World Citizenship, 1979–90; English New Educn Fellowship, 1979–86; Comparative Educn Soc. of GB, 1981–84; Assoc. of Colls of Further and Higher Educn, 1984–88; European Assoc. for Instnl Res., 1990–92; Univs of N of England Consortium for Internat. Develt, 1991–94; N of England Educn Conference, 1992; Inst. of Educn Soc., 1990–93; Soc. for Res. in HE, 1996–2001; Vice President: British Educnl Admin, and Management Soc., 1985–; Council for Internat. Educn, 1992–; Soc. for Res. in Higher Educn, 2002–. Chm., NFER/Nelson Publishing Co., 1985–86, 1987–99; Dir, Fenner plc, 1988–93. Trustee, Forbes Trust, 1987–88. Governor: Wye Coll., 1981–83; Hymers Coll., Hull, 1985–91; Westminster Coll., Oxford, 1991–96; Univ. of Glamorgan (formerly Poly. of Wales), 1991–2002; Sevenoaks Sch., 1994–97; Christ Church UC, Canterbury, 1996–2004; Mem. Council, Hong Kong Inst. of Educn, 1998–2004. Freeman, City of London, 1985. Yeoman, 1982–87, Liveryman, 1988–, Worshipful Soc. of Apothecaries of London. Hon. FCP 1977; Hon. FCCEA 1980. Hon. Fellow: Thames Polytechnic, 1991; Inst. of Educn, Univ. of London, 1995; Christ Church Canterbury UC, 2005. Hon. DSc Aston (Birmingham), 1977; Hon. LittD Leeds, 1979; Hon. DCL Kent, 1981; DUniv: Open, 1983; Ulster, 2000; Glamorgan, 2004; Hon. DLitt: Loughborough, 1984; Southampton, 1998; London, 1999; Leicester, 2004; Essex, 2004; Hon. LLD: Hull, 1992; Huddersfield, 1996; Bristol, 2001; Hon. DEd: Kingston, 1993; Oxford Brookes, 1993; Plymouth, 1993; UWE, 1994; Hong Kong Inst. of Educn, 2004; Hon. DSc (Educ) QUB, 1997. *Publications:* The Secondary Modern School, 1963; Society and the Education of Teachers, 1969; (ed with G. Baron) Educational Administration and the Social Sciences, 1969; Heading for Change, 1969; Planning and Policy in Post Secondary Education, 1972; Theory into Practice, 1972; Research Perspectives in Education, 1973; (ed with R. Farquhar and R. Thomas) Educational Administration in Australia and Abroad, 1975; Research and Reform in Teacher Education, 1978; (ed with B. Simon) Education in the Eighties: the central issues, 1981; (ed) Metaphors of Education, 1984; Universities Under Scrutiny, 1987; Policy and Strategy for Higher Education: collaboration between business and higher education, 1989; articles and papers in professional jls. *Recreations:* books, music.

**TAYLOR, William,** CBE 2001; QPM 1991; HM Chief Inspector of Constabulary for Scotland, 1999–2001; *b* 25 March 1947; *s* of late William Taylor and Margaret Taylor; *m* 1978, Denise Lloyd; two step *s*. *Educ:* Blairgowrie High Sch.; Nat. Police Coll. (8th Special Course and 16th Sen. Command Course). Joined Metropolitan Police Service, 1966; served Central London locations as Det. Constable, Sergeant and Inspector, and Chief Inspector, 1966–76; New Scotland Yard: Community Relations Branch, 1976–78; Det. Supt, Central Drugs Squad, 1978–79; Staff Officer to Comr of Police, 1980–82 (Det. Chief Supt); Comdr CID NE London, then Uniform Comdr, Hackney; Comdr Robbery Squad (Flying Squad) and Regional Crime Squad, 1982–85; Asst Comr, City of London Police, 1985–89; Dep. Chief Constable, Thames Valley Police, 1989–90; Asst Comr, Specialist Ops, Metropolitan Police, 1990–94; Comr, City of London Police, 1994–98; HM Inspector of Constabulary, 1998. Chm., Crime Cttee, ACPO, 1994–98; Mem. Exec. Cttee, Interpol, 1995–98; Dir, Police Extended Interviews, 1996–98. Police Long Service and Good Conduct Medal, 1988. *Recreations:* reading (travel, management and historical), hill walking, horse riding, collecting some Dalton ware.

**TAYLOR, His Honour William Edward Michael;** a Circuit Judge, Western Circuit, 1989–2006; Resident Judge for Plymouth, 1990–2006; *b* 27 July 1944; *s* of William Henry Taylor and Winifred Mary (*née* Day); *m* 1969, Caroline Joyce Gillies; two *d*. *Educ:* Denstone Coll., Uttoxeter, Staffs; Council of Legal Educn. Called to the Bar, Inner Temple, 1968; practised from 2 Harcourt Bldgs, Temple; a Recorder, 1987–89; Liaison Judge for Devon and Cornwall, 1999–2006; Hon. Recorder of Plymouth, 2004. Lectr, Council of Legal Educn, 1976–89. Chairman: Criminal Justice Strategy Cttee for Devon and Cornwall, 2000–06; Area Judicial Forum, 2004–06. Mem., Probation Cttees for Devon and Cornwall, 1995–2006. Hon. Pres., Univ. of Plymouth Law Soc., 1994–2018, now Emeritus. Governor: Blundell's Sch., Tiverton, 2000–15; Plymouth Univ., 2006–14 (Chm., 2012–14); Chairman: Blundell's Prep. Sch. Cttee, 2000–09; Hamoaze House, 2009–. Chm., River Yealm and Dist Assoc., 2008–11; Pres., Devon Safer Communities Trust. Patron, Twelve's Co. charity, Plymouth; Vice Patron, Drake Foundn, Plymouth. Hon. LLD Plymouth, 2005. *Recreations:* music, opera, fishing, vintage cars, wine. *Address:* Combined Court Service, Armada Way, Plymouth, Devon PL1 2ER. *Clubs:* Athenæum; English XX.

**TAYLOR, Sir William George, (Sir Bill),** Kt 2003; trainee independent researcher and writer; Managing Director, Improve Your Council consultancy, 2006–16; *b* 10 April 1952; *s* of late Colin Frey Taylor and Isobel Lauder Yule Taylor (*née* Selkirk, later Allsopp); *m* 1978, Anne Charles; one *s* one *d*. *Educ:* Church Road (Yardley) Primary Sch., Birmingham; Sheldon Heath Comprehensive Sch., Birmingham; Univ. of Lancaster (BA Hons 1973, MA 1985); Manchester Poly. (Advanced Cert Ed 1976). Detached Youth Worker, Young Unemployed People, Blackburn, 1973–74; Area Worker, Audley and Centre Manager, Accrington Rd, Youth Centre, Blackburn, 1974–77; Youth Tutor, Shadsworth HS, Blackburn, 1977–83; Youth Work Trainer Co-ordinator, Lancs, 1984–85; Youth Work Trainer/Manager, Blackburn, 1985–95; Youth Work Dist Team Manager, Ribble Valley, 1995–2006. Member: Bd, City Challenge, 1994–98; Bd, Elevate E Lancs Housing Mkt Restructuring Pathfinder, 2002–04; Chairman: Strategic Partnership Bd with Capita, 2001–04; Blackburn and Darwen Strategic Partnership Exec. (Local Strategic Partnership), 2002–04; E Lancs Partnership Forum, 2003–04. Associate Consultant: IDeA; Solace Enterprises; Nat. Youth Agency; Warwick Business Sch. Local Govt Centre. Member: NW Unitary Councils and Assoc. of Gtr Manchester Authorities, 2001–04; NW Regl Assembly and NW Constitutional Convention, 2001–04. Blackburn with Darwen Borough Council: Mem. (Lab), 1980–2004; Mayor, 1989–90, Dep. Mayor, 1990–91, of Blackburn; Dep. Leader, 1994–2001; Leader, 2001–04; Exec. Mem. for Educn and Lifelong Learning, 2000–01; Chairman of Committees: Recreation, 1984–86; Community and Leisure Services, 1986–89; Urban Prog., 1990–93; Urban Regeneration, 1993–94; Mgt and Finance, 1994–97; City Challenge, 1994; Educn and Trng, 1997–2000; Chairman: Early Years Sub-cttee, 1997–98; Ethnic Minorities Consultative Panel, 1990–91 and 1992–96; Vice-Chm., Exec. and Forum, Educn Action Zone, 1999–2001. Chairman: Mentor Enterprise for All, 2009–12; Third Sector Lancashire, 2009–10; Blackburn with Darwen NHS Teaching Health Care Trust Plus, 2010–13; NW Healthwatch Chairs and Chief Officers Gp, 2013–19; Chm. and Dir, Blackburn with Darwen NHS Healthwatch, 2013–19; Observer, Lancs and S Cumbria NHS Sustainability and Transformation Plan, 2016–19; Healthwatch rep., Lancs and S Cumbria Jt CCG, 2016–19. Non-executive Director: Vision Twenty One, 2006–09; Blackburn Community Business Partnership, 2006–19. Assoc. Lectr, Univ. of Cumbria (formerly St Martin's Coll.), 2006–08. Mem., 1995–2001, Chm., 1996–2001, Prince's Trust Volunteers Bd, Lancs; Vice-Chm., Prince's Trust Strategic Forum, Lancs, 2000–01. Governor, Blackburn Coll., 1981–93 and 2002–16 (Chm., 2008–16); Mem. Court, Lancaster Univ., 2008–; Trustee and Vice Chm., Lancaster Univ. Students Union, 2008–13. Hon. Fellow, Univ. of Lancaster, 2018. *Publications:* various in youth and community work, education, regeneration, leadership and local govt jls; regular blogger and occasional columnist in Lancashire Telegraph, Local Government Chronicle, Health Service Jl. *Recreations:* golf (off 20, now in abeyance!), sampling good wines and food, trying to engage with the world of digital technology, photography, proud grandad to Joshua and Alfie. *Address:* Lympstone, Pleasington Lane, Pleasington, Blackburn, Lancs BB2 5JH. *T:* (01254) 419268. *E:* sirbilltaylor@btinternet.com. *Club:* Blackburn Golf.

**TAYLOR, Rev. Canon Dr William Henry;** Vicar, St John's, Notting Hill, since 2002; *b* 23 Dec. 1956; *s* of Thomas Mather Taylor and Barbara Taylor (*née* Pitt). *Educ:* Westcott House, Cambridge. BA, MTh, MPhil; Sch. of Oriental and African Studies, Univ. of London (DPhil 2010). Ordained deacon, 1983, priest, 1984; Asst Curate, All Saints and St Philip with Tovil, Canterbury, 1983–86; Archbp's Advisor on Orthodox Affairs, Lambeth Palace, 1986–88; Sen. Curate, All Saints, Margaret St, London, 1986–88; Chaplain, Guy's Hosp., 1988; CMS 1988–91; Chaplain, Jordan Chaplaincy, 1988–91; Vicar, St Peter, Ealing, 1991–2000; Area Dean, Ealing, 1993–98; Provost, subseq. Dean, of Portsmouth, 2000–02. Chm., Anglican and Eastern Churches Assoc., 2001–; Mem., Internat. Commn of Anglican-Oriental Orthodox Dialogue, 2001–. Ecumenical Canon, Cath. of Holy Child, Manila, 2013–. FRAS 1982. Freeman, City of London, 1997. *Publications:* (ed) Christians in the Holy Land, 1994; Antioch and Canterbury, 2005; Narratives of Identity, 2013; (ed) Turkey, Looking Behind and Before, 2016; The Creativity Behind The Wall, 2018. *Recreations:* good wine, challenging travel. *Address:* 25 Ladbroke Road, W11 3PD. *T:* (020) 7727 3439, *T:* and *Fax:* (office) (020) 7727 4262. *E:* whtaylor@btconnect.com. *Club:* Nikaean.

**TAYLOR, William James;** QC (Scot.) 1986; QC 1998; *b* 13 Sept. 1944; *s* of Cecil Taylor and Ellen Taylor (*née* Daubney); civil partnership 2006, William Deas Roe, *qv*. *Educ:* Robert Gordon's College, Aberdeen; Aberdeen Univ. (MA Hons 1966; LLB 1969); Glasgow Univ. (Cert. in European Law (French) 1990). Admitted Faculty of Advocates, 1971; called to the Bar, Inner Temple, 1990. Standing Junior Counsel to DHSS, 1978–79, to FCO, 1979–86; Temp. Sheriff, 1997–99; part-time Sheriff, 2003–. Member: Criminal Injuries Compensation Bd, 1997–2001; Scottish Criminal Cases Review Commn, 1999–2005. Former Chairman: Traverse Th., Edinburgh; Fedn of Scottish Theatres; former Mem., TMA; former Member, Board: Scottish Ballet; Scottish Opera (Chm., 2004–07). Contested (Lab) Edinburgh W, Feb. and Oct. 1974; Regional Councillor (Lab), 1973–82. Hon. Prof., Univ. of St Andrews, 2018–. FRSA. *Recreations:* the arts, sailing, Scottish mountains, swimming, travel, restoring a garden, cooking. *Address:* Duirinish Oaks, Duirinish, by Kyle of Lochalsh, Ross-shire IV40 8BE. *T:* 07788 455545. *E:* qc@wjt.org.uk. *Clubs:* Traverse Theatre (Edinburgh); Plockton Sailing.

**TAYLOR, William McCaughey;** Chief Executive, Northern Ireland Police Authority, 1979–86; *b* 10 May 1926; *s* of William and Georgina Lindsay Taylor; *m* 1955, June Louise Macartney; two *s* two *d*. *Educ:* Campbell College, Belfast; Trinity College, Oxford (MA 1950). Lieut, Royal Inniskilling Fusiliers, 1944–47. International Computers Ltd, 1950–58; Lobitos Oilfields Ltd, 1958–60; HM Vice Consul, New York, 1960–63, HM Consul, 1963–65; NI Dept of Commerce, 1965–79. Chm., NI Coal Importers Assoc., 1986–91. *Publications:* After Our Heart Attacks, 2017. *Recreations:* golf, bridge, gardening, piano, musical compositions. *Address:* 1 Knocktern Gardens, Belfast BT4 3LZ. *Club:* Royal Belfast Golf.

**TAYLOR, William Rodney E.;** *see* Eatock Taylor.

**TAYLOR BRADFORD, Barbara;** *see* Bradford.

**TAYLOR-GOOBY, Prof. Peter Frederick,** OBE 2012; PhD; FBA 2009; FAcSS; Professor of Social Policy, University of Kent, since 1990; *b* Watford, 5 March 1947; *s* of John and Irene Taylor-Gooby; *m* 1999, Susan Lakeman; two *s* one *d*. *Educ:* Watford Grammar Sch.; Univ. of Bristol (BA Philos. and Eng. Lit. 1969); Univ. of York (Dip. Soc. Admin. (with dist.) 1972; MPhil Soc. Admin 1974; PhD Soc. Policy 1984). Lectr in Social Admin, Univ. of Manchester, 1974–79; Lectr, Sen. Lectr, then Reader in Social Policy, Univ. of Kent, 1979–89. Chairman: Social Work Social Policy Panel, RAE 2008; Social Work Social Policy Panel, REF 2014. Pres., Sociol. and Social Policy Section, BAAS, 2005–06. Co-Dir, Risk Res. Centre, Beijing Normal Univ., 2008–15. FAcSS (AcSS 2001). FRSA 2005. Lifetime Achievement Award, Social Policy Assoc., 2013; Univ. Research Achievement Award, Univ. of Kent, 2018. *Publications:* (jtly) Political Philosophy and Social Welfare, 1980, 2nd edn 2009; (with Jen Dale) Social Theory and Social Welfare, 1981; From Butskellism to the New Right, 1983; Public Opinion, Ideology and the Welfare State, 1985; (with Elim Papadakis) The Private Provision of Public Welfare, 1987; Social Change, Social Welfare and Social Science, 1991; (with Hartley Dean) Dependency

Culture, 1992; (ed jtly) Markets and Managers, 1993; (ed jtly) European Welfare Policy: squaring the welfare circle, 1996; (ed) Choice and Public Policy: the limits to welfare markets, 1998; (ed jtly) The End of the Welfare State?: responses to retrenchment, 1999; (jtly) European Welfare Futures, 2000 (rev. edn Korean, 2004); (ed) Risk, Trust and Welfare, 2000; (ed) Welfare States under Pressure, 2001; (ed) Making a European Welfare State?: convergences and conflicts over European social policy, 2004; (ed) New Risks, New Welfare: the transformation of the European welfare state, 2004 (trans. Chinese 2009); (ed) Ideas and Welfare State Reform in Western Europe, 2005; (ed jtly) Learning about Risk, 2006; (ed jtly) Risk in Social Science, 2006; Reframing Social Citizenship, 2009; (ed) New Paradigms in Public Policy, 2013; The Double Crisis of the Welfare State and What We Can Do About It, 2013; (ed jtly) The British Growth Crisis, 2015; The Baby Auction (novel), 2016; Ardent Justice (novel), 2017; After Austerity, 2017; Attitudes, Aspirations and Welfare, 2018; over 160 articles in jls and 125 book chapters. *Recreations:* hill-walking, cycling, socialism, writing, children. *Address:* School of Social Policy, Sociology and Social Research, University of Kent CT2 7NF. *E:* p.f.taylor-gooby@kent.ac.uk.

TAYLOR-JOHNSON, Samantha, OBE 2011; artist; *b* 4 March 1967; formerly Taylor-Wood; *m* 1997, Jeremy Michael Neal, (Jay), Jopling, *qv* (marr. diss. 2009); two *d*; *m* 2012, Aaron Johnson; two *d*. *Educ:* Goldsmiths' Coll., London (BA Hons Fine Art 1990; Hon. Fellow 2008). *Solo exhibitions include:* Sam Taylor-Wood: Killing Time, Showroom, London, 1994; Travesty of a Mockery, White Cube, London, 1995; Pent-Up, Chisenhale Gall., London, and Sunderland City Art Gall., 1996; 16mm, Ridinghouse Editions, London, 1996; Sam Taylor-Wood: Five Revolutionary Seconds, Barcelona, 1997; Sustaining the Crisis, LA, 1997; Milan, Seattle, 1998, Stuttgart, 1999, Warsaw, Madrid and NY, 2000; Directions, Washington, 1999; Mute, White Cube, London, 2001; Sam Taylor-Wood: Films and Photographs, Paris, 2001, Amsterdam, 2002; Hayward Gall., Montreal and Tokyo, 2002, Vienna, 2003, St Petersburg and Moscow, 2004; The Passion, NY, 2002; David, Nat. Portrait Gall., 2004; Strings, Edinburgh, 2004; Sorrow, Suspension, Ascension, NY, 2004; New Work, White Cube, 2004; Ascension, Chicago, 2004; Sex and Death and a Few Trees, Rome, 2005; Still Lives, Baltic, Gateshead, 2006; Yes I No, White Cube, 2008; Saatchi Gall., 2014; *group exhibitions include:* General Release, Venice Biennale, 1995; Brilliant! New Art from London, Walker Art Centre, Minneapolis, and Contemporary Art Mus., Houston, 1995; Sensation, RA, Hamburger Bahnhof, Berlin, and Brooklyn Mus., NY, 1997; work in public collections including: British Council, Contemp. Art Soc., Nat. Portrait Gall., Saatchi Collection, Tate Gall., London; Stedelijk Mus., Amsterdam; Bangkok Mus. of Contemp. Art; Fundacio "la Caixa", Barcelona; Royal Mus. of Fine Arts, Copenhagen; Collection Lambert, Geneva; Israel Mus., Jerusalem; Instituto de Arte Contemporânea, Lisbon; Walker Art Centre, Minneapolis; New Orleans Mus.; Guggenheim, NY; Robert Shiffler Collection, Ohio; Astrup Fearnley Mus., Oslo; Caldic Collection, Rotterdam; San Francisco Mus. of Mod. Art; Samsung Mus., Seoul. Director of films: Love You More, 2008; Nowhere Boy, 2009; Fifty Shades of Grey, 2015; A Million Little Pieces (also screenplay), 2019. Illy Caffè Prize for most promising young artist, Venice Biennale, 1997. *Publications:* Unhinged, 1996; Sam Taylor-Wood: third party, 1999; Contact, 2001; Sam Taylor-Wood, 2001; Sam Taylor-Wood: crying men, 2004; Second Floor, 2014. *Address:* White Cube, 144–152 Bermondsey Street, SE1 3TQ.

TAYLOR-SMITH, David James Benwell, MBE 2003; FRGS; Chief Executive Officer, PHS Group, since 2018; *b* Winchester, 16 Oct. 1961; *s* of late Maj. (retd) Alan Taylor-Smith and of Joy Taylor-Smith; *m* 1990, Jacqueline Ann Hunter Fletcher; two *d*. *Educ:* Tunbridge Wells Grammar Sch.; Southampton Univ. (BSc Hons Geog.); RMC Sandhurst. Pres., Student Union, Southampton Univ., 1984–85. Captain, 4th/7th Royal Dragoon Guards, 1985–89; Royal Dragoon Guards TA Officer, 1989–92. Director: Operation Raleigh, Zimbabwe, Botswana and Chile, 1989–94; Project Orbis, 1994–96; Corporate Affairs Dir, Jardine Pacific, 1996–98; Managing Director: Jardine Securicor Hong Kong, 1998–2002; Group 4 Securicor Justice Services, 2002–06; CEO, G4S (formerly Group 4 Securicor) UK and Ireland, 2006–10; Regl CEO, UK and Africa, 2010–12, Gp Chief Operating Officer, 2012, G4S plc; Regl Man. Dir, EMEA, Aggreko plc, 2013–16; CEO, VPS Gp, 2016–18. Mem. Bd, Hong Kong Business Envmt Council, 1998–2002. Mem. Council, Scientific Exploration Soc., 2006–08. Chm., RGS Hong Kong, 1995–2002. Trustee: WWF Hong Kong, 2001–02; WWF UK, 2005–11; Winston Churchill Meml Trust, 2017–. Chm., Westerham Soc., 2006–10. FRGS 1985. *Recreations:* walking, conservation, bee keeping, ski-ing.

TAYLOR-WOOD, Samantha; *see* Taylor-Johnson, S.

TAYLOUR, family name of **Marquess of Headfort**.

TAYTON, Lynn Margaret; QC 2006; **Her Honour Judge Tayton**; a Circuit Judge, since 2011; *b* 5 Feb. 1959; *d* of Gerald and Margaret Tayton; one *s*. *Educ:* Barr's Hill Sch., Coventry; University Coll. London (LLB Hons 1980); Council of Legal Educn. Called to the Bar, Gray's Inn, 1981; barrister, Nottingham, 1982–89; Sen. Lectr in Law, Nottingham Trent Poly., 1990–91; barrister, London, 1995–2011; a Recorder, 2009–11. Legal Assessor, GMC, 2010–11. Chair, Herts and Beds Bar Mess, 2007–11. Associate Lectr, OU, 2006; Mem., OU Law Prog. Cttee, 2007–13; Gray's Inn Advocacy Tutor; Judicial Coll. Tutor. *Recreations:* going to the theatre, cookery, variety of not too energetic physical pursuits, spending time with my family and other people who make me laugh. *Address:* Luton Crown Court, 7 George Street, Luton, Beds LU1 2AA.

TCHURUK, Serge; President and Chief Executive Officer, Joule Unlimited Technologies, Inc., 2014–15 (Director, 2014); *b* 13 Nov. 1937; *s* of Georges Tchuruk and Mathilde (*née* Dondikian); *m* 1960, Héléna Kalfus; one *d*. *Educ:* Ecole Nationale Supérieure de l'Armement; Ecole Polytechnique. With Mobil Oil in France, USA and Netherlands, 1968–80; Head, Mobil Oil BV, Rotterdam, 1979–80; with Rhône-Poulenc, 1980–86: Gen. Manager, Fertilizer Div., 1980–82; Mem., Exec. Cttee, 1981; Dep. Man. Dir, 1982–83; Man. Dir, 1983–86; Chm. Mgt Bd, 1986–87, Chm. and CEO, 1987–90, CDF Chimie, later ORKEM; Chm. and CEO, Total SA, Paris, 1990–95 (non-exec. Dir, 1995–2010); Dir, Thales, 1998–2009; Chm. and CEO, 1995–2006, Chm., 2006–08, Alcatel Alsthom, then Alcatel, later Alcatel-Lucent. Officier de la Légion d'Honneur, 1998. *Recreations:* music, ski-ing, tennis.

TE PAA-DANIEL, Dr Jennifer Louise Plane; JP; educational consultant, Auckland, since 2013; Senior Research Scholar, College of St John the Evangelist, Auckland, 2013 (Lecturer in Global Anglican Studies, Race Politics and Theological Education, 1992–2012, and Ahorangi (Principal), 1995–2012); Lay Canon, Holy Trinity Cathedral, Auckland, since 2005; *b* 19 Oct. 1953; *d* of Theodore Malcolm Plane and Wirihita (Zita) Te Paa; *m* (marr. diss.); one *s* one *d*; *m* 2012, Dr Roro Mana Daniel. *Educ:* Coll. of St John the Evangelist, Auckland (Dip. in Social Services 1990); Univ. of Auckland (BTh 1992; MEd Hons 1994); Graduate Theol Union, Berkeley (PhD 2001). Special Employment Liaison Officer, Auckland, 1981; Social Worker, Auckland, 1983–86; Sen. Vocational Trng Officer, Auckland, 1986–88; Tertiary Student Counsellor and Teacher, Auckland Inst. of Technol., 1988–90; Sen. Local Govt Policy Advr, 1990–92. Member: Internat. Anglican Indigenous Peoples Network, 1994–; Gen. Synod, 1998–2011; Social Justice Commn of Anglican Church, 2000–08; Inter-Anglican Internat. Theol Doctrinal Commn, 2001–08; Lambeth Commn, 2001–04; Archbishop of Canterbury's Commn on Theol Educn, 2001–; Internat. Anglican Women's Network, 2004–; Council, Internat. Women, Develt and Faith Alliance, 2007–; Nat. Complaints Assessment Cttee, NZ Teachers' Council, 2012–16; Moderator, Working Gp on Ecumenical Theol Educn, WCC, 2000–06; Mem., 1995, Global Convenor, 2001–12, Internat. Anglican Peace and Justice Network; Convenor, Nat. Anglican Church Centre for Women's Studies, 2005–11. Maori/Moriori Res. Fellow, 2013, Res., Affiliate, 2013–, Nat. Centre for Peace and Conflict Studies, Univ. of Otago; St Margaret's Vis. Prof. of Women in Ministry, Church Divinity Sch. of Pacific, Berkeley, Calif., 2014. Member: NZ Arts Council, 2007–09; South Pacific Assoc. of Theol Schs, 2008–. Member: Nat. Women's Adv. Cttee to Govt, 1981–86; Nat. Lotteries Distribution Cttee, 1981–86; Nat. Govtl Rev. Cttee on Tertiary Educn, 1986–88; Prisons Bd, 1987–97; Nat. Govtl Rev. Cttee on Prison Reform (Women), 1990; Human Rights Adv. Cttee, 1992–93. Cultural Advr to NZ Spirit of Adventure Trust, 2010; Trustee, Nat. Centre for Religious Diversity, 2016–; Trustee and Te Mareikura, Nat. Centre for Peace and Conflict Studies, Univ. of Otago, 2018–. JP NZ, 2014. Hon. DD: Episcopal Divinity Sch., Cambridge, 2003; Virginia Theol Seminary, Alexandria, 2008; Gen. Theol Seminary, NY, 2015; Hon. Dr Humane Letters, Church Divinity Sch. of Pacific, Univ. of Calif, Berkeley, 2014. Winston Churchill Fellowship Award, 1990; Distinguished Alumni Award, Univ. of Auckland, 2010; Alumni of Year Award, Grad. Theol. Union, Berkeley, 2010. *Publications:* What is the Family? A Cross Cultural Perspective, 1996; (contrib.) Growing Up Maori, 1999; (contrib.) Leadership Formation for a New World: an emergent indigenous Anglican Theological College, 2001; (contrib.) Thinking Outside the Square: church in Middle Earth, 2003; (contrib.) Theology Today, 2005; (contrib.) The Oxford Guide to the Book of Common Prayer Worldwide, 2005; (contrib.) Challenging Christian Zionism: theology, politics and the Israel-Palestine conflict, 2005; (contrib.) Other Voices, Other Worlds, 2006; (contrib.) Pursuing the Mind of Christ in Faith and Action: Njongonkulu Ndungane. Archbishop for the Church and the world, 2008; (jtly) Lifting Women's Voices: prayers to change the world, 2009; (jtly) In the Beginning was the Word: group bible studies on the Gospel of John, 2009; (contrib.) To the Church, To the World: Ki te Hahi, Ki te Ao, 2010; (contrib.) The Handbook of Theological Education in World Christianity, 2010; (contrib.) Tolerance - Respect - Trust, 2010; (ed with E. Fairbrother and contrib.) Our Place, Our Voice: explorations in contextual theology, 2012; (ed jtly and contrib.) Anglican Women on Church and Mission, 2013; (ed jtly and contrib.) Canterbury Studies in Anglicanism: Anglican women on Church and mission, 2013; (contrib.) The Reemergence of Liberation: models for the Twenty-First century, 2013; Whispers, Whisperers, Whispering in Whispers and Vanities: Samoan indigenous knowledge and religion, 2014; (contrib.) Wisdom and Imagination: religious progressives and the search for meaning, 2014; (contrib.) The Oxford Handbook of Anglican Studies, 2015; (contrib.) Postcolonial Practice of Ministry, 2016; Bible and Colonization: Aotearoa New Zealand in colonialism and the Bible—contemporary reflections from the global South, 2018; contribs to jls incl. Anglican Theol Rev., Circle, First Peoples Theology Jl, NZ Herald, Pacific Jl of Theology, Stimulus. *Recreations:* grandchildren, fishing, writing, researching and living into 'retirement' in Aitutaki, Cook Islands! *E:* jenzat1@gmail.com.

TEACHER, Michael John, FCA; Director: Ruralbridge, since 2010; PPF Europe, since 2015; *b* 2 June 1947; *s* of Charles and Ida Teacher; *m* 1972, Sandra Posner; three *s*. *Educ:* City Univ. (MSc Financial Mgt 1972). FCA 1969. Articled Clerk, Abey, Lish & Co., 1964–69; Audit Senior, Deloitte & Co., 1969–71; Corporate Finance Exec., Corinthian Holdings, then Welbeck Investment, 1973–76; Man. Dir, Holding Co. Ltd, Welbeck Investment Plc, 1976–82; Exec. Dir, Sir Joseph Causton Plc, 1983–84; Man. Dir, Pointon York Ltd, Venture Capital Co., 1984–87; Hillsdown Holdings PLC: Man. Dir, HIT Plc (Venture Capital subsid.), 1987–93; Exec. Dir, 1993–98; Chief Exec., 1998–99; Chief Executive: Unipoly Hldgs, 2001–06; Peek Hldgs, 2005–07; Ontex NV, 2006–13. Chairman: Avgol, 2013–18; Jeyes Hldgs Ltd, 2014–17; Ecoegg Ltd, 2018–. *Recreations:* tennis, soccer, running, charitable work.

TEAGLE, Vice-Adm. Sir Somerford (Francis), KBE 1994; Chief of Defence Force, New Zealand, 1991–95; *b* 9 June 1938; *s* of Leonard Herbert Teagle and Muriel Frances Teagle; *m* 1961, Leonie Marie Maire; one *s* one *d*. *Educ:* Christ's Coll., Christchurch, NZ; Royal Naval Coll., Dartmouth. Royal New Zealand Navy: Sea and Staff appts, 1958–85: Commanding Officer HMNZS: Manga, 1962–64; Taranaki, 1977; jssc, Canberra, 1977; CO HMNZS Canterbury, 1978–79; Captain, Naval Trng, 1981–84; ndc, Canada, 1983; Cdre, Auckland, 1986–87; Dep. Chief of Naval Staff, 1988–89; Chief of Naval Staff, 1989–91. *Recreation:* wine growing. *Address:* PO Box 84, Martinborough 5741, New Zealand. *Club:* Wellington (Wellington).

TEAGUE, David Norman, CMG 2011; Technical Lead, Foreign and Commonwealth Office, 2008–18; *b* Liverpool, 21 Aug. 1958; *s* of Norman Francis Teague and Patricia Teague; *m* 1982, Elizabeth Anne Kain; two *s*. *Educ:* Liverpool Blue Coat Sch.; Brasenose Coll., Oxford (BA Hons 1983). Various technical and leadership posts, FCO, 1983–2018. *Publications:* (jtly) papers on group theory. *Recreations:* vintage wireless—late valve, early transistor, British light music, mathematics, cookery.

TEAGUE, (Edward) Thomas (Henry); QC 2000; **His Honour Judge Teague**; a Circuit Judge, since 2006; *b* Weymouth, 21 May 1954; *s* of Harry John Teague and Anne Elizabeth Teague (*née* Hunt); *m* 1980, Helen Mary Howard; two *s*. *Educ:* St Francis Xavier's Coll., Liverpool; Christ's Coll., Cambridge (MA). Called to the Bar, Inner Temple, 1977; Mem., Wales and Chester Circuit, 1978–2006, Western Circuit, 2002–06; Asst Recorder, 1993–97; a Recorder, 1997–2006; Hon. Mem., Northern Circuit, 2007–. Legal Assessor, GMC, 2002–06. Chairman, Anthony Grainger Inquiry, 2016–19. FRAS 1991. *Recreations:* music, fly-fishing, astronomy. *Address:* Queen Elizabeth II Law Courts, Derby Square, Liverpool L2 1XA. *T:* (0151) 473 7373.

TEAPE, Angela Dawn; *see* Hatton, A. D.

TEAR, Rebecca, MA; Headmistress, Badminton School, since 2012; *b* Plymouth, 15 Nov. 1972; *d* of B. Warlow; *m* 1998, Richard Frederick John Tear; two *s*. *Educ:* Kelly Coll., Tavistock; Univ. of Exeter (BSc Chem. 1995); Inst. of Educn, Univ. of London (PGCE 1996; MA 2012). Hd, Jun. Sci., Hd of Lower Sixth, and Hd, Becket House, St George's, Ascot, 1998–2005; Hd of Sixth Form, 2005–08, Dep. Hd, 2008–12, Wycombe Abbey. *Recreations:* cooking, jogging, keeping fit with family, sailing, moorland walking, pilates, music (singing with choirs when possible). *Address:* Badminton School, Westbury Road, Westbury on Trym, Bristol BS9 3BA.

TEARE, Andrew Hubert; Chief Executive, Rank Group (formerly Rank Organisation) plc, 1996–98; *b* 8 Sept. 1942; *s* of late Arthur Hubert Teare and Rosalind Margaret Baker; *m* 1964, Janet Nina Skidmore; three *s*. *Educ:* Kingswood School, Bath; University College London (BA Hons Classics 1964). Turner & Newall, 1964–72; CRH, 1972–83 (Gen. Manager Europe, 1978–83); Rugby Group, 1983–90 (Asst Man. Dir, 1983–84; Man. Dir, 1984–90); Gp Chief Exec., English China Clays plc, 1990–95. Non-executive Director: Heiton Holdings, 1984–90; NFC, 1989–96; Prudential Corp., 1992–98. Pres., Nat. Council of Building Material Producers, 1990–92. CCMI. *Publications:* The Chairman (novel), 2005. *Recreations:* ski-ing, mountain walking, reading. *Address:* Turleigh Down House, Bradford-on-Avon BA15 2HF. *Club:* Hibernian United Service (Dublin).

**TEARE, His Honour Jonathan James**; a Circuit Judge, 1998–2014; Presiding Senior Judge, Sovereign Base Areas, Cyprus, 2007–14 (Deputy Senior Judge, 2001–06); b 13 Dec. 1946; y s of Prof. Donald Teare, MD, FRCP, FRCPath, DMJ and Kathleen Teare; m 1972, Nicola Jill, 2nd d of Lt-Col Peter Spittall, RM, CP and Peggy Spittall; two d. Educ: Pinewood Sch.; Rugby Sch. Called to the Bar, Middle Temple, 1970; practised, Midland and Oxford Circuit, 1971–98; Asst Recorder, 1985–90; Recorder, 1990–98. Member: Mental Health Review Tribunal, 2002–; Notts Probation Bd, 2004–11. Dir and Trustee, Egalitarian Trust, 2014–17; Nat. Justice Mus., 2017–. Served TA, HAC, 1965–69, RRF, 1970–72. Freeman, City of London, 1981; Liveryman, Soc. of Apothecaries, 1980–. High Sheriff, Notts, 2019–20. Recreations: gardening, shooting, travel, wine.

**TEARE, Hon. Sir Nigel (John Martin)**, Kt 2006; **Hon. Mr Justice Teare**; a Judge of the High Court of Justice, Queen's Bench Division, since 2006; a Presiding Judge, Western Circuit, 2013–16; Admiralty Judge, since 2011; b 8 Jan. 1952; s of Eric John Teare and Mary Rackham Teare; m 1975, Elizabeth Jane Pentecost; two s one d. Educ: King William's Coll., Isle of Man; St Peter's Coll., Oxford (BA 1973; MA 1975; Hon. Fellow, 2010). Called to the Bar, Lincoln's Inn, 1974, Bencher, 2004; practising barrister, 1975–2006; Jun. Counsel to Treasury in Admiralty matters, 1989–91; QC 1991; Asst Recorder, 1993–97; a Recorder, 1997–2006; a Dep. High Court Judge, 2002–06. Acting Deemster, IOM, 2000–06. Lloyd's Salvage Arbitrator, 1994–2000, Lloyd's Salvage Appeal Arbitrator, 2000–06. Recreations: collecting Manx paintings, tennis, golf. Address: Royal Courts of Justice, Strand, WC2A 2LL. Club: Royal Automobile.

**TEARLE, Katharine, (Katie), (Mrs Mark Pappenheim)**, MBE 2012; Director of New Music, Edition Peters Group, music publishers, since 2016; b Cheltenham, 12 Sept. 1961; d of Michael Victor Tearle and Sadie Catherine Tearle (née Bonstow); m 1988, Mark Pappenheim, qv; two s. Educ: Coloma Convent Girls Sch., Croydon; Univ. of Birmingham (BA 1st Cl. Hons Music, Drama and Dance 1983); Guildhall Sch. of Music and Drama and City Univ., London (MA Performance Studies (Vocal) 1985). Mktg Asst, Opera North, 1983–84; professional singer, contemp. repertoire, 1985–93; Hd of Educn, Glyndebourne Prodns Ltd, 1986–2011; Hd, Opera and Dance, Edition Peters Gp, 2012. Visiting Lecturer: Royal Holloway Coll., Univ. of London, 1984–87; City Univ., 1985–86. Mem., Arts Council England, SE, 2003–08. Chair, Eur. Network of Opera and Dance Educn, 2005–08. Mem. Council, Spitalfields Music, 2013–. Trustee, Michael Tippett Musical Foundn, 1998–. FRSA 2005. Recreations: singing, swimming, walking. Address: Peters Edition Ltd, 2–6 Baches Street, N1 6DN. T: (020) 7553 4003. E: katie.tearle@editionpeters.com.

**TEASDALE, Anthony Laurence**; Director General, European Parliamentary Research Service, European Parliament, since 2013; b Old Windsor, Berks, 4 June 1957; s of late John Stevenson Teasdale and Pauline Teasdale (née Tomlinson); m 2001, Jacqueline Louise Philips. Educ: Licensed Victuallers Sch., Slough; Slough Grammar Sch.; Balliol Coll., Oxford (BA 1st Cl. PPE 1978); Nuffield Coll., Oxford (MPhil Politics 1980). Lectr in Politics, Corpus Christi and Magdalen Colls, Oxford, 1980–82; Policy Advr, EDG, EP, 1982–86; Asst to Dir Gen. for Econ. and Financial Affairs, EC Council of Ministers, 1986–88; Special Adviser: to Foreign Sec., FCO, 1988–89; to Dep. Prime Minister, Lord Pres. of the Council and Leader of H of C, 1989–90; Res. Fellow, Nuffield Coll., Oxford, 1992–93; Hd, London Office, EPP Gp in EP, 1993–95; Special Advr to Chancellor of Exchequer, HM Treasury, 1996–97; Hd, London Office, 1997–2002, Hd, Policy Strategy, 2002–07, EPP Gp in EP; Hd of Strategy, 2007–12, Dep. COS, 2009–12, Office of Pres. of EP; Dir for EU Internal Policies, EP, 2012–13. Vis. Sen. Fellow, 2011–19, Vis. Prof. in Practice, 2019–, Eur. Inst., LSE. Hon. FAcSS 2016. Publications: (with T. Bainbridge) Penguin Companion to European Union, 1995, 4th edn 2012. Recreations: music, reading, cinema, travel. Address: DG EPRS, European Parliament, 60 rue Wiertz, Brussels 1047, Belgium. T: 22841678. E: anthony.teasdale@ep.europa.eu.

**TEASDALE, Sir Graham (Michael)**, Kt 2006; FRCP, FRCSE, FRCSGlas, FMedSci; Professor and Head of Department of Neurosurgery, University of Glasgow, 1981–2003; b 20 Sept. 1940; s of Thomas Teasdale and Eva Teasdale (née Elgey); m 1971, Dr Evelyn Muriel Arnott; two s one d (and one s decd). Educ: Johnston Grammar Sch., Durham; Durham Univ. Med. Sch. (MB BS 1963). MRCP 1966, FRCP 1988; FRCSE 1970; FRCSGlas 1981. Trng in medicine, surgery and specialisation in neurosurgery, 1963–75; University of Glasgow: Sen. Lectr in Neurosurgery, 1975–79; Reader in Neurosurgery, 1979–81; Associate Dean for Med. Res., 1999–2003. Pres., RCPSG, 2003–06. Chm. Bd, NHS Quality Improvement Scotland, 2006–10. President: Internat. Neurotrauma Soc., 1994–98; Eur. Brain Injury Consortium, 1993–2003; Soc. of British Neurological Surgeons, 2000–02. FMedSci 1999; FRSE 2001. Hon. FACS 2002; Hon. FRCS 2008. Hon. DM Athens 2002; Hon. DSc Sunderland, 2013. Publications: (jtly) Management of Head Injuries, 1982; (jtly) Current Neurosurgery, 1992; articles and papers on med. res., particularly on head injuries and the Glasgow Coma Scale, in med. jls. Recreations: water sports, hill walking and midge dodging in the West of Scotland, ski-ing, fly fishing. Address: Ardgryffe, Duchal Road, Kilmacolm PA13 4AY.

**TEASDALE, John Douglas**, PhD; FBA 2000; Special Scientific Appointment, MRC Cognition and Brain Sciences (formerly Applied Psychology) Unit, 1991–2004; b 1 Sept. 1944; s of George Eric Teasdale and Vera Joan Teasdale; m 1969, Jacqueline Blackburn; two s. Educ: Emmanuel Coll., Cambridge (BA 1965, MA); Inst. of Psychiatry, Univ. of London (Dip. Psych. 1966; PhD 1971). Lectr, Psychology Dept, Inst. of Psychiatry, Univ. of London, 1967–71; Principal Clin. Psychologist, University Hosp. of Wales, Cardiff, 1971–74; Sen. Res. Worker, Dept of Psychiatry, Univ. of Oxford, 1974–85; Sen. Scientist, MRC Applied Psychol. Unit, 1985–91. Vis. Prof., Inst. of Psychiatry, Univ. of London, 1995–2004. FMedSci 2000. Publications: (with P. J. Barnard) Affect, Cognition and Change, 1993; (with Z. V. Segal and J. M. G. Williams) Mindfulness-Based Cognitive Therapy for Depression, 2002, 2nd edn 2013; (jtly) The Mindful Way through Depression, 2007; (jtly) The Mindful Way Workbook, 2014; approx. 100 articles in books and learned jls. Recreations: sitting quietly, doing nothing. Address: 15 Chesterford House, Southacre Drive, Cambridge CB2 7TZ.

**TEATHER, Sarah Louise**; Director, Jesuit Refugee Service, UK, since 2016 (International Advocacy Consultant, 2015); b 1 June 1974. Educ: Leicester Grammar Sch.; St John's Coll., Cambridge (BA 1996). Policy analyst, Macmillan Cancer Relief, until 2003. Mem. (Lib Dem), Islington LBC, 2002–03. Contested (Lib Dem) Finchley & Golders Green, 2001. MP (Lib Dem) Brent E, Sept. 2003–2010, Brent Central, 2010–15. Lib Dem spokesman: on mental health, 2003–04; on London, 2004–05; on communities and local govt, 2005–06; on educn and skills, 2006–07; on innovation, univs and skills, 2007; on business, enterprise and regulatory reform, 2007–08; on housing, 2008–10; Minister of State, DFE, 2010–12. Chair, All Party Parliamentary Group: on Guantanamo Bay, 2006–10; on Refugees, 2012–15; Mem., Jt Cttee on Human Rights, 2014–15. FRSA 2007.

**TEBBIT**, family name of **Baron Tebbit**.

**TEBBIT, Baron** cr 1992 (Life Peer), of Chingford, in the London Borough of Waltham Forest; **Norman Beresford Tebbit**, CH 1987; PC 1981; Director: Sears (Holdings) PLC, 1987–99; British Telecommunications plc, 1987–96; BET, 1987–96; Spectator (1828) Ltd, 1989–2004; b 29 March 1931; 2nd s of Leonard and Edith Tebbit, Enfield; m 1956, Margaret Elizabeth Daines; two s one d. Educ: Edmonton County Grammar Sch. Embarked on career in journalism, 1947. Served RAF: commissioned GD Branch; qualif. Pilot, 1949–51; Reserve service RAuxAF, No 604 City of Middx Sqdn, 1952–55. Entered and left publishing and advertising, 1951–53. Civil Airline Pilot, 1953–70 (Mem. BALPA; former holder various offices in that Assoc.). Active mem. and holder various offices, Conservative Party, 1946–. MP (C) Epping, 1970–74, Chingford, 1974–92; PPS to Minister of State, Dept of Employment, 1972–73; Parly Under Sec. of State, Dept of Trade, 1979–81; Minister of State, Dept of Industry, 1981; Secretary of State for: Employment, 1981–83; Trade and Industry, 1983–85; Chancellor of the Duchy of Lancaster, 1985–87; Chm., Conservative Party, 1985–87. Former Chm., Cons. Members Aviation Cttee; former Vice-Chm. and Sec., Cons. Members Housing and Construction Cttee; Sec. House of Commons New Town Members Cttee. Dir, J. C. Bamford Excavators, 1987–91. Co-presenter, Target, Sky TV, 1989–98; columnist: The Sun, 1995–97; The Mail on Sunday, 1997–2001; blogger, Daily Telegraph, 2010–. Publications: Upwardly Mobile (autobiog.), 1988; Unfinished Business, 1991; The Game Cook, 2009; Ben's Story, 2014. Address: c/o House of Lords, SW1A 0PW.

**TEBBIT, Sir Kevin (Reginald)**, KCB 2002; CMG 1997; company director and strategic adviser; Permanent Secretary, Ministry of Defence, 1998–2005; b 18 Oct. 1946; s of R. F. J. Tebbit and N. M. Tebbit (née Nichols); m 1969, Elizabeth Alison, d of John and Elizabeth Tinley; one s one d. Educ: Cambridgeshire High Sch.; St John's Coll., Cambridge (Schol.; BA Hons 1969). Asst Principal, MoD, 1969–72; Asst Private Sec. to Sec. of State for Defence, 1973–74; Principal, MoD, 1974–79; First Sec., UK Delegn to NATO, 1979–82; transferred to FCO, 1982; E European and Soviet Dept, 1982–84; Hd of Chancery, Ankara, 1984–87; Dir, Cabinet of Sec. Gen. of NATO, 1987–88; Counsellor (Politico-Mil.), Washington, 1988–91; Hd, Econ. Relns Dept, FCO, 1992–94; Dir (Resources) and Chief Inspector, FCO, 1994–97; Dep. Under-Sec. of State, FCO, 1997; Dir, GCHQ, 1998. Exec. Vice Pres. (UK Defence and Govt), AECOM, 2015–; Chair, UK Security and Resilience Industries Community, 2018–; Sen. Vice Pres., Smiths Gp plc, 2019–. Chm., Finmeccanica UK, 2007–12; Sen. Advr, Hewlett Packard, 2013–15. Visiting Professor: QMUL, 2006–14; KCL, 2015–. Chm., Lifeboat Fund, 2004–10. Gov., Ditchley Foundn, 2004–; Member, Advisory Board: Centre for Social Justice, 2010–; Inst. for Security Sci. and Technol., Imperial Coll. London, 2009–; Sen. Associate Fellow, RUSI, 2012–. Trustee: British Friends of Aphrodisias, 1997–; Airey Neave Trust, 2006–. Recreations: music, countryside, archaeology, West Ham Utd. Club: Savile.

**TECKMAN, Jonathan Simon Paul**; Director, Fletcher Teckman Consulting Ltd, since 2002; b 27 May 1963; s of Sidney Teckman and late Stephanie Audrey Teckman (née Tresman); m 1997, Anne Caroline Fletcher; two s. Educ: Weston Favell Upper Sch., Northampton; Univ. of Warwick (BSc Hons Mgt Scis). Admin. trainee, 1984–86, HEO (Develt), 1986–90, DoE; Gp Finance Manager, Historic Royal Palaces Agency, 1990–93; Department of National Heritage, subsequently Department for Culture, Media and Sport: Principal, Nat. Lottery Div., 1993–95; Films Div., 1995–98 (Sec. to Adv. Cttee on Film Finance); Dep. Dir, 1998, Dir, 1999–2002, BFI; Public Sector Tutor, Ashridge Business Sch., 2004–09, Associate Tutor, 2009–; Chief Exec., Phoenix Educn Trust, 2011–13. Mem., BAFTA. Treas., BBFC, 2011–. Publications: Ordinary Joe, 2015. Recreations: cinema, reading, cricket, Rugby Union. Clubs: Bold Dragoon Cricket (Northampton); Aylesbury Rugby Football.

**TEDDER**, family name of **Baron Tedder**.

**TEDDER, 3rd Baron** cr 1946, of Glenguin, Co. Stirling; **Robin John Tedder**; Chairman, Vintage Capital Pty Ltd, since 1995; Proprietor, Glenguin Wine Co., since 1993; b 6 April 1955; er s of 2nd Baron Tedder and of Peggy Eileen Growcott; S father, 1994; m 1st, 1977, Jennifer Peggy (d 1978), d of John Mangan, NZ; 2nd, 1980, Rita Aristeia, yr d of John Frangidis, Sydney, NSW; two s one d. MW. Director: Glenguin Estate, 1993–; Blackwall Ltd, 2011–. Australian Ambassador, Singularity Univ., Calif, 2011–; Mentor, INCUBATE, Sydney Univ., 2015–. Fellow, Financial Services Inst. Heir: s Hon. Benjamin John Tedder, b 23 April 1985. Address: 11 Kardinia Road, Clifton Gardens, Sydney, NSW 2088, Australia.

**TEDSTONE, Dr Alison Elizabeth**; Deputy Director, Diet, Obesity and Physical Activity, and Chief Nutritionist, Public Health England, since 2013; b Worcs, 8 April 1961; m Alan; two c. Educ: N Bromsgrove High Sch.; Queen Elizabeth Coll.; St George's Hosp. Med. Sch. (BSc Hons Physiol. 1982; PhD Physiol. 1988). Res. Associate, George Washington Univ., 1982–83; Res. Asst, Dept of Clinical Pharmacology, Royal Free Hosp., 1983–84; Postdoctoral Res. Fellow, Univ. of Oxford, 1988–91; Lectr in Human Nutrition, Public Health Nutrition Unit, LSHTM, 1992–2001; Principal Nutritionist, Food Standards Agency, 2001–06; Hd of Nutrition Sci., Food Standards Agency, 2006–12, and DoH, 2010–12; Dep. Dir, Interim Nutrition Branch, DoH, subseq. PHE, 2012–13. Govt reports on nutrition, obesity, sugar and calorie reduction. FAfN 2012. Address: Public Health England, Wellington House, 133–155 Waterloo Road, SE1 8UG.

**TEGNER, Ian Nicol**, CA; Chairman, Control Risks Group, 1992–2000; b 11 July 1933; s of Sven Stuart Tegner, OBE, and Edith Margaret Tegner (née Nicol); m 1961, Meriel Helen, d of Brig. M. S. Lush, CB, CBE, MC; one s one d. Educ: Rugby School. CA. Clarkson Gordon & Co., Toronto, 1958–59; Manager 1959–65, Partner 1965–71, Barton Mayhew & Co., Chartered Accts; Finance Dir, Bowater Industries, 1971–86; Chm., Cayzer Steel Bowater, 1981–86; Dir, Gp Finance, Midland Bank, 1987–89. Chm., Crest Packaging, 1993–99; Director: Wiggins Teape Appleton, subseq. Arjo Wiggins Appleton, 1990–2000; Opera 80, subseq. English Touring Opera, 1991–99; TIP Europe plc, 1992–93; Teesside Power Ltd, 1993–2001; Coutts & Co., 1996–98. Institute of Chartered Accountants of Scotland: Mem. Council 1981–86; Pres., 1991–92; Mem., Accounting Standards Cttee of CCAB, 1984–86; Chm., Hundred Gp of Finance Dirs, 1988–90. Chm., Children of the Andes, 2001–03; Trustee, ClementJames Centre, 1996–2013. Publications: articles on accountancy in various jls and pubns. Recreations: book collecting, travel, hill-walking, choral singing, family life. Address: 7 Queensdale Walk, W11 4QQ.

**TEHRANI, Joanna Elizabeth**; see Glynn, J. E.

**TEICHMANN, Dr Sarah Amalia, (Mrs Jan-Felix Polonius)**, FMedSci; Head of Cellular Genetics, Wellcome (formerly Wellcome Trust) Sanger Institute, since 2016; Director, Research, Cavendish Laboratory, University of Cambridge, since 2016; b Karlsruhe, Germany, 15 April 1975; d of Hartmut Ernst Teichmann and Virginia Cranch Teichmann; m 2006, Jan-Felix Polonius; two d. Educ: European Sch., Karlsruhe; Trinity Coll., Cambridge (BA 1996; PhD 2000). Fellow, Trinity Coll., Cambridge, 1999–2015; MRC Prog. Leader, MRC Lab. of Molecular Biol., Cambridge, 2001–13; Gp Leader, EMBL-Eur. Bioinformatics Inst., 2013–16. FMedSci 2015. Publications: Teenage Detectives (with V. Teichmann), 1991; over 120 scientific papers in areas of computational biol. and genomics. *Recreations*: friends and family, tennis, cycling, ski-ing, basketball. *Address*: Wellcome Sanger Institute, Wellcome Genome Campus, Hinxton, Cambridge CB10 1SA. *T*: 07719 798717. *E*: st9@sanger.ac.uk.

**TEIKMANIS, Andris;** Ambassador of the Republic of Latvia to the United States of America, since 2016; *b* Rīga, Latvia, 29 Nov. 1959; *s* of Gunārs Teikmanis and Veronika Teikmane; *m* 1990, Inguna Peniķe; one *s* one *d*. *Educ*: Riga High Sch. No 5; Latvian Univ. (MA Law). Investigator, Police Bd, Riga City, 1983–88; Judge, Court of Kirov Dist, Riga City, 1988–90; Chm., Riga City Council, 1990–94; Mem., Supreme Council, Latvia, 1990–93, signed Declaration on Restoration of Independence of Republic of Latvia, 1990; Ambassador: to Council of Europe, 1994–98; to Germany, 1998–2002; Under-Sec. of State, Min. of Foreign Affairs, 2002–05; Ambassador to Russian Fedn, 2005–08; Sec. of State, Min. of Foreign Affairs, 2008–13; Ambassador to UK, 2013–16. Commemorative Medal for participation in barricades of 1991 (Latvia), 1996; Comdr, Order of Three Stars (Latvia), 2000; Hon. Medal, 2002, Commemorative Medal, 2004, Min. of Defence (Latvia); Cross of Recognition (Latvia), 2007; Commander: Prince Don Enrique Order (Portugal), 2003; Order of Merit (Italy), 2004; Grand Cross, Order of Merit (Germany), 2004; Grand Decoration of Honour in Gold with Star (Austria), 2013. *Recreations*: opera, classical music, jogging, cycling. *Address*: Embassy of the Republic of Latvia, 2306 Massachusetts Avenue, NW, Washington, DC 20008, USA. *E*: andris.teikmanis@mfa.gov.lv. *W*: www.twitter.com/teikmanis. *Club*: Cosmos (Washington, DC).

**TE KANAWA, Dame Kiri (Jeanette Claire),** CH 2018; ONZ 1995; DBE 1982 (OBE 1973); opera singer; *b* Gisborne, New Zealand, 6 March 1944; *m* 1967, Desmond Stephen Park (marr. diss. 1997); one *s* one *d*. *Educ*: St Mary's Coll., Auckland, NZ; London Opera Centre. Major rôles at Royal Opera House, Covent Garden, include: the Countess, in Marriage of Figaro; Elvira, in Don Giovanni; Mimi, in La Bohème; Desdemona, in Otello; Marguerite, in Faust; Amelia, in Simon Boccanegra; Fiordiligi, in Così Fan Tutte; Tatiana, in Eugene Onegin; title rôle in Arabella; Rosalinde, in Die Fledermaus; Violetta, in La Traviata; Manon, in Manon Lescaut. Has sung leading rôles at Metropolitan Opera, New York, notably, Desdemona, Elvira, and Countess; also at the Paris Opera, Elvira, Fiordiligi, and Pamina in Magic Flute, title rôle in Tosca; at San Francisco Opera, Amelia and Pamina; at Sydney Opera House, Mimi, Amelia, and Violetta in La Traviata; Elvira, with Cologne Opera; Amelia at La Scala, Milan; Countess in Le Nozze di Figaro at Salzburg Fest. Many recordings, incl. Maori songs. Estabd Kiri Te Kanawa Foundn, 2004. Hon. DMus: Oxford, 1983; Cambridge, 1997. Classical Brit Lifetime Achievement Award, 2010. Hon. AC 1990. *Publications*: Land of the Long White Cloud, 1989; Opera for Lovers, 1997. *Recreations*: golf, swimming, tennis.

**TELFER, Robert Gilmour Jamieson, (Rab),** CBE 1985; PhD; Executive Chairman, BSI Standards, 1989–92; Director, Manchester Business School, 1984–88; *b* 22 April 1928; *s* of late James Telfer and Helen Lambie Jamieson; *m* 1953, Joan Audrey Gunning; three *s*. *Educ*: Bathgate Academy (Dawson Trust Bursary); Univ. of Edinburgh (Mackay-Smith Prize; Blandfield Prize; BSc (Hons 1st cl.) 1950, PhD 1953). Shift Chemist, AEA, 1953–54; Chem. Lectr (pt-time), Whitehaven Tech. Coll., 1953–54; Imperial Chemical Industries Ltd: Res. Chemist, Billingham Div., 1954–58; Chem. Lectr (pt-time), Constantine Tech. Coll., Middlesbrough, 1955–58; Heavy Organic Chemicals Div., 1958–71; Fibre Intermediates Dir and R & D Dir, 1971–75; Div. Dep. Chm., 1975–76, Div. Chm., 1976–81, Petrochemicals Div.; Chm. and Man. Dir, 1981–84, Dir, 1984, Mather & Platt Ltd; Chm., European Industrial Services Ltd, 1988–89. Mem. Bd, Philips-Imperial Petroleum Ltd, 1975–81; Director: Renold PLC, 1984–98 (Chm., Audit Cttee, 1993–98); Volex PLC, 1986–98 (Chm., Audit Cttee, 1993–98); Teesside Hldgs Ltd, 1993–95. Sen. Vis. Fellow, Manchester Business Sch., 1988–. Group Chm., Duke of Edinburgh's Study Conf., 1974; Mem., ACORD for Fuel and Power, 1981–87; Chm., Adv. Council on Energy Conservation, 1982–84. Personal Adviser to Sec. of State for Energy, 1984–87. British Standards Institution: Mem. Main Bd, and Mem. Finance Cttee, 1988–92; non-exec. Chm., Standards Bd and Testing Bd, 1988–89. Member: Civil Service Coll. Adv. Council, 1986–89; HEFCE, 1992–97 (Chairman: Audit Cttee, 1993–97; Quality Assessment Cttee, 1996–98); Dir, Quality Assurance Agency for Higher Educn, 1997–98. Governor, Univ. of Teesside (formerly Teesside Polytechnic), 1989–97 (Chm., Govs, 1992–97; Chm., Resources Cttee, 1989–92). CCMI. Hon. MBA Manchester, 1989; Hon. LLD Teesside, 1998. *Publications*: papers in Jl Chem. Soc. and Chemistry and Industry. *Recreations*: walking, gardening, fossil hunting, decorative egg collecting, supporting Middlesbrough FC. *Address*: Downings, Upleatham Village, Redcar, Cleveland TS11 8AG.

**TELIČKA, Pavel;** Member (Alliance of Liberals and Democrats for Europe), European Parliament, 2014–19 (Vice-President, 2017–19); *b* 24 Aug. 1965; *s* of František Telička and Marie Teličková; *m* 1990, Eva Pašková; one *s* one *d*. *Educ*: Charles Univ., Prague (Dr of Law). Dir Gen. for Integration (EU, NATO and UN), 1996–98; Dep. Minister of Foreign Affairs, 1998–2000; State Sec. for European Affairs and 1st Dep. Minister of Foreign Affairs, 2000–03; Ambassador of Czech Republic to the EU, 2003–04; Mem., EC, 2004. Vice Pres., Alliance of Liberals and Democrats for Europe. Eur. Coordinator TEN-T: Rail Baltic(a), 2005–13; North Sea Baltic Corridor, 2014. Co-founder and Partner, BXL Consulting Ltd, 2005–13. President's Medal for contribn to integration process of Czech Republic into EU, 2003. *Publications*: How We Entered the EU, 2003.

**TELLER, Sadie;** see Coles, S.

**TEMIRKANOV, Yuri;** Music Director and Principal Conductor, St Petersburg (formerly Leningrad) Philharmonic Orchestra, since 1988; *b* 10 Dec. 1938. *Educ*: Leningrad Conservatory (graduated violinist, 1962, conductor, 1965). Musical Dir, Leningrad Symphony Orch., 1969–77; Artistic Dir and Chief Conductor, Kirov Opera, Leningrad, 1977–88; Principal Conductor, Royal Philharmonic Orch., 1978–98, now Conductor Laureate; Music Dir, Baltimore SO, 2000–06, now Emeritus; Music Dir, Teatro Regio di Parma, 2010–12. Principal Guest Conductor: Dresden Philharmonic Orch., 1994–98; Danish Nat. SO, 2004–08. Has conducted: Boston Symphony; Dresden Philharmonic; Danish Nat. Radio Symphony; Orch. of Santa Cecilia, Rome; Orch. Nat. de France; La Scala, Milan; Philadelphia Orch.; San Francisco Symphony; New York Philharmonic, etc. Recordings of major orchestral works of Tchaikovsky, Stravinsky, Prokofiev, Mussorgsky and Shostakovich. Abbiati Prize for best conductor, Italian Critics' Assoc., 2002. *Address*: c/o IMG Artists Europe, Capital Tower, 91 Waterloo Road, SE1 8RT. *T*: (020) 7957 5800.

**TEMKIN, Prof. Jennifer, (Mrs G. J. Zellick),** CBE 2018; LLD; FAcSS; Professor of Law, City, University of London (formerly City University London), since 2012; *b* 6 June 1948; *d* of late Michael Temkin and Minnie Temkin (*née* Levy); *m* 1975, Prof. Graham Zellick, *qv*; one *s* one *d*. *Educ*: S Hampstead High Sch. for Girls; LSE (LLB, LLM (Dist.), LLD); Inns of Court Sch. of Law. Called to the Bar, Middle Temple, 1971, Bencher, 2009; Lectr in Law, LSE, 1971–89; Prof. of Law and Dean, Sch. of Law, Univ. of Buckingham, 1989–92; Prof. of Law, 1992–2012, now Emeritus, and Dir, Centre for Legal Studies, 1994–96, Univ. of Sussex. Vis. Prof., Univ. of Toronto, 1978–79. Mem., Cttee of Heads of Univ. Law Schs, 1989–92, 1994–96. Member: Scrutiny Cttee on Draft Criminal Code, CCC, 1985–86; Home Sec's Adv. Gp on Use of Video Recordings in Criminal Proceedings, 1988–89; NCH Cttee on Children Who Abuse Other Children, 1990–92; External Reference Gp, Home Office Sex Offences Review, 1999–2000; Cttee of Experts on Treatment of Sex Offenders, Council of Europe, 2003–05; Expert Gp on Rape and Sexual Assault, Victims of Violence and Abuse Prevention Prog., DoH and Nat. Inst. for Mental Health in England, 2005–07; Home Office Biometrics and Forensics Ethics Gp (formerly Nat. DNA Database Ethics Gp), 2014–. Patron, Standing Cttee on Sexually Abused Children, 1993–96. Gov., S Hampstead High Sch. for Girls, 1991–99. FRSA 1989. FAcSS (AcSS 2009). Member: Editl Adv. Gp, Howard Jl of Criminal Justice, 1984–2016; Editl Bd, Jl of Criminal Law, 1986–2005. *Publications*: Rape and the Legal Process, 1987, 2nd edn 2002; Rape and Criminal Justice, 1995; (with Barbara Krahe) Sexual Assault and the Justice Gap: a question of attitude, 2008; articles in Mod. Law Rev., Criminal Law Rev., Cambridge Law Jl, Law Qly Rev., Internat. and Comparative Law Qly and other learned and professional jls. *Address*: City, University of London, Northampton Square, EC1V 0HB. *E*: jennifer.temkin.1@city.ac.uk.

*See also* A. D. R. Zellick.

**TEMKO, Edward James, (Ned);** writer, journalist and political analyst; Chief Political Correspondent, The Observer, 2005–08; *b* 5 Nov. 1952; *s* of late Stanley L. Temko and Francine Temko (*née* Salzman); *m* 1st, 1980, Noa Weiss (marr. diss. 1984); 2nd, 1986, Astra Bergson Kook; one *s*. *Educ*: Williams Coll., USA (BA Hons Pol Sci. and Econs). Reporter, Associated Press, Lisbon, 1976; United Press International: Europe, ME and Africa Editl Desk, Brussels, 1977; Correspondent, ME Office, Beirut, 1977–78; Christian Science Monitor: Chief ME Correspondent, Beirut, 1978–80; Moscow Correspondent, 1981–83; ME Correspondent, Jerusalem, 1984–85; SA Correspondent, Johannesburg, 1986–87; Sen. TV Correspondent for Europe, ME and Africa in London, World Monitor TV, 1989–90; Editor, Jewish Chronicle, 1990–2005. Regular appearances as political and current affairs analyst on UK and US television. *Publications*: To Win or To Die: a biography of Menachem Begin, 1987. *Recreations*: tennis, travel, technology, reading, writing, supporting perennially frustrating sports teams (the Washington Redskins and Tottenham Hotspur). *Address*: c/o The Observer, Kings Place, 90 York Way, N1 9GU.

**TEMMINK, Robert-Jan;** QC 2017; *b* London, 5 Feb. 1973; *s* of Harry and Ann Temmink; *m* 2002, Caroline Gill; one *s* one *d*. *Educ*: Merchant Taylors' Sch., Northwood; Trinity Coll., Cambridge (BA Hons 1995; MA 1998); Inns of Court Sch. of Law. FCIArb 2007. Called to the Bar: Middle Temple, 1996, Bencher, 2013; NI, 2007; Eastern Caribbean, 2018; in practice at the Bar, 1996–; arbitrator and mediator; Registered Practitioner, Dubai Internat. Financial Centre Courts, 2007–. Trustee: Temple Music Trust, 2010–; King's Singers Foundn, 2011–. Governor: Merchant Taylors' Sch., Northwood, 2009–; Sherborne Sch., 2016–. Liveryman, Merchant Taylors' Co., 2011– (Mem., Ct of Assts, 2017–); Under Renter Warden, 2017–18). *Publications*: (contrib.) Lissack & Horlick on Bribery, 2011, 2nd edn 2014; (contrib.) Gaeta on Investing in Emerging Markets, 2012. *Recreations*: singing, sailing, wine, cars, travel. *Address*: Quadrant Chambers, 10 Fleet Street, EC4Y 1AU. *E*: robert.temmink@quadrantchambers.com. *Clubs*: 67 Pall Mall, Royal Automobile.

**TEMPEST, Annie;** cartoonist; sculptor; *b* 22 Aug. 1959; *d* of Henry and Janet Tempest; *m* 1991, James McConnel, composer (marr. diss. 2006); one *d* (one *s* decd). *Educ*: Rye St Anthony Sch., Oxford; St Mary's Sch., Ascot. Cartoonist: The Yuppies, Daily Mail, 1985–93; Tottering-by-Gently, Country Life Magazine, 1994–; Senior Moments, WI Home & Country, 2005–06. Strip Cartoonist of the Year, Cartoonists' Club of GB, 1989; Pont Award for drawing the British Character, Cartoon Art Trust, 2009. *Publications*: Turbocharge Your Granny!, 1985; How Green are your Wellies?, 1985; Hooray Henry, 1986; Henry on Hols, 1987; Westenders, 1988; Tottering-by-Gently, vol. I, 1996, vol. II, 1998, vol. III, 2003; Tottering Hall, 2001; Lady Tottering's Journal, 2002; At Home with the Totterings, 2007; Out and About with the Totterings, 2010; The Tottering Annual, 2010; Drinks with the Totterings, 2010; In the Garden with the Totterings, 2011; She talks Venus, He talks Mars, 2011; Tottering Life, 2012; Tails of Tottering Hall, 2012; Tottering-by-Gently: the first twenty years, 2013; Lord Tottering: an English gentleman, 2013; *illustrator/contributor*: Publish and Be Damned!, 1988; Best Cartoons of the Year, 1988; Anneka Rice, The Recycled Joke Book, 1989; Mary Killen, Best Behaviour, 1991; Michael Seed, I Will See You in Heaven Where Animals Don't Bite..., 1991; Crime–check!, 1992; R. Rushbrooke, Where Did I Go Wrong?, 1992; Jonathan Ray, Berry's Best Cellar Secrets, 1998; Michael Seed, Will I See You in Heaven?, 1999; Alistair Sampson, The Guest from Hell, 2000; Robin Page, Why the Reindeer has a Velvet Nose, 2002. *Recreations*: inventing labour-saving devices, gardening, sculpting in all media, music, people watching, good wine, gory medical documentaries. *Address*: Tylers Barn, Wood Norton Road, Stibbard, Norfolk NR21 0EX. *E*: daffy@tottering.com. *Clubs*: British Cartoonists' Association, Sloane, Naval and Military; Muthaiga (Nairobi).

**TEMPEST, Kate;** see Calvert, K.

**TEMPIA, Nina Giuseppina;** a District Judge (Magistrates' Courts), since 2009; *b* London, 6 Aug. 1959; *d* of Orlando Tempia and Rina Angela Tempia (*née* Necchi-Ghiri). *Educ*: Sarah Siddons Comp. Sch., London; Univ. of Warwick (LLB); Guildford Coll. of Law. Admitted solicitor, 1987; Solicitor: Hogan Harris & Co., 1986–88; Jepson Goff & Co., 1988–89; Good Good & Co., 1989–98; Mackesys, 1998–2009; a Dep. Dist Judge (Magistrates' Courts), 2003–09. Member: Costs Cttee, Legal Services Commn, 1990–2009; Cttee, London Criminal Courts Solicitors' Assoc., 1998–2000. Chm., Soho Soc., 1998–2004. *Recreations*: theatre, cinema, reading, travelling, eating Italian food, drinking Merlot. *Address*: Westminster Magistrates' Court, 181 Marylebone Road, NW1 5BR.

**TEMPLE OF STOWE,** 9th Earl *cr* 1822; **James Grenville Temple-Gore-Langton;** Partner, Slade & Cooper, since 2002; *b* 11 Sept. 1955; *er s* of 8th Earl Temple of Stowe and Zilla Ray Temple-Gore-Langton (*née* Boxall) (*d* 1966); *S* father, 2013; *m* 2008, Julie Christine Mainwaring; one *s* one *d*. FCCA. Joined Slade & Cooper, 1994. *Heir*: *b* Hon. Robert Chandos Temple-Gore-Langton [*b* 22 Nov. 1957; *m* 1985, Susan Penelope Cavender; three *s* one *d*].

**TEMPLE, Anthony Dominic Afamado;** QC 1986; a Recorder, 1989–2015; *b* 21 Sept. 1945; *s* of Sir Rawden John Afamado Temple, CBE, QC and Jessie Margaret Wiseman Temple; *m* 1st, 1975 (marr. diss.); 2nd, 1983, Suzie Bodansky; two *d*. *Educ*: Haileybury and ISC; Worcester College, Oxford (Hon. Sec., OU Modern Pentathlon Assoc.). Called to the Bar, Inner Temple, 1968, Bencher, 1995; Crown Law Office, Western Australia, 1969; Assistant Recorder, 1982; a Dep. High Ct Judge, 1994–2014. Chm., Modern Pentathlon Assoc. of GB, 2004–16 (Vice-Pres., 2016–); Mem. Bd, Eur. Confedn Modern Pentathlon, 2012–. *Recreations*: modern pentathlon, travel, history. *Address*: 15 Lansdowne Walk, W11 3AH.

*See also* V. B. A. Temple.

**TEMPLE, Prof. (Isabel) Karen,** MD; FRCP; Professor of Medical Genetics, since 2006, and Director, Academic Unit of Human Development and Health, University of Southampton; *b* Kampala, Uganda, 3 April 1958. *Educ*: Sch. of Medicine, Univ. of Birmingham (MB BChir Hons 1981; MD 2004). FRCP 1995. Co-Lead, Wessex Genome Medicine Centre; Clin. Res. Lead, Wessex Imprinting Gp. Consultant, 1990–2006, Hon.

Consultant, 2006–, in Clin. Genetics, University Hosp. Southampton NHS Foundn Trust (formerly University Hosp. Southampton). Past Pres., Clin. Genetics Soc. *Address*: Faculty of Medicine, University of Southampton, University Road, Southampton SO17 1BJ. *E*: ikt@southampton.ac.uk.

**TEMPLE, Jane Rosemary;** *see* Ray, J. R.

**TEMPLE, Jill;** *see* Stansfield, J.

**TEMPLE, Prof. Sir John (Graham),** Kt 2003; FRCSE, FRCS, FRCPE, FRCP, FMedSci; Professor of Surgery, University of Birmingham, 1995–2003, now Emeritus; President, British Medical Association, 2017–18; *b* 14 March 1942; *s* of Joseph Henry Temple and Norah Temple; *m* 1966, Margaret Jillian Leighton Hartley; two *s* one *d*. *Educ*: William Hulme's Grammar Sch., Manchester; Liverpool Univ. Med. Sch. (MB ChB Hons; ChM). FRCSE 1969; FRCS 1970 (Hon. FRCS 2004); FRCP, FRCPE 1999; FRCPSGlas (*ad eundem*) 2003; FRCGP 2003; FRCEM (FFAEM 2003); FRCA 2005. Consultant Surgeon, Queen Elizabeth Hosp., Birmingham, 1979–98; Regl Postgrad. Dean, W Midlands, 1991–2000. Chm., Conf. Postgrad. Med. Deans UK, 1995–2000. Chair, Res. Council, Healing Foundn, 2002–17. Mem. Council, RCSE, 1997–2003 (Pres., 2000–03). Mem., Specialist Trng Authy, 1996–2006 (Chm., 2001–08); Hon. Col, 202 Field Hospital (V), 2004–09. FMedSci 1998; Fellow, Polish Soc. Surgeons, 1997; FFICM 2014. Hon. FHKCS 2001; Hon. FRACS 2002; Hon. FRCSI 2004. Hon. DSc Bristol, 2014. *Publications*: papers on postgraduate education and training. *Recreations*: off-shore sailing and racing, ski-ing. *Address*: Wharncliffe, 24 Westfield Road, Edgbaston, Birmingham B15 3QG.

**TEMPLE, Karen;** *see* Temple, I. K.

**TEMPLE, Mark Howard;** QC (Jersey) 2015; Solicitor General, Jersey, since 2015; *b* London, 28 Aug. 1966; *s* of John and Julienne Temple; *m* 1993, Silvia Gomez-Marcé; one *s* one *d*. *Educ*: King's Coll. Sch., Wimbledon; Selwyn Coll., Cambridge (BA Hist. 1988; MA 1992); Westminster Univ. (DipLaw). Admitted as solicitor, 1994; Solicitor Advocate, 2002. Solicitor: Ashurst Morris Crisp, 1992–2003; Mourant Ozannes, 2003–15 (Partner, 2007–15); Advocate, Royal Court of Jersey, 2005. *Recreations*: ski-ing, tennis, walking, family, Church (Anglican). *Address*: Law Officers' Department, Morier House, St Helier, Jersey, Channel Islands JE1 1DD. *T*: (01534) 441233, *Fax*: (01534) 441299. *E*: m.temple@gov.je. *Club*: Hurlingham.

**TEMPLE, Martin John,** CBE 2005; Chairman: EEF Ltd (formerly Engineering Employers Federation), 2008–16 (Director General, 1999–2008); Design Council, 2011–16 (Board Member, 2009–16); Health and Safety Executive, since 2016; *b* 30 Aug. 1949; *s* of John Douglas Temple and Kathleen Temple; *m* 1972, Lesley Imeson; one *s* one *d*. *Educ*: Bridlington Sch.; Univ. of Hull (BSc Hons 1970); Newcastle Poly. (Dip Mktg 1972); INSEAD (AMP 1991). Gen. Manager, British Steel Corp. Refractories Gp, 1979–85; Works Dir, GR-Stein Refractories, 1985–87; Dir, Sales and Mktg, British Steel Stainless, 1987–92; Avesta Sheffield: Dir, Mktg and Sales, 1992–95; Vice Pres., 1995–98. Bd Mem., Namtec Ltd, 2004–09; Dir, Vestry Court Ltd, 2000–14; Chm., 600 Gp plc, 2007–11. Chm., Transition Mgt Bd, Business Support Simplification Prog., BERR, later BIS, 2008–11. Chm., Warwick Business Sch., 2014–16. Board Member: Council of Eur. Employers of Metal, Engrg and Technology-based Industries, 1999–2009 (Chm., 2005–08); Women in Sci. and Engrg, 2001–08 (former Chm.); Engrg Develt Trust, 2000–07; Sci. Engrg Manufacturing Technol. Alliance, 2000–09; Engrg and Technol. Bd, 2002–08; Sheffield Teaching Hosp. Foundn Trust, 2013–; Great Exhibn of the North, 2016–19; Mem. Supervisory Bd, Sci., Engrg, Technol. and Maths Network, 2001–07. Mem. Council, Univ. of Warwick, 2011–16. Hon. FFOM 2008. Freeman, Co. of Cutlers, 1998. Hon. DSc Hull, 2011; Hon. Dr Sheffield Hallam, 2014. *Recreations*: Rugby, music, countryside, current affairs.

**TEMPLE, Nicholas John;** Chairman, Intela, since 2009; *b* 2 Oct. 1947; *s* of late Leonard Temple and of Lilly Irene Temple (*née* Thornton); *m* 1st; one *s* two *d*; 2nd, 2004, Lucinda (*née* Westmacott). *Educ*: King's Sch., Glos. Joined IBM, 1965; Chief Exec., 1992–94, Chm., 1994–96, IBM UK; Vice Pres., Industries, IBM Europe, 1995–96; mgt consultant, N. M. Rothschild & Sons, 1996. Chm., Hotelscene, 2008–13; non-executive Director: Electrocomponents PLC, 1996–2007; Blick plc, 1999–2004; Datacash, 2000–10; Datatec, 2002–. Council Mem., Foundn for Mfg and Ind., 1993–96. Chm., Action: Employees in the Community, 1993–96. Mem., President's Adv. Gp, Spastics' Soc., 1993–95. *Recreations*: rowing, ski-ing, opera. *Address*: 10 Markham Square, SW3 4UY. *T*: (020) 7581 2181.

**TEMPLE, Sir Richard (Carnac Chartier),** 5th Bt *cr* 1876, of The Nash, Kempsey, co. Worcester; Founder and Director, The Temple Gallery, since 1959; *b* 17 Aug. 1937; *er s* of Sir Richard Temple, 4th Bt, MC and Lucy Geils de Lotbinière; *S* father, 2007; *m* 1964, Emma Rose, 2nd *d* of Maj.-Gen. Sir Robert Laycock, KCMG, CB, DSO; three *d*. *Educ*: Stowe. PhD. Lieut, Royal Horse Guards (The Blues), 1958 (Gen. Service Medal, 1958). Lectr, Sch. of Traditional Arts, The Prince's Foundation, 1997–. *Publications*: Icons and the Mystical Origins of Christianity, 1991, 2nd edn 2001; Icons: divine beauty, 2004; The Art of Meditation, 2012; numerous scholarly articles and catalogues. *Recreations*: music, travel, philosophy. *Heir*: *nephew* Nicholas Christopher Lee Temple, *b* 3 Nov. 1986. *E*: richard@templegallery.com. *T*: (020) 7727 3809.

**TEMPLE, Victor Bevis Afoumado;** QC 1993; a Recorder of the Crown Court, 1989–2014; *b* 23 Feb. 1941; *s* of Sir Rawden John Afamado Temple, CBE, QC and Jessie Margaret Wiseman Temple; *m* 1974, Richenda Penn-Bull; two *s*. *Educ*: Shrewsbury Sch.; Inns of Court Sch. of Law. TA, Westminster Dragoons, 1960–61. Marketing Exec., 1960–68. Called to the Bar, Inner Temple, 1971, Bencher, 1996; Jun. Prosecuting Counsel to the Crown, 1985–91, Sen. Treasury Counsel, 1991–93, CCC. DTI Inspector into Nat. Westminster Bank Ltd, 1992. Mem. Panel of Chairmen, Police Discipline Tribunals, 1993–2014. *Recreations*: rowing, carpentry. *Address*: 21 College Hill, EC4R 2RP. *T*: (020) 3301 0910. *Club*: Thames Rowing (Pres., 2009–).

*See also* A. D. A. Temple.

**TEMPLE COX, Richard,** CBE 2002; Chairman: Birmingham and Solihull NHS Local Improvement Finance Trust, 2004–07; Community Regeneration Partnership, 2005–09; *b* 25 Dec. 1937; *s* of Richard G. Cox and Marianne A. Cox (*née* Ladbrook); *m* 1990, Caroline Mary Fauset Jefferson (*née* Welsh); one *s* two *d* from previous marriage. *Educ*: King Edward's Sch., Birmingham; Birmingham Sch. of Architecture (DipArch 1963). RIBA 1964. Secretary: Birmingham Civic Soc., 1964–71; Victorian Soc. W Midlands, 1969–71; Chm., Temple Cox Nicholls Architects, 1970–2000. Pres., Birmingham Architectural Assoc., 1983–84; Royal Institute of British Architects: Council Mem., 1987–93; Sen. Vice Pres., 1989–91; Chm., Educn Cttee, 1989–91. Mem., Construction Industry Council, 1991–94. Chm., Castle Vale HAT, 1992–2005. Mem., Community, Voluntary and Local Services, Cabinet Honours Selection Cttee, 2005–10. Trustee: Birmingham Pub Bombing Lord Mayor's Appeal, 1974; Sense in Midlands, 1988–92; Nat. Council, Deaf Blind Rubella Assoc., 1991–93; Birmingham Dogs Home, 2008–15 (Chm. Trustees, 2010–15); Chm.,

Birmingham Inst. for Deaf, 1976–94; Founder Chm., Access for Disabled, Birmingham, 1986. *Publications*: occasional contribs to RIBA Jl and Regeneration and Renewal. *Recreations*: travel, music, golf, gardening, after-dinner speaking, model railways, military history. *Clubs*: Aberdovey Golf; Droitwich Golf.

**TEMPLE-GORE-LANGTON,** family name of **Earl Temple of Stowe**.

**TEMPLEMAN, Miles Howard;** Director General, Institute of Directors, 2004–11; *b* 4 Oct. 1947; *s* of Robert James and Margot Elizabeth Templeman; *m* 1970, Janet Elizabeth Strang; two *s* one *d*. *Educ*: Haberdashers' Aske's Boys' Sch.; Jesus Coll., Cambridge (BA 1969, MA). Young & Rubicam, 1970–73; Beecham Foods, 1973–79; Levi Strauss, 1979–85; Whitbread, 1985–2000; Chief Exec., Bulmers, 2002–03; Eldridge Pope, 2002–04. Non-executive Director: Ben Sherman, 2000–03; Royal Mail, 2001–03; Shepherd Neame, 2002– (Chm., 2005–Oct. 2020); Portman Gp, 2003; non-exec. Chm., YO! Sushi, 2003–08. *Recreations*: tennis, golf, reading, opera. *Address*: Shepherd Neame, The Faversham Brewery, 17 Court Street, Faversham, Kent ME13 7AX. *Club*: Queen's.

**TEMPLER, Maj.-Gen. James Robert,** CB 1989; OBE 1978 (MBE 1973); Assistant Chief of Defence Staff (Concepts), Ministry of Defence, 1986–89; *b* 8 Jan. 1936; *s* of Brig. Cecil Robert Templer, DSO and Angela Mary Templer (*née* Henderson); *m* 1963 (marr. diss. 1979); two *s* one *d*, 1981, Sarah Ann Evans (*née* Rogers). *Educ*: Charterhouse; RMA Sandhurst. RCDS, psc. Commissioned Royal Artillery, 1955; Instructor, Staff Coll., 1974–75; Comd 42nd Regt, 1975–77; Comd 5th Regt, 1977–78; CRA 2nd Armd Div., 1978–82; RCDS 1983; ACOS Training, HQ UKLF, 1983–86. Man. Dir, Templers Gardening (formerly Templers Flowers), 1990–2017. Mem., British Cross Country Ski Team, 1958; European 3 Day Event Champion, 1962; Mem., British Olympic 3 Day Event Team, 1964. FCMI (FBIM 1988). *Recreations*: sailing, ski-ing, gardening, fishing, DIY. *Address*: Dayspring House, Great Durnford, Salisbury, Wilts SP4 6AZ.

**TEMPLETON, Prof. (Alexander) Allan,** CBE 2009; FRCOG, FRCP, FRCPE, FMedSci; Professor of Obstetrics and Gynaecology, University of Aberdeen, 1985–2012, now Emeritus (Regius Professor of Obstetrics and Gynaecology, 1985–2007); Clinical Director, Office of Research and Clinical Audit, Royal College of Obstetricians and Gynaecologists, 2007–14; *b* 28 June 1946; *s* of Richard and Minnie Templeton; *m* 1980, Gillian Constance Penney; three *s* one *d*. *Educ*: Aberdeen Grammar School; Univ. of Aberdeen (MB ChB 1969; MD Hons 1982). MRCOG 1974, FRCOG 1987; FRCPE 2005; FRCP 2006. Resident and Registrar, Aberdeen Hosps, 1969–75; Lectr and Sen. Lectr, Dept of Obst. and Gyn., Univ. of Edinburgh, 1976–85; Hd, Dept of Obst. and Gyn., Univ. of Aberdeen, 1985–2007. Chm., Soc. for the Study of Fertility, 1996–99; Mem., HFEA, 1995–2000. Hon. Sec., 1998–2004, Pres., 2004–07, RCOG. FMedSci 2002. *Publications*: The Early Days of Pregnancy, 1988; Reproductive Medicine and the Law, 1990; (ed jtly) Infertility, 1992; The Prevention of Pelvic Infection, 1996; Evidence-based Fertility Treatment, 1998; Management of Infertility, 2000; Models of Care in Women's Health, 2009; clinical and sci. articles on human infertility and *in vitro* fertilisation. *Recreations*: west coast of Scotland, mountains, photography. *Address*: Oak Tree Cottage, Leacnasaide, Gairloch, Wester Ross IV21 2AP. *T*: (01445) 741354.

**TEMPLETON, Dr Ian Godfrey;** Warden, Glenalmond College, Perth, 1992–2003; *b* 1 Feb. 1944; *s* of late Anthony Godard Templeton and Mary Gibson Templeton (*née* Carrick Anderson); *m* 1970, Elisabeth Aline Robin; one *s* one *d*. *Educ*: Gordonstoun Sch.; Edinburgh Univ. (MA); Bedford Coll., London Univ. (BA 1st cl. Hons Philosophy); Univ. of Edinburgh (PhD Simon Somerville Laurie 2010). Asst Master, 1969–71, Housemaster, 1971–73, Melville Coll.; Housemaster, Daniel Stewart's and Melville Coll., 1973–78; Asst Headmaster, Robert Gordon's Coll., Aberdeen, 1978–85; Headmaster, Oswestry Sch., 1985–92. *Recreations*: golf, choral singing, travel. *Address*: 18 Craigleith Crescent, Edinburgh EH4 3JL. *T*: (0131) 332 2449. *Clubs*: Royal & Ancient; Bruntsfield Links Golfing Society.

**TENBY,** 3rd Viscount *cr* 1957, of Bulford; **William Lloyd-George;** *b* 7 Nov. 1927; 2nd *s* of 1st Viscount Tenby, TD, PC, and Edna Gwenfron (*d* 1971), *d* of David Jones, Gwynfa, Denbigh; *S* brother, 1983; *m* 1955, Ursula Diana Ethel, *y d* of late Lt-Col Henry Edward Medlicott, DSO; one *s* two *d*. *Educ*: Eastbourne College; St Catharine's Coll., Cambridge (Exhibnr; BA 1949). Captain, Royal Welch Fusiliers, TA. PR Advr, Kleinwort Benson Gp, 1970–87; Consultant, Williams Lea & Co., 1988–93; Chm., St James Public Relations, 1990–93; non-exec. Dir, Ugland Internat. plc, 1993–96. House of Lords: Member: Cttee on Procedure, 1995–98; Cttee of Selection, 1998–2010; Sub-Cttee on Admin and Works, 1992–95; All Party Media Gp; elected Mem., H of L, 1999–2015. JP Hants (Chm., NE Hants (formerly Odiham) Bench, 1990–94). *Heir*: *s* Hon. Timothy Henry Gwilym Lloyd-George, *b* 19 Oct. 1962. *Address*: The White House, Dippenhall Street, Crondall, Farnham, Surrey GU10 5PE.

**TENCH, Leslie Owen;** Chairman, SIG plc, 2004–11 (Deputy Chairman, 2003–04). *Educ*: Univ. of Nottingham (BSc Metallurgy). Steetley plc; Twyfords Bathrooms; Reed International; Procter & Gamble; Managing Director: CRH UK, 1992–98; CRH Europe - Building Products, 1998–2002. Non-executive Director: Shepherd Bldg Gp, 1994–2004; Norcros plc, 2007–12; Tyman plc (formerly Lupus Capital plc), 2009–. *Recreations*: walking, theatre, music, travelling to unusual places.

**TENDLER, Prof. Saul Jonathan Benjamin,** PhD, DSc; Deputy Vice-Chancellor and Provost, University of York, since 2015 (Acting Vice-Chancellor and President, 2018–19); *b* Watford, 26 May 1961; *s* of late Arnold Tendler and Maxine Tendler; *m* 1991, Katherine Kraven; two *s* one *d*. *Educ*: Kingsbury High Sch.; Univ. of Manchester (BSc Pharmacy 1982); Aston Univ. (PhD 1986); Univ. of Nottingham (DSc 2007). MRPharmS 1983, FRPharmS 2000; FRSC 1993. Pre-registration Pharmacist, Westminster Hosp., London, 1982–83; MRC Trng Fellow, NIMR, Mill Hill, 1986–88; University of Nottingham: Lectr in Medicinal Chem., 1988–95; Reader in Biophysical Chem., 1995–98; Prof. of Biophysical Chem., 1998–2015; Dean, Graduate Sch., 1999–2003; Hd, Sch. of Pharmacy, 2003–09; Pro-Vice-Chancellor, 2009–15. Director: Nottingham Univ. Industrial and Commercial Enterprise Ltd, 2006–11; Biocity Ltd, 2006–12; York Sci. Park Ltd, 2016– (Chm., 2017–). Chairman: MRC/EPSRC/BBSRC Discipline Hopping Panel, 2005–12; EPSRC Analytical Sci. Rev., 2006; Member: Biological Methods Gp Cttee, RSC, 1990–96; BBSRC/EPSRC Biomolecular Scis Cttee, 1994–97; BBSRC Engrg and Physical Scis Cttee, 1995–97; BBSRC Engrg and Biological Systems Cttee, 1998–2001; Royal Soc./Royal Acad. of Engrg Nanotechnol. Wkg Gp, 2002–04; HEFCE Strategy Cttee for Res., 2003–08; BBSRC Tools and Resources Strategy Panel, 2006–10; BBSRC Biosci. Skills and Careers Strategy Panel, 2009–10; HEFCE/UUK/Dept for Employment and Learning, NI/GuildHE Quality in Higher Educn Gp, 2010–; UK Healthcare Educn Adv. Cttee, 2013–19. UK Rep., Nanosci. Cttee, 1999–2006, Domain Cttee: Materials, Physical and Nanoscis, 2006–09, EU COST. Non-exec. Dir, Notts Healthcare NHS Trust, 2010–15. Nuffield Foundn Sci. Res. Fellow, 1996–97. Theophilus Redwood Lectr, RSC, 2003. Lilly Prize for Pharmaceutical Excellence, 1994; Sci. Medal, British Pharmaceutical Conf., 1994; SAC Silver Medal, RSC, 1997; Pfizer Prize, 1998; GlaxoSmithKline Internat. Achievement Award, 2003. *Publications*: over 210 papers in learned jls. *Recreations*: sailing, running, walking the dog. *Address*: University of York, Heslington, York YO10 5DD. *T*: (01904) 322055. *E*: saul.tendler@york.ac.uk. *Clubs*: Athenæum; Attenborough Sailing.

**TENDULKAR, Sachin Ramesh,** Bharat Ratna 2014; Padma Vibhushan 2008 (Padma Shri 1999); Member, Rajya Sabha, India, 2012–18; Indian Test cricketer, 1989–2013; *b* Mumbai, 24 April 1973; *m* Anjali; one *s* one *d*. Youngest cricketer (aged 14) to play in Mumbai team in Ranji Trophy 1st cl. cricket tournament; youngest player (aged 15) to score a century in Ranji Trophy; only player to have scored a century on début in all of India's 1st cl. cricket tournaments – Ranji Trophy, Duleep Trophy and Irani Trophy; Test Cricket debut for India against Pakistan, 1989 (aged 16); 2nd youngest player to captain India in Test Cricket (aged 23); captained India in 25 Test matches and 73 limited overs Internats, 1996–97, 1999–2000; second youngest cricketer to have scored a century against England, 1990; first overseas player to play for Yorkshire CCC, 1992; highest aggregate run scorer (2278 runs) in World Cup cricket tournaments; leading run scorer in limited over internationals (18,126 in 463 matches); leading run scorer in Test Cricket (15,921 runs in 200 Tests); highest number of centuries in limited over internationals (49) and Test Cricket (51); first player to score 100 internat. centuries, 2012; first male cricketer to score a double hundred in limited over internationals, 2010. First sportsperson, and youngest person, awarded Bharat Ratna, 2014. Chatrapati Shivaji Award, 1990–91, Maharashtra Bhushan, 2001, Maharashtra State. Arjuna Award (India), 1994; Rajiv Gandhi Khel Ratna Award (India), 1998. *Publications:* Playing it My Way (autobiog.), 2014. *Address:* 19A Perry Cross Road, Bandra West, Mumbai 400050, India.

**TENENBAUM, Jane Elaine;** *see* Lush, J. E.

**TENET, George John;** Managing Director, Allen & Company LLC, since 2007; *b* 5 Jan. 1953; *m* A. Stephanie Glakas; one *s*. *Educ:* Georgetown Univ., Washington; Columbia Univ., NY (MIA 1978). Legislative Asst specialising in nat. security and energy issues, then Legislative Dir to Senator H. John Heinz, III; Designee to Vice Chm., Senator Patrick J. Leahy, 1985–86; Dir, Oversight of Arms Control Negotiations between Soviet Union and US, then Staff Dir, Senate Select Cttee on Intelligence, 1986–93; National Security Council: Mem., Presidential Transition Team, 1993; Special Asst to Pres. and Sen. Dir for Intelligence Programs, 1993–95; Dep. Dir, CIA, 1995–97; Dir, CIA, 1997–2004; Prof. of Diplomacy, Georgetown Univ., Washington, DC, 2004–07. Non-executive Director: Guidance Software, 2005–08; L-1 Identity Solutions, 2005–08; QinetiQ, 2006–08; QinetiQ North America, 2008. Presidential Medal of Freedom, USA, 2004. *Publications:* The Ability of US Intelligence to Monitor the Intermediate Nuclear Force Treaty; At the Center of the Storm: my years at the CIA (memoirs), 2007.

**TENISON;** *see* Hanbury-Tenison.

**TENISON;** *see* King-Tenison.

**TENNANT,** family name of **Baron Glenconner**.

**TENNANT, David;** *see* McDonald, D. J.

**TENNANT, Lady Emma;** Chairman, National Trust Gardens Advisory Panel, 1984–2001; Member, Council, National Trust, 1990–2002; *b* 26 March 1943; *d* of 11th Duke of Devonshire, KG, MC, PC and Dowager Duchess of Devonshire, DCVO; *m* 1963, Hon. Tobias William Tennant, *y s* of 2nd Baron Glenconner; one *s* two *d*. *Educ:* St Elphin's Sch., Darley Dale; St Anne's Coll., Oxford (BA History 1963). *Publications:* Rag Rugs, 1992. *Recreations:* gardening, painting. *Address:* Shaws, Newcastleton, Roxburghshire TD9 0SH. *T:* (01387) 376241.

**TENNANT, Helen Anne, (Lena);** Lecturer, Faculty of Education, University of Glasgow (formerly St Andrew's College, Glasgow), 1989–2004; *b* 15 Dec. 1943; *d* of late Joseph Dawson and Anna Dawson (*née* Giavarini); *m* 1975, Gerard E. Tennant; three *s* one *d*. *Educ:* St Mary's Acad., Bathgate; Notre Dame Coll. of Education, Glasgow (DipCE); RSAMD (Dip. Speech and Drama). Lectr in Speech and Drama, Notre Dame Coll. of Educn, Glasgow, 1969–75; extra-mural Lectr, St Peter's Seminary, Cardross, subseq. Glasgow, 1972–92; part-time Lectr, Coatbridge Coll., 1983–89. Member: Viewer's Consultative Council (Scotland), 1989–94; Radio Authy, 1995–2000. *Recreations:* theatre-going, playing church organ.

**TENNANT of Balfluig, Mark Iain;** Master of the Supreme Court, Queen's Bench Division, 1988–2005; Baron of Balfluig; *b* 4 Dec. 1932; *s* of late Major John Tennant, TD, KStJ and Hon. Antonia Mary Roby Benson, *d* of 1st Baron Charnwood and later Viscountess Radcliffe; *m* 1965, Lady Harriot Pleydell-Bouverie, *y d* of 7th Earl of Radnor, KG, KCVO; one *s* one *d*. *Educ:* Eton College; New College, Oxford (MA 1959). Lieut, The Rifle Brigade (SRO). Called to the Bar, Inner Temple, 1958, Bencher, 1984; Recorder, 1987–96. Restored Balfluig Castle (barony of Balfluig *cr* Charles II, 1650), dated 1556 in 1967 (the first to obtain a grant from Historic Bldgs Council for Scotland for bldg not inhabited or inhabitable). Chm., Royal Orchestral Soc. (formerly for Amateur Musicians), 1989–2009 (Pres., 2009–). *Recreations:* music, architecture, books. *Address:* Balfluig Castle, Aberdeenshire AB33 8EJ; 30 Abbey Gardens, NW8 9AT. *T:* (020) 7624 3200. *Club:* Brooks's.

**TENNANT, Michael Humphrey;** a District Judge, 1992–2008; President, Association of District Judges, 2007–08; *b* 11 Sept. 1942; *s* of Norman Humphrey Tennant and Marjorie Lillian Tennant (*née* Coles); *m* 1st, 1965, Kathleen Nicolette Chapman (marr. diss. 1998); two *d*; 2nd, 1998, June Mary Dixon. *Educ:* Bedford Modern Sch.; University College London (LLB Hons 1963). Admitted solicitor, 1966; Partner, Damant & Sons, 1969–84; High Court District Registrar and County Court Registrar, 1984; Asst Recorder, 1989; a Recorder, 1992. *Recreations:* music—listening to classical (mostly instrumental) and jazz and playing piano (classical), sailing—racing own National Sonata nationally and internationally, defending occasional hard-won sailing trophies, cruising wherever possible when time permits. *Address:* Chazey House, Salisbury Road, Sherfield English, Hants SO51 6FQ. *T:* (01794) 323344. *Clubs:* Sloane; Island Sailing (Cdre, 1989–92).

**TENNANT, Maj.-Gen. Michael Trenchard,** CB 1994; Army Adviser, British Aerospace, 1998–2001; *b* 3 Sept. 1941; *s* of Lt-Col Hugh Trenchard Tennant, MC and Mary Isobel Tennant (*née* Wilkie); *m* 1st, 1964, Susan Daphne (*d* 1993), *d* of late Lt-Col Frank Beale, LVO; three *s*; 2nd, 1996, Jacqueline Mary Parish (*née* ap Ellis), *widow* of David Parish; two step *d*. *Educ:* Wellington College. psc†. Commissioned RA 1961; served Bahrain, Aden, BAOR, Hong Kong, UK, 1962–71; Staff College, 1972–73; MoD, 1974–75; Bty Comdr, 127 (Dragon) Bty, BAOR, 1976–78; Directing Staff, Staff Coll., 1978–80; CO, 1 RHA, UK and BAOR, 1980–83; Comdr British Training Team, Nigeria, 1983–85; CRA 3 Armd Div., BAOR, 1985–87; CRA UKLF, 1988–91; Dir, RA, 1991–94. Hd of External Commns, Royal Ordnance Div., BAe, 1994–98. Col Comdt, RA, 1994–2005; Hon. Col, 1 RHA, 1994–99. Chm., CCF Assoc., 1996–2003. President: Army Cricket, 1992–93; RA Golf Soc., 1998–2012. *Recreations:* bridge, golf. *Clubs:* Fadeaways; Denham Golf, Rye Golf, Senior Golfers.

**TENNANT, Paul,** OBE 2015; Chief Executive, Law Society, since 2018 (Interim Chief Executive, 2017–18); *b* Sunderland, 21 April 1951; *s* of Alan and Frances Tennant; *m* Suzanne Foster; one *s* one *d*. *Educ:* St Aiden Sch. BA Hons. Sunderland BC, 1982–84; Guinness Trust, 1984–85; Orbit Gp, 1985–91; PMSL Ltd, 1991–94; Regl Dir, RBL Housing Assoc., 1994–97; Man. Dir, English Churches Housing Gp, 1997–2000; Chief Executive: Leeds Federated Housing Assoc., 2000–03; Orbit Gp, 2003–16. Formerly Chair, Housing Assocs Charitable Trust; Chair, Bd, Reallies, 2017; Co-Chair, Rethinking Social Housing, 2018. Pres., Chartered Inst. of Housing, 2013–14 (Mem. Bd, Canada). *Recreations:* Sunderland AFC fan, sport, music, reading. *Address:* Law Society, Law Society's Hall, 113 Chancery Lane, WC2A 1PL. *T:* (020) 8049 3996. *E:* paul.tennant@lawsociety.org.uk.

**TENNANT, Veronica,** CC 2003 (OC 1975); FRSC; ballet dancer, broadcaster and writer; *b* London, 15 Jan. 1947; *d* of Harry Tennant and Doris Tennant (Bassous); *m* 1969, Dr John Robert Wright; one *d*. *Educ:* Bishop Strachan Sch., Toronto; National Ballet Sch., Toronto. Prima Ballerina, Nat. Ballet of Canada, 1965–89; major performances include: début, Juliet in Romeo and Juliet, with Earl Kraul, 1965; Pulcinella, Triptych; Les Rendezvous; Solitaire; Swan Lake; The Lesson; Cinderella; Kraanerg (created leading rôle); Le Loup; La Sylphide; première perf. as Princess Aurora with Rudolf Nureyev in his Sleeping Beauty, 1972; La Sylphide, with Mikhail Baryshnikov, 1974; Giselle, with Rudolf Nureyev, 1974; Swanhilda in Coppelia, 1975; Washington Square, with Peter Schaufuss, 1978; La Fille Mal Gardée, 1979, and Le Corsaire Pas de Deux, 1980, with Peter Schaufuss; Napoli; The Dream, with Anthony Dowell, 1981; début, Tatiana in Onegin, with Raymond Smith, 1985; farewell perfs, Romeo and Juliet, with Raymond Smith and A Passion for Dance: Celebrating the Tennant Magic (gala tribute), 1989; film maker and writer, 1989–; host and consultant/writer, Sunday Arts Entertainment CBC TV, 1989–92; producer and dir for CBC Television and Bravo!FACT; founded Veronica Tennant Prodns, 1998; television producer: Salute to Dancers for Life, 1994; Margie Gillis: Wild Hearts in Strange Times, 1996; Governor General's Performing Arts Awards Gala, 2000; The Four Seasons, 2000; The Curse of Clara: a holiday tale, 2016; television producer and director: Mavis Staines— "Courage…", 1998; Karen Kain: Dancing in the Moment, 1999 (Internat. Emmy Award for Perf. Arts); Song of Songs, 1999; The Dancers' Story: the National Ballet of Canada, 2002; Northern Light: Visions and Dreams, 2003; A Pairing of SwanS, 2004; Shadow Pleasures, 2004; A Pair of RED Shorts, 2005; Celia Franca: Tour de Force, 2006; Vida y Danza, Cuba, 2008; Finding Body & Soul, 2009; conceived and Director: Something's Coming!, 2013; Niágara: a Pan-American Story, 2015. Dancers' Rep., Bd of Dirs, Nat. Ballet Co., 1972, 1984; Director: Ontario Arts Council, 1975–78; Toronto Arts Awards Foundn, 1988–90; Glenn Gould Foundn, 1989–92; Dancer Transition Centre, 1992–95; Governor General's Performing Arts Awards, 1992–95; Member, Board of Directors: City of Toronto Olympic Bid 2008, 1998 (Chm., Arts and Culture Cttee, 1998–2000); REEL Canada, 2010–. Adjunct Prof., Fine Arts, 1989–2004, Fellow, Winters Coll., 1991–99, York Univ. Nat. Ambassador for UNICEF, 1992–. FRSC 2006. Hon. DLitt: Brock, 1985; McGill, 2005; Hon. LLD: York, 1987; Simon Fraser, 1992; Toronto, 1992. Walter Carsen Prize for Excellence in the Performing Arts, 2000; Queen's Diamond Jubilee Medal, 2012. *Publications:* On Stage, Please, 1977; The Nutcracker, 1986; articles in Toronto Star, Dance International, Saturday Night Mag. and The Globe and Mail.

**TENNET, Michael John;** QC 2006; barrister; *b* 18 Jan. 1963; *s* of Brian and Margaret Tennet; *m* 1998, Jessica; two *s*. *Educ:* Solihull Sixth Form Coll.; New Coll., Oxford (MA 1st cl. Law 1984). Called to the Bar, Inner Temple, 1985; barrister, 1986–. *Publications:* (contrib.) Professional Negligence and Liability; (contrib.) International Trust Laws. *Recreations:* golf, tennis, Tottenham Hotspur Football Club. *Address:* Wilberforce Chambers, 8 New Square, Lincoln's Inn, WC2A 3QP. *T:* (020) 7306 0802. *E:* mtennet@wilberforce.co.uk.

**TENNYSON,** family name of **Baron Tennyson**.

**TENNYSON, 6th Baron** *cr* 1884; **David Harold Alexander Tennyson;** *b* 4 June 1960; *s* of James Alfred Tennyson, *ggs* of 1st Baron Tennyson, and of Beatrice Aventon (*née* Young); *S* cousin, 2006. *Educ:* Univ. of Canterbury, NZ (ME). *Heir: b* Alan James Drummond Tennyson [*b* 28 Jan. 1965; *m* 1998, Susanna Ruth Brow (marr. diss. 2006); one *s*; one *s* by Maria Elizabeth Walker].

**TENNYSON, Prof. (Charles) Jonathan (Penrose),** DPhil; FRS 2009; Massey Professor of Physics, University College London, since 2005 (Head, Department of Physics and Astronomy, 2004–11); Chief Scientist, Quantemol Ltd, since 2004; Chair, Blue Skies Space Ltd, since 2014; *b* Hitchin, 11 May 1955; *s* of late (Beryl) Hallam (Augustine) Tennyson and Margot Tennyson (*née* Wallach); *m* 1983, Janice Hopson; three *s* one *d*. *Educ:* Bootham Sch., York; King's Coll., Cambridge (BA 1977); Univ. of Sussex (DPhil 1980). Royal Soc. W Eur. Exchange Fellow, Univ. of Nijmegen, 1980–82; SO, SERC Daresbury Lab., 1982–85; University College London: Lectr, 1985–91; Reader, 1991–94; Prof., 1994–. Vis. Scientist, Inst. for Theoretical Atomic Molecular and Optical Physics, Harvard Univ., 1995–96. JILA Fellow, 1996. Chm., Hackney Chess Club, 2007–. *Publications:* Astronomical Spectroscopy, 2005, 3rd edn 2019; approx. 750 scientific papers. *Recreations:* chess, Tottenham Hotspurs. *Address:* Department of Physics and Astronomy, University College London, WC1E 6BT. *T:* (office) (020) 7679 7809, (home) (020) 8341 0923. *E:* j.tennyson@ucl.ac.uk.

**TENNYSON, Prof. Jonathan;** *see* Tennyson, Prof. C. J. P.

**TENNYSON-d'EYNCOURT, Sir Mark (Gervais),** 5th Bt *cr* 1930, of Carter's Corner Farm, Herstmonceux; *b* 12 March 1967; *o s* of Sir Giles Gervais Tennyson-d'Eyncourt, 4th Bt and of Juanita, *d* of late Fortunato Borromeo; *S* father, 1989. *Educ:* Charterhouse; Kingston Polytechnic (BA Hons Fashion). Freeman, City of London, 1989. *Heir:* none.

**TENREYRO, Prof. Silvana,** PhD; FBA 2018; Professor of Economics, London School of Economics and Political Science, since 2012; Member, External Monetary Policy Committee, Bank of England, since 2017; *b* Argentina, 6 Sept. 1973; *m* 2003, Francesco Caselli; two *s*. *Educ:* Nat. Univ. of Tucuman, Argentina (BA Econs *summa cum laude* 1997); Harvard Univ. (MA 1999; PhD Econs 2002). Economist, Fed. Reserve Bank of Boston, 2002–04; Lectr, 2004–07, Reader, 2008–12, LSE. Ext. Mem., Monetary Policy Cttee, Central Bank of Mauritius, 2012–14; Acad. Visitor, Bank of England, 2016–17. Mem. Council, Eur. Econ. Assoc., 2010–15; Royal Economic Society: Member: Council, 2015–; Exec. Cttee, 2016–17; Chair, Women's Cttee, 2016–17. *Publications:* contribs to jls incl. Jl Internat. Econs, Jl Econ. Perspectives, Amer. Econ. Rev., Qly Jl Econs. *Recreations:* family, sports, music, travelling, reading. *T:* 07891 181959. *E:* s.tenreyro@lse.ac.uk.

**TENZIN GYATSO; The Dalai Lama XIV;** spiritual and temporal leader of Tibet, since 1940; *b* 6 July 1935; named Lhamo Thondup; *s* of Chokyong Tsering and Diki Tsering. *Educ:* Monasteries of Sera, Drepung and Gaden, Lhasa; traditional Tibetan degree equivalent to Dr in Buddhist philosophy, 1959. Enthroned Dalai Lama, Lhasa, 1940; given name Jetsun Jampel Ngawang Losang Yeshi Tenzin Gyatso Sisum Wang-gyur Tsungpa Mepai De Pel Sangpo. Fled to Chumbi, South Tibet, on Chinese invasion, 1950; negotiated with China, 1951; fled to India after abortive revolt of Tibetan people against Communist Chinese, 1959, and established govt-in-exile in Dharamsala; stood down as political leader, 2011. Awards include: Magsaysay, Philippines, 1959; Lincoln, USA, 1960; Albert Schweitzer Humanitarian, USA, 1987; Congressional Gold Medal, USA, 2006; Templeton Prize, 2012; numerous other awards, hon. doctorates, hon. citizenships from France, Germany, India, Mongolia, Norway, USA; Nobel Peace Prize, 1989. *Publications:* My Land and My People (autobiog.), 1962; The Opening of the Wisdom Eye, 1963; An Introduction to Buddhism, 1965; Key to the Middle Way, 1971; Universal Responsibility and Good Heart, 1977; Four Essential Buddhist Commentaries, 1982; A Human Approach to World Peace, 1984; Kindness, Clarity and Insight, 1987; Freedom in Exile (autobiog.), 1990; The Good Heart, 1996; Ethics for the New Millennium, 1998; Ancient Wisdom, Modern World, 1999; A Simple Path, 2000; Advice on Dying, 2002; (jtly) The Art of Happiness at Work, 2003; (jtly) The Wisdom of Forgiveness, 2005; Beyond Religion: ethics for a whole world, 2012. *Address:* Thekchen Choeling, PO Mcleod Ganj, Dharamsala, HP 176219, India.

**TEO, Jan;** Managing Director, National Windscreens, since 2018; *b* Marylebone, London, Jan. 1970; *g d* of George Ernest Jeffs and Florence May Jeffs; *m* 2000, Charles Edward Watts. *Educ:* New Hall, Cambridge (BA Hist. 1992). Grad. trainee, 1992–94; Gen. Manager, Internat. Currency Exchange, 1994–98; Ops Manager, Investment Admin, Legal & General, 1998–2000; Product Gp Manager, Barclays, 2000–01; Hd, Customer Ops, RAC, 2001–04; Service Dir, Lex Transfleet, 2004–06; Business Transformation Dir, Fraikin, 2006–09; Chief Operating Officer, Business Services Europe, Deutsche Bank, 2009–14; CEO, Birmingham Royal Ballet, 2015–18. Director: Birmingham Mus Trust, 2012–; Birmingham Royal Ballet, 2014–15. Gov., Elmhurst Sch. for Dance, 2015–16. *Recreations:* history, museums and galleries, ballet, playing the piano, collecting things I don't need.

**TEO Eng Cheng, Michael;** High Commissioner of Singapore to Australia, 2011–14; *b* 19 Sept. 1947; *m* Joyce; one *s* one *d*. *Educ:* Auburn Univ., USA (BSc Business Admin); Fletcher Sch. of Law and Diplomacy, Tufts Univ., USA (MA). Joined Republic of Singapore Air Force, 1968: Comdr, 1985; Dist. Grad., USAF War Coll., 1985; Brig.-Gen., 1987; Chief of Air Force, 1990; High Comr to NZ, 1994–96; Ambassador, Republic of Korea, 1996–2001; High Comr to UK, and concurrently Ambassador to Ireland, 2001–11. FRAeS 2008. Gold Public Admin Medal (Mil.) (Singapore), 1989; Most Noble Order of Crown (Thailand), 1981; Outstanding Achievement Award (Philippines), 1989; Bintang Swa Bhuana Paksa Utama (Indonesia), 1991; Comdr, Legion of Merit (USA), 1991; Gwanghwa Medal (Korea), 2002. *Recreations:* golf, hiking, reading.

**TEPARAK, Pasan;** Ambassador of Thailand to the Court of St James's, 2012–14; *b* 30 Jan. 1961; *m* 1991, Paradee Tesavibul; two *s*. *Educ:* Satit Pathumwan Sch., Bangkok; Carlsbad High Sch., Carlsbad, Calif; Thammasat Univ., Bangkok (BA Internat. Relns; MA Public Admin). Joined Thai Foreign Service, 1984; Consul-Gen. of Thailand, Dubai, 2006–11; Minister, Royal Thai Embassy, Canberra, 2011; Ambassador attached to Min. of Foreign Affairs and assigned to the Prime Minister, 2011–12. Member, Board of Directors: Government Savings Bank, 2011–12; Krungthai Bank Public Co., 2012 (Mem., Bd of Exec. Dirs, 2012); EGCO Public Co., 2012–13 (Mem., Audit Cttee, 2012–13). Silver Medal (7th Class), Direkgunabhorn (Thailand), 2005; Kt Grand Cross (1st Class), Order of the White Elephant (Thailand), 2006; Chakrabarti Mala Medal (Thailand), 2009; Kt Grand Cordon (Special Class), Order of the Crown of Thailand, 2011; decorations from the Netherlands, Sweden, Brunei Darussalam and Denmark. *Recreations:* golf, reading. *Club:* Brocket Hall Golf.

**TERESHKOVA, Valentina Vladimirovna;** Russian cosmonaut; Chairman, Russian Association of International Co-operation, 1992–95; Head, Russian Centre for International Scientific and Cultural Co-operation, Russian Federation, 1994–2004; Deputy Chairman, Committee on International Affairs, State Duma, Russian Federation, since 2011; *b* Maslennikovo, 6 March 1937; *d* of late Vladimir Aksyonovich Tereshkov and of Elena Fyodorovna Tereshkova; *m*; one *d*. Formerly textile worker, Krasny Perekop mill, Yaroslavl; served on cttees; Sec. of local branch, Young Communist league, 1960; Member: CPSU, 1962–91; Central Cttee, CPSU, 1971–90; Deputy, 1966–90, Mem. of Presidium, 1970–90, USSR Supreme Soviet; Chairperson: Soviet Women's Cttee, 1968–87; Union of Soviet Societies for Friendship and Cultural Relns with Foreign Countries, 1987–92. Joined Yaroslavl Air Sports Club, 1959, and started parachute jumping; joined Cosmonaut Training Unit, 1962; became first woman in the world to enter space when she made 48 orbital flights of the earth in spaceship Vostok VI, 16–19 June 1963. Hero of the Soviet Union; Order of Lenin; Gold Star Medal; Order of October Revolution; Joliot-Curie Peace Medal; Nile Collar (Egypt), 1971; holds honours and citations from other countries. *Address:* 10 Granatny Pereulok, 123001 Moscow, Russia.

**TERFEL, Sir Bryn;** *see* Jones, Sir B. T.

**ter HAAR, Rev. Roger Eduard Lound;** QC 1992; a Recorder, and Deputy High Court Judge, since 2003; *b* 14 June 1952; *s* of late Dirk ter Haar and Christine Janet ter Haar; *m* 1st, 1977, Sarah Anne Martyn (marr. diss. 2012); two *s* one *d*; 2nd, 2014, Charlotte Mary Elizabeth Barney (*née* Raeburn). *Educ:* Felsted Sch.; Magdalen Coll., Oxford (BA 1973). Called to the Bar, Inner Temple, 1974, Bencher, 1992. Ordained deacon, 2006, priest, 2007; OLM, Bramley and Graffham, 2006–07; Asst Priest, Hascombe and Dunsfold, 2007–13. *Publications:* (ed jtly) Construction Insurance and UK Construction Contracts, 2nd edn 2008 to 3rd edn 2016; (jtly) Remedies in Construction Law, 2010, 2nd edn 2017. *Recreations:* gardening, reading. *Address:* Crown Office Chambers, 2 Crown Office Row, Temple, EC4Y 7HJ. *T:* (020) 7797 8100. *Clubs:* Brooks's, Garrick.

**TERRACCIANO, Pasquale;** Ambassador of Italy to Russia, since 2018; *b* Naples, 4 May 1956; *s* of late Silvio Terracciano and of Maria Terracciano (*née* Racana); *m* 1991, Karen Lawrence; two *s* one *d*. *Educ:* Univ. of Naples (law degree). Entered Italian Diplomatic Service, 1981; Second Sec., HR Directorate, Min. of Foreign Affairs, 1982–85; Consul, Rio de Janeiro, 1985–89; First Sec., later Counsellor, Perm. Repn of Italy to NATO, Brussels, 1989–93; Counsellor, Econ. Affairs Directorate, Min. of Foreign Affairs, 1993–95; Counsellor and Private Sec. to Foreign Minister, 1995–96; Counsellor, later First Counsellor, London and Alt. Exec. Dir for Italy, EBRD, 1996–2000; First Counsellor, Perm. Repn to Atlantic Council, Brussels, 2000–01; Dep. Hd of Cabinet to Foreign Minister, 2001–04; Hd, Inf. and Press Office, Min. of Foreign Affairs and spokesman for Foreign Minister, 2004–06; Ambassador to Madrid, also Andorra, 2006–10; Hd, Cabinet of Foreign Minister, 2010–11; Diplomatic Advr to Prime Minister and Prime Minister's G6 and G20 Sherpa Rep., 2011–13; Ambassador to UK, 2013–18. Cavaliere: Gran Croce di Giustizia Sacro Militare Ordine Costantiniano di San Giorgio, 2007; Gran Croce dell'Ordine al Merito della Repubblica Italiana, 2013. Gran Cruz, Orden de Isabel la Católica (Spain), 2011. *Recreations:* going to the opera, classical music. *Address:* Italian Embassy, Villa Berg, Denezhny Pereulok 5, 115127 Moscow, Russia. *E:* ambassador.mosca@esteri.it.

**TERRELL, Prof. (Richard) Deane,** AO 2002; PhD; Vice-Chancellor, 1994–2000, now Emeritus Professor and Visiting Fellow, College of Business and Economics, Australian National University; *b* 22 April 1936; *s* of Norman Walter Terrell and Dorothy Ismay Terrell; *m* 1961, Jennifer Anne Kathleen, *d* of Leonard Spencer and Margaret Rose Doman; two *s* one *d*. *Educ:* St Peter's Coll., Adelaide; Adelaide Univ. (Joseph Fisher Medal, 1958; Rhodes Scholar, 1959; BEc Hons); Oxford Univ.; ANU (PhD). Teaching appts, Univ. of Adelaide and MIT, 1959–64; Australian National University: Lectr, 1964–70; Sen. Lectr, Stats, 1970; Prof. of Econometrics, 1971–89; Dean, Faculty of Econs and Commerce, 1975–77, 1982–89; Head, Dept of Stats, 1979–82, 1989–91; Chm., Bd of Faculties, 1989–92; Acting Dep. Vice-Chancellor, and Dep. Vice-Chancellor, 1991–93; Mem., Adv. Bd, Centre for Arab Islamic Studies, 2001–. Visiting Professor: Pennsylvania, 1969; Princeton and LSE, 1972–73. Chm., Bd of Mgt, AARNet Pty Ltd, 2002–11; Vice-Pres., IDP Educn Australia, 1995–2004. Chm. Bd, IELTS (Aust.) Pty Ltd, 2002–07; Bd Mem., Gen. Sir John Monash Foundn, 2002–13 (Mem., Awards Cttee, 2002–13; Chm., Investment Cttee, 2002–13). Chm. and Principal Dir, Canberra Sch. of Music Foundn, 2004–; Chm., Canberra Symphony Orch., 2008–13 (Dep. Chm., 2006–08). Mem. Adv. Bd, Aust. Defence Coll., 2004–09. *Publications:* numerous articles in professional jls. *Recreations:* farming and grape growing, football, cricket. *Address:* c/o School of Finance, Actuarial Studies and Applied Statistics, Australian National University College of Business and Economics, CBE Building 26C, Kingsley Street, Canberra, ACT 0200, Australia. *Club:* Commonwealth (Canberra).

**TERRINGTON,** 6th Baron *cr* 1918, of Huddersfield, co. York; **Christopher Richard James Woodhouse,** FRCS; Professor of Adolescent Urology, University College London, 2005–11, now Emeritus; Consultant Urologist, Royal Marsden Hospital, 1981–2014; *b* 20 Sept. 1946; *s* of 5th Baron Terrington, DSO, OBE and Lady Davina Woodhouse (*née* Lytton), *widow* of 5th Earl of Erne; *S* father, 2001; *m* 1975, Hon. Anna Philipps, *d* of 3rd Baron Milford; one *s* one *d*. *Educ:* Winchester; Guy's Hosp. Med. Sch. (MB, BS 1970). FRCS 1975. Sen. Registrar in Urology, Inst. of Urology and St Peter's Hosps, 1977–81; Sen. Lectr in Urology, Inst. of Urology, 1981–97; Reader in Adolescent Urology, UCL, 1997–2005. Consultant Urologist, St George's Hosp., 1985–95; Clin. Dir of Urology, UCL Hosps, 2001–03. Hon. Consultant Urologist: Inst. of Urology, University Coll. London Hosps (formerly St Peter's Hosps), 1981–2012; Hosp. for Children, Great Ormond Street, 1981–2012. Vis. Professorships in Europe, USA and Australasia. Fellow, European Bd of Urology, 1993. Pres., Soc. of Genito-Urinary Reconstructive Surgeons, USA, 2002–03. Corresp. Member: German Assoc. of Urology, 2004; American Assoc. of Genito-Urinary Surgeons, 2005; Special Internat. Mem., Amer. Urological Assoc., 2012; Hon. Mem., Urological Soc. of Australia and NZ (formerly Australasian Urological Assoc.), 1999. Chm., Bd of Govs, Harris Acad. Sutton, 2018–. *Publications:* (with F. D. Thompson) Physiological Basis of Medicine: disorders of the kidney and urinary tract, 1987; Long Term Paediatric Urology, 1991; (jtly) Management of Urological Emergencies, 2004; Adolescent Urology and Long Term Outcomes, 2015; (with A. Kirkham) Radiology and Follow-Up of Urologic Surgery, 2017; contrib. to learned jls. *Recreations:* gardening, walking. *Heir:* *s* Hon. Jack Henry Lehmann Woodhouse, *b* 7 Dec. 1978. *Address:* Chelsea Urology, Lister House, Chelsea Bridge Road, SW1W 8RH. *T:* (020) 3701 7025. *E:* c.terrington@btinternet.com. *Club:* Leander (Henley-on-Thames).

*See also* Hon. N. M. J. Woodhouse.

**TERRY, Air Marshal Sir Colin George,** KBE 1998 (OBE 1983); CB 1995; DL; CEng; FREng; FRAeS; FCGI; FCILT; FIC; aerospace consultant; Executive Chairman, Centronic Group, 2016–18; non-executive Chairman, Centronic Ltd, 2016–18; *b* 8 Aug. 1943; *e s* of late George Albert Terry and Edna Joan Terry (*née* Purslow); *m* 1966, Gillian, *d* of late Conrad Glendor Grindley and Muriel Grace Grindley (*née* Duffield); two *s* one *d*. *Educ:* Bridgnorth Grammar Sch.; RAF Coll.; Imperial Coll., London (BScEng (Hons) 1965; FIC 2005). CEng; FRAeS 1986; FCGI 1997; FREng 2001. Commnd, Engr Br., RAF, 1962; served Abingdon, RAF Coll., Church Fenton, Leeming, Oakington, Finningley, RNAY Belfast, Laarbruch, Wildenrath, HQ Strike Comd; Student, RAF Coll., 1979; OC Eng Wing, RAF Coltishall, 1979–82; Eng Authy Staff, HQ Strike Comd, 1982–84; OC Eng Wing, RAF Stanley, 1982–83; Dep. Comd Engr, HQ Strike Comd, 1985–86; Station Comdr, RAF Abingdon, 1986–88; RCDS 1989; Dir, Support Management and Sen. Dir, MoD Harrogate, 1990–92; Dir Gen., Support Management, RAF, 1993–95; COS and Dep. C-in-C, Logistics Comd, RAF, 1995–97; AOC-in-C, Logistics Comd and Air Mem. for Logistics, RAF, 1997–99; Chief Engr (RAF), 1996–99. Chm., Safety Advisory Cttee, Military Aviation Authy, MoD, 2011–16. Gp Man. Dir, Inflite Engrg Services Ltd, 1999–2001; Adv. Bd, Kingfisher Airlines, Mumbai, 2006–10; non-executive Chairman: Meggitt plc, 2004–15; Avia Media Tech Ltd, 2013–16; Boxarr Ltd, 2017–; Conrad Grindley LLP, 2017–; non-executive Director: Fox Marble Plc, 2011–; Aveillant Ltd, 2014–17. Advr to Bd, Horton Internat., 2010–12. Chm., Engineering Council, 2002–06 (Mem. of Senate, 1999–2002); President: RAeS, 2005–06 (Mem. Council, 1999–2007; Chm., Learned Soc. Bd, 2003–06); Council of European Aerospace Socs, 2006–07; Member: ETB, 2002–06; Queen's Awards for Enterprise Cttee, 2002–06. FRSA; FILog. Commodore, RAF Sailing Assoc., 1994–99; Pres., Assoc. of Service Yacht Clubs, 1997–99; Flying Officer, RAFVR(T), 1999–2008. Pres., SSAFA Bucks, 2006–18. Member, Council: CGLI, 2004–08; Cranfield Univ., 2005–08 (Mem. Court, 1997–); Pres., C & G Coll. Assoc., 2003–04. Freeman, City of London, 2004. DL Bucks, 2005. *Recreations:* sailing, flying, ski-ing, modern languages, music, field sports. *Address:* c/o Royal Air Force Club, 128 Piccadilly, W1J 7PY. *Club:* Royal Air Force.

**TERRY, Ian Keith;** Mediator, One Essex Court, since 2016; Partner, Freshfields Bruckhaus Deringer (formerly Freshfields), 1986–2016; *b* 26 July 1955; *s* of late Keith Harold Terry and Shirley Margaret Terry; *m* 1993, Dr Elizabeth Ann Fischl; one *d*. *Educ:* Leeds Grammar Sch.; Keble Coll., Oxford (MA, BCL). Freshfields: trainee solicitor, 1978–80; admitted solicitor, 1980; Partner (Commercial Litigation), 1986–96; Managing Partner, worldwide, 1996–2001; Practice Gp Leader, Dispute Resolution, 2006–09. *Recreations:* shooting, ski-ing, theatre, opera.

**TERRY, John George;** professional footballer; Joint Assistant Head Coach, Aston Villa Football Club, since 2018; *b* Barking, 7 Dec. 1980; *s* of Ted and Sue Terry; *m* 2007, Toni Poole; one *s* one *d* (twins). Chelsea Football Club: mem., Youth Team, 1995–98, First Team, 1998–99 and 2000–17 (Captain, 2004–17); member, winning team: FA Cup, 2000, 2007, 2009, 2010, 2012; Premier League, 2005, 2006, 2010; League Cup, 2005, 2007; UEFA Champions League, 2012; UEFA Europa League, 2013; team mem., Nottingham Forest FC, 1999–2000; Capt., England Under 21s, 2001–02; team mem., England, 2003–12 (Captain, 2007–10 and 2011–12); Mem., England squad, Eur. Championships, 2004, 2012, World Cup, 2006, 2010; team mem., Aston Villa FC, 2017–18. Player of Year, PFA, 2005. *Publications:* John Terry: my winning season, 2005. *Address:* c/o Aston Villa Football Club, Villa Park, Birmingham B6 6HE.

**TERRY, (John) Quinlan,** CBE 2015; FRIBA 1962; architect in private practice, since 1967; *b* 24 July 1937; *s* of Philip and Phyllis Terry; *m* 1961, Christine de Ruttié; one *s* four *d*. *Educ:* Bryanston School; Architectural Association; Rome Scholar. Assistant to Raymond Erith, RA, FRIBA, 1962, Partner 1967–, Erith & Terry, subseq. Quinlan & Francis Terry, then Quinlan Terry; work includes: new Infirmary, Royal Hospital Chelsea; offices, shops and flats at Richmond Riverside; 20–32 Baker Street; 264–7 Tottenham Court Road; new retail bldgs in historic centre of Colonial Williamsburg, Va; six classical Villas in Regent's Park for Crown Estate Comrs; new Library, Lecture Theatre, and Residential Bldg, Downing Coll., Cambridge; new Brentwood Cathedral; restoration of the three State Drawing Rooms, 10 Downing Street; restoration of St Helen's, Bishopsgate, and Castletown Cox, Co. Kilkenny; Kilboy, Co. Tipperary; Queen Mother Sq., Poundbury for

Duchy of Cornwall. Mem., Royal Fine Art Commn, 1994–97. *Publications:* Architects Anonymous, 1994; Radical Classicism, 2006; The Practice of Classical Architecture, 2015. *Recreation:* the Pauline epistles. *Address:* Old Exchange, High Street, Dedham, Colchester, Essex CO7 6HA. *T:* (01206) 323186.

**TERRY, Sir Michael Edward Stanley I.;** *see* Imbert-Terry.

**TERRY, Quinlan;** *see* Terry, J. Q.

**TERZOPOULOS, Prof. Demetri,** PhD; FRS 2014; FRSC; Distinguished Professor, since 2012, Chancellor's Professor of Computer Science, since 2005, and Director, UCLA Computer Graphics and Vision Laboratory, since 2005, University of California, Los Angeles; Co-Founder and Chief Science Officer, VoxelCloud Inc., Los Angeles, since 2016. *Educ:* McGill Univ. (BEng Hons 1978; MEng 1980); Massachusetts Inst. of Technol. (PhD 1984). Res. Scientist, Artificial Intelligence Lab., MIT, 1984–85; Prog. Leader, Schlumberger Res., Palo Alto, 1985–89; University of Toronto: Associate Prof. of Computer Sci. and Associate Prof. of Electrical and Computer Engrg, 1989–95; Prof. of Computer Sci. and Prof. of Electrical and Computer Engrg, 1995–2005; Lucy and Henry Moses Prof. of Sci., and Prof. of Computer Sci. and Maths, Courant Inst., New York Univ., 2000–05. Consultant to: Hughes Aircraft Co.; Schlumberger Lab. for Computer Sci.; Ont. Hydro; Digital Equipment Corp.; NEC Res. Inst.; Intel Corp.; Almaden Res. Center, IBM; Honda R&D Americas. AI and Robotics Fellow, Canadian Inst. for Advanced Res., 1989–95; E. W. R. Steacie Meml Fellow, NSERC, 1996–98; Killam Res. Fellow, Canada Council for Arts, 1998–2000; Guggenheim Fellow, 2009–10; Okawa Fellow, 2011–12. FIEEE 2001; Mem., Eur. Acad. of Scis, 2002; FRSC 2006; Fellow, Assoc. for Computing Machinery, 2008. Gov. Gen.'s Academic Medal, 1973; Internat. Digital Media Award, 1994; Computer Animation Hon. Award, Prix Ars Electronica, 1995; Young Investigator Award, Canadian Image Processing and Pattern Recognition Soc., 1998; Tech. Achievement Award, Acad. of Motion Picture Arts and Scis, 2005; Computer Vision Dist. Researcher Award, IEEE, 2007; (jtly) Helmholtz Prize, IEEE Computer Soc., 2013; Award for Research Excellence, Canadian Image Processing and Pattern Recognition Soc., 2015. Founder Mem. of Editl Bds of eight sci. jls. *Publications:* (ed jtly) Real-Time Computer Vision, 1994; (ed jtly) Computer Animation and Simulation, 1995; (ed jtly) Deformable Models in Medical Image Analysis, 1998; (ed jtly) Distributed Video Sensor Networks, 2011; articles in sci. jls. *Address:* UCLA Computer Science Department, Los Angeles, CA 90095, USA. *W:* www.terzopoulos.com.

**TESLER, Brian,** CBE 1986; Deputy Chairman, LWT (Holdings) plc, 1990–94; Chairman: London Weekend Television Ltd, 1984–92 (Managing Director, 1976–90; Deputy Chairman, 1982–84; Deputy Chief Executive, 1974–76); The London Studios Ltd (formerly LWT Production Facilities Ltd), 1989–92; LWT International Ltd, 1990–92; LWT Programmes Ltd, 1990–92; *b* 19 Feb. 1929; *s* of late David Tesler and of Stella Tesler; *m* 1959, Audrey May Maclean; one *s*. *Educ:* Chiswick County School for Boys; Exeter Coll., Oxford (State Schol.; MA). Theatre Editor, The Isis, 1950–51; Pres., Oxford Univ. Experimental Theatre Club, 1951–52. British Forces Broadcasting Service, 1947–49; Producer/Director: BBC Television, 1952; ATV, 1957; ABC Television: Head of Features and Light Entertainment, 1960; Programme Controller, 1961; Dir of Programmes, 1962; Dir of Programmes, Thames Television, 1968. Chairman: ITV Superchannel Ltd, 1986–88; ITCA, 1980–82; Ind. TV Network Prog. Cttee, 1976–78, 1986–88; LWT Programme Adv. Bd, 1990–92; ITCA Cable and Satellite Television Wkg Party, 1981–88; ITV Film Purchase Cttee, 1989–90; The Magazine Business Ltd, 1992–96. Director: ITN Ltd, 1979–90; Channel Four Television Ltd, 1980–85; Oracle Teletext Ltd, 1980–92; Services Sound and Vision Corp. (formerly Services Kinema Corp.), 1981–2004. Chm., Lord Chancellor's Adv. Cttee on JPs, 1993–96 (Mem., 1991–96); Lay Interviewer for Judicial Appts, 1994–99; Ind. Assessor, OCPA, 2001–10. Member: British Screen Adv. Council, 1985–94 (Wkg Party on Future of British Film Industry, 1975–77; Interim Action Cttee on Film Industry, 1977–85); TRIC, 1979– (Pres., 1979–80; Companion, 1986); Vice-Pres., RTS, 1984–94 (FRTS 1992). Governor: Nat. Film and TV Sch. (formerly Nat. Film Sch.), 1977–95; BFI, 1986–95 (Dep. Chm., 1993–95). Daily Mail Nat. TV Award, 1954; Guild of Television Producers and Directors Award, 1957; Lord Willis Trophy for Outstanding Services to Television, Pye Television Award, 1986; Presidential Award, TRIC, 1991. *Recreations:* books, theatre, cinema, music.

**TESORIÈRE, (Harcourt) Andrew (Pretorius),** FRGS; HM Diplomatic Service; Head, European Union Border Assistance Mission to Moldova and Ukraine (in rank of Ambassador), since 2015 (Deputy Head, 2014–15); *b* 2 Nov. 1950; *s* of Pieter Ivan Tesorière and Joyce Margaret Tesorière (*née* Baxter); *m* 1987, Dr Alma Gloria Vasquez. *Educ:* Nautical Coll., Pangbourne; Britannia Royal Naval Coll., Dartmouth; University Coll. of Wales, Aberystwyth (BScEcon Hons); Ecole Nat. d'Admin, Paris. RNR, 1964–68; RN Officer, 1969–73; joined FCO, 1974; Persian lang. student, SOAS and Iran, 1975–76; Oriental Sec., Kabul, 1976–79; Third Sec., Nairobi, 1980–81; Second Sec., Abidjan (also accredited to Ouagadougou and Niamey), 1981–84; First Sec. and Hd of Chancery, later Chargé d'Affaires, Damascus, 1987–91; Hd, Field Ops, UN Office for Co-ordination of Humanitarian Assistance to Afghanistan, Afghanistan, 1994–95; Ambassador to Albania, 1996–98; Actg Hd of Mission and Sen. Pol Advr, UN Special Mission to Afghanistan, 1998–2000 (on secondment); Chargé d'Affaires *ai*, Kabul, 2001–02; Ambassador to Latvia, 2002–05; Ambassador to Algeria, 2005–07; Sen. Policy Advr to Internat. Security Assistance Force Comdr S, Afghanistan, 2007–08; OSCE Ambassador to Kyrgyzstan, 2008–12; FCO, 2012–14. Chm., Bd of Trustees, OSCE Acad., Bishkek, Kyrgyzstan, 2008–12. Sen. mentor, UK-US military exercises, 2012–13; led HMG triennial rev. of Westminster Foundn for Democracy, 2014. FRGS 1993. NATO Medal, ISAF, 2007; HM Operational Service Medal, Afghanistan, 2008; Sherektesh (Concord) Medal, Kyrgyz Republic, 2008. *Recreations:* travel, sport, foreign languages, art, countryside. *Address:* c/o Foreign and Commonwealth Office, King Charles Street, SW1A 2AH.

**TESSIER-LAVIGNE, Dr Marc,** FMedSci; FRS 2001; FRSC; President, Stanford University, since 2016; *b* 18 Dec. 1959; *s* of Sheila and Jacques Tessier-Lavigne; *m* 1989, Mary Alanna Hynes; two *s* one *d*. *Educ:* McGill Univ., Montreal (BSc 1st Cl. Hons Physics 1980); New Coll., Oxford (Rhodes Scholar; BA 1st Cl. Hons Phil. and Physiol., 1982; Hon. Fellow 2011); University Coll. London (PhD 1987; Schaffer Prize). FRSC 1999. University of California, San Francisco: Asst Prof., Dept of Anatomy, 1991–95; Associate Prof., 1995–97; Prof., Depts of Anatomy and Biochem. and Biophysics, 1997–2001; Asst Investigator, 1994–97, Investigator, 1997–2003, Howard Hughes Med. Inst.; Prof. of Biol Scis and Susan B. Ford Prof., Sch. of Humanities and Scis, Stanford Univ., 2001–03; Genentech Inc.: Sen. Vice-Pres., 2003–08; Exec. Vice-Pres., Research Drug Discovery, 2008–09; Exec. Vice-Pres., Research, and Chief Scientific Officer, 2009–11; Pres., and Carson Family Prof., Lab. of Brain Develt and Repair, Rockefeller Univ., 2011–16. Member: NAS, USA, 2005; Inst. of Medicine, NAS, USA, 2011; American Philosophical Soc., 2017; Amer. Acad. of Arts and Scis, 2013. FAAAS 2001; FMedSci 2004. Hon. Dr Medicine and Surgery, Pavia, Italy, 2006; Hon. DSc McGill, 2011; Hon. PhD UCL, 2014. McKnight Investigator Award, 1994; Charles Judson Herrick Award in Comparative Neurol., Amer. Assoc. Anatomists, 1995; Ameritec Foundn Prize, 1995; (jtly) Fondation IPSEN Prize for Neuronal Plasticity, 1996; Viktor Hamburger Award, Internat. Soc. for Develtl Neurosci., 1997; Young Investigator Award, Soc. for Neurosci., USA, 1997; (jtly) Wakeman Foundn Award for contribs in field of neuronal regeneration, 1998; Robert Dow Neurosci. Award, Oregon Health Sci. Univ., 2003; Reeve-Irvine Res. Medal, Univ. of Calif, Irvine, 2007; Ferrier Prize Lect., Royal Soc., 2007; Gill Dist. Award, Univ. of Indiana, Bloomington, 2010; (jtly) Alden Spencer Award, Columbia Univ., 2010; Meml Sloan-Kettering Medal for outstanding contribs to biomed. res., Meml Sloan-Kettering Cancer Center, 2011; W. Maxwell Cowan Award for outstanding achievement in develtl neurosci., Cajal Club, 2011; Henry G. Friesen Internat. Prize in Health Res., Canadian Acad. Health Scis and Friends of Canadian Insts Health Res., 2012; NY/NJ CEO Lifetime Achievement Award, Boston Biotech Confs, 2014. *Publications:* contribs in physiol. and develtl neurobiol. to scientific jls. *Recreations:* family, history. *Address:* Office of the President, Stanford University, Stanford, CA 94305–2061, USA.

**TESTINO, Mario,** Hon. OBE 2013; fashion photographer; *b* Lima, 1954. *Educ:* American Sch. of Lima; Univ. del Pacífico; Pontificia Univ. Católica del Perú; Univ. of San Diego, Calif. Photograph subjects include Naomi Campbell, Diana, Princess of Wales, Cameron Diaz, Elizabeth Hurley, Janet Jackson, Keira Knightley, Madonna, Kate Moss, Gwyneth Paltrow, Julia Roberts, Catherine Zeta-Jones, Prince Harry, Prince Charles and Duchess of Cornwall. Exhibitions include: NPG, 2002; Kensington Palace, 2005. *Publications:* Any Objections?, 1998; Front Row/Backstage, 1999; Alive, 2001; Portraits, 2002; Kids, 2003; Diana Princess of Wales, 2005; Let Me In, 2007; (ed) Lima Peru, 2007; Kate Moss, 2011. *Address:* c/o Art Partner, 1 Dekalb Avenue, 4th Floor, Brooklyn, NY 11201, USA.

**TETLEY, Ven. Joy Dawn,** PhD; Archdeacon of Worcester and Canon Residentiary of Worcester Cathedral, 1999–2008; Area Director of Ordinands, Diocese of Oxford, 2009–10 and 2012–13; *b* 9 Nov. 1946; *d* of Frederick and Mary Payne; *m* 1980, Rev. Brian Tetley, BA, FCA. *Educ:* Durham Univ. (BA 1968; PhD 1988); Leeds Univ. (CertEd 1969); St Hugh's Coll., Oxford (BA 1975; MA 1980); NW Ordination Course. Ordained deaconess 1977, deacon 1987, priest 1994; Deaconess: Bentley, 1977–79; St Aidan, Buttershaw, 1979–80; Durham Cathedral, 1980–83; Lectr, Trinity Coll., Bristol, and Deaconess, Chipping Sodbury and Old Sodbury, 1983–86; Deacon, 1987–89, Hon. Canon, 1990–93 (Canon Emeritus, 1993–), Rochester Cathedral, and Dio. Dir, Post-Ordination Trng, 1988–93; Principal, E Anglian Ministerial Trng Course, 1993–99; Actg Chaplain, Wadham Coll., Oxford, 2010. Lay Assessor, NHS, 2009–13. Columnist, Church Times, 1993–95. FRSA 2006. *Publications:* Encounter with God in Hebrews, 1995; Sunday by Sunday, 1995; A Way into Hebrews, 1998; Jonah, 2003; (jtly) Renewing the Eucharist, vol. 2: word, 2009; (contrib.) Apostolic Women, Apostolic Authority, 2010; (contrib.) Facing the Issues, 2012; (contrib.) Sermons on Difficult Subjects, 2013; (contrib.) Faith Matters, 2013; (contrib.) And With All Your Mind, 2015; God Speaking, 2015; Jesus' Women, 2016. *Address:* 23 Cripley Road, Oxford OX2 0AH. *T:* (01865) 250209. *E:* joy121tetley@btinternet.com. *Club:* National Liberal.

**TETLOW, Bernard Geoffrey;** QC 2011; *b* London, 31 July 1957; *s* of Brian and Agnes Tetlow; *m* 1991, Claire Hanika (marr. diss. 2008); two *s*. *Educ:* Thornleigh Salesian Coll.; S Bank Poly. (BA Hons Law); Hughes Hall, Cambridge (LLM 1983). Called to the Bar, Middle Temple, 1984; Lead Counsel, Lebanon Tribunal, 2010–. Legal Advr to Elgin and Arundel Garden Cttee, 2008–. *Recreations:* cricket, football, tennis, ski-ing, walking, reading, theatre, poker. *Address:* Garden Court Chambers, 57–60 Lincoln's Inn Fields, WC2A 3LJ. *E:* b_tetlow@hotmail.com. *Clubs:* Drones; Bolton Wanderers, South Bank Cricket, Holland Park Lawn Tennis.

**TETLOW, His Honour Christopher Bruce;** a Circuit Judge, 1992–2010; *b* 27 Feb. 1943; *s* of George Wilfred Tetlow and Betty Tetlow; *m* 1981, Rosalind Jane Cope; two *s* one *d*. *Educ:* Stowe Sch.; Magdalene Coll., Cambridge (MA). Called to the Bar, Middle Temple, 1969. *Clubs:* St James's (Manchester); Manchester Tennis and Racquet.

**TETT, Ann Laure, (Holly);** HM Diplomatic Service; High Commissioner to Malawi, since 2017; *b* London, 8 Aug. 1979; *d* of Elyot and Christine Tett; partner, Mark Kalch; four *c*. *Educ:* Lycée St Joseph, Avignon; Univ. of Sheffield (BSc Psychol.). Entered FCO, 2002; Desk Officer, Eur. Security and Defence Policy, FCO, 2002–03; Second Secretary: Addis Ababa, 2004–07; Tunis, 2007; Head: Public Diplomacy Partners Team, FCO, 2007–09; Iraq Enquiry Team, 2009–10; First Sec., Buenos Aires, 2011–16. *Address:* c/o Foreign and Commonwealth Office, King Charles Street, SW1A 2AH. *E:* holly.tett@fco.gov.uk.

**TETT, Gillian Romaine;** US Managing Editor, Financial Times, 2010–12 and since 2014; *b* 10 July 1967. *Educ:* Clare Coll., Cambridge (BA 1989; PhD Social Anthropol.). Financial Times, 1993–: Bureau Chief, Tokyo, 1997–2003; Dep. Hd, Lex Column, 2003; Asst Ed., 2012–14. Mem., Amer. Anthropological Assoc. Sen. Financial Journalist of Year, Wincott Awards, 2007; Business Journalist of Year, 2008, Journalist of Year, 2009, BPA; President's Medal, British Acad., 2011; Columnist of Year, Press Awards, 2014; Marsh Award for Anthropol. in World, RAI, 2014. *Publications:* Saving the Sun: a Wall Street gamble to rescue Japan from its trillion dollar meltdown, 2003; Fool's Gold: how unrestrained greed corrupted a dream, shattered global markets and unleashed a catastrophe, 2009; The Silo Effect: ordered chaos, the peril of expertise, and the power of breaking down barriers, 2015. *Address:* Financial Times, 330 Hudson Street, 8th Floor, New York, NY 10013, USA. *T:* (212) 6416503. *E:* Gillian.Tett@ft.com. *Club:* Overseas Press (New York).

**TETT, Holly;** *see* Tett, A. L.

**TEULINGS, Prof. Coenraad Nicolaas, (Coen),** PhD; Distinguished Professor, Utrecht University, since 2018; *b* Rijswijk, 13 Dec. 1958; *m* 1988, Salomé Bentinck; one *s* one *d*. *Educ:* Gymnasium β, Fons Vitae, Amsterdam; Univ. of Amsterdam (Master Econs cum laude 1985; PhD 1990). Jun., later Sen. Researcher, SEO Economic Res., 1985–91; Res. Fellow, Royal Dutch Acad. of Arts and Scis, 1991–95; Hd, Dept of Income Policy, Min. of Social Affairs, 1995–98; Prof. of Labour Econs, Univ. of Amsterdam, 1997–98; Dir, Tinbergen Inst., 1998–2004; Prof. of Labour Econs, Erasmus Univ., Rotterdam, 1998–2004; CEO, SEO Economic Res., 2004–06; Pres., CPB Netherlands Bureau for Econ. Policy Analysis, 2006–13; Montague Burton Prof. of Industrial Relations and Labour Econs, Univ. of Cambridge, 2013–18. Pt-time Prof., Univ. of Amsterdam, 2004–. Fellow, Tinbergen Inst., 1996; Member: CEPR, London; CES-IFO, Munich; IZA, Bonn. *Recreations:* sailing, cooking. *Address:* School of Economics, Utrecht University, PO Box 80125, 3508 TC Utrecht, Netherlands. *T:* 1653809549. *E:* c.n.teulings@outlook.com.

**TEVERSON,** family name of **Baron Teverson**.

**TEVERSON,** Baron *cr* 2006 (Life Peer), of Tregony, in the County of Cornwall; **Robin Teverson;** *b* 31 March 1952; *s* of Dr Crofton Teverson and Joan Teverson; *m* 1st, 1975, Rosemary Anne Young (marr. diss. 2005); two *d*; *m* 2nd, 2006, Terrye Lynn Jones. *Educ:* Exeter Univ. (BA Hons Econs). Managing Director: SPD Ltd and Dir, Exel Logistics, 1987–89; Supply Chain Consultancy (Rationale Ltd), 1989–94; Chm., Finance SW Ltd, 1999–2002; Chief Exec., Finance Cornwall, 2002–06. MEP (Lib Dem) Cornwall and West

Plymouth, 1994–99; contested (Lib Dem) SW Reg., 1999. Chair: H of L EU Select Cttee on Foreign Affairs, Defence and Develt, 2008–12; H of L Select Cttee on Arctic, 2014–15; Lib Dem spokesman on Energy and Climate Change, H of L, 2009–15. *Recreations:* history, riding, astronomy, travel, music. *Address:* House of Lords, SW1A 0PW.

**TEVERSON, Paul Richard**; Master of the Senior (formerly Supreme) Court, Chancery Division, since 2005; *b* 1 May 1953; *s* of late George Eric Teverson and Ailsa Betty Teverson (*née* Moor); *m* 1978, Hon. Joanna Rosamund Georgina, *d* of Baron Gore-Booth, GCMG, KCVO; two *s* one *d*. *Educ:* St Paul's Sch., London (Sen. Schol.); Corpus Christi Coll., Cambridge (Exhibnr; BA 1975). Called to the Bar, Inner Temple, 1976; in practice at Chancery Bar, 1978–2005. Dep. Chancery Master, 2000–05. *Publications:* (contrib.) The White Book, 2008–; (ed jtly) Tristram and Coote's Probate Practice, 31st edn, 2015. *Recreations:* reading, cycling (Mem., Barnes Bikers), theatre, opera. *Address:* Rolls Building, 110 Fetter Lane, EC4A 1BR. *Club:* Hurlingham.

**TEVIOT**, 2nd Baron *cr* 1940, of Burghclere; **Charles John Kerr**; genealogist; *b* 16 Dec. 1934; *s* of 1st Baron Teviot, DSO, MC, and Florence Angela (*d* 1979), *d* of late Lt-Col Charles Walter Villiers, CBE, DSO; *S* father, 1968; *m* 1965, Patricia Mary Harris; one *s* one *d*. *Educ:* Eton. Bus Conductor and Driver; genealogical and historical record agent. Director: Debrett's Peerage Ltd, 1977–83; Burke's Peerage Research, 1983–85; Burke's Peerage Ltd, 1984–85. Mem., Adv. Council on Public Records, 1974–83. Pres., Assoc. of Genealogists and Record Agents, 1997–2011. Fellow, Soc. of Genealogists, 1975. *Recreations:* reading, walking. *Heir:* *s* Hon. Charles Robert Kerr [*b* 19 Sept. 1971; *m* 1st, 2000, Yamaleth Molina Guillen (marr. diss.); one *d* (and one *d* decd); 2nd, 2012, Fiona, *d* of David Parry-Jones; one *d*]. *Address:* 28 Hazel Grove, Burgess Hill, West Sussex RH15 0BY. *T:* (01444) 242605.

**TEW, Dr Thomas**, FRSB; Chief Executive: Environment Bank, since 2011; Naturespace Partnership, since 2017; *b* London, 3 April 1963; *s* of Thomas Tew and Mary Tew (*née* Sidebottom); *m* 1990, Gillian Kerby; one *s* one *d*. *Educ:* Merchant Taylors' Sch., Northwood; Univ. of E Anglia (BSc Hons 1984); Wolfson Coll., Oxford (DPhil 1989). FRSB (FSB 2011). Postdoctoral res., Univ. of Oxford, 1989–92; Hd, Convention on Internat. Trade in Endangered Species, JNCC, 1994–97; Gen. Manager and Regl Dir, English Nature, 1998–2006; Dir, 2006–08, Exec. Dir and Chief Scientist, 2008–10, Natural England. Chm., Vincent Wildlife Trust, 2005–17. Trustee: HLF, then NLHF, 2014–; Nat. Trust, 2019–. FRSA 2010. *Publications:* contrib. scientific papers. *Recreations:* family, garden, walking, golf, football. *Address:* Heath Cottage, Ryhall Heath, Stamford, Lincs PE9 4EF. *T:* (01780) 754454, 07919 044936. *E:* tom.tew@hotmail.co.uk. *Club:* Rye Golf.

**TEWKESBURY, Bishop Suffragan of**, since 2016; **Rt Rev. Robert Wilfred Springett**; *b* Chelmsford, 15 Sept. 1962; *s* of late Jack and Patricia Springett; *m* 1991, Helen Bates; two *d*. *Educ:* Brentwood Sch.; Chelmsford Coll.; Lincoln Theological Coll.; Nottingham Univ.; King's Coll., London. Ordained deacon, 1989, priest, 1990; Curate: St James', Colchester, 1989; St Martin's, Basildon, 1992; Priest in Charge, South Ockendon and Belhus Park, 1994–2001; Area Dean, Thurrock, 1998–2001; Rector, Wanstead, 2001–10; Area Dean, Redbridge, 2008–10; Archdeacon of Cheltenham, 2010–16. Hon. Canon, Chelmsford, 2008–10. *Recreations:* travel, dog walking, ski-ing. *Address:* Bishop's House, 3 Hill Road, Gloucester GL4 6ST. *T:* (01452) 410022.

**TEWSON, Jane, (Mrs C. Lane)**, CBE 1999; Founder and Director, Igniting Change (formerly Pilotlight Australia), since 2000; *b* 9 Jan. 1958; *d* of Dr Tim Tewson, Oxford, and Dr Blue Tewson (*née* Johnston); *m* 1992, Dr Charles Lane; two *s*. *Educ:* Headington Sch., Oxford; Lord Williams' Sch., Thame. Project Co-ordinator, MENCAP, 1979–83; Founder and Chief Exec., Charity Projects and Comic Relief, 1984–96; Pilotlight UK, 1996–99; TimeBank, 1999. Trustee: Media Trust, 1996–99; Oxfam, 1996–99; Camelot Foundn, 1997–2000; Diana, Princess of Wales Meml Cttee, 1997–2000; St James Ethics Centre, 2000–; Reichstein Foundn, 2000–; Virgin Unite, 2005–. *Publications:* Dying to Know: bringing death to life, 2010 (Australian edn 2008). *Recreations:* travel, walking, gardening. *Address:* 35 Cressy Street, Malvern, Melbourne, Vic 3144, Australia.

**TEYNHAM**, 20th Baron *cr* 1616; **John Christopher Ingham Roper-Curzon**; *b* 25 Dec. 1928; *s* of 19th Baron Teynham, DSO, DSC, and Elspeth Grace (who *m* 2nd, 1958, 6th Marquess of Northampton, DSO, and *d* 1976), *e d* of late William Ingham Whitaker; *S* father, 1972; *m* 1964, Elizabeth, *yr d* of Lt-Col the Hon. David Scrymgeour-Wedderburn, DSO, Scots Guards (killed on active service 1944), and of Patricia, Countess of Dundee; five *s* five *d* (of whom one *s* one *d* are twins). *Educ:* Eton. A Land Agent. Late Captain, The Buffs (TA), formerly Coldstream Guards; active service in Palestine, 1948. ADC to Governor of Bermuda, 1953 and 1955; ADC to Governor of Leeward Islands, 1955; Private Secretary and ADC, 1956; ADC to Governor of Jamaica, 1962. Pres., Inst. of Commerce, 1972–; Vice Pres., Inst. of Export. Member of Council, Sail Training Association, 1964–69. OStJ. Lord of the Manors of South Baddesley and Sharpricks. *Recreations:* shooting, fishing. *Heir:* *s* Hon. David John Henry Ingham Roper-Curzon [*b* 5 Oct. 1965; *m* 1st, 1985, Lydia Lucinda (marr. diss. 2003), *d* of Maj.-Gen. Sir Christopher Airy, *qv*; two *s* one *d*; 2nd, 2003, Melanie Hayward; one *s* one *d* (twins)]. *Address:* Pylewell Park, Lymington, Hants SO41 5SJ. *Clubs:* Turf; House of Lords Yacht; Ocean Cruising; Puffin's (Edinburgh).

**THACKER, Prof. David Thomas**; theatre, film and television director; Associate Artistic Director, Octagon Theatre, Bolton, since 2015 (Artistic Director, 2009–15); Professor of Theatre, University of Bolton, since 2015; *b* 21 Dec. 1950; *s* of Thomas Richard Thacker and Alice May (*née* Beaumont); *m* 1983, Margot Elizabeth Leicester; three *s* one *d*. *Educ:* Wellingborough Grammar Sch.; Univ. of York (BA English and Related Lit.; MA Shakespeare). Theatre Royal, York: Asst Stage Manager, Dep. Stage Manager and Stage Manager, 1974–75; Asst Dir, 1975–76; Gateway Theatre, Chester: Arts Council Asst Dir, 1975–76; Associate Dir, 1977–78; Duke's Playhouse, Lancaster: Arts Council Associate Dir, 1978–79; Dir, 1980–84; Dir, Young Vic Theatre, 1984–93; Dir-in-Residence, RSC, 1993–95. Vis. Prof. of Dramatic Arts, Univ. of Bolton, 2009–15. *Theatre productions:* over 100 including: Young Vic: Ghosts, 1987; Who's Afraid of Virginia Woolf?, 1987; A Touch of the Poet, An Enemy of the People, 1989; The Winter's Tale, 1991; The Last Yankee, 1993; RSC: Pericles (Dir of the Year and Best Revival, Laurence Olivier Awards, 1991), The Two Gentlemen of Verona, 1991; As You Like It, 1992; The Merchant of Venice, 1993; Julius Caesar, Coriolanus, 1995; Bingo, The Tempest, 1995; Broken Glass, RNT, 1994, transf. Duke of York's, 1995; A View from the Bridge, Bristol Old Vic, 1994, transf. Strand, 1995; Death of a Salesman, RNT, 1996; The Price, Scarborough, 2011; Octagon: All My Sons, 2009; A Midsummer Night's Dream, Comedians, The Hired Man, A Streetcar Named Desire, Love on the Dole, 2010; Romeo and Juliet, The Price, Who's Afraid of Virginia Woolf?, Habeas Corpus, 2011; Alfie, The Winslow Boy, Lighthearted Intercourse, 2012; Of Mice and Men, Tull, The Glass Menagerie, An Inspector Calls, Long Day's Journey Into Night, 2013; Hobson's Choice, Twelfth Night, Journey's End, Early One Morning, 2014; A View from the Bridge, Hindle Wakes, The Ancient Secret of Youth and the Five Tibetans, Noises Off, 2015. *Television:* over 30 productions including: A Doll's House, 1992; Measure for Measure, 1994; Death of a Salesman, 1996; Broken Glass; The Scold's Bridle, 1998; Grafters; Kavanagh QC; The Vice; Waking the Dead; Murder in Mind; Blue Dove; The Mayor of Casterbridge, 2003; Faith, 2005. *Recreations:* sport, family, film and television, reading, politics. *Address:* 84 Ferme Park Road, N8 9SD.

**THACKER, Prof. Jonathan William**, PhD; King Alfonso XIII Professor of Spanish Studies, University of Oxford, since 2018; Fellow, Exeter College, Oxford, since 2018; *b* Cambridge, 20 Sept. 1967; *s* of Michael and Sarah Thacker; *m* 1991, Claire Lucie Chaplain; four *s*. *Educ:* Birkenhead Sch.; King's Coll. London (BA); Emmanuel Coll., Cambridge (PhD 1997). Lecturer in Spanish: Birkbeck Coll., Univ. of London, 1994–97; UCL, 1997–2001; Lectr, 2001–14, Prof. of Spanish Golden Age Lit., 2014–17, Merton Coll., Oxford. *Publications:* Rôle-play and the World as Stage in the Comedia, 2002; A Companion to Golden Age Theatre, 2007. *Recreations:* travel, theatre, birdwatching. *Address:* Exeter College, Oxford OX1 3BP. *T:* (01865) 279600. *E:* jonathan.thacker@mod-langs.ox.ac.uk.

**THACKRAY, John Richard Dominic**; QC 2019; **His Honour Judge Thackray**; a Circuit Judge, since 2019; *b* Leeds, 31 Jan. 1971; ; *m* 2008; one *s* two *d*. *Educ:* Kettlethorpe High Sch., Wakefield; Outwood Grange Sixth Form Coll., Wakefield; Leeds Univ. (LLB Hons 1993). Called to the Bar, Lincoln's Inn, 1994; a Recorder, 2016–19. *Recreations:* golf, running.

**THAKKER, Prof. Rajesh Vasantlal**, MD, ScD; FRCP, FRCPE, FRCPath, FMedSci; FRS 2014; May Professor of Medicine, and Fellow of Somerville College, University of Oxford, since 1999; *b* 27 Aug. 1954; *s* of late Vasantlal Gordhandas Thakker and of Indira Vasantlal Thakker; *m* 1980, Julie Claire Magee; one *d*. *Educ:* Pembroke Coll., Cambridge (MA, MB BChir, MD; ScD 2010); Middlesex Hosp. Med. Sch. MRCP 1983, FRCP 1993; FRCPE 1997; FRCPath 1998. Middlesex Hospital: House Physician, 1980–81; Registrar, 1983–85; MRC Trng Fellow and Hon. Sen. Registrar, 1985–88; Sen. House Physician, Northwick Park Hosp. and Hammersmith Hosp., 1981–83; MRC Clin. Scientist and Consultant Physician, Northwick Park Hosp., 1988–92; Sen. Lectr and Consultant Physician, 1988–94, Reader of Medicine, 1994–95, RPMS; Hd of MRC Molecular Endocrinology Gp, 1994–99, and Prof. of Medicine, 1995–99, RPMS, then ICSM, Univ. of London. NIHR Sen. Investigator, 2015–18. Chm., Efficacy, Mechanisms and Evaluations Bd, NIHR/MRC, 2008–16. Raine Vis. Prof., Perth, Australia, 2005. Lectures: WPU Jackson Meml, 1998, Bernard Pimstone Meml, 2003, 2016, Soc. for Endocrinology, Metabolism, and Diabetes of S Africa, 1998; Florence May McCredie, Melbourne, 2003; Endocrine Soc. (USA) Plenary, 2007; Yogesh C. Patel Meml, McGill Univ., Montreal, 2007; Jack W. Coburn Endowed, Amer. Soc. Nephrology, 2012; Erasmus, Univ. of Rotterdam, 2013; Arthur Broadus, Yale Univ., 2015. Gov., Oxford High Sch. (GDST), 2013–. Mem., Amer. Assoc. Physicians, 2013. Hon. Sen. Fellow, Harris Manchester Coll., Oxford, 2010. FMedSci 1999. Young Investigator Award, American Soc. for Bone and Mineral Research, 1988; Raymond-Horton Smith Prize, Cambridge Univ., 1994; Soc. for Endocrinol. Medal, 1995; Eur. Fedn of Endocrine Socs Prize, 1998; Graham Bull Prize, RCP, 1999; Louis V. Avioli Founders Award, Amer. Soc. for Bone and Mineral Res., USA, 2009; Parathyroid Medal, Fondazionefirmo, Florence, 2012; Internat. Res. Prize, Austrian Soc. for Bone and Mineral Res., 2015; Dale Medal, Soc. for Endocrinol. (UK), 2015; Hakan Ahlman Award for Translational Res., Eur. Neuroendocrine Tumours Soc., 2017. *Publications:* (ed) Genetic and Molecular Biological Aspects of Endocrine Disease, 1995, 2nd edn, 2018; (ed) Molecular Genetics of Endocrine Disorders, 1997; (ed) Transitional Endocrinology and Metabolism: neoplasia update, 2011; (ed) Genetics of Bone Biology and Skeletal Disease, 2013; articles in jls. *Recreations:* running, rambling, reading. *Address:* Somerville College, Oxford OX2 6HD. *Club:* Athenæum.

**THAKSIN SHINAWATRA**, PhD; Prime Minister of Thailand, 2001–06; *b* 26 July 1949; *m* Khunying Potjaman Shinawatra (marr. diss. 2008). *Educ:* Police Cadet Acad., Thailand; Eastern Kentucky Univ., USA (MA Criminal Justice 1975); Sam Houston State Univ., Texas (PhD Criminal Justice 1978). Royal Thai Police Department, 1973–87: Dep. Supt, Policy and Planning Subdiv.; Police Lt Col, 1987. Founder and Chm., Shinawatra Computer and Communications Gp, 1987–94. Minister of Foreign Affairs, Thailand, 1994–95; Leader, Palang Dharma Party, 1995–96; Dep. Prime Minister i/c of traffic and transportation, Bangkok, 1995–96; Dep. Prime Minister, 1997; MP (party list), 1998–2001; Founder and Leader, Thai Rak Thai Party, 1998–2006. Founder and Vice Chm., Thaicom Foundn, 1993–; Chm. Adv. Cttee, Pre-Cadet Class 10 and Police Cadet Class 26, 1994–; Honorary Member: Council, Police Cadet Acad.; Assoc. of Ex-Military Officers; President: Northerners' Assoc. of Thailand, 1998; Professional Golf Assoc. of Thailand; Honorary Advisor: Bangkok Club; Thai Northerners' Assoc. of Illinois, 1999; Northerners Club of Nontaburi. ASEAN Businessman of the Year Award, Asian Inst., Indonesia, 1992; Kiattiyod Jakdao Award in Economical Develt, Cttee of Armed Forces Prep. Sch. Foundn, 1992; 1993 Outstanding Telecom Man of Year Award, 1994; Outstanding Criminal Justice Alumnus Award, Sam Houston State Univ., 1996; Hon. Award, Mass Media Photographer Assoc. of Thailand, 1997. Kt Grand Cordon (Special Cl.), Order of Crown (Thailand), 1995, Order of White Elephant (Thailand), 1996; Kt Grand Cross (First Cl.), Order of Direkgunabhorn (Thailand), 2001; Grand Cross, Order of Sahametrei (Cambodia), 2001.

**THALMANN, Anton Meinrad Friedrich**; Ambassador of Switzerland to the Court of St James's, 2010–13; *b* Berne, 28 May 1948; *s* of Dr Ernesto Thalmann and Paula Thalmann (*née* Degen); *m* 1975, Dominique Andrée Schnyder-von-Wartensee; two *d*. *Educ:* Univ. of Geneva; Univ. of Berne (PhD 1975); Graduate Inst. for Advanced Internat. Studies, Geneva. Asst to gen. mgt, Swiss Bank Corp., Basle, 1974–77; diplomatic trainee, Swiss Mission to EC, Brussels, 1978–79; Legal Affairs Directorate, Fed. Dept of Foreign Affairs, 1979–83; Econ. Counsellor, Tokyo, 1983–87; Counsellor, Perm. Delegn of Switzerland to OECD, Paris, 1987–90; Hd, UN and Internat. Orgns Section, Fed. Dept of Foreign Affairs, 1990–95; Ambassador and Dep. Sec. Gen., Fed. Dept of Defence, Civil Protection and Sport, 1995–99; Ambassador: to Belgium and Hd, Mission to NATO, Brussels, 1999–2003; to Canada and the Bahamas, 2003–06; Ambassador and Dep. State Sec. and Political Dir, Fed. Dept of Foreign Affairs, 2006–10. Chm., UN Open-ended Wkg Gp on Marking and Tracing of Small Arms and Light Weapons, NY, 2004–05; Co-Chair, Geneva process on armed violence and develt, 2006–10. *Recreations:* ski-ing, windsurfing, golf, jogging, horse riding, classical music and jazz. *Clubs:* Athenæum, Travellers.

**THANE, Prof. Patricia Mary**, PhD; FBA 2006; FRHistS; Leverhulme Professor of Contemporary British History, Institute of Historical Research, University of London, 2001–10, now Professor Emerita; Research Professor in Contemporary History, King's College London, since 2010; *b* 17 Aug. 1942; *d* of John Lawrence Williams, RAF (killed in action, 1944) and of Violet (*née* Beckett); *m* 1966, John Sutherland Thane (separated 1982); one *d*. *Educ:* Convent of the Holy Family, Birkenhead; St Anne's Coll., Oxford (BA, MA Mod. Hist. 1964); LSE (DSA 1965; PhD 1970). FRHistS 1985. Asst Lectr, Lectr, Sen. Lectr, then Reader in Social Hist., Dept of Social Sci. and Admin, Goldsmiths' Coll., Univ. of London, 1967–94; Prof. of Contemp. Hist., Univ. of Sussex, 1994–2001. Hon. Treas., 1992–96, Vice-Pres., 2006–09, RHistS; Vice-Pres., Internat. Econ. Hist. Assoc., 1998–2001; Chair, 2001–08, Pres., 2017–, Social Hist. Soc., UK. Mem., Fawcett Soc., 2000–. *Publications:* (ed and contrib.) The Origins of British Social Policy, 1978; The Foundations of the Welfare State, 1982 (trans. Japanese), 2nd edn 1996 (trans. Japanese); (ed jtly and contrib.) The Power of the Past: essays for Eric Hobsbawm, 1984; (ed jtly) Essays in Social History, vol. 2, 1986; (ed with Gisela Book) Maternity and Gender Policies: women and the rise of the European welfare states 1880s–1950s, 1991; (ed with Paul Johnson) Old Age from Antiquity to Post-Modernity, 1998; (ed jtly) Labour's First

Century: the Labour Party 1900–2000, 2000; Old Age in English History: past experiences, present issues, 2000; (ed with Lynn Botelho) Women and Ageing in British Society since 1500, 2001; Companion to Twentieth Century British History, 2001; (ed) The Long History of Old Age, 2005; (ed) Unequal Britain: equalities in Britain since 1945, 2010; (ed with E. Breitenbach) Women and Citizenship in Britain and Ireland in the Twentieth Century: what difference did the vote make?, 2010; (with Tanya Evans) Sinners? Scroungers? Saints?: unmarried motherhood in twentieth-century England, 2012; Divided Kingdom: a history of Britain since 1900, 2018; numerous articles in learned jls and contribs to edited vols. *Recreation:* cooking. *Address:* 5 Twisden Road, NW5 1DL.

**THANE, Sarah Ann, (Mrs S. A. Wenban),** CBE 2003; JP; FRTS; Member, National Lottery Commission, 2005–13; *b* 21 Sept. 1951; *d* of John and Winifred Thane; *m* 1996, Peter Wenban; three step *s* two step *d*. *Educ:* Sutton Coldfield Grammar Sch. for Girls; Co. High Sch., Stourbridge; City of Birmingham Poly. (Dip. Communication Studies). Independent Television Commission: Dir of Public Affairs, 1990–96; Dir of Progs and Cable, 1996–2001; Dir of Progs and Advertising, 2001–03; Advisor: Content and Standards, Ofcom, 2004–05; (pt-time) to BBC Governors, 2005–06, to BBC Trust, 2007–08; Mem., Bd of Govs, Teachers' TV, 2008–10. Conducted exploratory review of the system of regulating child performances (reported, 2010). Non-exec. Dir, Films of Record, 2005–08. Vice-Chm., 1998–2000, Chm., 2000–02, RTS. Chm., Suffolk Craft Soc., 2014–. FRTS 1994. JP Suffolk, 2005 (Dep. Chm., W Suffolk Bench, 2012–14). DUniv Birmingham City, 2010. *Recreations:* music, visual arts and crafts, cooking, gardening, time with friends and family. *E:* sarahwenban@hotmail.com, chair@suffolkcraftsociety.org. *Club:* Reform.

**THANKI, Bankim;** QC 2003; *b* 19 April 1964; *s* of late B. D. Thanki and of Vijayalaxmi Thanki (*née* Modha); *m* 1988, Catherine Jane Margaret Spotswood (*d* 2015); three *s* one *d*. *Educ:* Owen's Sch., Herts (Hd of Sch.); Balliol Coll., Oxford (BA 1st cl. Hons Ancient and Modern History, 1986; MA 1989). Called to the Bar, Middle Temple, 1988 (Harmsworth Schol.), Bencher, 2008; in practice as barrister, specialising in commercial law, 1989–; Dep. Hd, 2013–18, Hd, 2018–, Fountain Court Chambers. Mem., Commercial Bar Assoc., 1989–. *Publications:* (jtly) Carriage by Air, 2000; (ed jtly) Commercial Court Procedure, 2001; (contrib.) Brindle & Cox, Law of Bank Payments, 2004, 4th edn 2010; (ed) Law of Privilege, 2006, 3rd edn 2018; (contrib.) Coppel, Information Rights, 4th edn 2014. *Recreation:* Manchester United FC. *Address:* (chambers) Fountain Court, Temple, EC4Y 9DH. *T:* (020) 7583 3335, *Fax:* (020) 7353 0329. *Clubs:* Athenæum, Royal Automobile.

**THANKI, (Frances) Jane;** *see* McIvor, F. J.

**THAPAR, Prof. Romila,** PhD; Professor of History, Jawaharlal Nehru University, New Delhi, 1970–91, now Professor Emeritus; *b* 30 Nov. 1931; *d* of Daya Ram Thapar and Kaushalya Khosla. *Educ:* Punjab Univ. (BA Hons Lit. 1952); Sch. of Oriental and African Studies, Univ. of London (BA Hons Hist. 1955; PhD Hist. 1958). Reader in Ancient Indian Hist., Delhi Univ., 1963–70. Kluge Vis. Prof., Library of Congress, 2003–04. Corresp. FBA 1999; Corresp. Fellow, RSE, 2006. Mem., Amer. Acad. of Arts and Scis, 2009. Hon. Fellow: Lady Margaret Hall, Oxford, 1986; SOAS, 1991; St Antony's Coll., Oxford, 2017. Hon. DLitt: Chicago, 1992; Oxford, 2002; Pretoria, 2017; Hon. DSc Edinburgh, 2004. Kluge Prize for Lifetime Achievement in the Humanities, 2008. *Publications:* Asoka and the Decline of the Mauryas, 1961, 3rd edn 2013; History of India, Vol. 1, 1966; Ancient Indian Social History: some interpretations, 1978, 2nd edn 2009; From Lineage to State, 1984, 2nd edn 2000 (14th impression 2013); Cultural Pasts, 2000 (9th impression 2010); Sakuntala, 2001 (3rd impression 2008); Early India, 2002 (2nd impression 2004); Somanatha, 2004 (3rd impression 2008); (ed) India: historical beginnings and the concept of the Aryan, 2006; The Aryan: recasting constructs, 2008 (3rd impression 2011); The Past Before Us: historical traditions of early North India, 2013; Readings in Early Indian History, 2013; The Past as Present, 2014; The Public Intellectual in India, 2015; Indian Society and the Secular, 2016; Talking History, 2017; The Historian and Her Craft, 2017; Indian Cultures as Heritage: contemporary pasts, 2018; for children: Indian Tales, 1961, 2nd edn 1993. *Recreations:* music, poetry, searching for unusual finger rings. *Address:* 23 B Road, Maharani Bagh, New Delhi 110065, India.

**THAROOR, Shashi,** PhD; Member (Congress) Thiruvananthapuram, Kerala, Lok Sabha, since 2009; *b* 9 March 1956; *s* of Chandran Tharoor and Lily Tharoor; *m* 1st, 1977, Tilottama Mukherji (marr. diss. 2000); two *s* (twins); 2nd, 2007, Christa Giles (marr. diss. 2010); 3rd, 2010, Sunanda Pushkar (*d* 2014). *Educ:* St Stephen's Coll.; Delhi Univ. (BA Hons); Fletcher Sch. of Law and Diplomacy, Tufts Univ. (MA 1976; MALD 1977; PhD 1978). United Nations High Commissioner for Refugees: Asst to Dir for External Affairs, 1978–81; Rep., Singapore, 1981–84; Dep. Chief of Secretariat, 1984–87; Exec. Asst to Dep. High Comr, 1987–89; United Nations Headquarters: Special Asst to Under-Sec.-Gen. for Peacekeeping, 1989–96; Exec. Asst to Sec.-Gen., 1997–98; Dir, Communications and Special Projs, 1998–2001; Under Sec.-Gen. for Commns and Public Inf., 2001–07. Chm., Afras Ventures, 2007–09. Union Minister of Ext. Affairs, India, 2009–10; Union Minister of State for Human Resource Develt, 2012–14. Chm., Parly Standing Cttee on Ext. Affairs, 2014–. Member Advisory Board: ICRC, Geneva; Indo-American Arts Council; Virtue Foundn; Breakthrough: the Vijay Amritraj Foundn. Fellow, NY Inst. of the Humanities. Bd of Overseers, Fletcher Sch. of Law and Diplomacy. Columnist: The Times of India; The Hindu; The Asian Age; Deccan Chronicle; The Mail Today; former Contrib. Editor, Newsweek Internat. Pravasi Bharatiya Samman, 2004. *Publications:* Reasons of State, 1982; The Great Indian Novel (novel), 1989; The Five-Dollar Smile and Other Stories, 1990; Show Business (novel), 1992; India: from midnight to the millennium, 1997, rev. edn as India: from midnight to the millennium and beyond, 2006; Nehru: the invention of India, 2003; Riot (novel), 2001; Bookless in Baghdad and Other Reflections on Literature, 2005; The Elephant, the Tiger and the Cellphone: reflections on India in the 21st century, 2007; (with Shaharyar Khan) Shadows Across the Playing Field: 60 years of India-Pakistan cricket, 2009; Pax Indica: India and the world in the 21st century, 2012; India Shastra: reflections on the nation in our time, 2015; Inglorious Empire: what the British did to India, 2017; Why I am a Hindu, 2018. *Recreations:* cricket, theatre, reading. *E:* office@tharoor.in. *Club:* India International Centre (New Delhi).

**THARP, Kenneth Olumuyiwa,** CBE 2017 (OBE 2003); Director, The Africa Centre, since 2018; *b* Croydon, 11 Feb. 1960; *s* of Prof. Gabriel O. Esuruoso and Pamela Tharp; partner, Luca Silvestrini. *Educ:* Perse Sch., Cambridge; Cambridge Coll. of Arts and Technol.; London Contemp. Dance Sch. (Professional Dip. Contemp. Dance; BA 1st Cl. Hons Contemp. Dance, Univ. of Kent, 1987). Dancer, London Contemp. Dance Th., 1981–94; freelance dancer, choreographer, teacher and dir, 1994–2007; dancer, rehearsal dir, Educn Co-ordinator, Arc Dance Co., 1994–2005; Artistic Dir, Sadler's Wells Youth Dance Co., 1994–2000; Dancer in Residence and Dir of Dance, Queens' Coll. Cambridge, 1998–2006; Asst to Dir and Hd of Contemp. Dance, Millennium Performing Arts, 1999–2007; Associate Artistic Dir, then Artistic Dir Designate, Nat. Youth Dance Co., 2002–04; Artistic Advr and Lead Artist, Royal Ballet Sch. Dance Partnership and Access Prog., 2005–07; Chief Exec., The Place, 2007–16. Vis. Prof. in Dance: Choreog. and Perf., Univ. of Lincoln, 2009–12. Member: Exec., Dance UK, 1995–2001; Adv. Bd, Royal Ballet, 1998–99; Dancers Career Develt, 2002–06; London 2012 Culture and Creativity Adv. Forum, 2006–08; Steering Gp, Cultural Learning Alliance, 2013–; Steering Gp, Knowledge Quarter, 2014–; Adv. Council, Creative Industries Fedn, 2015–. Trustee: Jazz Xchange Music and Dance Co., 1996–98; Creative Dance Artists Trust, 1999–2006; Royal Opera Hse, 2002–10 (Trustee, Benevolent Fund, 2009–); Phoenix Dance Th., 2006–07. Patron, Akademi, 2014–. Finalist Judge, BBC Young Dancer 2015. FRSA. *Publications:* contrib. articles to Dancing Times, Dance UK mag., Animated mag., Queens' Coll. Record, Arts Professional mag. *Recreations:* music, listening and playing (especially piano, Javanese gamelan, mbira), swimming, cycling, walking, nature, Buddhist studies, tennis, sea-kayaking.

**THARP, Lars Broholm;** ceramics historian; curator, speaker, broadcaster, since 1986; Director, Lars Tharp Ltd, ceramics and fine arts consultants, since 1993; Hogarth Curator, Foundling Museum, since 2010 (Director, 2008–10); *b* Copenhagen, 27 March 1954; *s* of Harry Tharp and Anne Marie Broholm; *m* 1983, Gillian Block; two *d*. *Educ:* Wyggeston Grammar Sch. for Boys, Leicester; Gonville and Caius Coll., Cambridge (BA Hons Archaeol. and Anthropol. 1976). Sotheby's, 1977–93: auctioneer, oriental and Eur. ceramics specialist; Hd, Ceramics, Oriental Works of Art; Dir, 1983–93. Freelance broadcaster; TV series include: The Antiques Roadshow, 1986–; Quizeum, 2015–16; presenter: Inside Antiques, 2004; Treasures of Chinese Porcelain, 2011; (and devisor) China in Six Easy Pieces, 2013; Hogarth: One Man and his Pug, 2014; Mem., winning team, Gonville and Caius Coll., alumni series, University Challenge, 2014; radio includes: chm. and writer, Hidden Treasures, 1998–2002; presenter, Out of the Fire, 2000, On the China Trail, 2007; columnist: Scandinavian Mag., 2010–; Ceramic Review, 2011–; The Spanner, 2011–. Guest Curator: Internat. Ceramics Fair and Seminar, Hogarth's China, 1997; York Mus, 2005–06. Vis. Prof. of Humanities, De Montfort Univ., 2008–12. Mem., Steering Cttee, York Museums' Trust for Centre of Ceramic Art, 2014–. Judge, Art Fund Prize, 2010, 2011. Listed NADFAS speaker; Guest Lecturer: Australia (ADFAS), 2010, 2013, 2016; NZ (NZDFAS), 2010, 2013. Dir/leader of tours to China and Europe, 2003–. Chm., Hogarth Gp, 2004–. Pres., Leicester Soc. of Artists, 2014–; Hon. Pres., Internat. Ceramics Fest., 2014–. Patron: Leicester Internat. Music Festival, 2006–; Framework Knitters' Mus., Wigston, 2007–. Trustee: Mus. of Worcester Porcelain, 1994–2000; William Hogarth Trust, 2009–14; Nat. Trust Champion for Stoneywell Cottage (Ernest Gimson), Leics, 2013. Freeman, City of London, 2003; Liveryman, Weavers' Co., 2005 (Mem., Ct of Assts, 2011). FSA 2011; FRSA 2000–11. Hon. DArt De Montfort, 2007; Hon. DLitt Leicester, 2016. *Publications:* The Little Brown Illustrated Encyclopaedia of Antiques (ed with Paul Atterbury), 1994; China in Hogarth's England, 1997; How to Spot a Fake, 1999; (ed) A-Z of 20th Century Antiques, 2000; contribs to various jls and newspapers. *Recreations:* 'cellist, choir, travel (Europe and China), museums. *T:* (office) (0116) 244 8788. *E:* lars@tharp.co.uk. *W:* www.tharp.co.uk.

**THARP, Twyla;** American dancer and choreographer; *b* 1 July 1941; *m* Peter Young (marr. diss.); *m* Robert Huot (marr. diss.); one *s*. *Educ:* Pomona Coll.; American Ballet Theatre Sch.; Barnard Coll. (BA Art History 1963). With Paul Taylor Dance Co., 1963–65; Founder, 1965, choreographer, 1965–87, Twyla Tharp Dance Foundn; Artistic Associate Choreographer, American Ballet Theatre, 1988–91; regrouped Twyla Tharp Dance, 1991; *modern dances/ballets* choreographed include: Tank Dive, 1965; Re-Moves, 1966; Generation, 1968; Medley, 1969; The One Hundreds, 1970; Eight Jelly Rolls, 1971; Deuce Coupe, Joffrey Ballet, 1973; As Time Goes By, Joffrey Ballet, 1973; Sue's Leg, 1975; Push Comes to Shove, American Ballet Theatre, 1976; Mud, 1977; Baker's Dozen, 1979; The Catherine Wheel, 1981; The Little Ballet, American Ballet Theatre, 1984; In the Upper Room, 1986 (Olivier Award, 1991); Everlast, 1989; The Rules of the Game, 1989; (with Mikhail Baryshnikov) Cutting Up, 1993; Demeter and Persephone, 1993; Mr Wordly Wise, Royal Ballet, Covent Garden, 1995; Heroes, Sweet Fields, 66, 1997; Known By Heart, 1998; The Beethoven Seventh, 2000; also dir, Movin' Out (Tony Award for best choreography), 2003; also dir, Come Fly Away (Drama Desk Award for outstanding choreography), 2010; 50th Anniversary Tour, 2015; Beethoven Opus 130, 2016; also dir, Twyla Tharp Dance, 2017; The Illustrated 'Farewell', Royal Ballet, 2017; *films* choreographed: Hair, 1978; Ragtime, 1980; Amadeus, 1984; White Nights, 1985; I'll Do Anything, 1994; *television* includes directing: Making Television Dance; The Catherine Wheel; Baryshnikov by Tharp. Hon. Mem., Amer. Acad. Arts and Letters, 1997. Creative Arts Award, Brandeis Univ., 1972; Astaire Award, 2003; Drama League Award for Sustained Achievement in Musical Theater, 2003; Nat. Medal of Arts, 2004; Jerome Robbins Award, 2008. *Publications:* Push Comes to Shove (autobiog.), 1992; The Creative Habit: learn it and use it for life, 2003; The Collaborative Habit: life lessons for working together, 2009; Keep It Moving: lessons for the rest of your life, 2019.

**THATCHER, Anthony Neville,** CEng, FIMechE; Vice Chairman, Thyssen-Bornemisza SAM, 1993–2007 (President and Chief Executive Officer, Thyssen-Bornemisza Group, 1991–92); *b* 10 Sept. 1939; *s* of Edwin Neville Thatcher and Elsie May Webster; *m* 1968, Sally Margaret Clark. *Educ:* Sir John Lawes Sch., Harpenden; Luton Tech. Coll.; Manchester Univ. (MSc). Student apprentice, Haywards Tyler & Co., Luton, 1956–64; Project Engineer, Smiths Industries, 1964–67; Ultra Electronics: Operations Res. Asst, Acton, 1967–69; Vice-Pres., Sales, USA, 1970–73; Marketing Dir, Acton, 1973–77; Managing Dir, Ultra Electronic Controls, 1977; Managing Director: Dowty Electronic Controls, 1978–82; Electronics Div., Dowty Gp, 1982; Dir, 1983–91, Chief Exec., 1986–91, Dowty Gp. Member: Avionics Cttee, Electronics and Avionics Requirements Bd, DTI, 1981–85; Council, Electronics Engineering Assoc., 1983–91 (Pres., 1986–87); RARDE Management Bd (Indust.), 1986–91; Council, SBAC, 1986–91; Innovation Adv. Bd, DTI, 1988–91; Engrg Markets Adv. Bd, DTI, 1988–90; Engrg Council, 1989–91. Council Mem., Cheltenham Ladies' Coll., 1988–91. Freeman, City of London; Liveryman and Trustee, Glass Sellers' Co. *Recreations:* art, jazz piano, opera, fishing, gardening, bird watching. *Clubs:* Athenæum, Carlton; Georgetown (Washington).

**THATCHER, Hon. Sir Mark,** 2nd Bt *cr* 1991, of Scotney in the County of Kent; *b* 15 Aug. 1953; *s* of Sir Denis Thatcher, 1st Bt, MBE, TD and Baroness Thatcher, LG, OM, PC, FRS; *S* father, 2003; *m* 1st, 1987, Diane Bergdorf (marr. diss. 2007), Dallas, Texas; one *s* one *d*; 2nd, 2008, Sarah-Jane (*née* Clemence), former wife of Lord Francis Russell; two step *s*. *Educ:* Harrow. *Heir: s* Michael Thatcher, *b* 28 Feb. 1989.

**THAW, Sheila, (Mrs John Thaw);** *see* Hancock, S.

**THEAKSTON, John Andrew;** Director, Black Sheep Brewery, 1992–2016; *b* 23 May 1952; *s* of late Robert Francis Theakston and Jane Hawley; *m* 1977, Elizabeth Jane Morgan; one *s* one *d*. *Educ:* Sedbergh Sch., Yorks; Worcester Coll., Oxford (MA Mod. History); Durham Univ. (MSc). Trainee, T. & R. Theakston, Brewers, 1975–77; Donald Macpherson Group: Corporate Planning Manager, 1977–81; Overseas Div. Manager, 1981–84; Higgs & Hill, subseq. Swan Hill Group, plc: Business Develt Manager, 1985–87; Gp Finance Dir, 1987–89; Jt Gp Man. Dir, 1989–90; Chief Exec., 1991–2004. Non-executive Director: ARCO Ltd, 2005–17 (non-exec. Chm., 2006–17); Halcrow Ltd, 2006–11. *Recreations:* sailing, walking, trout fishing, golf.

**THEAKSTON, Simon Francis Owen**; DL; Executive Director, T. & R. Theakston Ltd, since 2003; *b* Kingston upon Thames, 7 May 1957; *s* of Michael James Theakston and Jano Wynfor Theakston (*née* Owen); *m* 1980, Candida Patricia Mary, *yr d* of His Honour Stanley Sanderson Gill and Dr Patricia Gill; one *s* one *d*. *Educ*: Ashville Coll., Harrogate. T. & R. Theakston: Mktg Manager, 1981–85; Area Manager, Matthew Brown plc, 1986–90; Mktg Manager, Scottish & Newcastle Breweries, 1990–93; Sales Dir, T. & R. Theakston Ltd, 1993–95; Mktg Dir, John Smith's Ltd, 1995–2000; Nat. Account Controller, Caledonian Brewery, 2000–02; with brothers regained control of family business, T. & R. Theakston Ltd, 2003. Non-exec. Chm., Pub is the Hub, 2008–. Mem. (C), Harrogate BC, 2002–16 (Hon. Alderman, 2018). Trustee, Yorks Agricl Soc., 2002–16 (Chm., 2008–16). FCIM 2007. DL N Yorks, 2012. Liveryman, Brewers' Co., 2005– (Master, 2019–20). *Recreations*: reading, field sports, visiting National Trust properties, visiting pubs. *Address*: c/o T. & R. Theakston Ltd, The Brewery, Masham, Ripon, N Yorks HG4 4YD. *T*: (01765) 684315. *E*: simon.theakston@theakstons.co.uk.

**THEIS, Hon. Dame Lucy (Morgan)**, DBE 2010; **Hon. Mrs Justice Theis**; a Judge of the High Court of Justice, Family Division, since 2010; *b* 6 Nov. 1960; *d* of Michael and Jill Theis; *m* 1991, Andrew Firrell; one *s* one *d*. *Educ*: Birmingham Univ. (LLB 1981). Called to the Bar, Gray's Inn, 1982, Bencher, 2007; Asst Recorder, 1998–2000; Recorder, 2000–10; QC 2003; a Dep. High Ct Judge, Family Div., 2009–10; Sen. Family Liaison Judge, 2018–. Hd, Field Court Chambers, 1995–2010. Mem., Gen. Council of the Bar, 2010–; Vice-Chm., 2006–07, Chm., 2008–09, Family Law Bar Assoc. *Recreations*: gardening, riding, farming. *Address*: Royal Courts of Justice, Strand, WC2A 2LL.

**THELLUSSON**, family name of **Baron Rendlesham**.

**THEOCHAROUS, Archbishop Gregorios; His Eminence The Most Rev. Gregorios**; Greek Orthodox Archbishop of Thyateira and Great Britain, 1988–2019; *b* 2 Jan. 1929. *Educ*: High Sch., Lefkoniko, Famagusta; Pan Cyprian Gymnasium, Nicosia; Theol Faculty, Univ. of Athens. Monk in the Sacred Monastery, Stavrovouni, Cyprus; ordained: deacon, 1953; presbyter, 1959; asst parish priest and later parish priest, All Saints, Camden Town, 1959–69; Archdiocese of Thyateira: Chancellor, 1965–79; Asst Bishop of Tropaeou, 1970–88; locum tenens on death of Archbishop Athenagoras, 1979; spiritual oversight of Community of St Barnabas, Wood Green, 1970–84. Dr *hc* North London, 1993. *Address*: c/o Thyateira House, 5 Craven Hill, W2 3EN. *T*: (020) 7723 4787, *Fax*: (020) 7224 9301.

**THERBORN, Prof. Göran**, PhD; FAcSS; Professor of Sociology, 2006–08, now Emeritus, and Director of Research, Department of Sociology, 2008–10, University of Cambridge; Affiliated Professor of Sociology, Linnaeus University, Sweden, since 2011; *b* 23 Sept. 1941; *s* of Ragnar and Karin Therborn; *m* 1982, Sonia Piña; one *s* one *d*. *Educ*: Lund Univ. (PhD 1974). Reader in Sociol., Lund Univ., 1975–81; Professor: of Political Sci., Catholic Univ., Nijmegen, Netherlands, 1981–87; of Sociol., Gothenburg Univ., Sweden, 1987–2003; Dir, Swedish Collegium for Advanced Study in the Social Scis, Uppsala, 1996–2006. Eur. Prof. of Social Policy, Budapest, 1996; Visiting Professor: FLACSO Mexico, and ANU, 1978; Sorbonne, 1980; UCLA, 1991; Buenos Aires, 1992; L'Institut des scis politiques, Paris, 2004. FAcSS (AcSS 2010). Hon. DPhil Roskilde, 2007; Hon. FilDr Linnaeus, Sweden, 2010; Hon. Dr Pols Helsinki, 2011; Dr *hc*: Nacional de Educación a Distancia Madrid, 2014; Pretoria, 2016; Scientiae Medicae Dr *hc* Malmö, 2018. *Publications*: Science, Class and Society, 1976; What Does the Ruling Class Do When It Rules?, 1978; The Ideology of Power and the Power of Ideology, 1980; Why Some Peoples are More Unemployed than Others, 1986; European Modernity and Beyond, 1995; Between Sex and Power: family in the world 1900–2000, 2004; (ed jtly) Asia and Europe in Globalization, 2006; (ed) Inequalities of the World, 2006; From Marxism to Post-Marxism?, 2008; Les sociétés d'Europe du XXe au XXIe siècle, 2009; (ed jtly) Handbook of European Societies, 2010; The World, 2011; The Killing Fields of Inequality, 2013; Cities of Power, 2017. *Recreations*: travelling, arts, country house. *Address*: Byvägen 4, 38892 Ljungbyholm, Sweden. *T*: (480) 30613. *E*: gt274@cam.ac.uk.

**THÉRIAULT, Hon. Camille Henri**, CM 2018; President and Chief Executive Officer, Mouvement des Caisses Populaires Acadiennes, 2004–16; *b* 25 Feb. 1955; one *s* one *d*. *Educ*: Baie-Sainte-Anne High Sch.; Université de Moncton (BSocSc Political Sci.). Formerly: Vice-Pres., Corporate Affairs, United Maritime Fisherman's Co-operative; Manager, Kent Industrial Commn. Government of New Brunswick: MLA (L) Kent South, 1987–March 2001; Minister of: Fisheries and Aquaculture, 1991–94; Advanced Educn and Labour, 1994–95; Economic Develt and Tourism, 1995–98; Premier, 1998–99; Leader of the Opposition, 1999–2001. Chair: Public Accounts Cttee, 1987; Select Cttee on Representation and Electoral Boundaries; Jt Chair, Ministerial Cttee on Creating New Options; Member: Standing Cttee on Estimates, 1987; Cabinet Cttee on Policy and Priorities, 1994. Leader, NB Liberal Party, 1998–2001. Mem., 2001–, Chm., 2002–, Transportation Safety Bd.

**THEROUX, Louis Sebastian**; journalist; writer, documentary maker and presenter, BBC, 1996–2003 and since 2006; *b* Singapore, 20 May 1970; *s* of Paul Edward Theroux, *qv*; *m* 2012, Nancy Strang; three *s*. *Educ*: Westminster Sch.; Magdalen Coll., Oxford (BA 1st Cl. Hons Mod. Hist.). BBC documentary series include: Weird Weekends, 1998–2000; When Louis Met…, 2000–02; Louis Theroux's LA Stories, 2014; Dark States, 2017; Altered States, 2018; programmes include: Louis and The Brothel, Louis, Marin and Michael, Louis and the Nazis, 2003; Gambling in Las Vegas, The Most Hated Family in America, Under the Knife, 2007; Behind Bars, African Hunting Holiday, Law & Disorder in Philadelphia, Law & Disorder in Johannesburg, 2008; A Place for Paedophiles, The City Addicted to Crystal Meth, 2009; America's Medicated Kids, Law & Disorder in Lagos, 2010; Ultra Zionists, America's Most Hated Family in Crisis, Miami Megajail, America's Most Dangerous Pets, 2011; Extreme Love - Autism, Extreme Love - Dementia, Twilight of the Porn Stars, 2012; By Reason of Insanity, Transgender Kids, 2015; Drinking to Oblivion, A Different Brain, Savile, 2016; Talking to Anorexia, 2017; The Night in Question, Mothers on the Edge, Surviving America's Most Hated Family, Selling Sex, 2019; film, My Scientology Movie, 2016. *Publications*: The Call of the Weird, 2005; Gotta Get Theroux This, 2019. *Address*: c/o Anita Land Ltd, 10 Wyndham Place, W1H 2PU.

**THEROUX, Paul Edward**, FRSL; FRGS; writer; *b* 10 April 1941; *s* of Albert Eugene Theroux and Anne Dittami Theroux; *m* 1st, 1967, Anne Castle (marr. diss. 1993); two *s*; 2nd, 1995, Sheila M. L. Donnelly. *Educ*: Univ. of Massachusetts (BA). Lecturer: Univ. of Urbino, 1963; Soche Hill Coll., Malawi, 1963–65; Makerere Univ., Kampala, Uganda, 1965–68; Univ. of Singapore, 1968–71; Writer-in-Residence, Univ. of Virginia, 1972. Mem., AAAL (formerly AAIL), 1984. Hon. DLitt: Trinity Coll., Washington DC, 1980; Tufts Univ., Mass, 1980; Univ. of Mass, 1988. Patrons Gold Medal, RGS, 2015. *Publications*: novels: Waldo, 1967; Fong and the Indians, 1968; Girls at Play, 1969; Murder in Mount Holly, 1969; Jungle Lovers, 1971; Sinning with Annie, 1972; Saint Jack, 1973 (filmed, 1979); The Black House, 1974; The Family Arsenal, 1976; Picture Palace, 1978 (Whitbread Award, 1978); A Christmas Card, 1978; London Snow, 1980; The Mosquito Coast, 1981 (James Tait Black Prize, 1982; filmed, 1987); Doctor Slaughter, 1984 (filmed as Half Moon Street, 1987); O-Zone, 1986; My Secret History, 1989; Chicago Loop, 1990; Doctor de Marr, 1990; Millroy the Magician, 1993; My Other Life, 1996; Kowloon Tong, 1997; The Collected Short Novels, 1998; Hotel Honolulu, 2001; Blinding Light, 2005; The Elephanta Suite, 2007; A Dead Hand, 2009; The Lower River, 2012; Mother Land, 2017; *short stories*: The Consul's File, 1977; World's End, 1980; The London Embassy, 1982 (televised, 1987); The Collected Stories, 1997; The Stranger at the Palazzo d'Oro and Other Stories, 2003; Mr Bones: twenty stories, 2014; *play*: The White Man's Burden, 1987; *criticism*: V. S. Naipaul, 1972; *memoir*: Sir Vidia's Shadow, 1998; *travel*: The Great Railway Bazaar, 1975; The Old Patagonian Express, 1979; The Kingdom by the Sea, 1983; Sailing through China, illus. Patrick Procktor, 1983; Sunrise with Seamonsters: travels and discoveries 1964–84, 1985; The Imperial Way, 1985; Riding the Iron Rooster, 1988; Travelling The World, 1990; The Happy Isles of Oceania, 1992; The Pillars of Hercules, 1995; Fresh-Air Fiend, 2000; Dark Star Safari, 2002; Ghost Train to the Eastern Star: on the tracks of The Great Railway Bazaar, 2008; The Tao of Travel, 2011; The Last Train to Zona Verde, 2013; Deep South, 2015; Figures in a Landscape, 2018; On the Plain of Snakes, 2019; *screenplay*: Saint Jack, 1979; reviews in New York Times, etc. *Recreation*: paddling. *Address*: c/o Hamish Hamilton Ltd, 80 Strand, WC2R 0RC.

*See also* L. S. Theroux.

**THESIGER**, family name of **Viscount Chelmsford**.

**THETFORD, Bishop Suffragan of**, since 2009; **Rt Rev. Alan Peter Winton**; *b* London, 4 Sept. 1958; *s* of David John Winton and June Winton; *m* 1982, Philippa Mary Harrold; two *d*. *Educ*: Sheffield Univ. (BA Hons Biblical Studies 1983; PhD 1987); Lincoln Theol Coll. Ordained deacon, 1991, priest, 1992; Asst Curate, Christchurch, Southgate, 1991–95; Priest-in-charge, St Paul's, Walden with Preston, and Continuing Ministerial Educn Officer, Dio. of St Albans, 1995–99; Rector, Welwyn, 1999–2005; Team Rector, Welwyn Team Ministry, 2005–09. Hon. Canon, Cathedral and Abbey Church of St Alban, 2007–09. *Publications*: The Proverbs of Jesus, 1990. *Recreations*: reading, cricket. *Address*: Herfast House, 5 Vicar Street, Wymondham NR18 0PL. *T*: (01953) 528010. *E*: bishop.thetford@dioceseofnorwich.org.

**THEW, Rosemary Constance Evelyn**; Chief Executive, Driving Standards Agency, 2005–13; *b* 3 Nov. 1949; *d* of John Henry Thew and Enid Thew. *Educ*: Preston Manor County Grammar Sch. Civil Service: County Court Clerk, Lord Chancellor's Dept, 1967–70; Exec. Officer, IR, 1970–79; Manpower Services Commn, 1979–86; Regl Employment Manager, W Midlands, Dept of Employment, 1986–89; Implementation and Policy Manager, 1989–96, W Midlands Regl Dir, 1996–2001, Employment Service, Employment Dept Gp, then DfEE; Field Dir, W Midlands Jobcentre Plus, 2001–05. *Recreations*: gardening, walking, golf.

**THEWLES, Col (Francis) Edmund**, OBE 1989; Vice Lord-Lieutenant of Shropshire, 2007–17; *b* 11 Nov. 1942; *s* of Wing Comdr H. J. A. Thewles, OBE and Rhoda Frances Thewles (*née* Hulme); *m* 1969, Caroline, *y d* of Col R. W. B. Simonds, CBE and Laetitia (*née* Melsome); one *s* two *d*. *Educ*: Berkhamsted Sch.; RMA, Sandhurst. Commnd Worcestershire Regt, later Worcs and Sherwood Foresters Regt, 1964–93. Comdt, Shropshire ACF, 1997–2000; Chm., Shropshire AFC Trust, 2000–. DL Shropshire, 2004. *Recreations*: mountaineering, theatre, travel, classic cars. *Address*: The Merchant's House, 79 Coton Hill, Shrewsbury SY1 2DP. *T*: (01743) 353424, 07817 757835.

**THEWLIS, Sarah Anne**; Managing Director, Thewlis Graham Associates, since 2010; *b* 12 May 1958; *d* of Geoffrey Frank Bennett and Mollie Bennett (*née* Bates); *m* 1983, Rev. Canon Dr John Charles Thewlis. *Educ*: Dartford Grammar Sch. for Girls; Univ. of Hull (BA Hist. 1979); Relate Cert. in Marital and Couple Counselling; Univ. of Glasgow (MML 2008). MIPD 1991, FCIPD 1998. Marks and Spencer, 1979–91, Divl Personnel Controller for Distribution Centres; Dep. Sec., RCP, 1991–94; Chief Exec., RCGP, 1994–2002; Chief Exec. and Registrar, NMC, 2002–08; Principal Consultant, 2008–09, Man. Dir, 2009–10, GBR Search, subseq. Gundersen Partners. Lay Mem., Employment Tribunal Panel, 1999–2008. Member: Bishops' Equal Opportunities Cttee, 2001–09; Deployment, Remuneration and Conditions of Service Cttee, subseq. Remuneration and Conditions of Service Cttee, Archbishops' Council, 2006–11; Home Office Database Ethics Gp, 2007–15; Audit Cttee, RCGP, 2010–14; Bd Recruitment and Employment Confedn, 2013– (Chair, Employment Policy Cttee, 2018–). Non-exec. Dir, Phoenix Futures, 2007–16 (Mem., Audit Cttee, 2007–11; Vice Chm., 2011–). Chm., Assoc. of Exec. Recruiters, 2014–18. Mem. Bd, Internat. Women's Forum (UK), 2014–16. Chm., Mulberry Centre, 2016–. Governor: Deansfield Sch., Eltham; Horne Park Sch., Eltham; Queen Anne's Sch., Caversham, 2012– (Chm., Personnel Cttee, 2014–; Vice Chm., 2016–). Liveryman, Needlemakers' Co., 2010. FRSA 2001; FRSocMed 2006. Hon. FRCGP 2002. *Recreations*: horses, cats, people, current affairs. *Address*: Willow Cottage, Wellington Marsh, Herefordshire HR4 8DU. *T*: (01432) 830134. *E*: sat@thewlisgraham.com; Thewlis Graham Associates, Portland House, Bressenden Place, SW1E 5RS. *T*: (020) 7850 4781. *Club*: Royal Society of Medicine.

**THEWLISS, Alison Emily**; MP (SNP) Glasgow Central, since 2015; *b* 13 Sept. 1982; *m*; two *c*. *Educ*: Univ. of Aberdeen. Mem. (SNP), Glasgow CC, 2007–15. SNP spokesperson on cities, 2015–, on Treasury, 2017–. Mem., Communities and Local Govt Select Cttee, 2015–17. Mem., Scottish CND. *Address*: House of Commons, SW1A 0AA.

**THIAM, (Cheick) Tidjane**; Chief Executive, Credit Suisse, since 2015; *b* Abidjan, Côte d'Ivoire, 29 July 1962; *s* of Amadou Thiam and Marietou Sow; two *c*. *Educ*: Ecole Polytechnique de Paris (Engrg 1984); École Nationale Supérieure des Mines de Paris (Civil Engrg 1986); INSEAD (MBA 1988). McKinsey & Co.: internat. consultant, Paris, NY, EU, 1986–89; Young Professionals Prog., World Bank, Washington, DC (on sabbatical), 1989–90; Associate Dir, Financial Services Practice, Paris, 1991–94; CEO, 1994–98, Chm., 1998–99, Nat. Bureau for Tech. Studies and Develt, Côte d'Ivoire; Partner, McKinsey & Co., Paris, 2000–02; Aviva plc: Gp Strategy and Develt Dir, 2002–06; Man. Dir, Aviva Internat., 2006; CEO, Aviva Europe, 2006–07; Gp Chief Financial Officer, 2008–09, Gp Chief Exec., 2009–15, Prudential plc. Non-executive Director: Arkema, 2006–09; 21st Century Fox, 2014–. Member: Africa Progress Panel, 2007–; ODI, 2011–; Internat. Business Council, WEF; Prime Minister's Business Adv. Gp, 2012–; European Financial Round Table, 2013–; UK-ASEAN Business Council; Chairman: G20 High Level Panel for Infrastructure Investment, 2011; Assoc. of British Insurers, 2012–14; UKTI Strategic Adv. Gp; UKTI British Business Ambassador, 2014–15. Chevalier, Legion d'Honneur (France), 2011; Les Echos Grand Prix de l'Economie, 2013.

**THIAN, Robert Peter**; Reforming, Performance-enhancing Chairman; *b* 1 Aug. 1943; *s* of Clifford Peter Thian and Frances Elizabeth (*née* Stafford-Bird); *m* 1964, Liselotte von Borges; two *d*. *Educ*: Geneva Univ. (Lic. en Droit 1967). Called to the Bar, Gray's Inn, 1971. Glaxo Group plc: Legal Advr, 1967–71; Man. Dir, Portugal, 1972–80; Abbott Laboratories (USA): European Business Develt Dir, 1981–84; Regional Dir, Europe, 1985–87; Vice Pres., Internat. Operations, Novo Industri A/S (Denmark), 1987–89; Gp Chief Exec., North West Water Group, 1990–93; Founder and Chief Exec., Renex Ltd, 1993–; Chief Exec., The Stationery Office Gp, 1996–99; Chairman: IMO Gp, 1999–2000; Tactica Solutions Ltd, 1999–2001; Astron Gp, 2001–05; Orion Gp, 2001–04; Whatman Plc, 2002–07; Southern Water Gp (formerly Southern Water Services Ltd), 2003–07; Cardpoint plc, 2006–08; Equiniti Ltd (formerly Lloyds TSB Registrars), 2007–09; Dep.

Chm., Lansen Pharmaceutical Hldgs Ltd (Hong Kong), 2010–11. Mem., Mgt Adv. Bd, TowerBrook Capital Partners (UK) LLP, 2010–16. Non-executive Director: Celltech Gp, 1992–99; Medeval Ltd, 1995–98. *Recreations:* horses, golf, reading. *Address:* 15a Princes Gate Mews, SW7 2PS. *E:* bob.thian@renex.net. *Clubs:* Lansdowne; Chantilly Golf, Monte Carlo Golf; Black Diamond Golf (Fla).

**THICKNESSE, Cdre Philip John;** Clerk to Worshipful Company of Haberdashers, since 2013; *b* London, 6 June 1959; *s* of John D. Thicknesse and Anne M. Thicknesse (*née* Hardie); *m* 1985, Jane Elizabeth Bryant; three *s*. *Educ:* Downside Sch.; BRNC Dartmouth; Lancaster Univ. (BA Hons Hist. 1981); Royal Naval Coll., Greenwich (MA 1993). Joined RN 1978; Bridge Watch Keeper, HMS Fearless, Falklands War, 1982; Helicopter pilot, Fleet Air Arm, 1985–2011; 820 Naval Air Sqdn/HMS Ark Royal, 1986–87; Anti Submarine Warfare Officer, 1989; Principal Warfare Officer, HMS Birmingham, 1989–91; 829 Naval Air Sqdn/HMS Norfolk, 1991–93; 1st Lt, HM Yacht Britannia, 1993–95; CO, HMS Leeds Castle, 1996; Directing Staff, RMCS, 1997–99; CO, HMS Westminster, 2000–01; MA to 2nd Sea Lord, 2001–03; MoD Staff, 2003–06; Commanding Officer: Naval Transition Team, Iraq, 2006; Royal Naval Air Stn, Culdrose, 2006–08; Dir, Maritime Warfare Centre, 2009; Comdr, British Forces S Atlantic Is, 2009–11. Vis. Schol., Wolfson Coll., Oxford, 2012–13. Mem., Internat. Adv. Gp, Project for Study of 21st Century, 2014–. Chm., Navy Rugby Ltd, 2016–. FCMI 2012. Trustee: Royal Humane Soc., 2013–18; Surplus Fund of RN Club of 1765 and 1785, 2017–. Freeman, City of London, 2018. Bronze Star (US), 2006. *Publications:* (jtly) Brassey's Military Rotorcraft, 2nd edn 1999. *Recreations:* windsurfing, sailing, Real tennis, writing. *Address:* Haberdashers' Hall, 18 West Smithfield, EC1A 9HQ. *T:* (020) 7246 9988, *Fax:* (020) 7246 9989. *E:* clerk@haberdashers.co.uk. *Clubs:* Royal Navy of 1765 and 1785; Goldfish, Amphibians.

**THIELEMANN, Christian;** Principal Conductor, Sächsische Staatskapelle Dresden, since 2012; *b* Berlin, 1 April 1959. *Educ:* Orchestra Acad. of Berlin Philharmonic Orch. (violist). Rehearsal pianist, Deutsche Oper, Berlin, 1978; positions in Gelsenkirchen, Karlsruhe and Hanover; joined conducting staff of Rhine Opera, Dusseldorf, 1985; Generalmusikdirector: Nuremburg, 1988–97; Deutsche Oper, Berlin, 1997–2004; Munich Philharmonic, 2004–11. Conductor, 2000–, Music Dir, 2015–, Bayreuth Fest.; Artistic Dir, Salzburg Easter Fest., 2013–. Hon. RAM. Hon. Dr: Franz Liszt Coll. of Music, Weimar; Catholic Univ., Leuven. Conductor of the Year, Opernwelt mag., 2011. *Publications:* Christian Thielemann: Mein Leben mit Wagner, 2012 (trans. English, 2015). *Address:* Sächsische Staatskapelle Dresden, Theaterplatz 2, 01067 Dresden, Germany.

**THIESSEN, Gordon,** OC 2002; PhD; Chair, Canadian Public Accountability Board, 2002–07; *b* 14 Aug. 1938; *m* 1964, Annette Hillyar; two *d*. *Educ:* Univ. of Saskatchewan (BA 1960; MA 1961); London School of Economics (PhD 1972). Lectr in Economics, Univ. of Saskatchewan, 1962; joined Bank of Canada, 1963; Res., and Monetary and Financial Analysis Depts, 1963–79; Advr to Gov., 1979–84; Dep. Gov. (Econ. Res. and Financial Analysis), 1984–87; Sen. Dep. Gov., 1987–94; Gov., 1994–2001; Mem., Exec. Cttee, 1987–2001; Mem., 1987–2001, Chm., 1994–2001, Bd of Dirs. Vis. Economist, Reserve Bank of Australia, 1973–75. Gov., Ottawa Hosp., 2014–17.

**THIN, Andrew,** OBE 2014; Chairman: Scottish Canals, since 2014; Scottish Land Commission, since 2017; *b* Edinburgh, 21 Jan. 1959; *s* of James and Marjorie Thin; *m* 1985, Frances Elizabeth Clark; one *s* one *d*. *Educ:* Edinburgh University (BSc Hons 1982; MBA 1988; DipM 1991). Team leader, Highlands and Is Develt Bd, 1989–91; Chief Exec., Caithness and Sutherland Enterprise, 1991–95; Chm., John Muir Trust, 1997–2003; Convener, Cairngorms Nat. Park Authy, 2003–06; Chm., Scottish Natural Heritage, 2006–14. Mem. Bd, Crofters Commn, 2001–06. Non-exec. Dir, Scottish Govt, 2010–14. Mem. Bd, Children's Hearings Scotland, 2011–14. *Recreations:* long-distance running, canoeing, hill walking, climbing. *Address:* Wester Auchterflow Cottage, Munlochy, Ross-shire IV8 8PQ. *T:* (01463) 811632. *E:* andrew.thin@hotmail.co.uk.

**THIRLWALL, Prof. Anthony Philip,** PhD; FAcSS; Professor of Applied Economics, University of Kent, 1976–2004, now Emeritus; *b* 21 April 1941; *s* of Isaac Thirlwall and Ivy Florence Ticehurst; *m* 1st, 1966, Gianna Paoletti (marr. diss. 1986); one *s* one *d* (and one *s* decd); 2nd, 2011, Dr Penélope Pacheco-López; one *s*. *Educ:* Harrow Weald County Grammar Sch.; Univ. of Leeds (BA 1962; PhD 1967); Clark Univ. (MA 1963). Teaching Fellow, Clark Univ., 1962–63; Tutor, Cambridge Univ., 1963–64; Asst Lectr, Univ. of Leeds, 1964–66; Lectr and Reader, Univ. of Kent, 1966–76. Economic Adviser: ODM, 1966; Dept of Employment, 1968–70. Res. Associate, Princeton Univ., 1971–72; Visiting Professor: West Virginia Univ., 1967; Melbourne Univ., 1981, 1988; Vis. Scholar, King's Coll., Cambridge, 1979; Bye-Fellow, Robinson Coll., Cambridge, 1985–86; Dist. Vis. Fellow, La Trobe Univ., 1994. Consultant: Pacific Islands Develt Program, 1989–90, 1996; African Develt Bank, 1993–94 and 1999; Asian Develt Bank, 2003; UNCTAD, 2004–. Member: Council and Exec. Cttee, Royal Econ. Soc., 1979–89; Council, Business for Sterling, 1999–2006. Governor, NIESR, 1979–2018. Trustee, New Europe Res. Trust, 1999–2006. FAcSS 2001. Member, Editorial Board: Jl of Develt Studies, 1979–2008; Jl of Post Keynesian Econs, 1998–2016; African Develt Review, 1999–2016; Series Ed., Great Thinkers in Econs, 2007–. *Publications:* Growth and Development, 1972, 10th edn (with P. Pacheco-López) as Economics of Development, 2017 (trans. Chinese and Greek 2002); Inflation, Saving and Growth in Developing Economies, 1974 (trans. Spanish 1978); (with R. Dixon) Regional Growth and Unemployment in the UK, 1975; Financing Economic Development, 1976 (trans. Greek 1977, Spanish 1978, Turkish 1980); (with H. Gibson) Balance of Payments Theory and the UK Experience, 1980, 4th edn 1992; Nicholas Kaldor, 1987; (with S. Bazen) Deindustrialisation, 1989, 3rd edn 1997; Performance and Prospects of the Pacific Island Economies in the World Economy, 1991; (with J. McCombie) Economic Growth and the Balance of Payments Constraint, 1994; Economics of Growth and Development: selected essays, vol. 1, 1995; Macroeconomic Issues from a Keynesian Perspective: selected essays, vol. 2, 1997; The Euro and Regional Divergence in Europe, 2000; The Nature of Economic Growth: an alternative framework for understanding the performance of nations, 2002 (trans. Spanish and Japanese, 2003, Portuguese, 2005); Trade, the Balance of Payments and Exchange Rate Policy in Developing Countries, 2003; (with J. McCombie) Essays on Balance-of-Payments Constrained Growth: theory and evidence, 2004; (with P. Pacheco-López) Trade Liberalisation and The Poverty of Nations, 2008 (trans. Turkish 2010, Spanish 2011); Economic Growth in an Open Developing Economy: the role of structure and demand, 2013; Essays on Keynesian and Kaldorian Economics, 2015; numerous edited books, esp. on Lord Keynes and Lord Kaldor; articles in professional jls; *festschrift* Growth and Economic Development: essays in honour of A. P. Thirlwall, 2006. *Recreations:* athletics (rep. GB, European Veterans Athletics Champs (400m, 800m), 1982), tennis, gardening, travel. *Address:* 14 Moorfield, Canterbury, Kent CT2 7AN. *T:* (01227) 769904. *E:* at4@kent.ac.uk. *Club:* Royal Over-Seas League.

**THIRLWALL, Rt Hon. Dame Kathryn (Mary),** DBE 2010; PC 2016; **Rt Hon. Lady Justice Thirlwall;** a Lady Justice of Appeal, since 2016; Senior Presiding Judge for England and Wales, since 2019 (Deputy Senior Presiding Judge, 2017–19); *b* 21 Nov. 1957; *d* of Brian Edward Thirlwall and Margaret Thirlwall (*née* Earl); *m* 1984, Prof. Charles Kelly; one *s* one *d*. *Educ:* St Anthony's Sch., Sunderland; Bristol Univ. (BA Hons 1980); Newcastle Poly. (CPE 1981). Called to the Bar, Middle Temple, 1982; QC 1999; Recorder, 2000–10; a Judge of the High Ct, QBD, 2010–16. *Address:* Royal Courts of Justice, Strand, WC2A 2LL.

**THIRLWELL, Alison Catherine;** *see* Macdonald, A. C.

**THIRSK, Amanda Jane,** LVO 2013; Private Secretary and Comptroller to the Duke of York, since 2012; *b* London, 4 July 1965; *d* of late Michael Emanuel Reynolds, CBE and Susan Geraldine Reynolds (later Smith); *m* 1991, Jeremy David Thirsk (*d* 2007); three *d*. *Educ:* St Paul's Girls' Sch.; Selwyn Coll., Cambridge (BA Law 1987). Guinness Mahon & Co. Ltd: graduate trainee, 1987–88; Manager, Syndications Dept, 1988–91; COS to Dep. Chief Exec., 1991–94; Dep. Hd of Treasury, 1994–96; Dir, Banking Dept, 1996–98; Asst Private Sec., 2005–06, Dep. Private Sec., 2006–12, to the Duke of York. Director: Duke of York Youth Develt Ltd, 2012–; Pitch@Palace CIC, 2015–; Inspiring Digital Enterprise Award CIC, 2015–; Pitch@Palace Global Ltd, 2017–. Trustee, Prince Andrew Charitable Trust, 2012–. *Address:* Buckingham Palace, SW1A 1AA. *T:* (020) 7024 4227. *E:* amanda.thirsk@royal.uk.

**THIRUNAMACHANDRAN, Prof. Rama Shankaran,** FRGS; Vice-Chancellor and Principal, and Professor of Higher Education Policy, Canterbury Christ Church University, since 2013; *b* London, 26 Sept. 1966; *s* of Dr T. Thirunamachandran and S. Thirunamachandran; *m* 1994, Rachel Cottrell; one *s*. *Educ:* Downing Coll., Cambridge (BA 1989). Researcher, KCL, 1990–92; Sen. Asst Registrar, Univ. of Bristol, 1992–95; Hd of Res., Enterprise and Ext. Relns, Royal Holloway, Univ. of London, 1996–99; Regl Dir (SE), 1999–2001, Dir (Res., Innovation and Skills), 2002–08, HEFCE; Dep. Vice-Chancellor and Provost, Keele Univ., 2008–13. Director and Trustee: Higher Educn Acad., 2010–18 (Chm., 2015–18); UCAS, 2010–13; Mem. Bd, Universities UK, 2017–. Kent Ambassador, 2017–. FRGS 2013. *Recreations:* cricket, bridge, travel. *Address:* Vice-Chancellor's Office, Canterbury Christ Church University, Canterbury, Kent CT1 1QU. *T:* (01227) 782915. *E:* vc@canterbury.ac.uk.

**THISELTON, Prof. Rev. Canon Anthony Charles,** PhD, DD; FBA 2010; Professor of Christian Theology, University of Nottingham, 1992–2001 and 2006–11, now Emeritus (Head, Department of Theology, 1992–2001; Professor Emeritus in Residence, 2001–06); Canon Theologian: Leicester Cathedral, 1994–2011, now Emeritus; Southwell Minster, 2000–10, now Emeritus; *b* 13 July 1937; *s* of Eric Charles Thiselton and Hilda Winifred (*née* Kevan); *m* 1963, Rosemary Stella Harman; two *s* one *d*. *Educ:* City of London School; King's Coll., London (BD 1959; MTh 1964; FKC 2010); PhD Sheffield 1977; DD Durham 1993. Curate, Holy Trinity, Sydenham, 1960–63; Lectr and Chaplain, Tyndale Hall, Bristol, 1963–67, Sen. Tutor, 1967–70; Recognised Teacher in Theology, Univ. of Bristol, 1965–71; University of Sheffield: Sir Henry Stephenson Fellow, 1970–71; Lectr in Biblical Studies, 1971–79; Sen. Lectr, 1979–86; Principal, St John's Coll., Nottingham and Special Lectr in Theology, Univ. of Nottingham, 1986–88; Principal, St John's Coll. with Cranmer Hall, Univ. of Durham, 1988–92; Public Orator, Nottingham Univ., 1999–2001. British Acad. Res. Leave Award, 1995–96. Visiting Professor: Calvin Coll., Grand Rapids, USA, 1982–83; Regent Coll., Vancouver, 1983; Fuller Theol Seminary, Pasadena, Calif, 1984 and 2002; North Park Coll. and Seminary, Chicago, 1984; Res. Prof. of Christian Theology, Univ. of Chester (formerly Chester UC), 2003–; Scottish Jl of Theol. Lectures, 1994. Exam. Chaplain to Bishop of Sheffield, 1977–80, to Bishop of Leicester, 1979–89 and 1993–. Member: C of E Faith and Order Adv. Group, 1971–81, 1987–90; Doctrine Commn, 1977–90, 1996–2005 (Vice-Chm., 1987–90); Wkg Pty on Revised Catechism, 1988–89; Steering Gp, Revised Weekday Lectionary, 2004–05; Gen. Synod of C of E, 1995– (Mem., Theol. Educn and Trng Cttee, 1999–2005; Chm., Evangelical Gp, 1999–2004; Mem., Appts Cttee, 2005–); Crown Nominations (formerly Appts) Commn, 2000–10; Wkg Pty on Women in the Episcopate, 2001–06; C of E Evangelical Council, 2001–04; C of E Bd of Educn, 2005–10. Consultant, Clergy Discipline (Doctrine) Gp, 2000–04; Mem., Task Gp for Theol Educn in the Anglican Communion, 2003–06. Mem., HFEA, 1995–99. Council for National Academic Awards: Vice-Chm., Bd of Theol and Religious Studies, 1984–87; Mem., Cttee for Humanities, 1987–89. Pres., Soc. for the Study of Theology, 1998–2000. Adv. Editor, Jl for Study of NT, 1981–91; Editl Consultant, Ex Auditu (Princeton and Chicago), 1985–2010; Mem. Editl Bd, Biblical Interpretation (Brill, Leiden), 1992–2003, Internat. Jl Systematic Theol., 1999–2010. DD Lambeth, 2002; Hon. DTheol Chester, 2012. *Publications:* The Two Horizons: New Testament Hermeneutics and Philosophical Description, 1980; (with C. Walhout and R. Lundin) The Responsibility of Hermeneutics, 1985; New Horizons in Hermeneutics: theory and practice of transforming biblical reading, 1992; Interpreting God and the Postmodern Self, 1995; (with C. Walhout and R. Lundin) The Promise of Hermeneutics, 1999; First Corinthians: a commentary on the Greek text, 2000; Concise Encyclopedia of Philosophy of Religion, 2002; (ed jtly) Reading Luke: interpretation, reflection, formation, 2005; Thiselton on Hermeneutics: collected works, 2006; Shorter Exegetical and Pastoral Commentary on 1 Corinthians, 2006; The Hermeneutics of Doctrine, 2007; Hermeneutics, 2009; The Living Paul, 2009; Blackwell Commentary on 1 and 2 Thessalonians, 2010; The Last Things: a new approach, 2012; The Holy Spirit in Biblical Teaching: through the centuries, and today, 2012; The Thiselton Companion to Christian Theology, 2015; Systematic Theology, 2015; Discovering Romans, 2016; A Shorter Guide to the Holy Spirit, 2016; An Approach to the Philosophy of Religion, 2017; An Approach to the Study of Theology, 2017; Doubt, Faith and Certainty, 2017; Understanding Pannenberg: landmark theologian of the twentieth century, 2018; The Power of Pictures in Christian thought: the use and abuse of images in the Bible and theology, 2018; Puzzling Passages in Paul: forty conundrums calmly considered, 2018; contribs to learned jls and other books on New Testament, doctrine, and philosophical hermeneutics. *Recreation:* choral and organ music. *Address:* South View Lodge, 390 High Road, Chilwell, Nottingham NG9 5EG. *E:* thiselton@ntlworld.com.

**THISTLETHWAITE, Rev. Canon Dr Nicholas John;** Canon Residentiary and Precentor, Guildford Cathedral, 1999–2016, now Canon Emeritus (Sub Dean, 2006–16); a Chaplain to the Queen, since 2014; *b* Mansfield, Notts, 23 Oct. 1951; *s* of Peter and Joan Thistlethwaite; *m* 1980, Tessa North (*d* 2017); one *s*. *Educ:* Brunts Grammar Sch., Mansfield; Selwyn Coll., Cambridge (MA 1977; PhD 1981); Ripon Coll., Cuddesdon, Oxford (MA 1982). Ordained deacon, 1979, priest, 1980; Asst Curate, St Gabriel's, Heaton, 1979–82; Chaplain, 1982–90, Fellow, 1986–90, Dean's Vicar, 2019–, Gonville and Caius Coll., Cambridge; Vicar, Trumpington, Cambridge, 1990–99. Member: Cathedrals Fabric Commn for Eng., 2001–11; Fabric Adv. Cttee, Canterbury Cathedral, 2011–; Fabric Adv. Commn, Westminster Abbey, 2012–; Fabric Adv. Cttee, Norwich Cathedral, 2016–. Chm., British Inst. of Organ Studies, 1992–99 (Hon. Pres., 2017–). FSA 2019. Medal, RCO, 2015. *Publications:* The Organs of Cambridge, 1983, 2nd edn 2008; (contrib.) The New Grove Dictionary of Music and Musicians, 1985; The Making of the Victorian Organ, 1990; (ed jtly) The Cambridge Companion to the Organ, 1998; (contrib.) The Organ: an encyclopedia, 2006, 2nd edn 2015; (contrib.) Die Musik in Geschichte und Gegenwart, 2007. *Recreations:* political history, architecture and art, theatre, opera. *Address:* 16 Douglas Court, Ely, Cambs CB7 4SE. *T:* (01353) 663231. *Club:* Royal Over-Seas League.

**THOBURN, Prof. June,** CBE 2002; LittD; Professor of Social Work, University of East Anglia, Norwich, 1994–2004, now Emeritus; *b* 17 May 1939; *d* of late William Shuttleworth Bailey and Elizabeth Anne Bailey; *m* 1965, John Thomas Thoburn; two *s*. *Educ:* Univ. of Reading (BA Hons French); Oxford Univ. (Dip. Public and Soc. Admin); Univ. of East Anglia (MSW; LittD). Social worker, Social Services Depts of Leicester CC, RBK&C and Norfolk CC, 1964–79; University of East Anglia: Lectr in Social Work, 1979–94; Dean, Sch. of Social Work, 1998–2001. Non-exec. Dir, E Norfolk HA, 1994–98; Member: Pres. of Family Division's Adv. Gp, 1998–2004; Gen. Social Care Council, 2001–08; Advr on child protection and adoption to DoH, 1995–2004; Chairman: Jersey Child Protection Cttee, 2007–09; Norfolk Family Justice Bd, 2012–; Bd Mem., CAFCASS, 2009–12. FRSA 2001; AcSS 2002–06. Editor, Child and Family Social Work, 2002–04. *Publications:* Permanence in Child Care, 1986; Child Placement: principles and practice, 1988, 2nd edn 1994; Safeguarding Children with the Children Act 1989, 1999; Permanent Family Placement for Children of Minority Ethnic Origin, 2000; Family Support in Cases of Emotional Maltreatment and Neglect, 2000; Child Welfare Services for Minority Ethnic Families, 2004; Collaborative Practice with Vulnerable Children and Their Families, 2016. *Recreations:* dinghy sailing, films, travel. *Address:* School of Social Work, University of East Anglia, Norwich NR4 7TJ. *T:* (01603) 593566. *E:* j.thoburn@uea.ac.uk.

**THODAY, Jonathan Murray;** Founder and Joint Managing Director, Avalon Entertainment Ltd, since 1998; *b* 7 May 1961; *s* of Prof. John Marion Thoday, FRS and of Doris Joan Thoday; *m* 1996, Leanne Newman; one *s* one *d*. *Educ:* Corpus Christi Coll., Cambridge (BA Natural Scis 1983); University Coll. London (MSc Biotechnol. and Genetic Engrg 1984). Co-founding Managing Director: Avalon Promotions; Avalon Public Relns; Avalon Motion Pictures; Avalon Television; executive producer: The Frank Skinner Show; Fantasy Football League; TV Burp; Not Going Out; Russell Howard's Good News; Workaholics; Last Week Tonight with John Oliver; Catastrophe; Taskmaster; producer: Newman and Baddiel: live and in pieces, Wembley Arena, 1993; Jerry Springer: The Opera, NT and Cambridge Th., 2003, UK nat. tour, 2006. *Address:* Avalon, 4A Exmoor Street, W10 6BD. *T:* (020) 7598 8000; Avalon, 104 W 27th Street, 5th Floor, New York, NY 10001, USA; Avalon, 9171 Wilshire Blvd, Suite 320, Beverley Hills, CA 90210, USA.

**THOM, Dr Gordon;** Director, Nobasu Consulting Ltd, since 2014; *b* 18 May 1953; *m* 1977, Margaret Pringle; one *s* one *d*. *Educ:* Univ. of Aberdeen (PhD 1978). DoE, 1978; joined FCO, 1979; Second, subseq. First Sec., Tokyo, 1981; FCO, 1985–89; First Sec., New Delhi, 1989–93; Economic Counsellor, Tokyo, 1994–98; Man. Dir, Dyson Japan, 1998–2001; Internat. Man. Dir, Dyson Ltd, 2001–04; Chm., Dyson Japan, 2004–05; Pres., Dyson US, 2006–08; Dir, Thom Consulting, 2009–10; Man. Dir, Floor Care and Small Appliances, Electrolux Japan, 2009–12; Pres., Bodum Japan, 2012–14. *Address:* 75 Clearwater, Lower Mill Estate, Somerford Keynes, Cirencester, Glos GL7 6FN.

**THOM, James Alexander Francis;** QC 2003; a Recorder, since 2002; *b* 19 Oct. 1951; *s* of James Flockhart Thom and Elspeth Margaret Thom (*née* Macnaughton); *m* 1st, 1974, Theresa Lindsie Hawkins (marr. diss. 1997); two *s* one *d*; 2nd, 1999, Elisabeth Jane Campbell Mardall. *Educ:* Corpus Christi Coll., Oxford (MA, BCL). Called to the Bar, Middle Temple, 1974; admitted to Bar: of St Vincent and Grenadines, 1997; of British Virgin Islands, 2005. *Recreations:* walking, reading, cooking, wine.

**THOM, Kenneth Cadwallader;** HM Diplomatic Service, retired; *b* 4 Dec. 1922; *m* 1948, Patience Myra (*née* Collingridge); three *s* one *d*. *Educ:* University College School, London; St Andrews Univ. (MA (Hons)). Army Service, 1942–47; Assistant District Officer, then District Officer, Northern Nigerian Administration, 1950–59; 1st Secretary: FO, 1959; UK Mission to UN, NY, 1960–63; FO, 1963–66; Budapest, 1966–68; FCO, 1968–72; Counsellor, Dublin, 1972–74; Counsellor, FCO, 1974–78; Consul-General: Hanover, 1978–79; Hamburg, 1979–81; retired, and re-employed, FCO, 1981–85. *Address:* Heybrook, Lower Backway, Bruton, Somerset BA10 0EA.

**THOMAS;** *see* Elis-Thomas.

**THOMAS,** family name of **Barons Thomas of Cwmgiedd** and **Thomas of Gresford,** and **Baroness Thomas of Walliswood.**

**THOMAS OF CWMGIEDD,** Baron *cr* 2013 (Life Peer), of Cwmgiedd in the County of Powys; **Roger John Laugharne Thomas,** Kt 1996; PC 2003; Lord Chief Justice of England and Wales, 2013–17; *b* 22 Oct. 1947; *s* of Roger Edward Laugharne Thomas and Dinah Agnes Thomas, Cwmgiedd; *m* 1973, Elizabeth Ann, *d* of S. J. Buchanan, Ohio, USA; one *s* one *d*. *Educ:* Rugby School; Trinity Hall, Cambridge (BA; Hon. Fellow, 2004); Univ. of Chicago (Commonwealth Fellow; JD). Called to Bar, Gray's Inn, 1969, Bencher, 1992; QC 1984; a Recorder, 1987–96; a Judge of the High Court of Justice, QBD, 1996–2003; Judge of the Commercial Court, 1996–2003; Judge i/c Commercial Court List, 2002–03; a Lord Justice of Appeal, 2003–11; Vice-Pres., 2008–11, Pres., 2011–13, QBD; Dep. Hd of Criminal Justice, 2008–13. Presiding Judge, Wales and Chester Circuit, 1998–2001; Sen. Presiding Judge for England and Wales, 2003–06. Pres., Qatar Internat. Court, 2018–. Chairman: Financial Markets Law Cttee, 2017–; Commn on Justice in Wales, 2017–. Asst Teacher, Mayo College, Ajmer, India, 1965–66; Lord Morris of Borth-y-Gest Lectr, Univ. of Wales, 2000. Faculty Fellow, Law Sch., Univ. of Southampton, 1990. DTI Inspector, Mirror Gp Newspapers plc, 1992. Vice Pres., British Maritime Law Assoc., 1996–; President: British Insurance Law Assoc., 2004–06; Eur. Network of the Councils of the Judiciary, 2008–10. Chancellor, Aberystwyth Univ., 2018–. Hon. Fellow: Univ. of Wales, Aberystwyth, 2002; Univ. of Wales, Swansea, 2003; Cardiff, 2005; Bangor, 2008. Hon. LLD: Glamorgan, 2003; UWE, 2008; Cardiff Metropolitan, 2011. *Publications:* papers and articles on commercial, maritime and insurance law, the Welsh courts and devolution, constitutional and criminal law. *Recreations:* gardens, walking, travel. *Address:* House of Lords, SW1A 0PW.

**THOMAS OF GRESFORD,** Baron *cr* 1996 (Life Peer), of Gresford in the co. borough of Wrexham; **Donald Martin Thomas,** OBE 1982; QC 1979; a Recorder of the Crown Court, 1976–2002; *b* 13 March 1937; *s* of Hywel and Olwen Thomas; *m* 1st, 1961, Nan Thomas (*née* Kerr) (*d* 2000); three *s* one *d*; 2nd, 2005, Baroness Walmsley, *qv*. *Educ:* Grove Park Grammar Sch., Wrexham; Peterhouse, Cambridge (MA, LLB; Hon. Fellow, 2016). Solicitor at Wrexham, 1961–66; Lectr in Law, 1966–68; called to the Bar, Gray's Inn, 1967, Bencher, 1989; Barrister, Wales and Chester Circuit, 1968–; Dep. Circuit Judge, 1974–76; Dep. High Court Judge, 1985–2009. Mem., Criminal Injury Compensation Bd, 1985–93. Contested (L): W Flints, 1964, 1966, 1970; Wrexham, Feb. and Oct. 1974, 1979, 1983, 1987; Vice Chm., Welsh Liberal Party, 1967–69, Chm. 1969–74; President: Welsh Liberal Party, 1977, 1978, 1979; Welsh Liberal Democrats, 1993–97 (Vice-Pres., 1991–93). Lib Dem Shadow Attorney Gen., 2004–06, 2007–10 and 2015–, Shadow Lord Chancellor, 2006–07. Chairman: Marcher Sound, 1991–2000 (ind. local radio for NE Wales and Cheshire) (Vice Chm., 1983–91); Southbank Sinfonia Develt Council, 2003–08. President: London Welsh Choral, 2002–; Sirenian Singers, 2003–; Friends of Maelor Hosp., 2006–; Patron, Hong Kong Welsh Male Voice Choir, 2005–. *Recreations:* Rugby football, rowing, choral singing, harp and piano playing, fishing, cooking. *Address:* Hayman House, Gresford, Wrexham LL12 8RG. *T:* (01978) 852205. *Club:* Reform.

**THOMAS OF WALLISWOOD,** Baroness *cr* 1994 (Life Peer), of Dorking in the County of Surrey; **Susan Petronella Thomas,** OBE 1989; DL; a Deputy Speaker, House of Lords, 2002–07; Chairman, Surrey County Council, 1996–97 (Member (Lib Dem), 1985–97; Vice Chairman, 1993–96); *b* 20 Dec. 1935; *m* 1958, David Churchill Thomas, *qv*; one *s* two *d*. *Educ:* Cranborne Chase Sch.; Lady Margaret Hall, Oxford. NEDO, 1971–74; Chief Exec., British Clothing Industries Council for Europe, 1974–78. Chm. and Treas., Richmond Liberal Assoc., 1974–77; former Pres., Women Lib Dems. Chm., Highways and Transport Cttee, Surrey CC, 1993–96; Member: Surrey Probation Cttee, 1997–2001; Surrey Area Probation Bd, 2001–04. Contested: (Lib Alliance) Mole Valley, 1983 and 1987; (Lib Dem) Surrey, Eur. Parly elecns, 1994. Lib Dem spokesman, H of L, on transport, 1994–2001, on women, 2001–06, on Equality, 2007–09. Chm., Associate (formerly All-Party) Parly Gp on Sex Equality, 1998–2001; Mem., H of L European Select Cttee on EU, 2005–07 (Mem., Law and Instns Sub-Cttee, 2003–05; Chm., Social and Consumer Affairs Sub-Cttee, 2005–07). DL Surrey, 1996. *Address:* Hidden House, 15 Guilden Road, Chichester, W Sussex PO19 7LA. *T:* (01243) 780096.
*See also* Hon. D. W. P. Thomas.

**THOMAS OF WINCHESTER,** Baroness *cr* 2006 (Life Peer), of Winchester in the County of Hampshire; **Celia Marjorie Thomas,** MBE 1985; Head, Liberal Democrat (formerly Liberal) Whips' Office, House of Lords, 1977–2006; *b* 14 Oct. 1945; *d* of David and Marjorie Thomas. *Educ:* St Swithun's Sch., Winchester. Winchester Diocesan Bd of Finance, 1963–65; Winchester Cathedral Appeal, 1965–66; The Pilgrims' Sch., Winchester, 1967–72; Christ Church Cathedral Sch., Oxford, 1972–74; Asst in office of Rt Hon. Jeremy Thorpe, MP, 1975–76. Party Agent: (Lib) Winchester, Oct. 1974; (Lib/SDP Alliance, later Lib Dem) Brecon and Radnor, 1987 and 1992. House of Lords: Lib Dem spokesman for Work and Pensions, 2007–10, on Disability, 2016–. Chm., Delegated Powers and Regulatory Reform Cttee, 2010–15; Member: Merits of Statutory Instruments Select Cttee, 2006–10; Procedure Select Cttee, 2007–12, 2017–; Liaison Select Cttee, 2007–10; Refreshment Select Cttee, 2007–12; Equality and Disability Select Cttee, 2015–16; MCC Disability Access Cttee, 2015–. Vice-Pres., Lloyd George Soc., 2005–; Pres., Winchester Lib Dems, 2007–. Trustee, Muscular Dystrophy UK (formerly Campaign), 2010– (Vice Pres., 2008–). Patron: Winchester Churches Nightshelter, 2008–; Avonbrook Projects Abroad, 2008–; Thrive, 2011–; Pinotage Youth Develt Acad., 2012–; Driving Mobility, 2017–. *Recreations:* music, theatre, gardening, butterfly conservation, watching cricket. *Address:* House of Lords, SW1A 0PW. *T:* (020) 7219 3586. *E:* thomascm@parliament.uk. *Club:* Two Brydges.

**THOMAS, Abraham,** FSA; Fleur and Charles Bresler Curator-in-Charge, Renwick Gallery, Smithsonian American Art Museum, 2016–18; *b* Sunderland, 17 Oct. 1977; *s* of Dr Thomas Mathew and Dr Elizabeth Thomas; *m* 2015, Erin Elizabeth Kuykendall. *Educ:* Tiffin Sch.; Univ. of Leicester (BSc Computer Sci.). Analyst, Deutsche Bank, 2000–05; Curator, Designs, V&A Mus., 2005–13; Dir, Sir John Soane's Mus., 2013–15. Trustee, Blue Elephant Th., 2003–05. Gov., Newham Sixth Form Coll., 2003–05. FSA 2014. *Publications:* Owen Jones, 2009; 1:1 - Architects Build Small Spaces, 2010; Disrupting Craft: Renwick Invitational 2018, 2018. *Address:* Smithsonian American Art Museum, MRC 510 Box 37012, Washington, DC 20013–7012, USA.

**THOMAS, Prof. Adrian Tregerthen;** Professor of Music: Cardiff University (formerly University of Wales, Cardiff), 1996–2010, now Emeritus; Gresham College, 2003–06, Professor Emeritus, 2008; *b* 11 June 1947; *s* of Owen George Thomas and Jean Tregerthen. *Educ:* Univ. of Nottingham (BMus 1969); University Coll., Cardiff (MA 1971). Lectr in Music, 1973–82, Sen. Lectr, 1982–85, Hamilton Harty Prof. of Music, 1985–96, QUB. Hd of Music, BBC Radio 3, 1990–93. Medal of Polish Composers' Union, for Distinguished Service to Contemporary Polish Music, 1989; Order of Merit for Polish Culture, 1996; Lutosławski Medal, Lutosławski Soc., 2005; Gloria Artis Gold Medal, Polish Min. of Culture and Nat. Heritage, 2013. *Publications:* Grażyna Bacewicz: chamber and orchestral music, USA 1985; (contrib.) Cambridge Companion to Chopin, 1992; (contrib.) New Grove Dictionary of Opera, 1993; (contrib.) New Grove Dictionary of Women Composers, 1994; Górecki, 1997; (contrib.) New Grove Dictionary of Music and Musicians, 2nd edn 2000; Polish Music since Szymanowski, 2005; contrib. Music Rev., THES, Contemp. Music Rev., Music and Letters. *Recreations:* visual arts, poetry, oriental arts, entomology, Cornish landscape and history. *E:* adrianthomasmusic@me.com.

**THOMAS, Andrew Martin;** QC 2008; a Recorder, since 2008; a Deputy High Court Judge, since 2013; *b* Wrexham, 18 Oct. 1965; *s* of Martin and Nan Thomas; *m* 1995, Jodie Swallow; one *s* one *d*. *Educ:* Darland Comp. Sch., Rossett; Yale Sixth Form Coll., Wrexham; Peterhouse, Cambridge (BA 1987); Inns of Court Sch. of Law. Called to the Bar, Gray's Inn, 1989; barrister, 1990–; Hd of Chambers, Lincoln House, 2016–. Judge of First-tier Tribunal (Restricted Patient Panel) (pt-time), 2012–. *Recreations:* family, running, ski-ing. *Address:* c/o Lincoln House Chambers, Tower 12, The Avenue North, Spinningfields, 18–22 Bridge Street, Manchester M3 3BZ. *T:* (0161) 832 5701. *E:* andrew.thomas@lincolnhousechambers.com.

**THOMAS, Anne M.;** *see* Marsden Thomas.

**THOMAS, (Anthony) Richard,** CMG 1995; HM Diplomatic Service, retired; High Commissioner, Jamaica, and non-resident Ambassador to Haiti, 1995–99; *b* 11 July 1939; *s* of Frederick James Thomas and Winifred Kate Apthorpe Webb; *m* 1976, Ricky Parks Prado, London and Lima; one *s* one *d*. *Educ:* Ampleforth; Peterhouse, Cambridge (MA). FO 1962; served Caracas, Budapest, Washington, Madrid and FCO; Counsellor, Dep. Consul-Gen., Johannesburg, 1981; Minister Counsellor and Consul-Gen., Brasilia, 1985; FCO 1989; Ambassador to Angola, São Tomé and Príncipe, 1993. *Recreations:* listening to music, reading, theatre, visual arts, cooking. *Address:* c/o 83 Broxash Road, SW11 6AD.

**THOMAS, Hon. Barbara;** *see* Thomas Judge, Hon. Barbara Singer.

**THOMAS, Ven. Charles Edward;** Archdeacon of Wells, 1983–93; *b* 30 Dec. 1927. *Educ:* St David's College, Lampeter (BA 1951); College of the Resurrection, Mirfield. Deacon 1953, priest 1954; Curate of Ilminster, 1953–56; Chaplain and Asst Master, St Michael's Coll., Tenbury, 1956–57; Curate of St Stephen's, St Albans, 1957–58; Vicar, St Michael and All Angels, Boreham Wood, 1958–66; Rector, Monksilver with Elworthy, 1966–74, with Brompton Ralph and Nettlecombe, 1969–74 (Curate-in-charge of Nettlecombe, 1968–69); Vicar of South Petherton with the Seavingtons, 1974–83. RD of Crewkerne, 1977–82. *Address:* Geryfelin, Pentre, Tregaron, Ceredigion SY25 6ND. *T:* (01974) 298102.

**THOMAS, Prof. Christian David,** PhD; FRS 2012; Professor, Department of Biology, since 2004, and Director, Leverhulme Centre for Anthropocene Biodiversity, since 2019, University of York; *b* Croydon, 9 Sept. 1959; *s* of Ambler Thomas and Diana Thomas; *m* 1985, Dr Helen Billington; one *s* three *d*. *Educ:* Bradfield Coll.; Corpus Christi Coll., Cambridge (BA Natural Scis 1981); University Coll. of North Wales, Bangor (MSc Ecol. 1984); Univ. of Texas at Austin (PhD Zool. 1988). Scientist: Ecol. Div., DSIR, NZ, 1988–89; Dept of Conservation, Christchurch, NZ, 1989; Post-doctoral work, NERC Centre for Population Biol., Imperial Coll. London at Silwood Park, 1990–92; Lectr, Sch. of Biol Scis, Univ. of Birmingham, 1992–95; Res. Fellow, Dept of Biol., 1995–99, Prof.,

Sch. of Biol., 1999–2004, Univ. of Leeds. Pres., Royal Entomological Soc., 2018–June 2020. Hon. PhD Helsinki, 2014. *Publications:* Inheritors of the Earth, 2017; over 300 articles in scientific jls, edited book chapters. *Recreations:* wildlife gardening, natural history. *Address:* Department of Biology, University of York, York YO10 5DD. *T:* (01904) 328646. *E:* chris.thomas@york.ac.uk.

**THOMAS, (Christopher) Paul;** Deputy Chief Executive, Manchester Enterprises (formerly Manchester Training and Enterprise Council), 1998–2006; consultant, 2006–11; *b* 9 Feb. 1951; *s* of Donald Thomas and Rita Thomas (née Kershaw); *m* 1981, Colleen Doey. *Educ:* Hutton Grammar Sch.; Bridlington Sch.; Keble Coll., Oxford (MA PPE). Civil Service, 1973–97: Customs & Excise, HM Treasury, Cabinet Office, Dept of Employment, and DfEE; Regl Policy Advr, Yorks and Humberside TECs, 1997–98. Director: Sheffield Jazz, 2008– (Chair, 2016–); Jobsteps Employment Services Ltd, 2011–14 (Chm., 2012–14); Adsetts Partnership, 2012–14; Chevin Housing Assoc. Ltd, 2013–15; Together Housing Gp, 2015–. Gov., Hope Valley Coll., 2006–11 (Chm. Govs, 2009–11). *Recreations:* cricket, jazz, walking, ski-ing, reading, theatre, travel. *Address:* 11 Dore Road, Dore, Sheffield, S Yorks S17 3NA.

**THOMAS, Christopher Sydney;** QC 1989; PhD; FCIArb; a Recorder, 2000–14; *b* 17 March 1950; *s* of late John Raymond Thomas and of Daphne May Thomas; *m* 1979, Patricia Jane Heath; one *s* one *d. Educ:* King's Sch., Worcester; Univ. of Kent at Canterbury (BA Hons, 1st Cl.); Faculté International de Droit Comparé, Paris (Diplôme de Droit Comparé (avec mérite), 1972); King's Coll., London (PhD 1994). FCIArb 1994. Hardwick Scholar and Jenkins Scholar, Lincoln's Inn; called to the Bar, Lincoln's Inn, 1973; Asst Recorder, 1994–2000. Called to Gibraltar Bar, 1989. CEDR accredited Mediator, 1999. Dep. Hd, Keating Chambers, 2008–13. *Recreations:* farming, sailing. *Address:* Keating Chambers, 15 Essex Street, WC2R 3AA. *T:* (020) 7544 2600.

**THOMAS, Claire C.;** *see* Curtis-Thomas.

**THOMAS, Clarence;** Associate Justice of the Supreme Court of the United States, since 1991; *b* 23 June 1948. *Educ:* Yale Univ. (JD). Asst to Attorney Gen., State of Missouri, 1974–77; attorney in private practice, 1977–79; Legislative Asst, US Senate, 1979–81; Asst Sec. for Civil Rights, Dept of Educn, Washington, 1981–82; Chm., Equal Employment Opportunity Commn, Washington, 1982–90; Judge, US Court of Appeals, 1990–91. *Publications:* My Grandfather's Son: a memoir, 2007. *Address:* United States Supreme Court, 1 First Street NE, Washington, DC 20543, USA.

**THOMAS, Prof. David;** Professor of Geography, University of Birmingham, 1978–95, now Professor Emeritus; *b* 16 Feb. 1931; *s* of William and Florence Grace Thomas; *m* 1955, Daphne Elizabeth Berry; one *s* one *d. Educ:* Bridgend Grammar School; University College of Wales, Aberystwyth (BA, MA); PhD London. Asst Lectr, Lectr, Reader, University College London, 1957–70; Prof. and Head of Dept, St David's University College, Lampeter, 1970–78; Birmingham University: Head of Dept of Geography, 1978–86; Head of Sch. of Geog., 1991–93; Pro Vice-Chancellor, 1984–89. Pres., IBG, 1988 (Hon. Sec., 1976–78); Mem., Council, RGS, 1988–91. *Publications:* Agriculture in Wales during the Napoleonic Wars, 1963; London's Green Belt, 1970; (ed) An Advanced Geography of the British Isles, 1974; (with J. A. Dawson) Man and his world, 1975; (ed) Wales: a new study, 1977; (with P. T. J. Morgan) Wales: the shaping of a nation, 1984; articles in learned jls. *Recreations:* music, wine, spectating. *Address:* 3 Is-y-Coed, Wenvoe, Cardiff CF5 6DL. *T:* (029) 2059 2861.

**THOMAS, David;** strategy consultant, since 2012; Principal Ombudsman, Financial Ombudsman Service, 2000–12 (interim Chief Ombudsman, 2009–10); *b* 7 Nov. 1945; *s* of late Harold Bushell Thomas and Margaret Thomas; *m* 1st (marr. diss.); three *s* one *d*; 2nd, 2015, Jane Bibby. *Educ:* St Anselm's Coll., Birkenhead; Liverpool Univ. (LLB Hons 1966). Admitted Solicitor, England and Wales, 1969, Ireland, 1991; with F. S. Moore & Price, subseq. Lees Moore & Price, Birkenhead, then Lees Lloyd Whitley, Liverpool and London: Solicitor, 1969–71; Partner, 1971–84; Managing Partner, 1984–93; Chm., 1993–96; Banking Ombudsman, 1997–2000. Member: Accountancy and Actuarial Discipline (formerly Accountancy Investigation and Discipline) Bd, 2001–09; Bd, Office of Legal Complaints, 2009–15; Mem., Audit Adv. Cttee, 2007–11, Ind. Service Delivery Reviewer, 2012–14, Scottish Public Services Ombudsman; Chm., CI Financial Ombudsman, 2014–. Financial Redress Consultant, World Bank, 2011–. Mem., Regulatory Bd, ACCA, 2013–. Member: Steering Cttee, FIN-NET, 2006–11; Cttee, Internat. Network of Financial Services Ombudsmen, 2009–12. Dir, South West Mutual, 2019–. Sec., 1981–86, Vice-Pres., 1986–87, Pres., 1987–88, Liverpool Law Soc.; Member: Council, Law Soc., 1987–96; Cttee, City of London Law Soc., 2005–09. Mem., Council, QMUL, 2006–14. *Recreations:* modern history, theatre, naval aviation, walking.

**THOMAS, David Bowen,** PhD; Keeper, Department of Physical Sciences, Science Museum, 1984–87 (Keeper, Department of Physics, 1978–84); *b* 28 Dec. 1931; *s* of Evan Thomas and Florence Annie Bowen. *Educ:* Tredegar Grammar Sch.; Manchester Univ. (BSc). Research Fellow, Wayne Univ., Detroit, USA, 1955–57; Research Scientist, Min. of Agriculture, Fisheries and Food, Aberdeen, 1957–61; Asst Keeper, Science Museum, Dept of Chemistry, 1961–73; Keeper, Dept of Museum Services, 1973–78. Hon. FRPS 1985. *Publications:* The First Negatives, 1964; The Science Museum Photography Collection, 1969; The First Colour Motion Pictures, 1969. *Recreation:* country walking. *Address:* Tanglewood, Moushill Lane, Milford, Godalming, Surrey GU8 5BQ.

**THOMAS, David Churchill,** CMG 1982; HM Diplomatic Service, retired; Assistant Under Secretary of State, Foreign and Commonwealth Office, 1984–86; *b* 21 Oct. 1933; *o s* of late David Bernard Thomas and Violet Churchill Thomas (née Quicke); *m* 1958, Susan Petronella Arrow (*see* Baroness Thomas of Walliswood); one *s* two *d. Educ:* Eton Coll.; New Coll., Oxford (Exhibnr). Mod. Hist. 1st Cl., 1957. Army, 2nd Lieut, Rifle Brigade, 1952–54. Foreign Office, 1958; 3rd Sec., Moscow, 1959–61; 2nd Sec., Lisbon, 1961–64; FCO, 1964–68; 1st Sec. (Commercial), Lima, 1968–70; FCO, 1970–73; Head of South West European Dept, 1974; Asst Sec., Cabinet Office, 1973–78; Counsellor (Internal Affairs), Washington, 1978–81; Ambassador to Cuba, 1981–84. Advr on Overseas Scholarships Funding, FCO, 1989–2000. Mem., Marshall Aid Commemoration Commn, 1999–2005. Mem. Council, RIIA, 1988–94. Mem. Bd, Inst. of Latin American Studies, Univ. of London, 1988–93. Associate Fellow, Centre for Caribbean Studies, Warwick Univ., 1990–96. *Publications:* essays and review articles on Latin American affairs. *Recreations:* photography, listening to music. *Address:* Hidden House, 15 Guilden Road, Chichester, W Sussex PO19 7LA. *T:* (01243) 780096.

*See also* Hon. D. W. P. Thomas.

**THOMAS, David (Edward);** Member, Halesworth Town Council; *b* 12 Jan. 1955; *m* 1975, Janet Elizabeth Whatrup; one *s* one *d. Educ:* Univ. of East Anglia (BA). Served RN, 1972–80; Suffolk Constabulary, 1980–88. Mem. (Lab), Suffolk CC, 1993–95, 2000–09; Mem., Police Authy. MEP (Lab) Suffolk and SW Norfolk, 1994–99; contested (Lab) Eastern Reg., 1999.

**THOMAS, David Emrys,** OBE 1998; management and personnel consultant, 1991–2001; Member, Local Government Commission for England, 1992–98; *b* Ewell, 9 July 1935; *s* of Emrys and Elsie Florence Thomas; *m* 1957, Rosemary, *d* of Alexander and Kathleen De'Ath of Hampton, Middx; two *s* one *d. Educ:* Tiffin Grammar Sch., Kingston upon Thames. Dip. Mun. Admin; FCIPD. Local Govt Administrator, 1951–63; Indust. Relations Officer, LACSAB, 1963–68; Chief Admin. Officer, LGTB, 1968–69; Dep. Estab. Officer, Surrey CC, 1969–70; County Personnel Officer, Surrey, 1970–77; Under-Sec. (Manpower), AMA, 1977–81; Dep. Sec., 1981–87, Sec., 1987–91, LACSAB; Employers' Sec. to nat. jt negotiating councils in local govt, 1987–91; Official Side Sec., Police Negotiating Bd, 1987–91; Sec., UK Steering Cttee on Local Govt Superannuation, 1987–91. Founder Pres., Soc. of Chief Personnel Officers in Local Govt, 1975. *Recreations:* unskilled gardening, the musical theatre (Mem., Olivier Awards panel, 1998; Sec., Stage Musical Appreciation Soc., 1996–2006). *Address:* 13 Arum House, Essex Drive, Cranleigh, Surrey GU6 8GX. *T:* (01483) 548171. *E:* DEThomas41@aol.com.

**THOMAS, Prof. David Glyndor Treharne,** FRCSE, FRCP, FRCPGlas, FRCS; Professor of Neurosurgery, 1992–2006, Professor of Neurological Surgery, 2006, now Professor Emeritus, Institute of Neurology, University of London; Honorary Consultant Neurosurgeon, National Hospital for Neurology and Neurosurgery, Queen Square, since 1977; *b* 14 May 1941; *s* of Dr John Glyndor Treharne Thomas, MC and Ellen Thomas (née Geldart); *m* 1970, Dr Hazel Agnes Christina Cockburn, FFARCS; one *s. Educ:* Perse Sch., Cambridge; Gonville and Caius Coll., Cambridge (BA, MA); St Mary's Hosp. Med. Sch.; MB BChir Cantab. Hosp. appts at St Mary's to 1969 and Asst Lectr in Anatomy, 1967–68; Sen. House Officer in Surgery, 1970, Registrar in Cardio-Thoracic Surgery, 1970–71, RPMS; Registrar, Sen. Registrar and Lectr in Neurosurgery, Inst. of Neur. Scis, Glasgow, 1972–76; Sen. Lectr, 1976–92, Hd, Gough Cooper Dept of Neurological Surgery, 1995–2006, Inst. of Neurology; Consultant Neurosurgeon: Nat. Hosp. for Neurology and Neurosurgery and Northwick Park Hosp., Harrow, 1976–2006; St Mary's Hosp., 1994–2006. Vice-President: Eur. Assoc. of Neurosurgical Socs, 1991–95; Eur. Soc. for Stereotactic and Functional Neurosurgery, 1994–98; World Fedn of Neurosurgical Socs, 1995–99, 1999–2003 (Parliamentarian, 2010); Pres., Academia Neuroeurasiana, 1999–2003. Member: Medical Soc. of London; Harveian Soc. (Pres., 2013). *Publications:* (ed with D. I. Graham) Brain Tumours, 1980; (ed with M. D. Walker) Biology of Brain Tumour, 1986; (ed) Neuro-oncology: primary brain tumours, 1989; (ed) Stereotactic and Image Directed Surgery of Brain Tumours, 1993; (ed with D. I. Graham) Malignant Brain Tumours, 1995. *Recreation:* military and naval history. *Address:* Box 147, The National Hospital for Neurology and Neurosurgery, Queen Square, WC1N 3BG. *T:* (020) 3448 8993; 106 Globe Wharf, 205 Rotherhithe Street, SE16 5XX. *T:* (020)7237 0024. *Clubs:* Athenæum, Royal Society of Medicine.

**THOMAS, David Hugh;** Chief Executive, 1997–2002, non-executive Chairman, 2002–04, Morgan Grenfell & Co. Ltd, later DB UK Bank Ltd; *b* 6 Dec. 1951; *s* of late John William Hugh Thomas and Joyce Thomas (née Fox); *m* 1978, Frances Mary Brown; one *s* one *d. Educ:* Hertford GS; Corpus Christi Coll., Oxford (BA 1st cl. Hons Lit. Hum. 1974; Sec., then Librarian, Oxford Union Soc., 1973); St John's Coll., Oxford (MA; DPhil 1978). Joined Morgan Grenfell & Co. Ltd, 1978: Italian Export Credits, 1978–83; Eurobonds, 1983–84; Interest Rate and Currency Swaps, 1984–87; Dir, 1988–March 2002, Nov. 2002–2004; Market and Credit Risk Mgt, 1988–97; Global Head of Risk, Investment Banking Activities, Deutsche Bank Gp, 1995–98; Chief Exec., Bankers Trust Internat. PLC, 1999–2002 (non-exec. Chm., 2002–04); non-exec. Chm. and Partner, Altima Partners LLP, 2004–10; non-exec. Dir, Schroder & Co. Ltd, 2005–16. Mem. Council, 2008–09, Hon. Treas., 2009–15, Vice-Pres., 2015–, Soc. for Promotion of Hellenic Studies. Trustee, Oxford Lit. and Debating Union Trust, 2003–08. Gov., 1999–2009, Vice-Chm., 2002–09, Abbot's Hill Sch. *Publications:* (introd.) The Landmark Xenophon's Hellenika, 2009; (contrib.) Plato and Xenophon: comparative studies, 2018. *Recreations:* classical studies, especially Greek history, playing the piano (very badly).

**THOMAS, Prof. David John, (Dafydd),** MD; FRCP; Professor Emeritus of Clinical Neurosciences, Imperial College London, 2007 (Professor of Stroke Medicine, 2005–06); Chairman, St Mary's Therapy & Imaging Ltd, 2006–15; *b* 7 Dec. 1943; *s* of Jack and Rachel Lloyd Thomas, Cwmgorse; *m* 1966, Celia Margaret Barratt, *d* of Sir Charles and Lady Barratt; two *s* three *d. Educ:* Alleyn's Sch.; Clare Coll., Cambridge (BA Nat. Sci. 1966; BChir 1969; MA, MB 1970); Univ. of Birmingham Med. Sch. (MD 1977). MRCP 1972, FRCP 1985. Consultant Neurologist: King Edward VII Hosp., Windsor, Heatherwood Hosp., Ascot, Wexham Park Hosp., Slough and St Mark's Hosp., Maidenhead, 1978–2000; Sen. Consultant Neurologist, St Mary's Hosp., London, 1978–2006; Sen. Lectr in Neurology, Inst. of Neurology and Hon. Consultant Neurologist, Nat. Hosp. for Neurology and Neurosurgery, 1979–2006, and Chalfont Centre for Epilepsy, 1995–2006. Dir, D-Gen Ltd, 2000–. Sec. and Chm., Special Adv. Cttee on Neurology to RCP, 1985–91. Member: Council, Stroke Assoc., 1992–2008; Stroke Council, Amer. Heart Assoc., 1992–; European Stroke Council, 1993–. Chm., Charitable Assoc. Supplying Hosps, 1984–99 (Life Pres., 1999–2018). Governor, Nat. Soc. for Epilepsy, 2001–04; Trustee, Assoc. of British Neurologists, 2005–08 (Chm. of Fundraising, 2016–); Chm., St Mary's Develt Trust, 2016–; Pres., Med. Soc. of London, 2019– (Sec., 2016–18). *Publications:* Strokes and their Prevention, 1988; The Eye and Systemic Disease, 1989; Neurology: what shall I do?, 1990, 2nd edn 1997; papers on cerebrovascular disease and other neurological subjects. *Recreation:* photography. *Address:* 14 Queen Court, Queen Square, WC1N 3BG. *Clubs:* Athenæum, Royal Society of Medicine.

**THOMAS, Sir David (John Godfrey),** 12th Bt *cr* 1694, of Wenvoe, Glamorganshire; *b* 11 June 1961; *o s* of Sir Michael Thomas, 11th Bt and of Margaret Greta Thomas (née Cleland); *S* father, 2003; *m* 2004, Nicola Jane Lusty. *Educ:* Harrow; Ealing Coll. Health club owner. *Recreations:* squash, tennis. *Heir:* none. *Address:* 1 Waters Edge, Eternit Walk, SW6 6QU. *T:* and *Fax:* (020) 7381 4078. *Clubs:* Hurlingham, MCC, Escorts, Jesters.

**THOMAS, David Malcolm,** CBE 2000; LVO 2007; Chairman, In Kind Direct, 2004–07; *b* 20 Feb. 1944; *s* of Edward Reginald Thomas and Edna Thomas (née Lowcock); *m* 1969, Ursula Maria Brinkbaumer; one *s* one *d. Educ:* Burnage Grammar Sch.; Univ. of Manchester (BA Hons 1965); Manchester Business Sch. (Dip. Advanced Studies in Business Mgt); Harvard Business Sch. (AMP 1988). Mktg Controller, CWS, 1965–71; Regl Gen. Manager, Finefare, 1971–73; Regl Dir, Linfood, 1973–82; Regl Man. Dir, Grand Metropolitan, 1982–84; Whitbread: Regl Dir, 1984–89; Man. Dir, Whitbread Inns, 1989–91; Man. Dir, Restaurants and Leisure, 1991–97; Chief Exec., 1997–2004. Non-executive Director: Xansa, 2000–07; Sandown Park, 2004–14. Mem., Honours Selection Cttee (Economy), 2005–12. Trustee, Kids in Sport, 2009–19. *Recreations:* opera, ballet, gardening, horse racing, golf, wine, foreign travel. *E:* dmthomas44@gmail.com. *Clubs:* Sloane; Woking Golf.

**THOMAS, Prof. David Neville,** PhD; FRSB; FLSW; Professor of Marine Biology, since 2006, Head, School of Ocean Sciences, since 2016, and Interim Pro Vice-Chancellor for Research, since 2019, Bangor University (formerly University of Wales, Bangor); *b* Great Malvern, 12 Oct. 1962; *s* of Neville Norman and Christine Ruth Thomas; *m* 1st, 1983, Rosalind Mary Miller (marr. diss. 1998); two *d*; 2nd, 2002, Cornelia Metz. *Educ:* Prior Park

Coll., Bath; Guildford Coll. of Technol.; Univ. of Liverpool (BSc Envmtl Biol. 1984; PhD 1988). FRSB (FSB 2004). Royal Soc. Postdoctoral Res. Fellow (Eur. Exchange Prog.), Dept of Marine Botany, Univ. of Bremen, 1989–90; Researcher: Alfred Wegener Inst. for Polar and Marine Res., Bremerhaven, 1990–94; Inst. for Chem. and Biol. of the Sea, Univ. of Oldenburg, 1994–95; Centre for Tropical Marine Ecol., Bremen, 1996; Lectr, Sen. Lectr, Reader and Personal Chair, Sch. of Ocean Scis, Univ. of Wales, Bangor, 1996–2006; Acad. of Finland Dist. Prof. and Res. Prof., Finnish Envmt Inst., Marine Res. Centre, Helsinki, 2009–13, Vis. Res. Prof., 2014–; Docent, Helsinki Univ., 2010–; Prof. of Arctic Marine Biol., Arctic Res. Centre, Biosci. Dept, Aarhus Univ., Denmark, 2013; Dir, Sêr Cymru Nat. Res. Network for Low Carbon, Energy and the Envmt, 2013–19. Marine and Climate Fellowship, Hanse Inst. for Advanced Study, 2001–03. Mem., Sci. Bd, 2017–19, Mem., Sci. Commn, 2019–, NERC. Scientist for New Century Lect., Royal Instn of GB, 2001. FLSW 2018. Hon. CRC Fellow, Antarctic Climate and Ecosystems CRC, Univ. of Tasmania, 2004–07. *Publications:* Seaweeds, 2002; (ed jtly) Phytoplankton Productivity: carbon assimilation in marine and freshwater ecosystems, 2002; (ed with G. S. Dieckmann) Sea Ice, 2003, 3rd edn (sole ed.) 2017; Frozen Oceans: the floating world of pack ice, 2004; (ed jtly) Dissolved Organic Matter (DOM) in Aquatic Ecosystems, 2004; (jtly) Marine Ecology: processes, systems and impacts, 2005, 2nd edn 2011; Surviving Antarctica, 2007; (jtly) Biology of Polar Regions, 2008; (with D. G. Bowers) Introducing Oceanography, 2012; (jtly) Art Forms from the Abyss: Ernst Haeckel's images from the HMS Challenger Expedition, 2015; contrib. over 235 science-related pubns. *Recreations:* links between science and art, Worcestershire County Cricket Club, riding a bicycle when time permits. *Address:* School of Ocean Sciences, Bangor University, Menai Bridge, Anglesey LL59 5AB. *T:* (01248) 382878. *E:* d.thomas@bangor.ac.uk.

**THOMAS, Rev. Canon Prof. David Richard,** PhD; FBA 2018; Professor of Christianity and Islam, 2007–18, and Nadir Dinshaw Professor of Interreligious Relations, 2011–18, University of Birmingham, now Emeritus; Prebendary and Canon Theologian, Wells Cathedral, since 2017; *b* Neath, S Wales, 7 Aug. 1948; *s* of David James Haydn Thomas and Olive May Thomas (*née* Richards). *Educ:* Boys' Grammar Sch., Neath; Brasenose Coll., Oxford (BA 1971; MA 1974); Fitzwilliam Coll., Cambridge (BA 1975; MA 1980); Univ. of Lancaster (PhD 1983). Ordained deacon, 1980, priest, 1981; Curate: St Columba's Ch, Anfield, Liverpool, 1980–83; Our Lady and St Nicholas Ch, Liverpool, 1983–85; Chaplain, Corpus Christi Coll., Cambridge, 1985–90; Vicar, St Mark's Ch, Witton, Blackburn, 1990–93; Bishop's Advr on Interfaith Relns, Blackburn, 1990–93; Lectr, Centre for Study of Islam and Christian-Muslim Relns, Selly Oak, Birmingham, 1993–99; Sen. Lectr in Christianity and Islam, 1999–2004, Reader in Christianity and Islam, 2004–07, Univ. of Birmingham. *Publications:* Anti-Christian Polemic in Early Islam, 1992; Early Muslim Polemic against Christianity, 2002; Christian Doctrines in Islamic Theology, 2008; Christian-Muslim Relations: a bibliographical history, 14 vols, 2009–. *Recreations:* cinema, walking. *Address:* 25 The Liberty, Wells, Som BA5 2SZ. *T:* (01749) 677888. *E:* d.r.thomas.1@bham.ac.uk.

**THOMAS, David Richard Brynmor;** QC 2019; *b* Oxford, 6 Jan. 1964; *s* of Prof. David Brynmor Thomas and Elizabeth Elma Thomas (*née* Flanagan); *m* 1st, 1990, Margaret Turner Sinclair (marr. diss.); one *s* one *d*; 2nd, 2018, Lauren Elizabeth Downes. *Educ:* High Sch. of Dundee; Univ. of Edinburgh (MB ChB 1987); Coll. of Law, Guildford (CPE Dist. 1990; Law Soc. Finals 1st Cl Hons 1991). Jun. House Officer, Edinburgh Royal Infirmary, 1987–88; Jun. and Sen. House Officer posts, Glasgow Royal Infirmary, 1988–89; admitted as solicitor, 1993; Herbert Smith: trainee solicitor, 1991–93; Asst Solicitor, 1993–2000; Partner, 2000–11; called to the Bar, Middle Temple, 2011; in practice as barrister, 2011–. Hon. Sen. Lectr, 2013–15, Hon. Prof. of Law, 2015–, Sch. of Internat. Arbitration, Centre for Commercial Law Studies, QMUL. Chair, Bd of Trustees, CIArb, 2016 (Trustee, 2011–16; Dep. Chair, 2015–16); Trustee, Christ Church Spitalfields Restoration Trust, 2001–18. *Publications:* (ed with Prof. Stavros Brekoulakis) The Guide to Construction Arbitration, 2017, 2nd edn 2018. *Recreations:* various exercise, watching Rugby, golfing badly, ski-ing infrequently, reading history, in particular biography. *Address:* 39 Essex Chambers, 81 Chancery Lane, WC1A 1DD. *T:* (020) 7832 1111. *E:* david.brynmor.thomas@39essex.com. *Clubs:* New (Edinburgh); Royal and Ancient Golf (St Andrews).

**THOMAS, (David) Roger,** CMG 2000; HM Diplomatic Service, retired; Partner, Cley Energy Consultants, since 2003; Director, Eurasia Energy Ltd, since 2006; *b* 1 Jan. 1945; *s* of late Alun Beynon Thomas, FRCS, and Doreen Thomas. *Educ:* Leys Sch., Cambridge; Sch. of Oriental and African Studies, London Univ. (BA Hons Turkish). Entered Foreign Office, 1968: FO, 1968–71; Third Sec. (Chancery), Cairo, 1971–74; Second Sec. (Envmt), UK Repn to EEC, Brussels, 1974–78; Consul, Ankara, 1979–82; UN and EC Dept, FCO, 1982–86; Consul (Commercial), Frankfurt, 1986–90; Consul-Gen., Stuttgart, 1990–93; Non-Proliferation, FCO, 1993–97; Ambassador to Azerbaijan, 1997–2000; Consul-Gen., San Francisco, 2001–03. *Recreations:* gardening, ski-ing, sailing, photography. *E:* drthomas.mfh@gmail.com.

**THOMAS, Prof. David Stephen Garfield,** DPhil; Professor of Geography, University of Oxford, since 2004 (Head, School of Geography and Environment, 2008–12); Fellow of Hertford College, Oxford, since 2004; *b* Dover, 2 Oct. 1958; *s* of late Frederick Garfield Thomas and Ruth Muriel Thomas; *m* 1st, 1987, (Helen) Elizabeth Martin (*d* 1990); 2nd, 1992, Lucy Marie Heath; two *d*. *Educ:* Dover Grammar Sch. for Boys; Hertford Coll., Oxford (BA Hons 1980; PGCE 1981; DPhil 1984). Department of Geography, University of Sheffield: Lectr, 1984–93; Sen. Lectr, 1993–94; Prof., 1994–2004; Chm., 1997–2000; Dir, Sheffield Centre of Internat. Drylands Res., 1994–2004. Hon. Professor: Univ. of Cape Town, 2006–; Univ. of Witwatersrand, 2013–. Occasional Consultant, UNEP, 1990–; Lead Expert, UK Govt Foresight Project, Envmtl Drivers of Migration, 2009–12. Mem. Council, RGS, 2001–05 and 2011–16 (Hon. Sec., 2001–02; Vice Pres., 2002–05; Vice Pres., Res. and Higher Educn, 2013–16); Chm., British Geomorphological Res. Gp, 2002–03. Res. into long and short term envmtl change in drylands, dry land geomorphology, human-envmt interactions in drylands, esp. in Southern Africa. El-Baz Award for advances to desert sci., Geol Soc. of Amer., 2011. Editor, Jl of Arid Envmts, 1990–. *Publications:* Arid Zone Geomorphology, 1989, 3rd edn 2011; (with P. Shaw) The Kalahari Environment, 1991; (with N. Middleton) World Atlas of Desertification, 1992, 2nd edn 1997; (ed with R. Allison) Landscape Sensitivity, 1993; (with N. Middleton) Desertification: exploding the myth, 1995; (ed with A. Goudie) Dictionary of Physical Geography, 4th edn 2016; (with D. Sporton) Sustainable Livelihoods in Kalahari Environments, 2002. *Recreations:* Africa, Dover Athletic FC, running, gardening. *Address:* School of Geography and Environment, Oxford University Centre for the Environment, Dyson-Perrins Building, South Parks Road, Oxford OX1 3QY.

**THOMAS, David W.;** *see* Wynford-Thomas.

**THOMAS, Hon. David (William Penrose);** author, journalist; *b* 17 Jan. 1959; *s* of David Churchill Thomas, *qv* and Baroness Thomas of Walliswood, *qv*; *m* 1986, Clare Jeremy (marr. diss. 2016); one *s* two *d*. *Educ:* Eton; King's College, Cambridge (BA History of Art). Freelance journalist, 1980–84; Editor, The Magazine, 1984–85; Editor, Extra Magazine, Sunday Today, 1986; Asst Editor and Chief Feature Writer, You Magazine, Mail on Sunday, 1986–89; Ed., Punch, 1989–92; TV Critic, Sunday Express, 1991–96. Young Journalist of the Year (British Press Awards), 1983; Columnist of the Year (Magazine Publishing Awards), 1989. *Publications:* Not Guilty: in defence of the modern man, 1993; Great Sporting Moments, 1990; Girl (novel), 1995; Show Me The Money, 2000; Foul Play, 2003; Blood Relative (novel), 2011; Ostland, 2013; as Tom Cain: The Accident Man, 2007; The Survivor, 2008; Assassin, 2009; Dictator, 2010; Carver, 2011; Revenger, 2012; as David Churchill: Devil (The Leopards of Normandy), Vol 1, 2015; Duke, 2016, Conqueror, 2017; (with Wilbur Smith) War Cry, 2017; with Ian Irvine: Bilko: the Fort Baxter Story, 1985; Fame and Fortune, 1988; Sex and Shopping, 1988. *Recreations:* gardening, singing, yoga. *Address:* c/o LAW Ltd, 14 Vernon Street, W14 0RJ. *T:* (020) 7471 7900.

**THOMAS, Derek Gordon;** MP (C) St Ives, since 2015; *b* 20 July 1972; *m*; two *s*. Apprentice Cornish mason; community worker, Chapel St Methodist Ch, Penzance and Mustard Seed, Helston; proprietor, construction business. Founder, Survivealive, outdoor adventure project, 1997–. Former Mem. (C), Penwith DC. Member: Sci. and Technol. Select Cttee, 2015–17; Health and Social Care Select Cttee, 2018–. *Address:* House of Commons, SW1A 0AA.

**THOMAS, Derek John,** CBE 1996; DL; CPFA; Chief Executive, Surrey County Council, 1988–95; *b* 3 Dec. 1934; *s* of late James Llewellyn Thomas and Winifred Mary Thomas; *m* 1st (marr. diss.); three *d*; 2nd, 1978, Christine (*née* Brewer); one *s*. *Educ:* Hele's Sch., Exeter. Formerly: Treasurer's Depts: Devon CC; Corby Development Corporation; Bath CC; Taunton Bor. Council; Sen. Asst Bor. Treasurer, Poole Bor. Council; Asst County Treasurer, Gloucestershire CC; Principal Asst County Treasurer, Avon CC; County Treasurer, Surrey CC. Mem. Council, CIPFA, 1977–78, 1985–87; Mem. Cttee of Mgt, Schroder Exempt Property Unit Trust, 1981–2001. Chm., Local Management in Schools Initiative, 1988–93. Mem. Bd, Surrey TEC, 1990–95; Chm., Surrey First, 1996–2002. Chm., Disability Initiative, 1996–2011. Surrey University: Mem. Council, 1994–2004; Chm., F and GP Cttee, 1995–2004; Treas., 1997–2004; Mem., Finance Cttee, UCL, 2006–10. CCMI. DL Surrey, 1996. *Publications:* (ed jtly) A Fresh Start for Local Government, 1997. *Address:* Squirrels Leap, 14 Lime Avenue, Camberley, Surrey GU15 2BS. *T:* (01276) 684433.

**THOMAS, Sir Derek (Morison David),** KCMG 1987 (CMG 1977); HM Diplomatic Service, retired; *b* 31 Oct. 1929; *s* of K. P. D. Thomas and Mali McL. Thomas; *m* 1956, Lineke van der Mast; two *c*. *Educ:* Radley Coll., Abingdon; Trinity Hall, Cambridge (Mod. Langs Tripos; MA; Hon. Fellow, 1997). Articled apprentice, Dolphin Industrial Developments Ltd, 1947. Entered HM Foreign Service, 1953; Midshipman 1953, Sub-Lt 1955, RNVR; FO, 1955; 3rd, later 2nd, Sec., Moscow, 1956–59; 2nd Sec., Manila, 1959–61; UK Delegn to Brussels Conf., 1961–62; 1st Sec., FO, 1962; Sofia, 1964–67; Ottawa, 1967–69; seconded to HM Treasury, 1969–70; Financial Counsellor, Paris, 1971–75; Head of N American Dept, FCO, 1975–76; Asst Under Sec. of State, FCO, 1976–79; Minister Commercial and later Minister, Washington, 1979–84; Dep. Under Sec. of State for Europe and Political Dir, FCO, 1984–87; Amb. to Italy, 1987–89. European Advr to N. M. Rothschild & Sons, 1990–2004; Director: N. M. Rothschild & Sons, 1991–99; Nexus Marketing Consultancy, 1991–92. Chm., Liberalisation of Trade in Services Cttee, BI, 1992–96; Mem., Export Guarantees Adv. Cttee, 1992–97. Member, Council: RIIA, 1994–97; Reading Univ., 1991–99. Chm., British Inst. of Florence, 1987–89 and 1997–2002. Hon. LLD Leicester, 2003. *Recreations:* listening to people and music; being by, in or on water; grandfathering, gardening. *Address:* Flat 1, 12 Lower Sloane Street, SW1W 8BJ. *Club:* Leander.
*See also* Sir C. A. Gladstone, Bt.

**THOMAS, Donald Michael;** poet and novelist; *b* Redruth, Cornwall, 27 Jan. 1935; *s* of Harold Redvers Thomas and Amy (*née* Moyle); two *s* one *d*. *Educ:* Redruth Grammar Sch.; Univ. High Sch., Melbourne; New Coll., Oxford (BA 1st cl. Hons in English; MA). School teacher, Teignmouth Grammar Sch., 1959–63; Lectr, Hereford Coll. of Educn, 1964–78; full-time author, 1978–. *Publications: poetry:* Penguin Modern Poets 11, 1968; Two Voices, 1968; Logan Stone, 1971; Love and Other Deaths, 1975; The Honeymoon Voyage, 1978; Dreaming in Bronze, 1981; Selected Poems, 1983; Dear Shadows, 2004; Not Saying Everything, 2006; Unknown Shores, 2009; Flight & Smoke, 2009; Two Countries, 2011; Vintage Ghosts (verse novel), 2012; Mrs English and Other Women, 2014; Family Bible, 2015; Shadow Sonnets, 2017; *novels:* The Flute-Player, 1979; Birthstone, 1980; The White Hotel, 1981; Russian Nights, a quintet (Ararat, 1983; Swallow, 1984; Sphinx, 1986; Summit, 1987; Lying Together, 1990); Flying in to Love, 1992; Pictures at an Exhibition, 1993; Eating Pavlova, 1994; Lady with a Laptop, 1996; Charlotte, 2000; Hunters in the Snow, 2015; *play:* Hell Fire Corner, 2004; *translations:* Requiem and Poem without a Hero, Akhmatova, 1976; Way of All the Earth, Akhmatova, 1979; Bronze Horseman, Pushkin, 1982; Onegin, Pushkin, 2011; Ruslan and Ludmila, Pushkin, 2019; *memoirs:* Memories and Hallucinations, 1988; Bleak Hotel, 2008; *biography:* Alexander Solzhenitsyn: a century in his life, 1998. *Recreations:* travel, Russia and other myths, the culture and history of Cornwall, the life of the imagination. *Address:* The Coach House, Rashleigh Vale, Truro, Cornwall TR1 1TJ. *W:* www.dmthomasonline.net.

**THOMAS, Dudley Lloyd;** a District Judge (Magistrates' Courts) (formerly Stipendiary Magistrate), Somerset and Avon, 1999–2008, and Gloucestershire, 2004–08; Member: Family Proceedings Court Panel, 1991–2008; Youth Court Panel, 1994–2008; *b* 11 Jan. 1946; *s* of late Myrddin Lloyd Thomas and Marjorie Emily (*née* Morgan); *m* 1970, Dr Margaret Susan Early; two *s* (and one *s* decd). *Educ:* King Edward's Sch., Bath; Coll. of Law, London. Justices Clerk's Asst, 1966–71; admitted as solicitor, 1971; Partner, Trump & Partners, Bristol, 1973–88; called to the Bar, Gray's Inn, 1988; Metropolitan Stipendiary Magistrate, 1990–99. Formerly Mem., Western Circuit. Mem., Heritage in Wales. Friend, Royal Acad. of Arts. *Recreations:* Rugby football, cricket, music, theatre, travel, walking, swimming.

**THOMAS, Edward Stanley,** FIA; Pension Director, Law Debenture Corporation plc, 2002–08; *s* of Stanley Frederick Thomas and Kate Dickason Thomas; *m* 1974, Elizabeth Mary Helen Casson; three *s* one *d*. *Educ:* King Edward VI Grammar Sch., Stourbridge; Slough Grammar Sch.; Clare Coll., Cambridge (MA). FIA 1974. Teacher, Sherwood Coll., Naini Tal, India, 1965; Actuarial trainee, Prudential, 1968–70; joined Bacon & Woodrow, 1970, Partner, 1978–98; Nat. Sec., Nat. Council of YMCAs, 1998–2002. Liveryman, Actuaries' Co. *Club:* Royal Automobile.

**THOMAS, Sir Eric (Jackson),** Kt 2013; Vice-Chancellor, University of Bristol, 2001–15; *b* 24 March 1953; *s* of late Eric Jackson Thomas and Margaret Mary Thomas (*née* Murray); *m* 1976, Narell Marie Rennard; one *s* one *d*. *Educ:* Ampleforth Coll.; Univ. of Newcastle upon Tyne (MB BS 1976; MD 1987). MRCOG 1983, FRCOG 2001; FRCP 2004. Jun. hosp. posts, 1976–87; Res. Fellow, and Lectr, Univ. of Sheffield, 1984–87; Sen. Lectr, Univ. of Newcastle upon Tyne, 1987–90; Consultant Obstetrician and Gynaecologist: Newcastle Gen. Hosp., 1987–2000; Princess Anne Hosp., Southampton, 1991–2001; Southampton University: Prof. of Obstetrics and Gynaecol., 1991–2001; Hd of Sch. of Medicine, 1995–98; Dean, Faculty of Medicine, Health and Biol Scis, 1998–2000. Mem., Medicines Commn, 2002–03. Chm., 7th World Congress of Endometriosis, 2000. Mem.

Council, RCOG, 1995–2001 (Chm. Scientific Adv. Cttee, 1998–2000). Non-executive Director: Southampton Univ. Hosps NHS Trust, 1997–2000; Southampton and SW Hampshire HA, 2000–01. Dir, 2001–15, Chm., 2003–07, Worldwide Univs Network Ltd; Universities UK: Mem. Bd, 2006–11; Chm., Res. Policy Strategy Cttee, 2006–11; Chm., England and NI Council, 2009–11; Vice Pres., 2009–11; Pres., 2011–13. Mem. Bd, CASE (US), 2010–14; Chm., CASE Europe, 2010–14. Member: Bd, SW RDA, 2003–08; Regl Sports Bd, 2003–06; Bd, W of England LEP, 2014–15; Chairman: HERDA-SW, 2002–04; DfES Taskforce on Increasing Voluntary Giving in Higher Educn, 2003–04; ERIC (formerly Educn and Resources for Improving Childhood Continence), 2007–12 (Patron, 2013–); Marshall Aid Commn, 2010–13. Trustee: Nat. Endometriosis Soc., 1998–2000; RCOG, 2013–; IntoUniversity, 2013–; HRH Commonwealth Study Confs, 2015–. Mem., Court, UAL, 2015–. William Blair Bell Meml Lectr, RCOG, 1987. Founder FMedSci 1998. FRSA 1998. Fellow, Birkbeck, Univ. of London, 2015. Hon. Fellow, Univ. of Bristol, 2015. Mem., Soc. of Merchant Venturers, 2008–15. DL Bristol, 2005–15. Hon. LLD Bristol, 2004; Hon. DSc Southampton, 2006; Teesside, 2008; UWE, 2010; NSW, 2016; Hon. DCL Newcastle upon Tyne, 2016. *Publications:* (ed jtly) Modern Approaches to Endometriosis, 1991; articles on endometriosis and reproductive biology. *Recreations:* Newcastle United, golf. *Address:* Abbey Farm House, Oakley Road, Mottisfont, Romsey, Hants SO51 0LQ. *E:* Eric.Thomas@bristol.ac.uk. *Clubs:* Athenæum, Le Beaujolais; Mottisfont Social.

**THOMAS, Franklin Augustine;** lawyer, consultant; *b* 27 May 1934; *s* of James Thomas and Viola Thomas (*née* Atherley); *m* (marr. diss.); two *s* two *d. Educ:* Columbia College, New York (BA 1956); Columbia Univ. (LLB 1963). Admitted to NY State Bar, 1964; Attorney, Fed. Housing and Home Finance Agency, NYC, 1963–64; Asst US Attorney for Southern District, NY, 1964–65; Dep. Police Comr, charge legal matters, NYC, 1965–67; Pres., Chief Exec. Officer, Bedford Stuyvesant Restoration Corp., Brooklyn, 1967–77; Pres., Ford Foundn, 1979–96. Dir, Alcoa, 1977–2010. Chm., September 11th Fund, 2001–06. Hon. LLD: Yale, 1970; Fordham, 1972; Pratt Institute, 1974; Pace, 1977; Columbia, 1979; Witwatersrand, 2017. *Address:* 380 Lexington Avenue, New York, NY 10168, USA.

**THOMAS, Gareth;** barrister; *b* 25 Sept. 1954; *s* of William and Megan Thomas; *m*; one *s* one *d. Educ:* Rockferry High Sch., Birkenhead; UCW, Aberystwyth (LLB). ACII. Worked in insurance industry. Called to the Bar, Gray's Inn, 1977. Member (Lab), Flints CC, 1995–97. MP (Lab) Clwyd West, 1997–2005. Contested (Lab) Clwyd West, 2005. PPS to Sec. of State for Wales, 2001–02, to Sec. of State for NI, 2002–05. Member: Social Security Select Cttee, 1999–2001; Jt Human Rights Cttee, 2000–01. Bd Mem., N Wales Housing Assoc., 2006–. *Recreations:* walking, theatre, music. *Address:* Pine Lodge, Llanfwrog, Rhuthun, Denbighshire LL15 2LN; Atlantic Chambers, 4–6 Cook Street, Liverpool L2 9QU.

**THOMAS, Gareth Richard;** MP (Lab Co-op) Harrow West, since 1997; *b* 15 July 1967; *s* of Howard and Susan Thomas. *Educ:* UCW, Aberystwyth (BScEcons Hons Politics 1988); Univ. of Greenwich (PGCE 1991); KCL (MA Imperial and Commonwealth Hist. 1997). Teacher, 1992–97. Mem. (Lab) Harrow BC, 1990–97. PPS to Minister Without Portfolio and Party Chairman, 2001–02, to Sec. of State for Educn and Skills, 2002–03; Parly Under-Sec. of State, 2003–08, Minister of State, 2008–10, DFID; Parly Under-Sec. of State, 2007–08, Minister of State, 2008–09, BERR. Chm., Parly Renewable and Sustainable Energy Gp, 1998–2003. Chm., Co-op Party, 2000–. *Recreations:* arts (member of the Tate, theatre, etc.), road running, supporting Arsenal, Swansea City FC and Harrow Borough FC, watching London Welsh RFC. *Address:* House of Commons SW1A 0AA.

**THOMAS, Gareth Vaughan;** Chairman, Countrywide Farmers Plc, since 2016; *b* Belfast, 24 April 1957; *s* of Griff and Esther Thomas; *m* 1983, Sallie Campbell (marr. diss. 2013); two *s* one *d*; *m* 2017, Jessica Madge; one *s* one *d. Educ:* Royal Belfast Academical Instn; University Coll. of Wales, Aberystwyth (LLB Hons). Joined John Lewis as graduate trainee, 1979: Managing Director: Norwich, 1991–96; Bristol, 1996–98; Cribbs Causeway, 1998–2000; Director: Retail Ops, 2000–07; Design and Develt, 2007–08; Retail Dir, 2009–10. Non-executive Director: Share PLC Gp, 2014–; Co-op Gp; Ind. Dir, Shoppers Stop India, 2014–; Chm., Waterside Holiday Gp. Trustee: Save the Children, 2005–13; Tate, 2010–17; Tate Enterprises Ltd; American Mus. in Britain, 2012–. Chm., American Mus. *Recreations:* playing tennis, running, swimming, bodyboarding, watching live Rugby and F1. *Address:* 3 Combeside, Lyncombe Vale Road, Bath BA2 4LU. *E:* garethvthomas@me.com. *Club:* Bath Rugby.

**THOMAS, Dr Geoffrey Price;** Director, University of Oxford Department for Continuing Education, 1986–2007; President, Kellogg College (formerly Rewley House), 1990–2007, now President Emeritus (Hon. Fellow, 2008); *b* 3 July 1941; *s* of Richard Lewis Thomas and Aerona (*née* Pace); *m* 1965, Judith Vaughan, *d* of Arsul John Williams; two *d. Educ:* Maesteg Grammar Sch.; UC of Swansea (BSc 1st Cl. Hons Physics); Churchill Coll., Cambridge (PhD 1966); Univ. of Oxford (MA). Post-doctoral res., Cavendish Lab., Univ. of Cambridge, 1966–67; Staff Tutor, UC of Swansea, 1967–78; Dep. Dir, Dept of Ext. Studies, Univ. of Oxford, 1978–86; Fellow, Linacre Coll., Oxford, 1978–90, Hon. Fellow, 1990. Co-Chm., Council on Scientific Literacy, Chicago Acad. of Sci., 1993–. Mem., HEFCW, 2000–08. Visiting Scholar: Smithsonian Instn, 1986; Northern Illinois Univ., 1986; Univ. of Calif, Berkeley, 1993; Univ. of Washington, 1993; Harvard Univ., 1993; Univ. of Georgia, 1999. Chair, Global Teacher Educn Inc., 2014–. Gov., Univ. of Glamorgan, 2009–11; Chair, Univ. of Wales Trinity St David, 2010–14. Patron, David Mather Foundn, 2011–. Aelod, Gorsedd Beirdd Ynys Prydain, 2014. FLSW 2014. Hon. Fellow: Trinity Coll., Carmarthen, 2007; Swansea Metropolitan Univ., 2009. Paul Harris Fellow, Rotary Internat., 2007. Hon. DSc Wales Trinity St David, 2014. *Publications:* (ed jtly) The Nuclear Arms Race, 1982; (ed jtly) Science and Sporting Performance, 1982; (ed jtly) University Continuing Education 1981–2006, 2010; numerous articles on public understanding of science, and on continuing educn policy. *Address:* 102 Old Road, Headington, Oxford OX3 8SX.

**THOMAS, Prof. Geraint Wynn,** DPhil; Professor of Equity and Property Law, Queen Mary School of Law, University of London, 1999–2013, now Emeritus; *b* 10 Aug. 1948; *s* of David and Mair Thomas; *m* 1972, Janice Lilian Tilden; one *s* one *d* (and one *d* decd). *Educ:* Ardudwy Sch., Harlech; University Coll. of Swansea (BA 1969); Balliol Coll., Oxford (DPhil 1974). Called to the Bar, Inner Temple, 1976; in practice as barrister, specialising in trusts, estate, planning and pensions, 1981–2002; Lectr in Law, Univ. of Kent, 1976–91; Sen. Lectr in Law, QMW, 1995–99. Hon. QC 2015. *Publications:* Taxation and Trusts, 1981; Powers, 1998, 2nd edn 2010; (with A. Hudson) The Law of Trusts, 2004, 2nd edn 2010; (contrib.) International Trust Laws, ed J. Glasson, 2006. *Address:* School of Law, Queen Mary University of London, E1 4NS. *T:* (020) 7882 3603. *E:* g.w.thomas@qmul.ac.uk.

**THOMAS, Sir (Gilbert) Stanley,** Kt 2006; OBE 1994; Co-Founder and Chairman, TBI, airport owner and operator, 1993–2005; *b* 20 Sept. 1941; *s* of Thomas Stanley Thomas, MBE and Connie Thomas; *m* 1962, Shirley Mary Powell; two *s* one *d*. Food manufacturer; founder and Jt Man. Dir, Peter's Savoury Products Ltd, 1970–88, when co. sold. President: Boys' and Girls' Clubs of Wales, 1991–; Royal Welsh Agricl Soc., 2001–02; Cancer Aid Merthyr Tydfil, 2007; Pres., Noah's Ark Appeal, 2007– (Chm., 1999–2007); Chm., fund raising for NSPCC in Wales, 2006–16 (Chm., Full Stop Campaign, Wales, 2005–08); Nat. Vice Pres., NSPCC, 2015–. Patron, Merthyr Tydfil Rugby Club, 2009–. Freeman of Merthyr Tydfil, 2000. Hon. Fellow, Cardiff Univ., 2011. OStJ 1996. Chancellor's Medal, Univ. of Glamorgan, 2003. *Recreations:* Rugby, golf, sailing. *Address:* The Paddocks, Druidstone Road, St Mellons, Cardiff CF3 6XD. *T:* (029) 2079 5840. *Clubs:* Cardiff Rugby; La Moye Golf (Jersey); Aloha Golf (Marbella).

**THOMAS, Gwenda;** Member (Lab) Neath, National Assembly for Wales, 1999–2016; *b* 22 Jan. 1942; *d* of Hermas and Menai Evans (*née* Parry); *m* 1963, Morgan Thomas; one *s*. *Educ:* Pontardawe Grammar Sch. Clerical Officer, County Courts Br., LCD; Exec. Officer, Benefits Agency. Member: Gwaun Cae Gurwen Community Council, 1986–99 (Chm., 1988–89); Llanguicke Community Council, 1981–86; W Glamorgan CC, 1989–96 (Chm., Social Services Cttee); Neath Port Talbot CBC, 1996–99 (Chm., Social Services Cttee). Chm., review into services for vulnerable children, 2003–06 (report, Keeping Us Safe, 2006). Dep. Minister for Social Services, 2011–16, and for Children, 2011–16, Nat. Assembly for Wales. Mem., CPSA (Br. Chm., 1974–84).

**THOMAS, Gwyn;** *see* Thomas, R. G.

**THOMAS, Harvey,** CBE 1990; international public relations consultant, since 1976; Director of Presentation (formerly Director of Press and Communications), Conservative Party, 1985–91; Executive Director, African Enterprise UK, since 2011; *b* 10 April 1939; *s* of John Humphrey Kenneth Thomas and Olga Rosina Thomas (*née* Noake); *m* 1978, Marlies (*née* Kram); two *d. Educ:* Westminster School; Northwestern Bible College, Minneapolis; Univs of Minnesota and Hawaii. Billy Graham Evangelistic Assoc., 1960–75; Producer, Jeddah Economic Forum, 2006–07. Member, Board of Directors: London Cremation Co. plc, 1984– (Chm., 2014–18); Cameo Ltd, 2011–. Trustee: Trans World Radio UK, 2001– (Chm., 2002–18); Cremation Soc. of GB, 1983– (Chm., 2009–19). FCIPR, FCIJ, FRSA. *Publications:* In the Face of Fear, 1985; Making an Impact, 1989; If they haven't heard it—you haven't said it, 1995, 2nd edn 2000. *Recreations:* travel, family, trains. *Address:* 23 The Service Road, Potters Bar, Herts EN6 1QA. *T:* (01707) 649910. *E:* harvey@hthomas.net. *Club:* Institute of Directors.

**THOMAS, Heidi-Louise;** playwright and screenwriter, since 1986; *b* Liverpool, 13 Aug. 1962; *d* of Frederick Thomas and Marie-Louise Thomas; *m* 1990, Stephen McGann; one *s*. *Educ:* St Edmund's College Sch., Liverpool; Univ. of Liverpool (BA Hons Eng. Lang. and Lit.). Playwright: Shamrocks and Crocodiles, Liverpool Playhouse, 1986; Indigo, RSC, 1987; Some Singing Blood, Royal Court, 1992; The House of Special Purpose, Chichester Fest., 2009; Gigi, Neil Simon Th., NY, 2015; screenwriter: Madame Bovary, 1999; I Capture the Castle, 2002; Cranford, 2007; Return to Cranford, 2009; writer and executive producer for television: Lilies, 2006; Ballet Shoes, 2007; Upstairs Downstairs, 2010–12; Call the Midwife, 2012–; Little Women, 2017. *Publications:* Shamrocks and Crocodiles, 1988; Indigo, 1988; The Life and Times of Call the Midwife, 2012, 2nd edn 2013. *Recreations:* reading, theatre, cinema, ballet, Viennese art, English seaside, antique diamonds, new technology. *Address:* c/o The Agency, 24 Pottery Lane, Holland Park, W11 4LZ. *T:* (020) 7727 1346.

**THOMAS, Prof. Howard,** DSc; LKCSB Distinguished Professor of Strategic Management and Management Education, 2015, now Emeritus, and Director, Academic Strategy and Consulting Unit, Singapore Management University, 2015 (Professor of Strategic Management, and Dean, Lee Kong Chian School of Business, 2010–14); Ahmass Fakahany Distinguished Visiting Professor of Global Leadership, Questrom School of Business, Boston University, since 2015; *b* 31 Jan. 1943; *m* 1978. *Educ:* LSE (BSc 1964, MSc 1965); Univ. of Chicago (MBA 1966); Edinburgh Univ. (PhD 1970; DSc 2007). First Internat. Business Prog. Fellow, Grad. Sch. of Business, Univ. of Chicago, 1965–66; Lectr in Stats and Operational Res., Univ. of Edinburgh, 1966–69; Lectr, Sen. Lectr, then Adjunct Prof., London Business Sch., 1969–77; Foundn Prof. of Mgt, Australian Grad. Sch. of Mgt, Sydney, 1977–80; University of Illinois, Urbana-Champaign: James F. Towey Prof. of Strategic Mgt, Coll. of Business Admin, 1980–2000; Dean, Coll. of Business Admin, 1991–2000; Prof. Emer. and Dean Emer., 2000; Dean, Warwick Business Sch., 2000–10; Prof. Emeritus, Univ. of Warwick, 2010. Visiting Professor: Harvard Business Sch., 1970; USC, 1975; UBC, 1979; Sloan Sch. of Mgt, MIT, 1987; Kellogg Sch. of Mgt, Northwestern Univ., 1990. *Publications:* (with H. Behrend) Incomes Policy and the Individual, 1967; Decision Theory and the Manager, 1972; (with P. G. Moore) Case Studies in Decision Analysis, 1976; (with P. G. Moore) Anatomy of Decisions, 1976, 2nd edn 1988; (with G. M. Kaufman) Modern Decision Analysis, 1977; (with D. W. Bunn) Formal Methods in Policy Formulation, 1978; (with D. B. Hertz) Risk Analysis and its Applications, 1983; (with D. B. Hertz) Practical Risk Analysis, 1984; (with J. McGee) Strategic Management Research: an European perspective, 1986; (jtly) Managing Ambiguity and Change, 1988; (with R. Bettis) Risk and Strategy, 1990; (with H. Daems) Strategic Groups, Strategic Moves and Performance, 1994; (jtly) Building the Strategically–Responsive Organization, 1995; (jtly) Strategic Renaissance and Business Transformation, 1995; (jtly) Entrepreneurship: perspectives on theory building, 1995; (with W. C. Bogner) Drugs to Market, 1996; (with D. O'Neal) Strategic Integration, 1996; (jtly) Dynamics of Competence–Based Competition: theory and practice of competence–based competition, 1996; (jtly) Strategy, Structure and Style, 1997; (jtly) Strategic Discovery: competing in new arenas, 1997; (jtly) Auditing Organizations Through a Strategic Systems Lens, 1997; (jtly) Strategic Flexibility: managing in a turbulent environment, 1998; (jtly) Handbook of Strategy and Management, 2001; (jtly) Strategy: analysis and practice, 2005; (jtly) Strategic Leadership Processes in Business Schools, 2011; numerous articles in Jl Business Venturing, Jl Mgt Studies, Strategic Mgt Jl, Acad. of Mgt Jl, Acad. of Mgt Rev., Admin. Sci. Qly. *Recreations:* golf, Rugby (spectating), reading, swimming. *Address:* Lee Kong Chian School of Business, Singapore Management University, 50 Stamford Road, Singapore 178899. *T:* (65) 68280535, *Fax:* (65) 68280107. *E:* howardthomas@smu.edu.sg.

**THOMAS, Prof. Howard Christopher,** PhD; FRCP, FRCPGlas, FRCPath, FMedSci; Professor of Medicine, 1987–2011, now Emeritus Professor of Hepatology, Department of Medicine, Vice Chairman, Division of Medicine, 1997–2004, and Clinical Dean, 2001–04, Imperial College Faculty of Medicine (formerly St Mary's Hospital Medical School), London University; *b* 31 July 1945; *s* of Harold Thomas and Hilda Thomas; *m* 1975, Dilys Ferguson; two *s* one *d. Educ:* Univ. of Newcastle (BSc Physiol; MB, BS); PhD Glasgow. MRCPath 1983, FRCPath 1992; MRCP 1969, FRCP 1983; FRCPGlas 1984. Lectr in Immunology, Glasgow Univ., 1971–74; Royal Free Hospital Medical School, London: Lectr in Medicine, 1974–78; Sen. Wellcome Fellow in Clin. Sci., 1978–83; Reader in Medicine, 1983–84; Titular Prof. of Medicine, 1984–87; Chm., Dept of Medicine, St Mary's Hosp. Med. Sch., London Univ., 1987–97; Consultant Physician and Hepatologist, St Mary's Hosp., 1987–2011; Hd, Section (formerly Dept) of Hepatol. and Gastroenterol., Imperial Coll. Faculty of Medicine, Univ. of London, 2004–11. Non-exec. Dir, Riotech Pharmaceuticals, 2004– (Chm., 2009–). Member: Scientific Cttee, European Assoc. for Study of Liver, 1983–86; DoH Adv. Gp on Infected Health Care Personnel, 1994–2000; Australian Cttee to Review Nat. Hepatitis C Strategy, 2002–03; Nat. Expert Panel on New and Emerging Infections, 2003–09; Adv. Bd, German Network of Competence in

Medicine (viral hepatitis) (Hep-Net), 2003–10; British Liver Disease Clinical Interest Gp, 2007–10; RCP/DoH Ad Hoc Hepatology Expert Gp, 2007; Comprehensive UK Clinical Res. Network (Hepatology Nat. Specialist Gp), NIHR, 2009–11; 4th Internat. Adv. Cttee, Univ. of Mauritius, 2009; Service Configuration and Workforce Gp preparing Nat. Plan for Liver Services, 2010–11; Scientific Adv. Bd, Cholangiocarcinoma Charity, 2019–; Chairman: DoH Adv. Gp on Hepatitis, 1999–2009 (Mem., 1987–99); DoH Strategy Cttee on Hepatitis C, 2001–02; NW Thames Hepatology Network, 2004–08; Pan-London Hepatitis Commissioning Gp, 2004–06; Clinical Guidelines Gp for Chronic Hepatitis B, NICE, 2011–13; Co-Chm., Blood Borne Viruses Gp preparing Nat. Plan for Liver Services, 2010–11. Vice Pres., British Liver Trust, 2000– (Mem., Med. Adv. Cttee, 1990–96); Pres., British and Eur. Assocs for Study of the Liver, 1996–97; Mem., Assoc. of Physicians of GB and Ireland, 1983–; Member Council: RCP, 2002–04 (Mem., Nominations Cttee, 2002–07); British Soc. of Gastroenterol., 2002–05. Chm. of Trustees, Liver Res. Trust, 1987–; Trustee: Hepatitis B Foundn, 2007–; Caxton Trust, 2011–18; Mem., Liver Alliance, 2011–13. Dir, Skipton Fund Ltd, 2013–. Founder and Editor, Jl of Viral Hepatitis, 1993–. Lectures: Humphry Davy Rolleston, 1986; Cohen, Israel, 1988; Bushell, Australia, 1990; Hans Popper, Internat. Assoc. for Study of Liver, S Africa, 1996; Ralph Wright, Southampton, 1999; Sheila Sherlock, British Soc. of Gastroenterol., 2005. FMedSci 1999. British Soc. of Gastroenterol. Res. Medal, 1984; Hans Popper Internat. Prize for Distinction in Hepatology, 1989; Ivanovsky Medal of Russian Acad. of Med. Scis, 1997; Lifetime Recognition Award: British Assoc. for Study of the Liver, 2010; Eur. Assoc. for Study of the Liver for clin. and scientific contrib. in field of liver diseases, 2010; Kowsar Award, Univ. of Tehran, Iran, 2011; Imperial Coll. Medal, 2013. *Publications:* Clinical Gastrointestinal Immunology, 1979; (ed jtly) Recent Advances in Hepatology, vol. 1, 1983, vol. 2, 1986; (ed jtly) Viral Hepatitis, 1996, 4th edn 2013; (ed jtly) Hepatitis C, 2009; pubns on oral tolerance and in Hepatology. *Recreations:* fishing, golf. *Address:* Department of Hepatology and Gastroenterology, Imperial College Faculty of Medicine, St Mary's Hospital, Praed Street, W2 1PG. *T:* (020) 7725 6454. *Club:* Athenæum.

**THOMAS, Prof. Huw Jeremy Wyndham,** PhD; FRCP; Consultant Physician and Gastroenterologist, St Mary's Hospital, London, since 1994; Professor of Gastrointestinal Genetics, Imperial College London, since 2007; Physician to the Queen and Head of HM Medical Household, since 2014; *b* London, 25 Feb. 1958; *s* of late William John Thomas and of Enid Thomas (*née* James); *m* 1986, Caroline Susan Sayer; two *s* one *d*. *Educ:* Harrow Sch.; Trinity Coll., Cambridge (BA 1979; MA); London Hosp. Med. Coll. (MB BS 1982); University Coll. London (PhD 1991). FRCP 1997. Jun. appts, London Hosp., 1982–86; Registrar, Liver Unit, Royal Free Hosp., 1986–88; Clin. Res. Fellow, Imperial Cancer Res. Fund, 1988–91; Sen. Registrar, St Mary's Hosp., 1991–94; Physician, King Edward VII Hosp. for Officers, later King Edward VII Hosp. Sister Agnes, 1997–; Physician to Royal Household, 2005–14. Hon Consultant Physician, St Mark's Hosp., 1994–. *Publications:* contrib. chapters, reviews and papers to med. jls. *Address:* 5 Devonshire Place, W1G 6HL. *E:* huw.thomas@imperial.ac.uk.

**THOMAS, Huw Vaughan,** CBE 2018; Auditor General for Wales, 2010–18; *b* 23 Nov. 1948; *s* of Idris Thomas and Winifred Thomas; *m*; two *s*. *Educ:* Durham Univ. (BA Hons Mod. Hist. 1970); City Univ., London (MSc Admin. Scis 1971). Initial mgt postings, Dept of Employment, 1971–74; Manager, London Office, Professional and Exec. Recruitment, 1974–76; Private Sec. to Parly Under Sec. of State for Employment, 1976–77; Manpower Services Commission: Principal, Employment Rehabilitation Service, 1978–81; Industrial Relns Manager, 1982–83; Department of Employment: Regl Dir, SW England, 1984–88; Dir for Wales, 1988–91; Chief Executive: Gwynedd CC, 1991–96; Denbighshire CC, 1995–2001; Dir, Taro Consultancy Ltd, 2001–10. Dir, N Wales Trng and Enterprise Councils, 1991–98; Member: New Deal Adv. Taskforce for Wales, 1997–2000; HEFCW, 1998–2002; Commn on Powers and Electoral Arrangements of Nat. Assembly of Wales, 2002–04; Consumer Mem., Hearing Aid Council, 2000–10; Ind. Mem., Parole Bd of England and Wales, 2005–11; Chm., Nat. Registers of Communication Professionals working with Deaf and Deafblind People, 2010–15. Chm., Wales, Big Lottery Fund, 2004–10; Interim Mem. Bd, Olympic Lottery Distributor, 2005–06. Mem., Nat. Exec., Soc. of Local Authy Chief Executives, 1995–2001; Lay Mem. Council, Law Soc., 2001–05. Dir, Inst. of Welsh Affairs, 1994–97; Chm., Plas Glyn y Weddw Arts Centre, 1995–96; Member: Cttee for Wales, Nat. Trust, 1996–2000; Council for Wales, Prince's Trust, 2000–02; Trustee, RNID, 2000–06. FCIPD; CCMI. Hon. Mem. CIPFA. *Recreations:* cinema, art, travelling. *Address:* Glan Conwy, Colwyn Bay.

**THOMAS, Rev. (Hywel) Rhodri Glyn;** Member (Plaid Cymru) Carmarthen East and Dinefwr, National Assembly for Wales, 1999–2016; President, National Library of Wales, since 2016; *b* 11 April 1953; *s* of late Thomas Glyn Thomas and Eleanor Glyn Thomas; *m* 1975, Marian Gwenfair Davies; two *s* one *d*. *Educ:* Ysgol Morgan Llwyd, Wrexham; UCW, Aberystwyth, Bangor and Lampeter. Minister of Religion, St Clears Area, 1978–89 and 1992–; Man. Dir, Cwmni'r Gannwyll Cyf, 1989–95; Welsh Spokesman, Forum of Private Business, 1992–99; Dir, "Sgript" Cyf, 1992–. National Assembly for Wales: Shadow Minister for Agricl and Rural Affairs, 2002–03, for Envmt, Planning and the Countryside, 2003, for Health and Social Services, 2004–05; Minister for Heritage, 2007–08; Chairman: Agricl and Rural Affairs Cttee, 1999–2000; Culture Cttee, 2000–03; SW Wales Regl Cttee, 2001–02; HSS Cttee, 2006–07; Dep. Ldr, Plaid Cymru Assembly Gp, 2003–16. *Address:* Llanddwyn, Llangynin, St Clears, Carmarthenshire SA33 4JY.

**THOMAS, Prof. Hywel Rhys,** PhD; Professor of the Economics of Education, University of Birmingham, 1993–2015, now Emeritus; *b* 11 Jan. 1947; *s* of John Howard Thomas and Eva Beryl Thomas (*née* James); *m* 1st, 1968, Patricia Anne Beard (marr. diss.); 2nd, 1980, Christine MacArthur; one *s* two *d*. *Educ:* Llanelli Boys' Grammar Sch.; Univ. of Manchester (BA, MEd, PGCE); Univ. of Birmingham (PhD 1988). Parkinson Cowan Ltd, 1968–69; teacher: New Mills Sch., Derbys, 1970–73; Kersal High Sch., Salford, 1974–79; University of Birmingham: Lectr, 1979–89; Sen. Lectr, 1989–91; Reader, 1991–93; Hd, Sch. of Educn, 1993–2003; Dir of Lifelong Learning, 2000–02; Dir, Centre for Res. in Med. and Dental Educn, 2001–15. Sen. Educn Advr, British Council, 1997–2000. Chair, King Edward VI Acad. Trust, Birmingham, 2017–. Hon. FRCGP 2006. *Publications:* Managing Education: the system and the institution, 1985; Economics and Education Management, 1986; Education Costs and Performance, 1990; Financial Delegation and Local Management of Schools, 1990; Managing Resources for School Improvement, 1996; Schools at the Centre?, 1997; National Evaluation of Specialty Selection, 2010. *Address:* 30 Linden Road, Bournville, Birmingham B30 1JU.

**THOMAS, Prof. Hywel Rhys,** CBE 2017; PhD, DSc; FRS 2012; CEng, FREng; FICE; FGS; FLSW; Professor of Civil Engineering, Cardiff University (formerly University of Wales College of Cardiff), since 1995; *b* 20 April 1951; *s* of Howard Lionel Thomas and Elizabeth Sybil Thomas; *m*; one *s* two *d*. *Educ:* UC, Swansea (BSc 1st cl. Hons (Civil Engrg); PhD 1980); Imperial Coll., London (MSc (Soil Mechanics) 1973; DIC); Univ. of Wales (DSc 1994). CEng 1977; FICE 2000. Grad. engr, 1973–76, then Asst Resident Engr, 1976–78, Scott Wilson Kirkpatrick and Partners; Sen. Res. Asst, UC, Swansea, 1978–80; University College Cardiff, later University of Wales College of Cardiff, then Cardiff University: Lectr in Civil Engrg, 1980–90; Sen. Lectr, Sch. of Engrg, 1990–92; Reader, 1992–95; Cardiff School of Engineering: Dir, Geoenvmtl Res. Centre, 1996–2018; Sen. Dep. Hd, 1999–2002, Hd, 2002, Div. of Civil Engrg; Dir, 2002–10; Dep. Pro Vice-Chancellor, Innovation and Engagement, 2007–10; Pro Vice-Chancellor, Engagement and Internationalisation, 2010–12, Res., Innovation and Enterprise, 2013–18. MAE 2012. FGS 2001; FREng 2003; FLSW 2011. *Publications:* The Finite Element Method in Heat Transfer Analysis, 1996; numerous contribs to learned jls. *Address:* Cardiff University, Main Building Room 0.46, Park Place, Cardiff CF10 3AT. *T:* (029) 2087 0650, *Fax:* (029) 2087 0689. *E:* thomashr@cardiff.ac.uk.

**THOMAS, Jacqueline Louise, (Jacks), (Mrs Malcolm Edwards);** Director, London Book Fair and London Book and Screen Week, since 2013; *b* Taunton, 26 Jan. 1961; *d* of Norman Toby and Fay Games-Thomas; *m* 1988, Malcolm Edwards; one *s* one *d*. *Educ:* Bishop Fox's Grammar Sch., Taunton; St Helen's Sch., Northwood; Univ. of Hull (BA Hons French). Microphone Publicist, BBC Radio 3, 1983–84; Publishing Asst, Blackie Children's Books, 1984–85; PR and Promotions Manager, Victor Gollancz Ltd, 1985–90; Mktg Dir, Simon & Schuster, 1990–92; Founder and CEO, Jacks Thomas Consultancy, 1993–97; Dir of Communications, Reader's Digest Europe, 1993–2003; CEO and Partner, Midas PR, 2004–12. Co-Founder, Chiswick Book Fest., 2009. Mem., Oxford Brookes Industry Adv. Bd, 2015–. Mem., Book Brunch Adv. Bd, 2016–. Founder, W4 Cttee, NSPCC, 1998. *Recreations:* travel, reading, dinner parties, watching endless crime drama repeats. *Address:* 196–198 St Albans Avenue, W4 5JU; 9 Cedar Falls, Bishops Lydeard, Som TA4 3HR. *T:* 07887 895246. *E:* jackslouise@hotmail.com. *Clubs:* Soho House, Ivy.

**THOMAS, James Bowen,** CMG 1989; Senior Director, Global Security, Pfizer Inc., New York, 1999–2004; *b* 3 July 1942; *s* of William George Thomas and Rose Thomas (*née* Bowen); *m* 1966, Gaynor Margaret Wilkins (*d* 2005); one *s* one *d*. *Educ:* Queen Elizabeth I Grammar Sch., Carmarthen; University Coll. of Wales, Aberystwyth (BA Hons; MSc Econ. Internat. Politics). Lectr in Modern Chinese Hist., Oxford Poly., 1968–71; MoD, 1971–99; attached to FCO as First Sec., Washington, 1979–81. Trustee, Surrey Care Trust, 2008–09. *Recreations:* Rugby (Welsh), travel, the visual arts, giving TLC to old properties.

**THOMAS, Jane Elizabeth G.;** *see* Garland-Thomas.

**THOMAS, Dame Jean Olwen,** DBE 2005 (CBE 1993); ScD; FMedSci; FLSW; FRS 1986; Master of St Catharine's College, Cambridge, 2007–16; Professor of Macromolecular Biochemistry, University of Cambridge, 1991–2010, now Emeritus; *b* 1 Oct. 1942; *d* of John Robert Thomas and Lorna Prunella Thomas (*née* Harris). *Educ:* Llwyn-y-Bryn High School for Girls, Swansea; University Coll., Swansea, Univ. of Wales (BSc and Ayling Prize, 1964; PhD and Hinkel Research Prize, 1967 (Chem.)); MA Cantab 1969; ScD Cantab 1985. Beit Meml Fellow, MRC Lab. of Molecular Biology, Cambridge, 1967–69; Cambridge University: Demonstrator in Biochemistry, 1969–73; Lectr, 1973–87; Reader in the Biochemistry of Macromolecules, 1987–91; New Hall, Cambridge: Fellow, 1969–91, Professorial Fellow, 1991–2006; Coll. Lectr, 1969–91; Tutor, 1970–76; Vice-Pres., 1983–87; Hon. Fellow, 2007. Chm., Cambridge Centre for Molecular Recognition, 1993–2002. Member: SERC, 1990–94; Council, Royal Soc., 1990–92, 2007–13 (Biol Sec. and Vice Pres., 2008–13); EPSRC, 1994–97; Council and Scientific Adv. Cttee, ICRF, 1994–2001; Scientific Adv. Cttee, Lister Inst., 1994–2000; Sci. Adv. Council for Wales, 2015–18. President: Biochemical Soc., 2001–05 (Hon. Mem., 2007); Soc. of Biol., later Royal Soc. of Biol., 2014–18 (Hon. Fellow, 2013). Trustee: BM, 1994–2004; Wolfson Foundn, 2013–. Gov., Wellcome Trust, 2000–07; Pres., Techniquest, 2005–08. Chancellor, Swansea Univ., 2018–. Mem., EMBO, 1982; MAE 1991; FMedSci 2002; FLSW 2010. Hon. Fellow: UC Swansea, 1987; Cardiff Univ., 1998; Darwin Coll., Cambridge, 2007; Worcester Coll., Oxford, 2008; Aberystwyth Univ., 2009; Swansea Metropolitan Univ., 2011. Hon. Mem., Biophys. Soc., 2009. Hon. Bencher, Middle Temple, 2009. Hon. DSc: Wales, 1992; UEA, 2003; London, 2007. K. M. Stott Research Prize, Newnham Coll., Cambridge, 1976; Frances Hoggan Medal, Learned Soc. of Wales, 2016. *Publications:* Companion to Biochemistry: selected topics for further study, vol. 1, 1974, vol. 2, 1979 (ed jtly and contrib.); papers in sci. jls, esp. on chromatin structure and DNA-binding proteins. *Recreations:* reading, music, walking. *Address:* Department of Biochemistry, 80 Tennis Court Road, Cambridge CB2 1GA. *T:* (01223) 333670.

**THOMAS, Sir Jeremy (Cashel),** KCMG 1987 (CMG 1980); HM Diplomatic Service, retired; *b* 1 June 1931; *s* of Rev. H. C. Thomas and Margaret Betty (*née* Humby); *m* 1957, Diana Mary Summerhayes (*d* 2009); three *s*. *Educ:* Eton; Merton Coll., Oxford. 16th/5th Lancers, 1949–51. Entered FO, 1954; served Singapore, Rome and Belgrade; Dep. Head, Personnel Ops Dept, FCO, 1970–74; Counsellor and Head of Chancery, UK Mission to UN, NY, 1974–76; Head of Perm. Under-Sec.'s Dept, FCO, 1977–79; Ambassador to Luxembourg, 1979–82; Asst Under-Sec. of State, FCO, 1982–85; Ambassador to Greece, 1985–89. Chm., Chichester Harbour Trust, 2002–13. *Publications:* The Rhythm of the Tide: tales through the ages of Chichester Harbour, 1999. *Recreations:* sailing, fishing. *Address:* East Manor Farm, Pook Lane, East Lavant, near Chichester, West Sussex PO18 0AH. *T:* (01243) 531661. *Clubs:* Oxford and Cambridge; Itchenor Sailing, Bosham Sailing.

**THOMAS, Maj. Gen. Jeremy Hywel,** CB 2012; DSO 2007; PhD; consultant (part-time), since 2015; UK Representative of Thomson Reuters Special Services LLC, since 2018; Assistant Chief of Defence Staff (Intelligence Capability), Ministry of Defence, 2009–12; *b* 12 April 1957; *s* of Brian and Eslie Thomas; *m* 1978, Oenone French; one *s* one *d*. *Educ:* Worthing High Sch. for Boys; Worthing Sixth Form Coll.; Univ. of St Andrews (MLitt 2013); Univ. of Exeter (PhD 2017). Royal Marines: joined, 1975; Army Staff Coll., Camberley, 1989; OC L Company, 42 Commando, 1993–95; COS 3 Commando Bde, 1995–97; Comdr 45 Commando Gp, 1997–99; COS Jt Force HQ, 1999–2001; HCSC 2000; Dir Intelligence Ops, Defence Intelligence Staff, 2003–05; Commanded: 3 Commando Bde, 2006–07; UK Task Force in Afghanistan, Oct. 2006–April 2007; Sen. British Mil. Advr to HQ US Central Comd, Tampa, 2007–09. Security sector consultant (pt-time), 2012–. Rep. Col Comdt, RM, 2012–15. Chm. Trustees, RM Charitable Trust Fund, 2013–15. Hon. Fellow, Univ. of Exeter Strategy and Security Inst., 2012–15. *Recreations:* keeping fit, history and current affairs, gardening, active family holidays.

**THOMAS, Jeremy Jack,** CBE 2009; film producer; Chairman, Recorded Picture Co., since 1973; *b* 26 July 1949; *s* of late Ralph Philip Thomas, MC and Joy Thomas; *m* 1st, 1977, Claudia Frolich (marr. diss. 1981); one *s*; 2nd, 1982, Vivien Coughman; two *s*. *Educ:* Millfield. Has worked in most aspects of film prodn, esp. in editing dept before becoming a producer. Chm., BFI, 1993–97. Producer: Mad Dog Morgan, 1974; The Shout, 1977; Bad Timing, 1980; Merry Christmas, Mr Lawrence, 1982; Eureka, 1982; The Hit, 1984; Insignificance, 1985; The Last Emperor, 1987 (9 Acad. Awards incl. Best Film); Everybody Wins, 1990; The Sheltering Sky, 1990; The Naked Lunch, 1991; Little Buddha, 1992; Stealing Beauty, 1996; Blood and Wine, 1997; Brother, 1999; Sexy Beast, 2001; Young Adam, 2003; The Dreamers, 2003; Tideland, 2006; Fast Food Nation, 2007; Franklyn, 2008; Creation, 2009; Hara-Kiri: Death of a Samurai, 2011; A Dangerous Method, 2011; Dom Hemingway, 2013; Only Lovers Left Alive, 2014; High Rise, 2015; Tale of Tales, 2015; Blade of the Immortal, 2017; Dogman, 2018; First Love, 2019; Executive Producer: The Great Rock 'n Roll Swindle, 1979; Let Him Have It, 1991; Crash, 1995; The Brave, 1996; The Cup, 1999; Gohatto, 1999; Triumph of Love, 2001; Rabbit Proof Fence, 2002; Heimat 3 (TV series), 2004; Promised Land Hotel, 2004; Dreaming Lhasa, 2004; Don't Come Knocking, 2004; Glastonbury, 2005; Joe Strummer: the future is unwritten, 2007;

Essential Killing, 2010; Thirteen Assassins, 2010; Pina, 2011; The Man Who Killed Don Quixote, 2018; Prod./Dir, All The Little Animals, 1998. Special Award for Outstanding Contribn to Cinema, Evening Standard, 1990; Michael Balcon Award for Outstanding Contribn to Cinema, BAFTA, 1991; European Achievement in World Cinema, European Film Awards, 2006; Life Fellow, BFI, 1998. *Clubs:* Garrick, Royal Automobile.

**THOMAS, Dr John Anthony Griffiths;** Director and Trustee, Relate Avon, 2004–15 (Counsellor and Tutor, 1999–2004; Vice Chair, 2009–15); *b* 28 Aug. 1943; *s* of late William and Bernice Thomas; *m* 1965, Sylvia Jean Norman; two *d*. *Educ:* Leeds Univ. (BSc Chem. 1965); Univ. of Keele (PhD 1968); Open Univ. Mem., BPsS 2004. Teacher of Chemistry, Leeds Grammar Sch., 1968–69; Reed Business Publishing Ltd: Editor, 1969–75; Editorial Dir, 1975–77; Publishing Dir, 1977–84; Divisional Man. Dir, Med. Div., 1984–86; BBC Enterprises Ltd: Dir, BBC Magazines and Electronic Publishing Gp, 1986–93; Man. Dir, 1993–94; Managing Director: BBC Worldwide Television Ltd, 1994–95; BBC Worldwide Learning, 1995–97; Dep. Chm., BBC Worldwide Publishing, 1994–97; Dir, BBC Worldwide Ltd, 1994–97. Chairman: Redwood Publishing Ltd, 1988–93; Frontline Ltd, 1990–94; BBC Haymarket Exhibns Ltd, 1992–94; Galleon Ltd, 1993–94; Dir, Periodicals Publishing Assoc., 1989–94. Dir and Trustee, Bath Fests, 2007–13. Stanford Univ. Alumni, 1991. *Publications:* (ed) Energy Modelling, 1974; Energy Today, 1977; (ed) Energy Analysis, 1977; The Quest for Fuel, 1978. *Recreations:* psychology, reading, music, dance, walking, reading, jazz guitar.

**THOMAS, Prof. John David,** PhD; FBA 1989; Professorial Fellow in Papyrology, University of Durham, 1990–92, now Emeritus Professor; *b* 23 June 1931; *s* of Henry Thomas and Elsie Thomas (*née* Bruin); *m* 1st, 1956, Marion Amy Peach (*d* 2011); two *s*; 2nd, 2014, Angela Shaw. *Educ:* Wyggeston Grammar Sch., Leicester; Worcester Coll., Oxford (MA); PhD Wales. Lectr in Classics, UCW, Aberystwyth, 1955–66; University of Durham: Lectr, then Sen. Lectr in Palaeography, 1966–77; Reader in Papyrology, 1977–90. Vis. Fellow, Wolfson Coll., Oxford, 1981 (Life Mem. of Common Room, 2014). Member: Inst. for Advanced Study, Princeton, 1972; Comité Internat. de Papyrologie, 1983–95. Chancellor's Medal, Univ. of Durham, 2017. *Publications:* Greek Papyri in the Collection of W. Merton III, 1967; The Epistrategos in Ptolemaic and Roman Egypt, Pt I 1975, Pt II 1982; (with A. K. Bowman) Vindolanda: the Latin writing tablets, 1983; (with A. K. Bowman) The Vindolanda writing-tablets: Tabulae Vindolandenses II, 1994, III, 2003; contribs to the Oxyrhynchus Papyri XXXVIII, XLIV, XLVII, L, LVII, LXV–LXVII, LXX, LXXII, LXXIII, LXVII, LXXIX (Gen. Ed., Oxyrhynchus Papyri, LXVI, LXVII; Adv. Ed., LXVIII–); articles and reviews in learned jls. *Recreations:* music, bird watching, walking. *Address:* 43 Orchard House, New Elvet, Durham DH1 3DB. *T:* (0191) 386 1723. *Club:* Athenæum.

**THOMAS, Sir John Meurig,** Kt 1991; MA, PhD, DSc, ScD; FRS 1977; Distinguished Research Fellow, Department of Materials Science and Metallurgy, University of Cambridge, 1993–2002, now Hon. Professor in Solid State Chemistry; Master of Peterhouse, Cambridge, 1993–2002, Hon. Fellow, 2002; *b* Llanelli, Wales, 15 Dec. 1932; *s* of David John and Edyth Thomas; *m* 1st, 1959, Margaret (*née* Edwards) (*d* 2002); two *d*; 2nd, 2010, Prof. Jehane Ragai, Cairo. *Educ:* Gwendraeth Grammar Sch. (State Scholar); University College of Swansea (Hon. Fellow, 1985); Queen Mary Coll., London; DSc Wales, 1964; ScD Cantab, 1994. Scientific Officer, UKAEA, 1957–58; Asst Lectr 1958–59, Lectr 1959–65, Reader 1965–69, in Chemistry, UCNW, Bangor; Prof. and Head of Dept of Chemistry, UCW, Aberystwyth, 1969–78 (Hon. Fellow, 1996); Prof. and Head of Dept of Physical Chemistry, and Fellow of King's Coll., Univ. of Cambridge, 1978–86; Dir, Royal Instn of GB, and Davy Faraday Res. Lab., 1986–91; Resident Prof. of Chemistry, 1986–88, Fullerian Prof. of Chemistry, 1988–94, Prof. of Chemistry, 1994–2002, Emeritus Prof., 2002, Royal Instn of GB; Dep. Pro-Chancellor, Univ. of Wales, 1991–94. Visiting appointments: Tech. Univ. Eindhoven, Holland, 1962; Penna State Univ., USA, 1963, 1967; Tech. Univ. Karlsruhe, Germany, 1966; Weizmann Inst., Israel, 1969; Univ. of Florence, Italy, 1972; Amer. Univ. in Cairo, Egypt, 1973; IBM Res. Center, San José, 1977; Harvard, 1983; Ecole Nat. Sup. de Chimie de Paris, 1991; Scuola Normale Superiore, Pisa, 2003; USC, 2005–11; Cardiff, 2005–; Southampton, 2006–09; York, 2008–16; Monchot Prize Vis. Prof., Technische Universität, München, 2009; Vis. Prof., Hokkaido Univ., Japan, 2010; Adv. Prof., Jiao Tong Univ., Shanghai, 2010–; Dist. Vis. Lectr in Chem., NY Univ., 2014. Ind. Mem., Radioactive Waste Management Cttee, 1978–80; Member: Chem. SRC, 1976–78; SERC, 1986–90; Adv. Cttee, Davy-Faraday Labs, Royal Instn, 1978–80; Scientific Adv. Cttee, Sci. Center, Alexandria, 1979–2005; ACARD (Cabinet Office), 1982–85; COPUS, 1986–92; Bd of Governors, Weizmann Inst., 1982–2006; Academia Europaea, 1989. Mem., Royal Commn for Exhibn of 1851, 1995–2006 (Chm., Scientific Res. Cttee, 1996–2006). Chm., Chemrawn (Chem. Res. Applied to World Needs), IUPAC, 1987–93; Member, International Advisory Board: NSF Lab. of Molecular Sci., CIT, 1999–2010; Nat. Inst. of Informatics, Tokyo, 2000–17; President: Chem. Section, BAAS, 1988–89; London Internat. Youth Sci. Fortnight, 1989–93. Trustee: BM (Natural Hist.), 1987–92; Science Mus., 1990–95. Vice-President: Cambridge Univ. Musical Soc., 1994–; Cambridge Philosophical Soc., 1994–2000. Hon. Visiting Professor: in Physical Chem., QMC, 1986–2006; of Chem., Imperial Coll., London, 1986–91; Academia Sinica, Beijing, 1986–2005; Inst. of Ceramic Sci., Shanghai, 1986; Hon. Prof., Dalian Inst. Chem. Physics, Chinese Acad. of Scis, 2010. Pres., Nat. Eisteddfod of Wales, 2014. New mineral, meurigite, named in his honour, 1995. Lectures: BBC Welsh Radio Annual, 1978; Gerhardt Schmidt Meml, Weizmann Inst., 1979; Baker, Cornell Univ., 1982–83; Hund-Klemm, Max Planck Ges., Stuttgart, 1987; Christmas Lectures, Royal Instn, 1987 (televised, 1988); First Kenneth Pitzer, Coll. of Chem., Univ. of Calif, Berkeley, 1988; Van't Hoff, Royal Dutch Acad. of Arts and Scis, 1988; Bakerian, Royal Soc., 1990; Bruce Preller Prize, RSE, 1990; Sir Krishnan Meml, Delhi, 1991; Watson Centennial, CIT, 1991; Birch, ANU Canberra, 1992; Liversidge, Univ. of Sydney, 1992; Sir Joseph Larmor, Cambridge Philos. Soc., 1992; Patten, Indiana Univ., 1993; François Gault, Eur. Fedn of Catalyst Socs, 1995; Prettre, Lyons, 1996; Rutherford Meml (presented at seven locations in NZ), Royal Soc., 1997; Tetelman, Yale Univ., 1997; Pollack, Technion Haifa, 1998; Ziegler Centenary, Max Planck Inst., Mülheim, 1998; Linus Pauling, CIT, 1999; Taylor, Penn State, 1999; Major, Univ. of Connecticut, 2000; Miller, Univ. of Calif., Berkeley, 2000; Linus Pauling, Oregon State, 2000; John C. Polanyi Nobel Laureate Series Speaker, Univ. of Toronto, 2000; Griffiths Meml (250th anniv.), Hon. Soc. of Cymmrodorion, London, 2001; Debye, Univ. of Utrecht, 2001; Plenary Speaker, World Congress of Chemistry, Brisbane, 2001; Annual Public, Univ. of Surrey, 2002; Inst. of Appl. Catalysis Annual, UK, 2002; Linus Pauling (and Gold Medallist), Stanford Univ., 2003; Eyring, Arizona State Univ., 2003; Guggenheim, Reading Univ., 2003; Giulio Natta Centenary (and Centenary Gold Medallist), Italian Chem. Soc., 2003; Barrer, Penn State Univ., 2004; Ipatieff, Northwestern Univ., 2004; Discours Éminents, Geneva, 2005; David Lloyd George Meml, Criccieth Fest., 2005; Woodward, Yale, 2006; Golden Jubilee Dist., Hong Kong Baptist Univ., 2006; Max T. Rogers Dist., Michigan State Univ., 2007; Pirkey, Texas A & M Univ., 2007; A. S. Williams Dist., Univ. of S Carolina, 2007; Oersted, Danish Tech. Univ., 2007; Annual, Welsh Centre for Internat. Affairs, Cardiff, 2008; Solvay, Free Univ. of Brussels, 2009; English Public Lee, Amer. Univ. Cairo, 2009; Bragg Prize Lectr, British Crystallographic Assoc., 2010; Hassel, Univ.

of Oslo, 2010; Sven Breggen Prize Lectr, Royal Lund Acad. of Sci. and Technol., 2010; Gerhard Ertl Prize Lectr, Fritz-Haber Inst., Berlin, 2010; Areces Foundn Dist., Royal Acad. of Spain, 2011; J. J. Hermans, State Univ., N Carolina, 2011; Willard Gibbs Medal Centenary, Amer. Chem. Soc., 2011; Shipley, Clarkson Univ., NY, 2011; Waterloo Inst. of Nanosci., Canada, 2011; Stoner, Univ. of Leeds and Literary and Philos. Soc. of Leeds, 2011; Chemical Heritage Foundn, Philadelphia, 2011; 600th Anniv., Univ. of St Andrews, 2012; Jayne Prize, Amer. Philos. Soc., 2012. Founder FLSW 2010. Hon. FRSE 1993; Hon. FInstP 1999; Hon. FREng 1999. Hon. Fellow: Indian Acad. of Science, 1980; UMIST, 1984; UCNW, Bangor, 1988; RMS, 1989; Queen Mary and Westfield Coll., London, 1990; Foreign Fellow, INA, 1985; Hon. Foreign Member: Amer. Acad. of Arts and Scis, 1990; Venezuelan Acad. of Scis, 1994; Hon. For. Assoc., Engrg Acad. of Japan, 1991; Internat. Mem. (formerly Foreign Mem.), Amer. Philosophical Soc., 1993; Hon. Foreign Fellow: Russian Acad. of Scis, 1994; Hungarian Acad. of Sci., 1998; Polish Acad. of Arts and Scis, 1999; Amer. Carbon Soc., 1999; Göttingen Acad. of Natural Scis, 2003; Russian Chem. Soc., 2004; Accademia Nazionale dei Lincei, Rome, 2004; Royal Swedish Acad. Scis, 2013. Hon. Bencher, Gray's Inn, 1987. Hon. LLD Wales, 1984; Hon. DLitt CNAA, 1987; Hon. DSc: Heriot-Watt, 1989; Birmingham, 1991; Complutense, Madrid, 1994; Western Ontario, Glamorgan, 1995; Hull, 1996; Aberdeen, 1997; Hong Kong Baptist, 2008; DUniv: Open, 1997; Surrey, 1997; Dr *hc* Lyon, 1994; Eindhoven, 1996; American Univ., Cairo, 2002; Turin, 2004; Clarkson, NY, 2005; Sydney, 2005; Osaka Prefecture Univ., 2006; Bangor, 2009; St Andrews, 2012; S Carolina, 2013. Corday Morgan Silver Medal, Chem. Soc., 1967; first Pettinos Prize, American Carbon Soc., 1969; Tilden Medal and Lectr, Chem. Soc., 1973; Chem. Soc. Prizewinner in Solid State Chem., 1978; Hugo Müller Medal, RSC, 1983; Faraday Medal and Lectr, RSC, 1989; Messel Medal, SCI, 1992; Davy Medal, Royal Soc., 1994; Gibbs Gold Medal, ACS, 1995; Longstaff Medal, RSC, 1996; Hon. Medal, Polish Acad. of Scis, Warsaw, 1996; Semenov Centenary Medal, Russian Acad. of Sci., 1996; ACS Award for creative res. in homogeneous or heterogeneous catalysis (first recipient), 1999; Hon. Soc. of Cymmrodorion Medal, 2003; Sir George Stokes Gold Medal for innovation in analytical chem., RSC, 2005; Silver Medal for services to sci., Univ. of Siena, 2005; Dist. Achievement Award, Internat. Precious Metal Inst., 2007; Ahmed Zewail Gold Medal, Wayne State Univ., 2009; Kapitsa Gold Medal, Russian Acad. of Natural Scis, 2011; Blaise Pascal Medal for Material Sci., Eur. Acad. Scis, 2014; Menelaus Medal for Sci. and Technol., Learned Soc. Wales, 2015; Ahmed Zewail Gold Medal and Prize for Molecular Scis, Elsevier, 2015; Gold Medal for Outstanding Res., Univ. of Florence, 2016; Royal Medal, Royal Soc., 2016. Crystals and Lasers, TV series, 1987; Dylanwadau, radio series, 1990. Founding Editor: (jtly), Catalysis Letters, 1988; (jtly) Topics in Catalysis, 1992; (jtly) Current Opinion in Solid State and Materials Sci., 1996. *Publications:* (with W. J. Thomas) Introduction to the Principles of Heterogeneous Catalysis, 1967 (trans. Russian 1970); Pan edrychwyf ar y nefoedd, 1978; Michael Faraday and the Royal Institution: the genius of man and place, 1991 (trans. Japanese 1994, Italian 2007, Chinese 2013); (with K. I. Zamaraev) Perspectives in Catalysis, 1992; (with W. J. Thomas) Heterogeneous Catalysis: theory and practice, 1997, 2nd edn as Heterogeneous Catalysis: principles and practice, 2015; (with A. Zewail) 4D Electron Microscopy: imaging in space and time, 2010 (trans. Chinese 2013); Design and Applications of Single-Site Heterogeneous Catalysts: contributions to green chemistry, green technology and sustainability, 2012 (trans. Chinese 2013); numerous articles on solid state materials and surface chemistry, catalysis and influence of crystalline imperfections, in Proc. Royal Soc., Jl Chem. Soc., etc. *Recreations:* ancient civilizations, bird watching, hill walking, Welsh literature, music, reading other people's recreations in Who's Who. *Address:* Department of Materials Science and Metallurgy, University of Cambridge, 27 Charles Babbage Road, Cambridge CB3 0FS. *T:* (01223) 334300, *Fax:* (01223) 334567.

**THOMAS, Prof. Jonathan Paul,** DPhil; FBA 2002; Professor of Economics, University of Edinburgh, since 2002; *b* 28 May 1957; *s* of Berwyn Harold Thomas and Christine Erica Thomas (*née* Foden); *m* 1992, Ruth McFadyen; one *s*. *Educ:* Llanishen High Sch., Cardiff; St John's Coll., Cambridge (BA); MPhil 1981, DPhil 1989, Oxon. Res. Officer, Dept of Applied Econs, Univ. of Cambridge, 1982–84; temp. Lectr in Econs, Univ. of Bristol, 1984–85; Lectr, 1985–93, Sen. Lectr, 1993–96, Prof. of Econs, 1996–99, Univ. of Warwick; Prof. of Econs, Univ. of St Andrews, 1999–2002. Professorial Fellow, Univ. of Edinburgh, 2001–02. Hon. Prof., Univ. of Warwick, 1999. *Publications:* contribs to Econometrica, Rev. of Econ. Studies, Jl of Econ. Theory, American Econ. Review, etc. *Recreations:* tennis, golf, ski-ing. *Address:* School of Economics, University of Edinburgh, 31 Buccleuch Place, Edinburgh EH8 9JT. *E:* Jonathan.Thomas@ed.ac.uk.

**THOMAS, Julian Paul;** Master, Wellington College, since 2015; Chief Executive, Wellington College Group of Schools and Academies, since 2017; *b* Redbridge, 30 Dec. 1966; *s* of late Ronald Norman and of Sylvia Elsie Thomas; *m* 2001, Julia Wade; two *s*. *Educ:* Bancroft Sch.; King's Coll. London (BSc Hons Computer Sci.); Queens' Coll., Cambridge (PGCE Maths); Univ. of Hull (MBA Educnl Leadership). Teacher of Maths, Forest Sch., 1995–97; Hd of Year and Second in Charge of Maths, St Dunstan's Coll., 1997–2000; Dir of Studies, Portsmouth GS, 2000–03; Second Master, Hampton Sch., 2003–07; Headmaster, Caterham Sch., 2007–15. FRSA 2007. Gov., London Acad. of Excellence, 2012–15. Trustee: Wellington Coll. Multi-Acad. Trust, 2015– (Chm., 2017–); Crowthorne C of E Sch., 2015–. *Publications:* Foundation Mathematics Teacher's Resource, 1998; Intermediate Mathematics 2, 1998; Mathematics GCSE in a Year, 1999; Formula One Maths B1, 2001; Formula One Maths B2, 2001. *Recreations:* trekking/climbing (expedition to S Pole, Nov. 2014–Jan. 2015), running (Marathon des Sables, 2017), guitar, Leyton Orient FC, skydiving, rowing (Atlantic Ocean crossing, Dec. 2019). *Address:* Master's Lodge, Wellington College, Crowthorne, Berks RG45 7PU. *Club:* Hawks' (Cambridge).

**THOMAS, Dame Kathrin (Elizabeth), (Mrs E. V. Thomas),** DCVO 2018 (CVO 2002); JP; Lord-Lieutenant of Mid Glamorgan, 2003–19 (Vice Lord-Lieutenant, 1994–2002); *b* 20 May 1944; *d* of Dillwyn Evans and Dorothy Nelle (*née* Bullock); *m* 1967, Edward Vaughan Thomas (*d* 2006); two *s*. *Educ:* Cheltenham Ladies' Coll. Chairman: Mid Glamorgan FHSA, 1990–94; Mid Glamorgan HA, 1994–96; Bro Taf HA, 1996–99; Prince's Trust, Cymru, 1999–2001; Mem., Prince's Trust Council, 1996–2001; Pres., Royal Welsh Agricl Show, 2009. Hon. Col 203 (Welsh) Field Hosp. (V), 1998–2006 (Hon. Patron, 2008–). Mid Glamorgan: JP 1983; High Sheriff 1986–87; DL 1989. *Recreations:* family, travel, reading. *Address:* Gelli Hir, Nelson, Treharris CF46 6PL. *Club:* Army and Navy.

**THOMAS, Keith Garfield; His Honour Judge Keith Thomas;** a Circuit Judge, since 2004; *b* 10 Aug. 1955; *s* of Howard and Shirley Thomas; *m* 2003, Melinda Jane (*née* Vaughan). *Educ:* Mill Hill Sch.; Bristol Polytech. (LLB). Called to the Bar, Gray's Inn, 1977; Asst Provincial Stipendiary Magistrate, 1995; Asst Recorder, 1996–2000; Recorder, 2000–04; Resident Judge, Swansea Crown Court, 2011–19. Hon. Recorder, City and Co. of Swansea, 2011–19. *Recreations:* Rugby Union, cricket. *Address:* c/o Crown Court, St Helens Road, Swansea SA1 4PF. *Club:* Glamorgan Wanderers Rugby Football (Vice Chm., 1999–2008; Trustee, 2004–; Pres., 2018–).

**THOMAS, Sir Keith (Vivian)**, Kt 1988; FBA 1979; FLSW; Fellow of All Souls College, Oxford, 1955–57 and 2001–15, now Hon. Fellow; President of Corpus Christi College, Oxford, 1986–2000 (Hon. Fellow, 2000); *b* 2 Jan. 1933; *s* of late Vivian Jones Thomas and Hilda Janet Eirene Thomas (*née* Davies); *m* 1961, Valerie Little; one *s* one *d*. *Educ*: Barry County Grammar Sch.; Balliol Coll., Oxford (Brackenbury Schol.; 1st Cl. Hons Mod. History, 1955; Hon. Fellow 1984). Oxford University: Senior Scholar, St Antony's Coll., 1955; Fellow of St John's Coll., 1957–86 (Tutor, 1957–85; Hon. Fellow, 1986); Reader in Modern Hist., 1978–85; Prof. of Modern Hist., Jan.–Sept. 1986; Pro-Vice-Chancellor, 1988–2000; Mem., Hebdomadal Council, 1988–2000. Vis. Professor, Louisiana State Univ., 1970; Vis. Fellow, 1978, Lawrence Stone Vis. Prof., 2001, Princeton Univ.; Kratter Univ. Prof., Stanford Univ., 2004; Vis. Fellow, Heyman Center for the Humanities, Columbia Univ., 2008. Joint Literary Director, Royal Historical Soc., 1970–74, Mem. Council, 1975–78, Vice-Pres., 1980–84, Hon. Vice-Pres., 2001; Pres., British Acad., 1993–97. Member: ESRC, 1985–90; Reviewing Cttee on Export of Works of Art, 1989–92; Royal Commn on Historical Manuscripts, 1992–2002; Balzan Prize Cttee, 1995–2008. Trustee: Nat. Gall., 1991–98; British Museum, 1999–2008; Chairman: British Liby Adv. Cttee for Arts, Humanities and Social Scis, 1997–2002; Adv. Council, Warburg Inst., Univ. of London, 2000–08; Supervisory Cttee, Oxford DNB, 1992–2004. Delegate, OUP, 1980–2000 (Chm., Finance Cttee, 1988–2000). Judge, Wolfson Hist. Prize, 1975–2015 (Chm., 1996–2015). Lectures: Stenton, Univ. of Reading, 1975; Raleigh, British Acad., 1976; Neale, University Coll. London, 1976; G. M. Trevelyan, Univ. of Cambridge, 1978–79; Sir D. Owen Evans, University Coll. of Wales, Aberystwyth, 1980; Kaplan, Univ. of Pennsylvania, 1983; Creighton, Univ. of London, 1983; Ena H. Thompson, Pomona Coll., 1986; Prothero, RHistS, 1986; Merle Curti, Univ. of Wisconsin-Madison, 1989; Spinoza, Univ. of Amsterdam, 1992; Ford's in British History, Univ. of Oxford, 2000; British Acad., 2001; Menahem Stern, Jerusalem, 2003; Leslie Stephen, Univ. of Cambridge, 2004. FLSW 2010. MAE 1993 (Trustee, 1997–2001); For. Hon. Mem., Amer. Acad. of Arts and Scis, 1983; Hon. Mem., Japan Acad., 2009. Hon. Fellow: Univ. of Wales Coll. of Cardiff, 1995; Warburg Inst., Univ. of London, 2008. Hon. DLitt: Kent, 1983; Wales, 1987; Hull, 1995; Leicester, 1996; Sussex, 1996; Warwick, 1998; London, 2006; Hon. LLD: Williams Coll., Mass, 1988; Oglethorpe Univ., Ga, 1996; Hon. LittD: Sheffield, 1992; Cambridge, 1995; Columbia, 2011; Hon. PhD Uppsala, 2014. Norton Medlicott Medal, Histl Assoc., 2003; Lifetime Achievement Award, All-Party Parly Gp on Archives and Hist., 2015. Cavaliere Ufficiale, Ordine al Merito della Repubblica Italiana, 1991. Gen. Editor, Past Masters Series, OUP, 1979–2000. *Publications*: Religion and the Decline of Magic, 1971 (Wolfson History Prize, 1972); Rule and Misrule in the Schools of Early Modern England, 1976; Age and Authority in Early Modern England, 1977; (ed with Donald Pennington), Puritans and Revolutionaries, 1978; Man and the Natural World, 1983; (ed) The Oxford Book of Work, 1999; (ed with Andrew Adonis) Roy Jenkins: a retrospective, 2004; Changing Conceptions of National Biography, 2005; The Ends of Life, 2009; The Wolfson History Prize 1972–2012: an informal history, 2012; In Pursuit of Civility: manners and civilization in early modern England, 2018; contribs to historical books and jls. *Recreation*: looking for secondhand bookshops. *Address*: All Souls College, Oxford OX1 4AL; The Broad Gate, Broad Street, Ludlow, Shropshire SY8 1NJ.
*See also* E. J. Gowers.

**THOMAS, Kim**; *see* Gehrig, K.

**THOMAS, Dame Kristin S.**; *see* Scott Thomas.

**THOMAS, Leslie Letchworth**; QC 2014; *b* London, 1965; *s* of Godfrey and Sheila Thomas; one *s* one *d*. *Educ*: Kingston Univ. (LLB Hons 1987). Called to the Bar, Inner Temple, 1988, Bencher, 2015; barrister, specialising in public and administrative law, claims against the police and inquests: Wellington St Chambers, 1989–90; Garden Court Chambers, 1990– (Treas., 2012–17; Jt Hd of Chambers, 2017–). Mem., Bar Standards Bd, 2019–. Member, Bar: Dominica; Antigua and Barbuda; NI; Ireland. Lectr in Law, Westminster and Kingston Univs, 1988–92. Mem., Mgt Cttee, Central London Law Centre, 1989–2014 (Chair, 1999–2007). Mem., Standards Cttee for Public Life, Lewisham Council, 2008–. Mem., Mgt Cttee, Liberty, 1988–98. Hon. LLD Kingston, 2013. Legal Aid Barrister of Year, Legal Aid Practitioners' Gp, 2012, 2016 (for work on Hillsborough). *Publications*: (jtly) Inquests: a practitioner's guide, 2002, 3rd edn 2014; contrib. articles on devel ts in inquest law. *Recreations*: motorcycles, playing the tenor saxophone, jazz, Russian, travel. *Address*: Garden Court Chambers, 57–60 Lincoln's Inn Fields, WC2A 3LJ. *T*: (020) 7993 7600, *Fax*: (020) 7993 7700. *E*: info@gclaw.co.uk.

**THOMAS, Lynda, (Mrs Jon Branch)**; Chief Executive, Macmillan Cancer Support, since 2015 (Interim Chief Executive, 2014–15); *b* Coulsdon, 24 March 1965; *d* of late Bryn Thomas and of Vivienne Thomas (now Watson); *m* 1990, Jon Branch; one *s* two *d*. *Educ*: Univ. of Warwick (BA Hons Psychol. 1986). Commercial PR and mktg roles; PR Manager, NSPCC, 1996–2001; Macmillan Cancer Support (formerly Macmillan Cancer Relief): Hd of Media, 2001–03; Hd of Campaigns, Policy and Public Affairs, 2003–04; Dep. Dir, Communications, 2004–06; Director: External Affairs, 2007–11; Fundraising, 2011–14. *Recreations*: hiking, running, cycling, Arsenal. *Address*: Macmillan Cancer Support, 89 Albert Embankment, SE1 7UQ. *T*: (020) 7840 4923. *E*: lthomas@macmillan.org.uk.

**THOMAS, Mark David**; Owner and founder, TM Media, media consultancy, since 2007; *b* 1 March 1967; *s* of Rick and Jennie Thomas; *m*; two *s* two *d*; *m* 2009, Helen Morgan; one *s* one *d*. *Educ*: Rutlish Sch., London. News reporter, The People, 1988–94; News reporter, then Chief Reporter, News of the World, 1994–97; Features Ed., then Asst Ed., Daily Mirror, 1997–2001; Dep. Ed., Sunday Mirror, 2001–03; Ed., The People, 2003–07. *Address*: TM Media PR, 45 Circus Road, NW8 9JH. *T*: 07710 740468, (020) 7437 0474. *E*: mark@tm-media.co.uk.

**THOMAS, Martin Nicholas Caleb**; Chairman, BACIT (UK) Ltd, 2014–18; *b* Edinburgh, 1 June 1963; *s* of Prof. (Antony) Charles Thomas, CBE, FBA; *m* 1990, Miranda Jane Brett, *d* of Viscount Esher, *qv*; two *s* three *d*. *Educ*: Winchester Coll., Hants; St Anne's Coll., Oxford (BA Lit.Hum.; MA). Solicitor, Travers Smith and Clifford Chance; Sen. Legal Counsel, European Central Bank, 1996–2000; Dep. Chief Exec., Financial Law Panel, 2000–02; Sec., Financial Markets Law Cttee, Bank of England, 2002–06; Sec., Legal Certainty Gp, EC (on secondment), 2004–06; Chm., Landscape Hldgs Ltd, 2007–16; Partner, Altima Partners LLP, 2008–16. Dir, BACIT Ltd, 2012–16. Chairman: BACIT Foundn, 2012–18; Women for Women Internat. (UK), 2016–; Forward Arts Foundn, 2016– (Trustee, 2013–); Vice Chm., Med. Protection Soc., 2019–. *Address*: Ark Farm, Old Wardour, Tisbury, Wilts SP3 6RP. *T*: (020) 3397 3626.

**THOMAS, Martyn Charles**, CBE 2007; FREng; Director and Principal Consultant, Martyn Thomas Associates Ltd, IT consultancy and expert witness services, since 1998; *b* 13 Aug. 1948; *s* of late Leslie and Ruth Thomas; *m* 1980, Anne Rogers; one *s* one *d*. *Educ*: University Coll. London (BSc Biochem. 1969). FBCS 1980; CEng 1993; FIET (FIEE 1994); FREng 2007. Researcher, 1969–70, Systems Programmer, 1970–73, UCL; Designer, Standard Telephones & Cables, 1973–75; South West Universities Regional Computer Centre: Team Ldr, 1975–79; Systems Manager, 1979–83; Dep. Dir, 1980–83; Founder and Chm., Praxis plc, 1983–92; Partner, Deloitte & Touche, 1992–98. Visiting Professor: Univ. of Wales, Aberystwyth, 1993–; Bristol Univ., 1994–; Oxford Univ., 1999–2017; Manchester Univ., 2018–; Livery Co. Prof. of Inf. Technol., 2015–18, Dir and Mem. Academic Bd, 2015–, Council, 2016–, Gresham Coll. Chairman: Sci. and Engrg Assce Cttee, HSE, 2015–19; Risk and Audit Cttee, Office of Ind. Adjudicator for Higher Educn, 2015–17; Ind. Mem., EPSRC, 2002–05; Member: Defence Scientific Adv. Council, 2010–17; Expert Gp, Identity and Passport Service, 2010; Exec. Cttee, UK Computing Res. Cttee, 2013–; Cyber Experts Gp, Civil Contingencies Secretariat, 2016–; non-executive Director: Office of the Ind. Adjudicator for Higher Educn, 2010–17; SOCA, 2011–13; Health and Safety Lab., 2012–14; Health and Safety Exec., 2014–19; consultant, Nat. Crime Agency, 2013–15; Specialist Advr, Treasury Select Cttee, H of C, 2015–17. Mem., Engrg Policy Cttee, 2008–12, Vice-Pres., 2012–14, Chm., Ext. Affairs Cttee, 2012–15, Trustee, 2012–16, RAEng; Chm., IT Strategic Panel, IET, 2010–14. Assce and Innovation Dir, Aspect Assce Ltd, 2001–03. Chm., First Earth Ltd, 2001–03. Mem., Longitude Prize Cttee, 2013–15. Trustee, Canada-UK Council, 2018–. FRSA 1987. Hon. DSc: Hull, 1994; Edinburgh, 2004; City, 2005; Hon. DEng Bath, 2017. Achievement Medal in Computing and Control, IEE, 1993. *Publications*: (with M. Ould) The Fell Revival, 2000; (jtly) Harry Carter - Typographer, 2005; (with A. Rogers) Three Pieces, 2005; (ed jtly) Software for Dependable Systems: sufficient evidence?, 2007; (ed with A. Romanovsky) Industrial Deployment of System Engineering Methods, 2013; numerous papers, lectures and broadcasts. *Recreations*: researching and writing about typography and printing, art, backgammon, watching cricket at the Oval, walking, reading, theatre. *Address*: 72 Fentiman Road, SW8 1LA. *T*: (020) 7582 7169. *E*: martyn@thomas-associates.co.uk.

**THOMAS, Mervyn**; Executive Director, Cabinet Office, since 2018; *b* Cardiff, 8 May 1965; *s* of Richard Thomas and Hazel Thomas; civil partnership 2006, Malcolm Collingwood (*d* 2006). *Educ*: Open Univ. (MBA). Hd, Human Resources, European Investment Banking, Citigroup, 1998–2002; Hd, Human Resources, Corporate Banking Div., Royal Bank of Scotland, 2002–07; Director: Human Resources, DfT, 2007–12; Civil Service Resourcing, 2012–13; Gp Human Resources Dir, MoJ, 2014–17. *Recreations*: running, gym. *Address*: Richmond upon Thames, Surrey.

**THOMAS, Mervyn Lloyd Samuel**, CMG 2019; Founder, 1979, and Chief Executive, since 1999, Christian Solidarity Worldwide; *b* Grays, Essex, 14 May 1952; *s* of Sydney Herbert Thomas and Betty Mary Thomas (*née* Matthews); *m* 1992, Wendy Evans; one *s* and one step *d*. *Educ*: Grays Co. Tech. High Sch.; Thurrock Tech. Coll. Bank clerk, Westminster Bank, later Nat. Westminster Bank, 1968–78; Personnel Officer, Thames Board Mills, 1978–83; Dir, Dietary Foods Ltd, 1983–99. Ordained Assemblies of God Minister, 2001. Mem. (C), Thurrock BC, 1977–82. Trustee: CWR, 2005–20; Barfield Sch. Educnl Trust, 2008–17 (Chm., 2009–14); CURE Internat. UK, 2020–. Governor: Little Thurrock Co. Primary Sch., 1975–96 (Chm., 1980–96); Monkton Combe Sch., 2019–; Corporation Mem., Thurrock Coll., 1988–2003 (Chm., 1994–2003). Fellow, Inst. of Sales and Mktg Mgt 1993. *Publications*: Forbidden Faith, 2010; Standing Up, Speaking Out: 40 years fighting injustice, 2018. *Recreations*: reading (especially biography), attending Emmaus Road Church in Guildford, following Arsenal Football Club. *Address*: Christian Solidarity Worldwide, PO Box 99, New Malden, Surrey KT3 3YF. *T*: 07836 229020. *E*: mervynthomas@csw.org.uk. *Club*: National.

**THOMAS, Prof. (Meurig) Wynn**, OBE 2007; FBA 1996; FLSW, FEA; Professor of English, since 1995, and Emyr Humphreys Chair of Welsh Writing in English, since 2009, Swansea University (formerly University College of Swansea, then University of Wales, Swansea) (Director, Centre for Research into the English Literature and Language of Wales, 1998–2008); *b* 12 Sept. 1944; *s* of William John Thomas and Tydfil Thomas (*née* Rees); *m* 1975, Karen Elizabeth Manahan; one *d*. *Educ*: Gowerton Boys' Grammar Sch.; UCW, Swansea (BA 1965). University College of Swansea: Asst Lectr, 1966–69; Lectr in English, 1969–88; Sen. Lectr, 1988–94. Mem., British Library Adv. Cttee, Arts, Humanities and Social Scis, 2000–. Visiting Professor: Harvard, 1991–92; Univ. of Tübingen, 1994–95; Obermann Fellow, Univ. of Iowa, 1992. Mem., Welsh Arts Council and Chm., Literature Cttee, 1985–91; Vice-Chm., Welsh Language Section, Welsh Acad., 1996–97; Chairman: Univ. of Wales Press, 1998–2005; Welsh Books Council, 2005–; Mem., Wales Arts Review Panel, 2006. Sec., Univ. of Wales Assoc. for Study of Welsh Writing in English, 1983–96; Adjudicator, David Cohen Prize, 1996–97. Founding FLSW 2010 (Vice Pres., Arts, Humanities and Social Scis, 2010–17). Hon. Mem., Nat. Eisteddfod Gorsedd of Bards, 2000. Hon. Fellow, Coleg Cymraeg Cenedlaethol, 2012. Literary Executor, R. S. Thomas (unpublished work), 2000–; Chm., Saunders Lewis Meml Trust, 2008–. FEA 2005. *Publications*: Morgan Llwyd, 1984; The Lunar Light of Whitman's Poetry, 1987; (ed) Morgan Llwyd, Llyfr y Tri Aderyn, 1988; Emyr Humphreys, 1989; (ed) Emyr Humphreys, A Toy Epic, 1989; (ed) R. S. Thomas: y cawr awenydd, 1990; (ed) Wrenching Times: Whitman's Civil War poetry, 1991; Morgan Llwyd: ei gyfeillion a'i gyfnod, 1991 (Welsh Arts Council Prize, Vernam Hull Meml Prize, Ellis Griffith Meml Prize); Internal Difference: literature in twentieth-century Wales, 1992; (ed) The Page's Drift: R. S. Thomas at eighty, 1993; (ed) DiFfinio Dwy Lenyddiaeth Cymru (essays), 1995; (trans.) Dail Glaswellt, 1995; John Ormond, 1997; Corresponding Cultures: the two literatures of Wales, 1999; (ed) Gweld Sêr: Cymru a chanrif America, 2001; (ed) Emyr Humphreys: conversations and reflections, 2002; Kitchener Davies, 2002; (ed jtly) James Kitchener Davies: detholion o'i waith, 2002; (ed) R. S. Thomas, Residues, 2002; (ed) Welsh Writing in English, 2003; Transatlantic Connections: Whitman US-Whitman UK, 2005; In the Shadow of the Pulpit: literature and nonconformist Wales, 2011; R. S. Thomas: serial obsessive, 2013; The Nations of Wales, 1890–1914, 2016; All That is Wales: collected essays, 1996–2016, 2017 (Welsh Book of the Year, 2018); Cyfan-dir Cymru: ysgrifau 1996–2016, 2017; Emyr Humphreys, 2018; contrib. to jls and books. *Recreations*: reading, music, televiewing sport. *Address*: Department of English, Swansea University, Singleton Park, Swansea SA2 8PP. *T*: (01792) 295926.

**THOMAS, Prof. Michael**, PhD; Vice-Chancellor, University of Central Lancashire, 2015–18 (Professor and Deputy Vice-Chancellor, 2014–15); Co-Founder and Director, College for Military Veterans and Emergency Services, since 2014; *b* Bangor, N Wales, 21 July 1959; *s* of Hugh and Mair Ceinwen Thomas; *m* 2005, Mandy Drake; two *s* one *d*. *Educ*: Univ. of Manchester (BNSc); Univ. of Nottingham (PhD 2000); Liverpool John Moores Univ. (MA); Univ. of Leeds (Cert Ed). RMN 1985; RNT 1991. MBPsS 2003. Served RN (HM Submarines), 1975–80. Staff Nurse (Mental Health), Leighton Gen. District Hosp., Cheshire, and Wigan and Leigh Hosp., Lancs, 1982–92; Clin. Specialist, Prestwich Hosp., Manchester, and Sen. Nurse Tutor, Bolton and Salford Coll. of Nursing and Midwifery, 1992–96; Associate Dean, Univ. of Salford, 1996–2000; Prof. of Mental Health, and Dean, N Wales Inst., 2000–04; Prof. of Eating Disorders, and Hd, Biosci. and Psychol., Leeds Metropolitan Univ., 2004–06; University of Chester: Prof. of Eating Disorders, 2010–14; Exec. Dean, 2006–10; Pro Vice-Chancellor, 2010–14; Dir, Centre for Veterans, 2011–14. FHEA 2004. QARANC Medal for services to military veterans, 2014. *Publications*: Cognitive Behaviour Therapy Case Studies, 2012; Mental Health Across the Lifespan, 2016; contrib. articles and chapters. *Recreations*: music, gardening, family.

**THOMAS, Michael Christopher Pryce**; Legal Adviser to the European Union Committee, House of Lords, 2008–14; *b* 31 Oct. 1949; *s* of late David Hamilton Pryce Thomas, CBE and Eluned Mair Thomas (*née* Morgan); *m* 1978, Pauline Marie Buckman. *Educ*: St John's Coll., Oxford (BA); Univ. of Sussex (MA). Admitted solicitor, 1976; in private practice as asst solicitor, 1976–79; Legal Dept, MAFF, 1980–86; Law Officers' Dept, 1986–88; Grade 5, Legal Dept, MAFF, 1988–92; Legal Adviser: Dept of Transport, later DETR, 1993–97; European Secretariat, Cabinet Office, 1997–2004; Dir, Legal Services A, DTI, 2004–06; Legal Counsellor, FCO, 2006–07. *Recreations:* music, theatre. *E:* mc.pm.thomas@outlook.com.

**THOMAS, Michael David,** CMG 1985; QC 1973; barrister in private practice, 1958–2013; Attorney-General of Hong Kong, 1983–88; Member, Executive and Legislative Councils, Hong Kong, 1983–88; Chairman, Law Reform Commission, Hong Kong, 1983–88; Chairman, Qatar Regulatory Tribunal, 2011–13; *b* 8 Sept. 1933; *s* of late D. Cardigan Thomas and Kathleen Thomas; *m* 1st, 1958, Jane Lena Mary (marr. diss. 1978), *e d* of late Francis Neate; two *s* two *d*; 2nd, 1981, Mrs Gabrielle Blakemore (marr. diss. 1986); 3rd, 1988, Hon. Lydia Dunn (*see* Baroness Dunn). *Educ:* Chigwell Sch., Essex; London Sch. of Economics. LLB (Hons) 1954. Called to Bar, Middle Temple, 1955 (Blackstone Entrance Schol., 1952; Harmsworth Schol., 1957); Bencher, 1981. Nat. Service with RN, Sub-Lt RNVR, 1955–57. In practice at Bar from 1958. Junior Counsel to Minister of Defence (RN) and to Treasury in Admty matters, 1966–73. Wreck Commissioner under Merchant Shipping Act 1970; one of Lloyd's salvage arbitrators, 1974. Governor: Chigwell Sch., 1971–83; LSE, 2001–11. *Publications:* (ed jtly) Temperley: Merchant Shipping Acts, 6th edn 1963 and 7th edn 1974. *Recreations:* music, travel, tennis, art history. *Address:* Essex Court Chambers, 24 Lincoln's Inn Fields, WC2A 3EG; 19 Cadogan Square, SW1X 0HU. *Clubs:* Garrick, Queen's; Hong Kong (Hong Kong).

**THOMAS, Col Michael John Glyn;** private consultant in transfusion medicine, since 1995; Clinical Director, Blood Care Foundation, since 1995; Director, MG & SJ Enterprises, since 1995; *b* 14 Feb. 1938; *s* of Glyn Pritchard Thomas and Mary Thomas (née Moseley); *m* 1969, Sheelagh Thorpe; one *d*. *Educ:* Haileybury and ISC; Trinity College, Cambridge; St Bartholomew's Hosp. MA, MB, BChir, LMSSA, DTM&H. FRCPEd 1997. Qualified 1962; House Surgeon, Essex County Hosp. and House Physician, St James, Balham, 1963; Regtl MO, 2nd Bn The Parachute Regt, 1965; Trainee Pathologist, BMH Singapore, 1968; Specialist in Pathology, Colchester Mil. Hosp., 1971; Senior Specialist in Pathology, Army Blood Supply Depot, 1977; Exchange Pathologist, Walter Reed Army Inst. of Research, 1982–84; Officer in Charge of Leishman Lab., Cambridge Mil. Hosp., 1985–87; CO, Army Blood Supply Depot, 1987–95. Hon. Consultant Haematologist, UCH/Middlesex Hosp., 1987. Member: Council, BMA, 1974–82 (Chm., Junior Mems Forum, 1974–75; Chm., Central Ethical Cttee, 1978–82; Mem., expert panel on AIDS, 1986–; Mem., Bd of Sci. and Educn, 1987–93; Fellow, 1995); Cttee on Transfusion Equipment, BSI; Economic and Social Cttee, EEC, 1989–; Council, British Blood Transfusion Soc., 1998–2001 (Founder Chm., 1992–98, Sec., 1998–2004, Autologous Transfusion Special Interest Gp). Congress Pres., XXVIIIth Congress of Internat. Soc. of Blood Transfusion, 2004. *Publications:* contribs to ref. books, reports and jls on Medical Ethics, Haematology and Blood Banking, Malariology and subjects of general medical interest. *Recreations:* sailing, travel, photography, philately. *Address:* 8 Aveley Way, Maldon, Essex CM9 6YQ.

**THOMAS, Michael Stuart, (Mike);** management consultant; Chairman, Geospatial Insight Ltd, since 2019; *b* 24 May 1944; *s* of Arthur Edward Thomas. *Educ:* Latymer Upper Sch.; King's Sch., Macclesfield; Liverpool Univ. (BA). Pres., Liverpool Univ. Guild of Undergraduates, 1965–66; Past Mem. Nat. Exec., NUS. Head of Research Dept, Co-operative Party, 1966–68; Sen. Res. Officer, Political and Economic Planning (now PSI), 1968–73; Dir, Volunteer Centre, 1973–74; Dir of Public Relations and Public Affairs, Dewe Rogerson, 1984–88; Mem., BR Western Reg. Bd, 1985–92; Chairman: Corporate Communications Strategy, 1988–2000; Media Audits, 1990–2001; Fotorama (Holdings) Ltd, 1995–2000; Atalink Ltd, 1998–2001; SMF International, subseq. SMFI Ltd, 2000–12; Music Choice Europe, 2000–05; 422 Ltd, 2001–02; WAA Ltd, 2003–08; H. K. Wentworth Ltd, 2005–08; Utarget plc, 2007–08; Ad. IQ Global Ltd, 2008–10; VRL Financial News Publishing Ltd, 2011–12; PlasRecycle Ltd, 2015–16; Industrial Engrg Plastics Gp, 2014–17; Director: Lopex plc, 1998–2000; Metal Bulletin plc, 2000–02; Finance South East, 2008–10. Consultant to King Abdullah Fund for Develt (Jordan), and Inspirational Develt Gp, 2009–13. Site Moderator/Ed.-in-Chief, www.charter2010.co.uk, 2009–10. MP (Lab and Co-op 1974–81, SDP 1981–83) Newcastle upon Tyne E, Oct. 1974–1983. Mem., Select Cttee on Nationalised Industries, 1975–79; Chm., PLP Trade Gp, 1979–81; SDP spokesman on health and social services, 1981–83; Member: SDP Nat. Cttee, 1981–90; SDP Policy Cttee, 1981–90; Chairman: Organisation Cttee of SDP, 1981–88; By-election Cttee, SDP, 1984–88; SDP Finance Working Gp, 1988–90; a Vice-Pres., SDP, 1988–90; Mem., Alliance Strategy Cttee, 1983–87. Contested: (Lab and Co-Op) E Herts, 1970; (SDP) Newcastle upon Tyne East, 1983; (SDP/Alliance) Exeter, 1987. Founder of parly jl The House. *Publications:* Participation and the Redcliffe Maud Report, 1970; (ed) The BBC Guide to Parliament, 1979, 1983; (with Dr Peter Urbach) Commemorating Reform and Reformers, vol. 1, 2014, vol. 2, 2017; various PEP pamphlets, contribs, etc, 1971–; various articles, reviews, etc. *Recreations:* collecting pottery, medals and ephemera relating to elections (1650–), architectural and garden history, gardening, garden design, theatre, opera, music, cooking. *Address:* The Grove, 23 Temple Street, Brill, Bucks HP18 9SU. *E:* mikethomas77@gmail.com. *Club:* Reform.

**THOMAS, Michael T.;** *see* Tilson Thomas.

**THOMAS, Neil,** MBE 2016; RDI 2014; CEng; FIStructE; Chairman and Director, Atelier One Structural Engineers, since 1989; *b* Fordingbridge, 11 March 1959; *s* of Derek Francis Thomas and Rita Emily Thomas; *m* 2005, Sonia Pabla; one *s* three *d*. *Educ:* Rugeley Grammar Sch., Staffs; Univ. of Leeds (BSc Hons); Penn State Univ. CEng 1987; MIStructE 1987. Graduate Engr to Sen. Engr, Buro Happold, 1980–86; Resident Engr, Kuwait (on secondment), 1984–86; Associate, Anthony Hunt Associates, 1986–88; Founder and Dir, Hunt Projects, 1988–89; Co-founder, Atelier Ten, 1991. Visiting Professor: Yale Univ. 2010–14; MIT, 2015–. Ext. Examr, AA, 2012–. Mem., Steering Gp, Architectural Engrg course, Leeds Univ., 2015–. Hon. RIBA. *Publications:* Super Sheds, 1991; Remarkable Structures, 2002; Support and Resist, 2007; Liquid Threshold, 2009. *Recreations:* reading, swimming, scientific research, family. *Address:* Atelier One, 3 Charlotte Mews, W1T 4DZ. *T:* (020) 7323 3350. *E:* mail@atelierone.com.

**THOMAS, Neville;** *see* Thomas, R. N.

**THOMAS, Prof. Nicholas Jeremy,** PhD; FBA 2005; Professor of Historical Anthropology, and Director, Museum of Archaeology and Anthropology, University of Cambridge, since 2006; Fellow of Trinity College, Cambridge, since 2007; *b* 21 April 1960; *s* of Keith James Thomas and Sylvia Lawson; *m* 2004, Prof. Annie Coombes. *Educ:* Australian National Univ. (BA 1982; PhD 1986). Res. Fellow, King's Coll., Cambridge, 1986–89; Australian National University: Queen Elizabeth II Res. Fellow, 1990–92; Sen. Res. Fellow, 1993–96; Dir, Centre for Cross-Cultural Res., 1997–99; Prof. of Anthropology, Goldsmiths Coll., London, 1999–2006. Iris Foundn Award, 2015. *Publications:* Out of Time: history and evolution in anthropological discourse, 1989; Marquesan Societies: inequality and political transformation in eastern Polynesia, 1990; Entangled Objects: exchange, material culture and colonialism in the Pacific, 1991; Colonialism's Culture: anthropology, travel, and government, 1994; Oceanic Art, 1995; In Oceania: visions, artefacts, histories, 1997; Possessions: indigenous art/colonial culture, 1999; Discoveries: the voyages of Captain James Cook, 2003; Islanders: the Pacific in the age of empire, 2010 (Wolfson History Prize, 2010); (ed jtly) Art in Oceania: a new history, 2012 (Art Book Prize, 2014); The Return of Curiosity: what museums are good for in the twenty-first century, 2016; many articles in jls. *Address:* Museum of Archaeology and Anthropology, University of Cambridge, Downing Street, Cambridge CB2 3DZ. *T:* (01223) 333516.

**THOMAS, Nick,** MBE 2019; Chairman and Owner, Qdos Entertainment Group, since 1999; *b* Blandford Forum, Dorset, 16 Dec. 1959; *y s* of Douglas William and Mona Ellen Thomas; *m* 1985, Sandra Jane Finnigan; two *d*. *Educ:* Gladstone Rd Jun. Sch.; Scarborough Boys High Sch.; Graham Sch., Scarborough. Creator, Tommer Puppets (winner of ITV New Faces), 1975–80; owner: Nick Thomas Enterprises Ltd, 1981–91; HQ Theatres and Hospitality, HQ Collection, QVoice, QTalent, 1999–; CEO, Artist Mgt Gp Ltd, 1992–99. Vice Pres., Royal Variety Charity (formerly Entertainment Artistes Benevolent Fund), 2010–. Exec. Prod. at London Palladium: Cinderella, 2016; Dick Whittington, 2017 (Best Family and Entertainment, Olivier Awards, 2018); Snow White, 2018; Goldilocks and the Three Bears, 2019. *Recreations:* family, theatre, restaurants, motor cars, theatre memorabilia, fund raising for Great Ormond Street Hospital Children's Charity (Friend of Adeona, 2018–). *Address:* Qdos Entertainment Ltd, Queen Margaret's Road, Scarborough YO11 2YH. *T:* (01723) 500038. *E:* nthomas@qdosentertainment.co.uk. *Clubs:* Ivy, Arts, Groucho, Soho House.

**THOMAS, Norman,** CBE 1980; HM Chief Inspector of Schools (Primary Education), 1973–81; Specialist Professor in Primary Education, University of Nottingham, 1987–88; *b* 1 June 1921; *s* of Bowen Thomas and Ada Thomas (née Redding); *m* 1942, Rose Henshaw (*d* 2005); two *d*. *Educ:* Latymer's Sch., Edmonton; Camden Coll. Qual. Teacher, 1948. Commerce and Industry, 1937–47. Teacher, primary schs in London and Herts, 1948–56; Head, Longmeadow Jun. Mixed Sch., Stevenage, 1956–61; HM Inspector of Schools, Lincs and SE England, 1962–68; HMI, Staff Inspector for Primary (Junior and Middle) Schs, 1969–73. Chm., Cttee of Enquiry on Primary Educn in ILEA, 1983–84. Adviser to Parly Cttee on Educn, Science and Art, 1984–86, on Educn, 1994–97. Visiting Professor: NE London Polytechnic, 1984–86; Univ. of Herts (formerly Hatfield Poly.), 1991–; Hon. Prof., Univ. of Warwick, 1986–94. Hon. FCP 1988. Hon. DLitt Hertfordshire, 1998. *Publications:* Primary Education from Plowden to the 1990s, 1990; chapters in books and articles in professional jls. *Recreations:* photography, reading. *Address:* Kingsbury Manor, St Michael's, St Albans, Herts AL3 4SE.

**THOMAS, Owen John;** Member (Plaid Cymru) Central South Wales, National Assembly for Wales, 1999–2007; *b* 3 Oct. 1939; *s* of late John Owen Thomas and Evelyn Jane Thomas; *m* 1985, Siân Wyn Evans; twin *s*; three *s* one *d* by a previous marriage. *Educ:* Glamorgan Coll. of Educn (Cert Ed 1971); UC, Cardiff (MA 1990). Tax Officer, In and Revenue, 1956–61; Chemical Analyst, 1961–68; Primary Sch. Teacher, 1971–78; Dep. Headteacher, 1979–99. Shadow Minister for Culture, Sport and Welsh Lang., Nat. Assembly for Wales, 2001–07. Mem., Gorsedd of Bards, Royal Nat. Eisteddfod, 2001. *Recreations:* reading, socialising. *Address:* 4 Llwyn y Grant Place, Penylan, Cardiff CF23 9EX. *T:* (029) 2049 9868. *Club:* Ifor Bach (Cardiff).

**THOMAS, Patricia Ann;** environmental campaigner, author and journalist; *b* Los Angeles, Calif, 27 Oct. 1959; *d* of late William Shows and Patricia Gayle Thomas; *m* 1992, Jonathan Ralph Althelstan Savage (marr. diss. 1995); one *s*. *Educ:* Thousand Oaks High Sch., Calif; Centre for Counselling and Psychotherapy Educn, London (Dip. Psychotherapy and Counselling 1991). Record Sales Analyst, Record Business Mag., 1979–83; Asst Res. Manager, Music Div., Gallup Poll Ltd, 1983; Asst Producer, DJ Show, TVS, Southampton, 1984; freelance journalist and broadcaster, 1984–91; feature writer, Number One Mag., 1984–89; Editor: Insight mag., 1990–91; AIMS Jl, 1994–2004; Contrib. Editor, Wallace Press, 1994–2004; Editor, Proof!, 2003; Health Editor, 2004–07, Editor, 2007–09, Ecologist Mag.; Campaign Dir, Meat Free Monday, 2009–10 (Scientific Advr, 2010–); Campaign Manager, Cows Belong in Fields Campaign, Compassion in World Farming, 2010–11; Hd, Sustainability, 2011–12, Consultant, campaigns and sustainability projects, 2012–, Neal's Yard Remedies. Editor, NYR Natural News online, 2011–17; editor/owner, Natural Health News, 2017–. Dir, Beyond GM Ltd, 2014–. Host: British Airways in-flight entertainment, 1987–91; Deep Fried Planet, Resonance FM, London, 2010; reporter/interviewer: Capital Radio, London, 1989–90; Westwood One Radio Network, NY, 1989–90; producer/reporter, Ecostorm, 2016–. Trustee: Soil Assoc., 2012–14; Eyewitness Investigative Agency, 2013–18; Organic Res. Centre, 2015–17. Consultant, organic toiletries range, Stella McCartney Care, 2009. Mem., Guild of Health Writers, 2011. *Publications:* Every Woman's Birthrights, 1996; Every Birth is Different, 1997; The PROOF! Guide to Alternative First Aid, 1998; Choosing a Home Birth, 1998; Headaches: the common sense approach, 1999; Pregnancy: the common sense approach, 1999; You Can Prevent Cancer, 1999; Alternative Therapies for Pregnancy and Birth, 2000; Cleaning Yourself to Death: how safe is your home?, 2001; Living Organic, 2001; Your Birth Rights, 2002; What Works, What Doesn't: the guide to alternative healthcare, 2002; (contrib.) Failure to Progress: the contraction of midwifery, 2002; Living Dangerously: are everyday toxins making you sick?, 2003; Under the Weather: how weather and climate affect our health, 2004; What's in This Stuff?: the essential guide to what's really in the products you buy, 2006; (contrib.) A Slice of Organic Life, 2007; The 21st Century is Making You Fat, 2008; Skin Deep, 2008; Healthy, Happy Baby, 2008; Stuffed: positive action to prevent a global food crisis, 2010; Healing Foods: eat your way to a healthier life, 2013; Neal's Yard Remedies Beauty Book, 2015; Neal's Yard Remedies Essential Oils, 2016; Neal's Yard Remedies Complete Wellness, 2018; *for children:* First Look series: My Amazing Journey, 1998; My Family's Changing, 1998; My Brother, My Sister and Me, 2000; Stop Picking on Me!, 2000; I Miss You, 2000; My Friends and Me, 2000; Don't Call Me Special!, 2001; My Amazing Body, 2001; The Skin I'm In, 2003; I Can Be Safe, 2003; Is it Right to Fight?, 2003; My New Family!, 2003; Do I Have to Go to School?, 2006; My Manners Matter, 2006; Do I Have to Go to Hospital?, 2006; I'm Telling the Truth, 2006; Why Am I So Tired?, 2008; I Think I'm Going to Sneeze, 2008; Do I Have to Go to the Dentist?, 2008; Why is it So Hard to Breathe, 2008; I Can Make a Difference, 2010; Everyone Matters, 2010; Why Do I Feel Scared?, 2010; I Can Do It!, 2010; I Miss My Pet, 2012; Come Home Soon, 2012; This is My Family, 2012; First Look At series: I See Things Differently, 2014; Don't Call Me Fat, 2014; Leave Me Alone!, 2014. *Recreations:* cooking, foraging, photography, reading, music, walking, film, watersports, family. *Address:* c/o MBA Literary Agents, 62 Grafton Way, W1T 5DW. *T:* (020) 7387 2076. *E:* laura@mbalit.co.uk. *W:* www.howlatthemoon.org.uk.

**THOMAS, Patricia Anne,** CBE 2006; Commissioner for Local Administration in England, 1985–2005; Vice-Chairman, Commission for Local Administration in England, 1994–2005; *b* 3 April 1940; *d* of Frederick S. Lofts and Ann Elizabeth Lofts; *m* 1968, Joseph Glyn Thomas; one *s* two *d*. *Educ:* King's College London. LLB, LLM. Lectr in Law, Univ. of Leeds, 1962–63, 1964–68; Teaching Fellow, Univ. of Illinois, 1963–64; Sen. Lectr, then Principal Lectr, Head of Sch. of Law and Prof., Lancashire Polytechnic, 1973–85. Mem., Administrative Justice & Tribunals Council (formerly Council on Tribunals), 2005–10.

Mem., 1976–84, Vice-Pres., 1984, Pres., 1985, Greater Manchester and Lancashire Rent Assessment Panel; Chm., Blackpool Supplementary Benefit Appeal Tribunal, 1980–85. Non-exec. Dir, Univ. Hospitals of Morecambe Bay NHS Trust, subseq. Foundn Trust, 2009–12. Hon. Fellow, Lancashire Polytech., 1991. *Publications:* Law of Evidence, 1972.

**THOMAS, His Honour Patrick Anthony;** QC 1999; a Circuit Judge, 2008–18; Assistant Judge, St Helens Supreme Court, 2019; *b* 30 Oct. 1948; *s* of Basil and Marjorie Thomas; *m* 1978, Sheila Jones; two *d. Educ:* Rugby Sch.; Lincoln Coll., Oxford (BA). Called to the Bar, Gray's Inn, 1973, Bencher, 2005; Recorder, 1992–2008. Judicial Mem., Parole Bd, 2018–. *Recreations:* reading, theatre, walking, France.

**THOMAS, Paul;** *see* Thomas, C. P.

**THOMAS, Rear Adm. Paul Anthony Moseley,** CB 1998; FREng, FIMechE; Director, Environment, Health, Safety and Quality, British Nuclear Fuels plc, 2001–08; *b* 27 Oct. 1944; *s* of Glyn Pritchard Thomas and Mary (*née* Moseley); *m* 1972, Rosalyn Patricia Lee; one *s* two *d. Educ:* Haileybury; London Univ. (BSc(Eng) 1969); MSc CNAA 1971. CEng 1985, FREng (FEng 1998); FIMechE 1993; FCGI 2011. Joined RN, 1963; Asst Marine Engr Officer, HMS Renown, 1971–77; Sen. Engr Officer, HMS Revenge, 1977–82 (mentioned in despatches, 1979); Asst Dir, Reactor Safety, 1982–84; Naval Superintendent, Vulcan Naval Reactor Test Estabt, Dounreay, 1984–87; Chm., Naval Nuclear Technical Safety Panel, 1987–90; Dir, Nuclear Propulsion, 1990–94; Captain, RNEC Manadon, 1994–95; Chief Strategic Systems Exec., MoD (PE), 1995–98; AEA Technology Nuclear Engineering: Dir, Engrg Projects, 1999–2000; Dir, Strategic Develt, 2000–01. Chairman: Rail Safety and Standards Bd, 2008–15; Process Safety Forum, 2008–; Hazards Forum, 2009–17. Non-executive Director: NNB GenCo, 2011–18; Magnox Ltd, 2013–17. Pres., Nuclear Inst., 2008–10. Hon. FNucI (Hon. FINucE 2005); Hon. FSaRS 2011. *Recreations:* cycling, sailing, ballooning, railways. *Address:* Byway, Chapel Lane, Box, Corsham, Wilts SN13 8NU.

**THOMAS, Paul Huw;** QC 2003; **His Honour Judge Paul Thomas;** a Circuit Judge, since 2009; Resident Judge, Swansea Crown Court, since 2019; Hon. Recorder of Swansea, since 2019; *b* 25 June 1957; *s* of Hubert and Joan Thomas; *m* 1984, Mayda Elisabeth Jones; one *s* one *d. Educ:* Gowerton Sch.; Fitzwilliam Coll., Cambridge (MA). Called to the Bar, Gray's Inn, 1979, Bencher, 2008; Barrister, Iscoed Chambers, Swansea, 1980–2009; Jt Hd of Chambers, 2006–09; Asst Recorder, 1996–2000; Recorder, 2000–09; apptd to sit in Court of Appeal (Criminal Div.), 2018. Asst Boundary Comr for Wales, 2003–09. Citing Comr, Welsh Rugby Union, 2016–. Mem., Dermatology Council for Wales, 2005–10; Chm., Skin Care Cymru, 2006–. Trustee: Swansea Rugby Foundn, 1996–; Assoc. of Friends of Glynn Vivian Art Gall., 2006–10, 2012–16; Changing Faces, 2008–. *Recreations:* sport, especially Rugby, history, the arts, Rhossili. *Address:* Swansea Crown Court, St Helen's Road, Swansea SA1 4PF. *Clubs:* Swansea Rugby Football; Gowerton Cricket.

**THOMAS, Paul Roger;** Vice-President of Marketing, Ford of Europe, 2006–12; *m* Karen; two *c. Educ:* City Univ. (BSc). Joined Ford as trainee, 1974; sales and mktg posts with Ford of Britain, Ford Credit and Ford of Europe; Manager of Business Planning, Ford Credit, 1987–89; Gen. Field Manager, 1989–90, Mktg and Product Plans Manager, 1990–93, Ford of Britain; Vehicle and Derivative Progs Manager, Ford of Europe, 1993–95; Dist Manager, Midlands, Ford of Britain, 1995–99; Mktg Plans and Brand Develt Manager, Ford Product Develt Europe, 1999–2000; European Brand Manager, 2000–01; Dir of Sales, 2001–02, Man. Dir, 2002–06, Ford of Britain.

**THOMAS, Ven. Paul Wyndham;** Archdeacon of Salop, since 2011; Priest-in-charge, Forton, since 2011; *b* Llantwit Major, Vale of Glamorgan, 22 April 1955; *s* of Wyndham Ernest Clifford Thomas and Kathleen Mary Thomas; *m* June Garfield; three *s* two *d. Educ:* Cardiff High Sch. for Boys; Oriel Coll., Oxford; Wycliffe Hall, Oxford (BA Modern Hist. 1976; MA 1978; BA Theol. 1978; CTh 1979). Ordained deacon, 1979, priest, 1980; Curate, Llangynwyd with Maesteg, 1979–85; Team Vicar, Langport Area Churches, 1985–90; Priest-in-charge, Thorp Arch and Walton, 1990–93; Clergy Trng Officer, 1990–93; Vicar, Nether with Upper Poppleton, York, 1993–2004; Priest-in-charge, Doxey Stafford and Parish Develt Advr, 2004–11. *Recreations:* walking, theatre, music. *Address:* Archdeacon's House, The Vicarage, Tong, Shifnal, Shropshire TF11 8PW. *T:* (01902) 372622. *E:* paul.thomas@lichfield.anglican.org.

**THOMAS, Sir Philip (Lloyd),** KCVO 2003; CMG 2001; HM Diplomatic Service, retired; Senior Advisor: Shell International Ltd, 2006–09; Permian Global, 2010–15; *b* 10 June 1948; *s* of Gwyn Thomas and Eileen Thomas (*née* Jenkins); one *s. Educ:* Dulwich Coll.; St John's Coll., Cambridge (MA). Joined HM Diplomatic Service, 1972; Third Sec., FCO, 1972–74; Second Sec., Belgrade, 1974–77, FCO, 1977–80; First Secretary: (Commercial), Madrid, 1981–87; UK Perm. Representation to EU, Brussels, 1987–89; Cabinet Office, 1989–91; Counsellor (Politico-Military), Washington, 1991–96; Head, Eastern Dept, FCO, 1996–98; Consul Gen., Düsseldorf, and Dir-Gen. for Trade and Investment Promotion in Germany, 1999–2000; High Comr, Nigeria, 2001–04; Consul-Gen., New York, and Dir Gen., Trade and Investment in US, 2004–06. Mem. Bd, LPO, 2009–14.

**THOMAS, Prof. Phillip Charles,** FRSE; FRSB; FRAgS; Managing Director, Artilus Consultancy and Research, 1999–2010; Principal, 1990–99, now Emeritus Professor of Agriculture, Scottish Agricultural College; *b* 17 June 1942; *s* of William Charles Thomas and Gwendolen (*née* Emery); *m* 1967, Pamela Mary Hirst; one *s* one *d. Educ:* University College of North Wales, Bangor (BSc, PhD). FRSB (FIBiol 1983); FRSE 1993; FRAgS 1997. Lectr in animal nutrition and physiology, Univ. of Leeds, 1966–71; progressively, SSO to SPSO, Hannah Research Inst., 1971–87; Principal, West of Scotland Coll., 1987–90; Prof. of Agriculture, Univ. of Glasgow, 1987–99. Hon. Prof., Edinburgh Univ., 1990–; Vis. Prof., Univ. of Glasgow, 1999–2001. Chairman: Govt Adv. Cttee on Animal Feedingstuffs, 1999–2001; Animal Medicines Trng Regulatory Authy, 1999; Cumbria Foot and Mouth Disease Inquiry, 2002; Scottish Salmon Producers' Orgn, 2008–16; Tenant Farming Forum, Scottish Govt, 2010–; Member: Scottish Food Adv. Cttee, 2000–05; Scottish Natural Heritage Bd, 2005–11; Quality Meat Scotland Bd, 2008–14. Chm., Central Scotland Forest Trust, 2001–08. *Publications:* (with J. A. F. Rook) Silage for Milk Production, 1982; (with J. A. F. Rook) Nutritional Physiology of Farm Animals, 1983. *Club:* Farmers.

**THOMAS, Sir Quentin (Jeremy),** Kt 1999; CB 1994; President, British Board of Film Classification, 2002–12; Head of Constitution Secretariat, Cabinet Office, 1998–99; *b* 1 Aug. 1944; *s* of late Arthur Albert Thomas and Edith Kathleen Thomas (*née* Bigg); *m* 1969, Anabel Jane, *d* of late J. H. Humphreys; one *s* two *d. Educ:* Perse School, Cambridge; Gonville and Caius College, Cambridge. Home Office, 1966; Private Sec. to Perm. Under-Sec. of State, 1970; Crime Policy Planning Unit, 1974–76; Sec. to Royal Commn on Gambling, 1976–78; Civil Service (Nuffield and Leverhulme) Travelling Fellowship, 1980–81; Head, Broadcasting Dept, Home Office, 1984–88; Under Sec., 1988–91, Dep. Sec., then Political Dir, 1991–98, NI Office. Led Cabinet Office Review of BBC Monitoring, 2004–05; Chm., BBC Governors' Impartiality Review of BBC coverage of Israeli-Palestinian Conflict, 2005–06.
*See also* R. C. Thomas.

**THOMAS, Rachel Mary S.;** *see* Sandby-Thomas.

**THOMAS, Dr Raymond Tudor,** OBE 1994; Director, Brussels, British Council, 2003–06; *b* 19 May 1946; *s* of Edgar William Thomas and Lilian Phylis Thomas; *m* 1973, Gloria Forsyth; two *s. Educ:* King's Sch., Macclesfield; Jesus Coll., Oxford (BA Modern Hist. 1968); Inst. of Internat. Relns, Univ. of WI (Dip. 1970); Univ. of Sussex (DPhil 1976). Tutor, Davies's Ltd, 1969–70; Lectr, Inst. of Internat. Relns, Trinidad, 1970–71; British Council: Assistant Representative: Morocco, 1974–77; Pakistan, 1977–80; Malaysia, 1980–82; Regl Rep., Sabah, Malaysia, 1982–84; Projects Officer, London, 1984–85; Dep. Dir 1985–88, Dir 1988–90, Educnl Contracts Dept; Dir, EC Relns, Brussels, 1990–95; Regl Dir, subseq. Policy Dir, Middle East and N Africa, 1995–2000; Dir, Turkey, 2000–03. Chm., Renewable World (formerly Koru Foundn), 2010–12 (Trustee, 2008–12). *Publications:* Britain and Vichy: the dilemma of Anglo-French relations 1940–42, 1979. *Recreations:* family life, travel, reading, fly-fishing. *Address:* 52 St Anne's Crescent, Lewes, East Sussex BN7 1SD.

**THOMAS, Rev. Rhodri Glyn;** *see* Thomas, Rev. H. R. G.

**THOMAS, Richard;** *see* Thomas, A. R.

**THOMAS, Richard,** CMG 1990; HM Diplomatic Service, retired; *b* 18 Feb. 1938; *s* of late Anthony Hugh Thomas, JP and Molly Thomas, MBE; *m* 1966, Catherine Jane Hayes, Sydney, NSW; one *s* two *d. Educ:* Leighton Park; Merton Coll., Oxford (MA). Nat. Service, 2nd Lt, RASC, 1959–61. Entered CRO, later FCO, 1961; Accra, 1963–65; Lomé, 1965–66; UK Delegn NATO, Paris and Brussels, 1966–69; FCO, 1969–72; New Delhi, 1972–75; Asst Hd, Financial Relns Dept, FCO, 1976–78; FCO Visiting Res. Fellow, RIIA, 1978–79; Counsellor, Prague, 1979–83; Ambassador, Iceland, 1983–86; Overseas Inspector, 1986–89; Ambassador to Bulgaria, 1989–94; High Comr, Eastern Caribbean, 1994–98. Trustee: Leonard Cheshire Disability (formerly Leonard Cheshire), 1999–2005 (Internat. Chm., 2000–05; Vice Pres., 2005–14); Rye Arts Fest., 2003–10 (Chm., 2006–10); Mem. Adv. Bd, Peasmarsh Chamber Music Fest., 2012–. *Publications:* India's Emergence as an Industrial Power: Middle Eastern Contracts, 1982. *Recreations:* foreign parts, music, sketching, writing. *Address:* 4 Hiham Green, Winchelsea, E Sussex TN36 4HB. *Club:* Oxford and Cambridge.

**THOMAS, (Richard) Gwyn,** PhD; Chief Information Officer for Wales, and Director, Informatics for Health and Social Services, Welsh Government, 2009–13; Managing Director, Cogan Hall Consultancy, since 2013; *b* Treorchy, Rhondda, 14 Sept. 1949; *s* of Richard Lewis Thomas and Catherine Thomas; *m* 1971, Eirwen Birney; one *s* one *d. Educ:* Cowbridge Grammar Sch.; Univ. of Sheffield (BMet; PhD Metallurgy 1974); Univ. of Stirling (MSc Public Relns). Various sen. mgt posts and specialist positions, electricity supply industry, UK and Australia, 1974–92; Exec. Dir, Nottingham City Hosp., 1994–2000; Chief Executive Officer: NHS Information Authy, 2000–05; Informing Healthcare Prog., NHS Wales, 2005–09. Chm., Health Data Insight CIC, 2012–14. Vis. Prof., Sch. of Information Systems and Computing, Brunel Univ., 2003–06; Hon. Prof., Sch. of Medicine, Swansea Univ., 2013–. Chm., UK Council for Health Informatics Professionals, 2013–15. Sec., BCS Health, 2014–15. Life FBCS. *Recreations:* sitting, writing, walking, standing, staring, thinking, smiling. *E:* rgwyn.thomas@gmail.com.

**THOMAS, Richard James,** CBE 2009; Chairman, Administrative Justice and Tribunals Council, 2009–13; *b* 18 June 1949; *s* of Daniel Lewis Thomas, JP, and Norah Mary Thomas; *m* 1974, Julia Delicia, *d* of Dr E. G. W. Clarke; two *s* one *d. Educ:* Bishop's Stortford Coll.; Univ. of Southampton (LLB Hons); College of Law. Admitted Solicitor, 1973. Articled clerk and Asst Solicitor, Freshfields, 1971–74; Solicitor, CAB Legal Service, 1974–79; Legal Officer and Hd of Resources Gp, Nat. Consumer Council, 1979–86; Under Sec. and Dir of Consumer Affairs, OFT, 1986–92; Dir, Public Policy, Clifford Chance, 1992–2002; Information Comr, 2002–09. Vis. Prof., Northumbria Univ., 2007–13. Chm., British Univs N America Club, 1970–71; Member: Management Cttee, Royal Courts of Justice CAB, 1992–98; London Electricity Cons. Council, 1979–84; European Consumer Law Gp, 1981–86; European Commn Working Party on Access to Justice, 1981–82; Lord Chancellor's Adv. Cttee on Civil Justice Rev., 1985–88; Council, Office of Banking Ombudsman, 1992–2001; Adv. Cttee, Oftel, 1995–98; Advertising Adv. Cttee, ITC, 1996–2002; Bd, Financial Ombudsman Service, 1999–2002; Bd, NCC, 2001–02; Bd, Consumers Assoc., 2008–13 (Dep. Chm., 2009–13); Bd, Whitehall and Industry Gp, 2008–14; Cttee on Standards in Public Life, 2012–17; Adv. Cttee on Business Appts, 2018–. Advr, Centre for Information Policy Leadership, 2009–. Chair, Guernsey Data Protection Authy, 2018–. FRSA 1992–2015. Hon. LLD Southampton, 2007. Internat. Privacy Leadership Award, Internat. Assoc. of Privacy Professionals, 2008. *Publications:* reports, articles and broadcasts on range of legal, consumer, privacy, data protection and freedom of information issues. *Recreations:* family, maintenance of home and garden, travel. *Address:* 36 Park Lane, Reigate, Surrey RH2 8JX.

**THOMAS, Richard Peter;** Chief Financial Officer, British Council, since 2018; *b* Sutton, Surrey, 1962; *s* of Peter George Adrian Thomas and Mary Elizabeth Thomas; partner, Veronica Isobel Jean Gilmour; three *s* one *d. Educ:* Sherborne Sch.; Univ. of Manchester (BA Hons Hist.). ACA 1989. Deloitte Haskins & Sells, 1984–89; Revcom Gp, 1989–92; Finance Dir, British Pathé plc, 1992–97; BBC News, 1997–2008, Finance Dir, 2005–08; Chief Operating Officer, BBC World Service, 2008–15; Chief Finance Officer, Richmond CCG, 2015–17. *Recreations:* mountain trekking, football, Rugby, theatre. *Address:* British Council, 10 Spring Gardens, SW1A 2BN. *T:* (020) 3285 3112. *E:* richard.thomas@britishcouncil.org.

**THOMAS, Dr Robert Kemeys,** FRS 1998; Aldrichian Praelector and Reader in Physical Chemistry, University of Oxford, 2002–08, now Emeritus; Fellow, University College, Oxford, 1978–2008, now Emeritus; *b* 25 Sept. 1941; *s* of Preb. H. S. G. Thomas and Dr A. P. Thomas; *m* 1968, Pamela Woods; one *s* two *d. Educ:* Radley Coll., Abingdon; St John's Coll., Oxford (MA, DPhil 1968). Royal Soc. Pickering Fellow, 1970–75; Fellow, Merton Coll., Oxford, 1975–78; Lectr in Physical Chemistry, Univ. of Oxford, 1978–2002. Hon. Professor: Inst. of Chemistry, Chinese Acad. of Scis, Beijing, 1999–; China Petroleum Univ., Huangdao, 2005–. Dr *hc* Lund, 2012. *Publications:* contribs to chemical jls. *Recreations:* flora, funghi, music, Chinese language. *Address:* Physical and Theoretical Chemistry Laboratory, South Parks Road, Oxford OX1 3QZ.

**THOMAS, (Robert) Neville;** QC 1975; barrister-at-law; a Recorder of the Crown Court, 1975–82; *b* 31 March 1936; *s* of Robert Derfel Thomas and Enid Anne Thomas; *m* 1970, Jennifer Anne Brownrigg; one *s* one *d. Educ:* Ruthin Sch.; University Coll., Oxford (MA, BCL). Called to Bar, Inner Temple, 1962, Bencher, 1985. *Recreations:* fishing, walking, gardening, reading. *Address:* Milford Hall, Newtown, Powys SY16 3HF. *Club:* Garrick.

**THOMAS, Rt Rev. Roderick Charles Howell;** *see* Maidstone, Bishop Suffragan of.

**THOMAS, Roger;** see Thomas, D. R.

**THOMAS, Roger,** CBiol; Chief Executive, Countryside Council for Wales, 2002–13; b 26 Jan. 1953; s of Gerwyn and Daphne Thomas; m 1988, Jan Tyrer; one s twin d. Educ: NE London Poly. (BSc Hons); Henley Coll. of Mgt (MBA). MRSB; CBiol 1978. Various posts, incl. Lab. Manager, Welsh Water Scientific Directorate, 1976–92; Area Manager, NRA, 1992–95; Regl Gen. Manager, NRA Wales, 1995–96; Area Manager, 1996–98, Dir, 1998–2002, Envmt Agency Wales. Ind. Chair, Sci. and Liaison Gps, Skerries Tidal Turbine Array for SeaGen Wales, Marine Current Turbines Siemens, 2013–15. Associate, Welsh Inst. for Natural Resources, Bangor Univ., 2013–. Chairman: Coed Cymru, 2010–; Tir Coed, 2012–15; N Wales Wildlife Trust, 2014–; Wales Envmt Link, 2016–; Dir, Canolfan Beaumaris, 2014–. Trustee: Freshwater Habitats (formerly Ponds Conservation) Trust, 2006– (Chair, 2016–); Morgan Parry Foundn, 2014–; Centre for Alternative Technology, 2018–. Recreations: cycling, walking, junior Rugby coach, music, reading, sailing. Clubs: Bangor Rugby; Royal Anglesey Yacht; Beaumaris Rowing.

**THOMAS, Prof. Roger Christopher,** FRS 1989; Professor of Physiology, University of Cambridge, 1996–2006, now Emeritus (Head of Department, 1996–2006); Fellow, Downing College, Cambridge, 1996–2006; b 2 June 1939; e s of late Arthur Albert Thomas and Edith Kathleen (née Bigg); m 1964, Monica Mary, d of late Lt-Comdr William Peter Querstret, RN; two s. Educ: Perse Sch., Cambridge; Univ. of Southampton (BSc, PhD). Res. Associate, Rockefeller Univ., NY, 1964–66; Hon. Res. Asst, Biophysics, UCL, 1966–69; Bristol University: Lectr, 1969–77; Reader in Physiology, 1977–86; Prof. of Physiol., 1986–96; Hd of Dept of Physiol., 1985–90; Dean, Faculty of Science, 1990–93. Visiting Professor: Yale Univ., 1979–80; SISSA, Trieste, 2002–03. Scientific Ed., Physiology News, 2015–18. Publications: Ion-Sensitive Intracellular Microelectrodes, 1978; many papers on ion transport in learned jls. Recreations: cooking, walking, entertaining grandchildren. Address: Department of Physiology, Development and Neuroscience, University of Cambridge, Cambridge CB2 3EG. T: (01223) 333869, Fax: (01223) 333840. E: rct26@cam.ac.uk.
See also Sir Q. J. Thomas.

**THOMAS, Roger Christopher;** QC 2014; b Singapore, 1955; s of Victor Thomas and Rosina Thomas; m 1981, Jocelyn Anne Stoddard; one s. Educ: Portsmouth Grammar Sch.; St John's Coll., Oxford (MA; BCL). Called to the Bar, Lincoln's Inn, 1979; in practice as a barrister, 11 New Square, 1979–91, Pump Court Tax Chambers, 1991–. Publications: (ed) Halsbury's Laws of England, VAT, 4th edn, 1996, Customs and Excise, 4th edn, 1999; (ed jtly) Hill and Redman's Law of Landlord and Tenant, Stamp Taxes, 2013. Recreations: skiing, scuba diving, theatre. Address: 16 Bedford Row, WC1R 4EF. T: (020) 7414 8080. E: clerks@pumptax.com.

**THOMAS, Roger Geraint,** OBE 1997; DL; Chairman, Higher Education Funding Council for Wales, 2008–14; b Cardiff, 22 July 1945; s of Geraint Phillips Thomas and Doreen Augusta Thomas (née Cooke); m 1971, Rhian Elisabeth Kenyon Thomas. Educ: Univ. of Birmingham (LLB 1966). Admitted solicitor, 1969; Phillips & Buck, later Eversheds solicitors: Partner, then Jt Sen. Partner, 1969–87; Jt Regl Sen. Partner, 1987–95; Regl Sen. Partner, 1995–2000; consultant, 2000–06. Business partnership advr, Nat. Assembly for Wales, 1999–2002; Welsh Assembly: Mem., Ministerial Adv. Gp, Dept for Educn and Skills (formerly Dept for Children, Educn, Lifelong Learning and Skills), 2008–14; Mem., Rev. of Higher Educn in Wales, 2008–09. Chm., Chairs of Higher Educn Wales, 2004–08; Member: Gen. Adv. Council, BBC, 1992–95; Prog. Monitoring Cttee for Industrial S Wales Objective 2 Eur. Structural Funds, 1995–99; Chm.'s Gp, Cttee of Univ. Chairmen, 2003–08; Jt Negotiating Cttee for Higher Educn Staff, 2004–08; Wales Cttee, Leadership Foundn for Higher Educn, 2004–08; Dir, Univs and Colls Employers' Assoc., 2004–08. Mem., Welsh Council, CBI, 1987–97, 1998–2004, 2005–11. Chm., Penarth Headland Link, 2016–; Vice Chairman: Techniquest, 1988–2010; Business in Focus Ltd, 1998–2014. Mem. Court and Council, Nat. Mus. of Wales, 1983–2002 (Vice Pres., 2000–02); Director: Wales Millennium Centre, 1996–98; Welsh Nat. Opera Ltd, 2000–10 (Actg Chm., 2006). University of Glamorgan: Mem. Bd of Govs, 1994–2008; Chm., Audit Cttee, 1998–2001; Dep. Chm., 2001–02; Chm. and Pro-Chancellor, 2002–08; Mem. Council, Cardiff Univ., 2000–02. Judge, Provincial Court, Church in Wales, 2006–. CCMI 1996; FRSA 2000. High Sheriff, 2011–12, DL 2013, S Glamorgan. DUniv Glamorgan, 2008. OStJ 2003. Recreations: hill walking, music, travel. E: rgt@rgtpenarth.co.uk. Clubs: Cardiff and County; Penarth Yacht; Glamorganshire Golf.

**THOMAS, Roger Humphrey;** Chairman, Raymarine plc (formerly Raymarine Group Ltd), 2001–05; Chairman and Managing Director, Black & Decker, 1983–96; b 12 April 1942; s of Cyril Lewis Thomas and Phyllis Amy Thomas; m 1962, Myfanwy Ruth, (Nikki), Nicholas; three s. Educ: Slough Grammar School. FCCA. Black & Decker, 1970–96. Recreations: theatre, DIY, golf. Address: Stayes Wood, Northend, nr Henley-on-Thames, Oxon RG9 6LH. T: (01491) 638676.

**THOMAS, Roger Lloyd;** QC 1994; a Recorder, since 1987; b 7 Feb. 1947; s of David Eyron Thomas, CBE and Marie Lloyd Thomas; m 1974, Susan Nicola Orchard; one s one d. Educ: Cathays High Sch., Cardiff; University Coll. of Wales Aberystwyth (LLB). Called to the Bar, Gray's Inn, 1969. Recreations: tennis, music, reading. Club: Cardiff Lawn Tennis.

**THOMAS, Roger Martin;** QC 2000; **His Honour Judge Thomas;** a Circuit Judge, since 2004; b 18 Aug. 1954; s of Donald Thomas and Jessie Thomas (née Attwood); m 1981, Vanessa Julia Valentine Stirum; one s two d. Educ: Worksop Coll., Notts; Univ. of Hull (LLB). Called to the Bar, Inner Temple, 1976. Hon. Recorder of Bradford, 2012–17. Recreation: sport. Address: Sheffield Crown Court, 50 West Bar, Sheffield S3 8PH.

**THOMAS, Roger R.;** see Ridley-Thomas.

**THOMAS, Ronald Richard;** b 16 March 1929; m Lilian Audrey Jones; two s. Educ: Ruskin Coll. and Balliol Coll., Oxford (MA). Sen. Lectr, Econ. and Indust. Studies, Univ. of Bristol. Contested (Lab): Bristol North-West, Feb. 1974; Bristol East, 1987; MP (Lab) Bristol NW, Oct. 1974–1979. Former Mem., Bristol DC. Mem. UNITE (formerly ASTMS). Address: 64 Morris Road, Lockleaze, Bristol BS7 9TU.

**THOMAS, Rosemary,** OBE 2009; HM Diplomatic Service; Europe Directorate, Foreign and Commonwealth Office; b Liverpool, 17 July 1964; d of James and Madeleine O'Brien; m 1990, Alan Howard Thomas. Educ: Bellerive Convent Grammar Sch. for Girls, Toxteth, Liverpool; Univ. of Leeds (BA Hons Russian). Foreign and Commonwealth Office: joined 1990; Overseas Visits Sect., 1990–94; Research Analysts, 1994–97; Desk Officer: Asia-Europe Meeting Summit, 1997–98; Russian Sect., Eastern Dept, 1998–2001; Hd, Council of Europe Sect., OCSE/Council of Europe Dept, 2001–03; Hd, War Crimes Sect., Internat. Orgns Dept, 2003–05; Hd of Communications, EU Border Assistance Mission to Moldova and Ukraine, 2006–07; First Sec., Counter Narcotics, Kabul, 2007–08; Ambassador to Belarus, 2009–12; First Sec., Mexico, 2013; Dep. Dir, Eastern Europe and Central Asia, FCO, 2014; Hd of Communications, EU Border Assistance Mission, Ukraine, 2015; study leave, 2017. Recreations: ski-ing, walking, reading, music. Address: c/o Foreign and Commonwealth Office, King Charles Street, SW1A 2AH. Club: National Liberal.

**THOMAS, Prof. Sandra Mary,** OBE 2013; PhD; Director, Global Panel on Agriculture and Food Systems for Nutrition, since 2015; Professor of Science Policy, University of Sussex, 2005–06, Hon. Professor, since 2006; b 1 June 1951; d of late Alan Wallace Thomas and Josette Charlotte Jeanne Thomas (née Costa); m 1983 (marr. diss. 1993); one s one d. Educ: Dunsmore Sch. for Girls, Rugby; Westfield Coll., London (BSc 1971; PhD 1980); Brunel Univ. (MSc 1975). Tutor, Open Univ., 1978–90; Lectr, Goldsmiths' Coll., London, 1979–82, 1985–87; University of Sussex: Res. Fellow, 1987–94; Sen. Res. Fellow, 1994–2005; Professorial Fellow, 2005–06; Hon. Professorial Fellow, 2007–; Dir, Nuffield Council on Bioethics, 1997–2006; Dep. Dir, Govt Office for Sci. and Hd (formerly Dir) of Foresight, DTI, subseq. DIUS, later BIS, 2006–14; Dep. Dir, UK Space Agency, 2014–15. Member: Econ. and Social Cttee of EU, 1998–2002; Expert Adv. Gp on Genomes, DTI, 1999–2000; DFID Commn on IP Rights, 2000–02; UK Intellectual Adv. Cttee, 2000–05; Foresight Adv. Gp, 2000–02; Expert Adv. Gp on Clinical Res., Acad. Med. Scis, 2002–03; Expert Adv. Gp, MHRA, 2003–04; Ethics and Governance Council, UK Biobank, 2004–06; Sci. and Soc. Cttee, Royal Soc., 2004–06; Human Remains Adv. Gp, 2004–06; Steering Gp, Dept of Jobs, Enterprise and Innovation, Ireland, 2016–17; Vice Chm., Cttee on IP, Human Genome Orgn, 2003–08; Chair, Sci. Council, Food Standards Agency, 2017–. Dep. Chair, Adv. Gp, Sci Policy Res. Gp, Univ. of Sussex, 2017–. Trustee: Centre for Mgt of IP in Health R&D, 2003–07. Address: Global Panel on Agriculture and Food Systems for Nutrition, 20 Bloomsbury Square, WC1A 2NS.

**THOMAS, Sarah Joan;** Head of Bryanston School, since 2005; b 5 Sept. 1961; d of Raymond John Peter Thomas and Joan Mary Thomas (née Day); m 1985, Adrian Boote; two d. Educ: Birkenhead High Sch., GDST; Hertford Coll., Oxford (BA Lit.Hum. 1984); King's Coll. London (PGCE 1986). Classics Teacher, Sevenoaks Sch., 1986–99; Dep. Hd, Uppingham Sch., 1999–2005. Recreations: family, food, friends. Address: Bryanston School, Blandford, Dorset DT11 0PX. T: (01258) 452411.

**THOMAS, Simon;** Member (Plaid Cymru) Wales Mid and West, National Assembly for Wales, 2011–18; b Aberdare, 28 Dec. 1963; m 1997, Gwen Lloyd Davies; one s one d. Educ: UCW, Aberystwyth (BA Hons Welsh 1985); Coll. of Librarianship, Aberystwyth (Postgrad. DipLib 1988). Asst Curator, Nat. Liby of Wales, Aberystwyth, 1986–92; Policy and Res. Officer, Taff-Ely BC, 1992–94; Develt Officer, 1994–97, Manager, Jigso, 1997–2000, Wales Council for Voluntary Action. Mem. (Plaid Cymru) Ceredigion CC, 1999–2000. MP (Plaid Cymru) Ceredigion, Feb. 2000–2005. Contested (Plaid Cymru) Ceredigion, 2005. Mem., Standards and Privileges Cttee, H of C, 2003–05; Vice Chairman: Parly Envmt Gp, 2000–05; PRASEG, 2002–05; Mem., Envmtl Audit Cttee, 2000–05. Plaid Cymru: Member: Nat. Exec., 1995–98; Nat. Assembly Policy Gp, 1997–99; Policy Forum, 1999–2018 (Policy Co-ordinator for the Envmt); special advr on econ. develt and rural affairs, 2007–11. National Assembly for Wales: Shadow Minister for Energy, Climate Change and Rural Affairs, 2016–18; Chair, Finance Cttee, 2016–18. Vice-Chm., Global Legislators for a Better Environment, 2003–05. Publications: As Good as Our Words: guidelines for the use of Welsh by voluntary organisations, 1996; Plaid Cymru election manifestos, 1997, 1999; contrib. numerous articles in Welsh and English lang. jls. Recreations: culture and literature, cycling, family life.

**THOMAS, Sophie Lysandra;** Founding Director, Thomas.Matthews Ltd, since 1998; Director of Design, Useful Simple Ltd, since 2012; b Oxford, 25 June 1973; d of late Michael Thomas and of Pamela Thomas; m 2001, Daniel Epstein; one s one d. Educ: Oxford Brookes Univ. (Foundn in Art and Design); Central St Martin's Sch. of Art and Design (BA Hons Graphic Design 1995); Royal Coll. of Art (MA Communication Design 1997). Designer, Body Shop Internat., 1997–98; Co-Dir of Design, 2012–14, Dir of Circular Economy, 2014–16, RSA. Co-Founder: Three Trees Don't Make a Forest, 2007; Greengaged, 2008; The Great Recovery, 2012–16; Mem., London United. Trustee: Design Council, 2009–11; Useful Simple Trust, 2010–; WRAP UK, 2016–. Friend, St Bride's Liby. Hon. Lectr, UCL. MCIWM, 2014. FRSA. Hon. Fellow UAL, 2016. Publications: regular contribs to UK and internat. design press. Recreations: collecting plastic flotsam, letterpress and screen printing, growing vegetables, cheating at crosswords, choral singing. Address: Thomas.Matthews Ltd, First Floor, The Clove Building, 4 Maguire Street, Shad Thames, SE1 2NQ. T: (020) 7307 9292. E: sophie@thomasmatthews.com.

**THOMAS, Sir Stanley;** see Thomas, Sir G. S.

**THOMAS, Stephen Edward Owen; His Honour Judge Stephen Thomas;** a Circuit Judge, since 2019; b Shrewsbury, Shropshire, 5 April 1957; s of Elfed Howell Thomas and Eirlys Thomas; m 1983, Jennifer Olsen (d 2013); one s. Educ: Bridgnorth Grammar Sch.; Univ. of Exeter (LLB Hons). Called to the Bar, Gray's Inn, 1980; a Recorder, 2002–19. Recreations: squash, sailing. Address: Maidstone Crown Court, Barker Road, Maidstone ME16 8EQ. E: HHJ.Stephen.Thomas@ejudiciary.net.

**THOMAS, Sybil Milwyn; Her Honour Judge Thomas;** a Circuit Judge, since 2005; a Senior Circuit Judge, since 2014; Designated Family Judge for Birmingham, since 2014; d of late Terence Barrington Thomas and Ann Veronica Thomas. Educ: Edgbaston High Sch. for Girls, Birmingham; Univ. of Bristol (LLB Hons 1975). Called to the Bar, Gray's Inn, 1976, Bencher 2016; in practice, Midland and Oxford Circuit, 1977–2005; Asst Recorder, 1993–97; a Recorder, 1997–2005. Dep. Chancellor, Dio. of Lichfield, 2006–. Address: c/o Birmingham Family Court, 33 Bull Street, Birmingham B4 6DS.

**THOMAS, Trevor Anthony,** FRCA; Emeritus Consultant Anaesthetist, United Bristol Healthcare NHS Trust (formerly United Bristol Hospitals), since 2002 (Consultant Anaesthetist, 1972–2002); b 1939; s of Arthur William Thomas and Gladys Mary Gwendoline Thomas (née Hulin); m 1965, Yvonne Louise Mary Branch; one s. Educ: Bristol Grammar Sch.; Univ. of St Andrews (MB ChB 1964). FRCA (FFARCS 1969). Chm., Dept of Anaesthesia, United Bristol Hosps, 1977–80; Hon. Clin. Sen. Lectr, Bristol Univ., 1980–2002. SW Regl Assessor in Anaesthesia, 1978–2000, Central Assessor, 1999–2003, Confidential Enquiries into Maternal Deaths in UK (formerly Confidential Enquiry into Maternal Deaths in England and Wales). Chm., Med. Cttee, Bristol and Weston DHA, 1988–90. Mem. Council, 1989–96, Hon. Sec., 1994, Sect. of Anaesthetists, RSocMed; Obstetric Anaesthetists Association: Mem. Cttee, 1978–85; Minute Sec., 1980–81; Hon. Sec., 1981–85; Mem. Cttee and Pres. Elect, 1994–95; Pres., 1995–99; Society of Anaesthetists, SW Region: Mem. Cttee, 1975–85; Hon. Sec., 1985–88; Pres., 1997–98. Examr, Fellowship Exams, RCAnaes, 1985–96. Trustee, Special Trustees for United Bristol Hosps, 1992–99; Trustee and Mem. Council, St Peter's Hospice, 1996–2012. Asst Ed., 1975–76, Ed., 1976–80, Anaesthesia Points West. Publications: (with A. Holdcroft) Principles and Practice of Obstetric Anaesthesia and Analgesia, 2000; contrib. chapters to textbooks; contribs to learned jls, mainly on matters related to obstetric anaesthesia. Recreations: music, theatre, Tai Chi, genealogy, history relating to Spain and Spanish artists, bird watching. Address: 14 Cleeve Lawns, Downend, Bristol BS16 6HJ. Club: Bristol Savages.

**THOMAS, Victor Gerald B.;** see Bulmer-Thomas.

**THOMAS, Vivian Elliott Sgrifan,** CBE 1998 (OBE 1992); Chairman, British Standards Institution, 1992–2002; b 13 March 1932; s of William Edward Thomas and Cicely (née Elliott); m 1962, Valerie Slade Thomas; one s one d. Educ: Swindon High Sch., Southampton Univ. Engr Officer, Union Castle Line, 1953–58; with British Petroleum plc, 1959–92; Chief Exec. Officer, BP Oil UK Ltd, 1989–92. Director: Southern Water plc, 1992–96; Jaguar Ltd, 1993–2006; Gowrings Plc, 1992–2001. Recreations: golf, music, theatre. Address: Camelot, Bennett Way, West Clandon, Guildford, Surrey GU4 7TN. T: (01483) 222665. Club: Royal Automobile.

**THOMAS, (William) David;** QC 2002; b 20 Dec. 1958; s of John Lloyd Thomas and Kathleen Thomas; m 1987, Victoria Susan Cochrane; one s one d. Educ: The Heights; Midhurst Grammar Sch.; Wadham Coll., Oxford (MA). Called to the Bar, Middle Temple, 1982; in practice as barrister, 1983–. Publications: (contrib.) Keating on Construction Contracts, 8th edn 2006; (ed) Keating on NEC3, 2012. Recreations: gardening, cricket, wine, tennis. Address: Keating Chambers, 15 Essex Street, WC2R 3AA. E: dthomas@ keatingchambers.com. Clubs: MCC; Kirdford Cricket.

**THOMAS, William Ernest Ghinn,** FRCS; Consultant Surgeon, Sheffield Teaching Hospitals NHS Foundation Trust, 1986–2010, now Consultant Surgeon Emeritus (Clinical Director of Surgery, 1989–2008); Senior Vice President, Royal College of Surgeons of England, 2008–10; b London, 13 Feb. 1948; s of late Kenneth Dawson Thomas and of Monica Isobel Thomas; m 1973, Grace Violet Samways; two s three d. Educ: Dulwich Coll.; King's Coll. London (BSc 1969); St George's Hosp. Med. Sch., London (MB BS 1972); MS London 1980. MRCS 1972, FRCS 1976; LRCP 1972; ECFMG 1972. Consultant Surgeon, Royal Hallamshire Hosp., Sheffield, 1986–2010; Hon. Sen. Lectr in Surgery, Univ. of Sheffield, 1986–. Adjunct Prof., Faculty of Medicine, Univ. of Malaysia, 2018–. Phase 2 Assessor, GMC, 1999–2003. Royal College of Surgeons of England: Bernard Sunley Fellow, 1977; Arris and Gale Lect., 1981–82; Hunterian Prof., 1986–87; Mem., Court of Examrs, 1992–2000; Surgical Skills Tutor, 1994–2004; Mem., Council, 2002–12; Internat. Dir, 2002–08; Chm., Educn, 2003–08; Zachary Cope Meml Lect., 2005; Chm., Editl Bd, 2008–12. Member: Surgical Cttee, British Soc. of Gastroenterology, 1991–95; Intercollegiate Panel of Examrs, Gen. Surgery, 1995–2002; Internat. Bd of Dirs, Gastrointestinal Workshop, 2000–15; Pres., Surgical Section, RSocMed, 2000–01; Permanent Dean, Acad. of Educn, Internat. Soc. of Surgery, 2011–13. Hon. Sec., E Midlands Surgical Soc., 1994–99. Pres., Gideons Internat., 2013–16. Hon. FSACS 2006; Hon. Fellow: German Surgical Soc., 2010; Swiss Surgical Soc., 2015. Mem., Editl Bd, Hospital Doctor, 1987–2001; Chm. and Exec. Ed., Current Practice in Surgery, 1988–97; Series Ed. and Chm., Editl Bd, Surgery, 2000–17; Ed., Bulletin, RCS, 2002–08. Lectures: State of the Art, British Soc. of Gastroenterology, 1986; Martin Allgöwer, Internat. Soc. of Surgery, 2005; Heyendael Prize, Nijmegen, 2006. Award for bravery, Royal Humane Soc., 1974; Eur. Soc. for Surgical Res. Prize, 1981; Dr of the Year Award, BUPA Med. Foundn, 1985. Publications: Preparation and Revision for the FRCS, 1986; Self-Assessment Exercises in Surgery, 1986; (with E. Rhys Davies) Nuclear Medicine: applications in surgery, 1988; (with J. H. F. Smith) Colour Guide to Surgical Pathology, 1992; Basic Surgical Skills, 1996, 4th edn 2007; Preparation and Revision for MRCS, 1999, 2nd edn 2004; Specialist Registrar Skills in General Surgery, 1999; (with A. Aluwihare) Introduction to Surgical Skills, 2001; (with A. Wyman) The Abdomen, STEP Course Module VII, 2001; MCQs and Extended Matching Questions for the MRCS, 2002; (jtly) An Introduction to the Symptoms and Signs of Surgical Disease, 4th edn 2005 (1st Prize, BMA Med. Book Competition, 2006); (ed jtly) Anastomosis Techniques in the Gastro-Intestinal Tract, 2007; Short Stay Surgery, 2008; An Introduction to the Diagnosis and Management of Surgical Disease, 2010; (Sen. Ed.) Oxford Textbook of Fundamentals of Surgery, 2016; over 200 articles in learned jls. Recreations: ski-ing, oil painting, photography. Address: Ash Lodge, 65 Whirlow Park Road, Whirlow, Sheffield S11 9NN. T: (0114) 262 0852. E: wegthomas@ btinternet.com. W: www.wegthomas.com.

**THOMAS, Ven. William Jordison;** Archdeacon of Northumberland, 1983–92, Archdeacon Emeritus 1993; b 16 Dec. 1927; s of Henry William and Dorothy Newton Thomas; m 1954, Kathleen Jeffrey Robson, d of William Robson, Reaveley, Powburn, Alnwick. Educ: Holmwood Prep. School, Middlesbrough; Acklam Hall Grammar School, Middlesbrough; Giggleswick School; King's Coll., Cambridge (BA 1951, MA 1955); Cuddesdon College. National Service, RN, 1946–48. Assistant Curate: St Anthony of Egypt, Newcastle upon Tyne, 1953–56; Berwick Parish Church, 1956–59; Vicar: Alwinton with Holystone and Alnham and the Lordship of Kidland, 1959–70; Alston with Garrigill, Nenthead and Kirkhaugh, 1970–80, i/c Knaresdale, 1973–80; Industrial Chaplain, 1972–80; Team Rector of Glendale, 1980–82; RD of Bamburgh and Glendale, 1980–82. Travel leader, chaplain and lectr with leading pilgrimage, tour and cruise cos, 1992–2008. Hon. Chaplain: Actors' Church Union, 1953–56; Northumberland County NFU, 1978–2000. Harbour Comr, N Sunderland, 1990–92. Recreations: sailing own dinghy and other people's yachts, making pictures, travelling and making magic. Club: Victory Services.

**THOMAS, Sir William Michael,** 3rd Bt cr 1919, of Ynyshir, co. Glamorgan; b 5 Dec. 1948; er s of Sir William James Cooper Thomas, 2nd Bt, TD, and Freida Dunbar Thomas (née Whyte); S father, 2005. Educ: Harrow; Christ Church, Oxford. Heir: nephew Toby James Thomas, b 10 Oct. 1988.

**THOMAS, Wyndham,** CBE 1982; Chairman, Cambridge New Town Corporation PLC, 1999–2008; b 1 Feb. 1924; s of Robert John Thomas and Hannah Mary; m 1947, Elizabeth Terry Hopkin; one s three d. Educ: Maesteg Grammar School. Served Army (Lieut, Royal Welch Fusiliers), 1943–47. Schoolmaster, 1950–53; Director, Town and Country Planning Association, 1955–67; Gen. Manager, Peterborough New Town Develt Corp., 1968–83; Chm., Inner City Enterprises, 1983–92. Member: Land Commission, 1967–68; Commission for the New Towns, 1964–68; Property Adv. Gp, DoE, 1978–90; London Docklands Develt Corp., 1981–88. Chm., House Builders' Fedn Commn of Inquiry into Housebuilding and the Inner Cities, 1986–87 (report published 1987). A Vice-Pres., TCPA, 1992–. Mayor of Hemel Hempstead, 1958–59. Contested (Lab) SW Herts, 1955. Hon. MRTPI 1979 (Mem. Council, 1989–98). Freedom, City of Peterborough, 2012. Officer of the Order of Orange-Nassau (Netherlands), 1982. Publications: many articles on town planning, housing, etc, in learned jls. Recreations: collecting/restoring old furniture, writing. Address: 8 Westwood Park Road, Peterborough PE3 6JL. T: (01733) 564399.

**THOMAS, Wynn;** see Thomas, M. W.

**THOMAS, Zoë Siobhan;** see O'Sullivan, Z. S.

**THOMAS-DAVIES, Christine Mary;** see Tacon, C. M.

**THOMAS JUDGE, Hon. Barbara Singer, (Lady Judge),** CBE 2010; Chairman: UK Pension Protection Fund, 2010–16; Athene Capital LLP; Deputy Chairman, Financial Reporting Council, 2003–07; Chairman, UK Atomic Energy Authority, 2004–10, now Emeritus; b 28 Dec. 1946; d of Jules Singer and Marcia Bosniak; m 1978, Allen Lloyd Thomas (marr. diss. 2002); one s; m 2003, Sir Paul Rupert Judge (d 2017). Educ: Univ. of Pennsylvania (BA 1966); New York Univ. Sch. of Law (JD with Hons 1969). Partner, Kaye Scholer, Fierman, Hays & Handler, 1973–80; Comr, US Securities and Exchange Commn,

1980–83; Exec. Dir, Samuel Montagu & Co. Ltd, 1984–86; Sen. Vice Pres. and Gp Hd, Bankers Trust Co., 1986–90; Dir, News International plc, 1993–94; Chairman: Whitworths Gp Ltd, 1996–2000; Private Equity Investor plc, 2000–04 (Dir, 2004–); Astana Financial Services Authy; Dep. Chm., Friends Provident plc, 2001–09; non-executive Director: NV Belaert SA, 2007–; Magna International Inc., 2007–; Statoil, 2010–. Chairman: Hibob, 2016–; LoopUp, 2016–; SmartUp Ltd; Systemised Nomenclature of Medicine (Snomed) Internat.; Cambridge Code. Non-exec. Dir, DCA, 2004–06. Mem., Trilateral Commn, 2007–; Chm., Task Force on Nuclear Safety, 2014– (Dep. Chm., Tokyo Electric Power Co. Nuclear Reform Monitoring Cttee, 2014–); Mem., UAE Adv. Bd for Develt of Peaceful Nuclear Energy, 2012–. Mem. Bd of Dirs, Lauder Inst. of Internat. Mgt, Wharton Sch., Univ. of Pennsylvania, 1986–; Chm., Inst. of Dirs, 2015–18; Chm., Energy Inst., UCL, 2010–. Chm. Benjamin West Gp and Mem. Corporate Develt Bd, RA, 2000–; Mem., Council of Mgt, Ditchley Foundn, 2006–. Trustee: Wallace Collection, 2004–07; RA, 2005–. Governor, SOAS, 1997–2005 (Chm., 2006–10). Recreations: food, oriental porcelain. Address: 88 The Panoramic, 152 Grosvenor Road, SW1V 3JL. T: (020) 7919 0624. Clubs: Reform; Metropolitan (Washington, DC).

**THOMAS-SYMONDS, Nicklaus,** FRHistS; MP (Lab) Torfaen, since 2015; b Panteg, Torfaen, 26 May 1980; s of Jeffrey Symonds and late Pamela Symonds (née Thomas); m 2006, Rebecca Nelson; one s two d. Educ: St Alban's RC High Sch., Pontypool; St Edmund Hall, Oxford (MA PPE); Univ. of Glamorgan (DipLaw); Cardiff Univ. (BVC). FRHistS 2012. Tutor and Lectr in Politics, St Edmund Hall, Oxford, 2002–15; called to the Bar, Lincoln's Inn, 2004; in practice as barrister, 2004–15. Secretary: Blaenavan Lab. Party, 2004–15; Torfaen CLP, 2009–15. Shadow Minister for Work and Pensions, 2015–16; Shadow Solicitor-Gen., 2016–; Shadow Minister for Security, 2017–. Publications: Attlee: a life in politics, 2010; Nye: the political life of Aneurin Bevan, 2014; contrib. articles to British Hist., Llafur: Jl of Welsh People's Hist. Soc., Parly Affairs. Recreations: reading, watching football and Rugby. Address: House of Commons, SW1A 0AA. T: (020) 7219 4294. E: nick.thomassymonds.mp@parliament.uk. Club: Elgam Working Men's (Blaenavon).

**THOMASON, (Kenneth) Roy,** OBE 1986; Chairman, Charminster Estates Ltd, since 1998; director of other property companies; b 14 Dec. 1944; s of Thomas Roger and Constance Dora Thomason; m 1969, Christine Ann (née Parsons); two s two d. Educ: Cheney Sch., Oxford; London Univ. (LLB). Admitted Solicitor, 1969; Partner, 1970–91, Sen. Partner, 1979–91, Horden & George, Bournemouth. Mem., Bournemouth Council, 1970–92 (Leader, 1974–82; past Chm. Policy, Ways and Means, and Finance Cttees). Association of District Councils: Mem. Council, 1979–91; Leader, 1981–87; Chm., 1987–91; Chm., Housing and Environmental Health Cttee, 1983–87. Mem., Cons. Nat. Local Govt Adv. Cttee, 1981–97; various Cons. Party positions at constituency and area level, 1966–97 (Constituency Chm., 1981–82); contested (C) Newport E, 1983. MP (C) Bromsgrove, 1992–97. Member: Envmt Select Cttee, 1992–97; Jt Statutory Instrument Cttee, 1992–97; Chm., All-Party Export Gp, 1996–97 (Sec., 1993–96); Vice Chm., Cons. Parly Envmt Cttee, 1993–97. Fellow, Industry and Parlt Trust, 1996. Mem. Bd, London Strategic Housing, 2001–06 (Chm., 2002–06). Office holder, Dodford PCC, 2000–14; Lay Chm., St Laurence, Middleton St George PCC, 2017– (Treas., 2015–17). FRSA. Hon. Alderman, Bournemouth BC, 1993. Bailiff of the Court Leet and Court Baron of Bromsgrove, 2012–13 (Reeve, 2011–12; Ealdorman, 2013–). Recreations: walking, reading, architectural history, local activities. Address: The Old Chapel, Station Road, Middleton St George, Darlington DL2 1JG.

**THOMÉ, David Geoffrey C.;** see Colin-Thomé.

**THOMLINSON, Nicholas Howard,** FRICS; Chairman, Knight Frank Group, 2004–13; b 9 Jan. 1953; s of John and Lorna Thomlinson; m 2001, Lucy Joly de Lotbinière; two s, and three step s. Educ: Stowe Sch.; Keble Coll., Oxford (MA). FRICS 1978. With Knight Frank & Rutley, subseq. Knight Frank, then Knight Frank LLP, 1974–2013. Non-exec. Dir, Develt Securities plc, 2012–. Trustee, Hft (formerly Home Farm Trust), 2012–15. Recreations: making marmalade and chutney, bee-keeping, tennis. E: nick.thomlinson@ gmail.com. Clubs: Hurlingham; Wimbledon.

**THOMPSON;** see Grey-Thompson.

**THOMPSON, Prof. Alan James,** MD; FRCP, FRCPI, FMedSci; Consultant Neurologist, National Hospital for Neurology and Neurosurgery, Queen Square, since 1990; Garfield Weston Professor of Clinical Neurology and Neurorehabilitation, since 1998, and Dean, Faculty of Brain Sciences, since 2011, University College London; Chair, Neuroscience Programme, University College London Partners Academic Health Science Centre, since 2014; Senior Investigator, National Institute for Health Research, 2008–16, now Senior Investigator Emeritus; b Dublin, 29 Aug. 1955; s of late Frank and Maureen Thompson. Educ: Terenure Coll., Dublin; Trinity Coll. Dublin (MB BCh, BAO, BA 1979; MD 1985). FRCP 1994; FRCPI 1995. Hse officer, Meath Hosp., Dublin, 1979–80; SHO, then Registrar, Trinity Coll. and Dublin Hosps, 1980–82; Registrar in Neurol., 1982–83, Res. Registrar in Neurol., 1983–85, St Vincent's and Adelaide Hosps Dublin; Registrar in Neurol., London Hosp., 1985–87; Sen. Registrar in Neurol., Nat. Hosp. for Nervous Diseases, UCH, 1987–89; National Hospital for Neurology and Neurosurgery: Scarfe Lectr and Sen. Registrar, Dept of Clin. Neurol., 1989–90; Clin. Dir of Neurorehabilitation and Therapies, 1993–98; Dir, R&D, 1998–2006; Divl Clin. Dir, 2003–07; Consultant Neurologist, Whittington Hosp., London, 1990–98; Hd, Dept of Brain Repair and Rehabilitation, Inst. of Neurol., UCL, 2006–08; Dep. Dir, R&D Unit, 2006–08, Comprehensive Biomedical Res. Centre, 2006–10, Jt UCLH/UCL; Dir, Inst. of Neurol., 2008–11, and Vice-Dean and Dep. Hd, Faculty of Biomed., 2009–11, UCL; Clin. Lead for Neurol Diseases, Central and E London Clin. Res. Network, 2013–14. Series Ed., Queen Square Neurol Rehabilitation Series, 2003–; Ed.-in-Chief, Multiple Sclerosis Jl, 2006–; Member: Editl Bd, Lancet Neurol., 2003–; Adv. Bd, Current Med. Lit.: Multiple Sclerosis, 2009–11. Chm. and Mem. Bd, Internat. Med. and Scientific Bd, MS Internat. Fedn, 2005–15; Chm., Scientific Adv. Cttee, Internat. Progressive MS Alliance, 2012–; Member: Adv. Cttee for revision of ICD-10-neurol diseases, WHO, 2009–12; Res. Adv. Cttee, Nat. MS Soc., USA, 2009–. Brain Ambassador, Eur. Brain Council, 2014–. MAE 2018. FAAN 2009; FANA 2013; FMedSci 2015; FEAN 2018. Corresp. Mem., Amer. Neurol Assoc., 1997–2013. Guarantor, Brain, 2005–; Trustee: Nat. Hosp. Develt Foundn, subseq. Nat. Brain Appeal, 1998–; Patrick Berthoud Trust, 2004–09; Pewterers' Co. 500th Anniv. Trust, 2010–17. Friend: Almeida Th.; Wexford Opera Fest.; RA. Hon. Dr Hasselt, Belgium, 2008. Pioneer of the Nation, 2003. Biennial Prize for contrib. to res. in neurosci. and MS, Multiple Sclerosis Foundn of Madrid, 2016; John Dystel Prize for res. in MS, Amer. Acad. of Neurol., 2017; Lifetime Achievement Award, Consortium of MS Centers, USA, 2018. Publications: (ed jtly) Multiple Sclerosis: clinical challenges and controversies, 1997 (trans. Russian 2000); (ed jtly) Magnetic Resonance in Multiple Sclerosis, 1997 (trans. German 1998); (ed with I. McDonald) Key Advances in the Effective Management of Multiple Sclerosis, 1999; (jtly) Frontiers in Multiple Sclerosis, vol. 2, 1999; (ed) Neurological Rehabilitation of Multiple Sclerosis, 2006; (jtly) Multiple Sclerosis: the guide to treatment and management, 6th edn 2006; (jtly) Atlas of Multiple Sclerosis: multiple sclerosis resources in the world, 2008; (jtly) Multiple Sclerosis: recovery of function and neurorehabilitation,

2010; contrib. chapters in books and articles on MS, MRI, neurorehabilitation and outcome measurement to scientific jls. *Recreations:* music, theatre, reading, wine, Irish art. *Address:* UCL Institute of Neurology, Box 9, Queen Square, WC1N 3BG. *T:* (020) 3448 4152. *E:* alan.thompson@ucl.ac.uk. *Clubs:* Garrick; Trinity College Dublin Sports.

**THOMPSON, Amanda,** OBE 2012; Managing Director, Blackpool Pleasure Beach, since 2004 (Director, since 1988); President, Stageworks Worldwide Productions, since 1982; *b* 2 Sept. 1962; *d* of William Geoffrey Thompson, OBE, DL and Barbara Thompson; *m* 2003, Stephen Thompson. *Educ:* Badminton Sch., Bristol; Dover Brooks, Oxford. Ran dance studio; worked for Disney, Florida; produced first ice shows in Myrtle Beach, USA, 1982; Dep. Man. Dir, Blackpool Pleasure Beach, 2000–04. Producer/Dir of UK shows: Hot Ice Show; Mystique; Eclipse; Forbidden. Mem., Bd of Dirs, Internat. Assoc. of Amusement Parks and Attractions (Chm., EMEA); Patron: Grand Th., Blackpool; Blackpool Civic Trust. *Recreations:* shows, cinema, ski-ing, travel, fashion and interior design. *Address:* Blackpool Pleasure Beach, Ocean Boulevard, Blackpool FY4 1EZ. *T:* 0870 444 5588, *Fax:* (01253) 343958.

**THOMPSON, Prof. Andrew Stuart,** DPhil; Executive Chair, Arts and Humanities Research Council, since 2018 (Acting Chief Executive, 2015–17; Chief Executive, 2017–18); *b* Mansfield, Notts, 3 June 1968; *s* of John and June Thompson; *m* 1998, Sarah Jane Lenton; two *d. Educ:* Loughborough Grammar Sch.; Regent's Park Coll., Oxford (BA Modern Hist. 1990; MA 1991); Nuffield Coll., Oxford (DPhil Modern Hist. 1994). Fixed-term Tutorial Fellow in Modern Hist., Corpus Christi Coll., Oxford, 1993–97; University of Leeds: Lectr, 1997–2001; Sen. Lectr, 2001–05; Prof. of Imperial and Global Hist., 2005–11; Dean, Faculty of Arts, 2007–09; Pro-Vice Chancellor for Res., 2009–11; Prof. of Modern Hist., Univ. of Exeter, 2011–17. Hon. Prof., Univ. of S Africa, 2014–. Mem., AHRC, 2010–17. Gen. Ed., Studies in Imperialism series, 2014– (Co-Ed., 2011–14). *Publications:* Imperial Britain: the Empire in British politics, *c* 1880–1932, 2000; The Empire Strikes Back?: the impact of Imperialism on Britain from the mid-nineteenth century, 2005; Empire and Globalisation: networks of people, goods and capital in the British world, *c* 1850–1914, 2010; (ed) Britain's Experience of Empire in the Twentieth Century, 2011; Writing Imperial Histories, 2013. *Recreations:* distance running, Nottingham Forest FC, my Reliant Sabre sports car, Hanna-Barbera cartoons. *Address:* Arts and Humanities Research Council, Polaris House, North Star Avenue, Swindon SN2 1FL. *Club:* East India.

**THOMPSON, Anita Joy M.;** *see* Mauger-Thompson.

**THOMPSON, His Honour Anthony Arthur Richard;** QC 1980; a Circuit Judge, 1992–2003; Designated Civil Judge for Hampshire and Dorset, 1999–2003; *b* 4 July 1932; *s* of late William Frank McGregor Thompson and Doris Louise Thompson (*née* Hill); *m* 1958, Françoise Alix Marie Reynier; two *s* one *d* (and one *s* decd). *Educ:* Latymer Upper Sch.; University Coll., Oxford; La Sorbonne. FCIArb 1991. Called to the Bar, Inner Temple, 1957, Bencher, 1986; admitted to Paris Bar, 1988; a Recorder, 1985–92; Liaison Judge for Cornwall, 1993–99; Resident Judge for Cornwall, 1993–99. Chm., Bar European Gp, 1984–86 (Vice-Chm., 1982–84); Mem., Internat. Relations Cttee, Bar Council, 1984–86. QC: Singapore, 1985; Hong Kong, 1986; St Vincent and the Grenadines, 1986. Vice Pres., Cornwall Magistrates' Assoc., 1995–2005. Contested (Lab) Arundel and Shoreham, Oct. 1964. *Recreations:* food and wine, croquet, theatre, cinema, 19th century music, 20th century painting. *Clubs:* Garrick, Roehampton.

*See also* R. P. R. *Thompson*.

**THOMPSON, Anupama; Her Honour Judge Anupama Thompson;** a Circuit Judge, since 2019; *b* Trichur, India, 31 July 1972; *d* of Dr V. Gopinathan and Dr P. R. Gopinathan; *m* 2000, Lyall Thompson; one *s* two *d. Educ:* Westbourne Sch. for Girls, Glasgow; Univ. of Essex (LLB Hons). Called to the Bar, Inner Temple, 1994; Tenant, Castle Chambers, Harrow, 1997–2004; a Recorder, 2016–19. Asst Dir, Legal Services, NMC, 2008–16. Barrister Bd Mem., Bar Standards Bd, 2016–19. *Recreations:* theatre, Scottish country dancing, 90s Scottish music. *Address:* Harrow Crown Court, Hailsham Drive, Harrow, Middx HA1 4TU. *E:* hhj.anupama.thompson@ejudiciary.net.

**THOMPSON, Barnaby David Waterhouse;** film and television director and producer; Partner, Ealing Studios, since 2001 (Head of Studios, 2001–14); *b* London, 29 March 1961; *s* of late John Brian Thompson, CBE; *m* 1991, Christina Robert; one *s* one *d. Educ:* St Paul's Sch., London; Regent's Park Coll., Oxford (MA Hons Theol. and Philosophy). Producer and Dir, Refugees of Faith, 1984; Asst to Producer, Number One, 1985; Asst Producer, Witness in the War Zone, 1986; Man. Dir, World's End Prodns, 1987–90; Vice Pres., Creative Affairs, Broadway Video, NY, 1990–96; Chief Exec., Fragile Films, 1996–2001. Dir, Thin Blue Line, 1988; director and producer: Singing for Your Supper, 1988; Jimi Hendrix, 1989; producer: The Money Slaves, 1987; The Forgotten Holocaust, 1989; Dear Rosie, 1990; Spice World, 1997; An Ideal Husband, 1999; High Heels and Low Lifes, 2001; Lucky Break, 2001; The Importance of Being Earnest, 2002; Hope Springs, 2003; Imagine Me & You, 2005; Alien Autopsy, 2006; Fade to Black, 2006; I Want Candy, 2007; St Trinian's (also co-dir), 2007; Easy Virtue, 2008; St Trinian's 2: the Legend of Fritton's Gold (also co-dir), 2009; Dorian Gray, 2009; Burke and Hare, 2010; The D Train, 2015; Kids in Love, 2016; Associate Producer, Wayne's World, 1992; Co-Producer: Coneheads, 1993; Wayne's World 2, 1993; Lassie, 1994; Tommy Boy, 1995; Kids in the Hall: Brain Candy, 1996; Executive Producer: Kevin & Parry Go Large, 2000; Valiant, 2005; From Time to Time, 2009; (for TV) Maigret Sets a Trap, Maigret's Dead Man, 2016; Maigret—Night at the Crossroads, Maigret in Montmartre, 2017; Fisherman's Friends, 2019. Member: BAFTA; Acad. of Motion Picture Arts and Scis. *Recreations:* swimming, music, cycling. *Address:* Ealing Studios, Ealing Green, W5 5EP. *T:* (020) 8567 6655. *Clubs:* Soho House, MCC; Serpentine Swimming; Maidstone (E Hampton, Long Island, NY).

**THOMPSON, Bruce Kevin,** MA; Founding Head and Executive Principal, RDFZ King's College School, Hangzhou, China, since 2017; *b* 14 Nov. 1959; *s* of Keith Bruce Thompson, *qv*; two *d. Educ:* Newcastle High Sch., Newcastle-under-Lyme; New Coll., Oxford (MA Lit.Hum.). Asst Master, 1983–86, Head of Classics, 1986–94, Cheltenham Coll.; Dep. Rector, Dollar Acad., 1994–2000; Hd, Strathallan Sch., 2000–17. Chm., Scottish HMC, 2010–11. Schs' Rep., Scottish Rugby Council, 2010–16. *Recreations:* weight training, rowing, cycling, literature, music. *Club:* Leander (Henley-on-Thames).

**THOMPSON, Catriona Helen Moncrieff;** *see* Kelly, C. H. M.

**THOMPSON, Prof. Christopher,** MD; FRCP, FRCPsych; Chief Executive, Chris Thompson Consultants Ltd, since 2014; *b* 23 Sept. 1952; *s* of Derek and Margaret Thompson; *m* 1976, Celia Randall; three *d. Educ:* Lincoln Grammar Sch.; Strode's Sch., Egham; University Coll. London (BSc 1974; MB BS 1977; MD 1987). FRCPsych 1991; FRCP 1995; MRCGP 2000. Registrar in Psychiatry, Maudsley Hosp., 1978–81; Res. Fellow and Lectr, Inst. of Psychiatry, 1981–84; Sen. Lectr, Charing Cross Hosp. Med. Sch., 1984–88; University of Southampton: Prof. of Psychiatry, 1988–2003; Hd, Sch. of Medicine, 2000–03; CMO (formerly Dir of Healthcare), 2004–14, Dir of Public Affairs, 2012–14, Priory Gp. Royal College of Psychiatrists: Registrar, 1993–97; Vice Pres., 1997–99; Pres., Internat. Soc. for Affective Disorders, 2000–06. Mem. Bd, Depression Alliance, 2007–15. Mem. Council, UCL, 2007–13. Gold Medal, RCPsych, 1983. *Publications:* (ed and contrib.) Research Instruments in Psychiatry, 1989; (jtly) Caring for a Community, 1995; edited jointly and contributed: Psychological Applications in Psychiatry, 1985; The Origins of Modern Psychiatry, 1987; Learning Psychiatry through MCQ, 1988; Melatonin: clinical perspectives, 1988; Seasonal Affective Disorders, 1989; Violence: basic and clinical science, 1993; 3 official govt reports; over 100 scientific articles in learned jls. *Recreations:* classical and jazz guitar, golf.

**THOMPSON, Lt-Col Sir Christopher (Peile),** 6th Bt *cr* 1890; Equerry to HRH Prince Michael of Kent, since 1989 (Private Secretary, 1990–92); non-executive Chairman, Nuclear Decommissioning Ltd, 1995–2000 (Director, 1994–2000); *b* 21 Dec. 1944; *s* of Lt-Col Sir Peile Thompson, 5th Bt, OBE, and Barbara Johnson (*d* 1993), *d* of late H. J. Rampling; S father, 1985; *m* 1st, 1969, Anna Elizabeth (marr. diss. 1997), *d* of Major Arthur Callander; one *s* one *d*; 2nd, 2001, Penelope (*née* Allin), *widow* of 9th Viscount Portman. *Educ:* Marlborough; RMA Sandhurst. Commnd 11th Hussars (PAO), 1965; Tank Troop Leader and Reconnaissance Troop Leader, 11th Hussars, 1965–69; Gunnery Instructor, RAC Gunnery Sch., 1970–72; Sqdn Second i/c, A Sqdn, Royal Hussars, 1972–75; GSO 3 Intelligence, Allied Staff, Berlin, 1975–76; RMCS Shrivenham, 1977; Staff Coll., Camberley, 1978; DAAG (a) M2 (A) (Officer Manning), MoD, 1978–81; C Sqdn Ldr, Royal Hussars, 1981–83; GSO 2 (Operational Requirements), HQ DRAC, 1983–85; CO, Royal Hussars (PWO), 1985–87; SO1, Sen. Officers Tactics Div., 1987–90, retd. Director: Logical Security Ltd, 1996–98; Falcon Security Control (Overseas) Ltd, 2000–04; Nuclear Decommissioning Services Ltd, 2007–13 (Chm., 2006–11). Dir, Hyde Park Appeal, 1990–96; Trustee: Bike Aid, 1990–94; Queen Elizabeth Gate Appeal, 1990–96; Tusk, 1994–2002 (Patron, 2002–); Antigua Heritage Trust (UK), 1997–2000. Mem., Standing Council of the Baronetage, 2001–10. Patron, Earth 2000, 1997–2002. *Recreations:* travel, fishing, reading, golf, sailing. *Heir: s* Peile Richard Thompson, *b* 3 March 1975. *Clubs:* Cavalry and Guards; Mill Reef (Antigua).

**THOMPSON, Clive Hepworth,** CBE 1998; Director, Sustainable Governance Ltd, since 2009; *b* 7 July 1937; *s* of late Sidney Hepworth Thompson and Vera Wynne; *m* 1962, Joan Mary Kershaw; two *s. Educ:* Holywell Grammar Sch.; Manchester Univ. (BTech, MSc); Harvard Business Sch. BP Chemicals: Technical and Management appts; Works Gen. Manager, Barry Plant, 1975–78, Baglan Bay Plant, 1978–82; Gen. Manager, later Dir, Worldwide Petrochemicals, Production and Human Resources, 1982–90; Vice-Pres., Ops and Supply, Arco Chemical Europe, 1990–95. Mem., Audit Commn, 1990–97 (Dep. Chm., 1995–97). Creator, Science Opens Doors Project, 2013. Chm., Polymer Industry Skills Council, 2009–. Member: Welsh Water Authy, 1980–82; Chem. Industries Assoc. Cttees, 1985–; Chm., Inter-Company Productivity Group, 1987–90 (Mem., 1983–90). Non-exec. Dir, Frimley Park Hosp. NHS Trust, 1999–2002; Chm., Ashford and St Peter's Hosps NHS Trust, 2002–08. Creator, Science Open Doors, 2014–. Hon. FRSocMed 2008. Liveryman, Horners' Co. (Mem., Ct of Assts, 1995–). *Publications:* contribs to newspapers and learned jls, incl. Corporate Governance, on petrochemicals, environment policy and costs, management; articles on governance. *Recreations:* hill walking, opera, music, golf, reading history. *Address:* Dwr Golau, 13 Heronscourt, Lightwater, Surrey GU18 5SW. *T:* (01276) 476410. *Clubs:* Harvard Business School; Windlesham Golf.

**THOMPSON, Sir Clive (Malcolm),** Kt 1996; Chairman, Storm Financial Ltd, since 2003; Member, Industrial Advisory Panel, GVQ Investment Managers Ltd, since 2004; *b* 4 April 1943; *s* of Harry Louis Thompson and Phyllis Dora Thompson; *m* 1968, Judith Howard; two *s. Educ:* Clifton Coll.; Univ. of Birmingham (BSc). Marketing Executive: Royal Dutch Shell Gp, 1964–67; Boots Co. plc, 1967–70; Gen. Manager, Jeyes Gp Ltd, 1970–73; Managing Director: Aerosols Internat. Ltd, 1973–75; Jeyes Ltd, 1975–78; Health and Hygiene Div., Cadbury Schweppes, 1978–82; Gp Chief Exec. Designate, 1982, Gp Chief Exec., 1983–2003, Chm., 2002–04, Rentokil Initial (formerly Rentokil Gp) plc. Chm., Farepak, then Kleeneze, subseq. European Home Retail plc, 2001–06 (Dir, 1988–2006); Dep. Chm., Strategic Equity Capital plc, 2005–18; Director: Caradon plc, 1986–96; Wellcome plc, 1993–95; Sainsbury plc, 1995–2001; BAT Industries plc, 1995–98; Seeboard plc, 1995–96. Member: BOTB, 1997–99; Cttee on Corporate Governance, 1996–98; Dep. Chm., Financial Reporting Council, 1999–2001. Vice Pres., Chartered Inst. of Marketing, 1996–; Pres., CBI, 1998–2000 (Dep. Pres., 1997–98 and 2000–01). Treas., Imperial Soc. of Knights Bachelor, 2017–. MInstD. Hon. DSc Birmingham, 1999. *Recreations:* current affairs, stockmarket, golf, walking. *Address:* GVQ Investment Managers Ltd, 16 Berkeley Street, W1J 8DZ. *Clubs:* Royal Cinque Ports Golf; Wildernesse Golf (Sevenoaks).

**THOMPSON, Collingwood Forster James;** QC 1998; a Recorder, since 1997; *b* 19 Dec. 1952; *s* of Collingwood Forster James Thompson and Lillian Thompson; *m* 1985, Valerie Joyce Britchford. *Educ:* Merchiston Castle Sch., Edinburgh; University Coll. London (LLB Hons 1974). Called to the Bar, Gray's Inn, 1975; in practice at the Bar, 1977–. *Recreations:* fly-fishing (badly), hill walking (slowly), wine tasting (frequently), music, reading. *Address:* 7 Bedford Row, WC1R 4BS. *T:* (020) 7242 3555.

**THOMPSON, Damian Mark,** PhD; journalist and author; Editor-in-Chief, 2003–09 and since 2018, and Director, since 2003, The Catholic Herald; *b* 24 Jan. 1962; *s* of late Leonard Gilbert Thompson and Pamela Mary Thompson. *Educ:* Presentation Coll., Reading; Mansfield Coll., Oxford (MA); London Sch. of Econs (PhD). Religious Affairs Corresp., Daily Telegraph, 1990–94; freelance feature writer and television critic, 1994–; leader writer, 2003–14, Saturday columnist, 2011–14, Daily Telegraph; Ed., Telegraph Blogs, 2009–14; Associate Ed., Spectator, 2014–. Mem., Adv. Panel, INFORM, 2013– (Gov., 2003–13). *Publications:* The End of Time: faith and fear in the shadow of the millennium, 1996; (ed) Loose Canon: a portrait of Brian Brindley, 2004; Waiting for Antichrist: charisma and apocalypse in a Pentecostal Church, 2005; Counterknowledge: how we surrendered to conspiracy theories, quack medicine, bogus science and fake history, 2008; The Fix: how addiction is invading our lives and taking over your world, 2012. *Recreation:* playing the piano. *Address:* 19 Moorhouse Road, W2 5DH. *T:* 07968 119540. *Club:* Brooks's.

**THOMPSON, David,** QPM 2014; Chief Constable, West Midlands Police Authority, since 2016; *b* Manchester, 3 Jan. 1969; *s* of Bernard Thompson and Mrs Pamela Norman; *m* 1991, Carole; two *d. Educ:* Moorclose High Sch., Manchester; Univ. of Liverpool (LLB Hons). Constable to Asst Chief Constable, Gtr Manchester Police, 1990–2010; Dep. Chief Constable, W Midlands Police Authy, 2010–16. Lead for gangs, 2011–15, for criminal use of firearms, 2012–16, for finance, 2016, Nat. Police Chief Council. *Address:* West Midlands Police, Lloyd House, Colmore Circus Queensway, Birmingham B4 6NQ. *E:* b.godward@west-midlands.pnn.police.uk.

**THOMPSON, Sir David (Albert),** KCMG 2002; Vice-President, Royal Commonwealth Society for the Blind, since 2002 (Chairman, 1991–2001); *b* 28 Jan. 1932; *s* of Frederick Thompson and Mildred (*née* Dennis); *m* 1956, Doreen Jo Pryce (*d* 2014); one *s* one *d. Educ:* various UK schs. Nat. Service, Military Police, Germany, 1950–52. Served Northern Rhodesia Colonial Police, then with copper mining gp, Southern Rhodesia, 1953–58; sales and mktg posts with IBM UK, 1959–63; new product planning, IBM World Trade Corp., Ky, 1963–65; Rank Xerox, 1965–93: Sen. Mktg posts, London, 1965–67; Man. Dir, Rank Xerox Holland, Amsterdam, 1967–69; Sen. Mktg Exec., UK, 1969–72; Regl Dir for Australia, NZ, Hong Kong and Singapore, Sydney, 1972–74; Main Bd Dir, 1975–79; Pres., Xerox Latin America, 1979–83; Main Bd Dir, Rank Xerox Ltd, 1984–90; Chairman: Rank

Xerox Pensions Ltd, 1989–93; Rank Xerox (UK) Ltd, 1990–93; Xerox Engrg Systems (Inc.), USA, 1990–93; Dir, Lyell Hldgs (Inc.) USA, 1990–93; non-exec. Chm., Gestetner Hldgs Plc, 1993–95. Mem., Internat. Adv. Bd, Bank Austria Vienna, 1993–95. London Transport: Mem. (pt-time), London Transport Property Bd, 1991–95 (Vice Chm., 1993–95); Chm., London Buses, 1992–93; Mem., Audit, Safety, Remuneration and Design Cttees, 1992–95. Vice Chm., 1989–94, Chm., 1994–2001, Bd of Govs, Commonwealth Inst. Pres., Inst. Trng and Develt, 1992–94. Mem., President's Council, 1990–93, Overseas Trade Cttee, 1990–93, CBI. *Recreations:* reading, voluntary work. *Address:* 2 Ravenscroft Road, Henley-on-Thames, Oxon RG9 2DH. *Clubs:* Reform; Phyllis Court (Henley on Thames).

**THOMPSON, David Anthony Roland**, FCA; Deputy Chief Executive, Boots Co. plc, 2000–02; *b* 4 Sept. 1942; *s* of Harold Alfred Thompson and Olive Edna (*née* Marlow); *m* 1966, Stella Eunice Durow; two *s*. *Educ:* Burton Grammar Sch. FCA 1964. Joined Boots Co. plc, 1966: Gp Mgt Accountant, 1973–77; Vice-Pres. Finance, Boots Drug Stores, Canada, 1977–80; Finance Dir, Retail Div., 1980–89; Gp Financial Controller, 1989–90; Gp Finance Dir, 1990–2002; Jt Gp Man. Dir, 1997–2000. Non-executive Director: E Midlands Electricity, 1996–97; Cadbury Schweppes, 1998–2008; Nottingham Building Soc., 2002–14 (Chm., 2004–14). Chairman: Reach Learning Disability (formerly Southwell Care Project), 2002–; Nottingham Positive Futures Healthy Living Centre, 2003–05. *Recreations:* all sports (especially football), music, cinema, theatre.

**THOMPSON, David Brian**; Director, Cheveley Park Stud Ltd, since 1975; Chairman, Union Square plc, 1987–91; *b* 3 April 1936; *s* of Bernard Thompson and Rosamund Dee; *m* 1962, Patricia Henchley; one *s* two *d*. *Educ:* Haileybury and ISC. Jt Man. Dir, B. Thompson Ltd, 1960–70; Chm. and co-founder, 1974–84, Jt Chm., 1984–87, Dir, 1987–89, Hillsdown Holdings plc. *Recreations:* family, business, breeding and racing of bloodstock, swimming.

**THOMPSON, David George**; Member (SNP) Skye, Lochaber and Badenoch, Scottish Parliament, 2011–16 (Highlands and Islands, 2007–11); *b* 20 Sept. 1949; *s* of John Thompson and Doreen Thompson; *m* 1969, Veronica Macleod; one *s* three *d*. *Educ:* Lossiemouth High Sch.; Cert. in Legal Retrival., Dept of Trade, 1971; Dip. in Consumer Affairs, Trading Standards Inst., 1976; Inverness Coll. (HNC Gaelic 2004). Apprentice mechanic, Avery Scales, 1965–67; Trainee, then Trading Standards Officer, Banff, Moray and Nairn CC, 1967–73; Asst Chief Trading Standards Officer, Ross and Cromarty CC, 1973–75; Chief Trading Standards Officer, Comhairle Nan Eilean Siar, 1975–83; Dep. Dir of Trading Standards, 1983–86, Dir of Trading Standards, 1986–95, Highland Regl Council; Dir of Protective Services, Highland Council, 1995–2001. Chair, Bd, Voices for Scotland Ltd, 2019. Contested (SNP): Inverness, Nairn, Badenoch and Strathspey, 2005; Ross, Skye and Inverness W, Scottish Parlt, 2003. Convenor, Christians for Independence, 2009–; Elder, Church of Scotland, 2017–. Fellow, Chartered Trading Standards Inst., 2017 (Mem., 1971–). *Recreations:* DIY, hill walking.

**THOMPSON, David George Fossett**; Chief Executive, Anglia Maltings (Holdings) Ltd, since 2005; *b* 4 July 1954; *s* of late Edwin John and Helen Wilson Thompson; *m* 1980, Marika Ann Moran Davies; one *s* three *d*. *Educ:* Winchester Coll.; Magdalene Coll., Cambridge (Exhibnr; Schol.; BA 1975). Cons. Research Dept, 1975–76; Whitbread plc, 1976–77; Wolverhampton & Dudley Breweries, subseq. Marston's plc: various posts, 1977–86; Man. Dir, 1986–2001; Chm., 2001–13. Chm., Smiths Flour Mills, 2007–12; non-executive Director: Income & Growth Trust plc, 1994–2006 (Chm., 2005–06); Persimmon plc, 1999–2012; Warburtons Ltd, 2002–05; Caledonia Investments plc, 2003–13; Tribal Gp plc, 2004–09; Claverley Gp Ltd, 2017–18. Chm., Wolverhampton TEC, 1990–95; Dir, W Midlands Regl Develt Agency, 1998–2001.

**THOMPSON, David John**; economic consultant, since 2009; *b* 22 Nov. 1951; *s* of Cyril Thompson and Doris (*née* Savage). *Educ:* Cottingham Hallgate Primary Sch.; Beverley Grammar Sch.; Manchester Univ. (BA Econs 1973); London Sch. of Economics (MSc Econs 1977). Economist: DoE and Dept of Transport, 1973–83; Monopolies and Mergers Commn, 1984; Dir of Res. on Regulation, IFS, 1985–86; Economist: Dept of Transport, 1987–88; HM Treasury, 1989–91; Sen. Economic Advr, DfEE, 1992–98; Hd of Econs and Stats, MAFF, 1998–2001, DEFRA, 2001–04; Director: Central Analytical Directorate, DEFRA, 2004–05; Analysis and Strategy, later Analysis and Econs, DfT, 2005–09. Sen. Res. Fellow, London Business Sch., 1989–91. Dir, Economics Plus, 1996–98. *Publications:* contribs to books, articles in learned jls. *Recreations:* watching soccer, Rugby League and the Tour de France, rock and roll. *E:* 14thompson@14 thompson.karoo.co.uk. *T:* (020) 8863 9471, 07985 450157.

**THOMPSON, David Marcus**; Director, Origin Pictures Ltd, since 2008; *b* London, 18 July 1950; *s* of Louis and Cynthia Thompson. *Educ:* St Catharine's Coll., Cambridge (BA Hons English). English and Gen. Studies teacher, Bedales Sch.; joined BBC, 1975: Documentary Producer, Open Univ. Prodns, 1975–79; Producer, Everyman, 1979–85 (incl. first drama, Shadowlands (BAFTA and Emmy Awards)); BBC Drama, 1985–94 (created Screenplay series focusing on new talent); Exec. Producer, Single Drama, 1994–97; Hd of Films and Single Drama, BBC, 1997–2008. Exec. producer of films for cinema and TV incl. Shadowlands, 1985; Road, 1987; The Firm, 1988; Safe, 1993; Captives, 1994; Face, Woman in White, 1997; A Rather English Marriage, 1998; Wonderland, Mansfield Park, Ratcatcher, 1999; Nice Girl, Maybe Baby, Born Romantic, Last Resort, Liam, Billy Elliot, Madame Bovary, 2000; When I was 12, Perfect Strangers, Iris, 2001; Conspiracy, The Gathering Storm, Dirty Pretty Things, In this World, Morvern Callar, Out of Control, Tomorrow La Scala!, 2002; Heart of Me, The Lost Prince, I Capture the Castle, 2003; Mrs Henderson Presents, 2005; The History Boys, 2006; Miss Potter, Notes on a Scandal, 2007; Miss Austen Regrets, The Other Boleyn Girl, Brideshead Revisited, The Duchess, 2008; Freefall, Revolutionary Road, 2009. *Recreations:* family life, tennis.

**THOMPSON, (David) Robin (Bibby)**, CBE 1997; TD 1987; DL; Director, Bibby Line Ltd, 1974–87; Deputy Chairman, Rural Development Commission, 1992–96 (Member, 1986–96); *b* 23 July 1946; *s* of Noel Denis Thompson and Cynthia Joan (*née* Bibby); *m* 1971, Caroline Ann Foster (marr. diss. 1998); one *s* one *d*; *m* 1999, Jane Craddock; one *d*. *Educ:* Uppingham Sch.; Mons Officer Cadet Sch. Short service commn, QRIH, 1965; comd Queen's Own Yeomanry (TA), 1984–87; Hon. ADC to the Queen, 1987–90. Member: Council, Royal Agricl Soc. of England, 1985–91; Bd, Housing Corp., 1989–98; Chm., S Shropshire Housing Assoc., 1991–2000. Vice Chm., Pony Club, 2008–13. Shropshire: High Sheriff, 1989; DL, 2004. *Recreations:* ski-ing, horses, conservation. *Address:* Holly Bank Hadnall, Shrewsbury, Shropshire SY4 3DH. *Club:* Cavalry and Guards.

**THOMPSON, Dame Dianne**; *see* Thompson, Dame I. D.

**THOMPSON, Dr Dorothy Joan**, FBA 1996; Fellow, 1968–2006, now Life Fellow, and Lecturer in Classics and History, 1968–2006, Girton College, Cambridge; Isaac Newton Trust Affiliated Lecturer in Classics, University of Cambridge, 1992–2005; *b* 31 May 1939; *d* of late Frank William Walbank, CBE, FBA and Mary Woodward (*née* Fox); *m* 1st, 1966, Michael Hewson Crawford, *qv* (marr. diss. 1979); 2nd, 1982, John Alexander Thompson. *Educ:* Birkenhead High Sch.; Girton Coll., Cambridge (BA 1961; MA 1965; PhD 1966); Bristol Univ. (CertEd 1962). Girton College, Cambridge: Research Fellow, 1965–68; Grad. Tutor (Arts), 1971–81 and 1995–96; Sen. Tutor, 1981–92; Dir of Studies in Classics, 1983–2006; Clare College, Cambridge: Lectr in Classics, 1973–2006; Bye-Fellow, 2006–. Vis. Mem., IAS, Princeton, 1982–83; Vis. Prof., Princeton Univ., 1986; Fellow, Nat. Humanities Center, N Carolina, 1993–94; Leverhulme Trust Major Res. Fellowship, 2002–04. President: Assoc. Internationale de Papyrologues, 2001–07 (Hon. Pres., 2007–); Cambridge Philological Soc., 2002–04. James H. Breasted Prize, American Historical Assoc., 1989. Hon. DLitt Liverpool, 2013. *Publications:* Kerkeosiris: an Egyptian village in the Ptolemaic period, 1971; (jtly) Studies on Ptolemaic Memphis, 1980; Memphis under the Ptolemies, 1988, 2nd edn 2012; (with W. Clarysse) Counting the People in Hellenistic Egypt, 2 vols, 2006; (jtly) The Ptolemies, the Sea and the Nile: studies in waterborne power, 2013; (with T. Christensen and K. Vandorpe) Land and Taxes in Ptolemaic Egypt: an edition, translation and commentary for the Edfu land survey, 2017; numerous articles and reviews in learned jls. *Recreations:* reading, walking. *Address:* Girton College, Cambridge CB3 0JG. *T:* (01223) 338999.

**THOMPSON, Eloïse Mary Katherina Selina**; *see* Marshall, E. M. K. S.

**THOMPSON, Dame Emma**, DBE 2018; actor; *b* 15 April 1959; *d* of late Eric Norman Thompson and Phyllida Ann Law; *m* 2003, Greg Wise; one *d*. *Educ:* Newnham College, Cambridge (MA; Hon. Fellow, 1996). *Stage:* Footlights, Australia, 1982; Me and My Girl, Adelphi, 1984; Look Back in Anger, Lyric, 1989; King Lear, and A Midsummer Night's Dream, Renaissance Th. Co. world tour, 1989; Sweeney Todd, NY, 2014, Coliseum, 2015; *films:* Henry V, 1988; The Tall Guy, 1988; Impromptu, 1989; Dead Again, 1990; Howards End, 1992 (BAFTA Best Actress, Academy Award, Golden Globe Award, 1993); Peter's Friends, 1992; Much Ado About Nothing, 1993; The Remains of the Day, 1993; In the Name of the Father, 1993; Junior, 1994; Carrington, 1995; Sense and Sensibility (also wrote screenplay; BAFTA Best Actress); awards for screenplay incl. Academy Award), 1996; The Winter Guest, 1997; Judas Kiss, 1997; Primary Colors, 1998; Wit, 2001; Imagining Argentina, 2003; Love Actually, 2003; Harry Potter and the Prisoner of Azkaban, 2004; Nanny McPhee (also wrote screenplay), 2005; Stranger than Fiction, 2006; Harry Potter and the Order of the Phoenix, 2007; The Boat that Rocked, 2009; Last Chance Harvey, 2009; An Education, 2009; Nanny McPhee and the Big Bang, 2010; Harry Potter and the Deathly Hallows, Pt 2, 2011; Brave, 2012; Beautiful Creatures, Saving Mr Banks, 2013; Love Punch, Walking on Sunshine, Effie Gray (also wrote screenplay), 2014; A Walk in the Woods, The Legend of Barney Thomson, Adam Jones, Burnt, 2015; Alone in Berlin, 2016; Bridget Jones's Baby (also co-wrote screenplay), 2016; Beauty and the Beast, Alone in Berlin, 2017; The Meyerowitz Stories, 2017; The Children Act, 2018; Missing Link, Late Night, Men in Black: international, 2019; Last Christmas (also co-wrote screenplay), 2019; *television:* Alfresco, 1983; Tutti Frutti, 1986 (BAFTA Best Actress); Fortunes of War, 1986 (BAFTA Best Actress); Thompson, 1987; Angels in America, 2004; King Lear, 2018; Years and Years, 2019. Chm., Helen Bamber Foundn, 2007–. *Publications:* The Further Tale of Peter Rabbit, 2012; The Christmas Tale of Peter Rabbit, 2013; The Spectacular Tale of Peter Rabbit, 2014. *Recreations:* reading, walking, cooking, acting. *Address:* c/o Hamilton Hodell Ltd, 20 Golden Square, W1F 9JL.

**THOMPSON, Frazer Douglas**; Chief Executive Officer, Chapel Down Group plc, since 2001; *b* Christchurch, 30 July 1959; *s* of James Carr Thompson and Joan Diane Thompson (*née* Bush); *m* 1982, Susan Elizabeth Kelly; three *s*. *Educ:* Royal Grammar Sch., Newcastle upon Tyne; Univ. of Greenwich (BA Hons). Whitbread plc: Dir of Mktg, 1990–94; Strategy Develt Dir, 1994–96; Global Brand Dir, Heineken NV, Amsterdam, 1996–2001. Mem., Business Adv. Bd, SE LEP, 2009–. Chm., Inst. of Dirs, Kent, 2006–09. *Recreations:* wines, beers, food, hospitality, Rugby, theatre, modern art. *Address:* Sissinghurst Castle Farmhouse, Biddenden Road, Sissinghurst, Cranbrook, Kent TN17 2AB. *T:* (01580) 763033, *Fax:* (01580) 765333. *E:* frazer@chapeldown.com.

**THOMPSON, Geoffrey Austin**; DL; Head, Mill Hill County High School, 2004–19; *b* Belfast, 23 July 1952; *s* of Herbert, (Tommy), and Patricia Thompson; *m* 2000, Sally Mary (*née* Pulford); two step *s* one step *d*. *Educ:* Campbell Coll., Belfast; St Catharine's Coll., Cambridge (BA 1974); Stockwell Coll. (PGCE London 1978); South Bank Univ. (MBA Educn 1994). Teacher of English and Hist., Cannock Sch., 1974–77; Asst Dir of Music, Dir of Music, then Hd of Yr, Langley Park Boys' Sch., Beckenham, 1978–93; Dep. Hd, Downham Market High Sch., 1993–97; Hd, The Duchess's Community High Sch., Alnwick, 1997–2003. DL Greater London, 2019. *Recreations:* pianist, classical music, theatre, mountain sports, modern history. *E:* geoffreyandsally@btinternet.com.

**THOMPSON, Rt Rev. (Geoffrey) Hewlett**; an Hon. Assistant Bishop, Diocese of Carlisle, since 1999; *b* 14 Aug. 1929; *o s* of late Lt-Col R. R. Thompson, MC, RAMC; *m* 1954, Elisabeth Joy Fausitt, MA (Oxon), *d* of late Col G. F. Taylor, MBE and Dr Frances Taylor; two *s* two *d*. *Educ:* Aldenham Sch.; Trinity Hall, Cambridge (MA); Cuddesdon Theol College. 2nd Lieut, Queen's Own Royal West Kent Regt, 1948–49 (Nat. Service). Ordained deacon, 1954, priest, 1955; Curate, St Matthew, Northampton, 1954–59; Vicar: St Augustine, Wisbech, 1959–66; St Saviour, Folkestone, 1966–74; Bishop Suffragan of Willesden, 1974–79, Area Bishop of Willesden, 1979–85; Bishop of Exeter, 1985–99. Chairman: Community and Race Relations Unit, BCC, 1980–84 (Vice-Chm., 1976–80); Hospital Chaplaincies Council, 1991–97. Introduced into House of Lords, 1990. *Recreations:* fell walking, reading, gardening, music. *Address:* Low Broomrigg, Warcop, Appleby, Cumbria CA16 6PT. *T:* (017683) 41281. *Club:* Oxford and Cambridge.

**THOMPSON, (Gerald) Vincent (Bodenham)**, FCA; Vice Lord-Lieutenant of Essex, since 2019; *b* Margaretting, Essex, 7 Jan. 1951; *s* of Gerald and Margaret Thompson; *m* 1992, Diana Margaret O'Donnell; one *s* one *d*. *Educ:* Ampleforth Coll.; Jesus Coll., Cambridge (BA 1974; MA 1978). FCA 1983. Peat, Marwick, Mitchell & Co., 1974–78; Morgan Grenfell & Co. Ltd, 1978–90 (Dir, 1988–90); Dir, Hambros Bank Ltd, 1990–97; Man. Dir, Société Générale, 1997–2002; Partner, Macarthur & Co. Ltd, 2003–06; Associate, Corbett Keeling, 2007–09; Founding Partner, Easton Partners, 2009–. Non-executive Director: ProPhotonix, 2011–; Sandaire, 2018–. Mem., Investment Cttee, Jesus Coll., Cambridge, 2002–15. Trustee, Brentwood Diocesan Cathedral and Choral Trust, 1996–. Gov., St Mary's, Ascot, 2010–19. High Sheriff, 2015–16, DL 2016, Essex. *Recreations:* gardening, tennis, music, history, people. *Address:* Easton Glebe, Little Easton, Dunmow, Essex CM6 2JW. *T:* (01371) 872246. *E:* vincent.thompson@easton-partners.com. *Clubs:* Oxford and Cambridge; Essex.

**THOMPSON, Glenn**; *see* Thompson, J. McM. S. H. G.

**THOMPSON, Rt Rev. Gregory Edwin**; Bishop of Newcastle, NSW, 2014–17; *b* Muswellbrook, 1956. *Educ:* Ridley Coll. (ThL; DipMin; BTh Hons). Assistant: Nightcliff, 1982–83; St James Old Cathedral, 1984–85; ordained deacon, 1986, priest, 1986; Asst Curate, Heidelberg, 1986–88; Rector, Sanderson, 1988–89; Army Reserve Chaplain, 1989–95; State Sec., Bush Church Aid NSW, 1994–98; Gen. Licence, 1994–99; Bush Church Aid Nat. Res. Office, 1998–99; Rector, E Sydney, 1999–2004; Area Dean, Sydney City, 2001–04; Rector, Canberra, 2005–07; Bishop of the Northern Territory, 2007–13.

Pres., Council of Churches, Northern Territory, 2009–13. Chair: Anglicare Northern Territory, 2009–13; Gen. Synod Long Service Leave Fund, 2010; Member: Gen. Synod Aboriginal & Torres Strait Islander Task Gp and Standing Cttee, 2010–13; Australian Bishops Council of E Asia, 2011–13.

THOMPSON, (Henry) Antony Cardew W.; see Worrall Thompson.

THOMPSON, Rt Rev. Hewlett; see Thompson, Rt Rev. G. H.

THOMPSON, Howard; see Thompson, James H.

THOMPSON, (Hugh) Patrick; b 21 Oct. 1935; s of late Gerald Leopold Thompson and Kathleen Mary Lansdown Thompson; m 1962, Kathleen Howson. Educ: Felsted Sch., Essex; Emmanuel Coll., Cambridge (MA). Nat. Service, 2nd Lieut, KOYLI, 1957–59; TA, Manchester, 1960–65; Gresham's Sch., CCF, 1965–82 (CFM 1980); Major, retd. Engr, English Electric Valve Co., Chelmsford, 1959–60; Sixth Form Physics Master: Manchester Grammar Sch., 1960–65; Gresham's Sch., Holt, 1965–83. MP (C) Norwich North, 1983–97. Parliamentary Private Secretary: to Minister of State for Transport, 1987–88; to Minister of State, Dept of Social Security, 1988–89; to Minister for Health, 1992–94. Member: Parly and Scientific Cttee, 1983–97; Select Cttee, Educn, Science and the Arts, 1991–92; Select Cttee, Sci. and Technol., 1995–97; Speaker's Panel of Chairmen, 1994–97; Founder Mem., All Party Gp for Engrg Develt, 1985–97; Secretary: Cons. Back Bench Energy Cttee, 1986–87; Cons. Back Bench European Cttee, 1991–92. Publications: Elementary Calculations in Physics, 1963. Recreations: travel, music, gardening. Club: Norfolk (Norwich).

THOMPSON, Ian; Director, IKT Consulting Ltd, 2003–09; b 20 May 1951; s of Eber Edward Thompson and Edith (née Gilchrist); m 1st, 1972, Anne Rosalind Clouston (marr. diss. 1995); one d; 2nd, 1998, Karin Bell. Educ: Workington Grammar Sch.; Univ. of Hull (BSc); St Martin's Coll., Lancaster (PGCE). IPFA. VSO, Nigeria, 1973–74; with Humberside CC, 1974–80; Northamptonshire County Council, 1980–89: Chief Acct, 1986–88; Sen. Asst Educn Officer, 1988–89; Berkshire County Council: Sen. Asst Co. Treas., 1989–93; Co. Treas., 1993–96; Chief Finance and Property Officer, subseq. Dir of Finance and Property, then Dir of Resources, Swindon BC, 1997–2003. Recreations: playing guitar, playing squash, playing trains. Address: Ochor y Bryn, Hope, Leighton, Welshpool, Powys SY21 8HF. T: (01938) 555774.

THOMPSON, Dr (Ian) McKim; Vice President, British Medical Association, since 1998; b 19 Aug. 1938; s of late J. W. Thompson and Dr E. M. Thompson; m 1962, Dr Veronica Jane Richards (marr. diss. 1988); two s one d. Educ: Epsom Coll.; Birmingham Univ. (MB, ChB 1961). Lectr in Pathology, Univ. of Birmingham, 1964–67; Sen. Registrar, Birmingham RHB, 1967–69; Sen. Under Sec., 1969–85, Dep. Sec., 1985–96, BMA. Consulting Forensic Pathologist to HM Coroner, City of Birmingham, 1966–97. Part time Tutor, Dept of Adult and Continuing Educn, Keele Univ., 1985–2009; Tutor, Wedgwood Meml Coll., Barlaston, 1990–2009. Member: GMC, 1979–94; Royal Medical Foundn, 1998–2009 (Life Gov., 2009); Pres., Birmingham Med. Inst., 2003–10 (Fellow, 2010); Chm., Retired Members Forum, BMA, 2009–11 (Dep. Chm., 2007–09). Hon. MO, Inland Waterways Assoc., 1976– (Richard Bird Medallist, 2008). President: Sands Cox Soc., Univ. of Birmingham, 2006–07 (Vice-Pres., 2005–06); Russell Newbery Register, 2011–; Dudley Canal Trust, 2014–17. FRSocMed 1987. Hon. Collegian, Med. Colls of Spain, 1975. Publications: (ed) The Hospital Gazetteer, 1972; (ed) BMA Handbook for Hospital Junior Doctors, 1977, 5th edn 1990; (ed) BMA medical handbook for Trainee Doctors in General Practice, 1982, 3rd edn 1985; various medical scientific papers. Recreations: inland waterways, rambling. Address: Canal Cottage, Hinksford Lane, Kingswinford DY6 0BH. T: (01384) 294131.

THOMPSON, Dame (Ila) Dianne, DBE 2015 (CBE 2006); Chief Executive, Camelot Group plc, 2000–14 (Commercial Director, 1997–2000); b 31 Dec. 1950; d of Ronald Wood and Joan Wood (née Pinder); m 1972, Roger Thompson (marr. diss. 1992); one d. Educ: Batley Girls' Grammar Sch.; Manchester Poly. (BA Hons ext. London). Product Manager, CWS, 1972–74; Mktg Manager, ICI, 1974–79; Lectr, Manchester Poly., 1979–86; Mktg Dir, Sterling Roncraft, 1986–88; Man. Dir, Sandvik Saws & Tools, 1988–92; Marketing Director: Woolworths plc, 1992–94; Signet Gp, 1994–97. Chm., Walker Greenbank, 2019–; non-exec. Dir, Next plc, 2015–. Mem., Mktg Gp of GB, 1993. Mem., Press Complaints Commn, 2003–08. Chancellor, Manchester Metropolitan Univ., 2011–16. Owner, George Hotel, Yarmouth, IoW, 2014–. Pres., Mkt Res. Soc., 2014–17. FCIM 1988; Fellow, Mktg Soc., 1998; FRSA 2000; CCMI 2001. Veuve Cliquot Businesswoman of the Year, 2000; Marketer of the Year, Mktg Soc., 2001; Gold Medal, Chartered Mgt Inst., 2006. Recreations: theatre, cinema, entertaining, travel. Address: 3 Water's Edge, Yarmouth, Isle of Wight PO41 0XB.

THOMPSON, (James) Howard, OBE 1984; Programme Manager, Schistosomiasis Control Initiative, Imperial College London, 2002–08; b 26 March 1942; s of James Alan Thompson and Edna (née Perkins); m 1965, Claire Marguerite Dockrell; one s one d. Educ: Northampton Grammar Sch.; Magdalene Coll., Cambridge (BA); Stanford Univ. (MA). English Language Officer, British Council, Yugoslavia, 1966–69; Associate Prof., Punjab Univ., 1970–73; Dep. Representative, British Council, Kenya, 1974–78; Advr, Schs and Further Educn Dept, 1978–80; Educn Attaché, British Embassy, Washington, 1980–84; Dep. Controller, 1984–87, Controller, 1987–89, Science, Technology and Educn Div., British Council; Chm., Educn and Trng Export Cttee, 1988–89; British Council Director: Indonesia, 1989–92; Egypt, 1993–96; Brazil, 1997–2002. Vice Chm., Govs, Bentworth Prim. Sch., Hammersmith, 2008–12; Volunteer, Prison Advice and Care Trust, 2009–17. Publications: Teaching English, 1972. Recreations: photography, travel. Address: 1 Homefield Road, W4 2LN.

THOMPSON, Jan, OBE 2005; HM Diplomatic Service; Deputy High Commissioner, New Delhi, India, since 2018; b Bexleyheath, 25 Aug. 1965; d of late Thomas Henry Thompson and of Jean Thompson. Educ: Durham Univ. (BA Hons French and German); Postgrad. Dip. Interpreting and Translating. BBC World Service, 1989–90; joined FCO, 1990; Desk Officer, El Salvador, Honduras and Costa Rica, Latin Amer. Dept, 1990–91; German Min. of For. Affairs (on secondment), 1991–92; Second Sec. (Pol), Bonn, 1992–94; Hd of Section, E Adriatic Dept, FCO, 1994–97; First Sec. (Security Council), UK Mission to UN, NY, 1997–2000; Dep. Hd, UN Dept, FCO, 2000–02; Hd, Afghanistan Dept, FCO, 2002–05; Hd, British Embassy Office, Phuket, 2005; Sen. FCO Rep. in Scotland for G8 Summit, FCO, 2005; Dir, Comprehensive Spending Review Prog., FCO, 2005–07; UK Lead Negotiator, Internat. Climate Negotiations, DECC (on secondment), 2007–10; Head: Strategic Defence and Security Rev. Team, FCO, 2010; Libya Unit, FCO, 2011; Proj. Leader, Future of FCO Climate Diplomacy, FCO, 2012; lang. trng, 2012–13; Ambassador to the Czech Republic, 2013–17; Dep. High Comr, Ottawa, 2018. Recreations: theatre, travel. Address: c/o Foreign and Commonwealth Office, King Charles Street, SW1A 2AH.

THOMPSON, Janet, CB 2000; DPhil; Chief Executive, Forensic Science Service, 1988–2001; b 23 Oct. 1941; d of late Arthur Hugh Denison Fairbarns and Eleanor Mary Fairbarns (née Cattel); m 1999, Elliot Grant; one s one d, and one s from a former marriage. Educ: North London Collegiate Sch.; Brighton Coll. of Technol. (BSc 1963); Univ. of Oxford (DPhil 1968). CPhys, FInstP 1999. Chm., Science, Technol. and Mathematics Council, 1999–2001. Chm., European Network of Forensic Insts, 1997–99.

THOMPSON, Jeff; see Thompson, John J.

THOMPSON, Jeremy Gordon; Presenter, Live at Five, Sky News, 1999–2016; b 23 Sept. 1947; s of Gordon and Betty Thompson; m 1st, Nicky Wood (marr. diss. 1979); two s; 2nd, 1986, Lynn Bowland. Educ: Sevenoaks Prep. Sch.; Sevenoaks Sch.; King's Sch., Worcester. Reporter: Cambridge Evening News, 1967–71; BBC Radio Sheffield, 1971–74; BBC TV Look North, Leeds, 1974–77; N of England corresp., BBC TV News, 1977–82; ITN: Chief Sports Corresp., 1982–86; Asia Corresp., 1987–90; Africa Corresp., 1991–93; Sky News: Africa Corresp., 1993–95; USA Corresp., 1995–98; presenter, 1998–2016. Member: Press Golfing Soc.; Stage Golfing Soc. Gold Award for Best Internat. Reporter, NY Fest., 1992; Emmy Awards, 1992 and 1994 for reporting in Africa; Presenter of the Yr, RTS, 2005. Publications: Breaking News: an autobiography, 2017. Recreations: travelling, safaris, walking, golf, watching sport. E: jeremythompsonnews@gmail.com. Clubs: Cricket Writers', Rugby Writers'; Surrey CC; Harlequins Rugby; Hampton Court Palace Golf; Los Arqueros Golf (Spain).

THOMPSON, John, MBE 1975; HM Diplomatic Service, retired; Ambassador to Angola, and St Thomas and Prince, 2002–05; senior archival consultant, Foreign and Commonwealth Office, 2005–16; b 28 May 1945; s of late Arthur Thompson and Josephine (née Brooke); m 1966, Barbara Hopper (d 2018); one d. Educ: Whiteheath County Primary Sch., Ruislip, Middx; St Nicholas Grammar Sch., Northwood, Middx; Polytechnic of Central London (DMS 1975). Joined FO, 1964; Vice-Consul, Düsseldorf, 1966–69; Consular Officer, later Vice-Consul, Abu Dhabi, 1969–72; Vice-Consul, Phnom Penh, 1972–74; seconded to DTI, 1975–77; First Sec., FCO, 1977–79; First Sec., Hd of Chancery and Consul, Luanda, 1979–81; Consul (Commercial), São Paulo, 1981–85; Assistant Head: S Pacific Dept, FCO, 1985–87; Aid Policy Dept, FCO, 1987–88; High Comr to Vanuatu, 1988–92; Dep. Consul-Gen. and Dir of Trade, NY, 1992–97; Hd of Inf. Systems Dept and Library and Records Dept, FCO, 1997–99; Hd of Inf. Mgt Gp, FCO Services, FCO, 1999–2001. Recreations: philately, walking, reading, bridge.

THOMPSON, Sir John; see Thompson, Sir T. d'E. J.

THOMPSON, Prof. John Griggs, PhD; FRS 1979; Rouse Ball Professor of Mathematics, University of Cambridge, 1971–93, now Professor Emeritus; Fellow of Churchill College, Cambridge, 1968, now Fellow Emeritus; Graduate Research Professor, Department of Mathematics, University of Florida, since 1983; b Kansas, 13 Oct. 1932; s of John and Eleanor Thompson; m 1960, Diane Oenning (d 2013); one s one d. Educ: Yale (BA 1955); Chicago (PhD 1959); MA Cantab 1972. Prof. of Mathematics, Chicago Univ., 1962–68; Vis. Prof. of Mathematics, Cambridge Univ., 1968–70. Hon. DSc Oxon, 1987. Cole Prize, 1966; Field Medal, 1970; Berwick Prize, London Math. Soc., 1982; Sylvester Medal, Royal Soc., 1985; Wolf Prize, 1992; Poincaré Medal, 1992; (jtly) Abel Prize, Norwegian Acad. of Sci. and Letters, 2008. Address: 16 Millington Road, Cambridge CB3 9HP.

THOMPSON, John Handby, CB 1988; CVO 1994; Ceremonial Officer, Cabinet Office, and Secretary, Political Honours Scrutiny Committee, 1988–94; b 21 Feb. 1929; s of late Rev. John Thomas Thompson and Clara Handby; m 1st, 1957, Catherine Rose Heald (d 2014); two s one d; 2nd, 2015, Petra Laidlaw. Educ: Silcoates Sch., Wakefield; St John's Coll., Oxford (MA); Sheffield Univ. (PhD 1991). Served Intell. Corps, 1947–49. HM Inspector of Taxes, 1953–63; Dept of Educn and Science, 1964–88: Schs Council, 1971–73; Asst Sec., 1973; Mem., Prep. Cttee of European Univ. Inst., 1973–75; Dep. Accountant-Gen., 1976–78; Under Sec., 1978; Head of Schs Br. 1, 1978–80; Head of Further and Higher Educn Br. 1, 1980–84; Dir of Estabts and Orgn, 1985–88. Gov., Univ. (formerly Poly.) of N London, 1989–98 (Hon. Fellow, 1999). Pres., Chapels Soc., 1998–2001. Chm., Friends of the Congregational Library, 2001–06; Trustee: Congregational Meml Hall Trust, 2003–14; Lord Wharton's Charity, 2005–13. Publications: A History of the Coward Trust 1738–1988, 1998; Highgate Dissenters: their history since 1660, 2001; (contrib.) Modern Christianity and Cultural Aspirations, 2003; (contrib.) Who They Were in the Reformed Churches of England and Wales 1901–2000, 2007; The Free Church Army Chaplain 1830–1930, 2012; (contrib.) The Clergy in Khaki, 2013; (contrib.) Protestant Nonconformity and Christian Missions, 2014. Recreations: reading about Albania, Nonconformist history. Address: 2 Alwyne Villas, N1 2HQ. Club: Reform.

THOMPSON, Air Marshal John Hugh, CB 2000; FRAeS; Royal Air Force, retired; farmer, Lincolnshire, 2006–14; b 18 Sept. 1947; m 1969, Mary Elizabeth Emerson; two s one d. Educ: Fielding High Sch., NZ; RAF Coll., Cranwell. Hunter pilot, Bahrain, 1970–71; Harrier pilot, weapons instructor and Sqdn Comdr; Army Staff Coll., 1982; Station Comdr, Wittering, 1988–90; RCDS, 1991; Higher Comd and Staff Course, 1992; SASO, Rheindahlen, 1993–96; Office of the High Rep., Sarajevo, 1996; AOC and Comdt, RAF Coll., Cranwell, 1997–98; AOC No 1 Gp, 1998–2000; Defence Attaché and Head of British Defence Staff, Washington, 2000–02; Dir Gen., Saudi Armed Forces Project, 2002–06. FRAeS 2007. Recreations: golf, reading. Clubs: Royal Air Force; Berkshire Golf.

THOMPSON, Prof. John Jeffrey, (Jeff), CBE 1989; PhD; CChem, FRSC; Professor of Education, 1979–2005, and Director, Centre for the Study of Education in an International Context, 1992–2005, University of Bath, now Professor Emeritus; b 13 July 1938; s of late John Thompson and Elsie May Thompson (née Wright); m 1963, Kathleen Audrey Gough; three d. Educ: King George V Sch., Southport; St John's Coll., Cambridge (MA); Balliol Coll., Oxford (MA); PhD (CNAA); DipEd (Oxon). Asst Master, Blundell's Sch., 1961–65; Head of Chemistry, Watford Grammar Sch., 1965–69; Lectr in Educn, KCL, 1968–69; Shell Fellow, UCL, 1969–70; Lectr and Tutor, Dept of Educnl Studies, Oxford Univ., 1970–79; Lectr in Chemistry, Keble Coll., Oxford, 1970–76; Pro-Vice-Chancellor, Univ. of Bath, 1986–89. Chief Examr, Internat. Baccalaureate, 1970–89 (Chm., Bd of Chief Examrs, 1985–89); International Baccalaureate Organisation: Chm. Res. Cttee, 1998–2004; Dir for Internat. Educn, 2000–02; Academic Dir, 2003–04; Hd of Res. Unit, 2000–05; Chm., Examination Appeals Bd, 2003–13 (Dep. Chm., 1999–2003). Chairman: Assoc. for Science Educn, 1981; Nat. Curriculum Science Working Gp, 1987–88; Adv. Bd, Total Science Solutions, 2003–05; Chair: Alliance for Internat. Educn, 2001–09, 2011–; Curriculum Adv. Bd, Internat. Primary Curriculum and Internat. Middle Years Curriculum, 2002–; Adv. Bd, Internat. Teacher Educn for Primary Schs, 2013–. Mem., Council, 1988–92, Dep. Chm., 1989–92, School Exams and Assessment Council; Member: Nat. Commn on Educn, 1991–93; English Nat. Bd for Nursing, Midwifery and Health Visiting, 1993–2002. Pres., Educn Div., Royal Soc. of Chemistry, 1983–85; Dep. Chm., Educn Cttee, Royal Soc., 1995–98; British Association for the Advancement of Science: Vice Pres., 1996–2001; Vice Pres. and Gen. Sec., 1985–91; Chm. Council, 1991–96. Dir, Internat. Bd, United World Colls, 2005–11; Gov. and Mem. Council, United World Coll. of the Atlantic, 1992–2009; Governor: UWC Mostar, 2005–10; UWC Council of Admin, UWC Duino, Italy, 2009–; Chm., Bd of Govs, Oaktree Internat. Sch., Kolkata. Chair,

Internat. Schs (formerly British Internat. Schs) Award, 2016–. Hon. Mem., ASE, 1994; Hon. Fellow, British Sci. Assoc. (Hon. Fellow, BAAS, 2006). Mem. Council, Wildfowl Trust, 1981–91. FRSA 1983. Freeman, 1992, Liveryman, 1995, Goldsmiths' Co., 1992; Freeman, City of London, 1992. Gen. Editor, Bath Science series, age gps 16–19 (12 titles), and 5–16 (78 titles), 1990–2000; Ed.-in-Chief, Jl for Res. in Internat. Educn, 2002–06; Co-Ed., Internat. Sch. mag., 2014–. Hon DLitt Hertfordshire, 2000; Hon. EdD Bath, 2014. Distinguished Service Award: Internat. Schs Assoc., 2005; Eur. Council for Internat. Schs, 2005; Lifetime Achievement Award, Global Educn Forum, Dubai, 2016. *Publications:* Introduction to Chemical Energetics, 1967; European Curriculum Studies: Chemistry, 1972; (ed) Practical Work in Sixth Form Science, 1976; Foundation Course in Chemistry, 1982; Modern Physical Chemistry, 1982; (ed) Dimensions of Science (9 titles), 1986; The Chemistry Dimension, 1987; International Education: Principles and Practice, 1998; (ed) International Schools and International Education, 2000; (ed) International Education in Practice, 2002; (ed) A Handbook of Research in International Education, 2006, 2nd edn 2015; (jtly) International Schools: growth and influence, 2008; (ed) Taking the MYP Forward, 2011; (ed) Taking the DP Forward, 2011; (ed) Forward with the IPC, 2012; (ed) Taking the IB Continuum Forward, 2013; (ed) Assessment and Evaluation: issues in international education, 2016; (ed jtly) International Education (3 vols), 2016; (ed jtly) MYP: new directions, 2016; (ed jtly) International Schools: current issues and future prospects, 2016; (ed jtly) Taking the IB Career-related Programme Forward, 2017; (ed) Perspectives on Assessment and Evaluation in International Education, 2017; contrib. articles to res. jls and chapters in books on internat. educn. *Recreations:* music (brass bands and blue grass), North Country art, collecting sugar tongs. *Address:* University of Bath, Claverton Down, Bath BA2 7AY.

**THOMPSON, (John McMaster Samuel Hugh) Glenn,** CB 2001; Business Consultant, g thompson consulting, 2001–16; *b* 11 Nov. 1949; *s* of Hugh Glenn Thompson and Sarah (*née* McMaster); *m* 1971, Elizabeth McClements; two *d. Educ:* Regent House Grammar Sch., Newtownards. Clerk to Principal, NICS, 1967–86; Asst Sec., Industrial Develt Bd for NI, 1986–89; Regl Manager, 1989–92, Exec. Dir, 1992–96, Crestacare plc; Under-Sec., Civil Service, 1996–2001. *Recreations:* travel, Rugby Union.

**THOMPSON, John Michael Anthony,** FMA; museums and heritage consultant, since 1991; Associate Director, Barker Langham, 2007–12; *b* 3 Feb. 1941; *s* of George Thompson and Joan Smith; *m* 1965, Alison Sara Bowers; two *d. Educ:* William Hulme's Grammar Sch., Manchester; Univ. of Manchester. BA, MA; FMA 1980. Research Asst, Whitworth Art Gall., 1964–66; Keeper, Rutherston Collection, City Art Gall., Manchester, 1966–68; Director: North Western Museum and Art Gall. Service, 1968–70; Arts and Museums, Bradford City Council, 1970–74; Chief Arts and Museums Officer, Bradford Metropolitan Council, 1974–75; Dir, Art Galls and Museums, Tyne and Wear County Museums, 1975–91. Sen. Consultant, Prince Research Consultants Ltd, 1995–2007. Museums Association: Councillor, 1977–80, 1984–87 (Chm., Accreditation Cttee, 1978–80); Mentor and Reviewer, 1995–2013; Advisor to Arts and Recreation Cttee, AMA, 1981–91; Pres., Museums North, 1977, and 1991–92; Chm., Soc. of County Museum Dirs, 1982–86; Founder Mem. and Hon. Sec., Gp of Dirs of Museums in the British Isles, 1985–91. Dir, Museums and Galleries Consultancy Ltd, 1992–95; Mem. Bd, Jarrow 700 AD Ltd, 1992–2006. External Verifier: Museum Trng Inst., 1996–99; Qualifications for Industry, 1999–2006. Advr to UNESCO, 2001–06; Educn and Access Advr to Heritage Lottery Fund, 2005–. Chairman: Gosforth Adult Educn Assoc., 1994–2006; Friends of Shipley Art Gall., Gateshead, 2009–14. Vice Chm. Governors, Gosforth High Sch., 1997–99. Mem. Council, Tyne and Wear Building Preservation Trust, 2008– (Vice Chm., 2013–). Society of Friends (Quakers): Attender, Newcastle Local Meeting, 2009–16; Mem., 2016–; Trustee, Northumbria Area Meeting, 2017–Dec. 2020. *Publications:* (ed) The Manual of Curatorship: a guide to museum practice, 1984, 2nd edn 1993; Contracting Culture: museums and local government, 1994; articles in Museums Jl, Penrose Annual, Connoisseur, Printmaking Today, Quaker Voices. *Recreations:* classical guitar, running, walking. *Address:* 21 Linden Road, Gosforth, Newcastle upon Tyne NE3 4EY. *T:* (0191) 284 2797.

**THOMPSON, Prof. (John) Michael (Tutill),** FRS 1985; Professor of Nonlinear Dynamics, Department of Civil and Environmental Engineering, and Director, Centre for Nonlinear Dynamics and Its Applications, University College London, 1991–2002, now Emeritus Professor; Chairman, ES-Consult (Consulting Engineers), Copenhagen, since 1995; *b* 7 June 1937; *s* of John Hornsey Thompson and Kathleen Rita Thompson (*née* Tutill); *m* 1959, Margaret Cecilia Chapman; one *s* one *d. Educ:* Hull Grammar Sch.; Clare Coll., Cambridge (MA, PhD, ScD). FIMA; CMath. Research Fellow, Peterhouse, 1961–64; Vis. Res. Associate, Stanford (Fulbright grant), 1962–63; Lectr, 1964–68, Reader, 1968–77, Prof. of Structural Mechanics, 1977–91, UCL; Chm., Bd of Studies in Civil and Mech. Eng., Univ. of London, 1984–86. Vis. Prof., Faculté des Sciences, Univ. Libre de Bruxelles, 1976–78; Vis. Mathematician, Brookhaven Nat. Lab., 1984; Vis. Res. Fellow, Centre for Nonlinear Studies, Univ. of Leeds, 1987–97; Sen. Fellow, SERC, 1988–93; Hon. Fellow, Dept of Applied Maths and Theoretical Physics, Univ. of Cambridge, 2003–; a Sixth Century Prof. in Theoretical and Applied Dynamics (pt-time), Univ. of Aberdeen, 2006–16 (R. V. Jones Lectr, 2011; Hon. Prof., 2004). Organizer and Editor, IUTAM Symposium: on Collapse: the buckling of structures in theory and practice, 1982; on non-linearity and chaos in engrg dynamics, 1993; Ed., Phil. Trans Royal Soc., Series A, 1998–2007 (Actg Ed., 1990; Ed. and Organizer, first Theme Issue, 1990 and three Millennium Issues, 2000; Mem. Editl Bd, 2008–10); Chm. and Exec. Ed., Royal Soc. Trailblazing Project, 2008–10; sci. contribs to radio and TV, 1975–; Member Council: IMA, 1989–92 (Organizer, Conf. on Chaos, UCL, 1990); Royal Soc., 2002–03. MAE 2010. Hon. Mem., Hungarian Acad. Scis, 2010. Hon DSc Aberdeen, 2004. Cambridge University Prizes: Rex Moir, 1957; Archibald Denny, 1958; John Winbolt, 1960; OMAE Award, 1985, Lyapunov Award, 2013, ASME; James Alfred Ewing Medal, ICE, 1992; Gold Medal for Mathematics, IMA, 2004. *Publications:* (with G. W. Hunt) A general theory of elastic stability, 1973; Instabilities and catastrophes in science and engineering, 1982; (with G. W. Hunt) Elastic instability phenomena, 1984; (with H. B. Stewart) Nonlinear dynamics and chaos, 1986, 2nd edn 2002; (ed) Localisation and solitary waves in solid mechanics, 1999; Visions of the Future, vol. I, Astronomy and Earth Science, vol. II, Physics and Electronics, vol. III, Chemistry and Life Science, 2001; (ed) Advances in Astronomy: from big bang to the solar system, 2005; (ed) Advances in Earth Science: from earthquakes to global warming, 2007; Advances in Nanoengineering: electronics, materials and assembly, 2007; (ed with B. E. Launder) Geo-Engineering Climate Change: environmental necessity or Pandora's Box?, 2010; 200 articles in learned jls (and mem., editl bds). *Recreations:* walking, wildlife photography, badminton, tennis, astronomy with grandchildren. *Address:* 33 West Hill Road, Foxton, Cambs CB22 6SZ. *T:* (01223) 704354.

**THOMPSON, Sir Jonathan Michael,** KCB 2019; Chief Executive, Financial Reporting Council, since 2019; *b* 29 Dec. 1964; *s* of John and Jenny Thompson; *m* 1987, Dawn Warnes; three *s. Educ:* Earlham High Sch.; Norwich City Coll.; Suffolk Coll.; Anglia Poly. CIPFA 1989; CIMA 2014. Audit and accountancy posts, Norfolk CC, 1983–91; Superintendent, Eagle Star Gp, 1991–93; Manager, 1993–95, Sen. Manager, 1995–97, Ernst & Young; North Somerset Council: Finance Strategy Advr, 1997–2001; Hd, Corporate Finance, 2001–02; Dir, Finance and Resources, 2002–04; Dir of Finance, Ofsted, 2004–06; Dir Gen., Finance, DfES, May–July 2006; Dir Gen., Corporate Services, DfES, later DCSF, 2006–09; Hd, Govt Finance Profession, HM Treasury, 2008–11; Dir Gen. Finance, MoD, 2009–12; Permanent Sec., MoD, 2012–16; Chief Exec. and Permanent Sec., HMRC, 2016–19. *Recreations:* Church, community activities, movies, reading, cooking, wood-turning. *Address:* Financial Reporting Council, 125 London Wall, EC2Y 5AS.

**THOMPSON, Maj.-Gen. Julian Howard Atherden,** CB 1982; OBE 1978; Visiting Professor, Department of War Studies, King's College London, since 1997; *b* 7 Oct. 1934; *s* of late Major A. J. Thompson, DSO, MC and Mary Stearns Thompson (*née* Krause); *m* 1st, 1960, Janet Avery (*d* 2016), *d* of late Richard Robinson Rodd; one *s* one *d*; 2nd, 2017, Jane Diana Frieda, *e d* of late Dr George Exner. *Educ:* Sherborne School. 2nd Lieut RM, 1952; served 40, 42, 43, 45 Commandos RM, 1954–69; Asst Sec., Chiefs of Staff Cttee, 1970–71; BM, 3 Cdo Brigade, 1972–73; Directing Staff, Staff Coll., Camberley, 1974–75; CO 40 Cdo RM, 1975–78; Comdr 3 Cdo Brigade, 1981–83, incl. Falklands campaign (CB); Maj.-Gen. Comdg Trng Reserve Forces and Special Forces RM, 1983–86, retired. Sen. Res. Fellow in Logistics and Armed Conflict in the Modern Age, KCL, 1987–97. Chm., Idarat Maritime Ltd, 2010–. Life Vice-Pres., British Assoc. for Physical Training, 1998 (Pres., 1988–98). *Publications:* No Picnic: 3 Commando Brigade in the South Atlantic 1982, 1985; Ready for Anything: The Parachute Regiment at War 1940–1982, 1989; (contrib.) Military Strategy in a Changing Europe, 1991; (contrib.) Fallen Stars, 1991; The Lifeblood of War, 1991; (contrib.) The Observer at 200, 1992; The Imperial War Museum Book of Victory in Europe: North West Europe 1944–45, 1994; The Imperial War Museum Book of the War at Sea: the Royal Navy in the Second World War, 1996; (contrib.) Leadership and Command, 1997; The Imperial War Museum Book of War Behind Enemy Lines, 1998; (contrib.) Dimensions of Sea Power, 1998; The Royal Marines: from Sea Soldiers to a Special Force, 2000; (contrib.) Lightning Strikes Twice: the Great World War 1914–1945, 2000; (ed) The Imperial War Museum Book of Modern Warfare, 2002; The Imperial War Museum Book of the War in Burma 1942–1945, 2002; The Imperial War Museum Book of the War at Sea: 1914–1918, 2004; The Victory in Europe Experience, 2004; The 1916 Experience: Verdun and the Somme, 2006; (contrib.) Amphibious Assault: manoeuvre from the sea, 2007; Masters of the Battlefield, 2007; Dunkirk: retreat to victory, 2008; Call to Arms: great military speeches, 2009; Forgotten Voices of Burma, 2009; Forgotten Voices Desert Victory, 2011; The Second World War in 100 Objects, 2012; Gallipoli, 2015; The Royal Navy: 100 years of maritime warfare in the modern age, 2016; 1918: how the First World War was won, 2018. *Recreations:* sailing, shooting, history, cross-country ski-ing, ballet, opera, jazz. *Address:* c/o Lloyds Bank, Royal Parade, Plymouth, Devon PL1 1HB. *Clubs:* Army and Navy; Royal Marines Sailing.

**THOMPSON, Julian O.;** *see* Ogilvie Thompson.

**THOMPSON, Keith Bruce;** Vice-Chancellor, Staffordshire University, 1992–95, now Vice Chancellor Emeritus; *b* 13 Sept. 1932; *m* 1956, Kathleen Reeves; one *s* one *d. Educ:* Bishopshalt School, Hillingdon; New College, Oxford (Sec./Librarian, Oxford Union). PPE 1955, Dip Educn (distn), 1956, MA 1959; MEd Bristol, 1968. Schoolmaster, City of Bath Boys' School, 1956–62; Lectr, Newton Park Coll., Bath, 1962–67; Head of Dept, Philippa Fawcett Coll., Streatham, 1967–72; Principal, Madeley Coll. of Educn, 1972–78; Dep. Dir, 1978–86, Dir, 1986–92, N Staffs, later Staffs Poly. Chairman: Standing Conf. on Studies in Educn, 1980–82; Undergraduate Initial Training Bd (Educn), CNAA, 1981–85; Polytechnics Central Admissions System, 1989–93; Dep. Chm., UCAS, 1993–95; Mem. Bd, Nat. Adv. Body for Public Sector Higher Educn, 1983–88 (Chm., Teacher Educn Gp, 1983–85). Sec., British Philos. of Sport Assoc., 2002–05. Editor, Educn for Teaching, 1968–74. *Publications:* Education and Philosophy, 1972; (jtly) Curriculum Development, 1974; articles on educn, philosophy, physical educn, sport. *Recreations:* sport, music, books. *Address:* 3 Swindon Manor, Swindon Village, Cheltenham GL51 9TP. *T:* (01242) 698554. *See also* B. K. Thompson.

**THOMPSON, McKim;** *see* Thompson, I. McK.

**THOMPSON, Marjorie Ellis;** Media Adviser, Special Projects, Coram, 2017–19; *b* St Louis, Mo, 8 June 1957; *d* of John William Thompson, III and Janet Ann Thompson (*née* Neubeiser). *Educ:* Woodrow Wilson High Sch., Long Beach, California; Colorado Coll., Colorado Springs (BSc Hons 1978); LSE (MSc Econ 1979). Parly Officer, 1983–87, Vice Chm., 1987–90, Chm., 1990–93, Campaign for Nuclear Disarmament; Researcher for Ann Clwyd, MP, 1987; Royal College of Nursing, 1988–93; Dir, Communications and Res., CRE, 1993–97; Dir, Cause Connection, Saatchi & Saatchi, 1997–2001; Dir, Cause Related Marketing, Octagon Marketing, 2001–02; Dir (Campaigns, Communications, Cause-related marketing and imagination), 2002–, Campaigns Coach, 2017, C3i; Public Relations/Marketing: Shape Disability Arts, 2002; Neil Stewart Associates, 2005–09; Public Affairs and Media, Engage, 2010–11; Media Advr, Islam Channel, 2010–13; Sen. Advr, Media and Major Gifts, Mental Health Foundn, 2014–16; Dir, Policy, Campaigns and Communications, League Against Cruel Sports, 2016–17. Associate, Brands & Values, Bremen, 2008–13. Fellow: British-American Project, 1990–2012; Davos World Econ. Forum, 2000. Trustee: S London Maudsley Charitable Trust, 2006–07; Stand to Reason, 2008–10; Project Pressure, 2010–; Why Me?, 2011–16. Patron, London Welsh RFC, 2018–. *Publications:* (contrib.) Nursing: the hidden agenda, 1993; (with Hamish Pringle) Brand Spirit: how cause-related marketing builds brands, 1999; (with Christian Conrad) The New Brand Spirit: how communicating sustainability builds brands, reputations and profits, 2013; contrib. Market Leader, and Spectator and Guardian blogs. *Club:* Authors'.

**THOMPSON, Mark;** *see* Thompson, O. M.

**THOMPSON, Mark John Thompson;** President and Chief Executive, The New York Times Company, since 2012; *b* 31 July 1957; *s* of late Duncan John Thompson and Sydney Columba Corduff; *m* 1987, Jane Emilie Blumberg; two *s* one *d. Educ:* Stonyhurst Coll.; Merton Coll., Oxford (BA; Violet Vaughan Morgan English Prize; MA; Hon. Fellow, 2006). BBC Television: Research Asst Trainee, 1979–80; Asst Producer, Nationwide, 1980–82; Producer, Breakfast Time, 1982–84; Output Editor: London Plus, 1984–85; Newsnight, 1985–87; Editor: Nine O'Clock News, 1988–90; Panorama, 1990–92; Head of Features, 1992–94; Head of Factual Progs, 1994–96; Controller, BBC2, 1996–98; Dir of Nat. and Regl Broadcasting, 1998–2000; Dir of Television, 2000–01; Chief Exec., Channel Four, 2002–04; Dir Gen., BBC, 2004–12. Chm., Edinburgh Internat. TV Fest., 1996. Vis. Fellow, Nuffield Coll., Oxford, 2005. FRTS 1998; FRSA 2000. *Publications:* Enough Said: what's gone wrong with the language of politics?, 2016. *Recreations:* walking, cooking. *Address:* The New York Times Company, 620 Eighth Avenue, New York, NY 10018, USA. *Club:* Reform.

**THOMPSON, Very Rev. Matthew;** Dean of Birmingham, since 2017; *b* 10 Sept. 1968; *m* 2004, Michelle Lockhart; one *d. Educ:* Corpus Christi Coll., Cambridge (BA 1990; MA 1994; MPhil 1994); Ridley Hall, Cambridge. Ordained deacon, 1994, priest, 1995; Curate, Parish of the Ascension, Hulme, 1994–97; Curate, 1997–98, Team Vicar, 1998–2000, All Saints and Martyrs, Langley; Priest-in-charge, St Cross with St Paul, Clayton, 2000–08; Area Dean, Ardwick, 2003–08; Priest-in-charge, 2008–11, Vicar, 2011–17, St Peter and St

Philip, Bolton-le-Moors; Borough Dean of Bolton, 2010–17. Chair, House of Clergy, 2015–17. Chair, Birmingham Diocesan Bd of Educn, 2018–. Hon. Canon, Manchester Cathedral, 2012–17. *Recreations:* prayer, reading, running, cinema, music, theatre, school governance, hoping, dreaming. *Address:* Birmingham Cathedral, Colmore Row, Birmingham B3 2QB. *T:* (0121) 262 1840.

**THOMPSON, Michael,** FRAM; Professor of Horn, Royal Academy of Music, since 1985; Principal Horn, London Sinfonietta, since 1986; *m* 1975, Valerie Botwright; two *s* one *d.* *Educ:* Royal Acad. of Music. FRAM 1988. Principal Horn: BBC Scottish SO, 1972–75; Philharmonia Orch., 1975–85; internat. soloist and recording artist, 1985–. *Publications:* Warm-up Exercises, 1986; Schumann, Konzertstück: performing edition, 1988; Cadenzas for Haydn and Mozart Horn Concerti, 1990. *Recreations:* reading, walking, cooking. *Address:* 26 Presburg Road, New Malden, Surrey KT3 5AH. *T:* (020) 8241 8585.

**THOMPSON, Michael;** *see* Thompson, J. M. T.

**THOMPSON, Michael Jacques,** CMG 1989; OBE 1977; HM Diplomatic Service, retired; *b* 31 Jan. 1936; *s* of late Christopher Thompson and of Colette Jeanne-Marie Thompson; *m* 1967, Mary Susan (*née* Everard); one *s* one *d.* *Educ:* Uppingham; Christ's Coll., Cambridge (Law Tripos, 1956–60; MA). National Service, Kenya, Aden and Cyprus, 1954–56. HMOCS, Kenya, 1960–63; FCO, 1964; served Kuala Lumpur, Saigon, Lusaka and FCO, 1965–79; Counsellor, Kuala Lumpur, 1979–82; seconded to Comdr, British Land Forces, Hong Kong, 1982–85; Counsellor, FCO, 1985. Mem., Royal Asia Soc. Mem., Co. of Barbers. *Recreations:* tennis, golf, gardening. *Clubs:* Oxford and Cambridge; Huntercombe Golf.

**THOMPSON, Sir Michael (Warwick),** Kt 1991; DSc; FInstP; Deputy Chairman, Alliance & Leicester PLC, 1997–2000; Vice-Chancellor and Principal, University of Birmingham, 1987–96, Emeritus Professor, since 1996; *b* 1 June 1931; *s* of Kelvin Warwick Thompson and Madeleine Thompson; *m* 1st, Sybil (*née* Spooner) (*d* 1999); two *s*; 2nd, 2000, Jennifer (*née* Mitchell). *Educ:* Rydal Sch.; Univ. of Liverpool (BSc, DSc). Research scientist, AERE, Harwell, 1953–65; Sussex University: Prof. of Experimental Physics, 1965–80; Pro-Vice-Chancellor, 1973–77, actg Vice-Chancellor, 1976; Vis. Prof., 1980–86; Vice-Chancellor, UEA, 1980–86. Chairman: Physics Cttee, SRC, 1975–79; British Council Cttee for Academic Res. Collaboration with Germany, 1989–2000; Review of ISIS Neutron Source for Central Lab. of Res. Councils, 1997–98. Member: E Sussex Educn Cttee, 1973–78; E Sussex AHA, 1974–79; non-exec. Dir, W Midlands RHA, 1987–96; Chm., Review of London SHAs, 1993. Member: Council, Birmingham Chamber of Industry and Commerce, 1987–96; Council, CNAA, 1989–91; Council for Internat. Co-operation in Higher Educn, 1989–91; Council, CVCP, 1990–93, 1994–96 (Chm. Med. Cttee, 1994–96); Council for Industry and Higher Educn, 1991–96; Council, ACU, 1991–95; Standing Gp of Depts of Health and Educn on Undergrad. Med. and Dental Educn and Res., 1994–96. Director: Alliance & Leicester PLC (formerly Alliance Bldg Soc., then Alliance & Leicester Bldg Soc.), 1979–2000; Cobuild Ltd, 1987–96. Member Council: Eastbourne Coll., 1977–2000; QMW, 1996–2000 (Chm., Med. Sub-Cttee, 1996–2000). Trustee: Barber Inst. of Fine Arts, 1987–2007; St Bartholomew's Hosp. Med. Coll., 1998–2000. Mem., Birmingham Lunar Soc., 1991–96. President: Bodmin DFAS, 2000–11; Fowey River Assoc., 2001–07; Chm., Fowey Harbour Comrs Consultation Gp, 2010–13. Hon. Fellow, Univ. of Sussex, 2012. Hon. LLD Birmingham, 1997; Hon. DSc Sussex, 1998. Oliver Lodge Prizewinner, Univ. of Liverpool, 1953; Prizewinner, Materials Science Club, 1970; C. V. Boys Prizewinner, Inst. of Physics, 1972. Officer's Cross, Order of Merit (Germany), 1997. *Publications:* Defects and Radiation Damage in Metals, 1969; (jtly) Channelling, 1973; over 100 papers in sci. jls. *Recreations:* the arts, walking, sailing, fly fishing. *Address:* Readymoney Cottage, 3 Tower Park, Fowey, Cornwall PL23 1JD. *Clubs:* Athenæum; Royal Fowey Yacht.
*See also* P. W. Thompson.

**THOMPSON, Nathan James;** Chief Executive and Clerk of the Council, Duchy of Lancaster, since 2013; *b* Colwyn Bay, 15 June 1964; *s* of John Baragwanath Thompson and Helen May Saunders; *m* 1993, Lara; three *c.* *Educ:* Stonyhurst Coll.; Sheffield Hallam Univ. (BSc Urban Land Econs). MEPC plc, 1986–2000; JER Partners, 2000–04; Forth Ports plc, 2004–11, Man. Dir, Property Div., 2006–11. Trustee, Duke of Lancaster Housing Trust, 2013–. Mem., Assoc. of Lancastrians, 2013–. *Recreations:* family, sailing, golf, tennis. *Address:* Duchy of Lancaster, 1 Lancaster Place, Strand, WC2E 7ED. *T:* (020) 7269 1700, *Fax:* (020) 7269 1710. *E:* nthompson@duchyoflancaster.co.uk.

**THOMPSON, Neil;** *see* Thompson, R. N.

**THOMPSON, Nicholas,** RIBA; theatre architect in private practice; Director, 1974–2005, Leader, Arts Team, 1998–2005, Consultant, 2005–07, Renton Howard Wood Levin LLP; *b* 25 Feb. 1936; *s* of Eric Thompson and Dorothy (*née* Lake); *m* 1966, Clare Ferraby; two *s.* *Educ:* Christ's Hosp., Horsham; Oxford Sch. of Architecture (DipArch). RIBA 1961. Specialist in building design for performing arts, including: Crucible Th., Sheffield, 1971; Univ. of Warwick Arts Centre, 1973; Th. Royal and Royal Concert Hall, Nottingham, 1978–82; Old Vic, 1984; Alhambra, Bradford, 1986; Th. Royal, Newcastle, 1988; Lyceum Th., Sheffield, 1990; New Victoria Th., Woking, 1992; Donmar Warehouse, 1992; Anvil Concert Hall, Basingstoke, 1994; Bridgewater Concert Hall, Manchester, 1996; Sadler's Wells Th., 1998; masterplan and boarding houses for Christ's Hosp. Sch., 1998–2001; renovation of London Coliseum for ENO, 1999–2004; Dome Concert Hall and Mus., Brighton, 2002; theatre renovations for Sir Cameron Mackintosh, incl. Prince Edward Th., 1993 and 2004, Prince of Wales Th., 2004; refurbishment of Wigmore Hall, 2004; Wells Cathedral Sch., 2006–; *overseas projects* include: Concert Hall and Acad. of Music for Sultan of Oman, 1992; National Th., Damascus, 1993; Musik Th., Stuttgart, 1995; Musik Th., Duisburg, 1996; design consultant, Lazaristes Th. and Art Gall., Thessalonika, 1996; consultant: Athens Opera House, 1997–2004; Gennadius Lecture Th., American Sch. of Classical Studies, Athens, 2000; Montecasino Th., Johannesburg, 2005–07; (in association with Daniel Libeskind) interior architect, Grand Canal Th., Dublin, 2010. Dir, Paxos Fest. Trust, 1998–2017 (Chm., 2009–17). Goodwin & Wimperis Silver Medal, RIBA, 1964. *Publications:* articles in architectural press and lectures. *Recreations:* outdoors and active by day (travel, sailing, painting, making gardens), watching performances by night, collecting modern art. *Address:* 22 Lichfield Road, Richmond, Surrey TW9 3JR. *T:* and *Fax:* (020) 8948 0645. *E:* thomferr60@gmail.com. *Clubs:* Garrick, Architecture.

**THOMPSON, Sir Nicholas (Annesley Marler),** 2nd Bt *cr* 1963, of Reculver, co. Kent; solicitor with CMS Cameron McKenna LLP (formerly Cameron McKenna), 1997–2008; *b* 19 March 1947; *s* of Sir Richard Hilton Marler Thompson, 1st Bt and of Anne Christabel de Vere Marler Thompson (*née* Annesley); *S* father, 1999; *m* 1982, Venetia Catherine, *yr d* of Mr and Mrs John Heathcote; three *s* one *d.* *Educ:* King's Sch., Canterbury; Univ. of Kent at Canterbury (BA Law 1969). Admitted a solicitor, 1973. Mem. (C) Westminster City Council, 1978–86; Dep. Lord Mayor of Westminster, 1983–84. Contested (C) Newham South, 1983. Mem. Exec. Cttee, Standing Council of the Baronetage, 2003–12, 2014– (Chm., 2016–). *Recreations:* foreign travel, walking, theatre, reading, visiting historic houses and museums. *Heir: s* Simon William Thompson, *b* 10 June 1985. *Clubs:* Carlton (Member: Political Cttee, 2008–; Gen. Cttee, 2011–14, 2015–18, 2019–), United and Cecil (Mem., Cttee, 2008–16).

**THOMPSON, Sir Nigel (Cooper),** KCMG 2002; CBE 1996; CEng, FICE, FIStructE; Main Board Director, 1986–98, Deputy Chairman, 1998–2005, Ove Arup and Partners; Director, Trevor Estate, 1985–2011; *b* 18 June 1939; *s* of Henry Cooper Thompson and Beatrix Mary Cooper Thompson; *m* 1965, Nicola Jane Bonnett; one *s* two *d.* *Educ:* St Paul's Sch. CEng 1967; FIStructE 1985; FICE 2000. Joined Ove Arup and Partners, Consulting Engrs, 1960. Chm., St Helena Leisure Co., 2002–18. Chm., British Consulting Bureau, 1993–94. Chm., Construction Procurement Gp, DoE, 1993–96; Dep. Chm., British Airports Gp, DTI, 1996–98. Chairman: Govt/Private Sector Task Force for Kosovo, 1999–2000; Govt Task Force for Serbia and Montenegro, 2000–02. Mem., Business Adv. Council for Stability Pact for SE Europe, 2001. Founder Mem. Council, British Council of Offices, 1994; Mem. Council, CBI, 1993–96. Chairman: CPRE, 2003–08 (Mem. Cttee, Kennet Gp, 2000–10); BUILD - Building Understanding through Internat. Links for Develt, 2008–12. Major, Logistics Staff Corps, RE, 2001. Chm., Action for the River Kennet, 2003–12 (Pres., 2013–). Chm., Parish Council, Mildenhall, Wilts, 2004–19 (Vice-Chm., 2000–04). Liveryman, Engrs' Co., 2002–. Hon. Vice-Pres., Cambridge Univ. Land Soc., 2005. Gov., St Paul's Sch., 2007–11. Pres., Old Pauline Club, 2015–17. Chm., Claire Perry's Patrons Club, 2016–, Aldbourne and Ramsbury Br., 2019–, Devizes Cons. Assoc. Internat. Medal, ICE, 2000; Outstanding Contribn Award, ACE, 2001. *Recreations:* cricket, Rugby, landscape/estate gardening, farmer of pedigree Hampshire Down sheep. *Address:* Grove House, Stitchcombe, Marlborough, Wilts SN8 2NG. *Club:* Boodle's.

**THOMPSON, Nimble;** *see* Thompson, P. J. S.

**THOMPSON, Owen George;** *b* Glasgow; *s* of late Robert Thompson and of Margaret Thompson. *Educ:* Napier Univ. (BA Hons Accounting and Finance). Work for financial service cos. Mem. (SNP) Midlothian Council, 2005–15 (Dep. Leader, 2012–13; Leader, 2013–15). MP (SNP) Midlothian, 2015–17; contested (SNP) same seat, 2017. *Recreations:* football, computer games.

**THOMPSON, (Owen) Mark;** theatre designer; *b* 12 April 1957; *s* of late Owen Edgar Thompson and of Barbara Adele (*née* Lister). *Educ:* Radley Coll.; Birmingham Univ. (BA Hons Drama and Theatre Arts). Worked in rep. at Worcester, Exeter, Sheffield and Leeds; designs for: The Scarlet Pimpernel, Chichester, 1985 (transf. Her Majesty's); Cabaret, Strand, 1986; The Sneeze, Aldwych, 1988; Ivanov, and Much Ado About Nothing, Strand, 1989; A Little Night Music, Piccadilly, 1989; Shadowlands, Queen's, 1989 (transf. NY); Joseph and the Amazing Technicolor Dreamcoat, Palladium and Canadian, Australian and American tours, 1991 (Set Design Olivier Award, 1992); Company, Albery, 1996; Art, Wyndhams and NY, 1997; The Blue Room, Donmar Warehouse and NY, Dr Dolittle, Apollo Labbatts, 1998; Mamma Mia!, Prince Edward, 1999, Toronto, 2000, US tour, Australia, NY, 2001; Blast!, Apollo, 1999, NY, 2001; Lady in the Van, Queen's, 1999; (set only) Follies, NY, 2001; Bombay Dreams, Apollo Victoria, 2002, NY, 2004; And Then There Were None, Gielgud, 2005; Kean, Apollo, 2007; God of Carnage, Gielgud, 2008, NY, 2009; The Female of the Species, Vaudeville, 2008; Funny Girl, Chichester Festival Th., 2008; The Fastest Clock in the Universe, Hampstead, 2009; La Bête, Comedy, 2010, NY, 2010; The Children's Hour, Comedy, 2011; One Man Two Guvnors, NY, 2012; Charlie and the Chocolate Factory, Th. Royal, 2013 (Best Costume Olivier Award, 2014), NY, 2017; (set only) A Raisin in the Sun, NY, 2014; Electra, Old Vic, 2014; Welcome Home, Captain Fox!, Donmar Warehouse, 2016; Young Marx, Bridge Th., 2017; Tina - The Tina Turner Musical, Aldwych, 2018, Hamburg and NY, 2019; *for Royal Exchange Manchester:* Jumpers, 1984; The Country Wife, Mumbo Jumbo, 1986; The School for Scandal, 1990; *for RSC:* Measure for Measure, 1987; The Wizard of Oz, Much Ado About Nothing, 1988; The Comedy of Errors, 1990 (Set Design and Costume Design Olivier Awards, 1992); The Unexpected Man, 1998, NY, 2001; *for Almeida:* Volpone, 1990; Betrayal, Party Time, 1991; Butterfly Kiss, 1992; Rope, 2009; *for National Theatre:* The Wind in the Willows, 1990 (Olivier Award, Plays and Players Award, Critics Circle Award, 1991); The Madness of George III, 1991 (costume design for film, 1994); Arcadia, 1993; Pericles, 1994; What the Butler Saw, 1997; The Day I Stood Still, 1998; Life x 3, 2000, also NY, 2003; The Duchess of Malfi, 2003; Henry IV parts 1 and 2, 2005; The Alchemist, 2006; The Rose Tattoo, 2007; England People Very Nice, 2009; London Assurance, 2010; One Man Two Guvnors, 2011; She Stoops to Conquer, 2012; NT 50th, 2013; *for Royal Court:* Six Degrees of Separation, 1992 (transf. Comedy); Hysteria, 1994 (Olivier Award for Set Design); The Kitchen, 1995 (Critics' Circle Award); Mouth to Mouth, 2001; The Woman Before, 2005; Piano/Forte, 2006; Tribes, 2010; Birthday, 2012; *opera:* Montag aus Licht, La Scala, 1989 (costume design only); Falstaff, Scottish Opera, 1991; Peter Grimes, Opera North, 1989; Ariadne auf Naxos, Salzburg, 1991; Il Viaggio a Reims, Royal Opera, 1992; Hansel and Gretel, Sydney, 1992; The Two Widows, ENO, 1993; Queen of Spades, 1995, Macbeth, 2007, Metropolitan Opera, NY; Carmen, Opera Comique, Paris, 2009; The Mikado, Chicago Lyric Opera, 2010; *ballet:* Don Quixote, Royal Ballet, 1993. *Recreations:* cooking, gardening. *Address:* c/o Annette Stone, Arthouse B7–3, 1 York Way, N1C 4AT. *T:* (020) 3725 6893.

**THOMPSON, Patricia;** Commercial Partnerships Director, Special Olympics World Summer Games Abu Dhabi 2019, 2018; *b* Glasgow, 13 Oct. 1975; *d* of James and Alison Thompson; partner, Jamie Cunningham. *Educ:* Loughborough Univ. (BSc Physical Educn, Sports Sci. and Geog.). Account Manager, Bell Pottinger Sport, 1996–98; Hd of Events, Fast Track, 1998–2000; Mktg Consultant, Cricket NSW, 2001; Global Sponsorship Manager, SAP, 2003–05; Account Dir, The Works London, 2005–07; Hd, Arts and Sports, The Bigger Picture, 2007–12, Dir, Cycling Partnerships, 2012–14, BSkyB; Olympic and Strategic Partnerships Dir, Discovery Internat. and Eurosport, 2015–17. *Recreations:* active runner, cyclist and swimmer (completed London Marathon, 2012, Pinarello Bike Race, 2013, Gt North Swim, 2014, Ride London, 2015). *T:* 07800 932229.

**THOMPSON, Patrick;** *see* Thompson, H. P.

**THOMPSON, Patrick Miles; His Honour Judge Thompson;** a Circuit Judge, since 2016; *b* Liverpool, 22 Aug. 1968; *s* of Patrick Brian Thompson and Jaqueline Thompson; two *d.* *Educ:* St Edward's Coll., Liverpool; Univ. of Manchester (LLB Hons). Called to the Bar, Gray's Inn, 1990; a barrister, 1990–2016; a Recorder, 2009–16. *Recreation:* all sports (particularly football and Rugby Union). *Address:* Chester Crown Court, The Castle, Chester CH1 2AN. *T:* (01244) 317606. *E:* hhj.patrick.thompson@ejudiciary.net. *Club:* Chester City.

**THOMPSON, Sir Paul (Anthony),** 2nd Bt *cr* 1963; company director; *b* 6 Oct. 1939; *s* of Sir Kenneth Pugh Thompson, 1st Bt, and Nanne (*d* 1994), *yr d* of Charles Broome, Walton, Liverpool; *S* father, 1984; *m* 1971, Pauline Dorothy, *d* of Robert O. Spencer, Bolton, Lancs; two *s* two *d.* *Educ:* Aldenham School, Herts. *Heir: s* Richard Kenneth Spencer Thompson [*b* 27 Jan. 1976; *m* 2008, Hayley Watts, Auckland, NZ; one *s* one *d*]. *Address:* The Pines, 8 Vicarage Lane, Westhead, Ormskirk, Lancs L40 6HQ.

**THOMPSON, Prof. Paul Richard,** DPhil; social historian; Research Professor in Social History, University of Essex, 1988–2008, now Emeritus Professor; Founder and Trustee, National Life Stories (formerly National Life Story Collection), since 1987; *b* 1935; *m* 1st, Thea Vigne; one *s* one *d*; 2nd, Natasha Burchardt; one *d*; 3rd, Elaine Bauer. *Educ:* Bishop's Stortford Coll.; Corpus Christi Coll., Oxford (MA); The Queen's Coll., Oxford (Junior Research Fellow, 1961–64); DPhil Oxon 1964. University of Essex: Lectr in Sociology, 1964–69; Sen. Lectr, 1969–71; Reader, 1971–88; Sen. Res. Fellow, Nuffield Coll., Oxford, 1968–69; Vis. Prof. of Art History, Johns Hopkins Univ., 1972; Hoffman Wood Prof. of Architecture, Univ. of Leeds, 1977–78; Benjamin Meaker Prof., Univ. of Bristol, 1987. Dir, Qualidata, 1994–2001. Editor: Victorian Soc. Conf. Reports, 1965–67; Oral History, 1970–; Life Stories, 1985–89; International Yearbook of Oral History and Life Stories, 1992–96; Memory and Narrative, 1996–2002. Hon. DLitt: Aberdeen, 2007; Sussex, 2013; DUniv Essex, 2015. *Publications:* History of English Architecture (with Peter Kidson and Peter Murray), 1965, 2nd edn 1979; The Work of William Morris, 1967, 3rd edn 1991; Socialists, Liberals and Labour: the struggle for London 1880–1914, 1967; The Edwardians: the remaking of British Society, 1975, 2nd edn 1992; The Voice of the Past: Oral History, 1978, 4th edn 2017; Living the Fishing, 1983; I Don't Feel Old: the experience of later life, 1990; (with Raphael Samuel) The Myths We Live By, 1990; (with Gloria Wood) The Nineties, 1993; (with Hugo Slim) Listening for a Change, 1993; (with Cathy Courtney) City Lives, 1996; (with Daniel Bertaux) Pathways to Social Class, 1997; (jtly) Growing Up in Stepfamilies, 1997; (with Mary Chamberlain) Narrative and Genre, 1998; (with Daniel Bertaux) On Living Through Soviet Russia, 2004; (with Elaine Bauer) Jamaican Hands Across the Atlantic, 2006; Sea-change: Wivenhoe remembered, 2006. *Recreations:* cycling, drawing, music, friendship, travel. *Address:* 5 West Street, Wivenhoe, Essex CO7 9DE. *E:* paulth_wivenhoe@yahoo.co.uk.

**THOMPSON, Paul Warwick;** Vice-Chancellor (formerly Rector and Vice-Provost), Royal College of Art, since 2009; *b* 9 Aug. 1959; *s* of Sir Michael Thompson, *qv*; *m* 1984, Adline Finlay; one *s* one *d*. *Educ:* Bryanston Sch.; Univ. of Bristol (BA Jt Hons); Univ. of East Anglia (MA, PhD). Design Council, 1987–88; Design Museum, 1988–2001, Dir, 1992–2001; Dir, Smithsonian Cooper-Hewitt Nat. Design Mus., NY, 2001–09. Adjunct Prof., Imperial Coll. London, 2014–. Chm., Adv. Bd, Fabrica, Italy, 2012–15. Trustee, V&A Mus., 2009–. Visitor, Ashmolean Mus., 2010–18. *Recreations:* theatre, cinema, gardening. *Address:* Royal College of Art, Kensington Gore, SW7 2EU.

**THOMPSON, Sir Peter (Anthony),** Kt 1984; FCILT; President, Goldcrest Land PLC (formerly Goldcrest Homes plc), since 2014 (Chairman, 1998–2014); Chairman, BKP Property Holdings Ltd, since 2015; *b* 14 April 1928; *s* of late Herbert Thompson and Sarah Jane Thompson; *m* 1st, 1958, Patricia Anne Norcott (*d* 1983); one *s* two *d*; 2nd, 1986, Lydia Mary Kite (*née* Hodding); two *d*. *Educ:* Royal Drapers Sch.; Bradford Grammar Sch.; Leeds Univ. (BA Econ). Unilever, 1952–62; GKN, 1962–64; Transport Controller, Rank Organisation, 1964–67; Head of Transport, BSC, 1967–72; Group Co-ordinator, BRS Ltd, 1972–75; Exec. Vice-Chm. (Operations), Nat. Freight Corp., 1975–77; Chief Exec., Nat. Freight Corp., later Nat. Freight Co., 1977–80; Dep. Chm. and Chief Exec., 1980–82, Chm. and Chief Exec., 1982–84, Exec. Chm., 1984–90, Pres., 1991–93, NFC. Dir, 1989–90, Dep. Chm., 1989–90, Chm., March–July 1990, British & Commonwealth Hldgs; Chairman: Community Hospitals plc, 1981–96; Child Base Ltd, 1989–2005 (Pres., 2006–); FI Group plc, 1990–99; Douglas Stewart Ltd, 1992–2004; Phoenix Asset Mgt Ltd, 1998–2003, 2004–09; Stocktrade, 2000–01; Durabuild, 2001–02; OMG Ltd, 2001–02; Green Energy plc, 2001–17 (Dir, 2018–); Goodnights Enterprises, 2003–13; Milton Keynes Theatre Prodn Co. Ltd, 2004–08; Mill Manor Properties Ltd, 2003–15; Dep. Chm., Wembley plc, 1991–95; Director: Granville & Co. Ltd, 1984–90; Pilkington plc, 1985–93; Kenning Motor Group, 1985–86; Smiths Industries PLC, 1986–98; Meyer International, 1988–92; Aegis plc, 1993–99; Brewin Dolphin Gp, 1994–2000; Legal Document Co., 2001–07; Ecorider Ltd, 2006–07; Image Analysis, 2010–13; Pres., ProShare, 1994–99 (Chm., 1992–94). Mem., Nat. Trng Task Force, 1989–93. President: Inst. of Freight Forwarders, 1982–83; Inst. of Logistics and Distribn Management (formerly Inst. of Physical Distribn Management), 1988–93 (Chm., 1985–88); Vice-Pres., CIT, 1982–85; Chm., CBI Wider Share Ownership Task Force, 1990. Chm., Milton Keynes Theatre Gall. Trust, 1995–2003. CCMI. Hon. LLD: Leeds, 1991; Nottingham, 1991; Hon. DTech Bradford, 1991; Hon. DSc Cranfield Inst. of Technol., 1992. Hambro Businessman of the Year, 1983; BIM Gold Medal, 1991. *Publications:* Sharing the Success: the story of the NFC, 1990. *Recreations:* golf, walking, shooting, theatre, music. *Address:* The Mill House, Mill Street, Newport Pagnell, Bucks MK16 8ER. *Clubs:* Garrick, Royal Automobile.

**THOMPSON, Dr Peter Anthony,** FREng; FInstP, FRSC; Chief Executive Officer, National Physical Laboratory, since 2015; *b* Stoke-on-Trent, 5 July 1967; *s* of Brian George and Jean Marie Thompson; *m* 1993, Lindsay Jane Chisholm; one *s* one *d*. *Educ:* St Thomas More RC High Sch. and Sixth Form Coll., Stoke-on-Trent; Univ. of Salford (BSc Hons Applied Chem.); Cranfield Univ. (PhD Molecular Electronics). FInstP 2016; FRSC 2016; FREng 2018. Scientist, 1993–97; Programme Manager, DERA, 1998–2002; Gp Leader, 2002–04, Programme Leader, 2004–08, DSTL; Hd, Counter Terrorism Centre, MoD, 2008–09; Dir of Progs, DSTL, 2009–11; Strategic Advr to Chief Scientific Advr, MoD, 2011–12; Dep. Chief Exec., DSTL, 2012–15. Chm. Govs, S Wilts Univ. Tech. Coll., Salisbury, 2014–16 (Gov., 2013–14). *Recreations:* cricket and golf - more watching than playing these days; ski-ing once a year whilst my son is an instructor; travel. *Address:* Twin Ash, The Green, Pitton, Salisbury, Wilts SP5 1DZ. *T:* (01722) 712441. *E:* Peter.thompson@npl.co.uk. *Club:* Farley Cricket.

**THOMPSON, Peter James;** Owner, Peter Thompson Associates, since 1970; *b* Sheffield, 23 Feb. 1945; *s* of Andrew and Janet Thompson. *Educ:* Hurstpierpoint Coll.; Sussex Univ. (BA Hons). Founder, Peter Thompson Associates, PR agency, 1970. *Recreations:* food, drink, travel.

**THOMPSON, Peter John;** education and training consultant; *b* 17 April 1937; *s* of late George Kenneth Thompson and Gladys Pamela (*née* Partington), W Midlands; *m* 1961, Dorothy Ann Smith; one *s* three *d*. *Educ:* Aston Univ. (BSc 1st Cl. Hons MechEngrg; MSc); CNAA (DTech). Whitworth Soc. Prize. CEng, FIET; FIPD. With Tube Investments, 1952–61; Lectr 1961, Sen. Lectr 1968–70, Harris Coll., Preston; Sen. Sci. Officer, UKAEA, Preston, 1965–68; Prin. Lectr, Sheffield City Poly., 1970–77; Hd of Dept and Dean of Engrg, Trent Poly., Nottingham, 1977–83; Pro Rector, then Dep. Rector, Poly. of Central London, 1983–86; Professor, Trent Poly., 1980–83; Poly. of Central London, 1983–86; Chief Exec., NCVQ, 1986–91; Vis. Prof., Sch. of Mgt, Open Univ., 1991–94. School Inspector, OFSTED, 1984–2012. Partner, P & D Medallions, 1986–; Consultant, HR Services, 1997–. Mem., then Chm., Manufacturing Bd, CNAA, 1978–86; Mem., Cttee for Sci. and Technology, CNAA, 1982–86; Mem. then Chm., Cttee for Engrg in Polytechnics, 1981–86; Member: Engrg Adv. Cttee, NAB, 1980–84; Engrg Scis Divl Bd of IMechE, 1984–86; Chm., Materials Tech. Activities Cttee, IMechE, 1984–86; Mem., Council, Open Coll., 1987–90. Sen. Awards Consultant, C&G, 1992–95. Hon. Mem., C&G, 1991. FRSA. *Publications:* numerous papers on engrg manufacture and vocational educn and trng, 1968–, incl. papers on hydrostatic extension, lubrication, cutting tool wear and mechanics and metal forming; patents. *Recreations:* genealogy, numismatics, golf. *Address:* Berkhamsted, Herts HP4 3JJ. *T:* (01442) 865127.

**THOMPSON, His Honour Peter John;** a Circuit Judge, 1998–2013; *b* 30 Dec. 1943; *s* of late Eric Thompson and Olive Ethel Thompson (*née* Miskin); *m* 1969, Elizabeth Anne Granger Rees; one *s* two *d*. *Educ:* Glyn Grammar Sch.; St Catherine's Coll., Oxford (MA Jurisp.). Admitted Solicitor, 1970; Solicitor and Barrister, Supreme Court of Vic., Australia, 1972; Partner: Turner Martin & Symes, Solicitors, Ipswich, 1976–91; Eversheds, Solicitors, Ipswich, 1991–98. *Recreations:* jazz, playing and listening, soccer, playing and watching, jogging and walking in English and French countryside, family, literature, travel. *E:* pjthompson1943@gmail.com.

**THOMPSON, Peter John Stuart, (Nimble);** Chairman, N. G. Bailey Ltd, 2001–13; *b* 28 Sept. 1946; *s* of Douglas Thompson and Rene Thompson, OBE; *m* 1970, Morven Mary Hanscomb; one *s* one *d* (and one *s* decd). *Educ:* Rossall Sch.; Univ. of Leeds (LLB). MCIArb. Admitted solicitor, 1971; Managing Partner, Hepworth & Chadwick, 1989–94; Eversheds: Sen. Partner, Leeds and Manchester, 1994–99; Dep. Chm., 1995–98. Non-executive Director: TEP Electrical Distributors, 1975–; S. Lyles plc, 1994–99; Denney O'Hara Ltd, 1999–2011; Judicium plc, 2000–14; Rushbond plc, 2002–; Scarborough Building Soc., 2005–09; Institute of Dirs, 2009–16 (Regl Chm., Yorks, 2005–09; Dep. Chm., 2013–16); Skipton Building Soc., 2009–16 (Dep. Chm., 2013–16; Chm., Remuneration Cttee, 2013–16); Henderson Insurance Brokers Ltd, 2011–14. Chairman: Bd, Leeds Metropolitan Univ., 2000–06; Eureka!, the Mus. for Children, Halifax, 2003–07; Arch Resolution, 2017–; Governor: Giggleswick Sch., 1998–2015 (Vice Chm., 2002–07); Aysgarth Sch., 2016– (Chm., 2017–). Hon. FInstD, 2017. Hon. DLaws Leeds Metropolitan, 2006. *Recreations:* fishing, wine, family, friends, stalking. *Address:* The Grange, Kirkby Malzeard, Ripon, N Yorks HG4 3RY. *T:* (01765) 658398. *E:* Nimble@nimblet.co.uk. *Club:* Royal Automobile.

**THOMPSON, Peter Kenneth James;** Solicitor to Departments of Health and of Social Security, 1989–97; *b* 30 July 1937; *s* of Kenneth George Thompson and Doreen May Thompson; *m* 1970, Sandy Lynne Harper; two *d*. *Educ:* Worksop Coll.; Christ's Coll., Cambridge (MA, LLB). Called to the Bar, Lincoln's Inn, 1961; practised at Common Law Bar, 1961–73; Lawyer in Govt Service: Law Commission, 1973–78; Lord Chancellor's Dept, 1978–83; Under Sec., DHSS, 1983. General Editor: The County Court Practice, 1991–98; The Civil Court Practice, 1999–. Hon. QC 1997. *Publications:* The Unfair Contract Terms Act 1977, 1978; The Recovery of Interest, 1985; *radio plays:* A Matter of Form, 1977; Dormer and Grand-Daughter, 1978. *Recreation:* running a free legal advice service.

**THOMPSON, Rhodri William Ralph;** QC 2002; a Recorder, since 2010; *b* 5 May 1960; *s* of Ralph Kenneth Thompson and Dilys Grace Thompson (*née* Hughes); *m* 1989, Paula Mary Donaghy; one *s* one *d*. *Educ:* Eastbourne Coll.; University Coll., Oxford (BPhil, MA); City Univ. (Dip. Law). Called to the Bar, Middle Temple, 1989; in practice as barrister, 1989–; Monckton Chambers, 1990–2000 (Brussels, 1990–92, London, 1993–2000); Founder Mem., Matrix Chambers, 2000– (Chm., Mgt Cttee, 2004–06, 2014–16). Jt Chm., Jt Wkg Party of Bars and Law Socs of UK on Competition Law, 2012–; Hon. Treas., UK Assoc. of European Law, 2012–. *Publications:* (contrib.) Bellamy & Child, EC Law of Competition, 4th edn 1993 to 8th edn 2017; Single Market for Pharmaceuticals, 1994; UK Competition Law: the new framework, 2015. *Address:* Matrix Chambers, Griffin Building, Gray's Inn, WC1R 5LN. *T:* (020) 7611 9316. *E:* rhodrithompson@matrixlaw.co.uk.

**THOMPSON, Rear Adm. Richard Charles,** CBE 2014 (OBE 2007); CEng, FRAeS; Managing Director, Sealand Support Services Ltd, since 2018; *b* Reading, 12 Feb. 1966; *s* of George Albert Thompson and Josephine Anne Thompson; two *s* two *d*. *Educ:* Meadway Sch., Reading; Royal Naval Engrg Coll., Manadon; King's Coll. London (BEng Hons; MA Internat. Studies). CEng 2010, FRAeS 2014. Joined Royal Navy, 1985; 845 Sqn, 1989–91; 849 Sqn 1991–93; Merlin Project Team, 1994–97 and 2002–03; FONA Project Policy, 1997–98; acsc 1999; 820 Sqn, 2000–01; Strategic Planning Team, 2003–04; Jt Strike Fighter Project Team, 2004–06; Jt Helicopter Commd, 2006–07; Comdr Air Engrg, HMS Ark Royal, 2008–09; Hd, Customer Support Team (Fleet), Defence Equipment and Support, 2009–10; Chief Engr, 2010–13, Hd, 2013–16, Lightning II Project Team; Dir, Ops and Assce, Defence Safety Authy, 2016–18; Dir, Technical, Military Aviation Authy, 2016–18; Chief Naval Engr Officer, 2017–19. *Recreations:* mountain biking, dog walking, family.

**THOMPSON, (Richard) Neil;** Vice President Europe, Middle East and Africa, Microsoft Consumer Division, 2016–18; *b* Swansea, 23 Sept. 1966; *s* of Melvin and Joan Thompson; *m* 1994, Sarah Bruce; two *d*. *Educ:* Dwr-y-Felin Comprehensive Sch.; Loughborough Univ. (BSc Econs). Graduate trainee, Sea Containers Ltd, 1989–90; Direct Mktg Manager, Stena Line, 1990–92; Microsoft, 1992–: Mktg Manager, 1994–97, Hd of Communications, 1994–97, Microsoft UK; Eur. Communications Dir, 1997–2000; Eur. Mktg Dir, Xbox, 2000–03; Regl Dir, EMEA, 2003–05; General Manager: Entertainment Div., 2005–10; Consumer Channels Gp, 2011–13; Vice Pres., Retail Sales and Category Mgt, EMEA, 2013–16. Mem. Bd, Entertainment and Leisure Software Publishers Assoc., 2007–. *Recreations:* ski-ing, golf, travel.

**THOMPSON, Sir Richard (Paul Hepworth),** KCVO 2003; DM; FRCP; Physician to the Queen and Head of HM Medical Household, 1993–2005 (Physician to the Royal Household, 1982–93); Consultant Physician, St Thomas' Hospital, 1972–2005, now Emeritus Consultant, and Governor, 2004–05 and 2007–13, Guy's and St Thomas' NHS Trust; President, Royal College of Physicians, 2010–14; *b* 14 April 1940; *s* of Stanley Henry and Winifred Lilian Thompson; *m* 1974, Eleanor Mary Hughes. *Educ:* Epsom Coll.; Worcester Coll., Oxford (MA, DM; Hon. Fellow, 2010); St Thomas's Hosp. Med. Sch. MRC Clinical Res. Fellow, Liver Unit, KCH, 1967–69; Fellow, Gastroenterology Unit, Mayo Clinic, USA, 1969–71; Lectr, Liver Unit, KCH, 1971–72; Physician, King Edward VII Hosp. for Officers, 1982–2005. Mem., Lambeth, Southwark and Lewisham AHA, 1979–82. Examiner in Medicine: Soc. of Apothecaries, 1976–80; Faculty of Dental Surgery, RCS, 1980–86; Examr, 1991–2003, Censor, 1998–2000, Treas., 2003–10, RCP. Governor, Guy's Hosp. Med. Sch., 1980–82; Member Cttee of Management: Inst. of Psychiatry, 1981–95; King Edward VII Hosp. Fund, 1985–89, 1992–96 (Mem., Gen. Council, 1985–); Mem Council, Royal Med. Foundn of Epsom Coll., 2003–10. Member, Council: BHF, 2001–08 (Vice-Chm., 2001–08); British Cardiovascular Soc., 2008–14; Trustee: Thrive, 2001–10 (Patron, 2010–); Henry Smith Charity, 2007–15; Quit, 2011–15; Wellbeing of Women, 2014; Nat. Garden Scheme, 2014–; Patron, The Grange, 2014–. Hon. Associate Nightingale Fellow, 2004. *Publications:* Physical Signs in Medicine, 1980; Lecture Notes on the Liver, 1986; Curiosities from the College Museum, 2016; (with Louella Vaughan) Ever Persons Capable and Able: the physicians, 1660–2018, 2017; papers and reviews in med. jls. *Address:* 36 Dealtry Road, SW15 6NL. *T:* (020) 8789 3839.

**THOMPSON, Richard Paul Reynier,** OBE 2001; Partner, ARL Partners, since 2017; Director, Elvaston Global Ltd, since 2012; *b* 17 Aug. 1960; *s* of His Honour Anthony Arthur Richard Thompson, *qv*; *m* 1991, Louisa (*née* Yeates) (marr. diss.); two *s* one *d*. *Educ:* St Paul's Sch.; Exeter Univ. (LLB); Harvard Business Sch. Served Army, RGJ, 1978–88. Entered FCO, 1989; Second, later First Sec., Stockholm, 1991–93; First Secretary: FCO, 1993–96; UK Mission to UN, Geneva, 1996–99; Counsellor: Pristina, 1999–2000; FCO,

2000–04; Baghdad, 2004–05; FCO, 2006–07; Chief Constable, Civil Nuclear Constabulary, 2007–12. Vis. Fellow, KCL, 2012–. Hon. Fellow, Strategy and Security Inst., Univ. of Exeter, 2013–. CEO, Facewatch Ltd, 2014–16. *Recreations:* keeping fit, reading (politics and history).

**THOMPSON, Robert;** *see* Thompson, W. R.

**THOMPSON, Robin;** *see* Thompson, D. R. B.

**THOMPSON, Simon Robert;** Chairman: 3i Group plc, since 2015; Rio Tinto plc and Rio Tinto Ltd, since 2018 (non-executive Director, since 2014); *b* Bramhall, 16 June 1959; *s* of Robert Thompson and Patricia Thompson; *m* 1986, Fiona Graham-Bryce. *Educ:* Manchester Grammar Sch.; University Coll., Oxford (BA Geol. 1981); King's Coll. London (PhD Hist. 2018). Lloyds Bank Internat., 1981–85; N. M. Rothschild & Sons Ltd, 1985–94; Dir, S. G. Warburg & Co. Ltd, 1994–95; Minorco SA: Hd, Project Finance, 1995–97; Pres., Minorco Brasil, 1997–99; Anglo American plc: Hd, Zinc, 1999–2001; CEO, 2001–05, Chm., 2003–07, Base Metals Div.; Chm., Exploration Div., 2003–07; Chm., Tarmac, 2003–07; Exec. Dir, 2005–07. Chm., Tullow Oil plc, 2012–17; non-executive Director: AngloGold Ashanti, 2004–08; UC Rusal, 2007–09; Sandvik AB, 2008–15; Newmont Mining Corp., 2008–14; Amec plc, later Amec Foster Wheeler plc, 2009–15. Sen. Advr, Critical Resource, 2017–. Mem., Adv. Bd on Business and Sustainability, IFC, 2013–18; Vice Pres., Inst. of Business Ethics, 2017–. *Publications:* Unjustifiable Risk?: the story of British climbing, 2010; A Long Walk with Lord Conway, 2013. *Recreations:* mountaineering, writing. *Address:* 3i, 16 Palace Street, SW1E 5JD. *Clubs:* Athenæum, Alpine.

**THOMPSON, Steven Lim;** QC 2015; *b* London, 1969; *s* of John Quentin Thompson and Miao-Ling Thompson; *m* (marr. diss.); one *s* one *d*. *Educ:* Westminster Sch., London; St John's Coll., Cambridge (BA Hons 1990). Called to the Bar, Inner Temple, 1996; Chm., Internat. Cttee, Bar Council, 2019– (Vice-Chair, 2014–19). *Address:* XXIV Old Buildings, Lincoln's Inn, WC2A 3UP. *T:* (020) 7691 2424. *E:* clerks@xxiv.co.uk.

**THOMPSON, Sir (Thomas d'Eyncourt) John,** 6th Bt *cr* 1806, of Hartsbourne Manor, Hertfordshire; Managing Director, Rockspring Iberia, Madrid, since 2016 (Director, since 2006); *b* 22 Dec. 1956; *o s* of Sir (Thomas) Lionel Tennyson Thompson, 5th Bt and of Margaret Thompson (*née* Brown); *S* father, 1999; *m* 2002, Tanya, *d* of Michael Willcocks; one *s* two *d*. *Educ:* Eton; King's Coll., London (BA); Univ. of East London (MSc). MRICS (ARICS 1993). Associate Partner, Folkard & Hayward, London, 1984–90; Investment Surveyor, King Sturge, London, 1991–93, Brussels, 1994; Dir, Weatherall Green & Smith, Madrid, 1995–97; Partner, King Sturge, Madrid, 1997–2006. *Heir: s* Thomas Boulden Cameron Thompson, *b* 31 Jan. 2006. *Club:* East India.

**THOMPSON, Vincent;** *see* Thompson, G. V. B.

**THOMPSON, (William) Robert;** freelance cartoonist and illustrator, since 1992; *b* 21 July 1960; *s* of Wildon and Eileen Thompson; *m* 1993, Siobhán Maria Doyle; one *s* one *d*. *Educ:* Leeds Polytechnic (BA Hons Graphic Design). Art Dir, Camden Graphics, 1985–92. Contrib. cartoons/illustrations to The Guardian, The Times, Private Eye, The Spectator, The Oldie, FT, Mail on Sunday, Metro, Decanter, Radio Times, New Statesman, Real Deals, The Lady. *Publications:* Pointless Things to Do, 1995; illustrator: Private Eye's Cutting Humour, 1993; Can They Do That?, 2003; The Origins of Words and Phrases, 2007; QI Annual, 2009, 2010; Eyeballs, 2012. *Recreations:* walking my Jack Russell, growing vegetables, eating dark chocolate, drinking red wine, riding my bicycle. *E:* rtcartoonist@btinternet.com. *W:* www.robertthompsoncartoons.com.

**THOMPSON, Yvonne,** CBE 2003; Managing Director, ASAP Communications Ltd, 1995–2010; *b* 1957; one *d*. Phonogram; CBS; Founder: Positive Publicity, 1983–89; WM&P, 1990–94. Dir, Choice FM Radio. Member: Bd, Britain in Europe, 1999; Bd, London Develt Agency, 2000–07; Small Business Council, DTI, 2000–02; Economy Honours Cttee, 2013–; Comr, Local Govt Inf. Unit; Chairman: London Central LSC, 2000–08; Ethnic Minority Business Forum, DTI, 2000–06. Founder and Pres., Eur. Fedn of Black Women Business Owners, 1996–2011. Hon. DPhil London Metropolitan, 2005. *Publications:* 7 Traits of Highly Successful Women on Boards, 2014.

**THOMPSON-McCAUSLAND, Benedict Maurice Perronet;** Partner: Temax Associates, 1991–2018; Thompson Best, 2008–18; Group Chief Executive, National & Provincial Building Society, 1987–90; *b* 5 Feb. 1938; *s* of late Lucius P. Thompson-McCausland, CMG and Helen Laura McCausland; *m* 1964, Frances Catherine Fothergill Smith; three *d*. *Educ:* Eton Coll.; Trinity Coll., Cambridge (MA; Rowing Blue). FCA 1974–2003. Articled to Coopers & Lybrand, Chartered Accountants, 1961–64; Arbuthnot Latham & Co. Ltd, 1964–80: Asst to Dirs, 1964; Banking Manager, 1967; Dir, 1968; Dep. Chm., 1978; London Life Association Ltd: Dir, 1976–81; Vice-Pres., 1979–87; Chief Exec., 1981–87. Dir, Advanced Personnel Technology, 1993–2001; formerly Director: Western Trust & Savings Ltd; Concord Internat.; First National Finance Corp. plc. Chm., Lombard Assoc., 1979–81. Director: British Sch. of Osteopathy, 1991–2000 (Chm., 1996–2000); Harefield Hosp. NHS Trust, 1992–98. Mem. Council, 1987–2000, and Mem. Exec. Cttee, 1988–91, Industrial Soc. Mem., Council of Management, Arnolfini Gall., 1983–86. John Loxham Lectr, Inst. of Quality Assurance, 1997. *Publications:* (with Derek Biddle) Change, Business Performance and Values, 1985; (with J. Bergwerk) Leading to Success: how leaders unlock energy, 1994; articles in business jls. *Recreations:* rough gardening, military history. *Address:* 14 Alexander Street, W2 5NT. *T:* (020) 7221 7549. *Clubs:* Leander (Henley-on-Thames); Hawks (Cambridge).

**THOMSEN, Kim Stuart L.;** *see* Lerche-Thomsen.

**THOMSON,** family name of **Baron Thomson of Fleet**.

**THOMSON OF FLEET,** 3rd Baron *cr* 1964; **David Kenneth Roy Thomson;** Chairman: Thomson Reuters (formerly The Thomson Corporation), since 2002 (Director, since 1988); Woodbridge Co. Ltd; *b* 12 June 1957; *s* of 2nd Baron Thomson of Fleet and of Nora Marilyn (*née* Lavis); *S* father, 2006; *m* 1st, 1988, Mary Lou La Prairie (marr. diss. 1997); two *d*; 2nd, 2000, Laurie Ludwick (marr. diss. 2007); one *s*. *Educ:* Upper Canada Coll.; Selwyn Coll., Cambridge (MA). Chm., The Globe and Mail Inc. *Heir: s* Hon. Benjamin James Ludwick Thomson, *b* 10 March 2006. *Address:* Thomson Reuters, 333 Bay Street, Suite 400, Toronto, ON M5H 2R2, Canada.

**THOMSON, Sir Adam (McClure),** KCMG 2014 (CMG 2009); HM Diplomatic Service, retired; Director, European Leadership Network, since 2016; *b* 1 July 1955; *s s* of Sir John Adam Thomson, GCMG; *m* 1984, Fariba Shirazi; one *s* two *d*. *Educ:* Westminster Sch.; Trinity Coll., Cambridge (MA); Harvard Univ. (MPP). Joined FCO, 1978; Third, later Second Sec., Moscow, 1981–83; Second, later First Sec., UK delegn to NATO, Brussels, 1983–86; First Sec., FCO, 1986–89; Cabinet Office, 1989–91; First Sec. (Politico-Military), Washington, 1991–95; Counsellor (Political), New Delhi, 1995–98: Counsellor, Security Policy Dept, FCO, 1998–2002; Ambassador and Dep. Perm. Rep., UK Mission to UN, NY, 2002–06; Dir, South Asia and Afghanistan, FCO, 2006–09; High Comr to Pakistan, 2010–13; UK Perm. Rep., UK Delegn to NATO, 2014–16. *Address:* c/o European Leadership Network, Southbank House, Black Prince Road, SE1 7SJ.

**THOMSON, Andrew Francis;** Chairman and Joint Managing Director, D. C. Thomson & Co. Ltd, since 2005 (Director, since 1974); *b* Dundee, 14 Aug. 1942; *s* of C. Howard and Frances H. Thomson; *m* 1970, Bridget Ivory; two *s* one *d*. *Educ:* Ardvreck Sch.; Glenalmond Coll.; Churchill Coll., Cambridge (BA 1964). Dir, Alliance Trust plc, 1989–2001. Hon. LLD Dundee, 2006. *Recreations:* golf, travel, theatre. *Address:* 22 Meadowside, Dundee DD1 1LN. *T:* (01382) 223131.

**THOMSON, Prof. Andrew James,** OBE 2008; DPhil; FRS 1993; CChem, FRSC, FRSocMed; Professor of Chemistry, University of East Anglia, 1985–2007, Emeritus Professor of Chemistry and Biology, 2008; *b* 31 July 1940; *s* of late Andrew Henderson Thomson and Eva Frances Annie (*née* Moss); *m* 1966, Anne Marsden; two *s*. *Educ:* Steyning Grammar Sch.; Wadham Coll., Oxford (MA, DPhil; Hon. Fellow, 2012). FRSC 1990; FRSocMed 2008. Res. Asst Prof., Dept of Biophysics, Michigan State Univ., 1967; School of Chemical Sciences, University of East Anglia: Demonstrator, 1967–68; Lectr, 1968–77; Sen. Lectr, 1977–83; Reader, 1983–85; Hd of Inorganic Chem. Sector, 1984–97; Norwich Res. Park Prof., 1995–2007; Dean, Sch. of Chemical Scis and Pharmacy, 1999–2004; Dean, Faculty of Sci., 2004–07. Royal Society of Chemistry: Silver Medal for analytical chemistry, 1991; Hugo Muller Lectureship, 1997; Interdisciplinary Award, 2000; Chatt Lectureship, 2004. *Publications:* over 350 original papers in scientific jls. *Recreations:* walking, ballroom dancing, choral singing, gardening. *Address:* 12 Armitage Close, Cringleford, Norwich NR4 6XZ. *T:* (01603) 504623. *E:* a.thomson@uea.ac.uk, andrew33thomson@btinternet.com.

**THOMSON, Benjamin John Paget,** CBE 2018; FRSE; Chairman, Inverleith LLP (formerly Inverleith Capital LLP), since 2009; *b* London, 8 April 1963; *s* of David Paget Thomson, *qv*; *m* 1993, Lucy Juckes; two *s* two *d*. *Educ:* Bradfield Coll., Berks; Edinburgh Univ. (MA Hons Physics 1985); INSEAD (AMP). Researcher, H of C, 1981–82; Kleinwort Benson Ltd, 1985–90; Noble Group Ltd, 1990–2010: Dir, 1993; Chief Exec., 1997–2007; led mgt buy-out, 2000; Chm., 2007–10 (non-exec., 2008–10). Chairman: Reform Scotland, 2008–15; Barrington Stoke Ltd, 2008–16; Antonine Asset Mgt LLP, 2010–; Urbicus, 2011–17; Castle Capital Ltd, 2013–17; non-executive Director: Wellington Underwriting plc, 1993–97; Canmore Partnership, 1995–2003; CBS Private Capital SLP Ltd, 1996–2004; Roberts & Hiscox Gen. Partners Ltd, 1996–2011; PFI (NT) Ltd, 2001–05; Martin Currie Global Portfolio Trust (formerly Martin Currie Portfolio Investment Trust) plc (Sen. Ind. Dir), 2001–13; Oval Insce, 2003–06; Fidelity Special Values plc (Sen. Ind. Dir), 2008–15; Artisanal Spirits Co. Ltd, 2016–; HotHouse Brands Ltd, 2016–; Aye Ltd, 2016–. Non-executive Director: Scottish Financial Enterprise, 2001–08; Edinburgh Internat. Sci. Fest., 2008–15. Patron, 2003–09, Chm., 2009–17, Nat. Galls of Scotland. Mem., Speculative Soc. FRSE 2014. *Publications:* Higher Education Financial Yearbook, 1993; Further Education Financial Yearbook, 1993. *Recreations:* athletics, tennis, ski-ing, art, opera. *Address:* 33 Inverleith Terrace, Edinburgh EH3 5NU. *Clubs:* New (Edinburgh); Edinburgh Athletics.

**THOMSON, Caroline, (Lady Liddle);** Chair: Digital UK, since 2013 (non-executive Director, 2006–12); Trustees, Oxfam GB, since 2017 (Trustee, since 2017); *b* 15 May 1954; *d* of Baron Thomson of Monifieth, KT, PC; *m* 1st, 1977, Ian Bradley (marr. diss. 1980); 2nd, 1983, Roger John Liddle (*see* Baron Liddle); one *s*. Mary Datchelor Grammar Sch.; Univ. of York (BA Hons). BBC trainee, 1975–77; producer: Analysis, BBC Radio, 1978–81; Panorama, 1982; Political Advr to Rt Hon. Roy Jenkins, 1983; Commng Ed., Business and Sci., 1984–90, Hd, Corporate Affairs, 1991–95, Channel 4; Dep. Chief Exec., BBC World Service, 1995–2000; Dir, Public Policy, 2000–04, Strategy, 2004–06, Chief Operating Officer, 2007–12, BBC; Exec. Dir, English Nat. Ballet, 2013–16 (Trustee, 2016–). Non-executive Director: Pensions Regulator, 2005–09; NHS Trust Develt Authy, 2013–16; UK Govt Investments (formerly Shareholder Exec.), 2014– (Chm., Remuneration Cttee, 2016–); NHS Improvement, 2016–17 (Chm., Appts Cttee, 2016–17). Non-executive Director: CN Gp, 2012–18; Vitec plc, 2015 (Chm., Remuneration Cttee, 2015–); London First, 2016–18. Trustee: One World Broadcasting Trust, 2001–08; National Gall., 2008–16 (Dep. Chair, 2012–16); Tullie Hse Mus. and Gall., Carlisle, 2010–; The Conservatoire, 2016–. Mem. Council, Univ. of York, 2015–. Pres., Prix Italia, 2005–08. FRTS, 2007. Hon. Fellow, Univ. of Cumbria, 2015. DUniv York, 2013. *Recreations:* Italy, Cumbria, domesticity, singing.

**THOMSON, Catherine;** *see* Blee, C.

**THOMSON, Rev. Canon Celia Stephana Margaret;** Canon Residentiary, Gloucester Cathedral, since 2003; *b* Ripon, N Yorks, 19 Dec. 1955; *d* of late Duncan Thomson and Stephana Thomson. *Educ:* St Swithun's, Winchester; Lady Margaret Hall, Oxford (BA Modern History 1977); Birkbeck Coll., London (MA Renaissance Studies 1987); King's Coll., London (MA Religious Studies 1994); Salisbury and Wells Theol Coll. Eur. Res. Manager, Franklin Mint, 1978–85; self-employed in res. and public relns, 1985–89; ordained deacon, 1991, priest, 1994; Curate, St Barnabas, Southfields, 1991–95; Vicar, Christ Church, W Wimbledon, 1995–2003. Tutor in Ethics, SE Inst. of Theol Educn, 1995–2000; Vocations Advr, Lambeth Archdeaconry, 1995–2000. Mem., Gen. Synod, 2008–15 (Member: Clergy Discipline Commn, 2011–15; Cathedrals Fabric Commn for England, 2011–16). Mem., Exec. Cttee, Assoc. of English Cathedrals, 2016–. *Publications:* The Book of Ripon, 1978; (jtly) Gloucester Cathedral—Faith, Art and Architecture: 1000 years, 2010. *Recreations:* classical music especially opera and chamber music, singing, playing chamber music, walking, gardening, reading. *Address:* 3 Miller's Green, Gloucester GL1 2BN. *T:* (01452) 415824. *E:* celia.thomson@gloucestercathedral.org.uk.

**THOMSON, Sir David;** *see* Thomson, Sir F. D. D.

**THOMSON, Rt Rev. David,** DPhil, FSA, FRHistS; Bishop Suffragan of Huntingdon, 2008–18; an Honorary Assistant Bishop, Diocese of Hereford, since 2019; *b* 2 Feb. 1952; *s* of Canon Ronald and Coral Thomson; *m* 1974, Jean Elliot Douglas-Jones; two *s* two *d*. *Educ:* Keble Coll., Oxford (MA, DPhil 1978); Selwyn Coll., Cambridge (BA 1980, MA 1984); Westcott House, Cambridge. FSA 2008; FRHistS 2008. Lectr, Wentworth Castle Coll. of Educn, 1976–78. Ordained deacon, 1981, priest, 1982; Curate, Maltby Team Ministry, 1981–84; Team Vicar, Banbury, 1984–94; Team Rector, Cockermouth, 1994–2002; Archdeacon of Carlisle and Canon Residentiary, 2002–08; Interim Bishop of St Edmundsbury and Ipswich, 2013–15. Mem., Gen. Synod, 2013–15. Vice-Chair, Nat. Soc. and Bd of Educn, 2013–15; Chair, Schs Develt Gp, Nat. Soc., 2015–17. Sen. Mem., St Edmund's Coll., Cambridge, 2012–; Vis. Fellow, St John's Coll., Durham, 2015–; Hon. Fellow, Dept of Hist., Durham Univ., 2018–. Hon. Canon, Ely Cathedral, 2008–18. Gov., Trinity Sch., Carlisle, 2002–08 (Chair, 2003–05). Sec., Parish and People, 1984–93. Chair: Little Gidding Council of Reference, 2012–18; Cambs Historic Churches Trust, 2016–18. *Publications:* A Descriptive Catalogue of Middle English Grammatical Texts, 1979; An Edition of the Middle English Grammatical Texts, 1984; A Journey with John, 2004; Lent with Luke, 2005; Christmas by Candlelight, 2006; Ways to Pray, 2007; contribs to collaborative works; articles in learned jls on medieval and theol subjects. *Recreations:* medieval studies, detective fiction, crosswords, fine art. *Address:* 31 Apple Grove, Hereford HR4 0EA. *T:* 07771 864550. *E:* david@skypilots.co.uk.

**THOMSON, David;** writer and film critic; *b* London, 1941; *m* Lucy Gray; two *s. Educ:* Dulwich Coll.; London Sch. of Film Technique. Film studies teacher, then Hd, Film Studies, Dartmouth Coll., New Hants; Hd of Film, then Feature Producer, subseq. writer, BBC; various posts with Penguin. Contribs to Independent on Sunday, New York Times, New Republic, Sight and Sound, Film Comment, Movieline, Salon. *Publications:* Wild Excursions: the life and fiction of Laurence Sterne, 1972; A Biographical Dictionary of the Cinema, 1975, 5th edn, as The New Biographical Dictionary of Film, 2010; Suspects (novel), 1985; Warren Beatty and Desert Eyes: a life and a story, 1987; Silver Light (novel), 1990; Showman: life of David O. Selznick, 1993; Rosebud: the story of Orson Welles, 1996; 4–2, 1996; Big Sleep, 1997; Alien Quartet, 1998; Beneath Mulholland: thoughts on Hollywood and its ghosts, 1998; (with Lucy Gray) In Nevada: the land, the people, God and chance, 2000; Hollywood: a celebration!, 2001; The Whole Equation: a history of Hollywood, 2005; Nicole Kidman, 2006; Have You Seen…?, 2008; The Moment of Psycho: how Alfred Hitchcock taught America to love murder, 2010; The Big Screen: the story of the movies and what they did to us, 2012; Why Acting Matters, 2015; Warner Bros: the making of an American movie studio, 2017.

**THOMSON, David Michael;** QC (Scot.) 2017; *b* Glasgow, 1 Sept. 1973; *s* of Henry Geddes Thomson and Lucy Elliott Thomson; *m* 2008, Gayle Richardson; two *s. Educ:* Jordanhill Coll. Sch., Glasgow; Univ. of Glasgow (LLB Hons; DipLP). Admitted as solicitor, 1995; in practice as solicitor, 1995–2003; devil, 2003–04, Advocate, 2004–, Faculty of Advocates; Standing Junior Counsel: to Scottish Govt, 2005–09; to Advocate Gen. for Scotland, 2009–18. Scottish Ed., Mithani on Directors' Disqualification, 2014–. *Recreations:* Partick Thistle FC, sport, literature, friends. *Address:* Advocates' Library, Parliament House, Parliament Square, Edinburgh EH1 1RF. *T:* (0131) 226 5071. *E:* david.thomson@axiomadvocates.com. *Club:* Western (Glasgow).

**THOMSON, David Paget,** RD 1969; *b* 19 March 1931; *s* of Sir George Paget Thomson, FRS, Nobel Laureate, and Kathleen Buchanan Smith; *m* 1959, Patience Mary, *d* of Sir William Lawrence Bragg, CH, OBE, MC, FRS, Nobel Laureate; two *s* two *d. Educ:* Rugby Sch.; Grenoble Univ.; Trinity Coll., Cambridge (MA). Nat. Service, RN (Sub-Lieut), 1953–55; subseq. Lieut-Comdr RNR. Lazard Bros & Co., 1956, Director, 1965–86; seconded to HM Diplomatic Service, 1971–73, as Counsellor (Economic), Bonn. Dir Gen., BIEC, 1987–90. Chairman: Kleinwort, subseq. Dresdner RCM, Emerging Markets Trust, 1993–2002; Medical Sickness Annuity and Life Assce Soc. Ltd, 1995–97; Dep. Chm., Permanent Insce Co., 1995–97; Director: Finance Co. Viking, Zurich, 1969–87; Richard Daus & Co., bankers, Frankfurt, 1974–81; Applied Photophysics, 1976–87; Wesleyan Assce Soc. Ltd, 1997–2000; Foreign & Colonial European Investment Trust, 1998–2002. Mem., Monopolies and Mergers Commn, 1984–94. Member: Council, Brunel Univ., 1974–85; Court of Governors, Henley Management Coll., 1979–94. Hon. Treasurer, British Dyslexia Assoc., 1984–86. Chairman: Fitzwilliam Mus. Trust, Cambridge, 1988–93; Portsmouth Naval Base Property Trust, 1992–98; Royal Institution: Treasurer, 1976–81; Chm. Council, 1985. CC Oxon 1985–89. Master, Plumbers' Co., 1980–81. *Recreations:* hill-walking, gardening, real tennis. *Address:* Queens Croft, 16a Castle Street, Wallingford, Oxon OX10 8DW. *T:* (01491) 837161. *Club:* Athenæum (Chm., 1995–98).

*See also B. J. P. Thomson.*

**THOMSON, Maj.-Gen. David Phillips,** CB 1993; CBE 1989; MC 1965; Senior Army Member, Royal College of Defence Studies, 1992–95; *b* 30 Jan. 1942; *s* of Cyril Robert William Thomson and Louise Mary Thomson (*née* Phillips). *Educ:* Eastbourne Coll.; RMA Sandhurst. Commnd, Argyll and Sutherland Highlanders, 1962; despatches, 1968; Bde Major, 6th Armd Bde, 1975; Instr, Staff Coll., 1980; CO, 1st Bn, A and SH, 1982; Chief of Staff: RMCS, 1985; 1st Armd Div., 1986; Comdr, 1st Inf. Bde/UK Mobile Force, 1987; despatches, 1992. Col, Argyll and Sutherland Highlanders, 1992–2000. Captain, Royal Castle of Tarbert, 1992–2000. Chm., Sussex Combined Services Museum Trust, 1995–2007. FRGS 1993. *Recreations:* golf, historical research. *Address:* Home HQ, Argyll and Sutherland Highlanders, The Castle, Stirling FK8 1EH. *T:* (01786) 475165.

**THOMSON, Dick;** HM Diplomatic Service, retired; Consul General, Barcelona, 1999–2002; *b* 18 Dec. 1942; *s* of Adam and Janet Alexander Thomson; *m* 1972, Jacqueline Margaret Dunn (*d* 2003); one *s* one *d. Educ:* Port Glasgow High Sch.; Greenock High Sch. With Ministry of Transport, 1961–66; entered FCO, 1966; served: Havana, 1969–70; Athens, 1970–71; Rome, 1971–72; Warsaw, 1972–73; Personnel Dept, FCO, 1973–76; San Francisco, 1976–80; Consul, Algiers, 1980–83; Near East and N Africa Dept, FCO, 1984–87; First Sec., Copenhagen, 1988–92; Head of Parly Relns Unit, FCO, 1992–95; Ambassador to Dominican Republic, 1995–98. *Recreations:* mainly sport—soccer, tennis, swimming. *Address:* 202 Chesterfield Drive, Sevenoaks, Kent TN13 2EH.

**THOMSON, Duncan,** PhD; Keeper, Scottish National Portrait Gallery, 1982–97; *b* 2 Oct. 1934; *s* of Duncan Murdoch Thomson and Jane McFarlane Wilson; *m* 1964, Julia Jane Macphail; one *d. Educ:* Airdrie Acad.; Univ. of Edinburgh (MA 1956, PhD 1970; Hon. Fellow, 1998); Edinburgh Coll. of Art (Cert. of Coll.); Post-Dip. Scholarship); Moray House Coll. of Educn. Teacher of Art, 1959–67; Asst Keeper, Scottish National Portrait Gall., 1967–82. Scottish Arts Council: Mem., Art Cttee, 1983–89; Chm., Exhibn Panel, 1985–89. Chm., Mansfield Traquair Trust, 1996–. Vice-Pres., Art in Healthcare, 2007–14 (Mem. Bd, 2014–). Mem., Editl Bd, Scottish Cultural Resources Access Network, 1998–2004. *Publications:* The Life and Art of George Jamesone, 1974; Sir Henry Raeburn, 1994; Arikha, 1994; (jtly) The Skating Minister, 2004; A History of the Scottish National Portrait Gallery, 2011; *exhibition catalogues:* A Virtuous and Noble Education, 1971; Painting in Scotland 1570–1650, 1975; Eye to Eye, 1980; (jtly) John Michael Wright, 1982; (jtly) The Queen's Image, 1987; Raeburn: the art of Sir Henry Raeburn 1756–1823, 1997; (jtly) Avigdor Arikha From Life, 2006; contrib. to Burlington Mag., Walpole Soc., British Art Jl. *Recreation:* reading poetry (and thinking about writing it). *Address:* 3 Eglinton Crescent, Edinburgh EH12 5DH. *T:* (0131) 225 6430. *Club:* Scottish Arts (Edinburgh).

**THOMSON, Elaine Margaret;** Bid Manager, Absoft Ltd, 2014–16 (Logistics SAP Consultant, 1995–99; Support Centre Manager, 2003–09; Senior Public Sector Specialist, 2009–14); *b* 10 Aug. 1957; *d* of Dr Charles Thomson and Moira Thomson; partner, Archie Flockhart. *Educ:* Aberdeen Univ. (BSc Pure Sci.); Robert Gordon Univ. (Postgraduate Cert. in Corporate Communications and Public Affairs). Analyst/Programmer, ABB Vetco Gray UK Ltd, 1982–94. MSP (Lab) Aberdeen N, 1999–2003; contested same seat, 2003, 2007. Chair, Cornerstone (formerly Cornerstone Community Care), 2005–12 (non-exec. Dir, 2003–); Dir, Corners Turned, social enterprise co., 2008–12. *Recreations:* gardening, walking, learning French, reading, ski-ing. *E:* Elaine@elainethomson.com.

**THOMSON, Sir (Frederick Douglas) David,** 3rd Bt *cr* 1929; farmer; *b* 14 Feb. 1940; *s* of Sir James Douglas Wishart Thomson, 2nd Bt, and Evelyn Margaret Isabel, (Bettina), *d* of Lt-Comdr D. W. S. Douglas, RN; *S* father, 1972; *m* 1967, Caroline Anne (marr. diss. 1994), *d* of Major Timothy Stuart Lewis; two *s* one *d. Educ:* Eton; University College,

Oxford (BA Agric). Ben Line, 1961–89; Chairman: Through Transport Mutual Insce Ltd, 1983–2008 (Dir, 1973–2013); Britannia Steam Ship Insurance Assoc. Ltd, 1986–2008 (Dir, 1965–2008); S. A. Meacock, 1996–2019. Mem., Queen's Body Guard for Scotland, Royal Company of Archers. *Recreations:* shooting, music. *Heir: s* Simon Douglas Charles Thomson, *b* 16 June 1969. *Address:* Holylee, Walkerburn, Peeblesshire EH43 6BD. *T:* 07831 355691. *E:* sirdthomson@holylee.go-plus.net. *Club:* Boodle's.

**THOMSON, Jacqueline;** *see* Taylor, J.

**THOMSON, James Phillips Spalding;** Consultant Surgeon, St Mark's Hospital, 1974–99, now Emeritus (Clinical Director, 1990–97); Administrator, Priory Church of St Bartholomew the Great, 2000–02; Master, Sutton's Hospital in Charterhouse, 2001–12; *b* 2 Oct. 1939; *s* of late Peggy Marion Thomson (*née* Phillips) and James Laing Spalding Thomson, MB ChB, MRCGP; *m* 1968, Dr Anne Katharine (*née* Richards), MB BS, MRCP, DCH; one *s* three *d. Educ:* Haileybury and Imperial Service Coll.; Middlesex Hosp. Med. Sch., Univ. of London (MB BS 1962; MS 1974). LRCP, MRCS, 1962, FRCS 1969; DObst RCOG 1964. Jun. med. and surgical appts, 1962–71; Demonstrator, Dept of Anatomy, 1964–66, Lectr, Dept of Surgery, 1971–74, Middlesex Hosp. Med. Sch.; Consultant Surgeon: Royal Northern Hosp., 1975–77; Hackney Hosp., 1977–86; Homerton Hosp., 1986–90. Hon. Consultant Surgeon: St John's Hosp. for Diseases of the Skin, 1973–75; St Mary's Hosp., 1982–99; St Luke's Hosp. for the Clergy, 1976–99; Civil Cons. in Surgery, RAF, 1984–99, now Hon. Civil Cons.; Civilian Cons. in Colorectal Surgery, RN, 1986–99, now Emeritus Cons. in Surgery; Hon. Lectr in Surgery, Bart's Hosp. Med. Coll., 1977–94; Hon. Clin. Sen. Lectr in Surgery, Imperial Coll. Sch. of Medicine at St Mary's (formerly St Mary's Hosp. Med. Sch., Imperial Coll.), London, 1994–99. Hon. Cons. Advr in Surgery, Ileostomy Assoc., 1986–99. Examr in Surgery, Univs of Cambridge, Liverpool and London; Mem., Court of Examrs, RCS, 1986–92. Mem., UK Develt Cttee, Anglican Centre in Rome, 2013–18. President: Section of Coloproctology, RSocMed, 1994–95; Travelling Surgical Soc., 1998–2001; St Mark's Assoc., 1999; Hunterian Soc., 2001–02; Friends of St Mark's Hosp., 2006–18; Haileybury Soc., 2006–07; Patron and Fellow, Burgon Soc., 2002– (Pres., 2011–16); Patron, Walbrook Music Trust, 2011–. Chm., Notarial Adv. Bd, 2008–10. Vice-Chm. of Council and Trustee, 1992–2004, Vice Pres., 2016–, St Luke's Healthcare (formerly Hosp.) for the Clergy; Trustee: Med. Coll. of St Bartholomew's Hosp. Trust, 2002–11; St Andrew Holborn Church Foundn, 2003–11; Rev. Dr George Richards Charity, 2001–11; Tancred's Charities, 2001–11. Governor, Clergy Support Trust (formerly Corp. of Sons of the Clergy and Friends of the Clergy), 1988–. Ed., Kalendar of Holy Days approved for use in Dio. London, 2012–19. Liveryman: Apothecaries' Soc., 1980–; Barbers' Co., 1992–; Merchant Taylors' Co., 2014–. Mem., Order of Our Lady of Walsingham, 2010–. Hon. Fellow, QMUL, 2007. Frederick Salmon Medal, RSocMed, 1996; William Harvey Medal, QMUL, 2012; St Mellitus Medal, Dio. London, 2016. DM Lambeth, 1987. *Publications:* (jtly) Colorectal Disease, 1981; (jtly) Frontiers in Colorectal Disease, 1986; (jtly) Updates in Coloproctology, 1992; (jtly) Stained Glass Windows of Lambeth Palace Chapel: a guide, 2014; contribs to books and learned jls. *Recreations:* church music and architecture, heraldry, railways, canals, guide at Lambeth Palace. *Address:* Gallery House, 13 New Street, Holt, Norfolk NR25 6JJ. *T:* (01263) 711214, 07550 079522; 15 Nelson Terrace, N1 8DG. *T:* (020) 7253 1052. *E:* JamesPSThomson@aol.com. *Clubs:* Athenæum, Royal Society of Medicine.

**THOMSON, Rt Rev. John Bromilow;** *see* Selby, Bishop Suffragan of.

**THOMSON, Kenneth Andrew Lyons;** Director-General, Constitution and External Affairs (formerly Strategy and External Affairs, then Strategy and Operations), Scottish Government, since 2011; *b* 18 Oct. 1962; *s* of Andrew Leslie Thomson and Jennifer Thomson (*née* Lyons); *m* 1986, Ursula Schlapp; one *s* one *d. Educ:* Inch and Cramond Prim. Schs; Royal High Sch., Edinburgh; Univ. of St Andrews (MA Hons Music); Open Univ. (MBA). Supernumerary Lightkeeper, Northern Lighthouse Bd, 1980–83; Admin. Trainee, Civil Service, Scottish Office, 1988; Higher Exec. Officer (Develt) 1988–90; Pvte Sec. to Minister of State, Scottish Office, 1990–91; Principal Officer, 1991; Asst Dir, Scottish Financial Enterprise, 1991–93; project team, Setting Forth, 1993–96; Bill Manager, Crime and Punishment (Scotland) Act, 1996–97; work on white paper, 'Scotland's Parliament', 1997; Asst Sec., 1997; Principal Pvte Sec. to Sec. of State for Scotland, 1997–99, to First Minister of Scotland, 1999; Dir, Corporate Develt, 1999–2000, Hd, Health Improvement Strategy Div., 2000–02, Scottish Exec.; Dir, Corporate Services, Scottish Prison Service, 2002–05; Dir, Constitutional and Parly Secretariat, Scottish Exec., 2005–07; Dir, Constitution Law and Cts, 2007–10, Dir, Constitution, subseq. International and Constitution, Scottish Govt, 2010–11. Trustee, Dunedin Concerts Trust, 2007–12. *Recreations:* cooking, consort music, crosswords, cycling. *Address:* c/o Scottish Government, St Andrew's House, Edinburgh EH1 3DG.

**THOMSON, Malcolm George;** QC (Scot.) 1987; *b* 6 April 1950; *s* of late George Robert Thomson, OBE, and Daphne Ethel Thomson; *m* 1st, 1978, Susan Gordon Aitken (marr. diss. 2001); two *d*; 2nd, 2008, Maybel Hutton. *Educ:* Edinburgh Acad.; Edinburgh Univ. (LLB). Advocate 1974; called to the Bar, Lincoln's Inn, 1991. Standing Junior Counsel to Dept of Agriculture and Fisheries for Scotland and Forestry Commn in Scotland, 1982–87. Chm., NHS Tribunal (Scotland), 1995–2005; Mem., Scottish Legal Aid Bd, 1998–2006; Temp. Judge, Court of Session, 2002–17. Trustee, Nat. Liby of Scotland, 1995–2013. *Recreations:* sailing, ski-ing. *Address:* 12 Succoth Avenue, Edinburgh EH12 6BT. *T:* (0131) 337 4911. *Club:* New (Edinburgh).

**THOMSON, Mark Cameron Angus,** CMG 2015; OBE 2004; human rights defender; Secretary General, Association for the Prevention of Torture, 2001–18; *b* Redhill, 21 May 1956; *s* of Sir John Sutherland, (Sir Ian), Thomson, KBE, CMG, MBE (mil.) and Nancy Marguerite Thomson; *m* 1992, Catherine Girod; two *s* one *d. Educ:* Drasa Avenue Sch., Lautoka, Fiji; Grenville Coll., Bideford; Univ. of Essex (BA Latin Amer. Studies 1979); University Coll. London (MA Rural Develt in Latin America 1982). Coordinator, Nicaragua Solidarity Campaign, 1982–84; Community Educn Officer, Tower Hamlets Internat. Solidarity, 1984–88; Latin America and Caribbean Prog. Officer, World Univ. Service, 1988–91; Inter-govtl Orgns Coordinator, Amnesty Internat., 1991–92; Dep. Dir, Internat. Service for Human Rights, 1992–2001. *Recreation:* trying to keep my wife happy. *Address:* 33 Chemin de la Colline, Petit Lancy, 1213 Geneva, Switzerland. *T:* (22) 7924204. *E:* mcathomson@hotmail.com. *Club:* Mosquito Coasters Football.

**THOMSON, Sir Mark (Wilfrid Home),** 3rd Bt *cr* 1925, of Old Nunthorpe, Co. York; *b* 29 Dec. 1939; *s* of Sir Ivo Wilfrid Home Thomson, 2nd Bt and Sybil Marguerite, *yr d* of C. W. Thompson; *S* father, 1991; *m* 1st, 1976, Lady Jacqueline Rufus Isaacs (marr. diss. 1997), *o d* of 3rd Marquess of Reading, MBE, MC; three *s* one *d* (incl. twin *s*); 2nd, 2002, April MacKenzie Russell (*née* Arbon). *Heir: s* Albert Mark Home Thomson [*b* 3 Aug. 1979; *m* 2012, Olivia J. Hill; twin *s*].

**THOMSON, Michelle Rhonda;** Director, Momentous Change Ltd, since 2017; *b* 15 March 1965; *m* Peter Thomson; two *c. Educ:* Royal Scottish Acad. of Music and Drama; Abertay Univ. (MSc IT). Professional musician, 1985; Prog. Manager and Project Manager, Standard Life, 1991–2006; Prog. Manager and Portfolio Manager, Royal Bank of Scotland

Gp, 2006–08; Dir, Your Property Shop, 2009–15. Founder Mem. and Exec. Bd Mem., Business for Scotland, 2012–14; Bd Mem., Revive. MP for Edinburgh W, 2015–17 (SNP, May–Oct. 2015, Ind, Oct. 2015–2017). Mem., Business, Innovation and Skills Select Cttee, 2015; Ambassador, All Party Parly Gp for Fair Business Banking.

**THOMSON, Peter Alexander Bremner,** CVO 1986; HM Diplomatic Service, retired; *b* 16 Jan. 1938; *s* of Alexander Thomson, financial journalist, and Dorothy (*née* Scurr); *m* 1965, Lucinda Sellar; three *s*. *Educ:* Canford School; RN College, Dartmouth; Sch. of Oriental and African Studies, London (BA 1970; MPhil 1975; MA 1991). Sub Lieut and Lieut RN in HM Ships Albion, Plover, Tiger, Ark Royal, Eagle; Lt Comdr ashore in Taiwan and Hong Kong; joined Diplomatic Service, 1975; First Sec., FCO, Lagos, Hong Kong, 1975–84; Counsellor, Peking, 1984–87; High Comr, Belize, 1987–90; Counsellor, FCO, 1991–95; High Comr, Seychelles, 1995–97. *Publications:* Belize: a concise history, 2005. *Recreations:* sailing, walking. *Address:* The Red House, Charlton Horethorne, near Sherborne DT9 4NL.

**THOMSON, Prof. Richard Geoffrey,** FRCP, FFPH; Professor of Epidemiology and Public Health, Institute of Health and Society, since 1999, and Associate Dean for Patient and Public Engagement, Faculty of Medical Sciences, Newcastle Medical School, 2010–16, University of Newcastle upon Tyne; *b* 2 May 1958; *s* of Lesley Bambridge and Honor Thomson (*née* Gooding); *m* 1989, Tracy Robson; two *d*. *Educ:* Stamford Sch., Stamford; St Edmund Hall, Oxford (BA Physiol. 1979; BM BCh 1982); Univ. of Newcastle upon Tyne (MD 1990). FRCP 1996; FFPH 1996. Sen. House Officer, Medicine, Freeman Hosp., Newcastle upon Tyne, 1983–85; Res. Fellow, Newcastle upon Tyne Univ., 1985–88; Registrar, then Sen. Registrar in Public Health, 1988–89, Dir, Service Quality and Standards, 1989–92, Northern RHA; Sen. Lectr and Consultant in Public Health, Medical Sch., Newcastle upon Tyne Univ., 1992–99. Director: UK Quality Indicator Proj., 1997–2007; Epidemiology and Res., Nat. Patient Safety Agency, 2004–07. Mem., Steering Gp on Internat. Patient Safety Classification, WHO, 2005–07. Mem., 13th Club. Associate Editor, Quality and Safety in Health Care, 1991–2010. *Publications:* numerous articles in professional jls on risk communication and decision making, stroke epidemiology, health care quality and safety, and health services research. *Recreations:* tennis, literature, theatre, good food, fine wine, sitting with a fishing rod contemplating. *Address:* Institute of Health and Society, Newcastle University, Baddiley-Clark Building, Richardson Road, Newcastle upon Tyne NE2 4AX. *T:* (0191) 208 8760, *Fax:* (0191) 208 8422. *E:* richard.thomson@newcastle.ac.uk.

**THOMSON, Prof. Richard Ian,** PhD; FRSE; Watson Gordon Professor of Fine Art, University of Edinburgh, since 1996; *b* 1 March 1953; *s* of late Rev. George Ian Falconer Thomson and Mary Josephine Lambart Thomson (*née* Dixon); *m* 1978, Belinda Jane Greaves; two *s*. *Educ:* Shrewsbury Sch.; St Catherine's Coll., Oxford (Exhibnr; BA); Univ. of Oxford (Dip. Hist. of Art); Courtauld Inst. of Art, Univ. of London (MA; PhD 1989). FRSE 1998. Lectr, 1977–88, Sen. Lectr, 1988–95, Reader, 1995–96, in History of Art, Univ. of Manchester. Guest Scholar, J. Paul Getty Mus., Malibu, 1993; Van Gogh Vis. Fellow, Univ. of Amsterdam, 2007; Slade Prof. of Fine Art, Univ. of Oxford, 2008–09. Trustee, Nat. Galls of Scotland, 2002–10; Member, Comité Scientifique: Institut National d'Histoire de l'Art, Paris, 2008–14; Musée d'Orsay, Paris, 2010–17. Exhibitions curated or co-curated: Harold Gilman, 1981–82; Impressionist Drawings, 1986; The Private Degas, 1987; Camille Pissarro: impressionism, landscape and rural labour, 1990; Toulouse-Lautrec, 1991–92; Monet to Matisse: landscape painting in France 1874–1914, 1994; Seurat and the Bathers, 1997; Theo van Gogh, 1999; Monet 1878–1883: the Seine and the Sea, 2003; Toulouse-Lautrec and Montmartre, 2005; Degas, Sickert and Toulouse-Lautrec: London and Paris 1870–1910, 2005; Monet, 1840–1926, 2010–11; Dreams of Nature: Symbolist landscape from Van Gogh to Kandinsky, 2012–13; Splendeurs et Misères: Images de la prostitution en France, 1850–1910, 2015; Seurat's Circus Sideshow, 2017; Monet and Architecture, 2018. Commandeur, l'Ordre des Arts et des Lettres, 2018 (Officier, 2012). *Publications:* Toulouse-Lautrec, 1977; French Nineteenth Century Drawings in the Whitworth Art Gallery, 1981; Seurat, 1985; Degas, the Nudes, 1988; Edgar Degas, Waiting, 1995; (ed) Framing France, 1998; (ed jtly) Soil and Stone: impressionism, urbanism, environment, 2003; The Troubled Republic: visual culture and social debate in France 1889–1900, 2004; Vincent van Gogh: Starry Night, 2008; Art of the Actual, Naturalism and Style in Early Third Republic France 1880–1900, 2012. *Recreations:* gardening, jazz, hill walking. *Address:* History of Art, University of Edinburgh, Hunter Building, Lauriston Place, Edinburgh EH3 9DF. *T:* (0131) 650 4124, *Fax:* (0131) 650 6638. *E:* R.Thomson@ed.ac.uk.

**THOMSON, Robert James;** Chief Executive Officer, News Corporation, since 2013; *b* 11 March 1961; *s* of Jim and Gen Thomson; *m* 1992, Wang Ping; two *s*. *Educ:* Royal Melbourne Inst. of Technol. (BA Journalism). Finance and gen. affairs reporter, The Herald, Melbourne, then Sydney, 1979–83; Sen. Feature Writer, Sydney Morning Herald, 1983–85; Financial Times: Beijing corresp., 1985–89; Tokyo corresp., 1989–94; Foreign News Ed., 1994–96; Asst Ed., and Ed., Weekend FT, 1996–98; Man. Ed., based in NY, 1998–2002; Ed., The Times, 2002–07; Publisher, 2007–08, Ed.-in-Chief, 2008–12, Dow Jones & Co.; Man. Ed., Wall Street Journal, 2008–12. Dir, Soc. of Amer. Business Editors and Writers, 2001–02. *Publications:* The Judges: a portrait of the Australian judiciary, 1986; (jtly) The Chinese Army, 1990; (ed) True Fiction, 1998. *Recreations:* reading, tennis, cinema. *Address:* News Corporation, 1211 Avenue of Americas, New York, NY 10036, USA.

**THOMSON, Prof. Robert William,** PhD; FBA 1995; Calouste Gulbenkian Professor of Armenian Studies, University of Oxford, 1992–2001, now Professor Emeritus; Fellow of Pembroke College, Oxford, 1992–2001, now Supernumerary Fellow; *b* 24 March 1934; *s* of late David William Thomson and Lilian (*née* Cramphorn); *m* 1963, Judith Ailsa Cawdry; two *s*. *Educ:* George Watson's Boys' Coll., Edinburgh; Sidney Sussex Coll., Cambridge (BA 1955); Trinity Coll., Cambridge (PhD 1962). Halki Theol. Coll., Istanbul, 1955–56; Jun. Fellow, Dumbarton Oaks, Washington, 1960–61; Louvain Univ., 1961–62; Harvard University: Instructor, then Asst Prof. of Classical Armenian, Dept of Near Eastern Langs, 1963–69; Mashtots Prof. of Armenian Studies, 1969–92; Chm., Dept of Near Eastern Langs, 1973–78, 1980–81. Dir, Dumbarton Oaks, Washington DC, 1984–89. Hon. PhD Tübingen, 2003. *Publications:* (ed with J. N. Birdsall) Biblical and Patristic Studies in Memory of Robert Pierce Casey, 1963; Athanasiana Syriaca, 4 parts, 1965–77; Athanasius: Contra Gentes and De Incarnatione, 1971; The Teaching of Saint Gregory, 1971, 2nd edn 2001; Introduction to Classical Armenian, 1975; Agathangelos: history of the Armenians, 1977; (with K. B. Bardakjian) Textbook of Modern Western Armenian, 1977; Moses Khorenatsi: history of the Armenians, 1978, 2nd edn 2006; Elishe: history of Vardan, 1982; (ed with N. G. Garsoian and T. J. Mathews) East of Byzantium, 1982; (with B. Kendall) David the Invincible Philosopher, 1983; Thomas Artsruni: history of the Artsruni House, 1985; The Armenian Version of Dionysius the Areopagite, 2 vols, 1987; Lazar Parpetsi: history of the Armenians, 1991; Studies in Armenian Literature and Christianity, 1994; The Syriac Version of the Hexaemeron by Basil of Caesarea, 1995; A Bibliography of Classical Armenian Literature, 1995; Rewriting Caucasian History: the Armenian version of the Georgian Chronicles, 1996; (ed with J.-P. Mahé) From Byzantium to Iran: Armenian studies in honour of Nina G. Garsoian, 1997; (with J. Howard-Johnston) The Armenian History of Sebeos, 1999; The Lawcode of Mxit'ar Gosh, 2000; The Armenian Adaptation of the Ecclesiastical History of Socrates Scholasticus, 2001; Hamam: commentary on Proverbs, 2005; Nerses of Lambron: commentary on Revelation, 2007; The Lives of Saint Gregory, 2010; Saint Basil and Armenian Cosmology, 2012; Nonnus of Nisibis: commentary on Gospel of St John, 2014; Nersēs of Lambron: commentary on the dormition of Saint John, 2017; contribs to Jl Theol Studies, Le Muséon, Revue des études arméniennes, Dumbarton Oaks Papers, Oxford Dictionary of Byzantium, Encyclopedia Iranica, The Cambridge History of the Byzantine Empire.

**THOMSON, Roderick Nicol;** QC (Scot.) 2008; *b* Paisley, Scotland, 25 Aug. 1959; *s* of Frank William Thomson and Mabel Cockburn Thomson (*née* Nicol); *m* 1989, Catriona Mary McCraw; one *s* one *d*. *Educ:* Hitchin Boys' Grammar Sch.; Morrison's Acad.; Edinburgh Univ. (BCom 1980; LLB 1982; DipLP 1983). Admitted Advocate, 1990; Standing Junior Counsel in Scotland: to FCO, 2002–08; to HMRC, 2006–08. *Recreations:* fine art, painting, photography, cinema, fishing, golf, travel. *Address:* La Paillole Rouquette, St Pompon, Dordogne 24170, France. *T:* (5) 53281689. *E:* roddythomsonqc@gmail.com.

**THOMSON, Ross;** MP (C) Aberdeen South, since 2017; *b* Aberdeen; *s* of John and Roslyne Thomson. *Educ:* Balmedie Primary Sch.; Bridge of Don Acad.; Univ. of Aberdeen (MA Politics and Internat. Relns). Work in retail sector, 2009–10; customer advr, Bank of Scotland, 2010–11; Store Trainer, Debenhams, Aberdeen. Mem. (C) Aberdeen CC, 2012–17. Mem. (C) Scotland NE, Scottish Parlt, 2016–17. Mem., Scottish Affairs Cttee, H of C, 2017–. *Recreations:* travel, photography, family. *Address:* House of Commons, SW1A 0AA; (office) 192 Holburn Street, Aberdeen AB10 6DA. *T:* (01224) 592229. *E:* ross.thomson.mp@parliament.uk.

**THOMSON, Prof. Wendy,** CBE 2005; PhD; Vice-Chancellor, University of London, since 2019; *b* Montreal, 28 Oct. 1953; *d* of Shirley and Grace Thomson; *m* 1995, David Dorne (*d* 1999); two step *s*; one *d*. *Educ:* McGill Univ. (BSW; Masters of Social Work); Univ. of Bristol (PhD 1989). Asst Chief Exec., Islington BC, 1987–93; Chief Executive: Turning Point, 1993–96; Newham BC, 1996–99; Dir of Inspection, Audit Commn, 1999–2001; Prime Minister's Advr on Public Services Reform, Cabinet Office, 2001–05; Prof. and Dir, Sch. of Social Work, McGill Univ., Montreal, 2005–14; Man. Dir, Norfolk CC, 2014–19. Adviser: Office of Pres., Republic of Ghana, 2006–09; UNDP, 2006–08; Internat. Advr, Global Forum on Re-inventing Govt, 2007. Comr, Ontario Commn on Child Welfare, 2009–12; Chm., Expert Panel on Health Care Financing, Quebec Govt, 2012–14. Non-exec. Dir, Council, UEA, 2014–. Trustee: Norwich Univ. of Arts, 2017–; Diabetes UK, 2017. *Recreations:* yoga, gardening, theatre, travel, shopping, ski-ing, tennis. *Address:* Vice-Chancellor's Office, University of London, Senate House, Malet Street, WC1E 7HU.

**'t HOOFT, Prof. Dr Gerardus;** Professor of Theoretical Physics, Utrecht University, 1977–2011; *b* 5 July 1946; *s* of H. 't Hooft and M. A. van Kampen; *m* 1972, Albertha A. Schik, MD; two *d*. *Educ:* Dalton Lyceum Gymnasium beta, The Hague; Utrecht Univ. (PhD). Fellow, Theoretical Physics Div., CERN, Geneva, 1972–74; Asst Prof., Univ. of Utrecht, 1974–77. Heineman Prize, APS, 1979; Wolf Prize, Wolf Foundn, Israel, 1982; Franklin Medal, Franklin Inst., Philadelphia, 1995; (jtly) Nobel Prize for Physics, 1999; several decorations and 11 hon. doctorates. Commandeur in de Orde van de Nederlandse Leeuw, 1999. *Publications:* De bouwstenen van de Schepping, 1992 (In Search of the Ultimate Building Blocks, 1996); Under the Spell of the Gauge Principle, 1994; Playing with Planets, 2008; (with S. Vandoren) Tijd in Machten van Tien, 2011; The Cellular Automaton Interpretation of Quantum Mechanics, 2016; over 200 scientific pubns. *Address:* Institute for Theoretical Physics, Buys Ballotgebouw, Princetonplein 5, 3584 CC Utrecht, Netherlands; (postal) Postbus 80.089, 3508 TB Utrecht, Netherlands.

**THORBURN, Andrew,** BSc; FRTPI; Principal, Thorburns, since 1990; Chairman, Bow Street Partners, 1999–2005; Founder Chairman, Ringstall Ltd, since 2011; *b* 20 March 1934; *s* of James Beresford Thorburn and Marjorie Clara Burford; *m* Margaret Anne Crack; one *s* two *d*. *Educ:* Bridport Grammar Sch.; Univ. of Southampton (BSc). MRTPI 1959, FRTPI 1969. National Service, RN, 1954–56. Planning Asst, Kent CC, 1957–59; Planning Officer, Devon CC, 1959–63; Asst County Planning Officer, Hampshire CC, 1963–68; Dir, Notts and Derbyshire Sub-Region Study, 1968–70; Dep. County Planning Dir, Cheshire CC, 1970–73; County Planning Officer, E Sussex CC, 1973–83; Chief Exec., English Tourist Bd, 1983–85; Head of Tourism and Leisure Div., Grant Thornton, 1986–90. Pres., RTPI, 1982; Mem. Exec., Town and Country Planning Assoc., 1969–81. Founder Trustee, Sussex Heritage Trust, 1978–99; Dir and Trustee, Hants Assoc. for Care of the Blind, 2016–. Fellow, Tourism Soc., 1983–2008. *Publications:* Planning Villages, 1971; The Missing Museum, 2006. *Recreation:* thinking. *Club:* Fareham Sailing and Motor Boat.

**THORLEY, Giles Alexander;** Chief Executive, Development Bank of Wales, since 2017; *b* 29 June 1967; *s* of Hugh A. Thorley and Jillian E. Thorley; *m* 1st, 1993, Michelle Britt (marr. diss. 2018); three *s*; 2nd, 2018, Georgina Eclair-Heath; one *d*. *Educ:* Hereford Cathedral Sch.; QMC, Univ. of London (LLB); Inns of Court Sch. of Law. Called to the Bar, Inner Temple, 1990. Director: Nomura Internat. plc, 1990–98; Inntrepreneur Pub Co., 1998–99; Chief Exec., Unique Pub Co. plc, 1999–2001; Exec. Chm., 2001–03, Chief Exec., 2003–10, Punch Taverns plc; Chm., Tragus Hldgs, 2005–12; Operating Partner, TDR Capital LLP, 2010–16; Chief Exec., Finance Wales plc, 2016–17. Dir and Supervisory Bd Mem., Brewers and Licensed Retailers Assoc., subseq. British Beer and Pub Assoc., 1998–2010. *Recreations:* ski-ing, watersports, hockey, cycling, the family.

**THORLEY, Simon Joe;** QC 1989; International Judge, Singapore International Commercial Court, since 2015; *b* 22 May 1950; *s* of Sir Gerald Bowers Thorley, TD and of Beryl, *d* of G. Preston Rhodes; *m* 1983, Jane Elizabeth Cockcroft (*d* 2007); two *s* one *d*. *Educ:* Rugby Sch.; Keble Coll., Oxford (MA Jurisprudence). Called to the Bar, Inner Temple, 1972, Bencher, 1999 (Reader, 2012; Treas., 2013); pupilled to William Aldous; in practice at Intellectual Property Bar (formerly Patent Bar), 1972–2014; apptd by Lord Chancellor to hear Trade Mark Appeals, 1996–2003; Dep. High Court Judge, 1998–2014. Dep. Chm., Copyright Tribunal, 1998–2006. Chm., IP Bar (formerly Patent Bar) Assoc., 1995–99; Member: Gen. Council of the Bar, 1995–99; Council, British Gp, Internat. Assoc. for Protection of Industrial Property, 1993–95; Disciplinary Cttee, Eur. Patent Orgn, 2015–. Arbitrator and Mediator, 2014–. Trustee: Addenbrooke's Charitable Trust, 2015–; Med. Coll. of St Bartholomew's Hosp. Trust, 2015– (Chm., 2019–). *Publications:* (co-ed) Terrell on The Law of Patents, 13th edn 1982 to 16th edn 2005. *Recreations:* family, shooting, opera. *Address:* Brick Court Chambers, 7–8 Essex Street, WC2R 3LD. *T:* (020) 7379 3550.

**THORN, John Leonard,** MA; writer and educational consultant; Headmaster of Winchester College, 1968–85; *b* 28 April 1925; *s* of late Stanley and Winifred Thorn; *m* 1955, Veronica Laura (*d* 1999), *d* of late Sir Robert Maconochie, OBE, QC; one *s* one *d*. *Educ:* St Paul's School; Corpus Christi College, Cambridge. Served War of 1939–45, Sub-Lieutenant, RNVR, 1943–46. Asst Master, Clifton Coll., 1949–61; Headmaster, Repton School, 1961–68. Dir, Winchester Cathedral Trust, 1986–89. Dir, Royal Opera House, Covent Garden, 1971–76. Chm. Headmasters' Conference, 1981. Member: Bd, Securities

Assoc., 1987–91; Exec. Cttee, Cancer Res. Campaign, 1987–90; Chm., Hants Bldgs Preservation Trust, 1992–96 (Vice-Chm., 1989–92); Trustee: British Museum, 1980–85; Oakham Sch., 1985–89. Governor, Stowe Sch., 1985–90; Chm. of Governors, Abingdon Sch., 1991–94. *Publications:* (jtly) A History of England, 1961; The Road to Winchester (autobiog.), 1979; various articles. *Address:* 6 Chilbolton Avenue, Winchester SO22 5HD. *T:* (01962) 855990. *Club:* Garrick.

**THORN, His Honour Roger Eric;** QC 1990; a Circuit Judge, 2004–14; *b* 23 March 1948; twin *s* of late James Douglas 'Pat' Thorn and Daphne Elizabeth (*née* Robinson); *m* 2005, Clare (marr. diss.), *d* of late George Lillywhite, OBE and of Maureen Lillywhite. *Educ:* Mill Hill Sch.; Newcastle Univ. (LLB Hons). Called to the Bar, Middle Temple, 1970 (Harmsworth Schol. and Major Exhibn; Bencher, 1999); NE Circuit, 1970–2014; Asst Recorder, 1995–99; Recorder, 1999–2004; Dep. High Ct Judge, 1999–2014. Member: Bd of Faculty of Law, Newcastle Univ., 1990–94; Advocacy Studies Bd, Bar Council, 1996–2002; Panel of Arbitrators, Bar Council, 1999; Restricted Patients Panel, Mental Health Rev. Tribunal, 2000–11; Faculty, Middle Temple Advocacy, 2004–06. Hd of Mission to Kosovo, Bar Human Rights Cttee, 2000. Liaison Judge to Law Sch., 2004–10, Mem. Ct, 2006–10, Univ. of Hull. Life Gov., Mill Hill Sch., 1994. *Publications:* A Practical Guide to Road Traffic Accident Claims, 1987, 2nd edn 1991; legal contributor to Negotiating Better Deals, by J. G. Thorn (twin *b*), 1988; (jtly) Kosovo 2000: justice not revenge, 2000. *Recreations:* theatre, music, walking, local Amenity Society (Chairman, 1986–99). *Address:* Holly House, Main Street, Corbridge, Northumberland. *Clubs:* National Liberal; Old Millhillians.

**THORNBERRY, Rt Hon. Emily;** PC 2016; MP (Lab) Islington South and Finsbury, since 2005; *b* 27 July 1960; *d* of late Sallie Thornberry; *m* 1991, Christopher George Nugee (*see* Hon. Sir C. G. Nugee); two *s* one *d. Educ:* Univ. of Kent (BA 1982). Called to the Bar, Gray's Inn, 1983; in practice, specialising in criminal law, 1985–. Shadow Energy and Climate Change Minister, 2010; Shadow Health and Social Care Minister, 2010–11; Shadow Attorney Gen., 2011–14; Shadow Defence Minister, 2016; Shadow Sec. of State for Foreign and Commonwealth Affairs, 2016–; Shadow First Sec. of State, 2017–. *Address:* (office) 65 Barnsbury Street, N1 1EJ; House of Commons, SW1A 0AA. *E:* thornberrye@parliament.uk. *W:* www.emilythornberry.com.

**THORNBERRY, Prof. Patrick,** CMG 2006; PhD; Professor of International Law, Keele University, now Emeritus; *b* Middlesbrough, 4 Dec. 1944. *Educ:* Univ. of London (LLB); Univ. of Keele (LLM; PhD). Called to the Bar, Lincoln's Inn. Vis. Fellow, Kellogg Coll., Oxford. Mem., UN Cttee on Elimination of Racial Discrimination, 2001–14 (Rapporteur, 2002–08). Former Chm., Monitoring Rights Gp Internat. *Publications:* International Law and the Rights of Minorities, 1991; Indigenous Peoples and Human Rights, 2002; (with M. A. Estebanez) Minority Rights in Europe, 2004; (contrib.) The Rights of Minorities, 2005; (contrib.) Universal Minority Rights, 2007; The International Convention on the Elimination of All Forms of Racial Discrimination: a legal commentary, 2010; contribs to Human Rights Law Rev. *Address:* School of Politics, Philosophy, International Relations and Environment, Keele University, Keele, Staffs ST5 5BG.

**THORNBURGH, Richard Lewis;** Counsel, K&L Gates (formerly Kirkpatrick & Lockhart Nicholson Graham, then Kirkpatrick & Lockhart Preston Gates Ellis) LLP, 1994–2019; *b* 16 July 1932; *s* of Charles G. and Alice S. Thornburgh; *m* 1955, Virginia Hooton (decd); *m* 1963, Virginia Judson; four *s. Educ:* Yale Univ. (BEng 1954); Univ. of Pittsburgh Sch. of Law (LLB 1957). Staff Counsel, Aluminum Co. of America, 1957–59; Associate, Kirkpatrick, Pomeroy, Lockhart & Johnson, 1959–69; US Attorney, Western District, Pennsylvania, 1969–75; Asst Attorney General, Criminal Div., US Dept of Justice, 1975–77; Partner: Kirkpatrick Lockhart, Johnson & Hutchison, 1977–79; Kirkpatrick & Lockhart LLP, 1987–88 and 1991–92; Governor, Commonwealth of Pennsylvania, 1979–87; Attorney Gen. of the USA, 1988–91; Under-Sec.-Gen. for Admin and Management, UN, 1992–93. Dir, Inst. of Politics, John F. Kennedy Sch. of Govt, 1987–88. Numerous hon. degrees. *Publications:* Where the Evidence Leads (autobiog.), 2004, rev. edn 2010; Puerto Rico's Future: a time to decide, 2007; articles in professional jls. *Address:* 2540 Massachusetts Avenue NW, Washington, DC 20008, USA.

**THORNE, Jack;** screenwriter and playwright; *b* Bristol, 6 Dec. 1978; *s* of Mike and Maggie Thorne; *m* 2013, Rachel Mason; one *s. Educ:* St Bartholomew's Comprehensive Sch., Newbury; Pembroke Coll., Cambridge (BA Social and Pol Scis). Young Labour Officer for Newbury. Writer: *television:* Skins, 2007–09; (and creator) Cast Offs, 2009; This is England '86, 2010; (and creator) The Fades, 2011; (jtly) This is England '88, 2011; (and creator) Glue, 2014; This is England '90, 2015; The Last Panthers, 2016; National Treasure, 2016; Kiri, 2018; (jtly) The Virtues, 2019; The Light, 2019; (adaptation) His Dark Materials, 2019; *films:* The Scouting Book for Boys, 2009; A Long Way Down, 2014; Wonder, 2017; The Aeronauts, 2019; *theatre:* When You Cure Me, Bush, 2005; Bunny, nat. tour, 2011; (jtly) Greenland, NT, 2011; (adaptation) The Physicist, Donmar, 2012; (adaptation) Let the Right One In, Royal Court, 2013; The Solid Life of Sugar Water, NT, 2016; Harry Potter and the Cursed Child, Palace, 2016, transf. NY, 2018; Hope, Royal Court, 2016; (adaptation) Woyzeck, Old Vic, 2017; (adaptation) A Christmas Carol, Old Vic, 2017; the end of history..., Royal Court, 2019. Member: Writers' Guild of GB; Labour Party. *Publications:* When You Cure Me, 2005; Bunny, 2011; (jtly) Greenland, 2011; The Physicist, 2012; Let the Right One In, 2013; The Solid Life of Sugar Water, 2016; Harry Potter and the Cursed Child, 2016; Hope, 2016; Woyzeck, 2017. *Recreations:* walking, swimming, hiding at the back, local politics, watching plays, films and television. *Address:* c/o Casarotto, Waverley House, 7–12 Noel Street, W1F 8GQ.

**THORNE, Katherine Harriet, (Katy);** QC 2018; *b* Chiswick, 18 Oct. 1969; *d* of Maurice Richard Thorne and Eudora Anne Thorne; *m* 1998, Oliver Charles Aaron Lewis; two *s* one *d. Educ:* Waldegrave Sch., Twickenham; Richmond Coll.; Univ. of Leeds (BA French and Mgt Studies). Called to the Bar, Inner Temple, 1994; in practice as barrister, specialising in criminal law, 1994–. Mem. (Lab), Westminster CC, 1998–2002. Founder, Women in Criminal Law, 2017–. *Publications:* (ed jtly) Mason's Forensic Medicine for Lawyers, 6th edn 2015. *Recreations:* politics, wild swimming, casual feminism. *Address:* 54 Doughty Street, WC1N 2LS. *E:* k.thorne@doughtystreet.co.uk.

**THORNE, Prof. Michael Philip,** CBE 2016; PhD; education and business development consultant, since 2016; Vice Chancellor, Anglia Ruskin University, 2007–16; *b* 19 Oct. 1951; *m* 1975, Val Swift (*d* 2011); three *s. Educ:* Queen Mary Coll., Univ. of London (BSc Hons); Univ. of Birmingham (PhD 1979). Lecturer: SE Derbyshire Coll., 1973–75; UCL, 1978–79; UC Cardiff, 1979–88; Hd, Sch. of Computing, 1989–93, Pro Vice Chancellor, 1993–97, Univ. of Sunderland; Vice Principal, Napier Univ., 1998–2001; Vice Chancellor, Univ. of E London, 2001–06. Member: Foresight Panel (Leisure and Learning), OST, 1998–2001; Scottish Further Educn Funding Council, 1999–2003; Bd, Learning and Skills Network, 2006–11; Bd, Office of the Ind. Adjudicator, 2007–16; Sci. and Res. Adv. Bd, DCMS, 2009–10. Member, Board: London Thames Gateway Develt Corp., 2004–07; Gtr Cambridge and Gtr Peterborough LEP, 2012–16. Non-exec. Dir, Scottish Univ. for Industry, 1998–2004. Mem., 2009–16, Dep. Treas., 2016–18, Sir John Cass Foundn. Formerly Chair: Open Learning Foundn; Lead Scotland; Chm., Adv. Council on Libraries, 2007–10; Mem., Adv. Council, British Library, 2008–10. Formerly Member Board:

Northern Sinfonia; Northern Jun. Philharmonic; Learning World; Northern Informatics Applications Agency; Council of Administrators, Eur. Lifelong Learning Initiative. Chair, Music Therapy Trust, 2017–. Conductor: Easter Orchestral Soc., 1991–; Edinburgh Players Opera Gp, 2001–; Saffron Opera Gp, 2014–. Radio and TV progs. FIMA; FBCS. *Publications:* contrib. acad. papers and articles. *Recreations:* music (especially Wagner operas), theatre, hill-walking. *Address:* 18 Spencer Gate, St Albans, Herts AL1 4AD. *T:* 07768 542697. *E:* mthorne51@yahoo.co.uk. *Club:* Reform.

**THORNE, Sir Neil (Gordon),** Kt 1992; OBE 1980; TD 1969; DL; *b* 8 Aug. 1932; *s* of late Henry Frederick Thorne and Ivy Gladys Thorne. *Educ:* City of London Sch.; Coll. of Estate Mgt (BSc London Univ.). FCGI; FRICS. Asst Adjt, 58 Med. Regt, RA, BAOR, 1957–59 (Chief Negotiating Officer for creation of BAOR Mil. Trng Areas in Germany, 1958). Sen. Partner, Hull & Co., Chartered Surveyors, 1962–76. Mem. Bd, Jt Docklands Develt Corp., 1973–76. Councillor, London Borough of Redbridge, 1965–68, Alderman, 1975–78; Mem., GLC and Chm., Central Area Bd, 1967–73. Contested (C) Ilford South, 1974. MP (C) Ilford South, 1979–92; contested (C) same seat, 1992, 1997. Founder and first Chm., Unpaired Members Gp, 1982–85; Chairman: British Nepalese Parly Gp, 1983–92; British Korean Parly Gp, 1988–92; Vice Chm., UK Br., IPU, 1987–90; Member: Defence Select Cttee, 1983–92; Court of Referees, 1987–92. Chm., H of C Motor Club, 1985–91; Founder and Chairman: Armed Forces Parly Scheme, 1988–2015 (now Life Pres., Armed Forces Parly Trust); Police Service Parly Scheme, 1996–; Fire Service Parly Scheme, 2010–. Chm., World War II Widows Pension Gp, 1987–90. Chm., Britain-Nepal Soc., 1992–98 (Vice Pres., 1998–); Mem. Bd, British Chinese Armed Forces Heritage Project, 2015–18. Fellow, Industry and Parliament Trust, 1980 and 1990; Pres., Inst. of Civil Defence and Disaster Studies, 1996–2007; Chairman: Nat. Council for Civil Defence, 1982–86; St Edward's Housing Assoc., 1986–93; Ilford Age Concern, 1984–87, 1990–93; President: Redbridge Parkinson's Disease Soc., 1982–2001; Ilford Arthritis Care, 1986–2001; Gtr London Dist, St John Ambulance, 1992–2003; Redbridge Age Concern, 1993–2008; N and E London REME Assoc., 2000–15; Vice President: Ilford Tuberculosis and Chest Care Assoc., 1987–2000; Royal Soc. of St George, Chigwell, 2007–14; Royal British Legion, GLA City Hall, 2008–; Patron: Jubilee Club for Visually Handicapped, 1986–2000; Benevolent Fund for W Essex Hospices, 2001–06; Health Aid for Africa, 2008–17; Trustee: Children In Distress, 1986– (Life Pres., 2011); Meml Gates Trust, 1999–2009 (Hon. Dir of Develt for Constitution Hill Commonwealth War Meml); Amb., Girl Guiding, 2002–08; Chm., Emmeline Pankhurst Trust, 2018–20 (Hon. Dir, 2017). Chairman: Lord Mayor's £5 million Appeal for St Paul's Cathedral, 1993–94; Whitefriars Club, 2014–18. Founder Mem., Royal Artillery Firepower Mus., 2001–16. Mem., Mil. Educn Cttee, 1994–, and Court, 1995–2001, Univ. of Leeds. Prime Warden, Blacksmiths' Co., 2000–01. Member: TA, 1952–82; Metropolitan Special Constab. (HAC), 1983–92; Hon. Vice Comdt, HAC Specials, City of London Police, 2007–; CO, London Univ. OTC, 1976–80; Hon. Col, Leeds Univ. OTC, 1999–2007. DL Greater London, 1991; Rep. DL London Bor. of Brent, 2001–07. KStJ 1995 (Mem., Chapter Gen., 1989–97; Almoner, 1995–97). HQA (Pakistan), 1991; GDB (Nepal), 1991. *Publications:* Pedestrianised Streets: a study of Europe and America, 1973; Highway Robbery in the Twentieth Century: policy reform for compulsory purchase, 1990. *Address:* 13 Cowley Street, Westminster, SW1P 3LZ. *T:* (020) 7222 0480. *Clubs:* Honourable Artillery Company, Royal Air Force.

**THORNE, Nicholas Alan,** CMG 2002; HM Diplomatic Service, retired; International Relations Adviser to the Chief Executive Officer, Internet Corporation for the Assignment of Names and Numbers, California, 2008–11; independent consultant on issues related to governance of the Internet, since 2011; International Organisations Adviser to British Red Cross, since 2008; *b* 31 March 1948; *s* of late James Leslie Thorne and Grace Agnes Thorne; *m* 2003, Kristina Tronningsdal; one *s* one *d* by previous marriage. *Educ:* Chatham House Grammar Sch.; Westminster Univ. Joined HM Diplomatic Service, 1965; Yaoundé, 1971; UK Repn to EC, Brussels, 1974–78; UKMIS, UN, NY, 1980–83; Hd of Chancery, Manila, 1983–87; Dep. Hd, UN Dept and Hd, Human Rights, FCO, 1987–89; on secondment to Thorn/EMI, 1989–91; Counsellor and Dep. Hd of Mission, Helsinki, 1991–95; UKMIS, UN, NY, 1995–2003; Ambassador and UK Permanent Rep. to UN and other internat. orgns, Geneva, 2003–08. *Recreations:* travel, flying light aircraft, cooking, renovating old properties in France. *Address:* Les Augers, 16700 St Gourson, France. *E:* nicktny@aol.com. *Club:* Royal Over-Seas League.

**THORNE, Rosemary Prudence;** non-executive Director: Solvay SA, since 2014; Merrill Lynch International, since 2017; *b* Bristol, 12 Feb. 1952; *d* of Arnold Rex and Brenda Prudence Bishop. *Educ:* St Ursula's High Sch. for Girls; Warwick Univ. (BSc Hons Maths and Econs). FCMA 1984; FCT 1993. Finance Dir and Co. Sec., Harrods Ltd, 1986–90; Gp Financial Controller, Grand Metropolitan plc, 1990–92; Group Finance Director: J Sainsbury plc, 1992–99; Bradford & Bingley plc, 1999–2005; Ladbrokes plc, 2006–07. Non-executive Director: Royal Mail plc, 1998–2004; Cadbury Schweppes plc, 2004–07; Santander UK plc, 2006–15; Smurfit Kappa Gp plc, 2008–18; First Global Trust Bank plc, 2015–16. Member: Financial Reporting Rev. Panel, 1996–2006; Financial Reporting Council, 1998–2007. CCMI 1996; CGMA 2012. *E:* rosemary_thorne@btinternet.com.

**THORNE, Sam;** Director, Nottingham Contemporary, since 2016; *b* Eastbourne, 17 Nov. 1983; *s* of David and Helen Thorne. *Educ:* Univ. of Cambridge (BA English 2006; MA). Associate Ed., Frieze mag., 2009–14; Artistic Dir, Tate St Ives, 2014–16. Vis. Tutor, RCA, 2011–. Founding Dir, Open Sch. East, 2013–. *Publications:* School: a recent history of self-organised art education, 2017. *Recreations:* travel, museums, music, food. *Address:* Nottingham Contemporary, Weekday Cross, Nottingham NG1 2GB. *T:* (0115) 948 9750. *E:* samthorne@nottinghamcontemporary.org.

**THORNELY-TAYLOR, Rupert Maurice;** Consultant in Noise, Vibration and Acoustics, since 1968; Director: Rupert Taylor Ltd, since 1993; Saxtead Livestock Ltd, since 2013; farmer and bloodstock breeder; *b* Whalton, Northumberland, 21 May 1946; *s* of late Maurice Humphrey Taylor and Mary Patricia Stuart Taylor (*née* Wood); surname changed to Thornely-Taylor by Deed Poll, 1988; *m* 1st, 1964, Alison Grant, *d* of late Alistair Grant Saunders (marr. diss. 1987, she *d* 1999); 2nd, 1988, Frances Marion, *d* of late William John Lindberg. *Educ:* Harrow Sch. Acoustical engr, Burgess Products Co. Ltd, 1964–68; Dir, Rupert Taylor and Partners Ltd, 1970–81; Consultant to: London Underground, 1984–2001 and 2014–; LDDC, 1984–98; Crossrail, 1991–; Railtrack, 1999–2003; Associated British Ports, 2000–06; Network Rail, 2003–05; Transport for London, 2004–; Heathrow Airport Ltd (formerly BAA), 2007–13; HS2 Ltd, 2013–; res. contract, DoE, 1996. Consultant: New Victoria Th., N Staffs, 1984–2011; Railway Procurement Agency, Dublin, 2008–12; Shell E&P Ireland Ltd, 2010–13; ITV, 2015; Manchester Univ., 2015; London Bor. of Newham, 2016–. Expert witness for Sec. of State for Transport, H of C Select Cttee, High Speed Rail (London–W Midlands) Bill, 2013–16, (W Midlands–Crewe) Bill, 2018–, H of L Select Cttee, 2016–17. Member: Noise Adv. Council, 1970–80 (Chm., Wkg Gp on Noise Monitoring); ISO Wkg Gp on Groundborne Noise and Vibration from Rail Systems, 1998–; Project Bd, DEFRA, 2004–11; Ext. Rev. Gp, WHO Envmtl Noise Guidelines for Eur. Reg., 2018. Developer, FINDWAVE Finite-Difference-Time-Domain computer software, 1991–. Mem. Council, British Acoustical Soc., 1968–71; Founder Member and Hon. Treasurer: Assoc. Noise Consultants, 1970–74 (Vice Chm., 2001–03;

Chm., 2003–05; Pres., 2006–11; Hon. Mem., 2011; Outstanding Contribn Award, 2013); Inst. Acoustics, 1971–74 (Fellow, 1981; Dip. Examiner, 2010–14). Dir, Internat. Inst. Acoustics and Vibration, 2007–11, 2012–16 (Chm., Membership Cttee, 2011–; Sec., 2018–). Mem. (C) Wealden DC, 1995–2003 (Leader, 1999–2003). Member: E Sussex Econ. Partnership, 1999–2003; Inter-reg. Jt Monitoring Cttee, 1999–2001; SE England Regl Assembly, 1999–2003; Mem., Exec. Cttee, Wealden Constituency Cons. Assoc., 1993–2003; Chm., Wealden Constituency Business Gp, 2007–12. Breeder, Rumsden Herd of Pedigree Charolais Cattle (King's Trophy, Royal Smithfield Show, 2002; Reserve Breed Champion, Royal Show, 2009; Jun. Champion, Perth, 2010; Sen. Champion, Carlisle, 2010; Female Champion, Carlisle, 2011; Breed Champion and Interbreed Jun. Champion, Royal Welsh Show, 2011; Breed Champion and Interbreed Male Champion, S of England Show, 2011; Male Champion, Royal Highland Show, 2011, herd dispersed, 2012). Conservator, Ashdown Forest, 1997–2003 and 2006–13 (Chm., Finance and Gen. Purposes Cttee, 2007–09; Vice Chm., 2009–10, Chm., 2010–13, Bd of Conservators); Trustee, Ashdown Forest Conservation Trust, 2010–13. Mem., PCC, All Saints, Saxtead, 2013– (Churchwarden, 2015–). Churchill Fellow, USA, 1972. Hon. Treas., Nat. Pony Soc., 1991–97. Mem., Kennel Club. Winner (with F. M. Thornely-Taylor) of Best in Show: S Western Tibetan Spaniel Club Open Show, 2013; SE and E Anglia Tibetan Spaniel Club Open Show, 2014; Northern Tibetan Spaniel Club Championship Show, 2014 and Open Show, 2015; Tibetan Spaniel Assoc. Open Show, 2015; Reserve Best of Breed Richmond Championship Dog Show, 2015; Best of Breed: Midland Counties Canine Soc., 2016; British Utility Breeds Assoc., 2016; Best Opposite Sex Scottish Tibetan Spaniel Club Championship Show, 2017. Rayleigh Medal, Inst. of Acoustics, 2016. *Publications:* Noise, 1970, 4th edn 2001; Le Bruit et ses Méfaits, 1972; (ed) Noise Control Data, 1976; (jtly) Handbook of Noise Assessment, 1978; Electricity, 1979; (jtly) Measurement and Assessment of Groundborne Noise and Vibration, 2002, 2nd edn 2012; (illustrator) Perry the Perfect Puppy, 2000; contrib. papers to Proc. Inst. Acoustics, Internat. Inst. Acoustics and Vibration, Internat. Inst. Noise Control Engrg, Internat. Congress on Sound and Vibration. *Recreations:* painting, music, gardening, Tibetan Spaniels. *Address:* Saxtead Hall, Saxtead, Woodbridge, Suffolk IP13 9QT. *T:* (01728) 621521.

See also Rt Rev. H. V. Taylor.

**THORNETT, Gary Paul;** Master of the High Court, Queen's Bench Division, since 2016; *b* Warwickshire, 11 Feb. 1964; *s* of Harold and Marjorie Thornett; two *d*. *Educ:* King Edward VI Grammar Sch. for Boys, Stratford upon Avon; Royal Holloway Coll., Univ. of London (Organ Schol.; BMus 1985). ARCO; LRAM. Sub-Organist, St Finbarre's Cathedral, Cork, 1985–86; Lectr (pt-time), UC, Cork, 1985–86; admitted as solicitor, 1990; called to the Bar, Middle Temple, 1991; in practice as barrister, No 1 and No 5 Fountain Court, Birmingham, specialising in gen. civil law, then 12 King's Bench Walk, London, specialising in personal injury law; a Dep. Dist Judge, 2008–16. *Publications:* (Ed.) Sweet & Maxwell Weekly Personal Injury Bulletin, 2010–. *Recreations:* Baroque music (playing and listening), art and architecture, France and Italy. *Address:* Royal Courts of Justice, Strand, WC2A 2LL.

**THORNEYCROFT, Rev. Prebendary Pippa Hazel Jeanetta;** Prebendary of Lichfield Cathedral, 2000–09, now Prebendary Emeritus; Chaplain to the Queen, 2001–14; Minister-in-Charge, St Bartholomew's, Tong, Shifnal, since 2014; *b* 18 Feb. 1944; *d* of Philip Fitzgerald Mander and Priscilla Patricia (*née* Waller); *m* 1965, John Patrick Thorneycroft; two *s* two *d*. *Educ:* Cheltenham Ladies' Coll.; Exeter Univ. (BA Hons Theology 1965); W Midlands Ministerial Trng Course, Queen's Coll., Birmingham (GOE 1988). Ordained deacon, 1988, priest, 1994; Curate (non-stipendiary), St Mary Magdalene, Albrighton, 1988–90; asst deacon/priest (non-stipendiary), Badger, Beckbury, Kemberton, Ryton, Stockton and Sutton Maddock, 1990–96; Advr for Women in Ministry, Lichfield Dio., 1993–99; Priest-in-Charge: Shareshill, 1996–2009; Essington, 2006–09; Rural Dean of Penkridge, 2001–05; Interim Minister: Tettenhall Wood, Wolverhampton, 2010–12; Wellington and Hadley, 2012–13; Actg Team Rector, Central Telford, 2013–14; Associate Priest, Shifnal (Tong), 2014–. Mem., Skinners' Co., 1966–. *Recreations:* walking, cycling, bee-keeping. *Address:* Manor Cottage, High Street, Albrighton, nr Wolverhampton WV7 3JB. *T:* (01902) 375523.

**THORNHILL,** Baroness *cr* 2015 (Life Peer), of Watford in the County of Hertfordshire; **Dorothy Thornhill,** MBE 2012; Elected Mayor (Lib Dem) of Watford, since 2002; *m* 1st, Andrew Thornhill; one *s* one *d*; 2nd, Dr Iain Sharpe. Teacher, schools in Herts incl. Asst Hd, Queens Sch., Bushey. Spokesman on communities and local govt, H of L, 2015–. Mem. (Lib Dem), Watford BC, 1992–2002. Contested (Lib Dem) Watford, 2015. *Recreations:* avid Wales Rugby supporter and aficionado, Coronation Street. *Address:* House of Lords, SW1A 0PW.

**THORNHILL, Alan Russell,** PhD; Country Manager, Igenomix UK, and Senior Scientific Adviser, Igenomix International, since 2017; *b* Portsmouth, 12 Nov. 1966; *s* of late John Roger Thornhill and of Zandra Mary Knight (*née* Edwards); *m* 1999, Vikki Isobel Cookson (*d* 2014); one *s* two *d*. *Educ:* Royal Hospital Sch.; University Coll. London (BSc Hons Biol. 1989); Univ. of London (PhD Genetics 1996). High-complexity Clin. Lab. Dir, Amer. Bd of Bioanalysis, 2003; State Registered Clinical Scientist, 2005; Eur. Soc. of Human Reprodn and Embryol. Certified Sen. Clin. Embryologist, 2008. Res. Fellow, Molecular Embryology Unit, Inst. of Child Health, London, 1993–96; Clinical Embryologist, Assisted Conception Unit, King's Coll. Sch. of Medicine and Dentistry, London, 1996–98; Postdoctoral Res. Fellow, Dept of Obstetrics and Gynaecol., St Thomas' Hosp., London, 1999; IVF Lab. Dir, Mayo Clinic, Rochester, Minn, 2000–04; Scientific Dir, London Fertility Centre, 2005–06; Scientific Dir, 2007–13 and HFEA Person Responsible, 2010–13, London Bridge Fertility, Gynaecology and Genetics Centre, London; Consultant Clin. Res. Scientist, Assisted Conception Unit, Guy's Hosp., London, 2013; Associate Dir, Mkt Develt, Reproductive and Genetic Health, Illumina Inc., 2013–17. Hon. Sen. Lectr, UCL, 2004–08; Hon. Prof. in Reproductive Genetics, Dept of Bioscis, Univ. of Kent, Canterbury, 2015– (Hon. Reader, 2008–15). Sec., Alpha Scientists in Reproductive Medicine, 2004–13 (Chair, 2012–13). Mem., HFEA, 2009–15. *Publications:* (ed) Single Cell Diagnostics: methods and protocols, 2007; over 100 articles on assisted reproduction and genetics. *Recreations:* amateur dramatics, choral singing. *Club:* Victory Services.

**THORNHILL, Andrew Robert;** QC 1985; a Recorder, 1997–2004; *b* 4 Aug. 1943; *s* of Edward Percy Thornhill and Amelia Joy Thornhill; *m* 1971, Helen Mary Livingston; two *s* two *d*. *Educ:* Clifton Coll. Prep. Sch.; Clifton Coll.; Corpus Christi Coll., Oxford. Called to the Bar, Middle Temple, 1969, Bencher, 1995; entered chambers of H. H. Monroe, QC, 1969. Chm. Council, Clifton Coll., 1994–2010. *Publications:* (ed) Potter & Monroe: Tax Planning with Precedents, 7th edn 1974, to 9th edn 1982; (jtly) Tax Planning Through Wills, 1981, 1984; (jtly) Passing Down the Family Farm, 1982; (jtly) Passing Down the Family Business, 1984. *Recreations:* wooden boats, dinghy sailing, squash, walking. *Address:* Flat 4, Cavendish Lodge, 7 Percival Road, Clifton, Bristol BS8 3LE. *Clubs:* Oxford and Cambridge, Bar Yacht.

**THORNHILL, John Joseph Andrew,** OBE 2016; Chairman, Lay Observers' National Council, since 2018; Chairman, Magistrates' Association, 2008–11; *b* Liverpool, 1 July 1945; *s* of Walter Thornhill and Anne Margaret Thornhill; unmarried. *Educ:* St Francis Xavier's Coll., Liverpool; Univ. of Hull (BA Hons Classics 1967); Univ. of Edinburgh (Dip Ed Psych 1968); Manchester Metropolitan Univ. (Grad. Dip. Law 2001); Univ. of Wales, Aberystwyth (MPhil Law 2007). Teacher of Classics, Madras Coll., St Andrews, 1968–70; Hd, Classics, 1970–72, Dir of Studies, 1972–78, Notre Dame High Sch., Liverpool; Curriculum Develt Officer, ICT, Liverpool Poly., 1978–82; Sen. Lectr in IT, Liverpool Hope Univ., 1982–85; Teacher/Advr, ICT, Liverpool Educn Authy, 1985–94; Dir of ICT, Calderstones Sch., 1994–97. Ofsted Inspector, 1997–; consultant to DCSF, then DFE, 2007–; Nat. Leader of Governance, 2014–. Called to the Bar, Middle Temple, 2002. Mem., Judicial Appts Commn, 2012–14. Pres., Nat. Council of Ind. Monitoring Bds, 2013–17. E and W Rep., Eur. Network of Councils for Judiciary, 2010–15. Chm., Nat. Mock Trial Competition for Schs, 2013–. Chairman, Governors: Sudley Sch., Liverpool; All Saints Catholic High Sch., Kirkby, 2015–; Savio Coll., Sefton, 2017–. FRSA. Hon. LLD Manchester Metropolitan, 2013. JP Liverpool 1983–2015. *Publications:* (with D. A. Brodie) Microcomputing in Sport and Education, 1982; (contrib.) The Analysis of Practical Skills, 1985. *Recreations:* former professional referee Football and Rugby League, international athletics official, ski-ing, Scottish culture and country dancing, classical music (listening), spending time with sister Monica, niece Lucy and their families. *Address:* 5 Lynnbank Road, Calderstones, Liverpool L18 3HE. *T:* (0151) 722 1813, 07714 759466. *E:* johnjp@blueyonder.co.uk. *Clubs:* Army and Navy; Athenæum (Liverpool).

**THORNICROFT, Sir Graham (John),** Kt 2017; PhD; FRCPsych, FMedSci; Professor of Community Psychiatry, since 1996, and Director, WHO Collaborating Centre for Research and Training in Mental Health, since 2012, Institute of Psychiatry, Psychology and Neuroscience (formerly Institute of Psychiatry), King's College London; Consultant Psychiatrist, South London and Maudsley NHS Foundation Trust, since 1991; Director, NIHR Collaboration for Leadership in Applied Health Research and Care South London, since 2013; Chairman, Implemental (formerly Maudsley International), since 2014. *Educ:* Queens' Coll., Cambridge (BA 1st cl. Hons Soc. and Pol Sci. 1977); Guy's Hosp. Med. Sch., London (MB BS 1984); London Sch. of Hygiene and Tropical Medicine (MSc Epidemiol. 1989); Univ. of London (PhD 1995). MRCPsych 1988, FRCPsych 2000; MFPHM 1999. Mem., Health Services and Population Res. Dept, Inst. of Psychiatry, KCL, 1999– (Head, 1999–2013). Sen. Investigator, NIHR, 2007–. Vis. Scientist, Dept of Psychiatry, Univ. of Verona, 2000–; Vis. Prof., Dept of Epidemiol., Columbia Univ., NY, 2002–; Guest Prof., Peking Univ., 2016–. FMedSci 2005; FKC 2011; FRSA 2018. Hon. FRCPE 2014. *Publications:* (ed jtly) Measuring Mental Health Needs, 1992, 2nd edn 2001; (jtly) Emergency Mental Health Services in the Community, 1995; (with H. Knudsen) Mental Health Service Evaluation, 1996 (trans. Italian); (with G. Strathdee) Commissioning Mental Health Services, 1996; (with M. Tansella) Mental Health Outcome Measures, 1996, 3rd edn 2010; (jtly) London's Mental Health, 1997; (with D. Goldberg) Mental Health in Our Future Cities, 1998; (jtly) Camberwell Assessment of Need (CAN), 1999; (with M. Tansella) Common Mental Disorders in Primary Care: essay in honour of Professor Sir David Goldberg, 1999; (with M. Tansella) The Mental Health Matrix: a manual to improve services, 1999 (trans. Italian, Romanian, Russian, Spanish); (with A. Reynolds) Managing Mental Health Services, 1999 (trans. Italian, Portuguese); (with G. Szmukler) Textbook of Community Psychiatry, 2001; (jtly) Camberwell Assessment of Need for Adults with Developmental and Intellectual Disabilities (CANDID), 2003; (ed jtly) The Forensic CAN: a needs assessment for forensic mental health service users, 2006; (jtly) International Outcome Measures in Mental Health, 2006; Shunned: discrimination against people with mental illness, 2006 (Book of the Yr Award, Mental Health, BMA, 2007); Actions Speak Louder: tackling discrimination against people with mental illness, 2006; (ed jtly) Mental Health Policy and Practice Across Europe (Baxter Award, Eur. Health Mgt Assoc.), 2007; (ed jtly) Crisis Resolution and Home Treatment in Mental Health, 2008; (with M. Tansella) Better Mental Health Care, 2008; (jtly) Camberwell Assessment of Need: mother's version (CAN-M), 2008; (jtly) Oxford Textbook of Community Mental Health, 2011; (jtly) Community Mental Health: putting policy into practice globally, 2011; (jtly) Mental Illness, Discrimination and the Law: fighting for social justice, 2012; (jtly) A View from Inside, 2012; (jtly) Improving Mental Health Care: the global challenge, 2013; (jtly) Global Mental Health Trials, 2014; (jtly) Lancet Commission on Global Mental Health and Sustainable Development, 2018; over 520 peer-reviewed papers on mental health related stigma and discrimination, mental health needs assessment, the development of outcome scales, cost-effectiveness evaluation of mental health treatments and services, and global mental health. *Address:* Health Service and Population Research Department P029, Institute of Psychiatry, Psychology and Neuroscience, King's College London, De Crespigny Park, SE5 8AF. *T:* (020) 7848 0736, *Fax:* (020) 7277 1462. *E:* graham.thornicroft@kcl.ac.uk.

**THORNING-SCHMIDT, Helle;** Chief Executive Officer, Save the Children International, 2017–19; *b* Denmark, 14 Dec. 1966; *d* of Holger and Grete Thorning-Schmidt; *m* 1996, Stephen Nathan Kinnock, *qv*; two *d*. *Educ:* Univ. of Copenhagen (MA Political Sci.); Coll. of Europe (MA Eur. Studies). Internat. Advr to Confedn of Trade Unions. MEP (SDP) Denmark, 1999–2004; MP (SDP), 2005–15; Prime Minister of Denmark, 2011–15. Leader, SDP, Denmark, 2005–15.

**THORNTON,** Baroness *cr* 1998 (Life Peer), of Manningham in the co. of West Yorkshire; **Dorothea Glenys Thornton;** *b* 16 Oct. 1952; *e c* of Peter and Jean Thornton; *m* 1977, John Carr; one *s* one *d*. *Educ:* Thornton Secondary Sch., Bradford; LSE (BSc Econ 1976). Nat. Organiser, Gingerbread, 1976–78; N London Area Officer, Greater London CABx, 1978–79; Projects Dir, Inst. of Community Studies, 1979–81; Political Sec., Royal Arsenal Co-op. Soc., 1981–86; Public and Political Affairs Advr, CWS, 1986–92. Chm., Pall Mall Consult, 2001–07. Chm., Social Enterprise Coalition, 2001–07; Chief Exec., Young Foundn, 2015–. A Baroness in Waiting (Govt Whip), 2008–10; Parly Under-Sec. of State, DoH, 2010. Fabian Society: Gen. Sec., 1993–94; Develt Dir, 1994–96; Mem., Nat. Exec. Cttee, 1997–2000. Chm., Greater London Labour Party, 1986–91. Director: Labour Women's Network, 1990–; EMILY's List UK, 1993–; Improvement and Develt Agency, 1999–2007; Training for Life, 2003–07. Trustee, Fifteen Foundn, 2003–10. Gov., LSE, 2000–16, now Emeritus. FRSA 1999. *Recreations:* canoeing, hill-walking, Star Trek. *Address:* House of Lords, SW1A 0PW.

**THORNTON, Allan Charles,** OBE 2004; Chairman, Environmental Investigation Agency, since 1988 (Co-Founder and Director, 1984–86); *b* 17 Nov. 1949; *s* of Robert Charles Antoine Thornton and Jessie (Waldram) Thornton; *m* 1995, Polly Ghazi, journalist and author; two *d*. *Educ:* Banff Centre of Fine Art, Banff, Canada. Co-ordinator of Banff Centre Creative Writing Programme, 1976, 1977; established Greenpeace UK, 1977; Exec. Dir, 1977–81 and 1986–88; co-founder of Greenpeace vessel, Rainbow Warrior, 1978; co-founder, Greenpeace International, 1980; Internat. Project Co-ordinator with Greenpeace International, 1981. Albert Schweitzer Award, 1991; BBC TV Lifetime Achievement Award, 2000. *Publications:* To Save an Elephant, 1990. *Recreation:* viewing elephants and other wildlife in their natural habitat. *Address:* c/o Environmental Investigation Agency, 62–63 Upper Street, N1 0NY. *T:* (020) 7354 7960.

**THORNTON, His Honour Anthony Christopher Lawrence;** QC 1988; a Senior Circuit Judge, 1994–2015; a Deputy Judge of the Administrative Court and Queen's Bench Division, 2009–15; a Judge of the Crown Court, 2009–15; a Judge of the First-tier Tribunal (Mental Health), 2010–19; *b* 18 Aug. 1947; *s* of Richard Thornton and Margery Alice (*née* Clerk); *m* 1st, 1983, Lyn Christine Thurlby (marr. diss. 1998); one *s*; 2nd, 2006, Dawn Elisabeth Collins. *Educ:* Eton Coll.; Keble Coll., Oxford (BCL, MA). Called to the Bar, Middle Temple, 1970, Bencher, 1992. A Recorder, 1992–94; an official referee and Judge of the Technology and Construction Court of the High Court, 1994–2009. Mem. (pt-time), Parole Bd, 2002–10. Chairman: Fulham Legal Advice Centre, 1973–78; Hammersmith and Fulham Law Centre, 1975–78. External Moderator, Centre of Construction and Project Management, KCL, 1987–; Hon. Sen. Vis. Fellow, Centre for Commercial Law Studies, QMC, 1987–92. Mem., Gen. Council of the Bar, 1988–94 (Treas., 1990–92; Chm., Professional Standards Cttee, 1992–93). Dir, Apex Trust, 1991–94. Gov., Colfe's Sch., Lewisham, 2000–12. Liveryman, Leathersellers' Co., 1976– (Mem. Ct, 2002–; Master, 2015–16). Jt Editor, Construction Law Jl, 1984–94. *Publications:* (ed jtly) Building Contracts, in Halsbury's Laws of England, vol. 4, 1972; (contrib.) Construction Disputes: liability and the expert witness, 1989; contribs to Construction Law Jl. *Recreations:* football, opera, legal history, walking, companionship.

**THORNTON, Air Marshal Sir Barry (Michael),** KCB 2007 (CB 2004); CEng, FIMechE; FRAeS; engineering, aerospace and safety consultant; Chairman, Queen Mary Roehampton Trust, since 2017; *b* 19 Nov. 1952; *s* of Ronald Thornton and Enid Margaret Thornton (*née* Baxendale); *m* 1977, Delia Brown, barrister; two *s*. *Educ:* Baines Grammar Sch.; Nottingham Univ. (BSc); RMCS, Cranfield Univ. (MSc). CEng 1981; FIMechE 1994; FRAeS 2002. Joined RAF, 1971; initial and professional trng, 1974–75; aircraft and weapon systems appts at RAF Waddington, RAF Lyneham, RAF Abingdon and HQ RAF Germany, 1975–87; Advanced Staff Trng, 1988; OC Engrg and Supply Wing, RAF Honington, 1988–90; OC Engrg Wing, RAF Detachment Tabuk, Gulf War; Weapons Support Authy and Standardization, MoD, 1991–93; Combat Aircraft Test and Evaluation, DERA, MoD, 1994–96; rcds 1997; Dir Maritime Projects, MoD PE, 1998; Nimrod MRA4 Integrated Project Team Leader, Defence Procurement Agency, MoD, 1998–2000; Controller Aircraft RAF, and Exec. Dir, Defence Procurement Agency, MoD, 2000–03; Dir-Gen. Equipment Support (Air), 2003–04, Air Mem. for Logistics and Dir Gen. Logistics (Strike), 2004–06, Defence Logistics Orgn, MoD; Air Mem. for Personnel and C-in-C PTC, 2006–07; Air Mem. for Materiel and Chief of Materiel (Air), Defence Equipment and Support, 2007–09. Man. Dir, Ascent Flight Training Ltd, 2009–12; Co-Founder and Chm., SQEP Ltd, 2014–17. FCMI (FIMgt 1995). *Recreations:* golf, gardening, ski-ing. *Club:* Royal Air Force.

**THORNTON, Clive Edward Ian,** CBE 1983; FInstLEx, FCIB; corporate consultancy services, since 2003; Chairman: Melton Mowbray Building Society, 1991–2003 (Director, 1988–2003; Hon. President, 2003–09); Armstrong Capital Holdings Ltd, 1988–98; *b* 12 Dec. 1929; *s* of Albert and Margaret Thornton; *m* 1956, Maureen Carmine (*née* Crane); one *s* one *d*. *Educ:* St Anthony's Sch., Newcastle upon Tyne; Coll. of Commerce, Newcastle upon Tyne; College of Law, London; LLB 1977, BA Hons 1996, MA 1999, DipTh 2001, LLM 2005, London Univ. (ext.); Open Univ. (BSc Hons 1998, Dip. Geog. 1998); Heythrop Coll., Univ. of London (BD Hons (ext.) 2008; MTh 2010); Oxford Univ. (AdvDip English Local Hist. 2011); Univ. of Dundee (Postgrad. Dip. Family and Local Hist. 2013; MLitt 2016)). FInstLEx 1958; FCIB (FCBSI 1970). Solicitor. Associate, Pensions Management Inst., 1978. Articled to Kenneth Hudson, solicitor, London, 1959; admitted solicitor of Supreme Court, 1963. Asst Solicitor, Nationwide Building Soc., 1963; Solicitor, Cassel Arenz Ltd, Merchant Bankers, 1964–67; Abbey National Building Society: Chief Solicitor, 1967; Dep. Chief Gen. Man., 1978; Chief Gen. Manager, 1979–83; Dir, 1980–83; Partner, Stoneham Langton and Passmore, Solicitors, 1985–88. Chm., Metropolitan Assoc. of Building Socs, 1981–82. Chairman: Mirror Group Newspapers, 1984; Financial Weekly, 1985–87; Thamesmead Town Ltd, 1986–90; Gabriel Communications (formerly Universe Publications) Ltd, 1986–96; Dir, Investment Data Services Ltd, 1986–90. Proprietor, Thorndale Devon Cattle, 1983–2007; President: Devon Cattle Breeders Soc., 1997–98; Midland Columbarian Soc., 2011–13. Member: Law Soc. (Chm., Commerce and Industry Gp, 1974); Council, Chartered Bldg Socs Inst., 1973–81; Council, Building Socs Assoc., 1979–83; Bd, Housing Corp., 1980–86. Chairman: SHAC, 1983–86; Belford Hall Management Co. Ltd, 1990–93. Member: Council, St Mary's Hosp. Med. Sch., 1984–96; St Mary's Develt Trust, 1984–98. Freeman, City of London; Liveryman, Worshipful Co. of Bakers. *Publications:* Building Society Law, Cases and Materials, 1969, 3rd edn 1988; History of Devon Cattle, 1994; The Coaching Era, 2017. *Recreations:* music, reading, Modena pigeons, English local history, painting. *Address:* The Manor, The Green, Woughton on the Green, Milton Keynes MK6 3BE.

**THORNTON, Daniel;** Director of External Relations, Ark, since 2019; *b* Leeds, 6 Aug. 1969; *s* of Vernon and Frances Thornton; *m* 1998, Tasja Dorkofikis; one *s* one *d*. *Educ:* Wadham Coll., Oxford (BA PPE); London Sch. of Econs (MA Internat. Hist.). Oxford Analytica, 1990–91; FCO, 1991–97; Enron Europe, 1998; Cttee Specialist, Foreign Affairs Cttee, H of C, 1999–2001; HM Treasury, 2001–04; Private Sec. to Prime Minister, 2004–06; Principal Private Sec. to Sec. of State for Communities and Local Govt, 2006–07; Dir, Local Economic Develt and Renewal, DCLG, 2007–09; COS, 2009–13, Dir, Strategic Initiatives, 2013–15, GAVI Alliance; Prog. Dir, Inst. for Govt, 2015–18.

**THORNTON, Sir (George) Malcolm,** Kt 1992; Chairman: Value Based Solutions, since 2006; Birmingham Local Education Partnership, 2009–13; *b* 3 April 1939; *s* of George Edmund and Ethel Thornton; *m* 1st, 1962; (one *s* decd); 2nd, 1972, Shirley Ann, (Sue) (*née* Banton) (*d* 1989); 3rd, 1990, Rosemary (*née* Hewitt). *Educ:* Wallasey Grammar Sch.; Liverpool Nautical Coll. Liverpool Pilot Service, 1955–79 (Sen. 1st cl. Licence holder). Chairman: Keene Public Affairs Consultants Ltd, 1997–2009; Broadskill Ltd (formerly Intuition Gp Ltd), 2002–08; non-executive Director: Stack Computer Solutions, 2000–18; HB Villages Ltd, 2011–. Member: Wallasey County Borough Council, 1965–74 (Chm., Transport Cttee, 1968–69); Wirral Metropolitan Council, 1973–79 (Council Leader, 1974–77); Chairman: Merseyside Metropolitan Districts Liaison Cttee, 1975–77; Educn Cttee, AMA, 1978–79 (Mem., 1974–79); Council of Local Educn Authorities, 1978. Mem., Burnham (Primary and Secondary) Cttee, 1975–79. MP (C) Liverpool, Garston, 1979–83, Crosby, 1983–97; contested Crosby, 1997. PPS to Sec. of State for Industry, 1981–83, for the Environment, 1983–84. Chairman: Select Cttee on Educn, Sci. and the Arts, 1989–96 (Mem., 1985–96); Select Cttee on Educn and Employment, 1996–97. Pro Chancellor and Chm., Liverpool John Moores Univ., 2007–13 (Mem. Bd, 2001–13; Chm., Audit Cttee, 2003–07; Hon. Ambassador Fellowship, 2013). Trustee, Mersey Mission to Seafarers, 1999–2010 (Chm., 2002–10); Chm., Alder Hey Children's Hosp. Charitable Trust, 2017–18. Chm. Govs, Liscard Primary Sch., Wallasey, 1974–2011. Hon. Col 156 (NW) Transport Regt, RLC (V), 2000–05. FRSA. Hon. DEd De Montfort, 1994. *Recreations:* fishing, walking, cooking. *Address:* Meadow Brook, 79 Barnston Road, Heswall, Wirral CH60 1UE. *Club:* Heswall Golf.

**THORNTON, Helen Ann Elizabeth, (Mrs J. E. C. Thornton);** see Meixner, H. A. E.

**THORNTON, James Kevin;** Chief Executive Officer, ClientEarth, since 2006; *b* New York, 14 Feb. 1954; *s* of Peter William Thornton and Catherine Marion Thornton; *m* Martin John Goodman. *Educ:* Yale Univ. (BA Philos. *magna cum laude* 1976; Phi Beta Kappa); New York Univ. Sch. of Law (Juris Dr 1979). Member of the Bar, NY, 1981, US Supreme Court, 1987, Calif. 1989. Law Clerk, Judge John Wisdom, US Court of Appeals for 5th Circuit, New Orleans, 1979–80; Legal Fellow, Natural Resources Defense Council, NY, 1980–81; Lawyer, Paul, Weiss, Rifkind, Wharton and Garrison, NY, 1981–83; Lawyer, then Sen. Lawyer, Natural Resources Defence Council, 1983–91 (Founder: Citizen Enforcement Proj.; Los Angeles Office); Executive Director: Positive Futures, Santa Fe, 1992–99; Heffter Res. Inst., 1999–2006. Dir, Barbican Press, 2009–. Dir, Fundacja ClientEarth Poland, 2010–. Advr, Stranded Assets Prog., Smith Sch. of Enterprise and Envmt, Univ. of Oxford, 2014–. Mem., Task Force on Rule of Law and Ecol Civilization, China Council for Internat. Cooperation and Develt, 2015–. Mem., Law Soc., 2008; Mem., Wkg Gp on Model Statute Climate Change Remedies, Internat. Bar Assoc., 2015–. MInstCE. FZS; FRSA. Fellow, Ashoka, 2013–. Ordained Zen Buddhist priest, Soto sect, 2009. Editor in Chief, New York Univ. Law Rev., 1978–79. Leader of Year, Business Green, 2014, 2016; Special Achievement Award, FT Eur. Innovative Lawyer Awards, 2016; Sustainability Leader, edie Sustainability Leaders Awards, 2017; Outstanding Individual, Corporate Leadership, Global Good Awards, 2018. *Publications:* A Field Guide to the Soul, 1999; Immediate Harm (novel), 2010; (jtly) Environmental and Social Transparency under the Companies Act 2006: digging deeper, 2010; Sphinx: the second coming (novel), 2014; (jtly) Client Earth, 2017; The Feynman Challenge (poetry), 2017. *Recreations:* natural history of Pyrenees, playing the violin, composing poetry, koan practice, photographing London, wines of the Côtes du Rousillon Villages in situ. *Address:* ClientEarth, The Hothouse, 274 Richmond Road, E8 3QW. *T:* (020) 7749 5970. *E:* jthornton@clientearth.org. *W:* www.jamesthornton.org. *Clubs:* Conduit; Yale (New York).

**THORNTON, James Sebastian;** HM Diplomatic Service; Consul-General, Erbil, Iraq, since 2019; *b* Farnborough, Kent, 2 Nov. 1964; *s* of late Edward Alfred Thornton and of Mary Thornton (now Howard); *m* 1999, Anne Fiona Scrase; two *d*. *Educ:* Hampton Sch., Middx; Lycée Internat. de St Germain-en-Laye, France; King Edward VI Sch., Southampton; Lincoln Coll., Oxford (MA). UKAEA, 1986–89; entered FCO, 1989; Desk Officer, Envmt, Sci. and Energy Dept, 1990–91; Desk Officer, UKMIS to UN, NY, 1991; Second Sec., Algiers, 1992–94; Desk Officer, Near East and N Africa Dept, FCO, 1994–95; Perm. Under-Sec.'s Dept, FCO, 1995–96; Hd of War Crimes, Sect., UN Dept, FCO, 1997–99; Hd, Pol Sect., Mexico City, 2000–03; Dep. Hd of Mission, Abidjan, 2003–04; Dep. Hd, FCO/DFID Sudan Unit, 2005–07; Dep. Perm. Rep. to OECD, Paris, 2007–11; High Comr to Zambia, 2012–15; Ambassador to Bolivia, 2016–19. *Recreations:* running, hill walking, visiting art galleries. *Address:* c/o Foreign and Commonwealth Office, King Charles Street, SW1A 2AH. *E:* james.thornton@fco.gov.uk.

**THORNTON, Dame Janet (M.),** DBE 2012 (CBE 2000); PhD; FRS 1999; Senior Scientist, since 2001, and Director, 2001–15, now Director Emeritus, European Bioinformatics Institute, European Molecular Biology Laboratory; *b* 23 May 1949; *d* of James Stanley McLoughlin and Kathleen McLoughlin (*née* Barlow); *m* 1970, Alan D. Thornton; one *s* one *d*. *Educ:* Nottingham Univ. (BSc 1st Cl. Hons Physics); King's Coll. London and NIMR (PhD 1973). Research Assistant: Lab. of Molecular Biophysics, Oxford, 1973–78; Molecular Pharmacol., NIMR, 1978; Crystallography Department, Birkbeck College, London: SERC Advanced Fellow, 1979–83; Lectr, 1983–89; Sen. Lectr, 1989–90; Tutor, Open Univ., 1976–83; Prof. of Biomolecular Structure, and Dir, Biomolecular Structure and Modelling Unit, UCL, 1990–2001; Bernal Prof. of Crystallography, Birkbeck Coll., London, 1996–2001; Hd, Jt Res. Sch. in Molecular Scis, UCL and Birkbeck Coll., 1996–2001. Extraordinary Fellow, Churchill Coll., Cambridge, 2002–. Mem. Bd, Natural Hist. Mus., 2016–. For. Associate, NAS, USA, 2003. FMedSci 2014. *Publications:* contrib. numerous articles to jls incl. Jl Molecular Biol., Structure, Nature, Trends in Biochemical Scis, Proc. Nat. Acad. Sci., Protein Science. *Recreations:* reading, music, gardens, home. *Address:* European Bioinformatics Institute, European Molecular Biology Laboratory, Wellcome Genome Campus, Hinxton, Cambridge CB10 1SD. *T:* (01223) 492677.

**THORNTON, John Henry,** OBE 1987; QPM 1980; Deputy Assistant Commissioner, Metropolitan Police, 1981–86; *b* 24 Dec. 1930; *s* of late Sidney Thornton and Ethel Thornton (*née* Grinnell); *m* 1st, 1952, Norma Lucille (marr. diss. 1972; she *d* 1999), *d* of late Alfred and Kate Scrivenor; two *s*; 2nd, 1972, Hazel Ann (marr. diss. 1996), *d* of late William and Edna Butler; one *s* one *d* (and one *s* decd); 3rd, 1996, Mary Elizabeth, *d* of late John Patrick and Elizabeth Unity Jackson. *Educ:* Prince Henry's Grammar Sch., Evesham. RN 1949–50. Metropolitan Police, 1950; Comdr, 1976; Head of Community Relations, 1977–80; RCDS, 1981; Dep. Asst Commissioner, 1981; Dir of Information, 1982–83; Hd of Training, 1983–85; NW Area, 1985–86. Vice-Pres., British Section, Internat. Police Assoc., 1969–79. Chm., Breakaway Theatre Co., St Albans, 1987–94; Chm., St Albans Internat. Organ Fest., 1988–91. Chm. of Govs, Townsend C of E Sch., St Albans, 1990–96. Lay Canon and Cathedral Warden, St Albans, 1988–94; Churchwarden, St Leonard's, Bretforton, Worcs, 2002–18. Volunteer, Broadway Police Station, W Mercia Constabulary, 2005–14. CStJ 1984. *Recreation:* music. *Address:* c/o Barclays Bank, PO Box 300, St Albans, Herts AL1 3EQ.

**THORNTON, Prof. John Lawson;** Chairman: Barrick Gold Corporation, since 2014 (Director, since 2012; Co-Chairman, 2012–14); PineBridge Investments, since 2014; Professor and Director of Global Leadership, Tsinghua University, China, since 2003; Senior Adviser, Goldman Sachs Group, Inc., since 2003; *b* 2 Jan. 1954; *s* of John and Edna Thornton; *m* 1990, Margaret Bradham; two *s* one *d*. *Educ:* Hotchkiss Sch.; Harvard Coll. (AB); Oxford Univ. (MA); Yale Sch. of Mgt. Joined Goldman Sachs, 1980: Gen. Partner, 1988; Co-CEO, Goldman Sachs Internat. (Europe, ME and Africa), 1995–96; Chm., Goldman Sachs-Asia, 1996–98; Pres., and co-Chief Operating Officer, 1999–2003; Dir, Mem. Mgt Cttee, and Co-Chm., Partnership Cttee until 2003. Director: Laura Ashley plc, 1995–2003 (Chm., 1996–99); Ford Motor Co., 1996; Sky (formerly BSkyB) Gp plc; Pacific Century Gp, Inc., 2003–; Intel, 2003; News Corp., 2004–12; China Unicom Ltd, 2008. Mem., Council on Foreign Relns. Dir, Goldman Sachs Foundn. Member, Board of Trustees: Brookings Instn, 2000– (Chm., 2003–); Hotchkiss Sch.; Asia Soc.; Morehouse Coll.; Member: Investment Cttee, Yale Univ.; Adv. Bd, Yale Sch. of Mgt. *Address:* Tsinghua University, 1 Qinghuayuan, Beijing 100084, China.

**THORNTON, Sir Malcolm;** see Thornton, Sir G. M.

**THORNTON, Michael Douglas;** *b* Farnham, Surrey, 1 May 1952; *s* of Sir Peter Eustace Thornton, KCB and of Rosamond Hobart Thornton; *m* 1989, Peta Mary; one *d*. *Educ:* Charterhouse. FPC; CeMAP. Mktg manager, wholesale news and magazines, 1988–93; ind. financial advr and mortgage advr, 1993–2001; business develt manager, mortgage industry, 2001–08; local business bank manager, 2008–11; business develt manager for tax specialists, 2013. Member (Lib Dem): Eastleigh BC, 2007–15; Hants CC, 2017–. MP (Lib Dem) Eastleigh, March 2013–2015; contested (Lib Dem) same seat, 2015, 2017. Member:

Bishopstoke Parish Council, 2008–; Bishopstoke Good Neighbours, 2019–. Chair: Barrett's Oesophagus Campaign, 2015–17; 12th Eastleigh (Bishopstoke) Scouts, 2015–; Trustee, Eastleigh Asian Welfare and Cultural Assoc., 2015–. Gov., Wyvern Coll., 2016–. Street pastor, 2018–. *Recreations:* tennis, table tennis, country walks, squash, cricket, pubs.

**THORNTON, Neil Ross;** Director, Food and Green Economy, Department for Environment, Food and Rural Affairs, 2012–14; *b* 11 Feb. 1950; *s* of late George and Kay Thornton; *m* 1977, Christine Anne Boyes (marr. diss. 2006); two *d*; *m* 2009, Rachel Mary Haywood. *Educ:* Sedbergh Sch.; Pembroke Coll., Cambridge (BA Eng. 1971). Private Sec. to Perm. Sec., DoI, 1975; HM Treasury, 1979; Asst Sec., DTI, 1984; Principal Private Sec. to Sec. of State for Trade and Industry, 1988–90; Under Sec., 1990, Head, Europe Div., 1990–93, Exports to Europe and the Americas Div., 1993–96, DTI; Hd of Food, Drink and Marketing Policy Gp, 1996–99, Hd of Food Industry Competitiveness and Consumers, 1999–2000, MAFF; Hd of Animal Health Gp, MAFF, then Dir, Animal Health, DEFRA, 2000–03; Dir, Sustainable Consumption and Prodn and Waste (formerly Envmt Quality and Waste), DEFRA, 2003–09; Dir, Waste and Resources, and Dir, Delivery Transformation, DEFRA, 2009–12. *Recreations:* literature, choral singing, golf.

**THORNTON, Peter Anthony,** CEng; FRICS; FICE; Chief Executive, 1994–2018, and Chairman, 2008–18, Greycoat Real Estate LLP (formerly Greycoat Estates Ltd) (Consultant, 2018); *b* 8 May 1944; *s* of Robert and Freda Thornton; *m* 1st, 1969, Patricia Greenwood (marr. diss. 1987); one *s* two *d*, 2nd, 1997, Susan Harris. *Educ:* Bradford Grammar Sch.; Manchester Univ. (BSc). CEng 1971; FRICS 1984; FICE 1990. Engineer, Binnie & Partners (Consulting Engrs), 1967–71; self-employed, 1972–75; Commercial Manager, Sears Hldgs plc, 1975–79; Greycoat Plc, subseq. Greycoat Estates Ltd, then Greycoat Real Estate LLP, 1979–2018: Dir, 1981–99; Jt Man. Dir, 1986–94. *Recreations:* cars, tennis, water ski-ing. *Address:* Van Buren Cottage, Queen's Ride, Barnes Common, SW13 0JF. *T:* (020) 8788 1969. *Club:* Riverside Health and Racquet (Chiswick).

**THORNTON, His Honour Sir Peter (Ribblesdale),** Kt 2017; QC 1992; a Senior Circuit Judge, 2007–16; Chief Coroner, 2012–16; *b* 17 Oct. 1946; *s* of late Robert Ribblesdale Thornton, CBE; *m* 1981, Susan Margaret Dalal; one *s* one *d*. *Educ:* Clifton Coll.; St John's Coll., Cambridge (BA). Called to the Bar, Middle Temple, 1969, Bencher, 2001; Asst Recorder, 1994–97; Recorder, 1997–2007; Dep. High Ct Judge, 2003–16; Co-Hd, Doughty St Chambers, 2005–07. Chair: Fitness to Practise Appeals Panel, Royal Free and UC Med. Sch., 2003–07; Discipline Rev. Body, UCL, 2016–; Chairperson Arbitrator, Sports Dispute Resolution Panel, 2004–11. Vis. Prof., KCL, 2018–. Mem., Editl Bd, Criminal Law Review, 1997–. Chairman: NCCL, 1981–83; Civil Liberties Trust, 1991–95. Trustee, Howard League for Penal Reform, 2004–12. Consultant Ed., Jervis on Coroners, 2019–. *Publications:* (contrib.) Civil Liberties 1984, 1984; We Protest: Public Order Debate, 1985; The Civil Liberties of the Zircon Affair, 1987; Public Order Law, 1987; (contrib.) The Polygraph Test, 1988; Decade of Decline: Civil Liberties in the Thatcher Years, 1989; (ed jtly) Penguin Civil Liberty Guide, 1989; (jtly) Justice on Trial, 1992; (ed jtly) Archbold's Criminal Pleadings, Evidence and Practice, 1992–; (contrib.) Analysing Witness Testimony, 1999.

**THORNTON, Sally;** *see* Burgess, Sally.

**THORNTON, Dame Sara (Joanne),** DBE 2019 (CBE 2011); QPM 2006; Independent Anti-Slavery Commissioner, since 2019; *b* Poole, 27 Dec. 1962; *d* of Kenneth and Margreta Thornton; *m* 1st, 1986, Ewan McPhie (marr. diss. 1995); one *s*; 2nd, 1996, Daniel Haigh (marr. diss. 2004); one *s*. *Educ:* Durham Univ. (BA Philos. and Pols); Univ. of Cambridge (Dip. Applied Criminol.; MSt Applied Criminol., 2011). Metropolitan Police Service, 1986–2000; Thames Valley Police: Asst Chief Constable, 2000–03; Dep. Chief Constable, 2003–07; Chief Constable, 2007–15; Chair, Nat. Police Chiefs' Council, 2015–19. Dir, Police Nat. Assessment Centre, 2010–15. Vice Pres., ACPO, 2011–15. Hon. LLD Oxford Brookes, 2010; Hon. PhD Bucks New Univ., 2010. *Publications:* articles in Policing jl. *Recreations:* reading, dancing, keeping fit.

**THORNTON, Stephen,** CBE 2002; Chair, East of England Collaboration for Leadership in Applied Health Research and Care, since 2014; *b* 23 Jan. 1954; *s* of Harry Thornton and Alice Thornton (née Ainsworth); *m* 1976, Lorraine Anne Cassells; one *s* one *d*. *Educ:* Paston Sch., N Walsham, Norfolk; Manchester Univ. (BA Hons Politics and Mod. Hist.). DipHSM. NHS Nat. Mgt Trng scheme, 1979; Administrator: Prestwich Hosp., Manchester, 1980–82; Salford Royal Hosp., 1982–83; Fulbourn Hosp., Cambridge, 1983–85; Gen. Manager, Community Health Services, Cambs, 1985–89; Dir of Planning, E Anglia RHA, 1989–93; Chief Exec., Cambridge and Huntingdon HA, 1993–97; Cabinet Office Top Mgt Programme, 1996; Chief Executive: NHS Confedn, 1997–2002; The Health Foundn (formerly PPP Foundn), 2002–13. Member: NHS Modernisation Bd, 2000–01; Healthcare Commn (formerly Commn for Healthcare Audit and Inspection), 2002–06; NHS Nat. Quality Bd, 2009–14; NMC, 2013–. Non-executive Director: Monitor, 2006–14 (Dep. Chair, 2012–14); Eastern Academic Health Sci. Network, 2013–15; The Pathology Partnership, 2013–15; Senet Gp. 2016–. Mem. Council, Open Univ., 2003–06. Dir, Christian Blind Mission (UK), 2002–04. Trustee, Aquaid Lifeline Fund, 2001–. Hon. FRCP 2010. *Publications:* articles in Health Service Jl.

**THORNTON, Prof. Steven,** DM; FRCOG; Vice Principal for Health, Queen Mary University of London, since 2016; Consultant Obstetrician, Royal London Hospital, since 2016; *b* Lincoln, 4 Nov. 1959; *s* of Harry and Connie Thornton; *m* Georgina Hesling; one *s* one *d*. *Educ:* N Kesteven Comprehensive Sch.; Univ. of Southampton (BM 1983; DM 1989). MRCOG 1989, FRCOG 2004. MRC clinician scientist, Univ. of Cambridge, 1992–96; Prof. of Obstetrics, 1998–2010, Associate Dean (Res.), 2005–10, Univ. of Warwick; Dean: Peninsula Coll. of Medicine and Dentistry, 2010–12; Univ. of Exeter Med. Sch., 2012–15. Hon. Consultant Obstetrician, Royal Devon and Exeter Hosp., 2010–15. R&D Dir, Univ. Hosp. Coventry and Warwickshire NHS Trust, 2005–10; Clin. Dir, Comprehensive Local Res. Network, W Midlands (S), 2007–10; Res. Lead, W Midlands SHA, 2008–10. *Publications:* (ed) Pain in Obstetrics and Gynaecology, 2001; (ed) Hypertension in Pregnancy, 2003; (ed) Pre-term Labour, 2004; (ed) Pre-term Labour: best practice and research in clinical obstetrics and gynaecology, 2007; papers, research findings, letters and book chapters. *Recreations:* squash, running, motor sports, kite surfing. *Address:* Barford House, 4 Fieldgate Lane, Kenilworth, Warks CV8 1BT. *T:* 07771 747277; Queen Mary University of London, 2nd Floor, Dean Rees House, Charterhouse Square, EC1M 6BQ. *E:* steve.thornton@qmul.ac.uk. *Club:* Gynaecological Travellers.

**THORNTON, Rt Rev. Timothy Martin;** Bishop at Lambeth, since 2017; Bishop to the Forces, since 2017; an Honorary Assistant Bishop: Diocese of London, since 2017; Diocese of Portsmouth, since 2017; *b* 14 April 1957; *s* of John and Mary Thornton; *m* 1978, Siân Evans; one *s* one *d*. *Educ:* Southampton Univ. (BA Theol. 1978); St Stephen's House, Oxford (Cert. Theol.); KCL (MA Ecclesl Hist. 1997). Ordained deacon, 1980, priest, 1981; Asst Curate, Todmorden, Dio. Wakefield, 1980–83; Priest i/c, Walsden, 1983–85; Chaplain, UC Cardiff, 1985–87; Bishop's Chaplain: Wakefield, 1987–91; London, 1991–94; Principal, N Thames Ministerial Trng Course, 1994–98; Vicar of Kensington, 1998–2001; Area Bishop of Sherborne, 2001–08; Bishop of Truro, 2008–17. DL Dorset, 2007–08. *Address:* Lambeth Palace, SE1 7JU.

**THORNTON, Victoria Jane Dianne,** OBE 2012; Founding Director, Open-City, and Open House concept, 1992–2016; Founder and Chair, Open House Worldwide, since 2010; *b* Rochford, 12 Jan. 1953; *d* of Bill Thornton and Marianne Thornton (née Elliott); *m* 2007, Ken Allinson. *Educ:* Birkbeck, Univ. of London (MA 2009). Dir, Architectural Dialogue, 1983–2019; estabd RIBA Architecture Centre, 1994–98; Architecture Consultant to British Council VAD, 1998–2000; Advr, ALDEA Chile, 2017–. Member: Bd, Irish Architecture Foundn, 2005–13; Adv. Bd, Spacehive, 2012–; Res. Cttee, RIBA, 2013–; Council, AA, 2016– (Pres., 2018–). Trustee, Bath Preservation Trust, 2018–. Judge, Women in Architecture, 2012–. Freeman, Chartered Architects' Co., 2015–. Hon. FRIBA 2003. Hon. MA Metropolitan, 2005. *Publications:* (with K. Allinson) London's Contemporary Architecture: a visitor's guide, 2000, 6th edn as London's Contemporary Architecture: an explorer's guide, 2014; Open House London: 100 buildings, 2012. *Recreations:* architecture, hiking, food. *Address:* Quay House, 2c Kings Grove, SE15 2NB. *T:* 07525 934669. *E:* vthornton@urbandialogue.co.uk.

**THORNTON, Dr William Dickson,** CB 1990; Deputy Chief Medical Officer, Department of Health and Social Services, Northern Ireland, 1978–90, retired; *b* 9 July 1930; *s* of late William J. Thornton and Elfreda Thornton (née Dickson); *m* 1957, Dr Maureen Gilpin; one *s* three *d*. *Educ:* Portora Royal School; Trinity College Dublin (BA, MD). FFPH. General medical practitioner, 1955–65; NI Hospitals Authy, 1966–72; Dept of Health and Social Services (NI), 1973–90. Civil QHP, 1990–92. Chm., 1993–97, Vice-Pres., 2001–, Age Concern (NI). *Recreations:* boating, reading, gardening. *Address:* 54 Deramore Park South, Belfast BT9 5JY. *T:* (028) 9066 0186.

**THOROGOOD, Alfreda, (Mrs D. R. Wall),** FRAD; Artistic Director of Dance, Elmshurst School for Dance and the Performing Arts (formerly Elmhurst Ballet School), 1994–2004 (Senior Teacher, 1992–94); *b* Westminster, 17 Aug. 1942; *d* of Alfreda and Edward Thorogood; *m* 1967, David Richard Wall, CBE (*d* 2013); one *s* one *d*. *Educ:* Lady Eden's Sch.; Royal Ballet Sch., Jun. and Sen.; ARAD; Dip. PDTC. FRAD 2016. Royal Ballet Company: Soloist, 1965; Principal Dancer, 1968–80; Guest Repetiteur, 2018–19; Bush Davies School: Sen. Teacher, 1982–84; Dep. Ballet Principal, 1984–89; Dir, 1988–89; Artistic Advr, Royal Acad. of Dancing, 1989–92; Dance Consultant and Assessor, English Nat. Ballet Sch., 2004–19 (Gov., 2012–19). Guest Repetiteur, English Nat. Ballet Co., 2006–13. *Recreations:* music, art, reading, gardening, interior design, grandchildren. *Address:* 34 Croham Manor Road, S Croydon, Surrey CR2 7BE.

**THOROGOOD, Rev. Bernard George,** OBE 1992; General Secretary, United Reformed Church, 1980–92; *b* 21 July 1927; *s* of Frederick and Winifred Thorogood; *m* 1952, Jannett Lindsay Paton (née Cameron) (*d* 1988); two *s*; *m* 1991, Joan Tierney. *Educ:* Glasgow Univ. (MA); Scottish Congregational College. Ordained in Congregational Church, 1952; missionary appointment under London Missionary Society in South Pacific Islands, 1953–70; Gen. Sec., Council for World Mission, 1971–80. Moderator, Exec. Cttee, BCC, 1984–90; Mem., Central Cttee, WCC, 1984–91. DD Lambeth 1992. *Publications:* Not Quite Paradise, 1960; Guide to the Book of Amos, 1971; Our Father's House, 1983; Risen Today, 1987; The Flag and The Cross, 1988; No Abiding City, 1989; On Judging Caesar, 1990; One Wind Many Flames, 1991; Looking at Leisure: a European view, 1991; (ed) Gales of Change, 1994; Letters to Paul, 1999; Reef Passage, 2014; A Minister's Minutes, 2015; Shield of Faith, 2016; A Beginner's ABC of Christian History, 2017. *Recreation:* sketching. *Address:* Unit 1/12 Congham Road, West Pymble, NSW 2073, Australia. *T:* (2) 94987069.

**THOROLD, Sir (Anthony) Oliver,** 16th Bt *cr* 1642, of Marston, Lincolnshire; *b* 15 April 1945; *o s* of Captain Sir Anthony Thorold, 15th Bt, OBE, DSC and Jocelyn Elaine Laura Thorold (née Heathcote-Smith); *S* father, 1999, but his name does not appear on the Official Roll of the Baronetage; *m* 1977, Genevra Mercy Richardson, *qv*; one *s* one *d*. *Educ:* Winchester; Lincoln Coll., Oxford. Called to the Bar, Inner Temple, 1971. *Heir: s* Henry Lowry Thorold, *b* 6 Aug. 1981. *Address:* (chambers) 53–54 Doughty Street, WC1N 2LS; 8 Richmond Crescent, N1 0LZ.

**THORP, David;** Director, Livingbridge VC LLP (formerly ISIS Capital plc, then ISIS EP LLP), since 1995 (Chairman, 2001–04; Partner, 2005–14; Consultant, 2014–16; Managing Director, Friends Ivory & Sime Private Equity (formerly Ivory & Sime Baronsmead) plc, 1997–2001); Director, Sussex Place Ventures Ltd, since 2016 (Chairman, 2004–16); *b* 22 July 1945; *s* of late John and Kathleen Mary Thorp; *m* 1969, Christine Janice Kenyon; three *s*. *Educ:* Portsmouth Grammar Sch.; Queens' College, Cambridge (MA Natural Scis); London Business School (MBA). Alcan (UK), 1967–69; ICFC, then FFI, subseq. 3i plc, 1971–91, Dir, 1985–91; Dir-Gen., ESU, 1991–94. Chairman: Unipalm Ltd, 1992–94; Unipalm Gp plc, 1994–95; non-executive Director: Baronsmead VCT plc, 1995–2005; Patientline plc (formerly Patientline Ltd), 1998–2001 (Chm., Patientline Ltd, 1994–98); Job Opportunities Ltd, 2000–04; Assoc. of Investment Cos, 2007–16 (Dep. Chm., 2013–14). Mem. Council, 1997–2002, Chm., 2000–01, BVCA (formerly British Venture Capital Assoc.); Chm., AIC VCT Forum, 2006–16. Non-exec. Dir, Royal Surrey County Hosp., 1990–97. Liveryman, Glovers' Co., 2013–. *Recreations:* tennis, walking. *Address:* Larks Hill, 16 Longdown, Guildford, Surrey GU4 8PP. *T:* (01483) 561016.

**THORP, (Ian) Simon; His Honour Judge Thorp;** a Circuit Judge, since 2013. Called to the Bar, Inner Temple, 1988; a Recorder, 2002–13; a District Judge, 2008–13. *Address:* Worthing County Court, The Law Courts, Christchurch Road, Worthing, W Sussex BN11 1JD.

**THORP, Jeremy Walter,** CMG 2001; HM Diplomatic Service, retired; a Director, British Bankers' Association, and Secretary, Joint Money Laundering Steering Group, 2002–06; *b* 12 Dec. 1941; *s* of Walter and Dorothy Bliss Thorp; *m* 1973, Estela Lessa Guyer. *Educ:* King Edward VII Sch., Sheffield; Corpus Christi Coll., Oxford (MA). HM Treasury, 1963–67; DEA, 1967–69; HM Treasury, 1969–71; First Sec. (Financial), HM Embassy, Washington, 1971–73; HM Treasury, 1973–78; FCO, 1978–82; Head of Chancery, Lima, 1982–86; FCO, 1986–88; Dep. Hd of Mission, Dublin, 1988–92; Head of Resource and Finance, then Resource Planning, Dept, FCO, 1993–97; with Unilever PLC, 1997–98; Ambassador to Colombia, 1998–2001. Dir, British and Colombian Chamber of Commerce, 2003–; Mem., Exec. Cttee, Anglo-Colombian Soc., 2002– (Dep. Chm., 2004–06; Chm., 2006–10). Mem. Adv. Council, Farnham Castle Briefing and Conf. Centre, 2002–06. Trustee, Children Change Colombia (formerly Children of the Andes), 2002–15. *Recreations:* music, travel, looking at paintings, modern Irish history, walking, Latin America, Germany. *Address:* 9 Coutts Crescent, St Albans Road, NW5 1RF.

**THORP, Julia Anne L.;** *see* Lee-Thorp, J. A.

**THORP, Michelle;** Chief Executive Officer, Insolvency Practitioners Association, since 2018; *b* Birkenhead, 30 Sept. 1976; *d* of Leslie James Barlow and Rita Pardoe (née Burns). *Educ:* Bishops Bluecoat C of E High Sch.; Univ. of Edinburgh (MA Hons Hist. 1999); Saïd Business Sch., Univ. of Oxford (Maj. Projects Leadership Acad. 2016). Internat. and Eur. Criminal Justice Policy, and Spending Review Policy Team, Lord Chancellor's Dept, then DCA, 2000–02; Cabinet Cttee Sec., Econ. and Domestic Affairs Secretariat, Cabinet Office, 2002–03; Hd, Judicial Remuneration, 2003–04, Principal Speechwriter to Sec. of State, 2004–05, DCA; Sen. Manager, Deloitte CIS, 2006–07; Pte Sec. to Chm. of Judicial Appts Commn and Co. Sec. to Bd, MoJ, 2007–09, Dep. Dir, Projects, 2009–11, Min. of Justice; Dep. Dir, Major Projects Authy, 2011–13, Dir, 2013–15, Cabinet Office (Transformation Dir, Crown Commercial Service, 2014); Dir, NHS England (on secondment), 2015; Man. Dir, Global Transformation and Digital, Data and Technol., UKTI, then DIT, 2016–18. *Address:* Insolvency Practitioners Association, Valiant House, 1st Floor, 4–10 Heneage Lane, EC3A 5DQ. *E:* michelle.thorp@yahoo.com.

**THORP, Nicola Jayne Maria Louise**, FRCR; Consultant Clinical Oncologist, Clatterbridge Cancer Centre NHS Foundation Trust (formerly Clatterbridge Centre for Oncology NHS Foundation Trust), since 2001; *b* Shrewsbury, 11 April 1967; *d* of John Thorp and Elaine Thorp; *m* 1997, John Brennan; one *s* two *d*. *Educ:* Edgbaston High Sch. for Girls; Univ. of Leicester (MB ChB 1990). MRCP 1994; FRCR 1998. Junior doctor in Leicester, Liverpool and Clatterbridge. Chm., Brain Tumour Gp, 2013–; Mem. Exec., Children's Cancer and Leukaemia Gp, 2013–. Trustee, Nat. Mus Liverpool, 2011–. Gov., Belvedere Sch. GDST, 2006–09. *Recreations:* family, fell walking, Burgundy wine. *Address:* Clatterbridge Cancer Centre NHS Foundation Trust, Bebington, Wirral CH63 4JY. *T:* (0151) 334 1155, ext. 4859. *E:* nicky.thorp@clatterbridgecc.nhs.uk.

**THORP, Simon**; *see* Thorp, I. S.

**THORPE, Adrian Charles**, CMG 1994; MA; HM Diplomatic Service, retired; Ambassador to Mexico, 1999–2002; *b* 29 July 1942; *o s* of late Prof. Lewis Thorpe and Dr Barbara Reynolds; *m* 1968, Miyoko Kosugi. *Educ:* The Leys Sch., Cambridge; Christ's Coll., Cambridge (MA). HM Diplomatic Service, 1965–2002: Tokyo, 1965–70; FCO, 1970–73; Beirut, 1973–76 (Head of Chancery, 1975–76); FCO, 1976; Tokyo, 1976–81; FCO, 1981–85, Hd of IT Dept, 1983–85; Counsellor (Econ.), Bonn, 1985–89; Dep. High Comr, Kuala Lumpur, 1989–91; Minister, Tokyo, 1991–95; Ambassador to the Philippines, 1995–98. Man. Dir, Traviata Books Ltd, 2004–13. FRSA. *Publications:* articles in journals. *Recreations:* opera, travel, bookshops, comfort. *Address:* The Cider House, Over Compton, Sherborne, Dorset DT9 4QU. *Club:* Oxford and Cambridge.

**THORPE, Prof. Alan John**, OBE 2016; PhD; Director General, European Centre for Medium-Range Weather Forecasts, 2011–15; Visiting Professor of Meteorology, University of Reading, since 2006; *b* 15 July 1952; *s* of Jack Fielding Thorpe and Dorothy Kathleen Thorpe (*née* Davey); *m* 1979, Helen Elizabeth Edgar; one *s* one *d*. *Educ:* Univ. of Warwick (BSc Physics); Imperial Coll., London (PhD). Res. Asst, Imperial Coll., London, 1976–81; Scientist, Met. Office, 1981–82; University of Reading: Lectr, 1982–88, Reader, 1988–92, Prof., 1992–2006, Dept of Meteorol.; on leave of absence as Dir, Hadley Centre, Met. Office, 1999–2001; Dir, NERC Centres for Atmospheric Sci., 2001–05; Chief Exec., NERC, 2005–11. Hon. DSc Reading, 2017. *Publications:* over 100 papers in atmospheric sci. jls. *Recreation:* art appreciation.

**THORPE, Alexander Lambert**; QC 2017; *b* Salisbury, 4 June 1969; *s* of Rt Hon. Sir Mathew Alexander Thorpe, *qv; m* 1st, 2000 (marr. diss. 2010); one *s*; 2nd, 2010, Paloma Ucelay Ruiz; two *s*. *Educ:* Eton; King's Coll. London (BD). Called to the Bar, Inner Temple, 1995; in practice as barrister, specialising in matrimonial financial remedies. *Recreation:* food and wine. *Address:* Queen Elizabeth Building, Temple, EC4Y 9BS. *T:* (020) 7797 7837, *Fax:* (020) 7353 5422. *E:* a.thorpe@qeb.co.uk.

**THORPE, His Honour Anthony Geoffrey Younghusband**; a Circuit Judge, 1990–2008; *b* 21 Aug. 1941; *s* of G. J. Y. Thorpe, MBE; *m* 1966, Janet Patricia; one *d* (one *s* decd). *Educ:* Highgate School; Britannia Royal Naval College (scholarship); King's College London. Royal Navy: served HM Ships Hermes, Ark Royal, Vidal, Blake; Captain 1983; Chief Naval Judge Advocate, 1983–86; retired from RN 1990. Called to the Bar, Inner Temple, 1972 (Treasurer's Prize); Asst Recorder, 1984–89, Recorder, 1989–90; Resident Judge, Chichester Crown Ct, 2000–08. Pres., Ind. Tribunal Service, 1992–94 (Social Security, Medical, Disability, and Vaccine Damage Appeals, Child Support Appeals). Judicial Mem., Parole Bd for England and Wales, 2008–10. *Publications:* articles in learned jls incl. Ocean Develt and Internat. Law. *Recreation:* sailing. *Address:* 79 Bishopsgate Walk, Chichester, W Sussex PO19 6FQ.

**THORPE, Ian James**, AM 2019 (OAM 2001); swimmer; *b* Sydney, 13 Oct. 1982; *s* of Kenneth William and Margaret Grace Thorpe. *Educ:* East Hills Boys High Sch. Founder, Ian Thorpe's Fountain for Youth, charity, 2000–14. World Championships: Perth, 1998: Gold Medal: 400m freestyle; 4 x 200m freestyle relay; Fukuoka, 2001: Gold Medal: 200m freestyle; 400m freestyle; 800m freestyle; 4 x 100m freestyle relay; 4 x 200m freestyle relay; 4 x 100m medley relay; Barcelona, 2003: Gold Medal: 200m freestyle; 400m freestyle; 4 x 200m freestyle relay; Silver Medal, 200m individual medley; Bronze Medal, 100m freestyle; Commonwealth Games: Kuala Lumpur, 1998: Gold Medal: 200m freestyle; 400m freestyle; 4 x 100m freestyle relay; 4 x 200m freestyle relay; Manchester, 2002: Gold Medal: 100m freestyle; 200m freestyle; 400m freestyle; 4 x 100m freestyle relay; 4 x 200m freestyle relay; 4 x 100m medley relay; Silver Medal, 100m backstroke; Pan Pacific Championships: Sydney, 1999: Gold Medal: 200m freestyle; 400m freestyle; 4 x 100m freestyle relay; 4 x 200m freestyle relay; Yokohama, 2002: Gold Medal: 100m freestyle; 200m freestyle; 400m freestyle; 4 x 100m freestyle relay; 4 x 200m freestyle relay; Silver Medal, 4 x 100m medley relay; Olympic Games: Sydney, 2000: Gold Medal: 400m freestyle; 4 x 100m freestyle relay; 4 x 200m freestyle relay; Silver Medal, 100m freestyle; 4 x 100m medley relay; Athens, 2004: Gold Medal: 200m freestyle; 400m freestyle; Silver Medal, 4 x 200m freestyle relay; Bronze Medal, 100m freestyle. Aust. Male Athlete of the Year, 1999, 2000, 2001, 2004; Young Australian of the Year, 2000; American Internat. Athlete Trophy, 2001; Telstra People's Choice Award, 2001, 2002; Centenary Medal, 2001. *Publications:* The Journey, 2000; Live Your Dreams, 2002; This Is Me (autobiog.), 2012. *Recreations:* surfing, movies, going out with friends, charity work. *Club:* SLC Aquadot (Sydney).

**THORPE, Rt Hon. Sir Mathew Alexander**, Kt 1988; PC 1995; a Lord Justice of Appeal, 1995–2013; Deputy Head, Family Justice, and Head of International Family Justice, 2005–13; *b* 30 July 1938; *s* of late Michael Alexander Thorpe and Dorothea Margaret Lambert; *m* 1st, 1966, Lavinia Hermione Buxton (marr. diss. 1989); two *s* (and one *s* decd); 2nd, 1989, Mrs Carola Millar (marr. diss. 2013). *Educ:* Stowe; Balliol Coll., Oxford. Called to the Bar, Inner Temple, 1961, Bencher, 1985; QC 1980; a Recorder, 1982–88; a Judge of the High Court, Family Div., 1988–95. *Address:* 1 Hare Court, Temple, EC4Y 7BE.
See also A. L. Thorpe.

**THORPE, Nigel James**, CVO 1991; HM Diplomatic Service, retired; *b* 3 Oct. 1945; *s* of Ronald Thorpe and Glenys (*née* Robillard); *m* 1969 (marr. diss. 1976); two *s*; *m* 1978 (marr. diss. 2001); three *d*. *Educ:* East Grinstead Grammar Sch.; University Coll. of S Wales and Monmouthshire (BA Hons). Joined HM Diplomatic Service, 1969; Warsaw, 1970–72; Dacca, 1973–74; FCO, 1975–79; Ottawa, 1979–81; seconded to Dept of Energy, 1981–82; Asst Hd of Southern Africa Dept, FCO, 1982–85; Counsellor, Warsaw, 1985–88; Dep. High Comr, Harare, 1989–92; Head, Central European Dept, FCO, 1992–96; Sen. Directing Staff, RCDS (on secondment), 1996–97; Ambassador to Hungary, 1998–2003.

Chm., Vodafone Hungary Foundn, 2003; acting Dir, Vodafone Gp Foundn, 2005–06; Dir, Corporate Affairs, Vodafone Hungary, 2004–07. Pres., Friends of Hungarian Fine Arts Mus., 2007–08. Trustee: Liszt Acad. Network, 2001–; Personal Support Unit, 2010–13; Friends of the Connection, St Martin in the Fields (Sec., 2014); Chm., Respond, 2011–14 (Trustee, 2009–14). *Publications:* Harmincad Utca 6, a 20th Century History of Budapest, 1999. *Recreations:* gardening, carpentry, tennis (Sec., Old Coll. Lawn Tennis and Croquet Club, 2013–16).

**THORPE, Phillip Andrew**; Chairman and Chief Executive Officer, 2005–12, Advisor to Chairman, since 2012, Qatar Financial Centre Regulatory Authority; Advisor to Governor, Qatar Central Bank, since 2012; *b* 26 Aug. 1954; *s* of late Reginald Thorpe, OBE and of Fay Eglantine Thorpe; *m* 1st, 1976, Isabell Hanna Henkel (marr. diss. 1989); one *s* two *d*; 2nd, 1990, Melinda Kilgour Lewis (marr. diss. 1997); one *s* one *d*; 3rd, 1998, Jane Chunhae Kang. *Educ:* Victoria Univ., Wellington, NZ (BA Pol Sci., LLB); Univ. of Hong Kong (MSocSc Dist.). Admitted Barrister and Solicitor of Supreme Court of NZ and as Solicitor and Notary Public, Republic of Nauru. Solicitor, Beyer Christie O'Regan & Partners, Wellington, NZ, 1976–79; Legal Officer and Public Prosecutor, Govt of Republic of Nauru, 1979–81; Solicitor, Registrar-General's Dept, Hong Kong Govt, 1981–83; Hong Kong Securities Commission: Sen. Legal Advr, 1983–86; Asst Comr, 1986–88; Dep. Comr, 1988–89; Exec. Vice-Chm. and Chief Exec., Hong Kong Futures Exchange, 1987–89; Chief Exec., Assoc. of Futures Brokers and Dealers Ltd, 1989–91; Exec. Dir and Dep. Chief Exec., SFA Ltd, 1991–93; Exec. Dir and Chief Exec., London Commodity Exchange (1986) Ltd, 1991–92; Chief Exec., IMRO, 1993–98; Man. Dir, Authorisations, Enforcement, and Consumer Relns, FSA, 1998–2001; Pres., Futures Industry Inst., Washington, 2001–02; Chief Comr, Regulatory Agency, Dubai, then Chief Exec., Dubai Financial Services Authy, 2002–04. *Publications:* (Country Editor for Hong Kong) International Securities Regulation, 1986. *Recreations:* fishing, flying. *Address:* c/o PO Box 22989, Doha, Qatar.

**THORPE, Rt Rev. Richard Charles**; *see* Islington, Bishop Suffragan of.

**THORPE, Prof. Stephen Austen**, PhD; FRS 1991; Professor of Oceanography, University of Southampton, 1986–2003, now Emeritus. *Educ:* Rutherford Coll., Newcastle (BSc London 1958); Trinity Coll., Cambridge (BA 1961; PhD 1966). SPSO, Inst. of Oceanographic Scis, NERC, until 1986. Mem., NERC, 1991–94 (Mem., Marine Scis Cttee). Hon. Prof., Sch. of Ocean Scis, Univ. of Wales, Bangor, 2001–. Pres., RMetS, 1990–92; Vice-Pres., Scottish Assoc. for Marine Sci., 1993–2009, 2011–15. Walter Munk Medal, US Office of Naval Res. and Oceanography Soc., 1998; Fridtjof Nansen Medal, Eur. Geophysical Soc., 2000. *Publications:* (ed jtly) Oceanography, 1996; (ed jtly) Encyclopedia of Oceanography, 2001, 2nd edn 2009; The Turbulent Ocean, 2005; An Introduction to Ocean Turbulence, 2007; contribs to learned jls. *Address:* 1A Green Edge, Beaumaris, Anglesey LL58 8BY. *T:* (01248) 209579.

**THORPE-TRACEY, Stephen Frederick**; Controller, Newcastle Central Office, Department of Social Security (formerly of Health and Social Security), 1986–89, retired; *b* 27 Dec. 1929; *s* of Rev. and Mrs J. S. V. Thorpe-Tracey; *m* 1955, Shirley Byles; one *s* two *d*. *Educ:* Plymouth Coll. Emergency Commn, 1948; Short Service Commn, 1950; Regular Commn, DLI, 1952; Staff Coll., Camberley, 1960 (psc); GSO2, Defence Operational Res. Estabt, 1961–64; Training Major, 8 DLI (TA), 1964–65; Major, 1 DLI, 1965–66; GSO2, MoD, 1966–70; direct entry, Home Civil Service, 1970; Principal, DHSS, 1970; Asst Sec., 1977; Under Sec., 1986. Mem., Prescription Pricing Authy, 1990–93. Hon. Secretary: Mid Devon Div., SSAFA (formerly SSAFA and FHS, then SSAFA Forces Help), 1992–99; Uffculme Br., RBL, 1995–2013 (Chm., 2013–). Mem., Uffculme Parish Council, 1995–2003. Chm., Uffculme Soc., 1994–2002. Chairman: Trustees, Coldharbour Mill, 1996–2006 (Hon. Sec., 1994–96); Coldharbour Mill Ltd, 1998–2006. Chm., Tiverton Chess Club, 1994–; Pres., Devon County Chess Assoc., 2003–05, 2007–11. *Recreation:* chess. *Address:* 12 Carlton Court, Wells, Som BA5 1SF. *T:* (01749) 679985.

**THOULD, Anthony Julian**, MA; Head Master, King Edward VI School, Southampton, since 2002; *b* 16 June 1958; *s* of late Dr Anthony Keith Thould and of Bernine Thould; *m* 1984, Susan Jane Isabelle Rentoul; three *s* one *d*. *Educ:* King's Coll., Taunton; Pembroke Coll., Oxford (MA Hist.). Distribn Manager, H. P. Bulmer Plc, 1981–84; asst teacher, Westminster Sch., 1984–88; Hd of Hist., 1988–91, Dir of Studies, 1991–97, Cranleigh Sch.; Dir of Studies, King's Sch., Worcester, 1997–2002. *Recreations:* classical guitar, fencing. *Address:* King Edward VI School, Southampton SO15 5UQ. *E:* headmaster@kes.hants.sch.uk.

**THRASHER, Prof. Adrian James**, PhD; FRCP; FRCPCH; FRCPath; FRSB; FMedSci; Professor of Paediatric Immunology, since 2002, and Lead for Programme of Infection, Immunity, Inflammation and Physiological Medicine, since 2013, Great Ormond Street Institute of Child Health (formerly Institute of Child Health), University College London; *b* Shoreham-by-Sea, W Sussex, 27 May 1962; *s* of Paul and Isobel Thrasher; *m* 1991, Kanchan Pandurang Rege; two *s* one *d*. *Educ:* Brighton Coll.; St George's Hosp. Med. Sch. (MB BS 1986); PhD London 1995. MRCP 1989, FRCP 2004; MRCPCH 1998, FRCPCH 2011; FRCPath 2009; FRSB (FSB 2011). Hse physician, St Helier Hosp., Carshalton, 1986–87; hse surgeon, Ashford Hosp., Middx, 1987; Senior House Officer in Medicine: Broomfield Hosp., Chelmsford, 1987–88; Royal Surrey Co. Hosp., Guildford, 1988–89; Locum Registrar in Medicine, Royal Surrey Co. Hosp., then Dulwich Hosp., 1989; SHO in Thoracic Medicine, Brompton Hosp., 1989; University College Hospital: Registrar in Gen. Medicine, 1989–90; Sen. Registrar, 1992–93; University College London: Lectr in Molecular Medicine and Hon. Sen. Registrar in Medicine, 1990–91; Wellcome Clin. Trng Fellow and Hon. Sen. Registrar in Medicine, 1991–94; Lectr, Molecular Immunology Unit, Inst. of Child Health, 1994–98; Wellcome Trust Clin. Sci. Fellow, 1995–99, Sen. Fellow, 1999–2009; Sen. Lectr in Paediatric Immunol., 1998–2002; Dir, Centre for Immunodeficiency, Inst. of Child Health, 2006–13; Dir, Clin. Gene Therapy Prog., Gt Ormond St Hosp., 2001–. NIHR Sen. Investigator, 2008–16, now Emeritus. Hon. Consultant: Gt Ormond St Hosp. for Children NHS Trust, 1998–; UCL Hosps, 2000–; Vis. Specialist in Paediatric Immunol., Addenbrooke's Hosp. NHS Trust, 2004–. Co-Founder and Mem., Scientific Adv. Bd, Orchard Therapeutics, 2016–; Scientific Advisor: Rocket Pharmaceuticals; Generation Bio. Mem., Editl Bd, 2005–, Associate Ed., 2011–, Human Gene Therapy; Mem. Editl Bd, 2007–, Associate Ed., 2008–, Molecular Therapy. Member: British Soc. of Immunol., 1997–; Sci. Adv. Panel, Neuroblastoma Soc., 2003–11; Exec. Mem. Cttee, British Soc. for Cell and Gene Therapy (formerly British Soc. for Gene Therapy), 2004– (Pres., 2009–13); Bd Mem., Eur. Soc. for Cell and Gene Therapy, 2015–. Gov., London Acad. of Excellence, 2012–. FMedSci 2005. Descartes Prize for Res. and Sci., EU, 2005; Outstanding Achievement Award, Eur. Soc. of Gene and Cell Therapy, 2011; Gene Therapy Pioneer Award, Human Gene Therapy Jl, 2014. *Publications:* contrib. chapters in books including: Oxford Textbook of Medicine, 3rd edn 1995; Clinical Studies in Medical Biochemistry, 2nd edn 1998; Concise Oxford Textbook of Medicine, 2000; Encyclopedia of Life Sciences, 2001; Gene Therapy: the use of DNA as a drug, 2002; Blood and Bone Marrow Pathology, 2002; contrib. articles to jls incl. Jl Biol. Chem., Lancet, Qly Jl Medicine, Immunodeficiency, Nature, Biochem. Jl, Gene Therapy, Blood, British Jl Haematol., Eur. Jl Haematol.; Human Gene Therapy, British Jl Immunol., BMJ, Leukemia. *Recreations:* astronomy, cycling, cricket, photography. *Address:* Blaysworth Manor, Colmworth, Beds MK44 2LD. *E:* a.thrasher@ucl.ac.uk.

**THRELFALL, David**; actor; *b* 12 Oct. 1953. *Educ:* Wilbraham Comprehensive Sch.; Sheffield Art Coll.; Manchester Polytechnic Sch. of Theatre. Associate Artistic Dir, Royal Exchange Theatre, Manchester, 1998–2001. *Stage:* Bed of Roses, Royal Court; 3 years with RSC, incl. Savage Amusement, Nicholas Nickleby, 1980 (Clarence Derwent Award, British Theatre Assoc., SWET Award); Not Quite Jerusalem, Royal Court, 1982; Hamlet, Edinburgh Fest., 1986; Bussy D'Ambois, Old Vic, 1988; Wild Duck, Phoenix, 1990; Count of Monte Cristo, Royal Exchange, 1994; Richard II, Cottesloe, RNT, 1995; Hedda Gabler, Chichester, 1996; Present Laughter, Royal Exchange, 1997; The Rehearsal, NY, 1997; Peer Gynt, Royal Exchange, 1999; Tartuffe, RNT, 2002; The Entertainer, Derby Playhouse, 2003; Skellig, Young Vic, 2003; Someone Who'll Watch Over Me, New Ambassadors, 2005; Don Quixote, Swan, 2016, transf. West End, 2018; *television:* The Kiss of Death, 1976; Jumping the Queue, 1989; Clothes in the Wardrobe, 1993; Mary and Jesus, 1999; In the Beginning, 2000; series: Nicholas Nickleby, 1984; Paradise Postponed, 1985; The Marksman, 1988; Nightingales, 1990; Titmuss Regained, 1991; Statement of Affairs, Diana: Her True Story, 1993; Men of the World, 1994; Sex & Chips & Rock-'n'-Roll, 1999; Dinner of Herbs, 2000; Shameless (10 series; also dir 11 episodes), 2004–13 (North West Comedy Award, 2004; RTS Award, 2004, 2007, 2009, 2012); The Queen's Sister, 2005 (RTS Award); Constantine, Housewife 49 (BAFTA Award, 2007), 2006; Whistleblower, 2007; What Remains, 2013; Tommy Cooper: Not Like That, Like This, 2014; The Ark, Code of a Killer, Midwinter of the Spirit, 2015; Ripper Street, 2015; Troy: Fall of a City, 2018; *radio:* three series of Baldi; John Gabriel Borkman, 2015; Das Kapital, 2019; *films:* When the Whales Came, 1989; The Russia House, 1990; Patriot Games, 1992; Master and Commander, 2003; Alien Autopsy, 2006; Elizabeth: The Golden Age, Hot Fuzz, 2007; Black Sea, 2014. Hon. DArt: Manchester, 2013; Sheffield, 2014. Plays and Players Promising Newcomer, 1978. *Recreations:* motor bike, friends. *Address:* c/o Independent Talent Group Ltd, 40 Whitfield Street, W1T 2RH.

**THRIFT, Sir Nigel (John)**, Kt 2015; PhD, DSc; DL; FBA 2003; Vice-Chancellor, University of Warwick, 2006–16; Chair, Committee on Radioactive Waste Management, since 2018; *b* 12 Oct. 1949; *s* of Leonard John Thrift and Joyce Mary Wakeley; *m* 1978, Lynda Jean Sharples; two *d*. *Educ:* UCW, Aberystwyth (BA Hons); Univ. of Bristol (PhD 1979; DSc 1992); MA Oxon 2004. Research Fellow: Dept of Architecture, Univ. of Cambridge, 1975–76; Dept of Geog., Univ. of Leeds, 1976–78; Dept of Human Geog., ANU, 1979–81 (Sen. Res. Fellow, 1981–83); Lectr, 1984–86, Reader, 1986–87, St David's UC, Lampeter; Bristol University: Lectr, 1987–88; Reader, 1988–90; Prof. of Geography, 1990–2003, now Emeritus; Head, Dept of Geog., 1995–99; University of Oxford: Prof. of Geography, 2003–06; Hd, Div. of Life and Envmtl Scis, 2003–05; Student of Christ Church, 2004–06; Pro-Vice-Chancellor (Res.), 2005–06; Vis. Prof. of Geog., 2006–. Visiting Professor: Macquarie Univ., 1989; UCLA, 1992; Univ. of Vienna, 1998; Nat. Univ. of Singapore, 2002; Dist. Vis. Prof., Tsinghua Univ., Beijing, 2018–. Exec. Dir, Schwarzman Scholars, 2016–17. Mem., Geography Res. Assessment Panel, HEFCE RAE, 1997–2003; Chair, Main Panel H, 2008 RAE, 2004–06. FCO Marshall Fund Comr, 2010–15. Member: Bd, Higher Educn Stats Agency, 2008–15; Adv. Panel, Nat. Curriculum Rev., 2010–13; Governing Body, Eur. Inst. of Innovation and Technol., 2012–16; Monash Commn on Future of Aust. Higher Educn, 2017–18; Chair: IPPR Commn on Future of HE, 2011–12; Russell Gp A-level Content Adv. Bd, 2012–13. Dir, Nat. Centre for Univs and Business (formerly Trustee, Council for Industry and HE), 2012–14; Trustee: Liverpool Sch. of Tropical Medicine, 2013–15; Higher Educn Policy Inst., 2014–16; Mem., Bd of Trustees, Singapore Management Univ., 2018–. Fellow: Netherlands Inst. Advanced Study, 1993; Swedish Collegium for Advanced Study in Social Scis, 1999. FAcSS (AcSS 2001). DL W Midlands, 2014. Hon DLaws Bristol, 2010; Hon. LLD Monash, 2013. Heath Award, 1988, Victoria Medal, 2003, RGS; Medal, Univ. of Helsinki, 1999; Dist. Scholarship Honors, Assoc. of Amer. Geographers, 2007; Gold Medal, RSGS, 2009. *Publications:* (with D. N. Parkes) Times, Spaces, Places, 1980; (with D. K. Forbes) The Price of War, 1986; Spatial Formations, 1996; (with A. Leyshon) Money/Space, 1997; (jtly) Shopping, Place and Identity, 1998; (with A. Amin) Cities, 2002; Knowing Capitalism, 2005; Non-Representational Theory, 2007; (with P. Glennie) Shaping the Day, 2009; (with A. Amin) Arts of the Political, 2013; (with A. Amin) Seeing Like a City, 2016; numerous ed volumes; contrib. chapters in ed vols, and papers in learned jls. *Recreations:* reading, writing.

**THROUP, Margaret Ann**; MP (C) Erewash, since 2015; *b* W Yorks, 27 Jan. 1957. *Educ:* Univ. of Manchester (BSc Hons Biol.). Biomed. scientist, Calderdale HA; sales exec., product manager, mktg manager, business develt; Dir, In-Vitro Diagnostic Div., pharmaceutical co.; business consultant. PPS, DHSC, 2018–. Member: Health Select Cttee, 2015–18; Scottish Affairs Select Cttee, 2015–16. Mem., Parly Assembly, Council of Europe, 2017. *Address:* House of Commons, SW1A 0AA.

**THRUSH, Prof. Brian Arthur**, FRS 1976; Professor of Physical Chemistry, University of Cambridge, 1978–95, now Emeritus; Fellow, Emmanuel College, Cambridge, since 1960; *b* Hampstead Garden Suburb, 23 July 1928; *s* of late Arthur Albert Thrush and late Dorothy Charlotte Thrush (*née* Money); *m* 1958, Rosemary Catherine Terry (*d* 2016), *d* of late George and Gertrude Terry, Ottawa; one *d* (one *s* decd). *Educ:* Haberdashers' Aske's Sch.; Emmanuel Coll., Cambridge (Schol. 1946–50). BA 1949, MA, PhD 1953, ScD 1965. University of Cambridge: Demonstrator in Physical Chemistry, 1953; Asst Dir of Research, 1959; Lectr in Physical Chemistry, 1964, Reader, 1969; Hd of Dept of Physical Chemistry, 1986–88; Head of Dept of Chemistry, 1988–93; Tutor, 1963–67, Dir of Studies in Chemistry, 1963–78, Vice-Master, 1986–90 and Acting Master, 1986–87, Emmanuel Coll. Consultant Physicist, US Nat. Bureau of Standards, Washington, 1957–58; Sen. Vis. Scientist, Nat. Res. Council, Ottawa, 1961, 1971, 1980. Tilden Lectr, Chem. Soc., 1965; Vis. Prof., Chinese Acad. of Science, 1980–; Member: Faraday Division, Chem. Soc., 1976–79; US Nat. Acad. of Scis Panel on Atmospheric Chemistry, 1975–80; Lawes Agric. Trust Cttee, 1979–89; NERC, 1985–90; Council, Royal Society, 1989–91; NATO Panel on Global Change, 1989–92. Pres., Chemistry Sect., BAAS, 1986. Mem., Academia Europaea, 1990 (Mem., Council, 1992–98). M. Polanyi Medal, RSC, 1980; Rank Prize for Opto-Electronics, 1992. *Publications:* papers on gas kinetics and spectroscopy in Proc. Royal Soc., Trans Faraday Soc., etc. *Recreations:* wine, gardening. *Address:* Brook Cottage, Pemberton Terrace, Cambridge CB2 1JA. *T:* (01223) 357637.

**THUBRON, Colin Gerald Dryden**, CBE 2007; travel writer and novelist, since 1966; *b* 14 June 1939; *s* of late Brig. Gerald Ernest Thubron, DSO, OBE, and Evelyn (*née* Dryden); *m* 2011, Margreta de Grazia. *Educ:* Eton Coll. Editorial staff, Hutchinson & Co., 1959–62; freelance television film maker, Turkey, Japan, Morocco, 1962–64; Editorial staff, Macmillan Co., New York, 1964–65. FRSL 1969 (Vice-Pres., 2003–09; Pres., 2010–17); FRAS 1991. Hon. DLitt Warwick, 2002. Mungo Park Medal, RSGS, 2000; Lawrence of Arabia Meml Medal, RSAA, 2001; Travel Award, Soc. of Authors, 2008; Ness Award, RGS, 2011; Internat. Prize, Spanish Geographical Soc., 2014; Stanford Award for Outstanding Contrib. to Travel Writing. *Publications: non-fiction:* Mirror to Damascus, 1967; The Hills of Adonis, 1968; Jerusalem, 1969; Journey into Cyprus, 1975; The Royal Opera House, 1982; Among the Russians, 1983; Behind the Wall, 1987 (Thomas Cook Award, Hawthornden Prize, 1988); The Lost Heart of Asia, 1994; In Siberia, 1999 (Prix Bouvier, Fest. Saint-Malo, 2010); Shadow of the Silk Road, 2006; To a Mountain in Tibet, 2011; *novels:* The God in the Mountain, 1977; Emperor, 1978; A Cruel Madness, 1984 (Silver Pen Award, 1985); Falling, 1989; Turning Back the Sun, 1991; Distance, 1996; To The Last City, 2002; Night of Fire, 2016; contribs The Times, TLS, NY Rev. of Books. *Address:* 28 Upper Addison Gardens, W14 8AJ. *T:* (020) 7602 2522.

**THURLEY, Anna Julia**; *see* Keay, A. J.

**THURLEY, Dr Simon John**, CBE 2011; FSA; Senior Research Fellow, Institute of Historical Research, since 2015; Executive Director, Architrave Historical Services Ltd, since 2017; *b* 29 Aug. 1962; *s* of late Thomas Manley Thurley and of Rachel Thurley (*née* House); *m* 1st, 1998, Katharine (*née* Goodison) (marr. diss. 2007); 2nd, 2008, Anna Julia Keay, *qv*; one *s* one *d* (twins). *Educ:* Kimbolton Sch., Cambs; Bedford Coll., London (BA Hist.; Hon. Fellow, RHBNC, 2003); Courtauld Inst., London (MA, PhD Art Hist.). Inspector of Ancient Monuments, Crown Buildings and Monuments Gp, English Heritage, 1988–90; Curator, Historic Royal Palaces, 1990–97; Dir, Mus. of London, 1997–2002; Chief Exec., English Heritage, 2002–15. Vis. Prof. of Medieval London History, Royal Holloway, Univ. of London, 2000–06; Vis. Prof. of the Built Envmt, Gresham Coll., 2009–. Member: Cttee, Soc. for Court Studies, 1996– (Chm., 2005–11); Council, St Paul's Cathedral, 2001–15; Bd, British Liby, 2015–. President: City of London Archaeol Soc., 1997–2002; Huntingdonshire Local Hist. Soc., 2004–; London and Middlesex Archæol Soc., 2006–08; Vice-Pres., NADFAS, 2000–08; Patron, London Parks and Gardens Trust, 2001; Trustee: Dickens House Mus., 1998–2002; Canal and River Trust, 2011–16; Andrew Lloyd Webber Foundn, 2015–. FSA 2004; MCIfA (MIFA 1998); FRHistS 2006. Hon. RIBA 2006; Hon. RICS 2008. Writer and Presenter, TV series: The Lost Buildings of Britain, 2004; Buildings that Shaped Britain, 2006. *Publications:* (jtly) Henry VIII: images of a Tudor King, 1989; The Royal Palaces of Tudor England, 1993; Whitehall Palace, 1999; Hampton Court Palace: a social and architectural history, 2003; The Lost Buildings of Britain, 2004; Whitehall Palace, 2008; Somerset House, 2009; Men from the Ministry: how Britain saved its heritage, 2013; The Building of England: how the history of England has shaped our buildings, 2013; Houses of Power: the places that shaped the Tudor world, 2017; contribs to books and jls. *Recreation:* ruins. *E:* simon@kingstaithe.com.

**THURLOW, 9th Baron** *cr* 1792; **Roualeyn Robert Hovell-Thurlow-Cumming-Bruce**; chartered surveyor; Principal, RCB Advisors, since 2007; *b* London, 13 April 1952; *s* of 8th Baron Thurlow, KCMG and Yvonne Hovell-Thurlow-Cumming-Bruce (*née* Wilson); *S* father, 2013; *m* 1980, Bridget Anne Julia Insay Cheape; two *s* two *d*. *Educ:* 13 schs in 4 continents. MRICS 1979. Partner, 1985–99, Man. Dir, 1999–2007, Jones Lang Wootton, later Jones Lang LaSalle. Elected Mem., H of L, 2015. *Recreations:* country sports, Real tennis. *Heir: s* Hon. Nicholas Edward Decimus Hovell-Thurlow-Cumming-Bruce [*b* 16 Feb. 1986; *m* 2014, (Sophie) Joanna Heriot Maitland; one *s* one *d*]. *Address:* House of Lords, SW1A 0PW. *Clubs:* White's, Pratt's.

**THURLOW, Alan John**, FRCO; FRSCM; Organist and Master of the Choristers, Chichester Cathedral, 1980–2008; *b* 18 May 1947; *s* of John Edward Thurlow and Mary Bruce Thurlow (*née* Bennallack); *m* 1974, Christina Mary Perren. *Educ:* Bancroft's Sch., Woodford; Sheffield Univ. (BA 1st cl. Hons 1968); Emmanuel Coll., Cambridge. FRCO 1972; FRSCM 2007. Sub Organist, Durham Cathedral, 1973–80. Chairman: On Organ Fund, 1990–; Friends of Cathedral Music, 1990–2002; Organs Adv. Cttee, Council for the Care of Churches, 1997–2006; Chichester Diocesan Adv. Cttee, 2011–16; British Inst. of Organ Studies, 2011–; Organists Charitable Trust, 2015–; President: Cathedral Organists Assoc., 1995–96; IAO, 2009–13. DMus Lambeth, 2005. *Recreations:* walking, cycling. *Address:* 8 Old Bakery Gardens, Chichester, W Sussex PO19 8AJ. *T:* (01243) 533092. *Club:* Chichester City (Pres., 2004–11).

**THURSO, 3rd Viscount** *cr* 1952, of Ulbster; **John Archibald Sinclair**; Bt 1786; PC 2014; Chairman, VisitScotland, since 2016; Lord Lieutenant for Caithness, since 2017; *b* 10 Sept. 1953; *er s* of 2nd Viscount Thurso and Margaret Beaumont Sinclair (*née* Robertson); *S* father, 1995; *m* 1976, Marion Ticknor (*née* Sage); two *s* one *d*. *Educ:* Summerfields; Eton Coll. FIH (FHCIMA 1991); Master Innholder 1991. Savoy Hotel plc: Trainee, 1972; Gen. Manager and Dir, Lancaster Hotel, Paris, 1981–85; Gen. Manager and Dir, Cliveden, 1985–92; Chief Executive Officer: Granfel Hldgs, 1992–95; Champneys Gp Ltd, 1995–2001; Chm., Scrabster Harbour, 1997–2001; non-executive Director: Savoy Hotel plc, 1993–98; Lochdhu Hotels Ltd, 1975– (Chm., 1995–); Sinclair Family Trust Ltd, 1976– (Chm., 1995–); Thurso Fisheries Ltd, 1979– (Chm., 1995–); Ulbster Hldgs Ltd, 1994– (Chm., 1994–); Profile Selection and Recruitment Ltd, 1995–2002; Walker Greenbank PLC, 1997–2002 (Chm., 1999–2002); Royal Olympic Cruise Lines Inc. (USA), 1997–99; Mosimann's Ltd, 1998–2002. President: Licensed Victuallers Schs, 1997–98; Acad. of Food and Wine Service, 1998–. Patron: HCIMA, 1998–2003; IMS, 1998–2017. Lib Dem Spokesman on tourism, 1997–99, on food, 1998–99, H of L. MP (Lib Dem) Caithness, Sutherland and Easter Ross, 2001–15; contested (Lib Dem) same seat, 2015. Lib Dem Spokesman on Scottish matters, 2001–06, on transport, 2003–05, on business, innovation and skills (formerly business, enterprise and regulatory reform), 2009–10, H of C. Mem., H of C Commn, 2010–15; Chair, Finance and Services Cttee, H of C, 2010–15. Elected Mem., H of L, 2016. Member: Ind. Parly Standards Authy, 2015–16; VisitBritain, 2016–. FInstD 1997. *Recreations:* shooting, fishing, food and wine. *Heir: s* Hon. James Alexander Robin Sinclair [*b* 14 Jan. 1984; *m* 2010, Claire Rebecca, *e d* of John Schofield; one *s*]. *Address:* Thurso East Mains, Thurso, Caithness KW14 8HW. *Clubs:* Brooks's; New (Edinburgh).

**THWAITE, Ann Barbara**, DLitt; FRSL; writer; *b* London, 4 Oct. 1932; *d* of A. J. Harrop, LittD, PhD and H. M. Valentine of New Zealand; *m* 1955, Anthony Simon Thwaite, *qv*; four *d*. *Educ:* Marsden School, Wellington, NZ; Queen Elizabeth's Girls' Grammar Sch., Barnet; St Hilda's Coll., Oxford (MA 1959); DLitt Oxford 1998. FRSL 1987. Contributing Ed. and Mem., Editl Bd, Cricket Mag. Gp (US), 1974–2000. Vis. Prof., Tokyo Women's Univ., 1985–86; Helen Stubbs Meml Lectr, Toronto Public Library, 1990; Ezra Jack Keats Meml Lectr, Univ. of Southern Mississippi, 1992. Churchill Travelling Fellowship, 1993; Gladys Krieble Delmas Fellowship, British Library, 1998–99. Hon. Fellow, Univ. of Surrey Roehampton (Nat. Centre for Res. in Children's Literature), 2001. Regular reviewer of children's books: TLS, 1963–85; Guardian, TES. Vice-Pres., Tennyson Soc., 1997–. Governor: St Mary's Middle Sch., Long Stratton, Norfolk, 1990–2002; Hapton VC Primary Sch., Norfolk, 1995–2006. Hon. DLitt UEA, 2012. *Publications:* Waiting for the Party: the life of Frances Hodgson Burnett, 1974, reissued as Frances Hodgson Burnett: beyond the Secret Garden, 2007; (ed) My Oxford, 1977; Edmund Gosse: a literary landscape, 1984 (Duff Cooper Meml Prize, 1985); A. A. Milne: his life, 1990 (Whitbread Biography Award); (ed) Portraits from Life: essays by Edmund Gosse, 1991; The Brilliant Career of Winnie-the-Pooh, 1992; Emily Tennyson: the poet's wife, 1996; Glimpses of the Wonderful: the life of Philip Henry Gosse, 2002; Passageways: the story of a New Zealand family, 2009; Running in the Corridors: seven stories, 2014; Goodbye Christopher Robin: A. A. Milne and the making of Winnie-the-Pooh, 2017 (filmed 2017); *children's books* *include:* The Young Traveller in Japan, 1958; The House in Turner Square, 1960; Home and Away (US edn as The Holiday Map), 1967; The Travelling Tooth, 1968; The Camelthorn Papers, 1969; The Only Treasure, 1970; Tracks, 1978; (ed) Allsorts 1–7, 1968–75; (ed) Allsorts of Poems, 1978; The Ashton Affair, 1995; The Horse at Hilly Fields, 1996. *Recreations:* other people's lives, messing about on the river. *Address:* The Mill House, Low Tharston, Norfolk NR15 2YN. *T:* (01508) 489569. *Clubs:* Society of Authors, Royal Over-Seas League.

**THWAITE, Anthony Simon,** OBE 1990; FRSL; FSA; poet; Editorial Consultant, André Deutsch Ltd, 1992–95 (Director, 1986–92); *b* 23 June 1930; *s* of late Hartley Thwaite, JP, FSA, and Alice Evelyn Mallinson; *m* 1955, Ann Barbara Harrop (*see* A. B. Thwaite); four *d*. *Educ:* Kingswood Sch.; Christ Church, Oxford (MA). Vis. Lectr in English, Tokyo Univ., 1955–57; Producer, BBC, 1957–62; Literary Editor, The Listener, 1962–65; Asst Prof. of English, Univ. of Libya, 1965–67; Literary Editor, New Statesman, 1968–72; co-editor, Encounter, 1973–85. Henfield Writing Fellow, Univ. of East Anglia, 1972; Vis. Prof., Kuwait Univ., 1974; Japan Foundn Fellow, Tokyo Univ., 1985–86; Poet-in-Residence, Vanderbilt Univ., 1992. Member: Literature Adv. Cttee (formerly English Teaching Adv. Cttee), British Council, 1978–2002; Cttee, Royal Literary Fund, 1993–2014; Council, RSL, 2003–08. Chm. of Judges, Booker Prize, 1986. Pres., Philip Larkin Soc., 1995–. FRSL 1978; FSA 2000. Hon. Lay Canon, Norwich Cathedral, 2005–. Hon. Fellow, Westminster Coll., Oxford, 1990. Hon. DLitt: Hull, 1989; UEA 2007. Cholmondeley Poetry Award, 1983. *Publications: poetry:* Home Truths, 1957; The Owl in the Tree, 1963; The Stones of Emptiness, 1967 (Richard Hillary Memorial Prize, 1968); Penguin Modern Poets 18, 1970; Inscriptions, 1973; New Confessions, 1974; A Portion for Foxes, 1977; Victorian Voices, 1980; Poems 1953–1983, 1984; Letter from Tokyo, 1987; Poems 1953–1988, 1989; The Dust of the World, 1994; Selected Poems 1956–1996, 1997; A Different Country, 2000; A Move in the Weather, 2003; Collected Poems, 2007; Late Poems, 2010; Going Out (East Anglian Book Award for Poetry), 2015; *criticism:* Contemporary English Poetry, 1959; Poetry Today, 1973, rev. and expanded, 1985, 1996; Twentieth Century English Poetry, 1978; Six Centuries of Verse, 1984 (companion to Thames TV/Channel 4 series); Anthony Thwaite in Conversation with Peter Dale and Ian Hamilton, 1999; *travel:* (with Roloff Beny) Japan, 1968; The Deserts of Hesperides, 1969; (with Roloff Beny and Peter Porter) In Italy, 1974; (with Roloff Beny) Odyssey: Mirror of the Mediterranean, 1981; *editor:* (with Geoffrey Bownas) Penguin Book of Japanese Verse, 1964, rev. and expanded, 1998 and 2009; (with Peter Porter) The English Poets, 1974; (with Fleur Adcock) New Poetry 4, 1978; Larkin at Sixty, 1982; (with John Mole) Poetry 1945 to 1980, 1983; Collected Poems of Philip Larkin, 1988, rev. edn 2003; Selected Letters of Philip Larkin, 1992; Further Requirements: Philip Larkin, 2001; The Ruins of Time, 2006; Poet-to-Poet: John Skelton, 2008; Philip Larkin: letters to Monica, 2010; *for children:* Beyond the Inhabited World, 1976. *Recreations:* archaeology, antiquarian beachcombing, pottery. *Address:* The Mill House, Low Tharston, Norfolk NR15 2YN. *T:* (01508) 489569.

**THWAITES, Prof. Sir Bryan,** Kt 1986; MA, PhD; CMath, FIMA; Hon. Professor, Southampton University, since 1983; *b* London, 6 Dec. 1923; *e s* of late Ernest James and Dorothy Marguerite Thwaites; *m* 1948, Katharine Mary (*d* 1991), 4th *c* of late H. R. Harries and late Mrs L. Harries, Longhope, Glos; four *s* two *d*. *Educ:* Dulwich College (Fellow, 2006); Winchester College; Clare College, Cambridge (Wrangler, 1944). Scientific Officer, National Physical Laboratory, 1944–47; Lecturer, Imperial College, London, 1947–51; Assistant Master, Winchester College, 1951–59; Professor of Theoretical Mechanics, Southampton Univ., 1959–66; Principal, Westfield Coll., London, 1966–83 (Hon. Fellow, 1983; Hon. Fellow, QMW, 1990). Gresham Prof. in Geometry, City Univ., 1969–72. Co-founder and Co-Chm., Education 2000, 1982–86. Hon. Sec. and Treas., Dulwich College Mission, 1946–57; inventor of the Thwaites Flap, 1947. Chm. and Mem. ARC Cttees, 1948–69. Mem. Exec. Cttee, Internat. Commn on Math. Instruction, 1967–70. Special Lecturer, Imperial College, 1951–58. Chm., Southampton Mathematical Conf., 1961. Founding Director of the School Mathematics Project, 1961–75, Chm. of Trustees, 1966–83, Life Pres., 1984; Chm. of Internat. Mathematical Olympiad, first in UK, 1979; Chm. Adv. Council, ICL/CES, 1968–84. Member: Approved Sch. Cttee, Hampshire CC, 1954–58, 1961–66; US/UK (Fulbright) Commn, 1966–76; Davies Cttee on CSSB, 1969–70; Council, Kennedy Inst. of Rheumatology, 1969–71; Ct of London Univ., 1975–81; Council, Middlesex Hosp. Med. Sch., 1975–83; Court, Southampton Univ., 1981–94; Council, European Atlantic Gp, 2004–10. Chm., Collegiate Council, London Univ., 1973–76; Chm., Delegacy, Goldsmiths' Coll., 1975–80. Mem. Acad. Advisory Committee: Univ. of Bath, 1964–71; Open Univ., 1969–75. Chairman of: Council of C of E Colleges of Education, 1969–71; Church of England Higher Educn Cttee, 1974–76; Northwick Park Hosp. Management Cttee, 1970–74; Brent and Harrow AHA, 1973–82; Wessex RHA, 1982–88; King's Fund Enquiry into Sen. Management Trng in NHS, 1975–76; Nat. Staff Cttee for Admin. and Clerical Staff, NHS, 1983–86; Enquiry into Radiotherapy Incident, Exeter Hosp., 1988. Founding Chm., British False Memory Soc., 1993. Chairman: Govs, Heythrop Coll., 1978–82; Friends of Winchester Coll., 1989–91; Govs, More House, 1993–96; Trustee: Westfield Coll. Develt Trust, 1979–83; Southampton Med. Sch. Trust, 1982–88; Richmond Coll., 1987–93 (Academic Gov., 1992–2000); City Tech. Colls Trust, 1987–97; Forbes Trust, 1987–2009; Patron: Winchester Detached Youth Project, 1990–96; Winchester Coll., 2017–. Pres., Dulwich Prep. Coll. Old Boys, 2012–15. Mercier Lectr, Whitelands Coll., 1973; Foundn Lectr, Inst. of Health Policy Studies, Southampton Univ., 1987; 25th Anniv. Lectr, Nuffield Inst., Leeds Univ., 1988. Shadow Vice-Chancellor, Independent Univ., July–Nov. 1971. Hon. Life Mem., Math. Assoc., 1962. JP, Winchester City Bench, 1963–66. A Vice-Pres., Friends of GPDST, 1975–95. Mem. Council, 1964–94, Pres., 1966–67, Hon. Fellow, 2004, Institute of Mathematics and its Applications. Sponsor, Family and Youth Concern (formerly The Responsible Society), 1979–98 (Trustee, 1992–98). Founding Chm., 2001–04, Life Pres., 2004, Soc. of Our Lady at Winton. Founder, Millstream Forum, Bosham, 2009–19. *Publications:* (ed) Incompressible Aerodynamics, 1960; (ed) On Teaching Mathematics, 1961; The SMP: the first ten years, 1973; (ed) Hypotheses for Education in AD 2000, 1983; (ed) A Contemporary Catholic Commentary, 1998; numerous contributions to Proc. Royal Soc., Reports and Memoranda of Aeronautical Research Council, Quart. Jl of Applied Mech., Jl of Royal Aeronautical Soc., etc. *Recreations:* music, sailing, writing letters to The Times. *Address:* The Byre, Salthill Park, Fishbourne, W Sussex PO19 3PS. *T:* (01243) 790142. *E:* bryan.thwaites@btinternet.com. *Clubs:* Athenæum, Royal Air Force, Victory Services.

**THWAITES, Jacqueline Ann;** *see* Duncan, J. A.

**THWAITES, Ronald,** QC 1987; *b* 21 Jan. 1946; *e s* of Stanley Thwaites and Aviva Thwaites; *m* 1972, Judith Myers; three *s* one *d*. *Educ:* Richard Hind Secondary Tech. Sch.; Grangefield Grammar Sch., Stockton-on-Tees; Kingston Coll. of Technol. (subseq. Polytechnic, now Univ.); LLB London (external) 1968. Called to the Bar, Gray's Inn, 1970. *Recreations:* swimming, lighting bonfires. *E:* ronaldthwaites@icloud.com.

**THWAITES, Roy;** Deputy Director, South Yorkshire Branch, British Red Cross Society, 1990–96; *b* 13 Aug. 1931; *s* of Walter and Emily Alice Thwaites; *m* 1st, 1954, Margaret Anne (née Noble) (marr. diss.); one *s*; 2nd, 1991, Mary (née Appleby). *Educ:* Southey Green Secondary Sch.; Sheffield Central Technical Sch. City Councillor, Sheffield, 1965–74, Chief Whip and Chm. of Transport Cttee, 1969–74; South Yorkshire County Council: Councillor, 1973–86; Chief Whip and Chm. Passenger Transport Authority, 1973–78; Dep. Leader, 1978–79; Leader, and Chm. of Policy Cttee, 1979–86. Dep. Chm. and Dir, SYT Ltd, 1986–93. Member: E Midlands Airport Consultative Gp, 1982–86; Industrial Tribunals, 1987–2001. Vice-Chm., 1979–84, Dep. Chm., 1984–86, AMA; Member: Local Authorities' Conditions of Service Adv. Bd, 1979–86; Yorks and Humberside County Councils Assoc., 1983–86; Vice-Chm., 1982–85, Chm., 1985–86, NJC Local Govt Manual Workers Employers. Mem., Special Employment Measures Adv. Gp, MSC, 1983–86. Dep. Chm., Nat. Mining Mus. Trust (formerly Yorks Mining Mus. Trust), 1984–93 (Dir, 1986–92). Dep. Pres., Northern Racing Coll. (formerly Northern Racing Sch. Trust), 2004– (Dep. Chm., 1986–2004). Hon. Fellow, Sheffield City Poly., 1982. *Recreations:* walking, reading, photography.

**THYKIER, Claudia;** *see* Winkleman, C.

**THYNE, Malcolm Tod,** MA; FRSE; Headmaster, Fettes College, Edinburgh, 1988–98; *b* 6 Nov. 1942; *s* of late Andrew Tod and Margaret Melrose Thyne; *m* 1969, Eleanor Christine Scott; two *s*. *Educ:* The Leys Sch., Cambridge; Clare Coll., Cambridge (MA Nat. Scis with Pt II in Chem.; Cert. of Educn). FRSE 1994. Asst Master, Edinburgh Acad., 1965–69; Asst Master, Oundle Sch., 1969–72, Housemaster, 1972–80; Headmaster, St Bees School, 1980–88. Develt Dir, Arkwright Scholarship Trust, 1999–2000. Gov., St Bees Sch., Cumbria, 2000–05; Dir, Edinburgh Acad., 2000–07. Trustee: CLIC, 2000–03; Cumbria Cerebral Palsy, 2003–10. *Publications:* Periodicity, Atomic Structure and Bonding (Revised Nuffield Chemistry), 1976. *Recreations:* hillwalking, organic gardening, watercolours. *Address:* Tofts Close, 37 Uppleby, Easingwold, York YO61 3BD. *T:* (01347) 823063.

**THYNN,** family name of **Marquess of Bath**.

**THYNN, Alexander;** *see* Bath, Marquess of.

**THYSSEN, Marianne Leonie Petrus;** Member, European Commission, 2014–19; *b* Sint-Gillis-Waas, Belgium, 24 July 1956. *Educ:* Catholic Univ. of Leuven (law degree 1979). Res. asst, Faculty of Law, Catholic Univ. of Leuven, 1979–80; legal advr, Union of Self-employed Entrepreneurs and to Markant, 1980–88; Dir, Res. Dept, Union of Self-employed Entrepreneurs, 1988–91; Legal Associate, Sec. of State for Public Health, Belgium, 1986–88. MEP, 1991–2014. Pres., Christen-Democratisch en Vlaans Party, 2008–10.

**TIBBER, His Honour Anthony Harris;** a Circuit Judge, 1977–99; *b* 23 June 1926; *s* of Maurice and Priscilla Tibber; *m* 1954, Rhona Ann Salter (*d* 2016); three *s*. *Educ:* University College School, London; Magdalen College School, Brackley. Served in Royal Signals, 1945–48; called to the Bar, Gray's Inn, 1950; a Recorder of the Crown Court, 1976. Member: Matrimonial Causes Rule Cttee, 1980–84; Matrimonial Causes Procedure Cttee (Booth Cttee), 1983–85. Arbitrator and mediator, 2002–. *Recreations:* cultivating, idling, pottering. *Address:* 2 Osprey Court, 256 Finchley Road, NW3 7AA. *T:* (020) 7433 3234. *See also* P. H. Tibber.

**TIBBER, Peter Harris,** DPhil; HM Diplomatic Service, retired; Ambassador to Colombia, 2015–19; *b* 7 Sept. 1956; *s* of His Honour Anthony Harris Tibber, *qv*; *m* 1983, Eve Levy-Huet, MSc (Oxon); three *s*. *Educ:* Haberdashers' Aske's Sch.; University Coll., Oxford (MA; DPhil 1983). FCO, 1984–86; Paris, 1986–88; First Sec., FCO, 1988–90; Private Sec. to Minister of State, FCO, 1990–92; Ankara, 1993–96; Dep. Hd of Mission, Mexico City, 1996–2000; Trade Partners UK, subsequently UK Trade & Investment: Dir, Africa and ME, 2000–01; Internat. Mgt Directorate, 2001–02; Dir, Internat. Sectors (formerly Business) Gp, 2002–04; Consul-Gen., Dusseldorf, and Dir Gen., Trade and Investment, Germany, 2005–09; Dep. High Comr, Islamabad, Pakistan, 2009–11; Interim High Comr, Kenya, 2011–12; Ambassador to Sudan, 2012–15. *Recreations:* choral singing, piano, tennis, swimming, fiction. *E:* peter.tibber@gmail.com.

**TIBBITT, Rear Adm. Ian Peter Gordon,** CBE 2007; FRAeS; FIET; defence management consultant, since 2009; Managing Director, TDHB Ltd, since 2009; *b* 22 Oct. 1954; *s* of Peter Tibbitt and Daphne Tibbitt; *m* 1980, Marion Diane Lyons; two *d*. *Educ:* Arnold Sch.; Sidney Sussex Coll., Cambridge (BA 1976). MIET, CEng 1984; FRAeS 2003; FIET 2009. Joined RN as Air Engr Officer, 1973; Commando Helicopter and Sea Harrier Sqdns; acquisition, logistics and change mgt specialist, Merlin Mk 1 Project Manager, 1996–99; on staff of C-in-C Fleet, 2000–02; Dir Logistic Support (Air), 2002–03; Defence Logistics Orgn Restructuring Team Leader, 2003–04; Dir Logistics Rotary Wing, 2004–07; Dir Gen. Safety and Engrg, Defence Equipment and Support, MoD, 2007–09. Trustee, Fly Navy Heritage Trust, 2011–. *Recreation:* hockey (qualified hockey umpire). *T:* 07854 219409. *E:* mail@tdhb.co.uk.

**TIBBS, (Geoffrey) Michael (Graydon),** OBE 1987; Secretary of the Royal College of Physicians, 1968–86 (Secretary of Joint Faculty of Community Medicine, 1971–72, of Joint Committee in Higher Medical Training, 1972–86, and of Faculty of Occupational Medicine, 1978–86); *b* 21 Nov. 1921; *s* of Rev. Geoffrey Wilberforce Tibbs, sometime Chaplain RN and Vicar of Lynchmere, Sussex, and Margaret Florence Tibbs (née Skinner); *m* 1951, Anne Rosemary Wortley; two *s*. *Educ:* Berkhamsted Sch.; St Peter's Hall, Oxford. BA Hons Geography, 1948; MA 1952. FInstAM; MCIPD; FRGS. Served RNVR, Ordinary Seaman/Lieut, 1940–46 (despatches), HMS Cottesmore, HMS Sheffield, HM S/M Tantalus, HM S/M Varne. Sudan Political Service, Kordofan Province, 1949–55: seconded to MECAS, 1950; Dist Comr, Dar Messeria District, 1953. Various appointments in personnel, organisation and overseas services depts, Automobile Assoc., 1955–68. Hon. Mem., Soc. of Occupational Medicine, 1983; Hon. FRCP 1986; Hon. FFOM 1986; Hon. FFCM 1987. Freeman, City of London, 1986. *Publications:* Hello Lad, Come to join the Navy?, 2013; (with Anne Tibbs): A Look at Lynchmere, 1990; A Sudan Sunset, 2000; Another Look at Lynchmere, 2004. *Recreations:* producing pantomimes, parish affairs, preserving lowland heath, making bonfires. *Address:* Bunchfield, Lynchmere Ridge, Haslemere, Surrey GU27 3PP. *T:* (01428) 643120, 642176. *Club:* Naval.

**TICEHURST, David Keith; His Honour Judge Ticehurst;** a Circuit Judge, since 1998; Resident Judge, Taunton Crown Court, since 2013; *b* 1 May 1950; *s* of Frederick John and Barbara Elisabeth Ticehurst; *m* 1972, Gillian Shepherd; two *s* one *d*. *Educ:* Taunton's Grammar Sch., Southampton; Keynsham Grammar Sch., Bristol; Kingston Poly. (BA). Admitted solicitor, 1975; articled clerk, 1971–73, Solicitor, 1975–78, Lawrence & Co., Bristol; Solicitor, Osborne Clarke, Bristol, 1978–98 (Partner, 1980–98); Asst Recorder, 1991–94; Recorder, 1994–98. Founder Mem., Employment Lawyers' Assoc., 1992. Judicial Studies Board, later Judicial College, 2003–06; Equal Treatment Adv. Cttee, 2002–06; Tutor Judge, 2004–16. Gov., Sidcot Sch., 2002–07. Chm., Winscombe Youth Club, 2008–. Trustee, Fly 2Help, 2006–13. *Recreations:* cricket, watching Rugby, painting, reading. *Address:* Taunton Crown Court, Shire Hall, Taunton, Som TA1 4EU. *Clubs:* Winscombe Rugby Football (Vice-Pres.); Gloucestershire County Cricket (Life Mem.); Old Herpesians Cricket (Pres., 1998–).

**TICKELL, Prof. Adam Thomas,** PhD; Vice-Chancellor, University of Sussex, since 2016; b London, 14 Nov. 1964; s of Patrick Jocelyn Tickell and Diana Jane Tickell; m 1991, Bridget Kelly; two d. *Educ:* Warriner Comprehensive Sch.; Cheney Comprehensive Sch.; Univ. of Manchester (BA 1987; PhD 1992). Res. Fellow, Univ. of Manchester, 1989–91; Lecturer in Geography: Univ. of Leeds, 1991–94; Univ. of Manchester, 1994–97; Professor of Geography: Univ. of Southampton, 1997–2000; Univ. of Bristol, 2000–06; Prof. of Geography, 2006–11, Dean, Social Scis, 2006–09, Vice Principal, 2009–11, RHUL; Prof. of Geography, 2012–16, Pro Vice-Chancellor, Res., 2012–14, Provost, 2014–16, Univ. of Birmingham. *Publications:* Politics and Practice in Economic Geography, 2007; Globalisation in Practice, 2014; contrib. articles to learned jls. *Recreations:* hiking, family, arts. *Address:* Vice-Chancellor's Office, University of Sussex, Brighton BN1 9RH. *E:* vc@sussex.ac.uk.
*See also Dame O. C. Tickell, S. M. Tickell.*

**TICKELL, Lt Gen. Christopher Linley,** CBE 2011 (OBE 2003; MBE 2001); Deputy Chief of the General Staff, since 2019; b Epsom, 17 March 1964; s of Richard Tickell and Angela Tickell; m 1995, Fiona Gifford; two d. *Educ:* Wellington Coll.; Cranfield Univ. (MA Military Studies). Joined Army, 1983; Troop Comdr, Germany, NI, GB, Norway and Botswana, 1984–91; Adjt 39 Engr Regt, 1992–93; SO3 5 Airborne Bde, 1993–94; sc 1995; SO2 Operational Requirements, MoD, 1996–98; OC 9 Parachute Sqn, 1998–2000; Co. Comdr, RMA Sandhurst, 2001; SO1 Ops, HQ Land, 2002; CO 23 Engr Regt (Air Assault), 2003–05; Col Trng, Directorate of Trng, 2005–07; Comdr 8 Force Engr Bde, 2007–09; Dir, Army Div., 2010–12; GOC Army Recruiting and Trng Div., 2013–16; Dir, Capability, 2016–19. *Recreations:* walking, swimming, cycling, family.

**TICKELL, Dame Clare;** see Tickell, Dame O. C.

**TICKELL, Sir Crispin (Charles Cervantes),** GCMG 1989 KCVO 1983 (MVO 1958); HM Diplomatic Service, retired; Warden, Green College, Oxford, 1990–97 (Hon. Fellow, 1997); b 25 Aug. 1930; s of late Jerrard Tickell and Renée (née Haynes); m 1st, 1954, Chloë (marr. diss. 1976), d of late Sir James Gunn, RA, PRP; two s one d; 2nd, 1977, Penelope, d of late Dr Vernon Thorne Thorne. *Educ:* Westminster (King's Schol.; Hon. Fellow, 1993); Christ Church, Oxford (Hinchliffe and Hon. Schol.; 1st Cl. Hons Mod. Hist. 1952). FZS 2014. Served with Coldstream Guards, 1952–54; entered HM Diplomatic Service, 1954. Served at: Foreign Office, 1954–55; The Hague, 1955–58; Mexico, 1958–61; FO (Planning Staff), 1961–64; Paris, 1964–70; Private Sec. to successive Ministers responsible for British entry into the European Community, 1970–72; FCO, 1972–75; Fellow, Center for Internat. Affairs, Harvard Univ., 1975–76; Chef de Cabinet to Pres. of Commn of European Community, 1977–81; Vis. Fellow, All Souls Coll., Oxford, 1981; Ambassador to Mexico, 1981–83; Dep. Under-Sec. of State, FCO, 1983–84; Perm. Sec., ODA, 1984–87; British Perm. Rep. to UN, 1987–90. Director: IBM (UK), 1990–95 (Mem. IBM Adv. Bd, 1995–2000); BOC Envmtl Foundn, 1990–2003; Govett Mexican Horizons, 1991–96; Govett American Smaller Cos Trust, 1996–98; Govett Enhanced Income Investment Trust, 1999–2004. Member, Environment Committee: Friends Provident, 1995–99; F&C Asset Mgt, 1999–2007. Chairman: Internat. Inst. for Envmt and Develt, 1990–94; Climate Inst. of Washington, 1990–2002, 2012–; Earthwatch (Europe), 1990–97; Adv. Cttee on the Darwin Initiative for the Survival of Species, 1992–99. Director: Green Coll. Centre for Envmtl Policy & Understanding, Oxford, 1992–2006; Policy Foresight Prog., James Martin Inst. for Sci. and Civilisation, later James Martin 21st Century Sch., subseq. Oxford Martin Sch., Univ. of Oxford, 2006–. Sen. Vis. Fellow, Center for Envmt, Harvard Univ., 2002–03. Advr-at-Large to Pres., 2004–, Mem., Global Inst. of Sustainability, Arizona State Univ., 2007–. Chm., St Andrews Prize for Envmt, 1999–2015. Trustee: Baring Foundn, 1992–2001; Natural Hist. Mus., 1992–2001; WWF (UK), 1993–99; Royal Botanic Garden, Edinburgh, 1997–2001; Thomson Reuters (formerly Reuters) Foundn, 2000–14. President: Marine Biol. Assoc., 1990–2001; RGS, 1990–93; Nat. Soc. for Clean Air and Envmtl Protection, 1997–99; Gaia Soc., 1998–2001; Tree Aid, 2007–14. Convenor, Govt Panel on Sustainable Develt, 1994–2000; Member, Government Task Force: on Urban Regeneration, 1998–99; on Near Earth Objects, 2000. Chancellor, Univ. of Kent, 1996–2006. Mem., Global 500 (UN Roll of Honour for Envmtl Achievement), 1991. Minor planet named No 5971 Tickell, 2006. FLS 2008. Hon. Fellow: St Edmund's Coll., Cambridge, 1995; Royal Instn, 2002; Hon. FRIBA 2000. Mem. (Dr hc), Mexican Acad. of Internat. Law, 1983 (Orden Académico del Derecho, de la Cultura y de la Paz, 1989). Hon. LLD: Massachusetts, 1990; Bristol, Birmingham, 1991; Kent, 1996; Nottingham, 2013; Hon. DSc: UEA, 1990; Sussex, 1991; Cranfield, 1992; Loughborough, 1995; Exeter, 1999; Hull, Plymouth, 2001; St Andrews, Southampton, Oxford Brookes, Univ. du Littoral, 2002; Brighton, 2006; Dr hc: Central London Poly., Stirling, 1990; Sheffield Hallam, 1996; E London, 1998; Amer. Univ. of Paris, 2003; Univ. Juarez Autonoma de Tabasco, 2011; DUniv Open, 2006. Global Envmtl Leadership Award, Climate Inst., 1996; Patron's Medal, RGS, 2000. Officer, Order of Orange Nassau (Netherlands), 1958; Order of Aztec Eagle with sash (Mexico), 1994; Friendship Award (China), 2004. *Publications:* Climatic Change and World Affairs, 1977, 2nd edn 1986; Mary Anning of Lyme Regis, 1996; *contributed to:* The Evacuees, 1968; Life After Death, 1976; The United Kingdom/The United Nations, 1990; Sustaining Earth, 1990; Sir Francis Galton, 1991; Monitoring the Environment, 1992; Threats Without Enemies, 1993; Science for the Earth, 1995; The Changing World, 1996; Managing the Earth, 2002; Remaking the Landscape, 2002; Johannesburg Summit, 2002; A Parliament of Sciences, 2003; Roy Jenkins: a retrospective, 2004; Environmental Stewardship, 2005; China and Britain, 2005; Making the Difference: essays for Shirley Williams, 2011. *Recreations:* climatology; palæohistory; art, especially pre-Columbian and African. *Address:* Ablington Old Barn, Ablington, Cirencester, Glos GL7 5NU. *Clubs:* Brooks's, Garrick.

**TICKELL, Kathryn Derran,** OBE 2015; DL; musician, composer, educator and broadcaster; Director, Magnetic North East, since 2015; b Staffordshire, 8 June 1967; d of Michael Scott Tickell and Kathleen Tickell; two d. Professional musician, specialising in Northumbrian pipes and violin, 1986–; Leader, Kathryn Tickell Band. Lectr, Newcastle Univ., 2000–; Artistic Dir, Folkworks, 2009–. Recordings include 14 CDs. DL Northumberland, 2015. Hon. DCL Northumbria, 2007; Hon. MMus Durham, 2017. Queen's Medal for Music, 2008. MUniv Open, 2015. *Recreations:* playing music, reading, cooking. *W:* www.kathryntickell.com.

**TICKELL, Dame (Oriana) Clare,** DBE 2010; Chief Executive, Hanover Housing Association, 2014–18; Associate Director, Housing, Centre for Ageing Better; b 25 May 1958; d of Patrick Jocelyn Tickell and Diana Jane Tickell; m 1997, Edward Andres; two s. *Educ:* Bristol Univ. (CQSW 1986). Dep. Chief Exec., Centrepoint, 1986–89; Dir, Riverpoint, 1989–92; Chief Executive: Phoenix House, 1992–97; Stonham Housing Assoc., 1997–2004; Chief Exec., Nat. Children's Homes, then NCH, the children's charity, later Action for Children, 2004–13. Non-executive Director: Information Commn, 2003–10; Guinness Trust, 2010–14. Chair: Help the Hospices Commn into the Future of Hospice Care, 2011–13; Big Society Trust, 2018–; Mem., Community, Voluntary and Local Services Honours Cttee, 2011–18 (Chair, 2012–18). Member, Board: IPSO, 2014–15; Nat. Audit Office, 2018–. Chm., Early Intervention Foundn, 2015–. FRSA. Hon. FCGI. Hon. DLaws Bristol, 2012; DUniv Bishop Grosseteste, 2013. *Publications:* Tickell Review on the Early Years Foundation Stage, 2011. *Recreations:* swimming, literature, social media, art. *E:* Clare.tickell@icloud.com.
*See also A. T. Tickell, S. M. Tickell.*

**TICKELL, Sophia Mary;** Founder and Director, Meteos Ltd, since 2009; b London, 7 Oct. 1960; d of Patrick Jocelyn Tickell and Diana Jane Tickell; m 1989, James Painter; two d. *Educ:* Univ. of Birmingham (BA Hons 1983). Project Asst, Christian Aid, 1985–88; journalist, CEDOIN, Bolivia, 1988–92; Project Manager, Christian Aid, 1992–94; Advocacy Trainer, 1994–97, Hd, Private Sector Team, 1997–2003, Oxfam; Dir, 2004–05, Chm. Bd, 2005–09, Sustainability Ltd; Founder and Dir, PharmaFutures, 2003–. Member, Advisory Committee: Aviva Global Responsible Investments, 2007; Doughty Centre, Cranfield, 2008–17; Advisor: Bd Cttee on Corporate Social Responsibility, GlaxoSmithKline, 2008–10, 2013–19; Alliance Trust Sustainable Futures Funds, 2013–; Strategic Advr, Investing in a Just Transition, 2018–. Non-exec. Dir, Liontrust Asset Mgt, 2018–. Trustee, Green Alliance, 2008–17. *Publications:* (jtly) Mugged: poverty in your coffee cup, 2002; PharmaFutures reports. *Recreations:* singing, walking, gardening, literature, dance. *Address:* Meteos Ltd, Suite 282, 266 Banbury Road, Oxford OX2 7DL.
*See also Dame O. C. Tickell.*

**TICKLE, Prof. Cheryll Anne,** CBE 2005; PhD; FRS 1998; FRSE; Royal Society Foulerton Research Professor at University of Dundee, 2001–07, at University of Bath, 2007–10, now Professor Emeritus; b 18 Jan. 1945; d of Lewis Sidney Tickle and Gwendoline Muriel Tickle; m 1979, John Gray. *Educ:* Girton Coll., Cambridge (MA); Glasgow Univ. (PhD 1970). NATO Fellowship, Yale Univ., 1970–72; Middlesex Hospital Medical School, subseq. University College London Medical School: Research Fellow, Lectr, Sen. Lectr, 1972–87; Reader, 1987–91; Prof. of Developmental Biology, 1991–98; Prof. of Developmental Biology, Univ. of Dundee, 1998–2001. Mem. Council, BBSRC, 2001–07. FRSE 2000. *Address:* Department of Biology and Biochemistry, University of Bath, Bath BA2 7AY.

**TICKNER, Prof. Sylvia Elizabeth, (Lisa),** PhD; FBA 2008; Honorary Professor, Courtauld Institute of Art, University of London, since 2014 (Visiting Professor, 2007–14); b London, 21 Dec. 1944; d of Horace and Doris Warton; m Clive Tickner (marr. diss. 1981); partner, 1981, m 2006, Alexander Robert, (Sandy), Nairne, qv; one s one d. *Educ:* Wembley Co. Grammar Sch.; Hornsey Coll. of Art (BA Hons Fine Art); Univ. of Reading (PhD). Hornsey College of Art, later Middlesex Polytechnic, then Middlesex University: Lectr (pt-time), 1968–73; Sen. Lectr, then Principal Lectr, 1973–88; Reader, 1988–92; Prof., 1992–2007, now Emeritus. Vis. Fellow, Yale Centre for British Art, 1990; Kreeger Wolf Dist. Vis. Prof., Northwestern Univ., 1991; Leverhulme Res. Fellow, 1992–93; Leverhulme Emeritus Fellow, 2016–18; Vis. Fellow, Sterling and Francine Clark Inst., 2007. Paul Mellon Lectures, 1996. Mem., English Heritage Blue Plaques Panel, 2007–15; Trustee, The Art Fund, 2010–. Hon. DArt Kingston, 2005. *Publications:* The Spectacle of Women: imagery of the Suffrage Campaign 1907–1914, 1988; Modern Life and Modern Subjects: British art in the early twentieth century, 2000; Dante Gabriel Rossetti, 2003; Hornsey 1968: the art school revolution, 2008; *co-edited:* Mapping the Futures: local cultures, global change, 1993; Travellers' Tales: narratives of home and displacement, 1994; Future/Natural: nature, science, culture, 1996; The Block Reader in Visual Culture, 1996; British Art in the Cultural Field 1939–1969, 2012; London's New Scene: art and culture in the 1960s, 2020; catalogue essays, articles in acad. press and broadcasts. *Recreations:* gardening, Association Croquet. *E:* Lisa.Tickner@courtauld.ac.uk.

**TIDMARSH, Christopher Ralph Francis;** QC 2002; b 11 Dec. 1961; s of late Peter Francis Charles Tidmarsh and of Mary Elizabeth Tidmarsh; m 1992, Lorna Clare Johnson; three s one d. *Educ:* Merton Coll., Oxford (BA Hons Physics); Poly. of Central London (Dip. Law). Called to the Bar, Lincoln's Inn, 1985; Jun. Counsel to Inland Revenue, 1993. *Publications:* contrib. to various jls. *Recreations:* family, garden, surfing. *Address:* 5 Stone Buildings, Lincoln's Inn, WC2A 3XT. *T:* (020) 7242 6201.

**TIDMARSH, Prof. David H.,** PhD; CEng, FIMechE; Vice-Chancellor, Birmingham City University (formerly University of Central England), 2007–12. *Educ:* Lanchester Poly. (BSc, PhD). Joined Chrysler as grad. engr; British Leyland Technology; Head of Mech. Engrg, 1988, then Dir, Sch. of Engrg, Sheffield City Poly.; Dean of Engrg, 1993, Pro-Vice-Chancellor, 1998, Univ. of Central England; Vice-Chancellor, Anglia Poly. Univ., subseq. Anglia Ruskin Univ., 2004–07. FCMI.

**TIDMARSH, Sir James (Napier),** KCVO 2008; MBE 1989; Pro Chancellor, University of Bristol, 2007–14; Chairman, SouthWest One, 2008–11; Lord-Lieutenant, County and City of Bristol, 1996–2007; b 15 Sept. 1932; yr s of late Edward and Madeline Tidmarsh; m 1967, Virginia, y d of late Robin and Audrey Warren; two s. *Educ:* Taunton Sch. National Service: 1st Bn Duke of Cornwall's LI, 1952–54; TA 4/5 Bn Somerset LI, 1955–60. Factory manager, Dir, and Man. Dir, footwear industry, UK and Australasia, 1955–72; Man. Dir, Dycem Ltd, 1972–96; Director: Radio Avonside, 1979–83; Radio West, 1983–85; Founder Dir, GWR Radio plc, 1985–89. Director: Bristol Chamber of Commerce and Initiative, 1992–2015; Learning Partnership West (formerly Western Educn and Trng Partnership), 1995–99. Mem. Council, Royal Bath & West, 2012–. Vice-Chm., Nat. Assoc. Prison Visitors, 1966–69; Chm., Lord Chancellor's Adv. Cttee for Magistrates in Avon, 1997–2007. Patron: Young Bristol, 1999–2018; Avon Youth Assoc., 2000–16; Bristol Dist, Merchant Navy Assoc., 2005–; Teenage Parents (Bristol), 2007–17; West Country Br., Britain-Australia Soc., 2008–; Pres., Avon and Bristol Fedn of Clubs for Young People, 1994–98 (Chm., 1982–94). Mem. Council, Bristol Univ., 1994–2000. Governor, Colston's Collegiate Sch., 1986–94. Mem., Cook Soc., 1999–; Trustee: Bristol Benevolent Instn, 1973–; British Empire and Commonwealth Mus., 2003–14. Hon. Col, RM Reserve, SW England, 1998–2005. Mem., Soc. of Merchant Venturers, 1979– (Master, 1994–95). JP Bristol, 1977; High Sheriff, Avon, 1995–96. FRSA 2000. Hon. LLD: Bristol, 2002; UWE, 2003. KStJ 1997 (Pres., St John in Avon, 1998–2007). *Address:* 8 Prince's Buildings, Clifton, Bristol BS8 4LB. *T:* (0117) 973 0462. *Clubs:* Army and Navy, Royal Over-Seas League, Saintsbury; Clifton (Bristol).

**TIDMARSH, Janet;** see Legrand, J.

**TIDY, Morley David;** Assistant Under-Secretary of State (Personnel) (Air), Ministry of Defence, 1990–92; b 23 April 1933; s of James Morley and Winnie Tidy; m 1957, Wendy Ann Bennett; one s two d. *Educ:* Hove County Grammar School; Magdalene College, Cambridge (MA). National Service, RAF, 1951–53. Dept of Employment, 1956–57; HM Inspector of Taxes, Inland Revenue, 1957–66; MoD, 1966; Manchester Business School, 1967; First Sec. (Defence), UK Delegn to NATO, 1969–72; MoD, 1973; RCDS, 1977; Chief Officer, SBAA, Cyprus, 1980–83; Asst Under-Sec., Air Staff, MoD, 1984; Asst Under-Sec. (Ordnance), MoD, 1985; Asst Under-Sec., Defence Export Services, Administration, MoD, 1988. *Recreations:* cricket, golf, jigsaw puzzles.

**TIDY, William Edward, (Bill),** MBE 2001; freelance cartoonist, since 1958; writer, playwright, television and radio presenter; *b* 9 Oct. 1933; *s* of William Edward Tidy and Catherine Price; *m* 1960, Rosa Colotti; one *s* one *d* (and one *s* decd). *Educ:* Anfield Road Jun. Sch., Liverpool; St Margaret's Sen. Sch., Anfield, Liverpool. Shipping office boy, R. P. Houston, Liverpool, 1950–51. Served RE, 1952–55. Layout artist, Pagan Smith Advertising Agency, 1956–58. Cartoon strips: The Fosdyke Saga, Daily Mirror; The Cloggies, Private Eye; Gimbledon Down, New Scientist; Kegbuster, CAMRA; Dr Whittle, Gen. Practitioner. Presented for BBC TV: Tidy Up Walsall; Tidy Up Naples; My City; Draw Me; radio broadcasting includes: The News Quiz (also Guest Presenter); Midweek (also Guest Presenter); I'm Sorry I Haven't a Clue; Back to Square One; The Law Game; Trivia Test Match; Down Your Way; radio adaptation, The Fosdyke Saga (with John Junkin). After dinner speaker for many major cos; regular cruise lectr and after dinner entertainer, P&O. *Publications: (written and illustrated):* Sporting Chance, 1961; O Cleo, 1962; Laugh with Bill Tidy, 1966; Up the Reds, Up the Blues, 1968; Tidy's World, 1969; The Cloggies, 1969; Tidy Again, 1970; The Fosdyke Saga (14 vols), 1972–85; The Cloggies Dance Back, 1973; The Great Eric Ackroyd Disaster, 1976; The Cloggies Are Back, 1977; Mine's a Pint, What's Yours (The Kegbuster Story), 1981; Robbie and the Blobbies, 1982; Bill Tidy's Little Rude Book, 1984; A Day at Cringemound School, 1985; Bill Tidy's Book of Classic Cockups, 1985; The World's Worst Golf Club, 1987; The Incredible Bed, 1990; Draw me 387 Baked Beans in 10 seconds, 1991; Save Daring Waring with a pencil, 1993; Is there any news of the Iceberg? (autobiog.), 1995; (with P. Bahn) Disgraceful Archaeology, 1999; Bill Tidy's Book of Quotations, 1999, 2011; has also illustrated over seventy other books; contrib. to What's Brewing?, Classic FM Magazine, British Archaeology, Archaeology (USA). *Recreation:* cricket. *Address:* Terry Meadow Farm, Boylestone, Derbyshire DE6 5AB. *T:* (01335) 330858. *E:* bill@billtidy.com. *Clubs:* Cartoonist of Great Britain; Lord's Taverners (Pres., 2007–09).

**TIECH, Andrew C.;** *see* Campbell-Tiech.

**TIERNEY, Darren Christopher;** Director of Strategy, Department for International Trade, since 2017; *b* Belfast, 29 Jan. 1975; *s* of Patrick Tierney and Margaret Tierney; *m* 2001, Martha, *d* of Sir Louis Jacques Blom-Cooper, QC. *Educ:* St Columb's Coll., Derry; Queen's Univ., Belfast (BA Hons Business Admin and Mod. Langs 1997). Advertising sales exec., Daily Mail and Gen. Trust Gp, 1998–2000; Department of the Environment, Transport and the Regions, then Department of Transport, Local Government and the Regions, later Office of the Deputy Prime Minister: jun. policy roles in aviation, housing and land law, 2000–04; Bill Manager for Mental Capacity Bill, 2004–06; Private Sec. to Minister of State, MoJ, 2006–07; Dep. Principal Private Sec., 2007–09, Principal Private Sec., 2010–11, to the Lord Chancellor; Policy Manager for Legal Aid, Sentencing and Punishment of Offenders Act 2012, 2011–12; Director: of Youth Justice Policy (formerly of Strategy), MoJ, 2012–15; of CS Strategy and Efficiency, Cabinet Office, 2015–16; Interim Dir Gen., Prison Policy, MoJ, 2016. *Recreations:* cooking, cycling to burn the calories created by the cooking, reading contemporary fiction and political biographies. *Address:* Studio 44b, Limehouse Cut, 46 Morris Road, E14 6NQ. *T:* (020) 7517 9234. *E:* darren.tierney@hotmail.com.

**TIERNEY, James Kevin;** Sheriff of Grampian, Highland and Islands at Aberdeen, 2003–11; Consultant, Burness Paull (formerly Paull & Williamsons, then Burness Paull & Williamsons), since 2011; *b* 5 Oct. 1947; *s* of Edward Bird Tierney, schoolmaster, and Catherine Scanlan or Tierney; *m* 1971, Susan Mary Hubb; one *s* two *d*. *Educ:* St Aloysius' Coll., Glasgow; Edinburgh Univ. (LLB 1969). Admitted Law Soc. of Scotland, 1971; Partner: Littlejohns, Solicitors, Stirling, 1976–82; Paull & Williamsons, Advocates, Aberdeen, 1982–2000; Temp. Sheriff, 1987–92 and 1998–99; Sheriff of Tayside, Central and Fife at Perth, 2000. *Recreations:* golf, walking, gardening, European history, spectator sports. *Address:* Ardbeck, Banchory, Aberdeenshire AB31 4FE.

**TIERNEY, John;** caseworker, SDLP constituency office, Foyle, 2003; *b* 9 Dec. 1951; *s* of Paddy and Catherine Tierney; *m* 1972, Bernie Harkin; two *s* one *d*. *Educ:* St Joseph's, Derry. Mem. (SDLP), Derry City Council, 1981–2003, 2007–13; Mayor of Derry, 1984–85. Member: NI Forum, 1996–98; (SDLP) Foyle, NI Assembly, 1998–2003; SDLP Dep. Whip, 1999–2002, Whip, 2002–03. *Address:* 72 William Street, Derry BT48 9AD. *T:* (028) 7136 0700, *Fax:* (028) 7136 0808.

**TIETJEN, Tina, (Mrs G. R. Robertson),** OBE 2010; Chairman: East Thames Group, since 2010; Billing Code Board, since 2014, and Switch Guarantee Board, since 2016, Energy UK; *b* 10 June 1947; *d* of Arthur Tietjen and Mary Alice (*née* Storey); *m* 1972, Gordon R. Robertson (*d* 2019). *Educ:* Coloma Convent Grammar Sch. Jt Man. Dir, Video Arts Gp Ltd; Dir, MediaKey Gp, 1996–98; Chairman: WRVS, 1999–2005; Air Transport Users Council, 2003–11; Willow Foundn, 2008–10. Former non-executive Director: Phoenix Business Consultants; Michael Davey Financial Management; non-exec. Dir, L&Q Gp, 2016–. Mem. Bd, BITC, 1992–97. Membership Consultant, Business in the Community. Gov., Thames Valley Univ., 1999–2008. *Recreations:* travel, theatre, opera, gardening.

**TIKOISUVA, Pio Bosco;** High Commissioner of Fiji in the United Kingdom, also accredited to the Republic of Ireland, Denmark, Germany, Israel, Egypt and the Holy See, 2008–11; Director, Catholic Education, Archdiocese of Suva, 2014–17; *b* 13 March 1947; *m* 1973, Seniana Coalala; two *s* two *d*. *Educ:* St John's Coll., Fiji; Twickenham Coll. of Technol. (Dip. Printing 1976); Western Sydney Univ. (Postgrad. Cert. Mgt 2001). Government Printing Office, Fiji: apprentice, 1967–73; Tech. Asst, 1973–76; Sen. Tech. Asst, 1976–77; Fiji Institute of Technology: Hd, Sch. of Printing, 1977–82; Vice Principal, 1982–87; Dir, Min. of Youth and Sports, 1987–95; Regl Youth Develt Advr for S Pacific Commn, Noumea, New Caledonia, 1989–95; Govt Printer, Govt Printing Office, 1996–2000; Comr E Div., Min. of Regl Develt, 2000–02; CEO, Fiji Rugby Union, 2002–05, Acting CEO, 2011. Rugby: Vice Capt., Fiji Sec. Schs XV against NZ Vikings, 1966; Capt., St John's Coll. 1st XV team, 1966; Mem. Fiji Nat. rep. team, 1968–79; Internat. Invitation XV in NZ, 1972, in Tonga, 1972; played for: Harlequins Rugby Club, Surrey Dist Side, and British Barbarians Team, UK, 1973–76; Steel Bodgers XV v Cambridge, 1973–76; Steel Bodgers XV and Carwyn James XV, Newport Rugby Club Special Centenary Match, 1975; Capt., Fiji Nat. Team, 1977; Manager/Coach, Fiji Rugby 7s Team to Hong Kong, 1978–79; Coach, Nat. Juniors and Colts Team, 1983–84; Chm., Nat. Rugby Selectors, Fiji, 1989; Manager: Fiji XV Rugby Team, World Cup, France, 2007, NZ, 2011; Flying Fijians, Pacific Nations Cup, Fiji, 2007. Fiji Sports Hall of Fame Award, 2002; Fiji Sports Administrator Award, 2014; Lifetime Achievement Award, 2017, Life Member Award, 2019, Fiji RU.

**TILBIAN, Lorna Mona;** Chairman, Dowgate Capital, since 2019; *b* Nicosia; *d* of Berdge Tilbian and Mayda Tilbian (*née* Ouzounian); *m* 1992, Paul Dezelsky (marr. diss.). *Educ:* Cheltenham Ladies' Coll.; Univ. of Southampton (BA Jt Hons English and Hist.; PGCE). Agencies analyst, Sheppards and Chase, 1984–88; Dir, S. G. Warburg Securities, 1988–95; Executive Director: Panmure Gordon, 1995–2001; Numis Corp. plc, 2001–17 (Mem. Bd, 2005–17). Non-executive Director: Jupiter UK Growth Investment (formerly Primadona Growth) Trust plc, 2001–; ProVen VCT plc, 2013–; Finsbury Growth and Income Trust plc, 2017–; M&C Saatchi plc, 2018–; Euromoney Institutional Investor plc, 2018–; Rightmove plc, 2018–. *Recreations:* jewellery design, flower arrangement, Near Eastern cookery, travel. *Club:* Addison.

**TILBROOK, Richard James;** Prime Minister's Appointments Secretary for senior state appointments, since 2011; Deputy Appointments Secretary to the Prime Minister for senior ecclesiastical appointments, since 2014; Clerk of the Privy Council, since 2012 (Head of Honours and Appointments Secretariat, Cabinet Office, 2011–17); *b* 11 April 1962; 2nd *s* of late Dennis Frederick Tilbrook and Ann Elizabeth Tilbrook (*née* Knight); *m* 2017, Dr Paul Christopher Roberts. *Educ:* Royal Grammar Sch., Guildford; Queens' Coll., Cambridge (BA Classics 1983; MA 1987). Government Communications Headquarters, 1983–99: on secondment to Cabinet Office, 1995–98; Hd, London Office and Private Sec. to Perm. Sec., 1993–95; Department for International Development: Hd, Policy Coordination Unit, 1999–2000; Programme Manager: for Ukraine, Moldova and Belarus, 2000–01; for Afghanistan, 2002; policy posts, incl. secondment to Cabinet Office, 2002–08; Dep. Dir for Burma and corporate business, 2008; Dep. Chief of Assessments Staff, Cabinet Office, 2008–11. *Recreations:* singing (counter-tenor), gardening, village life, theatre, reading, writing pub reviews. *Address:* Honours and Appointments Secretariat, Cabinet Office, 1 Horse Guards Road, SW1A 2HQ. *Club:* Scribes.

**TILBY, Rev. Canon Angela Clare Wyatt;** Diocesan Canon, Christ Church Cathedral, Oxford, 2011–16, now Canon Emeritus; Canon of Honour and Hon. Chaplain, Portsmouth Cathedral; *b* 6 March 1950; *d* of Julian George Wyatt Tilby and Constance Mary (*née* Collier). *Educ:* North London Collegiate Sch.; Girton Coll., Cambridge (MA). Producer, Religious Programmes, BBC Radio, 1973–79, BBC TV 1979–94; Sen. Producer, Religious Programmes, BBC North, 1994–97. Ordained deacon, 1997, priest, 1998; NSM, St John the Evangelist, Cherry Hinton, 1997–2006. Tutor, 1997–2007, and Vice Principal, 2001–06, Westcott House, Cambridge; Vicar, St Benedict's, Cambridge, 2007–11; Diocesan Canon and Continuing Ministerial Develt Advr, Dio. of Oxford, 2011–16. Lectr in Spirituality and Early Ch History, Cambridge Theological Fedn, 1997–2011. Consultant, C of E Liturgical Commn, 2006–16 (Mem., 1998–2005). *Publications:* Teaching God, 1978; Won't You Join the Dance, 1984; Let There be Light, 1989; Science and the Soul, 1992; The Little Office Book, 1997; Son of God, 2001; God Before Breakfast, 2005; The Seven Deadly Sins: their origin in the spiritual teaching of Evagrius the Hermit, 2009. *Recreations:* history, psychology, music, travel, keeping fit. *Address:* 51 High Street, Portsmouth PO1 2LU. *T:* (023) 9275 2335.

**TILGHMAN, Prof. Shirley Marie,** OC 2014; PhD; FRS 1995; Professor of Molecular Biology, Princeton University (President, 2001–13, now President Emerita); *b* 17 Sept. 1946; *d* of Henry W. Caldwell and Shirley P. Carre; *m* (marr. diss.); one *s* one *d*. *Educ:* Queen's Univ., Kingston, Canada (BSc Hons 1968); Temple Univ., Philadelphia (PhD Biochem. 1975). Fogarty Internat. Fellow, NIH, Bethesda, 1975–77; Asst Prof., Temple Univ., 1978–79; Mem., Inst. for Cancer Res., Pa, 1979–86; Princeton University: Howard A. Prior Prof. of Life Scis, 1986–2001; Investigator, Howard Hughes Med. Inst., 1988–2001; Trustee, Jackson Lab., 1994–. Adjunct Associate Prof. of Human Genetics, Biochem. and Biophysics, Univ. of Pa, 1980–86; Adjunct Prof., Dept of Biochem., Univ. of Medicine and Dentistry of New Jersey-Robert Wood Johnson Med. Sch., NJ, 1988–2001. Ed. and Mem., Editl Bd, Molecular and Cell Biol., 1985–94; Member, Editorial Board: Jl Cell Biol., 1988–91; Genes and Develt, 1990–2001. Fellow, Inst. of Medicine, USA, 1995; Foreign Associate, Nat. Acad. of Scis, USA, 1996; Amer. Acad. of Arts and Scis, 1990; Amer. Phil Soc., 2000. Hon. DSc: Mt Sinai Coll. of Med., City Coll. of NY, 1994; Oxford, 2002; British Columbia, 2002; Dickenson Coll., 2002; Bard Coll., 2002; Queen's Univ., Kingston, Ont, 2002; Yale, 2002; Toronto, 2003; Western Ont, 2003; New York, 2005; Columbia, 2005; Univ. of Medicine and Dentistry of NJ, 2005; Rutgers, 2006; Rockefeller, 2006; Washington, 2007; Ryerson, 2007; Memorial Univ. of Newfoundland, 2007; Mills Coll., 2007; Amherst Coll., 2008; Rensselaer Polytechnic Inst., 2008; Hon. DLaws: Westminster Choir Coll., Rider Univ., 2002; Simon Fraser, 2002; Harvard, 2004; Hon. DHL Drew Univ., 2004. *Publications:* (ed with K. E. Davies) Genome Analysis: Vol. I 1990, Vols II and III 1991, Vol. IV 1992, Vols V and VI 1993; contrib. chapters in books; contrib. numerous articles and papers in Proc. Nat. Acad. Scis, USA, Jl Biol. Chem., Science, Nature, Genes Develt, Jl Cell Biol., Molecular Cell Biol. and others. *Recreations:* ski-ing, tennis, gardening, reading. *Address:* c/o Molecular Biology Faculty, Princeton University, 119 Lewis Thomas Laboratory, Washington Road, Princeton, NJ 08544–1014, USA.

**TILL, Prof. Geoffrey,** PhD; Professor of Maritime Studies, 1990, now Emeritus, and Chairman, Corbett Centre for Maritime Policy Studies, since 2014 (Director, 2007–14), King's College London; *b* 14 Jan. 1945; *s* of Arthur Till and Violet Dorothy Till (*née* Beech); *m* 1968, Cherry (*née* Austin) (decd); two *s* one *d*. *Educ:* King's Coll. London (BA Hons Mod. Hist. 1966; PGCE 1967; MA War Studies 1968; PhD 1976; FKC 2006). Lectr, then Sen. Lectr, Britannia RNC, 1968–72; Royal Naval College, Greenwich: Sen., then Prin., Lectr, 1972–89; Prof. of Hist. and Internat. Affairs, 1989–97; Dean of Academic Studies, JSCSC, Shrivenham, 1997–2006. Vis. Lectr, City Univ., 1973–85; Vis. Prof. in Maritime Studies, Nanyang Tech. Univ., Singapore, 2009–; Dist. Prof. of Maritime Studies, 2018, Dudley W. Knox Prof. of Naval Hist. and Strategy, 2018–, US Naval War Coll., Newport RI. Hon. Capt., RNR, 2009–14. *Publications:* Airpower and the Royal Navy, 1979; Maritime Strategy and the Nuclear Age, 1982; The Sea in Soviet Strategy, 1983; Naval Warfare and Policy, 1984; The Future of British Seapower, 1984; Modern Seapower, 1987; East–West Relations in the 1990s, 1990; Seapower: theory and practice, 1994; Seapower in the Millennium, 2001; Seapower: a guide for the 21st century, 2004, 4th edn 2018; The Development of British Naval Thinking, 2006; Seapower and the Asia Pacific, 2011; Asian Naval Expansion, 2013; Understanding Victory: naval operations from Trafalgar to the Falklands, 2014. *Recreations:* visiting country churches, bird watching, travel, extreme gardening. *Address:* Wansdyke Cottage, Allington, Devizes, Wilts SN10 3NL. *T:* (01380) 860176. *E:* geofftill45@gmail.com.

**TILL, Prof. James Edgar,** OC 1994; OOnt 2006; PhD; FRS 2000; FRSC; University Professor, University of Toronto, 1984–97, now Professor Emeritus; Senior Scientist, Ontario Cancer Institute, 1957–96, Emeritus, since 1997; *b* 25 Aug. 1931; *s* of William Till and Gertrude Ruth Till (*née* Isaac); *m* 1959, Marion Joyce Sinclair; one *s* two *d*. *Educ:* Univ. of Saskatchewan (BA Arts and Sci. 1952; MA Physics 1954); Yale Univ. (PhD Biophysics 1957). Postdoctoral Fellow, Connaught Med. Res. Labs, 1956–57; University of Toronto: Asst Prof., 1958–62, Associate Prof., 1962–65, Dept of Med. Biophysics; Prof., 1965–97; Associate Dean, Life Scis, Sch. of Grad. Studies, 1981–84; Hd, Div. of Biol Res., Ont. Cancer Inst., 1969–82. Sen. Fellow, Massey Coll., Toronto, 1985–2009. FRSC 1969. Internat. Award, Gairdner Foundn, 1969; Thomas W. Eadie Medal, RSC, 1991; Robert L. Noble Prize, 1993, R. M. Taylor Medal, 2001, Nat. Cancer Inst. of Canada; Canadian Medical Hall of Fame, 2004; Centenary Medal, RSC, 2005; (jtly) Albert Lasker Award, Lasker Foundn, 2005; Canadian Sci. and Engrg Hall of Fame, 2010. *Publications:* contrib. chapters in books and conf. proceedings; numerous contribs to refereed jls. *Address:* Princess Margaret Cancer Centre, University Health Network, 610 University Avenue, Room 9–416, Toronto, ON M5G 2M9, Canada. *T:* (416) 9462948.

**TILL, Prof. Jeremy William**, RIBA; Head, Central Saint Martins, and Pro Vice-Chancellor, University of the Arts London, since 2012; *b* 5 April 1957; *s* of late Barry Dorn Till; partner, Prof. Sarah Heath Wigglesworth, *qv. Educ:* Peterhouse, Cambridge (BA 1979); Poly. of Central London (DipArch 1983); Middlesex Univ. (MA 1999). RIBA 1995. Sen. Lectr and Sub-Dean, Bartlett Sch. of Architecture, UCL, 1991–99; University of Sheffield: Prof. of Architecture, 1999–2008; Head, Sch. of Architecture, 1999–2005; Dir of Architecture, 2005–08; Dean, Sch. of Architecture and the Built Envmt, Univ. of Westminster, 2008–12. Partner, Sarah Wigglesworth Architects, 1996–. Vis. Prof., Technical Univ., Vienna, 1995. *Publications:* (ed jtly) The Everyday and Architecture, 1998; (ed jtly) Architecture and Participation, 2005; Echo City, 2006; (jtly) Flexible Housing, 2007; Architecture Depends, 2009; (jtly) Spatial Agency, 2011; (jtly) The Design of Scarcity, 2014; numerous articles on architectl theory and educn. *Recreations:* growing, cooking and eating food. *Address:* Central Saint Martins, Granary Building, 1 Granary Square, N1C 4AA. *T:* (020) 7514 7444. *E:* jeremy@jeremytill.net.

**TILL, Stewart Myles**, CBE 2000; film, scripted television and theatre producer; *b* 24 April 1951; *s* of Ronald Leslie and Olive Till; *m* 1986, Lynda Helen Jones (marr. diss. 2017); one *s* one *d. Educ:* Dulwich Coll.; Univ. of Bath (BSc Hons Business Studies); Essex Univ. (MA American Politics). Account Executive: Leo Burnett Ltd, 1974–76; Saatchi & Saatchi, 1976–78; Marketing Dir, WEA Records, 1978–83; Vice-Pres., N Europe CBS/Fox Video, 1983–88; Dep. Managing Dir, Sky TV, 1988–92; President: International Polygram Filmed Entertainment, 1992–99; Universal Pictures Internat., 1999–2000; Pres. and Chief Exec., Signpost Films, 2001–02; Chm. and Chief Exec., United Internat. Pictures, 2002–06; Pres., Stadium Films, 2007–10; Chief Exec., 2009–11, Chair, 2011–12, Icon UK Gp; Dir, 2011–15, Chief Exec., 2012–14, Sonar Entertainment; Pres., Till Entertainment, 2014–. Chairman: UK Film Council, 2004–09 (Dep. Chm., 1999–2004); Silverfish, 2009–; non-exec. Chair, Picture Prodn Co., 2011–18; non-exec. Dir, Mediamorph, 2014–. Chm., Skillset, 2011–17 (Dep. Chm., 2002–10); Chm., Skills Action Gp, 2003–04. Trustee, Nat. Film and TV Sch., 1998–2005. Chm., Fife, 1997–2017. Mem., Develt Bd, Henley River and Rowing Mus., 2009–11. Mem., Adv. Bd, Sch. of Mgt, Univ. of Bath, 2000–05. Chm., 2006–08, Vice Chm., 2008–09, Millwall FC; Mem., Commercial Cttee, Football League, 2006–08. Gov., Dulwich Coll., 2008–09. Hon. Mem., Women in Film and TV, 2005–; Hon. Fellow, Goldsmiths, Univ. of London, 2004 (Vis. Prof., 2011–). FRSA 2001. DU Essex, 2006. *Recreations:* most British and American sports, including Millwall, NY Mets and LA Kings, enjoying time with my son and daughter and living the LA life. *Address:* 219 Mabery Road, Santa Monica, CA 90402, USA.

**TILLER, Ven. John**; Archdeacon of Hereford, 2002–04, now Emeritus; *b* 22 June 1938; *s* of Harry Maurice Tiller and Lucille Maisie Tiller; *m* 1961, Ruth Alison (*née* Watson); two *s* one *d. Educ:* St Albans Sch.; Christ Church, Oxford (MA, 2nd Cl. Mod. Hist.); Bristol Univ. (MLitt). Ordained deacon 1962, priest 1963, St Albans; Assistant Curate: St Cuthbert, Bedford, 1962–65; Widcombe, Bath, 1965–67; Chaplain and Tutor, Tyndale Hall, Bristol, 1967–71; Lectr in Church History and Worship, Trinity Coll., Bristol, 1971–73; Priest-in-Charge, Christ Church, Bedford, 1973–78; Chief Sec., ACCM, 1978–84; Chancellor and Canon Residentiary, Hereford Cathedral, 1984–2002; Diocesan Dir of Trng, Hereford, 1991–2000. Non-stipendiary Local Ministry and Mission Advr, Shrewsbury Episcopal Area, dio. Lichfield, 2005–10; Asst Chaplain, Meole Brace Holy Trinity, 2009. Hon. Canon of St Albans Cathedral, 1979–84. *Publications:* The Service of Holy Communion and its Revision (with R. T. Beckwith), 1972; A Modern Liturgical Bibliography, 1974; The Great Acquittal, 1980; Puritan, Pietist, Pentecostalist, 1982; A Strategy for the Church's Ministry, 1983; The Gospel Community, 1987; contribs to: The New International Dictionary of the Christian Church, 1974; Anglican Worship Today, 1980; New Dictionary of Christian Theology, 1988; The Parish Church?, 1988; (ed with G. E. Aylmer) Hereford Cathedral: a history, 2000; Archbishop William Sancroft: a troubled life, 2019. *Recreations:* walking, bird-watching, spuddling. *Address:* 2 Pulley Lane, Bayston Hill, Shrewsbury SY3 0JH. *T:* (01743) 873595. *E:* canjtiller@btinternet.com.

**TILLETT, Michael Burn**; QC 1996; a Recorder, since 1989; *b* 3 Sept. 1942; *s* of late Cyril Vernon Tillett and Norah Phyllis Tillett; *m* 1977, Kathryn Ann Samuel (marr. diss. 2008); two *d*; *m* 2011, Mary Kathleen Merrill. *Educ:* Marlborough Coll.; Queens' Coll., Cambridge (MA (Hons) Law). Called to the Bar, Inner Temple, 1965; in practice, 1966–2010; Asst Recorder, 1984–89. Legal Mem., Mental Health Rev. Tribunal, 2000–12. *Recreations:* golf, sailing, ski-ing. *Clubs:* Royal Automobile, Hurlingham, Royal Thames Yacht; Downhill Only; Seaview Yacht; Richmond Golf.

**TILLEY, Charles Basil**, OBE 2016; FCA, FCMA, CGMA; Executive Chairman, CGMA Research Foundation, since 2016 (Chief Executive, Chartered Institute of Management Accountants, 2001–16); *b* 22 Dec. 1950; *s* of Basil and Irene Tilley; *m* 1983, Sarah Anne Morgan; one *s* one *d*. CA 1973, FCA 2012; FCMA 2012; CGMA 2012. KPMG, 1974–88, Partner, 1986–88; Gp Finance Dir, Hambros plc, 1989–96; Hd of Finance and Ops, Granville Baird, 1997–2001. Mem. Bd, Ipswich Bldg Soc., 2008–15 (Chair, Audit Cttee, 2013–15); Mem. Bd, 2003–06, Chm., Professional requirements in Business Cttee, 2014–, IFAC; Mem. Bd, Gt Ormond St Hosp. Foundn Trust (formerly Gt Ormond St Hosp.), 2007–16 (Dep. Chm., 2012–16; Chm., Audit Cttee, 2008–16; Mem., Remuneration Cttee, 2007–16); non-exec. Dir, MORhomes plc, 2018–. Member: Accounting 4 Sustainability Project, 2008–; Internat. Integrated Reporting Council (formerly Cttee), 2010–. FRSA 2004. Hon. Dr: BPP University Coll., 2011; Edinburgh, 2017. *Recreations:* sailing, tennis, cycling, ski-ing, walking, golf. *Address:* Association of Certified International Professional Accountants, The Helicon, One South Place, EC2M 2RB. *E:* charles.tilley@aicpa-CIMA.com. *Clubs:* Sea View Yacht; Telford Park Tennis.

**TILLMAN, Harold Peter**, CBE 2010; entrepreneur; Chairman, British Fashion Council, 2008–14; *b* 15 Oct. 1945. CEO, Lincroft Kilgour plc, 1969–74; Vice Chm., Sumrie Clothes plc, 1979–82; non-executive Chairman: Honorbilt plc, 1987–90; BMB Menswear, 2000–03; Jaeger Ltd, 2003–12; Allders Croydon Ltd, 2005–10; First Restaurant Gp, 2006–; Complete Leisure Gp, 2007–10; Aquascutum, 2009–12. Chairman: Fashion Matters, Univ. of the Arts London, 2013–16 (Chm., Alumni Bd, 2008); Ethical Fashion Forum, 2016–; Ethical Fashion Gp, 2016–. Trustee, V&A Mus., 2012–14. Chm. and Founder, Patrons of Variety, the Children's Charity, 2014–; Chief Barker, Variety, 2019. Freeman, City of London, 2014.

**TILLMANN, Prof. Ulrike Luise**, PhD; FRS 2008; FIMA; Professor of Mathematics, University of Oxford, since 2000 (Deputy Head, Mathematical Institute, 2016–18); Fellow of Merton College, Oxford, since 1992; *b* Rhede, FRG, 12 Dec. 1962; *d* of Ewald and Marie-Luise Tillmann; *m* 1995, Jonathan Morris; three *d. Educ:* Gymnasium Georgianum, Vreden (Abitur 1982); Brandeis Univ. (BA 1985); Stanford Univ. (MA 1987; PhD 1990); Bonn Univ. (Habilitation 1996). SERC Res. Asst, Univ. of Cambridge, 1990–92; Jun. Res. Fellow, Clare Hall, Cambridge, 1990–92; CUF Lectr, Univ. of Oxford, 1992–2010; Tutor, 1992–2010, Subwarden, 2012–14, Merton Coll., Oxford. Member: Prog. Cttee, Internat. Centre for Mathematical Studies Edinburgh, 2005–17; Council, LMS, 2008–14 (Chm., Res. Meetings Cttee, 2011–14); Section Cttee, 2000, 2014, Prog. Cttee, 2018, Internat. Congress of Mathematicians; Vice Chair: Sci. Adv. Bd, Courant Res. Centre, Göttingen, 2007–; Scientific Adv. Bd, Oberwolfach, 2013–; Chair: Internat. Rev. Cttee, Mathematical Res. in Norwegian Univs, 2012; Scientific Adv. Bd, Hausdorff Centre for Maths, 2018–. Chaire de la Vallée Poussin, UCL Louvain, 2006–07. Fellow, Turing Inst., 2016– (Chair, Prog. Cttee, 2016–17). Vice-Pres., Royal Soc., 2018. Lectures: ICM, 2002; Emmy Noether, Deutsch Mathematiker Vereinigung, 2009; Ladyzhenskaya Vorlesung, Leipzig, 2011; Tondeur, Univ. of Illinois at Urbana-Champaign, 2017; Pinskey, Northwestern Univ., 2018. Ed., Topology, 2002–07; Founding and Man. Ed., Jl of Topology, 2008–17; Member, Editorial Board: Qly Jl Maths, 2000–; AGT, 2000–; LMS Pubns, 2007–11; Ergebnisse der Mathematik, 2015–; Geometry and Topol., 2017–; Jl of Amer. Mathematical Soc., 2018–. Mem., German Nat. Acad., Leopoldina, 2017. FAMS 2012; FIMA 2015. Whitehead Prize, 2004; Bessel Forschungspreis, 2007. *Recreations:* singing, baking, volleyball. *Address:* Mathematical Institute, University of Oxford, Andrew Wiles Building, Radcliffe Observatory Quarter, Woodstock Road, Oxford OX2 6GG.

**TILLMANS, Wolfgang**; artist and photographer; Professor of Fine Art, Städelschule, Frankfurt, 2003–09; *b* 16 Aug. 1968; *s* of Karl A. and Elisabeth Tillmans. *Educ:* Bournemouth & Poole Coll. of Art & Design. Guest Prof., Sch. of Fine Arts, Hamburg, 1998–99. Hon. Fellow, Arts Inst., Bournemouth, 2001. *Solo exhibitions* include: Kunsthalle, Zurich, 1995, 2012; Galerie Daniel Buchholz, Cologne, 2001, 2013, 2016, 2018; Andrea Rosen Gall., NY, Deichtorhallen Hamburg, and touring, Mus. Ludwig, Cologne, 2001; Regen Projects, LA, Maureen Paley Interim Art, London, 2002; Tate Britain, 2003; P.S.1 Contemp. Art Center, NY, 2006; Mus. of Contemp. Art, Chicago, 2006; Hamburger Bahnhof Mus. für Gegenwart, Berlin, 2008; Maureen Paley, London, 2008, 2013, 2016; Serpentine Gall., London, 2010; Walker Art Gall., London, 2010; Nat. Kunstgalerie Zachęta, Warsaw, 2011; Moderna Museet, Stockholm, and touring, Westfalen, Dusseldorf, 2012; Common Guild, Glasgow, 2012; Mus. de Arte Moderna, São Paulo, and touring, Bogatá, Lima and Santiago de Chile, 2012; Rencontres d'Arles, Arles, 2013; Wako Works of Art, Tokyo, 2014; Metropolitan Mus. of Art, NY, 2015; David Zwirner, NY, 2015; Museu Serralves - Museu de Arte Contemporânea, Porto, 2016; Tate Modern, 2017; Fondation Beyeler, Switzerland, 2017; Kunstverein Hamburg, 2017; David Zwirner, Hong Kong, 2018; Carré d'Art Contemporain, Nîmes, 2018; Musée d'Art Contemporain et Multimédias, Kinshasa, 2018; Irish Mus. of Mod. Art, Dublin, 2018; *group exhibitions* include: MOMA, NY, 1996; Berlin Biennale, 1998; Castello di Rivoli, Turin, Royal Acad. of Art, Tate Britain, 2000; Tate Modern, 2001; Tate Liverpool, 2002; Tokyo Opera City Art Gall., 2004; 53rd Venice Biennale, 2009; Fondation Beyeler, Riehen, Switzerland (also curator), 2014; Schirn Kunsthalle, Frankfurt/Main, Kunstmuseum, Bonn, Germany, Museu de Arte Moderna de São Paulo, Brazil, Walker Art Gall., Minneapolis, USA, Akureyri Art Mus., Iceland, Yokohama Mus. of Art, Japan, 2016; Seoul Mus. of Art, Walker Art Gall., Liverpool, Kunsthalle Wien, 2017; Nat. Gall., London, Kunsthaus Zürich, Musée des Beaux Arts, Rouen, 2018. Member: Akademie der Künste, Berlin, 2012; Royal Acad. of Arts, 2013. Trustee, Tate Gall., 2009–14. Ars viva Prize, Bundesverband der Deutschen Industrie, 1995; Böttcherstrasse Prize, Bremen, 1995; Turner Prize, 2000; Kulturpreis der Deutschen Gesellschaft für Photographie, Germany, 2009; Wollaston Award, Royal Acad., 2014; Internat. Award in Photography, Hasselblad Foundn, Sweden, 2015; Goslar Kaiserring Prize, 2018. *Publications: monographs:* Concorde, 1995; Burg, 1997; View from Above, 2001; Wolfgang Tillmans, 2002; (jtly) truth study center, 2005; Manual, 2007; Lighter, 2008; Abstract Pictures, 2011; FESPA Digital - Fruit Logistica, 2012; Neue Welt, 2012; Utoquai, 2013; Wako Book 5, 2014; Wolfgang Tillmans, 2014; The Cars, 2015; What's Wrong With Redistribution?, 2015; (ed with Brigitte Oetker) What is Different?, 2018; exhibn catalogues. *Address:* c/o Maureen Paley, 21 Herald Street, E2 6JT. *T:* (020) 7729 4112, *Fax:* (020) 7729 4113.

**TILLOTSON, Maj.-Gen. (Henry) Michael**, CB 1983; CBE 1976 (OBE 1970, MBE 1956); writer; *b* 12 May 1928; *er s* of late Henry and May Elizabeth Tillotson; *m* 1st, 1956, Angela Wadsworth Shaw (marr. diss.; she *d* 2012); two *s* one *d*; 2nd, 2006, Sybil Osborne. *Educ:* Chesterfield Sch.; RMA Sandhurst. Professional soldier, 1948–83: commnd E Yorks Regt, 1948; served: Austria, 1948–50; Germany and Berlin, 1951–52; Indo-China (attached French Union Forces), 1953 (Croix de Guerre with Palm); Malayan Emergency, 1953–55; Indonesian Confrontation, 1964–65; S Arabia, 1965–67 (despatches); MoD Intelligence, 1967–69; Inf. Bn Comdr, Cyprus, 1969–71; Col GS, Hong Kong, 1974–76; Chief of Staff UN Force, Cyprus, and Comdr British Contingent, 1976–78; research mission for UN Sec.-Gen. to UN Forces, Israel, Lebanon, Syria and Sinai, 1978; Dep. Dir, Army Staff Duties, and MoD rep., Cabinet Civil Contingencies Cttee, 1978–79; Chief of Staff (Maj.-Gen.) to C-in-C UKLF, 1980–83. Regl Dir SE Asia, Internat. Mil. Services Ltd, 1983–86. Col, PWO Regt of Yorks, 1979–86. Hon. Life Fellow, RSPB, 1993. *Publications:* Finland at Peace and War 1918–1993, 1993, 2nd edn 1996 (Finnish Gold Medal of Merit, 1996); With the Prince of Wales's Own, 1995; Dwin Bramall: the authorised biography of Field Marshal the Lord Bramall, 2005, rev. and reissued as The Fifth Pillar, 2006; (ed with Ian Brunskill and Guy Liardet) Great Military Lives in Obituaries, 2008; (ed) SOE and The Resistance as told in The Times Obituaries, 2011; occasional columnist in The Times, 2000–. *Recreations:* abroad, birds, listening to music. *Address:* West End House, Wylye, Wilts BA12 0QT. *Club:* Army and Navy.

**TILLSLEY, Gen. Bramwell Harold**; General of the Salvation Army, 1993–94; *b* 18 Aug. 1931; *s* of Harold Tillsley and Doris Tillsley (*née* Lawrence); *m* 1953, Maude Pitcher (*d* 2014); two *s* one *d. Educ:* Kitchener-Waterloo Collegiate; Univ. of Western Ontario (BA); Wycliffe Coll., Toronto; Salvation Army Trng Coll., Toronto. Social worker, Children's Aid Soc., Kitchener, Ont., 1952–55; Salvation Army: Windsor, Nova Scotia, 1956–58; Oakville, Ont., 1958–59; on staff, Salvation Army Coll., Toronto, 1959–65; Divl Youth Sec., Saskatchewan, 1965–66; N Toronto Congregation, 1966–71; Training Principal: Newfoundland, 1971–74; NY, 1974–77; Provincial Comdr, Newfoundland, 1977–79; Divl Comdr, Metro-Toronto, 1979–81; Trng Principal, London, 1981–85; Chief Sec., USA, South, 1985–89; Territorial Comdr, Australian Southern Territory, 1989–91; COS, Internat. HQ, London, 1991–93. Mem., Rotary Club, Toronto, Melbourne and London. Queen's Medal (Canada), 1978. *Publications:* Life in the Spirit, 1966; Life More Abundant, 1968; Manpower for the Master, 1970; This Mind in You, 1989; It Is Written: the collected works of Bramwell H. Tillsley, 2016. *Recreations:* music, golf, sports (ice hockey in youth). *Address:* 65 Spring Garden Avenue, Unit 604, North York, ON M2N 6H9, Canada.

**TILLYARD, James Henry Hugh**; QC 2002; a Recorder, since 1998; a Deputy High Court Judge, since 2004; *b* 7 March 1955; *s* of William Stephen Tillyard and Margaret Diana Tillyard; *m* 2000, Helen Patricia Scott; two *d*, and one *s* one *d* by a previous marriage. *Educ:* Sherborne Sch., Dorset; Leeds Univ. (BSc Chem. Eng). Called to the Bar, Middle Temple, 1978; Wales and Chester Circuit; specialises in family law. *Recreations:* boating, spending time with my wife and children. *Address:* 30 Park Place Chambers, Cardiff CF10 3BS. *T:* (029) 2039 8421. *E:* clerks@parkplace.co.uk. *Club:* Cardiff and County.

**TILSON, Joseph Charles, (Joe)**, RA 1991 (ARA 1985); painter, sculptor and printmaker; *b* 24 Aug. 1928; *s* of Frederick Albert Edward Tilson and Ethel Stapley Louise Saunders; *m* 1956, Joslyn Morton; one *s* two *d. Educ:* St Martin's School of Art; Royal Coll. of Art (ARCA); British School at Rome (Rome Scholar). RAF, 1946–49. Worked in Italy and Spain, 1955–59; Vis. Lectr, Slade Sch., Univ. of London and King's Coll., Univ. of Durham, 1962–63; taught at Sch. of Visual Arts, NY, 1966; Vis. Lectr, Staatliche Hochschule für Bildende Künste, Hamburg, 1971–72. Mem., Arts Panel, Arts Council,

1966–71. Exhib. Venice Biennale, 1964; work at Marlborough Gall., 1961–77, later at Waddington Galls; retrospective exhibitions: Boymans Van Beuningen Mus., Rotterdam, 1973; Vancouver Art Gall., 1979; Volterra, 1983; Castelbasso, 2001; RA, 2002. Biennale Prizes: Krakow, 1974; Ljubljana, 1985, 1995. Subject of TV films, 1963, 1968, 1974. *Recreation:* planting trees.

**TILSON THOMAS, Michael**; Music Director, 1995–June 2020, Music Director Laureate, from June 2020, San Francisco Symphony Orchestra; Conductor Laureate, London Symphony Orchestra, since 2016 (Principal Conductor, 1988–95; Principal Guest Conductor, 1995–2016); Artistic Director (formerly Artistic Adviser), New World Symphony, since 1988; concert pianist; *b* 21 Dec. 1944; *s* of Theodor and Roberta Thomas; *g s* of Boris and Bessie Thomashefsky, founders of Yiddish Theater, United States. *Educ:* Univ. of Southern California (Master of Music). Conductor, Young Musicians' Foundn Orchestra, LA, and conductor and pianist, Monday Evening Concerts, 1963–68; musical asst, Bayreuth, 1966–67; Koussevitzky Prize, Tanglewood, 1968; Asst then Principal Guest Conductor, Boston Symphony, 1969–74; NY début, 1969; London début, with LSO, 1970; Music Director: Buffalo Philharmonic, 1971–79; televised NY Philharmonic Young People's Concerts, 1971–77; Principal Guest Conductor, LA Philharmonic, 1981–85; Music Dir, Great Woods Festival, 1985; Co-Artistic Dir, Pacific Music Fest., Sapporo, Japan, 1990–; guest conductor with orchestras and opera houses in US and Europe; numerous recordings. Grammy Award: best orchestral recording, 1997, for Prokofiev's Romeo and Juliet with San Francisco SO; best classical album of the year, 1999, for Stravinsky's Firebird and Rite of Spring with San Francisco SO. *Address:* MTT Inc., 1645 Broadway, 20th Floor, New York, NY 10019, USA. *Club:* St Botolph (Boston).

**TILT, Sir (Robin) Richard**, Kt 1999; Social Fund Commissioner for UK, 2000–09; Director General, HM Prison Service, 1995–99; *b* 11 March 1944; *s* of late Francis Arthur Tilt and Mary Elizabeth Tilt (*née* Ashworth); *m* 1966, Kate Busby; two *s* one *d*. *Educ:* King's Sch., Worcester; Univ. of Nottingham (BA Hons); Open Univ. (Dip). HM Prison Service: Asst Governor, HM Borstal, Wellingborough, 1968–71; Tutor, Prison Service Staff Coll., 1971–74; Governor, HM Borstal, Pollington, 1974–75; Deputy Governor: Ranby, 1975–78; Gartree, 1978–80; Governor, Bedford, 1980–82; Hd, Manpower Section, HQ, 1982–84; Governor, Gartree, 1984–88; Dep. Regl Dir, Midlands, 1988–89; Hd, Industrial Relns, HQ, 1989–92; Hd of Finance, Police Dept, 1992–94; Dir of Services, 1994; Dir of Security and Progs, 1995. Chairman: Kettering Gen. Hosp. NHS Trust, 1999–2000; Northants HA, 2000–02; Leics, Northants and Rutland Strategic HA, 2002–06. Mem., Sentencing Adv. Panel, 1999–2002; Chairman: Social Security Adv. Cttee, 2005–11; Ind. Complaints Panel, Portman Gp, 2007–13; Internet Watch Foundn, 2012–17. Churchill Fellow, 1991. Friend of RA. *Recreations:* walking, reading, theatre, art. *Address:* Discovery House, Vision Park, Histon, Cambridge CB24 9ZR.

**TILTMAN, Sir John H.;** *see* Hessell Tiltman.

**TIMMER, Damien Gerard**; Managing Director, Mammoth Screen Ltd, since 2015 (Joint Managing Director, 2007–15); *b* London, 20 Oct. 1968; *s* of Maarten Timmer and Ann Timmer; *m* 1998, Rebecca Keane; two *s*. *Educ:* New Coll., Oxford (BA Mod. Hist. 1991). Script Editor, Central Films, 1994–95; Drama Develt Exec./Producer, Carlton TV, 1995–98; Exec. Producer, United Film and TV Prodns, 1998–2001; Hd of Drama, ITV Prodns, 2001–06. *Recreations:* theatre, piano, callisthenics. *Address:* Mammoth Screen Ltd, Third Floor, 142–144 New Cavendish Street, W1W 6YF. *T:* (020) 7268 0050.

**TIMMERMANS, Franciscus Cornelis Gerardus Maria;** Member and Vice-President, European Commission, since 2014; *b* Maastricht, 6 May 1964; *m* Irene; four *c*. *Educ:* Radbond Univ., Nijmegen (degree in French Lang. and Lit. 1985); Univ. of Nancy (postgrad. courses in Eur. Law and French Lit. 1985). Dep. Sec., Dutch Embassy, Moscow, 1990–93; Dep. Hd, EC Affairs Section, Min. for Develt Cooperation, 1993–94; staff mem. for EU Comr, Hans Van Den Broek, 1994–95; Sen. Advr and Private Sec. to High Comr on Nat. Minorities, OSCE, 1995–98; MP (Lab), Netherlands, 1998–2007 and 2010–12; Minister of Eur. Affairs, 2007–10, of Foreign Affairs, 2012–14. *Publications:* Gluck Auf: the story of a Limburg European, 2010; Broederschap, 2015. *Address:* European Commission, Rue de la Loi 200, 1049 Brussels, Belgium.

**TIMMINS, Col Sir John (Bradford),** KCVO 2002; OBE (mil.) 1973; TD 1968 (1st Clasp 1974); JP; Lord Lieutenant of Greater Manchester, 1987–2007; Chairman, Warburton Properties Ltd, since 1973; *b* 23 June 1932; *s* of John James Timmins and Janet Gwendoline (*née* Legg); *m* 1956, Jean Edwards; five *s* one *d*. *Educ:* Dudley Grammar Sch.; Wolverhampton Technical Coll.; Univ. of Aston-in-Birmingham (MSc). Building and Civil Engrg Industry, 1949–80; NW Regional Pres., Nat. Fedn of Building Trade Employers, 1974–75. Commnd RE, 1954; National Service, 1954–56; TA, 1956–80; comd 75 Eng. Regt(V), 1971–73, Hon. Col of the Regt, 1980–90; Hon. Colonel: Manchester and Salford Univ. OTC, 1990–98; Gtr Manchester ACF, 1991–2007. President: TA&VRA for NW England, 1994–99 (Vice-Chm., 1983–87; Vice-Pres., 1987–94, 1999–2007); EC&SM Wing ATC, 2007–12. ADC to the Queen, 1975–80. DL, 1981, High Sheriff, 1986–87, Gtr Manchester; JP Trafford, 1987. President, Greater Manchester: Order of St John, 1987–2007 (Chapter Gen., 1993–99); Royal Soc. of St George, 1988–2008 (Fellow, 2009). FRSA 1996. Hon. RNCM 1994. Hon. DSc Salford, 1990; Hon. LLD Manchester, 2001. KStJ 1988; KLJ 1990. *Recreations:* sailing, gardening. *Address:* 7 Little Heath Lane, Dunham Massey, Cheshire WA14 4TS. *Club:* Army and Navy.

**TIMMINS, Nicholas James Maxwell-;** chronicler and author; Public Policy Editor, Financial Times, 1996–2011; *b* 7 Sept. 1949; *s* of Rev. Leslie James and Audrey Maxwell-Timmins; *m* 1981, Elaine Barbara Brown; two *s* (twins) one *d*. *Educ:* Galleywall Road Prim. Sch., Bermondsey; Priors Court, Newbury; Kingswood Sch., Bath; Regent's Park Coll., Oxford (BA English Lang. and Lit. 1971). Reporter, Nature, 1971–74; Sci. and Medicine Corresp., 1974–78, Chief Labour and Industrial Corresp., 1978–79, Press Assoc.; gen. reporter, 1980, Health and Social Services Corresp., 1983–86, The Times; Health and Social Services Corresp., 1986–90, Political Corresp., 1990–95, The Independent; Public Policy Ed., 1995–96. Dist. Vis. Fellow, 1993, Mem. Adv. Council, 2001–03, Policy Studies Inst. Advr, Work, Income and Social Protection Cttee, Joseph Rowntree Foundn, 1994–98; Member Advisory Board: ESRC Centre for Analysis of Social Exclusion, 1997–2008; ESRC Centre for Market and Public Orgn, 2005–08; Member: Council, Pensions Policy Inst., 2001–; Phillis Cttee on Govt Communications, 2003–04; Exec. Cttee, Inst. for Fiscal Studies, 2015–. Visiting Professor: of Public Mgt, KCL, 2006–14; in Social Policy, LSE, 2012–. Sen. Associate, Nuffield Trust, 2008–; Senior Fellow: Inst. for Govt, 2011–; King's Fund, 2011–. Pres., Social Policy Assoc., 2008–11. Mem. Adv. Bd, Social Dimensions of Health Inst., Dundee and St Andrews Univs, 2005–11. Trustee, Think Ahead, 2017–. Hon. FRCP. Hon. DLitt Hull, 2016. *Publications:* The Five Giants: a biography of the welfare state, 1995, 3rd edn 2017; NHS 50th Anniversary: a history of the NHS, 1998; Rejuvenate or Retire?: views of the NHS at 60, 2008; Never Again: how and why the 2012 Health Act happened, 2012; The Wisdom of the Crowd: 65 views of the NHS at 65, 2013; Dying to Improve: the demise of the Audit Commission, 2014; (contrib.) The Coalition Effect, 2015; (jtly) Glaziers and Window Breakers: the role of the Secretary of State for Health, 2015; A Terrible Beauty: a short history of the National Institute for Health and Care Excellence, 2016; Universal Credit, 2016; The World's Biggest Quango: the first five years of NHS England, 2018. *Recreation:* kitchen talks. *T:* 07771 898094. *E:* nicholas.timmins@gmail.com.

**TIMMIS, Prof. Adam David,** MD; FRCP; Professor of Clinical Cardiology, Queen Mary (formerly Queen Mary and Westfield College), University of London, since 2002; Consultant Cardiologist, Barts Health NHS Trust (formerly Barts and the London NHS Trust), since 1987; *b* Harpenden, Herts, 3 July 1949; *s* of late Peter Timmis and Kathreen Timmis; *m* 1989, Naureen Bhatti; three *d*. *Educ:* Berkhamsted Sch.; Gonville and Caius Coll., Cambridge (BA 1970, MB BChir 1973; MD 1983); St Bartholomew's Hosp. Med. Coll. MRCP 1976, FRCP 1993. Res. and Clinical Fellow in Cardiol., Massachusetts Gen. Hosp., Boston, 1980–82; Sen. Registrar, Cardiol., Guy's Hosp., London, 1983–87. Clinical Dir, CVD Prevention, Barts Heart Centre, 2016–. Mem., Post-AMI, Chm., Chest Pain, Chm., Angina, Guideline Develt Gps, NICE, 2004–11. Member, Executive Committee: Nat. Inst. of Cardiovascular Outcomes Res., 2011–18; Farr Inst., 2013–18. Asst Sec., then Sec., 2002–04, Mem. Council, 2005–13, British Cardiac Soc. FESC 1994. Ed., Heart, 2006–13; Sen. Consulting Ed., Eur. Heart Jl, 2015–; Ed., Eur. Heart Jl: Quality of Care and Clinical Outcomes, 2016–. Mackenzie Medal, British Cardiovascular Soc., 2015. *Publications:* (contrib.) Hutchison's Clinical Methods, 20th edn 1995 to 22nd edn 2007; (contrib.) Oxford Textbook of Medicine, 5th edn 2010, 6th edn 2018; (contrib.) European Society of Cardiology Textbook of Cardiovascular Medicine, 3rd edn, 2018; over 300 papers in cardiovascular literature, major interests being cardiovascular outcomes research. *Recreations:* family and friends, cardiology, Arsenal FC, tennis. *Address:* Barts Heart Centre, West Smithfield, EC1A 7BE. *T:* (020) 7377 7000. *E:* a.d.timmis@qmul.ac.uk.

**TIMMIS, Prof. Kenneth Nigel,** PhD; FRS 2008; Professor, Institute of Microbiology, Technical University of Braunschweig, 1988, now Emeritus; *b* Blackpool, 16 Feb. 1946; *s* of Ernest Charles Timmis and Edith Primrose Timmis (*née* Holland); *m* 1964, Joan Kathleen Chalkley; one *s*. *Educ:* Kings Norton Grammar Sch., Birmingham; Univ. of Bristol (BSc Hons Microbiol.; PhD Microbiol. 1971); Free Univ. of Berlin (Habilitation in Microbiol. and Molecular Biol.). Postdoctoral posts, Yale Univ., 1972–73, Stanford Univ., 1973–76; Hd, Res. Gp, Max-Planck Inst. for Molecular Genetics, Berlin, 1976–81; Prof., Univ. of Geneva Med. Sch., 1981–88; Hd, Div. of Microbiol., Nat. Res. Centre for Biotechnol., Braunschweig, 1988–2011; Hd, Envmtl Microbiol. Lab., Helmholtz Centre for Infection Res., Braunschweig, 2006–11. Founding Editor: Envmtl Microbiol., 1999–; Microbial Biotechnol., 2008–; Envmtl Microbiol. Reports, 2009–. Mem., EMBO. Member: Amer. Acad. Microbiol.; Eur. Acad. Microbiol. Erwin Schrödinger Prize, German Assoc. for Promotion of Scis and Humanities, 2001. *Publications:* Handbook of Hydrocarbon and Lipid Microbiology, 2009; contrib. res. papers to learned jls. *Recreations:* family, reading, cooking, walking, gardening, cinema. *Address:* Institute of Microbiology, Technical University Braunschweig, Spielmannstrasse 7, 38106 Braunschweig, Germany. *E:* kntimmis@gmail.com.

**TIMMS, Kate;** *see* Gordon, V. K.

**TIMMS, Rt Hon. Stephen (Creswell);** PC 2006; MP (Lab) East Ham, since 1997 (Newham North East, June 1994–1997); *b* 29 July 1955; *s* of late Ronald James Timms and of Margaret Joyce Timms (*née* Johnson); *m* 1986, Hui-Leng Lim. *Educ:* Farnborough Grammar Sch.; Emmanuel Coll., Cambridge (MA, MPhil). Consultant, Logica, 1978–86; Ovum: Principal Consultant, 1986–94; Manager, Telecommunications Reports, 1994. Sec., Newham NE Labour Party, 1981–84. Newham Borough Council: Councillor (Lab), 1984–97; Chm., Planning Cttee, 1987–90; Leader, 1990–94. PPS to Minister of State, DFEE, 1997–98, to Sec. of State for NI, 1998; Parly Under-Sec. of State, DSS, 1998–99; Minister of State (Minister for Pensions), DSS, 1999; Financial Sec., HM Treasury, 1999–2001, 2004–05 and 2008–10; Minister of State: (Minister for School Standards), DFES, 2001–02; (Minister for e-commerce and Competitiveness, then for Energy, e-Commerce and Postal Services), DTI, 2002–04; (Minister for Pensions), DWP, 2005–06; Chief Sec. to HM Treasury, 2006–07; Minister of State: BERR, 2007–08; DWP, 2008; Parly Under-Sec. of State, BIS, 2009–10; Shadow Minister for Employment, 2010–15. Member: H of C Treasury Select Cttee, 1996–97; Educn Select Cttee, 2016; Select Cttee on Exiting the EU, 2016–; Chm., All Party Parly Gp on Faith and Society, 2012–; Mem. Council, 1996–98, Hon. Treas., 1997–98, Parly IT Cttee. Mem., Plaistow Christian Fellowship; Chm., Christians on the Left (formerly Christian Socialist Movement), 2012–16 (Vice-Chm., 1996–99); Labour Party Faith Envoy, 2007–. Trustee, Traidcraft Foundn, 2011– (Chm. Trustees, 2012–). Mem., Ramblers' Assoc. Hon. Pres., Telecommunications Users' Assoc., 1995–99. Hon. DEd E London, 2002. *Publications:* Broadband Communications: the commercial impact, 1986; ISDN: customer premises equipment, 1988; Broadband Communications: market strategies, 1992. *Address:* House of Commons, SW1A 0AA. *T:* (020) 7219 4000.

**TIMMS, Stephen John,** OBE 1997; CEng, CMarEng; Chief Operating Officer, Engineering and Technology Board, 2006–09; Trustee, Engineering Council UK, 2006–09; *b* Bristol, 25 March 1951; *s* of Ray Timms and Jean Timms; *m* 1973, Rosemary Kennedy; two *s*. *Educ:* Ashford Boys' Grammar Sch.; BRNC Dartmouth; RNEC Manadon (BSc Hons Mech. Engrg; MSc Marine Engrg); RNC Greenwich (Postgrad. Dip. Nuclear Reactor Technol.); Open Univ. (MBA). CEng 1982; MIMechE 1989; CMarEng 2007; FIMarEST 2007. Engineer Officer: HM Submarines Renown, Resolution, Repulse, 1976–79; HM Submarine Turbulent, 1984–88; Proj. Manager, Sub-surface Ballistic Nuclear reactor instrumentation and future Sub-surface Nuclear propulsion plant, 1988–91; Principal Lectr, Dept of Nuclear Sci. and Technol., 1991–93; JSDC, 1993–94; Dep. Captain Fleet Maintenance, Faslane, 1994–96; UK Mil. Rep. NATO HQ, Brussels, SO for Partnership for Peace, Mediterranean Dialogue, NATO-Russia, NATO-Ukraine, NATO enlargement, Arms Control and Peacekeeping, 1996–99; CSO (Support), British Forces Gibraltar and CO RN Gibraltar, 1999–2000; Naval Attaché, Brasilia, 2001–04; Dir, RNR and RN Youth Orgns, 2004–06. UK Rep. on wkg gp of Internat. Arctic Seas Assessment Proj., IAEA, Vienna, 1993–97. Mem. Bd, Naval Recruiting and Trng Agency, 2004–06. Mem. Cttee, Benelux Br., IMechE, 1997–99. Mem. Bd, Women in Sci., Engrg and Construction (formerly Women in Sci. and Engrg), 2008–09. Mem., RN Sailing Assoc. *Publications:* co-author of tech. papers for Internat. Arctic Seas Assessment Proj., IAEA, Vienna. *Recreations:* golf, sailing, cruise ship lecturing on naval and maritime history. *E:* sj_timms@hotmail.com.

**TIMMS, (Vera) Kate;** *see* Gordon, V. K.

**TIMNEY, Jacqueline Jill;** *see* Smith, Rt Hon. J. J.

**TIMPERLEY, Prof. Stuart Read;** Chairman: Stuart Timperley Associates, since 2002; GFM Ltd, since 2010; Partner, Stuart Slatter and Co., since 2002; Professor, Istituto Studi Direzionali, University of Milan, since 1998; *b* 30 July 1943; *s* of late Kenneth Read Timperley and Florence Timperley (*née* Burgess); *m* 1967, Veronica Parke; two *d*. *Educ:* Birkenhead Sch.; Univ. of Strathclyde (BA 1967; MBA 1968); Univ. of London (BSc 1967); Univ. of Liverpool (Shell Mex Res. Fellow, 1968; PhD 1971). Lectr, Univ. of Liverpool, 1970–72; London Business School: Lectr, 1972–80; Sen. Lectr, 1980–89; Dir,

Sloan Fellows Prog., 1976–80; Dir, Centre for Mgt Develt, 1984–91; Associate Prof., 1989–95; Sen. Associate, Judge Inst., Univ. of Cambridge, 1998–2002. Chm., Slatter Timperley Associates, 1990–2002. Vis. Prof., European Inst. for Advanced Studies in Mgt, Brussels, 1973–85. Chairman: Freightliner Ltd, 1988–91 (Dir, 1979); GSM Hldgs Ltd, 2009–; Director: Jermyn Hldgs Ltd, 1978–80; Intasun Ltd, 1983–87; ILG Ltd, 1986–89; Communisis plc, 2000–03; Pres., Consulteque.com SpA, 2000–03. Mem., Arts Council England, 2002–08; Chairman: Arts Council England, East (formerly Eastern Arts Bd), 1998–2008; English Regl Arts Bds, 2000–01. Chm., Watford FC, 1993–97, 2010– (Dir, 1990–97, 2009–10). Gov., London Business Sch., 1991–94. *Publications:* Personnel Planning and Occupational Choice, 1974; Humanisation of Work, 1982. *Recreations:* performing arts, football. *Address:* Stuart Timperley Associates, 3 Dorset Street, W1U 4EF. *T:* (020) 7486 1585.

**TIMPSON, (Anthony) Edward,** CBE 2018; *b* Knutsford, Cheshire, 26 Dec. 1973; *s* of Sir (William) John (Anthony) Timpson, *qv*; *m* 2002, Julia Helen Still; one *s* three *d*. *Educ:* Pownall Hall Sch.; Alderley Edge Co. Prim. Sch.; Stockport Grammar Jun. Sch.; Terra Nova Sch.; Uppingham Sch.; Durham Univ. (BA Hons Politics); Coll. of Law, London (LLB). Called to the Bar, Inner Temple, 1998; non-practising family law specialist. MP (C) Crewe and Nantwich, May 2008–2017; contested (C) same seat, 2017. PPS to Home Secretary, 2010–12; Parly Under-Sec. of State, 2012–15, Minister of State, 2015–17, DfE. Mem. Adv. Gp, Children's Comr for England, 2017–; Chair, CAFCASS, 2018–; Chair, Child Safeguarding Practice Review Panel, 2018–. *Recreations:* football (watching and playing), cricket, marathon running, travel, playing with my children.

**TIMPSON, Sir (William) John (Anthony),** Kt 2017; CBE 2004; Chairman, Timpson Ltd, since 1985; *b* 24 March 1943; *s* of Anthony and Hilda Timpson; *m* 1968, Alexandra Winkfield Dodd, MBE (*d* 2016); four *s* one *d*. *Educ:* Oundle Sch.; Nottingham Univ. (BA Hons Industrial Econs). Shoe shop asst, 1960–64; trainee, Clarks Shoes, 1964–65; Shoe Buyer, Timpson, 1965–68; Dir, William Timpson Ltd, 1968–73; Managing Director: Swears and Wells, 1973–75; William Timpson Ltd, 1975–83. Weekly business column, Ask John, Daily Telegraph, 2007–. Chair, Expert Adv. Panel on High Streets, 2018. Member: Footwear Wkg Party, NEDC, 1979–83; Women's Business Council, 2010–16. Pres., Footwear Distributors' Fedn, 1979–81. Chair of Governors: Brookway High Sch., 1980–86; Terra Nova Prep. Sch., 1994–2000; Gov., Delamere Primary Acad., 2008–; Trustee, Uppingham Sch., 2000–15. Trustee, ChildLine, 2003–08. Master, Pattenmakers' Co., 2011–12. *Publications:* Dear James, 2000; Cobbled Together, 2003; How to Ride a Giraffe, 2008; Upside Down Management, 2010; Ask John, 2014; High Street Heroes, 2015; Under Orders, 2016; Keys to Success, 2017; *for foster carers and adoptive parents:* A Guide to Attachment, 2009, 3rd edn 2015; How to Create a Positive Future, 2013; Looking After Looked After Children, 2016. *Recreations:* tennis, Real Tennis, golf, snooker, writing, garden but not gardening, holidays on Mustique. *E:* john@timpson.com. *Clubs:* Delamere Forest Golf (Captain, 2015–16); Manchester Tennis and Racquets.

*See also* A. E. Timpson.

**TIMS, Sir Michael (David),** KCVO 1992 (CVO 1984; LVO 1973 MVO 1963); Serjeant-at-Arms to HM The Queen, 1987–92, retired; *b* 14 Sept. 1931; *s* of late William Edward Tims and Eva Ida Tims; *m* 1959, Jacqueline Lily Clark; one *s*. *Educ:* Christ's Hosp.; Westminster Coll. Nat. Service Commn, Army Catering Corps, 1950–52. The Queen's Household: Dep. Comptroller of Supply, 1953–68; Asst to the Master of the Household, 1968–92. Mem., Bd of Green Cloth, 1988–. FRSA 1992. Donation Gov., Christ's Hosp., 2008–. JP Inner London, 1984–91. Freeman, City of London, 1986; Liveryman, Co. of Cooks, 1993–. Various hon. foreign awards. *Publications:* articles on fishing in national magazines. *Recreations:* battling with and painting big game fish, illustrated maps for anglers, also wildlife and Venice watercolours (exhibitor, Venice in Peril exhibns, London). *Address:* Clock Tower House, The Royal Paddocks, Hampton Court Road, E Molesey, Surrey KT8 9DA.

**TIMSON, Dame Penelope Anne Constance;** *see* Keith, Dame P. A. C.

**TIMSON, Dr Simon Edward;** Performance Director, Lawn Tennis Association, since 2016; *b* Leicester, 8 Dec. 1970; *s* of Frank and Margaret Timson; *m* 2007, Joanne Clarke; one *s* one *d*. *Educ:* Univ. of Exeter (BA(Ed) Hons Physical Educn); Univ. of Leeds (PhD Psychol. 2002). Accredited Sport and Exercise Scientist, BASES, 1999. Mem., British Bobsleigh Team, 1990–97; Teacher of PE, Richard Huish Coll., Taunton, 1994–96; Manager, Somerset CCC and SW Tennis Academies, 1996–2000; Performance Dir, British Skeleton, 2000–06; Hd, England Develt Prog. and Sci. Medicine, ECB, 2006–12; Dir of Performance, UK Sport, 2013–16. Hon. Dr: Bath, 2018; Exeter, 2018. *Publications:* (jtly) The Talent Lab, 2017; contribs to Sport and Exercise Psychol. Rev. *Recreations:* ski-ing, sport. *Address:* Lawn Tennis Association, National Tennis Centre, 100 Priory Lane, Roehampton, SW15 5JQ.

**TINCKNELL, Amanda Margaret,** CBE 2015; Chief Executive, Cranfield Trust, since 2000; *b* Uckfield, 12 July 1961; *d* of late Dr Ray Tincknell and of Margaret Tincknell; *m* 1997, Christopher Barrington Brown; one *s*. *Educ:* Beaconsfield High Sch.; Wycombe High Sch.; Leicester Univ. (BSc Hons); Cranfield Univ. (MBA 1989). Mkt Researcher, HR & H Market Res., 1984–85; Mkt Researcher, Lopex plc, 1985–86; Researcher, Bull Thompson Exec. Search, 1986–88; ind. consultant and researcher, 1989–2000. Volunteer Consultant and Trustee, Cranfield Trust, 1993–99. *Recreations:* family, gardening, books, sailing. *Address:* Cranfield Trust, Court Room Chambers, 1 Bell Street, Romsey, Hants SO51 8GY.

**TINCKNELL, Robert George;** Chief Executive Officer, Battersea Power Station Development Co., 2012–18; *b* 2 April 1967; *m* 1996, Rachel; one *s* one *d*. *Educ:* Allhallows Sch., Lyme Regis; De Montfort Univ., Leicester. MRICS 1997–2000. Commercial Manager, Connaught Gp plc, 1992–95; Man. Dir, Commercial, Berkeley Gp plc, 1995–2001; Develt Dir, Treasury Hldgs, 2002–05; Man. Dir, Treasury Hldgs (China) Ltd, 2006–08; Dir, China Real Estate Opportunities plc, 2006–08; CEO, Treasury Hldgs, 2008–12; Dir, Real Estate Opportunities plc, 2008–12. *Publications:* Battersea Power Station Community Charter: building a real place, brick by brick, 2014; (contrib.) Battersea Power Station: the placebook, 2014. *Recreations:* sailing, horse racing, music, practising Anglican.

**TINDALE, Gordon Anthony,** OBE 1983; Director of Government and Public Affairs, WH Smith (USA) Inc., 1995–99; *b* 17 March 1938; *s* of George Augustus Tindale and Olive Sarah Collier; *m* 1960, Sonia Mary Soper; one *d* (one *s* decd). *Educ:* Highgate Sch.; Trinity Coll., Oxford (BA (Mod. Hist)); Birkbeck Coll., London (MA (Internat. Relations)). Nat. Service, 1956–58. Joined British Council, 1961; postings in Iraq, Jordan, London and Egypt; Representative: Lesotho, Botswana and Swaziland, 1975–78; Zambia, 1979–83; Controller, Management Div., 1984–87; Representative, Egypt, 1987–89; Cultural Counsellor (formerly Cultural Attaché), Washington, 1989–94. *Recreations:* music, golf. *Address:* 26 Oppidans Road, Primrose Hill, NW3 3AG. *T:* (020) 7722 9343. *Club:* Hendon Golf.

**TINDALL, Gillian Elizabeth,** FRSL; novelist, biographer, historian; *b* 4 May 1938; *d* of D. H. Tindall and U. M. D. Orange; *m* 1963, Richard G. Lansdown; one *s*. *Educ:* Univ. of Oxford (BA 1st cl., MA). Freelance journalism: occasional articles and reviews for Observer, Guardian, London Evening Standard, The Times, Independent, Daily Telegraph, Financial Times and New York Times. Occasional broadcasts, BBC. JP (as Gillian Lansdown), Inner London, 1980–98. Chevalier de l'Ordre des Arts et des Lettres (France), 2001. *Publications: novels:* No Name in the Street, 1959; The Water and the Sound, 1961; The Edge of the Paper, 1963; The Youngest, 1967; Someone Else, 1969, 2nd edn 1975; Fly Away Home, 1971 (Somerset Maugham Award, 1972); The Traveller and His Child, 1975; The Intruder, 1979; Looking Forward, 1983; To the City, 1987; Give Them All My Love, 1989; Spirit Weddings, 1992; *short stories:* Dances of Death, 1973; The China Egg and Other Stories, 1981; Journey of a Lifetime and Other Stories, 1990; *biography:* The Born Exile (George Gissing), 1974; *other non-fiction:* A Handbook on Witchcraft, 1965; The Fields Beneath, 1977, 3rd edn 2011; City of Gold: the biography of Bombay, 1981, 2nd edn 1992; Rosamond Lehmann: an Appreciation, 1985; (contrib.) Architecture of the British Empire, 1986; Countries of the Mind: the meaning of place to writers, 1991; Célestine: voices from a French village, 1995 (Franco-British Soc. Award, 1996); The Journey of Martin Nadaud, 1999; The Man Who Drew London: Wenceslaus Hollar in reality and imagination, 2002; The House by the Thames and the People Who Lived There, 2006; Footprints in Paris: a few streets, a few lives, 2009; Three Houses, Many Lives, 2012; The Tunnel Through Time: a new route for an old London journey, 2016; The Pulse Glass: and the beat of other hearts, 2019. *Recreations:* keeping house, foreign travel, attempting to save London from undesirable commercial developments. *Address:* c/o Curtis Brown Ltd, 28/29 Haymarket, SW1Y 4SP.

**TINDALL, Sir Stephen (Robert),** GNZM 2019 (KNZM 2009; CNZM 2007); Founder and Managing Director, Warehouse Group, 1982–2004; *b* Devonport, Auckland, NZ, 5 May 1951; *s* of Robert George and Georgea Margaret Tindall; *m* 1973, Margaret Maria Murphy; three *s* two *d*. *Educ:* Bayswater Primary Sch.; Belmont Intermediate Sch.; Takapuna Grammar Sch.; Auckland Univ. of Technol. (Mgt Dip. 1976; Dip. Purchasing and Supply). Merchandise Dir, George Court & Sons, 1978–82. Founder, K-One W-One Ltd, venture capital co., 1994–. Founder, Tindall Foundn, 1994. Mem., World Business Council for Sustainable Develt, 1998. Founder, Kiwi Expat Assoc., 2001. Chair, Emirates Team NZ (Americas Cup Team), 2014–. *Publications:* The Tindall Foundation Story 1994–2017, 2018. *Recreations:* swimming, hiking, sailing, boating, travel, horseback mustering of sheep and cattle, golf, family time with wife, children and grandchildren. *Address:* PO Box 31.244, Milford, Auckland, New Zealand. *T:* 94883240. *E:* stephen@tindall.kiwi. *Clubs:* Royal New Zealand Yacht Squadron; Warkworth Golf.

**TINDLE, David,** RA 1979 (ARA 1973); painter; *b* 29 April 1932. *Educ:* Coventry Sch. of Art. MA Oxon 1985. Worked as scene painter and commercial artist, 1946–51; subseq. taught at Hornsey Coll. of Art; Vis. Tutor, Royal Coll. of Art, 1972–83, Fellow, 1981, Hon. FRCA, 1984; Ruskin Master of Drawing, Oxford Univ., and Professorial Fellow, St Edmund Hall, Oxford, 1985–87 (Hon. Fellow, 1988). RE, 1988–91. Hon. RBSA 1989. First showed work, Archer Gall., 1952 and 1953; regular one-man exhibns, Piccadilly Gall., from 1954; one-man exhibns at many public and private galleries in Gt Britain incl. Fischer Fine Art, 1985, 1989, 1992; Redfern Gall., London, 1994, 1996, 1998, 2000, 2001, 2003, 2004, 2005, 2007, 2009, 2016; Galerie du Tours, San Francisco and Los Angeles, 1964; Galleria Vinciana, Milan, 1968; Galleria Carbonesi, Bologna, 1968; Gallery XX, Hamburg, 1974, 1977, 1980; retrospective, Huddersfield Art Gall., 2016; rep. in exhibns at: Piccadilly Gall., 1954–; Royal Acad.; Internat. Biennale of Realist Art, Bruges, 1958 and Bologna, 1967; British Exhibn Art, Basel, 1958; John Moores, 1959 and 1961; Arts Council Shows: British Self-Portraits; Painters in East Anglia; Thames in Art; The British Art Show, 1979–80; Salon de la Jeune Peinture, Paris, 1967; Mostra Mercato d'Arte Contemporanea, Florence, 1967; British Painting 1974, Hayward Gall.; British Painting 1952–77, RA; Six English Painters—Eros in Albion, Arezzo, Italy, 1989; Portrait of the Artist, Tate Gall., 1989. Set of 3 Mural decorations for Open Univ., Milton Keynes, 1977–78. Designed sets for Iolanta, Aldeburgh Fest., 1988. Work rep. in numerous public and private collections, incl. Nat. Portrait Gall.; Chantrey Bequest purchases, 1974 and 1975, now in Tate Gall. Critic Prize, 1962; Europe Prize for Painting, 1969; Critics' Choice, Tooths, 1974; Waddington Prize, Chichester Nat. Art Exhibn, 1975; Johnson Wax Award, RA, 1983. *Address:* Via C. Barsotti, 194 Santa Maria Giudice, Lucca 55085, Italy; Redfern Gallery, 20 Cork Street, Mayfair, W1S 3HL.

**TINDLE, Sir Ray (Stanley),** Kt 1994; CBE 1987 (OBE 1973); DL; President, Tindle Newspapers Ltd, since 2017 (Chairman, 1972–2017); Chairman, Tindle Radio Holdings (formerly Tindle Radio) Ltd, since 1998; *b* 8 Oct. 1926; *s* of late John Robert Tindle and Maud Tindle; *m* 1949, Beryl Julia (*née* Ellis), MBE 2008, MA, DipEd; one *s*. *Educ:* Torquay Grammar Sch.; Strand Sch. FCIS; FCIArb. War service, Devonshire Regt (Captain), 1944–47. Asst to Dir, Newspaper Soc., 1952–58; Managing Director: Surrey Mirror Newspapers, 1959–63; Surrey Advertiser Newspapers, 1963–78 (Chm., 1978–97). Pres., Newspaper Soc., 1971–72; Vice Pres. and Chm. of Appeal, Newspaper Press Fund, 1990; Member: Newspaper Panel, Monopolies and Mergers Commn, 1987–93; Council, CPU, 1987–; Press Bd of Finance, 1990–. Founder, Tindle Enterprise Centres for the Unemployed, 1984–. Master, Stationers' and Newspaper Makers' Co., 1985–86. DL Surrey, 1989. Hon. DLitt Buckingham, 1999; DUniv Surrey, 2008. *Publications:* The Press Today and Tomorrow, 1975. *Recreations:* veteran cars, newspapers, boating. *Address:* Tindle Newspapers Ltd, Old Court House, Union Road, Farnham, Surrey GU9 7PT. *Clubs:* Royal Automobile, Veteran Car.

**TINER, John Ivan,** CBE 2008; non-executive Chairman, Ardonagh Group (formerly Towergate Insurance Group), since 2015; Partner, Resolution Operations LLP, 2008–13; *b* 25 Feb. 1957; *s* of Kenneth Tiner and late Joan Tiner; *m* 1978, Geraldine Kassell; two *s* one *d*. *Educ:* St Peter's Sch., Guildford; Kingston Poly. ACA 1980. Joined Arthur Andersen, 1976: Partner, 1988–2001; Managing Partner, Global Financial Services, 1997–2001; Financial Services Authority: Man. Dir, Consumer, Insce and Investment Directorate, 2001–03; Chief Exec., 2003–07. Director: Henderson New Star (formerly New Star Asset Management) Gp plc, 2008–09; Lucida plc, 2008–13; Credit Suisse Gp, 2009–; Resolution Ltd (formerly Friends Provident, then Friends Life Gp plc), 2009–14. Dir, Financial Services Skills Council, 2008–10. Trustee, Urological Foundn, 2009–. Vis. Fellow, Oxford Univ., 2008. Hon. DLitt Kingston, 2011. *Publications:* Accounting for Treasury Products, 1987, 2nd edn 1990. *Recreations:* family, tennis, sailing, golf, watching football and Rugby.

**TING, Prof. Samuel Chao Chung;** Thomas D. Cabot Institute Professor, Massachusetts Institute of Technology, since 1977; *b* 27 Jan. 1936; *s* of K. H. Ting and late T. S. Wang; *m*; two *d*; *m* 1985, Susan Carol Marks; one *s*. *Educ:* Univ. of Michigan (PhD). Ford Fellow, CERN, Geneva, 1963; Asst Prof. of Physics, Columbia Univ., 1965; Prof. of Physics, MIT, 1969–. Assoc. Editor, Nuclear Physics B, 1970; Mem. Editorial Board: Nuclear Instruments and Methods, 1977; Mathematical Modeling, 1980. Hon. Professor: Beijing Normal Coll., 1984; Jiatong Univ., Shanghai, 1987. Member: US Nat. Acad. of Science, 1976; European Physical Soc.; Italian Physical Soc.; Foreign Member: Pakistan Acad. of Science, 1984; Academia Sinica (Republic of China), 1975; Soviet Acad. of Science, 1988; Russian Acad. of Sci.; Hungarian Acad. of Sci.; Deutsche Akad. Naturforscher Leopoldina; For. Corresp.

Mem., Royal Spanish Acad. of Sci., 2003. Fellow, Amer. Acad. of Arts and Science, 1975. Hon. Fellow, Tata Inst. of Fundamental Res., Mumbai, 2004. Hon. ScD: Michigan, 1978; Chinese Univ. of Hong Kong, 1987; Bologna, 1988; Columbia, 1990; Univ. of Sci. and Technol. of China, 1990; Moscow State Univ., 1991; Bucharest, 1993; Nat. Tsinghua Univ., Taiwan, 2002; Nat. Jiatong Univ., Taiwan, 2003; Hon. Dr: HK Baptist, 2003; Rheinisch Westfälische Technische Hochschule, 2004; Dr *hc*: Nat. Central Univ., Taiwan, 2005; Hong Kong Univ. of Sci. and Technol., 2005. Nobel Prize for Physics (jt), 1976; Ernest Orlando Lawrence Award, US Govt, 1976; A. E. Eringen Medal, Soc. of Engineering Science, USA, 1977; Gold Medal in Science, City of Brescia, Italy, 1988; De Gasperi Prize, Italian Republic, 1988; Forum Engelberg Prize, 1996; Public Service Medal, NASA, 2001. *Publications:* articles in Physical Review and Physical Review Letters. *Address:* Department of Physics, Massachusetts Institute of Technology, 77 Massachusetts Avenue, Cambridge, MA 02139–4307, USA. *Club:* Explorers (New York).

**TINKER, Prof. Andrew,** PhD; FRCP, FMedSci; Professor of Cardiac Electrophysiology and Hon. Consultant, William Harvey Research Institute, Barts and the London and Queen Mary University of London, since 2011; *b* 12 June 1963; *s* of late Dr Jack Tinker, FRCP, FRCSGlas; *m* 1987, Janet Elizabeth Sweetnham (*née* Fricker); three *s* one *d*. *Educ:* Queen's Coll., Oxford (BA 1984); Royal Free Hosp., Univ. of London (MB BS Dist. 1987; PhD 1993). MRCP 1990, FRCP 2004. MRC Trng Fellow, Nat. Heart and Lung Inst., 1990–93; Postdoctoral Res. Fellow, UCSF, 1994–96; University College London: Wellcome Trust Sen. Res. Fellow, 1996–2001; Reader, 2001–04; Prof. of Molecular Medicine, 2004–; Hon. Consultant, Dept of Medicine, 2001–. FMedSci 2006. *Publications:* articles on ion channels, in particular in relation to their function in the heart and blood vessels. *Recreations:* running, chess, bridge. *Address:* Room 1.02, The Heart Centre, William Harvey Research Institute, Charterhouse Square, EC1M 6BQ. *T:* (020) 7882 5783. *E:* a.tinker@qmul.ac.uk.

**TINKER, Prof. Anthea Margaret,** CBE 2000; PhD; FAcSS; Professor of Social Gerontology, since 1988, Director, Age Concern Institute of Gerontology, 1988–98, King's College London; *b* 24 Oct. 1932; *d* of Lt-Comdr James Collins and Margaret Collins (*née* Herring); *m* 1956, Rev. Preb. Dr Eric Tinker, OBE (*d* 2011); two *s* one *d*. *Educ:* Univ. of Birmingham (BCom Econs, Pol., Sociol. 1953); City Univ. (PhD 1976). Asst Buyer, then Buyer, Boxfoldia Ltd, 1953–54; Res. Officer, BoT, 1954; HM Insp. of Factories, Min. of Labour, 1954–58; (pt-time) Res. Asst to Dir, Inst. of Local Govt Studies, and Lectr in Public Admin, Univ. of Birmingham, 1958–65; (pt-time) Lectr in Public Admin, Birmingham Sch. of Planning, 1958–65; (pt-time) Lectr in Social Policy, Extra-Mural Dept, Univ. of London, 1965–75; engaged in res., Royal Commn on Local Govt, 1967; Res. Fellow, City Univ., 1975–77; Sen., then Principal Res. Officer, DoE, 1977–88. Consultant: OECD, 1989–90; EU, 1991–2001; WHO, 2003–04. Exec. Mem., 1987–93, Fellow, 2008, British Soc. of Gerontology. Member: Cttee on Ageing, C of E Bd of Social Responsibility, 1988–89; Cttee on Long Term Care, Joseph Rowntree Foundn, 1995–96; Council, Assoc. of Res. Ethics Cttees, 2008–12; Chm., Res. Ethics Cttee, KCL, 2001–11; Chm. and Mem. of nat. and internat. adv. gps on ageing. Gov., Centre for Policy on Ageing, 1988–94. FRSocMed 1995 (Pres., Sect. of Geriatrics and Gerontology, 1998–2000); FKC 1998; FAcSS (Founder AcSS 1999). *Publications:* The Elderly in Modern Society, 1981, 4th edn as Older People in Modern Society, 1997; Staying at Home: helping elderly people, 1984; The Telecommunication Needs of Disabled and Elderly People, 1989; An Evaluation of Very Sheltered Housing, 1989; *jointly:* Women in Housing: access and influence, 1980; Families in Flats, 1981; A Review of Research on Falls among Elderly People, 1990; Falls and Elderly People: a study of current professional practice in England and innovations abroad, 1991; Life After Sixty: a profile of Britain's older population, 1992; Caring: the importance of third age carers, 1992; Homes and Travel: local life in the third age, 1992; The Information Needs of Elderly People, 1993; The Care of Frail Elderly People in the UK, 1994; Difficult to Let Sheltered Housing, 1995; Alternative Models of Care for Older People, Research Vol. 2, Royal Commn on Long Term Care, 1999; Home Ownership in Old Age, 1999; To Have and to Hold: the bond between older people and the homes they own, 1999; Eighty-five Not Out, 2001; University Research Ethics Committees: their role, remit and conduct, 2004; Facts and Misunderstandings about Pension and Retirement Ages, 2004; Improving the Provision of Information about Assistive Technology, 2005; UK Study of Elder Abuse and Neglect of Older People, 2008; An Age Friendly City: how far has London come?, 2015; pamphlets and booklets; numerous papers in learned and other jls. *Recreations:* family, houses. *Address:* 35 Theberton Street, N1 0QY. *T:* (020) 7359 4750.

**TINKER, Prof. Philip Bernard Hague,** OBE 2000; PhD, DSc; FRSB, FRSC, FRGS; FLS; author; Director of Terrestrial and Freshwater Science, Natural Environment Research Council, 1985–92; *b* 1 Feb. 1930; *s* of Philip and Gertrude Tinker; *m* 1955, Maureen Ellis (*d* 2005); one *s* one *d*. *Educ:* Rochdale High Sch.; Sheffield Univ. (BSc); PhD 1955; MA, DSc 1984, Oxon. FRSB (FIBiol 1974); FRSC 1985; FRGS 1989; FLS 1992. Overseas Res. Service, 1955–62; Sen. Scientific Officer, Rothamsted Experimental Stn, 1962–65; Lectr, Oxford Univ., 1965–71; Prof. of Agricultural Botany, Leeds Univ., 1971–77; Head of Soils Div., 1977–85, and Dep. Dir, 1981–85, Rothamsted Experimental Stn; Fellow, 1969–72, Sen. Res. Fellow, 1988–96, St Cross Coll., Oxford. Hon. Vis. Prof., Imperial Coll., 1992–95; Sen. Vis. Fellow, Plant Scis Dept, Oxford Univ., 1995–. Lectures: Regents, Univ. of California, 1979; Hannaford Meml, Adelaide, 1990; Francis New Meml and Medal, Fertilizer Soc., 1991. Chairman: UK Man and Biosphere Cttee, 1990–93; UK Cttee for Internat. Geosphere-Biosphere Prog., 1992–98; Biology Cttee, Palm Oil Res. Inst., Malaysia, 1995–98 (Mem., 1987–98). Member: UNESCO Adv. Cttee for Biosphere Reserves, 1992–96; IGBP Scientific Cttee, 1992–98. Pres., British Soil Sci. Soc., 1983–84; Gov., Macaulay Land Use Res. Inst., Aberdeen, 1990–2001. Fellow, Norwegian Acad. of Science and Letters, 1987; Hon. FRASE 1990; Hon. Member: Internat. Union of Soil Scis, 2002; World Soc. of Soil Sci., 2002. Busk Medal, RGS, 1994. *Publications:* (with R. H. V. Corley) The Oil Palm series, vol. 1, 1966 to vol. 5, 2015; (with F. E. Sanders and B. Mosse) Endomycorrhizas, 1975; (with P. H. Nye) Solute Movement in the Soil-root System, 1977; Soil and Agriculture—Critical Reviews, 1980; (with L. Fowden and R. M. Barrer) Clay Minerals, 1984; (with A. Läuchli) Advances in Plant Nutrition, vol. I, 1984, vol. II, 1986, vol. III, 1988; (with P. H. Nye) Solute Movement in the Rhizosphere, 2000; Shades of Green: a review of UK farming systems, 2000; *c* 175 papers. *Recreations:* reading, gardening, map collecting. *Address:* The Glebe House, Broadwell, Lechlade, Glos GL7 3QS. *T:* (01367) 860436. *Club:* Farmers.

**TINNISWOOD, Peter Maurice;** Head Master, Lancing College, 1998–2005; *b* 30 May 1951; *s* of late Maurice Owen Tinniswood; *m* 1975, Catharina Elizabeth Oeschger. *Educ:* Charterhouse; Magdalen Coll., Oxford (MA; PGCE Secondary); INSEAD (MBA 1981). Assistant Master: Repton Sch., 1974–76; Marlborough Coll., 1976–80; Sec. Gen., Franco-British Chamber of Commerce and Industry, Paris, 1981–83; Marlborough College: Asst Master, 1983–91; Head of Dept, 1983–86; Housemaster, 1985–91; Master, Magdalen Coll. Sch., Oxford, 1991–98. Governor: Dorset House Sch., 2000–06; Mowden Sch., 2002–05; St Paul's Sch., São Paulo, 2007–18. *Publications:* Marketing Decisions, 1981; Marketing and Production Decisions, 1991. *Address:* Samvara, Les Girvaysses, 81170 Noailles, France.

**TINSON, Dame Susan (Myfanwy),** DBE 1990; media consultant; Associate Editor and Director, External Relations, Independent Television News, 1989–2003; *b* 15 Jan. 1943; *d* of John and Kathleen Thomas; *m* 1968, Trevor James Tinson (marr. diss. 1979). *Educ:* South Hampstead High Sch.; Hull Univ. (BA Hons Social Studies). Independent Television News: Senior Editor, News at Ten and Asst Editor, ITN, 1982; consultant: ITV, 2003–06; ITN, 2003–. Non-executive Director: Asda plc, 1997–99; Yorkshire Building Soc., 1999–2006; Chime Communications plc, 2001–06; St Ives plc, 2004–07. Trustee, Heritage Lottery Fund, 1996–2001; Comr, Commonwealth War Graves Commn, 1999–2004; Mem. Cttee, Queen's Diamond Jubilee Pageant, 2012–13; Dir, HMS Victory Preservation Co., 2015–18. Mem., Adv. Bd, Pagefield Ltd, 2010–. FRTS 1996. *Address:* 170 Ebury Street, SW1W 8UP.

**TIPLER, Laura;** *see* Drysdale, L.

**TIPPER, Prof. Steven Paul,** DPhil; FBA 2007; Professor of Cognitive Psychology, University of York, since 2013; *b* 12 Sept. 1956; *s* of Malcolm Tipper and June Tipper; *m* 1987, Alison Warner; two *s* one *d*. *Educ:* Wolfson Coll., Oxford (BSc 1980; MSc 1981; DPhil 1985). Asst Prof., Mount Allison Univ., Canada, 1985–89; Associate Prof., McMaster Univ., Canada, 1989–93; Prof. of Cognitive Sci., 1993–2012, Dir, Wolfson Centre of Clinical and Cognitive Neurosci., 2004–12, Univ. of Wales, Bangor, later Bangor Univ. *Publications:* over 140 articles in learned jls, incl. Qly Jl of Exptl Psychology. *Recreations:* spending time with my family, discovering the history of York. *Address:* Department of Psychology, University of York, Heslington, York YO10 5DD. *T:* (01904) 323162.

**TIPPING, Rt Hon. Sir Andrew (Patrick Charles),** KNZM 2009 (DCNZM 2006); PC 1998; a Judge of the Supreme Court of New Zealand, 2004–12; *b* 22 Aug. 1942; *s* of Wing Comdr Patrick Alexander Tipping, RAF retd and Elizabeth Ayliffe Tipping; *m* 1st, 1967, Judith Ann Oliver (*d* 2010); two *s* one *d*; 2nd, 2012, Mary Jo Nicholson. *Educ:* Christ's Coll., Christchurch; Univ. of Canterbury (BA, LLB 1965; LLM 1st Cl. Hons 1966). Canterbury Dist Law Soc. Gold Medal, 1966; Sir Timothy Cleary Meml Prize, NZ Law Soc., 1967. Partner, Wynn Williams & Co., Barristers and Solicitors, 1967–86; Judge, High Court of NZ, 1986–97; Judge, Ct of Appeal of NZ, 1997–2004. Member of Council: Canterbury Dist Law Soc., 1976–84 (Pres., 1984); NZ Law Soc., 1982–84 (Mem., 1979–86, Chm., 1985–86, Courts and Tribunals Cttee). *Recreations:* gardening, fishing, tramping. *Address:* 256 Matapaua Bay Road, Opito RD 2, Whitianga 3592, New Zealand; 1803, 63 St Clair Avenue West, Toronto, ON M4V 2Y9, Canada. *Clubs:* Christchurch (Christchurch); Wellington (Wellington).

**TIPPING, Sir David Gwynne E.;** *see* Evans-Tipping.

**TIPPING, Simon Patrick, (Paddy);** Police and Crime Commissioner (Lab) for Nottinghamshire, since 2012; *b* 24 Oct. 1949; *m* 1970, Irene Margaret Quinn (*d* 2011); two *d*. *Educ:* Hipperholme Grammar Sch.; Nottingham Univ. (BA 1972; MA 1978). Social Worker, Notts, 1972–79; Project Leader, C of E Children's Soc., Nottingham, 1979–83. Mem. (Lab) Notts CC, 1981–93 (Chm., Economic Develt and Finance Cttees); Director: Notts Co-op. Develt Agency, 1983–92; Nottingham Develt Enterprise, 1987–93; REalliance, 2010–15; Chm., Notts Lift Cos, 2008–. MP (Lab) Sherwood, 1992–2010. Dep. Leader, H of C, 2007. Contested (Lab) Rushcliffe, 1987. Chm., Notts Community Foundn, 2010–. Vice Pres., Ramblers Assoc., 1995–. Trustee: Under One Roof, 2000–; Gedling Conservation Trust, 2010–; Rural Community Action Notts, 2013–. Gov., Notts Healthcare Trust, 2014–. *Recreations:* running, walking, gardening. *Address:* 14 Jarvis Avenue, Nottingham NG3 7BH.

**TIPPLER, John;** Director, Network, and Management Board Member, British Telecom, UK Communications Division, 1986–89, retired; *b* 9 Aug. 1929; *s* of George Herbert and Sarah Tippler, Spalding, Lincs; *m* 1st, 1952, Pauline Taylor (marr. diss. 1983); two *s*; 2nd, 1992, Martha Elisabet Berg (*d* 2014), psychoanalyst, Stockholm. *Educ:* Spalding Grammar School. Architect's Dept, Spalding RDC, 1945; Post Office Telephone Service, 1947; Royal Signals, 1949–50; Staff Mem., PO Central Engineering Sch., 1954–59; PO Engineering Develt, electronic and digital switching systems, 1959–80; Dep. Dir, System X Digital Exchange Develt, 1979–80; Dir, Exchange and Data Systems Op. and Develt, 1980; Dir of Engrg, BT, 1982–86. Dir, IT Inst., 1986–88. Mem., Youth Offending Community Panel, 2002–06. Mem., Exec. Cttee, 1997–2004, Trustee, 2004–08, Friends of Birzeit Univ. Advr, CAB, 1995–2002. *Recreations:* music, travel, cinema, theatre, reading, walking Tinkie the dog.

**TIPPLES, Amanda Jane;** QC 2011; a Recorder, since 2009; a Deputy High Court Judge, since 2013; a Lieutenant Bailiff, Guernsey, since 2016; *b* Pembury, 18 Dec. 1966; *d* of Bernard Sidney Tipples and Gillian Molly Tipples. *Educ:* Roedean Sch.; Gonville and Caius Coll., Cambridge (BA Zool. (Molecular Biol.) 1989); Council of Legal Educn. Called to the Bar, Gray's Inn, 1991; Bencher, Lincoln's Inn, 2014. Chm., Chancery Bar Assoc., 2016–18. *Address:* Maitland Chambers, 7 Stone Buildings, Lincoln's Inn, WC2A 3SZ. *T:* (020) 7406 1200, *Fax:* (020) 7406 1300.

**TIRAMANI, Jennifer Jane;** theatre designer and dress historian; Director, The School of Historical Dress, since 2009; *b* 16 Aug. 1954; *d* of Fredo Paulo Tiramani and Barbara Doreen Tiramani (*née* King); one *s* with Alastair Brotchie. *Educ:* Dartford Grammar Sch. for Girls; Central Sch. of Art and Design, London (Foundn course); Trent Poly., Nottingham (1st Cl. Dip. Theatre Design 1976). Designer, 7:84 England and 7:84 Scotland Th. Cos, 1978–84; Associate Designer, Theatre Royal, Stratford East, 1980–97; Designer, Renaissance Th. Co., 1988–90; Shakespeare's Globe: Associate Designer, 1997–2002; designs include: Henry V, 1997; Hamlet, 2000; Dir, Th. Design, 2003–05; designs include: Twelfth Night, 2003 (Olivier Award for Best Costume Design), 2012, transf. NY, 2013 (Tony Award for Best Costume Design of a Play, 2014); Measure for Measure, The Tempest, 2005; Richard III, 2012; West End prodns include: Steaming, Comedy, 1981; Much Ado About Nothing, Phoenix, 1988; designs for opera include: (stage and costume) Orlando, Opera Lille, 2010; La Clemenza di Tito, Aix-en-Provence Fest., 2011; (costume) Anna Bolena, Metropolitan Opera, NY, 2011; (costume) André Chenier, Royal Opera Hse, Covent Gdn, 2015; (costume) Le Nozze di Figaro, Opera Australia, Sydney, 2015 (Green Room Award for Best Design). Advr and contrib., Searching for Shakespeare exhibn, NPG, 2006. Vis. Prof., Sch. of Art and Design, Nottingham Trent Univ., 2008–11. Sam Wanamaker Award (jtly), Shakespeare's Globe, 2007. *Publications:* (contrib.) Shakespeare's Globe: a theatrical experiment, 2008; (jtly) Patterns of Fashion 4: the cut and construction of linen shirts, smocks, neckwear, headwear and accessories for men and women c1540–1660, 2008; (jtly) Seventeenth Century Women's Dress Patterns, Book 1, 2011, Book 2, 2012; (contrib.) Netherlandish Fashion in the Seventeenth Century, 2012; 17th Century Men's Dress Patterns 1600–1630, 2016; contribs to Costume. *Address:* The School of Historical Dress, 52 Lambeth Road, SE1 7PP. *E:* jtiramani@theschoolofhistoricaldress.org.uk.

**TIRVENGADUM, Sir Harry (Krishnan),** Kt 1987; Chevalier, Ordre National de la Légion d'Honneur 1986; Chairman and Managing Director, Air Mauritius, 1981–97, 2000–01; Managing Director, Air Afrique, 1997–99; *b* 2 Sept. 1933; *s* of late Govinden Tirvengadum and Meenatchee Sangeelee; *m* 1970, Elahe Amin Amin (*d* 2012); three *d*.

*Educ:* Royal College, Mauritius; Oxford Univ. Asst Sec., Min. of Works, 1952–67; Principal Assistant Secretary: Min. of Communications, in charge of Depts of Civil Aviation, Telecommunications, Marine Services, Posts & Telegraphs and Meteorological Services, 1968–72; Min. of Commerce and Industry, 1970; Air Mauritius: Gen. Manager, 1972–78; Dep. Chm. and Dep. Man. Dir, 1978–81. Chairman: Rodrigues Hotel, 1981–97; New Airport Catering Services, 1988–97; Mauritius Shopping Paradise Ltd, 1984–93; Director: Mauritius Hotels Gp, 1973–81; Plaisance Airlift Catering Unit, 1980–92; Mauritius Telecom, 1984–97; Mauritius Estate Development & Co., 1986–97; Mauritius Commercial Bank, 1989; State Bank Internat., 1990–97. Chm., Municipal Commn, Quatre-Bornes, 1974–77. Chief delegate of Mauritius, Triennial Assemblies, ICAO, 1971–; Rep. of Employers on Employment of Disabled Persons Bd, 1988–. Member: Exec. Cttee, IATA, 1988–91 (Chm., 1992–93); Nat. Educn Award Panel, 1988; Pres., African Airlines Assoc., 1995–96; Chm., Indian Ocean Regl Fund, 1999–2001. FCIT, FInstD. Citoyen d'Honneur, Town of Beau Bassin/Rose Hill, Mauritius, 1986. *Recreations:* bridge, swimming, walking. *Address:* Dr Arthur De Chazal Lane, Floréal, Mauritius. *T:* 6964455.

**TISDALL, Caroline Croft;** author; film maker; countryside campaigner and conservationist; racehorse owner; *b* Stratford-upon-Avon, 14 Dec. 1945; *d* of Frederick Mackenzie Tisdall and Elisabeth Croft Tisdall; *m* 1971, Angelo Bozzolla. *Educ:* Tiffin Girls' Sch.; Courtauld Inst. of Art, Univ. of London (BA Hons). Lectr in 20th Century Art Hist., Univ. of Reading, 1968–77; Art Critic, 1971–82, Corresp., Europe and Arab World, 1979–82, The Guardian. Ind. film writer and dir, 1982–, films include: The Last Post Run, Channel 4, 1982; Joseph Beuys, BBC, 1986; Marakele, The Making of a National Park, African Parks Foundn, 2001. Exhibns of photography incl. Mus. of Modern Art, NY, 1979, and Tate Modern, 2005. Vis. Prof., Oxford Brookes Univ., 2001. Member: Bd, Countryside Alliance, 1997–; Council, Nat. Trust, 2007–13; Co-Founder, 2000, UK Chm., 2005–14, African Parks Foundn. Trustee, John Muir Trust, 1994–2002; Trustee, Chiswick House and Gardens Trust, 2008–. MRHS (Founder FRHS, 2011). Mem., Internat. Dendrology Soc. Master of Hounds. 2006. Major Nat. Hunt wins include: French Champion Hurdle, 2015, Ultima Handicap Chase, 2016, 2017 (Un Temps pour Tout); Champion Nat. Hunt Flat Race, 2015 (Moon Racer); Becher Chase, 2016 (Vieux Lion Rouge). Hon. DArt Oxford Brookes, 1998. *Publications:* (with Angelo Bozzolla) Futurism, 1977, 4th edn 2006; Joseph Beuys: Coyote, 1976, 6th edn 2008; Joseph Beuys, 1979; (with Selim Nessib) Beirut: front-line story, 1983; (with Paul van Vlissingen) Witches Point, 1987; Joseph Beuys: we go this way, 1998. *Recreations:* National Hunt racing, scuba diving and marine research, dendrology, gardening, fishing, shooting, stalking, beagling. *Address:* Red Lion House, Chiswick Mall, W4 2PJ. *T:* 07792 930297. *E:* ctisdall@aol.com. *Clubs:* Kimbridge Fly Fishing; Silkie Scuba Diving and Fly Fishing.

**TISHLER, Gillian;** Director, Oxford Citizens' Advice Bureau, 2010–16; *b* 27 March 1958; *d* of Harry and Joyce Tishler. *Educ:* King Edward VI Sch., Morpeth; St Anne's Coll., Oxford (BA Hons Mod. Langs). Ministry of Agriculture, Fisheries and Food: fast stream trainee, 1979; Private Office (Private Sec. to Parly Sec.), 1986–87; Royal National Institute for the Blind: Parly Officer, 1987–89; Head of Public Affairs, 1989–93; Chief Exec., YWCA of GB, 1993–2007; Dir, Plymouth CAB, 2007–10. *Recreations:* theatre, singing, walking.

**TITCHENER, Alan Ronald,** CB 1993; Managing Director, Resource (Science and Technology Expertise) Ltd, 1993–96; *b* 18 June 1934; *s* of Edmund Hickman Ronald Titchener and Minnie Ellen Titchener; *m* 1959, Joyce Blakesley; two *s. Educ:* Harrow County Grammar Sch.; London School of Economics (BScEcon 1962). RAF, 1952. Colonial Office, 1954; Min. of Transport, 1962; Board of Trade, 1964; HM Consul New York, 1969; Dept of Trade, 1973; HM Consul-Gen., Johannesburg, 1978; Under Secretary, Department of Trade and Industry, 1982–93: Overseas Trade Div., 1982; Enterprise Initiative Div., 1987; Head of Personnel, 1991. *Club:* Royal Air Force.

**TITCHMARSH, Alan Fred,** MBE 2000; VMH; DL; writer and broadcaster; *b* 2 May 1949; *s* of Alan Titchmarsh and Bessie Titchmarsh (*née* Hardisty); *m* 1975, Alison Margaret Needs; two *d. Educ:* Ilkley County Secondary Sch.; Shipley Art and Tech. Inst.; Herts Coll. of Agric. and Hort. (Nat. Cert. Hort.); Royal Botanic Gardens, Kew (DipHort). FCIHort (FIHort 1998). Apprentice gardener, Parks Dept, Ilkley UDC, 1964–68; Supervisor, Staff Trng, Royal Botanic Gardens, 1972–74; Asst Editor, gardening books, Hamlyn Publishing, 1974–76; Asst Editor and Dep. Editor, Amateur Gardening, 1976–79; freelance writer and broadcaster, 1979–; gardening correspondent: Woman's Own, 1980–85; Daily Mail, 1985–99; Daily Express, and Sunday Express, 1999–; Radio Times, 1996–2001, 2004–07; gardening editor, Homes & Gardens, 1985–89; contrib. to BBC Gardeners' World Magazine, 1992–, Gardenlife, 2004–06; Country Life, 2011–; Sunday Telegraph, 2013–. BBC radio series include: You and Yours, Down to Earth, A House in a Garden, Alan Titchmarsh Show; numerous other progs incl. Alan Titchmarsh, Classic FM, 2012–; *BBC TV:* Nationwide, Breakfast Time, Open Air, Daytime Live; Chelsea Flower Show, 1983–97, 2001–13; Songs of Praise, 1989–94; Pebble Mill, 1991–96; Sweet Inspiration, 1993–94; Gardeners' World, 1995–2002; Ground Force, 1997–2003; How to be a Gardener, 2002–03; The Royal Gardeners, 2003; British Isles: a natural history, 2004; BBC Proms, 2004–08; 20th Century Roadshow, 2005; The Gardener's Year, 2006; The Great British Village Show, 2007; The Nature of Britain, 2007; Saving Planet Earth, 2007; *other TV includes:* Britain's Best, 2007; The Alan Titchmarsh Show, 2007–14; All the Queen's Horses, 2009; The Seasons, 2010; All the Queen's Men, 2010; Highgrove, 2010; Love Your Garden, 2011–; Prince Philip at 90, 2011; A Royal Year to Remember, 2011; Royal Windsor Jubilee Pageant, 2012; Prince Charles at Dumfries House, 2012; The Queen's Garden, 2014; Britain's Best Back Gardens, 2015; Titchmarsh on Capability Brown, 2015; Masterpiece, 2016–17; Winnie-the-Pooh: the world's most famous bear, 2016; Secrets of the National Trust with Alan Titchmarsh, 2017–; All Star Musicals, 2019; *theatre:* (narrator) The Wind in the Willows, Vaudeville, 2014; *album:* (music and poetry; with Debbie Wiseman) The Glorious Garden, 2018. Founder, Alan Titchmarsh's Gardens for Schools, 2001–11. Chancellor, Univ. of Winchester, 2015–. Vice-President: Wessex Cancer Trust, 1988–2013; Butterfly Conservation, 2000–; Arboricultural Assoc., 2000–; Patron: Rainbow Trust, 1993–2012; Kaleidoscope Theatre, 1995–; Seeds for Africa, 1999–2015; Treloar Trust, 1999–; Henry Spink Foundn, 2000–; Country Holidays for Inner City Kids, 2000–; Cowes Inshore Lifeboat, 2000–10; Writtle Coll., 2001–15; Horticap, 2002–; Hampshire and Wight Trust for Maritime Archaeology, 2005–; Royal Fund for Gardeners' Children (formerly Royal Gardeners' Orphan Fund), 2006–; Child Bereavement Charity, 2011–; Hon. Patron, Friends of the Castle of Mey, 2005–; Vice Patron, Jubilee Sailing Trust, 2000–12; Trustee: Nat. Maritime Mus., 2004–08; Garden Mus., 2008–; President: Gardening for Disabled Trust, 1989–; Telephones for the Blind, 1993–; London Children's Flower Soc., 2001–; Perennial (Gardeners' Royal Benevolent Soc.), 2005–; Plant Heritage, Nat. Council for the Conservation of Plants and Gardens, 2010–; Vice Pres., RHS, 2009–; Ambassador: Prince's Trust, 2003–; Prince's Countryside Fund, 2012–; RHS, 2013–. Mem., Consultative Cttee, Nat. Pinetum, 1996–2004. Comr, Royal Hosp., Chelsea, 2010–16. Freeman, City of London; Liveryman, Gardeners' Co. DL Hants, 2001; High Sheriff, IoW, 2008. Hon. FCGI 2000. Hon. DSc Bradford, 1999; DUniv: Essex, 1999; Leeds Metropolitan, 2003; Winchester, 2007. Gardening Writer of the Year, 1980, 1983; RHS Gold Medal, Chelsea Flower Show, 1985; Television Broadcaster of the Year, Garden Writer's Guild, 1997, 1998, 1999, 2000; Yorks Man of the Year, 1997, 2007; Lifetime Achievement Award, Garden Writers' Guild, 2004; Special Award, TRIC, 2004. VMH 2004. *Publications:* Starting With House Plants, 1976; Gardening Under Cover, 1979, 2nd edn 1985; Guide to Greenhouse Gardening, 1980; Climbers and Wall Plants, 1980; Everyone's Book of House Plants, 1981; (with R. C. M. Wright) Complete Book of Plant Propagation, 1981; Gardening Techniques, 1981; Pocket Indoor Gardener, 1982; Hamlyn Guide to House Plants, 1982; Pest-Free Plants, 1982; The Allotment Gardener's Handbook, 1982, 2nd edn 1993; The Rock Gardener's Handbook, 1983; How to be a Supergardener, 1983, 3rd edn 1999; (ed) 1,000 Handy Gardening Hints, 1983; Alan Titchmarsh's Avant Gardening, 1984, 2nd edn 1994; Alan Titchmarsh's Gardening Guides, 1984; The Gardener's Logbook, 1985; (ed) A–Z of Popular Garden Plants, 1985; Pocket Guide to Gardening, 1987; (cons. ed.) All Your Gardening Questions Answered, 1988; Daytime Live Gardening Book, 1990; The English River, 1993; Alan Titchmarsh's Favourite Gardens, 1995; (cons. ed) Ground Force Weekend Workbook, 1999; Gardeners' World Complete Book of Gardening, 1999; How to be a Gardener, 2001; Trowel and Error (memoirs), 2002; How to be a Gardener, Book 2, 2003; The Royal Gardeners, 2003; British Isles: a natural history, 2004; (ed and contrib.) Fill My Stocking (anthology), 2005; The Gardener's Year, 2005; Nobbut A Lad (memoir), 2006; The Nature of Britain, 2007; England, Our England (anthology), 2007; The Kitchen Gardener, 2008; Alan Titchmarsh's How to Garden: Vegetables and Herbs, 2009, Garden Design, 2009, Lawns, Paths and Patios, 2009, Pruning and Training, 2009, Container Gardening, 2009, Gardening in the Shade, 2009, Flowering Shrubs, 2010, Growing Fruit, 2010, Perennial Garden Plants, 2010, Climbers and Wall Shrubs, 2010, Greenhouse Gardening, 2010, Small Gardens, 2011, Pests and Problems, 2011, Growing Roses, 2011, Growing Bulbs, 2011, Small Trees, 2012, Allotment Gardening, 2012, Instant Colour, 2012, Weekend Gardening, 2012; Grow Your Own Plants, 2013; Water Gardening, 2013; Flowers and Foliage For Cutting, 2013; Knave of Spades (memoir), 2009; When I Was a Nipper (memoir), 2010; Tales from Titchmarsh, 2011; The Complete Countryman, 2011; Elizabeth: her life, our times, 2012; Love Your Garden, 2012; My Secret Garden, 2012; The Queen's Houses, 2014; *novels:* Mr MacGregor, 1998; The Last Lighthouse Keeper, 1999; Animal Instincts, 2000; Only Dad, 2001; Rosie, 2004; Love and Dr Devon, 2006; Folly, 2008; The Haunting, 2011; Bring Me Home, 2014; Mr Gandy's Grand Tour, 2016; The Scarlet Nightingale, 2018. *Recreations:* art, music, boating, theatre, movies, books. *Address:* c/o Arlington Enterprises, 3rd Floor, Great Portland Street, W1W 8QH. *T:* (020) 7580 0702. *Clubs:* Athenæum, Lord's Taverners, Royal Automobile.

**TITCHMARSH, Prof. John Michael,** DPhil; Royal Academy of Engineering Research Professor in Microanalytical Techniques for Structural Integrity Problems, University of Oxford, 1998–2005; Fellow, St Anne's College, Oxford, 1998–2005, now Senior Research Fellow; *b* 4 Sept. 1944; *s* of late Harold Titchmarsh and of Ada Titchmarsh; *m* 1967, Elaine Joy Knightley; two *d. Educ:* Christ's Coll., Cambridge (BA Nat. Sci. 1966; MA 1970); Wadham Coll., Oxford (DPhil 1969). Res. Asst, Univ. of Oxford, 1969–74; UKAEA, 1974–94; Philips Prof. in Materials Analysis, Sheffield Hallam Univ., 1994–98. Member of Committee: Inst. of Physics; RMS. Birks Award, Microbeam Analysis Soc., USA, 1995. *Publications:* papers in learned jls on electron microscopy. *Address:* Department of Materials, University of Oxford, Parks Road, Oxford OX1 3PH; St Anne's College, Oxford OX2 6JF.

**TITCOMB, Lesley Jane,** CBE 2019; Chief Executive, The Pensions Regulator, 2015–19; *b* Farnham Royal, Bucks, 16 June 1961; *d* of late Roy Thomas Titcomb and Claire Titcomb (*née* Belcher); *m* 1989, (Michael) Mark Prisk, *qv. Educ:* Oxford High Sch. GDST; St Anne's Coll., Oxford (MA Lit. Hum.). ACA 1990. Financial Services Authority: Dir of Authorisations, 2007–08; Dir, Small Firm Supervision, 2008–10; Actg Chief Operating Officer, 2010–13; Chief Operating Officer and Exec. Bd Mem., Financial Conduct Authy, 2013–15. Non-exec. Mem. Bd, Nat. Bank of Kuwait (Internat.) plc, 2016–. Trustee, StepChange. *Recreations:* singing, cooking, watching Rugby, theatre, ballet. *T:* 07966 216770. *E:* lesleytitcomb1@virginmedia.com.

**TITE, Prof. Michael Stanley,** DPhil; FSA; Edward Hall Professor of Archaeological Science and Director of Research Laboratory for Archaeology and History of Art, University of Oxford, 1989–2004, now Emeritus; Fellow of Linacre College, Oxford, 1989–2004, now Emeritus; *b* 9 Nov. 1938; *s* of late Arthur Robert Tite and Evelyn Frances Violet Tite (*née* Endersby); *m* 1967, Virginia Byng Noel; two *d. Educ:* Trinity Sch. of John Whitgift, Croydon; Christ Church, Oxford (MA, DPhil). FSA 1977. Research Fellow in Ceramics, Univ. of Leeds, 1964–67; Lectr in Physics, Univ. of Essex, 1967–75; Keeper, Dept of Scientific Res. (formerly Res. Lab.), British Museum, 1975–89. Pomerance Award for Sci. Contribs to Archaeol., Archaeol Inst. of America, 2008; Costa Navarino Internat. Archaeometry Award, Univ. of Peloponnese, Kalamata, 2013–14. *Publications:* Methods of Physical Examination in Archaeology, 1972; (with A. J. Shortland) Production Technology of Faience and Related Vitreous Materials, 2008; papers on scientific methods applied to archaeology in various jls. *Recreations:* travelling with "The Buildings of England", gardening. *Address:* 7 Kings Cross Road, Oxford OX2 7EU. *T:* (01865) 558422.

**TITFORD, Jeffrey William;** Member (UK Ind) Eastern Region, England, European Parliament, 1999–2009; *b* 24 Oct. 1933; *s* of Guy Frederick Titford and Queta Mehalah (*née* D'Wit); *m* 1956, Margaret Cheeld; one *s* three *d.* Dir, Titford Funeral Service Ltd, 1954–89, Man. Dir, 1970–89. Pres., Nat. Assoc. Funeral Dirs, 1975–76. UK Independence Party: Leader, 2000–02, 2010–11; Whip, 2009–; Life Pres., 2011. Contested: (Referendum) Harwich, 1997; (UKIP) Harwich, 2005. *Recreations:* fishing, walking, golf. *Address:* Bratton House, Charlton Gardens, Ditchling, E Sussex BN6 8WA.

**TITLEY, Gary;** Senior Consultant, Hume Brophy, 2011–15; Member (Lab) North West Region, England, European Parliament, 1999–2009 (Greater Manchester West, 1989–99); Leader, European Parliamentary Labour Party, 2002–09; *b* 19 Jan. 1950; *s* of Wilfred James and Joyce Lillian Titley; *m* 1975, Rosario, (Charo); one *s* one *d. Educ:* York Univ. (BA Hons Hist./Educn, 1973; PGCE 1974). TEFL, Bilbao, 1973–75; taught History, Earls High Sch., Halesowen, 1976–84; Personal Assistant to MEP, 1984–89. Mem., W Midlands CC, 1981–86 (Vice-Chair: EDC, 1981–84; Consumer Services Cttee, 1984–86). Dir, W Midlands Enterprise Bd, 1982–89; Chairman: W Midlands Co-op Finance Co., 1982–89; Black Country Co-op Develt Agency, 1982–88. Non-exec. Dir, Bolton PCT, 2009–12. Contested (Lab): Bromsgrove, 1983; Dudley W, 1987. Pres., Eur. Parlt delegn for relations with Finland, 1992–94; rapporteur, accession of Finland to EU. President: European Economic Area Jt Parly Assembly, 1994–95; Jt Parly Cttee for relns with Lithuania, 1999–2001; Cttee of Jt Parly Assembly and delegn presidents, 2001–02. Commander, White Rose (Finland), 1995; Golden Cross (Austria), 1996; Order of Grand Duke Gediminas (Lithuania), 2003. *Recreations:* family, reading, sport.

**TITLEY, Commandant Nursing Officer Jane,** CBE 1995; RRC 1990 (ARRC 1986); Director of Defence Nursing Services, 1992–95; *b* 22 April 1940; *d* of Louis and Phyllis Myra (Josephine) Titley. *Educ:* St Catherine's Convent, Nottingham; St Bartholomew's Hosp.; Sussex Maternity Hosp. SRN 1962; SCM 1963. Joined QARNNS, 1965; served in

Naval hosps and estabts in UK, Malta, Singapore, Naples and Gibraltar; Matron, 1986; Dep. Matron-in-Chief, 1988; Matron-in-Chief, 1990–94; QHNS, 1990–94. OStJ 1990. *Recreations:* 'to stand and stare', narrow-boating, genealogy. *Address:* Flat 10, 28 Pembridge Square, W2 4DS.

**TITTERINGTON, Prof. David Michael;** Professor of Organ, since 1991, and Head, Organ Studies, since 1996, Royal Academy of Music, and Professor, since 2017, University of London; concert organist, since 1986; *b* 10 Jan. 1958; *s* of Geoffrey Bridge Titterington and Claire Elizabeth Titterington (*née* Parsons). *Educ:* Pembroke Coll., Oxford (Organ Schol.; BA Hons 1980, MA 1984); Conservatoire de Rueil-Malmaison, Paris (1st Prize 1984, Prix d'Excellence 1985). Dir of Music, Dutch Ch, London, 1992–; Organ Consultant: Pembroke Coll., Oxford, 1993–95; Chapel Royal, HM Tower of London, 1997–2000; St Catharine's Coll., Cambridge, 2000–01; Sidney Sussex Coll., Cambridge, 2007–16; Canterbury Cathedral, 2007–; KCL, 2016–; Organ Curator, St John's Smith Square, 2012–. Vis. Prof. of Organ, Liszt Ferenc Acad. of Music, Budapest, 1997–; Hon. Prof., Liszt Ferenc State Univ., 1999; Dist. Vis. Prof., Tokyo Nat. Univ. of Arts, 2018; Vis. Prof., Yonsei Univ., Seoul, 2018. Fellow Commoner, Sidney Sussex Coll., Cambridge, 2016–. Gen. Ed., Organ Repertoire Series, 1987–97. Artistic Director: European Organ Fest. and Comp. (for FCO), 1992; Internat. Organ Fest., St Albans, 2007–. Solo recital début, RFH, 1986; *festival performances* include: Bicentennial Fest., Sydney, 1988; Hong Kong, Adelaide, NZ, Israel, Guelph, Prague Spring, Schleswig Holstein, Lahti, Granada, León, Brezice, BBC Proms, Cheltenham, City of London, Dartington, Belfast; *concerto performances* include: Berlin SO; BBC SO; Lahti SO; BBC Scottish SO; City of London Sinfonia; Britten Sinfonia; Guildhall String Ensemble; Allegri String Quartet. Freeman, Musicians' Co., 2017. Hon. Fellow, Bolton Inst. of Higher Educn, 1992; Hon. FRCO 1999; Hon. FKC 2018. Hon. RAM 2008. Hon. DMus Liszt Ferenc State, Budapest, 1999; DUniv Huddersfield, 2010; Hon. DArts Bolton, 2018. Arts Council of GB Award, 1984. *Publications:* (with J. Wainright) History of Pembroke College, Organs, 1995; (contrib.) Organs of Britain 1990–1995, 1996; (contrib.) New Grove Dictionary of Music and Musicians, 2000; article in RCO Jl. *Recreations:* silence, the sea, reading, friends. *Address:* Royal Academy of Music, Marylebone Road, NW1 5HT. *T:* (020) 7873 7339, *Fax:* (020) 7873 7439. *E:* d.titterington@ram.ac.uk. *Clubs:* Travellers, Savile.

**TITTERINGTON, Robert Mark;** QC (Guernsey) 2016; HM Comptroller (Solicitor-General), and Deputy Receiver General, Guernsey, since 2016; *b* Manchester, 20 Aug. 1958; *s* of Frank Kenneth and Sheila Titterington; *m* 1985, Lesley Ann Price; one *s* one *d.* *Educ:* Manchester Grammar Sch.; Leeds Univ. (LLB Hons); Univ. de Caen Basse-Normande (Cert. d'Etudes juridiques Françaises et Normande). Admitted as solicitor, 1983; Legal Asst, ICI, 1985–88; Crown Counsel, 1988–91, Sen. Crown Counsel, 1991–98, Principal Crown Counsel, 1998–2000, Falkland Is; Legislative Draftsman, 2000–05, Dir, Legislative Drafting, 2005–16, Guernsey; Advocate, Royal Court of Guernsey, 2004; Attorney Gen., Falkland Is, and S Georgia and S Sandwich Is, 2007; a Dep. Judge, Magistrates' Court, Guernsey, 2012–16. *Publications:* contrib. Jersey and Guernsey Law Rev. *Recreations:* football, golf, gardening. *Address:* Law Officers of the Crown, St James Chambers, St Peter Port, Guernsey GY1 2PA. *T:* (01481) 723355, *Fax:* (01481) 725439. *E:* robert.titterington@gov.gg. *Club:* Lansdowne.

**TIZARD, Dame Catherine (Anne),** ONZ 2002; GCMG 1990; GCVO 1995; DBE 1985; QSO 1996; Governor-General of New Zealand, 1990–96; *b* 4 April 1931; *d* of Neil Maclean and Helen Montgomery Maclean; *m* 1951, Rt Hon. Robert James Tizard, CNZM, PC (marr. diss. 1983; he *d* 2016); one *s* three *d.* *Educ:* Matamata College; Auckland University (BA). Tutor in Zoology, Univ. of Auckland, 1967–84. Member: Auckland City Council, 1971–83 (Mayor of Auckland, 1983–90); Auckland Regional Authy, 1980–83. Chair, NZ Historic Places Trust, 1996–2002; Trustee, NZ SO Foundn, 1996–2018; Trustee, Kiri te Kanawa Trust, 2004–14 (Dep. Chair, 2004–12); Trustee and Patron, Howard League for Penal Reform NZ, 2012–18. *Recreations:* music, reading, drama, cryptic crosswords. *Address:* 12A Wallace Street, Herne Bay, Auckland 1011, New Zealand.

**TIZARD, John Nigel;** independent strategic advisor and commentator on public policy and public services, since 2009; Director, John Tizard Ltd, since 2009; *b* Colchester, 16 Nov. 1954; *s* of Rodger Tizard and Angela Tizard; *m* 1995, Glenda Walker; one *s* one *d.* *Educ:* Colchester Royal Grammar Sch.; London Sch. of Econs (BScEcon). Spastics Soc., later Scope, 1977–97, Dir, Policy and Strategy, 1994–97; Gp Dir, Govt and Business Engagement, Capita Gp plc, 1997–2007; Dir, Centre for Public Services Partnerships, Univ. of Birmingham, 2008–10; Dir, Centre for Public Service Partnerships, Local Govt Inf. Unit, 2010–11. Founder and Convener, Voluntary Orgns Disability Gp, 1990–95; Exec. Advr to Public Services Strategy Bd, CBI, 2002–07 (seconded as Dir of Public Services (pt-time), 2005); Member: HM Treasury adv. panel on public sector perf. mgt, 2007; Adv. Panel, Govt's Rev. of Public Service Industry, 2008; Policy Adv. Bd, Social Market Foundn, 2008–15; Adv. Bd, Centre for Public Scrutiny, 2008–; CLG/LGA Local Innovations Awards Adv. Panel, 2009–10; non-executive Director: Social Investment Business, 2008–13; Resultsmark, 2014–; Chair: Collective Impact Capital CIC, 2016–; B-Side CIC, 2017–. Associate, GP Governance, 2016–. Interim Dir, 2012–13, Mem. Adv. Council, 2013–15, Collaborate, London S Bank Univ.; Chm. Govs, Aldridge Portland Community Acad., 2013–16. Evaluator, Eur. Public Service Awards, 2011, 2013, 2015, 2017. Speaker at UK and internat. confs. Contested (Lab): Arundel, 1979; Mid Beds, 1983. Mem., Beds CC, 1981–99 (Jt Leader, 1985–96). Non-exec. Dir, S Beds Community NHS Trust, 1990–94; Mem., Beds Police Authy, 1996–98. Mem., Council, Assembly of Eur. Regions, 1993–99 (Chm., Social Affairs Gp, 1993–99). Trustee: Adventure Capital Fund, 2007–; Nat. Assoc. for Voluntary and Community Action, 2010–16 (Vice Chm., 2012–13, 2015–16; Hon. Advr, 2016–18; Chm., 2018–19); Action Space, 2011– (Chm., 2015–); Tomorrow's People, 2011–18; Villiers Park Educn Trust, 2018–. Sen. Hon. Fellow, Univ. of Birmingham, 2010–13. Vis. Fellow, London S Bank Univ., 2012–15. FRSA. Mem., Guardian Local Govt Editl Bd, 2010–14. *Publications:* regular contribs to nat. and internat. media, incl. Municipal Jl, Huffington Post, Govt Opportunities, Third Sector. *Recreations:* cooking, reading, holidays in France and Europe. *Address:* John Tizard Ltd, 50 Ampthill Road, Shefford, Beds SG17 5BB. *E:* john@johntizard.com.

**TOAL, Rt Rev. Mgr Joseph;** *see* Motherwell, Bishop of, (RC).

**TOAL, Patrick Thomas,** CB 2007; Permanent Secretary, Department of Agriculture and Rural Development, Northern Ireland, 2003–07; *b* 8 March 1944; *s* of late Edward and Brigid Toal; *m* 1969, Bridget Macklin; one *s.* *Educ:* Abbey Grammar Sch., Newry; QUB. Appointed NI Civil Service, 1968; Department of Agriculture: admin trainee, 1976; various posts in Animal Health, Fisheries, Agricl Mktg and Co-opn, Horticulture, and Milk and Eggs Divs, 1976–83; Princ. Officer, Milk and Eggs Div., 1983–86; Head of Finance, 1986–89; Asst Sec., Hd of Animal Health and Welfare and Agric. Policy Divs, 1989–98; Dep. Sec., Agric. Policy, 1998–2003. Mem. Bd, Intervention Agency for Agricl Produce, 1998–2002. Mem. Council, Royal Ulster Agricl Soc., 2003–07. *Recreations:* golf (playing and admin), theatre, reading, amateur dramatics, gardening, Gaelic football, Rugby Union. *Clubs:* Fortwilliam Golf (Belfast) (Hon. Sec., 2007–12; Captain, 2013), Rosapenna Golf (Co. Donegal).

**TOASE, Philip Cursley,** CBE 2004; QFSM 2009; DL; Chief Fire Officer and Chief Executive, West Yorkshire Fire & Rescue Service, 2000–08; *b* 26 Sept. 1953; *s* of Gordon and Ray Toase; *m* 2003, Lorraine Robertson; one *s* one *d,* and one step *s.* *Educ:* Queen Elizabeth Grammar Sch., Wakefield; South Bank Univ. (BSc 1996). MCGI 1996. Joined W Yorks Fire Service as Fire fighter, Dewsbury, 1974; Station Officer, 1981; Asst Divl Officer, 1985; Divl Officer, 1987; Sen. Divl Officer, 1990; Asst Chief Fire Officer, 1995–99; Dep. Chief Fire Officer, 1999–2000. Chm. and Consultant, 3TC Software Ltd, 2008–18. DL W Yorks, 2008. Long Service and Good Conduct Medal, 1994. *Recreations:* Manchester United season ticket holder, cricket, Rugby, keeping fit. *Address:* Huddersfield, W Yorks.

**TOBIAS, Prof. Jeffrey Stewart,** MD; FRCP, FRCR; Consultant in Radiotherapy and Oncology, University College and Middlesex Hospitals, since 1981; Professor of Cancer Medicine, University College London, since 2002; *b* 4 Dec. 1946; *s* of late Gerald Joseph Tobias and of Sylvia Tobias (*née* Pearlberg); *m* 1st, 1973, Dr Gabriela Jill Jaecker (*d* 2008); two *s* one *d;* 2nd, 2011, Dr Susan Jacqueline Rachel Kiernan. *Educ:* Hendon Grammar Sch.; Gonville and Caius Coll., Cambridge (MA, MD, BChir); St Bartholomew's Hosp. Med. Sch. Junior hosp. posts, St Bartholomew's, Whittington, UCH and Hammersmith Hosps, 1971–74; Research Fellow in Oncology, Harvard Med. Sch., 1975–76; Fellow in Oncology, St Bartholomew's and Royal Marsden Hosps, 1976–80; Clinical Dir, Meyerstein Inst. of Oncology, Middlesex Hosp., 1992–97. Chairman: CRC New Studies Breast Cancer Working Party, 1990–2000; UK Co-ordinating Cttee for Cancer Research Head and Neck Working Party, 1990–2000; CRC Educn Cttee, 2000–02; Cancer Res. UK Tobacco Adv. Gp, 2003–06; Member: Nat. Adv. Gp for Screening in Oral Cancer, 1994–97; various MRC Adv. Gps. Advr, Audit Commn for Nat. Cancer Services, 2000. Founder Sec., British Oncological Assoc., 1986; Member Council: RCR, 1992–94; Cancer Res. UK (formerly CRC UK), 2000–12 (Trustee, 2002–12); Pres., British Assoc. of Head and Neck Oncologists, 1996–98; Chm., Annual British Cancer Res. Meeting, 2004. Lectures include: BAAS, 1997, 2006; Natalie Shipman, RCP, 2006; Centenary, RSocMed, 2011. *Publications:* (with M. J. Peckham) Primary Management of Breast Cancer, 1985; (with R. L. Souhami) Cancer and its Management, 1986, 7th edn (with D. Hochhauser) 2016; (with C. J. Williams) Cancer, a Colour Atlas, 1993; (with P. R. Thomas) Current Radiation Oncology, 3 vols, 1994, 1995, 1997; Cancer: what every patient needs to know, 1995, rev. edn 1999; (with A. C. Silverstone) Gynecologic Oncology, 1997; (with J. Houghton) Breast Cancer—New Horizons in Research and Treatment, 2000; (with L. Doyal) Informed Consent in Medical Research, 2001; (with K. Eaton) Living with Cancer, 2001; Clinical Governance and Revalidation: a practical guide, 2003; (ed jtly) Prevention and Screening for Cancer, 2018; many contribs to newspapers and learned jls about cancer management and medical ethics. *Recreations:* nothing too strenuous: music, cycling, ski-ing, reading, writing. *Address:* Department of Oncology, University College Hospital, NW1 2BU. *T:* (020) 3447 9088, *Fax:* (020) 3447 9055; 4 Canonbury Place, N1 2NQ. *E:* j.tobias100@btinternet.com. *Clubs:* Garrick, Royal Society of Medicine, Les Six; Albatross Wind and Water.

**TOBIN, Hon. Brian Vincent,** OC 2012; PC (Can.) 1993; Vice Chairman, BMO Financial Group, Bank of Montreal, since 2018 (Vice Chairman, BMO Capital Markets, 2013–18); *b* 21 Oct. 1954; *s* of Patrick Vincent Tobin and Florence Mary Tobin (*née* Frye); *m* 1977, Jodean Smith; two *s* one *d.* *Educ:* Meml Univ. of Newfoundland. MP (L): Humber-St Barbe-Baie Verte, 1980–96; Bonavista-Trinity-Conception, 2000–02; Parly Sec. to Minister of Fisheries and Oceans, 1981; Minister: of Fisheries and Oceans, 1993–96; of Industry, 2000–02; MHA (L) Bay of Islands, 1996–99, Straits and White Bay North, 1999–2000; Premier of Newfoundland and Labrador, 1996–2000. Leader, Liberal Party of NF, 1996–2000; Chair, Nat. Liberal Caucus, 1989. Sen. Business Advr, Dentons Canada (formerly Fraser Milner Casgrain) LLP, 2004–13; Exec. Chm., Consolidated Thompson Iron Mines Ltd, 2009–11. *Publications:* (jtly) All in Good Time (memoirs), 2002. *Recreations:* reading, music, sports.

**TOBIN, Patrick Francis John;** Administrator, Headmasters' and Headmistresses' Conference Projects in Central and Eastern Europe, 2003–12; *b* 4 Oct. 1941; *s* of Denis George and Una Eileen Tobin; *m* 1970, Margery Ann Sluce; one *s* three *d.* *Educ:* St Benedict's Sch., Ealing; Christ Church, Oxford (MA in Modern Hist.); London Univ. (PGCE). Head: of Econs, St Benedict's Sch., Ealing, 1963–71; of History, Christ Coll., Brecon, 1971–75; of History, Tonbridge Sch., 1975–81; Headmaster, Prior Park Coll., Bath, 1981–89; Principal, Mary Erskine Sch. and Daniel Stewart's and Melville Coll., Edinburgh, 1989–2000. Member: HMC, 1981– (Chm., 1998; Vice-Chm., 1999; Chm., Professional Develt Cttee, 1991–95); Governing Council, Scottish Council of Ind. Schs, 1990–94; Scottish Consultative Council for the Curriculum, 1991–95; Assessor, SHA Educnl Assessment Centres, 1991–95. Governor: Bryanston Sch., 2000–06; Portsmouth Grammar Sch., 2001–13; Ryde Sch., 2001–11; Magdalen Coll. Sch., Oxford, 2001–05; Our Lady's Convent Sen. Sch., Abingdon, 2004–11 (Chm., 2004–11); Bede's Sch., E Sussex, 2011–16; Advisory Governor: Ampleforth Coll., 2000–10; St Benedict's Ealing, 2000–06 (Chm., 2001–06); Downside Sch., 2001–03. Chm., Lower Park (Putney) Ltd, 2013–18. *Publications:* Sweet Wells, 1998; Making Good Teachers Better, 1994; Portrait of a Putney Pud: an unpredictable career in teaching (memoir), 2004. *Recreations:* reading, travelling, canal boats. *Address:* Glentruim, Ashlake Copse Lane, Kite Hill, Wootton, Ryde, Isle of Wight PO33 4LG. *Club:* East India.

**TOD, John Mackenzie,** OBE 1987; Director, France, British Council, and Cultural Counsellor, British Embassy, Paris, 1998–2004; *b* 24 Oct. 1944; *s* of John Alexander Tod and Eleanor May Tod (*née* Darrah); *m* 1970, Christiane Teytaud; two *s* one *d.* *Educ:* Calday Grange GS; King's Coll., Cambridge (BA English); Leeds Univ. (postgrad. Dip. TESL 1969); Inst. of Educn, London Univ. (MA Ed 1983). VSO, Malaita, Solomon Is, 1963–64; teacher, Ruffwood Comp. Sch., Kirby, 1965; joined British Council, 1968: Ghana, 1969–72; Brazil, 1972–74; Asst Dir (Educn), Kano, Nigeria, 1975–78; Asst Dir, Overseas Educnl Appts Dept, 1978–82; Rep., Senegal, 1983–88; Regl Dir and Supt Gen., Sociedade Brasileira de Cultura Inglesa, São Paulo, 1988–93; Dir of Arts, 1993–98. *Recreations:* choral music, literature, theatre, travel. *Address:* 35 rue du Tabellion, 1050 Brussels, Belgium. *T:* (2) 5340715.

**TOD, Vice-Adm. Sir Jonathan (James Richard),** KCB 1996; CBE 1982; Deputy Commander Fleet, 1994–97; *b* 26 March 1939; *e s* of late Col Richard Logan Tod and Elizabeth Allen Tod; *m* 1962, Claire Elizabeth Russell Dixon (*d* 2015); two *s.* *Educ:* Gordonstoun Sch. BRNC, Dartmouth, 1957–59; Flying trng, 1961; Hal Far (Malta), 1963; HM Ships: Ark Royal, Hermes, Eagle, RNAS, Lossiemouth, 1962–70; BRNC, Dartmouth, 1970–72; Exec. Officer, HMS Devonshire, 1972–74; Naval Staff, 1975–77; Comd HMS Brighton, 1978–80; Cabinet Office, 1980–82; RCDS 1983; Comd HMS Fife, 1984–85; Dir, Defence Programme, 1986–88; Comd HMS Illustrious, 1988–89; Flag Officer Portsmouth and Naval Base Comdr Portsmouth, 1989–90; ACDS (Policy and Nuclear), MoD, 1990–94. Chm., Sea Cadet Assoc., 1998–2005; Vice Chm., Marine Soc. and Sea Cadets, 2004–05 (Vice Pres., 2005); Mem. Council, RNLI, 2005–09 (Vice-Pres., 2009–). *Recreations:* electric boating, gardening. *Address:* c/o Naval Secretary, Fleet Headquarters, Whale Island, Portsmouth PO2 8BY.

**TODD, (Alan) James**; QC 2019; *b* Wrexham, 12 Sept. 1967; *s* of Ronald Stanley Todd and Gillian Margaret Todd (*née* Drinkwater); *m* 1995, Sian Hayley Griffiths; two *s*. *Educ*: King's Sch., Chester; St John's Coll., Cambridge (BA 1989). Called to the Bar, Gray's Inn, 1990; in practice as a barrister, specialising in personal injury and clinical negligence. *Recreations*: road cycling, ski-ing. *Address*: 39 Essex Chambers, 81 Chancery Lane, WC2A 1DD. *T*: (020) 7832 1111. *E*: james.todd@39essex.com.

**TODD, Prof. Christopher James**, PhD; FRCPE; Professor of Primary Care and Community Health, University of Manchester, since 2001 (Director of Research, School of Nursing, Midwifery and Social Work, 2003–13); Director, Policy Research Unit on Older People and Frailty, and Senior Investigator, National Institute for Health Research, since 2019; *b* Bournemouth, 1 Dec. 1956; *s* of Ernest James Todd and late Pamela Mary Todd (*née* Bramley); *m* 2001, Victoria Jane Brandon. *Educ*: Epsom Coll.; Univ. of Durham (BA Hons Psychol. 1978; MA 1980; PhD 1987). CPsychol 1989, AFBPsS 1990; FRCPE 2019. Temp. Lectr in Psychol., Dept of Soc. Scis, Sunderland Poly., 1980; Interviewer, PSI, London, 1986; Res. Officer, Centre for Applied Health Studies, Univ. of Ulster, Coleraine, 1987–90; University of Cambridge: Res. Associate, 1990–92, Sen. Res. Associate, 1992–93, Dir, 1993–2001, Health Services Res. Gp, Dept of Public Health and Primary Care; Affiliate Lectr, Fac. of Soc. and Pol Scis, 1994–2000; Co-Dir, Cambridge Res. Devlt Support Gp, Inst. of Public Health, 1997–2001; Wolfson College, Cambridge: Fellow, 1995–2001; Members' Steward, 1996–2000; Dir of Studies in Soc. and Pol Scis, 1999–2000. Director: EC Prevention of Falls Network Europe, 2003–11; EC Prevention of Falls Network for Dissemination, 2013–18. Associate Fellow, BPsS, 1990; Regl Fellow, RSM, 2009. *Publications*: contrib. to papers on palliative care, epidemiology of osteoporosis, falls prevention and health psychol. in jls. *Recreations*: sculling, walking, Pilates, wine tasting. *Address*: School of Health Sciences, University Place, University of Manchester, Oxford Road, Manchester M13 9PL. *T*: (0161) 306 7865, *Fax*: (0161) 306 7894. *E*: chris.todd@manchester.ac.uk. *Club*: Agecroft Rowing.

**TODD, Damian Roderic, (Ric)**; HM Diplomatic Service; Director, Parliamentary, Ministerial and Central Services, Foreign and Commonwealth Office, since 2017; *b* 29 Aug. 1959; *s* of late George Todd and Annette Todd. *Educ*: Lawrence Sheriff Grammar Sch., Rugby; Worcester Coll., Oxford (BA Hons History). Joined HM Diplomatic Service, 1980; Third Sec., then Second Sec., Pretoria and Cape Town, 1981–84; FCO, 1984–87; HM Consul and First Sec., Prague, 1987–89; FCO, 1989–91; First Sec. (Econ.), Bonn, 1991–95; on secondment to HM Treasury, 1995–97, Hd of Agric. Team, 1996–97; FCO, 1997–98; on loan to HM Treasury as Hd of EU Co-ordination and Strategy Team, 1998–2001; Amb. to the Slovak Republic, 2001–04; Finance Dir, FCO, 2004–07; Ambassador to Poland, 2007–11; Gov., Turks and Caicos Is, 2011–13; High Comr, Cyprus, 2014–16. *Address*: c/o Foreign and Commonwealth Office, King Charles Street, SW1A 2AH.

**TODD, Daphne Jane, (Mrs P. R. T. Driscoll)**, OBE 2002; PPRP (RP 1985); NEAC; artist; President, Royal Society of Portrait Painters, 1994–2000; *b* 27 March 1947; *d* of Frank Todd and Annie Mary Todd (*née* Lord); *m* 1984, Lt-Col (Patrick Robert) Terence Driscoll (*d* 2016); one *d*. *Educ*: Simon Langton Grammar Sch. for Girls, Canterbury; Slade Sch. of Fine Art, UCL (DFA 1969; HDFA 1971). Vis. Lectr, Byam Shaw Sch. of Art, 1971–75 and 1978–80; Dir of Studies, Heatherley Sch. of Fine Art, 1980–86. NEAC 1984; Royal Society of Portrait Painters: Mem. Council, 1986–90; Hon. Sec., 1990–91. Hon. Mem., Soc. of Women Artists, 1995. Tour Artist with TRH Prince of Wales and Duchess of Cornwall, S Africa and Tanzania, 2011. Judge, Big Painting Challenge, BBC TV, 2015. Work in exhibitions, including: Royal Acad. Summer Exhibns, 1969–; Critic's Choice, Tooth's, 1972; Slade Centenary, 1972; Slade Ladies, Mall Gall., 1991; President's Exhibn, Birmingham, 1995; solo retrospective exhibn, Morley Gall., London, 1989; solo exhibn, Messum's Gall., 2001, 2004, 2008, 2009, 2015; solo exhibn, Threadneedle Space, Mall Galleries, 2012. Work in private and public collections including: Royal Acad. (Chantrey Bequest); Lady Margaret Hall, UC, St Anne's Coll., Lincoln Coll. and Rhodes House, Oxford; Pembroke, St Catharine's, Girton, Clare and Sidney Sussex Colls, Cambridge; UCL; St David's Univ., Lampeter; De Montfort Univ.; Royal Holloway Mus. and Art Gall.; Bishop's Palace, Hereford; Wellington Barracks; BMA; ICE; NUMAST; Science Mus.; Nat. Portrait Gall.; Chapter House, St Paul's Cath.; Windsor Castle. Portrait commissions include: Grand Duke of Luxembourg; Lord Adrian; Dame Janet Baker; Spike Milligan; Sir Neil Cossons; Baron Klingspor; Sir Kirby and Lady Laing; Dr Stephen Spurr; Rt Rev. Graeme Knowles; Christopher Ondaatje; Dame Anne Mueller; Lord Sainsbury of Preston Candover; Lord Sharman; Prof. Marilyn Strathern; Lord Morris of Castle Morris, Sir Tom Stoppard; Lord Tugendhat; Lord Ashburton; Lord Armstrong of Ilminster; Lord and Lady Tebbit; Bill Packer; Lord Bledisloe; Viscount Mackintosh; Peter Scott; Lord Fellowes of West Stafford; Lady Armstrong; Sir Peter Gwynn-Jones, Garter King of Arms; Viscount Gage; HRH the Prince of Wales; Dame Sally Davies. Governor: Thomas Heatherley Educnl Trust, 1987–2014; FBA, 1994–2000. Treas., Friends of Argos Hill Windmill, 2009–11; Mem. Honour Cttee, Friends of Canterbury Mus, 2011–14. Freeman, Painter-Stainers' Co., 1997 (Hon. Liveryman, 2004). FRSA 1996. Ambassador for E Sussex, 2004–09. Hon. Fellow, Girton Coll., Cambridge, 2017. Hon. DArts: De Montfort, 1998; Kent, 2014. 2nd Prize, John Player Award, Nat. Portrait Gall., 1983 (Special Commendation, 1984); First Prize, Oil Painting of Year, Hunting Gp Nat. Art Prize, 1984; GLC Prize, Spirit of London, RFH, 1985; Ondaatje Prize for Portraiture and Gold Medal, 2001, Changing Faces Prize, 2017, Royal Soc. of Portrait Painters; 1st Prize, BP Portrait Award, Nat. Portrait Gall., 2010. *Publications*: contribs to The Artist. *Recreation*: gardening. *Address*: Salters Green Farm, Mayfield, E Sussex TN20 6NP. *T*: and *Fax*: (01892) 852472. *E*: daphne.todd@btinternet.com. *W*: www.daphnetodd.com. *Clubs*: Athenæum, Arts, Chelsea Arts.

**TODD, James**; *see* Todd, A. J.

**TODD, Jane Clare**, OBE 2013; DL; Chief Executive, Nottingham City Council, 2008–12; *b* 26 March 1951; *d* of Norman Henry Todd and Joyce Mary Todd; *m* (marr. diss.); two *s* one *d*. *Educ*: Nottingham Univ. (BA Social Policy). Nottingham City Council: Asst Chief Exec., Policy, 1992–97; Dir, Develt, 1997–2000; Dir, Develt and Envmtl Services, 2000–02; Regional Dir, Govt Office for the E Midlands, 2002–07. DL Notts, 2013. *Recreations*: walking, reading.

**TODD, Prof. Janet Margaret**, OBE 2013; PhD; President, Lucy Cavendish College, Cambridge, 2008–15; Professor of English Literature, University of Aberdeen, 2004–12; *b* 10 Sept. 1942; *d* of George and Elizabeth Dakin; *m* 1st, 1966 (marr. diss. 1983); one *s* one *d*; 2nd, 2001, Prof. D. W. Hughes. *Educ*: Newnham Coll., Cambridge (BA 1964; Hon. Fellow 2015); Univ. of Leeds; Univ. of Florida (PhD). Lectr, Univ. of Cape Coast, Ghana, 1966–67; Asst Prof. of English, Univ. of Puerto Rico, 1972–74; Asst, Associate, Full Prof. of English, Rutgers Univ., NJ, 1974–83; Fellow in English, Sidney Sussex Coll., Cambridge, 1983–89; Prof. of English Lit., UEA, 1990–2000; Francis Hutcheson Prof. of English Lit., Univ. of Glasgow, 2000–04. Vis. Prof. Univ. of Southampton, 1982–83. Bye-Fellow, Newnham Coll., Cambridge, 1998; Hon. Fellow, Lucy Cavendish Coll., Cambridge, 2000. General Editor: Complete Works of Jane Austen, 9 vols, 2005–06; Cambridge edn of Works of Jane Austen, 2005–09. Numerous awards. *Publications*: In Adam's Garden: a study of John Clare, 1973; Mary Wollstonecraft: an annotated bibliography, 1976; Women's Friendship in Literature, 1980; (jtly) English Congregational Hymns in the 18th Century, 1983; Sensibility, 1986; Feminist Literary History, 1988; The Sign of Angellica: women writing and fiction 1660–1800, 1989; (ed jtly) The Complete Works of Mary Wollstonecraft, 1989; (ed) A Dictionary of British Women Writers, 1989; (ed) The Works of Aphra Behn, 7 vols, 1992–96; (ed) Aphra Behn's Oroonoko, The Rover and Other Works, 1993; Gender, Art and Death, 1993; (ed) Aphra Behn Studies, 1996; The Secret Life of Aphra Behn, 1996, rev. edn as Aphra Behn: a secret life, 2017; (ed) Female Education, 6 vols, 1996; The Critical Fortunes of Aphra Behn, 1998; Mary Wollstonecraft: a revolutionary life, 2000; Rebel Daughters: Ireland in conflict 1798, 2003; (ed) Collected Letters of Mary Wollstonecraft, 2003; (ed) Oroonoko, 2003; (ed jtly) Cambridge Companion to Aphra Behn, 2004; (ed) Jane Austen in Context, 2005; Cambridge Introduction to Jane Austen, 2006; Death and the Maidens: Fanny Wollstonecraft and the Shelley Circle, 2007; (ed jtly) Jane Austen: the later manuscripts, 2008; Pride and Prejudice, 2011; (ed) Cambridge Companion to Pride and Prejudice, 2013; Jane Austen, Her Life, Times and Novels, 2013; Lady Susan Plays the Game, 2013; A Man of Genius, 2016; Radiation Diaries: cancer, memory and fragments of a life in words, 2018; (ed) Jane Austen's Sanditon, 2019. *Address*: Grange House, Selwyn Gardens, Cambridge CB3 9AX.

**TODD, Prof. John Andrew**, PhD; FRS 2009; Professor of Precision Medicine, University of Oxford, since 2016; Fellow, Brasenose College, Oxford, since 2016; *b* 23 June 1958; *s* of William and Elizabeth Todd; *m* 1988, Anne Nicola Roberts (marr. diss. 2012); two *s* one *d*. *Educ*: Coleraine Academical Instn; Edinburgh Univ. (BSc 1st cl. Hons 1980); Gonville and Caius Coll., Cambridge (PhD Biochemistry 1983). Research Fellow: Dept of Biochemistry, Cambridge Univ., 1983–85; MRC Molecular Biology Lab., Cambridge, 1984; SERC/NATO Res. Fellow, Dept of Microbiology and Immunology, Stanford Univ., Calif, 1985–88; Career Develt Award Fellow, Juvenile Diabetes Foundn Internat., 1988–90 (Grodsky Prize, 1998); University of Oxford: Sen. Scientist, Nuffield Dept of Surgery, 1988–90; Mem., Faculty of Medicine, 1989–98; Wellcome Trust Sen. Fellow in Basic Biomed. Sci., 1990–93; Univ. Res. Lectr, 1992–98; Wellcome Trust Prin. Res. Fellow, 1993–98; Prof. of Human Genetics, 1996–98; Prof. of Med. Genetics, Univ. of Cambridge, 1998–2016; Fellow, Gonville and Caius Coll., Cambridge, 1998–2016. Wellcome Vis. Prof., Louisiana State Univ., 1997. NIHR Sen. Investigator, 2009. Lectures: Balfour, Genetical Soc., 1994; Lilly, QUB, 1995; Dorothy Hodgkin, Diabetes UK, 2001. FMedSci 1998. Hon. MRCP 2000. Minkowski Prize, Eur. Assoc. for Study of Diabetes, 1995; Res. Prize, Boehringer Mannheim and Juvenile Diabetes Res. Foundn Internat., 1995; Biennial Biochem. Soc. Medal, Wellcome Trust, 1998; R. and B. Sackler Res. Award, 1998; Carter Medal and Lecture, Clin. Genetics Soc., 1999; NDRI Distinguished Scientist Award, 2008; David Rumbough Award for Scientific Excellence, Juvenile Diabetes Res. Foundn, 2011. *Publications*: articles in learned jls. *Recreations*: lateral thinking, study of natural selection and evolution, fly fishing, cycling, ski-ing, swimming, child minding. *Address*: Nuffield Department of Medicine, University of Oxford, Old Road Campus, Headington, Oxford OX3 7BN.

**TODD, Prof. John Francis James**, PhD; CEng, FInstMC; CChem, FRSC; Professor of Mass Spectroscopy, University of Kent at Canterbury, 1991–2000, now Emeritus; *b* 20 May 1937; *o s* of late Eric Todd and Annie Lewin Todd (*née* Tinkler); *m* 1963, Mavis Georgina Lee; three *s*. *Educ*: Leeds Grammar Sch.; Leeds Univ. (BSc, Cl. I Hons Chem.). Research Fellow: Leeds Univ., 1962–63; Yale Univ., USA, 1963–65; University of Kent at Canterbury: Asst Lectr in Chemistry, 1965–66; Lectr in Chemistry, 1966–73; Sen. Lectr, 1973–89; Reader in Physical Chemistry, Faculty of Natural Scis, 1990; Dir, Univ. Chemical Lab., 1991–94; Dep. Head, Chemistry Dept (Finance), 1996–97; Master of Rutherford Coll., 1975–85. CIL Distinguished Vis. Lectr, Trent Univ., Canada, 1988. J. B. Cohen Prizeman, Leeds Univ., 1963; Fulbright Research Scholar, 1963–65. Chm., Canterbury and Thanet HA, 1982–86. Chairman: Kent Section of Chem. Soc., 1975; British Mass Spectroscopy Soc., 1980–81 (Treas., 1990–93); Titular Mem., IUPAC Commn on Molecular Structures and Spectroscopy, 1979–91; Nat. Mem. Council, RSC, 1993–95. Mem., Kent Educn Cttee, 1983–88. Member: Clergy Orphan Corp., 1985–96; Council, Strode Park Foundn for the Disabled, 1986–90. Governor: S Kent Coll. of Technology, 1977–89; Canterbury Christ Church Univ. (formerly Canterbury Christ Church Coll., later UC), 1994–2007; Chm. of Govs, St Edmund's Sch., Canterbury, 1996–2006. Mem., Amer. Soc. of Sigma Xi, Yale Chapter. Jt Editor, Internat. Jl of Mass Spectrometry and Ion Processes, 1985–98. Hon. Life Mem., RSC, 2009. Hon. Fellow, Canterbury Christ Church Univ., 2008. Thomson Gold Medal, Internat. Mass Spectrometry Soc., 1997; Aston Medal, British Mass Spectrometry Soc., 2006. *Publications*: Dynamic Mass Spectrometry, vol. 4, 1975, vol. 5, 1978, vol. 6, 1981; Advances in Mass Spectrometry 1985, 1986; Practical Aspects of Ion Trap Mass Spectrometry, vols 1–3, 1995; Quadrupole Ion Trap Mass Spectrometry, 2005; Practical Aspects of Trapped Ion Mass Spectrometry, vol. 4, 2010, vol. 5, 2009; reviews and papers, mainly on mass spectrometry, in Jl of Chem. Soc. and Jl of Physics, etc. *Recreations*: music, travel, genealogy. *Address*: Ingram Building, School of Physical Sciences, University of Kent, Canterbury, Kent CT2 7NH; West Bank, 122 Whitstable Road, Canterbury, Kent CT2 8EG. *T*: (01227) 769552.

**TODD, Keith**; *see* Todd, T. K.

**TODD, Maree**; Member (SNP) Highlands and Islands, Scottish Parliament, since 2016; Minister for Children and Young People, since 2018; *b* Inverness, 27 Feb. 1973; *d* of John George Mackenzie and Christina Janet Mackenzie (now Mcgonigle); *m* 1998, John Alexander Todd; one *s* two *d*. *Educ*: Ullapool Primary Sch.; Ullapool High Sch.; Robert Gordon Univ., Aberdeen (BSc 1st Cl. Hons Pharmacy 1994; Postgrad. Dip. Clin. Pharmacy 1999); Univ. of Bedfordshire (Dip. Higher Educn (Antenatal Educn) 2009); Univ. of Strathclyde (Practice Cert. Ind. Prescribing 2016). Clin. Pharmacist, New Craigs Hosp., Inverness, 1996–2016; Antenatal Teacher, Nat. Childbirth Trust, 2009–16; Postgrad. Tutor, NHS Educn Scotland, 2014–15. *Recreations*: Rugby (watching not playing these days), running, travel, food, live music, reading. *Address*: Scottish Parliament, Edinburgh EH99 1SP; 12 HIgh Street, Dingwall, Ross-shire IV15 9RU.

**TODD, Sir Mark James**, KNZM 2013; CBE 1995 (MBE 1984); equestrian rider; *b* 1 March 1956; *s* of Norman Edward Todd and Lenore Adele Todd; *m* 1986, Carolyn Faye Berry; one *s* one *d*. *Educ*: Cambridge High Sch., NZ; Hamilton Tech. Inst. (Dip. Agric.). Three-day event wins: Badminton, 1980 (Southern Comfort), 1994 (Horton Point), 1996 (Bertie Blunt), 2011 (Land Vision); Burghley, 1987 (Wilton Fair, also runner up, on Charisma), 1990 (Welton Greylag), 1991 (Face the Music), 1997 (Broadcast News), 1999 (Diamond Hall Red); Olympic Games: Individual Gold Medal, 1984 (Charisma), 1988 (Charisma); Individual Bronze Medal, 2000 (Eye Spy II); NZ Team Bronze Medal, 2012; World Championships: NZ Team Gold Medal, 1990; Individual Silver Medal, 1998 (Broadcast News). New Zealand Sportsman of the Year, 1988; Event Rider of the Century, Internat. Equestrian Fedn, 1999; Equestrian Personality of the Century, Horse & Hound, 2000; Sportsman of the Century, Waikato, NZ, 2000; New Zealander of the Year, NZ Soc., 2000. *Publications*: Charisma; Mark Todd's Cross-Country Handbook, 1991; One Day Eventing, 1996; So Far, So Good, 1998; Second Chance (autobiog.), 2012. *Recreations*: ski-ing, swimming, tennis, squash, horse racing, music.

**TODD, Mark Wainwright**; Chair, Derbyshire Healthcare NHS Foundation Trust, 2014–15; *b* 29 Dec. 1954; *s* of Matthew and Viv Todd; *m* 1979, Sarah Margaret (*née* Dawson); one *s*. *Educ*: Sherborne Sch.; Emmanuel Coll., Cambridge (BA History 1976; MA). Longman Group, later Addison Wesley Longman, 1977–96: Man. Dir, Longman Industry and Public Service Mgt, 1988–92, Longman Cartermill, 1990–92; Dir, IT, 1992–94, Ops, 1994–96. MP (Lab) S Derbyshire, 1997–2010. Chair: NHS Derby City, 2010–13; NHS Derbyshire County, 2011–13. Chair of Trustees, Motor Neurone Disease Assoc., 2010–14.

**TODD, Michael Alan**; QC 1997; *b* 16 Feb. 1953; *y s* of Charles Edward Alan Todd and late Betty Todd (*née* Bromwich); *m* 1976, Deborah Collett. *Educ*: Kenilworth Grammar Sch.; Keele Univ. (BA 1976). Called to the Bar, Lincoln's Inn, 1977, Bencher, 2006; Jun. Counsel to the Crown, Chancery Div., 1992–97. Chm., Chancery Bar Assoc., 2007–10. Mem., Bar Council, 2007– (Vice-Chm., 2011; Chm., 2012). *Recreation*: equestrianism. *Address*: Erskine Chambers, 33 Chancery Lane, WC2A 1EN. *T*: (020) 7242 5532.

**TODD, Ric**; *see* Todd, D. R.

**TODD, Richard Frazer**; QC 2009; a Recorder, since 2010; a Deputy High Court Judge, since 2016; *b* Gosport, 21 Jan. 1965; *s* of late Alan Todd, RN and of Gillian Todd; *m* 1995, Elisabeth MacBean; two *s* two *d*. *Educ*: Royal Hosp. Sch.; Trinity Coll., Oxford (MA) Inns of Court Sch. of Law. Called to the Bar, Middle Temple, 1988, Bencher, 2016; in practice as barrister specialising in high value relationship generated disputes (mainly matrimonial finance cases); called (*ad hoc*) to the Bar: Cayman Islands, 2009; BVI, 2017; called to the Bar, Hong Kong SAR, 2014; on counsel list, Falkland Is; Counsel to Dept of Justice, Hong Kong. Mem., Law Commn Adv. Panels on Ancillary Relief, 2013, and Nuptial Agreements, 2014. Mem., Saving Faces/Head and Neck Cancer Audit. Member: Family Law Bar Assoc., 1988–; Gen. Council of the Bar, 1998–2002; Bar Cttee for Family Law; Prosecuting Counsel, Bar Standards Bd, 2002–. Mem., Royal Artillery Assoc., 1983–. Fellow, Internat. Acad. of Matrimonial Lawyers, 2009. Chambers and Partners Family Law Silk of the Year, 2010 and 2013; Family Law QC of Year, Economist/Law Monthly, 2011, 2012, 2014. *Publications*: (ed jtly) Practical Matrimonial Precedents, 2 vols, 1989, 44th edn 2015; At Court, 2000; The Essential Family Practice, 2 vols, 2000, 3rd edn 2003; (ed jtly) Jowitt's Dictionary of English Law, 2010; (ed with Elisabeth Todd) Todds' Relationship Agreements, 2013. *Recreations*: laws, wars and the great indoors. *Address*: 1 Hare Court, Temple, EC4Y 7BE. *T*: (020) 7797 7070, *Fax*: (020) 7797 7435. *E*: RTQC@1hc.com; Temple Chambers, 16/F One Pacific Place, Central, Hong Kong. *T*: 25232003, *Fax*: 28100302. *E*: todd@templechambers.com. *Club*: Athenæum.

**TODD, (Thomas) Keith**, CBE 2004; FCMA; Executive Chairman, KRM22 plc, since 2017; *b* 22 June 1953; *s* of Thomas William Todd and Cecilie Olive Todd; *m* 1979, Anne Elizabeth Hendrie; two *s* two *d*. FCMA 1985. Chief Accountant, Marconi Co. Ltd, 1978–81; Chief Financial Officer, Cincinnati Electronics, USA, 1981–86; Financial Dir, Marconi Co. Ltd, 1986–87; Dir, Finance and Business Strategy, 1987–96, Chief Exec., 1996–2000, ICL plc; Chm. and CEO, Dexterus Ltd 2001; Executive Chairman: FFastFill plc, 2002–17; ION Agency Business, 2015–17. Chairman: Ecsoft, plc, 2002–05; Broadband Stakeholder Gp, 2002–05; Easynet plc, 2002–06; Magic Lantern Prodns Ltd, 2006–18; Amino Technologies plc, 2007–12. Mem. Board, Camelot Gp plc, 1994–2000. Mem. Council, Open Univ., 1992–2000 (Hon. Treas., 1992–97). Life Mem., BAFTA, 2000. FRSA 1996. DUniv Open, 1999. *Recreation*: sports. *Address*: Granchester House, Manor Close, Penn, Bucks HP10 8HZ. *Clubs*: Royal Automobile, Eight; Beaconsfield Golf.

**TODD, Valerie Malvia May**, CBE 2014; Talent and Resources Director, Crossrail Ltd, since 2009; *b* Derby, 13 July 1962; *d* of Roy and Lucille Todd; one *d*. *Educ*: Hardwick Infant and Jun. Schs, Derby; Derby Sch.; Leicester Poly. (MA Hons Public Admin); Open Univ. (MBA). London Borough of Tower Hamlets: Programme Officer, 1986–87; Principal Finance and Contract Manager, 1987–90; Contract Services Manager, 1991–94; Hd of Support Services (Social Services), Havering LBC, 1994–99; Asst Dir, Social Services (Business Strategy and Support Services), Newham LBC, 1999–2003; Transport for London: Dir, Business Services (Surface Transport), 2004; Gp Dir, Equality and Inclusion, 2004–05; Man. Dir, Gp Services, 2005–09. Mem., Commn for Employment and Skills, 2008–17. Chm., Investors in People, UK, 2010–. Trustee, London Transport Mus., 2007–09. Gov., Univ. of W London, 2012–. DUniv Derby, 2013. *Recreations*: Caribbean cooking, art, culture. *Address*: Crossrail Ltd, 25 Canada Square, E14 5LQ. *T*: (020) 3229 9439. *E*: valerietodd@crossrail.co.uk.

**TODHUNTER, Michael John Benjamin**, MBE 2011; DL; Director, 1977–2009, Chairman, 2002–09, James Finlay Ltd; Director, 1989–2005, Chairman, 1999–2005, Kleinwort Capital Trust plc; *b* 25 March 1935; *s* of late Brig. Edward Joseph Todhunter and Agnes Mary (*née* Swire); *m* 1959, Caroline Francesca (MVO 2003), *d* of Maj. William Walter Dowding; one *s* two *d*. *Educ*: Eton Coll.; Magdalen Coll., Oxford (MA). 2nd Lieutenant, 11 Hussars, PAO, 1953–55. Banker; with Jessel Toynbee & Co. Ltd, 1958–84 (Dir, 1962, Dep. Chm., 1977); Chief Exec., Alexanders Discount plc, 1984–86; Dir, Mercantile House Hldgs plc, 1984–86; Man. Dir, PK English Trust Co. Ltd, 1986–89; London Advr, Yasuda Trust Banking Co. Ltd, 1989–98. Chm., Clyde Shipping Co. Ltd, 1978–2000. Dir, Newbury Racecourse plc, 1983–2004. Special Trustee, Gt Ormond St Hosp., 1979–96; Trustee: Missions to Seamen, 1980–96; Gift of Thomas Pocklington, 1990–99; Trustee and Gov., 2000–10, Fund Raiser, 2005–13, Prior's Court Foundn. High Sheriff, 1999, DL, 2005, Berks. Hon. Fellow, Inst. of Child Health, 1994. *Recreations*: travel, shooting. *Address*: The Old Rectory, Farnborough, Wantage OX12 8NX. *T*: (01488) 638298; (office) Swire House, 59 Buckingham Gate, SW1E 6AJ. *T*: (020) 7834 7717. *Clubs*: White's, Pratt's.

**TODIWALA, Cyrus Rustom**, OBE 2010 (MBE 2000); DL; Chef Patron, since 1995, and Co-owner, since 2004, Café Spice Namasté; Chef Patron: Mr Todiwala's Kitchen at Hilton, London Heathrow Terminal 5, since 2011, at Lincoln Plaza, London, since 2019; The Park Café, since 2013; Assado, since 2014; *b* Bombay, 16 Oct. 1956; *s* of Rustom Todiwala and Dowlat Todiwala; *m* 1984, Pervin Talati; two *s*. *Educ*: St Mary's Byculla, Bombay; Barnes High Sch., Bombay; Basant Kumar Somani Poly., Bombay (Dip. Hotel Admin and Food Technol. 1976). Commis Chef, 1976–78, Demi Chef, 1978–80, Chef de Partie, 1980–82, Taj Mahal Hotel, Bombay; Chef de Cuisine, Taj Holiday Village, Goa, 1982–84; Exec. Chef, Fort Aguada Beach Resort, 1984–86; Corporate Exec. Chef, Fort Aguada Beach Resort, Fort Aguada Hermitage, 1986–89; The Place, Poona, 1989–91; Chef/Manager, 1991–95, Chef Patron, 1993–95, Namasté Indian Restaurant. Presenter, TV series, The Incredible Spice Men, 2013. Former Member: NACETT; NHS Better Hosp. Food Prog. Panel. Director: Asian and Oriental Sch. of Catering, 1999–; London Food Bd, 2008–; Hospitality Skills Acad., 2008–; non-exec. Mem. Bd, Investors in People UK, 2004–10; Member: British Hospitality Assoc., 1995– (former Mem., Steering Cttee); Guild of Fine Food Retailers, 2002–; Campaign for Real Food, 2003–; Steering Cttee, Mutton Renaissance Movement, 2003–; Steering Cttee, Greener Food Britain, 2004–; Craft Guild of Chefs, 2004–; Royal Acad. (formerly Acad.) of Culinary Arts, 2004–; Scotch Beef Club, 2004–; London Adv. Bd, Springboard UK, 2006–; Chm., London Food Waste Cttee, 2008–. Pres., Time and Talents Assoc., 2000; Trustee, Learning for Life, 2000; Chef Ambassador, the Clink, 2013–; Founder, Zest Quest Asia, 2013–; Ambassador, Love British Food, 2019–. Patron, British Lop Pig Soc., 2014–. Hon. Prof., Univ. of W London (formerly Thames Valley Univ.), 2002–; Enterprise Champion, LeSoCo, 2013. FIH (FHCIMA 2007); Fellow: Epicurean World Master Chefs Soc., 1996; Master Chefs of GB, 2006; FRSA 2004. DL Gtr London, 2009. Hon. DBA London Metropolitan, 2009. Food Personality of the Year, BBC Radio 4 Food and Farming Awards, 2014. *Publications*: New Wave Indian Cooking, 1998; International Cuisine India, 2005; Indian Summer, 2008; Mr Todiwala's Bombay, 2013; (with Tony Singh) The Incredible Spice Men, 2013; Mr Todiwala's Spicebox, 2016. *Recreations*: travel, reading, cooking for friends, Zoroastrian history, animals and animal welfare, environment, sustainability all encompassing. *Address*: Café Spice Namasté, 16 Prescot Street, E1 8AZ. *T*: (020) 7488 9242. *E*: ctodiwala@yahoo.co.uk.

**TODNER, Karen Elizabeth**; Consultant Solicitor, GSG Law; *b* Sunderland, 10 April 1962; *d* of Urias Todner and Lilian Todner; *m* 1996, Ian Jobling; three *s*. *Educ*: Higham Lane Sch., Nuneaton; King Edward VI Sch., Nuneaton; Univ. of Exeter (LLB); Coll. of Law, Chester. Admitted solicitor, 1987. Man. Dir, Kaim Todner Ltd, 1990. Dir, Solicitors Disciplinary Tribunal, 2002 (Vice Pres., 2009); Pres., Mental Health Rev. Tribunal, 2003. *Recreations*: eating out, cinema, family, travel.

**TODOLÍ, Vicente**; Artistic Advisor, Pirelli HangarBicocca Foundation, since 2013; *b* 31 May 1958; *s* of Vicente and Julia Todolí; *m* 1998, Cristina Gimenez. *Educ*: Univ. of Valencia (Master of Geog. and Hist. 1980); Yale Univ. and CUNY (Fulbright Schol.; grad. studies in art). ISP Fellow, Whitney Mus. of American Art, NY, 1985; Chief Curator, 1986–88, Artistic Dir, 1988–96, Inst. Valenciano de Arte Moderno; Director: Museu Serralves, Porto, Portugal, 1996–2002; Tate Modern, 2002–10. Member, Advisory Boards: Museu d'Art Contemporani de Barcelona, 1998–; Manifesta Internat. Foundn, 2002–07; Serralves Foundn, 2003–; Botin Foundn, 2003–; Contemp. Art Soc., 2003–07; La Caixa Foundn, 2003–. Member: Adv. Cttee for Reina Sofia Nat. Mus. of Art, Madrid, 1993–96; Jury and Adv. Cttee, Carnegie Internat., 1995; Advr, for Future, Past, Present, Venice Biennale, 1997. Comendador, Orden de Santiago (Portugal), 2002.

**TODT, Jean Henri**; President, Fédération Internationale de l'Automobile, since 2009; *b* Pierrefort, Cantal, France, 25 Feb. 1946; *s* of Emmanuel Todt and Hilda Todt (*née* Benoliel); partner, Michelle Yeoh; one *s* by a previous marriage. *Educ*: Ecole des Cadres Sch. of Econs and Business, Paris. Rally co-driver, 1966–81. Dir, Peugeot Racing Activities, then PSA Peugeot-Citroën Sporting Activities, 1982–93; Team Principal, Scuderia Ferrari, 1993–2004; Mem., Bd of Dirs, 2001–09, Gen. Manager, 2004–06, CEO, 2006–08, Ferrari SpA. Member, Board of Directors: Edmond de Rothschild SA, 2008–; Gaumont, 2004–; Groupe Lucien Barriere, 2004–; Internat. Peace Inst., 2015–; Chm., Bd of Dirs, SUU Foundn, 2014–. Special Envoy of UN Sec. Gen. for Road Safety, 2015–. IOC Mem., Public Affairs and Social Develt through Sport Commn, 2017. Mem., Internat. Adv. Bd, Sotheby's, 2013–. Founder Mem., ICM Brain & Spine Inst. (formerly Inst. for Brain and Spinal Cord Disorders Foundn), 2002– (Vice Pres., 2017). Member: Académie des Technologies, 2004–; Académie des Sports, 2011–. Pres., E Safety Aware, 2009–. Mem., Bd of Trustees, Fedn Internat. de l'Automobile Foundn for the Automobile and Society, 2008–. Humanitarian of Year Award, UNA, NY, 2016. Commendatore (Italy), 2002; Dato Seri (Malaysia), 2006; Grand Croix, Légion d'Honneur (France), 2011; Mem., Order of Prince Yaroslav the Wise (Ukraine), 2011; Grand Officer, Ordre de Sainte Agathe (San Marino), 2012; Comdr, Nat. Order of Merit (Senegal), 2013; First Class Order Medal (Bahrain), 2014; Medal, Order of Friendship (Russia), 2015. *Publications*: 205: l'histoire d'un défi, 1985. *Recreation*: backgammon. *Address*: Fédération Internationale de l'Automobile, 8 Place de la Concorde, 75008 Paris, France, and 2 Chemin de Blandonnet, 1215 Genève 15, Switzerland. *T*: (1) 43124455. *E*: jtodt@fia.com. *Clubs*: Automobile Club de France, Polo de Paris.

**TOFFOLO, Rt Rev. Mgr Adrian Titian**; Parish Priest, The Sacred Heart, Kingsbridge, since 2012; *b* 22 Sept. 1944; *s* of Sante Battista Toffolo and Ethel Elizabeth (*née* Hannaford-Hill). *Educ*: St Boniface's Coll., Plymouth; Gregorian Univ., Rome (PhL, STL). Asst Priest, Penzance, 1969–72; Prof. of Theology, Oscott Coll., 1972–76; Assistant Priest: Torquay, 1976–80; Plymouth, 1980–84; Parish Priest: St Austell, 1984–85; Truro, 1985–91; Rector, Venerable English College, Rome, 1991–99; Parish Priest, Bovey Tracey and Chudleigh, 1999–2003; Episcopal Vicar for Formation, Dio. of Plymouth, 1999–2009; Parish Priest, Barnstaple, 2003–13; Episcopal Vicar: for Safeguarding, 2013–18; for Pastoral Services, 2014–18. Prelate of Honour, 1992. *Recreations*: mountain walking, music, DIY. *Address*: 19 Fosse Road, Kingsbridge, Devon TQ7 1NG. *T*: (01548) 852670.

**TOFT, Dr Anthony Douglas**, CBE 1995; LVO 2010; FRCPE; Consultant Physician, Royal Infirmary, Edinburgh, 1978–2009; Physician to the Queen in Scotland, 1996–2009; *b* 29 Oct. 1944; *s* of William Vincent Toft and Anne Laing; *m* 1968, Maureen Margaret Darling; one *s* one *d*. *Educ*: Perth Academy; Univ. of Edinburgh (BSc Hons, MD). FRCPE 1980; FRCP 1992; FRCPI 1993; FRCPGlas 1993; FRCSE (*ad hominem*), 1994. House Physician and House Surgeon, 1969–70, jun. med. posts, 1970–78, Royal Infirmary, Edinburgh. Chief Medical Adviser, Aegon (formerly Scottish Equitable Life Assurance Soc.), 1984–2015. Mem., Health Appointments Adv. Cttee, 1994–2000. Royal Coll. of Physicians of Edinburgh: Chm., Collegiate Members' Cttee, 1977; Mem. Council, 1986–88; Vice-Pres., 1990–91; Pres., 1991–94; Chm. Trustees, 1999–. Chairman: Scottish Royal Colls, 1993–94; Jt Cttee on Higher Med. Trng, 1994–96; Vice-Chm., UK Conf. of Med. Royal Colls, 1993–94. General Medical Council: Mem., 1999–2003; Occasional Chm., Professional Conduct Cttee, 1999–2004; Chm., Prof. and Linguistic Assessments Bd, 1999–2006. Pres., British Thyroid Assoc., 1997–99; Mem., Assoc. of Physicians of GB and Ireland, 1983–; Sec., Harveian Soc., 1980–94. Hon. Mem., Acad. of Medicine of Malaysia, 1993. Hon. FCPS (Pak) 1990; Hon. FACP 1993; Hon. FRACP 1993; Hon. FRCPC 1994; Hon. FRCGP 1994; Hon. FFPM 1994; Hon. Fellow, Acad. of Medicine of Singapore, 1994; Hon. FCPS (Bangladesh) 1995; Hon. FRCEM 1996; Hon. FFAEM 1997). *Publications*: Diagnosis and Management of Endocrine Diseases, 1982; papers on thyroid disease. *Recreations*: gardening, collecting art. *Address*: 41 Hermitage Gardens, Edinburgh EH10 6AZ. *T*: (0131) 447 2221.

**TÓIBÍN, Colm**; writer; Mellon Professor, Department of English and Comparative Literature, Columbia University, since 2012; *b* 30 May 1955; *s* of Mícheál Tóibín and Bríd O'Rourke. *Educ*: University Coll., Dublin (BA). Features Ed., In Dublin mag., 1981–82; Ed., Magill mag., 1982–85. Leonard Milberg Vis. Lectr in Irish Letters, Princeton Univ., 2009–11; Prof. of Creative Writing, Manchester Univ., 2011–12. Chancellor, Liverpool Univ., 2017–. *Publications*: *novels*: The South, 1990; The Heather Blazing, 1992; The Story of the Night, 1996; The Blackwater Lightship, 1999; The Master, 2004; Brooklyn, 2009; Testament of Mary (novella), 2012 (stage version, 2013); Nora Webster, 2014 (Hawthornden Prize, 2015); House of Names, 2017; *short stories*: Mothers and Sons, 2006; The Empty Family, 2010; *non-fiction*: Walking Along the Border, 1987, reissued as Bad Blood, 1994; Homage to Barcelona, 1990; The Trial of the Generals: selected journalism 1980–90, 1990; The Sign of the Cross: travels in Catholic Europe, 1994; Love in a Dark Time: gay lives from Wilde to Almodovar, 2001; (jtly) The Irish Famine: a documentary,

2001; Lady Gregory's Toothbrush, 2002; (ed) Synge: a celebration, 2005; New Ways to Kill Your Mother: writers and their families, 2012; Colm Tóibín on Elizabeth Bishop, 2015; Mad, Bad, Dangerous to Know: the fathers of Wilde, Yeats and Joyce, 2018. *T:* (1) 6768383. *E:* ctoibin@eircom.net.

**TOKSVIG, Sandra Birgitte, (Sandi),** OBE 2014; writer and comedian; *b* 3 May 1958; *d* of late Claus Bertel Toksvig and of Julie Anne Toksvig; one *s* two *d. Educ:* Mamaroneck High Sch., NY; Tormead, Guildford; Girton Coll., Cambridge (MA Hons). *Television* includes: No 73, 1980–86; Whose Line Is It Anyway?; Behind the Headlines, 1993; Great Journeys, 1993; The Big One, 1993; Island Race, 1995; Call My Bluff, 1996–2003; presenter: Fifteen to One, 2014–; QI, 2016–; co-presenter, The Great British Bake Off, 2017–; *stage* includes: (performer) Nottingham Playhouse Rep., 1980; Open Air Theatre, Regent's Park, 1980; (jt writer) The Pocket Dream, 1993; (performer and writer) Big Night Out at the Little Sands Picture Palace, 1995; (writer and performer) Sandi Toksvig's Christmas Cracker, Festival Hall, 2009; Sandi Toksvig Live (touring), 2012; Sandi Toksvig Live: politically incorrect (touring), 2016; (writer) Silver Lining, Rose Th. Kingston, 2017; National Trevor (touring), 2019; *radio* includes: Loose Ends, 1994–; I'm Sorry I Haven't a Clue, 1998–; Presenter: Midweek, 1996; Excess Baggage; Chair, The News Quiz, R4, 2006–15. Chancellor, Univ. of Portsmouth, 2012–17. Co-Founder, Women's Equality Party, 2015. *Publications: for children:* Tales from the Norse's Mouth, 1994; Unusual Day, 1997; If I Didn't Have Elbows, 1998; Super-saver Mouse, 1999; Super-saver Mouse to the Rescue, 2000; The Troublesome Tooth Fairy, 2001; Hitler's Canary, 2005; Girls Are Best, 2008; A Slice of the Moon, 2015; *plays:* The Pocket Dream, 1994; Bully Boy, 2011; *travel books:* Great Journeys of the World, 1994; (with John McCarthy) Island Race, 1995; *novels:* Whistling for the Elephants, 1999; Flying Under Bridges, 2001; Melted Into Air, 2006; Valentine Grey, 2012; *non-fiction:* The Chain of Curiosity, 2009; Peas and Queues: the minefield of modern manners, 2013; Between the Stops: the view of my life from the top of the number 12 bus, 2019. *Recreations:* golf, ski-ing, scuba diving, sewing. *Club:* Ivy.

**TOLAND, Prof. John Francis,** FRS 1999; FRSE; N. M. Rothschild & Sons Professor of Mathematical Sciences and Director, Isaac Newton Institute for Mathematical Sciences, University of Cambridge, 2011–16; Fellow, St John's College, Cambridge, 2011–16; *b* 28 April 1949; *s* of late Joseph Toland and Catherine Toland (*née* McGarvey); *m* 1977, Susan Frances Beck, *d* of late (James Henry) John Beck. *Educ:* St Columb's Coll., Derry (Alumnus Illustrissimus 2007); Queen's Univ., Belfast (BSc 1970, DSc 1993); Univ. of Sussex (MSc 1971, DPhil 1973). Batelle Advanced Studies Centre, Geneva, 1973; Lectr in Maths and Fellow of Fluid Mechanics Res. Inst., Univ. of Essex, 1973–79; Lectr in Maths, UCL, 1979–82; Prof. of Maths, Univ. of Bath, 1982–2011; EPSRC Sen. Res. Fellow, 1997–2002. Scientific Dir, Internat. Centre for Math. Scis, Edinburgh, 2002–10; Hon. Professor of Mathematics: Univ. of Edinburgh, 2003–10; Heriot-Watt Univ., 2003–10; Univ. of Bath, 2016–. Vis. lectr, Europe, Australia, USA. Chm., Mathematical Scis subpanel, REF 2014. Pres., LMS, 2005–07. FRSE 2003. Hon. Fellow, UCL, 2008. Hon. DSc: QUB, 2000; Edinburgh, 2007; Heriot-Watt, 2007; Bath, 2017; Sussex, 2017; DUniv Essex, 2009. Sen. Berwick Prize, LMS, 2000; Wolfson Res. Merit Award, 2008, Sylvester Medal, 2012, Royal Soc. *Publications:* mathematical research papers, mainly in nonlinear analysis. *Recreations:* horses, walking the dog. *Address:* 15 Lansdown Park, Bath BA1 5TG. *T:* (01225) 330996. *E:* jft26@cam.ac.uk.

**TOLEDANO, Daniel Ze'ev,** QC 2009; a Deputy High Court Judge, since 2017; *b* London, 2 Nov. 1969; *s* of Pinchas and Cynthia Toledano; *m* 1998, Dr Jan Raeburn; two *s* one *d. Educ:* Haberdashers' Aske's Sch., Elstree; Jesus Coll., Cambridge (BA 1st Cl. Hons 1992; MA). Called to the Bar, Inner Temple, 1993; in practice as barrister, specialising in commercial law, 1993–. *Recreations:* music and opera, theatre, running, cycling. *Address:* One Essex Court, Temple, EC4Y 9AR. *T:* (020) 7583 2000, *Fax:* (020) 7583 0118. *E:* dtoledano@oeclaw.co.uk.

**TOLER;** see Graham-Toler, family name of Earl of Norbury.

**TOLHURST, Jennifer Mary;** Lord-Lieutenant of Essex, since 2017; *b* Portadown, NI, 2 Dec. 1951; *d* of Brig. Denis Leonard Ormerod, CBE, DL and Frances Mary Ormerod (*née* Turner); *m* 1972, Philip John Tolhurst; two *s* one *d. Educ:* Army schs; Convent of Sacred Heart, Tunbridge Wells; secretarial coll. (Private Sec. Cert. 1969); Colchester Sch. of Art and Design (BA Hons Art and Design 2003). Res. at V&A Mus., 1970–71; Founder and Chm., Danbury and Little Baddow Br., NSPCC, 1976–82; involved with local Catholic ch and dio., 1976–. Mem. Bd, 1989–91, Vice Chm., 1991–93, Chm., 1993–96, Essex Prince's Youth Business Trust; Vice Chm., Lord Chancellor's Adv. Cttee in Essex, 2012–; Member: Council, High Sheriffs' Assoc., 2006–13; Court, Essex Univ., 2006–. Patron, Essex Community Foundn, 2017– (Vice Pres., 2006–17). Vice Chm. Govs, New Hall Sch., Chelmsford, 2006–12. JP, 1996–2005, High Sheriff, 2005–06, DL, 2006–17, Essex. *Recreations:* family, painting, sailing, Italy, music, gardening. *Address:* c/o Lord Lieutenant's Office, (01245) 809884. *E:* enquiries@essexlieutenancy.org.uk. *Clubs:* Royal Yacht Squadron (Lady Associate Mem.), Royal Thames Yacht.

**TOLHURST, Rear Adm. John Gordon,** CB 1995; FRAeS; defence consultant, retired; *b* 22 April 1943; *s* of Cdre Virgil George Tolhurst, CBE, VRD, RNR, and Elizabeth Mary Tolhurst. *Educ:* Sevenoaks Sch. Joined RN 1961; Commanding Officer: HMS Berwick, 1977; HMS Exeter, 1984; Asst Dir, Naval Warfare, 1986; Commodore, HMS Nelson, 1988; CO HMS Invincible, 1990; ADC to the Queen, 1990; Flag Officer: Sea Trng, 1992–96; Scotland, Northern England and NI, 1996–97; Mil. Dep. to Head of Defence Export Services, MoD, 1997–2002. Dir, Plafaisan Consultants, 2002–06; Man. Dir, JGT Associates Ltd, 2006–12. Chm., Aerospace & Defence Bd, Reed Exhibns, 2005–08. Chm., Clarion Defence and Security Ltd, 2008–12. Trustee: RNLI, 2002–12 (Vice Pres., 2012–; Chm., Ops Cttee, 2002–12); RNLI Heritage Trust, 2012–15. Vice Pres., Royal Internat. Air Tattoo, 2003–13. Dir, Royal Naval Club and Royal Albert Yacht Club, 2014–. Younger Brother, Trinity House. FRAeS 2004. *Recreations:* classic cars, travelling, gardening. *E:* jgtolhurst2@gmail.com.

**TOLHURST, Kelly Jane;** MP (C) Rochester and Strood, since 2015; Parliamentary Under-Secretary of State, Department for Business, Energy and Industrial Strategy, since 2018; *b* Borstal, Rochester, 23 Aug. 1978; *d* of Morris and Christine Tolhurst. *Educ:* Chapter High Sch. Dir, Skipper UK Ltd, Rochester, 2002–. Mem. (C) Medway Council, 2011–18. An Asst Govt Whip, 2018. Member: Eur. Scrutiny Select Cttee, 2015–16; Business, Innovation and Skills, subseq. Business, Energy and Industrial Strategy, Select Cttee, 2015–17. Contested (C) Rochester and Strood, Nov. 2014. *Address:* House of Commons, SW1A 0AA. *T:* (020) 7219 5387. *E:* kelly.tolhurst.mp@parliament.uk.

**TOLLEMACHE,** family name of **Baron Tollemache.**

**TOLLEMACHE, 5th Baron** *cr* 1876; **Timothy John Edward Tollemache,** KCVO 2015; Lord-Lieutenant of Suffolk, 2003–14 (Vice Lord-Lieutenant, 1994–2003); farmer and landowner; *b* 13 Dec. 1939; *s* of 4th Baron Tollemache, MC, DL, and Dinah Susan (*d* 1998), *d* of late Sir Archibald Auldjo Jamieson, KBE, MC; *S* father, 1975; *m* 1970, Alexandra Dorothy Jean, *d* of late Col Hugo Meynell, MC; two *s* one *d. Educ:* Eton. Commissioned into Coldstream Guards, 1959; served Kenya, Persian Gulf and Zanzibar, 1960–62; Course of Estate Management at Sandringham, Norfolk, 1962–64. President: E Anglian Productivity Assoc., 1984–88; Suffolk Agricl Assoc., 1988; Chm., CLA, Suffolk, 1990–93; Vice Pres., Suffolk Assoc. of Local Councils, 1996–2003 (Pres., 1978–96). Mem., Firearms Consultative Cttee, 1995–98. Chairman, Lord Chancellor's Advisory Committee: on JPs, 2003–14; on Gen. Comrs for Income Tax, 2003–10. Vice President: Cheshire Red Cross, 1980–; Suffolk Horse Soc., 2009–14; President: Friends of Ipswich Museums, 1980–96; CAB, Ipswich & dist, 1998–2005; Suffolk Historic Churches Trust, 2003– (Chm., 1996–2003); Music for Country Churches, Suffolk, 2003–14; Army Benevolent Fund, Suffolk, 2003–14; Suffolk Co. Scout Council, 2003–14; RLSS, Suffolk, 2003–14; Friends of Suffolk Record Office, 2003–14; Britain Australia Soc., Suffolk, 2003–14; E Anglia Reserve Forces and Cadets Assoc., 2003–; Suffolk Reserve Forces and Cadets Assoc., 2006–14. Jt Pres., NORCAS, 2006–14. Chairman: HHA (E Anglia), 1979–83; Bury St Edmunds Cathedral Appeal, 1986–90; Suffolk Family History Soc., 1988–2003; Suffolk Lieutenancy Honours Cttee, 2006–. Patron: Suffolk Accident Rescue Service, 1983–2014; E Suffolk Assoc. for the Blind, 1992–2006; Suffolk, BRCS, 2003–14; NSPCC, Suffolk, 2003–14; ACRE, Suffolk, 2003–14; Magistrates' Assoc., Suffolk, 2003–14; Suffolk Wildlife Trust, 2003–; Disability Care Enterprise, 2003–11; Help the Aged, Suffolk, 2003–14; Gainsborough House Mus., 2003–14; Friends of St Edmundsbury Cathedral, 2003–14; Suffolk Preservation Soc., 2003– (Vice Patron, 1992–2003); SSAFA (formerly SSAFA Forces Help), 2003– (Pres., 1996–2003); E Anglia Children's Hospices, 2005–14; St Matthew's Housing, 2005–14; Friends of Royal Hosp. Sch., 2006–14; St Nicholas Hospice, Bury St Edmunds, 2006–14; Suffolk Community Foundn, 2006–14; E Anglian Air Ambulance, 2006–14; Soc. of E Anglia Watercolourists (formerly RWS, E Anglia), 2006–14; Flatford Mill Campaign, 2007–14; Red Lodge Marine Detachment, 2009–14; East Coast Hospice, 2009–14; Suffolk Heraldry Soc., 2011–14; Guildhall Project, 2011–14; Ipswich Sch. Music Appeal, 2012–. Vice-Patron: Just 42, 2005–14; Almshouse Assoc., 2009–14; Ipswich Umbrella Trust, 2009–14. Gov., Framlingham Coll., 2003–14. Mem., 1996–2010, Trustee, 2000–10, SAS Regtl Assoc. DL Suffolk, 1984. KStJ 2004 (CStJ 1989) (Chm., 1982–89, Pres., 2003–13, St John's Council for Suffolk). *Recreations:* fishing, natural history. *Heir: s* Hon. Edward John Hugo Tollemache [*b* 12 May 1976; *m* 2007, Sophie, *d* of Iain Johnstone, *qv;* two *s* one *d]. Address:* Helmingham Hall, Stowmarket, Suffolk IP14 6EF. *Clubs:* White's, Pratt's, Special Forces.

**TOLLEMACHE, Sir Lyonel (Humphry John),** 7th Bt *cr* 1793, of Hanby Hall; JP, DL; FRICS; *b* 10 July 1931; *s* of Maj.-Gen. Sir Humphry Tollemache, 6th Bt, CB, CBE, DL and Nora Priscilla (*d* 1990), *d* of John Taylor; *S* father, 1990; *m* 1960, Mary Joscelyne, *d* of late Col William Henry Whitbread, TD; one *s* two *d* (and one *s* decd). *Educ:* Uppingham Sch.; RMA Sandhurst; RAC Cirencester. Major, Coldstream Guards, retd 1963. Member: Melton and Belvoir RDC, 1969–74, Melton BC, 1974–87 (Mayor, 1981–82); Leics CC, 1985–97. Gov., Royal Star and Garter Home, Richmond, 1985–2001. High Sheriff 1978–79, JP 1978, DL 1980, Leics. *Heir: s* Richard John Tollemache, JP [*b* 4 May 1966; *m* 1992, Amanda, *er d* of Gordon Phillips; one *s* two *d]. Address:* The Old Vicarage, Buckminster, Grantham NG33 5RT.

**TOLLERVEY, Prof. David,** PhD; FRS 2004; FRSE; Wellcome Trust Principal Research Fellow, since 1997, Professor of Cell Biology, since 2008, and Director, Wellcome (formerly Wellcome Trust) Centre for Cell Biology, since 2011, University of Edinburgh; *b* 19 Sept. 1955; *s* of Robert Muirhead Tollervey and late Isabella Stewart Tollervey (*née* Davidson); partner, Dr Hildegard Tekotte; three *s* one *d. Educ:* George Heriot's Sch., Edinburgh; Univ. of Edinburgh (BSc Hons 1977); Darwin Coll., Cambridge (PhD 1981). Postdoctoral Fellow, Univ. of Calif, San Francisco, 1980–83; Charge de Recherche, Institut Pasteur, Paris, 1984–88; Gp Leader, EMBL, Heidelberg, 1988–97. FRSE 2004. *Publications:* over 200 papers and reviews in scientific jls. *Recreations:* sailing, hill-walking. *Address:* Wellcome Centre for Cell Biology, University of Edinburgh, King's Buildings, Edinburgh EH9 3BF. *T:* (0131) 650 7092, *Fax:* (0131) 650 7040. *E:* d.tollervey@ed.ac.uk. *Club:* Fisherrow Yacht.

**TOLLEY, Carole Anne Bennett;** Director of Resources Head Office and Corporate Finance, Ministry of Defence, 2011–15; *b* 4 May 1955; *d* of Sidney and Monica Cox; *m* 1982, Graeme Neil Tolley; two *s. Educ:* Lady Margaret Hall, Oxford (BA Hons PPE 1977); University Coll. London (MSc Econs of Public Policy 1978). ACCA 1998. Joined MoD as admin trainee, 1978; Private Secretary: to Chief Scientific Advr, 1983; to Under-Sec. of State for Armed Forces, 1984–85; Assistant Director: Finance and Admin (Nuclear), 1985–86; Naval Pay and Conditions, 1987–88; Financial Mgt Develt Unit, 1988–89; Secretariat (Air Staff), 1989–92; Civilian Mgt, 1992–95; Dir, Intelligence Progs and Resources, 1995–97; rcds 1998; Director: Defence Mgt Trng, 1999–2001; Resources and Plans (Centre), 2001–04; Dir Gen., Financial Mgt, 2004–07; Dir Gen., subseq. Dir, Scrutiny, 2007–11. *Recreations:* music, hiking, wind-surfing, gardening, su doku.

**TOLLEY, David Anthony,** FRCS, FRCSEd; Consultant Urological Surgeon, and Director, Scottish Lithotriptor Centre, Western General Hospital, Edinburgh, 1980–2012; President, Royal College of Surgeons of Edinburgh, 2009–12; *b* Warrington, 29 Nov. 1947; *s* of Frank Stanley Tolley and Elizabeth Tolley (*née* Dean); *m* 1970, Judith Finn; three *s* one *d. Educ:* Manchester Grammar Sch.; King's Coll. Hosp. Med. Sch. (MB BS 1970). FRCS 1975; FRCSEd 1983; FRCPE 2006; FDSRCSE (*ad hominem*) 2007. House Surgeon and Physician, 1970–71, Sen. Surgical Registrar (Urol.), 1976–77, King's Coll. Hosp.; Sen. Urol Registrar, Yorks Regl Trng Scheme, 1977–80. Lectr in Human Morphol., Southampton Univ., 1971–72; Lectr in Anatomy and Fulbright Fellow, Univ. of Texas at Houston, 1972. Pres., Endourol. Soc., 2013–14. Royal College of Surgeons of Edinburgh: Mem. Council, 2000–05; Hon. Treas., 2006–09; King James Prof., 2009; Fellow, Faculty of Surgical Trainers, 2017. Mem. Council, British Assoc. of Urological Surgeons, 1978–79, 1995–2000; Founding Treas. and Trustee, FMCM, 2012–17. Hon. FCSHK 2010; Hon. FCSSL 2010; Hon. FAMM 2012; Hon. Fellow, Coll. of Surgeons of Indonesia, 2016. Coll. Medal, RCSEd, 2006; Gold Medal, British Assoc. of Urological Surgeons, 2012. *Publications:* Urinary Stones, 2002; contrib. *c* 150 articles on kidney stone disease, urinary tract cancer and urology. *Clubs:* New (Edinburgh); Luffness New Golf.

**TOLPUTT, John Nigel,** MA; Head, The Purcell School, 1999–2007; *b* 1 May 1947; *s* of Basil Tolputt and Betty Durrant; *m* 1971, Patta Davis; one *s* one *d. Educ:* St John's Coll., Cambridge (MA); Bristol Univ. (Cert Ed 1969). Teacher, Bromsgrove Sch., 1969–74; Head of English and Drama, Cranleigh Sch., 1974–87; Head, Rendcomb Coll., 1987–99. FRSA 1994. Hon. ARAM 2005. *Recreation:* theatre. *Address:* Mill End, Sir George's Place, Steyning, Sussex BN44 3LS.

**TOLSON, James;** Member (Lib Dem) Dunfermline West, Scottish Parliament, 2007–11; *b* 26 May 1965; *s* of Robert Archibald Tolson and Jane Wallace Tolson; *m* 1996, Alison Patricia Lord. *Educ:* Napier Univ., Edinburgh (BSc Hons Network Computing). Fitter/turner, Babcock Rosyth Defence Ltd, 1981–2000; Sales Advr, British Sky Broadcasting, 2003–07. Member (Lib Dem): Dunfermline DC, 1992–96; Fife Council, 1995–2007. Scottish Parliament: Lib Dem Shadow Minister for Communities and Sport, 2007–08;

Mem., Local Govt and Communities Cttee, 2007–11; Lib Dem spokesperson on Local Govt and Transport, 2008–11. Contested (Lib Dem) Dunfermline West, Scottish Parlt, 2011. *Recreations:* gardening, travel, cycling, charitable work (incl. Chm., Talking Tandems, 2013–17).

**TOLSON, Robin Stewart**; QC 2001; **His Honour Judge Tolson**; a Circuit Judge, since 2014; Designated Family Judge, Central Family Court, since 2015; *b* 21 June 1958; *s* of Trevor and Vivian Tolson; *m* 1987, Carol Atkinson (*d* 2011); two *d*. *Educ:* Hull Grammar Sch.; Jesus Coll., Cambridge (MA). Called to the Bar, Inner Temple, 1980; in practice as barrister, 1980–2014, specialising in family law and local govt admin. law; Asst Recorder, 1998–2000; Recorder, 2000–14; Dep. High Court Judge, 2004–14. *Publications:* Care Plans and the Human Rights Act, 1998. *Recreation:* tennis. *Address:* Central Family Court, 42–49 High Holborn, WC1V 6NP.

**TOM, Peter William Gregory**, CBE 2006; Chairman, Breedon Group plc (formerly Marwyn Materials, then Breedon Aggregates Ltd), 2008–19; *b* 26 July 1940; *s* of late John Gregory Tom and Barbara Tom (*née* Lambden); one *s* three *d* (and one *s* decd). *Educ:* Hinckley Grammar Sch. Joined Bardon Hill Quarries Ltd, 1956: Man. Dir, 1977; Chm. and Chief Exec., 1985; merged with: Evered plc, 1991, to form Evered Bardon; CAMAS, 1997, to form Aggregate Industries plc, Chief Exec., 1997–2005, non-exec. Chm., 2006–07. Chm., Jacksons CI Ltd; Director: Leicester FC plc, 1997–; Leicester Rugby Club Ltd, 1997–; Leicester Tigers Ltd, 1997–; Bardon Mill House Co., 2003–05; Tigers Events Ltd, 2003–; Aga Rangemaster Gp plc (formerly Aga Foodservice Gp plc), 2004–10; Rise Rocks Ltd, 2005–12; BPI Global Res. Ltd (formerly Global Botanical Res. Ltd), 2006–09; Nature's Defence (UK) Ltd, 2006–11; Nature's Defence Investments Ltd, 2006–11; Macquarie Growth Income Group, 2006–; Mayven UK plc, 2006–07; Mayven International Ltd, 2006–. Chm., Quarry Products Assoc., 1997.

**TOMALIN, Claire**; writer; *b* 20 June 1933; *d* of late Emile Delavenay and of Muriel Herbert; *m* 1st, 1955, Nicholas Osborne Tomalin (*d* 1973); one *s* two *d* (and one *s* one *d* decd); 2nd, 1993, Michael Frayn, *qv*. *Educ:* Hitchin Girls' Grammar Sch.; Dartington Hall Sch.; Newnham Coll., Cambridge (MA). Publishers' reader and editor, Messrs Heinemann, Hutchinson, Cape, 1955–67; Evening Standard, 1967–68; New Statesman: Asst Literary Editor, 1968–70; Literary Editor, 1974–77; Literary Editor, Sunday Times, 1979–86. Stage play, The Winter Wife, Nuffield, Southampton, 1991; CD, Songs of Muriel Herbert, 2009. Curator: Mrs Jordan, The Duchess of Drury Lane, Kenwood, 1995; Hyenas in Petticoats, Grasmere and NPG, 1997. Trustee, Nat. Portrait Gallery, 1992–2002. Registrar, Royal Literary Fund, 1984– (Mem. Cttee, 1974–99; Life Vice-Pres., 2000). Vice-Pres., English PEN, 1997–. Trustee, Wordsworth Trust, 2001–03 (Fellow, 2003–). FRSL 1974 (Mem. Council, 1993–2000; Vice-Pres., 2003–). Freeman, City of London, 2012. Hon., Mem., Magdalene Coll., Cambridge, 2003; Hon. Fellow: Lucy Cavendish Coll., Cambridge, 2003; Newnham Coll., Cambridge, 2004. Hon. LittD: UEA, 2005; Birmingham, 2005; Greenwich, 2006; Cambridge, 2007; Open, 2008; Goldsmiths, 2009; Roehampton, 2011; Portsmouth, 2012. Biographers Internat. Orgn Annual Award, 2016; Bodley Medal, 2018. *Publications:* The Life and Death of Mary Wollstonecraft, 1974; Shelley and his World, 1980; Parents and Children, 1981; Katherine Mansfield: a secret life, 1987; The Invisible Woman: the story of Nelly Ternan and Charles Dickens, 1990 (NCR, Hawthornden, and James Tait Black Prizes, 1991; filmed 2014); Mrs Jordan's Profession, 1994; Jane Austen: a life, 1997; (ed) Mary Shelley, Maurice, 1998; Several Strangers: writing from three decades, 1999; Samuel Pepys: the unequalled self, 2002 (Whitbread Prize, 2002; Samuel Pepys Award, 2003; Rose Mary Crawshay Prize, 2003); Thomas Hardy: the time-torn man, 2006; (ed) Selected Poems of Thomas Hardy, 2006; (ed) Selected Poems of John Milton, 2008; (ed) Selected Poems of John Keats, 2009; Charles Dickens: a life, 2011; (contrib.) Breaking Bounds: six Newnham lives, 2015; A Life of My Own, 2017; literary journalism. *Recreations:* walking, gardening, music. *Address:* c/o David Godwin, 55 Monmouth Street, WC2H 9DG.

**TOMALIN, Michael Hardwick**, CMG 2014; OBE 1990; Chairman, National Bank of Abu Dhabi Private Bank Suisse SA, Geneva, 2005–17; Board Advisor, National Bank of Abu Dhabi, since 2016 (Group Chief Executive, 1999–2013; Executive Director, 2012–13; non-executive Director, 2012–16); *b* London; *s* of Edward Thomas Tomalin and Florence Mary Tomalin; *m* 1980, Carolyn Anne Rowe; one *s* one *d*. *Educ:* Univ. of the Witwatersrand (BA Hons); Harvard Business Sch. (SMP). Investment Manager, N. M. Rothschild, London, 1972–76; Barclays Group: Hd, Planning, Johannesburg, 1976, London, 1977–80; Caribbean Dir, Barbados, 1980–82; Exec. Dir, Hong Kong, 1982–84; Man. Dir, Wellington, NZ, 1984–85; Country Manager, Tokyo, 1985–90; Chief Exec., Barclays Private Banking, London, 1992–99. Co-Chm., Finablr plc, 2019–; Chairman: ADIB Ltd, 2019–; Love Brand & Co., 2019–. Advisor: Abdul Lateef Jameel Gp, Jeddah, 2013–; PwC London, 2013–. Hon. DSc Banking and Finance, Sch. of Finance, IFS, 2015. *Recreations:* golf, bridge, travel. *Address:* Vinnicks, Highclere, Hants RG20 9SB; Trafalgar Gardens, W8. *Clubs:* Brooks's, Hurlingham.

**TOMBS**, family name of **Baron Tombs**.

**TOMBS**, Baron *cr* 1990 (Life Peer), of Brailes in the county of Warwickshire; **Francis Leonard Tombs**, Kt 1978; FREng; Chairman: Rolls-Royce, 1985–92 (Director, 1982–92); Old Mutual South Africa Trust, 1994–98; *b* 17 May 1924; *s* of Joseph and Jane Tombs; *m* 1949, Marjorie Evans (*d* 2008); three *d*. *Educ:* Elmore Green Sch., Walsall; Birmingham Coll. of Technology; BSc (Econ) Hons, London. GEC, 1939–45; Birmingham Corp., 1946–47; British Electricity Authority, Midlands, then Central Electricity Authority, Merseyside and N Wales, 1948–57; Gen. Manager, GEC, Erith, 1958–67; Dir and Gen. Man., James Howden & Co., Glasgow, 1967–68; successively Dir of Engrg, Dep. Chm., Chm., South of Scotland Electricity Bd, 1969–77; Chm., Electricity Council, 1977–80. Chairman: Weir Group, 1981–83; Turner & Newall, subseq. T & N, 1982–89; Director: N. M. Rothschild & Sons, 1981–94; Shell-UK, 1983–94. Pres., Molecule Theatre Ltd, 1993–96 (Chm., 1985–92). Member: Nature Conservancy Council, 1978–82; Standing Commn on Energy and the Environment, 1978–; SERC, 1982–85; Chairman: Engrg Council, 1985–88; ACARD, 1985–87 (Mem., 1984–87); ACOST, 1987–90. Mem., H of L, 1990–2015; Chm., H of L Select Cttee on Sustainable Develt, 1994–95; Mem., H of L Select Cttee on Sci. and Technol., 1997–2005. Pres., IEE, 1981–82; Vice-Pres., Fellowship of Engrg, 1982–85; Vice-Pres., Engineers for Disaster Relief, 1985–94. Chm., Assoc. of British Orchestras, 1982–86. FREng (FEng 1977); FRAeS 1994, Hon. FRAeS 1995; Hon. FIChemE 1985; Hon. FICE 1986; Hon. FIProdE 1986; Hon. FIMechE 1989; Hon. FIET 1990; Hon. FIEE 1991); Hon. FRSE 1996; Hon. Mem., British Nuclear Energy Soc. Pro-Chancellor and Chm. Council, Cranfield Inst. of Technol., 1985–91; Chancellor, Strathclyde Univ., 1991–97 (Hon. LLD 1976; DUniv 1991). Freeman, City of London, 1980; Liveryman, 1981–, and Prime Warden, 1994–95, Goldsmiths' Co. Hon. DTech Loughborough, 1979; Hon. DSc: Aston, 1979; Lodz, Poland, 1980; Cranfield, 1985; Bradford, 1986; City, 1986; Surrey, 1988; Nottingham, 1989; Warwick, 1990; Cambridge, 1990; DSc(Eng) QUB, 1986; DEd CNAA, 1989. KSG 2002. *Publications:* Power Politics, 2011. *Recreation:* music. *Address:* 1 Hancock House, Merlin Way, Warwick CV34 6TP.

**TOMBS, Sebastian Martineau**, FRIAS; Chief Executive, Architecture and Design Scotland, 2005–09; *b* 11 Oct. 1949; *s* of late Dr David M. Tombs and Joan (*née* Parley); *m* 1988, Eva Heirman; four *s* two *d*. *Educ:* Bryanston; Corpus Christi Coll., Cambridge (BArch, DipArch). ACIArb 1977, MCIArb 2002; FRIAS 1992. RMJM, Edinburgh, 1975–76; Roland Wedgwood, Edinburgh, 1976–77; Fountainbridge Housing Assoc., Edinburgh, 1977–78; Housing Corp., 1978–81; Housing Dept, Edinburgh DC, 1982–86; Depute Sec., 1986–94, Sec., 1995–2005, RIAS. Founder and first Sec., Scottish Ecological Design Assoc., 1991–94 (Chm., 1994–97); Founder and first Chm., Assoc. Planning Supervisors, 1995–97. Co-chair, Anthroposophical Soc. in GB, 2011–13. Chm., Lismore Community Trust, 2014–. Contested (Lib Dem): Edinburgh N and Leith, Scottish Parlt, 1999, 2003; Edinburgh N and Leith, 2001; Kilmarnock and Loudoun, 2010. *Recreations:* designing cartograms, choral music, doggerel, sketching, reverse cycling, house building (www.lismoreislandhome.com). *Address:* Baile Geamhraidh, Isle of Lismore, Argyll PA34 5UL.

**TOMEI, Anthony Laurence**, CBE 2013; Director, Salters' Institute, since 2015; *b* 1 June 1949; *s* of late Laurence Stephen Tomei and Dora Tomei (*née* Myring); *m* 1977, Nicola Bourn; one *s* two *d*. *Educ:* St Joseph's Coll., London; Univ. of Sussex (BSc); Univ. of Manchester (MSc). Physics teacher, VSO, Johore, Malaysia, 1970–72; teacher, William Ellis Sch., London, 1972–74; Nuffield Foundation: Research Grants Officer, 1977–82; Asst Dir, 1982–95; Dir, 1995–2012; on secondment to DCSF, 2007. Vis. Prof., Dept of Educn, KCL, 2012–. Mem., Royal Soc. Cttee on Maths Educn, 2019–. Trustee: Bristol Exploratory, 1983–86; Rutherford Trust, 1992–96; Integrated Educn Fund (NI), 1992–97. Governor: Nuffield Chelsea Curriculum Trust, 1980–88; Pensions Policy Inst., 2005– (Mem. Council, 2012–). Trustee: Bell Educnl Trust, 2012–; DEBRA, 2012–14; Assoc. of Charitable Foundns, 2015–; Bonnart Trust, 2017–. Governor: Parliament Hill Sch., London, 1992–2000; City and Islington Coll., 2013–. Liveryman, Salters' Co., 2015–. *Recreations:* tennis, family life, reading, walking. *Club:* MCC.

**TOMES, Susan Mary**; musician (pianist) and writer; *b* 26 May 1954; *d* of Albert Henry Tomes and Catherine Mary Tomes (*née* Brodie); one *d*; *m* 2004, Dr Robert Philip. *Educ:* RSAMD; King's Coll., Cambridge (BA 1975 (first woman to read Music), MA 1978). ARCM 1970. Solo recitalist and concerto soloist, 1979–; Founder Member: Domus Piano Quartet, 1979–95 (Gramophone Awards, 1985, 1995); Florestan Trio, 1995–2012 (Gramophone Award, Classic CD Award, 1999; Royal Philharmonic Soc. Award, 2000); Pianist, Gaudier Ensemble, 1993–. Prof., GSMD, 1995–; Faculty Mem., ChamberStudio, 2010–; Guest Prof., Eur. Chamber Music Acad., 2013–. Mem., internat. music competition juries, 2011–. Affiliate Artist, Centre for Musical Perf. and Creative Practice, Univ. of Cambridge, 2010–; presents annual masterclasses, London, 2010–. Contributor: The Guardian, 2000–; Financial Times, 2002–; book reviewer: The Independent, 2006–; The Guardian, 2008–. Writer and presenter of talks on music, BBC Radio 3 and Radio 4. Mem., Acad. Adv. Bd, Centre for Hist. and Analysis of Recorded Music, 2005–09. Cobbett Medal, Musicians' Co., 2013. *Publications:* Beyond the Notes: journeys with chamber music, 2004; A Musician's Alphabet, 2006; (contrib.) Cambridge Companion to Recorded Music, 2009; Out of Silence, 2010; Sleeping in Temples, 2014; Speaking the Piano, 2018. *Recreations:* reading, letter-writing, walking. *E:* susan@susantomes.com. *W:* www.susantomes.com.

**TOMIĆ, Dr Ivica**; Ambassador of the Republic of Croatia to the Court of St James's, 2009–12; *b* Split, Croatia, 13 March 1941; *s* of Jakov and Marija Tomić; *m* 1964, Jasna Berković; two *s*. *Educ:* Coll. of Maritime Studies, Univ. of Rijeka (Master Mariner 1966); Coll. of Foreign Trade, Univ. of Zagreb; Univ. of Wales Inst. of Sci. and Technol. (OECD Schol. 1974); Dept of Economy, Univ. of Zagreb (MBA 1977); Univ. of Oregon (Fulbright Schol. 1977); Faculty of Marine and Transportation Studies, Univ. of Rijeke (PhD 1983). Cadet, third, second and Chief Officer, Adriatic Shipping Co., Split, 1960–71; University of Zagreb: Institute of Transportation Studies: Res. Fellow and Project manager, 1972–83; teaching asst, Intercollegiate Transportation Studies, 1974–76; Hd, Transportation Technol., 1978–80; Asst Prof., Faculty of Maritime and Transportation Studies, Univ. of Rijeka, 1987. Asst Minister, Min. of Transportation and Maritime Affairs (Maritime sect.), 1983–93; Nat. Coordinator for Adriatic Danube Initiative, Min. of Foreign Affairs and Eur. Integration, 1993; Ambassador to: Slovakia, 1993–96; to Turkey, 1996–2000; Nat. Coordinator for Adriatic-Ionian Initiative, Min. of Foreign Affairs, 2000–01; Ambassador to Egypt, 2001–05; Asst Minister of Foreign Affairs, 2005–09; Perm. Rep. of Croatia to IMO, 2009–12. White Double Cross Order, 2nd class (Slovakia), 1997; Order of Prince of Branimir with Necklace (Croatia), 1998. *Publications:* Transportation Technology of Ports, 1986. *Recreations:* sailing, swimming, tennis, art, reading.

**TOMKA, Dr Peter**; Judge, International Court of Justice, since 2003 (Vice-President, 2009–12; President, 2012–15); *b* Banská Bystrica, 1 June 1956; *s* of Ján Tomka and Kornélia Tomková; *m* 1990, Zuzana Halgašová; one *s* one *d*. *Educ:* Charles Univ. Law Sch., Prague (LLM 1979; DJur 1981; PhD Internat. Law 1985). Lectr, Charles Univ., 1984–91; Asst Legal Advr, Min. of Foreign Affairs, Czechoslovakia, 1986–91; Legal Advr, Perm. Mission of Czechoslovakia to UN, NY, 1991–92; Ambassador and Dep. Perm. Rep., 1993–94, Actg Perm. Rep., 1994–97, of Slovakia to UN; Dir for Legal Affairs, 1997–98 and Dir-Gen. for Legal and Consular Affairs, 1998–99, Min. of Foreign Affairs, Slovakia; Ambassador and Perm. Rep. of Slovakia to UN, NY, 1999–2003; Agent of Slovakia before Internat. Court of Justice, 1993–2003. United Nations: Chm., Sixth (Legal) Cttee, Gen. Assembly, 1997; Mem., Internat. Law Commn, 1999–2003; Chm., Cttee of Legal Advrs on Public Internat. Law, Council of Europe, 2001–02; Member: Perm. Court of Arbitration, 1994–; American Soc., 2000–; Eur. Soc. Internat. Law, 2004–; Panel of Arbitrators, Annex VII, UN Law of the Sea Convention, 2004–; Panel of Arbitrators, Internat. Centre for Settlement of Investment Disputes, 2005–; Curatorium, Hague Acad. of Internat. Law, 2013–. Associate Mem., Inst. de droit internat., 2011–. Hon. Bencher, Middle Temple, 2013. *Recreations:* chess, ski-ing, art, history. *Address:* International Court of Justice, Peace Palace, Carnegieplein 2, 2517 KJ The Hague, Netherlands. *T:* 703022468, *Fax:* 703022420. *E:* p.tomka@icj-cij.org.

**TOMKINS, Adam**, FRSE; Member (C) Glasgow, Scottish Parliament, since 2016; John Millar Professor of Public Law, University of Glasgow, since 2003; *b* Newbury, Berks, 28 June 1969; *s* of Bill and Karen Tomkins; *m* 2004, Dr Lauren Apfel; three *s* one *d*. *Educ:* Gillingham Sch., Dorset; Univ. of E Anglia (LLB 1990); London Sch. of Econs and Pol Sci. (LLM 1991). Lectr, KCL, 1991–2000; Fellow, and Tutor in Law, St Catherine's Coll., Oxford, 2000–03. Fellow, Bingham Centre for Rule of Law, British Inst. of Internat. and Comparative Law, 2011–15. FRSE 2014. *Publications:* The Constitution After Scott, 1998; Public Law, 2003; Our Republican Constitution, 2005; British Government and the Constitution, 2011. *Recreation:* guitar music. *Address:* Scottish Parliament, Edinburgh EH99 1SP. *E:* adam.tomkins.msp@parliament.scot. *Clubs:* Arsenal Football, Rangers Football.

**TOMKINS, Patrick Lindsay**, QPM 2006; HM Chief Inspector of Constabulary for Scotland, 2007–09; *b* 20 Aug. 1960; *m* Susan; one *s* one *d*. *Educ:* Hastings Grammar Sch.; King's Coll., London (BA Hons); Royal Coll. of Defence Studies; Open Univ. (MA 2012).

With Sussex Police, 1979–93; Chief Superintendent, 1993–97, Comdr, 1997–99, Metropolitan Police; Asst Inspector of Constabulary, 1999–2002; Chief Constable, Lothian and Borders Police, 2002–07. *Recreations:* fly fishing, reading.

**TOMKYS, Sir (William) Roger,** KCMG 1991 (CMG 1984); DL; HM Diplomatic Service, retired; Master of Pembroke College, Cambridge, 1992–2004; *b* 15 March 1937; *s* of late William Arthur and Edith Tomkys; *m* 1963, Margaret Jean Abbey; one *s* one *d*. *Educ:* Bradford Grammar Sch.; Balliol Coll., Oxford (Domus Scholar; 1st cl. Hons Lit.Hum.). Entered Foreign Service, 1960; MECAS, 1960; 3rd Sec., Amman, 1962; 2nd Sec., FCO, 1964; 1st Sec., Head of Chancery, Benghazi, 1967; Planning Staff, FCO, 1969; Head of Chancery, Athens, 1972; Counsellor, seconded to Cabinet Office, 1975; Head of Near East and North Africa Dept, FCO, 1977–80; Counsellor, Rome, 1980–81; Ambassador: to Bahrain, 1981–84; to Syria, 1984–86; Asst Under Sec. of State and Principal Finance Officer, FCO, 1987–89; Dep. Under Sec. of State, FCO, 1989–90; High Comr, Kenya, 1990–92. Chm., Arab-British Chamber of Commerce, 2004–10. DL Cambridgeshire, 1996. Liveryman: Drapers' Co., 2003–; Merchant Taylors' Co., 2004–. Commendatore dell'Ordine al Merito, 1980; Order of Bahrain, 1st cl., 1984. *Address:* 41 New Road, Barton, Cambs CB23 7AY. *Clubs:* Royal & Ancient Golf (St Andrews); Royal Worlington and Newmarket Golf.

**TOMLIN, Rt Rev. Graham Stuart;** *see* Kensington, Area Bishop of.

**TOMLINSON,** Baron *cr* 1998 (Life Peer), of Walsall in the co. of West Midlands; **John Edward Tomlinson;** *b* 1 Aug. 1939; *s* of Frederick Edwin Tomlinson, headmaster, and Doris Mary Tomlinson. *Educ:* Westminster City Sch.; Co-operative Coll., Loughborough; Nottingham Univ. (Dip. Polit. Econ. Social Studies); MA (Industrial Relations) Warwick, 1982. Sec., Sheffield Co-operative Party, 1961–68; Head of Research Dept, AUEW, 1968–70; Lectr in Industrial Relations, 1970–74. MP (Lab) Meriden, Feb. 1974–1979; PPS to Prime Minister, 1975–76; Parly Under-Sec. of State, FCO, 1976–79, and ODM, 1977–79. Sen. Lectr in Industrial Relations and Management, later Hd of Social Studies, Solihull Coll. of Tech., 1979–84. MEP (Lab) Birmingham W, 1984–99; Eur. PLP spokesman on budgetary control, 1989–99. Member: EU Select Cttee, H of L, 1999–2002 and 2005–; Audit Cttee, H of L, 2009–12; H of L Rep., Convention on the Future of Europe, 2002–03; Mem., Jt Cttee on Conventions, 2006–. Chairman: Adv. Cttee, London Sch. of Commerce, 2004–; Assoc. of Ind. HE Providers, 2006–12; Bd, Anglia Ruskin Univ., 2010–; Assoc. Business Executives, 2011–. Mem., Council of Europe. Trustee, Industry and Parlt Trust, 1988–2007 (Pres., 2002–07). Pres., British Fluoridation Soc., 1998–2011. Contested (Lab) Warwicks N, 1983. *Publications:* Left, Right: the march of political extremism in Britain, 1981. *Address:* House of Lords, SW1A 0PW.

**TOMLINSON, David Redvers; His Honour Judge Tomlinson;** a Circuit Judge, since 2010; *b* Aylesbury, 6 April 1954; *s* of David Cecil Macalister Tomlinson and Audrey Tomlinson (*née* Freeman); *m* 1988, Jane Packer; one *s* two *d*. *Educ:* Lord Williams' Sch., Thame; Univ. of Leeds (LLB). Called to the Bar, Inner Temple, 1977; Asst Recorder, 1997–2000; Recorder, 2000–10. Gov., Waldegrave Sch., 2003–. *Recreations:* tennis, ski-ing, gardening, theatre, cinema. *Address:* Southwark Crown Court, English Grounds, Battlebridge Lane, SE1 2HU. *T:* (020) 7522 7221. *Club:* Garrick.

**TOMLINSON, Heather Ann;** Independent Consultant, SEND Transformation, Surrey County Council, since 2018; *b* 23 June 1953; *d* of Kenneth and Joan Veneear; two *d*; *m* Charles George Sisum. *Educ:* Cheshunt Grammar Sch.; Univ. of Sheffield (BEd Hons; MEd; DPSE). Teacher, Rotherham LEA, 1976–80; Teacher, 1981–88, Educn Advr, 1988–98, Sheffield LEA; Regl Advisory Teacher, S Yorks and Humberside LEAs, 1988–90; Asst Dir of Educn, Nottingham City LEA, 1998–2001; Corporate Dir of Educn, Nottingham CC, 2001–04; Dir of Educn and Lifelong Learning, 2004–05, Corporate Dir of Children and Young People's Services, 2005–09, Bristol CC; Interim Dir of Educn, Birmingham CC, 2009–10; Interim Strategic Dir, Children and Young People, Derby CC, 2011; Interim Exec. Dir, Brighton and Hove CC, 2012–13; Lead Internat. Associate (Saudi Arabia), Nat. Coll. for Teaching and Leadership, 2013–14; Interim Asst Dir of Educn, Merton LBC, 2015; Interim Hd of Learning, Southend BC, 2015–16; Ind. Strategic Lead for Inclusion, London Bor. of Newham, 2016–18. *Recreations:* sailing, photography, running. *Club:* St Mawes Sailing (Cornwall).

**TOMLINSON, Prof. Ian Philip Mark,** PhD; FRS 2019; FRCPath; FMedSci; Director, Cancer Centre, University of Edinburgh, since 2019; *b* Loughborough, 11 Sept. 1963; *s* of Philip and Margaret Tomlinson; *m* 1993, Lynda; three *d*. *Educ:* Loughborough Grammar Sch.; Sidney Sussex Coll., Cambridge (BA 1985; PhD 1998); Univ. of Bristol (BM 1st Cl. 1989); University Coll., Oxford (BM BCh 1992). FRCPath 1999. Gp Leader, London Res. Inst., CRUK, 1998–2008; Prof. of Molecular and Population Genetics, and Fellow, Queen's Coll., Univ. of Oxford, 2008–17; Dir, Inst. of Cancer and Genomic Scis, Univ. of Birmingham, 2017–19. Mem., EMBO, 2016–. FMedSci 2009. *Publications:* contribs to scientific jls. *Recreations:* hockey, gardening, several other sports.

**TOMLINSON, Ven. Jennifer Clare;** Archdeacon of Birmingham, since 2019; *b* London, 10 Aug. 1961; *d* of Vernon and Eunice Mills; *m* 1993, David Robert Tomlinson; two *d*. *Educ:* Rawlins Sch., Quorn, Leics; Trinity Hall, Cambridge (BA Hist. 1982; MA 1986); Ridley Hall, Cambridge; BA Theol. 1990. Ordained deacon, 1991, priest, 1994; Curate: St John the Baptist, Busbridge, 1991–95; St Peter and St Paul, Godalming, 1995–98; Assoc. Priest, St John's, Grays North, 1998–2008; Assoc. Priest, Saffron Walden and Villages Team Ministry, 2008–19; Proctor in Convocation, 2009–19; Mission and Ministry Advr, Dio. of Chelmsford, 2011–19. Chaplain, SW Essex PCT, 1999–2008. *Recreations:* choral music, gardening. *Address:* 1 Colmore Row, Birmingham B3 2BJ. *T:* (0121) 426 0441. *E:* jennyt@cofebirmingham.com.

**TOMLINSON, Sir John (Rowland),** Kt 2005; CBE 1997; operatic bass; *b* 22 Sept. 1946; *s* of Rowland and Ellen Tomlinson; *m* 1969, Moya (*née* Joel); one *s* two *d*. *Educ:* Accrington GS; Manchester Univ. (BSc Civil Engrg); Royal Manchester Coll. of Music. Since beginning career with Glyndebourne in 1970, has sung over 200 operatic bass roles with ENO, Royal Opera, Covent Garden, Opera North, Scottish Opera, and in Geneva, Lisbon, Bologna, Florence, Milan, Copenhagen, Amsterdam, Stuttgart, Bayreuth, Berlin, Dresden, Madrid, Santiago, Tokyo, Vienna, Paris, Bordeaux, Avignon, Aix-en-Provence, Orange, San Diego, San Francisco, Pittsburgh, Vancouver, NY, Munich, Chicago, Salzburg, Hamburg, Boston, Frankfurt, Barcelona, Rome, Antwerp and Sydney; also broadcasts and recordings; best known for interpretations of Wagner bass and bass-baritone rôles, incl. Hans Sachs, Wotan (Bayreuth, 1988–98), Wanderer, Hagen, Gurnemanz and The Flying Dutchman (Bayreuth, 2003, 2004, 2006), König Marke, König Heinrich; other rôles include: Boris Godunov, Figaro, Leporello, Sarastro, Fiesco, Arkel, Balstrode, Kingfisher, Dosifey, four villains in Hoffman, Méphistophélès, Zaccharia, Claggart, Bluebeard, Baron Ochs, Rocco, Golaud, Moses, Philip II, Attila, Oberto, Green Knight, The Minotaur and Borromeo, Tirésias, Varlaam, Thomas Becket, Ivan Susanin. Pres., RNCM, 2017– (Hon. FRNCM 1996); Hon. FGS 2011. Hon. Dr: Sussex, 1997; Manchester, 1998; Hon. DMus: Nottingham, 2004; Birmingham, 2004. Singer of the Year, Royal Philharmonic Soc., 1991, 1998, 2007; Grammy Award (for Bartok, Cantata Profana), 1993; Reginald Goodall Award, Wagner Soc., 1996; Evening Standard Opera Award, 1998; Southbank Show Opera Award, 1999; Society's Special Award, Laurence Olivier Awards, 2007; Gold Medal, Royal Philharmonic Soc., 2014. *Address:* c/o Music International, 13 Ardilaun Road, Highbury, N5 2QR. *T:* (020) 7359 5183. *W:* www.johntomlinson.org.

**TOMLINSON, Justin Paul;** MP (C) North Swindon, since 2010; Minister of State, Department for Work and Pensions, since 2019; *b* 1976. *Educ:* Harry Cheshire High Sch., Kidderminster; Oxford Brookes Univ. (BA Business and Mktg 1999). Sales and Mktg Manager, First Leisure, 1999–2000; Mktg Exec., Point to Point, 2000; Dir, TB Mktg Solutions Ltd, 2000–10. Mem. (C), Swindon BC, 2000–10. Parly Under-Sec. of State, DWP, 2015–16 and 2018–19. Mem., Public Accounts Cttee, 2012–14. Contested (C) N Swindon, 2005. *Address:* House of Commons, SW1A 0AA.

**TOMLINSON, Michael James;** MP (C) Mid Dorset and North Poole, since 2015; *b* Wokingham, 1 Oct. 1977; *s* of Howard and Heather Tomlinson; *m* 2000, Frances Mynors; one *s* two *d*. *Educ:* Univ. of London (BA Hons Classics). Called to the Bar, Middle Temple, 2002 (Queen Mother's Schol.). *Recreations:* all sports, reading, going to the beach with my family. *Address:* House of Commons, SW1A 0AA. *Clubs:* Hamworthy Cricket, Poole Hockey.

**TOMLINSON, Sir Michael (John),** Kt 2005; CBE 1997; Chairman, STEM Learning Ltd, (formerly Myscience Ltd), 2008–17; *b* 17 Oct. 1942; *s* of Edith Cresswell and Jack Tomlinson; *m* 1965, Maureen Janet; one *s* one *d*. *Educ:* Oakwood Technical High Sch., Rotherham; Bournemouth Boys' Sch.; Durham Univ. (BSc Hons Chem.); Nottingham Univ. (post-grad. Cert Ed (First Div.)). Chemistry teacher, Henry Mellish GS, Nottingham, 1965–69; Head of Chemistry, Ashby-de-la-Zouch GS, 1969–77; on secondment to ICI, 1977; Chief Inspector (Schools), HM Inspectorate of Schs, 1989–92; Dep. Dir, 1992–95, Dir of Inspection, 1995–2000, Office for Standards in Education; HM Chief Inspector of Schs, 2000–02; Chm., Hackney Educn Trust, 2002–07; Chief Advr for London Schs, DCSF, 2008–09. Educn Comr for Birmingham, 2014–16. Non-executive Director: RM plc, 2004–13; Piscari Ltd, 2008–10. Chair, 14–19 Govt Working Gp, 2003–04. Director: Sci. Yr 2002; Planet Science, 2003. Pres., ASE, 2005. Mem., Adv. Educn Bd, LSO, 2008–14. Chm., Basildon Excellence Panel, 2014–17. Trustee: Comino Foundn, 2002–11; Industrial Trust, 2003–07; Business Dynamics, 2004–07; Farming and Countryside Educn, 2008–13; Baker-Dearing Trust, 2010–; Oxford Trust, 2010–14. Chm. Govs, RSA Acad., 2008–12; Governor: Merchant Taylors' Sch., Northwood, 2012, 2014–; Mem. Ct, Univ. of Herts, 2009–14 (Gov., 2004–09). Pres., RASE, 2010–12. FRSA. Hon. FCGI 2009. Freeman, City of London, 2013; Liveryman, Merchant Taylors' Co., 2014 (Founding Mem., Educn Cttee, 2015–). Hon. DEd: Wolverhampton, 2004; De Montfort, Nottingham Trent, 2005; Durham, 2007; Manchester Metropolitan, 2008; Hon. DLitt Warwick, 2011; Hon. DCL: UEA, Northumbria, 2005; Leicester, 2006; Hon. Dr: Middlesex, 2005; York, 2012; Buckinghamshire, 2012; Birmingham City, 2016. Chem. Soc. Award in Chem. Educn (Bronze Medal), 1975. Silver Jubilee Medal, 1977. *Publications:* New Movements in the Study and Teaching of Chemistry, 1975; Organic Chemistry: a problem-solving approach, 1977; Mechanisms in Organic Chemistry: case studies, 1978; BP educn service contribs, 1974–78; 14–18: a new vision for secondary education, 2013; articles in professional jls. *Recreations:* gardening, fishing, food and wine, reading. *Address:* Brooksby, Mayhall Lane, Chesham Bois, Amersham, Bucks HP6 5NR. *T:* (01494) 726967.

**TOMLINSON, Prof. Richard Allan,** FSA; Director, British School at Athens, 1995–96; *b* 25 April 1932; *s* of James Edward Tomlinson and Dorothea Mary (*née* Grellier); *m* 1957, Heather Margaret Murphy (*d* 2009); three *s* one *d*. *Educ:* King Edward's Sch., Birmingham; St John's Coll., Cambridge (BA, MA). FSA 1970. Asst, Dept of Greek, Univ. of Edinburgh, 1957; University of Birmingham: Asst Lectr 1958, Lectr 1961, Sen. Lectr 1969, Prof., 1971–95, now Emeritus, Dept of Ancient History and Archaeology; Head of Sch. of Antiquity, 1988–91. British School at Athens: Editor, Annual, 1978–91; Chm. Managing Cttee, 1991–95; Vice-Pres., 2001–. *Publications:* Argos and the Argolid, 1972; Greek Sanctuaries, 1976; Epidaurus, 1983; (ed) Greek Architecture, by A. W. Lawrence, 5th edn 1996; (contrib.) Sir Banister Fletcher, A History of Architecture, 20th edn, 1996; Greek Architecture, 1989; The Athens of Alma-Tadema, 1991; From Mycenae to Constantinople, 1992; Greek and Roman Architecture, 1995; (jtly) A Gazetteer of the Cyrene Necropolis, 2009; articles in Annual of British Sch. at Athens, Jl of Hellenic Studies, Amer. Jl of Archaeology, etc. *Recreation:* architecture. *Address:* 15 Eymore Close, Birmingham B29 4LB.

**TOMLINSON, Prof. Sally,** PhD; Goldsmiths Professor of Policy and Management in Education, Goldsmiths College, London University, 1992–2000, now Emeritus; Honorary (formerly Senior) Research Fellow, Department of Education, University of Oxford, since 1998; *b* 22 Aug. 1936; *d* of Clifford Gilmore Entwistle and Alice Nora Stubbs; *m* 1957, Brian Joseph Tomlinson, Sqdn Ldr, RAF (retd); one *s* two *d*. *Educ:* Macclesfield Grammar Sch.; Liverpool Univ. (BA Hons); Birmingham Univ. (MSocSci); Warwick Univ. (PhD); Manchester Univ. (PGCE). Lectr and Sen. Lectr, West Midlands Coll. of Educn, 1970–74; Sen. Res. Fellow, Warwick Univ., 1974–78; Lectr, then Sen. Lectr, later Prof. of Educn, Lancaster Univ., 1978–91; Prof. of Educn, UC Swansea, 1991–92; Dean, Faculty of Educn, 1992–95, Pro Warden, 1994–97, Goldsmiths' Coll., London Univ. Sen. Associate Mem., St Antony's Coll., Oxford, 1984–85; Res. Associate, Centre for Res. in Ethnic Relns, 2002–10, Associate Fellow, Dept of Sociol., 2014–17, Univ. of Warwick. Vis. Prof., Univ. of Wolverhampton, 2008–11. Leverhulme Emeritus Fellow, 2009. Mem. Council, Adv. Centre for Educn, 1986–94 (Chm., 1991–93). Member: Court, Univ. of Bradford, 2001–04; Council, Univ. of Glos, 2000–09; Council, S Worcestershire Coll., 2011–15. Mem., Commn on Future of Multi-ethnic Britain, 1998–2000. Patron, Africa Educational Trust, 2012– (Trustee, 1992–2012; Vice-Chair, 2003–04; Chair, 2005–09); Trustee: Learning from Experience Trust, 1992–99; Educn Extra, 1992–2000. FRSA. *Publications:* (with John Rex) Colonial Immigrants in a British City, 1979; Educational Subnormality, 1981, reissued 2018; A Sociology of Special Education, 1982, repr. 2012; Ethnic Minorities in British Schools, 1983; Home and School in Multicultural Britain, 1984; (ed with Len Barton) Special Education and Social Interests, 1984; (with David Smith) The School Effect, 1989; (ed with A. Yogev) Affirmative Action and Positive Policies in the Education of Ethnic Minorities, 1989; Multicultural Education in White Schools, 1990; Educational Reform and its consequences, 1994; (jtly) The Assessment of Special Educational Needs: whose problem?, 1994; (ed with Maurice Craft) Ethnic Relations and Schooling, 1995; Education 14–19: critical perspectives, 1997; (ed jtly) School Effectiveness for Whom?, 1998; (jtly) Hackney Downs: the school that dared to fight, 1999; Education in a Post-Welfare Society, 2001, 2nd edn 2005; (with Tony Edwards) Selection isn't Working, 2002; Race and Education: policy and politics in Britain, 2008; (ed with T. Basit) Social Inclusion and Higher Education, 2012; Ignorant Yobs? Low Attainers in a Global Knowledge Economy, 2013; The Politics of Race, Class and Special Education, 2014; A Sociology of Special and Inclusive Education, 2017; Education and Race from Empire to Brexit, 2019; (with Danny Dorling) Rule Britannia: Brexit and the end of empire, 2019; many contribs to books and learned jls. *Recreations:* walking, politics. *Address:* Department of Education, University of Oxford, 15 Norham Gardens, Oxford OX2 6PY.

**TOMLINSON, Prof. Stephen,** CBE 2007; MD; FRCP; FMedSci; Provost, Cardiff University, 2006–10, now Professor Emeritus of Medicine (Hon. Fellow, 2019); Hon. Consultant Physician, Cardiff and Vale NHS Trust, since 2001; *b* 20 Dec. 1944; *s* of Frank Tomlinson and Elsie Tomlinson (*née* Towler); *m* 1970, Christine Margaret Hope; two *d. Educ:* Hayward GS, Bolton; Univ. of Sheffield (MB ChB Hons 1968; MD 1976). FRCP 1982. SHO and Registrar, Sheffield Royal Infirmary, 1969–72; Registrar, Middlesex Hosp., 1972–73; MRC Clin. Res. Fellow, 1973–75, Hon. Lectr, 1974–76, Middlesex Hosp. Med. Sch.; Sen. Registrar, Middlesex Hosp., 1975–76; Sir Henry Wellcome Travelling Fellow, MIT, 1976–77; Sheffield University: Wellcome Trust Sen. Res. Fellow in Clin. Sci., 1977–80; Wellcome Sen. Lectr, 1980–85; Hon. Reader in Medicine, 1982–85; Hon. Cons. Physician, Sheffield HA, 1977–85; Manchester University: Prof. of Medicine, 1985–2001; Dean of Med. Sch. and Faculty of Medicine, 1993–97, of Faculty of Medicine, Dentistry and Nursing, 1997–99; Hon. Consultant Physician, Manchester Royal Infirmary, 1985–2001; Vice-Chancellor, UWCM, 2001–04; Provost, Wales Coll. of Medicine, Biol., Life and Health Scis and Dep. Vice-Chancellor, Cardiff Univ., 2004–06. Mem., Ind. Rev. of Modernising Med. Careers (Tooke Inquiry), 2006. Mem. Bd, UK Res. Integrity Office, 2008–12. Chairman: Assoc. of Clin. Profs of Med., 1996–99; Fedn of Assocs of Clin. Profs, 1997–2000; Tropical Health and Educn Trust, 2007–10; ASH Wales, 2007–13; R&D Cttee, Velindre NHS Trust, 2002–12 (Mem. Bd, 2002–12); Wales for Africa Health Links Network, 2012–14 (Vice-Chm., 2011–12); Founder Chm., Vale for Africa, 2009–13. Pres., Assoc. of Physicians, 2002–03 (Hon. Sec. and Treas., 1988–98); Exec. Sec., Council of Heads of Med. Schs, 1997–99; Mem., GMC, 2001–03 (Mem., Educn Cttee, 1999). Member: Bd, QAA, 2003–07 (Chm., Wales Adv. Cttee, 2003–07); Bd, Nat. Coordinating Centre for Cancer, 2008–12 (Dep. Chm., 2010–12); HEFC Wales, 2013–16 (Mem., Res., Innovation and Educn Cttee, 2013–16); Adv. Council, UWC Atlantic Coll., 2013–; Council, Univ. of Exeter, 2013– (Mem., Univ. Ethics Cttee, 2013–); Biol Standards Cttee, Univ. of Cardiff, 2013–. Founder FMedSci, 1998. Hon. DSc Sheffield, 2012. *Publications:* papers on stimulus-response coupling and intracellular signalling in endocrine tissues; the orgn of health services for people with diabetes; international health. *Recreations:* arts and health, history of medicine, good food and wine (mine and others!). *Address:* Grasmere, 1 Newfield Gardens, South Road, Hagley DY9 0JT. *Club:* Medical Pilgrims (Hon. Sec., 1995–2012).

**TOMLINSON, Rt Hon. Sir Stephen (Miles),** Kt 2000; PC 2011; a Lord Justice of Appeal, 2010–17; *b* 29 March 1952; *s* of Enoch Tomlinson and Mary Marjorie Cecilia Tomlinson (*née* Miles); *m* 1980, Joanna Kathleen Greig; one *s* one *d. Educ:* King's Sch., Worcester (schol.); Worcester Coll., Oxford (schol.; Eldon Law Schol.; MA; Hon. Fellow, 2012). Called to the Bar, Inner Temple, 1974, Bencher, 1990 (Treas., 2014). Lectr in Law, Worcester Coll., Oxford, 1974–76. QC 1988; a Recorder, 1995–2000; a Dep. High Court Judge, 1996–2000; a Judge of the High Ct of Justice, QBD, 2000–10; Judge in Charge of Commercial Court, 2003–04. Chm., Assoc. of Average Adjusters, 2009. Gov., Shrewsbury Sch., 2003–12. *Recreations:* gardening, family, walking, ski-ing, cricket. *Clubs:* Garrick, MCC.

**TOMOS, Linda;** National Librarian, National Library of Wales, 2015–19; *b* Llanelli, 1 April 1952; *d* of Arthur Horatio Williams and Mary Eileen Williams; *m* 1974, Merfyn Wyn Tomos; two *s. Educ:* Didcot Girls' Grammar Sch.; Univ. of Wales, Aberystwyth (BLib Hist. and Librarianship). MCLIP 1975. Librarian: Coll. of Librarianship, Wales, 1974–76; Clwyd CC, 1976–79; Dir, Wales Information Network, 1990–2003; Dir, CyMAL: Museums Archives and Libraries Wales, Welsh Assembly Govt, later Welsh Govt, 2003–15. Chairman: BBC Educn Broadcasting Council Wales, 1999–2003; Liby and Information Services Council Wales, 2000–03; Mem., Welsh Adv. Council on Telecommunications, 1999–2003; Dir, Careers Wales NW, 2001–03. Chm., Adv. Bd for Wales, NT, 2016–. *Publications:* numerous reports and articles relating to electronic information management. *Recreation:* researching Welsh history and culture.

**TOMPKINS, Hon. Sir David (Lance),** KNZM 1999; Judge of the High Court of New Zealand, 1983–97, Acting Judge, 1998–2003; Judge, Court of Appeal of Kiribati, since 2001, of Vanuatu, since 2002, and of Tuvalu, since 2009; *b* 26 July 1929; *s* of Arthur Lance Tompkins, Judge, Supreme Court of NZ, and Marjorie Rees Tompkins (*née* Manning); *m* 1956, Erica Lya Felicity Ann Faris; two *s* one *d. Educ:* Whitiora Primary Sch.; Southwell Sch., Hamilton; King's Coll., Auckland; Auckland University Coll. (LLB 1951). Served 1st Field Regt, RNZA, TA, 1949–59 (Capt. 1958). Partner, Tompkins & Wake, Hamilton, 1953–71; Barrister, 1971; QC (NZ) 1974; Courts Martial Appeal Court Judge, 1982–83; Exec. Judge, Auckland High Court, 1989–92; Judge of the Privy Council and Court of Appeal of Tonga, 1995–; Judge, Criminal Appeal Div., Court of Appeal of NZ, 1996–97; Justice of Appeal, Court of Appeal of Fiji, 1997–2005; Judge, Supreme Court of Vanuatu, 1998–. Chairman: Council of Legal Educn, 1992–97; Nat. Case Mgt Cttee, 1994–97; Electricity Mkt Appeal, 1998–. Pres., Hamilton Dist Law Soc., 1969–71; Mem. Council, 1969–71, Vice Pres., 1979–81, NZ Law Soc.; Mem. Council, 1976–83, Life Mem., 1987, Law Asia; Pres., Auckland Medico-Legal Soc., 1994–95. Associate, Arbitrators' and Mediators' Inst., 1997; Mem., LEADR, 1997–. Pro-Chancellor, 1979–80, Chancellor, 1980–85, Waikato Univ. Outward Bound Trust: Vice-Pres., 1981–83; Pres., 1983–84; Guardian, 1992–. Chm., Chelsea Park Trust, 2002–. Hon. Dr Waikato Univ., 1986. Silver Jubilee Medal, 1977; Commemoration Medal (NZ), 1990. *Recreations:* sailing, croquet, ski-ing, computers, trout fishing, cooking. *Address:* 68/7 St Vincent Avenue, Remuera, Auckland 1050, New Zealand. *Clubs:* Hamilton (Life Mem.), Northern (Auckland).

**TOMPKINS, Steven Charles,** RIBA; Director, Haworth Tompkins Architects Ltd, since 1991; *b* 5 Oct. 1959; *s* of Keith and Patricia Tompkins; *m* 1986, Katherine Claire Tyndall; two *s. Educ:* Wellingborough Grammar Sch.; Univ. of Bath (BSc, BArch 1983). RIBA 1992. Arup Associates, London, 1984–86; Bennetts Associates, London, 1987–90. Major commissioned projects include: Royal Court Th., 2000; Coin St Housing, London, 2001; Regent's Park Open Air Th., 1998–2000; Almeida Th. at Gainsborough Studios, 2000, at King's Cross, 2001; Hayward Gall., 2005; Young Vic Th., 2006; Egg Th., Bath, 2006; Nat. Theatre Studio, 2008; Snape Maltings, 2009; London Liby, 2010; RCA, 2013; Everyman Th., Liverpool, 2014 (RIBA Stirling Prize); Chichester Fest. Th., 2014; NT Future project, 2015; Battersea Arts Centre, 2016; Bristol Old Vic, 2017; Bridge Th., 2017; Th. Royal Drury Lane, 2018; other Haworth Tompkins clients include: RCA; Aldeburgh Music; Donmar Th.; Grosvenor Estates; AXA; Peabody Trust; Chichester Fest. Th.; London Film Sch. Trustee: Young Vic Th.; Theatrum Mundi. Ambassador and Mem. Adv. Bd, Stephen Lawrence Trust. Hon. LLD. *Recreations:* painting, theatre, mountain walking. *Address:* Haworth Tompkins Ltd, 33 Greenwood Place, NW5 1LB. *T:* (020) 7250 3225, *Fax:* (020) 7267 1391. *E:* steve.tompkins@haworthtompkins.com.

**TOMPKINSON, Stephen Philip Patrick;** actor; *b* 15 Oct. 1965; *s* of Brian and Josephine Tompkinson; one *d* by former marriage. *Educ:* St Bede's RC High Sch., Lytham St Anne's; Central Sch. of Speech and Drama. *Theatre* includes: No One Sees the Video, Royal Court, 1990; Across the Ferry, Bush, 1991; Love's Labours Lost, Women Laughing, Manchester Royal Exchange, 1992; Tartuffe, nat. tour, 1997; Art, Wyndham's, 2000; Arsenic and Old Lace, Strand, 2003; Rattle of a Simple Man, Comedy Th., 2004; Cloaca, Old Vic, 2004; Charley's Aunt, nat. tour, 2007; The Revenger's Tragedy, Manchester Royal Exchange, 2008; Sign of the Times, nat. tour, 2009; Faith and Cold Reading, Live Th. Newcastle, 2011; Spamalot, Playhouse, 2012; Pig Farm, St James, 2015; The Red Lion, Live Th., Newcastle, Trafalgar Studios, 2017; Art, nat. tour, 2018; A Christmas Carol, Old Vic, 2018; *films* include: Treacle, 1987; Brassed Off, 1996; Hotel Splendide, 2000; Tabloid TV, 2001; Harrigan, 2013; A Dark Reflection, 2015; Hector, 2015; Walk Like a Panther, 2018; *television* includes: And a Nightingale Sang, 1989; The Deep Blue Sea, 1994; A Very Open Prison, 1995; First Signs of Madness; Flint Street Nativity, 1999; Lucky Jim, In Denial of Murder, 2003; Murder at the Vicarage, 2004; The Last Detective, New Tricks, Taming of the Shrew, Marian Again, 2005; Prime Suspect 7: The Final Act, 2006; Eric, Ernie and Me, 2017; *series:* Drop the Dead Donkey, 1990–98; All Quiet on the Preston Front, 1994 and 1995; Ballykissangel, 1996–98; Grafters, 1998; In Deep, 2001 and 2003; Bedtime, 2001; Ted and Alice; Wild at Heart, 2006–13; DCI Banks, 2010–16; Stephen Tompkinson's African Balloon Adventure, 2009; Stephen Tompkinson's Australian Balloon Adventure, 2010; Truckers, 2013; Trollied, 2014–18; Semi Detached, 2016; The Split, 2018. Hon. Fellow, Univ. of Central Lancashire, 1998. Hon DA Teeside, 2015. *Recreations:* cricket, swimming, cinema. *Address:* c/o Conway van Gelder Grant, Third Floor, 8/12 Broadwick Street, W1F 8HW. *T:* (020) 7287 0077. *E:* nick@conwayvg.co.uk. *Clubs:* Groucho, Gerry's.

**TOMPSETT, Dr Michael Francis,** FIEEE; materials and device physicist, inventor, integrated circuit developer, manager, software developer; *m* Dr Margaret. *Educ:* Brentwood Sch., Essex; Jesus Coll., Cambridge (BA 1962; PhD Physics and Engrg 1966). FIEEE 1986. Project Leader, EEV, Chelmsford, Essex, 1966–69; Supervisor, Bell Labs, NJ, 1969–89; Dir, Electronic Devices Div., US Army, 1991–97; Founder, 1997, Pres., 1997–2011, TheraManager LLC. Invented uncooled thermal imaging cameras, digital CCD imaging camera and integrated circuit video analog-to-digital converter. Mem., NAE, 2015. Chairman: Chatham Conservation Commn, 2013–; Chatham Community Preservation Cttee, 2015–. Hon. FRPS 2017. Lifetime Achievement Award, NJ Inventors' Hall of Fame, 2010; US Nat. Medal for Technol. and Innovation, 2010; Edison Gold Medal, IEEE, 2012; (jtly) Queen Elizabeth Prize for Engrg, 2017; Progress Medal, RPS, 2017. *Publications:* (with Carlo H. Sequin) Charge Transfer Devices, 1975 (trans. Japanese, 1977, Russian, 1978); refereed papers; 17 patents. *Address:* 17 Lake Shore Drive, Chatham, MA 02633, USA. *T:* (508) 2507448.

**TOMS, Edward Ernest;** Director, Studio Gallery, London, 1983–2002; Partner, Studio Gallery and Picture Framers, since 2003; *b* 10 Dec. 1920; *s* of Alfred William and Julia Harrington Toms; *m* 1946, Veronica Rose (*d* 2003), Dovercourt, Essex; three *s* one *d. Educ:* St Boniface's Coll.; Camel's Head 6th Form; HM Dockyard Sch., Devonport; Staff Coll., Camberley (psc), Nat. Defence Coll. (jssc). Electrical Engrg apprentice, HM Dockyard, Devonport, 1937–41; war service 1941–45; Trooper, Royal Tank Regt, Western Desert, PAIFORCE, Egypt, 1943; Captain Seaforth Highlanders; Special Forces, W Desert, Italy, Balkans, NW Europe; Regular Army, 1946, Seaforth Highlanders and QO Highlanders; Brigade Major, Berlin, 1959–61; Trng Major, 8th Bn Argyll and Sutherland Highlanders, 1961–63; CO QO Highlanders Depot, 1963–65; CO 3rd Bn Gordon Highlanders, 1965–67; Col GS (UK Cs-in-C Cttee), 1967–69. Principal, Home Civil Service, 1969; Asst Sec., Dept of Employment, 1973; seconded to Diplomatic Service as Counsellor, Bonn and Vienna, 1977–81; Internat. Labour Advr, FCO, 1981–83. Dir, Porcelain & Pictures Ltd, 1983–2002. *Recreations:* reading, writing, and dreaming of when I loved hill-walking and could do it. *Clubs:* Special Forces, Chelsea Arts, Civil Service, Army and Navy.

**TOMS, Sophie Jane;** a District Judge (Magistrates' Court), since 2018; *b* Pontypool, Torfaen, 17 Feb. 1976; *d* of Bernard William Toms and Ann Toms (*née* Gilfillan). *Educ:* Caerleon Comprehensive Sch.; Univ. of Glamorgan (LLB). Admitted as solicitor, 2001; solicitor, specialising in criminal defence, 2001–18; a Dep. Dist Judge (Magistrates' Court), 2012–18. *Recreations:* gardening, travel, cooking.

**TOMSETT, Alan Jeffrey,** OBE 1974; Director, Associated British Ports Holdings PLC, 1983–92 (Finance Director, 1983–87); chartered accountant; *b* 3 May 1922; *s* of Maurice Jeffrey Tomsett and Edith Sarah (*née* Mackelworth); *m* 1948, Joyce May Hill; one *s* one *d. Educ:* Trinity School of John Whitgift, Croydon; Univ. of London (BCom). JDipMA. Hodgson Harris & Co., Chartered Accountants, London, 1938. Served War, with RAF, 1941–46 (Middle East, 1942–45). Smallfield Rawlins & Co., Chartered Accountants, London, 1951; Northern Mercantile & Investment Corp. Ltd, 1955; William Baird & Co. Ltd, 1962–63. British Transport Docks Board, later Associated British Ports: Dep. Chief Accountant, 1963; Chief Accountant, 1964; Financial Controller, 1970; Bd Mem., 1974–87 (Finance Dir, 1974–85). Churchwarden, St John's, Shirley, 1988–92. FCA, FCMA, CPFA, FCIS, FCILT (Vice-Pres., 1981–82, Hon. Treasurer, 1982–88, CIT); FRSA 1969. *Address:* 14 Colts Bay, Craigwell on Sea, Bognor Regis, W Sussex PO21 4EH. *T:* (01243) 267211.

**TONBRIDGE, Bishop Suffragan of,** since 2018; **Rt Rev. Simon David Burton-Jones;** *b* Fleetwood, Lancs, 23 Dec. 1962; *s* of Harry and Dorothy Jones; *m* 1989, Julia Burton; one *s* one *d. Educ:* Fleetwood High Sch.; Emmanuel Coll., Cambridge (BA 1984; MA 1988); St John's Coll., Nottingham (BTh 1992; MA 1993). Res. Manager, Jubilee Centre, Cambridge, 1987–90; ordained deacon, 1993, priest, 1994; Vicar, St Mary's Church, Bromley, 1998–2005; Rector, St Nicholas Church, Chislehurst, 2005–10; Archdeacon of Rochester and Canon Res., Rochester Cathedral, 2010–18. *Recreations:* eating food with my family round the table, cricket, film, foreign fiction, the day of rest. *E:* simonburtonjones@btinternet.com.

**TONBRIDGE, Archdeacon of;** *see* Conalty, Ven. J. A.

**TONEGAWA, Prof. Susumu,** PhD; Picower Professor of Biology and Neuroscience, Department of Biology, Massachusetts Institute of Technology, since 2002; Director: RIKEN-MIT Center for Neural Circuit Genetics, since 2008; RIKEN Brain Science Institute, Japan, since 2009; *b* Nagoya, 5 Sept. 1939; *s* of Tsutomo and Miyoko Tonegawa; *m* 1985, Mayumi Yoshinari; one *s* one *d* (and one *s* decd). *Educ:* Kyoto Univ. (BS); Univ. of San Diego (PhD 1968). Postgraduate work: Univ. of California, San Diego, 1968–69; Salk Inst., San Diego, 1969–70; Mem., Basel Inst. of Immunology, 1971–81; Prof. of Biology and Neurosci., Center for Cancer Res., Dept of Biol., MIT, 1981–; Investigator, Howard Hughes Med. Inst., 1988–; Dir, Picower Center for Learning and Memory, MIT, 1994–2006. Avery Landsteiner Prize, Ges. für Immunologie, 1981; Gairdner Foundn Internat. Award, 1983; Nobel Prize for Physiology or Medicine, 1987. *Address:* Department of Biology, Massachusetts Institute of Technology, 77 Massachusetts Avenue, 46–5285, Cambridge, MA 02139–4307, USA.

**TONER, Charles Gerard;** Group Chairman, Barratt Developments PLC, 2002–08; *b* 20 Jan. 1942; *s* of Hugh and Sally Toner; *m* 1967, Valerie Anne Metcalfe; one *s* one *d. Educ:* Holy Cross Acad., Edinburgh. Mgt trainee in industry, 1959–64; Abbey National Plc, 1964–99: various mgt posts in branch network, 1969–86; Gen. Manager, branches and agencies, 1986–88; Ops Dir, 1988–92; Dir, Plc Bd and Man. Dir, New Business Div., 1992–93; Man. Dir, Retail Bank Div., 1993–96; Dep. Gp CEO, 1996–99, retd. Non-executive Director: NHBC, 1996–2002 (Dep. Chm., 1999–2002); MSB Internat. (Sen. non-exec. Dir), 1999–2002; FCE Bank Plc (Ford), 1999–2007. Trustee, Hospice of St

Francis, Berkhamsted, 2009–16 (Chm., 2010–16). *Recreations:* golf, tennis, travel. *Address:* Trundles, Crossfield Close, Shootersway, Berkhamsted, Herts HP4 3NT. *T:* (01442) 862985. *E:* charles.toner@btinternet.com. *Clubs:* Rotary (Berkhamsted Bulbourne); Berkhamsted Golf.

TONEY, Terence; Head of Business Development, Education and Society, British Council, 2015–18; *b* 23 Aug. 1952; *s* of Norman Toney and Margaret Toney (*née* Taglione); *m* 1977, Young Hae Kim; one *s*. *Educ:* Cardinal Hinsley Grammar Sch.; King's Coll. London (BA Hons German and Philosophy); Inst. of Educn, Univ. of London (PGCE); Univ. of Lancaster (MA). Lectr in English, British Centre, Sweden, 1975–76; English teacher, Dortmund, 1976–78; Lectr in English, Hokkaido Univ., Japan, 1980–82; British Council, 1983–2018: Asst Consultant, English Lang., London, 1983–85; Asst English Lang. Officer, Tokyo, 1985–87; English Lang. Officer, Colombia, 1987–90; Acad. Dir, Cultura Inglesa, São Paulo, 1990–94; Director: Korea, 1994–99; Japan, 1999–2002; Educnl Enterprises, 2002–04; Customer Services, 2004–06; Regl Dir, SE Europe, 2006–09; Hd of Business Transformation, 2009–11; Regl Dir, E Asia, 2011–15. Lay Mem. Council, Univ. of Durham, 2018–. *Recreations:* travelling, reading, foreign languages, walking, swimming, cycling. *Address:* 7 Buttercup Way, Stratford-upon-Avon CV37 7EQ.

TONGA, HM the King of; **King Lavaka Tupou VI;** *b* 12 July 1959; *s* of HM the King of Tonga, King Taufa'ahau Tupou IV and Halaevalu Mata'aho 'Ahome'e; *S* brother, 2012; *m* 1982, Heuifanga Nanasipau'u Vaea; two *s* one *d*. *Educ:* Leys Sch., Cambridge. Tongan Defence Services, 1982–98. Minister of Foreign Affairs and of Defence, 1998–2004; Prime Minister of Tonga, 2000–06; High Comr of Tonga to Australia, 2008–12. Former Chm., Tonga Communications Corp. *Heir:* s HRH Prince 'Ukukalala [*b* 1985; *m* 2012, Hon. Sinaitakala Fakafanua; one *s* one *d*]. *Address:* The Palace, Nuku'alofa, Tonga.

TONGE, family name of **Baroness Tonge**.

TONGE, Baroness *cr* 2005 (Life Peer), of Kew in the London Borough of Richmond upon Thames; **Jennifer Louise Tonge,** FRSPH; *b* 19 Feb. 1941; *d* of late Sidney Smith and Violet Smith (*née* Williams); *m* 1964, Dr Keith Angus Tonge (*d* 2013); two *s* (one *d* decd). *Educ:* Dudley Girls' High Sch.; University Coll. London (MB BS 1964). FRSPH (FRIPHH 1997). GP and family planning doctor, 1964–96; Hd, Women's Services, Ealing HA, 1983–89. Mem. (Lib Dem), Richmond on Thames LBC, 1981–90 (Chm., Social Services, 1983–89). Contested (Lib Dem) Richmond and Barnes, 1992. MP (Lib Dem) Richmond Park, 1997–2005. Lib Dem spokesman on internat. develt, 1997–2003, for children, 2003–04, for health, 2007–10. Hon. FFSRH (Hon. FFFP 2002); Hon. FRCOG 2015. *Address:* House of Lords, SW1A 0PW.

TONGE, Dr Gary James, FREng, FIET; consultant in electronic communications, since 2004; *b* 5 Sept. 1957; *s* of Dennis and Dorothy Tonge; *m* 1978, Fiona Margaret Mackintosh; two *s* two *d*. *Educ:* Univ. of Southampton (BSc 1st Cl. Hons Electronics; PhD Maths 1981). FREng 2001; FIET (FIEE 1993). Independent Broadcasting Authority: jun. engr, rising to Principal Engr, 1980–87; Hd, Engrg Secretariat, 1987–90; Independent Television Commission: Controller of Engrg, 1990–95; Dir, Engrg, 1995–2000; Dir, Technology, 2000–03. FRTS 1995. *Publications:* contrib. to IEEE Trans, RTS Jl, SMPTE Jl, Physics Rev. *Recreations:* Christian work, humanitarian projects. *E:* garytonge@yahoo.co.uk.

TONGE, Very Rev. Lister; Dean of Newport (formerly of Monmouth), since 2012; *b* Oldham, 23 Dec. 1951; *s* of Edward Tonge and Dorothy Tonge (*née* Clough). *Educ:* Heywood Grammar Sch.; Salford Grammar Sch.; King's Coll. London (AKC 1974); St Augustine's Coll., Canterbury; Loyola Univ., Chicago (Master of Pastoral Studies 1995). Ordained deacon, 1975, priest, 1976; Curate, Liverpool Parish Church, 1975–78; Precentor, Johannesburg Cathedral, SA, 1978–79; Community of the Resurrection, Mirfield, 1979–91; Chaplain: Community of St John Baptist, Windsor, then Oxford, 1996–; Ripon Coll., Cuddesdon, 2005–09. *Address:* The Deanery, 105 Stow Hill, Newport NP20 4ED. *T:* (01633) 259627. *E:* listertonge@gmail.com.

TONGE, Simon David; HM Diplomatic Service; High Commissioner to Papua New Guinea, 2014–18; *b* Oldham, Lancs, 18 Sept. 1969; *s* of Kenneth Tonge and Andrea Tonge (*née* Latchford); *m* 2012, Hera Lutsenko. *Educ:* Oldham Hulme Grammar Sch. for Boys; Lancaster Univ. (BSc Hons Mktg); Sheffield Univ. (MBA); Open Univ. (MA Envmt, Policy and Society; BSc Hons Geoscis). Entered FCO, 1996; Res. Analyst for SE Asia, FCO, 1996–97; Cttee Support Officer, UKMIS to UN, NY, 1997–98; Second Sec. (Political), Jakarta, 1998–2002; Regl Security Policy Advr, S Asia Gp, FCO, 2002–04; Hd of Section, Press Office, FCO, 2004; Hd, Governor's Office, Cayman Is, 2004–08; Dep. Hd of Mission, Baku, 2008–11; French lang. trng, 2012; Hd of Mission, Abidjan, 2012–14. Comdr, Nat. Order (Côte d'Ivoire), 2014. *Recreations:* hiking, photography, kitesurfing. *Address:* Foreign and Commonwealth Office, King Charles Street, SW1A 2AH. *E:* simondtonge@gmail.com.

TONGUE, Carole; adviser and lecturer on the media, broadcasting, culture and European affairs, since 1999; artistic producer; Founder and Chair, UK Coalition for Cultural Diversity, since 2005; Chair, European Coalitions for Cultural Diversity, since 2014; *b* 14 Oct. 1955; *d* of Muriel Esther Lambert and Walter Archer Tongue; *m* 1990, Chris Pond, *qv* (marr. diss. 1999); one *d*. *Educ:* Brentwood County High School; Loughborough University of Technology (BA Govt (Hons) and French). Asst Editor, Laboratory Practice, 1977–78; courier/guide in France with Sunsites Ltd, 1978–79; Robert Schuman scholarship for research in social affairs with European Parlt, Dec. 1979–March 1980; sec./admin. asst, Socialist Group of European Parlt, 1980–84. Consultant, Citigate Public Affairs, 2001–03; Associate Dir, Sovereign Strategy, 2003–10; Partner, CSPH Internat., 2010–. Advr, EUTOP, 2012–. MEP (Lab) London E, 1984–99; contested (Lab) London Reg., 1999. Dep. Leader, Eur. PLP, 1989–91. Bd Mem., Westminster Foundn for Democracy, 1990–93. Sen. Vis. Lectr, Dept European Studies, Loughborough Univ., 1995; Vis. Prof., Media Sch., Univ. of the Arts, London (formerly London Inst.), 2001; Vis. Lectr, City Univ., London, 2008. Hon. Vice Pres., Professional Land Reform Gp, 2005–. Member: Adv. Bd, Eur. Media Forum, 1996–99; Bd, London Film and Video Develt Agency, 1999–2003; Chair, UK Ind. Film Parlt, 2003–. Mem., Professional Conduct Cttee, 2001–06, Mem., Investigation and Registration Cttee, 2010–, GMC. Pres., Cities and Cinemas Europe, 1997–2000. Trustee and Vice Chair, Couper Art Collection, 2010–; Co-producer, The Fleeting Opera, 2000. Patron: Federal Trust, 1997–; Arts for All, 2011–; Pres., Arts à Parts, 2013–. Member: Fabian Soc.; BECTU; BAFTA. Trustee, CSV, 1995–. FRSA 2000. Hon. Dr Lincoln, 2005. *Publications:* chapters in books on European media; EP reports; articles on culture, film, citizenship, European affairs. *Recreations:* piano, cello, painting, horse riding, cinema, theatre, opera. *Address:* 1210 Whitehouse Apartments, 9 Belvedere Road, SE1 8YW. *E:* tonguec@btinternet.com.

TONKIN, Boyd Miles; Senior Writer, The Independent, 2013–16 (Literary Editor, 1996–2013); *b* 7 April 1955; *s* of Douglas George Marcus Tonkin and Joan Yvonne Tonkin (*née* Collis). *Educ:* Haberdashers' Aske's Sch., Elstree; Trinity Coll., Cambridge (MA English). Res. Student and pt-time Tutor, Univ. of Cambridge, 1978–81; Adult Educn Lectr, City Univ., 1981–83; Lecturer in English: Manchester Poly., 1983–84; West Sussex Inst., 1984–85; Staff Writer and Features Editor, Community Care mag., 1986–89; Social Affairs Editor, 1989–91, Literary Editor, 1991–96, New Statesman. Broadcaster, BBC Radio arts progs, 1995–. Judge: Whitbread Biography award, 1997; Booker Prize, 1999; Foreign Fiction Award, Independent, 2000–15 (also Convenor); David Cohen Prize for Literature, 2007; Chm. Judges, Man Booker Internat. Prize, 2016. *Publications:* (contrib.) Oxford Readers' Guide to Fiction, 2000; The 100 Best Novels in Translation, 2018; contribs to lit. guides and ref. works; essays in lit. jls in UK, US, France and Germany; articles in jls. *Recreations:* music, cinema, cricket, walking. *Address:* 104 Islington High Street, N1 8EG. *T:* (020) 7005 2656.

TONKIN, Derek, CMG 1982; HM Diplomatic Service, retired; *b* 30 Dec. 1929; *s* of Henry James Tonkin and Norah Wearing; *m* 1953, Doreen Rooke; one *s* two *d* (and one *s* decd). *Educ:* High Pavement Grammar Sch., Nottingham; St Catherine's Society, Oxford (MA). HM Forces, 1948–49; FO, 1952; Warsaw, 1955; Bangkok, 1957; Phnom Penh, 1961; FO, 1963; Warsaw, 1966; Wellington, 1968; FCO, 1972; East Berlin, 1976; Ambassador to Vietnam, 1980–82; Minister, Pretoria, 1983–86; Ambassador to Thailand, and concurrently to Laos, 1986–89. Chairman: Beta Viet Nam Fund Ltd, 1993–99; Beta Mekong Fund Ltd, 1994–2000; Network Myanmar, 2007–14. Director: Palais Angkor SA, 1998–2006; Euro-Thai Investments Ltd, 1999–2007. Chairman: Adv. Bd, Centre for SE Asia Studies, SOAS, 1990–93; Thai-British Business Assoc., 1991–93; Vietnam-Britain Business Assoc., 1993–94. Dir, Ockenden Internat. Bd of Trustees, 1999–2003. *Recreations:* tennis, music, linguistics. *Address:* Heathfields, Berry Lane, Worplesdon, Guildford, Surrey GU3 3PU. *Club:* Royal Over-Seas League.

TONKING, His Honour (Russel) Simon (William Ferguson); DL; a Circuit Judge, 1997–2015; *b* 25 March 1952; *s* of John Wilson Tonking and Mary Oldham Tonking (*née* Ferguson); *m* 1976, (Sylvia) Mithra McIntyre; one *s* one *d*. *Educ:* King's Sch., Canterbury; Emmanuel Coll., Cambridge (MA). Called to the Bar, Inner Temple, 1975, Bencher, 2011; barrister, Midland and Oxford Circuit, 1976–97; Asst Recorder, 1991–94; Recorder, 1994–97; Resident Judge at Stafford, 2006–15; Hon. Recorder of Stafford, 2008–15. Mem., Criminal Cttee, 2005–08, Jt Course Dir, 2008–13, Judicial Coll. (formerly Judicial Studies Bd). Lichfield Cathedral: Steward, 1978– (Head Steward, 1985–87, Pres. of Stewards, 2003–04); Mem., 2000–17, Chm., 2009–17, Cathedral Council (Mem. Transitional Council, 1998–2000); Dep. Chancellor, Diocese of Southwell, 1997–2005. DUniv Staffs, 2009. DL Staffs, 2006. *Publications:* (jtly) Crown Court Compendium, 2016. *Recreations:* many! *Address:* c/o Stafford Combined Court Centre, Victoria Square, Stafford ST16 2QQ. *T:* (01785) 610730. *Clubs:* TR Register; Outer Hebrides Tennis.

TONKINSON, Carole Willis, (Mrs B. F. Langford); Founding Publisher, Bluebird, Pan Macmillan, since 2014; *b* Philadelphia, Penn, 24 Dec. 1964; *d* of John Joseph Tonkinson and Christine Stewart Tonkinson; *m* 1993, Dr Barry Francis Langford; one *s*. *Educ:* Agnes Irwin Sch.; Univ. of Pennsylvania (BA *cum laude* 1986); Columbia Univ.; Inst. of Psychosynthesis, Middlesex Univ. (Dip. Counselling 2017). Editl Asst, William Morrow, 1986–87; Associate Ed., Art and Dance, Food and Wine, Elle mag., NYC, 1988–2000; Man. Ed., 1992–94, Editl Dir, 1994–95, Tricycle Books; Publisher, Harper Collins Nonfiction, overseeing HarperSport, HarperEntertainment, Thorsons, Element, HarperTrue and gen. commercial list, 1996–2014 (Mem. Bd, 2012–14). *Publications:* Big Sky Mind, 1996; Wake Up and Cook, 1997. *Recreations:* meditation (co-founder Zen Meditation Richmond, a weekly meditation group), yoga, cooking, theatre, reading, travel. *Address:* Bluebird, Pan Macmillan, 6 Briset Street, EC1M 5NR. *T:* 07799 067879, (020) 8948 5852. *E:* carolewillistonkinson@gmail.com.

TONRY, Prof. Michael; McKnight Presidential Chair in Law and Public Policy, since 2010, and Director, Institute on Crime and Public Policy, since 2005, University of Minnesota (Sonosky Professor of Law and Public Policy, 1990–2006; Bennett University Chair of Excellence, 2006–10); Senior Fellow, Netherlands Institute for the Study of Crime and Law Enforcement, Leiden, since 2003; *b* 9 June 1945; *s* of J. Richard Tonry and Frances Zimmerman Tonry (*née* Keedy); *m* 1st, 1966, Penelope Tyson (*d* 2010); two *s* two *d*; 2nd, 2012, Rossella Selmini. *Educ:* Univ. of N Carolina (AB Hist. 1966); Yale Univ. (LLB). Admitted to legal practice: Illinois, 1970; Pennsylvania, 1975; Maine, 1982. Lecturer in Law: Univ. of Chicago, 1971–73; Univ. of Birmingham, 1973–74; Dechert Price & Rhodes, Esqs, 1974–76; Prof. of Law, Univ. of Md, 1976–83; Pres., Castine Res. Corp., 1983–; Prof. of Law and Public Policy, and Dir, Inst. of Criminology, Univ. of Cambridge, 1999–2004. Vis. Prof. (Prof. avec indemnité), Univ. of Lausanne, 2001–. President: Amer. Soc. of Criminology, 2005–08; Eur. Soc. of Criminology, 2012–15. Scientific Mem., Max-Planck Soc., 2012–. Ed. and Publisher, The Castine Patriot, 1987–90. PhD *hc* Free Univ. Amsterdam, 2010. *Publications:* Sentencing Reform Impacts, 1987; Malign Neglect: race, crime and punishment in America, 1994; Sentencing Matters, 1996; Confronting Crime, 2003; Punishment and Politics: evidence and emulation in the making of English crime control policy, 2004; Thinking About Crime: sense and sensibility in American Penal Policy, 2004; Thinking About Punishment, 2009; Punishing Race, 2011; Why Punish? How Much?, 2011; Prosecutors and Politics in Comparative Perspective, 2013; Sentencing Fragments: penal reform in America, 1975–2025, 2016; *jointly:* Hypnotically Refreshed Testimony, 1985; Human Development and Criminal Behavior, 1991; *edited:* Ethnicity, Crime and Immigration, 1997; Intermediate Sanctions in Sentencing Guidelines, 1997; Handbook of Crime and Punishment, 1998; Penal Reform in Overcrowded Times, 2001; Crime, Punishment and Politics, 2007; The Oxford Handbook of Crime and Public Policy, 2009; The Oxford Handbook of Crime and Criminal Justice, 2011; Recidivism Has a Past—Has It A Future?, 2011; Politics and Prosecutors in Comparative Perspective, 2012; Sentencing Policies and Practices in Western Countries: comparative and cross-national perspectives, 2016; American Sentencing, 2019; Of One-Eyed and Toothless Miscreants, 2019; *edited jointly:* Reform and Punishment: essays on criminal sentencing, 1983; Communities and Crime, 1986; The Sentencing Commission: guidelines for criminal sanctions, 1987; Prediction and Classification, 1987; Managing Appeals in Federal Courts, 1988; Family Violence, 1990; Between Prison and Probation, 1990; Drugs and Crime, 1990; Modern Policing, 1992; Beyond the Law: crime in complex organisations, 1993; Intermediate Sanctions in Overcrowded Times, 1995; Building a Safer Society, 1995; Sentencing Reform in Overcrowded Times, 1997; Youth Violence, 1998; Prisons, 1999; Sentencing and Sanctions in Western Countries, 2001; Ideology, Crime and Criminal Justice, 2002; Reform and Punishment, 2002; Cross-national Studies in Crime and Justice, 2003; Youth Crime and Youth Justice, 2004; Crime and Justice in the Netherlands, 2007; Crime and Justice in Scandinavia, 2011; Crime and Justice in America, 1975–2025, 2013; Why Crime Rates Fall and Why They Don't, 2014; Oxford Handbook of Ethnicity, Crime and Immigration, 2014; Reinventing American Criminal Justice, 2017. *Address:* University of Minnesota, Law School, 312 Mondale Hall, 229–19th Avenue South, Minneapolis, MN 55455, USA.

TOOBY, Michael Bowen; curator, writer and researcher; *b* 20 Dec. 1956; *s* of Leslie and late Jill Tooby; *m* 1980, Jane Pare; one *s* one *d*. *Educ:* King Henry VIII Sch., Coventry; Magdalene Coll., Cambridge. Asst Curator, Kettle's Yard, Cambridge, 1978–80; Exhibns Orgnr, Third Eye Centre, Glasgow, 1980–84; Keeper, Mappin Art Gall., Sheffield, 1984–92; Founding Curator, Tate Gall. St Ives, and Curator, Barbara Hepworth Mus. and Sculpture Gdn, 1992–99; Dir, Nat. Mus. of Gall., Cardiff, 2000–04; Dir, Learning, Progs and Develt, Nat. Museums Wales, 2004–11. Chm., engage, (nat. assoc. for visual arts educn), 1999–2004. Vis. Prof. in Contemp. Curatorial Practice, Univ. of S Wales (formerly Univ. of Glamorgan), 2007–; Res. Prof., Bath Sch. of Art and Design, Bath Spa Univ., 2012– (Dean, Sch. of Art and Design, 2012–13); Sen. Res. Fellow, Henry Moore Inst., Leeds, 2014–15; Internat. Vis. Scholar, ANU Canberra, 2019. Academic Advr, Acad. of Visual Arts, Hong Kong Baptist Univ., 2016–19. Macready Lectr in Canadian Art, Art Gall. of Ontario, 1997; Ursula Hoff Lectr in Curating, Univ. of Melbourne, 2019. Trustee, Artes Mundi Internat. Art Prize, 2014–. Guest Curator, Journeys with 'The Waste Land', Turner Contemp., Margate, 2014–18. *Publications:* The True North: Canadian painting 1896–1939, 1988; monograph studies of: Lois Williams, 1996; Iwan Bala, 1999; David Nash, 2000; Trevor Bell, 2003; (contrib.) Kurt Jackson, 2010; Julian Stair, 2014. *Address:* c/o Bath School of Art and Design, Sion Hill, Bath BA1 5SF. *E:* mike.tooby@gmail.com.

**TOOKE, Sir John (Edward),** Kt 2007; DM, DSc; FRCP, FRCPI, FRCGP, FMedSci; Executive Chairman, Academic Health Solutions Ltd, since 2015; Professor of Medicine, since 2010, Vice-Provost (Health), 2010–15, and Head, School of Life and Medical Sciences and Head, Medical School, 2010–14, University College London; President, Academy of Medical Sciences, 2011–15; *b* 4 March 1949; *s* of Thomas Edward Tooke and Edna (*née* Wilgose); *m* 1972, Elizabeth Moore; one *s* one *d*. *Educ:* St John's Coll., Oxford (MA 1970; MSc 1972; BM BCh 1974; DM 1982; DSc 1998); King's Coll. Hosp. Med. Sch. FRCP 1993. Lectr in Medicine, Leeds Univ., 1979–82; BHF Res. Fellow, Karolinska Inst. Dept of Medicine, Sweden, 1982–83; Wellcome Trust Sen. Lectr in Medicine and Physiol., Charing Cross and Westminster Med. Sch., 1984–87; Sen. Lectr, 1987–92, Prof. of Vascular Medicine, 1992–2009, Univ. of Exeter; Inaugural Dean, Peninsula Med. Sch., 2000–09, Exec. Dean, Peninsula Coll. of Medicine and Dentistry, Univs of Exeter and Plymouth. Chm., Med. Schs Council (formerly Council of Hds of Med. Schs), 2006; former Chm., UK Healthcare Educn Adv. Cttee. Hon. Consultant Physician in diabetes and vascular medicine, Royal Devon and Exeter Healthcare NHS Trust, 1987–2009. Chm., Ind. Inquiry into Modernising Med. Careers, 2007–08. Chair, Centre for Advancement of Sustainable Med. Innovation, Univ. of Oxford and UCL, 2018– (Co-Chair, 2014–18). Hon. FMedSci 2000; Hon. FAcadMed. Camillo Golgi Award, Eur. Assoc. for Study of Diabetes, 1994. *Publications:* (ed with G. D. Lowe) A Textbook of Vascular Medicine, 1996; (ed) Diabetic Angiopathy, 1999. *Recreations:* angling, golf, sailing, le bricolage. *Address:* University College London, Gower Street, WC1E 6BT.

**TOOKEY, Richard William,** CBE 1984; Director and Group Public Affairs Co-ordinator, Shell International Petroleum Co. Ltd, 1984–93; *b* 11 July 1934; *s* of Geoffrey William Tookey, QC and Rosemary Sherwell Tookey (*née* Clogg); *m* 1st, 1956, Jill (*née* Ransford) (marr. diss. 1990); one *s* one *d* (and one *s* decd); 2nd, 1994, Colleen (*née* Channon) (*d* 2002); 3rd, 2006, Zoë (*née* Lambiris). *Educ:* Charterhouse. National Service, 2nd Lieut, 1st King's Dragoon Guards, 1952–54; Lanarkshire Yeomanry (TA), 1954–56; Inns of Court Regt/Inns of Court and City Yeomanry (TA), 1957–64. Joined Royal Dutch/Shell Group, 1954; posts in internat. oil supply and trading, 1954–73; Head of Supply Operations, 1973–75; Vice-Pres., Shell Internat. Trading Co., 1975–77; Man. Dir, Shell Tankers (UK) Ltd, 1978–79, Chm., 1980–84; Man. Dir, Shell Internat. Marine Ltd, 1980–84; Marine Co-ordinator, Shell Internat. Petroleum Co. Ltd, 1980–84. Part-time Mem., BRB, 1985–90; Mem., Gen. Cttee, Lloyd's Register of Shipping, 1978–85; Pres., Gen. Council of British Shipping, 1983–84. Liveryman, Shipwrights' Co., 1983–2018, Mem. Ct of Assts, 1987–96. *Recreation:* home. *Address:* 38 Mill Park Road, Mill Park, Port Elizabeth, 6001, South Africa. *T:* (41) 3745025. *E:* rwtookey@iafrica.com.

**TOOLEY, Prof. James Nicholas,** PhD; Professor of Educational Entrepreneurship and Policy, University of Buckingham, since 2019; *b* 21 July 1959; *s* of Arthur Henry Tooley and Barbara May Tooley (*née* Tubby); *m* 2018, Ekta Umedsinh Sodha. *Educ:* Kingsfield Sch., Bristol; Univ. of Sussex (BSc 1983; MSc 1986); PhD London 1994. Mathematics Teacher, Zimbabwe, 1983–86; Sen. Res. Officer, NFER, 1988–91; Res. Fellow, Univ. of Oxford, 1994–95; Sen. Res. Fellow, Univ. of Manchester, 1995–98; Prof. of Educn Policy, Univ. of Newcastle upon Tyne, 1998–2019 (on leave of absence as: Pres., Educn Fund, Orient Global, 2007–09; as Global Hd, Low Cost Schs, GEMS Educn, 2015–16; as Consultant, SABIS Educn, Lebanon and Dir, Cadmus Acads, Honduras, 2016–17). Member, Academic Advisory Council: IEA, 2005– (Dir, Educn Prog., 1995–2002); Centre for Market Reform of Educn, 2015–. Chairman: Omega Schs Franchise Ltd, Ghana, 2008–; Empathy Learning Systems Pvt Ltd, India, 2009–. Trustee, Omega Schs Foundn, Ghana, 2009–; Patron: Wilderspin Nat. Sch., 2010–; Assoc. of Formidable Educnl Develt, Nigeria, 2011–; Ind. Private Schs Assoc., Sierra Leone, 2014–; Chief Mentor, Nat. Ind. Schs Alliance, 2014–. Chm., Govg Body, Ind. Grammar Sch.: Durham. Adjunct Scholar, Cato Inst., 2009–; Visitor, Ralston Coll., 2013–; Vis. Prof., Beijing Normal Univ., 2013–; Res. Fellow, Independent Inst., USA, 2014–. *Publications:* Disestablishing the School, 1995; Education without the State, 1996; Educational Research: a critique, 1998; The Global Education Industry, 1999; The Seven Habits of Highly Effective Schools, 1999; Reclaiming Education, 2000; The Miseducation of Women, 2001; The Enterprise of Education, 2001; (ed) Buckingham at 25, 2002; (jtly) HIV and AIDS in Schools, 2002; (jtly) Private Schools for the Poor: a case study from India, 2003; (jtly) Delivering Better Education, 2003; (jtly) Government Failure: E. G. West on education, 2004; Could the Globalisation of Education Benefit the Poor?, 2004; (jtly) What Americans Can Learn from School Choice in Other Countries, 2005; (jtly) Private Education is Good for the Poor: a study of private schools serving the poor in low-income countries, 2005; E. G. West: economic liberalism and the role of government in education, 2008; The Beautiful Tree: a personal journey into how the world's poorest people are educating themselves, 2009; (jtly) Educational Equality: key debates in education policy, 2010; (jtly) The Private Schools Revolution in Bihar, 2012; From Village School to Global Brand: changing the world through education, 2012; Gandhi, RTE and the Denial of the Right to Education, 2014; (jtly) The Role and Impact of Private Education in Developing Countries: a response to the DFID-commissioned "rigorous literature review", 2015; Imprisoned in India: corruption and extortion in the world's largest democracy, 2016; (jtly) Education, War and Peace, 2017; Comeuppance: my experiences in an Indian prison, 2017. *Recreation:* walking in the foothills of Simonside. *Address:* University of Buckingham, Hunter Street, Buckingham MK18 1EG. *T:* (01280) 820210. *E:* james.tooley@buckingham.ac.uk. *Club:* Athenæum.

*See also* M. A. Tooley.

**TOOLEY, Sir John,** Kt 1979; arts consultant, since 1988; General Director, Royal Opera House, Covent Garden, 1980–88; *b* 1 June 1924; *yr s* of late H. R. Tooley; *m* 1st, 1951, Judith Craig Morris (marr. diss. 1965); three *d*; 2nd, 1968, Patricia Janet Norah Bagshawe (marr. diss. 1990), 2nd *d* of late G. W. S. Bagshawe; one *s*; 3rd, 1995, Jennifer-Anne (marr. diss. 2003). *Educ:* Repton; Magdalene Coll., Cambridge (Hon. Fellow, 2005). Served The Rifle Brigade, 1943–47. Sec., Guildhall School of Music and Drama, 1952–55; Royal Opera House, Covent Garden: Asst to Gen. Administrator, 1955–60; Asst Gen. Administrator, 1960–70; Gen. Administrator, 1970–80. Chairman: Nat. Music Council Executive, 1970–72; HEFCE Music Conservatories Adv. Gp, 1993–97. Director: Britten Estate Ltd, 1989–97; South Bank Bd, 1991–97 (Chm.); Compton Verney Opera Project, 1991–97; WNO, 1992–2000; David Gyngell & Co. Ltd, 1995–97; Almeida Th., 1997–2002 (Chm.), 1990–97); LPO, 1998–2010 (Mem., Adv. Council, 2014–); Chm., Monument Insurance Brokers Ltd, 1997–2002; Consultant: Internat. Management Gp, 1988–97; Ballet Opera House, Toronto, 1989–90; Trustee: Wigmore Hall, 1987–2001; SPNM; Australian Music Foundn, 1986–2014; Walton Trust, 1988–2000; Britten Pears Foundn, 1989–99; Dartington Summer Sch., 1989–2000; Purcell Tercentenary Trust, 1991–97; Performing Arts Labs, 1993–97; Sidney Nolan Trust, 1996– (Chm., 2005–14; Pres., 2014–). Pres., Salisbury Festival, 1988–2005; Chairman: Salisbury Cathedral Fabric Cttee, 1990–2005; Salisbury Cathedral Girl Choristers' Trust, 1995–2005; Chm., Rudolf Nureyev Foundn, 1995–2008. Gen. Advr, Istanbul Foundn for Culture and Arts, 1993–2008; Advr, Borusan Chamber Orch., Istanbul, 2005–08. Governor, Repton Sch., 1984–94. FGS. Hon. FRAM; Hon. RNCM. DUniv UCE, 1996. Queen Elizabeth II Coronation Award, RAD, 2005. Commendatore, Italian Republic, 1976. *Publications:* In House, 1999. *Recreations:* walking, theatre. *Address:* 18 Grange Court, Pinehurst, Grange Road, Cambridge CB3 9BD. *T:* (01223) 358737. *E:* tooley@btinternet.com.

**TOOLEY, Prof. Mark Arthur,** PhD; FRCP; FREng; Head, Medical Physics and Bioengineering, Director, Research and Development, and Consultant Clinical Scientist, Royal United Hospitals Bath NHS Foundation Trust, 2004–17, now Honorary Consultant Clinical Scientist; Specialist Scientific Advisor to Medical Directorate (part-time), NHS England and NHS Improvement, since 2019; *b* Bristol, 23 Dec. 1956; *s* of Arthur Henry Tooley and Barbara May Tooley (*née* Tubby); *m* 1992, Stella Mead; one *s* one *d*. *Educ:* Kingsfield Sch., Bristol; Univ. of Bath (BSc Elec. Engrg 1979); St Bartholomew's Hosp. Med. Coll., Univ. of London (MSc Med. Physics 1983; PhD Med. Physics 1990). CEng 1986; FIPEM 1996; FIET 1997; CSci 2006; FREng 2015. Asst Electronic Engr, Westinghouse Brake and Signal Co. Ltd, 1979–80; Med. Physicist, Royal United Hospital, Bath, 1980–84; Sen. Med. Physicist, St Bartholomew's Hosp., London, 1984–90; Principal Med. Physicist, Bristol Royal Inf., 1990–96; Consultant Sen. Lectr, Univ. of Bristol and Bristol Royal Inf., 1996–2004. Scientific Dir, Bristol Med. Simulation Centre, 1998–2009. Visiting Professor: UWE, 2009–; Univ. of Bath, 2014–18 (Hon. Prof., 2018). Member: EPSRC Peer Rev. Coll., 2000–; EPSRC Healthcare Technol. Strategy Adv. Team, 2013–16; Royal Soc. Univ. Fellowship Appt Panel, 2013–16. External Examiner: Med. Engrg, Cardiff Univ., 2004–06; Med. Phys and Bioengrg, UCL, 2015–. Director: Bristol Ensemble Ltd (formerly Emerald Ensemble Ltd), 1998–; Pentamed Ltd, 1998–2009; Inst. of Phys and Engrg in Medicine, 1997–2001, 2011–14 (Pres., 2017–); Assoc. of Clinical Scientists, 2000–03; Dir/Trustee, Designability (formerly Bath Inst. of Med. Engrg), 2002–. President Prize, SW Soc. of Anaesthetists, 2001; Essay Prize, RCP and Inst. of Phys and Engrg in Medicine, 2004; Dudley Buxton Medal, Royal Coll. of Anaesthetists, 2011; Lifetime Achievement Award, NHS Healthcare Science Awards, 2019. Member, Editorial Board: Physiological Measurement, 1999–2006; Jl of Med. Engrg and Technol., 2007–. *Publications:* (with Patrick Magee) The Physics, Clinical Measurement and Equipment of Anaesthetic Practice, 2005, 2nd edn 2011; articles in jls incl. BJA, Pacing and Electrophysiology. *Recreations:* marathon running, classical piano playing, camping, allotments. *E:* m.a.tooley@bath.ac.uk.

*See also* J. N. Tooley.

**TOOLEY, Dr Peter John Hocart;** consultant in pharmacovigilance, since 2017; General Practitioner, Twyford, Berks, 1966–90; pharmaceutical physician, since 1990; Director, PT Pharma Consultancy Ltd, Guernsey, 1998–2017; *b* St Helens, Lancs, 28 Feb. 1939; *s* of Dr Patrick Hocart Tooley and Margaret Brenda Tooley (*née* Williams); *m* 1st, 1966, Elizabeth Monica Roche (marr. diss. 1983); one *s* two *d*; 2nd, 1987, Diana Edith (*née* Sturdy); two step *d*. *Educ:* Elizabeth Coll., Guernsey; St George's Sch., Harpenden; London Hospital Med. Coll., Univ. of London (MB BS 1964; DObstRCOG 1965; DMJ (Clin.) 1981; DFFP 1993); Univ. of Wales Coll., Cardiff (LLM 1994). MRCS 1963; LRCP 1963; MRCGP 1971; MFPM (Dist.) 2012. HO Surgery, Connaught Hosp., London, 1963; HO Medicine, 1963–64, Resident Accoucheur, 1964, London Hosp.; SHO Gen. Surgery, Royal Sussex County Hosp., 1965; Jun. Registrar, Dept of Obstetrics and Gynaecol., London Hosp., 1966; Asst Dep. Coroner, Reading, 1984–89; Sen. Med. Advr and Med. Dir (Ireland), Janssen Pharmaceuticals, 1990–98. Consultant Med. Advr, Daiichi Sankyo (formerly Sankyo Pharma, 1998–2017). Member: Berks Local Med. Cttee, 1975–85; Berks Family Practitioner Cttee, 1975–85. FRSocMed 1990. Member: BMA, 1965–; Reading Pathol. Soc., 1967–; British Acad. of Forensic Sci., 1981–; Medico-legal Soc., 1982–2015; British Assoc. of Pharmaceutical Physicians, 1990–; Bolam Soc., 1996–. Freeman, City of London; Mem., Apothecaries' Soc., 1965 (Livery Cttee, 1994–2005; Sen. Warden, 2012; Master, 2013–14). Hon. Medical Officer: Oxfordshire RFU, 1970–97; Henley Rugby Club, 1970–97; Wasps RFC, 1993–98. Member: Vale Douzaine, Guernsey, 2005–17; Vale Commons, Guernsey, 2007–17. *Recreations:* Rugby, gardening, boating, family history, Guernsey history. *Address:* 4 Willow Way, Prior's Grange, Saxmundham, Suffolk IP17 1FR. *T:* (01728) 561702, 07738 409815. *E:* peter@pjtpharma.co.uk. *Club:* Guernsey Rugby Football.

**TOOPE, Prof. Stephen John,** OC 2015; PhD; Vice-Chancellor, University of Cambridge, since 2017; *b* Montreal, Canada, 14 Feb. 1958; *s* of Frank and Jocelyn Toope; *m* 1989, Paula Rosen; one *s* two *d*. *Educ:* Harvard Univ. (AB 1979); McGill Univ. (BCL/LLB 1983); Trinity Coll., Cambridge (PhD 1987; Hon. Fellow, 2016). Law Clerk to Chief Justice of Canada, 1986–87; McGill University: Asst Prof. of Law, 1987–93; Associate Prof. of Law, 1993–99; Dean, Faculty of Law, 1994–99; Prof. of Law, 1999–2006; Pres. and Vice-Chancellor, Univ. of BC, 2006–14; Dir, Munk Sch. of Global Affairs, Univ. of Toronto, 2015–17. Pres., Pierre Elliott Trudeau Foundn, 2002–06. Hon. Bencher, Middle Temple, 2017. *Publications:* Mixed International Arbitration, 1990; Legitimacy and Legality in International Law: an interactional account, 2010; contrib. articles to jls of internat. law and internat. relns. *Recreations:* classical music, theatre, literature. *Address:* Office of the Vice-Chancellor, University of Cambridge, The Old Schools, Trinity Lane, Cambridge CB2 1TN. *E:* stephen.toope@admin.cam.ac.uk.

**TOOTH, Sir (Hugh) John L.;** *see* Lucas-Tooth.

**TOOZE, Dr John,** FRS 1994; Vice President, Scientific and Facility Operations, Rockefeller University, 2005–13; *b* 16 May 1938; *s* of Reginald John Tooze and Doris Edith Tooze (*née* Bull); *m* 1st, 1962, Sarah Margaret Wynn (marr. diss.); two *s* one *d*; 2nd, 1983, Sharon Ann Queally; one *s* one *d*. *Educ:* Handsworth Grammar Sch., Birmingham; Jesus Coll., Cambridge (BA 1961); King's Coll. London (PhD 1965). Harvard Univ. Served Army, 1956–58. King's College London: Asst Lectr in Biophysics, 1961–65; Lectr, 1965–68; Wellcome Res. Fellow, Harvard Univ., 1965–67; Dep. Editor, Nature, 1968–70; Res. Administrator, ICRF, 1970–73; Exec. Sec., EMBO, Heidelberg, 1973–94; Associate Dir, EMBL, 1993–94; Dir, Support Services, ICRF, subseq. Res. Services, CRUK, 1994–2005. Editor: Trends in Biochemistry, 1979–85; EMBO Jl, 1982–2003. Trustee, Darwin Trust of Edinburgh, 1991–. EMBO Medal, 1986. *Publications:* Molecular Biology of Tumor Viruses, 1973; DNA Tumor Viruses, 1980; (with J. D. Watson) The DNA Story, 1982; (with C. I. Branden) Introduction to Protein Structure, 1991, 2nd edn 1999. *Recreations:* numismatics, English history, gardening. *Club:* Athenæum.

**TOPE,** family name of **Baron Tope.**

**TOPE,** Baron *cr* 1994 (Life Peer), of Sutton in the London Borough of Sutton; **Graham Norman Tope**, CBE 1991; Member (Lib Dem) London Assembly, 2000–08; *b* 30 Nov. 1943; *s* of late Leslie Tope, Plymouth and Winifred Tope (*née* Merrick), Bermuda; *m* 1972, Margaret East; two *s*. *Educ:* Whitgift Sch., S Croydon. Company Sec., 1965–72; Insce Manager, 1970–72; Dep. Gen. Sec., Voluntary Action Camden, 1975–90. Pres., Nat. League of Young Liberals, 1973–75 (Vice-Chm., 1971–73); Mem., Liberal Party Nat. Council, 1970–76; Exec. Cttee, London Liberal Party, 1981–84. Sutton Council: Councillor 1974–2014; Leader, Lib Dem (formerly Soc & Lib Dem) Group, 1974–99 (Liberal Gp, 1974–83, Liberal/SDP Alliance Gp, 1983–88); Leader of Opposition, 1984–86; Leader of Council, 1986–99; spokesperson on libraries, heritage, economic develt and community safety, arts and culture, 1999–2006, on community safety and cultural services, 2006–12; Vice Chm., Envmt and Neighbourhoods Cttee, 2012–14; Chm., Nonsuch Park Jt Mgt Cttee, 2012–13. Greater London Authority: Member: Metropolitan Police Authy, 2000–08; Mayor's Adv. Cabinet, 2000–04; Chm., Finance Cttee, 2000–08; Leader, Lib Dem Gp, 2000–06. MP (L) Sutton and Cheam, 1972–Feb. 1974; Liberal Party spokesman on environment, Dec. 1972–1974; contested (L) Sutton and Cheam, Oct. 1974. Lib Dem spokesman, H of L, on educn, 1994–2000, on communities and local govt, 2008–15; Mem., Select Cttee on Public Services and Demographic Change, 2012–13; Co-Chair, Lib Dem Communities and Local Govt Parly Cttee, 2010–15; Vice-Chm., All Party Parly Gp on Libraries, 1998–2014 (Chm., 2013–). President: London Lib Dems, 1991–2000; Sutton Bor. Lib Dems, 2015–; Lib Dem European and Internat. spokesperson, 1997–2014, Vice Pres., 2013–, Local Govt Assoc. Mem., Policy Cttee, AMA, 1989–97; Chm., Policy and Finance Cttee, London Boroughs Assoc., 1994–95. EU Committee of the Regions: UK Rep., 1994–2014; Mem. Bureau, 1996–2014; Vice Chm., UK Delegn, 1996–2014; Pres., European Lib Dem Reform Gp, 1998–2002; Chm., Constitutional Affairs Cttee, 2002–04 (First Vice Chm., 2004–06); Mem. Council of Europe, CLRAE, 1996–2004. Vice Chm., 1997–2000, Mem. Leaders' Cttee, 1995–2000, Assoc. of London Govt. Chm., Local Govt Gp for Europe, 2005–17. Pres., Save the Children, Sutton, 2009–; Patron, Arts Network Sutton, 2014–; Chair of Trustees: Whitgiftian Assoc., 2017– (Pres., 2016); Cityread London, 2017–. Freeman: City of London, 1998; London Bor. of Sutton, 2014; Liveryman, Needlemakers' Co., 1999–. *Publications:* (jtly) Liberals and the Community, 1974; (with Andrew Tope) A Life in Politics, 2010. *Address:* 88 The Gallop, Sutton, Surrey SM2 5SA. *T:* (020) 8642 5292; House of Lords, SW1A 0PW. *T:* (020) 7219 3098. *E:* topeg@parliament.uk.

**TÖPFER, Dr Klaus;** Founding Director, 2009, and Hon. Senior Fellow, since 2015, Institute for Advanced Sustainability Studies, Potsdam (Executive Director, 2009–15); *b* Waldenburg, Silesia, 29 July 1938; *m* Mechthildis; three *c*. *Educ:* König-Wilhelm-Gymnasium, Höxter, Weser; Univ. of Münster (DipEcon 1964; PhD 1968). Lectr, Econ. Acad., Hagen and Univ. of Bielefeld, 1965–71; Asst to Dir of Econ. Res., 1965–71, Hd, Econs Dept, 1970–71, Central Inst. for Regl Planning, Univ. of Münster; Lectr, Coll. of Admin. Scis, Speyer, 1971–78; Consultant in field of develt policy, Egypt, Malawi, Brazil and Jordan, 1971–78; Prof. and Dir, Inst. for Regl R&D, Univ. of Hanover, 1978–79; Associate Lectr in Envmtl and Resource Econs, Univ. of Mainz, 1985–86. Hd, Dept for Planning and Inf., State Chancellery of Saarland, 1971–78; State Sec., Min. for Social Affairs, Health and Envmt, 1978–85, Minister for Envmt and Health, 1985–87, Rhineland-Palatinate; Federal Minister for Envmt, Nature Conservation and Nuclear Safety, 1987–94; Mem. (CDU) Bundestag, 1990–98; Federal Minister for Regl Planning, Building and Urban Develt, and Co-ordinator for Transfer of Parlt and Federal Govt to Berlin and Compensation for Bonn Reg., 1994–98. Chm., UN Commn on Sustainable Develt, 1994–95; Under-Sec.-Gen., UN, 1998–2006; Dir-Gen., UN Office, Nairobi, 1998; Actg Exec. Dir, UN Centre for Human Settlements (Habitat), 1998–2000; Exec. Dir, UNEP, 1998–2006. Mem. Adv. Bd, Holcim Foundn for Sustainable Construction, Zurich, 2003–13. Joined Christian Democratic Union, 1972: Dist Chm., Saarbrücken and Mem., State Exec. Cttee, Saarland, 1977–79; Vice-Chm., Fed. Exec. Cttee on Envmtl Questions, 1983–87; Dist Chm., Rhine-Hunsrück, 1987–89; State Chm., Saarland, 1990–95; Mem., Presiding Cttee, 1992. Hon. Prof., Tongji Univ., Shanghai, 1997. Hon Dr: Free Univ., Berlin, 2002; Essen, 2002; Hannover, 2003. TÜV Rheinland Pfalz Envmt Award, 2000; Bruno H. Schubert Envmt Prize, 2002; German Envmt Prize, 2002; Wilhelm Weber Prize, 2003; Golden Steering Wheel Internat. Prize (Russia), 2003. OM (FRG), 1986; Comdr's Cross, 1989, Grand Cross, 1997, OM (FRG); Order of Southern Cross (Brazil), 2002; Danaker Order (Kyrgyz Republic), 2003. *Publications:* Die Beeinflussbarkeit privater Pläne dargestellt unternehmerischen Standortentscheidung, 1968; Regionalpolitik und Standortentscheidung, 1969; Standortentscheidung und Wohnortwahl, 1974; Die europäische Dimension der Umweltpolitik, 1989; Internationaler Umweltschutz, 1989; numerous contribs to books and to learned jls. *Recreations:* avid fan of card games, including Skat, football, fine wine.

**TOPP, Air Commodore Roger Leslie;** AFC 1950 (Bar 1955, 2nd Bar 1957); independent consultant, aviation and defence, 1988–99; *b* 14 May 1923; *s* of William Horace Topp and Kathleen (*née* Peters); *m* 1945, Audrey Jane Jeffery (*d* 1999); one *s* one *d*. *Educ:* North Mundham Sch.; RAF, Cranwell. Served War: Pilot trng, Canada, 1943–44, commissioned 1944; 'E' Sqdn Glider Pilot Regt, Rhine Crossing, 1945. Nos 107 and 98 Mosquito Sqdns, Germany, 1947–50; Empire Test Pilots' Sch. and RAE Farnborough, 1951–54; Commanded No 111 Fighter Sqdn (Black Arrows) Aerobatic Team, 1955–58; Allied Air Forces Central Europe, Fontainebleau, 1959; Sector Operational Centre, Brockzetel, Germany, 1959–61; jssc, Latimer, 1961–62; commanded Fighter Test Sqdn, Boscombe Down, 1962–64; Station Comdr, RAF Coltishall, 1964–66; Nat. Def. Coll., Canada, 1966–67; Opl Requirements, MoD (Air), London, 1967–69; Multi-role Combat Aircraft Project, Munich, 1969–70; HQ No 38 Gp, Odiham, 1970; Commandant, Aeroplane and Armament Experimental Estabt, Boscombe Down, 1970–72; Dep. Gen. Man., Multi-role Combat Aircraft Develt and Production Agency, Munich, 1972–78; retd from RAF, 1978. Consultant to Ferranti Defence Systems Ltd, Scotland (Aviation and Defence, FRG), 1978–88. *Recreations:* golf, sailing. *Club:* Royal Air Force.

**TOPPIN, Gilbert Anthony Lester;** independent advisor and non-executive director specialising in business issues, strategy and mergers and acquisitions, since 2010; *b* Barbados, 6 Nov. 1952; *s* of Herbert Lester Toppin and Betty Joan Toppin (*née* Mayers); *m* 2008, Donna Louise Reed; two *s* by a previous marriage. *Educ:* Univ. of Edinburgh (BSc Hons Civil Engrg 1975); Univ. of Southampton (MSc Irrigation Engrg 1976). MICE 1980; CEng 1981; MIStructE 1986; MCIWEM 1987; ACMA 1990; CGMA 2012. Researcher, Hydraulics Res. Station, 1976–77; Engineer: Binnie Black & Veatch, 1977–84; Stewart Lyons Partnership, 1984–86; Consultant, then Partner, Deloitte Consulting, 1986–2003; independent advr, 2004–07; CEO, EEF, 2008–09. Chm., ContactPartners Ltd, 2011–; Consulting Exec., Corporate Visions Inc., 2015–. FRSA 2009. *Publications:* (with Fiona Czerniawska) Business Consulting, 2005. *Recreations:* diving, family interests. *Address:* Old Potters, Pitch Place, Thursley, Godalming GU8 6QW. *T:* 07831 101144. *E:* gilbert@toppin.net.

**TOPPING, Rev. Frank;** actor, author, broadcaster and Methodist minister; Warden, John Wesley's Chapel (The New Room), Bristol, 2000–07; *b* 30 March 1937; *s* of late Frank and Dorothy Topping; *m* 1958, June Berry; two *s* one *d*. *Educ:* St Anne's Convent Sch., Birkenhead; St Anselm's Christian Brothers' Coll., Birkenhead; North West School of Speech and Drama; Didsbury Methodist Theol Coll., Bristol. Served RAF, Cyprus, 1955–57. Leatherhead Rep. Th., 1957–59; Royal Court, Chelsea, 1959; Wolverhampton Rep. Th., 1959; Granada TV, 1960–64; minister, Brighton, and Chaplain, Sussex Univ., 1967–70; freelance broadcaster, BBC Radio Brighton, 1967–70; ordained 1970; staff producer, BBC, 1970–80; Supt Methodist Minister, Barnet Circuit, 1997–2001. Song-writing partnership with Donald Swann, 1973–81; two-man show, Swann with Topping, Opera House, Jersey, fringe theatre, then at Ambassadors, London; presented three one-man plays, Edinburgh Fest. Fringe, 1986. TV series: Sunday Best, 1981; Topping on Sunday, 1982–84; The 5 Minute Show, TVS, 1989–90. Author of radio plays: On the Hill, 1974 (Grace Wyndham Goldie UNDA Dove award, 1975); A Particular Star, 1977. Formed Emmaus, later Topping Theatre Prodns with wife, 1985. *Publications:* Lord of the Morning, 1977; Lord of the Evening, 1979; Lord of my Days, 1980; Working at Prayer, 1981; Pause for Thought with Frank Topping, 1981; Lord of Life, 1982; The Words of Christ: forty meditations, 1983; God Bless You—Spoonbill, 1984; Lord of Time, 1985; An Impossible God, 1985, new edns 1997, 2011; Wings of the Morning, 1986; Act Your Age, 1989; Laughing in my Sleep (autobiog.), 1993; All the Days of my Life, 1994; Here I Stand…, 1997; Grappling with God on the M25, 1998; (ed) Daily Prayer, 2nd edn, 2003; Splinters of Light, 2008. *Recreations:* gardening, photography, travel. *Address:* Lamb Cottage, The Cross, Clearwell, Coleford, Glos GL16 8JU. *T:* (01594) 834278. *E:* franktopping@phonecoop.coop.

**TORLOT, Timothy Achille;** HM Diplomatic Service; Ambassador to Uzbekistan, since 2019; *b* 17 Sept. 1957; *s* of Sidney Achille Hodgson Torlot and Margaret Jane Torlot (*née* Read); *m* 1st, 1986, Bridie Morton (marr. diss. 2011); one *d*; 2nd, 2012, Jennifer Steil; one *d*. *Educ:* Worcester Coll., Oxford (BA Hons Modern Langs). Joined FCO, 1981; Arabic lang. trng, SOAS, 1982–84; Third Sec. (Pol/Inf./Aid), Muscat, 1984–87; Second Sec. (Political), Wellington, 1987–92; Head: of Section, Personnel Mgt Dept, FCO, 1992–95; Commonwealth Section, SE Asian Dept, FCO, 1995–97; Commercial Section, Santiago, 1997–2001; Multilateral Section, Counter-Terrorism Policy Dept, FCO, 2001; Dir, Advanced Technologies, UK Trade & Investment, 2002–05; Dep. Hd of Mission, Baghdad, 2005–06; Ambassador to Yemen, 2007–10; Hd of Section, Middle East Directorate, 2010–12; Ambassador and Hd, EU Delegn to Bolivia, European External Action Service (on secondment), 2012–16; Hd of Litigation, Middle East Directorate, FCO, 2016–18; Russian lang. trng, 2018–19. *Address:* c/o Foreign and Commonwealth Office, King Charles Street, SW1A 2AH.

**TORO-HARDY, Alfredo;** author, scholar; Ambassador of Venezuela to Singapore, 2009–17; *b* Caracas, 22 May 1950; *s* of Fernando Toro and Ofelia Toro (*née* Hardy); *m* 1st, 1972, Dinorah Carnevali (marr. diss. 1998); two *s* one *d*; 2nd, 2001, Gabriela Gaxiola. *Educ:* Central Univ. of Venezuela (LLB 1973; LLM Internat. Trade Law 1977); Univ. of Paris II (Comparative Law 1974); Internat. Inst. of Public Admin, Paris (Diplomatic Studies 1974); Univ. of Pennsylvania (LLM Corporate Law 1979). Simón Bolívar University, Caracas: Associate Prof., 1989–92; Co-ordinator, Latin American Studies Inst., and Dir, N American Studies Centre, 1989–91; Dir, Diplomatic Acad., with rank of Ambassador, Foreign Affairs Ministry, 1992–94; Ambassador: to Brazil, 1994–97; to Chile, 1997–99; to USA, 1999–2001; to the Court of St James's and concurrently to Republic of Ireland, 2001–07; to Spain, 2007–09. Advr to Minister of Foreign Affairs, 1992–94; Mem., Consultative Bd, Nat. Security and Defence Council, 1988–2000. Mem., Academic Bd on Social Responsibility, Univ. of Barcelona, 2003–; External Adviser, Univ. of Westminster Review Panel, 2004–. Vis. Schol. and Sen. Fulbright Schol., Princeton Univ., 1986–87; Hon. Prof., Univ. of Brasilia, 1996–97; Resident Schol., Rockefeller Foundn Bellagio Center, Sept. 2011, Oct. 2017; prof. and guest speaker in several univs and acad. instns in Venezuela, USA, Chile, Brazil, UK and others. Member: Inter-American Peace and Justice Commn, Santiago, 1997–; Windsor Energy Gp, London, 2002–; Global Dimensions, London, 2002–; RIIA, 2003–; Global Labor Orgn, 2017. Mem., Chairmans Club, 2003–. Weekly columnist and collaborator in numerous media publications, in Venezuela, Mexico, Brazil, Chile and Spain, including: El Universal, Caracas, 1994–; El Globo, Caracas, 1989–97. Holds several Venezuelan and foreign decorations. *Publications:* include: Los Libertadores de Venezuela, 1982; Rafael Caldera, 1982; Para qué una Política Exterior?, 1984; Venezuela, Democracia y Política Exterior, 1986; El Desafío Venezolano: Como Influir las Decisiones Políticas Estadounidenses, 1988; La Maldición de Sísifo: quince años de política exterior Venezolana, 1991; Bajo el Signo de la Incertidumbre, 1992; Las Falacias del Libre Comercio, 1993; De Yalta a Sarajevo: de la guerra fría a la paz caliente, 1993; Del Descalabro Mexicano a la Crisis Venezolana, 1995; El Desorden Global, 1996; The Age of Villages: the small village *vs* the global village, 2002; Iraky la Reconfiguración del Orden Mundial, 2003; La Guerra en Irak: causas y consecuencias, 2003; Tiene Futuro América Latina?, 2004; Los Estadounidenses, 2005; Hegemonía e Imperio, 2007; The World Upside Down: the complex partnership between China and Latin America, 2013; Understanding Latin America: a decoding guide, 2017; The Crossroads of Globalization: a Latin American view, 2018. *Address:* Callejón San Sebastian 25, Valle de Bravo, Edo. de Mexico, CP 51200, Mexico. *T:* 551018914. *E:* alfredotorohardy@hotmail.com.

**TORONTO, Archbishop of, (RC),** since 2007; **His Eminence Cardinal Thomas Collins,** STD; *b* 16 Jan. 1947. *Educ:* St Jerome's Coll., Waterloo, Ont. (BA 1969); St Peter's Seminary, London, Ont. (BTh 1973); Univ. of Western Ontario (MA 1973); Pontifical Biblical Inst., Rome (SSL 1978); Gregorian Univ., Rome (STD 1986). Ordained deacon, 1972, priest, 1973; Associate Pastor, Holy Rosary Parish, Burlington, Ont., and Christ the King Cath., Hamilton, Ont., 1973–75; Lectr, Dept of English, King's Coll., Univ. of Western Ontario, 1978–84; St Peter's Seminary: Lectr in Scripture, 1978–84; Gp Leader and Spiritual Dir, 1981–95; Associate Prof. of Scripture, 1985–97; Dean of Theol. and Vice-Rector, 1992–95; Rector, 1995–97; Bishop of St Paul, Alberta, 1997–99; Archbishop of Edmonton (Alberta), (RC), 1999–2007. Cardinal, 2012. President: Alberta Conf. of Catholic Bishops, 1999–2001; Assembly of Catholic Bishops of Ontario (formerly Ontario Conf. of Catholic Bishops), 2008–16 (Vice-Pres., 2016–; Mem., Permt Council, Canadian Conf. of Catholic Bishops, 1999–2003, 2007– (Chm., Nat. Commn of Theol., 1999–2001; Chm., 2001–03, Mem., 2003–05, Nat. Commn on Christian Unity); Member: Vatican Pontifical Council for Social Communications, 2010–16; Vatican Congregation for Catholic Educn, 2012–; Commn of Cardinals for oversight of Inst. for Works of Religion, 2014–; Vatican Congregation for Oriental Churches, 2015–. Member, Board of Directors: Caritas Health Gp, Edmonton, 1999–2007; Alberta Catholic Health Corp., 1999–2007; Chm., Bd of Dirs, Catholic Charities, Archdiocese of Toronto, 2007–; Trustee, Adv. Bd, Sharelife, 2007–. Chairman, Board of Governors: Newman Theol Coll., Edmonton, 1999–2007; St Joseph's Coll., Edmonton, 1999–2007; St Augustine's Seminary, Toronto, 2007–; Chancellor: Univ. of St Michael's Coll., Univ. of Toronto, 2007–; Pontifical Inst. of Mediaeval Studies, Toronto, 2007–; Chair, Bd of Dirs, Redemptoris Mater Missionary Seminary, Toronto, 2007–. Associate Ed., Discover the Bible, 1989–94; columnist, Bread of Life mag., 1987–89. *Publications:* The Eucharist: It is the Lord!, 2000; Reconciliation: Go in Peace, 2003; Pathway to Our Hearts: a simple approach to Lectio Divina with the Sermon on the

Mount, 2011; Cornerstones of Faith: reconciliation, Eucharist and stewardship, 2012; contrib. to Journey, Emmanuel, and Canadian Catholic Review. *Address:* 1155 Yonge Street, Toronto, ON M4T 1W2, Canada.

**TORPHICHEN,** 15th Lord *cr* 1564; **James Andrew Douglas Sandilands;** *b* 27 Aug. 1946; *s* of 14th Lord Torphichen, and Mary Thurstan, *d* of late Randle Henry Neville Vaudrey; *S* father, 1975; *m* 1976, Margaret Elizabeth, *o d* of late William A. Beale and of Mrs Margaret Patten Beale, Peterborough, New Hampshire, USA; four *d*. *Heir:* cousin Robert Powell Sandilands [*b* 10 Dec. 1950; *m* 1974, Cheryl Lynn Watson; one *s* one *d*]. *Address:* Calder House, Mid-Calder, West Lothian EH53 0HN.

**TORPY,** Air Chief Marshal Sir Glenn **(Lester),** GCB 2008 (KCB 2005); CBE 2000; DSO 1991; Senior Military Advisor, BAE Systems, 2011–18; *b* 27 July 1953; *s* of Gordon Torpy and Susan Torpy (*née* Lindsey); *m* 1977, Christine Jackson. *Educ:* Imperial Coll., London (BSc Eng). OC No 13 Sqn, 1989–92; PSO to AOC-in-C STC, 1992–94; Stn Comdr, RAF Bruggen, 1994–96; rcds 1997; ACOS Ops, Permanent Jt HQ, 1998–99; Dir Air Ops, MoD, 1999–2000; ACDS (Ops), 2000–01; AOC No 1 Gp, 2001–03; Dep. C-in-C Strike Command, 2003–04; Chief of Jt Ops, MoD, 2004–06; CAS, 2006–09; Air ADC to the Queen, 2006–09. Chm., Trustees, RAF Mus., 2013–19. Liveryman, Haberdashers' Co., 2006. FRAeS 2003; FCGI 2007. Officer, Legion of Merit (USA), 2003. *Recreations:* golf, sailing, military history, cabinet making. *T:* (01285) 821161. *E:* glenn.torpy@ btinternet.com.

**TORRANCE,** Very Rev. Prof. **Iain Richard,** KCVO 2019; Kt 2018; TD 1995; DPhil; FRSE; a Chaplain-in-Ordinary to the Queen in Scotland, 2001–19, an Extra Chaplain to the Queen, since 2019; Pro-Chancellor, University of Aberdeen, since 2013; Dean, Chapel Royal in Scotland, 2013–19; Dean of the Order of the Thistle, 2014–19; Hon. Professor of Early Christian Doctrine and Ethics, University of Edinburgh, since 2013; *b* 13 Jan. 1949; *yr s* of Very Rev. Prof. Thomas Forsyth Torrance, MBE, FBA and of Margaret Edith Spear; *m* 1975, Morag Ann MacHugh, *er d* of Francis John MacHugh and Wendy Anne Lang; one *s* one *d*. *Educ:* Edinburgh Acad.; Monkton Combe Sch., Bath; Edinburgh Univ. (MA Mental Philosophy, 1971); St Andrews Univ. (BD New Testament Langs and Lit., 1974); Oriel Coll., Oxford (DPhil 1980). Chaplain to the Moderator, Gen. Assembly of Church of Scotland, 1976–77; ordained, 1982; Minister, Northmavine, Shetland, 1982–85; Lecturer: in NT and Christian Ethics, Queen's Coll., Birmingham, 1985–89; in NT and Patristics, Birmingham Univ., 1989–93; Aberdeen University: Lectr in Divinity, 1993–97; Sen. Lectr, 1997–99; Prof. in Patristics and Christian Ethics, 1999–2004; Prof. Emeritus, 2004; Senate Assessor to Univ. Court, 1999–2003; Head, Dept of Divinity and Religious Studies, 2000–01; Dean, Faculty of Arts and Divinity, 2001–03; Master, Christ's Coll., Aberdeen, 2001–04; Pres., 2004–12, now Pres. Emeritus, and Prof. of Patristics, 2004–12, now Prof. Emeritus, Princeton Theological Seminary, New Jersey; Trustee, Center for Theological Inquiry, Princeton, 2004–12. Moderator, Gen. Assembly of Church of Scotland, 2003–04. TA Chaplain, 1982–97; ACF Chaplain, 1996–2000; Convener: Cttee on Chaplains to HM Forces, Gen. Assembly of C of S, 1998–2002; Theological Forum, Gen. Assembly of C of S, 2013–17. Select Preacher: Univ. of Oxford, 2004, 2017; Princeton Univ., 2005; Univ. of Aberdeen, 2009, 2013; St Andrews Univ., 2013; Univ. of Cambridge, 2016; Lectures: Willard, Charlotte, 2005; W. G. A. Wright, Sandhurst, 2005; Berger, Potomac, 2006; Stoner, Pittsburgh, 2008; Hoon-Bullock, San Antonio, 2009; Henderson, Pittsburgh Theological Seminary, 2013. Member: Dialogue between World Alliance of Reformed Churches and the Orthodox Church, 1992–2010 (Co-Chm., 2005–10); Acad. Internat. des Sciences Religieuses, 1997–; Benchmarking Panel for Degrees in Theology and Religious Studies, QAA, 1999–2000; Dialogue between World Communion of Reformed Churches and Anglican Communion, 2015–16. Sec., Soc. for Study of Christian Ethics, 1995–98; Hon. Sec., 1995–98, Hon. Pres., 1998–99, Aberdeen AUT. Judge, Templeton (UK) Award, 1994–99; Mem. Adv. Bd, Templeton Foundn, 2008–10. Trustee: Aberdeen Univ. Develt Trust, 2013–; Scotland's Churches Trust, 2017–; Edinburgh Quartet, 2018–; Edinburgh Walter Scott Soc., 2018– (Chm., Trustees, 2019–); Patron: Assoc. of Univ. Depts of Theol. and Religious Studies, 2013–; Elphinstone Inst., Univ. of Aberdeen, 2015–; Pluscarden Abbey South Range Appeal, 2016–. Co-ed., Scottish Jl of Theol., 1982–2015; Mem., Editl Bd, Ecclesiology, 2015–. Burgess of Guild, City of Aberdeen, 2004. FSAScot 1971; Corresp. FRSE 2007, FRSE 2013. OStJ 2015. Hon. DD: Aberdeen, 2005; St Andrews, 2005; Edinburgh, 2012; Hon. DTheol Reformed Theol Univ., Debrecen, Hungary, 2006; Hon. LHD King Coll., Tennessee, 2007. Hon. Black Belt, Nat. Karate Fedn, 2016. Friend for Life Award, Equality Network, 2004; Hon. Dist. Alumnus, 2012, Medal of Commendation for Christian Leadership, 2012, Princeton Theological Seminary; James I. McCord Award for Outstanding Contrib. to Ecumenical Scholarship, Center for Theological Inquiry, Princeton, 2012; Great Shogun Award, Order of Scottish Samurai, 2016. *Publications:* Christology after Chalcedon, 1989 (trans. Arabic 2015); (jtly) Human Genetics: a Christian perspective, 1995; Ethics and the Military Community, 1998; (ed jtly) To Glorify God: essays on modern reformed liturgy, 1999; (ed) Bioethics for the New Millennium, 2000; (ed jtly) The Oxford Handbook of Systematic Theology, 2007; (ed jtly) The Cambridge Dictionary of Christian Theology, 2011; The Correspondence of Severus and Sergius, 2011; many articles. *Recreation:* historical Scottish culture (buildings, literature, art). *Address:* (home) 25 The Causeway, Duddingston Village, Edinburgh EH15 3QA. *T:* (0131) 661 3092. *E:* irt@abdn.ac.uk. *Clubs:* New, Royal Scots (Edinburgh); Pilgrims (NY); Duddingston Golf (Edinburgh); Grange (Edinburgh).

**TORRANCE, Madeline Mary;** *see* Drake, M. M.

**TORRANCE, Monica;** *see* Ali, Monica.

**TORRANCE, Samuel Robert,** OBE 2003 (MBE 1995); professional golfer; *b* Largs, 24 Aug. 1953; *s* of late Robert Torrance and of June Torrance; *m* 1995, Suzanne Danielle; one *s* two *d*. Winner: Under-25 Match Play tournament Radici Open, 1972; Zambian Open, 1975; Martini Internat., Wales, 1976; Scottish PGA Championship, 1978, 1980, 1985, 1991, 1993, 1995; Colombian Open, 1979; Australian PGA Championship, 1980; Irish Open, 1981, 1995; Spanish Open, 1982; Portuguese Open, 1982, 1983; Scandinavian Open, 1983; Tunisian Open, 1984; Benson & Hedges Internat., England, 1984; Sanyo Open, Spain, 1984; Monte Carlo Open, 1985; Italian Open, 1987, 1995; German Masters, 1990; Jersey Open, 1991; Catalan Open, 1993; Kronenbourg Open, Italy, 1993; Honda Open, Germany, 1993; British Masters, 1995; French Open, 1998; Travis Perkins Senior Masters, 2004; European Senior Tour Order of Merit, 2005, 2006. Member: Dunhill Cup team, 1985–95 (winners, 1995); World Cup team, 1976–95; Mem., 1981–95, Captain, 2001–02, Ryder Cup team (winners, 1985, 1995, 2002). *Publications:* Sam (autobiog.), 2003; An Enduring Passion: my Ryder Cup years, 2010; Out of Bounds: legendary tales from the 19th hole, 2012. *Recreations:* snooker, tennis, all sport.

**TORRAVILLE,** Rt Rev. **David;** Priest-in-charge, White Bay, since 2016; *b* 29 May 1953; *s* of Rev. Canon Arnold Torraville and Nita Marie Torraville; *m* 1979, Karen Flemming; one *s* one *d*. *Educ:* Meml Univ. of Newfoundland (BA, BEd); Queen's Coll., St John's, Newfoundland (MDiv). Fellow in Pastoral Leadership Develt, Princeton Theol Seminary. Rector: Twillingate, 1985–89; Cathedral of St Martin, Gander, 1989–2000; Exec. Officer, Dio. Central Newfoundland, 2001–05; Bishop of Central Newfoundland, 2005–16. *Recreation:* flyfishing. *Club:* Kiwanis Internat.

**TORRENTS, Deborah Jane;** *see* Bronnert, D. J.

**TORRINGTON,** 11th Viscount *cr* 1721; **Timothy Howard St George Byng;** Bt 1715; Baron Byng of Southill, 1721; *b* 13 July 1943; *o s* of Hon. George Byng, RN (*d* on active service, 1944; *o s* of 10th Viscount) and Anne Yvonne Wood (*d* 2017) (she *m* 2nd, 1951, Howard Henry Masterton Carpenter; 3rd, 1990, Michael Ingram Bostock); *S* grandfather, 1961; *m* 1973, Susan, *d* of late Michael George Thomas Webster; three *d*. *Educ:* Harrow; St Edmund Hall, Oxford. Mem., Select Cttee on EEC, H of L, 1984–87 (Chm., Sub-Cttee B (Energy, Transport and Broadcasting), 1985–87). Chairman: Baltic Mills Ltd, 1995–; Lansdowne Oil & Gas plc, 2015– (Dir, 2005–). *Recreation:* travel. *Heir:* kinsman Colin Hugh Cranmer-Byng [*b* 10 Sept. 1960; *m* 1984, Lisa Anne Dallimore; two *s* four *d*]. *Address:* Belbins House, Whitehill, Mere, Wilts BA12 6BL. *Clubs:* White's, Pratt's; Muthaiga (Nairobi).

**TORRY,** Sir **Peter (James),** GCVO 2004; KCMG 2003; HM Diplomatic Service, retired; consultant; *b* 2 Aug. 1948; *m* 1979, Angela Wakeling Wood, *d* of late Joseph Neville Wood, CBE; three *d*. *Educ:* Dover Coll.; New Coll., Oxford (Open Schol.); BA 1970; Irvine Award, 1968; Rugby Blue, 1968, 1969). Joined FCO, 1970; Third Sec., Havana, 1971; Second Sec., Jakarta, 1974; First Sec., FCO, 1977; Bonn, 1981; First Sec., subseq. Counsellor, FCO, 1985; Washington, 1989; FCO, 1993–98, Dir (Personnel and Security), 1995–98; Ambassador: to Spain, 1998–2003; to the FRG, 2003–07. Senior Adviser: Celesio AG, 2007–10; Centrica PLC, 2008–; STAR Capital, 2009–; Cairn Capital, 2013–; Member, Supervisory Board: Blohm and Voss AG; Hertie Foundn, 2017–. Member, Advisory Board: Kiel World Economic Forum, 2007–; Betfair plc, 2011–; Sen. Advr, Global Counsel, 2017–. Policy Fellow, Bonn Inst. for Employment, 2009–. *Recreations:* golf, walking, ski-ing, books, antique furniture. *Address:* c/o Peter Torry Consultancy, 192 Emery Hill Street, SW1P 1PN. *Clubs:* Oxford and Cambridge; Vincent's (Oxford).

**TORTELIER, Yan Pascal;** Chief Conductor, Iceland Symphony Orchestra, since 2016; *b* 19 April 1947; *s* of late Paul Tortelier and of Maud (*née* Martin); *m* 1970, Sylvie Brunet-Moret; two *s*. *Educ:* Paris Conservatoire; general musical studies with Nadia Boulanger; studied conducting with Franco Ferrara in Sienna. Leader and Associate Conductor, Orchestre du Capitole de Toulouse, 1974–82; Principal Conductor and Artistic Dir, Ulster Orchestra, 1989–92; Principal Conductor: BBC Philharmonic, 1999–2002, now Conductor Emeritus; São Paulo SO, 2009–11, now Guest Conductor of Honour. Principal Guest Conductor: Pittsburgh SO, 2005–08; Royal Acad. of Music, London. Has conducted all major British orchestras and toured extensively in USA, Canada, Japan, Australia, Scandinavia, E and W Europe. Numerous recordings incl. complete symphonic works of Debussy and Ravel with Ulster Orch., and Hindemith and Dutilleux series with BBC Philharmonic. Hon. DLitt Ulster, 1992. *Publications:* Première orchestration of Ravel's Piano Trio, 1992. *Recreations:* ski-ing, windsurfing, scuba diving, nature. *Address:* c/o IMG Artists Europe, Capital Tower, 91 Waterloo Road, SE1 8RT.

**TORVILL, Jayne, (Mrs P. L. Christensen),** OBE 2000 (MBE 1981); professional ice skater; *b* 7 Oct. 1957; *d* of George Henry Torvill and Betty (*née* Smart); *m* 1990, Philip Lee Christensen; one adopted *s* one adopted *d*. *Educ:* Clifton Hall Grammar Sch. for Girls, Nottingham. Ice dancer, with Christopher Dean, *qv*; British Champions, 1978, 1979, 1980, 1981, 1982, 1983 and 1994; European Champions, 1981, 1982, 1984 and 1994; World Champions, 1981, 1982, 1983 and 1984; World Professional Champions, 1984, 1985, 1990, 1995 and 1996; Olympic Champions, 1984; Olympic Bronze Medallists, 1994. Trainer, choreographer and performer: Stars on Ice, USA, 1998–99, 1999–2000; Dancing on Ice, ITV, 2006–14; trainer, Ice Rink on the Estate, ITV, 2015; judge, Dancing on Ice, ITV, 2018. Hon. MA Nottingham Trent, 1994. *Publications:* (with Christopher Dean) Facing the Music, 1995; (with Christopher Dean) Our Life on Ice, 2014. *Recreations:* dance, theatre. *Address:* PO Box 32, Heathfield, E Sussex TN21 0BW. *T:* (01435) 867825.

**TOSELAND, Ronald James,** OBE 1991; Deputy Controller, National Air Traffic Services, 1988–91, retired; *b* 7 March 1933; *s* of W. M. and E. Toseland; *m* 1954, Joan Mary (*d* 2002), *d* of A. R. and D. M. Pickett; two *s*. *Educ:* Kettering Central School. RAF Navigator, 1951–61; Air Traffic Control Officer, 1961–91; i/c Heathrow ATC, 1981–83; Dir, Civil Air Traffic Ops, 1983–87; Joint Field Commander, NATS, 1987–88. *Recreations:* music, walking. *Address:* 1 Marshall Place, Oakley Green, Windsor SL4 4QD. *T:* (01753) 863313.

**TOSH, (Neil) Murray,** MBE 1987; Member (C) Scotland West, Scottish Parliament, 2003–07 (Scotland South, 1999–2003); *b* 1 Sept. 1950; *s* of late Neil Ferguson Tosh and of Mary Drummond Tosh (*née* Murray); *m* 1970, Christine Hind (*d* 2007); two *s* one *d*. *Educ:* Kilmarnock Acad.; Univ. of Glasgow (MA 2nd Cl. Hons); Jordanhill Coll. of Educn (Secondary Teaching Qualif.). Teacher of history, Ravenspark Acad., Irvine, 1975–77; principal teacher of history: Kilwinning Acad., 1977–84; Belmont Acad., Ayr, 1984–99. Mem. (C) Kyle and Carrick DC, 1987–96 (Convener, Housing Cttee and Vice Convener, Planning and Develt Cttee, 1992–96). Contested (C) Dumfries, Scottish Parlt, 2007. Scottish Parliament: Convener, Procedures Cttee, 1999–2003; Member: Transport and Envmt Cttee, 1999–2001; Subordinate Legislation Cttee, 2003–07; Dep. Presiding Officer, 2001–07. *Recreations:* hill-walking, reading (historical, political), historic buildings, touring holidays. *Address:* 14 Harleyburn Avenue, Melrose, Roxburghshire TD6 9JZ.

**TOTARO,** Prof. **Burt James,** PhD; FRS 2009; Professor of Mathematics, University of California, Los Angeles, since 2012; *b* 8 Aug. 1967. *Educ:* Princeton Univ. (AB 1984); Univ. of Calif at Berkeley (PhD 1989). Mem., Mathematical Scis Res. Inst., Berkeley, 1989–90; Dickson Instructor, 1990–93, Asst Prof., 1993–99, Dept of Maths, Univ. of Chicago; Mem., Inst. for Advanced Study, Princeton, 1994–95 and 2014–15; Lectr, Dept of Pure Mathematics and Mathematical Statistics, 1999, Lowndean Prof. of Astronomy and Geometry, 2000–13, Univ. of Cambridge. Eisenbud Prof., 2009, Vis. Mem., 2019, Mathematical Scis Res. Inst., Berkeley. Mem. Council, LMS, 2007–12. Ed., Proc. of LMS, 2003–08; Mem., Mgt Cttee, Jl of K-Theory, 2007–09; Man. Ed., Compositio Mathematica, 2008–18. Fellow, Amer. Mathematical Soc., 2019. Whitehead Prize, LMS, 2000; Prix Franco-Britannique, Acad. des Scis, 2001. *Recreation:* cats. *Address:* Mathematics Department, University of California, Los Angeles, PO Box 951555, Los Angeles, CA 90095-1555, USA.

**TOTNES, Archdeacon of;** *see* Dettmer, Ven. D. J.

**TOTTEN, William John;** Sheriff of Glasgow and Strathkelvin at Glasgow, 1999–2017; *b* 11 Sept. 1954; *s* of David and Sarah Totten; *m* 1985, Shirley Ann Morrison; one *s*. *Educ:* John Neilson Instn, Paisley; Univ. of Glasgow (LLB Hons 1977). Apprentice, Tindal, Oatts & Rodger, 1977–79; admitted solicitor, 1979; Procurator Fiscal Service, 1979–83; Asst, then Partner, Beltrami & Co., 1983–88; admitted to Faculty of Advocates, 1989; Advocate-Depute, 1993–96; Temp. Sheriff, 1998–99. *Recreations:* cycling, ski-ing, walking, reading, foreign travel.

**TOTTENHAM,** family name of **Marquess of Ely.**

**TÖTTERMAN, Richard Evert Björnson,** Kt Comdr, Order of the White Rose of Finland; Hon. GCVO 1976 (Hon. KCVO 1969); Hon. OBE 1961; Finnish Ambassador, retired; *b* 10 Oct. 1926; *s* of Björn B. Tötterman and Katharine C. (*née* Wimpenny); *m* 1953, Camilla Susanna Veronica Huber; one *s* one *d*. *Educ:* Univ. of Helsinki (Jur. lic.); Brasenose Coll., Oxford (DPhil; Hon. Fellow, 1982). Entered Finnish Foreign Service, 1952: served Stockholm, 1954–56; Moscow, 1956–58; Min. for For. Affairs, Finland, 1958–62; Berne, 1962–63; Paris, 1963–66; Dep. Dir, Min. for For. Affairs, Helsinki, 1966; Sec.-Gen., Office of the President of Finland, 1966–70; Sec. of State, Min. for For. Aff., 1970–75; Ambassador: UK, 1975–83; Switzerland, 1983–90, and (concurrently) to the Holy See, 1988–90. Chm. or Mem. of a number of Finnish Govt Cttees, 1959–75, and participated as Finnish rep. in various internat. negotiations; Chm., Multilateral Consultations preparing Conf. on Security and Co-operation in Europe, 1972–73. Holds numerous foreign orders (Grand Cross, Kt Comdr, etc). *Recreations:* music, outdoor life, international relations. *Address:* Parkgatan 9 A 11, 00140 Helsinki, Finland.

**TOUBE, Samantha Louise;** *see* Cohen, S. L.

**TOUCHE, Sir Eric MacLellan,** 3rd Bt *cr* 1962; *b* 22 Feb. 1960; *s* of Sir Rodney Gordon Touche, 2nd Bt and Ouida Ann Touche (*née* MacLellan); *S* father, 2017, but his name does not appear on the Official Roll of the Baronetage; *m* 1st, 1990, Leeanne Marie Stringer (marr. diss. 1998); one *s* one *d*; 2nd, 2005, Catherine Parenteau. *Heir: s* Braden Stringer, *b* 2 Oct. 1990.

**TOUCHE, Sir William George,** 4th Bt *cr* 1920; Vice Chairman, Deloitte UK, since 1993; *b* 26 June 1962; *s* of Sir Anthony George Touche, 3rd Bt and Hester Christina Touche (*née* Pleuger); *S* father, 2018; *m* 1st, 1987, Elizabeth Louise (marr. diss. 2005), *y d* of Allen Bridges; three *s* one *d*; 2nd, 2017, Donna Louise, *o d* of Alan Ward. *Educ:* Eton Coll.; Jesus Coll., Oxford (BA Modern Langs). Manager: Touche Ross, 1985–88; Deltec Banking Corp., 1989–90; Partner, Deloitte CIS, 1990–93. *Heir: s* Harry George Touche, *b* 3 June 1992.

**TOUGH, Sara Louise;** Executive Director, Children's Services, Norfolk County Council, since 2017; *b* London, 16 Sept. 1959; *d* of Josef and Iris Kardosh; *m* 1985, Stephen Tough; one *s*. *Educ:* Holland Park Sch., London; Goldsmiths' Coll., Univ. of London (BSc Hons Sociol.); University Coll., Swansea (CQSW 1983); Surrey Univ. (Dip. Play Therapy). Shropshire County Council: Social Worker, 1983; Sen. Social Worker, 1985; Team Manager, 1988; Service Manager, 1990; Dir, Sexual abuse Child Consultancy Service, 1995; Telford and Wrekin Borough Council: Change for Children Prog. Manager, 2002–07; Asst Dir, Sch. and Community Services, 2007–08; Integrated Services Dir, Children and Young People and Community Health, Swindon BC, 2008–14; Dir, Children's Services, 2014–17, Corporate Dir, Children, Adults and Communities, 2017, Dorset CC. Mem. Bd, 2011–15, Chair, Families, Communities and Young People Policy Cttee, 2019–, Assoc. of Dirs of Children's Services. *Recreations:* family, walking, music, films, fine food. *Address:* Norfolk County Council, County Hall, Martineau Lane, Norwich NR1 2DU. *T:* (01603) 222601. *E:* sara.tough@norfolk.gov.uk.

**TOUHIG,** family name of **Baron Touhig**.

**TOUHIG, Baron** *cr* 2010 (Life Peer), of Islwyn and Glansychan in the County of Gwent; **James Donnelly, (Don), Touhig;** PC 2006; *b* 5 Dec. 1947; *s* of Michael Touhig and Catherine Touhig (*née* Corten); *m* 1968, Jennifer Hughes (*d* 2014); two *s* two *d*. *Educ:* St Francis Sch., Aberyschan; E Monmouth Coll., Pontypool. Journalist, 1968–95; Editor, Free Press of Monmouthshire, 1976–90; General Manager: Free Press Gp, 1988–92; (Business Develt) Bailey Gp, 1992–93; Bailey Print, 1993–95. MP (Lab and Co-op) Islwyn, 1995–2010. PPS to Chancellor of the Exchequer, 1997–99; an Asst Govt Whip, 1999–2001; Parly Under-Sec. of State, Wales Office, 2001–05, MoD, 2005–06. Member: Welsh Select Cttee, 1996–97; Public Accounts Cttee, 2006–10; Chm., Members' Allowances Cttee, 2009–10 (Mem., Liaison Cttee, 2009–10); Chm., All-Party Alcohol Abuse Gp, 1996–99; Jt Sec., All-Party Police Gp, 1996–97; Hon. Sec., Welsh Gp, 1995–99, Mem., Backbench Cttee, 2007–10, PLP. Opposition spokesperson on defence, H of L, 2015–17. Lab. Party Parly Advr to Police Fedn of Eng. and Wales, 1996–98. KSS 1991. *Recreations:* reading, cooking for family and friends, walking. *Address:* House of Lords, SW1A 0PW.

**TOULMIN, (Ann) Camilla,** DPhil; FRSE; Senior Associate, International Institute for Environment and Development, since 2017 (Senior Fellow, 2002–03, 2015–17; Director, 2003–15); *b* Melbourne, 12 Aug. 1954; *d* of late Prof. Stephen Edelston Toulmin and Margaret Alison Toulmin (*née* Coutts); *m* 1983, Mark Ellis Powell Jones (*see* Sir Mark Jones); two *s* one *d*. *Educ:* English Sch., Addis Ababa; Oxford High Sch.; New Hall, Cambridge (BA Econs 1975); Sch. of Oriental and African Studies, Univ. of London (MSc Econs 1976); Somerville Coll., Oxford (DPhil Econs 1987). Lectr, Ahmadu Bello Univ., Zaria, 1977–79; Researcher: Internat. Livestock Centre for Africa, 1980–82; ODI, 1985–87; International Institute for Environment and Development: Prog. Dir, 1987–2002. Associate, Inst. for New Economic Thinking, 2018–. Member: French Min. of Foreign Affairs Steering Cttee on Land Tenure, 1996–; UK Govt Foresight Lead Expert Gp, Global Food and Farming Futures, 2009–11; Royal Soc. Wkg Gp on Reaping the Benefits, 2008–09, on Resilience, 2013–14; Adv. Council, Grantham Inst. for Climate Change Res., 2009–; Adv. Council, Envmtl Change Inst., Univ. of Oxford, 2013–; Rapporteur, Commn on Global Economic Transformation, 2018–. Trustee: Oxfam, 1986–88; WWF, 2004–10; Internat. Center for Agricl Res. in Dry Areas, 2008–15 (Chair, 2012–15); Franco-British Council, 2008–16; Chair, Television Trust for the Envmt, 2015–. Mem. Council, Royal Africa Soc., 2003–. Prof. in Practice, Univ. of Lancaster, 2016–. Open Soc. Fellow, 2016–17. FRSE 2019. *Publications:* Cattle, Women and Wells, 1992; Sustaining the Soil, 1996; Evolving Land Rights, Policy and Tenure in Africa, 2000; Dynamics of Resource Tenure, 2002; Towards a New Map of Africa, 2005; Climate Change in Africa, 2009; (contrib.) Why the Social Sciences Matter, 2014; (contrib.) New Directions for Smallholder Agriculture, 2014; (contrib.) The End of Desertification, 2016. *Recreations:* walking, family and friends. *Address:* International Institute for Environment and Development, 4 Hanover Street, Edinburgh EH2 2EN. *T:* (020) 3463 7399. *E:* camilla.toulmin@iied.org.

**TOULMIN, Timothy James;** Founder and Managing Director, Alder Media Ltd, since 2010; Specialist Partner, Issues and Crisis Management, Pagefield, since 2013; *b* 19 Jan. 1975; *s* of Michael Toulmin and Sandy Toulmin (*née* Rawkins). *Educ:* Repton Sch.; Peterhouse, Cambridge (MA Hist.); Cranfield Sch. of Mgt (MBA). Press Complaints Commission, 1996–2009: Dep. Dir, 2000–03; Acting Dir, 2004; Dir, 2004–09. Mem. Council, Friends of Peterhouse, 2005–09. Trustee: Action Against Abduction (formerly Parents and Abducted Children Together), 2013–16; Stonewall, 2015–. Mem. Bd, Brightwells Acad. Trust, 2016–. *Recreations:* sailing, hill walking, watching cricket. *Address:* Alder Media Ltd, 25 Sackville Street, W1S 3AX. *E:* tim.toulmin@alder-uk.com.

**TOULSON, Elizabeth, (Lady Toulson),** CBE 1999; DL; *b* 10 Nov. 1948; *d* of late Henry Bertram Chrimes and of Suzanne Isabel Chrimes (*née* Corbett-Lowe); *m* 1973, Roger Grenfell Toulson (Rt Hon. Lord Toulson, PC) (*d* 2017); two *s* two *d*. *Educ:* Liverpool Univ.; Clare Hall, Cambridge (LLB). Called to the Bar, Inner Temple, 1974. Women's Royal Voluntary Service: Trustee, 1981–; Vice-Chm., 1989–93; Nat. Chm., 1993–99. Director: Queen Elizabeth Foundn for Disabled People, 1999–; Surrey Voluntary Service Council, 1999–2002; Chm., Children's Soc., 2001–04. Chm. Council, 2011–, Lay Canon, 2013–, Guildford Cathedral. Trustee, Elizabeth Finn Trust, 2002–05. Vice-Patron: Guildford Choral Soc., 2001–; Vocaleyes, 2004–; Patron: Marriage Foundn, 2012–; Surrey Assoc. for Visual Impairment, 2013–; Pres., Surrey St John Ambulance, 2010–12. Advr, CAB, 2002–. Chairman: Nyika Vwaza Trust, 2003–08; Music of Life Foundn, 2003–04; Time for Families, 2006–10; Trustee, Guildford Community Family Trust, 2004–06. Governor: Charterhouse Sch., 1998–; Suttons Hosp., 2004–08. FRSA 2006. High Sheriff, 2009–10, DL 2009, Surrey. *Recreations:* reading, music, walking, tennis, swimming, ski-ing. *Address:* Billhurst Farm, White Hart Lane, Wood Street Village, Guildford, Surrey GU3 3DZ; 201 Rowan House, 9 Greycoat Street, SW1P 2QD.

**TOUMAZOU, Prof. Christofer,** PhD; FRS 2008; FREng, FMedSci; Regius Professor of Engineering, since 2013, Chief Scientist, Institute of Biomedical Engineering, since 2003 (Founding Director, 2003), and Director, Centre for Bio-Inspired Technology, Imperial College London; *b* Cheltenham, 5 July 1961; *s* of Markos and Andriana Toumazou; *m* 2003, Melanie Anne Joyce; two *s*; one *s* one *d* by previous marriage to Ann Mackenzie. *Educ:* Oxford Brookes Univ. (BSc Hons 1st Cl. 1983; PhD; Hon. DEng 2010). FIEEE 2002; FIET 2005; FREng 2008. Imperial College London: Lectr, 1986–92; Prof. of Circuit Design, 1992–2013; Hd, Bioengrg Dept, 1999–2004; Winston Wong Prof. of Biomedical Circuits, 2005–13. Chairman and Chief Technology Officer: Toumaz Technology, 2000–; Future Waves Ltd, 2003–; Chm. and CEO, DNA Electronics Ltd, 2004–; Founder and CEO, DnaNudge Ltd. MAE 2007. FCGI 2009; FMedSci 2013. Eur. Patent of Year Award, Eur. Patent Office, 2014. *Publications:* Analogue IC Design: the current-mode approach, 1990; (ed jtly) Switched-Currents: an analogue technique for digital technology, 1993; (ed jtly) Trade-Offs in Analog Circuit Design, 2004. *Recreations:* travelling, kendo, classical music. *E:* c.toumazou@ic.ac.uk.

**TOUT, Paul Edward H.;** *see* Hill-Tout.

**TOUYZ, Prof. Rhian Merry,** PhD; FRCPSGlas, FRSE; FMedSci; Professor of Medicine, since 2011, Director, Institute of Cardiovascular and Medical Sciences, since 2011, and British Heart Foundation Professor of Cardiovascular Medicine, since 2012, University of Glasgow; Hon. Consultant, Queen Elizabeth University Hospital, Glasgow, since 2011; *b* Johannesburg, 27 Jan. 1959; *d* of Arnold Glassman and Gertrude Glassman (*née* Libner); *m* 1st, 1981, Louis Touyz (marr. diss. 2009); one *s* one *d*; 2nd, 2014, David Andrew Koppel. *Educ:* Cyrildene Primary Sch., Johannesburg; Johannesburg High Sch. for Art, Ballet and Music; King David High Sch., Johannesburg; Univ. of Witwatersrand (BSc 1979; BSc Hons 1980; MB BCh 1984; MSc Med 1985; PhD 1992). FRCPSGlas 2012. Associate Prof., Dept of Medicine, Univ. of Montreal, 2002–07; Lab. Dir, Clin. Res. Inst. of Montreal, 2004–05; Prof., Dept of Medicine, Univ. of Ottawa, 2005–11; Consultant Physician, Hypertension Clinic, Nephrology, Ottawa Hosp., 2005–11; Sen. Scientist, Ottawa Hosp. Res. Inst., Ottawa, 2005–11; Canada Res. Chair in Hypertension, Univ. of Ottawa/Ottawa Hosp. Res. Inst., 2005–12. FAHA 2003; FCAHS 2012; FRSE 2013; FESC 2015; FMedSci 2017. *Publications:* (ed with E. L. Schiffrin) Hypertension, 2013; (ed with E. L. Schiffrin) Methods in Molecular Biology, 2016; contrib. chapters in books on cardiovascular medicine, hypertension, vascular biology and related topics; contribs to cardiovascular jls. *Recreations:* art, ballet, opera and music, travel. *Address:* Institute of Cardiovascular and Medical Sciences, BHF Glasgow Cardiovascular Research Centre, University of Glasgow, 126 University Place, Glasgow G12 0NX. *T:* (0141) 330 7775, 7774, *Fax:* (0141) 330 3360. *E:* rhian.touyz@glasgow.ac.uk. *Club:* Athenæum.

**TOVUE, Sir Ronald,** Kt 1987; OBE 1981; Commissioner, Constitution Review Commission, Papua New Guinea, 1995–97; Premier, Provincial Government of East New Britain Province, Papua New Guinea, 1981–87; Member of Provincial Assembly, 1979–87; *b* 14 Feb. 1933; *s* of Apmeledi ToPalanga and Rachael Waruruai; *m* 1971, Suluet Tinvil; two *s* one *d*. *Educ:* Pilapila Community Sch.; Kerevat High Sch. Teacher, 1957–65; Magistrate, 1965–74; Commissioner, 1974–76; businessman, 1977–. *Recreations:* golf, reading, gardening, fishing, church activities. *Address:* Ratavul, PO Box 354, Rabaul, Papua New Guinea. *Club:* Rabaul Golf (Rabaul).

**TOWE, Stewart Ronald,** CBE 2008; DL; Group Executive Chairman, Hadley Industries plc, since 2006; *b* Birmingham, 2 Aug. 1951; *s* of Ronald Towe and Margaret Towe; *m* 1978, Anne Westley; one *s* one *d*. *Educ:* Bromsgrove Sch. Accountant, Farmiloe & Co., 1972–76; Gp Accountant, 1976–78, Finance Dir, 1978–2006, Hadley Gp. Chairman: W Midlands Reg., Business in the Community, 2009–14; Black Country LEP, 2010–. Pro-Chancellor, Wolverhampton Univ., 2014– (Gov., 2008–14); Gov., Aston Univ., 2009–14; Chair of Governors: Ace Acad., Tipton, 2009–15; Bromsgrove Sch., 2010–16; Sandwell Acad., 2013–16. Patron, Prince's Trust, 2012–. High Sheriff 2012, DL 2013, W Midlands. *Recreations:* equestrian centre management, dressage, Rugby, endurance motorsport. *Address:* Hadley Industries plc, PO Box 92, Downing Street, Smethwick, W Midlands B66 2PA. *T:* (0121) 555 1300, *Fax:* (0121) 555 1301. *E:* stewart.towe@hadleygroup.com.

**TOWERS, John,** CBE 1995; FREng, FIMechE; Chairman, Phoenix Venture Holdings Ltd, 2000–11; Chairman, Rover Group Ltd, 2000–05; *b* 30 March 1948; *s* of Jack Towers and Florence Towers (*née* Abley); *m* 1990, Bethanie Williams; one *s* one *d*. *Educ:* Durham Johnston Sch.; Univ. of Bradford (BSc Hons Mech. Engrg). CEng 1974; FREng (FEng 1992); FIMechE 1992; FIIM 1989. Joined Perkins Engines as student apprentice, 1966: Quality Engr, later Mfg Dir and Gen. Manager, 1983–86; Vice-Pres., Internat. Services, Varity Corp. (Canada), 1986–87; Man. Dir, Massey Ferguson Tractors, 1987–88; Rover Group, 1988–96: Mfg Dir, Land Rover, 1988–89; Product Develt Dir, 1989–90; Dir, 1990–91; Man. Dir, Jan.–Dec. 1991, Product Supply; Gp Man. Dir, 1991–94; Gp Chief Exec., 1994–96; Chief Exec., Concentric Gp, 1996–2000. Director: Midland Bank, 1995–96; B. Elliott, 1996–2000; HatWel Ltd, 1996–2011. Vis. Prof., Warwick Univ., 1993. Mem., Council for Sci. and Technol., 1993–97. DUniv Central England in Birmingham, 1994. *Recreations:* golf, music, shooting.

**TOWL, Prof. Graham John,** DSc; FBPsS; FAcSS; Professor of Psychology, Durham University, since 2008 (Principal, St Cuthbert's Society, 2008–11; Pro-Vice-Chancellor and Deputy Warden, then Pro-Vice-Chancellor (Student Experience), 2011–16); *b* Boosbeck, 13 Aug. 1961; *s* of John Bruce Towl and Barbara Towl (*née* Moore); *m* 1993, Jacqueline Marie Walton. *Educ:* St Martin's Comp. Sch., Caerphilly; Durham Univ. (BA 1988; DSc 2008); Birkbeck Coll., Univ. of London (MSc 1990); Univ. of Birmingham (MBA 2000). FBPsS 2009; FAcSS (AcSS 2010). Psychologist, HM Prison Service, 1988–92; Hd, Psychology Dept, HMP and YOI Highpoint, 1992–95; Area Psychologist, East Anglia, 1995–98, Kent, 1998–2000, HM Prison Service; Hd, Psychological Services, Prisons and Probation, 2000–05; Chief Psychologist, Home Office, later MoJ, 2005–08. Visiting Professor: Univ. of Birmingham, 2000–08; Univ. of Portsmouth, 2001–08; Vis. Clinical Prof., Newcastle Univ., 2015–. Member: Audit Cttee, Acad. of Social Scis, 2013–15; HCPC, 2014–18; Ind. Adv. Panel, Deaths in Custody, 2014–18; Harris Rev. on deaths in custody of 18–24 year olds, 2014–15; Nat. Advr on Mental Health, Nightline, 2014–. Governor: New Coll. Durham, 2016–; Tees Esk and Wear Valley NHS Trust, 2017–18. PFHEA 2016. *Publications:* The Handbook of Psychology for Forensic Practitioners, 1996;

(ed jtly) Suicide in Prisons, 2000; Psychology in Prisons, 2003, 2nd edn 2008; Applying Psychology to Forensic Practice, 2004; Psychology in Probation Services, 2005; Psychological Research in Prisons, 2006; Dictionary of Forensic Psychology, 2008; Forensic Psychology, 2010, 2nd edn 2015; (jtly) Suicide in Prisons: prisoners' lives matter, 2017; Tackling Sexual Violence at Universities: an international perspective, 2019. *Recreations:* walking (our beauceron on the beach), watching films, martial arts, good food. *Address:* Psychology Department, Durham University, Science Laboratories, South Road, Durham DH1 3LE.

**TOWLE, Bridget Ellen,** CBE 2001; DL; Chair, Council, University of Leicester, 2013–19 (Member, 2000–19); *b* 19 April 1942; *d* of late William Henry Towle and Marjorie Louisa (*née* Hardstaff). *Educ:* Westonbirt Sch.; Univ. of Exeter (BA Gen. Hons, BA Hons); Leicester Poly. (Post Grad. Courses in Textile Technol. and Business Mgt). Teacher, VSO, Uganda, 1965–66; Towles plc: marketing mgt roles, 1966–94; Dir, 1972–94; Jt Man. Dir, 1980–94. Guide Association, later Girlguiding UK: various appts, incl. County Comr, Leics, 1985–92; Chief Guide, UK, and Chief Comr, Commonwealth Girl Guide Assocs, 1996–2001; Vice Pres., 2003–. Treas., Univ. of Leicester, 2009–13. Trustee: Coll. of Optometrists, 2004–10 (Chm., Lay Adv. Panel, 2007–10); Friends of Nyakasura Sch., Uganda, 2005–12; RAF Benevolent Fund, 2005–13. Mem. Council, Leicester Literary and Philosophical Soc., 2014–. Mem. PCC, All Saints, Loughborough, 2015– (Treas., 2016–). FRSA 1999. Hon. FCOptom 2013. Hon. LLD Exeter, 2000; Hon. DLitt Loughborough, 2002. Charity Trustee of the Year, Charity Times, 2000. DL Leics, 2013. *Recreations:* decorative arts, walking. *Address:* c/o University of Leicester, University Road, Leicester LE1 7RH. *Club:* Royal Air Force.

**TOWNELEY, Sir Simon (Peter Edmund Cosmo William),** KCVO 1994; Lord-Lieutenant and Custos Rotulorum of Lancashire, 1976–96; *b* 14 Nov. 1921; *e s* of late Col A. Koch de Gooreynd, OBE and Baroness Norman, CBE; assumed surname and arms of Towneley by royal licence, 1955, by reason of descent from *e d* and senior co-heiress of Col Charles Towneley of Towneley; *m* 1955, Mary, MBE (*d* 2001), 2nd *d* of Cuthbert Fitzherbert; one *s* six *d*. *Educ:* Stowe; Worcester Coll., Oxford (MA, DPhil; Ruffini Scholar). Served War of 1939–45, KRRC. Lectr in History of Music, Worcester Coll., Oxford, 1949–55. Mem., Agricultural Lands Tribunal, 1960–92. Dir, Granada Television, 1981–92. CC Lancs, 1961–64; JP 1956; DL 1970; High Sheriff of Lancashire, 1971. Mem. Council, Duchy of Lancaster, 1986–96. Patron: Nat. Assoc. for Mental Health (North-West); Emmaus Burnley, 2009–. Pres., NW of England and IoM TA&VRA, 1987–92; Chm., Northern Ballet Theatre, 1969–86; Member: Bd of Governors, Royal Northern Coll. of Music, 1961–98; Council, 1971–97, Court, 1971–98, Univ. of Manchester; Trustee: Historic Churches Preservation Trust, 1984–93; British Museum, 1988–93. Hon. Col, Duke of Lancaster's Own Yeomanry, 1979–88. CRNCM 1990; Hon. Fellow, Lancashire Polytechnic, 1987. Hon. DMus Lancaster, 1994. KStJ; KCSG. *Publications:* Venetian Opera in the Seventeenth Century, 1954 (repr. 1968); contribs to New Oxford History of Music. *Address:* Dyneley, Burnley, Lancs BB11 3RE. *T:* (01282) 423322. *Clubs:* Boodle's, Pratt's, Beefsteak.

*See also Sir P. G. Worsthorne.*

**TOWNEND, Ian Howard,** CEng, CMarSci, FREng; consultant on coast and estuary research, since 2014; Research Director, HR Wallingford Ltd, 2006–14; *b* Wolverhampton, 28 Feb. 1954; *s* of Gordon and Peggy Townend; *m* 1980, Mary Cranston; one *s* one *d*. *Educ:* Regis Sch., Wolverhampton; Exeter Univ. (BSc Engrg Sci. 1975). CEng 1980; CMarSci 2002. Joined Halcrow as Graduate Engr, 1975; Design Engr, 1975–81; Project Engr, 1981–91; Chief Coastal Engr, 1991–93; Man. Dir, ABPmer, 1993–2006. Visiting Professor: Univ. of Southampton, 2006–; East China Normal Univ., Shanghai, 2014–; Nanjing Hydraulic Res. Inst., Nanjing, 2014–. FREng 2010. *Recreations:* sailing, walking, music, sculpture, family.

**TOWNEND, John Coupe;** Director for Europe, Bank of England, 1999–2002; *b* 24 Aug. 1947; *s* of Harry Norman Townend and Joyce Dentith (*née* Coupe); *m* 1969, Dorothy Allister; three *s*. *Educ:* Liverpool Inst. High Sch. for Boys; London Sch. of Economics (BSc Econ; MSc). With Bank of England, 1968–2002: First Head, Wholesale Markets Supervision Div., 1986–90; Head, Gilt-Edged and Money Markets Div., 1990–94; Dep. Dir, 1994–98. Non-executive Director: LCH.Clearnet Ltd, 2004–12; LCH.Clearnet Gp, 2008–12; LCH.Clearnet SA, 2008–12. *Publications:* articles in econ. jls. *Recreations:* running, trekking, opera, birds, grandchildren.

**TOWNEND, His Honour John Philip;** a Circuit Judge, 1987–2001; *b* 20 June 1935; *o s* of Luke and Ethel Townend; *m* 1st, 1959; two *s* one *d*; 2nd, 1981, Anne Glover; one step *s* one step *d*. *Educ:* St Joseph's Coll., Blackpool; Manchester Univ. (LLB). National Service, 1957–58. Called to the Bar, Gray's Inn, 1959; Lectr in Law, Gibson and Weldon College of Law, 1960–65; Asst Legal Advr, Pilkington Bros, 1966–68; Legal Advr, Honeywell Ltd and G. Dew Ltd, 1968–70; joined chambers of Mr Stewart Oakes, Manchester, 1970. *Publications:* articles in various jls on legal topics. *Recreations:* classical music, jazz, food and wine, a decreasing number of active games, mountain walking. *Address:* c/o St John's Buildings, 24 St John Street, Manchester M3 4DJ.

**TOWNEND, Ven. Lee Stuart;** Archdeacon of Carlisle, since 2017; *b* Sheffield, 13 Jan. 1965; *s* of Keith Townend and Anne Townend; *m* 1986, Liz White; one *s* one *d*. *Educ:* St John's Coll., Durham Univ. (Dip. Theol. and Ministry 1998; MA Theol. and Ministry 2007). Ordained deacon, 1998, priest, 1999; Curate, Buxton Team Ministry, 1998–2001; Vicar: Loose, Canterbury, 2001–08; Ilkley, Bradford, 2008–12; Diocesan Missioner, Derby, 2012–17. *Recreation:* Sheffield Wednesday FC. *Address:* Church House, 19–24 Friargate, Penrith, Cumbria CA11 7XR. *T:* (01768) 807772. *E:* leethevicar@gmail.com.

**TOWNEND, Warren Dennis;** HM Diplomatic Service, retired; *b* 15 Nov. 1945; *s* of Dennis Jennings Townend and Mary Elizabeth Townend (*née* Knowles); *m* 1978, Ann Mary Riddle; three *s* one *d*. *Educ:* Netheredge Grammar Sch.; Abbeydale Grammar Sch. Joined Diplomatic Service, 1964; FO 1964–69; Vice Consul, Hanoi, 1969–70; Vice Consul (Commercial), Hamburg, 1970–73; Second Sec. (Commercial), Dacca, 1973–75; FCO, 1976–79; Second, later First, Sec., Bonn, 1979–84; First Sec. (Commercial), Bangkok, 1984–87; FCO, 1987–91; Dep. Consul-Gen. and Dep. Dir-Gen. for Trade and Investment Promotion in Germany, Düsseldorf, 1991–96; Consul-General: Shanghai, 1996–2000; Washington, DC, 2001–04. *Recreations:* DIY, travel. *E:* yes2eu@yahoo.com.

**TOWNER, Neena;** *see* Gill, N.

**TOWNLEY, Ven. Peter Kenneth;** Archdeacon of Pontefract, since 2008; *b* Manchester, 16 Nov. 1955; *s* of David Townley and Elsie Townley; *m* 1981, Moira Margaret Whitehorn; three *s*. *Educ:* Crab Lane Co. Primary Sch., Manchester; Moston Brook High Sch., Manchester; Univ. of Sheffield (BA 1978); Ridley Hall, Cambridge; Univ. of Manchester (Dip. Social and Pastoral Theol. 1986). Ordained deacon, 1980, priest, 1981; Asst Curate, Christ Church, Ashton-under-Lyne, 1980–83; Priest-in-charge, St Hugh's, Holts, Oldham, 1983–88; Rector, All Saints', Stretford, 1988–96; Vicar, St Mary-le-Tower, Ipswich, 1996–2008; Rural Dean, Ipswich, 2001–08. Member: Meissen Commn, 1991–2001; Gen. Synod, C of E, 1992–95, 2000–08; Porvoo Panel, 2003–. Chair, Diocesan Adv. Cttee; Clergy Develt Officer, Wakefield Episcopal Area. Hon. Canon: Dio. of St Edmundsbury and Ipswich, 2003–08; Ripon Cathedral, 2015–; Bradford Cathedral, 2015–. Diocesan Chaplain, Mothers' Union, 2016–. *Publications:* (contrib.) Spiritualitaet und innovative Unternehmensfuehrung, 2011; (contrib.) Prayer for the Day: 365 inspiring daily reflections, 2014, (contrib.) Prayer for the Day, vol. 2, 2016; (contrib.) Prayers To See You Through Each Day, 2017; various newspaper articles and obituaries. *Recreations:* the arts, travel, fun, still supporting The Tractor Boys, most of all, family and friends. *Address:* The Vicarage, Kirkthorpe, Wakefield, W Yorks WF1 5SZ. *T:* and *Fax:* (01924) 896327. *E:* archdeacon.pontefract@leeds.anglican.org. *Clubs:* Lansdowne, Nikaean.

**TOWNSEND, Prof. Alain Robert Michael,** PhD; FRS 1992; Professor of Molecular Immunology, since 1992, and Fellow of New College, since 1998, University of Oxford. *Educ:* St Mary's Hosp. Med. Sch., London Univ. (MB BS 1977); PhD London 1984; MA Oxon. MRCP 1979. Oxford University: Lectr in Clin. Immunology, 1985–92; Fellow, Linacre Coll., 1985–98. Louis-Jeantet Prize for Medicine, Geneva, 1992; Canada Gairdner Foundn Internat. Award, Toronto, 2000. *Address:* Weatherall Institute of Molecular Medicine, John Radcliffe Hospital, Headington, Oxford OX3 9DS. *T:* (01865) 222328; New College, Oxford OX1 3BN.

**TOWNSEND, Antony John;** Financial Regulators (formerly Services) Complaints Commissioner, since 2014; *b* London, 24 April 1957; *s* of Paul and Molly Townsend (*née* Ure); *m* 1st, 1984, Gillian Grice (marr. diss. 2006); two *s* two *d*; 2nd, 2006, Katherine Carter; two *s*. *Educ:* Bedales Sch.; Merton Coll., Oxford (MA English Lang. and Lit.). Civil Servant, Home Office, 1980–90; Hd of Conduct, then Dir, Standards and Educn, GMC, 1990–2001; Chief Executive: GDC, 2001–06; Solicitors Regulation Authy, 2006–14. Chair: UK and Ireland Regulatory Bd, RICS, 2013–; Regulatory Bd, ACCA, 2014–; Member: Bd, Professional Standards Authy for Health and Social Care, 2015– (Chm., Scrutiny Cttee, 2017–; Mem., Nominations Cttee, 2019–); Exec. Cttee, Ombudsman Assoc., 2018–; Determinations Panel, Pensions Regulator, 2018–. Trustee, Citizens Advice S Warwickshire (formerly Warwick Dist CAB), 2014–. *Recreation:* singing. *Address:* Office of the Complaints Commissioner, 23 Austin Friars, EC2N 2QP. *T:* (020) 7562 5530. *E:* complaintscommissioner@frccommissioner.org.uk.

**TOWNSEND, Bryan Sydney,** CBE 1994; Chairman, Midlands Electricity plc (formerly Midlands Electricity Board), 1986–96 (Chief Executive, 1990–92); *b* 2 April 1930; *s* of Sydney and Gladys Townsend; *m* 1951, Betty Eileen Underwood (*d* 2014); one *s* two *d*. *Educ:* Wolverton Technical Coll. CEng, FIET; FIMgt. Trainee, Northampton Electric Light & Power Co., 1946–50; successive appts, E Midlands, Eastern and Southern Electricity Bds, 1952–66; Southern Electricity Board: Swindon Dist Manager, 1966–68; Newbury Area Engr, 1968–70; Asst Chief Engr, 1970–73; Dep. Chief Engr, SE Electricity Bd, 1973–76; Chief Engr, S Wales Electricity Bd, 1976–78; Dep. Chm., SW Electricity Bd, 1978–86. Chm., Applecourt Develt. *Recreation:* golf.

**TOWNSEND, Dr Christina;** Chief Executive, Valuation Tribunal Service, 2007–09; *b* 10 Jan. 1947; *d* of Sidney Townsend and Vera (*née* Wallis). *Educ:* Dursley Grammar Sch., Glos; Leeds Univ. (BSc Psychol.); Birmingham Univ. (MSc); UWIST (PhD). Lectr, UWIST, 1973–75; Sen. Res. Officer, MSC, 1976–78; Asst Dir, Ashridge Mgt Coll., 1978–80; Hd of Div., Inst. of Manpower Studies, 1981–84; NHS Training Authority, subseq. Directorate: Dir, Res. Educn and Trng, 1984–88; Chief Exec., 1988–91; Nat. Trng Dir and Chief Exec., 1991–93; Chief Executive: Business & Technol. Educn Council, subseq. Edexcel Foundn, 1994–2002; Soc. of Chiropodists and Podiatrists, 2002–03; Appeals Service, 2003–06; Efficiency Dir, Tribunals Service, 2006–07. Dep. Chm., Personnel Standards Lead Body, 1991–94; Director: City Technol. Colls Trust, 1994–95; Mgt Charter Initiative, 1994–95; Further Educn Develt Agency, 1994–97; Member Council: Nat. Forum for Mgt Educn and Develt, 1994–99; Inst. for Employment Studies, 1998–; Mem. Bd, British Trng Internat., 1999–2001. Mem., Southwark PCT, 2007; Chm., Patient Participation Gp, Surrey Docks Health Centre, 2012–. Gov., Corp. of Cambridge Regl Coll., 1997–2003. Chm., Housing for Women, 2007–11. Trustee: Volunteer Reading Help, 2002–08; Age UK, 2015–17; Ind. Trustee, Police Dependants' Trust, 2015–18; Chair of Trustees, Citizens Advice Camden, 2017–. MInstD 1991 (Mem., Nat. Employment Cttee, 1991–97); CCMI (CIMgt 1994). JP City of Westminster, 2006. *Recreations:* travelling, hill-walking, theatre, bird watching. *Address:* 173 Rotherhithe Street, SE16 5QY.

**TOWNSEND, Christopher Peter,** OBE 2013; Commercial Director, Chelsea Football Club, since 2017; *b* Salisbury, Rhodesia, 25 May 1956; *s* of Gordon H. Townsend and Jean D. Townsend; two *s*. *Educ:* St Wilfred's RC Secondary Sch., Crawley; Newcastle Univ. (BSc Hons Geog. 1977); Nottingham Trent Univ. (MSc Mktg Mgt 1997). Grad. trainee and Sales Manager, EMI Records, 1977–80; Sales and Mktg Manager, Riva Computers, 1980–84; Mktg Controller, Laskys, 1984–86; Jt Man. Dir, DMB & B Direct, 1986–90; Marketing Director: BBC Subscription TV, BBC Enterprises, 1990–92; BSkyB, 1992–98; Dir, Interactive Services & Ecommerce, Telewest Broadband, 1999–2003; Gp Mktg Dir, TfL, 2003–06; Commercial Dir, LOCOG, 2006–12; Exec. Dir, and CEO, Broadband Delivery UK, DCMS, 2014–17. Associate Fellow, Green Templeton Coll., Oxford, 2006–; Vis. Fellow, Newcastle Univ. Business Sch., 2012–. Dir, Invictus Games, 2014–16. Mem., Develt Bd, Tusk, 2015–. *Recreations:* road cycling, circuit training, motor sport, rock concerts, classical concerts, ballet, collecting art, Manchester United. *Address:* Chelsea Football Club, Stamford Bridge, Fulham Road, SW6 1HS.

**TOWNSEND, Brig. Ian Glen,** CBE 2006; Director (formerly Secretary) General, Royal British Legion, 1996–2006; *b* 7 Feb. 1941; *s* of Kenneth Townsend and Irene (*née* Singleton); *m* 1st, 1964, Loraine Jean (marr. diss. 1988), *d* of late William A. H. Birnie, USA; twin *d*; 2nd, 1989, Susan Natalie, *d* of late Comdr Frank A. L. Heron-Watson, Dalbeattie; two step *s*. *Educ:* Dulwich Coll.; RMA, Sandhurst (psc †). Commnd RA, 1961; served UK, Norway, Singapore, Brussels and Germany, 1961–71; RMCS, 1971–72; Staff Coll., Camberley, 1972–73; MoD, BAOR and NATO, 1973–85; Comdr Artillery, 1st Armd Div., BAOR, 1986–88; ACOS, Trng, HQ UKLF, 1988–91. Hon. Col, 27 Field Regt, 1988–92. Dir, Sales and Marketing, Land Systems, 1991–93, Mil. Advr, 1993–96, VSEL; Director: Townsend Associates, 1993–96; Legion Enterprise Ltd, 1999; RBL Training Coll., 2000–. NMA Enterprise, 2004–08; Nat. Meml Arboretum, 2004–08. Mem., Nat. Meml Cttee for NI, 2004–08. Trustee: Officers' Assoc., 1996–2006; Mil. Mus. of the Pacific, 1997–; Desert Rats 7th Armd Div. Commemoration Fund, 1998–2008; Armed Forces Meml Trust, 2003–; Chm., Confedn of Service and Ex-Service Orgns, 2002–03; Vice-Pres., World Veterans' Fedn, 2006– (Chm., World Veterans' Fedn, Europe, 2002–09). Freeman, City of London, 1999. CCMI 2004 (FCMI) (FInstM 1988); FRSA 2006. Mem., ACEVO (formerly ACENVO), 1997–2006. Gov., Salisbury Coll., 2001–03. Gold Medal, World Veterans' Fedn, 2016. *Publications:* articles in professional jls. *Recreations:* walking, painting, music, theatre. *Clubs:* Army and Navy, Royal Over-Seas League.

**TOWNSEND, James Neville; His Honour Judge Townsend;** a Circuit Judge, since 2018; *b* London, 24 April 1957; *m* 1989; one *s* three *d*. *Educ:* Bedales Sch.; New Coll., Oxford (BA 1979; MA 1982). Called to the Bar, Inner Temple, 1980; in practice as barrister, Guildhall Chambers, Bristol, 1980–2018 (Hd of Chambers, 2015–17); a Recorder, 1999–2018. *Address:* The Law Courts, 10 Armada Way, Plymouth, Devon PL1 2ER.

**TOWNSEND, Mrs Joan,** MA, MSc; Headmistress, Oxford High School, GPDST, 1981–96; *b* 7 Dec. 1936; *d* of Emlyn Davies and Amelia Mary Davies (*née* Tyrer); *m* 1960, William Godfrey Townsend, Prof. Emeritus, Cranfield Univ.; two *d*. *Educ:* Somerville Coll., Oxford (Beilby Schol.; BA (Cl.I), MA); University College of Swansea, Univ. of Wales (MSc). School teaching and lecturing of various kinds, including: Tutor, Open University, 1971–75; Lectr, Oxford Polytechnic, 1975–76; Head of Mathematics, School of S Helen and S Katharine, Abingdon, 1976–81. FRSA 1986. *Publications:* paper in Qly Jl Maths and Applied Mech., 1965. *Address:* Silver Howe, 62 Iffley Turn, Oxford OX4 4HN. *T:* (01865) 715807.

**TOWNSEND, Martin;** Partner, Pagefield Communications, since 2019; *b* 11 July 1960; *s* of Ronald Norman Townsend and Margaret Annie Townsend (*née* Pattrick); *m* 1989, Jane O'Gorman; two *s* one *d*. *Educ:* Harrow Co. Grammar Sch.; London Coll. of Printing. Staff writer: Do It Yourself, 1979–81; Caravan, 1981–82; Sen. Writer, No 1, 1983–85; Co-creator, The Hit, 1985; Pop Ed., Today newspaper, 1986–87; freelance journalist, 1987–94; Showbusiness Ed., You mag., 1994–96; Ed., OK! mag., 1998–2001; Ed., Sunday Express, 2001–18. *Publications:* The Father I Had, 2007 (Mind Book of the Year, 2008). *Recreations:* listening to music, cycling, architecture, football, conversation. *Address:* Pagefield Communications, The Courtyard Studio, 18 Marshall Street, W1F 7BE. *E:* martin.townsend@pagefield.co.uk.

**TOWNSEND, Michael John,** OBE 2003; Principal Advisor, Conservation Advocacy, since 2013 (Senior Advisor, 2006–13); *b* 12 July 1957; *s* of John and Kathleen Townsend; *m* 1991, Amanda Adkins; two *s*. *Educ:* University Coll. of N Wales (BSc Hons Forestry 1986); Open Univ. (MA Envmt, Policy and Society 2007). MICFor 1990, FICFor 2002. Project leader, VSO, Kenya, 1980–83; Regl Manager, EFG plc, 1986–92; Michael Townsend Forestry & Landscapes, 1992–95; Woodland Trust: Woodland Ops Dir, 1995–97; Chief Exec., 1997–2004; Special Advr, 2006–. Trustee: Tree Aid, 2003–05; Herefordshire Wildlife Trust, 2018–. *Recreations:* bird-watching, gardening. *Address:* The Woodland Trust, The Elms, Eardisley, Hereford HR3 6PW.

**TOWNSEND, Prof. Paul Kingsley,** PhD; FRS 2000; Professor of Theoretical Physics, University of Cambridge, since 1998; *b* 3 March 1951; *m* Fátima Azpiroz; one *d*. *Educ:* Queens' Coll., Cambridge (BA 1972; MA); Brandeis Univ., Mass (PhD 1976). Postdoctoral Fellow, SUNY, 1976–79; UK Fellow, CERN, Geneva, 1980–81; Curie-Joliot Fellow, subseq. CNRS Vis. Fellow, Lab. de Physique Théorique, Ecole Normale Supérieure, Paris, 1982–83; Lectr, 1984–96, Reader, 1996–98, Dept of Applied Maths and Theoretical Physics, Univ. of Cambridge. *Address:* Department of Applied Mathematics and Theoretical Physics, University of Cambridge, Centre for Mathematical Sciences, Wilberforce Road, Cambridge CB3 0WA.

**TOWNSEND, Dr Ralph Douglas;** Headmaster, Winchester College, 2005–16; Chairman, Cothill Trust, since 2017; *b* 13 Dec. 1951; *s* of Harry Douglas Townsend and Neila Margaret McPherson; *m* 1973, Cathryn Julie Arnold; one *s* one *d*. *Educ:* Scotch Coll., WA; Univ. of Western Australia (BA 1973); Univ. of Kent at Canterbury (MA 1975); Keble Coll., Oxford (MA 1983; DPhil 1981). Assistant Master: Dover Coll., 1975–77; Abingdon Sch., 1977–78; Sen. Scholar, Keble Coll., Oxford, 1978–81; Jun. Res. Fellow and Dean of Degrees, Lincoln Coll., Oxford, 1983–85; Asst Master, then Head of English, Eton Coll., 1985–89; Head Master, Sydney Grammar Sch., Australia, 1989–99; Headmaster, Oundle Sch., 1999–2005. Governor: Mowden Hall Sch., Northumberland, 1999–2007; Old Buckenham Hall Sch., Suffolk, 1999–2006; Ardvreck Sch., Perthshire, 2001–06; Bramcote Lorne Sch., Notts, 2003–06; Ampleforth Coll., Yorks, 2003–06; Worth Sch., Sussex, 2004–10, 2016–19; St Swithin's Sch., Winchester, 2005–14; The Pilgrim's Sch., Winchester, 2005–14; Church Schs Co., 2005–11; Ct, Univ. of Southampton, 2005–14; St John's Sch., Old Windsor, 2008–17; Midhurst Rother Coll., W Sussex, 2008–16; Charterhouse Sch., 2016–19; Pres., Keio Acad. of NY, 2019–. Dir, 2012–14, Chm., 2014–16, Educn Fellowship (formerly Educn Trust); Adviser: United Learning Trust, 2005–11; African Leadership Acad., 2005–16; Nat. Coll. of Music, London, 2005–16; Sen. Consultant, China Europe Educn Res. Foundn, 2015–19; Sen. Advr, RSAcademics, 2016–17; Educn Advr, Manilla Gymnasium, Sweden, 2016–19. Trustee, St George's House, Windsor, 2015–19. Director: Lumia Skolan, Sweden, 2016–; Winton Consulting Ltd, 2017–. Hon. Liveryman, Grocers' Co., 2005. KHS 2011. *Recreations:* music, reading, walking. *Club:* Savile.

**TOWNSEND, Valerie Carol Marian;** *see* Vaz, V. C. M.

**TOWNSHEND,** family name of **Marquess Townshend.**

**TOWNSHEND, 8th Marquess** *cr* 1787; **Charles George Townshend;** Bt 1617; Baron Townshend, of Lynn Regis 1661; Viscount Townshend, of Raynham 1682; *b* 26 Sept. 1945; *s* of 7th Marquess Townshend and Elizabeth (*née* Luby, later Gault); *S* father, 2010; *m* 1st, 1975, Hermione (*d* 1985), *d* of Lt-Cdr R. M. D. Ponsonby and Mrs Dorothy Ponsonby; one *s* one *d*; 2nd, 1990, Mrs Alison Marshall, *yr d* of Sir Willis Combs, KCVO, CMG. *Educ:* Eton; Royal Agricultural College, Cirencester. Chm. and Dir, AIMS Ltd, 1977–87; Man. Dir, Raynham Workshops Ltd, 1986–94; Chm., Pera International, 1988–96. Gen. Comr, Income Tax, Norwich, 1989–97. Mem. Council, Design Gp Great Britain Ltd, 1984–90 (Chm., 1988). Mem. Council for Norfolk and Chief Steward, Royal Show, RASE, 1982–94. Patron: Gen. Townshend Club, Fakenham, 2004–; Upper Wensum Benefice, 2008–; Coxford Gp of Churches, 2008–; Pres., Fakenham and Dist Br., RBL. Churchwarden, St Mary's, East Raynham, and St Margaret's, West Raynham, 1991–. Hon. Mem., Cons. Club, Fakenham. *Heir: s* Viscount Raynham, *qv*. *Address:* Raynham Hall, Fakenham, Norfolk NR21 7EP. *E:* townshend@raynhamhall.com.

**TOWNSHEND, Prof. Charles Jeremy Nigel,** DPhil; FBA 2008; Professor of International History, University of Keele, 1987–2012, now Emeritus; *b* Nottingham, 27 July 1945; *s* of John Walter Henwood Townshend and Helen Betty Townshend; *m* 1978, Katherine Jane Lawley; two *s*. *Educ:* Oriel Coll., Oxford (BA 1967; DPhil 1973). Lectr in Hist., 1973–81, Sen. Lectr, 1981–87, Keele Univ. Olin Fellow, Nat. Humanities Center, N Carolina, 1987–88; Fellow, Woodrow Wilson Internat. Center for Scholars, Washington, 1991–92. *Publications:* The British Campaign in Ireland, 1975; Political Violence in Ireland: government and resistance since 1848, 1983; Britain's Civil Wars: counter insurgency in the twentieth century, 1986; Consensus in Ireland: approaches and recessions, 1988; Making the Peace: public order and public security in modern Britain, 1993; The Oxford Illustrated History of Modern War, 1997; Ireland: the 20th century, 1998; The State: historical and political dimensions, 1999; Terrorism: a very short introduction, 2002; Easter 1916: the Irish Rebellion, 2005; When God Made Hell: the British invasion of Mesopotamia and the creation of Iraq 1014–1921, 2010; The Republic: the fight for Irish independence 1918–1923, 2013 (Christopher Ewart-Biggs Meml Prize, 2014). *Recreation:* mountain biking. *Address:* 5 Church Plantation, Keele, Staffs ST5 5AY. *E:* c.j.n.townshend@keele.ac.uk.

**TOWNSHEND, Peter Dennis Blandford;** composer, performer, publisher, author; *b* London, 19 May 1945; *s* of Clifford and Betty Townshend; *m* 1st, 1968, Karen Astley (marr. diss. 2010); one *s* two *d*; 2nd, 2016, Rachel Fuller. *Educ:* Acton County Grammar Sch.; Ealing Art Coll. Mem., The Who, rock group, 1963–; Editor, Faber & Faber, 1983–90s; *recordings* include: with The Who: Tommy, 1969 (musical, filmed 1975, Grammy Award 1993, staged NY (Tony Award for best score), 1993, Toronto (Dora Mavor Moore Award), 1994, London, 1996 (Olivier Award, 1997)); Quadrophenia, 1973 (Classic Rock Award, 2011); Endless Wire, 2006; Quadrophenia: The Director's Cut, 2011; Who, 2019; singles: My Generation; I Can See For Miles; Can't Explain; Substitute; Pinball Wizard; solo: Empty Glass, 1980; Iron Man, 1989; Psychoderelict, 1993. Hon. DLitt W London, 2010. Ivor Novello Award, 1981; British Phonographic Industry Lifetime Achievement Award, 1983. BRIT Award for contribn to British Music, 1988; Living Legend Award, Internat. Rock Awards, 1991; Q Lifetime Achievement Award, 1997; Ivor Novello Lifetime Achievement Award, 2001; (jtly) Kennedy Center Honor, John F. Kennedy Center for Performing Arts, 2008; (jtly) Rock Honor, VH1, 2008; Les Paul Award, TEC Foundn, 2012. *Publications:* Horse's Neck, 1986; Who I Am (autobiog.), 2012; The Age of Anxiety (novel), 2019. *Recreation:* sailing.

**TOY, Rev. Canon John,** PhD; FSA; Chancellor of York Minster, 1983–99 (also Librarian and Guestmaster); Residentiary Canon, York Minster, 1983–99, now Emeritus; Prebendary of Laughton-en-le-Morthen, 1994–99; *b* 25 Nov. 1930; *e s* of late Sidney Toy, FSA and late Violet Mary (*née* Doudney), *m* 1963, Mollie, *d* of Eric and Elsie Tilbury; one *s* one *d*. *Educ:* Epsom County Grammar Sch.; Hatfield Coll., Durham (BA 1st cl. Hons Theol. 1953, MA 1962); PhD Leeds 1982. Ordained deacon, 1955, priest, 1956; Curate, St Paul's, Lorrimore Sq., Southwark, 1955–58; Student Christian Movement Sec. for S of England, 1958–60; Chaplain: Ely Theol Coll., 1960–64; St Andrew's Church, Gothenburg, Sweden, 1965–69; St John's College, York: Lectr in Theology, 1969; Sen. Lectr, 1972; Principal Lectr, 1979–83; Prebendary of Tockerington, 1983–94. FSA 2013. Kt, Royal Order of Polar Star, 1st cl. (Sweden), 2002. *Publications:* Jesus, Man for God, 1988; (jtly) A Pilgrim Guide to York, 1997; English Saints in the Medieval Liturgies of Scandinavian Churches, 2009; (jtly) The Office of St William of York, 2017; The Cult of St Olaf in England, 2017; contrib. to learned jls and cathedral booklets. *Recreations:* Scandinavia, history, architecture. *Address:* 15 Dulverton Hall, Esplanade, Scarborough, N Yorks YO11 2AR. *T:* (01723) 340115. *E:* johntoy@talktalk.net.

**TOYE, Bryan Edward;** JP; Chairman, Toye Group Holdings Ltd and associated companies, since 1969; *b* 17 March 1938; *s* of Herbert Graham Donovan Toye and late Marion Alberta Toye (*née* Montignani); *m* 1982, Fiona Ann, *d* of G. H. J. Hogg, Wellington, NZ; three *s* one *d*. *Educ:* St Andrew's Prep. Sch., Eastbourne; Stowe Sch. Joined Toye & Co., 1956; Dir, Toye Kenning & Spencer, 1962–; Dir, Toye & Co., 1966; Dep. Chm., Futurama Sign Gp Ltd, 1992–96; Mem. Adv. Bd, The House of Windsor Collection Ltd, 1994–95; non-executive Director: Trehaven Trust Ltd, 1990–97; DG HR (Navy) (formerly Naval Manning Agency), 1999–2005. Mem., Lloyd's, 1985–91. Member: Council, Advancing UK Aerospace Defence and Security Industries (formerly Defence Manufacturers Assoc.), 2005–10 (Chm., Clothing Interest Gp; Dep. Chm., Commercial Gp); Defence Sector Bd, 2010–. Alderman, Ward of Lime Street, City of London, 1983–96 (Past Pres., Lime St Ward Club); Master, Gold and Silver Wyre Drawers' Co., 1984; Liveryman, Goldsmiths' Co., 1985 (Prime Warden, 2004–05); Member, Court of Assistants: Broderers' Co. (Master, 1996–97); Guild of Freemen of City of London, 1986–97 (Mem., 1983). Member: United Wards Club, City of London; Tower Ward Club; Dowgate Ward Club. Pres., Royal Warrant Holders' Assoc., 1991–92 (Mem. Council, 1983–; Hon. Auditor, 1998–). Mem. Council, NSPCC, London, 1966–69; Chm., Greater London Playing Fields Assoc., 1988–90; Mem. Council, London Playing Fields Soc., 1990–92; Policy and Resources Cttee, King George's Fund for Sailors, 1990–92. Mem., W Midlands Council, CBI, 2010–. Trustee: (founder Mem.) Queen Elizabeth Scholarship Trust, 1990–96; Britain-Australia Bicentennial Trust; Black Country Museum (London Gp), 1991–97; British Red Cross, 1993– (Vice Pres. London Br., 1993–). Governor: City of London Sch., 1985–88; King Edward's Sch., Witley, 1988–93; Bridewell Royal Hosp., 1989–96; Christ's Hosp., 1989–96; City of London Freemen's Sch., 1993–96. Mem. Ct, RCA, 1983–86. Hon. Mem., Ct of Assts, HAC, 1986; Hon. Col 55 Ordnance Co. RAOC (V), 1988–93; Hon. Col, 124 Havering Petroleum Sqdn RLC (V), 1994–2000; Hon. Ordnance Officer, Tower of London, 1994–2008. Member: TA&VRA for Gtr London, 1992–99; City of London TA&VRA, 1992–99. Member: Royal Soc. of St George, London Br., 1981; Huguenot Soc., 1985; Cttee, Old Stoic Soc., 1985–92; Stewards' Enc., Henley Royal Regatta, 1980. FInstD 1966; FCMI (FIMgt 1983); FRSA 1985; MCIPS 1991. JP: City of London, 1983–96 (Chm. Bench, 1990–96); Hereford & Worcs, Supplemental list, 1996. OStJ 1980. *Recreations:* cricket, squash, shooting, sailing, swimming, tennis, gardening, classical music, Rugby, entertaining. *Address:* Toye Group Holdings Ltd, Newtown Road, Bedworth, Warwickshire CV12 8QR. *T:* (02476) 848800. *E:* brian.toye@toye.com. *Clubs:* Royal Automobile (Life Mem. 1968), City Livery (Pres., 1988–89), MCC; Middlesex Co. RFC; Wasps FC (Vice-Pres.); Leander (Henley).

**TOYE, Prof. John Francis Joseph;** Chairman, Advisory Council, Department of International Development, University of Oxford, since 2010; *b* 7 Oct. 1942; *s* of late John Redmond Toye and Adele Toye (*née* Francis); *m* 1967, Janet Reason; one *s* one *d*. *Educ:* Christ's Coll., Finchley; Jesus Coll., Cambridge (schol.; MA); Harvard Univ. (Frank Knox Vis. Fellow); Sch. of Oriental and African Studies, Univ. of London (MScEcon; PhD). Asst Principal, HM Treasury, 1965–68; Res. Fellow, SOAS, Univ. of London, 1970–72; Fellow (later Tutor), Wolfson Coll., Cambridge, 1972–80, and Asst Dir of Develt Studies, Cambridge Univ., 1977–80; Dir, Commodities Res. Unit Ltd, 1980–85; Prof. of Develt Policy and Planning and Dir, Centre for Develt Studies, University Coll. of Swansea, 1982–87; Dir, 1987–97, Fellow, 1987–98, Inst. of Develt Studies, Univ. of Sussex; Dir, Globalisation and Develt Strategies Div., UN Conf. on Trade and Develt, Geneva, 1998–2000; Dir, Centre for Study of African Economies, Oxford, 2000–03; Sen. Res. Associate, Queen Elizabeth Hse, Oxford, 2003–09. Hon. Fellow, Univ. of Birmingham, Inst. of Local Govt Studies, 1986. Member: Council, ODI, 1988–96; Adv. Cttee on Econ. and Social Res., ODA, 1989–95. Dir, Penn Club, 2010–12. *Publications:* (ed) Taxation and Economic Development, 1978; (ed) Trade and Poor Economies, 1979; Public Expenditure and Indian Development Policy 1960–70, 1981; Dilemmas of Development, 1987; (jtly) Does Aid Work in India?, 1990; (jtly) Aid and Power, 1991; Structural Adjustment and Employment Policy, 1995; Keynes on Population, 2000; (jtly) The UN and Global Political Economy, 2004; UNCTAD at Fifty: a short history, 2014; The Many Faces of Socioeconomic Change, 2017; numerous articles in acad. jls. *Recreations:* walking, music. *Address:* 6 Manor Court, Cambridge CB3 9BE.

**TOYNBEE, Polly;** columnist, The Guardian, 1977–88 and since 1998; writer; *b* 27 Dec. 1946; *d* of late Philip Toynbee, and of Anne Powell; *m* 1970, Peter Jenkins (*d* 1992); one *s* two *d*, and one step *d*. *Educ:* Badminton Sch.; Holland Park Comprehensive; St Anne's Coll., Oxford. Reporter, The Observer, 1968–71; Editor, The Washington Monthly, USA, 1972–73; Feature Writer, The Observer, 1974–76; Social Affairs Editor, News and Current Affairs, BBC, 1988–95; Associate Editor and columnist, The Independent, 1995–97. Vis. Fellow, Nuffield Coll., Oxford, 2004–12. Contested (SDP) Lewisham E,

1983. Gov., LSE, 1988–99. Member: Home Office Cttee on Obscenity and Censorship, 1980; DoH Adv. Cttee on the Ethics of Xenotransplantation, 1996; DoH Nat. Screening Cttee, 1996–2003; Mitochondria Consultation Gp, HFEA, 2012; NHS Assembly, 2019–. Mem. Bd, Political Qly, 2003–. President: Social Policy Assoc., 2005–09; Humanists UK (formerly British Humanist Assoc.), 2007–12, now Life Vice Pres.; Community Practitioners and Health Visitors Assoc., 2013–17. Chm. of Judges, Orange Prize, 2002; Chair, Brighton Dome and Fest., 2005–. Dir, Wise Gp, 2005–10; Trustee, Social Mobility Foundn, 2007–15. Hon. LLD: Essex, 2001; South Bank, 2002; Hon. DLitt: Loughborough, 2004; Sussex, 2006; DUniv: Stafford, 2004; Open, 2005; Kent, 2007; Hon. DLaws Leeds, 2004. Catherine Pakenham Award for Journalism, 1975; British Press Award, 1977, 1982, 1986, Columnist of the Year, 2007; BBC What the Papers Say Award, 1996 (Commentator of the Year); Magazine Writer of the Year, PPA, 1996; George Orwell Prize, 1997. *Publications:* Leftovers, 1966; A Working Life, 1970 (paperback 1972); Hospital, 1977 (paperback 1979); The Way We Live Now, 1981; Lost Children, 1985; Hard Work: life in low-pay Britain, 2003; with David Walker: Did Things Get Better? an audit of Labour's successes and failures, 2001; Better or Worse? Has Labour Delivered?, 2005; Unjust Rewards, 2008; The Verdict: did Labour change Britain?, 2010; Dogma and Disarray: Cameron at half time, 2012; Cameron's Coup: how the Tories took Britain to the brink, 2015; Dismembered: how the attack on the state harms us all, 2017. *Address:* The Guardian, Kings Place, 90 York Way, N1 9LG. *T:* (020) 7239 9556.

**TOYNE, Prof. Peter,** CBE 2009; Chairman, Friends of Cathedral Music, 2002–17; b 3 Dec. 1939; s of Harold and Doris Toyne; m 1969, Angela Wedderburn; one s. *Educ:* Ripon Grammar Sch.; Bristol Univ. (BA) The Sorbonne. Res. Asst, Univ. of Lille, 1964; Univ. of Exeter: Lectr in Geography, 1965–76; Sen. Lectr in Geography and Sub Dean of Social Studies, 1976–78; Dir, DES Credit Transfer Feasibility Study, 1978–80; Hd of Bishop Otter Coll., Chichester, and Dep. Dir (Academic), W Sussex Inst. of Higher Educn, 1980–83; Dep. Rector, NE London Polytechnic, 1983–86; Rector, Liverpool Poly., 1986–92, then Vice-Chancellor and Chief Exec., Liverpool John Moores Univ., 1992–2000 (Hon. Fellow, 2000). Sen. Inspector, Theol Colls, 1980–. Chm., Guidance Accreditation Bd, 1999–2002; Member: Council, Industrial Soc., 1997–2000; C of E Archbishops' Council, 1999–2006; Merseyside Bd, Nat. Probation Service, 2004–08. Chairman: Trustees, Rodolfus Choir, 1995–2001; Trustees, Liverpool St George's Hall, 1996–2000; Groundwork St Helens, Knowsley, Sefton & Liverpool, 1997–2001; Royal Liverpool Philharmonic Soc., 2000–03; Liverpool Culture Co., 2000–03; Liverpool Cathedral Develt Trust, 2002–08; Choirbook Trust, 2010–16; Thames Youth Orch., 2010–16; Trustee: Southwark Cathedral Educn Centre, 2012–; Young Organ Scholars Trust, 2016–. Chm., Woodlands Hospice, 2005–. Governor: Glyndŵr Univ., 2008–13; Liverpool Inst. of Performing Arts, 2008–13. Pres., Liverpool YMCA, 1997–2015. Hon. Life Pres., Liverpool Organists' Assoc., 2000–. DL 1990–2009, High Sheriff 2001, Merseyside. Hon. Col, 33 Signal Regt (V), 1999–2006. Hon. Freeman, City of Liverpool, 2010. FRSA; CCMI; FICPD; FRSCM 2018; Fellow, Eton Coll., 1996–2001. Hon. Fellow, Glyndŵr Univ., 2013. Hon. DEd CNAA, 1992. *Publications:* World Problems, 1970; Techniques in Human Geography, 1971; Organisation, Location and Behaviour, 1974; Recreation and Environment, 1974; Toyne Report: Credit Transfer, 1979; Toyne Report: Environmental Education, 1993; numerous articles in geographical, educnl jls, festschriften and popular press. *Recreations:* railways (model and real), liturgy, music (especially sacred). *Address:* 50 Commodore House, Juniper Drive, SW18 1TW. *E:* p.toyne@btinternet.com.

**TOYNE SEWELL, Maj.-Gen. Timothy Patrick;** DL; Director, Goodenough College (formerly The London Goodenough Trust for Overseas Graduates), 1995–2006; b 7 July 1941; s of late Brig. E P Sewell, CBE and E. C. M. Sewell, MBE (née Toyne); m 1965, Jennifer Lesley Lunt; one s one d. *Educ:* Bedford Sch.; Royal Military Acad., Sandhurst. Commnd KOSB, 1961; ADC to Governor of Aden, 1962–63; helicopter pilot, 2 RGJ and 2 Para, 1966–69; psc 1973; GSO 1, staff of CDS, 1979–81; CO, 1 KOSB, 1981–83; COS, British Forces Falkland Is, 1983–84; Sen. Directing Staff (Army), JSDC, 1984–85; Comdr, 19 Infantry Bde, 1985–87; rcds 1988; Comdr, British Mil. and Adv. Team, Zimbabwe, 1989–91; Comdt, RMA, 1991–94. Team Ldr, Tri Service Study into Services Recruiting Orgns, 1994–95. Col, KOSB, 1995–2001. Chairman: Exec. Cttee, Disability Sport England, 1998–99; Internat. Bd, United World Colls, 2006–12. Non-exec. Dir, Catalyst Investment Gp Ltd, 2007–12. Chm., Benjamin Britten Internat. Violin Competition, 2002–19. Life Gov., Haileybury, 1993; Chm. of Govs, Lambrook Haileybury Sch., 2003–08; Mem. Council, QMW, 1996–2005; Trustee: Med. Coll. of St Bartholomew's Hosp. Trust, 2000–05; Bedford Sch. Foundn, 2006–09; North-West Univ. (SA) Trust UK, 2004–08; Trichord Abrahamic Foundn, Poland, 2014–17; Lewis Pugh Foundn, 2017–; Mem. Bd, UWC Dilijan, Armenia, 2013–16; Chm., Supervisory Bd, Seeb Sch., Oman, 2011–18; Bd, British Internat. Sch., Casablanca, 2018–. Chm., Nether Wallop New Village Hall Trust, 2014–18. DL Greater London, 1999. Freeman, City of London, 2006. *Recreations:* racquet sports, golf, fishing, music. *Club:* Royal Over-Seas League (Mem. Council, 2002–09).

**TOZER, Stephanie,** QC 2019; b Wells, 1973; d of Ian and Mary Tozer; m 2012, Gordon Russell; one d. *Educ:* Godstowe Prep. Sch., High Wycombe; Badminton Sch., Bristol; St Swithun's Sch., Winchester; Keble Coll., Oxford (BA 1st Cl. Juris); Inns of Court Sch. of Law. Called to the Bar, Lincoln's Inn, 1996; Judge of First-Tier Tribunal (Property Chamber) (Land Registration), 2008–. *Publications:* (contrib.) The Law and Practice of Charging Orders on Land, 2013; (contrib.) The Electronic Communications Code and Property Law Practice and Procedure, 2018; (with C. Crampin) Mortgage Receivership Law and Practice, 2018. *Recreations:* family, ski-ing, dance. *Address:* Falcon Chambers, Falcon Court, EC4Y 1AA. *T:* (020) 7353 2484. *E:* tozer@falcon-chambers.com.

**TOZZI, Keith,** CEng, FICE; Executive Director: Tozzi Ltd, since 2011; The Bodyworks Ltd, since 2014; b 23 Feb. 1949; s of late Edward Thomas Tozzi and Winifred Tozzi (née Killick); m 2013, Fiona Begley; two s one d by a former marriage. *Educ:* Dartford Grammar Sch.; City Univ. (BSc Hons); Univ. of Kent (MA); Harvard Business Sch. (Internat. SMP). Civil Engr, Thames Water, 1973–75; Southern Water plc: Water Manager, 1975–81; Ops Manager, 1981–86; Engrg Manager, 1986–88; Divl Dir, 1988–92; Gp Technical Dir, 1992–96; Chm., Nat. Jt Utilities Gp, 1993–96; Chief Exec., BSI, 1997–2000; Gp Chief Exec., Mid-Kent Hldgs, subseq. Swan Gp plc, 2000–03; Chief Exec., Clifton Capital Investments, 2003–06; Chief Exec., 2005–06, Chm., 2006–10, Concateno plc; Dir, Ingemino Ltd, 2011–14. Chairman: RSVP.i (formerly IPID.com), 2000–; Inspicio plc, 2005–08; Kane Insce Gp, 2011–14; non-executive Director: Legal & General UK Select Investment Trust, 2000–03; Seal Analytical Ltd, 2004–09. Mem., CBI Southern Regl Council, 2000–04. Master, Water Conservators' Co., 2016–17. *Publications:* articles in newspapers and technical jls. *Recreations:* gardening, reading, classic cars. *Address:* The Top House, Chalfont Heights, Gerrards Cross, Bucks SL9 9TD. *T:* (01753) 889497.

**TOZZI, Nigel Kenneth,** QC 2001; b 31 Aug. 1957; s of Ronald Kenneth Tozzi and Doreen Elsie Florence Tozzi; m 1983, Sara Louise Clare Cornish; two s one d. *Educ:* Hitchin Boys' Grammar Sch.; Exeter Univ. (LLB 1st Cl. Hons); Inns of Court Sch. of Law (1st Cl.). Called to the Bar, Gray's Inn, 1980; in practice as Barrister and Arbitrator, specialising in commercial, insce and professional negligence litigation and internat. arbitration, 1980–. *Recreations:* playing hockey, watching cricket, theatre, cinema. *Address:* 4 Pump Court, Temple, EC4Y 7AN. *T:* (020) 7842 5555. *Clubs:* MCC; Sevenoaks Hockey.

**TRACE, Anthony John;** QC 1998; b 23 Oct. 1958; s of late Comdr Peter Trace, RD and bar, RNR, and Anne Trace (née Allison-Beer); m 1986, Caroline Tessa Durrant, e d of His Honour A. H. Durrant, qv; three s one d. *Educ:* Vinehall Prep. Sch.; Uppingham Sch.; Magdalene Coll., Cambridge (MA 1st Cl. Hons). Called to the Bar, Lincoln's Inn, 1981, Bencher, 2006. Dep. Managing Ed., Receivers, Administrators and Liquidators' Qly, 1993–2002. Vice-Chm., Chancery Bar Assoc., 2001–04 (Hon. Sec., 1997–2001). Mem., Internat. Editl Bd, Briefings in Real Estate Finance, 2000–02. Trustee, Uppingham Sch., 1999–2014. Churchwarden, St Helen's, Saddington, 2009–. Jt Organiser, Saddington Aid, 2013. Founder Member: Campaign for Real Gin, 1978; Plodda Falls Swimming Club, 2004; Friends of Turkey, 2006; CRAFT, Salcombe, 2013. Mem., Grand Order of Soc. for Protection of English Lang., 2014. Freeman, City of London, 1981; Liveryman, Musicians' Co., 1982. Jt winner, Observer Mace Debating Championship, 1981; winner: Commercial Litigation Silk of Year, Legal 500 UK Awards, 2013; UK Banking Barrister of Year, Finance Monthly Awards, 2016; Commercial Litigation Barrister of Year, Global Law Experts Awards, 2016. *Publications:* (contrib.) Butterworths European Law Service (Company Law), 1992; (contrib.) Butterworths Practical Insolvency, 1999. *Recreations:* stalking, shooting, fishing, the Turf, music, messing about in boats. *Address:* 4 Pump Court, Temple, EC4Y 7AN. *T:* (020) 7842 5555. *Clubs:* Athenæum, Garrick, Beefsteak; Pitt (Cambridge).

**TRACEY, Craig Paul;** MP (C) North Warwickshire, since 2015; b Durham, 21 Aug. 1974; s of Edward and Joyce Tracey; m 2014, Karen Mercer-West. *Educ:* Framwellgate Moor Comprehensive Sch. Owner, Dunelm Insce Brokers, 1996–2015. Dir, Dunelm Business Consultants, 2014–. Member: Southern Staffs Employment and Skills Bd, 2014–. Founder Trustee, Lichfield Garrick Th., 2012–16. *Recreations:* local football, ski-ing. *Address:* House of Commons, SW1A 0AA. *T:* (020) 7219 5646. *E:* craig.tracey.mp@parliament.uk.

**TRACEY, Prof. Ian Graham;** DL; Organist and Master of the Choristers, 1980–2007, Organist Titulaire, since 2008, Liverpool Cathedral; Professor, Fellow and Organist, Liverpool John Moores University (formerly Liverpool Polytechnic), since 1988; b 27 May 1955; s of William Tracey and Helene Mignon Tracey (née Harris). *Educ:* Trinity Coll. of Music, London (FTCL); St Katharine's Coll., Liverpool (PGCE). FRSCM 2008; FGCM 2009. Chorus Master, Royal Liverpool Philharmonic Soc., 1985–; Liverpool City Organist (formerly Consultant Organist, City of Liverpool), 1986–; Guest Dir of Music, BBC Daily Service, 1998–. Pres., Incorp. Assoc. of Organists of GB, 2001–03. Gov., Liverpool Coll., 1993–. DL Merseyside, 2015. FRSA 1988. Hon. FRCO 2004. Hon. DMus Liverpool, 2006. NW Arts Award for Classical Music, 1994. *Address:* Mornington House, Mornington Terrace, Upper Duke Street, Liverpool L1 9DY. *T:* and *Fax:* (0151) 708 8471. *E:* iantraceyenquiries@hotmail.co.uk. *W:* www.iantracey.com. *Club:* Artists' (Liverpool).

**TRACEY, Prof. Irene Mary Carmel,** DPhil; FRCA; FMedSci; Nuffield Professor of Anaesthetic Sciences, since 2007, Head, Nuffield Department of Clinical Neurosciences, since 2016, and Pro-Vice Chancellor, since 2018, University of Oxford; Warden, Merton College, Oxford, since 2019; b Oxford, 30 Oct. 1966; d of James Michael Tracey and Harriet (Irene) Beach Tracey (née Bell); m 1994, Prof. Myles Robert Allen, qv; two s one d. *Educ:* St Thomas More RC Primary Sch.; Gosford Hill Comprehensive Sch.; Merton Coll., Oxford (BA; MA; DPhil 1993). FRCA 2009. Postdoctoral Fellow, Harvard Med. Sch., 1994–96; University of Oxford: Postdoctoral Fellow, 1997–2001; Lectr and Fellow, Christ Church, 2001–07; Dir, Oxford Centre for Functional MRI of the Brain, 2005–15; Fellow, Pembroke Coll., 2007–19; Associate Hd of Med. Scis Div., 2014–16. FMedSci 2015. *Publications:* (ed jtly) Wall and Melzack's Textbook of Pain, 6th edn 2013; Pain, 2019; contrib. papers to peer-reviewed internat. jls; H-index 72. *Recreations:* running, tennis, mountaineering, playing piano. *Address:* Merton College, Merton Street, Oxford OX1 4JD. *T:* (01865) 276310. *E:* irene.tracey@ndcn.ox.ac.uk.

**TRACEY, Richard Patrick;** JP; strategic marketing and public affairs consultant, since 1997; b 8 Feb. 1943; o s of late P. H. (Dick) Tracey and Hilda Tracey; m Katharine Gardner; one s three d. *Educ:* King Edward VI Grammar Sch., Stratford-upon-Avon; Birmingham Univ. (LLB Hons). Leader Writer, Daily Express, 1964–66; Presenter/Reporter, BBC Television and Radio, 1966–78: internat. news and current affairs (The World at One, PM, Today, Newsdesk, 24 Hours, The Money Prog.); feature programmes (Wheelbase, Waterline, Motoring and the Motorist, You and Yours, Checkpoint); also documentaries (Colossus, Me and My Migraine); Public Affairs Consultant/Advisor, 1978–83. Non-executive Director: Tallack Golf Course Construction Ltd, 1987–91; Ranelagh Ltd, 1992–96. Member: Econ. Res. Council, 1981–2000; ISIS Assoc., 1981–92. Various Conservative Party Offices, 1974–81; Dep. Chm., Greater London Cons. Party, 1981–83; Mem., Cons. National Union Exec. Cttee, 1981–83. Contested (C) Northampton N, Oct. 1974. MP (C) Surbiton, 1983–97; contested (C) Kingston and Surbiton, 1997. PPS to Min. of State for Trade and Industry (IT), 1984–85; Parly Under Sec. of State, DoE (with special responsibility for sport), 1985–87. Member: Select Cttee on Televising H of C, 1988–92; Selection Cttee, 1992–94; Public Accounts Cttee, 1994–97. Chm., Cons. Parly Greater London MPs' Cttee, 1990–97 (Jt Sec., 1983–84); Sec., Cons. Parly Media Cttee, 1983–84. Mem., Exec. Cttee, Assoc. of Former MPs, 2007–. Mem. (C) Merton and Wandsworth, London Assembly, GLA, 2008–16 (Dep. Leader, 2009–16). Member: Metropolitan Police Authy, 2008–10; London Fire and Emergency Planning Authy, 2010–12 (Vice-Chm., 2010–12); Royal Marsden Patient Adv. Gp, 2017–; Chm., London Waste and Recycling Bd, 2012–16. Community Relns Advr, Battersea Power Station Proj., 2004–08; Chm., Pro-Active S London, Sport England, 2006–08; London Mayor's Ambassador for River Transport, 2009–16. Fellow, Industry and Parlt Trust, 1984. JP SW London (Wimbledon PSD), 1977. Freeman, City of London, 1984; Craft Owning Freeman, Watermen and Lightermen's Co., 2016. Mem., Inst. of Advanced Motorists, 1993. *Publications:* (with Richard Hudson-Evans) The World of Motor Sport, 1971; (with Michael Clayton) Hickstead—the first twelve years, 1972; articles, pamphlets. *Recreations:* riding, boating, debating. *E:* rdicktracey@msn.com.

**TRACEY, Stephen Frederick T.;** see Thorpe-Tracey.

**TRACY;** see Hanbury-Tracy, family name of Baron Sudeley.

**TRAEGER, Tessa,** FRPS; photographer of still life portraiture and landscape; b 30 April 1938; d of Thomas Cecil Grimshaw and Hannah Joan (née Dearsley); m 1st, 1965, Ronald S. Traeger (d 1968); 2nd, 2006, Patrick C. Kinmonth. *Educ:* Guildford High Sch. for Girls; Guildford Sch. of Art. FRPS 2018. Freelance photographer of private and commissioned work, 1975–91, incl. Vogue UK food series; 50 portraits of leading horticulturists commnd by NPG for main collection, 2000. Solo exhibitions: Photographers' Gall., 1978; Gall. Ratié, Paris, 1979; Neal St Gall., 1980; John Hansard Gall., Southampton, 1983; Sheffield Fine Art, 1988; M Gall., Hamburg, 1993; Ardèche Fest. des Arts, France, annually, 1994–98, 2003; Michael Hoppen Gall., London, 1997; Witkin Gall., NY, 1997; James Danziger Gall., NY, 1999; Association Gall., London, 2000; Foto Fest., Naarden, Holland, 2001; A Gardener's Labyrinth, NPG, 2003, Bradford, Hove and Scarborough, 2004, Bowes Mus., 2005, Port Eliot Fest., 2011, Boughton House, 2017; Voices of Vivarias, Purdy Hicks Gall.,

London, 2010, Oklahoma City Arts Centre, 2011; Chemistry of Light, 2013, Chemistry of Light Pt II, 2016, Purdy Hicks Gall., London; Calligraphy of Dance, Boughton House, 2014, Purdy Hicks Gall., London, 2015; Water Tank project, New York City, 2014–15; Wild is the Wind, Rossetti Studios, 2017; *group exhibitions*: Seeing Things, V&A, 2002; Credit Suisse Gall., Zürich, 2005; Garden of the Year, Christie's, London, 2010; L'Arbre et le photographe, Beaux-arts de Paris, 2012; Ardèche Fest. des Arts, 2013; 100 Years of Vogue, NPG, 2016, Manchester, 2016; Here We Are, Burberry, 2017; AOP 50, One Canada Square, London, 2018; New Art Centre, Salisbury, 2019; *collections*: V&A Mus.; Bibliothèque National, Paris; Metropolitan Mus. of Art, NY; Citibank Private Bank, London; NPG, London; Buhl Collection, USA; New Hall, Cambridge; RHS, London; Nat. Maritime Mus.; Lebedev Collection, and many private collections. Contrib. to Oral Hist. of British Photography for Nat. Sound Archive, British Liby, 1996. Silver Award, 1979, Gold Award, 1982, DAAD; Lion d'Or, Cannes Advertising Fest., 1994; Silver Award, Assoc. of Fashion, Advertising and Editorial Photographers, 1997 and 1998; Pink Lady Photographer of the Year Lifetime Achievement Award, 2014. *Publications*: (with A. Boxer) Summer Winter Cookbook, 1978; (with A. Boxer) A Visual Feast, 1991 (Andre Simon Award); (with M. Harrison) Ronald Traeger New Angles: a memoir (to accompany exhibn at V&A Mus.), 1999; (with P. Kinmonth) A Gardener's Labyrinth (to accompany exhibn at NPG), 2003; (with Lora Zarubin) I'm almost always hungry, 2003 (Gourmand World Cookbook Award; Best Cookbook Photography and Internat. Assoc. of Culinary Professionals awards, USA; Julia Child Award); (with Stewart Grimshaw) A Garden in Sussex, 2009; Voices of the Vivarais, 2010 (Photographic Book Prize, British Book Design and Prodn Awards); The Calligraphy of Dance, 2014; Fern Verrow, 2015; Sally Clarke: 30 Ingredients, 2015; (with Alastair Langlands) Robert Kime, 2015; The Loveliest Valley, 2016; (jtly) Wild is the Wind, 2017. *Recreations*: gardening, walking in N Devon, restoring 16th century manor house. *Address*: 68 Chesil Court, Chelsea Manor Street, SW3 5QS.
*See also Sir N. T. Grimshaw.*

**TRAFFORD, Dr Bernard St John;** writer, educationist, musician; Headmaster, Newcastle upon Tyne Royal Grammar School, 2008–17; Interim Head, Purcell School, 2018; *b* 23 May 1956; *s* of Peter and Josephine Trafford; *m* 1981, Katherine Potts; two d. *Educ*: All Hallows Prep. Sch.; Downside Sch.; St Edmund Hall, Oxford (BA Music, MA); Westminster Coll., Oxford (PGCE); Univ. of Birmingham (MEd; PhD; George Cadbury Prize). Teacher, Royal GS, High Wycombe, 1978–81; Wolverhampton Grammar School: Dir of Music, 1981–90; Hd of Sixth Form, 1987–90; Head, 1990–2008. Chair of Trustees, Sch. Councils UK, 2006–09; Equal Opportunities Officer, 2001–03, Pubns Officer, 2003–05, Assoc. of Sch. and Coll. Leaders. Chm., HMC, 2007–08 and 2008–09. Trustee, youngchoirs, 1984–2006 (Chm., 1998–2006); Trustee and Dir, Nat. Schs SO, 1998–2006. Regular columnist: TES online; Voice of the North blog. FRSA. Freeman, City of London, 2009; Liveryman, Merchant Taylors' Co., 2009. Winner, BBC Radio 3 Breakfast Christmas Carol Competition, 2017. *Publications*: Sharing Power in Schools: raising standards, 1993; Participation, Power-sharing and School Improvement, 1997; (ed) Diversity, Inclusivity and Equal Opportunities, 2002; (ed) Making the Most of It: management in schools and colleges, 2002; (jtly) What's It All About?, 2002; (ed) Two Sectors, One Purpose: independent schools in the system, 2002; School Councils, School Democracy, School Improvement: why, what, how, 2003; Raising the Student Voice, 2006; (jtly) The Personal Touch, 2006; (ed) i²=Independent and Innovative: examples of innovation in HMC schools, 2006; (jtly) Democratic Governance of Schools, 2007; Song for a Spy (novel), 2018; contribs to educn books and jls; *compositions*: Sir Christëmas (carol for SATB choir), 2018. *Recreations*: playing jazz, writing music, walking in Northumberland, running and cycling, trying to get thinner and fitter. *Address*: Oxford and Northumberland. *T*: 07866 604266. *E*: trafford.b@gmail.com.

**TRAFFORD, Hon. Mark Russell;** QC 2015; *b* Brighton, 27 July 1966; *s* of Baron Trafford and Helen Trafford (*née* Chalk); *m* 1995, Brigitte Anne Howe; two *s* two *d*. Called to the Bar, Lincoln's Inn, 1992 (Megarry Schol. 1992); in practice as barrister, 1992–. Associate Lectr, Oxford Inst. of Legal Practice, 1996–2013. Contested (C) Bradford E, 2017. *Publications*: contribs to Jl Internat. Banking and Financial Law. *Address*: Reform Chambers, 1st Floor, Cursitor Building, 38 Chancery Lane, WC2A 1EN.

**TRAHAR, Anthony John;** Chairman, Bartlett Resources LLP, since 2007; *b* 1 June 1949; *s* of Thomas Walter Trahar and Thelma Trahar (*née* Ashmead-Bartlett); *m* 1977, Patricia Jane; one *s* one *d*. *Educ*: St John's Coll., Johannesburg; Witwatersrand Univ. (BComm). Chartered Accountant (South Africa) 1973. Anglo American: joined as mgt trainee, Anglo American Corp. of S Africa Ltd, 1974; PA to Chm., 1976–77; Financial Dir, Anglo American Industrial Corp., 1982–86; Man. Dir, 1986–89, Exec. Chm., 1989–2000, Mondi Paper Co.; Exec. Dir, Anglo American Corp., 1991; Dep. Chm., Anglo American Industrial Corp., 1992–99; Exec. Dir, 1999–2007, CEO, 2000–07, Anglo American plc; Chm., Mondi Europe, 1993–2003. Chairman: S African Motor Corp., 1996–2000; AECI Ltd, 1999–2001; Langelade Projects Ltd, 2014–; Senior Adviser: Barclays Natural Resources, 2007–13; Macquarie Capital, 2013–17; Dir, LCV Hire Solutions Ltd, 2014–. Chm., Paleo-Anthropological Scientific Trust, 1999–2007. Hon. PhD Pretoria, SA, 2007. Gold Cross with Star, 1st cl. (Austria), 2004. *Recreations*: trout fishing, shooting, classic cars, music. *Clubs*: Royal Automobile; Rand (Johannesburg).

**TRAILL, Sir Alan (Towers),** GBE 1984; QSO 1990; arbitrator, expert witness and insurance consultant; Lord Mayor of London, 1984–85; *b* 7 May 1935; *s* of George Traill and Margaret Eleanor (*née* Matthews); *m* 1964, Sarah Jane (*née* Hutt); one *s*. *Educ*: St Andrew's Sch., Eastbourne; Charterhouse; Jesus Coll., Cambridge (MA). Underwriting Member of Lloyd's, 1963–89; Man. Dir, Colburn Traill Ltd, 1989–96; Divl Dir, First City Insurance Brokers Ltd, 1996–2000. Dir, Cayman Is Monetary Authy, 2003–06. British Insurance Brokers Association: Mem. Council, 1978–79; Chairman: Reinsurance Brokers Cttee, 1978–79; UK/NZ 1990 Cttee, 1989–90; Founder Mem. Cttee, ARIAS (Insce Arbitration Soc.), 1997–2012. Mem., Court of Common Council, City of London, 1970–2005; Alderman for Langbourn Ward, 1975–2005; Sheriff, City of London, 1982–83. Master: Cutlers' Co., 1979–80; Musicians' Co., 1999–2000. Vice-Pres., City Arts Trust, 2010– (Dir, 1980–2010). Trustee, Morden Coll., 1995–. Mem. Adv. Cttee, 1995–, Educn Cttee, 1998–, LSO. Patron, Treloar Coll. (Gov., 1986–2002); Hon. Gov., Christ's Hosp. Foundn, 2005–; Gov., Menuhin Sch., 2000–11 (Chm., 2006–11). KStJ 1985. *Recreations*: DIY, travel, opera, assisting education. *Address*: Wheelers Farm, Thursley, Godalming, Surrey GU8 6QE.

**TRAINOR, Sir Richard (Hughes),** KBE 2010; DPhil; FRHistS; FAcSS; Rector, Exeter College, Oxford, since 2014; Pro Vice-Chancellor, University of Oxford, since 2016; *b* 31 Dec. 1948; *s* of late William Richard Trainor and Sarah Frances (*née* Hughes); *m* 1980, Prof. Marguerite Wright Dupree; one *s* one *d*. *Educ*: Brown Univ. (BA); Princeton Univ. (MA); Merton Coll., Oxford (Rhodes Scholar; MA; Hon. Fellow, 2004); Nuffield Coll., Oxford (DPhil 1982). FRHistS 1990. Jun. Res. Fellow, Wolfson Coll., Oxford, 1977–79; Lectr, Balliol Coll., Oxford, 1978–79; University of Glasgow: Lectr in Econ. Hist., 1979–89; Sen. Lectr in Econ. and Social Hist., 1989–95; Prof. of Social Hist., 1995–2000; Dir, Design and Implementation of Software in Hist. Project, 1985–89; Co-Dir, Computers in Teaching Initiative Centre for Hist., Archaeol. and Art Hist., 1989–99; Dean, Faculty of Social Sci., 1992–96; Vice-Principal, 1996–2000; Vice-Chancellor and Prof. of Social Hist., Greenwich Univ., 2000–04; Principal and Prof. of Social History, KCL, 2004–14, now Emeritus Prof. (Fellow, 2004). Member: Jt Inf. Systems Cttee, 2001–05; HEFCE Cttee on Quality Assessment, Learning and Teaching, 2003–06; HEFCE Cttee on Leadership, Governance and Mgt, 2006–07; AHRC, 2006–11; HEFCE Rev. of Philanthropy in UK Higher Educn, 2012 (Mem., Implementation Gp, 2013); Commn on Future of Higher Educn, 2012–13. Universities UK: Mem. UK Bd, 2000–05, 2009–11; Treas., 2005–06; Pres., 2007–09; Co-Chm., UK/US Study Gp, 2008–09; Chm., Steering Gp, UUK/DfES Review of Student Services, 2002; Convenor, Steering Gp, Learning and Teaching Support Network, 2000–04. Chairman: London Metropolitan Network, 2002–06; Adv. Council, Inst. of Histl Res., 2004–09 (Hon. Fellow, 2009); Member: US-UK Fulbright Commn, 2003–09 (Patron, 2010); Bd, Higher Educn Acad., 2004–07. Governor: Henley Mgt Coll., 2003–05; St Paul's Sch., 2012–14; RAM, 2013–. Mem., Bd of Trustees, Univ. of London, 2010–13; Mem., Council, 2015–19, Chm., Conf. of Colls, 2017–19, Univ. of Oxford. Trustee, Museum of London, 2014–. Chair, Scholarship Cttee, Jardine Foundn, 2018–. Mem., Exec. Cttee, Pilgrims Soc. of GB, 2004–10. President: Glasgow and W of Scotland Br., HA, 1991–93; Econ. Hist. Soc., 2013–16 (Hon. Sec., 1998–2004; Vice Pres., 2016–). FAcSS (AcSS 2001). FRSA 1995. Hon. FTCL 2003; Hon. FRAM 2017. Hon. DCL Kent, 2009; Hon. DHL Rosalind Franklin Univ. of Medicine and Sci., 2012; DUniv Glasgow, 2014. Leadership Award, CASE Europe, 2011. *Publications*: (ed jtly) Historians, Computers and Data: applications in research and teaching, 1991; (ed jtly) Towards an International Curriculum for History and Computing, 1992; (ed jtly) The Teaching of Historical Computing: an international framework, 1993; Black Country Elites: the exercise of authority in an industrialised area 1830–1900, 1993; (ed with R. Morris) Urban Governance: Britain and beyond since 1750, 2000; (jtly) University, City and State: the University of Glasgow since 1870, 2000; contrib. numerous articles to books and jls. *Recreations*: parenting, observing politics, tennis. *Address*: Exeter College, Oxford OX1 3DP. *T*: (01865) 279605. *Club*: Athenæum.

**TRANHOLM-MIKKELSEN, Jeppe;** Secretary-General, Council of the European Union, since 2015; *b* Denmark, 30 Oct. 1962; *m*; two *c*. *Educ*: London Sch. of Econs and Pol Sci. (MSc Internat. Relns 1990); Univ. of Aarhus (Cand. Scient. Pol. 1992). Hd of Section, Min. of Foreign Affairs, Denmark, 1992–95; Sec., Embassy of Perm. Repn of Denmark to EU, 1995–98; Sen. Advr (EU Policy), Prime Minister's Office, 1998–2001; Hd, Dept of Gen. EU Policy, Min. of Foreign Affairs, 2001; Chief Advr (EU Policy), Prime Minister's Office, 2001–03; Ambassador and Dep. Perm. Rep. to EU, 2003–07; Ambassador to China and also to Mongolia and N Korea, 2007–10; Ambassador and Perm. Rep. to EU, 2010–15. *Address*: Council of the European Union, Rue de la Loi 175, 1048 Brussels, Belgium.

**TRAPIDO, Barbara Louise;** freelance writer, since 1982; novelist; *b* Cape Town, 5 Nov. 1941; *d* of Frits Johan Schuddeboom and Anneliese Schuddeboom (*née* Jacobsen); *m* 1963, Stanley Trapido (*d* 2008); one *s* one *d*. *Educ*: Natal Univ., Durban (BA Hons English); London Univ. Inst. of Educn (PGCE). Teacher: schs London, 1964–67; Coll. of Further Educn, Sunderland, and Remand Centre for Young Offenders, Co. Durham, 1967–70; Supervisor, Jericho Pre-School Playgroup, Oxford, 1970–82. *Publications*: Brother of the More Famous Jack, 1982; Noah's Ark, 1985; Temples of Delight, 1990; Juggling, 1994; The Travelling Hornplayer, 1999; Frankie & Stankie, 2003; Sex and Stravinsky, 2010. *Recreations*: concerts, opera, ballet, theatre, trawling fine art galleries (all spectator activities), cycling, dogs, family and friends. *Address*: c/o Victoria Hobbs, A. M. Heath & Co., 6 Warwick Court, WC1R 5DJ.

**TRAVERS, David;** QC 2010; *b* Durham City, 19 March 1957; *s* of late George Bowes Travers and Gertrude Colbert Travers (*née* Churnside); *m* 1984, Sheila Mary Killoran; one *s* two *d*. *Educ*: Spennymoor Sch.; King's Coll., London (Royal Instn Australian Sci. Schol., 1975; LLB; AKC 1979; LLM 1980); Regent's Coll.; Inns of Court Sch. of Law. Accredited Mediator 2000. Sabbatical Pres., Union of Students, KCL, 1979–80. Called to the Bar, Middle Temple, 1981 (Harmsworth Scholar 1982); in practice as a barrister, Manchester, 1981–88, Birmingham, 1988–2001, Temple, London, 2001–; Mem., Midland Circuit. Mem., Attorney Gen.'s Panel of Counsel (List A), 2002–10. Mem., Bar Council, 1995–2000 (Member: IT Cttee, 1996–98; Law Reform Cttee, 1996–98). Legal Assessor: Fitness to Practise Cttees (formerly Professional Conduct Cttees), GDC, 2002–; Fitness to Practise Cttees, GMC, 2003–12; Fitness to Practise Tribunals, MPTS, 2012–18. Lecturer: Accountancy Tuition Centre, Manchester and Liverpool, 1982–84; Sch. of Mgt Scis, UMIST, 1986–87; professional confs, 1992–; Central Law Trng, 1996–; Tutor, Dept of Biomed. Scis and Biomed. Ethics, Univ. of Birmingham, 1998–99. Vis. Prof. of Business Accountability, Newport Business Sch., Univ. of Wales, 2011–13; Vis. Prof., Univ. of South Wales, 2013–. Libel Reader, Daily Star and Daily Express, 1987–88. Member: Assoc. of Regulatory and Disciplinary Lawyers; Food Law Gp; Internat. Bar Assoc.; Health and Safety Lawyers Assoc.; Lex Anglo-Brasil; Planning and Envmt Bar Assoc.; UK Envmtl Law Assoc.; Chaîne des Rôtisseurs. Gov., Highclare Sch., 2004–10 (Chm., 2006–07). Student Mem., Gov. Body, KCL, 1977–78; Sabbatical Pres., Union of Students, KCL, 1978–79 (Hon. Life Mem., 1980). Hon. Fellow, Soc. of Food Hygiene and Technol., 2012. Editor, King's Counsel, jl of Sch. of Law, KCL, 1978. *Publications*: (jtly) Planning Law and Practice, 2013; (jtly) Planning Enforcement, 2015; articles on health, safety, envmtl and food and consumer law and related corporate governance matters. *Recreation*: 'finding the great in the small and the many in the few and practising difficult things while they are easy'. *Address*: 6 Pump Court, Temple, EC4Y 7AR. *T*: (020) 7797 8400. *E*: davidtravers@6pumpcourt.com.

**TRAVERS, William Morell Lindon,** OBE 2012; President, Born Free Foundation (UK), since 2014 (Chief Executive Officer, 1991–2014); *b* London, 4 Nov. 1958; *s* of late William, (Bill), Travers, MBE and of Virginia Travers (*née* McKenna), (Virginia McKenna, OBE); *m* 1989, Carolyne Baird (marr. diss. 2004); one *s* one *d*. *Educ*: Cranleigh Sch. Dir, Swan Productions, documentary films, 1979–86; Founder and Dir, Zoo Check Trust, 1984–90; Pres., Born Free USA, 2004–14, 2018–. Pres. and Chm. Bd, Species Survival Network, USA, 1994–; Mem., Species Survival Commn Reintroduction Specialist Gp, IUCN. FRGS. *Publications*: (ed jtly) Beyond the Bars, 1987. *Recreations*: travel, photography, wildlife, writing. *Address*: Born Free Foundation, Broadlands Business Campus, Langhurstwood Road, Horsham, W Sussex RH12 4QP. *T*: (01403) 240170. *E*: will@bornfree.org.uk. *W*: www.twitter.com/willtravers. *Club*: Special Forces.

**TRAVERSE-HEALY, Prof. Thomas Hector, (Tim),** OBE 1989; FCIPR, FPA; Director, Centre for Public Affairs Studies, since 1969; Senior Partner, Traverse-Healy Ltd, 1947–93; *b* 25 March 1923; *s* of John Healy, MBE, and Gladys Traverse; *m* 1946, Joan Thompson; two *s* three *d*. *Educ*: Stonyhurst Coll.; St Mary's Hosp., London Univ. DipCAM. Served War, Royal Marines Commandos and Special Forces, 1941–46. Chairman: Traverse-Healy & Regester Ltd, 1985–87; Charles Barker Traverse-Healy, 1987–89; non-exec. Dir, Charles Barker Hldgs, 1990–92. Mem., Public and Social Policy Cttee, National Westminster Bank, 1974–92; Professional Advr, Corporate Communications, 1990–92; Specialist Advr, CNAA, 1990–92. Prof. of Public Relns, Univ. of Stirling, 1988–97; Visiting Professor: Baylor Univ., Texas, 1988–97; Univ. of Wales, 1990–97; Advisor: Ball State Univ., USA; Westminster Univ. President: Internat. PR Res. and Educn Foundn, 1983–86; Internat. Foundn for PR Studies, 1987–89; Chm., (UK) PR

Educn Trust, 1990–92; Mem., Professional Practices Cttee, PR Consultants Assoc., 1987–91; Sec., PR Res. Network, 1994–97. Institute of Public Relations, later Chartered Institute of Public Relations: Mem. 1948, Fellow 1956; Pres. 1967–68; Tallents Gold Medal, 1985; Hon. Fellow 1988; Campbell-Johnson Medal, 2005; European PR Federation: Vice-Pres. 1965–69; International PR Association: Sec. 1950–61, Pres. 1968–73, Mem. Emeritus, 1982; Presidential Gold Medal, 1985; Chm., Coll. Emeriti, 2006–07. FRSA 1953; FIPA 1957. Member, US Public Affairs Council, 1975–91; Pres., World PR Congress: Tel Aviv, 1970; Geneva, 1973. Congress Foundn Lecture: Boston, 1976; Bombay, 1982; Melbourne, 1988; Istanbul, 2006. PR News Award, 1983; PR Week Award, 1987; Page Soc. Award, 1990; IPRA Award, 2008. *Publications:* numerous published lectures and articles in professional jls. *Recreations:* French politics, Irish Society. *Address:* 36 Belvedere House, Weston Acres, Banstead, Surrey SM7 3HB. *T:* (01737) 361705. *Clubs:* Athenæum; Philippics.

**TRAVIS, Prof. Simon Piers Leigh,** DPhil; FRCP; Professor of Clinical Gastroenterology, University of Oxford, since 2015; Fellow, Linacre College, Oxford, since 2001; Consultant Gastroenterologist, John Radcliffe Hospital, Oxford, since 2001; *b* Ivybridge, Devon, 27 March 1958; *s* of Roy and Marjorie Travis; *m* 1983, Pamela; two *d*. *Educ:* Winchester Coll.; St Thomas's Hosp. (MB BS Hons 1981); Univ. of Oxford (DPhil 1992). FRCP 1998. With Royal Navy, 1978–87 (Surg. Lt Comdr), Cdo MO, 1983–86 (Comdt Gen. RM's Commendation). House Physician, 1981–82, Registrar to Richard Thompson, Consultant Physician, 1988–89, St Thomas' Hosp., London; Lectr in Gastroenterology, Univ. of Oxford, 1989–92; Consultant Gastroenterologist, Plymouth, 1994–2001. Pres., Eur. Crohn's and Colitis Orgn, 2012–14. Hon. MA Oxon, 2002. Joanna and David B. Sachar Internat. Award, NY, 2015. *Publications:* (jtly) Gastroenterology, 1991; (jtly) Shared Care in Gastroenterology, 1997; Inflammatory Bowel Disease: rapid reference guide, 2004; IBD and IBS: novel mechanisms and future practice, 2010; Case Studies in Gastroenterology, 2010; contrib. 30 book chapters and 260 papers to peer-reviewed jls incl. 21 internat. guidelines; contrib. Nature Medicine, Lancet, Jl Exp. Med., Gastroenterology, Gut and other jls. *Recreation:* arboretum ex nihilo. *Address:* Translational Gastroenterology Unit, Nuffield Department of Experimental Medicine, John Radcliffe Hospital, Oxford OX3 9DU. *T:* (01865) 227552.

*See also Lord Hay.*

**TREACY, Rt Hon. Sir Colman Maurice,** Kt 2002; PC 2012; a Lord Justice of Appeal, 2012–18; *b* 28 July 1949; *s* of Dr Maurice Treacy and Mary Treacy; *m* (marr. diss.); one *s* one *d*; *m* 2002, Jane Ann, *d* of Edwin and Maureen Hooper; one step *d*. *Educ:* Stonyhurst Coll.; Jesus Coll., Cambridge (Open Scholar in Classics; MA; Hon. Fellow 2014). Called to the Bar, Middle Temple, 1971, Bencher, 1999; QC 1990; an Asst Recorder, 1988–91; a Recorder, 1991–2002; Head of Chambers, 1994–2000; a Judge of the High Court, QBD, 2002–12; a Presiding Judge, Midland Circuit, 2006–10. Mem., Mental Health Rev. Tribunal, 1999–2002; Asst Boundary Comr, 2000–02; Chm., Sentencing Council for England and Wales, 2013–18 (Mem., 2010–18); Judicial Comr, Investigatory Powers Commn, 2018–.

**TREACY, Philip Anthony,** Hon. OBE 2007; milliner; *b* Ballinasloe, Co. Galway, Ireland, 26 May 1967; *s* of late James Vincent Treacy and Katie Agnes Treacy. *Educ:* Nat. Coll. of Art and Design, Dublin (BA); Royal Coll. of Art (MDes; Sen. Fellow, 2002). Worked for designers incl. Rifat Ozbek, John Galliano and Victor Edelstein; former House Milliner to Marc Bohan and Victor Edelstein. Founder, Philip Treacy Ltd, 1990; first show in London, 1993, in New York, 1997, in Paris, 2000; hat manufacturer to designers incl. Karl Lagerfeld, Gianni Versace, Valentino, Rifat Ozbek, Givenchy, Alexander McQueen; designer for Debenhams, 1997–2001; launched accessory range, 1997; Design Dir, interiors, The G, Monogram Hotels, 2005; sports wear range for Umbro, 2006. Hon. DFA NUI, 2006. Accessory Designer of the Year, British Fashion Awards, 1991, 1992, 1993, 1996, 1997; Irish Fashion Oscar, 1992. *Address:* (office) 1 Havelock Terrace, SW8 4AS; (store) 69 Elizabeth Street, SW1W 9PJ.

**TREACY, Hon. Sir Séamus,** Kt 2007; **Hon. Lord Justice Treacy;** a Lord Justice of Appeal, Supreme Court of Judicature, Northern Ireland, since 2017; *b* 22 March 1956; *s* of late Joseph Treacy and Rose Veronica Treacy; *m* 1976, Viviane Jones; one *s* two *d*. *Educ:* St Malachy's Coll., Belfast; Queen's Univ., Belfast (LLB Hons). Called to the Bar: NI, 1979; Ireland (King's Inns), 1990; Inner Bar of Ireland, 2000; QC (NI) 1999; a Judge of the High Court of Justice, NI, 2007–17; PC, 2018. Mem., Panel of Arbitrators, Motor Insurers Bureau, 2005–07. *Recreations:* cycling, running, the arts. *Address:* Royal Courts of Justice, Chichester Street, Belfast BT1 3JF.

**TREADELL, Victoria Marguerite,** CMG 2010; MVO 1989; HM Diplomatic Service; High Commissioner to Australia, since 2019; *b* 4 Nov. 1959; *née* Jansz; *m* 1985, Alan Treadell. Entered FCO, 1978; Econ. Relns Dept, FCO, 1979–81; Visa Support Officer, Islamabad, 1981–83; Diary Sec., Perm. Under Sec.'s Office, 1983–85; Desk Officer, Western Europe Dept, 1985, FCO; Asst Mgt Officer, 1986–89, Commonwealth Heads of Govt Meeting and State Visits Officer, 1989–90, Kuala Lumpur; Asst Desk Officer, Resource Policy Dept, 1990–92, British Council Quinquennial Rev. Team, 1992–93, FCO; Dep. Hd, Export Services Section, FCO/DTI, 1993–96; Desk Officer, Latin America Dept, FCO, 1996–98; Hd, Professionalism in Trade Unit, FCO/DTI, 1998–99; Dep. Dir, Corporate Resources Gp, British Trade Internat., 1999–2002; Dir, NW of England, UK Trade and Investment, 2002–05; Dep. High Comr, Mumbai, 2006–10; High Commissioner: New Zealand, 2010–14; Malaysia, 2014–19. *Address:* c/o Foreign and Commonwealth Office, King Charles Street, SW1A 2AH.

**TREADGOLD, Sydney William,** CBE 1999; FCA; Secretary: Financial Reporting Council, 1990–98; Financial Reporting Review Panel, 1991–98; Accountancy Foundation, 2000–01; *b* 10 May 1933; *s* of Harold and Gladys Treadgold; *m* 1961, Elizabeth Ann White; two *s*. *Educ:* Larkmead Sch., Abingdon. Chartered accountant (ACA 1960, FCA 1970). Served RAF, 1951–53 (Navigator). Wenn Townsend, Chartered Accountants, 1954–62; Asst Finance Officer, Univ. of Liverpool, 1963–65; Principal: Min. of Aviation, 1965–67; Min. of Technol., 1967–71; Asst Sec., DTI, 1972–78; Under Secretary: Price Commn, 1978–79; Depts of Industry and Trade, 1979–83; DTI, 1983–89; Mem., Accounting Standards Task Gp, 1989–90; Secretary: Accounting Standards Bd, 1990–93; Regulation of Accountancy Profession Implementation Gp, 1999–2001. Mem., Certified Accountants' Disciplinary Panel, 1999–2003, Appointments Cttee, 2004–08. FRSA 1988. *Recreations:* Shakespeare, theatre, film, bridge. *Address:* 23 Sturges Road, Wokingham, Berks RG40 2HG.

**TREANOR, Most Rev. Noel;** *see* Down and Connor, Bishop of, (RC).

**TREASURE, Prof. Elizabeth Tulip,** PhD; Vice-Chancellor, Aberystwyth University, since 2017; *b* Glasgow, 17 Jan. 1958; *d* of Alexander, (Sandy) and Phyllis Maclaurin; *m* 1988, Patrick Treasure (*d* 1995); two *s* and one step *d*. *Educ:* Univ. of Birmingham (BDS 1979; PhD 1983). FRACDS 1994; FDSRCS 2000; FDSRCPSGlas 2011. HO, then SHO, 1980, Hon. SHO, 1980–82, Children's and Dental Hosps, Central Birmingham HA; Clinical Res. Fellow, Dept of Children's Dentistry and Orthodontics, Univ. of Birmingham, 1980–82; Community Dental Officer, 1982–85, Sen. Dental Officer, 1985–88, N Warwicks HA; Hon. Clinical Lectr, Community Dental Health Unit, Univ. of Birmingham, 1985–89; District Dental Officer, Kidderminster and District, and Bromsgrove and Redditch HAs, 1988–90; Lectr, 1990–93, Sen. Lectr, 1993–95, Dept of Community Dental Health, Univ. of Otago (Hd of Dept, 1994–95); Public Health Dentist (Specialist), Healthcare Otago Ltd (on contract), 1994–95; Univ. of Wales Coll. of Medicine, later Cardiff University, 1995–2017: Sen. Lectr in Dental Public Health, 1995–99; Prof., 2000–17; Vice Dean (Res.), 2003–06; Dean, Dental Sch., 2006–10; Dep. Vice Chancellor, 2010–17. Hon. Consultant in Dental Public Health: Cardiff and District Community NHS Trust, 1995–99; Cardiff and Vale District NHS Trust, 2000–10 (Gen. Manager, Dental Service Gp, 2006–10); Cardiff and Vale Univ. Local Health Bd, 2010–17. Scientific Advr, Dental and Optical Br., DoH, 2001–03. FLSW 2017. *Publications:* Essential Dental Public Health, 2002, 2nd edn 2013. *Recreations:* walking, cooking, travel, friends. *Address:* Aberystwyth University, Penglais, Aberystwyth SY23 3BF. *T:* (01970) 622010. *E:* vice-chancellor@aber.ac.uk.

**TREDINNICK, David Arthur Stephen;** MP (C) Bosworth, since 1987; *b* 19 Jan. 1950; *m* 1983, Rebecca Jane Shott (marr. diss. 2008); one *s* one *d*. *Educ:* Ludgrove Sch., Wokingham; Eton; Mons Officer Cadet Sch.; Graduate Business Sch., Cape Town Univ. (MBA); St John's Coll., Oxford (MLitt 1987). Trainee, E. B. Savoury Milln & Co., Stockbrokers, 1972; Account Exec., Quadrant International, 1974; Salesman, Kalle Infotec UK, 1976; Sales Manager, Word Processing, 1977–78; Consultant, Baird Communications, NY, 1978–79; Marketing Manager, Q1 Europe Ltd, 1979–81; Res. asst to Kenneth Warren, MP, and Angela Rumbold, CBE, MP, 1981–87; Dir, Malden Mitcham Properties (family business), 1985–. Contested (C) Cardiff S and Penarth, 1983. PPS to Minister of State, Welsh Office, 1991–94. Chm., Select Cttee on Statutory Instruments, 1997–2005; Member: Select Cttee on Health, 2010–15; Select Cttee on Sci. and Technol., 2013–15; Chairman: Jt Cttee on Statutory Instruments, 1997–2005; All-Party Parly Gp for Integrated Healthcare (formerly for Alternative and Complementary Medicine, then for Complementary and Integrated Medicine), 2006– (Treas., 1991–2002; Jt Chm., 2002–06); Treas., Parly Gp for World Govt, 1991–95; Secretary: Cons. backbench Defence Cttee, 1990–91; Cons. backbench Foreign Affairs Cttee, 1990–91. Chm., British Atlantic Gp of Young Politicians, 1989–91; Co-Chm., Future of Europe Trust, 1991–94; Chairman: Anglo East European Trade Co., 1990–97; Ukraine Business Agency, 1992–97. *Address:* House of Commons, SW1A 0AA. *T:* (020) 7219 4514.

**TREES,** family name of **Baron Trees.**

**TREES, Baron** *cr* 2012 (Life Peer), of The Ross in Perth and Kinross; **Alexander John Trees,** PhD; Professor of Veterinary Parasitology, University of Liverpool, 1994–2011, now Emeritus (Dean, Faculty of Veterinary Science, 2001–08); *b* 12 June 1946; *s* of John Trees and Margaret Trees (*née* Bell); *m* 1970, Frances Ann McAnally; one *d*. *Educ:* Univ. of Edinburgh (BVM&S 1969; PhD 1976). MRCVS 1969. Asst in gen. veterinary practice, Derby, 1970–71; Res. Asst, Univ. of Edinburgh, 1971–76; Elanco Products Ltd: Veterinary Advr for ME in Rome, 1977–80; Hd, Animal Sci., Rome (ME/N Africa), 1980; Liverpool School of Tropical Medicine, University of Liverpool: Lectr, Dept of Veterinary Parasitol., 1980–91; Sen. Lectr, 1991–94; Head: Veterinary Parasitol., 1992–2001; Parasite and Vector Biol. Div., 1994–97; Mem. Council, 1995–2004. Chm. Bd, Moredun Res. Inst., Edinburgh, 2011–. Member Council: RCVS, 2000–15 (Jun. Vice-Pres., 2008–09; Pres., 2009–10; Sen. Vice-Pres., 2010–11); RSTM&H, 1997–2009. Pres., Assoc. Veterinary Teachers and Res. Workers, 1996–97. Founding DipEVPC, 2003 (Vice-Pres., EVPC, 2006–09). Mem., Exec. Cttee, World Assoc. for Advancement of Veterinary Parasitol., 2007–17. Member: EU Sub-Cttee on Agric., Fisheries, Energy and Envmt, subseq. EU Energy and Envmt Sub-Cttee, H of L, 2014–17; EU Select Cttee, H of L, 2015–17. Hon. Fellow, Myerscough Coll., 2009. McCall Lect., 2011, Vis. Prof., 2012, Univ. of Glasgow. FMedSci 2019. Hon. FRSE 2016. Hon. DVetMed London; Hon. DVMS Glasgow, 2016. Selborne Medal for vet. res., Assoc. of Vet. Teachers and Res. Workers, 2005; Wooldridge Meml Medal and Lecture, BVA, 2009; Amoroso Award, British Small Animal Vet. Assoc., 2011; Queen's Medal, RCVS, 2019. Member, Editorial Board: Res. in Vet. Sci., 1991–2001; Trends in Parasitol. (formerly Parasitol. Today), 1992–2007; Vet. Ed.-in-Chief, Veterinary Record, 2011–. *Publications:* numerous peer-reviewed scientific papers and book chapters. *Recreations:* mountaineering, natural history, living life while I'm alive. *Address:* House of Lords, SW1A 0PW. *Club:* Farmers.

**TREFETHEN, Prof. Lloyd Nicholas, (Nick),** PhD; FRS 2005; Professor of Numerical Analysis, Oxford University, since 1997; Fellow, Balliol College, Oxford, since 1997; Global Distinguished Professor of Mathematics and Computer Sciences, New York University, since 2013; *b* 30 Aug. 1955; *s* of Lloyd McGregor Trefethen and Florence Newman Trefethen; *m* 1st, 1988, Anne Elizabeth Daman (marr. diss. 2008); one *s* one *d*; 2nd, 2011, Kate McLoughlin. *Educ:* Harvard Coll. (AB 1977); Stanford Univ. (MS Computer Sci./Numerical Analysis 1980; PhD 1982). NSF Post-doctoral Fellow and Adjunct Asst Prof., Courant Inst. of Mathematical Scis, New York Univ., 1982–84; Massachusetts Institute of Technology: Asst Prof. of Applied Maths, 1984–87; Associate Prof., 1987–91; Cornell University: Associate Prof., 1991–93; Prof. of Computer Sci., 1994–97. Pres., SIAM, 2011–12. Mem., NAE (US), 2007. *Publications:* Numerical Conformal Mapping, 1986; Numerical Linear Algebra, 1997; Spectral Methods in MATLAB, 2000; Schwarz-Christoffel Mapping, 2002; Spectra and Pseudospectra, 2005; Trefethen's Index Cards, 2011; Approximation Theory and Approximation Practice, 2013; Exploring ODEs, 2018; numerous technical articles. *Address:* Mathematical Institute, Oxford University, Woodstock Road, Oxford OX2 6GG.

**TREFGARNE,** family name of **Baron Trefgarne.**

**TREFGARNE, 2nd Baron** *cr* 1947, of Cleddau; **David Garro Trefgarne;** PC 1989; *b* 31 March 1941; *s* of 1st Baron Trefgarne and Elizabeth (*d* 2007), *d* of Charles Edward Churchill (she *m* 2nd, 1962, Comdr A. T. Courtney, from whom she obt. a divorce, 1966; 3rd, 1971, H. C. H. Ker (*d* 1987), Dundee); *S* father, 1960; *m* 1968, Rosalie, *d* of Baron Lane of Horsell; two *s* one *d*. *Educ:* Haileybury; Princeton University, USA. Opposition Whip, House of Lords, 1977–79; a Lord in Waiting (Govt Whip), 1979–81; Parly Under Sec. of State, DoT, 1981, FCO, 1981–82, DHSS, 1982–83, (Armed Forces) MoD, 1983–85; Minister of State: for Defence Support, 1985–86; for Defence Procurement, 1986–89; DTI, 1989–90; elected Mem., H of L, 1999. Chm., Assoc. of Cons. Peers, 2000–04. Dir of various companies. Chm., Sci., Engrg Manufacturing Technologies Alliance (formerly Engrg Trng Authority), 1994–2006. Dir, UK Skills, 1999–2005. Chm., Libyan British Business Council, 2003–13; Dep. Chm., Arab British Chamber of Commerce, 2004–. President: Popular Flying Assoc., 1992–97, 2000–03; Air Safety Gp, 2012–; Hon. President: British Assoc. of Aviation Consultants, 1994–; IEE, 2003–06; Welding Inst., 2006–08; Mem. Council, Air League, 1996–2006. Chm., Fairoaks Airport Consultative Cttee, 2009–. Vice Chm., ACF Assoc., 1992–2000. Gov., Guildford Sch. of Acting, 1992–2000; Mem. Council, Haileybury, 1993–2001, now Life Gov. Trustee, Mary Rose Trust, 1994–2001; Chm., Brooklands Mus. Trust, 2001–14. Patron, Catering Equipment Suppliers Assoc., 2005–. Hon. Fellow, Univ. of Central Lancs, 2004. DUniv Staffs, 2004.

Awarded Royal Aero Club Bronze Medal (jointly) for flight from England to Australia and back in light aircraft, 1963. *Recreation:* photography. *Heir: s* Hon. George Garro Trefgarne [*b* 4 Jan. 1970; *m* 2007, Camilla D'Arcy-Irvine; one *s* one *d*]. *Address:* House of Lords, SW1A 0PW.

**TREFUSIS,** *see* Fane Trefusis, family name of Baron Clinton.

**TREGEAR, Francis Benedict William;** QC 2003; a Recorder, since 2004; *b* 18 May 1957; *s* of late (George Herbert) Benjamin Tregear and of (Elisabeth) Bridget Tregear; *m* 1984, Elizabeth Anne Burke; one *s* one *d*. *Educ:* Lycée Français de Londres; Colet Court; St Paul's Sch.; St John's Coll., Cambridge (BA); Inns of Court Sch. of Law. Called to the Bar, Middle Temple, 1980; Mem., Lincoln's Inn, 1993, Bencher, 2010; called to the Bar, Eastern Caribbean Supreme Ct, 2004; Commercial Chancery practice. *Recreations:* running, music, London. *Address:* 24 Old Buildings, Lincoln's Inn, WC2A 3UP. *T:* (020) 7404 0946, *Fax:* (020) 7405 1360. *E:* francis.tregear@xxiv.co.uk.

**TREGEAR, (Vyvyan Alexander) Gordon;** Vice Lord-Lieutenant of West Sussex, 2009–14; *b* Karachi, 28 April 1944; *s* of Lt Col Vivian William Tregear and Virginia Doris Tregear (*née* Shrapnel-Smith); *m* 1981, Susan Alexandra Symington; three *d*. *Educ:* Cheltenham Coll.; Trinity Coll., Cambridge (BA Hons 1966; MA 2001). Admitted solicitor, 1970; Partner: Field Fisher & Martineau, 1974–76; Elbourne Mitchell & Co., 1976–82; est. own firm, Tregear & Co., 1982, merged with Bentleys Stokes & Lowless, 1986: Partner, 1986–95; Consultant, 1995–97. Owner and manager, S Lodge Estate, Horsham, 1982–. Mem., Legal and Parly Cttee, 1998–2003, Chm., Sussex Br., 1999–2001, CLA. Dir, Highland Soc. of London, 1980–82. Vice Pres., W Sussex Co. Scout Council, 2006–. High Sheriff, 2005–06, DL, 2008, W Sussex. *Publications:* (contrib.) Butterworth's Encyclopaedia of Forms and Precedents, 5th edn, 1989. *Recreations:* music (piano, bagpipes), shooting, family. *Address:* Long House, Long House Lane, Cowfold, W Sussex RH13 8AR. *T:* (01403) 864966. *E:* s.lodge.estate@btconnect.com. *Club:* Boodle's.

**TREGER, Julian Andre;** Chief Executive, Anglo Pacific Group, since 2013; *b* London, 22 Oct. 1962; *s* of John Walter Treger and Shirley Malca Treger; *m* 1996, Louisa Minna Westbury; one *s* two *d*. *Educ:* King David Sch.; Harvard Coll. (BA Hons); Harvard Business Sch. (MBA). J Rothschild Capital Mgt and RIT Capital, 1988–92; Partner: Active Value, 1993–2005; Audley Capital, 2005–. Trustee, Design Mus. Contributing Ed., Condé Nast House & Garden SA. *Recreation:* art and design collecting and supporting. *Address:* Anglo Pacific Group plc, 1 Savile Row, W1S 3JR. *W:* www.instagram.com/juliantreger.

**TREGILGAS-DAVEY, Marcus Ian; His Honour Judge Tregilgas-Davey;** a Circuit Judge, since 2016; *b* Liverpool, 21 Feb. 1967; *s* of Jenifer Hawkins; *m* 1998, Catherine Yates. *Educ:* Liverpool Blue Coat Sch.; Univ. of Southampton (LLB 1989); Darwin Coll., Cambridge (LLM 1990). Lectr in Law, Univ. of Southampton, 1991; called to the Bar, Gray's Inn, 1993; Army Prosecuting Authy, 1994–98; Pump Court Chambers, 1999–2016; a Recorder, 2009–16. Mem., Inns of Court Disciplinary Panel, 2012–. Mem., Helen's Book Club, 2016–. *Recreations:* canal boating, fine wines, malt whisky and pizza. *Address:* Northampton Crown Court, Lady's Lane, Northampton NN1 3HQ. *Club:* Richmond Bridge Boat (Mem., Bench Blisters Rowing).

**TREGLOWN, Prof. Jeremy Dickinson;** Professor of English, University of Warwick, 1993–2013, now Emeritus (Chairman, Department of English and Comparative Literary Studies, 1995–98); Senior Research Fellow, Institute of English Studies, School of Advanced Studies, University of London, since 2014; Chair, Arvon Foundation, since 2017; *b* 24 May 1946; *s* of late Rev. Geoffrey and Beryl Treglown; *m* 1st, 1970, Rona Bower (marr. diss. 1982); one *s* two *d*; 2nd, 1984, Holly Eley (*née* Urquhart) (*d* 2010); one *d* by Jennifer Lewis; 3rd, 2013, Maria Alvarez. *Educ:* Bristol Grammar Sch.; St Peter's Coll. and Hertford Coll., Oxford (MA, BLitt); PhD London. Lecturer: Lincoln Coll., Oxford, 1974–77; University College London, 1977–80; Times Literary Supplement: Asst Editor, 1980–82; Editor, 1982–90. Vis. Fellow: All Souls Coll., Oxford, 1986; Huntington Library, San Marino, Calif, 1988; Mellon Vis. Associate, Calif Inst. of Technol., 1988; Hon. Res. Fellow, UCL, 1991–; Ferris Vis. Prof., Princeton Univ., 1991–92; Jackson Brothers Fellow, Beinecke Liby, Yale, 1999; Leverhulme Res. Fellow, 2001–03; Mellon Fellow, Harry Ransom Humanities Res. Center, Univ. of Texas at Austin, 2002; Sokol Fellow, Cullman Center for Scholars and Writers, NY Public Liby, 2002–03; Fellow in Hist., Bogliasco Foundn, 2011, 2017; Fellow, Rockefeller Foundn Bellagio Center, 2011; Donald C. Gallup Fellow in Amer. Lit., Beinecke Liby, Yale, 2014; Leverhulme Emeritus Fellow, 2014–15. Mem. Council, RSL, 1989–96 and 2011–13; FRSL 1991; FRSA 1990; FEA 2001. Chairman of Judges: Booker Prize, 1991; Whitbread Book of the Year Award, 1998. Contributing Editor, Grand Street, NY, 1991–98. *Publications:* Roald Dahl, 1994; Romancing: the life and work of Henry Green, 2000; V. S. Pritchett: a working life, 2004; Franco's Crypt: Spanish culture and memory since 1936, 2013; edited: The Letters of John Wilmot, Earl of Rochester, 1980; Spirit of Wit: reconsiderations of Rochester, 1982; The Lantern Bearers, Essays by Robert Louis Stevenson, 1988; (with B. Bennett) Grub Street and the Ivory Tower: literary journalism and literary scholarship from Fielding to the Internet, 1998; (with D. McVea) Contributors to The Times Literary Supplement 1902–74: a biographical index, 2000; V. S. Pritchett: essential stories, 2005; Roald Dahl: collected stories, 2006; Mr Straight Arrow: the career of John Hersey, author of 'Hiroshima', 2019; various articles and book introductions. *Address:* Gardens Cottage, Ditchley Park, Enstone, Chipping Norton, Oxon OX7 4EP.

**TREGURTHA, Craig St John;** Group Managing Editor, Times Newspapers Ltd, since 2013; *b* London, 7 Aug. 1971; *s* of Eric and Maureen Tregurtha; *m* 1998, Joanna Stacey; two *s*. *Educ:* Quainton Hall Sch., Harrow; Merchant Taylors' Sch., Northwood. Trainee reporter, East Grinstead Courier, 1988–89; News Reporter, Crawley Observer, 1989–90; Dep. Gp Sports Ed., Crawley Observer and Mid-Sussex Times, 1990–92; Sports Ed., Sussex Express, 1992–93; Sports Reporter, Northants Evening Telegraph, 1993–95; The Sun; casual sport sub-ed., 1995–97; Asst Sports Ed., 1997–99; Online Sports Ed., 1999–2001; Associate Sports Ed., 2001–03; Sports Ed., Sunday Mirror, 2003–05; The Times: Football Ed., 2005–08; Dep. Sports Ed., 2008–10; Ed., Times Digital, 2010–11; Exec. Man. Ed., The Times, 2011–13. Mem. Bd of Dirs, Times Newspapers Ltd, 2013–. *Recreations:* football, motor racing, family, cinema, pizza. *Address:* The Times, News Building, 1 London Bridge Street, SE1 9GF. *T:* (020) 7782 5153. *E:* craig.tregurtha@thetimes.co.uk.

**TREISMAN, Sir Richard (Henry),** Kt 2016; PhD; FRS 1994; Head, Signalling and Transcription Laboratory, since 1988, and Director of Research, since 2015, Francis Crick Institute (formerly Imperial Cancer Research Fund Laboratories, later Cancer Research UK London Research Institute) (Director, 1999–2015); *b* 7 Oct. 1954; *s* of Woolf Benjamin Treisman and Marjorie Elizabeth (*née* Grounsell); *m* 1993, Kathleen Mary Weston; one *s* one *d*. *Educ:* Haberdashers' Aske's Sch.; Christ's Coll., Cambridge (BA 1977); ICRF/UCL (PhD 1981). Postdoctoral Fellow, Harvard Univ., 1981–84; Mem., Scientific Staff, Lab. of Molecular Biol., Cambridge, 1984–88. Mem., EMBO, 1987. Mem., Festiniog Railway Soc., Porthmadog, 1967–. EMBO Medal, 1995; Louis Jeantet Prize for Medicine, 2002. *Publications:* papers in scientific jls. *Recreations:* piano playing, fell-walking. *Address:* Signalling and Transcription Laboratory, Francis Crick Institute, 1 Midland Road, NW1 1AT.

**TRELAWNY, (James Edward) Petroc;** broadcaster, BBC Radio and Television; *b* Worcester, 27 May 1971; *s* of late Richard Trelawny and Jennifer Ann Trelawny (*née* Blackwood). *Educ:* Helston Sch. Presenter and reporter, BBC Radio Devon, 1989–91; presenter: British Forces Radio Hong Kong, 1991–92; Classic FM Radio, 1992–94; London Radio and LBC Radio, 1994–96; BBC Manchester, 1997; BBC Radio Three, 1998–; Cardiff Singer of the World, Leeds Piano Comp., BBC Proms and other progs, BBC TV, 1999–; contrib. to From Our Own Correspondent, BBC Radio 4, 2010–. Chm., 2005–15, Pres., 2015–, Lennox Berkeley Soc. President: Three Spires Singers, 2009–; Luton Music, 2015–; Vice President: London Cornish Soc., 1994–; Penlee House Gall., 2017–. Trustee, British Friends of Zimbabwe Acad. of Music, 2011–. *Publications:* occasional contribs to Spectator, Catholic Herald, Irish Times, Evening Standard, BBC Music Mag., Daily Telegraph. *Recreations:* music, theatre, travel, food, Zimbabwe, unusual rail journeys. *Address:* c/o BBC Radio Three, Broadcasting House, W1A 1AA. *E:* petroc.trelawny@bbc.co.uk. *Club:* Brydges Place.

**TRELAWNY, Sir John William Richard Salusbury-,** 14th Bt *cr* 1628, of Trelawny, Cornwall; *b* 30 March 1960; *o s* of Sir John Barry Salusbury-Trelawny, 13th Bt and Carol Knox (*née* Watson); *S* father, 2009; *m* 1st, 1980, Anita Snelgrove (marr. diss. 1986); one *s* one *d*; 2nd, 1987, Sandra Thompson (marr. diss. 1993); one *s*; 3rd, 2001, Laurian, *d* of Rev. Peter Adams; two *s*. *Heir: s* Harry John Salusbury-Trelawny, *b* 10 Dec. 1982.

**TRELAWNY, Petroc;** *see* Trelawny, J. E. P.

**TRELEAVEN, Prof. Philip Colin,** PhD; Professor of Computing, University College London, since 1985 (Pro-Provost, 1994–2008); *b* 15 March 1950; *s* of Frederick Colin and Evelyn Treleaven; *m* 1981, Isabel Gouveia-Lima. *Educ:* Brunel Univ. (BTech); Manchester Univ. (MSc, PhD). Research Fellow, Univ. of Newcastle upon Tyne, 1979–83; Sen. Res. Fellow, Reading Univ., 1983–85. Contested (C): Ealing Southall, 1992; SW London, Eur. Parly elecns, 1994. *Recreation:* politics. *Address:* Department of Computer Science, University College London, Gower Street, WC1E 6BT. *T:* (020) 7679 7288.

**TRELFORD, Prof. Donald Gilchrist;** journalist, Emeritus Professor in Journalism Studies, Sheffield University, since 2007; Editor, The Observer, 1975–93; *b* 9 Nov. 1937; *s* of late Thomas and Doris Trelford (*née* Gilchrist); *m* 1st, 1963, Janice Ingram; two *s* one *d*; 2nd, 1978, Kate Mark; one *d*; 3rd, 2001, Claire Bishop; one *s* one *d*. *Educ:* Bablake Sch., Coventry (School Captain, 1956); Selwyn Coll., Cambridge (Open exhibnr in English, MA; University Rugby and cricket). Pilot Officer, RAF, 1956–58. Reporter and Sub-Editor, Coventry Standard and Sheffield Telegraph, 1960–63; Editor, Times of Malawi, 1963–66; Correspondent in Africa for The Observer, The Times, and BBC, 1963–66; The Observer: Dep. News Editor, 1966; Asst Man. Editor, 1968; Dep. Editor, 1969; Chief Exec., The Observer Ltd, 1992–93; Prof. and Hd of Dept of Journalism Studies, 1994–2000, Vis. Prof., 2000–04, Sheffield Univ. Acting Editor, The Oldie, 1994; Sports columnist, Daily Telegraph, 1993–2008; columnist, Majorca Daily Bulletin, 2010–. Chm., The Baby Channel, 2000–01; Director: Optomen Television, 1988–97; Observer Films, 1989–93; Central Observer TV, 1990–93; Nat. Acad. of Writing, 2000–03; London Press Club, 2001–09 (Chm., 2002–07, Pres., 2007–12). Ind. Assessor, BBC TV Regl News, 1997. Member: British Executive Cttee, IPI, 1976–2000; Soc. of Editors, 1984–93; Guild of British Newspaper Editors, 1985–2000 (Mem., Parly and Legal Cttee, 1987–91); Council, Media Soc., 1981–2003 (Pres., 1999–2002); Defence, Press and Broadcasting Cttee, 1986–93; Competition Commn (newspaper panel), 1999–2006; Council, ASA, 2002–08; Vice-Pres., Newspaper Press Fund, 1992– (Appeals Chm., 1991). Chm., Eur. Fedn of Press Clubs, 2005–06; Pres., Internat. Assoc. of Press Clubs, 2006–07. Member, judging panel: British Press Awards, 1981–2002 (Chm., 2002); Scottish Press Awards, 1985; London Press Club Awards, 2002–12 (Chm., 2007–12); Mem., Olivier Awards Cttee, SWET, 1984–93; Judge: Whitbread Prize, 1992; Sony Radio Awards, 1994; George Orwell Prize, 1998. Mem. Adv. Bd, London Choral Soc., 1991–98; Chm., Soc. of Gentlemen, Lovers of Musick, 1996–2001. Vice-Pres., British Sports Trust, 1988–2002; Hon. Advr, NPFA, 1996–2004. Mem., Jurade de St Emilion, 1997–2003. Liveryman, Worshipful Co. of Stationers and Newspaper Makers, 1986; Freeman, City of London, 1986. FRSA 1988. Hon. DLitt Sheffield, 1990. Granada Newspaper of the Year Award, 1983, 1993; commended, Internat. Editor of the Year, World Press Rev., NY, 1984. Frequent broadcasts (writer, interviewer and panellist) on TV and radio; presenter: Running Late (C4); LBC Morning Report; TV interviews include: Rajiv Gandhi, Lord Goodman, Sir Leonard Hutton, Gromyko; speaker at internat. media confs in Spain, Egypt, W Germany, Italy, USA, India, Turkey, S Africa, Argentina, Kenya, Trinidad, Lebanon, Canada, Russia, Korea, Peru, Belgium, Singapore, Ethiopia and Dubai. *Publications:* Siege, 1980; (ed) Sunday Best, 1981, 1982, 1983; (contrib.) County Champions, 1982; Snookered, 1986; (contrib.) The Queen Observed, 1986; (with Garry Kasparov) Child of Change, 1987; (contrib.) Saturday's Boys, 1990; (contrib.) Fine Glances, 1991; Len Hutton Remembered, 1992; (contrib.) One Over Par, 1992; (ed) The Observer at 200, 1992; (with Daniel King) World Chess Championship, 1993; (contrib.) Animal Passions, 1994; W. G. Grace, 1998; Shouting in the Street, 2017. *Recreations:* snooker, tennis, watching Rugby and cricket. *Address:* Apartado 146, 07460 Pollenca, Majorca, Spain. *T:* 663453506, (UK) 07850 131742. *E:* donaldtrelford@yahoo.co.uk. *Clubs:* Garrick, London Press.

**TREMAIN, Rose,** CBE 2007; FRSL; novelist and playwright; *b* 2 Aug. 1943; *d* of late Viola Mabel Thomson and Keith Nicholas Home Thomson, MBE; *m* 1st, 1971, Jon Tremain (marr. diss.); one *d*; 2nd, 1982, Jonathan Dudley (marr. diss.); partner, Richard Gordon Heath Holmes, *qv*. *Educ:* Sorbonne, Paris; Univ. of East Anglia (BA Hons Eng. Lit.). Part-time Lectr, UEA, 1988–94, Chancellor, 2013–16, UEA. FRSL 1983. Dylan Thomas Prize, 1984; Giles Cooper Award, Best Radio Play, 1984. *Publications: novels:* Sadler's Birthday, 1976; Letter to Sister Benedicta, 1978; The Cupboard, 1981; The Swimming Pool Season, 1984; Restoration, 1989 (Sunday Express Book of the Year Award; filmed, 1996); Sacred Country, 1992 (James Tait Black Meml Prize, 1993; Prix Femina Etranger (France), 1994); The Way I Found Her, 1997; Music and Silence, 1999 (Whitbread Novel Award); The Colour, 2003; The Road Home, 2007 (Orange Broadband Prize for Fiction, Good Housekeeping Fiction of the Year Award, 2008); Trespass, 2010; Merivel: a man of his time, 2012; The Gustav Sonata, 2016 (Nat. Jewish Book Award, USA, 2016; Sky Arts Award for Literature, 2017); Islands of Mercy, 2020; *short stories:* The Colonel's Daughter, 1982; The Garden of the Villa Mollini, 1986; Evangelista's Fan, 1994; The Darkness of Wallis Simpson, 2005; The American Lover, 2014; *for children:* Journey to the Volcano, 1985; *memoir:* Rosie: scenes from a vanished life, 2018. *Recreations:* gardening, swimming, yoga. *Address:* 2 High House, South Avenue, Thorpe St Andrew, Norwich NR7 0EZ.

**TREMAINE, Prof. Scott Duncan,** PhD; FRS 1994; FRSC 1994; Richard Black Professor of Astrophysics, Institute for Advanced Study, Princeton, since 2007; *b* 25 May 1950; *s* of Vincent Joseph Tremaine and Beatrice Delphine (*née* Sharp). *Educ:* McMaster Univ. (BSc); Princeton Univ. (MA, PhD). Postdoctoral Fellow, CIT, 1975–77; Res. Associate, Inst. of Astronomy, Cambridge, 1977–78; Long-term Mem., Inst. for Advanced Study, Princeton, 1978–81; Associate Prof., MIT, 1981–85; University of Toronto: Prof. of Physics and Astronomy, 1985–97; Dir, Canadian Inst. for Theoretical Astrophysics, 1985–96; Prof. and Chm., Dept of Astrophysical Scis, Princeton Univ., 1998–2006, now Prof. Emeritus. Dir, Prog. in Cosmology and Gravity, Canadian Inst. for Advanced Res.,

1996–2002. Foreign Hon. Mem., Amer. Acad. of Arts and Scis, 1992; Mem., US NAS, 2003. *Publications:* (with J. J. Binney) Galactic Dynamics, 1987, 2nd edn 2008; papers in jls of physics and astronomy. *Address:* School of Natural Sciences, Institute for Advanced Study, Einstein Drive, Princeton, NJ 08540, USA. *T:* (609) 7348191.

**TREMBATH, Graham Robert;** QC 2003; *b* 18 May 1952; *s* of late Robert Edward George Trembath, MBE and Gladys Booth Trembath; *m* 1981, Ulrika Lillie Maria; one *s* one *d. Educ:* Cambusdoon Prep. Sch.; Fettes Coll.; Southampton Univ. (LLB Hons). Called to the Bar, Middle Temple, 1978; in practice specialising in serious crime defence. *Recreations:* golf, lifelong supporter of Chelsea Football Club, general sports fan. *Address:* 5 Paper Buildings, Temple, EC4Y 7HB. *T:* (020) 7583 6117, *Fax:* (020) 7353 0075. *E:* clerks@5pb.co.uk.

**TREMBERG, David;** His Honour Judge Tremberg; a Circuit Judge, since 2007; *b* London, 7 July 1961; *s* of late Philip Tremberg and of Sally Tremberg (now Firth); *m* 1987, Alison Jones; one *s. Educ:* Craven Park Prim. Sch.; JFS Sch.; Univ. of Hull (LLB Hons); Coll. of Europe, Bruges (Dip. Adv. Eur. Studies); Inns of Court Sch. of Law. Called to the Bar, Lincoln's Inn, 1985; Recorder, 2001–07. *Recreations:* watching and playing sport, spending time with family and friends, reading, cars. *Address:* Combined Court Centre, Lowgate, Hull, E Yorks HU1 2EZ.

**TREMLETT, Very Rev. Andrew;** Dean of Durham, since 2016; *b* Plymouth, 9 March 1964; *s* of Ven. Anthony Frank Tremlett; *m* 1988, Alison Louise Hills (separated 2016); two *s* one *d. Educ:* Plymouth Coll.; Pembroke Coll., Cambridge (BA 1986); Wycliffe Hall and Queen's Coll., Oxford (BA 1988); Exeter Univ. (MPhil 1996); University Coll., Chester (Postgrad. Cert. Church Sch. Educn 2003); Hebrew Univ., Jerusalem (Arabic Immersion 2014). Ordained deacon, 1989, priest, 1990; Asst Curate, St Matthias, Torquay, 1989–92; Asst Chaplain, Mission to Seamen and St Mary's, Rotterdam, 1992–95; Team Vicar, St Columba's, Fareham, 1995–98; Chaplain to the Bishop of Portsmouth, 1998–2003; Vicar, St Mary's, Goring-by-Sea, 2003–08; Residentiary Canon, Bristol Cath., 2008–10; Canon of Westminster, and Rector, St Margaret's, Westminster, 2010–16; Sub-Dean and Archdeacon, Westminster Abbey, 2014–16. Chm., Westminster Abbey Inst., 2013–16; Vice-Chm., Govs, Westminster City Sch., 2012–16. Trustee: Field Lane Foundn, 2012–16 (Chm., 2014–16); Mission to Seafarers, 2015–. Pres., St Cuthbert's Hospice, 2016–. Mem. Council, 2016–, Rector, St Chad's Coll., 2017–, Durham Univ. Mem., Exec. Cttee, Assoc. of English Cathedrals, 2018–. *Recreations:* running, playing the piano, languages. *Address:* The Deanery, The College, Durham DH1 3EQ. *T:* (0191) 374 4586.

**TREMLETT, George William,** OBE 1981; author, journalist and bookseller; Director, Corran Books Ltd, since 1981; Founder Chairman, George Tremlett Ltd, since 1965; *b* 5 Sept. 1939; *s* of late Wilfred George and of Elizabeth Tremlett; *m* 1971, Jane, *oc* of late Benjamin James Mitchell and Mrs P. A. Mitchell; three *s. Educ:* Taunton School; King Edward VI School, Stratford upon Avon. Member of Richmond upon Thames Borough Council, 1963–74; Chairman: Further Education Cttee, 1966–68; Barnes School Governors, 1967–73; Schools Cttee, 1972–73; Shene VIth Form Coll. Governors, 1973–74; Housing Cttee, 1972–74; Thames Water Authority, 1973–74. Greater London Council: Mem. (C) for Hillingdon, 1970–73, for Twickenham, 1973–86; Opposition Housing Spokesman, 1974–77; Leader of Housing Policy Cttee, 1977–81. Consultant: Nat. Assoc. of Voluntary Hostels, 1980–84; Local Govt Inf. Unit, 1985–86; Appeal Dir, SHAC and Help the Homeless National Appeal, 1985–87. Member: Housing Minister's Adv. Cttee on Co-operatives, 1977–79; Housing Consultative Council for England, 1977–81; Northampton Develt Corp., 1979–83; Stonham Housing Assoc., 1978–92; Chiswick Family Rescue Appeal Fund, 1979–80; Bd, Empty Property Unit, 1985–86; Adv. Panel, BBC Community Prog. Unit, 1985–87. Founder Chm., Dylan Thomas Meml Trust, 1985–90. Governor, Kingston Polytechnic and Twickenham Coll. of Technology, 1967–70; Court of City Univ., 1968–74. *Publications:* 17 biographies of rock musicians, 1974–77—on John Lennon, David Bowie, 10cc, Paul McCartney, The Osmonds, Alvin Stardust, Cat Stevens, Cliff Richard, Slade, The Who, David Essex, Slik, Gary Glitter, Marc Bolan, Rod Stewart, Queen and the Rolling Stones (published in many different countries); Living Cities, 1979; (with Caitlin Thomas) Life with Dylan Thomas, 1986; Clubmen, 1987; Homeless but for St Mungo's, 1989; Little Legs, 1989; Rock Gold, 1990; Dylan Thomas: in the mercy of his means, 1991; Gadaffi: the desert mystic, 1993; David Bowie, 1995; (with James Nashold) The Death of Dylan Thomas, 1997. *Recreations:* ornithology, exploring old churches, local history, rock 'n' roll music. *Address:* The Ship and Castle, King Street, Laugharne, Carmarthenshire SA33 4RY. *T:* (01994) 427444. *Club:* Laugharne RFC.

**TRENCH;** *see* Le Poer Trench, family name of Earl of Clancarty.

**TRENCH,** family name of **Baron Ashtown**.

**TRENCH, Jonathan Charles Stewart C.;** *see* Chenevix-Trench.

**TRENCHARD,** family name of **Viscount Trenchard**.

**TRENCHARD, 3rd Viscount** *cr* 1936, of Wolfeton; **Hugh Trenchard;** DL; Bt 1919; Baron 1930; Consultant, Simon Robertson Associates (formerly Robertson Robey Associates) LLP, since 2013; *b* 12 March 1951; *s* of 2nd Viscount Trenchard, MC and Patricia, *d* of Admiral Sir Sidney Bailey, KBE, CB, DSO; *S* father, 1987; *m* 1975, Fiona Elizabeth Morrison, *d* of 2nd Baron Margadale, TD, DL; two *s* two *d. Educ:* Eton; Trinity Coll., Cambridge (BA 1973). Captain, 4th Royal Green Jackets, TA, 1973–80. Entered Kleinwort Benson Ltd, 1973; Chief Rep. in Japan, 1980–85; Gen. Man., Kleinwort Benson Internat. Inc., Tokyo Br., 1985–88; Dir, Kleinwort Benson Ltd, 1986–96; Pres., 1988–95, Rep. in Japan, 1993–95, Dep. Chm., 1995–96, Kleinwort Benson Internat. Incorporated; Director: Robert Fleming & Co. Ltd, 1996–98; Robert Fleming Internat. Ltd, 1998–2000. Chm., Dejima Fund Ltd, 2001–09; Man. Dir, Mizuho Internat. plc, 2007–12; Director: KB Berkeley Japan Development Capital Ltd, 1987–97; Dover Japan Inc., 1985–87; ACP Hldgs Ltd, 1990–94; Berkeley Technology (formerly London Pacific Gp) Ltd, 1999–2011; AC European Finance Ltd, subseq. Westhall Capital Ltd, 2001–03; Dryden Wealth Mgt Ltd, 2004–05; Stratton Street PCC Ltd, 2006– (Chm., 2009–); Bache Global Series, 2008–15; Lotte Chemical UK Ltd, 2010–; Adamas Finance Asia Ltd, 2017–; Senior Adviser: Prudential Financial Inc., 2002–08; Rolls-Royce Power Engrg plc, 2014–15; Optum Health Solutions (UK) Ltd, 2014–18; Adamas Asset Mgt (HK) Ltd, 2014–17; Consultant and Sen. Advr, Mizuho Corporate Bank Ltd, 2013–14; Consultant, Japan Bank for Internat. Cooperation, 2017–; Sen. Advr to Govt on Japanese financial services, 2018–. Dir Gen., European Fund and Asset Mgt Assoc., 2006. Chm., Securities Cttee, 1993–95, Vice Chm. Council, 1995, European Business Community (Japan); Director: Japan Securities Dealers' Assoc., 1994–95; Bond Underwriters' Assoc. of Japan, 1994–95; Member: Japan Assoc. of Corporate Executives, 1987–95; Council, Japan Soc., 1992–93 and 1995–2004 (Vice-Chm., 1996–2000); Jt Chm., 2000–04; Hon. Vice Pres., 2013–). Vice-Chm., British-Japanese Parly Gp, 1997–99 and 2004–; Hon. Treas., H of L All-Party Defence Study Gp, 1992–93; elected Mem., H of L 2004–. Mem. Council, RAF Benevolent Fund, 1991–2003, 2006– (Chm., 2006–13; Dep. Chm., 2014–). Hon. Air Cdre, 600 (City of London) Sqn, RAuxAF, 2006–. DL Herts, 2008. Lieut, City of London, 2014. Order of the Rising Sun, Gold and Silver Star (Japan), 2014. *Heir: s* Hon. Alexander Thomas Trenchard [*b* 26 July 1978; *m* 2007, Mira, *d* of late Rainer Ostendorf; two *s*]. *Address:* Standon Lordship, Ware, Herts SG11 1PR. *Clubs:* Brooks's, Pratt's, Cavalry and Guards; Tokyo (Tokyo).

**TREND, Hon. Michael (St John),** CBE 1997; Executive Director: Relationships Foundation, 2008–18; Marriage Foundation, since 2012; *b* 19 April 1952; *e s* of Baron Trend, PC, GCB, CVO and Patricia Charlotte, *o d* of Rev. Gilbert Shaw; *m* 1987, Jill Elizabeth Kershaw; one *s* two *d. Educ:* Tormore Sch., Upper Deal, Kent; Westminster; Oriel Coll., Oxford; Greek Govt Scholar. Toynbee Hall, 1975–76; Sub-Editor, then Managing Editor, TLS, 1976–81; Editor: History Today, 1981–82; Parliamentary House Magazine, 1984–87; Home Editor, Spectator, 1987–90; Chief Leader Writer, Daily Telegraph, 1990–92. MP (C): Windsor and Maidenhead, 1992–97; Windsor, 1997–2005. PPS to Minister of State, DoH, 1993–94, to Sec. of State for Transport, 1994–95; Dep. Chm. and Dir Gen., Conservative Party, 1995–98; Chm., Cons. Party Internat. Office, 2000–05; Opposition frontbench spokesman on European affairs, 1998–99, on pensions, 1999–2000. Member: Select Cttee on Health, 1992–93, on Public Admin, 2000–05; Speaker's Adv. Cttee on Works of Art, 1993–2005. Asst Chm., Internat. Democrat Union, 1999–2005; Gov. and Vice-Chm., Westminster Foundn for Democracy, 1999–2005. Mem. Council of Reference, Zane. Mem. Bd, Victoria County History, 1992–98. *Publications:* The Music Makers, 1985. *Recreations:* music, hill walking.

**TRENEMAN, Ann Carolyn, (Mrs I. A. Berkoff);** journalist and author; columnist, The Times, since 2015 (Chief Theatre Critic, 2015–19); *b* Iowa City, USA, 6 Feb. 1956; *d* of Dr James Treneman and Beverly Treneman; *m* 2011, Ian Andrew Berkoff; two *d. Educ:* Univ. of Oregon (BA); Univ. of Kent at Canterbury (MA). Feature writer and sub-editor, Binghamton Evening Press, Binghamton, NY, 1980–84; freelancer, Kent Messenger Gp and nat. newspapers, 1985–88; Observer: Dep. Chief Sub-ed., 1988–91; Foreign Ed., 1992–96; feature writer, Independent, 1998–99; feature writer, 1999–2003, Parly sketchwriter, 2003–15, The Times. *Publications:* Annus Horribilis: the worst year in British politics, 2009; Dave and Nick: year of the honeymoon and beyond, 2011; Finding the Plot: 100 graves to visit before you die, 2013; All in This Together, 2015. *Recreations:* gardening, having fun. *Address:* Bakewell, Derbys DE45 1FG. *T:* 07775 711653. *E:* ann.treneman@thetimes.co.uk. *Club:* Groucho.

**TRENT, Steven Michael;** Founding Director, 1999, and Executive Director, since 2000, Environmental Justice Foundation; *b* London, 5 April 1963; *s* of Peter Trent and Jean Trent (*née* Clarke); partner, 1995, Juliette Williams; one *s. Educ:* Univ. of Kent at Canterbury (BA Hons Hist.). Campaign Dir, Envmtl Investigation Agency, 1989–99; Founder and Dir, Wildaid (USA), 1999–2012 (Pres., 2008–12); Mem., Internat. Bd, 2012–); Trustee and Chm., Wildaid UK, 2008–12. *Publications:* contrib. Envmtl Justice Foundn reports on envmtl security and human rights, climate refugees and ocean protection. *Recreations:* sailing, ski-ing, cycling, literature, modern politics, music, walking, wildlife. *Address:* c/o Environmental Justice Foundation, 1 Amwell Street, EC1R 1UL. *T:* (020) 7239 3310. *E:* steven.trent@ejfoundation.org.

**TRENTHAM, Dr David Rostron,** FRS 1982; Hon. Professor, Randall Centre for (formerly Division of) Cell and Molecular Biophysics, King's College London, since 2003; *b* 22 Sept. 1938; *s* of John Austin and Julia Agnes Mary Trentham; *m* 1966, Kamalini; two *s. Educ:* Univ. of Cambridge (BA Chemistry, PhD Organic Chemistry). Biochemistry Dept, University of Bristol: Jun. Research Fellow (Medical Research Council), 1966–69; Research Associate, 1969–72; Lectr in Biochemistry, 1972–75; Reader in Biochemistry, 1975–77; Edwin M. Chance Prof., Biochemistry and Biophysics Dept, Univ. of Pennsylvania, 1977–84; Hd of Physical Biochem. Div., NIMR, Mill Hill, 1984–2003. Colworth Medal, Biochemical Soc., UK, 1974; Wilhelm Feldberg Prize, Feldberg Foundn Bd for Anglo-German Scientific Exchange, 1990. *Publications:* numerous research papers in scientific jls. *Address:* Randall Centre for Cell and Molecular Biophysics, New Hunt's House, King's College London, Guy's Campus, SE1 1UL. *T:* (020) 7848 6434.

**TREPTE, Paul,** FRCO; Organist and Master of the Choristers, Ely Cathedral, 1990–2019; *b* 24 April 1954; *s* of Harry and Ruth Trepte; *m* 1981, Sally Lampard; one *d. Educ:* New College, Oxford (MA). Asst Organist, Worcester Cathedral, 1976; Dir of Music, St Mary's, Warwick, 1981; Organist and Master of the Choristers, St Edmundsbury Cathedral, 1985. Hon. FRSCM 2012; Hon. FGCM 2012. *Publications:* choral works. *Address:* 14b Back Hill, Ely CB7 4BZ. *T:* (01353) 660336.

**TRESCOWTHICK, Sir Donald (Henry),** AC 1991; KBE 1979; Chairman, Signet Group Holdings Pty Ltd, 1978–2005; Executive Director, Australian Olympic Committee, 1992–2001; *b* 4 Dec. 1930; *s* of Thomas Patrick and Elsie May Trescowthick; *m* 1952, Norma Margaret Callaghan; two *s* two *d.* FCPA. Chairman: Charles Davis Ltd, later Harris Scarfe Holdings Ltd, 1972–98; Harris Scarfe, 1976–93. Founder Chm., Victorian Div., Aust. Olympic Team Fund; Inaugural Chm., 1982, Chm., 1984–88 and 2000, Emeritus Chm., 2001, Prime Minister's Olympic Dinner; Mem., Selection Cttee, Sport Australia Hall of Fame, 1990; Treas. and Chm., 1996, Emeritus Chm., 1996–99, Sport Australia Hall of Fame Trust (Instigator of 'The Don Award', 1997); Chairman: Minus Children's Fund, 1975–98; Sir Donald and Lady Trescowthick Foundn; Inaugural Chm., 1972–88, Patron, 1972–, Melbourne to Hobart Yacht Race Cttee; Dir, Aust. Ballet Develt, 1978–93. Pres., Peter MacCallum Cancer Inst. Appeal, 1991–94; Patron: DOXA Youth Welfare Foundn; Special Olympics Australia, 1992–98; Team Equestrian Australia, 1993–2001. Olympic OM, 1981; CLJ 1982; Knight of Magistral Grace, SMO, Malta, 1984; KCSHS 1995. *Recreations:* golf, travel, reading, painting. *Address:* PO Box 93, Toorak, Vic 3142, Australia. *T:* (3) 98044600. *Clubs:* Athenæum, Victoria Racing (Melbourne); Geelong Football.

**TRESEDER, Sarah Louise,** OBE 2019; Chief Executive Officer, Royal Yachting Association, since 2010; *b* 1969; *d* of Hugh and Anna Treseder. *Educ:* Magdalen Coll., Oxford (BA Hons PPE 1991). Business Analyst, McKinsey & Co., 1991–93; Strategic Analyst, SEGA Europe, 1993–95; Gp Controller, Westminster Press, 1995–96; Man. Dir, Newsquest Buckinghamshire, 1996–99; Lead Strategist, Diageo, 2000–02; Man. Dir, Diageo Canaries, 2002–05; Global Dir, Diageo Reserve Brands, 2005–07; Man. Dir, The Admirable Crichton, 2008–10. Mem., Oxford and Cambridge Sailing Soc. *Recreations:* sailing (racing and cruising), cooking, reading, travel, dancing, seeing friends. *Address:* Royal Yachting Association, RYA House, Ensign Way, Hamble, Southampton SO31 4YA. *T:* (023) 8060 4102. *E:* sarah.treseder@rya.org.uk. *Clubs:* Royal Thames Yacht, Royal Southampton Yacht, Royal Southern Yacht, Oxford University Yacht.

**TRETHEWEY, Ven. Frederick Martyn;** Priest-in-charge, Christ Church, Brittany, 2013–16; *b* 24 Jan. 1949; *s* of Kendall and Winifred Trethewey; *m* 1971, Margaret (*née* Davidson); one *s* three *d. Educ:* Bedford Coll., London Univ. (BA (Hons) English, 1970); Inst. of Educn, London Univ. (PGCE 1971); Oak Hill Theol Coll. (DipTh 1977). Ordained deacon, 1978, priest 1979; Curate: St Mark with St Anne, Tollington Park, London, 1978–82; St Andrew, Whitehall Park, London, 1982–87; Team Vicar, Hornsey

Rise, Whitehall Park Team, 1987–88; Vicar, Brockmoor, W Midlands, 1988–2001; Chaplain, Dudley Gp of Hosps, 1988–2000; RD, Himley, 1996–2001; Archdeacon of Dudley, 2001–13. *Recreations:* sport, walking, gardening. *Address:* Finlock Bungalow, Redesdale Place, Moreton-in-Marsh GL56 0EQ.

**TREUHERZ, Julian Benjamin;** art historian and curator; Keeper of Art Galleries, National Museums Liverpool (formerly National Museums and Galleries on Merseyside) (Walker Art Gallery, Lady Lever Art Gallery and Sudley), 1989–2007; *b* 12 March 1947; *s* of late Werner Treuherz and Irmgard (*née* Amberg); partner, 1975, civil partnership, 2005, Peter de Figueiredo. *Educ:* Manchester Grammar Sch.; Christ Church, Oxford (MA); Univ. of East Anglia (MA). Dip. Museums Assoc. 1974. Manchester City Art Gallery: Trainee, 1971; Asst Keeper, 1972–74, Keeper, 1974–89, of Fine Art. Member: Victorian Soc. (Hon. Sec., Manchester Gp, 1972–79, Chm., 1980–83); Cttee, Whitworth Art Gall., 1993–2004; Cttee, Lakeland Arts (formerly Lake District Art Gall. and Mus.) Trust, 1997–2010; Burlington Mag. Consultative Cttee, 2003–. Hon. DLaws Liverpool, 2009. *Publications:* Pre-Raphaelite Paintings from the Manchester City Art Gallery, 1981; Hard Times: social realism in Victorian art, 1987; (with Peter de Figueiredo) Country Houses of Cheshire, 1988; Victorian Painting, 1993; (jtly) Sir Lawrence Alma-Tadema, 1996; (jtly) Dante Gabriel Rossetti, 2003; (jtly) The Railway: art in the age of steam, 2008; Ford Madox Brown, Pre-Raphaelite Pioneer, 2011; (with Peter de Figueiredo) 111 Places in Liverpool That You Shouldn't Miss, 2016; articles in art-historical jls. *Recreations:* playing the piano, cooking, opera, Sicily. *Address:* 1 Ingestre Road, Oxton, Wirral CH43 5TZ.

**TREVELYAN, Anne-Marie Belinda;** MP (C) Berwick-upon-Tweed, since 2015; Parliamentary Under-Secretary of State, Ministry of Defence, since 2019; *b* London, 6 April 1969; *d* of (Donald) Leonard Beaton and Katherine Beaton (*née* Bougarel); two *c*. *Educ:* St Paul's Girls' Sch., London; Oxford Poly. (BSc 2:1 Hons Maths 1990). CA 1993. Price Waterhouse, London, 1990–95; Blenheim Exhibns, 1995–97; financial consultancy, Newcastle upon Tyne, 1998–2014. Contested (C) Berwick-upon-Tweed, 2010. *Recreations:* hill walking, cooking for friends, tennis, reading Austen and Trollope. *Address:* House of Commons, SW1A 0AA. *T:* (020) 7219 4437. *E:* annemarie.trevelyan.mp@parliament.uk.

**TREVELYAN, Dennis John,** CB 1981; FCIPD; Principal, Mansfield College, Oxford, 1989–96, Hon. Fellow, 1997; *b* 21 July 1929; *s* of John Henry Trevelyan; *m* 1959, Carol Coombes; one *s* one *d*. *Educ:* Enfield Grammar Sch.; University Coll., Oxford (Scholar; MA). Entered Home Office, 1950; Treasury, 1953–54; Sec. to Parly Under-Sec. of State, Home Office, 1954–55; Principal Private Sec. to Lord President of Council and Leader of House, 1964–67; Asst Sec., 1966; Asst Under-Sec. of State, NI Office, 1972–76; Home Office: Asst Under-Sec. of State, Broadcasting Dept, 1976–77; Dep. Under-Sec. of State and Dir-Gen., Prison Service, 1978–83; First CS Comr and Dep. Sec., Cabinet Office, 1983–89, retd. Secretary: Peppiatt Cttee on a Levy on Betting on Horse Races, 1960; Lord Radcliffe's Cttee of Privy Counsellors to inquire into D Notice Matters, 1967. Vice-Chm., CS Sports Council, 1980–; Vice-Pres., Industrial Participation Assoc., 1987–98; Member: Bd of Management, Eur. Inst. of Public Admin, Maastricht, 1984–89; Council, City Univ. Business Sch., 1986–89; ECCTIS Adv. Group, 1990–98; Governor: Ashridge Management Coll., 1985–89; Contemporary Dance Trust, 1986–89; Oxford Centre for Hebrew and Jewish (formerly for Postgraduate Hebrew) Studies, 1992–2008 (Emeritus Gov., 2008); Trustee, Dancers Resettlement Fund, 1987–91. FRSA 1986. *Recreation:* music. *Address:* Lindfield, 1 Begbroke Lane, Begbroke, Oxon OX5 1RN. *Clubs:* Athenæum, MCC; Vincent's (Oxford).

**TREVELYAN, Edward Norman;** Statistician - Demographer, Population Division, Demographic Directorate, US Bureau of the Census, 2006–13; *b* 14 Aug. 1955; *e s* of Norman Irving Trevelyan, and of Jennifer Mary Trevelyan, *d* of Arthur E. Riddett; *m* 1993, Debbie Mullin-Trevelyan; one *s* one *d*. *Educ:* Univ. of Calif, San Diego (BA History 1981); Univ. of Calif, Santa Barbara (MA Political Sci. 1986; PhD Political Sci. 1998). Admissions Asst, Graduate Div., UCSB, 1990–99; Survey Statistician, Governments Div., Economic Directorate, US Census Bureau, 1999–2006. *Recreation:* sailing (Gold Medal, Soling Class, Olympic Games, 1984). *Address:* 25028 Maplewood Drive, St Michaels, MD 21663, USA. *T:* (410) 7452975.

**TREVELYAN, George Macaulay,** CB 2005; Chief Executive, Intervention Board, Ministry of Agriculture, Fisheries and Food, 1995–2001; *b* 1 April 1944; *s* of late (Charles) Humphry Trevelyan and Molly Trevelyan (*née* Bennett); *m* 1st, 1966, Susan Pearson; one *s* two *d*; 2nd, 1980, Valerie Preston; one *s*; 3rd, 2002, Julia Barker (*née* McDonald). *Educ:* Queen's Coll., Oxford (BA Mod. Hist.). Joined MAFF, 1967: Principal, 1971; UK spokesman on numerous agricl mgt cttees under Common Agricl Policy, 1973–81; Mem. of Cabinet, EC Commn for Social Affairs, Brussels, 1981–84; Head, Pesticides Safety, Plant Health, and Cereals/Set Aside Divs, 1984–95; Regl Dir (SE), 1989–91; Dir of Ops, Food and Mouth Disease, MAFF, subseq. DEFRA, 2001–02; Dir, Delivery Strategy Team, DEFRA, 2002–04; Managing Consultant, Hedra plc, 2005–06; Finance and Performance Manager, New Forest Nat. Park Authy, 2006–08. Pt-time Conciliator, EC Directorate Gen. for Agriculture, 2008–13. Councillor (Lab), London Borough of Camden, 1971–74 (Alderman; Chm., Planning and Communications, 1975–76). *Recreations:* sailing, cycling, walking, singing, reading. *Address:* 19 Leelands, Lymington, Hants SO41 8EY.
*See also* L. K. Trevelyan.

**TREVELYAN, Laura Kate;** anchor, BBC World News America, since 2012; *b* 21 Aug. 1968; *d* of George Macaulay Trevelyan, *qv*, and Susan (*née* Pearson); *m* 1998, James Goldston; three *s*. *Educ:* Parliament Hill Sch., London; Bristol Univ. (BA); Univ. of Wales Coll. of Cardiff (dip. newspaper journalism). Reporter, London Newspaper Gp, 1991; Researcher, A Week in Politics, Channel 4, 1991–92; BBC: Researcher, Breakfast News, 1993; Asst Producer, Newsnight, 1994; Reporter: On the Record, 1994–98; Today Prog., Radio 4, 1998–99; Political Corresp., 1999–2004; Political Corresp., Newsnight, 2000–01; Correspondent: N America, 2004–06; UN, 2006–09; BBC World Affairs Corresp., NY, 2009–12. Mem., Council on Foreign Relns, 2018–. Member, Board: CitySquash, 2015–; Brooklyn Kindergarten Soc., 2017–; Royal Oak Soc., 2018–. *Publications:* A Very British Family: the Trevelyans and their world, 2006; The Winchester: legend of the West, 2016. *Recreations:* hill-walking, tennis. *Address:* BBC News, 450 W 33rd Street, New York, NY 10001, USA. *Clubs:* Heights Casino, Century Association (New York).

**TREVELYAN, Sir Peter (John),** 6th Bt *cr* 1874, of Wallington, Northumberland; *b* 11 Sept. 1948; *o s* of Sir Geoffrey Washington Trevelyan, 5th Bt and Gillian Isabel (*née* Wood), MBE; *S* father, 2011; also sometime claimant to Trevelyan Baronetcy of Nettlecombe, Somerset, *cr* 1662, but claim no longer provable; *m* 1996, Diane Christine Terry; one *s*. *Educ:* Oundle; Trinity Coll., Cambridge (BA 1969; MA 1973). *Heir: s* Julian Miles Trevelyan, *b* 29 Oct. 1998.

**TREVELYAN, Rupert;** Regional Director, London, Jockey Club Racecourses, 2012–16; *b* Salisbury, Rhodesia, 20 July 1963; *s* of John and Patricia Trevelyan; *m* 1987, Sara; one *s* three *d*. *Educ:* Guinea Fowl Sch., Gweru, Rhodesia; Felsted Sch., Essex; Univ. of Westminster (MBA). Various posts with Centrica, 2000–04; Mktg and Passenger Services Dir, I of M Steampacket Co., 2004–08; Consultant, RHS, 2008–09; Man. Dir, Epsom Downs Racecourse, 2009–12. MCIM. *Address:* Weybrook, 51 Station Road, Gomshall, Guildford, Surrey GU5 9NP. *T:* 07826 050690.

**TREVELYAN, Vanessa Mary;** museum consultant and adviser, since 2013; Director, Norfolk Museums and Archaeology Service, 1999–2013; President, Museums Association, 2010–13; *b* London, 29 Sept. 1952; *d* of Frederick Cheetham and Ann Cheetham; *m* 1977, John Trevelyan. *Educ:* Notting Hill and Ealing High Sch. for Girls, London; Univ. of East Anglia (BA Hons); City Univ. (Dip. Arts Admin). Victoria and Albert Museum: Mus. Asst, 1975–79; Manager, Purchase Grant Fund for the Regions, 1979–89; Mus. Develt Officer, South Eastern Mus Service, 1989–94; Hd, Public Services and Registration, Mus and Galls Commn, 1994–98. Convenor, Ethic Cttee, Museums Assoc., 2001–09. Gov., Norwich University of the Arts (formerly Norwich University Coll. of the Arts), 2008–17. Pres., Norfolk Costume and Textiles Assoc., 2013–. Mem., E of England Regl Adv. Bd, Nat. Trust, 2013–19; Trustee, Mus. of East Anglian Life, 2013–. Member: Women Leaders in Mus Network, 2004–; Norwich Soc., 2013– (Exec. Cttee Mem., 2015–19; Chair, 2017–19); Founder Mem., Friends of Kett's Heights, 2015–. *Publications:* (ed) Dingy Places with Different Kinds of Bits: an attitudes survey of London museums amongst non-visitors, 1991; Fragments of Norwich City Walls, 2015; articles relating to museum standards and operations; ed articles in Miscellany jl. *Recreations:* gardening, early musicals, sketching, jogging, singing, visiting museums.

**TREVERTON-JONES, Gregory Dennis;** QC 2002; *b* 23 Nov. 1954; *s* of Paul and Margaret Treverton-Jones; *m* 1990, Tamsin Thomas; one *s* two *d*. *Educ:* Malvern Coll.; New Coll., Oxford (MA). Called to the Bar, Inner Temple, 1977. *Publications:* Imprisonment: the legal status of prisoners, 1989. *Recreations:* most sports including cricket, golf and tennis. *Address:* 39 Essex Chambers, 81 Chancery Lane, WC2A 1DD. *T:* (020) 7832 1111, *Fax:* (020) 7353 3978. *E:* gregtj@39essex.com. *Club:* MCC.

**TREVES, Vanni Emanuele,** CBE 2012; Chairman: Korn Ferry International, since 2004; *b* 3 Nov. 1940; *s* of Giuliano Treves (partisan, killed in action, 1944), and of Marianna Treves (*née* Baer); *m* 1971, Angela Veronica Fyffe; two *s* one *d*. *Educ:* St Paul's Sch. (Foundn Scholar); University Coll., Oxford (MA); Univ. of Illinois (LLM; Fulbright Scholar). Res. Fellow, Univ. of Illinois, 1961–62. Macfarlanes: articled clerk and Solicitor, 1963–68; Partner, 1970–2002; Sen. Partner, 1987–99. Vis. Attorney, White & Case, New York, 1968–69. Director: Oceonics Group, 1984–96; Saatchi & Saatchi, 1987–90; Chairman: BBA Gp plc, 1989–2000; McKechnie plc, 1991–2000; Fledgeling Equity and Bond Funds, 1992–2000; Dennis Gp (formerly Trinity Holdings) PLC, 1996–99; Channel 4 Television, 1998–2004; Equitable Life Assurance Soc., 2001–09; Intertek Gp plc, 2001–11; Director: Amplifon SpA, 2000–11; Amplifin SpA, 2000–; non-exec. Dir, Homerton Univ. Hosp. NHS Foundn Trust, 2011– (Chm., Risk Cttee, 2012–). Mem., Council for Industry and Higher Educn, 2003–06. Solicitor to Royal Acad., 1992–2017. Chm., Develt Cttee, Nat. Portrait Gall., 1991–99. Chairman: NSPCC Justice for Children Appeal, 1997–2000; NSPCC Organised Abuse Appeal, 2004–08; Fellow, NSPCC, 2009; Chm., Felix Project, 2018–. Trustee: J. Paul Getty Jr Charitable Trust, 1985–; 29th May 1961 Charitable Trust, 1970–; Prisoners Educn Trust, 2010–. Vice-Pres., London Fedn of Clubs for Young People (formerly of Boys' Clubs), 1991– (Hon. Treas., 1976–95). Gov., Sadler's Wells Foundn, 1999–2008 (Fellow, 2017). Chairman: Governors, London Business Sch., 1998–2006 (Gov., 1996–2006); Nat. Coll. of Sch. Leadership, 2004–12; Governor: Coll. of Law, 1999–2006; Hall Sch., Hampstead, 1983–94. Hon. Fellow, London Business Sch., 2006. Fellow, St Paul's Cathedral, 2012–. Mem., Editl Adv. Bd, Corporate Governance, 2001–. Knight, Order of the Star of Italy, 2014. *Recreation:* epicurean pursuits. *Address:* Ryder Court, 14 Ryder Street, SW1Y 6QB. *Club:* Boodle's.

**TREVETHIN,** 5th Baron *cr* 1921, **AND OAKSEY,** 3rd Baron *cr* 1947; **Patrick John Tristram Lawrence;** QC 2002; *b* 29 June 1960; *s* of 4th Baron Trevethin and Oaksey, (known as Lord Oaksey) and Victoria Mary (*née* Dennistoun); *S* father, 2012; *m* 1987, Lucinda, *e d* of Demetri Marchessini and Mrs Nicholas Peto; one *s* two *d*. *Educ:* Christ Church, Oxford. Called to the Bar, Inner Temple, 1985. Elected Mem., H of L, 2015–. *Heir: s* Hon. Oliver John Tristram Lawrence, *b* 17 May 1990. *Address:* 4 New Square, Lincoln's Inn, WC2A 3RJ. *T:* (020) 7822 2000.

**TREVETT, Peter George;** QC 1992; *b* 25 Nov. 1947; *s* of late George Albert Trevett and Janet Trevett; *m* 1972, Vera Lucia Dos Santos Ferreira; two *s* one *d*. *Educ:* Kingston Grammar Sch.; Queens' Coll., Cambridge (MA, LLM). Called to the Bar, Lincoln's Inn, 1971 (Mansfield Schol.), Bencher, 2000; in practice at Revenue Bar, 1973–. *Publications:* contribs to legal pubns. *Recreations:* golf, reading, collecting succulent plants, gardening.

**TREVIS, Diane Ellen;** theatre director; *b* 8 Nov. 1947; *d* of late Joseph Trevis and of Marjorie Trevis; *m* 1986, Dominic John Muldowney, *qv*; one *d*. *Educ:* Waverley Grammar Sch., Birmingham; Sussex Univ. Actress and dir, Glasgow Citizens' Theatre, 1972–80; Arts Council Associate Dir, Palace Theatre, Westcliff, 1982; Founder, The Workshop, Jerwood Studios, 2001, Dir, Jerwood Workshop, 2001–; Head of Directing, Drama Centre, Univ. of the Arts London, 2003–07; Artistic Dir, Rough Classics Th. Co., 2005–. Director: Royal Shakespeare Company: Taming of the Shrew, Happy End, 1985–86; The Revenger's Tragedy, 1987; Much Ado About Nothing, 1988; Elgar's Rondo, 1993; Royal National Theatre: Irish-Hebrew Lesson, 1981; The Mother, Yerma, School for Wives, A Matter of Life and Death, 1985–86; The Resistible Rise of Arturo Ui, 1991; Inadmissible Evidence, 1993; Happy Birthday Brecht, 1998; Remembrance of Things Past (adapted with Harold Pinter), 2000; Gawain, Royal Opera House, 1991; The Daughter in Law, 1996, The House of Bernarda Alba, 1997, Theatr Clwyd; Human Cannon, Ballad of California, 1997, Awake and Sing, Happy Birthday Brecht, 1998, Univ. of California; Masterclass, Th. Royal, Bath, 1999; Death of a Salesman, Birmingham Rep., 2000; The Voluptuous Tango, Pirate Jenny, Almeida Fest., 2000; Duchess of Malfi, 2005, Fears and Miseries of the Third Reich, 2006, Cochrane Th.; The Voluptuous Tango, As You Like It, 2006, Le Grand Meaulnes, 2007, Pittsburgh; Silverland, NY, 2007; An English Tragedy, The Dresser, Palace Th., Watford, 2008; London Cries, NY, 2008; Beaux Stratagem, Penn State Univ., 2011; Dracula, Cochrane Th., 2011; Romeo and Juliet, Akzent Th., Vienna, 2012. *Publications:* Remembrance of Things Proust, 2001; Being a Director : a life in the theatre, 2011. *Recreations:* Morocco, movies, mountain walks. *Address:* c/o National Theatre, South Bank, SE1 9PX.

**TREVOR,** 5th Baron *cr* 1880, of Brynkinalt, co. Denbigh; **Marke Charles Hill-Trevor;** *b* 8 Jan. 1970; *s* of 4th Baron Trevor and of Susan Janet Elizabeth, *o d* of Dr Ronald Bence; *S* father, 1997. *Educ:* Rannoch Sch., Perthshire. *Heir: b* Hon. Iain Robert Hill-Trevor [*b* 12 June 1971; *m* 1998, Kate, *yr d* of David Lord; one *s* one *d*]. *Address:* Brynkinalt Hall, Brynkinalt, Chirk, Wrexham LL14 5NS.

**TREVOR, Thomas Henry Llewellyn;** curator and writer on contemporary art; Artistic Director, Atlantic Project, Plymouth, since 2015; *b* 22 Nov. 1962; *s* of Tudor and Jean Trevor; *m* 1996, Zoë Shearman. *Educ:* Exeter Sch.; Exeter Coll.; Exeter Coll. of Art (Foundn); Pembroke Coll., Oxford (Ruskin Sch. Prize for Painting 1983); Goldsmiths' Coll., London (BA Hons 1986). Artist, musician and music producer for TV, 1986–94; independent curator, 1994–99, incl. projs at Inst. of Internat. Visual Arts, Wellcome Trust,

UCL, Camden Arts Centre and Freud Mus.; Dir, Spacex Gall., Exeter, 1999–2005, incl. two projs as part of Liverpool Biennial and Frieze Art Fair; Dir, Arnolfini, Bristol, 2005–13, incl. projects in Belgium, Germany, Italy, S Korea and Sweden; Associate Curator, Art Fund Internat. collection, Bristol Mus., 2008–12; Guest Curator: Devi Art Foundn, Delhi, India, 2013–14; Whitechapel Gall., London, 2015–17; Curatorial Consultant, 1st ARoS Triennial, ARoS Mus., Aarhus, Denmark, 2014; Artistic Dir, Dojima River Biennale, Osaka, 2014–15. Hon. Res. Fellow, Univ. of Exeter, 2014–. Founder Chair, Visual Arts South West (formerly Turning Point SW), 2010–13. Member: Internat. Assoc. of Curators of Contemp. Art, 2008–; Internat. Assoc. of Art Critics, 2010–; Steering Gp, Contemp. Visual Arts Network, 2010–13; Adv. Cttee, Gwangju Biennale, South Korea, 2012–14; Jury, Korea Artist Prize, South Korea, 2014; Internat. Biennial Assoc., 2014–. Hon. DLitt Exeter, 2014. *Recreations:* reading, walking, swimming in the sea. *E:* mail@tomtrevor.net. *W:* www.tomtrevor.net.

**TREVOR-JONES, Robert David; His Honour Judge Trevor-Jones;** a Circuit Judge, since 2008; *b* Bangor, N Wales, 29 March 1955; *s* of Robert Trevor-Jones and Elizabeth Trevor-Jones; *m* 1st, 1981, Elizabeth Anne Cheetham (marr. diss. 2003); three *d*; 2nd, 2016, Judith Fordham. *Educ:* Shrewsbury Sch.; Southampton Univ. (LLB); Coll. of Law. Called to the Bar, Gray's Inn, 1977; Asst Recorder, 2000; Recorder, 2000–08. *Recreations:* rowing, sailing, hill walking. *Address:* Liverpool Crown Court, Queen Elizabeth II Law Courts, Derby Square, Liverpool L2 1XA. *T:* (0151) 473 7373. *Clubs:* City; Royal Chester Rowing.

**TREW, Peter John Edward,** MICE; Director, Rush & Tompkins Group plc, 1973–90 (Chairman of Executive Committee, 1986–87); *b* 30 April 1932; *s* of late Antony Trew, DSC and Nora Trew (*née* Houthakker); *m* 1st, 1955, Angela (marr. diss. 1985; she *d* 1991), *d* of Kenneth Rush, CBE; two *s* one *d*; 2nd, 1985, Joan (*d* 2005), *d* of Allan Haworth; 3rd, 2011, Kuki Hahndel (*d* 2016), *d* of Zevi Gregor Bielsky. *Educ:* Diocesan Coll., Rondebosch, Cape. Royal Navy, 1950–54; served HMS Devonshire, Unicorn and Charity. Chartered Inst. of Secretaries Sir Ernest Clarke Prize, 1955. Contested (C) Dartford, 1966; MP (C) Dartford, 1970–Feb. 1974; Jt Sec., Cons. Parly Finance Cttee, 1972–74; Mem., Select Cttee on Tax Credits, 1972–73. Chm., Kent West Cons. European Constituency Council, 1978–80. Mem. Council, CBI, 1975–83 (Mem., Econ. and Fin. Policy Cttee, 1980–86). *Publications:* The Boer War Generals, 1999; Rodney and the Breaking of the Line, 2006. *Address:* 1 Painshill House, Cobham, Surrey KT11 1DL. *T:* (01932) 863315.

**TREWAVAS, Prof. Anthony James,** PhD; FRS 1999; FRSE; Professor of Plant Biochemistry, Edinburgh University, 1990–2004, now Emeritus; *b* 17 June 1939; *s* of Clifford John Trewavas and Phyllis (*née* Timms); *m* 1963, Valerie Leng; one *s* two *d*. *Educ:* Roan Grammar Sch.; University Coll. London (BSc 1961; PhD 1964). Sen. Res. Fellow, Univ. of East Anglia, 1964–70; University of Edinburgh: Lectr, 1970–84; Reader, 1984–90. Visiting Professor: Michigan State Univ., 1973; Univ. of Illinois, 1980; Univ. of Alberta, 1983; Univ. of Calif, Davis, 1985; Univ. of Mexico City, 1987; Univ. of Bonn, 1989; Univ. of Milan, 1996. Mem., Scottish Cttee, LEAF. Mem., Most Highly Cited Researcher gp, Inst. of Scientific Inf.; MAE 2002; Life Mem., Amer. Soc. of Plant Physiologists, 1999; Fellow, World Innovation Foundn, 2001; FRSE 1993. *Publications:* Molecular and Cellular Aspects of Calcium in Plant Development, 1985; (with David Jennings) Plasticity in Plants, 1986; Plant Behaviour and Intelligence, 2014; 250 res. papers. *Recreations:* music, reading, thinking, good wine. *Address:* Old Schoolhouse, Croft Street, Penicuik, Midlothian EH26 9DH. *T:* (01968) 673372.

**TREWEEK, Rt Rev. Rachel;** *see* Gloucester, Bishop of.

**TREWIN, Simon Courtenay;** literary agent, since 1993; Chief Executive Officer, Simon Trewin Creative, since 2019; *b* Highgate, 24 May 1966; *s* of late Ion Courtenay Gill Trewin and of Susan Harriet Trewin; *m* 1992, Helen Adie; one *s*. *Educ:* Highgate Sch.; Univ. of Kent (BA Hons Drama and Theatre Studies 1988). Mem., Equity, 1989–; actor and on prodn teams, Chichester Festival Th., Birmingham Rep Th., Royal Alexandra Th., Toronto and in West End; Literary Agent: Sheil Land Associates, 1993–99; Peter Fraser & Dunlop Ltd, 1999–2009; Hd of Literary, and Dir, United Agents Ltd, 2009–12; Partner, WME (William Morris Endeavour Entertainment Ltd), 2012–19. Founder, The Garage Press, London, 2018. Vis. Lectr, Southampton Univ., 2010–12. Trustee: Salisbury Playhouse Trust Ltd, 2011–14; Arvon Foundn, 2011–17. FRSA 2016. *Publications:* (jtly) Rock and Pop Elevens, 2009; (jtly) Shopping While Drunk, 2010; (jtly) The Encyclopedia of Guilty Pleasures, 2011. *Recreations:* classic cars, theatre, letterpress printing, collecting emerging artists. *Address:* Simon Trewin Creative, Adam House, 7 Adam Street, Royal Adelphi, WC2N 6AA. *E:* simon@simontrewin.co.uk. *Clubs:* Soho House, h, Old Cholmeleians.

**TREWSDALE, Janet Margaret,** OBE 2000; CStat, FSS; Senior Lecturer in Economics, Queen's University of Belfast, 1995–2004; *b* 8 May 1944; *d* of Keith and Joan Crush; *m* 1970, Dr John M. Trewsdale (*d* 1990). *Educ:* Univ. of York (BA Econs and Stats 1967). FSS 1969; CStat 1993. Lecturer in Economic Statistics: Univ. of Kent, 1969–70; Trent Poly., 1970–71; Lectr in Econs, QUB, 1972–95. Chm., NI Econ. Council, 1998–2006; Mem., Statistics Commn, 2000–08. Vice-Pres., Royal Statistical Soc., 1983–84. *Publications:* numerous contribs to books and learned jls. *Address:* 1 Belair Avenue, Newtownards, Co. Down, Northern Ireland BT23 4UD. *T:* (028) 9181 3542. *E:* j.trewsdale@gmail.com.

**TRICHET, Jean-Claude Anne Marie Louis;** European Chairman, Trilateral Commission, since 2012; Chairman of Board, Bruegel, since 2012; *b* 20 Dec. 1942; *s* of Jean Trichet and Georgette (*née* Vincent-Carrefour); *m* 1965, Aline Rybalka; two *s*. *Educ:* Ecole Nationale des Mines, Nancy; Inst. d'Etudes Politiques, Paris; Univ. de Paris (LèsSc Econ); Ecole Nationale d'Admin. Inspector of Finances, 1971–76; Sec.-Gen., Business Restructuring Interministerial Cttee, 1976–78; Advr, Ministry of Finance, 1978; counsellor on industry, energy and res. to the President (Valéry Giscard d'Estaing), 1978–81; Dep. Asst Sec., later Asst Sec., Treasury, 1981–86; Chief of Staff to Minister of Finance (Edouard Balladur), 1986–87; Under-Sec., Treasury, 1987–93; Governor, Bank of France, 1993–2003 (Hon. Gov., 2012–). Chairman: Paris Club (sovereign debt rescheduling), 1985–93; EC Monetary Cttee, 1992–93; Member, Board of Directors: BIS, 1993–2003, 2006–11; Eur. Central Bank (formerly Eur. Monetary Inst.), 1994–2011 (Pres., 2003–11); Chm., Ethics Cttee, 2015–); Gov., IBRD, 1993–95; Pres., Global Economy Meeting of Governors (formerly Gp of 10 Governors), 2003–11; Chm. and Chief Exec., Gp of Thirty, 2011–17 (Hon. Chm., 2017–). Mem., Bd of Dirs, Airbus Gp (formerly EADS), 2012–18. Mem., Acad. des Scis Morales et Politiques, 2010–. Hon. doctorates from Liège, Tel Aviv, Montréal, Stirling, Bologna and Sofia Univs. Policy-maker of the Year, Internat. Economy, 1991, 2007; Zerilli Marimo Prize, Acad. des Scis Morales et Politiques, 1999; Pico della Mirandola Prize, 2002; Franco-German Cultural Prize, 2006; Person of the Year, FT, 2007; Ludwig Erhard Meml Coin in Gold, 2007; Central Banker of the Year: Euromoney, 2008; The Banker, 2008; Internat. Charlemagne Prize of Aachen, 2011; (jtly) Global Economy Prize, Kiel Inst., 2011; Collier du Mérite Européen, Luxembourg, 2013; Lifetime Achievement Award, Nat. Assoc. of Business Economics, USA, 2014; Prize for Achievement, Monetärer Workshop, 2016. Commandeur, Légion d'honneur (France); Officier, Ordre National du Mérite (France); many foreign decorations, including Grand Cordon, Order of the Rising Sun (Japan), Grand Cross in the orders of The Netherlands, Germany, Austria, Poland and Commander in the Orders of Belgium, Brazil, Argentina, Portugal. *Publications:* articles on monetary policy, finance and economy. *Recreation:* poetry. *Address:* 7 Rue Rembrandt, 75008 Paris, France.

**TRICKER, Prof. Robert Ian,** DLitt; FCMA; Hon. Professor: Hong Kong Open University, since 2006; Director, International Corporate Policy Group (formerly Corporate Policy Group, Oxford), since 1979; *b* 14 Dec. 1933; *m* 1st, 1958, Doreen Murray (marr. diss. 1982); two *d*; 2nd, 1982, Gretchen Elizabeth Bigelow. *Educ:* King Henry VIII Sch., Coventry; Harvard Business Sch., USA; DLitt CNAA, 1983. FCA 1955–2002; FCMA 1959. Articled Clerk, Daffern & Co., 1950–55; Sub-Lt, RNVR, 1956–58; Controller, Unbrako Ltd, 1959–64; Directing Staff, Iron & Steel Fedn Management Coll., 1965; Barclays Bank Prof. of Management Information Systems, Univ. of Warwick, 1968–70; Director, Oxford Centre for Management Studies, 1970–79, Professorial Fellow, 1979–84 (P. D. Leake Res. Fellow, 1966–67); Res. Fellow, Nuffield Coll., Oxford, 1979–84 (Vis. Fellow, 1971–79); Dir, Management Develt Centre of Hong Kong, 1984–86; Prof. of Finance and Accounting, Univ. of Hong Kong, 1986–96. Hon. Professor: Univ. of Hong Kong, 1996–2006; Warwick Univ., 1996–2000. Institute of Chartered Accountants in England and Wales: Mem. Council, 1979–84; Mem. Educn and Trng Directorate, 1979–82; Chairman: Examination Cttee, 1980–82; Tech. and Res. Cttee, 1982–84. Member: Council, ICMA, 1969–72; Management and Industrial Relations Cttee, SSRC, 1973–75; Chm., Independent Inquiry into Prescription Pricing Authority for Minister for Health, 1976. Member: Nuffield Hosp. Management Cttee, 1972–74; Adv. Panel on Company Law, Dept of Trade, 1980–83; Company Affairs Cttee, Inst. of Directors, 1980–84; Standing Commn on CS Salaries and Conditions of Service, Hong Kong, 1989–96. Dep. Launching Authy, Torbay Lifeboat, 2001–05. Editor, Corporate Governance—an international review, 1992–2000 (Mem., Editl Bd, 2001–). CGMA 2012. *Publications:* The Accountant in Management, 1967; Strategy for Accounting Research, 1975; Management Information and Control Systems, 1976, 2nd edn 1982; The Independent Director, 1978; Effective Information Management, 1982; Governing the Institute, 1983; Corporate Governance, 1984; The Effective Director, 1986; The Director's Manual, 1990; International Corporate Governance, 1993; Harnessing Information Power, 1994; The Economist Pocket Director, 1996, 3rd edn 1999; The Economist Essential Director, 2003 (trans. Chinese and Russian 2003); Corporate Governance: principles, policies and practices, 2009, 4th edn 2019; Directors: an A-Z guide, 2009; (with Gretchen Tricker) Business Ethics: a stakeholder, governance and risk approach, 2014; Oxford Circus: the story of Oxford University and management education, 2015; (with Gregg Li) Understanding Corporate Governance in China, 2019. *Address:* The Hill House, 22/23 St Peter's Hill, Brixham, Devon TQ5 9TE. *E:* BobTricker@aol.com. *W:* www.bobtricker.co.uk. *Club:* Naval.

**TRICKETT, Jon Hedley;** MP (Lab) Hemsworth, since Feb. 1996; *b* 2 July 1950; *s* of Lawrence and Rose Trickett; *m* 1969 (marr. diss.); one *s* one *d*; *m* 1994, Sarah Balfour; one *d*. *Educ:* Hull Univ. (BA Politics); Leeds Univ. (MA Pol Sociol). Builder/plumber, to 1985. Joined Labour Party, 1971; Leeds City Council: Councillor, Beeston Ward, 1985–96; Chair: Finance Cttee, 1986–89; Housing Cttee, 1988–89; Leader, 1989–96. Chm., Leeds City Development Co., 1989–96; Member of Board: Leeds Development Corp., 1992–96; Leeds Health Care, 1992–96; Director: Leeds/Bradford Airport, 1988–96; Leeds Playhouse, 1988–96; Leeds Theatre Co., 1988–96. PPS to Minister Without Portfolio, 1997–98, to Sec. of State for Trade and Industry, 1998, to the Prime Minister, 2008–10; Shadow Minister of State, Cabinet Office, 2010–11; Shadow Minister for the Cabinet Office, 2011–13; Shadow Minister without Portfolio and Dep. Chair, Labour Party, 2013–15; Shadow Sec. of State for Communities and Local Govt, and Shadow Minister for Constitutional Convention, 2015–16; Shadow Sec. of State for Business, Innovation and Skills, 2016; Shadow Lord Pres. of the Council, 2016–; Shadow Minister for Cabinet Office, 2017–. Mem., Public Accounts Select Cttee, 2001–06. Mem., GMBATU. *Recreations:* cycling, sail-boarding. *Address:* Ground Floor, Moorthorpe Railway Station, Barnsley Road, South Kirkby, Pontefract, W Yorks WF9 3AT. *T:* (01977) 655695; House of Commons, SW1A 0AA. *Club:* Cyclists' Touring.

**TRICKEY, Very Rev. (Frederick) Marc;** Dean of Guernsey, 1995–2003; Rector of St Martin de la Bellouse, Guernsey, 1977–2002; Priest-in-charge of Sark, 1996–2003; *b* 16 Aug. 1935; *s* of Alan Paul Trickey and Isabella Livingston (*née* Gunn); *m* 1963, Elisabeth Marriette Plummer; one *s* one *d*. *Educ:* Bristol Grammar Sch.; St John's Coll., Univ. of Durham (BA (Hons) Psychol. 1962; DipTh 1964). Commercial trainee, Nat. Smelting Co. Ltd, Avonmouth, Bristol, 1954–59. Ordained deacon, 1964, priest, 1965; Asst Curate, St Lawrence, Alton, Hants, 1964–68; Rector of St John with Winnall, Winchester, 1968–77. Mem., General Synod of C of E, 1995–2000. Hon. Canon of Winchester Cathedral, 1995–2003, Canon Emeritus, 2003. States of Guernsey: Pres., Ecclesiastical Cttee, 1995–2003; Chairman: Panel of Appeal, Public Assistance Authy, 1985–96; RPI Steering Gp, 1996–; Member: Broadcasting Cttee, 1977–2004; Bd of Industry, 1982–95; States of Guernsey Ethics Cttee, 1993–2018; Housing Appeal Tribunal, 2005–15; States of Deliberation Code of Conduct Panel, 2007–16. Chairman: Guernsey Hard of Hearing Assoc., 1983–95 (Pres., 1995–); MIND, Guernsey, 1985–2002 (Pres., 2002–); Chm. of Trustees, Canacord Genuity Wealth Charitable Trust, 2004–. Chaplain: Guernsey Assoc. RN and RM, 1977–; St John Ambulance, Guernsey, 2004–. Mem. Cttee, Western Br., RBL, 2013–. *Publications:* Your Marriage, 1987. *Recreations:* singing, embroidery, walking, photography, philately (GB and Guernsey), saxophone. *Address:* L'Espérance, La Route des Camps, St Martin's, Guernsey GY4 6AD. *T:* (01481) 238441. *E:* fmt@cwgsy.net.

**TRICKEY, Jane Elizabeth;** *see* Hutt, J. E.

**TRIESMAN, Baron** *cr* 2004 (Life Peer), of Tottenham in the London Borough of Haringey; **David Maxim Triesman;** Chairman and Managing Director, Triesman Associates, since 2011; Director: Salamanca Group, since 2013; Gravity, since 2019; *b* 30 Oct. 1943; *s* of Michael Triesman and Rita (*née* Lubran); *m* 2004, Lucy Hooberman; one *d*. *Educ:* Stationers' Co. Sch., London; Univ. of Essex (BA Hons, MA Philosophy); King's Coll., Cambridge. FSS 1984. Res. Officer in Addiction, Inst. of Psychiatry, 1970–74; ASTMS secondment, 1974–75; Sen. Lectr and co-ord. postgrad. res., Poly. of S Bank, 1975–84; Dep. Sec. Gen. (Nat. Negotiating Sec.), NATFHE, 1984–93; General Secretary: AUT, 1993–2001; Lab. Party, 2001–03. Chairman: FA, 2008–10; England 2018 FIFA World Cup Bid, 2009–10. A Lord in Waiting (Govt Whip) and govt spokesman on energy, higher educn, transport and Europe, 2004–05; Parliamentary Under-Secretary of State: FCO, 2005–07; DIUS, 2007–08; Opposition Spokesman: for Business, 2010–11; for FCO, 2011–15. Co-Chm., British-St Lucia All-Party Parly Gp, 2012–; Vice Chm., All-Party Parly Gp on Chinese in Britain, 2012–; Member: All-Party Parly Univ. Gp, 2004–; All-Party Parly Gp on EU-US Trade and Investment, 2013–; EU Ext. Affairs Sub-cttee, 2015–. Mem., Eur. Leadership Network, 2015– (Mem., Exec. Bd, 2015–); Chm., Design Commn, 2015–17. Vis. Prof. in Social Econ., S Lawrence Univ., 1977; Vis. Fellow, Univ. of London Inst. of Educn, 1993–96; Visiting Fellow: in Econs, Wolfson Coll., Cambridge, 2000–; in Govt, LSE, 2005–; Sen. Associate Fellow, Sch. of Engrg, Warwick Univ., 2004–18. Member: Greater London Manpower Bd, 1981–86; Home Office Consultative Cttee on

Prison Educn, 1980–83; Burnham Further and Higher Educn Cttee, 1980–84; Univ. Entrance and Schs Exams Bd for Soc. Sci., 1980–84; Standing Cttee on Business and the Community, HEFCE, 1999–2002. Mem., Kensington, Chelsea and Westminster AHA, 1976–82. Member: Industrial Relns Public Appointments Panel, DTI, 1996–2001; Ind. Review of Higher Educn Pay and Conditions, 1998–99; Cabinet Office Better Regulation Task Force, 2000–01; Treasury Public Services Productivity Panel, 2000–02; British N American Cttee, 1999–2013; Chm., Cabinet Office Nat. Inq. into Housing Benefit, 2000–01. Non-executive Chairman: Mortgage Credit Corp., 1978–2001; Victoria Mgt Ltd, 2000–01; Templewood Student Investments, 2012–13; Chairman: ReGen World Develt, 2012–13; Funding Affordable Homes Housing Assoc. (formerly Funding Affordable Homes Investment Fund), 2014–19; Dir, One Ocean Ventures Ltd, 2015–18; non-exec. Dir, Havin Bank Ltd, 2013–; Chm., Bd of Advrs, Templewood Merchant Bank LLP, 2010–13; Member: Bd, Augur Buchler Partners, 2011–13; Advisory Board: UBS, 1987–2001; Joule Africa, 2011–; NextEnergy, 2012–13. Chm., Usecolor Foundn, 2001. Member: Fabian Soc., 1974–; Charles Rennie Mackintosh Soc., Glasgow, 1986–; Highgate Literary and Scientific Inst., 1990–; Bd, Chester Art Collections, 2012–13. Treas., Public Sector Reform Gp, 2007–09. Mem. Council, Ruskin Coll., Oxford, 2000–02; Mem. Governing Council and Hon. Fellow, Univ. of Northampton (formerly Nene Coll. of Higher Educn, then UC Northampton), 1996–; Chm., Internat. Bd, Hibernia Coll., 2012–15; Member, Board: Coll. of Haringey, Enfield and NE London, 2016–; Capital City Colleges Gp, 2017–. Patron, Tottenham Hotspur Foundn, 2007–; Trustee, Football Foundn, 2008–10. Mem. Bd, Wembley Nat. Stadium Ltd, 2008–10. Freeman: City of London, 2017; Stationers' Co., 2016 (Liveryman, 2017). FRSA 1990. Hon. DLaws South Bank, 2009; DUniv Essex, 2010. *Publications:* The Medical and Non-Medical Use of Drugs, 1969; (with G. Viani) Football Mania, 1972; Football in London, 1985; (jtly) College Administration, 1988; Managing Change, 1991; Can Unions Survive (Staniewski Meml Lect.), 1999; Higher Education for the New Century, 2000. *Recreations:* football, art, reading, walking, blues and rock guitar, family. *Address:* House of Lords, SW1A 0PW. *Clubs:* Library; Middlesex CC; Tottenham Hotspurs' Supporters.

**TRIFOGLI, Prof. Cecilia,** PhD; FBA 2014; Professor of Medieval Philosophy, University of Oxford, since 2008; Fellow, All Souls College, Oxford, since 1999; *b* Rome, 7 Feb. 1961. *Educ:* Univ. of Pisa (Laurea in Philosophy 1986; Laurea in Maths 1995); Univ. of Milan (PhD Maths 2001). Guest researcher (pt-time), Aristotle Latinus, De Wulf-Mansion Centrum, Univ. of Leuven, 1987, 1989–94, 1996, 1997–2000; Research Fellow: Foundn Ezio Franceschini, 1990–91; Alexander von Humboldt Stiftung, Thomas-Inst., Univ. of Cologne, 1995–96; Lectr in Medieval Philosophy, Univ. of Oxford, 1999–2008. Mem., Cttee for Edition of Medieval Latin Texts, British Acad., 2000– (Chm., 2008–). Pres., Latin Aristotle Commn, Internat. Soc. for Study of Medieval Philosophy, 2002–12. *Publications:* Oxford Physics in the XIIIth Century (ca. 1250–1270): motion, infinity, place and time, 2000; Liber Tertius Physicorum Aristotelis, Repertorio delle Questioni, Commenti Inglesi ca. 1250–1270, 2004; Liber Quartus Physicorum Aristotelis, Repertorio delle Questioni, Commenti Inglesi ca. 1250–1270, 2007; contribs to learned jls. *Address:* All Souls College, Oxford OX1 4AL.

**TRIGGER, His Honour Ian James Campbell;** a Circuit Judge, 1993–2014; *b* 16 Nov. 1943; *s* of late Walter James Trigger and Mary Elizabeth Trigger; *m* 1971, Jennifer Ann Downs; two *s. Educ:* Ruthin Sch.; UCW, Aberystwyth (LLB); Downing Coll., Cambridge (MA, LLM). Called to the Bar, Inner Temple, 1970 (major scholarship, 1967); Lectr in Law, UWIST, 1967–70; practice on Northern Circuit, 1970–93. Pt-time Pres., Mental Health Review Tribunal, 1995–2014; pt-time Chm., Immigration Appeal Tribunal, 1999–2005; pt-time Immigration Judge, 2005–08. Church in Wales: Lay Reader, 2005–; Judge, Provincial Court, 2006–19. Chm., Standards Cttee, Denbighshire CC, 2012–. Gov., Ruthin Sch., 2008–; Pres., Old Ruthinian Assoc., 2014–17. Chm., Clwyd W Conservative Constituency Assoc., 2015–. *Recreations:* gardening, walking, spending time with family. *Address:* Alyn Bank, Llanarmon-yn-lal, Denbighshire CH7 4QX.

**TRIMBLE,** family name of **Baron Trimble**.

**TRIMBLE,** Baron *cr* 2006 (Life Peer), of Lisnagarvey in the County of Antrim; **William David Trimble;** PC 1997; Member (UU) Upper Bann, 1998–2007, and First Minister, 1998–2002, Northern Ireland Assembly; *b* 15 Oct. 1944; *s* of William and Ivy Trimble; *m* 1978, Daphne Orr; two *s* two *d. Educ:* Bangor Grammar Sch.; Queen's University Belfast (LLB). Called to the Bar of Northern Ireland, 1969; Lectr, 1968, Sen. Lectr, 1977, Faculty of Law, QUB. Mem., Constitutional Convention, 1975–76. MP (UU) Upper Bann, May 1990–2005; contested (UU) same seat, 2005. Leader, Ulster Unionist Party, 1995–2005. Joined Cons. Party, 2007. (Jtly) Nobel Peace Prize, 1998. *Publications:* Northern Ireland Housing Law, 1986; To Raise up a new Northern Ireland, 2001; NI Law Reports, 1975–90. *Recreations:* music, reading. *Address:* House of Lords, SW1A 0PW.

**TRIMBLE, Dame Jenifer;** *see* Wilson-Barnett, Dame J.

**TRIMLESTOWN,** 21st Baron *cr* 1461 (Ire.), of Trimlestown, co. Meath; **Raymond Charles Barnewall;** *b* 29 Dec. 1930; *yr s* of 19th Baron Trimlestown and Muriel (*d* 1937), *d* of Edward Oskar Schneider; *S* brother, 1997. *Educ:* Ampleforth.

**TRIMMER, Sir Jon (Charles),** KNZM 1999; MBE 1974; Senior Artiste, Royal New Zealand Ballet, since 1993; *b* 18 Sept. 1939; *s* of Charles Trimmer and Lily Pamela (*née* Arrowsmith); *m* 1963, Jacqui de Joux Oswald. *Educ:* Wellington Tech. Coll. Art Sch., NZ. Joined Royal NZ Ballet, 1958; with Sadler's Wells, London, 1960–61; Australian Ballet, 1965–66; Royal Danish Ballet, 1969–71; has performed in 5 Royal Command Performances in NZ and overseas; rôles in dramatic plays on stage and TV. Patron, several arts and dance socs in NZ. Fulbright Scholar, NY, 1981. Turnovsky Award, NZ, 1986. Commemoration Medal (NZ), 1990. *Recreations:* pottery, gardening, writing short stories, painting. *Address:* 29 Ocean Road, Paekakariki, Kapiti Coast, New Zealand.

**TRIMMER, Stuart Alan;** QC 2006; a Recorder, since 2009; *b* 5 Oct. 1954; *s* of Alan and Vera Trimmer; *m* 1982, Fiona Hester; two *s* one *d. Educ:* Yeovil Sch.; Poly. of North London (LLB London 1976). Called to the Bar, Gray's Inn, 1977; Hd of Chambers, 4 Breams Buildings, 2010– (Jt Hd, 2006–10). *Recreations:* active Church member, youth activities organiser. *Address:* 4 Breams Buildings, Chancery Lane, EC4A 1HP. *T:* (020) 7092 1900, *Fax:* (020) 7092 1999. *E:* stuart.trimmer@4bb.co.uk.

**TRINDER, Frederick William;** Charity Commissioner, 1984–85; *b* 18 Nov. 1930; *s* of Charles Elliott Trinder and Grace Johanna Trinder (*née* Hoadly); *m* 1st, 1964, Christiane Friederike Brigitte Dorothea (*née* Hase) (*d* 1994); one *s*; 2nd, 2010, Vivien Margaret Neville (*née* Cox). *Educ:* Ruskin Coll., Oxford (Dip. Pols and Econs); LSE, Univ. of London (BSc). Admitted Solicitor, 1966; Legal Asst/Sen. Legal Asst, Charity Commn, 1966–74; Dep. Charity Comr, 1974–84. Mem., BBC and IBA Central Appeals Adv. Cttees, 1986–92. Trustee, Charities Official Investment Fund, 1988–2002. Mem. (Lab), Wandsworth BC, 1953–56, 1959–62. *Recreations:* travel, gardening, music. *Address:* 41 Parkview Road, Croydon CR0 7DF.

**TRINICK, Christopher John;** DL; Chairman, Qualifications and Curriculum Development Agency (formerly Qualifications and Curriculum Authority), 2008–12; Chief Executive, Lancashire County Council, 2002–08; *b* 26 Dec. 1948; *s* of George Herbert Trinick and Mary Elizabeth Trinick (*née* Burton); *m* 1976, Pamela May Hall; three *d. Educ:* Northumberland Coll. of Educn (Teacher's Cert. 1971); Univ. of Newcastle (BPhil 1980); Brunel Univ. (MA 1984). Teacher, Kelvin Hall, Hull, 1971–75; Head of House, Seaton Burn High Sch., N Tyneside, 1975–79; Professional Asst, Ealing LBC, 1979–82; Special Educnl Needs Prin. Officer, Bradford MBC, 1982–87; Dep. Chief Educn Officer, Salford City Council, 1987–91; Dir of Educn, Solihull MBC, 1991–96; Chief Educn Officer, then Dir of Educn and Cultural Services, 1996–2001, Exec. Dir for Change, 2001–02, Lancs CC. Clerk, Lancs Lieutenancy, 2002–08; Sec., Lancs Adv. Cttee, 2002–08. Director: E Lancs TEC, 1996–99; Adult Learning Inspectorate, 2001–07 (Vice Chm., 2005); Excellence NW, 2001–05. Mem. Bd, OFSTED, 2007–12 (Chm., Audit Cttee, 2007–12). Mem., All Souls Gp, 2002–04. Treasurer: Soc. of Educn Officers, 1997–2002; Schs Curriculum Award, 1997–2002; Sec., Primary Educn Study Gp, 1997–2002. Mem. Bd, Foundn for IT in Local Govt, 1992–2004; Chm., ACCE, 2007–08 (Vice Chm., 2006–07). Sec., Lord Chancellor's Adv. Cttee on Gen. Comrs of Income Tax, 2002–08. Pro-Chancellor, Edge Hill Univ., 2008–12. DL Lancs, 2008. *Recreations:* gardening, outdoors, fly fishing.

**TRINICK, (George) Marcus (Arthur);** QC 2010; Owner, Marcus Trinick QC (Solicitor's Practice), since 2016; *b* Redhill, 11 June 1952; *s* of Michael Trinick and Elizabeth Trinick; *m* 2009, Geraldine Mortimore; one *s* one *d. Educ:* Haileybury; Queen's Univ., Belfast (BA 1976). Bond Pearce, 1979–83; admitted solicitor, 1983; Coodes, solicitors, 1983–90; Bond Pearce, 1990–2008; Partner, Eversheds LLP, 2008–16. Member: Royal Instn of Cornwall, 1974–; Trevithick Soc., 1977–. *Recreations:* cricket, Roman history, sailing, walking, writing. *Address:* Crendell Cottage, Crendell, Fordingbridge, Hants SP6 3EB. *T:* (01725) 517091. *E:* mtrinick6@aol.com. *Club:* Lobster Cricket.

**TRIPP, Alan Charles Macdonald;** chartered accountant; *b* Edinburgh, 3 Feb. 1951; *s* of Charles Taylor Tripp and Agnes Tripp (*née* Macdonald); *m* 1974, Kathryn Margaret Morgan; two *s. Educ:* George Watson's Coll., Edinburgh; Univ. of Edinburgh (BCom Hons 1973). Chartered Accountant 1976. Student, then qualified Accountant, Deloitte & Co., 1973–77; Financial, then Chief Accountant, Vickers Oceanics Ltd, 1977–79; Hughes Microelectronics Ltd: Chief Accountant, 1979–83; Financial Controller, 1983–88; Co. Sec., 1985–91; Ops Dir, 1988–90; Dir and Gen. Manager, 1990–91; Man. Dir (EMEA), Hughes Identification Devices Inc., 1991–93; Gp Finance Dir, then Man. Dir (Customer Product Services), McQueen International Ltd, 1993–97; Man. Dir (CPS) and Sen. Vice Pres., Sykes Enterprises Inc., 1997–2000. Mem., Scottish Econ. Council, 1991–98; Member Board: Scottish Council for Res. in Educn, 1991–98; Scottish Further Educn Unit, 1994–2000; Scottish Higher Educn Funding Council, 2000–05; Vice Chair: Scottish Further Educn Funding Council, 1999–2005; Scottish Further and Higher Educn Funding Council, 2005–09. Member: Criminal Injuries Compensation Appeals Panel, later First Tier Tribunal, Criminal Injuries Compensation, 2000–; Social Security and Child Support Tribunal, 2011–. Mem. Bd, Glenrothes Coll., 1986–96. *Recreations:* Heart of Midlothian FC, golf, theatre, walking, history, cinema, reading, opera, walking football. *Address:* 66 Craigleith Road, Edinburgh EH4 2DU. *T:* (0131) 332 1983, *Fax:* (0131) 332 9831. *E:* alancmtripp@gmail.com.

**TRIPP, Prof. Charles Rees Howard,** PhD; FBA 2012; Professor of Politics with reference to the Middle East, School of Oriental and African Studies, University of London, 2007–17, now Emeritus; *b* Lui, Sudan, 8 March 1952; *s* of Peter Tripp and Rosemary Tripp; *m* 1991, Venetia Porter; two *d. Educ:* Winchester Coll.; New Coll., Oxford (BA); Sch. of Oriental and African Studies, Univ. of London (MSc; PhD 1984). Res. Associate, IISS, 1981–83; Dep. Dir, Prog. for Strategic and Internat. Security Studies, Institut Universitaire de Hautes Études Internationales et du Développement, Geneva, 1983–86; Lectr, 1986–92, Sen. Lectr, 1992–2001, Reader in Middle East Politics, 2001–07, SOAS, Univ. of London. Vice-Pres., British Acad. (British Internat. Res. Insts), 2018–. *Publications:* Iran and Iraq at War (with S. Chubin), 1988; A History of Iraq, 2000, 3rd edn 2007; Islam and the Moral Economy: the challenge of capitalism, 2006; The Power and the People: paths of resistance in the Middle East, 2013. *Recreations:* walking, reading, drawing. *Address:* School of Oriental and African Studies, University of London, Thornhaugh Street, WC1H 0XG. *E:* ct2@soas.ac.uk.

**TRIPP, Rt Rev. Howard George;** an Auxiliary Bishop in Southwark, (RC), 1980–2006, now Emeritus; Titular Bishop of Newport, 1980–2006; *b* 3 July 1927; *s* of late Basil Howard Tripp and Alice Emily Tripp (*née* Haslett). *Educ:* John Fisher School, Purley; St John's Seminary, Wonersh. Priest, 1953; Assistant Priest: Blackheath SE3, 1953–56; East Sheen, 1956–62; Asst Diocesan Financial Sec., 1962–68; Parish Priest, East Sheen, 1965–71; Dir, Southwark Catholic Children's Soc., 1971–80; VG, 1980–2006. Chm., London Churches Gp, 1993–98. *Address:* 35 St Catherine's Close, SW20 9NL. *T:* (020) 8542 4886. *E:* howardtripp@outlook.com.

**TRIPPIER, Sir David (Austin),** Kt 1992; RD 1983; JP; DL; Chairman, W. H. Ireland PLC, Stockbrokers, 1994–2008; *b* 15 May 1946; *s* of late Austin Wilkinson Trippier, MC and Mary Trippier; *m* 1975, Ruth Worthington, Barrister; three *s. Educ:* Bury Grammar School. Commnd Officer, Royal Marines Reserve, 1968 (qualif. parachutist, 1970; sc 1982). Member of Stock Exchange, 1968–; Chairman: Murray VCT, 1995–2005; Cambridgeshire Horizons Ltd, 2004–11. Mem., Rochdale Council, 1969–78, Leader Cons. Gp, 1974–76. MP (C) Rossendale, 1979–83, Rossendale and Darwen, 1983–92; contested (C) Rossendale and Darwen, 1992. Sec., Cons. Parly Defence Cttee, 1980–82; PPS to Minister for Health, 1982–83; Parliamentary Under-Secretary of State: (Minister for Small Firms and Enterprise) DTI, 1983–85; Dept of Employment, 1985–87; DoE, 1987–89; Minister of State (Minister for the Envmt and Countryside), DoE, 1989–92. Dep. Chm., Cons. Party, 1990–91. Nat. Vice Chm., Assoc. of Cons. Clubs, 1980–84. Chairman: Tepnel Diagnostics PLC, 1992–94; Envirosystems Ltd, 1992–99; Davenham Gp, 1994–96; Marketing Manchester Ltd, 1996–99; Vector Investments Ltd, 1996–2002; Director: Dunlop Heywood & Co., 1992–99; St Modwen Properties, 1992–2004; Sir David Trippier & Associates, 1992–2013; Murray Income plc, 1996–2005; Nord Anglia Educn PLC, 1996–2007; Camfil Air Filters Ltd, 1998–2000; UCG Ltd, 2001–03; ITV Granada (formerly Granada) Television Ltd, 2002–07; Consultant: Halliwell Landau, 1992–2006; Waste Management, 1992–97; Halliday Meecham, 1992–99. President: Manchester Chamber of Commerce and Industry, 1999–2000; Royal Lancs Agricl Soc., 1999–2000. Chm., Tidy Britain Gp, 1996–98. Governor, Manchester Grammar Sch., 1992–2005. President: Northern Reg., RM Assoc., 1988–93; Lancs RBL, 2004–07; Gtr Manchester SSAFA, 2012–16; Chm., NW of England Reserve Forces and Cadets Assoc., 2000–08; Vice-Chm., Council, RFCA (RM), 1999–2008. Hon. Col, RM Reserve, Merseyside, 1996–2010. Provincial Grand Master and Grand Superintendent for E Lancs, 2011–. FRSA 2006. JP Rochdale, 1975; DL Lancs, 1994, High Sheriff, Lancs, 1997–98. OStJ 2000. *Publications:* Defending the Peace, 1982; New Life for Inner Cities, 1989; Lend Me Your Ears (autobiog.), 1999. *Recreation:* gardening. *Address:* The Croft, 3 Heald Cottages, Lowerfold, Rochdale, Lancs OL12 7HS.

**TRITTON, Alan George**, CBE 1999; DL; Director, Barclays Bank Ltd, 1974–91; *b* 2 Oct. 1931; *s* of George Henton Tritton, Lyons Hall, Essex, and Iris Mary Baillie, Lochloy, Nairn; *m* 1st, 1958, Elizabeth Clare d'Abreu (marr. diss.; she *d* 2017); two *s* one *d*; 2nd, 1972, Diana Marion Spencer. *Educ*: Eton. Member of British Schools Exploring Soc. Expedn, Arctic Norway, 1949. Lt, 1st Batt. Seaforth Highlanders, active service Pahang, Malaya, 1950–52. Leader, S Orkneys Antarctic Survey Station, 1952–54, and Antarctic Relief Voyage, 1954, Falkland Islands Dependencies Survey; entered Barclays Bank Ltd, 1954; local Dir, 54 Lombard Street, 1964; Dir, Barclays Bank UK Management Ltd, 1972; India Adv., Barclays Bank, 1992–95. Dir, 1976–99, a Vice-Pres., 1983–99, Equitable Life Assce Soc.; Chairman: Plantation and Gen. Investments, 1994–96; University Life Assce Soc., 1994–99; Permanent Insurance Co. Ltd, 1995–99. A Vice-Pres., Royal Geographical Soc., 1983–86 (Mem. Council, 1975–96, Hon. Treas., 1984–96). Member: Cttee, British Trans-Arctic Expedn, 1966–69; Cttee, British Everest SW Face Expedn, 1974–75; Cttee of Management, Mount Everest Foundn, 1976–80; Friends' Cttee, Scott Polar Research Inst., 1976–80. Chairman: Westminster Abbey Investment Cttee, 1976–94; Calcutta Tercentenary Trust, 1989–2004; Member: Council, Internat. Chamber of Commerce, 1975–90 (Hon. Treas. 1985); Council, Foundn for Aviation and Sustainable Tourism, New Delhi, 1996–2005; Finance Cttee, 1997–, Council, 1999–2004, 2006–10, Royal Asiatic Soc.; Court, Essex Univ., 1995–2005. Pres., BACSA, 2010–16 (Vice-Pres., 2016–). Trustee: Brentwood Cathedral Trust, 1996–2010; Falkland Is Conservation Trust, 1998–2003. Mem. Cttee, Cuidich 'n Righ Club, 2015–. High Sheriff, 1992, DL 1993, Essex. *Publications*: The Half-Closed Door, 2009; When the Tiger fought the Thistle: the tragedy of Colonel William Baillie of the Madras Army, 2013; Scotland and the Indian Empire: politics, scholarship and the military in making British India, 2019. *Recreations*: travelling, writing. *Clubs*: Boodle's, Antarctic (Pres., 2012; Mem. Cttee, 2012–), Geographical, Essex (Pres., 2001); Tollygunge (Calcutta).

**TRITTON, Sir Jeremy Ernest**, 5th Bt *cr* 1905, of Bloomfield, Lambeth; *b* 6 Oct. 1961; *o s* of Major Sir Anthony John Ernest Tritton, 4th Bt and of Diana, *d* of Rear-Adm. St John Aldrich Micklethwait, CB, DSO; *S* father, 2012; *m* 2007, Mary Catherine Claydon; one *d*. *Educ*: Eton; Bristol Univ. (BSc). *Heir*: none. *Address*: 183 Old Brompton Road, SW5 0AN. *Club*: Boodle's.

**TROLLOPE, Andrew David Hedderwick**; QC 1991; a Recorder of the Crown Court, since 1989; *b* 6 Nov. 1948; *s* of late Arthur George Cecil Trollope and Rosemary (*née* Hodson); *m* 1978, Anne Forbes; two *s*. *Educ*: Charterhouse; Univ. of Nancy. Called to the Bar, Inner Temple, 1971, Bencher, 2002; Asst Recorder, 1985–89. Hd of Chambers, 1991–. Special Advr, NI Affairs Select Cttee, H of C, 2014–15. Chm., N London Bar Mess, 1998–2001. Member: South Eastern Circuit Cttee, 1990–93, 1994–97, 2006–09, 2013–; Cttee, Criminal Bar Assoc., 1991–2001; Internat. Relns Cttee, Bar Council, 2001–08; Mem. Council of Mgt, 2001–06, Mem. Adv. Council, 2006–, British Inst. of Internat. and Comparative Law. Fellow, Soc. of Advanced Legal Studies, 1998. *Recreations*: opera, jazz, swimming, tennis, sailing, travel. *Address*: 187 Fleet Street, EC4A 2AT. *T*: (020) 7430 7430, *Fax*: (020) 7430 7431. *Clubs*: Garrick, Hurlingham.
*See also* J. Trollope.

**TROLLOPE, Sir Anthony (Simon)**, 17th Bt *cr* 1642, of Casewick, Lincolnshire; *b* 31 Aug. 1945; *s* of Sir Anthony Owen Clavering Trollope, 16th Bt and of Joan Mary Alexis, *d* of Alexis Robert Gibbs; *S* father, 1987; *m* 1969, Denise, *d* of Trevern and Vida Thompson; two *d*. *Educ*: Univ. of Sydney (BA 1969); Univ. of New England (MBA 1998); Univ. of Western Sydney (BTeaching 2002). Worked in mktg mgt in major mgt positions for food producing companies, 1977–99; schoolteacher, retired. Breeder, in partnership with his wife, of Anglo-Arabian horses and Rhodesian Ridgeback dogs. Mem., Australian Marketing Inst., 1988–2002. *Heir*: *b* Hugh Irwin Trollope [*b* 31 March 1947; *m* 1971, Barbara Anne, *d* of William Ian Jamieson; one *s* two *d*]. *Address*: Casewick Park, 435 Golf Links Road, Glen Innes, NSW 2370, Australia. *Clubs*: Gordon Rugby, Arabian Horse Society of Australia (Sydney).

**TROLLOPE, Joanna**, CBE 2019 (OBE 1996); writer; *b* 9 Dec. 1943; *er d* of late Arthur George Cecil Trollope and Rosemary Trollope (*née* Hodson); *m* 1st, 1966, David Roger William Potter, *qv* (marr. diss. 1983); two *d*; 2nd, 1985, Ian Bayley Curteis, *qv* (marr. diss. 2001); two step *s*. *Educ*: Reigate County Sch. for Girls; St Hugh's Coll., Oxford (Gamble Scholar; MA 1972). Inf. and Research Dept, Foreign Office, 1965–67; teaching posts, 1967–79, incl. Farnham Girls' Grammar Sch., adult educn, English for foreigners and at Daneshill Sch. Writer in Residence, Victoria Magazine, USA, 1999. Chm., DNH Adv. Cttee on Nat. Reading Initiative, 1996–97; Member: Govt Adv. Body, Nat. Year of Reading, 1998; Adv. Bd, Costa Awards; Adv. Body, Sieghart Ind. Review of E-Lending in Public Libraries in England, DCMS, 2012; Govt Adv. Panel on public library service in England, 2014–. Judge: Melissa Nathan Awards, 2005–11; Sunday Times EFG Private Bank Short Story Award, 2012; Chief Judge, Orange Prize for Fiction, 2012. Vice President: Trollope Soc., 1995–; West Country Writers' Assoc., 1998–; Mem. Council, Soc. of Authors, 1997–. Member: Internat. PEN; Romantic Novelists Assoc. Trustee: Joanna Trollope Charitable Trust, 1995–; Royal Literary Fund, 2016–. Patron: Glos Community Foundn, 1994–2006; Mulberry Bush Sch., Witney, 2006–; Dementia UK (formerly for dementia); March Foundn; Chawton House Liby, 2016–; Cure Parkinson, 2019–; Ambassador: Meningitis Trust; RNIB (esp. Talking Books); Children's Reading Fund, Nat. Literary Trust, 2012–. DL Glos, 2002–06. *Publications*: Eliza Stanhope, 1978; Parson Harding's Daughter, 1979 (reissued under pseudonym Caroline Harvey, 1995); Leaves from the Valley, 1980; The City of Gems, 1981; The Steps of the Sun, 1983 (reissued under pseudonym Caroline Harvey, 1996); Britannia's Daughters: a study of women in the British Empire, 1983; The Taverners' Place, 1986 (reissued under pseudonym Caroline Harvey, 2000); The Choir, 1988 (televised, 1995); A Village Affair, 1989 (televised, 1994); A Passionate Man, 1990; The Rector's Wife, 1991 (televised, 1994); The Men and the Girls, 1992; A Spanish Lover, 1993; (ed) The Country Habit: an anthology, 1993; The Best of Friends, 1995; Next of Kin, 1996; Other People's Children, 1998 (televised, 2000); Marrying the Mistress, 2000 (dramatised for stage, 2005); Girl from the South, 2002; Brother and Sister, 2004; The Book Boy, 2006; Second Honeymoon, 2006; Friday Nights, 2008; The Other Family, 2010; Daughters-in-Law, 2011; The Soldier's Wife, 2012; Sense and Sensibility, 2013; Balancing Act, 2014; City of Friends, 2017; An Unsuitable Match, 2018; *as Caroline Harvey*: Legacy of Love, 1992; A Second Legacy, 1993; A Castle in Italy, 1993; The Brass Dolphin, 1997; contribs to newspapers and magazines. *Recreations*: reading, conversation, culture, travel. *Address*: c/o United Agents, 12–26 Lexington Street, W1F 0LE. *W*: www.joannatrollope.com.
*See also* A. D. H. Trollope.

**TROMANS, Stephen Richard**; QC 2009; *b* Birmingham, 2 Feb. 1957; *s* of Henry and Dorothy Tromans; *m* 1981, Caroline Frances Power; three *d*. *Educ*: Rowley Regis Grammar Sch.; Selwyn Coll., Cambridge (BA Law 1978); Norfolk Painting Sch. (Dip. Oil Painting, 2018). Admitted as solicitor, 1981; Lectr in Law, Dept of Land Econ., Univ. of Cambridge, and Fellow, Selwyn Coll., Cambridge, 1981–87; Partner: Wild Hewitson & Shaw, 1987–90; Simmons & Simmons, 1990–99; called to the Bar, Inner Temple, 1999; Jt Hd of Chambers, 39 Essex St, 2011–15. Chm., Environmental Law Foundn, 2010–14. Mem., Cttee on Radioactive Waste Mgt, 2016–. Mem. Council, English Nature, 1994–2000. Mem. Council, Ridley Hall, Cambridge, 2008–. Pres., Selwyn Coll. Alumni Assoc., 2017–18. Fellow, Centre for Energy and Envmtl Governance, Univ. of Cambridge, 2017–. FRSA. *Publications*: Commercial Leases, 1987, 2nd edn 1997; Planning Law, Practice and Precedents, 1990; The Environment Acts 1990–1995, 1991, 3rd edn 2003; The Law of Nuclear Installations, 1997, 2nd edn as Nuclear Law, 2010; Environmental Impact Assessment, 2003, 2nd edn 2012; Contaminated Land, 1994, 3rd edn 2019. *Recreations*: social tennis, industrial history, the great conductors, drawing, oil painting. *Address*: 39 Essex Chambers, 81 Chancery Lane, WC2A 1DD. *T*: (020) 7832 1111, *Fax*: (020) 7353 3978. *E*: stephen.tromans@39essex.com.

**TROMBETTA, Raffaele**; Commendatore, Ordine al Merito, Italy, 2011; Ambassador of Italy to the Court of St James's, since 2018; *b* Naples, 23 April 1960; *s* of Carlo Trombetta and Rita Aprea; *m* 1987, Victoria Jane Mabbs; one *s* one *d*. *Educ*: Univ. of Naples (BA Pol Sci.); London Sch. of Econs and Pol Sci. (MA Eur. Studies). Entered Diplomatic Service of Italy, 1985; Second, then First Sec., Bogota, 1987–90; Consul, London, 1990–95; Hd of Secretariat, Econ. Affairs Directorate, Rome, 1995; Office of Minister of Foreign Affairs, 1995–96; Counsellor, Office of Sec. Gen., 1997; Counsellor, then First Counsellor, Perm. Repn to EU in Brussels, 1998–2002; Dep. Hd of Mission, Beijing, 2002–06; Hd, Private Office of Minister of State for Foreign Affairs, 2006–08; Dep. Dir Gen. for Asia, Oceania, Pacific and Antarctic, Rome, and Dep. Dir Gen. for Eur. Integration, 2008–13; Dep. Dir Gen. for EU, and Principal Dir for Eur. Integration, Rome, 2010–13; Ambassador to Brazil, and also accredited to Suriname, 2013–16; Chief of Cabinet to Minister of Foreign Affairs, 2016–17; Personal Rep. and Sherpa of Pres., Council of Ministers for G7 Italian Presidency and G20, 2017. Grã-Cruz, Ordem Nacional do Cruzeiro do Sul (Brazil), 2016. *Recreations*: cinema, reading, football. *Address*: Embassy of Italy, 14 Three Kings Yard, W1K 4EH. *T*: (020) 7312 2200. *E*: sa.amblondra@esteri.it. *Clubs*: Athenæum, Travellers, National Liberal.

**TRONCHETTI PROVERA, Marco**; Chief Executive Officer, since 1992, and Executive Vice Chairman, since 2015, Pirelli & Co. SpA, Milan (Chairman, 2003–15); *b* Milan, 1948; *m*; three *c*. *Educ*: Bocconi Univ., Milan (grad. 1971). Founder, holding co. in field of maritime transportation, 1973–86; joined Pirelli Gp, 1986; Partner, Pirelli & Co., 1986–; Man. Dir and Gen. Manager, Société Internationale Pirelli SA, Basle, 1988–92; Chm., Prelios SpA (formerly Pirelli & Co. Real Estate SpA, Milan), 1991–2013; Pirelli SpA: Man. Dir and Gen. Manager, Finance and Admin and Gen. Affairs, 1991–92; Exec. Dep. Chm. and Man. Dir, 1992–96; Dep. Chm., 1995–99, Chm., 1999–2003, Pirelli & Co.; Chm. and CEO, Pirelli SpA, 1996–2003; Chairman: Olimpia SpA, 2001–07; Telecom Italia SpA, 2001–06; Dep. Chm. and Man. Dir, Olivetti SpA, 2001–08. Chm., CAMFIN SpA, Milan. Member: Internat. Adv. Bd, Allianz; Internat. Council, JP Morgan; European Adv. Cttee, NY Stock Exchange. Dep. Chm., Confindustria (Confedn of Italian Industries), 2000–. Board Member: Teatro alla Scala Foundn, 2001–05; Univ. Commerciale Luigi Bocconi; FC Internazionale SpA. Italian Chm., Council for US and Italy. Member: Assonime Steering Cttee; European Round Table of Industrialists; Italian Gp, Trilateral Commn. *Address*: Pirelli & Co. SpA, Viale Piero e Alberto Pirelli n. 25, 20126 Milan, Italy.

**TROOP, Patricia Ann, (Mrs P. A. Dittner)**, CBE 2001; FRCP, FFPH; Chief Executive, Health Protection Agency, 2003–08; independent consultant on public health and health policy, since 2005; *b* 5 April 1948; *d* of John Ronald Troop and Phoebe Margaret Troop; *m* 1979, Michael Dittner; one *s* one *d*. *Educ*: Manchester Univ. Med. Sch. (MB ChB 1971; MSc Community Medicine 1979); MA Cantab 1988. MFCM 1980, FFPHM (FFCM 1986); FRCP 2001. Dir of Public Health, Cambridge HA, 1988–91; Associate Lectr, Faculty of Medicine, Cambridge Univ., 1988–99; Chief Executive: Cambridge HA, 1990–93; Cambs Family Health Services, 1992–93; Director of Public Health: East Anglia RHA, 1993–95; Anglia and Oxford, then Eastern, Regl Office, NHS Exec., DoH, 1995–99; Dep. CMO, DoH, 1999–2003. Work for DoH, ECDC, WHO, 2008. Chm., Ind. Rev. of Incidents of Pseudomonas Infection in Neonatal Units in NI, 2012. Mem. and Vice-Chm., Cambs TEC, 1992–93. Chairman: Intercollegiate Gp on Nutrition, 2006–14; Internat. Cttee, Faculty of Public Health, 2011–13; Mem., Internat. Health Regulation Rev. Cttee, WHO, 2010–11. Non-exec. Dir, 2009–10, Sen. Ind. non-exec. Dir, 2010–13, Dep. Chm., 2013–15, Cambridge Univ. Hosps Foundn Trust. Vis. Prof., LSHTM, 2000–08; Hon. Prof., City Univ., 2003–14. Mem., Lucy Cavendish Coll., Cambridge, 1990–99. Hon. DSc: East Anglia, 2005; Cranfield, 2006. *Publications*: chapters and articles in various med. jls. *Recreations*: painting, yachting, golf. *Address*: 47a Lode Way, Haddenham, Ely, Cambs CB6 3UL. *T*: (01353) 741087.

**TROSS, Jonathan Edward Simon**, CB 2004; non-executive Director, UK Biobank, since 2013; *b* 21 Jan. 1949; *s* of late Francis Tross and Audrey (*née* Payne); *m* 1972, Ann Humphries; one *s* one *d*. *Educ*: Chislehurst and Sidcup Grammar Sch.; University Coll., Oxford (BA Hons Modern Hist., 1970). Teacher in Kenya, 1971; Department of Health and Social Security: grad. trainee, 1972; Principal, 1977–84; Asst Sec., Supplementary Benefits Review, 1984–87; Asst Dir, Corporate Div., Barclays Bank, on secondment, 1987–90; Pharmaceutical Industry Br., DoH, 1990–91; G3, Head of Planning and Finance Div., 1991–94, G2, Dir of Corporate Mgt, 1994–99, DSS; G2, Head of Constitution Secretariat, Cabinet Office, 1999–2001; Chief Exec., CAFCASS, 2001–04; Collaboration Proj. Dir, LGA, 2004–06. Non-exec. Dir, NICE, 2007–16. Comr (Non Operational), IPCC, 2009–15. Trustee and Treas., Citizens Advice, 2005–11; Treas., Garratt Park Allotment Soc., 2018–. *Recreations*: football, reading, theatre, walking, allotment. *Club*: Fulham Football.

**TROTMAN, Andrew Frederick**, MA; educational consultant and leadership coach, since 2011; *b* 9 Dec. 1954; *s* of late Campbell Grant Trotman and Audrey Trotman (*née* Simpson); *m* 1980, Mary Rosalind Spencer; one *s* one *d*. *Educ*: Alleyne's Grammar Sch., Stevenage; Balliol Coll., Oxford (MA English Language and Lit. 1977); Cert Ed Oxon 1978; Oxford Brookes Univ. (MA Coaching and Mentoring Practice 2013). Asst Master, Radley Coll., 1978–84; Housemaster, Abingdon Sch., 1984–90; Dep. Rector, Edinburgh Acad., 1991–95; Head Master, St Peter's School, York, 1995–2004; Warden, St Edward's Sch., Oxford, 2004–11; Acting Headmaster, Repton Sch., 2012. Governor: Cheam Sch., 2005–12; St Hugh's Sch., 2009–; Mem. Council, Malvern Coll., 2016–. Dir, Aspirance Leadership Services, 2013–. Educnl Advr, Clergy Support Trust (formerly Sons and Friends of Clergy), 2013–; Mem. Adv. Council, Winston Churchill Meml Trust, 2016–. MInstD 1997. FRSA. JP City of York, 1998–2004. *Recreations*: walking, rowing, music, bagpiping. *Address*: The Grey House, Grump Street, Ilmington, Shipston-on-Stour, Warwicks CV36 4LE. *E*: andrew@aspirance.co.uk.
*See also* J. G. Trotman.

**TROTMAN, John Grant**; Headmaster, Bishop's Stortford College, 1997–2011; *b* Silloth, Cumberland, 19 Sept. 1952; *s* of late Campbell Grant Trotman and Audrey Trotman (*née* Simpson); *m* 1st, 1977, Alexandra Kitchener-Payne (marr. diss. 2003); two *s*; 2nd, 2011, Melanie Carruthers (*née* Crawford). *Educ*: Alleyne's Grammar Sch., Stevenage; St Edmund Hall, Oxford (BA, MA, PGCE). Asst Master, Kent Coll., Canterbury, 1976–83; Head of English: Newcastle-under-Lyme Sch., 1983–85; St Edward's Sch., Oxford, 1985–92; Dep. Hd, The Leys, Cambridge, 1992–97. Dir, Isle of Wight Samaritans, 2015–18 (Chair, 2015). Gov., St Blasius Acad., Shanklin, 2013–18 (Dep. Chm., 2016–18). *Publications*: Both Brittle

and Beautiful (poems), 2015. *Recreations:* writing poetry, birds, wild places, school fiction of 1920s and 1930s, trees, trying to draw. *Address:* Brantwood House, 8 Pomona Road, Shanklin Old Village, Isle of Wight PO37 6PF. *T:* (01983) 863799. *E:* john.g.trotman@gmail.com.
*See also* A. F. Trotman.

**TROTT, Andrew James,** FRICS; Surveyor Member, Upper Tribunal (Lands Chamber) (formerly Lands Tribunal), since 2006; *b* 24 Dec. 1953; *s* of John and Lydia Trott; *m* 1981, Fiona Jane Maynard; three *s*. *Educ:* Sir Antony Browne's Sch., Brentwood; Poly. of South Bank (BSc Hons Estate Mgt); Open Univ. (BA, MBA). ARICS 1977, FRICS 1992. RICS Res. Fellow, Poly. of South Bank, 1979–80; Partner, John Trott and Son, 1980–82; Hd of Property Consultancy, London Transport, subseq. Transport for London, 1982–2005. *Recreations:* flying (private pilot's licence), football, golf, collecting modern first editions, Globe Theatre. *Address:* Upper Tribunal (Lands Chamber), Royal Courts of Justice, Strand, WC2A 2LL. *T:* (020) 7612 9725. *E:* uppertribunalmember.trott@ejudiciary.net.

**TROTT, Christopher John;** HM Diplomatic Service; Ambassador to the Republic of South Sudan, since 2019; *b* 14 Feb. 1966; *s* of John and Averil Trott; *m* 1992, Sunna Park; one *s* one *d*. *Educ:* Hawthorns Sch., Blechingley; Whitgift Sch., S Croydon; Bristol Univ. (BA Hons Hist. 1988); Sch. of Oriental and African Studies, Univ. of London (MA SE Asian Area Studies 1991). Entered FCO, 1991; Dep. Hd of Mission, Rangoon, 1993–96; First Secretary: (Commercial), 1996–99, (Political), 1999–2002, Tokyo; Dep. Hd of Mission, Kabul, 2002; FCO, 2003–07; Ambassador to Senegal and concurrently to Guinea-Bissau and Cape Verde, 2007–11, and concurrently to Mali, 2007–10; Consul Gen., Cape Town, 2011–15; Dean, Consular Corps, Cape Town, 2014–15; High Comr to Solomon Islands, Vanuatu and Nauru, 2016; Special Rep. for Sudan and South Sudan, and Hd, Jt Sudan Unit, FCO and DFID, 2016–19. Vice Pres., Whitgiftian Assoc., 2012–. Citizen of Honour, Commune of Timbuktu, 2010. *Recreations:* travel, reading, ski-ing, scuba-diving, season ticket holder at Crystal Palace FC. *Address:* Foreign and Commonwealth Office, King Charles Street, SW1A 2AH.

**TROTT, Philip David Anthony;** Partner, Bates Wells & Braithwaite London LLP, since 1992; *b* Exeter, 5 June 1952; *s* of Sydney Harold Trott and Ruth Lotte Trott; partner, Kate Edwards. *Educ:* Portsmouth Grammar Sch.; Oxford Poly. (HND Business Studies 1973); University Coll. London (LLB Hons 1976). Admitted solicitor, 1979; Partner: Lawford & Co., 1982–89; Thomson Snell & Passmore, 1989–92. Hon. Legal Advr, Holborn CAB, 1979–96; Advr, ArtLaw, 1983–84; Mem., Adv. Panel, Office of the Immigration Services Comr, 2001–06. Immigration Law Practitioners' Association: Co-Founder, 1984; Mem., Exec. Cttee, 1984–90, 1994–95, 2001–02; Convenor, Exec. Econ. Migration Sub-Cttee, 1984–2019; Chm., 1986–88. Brexit Taskforce, Law Soc. Editor, Immigration and Internat. Employment Law Jl, 1999–2000; Mem., Editl Bd and contrib., Lexis Nexis Immigration PSL, 2012–. *Publications:* (contrib.) Macdonald's Immigration Law and Practice, 3rd edn, 1991 to 7th edn, 2008; (contrib.) Jackson's Immigration Law and Practice, 2nd edn, 1999, 3rd edn, 2002. *Recreations:* sailing, cycling, walking, rowing, Southern Italian cookery, benefactor to the arts, VW Campervan enthusiast (Member, VW Owners' Club). *Address:* Bates Wells & Braithwaite London LLP, 10 Queens Street Place, EC4R 1BE. *T:* (020) 7551 7722, *Fax:* (020) 7551 7800. *E:* p.trott@bwbllp.com. *Clubs:* Lensbury, House of St Barnabas.

**TROTTER, Major Alexander Richard,** CVO 2013; JP; Lord-Lieutenant of Berwickshire, 2000–14; Chairman, Meadowhead Ltd (formerly Mortonhall Park Ltd), since 1974; *b* 20 Feb. 1939; *s* of late Major H. R. Trotter, TD, and of Rona Trotter (*née* Murray); *m* 1970, Julia Henrietta, *d* of Capt. Sir Peter McClintock Greenwell, 3rd Bt, TD; three *s*. *Educ:* Eton Coll.; City of London Tech. Coll. Served Royal Scots Greys, 1958–68; Manager, Charterhall Estate and Farm, 1969–; Vice Chm., Border Grain, Ltd, 1984–2003. Dir, Timber Growers GB Ltd, 1977–82. Scottish Landowners' Federation: Mem. Council, 1975–2004; Convener, 1982–85; Vice Pres., 1986–96; Pres., 1996–2001; Mem., NCC and Chm., Scottish Cttee, 1985–90; Mem., UK Cttee, Euro Year of the Envmt, 1986–88. Gen. Comr for Income Tax, Berwickshire, 1973–2010. Mem. (Ind.), Berwickshire CC, 1969–75 (Chm., Roads Cttee, 1974–75). Chm., Thirlstane Castle Trust, 1996–2007. Officer, Royal Co. of Archers. FRSA. DL 1987, JP 2000, Berwickshire. OStJ 2005. *Recreations:* golf, bridge, country sports. *Address:* Whinkerstones House, Duns, Berwickshire TD11 3RE. *T:* (home) (01890) 840555, (office) (01890) 840301. *E:* alex@charterhall.net. *Clubs:* Turf, Pratt's; New (Edinburgh).

**TROTTER, David;** *see* Trotter, W. D.

**TROTTER, Dame Janet (Olive),** DBE 2001 (OBE 1991); CVO 2018; Lord-Lieutenant for Gloucestershire, 2010–18; *b* 29 Oct. 1943; *d* of Anthony George Trotter and Joyce Edith Trotter (*née* Patrick). *Educ:* Derby Lonsdale Coll. of Educn (Cert Ed); BD (ext.) London Univ.; Inst. of Educn, London Univ. (MA); Henley Mgt Coll. (MSc Brunel Univ.). Teacher: St Leonards Secondary Sch., 1965–67; Chartham Secondary Sch., 1967–69; Rochester Grammar Sch. for Girls, 1969–73; Lectr, King Alfred's Coll., Winchester, 1973–84; Vice Principal, St Martin's Coll., Lancaster, 1985–86; Principal, St Paul and St Mary's Coll., Cheltenham, 1986–90; Principal, 1990–2006, Vice-Chancellor, 2002–06, Univ. of Gloucestershire (formerly Cheltenham and Gloucester Coll. of Higher Educn). Mem. and Chm., Glos HA, 1991–96; Chairman: S and W Reg., NHS Exec., DoH, 1996–2001; Glos Hosps NHS Foundn Trust (formerly NHS Trust), 2002–10. Chair, Nelson Trust. Member: HEFCE, 1992–97; TTA, 1994–99. DL Glos, 2006. Hon. Freeman, Cheltenham, 2002; Hon. Freewoman, Gloucester, 2018. Hon. DTech Pecs, Hungary, 1996; Hon. DEd: UWE, 2001; Brunel, 2004; Hon. DHum Elizabethtown Coll., Pa, 2002; Hon. DLaws Bristol, 2002. *Publications:* various articles. *Recreations:* cycling, music. *Address:* 1 Tivoli Court, Tivoli Road, Cheltenham, Glos GL50 2TD.

**TROTTER, Sir Neville (Guthrie),** Kt 1997; JP; DL; FCA; FRAeS, FCIT; Consultant, Thornton Baker, 1974–83, Grant Thornton, Chartered Accountants, 1983–2005; *b* 27 Jan. 1932; *s* of Captain Alexander Trotter and Elizabeth Winifred Trotter (*née* Guthrie); *m* 1983, Caroline, *d* of late Captain John Farrow, OBE, RN and Oona Farrow (*née* Hall); one *d*. *Educ:* Shrewsbury; King's Coll., Durham (BCom). Short service commn in RAF, 1955–58. Partner, Thornton Baker & Co., Chartered Accountants, 1962–74. Former Director: MidAmerican Energy Hldgs Co.; Wm Baird plc; Darchem Ltd; Romag plc. Mem. Council, NE Chamber of Commerce, 1998–2014; Regl Ambassador of NE in N America, UKTI and One Northeast, 2008–11; Chm., British-American Chamber of Commerce, NE of England, 1999–2014; Pres., 2000–12, Mem. Adv. Bd, 2012–19, Northern Defence Industries; Vice Pres., Soc. of Maritime Industries, 1996–. Former Member: East Coast Main Line (formerly Great North Eastern Railway, later National Express East Coast Main Line) Business Forum; Council, European Atlantic Gp. Mem., Newcastle City Council, 1963–74 (Alderman, 1970–74); Chm., Finance Cttee, Traffic Highways and Transport Cttee, Theatre Cttee). Mem., CAA Airline Users Cttee, 1973–79. Mem., Tyne and Wear Metropolitan Council, 1973–74; Vice-Chm., Northumberland Police Authority, 1970–74. MP (C) Tynemouth, Feb. 1974–1997. Chm., Cons. Party Shipping and Shipbuilding Cttee, 1979–85, 1994–97 (Vice-Chm., 1976–79); Secretary: Cons. Party Industry Cttee, 1981–83; Cons. Party Transport Cttee, 1983–84; Mil. Sec., Cons. Party Aviation Cttee, 1976–79; Member: Industry Sub-Cttee, Select Cttee on Expenditure, 1976–79; Select Cttee on Transport, 1983–92; Select Cttee on Defence, 1993–97; Parly Defence Study Group, 1980–97; Armed Forces Parly Scheme (RAF), 1990–91; formerly Chm., All-Party Gp for Prevention of Solvent Abuse. Private Member's Bills: Consumer Safety, 1978; Licensing Amendment, 1980; Intoxicating Substances Supply (Glue Sniffing), 1985. Pres., North Area Cons. Party, 1996–2003. Vice Pres., Soc. for Prevention of Solvent and Volatile Substance Abuse, 1989–. Former Parliamentary Consultant: British Transport Police Fedn; Go Ahead Gp; Bowrings. Former Member: Northern Economic Planning Council; Tyne Improvement Commn; Tyneside Passenger Transport Authority; Industrial Relations Tribunal; UK Defence Forum; Steering Cttee, Parly Maritime Gp; Member: Defence and Security Forum; Atlantic Council; Air League; RUSI (formerly Council Mem.); NE RFCA (formerly TAVRA), 1997–; US Naval Inst.; USAF Assoc.; US Navy League; Assoc. of US Army; Railway Studies Assoc. Pres., Tyneside Br., RM Assoc., 2001–16. Hon. Colonel: Royal Marine Reserve, 1998–2003; Durham ACF, 2003–05. Pres., TS Dauntless (formerly TS Rodney) Gosforth Sea Cadets, 2006–. Pres., Whitley Bay and Dist Scout Council, 2004–12. Council Member: Northumbria, Order of St John, 2005–12; High Sheriff's Assoc. of England and Wales, 2005–11. FRAeS 1998; FCIT 1998. Freeman, City of London, 1978; Member: Co. of Chartered Accountants, 1978; Hon. Co. of Air Pilots (formerly GAPAN), 2006–. JP Newcastle upon Tyne, 1973; DL 1997, High Sheriff, 2004–05, Tyne and Wear. *Recreations:* aviation, gardening, fell-walking, study of foreign affairs, defence and industry. *Clubs:* Royal Air Force; Northern Counties (Newcastle upon Tyne).

**TROTTER, Thomas Andrew,** FRCO; Organist, St Margaret's Church, Westminster Abbey, since 1982; Organist to the City of Birmingham, since 1983; *b* 4 April 1957; *s* of late His Honour Richard Stanley Trotter and Ruth Elizabeth Trotter. *Educ:* Malvern Coll.; Royal Coll. of Music, 1974–76 (schol.; ARCM) (organ schol., St George's Chapel, Windsor, 1975–76); King's Coll., Cambridge (organ schol., 1976–79; MA). John Stewart of Rannock Schol. in Sacred Music, Cambridge Univ., 1979; Countess of Munster schol. for further organ studies with Marie-Claire Alain in Paris. Début at Royal Fest. Hall, 1980; Prom. début, 1986; regular broadcasts for Radio 2 and Radio 3; has performed at fests throughout UK and in Europe; concert tours to Australia, USA and Far East; organ recordings. DUniv UCE, 2003; Hon. DMus Birmingham, 2006. Walford Davies Prize, RCM, 1976; First prize and Bach prize, St Albans Internat. Organ Competition, 1979; Prix de Virtuosité, Conservatoire Rueil-Malmaison, 1981; Instrumental Award, Royal Philharmonic Soc., 2001; Internat. Performer of the Year, NY Chapter, Amer. Guild of Organists, 2012; Medal, RCO, 2016. *Address:* c/o The Town Hall, Birmingham B3 3DQ.

**TROTTER, Prof. (Wilfred) David,** PhD; FBA 2004; King Edward VII Professor of English Literature, University of Cambridge, 2002–18; Fellow, Gonville and Caius College, Cambridge, since 2002; *b* 25 July 1951; *s* of late Wilfred Robert Trotter and Enid Beatrice Trotter (*née* Roulston). *Educ:* Gonville and Caius Coll., Cambridge (BA, PhD). Res. Fellow, Magdalene Coll., Cambridge, 1975–77; University College London: Lectr in English, 1977–87; Reader, 1987–90; Prof. of English, 1990–91; Quain Prof. of English Lang. and Lit., 1991–2002. Vis. Prof., CIT, 1988–89. *Publications:* The Poetry of Abraham Cowley, 1979; The Making of the Reader, 1984; Circulation: Defoe, Dickens and the economies of the novel, 1988; The English Novel in History 1895–1920, 1993; (jtly) A Companion to Edwardian Fiction, 1997; Cooking with Mud: the idea of mess in nineteenth century art and fiction, 2000; Paranoid Modernism, 2001; Cinema and Modernism, 2007; The Uses of Phobia: essays on literature and film, 2010; Literature in the First Media Age: Britain between the Wars, 2013. *Address:* Faculty of English, 9 West Road, Cambridge CB3 9DP.

**TROUBRIDGE, Sir Thomas (Richard),** 7th Bt *cr* 1799, of Plymouth; FCA; Partner, PricewaterhouseCoopers (formerly Price Waterhouse), 1989–2015; *b* 23 Jan. 1955; *s* of Sir Peter Troubridge, 6th Bt and of Hon. Venetia Daphne (who *m* 2nd, Captain W. F. E. Forbes, *qv*), *d* of 1st Baron Weeks; *S* father, 1988; *m* 1984, Hon. Rosemary Douglas-Pennant, *y d* of 6th Baron Penrhyn, DSO, MBE; two *s* one *d*. *Educ:* Eton College; Durham Univ. (BSc Eng). ACA 1980, FCA 1991. Joined Price Waterhouse, 1977. *Recreations:* sailing, ski-ing. *Heir:* *s* Edward Peter Troubridge [*b* 10 Aug. 1989; *m* 2017, Eleanor Jane Morse; one *s*]. *Address:* The Manor House, Elsted, Midhurst, W Sussex GU29 0JY. *T:* (01730) 825286. *Clubs:* White's, Hurlingham; Itchenor Sailing.

**TROUGHT, (Walter) Stuart;** President, States of Alderney, since 2011; *b* Cleethorpes, 12 Oct. 1950; *s* of Owen and Jane Trought; *m* 1990, Jane Maria Fraser; two *d*. *Educ:* Oakham, Plymouth. Master Mariner, 1978. Shell, 1967–78; Master, then Superintendent, Kuwait Oil Co., 1978–85; Dir, Gp Ops Bd, Lamnalco, 1985–2002; Dep. Gen. Manager, Abu Dhabi Petroleum Ports Operating Co., 2002–06; CEO and Chm., Alderney Renewable Energy, 2006–11. Guest Lectr, Gresham Coll., 2015. Chm., Alderney CPA, 2011–. Trustee: Cheape Charitable Trust, 2011–; Mignot Meml Hosp. Trust, 2011–; Patron: Alderney Cancer Relief, 2012–; Royal Channel Islands Yacht Club, 2011–; Chm., Alderney RNLI, 2012–; Guardian, Alderney Foundn, 2016–. Member: Honourable Co. of Master Mariners, 1987; Nautical Instn, 1987. Freeman, City of London. Queen's Diamond Jubilee Medal, 2012. *Recreations:* sailing, fishing, shooting, ski-ing. *Address:* 6 Little Street, Alderney, Channel Islands GY9 3TT. *T:* (01481) 823934, 07781 113099. *E:* strought@hotmail.com.

**TROUGHTON, James Michael;** Chairman, Tulliemet Ltd, since 1999; *b* Hambleden, 8 Nov. 1950; *s* of Sir Charles Hugh Willis Troughton, CBE, MC, TD and (Constance) Gillean (*née* Mitford), DL; *m* 1973, Sarah Campbell-Preston; one *s* two *d*. *Educ:* Radley Coll.; Trinity Coll., Cambridge (BA 1972; DipArch). RIBA 1975; ARIAS 1999. With Foster Associates, 1975–78; Richard Rogers and Partners, 1978–82; Founder Partner, Troughton McAslan, 1983–96; Chm., John McAslan and Partners, 1996–98. Troughton McAslan Architects completed works include: Derwent Valley Properties; Apple Computer Stockley Park; FC3 Canary Wharf; Jubilee line Stations, Canning Town and Stratford; De La Warr Pavilion, Bexhill; Yapi Kredi Bankasi HQ, Gebze, Istanbul; North End, Blair Castle, 1999 (jtly RIBA award). Trustee: Dunkeld Chapter House Mus., 2001–; Nat. Mus of Scotland, 2011–18. *Recreations:* hydro electric power generation, boats, art. *Address:* Blair Castle, Blair Atholl, Pitlochry PH18 5TJ. *T:* (01796) 481355. *Club:* Royal Highland Yacht.
*See also* P. J. C. Troughton, S. R. V. Troughton.

**TROUGHTON, Peter,** PhD; Chairman, 4RF Ltd, 1999–2012; *b* 26 Aug. 1943; *s* of late Frank Sydney Troughton and of Joan Vera Troughton (*née* Root); *m* 1967, Joyce Uncles; two *s*. *Educ:* City Univ. (BSc Eng); University College London (PhD). Technical apprentice, Plessey Co., then Post Office apprentice, 1959; PO scholarship, 1964; research for PhD, 1967; develt of microprocessor techniques for control of telephone switching systems, 1970; Dep. Gen. Manager, South Central Telephone Area, 1977; Head of Ops, Prestel, 1979; Gen. Manager, City Telephone Area, 1980; Regional Dir, British Telecom London, 1983; Man. Dir, British Telecom Enterprises, 1984–86; Dir and Partner, Alan Patricof Associates, 1986–88, non-exec. Dir, 1988–90; Man. Dir and Chief Exec. Officer, Telecom Corp. of NZ, 1988–92; Chairman: Trans Power (NZ National Power Grid) Estabt Bd, 1990–92; Marine Air Systems, then MAS Technology Ltd, 1993–98; Troughton, Swier and Associates, 1996–99. Director: Crown Health Enterprise Develt Unit, NZ, 1992–93; Electricity Supply Industry Reform Unit, Vic, Australia, 1993–95. Advr to NZ govt, 1993–94; Special Advr to Vic. Govt on reform and privatisation of electricity, gas and aluminium industries, 1995–99; Advr to Australian Davos Connection, World Econ. Forum, for conf. on energy in 21st century, 1998–2000. Mem., State Owned Enterprises Steering Cttee, 1992–93. Mem., NZ Business Round Table, 1988–92; Chm., Twyford and Dist Round Table, 1981–82. NZ Chief Exec. of the Year Award, 1991. NZ Commemoration Medal, 1990. *Publications:* articles and papers on microwave systems, computers, communications, and on restructuring, regulation and privatisation of utility industries. *Recreations:* travel, archaeology, bridge. *Club:* Wellington (NZ).

**TROUGHTON, Peter John Charles**, CBE 2015; Chairman, Lowland Investment Co. plc, 2012–17 (non-executive Director, since 1990); *b* 18 June 1948; *s* of Sir Charles Hugh Willis Troughton, CBE, MC, TD and (Constance) Gillean (*née* Mitford), DL; *m* 1977, Sarah Rose Colman (*see* S. R. Troughton); one *s* two *d*. *Educ:* Radley Coll.; Trinity Coll., Cambridge (MA Hons); Harvard Business Sch. (AMP 1987). Joined HM Diplomatic Service 1970; FCO, 1970–72; Jakarta, 1972–75; First Sec., FCO, 1975–79; W. H. Smith Gp plc, 1979–95: Managing Director: News, 1988–91; Retail, 1991–95; Dir, 1991–95; Chief Executive: Rothschild Asset Mgt Internat. Ltd, 1995–99; First Arrow Investment Mgt Ltd, 2000–04; Dir, J. Rothschild Services Ltd, 2005–10. Non-executive Director: Archant Ltd (formerly Eastern Counties Newspaper Gp), 1991–2016 (Vice-Chm., 2006–16); Waverton Global Investment Funds plc (formerly JOHIM Global Funds plc), 2011–17; Waverton Investment Funds plc, 2011–19; Waverton Investment Management Ltd, 2014–17. Partner, Spencer Hse Capital Mgt LLP, 2008–11. Mem., Salisbury Diocesan Bd of Finance, 2018–. Trustee: Nat. Gall., 1988–96 (Mem., Publications Cttee, 1982–88); Nat. Gall. Trust, 1996–2007 (Hon. Treas., 2001–07); Rothschild Foundn, 2004–11 and 2018–; Royal Opera House Endowment Fund, 2005–; Royal Collection Trust, 2007–16 (Chm., Audit Cttee, 2007–16; Chm., Future Prog. Bd, 2014–); Butrint Foundn, 2008–11; Swindon Mus. and Art Gall. Trust, 2015–19; Chm., National Gallery Publications Ltd, 1988–96. Mem., Adv. Cttee, Hillsborough Castle, 2016–. Mem. Council, 2005–19 (Chm., 2006–14), Pro Chancellor, 2013–19, Univ. of Bath. Gov., St Mary's Sch., Calne, 1992–2002. Mem., Soc. of Dilettanti, 2008–. *Recreations:* reading, walking, ski-ing. *Address:* The Lynch House, Upper Wanborough, near Swindon, Wilts SN4 0BZ. *T:* (01793) 790385. *Clubs:* Brooks's, Pratt's.
*See also* J. M. Troughton, S. R. V. Troughton.

**TROUGHTON, Sarah Rose;** Lord-Lieutenant of Wiltshire, since 2012; *b* London, 3 May 1953; *d* of Sir Timothy (James Alan) Colman, *qv*; *m* 1977, Peter John Charles Troughton, *qv*; one *s* two *d*. Lady-in-Waiting to Duchess of Kent, 1992–99. Member, Council: Friends of Tate Gall., 1983–89; Tate Patrons of British Art, 1985–90; American Mus. in Britain, 2001–09; Trustee, Chelsea Physic Garden, 2003–15 (Chm., 2009–15). Trustee and Patron, Wilts and Swindon Community Foundn, 2001–. Mem., Wiltshire House Hostel, 1989–2004. President or Patron, 2012–: Naomi House; Community First; Youth Action Wilts; Friends of Salisbury Cathedral; Wilts Victoria Co. Hist.; Wessex MS Centre; Relate; ABF The Soldiers' Charity; CPRE; Wilts Historic Churches Trust; Order of St John; Merchant's House, Marlborough; Wilts Mus., Devizes; Wilts Scouts; Prospect Hospice. DL Wilts, 2006. *Recreations:* painting, gardening, grandchildren, Scotland. *Address:* The Lynch House, Upper Wanborough, Swindon, Wilts SN4 0BZ. *T:* (01793) 790385.

**TROUGHTON, Simon Richard Vivian;** Deputy Chairman, Standard Life Aberdeen plc, since 2017; *b* Marlow, 23 Nov. 1953; *s* of Sir Charles Hugh Willis Troughton, CBE, MC, TD and (Constance) Gillean (*née* Mitford), DL; *m* 1983, Mary Elliot; two *s* one *d*. *Educ:* Radley Coll.; Selwyn Coll., Cambridge (MA Land Economy). Cazenove & Co., 1981–2003 (Partner, 1988–2000); Chief Operating Officer, Fanchier Partners, 2003–09; with Aberdeen Asset Mgt, 2009–17, Chm., 2017; Chm., Redburn Partners, 2010– (Chm., 2016). Lay Advr to RCS, 2012–. *Recreations:* country pursuits, golf. *Address:* Standard Life Aberdeen plc, 10 Queens Terrace, Aberdeen AB10 1YG. *E:* simon@troughton.com. *Clubs:* Whites, Pratts; Swinley Forest Golf, St Enodoc Golf.
*See also* J. M. Troughton, P. J. C. Troughton.

**TROUP, Sir (John) Edward (Astley),** Kt 2018; consultant; Executive Chairman and first Permanent Secretary, HM Revenue and Customs, 2016–17; *b* 26 Jan. 1955; *s* of Vice-Adm. Sir (John) Anthony (Rose) Troup, KCB, DSC, and of Cordelia Mary Troup; *m* 1978, Siriol Jane Martin; three *s* one *d*. *Educ:* Oundle Sch.; Corpus Christi Coll., Oxford (BA Maths 1976, MA; MSc Applied Maths 1977). ATII 1983. Admitted solicitor, 1981; joined Simmons & Simmons, 1979, Partner, 1985–95, 1997–2004; HM Treasury: Special Advr on Tax, 1995–97; Dir, Business and Indirect Tax, 2004–10; Dir-Gen., Tax and Welfare, 2010–12; Tax Assurance Comr and second Permanent Sec., HMRC, 2012–16. External Adviser: McKinsey; Frontier Economics. *Recreations:* cinema, art, London and the River Thames, the landscape, buildings and history of the British Isles.

**TROUSDELL, Lt Gen. Sir Philip (Charles Cornwallis),** KBE 2004; CB 2000; General Officer Commanding Northern Ireland, 2003–05; *b* 13 Aug. 1948; *s* of late Col Philip James Cornwallis Trousdell, OBE and Doreen Mary Trousdell (*née* Durdle); *m* 1986, Sally Caroline Slade Parker; one *s* two *d*. *Educ:* Berkhamsted; RMA, Sandhurst. Commnd Royal Irish Rangers, 1968: CO, 1st Bn, 1989–91; commanded 48 Gurkha Bde, 1992–93; Dir, Public Relns (Army), 1994–97; COS, HQ Land Comd, 1997–2000; Dep. Comdr (Ops) Stabilisation Force, Bosnia Herzegovina, 2000; Comdt, RMA Sandhurst, 2001–03. Col, Queen's Own Gurkha Transport Regt, 1993–2003; Dep. Col, 1996–2001, Col, 2001–13, Royal Irish Regt; Colonel Commandant: Media Ops Gp (Vol.), 2001–06; Bde of Gurkhas, 2003–07. Chm., Civil Nuclear Police Authy, 2011–16. Chm., Corporate Battlefields, 2007–13. Chairman: Gurkha Welfare Trust, 2003–07; Army Mus Ogilby Trust, 2012–; Dep. Chm., Help for Heroes Recovery Centres, 2017– (Trustee, 2012–; Chm., 2014–16). *Recreations:* reading, bicycling, wine. *Address:* Riverside House, Fordingbridge SP6 2JS. *Club:* Army and Navy.

**TROWELL, Stephen Mark;** QC 2015; a Recorder, since 2016; *b* Hemel Hempstead, 5 Oct. 1967; *s* of Peter Trowell and Judith Trowell; *m* 1997, Leila Habib; two *s* one *d*. *Educ:* Dame Alice Owen's Sch.; Keble Coll., Oxford (BA 1989); Wolfson Coll., Oxford (DPhil 1992). Called to the Bar, Middle Temple, 1995; in practice as barrister specialising in financial remedy work in matrimonial cases. *Recreations:* family, theatre, reading. *Address:* 1 Hare Court, Temple, EC4Y 7BE. *T:* (020) 1797 7070. *E:* clerks@1hc.com.

**TROWER, Hon. Sir William (Spencer Philip),** Kt 2019; **Hon. Mr Justice Trower;** a Judge of the High Court, Chancery Division, since 2019; *b* 28 Dec. 1959; *s* of late Anthony Gosselin Trower and Catherine Joan Trower (*née* Kellett); *m* 1986, Mary Louise Chastel de Boinville; four *d*. *Educ:* Eton Coll.; Christ Church, Oxford (MA); City Univ. (Dip. Law). Called to the Bar, Lincoln's Inn, 1983, Bencher, 2009; QC 2001; Dep. High Court Judge (Chancery Div.), 2007–19; Hd of Chambers, South Square, 2008–17. Non-exec. Dir, Insolvency Service, 2017–. Mem., Insolvency Rules Cttee, 2000–11. Mem. Council, Insolvency Lawyers' Assoc., 2005–18. *Publications:* (jtly) The Law and Practice of Corporate Administrations, 1994, 3rd edn as Corporate Administrations and Rescue Procedures, 2017; (contrib.) Montgomery and Ormerod on Fraud: Criminal Law and Procedure, 2008; (consultant ed.) Parry, Aycliffe and Shivji, Transaction Avoidance in Insolvencies, 2nd edn 2011 to 3rd edn 2018; (consultant ed.) O'Dea, Long and Smyth, Schemes of Arrangement: law and practice, 2012. *Recreations:* family, gardening, countryside, theatre. *Address:* Royal Courts of Justice, Strand, WC2A 2LL. *Club:* Garrick.

**TROWLER, Isabelle;** Chief Social Worker for England (Children and Families), since 2013; *b* Nantwich, Cheshire, 10 Oct. 1967; *d* of Dr Eric Trowler and Pat Trowler (*née* Fairclough, now Paxton); two *s*. *Educ:* Poly. of North London (BSc Sociol.); London Sch. of Econs and Pol Sci. (MSc Social Policy and Social Work). Social Worker, London Bor. of Lewisham, 1996–98; Commng Manager, London Bor. of Hackney, 1998–2001; Hd, Youth Support Develt, Royal Bor. of Kensington and Chelsea, 2001–05; Asst Dir, Children's Social Work, London Bor. of Hackney, 2005–11; Dir, Morning Lane Associates, 2010–13. *Publications:* (ed jtly) Social Work Reclaimed, 2011. *Recreations:* reading, writing and arithmetic.
*See also* R. Trowler.

**TROWLER, Rebecca;** QC 2012; a Recorder, since 2018; *b* Nantwich, Cheshire, 20 Oct. 1965; *d* of Dr Eric Trowler and Pat Trowler (*née* Fairclough, now Paxton); civil partnership 2008, Dr Alison Mears; one *d*. *Educ:* Manchester High Sch.; London Guildhall Univ. (BSc 1st Cl. Hons Psychol.). Called to the Bar, Gray's Inn, 1995, Bencher, 2017; in practice as a barrister, specialising in criminal law, 1996–. Internat. Dir, Criminal Bar Assoc., 2017–. *Publications:* (contrib.) Taylor on Criminal Appeals, 2nd edn 2012. *Recreations:* music, art, food, film. *Address:* Doughty Street Chambers, 53–54 Doughty Street, WC1N 2LS. *E:* r.trowler@doughtystreet.co.uk.
*See also* I. Trowler.

**TROWSDALE, Prof. John,** PhD; FMedSci; Professor of Immunology, and Head of Division of Immunology, Department of Pathology, University of Cambridge, 1997–2017, now Professor Emeritus; *b* 8 Feb. 1949; *s* of Roy R. Trowsdale and Doris Trowsdale (*née* Graham); *m* 1971, Susan Price; two *s* one *d*. *Educ:* Beverley Grammar Sch.; Univ. of Birmingham (BSc 1970; PhD 1973). European Fellow, Biochemical Soc., Gif-sur-Yvette, France, 1973–75; Res. Fellow, Scripps Clinic and Res. Foundn, Calif, 1975–78; SRC Res. Fellow, Genetics Lab., Univ. of Oxford, 1978–79; Imperial Cancer Research Fund: ICRF Fellow, 1979–82; Res. Scientist, 1982–85; Sen. Scientist, 1986–90; Prin. Scientist, 1990–97. Member: Council, European Fedn of Immunogenetics, 1995–98; Sci. Adv. Bd, Onyvax, 1997–; Chm., Histocompatibility and Immunogenetics Affinity Gp, British Soc. of Histocompatibility and Immunogenetics, 1996–99. FMedSci 2000. *Publications:* (jtly) Advanced Immunology, 1996; res. papers in science jls. *Recreations:* playing rock, jazz and classical music, painting. *Address:* Department of Pathology, Tennis Court Road, Cambridge CB2 1QP. *T:* (01223) 333711.

**TROY, Jill Mary; Her Honour Judge Troy;** a Circuit Judge, since 2013. *Educ:* Ralph Thoresby High Sch., Leeds; Lady Margaret Hall, Oxford (MA Juris.). Called to the Bar, Middle Temple, 1986; in practice as barrister, 1986–2013; a Dep. Dist Judge, 2008–13; a Recorder, 2008–13.

**TRUDEAU, Rt Hon. Justin (Pierre James);** PC (Can.) 2015; MP (L) Papineau, Montreal, since 2008; Prime Minister of Canada and Minister of Youth, since 2015; *b* Ottawa, 25 Dec. 1971; *s* of late Pierre Elliott Trudeau and of Margaret Trudeau; *m* 2005, Sophie Grégoire; two *s* one *d*. *Educ:* McGill Univ. (BA 1994); Univ. of British Columbia (BEd 1998). Teacher of French and Maths, West Point Grey Acad., then Winston Churchill Secondary Sch., Vancouver; Chair, Katimavik, 2002–06; Mem. Bd, Canadian Avalanche Foundn. Chair, Liberal Party Task Force on Youth Renewal, 2006; Leader, Liberal Party of Canada, 2013–. *Publications:* Common Ground (memoir), 2014. *Address:* Office of the Prime Minister, 80 Wellington Street, Ottawa, ON K1A 0A2, Canada.

**TRUDGILL, Prof. Peter John,** FBA 1989; Professor of English Linguistics, University of Fribourg, 1998–2005, now Emeritus; Hon. Professor of Sociolinguistics, University of East Anglia, since 2005; *b* 7 Nov. 1943; *s* of John Trudgill and Hettie Jean Trudgill (*née* Gooch); *m* 1980, Jean Marie Hannah. *Educ:* City of Norwich Sch.; King's Coll., Cambridge (BA; MA 1966); Edinburgh Univ. (Dip Gen Linguistics 1967; PhD 1971). Asst Lectr, Lectr, Reader, Prof., Dept of Linguistic Sci., Univ. of Reading, 1970–86; Reader, 1986–87, Prof. of Sociolinguistics, 1987–92, Essex Univ.; Prof. of English Linguistics, Univ. of Lausanne, 1993–98. Vis. Prof. at Univs of Hong Kong, Bergen, Aarhus, Illinois, Stanford, Osmania, Tokyo International Christian, ANU, Texas Austin, Toronto, Canterbury (NZ). Fellow: Norwegian Acad. of Sci and Letters, 1995; Royal Norwegian Acad. of Scis, 1996. Lifetime Hon. Mem., Linguistic Soc. of America, 2011. Hon. Dr: Uppsala, 1995; UEA, 2002; La Trobe, 2005; British Columbia, 2018; Patras, 2019. *Publications:* The Social Differentiation of English in Norwich, 1974; Sociolinguistics: an introduction, 1974, 4th edn 2000; Accent, Dialect and the School, 1975; Sociolinguistic Patterns in British English, 1978; (with A. Hughes) English Accents and Dialects, 1979; (with J. K. Chambers) Dialectology, 1980; (with J. M. Hannah) International English, 1982, 3rd edn 1994; On Dialect, 1983; Coping with America, 1983, 2nd edn 1985; Language in the British Isles, 1984; Applied Sociolinguistics, 1984; Dialects in Contact, 1986; The Dialects of England, 1990; (with J. K. Chambers) English Dialects: studies in grammatical variation, 1991; (with L. Andersson) Bad Language, 1991; Introducing Language and Society, 1992; Dialects, 1994; (with L. Bauer) Language Myths, 1998; Sociolinguistic Variation and Change, 2002; New Dialect Formation, 2004; In Sfakiá: passing time in the wilds of Crete, 2008, 2nd edn 2015; Sociolinguistic Typology: social determinants of linguistic complexity, 2011; (with George Dalidakis) Sfakia: a history of the region in its Cretan context, 2015; Dialect Matters: respecting vernacular language, 2016; Norwegian as a national language and other studies in Scandinavian linguistics, 2018. *Recreation:* Norwich City FC. *Address:* School of Language and Communication Studies, University of East Anglia, Norwich NR4 7TJ.

**TRUDINGER, Prof. Neil Sidney,** PhD; FRS 1997; FAA; Professor of Mathematics, Australian National University, 1973–2014, now Emeritus; *b* 20 June 1942; *s* of Laurence Robert Trudinger and Dorothy Winifred Trudinger. *Educ:* Univ. of New England, Australia (BSc Hons 1962); Stanford Univ., USA (MS 1965; PhD 1966). FAA 1978. Courant Instructor, New York Univ., 1966–67; Lectr, then Sen. Lectr, Macquarie Univ., Australia, 1967–70; Reader, then Prof., Univ. of Qld, 1970–73; Australian National University: Head, Dept of Pure Maths, 1973–78; Director: Commonwealth Special Res. Centre for Mathematical Analysis, 1982–90; Centre for Maths and its Applications, 1991–93; Dean, Sch. of Math. Scis, 1992–2000; Prof., Northwestern Univ., 1989–93. Hon. Professor: Univ. of Queensland, 2011–; Univ. of Wollongong, 2017–. Hon. DSc Univ. of New England, 2013. *Publications:* Elliptic Partial Differential Equations of the Second Order, 1977, 2nd edn 1983. *Address:* Mathematical Sciences Institute, Australian National University, Canberra, ACT 0200, Australia. *T:* (2) 61254568.

**TRUE,** family name of **Baron True**.

**TRUE, Baron** *cr* 2010 (Life Peer), of East Sheen in the County of Surrey; **Nicholas Edward True,** CBE 1993; Private Secretary to Leader of the Opposition, and Director, Opposition Whips' Office, House of Lords, 1997–2010; *b* 31 July 1951; *s* of Edward Thomas True and Kathleen Louise True (*née* Mather); *m* 1979, Anne-Marie Elena Kathleen Blanco Hood;

two s one d. *Educ:* Nottingham High Sch.; Peterhouse, Cambridge (BA Hons 1973; MA 1978). Mem., Cons. Res. Dept, 1975–82; Asst to Cons. Party Dep. Leader, 1978–82; Special Advr to Sec. of State for Health and Social Security, 1982–86; Dir, Public Policy Unit, 1986–90; Dep. Head, Prime Minister's Policy Unit, 1991–95; Special Advr, Prime Minister's Office, 1997. Councillor (C), Richmond-upon-Thames, 1986–90, 1998–2018 (Dep. Leader, 2002–06; Leader of Opposition, 2006–10; Leader, 2010–17). Mem., Leaders' Cttee, London Councils, 2010–17. Member: House Cttee, H of L, 2012–15; Procedure Cttee, H of L, 2015–18; Constitution Cttee, H of L, 2019–; Chm., Select Cttee on Intergenerational Fairness, H of L, 2018–19. Mem. Bd, Royal Parks Agency, 2012–17. Trustee: Olga Havel Foundn, 1990–94; Sir Harold Hood's Charitable Trust, 1996–; Richmond Civic Trust, 2006–10; Chm., Orleans House Trust, 2011–17. *Publications:* articles in newspapers, jls etc; pamphlets and papers on policy matters. *Recreations:* Byzantium, Italy, gardens, books. *Address:* 114 Palewell Park, East Sheen, SW14 8JH. *T:* (020) 8876 9628; Contrada Salino 15, San Ginesio, Macerata, Italy. *Clubs:* Beefsteak, Brooks's, Travellers.

**TRULUCK, Maj. Gen. Ashley Ernest George,** CB 2001; CBE 1997; Managing Director, Kerykeion Services (formerly Ashley Truluck Associates), since 2003; Managing Consultant, The Cultural Experience, since 2012; *b* 7 Dec. 1947; *s* of Maj. George William Truluck, RA and Elizabeth Truluck (*née* Kitchener); *m* 1976, Jennifer Jane Bell; one *s* one *d. Educ:* Harvey's Sch.; RMA Sandhurst; BA. Regtl duty, Bde of Gurkhas, Malaysia, Hong Kong, Nepal, 1969–74; ADC to Maj. Gen., Bde of Gurkhas, and Comdr FARELF, 1974–75; Commns Officer, Guards Armoured Bde, 1976–77; sc, 1978–79; GSO2, MoD, 1980–81; Comdr, 24th Airmobile Bde, BAOR, UK, 1982–84; Dir, Staff RMCS, 1984–86; Comdr, 3rd Armoured Div. Signals, BAOR, 1986–88; Col Army Staff Duties, 1989–90; HCSC, 1990; Comdt, Royal Sch. of Signals and Blandford Garrison, 1991–92; RCDS, 1993; Brig. Gen. Staff, UK Land Comd, 1994–96; Dir, Attack Helicopter, 1997–98; ACOS, SHAPE, 1998–2000. Chief Exec., Gtr London Magistrates' Courts Authy, 2001–03. Leader, Defence Information Mgt Study, 2004–05. Nat. Project Manager, Fire and Rescue Services Communications, 2005–10. Strategic Advr, IBM, 2010–14. Col Comdt, RCS, 2001–07; Adm., Royal Signals Yacht Club, 2003–12. Chm., London Criminal Justice Bd, 2001–03. Chairman: Royal Signals Trustee Ltd, 2001–14; Gurkha Welfare Trust (Wessex), 2010–; Chalke Valley Community Hub Ltd, 2013–16; Soc. for Army Historical Res., 2014–; Wilts Community Foundn; Dir, Armed Forces Charities Adv. Co., 2012–; Trustee, Armed Forces Common Investment Fund, 2012–. FInstD 2002; MRUSI 2004. High Sheriff Wilts, 2020. *Recreations:* offshore sailing, community projects, country pursuits, military history. *Clubs:* Army and Navy; Cape Horners.

**TRUMAN, Crispin Marshall,** OBE 2017; Chief Executive Officer, Campaign to Protect Rural England, since 2017; *b* Manchester, 7 Feb. 1964; *s* of late Anthony Barratt Truman and of Jill Estelle Truman; *m* 1996, Maria Luise Mehlstaeubl; three *s. Educ:* Ashton Park Comprehensive Sch., Bristol; St Peter's Coll., Oxford (BA Hons PPE; MSc Applied Social Studies). CQSW 1991. Residential Social Worker, London Bor. of Camden, 1986–89; Social Worker, Family Housing Assoc., 1991–93; Develt Worker, 1993–97, CEO, 1997–2003, Revolving Doors Agency; CEO, Churches Conservation Trust, 2003–17. Founder and Mem. Council, Future Religions Heritage (Europe), 2010–16. Chm., London Cycling Campaign, 1999–2004. Chm. Govs, Stoke Newington Sch. and Sixth Form, 2015–. *Recreations:* walking, cycling. *Address:* Campaign to Protect Rural England, 5–11 Lavington Street, SE1 0NZ. *E:* cmlvtruman@gmail.com.

**TRUMP, Donald John;** President of the United States of America, since 2017; *b* New York, 14 June 1946; *s* of Fred C. Trump and Mary Trump; *m* 1st, 1977, Ivana Zelnicek (marr. diss. 1991); two *s* one *d;* 2nd, 1993, Marla Maples (marr. diss. 1999); one *d;* 3rd, 2005, Melania Knauss; one *s. Educ:* New York Military Acad.; Wharton Sch. of Finance, Univ. of Pennsylvania (BS 1968). Joined father's co., Trump Organization, later Chm. and Pres.; Chm. and CEO, Trump Hotels & Casino Resorts, 1995–2004; Chm., Trump Entertainment Resorts Inc., 2005–16; holdings include: Trump Tower, Trump Palace, Trump Plaza, Trump World Tower, Trump International Hotel and Tower, New York; Trump Plaza, Mar-A-Lago, Florida; Trump Plaza Hotel Casino, Trump Castle Casino, Trump Taj Mahal Casino Resort, Atlantic City; acquired 50% stake in Empire State Bldg, 1994. Co-Exec. Prod. and host, TV series, The Apprentice, 2004–15. Launched Trump World Magazine, 2004. *Publications:* Trump: the way to the top, 2004; Crippled America: how to make America great again, 2015, repr. as Great Again: how to fix our crippled America, 2017; *jointly:* Trump: the art of the deal, 1988; Trump: surviving at the top, 1990; The Art of Survival, 1991; The Art of the Comeback, 1997; The America We Deserve, 2000; Trump: how to get rich, 2004; Trump: think like a billionaire, 2004; Trump Strategies for Real Estate, 2005; Why We Want You to Be Rich: two men - one message, 2006; Take Command, 2006; Trump University Real Estate 101, 2006; Trump University Marketing 101, 2006; Trump 101: the way to success, 2006; Trump University Entrepreneurship 101, 2007; Think Big and Kick Ass: in business and life, 2007; Trump - Never Give Up: how I turned my biggest challenges into success, 2008; Think Like a Champion: an informal education in business and life, 2009. *Address:* The White House, 1600 Pennsylvania Avenue NW, Washington, DC 20500, USA.

**TRUNDLE, Shirley Jean,** CBE 2004 (OBE 1999); Director, Wildlife, International, Climate and Forestry, Department for Environment, Food and Rural Affairs, since 2018; *b* 28 Feb. 1958; *d* of Derek and Jean Hayles; *m* 1979, John Malcolm Trundle; one *s* one *d. Educ:* Guildford High Sch.; Newnham Coll., Cambridge (MA); St Catharine's Coll., Cambridge (MPhil). Entered DES, 1981, subseq. DFE, then DFEE; Private Sec. to Sec. of State for Educn and Sci., 1986–87; Principal, 1987–93; Divl Manager, Higher Educn Policy and Funding, 1993–96; Sec. to Nat. Cttee of Inquiry into Higher Educn (Dearing Cttee), 1996–97; Head, Childcare Unit, 1998–99; Dir, Opportunity and Diversity Gp, 1999–2001; Department for Work and Pensions: Dir, Universal Banking Prog., 2001–03; Dir, Welfare Strategy and Performance, 2003–06; Dir, Benefit Strategy, 2006–08; Dir, Families, 2008–13, Care and Adoption, 2013–14, DCSF, subseq. DFE; Dir, Sustainable Land Mgt and Livestock Farming, 2014–15, Dir, Countryside and Nature, 2015–16, Dir, Natural Envmt Policy, 2016–18, DEFRA. *Recreations:* family, nature, travel, gardening, cooking. *Address:* Department for Environment, Food and Rural Affairs, 2 Marsham Street, SW1P 4DF.

**TRURO, Bishop of,** since 2018; **Rt Rev. Philip Ian Mounstephen;** *b* Crookham Village, Hants, 13 July 1959; *s* of Dennis Mounstephen and Ann Mounstephen; *m* 1984, Ruth Weston; one *d. Educ:* St Edward's Sch., Oxford; Southampton Univ. (BA 1980); Magdalen Coll., Oxford (PGCE 1981; BA 1987; CTh 1988). Ordained deacon, 1988, priest, 1989; Vicar, St James', W Streatham, 1992–98; Church Pastoral Aid Society: Hd, Pathfinders, 1998–2002; Hd of Ministry and Dep. Gen. Dir, 2002–06; Chaplain: St Michael's, Paris, 2007–12; RBL, Paris Br., 2007–12; Exec. Leader, CMS, 2012–18. Canon, Dio. of Europe, 2012–. Gov., Univ. of Glos, 2004–12 (Chair, Audit Cttee, 2007–12, Vice-Chair, Council, 2011–12; Hon. Fellow, 2013). Trustee: Send a Cow, 2015–18 (Vice Chm., 2016–18); Overseas Bishoprics' Fund, 2017–18; Archbp of Canterbury's Anglican Communion Fund, 2017–18. *Recreations:* music, theatre, cinema, gardening, record collecting. *Address:* Lis Escop, Feock, Truro TR3 6QQ. *T:* (01872) 862657. *E:* bishop@truro.anglican.org.

**TRURO, Dean of;** see Bush, Very Rev. R. C.

**TRUSCOTT,** Baron *cr* 2004 (Life Peer), of St James's in the City of Westminster; **Peter Derek Truscott;** parliamentarian, businessman, author and political analyst; *b* 20 March 1959; *s* of late Derek Truscott and of Dorothy Truscott; *m* 1991, Svetlana, *d* of late Col Prof. Nicolai Chernikov and Svetlana Chernikova. *Educ:* Newton Abbot Grammar Sch.; Exeter Coll., Oxford (History Prize; BA 1981, MA 1985, DPhil 1985, Modern History). Labour Party Organiser, 1986–89; NACRO, 1989–94. Councillor, Colchester Borough Council, 1988–92; contested (Lab) Torbay, 1992. Member: TGWU, 1986–2009; Co-op Party, 1987–2009; posts in Trade Union and Labour movements. MEP (Lab) Hertfordshire, 1994–99; contested (Lab) Eastern Reg., 1999. European Parliament: Labour spokesman on foreign affairs and defence, 1997–99; Vice-Pres., Cttee on Security and Disarmament, 1994–99; Mem., Foreign Affairs Cttee, 1994–99; Substitute Member: Regl Policy Cttee, 1994–97; Economic, Monetary and Industrial Policy Cttee, 1997–99. Deptl liaison peer, MoD, 2004–05; Mem., Select European Sub-Cttee C, H of L, 2005–06, 2007–09; Parly Under-Sec. of State for Energy, DTI, and DTI spokesman in H of L, 2006–07. Dir, Energy Enterprises Ltd, 2008–17; Man. Dir, Energy Enterprises 2 Ltd, 2017–; non-executive Director: Gulf Keystone Petroleum, 2008–12 (Member: Remuneration Cttee, 2008–12; Nomination Cttee, 2012; Audit Cttee, 2012 (Chm., 2010–12)); Eastern Petroleum Corp., 2008–11; African Minerals Ltd, 2008–09 (Consultant, 2009–12); 25 Jermyn Street St James's (RTM) Co. Ltd, 2012–17; Chm., 9 Lansdown Place West Ltd, 2014–15; Member, Advisory Board: OPUS Exec. Partners, 2008–11 (Chm., 2008–11); VAL Energy, 2009–11; Advr, Japan Bank for Internat. Cooperation, 2009–10; Chair, Adv. Bd, Russian Gold Fund, 2017–19; Advr to CEO, Thaler.One, 2018–. Associate Res. Fellow, IPPR, 2000–06; Associate Fellow, 2005–06, 2008–12, Mem., Internat. Adv. Bd, 2012–, RUSI. Fellow, Industry and Parlt Trust, 2005–. Mem., Internat. and Domestic Sub-Cttee, Labour Party NEC, 1996–97. Patron, Fire Safety Friends of Russia, 2016–. Sch. governor, 1988–92. *Publications:* Russia First, 1997; European Defence, 2000; Kursk, 2002; Putin's Progress, 2004; The Ascendancy of Political Risk Management, 2006; European Energy Security, 2009; numerous articles. *Recreations:* walking, music, theatre, swimming, travel. *Address:* House of Lords, SW1A 0PW. *Clubs:* Ritz, Farmers.

**TRUSCOTT, Ian Derek,** PhD; QC (Scot.) 1997; *b* 7 Nov. 1949; *s* of Derek and Jessie Truscott; *m* 1972, Julia Elizabeth Bland; four *s. Educ:* Edinburgh Univ. (LLB Hons 1971); Leeds Univ. (LLM 1974); Strathclyde Univ. (PhD 2004). Solicitor, 1973–87, 2013–17; Faculty of Advocates, 1988–2013, 2017–; called to the Bar, Gray's Inn, 1995; barrister, 1995–2014. Pt-time Judge (formerly Chm.), Employment Tribunals, England and Wales, 2002–. Vis. Prof. of Law, Strathclyde Univ., 1999–2010. *Recreations:* walking, snow dome collecting. *Address:* Advocates' Library, Parliament Square, Edinburgh EH1 1RF, *T:* (0131) 260 5683.

**TRUSCOTT, Sir Ralph (Eric Nicholson),** 4th Bt *cr* 1909, of Oakleigh, East Grinstead, Sussex; *b* 21 Feb. 1966; *o s* of Sir George James Irving Truscott, 3rd Bt and of Yvonne Dora Truscott (*née* Nicholson); *S* father, 2001, but his name does not appear on the Official Roll of the Baronetage. *Educ:* Sherborne Sch. *Heir:* none.

**TRUSS, Rt Hon. Elizabeth (Mary);** PC 2014; MP (C) South West Norfolk, since 2010; Secretary of State for International Trade and President of the Board of Trade, since 2019; Minister for Women and Equalities, since 2019; *b* Oxford, 26 July 1975; *d* of John Kenneth Truss and Priscilla Mary Truss; *m* 2000, Hugh O'Leary; two *d. Educ:* Roundhay Sch., Leeds; Merton Coll., Oxford (MA PPE). Commercial Analyst, Shell International, 1996–2000; Commercial Manager and Regulatory Econs Dir, Cable & Wireless, 2000–05; Divl Man. Dir, Communication Gp, 2005–07; Dep. Dir, Reform, 2007–09. Parly Under-Sec. of State, DFE, 2012–14; Sec. of State for Envmt, Food and Rural Affairs, 2014–16; Lord Chancellor and Sec. of State for Justice, 2016–17; Chief Sec. to the Treasury, 2017–19. Contested (C): Hemsworth, 2001; Calder Valley, 2005. *Recreations:* food, design, cinema. *Address:* House of Commons, SW1A 0AA. *T:* (020) 7219 7151. *E:* elizabeth.truss.mp@parliament.uk.

**TRUSS, Lynne;** writer; *b* 31 May 1955; *d* of Ernest Edward Truss and Joan Dorothy Truss. *Educ:* UCL (BA 1st cl. Hons (English Lang. and Lit.) 1977; Fellow 2004). Literary Ed., The Listener, 1986–90; columnist, TV Critic and Sports Columnist, The Times, 1990–2000. Writer, BBC drama series: Acropolis Now, 2000, 2002; A Certain Age, 2002, 2005; Inspector Steine, 2007, 2008, 2009, 2011. FRSL 2004. Hon. DLitt Brighton, 2005; DUniv Open, 2006; Hon. DFA, New York Sch. of Visual Arts, 2006. *Publications: novels:* With One Lousy Free Packet of Seed, 1994; Making the Cat Laugh, 1995; Tennyson's Gift, 1996; Going Loco, 1999; Cat Out of Hell, 2014; The Lunar Cats, 2016; A Shot in the Dark, 2018; The Man that Got Away, 2019; *non-fiction:* Tennyson and his Circle, 1999, rev. edn 2014; Eats, Shoots & Leaves, 2003 (Book of the Year, British Book Awards, and USA Today, 2004); Talk to the Hand, 2005; Get Her Off the Pitch, 2009; *drama scripts:* A Certain Age, 2007; Hell's Bells, 2012. *Address: c/o* David Higham Associates, 7th Floor, Waverley House, 7–12 Noel Street, W1F 8GQ. *T:* (020) 7434 5900, *Fax:* (020) 7437 1072. *E:* dha@davidhigham.co.uk, info@lynnetruss.com. *W:* www.lynnetruss.com.

**TRUSSLER, Lea;** see Paterson, L.

**TRUSTRAM EVE;** see Eve, family name of Baron Silsoe.

**TRUSWELL, Prof. (Arthur) Stewart,** AO 2001; MD, DSc, FRCP, FRACP; Professor of Human Nutrition, University of Sydney, 1978–99, now Emeritus; *b* 18 Aug. 1928; *s* of George Truswell and Molly Truswell (*née* Stewart-Hess); *m* 1st, 1956, Sheila McGregor (marr. diss. 1983); four *s;* 2nd, 1986, Catherine Hull; two *d. Educ:* Ruthin Sch., Clwyd; Liverpool Univ.; Cape Town Univ. (MB, ChB 1952, MD 1959); DSc Sydney 1998. FRCP 1975; FRACP 1980. Registrar in Pathology, Cape Town Univ., 1954; Registrar in Med., Groote Schuur Hosp., 1955–57; Research Bursar, Clin. Nutrition Unit, Dept of Med., Cape Town Univ., 1958 and 1959; Adams Meml Trav. Fellowship to London, 1960; Sen. Fellow, Clin. Nutrition, Tulane Univ., USA, 1961; Res. Officer, Clin. Nutrition Unit, Cape Town Univ., 1962; Sen. Mem., Scientific Staff, MRC Atheroma Research Unit, Western Infirmary, Glasgow, 1963 and 1964; full-time Lectr, then Sen. Lectr in Med. and Consultant Gen. Physician, Cape Town Univ. and Groote Schuur Hosp., 1965–71; Warden of Med. Students' Residence, Cape Town Univ., 1967–69; Prof. of Nutrition and Dietetics, Queen Elizabeth Coll., London Univ., 1971–78. Vice-Pres., Internat. Union of Nutritional Sciences, 1985–93; Member, numerous cttees, working parties, editorial bds and socs related to nutrition. *Publications:* Human Nutrition and Dietetics, 7th edn (with S. Davidson, R. Passmore, J. F. Brock), 1979; ABC of Nutrition, 1986, 4th edn 2003; (with J. I. Mann) Essentials of Human Nutrition, 1998, 5th edn 2017; History of Research on Diet and Coronary Heart Disease, 2010; numerous research papers in sci. jls on various topics in human nutrition. *Recreations:* gardening, walking. *Address:* 23 Woonona Road, Northbridge, NSW 2063, Australia; Human Nutrition Unit, School of Molecular Bioscience, Building G08, Sydney University, Sydney, NSW 2006, Australia. *T:* (2) 93513726. *E:* stewart.truswell@sydney.edu.au.

**TRUSWELL, Paul Anthony;** b 17 Nov. 1955; s of John and Olive Truswell; m 1981, Suzanne Clare Evans; two s. Educ: Firth Park Comprehensive Sch., Sheffield; Leeds Univ. (BA Hons 1977). Journalist, Yorkshire Post newspapers, 1977–88; Local Govt Officer, Wakefield MDC, 1988–97. Member: Leeds HA, 1982–90; Leeds FHSA, 1992–96. Mem. (Lab) Leeds CC, 1982–97, 2012–. MP (Lab) Pudsey, 1997–2010. Mem., Envmtl Audit Select Cttee, 1997–99. Hon. Vice Pres., Trading Standards Inst., 2008–13. Club: Belle Isle Working Men's.

**TRUSWELL, Stewart;** see Truswell, A. S.

**TRYON,** family name of **Baron Tryon**.

**TRYON, 4th Baron** cr 1940, of Durnford; **Charles George Barrington Tryon;** b 15 May 1976; s of 3rd Baron Tryon, OBE and Dale Elizabeth (née Harper); S father, 2018; m 2011, Dr Katherine Anne Lyon Carroll; one s two d. Heir: s Hon. Guy Aylmer George Tryon, b 30 Jan 2015.

**TSAI ING-WEN;** President of Taiwan, since 2016; b Taipei City, 1956. Educ: Nat. Taiwan Univ. (LLB 1978); Cornell Univ. Law Sch. (LLM 1980); London Sch. of Econs and Pol Sci. (PhD Law 1984). Associate Prof., then Prof. of Law, Nat. Chengchi Univ., 1984–90; Prof., Soochow Univ. Sch. of Law, 1991–93; Prof., Dept of Internat. Business, Nat. Chengchi Univ., 1993–2000. Senior Adviser: to Mainland Affairs Council, 1994–98 (Chm., 2000–04); to Nat. Security Council, 1999–2000. Chief Legal Advr, negotiations to gain admission to WTO, 1992–2000. Mem. (Democratic Progressive Party) Legislative Yuan, 2004–06; Vice Premier, 2006–07. Mem., Democratic Progressive Party, 2004–; Chair, 2008–10, 2010–12 and 2014–18. Address: Office of the President, No 122, Sec. 1, Chongqing South Road, Zhongzheng District, Taipei City 10048, Taiwan.

**TSANG, Sir Donald Yam-kuen,** KBE 1997 (OBE 1993); GBM 2002; Chief Executive, Hong Kong Special Administrative Region, 2005–12; b 7 Oct. 1944; m 1969, Selina Pou; two s. Educ: Harvard Univ. (MPA). Joined Govt of Hong Kong, 1967: Dep. Dir of Trade, responsible for trade with N America, 1984; Dep. Sec., Gen. Duties, responsible for Sino-British Jt Declaration, 1985; Dir of Admin, Office of Chief Sec., 1989–91; Dir-Gen. of Trade, 1991–93; Sec. for Treasury, 1993–95; Financial Sec., Hong Kong, 1995–2001; Chief Sec. for Admin, HKSAR, 2001–05. Grand Bauhinia Medal (HKSAR), 2002. Recreations: hiking, swimming, birdwatching. Address: c/o Office of Former Chief Executives, 28 Kennedy Road, Hong Kong.

**TSANGALIDIS, Ianthi Maria;** see Tsimpli, I. M.

**TSE, Simon;** Director, Customer Operations, Crown Commercial Service, since 2016; b Swansea, 30 May 1962; s of Phillip and Carol Ann Tse; m 1991, Elizabeth Ann Evans; two s. Educ: Bishopsgore Comprehensive Sch.; Halesowen Coll. (HND Mech. Engrg). Draughtsman, Unit Superheater Engrg, 1980–84; Dir, Welshglass Works Ltd, 1984–94; Man. Dir, MPlan Software Ltd, 1994–96; Man. Dir, 1996–2001, Business Services Dir, 2001–05, Virgin Media; mgt consultant, 2005–08; Chief Operating Officer, 2008–10, CEO, 2010–13, DVLA; Dir, Contracted Customer Services, DWP, 2013–16. Non-executive Director: Ty Hafan, 1998–2005; Phoenix, 2004–14; Maggie's Cancer Care Centre, 2008–14; Hill Community Develt Trust, Swansea, 2006–. Address: Crown Commercial Service, IB31 Concept House, Cardiff Road, Newport NP10 8QQ.

**TSELENTIS, Michael;** QC 2003; b 4 Nov. 1948; s of Anastasios and Helen Tselentis; m 1975, Jacqueline de Mowbray Niehaus; two s. Educ: Univ. of Cape Town (BA 1969; LLB 1971); Magdalen Coll., Oxford (Rhodes Schol. 1972; BCL 1975). Advocate, Supreme Court of South Africa, 1978; SC South Africa, 1989; Acting Judge, Supreme Court of South Africa, 1992; called to the Bar, Gray's Inn, 1995, Bencher, 2008; in practice at the Bar, specialising in international commercial law and arbitration, 1996–; Chartered Arbitrator, 2008. Chm. of, Johannesburg Bar Council, 1993–94. FCIArb. Recreations: squash, swimming, running, golf, reading, music, travelling. Address: 20 Essex Street, WC2R 3AL. T: (020) 7583 9294, Fax: (020) 7583 1341. E: mtselentis@20essexst.com. Clubs: Oxford and Cambridge; Rand (Johannesburg).

**TSIMPLI, Prof. Ianthi Maria,** PhD; Professor of English and Applied Linguistics, University of Cambridge, since 2015; Fellow, Fitzwilliam College, Cambridge, since 2016; b Athens, Greece, 2 Feb. 1964; d of Nikolaos and Angeliki Tsimpli; m 1998, Anastasios Tsangalidis; one s two d. Educ: Arsakeion Psichikou; Univ. of Athens (BA Philol. 1986); University Coll. London (Dip. Linguistics 1988; PhD Linguistics 1992). Lectr in Linguistics, Univ. of Newcastle upon Tyne, 1992–95; Asst Dir of Res., Res. Centre for English and Applied Linguistics, Univ. of Cambridge, 1995–97, (pt-time) 1997–2002; Sen. Mem., 1996–97, Fellow, 1997–2002, Darwin Coll., Cambridge; Aristotle University, Thessaloniki, Greece: Asst Prof., 1997–2000, Associate Prof., 2000–05, of Psycholinguistics; Prof. of Psycholinguistics: Lang. Acquisition and Lang. Disorders, 2005–15; Dir, Lang. Develt Lab., 2003–15; Prof. (pt-time) of Multilingualism and Cognition, Sch. of Psychol. and Clin. Lang. Scis, Univ. of Reading, 2013–15. Vis. Prof., Dept of English Studies, Univ. of Cyprus, 2006; Guest of the Rector Fellow, Netherlands Inst. of Advanced Study in Humanities and Social Scis, 2012. Publications: (with N. V. Smith) The Mind of a Savant: language learning and modularity, 1995 (trans. Japanese 1999); The Prefunctional Stage of First Language Acquisition: a crosslinguistic study, US edn 1996, UK edn 2013; (jtly) The Signs of a Savant: language against the odds, 2010; contribs to acad. jls incl. Lingua, Applied Psycholinguistics, Brain and Lang., Aphasiol., Second Lang. Res., Linguistic Approaches to Bilingualism. Recreations: family, cinema, theatre, walking, opera. Address: Department of Theoretical and Applied Linguistics, University of Cambridge, English Faculty Building, Cambridge CB3 9DA. T: (01223) 760809. E: imt20@cam.ac.uk.

**TS'ONG, Fou;** see Fou Ts'ong.

**TSUI, Prof. Daniel C.,** PhD; Arthur LeGrand Doty Professor, Department of Electrical Engineering, Princeton University, 1982, now Emeritus; b Henan, China, 1939; US citizen; m Linda Varland. Educ: Pui Ching Middle Sch., Hong Kong; Augustana Coll., Rock Island, Ill; Univ. of Chicago (PhD 1967). Res. Associate, Univ. of Chicago, 1967–68; Mem. Technical Staff, Bell Labs, Murray Hill, NJ, 1968–82. Fellow, AAAS; Mem., US NAS, 1987. Nobel Prize for Physics (jtly), 1998; Benjamin Franklin Award in Physics, 1998. Publications: contribs to jls. Address: Department of Electrical Engineering, Princeton University, Princeton, NJ 08544, USA.

**TSUI, Prof. Lap-Chee,** OC 1991; OOnt 2000; PhD; FRS 1991; FRSC 1989; President: Victor and William Fung Foundation, since 2014; Hong Kong Academy of Sciences, since 2015; Director, Qiushi Academy for Advanced Studies, since 2014 and Master, Residential College, Haining International Campus, since 2016, Zhejiang University; Emeritus University Professor, University of Toronto, since 2006; b 21 Dec. 1950; s of Jing-Lue Hsue and Hui-Ching Wang; m 1977, Lan Fong (Ellen); two s. Educ: Chinese Univ. of Hong Kong (BSc Biol. 1972; MPhil 1974); Univ. of Pittsburgh (PhD Biol Scis 1979). University of Toronto: Asst Prof. 1983–88, Associate Prof. 1988–90, Depts of Med. Genetics and Med. Biophysics; Prof., Dept of Molecular and Med. Genetics, 1990–2002, Univ. Prof., 1994–2006; Hospital for Sick Children, Toronto: Sen. Res. Scientist, 1983–2002; Sellers Chair in Cystic Fibrosis Res., 1989–2002; Dir, Cystic Fibrosis Res. Prog., 1995–99; Geneticist-in-Chief, 1996–2002; Dir, Centre for Applied Genomics, 1998–2002; Vice-Chancellor, 2002–14, Sen. Advr to the Pres., 2014, Univ. of Hong Kong. Mem. of team which identified first DNA marker linked to cystic fibrosis on chromosome 7, 1985; led team which isolated the gene responsible for cystic fibrosis and defined the principal mutation, 1989. Chairman: Gordon Res. Conf. on Human Molecular Genetics, 1995; Genome Canada Task Force, 1998–99; Internat. Sci. Prog. Cttee, Human Genome Meeting 2000, 1999–2000. Trustee, Educn Foundn, Fedn of Chinese Canadian Professionals, Ontario. Hon. Fellow, World Innovation Foundn, 2001. For. Associate, NAS, USA, 2004; For. Mem., Chinese Acad. of Scis, 2009. Hon. FRCP 2005. Hon. Fellow, Hughes Hall, Cambridge, 2012. Hon. DCL: Univ. of King's Coll., Halifax, 1991; St Francis Xavier, Antigonish, NS, 1994; Hon. DSc: New Brunswick, Fredericton, 1991; Chinese Univ. of Hong Kong, 1992; York Univ., Toronto, 2001; Tel Aviv, 2005; Toronto, 2007; Aberdeen, 2007; KCL, 2009; Edinburgh, 2010; Fudan, 2013; Western, 2013; Hong Kong Univ. of Sci. and Technol., 2015; Macau, 2015; Hong Kong, 2016. Paul di Sant'Agnese Distinguished Scientific Achievement Award, Cystic Fibrosis Foundn, USA, 1989; Gold Medal of Honor, Pharmaceutical Manufacturers' Assoc., Canada, 1989; Centennial Award, RSCan, 1989; Maclean's Honor Roll, 1989; Award of Excellence, Genetic Soc. Canada, 1990; Courvoisier Leadership Award, 1990; Gairdner Internat. Award, 1990; Cresson Medal, Franklin Inst., 1992; Mead Johnson Award, 1992; Sarsdedt Res. Prize, 1993; Sanremo Internat. Award, 1993; Lecocq Prize, Acad. des Scis, Inst de France, 1994; Henry Friesen Award, 1995; Medal of Honour, Canadian Med. Assoc., 1996; Community Service Award, Toronto Biotechnol. Initiative, 1998; Distinguished Scientist Award, MRC (Canada), 2000; Zellers Sen. Scientist Award, 2001; Killam Prize Award, Canada Council, 2002; Henry G. Friesen Internat. Prize, Friends of Canadian Inst. of Health Res., 2014; Warren Alpert Foundn Prize, Harvard Med. Sch., 2018. GBS (HKSAR) 2011; GBM (HKSAR) 2016. Publications: numerous papers in learned jls and invited papers and reviews. Recreations: cooking, travel, sightseeing. Address: Victor and William Fung Foundation, 33rd Floor, Alexandra House, 18 Chater Road, Central, Hong Kong. T: 28441051, Fax: 28441019.

**TSURUOKA, Koji;** Ambassador of Japan to the Court of St James's, since 2016; b 10 Aug. 1952; m Yooko. Educ: Univ. of Tokyo (BA Law); Harvard Law Sch. (LLM). Joined Min. of Foreign Affairs, Japan, 1976; Dir, First N America Div., 1998–2000; Minister, Indonesia, 2000–02; Prof., Nat. Grad. Inst. for Policy Studies, 2002–03; Dep. Dir-Gen., Foreign Policy Bureau, 2003–06; Director General: for Global Issues, 2006–08; Internat. Legal Affairs Bureau, 2008–10; Dep. Vice-Minister for Foreign Policy, 2010–12; Dep. Minister for Foreign Affairs, 2012–13; Chief Negotiator, Govt HQ for Trans-Pacific Partnership, 2013–16. Address: Embassy of Japan, 101–104 Piccadilly, W1J 7JT. T: (020) 7465 6500.

**TUAM, Archbishop of, (RC),** since 1995; **Most Rev. Michael Neary;** b 15 April 1946. Ordained priest, 1971; Titular Bishop of Quaestoriana and Auxiliary Bishop of Tuam, 1992–95. Address: Archbishop's House, Tuam, Co. Galway, Ireland. T: (93) 24166, Fax: (93) 28070.

**TUAM, KILLALA AND ACHONRY, Bishop of,** since 2011; **Rt Rev. Patrick William Rooke;** b 12 April 1955; s of late Rev. William Warburton Lloyd Rooke and Lucy Gwendoline Rosemary Rooke; m 1979, Alison Isobel Forsythe; one s two d. Educ: Sandford Park Sch., Dublin; Gurteen Agricl Coll., Roscrea; Salisbury and Wells Theol Coll.; Open Univ. (BA); Irish Sch. of Ecumenics, Trinity Coll. Dublin (MPhil). Ordained deacon 1978, priest 1979; Curate, Mossley, 1978–81; Ballwillan, Portrush, 1981–83; Rector: Craigs, Dunaghy and Killagan, 1983–88; Ballymore, Tandragee, 1988–94; Agherton, Portstewart, 1994–2006; Canon Preb., Lisburn Cathedral, 2001–05; Archdeacon of Dalriada, 2005–06; Dean of Armagh, and Keeper of the Robinson Public Library, 2006–11. Chm., Hard Gospel Cttee, Church of Ireland, 2005–09. Recreations: gardening, swimming, supporting Rugby. Address: Bishop's House, Breaffy Woods, Cottage Road, Castlebar, Co. Mayo F23 PW99, Ireland. T: (94) 9035703. E: bishop@tuam.anglican.org.

**TUCK, Anne Victoria, (Vicky);** Director-General, International School of Geneva, 2011–17; b 9 Jan. 1953; m 1977, Peter John Tuck; two s. Educ: Univ. of Kent (BA Hons French and Italian); Univ. of London Inst. of Educn (PGCE); Univ. de Lille et de Paris (Dip. Supérieur de Droit et de français des Affaires); Univ. of South Bank (MA). French and Italian teacher, Putney High Sch., 1976–81; Hd of Mod. Langs, Bromley High Sch., 1981–86; Lectr, Inst. of Educn, London Univ., 1991–94; Dep. Hd, City of London Sch. for Girls, 1994–96; Principal, Cheltenham Ladies' Coll., 1996–2011. Vice-Chm., ISC, 2009–10 (Chm., Educn Cttee, 2009–10). Pres., GSA, 2008. Mem. Council, GDST. Governor: Charterhouse Sch.; Westminster Sch.

**TUCK, Anthony;** see Tuck, J. A.

**TUCK, Sir Bruce (Adolph Reginald),** 3rd Bt cr 1910; b 29 June 1926; o s of Major Sir (William) Reginald Tuck, 2nd Bt, and Gladys Emily Kettle (d 1966), d of late N. Alfred Nathan, Wickford, Auckland, New Zealand, and widow of Desmond Fosberry Kettle, Auckland Mounted Rifles; S father, 1954; m 1st, 1949, Luise (marr. diss., in Jamaica, 1964), d of John C. Renfro, San Angelo, Texas, USA; two s; 2nd, 1968, Pamela Dorothy Nicholson, d of Alfred Nicholson, London; one d. Educ: Canford School, Dorset. Lieutenant, Scots Guards, 1945–47. Heir: s Richard Bruce Tuck, b 7 Oct. 1952. Address: Clopton House, 39 Mill Road, Ashley, Newmarket, Cambs CB8 9EE.

**TUCK, Prof. (John) Anthony,** MA, PhD; FRHistS; Professor of Medieval History, University of Bristol, 1990–93, now Emeritus; b 14 Nov. 1940; s of late Prof. John Philip Tuck and Jane Adelaide Tuck; m 1976, Amanda (marr. diss. 2003), d of late Dr L. J. Cawley, Carlton Husthwaite, near Thirsk, Yorks; two s. Educ: Newcastle upon Tyne Royal Grammar Sch.; Jesus Coll., Cambridge (BA, MA, PhD). FRHistS 1987. Lecturer in History, 1965–75, Sen. Lectr, 1975–78, Univ. of Lancaster; Master of Collingwood Coll., and Hon. Lectr in History, Univ. of Durham, 1978–87; Reader in Medieval History, Univ. of Bristol, 1987–90. Res. Associate, Oxford DNB, 1998–. Hon. Life Fellow, Collingwood Coll., Durham Univ., 1998. Clerk, Stapleford Parish Council, 2000–03. Publications: Richard II and the English Nobility, 1973; Crown and Nobility 1272–1461, 1985, 2nd edn 1999; (contrib.) Oxford DNB, 2004; (jtly) History of Newport, Victoria County History of Essex, 2015; contribs to various acad. jls and vols of essays. Recreations: walking, gardening, local history. Address: 8 Cherry Garden Lane, Newport, Saffron Walden, Essex CB11 3PZ.

See also R. F. Tuck.

**TUCK, Jonathan Philip;** Director of Library Services, 2008–17, Director of Academic Services, 2017–18, Royal Holloway, University of London (Interim Director of Library Services, 2019); b 6 Sept. 1952; s of Philip Charles Tuck and Janetta Margaret Tuck; m 1982, Ann Lambert; one s. Educ: Portsmouth Grammar Sch.; Univ. of Manchester (MA); MA Oxon 1998. MCLIP (ALA 1981). John Rylands University Library of Manchester: Asst Librarian, 1978–90; Sub-Librarian, 1990–94; Asst Dir and Head of Admin, 1994–96; Asst Dir and Dep. Univ. Librarian, 1996–97; Dep. to Dir, Univ. Liby Services, and to Bodley's Librarian, Oxford Univ., 1998–2002; Fellow, Wolfson Coll., Oxford, 1998–2002; Hd, British Collections, BL, 2002–08. Chairman: M25 Consortium of Academic Libraries, 2010–14; LIBER Wkg Gp on Leadership and Workplace Develt, 2016–18; Mem., LIBER

Leadership Progs Wkg Gp, 2019; Member, Board: SCONUL, 2014–17 (Chm., SCONUL Collaboration Strategy Gp, 2014–17); Senate House Liby, 2016–18. Trustee, Egham Mus., 2013–18. *Publications:* contrib. articles on aspects of librarianship, library collections, web archiving and e-books. *Recreations:* book collecting, sport, especially cricket, football, Portsmouth Football Club and Forest Green Rovers. *Address:* 14 Moors Close, Ducklington, Witney OX29 7TW. *T:* (01993) 705047.

**TUCK, Prof. Richard Francis,** PhD; FBA 1994; Frank G. Thomson Professor of Government, Harvard University, since 2002 (Professor of Government, 1995–2002); *b* 9 Jan. 1949; *s* of late Prof. John Philip Tuck and Jane Adelaide Tuck; *m* 1st, 1970, Mary Polwarth (marr. diss. 1993); two *s*; 2nd, 1993, Anne Malcolm; one *d*. *Educ:* Royal Grammar Sch., Newcastle upon Tyne; Jesus Coll., Cambridge (BA 1970; PhD 1976; Hon. Fellow 1997). Cambridge University: Research Fellow, 1970, Fellow, 1971–97, Jesus Coll.; Univ. Asst Lectr in History, 1973–77; Lectr in History, 1977–95; Reader in Political Theory, 1995. Vis. Fellow, Princeton Univ., 1989; Carlyle Lectr, Oxford, 1991. Foreign Hon. Mem., Amer. Acad. of Arts and Scis, 1992. *Publications:* Natural Rights Theories, 1979; Hobbes, 1989; Hobbes' Leviathan, 1991; Philosophy and Government 1572–1651, 1993; Hobbes on the Citizen, 1998; The Rights of War and Peace, 2001; Free Riding, 2008. *Recreations:* repairing houses, looking after children. *Address:* Department of Government, 1737 Cambridge Street, CGIS Knafel Building 404, Harvard University, Cambridge, MA 02138–3001, USA; 9 Park Terrace, Cambridge CB1 1JH.
*See also J. A. Tuck.*

**TUCK, Vicky;** *see* Tuck, A. V.

**TUCKER, Andrew Victor Gunn;** independent political analyst, since 2009; *b* 20 Dec. 1955; *s* of Kenneth Gunn Tucker and Megan Tucker; *m* 1986, Judith Anne Gibson. *Educ:* Calday Grange Grammar Sch., Wirral; University Coll., Oxford (BA Hons 1978; MA 1986). MCIL (MIL 1988). Jt Tech. Lang. Service, 1978–81; joined HM Diplomatic Service, 1981; lang. trng, SOAS, 1982; Second Sec., Dar es Salaam, 1982–85; First Secretary: on loan to Cabinet Office, 1985–87; and Press Attaché, Moscow, 1987–90; Dep. Hd, CSCE Unit, FCO, 1991–93; on loan to Auswärtiges Amt, 1993–94; Bonn, 1994–97; Dep. High Comr, Nairobi, and concurrently Alternate Perm. Rep. to UNEP and UN Centre for Human Settlements (Habitat), 1997–2000; Ambassador to Azerbaijan, 2000–03; Manager, Prism Prog., FCO, 2003–05; on interchange at GCHQ, 2005–09. Non-exec. Dir, Benenden Healthcare Soc., 2017– (Mem., Cttee of Mgt, 2016–17); Gov., Benenden Hosp. Trust, 2016–18; Trustee, Forty-Nine Thirteen Foundn, 2015–. Member: Friends of RSC; Winchester Russian Circle; Central Brittany Integration Assoc. *Recreations:* theatre, long walks, music, crosswords, cooking, general knowledge quizzes (finalist, BBC Brain of Britain, 2011; runner-up, BBC Mastermind, 2011; finalist, BBC Only Connect, 2012). *E:* andrewtucker@orange.fr.

**TUCKER, Clive Fenemore,** CB 1996; international education consultant; Director, International Affairs, Department for Education and Skills (formerly Department for Education and Employment), 1995–2006, and Department for Work and Pensions, 2001–06; *b* 13 July 1944; *s* of William Frederick Tucker and Joan Tucker; *m* 1978, Caroline Elisabeth Macready; two *d*. *Educ:* Cheltenham Grammar Sch.; Balliol Coll., Oxford (BA). Entered Ministry of Labour, 1965; Private Sec. to Perm. Sec., 1968–70; Department of Employment, later Department for Education and Employment: Principal, 1970; Asst Sec., 1978; Grade 4, 1986; Under Sec., 1987. Chm., EU Employment Cttee, 2001–03. Mem., Security Vetting Appeals Panel, 2009–15. Non-exec. Dir, RTZ Chemicals, 1987–90. Mem., Fulbright Commn, 1998–2006. Associate Dir, Specialist Schs and Acads Trust, 2006–12. *Publications:* (with C. Macready) Who Goes Where and Why: an overview and analysis of global education mobility, 2011. *Recreations:* opera, looking at pictures, tennis.

**TUCKER, Elizabeth Mary;** Head Mistress, Headington School, Oxford, 1982–96; *b* 20 July 1936; *d* of late Harold and Doris Tucker. *Educ:* Cheltenham Ladies' College; Newnham College, Cambridge (BA Classical Tripos 1958); King's College London (PGCE). Assistant Mistress, Queen Anne's School, Caversham, 1959–64; Head of Classics, Notting Hill and Ealing High School, GPDST, 1964–72; Head Mistress, Christ's Hospital, Hertford, 1972–82. Associate, Newnham Coll., Cambridge, 1986–99. Corporate Mem., Cheltenham Ladies' Coll., 1994. Trustee, Bloxham Project, 1982–2005; Mem., Channing Sch., Highgate, 2001– (Mem. Council, 1995–2000); Donation Gov., Christ's Hosp., 2002–. Eye-opener guide, Greeks, BM, 1997–. Commissary for Rt Rev. Dinis Sengulane, retired Bishop of Lebombo, Mozambique, 2010–. Chair, Enfield Chamber Orch., 2006–12. *Recreations:* music (piano, cello, church choir), friends and family. *Address:* 78 Manor Drive, N20 0DU. *Club:* University Women's.

**TUCKER, Jon(athan Leslie Tucker);** Faculty Operating Officer (formerly Director of Operations), Imperial College Business School, Imperial College London, since 2009; *b* 13 Oct. 1961; *s* of Leslie Harold Tucker and Marilyn Alice Tucker; *m* 1991, Janette Roe; one *s* one *d*. *Educ:* Fitzwilliam Coll., Cambridge (MA Sci. Tripos 1984). ACIB 1987. Lloyds Bank, subseq. Lloyds TSB: various managerial appts, Retail and Commercial Banking, 1984–96; Sen. Manager, Exec. Develt, 1997–98; Asst Dir, 1999–2002, Head, 2002–07, Science Mus.; Dir, Corporate Services, Nat. Mus. of Sci. and Industry, 2007–09. *Recreations:* science, museums and heritage, gardening, wildlife, military history. *Address:* Imperial College Business School, Imperial College London, South Kensington Campus, SW7 2AZ. *T:* (020) 7594 1246. *E:* j.tucker@imperial.ac.uk.

**TUCKER, Katherine Jane Greening; Her Honour Judge Tucker;** a Circuit Judge, since 2014; *b* Durham, 5 July 1969; *d* of Ian and Caroline Tucker; *m* 1997, Dr Julian Paul; three *d*. *Educ:* Framwellgate Moor Comprehensive Sch.; Leicester Univ. (LLB 1st Cl. French with Dist. in spoken French). Called to the Bar, Lincoln's Inn, 1993; fee-paid Employment Judge, 2004–09; full-time Employment Judge, 2009–14. *Publications:* (ed with S. George) Discrimination in Employment (looseleaf), 2006–. *Recreations:* family, riding, cycling, sailing, walking, literature, community. *E:* HHJ.Katherine.Tucker@ejudiciary.net.

**TUCKER, Prof. Maurice Edwin,** PhD; FGS; Professor of Geological Sciences, Durham University, 1993–2011, now Emeritus; Visiting Professor of Earth Sciences, University of Bristol, since 2011; *b* 6 Nov. 1946; *s* of Edwin Herlin and Winifred Tucker; *m* 1970, Vivienne; one *s* one *d*. *Educ:* Wanstead High Sch., Redbridge; Durham Univ. (BSc 1st cl. Hons Geol. 1968); Reading Univ. (PhD Sedimentol. 1971). CGeol; FGS 1973. Lecturer: Univ. of Sierra Leone, 1971–72; UC Cardiff, Univ. of Wales, 1973–74; Univ. of Newcastle, 1975–82; Lindemann Trust Fellow, Univ. of Calif, Berkeley, 1980–81; Durham University: Lectr, 1983–86; Sen. Lectr, 1986–88; Reader, 1988–93; Master, University Coll., 1998–2001. Pres., Internat. Assoc. of Sedimentologists, 1998–2002 (Hon. Mem., 2010); Hon. Fellow, Acad. of Scis and Arts, Croatia, 2009. Geological Society: Moiety of Lyell Fund, 1983; Coke Medal, 1994; Percy Allen Award, British Sedimentological Res. Gp, 2008; André Dumont Medal, Geol. Soc. of Belgium, 2009; Jean-Baptiste Lamarck Medal, Eur. Union of Geoscis, 2009. *Publications:* Sedimentary Petrology, 1981, 3rd edn 2001; Field Description of Sedimentary Rocks, 1982; Carbonate Sedimentology, 1990; Sedimentary Rocks in the Field, 1996, 4th edn 2011; Petrologia Sedimentar Carbonatica, 2017; *edited:* Modern and Ancient Lake Sediments, 1978; Techniques in Sedimentology, 1988; Carbonate Platforms, 1990; Carbonate Diagenesis, 1990; Calcretes, 1991; Dolomites, 1994; res. papers in carbonate sedimentol. and limestones. *Recreations:* sailing, modern art, North American auto licence plates, Roman stone. *Address:* School of Earth Sciences, University of Bristol, Bristol BS8 1RJ. *T:* (0117) 954 5400.

**TUCKER, Paul Geoffrey;** QC 2010; *b* Scarborough, 6 March 1967; *s* of late Geoffrey William Tucker and of Janet Victoria Tucker (*née* Nevitt); *m* 1993, Ursula McCormack; three *s*. *Educ:* Raincliffe Comp. Sch.; Scarborough Sixth Form Coll.; Selwyn Coll., Cambridge (BA Hons Law 1988). Called to the Bar, Gray's Inn, 1990; in practice as a barrister, specialising in planning and envmt, Kings Chambers, Manchester, 1991–; Associate Mem., Landmark Chambers, 2011–. Attorney Gen.'s Regl Panel, 2008–10. *Recreations:* guitar, archaeology, ski-ing, hill walking, travel, reading. *Address:* Kings Chambers, 36 Young Street, Manchester M3 3FT. *T:* (0161) 832 9082, *Fax:* (0161) 835 2139. *E:* ptucker@kingschambers.com.

**TUCKER, Sir Paul (Michael William),** Kt 2014; Chair, Systemic Risk Council, since 2015; Deputy Governor, Bank of England, 2009–13; *b* 24 March 1958; *s* of Brian William Tucker and late Helen May Tucker (*née* Lloyd). *Educ:* Trinity Coll., Cambridge (BA Maths, and Philosophy). Joined Bank of England, 1980; Bank Supervisor, 1980–84, and 1987; seconded to merchant bank as corporate financier, 1985–86; seconded to Hong Kong Govt as Advr to Hong Kong Securities Review Cttee, 1987–88; Mkts Area, 1988–89; Private Sec. to Gov., 1989–92; Gilt-Edged and Money Mkts Div., 1993–96 (Hd of Div., 1994–96); Hd of Monetary Assessment and Strategy Div., 1997–98; Dep. Dir, Financial Stability, 1999–2002; Exec. Dir, Markets, 2002–09; Member: Monetary Policy Cttee Secretariat, 1997–2002; Monetary Policy Cttee, 2002–13; Financial Policy Cttee (formerly Interim Financial Policy Cttee), 2011–13; Bd, Prudential Regulatory Authy, 2013; Bd, Bank for Internat. Settlements, 2009–13. Former Chairman: Basel Cttee on Payment and Settlement Systems; Resolution Gp, G20 Financial Stability Bd (former Mem., Steering Gp). Dir, Swiss Re, 2016–. Vis. Fellow, Nuffield Coll., Oxford, 2010–18; Fellow, Mossavar-Rahmani Center for Business and Govt, Harvard Kennedy Sch., 2015– (Sen. Fellow, 2013–15); Sen. Fellow, Harvard Business Sch., 2013–15. Pres., NIESR, 2019–. Gov., Ditchley Foundn. *Publications:* Unelected Power: the quest for legitimacy in central banking and the regulatory state, 2018. *Club:* Athenæum.

**TUCKER, Sir Richard (Howard),** Kt 1985; a Judge of the High Court of Justice, Queen's Bench Division, 1985–2000; *b* 9 July 1930; *s* of Howard Archibald Tucker (His Honour Judge Tucker), and Margaret Minton Tucker; *m* 1st, 1958, Paula Mary Bennett Frost (marr. diss. 1974); one *s* two *d*; 2nd, 1975, Wendy Kate Standbrook (*d* 1988); 3rd, 1989, Jacqueline Suzanne Rossvell Thomson, *widow* of William Thomson, artist. *Educ:* Shrewsbury Sch.; The Queen's Coll., Oxford (MA; Hon. Fellow, 1992). 2nd Lieut, RAOC, 1948–50. Called to Bar, Lincoln's Inn, 1954; Bencher, 1979; Treasurer, 2002. QC 1972; a Recorder, 1972–85; Mem. Senate, Inns of Court and the Bar, 1984–86; Dep. Leader, 1984–85, and Presiding Judge, 1986–90, Midland and Oxford Circuit. Member: Employment Appeal Tribunal, 1986–2000; Parole Bd, 1996–2003 (Vice-Chm., 1998–2000); Comr, Royal Ct of Jersey, 2003–10. Mediator, 2004–. Comr, Commn of Enquiry, Grand Cayman, 2008. *Recreations:* gardening, model railways, wood-turning. *Address:* Treasury Office, Lincoln's Inn, WC2A 3TL. *Club:* Garrick.

**TUCKER, William,** CVO 2019; Lord-Lieutenant of Derbyshire, since 2009; *b* Port Glasgow, 28 July 1945; *s* of William Tucker and Mary Tucker; *m* 1976, Jill Stanton; two *d*. *Educ:* Port Glasgow High Sch.; Co-operative Coll., Loughborough. Co-operative Movement, 1960–2005: non-exec. Chm., Co-operative Insce, 1994–2000; non-exec. Dir, Co-operative Bank, 1994–2000; Chief Exec., Midlands Co-operative Soc., 2000–05. Non-exec. Dir, Derby Hosps Foundn Trust, 2005–11. *Recreations:* gardening, reading, walking, travel. *Address:* Acacia House, Rectory Gardens, Aston on Trent, Derby DE72 2AZ. *T:* (01332) 792792. *E:* wtucker28@gmail.com.

**TUCKETT, Prof. Sir Alan (John),** Kt 2018; OBE 1995; Professor of Education, University of Wolverhampton, since 2015; *b* Brixham, 3 April 1948; *s* of Jack Tuckett and Joyce Tuckett (*née* Osborne); *m* 1st, 1969, Penny Allen (marr. diss. 1982); two *d*; 2nd, 2000, Toni Fazaeli; one *s* and one step *d*. *Educ:* Launceston Coll.; Univ. of E Anglia (BA 1st Cl. Hons English and American Lit. 1969). Principal: Brighton Friends Centre, 1973–81; Clapham-Battersea Adult Educn Inst., ILEA, 1981–88; CEO and Dir, Nat. Inst. of Adult Contg Educn, 1988–2011 (Hon. Life Mem., 2011; Emeritus Res. Fellow, 2012). Dist. Prof., Internat. Inst. for Adult and Lifelong Educn, New Delhi, 2014–; DAAD Prof., Univ. of Würzburg, 2019–20. Founding Chm., Nat. Fedn of Voluntary Literacy Schemes, 1977–79; Co-Chm., Lifelong Learning Bd, MLA, 2009–10; Vice-Chm., Centenary Commn on Adult Educn, 2019; Member: Nat. Adv. Cttee, Adult Literacy Resource Agency, 1975–77; Educn Adv. Council, BBC, 1987–92; Adv. Cttee on Educn for Adults with Disabilities, Prince's Trust, 1994–98; Bd, Basic Skills Agency, 1995–2003; Sustainable Develt Educn Panel, DfEE/DETR, 1998–2001; Bd, Leicester TEC, 1998–2001; Adult Learning Cttee, LSC, 2001–07; Council and Strategy Cttees, Open Univ., 2001–07; Govt Skills Alliance, 2003–07; Bd, Learning for Fourth Age, 2011–13; Bd, Cornwall Coll., 2012–17; UNESCO: Member: Learning Without Frontiers Task Force, 1996–97; Co-ordinating Cttee for NGOs working on Educn For All, 2011–12; Steering Cttee, Educn For All, 2012. Chm., Leicester Arts Centre, 2014–19. President: Internat. League for Social Commitment in Adult Educn, 1986–87; Pre-Sch. Learning Alliance, 1999–2003; Internat. Council for Adult Educn, 2011–15 (Treas., 2007–11); Friends Centre, 2017–. Ambassadorial Fellow, Assessors Guild, 2018. FCGI 2002. Hon. FCollT 2009; Hon. Fellow, UNESCO Inst. Lifelong Learning, 2016. DUniv: Open, 1999; Sheffield Hallam, 1999; Bradford, 2004; Staffs, 2005; Glamorgan, 2006; Hon. DCL Kent, 2004; Hon. DLitt: Brighton, 2005; Warwick, 2011. *Publications:* (jtly) The Learning Divide, 1997; Lifelong Learning in England and Wales, 1997; (with N. Sargant) Pandora's Box, 1997; (ed with A. McAulay) Demography and Older Learners, 2005; (ed) Participation and the Pursuit of Equality, 2007; (ed jtly) Lifelong Learning: a brave and proper vision, selected writings of Naomi Sargant, 2009; (with I. Nash) Seriously Useless Learning, 2014; contrib. chapters, articles to jls and reports in UK and internationally. *Recreations:* Leicester Tigers, Bob Dylan, allotment, grandchildren, Cornwall. *Address:* 14 Stonegate Avenue, Leicester LE2 3HE. *T:* (0116) 270 8566. *E:* alan.tuckett@gmail.com.

**TUCKETT, John Francis;** Immigration Services Commissioner, since 2019; *b* Welwyn Garden City, 9 Sept. 1951; *s* of Ronald Francis Tuckett and Elizabeth Mary Tuckett; *m* 2001, Tarja Teitto; two *s* three *d*. *Educ:* Aysgarth Sch.; Bootham Sch., York; King's Coll., Cambridge (BA Chem. Engrg 1974). Served RN, 1974–91: Commanding Officer: HMS Olympus, 1984–86; HMS Superb, 1988–89. Chief Executive Officer: Cleveland FHSA, 1991–92; Tees HA, 1992–99; Defence Secondary Care Agency, 2000–01; Programme Director: Defence Med. Services, 2002–04; Nat. Offender Mgt Services, Home Office, 2004–06; Dir, Major Projects, Office for Govt Commerce, 2006–11; Prog. Dir/Diocesan Sec., Dio. Leeds, 2012–14; CEO, Marine Mgt Orgn, 2015–19. *Recreations:* violin, mountain walking/biking, opera. *Address:* Office of the Immigration Services Commissioner, 5th Floor, 21 Bloomsbury Street, WC1B 3HF. *T:* (020) 7211 1500. *E:* john.tuckett@oisc.gov.uk. *Club:* Victory Services.

**TUCKETT, William Jonathan;** director and choreographer of theatre, film and opera, since 2005; occasional Principal Guest Artist, Royal Ballet; freelance arts consultant; *b* 3 Feb. 1969; *s* of John Tuckett and Gillian Gould; *m* Caro Howell; one *s*. *Educ:* Bristol Cathedral Sch.; Royal Ballet Upper Sch. Director and Choreographer: Sadler's Wells Royal Ballet, 1988–90; Royal Ballet, Covent Garden, 1990–2005; freelance, 2005–, working for orgns incl. Royal Ballet, English Nat. Ballet, Nat. Ballet of Canada, Sarasota Ballet, Fla, RSC, Shakespeare's Globe, Almeida Th., Royal Opera, Opera North, Welsh Nat. Opera, Grange Park Opera, Garsington Opera, Ilford Arts, Channel Four, BBC, Sky Arts, Vertigo Films, Sage Gateshead, KAAT Th., Japan, TATE Modern, Whitechapel Gall. *Recreations:* occasional kite flying, gardening, imagining, listening, watching, reading, pondering, wondering. *Address:* c/o Royal Opera House, Covent Garden, WC2E 9DD.

**TUCKEY, Andrew Marmaduke Lane;** Senior Adviser, Houlihan Lokey (formerly Quayle Munro), since 2012 (Chairman, 2010–12); Chairman, Teraco Data Environments, South Africa, since 2008; *b* 28 Aug. 1943; *s* of late Henry Lane Tuckey and Aileen Rosemary Newsom Tuckey; *m* 1st, 1967, Margaret Louise (*née* Barnes) (marr. diss. 1998); one *s* two *d*; 2nd, 1998, Tracy Elisabeth (*née* Long) (marr. diss. 2017); two *d*. *Educ:* Plumtree Sch., Zimbabwe. Chartered Accountant, 1966. Dixon Wilson, Chartered Accountants, 1962–66; British American Tobacco, 1966–68; Baring Brothers & Co., Ltd, 1968–95: Dir, 1973–81; Man. Dir, 1981–89; Chm., 1989–95; Dep. Chm., Barings plc, 1989–95; Adviser: Baring Brothers Ltd, 1995–96; Phoenix Securities Ltd, 1996–97; Senior Adviser: Donaldson, Lufkin & Jenrette, 1997–2000; Credit Suisse First Boston, 2000–01; Bridgewell, 2001–07 (Dir, 2003–05; Man. Dir, 2005–07); Academic Partnerships Internat., 2012–14; Vice Chm., Corporate Finance, Landsbanki Securities (UK) Ltd, 2007–08; Dep. Chm., Corporate Finance, 2008–09, Chief Exec., 2009–10, Quayle Munro. Director: Dillon, Read Holding Inc., 1991–95; Morris Homes Ltd, 2009–; Soak and Sleep, 2013–. Member: Federal Reserve Bank of New York Internat. Capital Markets Adv. Cttee, 1992–95; Financial Law Panel, 1993–97; Council, Baring Foundn, 1994–96. Director: Friends of Covent Garden, 1981–98 (Treas., 1981–96); Royal Opera House, 1992–95; City of London Fest., 2004–11; Watermill Th., 2005–. Gov., 2005–, Chm., 2007–, Central Sch. of Ballet (Chm., Develt Bd, 2002–05; Dep. Chm., 2008–). Trustee: Esmée Fairbairn Charitable Trust, 1986–99; Classic FM Charitable Trust, 1992–99. *Recreations:* opera, ballet, theatre. *Address:* Houlihan Lokey, 77 Shaftesbury Avenue, W1D 5DU. *Club:* White's.
*See also Rt Hon. Sir S. L. Tuckey.*

**TUCKEY, Rt Hon. Sir Simon (Lane),** Kt 1992; PC 1998; a Lord Justice of Appeal, 1998–2009; international arbitrator and mediator, 2009–18; Judge of Appeal, Gibraltar, 2010–12; *b* 17 Oct. 1941; *s* of late Henry Lane Tuckey and Aileen Rosemary Newsom Tuckey; *m* 1964, Jennifer Rosemary (*née* Hardie); one *s* two *d*. *Educ:* Plumtree School, Zimbabwe. Called to Bar, Lincoln's Inn, 1964, Bencher, 1989; QC 1981; a Recorder, 1984–92; a Judge of the High Court of Justice, QBD, 1992–98; a Judge, Employment Appeal Tribunal, 1993–98; Presiding Judge, Western Circuit, 1995–97; Judge in Charge, Commercial List, 1997–98. Chm., Review Panel, Financial Reporting Council, 1990–92. Mem., Judicial Studies Bd, 1993–95 (Chm., Civil and Family Cttee, 1993–95). *Address:* 23 High Point, North Hill, N6 4BA.
*See also A. M. L. Tuckey.*

**TUCKNOTT, John Anthony,** MBE 1990; HM Diplomatic Service; Deputy Ambassador to Iraq, since 2017; UK Trade Champion, since 2014; *b* 2 Jan. 1958; *s* of late Eric Tucknott and Ethel Tucknott (*née* Holland); *m* 2000, Riitta-Leena Irmeli Lehtinen; one *s*. *Educ:* Bournemouth Sch.; King's Coll. London (MA). Dept of Employment, 1975–77; joined HM Diplomatic Service, 1977; Communications Ops Dept, FCO, 1977–78; Lord Privy Seal's Office, 1978–80; Archivist, Rome, 1980–82; Cairo, 1982–85; N American Dept, 1985–87, W African Dept, 1987–88, FCO; Dep. Hd of Mission, Beirut, 1988–93; Hd of Section, Security Policy Dept, FCO, 1993–95; First Sec., UKMIS to UN, NY, 1995–98; Dep. Hd, Non-proliferation Dept, 1998–2000, UK Co-ordinator for War Crimes Issues, 2000–01, FCO; Dep. Hd of Mission and Counsellor (Trade and Investment Develt), Stockholm, 2002–05; Sen. Directing Staff (Civilian), RCDS, 2005–07; Dep. Hd of Mission, Baghdad, 2007–09; FCO, 2009–10; Ambassador to Nepal, 2010–13; Dep. High Comr, Karachi, and UKTI Dir for Pakistan, 2013–16. *Recreations:* walking, reading, music, travel. *Address:* c/o Foreign and Commonwealth Office, King Charles Street, SW1A 2AH.

**TUCKWELL, Anthony David,** MA; National Director, National Educational Assessment Centre, 2000–10; Headmaster, King Edward VI Grammar School, Chelmsford, 1984–99; *b* 4 July 1943; *s* of Alec William Tuckwell and Muriel Florence Tuckwell (*née* Green); *m* 1967, Kathleen Olivia Hatton. *Educ:* St Peter's Coll., Oxford (MA); Oxford Univ. Dept of Educn (DipEd); Leeds Metropolitan (MBA 1995); Essex Univ. (Cert. in Local History 2004). History Master, Southern Grammar Sch. for Boys, Portsmouth, 1966–69; St John's College, Southsea: Hd of Hist., 1970–73; Sen. Teacher (Curriculum Co-ordinator), 1973–78; Dep. Headmaster, Sale Co. Grammar Sch. for Boys, 1979–83. Headship Appt Consultant, ASCL, 1999–2009. Mem., Essex Rural Commn, 2008–09. Mem. Bd of Dirs, Chelmsford Cathedral Fest. Ltd, 1999–2008. Governor: Cobham Hall Sch., 2003–14; New Hall Sch., 2010–15. *Publications:* (contrib.) School Leadership in the 21st Century, 1996; (contrib.) Living Headship: voices, value, vision, 1999; That Honourable and Gentlemanlike House: a history of King Edward VI Grammar School, Chelmsford 1551–2001, 2000, 2nd edn, 2008; New Hall and its School: 'a true school of virtuous demeanour', 2006; Coming of Age: the life and times of Chelmsford Cathedral 1914–2014, 2013; Small is Beautiful: the story of Messing Village School 1837–2014, 2014; Life is for Living: the story of Acorn village, 2016; (contrib.) New Hall's Catholic Heritage in South Eastern Catholic History. *Recreations:* choral singing, literature, walking, travel. *Address:* 28 Oaklands Crescent, Chelmsford, Essex CM2 9PP.

**TUCKWELL, Barry Emmanuel,** AC 1992; OBE 1965; horn soloist, retired; conductor; Conductor and Music Director, Maryland Symphony Orchestra, 1982–98; *b* 5 March 1931; *s* of late Charles and Elizabeth Tuckwell, Australia; *m* 1st, 1958, Sally Eelin Newton; one *s* one *d*; 2nd, 1971, Hilary Jane Warburton; one *s*; 3rd, 1992, Susan Terry Levitan. *Educ:* various schs, Australia; Sydney Conservatorium. FRCM 1993. Melbourne Symph. Orch., 1947; Sydney Symph. Orch., 1947–50; Hallé Orch., 1951–53; Scottish Nat. Orch., 1953–54; Bournemouth Symphony Orch., 1954–55; London Symph. Orch., 1955–68; founded Tuckwell Wind Quintet, 1968; Chief Conductor, Tasmanian Symphony Orch., 1979–83; Guest Conductor, Northern Sinfonia, 1993–97. Mem. Chamber Music Soc. of Lincoln Center, 1974–81; Horn Prof., Royal Academy of Music, 1963–74; Pres., Internat. Horn Soc., 1969–77, 1992–94. Has played and conducted annually throughout Europe, GB, USA and Canada; has appeared at many internat. festivals, incl. Salzburg and Edinburgh; took part in 1st Anglo-Soviet Music Exchange, Leningrad and Moscow, 1963; toured: Far East, 1964 and 1975; Australia, 1970–95; S America, 1976; USSR, 1977; People's Republic of China, 1984. Many works dedicated to him; has made numerous recordings. Editor, complete horn literature for G. Schirmer Inc. Professorial Fellow, Univ. of Melbourne, 2005. Hon. RAM 1966; Hon. GSM, 1967. Hon. DMus Sydney. Harriet Cohen Internat. Award for Solo Instruments, 1968; George Peabody Medal, 1997; Andrew White Medal, Loyola Coll., 1998. *Publications:* Playing the Horn, 1978; The Horn, 1981. *Club:* Athenæum.

**TUDGE, Colin Hiram;** author; *b* 22 April 1943; *s* of late Cyril Tudge and Maisie Tudge; *m* 1st, 1966, Rosemary Shewan (marr. diss. 2001); one *s* two *d*; 2nd, 2001, Ruth West. *Educ:* Dulwich Coll.; Peterhouse, Cambridge (MA 1966). Writer on various magazines, 1965–80; staff writer, Farmers' Weekly, 1970–72; Features Ed., New Scientist, 1980–85; presenter, BBC Radio 3, 1985–90; freelance author and broadcaster, 1990–. Res. Fellow, Centre for the Philosophy of Social and Natural Scis, LSE, 1995–2005. Co-founder: Campaign for Real Farming, 2009; Oxford Real Farming Conf., 2010; Funding Enlightened Agriculture, 2012; Coll. for Real Farming and Food Culture, 2016. *Publications:* The Famine Business, 1977; (with M. Allaby) Home Farm, 1977; Future Cook, 1980; The Food Connection, 1985; Food Crops for the Future, 1988; Global Ecology, 1991; Last Animals at the Zoo, 1991; The Engineer in the Garden, 1993; The Day Before Yesterday, 1995; Neanderthals, Bandits and Farmers, 1998; The Second Creation, 2000; The Variety of Life, 2000; In Mendel's Footnotes, 2001; So Shall We Reap, 2003; The Secret Life of Trees, 2005; Feeding People is Easy, 2007; Consider the Birds, 2008; (with J. Young) The Link: uncovering our early ancestors, 2009; Good Food for Everyone Forever, 2011; Why Genes are Not Selfish and People are Nice, 2013; Six Steps Back to the Land, 2016. *Recreation:* working with farmers and activists to bring about a people's takeover of the world's food supply chain via the Campaign for Real Farming. *Address:* 20 Dove House Close, Wolvercote, Oxon OX2 8BQ. *E:* colin@colintudge.co.uk. *W:* www.colintudge.com.

**TUDHOPE, Maria-Jane Carmel;** *see* Lamb, M.-J. C.

**TUDOR, (Fiona) Philippa,** DPhil; Clerk of Committees, House of Lords, since 2011; *b* Shrewsbury, 15 Feb. 1958; *d* of (James) Brian Tudor and Rosaleen Tudor (*née* O'Connor); *m* 1989, David Richard Beamish (*see* Sir D. R. Beamish); one *d*. *Educ:* Sch. of SS Mary and Anne, Abbots Bromley; Somerville Coll., Oxford (MA, DPhil). FCIPD 2005; Dip. Corporate Governance, ACCA, 2006. House of Lords: Clerk, 1982; Sen. Clerk, 1986; Chief Clerk, 1993; seconded to Scotland Office as Hd, Parly and Constitl Div., 2001–03; Hd, Human Resources, 2003–07; Finance Dir, 2007–11. FRSA. *Publications:* Isobel Holst (née Harrison): Gustav Holst's other half, 2015. *Recreations:* historical research, classical music, walking. *Address:* House of Lords, SW1A 0PW. *T:* (020) 7219 3130. *E:* tudorfp@parliament.uk.

**TUDOR JOHN, William;** DL; Deputy Chairman, Nationwide Building Society, 2007–11; *b* 26 April 1944; *s* of Tudor and Gwen John; *m* 1st, 1967, Jane Clark (*d* 2007); three *d*; 2nd, 2014, Joanna Clayton. *Educ:* Cowbridge Sch., S Wales; Downing Coll., Cambridge (MA). Asst Solicitor, Allen & Overy, 1969–71; Banker, Orion Bank Ltd, 1971–72; Allen & Overy: Partner, 1972–2001; Head of Banking Dept, 1972–92; Man. Partner, 1992–94; Sen. Partner, 1994–2000; Chm. and Man. Dir, European Commitment Cttee, Lehman Brothers, 2000–08; Director: Lehman Brothers Europe Ltd, 2000–08; Lehman Brothers Internat. (Europe), 2000–08; Lehman Brothers European Mezzanine; SICAV, 2004–10; Man. Dir, Nomura Internat. plc, 2008–12. Non-executive Chairman: Sutton Seeds (Hldgs) Ltd, 1978–93; Horticultural & Botanical Hldgs Ltd, 1985–93; non-executive Director: Woolwich plc, 2000; Portman Bldg Soc., 2001–07 (Dep. Chm., 2004–06; Chm., 2006–07); Sun Bank plc, 2001–04; Grainger plc, 2005–10. Associate Fellow, Downing Coll., Cambridge, 1985–92, 1997–. Member: Law Soc., 1969–; City of London Solicitors' Co., 1974–; IBA, 1978–; Financial Law Panel, 1996–2002; Financial Mkts Law Cttee, 2002–09 (Vice-Chm., 2002–09); Chm., Wales in London, 2002–06. Chm., Law Foundn Adv. Council, Oxford Univ., 1998–2003; Member: Adv. Bd, Oxford Univ. Develt Prog., 1999–; Develt Bd, Nat. Mus. of Wales, 2007–18; Develt Bd, WNO, 2012–; Trustee, St Albans Abbey Fabric Trust, 2005–. Non-exec. Dir, Nat. Film and Television Sch., 2000–; Mem. Court, Univ. of Hertfordshire, 2006–. Steward of Appeal, BBB of C, 1978–. Freeman, City of London, 1994; Liveryman, Co. of Gunmakers, 1994–. High Sheriff, Herts, 2006–07; DL Herts, 2007. *Recreations:* Rugby football as an observer, music as a listener, shooting and reading as a participant, daughters' banker. *Address:* Willian Bury, Willian, Herts SG6 2AF. *T:* (01462) 683532. *E:* tjwillian@btinternet.com. *Club:* Cardiff and County (Cardiff).

**TUFFIN, David William,** FRICS; Consultant: Tuffin Ferraby Taylor LLP, since 2009; St Brides Fund Managers, since 2011; President, Royal Institution of Chartered Surveyors, 2007–08; *b* 11 June 1948; *s* of Reginald and Dorothy Tuffin; *m* 1968, Brenda King; one *s* one *d*. *Educ:* Portsmouth Northern Grammar Sch.; Raynes Park Co. Grammar Sch. FRICS 1979. Founding Partner, 1973–2004, Man. Partner, 2004–08, Tuffin Ferraby Taylor LLP. Royal Institution of Chartered Surveyors: Chairman: RICS Awards, 2012–16; Dispute Resolution Appts Bd, 2013–; Mem., Business Develt Bd, 2011–15. *Recreations:* shooting, socialising, unsuccessful angling. *Address:* Tuffin Ferraby Taylor LLP, 18 Holborn, EC1N 2LE. *T:* 07768 648266. *E:* dtuffin@tftconsultants.com.

**TUFFREY, Michael William;** Founder and Director, Corporate Citizenship Company, since 1997; *b* 30 Sept. 1959; *m*; one *s* two *d*. *Educ:* Douai Sch., Woolhampton; Durham Univ. (BA Hons Econ. Hist. and Econs 1981). ACA 1984. Accountant, Peat Marwick Mitchell & Co., London, 1981–84; Res. and Parly Officer, Lib/SDP whips office, H of L, 1984–87; Dir, Finance and Admin, Action Resource Centre, London, 1987–90; Community Affairs Consultant, Prima Europe, London, 1990–97. Mem. for Vauxhall: GLC, 1985–86 (Mem., Industry and Employment, Housing and Planning Cttees); ILEA, 1985–86; Mem. (Lib Dem), Lambeth LBC, 1990–2002 (Gp Leader, Lib Dem, 1990–98; de facto Jt Leader, Council, 1994–98). Contested: (L) Streatham, 1987; (Lib Dem) Vauxhall, June 1989, 1992. London Assembly, Greater London Authority: Mem. (Lib Dem), Feb. 2002–2012; Leader, Lib Dem Gp, 2006–10; Member: London Fire and Emergency Planning Authy, 2002–08 and 2010–12 (Leader, Lib Dem Gp, 2006–08); Budget Cttee, 2002–12; Environt Cttee, 2004–12. Mem., Assoc. of London Govt Leaders Cttee, 1994–2000 (Dep. Lib Dem Leader, 1994–2000); Lambeth Representative: AMA; LGA; Board Member: Business Link London, 1994–2000; London Develt Partnership, 1998–2000; 1994–98: Brixton City Challenge; Cross River Partnership, Central London Partnership; South Bank Partnership. Chm., Parly Lib Party Staff Assoc., 1986–87. Formerly: Nat. Treas., Gingerbread; Treas., then Chm., L'Arche Lambeth (former Nat. Bd Mem., L'Arche); founding Bd Mem., Vauxhall St Peter's Heritage Centre; Bd Mem., Vauxhall Cross Amenity Trust. Trustee: New Economics Foundn, 2016–; Restart Project, 2016–; Inst. of Business Ethics, 2017–. Editor, Corporate Citizen Briefing, 1991–. *Recreation:* licensed radio amateur. *Address:* 50 Lynette Avenue, SW4 9HD.

**TUFNELL, Col Greville Wyndham,** CVO 2002; DL; Development Officer, National Star Centre for Disabled Youth, 1982–95; Lieutenant, Queen's Body Guard of the Yeomen of the Guard, 1993–2002; *b* 7 April 1932; *s* of K. E. M. Tufnell, MC and E. H. Tufnell (*née* Dufaur); *m* 1st, 1962, Hon. Anne Rosemary Trench (*d* 1992), *d* of 5th Baron Ashtown, OBE and *widow* of Capt. Timothy Patrick Arnold Gosselin; two *d* (and one *d* decd), and one step *d*; 2nd, 1994, Susan Arnot Burrows (*d* 2018). *Educ:* Eton; RMA, Sandhurst. Commnd Grenadier Guards, 1952; Adjt, 2nd Bn, 1959–61; GSO 3, War Office, 1962–63; Staff Coll., 1964; Maj. 1965; DAQMG, London Dist, 1966–67; GSO 2, HQ 2 Div., 1969–71; Lt Col 1971; comdg 1st Bn, 1971–73 (despatches, 1972); Bde Maj., Household Div., 1974–76; Col 1976; Lt Col comdg Grenadier Guards, 1976–78; retd 1979. Queen's

Body Guard of Yeomen of the Guard: Exon, 1979; Ensign, 1985; Clerk of the Cheque and Adjutant, 1987. Freeman, City of London, 1961; Liveryman, Grocers' Co., 1965–. DL Glos, 1994. *Recreations:* shooting, fishing, gardening. *Address:* Arrow House, Church Road, Quenington, Glos GL7 5BN. *Clubs:* Cavalry and Guards, Sloane, Pitt, MCC.

TUFTON, family name of **Baron Hothfield**.

TUGE-ERECIŃSKA, Barbara; Ambassador of Poland to Cyprus, 2014–18; Titular Ambassador, Diplomatic Academy, Warsaw, since 2019; *b* 24 March 1956; *d* of Janusz Tuge and Jadwiga Duchnowska; one *s* by Andrzej Ereciński. *Educ:* Gdańsk Univ. (MA Scandinavian Studies). Staff mem., Foreign Dept, Nat. Bureau of Solidarity, 1981; Mem., Primate's Cttee for Assistance to Repressed Persons, 1982–87; Hon. Sec., Consular Agency of Sweden, Denmark and Norway, Gdynia, 1987–90; Plenipotentiary of City Bd for foreign contacts, Municipal Office to Gdańsk, 1990–91; Ambassador of Poland to Sweden, 1991–97; Ministry of Foreign Affairs: Dir, Europe-West Dept, 1997–98; Dir, Eur. Policy Dept, 1998–99; Under-Sec. of State, 1999–2001; Ambassador of Poland to Denmark, 2001–05; Sec. of State, Min. of Foreign Affairs, 2005–06; Ambassador of Poland to UK, 2006–12; Dir, Dept of Cooperation with Polish Diaspora, Min. of Foreign Affairs, 2012–14. Golden Cross, Order of Merit (Poland), 1997; Commander's Cross: Order of Merit (Italy), 2000; Order of Merit (Hungary), 2001; Order of the Dannebrog (Denmark), 2005. *Recreations:* reading books, walking (especially along the seashore). *E:* barbara.tuge-erecinska@msz.gov.pl.

TUGENDHAT, family name of **Baron Tugendhat**.

TUGENDHAT, Baron *cr* 1993 (Life Peer), of Widdington in the County of Essex; **Christopher Samuel Tugendhat**, Kt 1990; *b* 23 Feb. 1937; *er s* of late Dr Georg Tugendhat; *m* 1967, Julia Lissant Dobson; two *s*. *Educ:* Ampleforth Coll.; Gonville and Caius Coll., Cambridge (Pres. of Union; Hon. Fellow 1998). Financial Times leader and feature writer, 1960–70. MP (C) City of London and Westminster South, 1974–76 (Cities of London and Westminster, 1970–74); Mem., 1977–85, a Vice-Pres., 1981–85, EEC Commn. Director: Sunningdale Oils, 1971–76; Phillips Petroleum International (UK) Ltd, 1972–76; National Westminster Bank, 1985–91 (Dep. Chm., 1990–91); The BOC Group, 1985–96; Commercial Union Assce, 1988–91; LWT (Hldgs), 1991–94; Eurotunnel plc, 1991–2003; Rio Tinto plc, 1997–2004; Chairman: Abbey National plc, 1991–2002; Blue Circle Industries PLC, 1996–2001; Eur. Adv. Bd, Lehman Brothers, 2002–07. Chm., Imperial Coll. Healthcare NHS Trust, 2006–11. Member: Econ. Affairs Cttee, H of L, 2009–13, 2016–; EU Select Cttee, H of L, 2013–16 (Chm., Sub-Cttee on EU External Affairs, 2013–16). Chm., CAA, 1986–91. Chairman: RIIA (Chatham House), 1986–95; Adv. Council, European Policy Forum, 1998–; Governor, Council of Ditchley Foundn, 1986–2010; Vice-Pres., British Lung Foundn, 1986–2014. Chancellor, Univ. of Bath, 1998–2013. Hon. LLD Bath, 1998; Hon. DLitt UMIST, 2002. *Publications:* Oil: the biggest business, 1968; The Multinationals, 1971 (McKinsey Foundn Book Award, 1971); Making Sense of Europe, 1986; (with William Wallace) Options for British Foreign Policy in the 1990s, 1988; A History of Britain Through Books 1900–1964, 2019; various pamphlets and numerous articles. *Recreations:* being with his family, reading, conversation. *Address:* 35 Westbourne Park Road, W2 5QD. *Club:* Athenæum.

*See also* Hon. Sir M. G. Tugendhat.

TUGENDHAT, Hon. Sir Michael (George), Kt 2003; a Judge of the High Court of Justice, Queen's Bench Division, 2003–14; Judge in charge of Queen's Bench jury and non-jury lists, 2010–14; *b* 21 Oct. 1944; *s* of late Georg Tugendhat and Maire Littledale; *m* 1970, Blandine de Loisne; four *s*. *Educ:* Ampleforth Coll.; Gonville and Caius Coll., Cambridge (Scholar; MA); Yale Univ. Henry Fellowship. Called to the Bar, Inner Temple, 1969, Bencher, 1988; QC 1986; a Recorder, 1994–2003; a Dep. High Court Judge, 1995–2003; a Judge of the Courts of Appeal in Jersey and Guernsey, 2000–03. Mem., Bar Council, 1992–94. Chm., Civil Law Working Party on Corruption, 1999. Member, Mgt Cttee, Advice on Individual Rights in Europe Centre, 2000–03. Pres., Franco-British Lawyers Soc., 2011–14. Chm., Investment Cttee, Inner Temple, 2011–14. Mem., Exec. Bd, JUSTICE, 2016–. Fellow, Inst. Advanced Legal Studies, 1999–. Hon. Prof., Sch. of Law, Univ. of Leicester, 2013–16. *Publications:* (contrib.) Restitution and Banking Law, 1998; (contrib.) Yearbook of Copyright and Media Law, 2000; (ed jtly) The Law of Privacy and the Media, 2002, 2nd edn as Tugendhat and Christie: The Law of Privacy and the Media, 2011, 3rd edn 2016; (consulting ed.) Commercial Fraud Civil Liability, Human Rights, and Money Laundering, 2006; (contrib.) Halsbury's Laws of England, 4th edn; (contrib.) Thomas More's Trial by Jury, 2011; (consulting ed.) The Illicit Trade in Art and Antiquities, 2012; Liberty Intact: human rights in English law, 2016; Fighting for Freedom?, 2017; occasional contribs to legal jls. *E:* mt312@le.ac.uk. *Clubs:* Brooks's, Royal Automobile.

*See also* Baron Tugendhat, T. G. J. Tugendhat.

TUGENDHAT, Thomas Georg John, MBE 2010; MP (C) Tonbridge and Malling, since 2015; *b* 27 June 1973; *s* of Hon. Sir Michael George Tugendhat, *qv*; *m* Anissia; one *s* one *d*. *Educ:* Bristol Univ. (BA Theol. 1995); Gonville and Caius Coll., Cambridge (MPhil Islamic Studies 1996). CSV, 1991–92; journalist, Beirut, 1997–99; Fortune Promoseven, PR co., Lebanon, 1997–99; First Consulting Ltd, 2000–01; Bloomberg LP, 2001–03. Territorial Army, 2003–: Advr to Nat. Security Advr, Office of Nat. Security Council, Afghanistan, 2005–06; Advr to Gov., Helmand Province, 2006–07; Army Strategy Br., 2009–10; MA to CDS, 2010–13. Chm., Select Cttee on Foreign Affairs, 2017–; Mem., Admin and Constitutional Affairs Cttee, 2015–16. *Address:* House of Commons, SW1A 0AA.

TUGGEY, Lt Col Andrew Simon, CBE 2016; Vice Lord-Lieutenant of Gwent, since 2016; Chair, ScoutsCymru, since 2017; *b* Reading, 21 Oct. 1947; *s* of Bernard and Betty Tuggey; *m* 1974, Clare Main; three *s*. *Educ:* Reading Sch.; RMA, Sandhurst; RMCS, Shrivenham (BSc Eng). Commnd RE, 1968; Gurkha Engrs, 1969–70, 1975–76; BAOR, 1973–75, 1985–87; Queen's Gurkha Engrs, 1977–78, 1982–84; NI, 1978–80; Canada, 1987–89; CO, Royal Monmouthshire RE (Militia), 1990–92; MoD, 1992–94; NI, 1995–98; Defence Attaché, Riga, 1999–2002, Vilnius, 1999–2001. Chief Exec. and Sec., Commonwealth Party Assoc. UK, 2004–17. Chm., ABF The Soldier's Charity (formerly ABF), Gwent, 2005–. President: Newport Sea Cadets, 2016–; Monmouth Br., RBL, 2019–; Vice-President: Bridgend Male Choir, 2005–; Gwent Scouts, 2016–. Patron, Abergavenny Bridge to Cross Trust, 2016–. Pres., RE Assoc. Monmouth, 2015–. Trustee: Royal Monmouthshire RE (Militia), 2008–; Castle and Regtl Mus., Monmouth, 2017–; Community Foundn in Wales, 2018–. Mem., Wales Anti-Slavery Leadership Gp, 2019–. DL 2006, High Sheriff, 2015, Gwent; Mem. Council, High Sheriffs' Assoc. of England & Wales, 2017–. *Recreations:* country and outdoor pursuits, sailing, ski-ing, family, choral singing, ballet, opera, ice-cream tasting, travel. *Address:* Craig-y-Dorth, Monmouth, Gwent. *E:* vllgwent@monmouthshire.gov.uk, andrew.tuggey@scoutscymru.org.uk.

TUGHAN, John Charles Ronald; QC 2015; *b* Belfast, 9 Dec. 1968; *s* of Kenneth and Carole Tughan; *m* 2000, Louise Haddleton; two *d*. *Educ:* Campbell Coll., Belfast; Liverpool Univ. (LLB Hons). Called to the Bar, Inner Temple, 1991. *Address:* 4 Paper Buildings, Temple, EC4Y 7EX. *E:* jt@4pb.com.

TUGWELL, Very Rev. Simon Charles ffoster, DD, STD; OP; Fellow, Dominican Historical Institute, Rome, 1987–2016, now Emeritus Fellow (President, 1992–97); *b* 4 May 1943; *s* of Major Herbert Frederick Lewen Tugwell and Mary Brigit (*née* Hutchinson). *Educ:* Lancing Coll.; Corpus Christi Coll., Oxford (DD 1993); STD (Angelicum, Rome) 1987, STM (Dominican Order) 1993. Entered English Province of Dominican Order, 1965, ordained priest, 1971; Lectr and Tutor, Blackfriars, Oxford, 1972–92; Regent of Studies, English Dominicans, 1976–90; Mem., Faculty of Theol., Univ. of Oxford, 1982–92. Vis. Lectr, Angelicum, Rome, 1977–92; Flannery Prof. of Theol., Gonzaga Univ., Spokane, WA, 1982–83; Read-Tuckwell Lectr on human immortality, Bristol Univ., 1988. Emeritus Fellow, Blackfriars Hall, Oxford, 2016. Has lectured and preached in many parts of the world. Founding Ed., Dominican Hist. Newsletter, 1992–97. *Publications:* The Way of the Preacher, 1979; Early Dominicans, 1982; Ways of Imperfection, 1984; Albert and Thomas, 1988; The Apostolic Fathers, 1989; (ed) Letters of Bede Jarrett, 1989; Human Immortality and the Redemption of Death, 1990; (ed) Miraculi sancti Dominici mandato magistri Berengarii collecta, Petri Calo legendae sancti Dominici, 1997; (ed) Bernardi Guidonis scripta de sancto Dominico, 1998; (ed) Humberti de Romanis legendae sancti Dominici, 2008; Pelagius Parvus and his Summa, 2012; (ed) Petri Ferrandi legenda sancti Dominici, 2015; contribs to books and dictionaries; articles and reviews in learned jls. *Recreations:* teddy bears, writing silly verses. *Address:* Blackfriars, St Giles', Oxford OX1 3LY.

TUITE, Sir Christopher (Hugh), 14th Bt *cr* 1622; Senior Advisor, Carbon Fund, Conservation International, since 2008; *b* 3 Nov. 1949; *s* of Sir Dennis George Harmsworth Tuite, 13th Bt, MBE, and Margaret Essie, *d* of late Col Walter Leslie Dundas, DSO; *S* father, 1981; *m* 1976, Deborah Ann, *d* of A. E. Martz, Punxsutawney, Pa; two *s*. *Educ:* Univ. of Liverpool (BSc Hons); Univ. of Bristol (PhD). Research Officer, The Wildfowl Trust, 1978–81; Controller, The Nature Conservancy, Washington, DC, 1987–99; Director: Wildlife and Habitat Prog., IFAW, 1999–2004; USA, Green Belt Movement Internat., 2005–08. *Publications:* contribs to Jl of Animal Ecology, Jl of Applied Ecology, Freshwater Biology, Wildfowl. *Heir: s* Thomas Livingstone Tuite, *b* 24 July 1977. *Address:* c/o HSBC, 33 The Borough, Farnham, Surrey GU9 7NJ.

TUKE, Michael Antony, FREng; Chairman, MatOrtho Ltd, since 2011; *b* Carshalton, 28 Dec. 1947; *s* of Adrian Cyril Valentine and Muriel Tuke; *m* 1977, Ruth Mary Edwards; three *d*. *Educ:* Sutton East Co. Secondary Sch.; Croydon Tech. Coll. (HND Mech. Engrg). Engrg apprentice, Imperial Coll. Workshops, 1965–70; Res. Asst, Imperial Coll. London, 1970–78; Dir, Finsbury Instruments Ltd, 1978–90; Managing Director: Finsbury Orthopaedics, 1990–2009; Finsbury Develt, 1990–2009. FREng 2016. *Recreations:* classic cars, walking, family. *Address:* 21 Warwicks Bench, Guildford, Surrey GU1 3TF. *T:* (01483) 564439. *E:* mike.tuke@hotmail.co.uk.

TULETT, Louise Wendy, (Mrs J. L. W. Lee-Emery), CBE 2010; Director General, Finance, Ministry of Defence, 2015–17; *b* Dorking, 12 March 1960; *d* of Anthony and Valerie Linfield; *m* 1st, Barry Tulett; two *s*; 2nd, 2005, Jason L. W. Lee-Emery. *Educ:* Raleigh Primary Sch.; Howard of Effingham Co. Secondary Sch.; Southampton Inst. Higher Educn. CIPFA 1989. Clerical asst, Surrey CC, 1976–78; finance trainee, Waverley DC, 1978–87; trainee accountant, Woking BC, 1987–90; Asst Dir, Finance, NW Surrey HA, 1990–94; Dep. Dir, Finance, Frimley Park Hosp., 1994–2000; HM Treasury: Accountant, 2000–04; Team Leader, 2004–07; Gp Dir, Finance and Procurement, 2007–10; Finance Dir, MoD, 2010–15. Mem. Bd, UK Financial Investments Ltd, 2009–10. *Recreations:* relaxing with family and friends, walking the dogs, reading.

TULK, Catherine Jane; Her Honour Judge Tulk; a Circuit Judge, since 2017; *b* Altrincham, Cheshire, 24 Sept. 1957; *d* of Arthur Leslie Tulk and Irene Tulk; one *d*. *Educ:* Loreto Convent Grammar Sch., Altrincham; Manchester Poly. (BA Law with French). Admitted as solicitor, 1981; Legal Advr, Stockport Magistrates' Court, 1979–83, W Cumbria Magistrates' Court, 1983–84; Prosecuting Solicitor, Cambs, 1984–87; Solicitor, Metcalfe Copeman & Pettefar, Wisbech, 1987–88; Crown Prosecutor, Notts, 1988–90, Cambs, 1990–92; Legal Advr, Peterborough Magistrates' Court, 1998–2017; a Dep. Dist Judge (Magistrates' Courts), 2009–17; a Recorder, 2012–17. *Recreations:* cooking and eating, travel, Roxy Music. *Address:* Aylesbury Crown Court, Walton Street, Aylesbury, Bucks HP21 7FT. *E:* hhj.kate.tulk@ejudiciary.net.

TULLIBARDINE, Marquess of; Michael Bruce John Murray; Pre-Contracts Manager, Oktra; *b* 5 March 1985; *s* and *heir* of Duke of Atholl, *qv*.

TULLO, Carol Anne, OBE 2019; Director: The National Archives, 2006–17; Office of Public Sector Information, 2005–17; Controller of HM Stationery Office, Queen's Printer of Acts of Parliament and Government Printer for Northern Ireland, 1997–2017; Queen's Printer for Scotland, 1999–2017; Senior Consultant and Legal Counsel, The Trust Bridge, since 2017; *b* 9 Jan. 1956; *d* of Edward Alan Dodgson and late Patricia Dodgson; *m* 1979, Robin Brownrigg Tullo; one *s* one *d*. *Educ:* Hull Univ. (LLB Hons 1976); Inn of Courts Sch. of Law, City Univ. Called to the Bar, Inner Temple, 1977; Publishing Dir, Sweet & Maxwell Ltd, 1990–96; Consultant, Thomson Legal and Professional Gp, 1996–97. Chair, Law Publishers' Exec., 1995–2004, Bd Mem., Council of Acad. and Professional Publishers, 1996–2005, Publishers Assoc.; Mem., Exec. Cttee, Internat. Govt Printers and Publishers' Assoc., 1999–2009. Extended Chair, Eur. Forum of Official Gazettes, 2009–17. Mem., Jt Cttee on Legal Deposit, 2012–17. Non-exec. Advr and Consultant, Naomi Korn Associates, 2017–; Member: Bd, Trust Elevate, 2017–; Adv. Bd, Open Access Theory and Practice, 2018–; Advr, Civil Service Coll., 2017–. Vis. Prof., 2000–15, Mem., Ext. Adv. Panel, Centre for Inf. Leadership, 2009–17, Cass Business Sch., City Univ. Liveryman, Stationers' and Newspaper Makers' Co., 2015– (Ct Asst, 2016–); Mem., Masters and Wardens Cttee, 2015–16, 2017–18; Chair, Industry Cttee, 2017–). *Address:* Springhill, 21 Oakleigh Park South, N20 9JS.

TULLY, Sir (William) Mark, KBE 2002 (OBE 1985); freelance journalist and broadcaster, since 1994; *b* 24 Oct. 1935; *s* of late William Scarth Carlisle Tully, CBE and Patience Treby Tully; *m* 1960, Frances Margaret (*née* Butler); two *s* two *d*; partner, Gillian Wright. *Educ:* Twyford School, Winchester; Marlborough College; Trinity Hall, Cambridge (MA; Hon. Fellow, 1994). Regional Dir, Abbeyfield Soc., 1960–64; BBC, 1964–94: Asst, Appointments Dept, 1964–65; Asst, then Actg Rep., New Delhi, 1965–69; Prog. Organiser and Talks Writer, Eastern Service, 1969–71; Chief of Bureau, Delhi, 1972–93; South Asia Correspondent, 1993–94. Presenter: Something Understood, BBC Radio 4, 1995–2019; The Lives of Jesus, BBC TV series, 1996. Padma Shri (India), 1992; Padma Bhushan (India), 2005. *Publications:* (with Satish Jacob) Amritsar: Mrs Gandhi's last battle, 1985; (with Z. Masani) From Raj to Rajiv, 1988; No Full Stops in India, 1991; The Heart of India (short stories), 1995; The Lives of Jesus, 1996; (with Gillian Wright) India in Slow Motion, 2002; India's Unending Journey, 2007; India: the road ahead, 2011; Upcountry Tales: once upon a time in the heart of India, 2017. *Recreations:* fishing, bird watching, reading. *Address:* B26 Nizamuddin West, Delhi 110013, India. *T:* (11) 41033839. *Clubs:* Oriental; India International Centre, Gymkhana (Delhi), Bengal (Calcutta).

**TULVING, Prof. Endel**, OC 2006; PhD; FRS 1992; FRSC; Anne and Max Tanenbaum Chair in Cognitive Neuroscience, Rotman Research Institute, Baycrest Centre, Toronto and University of Toronto, 1992–2010, Scientist Emeritus, 2012; University Professor Emeritus in Psychology, University of Toronto, since 1992; *b* 26 May 1927; *s of* Juhan Tulving and Linda (*née* Soome); *m* 1950, Ruth Mikkelsaar; two *d*. *Educ:* Hugo Treffner Gymnasium; Univ. of Heidelberg; Univ. of Toronto (BA, MA); Harvard Univ. (Foundn Fellow, 1954–55; PhD). FRSC 1979. Teaching Fellow, Harvard Univ., 1955–56; University of Toronto: Lectr, 1956–59; Asst Prof. of Psychol., 1959–62; Associate Prof., 1962–65; Prof., 1965–70; Prof. of Psychol., Yale Univ., 1970–75; University of Toronto: Prof. of Psychol., 1972–92; Chm., Dept of Psychol., 1974–80; Univ. Prof., 1985–92. Vis. Scholar, Univ. of Calif., Berkeley, 1964–65; Fellow, Center for Advanced Study in Behavioural Scis, Stanford, Calif., 1972–73; Commonwealth Vis. Prof., Univ. of Oxford, 1977–78; Distinguished Res. Prof. of Neurosci., Univ. of Calif., Davis, 1993–98; Clark Way Harrison Dist. Vis. Prof. of Psychology and Cognitive Neurosci., Washington Univ., 1996–2007. Izaak Walton Killam Meml Scholarship, 1976; Guggenheim Fellow, 1987–88; William James Fellow, Amer. Psychol Soc., 1990; Montgomery Fellow, Dartmouth Coll. 1999. For. Hon. Mem., Amer. Acad. Arts and Scis, 1986; For. Associate, Nat. Acad. Scis, USA, 1988; Foreign Member: Royal Swedish Acad. Scis, 1991; Academia Europaea, 1996; Estonian Acad. of Scis, 2002. Hon. MA Yale, 1969; Hon. PhD: Umeå, Sweden, 1982; Haifa, Israel, 2003; Hon. DLitt: Waterloo, Canada, 1987; Laurentian, Canada, 1988; Hon. DPsych Tartu, Estonia, 1989; Hon. ScD: Queen's Univ., Ontario, 1996; Univ. of Toronto, 2002; Columbia Univ., NY, 2005. Warren Medal, Soc. of Exptl Psychologists, 1982; Dist. Scientific Contrib. Award, Amer. Psychol Assoc., 1983; Award for Dist. Contribs to Psychol. as a Science, Canadian Psychol Assoc., 1983; Izaak Walton Killam Prize in Health Scis, Canada Council, 1994; Gold Medal Award, Amer. Psychol Foundn, 1994; McGovern Award in the behavioral scis, AAAS, 1996; Wilhelm Wundt-William James Prize, Eur. Fedn of Psychologists' Assocs, 2003; Gairdner Internat. Award, Gairdner Foundn, 2005; Canadian Medical Hall of Fame, 2007; Pasteur-Weizmann/Servier Internat. Prize, 2009. Class II, Order of White Star (Estonia), 2000. *Publications:* Elements of Episodic Memory, 1983; (ed jtly) Organization of Memory, 1972; Memory Systems 1994, 1994; (ed) Memory, Consciousness, and the Brain: the Tallinn Conference, 1999; Oxford Handbook of Memory, 2000; articles in scientific jls. *Recreations:* golf, walking, chess, bridge. *Address:* 45 Bâby Point Crescent, Toronto, ON M6S 2B7, Canada. *T:* (416) 7623736.

**TUMPEL-GUGERELL, Gertrude**; Member, Executive Board, European Central Bank, 2003–11; *b* Kapelln, Austria, 11 Nov. 1952. *Educ:* grammar sch.; Univ. of Vienna (MSc Hons Econs and Soc. Scis 1975; Doctorate in Econs and Soc. Scis 1981). Economist, Econs Div., Oesterreichische Nationalbank, 1975–81; Econ. Policy Advr to Minister of Finance, and Mem. Supervisory Bd, Oesterreichische Laenderbank AG, 1981–84; Oesterreichische Nationalbank: Dep. Hd, Econs Div., 1985–86; Comptroller Gen. in charge of developing strategic planning and auditing, 1986–92; Dir, Area Corporate Planning and Mgt, 1992–97; Exec. Dir, Econs and Financial Markets Dept, 1997–2003; Vice-Gov., 1998–2003. Alternate Gov. of Austria to IMF, 1997–2003; European Union: Mem., Econ. and Finance Cttee, 1997–2003; Chm., Banking Adv. Cttee, 2002–03; European Central Bank: Member: Internat. Relns Cttee, 1999–2003; Banking Supervision Cttee, 1999–2003; Mem., Supervisory Bd, Financial Market Authy, Austria, 2002–03. Non-executive Director: Vienna Insurance Gp, 2012–; Commerzbank AG, 2012–; ÖBB Hldg AG, 2011–; Chm., Supervisory Bd, Austrian Res. Promotion Agency, 2011–. Consultant, Austrian Inst. of Econ. Res. Mem. Council, Univ. of Vienna, 2003–; Mem. Bd, Montanuniversität Leoben, 2013–. *Publications:* numerous articles and essays.

**TUNBRIDGE, William Michael Gregg**, MD; FRCP; Director of Postgraduate Medical Education and Training, Oxford University, 1994–2003; Professorial Fellow of Wadham College, Oxford, 1994–2003, now Fellow Emeritus; *b* 13 June 1940; *s of* Sir Ronald Ernest Tunbridge, OBE and of Dorothy (*née* Gregg); *m* 1965, Felicity Katherine Edith Parrish; two *d*. *Educ:* Kingswood Sch., Bath; Queens' Coll., Cambridge (MA, MD); University Coll. Hosp. House appointments: UCH, 1964–65; Mpilo Hosp., Bulawayo, 1965–66; Manchester Royal Infirmary, 1967–68; Tutor in Medicine, Univ. of Manchester, 1969–70; Registrar, Hammersmith Hosp., 1970–72; Sen. Res. Associate, Univ. of Newcastle, 1972–75; Sen. Registrar in Medicine, Durham, 1975–76; MRC Travelling Fellow, Liège, 1976–77; Consultant Physician, Newcastle Gen. Hosp. and Sen. Lectr in Medicine, Univ. of Newcastle upon Tyne, 1977–94; Consultant Physician, Radcliffe Infirmary, then Oxford Radcliffe Hosps, 1994–2005; Physician Emeritus, Nuffield Dept of Medicine, Oxford Univ., 2005–. President: Thyroid Club, 1994–96; Endocrine Section, Union of European Med. Specialists, 1994–98. *Publications:* (with P. D. Home) Diabetes and Endocrinology in Clinical Practice, 1991; Thyroid Disease: the facts, 3rd edn (with R. I. S. Bayliss) 1998, 4th edn (with M. P. J. Vanderpump) 2008; (ed) Rationing of Health Care in Medicine, 1993. *Recreations:* walking, golf. *Address:* Millstone, Ranmoor Lane, Hathersage, Hope Valley, Derbys S32 1BW. *T:* (01433) 650765. *Club:* Athenæum.

**TUNG Chee Hwa**; Chief Executive, Hong Kong Special Administrative Region, 1997–2005; Vice-Chairman, National Committee, Chinese People's Political Consultative Conference, since 2005; *b* 29 May 1937; *er s of* Tung Chao Yung and Koo Lee Ching; *m* 1961, Betty Tung Chiu Hung Ping; two *s* one *d*. *Educ:* Liverpool Univ. (BSc Marine Engrg 1960). Chm. and CEO, Orient Overseas (International) Ltd, 1986–96. Advr, Hong Kong Affairs, 1992–96; Member: Basic Law Consultative Cttee, 1985–90; Exec. Council, Hong Kong Govt, 1992–96; 8th Cttee, Chinese People's Political Consultative Conf., 1993–98, 10th Cttee, 2005–08, 11th Cttee, 2008–13, 12th Cttee, 2013–; Vice-Chm., Prep. Cttee, HKSAR, 1995–96. Member: Hong Kong/Japan Business Co-operation Cttee, 1991–96; Chm., Hong Kong/US Economic Co-operation Cttee, 1993–96; Founding Chm., China-US Exchange Foundn, 2008–. Hon. LLD Liverpool, 1997. *Recreations:* hiking, Tai Chi, swimming, reading.

**TUNNICLIFFE**, family name of **Baron Tunnicliffe**.

**TUNNICLIFFE**, Baron *cr* 2004 (Life Peer), of Bracknell in the County of Berkshire; **Denis Tunnicliffe**, CBE 1993; an Opposition Whip, House of Lords, since 2010; *b* 17 Jan. 1943; *s of* Harold Arthur and Nellie Tunnicliffe; *m* 1968, Susan Dale; one *s* (and one *s* decd). *Educ:* Henry Cavendish Sch., Derby; University Coll. London (State Schol.; BSc (Special)); College of Air Training, Hamble. Pilot, BOAC, 1966–72; British Airways, 1972–86; Chief Exec., International Leisure Group, Aviation Div., 1986–88; Man. Dir, London Underground Ltd, 1988–98; Mem. of Bd, 1993–2000, Chief Exec., 1998–2000, London Transport. Chairman: UKAEA, 2002–04; Rail Safety and Standards Bd, 2003–08; non-exec. Dir, Defence Equipment and Support (formerly Defence Logistics Orgn and Defence Procurement Agency), MoD, 2006–08. A Lord in Waiting (Govt Whip), 2008–10. Councillor, Royal Bor. of New Windsor, 1971–75; Councillor, Royal County of Berkshire, 1974–77; Dist Councillor, Bracknell, 1979–83. *Recreations:* flying, boating, church, travelling. *Address:* House of Lords, SW1A 0PW. *Clubs:* Royal Air Force, Royal Automobile.

**TUNNICLIFFE, Air Vice-Marshal Garry**, CVO 2019; Deputy Commandant, Royal College of Defence Studies, since 2019; *b* Plymouth, 14 Oct. 1966; *s of* John and Sandra Tunnicliffe; *m* 1992, Heidi Joan Manning; one *s* one *d*. *Educ:* Devonport High Sch. for Boys; Durham Univ. (BA Jt Hons Hist. and Politics 1988); King's Coll. London (MA Defence Studies 2001); Assoc. for Project Mgt qualification 2003; Inst. of Business Consulting Mgt (Consulting Dip. 2008); Inst. of Dirs (Dip. Co. Dir 2013). Commnd RAF, 1988; support rôles, RAF Germany, 1988–89; Accounting Officer, UK Support Unit, Ramstein, 1990–92; OC Personnel Mgt, RAF Buchan, 1992–93; Personnel SO, HQ 1 Gp, 1993–96; Op. Deny Flight, Italy, 1996; OC Stn Services Sqdn, RAF Coltishall, 1996–98; SO to SASO and DCS Ops, HQ Strike Comd, 1998–2000; acsc 2001; Business Change Manager, HQ RAF Infrastructure Orgn, 2001–03; OC Support Wing, RAF Coltishall, 2003–05; Defence Policy Planning Officer, MoD, 2005–06; Hd, Mgt Consultancy Services, HQ Strike Comd, 2006–08; Stn Comdr, RAF Halton, 2008–10; rcds 2011; Project Leader, New Employment Model (Conditions of Service), MoD, 2011–12; ACOS (Trng), HQ 22 (Trng) Gp, 2012–13; Hd, Armed Forces Remuneration, MoD, 2013–16; Defence Services Sec., and ACDS (Personnel Capability), MoD, 2016–19. *Recreations:* avid reader of military history, strategy and business change, adventurous travel, hiking. *Address:* Royal College of Defence Studies, Seaford House, 37 Belgrave Square, SW1X 8NS. *Club:* Royal Air Force.

**TUNSTALL, Sir Craig**, Kt 2014; Chief Executive (formerly Executive Headteacher), Gipsy Hill Federation, Lambeth, 2007–18; *b* Workington, Cumbria, 8 March 1971; *s of* Tom and Sarah Jane Tunstall; partner, Jeffrey Michael. *Educ:* Broughton Moor Primary Sch.; Netherhall Secondary Sch.; University Coll. of Ripon and York St John, Univ. of Leeds (BEd Hons); Greenwich Univ. (MA); Leicester Univ. (MBA). NPQH 2000. Teacher, Ayresome Jun. Sch., Middlesbrough, 1993–95; Torridon Jun. Sch., Lewisham, 1995–97; Sen. Teacher, Kender Primary Sch., Lewisham, 1997–99; Dep. Hd, Wyborne Primary Sch., Greenwich, 1999–2002; Headteacher: Kingswood Primary Sch., Lambeth, 2002; Executive Headteacher: Elm Wood Primary Sch., Lambeth, 2007; Paxton Primary Sch., Lambeth, 2009; Crawford Primary Sch., Southwark, 2011; Fenstanton Primary Sch., Lambeth, 2012; Mayflower Fedn, Southwark, 2013; Glenbrook Primary Sch., Lambeth, 2013. *Recreations:* classical music, theatre.

**TUNSTALL, Kathryn**; Strategic Director for Services to Children and Young People, Bradford Metropolitan District Council, 2007–14; *b* St Helens, Merseyside, 26 Nov. 1953; *d of* Eric Thomas Tunstall and Majorie Naomi Tunstall (*née* Guest); *m* 1992, Keith McKay Watson; one *s* one *d*, and two step *d*. *Educ:* Rivington Road Prim. Sch., St Helens; Cowley Girls' Grammar Sch., St Helens (Hd Girl); Univ. of Leeds (BA Hons Psychol./Sociol. 1975); Univ. of Hull (DipASS 1978; CQSW 1978). Qualified Social Worker, 1978, specialising in child protection; Sen. Manager, responsible for Community Social Work Services, Leeds CC, 1998–2002; Bradford Metropolitan District Council: Asst Dir for Children's Services, Social Services, 2002–05; Dir, Social Services, 2005–07. Chairman: Bradford Area Child Protection Cttee, 2002–06; Bradford Safeguarding Children Bd, 2006–13; Bradford Youth Offenders Services Bd, 2007–14; Bradford Children and Young People's Strategic Partnership, 2007–14. Non-exec. Dir, Disclosure and Barring Service, Home Office, 2015–19; Chm., Yorks and Humber Regl Adoption Bd, 2015–18. Trustee, Morrison Foundn, 2014–19; Dir and Trustee, Nell Bank Outdoor Centre, 2019–. *Recreations:* spending time with my own family, worldwide travel, understanding how families tick, indulging in quality food and wine, gardening, bird watching, Coronation Street, supporting St Helens Rugby League Football Club.

**TUOHY, Denis John**; broadcaster, writer and actor; *b* 2 April 1937; *s of* late John Vincent Tuohy and Anne Mary, (Nan), Tuohy (*née* Doody); *m* 1st, 1960, Moya McCann (marr. diss. 1988); two *s* two *d*; 2nd, 1998, Elizabeth Moran (marr. diss. 2007). *Educ:* Clongowes Wood Coll., Co. Kildare; Queen's Univ., Belfast (BA Hons Classics). Eisenhower Fellow, USA, 1967. BBC: Newscaster and Reporter, NI, 1960–64; Presenter, Late Night Line Up, 1964–67; Reporter and Presenter: 24 Hours, 1967–71; Panorama, 1974–75; Reporter, Man Alive, 1971–72; Presenter, Tonight, 1975–79; Thames Television: Reporter, This Week, 1972–74; Presenter, People and Politics, 1973–74; Presenter and Reporter: TV Eye, 1979–86; This Week, 1986–92; Newscaster, ITN, 1994–2001; Presenter: Something Understood, BBC Radio 4, 1995–99; Cards of Identity, RTE, 2002; A Living Word, RTE, 2003; Thought for the Day, BBC Radio Ulster, 2013–16; reporter/presenter on numerous documentaries, incl. for BBC and ITV: A Life of O'Reilly, 1974; Mr Truman, why did you drop the second bomb?, 1975; Do You Know Where Jimmy Carter Lives?, 1977; To Us a Child (prod jtly by Thames TV and UNICEF), 1986; The Blitz, 1991; The Real Dad's Army, 1998; The Law and the "Lunatic", 1999; for UTV: The Troubles I've Seen, 2008, 2012, 2014, 2015; UTV at Fifty, 2009; Belfast Blitz Anniversary, 2011; Thatcher's Ireland, 2013; October 1968: Brink of Chaos, 2018. Actor: Fair City, and The Clinic, RTE TV series, 2003; Fallout, RTE TV drama, 2006; The Tempest, Cork Midsummer Fest., 2006; Strength and Honour (film), 2007; Killinaskully, RTE TV series, 2007–08; Scapegoat, 2009, Betrayal of Trust, 2011, BBC NI TV drama; Blackness After Midnight, Belfast City Hall, 2012; The Week Before, Belfast, 2016. *Publications:* Wide-eyed in Mediaeval (memoirs), 2005; articles in Irish Times, Sunday Independent, Belfast Telegraph, Irish News, Scotsman, Independent, New Statesman, The Tablet, The Oldie, etc. *Recreations:* walking in the Mournes, theatre, cinema, watching Rugby and cricket. *Address:* 16 Aurora na Mara, Shore Road, Rostrevor, Co. Down BT34 3UP.

**TUPPER, Sir Charles Hibbert**, 6th Bt *cr* 1888, of Armdale, Halifax, Nova Scotia; *b* 10 July 1964; *o s of* Sir Charles Hibbert Tupper, 5th Bt and of Bernice Yvonne (*née* Quinn, now Elderkin); *S* father, 2008, but his name does not appear on the Official Roll of the Baronetage; *m* 1987, Elizabeth Ann Heaslip; one *d*. *Heir:* cousin Charles Reginald Hibbert Tupper, *b* 20 Dec. 1947.

**TURCAN, Henry Watson**; a Recorder of the Crown Court, 1985–2013; *b* 22 Aug. 1941; *s of* late Henry Hutchison Turcan and Lilias Cheyne; *m* 1969, Jane Fairrie Blair; one *s* one *d*. *Educ:* Rugby School; Trinity College, Oxford (BA, MA). Called to the Bar, Inner Temple, 1965, Bencher, 1992. Legal Assessor to General Optical Council, 1983–2003. Special Adjudicator, Immigration Appeals, 1998–2005; an Immigration Judge, 2005–11. *Recreations:* shooting, fishing, golf, National Hunt racing. *Address:* Cairney Hall, Newburgh, Fife KY14 6JB. *T:* (01337) 810302. *Clubs:* New (Edinburgh); Royal and Ancient Golf (St Andrews), Hon. Company of Edinburgh Golfers (Muirfield). New Zealand Golf (Chm., 1997–2011; Pres., 2011–).

**TURCAN, William James**; Chief Executive, Elementis (formerly Harrisons & Crosfield plc), 1994–98; *b* 4 Jan. 1943; *m* 1967, Elisabeth Margaret Stewart; three *s* one *d*. *Educ:* Rugby Sch.; Trinity Coll., Oxford (MA). Binder Hamlyn, 1965–70; Pauls Malt, 1970–86; Finance Dir, Pauls plc, 1986–88; Finance Dir, Harrisons & Crosfield, 1988–94. Bd Mem., Glenrothes New Town Develt Corp., 1983–86.

**TURING, Sir John Dermot**, 12th Bt *cr* 1638 (NS), of Foveran, Aberdeenshire; Partner, Clifford Chance, Solicitors, since 1999; *b* 26 Feb. 1961; *s of* John Ferrier Turing (*d* 1983) and of Beryl Mary Ada, *d of* late Herbert Vaughan Hann; *S* kinsman, Sir John Leslie Turing, 11th Bt, 1987; *m* 1986, Nicola J., *er d of* M. D. Simmonds; two *s*. *Educ:* Sherborne Sch., Dorset; King's Coll., Cambridge (BA 1982; MA 1986); New Coll., Oxford (DPhil 1986). Admitted solicitor, 1991. Trustee, Bletchley Park Trust, 2012–. *Heir: s* John Malcolm Ferrier Turing, *b* 5 Sept. 1988. *Address:* 68 Marshalswick Lane, St Albans AL1 4XF.

**TÜRK, Dr Danilo**, Hon. GCB 2008; President, Republic of Slovenia, 2007–12; Chairman, Global Fairness Initiative, since 2014; *b* Maribor, 19 Feb. 1952; *m* 1976, Barbara Miklič; one *d*. *Educ:* elementary and grammar sch., Maribor; Univ. of Ljubljana (law degree 1975; Dr 1982); Univ. of Belgrade (LLM 1979). Prof. of Internat. Law, 1981–92, Hd, Inst. of Internat. Law and Internat. Relns, 1983–92, Univ. of Ljubljana; Ambassador of Slovenia to UN, 1992–2000; Rep. of Slovenia on UN Security Council, 1998–99; Asst of UN Sec.-Gen. for Political Affairs, 2000–05; Prof. of Internat. Law, 2005–08, now Emeritus, Vice-Dean, 2006–07, Univ. of Ljubljana. Vis. Prof. of Law, Columbia Univ., NY, 2015. Mem., UN Sub-Commn on Prevention of Discrimination and Protection of Minorities, 1984–92; UN Special Rapporteur on Realization of Econ., Social and Cultural Rights, 1986–92; Mem., Slovene Delegn at Conf. of Yugoslavia, 1991–92. *Publications:* Načelo neintervencije v mednarodnih odnosih in v mednarodnem pravu (The Principle of Non-intervention), 1984; Temelji mednarodnega prava (Foundations of International Law), 2007; contrib. articles to law jls. *Recreations:* nordic walking, cross-country ski-ing, ski-ing.

**TURLEY, Anna Catherine**; MP (Lab Co-op) Redcar, since 2015; *b* Dartford, 9 Oct. 1978. *Educ:* Ashford Sch., Kent; Greyfriars Hall, Oxford (BA Hons Hist.). Civil Servant, Home Office, 2001–05; Special Adviser: to Sec. of State for Work and Pensions, 2005; to Chancellor of Duchy of Lancaster, 2006–07; Dep. Dir, New Local Govt Network, 2007–10. *Address:* House of Commons, SW1A 0AA. *T:* (020) 7219 5441. *E:* anna.turley.mp@parliament.uk.

**TURMEAU, Prof. William Arthur**, CBE 1989; PhD; FRSE; CEng, FIMechE; Chairman, Scottish Environment Protection Agency, 1995–99; Principal and Vice-Chancellor, Napier University, 1992–94 (Principal, Napier College, subseq. Napier Polytechnic of Edinburgh, 1982–92); *b* 19 Sept. 1929; *s* of Frank Richard Turmeau and Catherine Lyon Linklater; *m* 1957, Margaret Moar Burnett, MA, BCom; one *d*. *Educ:* Stromness Acad., Orkney; Univ. of Edinburgh (BSc); Moray House Coll. of Educn; Heriot-Watt Univ. (PhD). FIMechE, CEng, 1971; FRSE 1990. Royal Signals, 1947–49. Research Engr, Northern Electric Co. Ltd, Montreal, 1952–54; Mechanical Engr, USAF, Goose Bay, Labrador, 1954–56; Contracts Manager, Godfrey Engrg Co. Ltd, Montreal, 1956–61; Lectr, Bristo Technical Inst., 1962–64; Napier College: Lectr and Sen. Lectr, 1964–68; Head, Dept of Mechanical Engrg, 1968–75; Asst Principal and Dean, Faculty of Technology, 1975–82. Member: CICHE, British Council, 1982–92; CVCP, 1992–94 (Mem., Cttee of Dirs of Polytechnics, 1982–92); Standing Conf. of Rectors and Vice-Chancellors of European Univs, 1990–94; Cttee of Scottish Univ. Principals, 1992–94; Scottish Div. Cttee, Inst. of Dirs, 1992–94; Acad. Standards Cttee, IMechE, 1994–2004. Dir, ASH Scotland, 1996–. Trustee, Dynamic Earth Charitable Trust, 1994–2000. Mem. Court, Edinburgh Acad., 1993–99. Dr *hc* Edinburgh, 1992; DEd *hc* Napier, 1995. *Publications:* various papers relating to higher educn. *Recreations:* modern jazz, Leonardo da Vinci. *Address:* 132 Victoria Street, Stromness, Orkney KW16 3BU. *T:* (01856) 850500. *E:* profwaturmeau@aol.com.

**TURNAGE, Mark-Anthony**, CBE 2015; composer; *b* 1960. *Educ:* Royal College of Music. Mendelssohn Scholar, Tanglewood, USA, 1983. Composer in Association: City of Birmingham Symphony Orchestra, 1989–93; ENO, 1995–2000; Associate Composer, BBC SO, 2000–03; Mead Composer in Residence, Chicago SO, 2006–10; Composer in Residence, LPO, 2006–11. *Compositions include: stage:* Greek, 1988 (BMW prizes for best opera and best libretto, Munich Biennale, 1988); The Silver Tassie (opera), 2000 (Outstanding Achievement in Opera (jtly), Laurence Olivier Awards, and South Bank Show Award for opera, 2001); Anna Nicole (opera), 2011; Strapless (ballet), 2016; Coraline, 2018; *vocal:* Lament for a Hanging Man, 1983; Greek Suite, 1989; Some Days, 1989; Twice Through The Heart, 1997; A Relic of Memory, 2003; The Torn Fields, 2004; Two Baudelaire Songs, 2004; About Water, 2007; At Sixes and Sevens, 2013; *orchestral:* Night Dances, 1981; Three Screaming Popes, 1989; Momentum, 1991; Drowned Out, 1993; Your Rockaby (saxophone concerto), 1994; Dispelling the Fears, 1995; Silent Cities, 1998; Evening Songs, 1999; Another Set To, 2000; Dark Crossing, 2001; Etudes and Elegies, 2002; On Opened Ground (viola concerto), 2002; Scherzoid, 2005; Yet Another Set To (trombone concerto), 2005; From All Sides, 2006; Chicago Remains, 2007; Mambo, Blues and Tarantella (violin concerto), 2008; Five Views of a Mouth, 2009; Texan Tenebrae, 2010; Hammered Out, 2010; Undance (ballet score), 2011; Canon Fever, 2012; Cello Concerto, 2012; Trespass (ballet score), 2012; Speranza, 2013; Frieze, 2013; Piano Concerto, 2013; Erskine, 2013; Passchendale, 2014; Håkan, 2015; Dialogue, 2015; Remembering: In Memoriam Evan Scofield, 2017; Martland Memorial, 2017; Refugee, 2019; *ensemble:* On All Fours, 1985; Kai, 1990; Three Farewells, 1990; Blood on the Floor, 1996; About Time, 1999; Bass inventionS, 2000; Slide Stride, 2002; Eulogy, 2003; No Let Up, 2004; Crying Out Loud, 2004; A Prayer Before Stillness, 2007; A Constant Obsession, 2009; *instrumental:* Sleep on, 1992; Two Elegies framing a Shout, 1994; True Life Stories, 1995–99; Two Memorials, 1995–2000; Riffs and Refrains (solo clarinet), 2003; A Few Serenades, 2004; A Slow Pavane, A Fast Stomp, A Short Procession (piano trios), 2005; Twisted Blues with Twisted Ballad, 2008; Contusion, 2014; Duetti d'Amore, 2015; Power Play, 2015; Shroud (string quartet), 2016. *Relevant publication:* Mark-Anthony Turnage, by Andrew Clements, 2000. *Address:* c/o Cathy Nelson Artists and Projects, The Court House, Dorstone, Herefordshire HR3 6AW. *T:* (01981) 551903.

**TURNBERG**, family name of **Baron Turnberg**.

**TURNBERG**, Baron *cr* 2000 (Life Peer), of Cheadle in the county of Cheshire; **Leslie Arnold Turnberg**, Kt 1994; MD; FRCP, FMedSci; Chairman: National Centre for Replacement, Refinement and Reduction of Animals in Research, 2004–07; Medical Advisory Board, Nations Health Care, 2004–07; *b* 22 March 1934; *s* of Hyman and Dora Turnberg; *m* 1968, Edna Barme; one *s* one *d*. *Educ:* Stand Grammar Sch., Whitefield; Univ. of Manchester (MB, ChB 1957, MD 1966). MRCP 1961, FRCP 1973; FRCPE 1993; FRCP(I) 1993; FRCPSGlas 1994; FRCS 1996; FCPS (Pak). Junior medical posts: Manchester Jewish Hosp.; Northern Hosp.; Ancoats Hosp.; Manchester Royal Infirmary, 1957–61 and 1964–66; Registrar, UCH, 1961–64; Lectr, Royal Free Hosp., 1967; Res. Fellow, Univ. of Texas South-Western Med. Sch., Dallas, Texas, 1968; University of Manchester: Lectr, then Sen. Lectr, 1968–73; Dean, Fac. of Medicine, 1986–89; Prof. of Medicine, 1973–97. Chm., Specialist Training Authy, 1996–98. Hon. Consultant Physician, Salford HA, 1973–97. Member: Salford HA, 1974–81 and 1990–92; NW RHA, 1986–89. Chairman: PHLS Bd, 1997–2002; Health Quality Service, 2000–04; UK Forum on Genetics and Insurance, 2002–07. Mem. Bd, Renovo Gp, 2005–11. Mem., Select Cttee on sci. and technol., H of L, 2001–05. Scientific Advr, Assoc. Med. Res. Charities, 1997–2016. Royal College of Physicians: Mem. Council, 1989–92; Pres., 1992–97; Chairman: Educn Cttee, 1990–92; Wkg Gp on Communication, 1991–92; British Society of Gastroenterology: Mem. Council, 1989–92; Chm., Res. Cttee, 1991–92; Pres., 1999–2000; President: Med. Section, Manchester Med. Soc., 1992–93; Medical Protection Soc., 1997–2007. Trustee: Wolfson Foundn, 1997–; Hadassah UK, 2000–12; Ovarian Cancer Action, 2008–17; Weizmann UK, 2010–. Founder FMedSci 1998 (Vice Pres., 1998–2004). Hon. FFOM 1993; Hon. FRACP 1994; Hon. FRCOphth 1996; Hon. FRCOG 1996; Hon. FFPM 1997; Hon. Fellow: Acad. of Medicine, Singapore, 1994; Coll. of Medicine, S Africa, 1994. Hon. DSc: Salford, 1996; Manchester, 1998; Imperial Coll. London, 2000; Keele, 2008. *Publications:* Electrolyte and Water Transport Across Gastro-intestinal Epithelia, 1982; Clinical Gastroenterology, 1989; Forks in the Road, 2014; Beyond the Balfour Declaration, 2017; pubns on mechanisms of intestinal absorption and secretion in health and disease and on clinical gastroenterology. *Recreations:* reading, writing, Middle East history, antiquarian books, painting, walking, talking. *Address:* House of Lords, SW1A 0PW.

**TURNBULL**, family name of **Baron Turnbull**.

**TURNBULL**, Baron *cr* 2005 (Life Peer), of Enfield in the London Borough of Enfield; **Andrew Turnbull**, KCB 1998 (CB 1990); CVO 1992; Secretary of the Cabinet and Head of the Home Civil Service, 2002–05; *b* 21 Jan. 1945; *s* of Anthony and Mary Turnbull; *m* 1967, Diane Clarke; two *s*. *Educ:* Enfield Grammar Sch.; Christ's Coll., Cambridge (BA). ODI Fellow working as economist, Govt of Republic of Zambia, Lusaka, 1968–70; Asst Principal, 1970–72, Principal, 1972–76, HM Treasury; on secondment to staff of IMF, 1976–78; Asst Sec., HM Treasury, 1978–83; Private Sec. to the Prime Minister, 1983–85; Hd of Gen. Expenditure Policy Gp, HM Treasury, 1985–88; Principal Private Sec. to Prime Minister, 1988–92; Dep. Sec. (Public Finance), 1992, Second Permanent Sec. (Public Expenditure), 1993–94, HM Treasury; Permanent Secretary: DoE, later DETR, 1994–98; HM Treasury, 1998–2002. Chair, BH Global Ltd, 2008–12; non-executive Director: Prudential plc, 2006–15; British Land Co. plc, 2006–17; Frontier Economics Ltd, 2006–15. Chair, Zambia Orphans Aid, 2006–; Trustee, Global Warming Policy Foundn, 2009–. Chair of Govs, Dulwich Coll., 2009–15. *Recreations:* walking, sailing, opera, golf. *Address:* House of Lords, SW1A 0PW. *Club:* Tottenham Hotspur.

**TURNBULL, Hon. Lord; Alan D. Turnbull;** a Senator of the College of Justice in Scotland, since 2006. *Educ:* Univ. of Dundee (LLB 1979). Admitted to Faculty of Advocates, 1982; in practice at the Bar; Advocate Depute, 1995–97; QC (Scot.) 1996; Principal Advocate Depute, 2001–06. *Address:* Court of Session, Parliament House, Edinburgh EH1 1RQ.

**TURNBULL, Alan**, OBE 2016; PhD; FRS 2013; FREng; Senior Fellow, National Physical Laboratory, since 2011 (Fellow, since 1989); *b* Glasgow, 4 Sept. 1949; *s* of Alexander Stewart Turnbull and Mary Turnbull; *m* 1971, Ruth Jane Bolton (*d* 2009); two *d*. *Educ:* St Augustine's Sch., Glasgow; Univ. of Strathclyde (BSc 1st Cl. Hons 1970); Univ. of Bristol (PhD 1974). FICorr 1986; FIMMM 1999; FREng 2011. Joined Materials Div., NPL, 1973. Vis. Scientist, MIT, 1989. Fellow, 2008, Whitney Award, 2009, Nat. Assoc. of Corrosion Engrs Internat.; T. P. Hoar Prize, ICorr, 1987 and 2011; Bengough Prize and Medal, Inst. of Materials, 1994 and 2018; Cavallaro Medal, Eur. Fedn of Corrosion, 2002; U. R. Evans Award, ICorr, 2004; Alec Hough-Grassby Award, Inst. of Measurement and Control, 2013; Lee Hsun Lect. Award, Inst. of Metal Res., Shenyang, Chinese Acad. of Scis, 2017; China Dist. Materials Scientist Award, Univ. of Sci. and Technol., Beijing, 2017. *Publications:* scientific papers in Corrosion, Corrosion Sci., Materials Sci. and Engrg. *Recreations:* golf, hiking, gardening, watching football. *Address:* 1 Kingsmead Avenue, Sunbury TW16 5HW. *T:* (work) (020) 8943 7115. *E:* alan.turnbull@npl.co.uk.

**TURNBULL, Alan D.;** *see* Turnbull, Hon. Lord.

**TURNBULL, Rt Rev. (Anthony) Michael (Arnold);** *see* Turnbull, Rt Rev. M.

**TURNBULL, David Knight Thomas**, FCA; Director: XXX Building Ltd, since 1999; Helpcards Ltd, since 2007; *b* 13 Dec. 1948; *s* of Stanley Thomas Turnbull and Lalla Turnbull (*née* Knight); *m* 1972, Monica Belton; one *s* one *d*. *Educ:* Stationers' Co. Sch.; Westfield Coll., London Univ. (BSc). FCA 1975. With Coopers & Lybrand, Sheffield and Iran, 1972–79; Amalgamated Metal Corporation plc: Gp Chief Acct, 1980–84; Corporate Controller, 1984–86; Gen. Manager, Business Develt, 1986–89; Finance Director: PO Counters Ltd, 1989–94; British Council, 1994–2000; Army Benevolent Fund, 2001–06. Sec., Interstate Programmes Ltd, 2000–12. *Recreations:* anything old, watching Rugby. *Address:* Halfway Grange, Chantry View Road, Guildford, Surrey GU1 3XR.

**TURNBULL, Hon. Malcolm Bligh;** MHR (L) Wentworth, New South Wales, 2004–18; Prime Minister of Australia, 2015–18; Leader of the Liberal Party, Australia, 2015–18; *b* 24 Oct. 1954; *s* of late Bruce Bligh Turnbull and Coral (*née* Lansbury); *m* 1980, Lucinda Mary Forrest Hughes, AO, *d* of Hon. Thomas Hughes, AO, QC; one *s* one *d*. *Educ:* Sydney Grammar Sch.; Sydney Univ. (BA, LLB); Brasenose Coll., Oxford (Rhodes Schol. (NSW) 1978, BCL 1980). Journalist, Nation Review, 1975; Political Correspondent: TCN–9, Sydney, 1976; The Bulletin, 1977–78; Journalist, Sunday Times, London, 1979; admitted to NSW Bar, 1980; Barrister, Sydney, 1980–83; Gen. Counsel and Secretary, Consolidated Press Holdings Ltd, 1983–86; Partner: Turnbull McWilliam, Solicitors, Sydney, 1986–87; Turnbull & Co., Solicitors, 1987–90; Jt Man. Dir, Whitlam Turnbull & Co. Ltd, Investment Bankers, Sydney, 1987–90; Man. Dir, Turnbull & Partners Pty Ltd, Investment Bankers, 1987–97; Man. Dir and Chm., Goldman Sachs Australia, 1997–2001; Partner, Goldman Sachs & Co., 1998–2001. Chm., Australian Republican Movement, 1993–2000 (Dir, 1991–2002); Delegn, Constitutional Convention, 1998; Hon. Federal Treas., Liberal Party of Australia, 2002–03. Parly Sec. to PM of Australia, 2006–07; Minister for the Envmt and Water Resources, 2007; Federal Shadow Treas., 2007–08; Leader, Parly Liberal Party and Leader of the Opposition, 2008–09; Shadow Minister for Communications and Broadband, 2010–13; Minister for Communications, 2013–15. Chairman: FTR Holdings, then WebCentral Gp, Ltd, 1995–97, 2001–04 (Dir, 1995–2004); OzEmail Ltd, 1995–99 (Dir, 1995–99); Dir, Reach Ltd, 2001–04. Chm., Menzies Res. Centre, 2002–04. Centenary Medal, Australia, 2003. *Publications:* The Spycatcher Trial, 1988; The Reluctant Republic, 1993; Fighting for the Republic, 1999. *Recreations:* walking, swimming, kayaking, sailing. *Clubs:* Athenæum (Philadelphia); Australian, Tattersall's (Sydney); Royal Prince Edward Yacht, Royal Motor Yacht; North Bondi Surf Life Saving (Sydney).

**TURNBULL, Rt Rev. Michael**, CBE 2003; DL; Bishop of Durham, 1994–2003; an Honorary Assistant Bishop: Diocese of Canterbury, since 2003; Diocese of Europe, since 2003; Diocese of Rochester, since 2010; *b* 27 Dec. 1935; *s* of George Ernest Turnbull and Adeline Turnbull (*née* Awty); *m* 1963, Brenda Susan Merchant; one *s* two *d*. *Educ:* Ilkley Grammar Sch.; Keble Coll., Oxford (MA); St John's Coll., Durham (DipTh). Ordained deacon, 1960; priest, 1961; Curate: Middleton, 1960–61; Luton, 1961–65; Domestic Chaplain to Archbishop of York, 1965–69; Rector of Heslington and Chaplain, York Univ., 1969–76; Chief Secretary, Church Army, 1976–84; Archdeacon of Rochester, also Canon Residentiary of Rochester Cathedral and Chm., Dio. Bd for Mission and Unity, 1984–88; Bishop of Rochester, 1988–94. Entered H of L, 1994. Mem., General Synod, C of E, 1970–75, 1987–2003; Vice-Chm., Central Bd of Finance, C of E, 1990–98; Member: Bd, Church Commissioners, 1989–98; Archbishops' Council, 1998–2000 (Chm., Ministry Div., 1999–2000); Archbps' Commn on Cathedrals, 1992–93; Chairman: Archbps' Commn on orgn of C of E, 1994–96; Foundn for Church Leadership, 2003–06. Chairman: NE Constitutional Convention, 1999–2003; Campaign for English Regs, 2000–03. Chairman: Bible Reading Fellowship, 1985–94; Coll. of Preachers, 1990–98. Lectr, Swan Hellenic, 2003–15; Pilgrimage Leader, 2003–15. Mem. Bd, Pilgrims Hospices, 2016–. DL Kent, 2005. Hon. Fellow, St Chad's Coll., Durham, 2002. Hon. DLitt Greenwich, 1994; Hon. DD Dunelm, 2003. *Publications:* (contrib.) Unity: the next step?, 1972; God's Front

Line, 1979; Parish Evangelism, 1980; Learning to Pray, 1981; 100 Minute Bible Reflections, 2007; The State of the Church and the Church of the State, 2012. *Recreations:* cricket, family life, allotment. *Address:* 3 Gardners Quay, Upper Strand Street, Sandwich, Kent CT13 9DH. *T:* (01304) 611389. *E:* amichaelturnbull@yahoo.co.uk. *Club:* MCC.

TURNBULL, Rev. Dr Richard Duncan, PhD; FRHistS; Director, Centre for Enterprise, Markets and Ethics, since 2012; *b* 17 Oct. 1960; *s of* Alan Allgood Turnbull and late Kathleen Turnbull; *m* 1986, Caroline Andrew; one *s* three *d*. *Educ:* Moseley Grammar Sch.; Normanton High Sch.; Univ. of Reading (BA 1982); Univ. of Durham (BA 1992; PhD 1997); Univ. of Oxford (MA 2005). CA 1985. Supervisory and trng posts, 1982–87, Manager, 1987–90, Ernst and Young, chartered accountants; ordination trng, Cranmer Hall, Durham, 1990–94; ordained deacon, 1994, priest, 1995; Curate, Christ Church, Portswood, Southampton, 1994–98; Vicar, Christ Church, Chineham, Basingstoke, 1998–2005; Principal, Wycliffe Hall, Oxford, 2005–12 (Hon. Res. Fellow, 2012–); Mem., Faculty of Theology, Univ. of Oxford, 2005–. Member: Gen. Synod, 1995–2005 (Chm., Business Cttee, 2004–05); Archbishops' Council, 2003–05. FRHistS 2014. *Publications:* Anglican and Evangelical?, 2007; Shaftesbury: the great reformer, 2010; Reviving the Heart, 2012; A Passionate Faith, 2012; Quaker Capitalism: lessons for today, 2014; (ed) Quakers, Business and Corporate Responsibility, 2019; articles on Evangelicalism in Churchman and Anvil; contrib. dictionary entry on 7th Earl of Shaftesbury to Theologische Realenzyklopädie, 1999. *Recreations:* walking, reading, visiting historic houses, Real tennis. *Address:* Centre for Enterprise, Markets and Ethics, 1st Floor, 31 Beaumont Street, Oxford OX1 2NP. *T:* (01865) 513453. *E:* richard.turnbull@theceme.org.

TURNBULL, Sara Kate McConnell, CEnv; Founder and Director, Work Wild Ltd, since 2016; *b* 3 Nov. 1980; *d of* Susan Turner (later MacBride Stewart), step *d of* Aidan MacBride Stewart and *d of* Stephen Turnbull. *Educ:* United World Coll. of the Atlantic; Royal Holloway, Univ. of London (BA Hons Drama and Japanese); Univ. of E London (MSc Arch.). CEnv 2010. Interim Chief Exec., Creative Land Trust, 2019–. Non-exec. Dir, Covent Gdn Mkt Authy, 2016–. Ind. Panel Mem., HS2 Business, Community and Envmt Funds, 2016–. Chair, Workspace Providers Bd, GLA, 2017–. Mem., Energy Inst., 2010. *Publications:* Working Wild, 2019. *Recreations:* swimming anywhere (ideally outdoors and naked), sailing anything (preferably wooden), riding waves (and bikes), dancing (barefoot). *Address:* Work Wild Ltd, 25 Lavington Street, SE1 0NZ. *T:* 07972 103966. *E:* sara@workwild.space.

TURNER, family name of Barons Netherthorpe and Turner of Ecchinswell.

TURNER OF ECCHINSWELL, Baron *cr* 2005 (Life Peer), of Ecchinswell in the County of Hampshire; (Jonathan) Adair Turner; Senior Fellow, Institute for New Economic Thinking, 2013–19 and since 2019 (Chairman, Governing Board, 2015–19); *b* 5 Oct. 1955; *s of* Geoffrey Vincent Turner and Kathleen Margaret (*née* Broadhurst); *m* 1985, Orna Ní Chionna, *qv*; two *d*. *Educ:* Gonville and Caius Coll., Cambridge (MA Hist. and Econs 1978; Hon. Fellow, 2011). Chm., Cambridge Univ. Cons. Assoc., 1976; Pres., Cambridge Union Soc., 1977. BP, 1979; with Chase Manhattan Bank, 1979–82; McKinsey & Co., 1982–95: Principal, 1988; Dir, 1994–95; Dir Gen., CBI, 1995–99; Vice Chm., Merrill Lynch Europe, 2000–06. Mem., Ct of Dirs, 2008–13, Interim Financial Policy Cttee, 2011–13, Bank of England. Chairman: Chubb European Gp Ltd, 2017–; Chubb Underwriting Agencies Ltd, 2017–; non-executive Director: United Business Media, 2000–08; Siemens plc, 2006–08; Paternoster UK Ltd, 2006–08; Standard Chartered plc, 2006–08; Prudential, 2015–19; Ind. Dir, 2014–17, Sen. Advr, 2017–, Oak North; Advr, Bd, Envision Energy Internat., 2018–. Chairman: Low Pay Commn, 2002–06; Pension Commn, 2003–06; ESRC, 2007–08 (Mem., 2003–08); Climate Change Cttee, 2008–12; Supervisory and Regulatory Cttee, Internat. Financial Stability Bd, 2009–13; Energy Transitions Commn, 2016–. Vis. Prof., 1999–, and Chair, Policy Cttee, Centre for Economic Performance, 1999–2007, LSE; Vis. Prof., Cass Business Sch., 2004–. Vis. Fellow, Nuffield Coll., Oxford, 2008–; Sen. Fellow, Centre for Financial Studies, Frankfurt, 2013–; Vis. Prof., INCEIF Global Univ. of Islamic Finance, 2015–17. Mem., Adv. Council, Bank of China's Sch. of Finance, Tsinghua Univ., 2015–. Trustee: Cambridge Foundn, 2002–08; WWF, 2001–07; Save the Children, 2006–08; BM, 2013– (Chm., Audit Cttee, 2013–). Hon. FRSE 2010; Hon. FRS 2016; Hon. Inst. and Faculty of Actuaries, 2018. Hon. DSc City, 2002; Hon. LLD Cambridge, 2017. *Publications:* Just Capital: the liberal economy, 2001; Economics after the Crisis: objectives and means, 2012; Between Debt and the Devil: money, credit and fixing global finance, 2015. *Recreations:* ski-ing, opera. *Address:* House of Lords, SW1A 0PW.

TURNER OF ECCHINSWELL, Lady; *see* Ní Chionna, O.

TURNER, Amédée Edward; QC 1976; *b* 26 March 1929; *s of* Frederick William Turner and Ruth Hempson; *m* 1960, Deborah Dudley Owen; one *s* one *d*. *Educ:* Temple Grove, Heron's Ghyll, Sussex; Dauntsey's Sch., Wilts; Christ Church, Oxford (MA). Called to Bar, Inner Temple, 1954; practised patent bar, 1954–57; Associate, Kenyon & Kenyon, patent attorneys, NY, 1957–60; London practice, 1960–2009; Senior Counsel: APCO Europe, Brussels, 1995–98; WorldSpace Ltd, 1999–2001; of Counsel, Oppenheimer Wolff and Donnelly, Brussels, 1994–2003. Dir, CJA Consultants Ltd, 1999– (Chm., 2004–). Hon. Sec., ME Gp, Cons. Commonwealth Council, 1954–57, 1960 and 1979. Contested (C) Norwich N, gen. elections, 1964, 1966, 1970. European Parliament: MEP (C) Suffolk, 1979–94; contested (C) Suffolk and SW Norfolk, 1994; Hon. MEP, 1994; EDG spokesman on energy res. and technol., 1984–89; Chief Whip, EDG, 1989–92; joined EPP Gp, 1992; Mem., EPP Gp Bureau, 1992–94; Chm., Civil Liberties and Internal Affairs Cttee, 1992–94; Vice Chm., Legal Cttee, 1979–84; Member: Economic and Monetary Cttee, 1979–84; ACP Jt Assembly, 1980–94; Transport Cttee, 1981–84; Energy Cttee, 1984–94; Legal Affairs Cttee, 1984–89. PHARE Advr to Macedonian Parlt on improving legislature and democratic effectiveness, 2001–02 (manual, The Approximation of EU Law, 2002). Mem., Exec. Cttee, European League for Econ. Co-operation, 1996–2000. Mem., Adv. Council to Anglican Observer, UN, 2002–06; organised and prepared report, Muslim Grass-roots in the West Discuss Democracy, 2007, campaign of over 140 speaking engagements on report, Britain, USA, Canada, Brussels and Istanbul, 2007–15; Lay Muslims roundtable discussions on compatibility of Islam and democracy, Canada, Italy, France, Germany and Spain, 2009–15; Founder and Mem., IDDEX, Innovation Mgt, speaking engagements on patent litigation insurance, 2012. Mem., Soc. of Cons. Lawyers, 1960–. Mem., Salzburg Global Fellowship, 2008–. *Publications:* The Law of Trade Secrets, 1962, supplement, 1968; The Law of the New European Patent, 1979; many Conservative Party study papers, 1950–70, on defence, oil and Middle East; reports on patent litigation inscr for EC, 2003, 2006; A Qur'an Paper: everything that is actually in the Qur'an as described by a Non-Muslim Westerner for Non-Muslims, 2015; (with Davide Tacchini) Islam and Democracy: voices of Muslims amongst us, 2019. *Recreations:* designing historical themes in 13 acre garden at Westleton, Suffolk, art deco collection, oil painting. *Address:* Penthouse 7, Bickenhall Mansions, 63–104 Bickenhall Street, W1U 6BS. *T:* (020) 7935 2949, *Fax:* (020) 7935 2950; 5 New Square, Lincoln's Inn, WC2A 3RJ. *T:* (020) 7404 0404; The Barn, Westleton, Saxmundham, Suffolk IP17 3AN. *T:* (01728) 648235; La Combe de la Boissière, St Maximin, Uzès 30700, France. *T:* 466220393; 15 La Bastide d'Uzes, Chemin de l'Escalette, 30700 Uzes (2720), France. *T:* 466372567. *E:* amedee.turner@btinternet.com. *Club:* Coningsby.

TURNER, Andrew John; *b* Coventry, 24 Oct. 1953; *s of* late Eustace Albert Turner and Joyce Mary Turner (*née* Lowe). *Educ:* Rugby Sch.; Keble Coll., Oxford (BA 1976, MA 1981); Birmingham Univ. (PGCE 1977); Henley Mgt Centre. Teacher of Econs and Geog., Rushden Boys' Comp. Sch., 1977, Lord Williams's Sch., Thame, 1978–84; Res. Officer, Cons. Central Office, 1984–86; Special Advr to Sec. of State for Social Services, 1986–88; Dir, Grant-maintained Schools Foundn, 1988–97; Dep. Dir, Educn Unit, IEA, 1998–2000; Head of Policy and Resources, Educn Dept, Southwark BC, 2000–01. Educn Consultant, 1997–2001, Dir, 2000–02, Empire Packet Co. MP (C) Isle of Wight, 2001–17. A Vice-Chm., Conservative Party, 2003–05; Opposition front bench spokesman on charities, 2005–06. Member: European Scrutiny Cttee, 2015–17; Public Admin and Constitl Affairs Cttee, 2015–17. FRSA. *Recreations:* walking, the countryside, old movies, avoiding gardening. *Address:* Seal House, Sea Street, Newport, Isle of Wight PO30 5BW.

TURNER, Prof. (Andrew) Neil, PhD; FRCP, FRCPE; Professor of Nephrology, since 1998, and Dean of Undergraduate Teaching, College of Medicine and Veterinary Medicine, since 2012, University of Edinburgh; Hon. Consultant Nephrologist, Edinburgh Royal Infirmary, since 1998; *b* 28 April 1956; *s of* Rodney Turner and Eileen (*née* Wade); *m* 1984, Helen Cameron; three *s*. *Educ:* Downing Coll., Cambridge (MA 1977); Lincoln Coll., Oxford (BM BCh 1980); PhD London 1992. FRCP 1996; FRCPE 1997. Med. trng in Oxford, Croydon, Northampton, Liverpool, Norwich and York, 1980–85; renal trng, Oxford, 1983, and Hammersmith, 1985–92; NKRF Sen. Res. Fellow, 1990; Hon. Consultant, Hammersmith Hosp. and Sen. Lectr, RPMS, 1993; Sen. Lectr in Medicine and Nephrology, Univ. of Aberdeen and Aberdeen Royal Hosp., 1994–98. Chm., Kidney Res. UK, 2008–. ILTM 2000. Editor: www.edren.org, 2000–; www.patientview.org, 2005–. *Publications:* (contrib.) Oxford Textbook of Medicine, 4th edn 2005, 5th edn 2018; (ed jtly) Oxford Textbook of Clinical Nephrology, 4th edn 2015; (contrib.) Davidson's Principles and Practice of Medicine, 22nd edn 2014; papers in learned jls on autoimmunity, antigen processing, renal disease, teaching, information technology and health. *Recreations:* art, the outdoors, dance, music. *Address:* Renal Medicine, Royal Infirmary, Little France, Edinburgh EH16 4SA. *T:* (0131) 242 9167. *E:* neil.turner@ed.ac.uk.

TURNER, Anna; JP; Lord-Lieutenant of Shropshire, since 2019; *b* Market Drayton, 8 Aug. 1958; *d of* Bill and Jane Tellwright; *m* 1980, Jonathon Turner; one *s* one *d*. Samaritan, 1980–83. Mem., Bd of Visitors, Stoke Heath Prison, 1984–94. JP 1990, High Sheriff, 2009, DL 2010, Shropshire. *Recreations:* riding, hunting, stalking, walking. *Address:* Heath Paddocks, Prees Heath, Whitchurch, Shropshire SY13 2AF. *T:* (01948) 663527. *E:* annaturner123@yahoo.co.uk. *Club:* Turf.

TURNER, Ven. Antony Hubert Michael; Archdeacon of the Isle of Wight, 1986–96, now Archdeacon Emeritus; *b* 17 June 1930; *s of* Frederick George and Winifred Frances Turner; *m* 1956, Margaret Kathleen (*née* Phillips) (*d* 2016); one *s* two *d*. *Educ:* Royal Liberty Grammar School, Romford, Essex; Tyndale Hall, Bristol. FCA 1963 (ACA 1952); DipTh (Univ. of London), 1956. Ordained deacon, 1956, priest, 1957; Curate, St Ann's, Nottingham, 1956–59; Curate in Charge, St Cuthbert's, Cheadle, Dio. Chester, 1959–62; Vicar, Christ Church, Macclesfield, 1962–68; Home Sec., Bible Churchmen's Missionary Soc., 1968–74; Vicar of St Jude's, Southsea, 1974–86; RD of Portsmouth, 1979–84; Priest i/c, St Mary, Rotterdam, 1999–2000. Church Commissioner, 1983–93. Vice Chm., C of E Pensions Bd, 1988–97. *Recreations:* photography, caravanning. *Address:* 15 Avenue Road, Hayling Island, Hants PO11 0LX. *T:* (023) 9246 5881.

TURNER, Barry Horace Page, PhD; writer and editor; *b* 4 Oct. 1937; *o s of* Laurence and Esther Turner; *m* 1st, 1965, Sandra Hogben (marr. diss. 1972); 2nd, 1974, Gunilla Nordquist (marr. diss. 1986); one *s* one *d*; 3rd, 1997, Mary Elizabeth Fulton. *Educ:* King Edward VI Grammar Sch., Bury St Edmunds; London School of Economics (BSc Econs 1961; PhD 1966); Inst. of Educn, London Univ. (DipEd 1962). Dep. Editor, New Education, 1966–68; Educn Corresp., Observer, 1969–71; Reporter and Presenter, BBC Current Affairs, Thames TV, Yorkshire TV, Granada TV, 1969–77; Mktg Dir, Macmillan Press, 1977–81. Chm., Nat. Acad. of Writing, 2003–09. Vis. Prof., Birmingham City Univ. (formerly UCE), 2006–13. Editor: The Writer's Handbook, annually 1988–2011; The Statesman's Yearbook, annually 1997–2014. *Plays:* (jtly) Henry Irving, 1995; Agate, 1997; Novello, 2011. *Publications:* (jtly) Adventures in Education, 1969; Free Trade and Protection, 1971; Equality for Some, 1974; A Place in the Country, 1974; Sweden, 1976; The Other European Community, 1982; (jtly) The Playgoer's Companion, 1983; A Jobbing Actor, 1984; Richard Burton, 1987; East End, West End, 1990; Marks of Distinction, 1988; ...And the Policeman Smiled, 1991; The Long Horizon, 1993; Quest for Love, 1994; (jtly) When Daddy Came Home, 1995; The Writer's Companion, 1996; One Small Suitcase (for children), 2003; Countdown to Victory, 2004; Suez 1956: the inside story of the first oil war, 2006; Outpost of Occupation: how the Channel Islands survived Nazi rule, 1940–45, 2010; Beacon for Change: how the Festival of Britain shaped the modern age, 2011; The Victorian Parson, 2015; Karl Doenitz and the Last Days of the Third Reich, 2015; The Berlin Airlift: the relief operation that defined the Cold War, 2017; Men of Letters: the story of Garrick writers, 2019; Waiting for War: Britain 1939–1940, 2019; contribs to The Times, Daily Mail. *Recreation:* revisiting old books and movies. *Address:* 34 Ufton Road, N1 5BX. *T:* (020) 7241 0116; Le Bernet, 32480 La Romieu, France. *T:* 562288841. *Clubs:* Garrick, Chelsea Arts.

TURNER, Brian James, CBE 2002; chef, restaurateur; *b* 7 May 1946; *s of* Lawrence and Lily Turner; *m* 1973, Denise Parker; two *s*. *Educ:* Morley Grammar Sch.; Leeds Coll. of Food Technol. Chef: Simpson's, Strand, 1963–65; Savoy Grill, 1965–68; Beau Rivage Palace, Lausanne, 1969; Claridge's, London, 1970–71; Capital Hotel/Restaurant, London, 1971–86; Turner's Restaurant, London, 1986–2001; Brian Turner's Restaurant, Crowne Plaza Hotel, NEC Birmingham, 2001–05; Turner's Grill, Slough, 2006–08; Turner's Grill, Birmingham, 2006–08; Chef/Patron, Brian Turner Mayfair, 2003–08; Dir, Foxtrot Oscar, 2001–03. *Television* includes: This Morning, 1992–2000 and 2003–; Food and Drink, 1992–2000; Ready Steady Cook, 1992–; Great Food Live, 2003–; Saturday Kitchen, 2005–; Saturday Cooks, 2006–; Daily Cooks, 2007–; A Taste of Britain, 2014. Member: Royal Acad. (formerly Acad.) of Culinary Arts, 1987– (Chm., 1993–2004; Pres., 2004–); Hospitality Skills, 2001–; UK Skills, 2002–; Prince's Trust, 2002–; Les Disciples D'Auguste Escoffier, 2010–. Honorary Professor: Thames Valley Univ., 2001; Univ. Coll. Birmingham, 2017. FCGI 2005; FRSA 2006. Hon. DSc Leeds Metropolitan, 2006; DUniv Sheffield Hallam, 2008. Chef of Year Award, 1997; Special Award, 2004, Caterer and Hotelkeeper; Special Award, Craft Guild of Chefs, 1997; Wedgwood Award, 1997; Nestlé Toque d'Or, 2003; Ambassadorial Award, Yorks Life Food and Drink Awards, 2004; Special Award, Springboard Awards for Excellence, 2004; Lifetime Achievement Award, Yorks TV Awards, 2005; British Hospitality Assoc. Award, 2006; Award for Outstanding Contrib. to British Food Industry, Nat. Assoc. of Catering Butchers, 2007; Hon. Apprenticeship Award, Apprenticeship Ambassadors Network, 2009; Yorkshire Powerhouse Business Award, 2016. *Publications:* Campaign for Great British Food, 1990;

Sunday Best, 1995; Out to Lunch, 2 vols, 1996 and 1997; (with A. Worrall Thompson) Ready Steady Cook, Book 1, 1997; The Big Ready Steady Cookbook, 1997; Grills and Barbecues, 1997; A Yorkshire Lad: my life with recipes, 2000; Brian Turner's Favourite British Recipes, 2003; Ready Steady Cook: the top 100 recipes, 2003; Great British Grub, 2009; A Taste of Summer, 2011. *Recreations:* sport, brass band music, opera, travel. *Address:* 212 Central Meat Market, Smithfield, EC1A 9LH. *T:* (020) 7248 1005. *E:* turnerrest@aol.com. *W:* www.brianturner.co.uk.

**TURNER, Prof. Bryan Michael,** PhD; FRS 2015; Professor of Experimental Genetics, University of Birmingham, 1996–2015, now Emeritus; *b* Dartford, 11 Feb. 1948; *s* of Alfred and Audrey Turner; *m* 1970, Virginia Lawrence; two *s*. *Educ:* Dartford Grammar Sch.; University Coll. London (BSc Biochem. 1969; PhD 1973). Asst Prof., Mt Sinai Sch. of Medicine, NY, 1973–78; MRC Scientist, NIMR, Mill Hill, 1978–81; Medical School, University of Birmingham: Lectr, 1981–88; Sen. Lectr, 1989–95; Reader, 1995–96. *Publications:* Chromatin and Gene Regulation, 2001; contribs to scientific jls. *Recreations:* theatre, music, gardening. *Address:* Institute of Cancer and Genomic Sciences, University of Birmingham, Vincent Drive, Edgbaston, Birmingham B15 2TT. *T:* (0121) 414 6824. *E:* b.m.turner@bham.ac.uk.

**TURNER, Prof. Bryan Stanley,** PhD, DLitt, LittD; Presidential Professor of Sociology, Graduate Center, City University of New York, 2010–17, now Emeritus Professor of Sociology (Director, Committee on Religion, 2010–18); Professor of Sociology, Australian Catholic University, since 2013; *b* 14 Jan. 1945; *s* of Stanley W. Turner and Sophia (*née* Brookes); *m* 2008, Nguyen Kim Hoa; one *d*. *Educ:* Univ. of Leeds (BA 1966; PhD 1970); Flinders Univ. (DLitt 1976); Univ. of Cambridge (MA 2002; LittD 2009). Lecturer: Univ. of Aberdeen, 1969–74; Univ. of Lancaster, 1974–78; Sen. Lectr, 1979–80, Reader, 1980–82, Univ. of Aberdeen; Prof. of Sociology, Univ. of Flinders, 1982–88; Prof. of Gen. Social Sci., Univ. of Utrecht, 1988–90; Professor of Sociology: Univ. of Essex, 1990–92; Deakin Univ., 1992–98; Cambridge Univ., 1998–2005; Fellow of Fitzwilliam Coll., Cambridge, 2002–05; Prof. of Sociology and Res. Leader, Asia Res. Inst., Nat. Univ. of Singapore, 2005–09; Prof. of Social and Political Thought, Univ. of Western Sydney, 2009; Alona Evans Dist. Vis. Prof. of Sociology, Newhouse Center for Humanities, Wellesley Coll., Mass, 2009–10. Hon. Prof. of Sociol., 2015–, Dir, Centre for Citizenship, Social Pluralism and Religious Diversity, 2016–, Univ. of Potsdam (Max Planck Res. Award, 2015); Dist. Hon. Fellow, Edward Cadbury Centre, Univ. of Birmingham, 2017–. FASSA 1988. Editor: (jtly) Body & Society, 1994–; Citizenship Studies, 1997–; (jtly) Jl of Classical Sociology, 2001–. *Publications:* Weber and Islam, 1974; For Weber, 1981; Religion and Social Theory, 1983; The Body and Society, 1984; Citizenship and Capitalism, 1986; Medical Power and Social Knowledge, 1987; Regulating Bodies, 1992; Orientalism, Postmodernism and Globalism, 1994; (ed) The Blackwell Companion to Social Theory, 1996; Classical Sociology, 1999; Islam: critical concepts in sociology, 2003; The New Medical Sociology, 2004; (ed jtly) International Handbook of Sociology, 2005; The Cambridge Dictionary of Sociology, 2006; Vulnerability and Human Rights, 2006; (ed with Patrick Baert) Pragmatism and European Social Theory, 2007; Rights and Virtues: political essays on citizenship and social justice, 2008; (ed) The Routledge International Handbook of Globalization Studies, 2010; (with Habibul Haque Khondker) Globalization East and West, 2010; Religion and Modern Society, 2011; (with Anthony Elliott) On Society, 2012; The Religious and the Political, 2013; (with Kamaludeen M. Nasr) The Future of Singapore, 2014; (with Oscar Salemink) The Routledge Handbook of Religions in Asia, 2015; (ed jtly) Religions, Nations and Transnationalism in Multiple Modernities, 2017; (Chief Ed.) Blackwell-Wiley Encyclopedia of Social Theory, 5 vols, 2018. *Recreations:* gardening, tourism, walking, collecting books. *Address:* Thomas More Law School, Australian Catholic University, 8–20 Napier Street, North Sydney, NSW 2060, Australia.

**TURNER, Dr Christian Philip Hollier,** CMG 2012; HM Diplomatic Service; High Commissioner to Pakistan, since 2019; *b* Crawley, 19 Aug. 1972; *s* of Andrew and Caroline Turner; *m* 2003, Claire Barber; one *s* one *d*. *Educ:* Marlborough Coll.; Univ. of Manchester (BA Hons English Lang. and Lit. 1994); Univ. of York (DPhil English and Related Lit. 1998). Tutor, Univ. of York, 1996–98; researcher, Videotext Communications, 1998; Cabinet Office: Sec. to Better Regulation Taskforce, 1998–99; Sec. to Econ. and Domestic Cttees of Cabinet, 1999–2000; Private Sec. to Minister of State, 2001–02; Dep. Team Leader, Prime Minister's Strategy Unit, 2002–03; First Sec., Washington, 2003–06; entered FCO, 2005; Private Sec. to Prime Minister, 2007; Dep. Dir, 2008–09, Dir, 2009–12, Middle East and N Africa, FCO; High Comr, Kenya, 2012–15; Dir, London Syria Conf., Cabinet Office, 2016; Dir Gen., Middle East and Africa, FCO, 2016–17; Prime Minister's Internat. Affairs Advr and Dep. Nat. Security Advr, Cabinet Office, 2017–19. Mem. Bd, FCO, 2016–. Trustee, Latitude Global Volunteering, 2009–12. *Recreations:* choral singing, walking, opera, family, medieval history. *Address:* c/o Foreign and Commonwealth Office, King Charles Street, SW1A 2AH.

**TURNER, Rev. Christopher Gilbert;** Minister with permission to officiate, Oxford Diocese, 2000–Jan. 2020; Headmaster, Stowe School, 1979–89; *b* 23 Dec. 1929; *s* of late Theodore F. Turner, QC; *m* 1961, Lucia, *d* of late Prof. S. R. K. Glanville (Provost of King's Coll., Cambridge); one *s* one *d* (and one *d* decd). *Educ:* Winchester Coll. (Schol.); New Coll., Oxford (Exhibnr, MA), Oxford Ministry Course. Asst Master, Radley Coll., 1952–61; Senior Classics Master, Charterhouse, 1961–68; Headmaster, Dean Close Sch., 1968–79. Schoolmaster Student at Christ Church, Oxford, 1967. Foundation Member of Council, Cheltenham Colleges of Educn, 1968. Mem., HMC Cttee, 1974–75, 1987–88; Chm., Common Entrance Cttee, 1976–80; Gov., Chipping Norton Sch., 1996–2006. Ordained deacon, 1992, priest, 1993. *Publications:* chapter on History, in Comparative Study of Greek and Latin Literature, 1969; chapter on Dean Close in the Seventies, in The First Hundred Years, 1986; (contrib.) Encounters, 2007. *Recreations:* music (violin-playing), reading, walking, different forms of manual labour; OUBC 1951. *Address:* Rosemullion, High Street, Great Rollright, near Chipping Norton, Oxon OX7 5RQ. *T:* (01608) 737359.

**TURNER, Dr Christopher John Bridgman;** Editor, Cabinet Magazine, since 2004; Keeper of Design, Architecture and Digital, Victoria and Albert Museum, since 2017; *b* Ascot, 10 Dec. 1972; *s* of Alan John Turner and Mary Frances Turner; two *d*. *Educ:* Eton Coll.; Peterhouse, Cambridge (Schol.; BA Double 1st Cl. 1995); Birkbeck, Univ. of London (PhD 2001). Res. Fellow, Central Cities Inst., Univ. of Westminster, 2001–03; Dramaturge on Stuff Happens, NT, 2003; Vis. Schol., Columbia Univ., 2003–04; Ed.-in-Chief, Modern Painters, 2007–09; Ed., Icon Mag., 2010–14; Dep. Dir, London Design Fest., 2015–17; Dir, 2015–17, Artistic Dir, 2017–18, London Design Biennale. Lectr, AA, 2015–16. Jerwood Prize, RSL, 2005. *Publications:* Adventures in the Orgasmatron: how the sexual revolution came to America, 2011; contribs to London Rev. of Books, TLS, Guardian, Tate Etc, Apollo, Architectural Record. *Recreations:* travel, architecture, flying, Norfolk. *Address:* 9 Aberdeen Mansions, Kenton Street, WC1N 1NL. *E:* drchristopherturner@gmail.com.

**TURNER, Colin Francis;** Senior District Judge (formerly Senior Registrar), Family Division of High Court, 1988–91, retired (Registrar, 1971–88); *b* 11 April 1930; *s* of Sidney F. and Charlotte C. Turner; *m* 1951, Josephine Alma Jones (*d* 2013); two *s* one *d*. *Educ:* Beckenham Grammar Sch.; King's Coll., London. LLB 1955. Entered Principal Probate Registry, 1949; District Probate Registrar, York, 1965–68. MBOU. Hon. Mem., London Nat. History Soc., 1998. *Publications:* (ed jtly) Rayden on Divorce, 9th, 11th, 12th and 13th edns, consulting editor to 14th edn; an editor of Supreme Court Practice, 1972–90; (jtly) Precedents in Matrimonial Causes and Ancillary Matters, 1985. *Recreations:* birding, fishing, entomology. *Address:* Lakers, Church Road, St Johns, Redhill, Surrey RH1 6QA. *T:* (01737) 761807.

**TURNER, Colin William;** Rector, Glasgow Academy, 1983–94; *b* 10 Dec. 1933; *s* of William and Joyce Turner; *m* 1958, Priscilla Mary Trickett; two *s* two *d*. *Educ:* Torquay Grammar Sch.; King's Coll., London (BSc; AKC). Edinburgh Academy: Asst Master, 1958–82; OC CCF, 1960–74; Head, Maths Dept, 1973–75; Housemaster, 1975–82. *Recreations:* mountaineering, gardening, local history. *Address:* Leat, Lowerdown, Bovey Tracey, Devon TQ13 9LF. *T:* (01626) 832266.

**TURNER, David Andrew;** QC 1991; a Recorder of the Crown Court, 1990–2019; *b* 6 March 1947; *s* of late James and Phyllis Turner; *m* 1978, Mary Christine Moffatt (*d* 2012); two *s* one *d*. *Educ:* King George V Sch., Southport; Queens' Coll., Cambridge (MA, LLM). Cambridge Footlights, 1967–69. Called to the Bar, Gray's Inn, 1971, Bencher, 2001; Asst Recorder, 1987–90; Panel Deemster, IOM, 2008–17. *Recreation:* music.

**TURNER, David George Patrick;** QC 2000; **His Honour Judge Turner;** a Circuit Judge, since 2004; Deputy Designated Family Judge for London, 2005–13; *b* 11 July 1954; *s* of George P. Turner and Elsie B. Turner (*née* McClure); *m* 1978, Jean Patricia Hewett; two *s*. *Educ:* Foyle Coll., Londonderry; King's Coll. London (LLB, AKC 1975). Called to the Bar, Gray's Inn, 1976, Bencher, 2015; in practice at the Bar, 1976–2004; Asst Recorder, 1997–2000; a Recorder, 2000–04; Head of Chambers, 2003–04. Judicial Member: Essex Courts Bd, 2004–07; Beds, Essex, Herts Courts Bd, 2007–09; Magistrates' Area Trng Cttee for London, 2006–13. Chancellor, dio. of Chester, 1998–; Dep. Chancellor, dio. of Liverpool, 2001–02, and of London, 2002–; Mem., Legal Adv. Commn, C of E, 2007–10; Chair of Tribunals under Clergy Discipline Measure, 2007–. Reader, 1981–; Churchwarden, 1983–2006, All Souls, Langham Place. Trustee: Langham Partnership, 1978–; London Lectures Trust, 1990–; Vice-Pres., Nature in Art Trust, 2010–. Mem., Patron's Circle, Sir John Soane's Mus., 2009–14. Pres., Foyle Coll. Former Pupils' Assoc., 2016–17. *Address:* c/o Crown Court, New Street, Chelmsford, Essex CM1 1EL.

**TURNER, David John;** Chairman, Wellhopped Ltd, since 2017; *b* 7 Feb. 1945; *s* of late Frederick and Sheila Margaret Turner; *m* 1991, Julia Anne Thompson; two *s* three *d*. FCA 1969. Cook & Co., Liverpool, 1963–67; Touche Ross & Co., London, 1967–69; Mgt Auditor, Mobil Oil Corp., 1969–71; Chief Accountant, Mobil Servs Ltd, 1971–73; Special Projects Co-ordinator, Mobil Europe Inc., 1973–74; Finance Director: Booker Agriculture, 1975–84; Booker McConnell Ltd, subseq. Booker plc, 1984–93; GKN plc, 1993–2001; Chief Financial Officer, 2001–03, CEO, 2003–07, Brambles Industries plc. Dep. Chm., 2007–08, Chm., 2008–10, Cobham plc; Chm., Commonwealth Bank of Australia, 2010–16 (non-exec. Dir, 2006–10); non-exec. Dir, Whitbread plc, 2001–06. Dir, O'Connell Street Associates Pty Ltd, 2007–16; Ind. Mem. Bd, Ashurst, 2013–. Dir, Great Barrier Reef Foundn, 2007–18. *Recreations:* tennis, fishing, ski-ing, opera. *Club:* Boodle's.

**TURNER, Prof. David Warren,** FRS 1973; Fellow of Balliol College, Oxford, 1967–94, now Emeritus Fellow; Professor of Electron Spectroscopy, Oxford, 1985–94, now Emeritus Professor; *b* 16 July 1927; *s* of Robert Cecil Turner and Constance Margaret (*née* Bonner); *m* 1954, Barbara Marion Fisher; one *s* one *d*. *Educ:* Westcliff High Sch.; Univ. of Exeter. MA, BSc, PhD, DIC. Lectr, Imperial Coll., 1958; Reader in Organic Chemistry, Imperial Coll., 1965; Oxford University: Lectr in Physical Chem., 1968; Reader in Physical Chemistry, 1978; Reader in Electron Spectroscopy, 1984. Lectures: Kahlbaum, Univ. of Basle, 1971; Van Geuns, Univ. of Amsterdam, 1974; Harkins, Chicago Univ., 1974; Kistiakowsky, Harvard, 1979; Liversidge, RSC, 1981–82. Tilden Medal, Chemical Soc., 1967; Harrison Howe Award, Amer. Chem. Soc., 1973. Hon. DTech, Royal Inst., Stockholm, 1971; Hon. DPhil Basle, 1980; Hon. DSc Exeter, 1999. *Publications:* Molecular Photoelectron Spectroscopy, 1970; contrib. Phil. Trans Royal Soc., Proc. Royal Soc., Jl Chem. Soc., etc. *Recreations:* music, gardening, tinkering with gadgets. *Address:* Balliol College, Oxford OX1 3BJ.

**TURNER, Prof. Denys Alan,** DPhil; Horace Tracy Pitkin Professor of Historical Theology, and Professor of Religious Studies, Yale University, 2005–14; *b* 5 Aug. 1942; *s* of Alan Turner and Barbara Turner (*née* Mason); two *s* one *d*; *m* 2015, Courtney Palmbush. *Educ:* Nat. Univ. of Ireland (BA 1962; MA 1965); St Edmund Hall, Oxford (DPhil 1975). Asst Lectr, 1967–74, Coll. Lectr, 1974–76, in Philosophy, UC, Dublin; Lectr, 1976–89, Sen. Lectr, 1989–95, in Philosophy of Religion, Dept of Theology and Religious Studies, Univ. of Bristol; H. G. Wood Prof. of Theology, Univ. of Birmingham, 1995–99; Norris Hulse Prof. of Divinity, Cambridge Univ., and Fellow of Peterhouse, Cambridge, 1999–2005 (Emeritus Fellow, 2005–). Hon. DLitt UCD, 2011; Hon. DHumLit Albertus Magnus Coll., 2014. *Publications:* Marxism and Christianity, 1983; Eros and Allegory: medieval exegesis of the Song of Songs, 1995; The Darkness of God: negativity in Christian mysticism, 1995; Faith Seeking, 2002; Faith, Reason and the Existence of God, 2004; Julian of Norwich, Theologian, 2011; Thomas Aquinas: a portrait, 2013; God, Mystery and Mystification, 2019. *Recreations:* mediaeval church architecture, classical music from Ockeghem to Mahler, gardens. *Address:* 48 Model Avenue, Hopewell, NJ 08525, USA.

**TURNER, Derek,** CBE 2003; FREng; consultant, since 2013; Director, Network Delivery and Development (formerly Traffic Operations, then Network Operations Director), 2005–13, and Deputy Chief Executive, Highways Agency, 2009–13; *b* 8 May 1953; *s* of Edgar and Maud Turner; *m* 1977, Maggy Sporne (marr. diss. 2005); one *d*, and one step *s*. *Educ:* Hinchley Wood Co. Secondary Sch.; Sheffield Univ. (BEng Hons). CEng 1979; FICE 1991; FCIHT (FIHT 1991); FCILT (FILT 1995); FREng 2005. Asst Engr, Herts CC, 1974–80; Professional Officer, GLC, 1980–82; Principal Engr, Hackney, 1982–85; Gp Planner, Islington, 1985–86; Dep. Bor. Engr, Wandsworth, 1986–90; Bor. Engr and Surveyor, Haringey, 1990–91; Traffic Dir for London, 1991–2000; Man. Dir, Street Mgt, Transport for London, 2000–03. Principal, Derek Turner Consultancy, 2003–05. Vis. Prof. of Civil and Envmtl Engrg, UCL, 2003–08, 2016–. Non-executive Director: Infocell Hldgs Ltd, 2003–05; EGS Ltd, 2007–08; Bd Dir, Colin Buchanan and Partners, 2004–05; Co-Chair, Highways UK Adv. Bd, 2015–19; non-exec. Chm., Zenzic UK Ltd (formerly Meridian Mobility Ltd), 2018–. Tech. Advr to Saudi Arabia Min. of Transport, UN, 2019. MCIM 1985; FRSA 1993. AA Award for Red Route 2000; European Transport Planner of Year, European Transport Cttee (ETC), 2003; Transport Planner of Year, Transportation Planning Soc., 2003. *Publications:* contribs to Jl ICE (Webb Prize 1997), Traffic Engrg and Control, Amer. Soc. of Civil Engrs. *Recreations:* classical music, walking, countryside, travel. *T:* 07920 096150. *E:* derek-turner@hotmail.co.uk.

**TURNER, Dr Desmond Stanley**; b 17 July 1939; s of Stanley and Elsie Turner; m 1st, 1966, Lynette Gwyn-Jones (marr. diss. 1987); one d; 2nd, 1997, Lynn Rogers. Educ: Luton Grammar Sch.; Imperial Coll., London (BSc); University Coll. London (MSc); PhD London; Brighton Univ. (PGCE). ARCS. Junior posts, Royal Free and St Mary's Hosps Schs of Medicine, 1963–67; Research Associate and Hon. Lectr, Guy's Hosp. Med. Sch., 1967–71; Research Fellow and Hon. Lecturer: Univ. of Surrey, 1971–76; Univ. of Sussex, 1974–78; Chm. and Man. Dir, Martlet Brewery, 1979–83; science teacher, 1984–95. MP (Lab) Brighton Kemptown, 1997–2010. R. D. Lawrence Meml Fellowship, British Diabetes Assoc., 1970–72. Publications: research papers and reviews. Recreations: sailing, fencing. Address: 49 Queen's Park Terrace, Brighton BN2 2YZ. T: (01273) 687732.

**TURNER, Geoffrey Howard**; Chief Executive, Securities Institute, 1997–2003; b 1945; s of Charles William Turner and Evelyn Doris; m 1975, Margaret Linda Donaldson; two d. Educ: King's Sch., Chester; St Edmund Hall, Oxford (BA, MA; Special Dip. Social Studies). With Simon & Coates, stockbrokers, 1968–70; British India Steam Navigation Co., 1970–73; Stock Exchange, 1973–90: Asst Manager, 1973–75, Manager, 1975–78, Membership Dept; Secretary: Wilson Evidence Cttee, 1978; Planning Cttee, 1977–78; Restrictive Practices Case Cttee, 1978–83; Head of Membership, 1983–86; Dir of Membership, 1986–90; Dir of Authorisation, Securities Assoc., 1986–92; Dir of Public Affairs, SFA, 1993–94; Chief Exec., Assoc. of Private Client Investment Managers and Stockbrokers, 1994–97. External Examr, London Guildhall Univ., 1996–2000. Mem. (C), St Albans DC, 2006–18. Mem., Harpenden Village Rotary Club. Hon. Alderman, City and Dist of St Albans, 2018. Recreations: visiting country churches, collecting prints and ephemera. Clubs: Vincent's (Oxford); Leander (Henley).

**TURNER, Rt Rev. Geoffrey Martin**; Bishop Suffragan of Stockport, 1994–2000; an Hon. Assistant Bishop, Diocese of Chester, since 2002; b 16 March 1934; s of Ernest Hugh Turner and Winifred Rose Turner (née Martin); m 1959, Gillian Chope; two s one d. Educ: Bideford Grammar Sch.; Sandhurst; Oak Hill Theol Coll. Commnd RA, 1954; 25 Field Regt, 1954–57; Trucial Oman Scouts, 1957–59; Jun. Leader Regt RA, 1959–60. Ordained deacon, 1963, priest, 1964; Assistant Curate: St Stephen, Tonbridge, 1963–66; St John, Heatherlands, dio. of Salisbury, 1966–69; Vicar: St Peter, Derby, 1969–73; Christ Church, Chadderton, dio. of Manchester, 1973–79; Rector of Bebington, 1979–93; Rural Dean, Wirral North, 1989–93; Hon. Canon, Chester Cathedral, 1989–93; Archdeacon of Chester, 1993–94. Recreations: sport, literature. Address: 18 Gracey Court, Woodland Road, Broadclyst, Exeter EX5 3GA. T: (01392) 465269.
See also M. Turner.

**TURNER, George**, PhD; b 9 Aug. 1940; s of late George and Jane Turner; m Lesley Duggan; two d, and one step s one step d. Educ: Laxton Grammar Sch.; Imperial Coll., London (BSc Hons); Gonville and Caius Coll., Cambridge (PhD Physics 1967). Formerly Lectr in electronic engrg, Univ. of E Anglia. Mem. (Lab) Norfolk CC, 1977–97. Contested (Lab) Norfolk NW, 1992; MP (Lab) Norfolk NW, 1997–2001; contested same seat, 2001. Founding Man. Dir, 2001–10, Chm., 2010–, Cranberry Commns Ltd (formerly Datasharp Telecom Ltd); Chm., Oxicoco Ltd, 2011–.

**TURNER, Prof. Grenville**, FRS 1980; Professor of Isotope Geochemistry, 1988–2002, Research Professor, 2002–12, Manchester University, now Professor Emeritus; b 1 Nov. 1936; o s of Arnold and Florence Turner, Todmorden, Yorks; m 1961, Kathleen, d of William and Joan Morris, Rochdale, Lancs; one s one d. Educ: Todmorden Grammar Sch.; St John's Coll., Cambridge (MA); Balliol Coll., Oxford (DPhil). Asst Prof., Univ. of Calif at Berkeley, 1962–64; Lectr, Sheffield Univ., 1964–74, Sen. Lectr, 1974–79, Reader, 1979–80, Prof. of Physics, 1980–88. Vis. Associate in Nuclear Geophysics, 1970–71, Vis. Associate in Geochem., 2013, Calif Inst. of Technol. Mem. Council, Royal Soc., 1990–92. Fellow: Meteoritical Soc., 1980 (Leonard Medal, 1999); American Geophysical Union, 1998; Geochemistry Fellow, Geochemical Soc. and European Assoc. of Geochemistry, 1996. Rumford Medal, Royal Soc. 1996; Urey Medal, Eur. Assoc. of Geochemistry, 2002; Gold Medal for Geophysics, RAS, 2004. Hon. Citizen, Todmorden, 2013. Publications: scientific papers on applications of isotope geochem. to understanding the evolution of the earth and solar system, and on earliest development of the widely used Ar-Ar dating method. Recreations: photography, walking, theatre. Address: 42 Edgehill Road, Sheffield S7 1SP. E: grenville.turner@manchester.ac.uk.

**TURNER, Harry Edward**; Chairman, Amcom Resources plc, 1995–2000; b 28 Feb. 1935; s of Harry Turner and Bessie Elizabeth Jay; m 1956, Carolyn Bird; one s one d. Educ: Sloane Grammar Sch., Chelsea. Served Middlesex Regt, Austria, 2nd Lieut, 1953–55. Sales Representative, Crosse & Blackwell Foods, 1955–56; Advertising Executive: Daily Herald, 1956–58; Kemsley Newspapers, 1958–60; Feature Writer and Advtsg Manager, TV International Magazine, 1960–62; Sales Dir, Westward Television, 1962–80; Dir of Marketing, 1980–85, Man. Dir, 1985–92, Television South West; Dir, ITN, 1987–92. Dir, Prince of Wales Trust, 1988–. FRSA 1986. Mem., Middx Regtl Assoc., 1955–. Mem., Solus Club, 1986–. Publications: The Man Who Could Hear Fishes Scream (short stories), 1978; The Gentle Art of Salesmanship, 1985; So You Want To Be a Sales Manager, 1987; Innocents in the Boardroom, 1991; The Venetian Chair, 1998; Poems of the Peninsular, 2001; Poems of Nelson's Navy, 2002; Wrapped in Whirlwinds, 2005; Growing Up in Fulham, 2005; Urban Legends, 2006; Zen and the Art of Gentle Retirement, 2009; Heaven's Anvil, 2010. Recreations: tennis, riding, ski-ing, literature, travel. Address: Old Boathouse View, 5 Admiral Stirling Court, Weybridge, Surrey KT13 8XX. T: (01932) 821465. Clubs: Garrick; Ackosando (NY).

**TURNER, James**; QC 1998; b 23 Nov. 1952; s of late James Gordon Melville Turner, GC and of Peggy Pamela Hare (née Masters); m 1979, Sheila Green (marr. diss. 2016); three s two d. Educ: Robertsbridge Co. Secondary Modern Sch.; Bexhill Grammar Sch.; Univ. of Hull (LLB Hons). Called to the Bar, Inner Temple, 1976, Bencher, 2006. Publications: (contrib. editor) Archbold: Criminal Pleading, Evidence and Practice, annually, 1992–2018. Recreations: eating, reading, cinema, soul music. Address: 1 King's Bench Walk, Temple, EC4Y 7DB. T: (020) 7936 1500, Fax: (020) 7936 1590. E: jturner@1kbw.co.uk.

**TURNER, James Edward**; Chief Executive, Sutton Trust, since 2019; b Kettering, 6 March 1978; s of Chris and Ann Turner; m 2004, Victoria Read; two s. Educ: Bishop Stopford Comprehensive Sch.; Churchill Coll., Cambridge (MA English 1999). Exec. Officer, Charity Commn, 2002–04; Sutton Trust: researcher, 2004–06; Policy Dir, 2007–09; Dir, Progs, 2010–15; Dep. CEO, Educn Endowment Foundn, 2015–19. Trustee: Brilliant Club; 2011–; Centre for Homelessness Impact, 2018–. Recreations: cricket, cooking, design, family. Address: Sutton Trust, Millbank Tower, SW1P 4QP.

**TURNER, Prof. James Johnson**, FRS 1992; Research Professor in Chemistry, University of Nottingham, 1995–97, now Emeritus (Professor of Inorganic Chemistry, 1979–95); b 24 Dec. 1935; s of Harry Turner and Evelyn Turner (née Johnson); m 1961, Joanna Margaret Gargett; two d. Educ: Darwen Grammar Sch.; King's Coll., Cambridge (MA, PhD 1960; ScD 1985). CChem; FRSC. Research Fellow, King's Coll., Cambridge, 1960; Harkness Fellow, Univ. of Calif, Berkeley, 1961–63; University of Cambridge: Univ. Demonstrator, 1963–68; Univ. Lectr, 1968–71; College Lectr, 1963–71, Admissions Tutor, 1967–71, King's Coll.; Prof. and Head of Dept of Inorganic Chemistry, Univ. of Newcastle upon Tyne, 1972–78; Nottingham University: Hd of Chem. Dept, 1982–85, 1991–93; Pro-Vice-Chancellor, 1986–90. Science and Engineering Research Council (formerly SRC): Mem., 1974–77, Chm., 1979–82, Chemistry Cttee; Mem., Science Bd, 1979–86; Mem. Council, 1982–86. Royal Society of Chemistry: Mem., 1974–77, Vice-Pres., 1982–84 and 1991–93, Pres., 1993–95, Dalton Council; Tilden Lectr, 1978; Liversidge Lectr, 1991; Mem. Council, Royal Soc., 1997–99. Publications: papers mainly in jls of Chem. Soc. and Amer. Chem. Soc. Recreations: walking, music, theatre. Address: 7 Hallams Lane, Chilwell, Nottingham NG9 5FH. T: 07535 560334.

**TURNER, James Michael**; QC 2013; b London, 28 Sept. 1967; s of Sir Michael John Turner and of (Frances) Deborah Turner; m 1994, Franca Edelaar; three s one d. Educ: Radley Coll.; Univ. of Durham (BA Law); Tübingen Univ. (LLM). Called to the Bar, Inner Temple, 1990; in practice as a barrister, specialising in internat. commercial and shipping law, 1992–. Publications: (with Sarah Derrington) Law and Practice of Admiralty Matters, 2007. Recreations: photography, wine, music.

**TURNER, Janet Mary, (Mrs Paul Griffin)**; QC 1996; barrister; Co-founder and Director, Minerva Smart Cities Ltd, since 2016; b 16 Nov. 1957; d of Cecil Sidney Turner and Gwendoline Joyce Turner (née Loseby); m 1983, Paul Griffin; one s one d. Educ: Wycombe Abbey Sch.; Bristol Univ. (LLB 1st cl. Hons). Called to the Bar, Middle Temple, 1979 (Harmsworth Schol.); practising in field of commercial litigation, 1979–2000; legal consultant, 2000–07; partner (charities and not for profit), Taylor Vinters, 2007–12; Hd, Not for Profit Solutions, Berwin Leighton Paisner LLP, 2012–16. Member: London Common Law and Commercial Bar Assoc., 1986–99 (Sec., 1990–97); Commercial Bar Assoc., 1989–99; Charity Law Assoc., 2007–. Non-exec. Dir, Norwich and Peterborough Building Soc., 2007–11. Trustee: Wothorpe Towers Preservation Trust, 2005–; Cambridge Union Soc., 2010–17. Recreations: heritage conservation, food and wine, collecting ephemera, landscape gardening. E: jmtqc@btconnect.com.

**TURNER, Jean McGiven**; Executive Director, Scotland Patients Association, 2007–14; b Glasgow, 1939. Educ: Hillhead High Sch., Glasgow; Aberdeen Univ. (MB ChB 1965; DA 1970). Anaesthetist: Aberdeen Royal Infirmary; Southern Gen. Hosp., Glasgow; GP, Springburn, Glasgow, 1975–2000. Vocational Studies Tutor (pt-time) on gen. practice, Glasgow Univ., 1999–2003. MSP (Ind) Strathkelvin and Bearsden, 2003–07; contested same seat, 2007. Mem., Health Cttee, Scottish Parlt, 2003–07.

**TURNER, John**, CB 1999; Under Secretary, Department for Education and Employment (formerly Department of Employment), 1988–99; Member, Civil Service Appeal Board, 2000; b 22 April 1946; s of late William Cecil Turner and Hilda Margaret Turner; m 1971, Susan Georgina Kennedy; two s one d. Educ: Ramsey Abbey Grammar Sch.; Northwood Hills Grammar Sch. Entered Civil Service, 1967; Principal, DoI, 1979; MSC, 1981–84; Asst Sec., Dept of Employment, 1985; Prin. Pvte Sec. to Rt Hon. Lord Young of Graffham and Rt Hon. Norman Fowler, 1986–87; Small Firms and Tourism Div., Dept of Employment, 1989; Dep. Chief Exec., Employment Service, 1989–94; Govt Regl Dir for Eastern Reg., 1994–96; Dir of Jobcentre Services, Employment Service, 1997–99. Trustee, Rathbone Trng, 2001. Non-exec. Dir, Sheffield Children's NHS Trust, 2002–12. Recreations: music, reading, the outdoors.

**TURNER, Rt Hon. John Napier**; PC (Can.) 1965; CC (Can.) 1995; QC (Can.); Leader of the Liberal Party of Canada, and Leader of the Opposition, 1984–90; Partner, Miller Thomson, Toronto, 1990–2013; b 7 June 1929; s of Leonard Turner and Phyllis Turner (née Gregory); m 1963, Geills McCrae Kilgour; three s one d. Educ: Normal Model Public Sch., Ottawa, Ont.; Ashbury Coll., 1939–42; St Patrick's Coll., 1942–45; Univ. of BC (BA Hons Pol Sci. 1949); Oxford Univ. (Rhodes Scholar; BA Juris. 1951; BCL 1952; MA 1957). Joined Stikeman, Elliott, Tamaki, Mercier & Turner, Montreal, Quebec; practised with them after being called to English Bar, 1953, Bar of Quebec, 1954 and Bar of Ont., 1968; QC (Ont and Que) 1968; with McMillan Binch, Toronto, 1976–84. MP for Montreal-St Lawrence-St Georges, 1962–68, Ottawa-Carleton, 1968–76, Vancouver Quadra, 1984–93; Parly Sec. to Minister of Northern Affairs and Nat. Resources, 1963–65; Minister without Portfolio, Dec. 1965–April 1967; Registrar-Gen. of Canada, April 1967–Jan. 1968; Minister of Consumer and Corporate Affairs, Dec. 1967–July 1968; Solicitor-Gen., April–July 1968; Minister of Justice and Attorney-Gen. of Canada, July 1968–Jan. 1972; Minister of Finance, Jan. 1972–Sept. 1975; resigned as MP, Feb. 1976; Prime Minister of Canada, June–Sept. 1984. Barbados Bar, 1969; Yukon and Northwest Territories, 1969; Trinidad Bar, 1969; British Columbia, 1969. Hon. LLD: Univ. of New Brunswick, 1968; York Univ., Toronto, 1969; Univ. of Toronto, 1996; Hon. DCL Mt Allison Univ., NB, 1980. Publications: Senate of Canada, 1961; Politics of Purpose, 1968. Recreations: tennis, canoeing, ski-ing; Canadian Track Field Champion 1948, Mem. English Track and Field Team. Address: 59 Oriole Road, Toronto, ON M4V 2E9, Canada.

**TURNER, Prof. (John) Stewart**, FAA 1979; FRS 1982; Foundation Professor of Geophysical Fluid Dynamics, Australian National University, 1975–95, now Emeritus; b Sydney, Aust, 11 Jan. 1930; s of Ivan Stewart Turner and Enid Florence (née Payne); m 1959, Sheila Lloyd Jones; two s one d. Educ: North Sydney Boys' High Sch.; Wesley Coll., Univ. of Sydney (BSc, MSc); Trinity Coll., Univ. of Cambridge (PhD). FInstP 1969. Research Officer, CSIRO cloud physics group, 1953–54 and 1960–61; 1851 Exhibition Overseas Schol., 1954–57; postdoctoral research post, Univ. of Manchester, 1958–59; Rossby Fellow, then Associate Scientist, Woods Hole Oceanographic Instn, 1962–66; Asst Director of Research, then Reader, Dept of Applied Mathematics and Theoretical Physics, Univ. of Cambridge, 1966–75; Fellow of Darwin Coll., Cambridge, 1974; Overseas Fellow, Churchill Coll., Cambridge, 1985; Fairchild Scholar, CIT, 1993. Matthew Flinders Lectr, Aust. Acad. of Science, 1990. Member, Australian Marine Sciences and Technologies Adv. Cttee (AMSTAC), 1979–84. Associate Editor, Journal of Fluid Mechanics, 1975–95; Mem. Editorial Adv. Board, Deep-Sea Research, 1974–84. Publications: Buoyancy Effects in Fluids, 1973, paperback 1979; papers in various scientific jls. Recreations: reading, photography.

**TURNER, Jonathan Richard**; QC 2006; a Deputy High Court Judge, since 2017; b 13 Sept. 1963; s of Norman Asher Turner and Annette Suzanne Turner; m 1991; one s three d. Educ: Trinity Coll., Cambridge (BA 1986). Harvard Law Sch. (LLM 1987); Inns of Court Sch. of Law. Called to the Bar, Middle Temple, 1988, Bencher, 2018; Mem., NY Bar, 1988; in practice, 1988–, specialising in competition, European, public and admin., envmtl, and commercial law. Standing Counsel, OFT, 1997–2006; Crown A Panel of Treasury Counsel, 2001–06. Publications: (contrib.) Bellamy & Child Common Market Law of Competition, 3rd edn 1987, 4th edn 1993, 7th edn as Bellamy & Child, European Union Law of Competition, 2013, (consultant ed) Supplement to 7th edn, 2014, rev. edn 2015. Recreations: squash, literature, social and political theory, family. Address: Monckton Chambers, 1 Raymond Buildings, Gray's Inn, WC1R 5NR. T: (020) 7405 7211, Fax: (020) 7405 2084. E: jturner@monckton.com.

**TURNER, Karl**; MP (Lab) Kingston upon Hull East, since 2010; *b* East Hull, 15 April 1971; *s* of Ken Turner and Pat Turner. *Educ:* Bransholme High Sch.; Hull Coll.; Hull Univ. YTS, Hull CC; self-employed antiques dealer; called to the Bar, Middle Temple, 2005; in practice as a barrister, Max Gold Partnership, Hull, 2005–09, Wilberforce Chambers, Hull, 2009–. An Opposition Asst Whip, 2013–15; Shadow Solicitor-Gen., 2014–16; Shadow Minister for Justice, 2015–16; Shadow Attorney Gen., 2016; an Opposition Whip, 2016–17; Shadow Minister for Transport, 2017. *Address:* House of Commons, SW1A 0AA.

**TURNER, Kerry**; *see* Turner, R. K.

**TURNER, Leigh**; *see* Turner, R. L.

**TURNER, Mark**; Head of School, St Michaels University School, Victoria, BC, since 2018; *b* Hampstead, 19 Sept. 1961; *s* of Rt Rev. Geoffrey Martin Turner, *qv*; *m* 1987, Elizabeth Jane Gugan; two *s*. *Educ:* Rossall Sch.; Mansfield Coll., Oxford (BA 1984); RMA Sandhurst; Hughes Hall, Cambridge (PGCE 1987). Short service commn RA, 1984–87. Asst Master, 1988–89, Hd of Dept, 1989–90, Housemaster, Laxton House, 1990–95, Oundle Sch.; Headmaster: Kelly Coll., Tavistock, 1995–2001; Abingdon Sch., 2002–10; Shrewsbury Sch., 2010–18. Inspector, ISI, 1997–2018. Governor: Packwood Haugh Sch., 2010–18; Abberley Hall Sch., 2010–18; Prestfelde Sch., 2010–18. *Recreations:* deer stalking, fly fishing. *Address:* St Michaels University School, 3400 Richmond Road, Victoria, BC V8P 4P5, Canada. *Club:* East India.

**TURNER, Hon. Sir Mark (George)**, Kt 2013; **Hon. Mr Justice Turner**; a Judge of the High Court of Justice, Queen's Bench Division, since 2013; a Presiding Judge, Northern Circuit, 2013–17; *b* 27 Aug. 1959; *s* of Jeffrey Turner and Joyce Turner; *m* 1988, Caroline Sophia Bullock; three *d*. *Educ:* Sedbergh Sch.; Queen's Coll., Oxford (BA). Called to the Bar, Gray's Inn, 1981, Bencher, 2004; in practice as barrister, Northern Circuit, 1982–2013; Asst Recorder, 1997–2000; QC 1998; a Recorder, 2000–13; a Dep. High Ct Judge, 2007–13. Patron, New Beginnings charity for homeless children, 1999–. *Publications:* Occupational Rhinitis, 1998; Occupational Asthma, 1998; Occupational Stress, 2007. *Recreations:* quizzes, computers, classical music, history. *Address:* Royal Courts of Justice, Strand, WC2A 2LL. *T:* (020) 7947 6955.

**TURNER, Rev. Martin Hugh**; Supernumerary Methodist Minister, St Michael's Whaddon, Cheltenham, since 2015; *b* Loughton, Essex, 13 July 1948; *s* of Percy and Dorothy Turner; *m* 1976, Biddy Bazlinton; one *s* two *d*. *Educ:* Brentwood Coll. of Educn (Cert Ed); Wesley Coll., Bristol; West Hill, Birmingham (Postgrad. Cert. Youth and Community Work). Ordained Methodist Minister, 1978; Methodist Chaplain, Bradford Univ., and Asst Minister, Bradford Mission, 1977–80; Minister: St Andrew's Church and Community Centre, Halifax, 1980–86; St Albans Circuit, and Regl Chaplain, NCH, 1986–97; Superintendent Minister, Hemel Hempstead Circuit, and Methodist Chaplain, HM Prison Bovington (Mount Prison), 1997–2001; Superintendent Minister and Team Leader, Methodist Central Hall, Westminster, 2001–15; Chaplain, Methodist Parly Fellowship, 2001–15. Mem. College, Westminster Abbey, 2008–15. Member: Methodist Conference, 1982, 1984, 1988, 1990–91, 1993–2008, 2010–14; Methodist Council, 2000–06; Methodist Strategy and Resources Cttee, 2000–06. *Publications:* (contrib.) Digging for Treasure, 2009; (contrib.) As a Fire by Burning, 2013; contrib. to Scripture Union Bible notes. *Recreations:* antiques, fishing, gardening, West Ham Utd, Cheltenham Town FC, friends and family. *Address:* 22 Noverton Lane, Prestbury, Cheltenham GL52 5BB. *T:* (01242) 300761. *E:* revmartinturner@gmail.com.

**TURNER, Michael John**, CBE 1999; FRAeS; Chairman: Babcock International Group plc, 2008–19 (non-executive Director, 2008); GKN plc, 2012–18 (Senior Independent non-executive Director, 2009–12); *b* 5 Aug. 1948; *s* of Thomas Turner and Hilda Turner (*née* Pendlebury); *m* 1st, 1972, Rosalind Thomas (marr. diss.); two *s*; 2nd, 1985, Jean (*née* Crotty); two step *d*. *Educ:* Didsbury Tech. High Sch.; Manchester Poly. (BA). ACIS 1973; FRAeS 1991. With British Aerospace, subsequently BAE SYSTEMS, 1966–2008: undergrad. apprentice, Hawker Siddeley Aviation, Manchester, 1966; Contracts Manager (Mil.), 1978–80; Exec. Dir, Admin, 1981–84, Manchester Div.; Division Director and General Manager: Kingston and Dunsfold, 1984–86; Weybridge, Kingston and Dunsfold, 1986–87; Exec. Vice-Pres., Defence Mktg, 1988–92; Chm. and Man. Dir, Regl Aircraft, 1992–99; Main Bd Dir, 1994; Gp Man. Dir, 1997–98; Exec. Dir, 1998–99; Chief Operating Officer, 1999–2002; Chief Exec., 2002–08; Mem., Supervisory Bd, Airbus, 1998–2006. Chairman: Aerospace Innovation and Growth Team, DTI, 2005; Defence Industries Council, 2007–10; Jt Chm., Nat. Defence Industries Council, 2007–10. Non-executive Director: Lazard Ltd, 2006–; Barclays, 2018–19. President: SBAC, 1996–97; AeroSpace and Defence Industries Assoc. of Europe, 2003–04. Hon. DAdmin Manchester Metropolitan, 2006; Hon. DSc: Cranfield, 2007; Loughborough, 2007. *Recreations:* golf, cricket, Rugby, Manchester United.

**TURNER, Neil**; Chair, Wigan and Leigh Housing Company, 2011–17; non-executive Director, Wrightington, Wigan and Leigh Hospital Foundation Trust, 2010; *b* 16 Sept. 1945; *m* 1971, Susan Beatrice; one *s*. Quantity surveyor, AMEC Construction, 1963–92. Member (Lab): Wigan CBC, 1972–74; Wigan MBC, 1975–2000 (Chairman: Highways and Works Cttee, 1980–97; Best Value Rev. Panel, 1998–2000). MP (Lab) Wigan, Sept. 1999–2010. Sec., All Party Parly Gp on Rugby League, 2005–10; founder and Vice-Chair, All Pty Orthopaedic Alliance of MPs, 2004–10; Chair, SIGOMA Gp of MPs, 2005–10. Chairman: Public Services Cttee, AMA, 1995–97; Quality Panel, LGA, 1997–99. *Club:* Marsh Green Labour (Marsh Green, Wigan).

**TURNER, Neil**; *see* Turner, A. N.

**TURNER, Pamela Ann**; *see* Major, P. A.

**TURNER, Ven. (Peter) Robin**, CB 1999; DL; Hon. Canon of Southwell Minster, 2002–12, now Canon Emeritus; Chaplain to Sector Ministries, Diocese of Southwell and Nottingham, 2004–12; Hon. Canon Pastor, Southwell Minster, 2014–16; *b* 8 March 1942; *s* of late Ronald James Turner and Irene Bertha (*née* Stocker); *m* 1967, Elizabeth Mary Kennen; two *s*. *Educ:* Dulwich Coll.; King's Coll. London (AKC); St Luke's Coll., Exeter (PGCE); Open Univ. (BA); Westminster Coll., Oxford (MTh). Ordained deacon, 1966, priest, 1967; Asst Curate, Crediton, 1966–69; Chaplain, RAF: Locking, 1970; Waddington, 1971–72; Nicosia, 1972–74; Little Rissington, 1975–76; Coltishall, 1976–78; Chaplains' Sch., 1978–81; Religious Progs Advr, British Forces Broadcasting Service, Germany, 1981–84; Chaplain, RAF: Odiham, 1984–85; Gütersloh, 1985–88; RAF Coll. Cranwell, 1988–89; Assistant Chaplain-in-Chief: RAF, Germany, 1989–91; RAF Strike Command, 1991–93; QHC, 1991–98; Principal, RAF Chaplains' Sch., 1993–95; Chaplain-in-Chief and Archdeacon, RAF, 1995–98, now Archdeacon Emeritus; non-residentiary Canon, Lincoln, 1995–98; Chaplain: Dulwich Coll., 1998–2002; to Bp of Southwell, subseq. Bp of Southwell and Nottingham, 2002–07; Notts Fire and Rescue Service, 2008–17. Hon. Chaplain to the Queen, 1998–. Freeman, City of London, 2001; Liveryman, Musicians' Co., 2003–. President: Friends of St Clement Danes Ch (Central Ch of RAF), 2005–13; Notts, RBL, 2007–19; Alleyn Club, 2007–08. Trustee, Dulwich Estate, 2005–15; Chairman: St Boniface Trust, 2005–; Bereavement Trust, 2012–; Southwell Minster Choir Assoc., 2017–. FRSA 2000–18. DL Notts, 2007. OMLJ 2017. *Recreations:* choral singing, classical music, reading history and biography, armchair cricket, wine and its enjoyment. *Address:* 12 Chimes Meadow, Southwell, Notts NG25 0GB. *T:* (01636) 812250, 07890 633137. *E:* pr.turner@lineone.net. *Clubs:* Royal Air Force, Victory Services; Nottingham and Notts United Services.

**TURNER, Phil**; Member, 1971–2006, and Executive Member, Culture, 2005–06, Camden Borough Council; *b* 7 June 1939; *s* of William Morris Turner and Eileen Lascelles Turner; *m* 1st, 1963, Gillian Sharp (*d* 1988); one *s* two *d* (and one *s* decd); 2nd, 2007, Maureen Alcock; two step *s* (and one step *s* decd). *Educ:* Beckenham and Penge Grammar School for Boys; University Coll. London (BScEcon). National Coal Board, later British Coal: Management Trainee, 1961–63; Hd of Information, Purchasing and Stores, 1963–65; O & M Officer, 1965–66; Hd of Admin, R & D Dept, 1966–68; Hd of Manpower Planning, 1968–73; Staff Manager, Opencast Exec., 1973–78; Hd of Conditions of Service, 1978–80; Dep. Dir of Staff Pay and Conditions, 1980–86; Head of Employment Policy, 1986–89. Joined Labour Party, 1963; Chair, Hampstead Labour Party, 1968–70; Camden Borough Council, 1971–2006: Chair: Building Works and Services Cttee, 1978–80 and 1986–89; Staff and Management Services Cttee, 1990–93; Leisure Services Cttee, 1993–97, 1998–2001; Corporate Services Cttee, 1997–98; Exec. Mem., Leisure and Community Services, 2001–05; Leader of Council, 1982–86, Dep. Leader, 1992–93, 1994–95 and 2003–06. Member: Assoc. of London Authorities, 1983–86; Policy Cttee, AMA, 1984–86; Vice Chair, Assoc. of London Govt Arts and Leisure Cttee, 1995–2000; Chair: London Steering Gp, Euro '96, 1995–96; London Sport Bd, 1996–2000. Contested (Lab): Cities of London and Westminster South, Feb. and Oct. 1974; (Lab) Hampstead and Highgate, 1987. Board Member: Kingsgate Community Assoc., 2006–10; Winchester Project, 2006–15 (Chair, Bd of Trustees, 2009–15). Sec., Camden Co-op. Party, 2009–. Trustee: Community Assoc. of W Hampstead, 2016–18 (Chm. Trustees, 2018); Hampstead Community Centre, 2019–. *Recreations:* family, travelling, book collecting, contemplating the eternal verities, creative writing group, U3A. *Address:* 33 Minster Road, NW2 3SH. *T:* (020) 7692 0439.

**TURNER, Richard Keith**, OBE 2007; CEng, FCIHT; Chief Executive, Freight Transport Association, 2001–07; *b* 2 Oct. 1944; *s* of Richard Louis Turner and Queenie Kate Turner; *m* 1968, Jenny Georgina Whitehead; two *s* one *d*. *Educ:* E Barnet Grammar Sch.; Leeds Univ. (BSc Civil Engrg 1965); Bradford Univ. (MSc Traffic Engrg Planning 1972). CEng 1972. Grad. Engr, Herts CC, 1965–67; Sen. Engr, Leeds CC, 1967–73; Freight Transport Association: Highways and Traffic Advr, 1973–83; Dir of Planning, 1983–95; Dep. Dir Gen., 1995–2000. Member: Commn for Integrated Transport, 2004–10; Planning Cttee, London Thames Gateway Develt Corp., 2007–12. FCIHT (FIHT 1980); FCILT (FILT 1993); MICE 1972. *Publications:* numerous papers on transport planning and freight. *Recreations:* big DIY, cycling, swimming.

**TURNER, Richard Timmis**, CMG 2002; OBE 1978; FRAeS; Group Marketing Director, 1991–2002, Director, 1992–2002, Rolls-Royce plc; *b* 17 Aug. 1942; *s* of late Dr John Richard Timmis Turner and of Alison Elizabeth Turner; *m* 1982, Margaret Corbett; two *d*. *Educ:* Shrewsbury Sch.; Univ. of Manchester (BA Politics and Mod. Hist.). FRAeS 1993. Joined Rolls-Royce Ltd, 1965; Commercial Manager, NY, 1971–74; Mktg Exec., Civil Engines, 1977–88; Commercial Dir, Civil Engines, Rolls-Royce plc, 1988–89; Gp Mktg Dir, 1988–91, Dir, 1989–91, STC plc; rejoined Rolls-Royce plc, 1991. Non-executive Director: British Steel, 1994–99; Corus Gp plc, 1999–2004; Senior plc, 1996–2004. Member: BOTB, 1997–99; Bd, British Trade Internat., 1999–2003 (Chm., Business Adv. Panel, 1999–2003). Member: Council, SBAC, 1992–2002 (Pres., 1994–95); Ext. Affairs Bd, Royal Aeronautical Soc., 2006–13. Dep. UK Chm., Singapore British Business Council, 1996–2002; Mem., Indonesian British Business Council, 1997–2002. Mem. Adv. Council, British Expertise (formerly British Consultants and Contractors Bureau), 2001–14. Board Member: Nat. Campaign for Arts, 2006–13; Bath Fests, 2009–; Manning Camerata, 2013–. Trustee, Swordfish Heritage Trust (RN), 1998–2002. *Recreations:* music, opera, Rugby football. *Address:* 6 Widcombe Terrace, Bath BA2 6AJ. *T:* 07770 442333. *E:* Richardturner45@yahoo.co.uk. *Club:* Athenæum.

**TURNER, Robert Edward, (Ted)**; American broadcasting company executive; Chairman and President, Turner Broadcasting System Inc., 1970–96; Founder and Chairman, Turner Foundation Inc., since 1991; *b* 19 Nov. 1938; *s* of Robert Edward Turner and Florence Turner (*née* Rooney); *m* 1st, Judy Nye (marr. diss.); one *s* one *d*; 2nd, 1965, Jane Shirley Smith (marr. diss. 1988); one *s* two *d*; 3rd, 1991, Jane Fonda (marr. diss. 2001). *Educ:* Brown Univ. Gen. Manager, Turner Advertising, 1960–63; Pres. and Chief Exec. Officer, various Turner cos, 1963–70; founded Turner Enterprises, 1976; Dir, 1996–2006, Vice Chm., 1996–2003, Time Warner Inc., then AOL Time Warner, subseq. Time Warner; launched Ted's Montana Grill, 2002. Pres., Atlanta Braves, 1976–96; Chm. of Bd, Atlanta Hawks, 1977–96. Won America's Cup in yacht Courageous, 1977. Pres.'s Award, 1979, 1989, Ace Special Recognition Award, 1980, Nat. Cable TV Assoc.; Special Award, Edinburgh Internat. TV Fest., 1982; Lifetime Achievement Award, NY Internat. Film and TV Fest., 1984; Tree of Life Award, Jewish Nat. Fund, 1985. *Publications:* (jtly) The Racing Edge, 1979.

**TURNER, Prof. (Robert) Kerry**, CBE 2000; Professorial Research Fellow, since 2010, and Director, Centre for Social and Economic Research on Global Environment, since 2016, University of East Anglia, since 2010 (Professor of Environmental Sciences, 1991–2010); *b* 10 Aug. 1948; *s* of Ben Rees Turner and Eunice Ann Turner; *m* 1971, Merryl Noreen Eborne; one *s*. *Educ:* UC, Swansea (BSc Econs 1970); UC, Cardiff (Cert Ed 1971); Leicester Univ. (MA (Dist) 1972). Lectr in Econs, Coventry Poly., 1974–76; Sen. Res. Fellow, Dept of Econs, Leicester Univ., 1976; Lectr, 1977–88, Sen. Lectr, 1989–91, Sch. of Envmtl Scis, UEA. Chair, Foresight Panel on Natural Resources and the Envmt, OST/DTI, 1995–99; Co-Chair, UK Nat. Ecosystem Assessment, 2012–14; Member: Bd, NRA, 1991–96; Regl Envmtl Protection Agency Cttee (Anglian Reg.), Envmt Agency, 1996–2002; Chair: Broads Authy, 2003–08 (Mem., 1996–2008, Vice Chair, 1996–2000, Chair, 2000–02, Envmt Cttee; Chm., Standards Cttee, 2002–03); Broads Climate Partnership, 2008–. Hon. Prof., Univ. of Exeter, 2016. Ed.-in-Chief, Envmtl and Resource Econs Jl, 1999–2012; Jt Ed., Regl Envmtl Change Jl, 1999–2002. FRSA 1991. Hon. FCIWEM. Hon. DSc Hull, 2014. *Publications:* Household Waste: separate collection recycling, 1983; *jointly*: Economics of Planning, 1977; Environmental Planning and Management, 1983; Economics of Natural Resources and the Environment, 1990 (trans. Italian 1992, Spanish 1995); Elementary Environmental Economics, 1994; Blueprint III, 1993; *edited*: Sustainable Environmental Management: principles and practice, 1988, 2nd edn 1993; *edited jointly*: Bibliography of Environmental Economics, vols 1 and 2, 1976; Progress in Resource Management and Environmental Planning, vol. 2, 1980, vol. 3, 1981, vol. 4, 1983; Wetlands: market and intervention failure, 1991; Economic Incentives and Environmental Policy, 1994; Ecosystems and Nature, 1999; Perspectives on Integrated Coastal Zone Management, 1999; Economics of Coastal and Water Resources, 2000; Managing a Sea: the ecological economics of the Baltic Sea, 2000; Managing Wetlands: an ecological economics approach, 2003; Managing European Coasts: past, present and future, 2005; Valuing Ecosystem Services: the case of multifunctional wetlands, 2008; Coastal

Zones Ecosystem Services, 2015; Routledge Handbook of Ecosystem Services, 2016; over 300 contribs to books, articles in jls and reports. *Recreations:* outdoor environment, tennis. *Address:* School of Environmental Sciences, University of East Anglia, Norwich NR4 7TJ. *T:* (01603) 592551.

**TURNER, (Robert) Leigh,** CMG 2014; HM Diplomatic Service; Ambassador to Austria, and UK Permanent Representative to the United Nations, Vienna, since 2016; *b* 13 March 1958; *s* of late John Turner and of Susan Turner; *m* 1992, Pamela Ann Major, *qv*; one *s* one *d*. *Educ:* Downing Coll., Cambridge (BA Geog. 1979). Admin. Trainee, Freight Central Div., Dept of Transport, 1979; Asst to Regl Dir, Germany, PSA, 1980; HEO (Develt), Housing Policy, Pvte Rented Sector, DoE, 1981; IC2/IA3 Div., Supply Side Policy, HM Treasury, 1982; entered FCO, 1983; Second Sec., Vienna, 1984–87; FCO, 1987–92; First Sec., Moscow, 1992–95; FCO, 1995–98; Counsellor, EU and Econ., Bonn and Berlin, 1998–2002; special unpaid leave, 2002–06: writer, 2002–06; freelance journalist, FT, Boston Globe, Die Welt, Berliner Morgenpost, Philadelphia Inquirer, 2003–06; Dir, Overseas Territories, FCO, 2006–08; Ambassador to Ukraine, 2008–12; Consul Gen., Istanbul, and Dir-Gen. of Trade and Investment for Turkey, Ukraine, S Caucasus and Central Asia (formerly Dir of Trade for Turkey and Central Asia), 2012–16. *Recreations:* writing (novels and short stories), Lundy Island. *Address:* c/o Foreign and Commonwealth Office, King Charles Street, SW1A 2AH. *W:* http://blogs.fco.gov.uk/leighturner, www.twitter.com/LeighTurnerFCO, www.instagram.com/leighturnerFCO.

**TURNER, Robert Lockley,** FSA; Senior Master of the Supreme Court, Queen's Bench Division, and Queen's Remembrancer, 1996–2007; *b* 2 Sept. 1935; *s* of James Lockley Turner, OBE and Maud Beatrice Turner; *m* 1963, Jennifer Mary Leather; one *s* one *d*. *Educ:* Clifton Coll.; St Catharine's Coll., Cambridge (BA 1957, MA 1973). Called to the Bar, Gray's Inn, 1958, Bencher, 2000. Commnd Gloucestershire Regt (28th/61st), 1959 (2nd Lieut); transf. to Army Legal Services, 1960 (Captain); Major 1962; retd from Army, 1966 (GSM with clasp South Arabia, 1966). Practised at Common Law Bar in London and on Midland and Oxford Circuit, 1967–84; a Recorder of the Crown Court, 1981–84; Master of Supreme Court, QBD, 1984–96. Prescribed Officer for Election Petitions, 1996–2007. Advisor to Law Reform Commn, Malta, 1993–99. Assessor, Access to Justice Inquiry, 1994–96. Mem., Notarial Bd, 1999–2012. President: Inst. of Credit Mgt, 2003–10 (Hon. FCICM (Hon. FICM 1997)); High Court Enforcement Officers Assoc., 2007–10. Chm., Sherbert Foundn, 2008–15. Vis. Fellow, Inst. of Internat. Maritime Law, Malta, 1998–99; Visiting Professor: Univ. of Glos, 2007–; Univ. of Cambridge, 2011–. FSA 2018. Hon. Sen. Steward, Westminster Abbey, 2003–07 (Hon. Steward, 1985–2003); Churchwarden, St Matthew's, Midgham, 1990–94. Freeman, City of London, 1997; Liveryman: Scriveners' Co., 1999–2010; Goldsmiths' Co., 2007–. Warden, Hon. Co. of Glos, 2010–11. Trustee: Glos Regt, 2005–11; Soldiers of Gloster Mus., 2005–11. Chief Advisory Ed., Atkin's Court Forms, 1997–2009; Sen. Ed., Civil Procedure, 1999–2007. Hon. LLD West of England, 2006. *Publications:* (ed jtly) Supreme Court Practice, 1988–99; The Office of the Queen's Bench Master, 1990; (ed jtly) Chitty and Jacob, Queen's Bench Forms, 1992; (ed jtly) High Court Litigation Manual, 1992; Annual Practice, 1995; Ars Magistri, 1996; Queen's Bench Guide, 2000; Within the Permitted Variation, 2007; (jtly) Awards to Children and Protected Parties, 2007; Civil Procedure Rules 10 Years On, 2009; Recollections of a Remembrancer, 2010; Civil Justice, 2011; Improving Quality of Civil Justice, 2013; The English Notary: his place in history, 2013; Medieval Shields of Westminster Abbey, 2014; Of Pennies and the Pyx, 2016; Evidence in European Civil Procedure, 2016; The Circle in the Stone, 2017. *Recreation:* Drosselmeyer to grandchildren. *E:* robertturner1935@gmail.com. *Club:* Army and Navy.

**TURNER, Ven. Robin;** *see* Turner, Ven. P. R.

**TURNER, Stephen Edward;** HM Diplomatic Service, retired; Consul General, Auckland, and Director, Trade Development, New Zealand, 2002–05; *b* 25 March 1946; *s* of Leslie and Kathleen Turner; *m* 1966, Maureen Ann Dick; two *s* two *d*. *Educ:* John Ruskin Grammar Sch., Croydon. Entered FCO, 1963; served: Jakarta, 1968–72; Kuala Lumpur, 1972–75; FCO 1975–78; Malta, 1978–83; Jakarta, 1983–87; FCO, 1987–90; Consul, Seattle, 1990–95; Dep. Hd of Mission and Consul Gen., Hanoi, 1995–98; Dep. High Comr, Dhaka, 1998–2002. *Recreations:* entomology, ornithology, gardening, travel, the study of the life of Alfred Russel Wallace, hiking. *Address:* 38a Mar Tirreno, Tarifa E11380, Cadiz, Spain.

**TURNER, Stewart;** *see* Turner, J. S.

**TURNER, Ted;** *see* Turner, R. E.

**TURNER, Dr William;** Regional Medical Officer, Yorkshire Regional Health Authority, 1976–86, retired; *b* 23 Feb. 1927; *s* of Clarence and Mabel Turner; *m* 1950, Patricia Bramham Wilkinson; one *s* two *d*. *Educ:* Prince Henry's Grammar Sch., Otley, Yorks; Leeds Univ. MB, ChB; DPH, FFCM; LLB. House Officer, Leeds Gen. Infirmary, 1950–51; RAMC, 1951–53; Gen. Practitioner, 1953–55; Public Health Trng, 1955–60; Medical Officer of Health: Hyde, 1960–63; Huddersfield, 1963–67; Bradford, 1967–74; Area MO, Bradford, 1974–76. Member: Standing Med. Adv. Cttee, 1978–82; NHS Steering Gp on Health Services Inf., 1979–84. *Publications:* contrib. BMJ, Medical Officer. *Address:* Bentcliffe, 1 Premiere Park, Ilkley, West Yorks LS29 9RQ. *T:* (01943) 600114.

**TURNER LAING, Sophie Henrietta, (Mrs C. Comninos),** OBE 2018; Chief Executive Officer, Endemol Shine Group, since 2014; *b* 7 Sept. 1960; *d* of late Graham Turner Laing and of Gillian Vera Turner Laing (*see* G. V. Drummond); *m* 1987, Carlo Comninos; one *s* one *d*. *Educ:* Oakdene Sch., Bucks. Variety Club of GB, 1979–80; KM Campbell Pty Ltd, Australia, 1980–82; Sales Exec., 1982–85, Sales Dir, 1986–89, Henson Internat. TV; Jt Founder and Dep. Man. Dir, Hit Entertainment, 1989–95; Vice Pres., Broadcasting, Flextech TV, 1995–98; BBC: Controller, Programme Acquisition, 1998–2003; Acting Dir, Marketing and Communications, 2001; Acting Dir, BBC TV, 2002; British Sky Broadcasting Ltd: Dir, Film Channels and Acquisitions, 2003–04; Dep. Man. Dir, Sky Networks, 2004–07; Man. Dir, Content (formerly Entertainment, News and Broadcast Ops), 2007–14. Non-exec. Dir, Debenhams plc, 2009–15. Gov., Nat. Film and TV Sch., 2004–16. Mem., BAFTA, 2000– (Trustee, 2006–10; Vice Pres., TV, 2010–15); Trustee, Media Trust, 2010–14. *Recreations:* film, theatre, ski-ing.

**TURNER-WARWICK, Richard Trevor,** CBE 1991; MA, MSc, DM Oxon, MCh; Hon. DSc; FRCP, FRCS, FRCOG, Hon. FACS; Hon. FRACS; specialist in reconstruction and functional restoration of the urinary tract; Emeritus Surgeon and Urologist to the Middlesex Hospital (Senior Surgeon, 1969–90); Hon. Senior Lecturer, London University Institute of Urology, since 1962; Hon. Consultant Urologist, Royal Prince Alfred Hospital, Sydney, since 1980; Robert Luff Foundation Fellow in Reconstructive Surgery, 1990; *b* 21 Feb. 1925; *s* of W. Turner Warwick, FRCS; *m* 1950, Margaret Elizabeth Harvey Moore, (Prof. Dame Margaret Turner-Warwick, DBE) (*d* 2017); two *d*. *Educ:* Bedales School; Oriel Coll., Oxford; Middlesex Hosp. Medical School. Pres. OUBC, 1946; Mem. Univ. Boat Race Crew, Isis Head of River crew and Univ. Fours, 1946; Winner OU Silver Sculls, 1946; BSc thesis in neuroanatomy, 1946. Sen. Broderip Sch., Lyell Gold Medallist and Freeman Sch., Middx Hosp., 1949; surgical trng at Middx Hosp. and St Paul's Hosp., London, and Columbia Presbyterian Med. Centre, NY, 1959. Hunterian Prof. of RCS, 1957, 1976; Comyns Berkeley Travelling Fellowship to USA, 1959. British Assoc. of Urological Surgeons: Mem. Council, 1975–78 and 1982–92; Pres., 1988–90; Fellow, 1961; St Peter's Medal, 1978; Member: Council, Royal Coll. of Surgeons, 1980–92; RCOG, 1990–92; Internat. Soc. of Urology, 1966–; European Soc. of Urology; Soc. of Pelvic Surgeons, 1963; Founder Mem., 1969, Pres., 1985, Internat. Continence Soc.; Corresp. Member: Amer. Assoc. of Genito Urinary Surgeons, 1972 (Harry Spence Medal, 1998); American and Australasian Urological Assocs. Fellow UCL, 1992. Fellow: Assoc. of Surgeons of GB and Ireland, 1960; Australasian Soc. Urology, 1989; Hon. FRACS 1981; Hon. FACS 1997; Hon. FRSocMed 2003. Hon. DSc New York, 1985. Moynihan Prize of Assoc. of Surgeons, 1957; Victor Bonney Prize, RCOG, 1987; Valentine Medal, NY Acad. of Medicine, 1992. *Publications:* (with Christopher Chapple) Functional Reconstruction of the Female Genito-Urinary Tract, 2002; various articles in scientific jls, contributing to surgery, to develt of operative procedures for the reconstruction and restoration of function of the urinary tract, and to design of surgical instruments. *Recreations:* water, family, fishing, gardening. *Address:* Pynes House, 9 Silver Street, Thorverton, Exeter EX5 5LT. *T:* (01392) 861173, *Fax:* (01392) 860940. *Clubs:* Vincent's (Oxford); The Houghton (Stockbridge); Leander (Henley); Ottery St Mary Fly Fishers.

**TURNOCK, Graham,** PhD; Chief Executive, UK Space Agency, since 2017; *b* Aberdeen, 30 July 1968; *s* of David Turnock and Edith Marion Turnock; *m* 2002, Cheryl Smith. *Educ:* St Catharine's Coll., Cambridge (BA 1989; PhD 1993); Ecole Nationale d'Administration (Diplôme d'Admin Publique 1997). HM Treasury: fast stream trainee, 1992–97; Principal, European Communities Budget, 1997–99, Public Enterprise Partnerships, 1999–2002; Dir, British Energy Team, DTI, 2002–03; Dir, Gershon Efficiency Rev., Cabinet Office, 2003–04; Leader, Transport Team, HM Treasury, 2004–08; Dir, Programmes, DCMS, 2008–11; Chief Exec., Better Regulation Exec., BIS, then BEIS, 2011–17. Leader, triennial Rev. of UK Sport and Sport England, 2014–15. Trustee, YHA England and Wales, 2015–. *Publications:* papers on particle physics. *Recreations:* cycling, exploring France, wine. *Address:* UK Space Agency, Polaris House, North Star Avenue, Swindon, Wilts SN2 1SZ. *Club:* Finsbury Park Cycling.

**TURNOUR,** family name of **Earl Winterton**.

**TURNQUEST, Sir Orville (Alton),** GCMG 1995; QC (Bahamas) 1992; Governor-General of the Bahamas, 1995–2001; *b* 19 July 1929; *y s* of late Robert Turnquest and Gwendolyn Turnquest; *m* 1955, Edith Louise Thompson; one *s* two *d*. *Educ:* Govt High Sch.; Univ. of London (LLB). Articled 1947–53; called to Bahamas Bar, 1953; called to the Bar, Lincoln's Inn, 1960 (Hon. Bencher); Counsel and Attorney of Supreme Ct; Notary Public; private practice, 1953–92; stipendiary and circuit magistrate and coroner, 1959; law tutor and Mem., Exam. Bd, Bahamas Bar, 1965–92. Chancellor, Dio. of Nassau and Bahamas. Sec.-Gen., Progressive Liberal Party, 1960–62; MP South Central, Nassau, 1962–67, Montagu, 1982–94; Opposition Leader in Senate, 1972–79; Dep. Leader, Free Nat. Movement, 1987–94; Attorney-Gen., 1992–94; Minister of Justice, 1992–93, of Foreign Affairs, 1992–94; Dep. Prime Minister, 1993–94. Pres., Bahamas Bar Assoc.; Chm., Bahamas Bar Council, 1970–72. Pres., CPA, 1992–93. Chm., One Bahamas Foundn. Member: Anglican Central Educnl Authy; Nat. Cttee of United World Colls; Bd of Govs, St John's Coll. and St Anne's High Sch. Trustee, Governor-General's Youth Award (Bahamas), 2007–17. *Publications:* What Manner of Man is This?: the Duke of Windsor's years in the Bahamas, 2016. *Recreations:* swimming, music, reading. *Address:* Kalamalka, Skyline Drive, PO Box N–8181, Nassau, Bahamas.

**TUROK, Prof. Neil Geoffrey,** Hon. OC 2018; PhD; FRSC; Executive Director, 2008–18, now Director Emeritus, and Mike and Ophelia Lazaridis Niels Bohr Professor, since 2013, Perimeter Institute for Theoretical Physics, Canada; *b* 16 Nov. 1958; *s* of Benjamin and Mary Turok; *m* 1992, Corinne Francesca Squire; one *d*. *Educ:* Churchill Coll., Cambridge (BA); Imperial Coll., London (PhD). Postdoctoral Fellow, Univ. of California, Santa Barbara, 1983–85; Advanced Res. Fellow, 1985–87, Reader in Theoretical Physics, 1991–92, Imperial Coll.; Associate Scientist, Fermilab, Ill, 1987–88; Asst Prof., 1988–91, Associate Prof., 1992–95, David and Lucile Packard Fellow, 1992–97, Prof., 1995, Princeton Univ.; Prof. of Math. Physics, Univ. of Cambridge, 1996–2008. Founder, African Inst. for Mathematical Scis, 2003. James Clerk Maxwell Prize, Inst. of Physics, 1992. *Publications:* over 100 articles in Nuclear Physics B, Phys. Review, Phys. Review Letters, New Scientist, Scientific American. *Recreations:* jazz, nature, playing with Ruby. *Address:* Perimeter Institute for Theoretical Physics, 31 Caroline Street North, Waterloo, ON N2L 2Y5, Canada.

**TURRELL, David Geoffrey,** CBE 2009; Executive Headteacher, Sir Bernard Lovell School, 2009–14 (Headteacher, 1995–2009); *b* 6 Feb. 1951; *s* of Stuart Turrell and Catherine Turrell; *m* 2013, Jane Gardner; one *s* one *d*, and two step *d*. *Educ:* Univ. of London (BA, MA). Chair, Nat. Baccalaureate Trust. *Publications:* (contrib.) Developing Quality Schools, 1994. *Recreations:* walking, theatre, politics, travelling, family.

**TURTON, Eugenie Christine, (Genie),** CB 1996; *b* 19 Feb. 1946; *d* of late Arthur Turton and Georgina (*née* Fairhurst). *Educ:* Nottingham Girls' High Sch. (GPDST); Girton Coll., Cambridge (schol.; MA). Research student (G. C. Winter Warr Studentship), Univ. of Cambridge, 1967–70; joined CS as Asst Principal, MoT, later DoE, 1970; Private Sec. to Parly Under Sec. of State, 1973–74; Principal, 1974–80; Prin. Private Sec. to successive Secretaries of State for Transport, 1978–80; Asst Sec., 1980–86; seconded to Midland Bank International, 1981–82, and to Cabinet Office/MPO (Machinery of Govt Div.), 1982–85; Under Sec., DoE, 1986–91; Director: Heritage and Royal Estate (formerly Ancient Monuments and Historic Bldgs), 1987–90; Inner Cities, 1990–91; Dep. Sec., DoE, 1991–94; Dir, Citizen's Charter Unit, Cabinet Office, 1994–97; Dir, Govt Office for London, 1997–2000; a Director General: DETR, then DTLR, 2000–02; ODPM, 2002–04. Non-executive Director: Woolwich Building Soc., 1987–91; Wates Gp, 2004–13; Rockpools Ltd, 2005–; Cognatum Trust, 2011–13; Member, Board: Genesis Housing Gp, 2009–18; Optivo Housing, 2018–; Associate, Critical Eye, 2009–. Advr to Min. of Public Admin, Govt of Trinidad and Tobago, 2010–16. Mem., Adv. Council, Radioactive Waste Mgt, 2018–. Trustee: Pilgrim Trust, 1991–2008; Horniman Mus., 2002–12; Dulwich Picture Gall., 2004–15; AA Motoring Trust, 2005–07; Sir Edward Heath Charitable Foundn, 2007–17; Wessex Archaeology, 2008–17 (Chm., 2013–17). Mem. Council, City Univ., 2000–04. Lay Canon and Mem. Chapter, Salisbury Cath., 2007–19, now Canon Emeritus. *Recreations:* books, music, painting, gardening. *Club:* Athenæum.

**TURVEY, Garry,** CBE 1991; Director-General, Freight Transport Association, 1984–93; *b* 11 Oct. 1934; *s* of Henry Oxley Turvey and Annie Maud Braley; *m* 1960, Hilary Margaret Saines; three *s*. *Educ:* Morecambe Grammar School. FCIS. Metropolitan Vickers Ltd, Manchester, 1956–58; AEI Manchester Ltd, 1958–60; Asst Sec., 1960–67, Sec., 1967–69, Traders' Road Transport Assoc.; Sec., 1969–84 and Dep. Dir-Gen., 1974–84, Freight Transport Assoc. Freeman, City of London, 1994; Liveryman, Carmen's Co., 1994. *Recreations:* cricket, fly-fishing, gardening. *Address:* 139 Imberhorne Lane, East Grinstead, West Sussex RH19 1RP. *T:* (01342) 325829. *Club:* MCC.

**TUSA, Sir John,** Kt 2003; Managing Director, Barbican Centre, 1995–2007; Chair, Clore Leadership Foundation, 2009–14; b 2 March 1936; s of late John Tusa, OBE and Lydia Sklenarova; m 1960, Ann Hilary Dowson; two s. Educ: Trinity Coll., Cambridge (BA 1st Cl. Hons History). BBC general trainee, 1960; Producer, BBC External Services, 1962; freelance radio journalist, 1965; Presenter: BBC Radio 4 The World Tonight, 1968; BBC2 Newsnight, 1979–86; Man. Dir, World Service, BBC, 1986–92; Presenter, One O'Clock News, BBC TV, 1993–95. Chm., London News Radio, 1993–94. Pres., Wolfson Coll., Cambridge, 1993. Chairman: Adv. Cttee, Govt Art Collection, 1993–2003; BBC Marshall Plan of the Mind Trust, 1992–99; Wigmore Hall Trust, 1999–2011 (Trustee, 1993–95); Dep. Chm. Trustees, BM, 2004–09 (Trustee, 2000–04); Member: Council, RIIA, 1984–90, 1991–95; Board, Public Radio Internat. (formerly American Public Radio), 1990–99; Adv. Cttee, London Internat. String Quartet Competition, 1991–2009 (Vice-Chm. of Board, 1995–2009); Board, ENO, 1996–2003; British Architecture Trust Bd, 2014–17; Trustee: Nat. Portrait Gall., 1988–2000; Thomson Foundn, 1992–95; Design Mus. Trust, 1999–2000; Somerset House Trust, 2004–06; Turquoise Mountain Trust, 2006–; New Deal of the Mind, 2009–12; EU Youth Orch., 2014–; Royal Fine Art Commn, 2015–; Hon. Chm., www.theartsdesk.com, 2009–13. Chm. of Govs, Univ. of the Arts, London, 2007–13. Hon. FRIBA 2001; Hon. RAM 1999; Hon. GSMD 1999; Hon. Mem., ISM, 2001; Hon. FRA, 2011. Hon. LLD London, 1993; DUniv Heriot-Watt, 1993; Hon. DLitt City, 1997; DU: Essex, 2006; Kingston, 2007; Kent, 2008; Hon. Dr Univ. of the Arts, London, 2014. TV Journalist of the Year, RTS 1983; Richard Dimbleby Award, BAFTA, 1984; BPG Award for outstanding contribn to radio, 1991; Presenter of the Year, RTS, 1995. Knight First Class, Order of the White Rose (Finland), 1998; Silver Medal, Order of Jan Masaryk (Czech Republic), 2018. Publications: Conversations with the World, 1990; A World in Your Ear, 1992; (with Ann Tusa) The Nuremberg Trial, 1983; The Berlin Blockade, 1988; Art Matters: reflecting on culture, 1999; On Creativity, 2003; The Janus Aspect: artists in the twenty first century, 2005; Engaged with the Arts: writings from the front line, 2007; Pain in the Arts, 2014; Making a Noise, 2018. Recreations: tennis, chamber music, listening, travel. Address: 16 Canonbury Place, N1 2NN. T: (020) 7704 2451.

**TUSHINGHAM, Rita;** actress; b 14 March 1942; d of John Tushingham; m 1962, Terence William Bicknell (marr. diss. 1976); two d; m 1981, Ousama Rawi (marr. diss. 1996). Educ: La Sagesse Convent, Liverpool. Student, Liverpool Playhouse, 1958–60. Associate, London Film Sch., 2011. Hon. Fellow, Liverpool John Moores Univ., 2009. BBC Personality of the Year, Variety Club of GB, 1988. Stage appearances: Royal Court Theatre: The Changeling, 1960; The Kitchen, 1961; A Midsummer Night's Dream, 1962; Twelfth Night, 1962; The Knack, 1962; other London theatres: The Giveaway, 1969; Lorna and Ted, 1970; Mistress of Novices, 1973; My Fat Friend, 1981; Children, Children, 1984; Vagina Monologues, 2003. Films: A Taste of Honey, 1961 (Brit. Film Acad. and Variety Club awards for Most Promising Newcomer, 1961; NY Critics, Cannes Film Festival and Hollywood Foreign Press Assoc. awards); The Leather Boys, 1962; A Place to Go, Girl with Green Eyes (Variety Club award), 1963; The Knack, 1964 (Silver Goddess award, Mexican Assoc. of Film Corresps); Dr Zhivago, 1965; The Trap, 1966; Smashing Time, Diamonds For Breakfast, 1967; The Guru, 1968; The Bed-Sitting Room, 1970; Straight on till Morning, 1972; Situation, 1972; Instant Coffee, 1973; Rachel's Man, 1974; The Human Factor, 1976; Pot Luck, State of Shock, 1977; Mysteries, 1978; Incredible Mrs Chadwick, 1979; The Spaghetti House Siege, 1982; Flying, 1984; A Judgement in Stone, Single Room, 1986; Resurrected, Dante and Beatrice in Liverpool, 1989; Hard Days' Hard Nights, 1990; Paper Marriage, Rapture of Deceit, 1991; Desert Lunch, 1992; An Awfully Big Adventure, 1994; The Boy from Mercury, 1995; Under The Skin, 1996; Swing, Out of Depth, 1998; Home Ground, 2000; Being Julia, 2003; Loneliness and the Modern Pentathlon, 2004; The Hideout, 2006; Puffball, Come Here Today, 2008; Telstar, Broken Lines, The Calling, 2009; One of the Things that makes me Doubt (film art installation), Seamonsters, 2011; Outside Bet, The Wee Man, 2012; My Name is Lenny, 2017. TV appearances include: Red Riding Hood (play), 1973; No Strings (own series), 1974; Don't Let Them Kill Me on Wednesday, 1980; Confessions of Felix Krull, 1980; Seeing Red, 1983; Pippi Longstocking, 1984; The White Whale—The Life of Ernest Hemingway (film), 1987; cameo appearance in Bread, 1988; Sunday Pursuit; Gütt, Ein Journalist, 1991; Hamburg Poison, 1992; Family Secrets (film), 1995; I Was Eddie Mostyn, 1995; Shadow Play, 2001; Margo beyond the Box, 2003; New Tricks, 2005; Miss Marple: The Sittaford Mystery, 2005; Angel Cake, 2006; Bedlam, 2011; In the Flesh, 2013–14; Patty and Chips with Scraps (BBC radio play), 1997; voiceover for documentary celebrating 50th anniversary of 'A Hard Day's Night', 2014; Neil Gaiman Likely Stories, 2016; Vera, 2018. Recreations: interior decorating, cooking, watercolour painting. Address: c/o Michele Milburn, Milburn Browning Associates, The Old Truman Brewery, 91 Brick Lane, E1 6QL.

**TUSK, Donald Franciszek;** President of the European Council, 2014–19; b Gdańsk, Poland, 22 April 1957; s of late Donald and Ewa Tusk; m Małgorzata; one s one d. Educ: Univ. of Gdańsk. Manual labourer, Świetlik co-operative; journalist, Maritime Publishing House; Dep. Ed., Gazeta Gdańska, 1989; Founder and Ed., Przegląd Polityczny. Mem., Solidarity Trade Union, 1980–89. Leader, 1989, Chair, 1991–94, Congress of Liberals, later Liberal-Democratic Congress; Vice-Chair, Freedom Union, 1994. MP (Freedom Union), 1991–93, 2001–14; Dep. Marshal of Sejm, 2001–05; Senator and Vice Marshal of Senate, 1997–2001; Leader of Opposition, 2001–07; Prime Minister of Poland, 2007–14. Co-Founder, 2001, Leader, 2003–14, Civic Platform. Publications: Kashubian Lake District, 1985; Once There Was Gdańsk, 1996; Gdańsk 1945, 1998; Old Sopot, 1998; Ideas of Gdańsk's Liberalism, 1998.

**TUSTIN, Rt Rev. Dr David;** Hon. Assistant Bishop of Lincoln, since 2001; Bishop Suffragan of Grimsby, 1979–2000; b 12 Jan. 1935; s of John Trevelyan Tustin and Janet Reynolds; m 1964, Mary Elizabeth (née Glover) (d 2014); one s one d. Educ: Solihull School; Magdalene Coll., Cambridge (MA Hons); Geneva Univ. (Cert. in Ecumenical Studies); Cuddesdon Coll., Oxford. Philip Usher Memorial Scholar (in Greece), 1957–58; deacon 1960, priest 1961; Curate of Stafford, 1960–63; Asst Gen. Sec., C of E Council on Foreign Relations and Curate of St Dunstan-in-the-West, Fleet St, 1963–67; Vicar of S Paul's, Wednesbury, 1967–71; Vicar of Tettenhall Regis, 1971–79; RD of Trysull, 1977–79. Canon and Prebendary of Lincoln Cathedral, 1979–2000. Co-Chm., Anglican/Lutheran Internat. Commn, 1986–98; Pres., Anglican/Lutheran Soc., 1986–99; Mem., Gen. Synod of C of E, 1990–2000 (Chm., Council for Christian Unity, 1993–98). Trustee, Mus. of Timekeeping (formerly British Horological Inst. Mus.), Upton Hall, 2015–. DD Lambeth 1998. Comdr, Royal Order of Polar Star (Sweden), 2000. Publications: A Bishop's Ministry: reflections and resources for church leadership, 2013. Recreations: music, family life, languages, travel, horology. Address: The Ashes, Tunnel Road, Wrawby, Brigg, N Lincs DN20 8SF.

**TUTT, Prof. Norman Sydney,** OBE 2002; Executive Director of Housing and Social Services, London Borough of Ealing, 2001–03 (Director of Social Services, 1999–2001); b 8 June 1944; s of Sydney Robert Tutt and Stella May Tutt; m 1966, Diana Patricia Hewitt; two s. Educ: Chislehurst and Sidcup Grammar Sch.; Univ. of Keele (BA); Univ. of Leeds (MSc); Univ. of Nottingham (PhD). Clin. Psychologist, Nottingham, 1966–69; Resident Psychologist, St Gilbert's Approved Sch., 1969–73; Professional Advr, Northampton Social Services, 1973–74; Sen. Develt Officer, London Boroughs Children Reg. Planning Cttee, 1974–75; Principal Social Work Services Officer, DHSS, 1975–79; Prof. of Applied Social Studies, 1979–92 (on leave of absence, 1989–92), and Hon. Prof., 1992–95, Lancaster Univ.; Dir of Social Services, Leeds CC, 1989–93; Exec. Dir, Social Information Systems, 1993–98. Man., Gulbenkian Commn on Violence to Children, 1995–96. Vis. Prof., Faculty of Community Health Scis, Univ. of Wales Inst. at Cardiff (formerly Cardiff Inst.), 1994–2000. Mem. Council, ASA, 1996–2002. Mem. Bd, Hanover Housing Assoc., 1996–99. Publications: Care or Custody, 1975; (ed) Violence, 1975; (ed) Alternative Strategies for Coping with Crime, 1978; (ed) A Way of Life for the Handicapped, 1983; Children in Custody, 1987; (ed) Children and Homicide, 1996; contributor to other pubns. Recreations: work, wine, walks, cracking jokes. Address: Chateau Milhau, 34620 Puisserguier, France. T: (4) 67893275. Clubs: as with Groucho Marx he would not join a club which would have him as a member.

**TUTTE, John Frederick;** Chairman, Redrow plc, since 2019 (Group Chief Executive, 2014–19); b Stetchworth, Cambs, 24 June 1956; s of Joe and Doreen Tutte; m 1978, Yvonne; two s. Educ: King's Coll. London (BSc Hons Civil Engrg). Chief Exec., Wilson Connolly plc, 1999–2001; Regl Chm., 2002–09, Gp Man. Dir, 2009–14, Redrow plc. Mem. Bd, Home Builders Fedn, 2015–. Chm., Homebuilding Skills Partnership, 2016–. Recreations: family, gardening, art. Address: Redrow plc, Redrow House, St David's Park, Ewloe, Flintshire CH5 3RX. T: (01244) 520044, 07713 507135. E: john.tutte@redrow.co.uk.

**TUTTLE, Hon. Robert Holmes;** Joint Managing Partner, Tuttle-Click Automotive Group, 1989–2005 and since 2009; b 1944; s of Holmes Tuttle; m Maria Denise Hummer; two d from former marr. Educ: Stanford Univ. (BA 1965); Univ. of Southern Calif (MBA 1968). Special Asst to President of USA, 1982–85, Dep. Asst, 1985–88, Asst, 1988–89; Dir, Presidential Personnel, 1985–89; Ambassador of USA to the Court of St James's, 2005–09. Director: Arizona Bank, 1989–99 (Chm., Exec. Cttee, 1994–98); City Nat. Corp., 2002–05, 2010–.

**TUTU, Most Rev. Desmond Mpilo,** Hon. CH 2015; Archbishop of Cape Town and Metropolitan of Southern Africa, 1986–96, now Archbishop Emeritus; Chair, Truth and Reconciliation Commission, 1995–99; Co-Founder, Desmond Tutu Peace Centre, 1998; b Klerksdorp, Transvaal, 7 Oct. 1931; s of Zachariah and Aletta Tutu; m 1955, Leah Nomalizo Shenxane; one s three d. Educ: Johannesburg Bantu High Sch.; Bantu Normal Coll., Pretoria (Higher Teachers' Dip. 1953); Univ. of S Africa (BA 1954); St Peter's Theol Coll., Johannesburg (LTh 1960); King's Coll. London (BD 1965, MTh 1966; FKC 1978). Schoolmaster: Madibane High Sch., Johannesburg, 1954; Munsieville High Sch., Krugersdorp, 1955–57. Theological coll. student, 1958–60; deacon 1960, priest 1961, St Mary's Cathedral, Johannesburg. Curate: St Alban's Church, Benoni, 1960–61; St Philip's Church, Alberton, 1961–62; St Alban's, Golders Green, London, 1962–65; St Mary's, Bletchingley, Surrey, 1965–66; Lecturer: Federal Theol Seminary, Alice, CP, 1967–69; Univ. of Botswana, Lesotho and Swaziland, Roma, Lesotho, 1970–72; Associate Dir, Theol Education Fund (WCC) based in Bromley, Kent, and Hon. Curate, St Augustine's, Grove Park, 1972–75; Dean of Johannesburg, 1975–76; Bishop of Lesotho, 1976–78; Gen. Sec., South African Council of Churches, 1978–85; Rector, St Augustine's Parish, Soweto, 1981–85; Bishop of Johannesburg, 1985–86. Woodruff Vis. Prof., Emory Univ., 1998–2000. Chancellor, Univ. of Western Cape, Cape Town, 1988–2010. Pres., All Africa Conference of Churches, 1987–97. Mem., The Elders. Trustee, Phelps Stoke Fund, New York. Holds over fifty hon. degrees from academic institutions in UK, Europe and USA. Athena Prize, Onassis Foundation, 1980; Nobel Peace Prize, 1984; Albert Schweitzer Humanitarian Award, Emmanuel Coll., Boston, 1988; Mo Ibrahim Foundn Award, 2012; Templeton Prize, Templeton Foundn, 2013. Order of Meritorious Service, Gold (S Africa), 1996; Order of Southern Cross (Brazil), 1987; Order of Merit of Brasilia (Brazil), 1987; Grand Cross of Merit (Germany), 1996; Presidential Medal of Freedom (USA), 2009; BGCStJ, 2017. Publications: Crying in the Wilderness, 1982; Hope and Suffering, 1983; The Words of Desmond Tutu, 1989; The Rainbow People of God, 1994; No Future Without Forgiveness, 1999; God Has a Dream: a vision of hope for our time, 2004; Made for Goodness: and why this makes all the difference, 2010; God Is Not a Christian: speaking truth in times of crisis, 2011; (with M. Tutu) The Book of Forgiving: the fourfold path for healing ourselves and our world, 2014; In God's Hands, 2014; (with Dalai Lama) The Book of Joy, 2016; articles and reviews. Recreations: music, reading, jogging.

**TUYMANS, Luc;** artist; b Belgium, 14 July 1958. Solo exhibitions worldwide, 1985–, including: David Zwirner, New York; Zeno X Gall., Antwerp; White Cube, London, 1999, 2001; Tokyo Opera Art Gall., 2000; Venice Biennale, 2001; Helsinki Kunsthalle, 2003; Pinakothek der Moderne, Munich, 2003; Tate Modern, 2004; Fundação de Serralves, 2006; Kunsthalle Budapest, 2007; Haus der Kunst, Munich, 2008; Wiels, Brussels, 2008; Wexner Center for the Arts, Ohio, 2008; Baibakov Art Projects, Moscow, 2009; Moderna Museet, Malmö, 2009; San Francisco Mus. of Modern Art, 2010; Dallas Mus. of Art, 2010; Mus. of Contemporary Art, Chicago, 2010; Paleis voor Schone Kunsten, Brussels, 2011; Kunsthalle Bremerhaven, 2012; Menil Collection, Houston, 2013; Qatar Museums Gall. Al Riwaq, Doha, 2015; Talbot Rice Gall., Edinburgh, 2015; Mus. aan de Stroom, Antwerp, 2016. Address: c/o Zeno X Gallery, Godtsstraat 15, 2140 Antwerp Borgerhout, Belgium. E: info@zeno-x.com.

**TVEIT, Rev. Dr Olav Fykse;** General Secretary, World Council of Churches, 2010–March 2020. Educ: Norwegian Sch. of Theol., Oslo (MTh 1986; Practicum 1987; DTh 2002). Army chaplain, Sessvollmoen (nat. service), 1987–88; parish priest, Haram, Møre dio., 1988–91; Consultant and Sen. Consultant for theol issues, Ch of Norway Council on Ecumenical and Internat. Relns, 1991–96; res. schol., Res. Council of Norway and Norwegian Sch. of Theol., 1996–2001; Church of Norway: Sec., Doctrinal Commn, 1999–2000; Sec., Commn on Church-State Relns, 2001–02; Gen. Sec., Council on Ecumenical and Internat. Relns, 2002–09. Moderator: Ecumenical Mt of Olive Foundn, Norway, 2002; Ch of Norway-Islamic Council of Norway contact gp, 2005–09; Ch of Norway-Jewish Congregation in Norway contact gp, 2005–09. Member: Bd of Dirs and Exec. Cttee, Christian Council of Norway, 2002–09; Exec. Cttee, Commn for Cooperation between parishes and missionary orgns, 2005–09; Inter-Faith Council of Norway, 2006–09; Faith and Order Plenary Commn, WCC, 2007–09; Mt of Olive Land Develt Cttee, Jerusalem, 2008–09; Mem., Bd of Trustees, Norwegian Ch Aid, 2007–09. Recreation: ski-ing. Address: World Council of Churches, PO Box 2100, 1211 Geneva 2, Switzerland. T: (22) 79162885, Fax: (22) 7916535. E: dcb@wcc-coe.org.

**TWEDDLE, Dr Dominic;** Director General, National Museum of the Royal Navy, since 2009; b Westow, N Yorks, 16 March 1954; s of Wilfrid and Pauline Mary Tweddle. Educ: Stowmarket Grammar Sch.; Univ. of Southampton (BA Hons Archaeol. and Hist. 1975); Emmanuel Coll., Cambridge; University Coll. London (PhD 1986). Res. Asst, BM, 1978–79; Asst Dir, York Archaeol Trust, 1979–95; Chief Executive Officer: Past Forward Ltd, 1995–2000; Continuum Gp, 2000–08. Hon. Fellow, Dept of Hist., Univ. of York, 1991–96; Hon. Lectr, 2004–08, Hon. Prof., 2008–18, Inst. of Archaeol., Univ. Coll. London; Hon. Prof., Univ. of Portsmouth, 2010–. Publications: Growing Up in Viking

Times, 1993; Corpus of Anglo Saxon Stone Sculpture IV: South-East England, 1995; (contrib.) The Archaeology of York. *Recreations:* travel, collecting art and antiques, gardening. *Address:* National Museum of the Royal Navy, Portsmouth Historic Dockyard, HM Naval Base PP66, Portsmouth PO1 3NH. *T:* (023) 9289 1370, ext. 2018. *E:* director-general@nmrn.org.uk. *Club:* Army and Navy.

**TWEEDALE, (John) Christopher;** Chief Executive, GEP Academies, since 2018; *b* Rochdale, 15 Dec. 1956; *s* of late Austen Tweedale and of Bernadette Tweedale; *m* 1985, Jacqueline Sullivan; two *s*. *Educ:* Bishop Henshaw High Sch., Rochdale; Univ. of Leicester (BSc Hons Geol. 1978; PGCE 1979); Keele Univ. (MBA 2000). Teacher: Cardinal Wiseman High Sch., Ealing, 1979–82; John F. Kennedy High Sch., Herts, 1982–86; Sen. Teacher, Therfield Sch., 1986–89; Dep. Principal, Okehampton Coll., 1989–96; Headteacher, John Masefield High Sch., Herefordshire, 1996–2004; Sen. Policy Advr, 2004–07, Dep. Dir, 14–19 Educn, 2007–09, DfES, later DCSF; Dir, Schs and Young People (formerly Children, Young People and School Effectiveness), Welsh Govt (formerly Welsh Assembly Govt), 2009–13; UK Dir, 2013, CEO and Schs Dir, 2014–16, CfBT Schs Trust; CEO, Aldridge Educn, 2016–18. FRSA. *Recreations:* golf, walking, music, arts, travel. *Address:* GEP Academies, Woodruff Avenue, Guildford, Surrey GU1 1XX. *E:* ctweedale@gepacademies.com. *Clubs:* Royal Over-Seas League; Ross-on-Wye Golf; Wormcatchers Golf Soc. (Glos).

**TWEEDDALE, 14th Marquis of,** *cr* 1694; **Charles David Montagu Hay;** Lord Hay of Yester, 1488; Earl of Tweeddale, 1646; Viscount Walden, Earl of Gifford, 1694; Baron Tweeddale (UK), 1881; Hereditary Chamberlain of Dunfermline; *b* 6 Aug. 1947; *yr* twin *s* of 12th Marquis of Tweeddale, GC and of Hon. Sonia Mary, *d* of 1st Viscount Ingleby, PC; *S* brother, 2005. *Educ:* Milton Abbey, Blandford, Dorset; Trinity Coll., Oxford. *Heir: b* (Lord) Alistair James Montagu Hay, DPhil, *b* 4 Nov. 1955; does not use courtesy title.

**TWEEDIE, Prof. Sir David (Philip),** Kt 1994; Chairman, International Valuation Standards Board, since 2012; President, Institute of Chartered Accountants of Scotland, 2012–13 (Senior Vice-President, 2011–12; Junior Vice-President, 2010–11); *b* 7 July 1944; *s* of Aidrian Ian Tweedie and Marie Patricia Tweedie (*née* Phillips); *m* 1970, Janice Christine Brown; two *s*. *Educ:* Grangemouth High Sch.; Edinburgh Univ. (BCom, PhD). CA 1972. Accountancy trng, Mann, Judd, Gordon (Glasgow), 1969–72; Edinburgh University: Lectr in Accounting, 1973–78; Associate Dean, Fac. of Social Scis, 1975–78; Technical Dir, Inst. of Chartered Accountants, Scotland, 1978–81; Nat. Res. Partner, KMG Thomson McLintock, 1982–87; Nat. Tech. Partner, KPMG Peat Marwick McLintock, 1987–90; Chairman: Accounting Standards Bd, 1990–2000; Internat. Accounting Standards Bd, 2000–11. Visiting Professor of Accounting: Univ. of Lancaster, 1978–88; Univ. of Bristol, 1988–2000; Edinburgh Univ., 1999–; Univ. of Strathclyde, 2017–. UK and Irish Representative: Internat. Auditing Practices Cttee, 1983–88; Internat. Accounting Standards Cttee, 1995–2000; Auditing Practices Committee, Consultative Committee of Accountancy Bodies: Mem., 1985–90; Vice-Chm., 1986–88; Chm., 1989–90. Institute of Chartered Accountants in England and Wales: Mem. Council, 1989–91; Mem., Financial Reporting Council, 1990–2000; Chm., Urgent Issues Task Force, 1990–2000. FRSE 2001. Hon. FIA 1999; Hon. FSIP 2004; Hon. FCCA 2005; Hon. CPA (Aust.) 2012. Freeman, City of London, 2014. Hon. DSc (Econ) Hull, 1993; Hon. LLD: Lancaster, 1993; Exeter, 1997; Dundee, 1998; Hon. DLitt Heriot-Watt, 1996; Hon. DBA: Napier, 1999; Oxford Brookes, 2004; Lincoln, 2012; Hon. DSc (SocSci) Edinburgh, 2001. Centenary Award, Chartered Accountants Founding Socs, 1997; CIMA Award, 1998; IFAC Internat. Gold Service Award, 2011; Accounting Hall of Fame, 2013. *Publications:* (with T. A. Lee) The Private Shareholder and the Corporate Report, 1977; Financial Reporting, Inflation and the Capital Maintenance Concept, 1979; (with T. A. Lee) The Institutional Investor and Financial Information, 1981; (with G. Whittington) The Debate on Inflation Accounting, 1984; contribs to professional and acad. accounting jls and books. *Recreations:* athletics and Rugby (watching, not participating, sadly), walking, gardening. *Address:* International Valuation Standards Council, 4 Lombard Street, EC3V 9AA.

**TWEEDSMUIR, 4th Baron** *cr* 1935, of Elsfield, Oxford; **John William Howard de l'Aigle, (Toby), Buchan;** *b* 25 May 1950; *s* of 3rd Baron Tweedsmuir and Barbara, 2nd *d* of Ernest Nash Ensor; *S* father, 2008; *m* 1st, 1977, Amanda Jocelyn, *d* of Sir Gawain Westray Bell, KCMG, CBE; two *s*; 2nd, 2001, Dominique, *d* of late Dennis Joseph Enright, OBE; one *s* two *d*. *Educ:* Magdalen Coll. Sch., Oxford. *Heir: s* Hon. John Alasdair Gawain Buchan, *b* 20 Nov. 1986.

**TWEEDY, Colin David,** LVO 2003; OBE 2000; Chief Executive: The Building Centre, since 2012; Built Environment Trust, since 2015; *b* 26 Oct. 1953; *s* of late Clifford Harry Tweedy, of Abbotsbury, Dorset and Kitty Audrey (*née* Matthews); *m* 2008, Campbell Guthrie Gray. *Educ:* City of Bath Boys' Sch.; St Catherine's Coll., Oxford (MA). Manager, Thorndike Theatre, Leatherhead, 1976–78; Corporate Finance Officer, Guinness Mahon, 1978–80; Asst Dir, Streets Financial PR, 1980–83; Dir Gen., Assoc. for Business Sponsorship of the Arts, later Chief Exec., Arts & Business, 1983–2012. Chm., Comité Européen pour le Rapprochement de l'Economie et de la Culture; Mem. Council, Japan Festival, 1991; Director: Covent Garden International Festival, 1995–2001; Headlong Th. Co. (formerly Oxford Stage Co.), 1985–2012; Crusaid, 1987–2004; Mariinsky Theatre Trust, 1999–; Mem. Council, Nat. Musicians' Symphony Orch., 2001–; Member: UK Nat. Cttee, European Cinema and TV Year, 1988–89; Council for Charitable Support, 1998–2008; Design Council Sounding Bd, 2013–. Co-Founder, Stonewall Equality Trust, 1989; Founder, 2002, and Trustee, Prince's Foundn for Children and the Arts (formerly Prince of Wales Arts & Kids Foundn), 2000–15; Trustee: Serpentine Gall., 1990–; The Ideas Foundn, 2003–; Next Generation Foundn, 2003–08. Selector, Discerning Eye 2000 exhibn; a Judge: PR Week Awards, 2000; Art & Work Awards, 2002; Mem. Adv. Panel, Costa (formerly Whitbread) Bk Awards, 1998–. Gov., Univ. of Creative Arts, 2009–. Freeman, City of London, 1978. CCMI 2002; FRSA. Hollis Sponsorship Personality of the Year, 2003. *Publications:* A Celebration of Ten Years' Business Sponsorship of the Arts, 1987. *Recreations:* the arts in general, opera, theatre and contemporary art in particular, Italy, food, travel. *Address:* The Building Centre, 26 Store Street, WC1E 7BT. *T:* (020) 7692 4000. *E:* c.tweedy@buildingcentre.co.uk. *Club:* Groucho.

**TWELFTREE, Dame Marcia (Anne),** DBE 2010; part-time education consultant, since 2009; *b* Walsall Wood, 31 March 1950; *d* of Bernard Harold Daffern and Sylvia May Daffern (*née* Booth); *m* 1983, Michael Richard Twelftree; one *s* one *d*. *Educ:* King Edward VI High Sch. for Girls, Birmingham; Bristol Univ. (BSc Hons Chem. 1971); St John's Coll., Oxford (PGCE 1972). Teacher: Oxford Sch., 1972–73; Burford Sch., 1973–74; Lectr, Swindon Coll., 1979–84; Sen. Teacher, Ridgeway Sch., Wroughton, 1984–90; Dep. Headteacher, Sheldon Sch., Chippenham, 1990–93; Head Teacher: John O'Gaunt Sch., Hungerford, 1993–97; Charters Sch., Sunningdale, 1997–2009. Association of School and College Leaders: Salaries Condition of Service Officer, 1995–97; Mem., Nat. Council, 1999–2009. Mem., Implementation Rev. Unit, 2003–09. Mem. Bd, Sch. Food Trust, 2007–11. Trustee, Prince Philip Trust, 2011–. Chair: Govs, Burnham Park Acad., 2012–15; Interim Exec. Bd, Wye Valley Sch., 2013–14; Interim Exec. Bd, Parker EACT Acad., Daventry, 2014. Regl Dir, CfBT Educn Trust, 2015–17. *Recreations:* being a 'mad' grandma to 6 grandsons, travel to far-flung places, touring Europe in a camper-van, theatre, cinema, walking, aqua-aerobics. *Address:* Rose Cottage, 117 Rowtown, Addlestone, Surrey KT15 1HQ. *T:* (01932) 888908. *E:* twelftreem@gmail.com.

**TWELVETREE, Eric Alan;** County Treasurer, Essex County Council, 1974–87; *b* 26 Dec. 1928; *m* 1953, Patricia Mary Starkings; two *d*. *Educ:* Stamford Sch., Lincs; qualif. IPFA and ACCA. Served with Borough Councils: Gt Yarmouth, Ipswich, Stockport, Southampton; County Councils: Gloucestershire, Kent. Pres., Soc. of County Treasurers, 1986–87. Dir, Chelmsford Hospice, then Farleigh Hospice, Chelmsford, 1991–99. Mem., Exec. Cttee, Field Studies Council, 1978–2001. *Recreations:* watercolours, history of Tetbury Society. *Address:* 12 Cherry Orchard Road, Tetbury, Glos GL8 8HX.

**TWIGG, (John) Derek;** MP (Lab) Halton, since 1997; *b* 9 July 1959; *s* of Kenneth and Irene Twigg; *m* 1988, Mary Cassidy; one *s* one *d*. *Educ:* Bankfield High Sch., Widnes; Halton Coll. of Further Educn. Civil service posts, Department of Employment, and DFE, then DFEE, 1975–96; political consultant, 1996–97. Member (Lab): Cheshire CC, 1981–85; Halton DC, 1983–97. PPS to Minister of State, DTI, 1999–2001, to Sec. of State, DTLR, 2001–02; an Asst Govt Whip, 2002–03; a Lord Comr of HM Treasury (Govt Whip), 2003–04; Parliamentary Under-Secretary of State: DFES, 2004–05; DfT, 2005–06; MoD, 2006–08; Shadow Health Minister, 2010–11. Mem., Public Accounts Cttee, 1998–99. *Recreations:* hill walking, reading military history. *Address:* House of Commons, SW1A 0AA. *T:* (020) 7219 3000.

**TWIGG, Stephen;** MP (Lab and Co-op) Liverpool West Derby, since 2010; *b* 25 Dec. 1966; *s* of late Ian David Twigg and Jean Barbara Twigg. *Educ:* Southgate Comprehensive Sch.; Balliol Coll., Oxford (BA Hons). Pres., NUS, 1990–92; Parliamentary Officer: British Sect., Amnesty Internat., 1992–93; NCVO, 1993–94; researcher, office of Margaret Hodge, MP, 1994–96. Mem. (Lab), Islington LBC, 1992–97. Gen. Sec., Fabian Soc., 1996–97 (Mem. Exec., 1997–2015). MP (Lab) Enfield, Southgate, 1997–2005; contested (Lab) same seat, 2005. Parly Sec., Privy Council Office, 2001–02; Parly Under-Sec. of State, DfEE, 2002–04, Minister of State, DfES, 2004–05; Shadow Sec. of State for Educn, 2011–13. Member: Select Cttee on Modernisation of H of C, 1998–2000; Select Cttee on Educn and Employment, 2000–01; Chm., Select Cttee on Internat. Develt, 2015–; Member: H of C Liaison Cttee, 2015–; Jt Cttee on Nat. Security Strategy, 2015–. Dir, Foreign Policy Centre, 2005–10 (Bd Mem., 1998–2005). Chairman: Labour Campaign for Electoral Reform, 1998–2001; Lab. Friends of Israel, 1998–2001. Dir, Crime Concern, 1997–2000. Dir, Special Projects, AEGIS Charitable Trust, 2005–10; Chm., Young People Now Foundn, 2006–08. Trustee, WEA, 2006–08 (Patron, 2008–); Chair of Trustees, Merseyside Domestic Violence Services, 2008–14 (Patron, 2014–). Patron: Merseyside Motor Neurone Disease Assoc., 2011–; Amputees and Carers Support In Liverpool, 2011–. Mem., USDAW. Gov., Jubilee Primary Sch., 2006–07. *Address:* House of Commons, SW1A 0AA.

**TWIGGER, Andrew Mark;** QC 2011; *b* Cuckfield, 23 Oct. 1968; *s* of Alan and Gillian Twigger; *m* 1997, Harriet Leeper; two *s* one *d*. *Educ:* Aylesbury Grammar Sch.; St John's Coll., Oxford (BA Lit.Hum. 1991); City Univ. (DipLaw). Called to the Bar, Inner Temple, 1994; in practice as barrister, specialising in chancery and commercial litigation, esp. banking and finance. *Recreations:* music, history. *Address:* Maitland Chambers, 7 Stone Buildings, Lincoln's Inn, WC2A 3SZ. *T:* (020) 7406 1200. *E:* atwigger@maitlandchambers.com.

**TWIGGER, Robert James,** OBE 2016; Acting Serjeant at Arms, House of Commons, 2015–16; *b* Hornchurch, 27 July 1958; *s* of late Ernest Twigger and of Marion Twigger (*née* Riley); *m* 1st, 1990, Corinne Lethieullier (*d* 1996); one *s* one *d*; 2nd, 2016, Emma-Jane Netta Garnett (*née* Bird). *Educ:* Royal Liberty Sch., Romford; Univ. of Birmingham (BSocSc Mathematical Econs). House of Commons Library: Statistician, 1979–93; Hd, Econ. Policy and Statistics Section, 1993–2000; House of Commons: Dir, Parly and Reference Services, 2000–04; Hd, Office of the Clerk, 2004–08; Dir, Information Services for Members, 2008–12; Sec., House of Commons Commn, 2012–15; Associate Serjeant at Arms, 2008–15. *Recreations:* family, church, sailing, railways.

**TWIGGER, Terence;** Chief Executive, Meggitt plc, 2001–13 (Finance Director, 1993–2000); *b* 21 Nov. 1949; *s* of Gilbert and Elizabeth Twigger; *m* 1973, Elizabeth Kimberley; two *d*. *Educ:* King Edward VI Grammar, Nuneaton; Bristol Univ. (BSc). FCA; FRAeS. Touche Ross & Co., 1971–76; various appts, 1977–90, Finance Dir, 1990–93, Lucas Aerospace. *Recreations:* reading, shooting, fishing. *Address:* The Walled Garden, Holly Hill Lane, Sarisbury Green, Southampton SO31 7AH.

**TWIGGY;** *see* Lawson, Dame Lesley.

**TWIN, Prof. Peter John,** OBE 1991; FRS 1993; Professor of Experimental Physics, University of Liverpool, 1987–2001, Emeritus Professor and Senior Fellow, since 2001; *b* 26 July 1939; *s* of Arthur James and Hilda Ethel Twin; *m* 1st, 1963, Jean Esther Leatherland (*d* 2012); one *s* one *d*; 2nd, 2013, Sally Shand. *Educ:* Sir George Monoux Grammar Sch., Walthamstow; Univ. of Liverpool (BSc Hons, PhD). University of Liverpool: Lectr, 1964–73; Sen. Lectr, 1973–79; Reader, 1979–85; Head, Nuclear Structure Facility, Daresbury Lab., SERC, 1983–87. Vis. Prof., Univ. of Alberta, 1968–69. Reader, dio. of Chester, 1991–. Tom Bonner Prize, APS, 1991; John Price Wetherill Medal, Benjamin Franklin Inst., USA, 1991; Lisa Meitner Prize, Eur. Physical Soc., 2004. *Publications:* numerous papers in learned jls. *Address:* Oliver Lodge Laboratory, University of Liverpool, Liverpool L69 3BX. *T:* (0151) 794 3378.

**TWINE, Derek Milton,** CBE 2007; Chief Executive, Scout Association, 1996–2013; *b* 1 May 1951; *s* of late Edward Montague Twine and Winifred May Twine (*née* Milton); *m* 1974, Rhoda, *d* of Very Rev. R. J. N. Lockhart; one *s* one *d*. *Educ:* Reigate GS; UCNW, Bangor (BA Hons Educn 1st cl.). Researcher, 1973–75, Lectr in Education, 1975–76, Univ. of Wales; Scout Association: Dir, Venture Scout Trng, 1976–79; Dir of Programme, 1979–85; Exec. Comr (Programme and Trng), 1985–96. Member: Youth Panel, Nat. Trust, 1978–85; Voluntary Sector Panel, RSA, 1990–96; Mgt Cttee, Educn and Standards, Nat. Youth Agency, 1991–95 (Chm., 1993–95); Strategic Adv. Panel, British Youth Council, 2007–; Council, Nat. Trust, 2013–18; Council, Bradford Cathedral, 2013– (Chm., 2014–); National Society for Voluntary Youth Service: Mem., Exec. Cttee, 1979–82; Chm., Develt Project, 1979–82; Chm., Trng Managers' Gp, 1990–96. Trustee: Whitechapel Foundn, 1996–2012; Croatia Sunrise City Support, 1996–99; Church Urban Fund, 2008–18 (Vice Chm., 2009–18). Gov., Davenant Foundn Sch., 1994–2012. Hon. Lay Canon, Bradford Cathedral, 2017–. FITD, subseq. FCIPD, 1987–2013; FRSA 2002. *Publications:* various articles in youthwork and educnl jls. *Recreations:* church activities, theatre, cooking. *Address:* 14 Rose Bank, Burley-in-Wharfedale, W Yorks LS29 7PQ.

**TWINING, Alexandra Mary;** *see* Hall Hall, A. M.

**TWINING, James Douglas Robert**; Partner, Greycoat Place, since 2016; Chief Executive, Kingsbridge Group, since 2017; *b* Watford, 13 Dec. 1972; *s* of Robert Ernest Twining and Ann Carolyn Twining; *m* 2002, Victoria Laura Toft; one *s* two *d*. *Educ*: Merchant Taylors' Sch., Northwood; Christ Church, Oxford (MA). Associate Dir, UBS Warburg, 1995–99; Finance Dir, GroupTrade, 1999–2002; Man. Dir, Se7en Mile Ltd, 2002–04; Associate Principal, McKinsey & Co., 2004–11; Gp Commercial Dir, Jardine Lloyd Thompson plc, 2011–16. Chm., English Heritage Foundn, 2011–15; Trustee, English Heritage Trust, 2015– (Dep. Chm., 2019–). Governor: St Christopher's Sch., 2010–19; Merchant Taylors' Sch., Northwood, 2018–. *Publications*: novels: The Double Eagle, 2005; The Black Sun, 2006; The Gilded Seal, 2007; The Geneva Deception, 2009. *Recreations*: the past, collecting safe plates, trivia, geocoaching. *Address*: c/o Curtis Brown, 28–29 Haymarket, SW1Y 4SP. *E*: mail@jamestwining.com.

**TWINING, Prof. William Lawrence**, FBA 1997; Quain Professor of Jurisprudence Emeritus, University College London, since 2004 (Quain Professor of Jurisprudence, 1983–96; Research Professor of Law, 1996–2004); *b* 22 Sept. 1934; *s* of Edward Francis Twining and Helen Mary Twining (*née* Dubuisson); *m* 1957, Penelope Elizabeth Wall Morris; one *s* one *d*. *Educ*: Charterhouse School; Brasenose College, Oxford (BA 1955; MA 1960; DCL 1990); Univ. of Chicago (JD 1958). Lectr in Private Law, Univ. of Khartoum, 1958–61; Sen. Lectr in Law, University Coll., Dar-es-Salaam, 1961–65; Prof. of Jurisprudence, The Queen's Univ., Belfast, 1965–72; Prof. of Law, Univ. of Warwick, 1972–82. Mem., Cttee on Legal Educn in N Ireland, 1972–74; President: Soc. of Public Law Teachers of Law, 1978–79; UK Assoc. for Legal and Social Philosophy, 1980–83; Chairman: Bentham Cttee, 1982–2000; Commonwealth Legal Educn Assoc., 1983–93; vis. appts in several Univs. Foreign Mem., Amer. Acad. of Arts and Scis, 2007. FAcSS 2013. Hon. QC 2002. Hon. LLD: Univ. of Victoria, BC, 1980; Edinburgh, 1999; QUB, 1999; Southampton Inst., 2000; York Univ., Toronto, 2002; Windsor, Ont, 2009; Coll. of Law, London, 2011. General Editor: Law in Context series, 1966–; Jurists series, 1979–. *Publications*: The Karl Llewellyn Papers, 1968; Karl Llewellyn and the Realist Movement, 1973, 2nd edn 2012; (with David Miers) How to Do Things with Rules, 1976, 5th edn 2010; (with J. Uglow) Law Publishing and Legal Information, 1981; (ed) Facts in Law, 1983; Theories of Evidence, 1985; (ed) Legal Theory and Common Law, 1986; (ed with R. Tur) Essays on Kelsen, 1986; (ed jtly) Learning Lawyers' Skills, 1989; (ed jtly) Access to Legal Education and the Legal Profession, 1989; Rethinking Evidence, 1990, 2nd edn 2006; (ed) Issues of Self-determination, 1991; (with T. Anderson) Analysis of Evidence, 1991, 2nd edn (with T. Anderson and D. Schum) 2005; (with E. Quick) Legal Records in the Commonwealth, 1994; Blackstone's Tower: the English Law School, 1994; Law in Context: enlarging a discipline, 1997; Globalisation and Legal Theory, 2000; The Great Juristic Bazaar, 2002; (ed jtly) Evidence and Inference in History and Law, 2003; General Jurisprudence, 2009; (ed) Human Rights: southern voices, 2009; (with P. Dawid and M. Vasilaki) Evidence, Inference and Enquiry, 2011; Globalisation and Legal Scholarship, 2011; (ed jtly) Legal Fictions in Theory and Practice, 2015; Jurist in Context: a memoir, 2019. *Address*: 10 Mill Lane, Iffley, Oxford OX4 4EJ.

**TWINN, Ian David**, CBE 2018; PhD; Director of Public Affairs, Incorporated Society of British Advertisers, 1998–2017; *b* 26 April 1950; *s* of late David Twinn and of Gwynneth Irene Twinn; *m* 1973, Frances Elizabeth Holtby; two *s*. *Educ*: Netherhall Secondary Modern School, Cambridge; Cambridge Grammar School; University College of Wales, Aberystwyth (BA hons); University of Reading (PhD). Senior Lecturer in Planning, Polytechnic of the South Bank, 1975–83. MP (C) Edmonton, 1983–97; contested (C) same seat, 1997. PPS to Minister of State for Industry, 1985–86, to Dep. Chm. of Cons. Party, 1986–88, to Minister of State for Energy, 1987–90, to Minister of State for the Environment, 1990–92, to Paymaster Gen., 1992–94. MEP (C) London Reg., Oct. 2003–2004; contested (C) London Reg., EP elecns, 1999, 2004, 2009. Chm., London Reg., Cons. Party, 2014–17. Vice Chm., British Caribbean Assoc., 1986–. FRSA 1989; FRGS (MIBG 1972). Comdr, Order of Honour (Greece), 2000. *Recreations*: collecting secondhand books, renovating antique furniture. *Address*: 85 Calton Avenue, SE21 7DF. *T*: (020) 8299 4210.

**TWISLETON-WYKEHAM-FIENNES;** *see* Fiennes.

**TWIST, Kenneth Lyndon**; HM Chief Inspector of Mines and Quarries, 1992–96; *b* 13 Jan. 1938; *s* of Joseph and Sarah Ellen Twist; *m* 1959, Emily Owens; three *s*. *Educ*: Wigan and Dist Mining & Technical Coll. (Dip. Mining Engrg). Colliery Manager's Cert., 1963. FIMinE 1979. Dep. General Manager, Agecroft, 1969–76; Health and Safety Executive: Inspector of Mines, 1976–87; Principal Dist Inspector of Mines, 1987–91; Dep. Chief Inspector of Mines, 1991–92. Chm., Safety in Mines Res. Adv. Bd, HSC, 1992–96. *Publications*: papers in Mining Engineer, Jl of Instn of Mining Engrs. *Recreations*: gardening, reading, photography, computing, golf. *Address*: Ridgeway, Sunnyridge Avenue, Marford, Wrexham LL12 8TE. *T*: (01978) 855638.

**TWIST, Mary Elizabeth, (Liz);** MP (Lab) Blaydon, since 2017; *m* Charles Twist (*d* 2000). Worked for UNISON, Northern Reg., incl. Regl Hd of Health; case worker, office of David Anderson, MP. Mem. (Lab), Gateshead Council, 2012–. Member: Petitions Cttee, 2017–; Housing, Communities and Local Govt Cttee, 2017–19; Cttee on Privileges, 2019–; Cttee of Standards, 2019–. Listener, Samaritans of Gateshead. *Address*: House of Commons, SW1A 0AA.

**TWITE, Robin**, OBE 1982; Director, Department of Environmental Diplomacy, Arava Environmental Institute, Ketura, Israel, since 2015; *b* 2 May 1932; *s* of Reginald John Twite and May Elizabeth Walker; *m* 1st, 1958, Sally Randall (marr. diss.); 2nd, 1980, Sonia Yaari (*d* 2016); one *s* three step *d*. *Educ*: Lawrence Sheriff School, Rugby; Balliol College, Oxford (BA History 1955). Asst Editor, Schoolmaster, weekly jl of NUT, 1956–58; British Council, 1958–73: served in Israel and London as Sec., Overseas Students Fees Awards Scheme; Sec., Open Univ. of Israel, 1973–76; British Council, 1976–88: adviser on adult and further educn, 1977–79; regional rep., Calcutta, 1980–84; Controller, Books, Libraries and Inf. Div., 1984–88. Hebrew University, Jerusalem: Advr to Chm., Res. Authy, 1988–91; Develt Advr, Truman Res. Inst. for Peace, 1991–93; Director: Conflict Resolution Project, Leonard Davis Inst. for Internat. Relns, 1994–97; Envmtl Prog., Israel-Palestine Center for Res. and Inf., Jerusalem, 1997–2014. *Publications*: (ed) The Future of Jerusalem, 1993; (ed) Israeli-Arab Negotiations, 1993; (ed) Our Shared Environment: environmental problems of Israel, the West Bank and Gaza, 1994. *Recreations*: music making, environmental activism. *Address*: Flat 5, Hildesheimer Street, Jerusalem 9311507, Israel. *T*: 0522272476.

**TWO CITIES, Archdeacon for the;** *no new appointment at time of going to press.*

**TWOMLOW, Richard William; His Honour Judge Twomlow;** a Circuit Judge, since 2011; *b* Loughborough, 19 Nov. 1953; *s* of William Henry and Mavis Millicent Twomlow; *m* 1995, Laura Jane; one *d*. *Educ*: Whitchurch High Sch., Cardiff; Trinity Coll., Cambridge (BA 1975). Called to the Bar, Gray's Inn, 1976; Recorder, 1997–2011. *Recreations*: reading, travel, music, watching sport (especially cricket and Association Football), military history. *Address*: Merthyr Tydfil Combined Court Centre, Glebeland Place, Merthyr Tydfil CF47 8BH.

**TWYCROSS, Fiona Ruth**, PhD; Member (Lab), London Assembly, Greater London Authority, since 2012; Deputy Mayor for Fire and Resilience, since 2018; *b* London, 29 May 1969; *d* of Robert Geoffrey Twycross, *qv*; *m* 2017, Jan Thomas Moldung. *Educ*: Cheney Sch., Oxford; Univ. of Edinburgh (MA Hons Scandinavian Studies 1992; PhD 1997); Birkbeck Coll., Univ. of London (MSc Public Policy and Mgt 2004). Labour Party: Cttee Officer, 1998–2001; Regl Organiser, 2001–03; Dep. Regl Dir, 2003–05; Regl Dir, 2005–08; Diabetes UK: Hd, Campaigns and Volunteer Develt, 2008–09; Hd, Governance, 2009–12. Mem., London Fire and Emergency Planning Authy, 2012–18 (Chm., 2016–18). *Address*: Greater London Authority, City Hall, The Queen's Walk, More London, SE1 2AA. *T*: (020) 7084 2567. *E*: fiona.twycross@london.gov.uk.

**TWYCROSS, Dr Robert Geoffrey**, FRCP, FRCR; Macmillan Clinical Reader in Palliative Medicine, Oxford University, 1988–2001, now Emeritus; Director, palliativedrugs.com, 2000–18; *b* 29 Jan. 1941; *s* of Jervis and Irene Twycross; *m* 1964, Deirdre Maeve, *d* of John Richard Campbell; two *s* three *d*. *Educ*: St John's Sch., Leatherhead; St Peter's Coll., Oxford (BA 1962; BM BCh 1965; MA 1965; DM 1977). MRCP 1969, FRCP 1980; FRCR 1996. Hosp. appts, Oxford, Lancaster, Epsom and Manchester, 1966–71; Res. Fellow, St Christopher's Hospice, London, 1971–76; Vis. MO, St Joseph's Hospice, London, 1971–76; Consultant Physician, Sir Michael Sobell House, Churchill Hosp., Oxford, 1976–2001; Fellow of St Peter's Coll., Oxford, 1987–2001, now Emeritus; Hd, WHO Collaborating Centre for Palliative Care, 1988–2005; Academic Dir, Oxford Internat. Centre for Palliative Cancer Care, 1992–2005. Visiting Professor: RSocMed of USA Foundation, 1979; Sir Ernest Finch, Sheffield, 1994; Univ. del Salvador, Buenos Aires, 1999–2005; Amrita Inst. of Med. Scis, Kochi, India, 2003–06. Mem., WHO Expert Adv. Panel on Cancer, 1985–2005. Hon. Life Mem., British Lymphology Soc., 2004; Hon. Member: Polish Soc. of Palliative Medicine, 2011; Paliativos Sin Fronteras, Spain, 2011. Trustee, Foundn for Palliative Care Educn. Aid and Co-operation Medal, Poland, 1993; Founder's Award, Nat. Hospice Orgn, USA, 1994; Serturner Prize, Serturner Soc., 1995; Vittorio Ventafridda Award, Internat. Assoc. for Hospice and Palliative Care, 2006; Lifetime Achievement Award: Amer. Acad. of Hospice and Palliative Medicine, 2008; Indian Assoc. for Palliative Care, 2008; Plaque of Honour, Indian Assoc. of Palliative Care, 2012. *Publications*: The Dying Patient, 1975; (ed) Pain Relief in Cancer, vol. 3 No 1, 1984; A Time to Die, 1984; (ed) Edinburgh Symposium on Pain Control and Medical Education, 1989; Pain Relief in Advanced Cancer, 1994; Introducing Palliative Care, 1995, 5th edn (with A. Wilcock) 2016; Symptom Management in Advanced Cancer, 1995, 4th edn (with A. Wilcock and C. Stark Toller) 2009; (jtly) Palliative Care Formulary, 1998, 6th edn 2017 (ed jtly), Italian edn 2004, German edn 2005, USA edn, as Hospice and Palliative Care Formulary, 2006, 2nd edn 2008, Canadian edn 2010, Polish edn 2011); (ed jtly) Lymphoedema, 2000; with S. A. Lack: Symptom Control in Far-Advanced Cancer: pain relief, 1983; Therapeutics in Terminal Cancer, 1984; Oral Morphine in Advanced Cancer, 1984, (sole author) 5th edn 2009; Control of Alimentary Symptoms in Far-Advanced Cancer, 1986; Oral Morphine: information for patients, families and friends, 1987, (sole author) 2nd edn, as Morphine and the relief of cancer pain, 1999; (ed jtly) Pruritus in advanced disease, 2004; (jtly) Palliative Medicine (Chinese edn), 2005; (with J. Li) Palliative Medicine: cancer pain and symptom management (Chinese edn), 2009; contribs to learned jls. *Recreations*: gardening, walking, reading. *Address*: Tewsfield, Netherwoods Road, Oxford OX3 8HF. *E*: robttwy@gmail.com.

*See also* F. R. *Twycross*.

**TWYFORD, Donald Henry**, CB 1990; Under Secretary, Export Credits Guarantee Department, 1981–89, Director and Chairman of Project Group Board, 1986–89; *b* 4 Feb. 1931; *s* of Henry John Twyford and Lily Hilda (*née* Ridler); *m* 2006, Maria Dolores Quintero Hernández. *Educ*: Wembley County School. Joined Export Credits Guarantee Dept, 1949; Principal, 1965; seconded to Dept of Trade: Principal (Commercial Relations with East Europe), 1972–75; Asst Secretary (Country Policy), 1976; Establishment Officer, 1979–81; Under Secretary, Head of Services Group (internat. and country policy), ECGD, 1981–85; Hd of Project Underwriting Gp, 1985–89. Chairman, European Policy Co-ordination Group, 1981. President: Jávea Fest. Cttee, 2000; Jávea Internat. Civic Soc., 2001–02. Mem. Founding Cttee, Nueva Jávea party, 2006. *Recreations*: gardening, music, travel. *Address*: Cami de la Sabatera 33, Jávea 03739, Alicante, Spain.

**TWYMAN, Paul Hadleigh;** management consultant; Director: Nationwide (formerly Nationwide Anglia) Building Society, 1987–2002 (Anglia Building Society, 1983–87); Connex Transport UK Ltd, 1999–2002; *s* of late Lawrence Alfred Twyman and Gladys Mary (*née* Williams). *Educ*: Leyton County High Sch.; Chatham House Sch., Ramsgate; Univ. of Sheffield (BAEcon); London Sch. of Econs and Pol Science (MScEcon). Schoolteacher, 1964; Asst Principal, BoT, 1967; Secretariat, Commn on Third London Airport, 1969; Private Sec. to Sec. of State for Trade and Industry, 1971; Dept of Industry, 1975; Anti-Dumping Unit, Dept of Trade, 1976; Asst Sec., and Head of Overseas Projects Group, Dept of Trade, 1978; Dept of Transport, 1983; Cabinet Office, 1984; Under Sec., and Dir, Enterprise and Deregulation Unit, Dept of Employment, 1985. Econ. Adviser to Chm. of Conservative Party, and Head of Econ. Section, Cons. Res. Dept, 1987. Chm., Policy Strategy Unit, 1988–2006. Contested (C) Greater Manchester W, European Parly elecn, 1989. Dir, D'Arcy Masius Benton & Bowles, 1990–96; Corporate Strategy Dir, Bates Dorland Ltd, later Bates UK, 1996–99. Mem., Central London LSC, 2001–05. Chm., Consultative Cttee, Kent Internat. Airport, 2006–14; Member: Thanet Dist Police Adv. Cttee, 1989–99; Thanet DC, 1991–95. Mem., Lambeth Community Police Consultative Gp, 1996–2002 (Hon. Comptroller, 1998–99; Vice-Chm., 1999–2001). Associate Mem., Kensington, Chelsea and Westminster HA, 1996–2002. Trustee, Opportunity Internat. (UK), 1995–2002. Gov., City of Westminster Coll., 1999–2002. Member: RIIA; FRSA. Mem., Royal African Soc. *Recreations*: family and friends, gardening, hill walking, observing gorillas.

**TYACKE, Sarah Jacqueline, (Mrs Nicholas Tyacke)**, CB 1998; FSA; FRHistS; Chief Executive, National Archives (formerly Chief Executive and Keeper of Public Records, Public Record Office), 1992–2005 and Historical Manuscripts Commissioner, 2003–05; *b* 29 Sept. 1945; *d* of late Colin Walton Jeacock and Elsie Marguerite Stanton; *m* 1971, Nicholas, *s* of Maj.-Gen. David Noel Hugh Tyacke, CB, OBE; one *d*. *Educ*: Chelmsford County High Sch.; Bedford Coll., London (BA Hons History). FSA 1985; FRHistS 1994. Asst Keeper, Map Room, BM, 1968; Dep. Map Librarian, British Liby, 1973–85; undertook govt scrutiny of BL preservation (under Efficiency Unit, Cabinet Office), 1985–86; Director of Special Collections, British Library, 1986–91. Chm., European Co-ordinating Bd, 1992–96, a Vice-Pres., 1996–2000, Internat. Council on Archives; Vice-Chm., Professional Bd, IFLA, 1987–89. Vice-Pres., 1995–97 and 2002–, Trustee, 2004–, Hakluyt Soc. (Jt Hon. Sec., 1984–95; Pres., 1997–2002); a Vice-Pres., RHistS, 2000–03 (Hon. Vice-Pres., 2004–). Dir, Imago Mundi, 1987–; Trustee, Mappa Mundi, 1989–96; Chm. Trustees, Internat. Records Mgt Trust, 2004–; Chm., Harley Trustees, 2007–; Chair: Mount Everest Foundn, 2009–13 (Trustee, 2011–12); Fund for Internat. Develt of Archives/Internat. Council on Archives, 2010–16; Internat. Soc. for the History of the Map, 2015–16 (Hon. Sec., 2011–15). Mem. Council, RHBNC, 2003–13 (Hon. Fellow, 1999); Gov., London Metropolitan Univ., 2004–09. Mem., Hillsborough Ind. Panel, 2010–12. Sandars Lectures, Cambridge, 2007; Leverhulme Emeritus Fellowship, 2005–07.

Sen. Res. Fellow, Sch. of Advanced Study, Univ. of London, 2005–. Fellow, ICA, 2016. Hon. DPhil: Guildhall, 1996; Essex, 2005; Hon. DLitt London, 2006. President's Medal, British Acad., 2010. *Publications:* Copernicus and the New Astronomy (with H. Swiderska), 1973; (ed jtly with H. M. Wallis) My Head is a Map: essay and memoirs in honour of R. V. Tooley, 1973; London Map-Sellers 1660–1720, 1978; (with John Huddy) Christopher Saxton and Tudor map-making, 1980; (ed) English map-making 1500–1650: historical essays, 1983; Catalogue of maps, charts and plans in the Pepys Library, Magdalene College, Cambridge, 1989; The History of Cartography, vol. 3 (contrib.), 2007, vol. 4, 2019 (Associate Ed.); contribs to archival, library and cartographic jls, incl. The Library, Imago Mundi, Cartographic Jl. *Recreations:* the sea, travel, hill-walking, painting. *Address:* 1a Spencer Rise, NW5 1AR.

**TYDEMAN, John Peter,** OBE 2003; Head of BBC Radio Drama, 1986–94; *b* 30 March 1936; *s* of George Alfred Tydeman and Gladys (*née* Johnson). *Educ:* Feltonfleet; Hertford GS; Trinity Coll., Cambridge (MA). Nat. Service, 2 Lieut RA, 1954–56. Joined BBC, 1959; producer, 1962–80; Asst Head, Radio Drama, 1980–86. Dir of stage, radio and television plays. Prix Italia, 1970; Prix Futura, 1979 and 1983; Broadcasting Press Guild Award, 1983; Sony Special Award for Services to Radio, 1994; Lifetime Achievement Award, Radio Acad., 2010. *Recreations:* theatre, travel, reading, the company of friends. *Address:* Bay Tree Cottage, 28 The Street, North Lopham, Diss, Norfolk IP22 2NB. *T:* (01379) 687339, 07931 547070. *Club:* Garrick.

**TYE, Alan Peter,** RDI 1986; Partner, Tye Design (formerly Alan Tye Design (Industrial & Product Designers), 1962–2017; *b* 18 Sept. 1933; *s* of Chang Qing Tai and Emily Tai (*née* Thompson); *m* 1966, Anita Birgitta Göethe Tye; three *s* two *d*. *Educ:* Regent Street Polytechnic Sch. of Architecture. RIBA 1959; FCSD (FSIAD 1979). Qualified as architect, 1958; with Prof. Arne Jacobsen, Copenhagen, 1960–62; formed Alan Tye Design, 1962; incorporated HID Ltd, 1977; launched Healthy Individual Design Practice Method (HID), 1992. Mem., Selection Cttee, Council of Industrial Design, 1967; Civic Trust Award Assessor, 1968, 1969; Vis. Tutor, RCA, 1978–83; External Examr, 1987–90; Specialist Adviser on Industrial Design, CNAA, 1980; London Region Assessor, RIBA, 1981 and 1988; RSA Bursary Judge, 1983–; External Examr, Design Res. for Disability, London Guildhall Univ., 1998–2002. Convenor, Faculty of RDI, RSA, 1991–. Guest Prof., Royal Danish Acad. of Fine Arts, 1996. Hon. FRCA 2012. Internat. Design Prize, Rome, 1962; Council of Industrial Design Award, 1965, 1966, 1981; British Aluminium Design Award, 1966; 1st Prize, GAI Award, 1969; Observer (London) Design Award, 1969; Ringling Mus. of Art (Fla) Award, 1969; Gold Medal, Graphic Design, 1970; 1st Prize, GAI Award, Internat. Bldg Exhibn, 1971; British Aluminium Eros Trophy, 1973; 4 Awards for Design Excellence, Aust., 1973; Commendation for Arch., 1977; Internat. Award, Inst. of Business Designers (NY), 1982; Internat. Bldg Exhibits Top Design Award, 1983, 1985; Resources Council of America Design Award, 1987; Prince Philip Duke of Edinburgh Designer of the Year Finalist, 1993, 1999; RIBA Regl Design Award, 1995; other design awards. *Publications:* (with Dermot O'Flynn) Healthy Industrial Design, 1995. *Recreations:* tai chi, aikido. *Address:* The Red House, Great West Plantation, Tring, Herts HP23 6DA. *T:* (01442) 823325.

**TYLER,** family name of **Baron Tyler**.

**TYLER,** Baron *cr* 2005 (Life Peer), of Linkinhorne in the county of Cornwall; **Paul Archer Tyler,** CBE 1985; PC 2014; journalist and public affairs consultant; *b* 29 Oct. 1941; *s* of Oliver Walter Tyler and Ursula Grace Gibbons Tyler (*née* May); *m* 1970, Nicola Mary Ingram; one *s* one *d*. *Educ:* Mount House Sch., Tavistock; Sherborne Sch.; Exeter Coll., Oxford (MA). Pres., Oxford Univ. Liberal Club, 1962. Royal Inst. of British Architects: Admin. Asst, 1966; Asst Sec., 1967; Dep. Dir Public Affairs, 1971; Dir Public Affairs, 1972. Man. Dir, Cornwall Courier newspaper gp, 1976–81; Exec. Dir, Public Affairs Div., 1982–84, Dir, 1985–88, Good Relations plc; Chief Exec., 1984–86, Chm., 1986–87, Good Relations Public Affairs Ltd; Sen. Consultant, Good Relations Ltd, 1987–92; Dir, 1987–95, Man. Dir, 1987–92, Western Approaches Public Relns Ltd, Launceston, Cornwall. County Councillor, Devon, 1964–70; Mem., Devon and Cornwall Police Authority, 1965–70; Vice-Chm., Dartmoor Nat. Park Cttee, 1965–70; Chm., CPRE Working Party on the Future of the Village, 1974–81; Mem. Bd of Shelter (Nat. Campaign for the Homeless), and rep. in Devon and Cornwall, 1975–76; Advr to Bd, SW Ambulance Service NHS Trust, 2014–17. Chm., Faiths and Civil Soc. Unit, Anglia Ruskin Univ., then at Goldsmiths, Univ. of London, 2006–. Sec., L/SDP Jt Commn on Employment and Industrial Recovery, 1981–82. Chm., Devon and Cornwall Region Liberal Party, 1981–82; Chm., Liberal Party NEC, 1983–86. Campaign Adviser to Rt Hon. David Steel, and Mem., Alliance Campaign Planning Gp, 1986–87. Contested (L): Totnes, 1966; Bodmin, 1970, 1979; Beaconsfield, 1982; contested (Soc & Lib Dem) Cornwall and Plymouth, European Parly Election, 1989. MP: (L) Bodmin, Feb.–Sept. 1974; (Lib Dem) North Cornwall, 1992–2005. Parly Liberal spokesman on housing and transport, 1974; Parly adviser to RIBA, 1974; Lib Dem spokesman on agriculture and rural affairs, 1992–97, on transport, 1994–95, on food, 1997–99, on constitutional affairs, 2001–05; Lib Dem Chief Whip, 1997–2001; Shadow Leader of House, 1997–2005. Member: Select Cttee on Modernisation of H of C, 1997–2005; Jt Select Cttee on Parly Privilege, 1997–99, on H of L Reform, 2002–05, on Conventions, 2006–07, on Draft Constitutional Renewal Bill, 2008, on Draft Lords Reform Bill, 2011–12, on Delegated Powers and Regulatory Reform, 2017–19. Lib Dem spokesman on constitutional affairs, 2006–15, on constitutional and political reform, 2015–. Dir, Make Votes Count, 2006–; Vice Chm., Hansard Soc., 2008–18. DL Cornwall, 2005–10. *Publications:* A New Deal for Rural Britain (jtly), 1978; Country Lives, Country Landscapes, 1996; Parliament's Last Chance, 2003; Britain's Democratic Deficit: constitutional reform - unfinished business, 2003; (jtly) Reforming the House of Lords: breaking the deadlock, 2005; (jtly) Funding Democracy: breaking the deadlock, 2013; Who Decides?, 2014. *Recreations:* gardening, walking, Cornish ancestry. *Address:* House of Lords, SW1A 0PW.

**TYLER OF ENFIELD,** Baroness *cr* 2011 (Life Peer), of Enfield in the London Borough of Enfield; **Claire Tyler;** *b* 4 June 1957. *Educ:* Latymer Grammar Sch.; Univ. of Southampton (BSc Law and Politics); South Bank Poly. (Postgrad. Dip. Mgt Studies). With GLC/ILEA, 1978–88; mgt posts, Dept of Employment, 1988–92; Divl Manager, DFES, 1992–97; Hd, Connexions Unit, 1998–2000; Dep. Chief Exec., Connexions Nat. Unit, 2000–02; Dir, Social Exclusion Unit, Cabinet Office, then OPDM, subseq. DCLG, 2002–06; Dir, Vulnerable Children Gp, DFES, 2006–07; CEO, Relate, 2007–12 (Vice Pres., 2012); Chm., CAFCASS, 2012–18. Lib Dem spokesperson on mental health, H of L, 2015–. Mem., H of L Select Cttee on Public Service and Demography, 2012–13, on Affordable Childcare, 2014–15, on Social Mobility, 2015–16; Chair, H of L Select Cttee on Financial Exclusion, 2016–17; Co-Chair, All Party Parly Gp on Social Mobility, 2015–, on Wellbeing Economics, 2015–; Vice-Chair, All-Party Parly Gp on Wellbeing, 2012–15; Chair, Lib Dem Policy Working Gp on Balanced Working Life, 2012–13; Co-Chair, Growing Giving Parly Inquiry, 2013–15. Chair, Values-based Child and Adolescent Mental Health System Commn, 2015–16. Co-Chair, Social Policy Forum, 2005–10; Chair, Making Every Adult Matter Coalition of Charities, 2013–; Mem. Bd, Think Ahead Sub Cttee, 2014–16. Pres., Nat. Children's Bureau, 2012–; Vice-Pres., Relate, 2012–. *Address:* House of Lords, SW1A 0PW.

**TYLER, Andrew Oliver,** CBE 2012; PhD; CMarSci, CEng; FIMarEST, FREng, FRAeS, RCNC; Group Chief Executive Officer, Algeco Group, since 2018; Director, Ancient Horse Ltd, since 2013; *b* 22 June 1967; *s* of Thomas Tyler and Patricia Tyler; *m* 1995, Emma Tyler (marr. diss. 2008); two *s* two *d*; partner, Mrs Jennifer Parker. *Educ:* Univ. of Plymouth (BSc 1st cl. Hons Nautical Studies 1989; PhD Marine Sci. 1999); London Business Sch. (MBA Distn 2001). MRICS 1991; FIMarEST 2002; CMarSci 2003; RCNC 2007; CEng, FREng 2010; FRAeS 2015. British Maritime Technology Group: oceanographer and marine scientist, 1989–96; Man. Dir, BMT Marine Information Systems, 1996–2001; Man. Dir, BMT Defence Services, 2001–05; Chief Exec., BMT Defence, 2005–06; Dir Land and Maritime, Defence Procurement Agency, 2006–07; Dir Gen. Ships, 2007–08, Chief Operating Officer, 2008–11, Defence Equipment and Support, MoD; Chief Exec., Marine Current Turbines, 2011–13; Chief Exec., Northrop Grumman Europe, 2013–18. Chm., Kite Power Systems, 2017–. *Publications:* several papers in field of marine pollution science. *Recreations:* running, powerlifting, yoga, progressive/heavy rock and ecclesiastical choral music, bass guitar, hill walking, supporting England's great test cricket team. *Address:* Ancient Horse Ltd, Bakers Orchard, 7 Huntingdon Street, Bradford-on-Avon, Wilts BA15 1RF.

**TYLER, Anne;** writer; *b* 25 Oct. 1941; *d* of Lloyd Parry Tyler and Phyllis Mahon Tyler (*née* Mahon); *m* 1963, Taghi M. Modarressi, MD (*d* 1997); two *d*. *Educ:* Duke Univ. (BA). Mem., AAIL. AAIL Award for Literature, 1977; Nat. Book Critics Circle Award for fiction, 1985; Sunday Times Award for Literary Excellence, 2012. *Publications:* If Morning Ever Comes, 1964; The Tin Can Tree, 1965; A Slipping Down Life, 1970; The Clock Winder, 1972; Celestial Navigation, 1974; Searching for Caleb, 1976; Earthly Possessions, 1977; Morgan's Passing, 1980; Dinner at the Homesick Restaurant, 1982; The Accidental Tourist, 1985; Breathing Lessons, 1988 (Pulitzer Prize for fiction, 1989); Saint Maybe, 1991; Tumble Tower (for children), 1993; Ladder of Years, 1995; A Patchwork Planet, 1998; Back When We Were Grownups, 2001; The Amateur Marriage, 2004; Timothy Tugbottom Says No (for children), 2005; Digging to America, 2006; Noah's Compass, 2010; The Beginner's Goodbye, 2012; A Spool of Blue Thread, 2015; Vinegar Girl, 2016; Clock Dance, 2018. *Address:* 8 Roland Green, Baltimore, MD 21210, USA.

**TYLER, Antony Nigel;** Director General and Chief Executive Officer, International Air Transport Association, 2011–16; *b* Moascar, Egypt, 27 April 1955; *s* of Maj.-Gen. Sir Leslie Norman Tyler, KBE, CB and late Sheila Tyler (*née* Field); *m* 1st, 1980, Jane Douglas Blackley (marr. diss. 2008); two *s* one *d*; 2nd, 2012, Charlotte Andsager. *Educ:* Worth Sch.; Brasenose Coll., Oxford (BA Juris. 1977). FRAeS 2012. John Swire & Sons Ltd, 1977–2011; Chief Operating Officer, 2005–07, Chief Exec., 2007–11, Cathay Pacific Airways; Chm., Dragonair, 2007–11. Non-executive Director: NATS, 2013–16; BOC Aviation, 2016–; Bombardier Inc., 2017–; Trans-Maldivian Airways, 2018–; Qantas Airways, 2018–. Mem., Hong Kong Develt Commn, 2012–15. *Recreations:* ski-ing, scuba diving, music. *Address:* 4F Scenic Villas, Pokfulam, Hong Kong. *Clubs:* Royal Automobile; Hong Kong, Hong Kong Country, Hong Kong Foreign Correspondents' (Hong Kong).
*See also* Maj.-Gen. T. N. Tyler.

**TYLER, David Alan;** Chairman: Hammerson plc, since 2013; Hampstead Theatre, since 2012; Domestic and General Ltd, since 2015; *b* Woking, 23 Jan. 1953; *s* of Alan and Jill Tyler; *m* 1st, 1977, Sharon Lantin (marr. diss. 2011); one *s* one *d*; 2nd, 2017, Margaret Fingerhut. *Educ:* Trinity Hall, Cambridge (BA Econs 1974). FCMA 1983; MCT 1991. Unilever plc, 1974–86; County NatWest Ltd, 1986–89; Finance Director: Christie's International plc, 1989–96; GUS plc, 1997–2007. Chairman: 3i Quoted Private Equity plc, 2007–09; Logica plc, 2007–12; J. Sainsbury plc, 2009–19; non-executive Director: Burberry Gp plc, 2002–15; Experian plc, 2006–12; Reckitt Benckiser Gp plc, 2007–09. *Recreations:* enjoying barn in Sussex, family, friends, theatre, current affairs, jogging, cycling, listening to music, washing up. *Address:* Hammerson plc, Kings Place, 90 York Way, N1 9GE.

**TYLER, Ian Paul;** Chairman: Bovis Homes, since 2013; Cairn Energy PLC, since 2014 (non-executive Director, since 2013); Amey plc, since 2018; *b* 7 July 1960; *s* of Ray and Peggy Tyler; *m* Janet; two *d*. *Educ:* Univ. of Birmingham (BCom). ACA. Arthur Andersen & Co., 1982–88; Gp Treas./Financial Controller, Storehouse Plc, 1988–91; Financial Comptroller, Hanson Plc, 1991–93; Finance Dir, ARC Ltd, 1993–96; Finance Dir, 1996–2002, Chief Operating Officer, 2002–05, Chief Exec., 2005–13, Balfour Beatty plc. Non-executive Director: BAE Systems, 2013–; Mediclinic Internat., 2016–17. *Recreations:* private pilot, keeping fit.

**TYLER, Prof. Lorraine Komisarjevsky,** PhD; FBA 1995; MRC Professor of Cognitive Neuroscience, University of Cambridge, since 1998, and Director (formerly Co-Director), Centre for Speech, Language and the Brain, since 1990; Fellow, Clare College, Cambridge, since 2000; *b* 11 Jan. 1945; *d* of James and Anne Komisarjevsky; *m* 1982, William D. Marslen-Wilson, *qv*; one *s* one *d*. *Educ:* Leicester Univ. (BA); Chicago Univ. (PhD 1977). Sen. Res. Fellow, Max Planck Inst. for Psycholinguistics, 1977–85; Lectr, Dept of Psychology, Cambridge Univ., 1985–90; Prof. of Psychology, Birkbeck Coll., Univ. of London, 1990–98. *Publications:* Spoken Language Comprehension, 1992; contrib. Brain and Lang., Jl of Cognitive Neurosci., Cerebral Cortex, Psychological Rev., Cognition, etc. *Address:* Department of Psychology, University of Cambridge, Downing Street, Cambridge CB2 3EB. *T:* (01223) 766457.

**TYLER, Prof. Nicholas Andrew,** CBE 2011; PhD; FREng, FICE, FCIHT; Chadwick Professor of Civil Engineering, since 2003, and Director, UCL Centre for Transport Studies, since 2017, University College London; *b* Harrow, Middx, 3 Sept. 1954; *s* of Douglas Eric Rhodes Tyler and Joan Priscilla Tyler (*née* Hill); *m* 1988, Katrina Hoogendam. *Educ:* University College Sch.; Royal Coll. of Music (ARCM 1975); Poly. of Central London (MSc 1987); University Coll. London (PhD 1992). FICE 2004; FREng 2014; FCIHT 2017. Freelance musician, 1975–82; Mgt Trainee, BEREC Gp, 1982–84; Ops Manager, Unichem Ltd, 1984–85; Mentor, Community Aid, 1985–86; University College London: Res. Asst, 1987–92, Lectr, 1992–97, Sen. Lectr, 1997–99, Reader, 1999–2002, in Transport Studies; Prof. of Communities and Transport, 2002–03; Hd of Dept, Civil, Envmtl and Geomatic Engrg, 2003–13; Pro Provost, E and S Asia, 2011–15. Prof. Honorario de Ingeniería, Pontificia Universidad Católica del Peru, 2008–. *Publications:* (ed) Accessibility and the Bus System: from concepts to practice, 2002, 2nd edn as Accessibility and the Bus System: transforming the World, 2015; articles in New England Jl of Medicine, Transportation Res., Transportation Planning and Technol., Jl Transport Geog., Healthcare Technol. Letters, Safety Sci., Transportation Res. Record, Proc. ICE, Transportation, Sustainability. *Recreation:* music (oboe playing). *Address:* Department of Civil, Environmental and Geomatic Engineering, University College London, Gower Street, WC1E 6BT. *T:* (020) 7679 1562. *E:* n.tyler@ucl.ac.uk.

**TYLER, Paula Margot; Her Honour Judge Tyler;** a Circuit Judge, since 2012; *b* Manchester, 18 Sept. 1961; *d* of Joseph Paul Tyler and Margaret Tyler; partner, Jai Penna, *qv*. *Educ:* Stand Grammar Sch. for Girls; University Coll. London (BSc Hons Anthropol.). Admitted solicitor, 1989; transferred to the Bar, Middle Temple, 1997; a Recorder, 2005–12. *Recreations:* crime fiction, film, a range of sports, all things Italian.

**TYLER, Richard Herbert;** executive coach and business consultant; Director: Dick Tyler Consultancy LLP, since 2014; Tyler Wilson Ltd, since 2016; Senior Partner, 2011–14, Consultant, 2014–15, CMS Cameron McKenna LLP; *b* Cheltenham, 19 Feb. 1959; *s* of Peter Anthony Tyler and late Barbara Margaret Tyler (*née* Wilson); *m* 1985 (marr. diss. 2011); two *d. Educ:* Cheltenham Grammar Sch.; Fitzwilliam Coll., Cambridge (BA 1982; MA 1985). Admitted solicitor, 1985; McKenna & Co., later CMS Cameron McKenna LLP: joined 1983; Partner, 1992–2014; Man. Partner, 2000–08; Exec. Partner, CMS Legal Services EEIG, 2008–11. Mem. Bd, London Legacy 2020, 2006–12. Faculty Mem., Meyler Campbell Ltd, 2011–; Dir/Trustee, PRIME, 2012–15. Dir, Varsity Match Co. Ltd, 2015–. President: Old Patesians RFC, 2006–; Fitzwilliam Soc., 2012–13. Member: Cttee, City of London Law Soc., 2012–15; Court, City of London Solicitors' Co., 2016–18. Mem., Develt Cttee, Fitzwilliam Coll., Cambridge, 2014–18. Chm., Cambridge Univ. RFU, 2016–. *Recreations:* watching Rugby and other sport, fitness, performing arts, choral singing (Barts Choir). *Address:* c/o Dick Tyler Consultancy LLP, First Floor, York House, 74–82 Queen Victoria Street, EC4N 4SJ. *T:* (020) 7282 0101. *E:* dick@dicktyler.com. *Club:* Hawks' (Cambridge).

**TYLER, Maj.-Gen. Timothy Nicholas,** CB 2008; Director, Kilmeston Consulting, since 2012; *b* 15 Dec. 1953; *s* of Maj.-Gen. Sir Leslie Norman Tyler, KBE, CB and Sheila Tyler; *m* 1976, Johanna Lee Weston; three *s* six *d. Educ:* Worth Sch.; Christ's Coll., Cambridge (MA 1979). Commnd REME, 1972; Commander: Equipment Support, 1st Armoured Div., 1992–93; REME Trng Gp, 1997–99; Director: Army Staff Duties, 1999–2001; Army Resources and Plans, 2001–02; rcds 2002; COS HQ Adjt Gen., 2003; Dep. Adjt Gen., 2004–05; Quartermaster Gen., 2006–07; Dir Gen. Logistics (Land), 2006–07; Dir Gen. Land Equipment, 2007–08. Dir, Serco Gp plc, 2009–12. Asst Col Comdt, AGC, 2004–05; Colonel Commandant: REME, 2005–12; Corps of Army Music, 2005–09. Chair of Govs, Royal Star and Garter Homes, 2015–. *Recreations:* singing, sailing.
*See also A. N. Tyler.*

**TYLER, William John;** QC 2014; a Recorder, since 2012; a Deputy High Court Judge (Family Division), since 2016; part-time Deemster and High Bailiff, Isle of Man, since 2017; *b* Northampton, 25 May 1974; *s* of late John Douglas Tyler and of Gillian Mary Tyler (*née* Haig); *m* 1999, Charlotte Taylor-Hunt; one *s* two *d. Educ:* Stoneygate Sch., Leicester; Oundle Sch.; Worcester Coll., Oxford (BA Hons Juris. 1995; MA). Called to the Bar, Inner Temple, 1996; in practice as a barrister, specialising in children's law, 1996–. *Recreations:* gastronomy, gardening, cycling, opera. *Address:* 36 Group, 4 Field Court, Gray's Inn, WC1R 5EF. *T:* (020) 7421 8000. *Club:* Oxford and Cambridge.

**TYLER-HAYWOOD, (June) Sandra;** HM Diplomatic Service, retired; Head of Governor's Office, Falkland Islands, 2012–17; *b* Nuneaton, 5 March 1957; *d* of late Herbert Sidney Kirk and of Cynthia Ruby Kirk (*née* Hartshorn); *m* 1991, Ian Haywood; one *s* one *d. Educ:* Manor Park Grammar Sch.; Open Univ. (BSc). Entered FCO, 1989; Admin. Officer, FCO, 1989–92; Third Secretary: FCO, 1992–94; Beijing, 1994–97; Lisbon, 1998–2002; Second Sec., FCO, 2002–05; First Secretary: Eastern Caribbean, 2005–07; Basra, 2008–09; Ambassador to Eritrea, 2010–12. *Recreations:* photography, golf.

**TYMKEWYCZ, Stefan;** Member (SNP) Edinburgh City Council, 2007–17; *b* 18 Sept. 1959; *s* of Bohdan and Jean Tymkewycz; *m* Morag Allard. *Educ:* St David's Primary and Secondary Schs, Dalkeith; Esk Valley Coll., Dalkeith. Apprentice engr, 1976–80; traveller, 1980–84; Metropolitan Police Officer, 1984–2001; property landlord, 2001–. MSP (SNP) Lothians, May–Aug. 2007. Patron, Alma Project, 2012– (Chair Trustees, 2018–). *Recreations:* travelling, keeping fit, cycling, theatre and cinema, hill walking, football (season ticket holder at Hibernian FC), Scrabble. *E:* stymkewycz@btinternet.com.

**TYMMS, Prof. Peter Booth,** PhD; FAcSS; Professor of Education, Durham University, since 1999; *b* Springs, S Africa, 21 Jan. 1949; *s* of Wilfrid Widdas Tymms and Dorothy Tymms (*née* Booth); *m* 1974, Beena Rose Steaphen; two *s. Educ:* Giggleswick Sch.; Christ's Coll., Cambridge (BA 1970; MA 1975); Newcastle Univ. (PGCE 1971; MEd 1986); PhD Cantab 1997. Teacher of Sci. and Housemaster, Nchelenge Secondary Sch., Zambia, 1971–75; Teacher of Chemistry, Ulverston High Sch., 1975; Teacher of Chemistry, 1975–78, Hd of Chemistry, 1978–84, Easington Secondary, subseq. Comprehensive Sch.; Lectr in Chemistry with Physics, Peterlee Coll., 1985–90; on secondment as Res. Associate, Univ. of Newcastle upon Tyne, 1987–90; Lectr, Moray Hse Inst. of Educn, Heriot-Watt Univ., 1990–92; Lectr, 1992–95, Dir for Res., 1994–95, Dept of Educn, Univ. of Newcastle upon Tyne; Durham University: Reader, 1996–99; Dir, Centre for Evaluation and Monitoring, 2003–10; Hd of Dept, Sch. of Educn, 2010–13. Gov., Elemore Sch., 2019–. FAcSS 2010. *Publications:* Baseline Assessment and Monitoring in Primary Schools, 1999; (ed jtly) Techniques for Monitoring the Comparability of Examination Standards, 2007; (with F. Ndaji) The P Scales: assessing the progress of children with special educational needs, 2009; contrib. chapters in books and articles, res. reports and reviews in jls. *Recreations:* croquet, gardening, reading. *Address:* School of Education, Durham University, Leazes Road, Durham DH1 1TA. *T:* (0191) 334 8413. *E:* peter.tymms@gmail.com.

**TYNAN, Prof. Michael John,** MD, FRCP; Professor of Paediatric Cardiology, Guy's Hospital, 1982–99; *b* 18 April 1934; *s* of late Jerry Joseph Tynan and Florence Ann Tynan; *m* 1958, Eirlys Pugh Williams. *Educ:* Bedford Modern School; London Hospital. MD, BS. Senior Asst Resident, Children's Hosp., Boston, Mass, 1962; Registrar, Westminster Hosp., 1964; Registrar, later Lectr, Hosp. for Sick Children, Great Ormond St, 1966; consultant paediatric cardiologist, Newcastle Univ. Hospitals, 1971, Guy's Hosp., 1977. *Publications:* (jtly) Paediatric Cardiology, a textbook, 1983; articles on nomenclature and classification of congenital heart disease and on heart disease in children. *Recreations:* singing, watching cricket, playing snooker. *Address:* 5 Ravensdon Street, SE11 4AQ. *T:* (020) 7735 7119. *Clubs:* Athenæum; Roehampton Golf.

**TYNAN, Sarah Jane,** FRAM; opera singer, since 2003; *b* London, 30 April 1976; *d* of James and Caroline Tynan; *m* 2007, Leigh Melrose; one *s* one *d. Educ:* Royal Northern Coll. of Music (BMus 2000); Royal Acad. of Music (Dip. RAM 2003; LRAM 2003; FRAM 2019). Principal rôles: Rosina, Adina, Partenope Ilia, Tytania, Lucia, Hanna Glawari, Euridice, ENO, 2003–19; Cleopatra, Opera North, 2012; Henze's Manon, WNO, 2014; Merab, Glyndebourne on Tour, 2015; Fiorilla, Garsington, 2017; Pat Nixon, Danish Opera, 2019; has performed at: Les Illuminations, Aldeburgh Fest., 2016; Brahms Requiem and Beethoven 9, Maggio Musicale Fiorentino, Florence, 2017; Haydn Creation, Edinburgh Fest., 2018. *Recreations:* family, travel, teaching, cycling, gin. *Address:* Groves Artists Management, 7 St George's Court, 131 Putney Bridge Road, SW15 2PA. *T:* (020) 8874 3222. *E:* sarah@sarahtynan.com.

**TYNAN, William;** part-time researcher for John Robertson, MP, 2005–15; *b* 18 Aug. 1940; *s* of late James and Mary Tynan; *m* 1964, Elizabeth Mathieson; three *d. Educ:* St Joseph's Sch.; St Mungo's Acad.; Stow Coll. Press toolmaker, 1961–88. Joined AEU (subseq. AEEU), 1966: shop steward and convener, 1966; Member: Mid Lanark Dist Cttee, 1969; Divl Cttee, 1976; Nat. Cttee, 1977–88; full-time Union Official, 1988–99: Dist Sec., 1988–96; Regl Officer, 1996–99; Political Officer, 1991; Scottish Political Sec., 1993. MP (Lab) Hamilton South, Sept. 1999–2005. Member: Parly Select Cttee on NI, 2001–05; European Scrutiny Cttee, 2001–05; Convenor, Scottish Gp of MPs, 2001–02; Special Advr, All Party Parly Gp on Nuclear Energy, 2005– (Chm., 2001–05). Joined Labour Party, 1969: Mem. Exec. and Gen. Mgt Cttee, Hamilton N and Hamilton S Constituency Parties, 1979–2005; Chm., Hamilton S CLP, 1987; Member: Scottish Labour Policy Forum, 1998; Scottish Exec., 1982–88. Nat. Coordinator, Trade Unions for Safe Nuclear Energy, 2006–. Board Member: SoLVE, S Lanarkshire, 2006–; VASLAN, 2011–. *Recreations:* golf, swimming, gardening, DIY. *Address:* 6 East Scott Terrace, Hamilton ML3 6SF. *T:* (01698) 421660.

**TYNDALL, Rev. Canon Timothy;** Chief Secretary, Advisory Council for the Church's Ministry, 1985–90; *b* 24 April 1925; *s* of Rev. Denis Tyndall and Nora Tyndall; *m* 1953, Dr Ruth Mary Turner (*d* 1998); two *s* twin *d. Educ:* Jesus Coll., Cambridge (BA). Parish Incumbent: Newark, 1955; Nottingham, 1960; Sunderland, 1975. *Address:* Flat 16, 2B Bollo Lane, Chiswick, W4 5LE. *T:* (020) 8994 4516.

**TYNER, Sarah Frances;** *see* Jones, S. F.

**TYRE, Hon. Lord; Colin Jack Tyre,** CBE 2010; a Senator of the College of Justice in Scotland, since 2010; *b* 17 April 1956; *s* of James Harrison Tyre and Lilias Carmichael Tyre (*née* Kincaid); *m* 1982, Elaine Patricia Carlin (*d* 2010); one *s* two *d. Educ:* Dunoon Grammar Sch.; Univ. of Edinburgh (LLB Hons); Université d'Aix-Marseille (DESU). Admitted Solicitor, 1980; admitted to Faculty of Advocates, 1987; QC (Scot.) 1998. Lectr in Law, Univ. of Edinburgh, 1980–83; Tax Editor, CCH Editions Ltd, 1983–86; Standing Junior Counsel: MoD (PE), 1991–95; Scottish Office Envmt Dept (in planning matters), 1995–98; Comr (pt-time), Scottish Law Commn, 2003–09. Pres., CCBE, 2007 (Hd, UK Delegn, 2004). Chm., Bd of Govs, Fettes Coll., Edinburgh, 2012–18; Mem., Bd of Trustees, Acad. of Eur. Law, Trier, 2012–. Mem., Exec. Bd, Eur. Network of Judicial Councils, 2016–18. Grand Decoration of Honour, Austria, 2009. *Publications:* CCH Inheritance Tax Reporter, 1986; (jtly) Tax for Litigation Lawyers, 2000; contrib. Stair Memorial Encyclopaedia, learned jls. *Recreations:* mountain walking, golf, orienteering, music (especially popular). *Address:* Parliament House, Edinburgh EH1 1RQ. *T:* (0131) 225 2595.

**TYRELL-KENYON;** *see* Kenyon.

**TYRER, His Honour Christopher John Meese;** DL; a Circuit Judge, 1989–2011; Resident Judge, Aylesbury Crown Court, 2005–11; *b* 22 May 1944; *s* of late Jack Meese Tyrer and of Margaret Joan Tyrer (*née* Wyatt); *m* 1974, Jane Beckett, JP, LLB, MA, barrister; one *s* one *d. Educ:* Wellington College; Bristol University. LLB Hons. Called to the Bar, Inner Temple, 1968. Asst Recorder, 1979–83; a Recorder, 1983–89; Designated Family Judge, Bucks 1991–97, London 1998–2005. Governor: St John's Sch., Lacey Green, 1984–92; Speen Sch., 1984–96 (Chm., 1989–91 and 1995–96); Misbourne Sch., 1993–2007 (Vice Chm., 1995–2000, Chm., 2000–07). Mem., Bucks Assoc. of Govs of Primary Schs, 1989–90. Patron, Law Soc., Buckinghamshire New Univ. (formerly Buckinghamshire Chilterns University Coll.), 2002–12; Vice Patron, Oasis Partnership, 2014–. Chair, New Leaf Charity for supporting ex-offenders, 2011–. Trustee: Thames Valley Partnership, 2011–; New Mozart Orch., 2017; Chiltern Arts Fest., 2017–. Hon. Recorder of Aylesbury, 2010–11. DL Bucks, 2008. Hon. Dr Bucks New, 2011. Ed., Clarke Hall and Morrison on Children, 2003–07. *Recreations:* grandchildren, sponsored children in Nicaragua and The Philippines, music, boating, following Wycombe Wanderers Football Club. *Address:* Randalls Cottage, Loosley Row, Princes Risborough, Bucks HP27 0NU. *T:* (01844) 344650.

**TYRER, Prof. Peter Julian,** MD; Professor of Community Psychiatry, Imperial College London (formerly Imperial College of Science, Technology and Medicine), 1991–2016, now Emeritus; Honorary Professor, University of Nottingham, since 2006; *b* 13 Aug. 1940; *s* (identical twin) of Frank Herbert Tyrer and Mary (May) Jane Tyrer; *m* 1st, 1967, Ann Anderson (marr. diss. 2003); one *s* two *d*; 2nd, 2010, Helen Seivewright (*née* Bown). *Educ:* King Edward Sch., Birmingham; Gonville and Caius Coll., Cambridge (BA 1962; MB, BChir 1966; MD 1975); St Thomas's Hosp. Med. Sch., London. FRCPsych 1979, Hon. FRCPsych 2014; FRCP 1993; FFPH (FFPHM 1999). House Officer in Psychological Medicine, St Thomas' Hosp., 1966–67; Sen. House Officer in Medicine, Burton-on-Trent Gen. Hosp., 1967–68; Registrar in Psychiatry: St John's Hosp., Aylesbury, 1968–69; Maudsley Hosp., 1969–70; MRC Clin. Res. Fellow, 1970–73; Sen. Lectr in Psychiatry, Univ. of Southampton, 1973–79; Cons. Psychiatrist, Mapperley Hosp., Nottingham, 1979–88; Sen. Lectr in Community Psychiatry, St Mary's Hosp. Med. Sch., 1988–91; Hd, Dept of Public Mental Health, 1997–2002, Dept of Psychol Medicine, 2002–05), ICSTM. Andrew Woods Prof., Univ. of Iowa, 1986. Milroy Lectr, RCP, 2007. Ed., British Jl of Psychiatry, 2003–13. European Pres., Internat. Soc. for Study of Personality Disorders, 1995–98; Founding Pres., British and Irish Gp for the Study of Personality Disorders, 1999; Chairman: Sect. on Personality Disorders, World Psychiatric Assoc., 2008– (Co-Chm., 2002–08); Working Gp for Revision of Personality Disorders, WHO, 2010–15. Chair, Nidus-UK, 2013–. FMedSci 1999. Gaskell Bronze Medal and Res. Prize, 1973, Lifetime Achievement Award, 2015, RCPsych. *Publications:* The Role of Bodily Feelings in Anxiety, 1976; Insomnia, 1978; Stress, 1980, 2nd edn 2003; (ed) Drugs in Psychiatric Practice, 1982, 2nd edn 1997; How to Stop Taking Tranquillisers, 1986; Models for Mental Disorder (with D. Steinberg), 1987, 5th edn (sole author) 2013; Personality Disorders: diagnosis, management and course, 1988, 2nd edn 2000; (ed) Psychopharmacology of Anxiety, 1989; Classification of Neurosis, 1989; (with C. Freeman) Research Methodology in Psychiatry: a beginner's guide, 1989, 3rd edn 2006; (with B. Puri) Sciences Basic to Psychiatry, 1992, 2nd edn 1998; (with P. Casey) Social Function in Psychiatry: the hidden axis of classification exposed, 1993; Anxiety: a multidisciplinary review, 1999; (with K. Silk) Cambridge Textbook of Effective Treatments in Psychiatry, 2008; Nidotherapy: harmonising the environment with the patient, 2009, 2nd edn 2018; (with K. R. Silk) Effective Treatments in Psychiatry, 2011; The Death of King John (play), 2016, 2nd edn 2017; Taming the Beast Within: shredding the stereotypes of personality disorder, 2018; The Watermeadow Mystery (novel), 2018. *Recreations:* jousting with social workers, writing eye-openers, doggerel, composing operettas. *Address:* The Poplars, Cotham Lane, Hawton, Newark, Notts NG24 3RL. *T:* (01636) 679245.

**TYRIE,** Baron *cr* 2018 (Life Peer), of Chichester in the County of West Sussex; **Andrew Guy Tyrie;** PC 2015; Chairman, Competition and Markets Authority, since 2018; *b* 15 Jan. 1957; *s* of late Derek and Patricia Tyrie. *Educ:* Felsted Sch.; Trinity Coll., Oxford (MA); Coll. of Europe, Bruges (MDip. Econ. Studies); Wolfson Coll., Cambridge (MPhil). BP, 1981–83; Cons. Res. Dept, 1984–85; Special Advr to Chancellor of the Exchequer, 1986–90; Fellow, Nuffield Coll., Oxford, 1990–91; Woodrow Wilson Scholar, Washington, 1991; Sen. Economist, EBRD, 1992–97. Contested (C) Houghton and Washington, 1992. MP (C) Chichester, 1997–2017. Shadow Financial Sec., 2003–04; Shadow Paymaster Gen., 2004–05. Chairman: Treasury Select Cttee, 2010–17 (Mem., 2001–03, 2009–10); Parly Commn on Banking Standards, 2012–13; Liaison Cttee, 2015–17; Member: Select Cttee on Public Admin, 1997–2001; Justice Cttee (formerly Constitutional Affairs Select Cttee), 2005–10; Public Accounts Commn, 1997–2017 (Chm., 2010–11); Exec. Cttee, 1922 Cttee, 2005–06. *Publications:* The Prospects for Public

Spending, 1996; Sense on EMU, 1998; Reforming the Lords, 1998; (jtly) Leviathan at Large, 2000; Mr Blair's Poodle, 2000; (jtly) Statism by Stealth, 2002; Mr Blair's Poodle Goes to War, 2004; (jtly) Account Rendered, 2011; many pamphlets on econ. and parly issues. *Recreation:* golf. *Clubs:* Garrick, MCC, Royal Automobile.

**TYRIE, Peter Robert,** MBE 2010; Managing Director, Eton Group, 1999–2009; *b* 3 April 1946; *m* 1972, Christine Mary Tyrie; three *s* (and one *d* decd). *Educ:* Westminster College Hotel Sch. (BSc Hotel Admin). Manager, Inverurie Hotel, Bermuda, 1969–71; Resident Manager, Portman Hotel, London, 1971–73; Project Dir, Pannell Kerr Forster, 1973–77; Operations Dir, Penta Hotels, 1977–80; Managing Director: Gleneagles Hotels plc, 1980–86; Mandarin Oriental Hotel Gp, 1986–89; Balmoral Internat. Hotels, 1989–98. Director: Bell's Whisky, 1983; Dragon Trust, Edinburgh Fund Managers, 1989–2010; Aberdeen Asset Managers Dragon Fund, 1989–2010. FIH (FHCIMA 1977). *Recreations:* squash, shooting, fishing, Rugby, classic cars. *Address:* Popple Meadows, Graffham, Petworth, W Sussex GU28 0QF.

**TYRONE, Earl of;** Richard John de la Poer Beresford; *b* 19 Aug. 1987; *er s* and *heir* of Marquess of Waterford, *qv*. *Educ:* Harrow.

**TYRONE, Polly Janet;** *see* Mackenzie, P. J.

**TYROR, John George,** OBE 1999; JP; Director of Safety, United Kingdom Atomic Energy Authority, 1990–92, retired; *b* 5 Nov. 1930; *s* of John Thomas Tyror and Nora Tyror (*née* Tennant); *m* 1956, Sheila Wylie; one *s* one *d*. *Educ:* Manchester Univ. (BSc 1st cl. Hons Maths, MSc); Trinity Hall, Cambridge. FInstP. Asst Lectr, Univ. of Leeds, 1955–56; AEA Harwell, 1956–59; Atomic Energy Estabt, Winfrith, 1959–63; Reactor Develt Lab., Windscale, 1963–66; Winfrith, 1966–87 (Asst Dir, 1979–87); Dir, Safety and Reliability Directorate, Culcheth, 1987–90. Member: Eur./Amer. Cttee on Reactor Physics, 1960–72; Adv. Cttee for Transport of Radioactive Materials, 1981–84; Adv. Cttee on Safety of Nuclear Installations, HSC, 1992–95; Nuclear Safety Adv. Cttee, HSC, 1995–98. Chm., Compensation Scheme for Radiation-Linked Diseases, 2001–07. JP Poole, 1976, Macclesfield, 1988. *Publications:* An Introduction to the Neutron Kinetics of Nuclear Power Reactors, 1970. *Recreations:* bridge playing and teaching, food and wine, grandfather.

**TYRRELL, Robert James;** Principal, Bob Tyrrell and Co., since 2000; Chairman, Demos, 2002–06 (Member, Advisory Council, since 1992); *b* 6 June 1951; *s* of Peter John Tyrrell and Mair (*née* Harries); *m* 1983, Jean Linda McKerrow; two *d*. *Educ:* St Peter's Coll., Oxford (MA, PPE), LSE (MSc Phil with dist.). Academic research, Sussex and Glasgow Univs, 1972–74; joined James Morrell & Associates, 1974; Perkins Engines, 1977; Futures Group, USA, 1980; Man. Dir, 1986–92, Chief Exec., 1992–95, Exec. Chm., 1995–96, Henley Centre for Forecasting. Develt Partner, Cognosis Strategy Consultants, 1999–2003. Chm., Global Future Forum Europe, 2001–03. Vis. Prof., City Univ. Business Sch., 1994–2001. Director: New Solutions, 1997–2000; La Table du Pain, Luxembourg, 1999–2007; Archial (formerly SMC) Gp plc, 2005–09; non-exec. Dir, Trajectory Ltd, 2011–; Chm., Sociovision, UK, 2001–03. Associate and Consultant, Milligan Retail, 2005–. Member: Steering Cttee, Econ. Beliefs and Behaviour Prog., ESRC, 1994–99; Council, Conservative Party Policy Forum, 1999–2002. Assoc. Mem., BUPA, 2004–. Trustee and Dir, Golden Oldies, 2007–09. Presenter: Opinions, C4, 1994; Analysis, BBC Radio, 1997–2007. FRSA. *Publications:* (ed jtly) Britain in the 1980s, 1974; (ed jtly) Britain 2001, 1977; (ed jtly) Planning for Social Change, annually, 1983–93; Things Can Only Get... Different, 2001. *Recreations:* reading, sailing, fly-fishing, cycling, walking, theatre, guitar, meditating, lindy hop dancing. *Address:* Warberry Lodge, Lansdown Road, Bath BA1 5RB.

**TYRWHITT, Sir Reginald (Thomas Newman),** 3rd Bt *cr* 1919; DL; *b* 21 Feb. 1947; *er s* of Admiral Sir St John Tyrwhitt, 2nd Bt, KCB, DSO, DSC and Bar (*d* 1961), and Nancy (Veronica) Gilbey (who *m* 1965, Sir Godfrey Agnew, KCVO, CB; she *d* 2010); *S* father, 1961; *m* 1972, Sheila Gail (marr. diss. 1980 and annulled 1984), *d* of William Alistair Crawford Nicoll, Liphook, Hants; *m* 1984, Charlotte, *o d* of late Captain and the Hon. Mrs Angus Hildyard, Goxhill Hall, Goxhill, N Lincs; one *s* one *d*. *Educ:* Downside. Served in Royal Artillery 1966–69. Career spent subseq. in UK paper industry. DL Lincs, 2014. *Recreations:* shooting, fishing, drawing. *Heir: s* Robert St John Hildyard Tyrwhitt [*b* 15 Feb. 1987; *m* 2016, Anneke, *d* of Prof. Kieran Hodnett and Eveline van Ijssel, Lisnagry, Co. Limerick].

**TYSON, Elisabeth;** *see* Murdoch, E.

**TYSON, Prof. Laura D'Andrea,** PhD; Dean of London Business School, 2002–06; Director, Institute for Business and Social Impact, since 2013, and Distinguished Professor, Graduate School, since 2016, Haas School of Business, University of California at Berkeley (Professor of Business, Administration and Economics, 1992–2016, now Emeritus); *b* 28 June 1947; *m* Erik Tarloff; one *s*. *Educ:* Smith Coll. (BA 1969); MIT (PhD 1974). Asst Prof., Dept of Econs, Princeton Univ., 1974–77; University of California, Berkeley: Prof. of Econs, 1977–2002; Prof., 1990–2002, Dean, 1998–2002, Prof. of Econs and Business Admin, 2007–08, S. K. and Angela Chan Chair in Global Mgt, 2008–13, Haas Sch. of Business; Dir, Inst. of Internat. Studies, 1990–92; Dir of Res., Berkeley Roundtable on Internat. Economy, 1988–92; Dist. Teaching Award, 1982. Chairman: US President's Council of Econ. Advrs, 1993–95; Nat. Econ. Council, 1995–96; Principal, Law and Econs Consulting Gp, 1997–2000; Mem., Council on Foreign Relations, 1997–. Member Board: Eastman Kodak Co., 1997–; Morgan Stanley Co., 1998–; SBC Communications, 1999–; Bruegel, 2005–. Columnist, Business Week. Fellow, Nat. Fellows Prog., Hoover Inst., 1978–79. *Publications:* The Yugoslav Economic System and its Performance in the 1970s, 1980; (ed with Egon Neuberger) The Impact of External Economic Disturbances on the Soviet Union and Eastern Europe, 1980; (ed with John Zysman) American Industry in International Competition: political and economic perspectives, 1983; Economic Adjustment in Eastern Europe, 1984; (ed with Ellen Comisso) Power, Purpose and Collective Choice: economic strategy in socialist states, 1986; (ed with William T. Dickens and John Zysman) The Politics of Productivity: the real story of why Japan works, 1989; Who's Bashing Whom? trade conflict in high technology industries, 1992; articles in professional jls. *Address:* Haas School of Business, 545 Student Services #1900, University of California at Berkeley, Berkeley, CA 94720–1900, USA.

**TYSZKIEWICZ, Zygmunt Jan Ansgary,** CMG 1998; President, Lanckoronski Foundation, 1996–2014; *b* 4 Feb. 1934; *s* of Count Jan Michal Tyszkiewicz and Anna Maria Tyszkiewicz (*née* Princess Radziwill); *m* 1958, Kerstin Barbro Ekman; two *s* two *d*. *Educ:* Downside Sch.; Sidney Sussex Coll., Cambridge (BA Hons Mod. and Medieval Langs). Officer, XII Royal Lancers, 1956–57. Joined Shell International Petroleum, 1957: Man. Dir, Shell-BP Tanzania, 1970–73; Gen. Manager, Shell Hellas, 1979–85; Sec. Gen., UNICE, Brussels, 1985–98. Member: Bd, Eur. Foundn for Mgt Develt, Brussels, 1985–98; Adv. Council, Involvement and Participation Assoc., London, 1998–2005. Gov., Eur. Policy Forum, London, 1998–2011. Hon. DBA Robert Gordon Univ., 2000. KM 1994; Grand Cross ad Merito Melitensi, SMO Malta, 2002; Kt, Order of Dannebrog (Denmark), 1997; Comdr, Order of Leopold (Belgium), 1998. *Publications:* contrib. numerous articles on European and business issues in UK and European jls. *Recreations:* family holidays with grandchildren, European Union and Polish politics. *Address:* 5 Champneys Walk, Cambridge CB3 9AW. *T:* (01223) 302816. *E:* zygmunttysz@hotmail.co.uk.

**TYTE, David Christopher,** CB 1997; PhD; Director Rationalisation, Defence Evaluation and Research Agency, Ministry of Defence, 1991–97; *b* 19 Aug. 1937. *Educ:* Dulwich Coll.; Imperial Coll., London (PhD, BSc). CEng, FInstP. NRC Post Doctoral Fellow, Univ. of Western Ontario, 1962–65; Asst Prof., York Univ., Toronto, 1965–67; joined MoD, 1967; Dep. Dir (Underwater), Admiralty Res. Estabt, 1987–89; Technical Dir, DRA, 1989–91.

**TYZACK, His Honour David Ian Heslop;** QC 1999; a Circuit Judge, 2000–14; Designated Family Judge, Exeter, 2010–14; Nominated Judge of the Court of Protection, 2011–14; *b* 21 March 1946; *s* of late Ernest Rudolf Tyzack and Joan Mary Tyzack (*née* Palmer); *m* 1973, Elizabeth Anne Cubitt; one *s* one *d*. *Educ:* Allhallows Sch., Rousdon; St Catharine's Coll., Cambridge (MA 1969). Called to the Bar, Inner Temple, 1970, Bencher, 2007; in practice at the Bar, Western Circuit, 1971–2000; Asst Recorder, 1996–2000; Recorder, 2000; a Dep. High Ct Judge, 2000–14; Designated Family Judge, Plymouth, 2003–09. Chm., Devon and Cornwall Br., Family Law Bar Assoc., 1992–2000. Mem., Devonshire Assoc. Churchwarden, Farringdon Ch, Devon, 1992–2010. *Publications:* (contrib.) Essential Family Practice, 2001. *Recreations:* gardening, ski-ing, church, house in France. *Address:* Magdalen Chambers, Victory House, Dean Clarke Gardens, Exeter EX2 4AA. *Club:* Devon and Exeter Institution.

# U

**UCHIDA, Dame Mitsuko**, DBE 2009 (CBE 2001); pianist; *b* 20 Dec. 1948; *d* of Fujio and Yasuko Uchida. *Educ*: Hochschule für Musik, Vienna. First recital at age of 14 in Vienna; performs regularly with orchestras worldwide incl. Berlin Philharmonic, Vienna Philharmonic, Cleveland, etc.; performed complete Mozart piano sonatas in London, 1982, Tokyo, 1983, and NY, 1991; Schubert and Schoenberg recitals in Salzburg, London, Vienna, NY, Tokyo, etc, 1994–96; complete Mozart piano concertos with Cleveland Orch., 2003–08; five Beethoven piano concertos with Berlin Philharmonic, 2010; repertoire ranges from Bach to Boulez. Co-Dir, Marlboro Music Fest., Vermont, USA, 2000–; Founder Mem., Borletti-Buitoni Trust, 2003–. Mem., American Philosophical Soc. Recordings include: complete piano sonatas and concertos of Mozart; Beethoven's piano concertos; Debussy's Etudes; Schumann's Carnaval; Schoenberg piano concerto; Beethoven's last five piano sonatas. Has won many prizes for recordings. Hon. DMus: Oxford, 2009; Cambridge, 2014. *Recreations*: sleeping, listening to music. *Address*: c/o Victoria Rowsell Artist Management, 34 Addington Square, SE5 7LB. *T*: (020) 7701 3219. *E*: management@victoriarowsell.co.uk.

**UDAL, Rev. Canon Joanna Elizabeth Margaret;** Archbishop of Canterbury's Secretary for Anglican Communion Affairs, 2009–14; Chaplain, Southwark Cathedral, since 2011; *b* London, 27 Dec. 1964; *d* of John Udal and Ann Hopkins-Clarke. *Educ*: Sherborne Sch. for Girls; Univ. of Durham (BSc Maths 1986; PGCE 1987); Ripon Coll., Cuddesdon (BTh Theol. Oxon 1997). Admin. Asst, Internat. Chamber of Shipping, 1987–89; Chamber of Shipping: Admin. Asst, 1989–91; Asst Manager, 1991–94; Manager, Internat. Policy, 1994. Ordained deacon, 1997, priest, 1998; Asst Curate, St Augustine of Canterbury, Whitton, London, 1997–2000; Asst to Archbishop of Sudan, 2001–09. Provincial Canon, All Saints' Cathedral, Juba, Sudan, 2007–. Cross of St Augustine, 2018. *Publications*: contrib. article in Ecumenical Rev. *Recreations*: choral singing, opera, Sudan Archaeology Society (Sec., 2005–09).

**UDALL, Jan;** *see* Beaney, J.

**UDDIN**, family name of **Baroness Uddin**.

**UDDIN**, Baroness *cr* 1998 (Life Peer), of Bethnal Green in the London Borough of Tower Hamlets; **Pola Manzila Uddin;** *b* Bangladesh, 17 July 1959; *m* 1976, Komar Uddin; four *s* one *d*. Youth and Community Worker, YWCA, 1980–82; Liaison Officer, Tower Hamlets Social Services, 1982–84; Manager: Women's Health Project, 1984–88; Asian Family Counselling Service, 1989–90; Social Worker, Manager and subseq. Mgt Consultant, London Borough of Newham Social Services, 1993–98. Mem. (Lab), Tower Hamlets LBC, 1990–98 (Dep. Leader, Lab Gp, 1993–94; Dep. Leader, Council, 1994–96). House of Lords: former Chairman: Home Office Wkg Gp; Wkg Gp on Pol and Community Leadership; European Select Cttee; Chair, Govt Cttee on Forced Marriage; Mem., Community Cohesion Bd. Non-exec. Dir, Carlton TV (Chm., London Licensing Bd). Member: CPA; IPU; former Mem., CETSW. Member, Board: Autism Speak UK; St Katharine and Shadwell Trust. Patron: Bethnal Green and Victoria Park Housing Assoc.; Orbis International; Tower Hamlets Women's Aid; Royal Coll. of Speech and Language Therapy; Disability Trust; Attlee Foundn; Social Action for Health. *Address*: House of Lords, SW1A 0PW. *T*: (020) 7219 8506.

**UDEN, Martin David;** HM Diplomatic Service, retired; Group Government Affairs, HSBC, 2015–17; *b* 28 Feb. 1955; *s* of late Rodney Frederick Uden and Margaret Irene Uden (*née* Brunt); *m* 1982, Fiona Jane Smith; two *s*. *Educ*: Ravensbourne Sch. for Boys; Queen Mary Coll., London Univ. (LLB). Called to the Bar, Inner Temple, 1977; joined FCO, 1977; Second Sec., Seoul, 1978–81; Second, later First Sec., FCO, 1981–86; First Sec., Bonn, 1986–90; FCO, 1990–93; Dep. Head, CSCE Unit, FCO, 1993–94; Pol Counsellor and Consul-Gen., Seoul, 1994–97; Econ., then Trade/Econ., Counsellor, Ottawa, 1997–2001; Internat. Dir, Invest-UK, 2001–03; Consul-Gen., San Francisco, 2003–07; Ambassador to South Korea, 2008–11; Man. Dir, British Business Embassy, UK Trade & Investment, 2012; Coordinator, Security Council Panel of Experts on the Democratic People's Rep. of Korea, UN, 2012–14; Dep. High Comr, Lagos, 2015. Internat. Partnerships Advr, QMUL, 2017–. Chm., British Korean Soc., 2018–. Trustee, USPG, 2018–. *Publications*: (with T. Bennett) Korea: caught in time, 1997; Times Past in Korea, 2003.

**UDNY-LISTER, Sir Edward Julian;** *see* Lister, Sir E. J. U.

**UFF, Prof. John Francis**, CBE 2002; QC; PhD; FREng, FICE, FCIArb; international arbitrator, advocate and engineer; Nash Professor of Engineering Law, University of London, 1991–2003, now Emeritus Professor; a Recorder, 1998–2005; *b* 30 Jan. 1942; *s* of Frederick and Eva Uff; *m* 1967, Diana Muriel Graveson; two *s* one *d*. *Educ*: Stratton Sch.; King's College London (BSc (Eng), PhD; FKC 1997). Asst engineer, Rendel Palmer & Tritton, 1966–70; Vis. Lectr in civil engineering, 1963–68; called to the Bar, Gray's Inn, 1970, Bencher, 1993 (Vice-Treas. 2010; Treas., 2011); practice at Bar, Keating Chambers, 1970–, Head of Chambers, 1992–97; Asst Recorder, 1993–98; a Dep. Judge, Technology and Construction Court, 1999–2005. Dir, Centre of Construction Law and Management, KCL, 1987–99; arbitrator in construction disputes; lectr to professional bodies in engineering law and arbitration. Vice-Pres., London Court of Internat. Arbitration, 2003–08. Member: Standing Cttee on Structural Safety, 1984–90; Bldg Users Insurance against Latent Defects Cttee, DoE, 1986–88; Adv. Cttee on arbitration law, DTI, 1993–95. Chairman: Ind. Commn of Inquiry into Yorks Water, 1996; Public Inquiry into Southall Rail Accident, 1997–99; Commn of Enquiry into Public Construction Sector, Trinidad and Tobago, 2008–10; Jt Chm., Public Inquiry into Rail Safety Systems, 1999–2000; Ind. Reviewer of UK Professional Engrg, ICE, IET and IMechE, 2016. Mem. Council, ICE, 1982–85; Mem. and Trustee, Bd of Trustees, Engrg Council, 2012–15; President: Engrg Section, BAAS, 2003–04; Soc. of Construction Arbitrators, 2004–07; Bar Music Soc., 2008–. Vice-President: KCL Assoc., 1993–95; Acad. of Experts, 2019. FREng (FEng 1995). Master, Arbitrators' Co., 2014–15. Prin. Ed., book series of Centre of Construction Law and Mgt, KCL, on construction law, management, environment law and dispute resolution, 1988–. President's Medal, Soc. Construction Law, 2000; Gold Medal, ICE, 2002. *Publications*: Construction Law, 1974, 12th edn 2016; (contrib.) Keating on Building Contracts, 4th edn 1978 to 10th edn 2016; (jtly) ICE Arbitration Practice, 1986; (jtly) Methods of Procurement in Ground Investigation, 1986; (principal draftsman) Construction Industry Model Arbitration Rules, 1998; (contrib.) Chitty on Contracts, 28th edn 1999, 31st edn 2012; (principal draftsman) ICC Form of Contract, 2014; technical papers in civil engineering; papers and articles in engineering law and procedure. *Recreations*: playing with violins, painting, walking. *Address*: 15 Essex Street, WC2R 3AU. *T*: (020) 7544 2600; Pale Farm, Chipperfield, Herts WD4 9BH. *Clubs*: Athenæum, Ronnie Scott's.

**UFFEN, Kenneth James,** CMG 1977; HM Diplomatic Service, retired; UK Permanent Representative to OECD, Paris, 1982–85; *b* 29 Sept. 1925; *s* of late Percival James Uffen, MBE, former Civil Servant, and late Gladys Ethel James; *m* 1954, Nancy Elizabeth Winbolt; one *s* two *d*. *Educ*: Latymer Upper Sch.; St Catharine's Coll., Cambridge. HM Forces (Flt-Lt, RAFVR), 1943–48; St Catharine's Coll., 1948–50; 3rd Sec., FO, 1950–52; Paris, 1952–55; 2nd Sec., Buenos Aires, 1955–58; 1st Sec., FO, 1958–61; 1st Sec. (Commercial), Moscow, 1961–63; seconded to HM Treasury, 1963–65; FCO, 1965–68; Counsellor, Mexico City, 1968–70; Economic Counsellor, Washington, 1970–72; Commercial Counsellor, Moscow, 1972–76; Res. Associate, IISS, 1976–77; Ambassador to Colombia, 1977–82. *Recreations*: music, gardens. *Address*: 40 Winchester Road, Walton-on-Thames, Surrey KT12 2RH.

**UGANDA, Archbishop of,** 2012–March 2020; **Most Rev. Stanley Ntagali;** *b* Kabale, Uganda, 1 March 1955; *s* of late Ernest Ntagali and of Molly Ntagali; *m* 1978, Beatrice; four *s* one *d*. *Educ*: Bishop Turker Theol Coll. (CTh 1981); Kilimanjaro Christian Med. Centre, Moshi, Tanzania (CertCPE 1983); St Paul's Univ., Limuru, Kenya (BD 1993); Oxford Centre for Mission Studies (MA Theol. and Develt 2000). Missionary, Karamoja, 1977–86; Archdeacon of Masindi, 1994–99; Diocesan Sec., Dio. of Bunyoro-Kitara, 2000–02; Provincial Sec., Church of Uganda, 2003–04; Bishop, Dio. of Masindi-Kitara, 2004–12. *Publications*: More than One Wife: polygamy and grace, 2012. *Address*: Church of Uganda, PO Box 14123, Kampala, Uganda. *E*: bishopntagali@yahoo.com.

**UIST, Hon. Lord; Roderick Francis Macdonald;** a Senator of the College of Justice in Scotland, since 2006; *b* 1 Feb. 1951; *s* of late Finlay Macdonald and Catherine Maclean. *Educ*: St Mungo's Acad., Glasgow; Glasgow Univ. (LLB Hons). Admitted advocate, 1975; Advocate-Depute (Crown Counsel), 1987–93; QC (Scot.) 1988; Home Advocate-Depute (Sen. Crown Counsel), 1990–93; called to the Bar, Inner Temple, 1997. Legal Chm., Pension Appeal Tribunals for Scotland, 1995–2001; Member: Criminal Injuries Compensation Bd, 1995–2000; Criminal Injuries Compensation Appeals Panel, 1997–99. *Recreations*: walking, Provence. *Address*: Court of Session, Parliament House, Edinburgh EH1 1RQ. *T*: (0131) 225 2595.

**ULLMAN, Jennifer Margaret;** landscape and heritage management consultant, since 2009; *b* Boston, Mass, 19 Dec. 1964; *d* of Richard Ullman and Yoma Ullman; *m* 1994, John G. Curtin. *Educ*: Oberlin Coll. (BA Hons Hist. of Art); Yale Univ. (Master and MPhil Hist. of Art); Inchbald Sch. of Design (Dip. Garden Design 1994). Manager, Historic Morven, New Jersey, 1995–97; Wandsworth Council: Manager, Battersea Park, 1998–2000; Asst Chief Parks Officer, 2000–02; Chief Parks Officer, 2002–08. Chm., Bd of Dirs, Greenspace, 2002–03; Member: Managing Cttee, London Parks and Gardens Trust, 2003–09; London Cttee, Heritage Lottery Fund, 2012–17; Council, RSPB, 2014–; SE Regl Adv. Bd, NT, 2019–. Trustee, Royal Botanic Garden, Kew, 2008–16. Judge, Green Flags Awards, 2001–11. *Publications*: Battersea Park, 2016. *Recreations*: gardening, cycling, birdwatching, walking. *Address*: 63 Amerland Road, SW18 1QA. *T*: 07771 983842. *E*: jennifer@jenniferullman.com.

**ULLMAN, Tracey;** actress, writer and producer; *b* Slough, 30 Dec. 1959; *m* 1983, Allan McKeown (*d* 2013); one *s* one *d*. *Educ*: Italia Conti Acad. of Theatre Arts. Actress, 1980–; *television series* include: Mackenzie, 1980; A Kick Up the Eighties, 1981; Three of a Kind, 1981–83 (BAFTA TV Award, 1984); Girls on Top, 1985–86; The Tracey Ullman Show, 1987–90; The Little Lulu Show, 1995; Tracey Takes On (also creator and exec. prod.), 1996–99; Ally McBeal (Emmy Award, 1999); State of the Union (also creator and exec. prod.), 2008–10; Tracey Ullman's Show (also exec. prod.), 2016, 2017; Howards End, 2017; Tracey Breaks The News, 2017, 2018; *films* include: Small Time Crooks, 2000; Corpse Bride (voice), 2005; Into the Woods, 2014. *Address*: c/o Hamilton Hodell, 20 Golden Square, W1F 9JL. *T*: (020) 7636 1221, *Fax*: (020) 7636 1226. *E*: info@hamiltonhodell.co.uk.

**ULLMANN, Sir Anthony (James),** Kt 2015; Chairman and Chief Executive Officer, Shackletons Group Ltd, since 2018; *b* London, 15 June 1954; *s* of Jean-Jacques and Bella Ullmann; *m* 1983, Riva Benson; two *s* one *d*. *Educ*: Bradford Grammar Sch. Dir, Ullmann & Bamforth Ltd, 1976–79; Chm., Ullmann Internat. Ltd, 1980–2005; Man. Dir, 1995–2015, non-exec. Chm., 2016–17, Autofil Worldwide Ltd. Chm., Volfortis Consulting Ltd, 2015–. Non-exec. Dir, Connect Yorks, 2018–. Advr to Rt Hon. Nicholas Clegg, MP, 2000–17. Mem., Lib Dem Business Adv. Gp, 2014–. *Recreations*: family, travel, theatre, golf. *Club*: Ivy.

**ULLMANN, Liv (Johanne);** actress; *b* Tokyo, 16 Dec. 1938; *d* of late Viggo Ullmann and of Janna (*née* Lund), Norway; *m* 1st, 1960, Dr Gappe Stang (marr. diss. 1965); 2nd, 1985, Donald Saunders (marr. diss. 1995). *Educ*: Norway; London (dramatic trng). Stage début, The Diary of Anne Frank (title role), Stavanger, 1956; major roles, National Theatre and Norwegian State Theatre, Oslo; Amer. stage début, A Doll's House, New York Shakespeare Festival, 1974–75; Anna Christie, USA, 1977; The Bear, La Voix humaine, Australia, 1978; I Remember Mama, USA, and Ghosts (Ibsen), Broadway, 1979; British theatre début, Old Times, Guildford, 1985; dir, A Streetcar Named Desire, Sydney Th. Co., Sydney and NY, 2009. Wrote and dir. short film, Parting, 1981. Twelve hon. doctorates, including Brown, Smith Coll., Tufts and Haifa. *Films*: Pan, 1965; The Night Visitor, 1971; Pope Joan, 1972; The Emigrants, 1972 (Golden Globe Award); The New Land, 1973 (Best Actress, Nat. Soc. of Film Critics, USA); Lost Horizon, 1973; 40 Carats, 1973 (Golden Globe Award); Zandy's Bride, 1973; The Abdication, 1974; The Wild Duck, 1983; The Bay Boy, 1985; Let's Hope it's a Girl, 1987; Mosca Addio, 1987; Time of Indifference, 1987; La Amiga, 1987; The Ox, 1993; *director*: Sophie, 1993; Kristin Lavransdatter (also wrote screenplay), 1995; Private Confessions, 1996; Faithless, 2000;

Miss Julie, 2015; (dir. by Ingmar Bergman): Persona, 1966; The Hour of the Wolf, 1968 (Best Actress, Nat. Soc. of Film Critics, USA); Shame, 1968 (Best Actress, Nat. Soc. of Film Critics, USA); The Passion of Anna, 1969; Cries and Whispers, 1972; Scenes from a Marriage, 1974; Face to Face, 1976; The Serpent's Egg, 1977; The Autumn Sonata, 1978 (5 NY Film Critics awards); Saraband, 2005. Goodwill Ambassador, UNICEF, 1980–; Vice Pres., Internat. Rescue Cttee. Peer Gynt Award, Norway (1st female recipient). Commander with Star, Order of St Olav (Norway), 2005 (Commander, 1994). *Publications:* (autobiog.) Changing, 1977; Choices, 1984.

**ULLMANN, Phillip Lionel,** FCA; Chief Energiser, Cordant Group plc, since 1996; *b* London, 22 Dec. 1964; *s* of Jack and Marianne Ullmann; *m* 1989, Deborah Broza; two *s* two *d*. *Educ:* Hasmonean High Sch.; Gonville and Caius Coll., Cambridge (MA Engrg); Brunel Univ. (MBA). FCA 2003. Chiswell Wire Co., 1988–90; KPMG, 1991–93; Sainsbury's, 1993–94; Wace Creative Imaging, 1994–95. *Recreations:* keen sportsman, Arsenal fan, cricket, tennis, family, reading, energising people. *Address:* Cordant Group plc, 346 Long Lane, Hillingdon, Middx UB10 9PF. *T:* (01895) 201800. *E:* phillip.ullmann@cordantgroup.com.

**ULLRICH, Kay Morrison;** Member (SNP) West of Scotland, Scottish Parliament, 1999–2003; *b* 5 May 1943; *d* of John Dallas Morrison and Charlotte McMillan Morrison (*née* Neil); *m* 1st, 1964, Andrew Jofre (marr. diss.); one *s* one *d*; 2nd, 1976, Grady Ullrich. *Educ:* Ayr Acad.; Queen's Coll., Glasgow (CQSW). Butlin's Redcoat, 1961–64; schools swimming instructor, N Ayrshire, 1973–81; sch. social worker, 1984–86, hosp. social worker, 1986–92, Strathclyde; sen. court social worker, E Ayrshire, 1992–97. Scottish Parliament: Spokesperson on health and community care, 1999–2000; SNP Chief Whip, 2000–03; Mem., Standards and Equal Opportunities Cttees, 2000–03. Vice-Pres., SNP, 1997–99. Contested (SNP): Cunninghame S, 1983 and 1987; Motherwell S, 1992; Monklands E, June 1994. *Recreations:* swimming, travel, meeting friends. *Address:* Tulsa, Montgomeryfield, Dreghorn, Irvine KA11 4HB. *T:* (01294) 213331.

**ULLSTEIN, Augustus Rupert Patrick Anthony;** QC 1992; a Recorder, since 1999; *b* 21 March 1947; *s* of late Frederick Charles Leopold Ullstein and Patricia (*née* Guinness); *m* 1970, Pamela Margaret Wells; two *s* two *d*. *Educ:* Bradfield Coll., Berks; LSE (LLB Hons). Called to the Bar, Inner Temple, 1970, Bencher, 2006; in practice as barrister, 1970–2017; an Asst Recorder, 1993–99. Liveryman, Bowyers' Co., 1980–2009. *Publications:* (Supervising Editor) Pelling and Purdie, Matrimonial Injunctions, 1982; Compensation for Personal Injury in England, Germany and Italy, 2005. *Recreations:* my children, after dinner speaking.

**ULLSWATER,** 2nd Viscount *cr* 1921, of Campsea Ashe, Suffolk; **Nicholas James Christopher Lowther,** LVO 2002; PC 1994; Private Secretary, Comptroller and Equerry to Princess Margaret, Countess of Snowdon, 1998–2002; *b* 9 Jan. 1942; *s* of Lieut John Arthur Lowther, MVO, RNVR (*d* 1942), and Priscilla Violet (*d* 1945), *yr d* of Reginald Everitt Lambert; *S* great-grandfather, 1949; *m* 1967, Susan, *d* of James Howard Weatherby; two *s* two *d*. *Educ:* Eton; Trinity Coll., Cambridge. Captain, Royal Wessex Yeomanry, T&AVR, 1973–78. A Lord in Waiting (Govt Whip), H of L, 1989–90; Parly Under-Sec. of State, Dept of Employment, 1990–93; Capt. of Corps of Gentlemen at Arms (Govt Chief Whip), H of L, 1993–94; Minister of State (Minister for Construction and Planning), DoE, 1994–95; elected Mem., H of L, 2003. *Heir: s* Hon. Benjamin James Lowther [*b* 26 Nov. 1975; *m* 2007, Theresa Schoeman; one *s* two *d*.] *Address:* Whiteacres, Cross Lane, Brancaster, King's Lynn, Norfolk PE31 8AE. *T:* (01485) 210488.

**ULPH, Prof. David Tregear,** CBE 2016; FRSE; Professor of Economics, University of St Andrews, since 2006 (Head, School of Economics and Finance, 2006–10); Director, Scottish Institute for Research in Economics, 2010–17; *b* 26 Oct. 1946; *s* of late Cyril Ulph and Myra Ulph; *m* 1971, Elizabeth Mackie; two *d*. *Educ:* Univ. of Glasgow (MA); Balliol Coll., Oxford (BLitt). FRSE 2010. Lectr in Econs, Univ. of Stirling, 1971–78; Lectr, then Reader in Econs, UCL, 1978–84; Professor of Economics: Univ. of Bristol, 1984–92; UCL, 1992–2001; Chief Economist and Dir, Analysis and Res., subseq. Analysis, HM Inland Revenue, then HMRC, 2001–06. Member: NHS Pay Rev. Body, 2015–; Competition Appeal Tribunal, 2017–; Scottish Fiscal Commn, 2018–. FRSA 2001. *Publications:* over 90 articles in refereed jls and books. *Recreations:* bridge, cinema, travel, cooking. *Address:* School of Economics and Finance, The Scores, University of St Andrews, St Andrews, Fife KY16 9AL. *T:* (01334) 462420.

**ULRICH, Walter Otto;** Deputy Secretary, Department of Education and Science, 1977–87; *b* 1 April 1927. Ministry of Works: Asst Principal, 1951; Principal, 1955; Treasury 1958–60; Principal Private Sec. to Minister of Public Building and Works, 1963–65; Asst Sec., 1965; Min. of Housing and Local Govt, 1966; DoE, 1970; Under-Sec., 1972; Cabinet Office, 1974–76. *Address:* 46 Grinstead Lane, Lancing, W Sussex BN15 9DZ. *T:* (01903) 762169.

**ULSTER, Earl of; Alexander Patrick Gregers Richard Windsor;** *b* 24 Oct. 1974; *s* of HRH The Duke of Gloucester and HRH The Duchess of Gloucester; *m* 2002, Dr Claire Alexandra, *d* of Mr and Mrs Robert Booth; one *s* one *d*. *Educ:* Eton Coll.; King's Coll., London Univ. (BA War Studies 1996); RMA, Sandhurst. Commnd King's Royal Hussars, 1998; Captain, 2000. *Heir: s* Lord Culloden, *qv*.
*See under Royal Family.*

**UMUNNA, Chuka;** MP for Streatham, since 2010 (Lab, 2010–19; Ind, 2019; Lib Dem, since 2019); *b* 17 Oct. 1978; *m* 2016, Alice Sullivan; one *d*. *Educ:* St Dunstan's Coll., Catford; Univ. of Manchester (LLB English and French Law); Univ. of Burgundy; Nottingham Law Sch. Admitted Solicitor, 2004; with Herbert Smith, London, 2002–06, Rochman Landau, 2006–10. Shadow Sec. of State for Business, Innovation and Skills, 2011–15. Member: Treasury Select Cttee, 2010–11; Home Affairs Select Cttee, 2015–17; Vice Chairman, All Party Parliamentary Group: on Nigeria, 2010–15; on Thameslink, 2010–15. Lib Dem spokesman on Treasury and business, 2019–. Member: GMB; Unite; Fabian Soc.; Compass. *Publications:* (ed) Owning the Future: how Britain can make it in a fast-changing world, 2014. *Address:* House of Commons, SW1A 0AA.

**UNDERHILL, Prof. Allan Edward,** PhD, DSc; CChem, FRSC; Professor of Inorganic Chemistry, University College of North Wales, then University of Wales, Bangor, 1983–99, now Emeritus; *b* 13 Dec. 1935; *s* of Albert Edward Underhill and Winifred Underhill (*née* Bailey); *m* 1960, Audrey Jean Foster; one *s* one *d*. *Educ:* Univ. of Hull (BSc 1958; PhD 1962); DSc Wales 1983. Res. Chemist, ICI Ltd, 1961–62; Lectr, Loughborough CAT, 1962–65; University College of North Wales (Bangor): Lectr, 1965–74; Sen. Lectr, 1974–83; Dean, Faculty of Sci., 1985–87, 1994–95; Pro-Vice-Chancellor, 1995–99. Restoration Project Coordinator, St George's Ch, Shrewsbury, 2012–. *Publications:* over 250 res. papers in RSC jls, Nature, etc. *Recreations:* theatre, bridge, walking, photography.

**UNDERHILL, Prof. Michael James,** PhD; FREng; Professor of Electronics, 1992–2004, part-time Lecturer, since 2004, University of Surrey; Chief Executive Officer, Underhill Research Ltd, since 2007; *b* 22 March 1939; *s* of Gp Capt. (retd) Rev. Wilfrid Underhill, DSC and Barbara Nowell Underhill (*née* James); *m* 1977, Gillian Brown; two *s*. *Educ:* St John's Sch., Leatherhead; Oriel Coll., Oxford (Schol.; Bible Schol.; Capt. of Boats, 1959–60; BA Physics 1960; MA); Univ. of Surrey (PhD Electronics 1972). FIET (FIEE 1982); FREng (FEng 1982). Philips Res. Labs (formerly Mullard Res. Labs), 1960–84 (Head of Systems Div., 1982–84); Tech. Dir, MEL (Philips), 1984–90; Engrg Dir, Thorn EMI Sensors Div., 1990–91; Head of Dept, Electronic and Electrical Engrg, 1992–96, Dean of Engrg, 1996–97, Univ. of Surrey (Vis. Lectr on Systems Engrg, 1996–82; Vis. Prof., 1984–90). Chm., European Frequency and Time Forum, 1996. Member: NATS Res. Adv. Council, 1996–99; Defence Science Adv. Council, 1982–96 (Chm., various bds and cttees). Founder and Res. Dir, Toric Ltd, 2001–10. Chm., Sussex IET, 2007–09. Institution of Electrical Engineers, subseq. of Engineering and Technology: Mem. Council, 1992–2007; Chm., Electronics Div., 1993–94; Chm., Surrey Centre, 1996–97; P. Perring Thoms Award, 1981; J. J. Thomson Award, 1993. Parish Councillor, Rusper, 1977–83. FRSA 1992. *Publications:* 66 patents; 126 papers on frequency control, phase noise, time jitter, electronics, antennas and propagation, electromagnetic strings, pulsars, gravity and gravity waves, dark matter/energy, an electromagnetic theory of everything, and age of universe. *Recreations:* licensed radio amateur and Member of Radio Society of Great Britain since 1956, amateur dramatics (Holding Trustee and Pres., Ifield Barn Theatre Soc.), playing jazz piano, ski-ing, travel, hack and bash gardening. *Address:* Hatchgate, Tandridge Lane, Lingfield, Surrey RH7 6LL. *T:* (01342) 892154.

**UNDERHILL, Rt Hon. Sir Nicholas Edward,** Kt 2006; PC 2013; **Rt Hon. Lord Justice Underhill;** a Lord Justice of Appeal, since 2013; Vice-President, Court of Appeal (Civil Division), since 2018; *b* 12 May 1952; *s* of late Judge Underhill, QC and Rosalie Jean Underhill (who *m* 1989, William Anderson Beaumont, CB, OBE, AE); *m* 1987, Nina Grunfeld; two *s* two *d*. *Educ:* Winchester Coll.; New Coll., Oxford (MA Hons; Hon. Fellow, 2015). Called to the Bar, Gray's Inn, 1976, Bencher, 2000. QC 1992; a Recorder, 1994–2006; Attorney Gen. to the Prince of Wales, 1998–2006; a Dep. High Court Judge, 1998–2006; a Judge of the High Ct of Justice, QBD, 2006–13; a Judge of the Employment Appeal Tribunal, 2000–03 and 2006–13; Pres. of the Employment Appeal Tribunal, 2009–11. Chm., Bar Pro Bono Unit, 2002–05. Trustee: St John's Smith Square, 1996–2014 (Chm., 2010–13); London Library, 2008–12 (Vice-Chm., 2011–12). *Publications:* The Lord Chancellor, 1978. *Address:* Royal Courts of Justice, Strand, WC2A 2LL.

**UNDERWOOD, Ashley Grenville;** QC 2001; *b* 28 Dec. 1953; *s* of Dennis William Underwood and Brenda Margarita Underwood; *m* 1982, Heather Kay Leggett; one *d*. *Educ:* London Sch. of Econs (LLB Hons). Called to the Bar: Gray's Inn, 1976; NI, 2014; Hd of Chambers, 1999–2006. *Recreations:* motorcycling, classic cars, conversation. *Address:* Cornerstone Barristers, 2–3 Gray's Inn Square, WC1R 5JH.

**UNDERWOOD, Prof. Graham James Charles,** DPhil; Professor of Marine and Freshwater Biology, University of Essex, since 2004 (Executive Dean, Faculty of Science and Health, 2013–19); *b* Leicester, 31 March 1964; *s* of John Underwood and Valerie Underwood; *m* 1990, Dr Nicola Jane Durward Slee; one *s* one *d*. *Educ:* Beauchamp Coll., Oadby; Univ. of Reading (BSc Zool. 1986); Univ. of Sussex (DPhil 1989). Department of Biological Sciences, University of Essex: Lectr, 1992–98; Sen. Lectr, 1998–2002; Reader, 2002–04. Mem., Regl Flood Coastal Commn, Envmt Agency, 2012–. Natural Environment Research Council: Member: Panel of Chairs, 2009–14; Sci. and Innovation Strategy Bd, 2011–14; Sci. Cttee, 2019–; Chm., Strategic Progs Adv. Gp, 2015–19; Member: Marine Protected Areas Sci. Adv. Panel, DEFRA, 2009–12; Individual Merit Promotion Panel, Res. Councils, 2015–. Adjunct Prof., Michigan Technol Univ., 2001–17. Governor: N Essex Partnership Univ. NHS Foundn Trust, 2013–16; Essex Partnership Univ. NHS Foundn Trust, 2017–19. *Publications:* contribs to Limnology and Oceanography, Procs of NAS, Jl of Phycology, Jl Internat. Soc. Microbial Ecol., Nat. Clin. Change. *Recreations:* gardening, morris dancing, history, sailing, natural history. *Address:* Faculty of Science and Health, University of Essex, Wivenhoe Park, Colchester, Essex CO4 3SQ. *T:* (01206) 873337. *E:* gjcu@essex.ac.uk.

**UNDERWOOD, Sir James (Cresseé Elphinstone),** Kt 2005; MD; FRCP, FRCPath, FMedSci; Joseph Hunter Professor of Pathology, University of Sheffield, 1984–2006, now Emeritus Professor (Dean, Faculty of Medicine, 2006); *b* 11 April 1942; *s* of John and Mary Underwood; *m* 1st, 1966 (marr. diss. 1986); one *s* one *d*; 2nd, 1989, Alice Cameron Underwood; one *s*. *Educ:* Downside Sch.; St Bartholomew's Hosp. Med. Coll. (MB BS 1965; MD 1973). MRCS, LRCP 1965; MRCPath 1972, FRCPath 1984; FRCP 2004; FRCPI 2004. SHO, then Registrar in Pathology, St Bartholomew's Hosp., London, 1966–69; University of Sheffield: Lectr in Pathology, 1969–73; Sen. Lectr, 1974–82; Reader, 1983. MRC Clinical Res. Fellow, Chester Beatty Res. Inst., London, 1973–74; Wellcome-Ramaciotti Res. Fellow, Univ. of Melbourne, 1981. Consultant Histopathologist, Sheffield AHA(T), subseq. Central Sheffield Univ. Hosps NHS Trust, later Sheffield Teaching Hosps NHS Foundn Trust, 1974–2006; Hon. Civilian Consultant Histopathologist, RAF, 2002–09. President: RCPath, 2002–05 (Vice-Pres., 1999–2002); British Div., Internat. Acad. Pathology, 2000–02. Ed., Histopathology, 1995–2002. FMedSci 2005. Hon. Member: Japanese Soc. Pathology, 1996; Hungarian Soc. Pathologists, 1996. Hon. FCPath: Hong Kong, 2001; S Africa, 2006. Cunningham Medal, British Div., Internat. Acad. of Pathology, 2005; Doniach Award, Pathol Soc., 2008. *Publications:* Introduction to Biopsy Interpretation and Surgical Pathology, 1981, 2nd edn 1987; General and Systematic Pathology, 1992, 5th edn 2009; papers on tumour pathology, chronic liver disease and the autopsy. *Recreations:* music, art, photography, fell-walking, local history. *Address:* Cliburn Mill, Cliburn, Cumbria CA10 3AW. *Club:* Athenæum.

**UNDERWOOD, John Morris;** Chief Executive, Freshwater Group, since 2017 (Deputy Chief Executive, 2009–17); Director, Centre for Health Communication Research and Excellence, and Visiting Professor, Buckinghamshire New University, since 2011; *b* 8 Nov. 1953; *s* of John Edward Underwood and Ella Lillian Morris Underwood; *m* 1987, Susan Clare Inglish; two *s*. *Educ:* Univ. of Sheffield (BSc Hons); University Coll., Cardiff (Graduate Dip. in Journalism). BBC trainee journalist, 1976–78; regional TV reporter, 1978–80; TV reporter, ITN, 1980–82; home affairs corresp., ITN, 1982–83; freelance TV producer and presenter, 1983–89; Exec. Producer, House of Commons Cttee TV, 1989–90; Dir of Campaigns and Communications, Labour Party, 1990–91; Partner, subseq. Dir, Clear Communication, 1991–2006. Mem., Mgt Bd, Catalyst think tank, 1998–2005 (Chm., 2001–05). Chm. Trustees, Alcohol Change UK (formerly Alcohol Research UK), 2018– (Trustee, 2013–18). Hon. Prof., Univ. of Glasgow, 2016–18. Editor, New Century, 1993–95. *Publications:* The Will to Win: John Egan and Jaguar, 1989. *Recreations:* theatre, walking. *Address:* 10 Percival Road, SW14 7QE. *T:* 07730 955689.

**UNDERWOOD, Susan Lois,** OBE 2006; FMA; Director, Qatar Children's Museum, 2009–16; *b* 6 Aug. 1956; *d* of John and Lois Underwood; two *s* one *d*. *Educ:* Univ. of St Andrews (MA Hons); Univ. of Leicester (Mus. Studies Grad. Cert.). FMA 1994. Curator, Nat. Railway Mus., York, 1983–85; Keeper of Local Hist., Scunthorpe Mus. and Art Gall., 1985–88; Dep. Dir, N of England Museums Service, 1989–90; Dir, N of England Museums Service, subseq. NE Museums, then Chief Exec., NE MLA, 1990–2005; Dir, Sharjah Mus, 2005–08; Advr for Mus to Ruler of Sharjah, UAE, 2008–09. Comr, English Heritage, 1997–2003. Mem. Bd, One NorthEast, 2005. Trustee, North Music Trust, 2016–. *Recreations:* my family, museums, galleries and heritage, walking, travelling.

**UNERMAN, Sandra Diane**, CBE 2002; Solicitor and Legal Adviser, Department for Communities and Local Government (formerly Office of the Deputy Prime Minister), 2004–08; Lawyer (part-time), Treasury Solicitor's Department, 2008–10; *b* 23 Aug. 1950; *d* of Cecil Unerman and Renee Unerman (*née* Goldberg). *Educ*: Gartlett Sch.; Orange Hill Grammar Sch.; Bristol Univ. (BA Hons History); Middx Univ. (MA Creative Writing 2013). Called to the Bar, Inner Temple, 1973; Legal Dept, DoE, later DETR, then DTLR, subseq. ODPM, now DCLG, 1974–2010; Dep. Solicitor, 1992–2004. UK Civil Service Fellow, Humphrey Inst., Univ. of Minnesota, 1989–90. *Publications*: novels: Trial of Three, 1979; Spellhaven, 2017; Ghosts and Exiles, 2018. *Recreations*: writing, reading, listening to music, theatre going, folklore, conversation.

**UNGER, Michael Ronald**; Chief Executive, Roy Castle Lung Cancer Foundation, 2002–08; Chairman, Piccadilly Radio Ltd, 2006–08; *b* 8 Dec. 1943; *s* of late Ronald Unger, CBE and of Joan Maureen Unger; *m* 1st, 1966, Eunice Dickens (marr. diss. 1992); one *s* (one *d* decd); 2nd, 1993, Noorah Ahmed (marr. diss. 2005; she *d* 2013). *Educ*: Wirral Grammar School. Trainee journalist, Thomson Regional Newspapers, Stockport, 1963; Reading Evening Post, 1965–67; Perth Daily News, W Australia, 1967–71; Daily Post, Liverpool, 1971, Editor, 1977–82; Editor: Liverpool Echo, 1982–83; Manchester Evening News, 1983–97; Gen. Manager, Jazz FM (NW), 2000–02. Dir, Guardian Media Gp plc (formerly Guardian and Manchester Evening News plc), 1983–97; non-executive Director: Kenyon Fraser PR Ltd, 2009–11; HM Partnerships Ltd, 2009–13. Chm., NW Arts Bd, 1991–93; Mem., Broadcasting Standards Commn, 1999–2000. Chm., Eternal Forest Trust, 2005–10; Trustee: Scott Trust, 1986–97; The Lowry, 1994–2003; Youth Charter for Sport, 1994–2000; NW Film Archives, 1998–2004; All Together Now, 2005–13; Hoylake Cottage Trust, 2010–13; Cheshire W CAB, 2012–13. *Publications*: (ed) The Memoirs of Bridget Hitler, 1979; The Hitlers of Liverpool, 2011; (contrib.) Posts and Echoes, 2017; Malin Head, 2018. *Recreations*: art, reading, walking, gardening.

**UNGLEY, John Guilford Gordon**; Master of the Supreme Court, Queen's Bench Division, 1997–2008; Master assigned to clinical negligence cases, 1999–2008; *b* 30 Jan. 1939; *s* of Harold Gordon Ungley and Ella Gwyneth Reay Ungley (*née* Heslop); *m* 1976, Elizabeth Metcalfe (*née* Mayall) (*d* 2018); one *d*, and two step *d*. *Educ*: Charterhouse. Queen's Royal Irish Hussars, 1960–61. Called to the Bar, Gray's Inn, 1965; in practice at the Bar, Western Circuit, 1966–97; Asst Recorder, 1986–89, Recorder, 1989–2004. *Recreations*: sailing, learning to garden and cook in retirement, bellringing, certified watchkeeper Portland Bill National Coastwatch Institution. *Clubs*: Cavalry; Bar Yacht, Royal Solent Yacht.

**UNRUH, Prof. William George**, PhD; FRS 2001; FRSC 1984; Professor of Physics, University of British Columbia, since 1984; Fellow, Canadian Institute for Advanced Research, since 1987; *b* 28 Aug. 1945; *s* of Benjamin Unruh and Anne Unruh (*née* Janzen); *m* 1974, Patricia Truman; one *s*. *Educ*: Univ. of Manitoba (BSc Hons 1967); Princeton Univ. (MA 1969; PhD 1971). FAPS 2000. NSERC (Rutherford) Post Doctoral Fellow, Birkbeck Coll., 1971–72; Miller Fellow, Univ. of Calif, Berkeley, 1973–74; Asst Prof., McMaster Univ., 1974–76; Asst Prof., Univ. of BC, 1976–81; Dir, Cosmology Prog., Canadian Inst. for Advanced Res., 1987–97. Hon. Foreign Mem., American Assoc. of Arts and Scis, 2003. Hagler Fellow, Hagler Inst. for Advanced Study, Texas A&M Univ., 2018; Helmholtz Fellow, 2019. Hon. DSc McMaster, 2008. Sloan Medal, Sloan Foundn, 1978; Rutherford Medal, RSC, 1982; Herzberg Medal, 1983, Medal of Achievement, 1996, Canadian Assoc. of Physicists; Steacie Prize, Steacie Foundn, 1984; Sci. and Engrg Gold Medal, Sci. Council of BC, 1990; Killam Prize in Natural Scis, Canadian Council, 1995; Mathematical Physics Prize, Canadian Assoc. of Physicists and Centre Recherche du Mathématique, 1996. *Publications*: (ed with G. Semenoff) The Early Universe, 1987; contrib. numerous papers to scientific jls. *Address*: Department of Physics and Astronomy, University of British Columbia, Vancouver, BC V6T 1Z1, Canada. *T*: (604) 8223273.

**UNSWORTH, Prof. Anthony**, PhD, DEng; CEng, FREng, FIMechE; Professor of Engineering, Durham University, 1989–2015, now Emeritus; *b* 7 Feb. 1945; *s* of late James Unsworth and Annie Unsworth; *m* 1967, Jill Chetwood. *Educ*: Salford Univ. (BSc 1967); Leeds Univ. (MSc 1968; PhD 1972; DEng 1990). CEng 1972; FIMechE 1984; FREng 1996. Res. Engr, David Brown Industries, 1967–69; University of Leeds: Res. Fellow, 1969–71; Lectr, 1971–76; University of Durham: Lectr, 1976–79; Sen. Lectr, 1979–84; Reader, 1984–89; Dir, Centre for Biomedical Engrg, 1989–2012; Hd, Sch. of Engrg and Applied Sci., then Sch. of Engrg and Computer Sci., 1990–94; Dep. Dean of Sci., 1994–97; Dean of Sci., 1997–2000; Hd, Sch. of Engrg, 2000–06; Dir of Res., Faculty of Sci., 2006–10. Vis. Scientist, Cornell Univ., 1981. Dir, Action Research, 1992–95; non-exec. Dir, S Durham HA, 1993–96. Chm., NHS Res. Ethics Cttee, 1995–96; Chm., Engrg in Medicine Gp, 1989–92, Vice-Pres., 2011, Chair, Pubns Bd, 2010–, IMechE; Member: Panel 30, 2001 RAE; Panel 28, 2008 RAE; Bd, Engrg Council, 2008–13. Editor: Pt H, Proc. IMechE; Jl Engrg in Medicine. Hon. Lifetime Mem., Internat. Soc. for Technol. in Arthroplasty, 2011. Silver Medal in Tribology, 1972, Donald Julius Groen Prize in Tribology, 1991, James Clayton Prize, 1999, IMechE; James Alfred Ewing Medal, ICE, 2005; Best Paper Prize, Professional Engrg Publishing, 2009; Lifetime Achievement Award, Internat. Soc. for Technol. in Arthroplasty, 2011; Duncan Dowson Prize, IMechE, 2014; Chancellor's Medal, Durham Univ., 2018. *Publications*: (contrib.) Tribology of Natural and Artificial Joints, 1981; (contrib.) Introduction to Biomechanics, 1981; (contrib.) Mechanics of Joints, 1993; (contrib.) Oxford Textbook of Rheumatology, 2001; over 325 papers in internat. jls in tribology and biomed. engrg; numerous presentations at internat. confs. *Recreation*: singing sacred music and light opera. *Address*: Department of Engineering, University of Durham, Science Laboratories, South Road, Durham DH1 3LE. *T*: (0191) 334 2521. *E*: tony.unsworth@durham.ac.uk.

**UNSWORTH, Francesca Mary**; Director, News and Current Affairs, BBC News, since 2018; *b* Stoke-on-Trent, 29 Dec. 1957; *d* of John and Phyllis Unsworth. *Educ*: St Dominic's High Sch. for Girls; Univ. of Manchester. Joined BBC, 1980; worked in local radio, Bristol and Leicester; Producer: Newsbeat, Radio 1; World at One, PM, Radio 4; Home News Ed.; Head: Political Progs, 2001–05; Newsgathering, 2005–12; Actg Dir, 2012–13, Dep. Dir, 2013–14, News and Current Affairs; Dir, World Service Gp, 2014–18. Mem. Bd, BBC, 2019–. Mem. Bd, Soc. of Editors (Pres., 2011–12). *Address*: BBC Broadcasting House, Portland Place, W1A 1AA.

**UNSWORTH, Ian Stephen**; QC 2010; a Recorder, since 2018; *b* Billinge, Lancs, 7 Dec. 1966; *s* of William Unsworth and Jean Unsworth; *m* 1996, Michelle Cown; two *s* one *d*. *Educ*: Ashton-in-Makerfield Grammar Sch.; Alsager Sch.; Univ. of Huddersfield (LLB Hons Business Law). Called to the Bar, Lincoln's Inn, 1992; in practice as barrister, specialising in criminal law: Exchange Chambers, 2000–10; 7 Harrington Street Chambers, 2010–; apptd to Attorney Gen.'s A List, 2007. Chm., Disciplinary Appeals Panel, RFU, 2010–; Judicial Officer, 6 Nations Rugby Championship, 2014–. *Recreations*: golf, running, triathlon, Rugby Union, family life, concerts, debating. *Address*: 7 Harrington Street Chambers, 7 Harrington Street L2 9YH. *T*: (0151) 242 0707, *Fax*: (0151) 236 2800; Farrars Building, Temple, EC4Y 7BD. *T*: (020) 7583 9241, *Fax*: (020) 7583 0090. *Club*: Royal Liverpool Golf.

**UNWIN, Sir Brian**; *see* Unwin, Sir J. B.

**UNWIN, David Charles**; QC 1995; *b* 12 May 1947; *s* of Peter Unwin and Rosemary (*née* Locket); *m* 1969, Lorna Bullivant; one *s* one *d*. *Educ*: Clifton Coll.; Trinity Coll., Oxford. Called to the Bar, Middle Temple, 1971; Jun. Counsel to Attorney Gen. in charity matters, 1987–95. Charity Comr, 2002–07. *Recreations*: music, mountaineering, cycling. *Club*: Climbers'.

**UNWIN, Eric Geoffrey**; Chairman, Advisory Board, Palamon Capital Partners, since 2015; Chairman: Tryzens Holdings Ltd, since 2014; RemCom, since 2014; Verastar, since 2015; GNS, since 2016; Hastee Pay, since 2019; *b* 9 Aug. 1942; *s* of Maurice Doughty Unwin and Olive Milburn (*née* Watson); *m* 1967, Margaret Bronia Element; one *s* one *d*. *Educ*: Heaton Grammar School, Newcastle upon Tyne; King's College, Durham Univ. (BSc Hons Chemistry). Cadbury Bros, 1963–68; joined John Hoskyns & Co., 1968; Managing Dir, Hoskyns Systems Development, 1978; Dir, 1982, Man. Dir, 1984, Exec. Chm., 1988–93, Hoskyns Group; Chief Operating Officer, 1993–2000, and Vice Chm., Exec. Bd, 1996–2000, Cap Gemini Sogeti, then Cap Gemini; CEO, Cap Gemini, then Cap Gemini Ernst and Young, 2000–01. Chairman: Cap Programmator AB, 1993–2000; United Business Media, 2002–07; Halma plc, 2003–13 (Dep. Chm., 2002–03); Cloud Networks Ltd, 2005–06; Liberata, 2003–11; Omnibus Systems Ltd, 2005–10; Taptu Ltd, 2007–12; Alliance Medical, 2008–10; ReD, 2011–14; OpenCloud, 2011–14; XChanging plc, 2012–16; non-executive Director: Volmac Software Groep NV, 1992–; Gemini Consulting Hldg SA, 1994–2000; United News & Media plc, 1995–2002; Towry Hldgs Ltd, 2014–16; Mem. Bd, Cap Gemini SA, 2000–12. Pres., Computing Services Assoc., 1987–88. Mem., ITAB, 1988–91. CCMI (CBIM 1984; Mem. Bd, 1990–94). Freeman, City of London, 1987; Founder Mem., and Liveryman, Co. of Information Technologists, 1987. *Recreations*: golf, ski-ing. *Address*: 204 The Chilterns, 24 Paddington Street, W1U 5QY. *Clubs*: Royal Automobile; Hunstanton Golf, Royal West Norfolk Golf, Morfontaine Golf (France).

**UNWIN, Sir (James) Brian**, KCB 1990 (CB 1986); President, European Investment Bank, 1993–99, now Hon. President; President, European Centre for Nature Conservation, 2001–13, now Hon. President; *b* 21 Sept. 1935; *s* of Reginald Unwin and Winifred Annie Walthall; *m* 1964, Diana Susan, *d* of Sir David Aubrey Scott, GCMG; three *s*. *Educ*: Chesterfield School; New College, Oxford (MA; Hon. Fellow, 1997); Yale University (MA). Nat. service, 2nd Lieut, Northants Regt, 1953–55. Asst Principal, CRO, 1960; Private Sec. to British High Commissioner, Salisbury, 1961–64; 1st Secretary, British High Commission, Accra, 1964–65; FCO, 1965–67; transferred to HM Treasury, 1968; Private Sec. to Chief Secretary to Treasury, 1970–72; Asst Secretary, 1972; Under Sec., 1976; seconded to Cabinet Office, 1981–83; Dep. Sec., HM Treasury, 1983–85; Dir, Eur. Investment Bank, 1983–85; Dep. Sec., Cabinet Office, 1985–87; Chm., Bd of HM Customs and Excise, 1987–93; Chm., Supervisory Bd, European Investment Fund, 1994–99; Gov., EBRD, 1993–99; Chm., European Task Force on Banking and Biodiversity, 2002–10. Dir, Dexia SA, 2000–10; Chairman: Asset Trust Housing Ltd, 2003–12; Asset Trust Housing Assoc., 2012–14. Pres., Customs Co-operation Council, 1991–92. Chm., Civil Service Sports Council, 1989–93. Member: IMPACT Adv. Bd, 1990–93; Bd of Dirs, ENO, 1993–94, 2000–08 (Sec., 1987–93); Bd, Centre d'Etudes Prospectives, 1996–2000; Bd, Foundation Pierre Werner, 1998–2000. Mem. Council, Federal Trust for Educn and Res., 2003–. Pres., New Coll. Soc., 2003–08. Hon. Pres., Euronem, Athens, 2000–10. Gold Medal, Fondation du Mérite Européen, 1995. Comdr, Order of Ouissam Aloui (Morocco), 1998; Grand Officier, Ordre de la Couronne (Belgium), 2001; Grand Croix, Ordre Grand-Ducal de la Couronne de Chêne (Luxembourg), 2002. *Publications*: Terrible Exile: the last days of Napoleon on St Helena, 2010; (jtly) Financial Regulation: Britain's next European challenge, 2010; A Tale in Two Cities: Fanny Burney and Adele, Comtesse de Boigne, 2013; With Respect, Minister: a view from inside Whitehall, 2017. *Recreations*: opera, bird watching, Wellingtoniana, cricket. *Club*: Reform.

**UNWIN, Julia**, CBE 2006 (OBE 2000); consultant, since 2017; Chief Executive (formerly Director), Joseph Rowntree Foundation, 2007–16; *b* 6 July 1956; *d* of Peter William Unwin, *qv*; partner, Patrick Kelly; two *d*. *Educ*: Univ. of Liverpool (BA 1978); London Sch. of Econs (MSc 1991). Dir, Homeless Network, 1986–92; consultant, 1992–2006. Member: Bd, Housing Corporation, 1992–2001; Charity Commn, 1998–2003; Dep. Chm., Food Standards Agency, 2003–06. Chairman, Committee of Reference: ISIS Asset Mgt, 2004–06; Friends Provident, 2004–06. Non-executive Director: Mears Gp plc, 2016–; Yorkshire Water, 2017–; Financial Reporting Council, 2018–. Chm., Ind. Inquiry into Civil Society Futures in England, 2017–19. Lectures: York Ebor, 2011; Gresham Coll., 2012; CREW Regeneration Wales and Univ. of Glamorgan, 2013; Beveridge, Toynbee Hall, 2013. Trustee, Dartington Hall Trust, 2017–. Fellow, Carnegie UK Trust, 2017–18. Mem. Council, Univ. of York, 2009– (Pro-Chancellor, 2016–18). FRSA; FCGI 2012. Hon. DLaws: York St John, 2012; Bristol, 2016; DUniv S Wales, 2014. Lifetime Achievement Award, Chartered Mgt Inst., 2019. *Publications*: The Grant Making Tango, 2004; Fruitful Funding, 2005; Why Fight Poverty, 2013. *W*: www.juliaunwin.com.

**UNWIN, Ven. Kenneth**; Archdeacon of Pontefract, 1981–92, now Emeritus; *b* 16 Sept. 1926; *s* of Percy and Elsie Unwin; *m* 1958, Beryl Riley (*d* 2017); one *s* four *d*. *Educ*: Chesterfield Grammar School; St Edmund Hall, Oxford (MA Hons); Ely Theological Coll. Assistant Curate: All Saints, Leeds, 1951–55; St Margaret, Durham City (in charge, St John's, Neville's Cross), 1955–59; Vicar: St John Baptist, Dodworth, Barnsley, 1959–69; St John Baptist, Royston, Barnsley, 1969–73; St John's, Wakefield, 1973–82. Hon. Canon, Wakefield Cathedral, 1980–92. RD of Wakefield, 1980–81. Proctor in Convocation, 1972–82.

*See also* Sir D. D. Acland, Bt.

**UNWIN, Nigel**; *see* Unwin, P. N. T.

**UNWIN, Peter Francis**, CB 2011; Chief Executive, Whitehall and Industry Group, 2015–19; *b* 8 June 1954; *s* of late Francis Charles Unwin, MBE and Margaret (Marjorie) Unwin (*née* Caskey); *m* 1978, Margaret Elizabeth Wiseman; two *s* one *d*. *Educ*: George Watson's Coll., Edinburgh; Pembroke Coll., Cambridge (BA Hons Maths 1975; Dip. Mathematical Stats 1976). Asst Statistician, Capital and Co. Taxation, Inland Revenue, 1976–79; Private Sec. to Hd, Govt Statistical Service, 1979–81; Principal, Gen. Finance Div., MoD, 1981–84; Statistician, Local Authy Statistics Div., 1984–87; Principal, Local Authy Capital Finance Div., 1987–90; Hd, Inner Cities Policy Unit, 1990–93, Internat. Envmt Div., 1993–97, DoE; Hd, Global Atmosphere Div., DoE, then DETR, 1997–98; Principal Private Secretary: to Dep. Prime Minister, 1998–2001; to Sec. of State for Local Govt, Transport and the Regions, 2001; Director: Central Policy Gp, Cabinet Office, 2001–02; Corporate Strategy and Resources, ODPM, 2002–04; Dir Gen., Corporate Strategy and Resources Gp, ODPM, 2004–06; Corporate Delivery Gp, DCLG, 2006–07; Department for Environment, Food and Rural Affairs: Dir Gen., Natural Envmt Gp, later Envmt and Rural Gp, 2007–12; Acting Perm. Sec., 2011; Dir Gen., Policy Delivery Gp, 2012–15. Mem., Aldersgate Gp, 2018–. *Recreations*: golf, ski-ing, travel, hill walking, wine. *E*: peter.unwin56@gmail.com. *Club*: Chislehurst Golf (Captain, 2019–20).

**UNWIN, Dr (Peter) Nigel (Tripp),** FRS 1983; Scientist, Medical Research Council Laboratory of Molecular Biology, Cambridge, 1968–80 and since 1987; Senior Research Fellow, Trinity College, Cambridge, since 1988; *b* 1 Nov. 1942; *s* of Peter Unwin and Cara Unwin (*née* Pinckney); *m* 1968, Janet Patricia Ladd; one *s* one *d*. *Educ:* Univ. of Otago, NZ (BE); Univ. of Cambridge (PhD 1968). Prof. of Structural Biol., then Cell Biol., Stanford Univ. Sch. of Medicine, Calif, 1980–87. Royal Soc. Croonian Lectr and Medal, 2000. Founder FMedSci 1998. Hon. FRMS 1989. Ernst Ruska Award, Ernst Ruska Foundn, 1980; Rosenstiel Award, Brandeis Univ., Mass, 1991; Louis Jeantet Prize for Medicine, Jeantet Foundn, Geneva, 1996; Gregori Aminoff Prize, Royal Swedish Acad. of Scis, 1999; Gjønnes Medal in Electron Crystallography, Internat. Union of Crystallography, 2017. *Recreation:* mountaineering. *Address:* 19/20 Portugal Place, Cambridge CB5 8AF.

**UNWIN, Prof. (Peter) Timothy (Holt),** CMG 2016; PhD; UNESCO Chair in Information and Communication Technologies for Development, Royal Holloway and Bedford New College, University of London, since 2007 (Professor of Geography, 1999–2011, now Emeritus); *b* 11 July 1955; *s* of Thomas Peter Farrer Unwin and Rhoda Patricia Unwin (*née* Vare); *m* 1981, Pamela Julie Cottam; one *s* two *d*. *Educ:* St John's Coll., Cambridge (BA 1976, MA 1980); Univ. of Durham (PhD 1980). Bedford College, subseq. Royal Holloway and Bedford New College, University of London: Lectr, 1981–92; Sen. Lectr, 1992–93; Reader in Geog., 1993–99; Hd, Dept of Geog., 1999–2001; on secondment as Leader, Imfundo: Partnership for Inf. Technol. in Educn, DFID, 2001–04. CEO, 2011–12, Sec. Gen., 2012–15, Commonwealth Telecommunications Orgn. Prog. Dir, 2007, Sen. Advr, 2008–11, Partnerships for Educn, World Economic Forum; Chair, Commonwealth Scholarship Commn in UK, 2009–14 (Commonwealth Scholarship Comr, 2004–14). Dir and Chair, Intellectual Leadership Team, Res. and Innovation Hub on Technol. for Educn, 2019–. Member: Adv. Bd, m-Powering Develt, ITU, 2013–18; Digital Adv. Panel, DFID, 2013–; Steering Cttee, World Economic Forum Internet for All Initiative, 2015–18; Internat. Adv. Bd, UN Univ. Inst. on Computing and Soc., 2015–. Vis. Scholar, Peking Univ., 2011; Hon. Prof., Lanzhou Univ., 2011–. Hon. Sec., RGS (with IBG), 1995–97. Academic Advr and Ext. Examiner, Inst. of Masters of Wine, 2004–12. Hon. Mem., Estonian Geographical Soc., 2002. Cuthbert Peek Award, RGS, 1992. *Publications:* Wine and the Vine: an historical geography of viticulture and the wine trade, 1991 (trans. Italian, Greek and Spanish); The Place of Geography, 1992 (trans. Spanish); (ed) Atlas of World Development, 1996; (ed jtly) Environmental Management, 1997; (ed) A European Geography, 1998; (ed jtly) European Landscapes, 2003; (ed) Information and Communication Technology for Development, 2009; Reclaiming Information and Communication Technologies for Development, 2017. *Recreations:* wine, photography, walking, gardening. *Address:* Department of Geography, Royal Holloway, University of London, Egham, Surrey TW20 0EX. *W:* http://unwin.wordpress.com. *Clubs:* Athenæum, Geographical.

**UNWIN, Peter William,** CMG 1981; HM Diplomatic Service, retired; writer; Chairman, David Davies Memorial Institute of International Studies, 2001–07 (Director, 1995–2001); *b* 20 May 1932; *s* of Arnold and Norah Unwin; *m* 1955, Monica Steven; two *s* two *d*. *Educ:* Ampleforth; Christ Church, Oxford (history scholar). Army, 1954–56; FO, 1956–58; British Legation, Budapest, 1958–61; British Embassy, Tokyo, 1961–63; FCO, 1963–67; British Information Services, NY, 1967–70; FCO, 1970–72; Bank of England, 1973; British Embassy, Bonn, 1973–76; Head of Personnel Policy Dept, FCO, 1976–79; Fellow, Center for Internat. Affairs, Harvard, 1979–80; Minister (Economic), Bonn, 1980–83; Ambassador to: Hungary, 1983–86; Denmark, 1986–88; a Dep. Sec. Gen. of the Commonwealth, 1989–93. Chairman: British-Hungarian Soc., 1993–2000 (Pres., 2000–04); Abbeyfield Internat., 1996–2002; Vice Chm., UK Cttee, UNICEF, 1996–2000. Order of Merit (Hungary), 1996. *Publications:* Voice in the Wilderness: Imre Nagy and the Hungarian Revolution, 1991; Baltic Approaches, 1996; Hearts, Minds & Interests: Britain's place in the world, 1998; Where East Met West: a Central European journey, 2000; The Narrow Sea: the history of the English Channel, 2003; 1956: power defied, 2006; (ed) Newcomers' Lives: the story of immigrants as told in obituaries from The Times, 2013; contrib. The European, Evening Standard, Guardian, Independent, Independent on Sunday, International Affairs, International Relations, The Observer, The Times and The Tablet. *Address:* 4 Airedale Road, SW12 8SF. *T:* (020) 8675 6629.

*See also* J. Unwin, S. J. Unwin.

**UNWIN, Stephen James;** theatre and opera director, playwright, writer, translator, teacher, strategist, campaigner for disabled children; *b* Budapest, 29 Dec. 1959; *s* of Peter William Unwin, *qv*; two *s* one *d*. *Educ:* Downing Coll., Cambridge (BA Hons 1982). Trainee Dir, Almeida, 1982; Associate Dir, Traverse Th., Edinburgh, 1985–88; Resident Dir, NT Studio, 1992; Founding Dir, English Touring Th., 1993–2008; Artistic Dir and Chief Exec., Rose Th., Kingston, 2008–14; freelance dir, NT, Royal Court, ENO, Covent Gdn, Th. Royal, Bath. Chm., KIDS, 2016–; Mem., Whitefield Acad. Trust, 2017–. Judith E. Wilson Fellow, Cambridge Univ., 2001; Halle Dist. Fellow, Emory Univ., 2014; Lectr, RCM, LAMDA, Guildhall, Univ. of S Carolina. *Publications:* Pocket Guide to Shakespeare's Plays, 1998; So You Want to be a Theatre Director?, 2004; A Guide to the Plays of Bertolt Brecht, 2007; The Well Read Play, 2011; All Our Children (play), 2017; *translations:* La Ronde, 2007; Lady From the Sea, 2012; Ghosts, 2013. *Recreations:* reading, travel, disability campaigning, music, family. *Address:* 9 Clapton Terrace, E5 9BW. *E:* steveunwin@btinternet.com. *W:* www.stephenunwin.uk.

*See also* J. Unwin.

**UNWIN, Timothy;** *see* Unwin, P. T. H.

**UPPAL, Paul Singh;** Small Business Commissioner, since 2017; *b* Birmingham, 14 June 1967; *s* of Surjit and Balbir Uppal; *m* 1991, Kashmir Matto; one *s* two *d*. *Educ:* Harborne Hill State Sch.; Warwick Univ. (BA Pol. 1st cl.). Owner of own business. MP (C) Wolverhampton SW, 2010–15; contested (C) same seat, 2015, 2017. *Recreations:* running, reading, theatre and, very rarely, cooking.

**UPRICHARD, Dame Mary (Elizabeth),** DBE 1998 (OBE 1983); President, UK Central Council for Nursing, Midwifery and Health Visiting, 1993–98 (Member of Council, 1980–93); *b* 23 March 1938; *d* of late Norman Uprichard and Rebecca Uprichard (*née* Gracey). *Educ:* Grosvenor Grammar Sch., Belfast. RSCN, RGN, RM, MTD. Sch. of Midwifery, Belfast, 1974–83; Dir of Midwifery Educn, NI Coll. of Midwifery, 1983–97. Chairman: Nat. Bd for Nursing, Midwifery and Health Visiting, 1988–93 (Mem. Bd, 1980–93); Nurses Welfare Service, 1999; Member: EC Adv. Cttee on Training of Midwives, 1984–98; Council for Professions Supplementary to Medicine, 1997; Council on Social Responsibility, Methodist Church in Ireland, 1994.

**UPSHAW, Dawn;** American soprano; Charles Franklin Kellogg and Grace E. Ramsey Kellogg Professor of the Arts and Humanities, and Artistic Director, Graduate Vocal Arts Program, Bard College Conservatory of Music, since 2004; *b* 17 July 1960; *m* Michael Nott; two *c*. *Educ:* Illinois Wesleyan Univ. (BA Music 1982); Manhattan Sch. of Music (MA 1984). Joined NY Metropolitan Opera, 1984; début, Rigoletto, 1984; other productions include: Magic Flute, Wolf Trap Fest., 1985, Aix-en-Provence Fest., 1988; Death in the Family, Opera Co. of St Louis, 1986; Béatrice et Bénédict, 1993, Theodora, 1996, Glyndebourne Fest.; The Rake's Progress, Stravinsky Fest., Paris, 1996; El Niño, Châtelet, Paris, 2000; Cunning Little Vixen, Royal Opera House, Covent Garden, 2003; numerous recitals and concerts with major orchestras and chamber gps. Numerous recordings (Grammy Awards). (Jtly) Winner, Naumburg Competition, 1985.

**UPTON, Anna Louise;** *see* McKenna, A. L.

**UPTON, Prof. Graham,** PhD; DL; educational consultant; Director, GU Consultants Ltd, since 2009; *b* 30 April 1944; *m* 1st, 1966, Jennifer Ann Clark (marr. diss. 1984); one *s* one *d*; 2nd, 1986, Bebe Speed; one *s* one *d*. *Educ:* Univ. of Sydney (BA, Dip Educn 1966); MA 1969); Univ. of New South Wales (MEd 1973); UC Cardiff, Univ. of Wales (PhD 1978). CPsychol 1988; FBPsS 1996. Teacher, New South Wales, 1966–70; Lectr in Educn, Sydney Teachers' Coll., 1970–71; Lectr in Special Educn, Leeds Poly., 1972–74; University College, Cardiff, 1974–88: Lectr; Sen. Lectr; Reader; Hd of Dept of Educn; Dean, Collegiate Faculty of Educn; Dean, Faculty of Educn and Prof. Studies; University of Birmingham: Prof. of Educnl Psychology and Special Educn and Hd, Sch. of Educn, 1988–93; Pro-Vice-Chancellor, 1993–97; Vice-Chancellor: Oxford Brookes Univ., 1997–2007; Univ. of Cumbria, 2010–11; interim Vice-Chancellor, Glyndŵr Univ., 2015–16; Vice-Chancellor, Birmingham City Univ., 2016–17; interim Vice-Chancellor, Bangor Univ., 2018–19. Oxford Playhouse: Mem. Bd, 2001–09; Chm., 2004–09; Pres., 2009–15. Chm., Oxford Expression Technologies, 2009– (non-exec. Dir, 2008–). Mem. Adv. Council, Oxford Trust, 2001–07. Chairman: Oxford Community Partnership, 2002–07; Experience Oxfordshire, 2013–18; Bd of Trustees, Pegasus Th., 2016–19. Governor, Headington Sch., 1999–2007; Member: Bd of Govs, UWE, 2009–15; Council, Univ. of Bangor, 2016–19. Internat. Assoc., UK Leadership Foundn for Higher Educn, 2009–11. AcSS 2000. FRSA 1999. Hon. Fellow: Birmingham Coll. of Food, Tourism and Leisure Studies, 1991; Univ. of Cumbria, 2012; Glyndŵr Univ., 2016. DUniv Oxford Brookes, 2009. Under Sheriff, 2012–13, High Sheriff, 2013–14, DL 2014, Oxfordshire. *Publications:* Physical and Creative Activities for the Mentally Handicapped, 1979; Behaviour Problems in the Comprehensive School, 1980; Educating Children with Behaviour Problems, 1983; Staff Training and Special Educational Needs, 1991; Special Educational Needs, 1992; Special Education in Britain After Warnock, 1993; Emotional and Behavioural Difficulties in Schools, 1994; The Voice of the Child, 1996; Pupils with Severe Learning Difficulties who Present Challenging Behaviour, 1996; Stresses in Special Educational Needs Teachers, 1996; Sound Practice, 1997; Effective Schooling for Pupils with Emotional and Behavioural Difficulties, 1998. *Recreations:* good food, DIY, cycling.

**UPTON, (James) William (David);** QC 2019; *b* Bowden, Scotland, 13 Dec. 1965; *s* of late James, (Dan), Upton and of Eve Upton (*née* Wade); *m* 2003, Melanie Ragge. *Educ:* Trinity Coll., Cambridge (BA 1988; LLM 1989). Called to the Bar, Inner Temple, 1990; Member: Attorney Gen.'s Panel of Jun. Counsel to the Crown (Civil), 2003–13; List of Regulatory Advocates in Health and Safety Envmtl Law, 2013–19. Sec., Planning and Envmt Bar Assoc., 2013–18. Mem., Court of Common Council, City of London Corp. (Ward of Farringdon Without), 2017–. *Publications:* (ed) Environmental Law, 2000, 2nd edn 2009. *Recreations:* classical music, art galleries, photography, fishing, bridge. *Address:* 6 Pump Court, Temple, EC4Y 7AR. *T:* (020) 7797 8400. *E:* william.uptonqc@6pumpcourt.co.uk.

**UPTON, Robert Ian William,** CBE 2009; strategic policy and planning consultant, since 2014; Senior Examining Inspector, National Infrastructure Division, Planning Inspectorate, 2012–14; *b* 20 Aug. 1951; *s* of late Ronald Alfred Upton and Iris Aveline Upton; *m* 1987, Mary Faith Higgins; one *d* (and one *d* decd). *Educ:* Dulwich Coll.; Magdalene Coll., Cambridge (MA); Harvard Business Sch. Hong Kong Government, 1972–91: Clerk of Councils, 1982–84; Sec., Educn Commn, 1985–86; Dep. Sec. for Security, 1986–89; Dir of Planning, 1989–91. Chief Exec., Rushmoor BC, 1992–96; Sec.-Gen., Royal Town Planning Inst., 1996–2009; Jt Deputy Chair, Infrastructure Planning Commn, 2009–12. Vis. Prof., Sheffield Univ., 2013–11. Mem., Adv. Council on Radioactive Waste Mgt, 2017–. FAcSS (AcSS 2010). Hon. MRTPI 2006; Hon. Mem., HK Inst. of Planners, 2014. Hon. LittD Sheffield, 2011. Jt Ed., Planning Theory & Practice, 1999–; Series Ed., RTPI Library Series, 1999–. *Recreations:* reading, walking, book-hunting, Newfoundland dogs.

**UPTON, Rt Hon. Simon (David);** PC 1999; FRSNZ 1999; Parliamentary Commissioner for the Environment, New Zealand, since 2017; *b* 7 Feb. 1958; *s* of Thomas Wilson Upton and Dorothy Vernon Upton (*née* Hosking); *m* 1984, Bhaady Jane Miller; one *s* one *d*. *Educ:* Southwell Prep. Sch., Hamilton, NZ; St Paul's Collegiate Sch.; Auckland Univ. (BA, LLB Hons); Wolfson Coll., Oxford (Rhodes Schol.; MLitt). MHR (Nat.): Waikato, then Raglan, 1981–96; party list, 1996–99; Minister: for the Envmt, 1990–91 and 1993–99; of Res., Sci. and Technol., 1990–96; of Health, 1990–93; for Crown Res. Insts, 1991–99; of Biosecurity, 1996–97; of State Services, 1998–99; of Cultural Affairs, 1998; Associate Minister of Foreign Affairs, 1996–99. Chm., Round Table on Sustainable Envmt, 1998–2015, Dir, Envmt, 2010–17, OECD. Dir, Global Subsidies Initiative, Internat. Inst. for Sustainable Develt, 2007–08; Mem., China Council for Internat. Cooperation on Envmt and Develt, 2013–17. Dir, Holcim (NZ) Ltd, 2007–10. Advr on climate change to PricewaterhouseCoopers (NZ), 2005–10. Chm., 7th Session of UN Commn on Sustainable Develt, 1999. *Publications:* The Withering of the State, 1986. *Recreations:* gardening and landscaping, NZ geology and botany, music, ski-ing, trail-running. *Address:* Parliamentary Commissioner for the Environment, PO Box 10–241, Wellington, New Zealand. *Club:* Wellington (Wellington, NZ).

**UPTON, William;** *see* Upton, J. W. D.

**UPWARD, Mrs Janet;** Chair, Birmingham and Solihull Mental Health Patients' Forum, 2007–08 (Member, 2004–08). *Educ:* Newnham College, Cambridge (BA (Geog. Hons) 1961; MA 1966); Univ. of Birmingham (MSocSci 1993). Sec., Nat. Fedn of Consumer Gps, 1972–82; Mem., 1978–84, Dep. Chm., 1978–83, Domestic Coal Consumers' Council; Chm., Nat. Consumer Congress, 1981–83; Chief Officer, S Birmingham CHC, 1982–90; Project Manager, Birmingham FHSA, 1991–96. Chair, Bromsgrove Concert Club, 2010–18.

**URBAN, Mark Lee;** Diplomatic and Defence Editor, BBC Newsnight, since 1999; *b* London, 26 Jan. 1961; *s* of Harry and Josephine Urban; *m* 1993, Hilary Jane Rosen; one *s* two *d*. *Educ:* King's College Sch., Wimbledon; London Sch. of Economics (BSc (Econ) Internat. Relns). Asst producer, BBC TV, 1983–86; Defence Corresp., Independent, 1986–90; BBC Television: reporter, Newsnight, 1990–93; Middle East Corresp., 1993–94; Diplomatic Corresp., Newsnight, 1995–98. Trustee: Royal Armouries, 2012–18; Imperial War Mus., 2018–. *Publications:* Soviet Land Power, 1983; War in Afghanistan, 1987; Big Boys' Rules: the secret struggle against the IRA, 1992; UK Eyes Alpha: the inside story of British Intelligence, 1996; The Illegal, 1996; The Linguist, 1998; The Man Who Broke Napoleon's Codes, 2001; Rifles: six years with Wellington's legendary sharpshooters, 2003; Generals: ten British commanders who shaped the world, 2005; Fusiliers: eight years with the Redcoats in America, 2007; Task Force Black: the explosive true story of the SAS and the secret war in Iraq, 2010; The Edge: is the military dominance of the West coming to an end?, 2015; The Skripal Files: the life and near death of a Russian spy, 2018. *Recreations:* good food, reading, trying to keep fit, ski-ing. *Address:* c/o Newsnight, BBC News Centre, Broadcasting House, Portland Place, W1A 1AA.

**URCH, Lt Gen. Tyrone Richard,** CBE 2011 (OBE 2005; MBE 2000); Commander Home Command, since 2018; Chief Royal Engineer, since 2018; *b* Malta, 12 June 1965; *s* of Christopher Urch and Carole Urch; *m* 1987, Gillian Elizabeth Tidd; one *s* one *d*. *Educ:* Warminster Sch.; Wellbeck Coll.; Cranfield Univ. (BEng Civil Engrg); King's Coll. London (MA). CEng 1997; FICE 2005; FInstRE 2010. Commnd RE, 1984; Regtl duty and on Army Staff, 1984–2003; CO 22 Engr Regt, 2003–05; Comdr, 1st Mechanized Bde, 2008–10; ACOS Ops PJHQ, 2010–12; operational deployments to NI, Bosnia, Iraq; COS Land Forces, Army HQ, 2012–15; GOC Force Troops Comd, 2015–17. *Recreations:* family, squash, Rugby, mountaineering, dog walking, keeping fit, reading, travel. *Address:* HQ Home Command, Montgomery House, Queen's Avenue, Aldershot, Hants GU11 2JN.

**URE, James Mathie,** OBE 1969; British Council Representative, India, and Minister (Education), British High Commission, New Delhi, 1980–84; *b* 5 May 1925; *s* of late William Alexander Ure, and Helen Jones; *m* 1950, Martha Walker Paterson; one *s* one *d*. *Educ:* Shawlands Acad., Glasgow; Glasgow Univ. (MA); Trinity Coll., Oxford (BLitt). Army Service, 1944–47. Lectr, Edinburgh Univ., 1953–59; British Council: Istanbul, 1956–57; India, 1959–68; Dep. Controller, Arts Div., 1968–71; Rep., Indonesia, 1971–75; Controller, Home Div., 1975–80. *Publications:* Old English Benedictine Office, 1952; (with L. A. Hill) English Sounds and Spellings, 1962; (with L. A. Hill) English Sounds and Spellings—Tests, 1963; (with J. S. Bhandari and C. S. Bhandari) Read and Act, 1965; (with C. S. Bhandari) Short Stories, 1966.

**URE, Sir John (Burns),** KCMG 1987 (CMG 1980); LVO 1968; HM Diplomatic Service, retired; author; *b* 5 July 1931; *s* of late Tam Ure; *m* 1972, Caroline, *d* of late Charles Allan, Roxburghshire; one *s* one *d*. *Educ:* Uppingham Sch.; Magdalene Coll., Cambridge (MA); Harvard Business Sch. (AMP). Active Service as 2nd Lieut with Cameronians (Scottish Rifles), Malaya, 1950–51; Lieut, London Scottish (Gordon Highlanders) TA, 1952–55. Book publishing with Ernest Benn Ltd, 1951–53; joined Foreign (subseq. Diplomatic) Service, 1956; 3rd Sec. and Private Sec. to Ambassador, Moscow, 1957–59; Resident Clerk, FO, 1960–61; 2nd Sec., Leopoldville, 1962–63; FO, 1964–66; 1st Sec. (Commercial), Santiago, 1967–70; FCO, 1971–72; Counsellor, and intermittently Chargé d'Affaires, Lisbon, 1972–77; Head of South America Dept, FCO, 1977–79; Ambassador to Cuba, 1979–81; Asst Under-Sec. of State for the Americas, FCO, 1981–84; Ambassador to Brazil, 1984–87, to Sweden, 1987–91. UK Comr Gen., Expo 92, 1990–92. Director: Thomas Cook Group, 1991–99; Sotheby's Scandinavia AB, 1991–99; CSE Aviation, 1992–94; Consultant: Robert Fleming & Co. (merchant bankers), 1995–98; Ecosse Films, 1997–99; European Risk Mgt Consultants, 1997–2000; Sotheby's Scandinavia, 1999–. Chairman: panel of judges, Thomas Cook Travel Book of the Year Award, 1991–2000; Anglo-Swedish Soc., 1992–96; Anglo-Brazilian Chamber of Commerce, 1994–96. Pres., Weald of Kent Protection Soc., 2005–11. Trustee, Leeds Castle Foundn, 1995–2006. Life Fellow and Mem. Council, RGS, 1982–84. Comdr, Mil. Order of Christ, Portugal, 1973. *Publications:* Cucumber Sandwiches in the Andes, 1973 (Travel Book Club Choice); Prince Henry the Navigator, 1977 (History Guild Choice); The Trail of Tamerlane, 1980 (Ancient History Club Choice); The Quest for Captain Morgan, 1983; Trespassers on the Amazon, 1986; Central and South America sections, in RGS History of World Exploration, 1990; A Bird on the Wing: Bonnie Prince Charlie's flight from Culloden retraced, 1992; Diplomatic Bag, 1994; The Cossacks, 1999; In Search of Nomads, 2003; Pilgrimage: the great adventure of the Middle Ages, 2006; (contrib.) The Seventy Great Journeys in History, 2006; Shooting Leave: spying out Central Asia in the Great Game, 2009; (contrib.) The Great Explorers, 2010; Sabres on the Steppes, 2012; Beware the Rugged Russian Bear, 2015; travel articles in Daily and Sunday Telegraph; book reviews in TLS and Country Life; biographies for Oxford DNB. *Recreation:* travelling uncomfortably in remote places and writing about it comfortably afterwards. *Address:* Netters Hall, Hawkhurst, Kent TN18 5AS. *T:* (01580) 752191. *Clubs:* White's, Beefsteak, Pilgrims.

**URQUHART, Sir Brian (Edward),** KCMG 1986; MBE 1945; Scholar-in-Residence, Ford Foundation, 1986–96; an Under-Secretary-General, United Nations, 1974–86; *b* 28 Feb. 1919; *s* of Murray and Bertha Urquhart; *m* 1st, 1944, Alfreda Huntington (marr. diss. 1963); two *s* one *d*; 2nd, 1963, Sidney Damrosch Howard; one *s* one *d*. *Educ:* Westminster; Christ Church, Oxford (Hon. Student, 1985). British Army: Dorset Regt and Airborne Forces, N Africa, Sicily and Europe, 1939–45; Personal Asst to Gladwyn Jebb, Exec. Sec. of Preparatory Commn of UN, London, 1945–46; Personal Asst to Trygve Lie, 1st Sec.-Gen. of UN, 1946–49; Sec., Collective Measures Cttee, 1951–53; Mem., Office of Under-Sec.-Gen. for Special Political Affairs, 1954–71; Asst Sec.-Gen., UN, 1972–74; Exec. Sec., 1st and 2nd UN Conf. on Peaceful Uses of Atomic Energy, 1955 and 1958; active in organization and direction of UN Emergency Force in Middle East, 1956; Dep. Exec. Sec., Preparatory Commn of Internat. Atomic Energy Agency, 1957; Asst to Sec.-Gen.'s Special Rep. in Congo, July–Oct. 1960; UN Rep. in Katanga, Congo, 1961–62; responsible for organization and direction of UN peace-keeping ops and special political assignments. Hon. LLD: Yale, 1981; Tufts, 1985; Grinnell, 1986; State Univ. NY, 1986; Warwick, 1989; DUniv: Essex, 1981; City Univ. NY, 1986; Hon. DCL Oxford, 1986; Hon. DHL Colorado, 1987; Hon. DLitt: Keele, 1987; Cambridge, 2005; Brown, 2006, Amherst, 2008. *Publications:* Hammarskjold, 1972; A Life in Peace and War (autobiog.), 1987; Decolonization and World Peace, 1989; (with Erskine Childers) A World in Need of Leadership: tomorrow's United Nations, 1990; Ralph Bunche: an American life, 1993; (with Erskine Childers) Renewing the United Nations System, 1994; A World in Need of Leadership: tomorrow's United Nations, a fresh appraisal, 1996; various articles and reviews on internat. affairs. *Address:* PO Box 384, Tyringham, MA 01264, USA. *T:* (212) 6796358. *Club:* Century (New York).

**URQUHART, Rt Rev. David Andrew;** *see* Birmingham, Bishop of.

**URQUHART, Lawrence McAllister,** CA; Chairman, BAA plc, 1998–2002 (Director, 1993–2002); *b* 24 Sept. 1935; *s* of Robert and Josephine Urquhart; *m* 1961, Elizabeth Catherine Burns; three *s* one *d*. *Educ:* Strathallan; King's Coll., London (LLB). CA 1961. Price Waterhouse & Co., 1957–62; Shell International Petroleum, 1962–64; P. A. Management Consultants, 1964–68; Charterhouse Gp, 1968–74; TKM Gp, 1974–77; Burmah Oil, subseq. Burmah Castrol, 1977–99: Gp Man. Dir, 1985–88; Chief Exec., 1988–93; Chm., 1990–98; non-exec. Dir, 1998–99. Chairman: English China Clays, 1995–99 (Dir, 1991–99); Scottish Widows plc (formerly Scottish Widows' Fund and Life Assurance Soc.), 1995–2001 (non-exec. Dir, 1992–95); non-executive Director: Imerys SA, 1999–2002; Lloyds TSB Bank plc, 2000–02; Lloyds TSB Group plc, 2000–02. *Recreations:* piano, orchestral concert going.

**URQUHART, Linda Hamilton,** OBE 2012; Chairman, Morton Fraser, 2011–17; *b* Edinburgh, 21 Sept. 1959; *d* of Douglas Hamilton Urquhart and Ina Allan Urquhart; *m* 1988, David Spencer Burns; two *d*. *Educ:* James Gillespie's High Sch.; Univ. of Edinburgh (LLB, DipLP). Admitted as solicitor, 1982; Partner, 1985–99, Chief Exec., 1999–2011, Morton Fraser. Non-executive Director: ESPC Gp of cos, 2005–09; Remarkable (formerly Investors in People Scotland), 2011–19 (Chm., 2011–19); Adam Bank, 2012–18; Edinburgh Airport, 2013–; Coutts, 2018–. Member, Board: Scottish Enterprise, 2011–16; CBI, 2011–17 (Chm., CBI Scotland, 2009–11). Mem., Develt Bd, Prince's Trust Scotland, 2011–13. Trustee: Royal Scottish Acad. Foundn, 2013–19; Marie Curie (formerly Marie Curie Cancer Care), 2014–. Co-Chair, Fair Work Convention, 2015–17. Ambassador, Girlguiding UK, 2008–17 (Pres., Girlguiding Scotland, 2017–). Co-Ed., Green's Property Law Bulletin, 1997–2016. Mem., Soc. of WS, 1985–. *Recreations:* sailing, walking, ski-ing, golf, singing. *Club:* Royal Highland Yacht.

**URQUHART, His Honour Peter William Gordon;** a Circuit Judge, 1992–2001; *b* 18 March 1934; *s* of Gordon Eldridge Urquhart and Constance Margaret (née Taylor); *m* 1965, Carolyn Hemingway Hines; one *s* one *d*. *Educ:* Liverpool Coll.; Peterhouse, Cambridge (MA, LLB). Admitted solicitor, 1960. Member: Lord Chancellor's Legal Aid Adv. Cttee, 1974–80; Equal Opportunities Commn, 1977–82. *Recreations:* book collecting, reading, gardening, early music, jazz. *Address:* Braehead, 19 Poplar Road, Prenton, Merseyside CH43 5TB. *T:* (0151) 652 4043. *Club:* Athenæum (Liverpool).

**URQUHART IRVINE, Oliver Henry,** MVO 2018; FSA, FRAS; Director of Library and Learning Services, School of Oriental and African Studies, University of London, since 2019; *b* Carlisle, 11 Jan. 1974; *s* of Robert John Macferson Irvine and Lesley Marian Irvine (née Urquhart); one *s* one *d*. *Educ:* Courtauld Inst., Univ. of London (BA 1996); Univ. of Amsterdam (MA 1997); Coll. of Law (Grad. Dip. Law 2005); Inst. of Art Law (Postgrad. Dip. Art Law 2007; Dip. Art Profession Law and Ethics 2008). Specialist, Books and MSS Dept, Christie's, 1997–99; antiquarian bookseller, Maggs Bros Ltd, 1999–2005; British Library: Cultural Property Manager, 2005–10; Hd, Asian Middle Eastern and African Dept, 2010–12; Hd, BL Qatar Foundn Partnership, 2011–14; Librarian, Royal Liby, 2014–19, and Asst Keeper, 2014–18, Dep. Keeper, 2018–19, Royal Archives. Mem., Spoliation Adv. Panel, 2015–. Sen. Associate Mem., Hughes Hall, Cambridge, 2012–. Trustee and Mem. Council of Mgt, Windsor Fest., 2016–19. Gov., Tottenhall Infants Sch., 2012–14. FSA 2008; FRAS 2013. Freeman: City of London, 2017; Stationers' and Newspaper Makers' Co., 2017 (Liveryman, 2018); Goldsmiths' Co., 2018. *Recreation:* running. *Address:* School of Oriental and African Studies, University of London, 10 Thornhaugh Street, Russell Square, WC1H 0XG. *T:* (020) 7898 4161. *E:* ou2@soas.ac.uk. *Clubs:* Athenæum, Savile.

**URSELL, Rev. Canon Philip Elliott;** Principal, Pusey House, Oxford, 1982–2003 (Governor, 2006–13); Fellow, St Cross College, Oxford, 1982–2003; Warden, Society of The Most Holy Trinity, Ascot Priory, 1984–2013; *b* 3 Dec. 1942; *o s* of late Clifford Edwin Ursell and Hilda Jane Ursell (née Tucker). *Educ:* Cathays High Sch.; University Coll. Cardiff (Craddock Wells Exhibnr; BA); St Stephen's House, Oxford. MA Oxon. DD Nashotah House, Wisconsin. Curate of Newton Nottage, Porthcawl, 1968–71; Asst Chaplain of University Coll. Cardiff, 1971–77; Chaplain of Polytechnic of Wales, 1974–77; Chaplain, Fellow and Dir of Studies in Music, Emmanuel Coll., Cambridge, 1977–82. Bishop's Commissary for Province of Canterbury, and Canon of Rio Grande, 2005–. Select Preacher, Harvard Univ., 1982, 1983, 1996, 1997; Univ. Preacher, Harvard Summer Sch., 1985. Examining Chaplain to the Bishop of London, 1987–2010. Trustee, Number 1 Trust Fund, 1983–2017 (Chm., 1991–2002); Chairman: Soc. for Maintenance of the Faith, 1995–; Anglo-Catholic Ordination Candidates Fund, 2000–. Gov., Heathfield Sch., 2008–. Mem. Governing Body, Church in Wales, 1971–77. *Recreations:* fine wines, opera, championing lost causes. *Address:* 273 Hayes Apartments, Cardiff CF10 1BZ. *T:* (029) 2132 8359. *Club:* Clifton (Bristol).

**URWIN, Rt Rev. Lindsay Goodall,** OGS; Vicar, Christ Church, Brunswick, since 2015; Bishop with responsibility for the care of Anglican Schools, Diocese of Melbourne, since 2015; an Hon. Assistant Bishop, Diocese of Norwich, since 2009; *b* 13 March 1956. *Educ:* Camberwell GS, Australia; Ripon Coll., Cuddesdon; Heythrop Coll., Univ. of London (MA 2003). Ordained deacon, 1980, priest, 1981; Curate, St Peter, Walworth, 1980–83; Vicar, St Faith, N Dulwich, 1983–88; Diocesan Missioner, Chichester, 1988–93; Area Bishop of Horsham, 1993–2009; Guardian, 2006–15, Administrator, 2009–15, Shrine of Our Lady of Walsingham, Norfolk, now Guardian Emeritus. Honorary Assistant Bishop: Dio. of Chichester, 2009–15; Dio. of Peterborough, 2011–15; Dio. of Ely, 2011–15. Nat. Chm., Church Union, 1995–98. Member: OGS, 1991– (UK Provincial, 1996–2005); Coll. of Evangelists, 1999–. Provost, Southern Region, Woodard Corp. of Schs, 2006–15. Hon. DD Nashotah House, Wisconsin, 2011. *Publications:* (ed jtly) Youthful Spirit, 1999. *Address:* Christ Church, 8 Glenlyon Road, Brunswick, Vic 3056, Australia. *T:* (3) 93801064.

**URWIN, Peter;** *see* Urwin, T. P.

**URWIN, Roger John,** CBE 2007; PhD; FREng, FIET; Chairman, Utilico Investments Ltd (formerly Utilico Ltd), 2010–15; *b* 8 Feb. 1946. *Educ:* Watford Grammar Sch.; Weston-super-Mare Grammar Sch.; Southampton Univ. (BSc 1964; PhD 1971). CEng; FIET (FIEE 1990). Various appts with CEGB, 1971–85; Dir of Engrg, Midlands Electricity Bd, 1985–90; Man. Dir, subseq. Chief Exec., London Electricity, 1990–95; Dir, 1995–2001, Chief Exec., 2001–02, Nat. Grid Gp; Chief Exec., Nat. Grid Transco plc, 2002–06. Chm., Alfred McAlpine plc, 2007–08 (non-exec. Dir, 2006–08); non-executive Director: Special Utilities Investment Trust plc, 1993–2003; TotalFinaElf Exploration UK plc, 1996–2003; Utilico Investment Trust plc, 2003–10; Canadian Utilities Ltd, 2007–. FREng (FEng 1998).

**URWIN, (Terence) Peter;** public sector consultant, since 2001; Director of Administration and County Solicitor, Northumberland County Council, 1990–2000; *b* 28 Oct. 1948; *s* of John Robson Urwin; *m* 1971, Mary Theresa Smith; one *d*. *Educ:* Durham Johnston Sch.; Liverpool Univ. (LLB Hons). Solicitor. Durham County Council: Asst Solicitor, 1973–74; Asst Clerk of the Council, 1974–86; Dep. County Solicitor, 1986–90. Clerk to the Lieutenancy, Northumberland, 1990–2000. Secretary, Northumberland Advisory Committee: Justices of the Peace, 1990–2000; Gen. Comrs of Income Tax, 1990–2000. Mem. Council, Law Soc., 1997–2001. *Recreations:* Rugby, walking, crosswords, motorcycling. *Address:* Buckburns, Brancepeth Village, Durham City DH7 8DT. *T:* (0191) 378 3086.

**USBORNE, (Thomas) Peter,** MBE 2011; Founder and Managing Director, Usborne Publishing Ltd, since 1973; *b* 18 Aug. 1937; *s* of Thomas George Usborne and Gerda (née Just); *m* 1964, Cornelie Tücking; one *s* one *d*. *Educ:* Summer Fields Sch., Oxford; Eton Coll.; Balliol Coll., Oxford (BA); INSEAD, Fontainebleau, France (MBA 1966). Co-Founder and Man. Dir, Private Eye mag., 1962–65; Sen. Scientist, Metra Sigma Martech, 1967–68; Asst to Chm., BPC Publishing Ltd, 1969–70; Publishing Dir, Macdonald Educnl, 1970–73. *Recreations:* flying, gardening, France. *Clubs:* Garrick, Groucho.

**USHER, Sir Andrew (John),** 8th Bt *cr* 1899, of Norton, Ratho, Midlothian and of Wells, Hobkirk, Roxburghshire; interior decorator and builder; *b* 8 Feb. 1963; *er s* of Sir John Usher, 7th Bt and of Rosemary Margaret, *d* of Col Sir Reginald Houldsworth, 4th Bt, OBE, TD; *S* father, 1998; *m* 1987, Charlotte Louise Alexandra, *o d* of R. B. Eldridge; two *s*. *Educ:* Hilton Coll., S Africa. *Recreations:* golf, fishing. *Heir: s* Rory James Andrew Usher, *b* 11 June 1991.

**USHER, Rt Rev. Graham Barham;** *see* Norwich, Bishop of.

**USSHER, Kitty;** Teacher of Mathematics, Now Teach career-change programme, since 2017; *b* 18 March 1971; *d* of Patrick Ussher and Susan (née Bottomley, now Whitfield); *m* 1999, Peter Colley; one *s* one *d*. *Educ:* Balliol Coll., Oxford (PPE 1993); Birkbeck Coll., London (MSc Econs 1998); Goldsmiths, Univ. of London (PGCE 2018). Researcher,

**UTEEM, Cassam;** Labour Party, 1994–97; Economist: EIU, 1997–98; Centre for European Reform, 1998–2000; Chief Economist, Britain in Europe Campaign, 1999–2001; Special Advr to Rt Hon. Patricia Hewitt, MP, at DTI, 2001–04. Mem. (Lab), Lambeth LBC, 1998–2002. MP (Lab) Burnley, 2005–10. Economic Sec., 2007–08, Exchequer Sec., 2009, HM Treasury; Parly Under-Sec. of State, DWP, 2008–09. Dir, Demos, 2010–11; Chief Econ. Advr, Portland Communications, 2013–16; Man. Dir, Tooley Street Research, 2014–18. Mem., Financial Services Consumer Panel, 2015–17. Chair, Labour in the City, 2012–17; Mem., Ind. Economists Gp, TheCityUK, 2012–17. *Publications:* pamphlets for Demos, Centre for European Reform, Smith Inst., Social Market Foundn, Centre for London. *Recreations:* hill walking, supporting Burnley Football Club. *Address:* c/o Now Teach, Ark, 65 Kingsway, WC2B 6TD.

**UTEEM, Cassam;** President, Republic of Mauritius, 1992–2002; *b* 22 March 1941; *s* of Omar and Aisha Uteem; *m* 1967, Zohra Uteem; one *s* one *d* (and one *s* decd). *Educ:* Univ. of Mauritius (Dip. Soc. Work); Univ. of Paris VII (LèsL, MPsychol). Mem., Municipal Council, Port Louis, 1969, 1977–79, 1986–88 (Lord Mayor, 1986); MLA Port Louis East/Maritime, 1982–92; Minister of Employment, Social Security and National Solidarity, 1982–83; Opposition Whip, 1983–87; Chm., Public Accounts Cttee, 1988–90; Dep. Prime Minister and Minister of Industry and Industrial Technol., 1990–92. UN Special Envoy and Hd of Electoral Observation Mission, Burundi, 2015. Mem. Bd, Internat. Inst. for Democracy and Electoral Assistance. Hon. DCL Mauritius, 1994; Dr *hc* Aix Marseilles III, 1994. Grand Commander, Order of Star and Key of the Indian Ocean (Republic of Mauritius), 1993. *Recreations:* reading, walking. *Address:* c/o State House, Le Reduit, Mauritius. *T:* 4543021.

**UTTERSON, Joanna;** *see* Mackle, J.

**UTTING, Sir William (Benjamin),** Kt 1991; CB 1985; President, Mental Health Foundation, 1999–2014 (Trustee, 1988–97; Vice-President, 1997–99); *b* 13 May 1931; *s* of John William Utting and Florence Ada Utting; *m* 1954, Mildred Jackson; two *s* one *d*. *Educ:* Great Yarmouth Grammar Sch.; New Coll., Oxford (Exhibnr; MA; Hon. Fellow, 1996); Barnett House, Oxford. Probation Officer: Co. Durham, 1956–58; Norfolk, 1958–61; Sen. Probation Officer, Co. Durham, 1961–64; Principal Probation Officer, Newcastle upon Tyne, 1964–68; Lectr in Social Studies, Univ. of Newcastle upon Tyne, 1968–70; Dir of Social Services, Kensington and Chelsea, 1970–76; Chief Social Work Officer, DHSS, 1976–85; Chief Inspector, Social Services Inspectorate, DHSS, subseq. DoH, 1985–91. Member: Chief Scientist's Res. Cttee, DHSS, 1973–76; SSRC, 1979–83; ESRC, 1984; Cttee on Standards in Public Life, 1994–2001. Chm., 1991–97, Pres., 1997–2002, NISW. Chairman: Mary Ward House Trust, 1997–2006; Forum on Children and Violence, 1997–2000; Vice-Pres., Nat. Children's Bureau, 2002–07; Member of Council: Caldecott Foundn, 1998–2002; Goldsmiths Coll., London Univ., 1993–2006 (Chair, 2000–06, Hon. Fellow, 2007); Trustee: Joseph Rowntree Foundn, 1991–2006 (Dep. Chm., 2001–05; Chm., 2005–06); CSV, 1991–97; Family Fund Trust, 1996–2000. Pres., New Coll. Soc., 2002–03. Fellow, Centre for Social Policy, Dartington, 2001. Hon. DLitt: UEA, 1992; East London, 1998; Hon. DCL Northumbria, 1997; Hon. DSc Kingston, 2000. *Publications:* Children in the Public Care, 1991; People Like Us, 1997; contribs to professional jls. *Recreations:* literature, music, art. *Address:* 76 Great Brownings, SE21 7HR. *T:* (020) 8670 1201.

**UXBRIDGE, Earl of; Benedict Dashiel Thomas Paget;** *b* 11 April 1986; *s* and *heir* of Marquess of Anglesey, *qv*; *m* Katherine Rose.

# V

**VADERA**, Baroness *cr* 2007 (Life Peer); **Shriti Vadera**; PC 2009; Chair, Santander UK, since 2015; *b* Uganda. *Educ:* Somerville Coll., Oxford. With S. G. Warburg, later UBS, 1984–99; Mem. Council of Econ. Advrs, HM Treasury, 1999–2007; Parliamentary Under-Secretary of State: DFID, 2007–08; BERR, later BIS, and in Cabinet Office, 2008–09. Advr to S Korean Presidency of G20 Gp of Nations, 2009–10. Non-executive Director: BHP Billiton, 2011–15 (Sen. Ind. Dir, 2015–); Astra Zeneca, 2011–18. Trustee, Oxfam, 2000–05. *Address:* House of Lords, SW1A 0PW.

**VADGAMA, Prof. Pankaj Maganlal**, PhD; FRCPath; FRSC; FInstP; FIMMM; FRSB; Professor of Clinical Biochemistry, and Director, Interdisciplinary Research Centre in Biomedical Materials, Queen Mary University of London, since 2000; *b* 16 Feb. 1948; *s* of Maganlal Vadgama and Champaben Vadgama (*née* Gajjar); *m* 1977, Dixa Bakrania; one *s* two *d*. *Educ:* Orange Hill Co. Grammar Sch.; Univ. of Newcastle upon Tyne (MB BS, BSc 1st cl. Hons; PhD 1984). FRCPath 1989; FRSC 1996; FInstP 2000; FIMMM 2001; FRSB (FSB 2012). MRC Trng Fellow, Newcastle Univ., 1978–81; Sen. Registrar in Clin. Biochem., Newcastle Gen. Hosp., 1981–83; Dir, Biosensor Gp, Newcastle Univ., 1983–88; Manchester University: Prof. of Clin. Biochem., 1988–2000; Prof. of Biomed. Materials, 1999–2000. Hon. Consultant Chemical Pathologist: Royal Victoria Infirmary, Newcastle, 1983–88; Hope Hosp., Salford, 1988–2000; Barts Health NHS Trust (formerly Barts and the London NHS Trust), 2000–15. *Publications:* (ed) Surfaces and Interfaces for Biomaterials, 2005; contribs on biosensors, *in vivo* monitoring, biomaterials, biocompatibility and membrane technol. *Recreations:* reading, walking. *Address:* 16 Wellfields, Loughton, Essex IG10 1NX. *T:* (office) (020) 7882 5151, *Fax:* (020) 7882 3390. *Club:* Athenæum.

**VAILE, Hon. Mark Anthony James**, AO 2012; Chairman: CBD Energy Ltd, 2008–13; Whitehaven Coal, since 2012; *b* 18 April 1956; *s* of George and Sue Vaile; *m* 1976, Wendy Duff; three *d*. *Educ:* Taree High Sch., NSW. Jackaroo, 1973–75; farm machinery retailer, 1975–78; stock, station and real estate agent and auctioneer, 1978–92. Greater Taree City Council: Alderman, 1985–93; Dep. Mayor, 1986–87, 1991–92, 1992–93. Mem., National Party, 1978– (Chm., Wingham Br., 1982–86); Sec., Lyne Electorate Council, 1984–90. MP (National) Lyne, NSW, 1993–2008. Minister: for Transport and Regl Develt, 1997–98; for Agric., Fisheries and Forestry, 1998–99; for Trade, 1999–2006; for Transport and Regl Services, 2006–07; Dep. Prime Minister, 2005–07. Asst Nat. Party Whip, 1994–96; Nat. Party Whip, 1996–97; Dep. Leader, 1999–2005, Leader, 2005–07, Fed. Parly Nat. Party, Australia. Palisade Investment Partners: Chm., Regl Infrastructure Fund, 2008–; Chm., Investor Adv. Gp, 2008–; Mem., Adv. Bd, 2014–. Chm., Aston Resources Ltd, 2009–12; non-executive Director: Virgin Australia (formerly Blue) Hldgs Ltd, 2008–; Stamford Land Ltd, 2009–; Servcorp Ltd, 2011–; HostPlus Investments Pty Ltd, 2012–. Co-Chm., Australia America Leadership Dialogue. Chm., Australia Korea Business Council. *T:* (4) 18229227. *E:* mav@vaileassoc.com.

**VAISEY, David George**, CBE 1996; FSA; FRHistS; Bodley's Librarian, Oxford, 1986–96, now Emeritus; Keeper of the Archives, Oxford University, 1995–2000; Professorial Fellow then Fellow by Special Election, Exeter College, Oxford, 1975–2000, now Emeritus; *b* 15 March 1935; *s* of William Thomas Vaisey and Minnie Vaisey (*née* Payne); *m* 1965, Maureen Anne (*née* Mansell); two *d*. *Educ:* Rendcomb Coll., Glos (schol.); Exeter Coll., Oxford (Exhibnr; BA Mod. Hist., MA). 2nd Lieut, Glos Regt and KAR, 1955–56. Archivist, Staffordshire CC, 1960–63; Asst then Sen. Asst Librarian, Bodleian Liby, 1963–75; Dep. Keeper, Oxford Univ. Archives, 1966–75; Keeper of Western Manuscripts, Bodleian Liby, 1975–86. Vis. Prof., Liby Studies, UCLA, 1985. Hon. Res. Fellow, Dept of Library, Archive and Information Studies, UCL, 1987–. Member: Royal Commn on Historical Manuscripts, 1986–98; Adv. Council on Public Records, 1989–94; Expert Panel on Museums, Libraries and Archives, Heritage Lottery Fund, 1999–2005; Archive, Libraries and Information Adv. Cttee, English Heritage, 1999–2002; Chm., Nat. Council on Archives, 1988–91. Vice-Pres., British Records Assoc., 1998–2006; Pres., Soc. of Archivists, 1999–2002. FRHistS 1973; FSA 1974. Hon. Fellow, Kellogg Coll., Oxford 1996. Encomienda, Order of Isabel the Catholic (Spain), 1989. *Publications:* Staffordshire and The Great Rebellion (jtly), 1964; Probate Inventories of Lichfield and District 1568–1680, 1969; (jtly) Victorian and Edwardian Oxford from old photographs, 1971; (jtly) Oxford Shops and Shopping, 1972; (jtly) Art for Commerce, 1973; Oxfordshire: a handbook for students of local history, 1973, 2nd edn 1974; The Diary of Thomas Turner 1754–65, 1984; Bodleian Library Treasures, 2015; articles in learned jls and collections. *Address:* 3 Stonehill Lane, Southmoor, Oxon OX13 5HU.

**VAITILINGAM, Adam Skanda**; QC 2010; a Recorder, since 2004; *b* Clevedon, 29 Nov. 1963; *s* of Skanda Vaitilingam and Angela Vaitilingam; *m* 2012, Sarah Gibson; one *d*. *Educ:* Bristol Grammar Sch.; King's Coll., Cambridge (BA 1986). Called to the Bar, Middle Temple, 1987. *Publications:* (jtly) The Rough Guide to Jamaica, 1995. *Recreations:* ski-ing, cricket, Bristol City FC. *Address:* Albion Chambers, Broad Street, Bristol BS1 1DR. *T:* (0117) 927 2144.

**VAIZEY, Lady; Marina Vaizey**, CBE 2009; writer, lecturer and art critic; Editor, National Art Collections Fund Publications, 1991–94 (Editorial Consultant, 1994–98); *b* 16 Jan. 1938; *o d* of late Lyman and Ruth Stansky; *m* 1961, Baron Vaizey (*d* 1984); two *s* one *d*. *Educ:* Brearley Sch., New York; Putney Sch., Putney, Vermont; Radcliffe Coll., Harvard Univ. (BA Medieval History and Lit.); Girton Coll., Cambridge (BA, MA). Art Critic: Financial Times, 1970–74; Sunday Times, 1974–92; Dance Critic, Now!, 1979–81. Member: Arts Council, 1976–79 (Mem. Art Panel, 1973–79, Dep. Chm., 1976–79); Advisory Cttee, DoE, 1975–81; Paintings for Hospitals, 1974–90; Cttee, Contemporary Art Soc., 1975–79 1980–94 (Hon. Sec., 1988–94); Hist. of Art and Complementary Studies Bd, CNAA, 1978–82; Photography Bd, CNAA, 1979–81; Fine Art Bd, CNAA, 1980–83; Passenger Services Sub-Cttee, Heathrow Airport, 1979–83; Visual Arts Adv. Cttee, British Council, 1987–2004; Crafts Council, 1988–94; Art Wkg Gp, National Curriculum, DES, 1990–91; Cttee, 20th Century Soc., 1995–98; Gov., South Bank Bd, 1993–2003; Governance Forum, Mus. Assoc., 2003–09; Trustee: Nat. Mus and Galls on Merseyside, 1986–2001; Geffrye Mus., London, 1990–2010; Imperial War Mus., 1991–2003; London Open House, 1996–2008; Internat. Rescue Cttee UK, 1997–2007; The Musical Brain, 2010–19; Contemp. Applied Arts, 2014–16; Mem. Council, Friends of the V&A, 2001–13 (Chm., 2006–13); Gov., Nat. Army Mus., 2001–08 (Mem. Council, Friends of Nat. Army Mus., 2003–06); Exec. Dir, Mitchell Prize for the Hist. of Art, 1976–87. Governor: Camberwell Coll. of Arts and Crafts, 1971–82; Bath Acad. of Art, Corsham, 1978–81. Curated: Critic's Choice, Tooth's, 1974; Painter as Photographer, touring exhibn, UK, 1982–85; Shining Through, Crafts Council, 1995. Turner Prize Judge, 1997. *Publications:* 100 Masterpieces of Art, 1979; Andrew Wyeth, 1980; The Artist as Photographer, 1982; Peter Blake, 1985; Christiane Kubrick, 1990; Christo, 1990; Sorensen, 1994; Picasso's Ladies, 1998; Sutton Taylor, 1999; Felim Egan, 1999; (with Charlotte Gere) Great Women Collectors, 1999; (ed) Art, the Critics' Choice, 1999; Magdalene Odundo, 2001; The British Museum Smile, 2002; Colin Rose, 2003; Wendy Ramshaw, 2004; Andrew Logan, 2009; Room of Dreams, 2012; Being Tracey, 2012; Lucian Freud: mapping the human, 2012; Documents and Dreams, 2013; Between Dream and Nightmare: a view of modern German art, 2014; Through the Lens: studies in photography, 2015; Painted Lives: Vanessa Bell and David Hockney, 2017; Munch and Van Gogh: life, love, death, 2019. *Address:* 41 Brackley Road, Chiswick, W4 2HW. *T:* (020) 8994 7994. *E:* marinavaizey@virginmedia.com. *Club:* Athenæum.
See also Rt Hon. E. H. B. Vaizey.

**VAIZEY, Rt Hon. Edward Henry Butler, (Rt Hon. Ed)**; PC 2016; MP for Wantage, since 2005 (C, 2005–19; Ind, since 2019); *b* 5 June 1968; *s* of Baron Vaizey and of Lady Vaizey, *qv*; *m* 2005, Alexandra Mary Jane Holland; one *s* one *d*. *Educ:* St Paul's Sch., London; Merton Coll., Oxford (BA 1989, MA 2004); City Univ. (Dip. Law 1992). Desk Officer, Conservative Res. Dept, 1989–91; called to the Bar, Middle Temple, 1993, practised as barrister, 1993–96; Director: Public Policy Unit, 1996–97; Politics Internat., 1997–98; Consolidated Communications, 1998–2003; Chief Speech Writer to Leader of the Opposition, 2004. Opposition frontbench spokesman on the arts, 2006–10; Parliamentary Under-Secretary of State: BIS, 2010–11; DCMS, 2010–14; Minister of State, DCMS and BIS, 2014–16; Prime Minister's Trade Envoy to Vietnam, Cambodia and Laos, 2017–. Contested (C) Bristol East, 1997. Exec. Dir, Edexcel Ltd, 2007–10; Exec. in Residence, LionTree LLC, 2017–. Visiting Professor: KCL, 2017–; Newcastle Univ., 2018–. Advr, Digital Th., 2017–; Member, Advisory Board: NEC Europe, 2017–19; Salary Finance, 2019–; News Guard, 2019–; FTI Consulting, 2019–. Vice-Chm., British Exports Assoc., 2016–. Vice-Chm., National Churches Trust, 2008–10; Trustee: Heritage of London Trust, 2009–10; Documentary Society, 2016–; Nat. Youth Th., 2016–; London Music Masters, 2018–. Member Board: Bush Th., 2009–10; NYT, 2016–. Pres., Didcot Town FC, 2005–. Fellow, Radio Acad., 2015. Hon. FRIBA 2010. *Publications:* (ed with M. Gove and N. Boles) A Blue Tomorrow, 2001; (ed with M. McManus) The Blue Book on Transport, 2002; (ed) The Blue Book on Health, 2002. *Address:* House of Commons, SW1A 0AA. *T:* (020) 7219 3000. *E:* vaizeye@parliament.uk. *Club:* Soho House.

**VAJDA, Christopher Stephen**; a Judge of the Court of Justice of the European Union, since 2012; *b* 6 July 1955; *s* of late Stephen Vajda and of Heidi Vajda (*née* Schmalhorst); *m* 2012, Brenda Wing-Yin Chow; one *s*. *Educ:* Winchester Coll.; Corpus Christi Coll., Cambridge (MA); Inst d'Etudes Européennes, Brussels (Licence spéciale en droit européen). Called to the Bar, Gray's Inn, 1979 (Bencher 2004), NI, 1996; QC 1997; a Recorder, 2002–12. Mem., Supplementary Panel, Treasury Counsel, 1993–97. *Publications:* (contrib.) Bellamy & Child, Common Market Law of Competition, 3rd edn 1987 to 6th edn 2008. *Recreation:* spending time with the family. *Address:* Court of Justice of the European Union, L-2925 Luxembourg. *Club:* Royal Automobile.

**VALE, Brian**, CBE 1994 (OBE 1977); Regional Director for Middle East and North Africa, British Council, 1995; retired; *b* 26 May 1938; *s* of Charles Vale (*née* Knowles); *m* 1966, Margaret Mary Cookson; two *s*. *Educ:* Sir Joseph Williamson's Mathematical Sch., Rochester; Keele Univ. (BA, DipEd); King's Coll., London (MPhil). HMOCS, N Rhodesia, 1960–63; Assistant to Comr for N Rhodesia, London, 1963–64; Educn Attaché, Zambia High Commn, London, 1964–65; British Council: Rio de Janeiro, 1965–68; Appts Div., 1968–72; Educn and Sci. Div., 1972–75; Rep., Saudi Arabia, 1975–78; Dep. Controller, Educn and Sci. Div., 1978–80; Dir Gen., Tech. Educn and Trng Orgn for Overseas Countries, 1980–81; Controller, Sci., Technol. and Educn Div., 1981–83; Rep. in Egypt, and Cultural Counsellor, British Embassy, Cairo, 1983–87; Asst Dir Gen., 1987–90; Dir, Spain, and Cultural Attaché, British Embassy, Madrid, 1991–95. Chm., Internat. Family Health, 1998–2005; Vice Pres., Navy Records Soc., 2009–13 (Mem. Council, 2005–09, 2013–17). Chm., St Alfege Develt Cttee, Greenwich, 2004–10. Medalha Merito Tamandaré (Brazil), 1997. *Publications:* Independence or Death: British sailors and Brazilian independence, 1996; A War Betwixt Englishmen: Argentina versus Brazil in the River Plate 1825–30, 1999; A Frigate of King George: life and duty on HMS Doris 1807–1829, 2001; The Audacious Admiral Cochrane, 2004; Cochrane in the Pacific: fortune and freedom in Spanish America, 2007; (with Prof. Griffith Edwards) Physician to the Fleet: the life and times of Thomas Trotter, 1760–1832, 2011; contribs to specialist jls on naval hist. *Recreations:* reading, talking, naval history. *Address:* 40 Gloucester Circus, SE10 8RY. *T:* (020) 8858 6233.

**VALENTIA, 16th Viscount** *cr* 1622 (Ire.); **Francis William Dighton Annesley**; Bt 1620; Baron Mountnorris 1628; *b* 29 Dec. 1959; *s* of 15th Viscount Valentia and of Anita Phyllis Annesley (*née* Joy); *S* father, 2005; *m* 1982, Shaneen Therese Hobbs; two *d*. *Educ:* Falcon Coll., Bulawayo (DipAgr; BCom (Mktg)). *Recreations:* golf, scuba diving. *Heir: b* Hon. Peter John Annesley [*b* 18 Dec. 1967; *m* 1997, Deborah Ann Coelen; five *s*]. *Address:* 3 Ruby Close, Wokingham, Berks RG41 3TX. *T:* (0118) 989 0258. *E:* fwd.annesley@live.co.uk.

**VALENTIN, Ben Matthew**; QC 2016; *b* St Albans, 16 Jan. 1971; *s* of David Charles Valentin and Gwendoline Ann Valentin; *m* 1995, Larisa Malakoff (marr. diss.); one *s* one *d*; partner, Lynn Dunne; two *s*. *Educ:* Bedford Sch.; Worcester Coll., Oxford (BA 1992; BCL 1993); Cornell Law Sch. (LLM 1994). Called to the Bar, Inner Temple, 1995; in practice as barrister, specialising in commercial law, 1995–. *Recreations:* family, ski-ing, sailing, travel. *Address:* Fountain Court Chambers, Temple, EC4Y 9DH. *T:* (020) 7583 3335. *E:* bv@fountaincourt.co.uk. *Club:* Athenæum.

**VALENTINE,** Baroness *cr* 2005 (Life Peer), of Putney in the London Borough of Wandsworth; **Josephine Clare Valentine;** Project Director, Blackpool, Business in the Community, since 2017; Chief Executive, London First, 2003–16; *b* 8 Dec. 1958; *d* of Michael and Shirley Valentine; *m* 1990, Simon Acland; two *d*. *Educ:* St Hugh's Coll., Oxford Univ. (BA Hons Maths and Philosophy). Manager, Corporate Finance, Barings, 1981–88; Chief Exec., Blackburn Partnership, 1988–90; Sen. Manager, Planning and Corporate Finance, BOC Gp, 1990–95; Chief Exec., Central London Partnership, 1995–97; London First, 1997–2016. Comr, Nat. Lottery, 2001–05. Chm., Heathrow Southern Rlwy, 2017–. Mem. Bd, Peabody, 2012–17; non-exec. Dir, HS2 Ltd, 2014–18. Mem. Council, UCL, 2014– (Vice Chm., 2018–). *Recreations:* piano, bridge, travel, logic puzzles.

**VALENTINE, Caroline, (Mrs Malcolm Valentine);** *see* Charles, Caroline.

**VALIANT, Prof. Leslie Gabriel,** FRS 1991; T. Jefferson Coolidge Professor of Computer Science and Applied Mathematics, Harvard University, since 2001; *b* 28 March 1949; *s* of Leslie Valiant and Eva Julia (*née* Ujlaki); *m* 1977, Gayle Lynne Dyckoff; two *s*. *Educ:* Tynemouth High Sch.; Latymer Upper Sch.; King's Coll., Cambridge (MA; Hon. Fellow, 2013); Imperial Coll., London (DIC); Warwick Univ. (PhD). Vis. Asst Prof., Carnegie Mellon Univ., Pittsburgh, 1973–74; Lecturer: Leeds Univ., 1974–76; Edinburgh Univ., 1977–81, Reader 1981–82; Gordon McKay Prof. of Computer Sci. and Applied Maths, Harvard Univ., 1982–2001. Vis. Prof., Harvard Univ., 1982; Vis. Fellow, Oxford Univ. Computing Lab. and Merton Coll., Oxford, 1987–88; Guggenheim Fellow, 1985–86. Fellow, Amer. Assoc. for Artificial Intelligence, 1992; Mem., US NAS, 2001. Dr *hc* École Normale Supérieure, Lyon, 2012; Hon. DSc Warwick, 2013; DMath Waterloo, 2013; DEng Leeds, 2018. Nevanlinna Prize, IMU, 1986; Knuth Prize, ACM/IEEE, 1997; Eur. Assoc. for Theoretical Comp. Sci. Award, 2008; A. M. Turing Award, 2010. *Publications:* Circuits of the Mind, 1994; Probably Approximately Correct, 2013; research papers in scientific jls. *Address:* School of Engineering and Applied Sciences, Harvard University, 33 Oxford Street, Cambridge, MA 02138, USA. *T:* (617) 4955817.

**VALIN, Reginald Pierre;** business consultant; *b* 8 March 1938; *s* of Pierre Louis Valin and Molly Doreen Valin; *m* 1960, Brigitte Karin Leister; one *d*. *Educ:* Emanuel School. Bank of America, 1959–60; Charles Barker & Sons Ltd, later Charles Barker City, 1960–79: Dir, 1971–73; Man. Dir, 1973–76; Chief Exec., 1976–79; Founder Dir, Valin Pollen, subseq. The VPI Gp: Chm. and Chief Exec., 1979–89, Dep. Chm., 1989–90. *Publications:* Echoes of a Past (as Sophie Vitesse), 2010; Not as Planned: recollections, 2017. *Address:* 38 Monckton Court, Melbury Road, W14 8NF. *T:* (020) 7371 1872.

**VALIOS, Nicholas Paul;** QC 1991; a Recorder of the Crown Court, 1986–2016; *b* 5 May 1943; *s* of Nicholas William and Elizabeth Joan Valios; *m* 1967, Cynthia Valerie Horton; one *s* one *d*. *Educ:* Stonyhurst Coll., Lancs. Called to the Bar, Inner Temple, 1964; Mem., SE Circuit. *Recreations:* windsurfing, golf, reading, computers, scuba diving.

**VALK, Antoine Jan Macgiel,** CBE 2014; Managing Director, Valk Management and Advice Ltd, since 2013; *b* Surabaya, Dutch Indies, 12 Dec. 1949; *s* of Anthony and Betsy Valk; *m* 1st, 1977, Martine Elisabeth Kolff (*d* 1991); three *d*; 2nd, 2013, Tine Emilie Stikker. *Educ:* Delft Univ. of Technol. (Engrg degree Metallurgy). Product Manager, Philips Electronics, 1982–86; Vice Pres., Optimage Interactive Services, Chicago, 1986–89; Vice Pres., Mktg, KPN Telecom, 1990–94; Product Line Dir, ATsT-Unisource, 1995–98; Commercial Dir, Ned Train, 1998–2001; CEO, Abellio Hldgs, 2001–12. Mem., British Transport Police Authy, 2012–17. Mem. Bd, British Quality Foundn, 2011–19. Chm., Adv. Bd, Nat. Rlwy Mus., 2019–. Chm., Netherlands British Chamber of Commerce, 2013–. Chm., Dutch Nat. Trust, 2014–. Vice Chm., Dutch Maritime Mus., 2014–; Trustee, Science Mus., 2015–; Chm., Eden Holland Foundn, 2017–. Liveryman, Co. of Carmen, 2011. Officer, Order of Orange Nassau (Netherlands), 2014. *Recreations:* opera, classical music, golf. *Address:* Valk Management and Advice Ltd, 7 Queen Square, Brighton BN1 3FD. *T:* 07747 563074. *E:* anton@valk-consult.com. *Club:* Reform.

**VALLANCE,** family name of **Baron Vallance of Tummel**.

**VALLANCE OF TUMMEL,** Baron *cr* 2004 (Life Peer), of Tummel in Perth and Kinross; **Iain David Thomas Vallance,** Kt 1994; Chairman, Edinburgh Business School, Heriot-Watt University, since 2017; *b* 20 May 1943; *s* of late Edmund Thomas Vallance and Janet Wright Bell Ross Davidson; *m* 1967, Elizabeth Mary McGonnigill (*see* E. M. Vallance); one *s* one *d*. *Educ:* Edinburgh Acad.; Dulwich Coll.; Glasgow Acad.; Brasenose Coll., Oxford (Hon. Fellow, 1997); London Grad. Sch. of Business Studies (MSc). FCIBS 2002. Joined Post Office, 1966; Director: Central Finance, 1976–78; Telecommunications Finance, 1978–79; Materials Dept, 1979–81; British Telecommunications: a Corp. Dir, 1981–2001; Board Mem. for Orgn and Business Systems, 1981–83; Man. Dir, Local Communications Services Div., 1983–85; Chief of Operations, 1985–86; Chief Exec., 1986–95; Chm., 1987–2001 (part-time 1998–2001); Pres. Emeritus, 2001–02. Dir, 1993–2005, Vice-Chm., 1994–2005, Royal Bank of Scotland; Dir, Mobil Corp., 1996–99. Chairman: Nations Healthcare Ltd, 2005–07; Amsphere Ltd, 2006–16. Pres., CBI, 2000–02 (Mem., Pres.'s Cttee, 1988–2008); Member, President's Committee: (also Adv. Council), BITC, 1988–2002; Eur. Foundn for Quality Management, 1988–96. Chairman: Eur. Adv. Cttee, New York Stock Exchange, 2000–02 (Mem., 1995–2005); European Services Forum, 2003–07; Dep. Chm., Financial Reporting Council, 2001–02. Member: Internat. Adv. Bd, British-American Chamber of Commerce, 1991–2002; Bd, Scottish Enterprise, 1998–2001; Internat. Adv. Bd, AllianzSE, 1998–2016; Supervisory Bd, Siemens AG, 2003–13; European Adv. Council, Rothschild Gp, 2003–09. Chm., H of L Econ. Affairs Cttee, 2008–10 (Mem., 2005–07); Member: H of L Sub Cttee A, Econ. and Financial Affairs and Internat. Trade, 2010–15; H of L Select Cttee on Sci. and Technol., 2015–. Vice Pres., Princess Royal Trust for Carers, 1999–2012 (Chm., 1991–98); Trustee, Monteverdi Trust, 1993–2001; Patron, Loughborough Univ., 1996–; Chm., Royal Conservatoire of Scotland, 2006–16. Freeman, City of London, 1985; Liveryman, Wheelwrights' Co., 1986–. Hon. Gov., Glasgow Acad., 1993–. Fellow, London Business School, 1989. Hon. DSc: Ulster, 1992; Napier, 1994; City, 1996; Hon. DTech: Loughborough, 1992; Robert Gordon, 1994; Hon. DBA Kingston, 1993; Hon. DEng Heriot-Watt, 1995; Hon. Dr Royal Conservatoire of Scotland, 2016. *Recreations:* hill walking, music. *Address:* House of Lords, SW1A 0PW.

**VALLANCE OF TUMMEL, Lady;** *see* Vallance, E. M.

**VALLANCE, Air Vice-Marshal Andrew George Buchanan,** CB 2003; OBE 1987; FRAeS; Secretary, Defence Press and Broadcasting Advisory Committee, 2004–16; *b* 7 April 1948; *s* of George Charles Buchanan Vallance and Dorothy Mabel Vallance (*née* Wooton); *m* 1972, Katharine Ray Fox; one *s* one *d*. *Educ:* RAF Coll., Cranwell; RAF Staff Coll. (psa 1980); Queens' Coll., Cambridge (MPhil Internat. Relns 1988). Commnd RAF, 1969; sqdn pilot with Nos 9, 617 and 27 Sqdns; Flight Comdr, No 50 Sqdn, 1977–79; Personal SO to Air Mem. for Personnel, 1981; OC No 55 Sqdn, 1982–84; Personal SO to CAS, 1984–87; Dir of Defence Studies 1988–90; Chief of Mil. Co-op., SHAPE, 1991–93; OC RAF Wyton, 1993–95; Dep. Dir, Nuclear Policy, MoD, 1995; Chief, Special Weapons Br., SHAPE, 1996–98; COS, Reaction Forces Air Staff, NATO, 1998–2000; COS and Dep. C-in-C, RAF Personnel Trng Comd, 2000; Exec. Asst to COS, Comd Gp, SHAPE, 2000–04. Chm., Services Sound and Vision Corp., 2009–19. FRAeS 1999. Member: RUSI, 1988–; IISS, 1988–. *Publications:* Air Power, 1989; RAF Air Power Doctrine, 1990; The Air Weapon, 1995; contrib. numerous articles to various defence jls. *Recreations:* military history, classical music, structural gardening, strategic studies. *Club:* Royal Air Force.

**VALLANCE, Dr Elizabeth Mary, (Lady Vallance of Tummel);** JP; Founder and Chairman, me too, since 1999; Chairman: Centre for Mental Health, 2010–18; Young Minds, since 2017; *b* 8 April 1945; *e d* of William Henderson McGonnigill and Hon. Jean, *d* of 1st Baron Kirkwood; *m* 1967, Iain David Thomas Vallance (*see* Baron Vallance of Tummel); one *s* one *d*. *Educ:* Univ. of St Andrews (MA Philosophy and Politics (1st Cl. Hons)); London Sch. of Econs and Pol Sci. (MSc Dist.); Univ. of London (PhD); London Business Sch. (Sloan Fellow; sen. mgt course); Harvard Business Sch. (sen. mgt course). Queen Mary College, later Queen Mary and Westfield College, University of London: Asst Lectr, Lectr, Sen. Lectr, Reader in Govt and Politics, 1968–85; Head, Dept of Politics, 1985–88; Vis. Prof., 1990–96; Hon. Fellow, 1997. Chm., St George's Healthcare NHS Trust, 1993–99; Director: HMV Group, 1990–97; Norwich Union plc, 1995–2000; Charter European Trust (formerly Charter Pan-European Trust) plc, 1998–2012 (Sen. Ind. Dir, 2006–12); Health Foundn (formerly PPP Healthcare Medical Trust), 1999–2008 (Vice-Chm., 2003–08); Aviva plc (formerly CGNU) plc, 2000–05; Medical Protection Soc., 2005–13. Chm., NHS Adv. Cttee on Distinction, then Clin. Excellence, Awards, 2000–05; Mem., Cttee on Standards in Public Life, 2004–11. Chairman: I CAN, 2007–15; CEDR, 2011–17; Nat. Autism Project, 2015–18. Chm. of Govs, James Allen's Girls' Sch., 1991–94; Chm. Council, Inst. of Educn, Univ. of London, 2000–09; Governor: Sutton Valence Sch., 2006– (Chm., 2015–); LSE, 2016–. Member: Adv. Council, Citizenship Foundn, 1988–; Council, Dulwich Picture Gallery Trust, 1995–2000; Council, RSA, 1997–2002; Adv. Council, NCVO, 1998–; Press Complaints Commn Appts Commn, 2009–11. Vice-Pres., Autistica, 2010–. Trustee: Royal Anniversary Trust, 1994–2004; St George's Hosp. Special Trustees, 1999–2001; Playing Alive Foundn, 2004–08; Autism Speaks, 2006–10. Patron: Donaldson Coll., Edinburgh, 1998–2004; Marlow Theatre Develt Trust, 2007–; Sheriffs' and Recorders' Fund, 2008–; Pitlochry Fest. Th., 2011–. Kent Ambassador, 2012–. FRSA 1991; FCGI 2004; Hon. Fellow, Inst. of Educn, 2010; Hon. FCollT 2010. JP Inner London, 1993; High Sheriff, Greater London, 2008–09. Hon. DCL Kent, 2013. Carrington Award, Hon. Co. of Educators, 2014. *Publications:* (ed) The State, Society and Self-destruction, 1975; Women in the House, 1979; (with Davies) Women of Europe, 1982; (with Radice and Willis) MP: the job of a backbencher, 1988; (with Mahoney) Business Ethics in a New Europe, 1992; Business Ethics at Work, 1995; contribs to other books, academic articles, journalism. *Recreations:* writing, reading novels, ski-ing, opera. *Address:* Young Minds, Suite 11, Baden Place, Crosby Row, SE1 1YW. *T:* (020) 7089 5050.

**VALLANCE, Sir Patrick (John Thompson),** Kt 2019; MD; FRS 2017; FRCP; FMedSci; Chief Scientific Adviser to the Government, and Head, Government Office for Science, since 2018; *b* 17 March 1960; *s* of Peter John Vallance and Barbara Bickford Vallance (*née* Thompson); *m* 1986, Sophia Ann Dexter; two *s* one *d*. *Educ:* Truro Sch.; St George's Hosp. Med. Sch., Univ. of London (BSc 1981; MB BS with Dist. 1984; MD 1990). MRCP 1987, FRCP 1995. Lectr, 1986–90, Sen. Lectr and Consultant Physician, 1990–95, St George's Hosp. Med. Sch.; Prof. of Clin. Pharmacol. and Consultant Physician, 1995–2002, Prof. of Medicine and Hd, Div. of Medicine, 2002–06, UCL; GlaxoSmithKline: Hd of Drug Discovery, 2006–10; Sen. Vice-Pres. and Hd of Medicines Discovery and Develt, 2010–12; Pres., R&D, 2012–18. Goulstonian Lectr, RCP, 1996. Chm., Wellcome Trust Pharmacol. and Physiology Panel, 2002–05. FMedSci 1999 (Registrar, 2003–06). Hon. Fellow: Faculty of Medicine, Imperial Coll. London, 2006; UCL, 2007. Hon. DSc: London, 2007; Imperial Coll. London, 2016; York, 2016; Glasgow, 2017. Graham Bull Prize, RCP, 2002. *Publications:* (ed jtly) Endothelial Function in Hypertension, 1987; (ed jtly) Endothelium in Human Physiology and Pathophysiology, 1989; contribs to learned jls on pharmacol., vascular biol., and exptl and clin. medicine. *Recreations:* mushrooming, cooking, gardening, playing tennis badly. *Address:* Government Office for Science, 10 Victoria Street, SW1H 0NN.

**VALLANCE, Philip Ian Fergus;** QC 1989; in-house counsel, Berrymans Lace Mawer, 2002–17; *b* 20 Dec. 1943; *o s* of Aylmer Vallance and Helen Gosse; *m* 1973, Wendy, *d* of J. D. Alston; one *s* one *d*. *Educ:* Bryanston; New Coll., Oxford (BA Mod. Hist). Called to the Bar, Inner Temple, 1968. *Recreation:* dining on trains. *Club:* Travellers (Chm., 2006–10).

**VALLANCE WHITE, James Ashton,** CB 1997; Fourth Clerk at the Table and Clerk of the Judicial Office, House of Lords, 1983–2002; Clerk to Committee for Privileges (Peerage Claims) 1983–2002; Registrar of Lords' Interests, 1996–2002; *b* 25 Feb. 1938; *s* of Frank Ashton White and Dieudonnée Vallance; *m* 1987, Anne O'Donnell. *Educ:* Allhallows School; Albert Schweitzer College, Switzerland; St Peter's College, Oxford (MA). Clerk, House of Lords, 1961; Clerk of Committees, 1971–78; Chief Clerk, Public Bill Office, 1978–83. *Address:* 14 Gerald Road, SW1W 9EQ. *T:* (020) 7730 7658; Biniparrell, San Luis, Menorca. *T:* (971) 151476. *Clubs:* Brooks's, Beefsteak.

**VALLAT, Richard Justin;** QC 2018; *b* Merton, London, 31 May 1973; *s* of John Vallat and Clare Vallat (*née* Rowlandson); *m* 2002, Clarissa Levi; one *s* one *d*. *Educ:* Winchester Coll.; Merton Coll., Oxford (MA); City Univ. (DipLaw); Open Univ. (BSc Hons). Called to the Bar, Gray's Inn, 1997; in practice as barrister specialising in revenue law, 1998–. *Recreations:* Real tennis, rackets, ski-ing, cooking. *Address:* Pump Court Tax Chambers, 16 Bedford Row, WC1R 4EF. *T:* (020) 7414 8080. *E:* clerks@pumptax.com. *Clubs:* Queen's, Jesters.

**VALLELY, Paul,** CMG 2006; writer, broadcaster and consultant in organisational ethics and philanthropy; Visiting Professor in Public Ethics and Media, University of Chester, since 2013; Senior Honorary Fellow, Global Development Institute (formerly Brooks World Poverty Institute), University of Manchester, since 2013; Managing Director, Paul Vallely Consulting Ltd, since 2013; *b* 8 Nov. 1951; *s* of late Victor Terence Vallely and Mary Frances Mannion; *m* 1st, 1972, Heather Cecilia Neil (marr. diss.); one *d*; 2nd, 2000, Christine Lesley Morgan, *qv*; one *s*. *Educ:* St Mary's Coll. Grammar Sch., Middlesbrough; Univ. of Leeds (BA Philosophy and English). Reporter, Feature Writer, Theatre Critic, Yorkshire Post, 1974–80; Asst Features Editor, Sunday Telegraph Magazine, 1980–82; Radio Critic, The Listener, 1980–82; Feature Writer, Mail on Sunday, 1982–84; Home News Reporter and Corresp. in Africa, Belfast and NY, The Times, 1984–89; Sen. Foreign Writer, Religious Affairs Editor, News Editor and Asst Editor, Sunday Correspondent, 1989–90; Land Reform Study, Philippines, Brazil, Eritrea, Christian Aid, 1990; Editor of Irish edn, Sunday Times, 1991–92; Oped Feature Writer, Daily Telegraph, 1992–94; Dep. Editor, The European, 1994; Editor, News Review, Sunday Times, 1994–95; Feature Writer and Leader Writer, The Independent, 1995–2013 (Associate Editor, 2000–13); Exec. Editor, Independent on Sunday, 1999–2000; seconded to PM's Commn for Africa, 2004–05 (co-author report, Our Common Interest, 2005). Columnist: The Tablet, 1996–99 (Dir, 2006–; Trustee, 2018–); Third Way, 1995–2016; Church Times, 2002–; Independent on Sunday, 2008–16; contributor to: New York Times, 2013–; Guardian,

2013–. Editl Advr, Catholic Bishops' Conf. of England and Wales, 2004, 2011. Lectures: La Casas, Blackfriars, Oxford, 2000; Gilpin, Durham, 2004; Newman, London, 2008; Anthony Storey Meml, 2008, 2014; Greenbelt, 2013, 2015; Ushaw, 2013; Patrick Finn, Dublin, 2014; Fisher, Cambridge, 2014; Seattle, 2015; Inaugural, Chester, 2015; The Tablet, London, 2015; Fordham, NY, 2015; Harvard Law Sch., 2015; Boston Coll., 2015; Virginia Theol Seminary, 2015; Catenian Centenary, Middlesbrough, 2016; Newman, Manchester, 2016; Milwaukee Red Mass, 2016; Westminster Dio., 2017; Nat. Sch. of Formation, 2018. Chair, Catholic Inst. for Internat. Relations, 1995–2001 (Trustee, 1993–2001). Mem., Bd of Corporate Social Responsibility, Waitrose, 2014–17. Media Adviser: Christian Aid, 1990–92; CAFOD, 1993–2001; Trustee, Traidcraft, 1992–95; Chair, Traidcraft Exchange, 1995–99. FRSA 1996. Hon. Res. Fellow, Univ. of Manchester, 2009–. Hon. Ecumenical Lay Canon, 2018–, Mem., Cathedral Council, 2019–, Manchester Cathedral. Gov., St Joseph's RC Primary Sch., Sale, 2005–09 (Chair, 2006–09). *Publications:* (with David Blundy) With Geldof in Africa, 1985; (with Bob Geldof) Is That It?, 1986; Bad Samaritans: First World ethics and Third World debt, 1990; Promised Lands: stories of power and poverty in the Third World, 1992; (for children) Daniel and the Mischief Boy, 1993; (ed) The New Politics: Catholic social teaching for the 21st century, 1999; The Church and the New Age, 2000; (ed) A Place of Redemption: a Christian approach to punishment and prison, 2004; The Fifth Crusade: George Bush and the Christianisation of the war in Iraq, 2004; (with Bob Geldof) Geldof in Africa, 2005; Hello World: the official Live8 book, 2005; New Labour and the New World Order in Remoralising Britain, 2008; Catholic Social Teaching and The Big Society, 2011; Pope Francis: untying the knots, 2013; Pope Francis: the struggle for the soul of Catholicism, 2015; A History of Philanthropy, 2020. *Recreation:* Thomas. *Address:* Paul Vallely Consulting Ltd, PO Box 165, Sale, Cheshire M33 2YA. *T:* (0161) 973 3456. *E:* paul@paulvallely.com. *W:* www.paulvallely.com. *Club:* Manchester United.

**van ANDEL, Dr Katharine Bridget, (Mrs T. H. van Andel);** *see* Pretty, Dr K. B.

**van BEURDEN, Bernardus Cornelis Adriana Margriet, (Ben);** Chief Executive Officer, Royal Dutch Shell, since 2014; *b* Roosendaal, 23 April 1958; *m* 2008, Stacey Dickson; one *s* three *d*. *Educ:* Delft Univ. of Technol. (Masters degree Chem. Engrg). Royal Dutch Shell: joined 1983; Private Asst to Chm., 2002; Vice Pres., Manufacturing Excellence, 2005–06; Exec. Vice Pres., Chemicals, 2006–12; Downstream Dir, 2013. *Recreations:* reading, running. *Address:* Royal Dutch Shell, Carel van Bylandtlaan 16, 2596 HR The Hague, The Netherlands. *T:* (70) 3779111, *Fax:* (70) 3772780.

**VAN BUEREN, Prof. Geraldine;** Professor of International Human Rights Law, School of Law, Queen Mary (formerly Queen Mary and Westfield College), University of London, since 1998; *b* Hackney, London, 1955; *d* of Sidney and Ann Van Bueren; *m* 1995, James Michael. *Educ:* LLB Wales; University Coll. London (LLM). Called to the Bar, Middle Temple, Bencher, 2012. WP Schreiner and Internat. Human Rights Law Prof., Univ. of Cape Town, 2002–06. Fellow, Goodenough Coll., London. Visiting Professor: Univ. of Cape Town, 1999; Northwestern Univ., 2005; Vis. Fellow, Kellogg Coll., Oxford, 2013–; Vis. Schol., Baldy Center, SUNY, 1995. Associate Tenant, Doughty St Chambers. Mem., Equality and Human Rights Commn, 2009–12. Non-exec. Dir and Trustee, Save the Children, 2005–09. Co-founder, INTERIGHTS (represented Amnesty Internat. at UN during drafting of Convention on Rights of the Child and UN Rules for Protection of Juveniles Deprived of their Liberty). Member, Advisory Board: Human Rights Watch (Children's Rights Project); British Inst. of Human Rights; René Cassin. Hon. QC 2013. Child Rights Lawyer Award, UNICEF, 2003. *Publications:* The International Law on the Rights of the Child, 1995; Child Rights in Europe, 2008; Law's Duty to the Poor, 2010. *Recreations:* breakfasts in bed, tracking wildlife in the bush. *Club:* Athenæum.

**VANCOUVER, Archbishop of, (RC),** since 2009; Most Rev. John Michael Miller, CSB; *b* Ottawa, 9 July 1946; *s* of Albert Henry Miller and Katharine Beatrice Miller (*née* Robb). *Educ:* Univ. of Toronto (BA 1969); Univ. of Wisconsin (MA 1970); Univ. of St Michael's Coll., Toronto (MDiv 1974); Pontifical Gregorian Univ., Rome (STL 1976; STD 1979). Ordained priest, 1975; Prof. of Theol., Univ. of St Thomas, Houston, 1979–90; Vice Pres., Academic Affairs, Univ. of St Thomas, Houston, 1990–92; Asst, Secretariat of State, Holy See, 1992–97; Pres., Univ. of St Thomas, Houston, 1997–2003; apptd Archbishop, 2003; Sec., Congregation of Catholic Educn, Holy See, 2003–07; Coadjutor Archbishop of Vancouver, 2007–09. *Publications:* The Divine Right of the Papacy in Recent Ecumenical Theology, 1980; What Are They Saying about Papal Primacy?, 1983; Life's Greatest Grace: why I belong to the Catholic Church, 1993; The Shepherd and the Rock: origin, development and mission of the papacy, 1995; (ed) The Encyclicals of John Paul II, 1996, 2nd edn 2001; (ed) The Post-Synodal Apostolic Exhortations of John Paul II, 1998; contribs to jls incl. Seminarium, America, Catholic Higher Education in Europe, Crisis, Canadian Catholic Review, Current Issues in Catholic Higher Education. *Address:* Chancery Office, Archdiocese of Vancouver, 4885 Saint John Paul II Way, Vancouver, BC V5Z 0G3, Canada. *T:* (604) 6830281, *Fax:* (604) 6834288. *E:* chancery@rcav.org.

**VAN CULIN, Rev. Canon Samuel;** Residentiary Canon, Washington National Cathedral; Secretary General, Anglican Consultative Council, 1983–94; Organising Secretary, Lambeth Conference of Anglican Bishops, 1988; *b* 20 Sept. 1930; *s* of Samuel Van Culin and Susie (*née* Mossman). *Educ:* High School, Honolulu; Princeton University (AB); Virginia Theological Seminary (BD). Ordained 1955; Curate, St Andrew's Cathedral, Honolulu, 1955–56; Canon Precentor and Rector, Hawaiian Congregation, 1956–58; Asst Rector, St John, Washington DC, 1958–60; Gen. Sec., Laymen International, Washington, 1960–61; Asst Sec., Overseas Dept, Episcopal Church, USA, 1962–68; Sec. for Africa and Middle East, Episcopal Church, USA, 1968–76; Executive, World Mission, 1976–83. Hon. Canon: Canterbury Cathedral, 1983; Ibadan, Nigeria, 1983; Jerusalem, 1984; Southern Africa, 1989; Honolulu, 1991. Hon. DD: Virginia Seminary, 1977; Gen. Theol Seminary, 1983. *Recreations:* music, swimming. *Address:* 3900 Watson Place, NW, #5D–B, Washington, DC 20016, USA. *Clubs:* Athenæum, Huguenot Society; Princeton (New York).

**VandeLINDE, Prof. (Vernon) David,** PhD; Vice-Chancellor, 2001–06, Vice-Chancellor Emeritus, 2011, University of Warwick; *b* Charleston, W Virginia, 9 Aug. 1942; *s* of Vernon Geno VandeLinde and Ava Mae (*née* Scott); *m* 1964, Marjorie Ann Park (*d* 2017); two *s*. *Educ:* Carnegie Mellon Univ. (BS 1964; MS 1965; PhD 1968). Johns Hopkins University: Asst Prof., Elec. Engrg, 1967–74; Associate Prof., 1974–77; Prof., 1977–92; Dean, Sch. of Engrg, 1978–92; Vice-Chancellor, Univ. of Bath, 1992–2001. Chairman: Overseas Res. Students Awards Scheme Cttee, UUK (formerly CVCP), 1993–2005; Better Regulation Review Gp, DfES, 2003–04; Mem., Council for Science and Technology, 2000–03. Non-exec. Dir, W Midlands S Strategic HA, 2003–06. Hon. LLD Bath, 2001; Hon. DEd West of England, 2001; Hon. LLD Warwick, 2007. Distinguished Alumni Award, Carnegie Mellon Univ., 2008. *Address:* 2180 Waterview Drive, Unit 721, North Myrtle Beach, SC 29582, USA.

**VANDEN-BEMPDE-JOHNSTONE;** *see* Johnstone.

**van den BERGH, Maarten Albert;** Chairman, Supervisory Board, Akzo Nobel nv, 2006–09 (Deputy Chairman, 2005–06); *b* 19 April 1942; *s* of Sidney James van den Bergh and Maria van den Bergh (*née* Mijers); *m* 1965, Marjan Désirée Kramer; two *d*. *Educ:* Univ. of Groningen (Drs Econs). Joined Shell Gp, 1968; East and Australasia Area Co-ordinator, 1981–84; Dep. Gp Treas., Shell Internat., 1984–86; Chm., Shell cos in Thailand, 1987–89; Regl Co-ordinator, Western Hemisphere and Africa, Shell Internat., 1989–92; Royal Dutch/Shell Group plc: Gp Man. Dir, 1992–2000; Dir of Finance, 1994–98; Vice-Chm., Cttee of Man. Dirs, and Pres., Royal Dutch Petroleum Co., 1998–2000; non-exec. Dir, 2000–09. Dep. Chm., 2000–01, Chm., 2001–06, Lloyds TSB Gp plc; non-executive Director: British Telecommunications plc, 2000–01; BT Group plc, 2001–09 (Dep. Chm., 2006–09); British Airways Plc, 2002–11. Advr to Chief Exec., HKSAR, 1998–2002. Member: Internat. Bd of Advisers to Pres. of Philippines, 2001–09. Adv. Council, Amsterdam Inst. of Finance, 2001–05. Mem., Steering Bd, and Dutch Co-Chm., Apeldoorn Conf., 2003–09. Advr, Rembrandt Soc., 2001–05. Fellow and Vice-Pres., Inst. of Financial Services, 2001–06; Mem., Guild of Internat. Bankers, 2001–06. *Recreation:* European history. *Club:* Soc. De Witte (The Hague).

**van den BERGH, Prof. Sidney,** OC 1994; FRS 1988; astronomer, Dominion Astrophysical Observatory, Victoria, British Columbia, 1977–2012; *b* 20 May 1929; *s* of S. J. van den Bergh and S. M. van den Berg; *m* 1st, 1957, Roswitha Koropp (marr. diss.); one *s* two *d*; 2nd, 1978, Gretchen Krause (*d* 1987); 3rd, 1990, Paulette Brown. *Educ:* Princeton Univ. (AB); Ohio State Univ. (MSc); Göttingen Univ. (Dr rer. nat.). Asst Prof., Ohio State Univ., 1956–58; progressively, Asst Prof., Associate Prof., Univ. of Toronto, 1958–77; Dir, Dominion Astrophys. Observatory, 1977–86. Adjunct Prof., Univ. of Victoria, 1978–2009. Res. Associate, Mt Wilson and Palomar Observatories, 1967–68. ARAS 1984. Hon. DSc: St Mary's Univ., 1995; Univ. of Victoria, 2001. NRCC President's Research Medal, 1988; Killam Laureate, Killam Trust, 1990; Henry Norris Russel Prize Lecture, Amer. Astron. Soc., 1990; Carlyle S Beals Award, 1998, R. M. Petrie Prize, 1999, Can. Astron. Soc.; Catherine Wolfe Bruce Gold Medal, Astron. Soc. Pacific, 2008; Canadian Hall of Fame for Sci. and Technol., 2012; Gruber Cosmology Prize, Peter Gruber Foundn, 2014. *Publications:* approx. 900 articles in various scholarly jls. *Recreation:* archaeology.

**van den BROEK, Hans,** Grand Cross Order of Oranje Nassau; Hon. GCMG; President, Netherlands Institute for International Relations, 2000–07; Honorary Minister of State, Netherlands, since 2005; *b* 11 Dec. 1936; *m* 1965, Josephine van Schendel; two *d*. *Educ:* Univ. of Utrecht (Law degree). Lawyer, Rotterdam, 1965–68; Enka Bv., Arnhem: Sec., Mgt Bd, 1969–73; Commercial Manager, 1973–76. Member: Lower House of Parliament, Netherlands, 1976–78; Exec., Catholic People's Party, 1978–81; State Sec. for Foreign Affairs, 1981–82; Minister for Foreign Affairs, 1982–93. Mem., CEC, later EC, 1993–99. Chm., Radio Netherlands Internat., 2000–; Member: Supervisory Bd, Schiphol Gp, 2000–; Supervisory Council, Utrecht Univ., 2000–07. Pres., Carnegie Foundn, 2000–07; Founding Mem., Global Leadership Foundn, 2000–. Grand Cross: Order of Merit (Italy); Order of Isabel la Católica (Spain); Nat. Order of Merit (France); Order of Merit (Germany); Order of the Rising Sun (Japan). *Address:* Zwiepseweg 158, 7241 PV Lochem, The Netherlands.

**VAN DEN HOVEN, Helmert Frans;** *see* Hoven.

**VAN der BIJL, His Honour Nigel Charles;** a Circuit Judge, 2001–16; *b* 28 April 1948; *s* of late Nicholas Alexander Christian Van der Bijl and of Mollie Van der Bijl; *m* 1974, Loba Nassiri; one *s* one *d*. *Educ:* Trinity Coll., Dublin (MA Classics, LLB). Called to the Bar, Inner Temple, 1973; Co. Sec., Internat. Div., Beecham Pharmaceutical, 1973–74; Legal Manager, Shahpur Chemical Co. Ltd and Nat. Iranian Oil Co., Tehran, 1974–77; in private practice as barrister, specialising in crime and in European and human rights law, 1977–2001; a Recorder, 1996–2001. Recorder of the City of Canterbury, 2004–16. Friend, British Sch. of Athens, 1996–. *Recreation:* cycling.

**van der EEMS, Jeffrey Peter;** Chairman, Continental Bakeries, since 2016; *b* Canada, 5 Nov. 1962; *s* of Jan and Eugenie van der Eems; *m* 1993, Beth Baumgartner; one *s* one *d*. *Educ:* Univ. of Calif, Irvine (BA); Thunderbird Sch. of Global Mgt (Masters Internat. Mgt). Vice Pres., M&A, Chemical Bank, 1990–93; Chief Financial Officer, EMEA, 1999–2000, UK, 2000–05, PepsiCo; United Biscuits: Chief Financial Officer, 2005–07; Chief Operating Officer, 2007–13; CEO, Internat., 2013–15; CEO, 2015–16. Gov., King's House Sch., Richmond, 2016–. Mem., Phi Beta Kappa. *Recreations:* travel, coaching youth football, sailing, ski-ing.

**VANDERMARK, Simone;** *see* Hochgreb, S.

**van der MEER, Tobias;** Chief Executive Officer, Hastings Insurance Group plc, since 2018; *b* Delft, Netherlands, 16 March 1977; *s* of Alfred and Sandy van der Meer; *m* 2009, Kate; three *c*. *Educ:* St Edmund Hall, Oxford (BA Hons Econs and Mgt 1997). Strategy Consultant, Monitor Co., 1997–2000; commercial and strategy rôles, Egg, 2000–05; UK Mktg Dir, Citigroup, 2005–06; UK Retail Bank Hd (Citibank and Egg), Citigroup, 2006–08; Hd, Retail Banking, Anglo Irish Bank, 2008–09; Managing Director: (Money and Ops), Moneysupermarket Plc, 2009–11; Hastings Insce Gp, 2011–18.

**VANDERMERWE, Prof. Sandra,** DBA; Extraordinary Professor, specialising in Customer Centric Transformation in a Digital World, Gordon Institute of Business Science, South Africa, since 2010; *b* 8 Aug. 1946; *d* of late David Fortes and Myra Fortes; two *d*. *Educ:* Univ. of Cape Town (BA 1966); Grad. Sch. of Business, Univ. of Cape Town (MBA 1972); Grad. Sch. of Business, Univ. of Stellenbosch (DBA 1974). Senior Lecturer: Dept of Business Sci., Univ. of Cape Town, 1973–76; Grad. Sch. of Business, Univ. of Stellenbosch, 1976–79; Prof., and Head of Mktg Dept, Univ. of Witwatersrand, 1979–82; Prof. of Internat. Mktg, Internat. Mgt Inst., Geneva, 1983–85; Prof. of Internat. Mktg and Services, IMD-Internat. Inst. for Mgt Develt, Lausanne, 1986–96 (also Dir, several exec. progs); Prof., 1996–2005, Vis. Prof. and Strategic Associate, 2006–13, specialising in Customer Focused Transformation, Imperial Coll. (formerly Tanaka) Business Sch., Imperial Coll. of Sci., Technol. and Medicine. Adjunct Prof., European Sch. of Mgt and Technol., Germany, 2006–10. Mem. Bd, Internat. Health Insurance, 2000–05. Sen. Associate, Deloitte Consulting, 2014–. Consultant globally on implementing customer-centric growth and transformation and impact technol., major internat. cos; speaker on Executive progs for business schs incl. INSEAD, London Business Sch., and Templeton Coll., Oxford. Board Member: Internat. Women's Forum, 2010–13; Handspring Puppet Trust, 2011–16. Trustee, Wendy Appelbaum Foundn, 2009–. Mem., editl bds, and reviewer for internat. academic and mgt jls. FRSA 1996. Several awards. *Publications:* From Tin Soldiers to Russian Dolls: creating added value through services, 1993; (jtly) Cases in European Marketing Management, 1994; (jtly) Competing Through Services, 1994; The 11th Commandment: transforming to 'own' customers, 1995; Customer Capitalism: getting increasing returns in new market spaces, 1999; Breaking Through: implementing customer focus in enterprises, 2004 (trans. Japanese 2009), 2nd edn as Implementing Disruptive Customer Centricity, 2014; numerous articles in prof. jls. *Recreations:* animal healing, hiking, arts. *Address:* 14 Roseberry Avenue, Oranjezicht, Cape Town 8001, South Africa.

**VANDERSTEEN, Martin Hugh;** Chairman, Bart's and The London NHS Trust, 2001–03; *b* 9 Aug. 1935; *s* of William Martin Vandersteen and Dorothy Margaret Vandersteen (*née* Leith); *m* 1967, Catherine Susan Mary Webb; two *s. Educ:* Harrow Co. Grammar Sch. for Boys; Open Univ. (BSc 2004). Chartered Accountant, 1957; Allen, Attfield & Co. Chartered Accountants, 1951–57; Andersen Consulting, 1957–97: Partner, 1968; Man. Partner UK, 1973–86; Man. Partner Regl, 1989–94; Man. Partner Resources and Quality, 1994–97. Non-exec. Dir, 1999–, Chm., 2000, Kingston Hosp. NHS Trust. *Recreations:* sailing, fishing, golf, swimming, science. *Address:* 16 Wildcroft Manor, Wildcroft Road, SW15 3TS. *T:* (020) 8788 9026. *E:* mvanderstn@aol.com. *Clubs:* Royal Ocean Racing; Royal Southern Yacht; Otter Swimming.

**van der VEEN, Air Vice-Marshal Marten;** Senior Bursar, 2000–05 (Bursar, 1998–2000) and Fellow, 1999–2005, Balliol College, Oxford; *b* 22 Jan. 1946; *s* of late Lourens Jan van der Veen and Esmé Lily van der Veen (*née* Edwards); *m* 1968, Susan Mary Wallers; two *s. Educ:* King's Coll. Sch., Wimbledon; Magdalen Coll., Oxford (MA Engrg Sci. and Econs); RAF Coll., Cranwell (Aerosystems course). Exchange Officer with French Air Force, Paris, 1978–79; RAF Staff Coll., 1980; Dir of Defence Studies, RAF, 1985–88; Station Comdr, RAF Cosford, 1989–90; Dir, Support Policy, RAF, 1991–93; Station Comdr, RAF St Athan and Air Officer, Wales, 1994–95; last Commandant, RAF Staff Coll., Bracknell, 1996; DG Support Mgt, RAF, 1997. Gov., Stowe Sch., 2002–12 (Vice-Chm., 2007–12). Chm., RAF Oxford and Cambridge Soc., 2009–12. *Recreations:* travel, classical music, opera, inevitable DIY. *Clubs:* Royal Air Force; Phyllis Court (Henley).

**VAN der VEER, Jeroen;** Chairman, Supervisory Board: Philips, since 2011 (Member, since 2009); Royal Boskalis Westminster NV, since 2018 (Member, since 2015); President, Royal Dutch Petroleum NV, 2000–09; a Group Managing Director, 1997–2009, Chairman, Committee of Managing Directors, 2004–09, and Chief Executive, 2004–09, Royal Dutch/Shell Group (Vice-Chairman, 2000–04; non-executive Director, 2009–13); *b* 1947; *m*; three *d. Educ:* Delft Univ. (MMechE 1971); Rotterdam Univ. (MEcons 1976). Joined Shell Internat. BV, 1971; Refining, Curaçao, 1978; Marketing, UK, 1981; Corporate Planning, UK, 1984; Area Officer, 1990; Pres. and CEO, Shell Chemicals Co., Houston, 1995–97; Gp Res. Advr, 1997. Chm., Supervisory Bd, ING, 2011–18 (Mem., 2009–18); Vice Chm., Unilever, 2009–11 (non-exec. Dir, 2002–09); non-exec. Dir, Equinor ASA, 2016–. *Recreations:* golf, sailing, ski-ing, visiting museums.

**van der WERFF, His Honour Jonathan Ervine;** a Circuit Judge, 1986–2007; Resident Judge, Inner London Crown Court, 1993–2007; *b* 23 June 1935; *s* of H. H. J. van der Werff; *m* 1968, Katharine Bridget (*d* 2014), *d* of Major J. B. Colvin, Withypool, Som; two *d. Educ:* St Piran's Sch., Maidenhead; Harrow; RMA, Sandhurst. Commnd in Coldstream Guards, 1955; Adjt 1st Bn, 1962–63; Major 1967, retired 1968. Called to Bar, Inner Temple, 1969; a Recorder, 1986; Resident Judge, Croydon Law Courts, 1989–93; Sen. Circuit Judge, 1993. *Clubs:* Boodle's, Pratt's, Something.

**VANDER ZALM, Hon. William N.;** Premier of the Province of British Columbia, 1986–91; MLA (Social Credit Party) for Richmond, British Columbia; *b* Noordwykerhout, Holland, 29 May 1934; *s* of Wilhelmus Nicholaas van der Zalm and Agatha C. Warmerdam; *m* 1956, Lillian Mihalic; two *s* two *d. Educ:* Phillip Sheffield Sen. Secondary Sch., Abbotsford, BC. Purchased Art Knapp Nurseries Ltd, and became Co. Pres., 1956. Alderman 1965, Mayor 1969, Surrey Municipal Council. Minister of Human Resources, BC, 1975; Minister of Municipal Affairs and Minister responsible for Urban Transit Authority, 1978; Minister of Educn and Minister responsible for BC Transit, 1982; Leader, BC Social Credit Party, 1986–. Established Fantasy Garden World, major tourist attraction in Richmond, BC, 1983–. Hon. Dr Law Univ. of the North, Prince George, BC, 2004. *Publications:* The Northwest Gardener's Almanac, 1982; Bill Vander Zalm For the People: hindsight, insight, foresight (autobiog.), 2008; HST—The People for Democracy, 2013. *Recreations:* gardening, fishing, soccer. *Address:* 3553 Arthur Drive, Ladner, BC V4K 3N2, Canada.

**van der ZYL, Marie Sarah;** Partner, The Ince Group (formerly Gordon Dadds, then Ince Gordon Dadds) LLP, since 2016; President, Board of Deputies of British Jews, since 2018 (a Deputy, since 2012); *b* London, 7 Nov. 1965; *d* of Barry Benjamin Kaye and Szusanne Kaye; *m* 1998, Darrell David van der Zyl; two *d. Educ:* Woodbridge High Sch., Woodford Green; Liverpool Poly. (LLB Hons 1988); Chester Law Sch. Admitted as solicitor, 1991; trainee, Courts and Co., 1993; Solicitor, 1993–95, Employment Lawyer and Partner, 1995–97, Booth and Blackwell; Partner, Kingsford Stacey Blackwell, 1997–2001; Partner, then Hd of Employment, Davenport Lyons, 2001–14; Consultant, Gordon Dadds, 2014–16. *Recreations:* reading, going to the theatre, sewing, antiques, Zumba.

**VANDEVELDE, Luc Emile;** Founder and Chairman, Change Capital Partners, since 2002; *b* Belgium, 26 Feb. 1951; *s* of Emile Vandevelde and Sylvie Vandevelde (*née* Jacobs); *m* Monique Sapin; one *s.* Administrator, Kraft NV SA, Brussels, 1971–80; Finance Dir, Kraft Leonesas SA, Madrid, 1980–83; Vice-Pres. of Develt and Planning, Kraft Europe, Lausanne, 1983–86; Dir of Finance and Admin, Kraft GmbH, Germany, 1986–88; Vice-Pres. of Finance and Admin, Kraft Internat., USA, 1988–90; Vice-Pres. of Admin and Develt, Kraft General Foods Internat., NY, 1989–90; CEO, France, 1989–93, Italy, 1994–95, Kraft Jacobs Suchard; Pres. and Chief Operating Officer, 1995–99, Chm., 1999–2000, Promodès; Chief Exec., 2000–02, Chm., 2000–04, Marks and Spencer plc; Dir, 2004–07, Chm., 2005–07, Carrefour. Chm., Majid Al Futtaim Ventures, 2014–; non-exec. Dir, Société Générale, 2006–12; Sen. non-exec. Dir, Vodafone, 2012–15 (non-exec. Dir, 2003–12). *Address:* Change Capital Partners, 91 Wimpole Street, W1G 0EF.

**van de VEN, Prof. Johan Jacob, (Hans),** PhD; FBA 2013; Professor of Modern Chinese History, University of Cambridge, since 2004; Fellow of St Catharine's College, Cambridge, since 1988; *b* The Hague, 10 Jan. 1958; *s* of Henk van de Ven and Reina van de Ven (*née* Jonker Roelants); *m* 1983, Susan Kerr; three *s. Educ:* Leiden Univ. (BA 1980); Harvard Univ. (PhD 1987). University of Cambridge: Lectr, 1988–2000; Sen. Lectr, 2000–02; Reader, 2002–04. Dir, Melbourne Village College Acad., 2011–13. *Publications:* From Friend to Comrade: the founding of the Chinese Communist Party, 1991; (ed) Warfare in Chinese History, 2000; War and Nationalism in China, 2003; (ed jtly) The Battle for China, 2010; Breaking with the Past, 2014; China at War, 1937–1952, 2017. *Recreations:* sailing, tennis. *Address:* St Catharine's College, Trumpington Street, Cambridge CB2 1RL.

**VAN de WALLE, Leslie;** non-executive Chairman, Euromoney, since 2019; Chief Executive, Rexam PLC, 2007–09; *b* 27 March 1956; *s* of Philippe Van de Walle and Luce Van de Walle; *m* 1982, Domitille Noel; two *d. Educ:* Hautes Etudes Commerciales, Paris. Managing Director: Schweppes Benelux, 1990–92; Schweppes France and Benelux, 1992–93; Schweppes Spain and Portugal, 1993–94; Snacks Div., Continental Europe UB, 1994–95; Chief Executive Officer: UB Continental Europe, 1996–97; McVitie's Gp, 1998; Chief Exec., United Biscuits Gp, 1999–2000; CEO, Shell South America and Africa, 2001; Pres., Shell Europe Oil Products; Exec. Vice-Pres., Global Retail, Royal Dutch Shell, 2004–06. Non-executive Director: Aegis Gp plc, 2003–09; Aviva plc, 2009–12; DCC plc, 2010–; La Seda de Barcelona, 2011–; Cape plc, 2012; Dep. Chm. and Sen. Ind. Dir, Crest Nicholson, 2018–; non-executive Chairman: SIG plc, 2011–17 (non-exec. Dir, 2010); Robert Walters plc, 2012–18. *Recreations:* golf (handicap 4), travel. *Address:* 65 Rose Square, Fulham Road, SW3 6RS. *Club:* Lambourne Golf.

**van DUIJN, Prof. Cornelia Marja,** PhD; Professor of Epidemiology, Nuffield Department of Population Health, University of Oxford, since 2018; Fellow, St Cross College, Oxford, since 2018; *b* Katwijk, Netherlands, 11 April 1962; *d* of Cornelis van Duijn and Pietje van Duijn-van der Bent; *m* 2014, Eveline van de Hoek. *Educ:* Agricl Univ. of Wageningen, Netherlands (MSc Human Nutrition 1987); Erasmus Univ., Rotterdam (PhD Genetic Epidemiol. 1991). Res. Fellow, Dutch Childhood Leukaemia Study Gp, The Hague, 1987–88; Hd, Genetic Epidemiol., 1993–2001, Prof. of Genetic Epidemiol., 2001–18, Erasmus MC, Rotterdam; Prof. of Translational Epidemiol., Leiden Univ., 2016–18. *Publications:* contrib. papers to internat. scientific jls. *Recreations:* literature, art and architecture, golf and outdoor activities, swimming, fitness. *Address:* Nuffield Department of Population Health, University of Oxford, Big Data Institute, Li Ka Shing Centre for Health Information and Discovery, Old Road Campus, Headington, Oxford OX3 7FZ. *T:* (01865) 289403. *E:* Cornelia.vanDuijn@ndph.ox.ac.uk.

**VANE;** *see* Fletcher-Vane, family name of Baron Inglewood.

**VANE,** family name of **Baron Barnard**.

**VANE, Amber;** *see* Feldman, S. J.

**VANE-TEMPEST-STEWART,** family name of **Marquess of Londonderry**.

**VANE-WRIGHT, Richard Irwin;** Keeper of Entomology, 1998–2004, Scientific Associate, since 2004, Natural History Museum; *b* 26 July 1942; *s* of late Gerald, (James), Vane Wright, and Jessie Margaret (*née* Baldwin); *m* 1987, Hazel June Whitehead; two *d. Educ:* University Coll. London (BSc 1st Cl. Hons Zool. 1967). British Museum (Natural History), subseq. Natural History Museum: Asst (Scientific), 1961–63; SO, Dept Entomology, 1967–84; Dep. Keeper of Entomology, 1984–90; Individual Merit Researcher (Band 2), 1990–98. Chair: Scientific Names Cttee, N Amer. Butterfly Assoc., 2011–; Friends of Westgate Parks (Canterbury), 2012–14 (Hon. Treas., 2016–; Trustee, 2018–); Hon. Curator, Westgate Parks Invertebrate Resource, 2011–. Fellow: Wissenschaftskolleg, Berlin, 1993–94; NESTA, 2005–08; Vis. Sen. Res. Fellow, Ecol. Res. Gp, Sch. of Human and Life Scis, Canterbury Christ Church Univ., 2010–. Hon. Prof. of Taxonomy, Univ. of Kent, Canterbury, 2006–18 (Hon. Res. Associate, 2018–). Hon. Fellow, Royal Entomol Soc. of London, 2004. Hon. Advr, Swallowtail and Birdwing Butterfly Trust, 2018–. Sec., South Canterbury Residents Assoc., 2009–14; Chair, Oaten Hill and South Canterbury Assoc., 2016–18. Pres., Kent Field Club, 2017–19. Hon. DSc Copenhagen, 2003. Karl Jordan Medal, Lepidopterists' Soc., USA, 1989; Jacob Hübner Award, Assoc. for Tropical Lepidoptera, 2005. *Publications:* (with P. R. Ackery) The Biology of Butterflies, 1984, 2nd edn 1989; (with P. R. Ackery) Milkweed Butterflies, 1984; (ed jtly) Phylogenetics and Ecology, 1994; (ed jtly) Systematics and Conservation Evaluation, 1994; (jtly) Carcasson's African Butterflies, 1995; Butterflies, 2003, 2nd edn 2015; (with Harold Hughes) The Seymer Legacy: Henry Seymer and Henry Seymer Jnr of Dorset, and their entomological paintings, 2005; (ed and contrib.) The Role of Behaviour in Evolution, 2014; numerous contribs to books and science jls. *Recreations:* jazz, walking, woodwork, books, clocks, craneflies, butterflies, conservation. *Address:* Department of Life Sciences, Natural History Museum, Cromwell Road, SW7 5BD. *Club:* Tetrapods (Chair, 2002–18).

**VANEZIS, Prof. Peter Savvas,** OBE 2001; MD, PhD; FRCPath, FRCPGlas, FFFLM, FCSFS, FAFMS; Director, Cameron Forensic Medical Sciences, Barts and the London School of Medicine and Dentistry, Queen Mary University of London, 2006–18, now Professor Emeritus; Director and Principal, Academy of Forensic Medical Sciences, since 2011; *b* 11 Dec. 1947; *s* of Savvas Vanezis and Efrosini Vanezis; *m* 1981, Maria Galatariotis; one *s* one *d. Educ:* Wanstead High Sch.; Bristol Univ. (MB ChB, MD); PhD London; DMJ Path. FFFLM 2006; FCSFS (FFSSoc 2011); FAFMS 2011. Jun. appt, St Olave's Hosp. (Guy's), 1973–74; Jun. Lectr, Lectr and Sen. Lectr in Forensic Medicine, London Hosp. Med. Coll., 1974–90; Reader and Head of Dept of Forensic Medicine and Toxicology, Charing Cross and Westminster Med. Sch. and Hon. Consultant, Riverside AHA, 1990–93; Regius Prof. of Forensic Medicine and Sci., 1993–2003, and Dir, Human Identification Centre, 1994–2003, Univ. of Glasgow; Dir Gen., Centre for Internat. Forensic Assistance, 2001–03; Chief Forensic Med. Officer, Forensic Sci. Service, 2003–06; CMO, iGene London Ltd, 2013–16. External Examiner in Forensic Pathology: Postgrad. Med. Inst., Sri Lanka, 1995–; Coll. of Pathologists, Hong Kong, 1999–; Ext. Examiner in Forensic Medicine, Univ. of Malaysia, 2001–. Visiting Professor: Inst. of Forensic Medicine, Singapore, 2000–; London South Bank (formerly S Bank) Univ., 2001–; Univ. of Glasgow, 2003–; Leicester Univ., 2010–12; UCL, 2015–; Vis. Prof. Laureate, European Univ. of Cyprus, 2014–; Hon. Prof., Dept of Pathology, Univ. of HK, 2003–. Hon. Consultant: Tower Hamlets AHA, 1982–90; the Armed Forces, 1992–2010; Gtr Glasgow Health Bd, 1993–; Medico-legal Inst., Santiago, 1994–; Govt of Republic of Cyprus, 1984–. Advr in Forensic Medicine to: ICRC, 2006–; Govt of Malaysia, 2009–. President: British Acad. of Forensic Scis, 1996–97; British Assoc. in Human Identification, 2001–03; mem., numerous forensic science socs, UK and USA. Mem. Adv. Cttee, Action Against Medical Accidents, 2010–. Mem., Editl Bds (Path), Science and Justice, Jl of Clinical Path, Amer. Jl Forensic Medicine & Path; Ed.-in-Chief, Medicine, Science and the Law, 2009–15 and 2018. *Publications:* Pathology of Neck Injury, 1989; Suspicious Death-Scene Investigation, 1996; Essential Forensic Medicine, 2019; Sharp Force Trauma, 2020; articles on forensic medicine and science in learned jls. *Recreations:* painting, golf. *Address:* The Shrubbery, High Road, Thornwood Epping, Essex CM16 6LU.

**VAN GELDER, Daniel Nathan;** Co-Founder and Director, Exemplar Properties, 2003–18; *b* London, 4 July 1973; *s* of Stanley Malcom Van Gelder and Beverley Anne Van Gelder; *m* 1994, Daniela Davidson; two *d. Educ:* Harrow Sch. (Scholar); Univ. of Bristol (BSc Hons Valuation and Estate Mgt). FRICS 2016. Director: CB Richard Ellis, 1993–95; Development Securities plc, 1995–2003. CEO, Prestige Yachting, 2012–18. Chm., Westminster Property Assoc., 2013–16. Freeman, City of London, 2018. *Recreations:* sailing, shooting, backgammon. *Clubs:* Royal Thames Yacht, Royal Southern Yacht.

**van GELDER, Prof. Gerard Jan Henk,** PhD; FBA 2005; Laudian Professor of Arabic, University of Oxford, 1998–2012, now Emeritus; Fellow, St John's College, Oxford, 1998–2012, now Emeritus; *b* 10 June 1947; *s* of Gerard Jan van Gelder and Hendrika Venmans; *m* 1973, Sheila Maureen Ottway; two *d. Educ:* Univ. of Amsterdam (doctoral); Univ. of Leiden (PhD 1982). Librarian, Inst. for Modern Near East, Univ. of Amsterdam, 1973–75; Lectr in Arabic, Univ. of Groningen, 1975–98. Mem., Royal Netherlands Acad. of Arts and Scis, 1997. *Publications:* Beyond the Line: classical Arabic literary critics on the coherence and unity of the poem, 1982; Two Arabic Treatises on Stylistics, 1987; The Bad and the Ugly: attitudes towards invective poetry (Hijā') in classical Arabic literature, 1989; Of Dishes and Discourse, 2000; Close Relationships: incest and inbreeding in classical Arabic literature, 2005; (with Marlé Hammond) Takhyīl: the imaginary in classical Arabic poetics, 2008; Sound and Sense in Classical Arabic Poetry, 2012; Classical Arabic Literature:

a library of Arabic literature anthology, 2013; (ed and trans. with G. Schoeler) al-Ma'arri, Risalat al-ghufran, 2014; books in Dutch; contrib. articles in learned jls and encyclopaedias. *Recreations:* music and musicology, especially early music. *Address:* Middelhorsterweg 40, 9751 TG Haren, The Netherlands.

**VAN HAEFTEN, John Henry;** Chairman and Managing Director, Johnny Van Haeften Ltd, since 1977; *b* London, 22 June 1952; *s* of John Francis Henry Van Haeften and Barbara Joan Van Haeften; *m* 1977, Sarah Anne Rowley; one *d. Educ:* Eton. Liaison, Postage Stamp Dept, later Asst Press Officer, Christie's, 1969–77. Mem., Reviewing Cttee on Export of Works of Art and Objects of Cultural Interest, 2001–11. Mem. Council, British Antique Dealers Assoc., 1989–92; Vice Chm., Soc. of London Art Dealers, 1998–2000, 2001–02. Mem., Exec. Cttee, Eur. Fine Art Foundn, 1989–2016; Trustee, Dulwich Picture Gall., 2010–. *Recreations:* philately, pop music. *Address:* Beaufort House, Ham Street, Ham, Richmond, Surrey TW10 7HL. *T:* (020) 7930 3062. *E:* paintings@johnnyvanhaeften.com. *Club:* Carlton.

**VANHANEN, Matti;** MP (Centre Party) Uusimaa, Finland, since 2015; *b* Jyväskylä, Finland, 4 Nov. 1955; *s* of Tatu and Anni Vanhanen; *m* (marr. diss.); one *s* one *d. Educ:* Helsinki Univ. (Master Soc. Scis). Journalist, 1985–88, Ed.-in-Chief, 1988–91, Kehäsanomat (local newspaper). Exec. Dir, Finnish Family Firms Assoc., 2010–14. MP (Centre Party) Uusimaa, Finland, 1991–2010. Vice Chairman: Parly Envmt Cttee, 1991–95; Parly Gp, Centre Party, 1994–2001; Chm., Parly Grand Cttee, 2000–01; Rep. of Parlt, European Convention on Future of EU, 2002–03; Minister of Defence, 2003; Prime Minister, 2003–10. Centre Party: Mem. or Dep. Mem., Party Delegn, 1976–2000; Chm., Youth League, 1980–83; Bd Mem., 1980–83; Vice Chm., 2000–03; Chm., 2003–10. Espoo City Council, 1981–84; Nurmijärvi Municipal Council, 1989–; Board Member: Helsinki Met. Area Council YTV, 1983–84; Uusimaa Regl Council, 1991–2000. Member Supervisory Board: Neste/Fortum, 1991–2003; Helsingin Osuuskauppa (Cooperative), 2002–03. Chairman: State Youth Council, 1987–90; Housing Foundn for the Young, 1998–2003 (Vice Chm., 1981–97); Union for Rural Educn, 1998–2003; Vice Chairman: Housing Council, 1991–2003; Pro Medi-Heli Assoc., 1995–2003. *Address:* Parliament of Finland, 00102 Eduskunta, Finland.

**VANHEGAN, Joanna Angela;** see Smith, J. A.

**VANHEGAN, Mark James;** QC 2009; barrister, since 1990; *b* Oxford, 27 March 1966; *s* of Dr Robert Ian Vanhegan and late Valerie Vanhegan; *m* 1994, Joanna Angela Smith, *qv;* two *d. Educ:* Abingdon Sch.; Trinity Coll., Cambridge (BA Nat. Sci. and Law 1989). Called to the Bar, Lincoln's Inn, 1990. *Recreations:* walking, tennis, gardening, travel. *Address:* 11 South Square, Gray's Inn, WC1R 5EY. *T:* (020) 7405 1222, *Fax:* (020) 7242 4282. *E:* mark@vanhegan.org. *Club:* TSSC.

**van HEYNINGEN, Joanna,** OBE 2016; architect; Consultant, van Heyningen and Haward Architects, since 2012 (Joint Principal, then Partner, 1982–2012); *b* 22 July 1945; *d* of William Edward Kits van Heyningen and Ruth Eleanor van Heyningen (*née* Treverton); *m* 1977, Birkin Anthony Christopher Haward, *qv;* one *s* one *d. Educ:* Oxford High Sch. for Girls; St Anne's Coll., Oxford (BA (French and Russian) 1967); New Hall, Cambridge (BA (Architecture) 1971); Darwin Coll., Cambridge (Dip Arch 1973). RIBA 1981. Estab. private practice, 1977; formed van Heyningen and Haward Architects, 1982. Mem., Awards Gp, RIBA, 2000–04, 2017–. Co-Chair, Oxford and London Design Rev. Panels, Design Council CABE, 2014–; Mem., New Bermondsey Quality Team, 2011–16. Governor: Building Centre Trust, 1998–2016; Purcell Sch. of Music, 2012– (Chair, Bldg Cttee, 2012–). Trustee, Find Your Feet, 2013–16; Founder, CoHo (Dartmouth Park Co-housing), 2014–. BDA Assessor, 2007–15; External Examiner: Cambridge Univ. Sch. of Architecture, 2009–11; Cardiff Sch. of Architecture, 2014–16; Stirling Prize Assessor, 2012. Award winning buildings include: Haward House, London, 1976; Newnham Coll. Rare Books Liby, Cambridge, 1981; 2nd Haward House, London, 1986; Clovelly Visitor Centre, 1989; Wilson Court, Cambridge, 1994; Jacqueline du Pré Music Building, Oxford, 1995; King Alfred's Sch., London, 1997; Gateway to the White Cliffs (NT), Dover, 1999; West Ham Station, Jubilee Line Extension, 1999; Nat. Centre for Early Music, York, 2000; Polhill Information Centre, Bedford, 2000; Khoan & Michael Sullivan Chinese Painting Gall., Ashmolean Mus., Oxford, 2001; Sutton Hoo Visitor Centre (NT), 2002; RSPB Envmt and Educn Centre, Rainham, 2006; Lewisham Children and Young People's Centre, 2006; Centre for Classical and Byzantine Studies, Oxford Univ., 2006; Trinity Events Centre, Suffolk Showground, 2006; Ysol Ifor Bach, Caerphilly, 2007; Performing Arts Centre, Latymer Sch., 2008; Dennis Sciama Building, Portsmouth Univ., 2008; Gillespie Court, Clare Coll., Cambridge, 2008; Market Hall, Bolton, 2008; Corfield Court, St John's Coll., 2009; National Museums at Chatham, 2009; Edward Alleyn Bldg, Alleyn's Sch., 2010; Latymer Sci. and Library Building, 2010; New N London Synagogue, 2011; Performance Buildings, Hornsey, 2011. Exhibitions: Kent Design, Maidstone, 2000; University Challenge: buildings for higher educn, Building Centre, 2001; New Connections, Municipal Arts Soc. of NY, NY, 2001; Winning Designs, Bristol Arch. Centre, RIBA, and Cube Gall., Manchester, 2002; Diverse City, RIBA, 2003; Celebration of Architectural Competitions, Cube Gall., Manchester, 2003, RIAS, Edinburgh, 2004; Women in Architecture, Paris, 2004. *Recreations:* visiting buildings and places, making things, painting, seeing friends. *Address:* 1c Laurier Road, NW5 1SD. *T:* (020) 7482 5146. *E:* joannavanh@gmail.com.

**van HEYNINGEN, Prof. Veronica,** CBE 2010; DPhil; FRS 2007; FRSE; FMedSci; research scientist in human genetics, retired; Group Leader and Section Head, MRC Human Genetics Unit, Edinburgh, 1992–2012; Hon. Professor: Institute of Ophthalmology, University College London, since 2012; University of Edinburgh, since 2013; *b* 12 Nov. 1946; *d* of Laszlo and Anna Daniel; *m* 1968, Simon van Heyningen; one *s* one *d. Educ:* Girton Coll., Cambridge (BA 1968, MA 1971); Northwestern Univ. (MS 1970); DPhil Oxon 1973. Beit Meml Fellow, Oxford and Edinburgh Univs, 1973–76; MRC Human Genetics Unit: postdoctoral scientist, 1977–81; Scientist with tenure, 1981–86; Sen. Scientist, 1986–91; Special Appt grade, 1991. President: Eur. Soc. of Human Genetics, 2003; Genetics Soc., 2009–12. Mem., Human Genetics Commn, 2000–06. Trustee, Nat. Museums of Scotland, 1994–2000; Trustee Dir, Earlham Inst. (formerly Genome Analysis Centre), 2013–19. Patron, Aniridia Network UK, 2013–. Pres., Galton Inst., 2014–. Mem., EMBO, 2002. FRSE 1997; FMedSci 1999. *Publications:* contribs to scientific jls. *Recreations:* museums, theatre, feeding people, travelling, novels. *E:* veronica.vanheyningen@igmm.ed.ac.uk.

**VAN INGEN, Alexander Charles;** Artistic Director, Champs Hill Records, since 2009; Chief Executive, Academy of Ancient Music, since 2017; *b* Clatterbridge, Wirral, 1981; *s* of Charles Frederick Van Ingen and Judith Suzanne Van Ingen (*née* Aggett); partner, Stephanie Michelle Oade. *Educ:* Birkenhead Sch.; Univ. of Surrey. Recording producer, engr and editor, 2002–; Exec. Producer, Decca/Universal, 2012–17. Vis. Lectr, RNCM, 2008–16. *Recreations:* music, sailing, opera, politics, travel. *Address:* Academy of Ancient Music, 11b Kings Parade, Cambridge CB2 1SJ. *E:* avi@vaningen.net.

**VAN KLAVEREN, Adrian;** Head, Strategic Change, BBC News, 2014–18; *b* 31 Dec. 1961; *s* of late Arthur Van Klaveren and Thelma Van Klaveren; *m* 1990, Julie Stringer; two *s. Educ:* Bristol Grammar Sch.; St John's Coll., Oxford (BA Modern Hist.). Joined BBC, 1983; news trainee, 1983–85; producer, TV News, 1985–90; Sen. Producer, Panorama, 1990–91; Deputy Editor: Nine O'Clock News, 1992–94; Newsnight, 1994; Hd, Local Progs, BBC W Midlands, 1995–96; News Ed., 1996–2000, Hd, 2000–05, Newsgathering, Dep. Dir and Controller of Prodn, 2005–08, BBC News; Controller, BBC Radio 5 Live and 5 Live Sports Extra, 2008–12; Controller, World War One Centenary, BBC, 2013–14. *Recreations:* football (especially Spurs), cricket, political biography.

**van KOOTEN, Prof. George,** PhD; Lady Margaret's Professor of Divinity, University of Cambridge, since 2018; Fellow, Clare Hall, Cambridge, since 2018; *b* Delft, 8 Nov. 1969; *s* of Geurt van Kooten and Annie van Kooten (*née* Kok); *m* 1999, Marike Kerssen; three *s. Educ:* Univ. of Durham (MA New Testament Studies 1995); Univ. of Leiden (MA Theol. 1995; PhD 2001); Christ Ch, Oxford (MSt Jewish Studies in Graeco-Roman Period 1996). University of Groningen: Lectr, 2002–06; Prof. of New Testament and Early Christianity, 2006–18; Dean, Faculty of Theol. and Religious Studies, 2008–13. Visiting Fellow: Clare Hall, Cambridge, 2013–14; Georg-August-Univ., Göttingen, 2015. Series Ed., Ancient Philosophy & Religion, 2017–. *Publications:* Cosmic Christology in Paul and the Pauline School, 2003; Paul's Anthropology in Context, 2008; (ed jtly) The Star of Bethlehem and the Magi, 2015; (ed jtly) Saint Paul and Philosophy, 2017; (ed jtly) Intolerance, Polemics and Debate in Antiquity, 2019. *Recreations:* cycling, walking, swimming, tennis, music, art. *Address:* Faculty of Divinity, University of Cambridge, West Road, Cambridge CB3 9BS. *T:* (01223) 763018. *E:* gv258@cam.ac.uk.

**van KUFFELER, John Philip de B.;** see de Blocq van Kuffeler.

**VAN LAAST, Anthony Vivian,** CBE 2019 (MBE 1999); choreographer; *b* Bognor Regis, 31 May 1951; *s* of Lt Col J. V. Hawkins and M. D. Hawkins; *m* 1998, Annette Stone; one *s* one *d. Educ:* Tonbridge Boys' Sch.; King Alfred Sch.; London Sch. of Contemp. Dance. Dancer, London Contemp. Dance Th., 1971–80; choreographer: *theatre* includes: Song and Dance, Palace, 1982; The Mikado, ENO, 1986; Joseph and the Amazing Technicolour Dreamcoat, London Palladium, 1991, NY, 1994; Mamma Mia!, Prince Edward, 1999, NY, 2001, transf. Prince of Wales, 2004, transf. Novello, 2012; Jesus Christ Superstar, NY, 2001; Sister Act, London Palladium, 2009, NY, 2011; Tina The Musical, Aldwych, 2018, NY, 2019; *films:* Joseph and the Amazing Technicolour Dreamcoat, 1991; Mamma Mia!, 2008; Harry Potter and the Deathly Hallows: Part 1, 2010; Beauty and the Beast, 2017; Mamma Mia! Here We Go Again, 2018. Patron: The Place; Urdang Acad.; Midlands Acad. of Dance and Drama. *Recreations:* mountain biking, hiking, collecting art, white goods shopping. *Address:* c/o Alison Jenkins, The Manor House, Sibford Gower, Banbury, Oxon OX15 5RX. *T:* (01295) 780741. *E:* alison@alisonjenkins.com.

**van LEUVEN, (John) Nikolas;** QC (Guernsey) 2002; Director General, Guernsey Financial Services Commission, 2009–13; *b* 17 July 1947; *s* of John van Leuven and Catherine van Leuven; *m* 1st, 1976, Anne Loveridge (marr. diss.); 2nd, 1997, Wendy Sheppard (*d* 2012); two *s* one *d;* 3rd, 2017, Diana Mortimer. *Educ:* Elizabeth Coll., Guernsey; Trinity Hall, Cambridge (MA); Caen Univ. (Cert. d'Etudes Juridiques Françaises et Normandes). NP 1989. Called to the Bar, Inner Temple, 1970; called to the Guernsey Bar, 1971; Batonnier, Guernsey Bar, 1994–96; in private practice, Guernsey, 1971–2002; Sen. Partner, Ozannes, 1983–2002; HM Procureur (Attorney Gen.) and HM Receiver Gen., Guernsey, 2002–09. Mem., Chief Pleas of Sark, 1997–2002; Mem., Guernsey States of Deliberation, 2002–09. Mem., British Acad. of Forensic Sci., 1981. FCIArb 1999. Chm., Guernsey St John Council, 2001–08; Knight Comdr, Commandery of Order of St John, Bailiwick of Guernsey, 2013–16. KStJ 2012 (CStJ 2010; OStJ 2000). Mem., Edit Bd, Jersey and Guernsey Law Rev., 2006–. *Recreations:* book collecting, local history. *Address:* Portland, Domaine de Beauport, Hauteville, St Peter Port, Guernsey GY1 1DL. *Clubs:* Royal Automobile; Sark Yacht; Royal Guernsey Golf.

**van LINT, Prof. Theo Maarten,** PhD; Calouste Gulbenkian Professor of Armenian Studies, University of Oxford, and Fellow, Pembroke College, Oxford, since 2002; *b* 15 June 1957; *s* of Henk and Coby van Lint. *Educ:* Leiden Univ. (MA Slavic Langs and Lits, 1988; MA Indo-European Comparative Linguistics 1988; PhD Armenian Studies 1996). Researcher: Netherlands Orgn for Scientific Res., 1996–99; Deutsche Forschungsgemeinschaft, Westfälische Wilhelms-Universität, Münster, 1999–2001. Mem., Assoc. Internat. des Études Arméniennes, 1986–. *Publications:* articles in Revue des Études Arméniennes. *Recreations:* volleyball, literature. *Address:* The Oriental Institute, University of Oxford, Pusey Lane, Oxford OX1 2LE.

**VANN, Ven. Cherry Elizabeth;** Archdeacon of Rochdale, since 2008; Prolocutor of the Lower House, Convocation of York, since 2013; *b* Whetstone, Leicester, 29 Oct. 1958; *d* of Maurice and Jean Vann. *Educ:* Lutterworth Upper Sch.; Royal Coll. of Music (ARCM 1978; GRSM 1980); Westcott House. Ordained deacon, 1989, priest, 1994; Parish Deacon, St Michael, Flixton, 1989–92; Parish Deacon, 1992–94, Asst Curate, 1994–98, Bolton-le-Moors; Team Vicar, 1998–2004, Incumbent, 2004–08, E Farnworth and Kearsley; Area Dean, Farnworth, 2005–08. Chaplain: Colleges of Higher Educn and Further Educn, Bolton, 1992–98; Deaf Community, 1998–2004. Hon. Canon, Manchester Cathedral, 2007–. *Recreations:* music, gardening, hill-walking. *Address:* 57 Melling Road, Oldham OL4 1PN. *T:* (0161) 678 1454. *E:* archrochdale@manchester.anglican.org.

**VANNECK,** family name of **Baron Huntingfield**.

**VANNET, Alfred Douglas;** Sheriff of South Strathclyde, Dumfries and Galloway at Airdrie, 2003–09, part-time, since 2009; Senior Tutor in Criminal Litigation, and Hon. Professorial Teaching Fellow, School of Law, University of Glasgow, since 2010; *b* 31 July 1949; *s* of William Peters Vannet and Jean Farquhar Low or Vannet; *m* 1979, Pauline Margaret Renfrew; one *s* one *d. Educ:* High Sch. of Dundee; Univ. of Dundee (LLB 1973). Solicitor in private practice, Oban, 1973–76; Procurator Fiscal Depute, Dundee, 1976–77; Procurator Fiscal Depute, then Sen. Procurator Fiscal Depute, Glasgow, 1977–84; Crown Office, Edinburgh: Head of Appeals Section, 1984–87; Asst Solicitor, Law Officers' Secretariat, 1987–88; Dep. Crown Agent, 1990–94; Solicitor to Public Inquiry into Piper Alpha Disaster, 1988–90; Regional Procurator Fiscal: Grampian Highland and Islands, 1994–97; Glasgow and Strathkelvin, 1997–2000; floating Sheriff, all Scotland, 2000–01; Sheriff at Airdrie and Lanark, 2001–03. Mem., Criminal Courts Rules Council, 1997–2000. Member: Forensic Sci. Soc., 1985–2000; Internat. Assoc. of Prosecutors, 1997–2000; Council, Scottish Medico-Legal Soc., 1997–2000. Hon. Mem., Royal Faculty of Procurators in Glasgow, 1997. FRSA 1995. *Recreations:* music, dog walking, curling. *Address:* Sheriff Court House, Graham Street, Airdrie ML6 6EE. *T:* (01236) 751121. *E:* alfred.vannet@glasgow.ac.uk.

**VAN ORDEN, Brig. Geoffrey Charles,** CBE 2019 (MBE 1973); Member (C) Eastern, European Parliament, since 1999; *b* 10 April 1945; *s* of Thomas and Mary Van Orden; *m* 1974, Frances Elizabeth Weir; three *d. Educ:* Sandown Sch.; Mons OCS; Univ. of Sussex (BA Hons Pol Sci.); Indian Defence Services Staff Coll. (psc). Commnd Intelligence Corps, 1964; operational service in Borneo, NI and BAOR; Directing Staff, Führungs Akademie der Bundeswehr, 1985–88; COS and ACOS, G2 Berlin (British Sector), 1988–90; Assessment Staff, Cabinet Office, 1990; Res. Associate, IISS and Service Fellow, Dept of War Studies, KCL, 1990–91; Head, Internat. Mil. Staff Secretariat, NATO HQ, 1991–94; retd and trans. to Regular Reserve, 1994; Sen. Official, EC (Directorate-Gen. Ext. Relations), 1995–99. European Parliament: Cons. Defence Spokesman, 1999–; Mem., Foreign Affairs Cttee, 1999– (Vice-Chm., 2002–06). Vice Chairman: ECR, 2009–; Special Cttee on Terrorism, 2018–; Chm., Delegn for Relns with India, 2014–. Mem., IISS, 1991–. Founder Mem., Anglo-German Officers' Assoc., 1991. Chairman: Friends of Zimbabwe, 2004–; Europe-India Chamber of Commerce, 2010–14; Friends of Sri Lanka, 2010–; Founder Mem., Friends of India, 2003–; Founding Pres., New Direction - The Foundn for Eur. Reform, 2010–; Member: Countryside Alliance, 1999–; Bow Gp, 1999–. Freeman, City of London, 1991; Freeman, Co. of Painter-Stainers, 1991. *Publications:* various articles on foreign and security policy issues. *Address:* 88 Rectory Lane, Chelmsford, Essex CM1 1RF; European Parliament, Rue Wiertz, 1047 Brussels, Belgium. *T:* (2) 2847332. *Club:* Army and Navy.

**van OSS, Dame Angela Ruth;** *see* McLean, Dame A. R.

**VAN REENEN, Prof. John Michael,** OBE 2017; PhD; FBA 2010; Gordon Y. Billard Professor in Management and Economics, and Professor of Applied Economics, Massachusetts Institute of Technology, since 2016; *b* 26 Dec. 1965; *s* of Lionel and Anne Van Reenen; *m* 2001, Sarah Chambers; one *d*. *Educ:* Queens' Coll., Cambridge (BA 1988; Joshua King Prize, 1988); LSE (MSc 1989; Automation Prize, 1989); University Coll. London (PhD 1992). Res. Fellow, Inst. for Fiscal Studies, 1993–95; Prof., Dept of Econs, UCL, 1995–2003; Dir, Centre for Econ. Performance, 2003–16, Prof., Dept of Econs, 2003–, LSE. Visiting Professor: Univ. of Calif, Berkeley, 1998–99; Stanford Univ., 2008–09; Harvard Univ., 2013–14. Sen. Policy Advr to Sec. of State, DoH, 2000–01. Research Fellow: Centre for Econ. Policy Res., 1996–; Nat. Bureau of Econ. Res., 2006–; Inst. for the Study of Labor, 2010–. Fellow: Econometric Soc., 2012; Soc. for Labor Economists, 2013. Yrjö Jahnsson Award, 2009; Arrow Prize, Internat. Assoc. of Health Econs, 2011; (jtly) EIB Prize for Excellence in Econ. and Social Res., 2014; Harvard Business Rev.-McKinsey Prize for best mgt article of year, 2017; Nat. Inst. for Health Care Mgt Foundn Award for res. into healthcare, 2019. *Publications:* over 100 articles in American Econ. Rev., Qly Jl of Econs, Rev. of Econ. Studies and many others. *Recreations:* music, cooking, film, reading, arguing, politics. *Address:* 161 Fentiman Road, SW8 1JZ. *T:* (020) 7955 6976. *E:* vanreene@mit.edu. *Clubs:* Black's, Tuesday.

**VAN ROMPUY, Herman;** President of the European Council, 2009–14; President, European Policy Centre; *b* Etterbeek, Belgium, 31 Oct. 1947; *s* of Prof. Vic Van Rompuy and Germaine Geens; *m* Geertrui Windels; two *s* two *d*. *Educ:* St-Jan Berchmanscollege, Brussels; Katholieke Universiteit Leuven (Bachelor of Philos. 1968; Master Applied Econs 1971). Attaché Internal Affairs, Nat. Bank of Belgium, 1972–75; Adviser to Cabinet of Prime Minister of Belgium, 1975–78, of Minister of Finance, 1978–80; Dir, Centrum voor Politieke, Economische en Sociale Studies, 1980–88; Lecturer: Handelshogeschool, Antwerp, 1980–87; Vlaamse Economische Hogeschool, Brussels, 1982–2008. Vice-Prime Minister and Minister of Budget, 1993–99; MP (Christian Democratic and Flemish), 1995–2009; Speaker, House of Representatives, 2007–08; Royal Explorer, 2007; Royal Conciliator, 2007; Prime Minister, 2008–09. Grootlint in de Leopoldsorde (Belgium), 2009. *Publications:* De kentering der tijden, 1979; Hopen na 1984, 1984; Het christendom: een moderne gedachte, 1990; Vernieuwing in hoofd en hart: een tegendraadse visie, 1998; De binnenkant op een kier: avonden zonder politiek, 2000; Dagboek van een vijftiger, 2004; Op zoek naar wijsheid, 2007; Haiku, 2010; In de wereld van Herman Van Rompuy, 2010; Haiku 2, 2014.

**van SCHOONHETEN, Baron Willem Oswald B.;** *see* Bentinck van Schoonheten.

**VÄNSKÄ, Osmo;** Music Director, Minnesota Symphony Orchestra, 2003–13 and since 2014; *b* Finland, 1953. *Educ:* trained as clarinettist; Sibelius Acad., Helsinki (conducting, under Jorma Panula). Formerly co-principal clarinettist, Helsinki Philharmonic Orch.; Music Dir, 1988–2008, Conductor Laureate, 2008–, Lahti SO; Chief Conductor: Icelandic SO, 1993–96 (Principal Guest Conductor, 2014–); BBC Scottish SO, 1996–2002; Guest Conductor of orchestras in Europe, USA, Australia and Japan. First Prize, Internat. Young Conductors' Competition, Besançon, 1982. *Address:* c/o HarrisonParrott Ltd, The Ark, 201 Talgarth Road, W6 8BJ.

**van STEENIS,** family name of **Baroness Cavendish of Little Venice.**

**van STEENIS, Jonkheer Huw John;** Group Managing Director, Investor Relations and Chair, Sustainable Finance Committee, UBS, since 2019; *b* 25 Sept. 1969; *s* of Jonkheer Dr Dick van Steenis and Christine van Steenis (née Hopkins); *m* 1999, (Hilary) Camilla Cavendish (*see* Baroness Cavendish of Little Venice); three *s*. *Educ:* Trinity Coll., Oxford (MA PPE; Stirling Boyd Prize); INSEAD (Louis Franck Schol.; MBA). Sen. Manager, Boston Consulting, 1995–99; Hd, Diversified Financial Res., JP Morgan, 1999–2002; Global Hd, Financial Services Res., Morgan Stanley, 2002–16; Global Hd of Strategy and Mem., Gp Mgt Cttee, Schroders plc, 2016–18; Sen. Advr to Gov., Bank of England, 2018–19. Member: Agenda Council on Banking, 2014–, Disruptive Innovation in Financial Services Gp, 2014–, WEF; Adv. Council on Financial Stability, Eur. Central Bank, 2014–; Mkt Monitoring Gp, Inst. of Internat. Finance, 2016–. Mem. Bd, ENO, 2015– (Chair, Adv. Bd, 2019–). FRSA 1999. Creator of Asset Mgt Barbell. Chm., Hope for Grenfell Gala, Rugby Portobello Trust, 2018. Author, report of Future Finance Rev., Bank of England, 2019. *Publications:* contrib. articles on financial services and central banking policy. *Recreations:* opera, running, tennis, ski-ing. *Address:* 16 Hamilton Terrace, NW8 9UG. *Club:* Mardens (Klosters).

**VANSTONE, Hugh;** freelance lighting designer; Associate Artist, Old Vic, since 2015; *b* Exeter, 8 Aug. 1965; *s* of Jeremy and Marion Vanstone; civil partnership 2006, George Stiles. *Educ:* Exeter Sch. Has designed lighting for over 200 prodns for UK nat. cos and in NY; *productions* include: The Blue Room, Donmar, and transf. NY, 1998, and The Unexpected Man, RSC, 1998 (Olivier Award); The Cherry Orchard, NT, 2000, and The Graduate, Gielgud, 2000 (Olivier Award); Blast, NY, 2001 (Nat. Broadway Th. Award, 2002); Pacific Overtures, Donmar, 2003 (Olivier Award, 2004); Spamalot!, NY, 2005, Palace, 2006; The Wizard of Oz, London Palladium, 2011 (Kt of Illumination Award); Shrek, Th. Royal Drury Lane, 2011, and UK tours; Ghost, Manchester Opera Hse, then Piccadilly, 2011 (What's On Stage Award, 2012), transf. NY, 2012 (Outer Circle Critics Award); Matilda, Cambridge Th., 2011, transf. NY, 2013 (Tony Award), Australia, 2015 and tours; Le Bal des Vampires, Paris, 2014 (jtly) Molière Award); Don Quixote, Royal Ballet, 2014; The Red Lion, NT, 2015; An Act of God, NY, 2015; Closer, 2015, Welcome Home, Captain Fox, 2016, Donmar; Tanz der Vampire, Europe and Russia, 2016; Dreamgirls, Savoy, 2016; Venus in Fur, Haymarket, 2017; The Boys in the Band, NY, 2018; The Birthday Party, Pinter, 2018; Exit the King, NT, 2018; The Height of the Storm, Wyndham's, 2018, transf. NY, 2019; Hillary and Clinton, NY, 2019; (co-designer) Mary Poppins, Prince Edward Th., 2019; (co-designer) Back to the Future, Manchester Opera House, 2020; *Old Vic productions* include: The Real Thing, 2010; Future Conditional, 2015; Art, 2016, and UK tour; No's Knife, 2016; Groundhog Day, 2016, transf. NY, 2017; The Master Builder, 2016; A Christmas Carol, 2017, 2018; Present Laughter, 2019. *Address:* c/o Judy Daish Associates Ltd, 2 St Charles Place,, W10 6EG. *T:* (020) 8964 8811. *W:* hughvanstone.com. *Club:* Soho House.

**van WACHEM, Lodewijk Christiaan;** Knight, Order of the Netherlands Lion, 1981; Commander, Order of Orange-Nassau, 1990; Hon. KBE 1988 (Hon. CBE 1977); *b* Pangkalan Brandan, Indonesia, 31 July 1931; *m* 1958, Elisabeth G. Cristofoli; two *s* one *d*. *Educ:* Univ. of Technol., Delft (mech. engr). Joined Royal Dutch/Shell Gp, 1953; worked in Latin America, Africa, FE and Europe; Royal Dutch Petroleum Co.: Man. Dir, 1976–82; Pres., 1982–92; Chm., Supervisory Bd, 1992–2002. Member, Supervisory Board: Akzo Nobel NV, 1992–2002; BMW AG, 1994–2002; Bayer AG, 1997–2002; Chm., Bd of Dirs, Global Crossing Ltd, 2003–11; Member, Board of Directors: Credit Suisse Hldg, 1992–96; IBM Corp., 1992–2002; Philips Electronics NV, 1993–2005 (Chm., 1999–2005); Atco Ltd, 1993–2009; Zurich Financial Services, 1993–2005 (Vice-Chm., 2001–02; Chm., 2002–05). Hon. Citizen, Singapore, 2004.

**van ZWANENBERG, Zoë;** Management Consultant: Zwan Consulting, since 2008; Associate Centre for Confidence and Well-Being, since 2008; research consultant, Churches Together in Britain and Ireland, 2011; *b* Ipswich, 20 Dec. 1952; *d* of David Francis and Aldyth Vincent van Zwanenberg; *m* 1986, Stephen Thompson (marr. diss. 1995); two step *d*. *Educ:* Univ. of Birmingham (BA Eng. Lang. and Lit.); Univ. of Sussex (MA Hist. of Art). MCIPD 1987; MIHM 1984. Gen. mgt, NHS, 1979–86; Force Personnel Officer, Suffolk Constabulary, 1987–90; Dir, Personnel and Trng, Life Span Healthcare, 1990–92; Mgt and Employee Develt Advr, InterCity, 1992–93; Dir, HR, Anglia Railways, 1993–96; Orgn Develt Advr, EA, 1996–99; Hd, Strategic Change Unit, NHS in Scotland, 1999–2001; Chief Exec., Scottish Leadership Foundn, 2001–08. Non-exec. Dir, Scottish Prison Service, 2009–. Chairman: Scottish Youth Dance, 2000–06, 2010– (Dir, 2007); Scottish Ballet, 2004–13; Lamp of Lothian, 2013–; Diocesan Standing Cttee, 2013–; Dir, Scottish Sculpture Trust, 2001–04. Hon. Professor: Queen Margaret Univ., 2007–12; De Montfort Univ., 2007–13. *Recreations:* arts and culture, European travel, ballet, opera, reading, gardens. *Address:* 10 Bielside Gardens, West Barns, Dunbar, Scotland EH42 1WA. *E:* zoe_van_zwanenberg@hotmail.com.

**VARA, Shailesh Lakhman;** MP (C) North West Cambridgeshire, since 2005; *b* 4 Sept. 1960; *s* of Lakhman Arjan Vara and Savita Vara (née Gadher); *m* 2002, Beverley Deanne Fear; two *s*. *Educ:* Aylesbury Grammar Sch.; Brunel Univ. (LLB; Hon. Fellow, 2010); Guildford Coll. of Law. Admitted Solicitor, 1990; articled, Richards Butler, 1988–90; Crossman Block, 1991–92; Payne Hicks Beach, 1992–93; CMS Cameron McKenna, 1994–2001. Shadow Dep. Leader of the H of C, 2006–10; an Asst Govt Whip, 2010–12; Parly Under-Sec. of State, MoJ, 2013–16, DWP, 2015–16; Parly Under-Sec. of State, 2018, Minister of State, 2018, NI Office. Mem., Select Cttee on Envmt, Food and Rural Affairs, 2005–06, on Admin, 2010–11, on Finance and Services, 2011–13. Mem., Exec. Cttee, Commonwealth Parly Assoc., 2017–18 (Mem., Finance, Audit and Remuneration Cttee, 2017–18). Chm., Cons. Parly Friends of India, 2008–10; Jt Chm., Cons. Friends of India, 2016–17. A Vice-Chm., Cons. Party, 2001–05. Contested (C): Birmingham Ladywood, 1997; Northampton S, 2001. Treas., 2001–04, Vice Chm., 2006–09, Exec. Cttee, Soc. of Cons. Lawyers. Mem., Campaign Exec. Gp, Great Fen Project, 2005–10. Gov., Westminster Kingsway Coll., 2002–05. Vice-Pres., Huntingdonshire CCC, 2007–. Pravasi Bharatiya Samman Award, India, 2014. *Recreations:* travel, cricket, tae kwon do. *Address:* House of Commons, SW1A 0AA. *T:* (020) 7219 3000. *E:* varas@parliament.uk.

**VARADHAN, Prof. Srinivasa,** PhD; FRS 1998; Professor of Mathematics, Courant Institute of Mathematical Sciences (formerly Courant Institute), New York University, since 1972; *b* 2 Jan. 1940; *s* of S. V. Rangaiyengar and S. R. Janaki; *m* 1964, Vasundara Narayanan; two *s*. *Educ:* Madras Univ. (BSc Hons, MA); Indian Statistical Inst. (PhD 1963). Courant Institute, New York University: Vis. Member, 1963–66; Asst Prof., 1966–68; Associate Prof., 1968–72; Dir, 1980–84 and 1992–94. Fellow, Amer. Acad. Arts and Sci., 1988; Associate Fellow, Third World Acad. Scis, 1988; Mem., NAS, 1995. *Publications:* Multi-dimensional Diffusion Processes, 1979; On Diffusion Problems and Partial Differential Equations, 1980; Large Deviations and Applications, 1984; Probability Theory, 2001; Stochastic Processes, 2007. *Recreations:* travel, tennis, squash, bridge. *Address:* Courant Institute of Mathematical Sciences, New York University, 251 Mercer Street, New York, NY 10012, USA. *T:* (212) 9983334.

**VARAH, Kate Elizabeth, (Mrs M. J. S. Booth);** Executive Director, Old Vic, since 2015; *b* Leics, 11 June 1976; *d* of George Peter Michael Varah and Sally Anne Varah; *m* 2005, Matthew James Spencer Booth; three *s*. *Educ:* Guildford High Sch. for Girls; Keble Coll., Oxford (BA Hons Theol. 1997; MA); Coll. of Law (CPE (Merit); Legal Practice Course (Dist.)). Admitted Solicitor, 2001. Solicitor Advocate, 2001–05, Community Investment Manager, 2004–06, Linklaters; Solicitors' Higher Courts Advocate Accreditation, 2002; Dir, Business Develt, Chickenshed, 2006–08; Business Dir, then Chief Operating Officer, Old Vic, 2009–15. Mem., Chad Varah Meml Appeal Taskforce, Samaritans, 2007–08. Chm., Parents in the Performing Arts, 2016–17. Founder and Trustee, Michael Varah Meml Fund, 2007–; Trustee, Chickenshed, 2010–16. Co-Chairman: Garden House Parents' Assoc. Fundraising, BookTrust/Royal Hosp. Chelsea, 2015–16; Westminster Cathedral Choir Sch. Parents' Assoc., 2018–20. *Recreations:* anything, anywhere, with my children. *Address:* The Old Vic, The Cut, SE1 8NB. *E:* Kate.varah@oldvictheatre.com. *Club:* Soho House.

**VARCOE, (Christopher) Stephen;** baritone and teacher; *b* 19 May 1949; *s* of Philip William and Mary Northwood Varcoe; *m* 1972, Melinda Davies; two *s* two *d* (and one *s* decd). *Educ:* King's School, Canterbury; King's College, Cambridge (MA); University of York (PhD). Freelance concert and opera singer, 1970–; on teaching staff, Royal Coll. of Music, 2003–. Fellow, Murray Edwards Coll., Cambridge, 2009–10. Calouste Gulbenkian Foundation Fellowship, 1977. *Publications:* Sing English Song: a practical guide to the language and repertoire, 2000; (contrib.) Cambridge Companion to Singing, 2000; (contrib.) New Percy Grainger Companion, 2010. *Recreations:* painting, gardening, building.

**VARCOE, Jeremy Richard Lovering Grosvenor,** CMG 1989; HM Diplomatic Service, retired; part-time Immigration Judge (formerly Adjudicator), 1995–2007; *b* 20 Sept. 1937; *s* of late Ronald A. G. Varcoe and Zoe E. Varcoe (née Lovering); *m* 1st, 1961, Wendy Anne Moss (*d* 1991); two *d*; 2nd, 1995, Ruth Murdoch (née Wallis). *Educ:* Charterhouse; Lincoln Coll., Oxford (MA). National Service, Royal Tank Regt, 2nd Lieut, 1956–58. HMOCS: District Officer, Swaziland, 1962–65. Called to the Bar, Gray's Inn, 1966; Lectr in Law, Univ. of Birmingham, 1967–70; joined HM Diplomatic Service, 1970; FCO, 1970–72; Dep. Secretary General, Pearce Commn on Rhodesian Opinion, 1972; First Sec., Ankara, 1972–74, Lusaka, 1974–78; FCO, 1978–79; Counsellor, Kuala Lumpur, 1979–82; Head of Southern African Dept, FCO, 1982–84; Counsellor, Ankara, 1984–85; on special leave with Standard Chartered Bank, Istanbul, 1985–87; Ambassador to Somalia, 1987–89; Minister/Dep. High Comr, Lagos, 1989–90; Asst Under-Sec. of State, FCO, 1990–91. Co-ordinator, London Economic Summit, 1991. Dir Gen., United World Colls, 1992–94; Dep. Dir, Develt Office, Oxford Univ., 1995–96. *Publications:* Legal Aid in Criminal

Proceedings—a Regional Survey, 1970. *Recreations:* walking, playing at golf, local issues in Cornwall, tilting at wind turbines. *Address:* Dozmary, Rock Road, Rock, Wadebridge, Cornwall PL27 6PW. *Club:* St Enodoc Golf.

**VARCOE, Stephen;** *see* Varcoe, C. S.

**VARDAXOGLOU, Prof. John Costas, (Yiannis),** PhD; CEng, FIET, FREng, FIEEE; Professor of Wireless Communications, Loughborough University, since 1998 (Dean, School of Electronic, Electrical and Systems Engineering, 2006–12); *b* Athens, 3 Sept. 1959; *s* of Costas and Evangelia Vardaxoglou; *m* 1987, Rachel McQuail; two *s*. *Educ:* First Sch. of Kalamaki, Alimos, Athens; Univ. of Kent (BSc Math. Physics 1982; PhD Electronics 1985). CEng 2011; FIET 2011; FREng 2011; FIEEE 2012. Res. Asst, Univ. of Kent, 1985–88; Lectr, 1988–92, Sen. Lectr, 1992–98, Loughborough Univ. of Technol., later Loughborough Univ. Founder Dir, Antrum Ltd, 2011–. *Publications:* Frequency Selective Surfaces: analysis and design, 1997. *Address:* 38 Fairmount Drive, Loughborough, Leics LE11 3JR. *T:* (01509) 560625, (office) (01509) 227001, *Fax:* (01509) 227008. *E:* j.c.vardaxoglou@lboro.ac.uk.

**VARDY, Prof. Alan Edward,** PhD, DEng, DSc; FREng, FICE, FRSE; Professor of Civil Engineering, 1979–95, Research Professor of Civil Engineering (part-time), 1995–2016, now Professor Emeritus, University of Dundee; Engineering Consultant, Dundee Tunnel Research, since 1995; *b* Sheffield, 6 Nov. 1945; *s* of John Moreton Vardy and Margaret Vardy (*née* Thompson); *m* 1991, Susan Janet Upstone; two *s* one *d*. *Educ:* Univ. of Leeds (BSc 1st Cl. Hons Civil Engrg 1967; PhD Civil Engrg 1971; DEng Tunnel Safety 1997); Univ. of Dundee (DSc Transient 1-D Flows 2007). FICE 1989 (MICE 1975); Eur Ing 1989; FRSE 2002; FREng 2007. Res. Officer, 1971–72, Lectr in Civil Engrg, 1972–75, Univ. of Leeds; Royal Soc. Warren Res. Fellow, Univ. of Cambridge, 1975–79; University of Dundee: Hd, Dept of Civil Engrg, 1979–85; Dir, Wolfson Bridge Res. Unit, 1980–90; Dep. Principal, 1985–88; Dep. Principal and Vice Principal, 1988–89; Royal Soc./SERC Industrial Fellow, 1990–94; Dir, Lightweight Structures Unit, 1998–2004. FASCE 1995 (MASCE 1980). FRSA 1980; FHEA 2007. *Publications:* Fluid Principles, 1990; 200 papers in jls and confs. *Recreations:* wine, wife, walking. *Address:* Dundee Tunnel Research, Kirkton, Abernyte, Perthshire PH14 9SS. *T:* (01828) 686241.

**VARDY, Sir Peter,** Kt 2001; DL; Chairman: Vardy Foundation, since 1989; Vardy Property Group, since 2006; Peter Vardy Ltd, since 2006; *b* 4 March 1947; *s* of late Reginald Vardy and of Sarah Vardy; *m* 1971, Margaret; two *s* one *d* (and one *s* decd.). *Educ:* Chorister Sch.; Durham Sch. Began work in family business, Reg Vardy Ltd (motor dealership), at age of 16; built co. to become one of largest UK motor retail gps; CEO, 1982–2006; floated on Stock Exchange, 1989; sold to Pendragon Plc, 2006. Dir, SONIK Sports Ltd, 2009–. Sponsor Chairman: Emmanuel Coll., Gateshead (City Tech. Coll.), 1990–2010; Kings Acad. (City Acad.), Middlesbrough, 2003–10; Trinity Acad. (City Acad.), Doncaster, 2005–10; Bede Acad. (City Acad.), Blyth, 2009–10. Founder Chm., Safe Families for Children in the UK, 2012–18; Dir, Durham and Tees Valley Community Rehabilitation Co., 2016–. Director: Foundn of Light, 2012–18; Achieving Real Change in our Communities, 2014–. DL Tyne and Wear, 2002. Freedom of the City of Sunderland, 2011. Hon. DBA Sunderland, 1995; Hon. DLaws Pennsylvania, 2009. Beacon Award for Philanthropy, 2015. *Address:* Vardy Family Office, Regus House, 4 Admiral Way, Doxford International Business Park, Sunderland, Tyne and Wear SR3 3XW.

**VARDY, Peter Christian,** PhD; Vice-Principal, 1999–2011, and Senior Lecturer, 1983–2011, Heythrop College, London; *b* 29 July 1945; *s* of Mark and Christa Vardy; *m* 1st, 1974, Anne Moore (marr. diss. 2004); two *s* four *d*; 2nd, 2009, Charlotte Vardy (*née* Fowler); two *d*. *Educ:* Charterhouse; Univ. of Southampton (BA 1979); W Sussex Inst. of Higher Educn (PGCE 1980); KCL (MTh 1982; PhD 1985). FCA 1967. Chm., H. Young Holdings plc, 1979–83. Dir, Candle Conferences Ltd and Candle Resources Ltd, 2010–19. Chm., Bd of Theology, Univ. of London, 1990–93. Pres., London Soc. for the Study of Religion, 1996–98. Ed., Dialogue Australasia, 1997–2009; Mem. Bd, Dialogue Australasia Network, 2001–13. *Publications:* The Puzzle of God, 1989, 4th edn 1999; (jtly) The Puzzle of Ethics, 1990, 4th edn 1999; The Puzzle of Evil, 1991, 2nd edn 1997; The Puzzle of Sex, 1993, 2nd edn 2009; (jtly) The Puzzle of the Gospels, 1994; (ed) Great Christian Thinkers, 1995; What is Truth, 1999, 2nd edn 2003; (jtly) The Thinker's Guide to Evil, 2003; (jtly) The Thinker's Guide to God, 2003; Being Human, 2003; Kierkegaard, 2008; (jtly) Good and Bad Religion, 2010; (jtly) Ethics Matters, 2012; (jtly) God Matters, 2013; (jtly) Bible Matters, 2014; The Puzzle of Christianity, 2016; Beyond the Cave, 2019. *Recreations:* philosophy, reading, writing, stillness and preparing for death. *T:* (01423) 755048. *E:* petervardy@ymail.com.

**VARGAS LLOSA, Mario;** writer; *b* Arequipa, Peru, 28 March 1936; *m* 1st, 1955, Julia Urquidi (marr. diss. 1964); 2nd, 1965, Patricia Llosa Urquidi; two *s* one *d*. *Educ:* Univ. Nacional Mayor de San Marcos, Lima (BA); Univ. of Madrid (PhD 1971). Journalist and broadcaster, Lima and Paris; Lectr, QMC, 1967; Writer in Residence, Wilson Center, Smithsonian Instn, 1980; Vis. Fellow, Wissenschaftskolleg, Berlin, 1991–92; Dist. Writer-in-Residence, Georgetown Univ., Washington DC, 2003; Visiting Professor: Washington State Univ., 1968; KCL, 1969; Univ. de Puerto Rico, 1969; Columbia Univ., 1975; Cambridge Univ., 1977; Syracuse Univ., 1988; Florida Internat. Univ., 1991; Harvard Univ., 1992–93; Princeton Univ., 1993; Georgetown Univ., 1994, 1999; Oxford Univ., 2000. Founder of political party, Movimiento Libertad, 1988; Presidential candidate, Peru, 1990. Pres., PEN Club Internat., 1976–79. Member: Acad. Peruana de la Lengua, 1975; Royal Spanish Acad., 1994; Internat. Acad. of Humanism, 1996. Hon. FKC 2007. Holds numerous honorary doctorates. Biblioteca Breve prize (Spain), 1963; Rómulo Gallegos Internat. Literature prize (Venezuela), 1967; Ritz Paris Hemingway prize (France), 1985; Asturias prize (Spain), 1986; Planeta prize (Spain), 1993; Cervantes prize (Spain), 1994; Jerusalem prize (Israel), 1995; Pluma de Oro Award, Club de la Escritura, Madrid, 1997; Crystal Award, World Econ. Forum, 2001; Americas Award, Americas Foundn, 2001; Nabokov Prize, PEN American Center, 2002; Budapest Prize (Hungary), 2003; Premio Mercosur a las Letras, Konex Foundn (Argentina), 2004; Premio a la libertad, Friedrich Naumann Foundn (Germany), 2009; Nobel Prize in Literature, 2010. Congressional Medal of Honour (Peru), 1981; Gran Cruz, Orden El Sol (Peru), 2001; Medal of Honor of Peruvian Culture (Peru), 2004; Légion d'honneur (France), 1985; Commandeur, Ordre des Arts et des Lettres (France), 1993; Gran Cruz, Order of Rubén Darío (Nicaragua), 2006. *Publications:* Los jefes (short stories), 1959; Mario Vargas Llosa: obras completas, vol. I Narraciones y novelas (1959–1967), 2004, vol. II Novelas (1969–1977), 2004, vol. III Novelas y Teatro (1981–1986), 2005; Diálogo de damas (poems), 2007; Fonchito y la luna (children's story), 2010; *novels:* La ciudad y los perros, 1963; La casa verde, 1966; Los cachorros, 1967; Conversación en la Catedral, 1969; Historia secreta de una novela, 1971; Pantaleón y las visitadoras, 1973; La tía Julia y el escribidor, 1977 (filmed as Tune in Tomorrow, 1990); La guerra del fin del mundo, 1981; La historia de Mayta, 1984; ¿Quién mató a Palomino Molero?, 1986; El hablador, 1987; Elogio de la madrastra, 1988; Lituma en los Andes, 1993; Los cuadernos de Don Rigoberto, 1997; La fiesta del chivo, 2000 (filmed as The Feast of the Goat, 2006); El paraíso en la otra esquina, 2003; Travesuras de la niña mala, 2006; El sueño del celta, 2010; El Héroe Discreto, 2015; Cinco Esquinas, 2016 (trans. English as The Neighbourhood, 2018); *plays:* La señorita de Tacna, 1981; Kathie y el hipopótamo, 1983; La Chunga, 1986; El loco de los balcones, 1993; Odiseo y Penélope, 2007; Al pie del Támesis, 2008; Las mil noches y una noche, 2009; *non-fiction:* Contra viento y marea (essays), vols I and II, 1986, vol. III, 1990; La verdad de las mentiras (essays), 1990, new edn 2002; El pez en el agua (autobiog.), 1993; Desafíos a la libertad (essays), 1994; Making Waves (essays), 1996; Touchstones: essays on literature, art and politics, 2007; Wellsprings (essays), 2008; Sables y utopías: visiones de América Latina (essays), 2009; Notes on the Death of Culture, 2015; articles for El País and Letras Libres. *Address:* Las Magnolias 295-6° Piso, Barranco, Lima 04, Peru. *Fax:* (1) 4773518; c/o Faber & Faber Ltd, Bloomsbury House, 74–77 Great Russell Street, WC1B 3DA. *Fax:* (020) 7927 3801.

**VARLEY, John Christian,** OBE 2016; TD 1991, and bar 1997; FRAgS; FCIM; Estates Director, Clinton Devon Estates, since 2000; *b* Leeds, 5 Oct. 1960; *s* of late Maurice Varley and of Audrey Varley; *m* 1995, Rebecca Warner (marr. diss. 2018); one *s* two *d*. *Educ:* Leeds Grammar Sch.; Univ. of Leeds (BA Hons); McGill Univ., Montreal (MBA); INSEAD, Paris (Dip.). Mktg Exec., Dunlop Hldgs, 1982–84; Product Manager, Gestetner Internat., 1984–86; British Telecom: Mktg Manager, IDD, 1986–90; Manager: IDD Strategy, 1990–92; Internat. Telephony, 1992–95; Sen. Customer and Field Ops Manager Scotland, 1995–98; Gen. Manager, Corporate Clients, 1998; Prog. Dir, AT&T/BT Global Venture, 1998–99; Dir, Project Heritage, 1999–2000. Chm., Rural Cttee, 2008–14, Gp Chm., 2015–17, Estates Business Gp. Member, Board: Countryside Agency, 2002–06; Commn for Rural Communities, 2006–09; Envmt Agency, 2009– (Chm., Envmt Agency Pension Fund, 2012–15); Natural England, 2015–17; Member: Govt Wildlife Network Rev. Panel, 2009–10; Govt Ind. Forestry Panel, 2011–12; Chm., Govt Network Rail Vegetation Mgt Rev., 2018–19. Officer, RA, TA, 1978–2000. FCIM 2004; FRAgS 2014. *Recreations:* walking, travel, family, keeping a global perspective. *Address:* c/o Clinton Devon Estates, Bicton Arena, East Budleigh, Budleigh Salterton, Devon EX9 7BL. *T:* (01395) 441141/2. *E:* mail@clintondevon.com. *Clubs:* Farmers, Cavalry and Guards.

**VARLEY, John Silvester;** Group Chief Executive, Barclays Bank plc, 2004–10; *b* 1 April 1956; *m* 1981, Carolyn Thorn Pease; one *s* one *d*. *Educ:* Downside Sch.; Oriel Coll., Oxford (MA 1st cl. Hons History). Admitted Solicitor, 1979; Commercial Law Dept, Frere Cholmeley, Solicitors, 1979–82; Asst Dir, Corporate Finance Dept, Barclays Merchant Bank, 1982–86; Barclays de Zoete Wedd: Corporate Finance Div., 1986–89; Man. Dir, BZW Asia, 1989–91; Dep. Chief Exec., Global Equities Div., 1991–94; Dir, Odey Asset Management, 1994–95; Chairman: BZW Asset Management, 1995–96; BZW Property Investment Management, 1995–96; Dir, Barclays Global Investors, 1995–96; Chm., Barclays Asset Management Gp, 1996–98; Barclays Bank plc: Dir, 1998–; Chief Exec., Retail Finance Services, Barclays Bank plc, 1998–2000; Gp Finance Dir, 2000–03. Non-executive Director: BlackRock, 2009–; AstraZeneca (Sen. Ind. Dir, 2012–15); Rio Tinto, 2011–17 (Sen. Ind. Dir, 2012–17). Chm., Marie Curie Cancer Care, 2011–17; Trustee, Prince of Wales's Charitable Foundn, 2011–. Fellow, Eton Coll., 2011–. *Clubs:* Brooks's, Army and Navy, White's.

**VARLEY, Rosemary Margaret, (Rosie),** OBE 2007; Chairman: Public Guardian Board, 2007–12; General Social Care Council, 2008–12; *b* 22 Dec. 1951; *d* of late Ratcliffe Bowen Wright, MD, FRCOG and of Dr Margaret Bowen Wright (*née* Williams); *m* 1976, Andrew Iain Varley (*d* 2005); one *s* one *d*. *Educ:* New Hall, Chelmsford; Durham Univ. (BA Hons); Manchester Univ. (MA Econ). Various acad. posts, Manchester Univ., 1978–83; Mem., W Suffolk HA, 1984–92; Chairman: Mid Anglia Community NHS Trust, 1992–97; Anglia and Oxford, then Eastern, Reg., NHS Exec., DoH, 1997–2001; NHS Appointments Comr, Eastern Reg., 2001–06. Ind. Mem., E of England Regl Assembly, 1999–2001. Non-exec. Dir, W Suffolk Hospital NHS Trust, 2011–18. Member: Mental Health Rev. Tribunal, 1995–2017; Disability Appeal Tribunal, 1992–2017. Chm., General Optical Council, 1999–2009; Mem., Council for Healthcare Regulatory Excellence (formerly Council for the Regulation of Healthcare Professionals), 2002–08 (Actg Chm., 2007–08); Mem., NMC Appts Bd, 2007–09; Ind. Public Appts Assessor, 2012–; Chair, Statutory Panellists Assce Cttee, GDC, 2014–. Chair, Special Educn and Disability Acad. Trust, 2017–. Governor: Priory Sch., Bury St Edmunds, 2007–17; St Benedict's RC Sch., Bury St Edmunds, 2011–17. FRSocMed 1999; Hon. Fellow, Coll. of Optometrists, 2009. Freeman, City of London, 2005; Liveryman, Co. of Spectacle Makers, 2006–. DUniv: East Anglia, 2009; Essex, 2009. *Publications:* contrib. various articles in health jls and mgt textbooks. *Recreations:* walking, all things Italian, bridge, extended family. *Address:* Avon House 40/41, The Green, Barrow, Suffolk IP29 5AA. *T:* (01284) 811257. *E:* rosievarley@btinternet.com, rosievarley@gmail.com.

**VARMUS, Prof. Harold Eliot,** MD; Lewis Thomas University Professor of Medicine, Cornell University, since 2015; Senior Associate Member, New York Genome Center, since 2015; *b* 18 Dec. 1939; *s* of Frank Varmus and Beatrice Barasch Varmus; *m* 1969, Constance Louise Casey; two *s*. *Educ:* Freeport High Sch., NY; Amherst Coll., Mass (BA 1961); Harvard Univ. (MA 1962); Columbia Univ., NY (MD 1966). Surgeon, US Public Health Service, 1968–70; Dept of Microbiology, Univ. of California Medical Center, San Francisco: Lectr, 1970–72; Asst Prof., 1972–74; Associate Prof., 1974–79; Prof. of Microbiology and Immunology, 1979–93 (Dept of Biochem. and Biophys, 1982–93); Amer. Cancer Soc. Prof. of Molecular Virology, 1984–93; Dir, NIH, Bethesda, Md, 1993–99; Pres. and CEO, Memorial Sloan-Kettering Cancer Center, NY, 2000–10; Dir, Nat. Cancer Inst., Md, 2010–15. Scientific Consultant, Chiron Corp., 1982–87; Member, Scientific Adv. Bd: Merck Corp., 1985–88; Gilead Corp., 1988–. Co-Chm., US President's Council of Advrs on Sci. and Technol., 2009–. Associate Editor: Cell, 1974–78, 1979–; Virology, 1974–84; Genes and Develt, 1986–; Editor, Molecular and Cellular Biol., 1984–88; Mem., Editl Bd, Trends in Genetics, 1989–. Member: Special Grants Cttee, Calif. Div., Amer. Cancer Soc., 1973–76; Breast Cancer Virus Wkg Gp, Virus Cancer Program, 1973–74; Bd of Scientific Counselors, Div. of Cancer Biol. and Diagnosis, 1983–87, Nat. Cancer Inst.; Virology Study Section, NIH, 1976–80. Member: AAAS; Amer. Soc. Microbiology; Amer. Soc. Biochem. and Molecular Biol; Amer. Soc. Virology; Nat. Acad. Scis, 1984; Amer. Acad. Arts and Scis, 1988. Foreign Mem., Royal Soc., 2005. Hon. DSc: Amherst Coll., 1984; Columbia Univ., 1990. Numerous awards and prizes incl. (jtly) Nobel Prize for Physiology or Medicine, 1989. *Publications:* The Art and Politics of Science (memoirs), 2009. *Address:* Weill Department of Medicine, Cornell University, 525 East 68th Street, Box 130, New York, NY 10065, USA.

**VARNEY, Sir David (Robert),** Kt 2006; Chairman, Packt Ltd, 2012–18; *b* 11 May 1946; *s* of Robert Kitchener Frederick Varney and Winifred Gwendolen Williams; *m* 1971, Patricia Ann Billingham; one *s* one *d*. *Educ:* Brockley County Grammar Sch.; Surrey Univ. (BSc); Manchester Univ. (MBA; Alumnus of the Year, 2005). Joined Shell Refining Co., 1968; various appts in UK, Australia, Holland and Sweden, 1968–90; Head of Mkting, Branding and Product Develt, SIPCO, 1990–91; Man. Dir, Downstream Oil, Shell UK, 1991–95; Dir (responsible for Shell's oil products business in Europe), Shell Internat. Petroleum Co., 1996; Chief Exec., BG Group plc, 1997–2000; Chairman: BT Wireless, subseq. mmO$_2$, 2001–04; HM Revenue and Customs, 2004–06. Non-executive Director: Cable and Wireless, 1999–2000; HM Treasury, 2004–07; Civil Service Steering Bd, 2007–09. PM's Advr on Public Service Transformation, 2007–09. Member: Bd, Oil, Gas and Petrochemicals Supplies Office, 1997–99; Public Service Productivity Panel, 2000–01; Policy Commn on Future of Farming and Food, 2001–02. Chm., BITC, 2002–04.

President: Inst. of Employment Studies, 2003–07; Chartered Mgt Inst., 2005–06. Interim Chm., Barking, Havering and Redbridge Univ. Hosps NHS Trust, 2010. Pro Chancellor, Univ. of Surrey, 2016– (Mem., 1994–2002, Vice-Chm., 2001–02, Council; Chm., Annual Fund Disbursement Cttee, 2012–15). Chm., Stroke Assoc., 2013–16. Chm., Nat. Assoc. of Citizens Advice Bureaux, 2015–18. Hon. DTech London Metropolitan, 2005; Hon. LLD Bath, 2006; DUniv Surrey, 2007. *Recreations:* opera, Formula 1 motor racing, Rugby. *Address:* 5 College Road, Dulwich, SE21 7BQ. *Clubs:* Athenæum, Royal Society of Medicine (Mem. Council, 2003–05).

**VARNISH, Peter,** OBE 1982; FREng, FIET; Director, since 2001, and Chief Executive, since 2006, Geopolitical (formerly International Geopolitical) Solutions Ltd; *b* 30 May 1947; *s* of John Varnish and Ilma Varnish (*née* Godfrey); *m* 1968, Shirley-Anne Bendelow; two *s*. *Educ:* Warwick Sch.; UCNW, Bangor (BSc Hons 1968). CEng 1987; FIET (FIEE 1989); FREng (FEng 1995). Res., Services Electronics Res. Lab., Baldock, 1968–75; Scientific Advr to MoD, British Embassy, Washington, 1975–79; Res. Area Co-ordinator for Electrical Warfare in UK, ASWE Portsdown, 1979–81; Officer i/c, ASWE Funtington, 1981–84; Head: Radar Div., ASWE Portsdown, 1984–86; Signature Control, ARE Funtington, 1986–88; Electronic Warfare and Weapons Dept, ARE Portsdown, 1988–90; Dir, Above Water Weapons, DRA, 1990–92; RCDS 1992; Dir, SDI Participation Office, 1993; Dir of Sci. for Ballistic Missile Defence, MoD, 1993–95; Defence Evaluation and Research Agency: Dir, Internat. Business Develt, 1995–2000; Dir of Technology (Partnership), 2000–01; Chief Exec., S3T Ltd, 2001–05; Man. Dir, World Wide Water Ltd, 2019–. Vis. Prof., Univ. of Coventry, 2018–. Chairman: Definition International Ltd, 2002–09; AeroGB Ltd, 2010–; Director: CMB Ltd, 2001–04; Sparks Technology Ltd, 2001–06; Charteris, Mackie, Baillie, 2001–05; Closed Solutions Ltd, 2002–16; Table 27 Ltd, 2004–07; QTEL Europe Plc, 2005–06; Consols Ltd, 2006–08; Blue Star Capital, 2008–13; Trango Ltd, 2009–11; Cambridge Global Capital UK Ltd, 2013–; ITC Gp, 2015–; TUK Trading Ltd, 2019–. Mem., Defence Scientific Adv. Council, 1991–99; Adviser: Home Office, 2003–11; MoD Faraday Initiative, 2004–; FBM Babcock, 2005–08; to Shadow Minister for Defence Procurement, 2007–11; Aerospace Resources, 2008–15; Foreign and Commonwealth Office, 2009–14; Northrop Grumman, 2009–14; Lockheed Martin, 2009–15; Broadcast Networks Ltd, 2012–14; Sen. Advr, Tayrona UK Ltd, 2015–19. Chairman: Common Defence Forum, 1988–2004; Military Microwaves, 1990; Stealth Conf., 1990, 2003, 2004; Milcon, Abu Dhabi, biennially, 1995–2003; Singapore Internat. Defence Conf., 1997, 1999, 2005; Air Missile Conf., 2001–05; Global Security Conf., 2002; Interoperability Conf., 2002–05; Asymmetric Warfare, 2004–06; Homeland Defence Conf., Dubai, 2005–06; Internat. Security Nat. Resilience, London, 2007; EW-AOC, Interlaken, 2007; Networked Public Safety, London, 2008; Owning the Night, Bisley, 2009, 2011; CNi, Expo London, 2010; Vice-Chm., Global Security, Asia Conf., Singapore, 2005, 2007. Mem., Cttee, RM Mus. Appeal (Seamore), 2014–. Mem., Sainsbury Award Cttee, Royal Acad. of Engrg, 2010–. Mem. Assoc. of Old Crows, later Assoc. of Electronic Warfare, 1978–. Pres., Old Warwickian Assoc., 2020–. TV appearances, Horizon and Discovery. Liveryman, Coachmakers' and Coach Harness Makers' Co., 2008–; Freeman, City of London, 2009. SMIEE; MInstD 1995. FRSA 1996. Several patents on stealth technology, electronic devices, radar. *Publications:* numerous papers on electron bombarded semiconductor devices, radar, electronic warfare, Stealth, ballistic missile defence and res. policy, engrg higher educn, defence globalisation, technol. of modern warfare, cyber warfare and defence; articles in London papers on cyber security and 5G. *Recreations:* Rugby football, classical music, cyber-security, furtherance of science in UK. *Address:* 1 Greatfield Way, Rowlands Castle, Hants PO9 6AG. *T:* (023) 9241 2440. *E:* peter.varnish@btinternet.com. *Clubs:* Army and Navy, Brooks's.

**VÁSÁRY, Tamás;** pianist and conductor; Principal Conductor, Budapest Symphony Orchestra, 1993–2004, now Lifetime Hon. Chief Conductor; Music Director and Conductor, Kodály-Bartók World Youth Orchestra, since 2006; *b* 11 Aug. 1933; *s* of Jozsef Vásáry and Elizabeth (*née* Baltazár); *m* 1967, Ildiko (*née* Kovàcs). *Educ:* Franz Liszt Acad. of Music, Budapest. First concert at age of 8 in Debrecen, Hungary; First Prize, Franz Liszt Competition, Budapest, 1947; prizes at internat. competitions in Warsaw, Paris, Brussels, Rio de Janeiro; Bach and Paderewski medals, London, 1961; début in London, 1961, in Carnegie Hall, NY, 1961; plays with major orchestras and at festivals in Europe, USA, Australasia and Far East; 3 world tours. Conducting debut, 1970; Musical Dir, Northern Sinfonia Orch., 1979–82; Principal Conductor, 1989–97, Conductor Laureate, 1997–98, Bournemouth Sinfonietta; conducts worldwide. Records Chopin, Debussy, Liszt, Rachmaninov (in Germany), Brahms, Mozart, Honegger, Respighi, Martinu, Beethoven. *Publications:* A zenén túl, 2003. *Recreations:* yoga, writing, sports. *Address:* c/o Magyar Rádió Zenekari Iroda, Bródy Sándor u. 5–7, 1800 Budapest, Hungary.

**VASELLA, Dr Daniel L.;** Chairman, Novartis AG, 1999–2013 (President and Head of Executive Committee, 1996–99; Chief Executive Officer, 1999–2010); *b* 15 Aug. 1953; *m*; two *s* one *d*. *Educ:* Univ. of Berne (MD 1979). Former resident physician: Waid Hosp., Zurich; Univ. Hosp., Berne; Inst. of Pathology, Univ. of Berne; attendant physician, C. L. Lory Haus, Univ. Hosp., Berne, 1984–88; Sandoz Group: consecutively, mkt res. and sales, Product Manager for Sandostatin, then Dir of special project mkting, Sandoz Pharmaceuticals Corp., USA, 1988–92; Asst Vice-Pres., 1992; Head of Corp. Mkting, 1993; Sandoz Pharma Ltd: Sen. Vice-Pres. and Hd of Worldwide Develt, 1994; Chief Operating Officer, 1994; CEO, 1995–96. Member, Board of Directors: PepsiCo, Inc., 2002–; American Express Co., 2012–; XBiotech, 2014–18; mPharma, 2019–. Member: Internat. Bd of Govs, Peres Center for Peace in Israel; Bd of Trustees, Carnegie Endowment for Internat. Peace; Internat. Business Leaders Adv. Council for Mayor of Shanghai.

**VASEY, Terence,** CMG 2004; Chief Executive, British Leprosy Relief Association, 1991–2010; *b* 5 Sept. 1944; *s* of Thomas William Vasey and Hannah Mary Vasey (*née* Wilkinson); *m* 1976, Margarita Pradera de Mendivil. *Educ:* Heythrop Coll., London (BA (Philos. and Theol.) 1968); Southampton Univ. (Dip. Social Work). CQSW 1976. Principal Social Worker, Emergency Services, London Borough of Hackney, 1969–82; Hd of Therapy and Social Work Co-ordinator, Dartmouth House Centre, London, 1982–85; Country Co-ordinator, Bolivia and Brazil, UNA Internat Service, 1985–90. KLJ 2005 (CLJ 1998). *Recreation:* diving. *Address:* 4 Irvine Road, Colchester, Essex CO3 3TR. *T:* 07709 955412.

**VASSALL-ADAMS, Guy Luke;** QC 2016; *b* London, 11 Oct. 1969; *s* of Dr Paul Rory Vassall-Adams and Dr Nicola Vassall-Adams (*née* Lissau); *m* 2005, Mariana Goetz; one *s* one *d*. *Educ:* St Catherine's Coll., Oxford (BA Hons PPE 1992); Univ. of Essex (LLM Internat. Human Rights Law); Coll. of Law. Researcher: LWT, 1992–93; Oxfam GB, 1993–94; Humanitarian Affairs Officer, UN, 1995–97; called to the Bar, Middle Temple, 2000; in practice as barrister, specialising in media law, 2000–. *Publications:* Rwanda: an agenda for international action, 1994. *Recreations:* family, travel, music, running, ski-ing. *Address:* Matrix Chambers, Griffin Building, Gray's Inn, WC1R 5LN. *T:* (020) 7404 3447. *E:* guyvassall-adams@matrixlaw.co.uk.

**VASSAR-SMITH, Sir John (Rathborne),** 4th Bt *cr* 1917, of Charlton Park, Charlton Kings, Co. Gloucester; Headmaster, St Ronan's Preparatory School, 1972–97; *b* 23 July 1936; *o s* of Major Sir Richard Rathborne Vassar-Smith, 3rd Bt and Mary Dawn, *d* of Sir Raymond Woods, CBE; *S* father, 1995; *m* 1971, Roberta Elaine, *y d* of Wing Comdr N. Williamson; two *s*. *Educ:* Eton. *Heir: s* Richard Rathborne Vassar-Smith [*b* 29 Dec. 1975; *m* 2013, Lydia Newhouse; two *d*]. *Address:* 24 Haywards Close, Wantage, Oxon OX12 7AT.

**VASSILIOU, Androulla;** Member, European Commission, 2008–14; *b* Pafos, Cyprus, 30 Nov. 1943; *d* of Evelthon and Lucia Géorgiades; *m* 1966, Dr George Vassos Vassiliou, *qv*; one *s* two *d*. *Educ:* London Inst. of World Affairs (Dip. Internat. Affairs 1966). Called to the Bar, Middle Temple, 1964; in practice as a barrister, 1968–88; Legal Advisor: Standard Chartered Bank, 1970–80; Bank of Cyprus, 1980–93. President: UN Assoc. of Cyprus, 1978–92; World Fedn of UN Assocs, 1991–95 (Hon. Pres., 1995); Mem., Select Internat. Gp on occasion of 50th Anniv. of UN, 1995. Pres., Cyprus Fedn of Business and Professional Women, 1996–2000. MP (United Democrats), Cyprus, 1996–2006; Alternate Rep. of Cyprus Parlt to Convention on Future of Europe, 2001–03. Vice Pres., ELDR, 2001–06. Chm., Eur. Liberal Women's Network, 2001–06. Chm., Bd of Trustees, Bank of Cyprus Oncology Centre, 2002–08. *Recreations:* listening to music, walking, swimming, reading, travelling.

**VASSILIOU, Dr George Vassos;** President of Cyprus, 1988–93; Chairman: Middle East Marketing Research Bureau Ltd, since 1963; Ledra Advertising Agency, since 1967; Aetheria Heights, since 2017; *b* 20 May 1931; *s* of Vassos Vassiliou and Fofo Vassiliou; *m* 1966, Androulla Georgiades (*see* A. Vassiliou); one *s* two *d*. *Educ:* Univs of Geneva, Vienna and Budapest (DEcon). Market researcher, Reed Paper Group, UK; Founder: Middle East Marketing Research Bureau, 1963; Ledra Advertising Agency, 1967; Middle East Centre for Management and Computing Studies, 1984; Cyprus Branch, Inst. of Directors (Hon. Sec.). Vis. Prof., Cranfield School of Management, 1985–2012. MP (United Democrats), Cyprus, 1993; Leader, Free Democrats Movt, later United Democrats, Cyprus, 1993–2005. Head, Cyprus negotiating team for accession to EU, 1998–2003. Member: Bd and Exec. Cttee, Bank of Cyprus, 1981–88; Econ. Adv. Council, Church of Cyprus, 1982–88; Educn Adv. Council, 1983–88; Inter Action Council, 1994–; Club de Monaco, 1995–2012; Trilateral Commn, 2000–. Chm. Bd, World Inst. for Develt Econ. Res. of UN Univ., Helsinki, 1999–2000 (Mem., 1995–). Mem., Bd of Govs, Shimon Peres Inst. for Peace, 1997–. Dr *hc*: Univ. of Athens; Univ. of Econs, Budapest; Univ. of Salonica; Univ. of Cyprus; Cyprus Inst. of Internat. Mgt; Univ. of Aegean, Rhodes. Grand Cross of Order of Merit (Cyprus), 2002. Grand Cross: Legion of Honour (France); Order of the Saviour (Greece); Order of Republic of Italy; Standard (Flag) Order (Hungarian People's Republic); Grand Collar, Order of Austria. *Publications:* Marketing in the Middle East, 1976; The Middle East Markets up to 1980, 1977; Towards the Solution of the Cyprus Problem, 1992; Modernisation of the Civil Service, 1992; (with Klaus Schwab) Overcoming Indifference, 1994; Towards a larger, yet more effective European Union, 1999; Cyprus—European Union: from the first steps to the accession, 2004; The Accession Story: the enlargement of the EU from 15 to 25 members, 2007; Pragmatism vs Popularism: the vision and the performance of the government (1988–1993), 2007; From the President's Office: a journey towards reconciliation in a divided Cyprus, 2010; Responsibilities Ahead: a collection of articles, speeches and interviews (1998–2009), 2010; A Contemporary Odyssey (autobiog.), 2013; Reflections for Yesterday and Tomorrow, 2014; Presidency: building the future (autobiog.), 2017; numerous articles and contribs in internat. media. *Address:* 21 Academia Avenue, Aglandjia, PO Box 22098, Nicosia 1583, Cyprus.

**VASSYLENKO, Volodymyr;** Professor of International Public Law, National University of Kyiv-Mohyla Academy, since 2010; Member, Constitutional Commission, since 2015; Auditor, Ukraine External Control Commission, National Anti-Corruption Bureau, since 2018; *b* Kyiv, Ukraine, 16 Jan. 1937; *m*; one *s* one *d*. *Educ:* Kyiv State Univ. (PhD 1964; LLD 1977). Teaching Public Internat. Law, Human Rights Law, Internat. Humanitarian Law and Law of Internat. Orgn, Ukrainian Inst. Internat. Relns, Kyiv State Univ., 1964–93 (Prof. 1978); Legal Advr to Min. of Foreign Affairs, Ukraine, 1972–93; Sen. Legal Advr to Parliament of Ukraine and Mem., Constitutional Commn, 1991–93; Ambassador to Belgium, The Netherlands and Luxembourg, and Rep. to EU and N Atlantic Co-operation Council, 1993–95; Ambassador-at-Large, Min. of Foreign Affairs, 1995–98; Ambassador to UK and (non-resident) to Ireland, 1998–2002; Permanent Rep. to IMO, 1999–2002; Judge *ad litem*, Internat. Criminal Tribunal for Former Yugoslavia, 2002–05; Advr, Minister of Foreign Affairs, Ukraine, 2005–10. Rep. of Ukraine to internat. confs; Rep. to UN Commn on Human Rights, 1989–91, 1996–98, 2005; Rep. to UN Human Rights Council, 2006–10; Mem., Ukrainian Delegn to CIS summits, 1991, 1992; Agent of govt of Ukraine, UN Internat. Court of Justice (maritime delimitation in Black Sea), 2007–09. Chm., Presidential Selection Commn for High Council of Justice of Ukraine, 2015–18. Member: Consultative Council to Min. of Justice, Ukraine; Supervisory Bd, Ukrainian Legal Foundn. Sec., Adv. and Governing Councils, 1972–78, Mem., 1978–92, Inst. Internat. Relns, Kyiv State Univ. Mem., Grand Council, Democratic People's Movement of Ukraine, 1969–91. Vice-Pres., Ukrainian Assoc. for UN, 1989–98; Co-Founder and Dep. Chm., NGO, For Ukraine in NATO, 2015–. *Publications:* International Law, 1971; *monographs:* (jtly) State Responsibility for International Offences, 1976; Sanctions in International Law, 1982; Legal Aspects of Participation of the Ukrainian SSR in International Relations, 1985; Protection Mechanisms for International Law and Order, 1986; (jtly) Fundamentals of International Law, 1988; The Ukrainian Holodomor of 1932–1933 as a Crime of Genocide: a legal assessment, 2009; Main Trends in the Development of International Human Rights Law, 2013; The Geopolitical and National Dimensions of the Language Situation in Ukraine, 2013; A War Against the Ukrainian Language, 2013; The 2014 Russo-Ukrainian War, 2014; At War As At War: tertium non datur, 3 vols, 2019; contrib. numerous articles in public internat. law and constitutional protection of human rights. *Address:* 4/6 Antonovych St, Apt 23, 01004 Kyiv, Ukraine. *T:* (050) 3859453, (44) 5262774, 4256073.

**VATER, John Alistair Pitt;** QC 2012; *b* Wallasey, 23 July 1971; *s* of Gordon Vater and Joan Vater; *m* 2002, Chloe Hubbert; one *s*. *Educ:* Birkenhead Sch.; St Peter's Coll., Oxford (Domus Scholar; BA Juris. 1993). Called to the Bar, Gray's Inn, 1995 (Lord Justice Holker Scholar); in practice as a barrister, Harcourt Chambers, specialising in family law, 1995–. Member: Midland Circuit; Family Law Bar Assoc. *Publications:* (jtly) Contact: the new deal, 2006; (jtly) The Public Law Outline: a case management compendium, 2008. *Recreations:* playing it by ear, keeping my head down, game fishing, shooting, travelling, Liverpool FC. *Address:* Harcourt Chambers, 2 Harcourt Buildings, Temple, EC4Y 9DB. *T:* (020) 7353 6961, *Fax:* (020) 7353 6968. *E:* jvater@harcourtchambers.law.co.uk.

**VAUGHAN,** family name of **Earl Lisburne.**

**VAUGHAN, Dr David Glyn,** OBE 2017; Director of Science, British Antarctic Survey; *b* Akrotiri, Cyprus, 23 Oct. 1962; *s* of Robert Garrick Vaughan and Mary Wilson Vaughan (*née* Rye); *m* Jacqueline Deborah Balchin. *Educ:* Yateley Sch., Hants; Ivybridge Sch., S Devon; Churchill Coll., Cambridge (BA Natural Scis 1984); Univ. of Durham (MSc Geophysics 1985); Open Univ. (PhD 1995). British Antarctic Survey, 1985–, incl. leading 10 field campaigns in Antarctica. Hon. Prof., Sch. of Envmt and Society, Swansea Univ., 2006–. Prog. Coordinator, EU Framework 7 Prog., ice2sea, 2009–13. Mem., Sci. Bd, NERC, 2015–. Lead author, Third Assessment Report of IPCC, 1998–2001; Coordinating

Lead Author: IPCC Fourth Assessment Report, 2004–07; IPCC Fifth Assessment Report, 2008–13. Mem., Internat. Glaciol Soc.; Hon. Mem., Royal Instn of GB. Polar Medal, 2004. *Publications:* contribs to peer-reviewed scientific jls. *Recreations:* swimming, horse-riding, sailing, leatherwork, making stuff and getting dirty. *Address:* British Antarctic Survey, Madingley Road, Cambridge CB3 0ET. *T:* (01223) 221400. *E:* dgvaughan01@gmail.com.

**VAUGHAN, Derek,** CBE 2019; Member (Lab) Wales, European Parliament, 2009–19; *b* 2 May 1961; *s* of Ivor and Marlene Vaughan; *m* 1998, Eirlys Herbert; one *s* one *d*. *Educ:* Swansea Univ. (BSc Econ. Hons). Engr, Hoover Ltd, 1977–81; civil servant, Valuation Office Agency, 1981–92; official, Public Services, Tax and Commerce Union, later PCS trade union, 1992–2004. Mem. (Lab) Neath Port Talbot BC, 1995–2010 (Leader, 2004–09). Leader, Welsh LGA, 2005–08. *Recreation:* sport (obtained 5 Welsh schoolboy caps at football).

**VAUGHAN, Elizabeth, (Mrs Ray Brown),** FRAM, FRWCMD; international operatic mezzo-soprano (formerly soprano); *b* Llanfyllin, Montgomeryshire; *m* 1968, Ray Brown (former Gen. Manager, D'Oyly Carte Opera) (*d* 2015); one *s* one *d*. *Educ:* Llanfyllin Grammar Sch.; RAM (ARAM, LRAM); Kathleen Ferrier Prize. Joined Royal Opera House; rôles in: Benvenuto Cellini; La Bohème; Midsummer Night's Dream; Madama Butterfly; Rigoletto; Simon Boccanegra; La Traviata; Il Trovatore; Turandot; Don Giovanni; Un Ballo in Maschera; Ernani; Nabucco; Aida; Cassandra; La Forza del Destino; Tosca; Idomeneo; Macbeth; Gloriana; Salome; Katya Kabanova; Hansel and Gretel; The Carmelites; Suor Angelica. Frequent appearances with: ENO; WNO; Opera North; Scottish Opera; Vienna State Opera; Deutsche Oper, Berlin; Hamburg State Opera; Metropolitan Opera, NY; Paris Opera. Professor of Singing: Guildhall School of Music, 1989–92; RNCM, 1994–96. Has toured in: Europe; USA; Australia; Canada; Japan; S America. Hon. DMus: Wales, 1987. *Recreations:* tapestry, antiques, cookery.

**VAUGHAN, Prof. John Patrick,** CBE 1998; MD; FRCPE, FFPH; Professor of Epidemiology and Public Health (formerly Health Care Epidemiology), London School of Hygiene and Tropical Medicine, University of London, 1987–2000, now Emeritus; consultant in international health; *b* 27 Dec. 1937; *s* of Thomas Frances Gerald Vaughan and Ellaline (*née* Norwood); *m* 1st, 1960, Patricia Elspeth Pooley; two *s*; 2nd, 1975, Pauline Winifred Macaulay; two step *s* one step *d*. *Educ:* Bishop Wordsworth GS, Salisbury (Holgate and Folliott Prizes); Guy's Hosp. Med. Sch. (MB BS 1961; MD 1978); London Sch. of Hygiene and Tropical Medicine (Dip. Clin. Tropical Med. 1964; Dip. Tropical Public Health (Dist.) 1969). FRCPE 1982; FFPH (FFPHM 1988). Specialist physician, Papua New Guinea, 1966–68; Head, Dept of Epidemiology and Biostats, Univ. of Dar es Salaam, 1969–73; Sen. Lectr in Epidem. and Public Health, Med. Sch., Nottingham, 1973–75; London School of Hygiene and Tropical Medicine: Sen. Lectr, 1975–83; Director: Trop. Epidem. Unit, 1975–79; Evaluation and Planning Centre, 1980–89; Reader, 1983–87; Head of Dept of Public Health and Policy, 1989–93; on secondment as Dir, Public Health Scis Div., Internat. Centre for Diarrhoeal Disease Res., Dhaka, 1995–98. Visiting Professor: Federal Univ. of Pelotas, Brazil, 1986–90 (Hon. Prof. 2013); Andalucian Sch. of Public Health, Spain, 1990–94; Aga Khan Univ. of E Africa, Faculty of Health, Nairobi, Kenya, 2015–. Specialist Advr in Public Health to World Bank, 1989; hon. consultancies include: NHS, 1975–; MRC; WHO, in foreign countries; Sen. Health and Population Advr, DFID, 1998–99; Adviser in Public Health: Perf. and Innovation Unit, Cabinet Office, 2000–01; WHO Geneva staff, 2001–02. Member: Amnesty Internat.; WWF; Dorset Trust for Nature Conservation; Trustee: Malaria Consortium (UK), 2002–07; BBC World Service Trust (UK), 2003–10; BRAC UK, 2006–10; HealthProm, 2012–. Founder and Editor, Health Policy and Planning Jl, 1985–93. Okeke and William Simpson Prizes for best student, LSHTM, 1969. *Publications:* (jtly) Community Health, 1981; (ed jtly and contrib.) Refugee Community Health Care, 1983; (jtly) Community Health Workers: the Tanzanian experience, 1987; (jtly) In the Shadow of the City: community health and the urban poor, 1988; (with R. Morrow) Manual of Epidemiology for District Health Management, 1989 (trans. French, Portuguese, Spanish, Turkish); (jtly) Health System Decentralization: concepts, issues and country experience, 1990 (trans. French, Spanish, Indonesian); (ed with C. Normand) Europe without Frontiers: the implications for health, 1993; (contrib.) Disease Control Priorities in Developing Countries, 1993; monographs on health and medicine; over 120 contribs to learned jls on internat. health and epidemiology. *Recreations:* travel, yachting, reading, art history, wild life, natural history. *Address:* Department of Public Health and Policy, London School of Hygiene and Tropical Medicine, Keppel Street, WC1E 7HT. *T:* (020) 7636 8636. *E:* jpatrickvaughan@aol.com.

**VAUGHAN, Jonathan Randal, (Johnny);** broadcaster; presenter: Capital Breakfast, London, Capital FM radio, 2004–11; Radio X, since 2015; *b* Barnet, 16 July 1966; *s* of Randal John Vaughan and Lilius Fay Vaughan; *m* 1999, Antonia Davies (marr. diss.); one *s* one *d*. *Educ:* Uppingham Sch., Rutland. *Television:* presenter: Moviewatch, 1994; Here's Johnny, 1997; The Big Breakfast, 1997–2001; Johnny Vaughan Film Show, 1999; helped launch BBC 3, 2003–04; Superstars, 2003; Johnny Vaughan Tonight, 2003; Live at Johnny's, 2004; Johnny and Denise, 2004; Passport to Paradise, 2004; My Kind of Town, 2005; Space Cadets, 2005; Car of the Year, 2008; Mud Men, 2011–13; writer: Orrible (also actor), 2001; Dead Casual, 2002; Top Buzzer, 2004; *radio:* presenter: Fighting Talk, 2003; The Warm Up with Johnny Vaughan, 2013–15. *Publications:* (with C. Murray) Fighting Talk, 2008. *Address:* c/o Independent Talent Group Ltd, 40 Whitfield Street, W1T 2RH. *T:* (020) 7636 6565. *E:* jessicastone@independenttalent.com. *Club:* Coombe Hill Golf.

**VAUGHAN, Karen;** *see* Vaughan, M. K.

**VAUGHAN, Kieran Patrick;** QC 2012; *b* Birmingham, 13 March 1970; *s* of Carmel and Damzen Vaughan; *m* 2001, Barbara; two *d*. *Educ:* St Patrick's Coll., Armagh; Univ. of Kent at Canterbury (LLB Hons). *Recreations:* Gaelic football, ski-ing. *Address:* 2 Bedford Row, WC1R 4BU.

**VAUGHAN, Michael Paul,** OBE 2006; cricketer; sports commentator and journalist; *b* 29 Oct. 1974; *s* of Graham Vaughan and Deirdre Vaughan (*née* Greenhaugh); *m* 2003, Nichola Shannon; one *s* two *d*. *Educ:* Silverdale Comprehensive Sch., Sheffield. Cricketer (right-handed batsman): Yorks CCC, 1993–2009; England: début, 1999; apptd Captain, One Day Internat. and Test teams, 2003, World Cup team, 2003; won Test series: *v* Bangladesh, 2003, 2005; *v* W Indies (home and away), 2004; *v* NZ, 2004; *v* S Africa, 2004–05; *v* Australia, 2005; resigned as Test Captain, 2008. Ranked world number one batsman, 2003. *Publications:* A Year in the Sun, 2003; Calling the Shots: the Captain's story, 2005. *Address:* c/o Phoenix Management Group Ltd, Unit 3, Owen House Farm, Wood Lane, Knutsford, Cheshire WA16 7NY.

**VAUGHAN, (Moira) Karen,** FRAM; Co-principal harp, London Symphony Orchestra, 1984–2015; Professor, since 2004, and Head of Harp, since 2010, Royal Academy of Music; Associate Artistic Director, World Harp Congress, since 2011; *b* Kirkby Lonsdale, 18 March 1950; *d* of (Douglas) Brian Vaughan and (Ethel) Moira Vaughan (*née* Kneale); *m* 1979, Adrian Evett (marr. diss. 1989); one *s*. *Educ:* James Allen's Girls' Sch., Dulwich; Alice Ottley Sch., Worcester; Royal Acad. of Music (LRAM; Performance Dip.). FRAM 2014. Harpist: Scottish Chamber Orch., 1974–78; Royal Scottish Nat. Orch., 1978–84; Prof., RSAMD, 1999–2008. Mem., Bd of Dirs, 2002–, Corp., 2011–, World Harp Congress.

*Publications:* contrib. articles to UK Harp Assoc. mag. *Recreations:* theatre, opera, home, family, friends. *Address:* Royal Academy of Music, Marylebone Road, NW1 5HT. *E:* k.vaughan@ram.ac.uk.

**VAUGHAN, Prof. Peter James,** QPM 2013; DL; Professor, and Director of Strategic Projects: Policy and Security, University of South Wales, since 2018; Lord-Lieutenant of Mid Glamorgan, since 2019 (Vice Lord-Lieutenant, 2018–19); *b* Merthyr Tydfil, 7 Sept. 1962; *s* of Cyril and June Vaughan; *m* 1986, Suzanne Journeaux; one *s* one *d*. *Educ:* Univ. of Wales, Swansea (BSc Hons); Fitzwilliam Coll., Cambridge (Dip. Applied Criminol.). Joined S Wales Police, 1984; Sgt, 1990; Insp., 1992; Chief Insp., 1996; Supt, 1997; Chief Supt, 2001; Asst Chief Constable, Wilts Police, 2003–07; Asst Chief Constable, 2007, Dep. Chief Constable, 2007–09; Chief Constable, 2010–18, S Wales Police. Chm., Acquisitive Crime Cttee, 2010–14, Vice Pres., 2013–15, ACPO; Vice Pres., Nat. Police Chiefs Council, 2015–17. Mem., Commn on Justice in Wales, 2018–. Mem. Council, Prince's Trust, Cymru, 2010–17. Chairman: Jt Emergency Services Gp Wales, 2013; All Wales Criminal Justice Bd, 2012–15. Ind. Trustee, St John's Cymru, 2014–18 (Vice Chancellor, 2017–18). DL Mid Glamorgan, 2013. Hon. Fellow, Cardiff Univ., 2014. Hon. Dr S Wales, 2015; Hon. DSc Swansea, 2016. CStJ 2016 (OStJ 2013). *Recreations:* fitness, surfing, holidays, family.

**VAUGHAN, Rt Rev. Peter St George;** Area Bishop of Ramsbury, 1989–98; Hon. Assistant Bishop, Dioceses of Gloucester and Bristol, 2002–11; *b* 27 Nov. 1930; *s* of late Dr Victor St George Vaughan and Dorothy Marguerite Vaughan; *m* 1961, Elisabeth Fielding Parker; one *s* two *d*. *Educ:* Charterhouse; Selwyn Coll., Cambridge (MA Theology 1959); Ridley Hall, Cambridge; MA Oxon (by incorporation) 1963. Nat. Service, 1949–51, Lt RAPC. Ordained deacon 1957, priest 1958; Asst Curate, Birmingham Parish Church, 1957–62; Chaplain to Oxford Pastorate, 1963–67; Asst Chaplain, Brasenose Coll., Oxford, 1963–67; Vicar of Christ Church, Galle Face, Colombo, 1967–72; Precentor of Holy Trinity Cathedral, Auckland, NZ, 1972–75; Principal of Crowther Hall, CMS Training Coll., Selly Oak Colleges, Birmingham, 1975–83; Archdeacon of Westmorland and Furness, 1983–89. Hon. Asst Bishop, Dio. of Bradford, 1998–2001; Hon. Canon: Carlisle Cathedral, 1983–89; Salisbury Cathedral, 1989–98, now Emeritus; Bradford Cathedral, 1998–2001. Commissary for Bishop of Colombo, 1984–2011. Mem., Third Order Of St Francis, 2006. *Recreations:* gardening, reading, people. *Address:* Willowbrook, Downington, Lechlade-on-Thames, Glos GL7 3DL. *T:* (01367) 252216. *E:* e.vaughan786@btinternet.com.

**VAUGHAN, Prof. Robert Charles,** FRS 1990; Professor of Mathematics, Pennsylvania State University, since 1999; *b* 1945. Imperial College, London, 1972–97: Prof. of Pure Maths, 1980–97; EPSRC (formerly SERC) Senior Fellow, 1992–96; Vis. Prof. of Maths, Univ. of Michigan, Ann Arbor, 1997–98; Dist. Vis. Prof., Univ. of York, 2008; Frederick W. and Lois B. Gehring Vis. Prof. of Maths, Univ. of Michigan, 2013–14. *Publications:* The Hardy-Littlewood Method, 1981, 2nd edn 1997; (with H. L. Montgomery) Multiplicative Number Theory I: classical theory, 2006. *Address:* Department of Mathematics, McAllister Building, Pennsylvania State University, University Park, PA 16802, USA.

**VAUGHAN, Roger,** PhD; FREng; FRINA; Chairman, Safinah Ltd, 1998–2018; *b* 14 June 1944; *s* of late Benjamin Frederick Vaughan and Marjorie (*née* Wallace); *m* 1st, 1968 (marr. diss.); three *s* two *d*; 2nd, 1987, Valerie (*née* Truelove); one step *s* (and one step *s* decd). *Educ:* Manchester Grammar Sch.; Newcastle Univ. (BSc Hons Naval Architecture and Shipbuilding 1966, PhD 1971). FREng (FEng 1990). Student apprentice, Vickers Gp, 1962; Shipbuilding Develt Engr, Swan Hunter Shipbuilders Ltd, 1970–71; Dir, 1971–81, Man. Dir, 1978–81, A&P Appledore Ltd; Dir, Performance Improvement and Productivity, British Shipbuilders, 1981–86; took part in privatisation of Swan Hunter, 1986; Joint Chief Exec., Swan Hunter, 1988–93; Chief Exec., Sch. of Mgt, Newcastle Univ., 1995–99. Non-exec. Dir, Newcastle City Health NHS Trust, 1996–2001; Dir, Northern Sinfonia Concert Soc. Ltd, 1996–2002. Vis. Prof., 2000–01, 2005–10, Res. Fellow, 2001–05, Business Sch. (formerly Sch. of Mgt), Univ. of Newcastle. Member: Nat. Curriculum Council, 1992–94; Council, Newcastle Univ., 1992–95 (Chm., Engrg Design Centre, 1990–94). Dir, Three Rivers Learning Trust, 2011–17 (Chm., 2011–14; Mem., 2011–). Pres., Shipbuilders and Shiprepairers Assoc., 1991–93. FRSA 1993. Shipbuilding Gold Medal, NECInst, 1969. *Recreations:* music, theatre, ballet, opera, sailing, walking, reading. *Address:* Correslaw, Netherwitton, Morpeth, Northumberland NE61 4NW.

**VAUGHAN, Roger Davison,** OBE 1986; FREng; General Manager, Fast Reactor Projects, National Nuclear Corporation Ltd, 1977–88, retired; Director, Fast Reactor Technology Ltd, 1984–88; *b* 2 Oct. 1923; *s* of late David William and Olive Marion Vaughan; *m* 1951, Doreen Stewart (*d* 2016); four *s*. *Educ:* University High Sch., Melbourne; Univ. of Melbourne, Aust. (BMechE). Engineer Officer, RAAF, 1945–46. Chemical Engr, Commonwealth Serum Laboratories, 1946–47; Works apprenticeship, C. A. Parsons & Co., 1948–49; Chief Engr, C. A. Parsons Calcutta, 1950–53; AERE, Harwell, 1954; Chief Engineer: Nuclear Power Plant Co., 1955–59 (Director, 1958); The Nuclear Power Group, 1960–75 (Dir, 1960–75); Manager, Technology Div., Nuclear Power Co., 1976–77. Chairman: Gas-cooled Breeder Reactor Assoc., Brussels, 1970–78; Forum on Cabinet Office Energy Review, 2002; Member: Bd, BSI, 1989–92 (Chm., BSI Engineering Council, 1983–88); BSI Standards Bd, 1992–96. FIMechE (Mem. Council, 1977–81, 1985–89; Chairman: Power Industries Div., 1985–89; Energy Jt Venture Study Gp, Engrg Council, 1996–98); FREng (FEng 1981). *Publications:* papers in jls of IMechE, Brit. Nuc. Energy Soc., World Energy Conf. *Recreations:* ski-ing, mountain walking, questionable performer on piano and clarinet. *Address:* Otterburn House, Manor Park South, Knutsford, Cheshire WA16 8AG. *T:* (01565) 632514. *Club:* Himalayan (Bombay).

**VAUGHAN, Tom;** *see* Phillips, Sir T. R. V.

**VAUGHAN JONES, Sarah Jane;** QC 2008; a Recorder, since 2004; *b* London, 20 July 1961; *d* of Dr Ronald Vaughan Jones and Pamela Vaughan Jones; three *d*. *Educ:* Trinity Hall, Cambridge (BA Law 1982). Called to the Bar, Middle Temple, 1983; in practice as barrister specialising in clinical negligence and medical law. *Recreation:* walking the Cornish cliffs. *Address:* 2 Temple Gardens, EC4Y 9AY. *T:* (020) 7822 1200. *E:* svj@2tg.co.uk.

**VAUX OF HARROWDEN,** 12th Baron *cr* 1523; **Richard Hubert Gordon Gilbey;** *b* London, 16 March 1965; *s* of 11th Baron Vaux of Harrowden and of Beverley Anne Gilbey (*née* Walton); *S* father, 2014; *m* 1996, Elizabeth Frances Worsley; two *s*. *Educ:* Ampleforth Coll.; Univ. of Aberdeen (MA Hons). ACA 1991. Sen. Manager, Price Waterhouse, 1987–97; Sen. Investment Officer, Indochina Asset Mgt, 1997–2000; Chief Financial Officer, Reech Capital plc, 2001–04; Man. Dir, Corp. Develt, Sungard, 2004–16. Elected Mem., H of L, 2017–. *Recreations:* ski-ing, walking, fishing, shooting, dogs. *Heir:* s Hon. Alexander John Charles Gilbey, *b* 17 June 2000. *Address:* House of Lords, SW1A 0PW. *E:* vaux@parliament.uk. *Club:* Kandahar Ski.

**VAUX, John Esmond George,** CBE 2009; Speaker's Counsel, House of Commons, 2000–08; *b* 3 Sept. 1948; *s* of Arthur Ernest Vaux and Marjory May Vaux; *m* 1980 Jenny Lennox; one *s* one *d*. *Educ:* Gosport Co. Grammar Sch.; Selwyn Coll., Cambridge (MA).

Legal Dept, MAFF, 1979–90 (on secondment to EC, 1983–85); Cabinet Office Legal Advr, and Hd, European Div., Treasury Solicitor's Dept, 1990–97; Speaker's Counsel (European Legislation), H of C, 1997–2000.

**VAUX, Maj.-Gen. Nicholas Francis**, CB 1989; DSO 1982; DL; Major General Royal Marines Commando Forces, 1987–90, retired; *b* 15 April 1936; *s* of late Harry and Penelope Vaux; *m* 1st, 1966, Zoya Hellings (*d* 2012); one *s* two *d*; 2nd, 2017, Mrs Hilary Smart. *Educ*: Stonyhurst College. Commissioned RM, 1954; served Suez, 1956; Far East, 1958–61; West Indies Frigate, 1962–64; Staff Coll., Camberley, 1969; MoD (Army), 1975–77; Special Advisor, USMC, 1979–81; CO 42 Commando RM, 1981–83; Falklands, 1982; RCDS, 1985. Consultant and Man. Dir, UK-Russia Security Gp, subseq. Internat. Security Co., 1993. Chm., Exeter Racecourse, 2003–11. DL Devon, 2003. *Publications*: March to the South Atlantic, 1986. *Recreation*: field sports. *Address*: National Westminster Bank, Old Town Street, Plymouth PL1 1DG. *Club*: Farmers.

**VAVALIDIS, Barbara Joan**; *see* Donoghue, B. J.

**VAVASOUR, Sir Eric (Michel Joseph Marmaduke)**, 6th Bt *cr* 1828, of Haslewood, Yorkshire; Engineer, Schneider Electric Ltd, 2012–19; *b* 3 Jan. 1953; *s* of Hugh Bernard Moore Vavasour (*d* 1989) and Monique Pauline Marie Madeleine (*née* Beck) (*d* 1982); *S* kinsman, 1997; *m* 1976, Isabelle Baudouin Françoise Alain Cécile Cornelie Ghislaine (*née* van Hille); two *s* one *d*. *Educ*: St Joseph's Coll., Stoke-on-Trent; Manchester Univ. (BSc). BCRA, 1977; Matthey Printed Products Ltd, 1979; BAL (UK) Ltd, 1985–2009: Sen. Engr, then Chief Engr, 1997–2009, Tech. Consultant, 2009, BAL Broadcast Ltd (Dir, 2001–08); Director: Faraday Technol. Hldgs Ltd, 2001–08; Hilltop Design Ltd, 2009–17. *Heir*: *s* Joseph Ian Hugh André Vavasour, *b* 22 Jan. 1978. *Address*: 15 Mill Lane, Earl Shilton, Leicester LE9 7AW.

**VAVER, Prof. David**, CM 2016; FRSC; Professor of Intellectual Property Law, Osgoode Hall Law School, York University, Canada, since 2009; *b* 28 March 1946; *s* of Ladislav and Pola Vaver; *m* 1978, Judith Maxine McClenaghan; one *s* one *d*. *Educ*: Auckland Grammar Sch.; Univ. of Auckland (BA French 1969; LLB Hons 1970); Univ. of Chicago (JD 1971); MA Oxon 1998. Called to the Bar, NZ, 1970; Asst Prof. of Law, Univ. of BC, 1971; Lectr, 1972–74, Sen. Lectr in Law, 1974–78, Univ. of Auckland; Res. Dir, later Dir, Legal Res. Foundn, Auckland, 1972–78; Associate Prof. of Law, Univ. of BC, 1978–85; Prof. of Law, Osgoode Hall Law Sch., York Univ., Toronto, 1985–98; Reuters Professor of Intellectual Property and Inf. Technol. Law, Univ. of Oxford, 1998–2008, now Emeritus; Fellow, St Peter's Coll., Oxford, 1998–2008, now Emeritus; Dir, Oxford Intellectual Property Res. Centre at St Peter's Coll., 1998–2008. Assoc. Mem., Chambers of Ian Purvis, QC (formerly of Michael Silverleaf, QC), 11 South Square, 2008–. NZ Law Foundn Dist. Vis. Fellow, 2000. Editor-in-Chief, Intellectual Property Jl, 1984–98, 2010–. Consultant on copyright law reform to Dept of Canadian Heritage, 1989–98; Mem., Intellectual Property Adv. Cttee to Minister of Trade and Industry, 2001–08. FRSC 2018. Pattishall Medal, Internat. Trademark Assoc., 2012. *Publications*: Intellectual Property Law: copyright, patents, trademarks, 1997, 2nd edn 2011; Copyright Law, 2000; numerous contribs to edited books and legal jls on intellectual property and contract law. *Recreations*: music, art, wine.

**VAVRECKA, David; His Honour Judge Vavrecka**; a Circuit Judge, since 2015; Designated Family Judge for Hertfordshire, since 2017; *b* Prague, Czechoslovakia, 7 Nov. 1967; *s* of late Dr Milan Vavrecka and Olga T. Vavrecka (*née* Simek); *m* 1995, Annabel Adcock; three *s*. *Educ*: Brentwood Sch., Essex; University Coll. London (LLB 1990; LLM 1991). Called to the Bar, Middle Temple, 1992; in practice at the Bar, specialising in family law, 1992–2015; a Recorder, 2012–15. *Recreations*: jazz, architecture, tennis, walking. *Address*: c/o Watford Family and County Court, 3rd Floor, Cassiobury House, 11–19 Station Road, Watford WD17 1EZ.

**VAYANOS, Prof. Dimitri**, PhD; FBA 2014; Professor of Finance, and Director, Paul Woolley Centre for Study of Capital Market Dysfunctionality, since 2004, and Director, Financial Markets Group, since 2017, London School of Economics and Political Science. *Educ*: Ecole Polytechnique, Paris (Dip. d'Ingenieur); Massachusetts Inst. of Technol. (PhD 1993). Asst Prof. of Econs, Stanford Univ. Grad. Sch. of Business, 1993–97; Asst Prof. of Finance, 1997–2001, Associate Prof. of Finance, 2001–04, MIT Sloan Sch. of Mgt. Dir, Financial Econs Prog., then Res. Fellow, Centre for Econ. Policy Res., 2005–11. Dir, Amer. Finance Assoc., 2012–15. *Publications*: contrib. papers to jls incl. Rev. Econ. Studies, Rev. Financial Studies, Jl Finance, Jl Econ. Theory, Qly Jl Econs, Jl Financial Econs. *Address*: Department of Finance, London School of Economics and Political Science, Houghton Street, WC2A 2AE.

**VAZ, Rt Hon. (Nigel) Keith (Anthony Standish)**; PC 2006; MP (Lab) Leicester East, since 1987; *b* Aden, 26 Nov. 1956; *s* of late Anthony Xavier Vaz and Merlyn Verona Vaz; *m* 1993, Maria Fernandes; one *s* one *d*. *Educ*: St Joseph's Convent, Aden; Latymer Upper Sch., Hammersmith; Gonville and Caius Coll., Cambridge (BA 1979); Coll. of Law, Lancaster Gate. Solicitor, Richmond-upon-Thames BC, 1982; Senior Solicitor, Islington BC, 1982–85; Solicitor, Highfields and Belgrave Law Centre, Leicester, 1985–87. Contested (Lab): Richmond and Barnes (gen. election), 1983; Surrey W (European Parlt election), 1984. Opposition front bench spokesman on inner cities and urban areas, 1992–97; PPS to Attorney Gen. and Solicitor Gen., 1997–99; Parly Sec., Lord Chancellor's Dept, 1999; Minister of State (Minister for Europe), FCO, 1999–2001. Member: Home Affairs Select Cttee, 1987–92 (Chm., 2007–16); Constitutional Affairs Select Cttee, 2002–07; Jt Cttee on Nat. Security Strategy, 2010–16; Justice Cttee, 2016–17; Internat. Trade Cttee, 2017–. Chairman: All Party Hosiery and Knitwear Gp, 1987–92; Unison Gp of MPs, 1996–99; Indo-British Parly Gp, 1997–99 (Vice Pres., 1999–); Yemen All Party Parly Gp, 1997–99, 2001–; All Party Parly Gp on Diabetes, 2015–; All Party Parly Gp on Immigration and Visas, 2017–; Vice Chairman: Tribune Gp of MPs, 1992 (Treas., 1994); PLP Internat. Develt Gp, 1997–99; All Party Parly Gp to Holy See, 2006; Treas., All Party Parly Race and Community Gp, 2006; Founder, All Party Parly Tamil Gp, 2008. Labour Party: Mem., Regl Exec., 1994–96; Chm., Ethnic Minority Taskforce, 2006–; Mem., NEC, 2007–; Trustee, Pension Regulator, 2008. Pres., India Develt Gp (UK) Ltd, 1992–. Chm., City 2020, Urban Policy Commn, 1993–99; Mem., Nat. Adv. Cttee, Crime Concern, 1989–93; Vice Chm., British Council, 1998–99. Mem., Clothing and Footwear Inst., 1998–94. Vice Pres., Assoc. of Dist Councils, 1993–97. Patron: Gingerbread, 1990–; Labour Party Race Action Gp, 2000–. Founder Patron: Naz Project London, 1999–; Next Steps Foundn, 2003; Silver Star Appeal, 2006. Jt Patron, UN Year of Tolerance, 1995; EU Ambassador, Year of Intercultural Dialogue, 2008. President: Leicester and S Leics RSPCA, 1988–99; Leicester Kidney Patients Assoc., 2000. Former Columnist: Tribune; Catholic Herald; New Life (Gujarat Samachar). *Address*: 144 Uppingham Road, Leicester LE5 0QF. *T*: (0116) 212 2028. *Club*: Scraptoft Valley Working Men's.

*See also* Rt Hon. V. C. M. Vaz.

**VAZ, Rt Hon. Valerie (Carol Marian)**; PC 2019; MP (Lab) Walsall South, since 2010; *b* Aden, 7 Dec. 1954; *d* of late Anthony Xavier Vaz and Merlyn Verona Vaz (*née* Pereira); *m* 1992, Paul John Townsend; one *d*. *Educ*: Twickenham Co. Grammar Sch.; Bedford Coll., Univ. of London (BSc); Coll. of Law (CPE and Law Soc. final exam.). Articled clerk, Herbert Smith, 1982–84; admitted solicitor, 1984; local govt solicitor, London Bors of Brent and Hammersmith and Fulham, 1985–92; Townsend Vaz Solicitors, 1992–2001; Dep. Dist Judge, 1996–2000; Treasury Solicitor's Dept, 2001–10; MoJ, 2008–09 (on secondment). Mem. (Lab) Ealing LBC, 1986–90 (Dep. Leader, 1988–89). Shadow Leader, H of C, 2016–. Member: Health Select Cttee, 2010–15; Regulatory Reform Cttee, 2010–15; H of C Governance Cttee, 2014–15; Panel of Chairs, 2015–16; Sci. and Technol. Select Cttee, 2015–16; Envmt, Food and Rural Affairs Select Cttee, 2016; H of C Commn, 2016–; Chm., All Party Parly Gp on Epilepsy, 2015–; Mem., All Party Parly Gp on Burma, on Music (Vice-Chm.); Vice-Chair, Parly Labour Party, 2010–16. Mem., Lay Adv. Panel, Coll. of Optometrists, 2007. Presenter, Network East, BBC TV, 1987. Mem., Law Soc. *Recreations*: music, playing piano and guitar, gardening, member of National Trust and Kew Gardens, Friend of New Art Gallery Walsall. *Address*: House of Commons, SW1A 0AA. *T*: (020) 7219 7176, *Fax*: (020) 7219 5045. *E*: valerie.vaz.mp@parliament.uk.

*See also* Rt Hon. N. K. A. S. Vaz.

**VEAL, Kevin Anthony**; Sheriff of Tayside Central and Fife, 1993–2014; *b* 16 Sept. 1946; *s* of George Algernon Veal and Pauline Grace Short; *m* 1969, Monica Flynn; two *s* two *d*. *Educ*: St Joseph's Primary Sch., Dundee; Lawside Acad., Dundee; Univ. of St Andrews (LLB 1966). Partner, Burns Veal & Gillan, Dundee, 1971–93; Temp. Sheriff, 1984–93. Dean, Faculty of Procurators and Solicitors in Dundee, 1991–93; part-time Tutor, Dept of Law, Univ. of Dundee, 1978–85. Mem., Court, Abertay Dundee Univ., 1998–2009 (Hon. Fellow, 2010). Musical Dir, Cecilian Choir, Dundee, 1975–; Hon. Pres., Dundee Operatic Soc., 2003–14. President: Tayside Organists' Soc., 1976–77 and 1982–83; Scottish Fedn of Organists, 2017–18. KC★HS 2007 (KCHS 1998; KHS 1989); KSG 1993. *Recreations*: choral music, organ playing, classical music. *Address*: Viewfield, 70 Blackness Avenue, Dundee DD2 1JL. *T*: (01382) 668633.

**VEALE, Sarah**, CBE 2006; Head, Equality and Employment Rights, Trades Union Congress, 2003–15; *b* Oxford, 6 June 1953; *d* of John Veale and Diana Veale; *m* 1989, Roy Collins; two *d*. *Educ*: Milham Ford Sch.; Oxford Brookes Univ. (BA Hons Eng.); Goldsmiths' Coll., London (PGCE). Vice Pres., NUS, 1982–84; various policy positions, 1985–93, Sen. Employment Rights Officer, 1994–2003, TUC. Member: Council, ACAS, 2004–11; Regulatory Policy Cttee, 2009–18; Bd, HSE, 2012–15; Bd, Equality and Human Rights Commn, 2013–17. FRSA. Hon. LLD Oxford Brookes, 2011. *Publications*: (contrib.) Adding Value Through Information and Consultation, 2005; (jtly) Statutory Regulation and Employment Relations, 2013. *Recreations*: reading, music, politics, art.

**VEASEY, Josephine**, CBE 1970; opera singer (mezzo soprano), retired; vocal consultant to English National Opera, 1985–94; *b* London, 10 July 1930; *m* (marr. diss.); one *s* one *d*. Joined chorus of Royal Opera House, Covent Garden, 1948; a Principal, on tour, in opera, for Arts Council; a Principal, Royal Opera House, Covent Garden, 1955–. Teacher of voice production, RAM, 1983–84. Has sung at Royal Opera House, Glyndebourne, Metropolitan (NY), La Scala, and in France, Germany, Spain, Switzerland, South America; operatic Roles include: Octavian in Der Rosenkavalier; Cherubino in Figaro; name role in Iphigénie; Dorabella in Così fan Tutte; Amneris in Aida, Fricka in Die Walküre; Fricka in Das Rheingold; name role in Carmen; Dido and Cassandra in the Trojans; Marguerite in The Damnation of Faust; Charlotte in The Sorrows of Werther; Eboli, Don Carlos; name role, Orfeo; Adalgisa in Norma; Rosina in The Barber of Seville; Kundry in Parsifal; Gertrude in Hamlet, 1980. Concerts, 1960–70 (Conductors included Giulini, Bernstein, Solti, Mehta, Sargent). Verdi's Requiem; Monteverdi's Combattimento di Tancredi e Clorinda, Aix Festival, 1967; various works of Mahler; two tours of Israel (Solti); subseq. sang in Los Angeles (Mehta); then Berlioz: Death of Cleopatra, Royal Festival Hall, and L'enfance du Christ, London and Paris; Rossini's Petite Messe Solennelle, London and Huddersfield (with late Sir Malcolm Sargent); Handel's Messiah, England, Munich, Oporto, Lisbon; Berlioz's Romeo and Juliette, London, and Bergen Festival; Rossini's Stabat Mater, Festival d'Angers and London, 1971; Berlioz's Beatrice and Benedict, NY, and London; Emperor in 1st perf. Henze's We Come to the River, Covent Garden, 1976. Has sung Elgar's Dream of Gerontius all over England. Hon. RAM 1972.

**VEAZEY, Janis Mary**; *see* Kelly, J. M.

**VEDERAS, Prof. John Christopher**, PhD; FRS 2009; FRS(Can) 1997; University Professor of Chemistry, University of Alberta, since 2000; *b* Detmold, Germany, 19 Feb. 1947; *s* of Joseph and Irene Vederas; *m* 1991, Andrea A. Opgenorth; one *s*. *Educ*: Stanford Univ. (BSc); Massachusetts Inst. of Technol. (PhD). Postdoctoral Fellow: Univ. of Basel, 1973–76; Purdue Univ., 1976–77; Asst Prof., 1977–82, Associate Prof., 1982–87, Prof., 1987–, Univ. of Alberta; Canada Res. Chair in Bioorganic and Medicinal Chem., 2001–. Pres., Canadian Soc. for Chem., 2002–03. Mem. Council, NSERC, 2001–04. Chair: CIC, 2015–16; Amer. Peptide Symposium, 2017. *Publications*: contribs to Desktop Edns in Chem., Topics in Current Chem., and major scientific jls; 23 patents. *Recreations*: music, film, travel, literature. *Address*: Department of Chemistry, University of Alberta, Edmonton, AB T6G 2G2, Canada. *T*: (780) 4925475, *Fax*: (780) 4928231. *E*: john.vederas@ualberta.ca.

**VEDI, Anu Kiran**, CBE 2005; strategic and property consultant, since 2009; Group Chief Executive, Genesis Housing Group, 1999–2009; *b* 10 Feb. 1955; *s* of late Jagjeet Singh Vedi and Bimla Vedi; *m* 1980, Shobhana Chadha; two *s*. *Educ*: Duke of Gloucester Sch., Nairobi; Cranford Sch., Middlesex. Chartered Accountant, 1980; Director of Finance: Ealing Family Housing Assoc., 1982–86; Sanctuary Housing Assoc., 1986–88; Paddington Churches Housing Assoc., 1988–99. Member: Adv. Bd, Relationships Foundn, 2005–; Bd, Dolphin Square Foundn, 2005–10. Trustee, World Child Cancer, 2010–. *Recreations*: sports, reading, family. *Address*: Silver Springs, Over The Misbourne, Denham UB9 5DR. *E*: a1akv@hotmail.co.uk.

**VEDRINE, Hubert Yves Pierre**; Managing Partner, Hubert Vedrine Conseil, since 2003; *b* 31 July 1947; *s* of Jean and Suzanne Vedrine; *m* 1974, Michèle Froment; two *s*. *Educ*: Lycée Albert-Camus; Univ. of Nanterre; Institut d'Etudes Politiques; Ecole Nationale d'Administration. Chargé de mission, Min. of Culture, 1974–78; Head, Dept of Architecture, Min. of the Envmt, 1978–79; Co-ordinator, Cultural Relations, Near and Middle East, Min. of Foreign Affairs, 1979–81; Head, Dept for Technical Co-operation on Health, Housing, Public Admin and Human Science, 1979–81; Technical Advr on External Affairs (diplomatic and visa), Office of Sec.-Gen. of the Pres., 1981–86; Maître des requêtes, Conseil d'Etat, 1986; Advr and Spokesman, 1988–91, Sec.-Gen., 1991–95, Office of the Pres.; Partner, Jeantet & Associés, barristers, 1996–97; Minister of Foreign Affairs, 1997–2002. *Publications*: Mieux aménager sa ville, 1979; Les Mondes de François Mitterrand, 1996; (with D. Moïsi) Les Cartes de la France à l'Heure de la Mondialisation, 2000; Face à l'hyperpuissance, 2003; François Mitterrand: un dessein, un destin, 2005; Continuer l'Histoire, 2007; Le temps des chimères, 2010; Dans la mêlée mondiale: 2009–12, 2012; La France au défi, 2014; Le monde au défi, 2016; Comptes à rebours, 2018; Face au chaos: sauver l'Europe!, 2019; with P. Boniface: Atlas du Monde Global, 2008; Atlas des crises et des conflits, 2009; Atlas de la France, 2011. *Address*: 15 Rue de Laborde, 75008 Paris, France.

**VEEDER, Van Vechten;** QC 1986; *b* 14 Dec. 1948; *s* of John Van Vechten Veeder and Helen Letham Townley; *m* 1st, 1970; one *s* one *d*; 2nd, 1991, Marie Lombardi; one *d*. *Educ:* Ecole Rue de la Ferme, Neuilly, Paris; Clifton College, Bristol; Jesus College, Cambridge. Called to the Bar, Inner Temple, 1971, Bencher, 2000; a Recorder, 2000–06. *Recreations:* sailing, travelling, reading. *Address:* Essex Court Chambers, 24 Lincoln's Inn Fields, WC2A 3EG. *T:* (020) 7813 8000, *Fax:* (020) 7813 8080. *Clubs:* Garrick; Myopia (Mass).

**VEITS, Peter John;** a District Judge (Magistrates' Courts), since 2011; *b* Liverpool, 18 July 1958; *s* of Arthur and Patricia Veits; *m* 1976, Catherine Fabian; two *d*. *Educ:* Litherland High Sch., Liverpool; Manchester Poly. (Dip. Magisterial Law 1982). Called to the Bar, Gray's Inn, 1985; Magistrates' Court Clerk, Liverpool, Ripon, S Sefton and Nottingham, 1977–89; Dep. Justices' Clerk, 1989–91, Justices' Clerk, 1991–2011, Lincoln; a Dep. Dist Judge, 2000–11. Pres., Justices' Clerks' Soc., 2007–08. Asst Ed., Wilkinson's Road Traffic Offences, 2011–. *Recreations:* hill-walking, family, grandchildren. *Address:* Lincoln Magistrates' Court, 358 High Street, Lincoln LN5 7QA.

**VEL, Mary Elaine;** *see* Hammond, M. E.

**VELTMAN, Prof. Dr Martinus Justinus Godefridus;** McArthur Professor of Physics, University of Michigan, 1981–97, Emeritus Professor, since 1997; *b* Netherlands, 27 June 1931; *s* of Gerard P. H. Veltman and Goverdina Veltman; *m* 1960, Anna M. M.; two *s* one *d*. *Educ:* Univ. of Utrecht (PhD 1963). Fellow and Staff Mem., CERN, Geneva, 1961–66; Prof. of Theoretical Physics, Univ. of Utrecht, 1966–81. High Energy Physics Prize, Eur. Physics Soc., 1993; Nobel Prize for Physics, 1999. Comdr, Order of Dutch Lion (Netherlands), 1999; Officier, Légion d'Honneur (France), 2000. *Publications:* Diagrammatica, 1994; Facts and Mysteries in Particle Physics, 2002. *Recreation:* billiards. *Address:* Nikhef, PO Box 41882, 1009 DB Amsterdam, Netherlands. *Club:* Probus '83 (Bilthoven, Netherlands).

**VENABLES, Prof. Anthony James,** CBE 2009; DPhil; FBA 2005; BP Professor of Economics and Director, Oxford Centre for the Analysis of Resource Rich Economies, University of Oxford, since 2007; Fellow of New College, Oxford, since 2007; *b* 25 April 1953; *s* of John Stuart Venables and Phyllis (*née* Cox); *m* 1983, Patricia Rice, *qv*; one *s* one *d*. *Educ:* Clare Coll., Cambridge (MA); St Antony's Coll., Oxford (BPhil); Worcester Coll., Oxford (DPhil 1984). Lecturer in Economics: Univ. of Essex, 1978–79; Univ. of Sussex, 1979–88; Eric Roll Prof. of Econ. Policy, Univ. of Southampton, 1988–92; Prof. of Internat. Econs and Dir, Globalization Prog., Centre for Econ. Perf., LSE, 1992–2007. Ed., Eur. Econ. Rev., 1991–95. Res. Manager, Trade Gp, World Bank, Washington, 1998–99; Chief Economist, DFID, 2005–08. Res. Fellow, 1984–, Co-Dir, Internat. Trade Prog., 1994–2003, Trustee, 2013–, Centre for Econ. Policy Res., London. Specialist Advr, H of L Select Cttee on Econ. Affairs, 2001–02; Adviser: HM Treasury, 2001–02; DfT, 2014–. Member: Econs Res. Adv. Bd, GLA, 2003–; Adv. Bd, Regl Growth Fund, 2011–; Council, British Acad., 2013–. Fellow: Econometric Soc., 2003; Regl Sci. Assoc. Internat., 2009. *Publications:* (jtly) The Spatial Economy: cities, regions and international trade, 1999; (jtly) Multinational Firms in the World Economy, 2004; contrib. acad. jls in internat. econs, econ. geography, develt econs and resource econs. *Address:* Department of Economics, Manor Road, Oxford OX1 3UQ.

**VENABLES, Rt Rev. Cameron David;** an Assistant Bishop, Diocese of Brisbane, since 2014; *b* Bangor, NI, 15 March 1965; *s* of Peter Arthur Goode Venables and Jennifer Anne Venables (*née* Davidson); *m* 1998, Katherine Rebecca Doulin; one *s* two *d*. *Educ:* Wilson's Grammar Sch.; Wolverhampton Poly. (BA Hons); Brisbane Coll. of Theology (BTh). Ordained deacon, 1993, priest, 1995; Asst Curate, Bundaberg, 1994–95; Foundn Chaplain, St Luke's Anglican Sch., 1994–95; PNG-Popondota Diocesan Youth Co-ordinator, 1996–2000; Associate Priest, Lismore, 2000–03; Anglican Chaplain, Lismore Campus, Southern Cross Univ., 2001–03; Ministry Co-ordinator, Fitzroy Ministry Cluster, 2004–05; Rector, All Saints' Community, Anglican Parish of N Rockhampton, 2005–14; Canon, St Paul's Cathedral, Rockhampton, 2008–12; Chaplain, Rockhampton Grammar Sch., 2010–14; Archdeacon and Vicar Gen., Dio. of Rockhampton, 2012–14. Member: Anglican Bd of Mission Develt Cttee, 2002–14; Sanctuary, Central Queensland, 2005–14; Sudanese Anglican Council, Anglican Ch of Southern Qld, 2015–; Community Services Commn, Anglican Ch of Southern Qld, 2016–; Toowoomba Interfaith Wkg Gp, 2016–. *Recreations:* piano, guitar, reading, gardening, walking. *Address:* PO Box 2600, Toowoomba, Qld 4350, Australia. *T:* (7) 46147050, 0419784456. *E:* cvenables@anglicanchurchsq.org.au. *W:* www.facebook.com/Cam Venables. *Club:* United Service (Brisbane).

**VENABLES, Most Rev. Gregory James;** *see* Argentina, Bishop of.

**VENABLES, Jean,** CBE 2010 (OBE 2004; MBE 1997); CEng, FREng; FICE; Director, Venables Consultancy Services Ltd, since 1988; *b* 11 June 1948; *d* of Denis and Zena Edwards; *m* 1970, Roger Kendrick Venables; two *s*. *Educ:* Imperial College, London (BSc(Eng); MSc). CEng 1974, FREng 2006; MCIWEM 1995; FICE 1998; CEnv 2004. Sen. Lectr in Civil Engrg, Kingston Poly., 1975–94; Chm., Crane Envmtl, 1994–2016; Chief Exec., Assoc. of Drainage Authorities, 2003–15. Non-exec. Dir, Hydraulics Res. Wallingford, 2011–17. Visiting Lecturer: Southampton Univ., 2006–14; Imperial Coll., London, 2007–16; Strathclyde Univ., 2008–11; Vis. Prof., Coventry Univ., 2017–. Chairman: Thames Regl Flood Defence Cttee, 1994–2003; Thames Estuary Partnership, 2003–10; Customer Challenge Gp, Sutton and E Surrey Water, 2012–16; Nuclear Liabilities Fund, 2014–16; Mem., Anglian (Central) Regl Flood and Coastal Cttee, Envmt Agency, 2018–. Mem., Technical Commn, 2010–, Council, 2013–, RNLI. Vice Pres., 2007–08, Pres., 2008–09, Chair, Professional Conduct Panel, ICE, 2010–16; Mem. Council, 2010–14, Mem. Educn Cttee, RAEng, 2014–18. Pres., IESF, 2018. Chair, Civil Engrs Club, 2015–18. FCGI 2002. Foundn Gov., Tiffin Sch., Kingston upon Thames, 2010–16. Liveryman, Co. of Engrs, 2006– (Mem., Ct of Assts, 2009–16). Hon. DSc: Nottingham, 2005; Kent, 2012; Abertay, 2018; Hon. DEng Kingston, 2006. *Publications:* Preparing for the Professional Reviews of the ICE, 1995. *Recreations:* walking, gardening, seeing friends and family, travelling. *Address:* Brackendale, Clay Close Lane, Impington, Cambridge CB24 9NE.

**VENABLES, Patricia;** *see* Rice, P.

**VENABLES, Robert;** QC 1990; *b* 1 Oct. 1947; *s* of Walter Edwin Venables, MM, and Mildred Daisy Robson Venables. *Educ:* Merton Coll., Oxford (MA); London School of Economics (LLM). FTII. Called to Bar, Middle Temple, 1973, Bencher, 1999; private practice as barrister, 1976–. Lecturer: Merton Coll., Oxford, 1972–75; UCL, 1973–75; Official Fellow and Tutor in Jurisprudence, St Edmund Hall, Oxford, and CUF Lectr, Oxford Univ., 1975–80; Fellow, St Edmund Hall, Oxford, 1992–. Chartered Institute of Taxation: Council Mem, 1999–2011; Chartered Tax Adviser, 1999. Chm., Revenue Bar Assoc., 2001–05. Pres., Key Haven Pubns Ltd (formerly Key Haven Pubns plc), 1990–. Treasurer, CRUSAID, 1991–96 (Pres. Council, 1996–); Director: Yves Guihannec Foundn, 1992–; Temple Music Foundn, 2004–; Trustee, Morris Venables Charitable Foundn, 2004–. Consulting Editor: Personal Tax Planning Review; Corporate Tax Review; Offshore and Internat. Taxation Review; EC Tax Jl; Taxation Ed., Charities Law and Practice Review. *Publications:* Inheritance Tax Planning, 1986, 4th edn 2000; Preserving the Family Farm, 1987, 2nd edn 1989; Non-Resident Trusts, 1988, 8th edn 2000; Tax Planning and Fundraising for Charities, 1989, 3rd edn 2000; Hold-Over Relief, 1990; The Company Car, 1990; Tax Planning Through Trusts—Inheritance Tax, 1990; National Insurance Contributions Planning, 1990; Capital Gains Tax Planning for Non-UK Residents, 1991, 3rd edn 1999; The Family Home, 2002; The Taxation of Trusts, 2006, 3rd edn 2009; The Taxation of Foundations, 2010; The Taxation of Trusts, 2010. *Recreation:* music making. *Address:* Tax Chambers, 15 Old Square, Lincoln's Inn, WC2A 3UE. *T:* (020) 7242 2744, *Fax:* (020) 7831 8095. *E:* taxchambers@15oldsquare.co.uk. *Club:* Athenæum.

**VENABLES, Robert Michael Cochrane;** Consultant, Bircham Dyson Bell (formerly Bircham & Co.), Solicitors, 1997–2007; *b* 8 Feb. 1939; *s* of late Cdre Gilbert Henry Venables, DSO, OBE, RN and Muriel Joan Haes; *m* 1972; two *s* two *d*. *Educ:* Portsmouth Grammar Sch. Admitted solicitor, 1962; in private practice, London, Petersfield and Portsmouth, 1962–70; Treasury Solicitor's Department: Legal Asst, 1970; Sen. Legal Asst, 1973; Asst Treasury Solicitor, 1980; Charity Comr, 1989–97. Adminr, Cobbe Collection Trust, 1997–99. Mem. Council, Law Soc., 1993–2001; Pres., City of Westminster Law Soc., 1997–98. Trustee: Incorp. Council of Law Reporting for Eng. and Wales, 1999–2010; LawCare (formerly SolCare), 1997– (Chm., 1998–2003, 2005–07); Old Portmuthian Charity, 1999–2018. Mem., FDA, 1974–97 (Chm., Legal Sect., 1981–83; Mem., Exec. Cttee, 1981–83, 1987–92). Ind. Co-opted Mem., Standards Cttee, E Hants DC, 2002–12 (Chm., 2004–12). Vis. Prof. of Charity Law, London S Bank Univ., 2005–08. Pres., Petersfield Dist, Scout Assoc., 2013– (Dist Sec., 2009–11). Trustee: Helios Foundn for Sustainable Energy, 2010–16; Winton House Centre (formerly Trust), 2011–; Steep Allotments Charity, 2012–16; E Hants CAB, 2012–17. FRSA 1995. *Recreations:* opera, theatre, collecting domestic anachronisms. *Address:* c/o Bircham Dyson Bell LLP, 50 Broadway, SW1H 0BL.

**VENABLES, Terence Frederick;** Owner, Hotel La Escondida, Alicante; Assistant Coach, England football team, 2006–07; *b* 6 Jan. 1943; *m* Yvette; two *d*. *Educ:* Dagenham. Played at football clubs: Chelsea, 1958–66 (Captain, 1962); Tottenham Hotspur, 1966–68 (winners FA Cup 1967); Queen's Park Rangers, 1968–73; represented England at all levels; Club Manager: Crystal Palace, 1976–80 (took club from 3rd Div. to top of 1st Div.); QPR, 1980–84 (won 2nd Div. title, 1980); Barcelona, 1984–87 (won Spanish championship, 1984); Tottenham Hotspur, 1987–93 (won FA Cup, 1991; Chief Exec., 1991–93); Coach: England football team, 1994–96; Australian football team, 1996–98; Chm., Portsmouth FC, 1996–98; Head Coach, Crystal Palace FC, 1998–99; Coach, Middlesbrough FC, 2000–01; Manager, Leeds Utd FC, 2002–03. Chm., Acad. of Dreams, 2012. *Publications:* They Used to Play on Grass, 1971; (with Gordon Williams) TV detective series Hazell: Hazell plays Solomon, 1974; Hazell and the Three Card Trick, 1975; Hazell and the Menacing Jester, 1976; (with Neil Hanson) Terry Venables: the Autobiography, 1994; (with Jane Nottage) Venables' England, 1996; The Best Game in the World, 1996; Born to Manage, 2014.

**VENABLES-LLEWELYN, Sir John (Michael) Dillwyn-,** 4th Bt *cr* 1890; farmer, since 1975; *b* 12 Aug. 1938; *s* of Sir Charles Michael Dillwyn-Venables-Llewelyn, 3rd Bt, MVO, and Lady Delia Mary Dillwyn-Venables-Llewelyn, *gd* of 1st Earl St Aldwyn; *S* father, 1976; *m* 1st, 1963, Nina (marr. diss. 1972), *d* of late Lt J. S. Hallam; two *d*; 2nd, 1975, Nina Gay Richardson Oliver (*d* 1995); one *d* decd; 3rd, 2005, Carolyn I'Anson. *Recreation:* racing vintage cars. *Address:* Llysdinam, Newbridge-on-Wye, Llandrindod Wells, Powys LD1 6NB.

**VENDLER, Helen Hennessy,** PhD; author and poetry critic; Porter University Professor, Harvard University, 1990–2018, now Professor Emerita; *b* Boston, Mass, 30 April 1933; *d* of George and Helen Hennessy (*née* Conway). one *s*. *Educ:* Emmanuel Coll., Boston, Mass (AB 1954); Harvard Univ. (PhD 1960). Instructor, Cornell Univ., 1960–63; Lectr, Swarthmore Coll. and Haverford Coll., Pa, 1963–64; Asst Prof., Smith Coll. Northampton, Mass, 1964–66; Associate Prof., 1966–68, Prof., 1968–85, Boston Univ.; Harvard University: Kenan Prof., 1985–90; Associate Acad. Dean, 1987–92; Sen. Fellow, Harvard Soc. Fellows, 1981–93. Fulbright Lectr, Univ. of Bordeaux, 1968–69; Vis. Prof., Harvard Univ., 1981–85. Poetry Critic, New Yorker, 1978–95. Member: Educnl Adv. Bd, Guggenheim Foundn, 1991–2001; Pulitzer Prize Bd, 1991–2000. Jefferson Lectr, NEH, 2004. Overseas Fellow, Churchill Coll., Cambridge, 1980; Stewart Parnell Fellow, Magdalene Coll., Cambridge, 1996, Hon. Fellow, 1996. Holds numerous hon. degrees, including: DLitt: Columbia, 1990; Harvard, Washington, 1991; DHL: Toronto, 1992; TCD, 1993; Cambridge, 1997; NUI, 1998; QUB, 2010. Awards include: Nat. Book Critics Award, 1980; Keats-Shelley Assoc. Award, 1994; Truman Capote Award, 1996; Jefferson Medal, APS, 2000. *Publications:* Yeats's Vision and the Later Plays, 1963; On Extended Wings: Wallace Stevens' longer poems, 1969; The Poetry of George Herbert, 1975; Part of Nature, Part of Us, 1980; The Odes of John Keats, 1983; Wallace Stevens: words chosen out of desire, 1984; (ed) Harvard Book of Contemporary American Poetry, 1985; Voices and Visions: the poet in America, 1987; The Music of What Happens, 1988; Soul Says, 1995; The Given and the Made, 1995; The Breaking of Style, 1995; Poems, Poets, Poetry, 1995; The Art of Shakespeare's Sonnets, 1997; Seamus Heaney, 1998; Coming of Age as a Poet, 2003; Poets Thinking, 2004; Invisible Listeners, 2005; Our Secret Discipline, 2007; Last Looks, Last Books, 2010; Dickinson: selected commentaries, 2010; The Ocean, the Bird, and the Scholar, 2015. *Address:* Department of English, Harvard University, Barker Center, 12 Quincy Street, Cambridge, MA 02138–3929, USA.

**VENESS, Sir David (Christopher),** Kt 2005; CBE 2000; QPM 1994; Under-Secretary-General for Safety and Security, United Nations, 2005–09; *b* 20 Sept. 1947; *m*; three *c*. *Educ:* Raynes Park Co. Grammar Sch.; Trinity Coll., Cambridge (BA 1975; LLB 1976). Joined Metropolitan Police, 1966; CID officer, 1969; detective in N, E and Central London; Detective Chief Supt in Fraud Squad and Crime Ops Gp; Comdr, 1987, served with Royal and Diplomatic protection, until 1990; rcds, 1990; Comdr, Public Order, Territorial Security and Operational Support; a Dep. Asst Comr, 1991–94; an Asst Comr, 1994–2005. Co-Chm., Consultative Bd, CSSC, 2011–.

**VENGEROV, Maxim;** violinist, conductor and teacher; Polonsky Visiting Professor of Violin, Royal College of Music, since 2016; *b* 1974; *s* of Alexander Vengerov, oboist, and Larissa Vengerov; studied with Galina Turtschaninova, then Zakhar Bron; *m* 2011, Olga Gringolts; two *d*. Has performed in recitals worldwide; has appeared with major orchestras throughout the world, including: NY Philharmonic, 1991; Berlin Philharmonic; LSO; Chicago SO; LA Philharmonic; Vienna Philharmonic; San Francisco SO; Concertgebouw. Menuhin Prof. of Music, RAM, 2012–15. Ambassador for UNICEF, 1997–. Numerous recordings. First Prize: Jun. Wieniawski Competition, Lublin, 1985; Carl Flesch Internat. Violin Competition, London, 1990; Grammy Award, best instrumental soloist, 2004.

**VENKITARAMAN, Prof. Ashok,** FMedSci; Ursula Zoellner Professor of Cancer Research, University of Cambridge, since 1998; Fellow, Pembroke College, Cambridge, since 2007; Director, Medical Research Council Cancer Unit, Cambridge, since 2010 (Deputy Director, 2001–06; Co-Director, 2006–10); *s* of Prof. Avittathur R. Venkitaraman and Vasanti Venkitaraman; *m* 1984, Dr Rajini Ramana; one *s* one *d*. *Educ:* Christian Med. Coll., Vellore, India (MB BS 1984); University Coll. London (PhD 1988); MA Cantab

1993. House Physician, Christian Med. Coll. Hosp., Vellore, India, 1983–84; Fellow, Lady Tata Meml Trust, UCL and Charing Cross and Westminster Med. Sch., 1985–88; MRC Laboratory of Molecular Biology, Cambridge: Fellow, Beit Meml Trust, 1988–91; Mem., Scientific Staff, 1991–98; Fellow, New Hall, Cambridge, 1991–2007, now Emeritus. Mem., EMBO European Acad., 2004–. FMedSci 2001. *Publications:* numerous contribs to scientific and med. jls. *Address:* Medical Research Council Cancer Unit, University of Cambridge, Hills Road, Cambridge CB2 0XZ. *T:* (01223) 336901.

**VENNE, Roger André;** Queen's Coroner and Attorney, Master of the Crown Office, Registrar of Criminal Appeals, Registrar of the Courts-Martial Appeal Court and a Master of the Queen's Bench Division, 2003–11; *b* 11 June 1946; *s* of Georges and Rose Ellen Venne; *m* 1970, Katherine Winter; one *s* one *d* (and one *d* decd). *Educ:* St Mary's Coll., Southampton; Inns of Court Sch. of Law. Called to the Bar, Gray's Inn, 1972, Bencher, 2000; Legal Asst, Criminal Appeal Office, 1973–78; Sen. Legal Asst and Legal Sec. to Lord Chief Justice, 1978–80; Crown Office, 1980; Asst Registrar, Criminal Appeal Office, 1981–87; Hd, Crown Office, 1987–89; Sen. Lawyer, Civil Appeals Office, and Legal Sec. to Master of the Rolls, 1989; Lord Chancellor's Department: Head: Law Reform and Adv. Div., 1990–93; Judicial Appts Div. 2, 1993–96; Dep. Sec. of Commns, 1996–99; Hd, Civil Appeals Office, and Master, 1999–2003. Mem., Criminal Cttee, Judicial Studies Bd, 2003–08. Dep. Ed.-in-Chief, Administrative Court Digest (formerly Crown Office Digest), 1988–; an Ed., Civil Procedure (formerly Supreme Court Practice), 1989–2011. Hon. QC 2011. *Publications:* (jtly) Alderney Annals, 1992; contribs to legal jls. *Recreations:* sailing, book-collecting. *Address:* 14 St James Terrace, Winchester SO22 4PP. *Clubs:* Royal Cruising, Bar Yacht; Alderney Sailing.

**VENNER, Rt Rev. Stephen Squires;** DL; Bishop for the Falkland Islands, 2007–14; Bishop to the Forces, 2009–14; an Honorary Assistant Bishop: Diocese of Rochester, since 2010; Diocese of Europe, since 2011; Diocese of St Albans, since 2013; *b* 19 June 1944; *s* of Thomas Edward Venner and Hilda Lester Venner; *m* 1972, Judith Sivewright Johnstone; two *s* one *d*. *Educ:* Hardyes Sch., Dorchester; Birmingham Univ. (BA); Linacre Coll., Oxford (MA); London Univ. (PGCE). Curate, St Peter, Streatham, 1968–71; Hon. Curate: St Margaret, Streatham Hill, 1971–72; Ascension, Balham, 1972–74; Head of RE, St Paul's Girls' Sch., Hammersmith, 1972–74; Vicar, St Peter, Clapham and Bishop's Chaplain to Overseas Students, 1974–76; Vicar: St John, Trowbridge, 1976–82; Holy Trinity, Weymouth, 1982–94; RD of Weymouth, 1988–94; Canon and Prebendary of Salisbury Cathedral, 1989–94; Bishop Suffragan of Middleton, 1994–99; Bishop Suffragan of Dover and Bishop in Canterbury, 1999–2009. Chaplain to Lord Warden of Cinque Ports, 2004–09. Pro-Chancellor, Canterbury Christ Church Univ., 2005–09. Vice Pres., Woodard Corp., 1995–98 (Pres., 1999–2002); Co-Chm., Church of England/Moravian Contact Gp, 1996–99. Non-exec. Dir, Abbeyfield Soc., 2015–. Ambassador, Chatham Historic Dockyard, 2013–. DL Kent, 2009. Mem. Council, Greater Manchester, 1996–99, Kent, 2000–09, Order of St John. Hon. DD Birmingham Univ., 2009; DUniv Canterbury Christ Church, 2010. *Recreations:* enjoying family and friends, U3A activities, holidays and subsequent photobooks. *Address:* 81 King Harry Lane, St Albans AL3 4AS. *T:* (01727) 831704. *E:* stephen@venner.org.uk.

**VENNING, Philip Duncombe Riley,** OBE 2003; FSA; Secretary, Society for the Protection of Ancient Buildings, 1984–2012; *b* 24 March 1947; *s* of late Roger Venning and Rosemary (*née* Mann); *m* 1987, Elizabeth Frances Ann, *d* of M. A. R. Powers; two *d*. *Educ:* Sherborne Sch.; Trinity Hall, Cambridge (MA). Times Educational Supplement, 1970–81 (Asst Editor, 1978–81); freelance journalist and writer, 1981–84. Mem., Westminster Abbey Fabric Commn, 1998–. Member: Council, Nat. Trust, 1992–2001; Expert Panel, 2005–11, E of England Cttee, 2013–19, Heritage Lottery Fund. Vice-Pres., Nat. Churches Trust (formerly Historic Churches Preservation Trust), 2005–08; Founder Trustee, Heritage Link, 2002–03. Accredited lectr, Arts Soc. (formerly NADFAS), 2013–. FSA 1989; FRSA 1990. Queen Mother Meml Medal for Contribution to Craftmanship, SPAB, 2011. *Publications:* contribs to books and other pubns on educn and on historic buildings. *Recreations:* exploring Britain, book collecting. *Address:* Wyke House, Mill Lane, Docking, Norfolk PE31 8NX.

**VENNING, Robert William Dawe;** Principal Establishment and Finance Officer, Cabinet Office, 1993–96; *b* 25 July 1946; *s* of Tom William Dawe and Elsie Lillian Venning; *m* 1969, Jennifer Mei-Ling Jackson; one *s* one *d*. *Educ:* Midhurst Sch.; Univ. of Birmingham (BA Special Hons Philosophy 1968). Tutor in Philosophy, Univ. of Birmingham, 1968; Lectr in Logic and Scientific Method, Lanchester Polytechnic, 1969; Department of Health and Social Security: Admin. Trainee, 1971; Private Sec. to Minister for Disabled, 1974; Principal, 1975; Private Sec. to Minister for Health, 1981; Asst Sec., 1983; Under Sec., HA Personnel Div., DoH, 1990–93. Non-exec. Dir, Compel plc, 1990–93. *Recreations:* playing classical and flamenco guitar; electronics and computing. *Address:* 85 Oaks Avenue, Shelly Beach, NSW 2261, Australia.

**VENTER, J. Craig,** PhD; Founder, Chairman and Chief Executive Officer, J. Craig Venter Institute, since 2006; Co-Founder, Chairman and Co-Chief Scientist, Synthetic Genomics, since 2005; *b* 14 Oct. 1946; *m* Claire Fraser. *Educ:* UCSD (BS; PhD 1975). Served US Navy, Vietnam, 1967. Asst Prof., subseq. Prof., of Pharmacol. and Therapeutics, SUNY, 1976–84; Section and Lab. Chief, NIH, 1984–92; Founder, Chm. and Chief Scientist, Inst. for Genomic Res., 1992–2006; President and Chairman: Inst. for Biol Energy Alternatives, 2002–06; Center for the Advancement of Genomics, 2002–06; J. Craig Venter Sci. Foundn, 2002–06; Founder, 1998, Pres. and CSO, 1998–2002, Chm., Scientific Adv. Bd, 2002, Celera Genomics Corp.; Co-founder, 2014, CEO 2014–17, Chm., 2014–18, Human Longevity Inc. *Publications:* A Life Decoded (autobiog.), 2007; Life at the Speed of Light: from the double helix to the dawn of digital life, 2013; articles in learned jls. *Address:* J. Craig Venter Institute, 9704 Medical Center Drive, Rockville, MD 20850–3343, USA.

**VENTERS, Ewan Andrew;** Chief Executive Officer, Fortnum & Mason plc, since 2012; *b* Dunfermline, Fife, 24 Aug. 1972; *s* of Alexander Venters and Josephine Venters; *m* 1998, Jane Houghton; two *d*. *Educ:* St Serf's Sch., Edinburgh. Sainsbury's Supermarkets Ltd: Mgt trainee to Dept Manager, Fresh Produce, 1989–91; New Store Logistics Controller, 1991–92; PA to Northern Regl Dir, 1992–94; PA to Dep. Chm., J. Sainsbury plc, 1994–97; Food Buyer, Sainsbury's Supermarkets Ltd, 1997–99; Brake Bros Ltd, later Brakes: Buying Controller, 1999–2001; Commercial Dir, 2001–03; Sales Ops Dir, 2003; UK Nat. Account Dir, 2003–04; Man. Dir, White Tablecloths, 2005; Dir, Food and Restaurants, Selfridges, 2005–12. *Recreations:* food and entertaining, theatre, shooting. *Address:* Fortnum & Mason plc, 181 Piccadilly, W1A 1ER. *T:* (020) 7973 5619. *E:* Ewan.Venters@FortnumandMason.co.uk.

**VENTERS, June Marion, (Mrs R. P. Brown);** QC 2006; Senior Partner, Venters Solicitors, since 1991; a Recorder, since 1998; *b* 25 March 1957; *o d* of Douglas William Walter Venters and Lily Lydia Venters (*née* Grimwood); *m* 1994, Robin Perry Brown; one *d*. *Educ:* Honor Oak Grammar Sch.; College of Law. Admitted solicitor, 1984. Family and Civil Mediator, 2007; Resolution Accredited Specialist—domestic abuse and children advocacy, 2010–, and internat. child abduction, 2011–. Mem., Family Law Cttee, Law Soc., 2013–. Legal Business Woman of the Year, Law Soc. and Assoc. of Women Solicitors, 2009. *Publications:* Standard Letters and Forms, 1995; (contrib.) Child Care Management Practice, 2009. *Recreation:* my family. *Address:* Venters Solicitors, 7a West Street, Reigate, Surrey RH2 9BL. *T:* (01737) 229610, *Fax:* (01737) 244520. *E:* j.ventersqc@venters.co.uk.

**VENTRESS, Peter John;** Chairman: Galliford Try plc, since 2016; Bunzl plc, from April 2020 (non-executive Director, since 2019); *b* England, 3 Dec. 1960; *s* of Gordon Denis and Pauline Marie Ventress; *m* 1988, Karen Morris; three *d*. *Educ:* St Joseph's Coll., Beulah Hill, London; Greyfriars, Oxford (BA Modern Hist. and Modern Langs 1983; MA); Open Univ. (MBA 1993). Exec., NatWest Internat., 1984–86; Mktg Dir, McNaughton Paper Gp, 1986–93; Sales and Mktg Dir, Guppy Paper plc, 1993–95; Business Develt Dir, UK Paper plc, 1995–97; Man. Dir, Guppy Paper plc 1997–99; President: Buhrmann France, 1999–2002; Corporate Express Canada, 2003–05; Corporate Express Europe, 2005–07; CEO, Corporate Express NV, 2007–08; Pres., Staples Internat., 2008–09; CEO, Davis Service Group plc, then Berendsen plc, 2010–15. Non-executive Director: Premier Farnell plc, 2013–16; Softcat plc, 2015–19; BBA Aviation plc, 2016– (Sen. Ind. Dir, 2019–). *Recreations:* golf, theatre, opera, tennis. *Clubs:* Oxford and Cambridge, Farmers.

**VENTRY,** 8th Baron *cr* 1800 (Ire.); **Andrew Wesley Daubeny de Moleyns;** Bt 1797; Managing Director, Ventry Estates, since 2007; *b* 28 May 1943; *s* of Hon. Francis Alexander Innys Eveleigh Ross de Moleyns (*d* 1964) (2nd *s* of 6th Baron) and Joan (later Joan Springett), *e d* of Harold Wesley; assumed by deed poll, 1966, surname of Daubeny de Moleyns; *S* uncle, 1987; *m* 1st, 1963, Nelly Renée (marr. diss. 1979), *d* of Abel Chaumillon; one *s* two *d*; 2nd, 1983, Jill Rosemary, *d* of C. W. Oram; one *d*. *Educ:* Edge Grove; Aldenham; Berks Coll. of Agric. Farmer, 1961–81; Man. Dir, Burgie Lodge Farms Ltd, 1968–79; Sen. Partner, Scott Co. Farms Ltd, 1980–85; Pres., GlenScott Motor Controls Inc., 1986–95; Marketing Manager, Unico (UK) Ltd, 1995–2000; Real Estate Manager, Savills Riviera Estates, 2000–07. *Recreations:* shooting, stalking, photography, sailing, skiing. *Heir: s* Hon. Francis Wesley Daubeny de Moleyns, *b* 1 May 1965.

**VERANNEMAN de WATERVLIET, Jean-Michel;** historian; Ambassador of Belgium to Portugal, 2010–12; *b* Bruges, 11 July 1947; *s* of Raymond Veranneman de Watervliet and Manuela van den Bogaerde de Terbrugge; *m* 1981, Maria do Carmo; three *s*. *Educ:* Paris Inst d'Etudes Politiques; Army Reserve Officers course, Chasseurs Ardennais Regt; Univ. Libre de Bruxelles (Soc. Scis degree); Vrije Univ. Brussel (Press and Communication Scis degree). Intern, EC, Brussels, 1976; joined Diplomatic Service, 1976; trng, Foreign Min., Brussels, 1976–77 and 1977–78; Third Sec., Bonn, 1977; Dep. Hd of Mission, Brasilia, 1978–80 and 1980–81; Chargé d'Affaires, La Paz, 1980; Dep. Hd, Pol Mil. Desk, 1981–83; Ambassador, Mozambique and Swaziland, 1983–86; First Secretary: UN, NY, 1986–89; EC, Brussels, 1989–91; Consul Gen., São Paulo, 1991–94; Minister Plenipotentiary and Dep. Hd of Mission, London, 1994–97; Africa Dir, 1997–2000; Ambassador: Brasilia, 2000–03; Tel Aviv, 2003–06; Court of St James's, 2006–10. Professor: Univ. Católica de Lisboa, 2012–14; Univ. Nova de Lisboa, 2013–14. Grand Officier, Ordre de Léopold II; Commandeur: Ordre de Léopold; Ordre de la Couronne; Croix Civique de Première Classe; Grand Cross, Order of Southern Cross (Brazil); Grand Cross, Order of Merit (Portugal). *Publications:* Is the Sovereign Nation State Obsolete?, 1997; History of Africa, 2003; The Ally We All Forgot: Brazil in World War Two, 2011; Belgium in the Second World War, 2014; Belgium in the Great War, 2018. *Recreations:* reading history books, archery, ship models, yachting. *Address:* Rua Joseph Bleck 48–2A, 1494–724 Dafundo-Oeiras, Portugal; Château de Wodémont, 4608 Dalhem-Neufchâteau, Belgium. *Clubs:* Royal Anglo-Belgian; Cercle Gaulois Artistique et Littéraire (Brussels).

**VERCOE, Miranda Lucy Mary;** *see* Carruthers-Watt, M. L. M.

**VERDAN, (Hilaire) Alexander;** QC 2006; a Recorder, since 2004; a Deputy High Court Judge (Family Division), since 2009; *b* 24 May 1963; *s* of Jean Pierre Verdan and late Sonya de Vries (*née* Beasley); *m* 1987, Alexandra Mutch; three *s*. *Educ:* W London Inst. of Higher Educn (BA Hons); Poly. of Central London (Dip. Law). Called to the Bar, Inner Temple, 1987; in practice as a barrister, 1987–, specialising in family law (children). *Recreations:* cycling, ski-ing, reading, theatre, cinema, eating and drinking. *Address:* 4 Paper Buildings, Temple, EC4Y 7EX.

**VERDI, Prof. Richard Frank,** OBE 2007; PhD; Professor of Fine Art, 1989–2007, and Director, Barber Institute of Fine Arts, 1990–2007, University of Birmingham; *b* 7 Nov. 1941; *s* of Frank and Anne Verdi. *Educ:* Univ. of Michigan (BA 1963); Univ. of Chicago (MA 1966); Courtauld Inst. of Art, Univ. of London (PhD 1976). Lectr in Hist. of Art, Univ. of Manchester, 1969–71; Lectr, 1971–81, Sen. Lectr, 1981–89, in Hist. of Art, Univ. of York. FRSA 1999. *Publications:* Klee and Nature, 1984; Cézanne and Poussin: the classical vision of landscape, 1990; Cézanne, 1992; Nicolas Poussin 1594–1665, 1995; Saved! 100 Years of the National Art Collections Fund, 2003; The Parrot in Art, 2007; Rembrandt's Themes: life into art, 2014; Poussin as a Painter: from classicism to abstraction, 2019. *Recreations:* music, literature, natural history. *Address:* 42 Upland Road, Selly Park, Birmingham B29 7JS.

**VERDIRAME, Prof. Guglielmo,** PhD; QC 2019; Professor of International Law, King's College London, since 2011; *b* Reggio Calabria, Italy; *s* of Giuseppe and Antonia Verdirame. *Educ:* Univ. of Bologna (Laurea in Giurisprudenza); Sch. of Oriental and African Studies, Univ. of London (LLM); London Sch. of Econs and Pol Sci. (PhD); MA Oxon. Res. Officer, Refugee Studies Centre, Univ. of Oxford, 1997–98; Jun. Res. Fellow, Merton Coll., Oxford, 2000–02; Lectr, Univ. of Cambridge, 2003–11; called to the Bar, Inner Temple, 2006. Vis. Prof., Columbia Law Sch., 2015. Founding Co-Chair, Africa and ME Refugee Assistance, 2003–12. Trustee, Bridges to the Future, 2014–. *Publications:* Rights in Exile, 2005; The UN and Human Rights, 2011. *Recreations:* theatre, art, crossfit, travel, thermae. *Address:* 20 Essex Street, WC2A 3AL. *E:* gverdirame@20essexst.com. *Clubs:* Travellers, Beefsteak.

**VERE OF HANWORTH, Lord; James Malcolm Aubrey Edward de Vere Beauclerk;** *b* 2 Aug. 1995; *s* and *heir* of Earl of Burford, *qv*. *Educ:* Uppingham Sch.; Univ. of Kent. Model, represented by Next Models, London.

**VERE OF NORBITON,** Baroness *cr* 2016 (Life Peer), of Norbiton in the Royal London Borough of Kingston upon Thames; **Charlotte Sarah Emily Vere;** Parliamentary Under Secretary of State, Department for Transport, since 2019; *b* Malacca, Malaysia, 9 March 1969; *d* of Col Roger Vere and Karin Vere (*née* Naylor, now Terry); *m* 1st (marr. diss.); one *s* one *d*; 2nd, 2017, Michael Chattey, OBE. *Educ:* Stover Sch.; University Coll. London (BSc (Eng) Hons 1989); Kellogg Grad. Sch. of Mgt, Northwestern Univ., Ill (MBA 1997). Associate, financial services industry, 1989–99; Financial Dir, Recruit Media, 2005–07; CEO, Big White Wall Ltd, 2007–09: Finance Dir, No2AV, 2010–11; Exec. Dir, GSA, 2012–16; Interim Gen. Sec., ISC, 2014–15; Exec. Dir, Conservatives IN, 2016. A Baroness in Waiting (Govt Whip), 2016–19. Mem., Develt Bd, Oxford Mindfulness Centre, Univ. of Oxford, 2012–16. Gov., Shrewsbury Ho. Sch., 2015–19. *Recreations:* running (infrequently and slowly), singing (enthusiastically and badly). *Address:* House of Lords, SW1A 0PW. *T:* 07990 574459. *E:* charlotte@charlottevere.com.

**VERE-HODGE, Michael John Davy;** QC 1993; a Recorder, since 1989; *b* 2 July 1946; *s* of late Nicholas and Ann Vere-Hodge; *m* 1st; one *s* one *d*; 2nd, 2004, Nicola Anne Heron. *Educ:* Winchester Coll.; Grenoble Univ. Called to the Bar, Gray's Inn, 1970, Bencher, 2005. Head of Chambers, 2001–05. *Recreations:* shooting (GB Helice Shooting team, 2006; Veteran World Champion, 2015), fishing. *Address:* 3 Paper Buildings, Temple, EC4Y 7EU.

**VEREKER,** family name of **Viscount Gort.**

**VEREKER, Sir John (Michael Medlicott),** KCB 1999 (CB 1992); Independent Director: XL Group plc, since 2007; Catlin UK, since 2016; *b* 9 Aug. 1944; *s* of late Comdr C. W. M. Vereker and M. H. Vereker (*née* Whatley); *m* 1971, Judith Diane, *d* of Hobart and Alice Rowen, Washington; one *s* one *d*. *Educ:* Marlborough Coll.; Keele Univ. (BA Hons 1967). Asst Principal, ODM, 1967–69; World Bank, Washington, 1970–72; Principal, ODM, 1972; Private Sec. to successive Ministers of Overseas Develt, 1977–78; Asst Sec., 1978; Prime Minister's Office, 1980–83; Under Sec., 1983–88, and Principal Finance Officer, 1986–88, ODA, FCO; Dep. Sec., DES, then DFE, 1988–93; Perm.-Sec., ODA, subseq. DFID, 1994–2002; Gov. and C-in-C of Bermuda, 2002–07. Chm., Students Loans Co. Ltd, 1989–91. Independent Director: XL Insce Co. Ltd, 2008–15; MWH Global, 2009–15. Mem. Council, Inst. of Manpower Studies, 1989–92; Member Board: British Council, 1994–2002; IDS, 1994–2001; VSO, 1994–2002; Mem. Adv. Council, British Consultants and Construction Bureau, 2000–05; Mem., Volcker Commn on World Bank, 2007–; Gov., Ditchley Foundn for Internat. Relations, 2007–. Hon. Vice-Pres., Raleigh Internat., 2002–15. Trustee, Internat. Assoc. for Digital Pubns, 2004–09. CCMI (CIMgt 1995). FRSA 1999. KStJ 2002. Hon. DLitt Keele, 1997. *Publications:* Blazing the Trail, 2002; tech. papers for Commonwealth Secretariat and World Bank.

**VEREY, Sir David (John),** Kt 2015; CBE 2004; Chairman, Sofina SA, since 2014 (Director, since 2004); *b* 8 Dec. 1950; *s* of late Michael John Verey, TD and Sylvia Mary Verey; *m* 1st, 1974, Luise Jaschke (marr. diss. 1990); two *s* one *d*; 2nd, 1990, Emma Katharine Broadhead (*née* Laidlaw). *Educ:* Eton College; Trinity College, Cambridge (MA). Lazard Brothers: joined 1972; Dir, 1983–2001; Dep. Chief Exec., 1985–90; Chief Exec., 1990–2001; Chm., 1992–2001; Dep. Chm., Cazenove Gp Plc, 2001–02. Chairman: Blackstone Gp UK, 2004–08; Thames River Capital Ltd, 2009–10. Director: Pearson plc, 1996–2000; Daily Mail and Gen. Trust plc, 2004–14; Mem., Supervisory Bd, Bank Gutmann AG, 2002–16; Sen. Advr, Lazard & Co. Ltd, 2010–. Lead non-exec. Dir, DCMS, 2011–16. Mem., Financial Services Practitioner Panel, 2002–05. Chm., The Art Fund, 2004–14. Special Advr, Fresh Minds Ltd, 2004–10. Trustee: Tate Gall., 1992–2004 (Chm., Bd of Trustees, 1998–2004); Pilgrim Trust, 2008–14; Teaching Awards Trust, 2009–14; British Council, 2014–; West London Zone, 2016–; Chairman: Adv. Bd, Govt Art Collection, 2013–; Friends of Leighton House Mus., 2016–. Fellow, Eton Coll., 1997–2012. *Recreations:* stalking, bridge, gardening, travel.

**VERHAGEN, Maxime Jacques Marcel;** Chairman, Bouwend Nederland, since 2013; *b* Maastricht, 14 Sept. 1956; *m* Annemieke Beijlevelt; three *c*. *Educ:* Univ. of Leiden (degree in History 1986). Christian Democratic Alliance: Asst to an MP, 1984–87; joined parly staff with responsibility for Eur. affairs, develt cooperation and trade policy. Mem. (CDA) Oegstgeest Municipal Council, 1986–90 (Leader, CDA Gp, 1986–89). Mem., European Parlt, 1989–94. Mem., House of Representatives, Netherlands, 1994–2007 (Leader, CDA Parly Party, 2002–07). Minister of Foreign Affairs, Netherlands, 2007–10; Dep. Prime Minister and Minister of Economic Affairs, Agriculture and Innovation, Netherlands, 2010–12. Vice Chairman: ACP-EU Jt Assembly; Perm. Parly Cttee on Foreign Affairs. Member Board: Eduardo Frei Foundn; Netherlands Atlantic Assoc., 1996–2003; European Movement, 1996–2003; Parly Hist. Foundn, Nijmegen Univ.; Member, Supervisory Board: Free Voice; Chemelot Campus BV, 2013–. Grand Officer, Order of the Legion of Merit of O'Higgins (Chile); Grand Cross: Order of Merit (Germany), 2007; Order of the Southern Cross (Brazil), 2008; Officer, Order of Orange Nassau (Netherlands), 2012.

**VERHEUGEN, Günter,** Hon. GCVO 1998; non-executive Managing Director, European Experience GmbH, since 2010; Board Member: Ford Otosan, Turkey; Löwen Entertainment, Germany; Honorary Professor, Viadrina University, Frankfurt; *b* Bad Kreuznach, 28 April 1944; *s* of Leo Verheugen and Leni (*née* Holzhäuser); *m* 1st, Helga (*d* 1983); 2nd, 1987, Gabriele (*née* Schäfer) (marr. diss. 2011). *Educ:* studied history, sociol. and politics in Cologne and Bonn. Trainee, Neue Rhein-Neue Ruhr Zeitung, 1963–65; Head: Public Relns Div., Min. of Interior, W Germany, 1969–74; Analysis and Inf. task force, Foreign Office, 1974–76; Federal Party Manager, 1977–78, Gen. Sec., 1978–82, FDP. Mem. (SPD) Bundestag, 1983–99 (Mem., Foreign Affairs Cttee, 1983–99; Chm., EU special cttee, 1992). Chm., Socialist Internat. Peace, Security and Disarmament Council, 1997–99. Chm., Radio Broadcasting Council, Deutsche Welle, 1990–99. Joined SPD, 1982: spokesman of Nat. Exec., 1986–87; Editor-in-Chief, Vorwärts (SPD newspaper), 1987–88; Dep. foreign policy spokesman and Chm., UN wkg gp of parly gp, 1991–93; Chm., Bavarian SPD gp in Bundestag, 1993–95; Sec., parly gp, 1993; Fed. Party Manager, 1993–95; Dep. Chm., parly gp for foreign, security and develt policy, 1994–97; Chm., Kulmbach-Lichtenfels dist, 1996–99; Mem., Upper Franconia regl exec., 1996–99; Co-ordinator for internat. relns of SPD and SPD parly gp, 1997–99; Mem., Nat. Exec., 1997–. European Commission: Mem., 1999–2010; Vice-Pres., 2004–10; Co-chair, Trans Atlantic Econ. Council, 2007–10. Mem., Club for Envmt and Develt, Protestant Ch, Germany, 1998–. Dr *hc:* Vilnius; Szczecin; Wroclaw; Bratislava; Prague; Ljubljana; Cluj; Timisoara. Prizes: Schumpter, 2004; Hoegner, 2005; Polish Business Oscar, 2011; German SME, 2011; Jadwiga of Silesia, 2013. Officer's Cross, Order of Merit (Germany), 1994; Order of Merit (Bavaria), 1997; Kt Comdr's Cross, Order of Merit (Italy), 1982; Commandeur de la Légion d'Honneur (France). *Publications:* Zukunft für Deutschland, 1980; Der Ausverkauf: Macht und Verfall der FDP, 1984; (jtly) Halbzeit in Bonn: die BRD zwei Jahre nach der Wende, 1985; Apartheid, Südafrika und die deutschen interessen am Kap, 1986; Europa in der Krise, 2005; and numerous others.

**VERHOFSTADT, Guy;** Member (Lib Dem), European Parliament, since 2009; Leader, Alliance of Liberals and Democrats for Europe, since 2009; Prime Minister of Belgium, 1999–2008; *b* 11 April 1953; *s* of Marcel Verhofstadt and Gaby (*née* Stockmans); *m* 1981, Dominique Verkinderen; one *s* one *d*. *Educ:* Koninklijk Atheneum, Ghent; Univ. of Ghent (LLM 1975). Attorney, Ghent Bar, 1975–94. Pol Sec. to Nat. Pres., Party for Freedom and Progress, 1977–81; Mem. (Party for Freedom and Progress) Ghent-Ekklo, House of Reps, Belgium, 1978–84, 1985–95; Dep. Prime Minister and Minister for the Budget, Scientific Res. and the Plan, 1985–88; Pres., shadow cabinet, 1988–91; Minister of State, 1995–2008; Senator (Flemish Liberals and Democrats), and Vice Pres., Senate, 1995–99. Mem., City of Ghent Council, 1976–82, 2007–. Nat. Pres., Party for Freedom and Progress, 1982–85, 1989–92; Nat. Pres., Flemish Liberals and Democrats, 1992–95, 1997–99. Vice-Pres. and Rapporteur, Rwanda Investigation Commn, Senate, 1996–97. *Publications:* Angst, afgunst en het algemeen belang, 1994; De Belgische ziekte, 1997; De Vierde Golf, 2002; De Verenigde Staten van Europa, 2005; Het Vierde Burgermanifest, 2006; pamphlets, articles, contribs to books. *Address:* European Parliament, 60 rue Wiertz, 1047 Brussels, Belgium.

**VERITY, Anthony Courtenay Froude,** MA; Master, Dulwich College, 1986–95; *b* 25 Feb. 1939; *s* of Arthur and Alice Kathleen Verity; *m* 1962, Patricia Ann Siddall; one *s* one *d*. *Educ:* Queen Elizabeth's Hosp., Bristol; Pembroke Coll., Cambridge (MA). Assistant Master: Dulwich Coll., 1962–65; Manchester Grammar Sch., 1965–69; Head of Classics, Bristol Grammar Sch., 1969–76; Headmaster, Leeds Grammar Sch., 1976–86. Educnl Advr to Emir of Qatar, 1996. Chm., Schools' Arabic Project, 1988–96. Trustee, Dulwich Picture Gallery, 1994–96. Gov., Stonyhurst Coll., 2004–15. Editor, Greece and Rome, 1971–76. *Publications:* Latin as Literature, 1971; (trans.) The Idylls of Theocritus, 2002; (trans.) The Odes of Pindar, 2007; (trans.) Homer, The Iliad, 2011; (trans.) Homer, The Odyssey, 2016; contribs to Jl of Arabic Lit., Greece & Rome. *Recreations:* music, fell-walking, classics, the Middle East. *Address:* 14 Duncombe Hill, SE23 1QB. *Club:* Athenæum.

**VERITY, Edward Robert;** Editor, Mail on Sunday, since 2018; *b* Bradford, 19 Aug. 1965; *s* of Alan and Rowan Verity; *m* 2011, Joanne Hegarty; one *s*. *Educ:* Bradford Grammar Sch.; Corpus Christi Coll., Oxford (BA PPE 1987). Royal reporter, 1993–95, Femail Ed., 1996–99, Daily Mail; Editorial Dir, Associated New Media, 2000–02; Associate Ed., Mail on Sunday, 2002–04; Ed.-in-Chief, Associated Newspapers Ireland, 2004–08; Dep. Ed., Mail on Sunday, 2010–12; Associate Ed., 2012–16, Dep. Ed., 2016–18, Daily Mail. *Recreations:* football, wine, food, travel, spy novels. *Address:* Mail on Sunday, 2 Derry Street, W8 5TT. *T:* (020) 7938 6000. *E:* ted.verity@dailymail.co.uk.

**VERJEE, Baron** *cr* 2013 (Life Peer), of Portobello in the Royal Borough of Kensington and Chelsea; **Rumi Verjee,** CBE 2009; Owner and Chairman, Thomas Goode & Co., since 1995; *b* Uganda, 1957. *Educ:* Haileybury Sch.; Downing Coll., Cambridge (BA Law 1978; Hon. Fellow). Called to the Bar, Middle Temple, 1979. Founder in UK, Domino's Pizza, 1985–89. Co-Owner, Watford FC, 1993–97. Chairman: Brompton Capital Ltd, 1996–; Ipanema Properties, Brazil. Mem., Adv. Bd for 2012 London Olympic Games, British Olympic Assoc., 2007–12. Member: World Presidents' Orgn, 2008–; Chief Executives' Orgn, 2011–; Global Leadership Foundn, 2013–. Founder, Rumi Foundn, 2006. Chm., WE (formerly Free the Children) UK, 2015– (Co-Chm., WE Day UK, 2014–). Patron, Think Equal, 2016–. *Address:* Rumi Foundation, Clutha House, 10 Storey's Gate, SW1P 3AY.

**VERMA,** Baroness *cr* 2006 (Life Peer), of Leicester in the County of Leicestershire; **Sandip Verma;** *b* 30 June 1959; *d* of S. S. and R. Rana; *m* 1977, Ashok Kumar Verma; one *s* one *d*. *Educ:* locally. Senior Partner, Domiciliary Care Services, 2000. Contested (C): Hull E, 2001; Wolverhampton SW, 2005. House of Lords: Opposition spokesperson on health, educn and skills, 2006–07, on innovation, univs and skills, 2007–10, on children, schs and families, 2007–08, 2009–10; an Opposition Whip, 2006–10; a Baroness in Waiting (Govt Whip), 2010–12; govt spokesman for Cabinet Office, 2010–12, internat. develt, 2010–11, women and equalities, 2010–12, business, innovation and skills, 2011–12; Parly Under-Sec. of State, DECC, 2012–15, DFID, 2015–16. Advr, Bright Distributors Ltd, 2006–10. Exec. Mem., Ethnic Diversity Council, 2005–. Chm. (Political), Leics South Cons. Assoc., 2006–08; Pres., City of Leics Cons. Assoc., 2008–09, 2010–11. Champion, Roko Breast Cancer, 2006–; Patron: Tory Reform Group, 2006–; Cons. British Asian Link, 2006–; Pakistan-India Friendship Soc., 2006–; Bucks Punjabi Internat. Soc., 2006–. *Recreations:* socialising, reading, walking, going to different parts of the world, arranging events, watching cricket. *Address:* House of Lords, SW1A 0PW. *T:* (office) (020) 7219 5216, (home) (0116) 270 1686, *Fax:* (0116) 270 1603. *E:* Vermas@parliament.uk.

**VERMONT, Christopher John;** Chairman, BPL (Holdings) Ltd, since 2019; *b* London, 16 Dec. 1959; *s* of David Neville Vermont and Ann Marion Vermont (*née* Wilson); *m* 1987, Sarah Webster; one *s* three *d*. *Educ:* St Paul's Sch., Barnes; Magdalene Coll., Cambridge (BA Social and Pol Scis 1982; MA). Manager, Internat., ANZ Grindlays Bank, London, Calcutta, Delhi, 1982–90; Head: Origination and Syndication, ANZ Bank Ltd, 1991–2000; Primary Mkts, 2001, Project and Structured Finance, 2002–03, Debt Solutions, 2003–04, ANZ Investment Bank; Head, Debt Capital Markets, then Head of GuarantCo, later CEO, GuarantCo, Frontier Markets Fund Managers, 2007–16. Non-executive Director: Art Circuit, 2007–; BPL Global Ltd, 2008–; Charity Bank Ltd, 2010–16 (Trustee, 2010–); Chm., Assets and Liabilities Cttee, 2010–13; Mem., Adv. Panel, 2016–); Long Acre Estates Ltd, 2013–17; InfraCredit Nigeria Ltd, 2017– (Chm., New Business Cttee and Credit Cttee). Sen. Expert in connection with setting up of Eur. Fund for Sustainable Develt, EC, 2017–18. Gov., St Paul's Sch., Barnes, 2010– (Member: Educn Cttee, 2011–14; Investment Sub-Cttee, 2013–; Finance Cttee, 2014– (Chm., 2018–); Chm., Treasury Cttee, 2017–). Mem. Ct, Mercers' Co., 2014– (Member: Finance Cttee, 2007–; Investment Sub-Cttee, 2009–13; Upper Warden, 2019–). *Recreations:* gardening (vegetables), log splitting, tennis, swimming, classic cars. *E:* chris@chrisvermont.com.

**VERMUNT, Prof. Jan Dominicus Hyacinthus,** PhD; Professor of Learning and Innovation, Eindhoven University of Technology, Netherlands, since 2018; *b* Breda, Netherlands, 16 Feb. 1957; *s* of Kees and Corrie Vermunt; *m* 1984, Margaret Hylkema; one *s* one *d*. *Educ:* Tilburg Univ. (MSc Psychol. and Educn (*cum laude*) 1984; PhD Psychol. (*cum laude*) 1992). Tilburg University: Res. Asst, 1984–86; Asst Prof., 1986–95; Associate Prof., Leiden Univ., 1995–99 and 2002–04; Professor: Maastricht Univ., 1999–2002; Utrecht Univ., 2004–12; Prof. of Educn, Univ. of Cambridge, 2012–18; Fellow, Wolfson Coll., Cambridge, 2013–18. Vis. Prof., Hasselt Univ., Belgium, 2002–03; Res. Fellow, Univ. of Amsterdam, 1992–95. Hon. Dr Antwerp, 2016. *Publications:* (ed jtly) Learning Patterns in Higher Education, 2014; contribs to learned jls incl. Learning and Instruction, British Jl Educnl Psychol., Learning and Individual Differences, Studies in Higher Educn, Teaching and Teacher Educn, Internat. Jl Sci. Educn, Educnl Psychol. Rev. *Recreations:* travel, cycling, music, chess. *Address:* Eindhoven School of Education, Eindhoven University of Technology, Groene Loper 3, 5612 AE Eindhoven, Netherlands. *T:* 402476197. *E:* j.d.h.m.vermunt@tue.nl.

**VERNEY,** family name of **Baron Willoughby de Broke.**

**VERNEY, Sir Edmund Ralph,** 6th Bt *cr* 1818, of Claydon House, Buckinghamshire; *b* 28 June 1950; *o s* of Sir Ralph Bruce Verney, 5th Bt, KBE and Mary (*née* Vestey); *S* father, 2001; *m* 1982, Daphne Fausset-Farquhar; one *s* one *d*. *Educ:* Harrow; York Univ. FRICS. Mem., Nat. Council, CLA, 1990–2001 (Chm., Bucks Br., 1996–99). Prime Warden, Dyers' Co., 2000–02. High Sheriff, Bucks, 1998–99. *Heir: s* Andrew Nicholas Verney [*b* 9 July 1983; *m* 2013, Alexandra Edwina Luttrell; *d* of Ronald Munro Ferguson; one *s*]. *Address:* Claydon House, Middle Claydon, Bucks MK18 2EX.

**VERNEY, (Sir) (John) Sebastian,** (3rd Bt *cr* 1946, of Eaton Square, City of Westminster; *S* father, 1993, but does not use the title and his name does not appear on the Official Roll of the Baronetage). *Heir:* none.

**VERNON,** family name of **Baron Lyveden.**

**VERNON,** 11th Baron *cr* 1762; **Anthony William Vernon-Harcourt;** founder and Chairman, Monks Partnership Ltd, 1980–2002; *b* 29 Oct. 1939; *s* of William Ronald Denis Vernon-Harcourt, OBE and Nancy Everil (*née* Leatham); *S* kinsman, 2000; *m* 1966, Cherry Stanhope, *er d* of T. J. Corbin; three *s* one *d*. *Educ:* Eton; Magdalene Coll., Cambridge. *Publications:* Archibald Sturrock: pioneer locomotive engineer, 2007; Yorkshire Engine Company: Sheffield's locomotive manufacturer, 2008; Leveson Francis Vernon-Harcourt, Civil Engineer, 2012. *Recreations:* Church of England, railway history, cycling, gardening.

*Heir: s* Hon. Simon Anthony Vernon-Harcourt [*b* 24 Aug. 1969; *m* 1999, Jessica Jane, *e d* of William Eric Faber; two *d*]. *Address:* Monks Farm, Debden Green, Saffron Walden, Essex CB11 3LX.

**VERNON, Annette**; *see* Sharkey, A.

**VERNON, David Bowater**; Under Secretary, Inland Revenue, 1975–84; *b* 14 Nov. 1926; *s* of Lt-Col Herbert Bowater Vernon, MC, and Ivy Margaret Vernon; *m* 1954, Anne de Montmorency Fleming, *d* of late John and Margaret Fleming; three *s* three *d*. *Educ:* Marlborough Coll.; Oriel Coll., Oxford (MA). RA, 1945–48 (Lieut). Inland Revenue, 1951–84. *Recreation:* gardening. *Address:* 6 Hurstwood Park, Tunbridge Wells, Kent TN4 8YE.

**VERNON, Diana Charlotte**; Principal, Methodist Ladies' College, Melbourne, since 2014; *b* 30 April 1961; *d* of Roderick W. P. Vernon and late Jennifer F. F. Vernon (*née* Tyrrell). *Educ:* St Michael's, Burton Park; St Mary's Coll., Durham Univ.; King's Coll., London (PGCE). Editl Asst, John Wiley & Sons Ltd, 1982–84; Account Executive: Business Image PR, 1984–85; Grayling, 1985–87; Corporate Communications Executive: Thorn EMI, 1987–89; London Internat. Gp, 1989–93; Housemistress and Dir of PR, Downe House, Newbury, 1994–2000; Headmistress: Woldingham Sch., 2000–07; City of London Sch. for Girls, 2007–14. *Governor:* Lilian Baylis, London, 1985–2002; Flexlands Sch., Chobham, 1994–2003; St Christopher's, Hampstead, 2003–14; Conifers, Sussex, 2003–06; Notting Hill Prep. Sch., 2007–14. *Recreations:* theatre, cookery, travel, walking, cycling. *Address:* Methodist Ladies' College, 207 Barkers Road, Kew, Vic 3101, Australia.

**VERNON, Sir James (William)**, 5th Bt *cr* 1914, of Shotwick Park, Chester; business consultant; *b* 2 April 1949; *s* of Sir Nigel Vernon, 4th Bt and Margaret Ellen Vernon (*née* Dobell); *S* father, 2007; *m* 1981, Davinia Elizabeth Howard; two *s* one *d*. *Educ:* Shrewsbury. FCA. *Recreations:* shooting, fishing, vintage cars, gardening. *Heir: s* George William Howard Vernon, *b* 25 July 1987. *Address:* The Hall, Lygan-y-Wern, Pentre Halkyn, Holywell, Flintshire CH8 8BD. *Clubs:* Army and Navy, Honourable Artillery Company; Liverpool Artists; Chester City; Bentley Drivers, Vintage Sports Car.

**VERNON, Kenneth Robert**, CBE 1978; Deputy Chairman and Chief Executive, North of Scotland Hydro-Electric Board, 1973–88; *b* 15 March 1923; *s* of late Cecil W. Vernon and Jessie McGaw, Dumfries; *m* 1946, Pamela Hands, Harrow; one *s* three *d* (and one *d* decd). *Educ:* Dumfries Academy; Glasgow University. BSc, FREng, FIET, FIMechE. BTH Co., Edinburgh Corp., British Electricity Authority, 1948–55; South of Scotland Electricity Bd, 1955–56; North of Scotland Hydro-Electric Bd, 1956; Chief Electrical and Mech. Engr, 1964; Gen. Man., 1966; Bd Mem., 1970. Dir, British Electricity International Ltd, 1976–88; Mem. Bd, Northern Ireland Electricity Service, 1979–85. *Publications:* various papers to technical instns. *Recreations:* fishing, gardening. *Address:* 10 Keith Crescent, Edinburgh EH4 3NH. *T:* (0131) 332 4610.

**VERNON-HARCOURT**, family name of **Baron Vernon**.

**VERPLAETSE, Viscount Alfons Remi Emiel**; Governor, National Bank of Belgium, 1989–99, now Hon. Governor; *b* Zulte, Belgium, 19 Feb. 1930; created Viscount, 1999; *s* of Leon Verplaetse and Alida Baert; *m* 1954, Odette Vanhee; three *s* two *d*. *Educ:* Catholic Univ. of Louvain (Licentiate of Commercial and Consular Scis). Joined National Bank of Belgium, 1953: Attaché, 1960–62; Asst Advr, 1962–66; Advr, 1966–74; Inspector Gen., 1974–80; Sen. Economist, 1980–82; on secondment to Social and Econ. Cabinet of Prime Minister as Dep. Chief of Cabinet, 1982–83, Chief of Cabinet, 1983–88; Dir, 1985–88; Vice-Governor, 1988–89. Gov., IMF, 1989–99; Deputy Governor: IBRD, 1989–99; IFC, 1989–99; IDA, 1989–99. Dir, European Fund for Monetary Co-operation, 1989–94; Mem. Council, European Monetary Inst., 1994–99. Grand Officier, Ordre de la Couronne (Belgium), 1991; Grande Ufficiale, Ordine al Merito (Italy), 1986; Officier de la Légion d'Honneur (France), 1994. *Address:* National Bank of Belgium, Boulevard de Berlaimont 14, 1000 Bruxelles, Belgium. *T:* (2) 2214777.

**VERSACE, Donatella**; Vice-President and Creative Director, Gianni Versace Group, since 1997; *b* 2 May 1955; *d* of Antonio Versace and Francesca Versace; *m* Paul Beck (marr. diss.); one *s* one *d*. *Educ:* Univ. of Florence. Joined Versace, 1978; designer: Versace Young, 1993; Versus; Isante; launched fragrance, Versace Woman, 2001. *Address:* Gianni Versace SpA, Via Borgospesso 15/A, 20121 Milan, Italy.

**VERTOVEC, Prof. Steven Allen**, DPhil; Director, Max Planck Institute for the Study of Religious and Ethnic Diversity, Göttingen, since 2007; Hon. Joint Professor of Sociology and Ethnology, University of Göttingen, since 2007; *b* 2 July 1957; *s* of Frank J. Vertovec and Dorothea M. Vertovec; *m* 1994, Astrid Gräfe; one *s* one *d*. *Educ:* Immaculate Conception High Sch., Elmhurst, Ill; Univ. of Colorado, Boulder (BA); Univ. of Calif, Santa Barbara (MA); Nuffield Coll., Oxford (DPhil 1988). Res. Fellow, Sch. of Geography, Oxford Univ., 1991–93; Principal Res. Fellow, Centre for Res. in Ethnic Relns, Univ. of Warwick, 1994–97; Dir, ESRC Transnat. Communities Res. Prog., 1997–2003; University of Oxford: Res. Reader in Anthropology, 1997–2002; Prof. of Transnational Anthropology, 2002–07; Dir, Centre on Migration, Policy and Society, 2003–07; Jt Dir, Internat. Migration Inst., 2006–07; Sen. Res. Fellow, Linacre Coll., Oxford, 1997–2007. Regents' Fellow, Univ. of Calif, 1980–82; Overseas Res. Student Award, CVCP, 1983–86; Res. Fellow, Alexander von Humboldt-Stiftung, 1993–94; Vis. Fellow, Inst. Ethnology, Free Univ., Berlin, and Inst. Eur. Ethnology, Humboldt Univ., Berlin, 1993–94. *Publications:* (jtly) South Asians Overseas: migration and ethnicity, 1990; Aspects of the South Asian Diaspora, 1991; Hindu Trinidad: religion, ethnicity and socio-economic change, 1992; (with A. Rogers) The Urban Context: ethnicity, social networks and situational analysis, 1995; (with C. Peach) Islam in Europe: the politics of religion and community, 1997; (with A. Rogers) Muslim European Youth: reproducing religion, ethnicity and culture, 1998; Migration and Social Cohesion, 1999; (with R. Cohen) Migration, Diasporas and Transnationalism, 1999; The Hindu Diaspora: comparative patterns, 2000; (with R. Cohen) Conceiving Cosmopolitanism, 2002; (with B. Parekh) Culture and Economy in the Indian Diaspora, 2003; (with D. Posey) Globalization, Globalism, Environments and Environmentalism, 2004; (with W. Schiffauer) Civil Enculturation, 2004; (jtly) Citizenship in European Cities, 2004; Transnationalism, 2008; (ed) Anthropology of Migration and Multiculturalism, 2009; (ed jtly) The Multicultural Backlash: European discourses, policies and practices, 2010; (ed) Migration and Diversity, 2014; (ed) Routledge International Handbook of Diversity Studies, 2015; (ed) Diversities Old and New: migration and socio-spatial patterns in New York, Singapore and Johannesburg, 2015; (ed jtly) Comparing Super-diversity, 2015; Diversities Old and New, 2015; contrib. articles to Religion, Ethnic and Racial Studies, Social and Economic, Ethnology, New Community, Etnolog, Contribs to Indian Sociology, Social Compass, Internat. Social Sci. Jl; Jl of Ethnic and Migration Studies; Internat. Migration Review. *Address:* Max Planck Institut zur Erforschung multireligioser und multiethnischer Gesellschaften, Hermann Foge Weg 11, 37073 Göttingen, Germany.

**VERULAM, 7th Earl of**, *cr* 1815; **John Duncan Grimston**; Bt 1629; Baron Forrester (Scot.), 1633; Baron Dunboyne and Viscount Grimston (Ire.), 1719; Baron Verulam (Gt. Brit.), 1790; Viscount Grimston (UK), 1815; *b* 21 April 1951; *s* of 6th Earl of Verulam and Marjorie Ray (*d* 1994), *d* of late Walter Atholl Duncan; *S* father, 1973; *m* 1976, Dione Angela (*see* Countess of Verulam), *e d* of Jeremy Fox Eric Smith, *qv*; three *s* one *d*. *Educ:* Eton; Christ Church, Oxford (MA 1976). Dir, Baring Brothers, 1987–96; Man. Dir, ABN-AMRO Bank, 1996–2000; Dir, Kleinwort Benson Private Bank, 2001–08. Chm., Grimston Trust Ltd, 1982–. *Heir: s* Viscount Grimston, *qv*. *Clubs:* White's, Beefsteak.

**VERULAM, Countess of; Dione Angela Grimston**, CVO 2019; artist; Lord Lieutenant of Hertfordshire, 2007–17; *b* 19 July 1954; *d* of Jeremy Fox Eric Smith, *qv*; *m* 1976, Earl of Verulam, *qv*; three *s* one *d*. *Educ:* Benenden Sch.; Exeter Univ. (BA Hons Hist. and Archaeol.). Stencilling commns, 1981–2001; solo exhibitions: Fleming Collection, 2007; Sladmore Gall., 2010; Mount St Gall., 2013; Rebecca Hossack Art Gall., 2015; Cricket Fine Art, 2019. Mem., Panel of Acceptance in Lieu, DCMS, 2001–06. Mem., Regl Cttee, NT, 1991–98. Liveryman, Goldsmiths' Co., 2005–. High Sheriff, 2002–03, DL 2003–07, Herts. Trustee, St Albans Cathedral Fabric Trust, 1995–2004. Pres. or Patron of various orgns in Herts. Hon. DArts Herts, 2017. *Publications:* (ed) Memories of Strathvaich, 1992; Gorhambury Gardens Guide, 1993. *Recreations:* ski-ing, golf, theatre, opera, reading, sewing, painting, Gorhambury. *Clubs:* Boodle's Ladies' Side, Chelsea Arts; Northern Meeting (Inverness).

**VESEY**, family name of **Viscount de Vesci**.

**VESSEY, Prof. Martin Paterson**, CBE 1994; FRS 1991; FMedSci; Professor of Public Health (formerly Social and Community Medicine), University of Oxford, 1974–2000, now Emeritus; Fellow of St Cross College, Oxford, since 1973; *b* 22 July 1936; *s* of Sidney J. Vessey and Catherine P. Vessey (*née* Thomson); *m* 1959, Anne Platt; two *s* one *d*. *Educ:* University College Sch., Hampstead; University Coll. London (Fellow, 1992); University Coll. Hosp. Med. Sch., London. MB, BS London 1959; MD London 1971; FFCM RCP 1972; MA Oxon 1974; MRCPE 1978; FRCPE 1979; FRCGP 1983; FRCP 1987; FRCOG 1989; FFSRH (FFFP 1995). Scientific Officer, Dept of Statistics, Rothamsted Exper. Stn, 1960–65; House Surg. and House Phys., Barnet Gen. Hosp., 1965–66; Mem. Sci. Staff, MRC Statistical Research Unit, 1966–69; Lectr in Epidemiology, Univ. of Oxford, 1969–74. Advr to WHO Human Reproduction Prog., 1972–96; Chairman: Adv. Cttee on Breast Cancer Screening, DHSS, subseq. DoH, 1987–99; Adv. Cttee on Cervical Cancer Screening, DoH, 1996–2006; Adv. Cttee on Bowel Cancer Screening, DoH, 2008–11; Member: Cttee on Safety of Medicines, 1980–92, 1996–98; Royal Commn on Environmental Pollution, 1984–89. Founder FMedSci 1998. *Publications:* many sci. articles in learned jls, notably on med. aspects of fertility control, safety of drugs, epidemiology of cancer and women's health. *Recreations:* fine arts, conservation, model engineering. *Address:* Clifden Cottage, Burford Road, Fulbrook, Burford OX18 4BL.

**VESTAGER, Margrethe**; Member, European Commission, since 2014; *b* Denmark, 13 April 1968; *d* of Hans Vestager and Bodil Tybjerg; *m* 1994, Thomas Jensen; three *d*. *Educ:* Univ. of Copenhagen (MSc Econs 1993). Hd of Section, Min. of Finance, Denmark, 1993–95; Special Consultant, 1995–97, Hd of Secretariat, 1997–98, Agency for Financial Mgt and Admin. Affairs: Minister of Ecclesiastical Affairs, 1998–2000, of Educn, 1998–2001; MP (Social Liberal) Frederiksborg, 2001–07, N Zealand, 2007–14, Denmark; Minister for Econ. Affairs and Interior, 2011–14; Dep. Prime Minister, 2011–14. Leader, Social Liberal Party, 2011–14. *Address:* European Commission, 200 rue de la Loi, 1049 Brussels, Belgium. *T:* (2) 2955136. *E:* margrethe-vestager@ec.europa.eu.

**VESTEY**, family name of **Baron Vestey**.

**VESTEY, 3rd Baron** *cr* 1922, of Kingswood; **Samuel George Armstrong Vestey**, GCVO 2018 (KCVO 2009); DL; Bt 1913; Master of the Horse, 1999–2018; a Permanent Lord in Waiting to the Queen, since 2019; *b* 19 March 1941; *s* of late Captain the Hon. William Howarth Vestey (killed in action in Italy, 1944; *e s* of 2nd Baron Vestey and Frances Sarah Howarth) and Pamela Helen Fullerton, *d* of George Nesbitt Armstrong; *S* grandfather, 1954; *m* 1st, 1970, Kathryn Mary (marr. diss. 1981; she *d* 2017), *er d* of John Eccles, Moor Park, Herts; two *d*; 2nd, 1981, Celia Elizabeth, *d* of late Major Guy Knight, MC, Lockinge Manor, Wantage, Oxon; two *s* one *d*. *Educ:* Eton. Lieut, Scots Guards. Chairman: Steeplechase Co. (Cheltenham), 1990–2011; Vestey Group Ltd, 1995–2015. Chm., Meat Training Council, 1991–95. President: London Meat Trade and Drovers Benevolent Assoc., 1973; Inst. of Meat, 1978–83; Three Counties Agricl Soc., 1978; Royal Bath and W of England Soc., 1994; BHS, 1994–97; Old Etonian Assoc., 2018. Chm., Royal Agricl Soc. of the Commonwealth, 1998–. Patron, Glos CCC, 1997–2014. Liveryman, Butchers' Co. DL Glos, 1982. Queen's Golden Jubilee Medal, 2002; Queen's Diamond Jubilee Medal, 2012. GCStJ 1987 (Chancellor of the Order, 1988–91, Lord Prior, 1991–2002). *Recreations:* racing, shooting, cricket. *Heir: s* Hon. William Guy Vestey [*b* 27 Aug. 1983; *m* 2012, Violet Gwyneth, *o d* of late Gavin Henderson; one *s* one *d*. Page of Honour to the Queen, 1995–97]. *Address:* Stowell Park, Northleach, Glos GL54 3LE. *Clubs:* White's, Turf, MCC; Jockey (Newmarket); I Zingari; Melbourne (Melbourne); South Cerney Golf.

**VESTEY, Sir Paul (Edmund)**, 3rd Bt *cr* 1921, of Shirley; *b* 15 Feb. 1944; *s* of Sir (John) Derek Vestey, 2nd Bt and Phyllis Irene Vestey (*née* Brewer); *S* father, 2005; *m* 1971, Victoria Anne Scudamore, *d* of John Salter; three *d*. *Educ:* Radley. *Heir: cousin* James Patrick Vestey [*b* 13 April 1954; *m* 1981, Nicola Jane Knight]. *Address:* Manor House Farm, Bishops Sutton, Alresford, Hants SO24 0BA.

**VETTRIANO, Jack**, OBE 2003; artist, since 1988; Founder, Jack Vettriano Publishing Ltd, 2015; *b* Fife, 17 Nov. 1951; *s* of William and Catherine Hoggan, *né* Jack Hoggan. Mining engr, 1966–70; variety of middle mgt posts, 1970–88. Co-Founder, Heartbreak Publishing Ltd, 2008–17. Self-taught artist; solo exhibitions: Edinburgh, London, Hong Kong, Johannesburg; Portland Gall., London, 2004, 2006; Homage a Tuiga, Monaco Yacht Club, 2009; Days of Wine and Roses, Kirkcaldy Mus., Fife and Heartbreak Gall., London, 2010; The Ballroom Spy, Heartbreak Gall., London, and Royal West Acad., Bristol, 2011; retrospective, Kelvingrove Art Gall. and Mus., Glasgow, 2013; A Celebration, Heartbreak Gall., London, 2014. Represented by Portland Gall., 1994–2007, by Heartbreak Gall., London, 2009–14. Hon. DLitt St Andrews, 2003; DUniv Open, 2004. *Publications:* (with W. Gordon Smith) Fallen Angels, 1996; Man's World, 2009; Women in Love, 2009; (with Anthony Quinn): Lovers and Other Strangers, 2000; Jack Vettriano: a life, 2004; Studio Life, 2008; Jack Vettriano: a retrospective, 2013. *Recreations:* music, film, ballroom dancing.

**VIALA, Prof. Alain Bernard Jean**; Professor of French Literature, University of Oxford, 2002–15, now Emeritus; Fellow, Lady Margaret Hall, Oxford, 2002–15, now Emeritus; Professor of French Literature, University of Paris III, Sorbonne Nouvelle, since 1985; *b* 20 Nov. 1947; *s* of Ernest and Marie Viala. *Educ:* Ecole Normale Supérieure, Cachan; (Agrégé des lettres; DèsL). Lecturer: Ecole Nationale de Chimie, 1972–78; Ecole d'Artillerie, 1973–74; Asst Prof., Univ. Sorbonne Nouvelle, 1978–84; Prof. of French Studies and Fellow, Wadham Coll., Univ. of Oxford, 1997–2002. Guest Professor: Univ. de Liège, 1988; Univ. of Tel Aviv, 1996. Pres., Commn des Programmes de Lettres, Min. of Educn, France, 1993–2002. Member: Lit. Cttee, Presses Universitaires de France, 2007–; Steering Cttee, 2013–, and Comité de Pilotage Scientifique, Agence Nat. de la Recherche, France, 2014–18. Co-convenor, Rencontres recherche et Création, Fest. d'Avignon, 2014–. Chevalier des Palmes Académiques (France), 1988; Chevalier, Ordre National du Mérite

(France), 2006. *Publications:* Savoir-lire, 1982; Naissance de l'écrivain, 1985; Racine: la stratégie du caméléon, 1990; Approches de la réception, 1993; Le théâtre en France, 1996, 5th edn 2016; Le Dictionnaire du Littéraire, 2002; Le Tragique, 2002; De la Publication, 2002; Lettre à Rousseau sur l'intérêt littéraire, 2005; Histoire du théâtre, 2006, 4th edn 2012; La France galante, 2008 (R. H. Gapper Prize, Soc. for French Studies, 2009); La culture littéraire, 2009; (with Daniel Mesguich) Le Theatre, 2011; Histoire de la littérature française, 2012; (ed jtly) Mises en intrigue, 2016; De la Révolution à la Belle Epoque, 2017. *Address:* Lady Margaret Hall, Oxford OX2 6QA.

**VICARY-SMITH, Peter David;** Director, Theconsumerfirst Ltd, since 2018; *b* 31 May 1962; *s* of James David Smith and Valerie Ann Smith; changed name by deed poll to Vicary-Smith on marriage, 1991; *m* 1991, Susan Joy Vicary; two *d*. *Educ:* Dulwich Coll.; Queen's Coll., Oxford (BA PPE 1984; MA PPE 1994). Various mktg appts, Procter and Gamble, Mars Confectionery and Kenner Parker, 1984–88; McKinsey & Co., 1988–91; Hd of Appeals, Oxfam, 1991–96; Dir of Fundraising and Communications, ICRF, 1996–2002; Commercial Dir, Cancer Research UK, 2002–04; Chief Exec., Which?, 2004–18. Non-exec. Dir, Oxfordshire Learning Disabilities NHS Trust, 1994–96. Member: Fundraising Standards Bd, 2006–08; Commercial Panel, Nat. Trust Enterprises, 2007–15. Pres., BEUC, Eur. Consumers' Orgn, 2012–14. Trustee: Methodist Homes for the Aged, 2003–06; Marie Curie Cancer Care, 2012–13. *Recreations:* gardening, history. *Club:* Lansdowne.

**VICK, Graham,** CBE 2009; Founder, 1987, and Artistic Director, Birmingham Opera Company (formerly City of Birmingham Touring Opera); *b* 30 Dec. 1953. Trained as a singer and conductor. Associate Dir, English Music Theatre; Director of Productions: Scottish Opera, 1984–87; Glyndebourne Fest. Opera, 1994–2000. Hambro Vis. Prof. of Opera Studies, Oxford Univ., 2002–03; Hon. Prof. of Music, Univ. of Birmingham. Work in a wide repertoire from Monteverdi to Berio includes productions for: Royal Opera House, Covent Garden; ENO; Glyndebourne Fest. Opera; Opera North; Scottish Opera; Metropolitan Opera, NY; Chicago Lyric Opera; San Francisco Opera; La Scala, Milan; Opéra Nationale de Paris; Vienna State Opera; Bavarian State Opera; Maggio Musicale, Florence; Netherlands Opera; Deutsche Oper, Berlin; Teatro Real, Madrid; Gran Teatre del Liceu, Barcelona; Mariinsky Theatre, St Petersburg. *Address:* Birmingham Opera Company, 205 The Argent Centre, 60 Frederick Street, Birmingham B1 3HS; Groves Artists, 7 St George's Court, 131 Putney Bridge Road, SW15 2PA.

**VICKERMAN, Jill Margaret;** National Director (Scotland) (formerly Scottish Secretary), British Medical Association, since 2013; *b* Edinburgh, 18 June 1965; *d* of William Justice Vickerman and Seonaid Mairi Grant Vickerman. *Educ:* Edinburgh Univ. (BSc Maths and Stats). Statistician, Scottish Office, 1987–2004; Scottish Government: Hd, Analytical Services for Health and Social Care, 2004–09; Dep. Dir for Healthcare Planning, 2009–10; Policy Dir for Health and Social Care, 2010–13. Trustee, Erskine Hosp., 2012–. *Recreations:* golf, ski-ing, hill-walking, piano, fiddle. *Address:* 14 Queen Street, Edinburgh EH2 1LL. *T:* (0131) 247 3016, *Fax:* (0131) 247 3001. *E:* jvickerman@bma.org.uk.

**VICKERS, Andrew Julian;** Attending Research Methodologist, Memorial Hospital for Cancer and Allied Diseases, New York, since 2012 (Assistant Attending Research Methodologist, 1999–2006; Associate Attending Research Methodologist, 2006–12); Professor of Healthcare Policy and Research, Weill Cornell Medical College, since 2014; *b* 11 Feb. 1967; *s* of Jeffrey Vickers and Angela Vickers; *m* 1996, Caroline Batzdorf; one *s* one *d*. *Educ:* Girton Coll., Cambridge (BA 1989); Green Coll., Oxford (DPhil 1999). Joined Res. Council for Complementary Medicine, 1993; Dir of Res., 1997–99; estabd registry of randomised trials in complementary medicine for Cochrane Collaboration, 1995; Asst Mem., 1999–2006, Associate Mem., 2006–12, Mem., 2012–, Meml Sloan Kettering Cancer Center; Asst Prof. of Public Health, 2004–07, Associate Prof., 2007–13, Prof. of Public Health, 2013, Weill Med. Coll., Cornell Univ. Ed., Complementary Therapies in Medicine, 1996–99. Principal investigator, NHS funded trial of acupuncture for headache, 1998. Mem., R&D Cttee, Prince of Wales initiative for Integrated Medicine, 1996–98. *Publications:* Complementary Medicine and Disability, 1993; Health Options: complementary therapies for cerebral palsy and related conditions, 1994; Massage and Aromatherapy: a guide for health professionals, 1996; (ed) Examining Complementary Medicine: the sceptical holist, 1998; (jtly) ABC of Complementary Medicine, 2000; What is a p value anyway?, 2010; contrib. numerous papers to peer-reviewed health-related jls. *Recreations:* cooking, Ultimate Frisbee, running, guitar. *E:* andrewline@earthlink.net.

**VICKERS, Andrew Robert;** a District Judge (Magistrates' Courts), 2004–16; *b* 18 Jan. 1951; *s* of late Francis Albert Vickers and Barbara Winifred Vickers (*née* Tappenden); *m* 1973, Alison Ayres; one *s* two *d*. *Educ:* Windsor Grammar Sch.; Univ. of London (ext. BA 1976). Called to the Bar, Gray's Inn, 1987. Assistant: Chamberlain's Dept, City of London Corp., 1977–78; Mansion House and Guildhall Justice Rooms, 1978–83; PSDs, Slough and Windsor, 1983–86; Principal Court Clerk, Hounslow PSA, 1986–89; Dep. Justices' Clerk, Enfield PSA, 1989–92; Clerk to the Justices, Kingston upon Thames PSA, 1992–2004; Justices' Chief Exec., Kingston upon Thames MCC, 1995–2001; Regl Justices' Clerk for Hounslow, Ealing, Richmond, Wimbledon, W London and S Western PSAs, 2003–04. *Recreations:* avid supporter of Brentford FC, reading, music, Nat. Trust volunteer at Osterley Park.

**VICKERS, Sir Brian (William),** Kt 2008; PhD, LittD; FBA 1998; Professor of English Literature, and Director, Centre for Renaissance Studies, ETH Zürich, 1975–2003, now Emeritus Professor; *b* 13 Dec. 1937; *s* of William Morgan Davies and Josephine Davies (*née* Grant); *m* 1st, 1962, Ilse-Renate Freiling (marr. diss. 1989; she *d* 2019); two *d*; 2nd, 1989, Sabine Köllmann; one *s* one *d*. *Educ:* St Marylebone Grammar Sch.; Trinity Coll., Cambridge (BA 1st Cl. Hons English 1962; Charles Oldham Shakespeare Schol., 1961; Sen. Schol., 1962); PhD 1967, LittD 1996 Cantab. Cambridge University: Res. Fellow, Churchill Coll., 1964–65; Asst Lectr in English, 1964–68; Fellow and Dir of Studies in English, Downing Coll., 1966–71; Univ. Lectr in English, 1968–72; Prof. of English Lit., Univ. of Zürich, 1972–75. Vis. Fellow, All Souls Coll., Oxford, 1980–81; Fellow, Wissenschaftskolleg zu Berlin, 1986–87; Vis. Prof. of English Lit., UCL, 2012–. Lectures: Shakespeare, British Acad., 1992; John Coffin, London Univ., 2001; Sam Wanamaker Fellowship, Shakespeare's Globe, 2015. Pres., Internat. Soc. for History of Rhetoric, 1977–79; Chm., Soc. for Renaissance Studies, 2004–07. Dist. Sen. Fellow, Sch. of Advanced Study, Univ. of London, 2003–; Sen. Res. Fellow, Inst. of English Studies, 2004–. Hon. Fellow, Downing Coll., Cambridge, 2008. Hon. Foreign Mem., Amer. Acad. of Arts and Scis, 2007. Hon. Pres., Old Philologians Assoc., 2004–. Member of Editorial Board: Renaissance Studies, 1994–98; Annals of Science, 1995–2016; Isis, 1999–2002; Early Science and Medicine, 2009–; Interdisciplinary Science Reviews, 2011–. Dir, The Oxford Francis Bacon, 2009–17 (Chm. Adv. Bd, 2005–09); Gen. Ed., The Complete Works of John Ford, 2005–. Dr *hc* Fribourg, 2003; Hon. DLit London, 2009. *Publications:* (ed) Henry Mackenzie, The Man of Feeling, 1967, 2nd edn 2001; Francis Bacon and Renaissance Prose, 1968; The Artistry of Shakespeare's Prose, 1968, rev. edn 1979; (ed) Essential Articles for the Study of Francis Bacon, 1968; (ed) The World of Jonathan Swift, 1968; (ed) Seventeenth Century Prose, 1969; Classical Rhetoric in English Poetry, 1970, rev. edn 1989 (trans. German 2008); Towards Greek Tragedy, 1973; (ed) Shakespeare: the critical heritage, 6 vols, 1623–1692, 1974, 1693–1733, 1974, 1733–1752, 1975, 1753–1765, 1976, 1765–1774, 1979, 1774–1801, 1981; (ed jtly) Hooker: the laws of ecclesiastical polity, 1976; Shakespeare's Coriolanus, 1976; (ed) Rhetoric Revalued, 1982; (ed) Occult and Scientific Mentalities in the Renaissance, 1984 (trans. Spanish 1980); (ed) Arbeit, Musse, Meditation: Betrachtungen zur Vita activa und Vita contemplativa, 1985, rev. edn 1991; (ed) Public and Private Life in the Seventeenth Century: the Mackenzie-Evelyn debate, 1986; (ed) English Science: Bacon to Newton, 1987; In Defence of Rhetoric, 1988 (trans. Italian 1994), rev. edn 1997; Returning to Shakespeare, 1989; Appropriating Shakespeare: contemporary critical quarrels, 1993; (ed) Francis Bacon: the major works, 1996, 2nd edn 2002; (ed) Francis Bacon: history of the reign of King Henry VII, 1998; (ed) Francis Bacon: the essays and counsels, civil and moral, 1999; (ed) English Renaissance Literary Criticism, 1999; Counterfeiting Shakespeare: evidence, authorship and John Ford's Funerall Elegye, 2002; Shakespeare, Co-Author: a historical study of five collaborative plays, 2002; Shakespeare, A Lover's Complaint, and John Davies of Hereford, 2007; (with S. Köllmann) Mächtige Worte—Antike Rhetorik und europäische Literatur, 2008; (jtly) The Collected Works of John Ford, vol. I, 2011, vols 2 and 3, 2017; The One King Lear, 2016; (Gen. Ed.) series, Shakespeare: the critical tradition: King John, 1996; Richard II, 1998; A Midsummer Night's Dream, 1999; Measure for Measure, 2001; Coriolanus, 2004; The Merchant of Venice, 2005; articles and reviews in learned jls. *Recreations:* music, sport, film. *Address:* 7 Abbot's Place, NW6 4NP. *T:* (020) 7624 7217.

**VICKERS, Edmund Benedict Blyth;** QC 2017; *b* 22 Aug. 1969; *s* of late Michael Vickers and Anne Vickers (*née* Blyth-Praeger); *m* 1998, Laura Polk; two *s* one *d*. *Educ:* Ampleforth Coll.; Durham Univ. (BA Hons Hist.); City Univ. (DipLaw); Inns of Court Sch. of Law. Called to the Bar, Middle Temple, 1993; in practice as barrister, specialising in criminal law, 1993–; Advocacy Trainer, Hon. Soc. Middle Temple, 2000–; Lead Facilitator, Vulnerable Witness Advocacy Trainer, Inns of Court Coll. of Advocacy, 2016–. Mem., Exec. Cttee, 2007–12, Treas., 2010–12, Criminal Bar Assoc.; Mem., Ethics Cttee, Bar Council, 2016–; Mem., Scholarship Panel, Hon. Soc. Middle Temple, 2009–. Trustee, 2015–, Treas., 2016–, Kalisher Trust. Liveryman, Goldsmiths' Co., 2010. *Recreations:* theatre, ski-ing, golf, cricket. *Address:* Red Lion Chambers, 18 Red Lion Court, EC4A 3EB. *T:* (020) 7520 6000. *E:* clerks@18rlc.co.uk. *Club:* Islay Golf.

**VICKERS, Hilary Anne;** see Taylor, H. A.

**VICKERS, Hugo Ralph;** DL; author, lecturer and broadcaster; Chairman, Commonwealth Walkway (formerly Outdoor) Trust, since 2012; *b* 12 Nov. 1951; *s* of late Ralph Cecil Vickers, MC, and Dulcie (*née* Metcalf); *m* 1995, Elizabeth Anne Blyth Vickers (marr. diss. 2014), *y d* of late (Dennis) Michael Vickers, Montaillac, France; two *s* one *d*. *Educ:* Eton; Strasbourg Univ. St George's Chapel, Windsor Castle: Lay Steward, 1970–; Capt., 2014–; Mem., Adv. Council, later Mgt Cttee, Friends of St George's, 2001–04, 2005–11. Worked with London Celebrations Cttee, Queen's Silver Jubilee, 1977; Administrator, Great Children's Party, Hyde Park, 1979. Chm., Jubilee Walkway Trust, 2002–12; Member: Prince of Wales' Royal Parks Tree Appeal, 1987–2003; Council of Mgt, Windsor Fest., 1999–2017. Broadcaster including: studio guest, weddings of Prince of Wales and Duke of York, funeral of Diana, Princess of Wales; asstd with commentaries: wedding of Earl of Wessex, Queen Mother's 100th birthday and funeral, wedding of Duke of Sussex. Producer and writer, one-man play, The Immortal Dropout, Jermyn St Th., 2008; Historical Adviser: The King's Speech (film), 2010; Titanic (TV), 2012; Victoria and Abdul (film), 2017. Golo Mann Dist. Lectr, Claremont McKenna Coll., 2007. Trustee, Age Unlimited, 2010–. Patron, Me2 Club, 2012–. Liveryman, Co. of Musicians, 1978. DL Berks, 2010. *Publications:* We Want the Queen, 1977; Gladys, Duchess of Marlborough, 1979; Debrett's Book of the Royal Wedding, 1981; (ed) Cocktails and Laughter, 1983; Cecil Beaton, 1985; Vivien Leigh, 1988; Royal Orders, 1994; Loving Garbo, 1994; The Private World of the Duke and Duchess of Windsor, 1995; The Kiss (Stern Silver Pen for non-fiction), 1996; Alice, Princess Andrew of Greece, 2000; (ed) The Unexpurgated Beaton, 2002; (ed) Beaton in the Sixties, 2003; (ed) Alexis: the memoirs of the Baron de Redé, 2005; Elizabeth, The Queen Mother, 2005; (ed) The Rich Spoils of Time, 2006; (ed) Horses and Husbands, 2007; St George's Chapel, Windsor Castle, 2008; Behind Closed Doors, 2011; A Walk for the Queen, 2012; Coronation, 2013; (ed) Jeffrey, 2014; (ed) Cecil Beaton: portraits and profiles, 2014; The Lay Stewards of St George's Chapel, Windsor Castle, 2016; The Crown: truth and fiction, 2017; (ed) The Quest for Queen Mary, 2018. *Recreations:* reading, travel, photography, walking. *Address:* 62 Lexham Gardens, W8 5JA. *T:* 07774 671540; The Manor House, East Chisenbury, Wilts SN9 6AQ. *E:* hugovickers@wyeford.co.uk. *W:* www.hugovickers.co.uk. *Club:* Beefsteak.

**VICKERS, Sir John (Stuart),** Kt 2005; DPhil; FBA 1998; Warden, All Souls College, Oxford, since 2008 (Fellow, 1991–2008); *b* 7 July 1958; *s* of Aubrey and late Kay Vickers; *m* 1991, Maureen Freed; one *s* two *d*. *Educ:* Eastbourne Grammar Sch.; Oriel Coll., Oxford (BA PPE 1979; Hon. Fellow 2005); MPhil Econs Oxon 1983; DPhil Econs Oxon 1985. Financial Analyst, Shell UK, 1979–81; Fellow, All Souls Coll., Oxford, 1979–84; Roy Harrod Fellow in Economics of Business and Public Policy, Nuffield Coll., Oxford, 1984–90; Drummond Prof. of Political Economy, Univ. of Oxford, 1991–2008 (on leave, 1998–2005); Exec. Dir, Chief Economist, and Mem. Monetary Policy Cttee, Bank of England, 1998–2000; Dir Gen., 2000–03, Chm., 2003–05, OFT. Chm., Ind. Commn on Banking, 2010–11. Vis. Fellow, Princeton, 1988; Vis. Lectr, Harvard, 1989, 1990; Vis. Prof., London Business Schs., 1996. President: Inst. for Fiscal Studies, 2003–07; REconS, 2007–10; Eur. Assoc. Res. in Industrial Econs, 2018–20. Rhodes Trustee, 2006–11. Fellow, Econometric Soc., 1998. Hon. DLitt UEA, 2001. *Publications:* (jtly) Privatization: an economic analysis, 1988; (jtly) Regulatory Reform, 1994; articles in econ. jls on industrial organisation, regulation, competition, monetary policy. *Address:* All Souls College, Oxford OX1 4AL. *T:* (01865) 279379.

**VICKERS, Martin John;** MP (C) Cleethorpes, since 2010; *b* Cleethorpes, 13 Sept. 1950; *m* 1981, Ann Gill; one *d*. *Educ:* Havelock Sch.; Grimsby Coll.; Univ. of Lincoln (BA Hons Politics 2004). In printing industry, 1967–78; in retail trade, 1978–94; Constituency Agent to Edward Leigh, MP, 1994–2010. Member (C): Great Grimsby BC, 1980–94; NE Lincs Council, 1999–2011 Cabinet Mem., 2003–09). Contested (C) Cleethorpes, 2005. *Address:* House of Commons, SW1A 0AA.

**VICKERS, Rt Rev. Michael Edwin;** Area Bishop of Colchester, 1988–94; an Assistant Bishop, Diocese of Blackburn, 1994–2013; *b* 13 Jan. 1929; *s* of William Edwin and Florence Alice Vickers; *m* 1960, Janet Cynthia Croasdale; three *d*. *Educ:* St Lawrence Coll., Ramsgate; Worcester Coll., Oxford (BA Mod. History 1952; MA 1956); Cranmer Hall, Durham (DipTheol with distinction, 1959). Company Secretary, Hoares (Ceylon) Ltd, 1952–56; Refugee Administrator for British Council for Aid to Refugees, 1956–57; Lay Worker, Diocese of Oklahoma, 1959; Curate of Christ Church, Bexleyheath, 1959–62; Sen. Chaplain, Lee Abbey Community, 1962–67; Vicar of St John's, Newland, Hull, 1967–81; Area Dean, Central and North Hull, 1972–81; Archdeacon of E Riding, 1981–88. Chm., York Diocesan House of Clergy, 1975–85; Canon and Prebendary of York, 1981–88. Mem., Gen. Synod, 1975–88 (Proctor in Convocation, 1975–85). *Recreations:* gardening, walking, travel, drama. *Address:* 137 Canalside, Redhill, Surrey RH1 2FH. *T:* (01737) 642984.

**VICKERS, Prof. Michael John**, DLitt; FSA 1978; Professor of Archaeology, University of Oxford, 2002–10, now Emeritus (Reader in Archaeology, 1996–2002); Dean of Degrees, Jesus College, Oxford, since 2002 (Garden Master, 2002–08; Senior Research Fellow in Classical Studies, 1996–2010, now Emeritus Fellow); Senior Assistant Keeper, Department of Antiquities, Ashmolean Museum, 1988–2010 (Assistant Keeper, 1971–88); *b* 17 Feb. 1943; *s* of late John Fletcher and Agnes Mary Vickers; *m* 1st, 1966, Marie Moley (marr. diss. 1982); one *s* one *d*; 2nd, 1982, Susan Brandes (*d* 1998); two *s*; 3rd, 2001, Manana Odisheli. *Educ*: St Bede's Coll., Manchester (jun. high jump champion, Lancs, 1960); UCNW Bangor (BA (Classics) 1964); Corpus Christi Coll., Cambridge (Dip. Classical Archaeol. 1965); Univ. of Wales (DLitt 1999). Asst Lectr in Ancient Hist. and Classical Archaeol., University Coll., Dublin, 1966–69; Lectr in Archaeol., Univ. of Libya, Benghazi, 1969–70. Vis. Mem., University Coll., Cambridge, 1970–71; Mem., Inst. for Advanced Study, Princeton, 1976; Vis. Lectr, Univ. of Texas, 1979–80; George Tait Meml Lectr, Eton Coll., 1987; Visiting Scholar: Inst. for Advanced Studies, Hebrew Univ., Jerusalem, 1993; Getty Villa, Malibu, 2013; Visiting Professor: Univ. of Catania, 2002; Univ. of Colorado at Boulder, 2003 and 2013; Tbilisi State Univ., 2012; Kress Lectr, Archaeol Inst. of America, 2002–03. Co-Dir, excavations at Pichvnari, Georgia, 1998–2010. Chm., Friends of Academic Res. in Georgia, 2005–10. Corresponding Member: German Archaeol Inst., 1978; Archaeol Inst. of America, 2010; Hon. Mem., Vani Expedn, Centre for Archaeol Studies, Georgian Acad. of Scis, 1995. Hon. Dr Batumi State Univ., 2008. *Publications*: The Roman World, 1977, 2nd edn as Ancient Rome, 1989; Greek Vases, 1978, 3rd edn 1989; Greek Symposia, 1978; Scythian Treasures in Oxford, 1979; (with K. Branigan) Hellas, 1980; (jtly) From Silver to Ceramic: the potter's debt to metalwork in the Greco-Roman, Chinese and Islamic worlds, 1986; (ed) Pots and Pans, 1986; The Ancient Romans, 1992; (ed with M. Henig) Cameos in Context: the Benjamin Zucker lectures 1990, 1993; (with D. W. J. Gill) Artful Crafts: Ancient Greek silverware and pottery, 1994, 2nd edn 1996; Pericles on Stage: political comedy in Aristophanes' early plays, 1997; Ancient Greek Pottery, 1998; Images on Textiles: the weave of fifth-century Athenian art and society, 1999; Skeuomorphismus, oder die Kunst aus wenig viel zu machen, 1999; Scythian and Thracian Antiquities in Oxford, 2002; (with A. Kakhidze) Pichvnari I, Pichvnari 1998–2002: Greeks and Colchians on the East Coast of the Black Sea, 2004; Oedipus and Alcibiades in Sophocles, 2005; The Arundel and Pomfret Marbles in Oxford, 2006; Sophocles and Alcibiades: Athenian politics in Ancient Greek literature, 2008; Aristophanes and Alcibiades: echoes of contemporary history in Athenian comedy, 2015; Parerga: selected essays on literature, art and archaeology, 2019; articles in jls. *Recreation*: classical philology. *Address*: 20 Stone Meadow, Oxford OX2 6TQ. *E*: michael.vickers@jesus.ox.ac.uk.

**VICKERS, Lt-Gen. Sir Richard (Maurice Hilton)**, KCB 1983; CVO 1998 (LVO 1959); OBE 1970 (MBE 1964); an Extra Gentleman Usher to the Queen, since 1998 (a Gentleman Usher, 1986–98); *b* 21 Aug. 1928; *s* of Lt-Gen. W. G. H. Vickers, CB, OBE; *m* 1957, Gaie, *d* of Maj.-Gen. G. P. B. Roberts, CB, DSO, MC; three *d*. *Educ*: Haileybury and Imperial Service Coll.; RMA. Commissioned Royal Tank Regt, 1948; 1st RTR, BAOR, Korea, Middle East, 1948–54; Equerry to HM The Queen, 1956–59; Brigade Major, 7 Armd Bde, 1962–64; 4th RTR, Borneo and Malaysia, 1964–66; CO The Royal Dragoons, 1967–68, The Blues and Royals, 1968–69; Comdr, 11th Armd Brigade, 1972–74; Dep. Dir of Army Training, 1975–77; GOC 4th Armoured Div., 1977–79; Comdt, RMA, 1979–82; Dir-Gen. of Army Training, 1982–83. Dir Gen., Winston Churchill Meml Trust, 1983–93. *Recreation*: flyfishing.

**VICKERS, Sir Roger (Henry)**, KCVO 2010; FRCS; Orthopaedic Surgeon, 1992–2010, and Serjeant Surgeon, 2006–10, to the Queen; Consultant Orthopaedic Surgeon: St George's Hospital, 1980–2008; King Edward VII's Hospital Sister Agnes (formerly King Edward VII Hospital for Officers), 1992–2011; Civilian Consultant Orthopaedic Surgeon to the Army, 1992–2008; *b* 26 July 1945; *s* of late Dr H. Renwick Vickers, FRCP and of Penelope Evelyn (*née* Peck); *m* 1972, Joanna, *d* of late John Francis Mordaunt; two *s* two *d*. *Educ*: Winchester Coll.; Magdalen Coll., Oxford (MA); St Thomas's Hosp. (BM, BCh 1970). FRCS 1975. Sen. Orthopaedic Registrar, Charing Cross, St Mary's and Royal Nat. Orthopaedic Hosps, 1977–80; Consultant Orthopaedic Surgeon, St James' Hosp., London, 1980–88. Mem. Council, Med. Defence Union, 1983–2016; Mem., Adv. Bd, Med. Sickness Soc., subseq. Wesleyan Med. Sickness, 1998–2011. Trustee, RNLI, 2006–13. Master, Barbers' Co., 2014–15. *Recreations*: sailing, Real tennis. *Address*: Creek Cottage, Woodgaston Lane, Hayling Island PO11 0RL. *Clubs*: Garrick, Hurlingham; Royal Yacht Squadron.

**VICKERS, Dr Tony**; Project Manager, UK Human Genome Mapping Project, 1990–92. *Educ*: Manchester Grammar Sch.; Sidney Sussex Coll., Cambridge (MA, PhD). University of Cambridge: Demonstrator, 1956–61; Lectr in Physiology, 1961–72; Fellow, Sidney Sussex Coll., 1956–70; Headquarters Office, MRC, 1972–84 (Head of Medical Div., 1980–84); UK Administrator, Ludwig Inst. for Cancer Res., 1985–89. Member of Council: BAAS, 1969–72, 1982–85 (Pres., Biomed. Scis Sect., 1977); Cancer Res. Campaign, 1980–85 (Mem., Scientific Cttee, 1979–85); Paterson Labs, Manchester, 1984–85. Chm., Tenovus Sci. Adv. Cttee, 1987–91; Mem. Res. Cttee, Clatterbridge Centre for Oncology and Cancer Res. Trust, 1994–99. Governor, Beatson Inst., Glasgow, 1983–85.

**VICKERY, Prof. Amanda Jane**, PhD; Professor of Early Modern History, Queen Mary University of London, since 2011; *b* Preston, Lancs, 8 Dec. 1962; *d* of Derek Vickery and Renée Grant; *m* 1994, Prof. John Styles; three *d*. *Educ*: Penwortham Girls Grammar Sch., Preston; Bedford Coll., Univ. of London (BA 1984); Royal Holloway and Bedford New Coll., Univ. of London (PhD 1991). Res. Fellow, Churchill Coll., Cambridge, 1989; Royal Holloway, University of London: Lectr in Mod. Brit. Women's Hist., 1992–99, Reader, 1999–2009; Prof. in Mod. Brit. Hist., 2009–10. Leverhulme Major Res. Fellow, 2004–07. Vis. Prof., Historicum, Ludwig Maximilians Univ., Munich, 2007; Kratter Prof., Stanford Univ., 2010. Writer and presenter: television: The Trouble with Love, 2002; At Home with the Georgians, 2010; The Many Lovers of Jane Austen, 2011; The Story of Women and Art, 2014; Suffragettes Forever, 2015; La Traviata: Love, Death and Divas, 2015; radio: A History of Private Lives, 2009; Voices from the Old Bailey, 2010, 2011; A History of Men, 2012. *Publications*: The Gentleman's Daughter: women's lives in Georgian England (Longman-History Today Prize; Whitfield Prize, RHistS; Wolfson Prize), 1998; (ed) Women, Privilege and Power: British politics, 1750 to the present, 2001; (ed jtly) Gender, Taste and Material Culture in Britain and North America, 1700–1830, 2006; Behind Closed Doors: at home in Georgian England, 2009. *Recreations*: culture, clothes, chat. *Address*: School of History, Queen Mary University of London, Mile End Road, E1 4NS.

**VICTORY, Louis Eamonn Julian**; artist, photographer and designer; community activist; consultant, public interest consultancy, since 2004; *b* 14 Feb. 1948; *s* of Gerald Louis Victory and Doris Mabel Victory; *m* 1st, 1969, Sian Anne Bees Davies (marr. diss. 1996; she *d* 2002); three *d*; 2nd, 2004, Mary Reville. *Educ*: Cambridge Grammar Sch.; Christ's Coll., Cambridge (MA). DipArch; RIBA 1974. Architect in public and private practice, Birmingham, Oxon and Dyfed, 1972–90; Nottinghamshire County Council: Dep. Co. Architect, 1990; Dep. Dir, 1991, Dir, 1992–95, Construction and Design; Dir, Envmt, 1995–2000; Chief Exec., Cumbria CC, 2000–04. Chm., Avon Ambulance NHS Trust, 2005–06. Trustee: Portland Coll., 1994–; Totnes Trust, 2013–18. Exhibiting photographer and artist. *Recreation*: observing, enhancing and commenting creatively on the visual world.

**VIDYASAGAR, Prof. Mathukumalli**, PhD; FRS 2012; Distinguished Professor and Science and Engineering Research Board Distinguished Fellow, Indian Institute of Technology Hyderabad, since 2015; *b* Guntur, India, 29 Sept. 1947; *s* of late Mathukumalli Venkata Subbarao. *Educ*: Univ. of Wisconsin, Madison (BS Electrical Engrg 1965; MS 1967; PhD 1969). Assistant Professor of Electrical Engineering: Marquette Univ., Milwaukee, 1969–70; Concordia Univ., Montreal, 1970–80; Prof. of Electrical Engrg, Univ. of Waterloo, 1980–89; Dir, Centre for Artificial Intelligence and Robotics, Bangalore, 1989–2000; Exec. Vice Pres., Tata Consultancy Services, Hyderabad, 2000–09; Cecil and Ida Green Prof. of Systems Biol. Sci., 2009–19, Founder Hd, Dept of Bioenrgg, 2010, Univ. of Texas, Dallas. FIEEE 1983; FIASc 1992; Fellow: Indian Nat. Acad. of Engrg, 1992; Indian Nat. Acad. of Sci., 1994; FInstP 2012. Control Systems Award, IEEE, 2008; Rufus Oldenburger Medal, ASME, 2012. *Publications*: Feedback Systems: input-output properties (jtly), 1975; Nonlinear Systems Analysis, 1978, 2nd edn 1993; Input-Output Analysis of Large-Scale Interconnected Systems, 1981; Control System Synthesis: a factorization approach, 1985; (jtly) Robot Dynamics and Control, 1989; A Theory of Learning and Generalization: with applications to neural networks and control systems, 1997, 2nd edn 2003; (jtly) Robot Modeling and Control, 2006; Computational Cancer Biology: an interaction networks approach, 2012; articles in jls. *Address*: Indian Institute of Technology Hyderabad, Main Road, Near NH-65, Sangareddy, Kandi, Telangana 502285, India.

**VIGARS, Anna Lilian**; QC 2017; *b* Kendal, Westmorland, 3 Aug. 1972; *d* of Colin Weir and Angela Weir; *m* 1996, Christopher Vigars; one *s*. *Educ*: St Edmund Hall, Oxford (BA Mod. Hist.); City Univ. (DipLaw). Called to the Bar, Gray's Inn, 1996; in practice as barrister, specialising in criminal law; a Recorder, 2012–. Chm., Govs, St Werburgh's Primary Sch. *Recreations*: family, church, cookery, theatre. *E*: anna.vigars@guildhallchambers.co.uk.

**VIGARS, Della, (Mrs Paul Vigars)**; *see* Jones, Della.

**VIGGERS, Lt-Gen. Sir Frederick (Richard)**, KCB 2007; CMG 2004; MBE 1988; DL; Gentleman Usher of the Black Rod and Serjeant-at-Arms, House of Lords, and Secretary to the Lord Great Chamberlain, 2009–11; *b* 29 June 1951; *m* Jane; one *s* one *d*. Commnd RA, 1972; served in Germany and UK; psc 1983; Comdr, Gun Battery, 3rd Regt, RHA, 1984–85; COS, 1st Infantry Bde, UK Mobile Force, 1986; Staff Coll. Directing Staff, Camberley, 1988; Comdr, 3 RHA, Germany, 1989; 19 Infantry Bde, Colchester, 1990; Central Staff Directorate of Defence Policy, MoD, 1991–93; Defence Costs Study Secretariat, MoD, 1993; Comdr Artillery, 3rd UK Div., 1994; hcsc; Dir of Manning (Army), 1997; Comdr, Multi-Nat. Div. (SW), Stabilisation Force, Bosnia Herzegovina, 1999–2000; COS, HQ Land Comd, 2000–03; Dep. Comdg Gen., Combined Jt Task Force 7, and Sen. British Mil. Rep., Iraq, 2003; Mil. Sec. and Chief Exec., Army Personnel Centre, 2003–05; Adjutant Gen., 2005–08. DL Hants, 2008. *Address*: c/o NatWest, 12 Fore Street, Wellington, Somerset TA21 8AL.

**VIGGERS, Sir Peter (John)**, Kt 2008; *b* 13 March 1938; *s* of late J. S. Viggers and E. F. Viggers (later Mrs V. E. J. Neal), Gosport; *m* 1968, Jennifer Mary McMillan, MB, BS, LRCP, MRCS, DA, *d* of late Dr R. B. McMillan, MD, FRCP, Guildford, and late Mrs J. T. C. McMillan, MA, MIB; two *s* one *d*. *Educ*: Portsmouth Grammar Sch.; Trinity Hall, Cambridge (MA 1961). Chm., Cambridge Univ. Cons. Assoc., 1960. Solicitor 1967. Royal Canadian Air Force (pilot), 1956–58; commnd 457 (Wessex) Regt, RA (TA), 1963. MP (C) Gosport, Feb. 1974–2010. PPS to Solicitor-General, 1979–83, to Chief Sec. of HM Treasury, 1983–85; Parly Under-Sec. of State (Industry Minister), NI Office, 1986–89. Chm., Select Cttee on Armed Forces Bill, 1986, 1996; Member: Select Cttee on Members' Interests, 1991–93; Select Cttee on Defence, 1992–97, 2000–01, 2003–05 (Vice-Chm., 2000–01, 2003–05); Exec., British-American Parly Gp, 2000–10 (Jt Treas., 2003–09); Vice-Chm., British-Japanese Parly Gp, 1999–2010 (Chm., 1992–99); UK Delegate: Jt IPU and UN Conf. on Conventional Disarmament, Mexico City, 1985; N Atlantic Assembly, 1981–86, 1992–2010 (Vice-Chm., Political Cttee, 1995–97; Chm., 2000–04). Chm. and dir of public and private cos, 1972–. Underwriting Member of Lloyd's (Council Mem., 1992–96); Chm. Trustees, Lloyd's Pension Fund, 1996–2010. Mem., Management Cttee, RNLI, 1979–89, Vice-Pres., 1989–2008. Dir and Trustee, HMS Warrior 1860, 1995–2004. *Publications*: Vigorous Times, 2014. *Recreations*: opera, travel, trees, Burgundy. *Address*: 30 Smith Square, SW1P 3HF. *T*: (020) 7222 2775. *Clubs*: Boodle's, Royal Air Force.

**VIGNOLES, Prof. Anna Frances**, CBE 2019; PhD; FBA 2017; Professor of Education (1938), University of Cambridge, since 2012; Fellow, Jesus College, Cambridge, since 2014; *b* 1969; *d* of Phil and Lucy Vignoles; *m* Robin Griffiths; one *s* one *d*. *Educ*: Sch. of Oriental and African Studies, Univ. of London (BA 1st Cl. Econs with Politics 1991); Univ. of Newcastle upon Tyne (PhD Econs 1998). Res. Fellow, LSE, 1998–2003; Prof. of Econs of Educn, Inst. of Educn, Univ. of London, 2003–12; Res. Fellow, IFS, 2011–. Economist Mem., NHS Pay Rev. Body. Mem., ESRC, 2018– (Mem., Evaluation Cttee, 2013–). Trustee, Nuffield Foundn, 2015–. *Publications*: (with S. Machin) What's the Good of Education?: the economics of education in the UK, 2005; contribs to Jl Royal Statistical Soc., Series A, Oxford Rev. of Educn, Oxford Econ. Papers, Economica, Econs of Educn Rev. *Recreations*: sailing, travel. *Address*: Faculty of Education, University of Cambridge, 184 Hills Road, Cambridge CB2 8PQ. *T*: (01223) 767600, *Fax*: (01223) 767602. *E*: av404@cam.ac.uk.

**VIGNOLES, Roger Hutton**, ARCM; pianoforte accompanist; *b* 12 July 1945; *s* of late Keith Hutton Vignoles and of Phyllis Mary (*née* Pearson); *m* 1st, 1972, Teresa Ann Elizabeth Henderson (marr. diss. 1982); 2nd, 1982, Jessica Virginia, *d* of late Prof. Boris Ford; one *s* one *d*. *Educ*: Canterbury Cathedral Choir Sch.; Sedbergh Sch.; Magdalene Coll., Cambridge (BA, BMus; Hon. Fellow, 2009); Royal College of Music, London (ARCM). Accompanist of internat. reputation, regularly appearing with the most distinguished internat. singers and instrumentalists (Sir Thomas Allen, Dame Kiri te Kanawa, Dame Felicity Lott, Sarah Walker, etc.), both in London and provinces and at major music festivals (e.g. Aldeburgh, Cheltenham, Edinburgh, Brighton, Bath, Salzburg, Prague, etc.) and broadcasting for BBC Radio 3 and television. International tours incl. USA, Canada, Australia–New Zealand, Hong Kong, Scandinavia, and recitals at Opera Houses of Cologne, Brussels, Frankfurt, Lincoln Center, NY, San Francisco, Tokyo, Carnegie Hall, NY, Venice, Paris, Munich, Berlin, etc. Repetiteur: Royal Opera House, Covent Garden, 1969–71; English Opera Group, 1968–74; Australian Opera Company, 1976. Professor of Accompaniment, 1974–81, Prince Consort Prof. of Piano Accompaniment, 1996–, RCM; Consultant Prof. of Accompaniment, RAM, 1989–. Masterclasses for singers and pianists in Aarhus, Amsterdam, Barcelona, Copenhagen, Stockholm, Vienna, Toronto, Montreal, Ravinia Fest., Santa Fe Opera, Britten-Pears Sch., Snape. Extensive discography of vocal and chamber music. Hon. RAM 1984; Hon. FRCM 1997. *Recreations*: drawing, painting, looking at pictures, swimming, sailing. *Address*: 130 Mercers Road, N19 4PU. *T*: (020) 7272 5325, *Fax*: (020) 7281 1840.

**VIJAYRAGHAVAN, Prof. Krishnaswamy**, PhD; FRS 2012; Principal Scientific Advisor, Government of India, since 2018; Distinguished Professor, National Centre for Biological Sciences, Tata Institute of Fundamental Research, Bangalore, since 2012; *b* 3 Feb. 1954; *m* Usha; one *s*. *Educ*: Indian Inst. of Technol., Kanpur (BTech Chem. Engrg 1975; MTech); Bombay Univ. (PhD Molecular Biol.). Res. Fellow, 1984–85, Sen. Res. Fellow, 1986–88, Calif Inst. of Technol.; joined Tata Inst. of Fundamental Res., 1988, joined Nat. Centre for Biol Scis, Bangalore, 1992, Sen. Prof. and Dir, 1998–2012; Sec. Dept of Biotechnol., Ministry of Sci. and Technol., India, 2013–18. Mem., Sci. Adv. Council to Prime Minister of India, 2005–. Mem., Adv. Cttee, Howard Hughes Med. Inst. Janelia Farm Res. Campus, 2009–. Mem., Bd of Govs, Okinawa Inst. of Sci. and Technol. Sch. Corp., 2011–. FASc 1997; FNA 1999. Foreign Associate: EMBO; NAS, USA, 2014. Shanti Swarup Bhatnagar Prize, 1998; Infosys Prize in Life Scis, 2009. Padma Shri (India), 2013. *Address*: National Centre for Biological Sciences, Tata Institute of Fundamental Research, Bellary Road, Bangalore 560065, Karnataka, India.

**VILE, Prof. Maurice John Crawley**; Professor Emeritus of Political Science, University of Kent; *b* 23 July 1927; *s* of Edward M. and Elsie M. Vile; two *s*; *m* Nancy Gaffield. *Educ*: London Sch. of Economics (BSc (Econ) 1951); PhD London, 1954; MA Oxford, 1962. FRHistS 1989. Lectr in Politics, Univ. of Exeter, 1954–62; Fellow of Nuffield Coll., Oxford, 1962–65; Lectr in Politics, Magdalen Coll., Oxford, 1963–64; University of Kent: Reader in Politics and Govt, 1965–68; Prof. of Political Sci., 1968–84; Dir of Internat. Progs, 1984–87; Dean of Faculty of Social Scis, 1969–75; Pro-Vice-Chancellor, 1975–81; Dep. Vice-Chancellor, 1981–84; Dir of British Progs, Boston Univ., 1989–94; Dir of Res., Canterbury Christ Church Coll., 1994–99. Visiting Professor: Univ. of Massachusetts, 1960; Smith College, Mass., 1961. Royer Lectr, Univ. of Calif., Berkeley, 1974. Hon. Fellow, Canterbury Christ Church UC, 2003. Hon. DCL Kent, 1993. *Publications*: The Structure of American Federalism, 1961; Constitutionalism and the Separation of Powers, 1967, 2nd edn 1998; Politics in the USA, 1970, 6th edn 2007; Federalism in the United States, Canada and Australia (Res. Paper No 2, Commn on the Constitution), 1973; The Presidency (Amer. Hist. Documents Vol. IV), 1974.

**VILIKOVSKÝ, Ján**, PhD; Head: Slovak Centre for Literary Translation, 1997–2002; Centre for Information on Literature, 2001–02; Dean, Philological Faculty, Matej Bel University, Banská Bystrica, 2001–04; *b* 13 July 1937; *s* of late Prof. Ján Vilikovský and Dr Júlia Vilikovská (*née* Bárdošová); *m* 1st, 1962, Božica Šturová (*d* 1985); two *d*; 2nd, 1992, Mária Horváthová. *Educ*: Comenius Univ., Bratislava (BA 1959; MA 1975; PhD 1982). Editor, Slovak Writers' Publishing House, 1959–70; Asst Prof., Inst. of Translators, 1970–74; Asst Prof., Dept of English and American Studies, Comenius Univ., 1974–90; Sec.-Gen., Slovak Translators' Assoc., 1986–90; Dir, Tatran Publishers, 1990–92; Ministry of Foreign Affairs, 1992–96; Ambassador of Czechoslovakia, 1992; Ambassador of Slovak Republic to UK, 1993–96. Asst Gen. Sec., RECIT (European Network of International Centres of Literary Translators), 2000–04. Hon. Dr Constantine the Philosopher Univ., Nitra, 2007. Ján Hollý Prize for Translation, 1969, 1980, 2003. *Publications*: Slovak-English Dictionary, 1959, 5th edn 1992; Preklad ako tvorba (Translation as a creative process), 1984; Shakespeare u nás (Shakespeare in Slovakia), 2014; contribs to learned jls; translations from English and American literature. *Recreations*: classical music, reading, talking. *Address*: Žalužická 7, 821 01 Bratislava, Slovakia.

**VILJOEN, His Honour (Theo) Leon**; a Circuit Judge, 1992–2007; *b* 25 Aug. 1937; *s* of Robert Bartlett Viljoen and Cecilia Jacoba Viljoen (*née* van der Walt); *m* 1967, Dorothy Nina Raybould (*d* 2014), *d* of late Prof. S. G. Raybould; two *d*. *Educ*: Afrikaanse Hoër Seunskool; Univ. of Pretoria. Called to the Bar, Middle Temple, 1972; a Recorder, 1991–92; a Deputy High Court Judge, 1993–2007. Legal Assessor, UKCC, 1987–92. Mem., 1997–2003, 2004–10, Appraiser, 2005–10, Parole Bd. Life Pres., Les Planes Tractor Co-op., Gard, France. *Recreations*: walking, gardening, wine. *Address*: c/o 2 Harcourt Buildings, Temple, EC4Y 9DB. *T*: (020) 7583 9020.

**VILLAGE, Peter Malcolm**; QC 2002; *b* 3 Feb. 1961; *s* of late Malcolm Rowland Village and of Margaret Village; *m* 1992, Alison Helen Wallis; one *s* two *d*. *Educ*: Repton Sch.; Univ. of Leeds (LLB Hons); Inns of Court Sch. of Law. Called to the Bar, Inner Temple, 1983, Bencher, 2011, NI, 1997; barrister specialising in planning, compulsory purchase and judicial review, 1985–. Legal Counsel (pt-time), Commercial Estates Gp, 2015–. Dir, Carlyle Land Ltd, 2014–. Gov., Repton Sch., 1998–2015. *Recreations*: salmon fishing, shooting, ski-ing, walking the dog. *Address*: 39 Essex Chambers, 81 Chancery Lane, WC2A 1DD. *T*: (020) 7832 1111. *E*: peter.village@39essex.com. *Club*: Brooks's.

**VILLEROY DE GALHAU, François**; Officier de la Légion d'Honneur, 2014; Governor, Banque de France, since 2015; Chairman, Autorité de contrôle prudentiel et de résolution; *b* Strasbourg, 24 Feb. 1959; *s* of Claude Villeroy de Galhau and Odile de Calan; *m* 1981, Florence de Vautibault; five *c*. *Educ*: Ecole Polytechnique; Ecole Nat. d'Admin. Inspector of Finance, 1984–87; French Treasury, 1988–90; Eur. Advr to Minister of Finance and Prime Minister, 1990–93; French Treasury, 1993–96; Financial Advr, Perm. Representation of France to EU, Brussels, 1996–97; COS to Minister of Economy, Finance and Industry, 1997–2000; Hd, Gen. Tax Directorate, 2000–03; CEO, Cetelem, 2003–08; Hd, Retail Banking Activities, BNP Paribas, 2008–11; Chief Operating Officer, BNP Paribas Gp i/c Eur. Domestic Mkts and Corporate Social Responsibility, 2011–15; French Prime Minister's assignment on corporate investment financing, 2015. *Publications*: 18 leçons sur la politique économique, 2003, 2005; L'Espérance d'un Européen, 2014. *Address*: Banque de France, 31 rue Croix-des-Petits-Champs, 75001 Paris, France. *T*: (1) 42922001, *Fax*: (1) 42922010. *E*: sec.gouverneur@banque-france.fr.

**VILLIERS**; see Child Villiers, family name of Earl of Jersey.

**VILLIERS**; see de Villiers.

**VILLIERS**, family name of **Earl of Clarendon**.

**VILLIERS, Viscount; George Henry William Child-Villiers**; *b* 1 Sept. 2015; *s* and heir of Earl of Jersey, *qv*.

**VILLIERS, Charles Nigel**, FCA; Deputy Chairman, Abbey National plc, 1999–2001; *b* 25 Jan. 1941; *s* of Robert Alexander and Elizabeth Mary Villiers; *m* 1970, Sally Priscilla Magnay; one *s* one *d*. *Educ*: Winchester Coll.; New Coll., Oxford (MA German and Russian); Harvard Business Sch. (AMP). Arthur Andersen & Co., 1963–67; ICFC, 1967–72; County Bank Ltd, 1972–86; Dir, 1974; Dep. Chief Exec., 1977; Chm. and Chief Exec., 1984–85; Exec. Chm., 1985–86; Exec. Dir, National Westminster Bank, 1985–88; Chief Exec., NatWest Investment Bank Ltd (estab. June 1986 incorporating the business of County Bank Ltd), 1986–88; Chm., County NatWest Ltd, 1986–88; Man. Dir of Corporate Develt, Abbey National plc (formerly Abbey Nat. Bldg Soc.), 1988–99. Non-exec. Dir, DTZ Hldgs, 1997–2004. Treas., E Thames Housing Gp, 2001–08. *Recreations*: opera, ski-ing, European history, tennis. *Club*: Reform.

**VILLIERS, Rt Hon. Theresa (Anne)**; PC 2010; MP (C) Chipping Barnet, since 2005; Secretary of State for Environment, Food and Rural Affairs, since 2019; *b* 5 March 1968; *d* of late George Villiers and of Virginia Villiers; *m* 1999, Sean David Henry Wilken, *qv* (marr. diss.). *Educ*: Univ. of Bristol (LLB Hons 1990); Jesus Coll., Oxford (BCL Hons 1991). Called to the Bar, Inner Temple, 1992; Barrister specialising in chancery, insolvency and entertainment law, 1994–95; Lectr in Law, King's Coll., London, 1995–99. MEP (C) London Region, 1999–2005. Treas. and economic spokesman, 1999–2004, Dep. Leader, 2001–02, Cons. delegn to EP; EP Rapporteur for Investment Services Directive, 2002–05. Shadow Chief Sec. to HM Treasury, 2005–07; Shadow Sec. of State for Transport, 2007–10; Minister of State, DfT, 2010–12; Sec. of State for NI, 2012–16. *Publications*: (with Sean Wilken) Waiver, Variation and Estoppel, 1998; Tax Harmonisation: the impending threat, 2001; various articles in legal jls, incl. Lloyd's Maritime and Commercial Law Qly. *Address*: House of Commons, SW1A 0AA. *Club*: Middlesex CC.

**VINCENT, Prof. Angela Carmen**, FRS 2011; Professor of Neuroimmunology, University of Oxford, 1998–2008, now Emeritus; Fellow, Somerville College, Oxford, 1992–2008, now Emeritus; *b* Woking, Surrey, 30 Sept. 1942; *d* of Sir Joseph Molony, KCVO and Carmen Mary Molony (*née* Dent); *m* 1967, Philip Vincent; two *s* two *d*. *Educ*: St Mary's Convent, Ascot; Westminster Hosp. Med. Sch., London Univ. (MB BS 1966); University Coll. London (MSc Biochem. 1969). MRCPath 1991. Lectr in Clin. Neuroimmunol., Univ. of Oxford, 1992–98; Hon. Consultant in Immunol., John Radcliffe Hosp., Oxford, 1992–2016. FMedSci 2002. Hon. PhD Bergen, 2004. *Publications*: (ed jtly) Clinical Neuroimmunology, 2005; (ed with R. C. Dale) Inflammatory and Autoimmune Disorders of the Nervous System in Children, 2010; (ed with S. J. Pittock) Autoimmune Neurology, 2016; over 500 articles and chapters on autoimmune diseases of the nervous system. *Recreations*: children and grandchildren, occasional tennis and opera. *Address*: Taverners, Woodeaton, Oxon OX3 9TH. *T*: (01865) 559636. *E*: angela.vincent01@gmail.com.

**VINCENT, Anthony Lionel**; Legal Adviser, Department of Foreign Affairs and Trade, Canberra, 1993–97; *b* 18 Oct. 1933; *s* of Harold Francis Vincent and Lesley Allison Vincent; *m* 1958, Helen Frances Beasley; one *s* one *d*. *Educ*: Univ. of Western Australia, Perth (LLB); Univ. of Oxford (BCL). Joined Dept of Foreign Affairs, Aust., 1958; served: Karachi, 1959–61; Hong Kong, 1963–66; Singapore, 1966–69; Belgrade, 1972–74; Paris, 1977–80; Australian Ambassador to: Iraq, 1981–83; GDR, 1984; Dep. High Comr in London, 1984–87; Asst Sec., Treaties and Sea Law Br., 1987–89, Intelligence and Defence Br., 1989–90, Dept of Foreign Affairs and Trade, Canberra; Ambassador to Czech and Slovak Federal Republic, subseq. to Czech and Slovak Republics, 1990–93. *Recreations*: drawing, painting, reading. *Address*: 56 Blackwall Reach Parade, Bicton, WA 6157, Australia.

**VINCENT, Catherine Beatrice Margaret, (Katie)**; *see* Derham, C. B. M.

**VINCENT, Prof. Colin Angus**, OBE 2003; Professor of Electrochemistry, 1989–2003, Master of the United College, 1996–2003 and Deputy Principal, 2001–03, University of St Andrews; *b* 4 March 1938; *s* of Harold Frederick Vincent and Helen McEachern Vincent; *m* 1964, Doris Susan Cole; one *s* one *d*. *Educ*: Oban High Sch.; Univ. of Glasgow (BSc 1960; PhD 1963; DSc 1987); Univ. of St Andrews (MA 2008). MIEE; CChem, FRSC 1976; FRSE 1992. Assistant, Univ. of Glasgow, 1963–65; Lectr, Univ. of Illinois, 1965–67; University of St Andrews: Lectr, 1967–76; Sen. Lectr; 1976–84; Reader, 1984–89; Head, School of Chemistry, 1990–97; Vice-Principal, 1996–2001; Vice-Chancellor and Acting Principal, 2000. Hon. LLD St Andrews, 2003. Galvani Medal, Italian Chem. Soc., 1998. *Publications*: (jtly) Alkali Metal, Alkaline Earth Metal and Ammonium Halides in Amide Solvents, 1980; Modern Batteries, 1984, 2nd edn 1997; Polymer Electrolyte Reviews, vol. 1, 1987, vol. 2, 1989; more than 120 papers in learned jls. *Recreations*: hill walking, opera. *Address*: 1 Station Brae, Newport-on-Tay, Fife DD6 8DQ. *T*: (01382) 543156.

**VINCENT, Dr Jean-Paul**, FRS 2013; FMedSci; Group Leader, Francis Crick Institute, since 2015; *b* Kinshasa. *Educ*: Univ. of Louvain (BSc Applied Physics); Univ. of California, Berkeley (Fulbright Fellow; MA Biophysics; PhD 1982). Damon Runyon Fellow, Med. Center, Univ. of Calif, San Francisco, 1987–93; Res. Gp Leader, MRC Lab. of Molecular Biol., Cambridge, 1993–97; Gp Leader, 1997–2012, Jt Hd of Div., 2012–15, MRC NIMR. Co-founder, VASTox, later Summit Corp. plc, 2001 (Mem., Scientific Adv. Bd). Mem., EMBO, 2006. Member: British Soc. Develtl Biol.; British Soc. for Cell Biol.; British Genetics Soc. FMedSci 2010. *Publications*: contribs to learned jls incl. Sci. Signalling, Cell, Proc. NAS, Nature Cell, Develt. *Address*: Francis Crick Institute, 1 Midland Road, NW1 1AT.

**VINCENT, Rev. Dr John James**; writer and lecturer; Methodist Minister, Sheffield Inner City Ecumenical Mission (Superintendent, 1970–97); Director, Urban Theology Union (formerly Unit), 1969–97, Director Emeritus, since 1997; President of the Methodist Conference, 1989–90; *b* 29 Dec. 1929; *s* of late David Vincent and Ethel Beatrice Vincent (*née* Gadd); *m* 1958, Grace Johnston, *d* of late Rev. Wilfred Stafford, Bangor, Co. Down; two *s* one *d*. *Educ*: Manchester Grammar Sch.; Richmond Coll.; London Univ. (BD 1954); Drew Univ., USA (STM 1955); Basel Univ., Switzerland (DTheol 1960). Sgt, RAMC, 1948–49. Minister, Manchester and Salford Mission, 1956–62; Supt, Rochdale Mission, 1962–69; Founder and Leader, The Ashram Community, 1967–. Visiting Professor of Theology: Boston Univ., and New York Theol Seminary, 1969–70; Drew Univ., 1977; Adjunct Prof. of Theol., New York Theol Seminary, 1979–88. Hon. Lectr in Biblical Studies, 1990–; supervisor, doctoral prog. in Contextual, Urban and Liberation Theologies, 1993–, Sheffield Univ.; Hon. Lectr in Theol. and doctoral supervisor, Birmingham Univ., 2003–. Chairman: NW Campaign for Nuclear Disarmament, 1957–63; Alliance of Radical Methodists, 1970–76; Urban Mission Trng Assoc., 1982–90; Trustee Savings Bank Depositors Assoc. (also litigant in High Court and H of L, TSB *v* Vincent), 1986; Jt Co-ordinator, British Liberation Theol. Inst., 1990–; Co-Chair, Urban Theologians Internat., 1993–; Member: Studiorum Novi Testamenti Societas, 1961–; Council, Christian Orgns for Social, Political and Econ. Change, 1981–91; Exec., Assoc. of Centres of Adult Theol. Educn, 1984–90. Fellow, St Deiniol's Library, Hawarden, 2003. Jt Ed., British Liberation Theology series, 1995, 1997, 1999, 2001. Centenary Achievement Award, Sheffield Univ., 2005. *Publications*: Christ in a Nuclear World, 1962; Christian Nuclear Perspective, 1964; Christ and Methodism, 1965; Here I Stand, 1967; Secular Christ, 1968; The Race Race, 1970; The Jesus Thing, 1973; Stirrings: essays Christian and Radical, 1975; Alternative Church, 1976; Disciple and Lord: discipleship in the Synoptic Gospels, 1976; Starting All Over Again, 1981; Into the City, 1982; OK, Let's Be Methodists, 1984; Radical Jesus, 1986, 2nd edn 2004; Mark at Work, 1986; Britain in the Nineties, 1989; Discipleship in the Nineties, 1991; A Petition of Distress from the Cities (to the Queen and Govt), 1993; (ed jtly) The Cities: Methodist report, 1997; Hope from the City, 2000; (ed jtly) Bible and Practice, 2001; (ed jtly) Methodist and Radical, 2003; (ed) Faithfulness in the City, 2003; (ed) Mark: gospel of action, 2006; (ed) Primitive Christianity, 2007; (jtly) The City in Biblical Perspective, 2009; A Lifestyle of Sharing, 2009; (jtly) The Drama of Mark, 2010; (ed) Stilling the Storm, 2011; (ed) Christian Communities, 2011; (ed) Acts in Practice, 2012; (ed) British Liberation Theology: for Church and Nation, 2012; Christ in the City: the dynamics of Christ in urban theological practice, 2013; Methodism Unbound: Christ and Methodism for the 21st century, 2015; (ed) Radical Christianity: roots and fruits, 2016; (ed) The Servant of God in Practice, 2017; (with Grace Vincent) Inner City Testament, 2017; *relevant publication*: Urban Christ: responses to John Vincent, ed I. K.

Duffield, 1997. *Recreations:* jogging, writing. *Address:* 7 College Court, Sheffield S4 7FN. *T:* (0114) 243 6688, *T:* and *Fax:* (Urban Theology Union) (0114) 272 9907. *E:* office@utusheffield.org.uk.

**VINCENT, Prof. John Russell;** Professor of History, University of Bristol, 1984–2002, now Emeritus Professor; *b* 20 Dec. 1937; *s* of late Prof. J. J. Vincent and M. Monica Vincent, MSc, PhD (*née* Watson); *m* 1972, Nicolette Elizabeth Kenworthy; one *s* (and one *s* decd). *Educ:* Bedales Sch.; Christ's Coll., Cambridge. Fellow, Peterhouse, Cambridge, 1962–70; Lectr in Modern British History, Cambridge Univ., 1967–70; Prof. of Modern History, Univ. of Bristol, 1970–84. Vis. Prof., UEA, 2003–08. Chm., Bristol Br., NCCL, 1972–74. *Publications:* The Formation of the Liberal Party, 1966 (2nd edn as The Formation of the British Liberal Party 1857–68, 1980); Poll Books: how Victorians voted, 1967; (ed with A. B. Cooke) Lord Carlingford's Journal, 1971; (ed with M. Stenton) McCalmont's Parliamentary Poll Book 1832–1918, 1971; (with A. B. Cooke) The Governing Passion: Cabinet Government and party politics in Britain 1885–86, 1974; (ed) Disraeli, Derby and the Conservative Party: the political journals of Lord Stanley 1849–69, 1978; Gladstone and Ireland (Raleigh Lecture), 1979; (ed) The Crawford Papers: the journals of David Lindsay, Twenty-Seventh Earl of Crawford and Tenth Earl of Balcarres during the years 1892 to 1940, 1984; Disraeli, 1990; (ed) The Derby Diaries 1869–1878, 1995; (contrib.) Twentieth-Century Britain: an encyclopaedia, 1995; An Intelligent Person's Guide to History, 1995; (contrib.) Why Tory Governments Fall, 1996; (ed) The Derby Diaries 1878–1893, 2003. *Recreation:* journalism. *Address:* University of Bristol, Senate House, Bristol BS8 1TH.

**VINCENT, Matthew Philip Jude;** Lombard Columnist, Financial Times, since 2017; *b* 28 Oct. 1966; *s* of Dudley Joseph and Claire Vincent. *Educ:* Salvatorian Coll., Harrow Weald; Univ. of Manchester (BA Hons English Lang. and Lit.). Prodn asst, BBC TV, 1988–89; staff writer: Stately Homes and Gardens mag., 1989–90; Money mag., 1990; Moneywise magazine: staff writer, 1990–92; Chief Sub-ed./Associate Ed., 1992–95; Ed., 1995–2000; Hd of Content, Investors Chronicle Online and FT Business, 2000–02; Editor: Investors Chronicle, 2002–07; FT Business, 2002–07; FT Personal Finance, 2007–12; UK Companies Ed., 2012–14; Dep. Companies Ed., 2014–16. BBC TV: reporter, Short Change, 1994; presenter, Pound For Pound, 1998. *Publications:* contrib. articles to various financial jls. *Recreations:* poetry, cricket, sherry. *Address:* Financial Times, Bracken House, 1 Friday Street, EC4M 9BT. *Club:* Blackheath Cricket.

**VINCENT, Prof. Nicholas Charles,** DPhil; FBA 2010; Professor of Medieval History, University of East Anglia, since 2003; *b* Sittingbourne, 20 Oct. 1961; *s* of Roy Charles Vincent and Joan Mary Vincent (*née* Biart); *m* Juliet Tyson; one *s* two *d*. *Educ:* Borden Sch.; Kent Jun. Music Sch.; St Peter's Coll., Oxford (BA Hons 1st Cl. 1983; MPhil 1987; DPhil 1993). House Tutor, Clifton College Prep. Sch., 1983–84; History Master: Stowe Sch., Buckingham, 1986; Gstaad Internat. Sch., 1986–87; William Stone Res. Fellow, 1990–95, Bye Fellow, 1994, Peterhouse, Cambridge; Reader, 1995–99, Prof., 1999–2003, Christ Church Coll., Canterbury. Visiting Fellow: All Souls Coll., Oxford, 1999–2000; Peterhouse, Cambridge, 2000–01; École Nationale des Chartes, Paris, 2002; Université de Poitiers, 2009. FRHistS 1995; FSA 1999. Hon. Sec., Pipe Roll Soc., 1994. Mem., Adv. Bds incl. English Historical Review, Cahiers de Civilisation Médiévale, Annales du Midi. *Publications:* (trans. with A. Alikhani) Asadollah Alam, The Shah and I: the confidential diary of Iran's Royal Court, 1969–1977, 1991; English Episcopal Acta IX: Winchester 1205–1238, 1994; Peter des Roches, 1996; The Letters and Charters of Cardinal Guala Bicchieri, 1996; Acta of Henry II and Richard I, 1996; The Holy Blood, 2001; The Magna Carta, 2007; (ed with C. Harper-Bill) Henry II: new interpretations, 2007; (ed) Records, Administration and Aristocratic Society in the Anglo-Norman Realm, 2009; A Brief History of Britain 1066–1485, 2011; Magna Carta: a very short introduction, 2012; Norman Charters from English Sources, 2013; Magna Carta: the foundation of freedom, 2014; Magna Carta: origins and legacy, 2015; King John, an Evil King, 2019; approx. 100 academic articles. *Recreations:* music, 19th century literature. *Address:* School of History, University of East Anglia, Norwich NR4 7TJ. *T:* (01603) 592745. *E:* n.vincent@uea.ac.uk.

**VINCENT, Prof. Nigel Bruce,** FBA 2006; Mont Follick Professor of Comparative Philology, University of Manchester, 1987–2011, now Professor Emeritus of General and Romance Linguistics; *b* 24 Sept. 1947; *s* of Denis George Vincent and Peggy Eliza Vincent; *m* 1st, 1971, Janet Elizabeth Hutchinson (marr. diss. 1999); two *d*; 2nd, 1999, Merethe Damsgård Sørensen; one *d*. *Educ:* Sexey's Sch., Bruton; Trinity Hall, Cambridge (BA 1st cl. hons Mod. and Medieval Langs 1970); Darwin Coll., Cambridge (Dip. Linguistics 1971). Lecturer: Birkbeck Coll., London, 1973–74; Univ. of Lancaster, 1974–76; Univ. of Hull, 1976–81; Univ. of Cambridge, 1981–87 (Fellow, Trinity Hall, 1983–87); University of Manchester: Res. and Graduate Dean of Arts, 1992–96; Associate Dean, Postgrad. Res. in Humanities, 2004–06; Associate Vice-Pres., Graduate Educn, 2006–11. British Acad. Res. Reader, 1996–98. Visiting Professor: Univ. of Pavia, 1983; Univ. of Rome, 1986; Ecole Pratique des Hautes Etudes, Paris, 1993; Australian Linguistic Inst., La Trobe Univ., 1994; Univ. of Copenhagen, 1997; Melbourne Univ., 2000; Erskine Fellow, Univ. of Canterbury, NZ, 2000. Member: Res. Grants Bd, ESRC, 1988–91; Council, Philological Soc., 1982–86, 1989–94, 1995–99 (Pres., 2000–03); Res. Gp Leader, EUROTYP Project, ESF, 1990–94; Humanities Res. Bd, 1994–96; Chm., Res. Assessment Panels, HEFCE, 1992, 1996, 2005–08; Vice-Pres. for Res. and Higher Educn Policy, British Acad., 2010–14; Pres., MHRA, 2013. Vice Pres., Società di Linguistica Italiana, 1990–92; President: Internat. Soc. of Historical Linguistics, 1993–95; Perm. Internat. Cttee of Linguists, 2013–14. Mem. Bd, British Inst. in Paris, 1999–2002. MAE 2013. Editor, Jl of Linguistics, 1984–93. *Publications:* (jtly) Studies in the Romance Verb, 1982; (jtly) The Romance Languages, 1988; (jtly) Parameters of Morphosyntactic Change, 1997; (jtly) Linguistic Areas, 2006; (jtly) Dialects and Diachrony, 2014; (jtly) Early and Late Latin: continuity or change?, 2016; articles in jls. *Recreations:* wine, all things Italian. *Address:* Holsteinborgvej 215, Bisserup, 4243 Rude, Denmark. *T:* 07932 770508. *E:* nigel.vincent@manchester.ac.uk.

**VINCENT, Robert Warden,** CBE 2010; Chief Executive, Doncaster Metropolitan Borough Council, 2010–11; Electoral Commissioner, since 2016; *b* 27 Sept. 1951; *s* of Stanley and Joan Vincent; *m* 1974, Heather Hitchen; two *s* two *d*. *Educ:* King's Coll., Wimbledon; Univ. of Liverpool (BEng 1973; MCD 1975). MRTPI 1977. Town planning and policy posts, Dorset CC, 1973–78 and Tameside MBC, 1978–87; Kirklees Metropolitan Council: Asst Dir of Educn, 1987–90; Hd of Resources, 1990–94; Chief Educn Officer, 1994–98; Exec. Dir and Dep. Chief Exec., 1998–2004; Chief Exec., 2004–10. Non-executive Director: DCLG, 2008–10; Bradford Dist Care Trust, 2013– (Dep. Chair, 2014–); Adviser: to DoH, 2012–15; to Public Health England, 2013–15. Chair, Kirklees Theatre Trust, 2013–16. Hon. Dr Huddersfield, 2016. *Recreations:* looking at buildings, making furniture.

**VINCENT, Simon Robert,** OBE 2015; Executive Vice President, and President, Europe, Middle East and Africa, Hilton (formerly Hilton Worldwide), since 2007 (Member, Executive Committee, since 2007); *b* Lymington, 28 May 1963; *s* of Leonard Roy Vincent and Mary Sheila Vincent; *m* 1994, Charlotte Helen; two *c*. *Educ:* Priestlands Sch., Lymington; Brockenhurst Coll.; City Univ., London (BSc Banking and Internat. Finance 1985). With Midland Bank Internat., 1985–88; Thomas Cook, 1989–2002: Man. Dir, Tour Ops, 1997–99; Chief Operating Officer, UK Travel, 1999–2002; CEO, Opodo, 2004–06. Mem., Pi Capital. Non-exec. Dir, Fortnum and Mason, 2014–. *Recreations:* golf, tennis, sailing. *E:* vincentsr1@aol.com. *Clubs:* 5 Hereford Street; Walton Heath Golf.

**VINCENT, Sir William (Percy Maxwell),** 3rd Bt *cr* 1936; Managing Director, Cambridge Associates Ltd, 1995–2015; *b* 1 Feb. 1945; *o s* of Sir Lacey Vincent, 2nd Bt, and Helen Millicent, *d* of Field Marshal Sir William Robert Robertson, 1st Bt, GCB, GCMG, GCVO, DSO; *S* father, 1963; *m* 1976, Christine Margaret, *d* of Rev. E. G. Walton; three *s*. *Educ:* Eton College. 2nd Lieutenant, Irish Guards, 1964–67. Director: Save and Prosper Investment Mgt, 1980–85; Touche Remnant & Co., 1985–92; M & G (N America) Ltd, 1992–95. *Recreations:* water ski-ing, sailing. *Heir: s* Edward Mark William Vincent, *b* 6 March 1978. *Address:* Battlegreen, Green Lane, Hambledon, Hants PO7 4TB.

**VINE, Prof. Frederick John,** FRS 1974; Emeritus Professor, School of Environmental Sciences, University of East Anglia, since 2004 (Professor, 1974–98; Professorial Fellow, 1998–2004); *b* 17 June 1939; *s* of Frederick Royston Vine and Ivy Grace Vine (*née* Bryant); *m* 1964, Susan Alice McCall; one *s* one *d*. *Educ:* Latymer Upper Sch., Hammersmith; St John's Coll., Cambridge (BA, PhD). Instructor, 1965–67, and Asst Professor, 1967–70, Dept of Geological and Geophysical Sciences, Princeton Univ., NJ, USA; Reader, 1970–74, Dean, 1977–80 and 1993–98, School of Environmental Sciences, UEA. Arthur L. Day Medal, Geol Soc. of America, 1968; Henry Bryant Bigelow Medal, Woods Hole Oceanographic Instn, 1970; J. J. Bigsby Medal, Geol Soc. of London, 1971; (jtly) S. Chapman Medal, RAS, 1973; (jtly) Arthur L. Day Prize, US NAS, 1975; (jtly) Charles Chree Medal, Inst. of Physics, 1977; (jtly) Balzan Foundn Prize for Geology and Geophysics, 1981; (jtly) Hughes Medal, Royal Soc., 1982; Prestwich Medal, Geol Soc. of London, 2007. *Publications:* (jtly) Global Tectonics, 1990, 3rd edn 2009; articles in Nature, Science, Phil. Trans Roy. Soc. London, etc. *Recreations:* walking, travel.

**VINE, Jeremy;** Presenter: Jeremy Vine Show, BBC Radio Two, since 2003; Eggheads, BBC2, since 2008; Jeremy Vine, Channel 5, since 2018; *b* 17 May 1965; *s* of late Dr Guy and of Diana Vine; *m* 2002, Rachel Schofield; two *d*. *Educ:* Epsom Coll.; Durham Univ. (BA Hons English Lit. 1986). Coventry Evening Telegraph, 1986–87; joined BBC, 1987: News Trainee, 1987–89; Programme Reporter, Today, 1989–93; Political Corresp., 1993–97; Africa Corresp., 1997–99; Presenter: Newsnight, 1996–2002, full-time, 1999–2002; Politics Show, BBC TV, 2003–05; Panorama, BBC1, 2007–10; Crimewatch, BBC1, 2016–17; Points of View, BBC1, 2008–18. *Publications:* It's All News to Me, 2012; What I Learnt: what my listeners say and why we should take notice, 2017. *Address:* c/o BBC Radio 2, Western House, W1A 1AA. *T:* (020) 7765 2129. *Clubs:* Reform, Soho House; Chelsea Football.

**VINEALL, Sir Anthony (John Patrick),** Kt 2002; Chairman, School Teachers' Review Body, 1996–2002; *b* 17 March 1932; *s* of George John Charles Vineall and Helen Fairley Vineall (*née* Bradshaw); *m* 1962, Dorothy Earnshaw; two *s*. *Educ:* Leeds Grammar Sch.; New Coll., Oxford (MA PPE). FCIPD (FIPD 1982). Nat. Service, commnd RA, 1951. Unilever: personnel posts in Animal Foods, Frozen Food, and in Ghana, 1955–67; Co. Personnel Manager, Walls Meat, 1967–70; Personnel Dir, SSC&B Lintas, 1970–75; Dir, Unilever UK Hldgs and Nat. Personnel Manager, 1975–81; Head of Corporate Mgt Develt, 1981–92. Chm., Tavistock and Portman NHS Trust, 1993–99. Member: Council, Foundn for Mgt Educn, 1976–92; Doctors' and Dentists' Pay Review Body, 1990–93; Review of Armed Forces Career and Rank Structure, 1994–95; Chairman: Exec. Cttee, Industrial Soc., 1982–85; Careers Res. Adv. Centre, 1991–96 (Mem. Council, 1981–); Vice Pres., Centre for Internat. Briefing, Farnham Castle, 1996– (Chm. Govs, 1987–96). Vice Chm. of Govs, Guildford Royal Grammar Sch., 2004–08 (Gov., 1994–). *Recreations:* gardening, travel, bridge. *Address:* Ways End, 34 Abbotswood, Guildford GU1 1UZ.
See also N. E. J. Vineall.

**VINEALL, Nicholas Edward John;** QC 2006; a Deputy High Court Judge, since 2017; *b* 1 May 1963; *s* of Sir Anthony John Patrick Vineall, *qv*; *m* 1992, Kate Jenkins; two *s* one *d*. *Educ:* Royal Grammar Sch., Guildford; Christ's Coll., Cambridge (BA Natural Sci. 1985); Univ. of Pittsburgh (MA Hist. and Philosophy of Sci.); City Univ. (Dip. Law). Harkness Fellow, Univ. of Pittsburgh, 1985–86. Called to the Bar, Middle Temple, 1988, Bencher, 2015; in practice as barrister, 4 Pump Court specialising in commercial and construction law (Jt Hd of Chambers, 2017–). Mem., Council of Legal Educn, 1990–96. Member: Bar Council, 1990–96 and 2016– (Chm., Young Bar, 1994); Exec. Cttee, Soc. of Cons. Lawyers, 1999–2007, 2009–12 (Chm., Res., 2003–05); Standards Cttee, Bar Standards Bd, 2010–14. Trustee: Harold G. Fox Educn Fund, 2017–; Inns of Court Bar Educnl Trust, 2018–. Mem. (C) Southwark LBC, 2006–10 (Chm., Dulwich Community Council, 2006–10). Chm., Dulwich and W Norwood Cons. Assoc., 2000. Contested (C) Dulwich and W Norwood, 2001, Morley and Rothwell, 2005. Governor: Waverley Sch. and Harris Girls' Acad., E Dulwich, 1998–2008; Royal Grammar Sch., Guildford, 2011–. Chm., Free Representation Unit, 1988. Mem., St Stephen's Dulwich PCC, 2017–. Ed., Lloyd's Law Reports (Financial Crime), 2008–14. *Recreations:* music, microscopy, tennis, bridge. *Address:* 4 Pump Court, Temple, EC4Y 7AN. *T:* (020) 7842 5555.

**VINEN, William Frank, (Joe),** FRS 1973; Poynting Professor of Physics, 1962–74, Poynting Professor of Physics, 1974–97, University of Birmingham, now Emeritus Professor of Physics; *b* 15 Feb. 1930; *o s* of Gilbert Vinen and Olive Maud Vinen (*née* Roach); *m* 1960, Susan-Mary Audrey Master; one *s* one *d*. *Educ:* Watford Grammar Sch.; Clare College, Cambridge. Research Fellow, Clare College, 1955–58. Royal Air Force, 1948–49. Demonstrator in Physics, Univ. of Cambridge and Fellow of Pembroke Coll., 1958–62 (Hon. Fellow, 2014). Hon. Life Fellow, Coventry Univ. (formerly Poly.), 1989. Hon. FInstP, 2002. Hon. Dr Charles Univ., Prague, 2008. Simon Meml Prize, Inst. of Physics, 1963; Holweck Medal and Prize, Inst. of Physics and French Physical Soc., 1978; Rumford Medal, Royal Soc., 1980; Guthrie Medal and Prize, Inst. of Physics, 2005. *Recreation:* good food. *Address:* 52 Middle Park Road, Birmingham B29 4BJ. *T:* (0121) 475 1328. *E:* w.f.vinen@bham.ac.uk.

**VINES, Prof. David Anthony,** PhD; Professor of Economics, University of Oxford, 2000–17; Fellow in Economics, Balliol College, Oxford, 1992–2017, now Emeritus Fellow; Adjunct Professor of Economics, Research School of Economics, Australian National University, 1991; *b* 8 May 1949; *s* of Robert Godfrey and Vera Frances Vines; *m* 1st, 1979, Susannah Lucy Robinson (marr. diss. 1992); three *s*; 2nd, 1995, Jane Elizabeth Bingham; two step *s*. *Educ:* Scotch Coll., Melbourne; Melbourne Univ. (BA 1971); Cambridge Univ. (BA 1974; MA 1977; PhD 1984). Cambridge University: Fellow, Pembroke Coll., 1976–85; Res. Officer and Sen. Res. Officer, Dept of Applied Econs, 1979–85; Adam Smith Prof. of Political Economy, Univ. of Glasgow, 1985–92; Reader in Econs, Oxford Univ., 1997–2000; Res. Fellow, Centre for Econ. Policy Res., London, 1985–. Board Member: Channel 4 Television, 1987–92; Glasgow Develt Agency, 1990–92. Economic Consultant to Sec. of State for Scotland, 1987–92; Consultant, IMF, 1988, 1989. Economic and Social Research Council: Member: Econ. Affairs Cttee, 1985–87; Res. Progs Bd, 1992–93; Dir, Res. Prog. on Global Econ. Instns, 1994–2000. Mem. Academic Panel, HM Treasury, 1986–95. Mem. Council, Royal Economic Soc., 1988–92. Bd Mem., Analysys, 1989–2002. Comr, BFI Enquiry into the Future of the BBC, 1992. Houblon Norman Fellow, Bank of England, 2002. Res. Dir, Politics and Econs of Global

Governance Eur. Div. Res. Prog., Framework Seven, EU, 2008–12. Bd Mem., Scottish Early Music Consort, 1990–91. *Publications:* (with J. E. Meade and J. M. Maciejowski) Stagflation, Vol. II: Demand Management, 1983; (with D. A. Currie) Macroeconomic Interactions Between North and South, 1988; (jtly) Macroeconomic Policy: inflation, wealth and the exchange rate, 1989; (with G. Hughes) Deregulation and the Future of Commercial Television, 1989; (with A. Stevenson) Information, Strategy, and Public Policy, 1991; (with D. A. Currie) North South Interactions and International Macroeconomic Policy, 1995; (with Peter Drysdale) Europe, East Asia and APEC, 1998; (ed with Alan Montefiore) Integrity in the public and private domains, 1998; (jtly) The Asian Financial Crises, 1999; (with Chris Gilbert) The World Bank: structure and policies, 2000; (with Chris Gilbert) The IMF and its Critics: reform of global financial architecture, 2004; (with Peter Temin) The Leaderless Economy: why the world economic system fell apart and how to fix it, 2013; (with Peter Temin) Keynes: useful economics for the world economy, 2014; (with Nicholas Morris) Capital Failure: rebuilding trust in the financial system, 2014; papers on international macroeconomics, macro-economic policy, in professional jls. *Recreations:* hillwalking, music. *Address:* Balliol College, Oxford OX1 3BJ. *T:* (01865) 271067, *Fax:* (01865) 271094.

**VINET, Dr Luc;** Aisenstadt Professor of Physics, and Director, Centre de Recherches Mathématiques, 1993–99 and since 2013, University of Montreal; *b* 16 April 1953; *m* Letitia Muresan; three *s* one *d. Educ:* Univ. of Montreal (BSc Hons Physics 1970; MSc Theoretical Physics 1974; PhD Theoretical Physics 1980); Dr in Theoretical Physics, Univ. Pierre & Marie Curie, 1979. Res. Associate, Center for Theoretical Physics, MIT, 1980–82; Department of Physics, University of Montreal: NSERC Res. Fellow, 1982–87; Asst Prof., 1987–88; Associate Prof., 1987–88; Prof., 1992–99; Associate Mem., Centre de recherches mathématiques, 1999–2002; Pres., Network for Computing and Mathematical Modelling (rcm2), 1996–99; Chief Exec., Bell Energis Univ. Lab., 1998; McGill University: Prof., Dept of Maths and Stats and Dept of Physics, 1999–2005; Vice-Principal (Acad.), 1999–2005; Provost, 2001–05; Rector, Univ. of Montreal, 2005–10. Chair: Panel of Experts, Canadian Foundn for Innovation; Conf. des Recteurs et des Principaux des Univs du Québec; Member: Groupe de travail sur les affaires médicales; Gen. Physics Steering Cttee; Inst. de finance mathématique de Montréal; Bd, Canadian Inst. for Telecommunications Res.; Comité Ministériel sur la pondération des activités; Bd, Maths of Information Technol. and Complex Systems; Bd, Ouranos; Bd, Industries de la science de la vie et biotechnologies. Member: Soc. for Industrial and Applied Maths; Canadian Assoc. Physicists; Canadian Mathematical Soc. Hon. Mem., Golden Key Nat. Honor Soc., 2000. Officier, Ordre des Palmes Académiques (France), 2009. *Address:* Mathematical Research Center, University of Montreal, PO Box 6128, Station Centre-Ville, Montreal, QC H3C 3J7, Canada.

**VINEY, Anne Dorothy;** Chief Executive, Cruse Bereavement Care, 2002–08; *b* 29 March 1948; *d* of Edward Walter Totman and Margaret Totman (*née* Fulljames); *m* 1970, Stephen John Viney. *Educ:* Bristol Univ. (BA Hons (French) 1969); King's Coll. London (PGCE 1970); Goldsmiths Coll., London (CQSW 1986); Open Univ. (MBA 2000). Teacher: London Borough of Sutton, 1970–71; Essex CC, 1971–75; London Borough of Barnet, 1975–76; Sec., NABC, 1976; Age Concern, Westminster: Sec., 1977; Welfare Worker, 1977–79; Dep. Organising Sec., 1979–85; Social Worker, Camden Social Services, at Gt Ormond St Hosp., 1986–87; Asst Dir, 1987–99, Hd of R&D, 1999–2001, Victim Support. *Recreations:* music, films, theatre. *E:* anne.viney@runbox.com. *Club:* Royal Society of Medicine.

**VINGT-TROIS, His Eminence Cardinal André Armand;** Archbishop of Paris (RC), 2005–18, now Emeritus; Officier de la Légion d'Honneur; Officier de l'Ordre National du Mérite; *b* 7 Nov. 1942; *s* of Armand Vingt-Trois and Paulette (*née* Vuillamy). *Educ:* Lycée Henri IV, Paris; St Sulpice Seminary, Issy-les-Moulineaux; Institut Catholique, Paris (BTh 1962). Military service, Germany, 1964–65; ordained priest, 1969; Asst Pastor, St Jeanne de Chantal, Paris, 1969–74; Dir and Prof. of Sacramental and Moral Theology, St Sulpice Seminary, Issy-les-Moulineaux, 1974–81; Vicar Gen., Archdiocese of Paris, 1981–99; ordained Aux. Bishop of Paris, 1988; Metropolitan Archbishop of Tours, 1999. Cardinal, 2007. French Bishops' Conference: Member: Episcopal Cttee for Charismatic Renewal, 1988–96; Permt Cttee for Information and Communications, 1988–97; Permt Cttee for Econ. Affairs, 1997–99; Pres., Cttee for the Family, 1998–2005; Pres., 2007–13. Mem., Presidency Cttee, Pontifical Council for the Family and Congregation of Bishops, 2006–, and for the Pastoral Care of Migrants and Itinerant People, 2008–. Member: Congregation for the Clergy, 2010–; Congregation of the Oriental Churches, 2012–. Grand Cross Knight, Equestrian Order of the Holy Sepulchre, 2012. *Publications:* A Year of Blessings, 2000; To Know the Catholic Faith, 2000; Catecheses for the Jubilee Year, 2001; The Family: 15 questions to the Church, 2003; To Believe, to Hope, to Love, 2007; The Signs that God Sends Us, 2007; Freedom in Faith, 2008; Bishops, Priests and Deacons, 2009; A Mission for Liberty, 2010; Prayer: why? how?, 2010; Family Life: building happiness, 2011; What Kind of a Society Do We Want?, 2012; God Opens New Paths, 2015; Discovering Jesus in Mark's Gospel, 2016; The Word Does What It Says: listening to Luke's gospel, 2017; The Beloved Disciple as Instructor: the teaching of John's gospel, 2017. *Address:* c/o Diocese de Paris, 10 rue du Cloître-Notre-Dame, 75004 Paris, France.

**VINJAMURI, Dr Leslie;** Head, US and Americas Programme, and Dean, Queen Elizabeth II Academy, Chatham House, Royal Institute of International Affairs, since 2018 (Member, Council, since 2015); Director, Centre on Conflict, Rights and Justice, since 2016, and Reader in International Relations, since 2018, School of Oriental and African Studies, University of London (Co-Director, 2011–16); *b* New Jersey, USA, 25 July 1968; *d* of Sudhir Kumar Vinjamuri and Carol Vinjamuri; *m* 1993, Oliver Wright; two *s* one *d. Educ:* Wesleyan Univ. (BA 1991); London Sch. of Econs and Pol Sci. (MSc (Econs) Dist. 1992); Columbia Univ. (MPhil 1997; PhD 2001). Foreign Affairs Associate, Congressional Res. Service, 1992; Res. Associate, US Agency for Internat. Develt, 1992–94; Fellow, John M. Olin Inst., Harvard Univ., 1999–2000; Vis. Fellow, Centre for Internat. Studies, 2000–01, Centre for Study of Human Rights, 2006–07, LSE; Asst Prof., Sch. of Foreign Service, Georgetown Univ., 2002–07; Sen. Lectr, SOAS, Univ. of London, 2007–18. Vis. Sen. Fellow and Mem., Adv. Bd, LSE IDEAS, 2017–. Mem., Marshall Commn, 2019–. Regular appearances on networks incl. CNN, Bloomberg TV, BBC. Life Mem., Council on Foreign Relns, 2015. Mem., Bd of Dirs, Inst. for Integrated Transitions, 2015–. Trustee, Gilbert Murray Trust, 2011–16. *Publications:* (ed jtly) Human Rights Futures, 2017; contribs to Ethics and Internat. Affairs, Annual Rev. of Political Sci., Internat. Security, Daedalus, Telegraph, Independent, CNN (online). *Recreations:* theatre, travel, running. *Address:* Royal Institute of International Affairs, Chatham House, 10 St James's Square, SW1Y 4LE. *E:* lv@soas.ac.uk; 5 England's Lane, NW3 4YA.

**VINKEN, Adrian Charles,** OBE 2006; DL; Chief Executive, Theatre Royal Plymouth, since 1990; *b* London, 14 May 1953; *s* of Joseph and Esther Vinken; *m* 1985, Elaine Gibbs; two *d. Educ:* Gunnersbury Grammar Sch., London; Univ. of Sheffield (BA Hons 1976). Res. and tutoring, Univ. of Sheffield, 1976–80; Founding Dir, Leadmill Arts Centre, Sheffield, 1980–90. Chair: Nat. Assoc. of Arts Centres, 1985–88; Arts Develt Assoc. 1988–90; Culture SW, 2000–07; Touring Partnership Ltd, 2001–; Plymouth Culture Bd, 2009–; Mayflower 400, 2014–. Dir, Lowry Trust, Salford, 2005–. Hon. DArts Plymouth, 2011. DL Devon, 2019. *Recreations:* fell-running, mountaineering, theatre, classic car maintenance, family. *Address:* Theatre Royal, Royal Parade, Plymouth PL1 2TR. *T:* (01752) 230336. *E:* adrian.vinken@theatreroyal.com.

**VINNEY, Prof. John Edward;** DL; PhD; CEng, FIMechE; FHEA; Professor and Vice-Chancellor, Bournemouth University, since 2010; *b* Croydon, 15 April 1965; *s* of Edward Vinney and Shirley Vinney (*née* Packer); *m* 1987, Maria Tiffany Rollason; three *d. Educ:* Dorset Inst. of Higher Educn (HND 1986); Bristol Poly. (BEng Hons 1990); Univ. of West of England (PhD 1998; PGCE 2001). FIMechE 2003. Projects Engr, Vickers Shipbuilding and Engrg Ltd, 1986–90; Design Engr, British Aerospace (Space Systems) Ltd, 1990–91; Lectr, Coventry Univ., 1991–92; University of the West of England: Sen. Lectr, 1992–99; Principal Lectr, 1999–2001; Hd of Sch., 2001–03; Associate Dean, 2003–05; Dean, 2005–06; Bournemouth University: Dean, 2006–08; Pro Vice-Chancellor, Resources, 2008–09, Educn and Professional Practice, 2009–10. FHEA 2004. DL Dorset, 2019. *Publications:* articles in learned jls. *Recreations:* badminton, cycling, walking. *Address:* Bournemouth University, Talbot Campus, Fern Barrow, Poole, Dorset BH12 5BB. *T:* (01202) 965006, *Fax:* (01202) 965069. *E:* vice-chancellor@bournemouth.ac.uk.

**VINSON,** family name of **Baron Vinson.**

**VINSON,** Baron *cr* 1985 (Life Peer), of Roddam Dene in the County of Northumberland; **Nigel Vinson,** LVO 1979; DL; entrepreneur; Founder, 1952, Chairman, 1952–72, Plastic Coatings Ltd; Founder Director, Centre for Policy Studies, 1974–80; *b* Nettlestead Place, Kent, 27 Jan. 1931; *s* of late Ronald Vinson and Bettina Vinson (*née* Southwell-Sander); *m* 1972, Yvonne Ann Collin; three *d. Educ:* Pangbourne Naval Coll. Lieut, Queen's Royal Regt, 1949–51. Plastic Coatings Ltd: started in a Nissen hut, 1952, flotation, 1969; Queen's Award to Industry, 1971. Director: Fleming High Income Growth Trust (formerly Fleming Tech. Trust), 1972–2001; BAA, 1973–80; Electra Investment Trust, 1975–98 (Dep. Chm., 1990–98); Barclays Bank UK, 1982–88. Mem., H of L Select Cttee on Econ. Affairs, 2001–03. Member: Crafts Adv. Cttee, 1971–77; Design Council, 1973–80; Dep. Chm., CBI Smaller Firms Council, 1979–84; Chairman: CoSIRA, 1980–82; Rural Develt Commn, 1980–90 (Mem., 1978–90); Industry Year Steering Cttee, RSA, 1985–87; Pres., Industrial Participation Assoc., 1979–89 (Chm., 1971–78). Institute of Economic Affairs: Trustee, 1972–2004; Chm. of Trustees, 1989–95; Life Vice-Pres., 1998. Trustee, Civitas, 2005–. Hon. Dir, Queen's Silver Jubilee Appeal, 1976–78; Member: Northumbrian Nat. Parks Countryside Cttee, 1977–89; Regional Cttee, Nat. Trust, 1977–84. Chm., NE Region, PYBT, 1995–98; Pres., NE Civic Trust, 1999–2001. Council Mem., St George's House, Windsor Castle, 1990–96. Foundation Donor: Martinmere Wildfowl Reserve, 1972; Buckingham Univ. Vinson Centre for Liberal Econs, 2016; gifted a village green to Holburn, Northumberland, 2006. Trustee, Chillingham Wild Cattle, 1989. FRSA. DL Northumberland, 1990. *Publications:* Personal and Portable Pensions for All, 1984; Owners All, 1985; Take upon Retiring, 1998. *Recreations:* fine art and craftsmanship, horses, farming. *Address:* 34 Kynance Mews, SW7 4QR. *T:* (01668) 217230. *Clubs:* Boodle's, Pratt's.

**VINTER, Anne Elizabeth;** *see* Baldock, A. E.

**VINTON, Alfred Merton;** Chairman, Electra Partners Ltd (formerly Electra Kingsway Managers, then Electra Fleming Ltd), 1995–2009; *b* 11 May 1938; *s* of Alfred Merton Vinton and Jean Rosalie Vinton (*née* Guiterman); *m* 1st, 1963, Mary Bedell Weber; two *s* one *d;* 2nd, 1983, Anna-Maria Hawser (*née* Dugan-Chapman); one *s* one *d. Educ:* Harvard College (AB Econs 1960). US Navy Lieut (JG), 1960–62. J. P. Morgan, 1962–88; Chief Operating Officer, N. M. Rothschild & Sons, 1988–92; Chief Exec. Officer, Entreprises Quilmes SA, 1992–94; Director: Sand Aire Investments plc, 1995–2005; Sagitta Investment Advrs Ltd, 1996–2001; Unipart Ltd, 1998–2014 (Dep. Chm.); Amerindo Internet Fund plc, 2000–06; Lambert Howarth Gp plc, 2000–07; GP Investments Ltd, 2006–; Alantra Partners SA, Spain, 2016–; Sen. Ind. Dir, European Goldfields Ltd, 2010–12; Chm., N+1 Singer, 2016–. *Recreations:* golf, tennis, riding, music. *Address:* Stoke Albany House, Market Harborough, Leics LE16 8PT. *T:* (01858) 535227. *Clubs:* White's; Sunningdale Golf; Harvard (New York).

**VIÑUALES, Prof. Jorge Enrique;** Harold Samuel Professor of Law and Environmental Policy, University of Cambridge, since 2013 (Founder and Director, Cambridge Centre for Environment, Energy and Natural Resource Governance, 2014); *b* Buenos Aires, 7 Jan. 1976; *s* of Ricardo Miguel Viñuales and Margit Viñuales (*née* Juhasz). *Educ:* Nat. Univ. of Central Buenos Aires (LLB); Univ. of Freiburg (LLB); Univ. of Geneva (BA; MA); Inst Universitaire de Hautes Études Internationales (BA, MA); Harvard Law Sch. (LLM); Sciences Po Paris (Dr ès sciences politiques, 2008). Of Counsel: Lévy Kaufmann-Kohler, Switzerland, 2008–11; Lalive, Switzerland, 2015–19; Pictet Chair of Internat. Envmtl Law, Grad. Inst., Geneva, 2009–13. Country Expert, Amnesty Internat., Swiss Section, 2003–05; Vis. Expert, Internat. Develt Law Orgn and UNESCO Chair (Burundi), 2007–08. Exec. Dir, 2006–12, Dir-Gen., 2016–, Latin American Soc. of Internat. Law. Chm., Water Compliance Cttee, UNECE/WHO-Europe Protocol on Water and Health, 2017–. *Publications:* (ed jtly) Diplomatic and Judicial Means of Dispute Settlement, 2012; Foreign Investment and the Environment in International Law, 2012; (ed jtly) Harnessing Foreign Investment to Promote Environmental Protection, 2013; (ed jtly) Unity and Diversity of International Law, 2014; (ed jtly) The Foundations of International Investment Law, 2014; (ed) The Rio Declaration on Environment and Development: a commentary, 2015; (with P. M. Dupuy) International Environmental Law, 2015, 2nd edn 2018. *Recreations:* Kung Fu (Baji style), travelling, cinema, art, cooking. *Address:* Cambridge Centre for Environment, Energy and Natural Resource Governance, University of Cambridge, 19 Silver Street, Cambridge CB3 9EP. *T:* (01223) 337147, *Fax:* (01223) 337130. *E:* jev32@cam.ac.uk.

**VIRDEE, Sir Tejinder Singh,** Kt 2014; PhD; FRS 2012; FInstP; Professor of Physics, Imperial College London, since 1996; *b* Nyeri, Kenya, 13 Oct. 1952; *s* of late Sardar Chain Singh and of Bibi Udham Kaur; *m* 1983, Vatsala Oza; one *s* one *d. Educ:* Kings Norton Boys Grammar Sch., Birmingham; Queen Mary Coll., Univ. of London (BSc 1974); Imperial Coll. London (PhD 1979). FInstP 2012. Joined CERN as Fellow, Experimental Physics Div., 1979; Co-founder, 1990, Dep. Spokesperson, 1993–2006, Spokesperson (Leader), 2007–10, Compact Muon Solenoid Collaboration, CERN Large Hadron Collider. High Energy Physics Prize, 2007, Chadwick Prize and Medal, 2009, Glazebrook Prize and Medal, 2015, Inst. of Physics; Sikh Award (Educn), 2010; Fundamental Physics Prize, Milner Foundn, 2012; India Internat. Award (Sci.), 2013; High Energy and Particle Physics Prize, Eur. Physical Soc., 2013; Person of Year, GG2 Asian Leadership Awards, 2013; W. K. H. Panofsky Prize in Exptl Particle Physics, APS, 2015; Outstanding Achievement in Sci. and Technol., Asian Awards, 2015. Hon. DSc: QMUL, 2013; Univ. Claude Bernard, 2013; Panjab, Chandigarh, 2017. *Address:* Blackett Laboratory, Physics Department, Imperial College London, Prince Consort Road, SW7 2AZ; CERN, 1211 Geneva 23, Switzerland.

**VIRLEY, Simon James,** CB 2014; Head, Energy and Natural Resources, KPMG UK, since 2015; *b* 7 June 1969; *s* of Brian Michael Virley and Jean Barbara (*née* Lofts); *m* 2005, Kate Jaggar; two *s. Educ:* Jesus Coll., Oxford (BA Hons PPE 1990, MA 1994); London Sch. of Econs (MSc Econs 1995). Econs tutor, Green Coll., Oxford, 1990–91; Economist, Dept of Transport, 1991–93; Policy Advr, 1993–99, Team Leader, 1999–2000, HM Treasury; Private Sec. (Econ. Affairs) to Prime Minister, 2000–03; Dir, Better Regulation Exec.,

Cabinet Office, 2003–05; Dir, Corporate Finance, KPMG (on secondment from Cabinet Office), 2005–07; Hd, Renewable Energy and Innovation Unit, later Chief Exec., Office for Renewable Energy Deployment, BERR, later DECC, 2008–09; Actg Dir Gen., Nat. Climate Change and Consumer Support, 2009, Dir Gen., Energy Markets and Infrastructure, 2009–15, DECC. Mem., ICAEW, 2015–; FEI 2016. Member: Energy Policy Debates Mgt Cttee, Energy Inst., 2015–; Adv. Bd, Energy 2050, Univ. of Sheffield, 2015–; Energy and Climate Change Cttee, CBI, 2017–. *Publications*: contrib. to jls incl. Econ. Briefing, Treasury Occasional Papers, Transport Policy. *Recreations*: cricket, football, ski-ing, golf, tennis. *Address*: KPMG LLP, 15 Canada Square, E14 5GL.

**VISCHER, Vivienne;** *see* Cox, V.

**VISSCHER, Stephen Hendrick,** CBE 2013; Director of Strategic Partnerships and Chief Operating Officer, Global Institute for Food Security, Saskatchewan, since 2019 (non-executive Director, 2015–18; Interim Executive Director and Chief Executive Officer, 2018–19); *b* Northampton, 12 Jan. 1955; *s of* Johannes Visscher and Marjorie Visscher; *m* 1979, Ann Patricia Bowles; two *s*. *Educ*: FCMA 1995. Biotechnology and Biological Sciences Research Council: Director: Finance and Estates, 1994–2000; Finance and Admin, 2000–05; Exec. Dir, 2005–07; Interim Chief Exec., 2007–08; Dep. Chief Exec. and Chief Operating Officer, 2008–15; Dep. Chief Exec. - Internat., 2015–18. Dir, Norwich Research Partners LLP, 2012–19; Partner, William Cowley Parchment and Vellum Manufrs, 1997–. Trustee, Med. Res. Foundn, 2012–19; Dir, Life Arc (formerly MRC Technology), 2017–. FIIA 1996; FRSB (FSB 2013); FRSA. *Recreations*: walking, ski-ing, gardening, tennis, travel. *Address*: Global Institute for Food Security, University of Saskatchewan, Gymnasium Place, Saskatoon, SK S7N 0W9, Canada. *T*: 3069663701. *E*: steve.visscher@gifs.ca. *Club*: Farmers.

**VISSER, John Bancroft;** Associate Member, Powell's School, Cirencester, 2013–15 (Governor, 1992–2013; Chairman, 1999–2005); Trustee, Enrichment Fund, Cirencester Deer Park School, since 2011 (Governor, 1998–2010; Associate Member, 2010–18); Trustee, since 1991, and Chairman, since 2018, Powell's Educational Foundation and associated charities (Vice-Chairman, 2008–18); *b* 29 Jan. 1928; *o s of* late Gilbert and Ethel Visser; *m* 1955, Astrid Margareta Olson; two *s* one *d*. *Educ*: Mill Hill Sch.; New Coll., Oxford (Exhibnr). Entered Civil Service, Asst Principal, Min. of Supply, 1951; Principal, 1956; Min. of Aviation, 1959; Admin. Staff Coll., 1965; Asst Sec., 1965; Min. of Technology, 1967; Royal Coll. of Defence Studies, 1970; Civil Service Dept, 1971; Procurement Exec., MoD, 1971; Under-Sec., 1974; Sec. of Nat. Defence Industries Council, 1971–74; Dir of Admin, SRC, then SERC, 1974–88. *Recreations*: sport, music, gardening, art and antiques, heritage steam railways. *Address*: 79 Corinium Gate, Cirencester, Glos GL7 2PX. *T*: (01285) 652626. *Club*: Old Millhillians.

**VITA-FINZI, Dr Claudio,** FBA 2012; Scientific Associate, Department of Earth Sciences (formerly Mineralogy), Natural History Museum, since 2001; *b* Sydney, 21 Nov. 1936; *s of* Paolo Vita-Finzi and Nadia Vita-Finzi (*née* Touchmalova); *m* 1969, Penelope; one *s*. *Educ*: Quintin Sch.; St John's Coll., Cambridge (BA 1958; PhD 1962; ScD 1988). Res. Fellow, St John's Coll., Cambridge, 1961–64; University College London: Lectr in Geog., then Geology, 1964–87; Prof. of Neotectonics, 1987–2001, now Emeritus. Mem., Amer. Philosophical Soc., 1997–. G. K. Warren Prize, US NAS, 1994. *Publications*: The Mediterranean Valleys, 1969; Recent Earth History, 1973; Archaeological Sites, 1978; Recent Earth Movements, 1986; Monitoring the Earth, 2002; Planetary Geology, 2005; The Sun: a user's manual, 2008; Solar History, 2012; A History of the Solar System, 2016; The Sun Today, 2018; papers in scientific jls. *Recreation*: clarinet trios for two. *Address*: 22 South Hill Park, NW3 2SB. *T*: (020) 7794 4415, 07713 886687. *E*: cvitafinzi@aol.com.

**VITMAYER, Dame Janet,** DBE 2018 (CBE 2011); Chief Executive, Horniman Museum and Gardens, 1998–2018; *b* 2 Sept. 1952; *d of* Arnost Vitmayer and Maria (*née* Pichler); one *s* one *d*. *Educ*: Univ. of Keele (BA Hons Hist. and American Studies 1976); City Univ. (MA Mus. and Gall. Mgt 1990). Imperial War Mus., 1976–83; Dir, Livesey Mus., 1983–93; Hd, Public Services, Horniman Mus. and Gardens, 1993–98. Visitor, Pitt Rivers Mus., Univ. of Oxford, 2000–15. Chair, Medicine, History and Society Capital Awards Cttee, Wellcome Trust, 2008, 2009, 2011–13. Trustee: London Transport Mus., 2008–14; Collections Trust, 2008–15; Hunterian Collection, 2013–; Florence Nightingale Mus., 2016–. *Recreations*: family pursuits, travel.

**VITORIA, Dr Mary Christine;** QC 1997; *m* Prof. Clive Ashwin. *Educ*: Bedford Coll., London (BSc, PhD Chemistry); LLB (ext.), BA Spanish and Latin American Studies (ext.), London Univ. Called to the Bar, Lincoln's Inn, 1975, Bencher, 2004; Lectr in Law, QMC, 1977; in practice at the Bar, 1978–2008. Editor: Reports of Patent Cases, 1995–2011; Fleet Street Reports, 1995–2011. *Publications*: (jtly) Modern Law of Copyright and Designs, 1980, 4th edn 2011; (contrib.) Halsbury's Laws of England, 4th edn. *Recreations*: opera, bird watching. *Address*: 8 New Square, Lincoln's Inn, WC2A 3QP. *T*: (020) 7405 4321.

**VITORINO, António;** Director General, International Organization for Migration, since 2018; *b* 12 Jan. 1957; *m*; two *s*. *Educ*: Lisbon Law Sch. (law degree 1981; Master in Law and Pol Sci. 1986). Lawyer, 1982; Asst Prof., Lisbon Law Sch., 1982; Prof., Lisbon Autonomous Univ., 1986; Judge, Constitutional Court of Portugal, 1989–94; Vice-Pres., Portugal Telecom Internacional, 1998–99; Prof., Internat. Univ., 1998–99. Deputy (Socialist Party) Portuguese Parlt, 1980–83, 1985–89; Sec. of State for Parly Affairs, 1984–85, for Admin and Justice, Macao govt, 1986–87; Dep. Prime Minister and Minister of Defence, 1995–97; Mem., European Parlt, 1994–96; Mem., Eur. Commn, 1999–2004. Member: Jt EP and Portuguese Parlt Cttee on European Integration, 1980–84; Sino-Portuguese Jt Liaison Gp on Macao, 1987–89. Partner, Cuatrecascas, Gonçalves, Pereira & Associates, Lisbon, 2005–18. Pres., Gen. Assembly, Santander Totta Bank, 2005–. Pres., Notre Europe, 2011–16. Former Chm., Eur. Policy Centre. *Publications*: books on European affairs, constitutional law and pol sci.

**VIVIAN,** family name of **Barons Swansea** and **Vivian**.

**VIVIAN,** 7th Baron *cr* 1841; **Charles Crespigny Hussey Vivian;** Bt 1828; *b* 20 Dec. 1966; *s of* 6th Baron Vivian and his 1st wife, Catherine Joyce (*née* Hope) (now Countess of Mexborough); *S* father, 2004. Co-founder, Pelham Public Relations, 2018. Dir, Tavistock Communications, 2017–. *Recreations*: Rugby, water ski-ing. *Heir*: nephew Thomas Crespigny Brabazon Vivian [*b* 17 Jan. 1971; *m* 2001, Victoria Ruth Ambrahams; one *s* one *d*]. *Address*: 28 Walpole Street, SW3 4QS. *Clubs*: White's, 5 Hertford Street.

**VIVIAN, James Antony,** FRCO; Director of Music, St George's Chapel, Windsor, since 2013; *b* Worcester, 19 June 1974; *s of* Roy John Vivian and Pamela Ann Vivian (*née* Bromley); *m* 2004, Ann Elise Smoot; one *s* one *d*. *Educ*: Malvern Coll. (Music Scholar); King's Coll., Cambridge (BA 1996; MA 1999). FRCO 1994. Actg Asst Organist, Lincoln Cath., 1992–93; A. H. Mann Organ Scholar, King's Coll., Cambridge, 1993–97; Temple Church: Suborganist, 1997–2004; Organist, 2004–13; Dir of Music, 2006–13. Various broadcasts; recordings on EMI, Decca, Hyperion, Priory, Signum, Sony BMG. *Recreations*: American history, cooking, baseball.

**VLESSING, Suzanna;** *see* Taverne, S.

**VLIEGHE, Dr Gertjan Willem;** External Member, Monetary Policy Committee, Bank of England, since 2015; Executive Fellow, London Business School, since 2016; *b* Amsterdam, 1971; *m* 1996, Shakeh Harikian; one *s* one *d*. *Educ*: Vesalius Coll., Belgium (BA Business Econs 1993); Univ. of Sussex (DipEcon); London Sch. of Econs and Pol Sci. (MSc Econs 1998; PhD Econs 2005). Analyst and Associate, J P Morgan (Belgium), 1994–96; Bank of England: economist, 1998–2004; Econ. Asst to Gov., 2004–05; Dir, Deutsche Bank, 2005–07; Partner and Sen. Economist, Brevan Howard Asset Mgt, 2007–15. *Address*: c/o Bank of England, Threadneedle Street, EC2R 8AH.

**VOAKE, Charlotte Elizabeth Mary;** freelance author and illustrator; *b* 9 Jan. 1957; *d of* Colin and Margaret Voake; *m* 1983, Robert Atkins; one *s* one *d*. *Educ*: Birkenhead High Sch., GPDST; University Coll. London (BA Hons Hist. of Art). *Publications*: illustrator: The Best of Aesop's Fables by Margaret Clark, 1990; Elsie Piddock Skips in Her Sleep by Eleanor Farjeon, 2000; A Child's Guide to Wild Flowers by Kate Petty, 2004; Collected Poems by Allan Ahlberg, 2008; The Further Adventures of the Owl and the Pussycat by Julia Donaldson, 2013; The Owl and the Pussy-cat by Edward Lear, 2014; Say It by Charlotte Zolotow, 2015; Beatrix Potter and the Unfortunate Tale of a Borrowed Guinea Pig by Deborah Hopkinson, 2015; The Things That I Love About Trees by Chris Butterworth, 2018; author and illustrator: Ginger, 1997 (Smarties Award, 1997); Pizza Kittens, 2002 (Smarties Award, 2002); Ginger Finds a Home, 2003; Hello Twins, 2006 (Best Illustrated Children's Bks Award, NY Times, 2006); Tweedle Dee Dee, 2008; A Little Guide to Trees, 2009; Ginger and the Mystery Visitor, 2010; Melissa's Octopus, 2014; *Recreations*: gardening, piano, violin.

**VOBE, Helen Mary;** *see* Jones, H. M.

**VOGEL, Dr Dieter H.;** Founder and Chairman, Lindsay Goldberg Vogel GmbH, since 1998; *b* 14 Nov. 1941; *m* 1970, Ursula Gross; two *c*. *Educ*: primary sch., Berchtesgaden; secondary sch., Frankfurt; Tech. Univ. of Darmstadt (Dip. Mech. Engrg); Tech. Univ. of Munich (Dr.Ing). Asst Prof., Thermic Turbo Engines, Tech. Univ. of Munich, 1967–69; Vice-Pres., Printing Div., Bertelsmann AG, 1970–74; Pegulan Ag, 1975–85 (Chm., 1978); Vice-Chm., Mgt Bd, Batig (BAT Industries), 1978–85; Thyssen Group, 1986–98: Chm., Thyssen Handelsunion AG, 1986–96; Mem., Exec. Bd, 1986–91; Dep. Chm., 1991–96, Chm., 1996–98, Thyssen AG; Chm., Deutsche Bahn AG, 1998–2001. Chairman, Supervisory Board: Mobilcom AG, 2003–07; Bertelsmann AG, 2004–07; Klöckner & Co., 2006–. Chm., Bd of Trustees, Bertelsmann Foundn, 2007–11. *Publications*: M & A—Ideal und Wirklichkeit, 2002. *Recreation*: ski-ing. *Address*: Lindsay Goldberg Vogel GmbH, Neuer Stahlhof, Breite Straße 69, 40213 Düsseldorf, Germany.

**VOGEL, Hans-Jochen,** Hon. CBE; Dr jur; Chairman: Social Democratic Party (SPD), Federal Republic of Germany, 1987–91; Gegen Vergessen-Für Demokratie eV, 1993–2001; *b* 3 Feb. 1926; *s of* Dr Hermann Vogel and Caroline (*née* Brinz); *m* 1st, 1950, Ilse Leisnering (marr. diss. 1972); one *s* two *d*; 2nd, 1972, Liselotte Biersack. *Educ*: Göttingen and Giessen; Univs of Marburg and Munich (Dr jur 1950). Army service, 1943–45 (PoW). Admitted Bavarian Bar, 1951; Legal Asst, Bavarian Min. of Justice, 1952–54; District Court Counsel, Traunstein, 1954–55; staff of Bavarian State Chancellery, 1955–58; Munich City Council, 1958–60, Oberbürgermeister (Chief Executive), Munich, 1960–72 (re-elected, 1966); Vice-Pres., Org. Cttee, Olympic Games, 1972. Mayor of West Berlin, Jan.–June 1981, leader of opposition, 1981–83. Chm., Bavarian SPD, 1972–77; Mem. (SPD) Bundestag, 1972–81, 1983–94; Minister of regional planning, housing and urban devel, 1972–74; Minister of Justice, 1974–81; Leader of the Opposition, 1983–91. Bundesverdienstkreuz; Bavarian Verdienstorden. *Publications*: Städte im Wandel, 1971; Die Amtskette: Meine 12 Münchner Jahre, 1972; Reale Reformen, 1973; Nachsichten, 1996; Demokratie lebt auch vom Widerspruch, 2001; Politik und Anstand, 2005; Deutschland aus der Vogel Perspektive, 2007; Wie wollen wir leben?, 2011; Nach Was zusammengehört: die SPD und die deutsche Einheit 1989/1990, 2014; Es gilt das gesprochene Wort, 2016. *Recreations*: mountaineering, swimming, reading history. *Address*: Gegen Vergessen-Für Demokratie eV, Stauffenbergstrasse 13–14, 10785 Berlin, Germany.

**VOGEL, Prof. Johannes Christian,** PhD; Director General, Museum für Naturkunde, Berlin, and Professor of Biodiversity and Public Science, Humboldt University, Berlin, since 2012; *b* 15 May 1963; *s of* late Erich Vogel and Edith Vogel (*née* Fröböse); *m* 2003, Dr Sarah Catherine Darwin; two *s*. *Educ*: Ratsgymnasium, Bielefeld; Bielefeld Univ. (Vordiplom Biol. 1986); Peterhouse, Cambridge (PhD 1996). Served Armed Forces, FRG, 1982–84. Researcher, Alpeninstitut, Munich, 1989–90; Natural History Museum: Researcher, Dept of Botany, 1995–2004; Hd, UK Biodiversity Prog., 1999–2004; Keeper of Botany, 2004–11. Chm., European Citizen Sci. Assoc., 2014–; Dep. Chm., German BioEconomy Council, 2012–; Chm., Open Sci. Policy Platform, EU Commn, 2016–. Member: UK Biodiversity Gp, 1999–2001; Biodiversity Res. Adv. Gp, 2001–07; DCMS Sustainable Develt Forum, 2001–05; Darwin Expert (formerly Initiative Adv.) Cttee, 2005–11; Interdisciplinary Panel on Plant Genomics, ESRC Genomic and Policy Forum, 2005–09; Scientific Adv. Cttee, Chelsea Physic Garden, 2008–12; Leopoldina AG Taxonomie, 2012–14; Expert Rev. Panel, Volkswagenstiftung, 2013–14. Member Board: Naturwissenschaftlicher Verein für Bielefeld und Umgegend e.V., 1985–90; Dachverband Naturwissenschaftlicher Vereine Deutschlands, 1995–2008; Landesverband der Museen zu Berlin, 2012–; Council Mem., Systematics Assoc., 1995–98. Trustee: Radio Bielefeld, 1988–2004; Nat. Biodiversity Network, 1999–2011. Expert Rev. Panel, Deutsche Forschungsgemeinschaft, 2000–08. Spokesperson, Leibnizverbund Biodiversity, 2012–. FLS 1994; FAAAS 2010. Strasburger Preis, Deutsche Botanische Gesellschaft, 1996. *Publications*: papers on role of natural history museums in science and society; scientific papers on plant evolution, genetics, biogeography, systematics and biodiversity conservation in range of learned scientific jls. *Recreations*: natural history, walking, photography, music. *Address*: Stiftung Museum für Naturkunde, Leibniz-Institut für Evolutions- und Biodiversitätsforschung an der Humboldt-Universität zu Berlin, Invalidenstraße 43, 10115 Berlin, Germany. *T*: (30) 8891408544, *Fax*: (30) 8891408561. *E*: generaldirektor@mfn.berlin.

**VOGEL, Julian Andrew;** Chief Creative Officer, Modus BPCM (formerly Modus Publicity), since 1989; Communication Consultant, If You Knew, since 2011; *b* London, 6 May 1966; *s of* Peter and Juliet Vogel; *m* 1998, Sally Mackereth (marr. diss. 2019); one *s* one *d*. *Educ*: Mill Hill Sch.; Middlesex Univ. (BA Hons Business Studies); Inst. of Marketing (Dip. 1987). Associate Producer, Vidal Sassoon: The Movie, 2007–12; Producer, Out Takes: Vidal Sassoon exhibn, Somerset Hse, 2012. Member: Art Plus Cttee, Whitechapel Gall., 2006–13; Develt Cttee, Design Mus., 2007–12 (Trustee, 2012–); Develt Cttee, V&A Mus., 2011–; Adv. Panel, Southampton Solent Univ., 2016–19. Co-Chair, Mending Broken Hearts, BHF, 2010–17. Gov., St Christopher's Sch., Hampstead, 2009–15. Mem., Assoc. of Lighthouse Keepers, 2007–. *Recreations*: film, photography, art, family, architecture, travel, writing, cycling, running. *Clubs*: Soho House, George, 5 Hertford Street, Annabel's.

**VOGENAUER, Prof. Stefan;** Director, Max Planck Institute for European Legal History, Frankfurt, since 2015; *b* 4 Aug. 1968; *s of* Gottfried Dieter Vogenauer and Brigitte Maria (*née* Franz); *m* 1997, Jutta Greive; two *s* one *d*. *Educ*: Johann-Heinrich-Voß-Gymnasium, Eutin; Kiel Univ. (First State Exam. in Law 1994); Trinity Coll., Oxford (MJur 1995;

Clifford Chance Prize; HLA Hart Prize); Regensburg Appeal Court (Second State Exam. in Law 2000). Res. Asst and Lectr (pt-time), Univ. of Regensburg, 1997–2002; Res. Fellow, Max-Planck-Inst. for Foreign Private Law and Private Internat. Law, Hamburg, 2002–03; Lectr (pt-time), Bucerius Law Sch., Hamburg, 2002–04; Prof., later Linklaters Prof. of Comparative Law, 2003–15, Dir, Inst. of European and Comparative Law, 2004–15, Univ. of Oxford; Fellow, Brasenose Coll., Oxford, 2003–15. Scientific Mem., Max Planck Soc., 2014–. Fellow, Acad. of Scis and Letters, Mainz, 2016–. Humboldt Res. Award, 2012. *Publications:* Die Auslegung von Gesetzen in England und auf dem Kontinent, 2001 (Max Weber Prize, Bavarian Acad. of Scis and Humanities, 2002; Otto Hahn Medal, Max Planck Soc., 2002; Prize of German Legal History Conf., 2008); Commentary on the UNIDROIT Principles of International Commercial Contracts, 2009, 2nd edn 2015; Englisch als Vertragssprache, 2018; articles on comparative law, European legal hist., German, English and European private law and legal method. *Address:* Max Planck Institute for European Legal History, Hansaallee 41, 60323 Frankfurt/Main, Germany. *T:* (69) 789780, *Fax:* (69) 78978169. *E:* vogenauer@rg.mpg.de.

**VOGTHERR, Dr Christoph Martin;** Director, Hamburger Kunsthalle, since 2016; *b* Uelzen, Germany, 17 Jan. 1965; *s* of Dr Hans-Jürgen Vogtherr and Susanne Vogtherr. *Educ:* Freie Universität, Berlin (MA 1992; PhD 1996); Ruprecht-Karls Universität, Heidelberg; Trinity Coll., Cambridge. Res. Asst, Preussische Akademie der Künste Berlin-Brandenburg, Berlin, 1995–96; Curatorial Asst, 1996–98, Curator, 1998–2007, Stiftung Preussische Schlösser und Gärten Berlin-Brandenburg, Potsdam; Curator, 2007–11, Dir, 2011–16, Wallace Collection, London. Trustee, Wigmore Hall, 2014–16. *Address:* Hamburger Kunsthalle, Glockengießerwall 5, 20095 Hamburg, Germany. *E:* vogtherr@hamburger-kunsthalle.de.

**VOLCKER, Paul A.;** Frederick H. Schultz Professor of International Economic Policy, Princeton University, 1988–96, now Emeritus; Chairman: James D. Wolfensohn Incorporated, 1988–96; Volcker Alliance, since 2013; *b* Cape May, New Jersey, 5 Sept. 1927; *s* of Paul A. Volcker and Alma Louise Klippel; *m* 1st, 1954, Barbara Marie Bahnson (*d* 1998); one *s* one *d*; 2nd, 2010, Anke Maria Dening. *Educ:* Princeton Univ. (AB *summa cum laude*); Harvard Univ. (MA); LSE. Special Asst, Securities Dept, Fed. Reserve Bank, NY, 1953–57; Financial Economist, Chase Manhattan Bank, NYC, 1957–62; Vice-Pres. and Dir of Forward Planning, 1965–69; Dir, Office of Financial Analysis, US Treasury Dept, 1962–63; Dep. Under-Sec. for Monetary Affairs, 1963–65; Under-Sec. for Monetary Affairs, 1969–74; Senior Fellow, Woodrow Wilson Sch. of Public and Internat. Affairs, Princeton Univ., 1974–75; Pres. NY Federal Reserve Bank, 1975–79; Chairman: American Federal Reserve Board, 1979–87; J. Rothschild, Wolfensohn & Co., 1992–95. Chairman: Group of Thirty, 1989–2000; Trilateral Commn, 1992–2001; Internat. Accounting Standards Cttee, IASC Foundn, 2001–06; Independent Inquiry Cttee into UN Oil for Food Prog., 2004–06; President's Econ. Recovery Adv. Bd, 2009–11. *Publications:* (with Christine Harper) Keeping At It: the quest for sound money and good government, 2018. *Address:* 151 E 79th Street, New York, NY 10075, USA.

**VOLFING, Prof. Annette Marianne,** DPhil; FBA 2015; Professor of Medieval German Literature, University of Oxford, since 2008; Fellow in German, Oriel College, Oxford, since 1994; *b* Copenhagen, 5 Feb. 1965; *d* of Ole and Anne Volfing; *m* 1987, David Thomas. *Educ:* Internat. Sch. of Geneva; St Edmund Hall, Oxford (BA Philosophy and German 1985; DPhil Modern Langs (German) 1993). Lectr in Medieval German Lit., 1994–2006, Reader, 2006–08, Univ. of Oxford. Mem., Kommission für Deutsche Literatur des Mittelalters, Bavarian Acad. of Sci. and Humanities, 2014. *Publications:* Heinrich von Mügeln, Der Meide Kranz: a commentary, 1997; John the Evangelist and Medieval German Writing: imitating the inimitable, 2001; Medieval Literature and Intertextuality in Middle High German: reading and writing in Albrecht's Jüngerer Titurel, 2007; The Daughter Zion Allegory in Medieval German Religious Writing, 2017. *Recreations:* running, writing poetry. *Address:* Oriel College, Oxford OX1 4EW. *T:* (01865) 276555. *E:* Annette.Volfing@oriel.ox.ac.uk.

**VOLHARD, Christiane N.;** *see* Nüsslein-Volhard.

**VOLLAND, Rev. Dr Michael;** Principal, Ridley Hall Theological College, Cambridge, since 2017; *b* Reading, 2 May 1974; *s* of John Volland and Eileen Volland; *m* 1998, Rachel Hall; two *s* one *d*. *Educ:* Northumbria Univ. (BA Hons Fine Art 1996); King's Coll. London (MA Theol Educn 2002); Cambridge Univ. (CTh 2006); Durham Univ. (DThM 2013). Ordained deacon, 2006, priest, 2007; Asst Curate, Gloucester Cathedral, 2006–09; Dir of Mission, Cranmer Hall, Durham, 2009–15; Area Dean, Easington, 2014–15; Dir, Context-based Training, Ridley Hall Theol Coll., Cambridge, 2015–17. Part-time Chaplain, Durham Army Cadet Force, 2013–. *Publications:* God on the Beach, 2005; Through the Pilgrim Door, 2009; The Minister as Entrepreneur: leading and growing the church in an age of rapid change, 2015. *Recreations:* running, theatre, art, music, family, walking. *Address:* Ridley Hall Theological College, Ridley Hall Road, Cambridge CB3 9HG. *T:* (01223) 741070. *E:* mjv22@cam.ac.uk.

**VOLLMER, Patrick Matthias;** Director, Library Services, since 2015, and Librarian, since 2016, House of Lords; *b* Bonn, Germany, 18 Aug. 1969; *s* of Dr Rudolf Vollmer and Irene Vollmer (*née* Kirby); *m* 2003, Sarah Gaffey; one *d*. *Educ:* Peter Joerres Gymnasium, Ahrweiler, Germany; Univ. of Warwick (LLB; LLM). Sub-ed., Halsbury's Laws of England, 2000–02; House of Lords: Liby Clerk, 2002–05; Sen. Liby Clerk, 2005–13; Hd of Res., 2013–15. *Recreations:* cooking, Munich, photography, theatre. *Address:* Library, House of Lords, SW1A 0PW. *T:* (020) 7219 5420. *E:* vollmerp@parliament.uk.

**VOLLRATH, Prof. Lutz Ernst Wolf;** Professor of Histology and Embryology, University of Mainz, Germany, 1974–2004, now Emeritus; *b* 2 Sept. 1936; *s* of Pastor Richard Hermann Vollrath and Rita (*née* Brügmann); *m* 1963, Gisela (*née* Dialer); three *d*. *Educ:* Ulrich-von-Hutten Schule, Berlin; Univs of Berlin, Kiel (Dr med 1961), and Tübingen. Wissenschaftlicher Assistent, Dept of Anatomy, Würzburg, Germany, 1963; Res. Fellow, Dept of Anatomy, Birmingham, 1964; Wissenschaftlicher Assistent, Dept of Anatomy, Würzburg, 1965–71 (Privatdozent, 1968; Oberassistent, 1969; Universitätsdozent, 1970); King's College London: Reader in Anatomy, 1971; Prof. of Anatomy, 1973–74. Hon. Mem., Romanian Soc. of Anatomists, 1996; Corresp. Mem., Saxonian Acad. of Scis in Leipzig, 1998; Hon. Mem., Anatomy Assoc., Costa Rica, 1999. Editor: Cell & Tissue Research, 1978–96; Annals of Anatomy, 1992–2010. Hon. DM Halle-Wittenberg, 2008. *Publications:* (co-editor) Neurosecretion: the final neuroendocrine pathway, 1974; The Pineal Organ, 1981; (ed) Handbook of Microscopic Anatomy (formerly Handbuch der mikr. Anat. des Menschen) (series), 1978–; research publications on histochemistry and ultrastructure of organogenesis and various aspects of neuroendocrinology, in Annals of Anatomy, Z Zellforsch., Histochemie, Phil. Trans Royal Society B, Erg. Anat. Entw.gesch. *Recreation:* gardening. *Address:* c/o Institut für Mikroanatomie und Neurobiologie, Universitaetsmedizin Mainz, Building 708, Langenbeckstr. 1, 55131 Mainz, Germany.

**VOLPE, Michael;** General Director, Opera Holland Park, since 1989; *b* London, 29 May 1965; *s* of Francesco Volpe and Lidia Volpe (*née* Perillo); *m* 2011, Sally Connew; one *s* two *d*. *Educ:* Woolverstone Hall Grammar Sch., Ipswich. Travel Features, London Newspaper Gp, 1983–86; Internat. Exhibns and Events Manager, Utell International, 1986–89. Hon. DMus Oxford Brookes, 2016. *Publications:* Noisy At The Wrong Times (memoir), 2015. *Recreations:* opera, jazz, sports, boxing, literature, film, ski-ing, art, cooking, Chelsea Football Club, whisky. *Address:* Opera Holland Park, 37 Pembroke Road, W8 6PW. *T:* (020) 3846 6220. *E:* Michael.volpe@operahollandpark.com.

**VOLTERRA, Robert Gustavo;** Partner, Volterra Fietta, since 2011; *b* Toronto, 20 Sept. 1964. *Educ:* Univ. of Western Ontario (Lt-Gov. of Ontario Schol.; BA Internat. Relns 1987); Osgoode Hall Law Sch., York Univ., Toronto (LLB 1989); Trinity Hall, Cambridge (Commonwealth Schol.; LLM 1992). Called to the Bar and admitted as solicitor, Ontario; admitted as solicitor and Solicitor Advocate (Higher Rights of Audience (Civil)), England and Wales. Junior, public internat. law practice of Prof. Sir Elihu Lauterpacht, 1994–96; Fellow, Curso de Direcho Internacional, OAS, Rio de Janeiro, 1995; Associate, Freshfields Bruckhaus Deringer, 1996–2001; Partner: Herbert Smith, 2001–05; Latham & Watkins, 2005–11. Mem., Attorney Gen.'s A Panel of public internat. law counsel. Vis. Prof. of Internat. Law, UCL; Vis. Sen. Lectr, KCL. *Publications:* (contrib.) Stress Testing the Law of the Sea, 2018; contrib. to Financier Worldwide. *Address:* Volterra Fietta, 8 Mortimer Street, Fitzroy Place, W1T 3JJ. *T:* (020) 7380 3890. *E:* Robert.Volterra@volterrafietta.com.

**von BERTELE, Maj. Gen. Michael James,** CB 2012; OBE 1994; FRCP; non-executive Director, Salisbury NHS Foundation Trust, since 2016; *b* 23 Aug. 1956; *s* of late Otto Bertele von Grenadenberg and Monica von Bertele (*née* Barrett); *m* 1985, Frances Mary Buist Loudon; one *s* two *d*. *Educ:* St Mary's, Darlington; Welsh Nat. Sch. of Medicine, Cardiff (MB BCh 1979); London Sch. of Hygiene and Tropical Medicine (DAvMed 1986; DIH 1989). MFOM 1991; FRCP 2013. Peripatetic drayman, Schwechat Brewery, Vienna, 1974–76; commnd RAMC, 1976; MO, Parachute Field Ambulance, 1980–83; Specialist in Aviation Medicine, 1983–91; Consultant in Occupational (Aviation) Medicine, 1991; Commanding Officer: 5 Armd Field Ambulance, 1992–94; British Med. Bn, UN Protection Force, 1993; Comdr, Med. 3 (UK) Div., 1996–98; rcds 2000; Col, Employment Policy (Army), 2001–03; Dir, Med. Operational Capability, MoD, 2004–06; Chief Exec., Defence Medical Educn and Trng Agency, 2006–08; Comdr, Jt Med. Comd, 2008–09; Dir Gen. Army Med. Services, 2009–12. Chief Exec., Picker Inst. Europe, 2012–13; Humanitarian Dir, Save the Children Internat., 2013–15. QHS 2008–12. Non-exec. Dir, Proton Partners Internat., 2015–. *Recreation:* walking with family and border terrier. *Address:* The Old Bakery, Old Coach Road, Bulford, Salisbury, Wilts SP4 9DA. *E:* michaelvonbertele@hotmail.com.

**von DOHNÁNYI, Christoph;** Principal Conductor, Philharmonia Orchestra, London, 1997–2008, now Honorary Conductor for Life; Chief Conductor, NDR Symphony Orchestra, Hamburg, 2004–10; *b* 8 Sept. 1929; *m* 1st, 1957, Renate Zillessen (marr. diss.); one *s* one *d*; 2nd, 1979, Anja Silja, *qv* (marr. diss.); one *s* two *d*; 3rd, Barbara Koller. *Educ:* 2 years' law study; Musikhochschule, Munich; Florida State Univ.; with grandfather Ernst von Dohnányi in USA. Coach and asst conductor, Frankfurt Opera, 1953; Gen. Music Dir, Lübeck and Kassel, 1957–63; Chief Conductor, Radiosymphonie Orch., Cologne, 1964–70; London début with LPO, 1965; Gen. Music Dir, Frankfurt Opera, 1968–77; Dir, Städtische Bühnen, Frankfurt, 1972–77; Intendant and Chief Conductor, Hamburg Opera, 1977; Music Dir, Cleveland Orch., 1984–2002; Music Dir Laureate, 2002–. Guest Conductor of major orchestras and opera houses in Europe, Israel and USA; Artistic Advr, l'Orchestre de Paris, 1998–2000. Numerous recordings; honours, music prizes and hon. doctorates. *Address:* c/o HarrisonParrott, The Ark, 201 Talgarth Road, W6 8BJ.

**von ETZDORF, Georgina Louise,** RDI 1997; freelance designer of textiles, ceramics and life style; painter; Artistic Director, Georgina von Etzdorf, 1981–2006; Founder and Artistic Director, nice work if you can get it, since 2008; *b* 1 Jan. 1955; *d* of late Roderick Rudiger von Etzdorf and Audrey von Etzdorf (*née* Catterns). *Educ:* Downe House; St Martin's Sch. of Art; Camberwell Sch. of Art (BA Hons 1977). Freelance textile designer, 1978–79; freelance designer, developing designs from paper work and silk screens on to fabric, 1979–80; Founder, Georgina von Etzdorf Partnership, 1981; artistic dir of team producing biannual collections of clothing and accessories, 1992–. Lectures and teaching posts: Cooper Hewitt Mus., NYC; Nova Scotia Sch. of Art and Design; Glasgow Coll. of Art; St Martin's Sch. of Art; Royal Coll. of Art; Crafts Council. *Exhibitions:* Smithsonian Instn's Nat. Mus. of Design, Washington; Cooper Hewitt Mus., NY; V&A; Manchester City Art Gall. (25 yr retrospective), 2006. Gov., Univ. of the Arts, 2005. Hon. Fellow, London Inst., 2003. Hon. DDes Winchester Sch. of Art, Univ. of Southampton, 1996. Enterprise Award for Small Businesses, Radio 4, 1984; British Apparel Export Award, 1986; Manchester Prize for Art and Industry, British Gas Award, 1988. *Recreations:* singing, dancing, playing the ukelele. *Club:* Chelsea Arts.

**VON FRIESENDORFF, Baron Sir (Rickard) Fredrik (Knut),** 11th Bt *cr* 1661, of Herdick; *b* Örebro, Sweden, 16 Dec. 1937; *s* of Baron Sir (Claes) Fredrik (Wilhelm) von Friesendorff, *de jure* 10th Bt and Margareta Dahlquist; Btcy became dormant 1670; *S* father, 1974; *m* 1965, Siv Monika Eriksson (marr. diss. 1972); one *s*. Joined Swedish military as troop instructor, 1954; curator, 1980; retired as Captain, 1998. Tour guide, Swedish mountains, 1974–77. *Heir: s* Johan Frederik von Friesendorff [*b* 19 April 1966; *m* 1995, (Maud) Charlotte Johansson; three *s* (incl. twins)]. *Address:* Svarta Bangatan 6, 702 32 Örebro, Sweden. *T:* 723008154. *E:* johan.frisen@hotmail.se.

**von HASE, Bettina Ilse Friederike;** Founder and Director, Nine AM Ltd, art advisory, since 1998; *b* Bonn, 24 Jan. 1957; *d* of Karl-Günther von Hase, *qv*. *Educ:* Francis Holland Sch., Clarence Gate; Marlborough Coll.; Lady Margaret Hall, Oxford (BA 1978). Graduate trainee scheme, Reuters, 1978–81; assistant producer: Enigma Productions Ltd, 1981–82; CBS News, London, 1982–83; producer, ARD German Television, 1983–86; Hubert Burda Media, 1987–88; Proj. Dir Arts, SRU Ltd, mgt consulting, 1988–93; Hd, Develt, Nat. Gall., London, 1993–94; Dir, New World Vision, Hubert Burda Media, 1994–97. *Recreations:* art, ocean, walking, reading, film.

**von HASE, Karl-Günther,** Hon. GCVO 1972; Hon. KCMG 1965; Hon. President, Deutsch-Englische Gesellschaft, Düsseldorf, since 1993 (Chairman, 1982–93); *b* 15 Dec. 1917; *m* 1945, Renate Stumpff; five *d*. *Educ:* German schools. Professional Soldier, 1936–45; War Academy, 1943–44; Training College for Diplomats, 1950–51; Georgetown Univ., Washington DC, 1952. German Foreign Service: German Embassy, Ottawa, 1953–56; Spokesman, Foreign Office Bonn, 1958–61; Head, West European Dept, 1961–62; Spokesman of German Federal Government, 1962–67; State Secretary, Min. of Defence, German Federal Govt, 1968–69; German Ambassador to the Court of St James's, 1970–77; Dir-Gen., Zweites Deutsches Fernsehen, 1977–82. Hon. LLD Manchester, 1987. Holds German and other foreign decorations. *Recreations:* shooting, music. *Address:* Am Stadtwald 60, 53177 Bonn, Germany.
*See also* B. I. F. von Hase.

**von HIPPEL, Dr Karin Lisa;** Director-General, Royal United Services Institute, since 2015; *b* Iowa City, USA; *d* of Arndt and Marianne von Hippel. *Educ:* Yale Univ. (BA Psychol. 1987); St Peter's Coll., Oxford (MSt Modern Hist. 1988); London Sch. of Econs and Political Sci. (PhD Internat. Relns 1993). Consultant on Governance, Somalia Unit, EC, Nairobi, 1996–97; Political Advr to Rep. of Secretary Gen., UN Political Office for Somalia, Nairobi, 1998–99; Dir, Office of Community Affairs, Dept of Local Admin, UN

Interim Admin Mission in Kosovo, 2000; Sen. Res. Fellow, Centre for Defence Studies, KCL, 2001–05; Sen. Fellow and Co-Dir, Post-Conflict Reconstruction Project, Center for Strategic and Internat. Studies, Washington, 2005–10; US Department of State, Washington: Sen. Advr, Office of Coordinator for Counter-terrorism, 2010–11; Transition Team Lead, 2011; Dep. Asst Sec. of State, Bureau of Conflict and Stabilization Ops, 2012–14; COS, Office of Special Presidential Envoy for Global Coalition to Counter ISIL, 2014–15. *Publications:* (contrib.) Brassey's Defence Yearbook, 1977, 1999; Democracy by Force: US intervention in the post cold war world, 2000; Europe Confronts Terrorism, 2005; (ed with J. Alterman) Understanding Islamic Charities, 2007; Center for Strategic and Internat. Studies pubns; contrib. chapters in books; contribs to jls incl. Annals Amer. Acad. Political and Social Sci., Conflict, Security and Develt, Political Qly; Jl N African Studies, Jl Modern African Studies. *Address:* Royal United Services Institute, Whitehall, SW1A 2ET. *E:* director@rusi.org. *Club:* National Liberal.

**von KLITZING, Prof. Klaus,** PhD; Director, Max-Planck-Institut für Festkörperforschung, Stuttgart, since 1985; *b* 28 June 1943; *s* of Bogislav and Anny von Klitzing; *m* 1971, Renate Falkenberg; two *s* one *d*. *Educ:* Technische Univ., Braunschweig (Dipl Phys); Univ. of Würzburg (PhD; Habilitation (univ. teaching qual.)). Prof., Technische Univ., München, 1980–84; Hon. Prof., Univ. of Stuttgart, 1985. Foreign Mem., Royal Soc., 2003. Hon. FInstP 2002. Nobel Prize for Physics, 1985. *Address:* Max-Planck-Institut für Festkörperforschung, Heisenbergstrasse 1, 70569 Stuttgart, Federal Republic of Germany. *T:* (711) 6891570.

**von MALLINCKRODT, George Wilhelm,** Hon. KBE 1997; President, Schroders plc, 1995–2017 (Chairman, 1984–95; Director, 1977–2008); Chairman, Schroders Incorporated, New York, 1985–2017; Chairman, J. Henry Schroder Bank AG, Zurich, 1984–2003; *b* 19 Aug. 1930; *s* of Arnold Wilhelm von Mallinckrodt and Valentine von Mallinckrodt (*née* von Joest); *m* 1958, Charmaine Schroder; two *s* two *d*. *Educ:* Salem, West Germany. Agfa AG Munich, 1948–51; Münchmeyer & Co., Hamburg, 1951–53; Kleinwort Sons & Co., London, 1953–54; J. Henry Schroder Banking Corp., New York, 1954–55; Union Bank of Switzerland, Geneva, 1956–57; J. Henry Schroder Banking Corp., NY, 1957–60; J. Henry Schroder & Co., subseq. J. Henry Schroder Wagg & Co., London, 1960–85, Director, 1967–2000; Schroders Incorp., NY, 1977–2008; Chm. and Chief Exec. Officer, J. Henry Schroder Bank & Trust Co., NY, 1984–86. Director: Schroder Asseily & Co., 1981–2000; Schroders Australia Hldgs Ltd, Sydney, 1984–2001; NM UK, 1986–90; Schroder Internat. Merchant Bankers, 1988–2000; Director: Allianz of America Inc. (NY), 1978–84; Banque Privée de Gestion Financière (Paris), 1980–83; Siemens plc, 1989–2000; Euris SA, Paris, 1989–98; Foreign & Colonial German Investment Trust PLC, 1992–98; British Invisibles, 1995–98. Vice-Pres., German-British Chamber of Industry and Commerce in UK, 1996–2017 (Dir, 1971–91, Pres., 1992–95); Advr, McGraw Hill Inc., USA, 1986–89; Advr, Bain & Co., 1997–2005; Dir, Eur. Arts Foundn, 1987–2002. Member: British N American Cttee, 1988–2013; City Adv. Gp, CBI, 1990–; World Economic Forum (Chm. Council, 1995–97). Pres., German YMCA, London, 1961–2017; Member: Ct of Benefactors, Oxford Univ., 1990–; Nat. Art Collection Develt Fund, 1995–2005; BM Develt Trust, 1995–; INSEAD Circle of Patrons, 1995–; Finance Cttee, St George's Coll. Foundn, and Adv. Cttee on Finance to Dean and Canons, Windsor, 2003–17; Council, John F. Kennedy Sch. of Govt, Harvard Univ., 2005–; Trustee: Prague Heritage Fund, 1992–2004; Christian Responsibility in Public Affairs, 1994–; Patron, Three Faiths Forum, 2005–. Freeman, City of London, 2004. FRSA 1986; CCMI (CBIM 1986). Hon. DCL: Bishop's Univ., Canada, 1994; Washington Univ., St Louis, Mo. Verdienstkreuz am Bande, 1986, Verdienstkreuz 1 Klasse, 1990, Grosse Verdienstkreuz, 2001, des Verdienstordens (Germany). Awarded Annual Sternberg Interfaith Award, 2005. KCSG 2012. *Recreations:* music, libraries.

**von MOLTKE, Gebhardt;** Chairman, Deutsch-Britische Gesellschaft, 2003–13; *b* 28 June 1938; *s* of late Hans-Adolf von Moltke and Davida, Gräfin Yorck von Wartenburg; *m* 1965, Dorothea Bräuer; one *s* one *d*. *Educ:* Univs of Grenoble, Berlin, Freiburg (Law); qualified as lawyer, 1967. German Trade Unions, 1967–68; Fed. Republic of Germany Diplomatic Service, 1968–2003: served Liverpool, Cabinet of Foreign Minister, Moscow, Jaoundé/Cameroon, and Foreign Office Personnel Dept; Washington Embassy, 1982–86; Head, US Desk, Foreign Office, 1986–91; Asst Sec.-Gen. for Political Affairs, NATO HQ, Brussels, 1991–97; Ambassador to UK, 1997–99; Perm. Rep. to NATO, 1999–2003. *Recreations:* music, art (Italian drawings), reading, tennis.

**von OTTER, Anne Sofie;** singer (mezzo-soprano); *b* Stockholm, 9 May 1955. *Educ:* Stockholm Acad. of Music; GSMD; vocal studies with Vera Rozsa, 1981. With Basle Opera, 1983–85; freelance, 1985–; appearances at most major opera houses incl. Royal Opera, Covent Garden, 1985–; Metropolitan Opera, 1985–; La Scala, Milan, 1987–; Glyndebourne, Geneva, Aix-en-Provence, Paris, Vienna, Chicago, Berlin and Munich; has also given recitals worldwide. Rôles include: Mozart: Cherubino, Sextus, Idamante, Dorabella, Ramiro; Strauss: Octavian, Clairon, Componist; Bellini: Romeo; Rossini: Tancredi, Cenerentola; Bizet: Carmen; Gluck: Orfeo; Monteverdi: Nerone; Handel: Ariodante, Xerxes. Major recordings include: Cosi fan tutte; Orfeo ed Euridice; Hansel and Gretel; Der Rosenkavalier; Le Nozze di Figaro; Idomeneo; Ariodante; Werther; Les Contes d'Hoffmann; La Damnation de Faust; Nuits d'Eté, Mahler cycles, and lieder by Mahler, Brahms, Grieg, Wolf, etc. Hon. RAM 2002. *Address:* c/o HarrisonParrott Ltd, The Ark, 201 Talgarth Road, W6 8BJ.

**von PLOETZ, Dr Hans-Friedrich;** Ambassador of Germany to the Russian Federation, 2002–05; advisor to companies on strategy in Russian and other Commonwealth of Independent States markets, since 2005; *b* 12 July 1940; *m* 1971, Päivi Leinonen; two *s*. Diplomatic posts in: Morocco, 1967–68; Helsinki, 1968–73; Min. for Foreign Affairs, 1973–78; Washington, 1978–80; Min. for Foreign Affairs, 1980–88; Dep. Perm. Rep. of Germany, 1988–89, Ambassador and Perm. Rep. of Germany, 1989–93, on NATO Council; Dir-Gen. for Eur. Integration, Bonn, 1993–94; State Sec., Min. for Foreign Affairs, Bonn, 1994–99; Ambassador to UK, 1999–2002. Mem., Expert Gp on New Strategic Concept for NATO, 2009–10. Mem., Supervisory Bd, Robert Bosch GmbH, 2008–12; Sen. Advr, Wermuth Asset Mgt, Moscow and Frankfurt, 2009–; Mem., Supervisory Council, Baltic Internat. Bank, Riga, 2016–. Chairman: Foundn on German-Russian Youth Exchange, 2006–11; Investment Adv. Council, Green Gateway Fund, 2011–; Adv. Bd, Center for Global Politics, Free Univ. Berlin, 2010–. *Recreations:* music, golf, gardening. *Address:* Schloßstrasse 5, 14059 Berlin, Germany.

**von PRONDZYNSKI, Prof. Ferdinand Victor René,** PhD; Principal and Vice-Chancellor, Robert Gordon University, Aberdeen, 2011–18; *b* Bevensen, Germany, 30 June 1954; *s* of Hans von Prondzynski and Irene von Prondzynski (*née* Countess Grote); *m* 1985, Heather Ingman; two *s*. *Educ:* Headfort Sch., Kells, Co. Meath; Schule Schloss Salem; Thomas Morus Gymnasium, Oelde; Trinity Coll. Dublin (BA; LLB 1978); Christ's Coll., Cambridge (PhD 1983). Bank official, Dresdner Bank AG, Germany, 1972–74; Lectr, TCD, 1980–90; Prof. of Law, Univ. of Hull, 1991–2000; Pres., Dublin City Univ., 2000–10. Chair, Rev. of Higher Educn Governance in Scotland, 2011–12. MRIA 2006; Mem., Royal Dublin Soc., 2011. KLJ 2010. *Publications:* Employment Law in Ireland (with C. McCarthy), 1984, 2nd edn 1987; Freedom of Association and Industrial Relations, 1986; contrib. articles and book chapters. *Recreations:* photography, English, Scottish and Irish literature, football. *Address:* North Ythsie Farm, Tarves, Ellon, Aberdeenshire AB41 7LS. *T:* (01651) 851745. *E:* f.von-prondzynski@rgu.ac.uk; Knockdrin Castle, Mullingar, Ireland.

**von REITZENSTEIN, Hans-Joachim Freiherr;** *see* Leech, John.

**von RICHTHOFEN, Baron Hermann,** Hon. GCVO 1992; Permanent Representative of the Federal Republic of Germany to NATO, 1993–98; *b* 20 Nov. 1933; *s* of Baron Herbert von Richthofen and Baroness Gisela von Richthofen (*née* Schoeller); *m* 1966, Christa, Countess von Schwerin; one *s* two *d*. *Educ:* Univs of Heidelberg, Munich and Bonn; Dr in law Cologne Univ. 1963. Joined Diplomatic Service of FRG, 1963; served Boston, Mass, 1963–64; FO, 1964–66; Saigon, 1966–68; Jakarta, 1968–70; FO, 1970–74; Dep. Hd, Sect. for Internat. Law, FO, 1974; Hd, Sect. for Pol. Policy, Perm. Mission to GDR, 1975–78; Hd of Dept for German and Berlin Affairs, FO, 1978–80; seconded to Fed. Chancellery as Hd of Intra-German Policy Unit, 1980–86; Dir Gen. of Legal Div., 1986, of Political Div., and Political Dir, 1986–88, FO; Ambassador to UK, 1988–93. Chm., British-German Assoc., Berlin, 1998–2003 (Hon. Mem.). Gov., Ditchley Foundn, 1988–93, 1996–2015. Trustee, 21st Century Trust, 1998–2009. Hon. Prof., Central Connecticut State Univ., 2001. Hon. LLD Birmingham, 2000. ER 1961, RR 1985, Johanniter Orden; Officer's Cross, Order of the Knights of Malta, 1967; Commander's Cross: Order of Merit (Italy), 1979; Legion of Honour (France), 1987; Grand Officer's Cross, Order of Infante D. Henrique (Portugal), 1988; Knight Commander's Cross, 2nd class (Austria), 1989; Grand Cross, Order of Merit (FRG), 1999; Grand Cross, Order of Merit (Luxembourg), 2000; Commander's Cross, Order of Merit (Poland), 2003; Order of Merit of Land Brandenburg (Germany), 2000. *Recreations:* reading history, arts. *Address:* Beckerstrasse 6a, 12157 Berlin, Germany.

**von SCHIRNDING, Nicholas Kurt;** Executive Chairman, Arc Minerals (formerly Ortac Resources), since 2017; *b* 4 Aug. 1962; *s* of Kurt von Schirnding and Gisela von Schirnding; *m* 1993, Jessica Pudney; two *s* one *d*. *Educ:* Univ. of Cape Town (LLB 1985). Sub-Lieut, S African Navy, 1986–87; Treasury, Gold Finance, Anglo American Corp. SA, 1988–92; Indian Desk, De Beers, 1992–93; Finance Div., Minorco, 1994–98; Hd, Investor and Corporate Affairs, Anglo American plc, 1999–2011; Exec., 2011–12, CEO, 2013–14, Bumi plc, then Asia Resource Minerals plc; CEO, Carajas Copper Co., 2014–16. Consultant, Apollo Global Mgt LLC, 2019–. Vice Chm., PT Berau Coal Energy, 2014; Chm., Fodere Gp, 2017–; non-executive Director: Garrison Capital, 2016–17; Jangada plc, 2017–. *Recreations:* running, golf. *E:* non@vonschirnding.com. *Clubs:* Goodwood Kennels; Wimbledon Park Golf; Kelvin Grove (South Africa).

**von STUMM, Johannes,** FRSS; PPRBS; sculptor; *b* Munich; *s* of Nikolaus and Ursula von Stumm; *m* 1992, Carolyn Wroughton; one *s* one *d*. *Educ:* Gymnasium Monastery Ettal; Oskar von Miller Gymnasium; Ludwig Maximilians Univ., Munich (Law and Politics); Acad. of Fine Arts, Munich. Self-employed sculptor, Munich, 1988–95; work with Peter Layton, London, Clifford Reney, London and at Exptl Glass Workshop, NY, 1989; teacher of sculpture, studio Keferloh, Munich, 1990–95; asst teacher, Bildwerk, Frauenau, 1993–95; opened studio, S Fawley, Wantage, Oxon, 1995. Guest Lecturer: Art Inst., Bournemouth, 2004; Christ Ch UC, Canterbury, 2005; Imperial Coll. London, 2016; Central St Martin's, London, 2006; Newbury Coll., 2010; Jesus Coll., Oxford, 2017. Royal Society of British Sculptors, later Royal Society of Sculptors: Mem., 1997–; Mem. Council, 2003–12; Treas. 2004–09; Pres., 2009–12; Mem., Oxford Art Soc., 1999– (Pres., 2014–); Pres., Open Studios W Berks and N Hants, 2015–; Trustee, Reading Art Foundn, 2017. Founding Mem., Sculpture Network Europe, 2003; Mem., Deutscher Kuenstlerbund, 2005–. Solo exhibitions include: Turtle Key Gall., London, Film Hochschule, Munich, 1995; Mus. of Oxford, 1996; Watermill Th., Newbury, Galerie Neuendorf, Memmingen, Germany, 1997; Curwen Gall., London, 1998, 2000, 2002, 2004; Galerie Vromans, Amsterdam, 2001; Orangerie, Munich, 2003; Galerie Besch, Illingen, Germany, 2016; Galerie Verbeeck, Brussels, 2019; Galerie Alte Lateinschule, Illingen, 2019; *group exhibitions* include: James Colman Fine Art Gall., London, Art '97, London, 20th Century Art Fair, London, 1997; Hannah Peschar Gall., Surrey, 1997, 1999, Sussex, 2001; Galerie 410, Frankfurt, 1998; City of Munster, out of door sculpture, Germany, 1998, 2002; Open Studios, Newbury, 1998, 2000, 2002, 2004, 2014; Art '99, London, Kanazawa, Japan, Oxford Art Soc., Abingdon, 1999; Art 2000, London, Zürich Art Fair, Switzerland, Artfair, Brussels, 2000; RSBS, 2000, 2002, 2003, 2005, 2006; Mall Gall., London, 2001; Gall. Beaux Art, Bath, 2001, 2003; Goodwood Sculpture Park, 2001, 2004; Affordable Art Fair, NY, Haus der Deutschen Industrie, Berlin, Manchester Art Gall., Art 2002, London, 2002; Leicester Univ. Botanic Gdn, 2002, 2003; Cass Sculpture Foundn, 2004; Thompson's Gall., London, 2004, 2005, 2006, 2008, 2010, 2011, 2017; Royal Acad., London, Daniel Katz Gall., London, Sidney Cooper Gall., Canterbury, Wiseman Gall., Oxford, Art Fair, Chicago, 2005; Robert Bowman Gall., then Robert Bowman Contemp., later Modern, subseq. Bowman Sculpture, London, 2005, 2006, 2007, 2008, 2010, 2011, 2013, 2016; Curwen Gall., London, 2006, 2009, 2017; Jenny Granger Gall., Whitstable, Galerie Thiess, Munich, Fusion Gall., Altea, Spain, Abbey Hse Gdns, Malmesbury, Chichester Cathedral, 2007; Puthall Sculpture Park, 2008; Galerie Marschall, Bernried, Germany, 2012, 2017; Mus. für Konkrete Kunst, Freiburg, Fitzwilliam Mus., Cambridge, RWA, 2009; Aventurijn Galerie, Epe, Netherlands, Garden Gall., Broughton, 2010; Eton Coll., 2012; Patrick Heide Gall., London, 2014, 2018; Garden Gall., Broughton, OnForm, Asthall Manor, 2014; Jarfo Gall., Kyoto, Japan, 2014, 2015, 2017; Soul Gall., Winnipeg, Canada, 2015, 2018; Changsha Sculpture Park, 2015; Minster Gall., Winchester, 2016; Galerie Root, Berlin, 2017; art 3f, Paris Expo, Galeria Gaudi, Madrid, Galerie Verbeeck, Antwerp, Gall. Hignell, London, Salisbury Mus., Tefaf Maastricht, 2018; *commissions* include: Prior's Court Sch., Newbury sculpture gdn, 2001; Prudential Corp. plc, Accel Venture Capital, 2002; public sculpture, Wantage, Oxon, 2003; public sculpture, Newbury, 2005; Slater Centre, New Greenham Common 2009. FRSS (FRBS 2004). *Address:* Wellhill House, South Fawley, Wantage, Oxon OX12 9NL. *T:* (01488) 638194, *Fax:* (01488) 638195. *E:* vonstumm@aol.com. *Club:* Chelsea Arts.

**von WINTERFELDT, (Hans) Dominik;** Partner, Boyden World Corporation, New York, 1996–2007; *b* 3 July 1937; *s* of late Curt von Winterfeldt and Anna Franziska Margaretha Luise (*née* Petersen); *m* 1966, Cornelia Waldthausen; one *s* one *d*. *Educ:* German schools; Stanford-INSEAD, Fontainebleau (Industriekaufmann). DipICC. Joined Hoechst AG, Frankfurt/Main, 1957; Asst Manager, Hoechst Colombiana Ltda, 1960; Commercial Manager, Pharmaceuticals, Hoechst Peruana SA, 1963; General Manager, Hoechst Dyechemie W. L. L., Iraq, 1965; Man. Dir, Hoechst Pakistan Ltd and Hoechst Pharmaceuticals Ltd, 1967; Hoechst UK Ltd: Dep. Man. Dir, 1972; Man. Dir and Chief Exec., 1975; Exec. Chm., 1984; Dir (Corporate PR and Communications), Hoechst AG, Frankfurt/Main, 1987–94; Dir, Cassella AG, 1994–95. Dir, GML Consulting Ltd, Hong Kong, 2006–17. Mem., British Assoc. for Shooting and Conservation, 1979–. Mem., Rotary Club, Frankfurt, 1990–. KStJ 2008. *Recreations:* music, deer stalking. *Address:* Scheffelstrasse 40a, 22301 Hamburg-Winterhude, Germany.

**VORDERMAN, Carol Jean,** MBE 2000; broadcaster and author; *b* 24 Dec. 1960; *d* of Anton Joseph Maria Vorderman and Edwina Jean Vorderman; *m* 1st, 1985 (marr. diss. 1987); 2nd, 1990 (marr. diss. 2002); one *s* one *d*. *Educ:* Blessed Edward Jones High Sch., Rhyl; Sidney Sussex Coll., Cambridge (MA). Member: Action into Engrg Task Force, DTI, 1995; Home Office Internet Task Force, 2001–02. Founder Mem. and Trustee, NESTA, 1998–2001. Television programmes include: Countdown, 1982–2008; World Chess Championship (Kasparov *v* Short), 1993; Tomorrow's World, 1994–95; Computers Don't Bite, 1997; Mysteries with Carol Vorderman, 1997–98; Carol Vorderman's Better Homes, 1999–2003; Find a Fortune, 1999–2001; Star Lives (formerly Stars and Their Lives), 1999–2002; Tested to Destruction, 1999; Better Gardens, 2000; Pride of Britain Awards, 2000–; Britain's Brainiest Kids, 2001–02; Vorderman's Sudoku Live, 2005; Golden Lot, 2005; Loose Women, 2011–; Food Glorious Food, 2013. Columnist: Daily Telegraph, 1996–98; Mirror, 1998–2004. FRSA 1997. Hon. Fellow, Univ. of Wales, Bangor, 1999. Hon. MA Bath, 2000. *Publications:* Dirty, Loud and Brilliant, 1988; Dirty, Loud and Brilliant Too, 1989; How Mathematics Works, 1996; (with R. Young) Carol Vorderman's Guide to the Internet, 1998, 2nd edn 2001; Maths Made Easy, 1999; Science Made Easy, 2000; English Made Easy, 2000; Educating and Entertaining Your Children Online with Carol Vorderman, 2001; (with Ko Chohan) Detox for Life, 2001; Carol Vorderman's Summer Detox, 2003; Carol Vorderman's Detox Recipes, 2003; Carol Vorderman's 30 Day Cellulite Plan, 2004; Carol Vorderman's How to do Sudoku, 2005; Super Brain, 2007; It All Counts (autobiog.), 2009. *Address:* c/o John Miles Organisation, Cadbury Camp Lane, Clapton-in-Gordano, Bristol BS20 7SB. *T:* (01275) 854675.

**VORHAUS, Jennifer;** *see* Dixon, Jennifer.

**VOS, Rt Hon. Sir Geoffrey (Charles),** Kt 2009; PC 2013; Chancellor of the High Court, since 2016; *b* 22 April 1955; *s* of late Bernard Vos and Pamela Celeste Rose (*née* Heilbuth); *m* 1984, Vivien Mary Fieldhouse (*née* Dowdeswell); one *d* and two step *d* (and one step *s* decd). *Educ:* University College Sch., London; Gonville and Caius Coll., Cambridge (BA, MA; Hon. Fellow, 2015). Called to the Bar, Inner Temple, 1977, Bencher, 2009; Bencher, Lincoln's Inn, 2000 (Master of the Walks, 2019); QC 1993; Judge of Cts of Appeal of Jersey and Guernsey, 2005–09; Judge of Ct of Appeal of Cayman Islands, 2008–09; a Judge of the High Ct of Justice, Chancery Div., 2009–13; a Lord Justice of Appeal, 2013–16. Mem., LawTech Delivery Panel, Law Soc., 2018– (Chm., UK Jurisdiction Taskforce, 2018–). Chm., Chancery Bar Assoc., 1999–2001 (Hon. Sec., 1994–97; Vice-Chm., 1997–99). Bar Council: Chm., Fees Collection Cttee, 1995–2004; Vice Chm., 2001–03, Chm., 2004–05, Professional Standards Cttee; Mem., Gen. Mgt Cttee, 2004–07; Vice Chm., 2006; Chm., 2007. Member: Panel on Fair Access to the Professions, 2009; Judicial Exec. Bd, 2016–. Pres., Eur. Network of Councils for the Judiciary, 2015–16. Trustee: Social Mobility Foundn, 2007–11 (Chm., 2008–11); Slynn Foundn, 2009–. *Recreations:* farming, wine. *Address:* Royal Courts of Justice, Strand, WC2A 2LL. *Clubs:* Oxford and Cambridge; Worcestershire Golf.

**VOS, His Honour Geoffrey Michael;** a Circuit Judge, 1978–94; *b* 18 Feb. 1927; *s* of Louis and Rachel Eva Vos; *m* 1955, Marcia Joan Goldstone (marr. diss. 1977); two *s* two *d*; *m* 1981, Mrs Anne Wilson. *Educ:* St Joseph's College, Blackpool; Gonville and Caius College, Cambridge (MA, LLB). Called to the Bar, Gray's Inn, 1950. A Recorder of the Crown Court, 1976–78. *Recreations:* swimming, walking. *Address:* c/o The Crown Court, The Law Courts, Quayside, Newcastle upon Tyne NE1 3LA. *T:* (0191) 201 2000.

**VOSPER, Christopher John;** QC 2000; **His Honour Judge Vosper;** a Circuit Judge, since 2006; *b* 4 Oct. 1952; *s* of John Darvel Vosper and Hettie Vosper; *m* 1982, Ann Prosser Bowen; one *s* one *d*. *Educ:* Cowbridge Grammar Sch.; Pembroke Coll., Oxford (MA). Called to the Bar, Middle Temple, 1977; in practice as barrister, 1977–2006; a Recorder, 1998–2006. *Address:* Swansea Civil Justice Centre, Caravella House, Quay West, Quay Parade, Swansea SA1 1SP.

**VOSS, Karen;** *see* Holford, K.

**VOSS, Robert Andrew,** CBE 2014; Lord-Lieutenant for Hertfordshire, since 2017; Chairman, Voss International Ltd, 1987–2015; Venture Partner, Octopus Investments Ltd, since 2008; *b* London, 9 Feb. 1953; *s* of Richard Voss and Renate Voss; *m* 1975, Celia Gerard; two *s* one *d*. *Educ:* University College Sch., London; Univ. of Manchester (BSc Hons Mgt Sci.). Trading Manager, Brookside Metal Co. Ltd, 1975–80; Dir, Metramet Ltd, 1980–87; Chm., Advanced Steel Products Ltd, 1991–2011. Pres., Eurometrec, 1994–98 and 2006–14. Mem. Bd, 1986–2015, Chm., Internat. Trade Council, 2006–15, Bureau of Internat. Recycling, Brussels. Pres., British Secondary Metals Assoc., 1984–86. Vice-Pres., Tring Park Sch. for Performing Arts, 2018–; President: St John's Co. Priory Gp, 2017–; Herts Community Foundn, 2019–; Scouts Herts, 2019–. Trustee, Young Person of the Year, 2016–; Founder, JC Young Entrepreneurs Awards, 2012–; Judge, Young Enterprise, 2013–. Patron: Cure Parkinson's Trust, 2018–; Peace Hospice, 2018–; Future Living Herts, 2018–; Hospice of St Francis, 2019–. Gov., Univ. of Hertfordshire, 2016–. DL Herts, 2015–17. *Publications:* articles on internat. trade of metals and recycling. *Recreations:* golf, watching Rugby, soccer, cricket, music, travel, family, food, Europe, Young Entrepreneurs. *Address:* Greenway, Loudwater Drive, Loudwater, Herts WD3 4HJ. *T:* 07785 227933. *E:* robert@voss.uk.com. *Clubs:* MCC; Moor Park Golf; Middlesex CC; Lord's Taverners.

**VOUSDEN, Prof. Karen Heather, (Mrs R. Ludwig),** CBE 2010; FRS 2003; FRSE; FMedSci; Chief Scientist, Cancer Research UK, since 2016; *b* 19 July 1957; *d* of William and Erna Vousden; *m* 1986, Robert Ludwig; one *d*. *Educ:* Queen Mary Coll., Univ. of London (BSc 1978; PhD 1982). Post-Doctoral Fellow, Inst. of Cancer Res., London, 1981–85, Nat. Cancer Inst., USA, 1985–87; Hd, Human Papillomavirus Gp, Ludwig Inst. for Cancer Res., 1987–95; Dir, Molecular Virology and Carcinogenesis Lab., Advanced Biosci. Lab. Basic Res. Prog., USA, 1995–99; Chief, Regulation of Cell Growth Lab., Nat. Cancer Inst., USA, 1999–2002; Dir, Beatson Inst. for Cancer Res. and Prof., Glasgow Univ., 2002–16. MNAS 2019. FRSE 2004; FMedSci 2006. *Publications:* contrib. numerous articles to learned jls. *Recreation:* hill-walking. *Address:* Francis Crick Institute, 1 Midland Road, NW1 1AT. *T:* (020) 3796 3444. *E:* karen.vousden@crick.ac.uk.

**VRAALSEN, Tom;** Commander, Royal Order of Saint Olav 1987; Ambassador and Special Advisor to Norwegian Ministry of Foreign Affairs, 2004–12; *b* 26 Jan. 1936; *m* 1977, Viebecke Strøm; two *d*. *Educ:* Arhus Sch. of Econs and Business Admin, Denmark (MEcon). Entered Norwegian Foreign Service, 1960; served Peking, Cairo, Manila, 1960–71; Head of Div., Min. of Foreign Affairs, 1971–75; Minister-Counsellor, Perm. Mission of Norway to UN, NY, 1975–81; Dir-Gen., Min. of Foreign Affairs, 1981–82; Ambassador, Perm. Mission of Norway to UN, NY, 1982–89; Minister of Develt Assistance, 1989–90; Dir of Information, Saga Petroleum, 1991–92; Asst Sec. Gen., Min. of Foreign Affairs, 1992–94; Ambassador to: UK, 1994–96; USA, 1996–2001; to Finland, 2001–03. Special Envoy of UN Sec.-Gen. for humanitarian affairs, Sudan, 1998–2004. Chairman: Assessment and Evaluation Commn, Khartoum, 2005–08; Task Force for Internat. Cooperation on Holocaust Educn, Remembrance and Res., 2009–10.

**VU QUANG MINH;** Ambassador of Vietnam to Cambodia, since 2018; *b* Hanoi; *m*; two *s*. *Educ:* Moscow International Relations Inst. (BA 1988); Princeton Univ. (MPA 1995). Joined Ministry of Foreign Affairs, Vietnam, 1990; worked in several depts incl. Dept for Soviet Union, UNESCO Nat. Secretariat, ASEAN Nat. Secretariat, Office of the Minister, and Multilateral Econ. Cooperation Dept, 1990–97; Personal Sec. to Dep. Prime Minister and Foreign Minister, Office of the Govt of Vietnam, 1997–2002; Counsellor, Hd of Econ. Section, USA, 2002–06; Director General: Multilateral Econ. Cooperation Dept, 2007–08; Econ. Affairs Dept, 2008–10; Asst Minister, 2011; Ambassador to UK, 2011–14; Dir-Gen., Econ. Affairs Dept, 2014–18. *Recreations:* music, literature, movies, chess, table tennis, swimming. *Address:* Embassy of Vietnam, 436 Monivong, Phnom Penh, Cambodia.

**VUATHA, Sir Tipo,** Kt 2016; LVO 2007; MBE 1998; Official Secretary to Governor Generals of Papua New Guinea, until 2016; *b* Port Moresby, PNG, 5 Feb. 1952; *s* of Vuatha and Lama; *m* Avu; three *s* two *d*. *Educ:* Dip. Public Finance and Accountancy. Civil Servant, PNG, 1972–2016; with Dept of Agric. and Livestock, 1972. *Recreation:* annual leaves. *Address:* PO Box 1277, Waterfront, Port Moresby, Papua New Guinea.

**VULLIAMY, Edward Sebastian;** Senior Correspondent and writer, The Guardian and The Observer, since 1986; *b* 1 Aug. 1954; *s* of late John Sebastian Papendiek Vulliamy and of Shirley Hughes, *qv*; separated; two *d*. *Educ:* University Coll. Sch., London; Univ. di Firenze (Dip. Italian and Renaissance Studies 1973); Hertford Coll., Oxford (MA PPE 1976). Researcher, World in Action, Granada TV, 1979–85; The Guardian: gen. reporter, 1986–89; corresp. in Italy and Balkans, 1990–96; US corresp., Guardian and Observer, 1994–95 and 1997–2003. RTS Award, 1985; Internat. Reporter of Year, British Press Awards, 1992, 1997; Foreign Corresp. of Year, Granada/What the Papers Say Awards, 1992; Amnesty Internat. Award, 1992; James Cameron Meml Award, 1994; Ryszard Kapuściński Award for literary reportage, 2013. *Publications:* Seasons in Hell: understanding Bosnia's war, 1994; (with David Leigh) Sleaze: the corruption of Parliament, 1996; Amexica, 2010; The War is Dead, Long Live the War: Bosnia, the reckoning, 2012; (with M. Jacobs) Everything is Happening: journey into a painting, 2014; contrib. chapters in books, incl. Crimes of War, ed Gutman and Reiff; contribs to jls incl. Internat. Affairs, Colombian Journalism Rev., Nat. Geographic. *Recreations:* opera, classical music, rock blues, jazz, history of painting, especially Italian Renaissance, Italy, football, politics, current affairs. *Address:* c/o The Guardian, Kings Place, 90 York Way, N1 9AG. *E:* ed.vulliamy@guardian.co.uk. *Club:* Frontline.

**VULLIAMY, Shirley, (Mrs J. S. P. Vulliamy);** *see* Hughes, S.

**VULLO, Stephen;** QC 2014; *b* London, 2 July 1967; *s* of Antonino Vullo and Jill Vullo; *m* 2004, Camilla Rasumund Hester Church; two *s* one *d*. *Educ:* St Gregory's High Sch., Kenton; City of London Poly. (LLB Hons Business). Called to the Bar, Middle Temple, 1996; in practice as a barrister, 2 Bedford Row, 2006–. *Recreations:* family, cooking, attempting to grow the perfect tomato in our mountain top house in Sicily. *Address:* 2 Bedford Row, WC1R 4BU. *T:* (020) 7440 8888. *E:* svullo@2bedfordrow.co.uk.

**VUNAGI, Most Rev. David,** GCMG 2019; Governor General of the Solomon Islands, since 2019; *b* Samasodu, St Ysabel, 5 Sept. 1950; *s* of late Douglas Vunagi and Rositer Vunagi; *m* 1978, Mary; two *s* one *d*. *Educ:* Univ. of the S Pacific (DipEd Sci. 1976); Univ. of PNG (BEd Biol. 1982); Melbourne Coll. of Divinity (BTh 1990); Vancouver Sch. of Theology (MTh 1998). Principal, Selwyn Coll., 1985–86; Founding Co-ordinator of Distance Educn, Solomon Islands Coll. of HE, 1991; Lectr in Biblical Studies, Bishop Patteson Theol Coll., Kohimarama, 1992; Principal, Selwyn Coll., 1993–96 and 1999; Sen. Priest, Lawe Region, Dio. of Ysabel, 1998; Mission Sec., Church of Melanesia, 2000; Bishop, Dio. of Temotu, 2001–09; Archbishop of Melanesia, 2009–15. *Recreations:* reading, listening to radio news. *Address:* Office of the Governor General, Government House, PO Box 252, Honiara, Solomon Islands. *E:* dvunagi@comphq.org.sb.

**VUONG THUA PHONG;** Ambassador of Vietnam to Belgium, 2015–18; *b* 25 Oct. 1956; *m* Ngo Thi Phi Nga; two *s*. *Educ:* Soviet Union. Dep. Dir, Policy Planning Dept, Min. of Foreign Affairs, Vietnam; Private Sec. to Foreign Minister, 1994–98; Ambassador: to UK, 1998–2003; to Czech Republic, 2007–10; Dep. Dir, Commn for Ext. Affairs, Communist Party Central Cttee, Vietnam. Member: RIIA; London Diplomatic Assoc. *Recreation:* golf. *Club:* London Golf.

**VYSE, Prof. Timothy James,** PhD; FRCP; FMedSci; George Koukis Professor of Molecular Medicine, King's College London, since 2010; *b* Derby, 27 Jan. 1961; *s* of James and Teresa Vyse; *m* 1990, Varsha Jani; two *s*. *Educ:* Trinity Hall, Cambridge (BA 1982); Guy's Hosp. Med. Sch. (MB BS 1985); Royal Postgrad. Med. Sch., Univ. of London (PhD 1994). MRCP 1989, FRCP 2012. Fulbright Res. Fellow, Nat. Jewish Center for Immunol., Denver, Colo, 1994–98; Wellcome Trust Sen. Clin. Res. Fellow, 1998–2007, Prof. of Rheumatol., 2007–10, Imperial Coll. London. FMedSci 2013. *Address:* Department of Medical and Molecular Genetics, King's College London, Guy's Hospital, SE1 9RT. *T:* (020) 7188 8431. *E:* timothy.vyse@kcl.ac.uk.

**VYVYAN, Maj.-Gen. Charles Gerard Courtenay,** CB 1998; CBE 1990 (MBE 1974); Gentleman Usher of the Scarlet Rod, Order of the Bath, 2006–18; Defence Attaché and Head, British Defence Staff, Washington, 1997–2000; *b* 29 Sept. 1944; *er s* of John Michal Kenneth Vyvyan and Elizabeth Mary Lowder Vyvyan; *m* 1989, Elizabeth Frances (LVO 1998), 3rd *d* of Sir John Paget, 3rd Bt, Haygrass, Taunton. *Educ:* Winchester Coll.; Balliol Coll., Oxford (BA Mod. Hist. 1966; MA 1991). Nat. Defence Coll., Pakistan (MSc, Defence and Strategic Studies). Commnd, Royal Green Jackets (Rifle Bde), 1967; Sultan of Oman's Armed Forces, 1975–76; Staff Coll., 1978; CO 1st Bn RGJ, 1984–86; Col GS Mil. Ops, 1986–87; Comdr 3 Inf. Bde, 1988–90; student, Nat. Defence Coll., Pakistan, 1990–91; DCS, HQ UKLF, 1991–94; COS, HQ UKLF, later Land Command, 1994–97. Col Comdt, 1 RGJ, 1994–2000. Vis. Fellow, Eisenhower Inst., Washington, 2002–06. Gov., Cranleigh Sch., 2000–10. *Recreations:* mountains, gardens, travel, fishing, Alexander the Great. *Clubs:* Boodle's (Chm., 2007–10), Beefsteak.

**VYVYAN, Sir (Ralph) Ferrers (Alexander),** 13th Bt *cr* 1645, of Trelowarren, Cornwall; DL; *b* 21 Aug. 1960; *s* of Sir John Stanley Vyvyan, 12th Bt and of his 3rd wife, Jonet Noël, *e d* of Lt-Col Alexander Hubert Barclay, DSO, MC; *S* father, 1995, but his name does not appear on the Official Roll of the Baronetage; *m* 1986, Victoria Arabella, *y d* of M. B. Ogle; five *s*. *Educ:* Charterhouse; Sandhurst; Architectural Assoc. High Sheriff 2008, DL 2010, Cornwall. *Heir:* *s* Joshua Drummond Vyvyan, *b* 10 Oct. 1986. *Address:* Trelowarren, Mawgan, Helston, Cornwall TR12 6AF.

# W

**WABOSO, David Gogo,** CBE 2014; CEng, FREng; FICE; Managing Director, Group Digital Railway, Network Rail, 2016–19; *b* London, 19 March 1956; *s* of Dr Marcus Feyi Waboso and Mrs Margaret Waboso (later Sheldrick); *m* 2009, Angela Bucknor; one *s* two *d*. *Educ:* Crypt Sch., Gloucester; Coventry Univ. (BSc 1978); Imperial Coll. London (MSc; DIC 1980); Templeton Coll., Oxford (AMP 1995). CEng 1985; FICE 1999; FREng 2009. Grad. engr, Ove Arup and Partners, 1982–84; Design Engr, Pell Frischmann Partners, 1984–86; Sen. Engr, Parkman Consulting Engrg, 1986–89; Nichols Gp Project Manager, DLR, 1990–95; Sen. Supervising Engr, Jubilee Line Extension, 1996–99; Sen. Vice Pres., Bechtel, 2000; Prog. Dir, Eur. Rail Traffic Mgt System, 2001–03; Tech. Dir, Strategic Rail Authy and non-exec. Dir, Rail Safety and Standards Bd, 2003–05; Dir of Engrg, 2005–09, of Capital Progs, 2010–16, London Underground. Pres., Assoc. for Project Mgt, 2015–. FIRSE 2002; FCGI 2010; FAPM 2011. Leader of the Year, Manufrg and Infrastructure, Black British Business Awards, 2014. *Publications:* contribs to tech. press incl. Railway Technology Magazine, Modern Railway, Construction Engineer. *Recreations:* jazz and guitar, football (West Ham), family, gardening, walking. *Address:* (office) The Quadrant: MK, Elder Gate, Milton Keynes Central, Bucks MK9 1EN. *T:* (01908) 782546. *E:* David.Waboso@networkrail.co.uk. *Clubs:* Old Cryptians; Woodford Wells.

**WACE, Emma;** *see* Chichester Clark, E.

**WADDAMS, Prof. Catherine Mary,** PhD; Professor, Norwich Business School, University of East Anglia, 2000–18, now Emeritus; *b* Lambeth, 12 July 1948; *d* of Herbert Waddams and Margaret Waddams (*née* Burgess); *m* 1st, 1970, F. Christopher Price (marr. diss. 1992); one *s* one *d*; 2nd, 1994, Morten Hviid. *Educ:* Simon Langton Grammar Sch. for Girls, Canterbury; Univ. of Nottingham (BSc Maths and Econs 1969; PhD Econs 1973). Lecturer in Economics: Lanchester Poly., 1972–73; Leicester Poly., 1974; Leicester Univ., 1979–95 (Dean, Social Scis, 1989–94); Prof., Warwick Business Sch. and Dir, Centre for Mgt Under Regulation, 1995–2000; Dir, Centre of Competition and Regulation, subseq. Centre for Competition Policy, 2000–11, UEA. Visiting Fellow: Dept of Applied Econs and Clare Hall, Cambridge, 1993; Univ. of Copenhagen, 1999; Univ. of Calif. Energy Inst., 2003, 2006. Mem., Competition Commn, 2001–09; nonexec. Dir, Ofwat, 2013–. Reader, Dio. Norwich, licensed to St George Colegate, 2014–. *Publications:* Welfare Economics in Theory and Practice, 1977; (ed jtly) Privatisation and Regulation: a review of the issues, 1994; (ed jtly) Utility Privatization and Regulation: a fair deal for consumers?, 2003; articles in acad. jls and policy contribs on privatisation, regulation, introduction of competition, consumer choice and distributional effect of reform, particularly in energy. *Recreations:* choral singing, canoeing, gardening. *Address:* Centre for Competition Policy, University of East Anglia, Norwich NR4 7TJ. *T:* (01603) 593715, *Fax:* (01603) 591622. *E:* c.waddams@uea.ac.uk.

**WADDELL, Bruce;** *b* 18 March 1959; *s* of Ken and Christina Ann Waddell; *m* 1994, Cathy Cullis; one *s*. Johnston Newspapers, 1977–87; Sub Ed., then Chief Sub Ed., Scottish Sun, 1987–90; Dep. Ed., Sunday Scot, 1990–91; Mktg and Sales Exec., Murray Internat., 1991–93; Dep. Ed., 1993–98, Ed., 1998–2003, Scottish Sun; Ed., Daily Record, 2003–09; Ed.-in-Chief, Scottish Daily Record and Sunday Mail Ltd, 2009–11; Dir of Media, BIG Partnership, 2012–13. *Recreations:* football, classic cars, cinema, golf.

**WADDELL, Rear-Adm. William Angus,** CB 1981; OBE 1966; *b* 5 Nov. 1924; *s* of late James Whitefield Waddell and Christina Waddell (*née* Maclean); *m* 1950, Thelma Evelyn Tomlins (*d* 2007); one *s* one *d*. *Educ:* Glasgow Univ. (BSc (Hons) Maths and Nat. Phil.; Cleland Gold Medal). Midshipman, Sub Lieut RNVR (Special Branch), HMS Ranee, HMS Collingwood, 1945–47; Instr Lieut, HMS Collingwood, HMS Glasgow, HMS Siskin, HMS Gambia, 1947–59 (RMCS 1956–57); Instr Comdr, HMS Albion, 1959–61; Staff of Dir, Naval Educn Service, 1961–63; Sen. British Naval Officer, Dam Neck, Virginia, 1963–66; Officer i/c RN Polaris Sch., 1966–68; Instr Captain, Staff of SACLANT (Dir, Inf. Systems Gp), 1969–72; Dean, RN Coll., Greenwich, 1973–75; Dir Naval Officer Appointments (Instr), 1975–78; Rear-Adm. 1979; Chief Naval Instructor Officer, 1978–81 and Flag Officer, Admiralty Interview Bd, 1979–81. ADC to HM the Queen, 1976–79. Assoc. Teacher, City Univ., 1973–75; Sec. and Chief Exec., RIPH&H, 1982–90. Hon. FRSPH (Hon. FRIPHH 1990). *Publications:* An Introduction to Servomechanisms (with F. L. Westwater), 1961, repr. 1968. *Address:* c/o National Westminster Bank, 80 Lewisham High Street, SE13 5JJ.

**WADDINGTON, Prof. David James;** Professor of Chemical Education, University of York, 1978–2000, now Emeritus; *b* 27 May 1932; *s* of late Eric James and Marjorie Edith Waddington; *m* 1957, Isobel Hesketh; two *s* one *d*. *Educ:* Marlborough College; Imperial College, Univ. of London (BSc, ARCS, DIC, PhD). Head of Chemistry Dept, 1959, Head of Science Dept, 1961, Wellington College; York University: Sen. Lectr, 1965; Head Chemistry Dept, 1983–92; Pro-Vice-Chancellor, 1985–91. Hon. Prof., Mendeleev Univ. of Chem. Technol., Moscow, 1998–; Vis. Prof., Inst. für die Pädagogik der Naturwissenschaften, Univ. Kiel, 2000–. President: Educn Div., Royal Soc. of Chem., 1981–83; Inst. of Sci. Technol., 1995–2000; Sec., 1977, Chm., 1981–86, Cttee on Teaching of Chemistry, IUPAC; Sec., 1986–89, Chm., 1990–94, Cttee on Teaching of Science, ICSU. Liveryman, Salters' Co., 2001–; Freedom, City of London, 2001. Nyholm Medal, RSC, 1985; Brasted Award, ACS, 1988. Nat. Order of Scientific Merit (Brazil), 1997; ACS-CEI Award, 2012. Ed. and co-author, Essential Chemical Industry online, 2011–. *Publications:* Organic Chemistry, 1962, 4th edn 1969; (with H. S. Finlay) Organic Chemistry Through Experiment, 1965, 4th edn 1985; (with R. O. C. Norman) Modern Organic Chemistry, 1972, 4th edn 1987; (with A. Kornhauser and C. N. R. Rao) Chemical Education in the 70s, 1980; (ed) Teaching School Chemistry, 1985; (jtly) The Essential Chemistry Industry, 1985, 5th edn 2011; (ed) Education, Industry and Technology, 1987; (jtly) Introducing Chemistry: the Salters' approach, 1989; Chemistry: the Salters' approach, 1990; (jtly) Salters' Advanced Chemistry, 1994, 2nd edn 2000; (ed) Science for Understanding Tomorrow's World: global change, 1994, 2nd edn 2000; Global Environmental Change Science: education and training, 1995; (with J. N. Lazonby) Partners in Chemical Education, 1996; (jtly) Salters' Higher Chemistry, 1999; Evaluation as a Tool for improving Science Education, 2005; Context Based Learning of Science, 2005; Standards in Science Education, 2007. *Recreation:* gardening. *Address:* Department of Chemistry, University of York, York YO10 5DD.

**WADDINGTON, Hon. James Charles;** QC 2015; a Recorder, since 2004; *b* Preston, 12 Oct. 1960; *s* of Baron Waddington, GCVO, PC, QC; *m* 1st, 1990, Anne Miller (marr. diss. 2008); one *s* one *d*; 2nd, 2017, Anne Mannion. *Educ:* Aysgarth Prep. Sch.; Radley Coll.; Exeter Univ. (LLB). Called to the Bar, Gray's Inn, 1983; in practice as a barrister, specialising in commercial fraud. Member: SE Circuit; Criminal Bar Assoc. *Recreations:* cricket, theatre, cinema, art, travel. *Address:* Foundry Chambers, Quality House, 5–9 Quality Court, Chancery Lane, WC2A 1HP. *T:* (020) 7400 1800, *Fax:* (020) 7404 1405. *Club:* Travellers.

**WADDINGTON, Susan Andrée;** European Programme Director, National Institute of Adult Continuing Education, 2000; *b* 23 Aug. 1944; *m* 1966, Ivan Waddington; one *s* one *d*. *Educ:* Blyth GS, Norwich; Leicester Univ. (BA; MEd). Assistant Director of Education: Derbys CC, 1988–90; Birmingham CC, 1990–94. Pres., European Assoc. for Educn of Adults, 2008–13. Member (Lab): Leics CC, 1973–91; Leicester CC, 2003–07, 2011–. MEP (Lab) Leicester, 1994–99. Contested (Lab): Leics NW, 1987; E Midlands Reg., EP, 1999. *Address:* 5 Roundhill Road, Leicester LE5 5RJ. *E:* susan.waddington@ntlworld.com.

**WADE, His Honour Charles;** *see* Wade, His Honour R. C. B.

**WADE, Clare Catherine;** QC 2018; *b* Middlesbrough, 4 Oct. 1965; *d* of Michael John Wade and Doreen Margaret Wade; one *s* one *d*. *Educ:* Durham Univ. (BA 1st Cl. Hons English Lang. and Lit.); City Univ. (DipLaw). Called to the Bar, Inner Temple, 1990; in practice as barrister specialising in criminal defence. *Recreations:* literature, family, feminism, Justice for Women campaigning. *Address:* Garden Court Chambers, 57–60 Lincoln's Inn Fields, WC2A 3LJ. *T:* (020) 7993 7600. *E:* info@gclaw.co.uk.

**WADE, Gillian Anne;** QC (Scot.) 2013; Sheriff of Tayside Central and Fife at Perth, since 2016; *b* Glasgow, 26 April 1966; *d* of Kenneth William Eadie and Elizabeth Johnstone Eadie; *m* 1st, 1994, Paul Francis Joseph Wade (*d* 2011); 2nd, 2016, John Mauchline. *Educ:* Craigholme Sch.; Univ. of Glasgow (LLB Hons; DipLP). Solicitor: Scotland, 1989–98; England and Wales, 1992–98; Mem., Faculty of Advocates, 1998–; Mem., Mental Health Tribunal for Scotland, 2004–; Advocate Depute, 2008–; Sen. Advocate Depute, 2010–; Sheriff of Tayside Central and Fife at Stirling, 2015–16; Temp. Judge, Court of Sessions, 2019. Hd, Nat. Sexual Crimes Unit, 2011–13. Asst Ed., Tolley's Jl of Media Law, 1987–98. *Recreations:* reading, writing, walking, cooking, music. *Address:* Dornoch Mill, Crieff, Perthshire PH7 3QN. *T:* 07739 639319. *E:* gillian.a.wade@btinternet.com.

**WADE, Helena;** *see* Mills, H.

**WADE, Ian;** QC 2010; Assistant Coroner: East London, since 2014; Buckinghamshire and Berkshire, since 2016; *b* Chelmsford, 7 Sept. 1954; *s* of George Richard Wade and Alice Wade (*née* Lorentzen); *m* 1981, Paula Fernandes; two *d*. *Educ:* King Edward VI Sch., Norwich; Pembroke Coll., Cambridge (BA 1976). Called to the Bar, Gray's Inn, 1977; Asst Dep. Coroner, W London, 2012–14. Mem., Standards Cttee, Bar Standards Bd, 2012–15. *Recreation:* good books. *Club:* Hurlingham.

**WADE, Dr Joanne,** OBE 2018; Deputy Director, Association for Decentralised Energy, since 2019; *b* Preston, 3 Sept. 1966; *d* of late Harrold Anderton Wade and of Betty Wade; *m* 1996, Matthew Adrian Leach; two *d*. *Educ:* Imperial Coll. London (BSc Chemistry with Mgt Sci. 1987; MSc Envmtl Technol. 1988; PhD 1996). Analyst, Price Waterhouse, 1988–90; Researcher, Envmtl Change Inst., Univ. of Oxford, 1994–95; Res. Dir, Assoc. for Conservation of Energy, 1995–2004; CEO, Impetus Consulting, 2004–09; ind. consultant, 2009–14; CEO, Assoc. for Conservation of Energy, subseq. Assoc. for Decentralised Energy, 2014–19. Chair, Adv. Bd, Centre for Res. on Energy Demand Solutions, 2018–; Mem. Council, Energy Inst., 2015–. Vice Pres., Eur. Council for an Energy Efficient Economy, 2016–19. FEI 2002. *Address:* Association for Decentralised Energy, 10 Dean Farrar Street, SW1H 0DX. *T:* (020) 3031 8740. *E:* joanne.wade09@gmail.com.

**WADE, Kathryn Jean, (Mrs H. P. Williams),** FRAD; freelance ballet teacher and adjudicator; Director, English National Ballet School, 1990–2002; Principal, Outreach Programme, Royal Ballet School, 2005–10; *b* 27 Dec. 1945; *d* of George Wade Brown and Sheila (*née* Gilbourne-Stenson); adopted surname Wade, 1965; *m* 1981, Hugh Patrick Williams, FRCS. *Educ:* Royal Ballet Sch., Jun. and Sen. With Royal Ballet Co., 1965–70; Sen. Soloist, London Fest. Ballet, 1970–72; Soloist, Royal Ballet Co., 1970–75; teacher, Royal Ballet Sen. Sch., 1975–88; Ballet Administrator, Jun. and Sen. Royal Ballet Schs, 1988–92. Internat. teacher and adjudicator at internat. ballet and dance comps. Mem., Exec. Cttee, Royal Acad. of Dance (formerly of Dancing), 1990–2016 (Trustee, 2009–16). Trustee: Dance Teachers' Benevolent Fund, 1996–2016; Voices of British Ballet, 2002–; Ashton Trust, 2006–08; Dancers' Career Develt, 2011–16; Dame Margot Fonteyn Scholarship Fund, 2012–. FRAD 2016. Adeline Genée Gold Medal, Royal Acad. of Dancing, 1965. *Publications:* (contrib.) The Ballet Goers' Guide, 1981; (tech. advr) My Ballet Book, 1988; contrib. to Dancing Times, Dance Now. *Recreations:* all performing arts, travelling. *E:* kathrynwadewilliams@yahoo.co.uk.

**WADE, Laura Joanne;** playwright; *b* Bedford, 16 Oct. 1977; *d* of Stuart Wade and Tina Wade (*née* Wingrove); partner, Samuel Alexander Joseph West, *qv*; two *d*. *Educ:* Univ. of Bristol (BA Hons Drama 1999). *Plays:* Limbo, Sheffield Crucible, 1996; 16 Winters, Bristol Old Vic Basement, 2000; Young Emma, Finborough Th., 2003; Colder Than Here, Soho Th., 2005; Breathing Corpses, Royal Court, 2005; Other Hands, Soho Th., 2006; Posh, Royal Court, 2010, Duke of York's Th., 2012, film adaptation as The Riot Club, 2014, Oxford Playhouse and UK tour, 2019; Alice, Sheffield Crucible, 2010; Kreutzer v Kreutzer, Sydney Opera Hse and Australian tour, 2010; Tipping the Velvet, Lyric, 2015; Home, I'm Darling, Th. Clwyd, NT, 2018, transf. Duke of York's, 2019; The Watsons, Minerva Th., Chichester, 2018, transf. Menier Chocolate Factory, 2019;

radio plays: Otherkin, 2007; Coughs and Sneezes, 2009; Hum, 2009. *Publications:* Colder Than Here, 2005; Breathing Corpses, 2005; Other Hands, 2006; Posh, 2010; Alice, 2010; Plays One, 2012; Tipping the Velvet, 2015; Home, I'm Darling, 2018; The Watsons, 2018. *Recreation:* birdwatching. *Address:* c/o Knight Hall Agency Ltd, Lower Ground Floor, 7 Mallow Street, EC1Y 8RQ. *T:* (020) 3397 2901. *E:* office@knighthallagency.com.

**WADE, Martyn John,** OBE 2015; National Librarian, 2002–14, and Chief Executive, 2008–14, National Library of Scotland; *b* 24 March 1955; *s* of Albert R. Wade and Nancy Joan Wade; *m* 1978, Anne Patterson. *Educ:* Newcastle Poly. (BA); Univ. of Wales, Aberystwyth (MLib; Hon. Fellow 2010). MCLIP (ALA 1978). Trainee librarian, Northumberland, 1976–78; br. librarian, Sunderland MBC, 1978–81; br. librarian and librarian i/c, Sutton LBC, 1981–87; librarian, Northumberland CC, 1987–91; Area Librarian, Leics CC, 1991–93; Area Library Officer, Cambridgeshire CC, 1994–99; Hd, Libraries, Inf. and Learning, Glasgow CC, 1999–2002. Mem., NLHF (formerly HLF) Cttee for Scotland, 2016–. Chair, Cttee on Freedom of Access to Inf. and Freedom of Expression, 2013–19, Cttee on Copyright and Other Legal Matters, 2019–, Internat. Fedn of Liby Assocs and Instns. Trustee, 2013–, Chair of Council, 2014–17, CILIP. Vice Chm., Edinburgh UNESCO City of Literature Trust, 2008; Associate, Carnegie UK Trust, 2017–. Hon. Prof., Dept of Information Mgt, Robert Gordon Univ., Aberdeen, 2011–; Hon. Res. Fellow, Strathclyde Univ., 2017–. Chair, Govs, Mortification of Innerpeffray, 2014–. FRSA 2006. *Recreations:* motorcycling, reading, the arts, cooking. *Address:* 10 Beechwood, Linlithgow EH49 6SF. *E:* martynwade315@gmail.com. *Club:* Scottish Motorcycle.

**WADE, Michael John,** OBE 2018; Senior Adviser, Cabinet Office, since 2015 (Crown Representative, Insurance, 2013–15); *b* Woking, 22 May 1954; *s* of late Peter Wade and Lorna Wade (*née* Harris); *m* 1997, Caroline Dashwood; one *s*. *Educ:* Royal Russell Sch.; N Staffs Coll. C. E. Heath Aviation Syndicate, Lloyd's, 1975; Hartley Cooper, Lloyd's, 1975–80; Founder and CEO, Holman Wade Ltd, Lloyd's Brokers, 1980–93, merged with Horace Clarkson, 1986; Founder and CEO, CLM Insce Fund plc, 1993–2000; Founder and CEO, Rostrum Gp, 2000–05; Founder and Chm., Optex Gp, 2006, merged into Besso, 2011, sold 2012. Member: Lloyd's Task Force, 1991; Council of Lloyd's, 1988–92. Sen. Advr, Swiss Re, 2016–; Sen. non-exec. Dir, Neon Underwriting Ltd, Lloyd's, 2017–; non-exec. Chm., TigerRisk Capital Markets & Advisory (UK) Ltd, 2017–. Chm., London Fest. Opera, 1991–; Trustee, Salisbury Cathedral Girls Choral Trust, 2003–. Made recording of Saint-Saëns Organ Symphony, as conductor, 2014. Freeman, Insurers' Co., 2016. *Publications:* Lloyd's: a route forward, 1992; contrib. Financial Times. *Recreations:* music, architecture, economics, Trafalgar Park. *Address:* 87 Vincent Square, SW1P 2PQ. *T:* (020) 7821 0675. *E:* michaeljwade@hotmail.com. *Club:* Brooks's.

**WADE, Rebekah;** *see* Brooks, R.

**WADE, Richard,** PhD; CEng; FIET; CPhys, FInstP; Consultant, Richard Wade Associates Ltd, since 2013; *b* North Ferriby, 15 May 1954; *s* of Alan Wade and Kathleen Wade; *m* 1976, Elaine Rolfe; two *s*. *Educ:* Univ. of Essex (BSc Physics); Imperial Coll. London (PhD Physics 1979). CEng 1993; FIET 1997; FInstP 2010. Res. Scientist, Royal University, Edinburgh, 1980–89; Associate Dir, Jt Astronomy Centre, Hawaii, 1989–92; Hd, Engrg, Rutherford Appleton Lab., 1992–2001; Dir, Progs, PPARC, 2001–07; Chief Operating Officer and Dep. Chief Exec., STFC, 2007–12. Pres., Council, Eur. Southern Observatory, 2005–08; Vice Pres., Council, CERN, 2011–12. Vis. Prof. in Physics, Univ. of Oxford, 2007–12. *Publications:* over 50 papers in learned jls. *Recreations:* ski-ing, walking, keeping fit, running (completed London, Paris and NYC Marathons). *Address:* 44 Henleys Lane, Drayton, Abingdon OX14 4HU. *T:* 07788 971048. *E:* richard.wade6@btinternet.com.

**WADE, His Honour (Richard) Charles (Bathurst);** a Circuit Judge, 2000–11; a Designated Family Judge, Swindon, 2006–11; *b* 16 Dec. 1946; *s* of David Ison Wade and Margaret Elizabeth Lucy Wade (*née* Wainwright); *m* 1972, Juliet Ann Jehring; one *s* three *d*. *Educ:* Malvern Coll. Admitted Solicitor, 1972; in private practice, 1972–89; County Court Registrar, 1989–91; Dist Judge, 1991–2000. Trustee: Gloucester Acad. of Music and Performing Arts, 1992–99; Harnhill Centre of Christian Healing, 2001–05; Community Foster Care and Community Family Care, 2014–. Mem. Council, Cheltenham and Gloucester Coll. of Higher Educn, 1999–2000. Pres., Foundn Fellows, Univ. of Gloucestershire, 2002–08, Hon. Vice-Pres., 2008–. *Recreations:* gardening, music, walking.

**WADE, Richard Lawrence;** writer, photographer; *b* 5 July 1938; *s* of Wilfred George Wade and Frances Mary (*née* Smith); *m* 1st, 1962, Angela Lee Mikhelson (marr. diss. 1995); two *d*; 2nd, 1996, Angela Claire Mills (*née* Thomson). *Educ:* Bedford Sch.; New Coll., Oxford (MA Oriental Studies (Arabic and Persian); Pres., OU Gymnastics Club (Half Blue)). Management Trainee, Unilever Ltd, 1961–63; BBC TV, 1963–75: dir and producer, 1963–70; Editor, Tomorrow's World, 1970–75; Chief Asst, Radio 4 and Hd of Radio 4, 1975–83; Chief Asst to Man. Dir, BBC Radio, 1983–86; Dir, Foster Associates Ltd, 1986; Marketing Dir, BITC, 1986–88; Man. Dir, Business in the Cities, 1988–89; Dir Gen., Advertising Assoc., 1990–93; Fellow and Dir of Develt, St Edmund Hall, Oxford, 1993–96. Founder, Freespeling.com, 2001. Chm., Direct Marketing Assoc. (UK) Ltd, 1991–92. Mem., Calderdale Partnership, Halifax, 1987–89. Mem., BAFTA, 1968–. Freeman, City of London, 1988. *Recreations:* conversation, photography. *Address:* 49 Park Town, Oxford OX2 6SL. *T:* (01865) 511984. *Club:* Oxford and Cambridge.

**WADE, (Sarah) Virginia,** OBE 1986 (MBE 1969); tennis player; commentator: BBC Television, since 1980; British Eurosport; *b* 10 July 1945; *d* of late Eustace Holland Wade and of Joan Barbara Wade. *Educ:* Sussex Univ. (BSc). Won tennis championships: US Open, 1968; Italian, 1971; Australian, 1972; Wimbledon, 1977; played for GB in Wightman Cup and Federation Cup 20 times (record); Captain, GB team. Mem. Cttee, All England Lawn Tennis Club, 1983–91. Hon. LLD Sussex, 1985. Elected into Internat. Tennis Hall of Fame, 1989. *Publications:* Courting Triumph, 1978; Ladies of the Court, 1984. *Address:* c/o Once Upon A Time, Golden House, 30 Great Pulteney Street, W1F 9NN.

**WADE-GERY, Laura;** Executive Director of multichannel and e-commerce, 2011–16, and of UK Retail, 2014–16, Marks and Spencer; *b* London, 26 Jan. 1965; *d* of Sir Robert Lucian Wade-Gery, KCMG, KCVO and of Sarah Wade-Gery (*née* Harris); *m* 2005, Simon Roberts; one *d*. *Educ:* Magdalen Coll., Oxford (BA Modern Hist.); INSEAD, Fontainebleau (MBA). Kleinwort Benson Ltd, 1987–91; Gemini Consulting, 1993–97; Tesco: Targeted Mktg Dir, 1997–2000; Strategy Dir, 2000–03; CEO, Tesco.com and Tesco Direct, 2003–11. Non-executive Director: Trinity Mirror plc, 2006–12; British Land plc, 2015–; John Lewis Partnership, 2017–; Immunocore Ltd, 2017–. Non-exec. Dir, NHS Improvement, 2018–. Mem. Council, Aldeburgh Music; Mem., Bd of Trustees, Royal Opera House, 2012–. *Recreations:* gardening, running, opera.

**WADHAM, John;** solicitor and independent human rights consultant, since 2014; *b* 24 Jan. 1952; *s* of late Ernest George Wadham and Unity Winifred Wadham (*née* Errington). *Educ:* London School of Economics (BSc 1974); Surrey Univ. (CQSW 1978; MSc 1979); Coll. of Law (CPE 1989). Legal Advr, Wandsworth Law Centres, 1978–86; articled clerk, Birnberg & Co., Solicitors, 1987–90; admitted Solicitor, 1989; Legal Officer, 1990–92, Dir of Law, 1992–95, Dir, 1995–2003, NCCL, later Liberty; Dep. Chm., Ind. Police Complaints Commn, 2003–07; Gen. Counsel (formerly Gp Dir, Legal), Equality and Human Rights Commn, 2007–13; Exec. Dir, INTERIGHTS (Centre for Legal Protection of Human Rights), 2013–15; Associate Mem., Doughty St Chambers, 2014–. Expert for orgns incl. Council of Europe, UNDP and Commonwealth Secretariat. Mem., Human Rights Act Task Force, 1999–2001; Chairman: Forum for Preventing Deaths in Custody, 2006–09; UK Human Rights Coalition, 2001–03; Internat. Network for Ind. Oversight of Policing, 2006–07; UK Nat. Preventative Mechanism, 2016–. Member: Rule of Law Panel, Commonwealth Secretariat, 2015–; Sexual Orientation and Gender Identity Panel, Council of Europe, 2015–; Ind. Adv. Panel on Deaths in Custody, 2018–. Mem., Human Rights Cttee, Law Soc. of England and Wales, 2015–. Hon. Fellow of Law, Univ. of Kent at Canterbury, 1992–2003; Hon. Lectr in Law, Univ. of Leicester, 2000–; Vis. Lectr in Law, Univ. of Auckland, 2012–; Visiting Fellow: Univ. of Bristol, 2014–; KCL, 2014–. Series Editor, Blackstone's Human Rights Act series, 2000–04. *Publications:* (contrib.) The Penguin Guide to the Law, 3rd edn, 1992, 4th edn, 2001; (ed) Your Rights: the Liberty guide, 5th edn 1994 to 7th edn 2000; Blackstone's Guide to the Human Rights Act 1998, 1999, 7th edn 2015; Blackstone's Guide to the Freedom of Information Act 2000, 2001, 5th edn 2013; Blackstone's Guide to the Identity Cards Act 2006, 2006; Blackstone's Guide to the Equality Act 2010, 2010, 3rd edn 2016. *Recreation:* flying (private pilot). *Address:* 45 Cambridge Road, Stansted, Essex CM24 8BX.

**WADHAMS, Prof. Peter,** ScD; FRGS; Professor of Ocean Physics, Department of Applied Mathematics and Theoretical Physics, Cambridge University, 2003–15, now Emeritus (Scott Polar Research Institute, 2001–02); Fellow, Clare Hall, Cambridge, 2013–15, now Emeritus; Professeur Associé Recherche, Université Pierre et Marie Curie, Paris, since 2007; Professor, Università Politecnica delle Marche, Ancona, since 2016 (Visiting Professor, 2013–16); *b* 14 May 1948; *s* of late Frank Cecil Wadhams and Winifred Grace Wadhams (*née* Smith); *m* 1980, Maria Pia Casarini. *Educ:* Palmer's Sch., Grays, Essex; Churchill Coll., Cambridge (BA Phys. 1969; MA 1972; ScD 1994); graduate res., Scott Polar Res. Inst. (PhD 1974). Res. Scientist, Bedford Inst. of Oceanography, Dartmouth, Canada, 1969–70 (asst to Sen. Scientist on Hudson '70 expedn, first circumnavigation of Americas); Fellow, NRC Canada, 1974–75 (Inst. Ocean Scis, Victoria, BC); Cambridge University: Scott Polar Research Institute, 1976–2002: leader, Sea Ice Gp, 1976; Asst Dir of Res., 1981; Dep. Dir, 1983–87; Dir, 1987–92; Sen. Res. Fellow, Churchill Coll., 1983–93; Reader in Polar Studies, 1992–2001. Leader, 49 field ops in Arctic, 5 in Antarctic; UK Deleg., Arctic Ocean Scis Bd, 1984–; Member: IAPSO Commn on Sea Ice, 1987– (Pres., 1999–); SCAR Gp of specialists in Antarctic Sea Ice, 1989–; IASC Wkg Gp on Global Change, 1992–; Co-ordinator, Internat. Prog. for Antarctic Buoys, World Climate Res. Prog., 1999–; Member: Scientific Cttee, EEA, Copenhagen, 2004–12; Scientific Commn for the Holy Shroud, Dio. of Turin, 2009–. Vis. Prof., Naval Postgrad. Sch., Monterey, 1980–81; Green Schol. Scripps Instn, 1987–88 and 2016–17; Walker-Ames Vis. Prof., Univ. of Washington, WA, 1988; Vis. Prof., Nat. Inst. of Polar Res., Tokyo, 1995, 1996–97. Fellow, Scottish Assoc. of Marine Science, 2003–06; For. Mem., Finnish Acad. of Sci. and Letters, 2006. W. S. Bruce Prize, RSE 1977; Polar Medal, 1987; Italgas Prize for Envmtl Scis, 1990. *Publications:* (contrib.) The Nordic Seas, 1986; (contrib.) The Geophysics of Sea Ice, 1986; (ed) Ice Technology for Polar Operations, 1990; (contrib.) Microwave Remote Sensing of Sea Ice, 1992; (ed) Advances in Ice Technology, 1992; Marine, Offshore and Ice Technology, 1994; (ed) The Arctic and Environmental Change, 1996; Ice in the Ocean, 2000; Arctic Sea Ice Thickness: past, present and future, 2007; The Great Ocean of Truth, 2009; A Farewell to Ice: a report from the Arctic, 2016; numerous sci. papers on glaciology and polar oceanography. *Recreations:* painting, music, sailing. *Address:* Centre for Mathematical Sciences, Wilberforce Road, Cambridge CB3 0WA.

**WADHWANI, Sushil Baldev,** CBE 2002; PhD; Chief Investment Officer, QMA Wadhwani, since 2019 (Chairman and Chief Executive Officer, Wadhwani Asset Management LLP, 2002–18); *b* 7 Dec. 1959; *s* of Baldev and Meena Wadhwani; *m* 1st, 1991, Anjali Mirgh (marr. diss. 1994); 2nd, 1996, Renu Sakhrani; one *s* one *d*. *Educ:* London Sch. of Economics (BSc Econs; MSc Econs 1982; PhD 1986). Lectr, 1984–91, Reader, 1991–92, in Economics, LSE; Dir of Equity Strategy, Goldman Sachs Internat. Ltd, 1991–95; Dir of Res. and Partner, Tudor Gp, 1995–99; Mem., Monetary Policy Cttee, Bank of England, 1999–2002. Partner, Caxton Associates, 2012–16. Visiting Professor: Sir John Cass Business Sch., City of London (formerly City Univ. Business Sch.), 2000–; LSE, 2000– (Emeritus Gov.). Asst Ed., Economic Policy, 1987–89; Mem. Editl Bd, New Economy, 1996–. *Publications:* articles in academic jls. *Address:* (office) 9th Floor, Orion House, 5 Upper St Martin's Lane, WC2H 9EA. *T:* (020) 7663 3400.

**WADIA, Jim,** FCA; Chief Operating Officer, Linklaters, 2001–04; *b* 12 April 1948; *m* 1972, Joelle Garnier; one *s* one *d*. *Educ:* Le Rosey, Rolle, Switzerland; Inns of Court Sch. of Law. Called to the Bar, Inner Temple, 1969. Arthur Andersen: Partner, 1982–2000; Hd, London Tax, 1989–93; Man. Partner, UK, 1993–97; Worldwide Man. Partner, 1997–2000. FRSA 1993. *Recreations:* tennis, theatre. *Address:* 28 Eldon Road, W8 5PT. *T:* (020) 7937 7045.

**WADKINS, Lanny;** golfer; *b* 5 Dec. 1949; *s* of Jerry Lanston Wadkins and late Frances Ann Wadkins (*née* Burnett); *m* 1971, Rachel Irene Strong (marr. diss.); one *d*; *m* 1978, Penelope Elizabeth Atwood; two *s*. *Educ:* Wake Forest Univ., USA. US Amateur Champion, 1970; tournament wins include: US World Series and US PGA, 1977; Tournament Players' Champion, 1979, 1982, 1983; Hawaiian Open, 1988, 1991; mem., US Ryder Cup Team, 1977, Captain, 1995. *Address:* c/o Professional Golfers' Association America/Senior Tour, 100 Avenue of the Champions, PO Box 109601, Palm Beach Gardens, FL 33410–9601, USA.

**WADLEY, Veronica Judith Colleton,** CBE 2018; Chair, London Regional Council, and Member of Council, Arts Council England, 2010–18; Senior Advisor to Mayor of London (Team London, Volunteering and Charities), 2012–16; *b* 28 Feb. 1952; *d* of Neville John Wadley and late Anne Colleton Wadley (*née* Bowring); *m* 1985, Thomas Michael Bower, *qv*; one *s* one *d* and two step *s*. *Educ:* Francis Holland Sch., London; Benenden Sch., Kent. Condé Nast Pubns, 1971–74; Telegraph Mag., 1978–81; Mail on Sunday, 1982–86; Daily Telegraph: Features Ed., 1986–89; Asst Ed., 1989–94; Dep. Ed., 1994–95; Daily Mail: Associate Ed., 1995–98; Dep. Ed., 1998–2002; Ed., Evening Standard, 2002–09. Ind. Dir, Times Newspapers Hldgs, 2011–; non-exec. Dir, Berkeley Gp, 2012–. Chair, Expert Panel for Modern Music Curriculum, DfE, 2018–; Member: Adv. Council, Arts & Business, 2009–11; GLA Music Educn Adv. Council, 2009–16; Bd, City of London Educn Bd, 2016–; Council, RCM, 2018–; Trustee: Northern Ballet, 2009–14; and Co-Founder, London Music Fund (formerly Mayor of London's Fund for Young Musicians), 2011– (Chair, 2014–16); Governor: (formerly Dir), Yehudi Menuhin Sch., 2012–; Shoreditch Park Acad., 2019–. Chair, London Music Awards, 2014–16. Ambassador, For Jimmy, 2016–18. FRSA. *Recreations:* going to the theatre, listening to music, walking, ski-ing, swimming, cooking for friends and family. *E:* veronica@veronicawadley.com.

**WADSWORTH, Antony Ronald,** CBE 2011; Chairman, British Phonographic Industry, since 2007; *b* Bolton, Lancs, 21 Oct. 1956; *s* of Ronald and Margaret Wadsworth; *m* 1987, Susan Elizabeth Thornley; one *s* one *d*. *Educ:* Bolton Sch.; Univ. of Newcastle-upon-Tyne (BA Econs). Musician, 1978–79; Production Manager: Warwick Records, 1979–80; Transatlantic Records, then Logo Records, 1980–81; RCA Records, 1981–82; Production

Manager, 1982–84; Gen. Manager, Strategic Mktg, 1984–87, EMI Records UK; Mktg Dir, 1987–92, Man. Dir, 1992–98, Parlophone Records; Chm. and CEO, EMI Music UK, 1998–2008. Vis. Prof., Univ. of Newcastle upon Tyne, 2007–. Chm., Brit Awards Ltd, 2007–. Chm., Julie's Bicycle, 2009–. Trustee: EMI Archive Trust, 1998–; Brit Trust, 1998–; Music Sound Foundn, 2004–. Hon. DMus Gloucestershire, 2009. *Recreations:* music, theatre, art, walking, reading. *Address:* British Phonographic Industry, Riverside Building, County Hall, Westminster Bridge Road, SE1 7JA. *T:* (020) 7803 1300. *E:* tony.wadsworth@bpi.co.uk. *Club:* Soho House.

**WADSWORTH, Brian;** transport and public affairs consultant, since 2008; *b* 18 Jan. 1952; *s* of George David Brian Wadsworth and Betty (*née* Metcalfe); *m* 1987, Anne Jacqueline Beuselinck (OBE 2014). *Educ:* Univ. of British Columbia (BA Hons Eng. Lit. 1973). FILog 1998; FCILT 1999; FRIN 2010. Entered Department of Transport, 1974; Sec., Review of Main Line Rly Electrification, 1978–79; Sec. to Chief Exec., LB of Hounslow, 1981; Principal: Transport Policy Rev. Unit, 1981–83; London Transport Finance, 1984; Pvte Sec. to Minister of State, 1985; Finance Transport Industries (BA, BAA, NBC privatisations), 1986–89; Sec. to BA plc, 1989–91; Asst Sec., Rlys Policy (BR privatisation), 1991–95; Sec. to British Oxygen plc, 1995; Under Sec., Dir of Finance, 1995–97; Dir, Freight Distribn and Logistics, DETR, 1997–99; Dir, Logistics and Maritime Transport, DETR, subseq. DTLR, then DfT, 1999–2007; Dir, Strategic Roads, Planning and Nat. Networks, DfT, 2007–08. Chm. Admin. Bd, European Maritime Safety Agency, 2003–09. Dir, Road Ahead Gp, 2011–. Freeman, City of London, 1997; Liveryman: Co. of Carmen, 1997– (Master, 2009–10); Co. of Plumbers, 2013– (Master, 2016–17). *Publications:* Best Methods of Railway Restructuring and Privatisation, 1995. *Recreations:* travel, boating, music. *Address:* 211 Ashley Gardens, Emery Hill Street, SW1P 1PA; 29 Swinnerton House, Phyllis Court Drive, Henley-on-Thames RG9 2HU. *E:* wadsworth.brian@btinternet.com. *Clubs:* United Wards (Pres., 2019–20), Castle Baynard Ward and Bridge Ward; Phyllis Court (Henley).

**WADSWORTH, His Honour James Patrick;** QC 1981; a Circuit Judge, 2000–10; *b* 7 Sept. 1940; *s* of Francis Thomas Bernard Wadsworth, Newcastle, and Geraldine Rosa (*née* Brannan); *m* 1963, Judith Stuart Morrison, *e d* of Morrison Scott, Newport-on-Tay; one *s* one *d*. *Educ:* Stonyhurst; University Coll., Oxford (MA). Called to the Bar, Inner Temple, 1963, Bencher, 1988; a Recorder, 1980–2000. Member: Mental Health Rev. Tribunal, 1995–2012; Parole Bd, 2006–12. Member: Bar Council, 1992–95; Bar Professional Standards Cttee, 1993–95. *Recreations:* eating and idling. *Address:* 9½ Compton Avenue, N1 2XD.

**WADSWORTH, Prof. Michael Edwin John,** PhD; FFPH, FAcSS; Director, Medical Research Council National Survey of Health and Development, 1985–2006, now Hon. Senior Scientist, Lifelong Health and Ageing Unit, and Professor of Social and Health Life Course Research, Department of Epidemiology and Public Health Medicine, 2003–06, now Emeritus, Royal Free and University College Medical School, University College London (formerly University College London Medical School); *b* 20 Jan. 1942; *s* of Cecil and Amelia Wadsworth; *m* 1st, 1966, Jane Arnott (marr. diss. 1991); one *s* one *d*; 2nd, 2001, Kit Leighton-Kelly; one *d*. *Educ:* Leeds Univ. (BA, MPhil); London Sch. of Econs (PhD 1976). FFPH 2006 (Hon. MFPHM 1993); FAcSS 2014. Research Asst, Dept of Medicine, Guy's Hosp. Med. Sch., 1963–65; Res. Fellow, Dept of Gen. Practice, Univ. of Edinburgh Med. Sch., 1965–68; Res. Scientist, MRC Nat. Survey Health and Develt, 1968–2007. *Publications:* (jtly) Health and Sickness, 1971; Roots of Delinquency, 1976; (ed with D. Robinson) Studies in Everyday Medical Life, 1976; (ed with U. Gerhardt) Stress and Stigma, 1985; The Imprint of Time, 1991; (ed with M. G. Marmot) Fetal and Early Childhood Development, 1997; (ed jtly) Changing Britain, Changing Lives, 2003; (ed jtly) Epidemiological Methods in Life Course Research, 2007; (ed with J. Bynner) A Companion to Life Course Studies, 2011; numerous chapters and articles in learned jls in medicine and social scis. *Recreations:* music, living. *Address:* 12C Kingsdown Parade, Bristol BS6 5UD. *T:* (0117) 924 4906.

**WADVANI, Sanjay Mark,** OBE 2007; HM Diplomatic Service; Head of Transformation, Knowledge and Technology Directorate, Foreign and Commonwealth Office, since 2017; *b* Calcutta, 6 Dec. 1966; *s* of late Moti Shamdas Wadvani and of Jeanne Wadvani; *m* 2011, Rochele Irene Selwyn; one *d*. *Educ:* Taunton Sch.; Poly. of Central London. Entered FCO, 1987; Registry Officer: Hong Kong Dept, FCO, 1987–88; Beijing, 1989–91; Clearance Officer, then Mgt Officer, later Third Sec., Damascus, 1991–94; Resource Mgt Officer, Africa and Commonwealth Comd, FCO, 1995–98; Second Sec. (Commercial), Santiago, 1998–2002; Dep. Consul-Gen. and Hd, Trade and Investment, Guangzhou, 2002–05; Hd, China (Ext.) policy team, Far Eastern Dept, FCO, 2006–09; Dep. High Comr, Kolkata, 2009–13; Ambassador to Turkmenistan, 2013–16. *Recreations:* sport, theatre, reading, travel. *Address:* c/o Foreign and Commonwealth Office, King Charles Street, SW1A 2AH. *E:* sanjay.wadvani@fco.gov.uk.

**WAENA, Sir (Rahumaea) Nathaniel,** GCMG 2005; CSI 2005; Governor General, Solomon Islands, 2004–09; *b* 1 Nov. 1945; *s* of Joseph Talo and Matilda Tahalata; *m* 1972, Alice Ole; three *s* three *d*. *Educ:* Alangaula, Pawa and Lae Tech. Trng Inst. Provincial Sec., 1978–82; Chief Admin. Officer, 1982–84; Perm. Sec., 1984–87. MP Solomon Is, 1987–2004; Minister: Provincial Govt and Rural Develt, 1989–90, 2000–01; Health and Medical Services, 1993–94; Nat. Unity, Reconciliation and Peace, 2001–04. Chm., Eminent Persons Adv. Council, Constitutional Reform Prog., Solomon Is Govt, 2017–. Vice-Pres., Honiara Town Council, 1984–86. Chm. Council, Solomon Is Coll. of Higher Educn, then Chm. and Pro-Vice-Chancellor, Solomon Is Nat. Univ., 2011. KStJ 2005. *Recreations:* gardening, reading, watching sports competitions. *Address:* c/o Government House, Honiara, Solomon Islands. *T:* 21777, *Fax:* 22533.

**WAGERMAN, Anthony;** Chief Executive Officer, Travelex Ltd, 2015–17; *b* London, 17 Sept. 1961; *s* of late Peter Henry Wagerman and Josephine Miriam Wagerman, OBE; *m* 1986, Danielle Polak; two *d*. *Educ:* Hasmonean Grammar Sch.; JFS Sch., Harrow; City Univ., London (BSc (Hons) Chem.; MBA). Travelex Ltd: Hd of Gp Mktg, 2000–05; Hd, Gp Retail, 2005–06; Man. Dir, Retail/Currency Services Div., 2006–11; Man. Dir, Europe and Americas, 2011–13; Dep. CEO, 2013–15. *Recreations:* reading, walking.

**WAGGOTT, Shuna Taylor;** *see* Lindsay, S. T.

**WAGNER, Arnold,** OBE 2003; Chair, Pension Protection Fund, since 2016 (non-executive Director, since 2011); *b* Manchester, 25 Sept. 1949; *s* of Herman and Toby Wagner; *m* 1975, Sandra Wineman; one *s* three *d*. *Educ:* Salford Grammar Sch.; Middlesex Poly. (BA Hons Business Studies 1972); London Sch. of Econs and Pol Sci. (MSc(Econ) Industrial Relns 1973). Res. Fellow, Manchester Business Sch., 1973–76; Lectr in Industrial Relns, Manchester Poly., 1976–78; UK Personnel Dir, Internat. Computers Ltd, 1978–86; Personnel Dir, Fisons Scientific Equipment, 1986–94; Group HR Director: Bunzl plc, 1994–2003; Smiths Gp plc, 2003–09. Non-executive Director: Renew Hldgs plc, 2003–06; UKAEA, 2006–10; CIFAS, 2017–. Hon. Vice Chm., Jewish Care, 2012–. Hon. Chm. Govs, JFS Sch., 1993–2003. *Recreations:* cricket, football, theatre, opera. *Address:* Pension Protection Fund, 12 Dingwall Road, Croydon CR0 2NA. *T:* (020) 8633 4936, *Fax:* arnold.wagner@ppf.co.uk.
*See also* L. *Wagner.*

**WAGNER, Erica Augusta;** writer; Lecturer in Creative Writing, Goldsmiths, University of London, since 2016; Literary Editor, The Times, 1996–2013; *b* NYC; *d* of Arthur Wagner and Ellen Wagner; *m* 1993, Francis Jonathan Gilbert; one *s*. *Educ:* Brearley Sch., NYC; St Paul's Girls' Sch., London; Corpus Christi Coll., Cambridge (BA Hons 1989); UEA (MA Creative Writing 1991). Freelance editor/researcher/journalist, 1992–95; The Times: Asst to Literary Editor, 1995; Dep. Literary Editor, 1996. Consulting Literary Ed., Harper's Bazaar UK, 2014–; Contributing Writer, New Statesman, 2014–. A Judge, Man Booker Prize, 2002 and 2014. Hon. PhD UEA, 2015. *Publications:* Gravity: stories, 1997; Ariel's Gift: Ted Hughes, Sylvia Plath and the story of Birthday Letters, 2000; Seizure, 2007; First Light: a celebration of Alan Garner, 2016; Chief Engineer: Washington Roebling, the man who built the Brooklyn Bridge, 2017. *Recreations:* bridges, cooking. *Address:* c/o Antony Harwood Ltd, 103 Walton Street, Oxford OX2 6EB. *T:* (01865) 559615.

**WAGNER, Dame Gillian (Mary Millicent), (Lady Wagner),** DBE 1994 (OBE 1977); Chairman: Carnegie UK Trust, 1995–2000 (Trustee, 1980–2002); Residential Forum, since 1994; *b* 25 Oct. 1927; *e d* of late Major Henry Archibald Roger Graham, and of Hon. Margaret Beatrix, *d* of 1st Baron Roborough; *m* 1953, Sir Anthony Wagner, KCB, KCVO; two *s* one *d*. *Educ:* Cheltenham Ladies' Coll.; Geneva Univ. (Licence ès Sciences Morales); London Sch. of Economics (Dip. Social Admin). PhD London 1977. Mem. Council, Barnardo's, 1969–97 (Chm., Exec./Finance Cttee, 1973–78; Chm. Council, 1978–84); Chairman: Nat. Centre for Volunteering (formerly Volunteer Centre), 1984–89 (Pres., 1990–2002); Review of Residential Care, 1986–88; Ct of Govs, Thomas Coram Foundn for Children, 1990–95; The Leche Trust, 1992–97; Chair, Community Care Inquiry for people with learning difficulties, Mental Health Foundn, 1995–96; President: Skill: Nat. Bureau for Students with Disabilities, 1978–91; IAPS, 1985–90; Abbeyfield UK, 2003–09; Patron, Abbeyfield Soc., 2010– (President, 1995–2002); Trustee, Princess Royal Trust for Carers, 1992–2002. Mem. Exec. Cttee, Georgian Gp, 1970–78. Chm. of Governors, Felixstowe Coll., 1980–87; Governor: Nat. Inst. for Social Work, 1988–96; LSE, 1991–96. FRSA 1995. Hon. DSc Bristol, 1989; Hon. LLD Liverpool, 1990. *Publications:* Barnardo, 1979; Children of the Empire, 1982; The Chocolate Conscience, 1987; Thomas Coram, Gent., 2004; Miss Palmer's Diary: the secret journals of a Victorian lady, 2017; various articles on residential care. *Recreations:* travelling, swimming. *Address:* Flat 31, 55 Ebury Street, SW1W 0PA. *T:* (020) 7730 0040; 46 Lee Road, Aldeburgh, Suffolk IP15 5HG. *T:* (01728) 454550. *E:* gillianwagner27@gmail.com. *Club:* Athenæum.

**WAGNER, Prof. Leslie,** CBE 2000; MA(Econ); Vice-Chancellor (formerly Principal and Chief Executive), and Professor, Leeds Metropolitan University, 1994–2003; *b* 21 Feb. 1943; *s* of Herman and Toby Wagner; *m* 1967, Jennifer Jean Fineberg; one *s* one *d*. *Educ:* Salford Grammar Sch.; Manchester Univ. (MA (Econ)). Economic Asst and Economic Advr, DEA, 1966–69; Economic Advr, Min. of Technology, 1969–70; Lectr in Econs, Open Univ., 1970–76; Hd of Social Sciences, 1976–82, Prof., 1980, Polytechnic of Central London; Asst Sec. (Academic), Nat. Adv. Body for Local Authy Higher Educn, 1982–85; Dep. Sec., Nat. Adv. Body for Public Sector Higher Educn, 1985–87; Dir, Poly. of N London, 1987–92, then Vice-Chancellor and Chief Exec., Univ. of N London, 1992–93. Member: Bd, Open Learning Foundn, 1990–96 (Chm., 1990–93); Bd, HEQC, 1992–97; Council for Industry and Higher Educn, 1992–2003; Leeds TEC, 1997–2001; DFEE Skills Task Gp, 1998–2000. Chairman: SRHE, 1994–96; Higher Educn for Capability, 1994–98; Yorks and Humberside Univs Assoc., 1996–99; UUK Wider Participation and Lifelong Learning Gp, 1998–2003; Leeds Common Purpose Adv. Gp, 2000–03; Univ. Vocational Awards Council, 2001–03; Higher Educn Acad., 2003–07; Foundn Degree Task Force, 2003–04; Educn Leeds, 2004–07. Councillor (Lab) London Bor. of Harrow, 1971–78, Chm., Educn Cttee, 1972–74. Contested (Lab) Harrow W, Feb. 1974. Dir, Leeds Business Services Ltd, 2001–03; Mem., Leeds Cares Leadership Gp, 2000–01. Vice-Pres., Utd Synagogue, 1992–93; Chairman: Jewish Community Allocations Bd, 1994–96; Commn on the Future of Jewish Schs, 2007–08; Vice-Chm., Inst. for Jewish Global Affairs, Jerusalem, 2010–; Mem. Bd, Jewish Chronicle Trust, 1999–2008. Trustee, Chief Rabbinate Trust, 2003–11. Chancellor, Univ. of Derby, 2003–08. Mem. Council, Open Univ., 2005–08. Fellow, Jerusalem Centre for Public Affairs, 2011–. Hon. Dr of Univ. Middlesex, 2003; DUniv: Leeds Metropolitan, 2003; Open, 2006; Derby, 2008; Hon. DCL Huddersfield, 2003. *Publications:* (ed) Readings in Applied Microeconomics, 1973, 2nd edn 1981; (ed) Agenda for Institutional Change in Higher Education, 1982; The Economics of Educational Media, 1982; (jtly) Choosing to Learn: a study of mature students, 1987. *E:* vcwagner@hotmail.com.
*See also* A. *Wagner.*

**WAGONER, G. Richard;** Chief Executive Officer, 2000–09, and Chairman, 2003–09, General Motors Corporation; *b* Wilmington, Delaware, 9 Feb. 1953. *Educ:* Duke Univ. (BS 1975); Harvard Univ. (MBA 1977). General Motors Corporation: analyst in treasurer's office, Manager, Latin American financing, Dir, Canadian and overseas borrowing, then Dir, capital analysis and investment, NY, 1977–81; Treas., 1981–84; Exec. Dir of Finance, 1984–87; São Paulo, Brazil; Vice-Pres. and Financial Manager, 1987–88, Gp Dir of strategic business planning, 1988–89, Canada; Vice-Pres. of Finance, Zurich, 1989–91; Pres. and Man. Dir, Brazil, 1991–93; Chief Financial Officer, 1992–94, and Head of Worldwide Purchasing Gp, 1993–94; Exec. Vice-Pres. and Pres. of N American ops, 1994–98; Chief Operating Officer, 1998–2000; Pres., 1998–2003; Mem., Bd of Dirs, 1998–2009; Dir, Graham Hldgs (formerly The Washington Post) Co., 2010–.

**WAGSTAFF, Ven. Christopher John Harold;** Archdeacon of Gloucester, 1982–2000, now Emeritus; *b* 25 June 1936; *s* of Harold Maurice Wagstaff and Kathleen Mary Wagstaff (*née* Bean); *m* 1964, Margaret Louise (*née* Macdonald); two *s* one *d*. *Educ:* Bishop's Stortford College, Herts; Essex Inst. of Agriculture, Chelmsford (Dipl. in Horticulture 1959); St David's Coll., Lampeter (BA 1962, Dipl. in Theol. 1963). Deacon 1963, priest 1964; Curate, All Saints, Queensbury, 1963–68; Vicar, St Michael's, Tokyngton, Wembley, 1968–73; Vicar of Coleford with Staunton, 1973–83; RD, South Forest, 1975–82. Diocese of Gloucester: Chairman: House of Clergy, 1983–95; Bd of Social Responsibility, 1983–96; Diocesan Trust, 1983–2000; Diocesan Assoc. for the Deaf, 1989–94; DAC, 1988–2000; Adv. Council for Ministry, 1996–2000. Mem., General Synod, 1988–98. Hon. Canon, St Andrew's Cathedral, Njombe, Tanzania, 1993–. Freeman, City of London; Liveryman, Co. of Armourers and Brasiers (Master, 2000–01). *Recreations:* gardening, entertaining, travel. *Address:* Karibuni, 1 Collafield, Littledean, Glos GL14 3LG. *T:* (01594) 825282.

**WAGSTAFF, David St John Rivers;** a Recorder of the Crown Court, 1974–94; barrister, retired; *b* 22 June 1930; *s* of late Prof. John Edward Pretty Wagstaff and Dorothy Margaret (*née* McRobie); *m* 1970, Dorothy Elizabeth Starkie; two *d*. *Educ:* Winchester Coll. (Schol.); Trinity Coll., Cambridge (Schol., MA, LLB). Called to Bar, Lincoln's Inn, 1954; practised on N Eastern Circuit. *Publications:* Man's Relationship with God, or Spiritual Adventure, 1996. *Recreations:* mountaineering, fencing. *Address:* 8 Breary Lane East, Bramhope, Leeds LS16 9BJ. *Clubs:* Alpine; Fell and Rock Climbing (Lake District).

**WAGSTAFF, Sheena Vanessa;** Leonard A. Lauder Chairman (formerly Chairman), Modern and Contemporary Art, Metropolitan Museum of Art, New York, since 2012; *b* 30 Aug. 1956; *d* of Walton Wynter Wagstaff and Patricia (*née* Hugonin); *m* 1983, Mark Michael Peregrine Francis; one *s* one *d*. *Educ*: Univ. of East Anglia (BA Hons Hist. of Art and Arch. 1980). Postgraduate Fellow, Whitney Mus. of American Art, NY, 1982–83. MOMA, Oxford, 1976–77; Whitechapel Art Gall., 1980–82; Lisson Gall., 1983–84; freelance curator, 1984–93; curated exhibitions for: Whitney Mus. of American Art, NY; Kettle's Yard Gall., Cambridge; ICA, London; Centre Culturel de Courbevoie, Paris; Mattress Factory, Pittsburgh; Dir of Collection, Exhibns and Educn, Frick Art Mus., Pittsburgh, 1993–98; Hd of Exhibns and Displays, Tate Britain, 1998–2001; Chief Curator, Tate Modern, 2001–12. Mem., Design Rev. Panel, Southwark LBC, 2006–08. Member: Adv. Bd, Delfina Foundn, 2007–; Bd, Bidoun Mag., 2009–18; Mayor of London's Adv. Bd, Shubbak Fest., 2010–11; Internat. Adv. Bd, Istanbul Modern, 2011–; US Nomination Bd, Praemium Imperiale, 2013–18; Professional Fine Arts Cttee, Foundn for Art and Preservation in Embassies, 2016–. Mem., Cranium. *Publications*: numerous exhibition catalogues. *Recreations*: ancient and modern art, architecture, music, dance, literature, walking, gardening. *Address*: Metropolitan Museum of Art, 1000 Fifth Avenue, New York, NY 10028–0198, USA. *T*: (212) 3965192.

**WAGSTAFFE, Christopher David;** QC 2011; *b* Glossop, Derbys, 1967; *s* of David and Margaret Wagstaffe; *m* 1987, Vikki Ryder; two *s* two *d*. *Educ*: Glossop Sch., Derbys; Univ. of Essex (LLB Hons); Inns of Court Sch. of Law. Called to the Bar, Inner Temple, 1992. Mem., Derbys Police Authy, 1994–96. Member: Family Law Bar Assoc., 1995–; S Eastern Circuit, 2008–. *Publications*: (ed jtly) Cohabitation and Trusts of Land, 2006, 2nd edn 2009; contrib. articles to Family Law, Trusts and Trustees. *Recreations*: sport, reading, theatre and cinema. *Address*: 29 Bedford Row, WC1R 4HE. *T*: (020) 7404 1044. *E*: cwagstaffe@29br.co.uk.

**WAIN, Peter;** a District Judge (Magistrates' Courts), 2004–11, a Deputy District Judge, 2011–14; *b* 3 Sept. 1947; *s* of late Frank and Margaret Wain; *m* 1972, Mary Carolyn Hilditch; two *s* one *d*. *Educ*: Bemrose Sch., Derby; Stamford Sch., Lincs; Univ. of Leeds (LLB Hons 1969). Called to the Bar, Gray's Inn, 1972; Clerk to the Felixstowe, Ipswich and Woodbridge Justices, 1978–87; practising barrister, 1987–2004. Pt-time Legal Mem., Mental Health Review Tribunal, 1995–2005. *Recreations*: bird watching, sculling on the River Deben, researching the lost medieval port of Goseford. *Clubs*: Bawdsey Bird; Felixstowe Ferry Sailing.

**WAINE, Rt Rev. John,** KCVO 1996; Bishop of Chelmsford, 1986–96; Clerk of the Closet to the Queen, 1989–96; an Honorary Assistant Bishop, Diocese of St Edmundsbury and Ipswich, since 2008; *b* June 1930; *s* of late William and Ellen Waine; *m* 1957, Patricia Zena Haikney; three *s*. *Educ*: Prescot Grammar Sch.; Manchester Univ. (BA); Ridley Hall, Cambridge. Deacon 1955, Priest 1956; Curate of St Mary, West Derby, 1955–58; Curate in Charge of All Saints, Sutton, 1958–60; Vicar of Ditton, 1960–64; Vicar of Holy Trinity, Southport, 1964–69; Rector of Kirkby, 1969–75; Bishop Suffragan of Stafford, 1975–78; Bishop of St Edmundsbury and Ipswich, 1978–86. Chm., Churches Main Cttee, 1991–96. Mem., Press Complaints Commn, 1997–2010. Chairman: Council, Univ. of Essex, 1995–2001; Foundn, Univ. of Essex, 2001–07. Master, Glass Sellers' Co., 1999–2000. Entered H of L, 1985. DUniv Essex, 2002. GCStJ 1999 (ChStJ 1983; Prelate, 1999–2007). *Recreations*: music, gardening. *Address*: Broadmere, Ipswich Road, Grundisburgh, Woodbridge, Suffolk IP13 6TJ. *T*: (01473) 738296. *Club*: Royal Air Force.
See also Very Rev. S. J. Waine.

**WAINE, Peter Edward;** Chairman, Campaign to Protect Rural England, 2008–14; Co-founder, Hanson Green, 1989–2016; *b* Rugby, 27 June 1949; *s* of late Dr Theodore Edward Waine and Mary Florence Waine; *m* 1973, Stefanie Vuikaba Snow; one *d*. *Educ*: Bilton Grange; Worksop Coll.; Bradford Univ. (BSc 1970). Divisional Level Human Resources roles: GEC, 1970–74; Cape Industries, 1974–79; Coopers and Lybrand, 1979–83; Dir, CBI, 1983–88; CEO, Directorship Appointments Ltd, 1988–89. Chm., Core Care Ltd, 1990–92; non-executive Director: W. R. Royle & Sons Ltd, 1988–96; SSK Ltd, 1994–98; Wild Wiki Ltd, 2011–14; Sen. non-exec. Dir, Quarto Gp plc, 1998–2013. Non-executive Director: E Herts DHA, 1990–92; E Herts Trust, 1992–96. Mem., ICC, 1994–2005; Chairman: Tree Council, 1996–98 (Vice Pres., 1998–2000); Brogdale Horticl Trust, 2001–06; Spectrum, 2016–; Housman Soc., 2017–; Trustee: ROH, 1999–2001; Gardens Trust, 2016–; Mem., Jt Cttee, Nat. Amenity Socs, 2018–. Visiting Professor: Warwick Business Sch., 2004–10; Cass Business Sch., 2004–10. Member Council: BIM, 1979–81; Eur. Business Sch., 1983–90. Vice Chm., Bow Gp, 1972 (Chm., Birmingham Gp 1971). Mem., Rugby DC, 1973–77. Contested (C) Nottingham N, 1979. Member, Judging Panel: Contrarian Prize, 2013–; Wainwright Literary Prize, 2017, 2018. Gov. and Chm. of Foundn, Bilton Grange Sch., Rugby, 2014–18. Liveryman, Gardeners' Co., 2007 (Mem. Ct, 2013–). Chm., Welwyn Gdn City Centenary Foundn, 2018–. *Publications*: (with David Clutterbuck) The Independent Board Director, 1993; (with Mike Walker) Takeover, 2000 (trans. five langs); The Board Game, 2002; Under a Passing Sky: a poetry collection, 2011; (with O. Hilliam) 22 Ideas That Saved the English Countryside, 2016; various mags, newspapers incl. weekly columnist under pseudonym for London newspaper, 1984–87. *Recreation*: English countryside. *Club*: MCC.

**WAINE, Very Rev. Stephen John;** Dean of Chichester, since 2015; *b* 1959; *s* of Rt Rev. John Waine, *qv*; one *s* one *d*; *m* 2015, Elizabeth Rowe; two step *d*. *Educ*: Univ. of E Anglia (BA Econ. and Social Studies); Westcott House, Cambridge. Ordained deacon 1984, priest 1985; Asst Curate, St Peter's, Wolverhampton, 1984–88; Minor Canon and Succentor, St Paul's Cathedral, 1988–93; Vicar, St Edward the Confessor's, Romford, 1993–2010; Priest-in-charge, St John's, Romford, 2002–10; Archdeacon of Dorset, 2010–15; Canon and Prebendary, Sarum Cathedral, 2010–15. *Recreations*: music (singing and listening), cooking, walking, DIY, reading, sailing, armchair football and cricket. *Address*: The Deanery, Canon Lane, Chichester, W Sussex PO19 1PX. *E*: dean@chichestercathedral.org.uk.

**WAINE, His Honour Stephen Phillip;** a Circuit Judge, 2001–13; Designated Family Judge, Northampton, 2006–13; *b* 9 June 1947; *s* of late Dr Theodore Edward Waine and Mary Florence Waine; *m* 1st, 1976 (marr. diss.); 2nd, 1981, Clare (*née* Pryor); one *s* one *d*. *Educ*: Rugby Sch.; Southampton Univ. (LLB). Called to the Bar, Lincoln's Inn, 1969; a Recorder, Midland and Oxford Circuit, 1992–2001. Chm., Mental Health Tribunals, 2002–. Chm. and Trustee, Equata, 2013–19; Trustee, Kidsaid Northampton, 2013–17. FCIArb 1999–2015. *Recreations*: golf, gardening, watching sports, reading, woodland restoration. *Address*: c/o Northampton Combined Court Centre, 85–87 Lady's Lane, Northampton NN1 3HQ. *Clubs*: MCC; Wellingborough Golf.
See also P. E. Waine.

**WAINWRIGHT, Elizabeth-Anne;** see Gumbel, E.-A.

**WAINWRIGHT, (Elizabeth) Jane,** MA; Co-Founder and Educational Consultant, Education Oxford, 2011–15; *b* 27 Sept. 1950; *d* of Eric Foster Wainwright and Marie Wainwright; civil partnership 2006, Kate Watkins. *Educ*: St Hugh's Coll., Oxford (MA; PGCE); Sch. of Oriental and African Studies, Univ. of London (MA); Open Univ. (Advanced Dip. Educnl Mgt 1987; BSc Hons 1st cl. 2017). Geography teacher: Sandford Sch., Addis Ababa, 1975–77; Peers Sch., Oxford, 1977–82; Hd of Geog., Plymouth High Sch., 1982–88; Dep. Hd, Lancaster Girls' GS, 1988–92; Headteacher: Aylesbury High Sch., 1992–2002; Wycombe High Sch., 2002–08. *Publications*: contrib. Jl of Res. on NE Africa. *Recreations*: travel, feminism, friends, field geology. *E*: jane_wainwright@btinternet.com.

**WAINWRIGHT, Faith Helen, (Mrs K. J. Glynn),** MBE 2012; FREng, FICE, FIStructE; Director, Ove Arup and Partners, since 1998; *b* Dunfermline, Fife, 25 May 1962; *d* of Comdr Brian Hebden Wainwright, RN and Anne Vera Wainwright (*née* Temple); *m* 1988, Kieran J. Glynn; one *s* two *d*. *Educ*: Queen Anne's Sch., Caversham; St Edmund Hall, Oxford (BA; Hon. Fellow, 2015). MIStructE 1987, FIStructE 2003; FREng 2003; FICE 2003. Joined Arup, 1983; projects include: ITN London, 1990; Western Morning News, Plymouth, 1992; Lycée Albert Camus, Frejus, 1994; American Air Mus., Duxford, 1996; Tate Modern, London, 2000; Hongkong and Shanghai Banking Corp. HQ, Canary Wharf, 2002; London Bridge Tower, 2003; Dean, 2011–13, Hd of Tech. Skills, 2013–, Arup Univ. Non-exec. Dir, Knowledge Transfer Network Ltd, 2014–18. Member: Standing Cttee on Structural Safety, 2001–07; Council, IStructE, 2003–06 (Pres., 2018); Adv. Council, BL, 2004–11; Council, RAEng, 2010–13; Vice Chairman: Cttee for Safety in Tall Buildings, 2001–03; Jt Bd of Moderators, 2004–10. Juror: BBC Design Awards, 1996; OASYS Design Awards, 2001. Mem., Smeatonian Soc., 2018–. MInstD; MInstKT 2009. FRSA. Hon. DEng Bath 2014. Trustee, Ove Arup Foundn, 2018–. *Publications*: (contrib. jtly) Fire Safety Engineering and the Case for Dynamic Robustness in the Design of Tall Buildings, 2002; (contrib. jtly) Extreme Event Mitigation in Buildings, 2006; (contrib.) Making Knowledge Management Work for your Organisation, 2012; contribs to learned jls on structural robustness and building projects, incl. Jl IStructE, Planning and Guidance, Ingenia, Structural Engineer. *Recreations*: family, sailing. *Address*: Arup, 13 Fitzroy Street, W1T 4BQ. *T*: (020) 7755 2061, *Fax*: (020) 7755 2150. *E*: faith.wainwright@arup.com.

**WAINWRIGHT, Jane;** see Wainwright, E. J.

**WAINWRIGHT, Lisa Jayne;** Chief Executive, Sport and Recreation Alliance, since 2019; *b* Barnsley, 14 Oct. 1970; *d* of Colin and Audrey Wainwright; *m* 2019, Karena Thomas; two *d*. *Educ*: Royston Comprehensive Sch.; Barnsley Sixth Form Coll.; Univ. of Warwick (BA Hons Physical Educn with QTS 1993); De Montfort Univ. (MA Learning and Teaching 1998). Sports Officer, Univ. of Warwick Students Union, 1993–94; E Reg. Netball Develt Officer, 1994–98; Nat. Youth Develt Officer, England Netball, 1998–2000; Sen. Governing Body Manager, Sport England, 2000–02; Membership Services Dir, England Netball, 2002–04; Sport Develt Manager (Volunteers), 2004–06, Hd, Nat. Sport, 2006–08, Sport England; Chief Executive Officer: Volleyball England, 2008–16; British Basketball Fedn, 2016–18; Interim Chair, Swim England, 2015. Tech. Dir, Internat. Volleyball Fedn, 2018–; Mem., Governance Commn, Internat. Basketball Fedn, 2018–. Director: Wallace Gp, 2016–; British Olympic Assoc., 2017–18. Chair, Inst. of Swimming, 2013–. Trustee, Samworth Brothers Sport Opportunity Fund, 2013–. Fellow, Chartered Inst. for Mgt of Sport and Physical Activity, 2012. Hon. DSc Beds, 2019. *Recreations*: swimming, camping, family, outdoor activities, equality. *Address*: Sport and Recreation Alliance, 5th Floor, Holborn Tower, 137–144 High Holborn, WC1V 6PL. *T*: 07836 032417. *E*: lwainwright@sportandrecreation.org.uk.

**WAINWRIGHT, Prof. Mark Sebastian,** AM 2004; PhD, DSc; FTSE, FIChemE, FIEAust, FRACI; Professor of Chemical Engineering, 1989–2009, now Emeritus, and Vice-Chancellor and President, 2004–06, University of New South Wales; Chairman: Smart Services Co-operative Research Centre, since 2010 (Director, since 2009); Foundation for Australian Studies in China, since 2012; *b* 20 Oct. 1943; *s* of William Edward and Marjorie Wanda Wainwright; *m* Irene Eve Ruffio; two *d*. *Educ*: S Australia Inst. of Technol. (BAppSc Hons); Univ. of Adelaide (MAppSc); McMaster Univ. (PhD Chem. Engrg); Univ. of S Australia (DSc). University of New South Wales: School of Chemical Technology: Lectr in Industrial Chem., 1974–77; Sen. Lectr, 1978–80; School of Chemical Engineering and Industrial Chemistry: Associate Prof., and Hd, Dept of Industrial Chem., 1981–88; Hd, Dept of Chem. Engrg, 1989–91; Dean, Faculty of Engrg, 1991–2000; Actg Pro-Vice-Chancellor (Inf. Services), 1994; Pro-Vice-Chancellor (Res.), 1998–2000; Dep. Vice-Chancellor (Res. and Internat.), 2001–04. Chairman: Australia-China Council, 2006–11; Nat. Computational Infrastructure Steering Cttee, 2007–; INTERSECT Australia Ltd, 2008–; Nat. Inst. for Promotion of ICT in Health. Mem. Bd, Engrg Aid Australia. Mem. Council, Univ. of Qld, 2009–. *Publications*: contrib. numerous papers; patents published. *Recreation*: golf. *Club*: Coast Golf.

**WAINWRIGHT, Richard Barry;** European Law consultant, FIPRA International, since 2008; Principal Legal Adviser, European Commission, 1992–2005; *b* 10 June 1940; *s* of Denys and Shelagh Wainwright; *m* 1966, Linda Sully; three *s* one *d*. *Educ*: Trinity Coll., Oxford (BA Hons). Inns of Court Sch. of Law. In practice as barrister, 1966–68; Solicitor's Office, Inland Revenue, 1968–69; Legal Advr, British Petroleum Co., 1969–73; with Legal Service, EC, 1973–2005. European Law consultant, Allen and Overy, London and Brussels, 2005–08. *Publications*: contribs to Common Market Law Rev., European Law Rev., Oxford Yearbook of European Law, Revue du Marché Commun. *Recreations*: music, reading, sailing, ski-ing, tennis, golf, walking. *Club*: Château Ste Anne (Brussels).

**WAINWRIGHT, Sir Robert Mark,** KCMG 2018; Senior Partner, Cyber Security, North West Europe, Deloitte, since 2018; *b* Carmarthen, 17 Sept. 1967; *s* of Victor and Christine Wainwright; *m* 1994, Suzanne; one *s* two *d*. *Educ*: London Sch. of Econs and Pol Sci. (BSc (Econ) Internat. Relns 1989). Security Service: Desk Officer, 1989–94; Ops Team Leader, 1994–97; Dep. Hd, Serious Crime Section, 1997–2000; Chief, UK Liaison Bureau, Europol, 2000–03; International Director: Nat. Criminal Intelligence Service, 2003–06; SOCA, 2006–09; Dir, Europol, 2009–18. *Recreations*: sport, history, family. *Address*: Deloitte, Gustav Mahlerlaan 2970, 1081 LA Amsterdam, Netherlands.

**WAINWRIGHT, Sam,** CBE 1982; Post Office Corporation: Member of Board, 1977–85; Deputy Chairman, 1981–85; Managing Director, National Girobank, 1977–85; Director, Postel Investment Ltd, 1982–85; *b* 2 Oct. 1924; *m* Ruth Strom; three *s* one *d*. *Educ*: Regent Street Polytechnic; LSE (MSc Econ). Financial journalist, Glasgow Herald, 1950; Deputy City Editor, 1952–55; Head of Research: Grieveson Grant, 1955–58; W. Greenwell, 1958–60; Director: Rea Brothers Ltd (Merchant Bankers), 1960–77 (Managing Dir, 1965–77); Furness Withy & Co. Ltd, 1971–77; Stothert & Pitt Ltd, 1970–77 (Chm., 1975–77); Dundee, Perth and London, 1974–76; Aeronautical & General Instruments Ltd, 1968–77; Manders (Hldgs), 1972–87 (Dep. Chm., 1985–86; Chm., 1986–87); BICC, 1985–90 (Chm., Audit Cttee, 1986–90); Lancashire & London Investment Trust Ltd, 1963–77; Scottish Cities Investment Trust Ltd, 1961–77; Scottish & Mercantile Investment Co. Ltd, 1964–77; AMDAHL (UK), 1987–93. Member: Post Office Audit Cttee, 1978–80; Monopolies and Mergers Commn, 1985–91. Chm., Jigsaw Day Nurseries, 1991–95. Mem. Council, Soc. of Investment Analysts, 1961–75, Fellow, 1980. Hon. Editor, The Investment Analyst, 1961–74. *Publications*: articles in various Bank Reviews. *Recreations*: reading, bridge, walking. *Address*: Flat 5, 29 Warrington Crescent, W9 1EJ. *T*: (020) 7286 8050. *Club*: Reform.

**WAINWRIGHT, Timothy John**; Chief Executive, WaterAid UK, since 2017; *b* Farnborough, Kent, 2 Jan. 1964; *s* of David Wainwright and Judith Wainwright (*née* Hyde); *m* 1993, Alison Vickers; two *d*. *Educ*: Sidney Sussex Coll., Cambridge (BA Maths 1985); Lancaster Univ. (MSc Operational Res. 1987). Brand Develt Manager, British Airways plc, 1987–96; Fundraising Develt Manager, 1996–2001, Regl Manager, Southern Africa, 1999, Oxfam GB; Country Dir, VSO China, 2001–04; Regl Prog. Manager, Oxfam GB, 2004–07; Dir, English Regions, Equality and Human Rights Commn, 2008–10; CEO, ADD Internat., 2010–17. Chm., Bond, 2015–17. *Recreations*: gardening, singing.

**WAIT, His Honour John James**; a Circuit Judge, 1997–2017; *b* 19 Sept. 1949; *s* of Eric James Wait and Rachel Wait; *m* 1986, Patricia, (Tricia), Ann Hitchcock; two *s*. *Educ*: Queen Mary's Grammar Sch., Walsall; Nottingham Univ. (LLB 1971). Called to the Bar, Inner Temple, 1972, Bencher, 2011; Lectr in Law, UCW, Aberystwyth, 1972–74; in practice at the Bar, 1974–97; Asst Recorder, 1989–93; a Recorder, 1993–97; Midland and Oxford Circuit; Resident Judge, Derby Combined Court, 2000–08. Jt Dir, Criminal Induction Course, Judicial Studies Bd and Judicial Coll., 2008–13.

**WAITE, Rt Hon. Sir John (Douglas)**, Kt 1982; PC 1993; a Lord Justice of Appeal, 1993–97; *b* 3 July 1932; *s* of late Archibald Waite and Betty, *d* of late Ernest Bates; *m* 1966, Julia Mary, *er d* of late Joseph Tangye; three *s* two step *s*. *Educ*: Sherborne Sch.; Corpus Christi Coll., Cambridge (MA). President of Cambridge Union, 1955. Nat. Service, 2nd Lieut, RA, 1951–52. Called to Bar, Gray's Inn, 1956, Bencher, 1981; QC 1975; a Judge of the High Court of Justice, Family Div., 1982–93; Presiding Judge, North Eastern Circuit, 1990–93; Judge, Gibraltar Court of Appeal, 1997–2000. Pres., Employment Appeal Tribunal, 1983–85. Co-Chm., Ind. Asylum Commn, 2006–08. Chairman: UNICEF (UK), 1997–2004; Special Trustees, Middx and UC Hosps, 1997–2004; UCL Hosps Charitable Foundn, 1999–2004. *Recreations*: reading (haphazardly), sailing (uncertainly), gardening (optimistically). *Address*: 54 Church Street, Orford, Woodbridge, Suffolk IP12 2NT; Flat 19, Wentworth Mansions, Keats Grove, NW3 2RL. *Clubs*: Athenæum; Orford Sailing.

**WAITE, Jonathan Gilbert Stokes**; QC 2002; *b* 15 Feb. 1956; *s* of late Capt. David Waite, RN, and Joan Waite (*née* Paull). *Educ*: Sherborne Sch.; Trinity Coll., Cambridge (MA). Called to the Bar, Inner Temple, 1978; in practice, specialising in personal injury, industrial diseases and pharmaceutical product liability law, 1979–. *Recreations*: golf, ski-ing, bridge, wines of Bordeaux. *Address*: 76 Forthbridge Road, Battersea, SW11 5NY; Crown Office Chambers, 2 Crown Office Row, Temple, EC4Y 7HJ. *T*: (020) 7228 4488, *Fax*: (020) 7797 8100. *E*: waite@crownofficechambers.com; Fauret, 82110 Bouloc, Tarn-et-Garonne, France. *Clubs*: Woking Golf, Aldeburgh Golf, Rye Golf, Royal St George's Golf.

**WAITE, Judith Mary;** *see* Rowe, J. M.

**WAITE, Stephen**, DPhil; Principal and Chief Executive Officer, Writtle University College (formerly Writtle College), 2013–17; *b* Willesden, London, 25 Aug. 1954; *s* of Frederick John Waite and Gladys Violet Waite; *m* 1981, Alison Jean Mitchard; two *d*. *Educ*: Bishopsfield Secondary Modern Sch., Fareham; Fareham Technical Coll.; Univ. of Sussex (BSc Hons 1st Cl. Biol Scis; DPhil 1980); Open Univ. (BA Maths). MCIEEM (MIEEM 1992). Lectr in Ecol. and Plant Scis, Poly. of Central London, 1979–91; Brighton Polytechnic, later University of Brighton: Sen. Lectr in Ecol. and Envmtl Scis, 1991–95; Principal Lectr in Biol., 1995–2009; Dep. Hd, Sch. of Pharmacy and Molecular Sci, 2004–09; Vice Principal (HE) and Dean, Hartpury Coll., 2009–13. Course Dir, Cert. and Dip. in Field Biol., Birkbeck Coll., Univ. of London, 1991–98. *Publications*: Pollution: ecology and biotreatment, 1993; Statistical Ecology in Practice: a guide to analysing environmental and ecological field data, 2000; numerous articles on plant and landscape ecol. in learned jls. *Recreations*: science, reading, music, guitar, swimming, DIY. *Club*: Mid Sussex Marlins (Masters).

**WAITE, Terence Hardy**, CBE 1992 (MBE 1982); writer and lecturer; Adviser to Archbishop of Canterbury on Anglican Communion Affairs, 1980–92 (taken captive and held hostage in Lebanon, Jan. 1987–19 Nov. 1991); Fellow Commoner, Trinity Hall, Cambridge, 1992–93, now Emeritus; *b* 31 May 1939; *s* of Thomas William Waite and Lena (*née* Hardy); *m* 1964, Helen Frances Watters; one *s* three *d*. *Educ*: Wilmslow and Stockton Heath, Cheshire; Church Army Coll., London. Lay training adviser to Bishop and Diocese of Bristol, 1964–68; Adviser to Archbishop of Uganda, Rwanda and Burundi, 1968–71; Internat. Consultant working with Roman Catholic Church, 1972–79. Member, National Assembly, Church of England, 1966–68 (resigned on moving to Africa); Co-ordinator, Southern Sudan Relief Project, 1969–71. Vis. Fellow, Magdalen Coll., Oxford, 2006. Founder-Chairman: Y Care International, 1985–2000 (Pres., 2000–); Hostage UK, 2005–; Pres., Emmaus UK, 1998–. Chm., Prison Video Trust, 1998–2016. Pres., Llangollen Internat. Musical Eisteddfod, 2006–; Vice President: Suffolk Assoc. of Local Councils, 1999–; E Cheshire Hospice, Macclesfield, 2001–; English Music Fest., 2006–; Chester Music Soc., 2011–. Trustee, Butler Trust, 1986–2010 (Patron, 2010–). Patron: Bury St Edmunds Volunteer Centre, 1994–; Warrington Male Voice Choir, 1996–; Romany Soc., 1997–2014; W Suffolk Voluntary Assoc. for the Blind, 1998–; Suffolk Far East Prisoners of War (Pres.); Save our Parsonages, 1999–; Bridge Project, Sudbury, 1999–; Children (and Families) of Far Eastern Prisoners of War, 1999–; Friends of the Samaritans, Bury St Edmunds; One to One Children's Fund, 2001–; Under-Privileged Children's Charity, Bristol, 2003–; British Friends of Neve Shalom/Wahat al-Salam, 2003–; Habit for Humanity, 2004–; Children with Aids Charity, 2004–; Rapid UK, 2004–; Sunderland Counselling Services, 2004–; Tymes Trust, 2005–; Storybook Dads, 2007–; Henry Spink Foundation, 2009–; Escaping Victimhood, 2011–; Asylum Aid, 2012–. Ambassador for WWF, 2000–. Hon. DCL: Kent at Canterbury, 1986; City, 1992; Hon. LLD: Liverpool, 1992; Durham, 1992; Sussex, 1992; Yale, 1992; Robert Gordon, 2007; Hon. DHL Virginia Commonwealth Univ., 1996; Hon. LHD Wittenberg, 1992; Hon. DHumLit Southern Florida, 1992; Hon. DPhil Anglia Polytech. Univ., 2001; Hon. DLitt: Nottingham Trent, 2001; De Montfort, 2005; Chester, 2008; Open, 2009. Templeton UK Award, 1985; Franklin D. Roosevelt Four Freedom Award, 1992. *Publications*: Taken on Trust, 1993; Footfalls in Memory, 1995; Travels with a Primate, 2000; The Voyage of the Golden Handshake (novel), 2015; Out of Silence: memories, poems, reflections, 2016; Solitude: memories, people, places, 2017; Travels with a Primate: around the world with Robert Runcie, 2019. *Recreations*: music, travel (esp. in remote parts of the world), Jungian studies, international affairs. *Address*: Trinity Hall, Cambridge CB2 1TJ. *Clubs*: Travellers; Empire (Toronto).

**WAKE, Sir Hereward Charles**, 15th Bt *cr* 1621; *b* 22 Nov. 1952; *s* of Sir Hereward Wake, 14th Bt, MC and Julia Rosemary Wake (*née* Lees); *S* father, 2017; *m* 1st, 1977, Lady Doune Ogilvy, *e d* of Earl of Airlie, *qv* (marr. diss. 1995); two *s* one *d* (and one *s* decd); 2nd, 1998, Mrs Joan Barrow. High Sheriff, Northants, 2005. *Heir*: *s* John Hereward, *b* 6 Oct. 1978.

**WAKEFIELD, Area Bishop of**, since 2014; **Rt Rev. Anthony William Robinson**; *b* 25 April 1956; *m* 1981, Susan Boddy; two *s* one *d*. *Educ*: Bedford Modern Sch.; Salisbury and Wells Theol. Coll. Ordained deacon, 1982, priest, 1983; Asst Curate, St Paul, Tottenham, 1982–85; Team Vicar, 1985–89, Team Rector, 1989–97, Resurrection, Leicester; Archdeacon of Pontefract, 1997–2003; Bishop Suffragan of Pontefract, 2002–14. Rural Dean, Christianity North, Leicester, 1992–97; Hon. Canon, Leicester Cathedral, 1994–97. *Address*: Pontefract House, 181a Manygates Lane, Wakefield WF2 7DR. *T*: (01924) 250781. *E*: bishop.tony@leeds.anglican.org.

**WAKEFIELD, Dean of;** *see* Cowling, Very Rev. S. C.

**WAKEFIELD, Her Honour Anne Prudence;** a Circuit Judge, 1999–2005; *b* 25 May 1943; *d* of John Arkell Wakefield and Stella Adelaide Wakefield; *m* 1974, James Robert Reid, *qv* (marr. diss. 2002); two *s* one *d*. *Educ*: London Sch. of Economics and Political Science (LLB); Newnham Coll., Cambridge (LLM 1969). Called to the Bar, Gray's Inn, 1968; in practice, 1970–75 and 1987–99; Asst Recorder, 1991–95; a Recorder, 1995–99. Lecturer in Law: LSE, 1969–70; pt-time, QMC, 1983–87. Pt-time Chm., Industrial Tribunals, 1992–99; a Judge of the Employment Appeal Tribunal, 2000–05. Associate, Newnham Coll., Cambridge, 2002–05.

**WAKEFIELD, Sir (Edward) Humphrey (Tyrrell)**, 2nd Bt *cr* 1962; *b* 11 July 1936; *s* of Sir Edward Birkbeck Wakefield, 1st Bt, CIE, and Constance Lalage, *e d* of Sir John Perronet Thompson, KCSI, KCIE, and *nephew* of 1st Baron Wakefield of Kendal; *S* father, 1969; *m* 1st, 1960, Priscilla (marr. diss. 1964), *e d* of O. R. Bagot; 2nd, 1966, Hon. Elizabeth Sophia (from whom he obt. a divorce, 1971), *e d* of 1st Viscount De L'Isle, VC, KG, PC, GCMG, GCVO, and former wife of G. S. O. A. Colthurst; one *s*; 3rd, 1974, Hon. Katharine Mary Alice Baring, *d* of 1st Baron Howick of Glendale, KG, GCMG, KCVO, and of Lady Mary Howick; one *s* one *d* (and one *s* decd). *Educ*: Gordonstoun; Trinity Coll., Cambridge (MA Hons). Formerly Captain, 10th Royal Hussars. Exec. Vice-Pres., Mallett, America Ltd, 1970–75; Chm., Tyrrell & Moore Ltd, 1978–92; Director: Mallett & Son (Antiques) Ltd, 1971–78; Tree of Life Foundn, 1976–. Dir, Spoleto Fest. of Two Worlds, USA and Italy, 1973–80. Chm., Wilderness Trust, 1999–2006 (Patron, 2011–); President: Northumberland Nat. Park Mountain Rescue (formerly Northumberland Nat. Park Search and Rescue) Team; Avison Trust; Tibetan Spaniel Assoc.; Patron: Action North East; Medicine and Chernobyl; Centre for Search Res. UK; Shadow Dance UK, etc; formerly Appeals Consultant, London Br., British Red Cross Soc. Mem., Standing Council of Baronetage. Mem., Soc. of Dilettante. Fellow, Pierpont Morgan Library. Joined NZ Everest Team, 1990, and also in their first ascent of Mount Wakefield; Mem., Norman Vaughan Antarctic Expedn, 1993. Life Mem., Scott-Polar Inst. FRGS. Order of Nat. Inst. (Greece), 1954. *Recreations*: riding, writing, music, shooting. *Heir*: *s* Capt. Maximilian Edward Vereker Wakefield [*b* 22 Feb. 1967; *m* 1994, Lucinda Katharine Elizabeth, *d* of Lt-Col and Mrs David Pipe; two *s*. *Educ*: Milton Abbey; RMA Sandhurst]. *Address*: Chillingham Castle, Chillingham, Northumberland NE66 5NJ. *Clubs*: Beefsteak, Cavalry and Guards, Turf; Harlequins Rugby Football (Twickenham) (Hon. Life Mem.).

*See also* G. H. C. Wakefield.

**WAKEFIELD, Gerald Hugo Cropper, (Hady)**; Chairman, J & H Marsh & McLennan (Holdings) Ltd (formerly Bowring Group), 1996–99; *b* 15 Sept. 1938; *s* of Sir Edward Wakefield, 1st Bt, CIE, and (Constance) Lalage, *e d* of Sir John Perronet Thompson, KCSI, KCIE; *m* 1971, Victoria Rose Feilden; one *s*. *Educ*: Eton; Trinity Coll., Cambridge (MA). Started at Lloyd's, 1961; joined C. T. Bowring & Co., 1968, Dir 1983; Guy Carpenter & Co., NY: Dep. Chm., 1990; Pres., 1993; Chm., 1996. *Recreations*: fishing, shooting, ski-ing, opera. *Address*: Bramdean House, Alresford, Hants SO24 0JU. *T*: (01962) 771214. *Clubs*: White's, Cavalry and Guards, Beefsteak; The Brook (NY).

**WAKEFIELD, Sir Humphrey;** *see* Wakefield, Sir E. H. T.

**WAKEFIELD, Sir Norman (Edward)**, Kt 1988; Chairman, Y. J. Lovell (Holdings) plc, 1987–90; *b* 30 Dec. 1929; *s* of Edward and Muriel Wakefield; *m* 1953, Denise Mary Bayliss (*d* 1998); two *s* four *d*. *Educ*: Wallington County Sch.; Croydon and Brixton Technical Colls. Articled student, Wates Ltd, 1947; Man. Dir, Wates Construction Ltd, 1967; Pres., jt venture co., USA, between Wates and Rouse Co., 1970–73; Man. Dir, Holland, Hannen & Cubitts, 1973; Chief Exec., 1977–83, Chm. and Chief Exec., 1983–87, Y. J. Lovell (Holdings). Dep. Chm., Housing Corp., 1990–94. Director: Lloyds Abbey Life, 1986–93; English Estates, 1990–94. Pres., CIOB, 1985–86. Chm., 1995–2003, Dep. Chm., 2003–08, Nelson House Recovery Trust. Charity consultant, 1995–2010. *Recreations*: opera, walking, gardening. *Address*: 12 Rosemary Gate, Esher Park Avenue, Esher, Surrey KT10 9NZ. *Club*: Arts.

**WAKEFIELD, His Honour Robert;** a Circuit Judge, 1996–2011; *b* 14 Feb. 1946; *s* of Dudley James Wakefield and Violet Harriette Hart; *m* 1977, Anne Jennifer Gregory. *Educ*: Birmingham Univ. (LLB); Brasenose Coll., Oxford (BCL). Called to the Bar, Middle Temple, 1969; Recorder, 1993–96.

**WAKEFIELD, Victoria Elizabeth Livesey**; QC 2019; *b* Birkenhead, 20 Aug. 1979; *d* of Richard Wakefield and Christina Wakefield and step *d* of Jennifer Nicholson; partner, Matthew Ashton; one *s* one *d*. *Educ*: Tapton Comprehensive Sch., Sheffield; Trinity Coll., Cambridge (BA 1st Cl. Hons Law 2001); Univ. Libre de Bruxelles (DES Droit Eur. 2002); Inns of Court Sch. of Law (BVC 2003). Called to the Bar, Gray's Inn, 2003; in practice as a barrister, specialising in EU, public and commercial law, Brick Court Chambers. *Recreations*: singing, dancing, drinking beer, seeing friends and family. *Address*: Brick Court Chambers, 7–8 Essex Street, WC2R 3LD. *T*: (020) 7379 3550. *E*: clerks@brickcourt.co.uk.

**WAKEFIELD, William Barry**, CB 1990; Deputy Director (Research), National Commission on Education, 1991–95; *b* 6 June 1930; *s* of Stanley Arthur and Evelyn Grace Wakefield; *m* 1953, Elizabeth Violet (*née* Alexander); three *s* one *d*. *Educ*: Harrow County Grammar Sch.; University Coll., London. BSc; FSS. Statistician, NCB, 1953–62; DES, 1962–67; Chief Statistician, MoD, 1967–72, CSO, 1972–75; Asst Dir, CSO, Cabinet Office, 1975–79; Dir of Statistics, DES, 1979–90. Member, United Reformed Church. *Recreations*: horse racing, gardening, family history. *Address*: Egg Hall Cottage, 14 Birch Street, Nayland, Colchester CO6 4JA.

**WAKEFORD, David Ewing**, MBE 1992; External Trade Director, Africa Invest Fund Management Ltd, 2009–10; Managing Director, Global Trade Knowledge, 1999–2000 and 2006–11; *b* 30 Oct. 1944; *s* of Arthur Ewing Wakeford and late Gertrude Ada Wakeford (*née* Hall); *m* 1st, 1968 (marr. diss. 2006); three *s*; 2nd, 2007, SallyAnn Jackson. *Educ*: Hadham Hall Sch.; St Mary's Sch., Welwyn; Univ. of Manchester (MSc Polymer and Fibre Sci.). ICI, 1963–99: Res. Chemist, Plastics Div., 1963–78; Purchasing Manager, Petrochemicals and Plastics, 1978–85; Internat. Trade Manager, Head Office, 1985–99; Chief Exec., Simpler Trade Procedures Board, then SITPRO Ltd, 2000–05; Internat. Trade Dir, Commonwealth Business Council, 2006–09. Dir, Dorset Advocacy, 2014– (Vice Chm., 2014–). *Recreations*: sailing, bird-watching, country pursuits.

**WAKEFORD, Sir (Geoffrey) Michael (Montgomery)**, Kt 2004; OBE 1995; Clerk to the Worshipful Company of Mercers, 1974–98; Barrister-at-Law; *b* 10 Dec. 1937; *o s* of late Geoffrey and Helen Wakeford; *m* 1966, Diana Margaret Loy Cooper, *y d* of late Comdr W. G. L. Cooper and of Patricia Cooper (*née* Fforde), Aislaby, N Yorks; two *s* two *d*. *Educ*: Downside; Clare Coll., Cambridge (Exhibnr; MA, LLB). Called to Bar, Gray's Inn and

South Eastern Circuit, 1961; practised at Common Law Bar until 1971. Apptd Dep. Clerk to the Mercers Co., 1971. Director: Portman Settled Estates Ltd, 1998–2007; Alto Film Prodn LLP, 2002–16. Clerk to Govs, St Paul's Schs, 1971–98; Governor: London Internat. Film Sch., 1981–85, 1990–2017 (Vice Chm., 1997–2010; Hon. Associate, 2009); Molecule Theatre, 1986–; Unicorn Children's Theatre, 2005–11; Thomas Telford Sch., 1990–2001 (Chm., 1997–2001); Abingdon Sch., 2000–07; Guardian Angels RC Primary Sch., Tower Hamlets, 2000–07, 2011–15 (Chm., 2000–07; Associate, 2007–11, 2016–19); Walsall Acad., 2001–09 (Chm., 2001–09). *Club:* Travellers.

**WAKEFORD, Richard George;** rural strategy consultant, since 2011; *b* 6 Oct. 1953; *s* of (Henry) Eric Wakeford and Mary Elisabeth Wakeford (*née* Parsons); *m* 1976, Susan Mary Beacham; three *s*. *Educ:* Chichester High Sch. for Boys; King's Coll., London (BSc Maths and Physics). Exec. Officer, 1975–80, Asst Private Sec. to Minister of State, 1979–80, DoE; HEO posts, DoE and Dept of Transport, 1980–83; Department of the Environment: Private Sec. to Permt Sec., 1983–85; Planning Inspectorate, 1985; Develt Control, 1985–87; Bill Manager, Water Privatisation, 1988–89; Principal, Envmt White Paper Team, 1990; (last) Chief Exec., Crown Suppliers, 1991; Head of Develt Plans and Policies, 1991–94; Asst Sec., Economic and Domestic Secretariat, Cabinet Office, 1994–96; Chief Executive: Countryside Commn, 1996–99; Countryside Agency, 1999–2004; Hd, Scottish Exec. Envmt and Rural Affairs Dept, later Dir-Gen. Envmt, Scottish Govt, 2005–09; Dir-Gen. Rural Futures, Scottish Govt, 2009–10. UK Sustainable Develt Comr, 2000–04; Chm., UK Sustainable Develt Res. Network, 2011. Chairman: Rural Wkg Party, OECD, 2007–12; EC Adv. Cttee on priorities for food security, rural and marine res., 2016–18; Heating Equipment Testing and Approvals Scheme, 2017–. Non-exec. Bd Mem., DEFRA, 2001–04. Mem., Cotswolds Area of Outstanding Natural Beauty, 2012–18; Chair, Glos Market Towns Forum, 2017–. Mem., Winchcombe Town Council, 2012–. Trustee, RICS Trust, 2013–; Chair, RICS Res. Trust, 2017–. Mid Career Fellow, Princeton Univ., 1987–88; Vis. Prof., Birmingham City Univ., 2013–. FAcSS 2018. Hon. MRTPI. Hon. Dr Glos. *Publications:* Speeding Planning Appeals, 1986; American Development Control: parallels and paradoxes from a British perspective, 1990. *Recreations:* gardening, photography, built and natural landscape, cycling. *Address:* Charingworth Court, Broadway Road, Winchcombe, Glos GL54 5JN. *T:* (01242) 603033, 07557 057047.

**WAKEHAM,** family name of **Baron Wakeham**.

**WAKEHAM, Baron** *cr* 1992 (Life Peer), of Maldon in the County of Essex; **John Wakeham;** PC 1983; JP; DL; FCA; Chairman, Press Complaints Commission, 1995–2002; *b* 22 June 1932; *s* of late Major W. J. Wakeham and Mrs E. R. Wakeham; *m* 1st, 1965, Anne Roberta Bailey (*d* 1984); two *s*; 2nd, 1985, Alison Bridget Ward, MBE, DL, *d* of late Ven. E. J. G. Ward, LVO; one *s*. *Educ:* Charterhouse. Chartered Accountant. MP (C) Maldon, Feb. 1974–1983, Colchester South and Maldon, 1983–92; Asst Govt Whip, 1979–81; a Lord Comr of HM Treasury (Govt Whip), 1981; Parly Under-Sec. of State, DoI, 1981–82; Minister of State, HM Treasury, 1982–83; Parly Sec. to HM Treasury and Govt Chief Whip, 1983–87; Lord Privy Seal, 1987–88; Leader of the H of C, 1987–89; Lord Pres. of the Council, 1988–89; Sec. of State for Energy, 1989–92; Minister responsible for co-ordinating develt of presentation of govt policies, 1990–92; Lord Privy Seal and Leader of the H of L, 1992–94. Chm., Royal Commn on Reform of H of L, 1999. Chm., British Horseracing Bd, 1996–98 (Mem., 1995–98). Chancellor, Brunel Univ., 1998–2012, Chancellor Emeritus, 2013. Mem., Cttee of Mgt, RNLI, 1995–2005. JP Inner London, 1972; DL Hants, 1997. Hon. PhD Anglia Poly. Univ., 1992; DUniv Brunel, 1998. *Recreations:* sailing, racing, reading. *Address:* House of Lords, SW1A 0PW. *Clubs:* Carlton (Chm. 1992–98), Buck's, Garrick; Royal Yacht Squadron.

**WAKEHAM, Sir William (Arnot),** Kt 2009; FREng; Chairman: Exeter Science Park, since 2009; South East Physics Network, since 2009; *b* 25 Sept. 1944; *s* of Stanley William Wakeham; *m* 1st, 1969, Christina Marjorie Stone (marr. diss. 1974); one *s*; 2nd, 1978, Sylvia Frances Tolley; two *s*. *Educ:* Univ. of Exeter (BSc 1966; PhD 1969; DSc 1985). FREng (FEng 1997). Research Associate, Brown Univ., USA, 1969–71; Imperial College, London University: Lectr in Transport Processes, Dept of Chem. Engrg, 1971–78; Reader in Chemical Physics, 1978–85; Prof. in Chemical Physics, 1985–2001; Hd of Dept of Chem. Engrg and Chem. Technology, 1988–96; Pro Rector (Research), 1996–2001; Dep. Rector, 1997–2001; Vice-Chancellor, Univ. of Southampton, 2001–09. Chm., Commn of IUPAC, 1993–98. Mem., EPSRC, 2005–11. Treas., Euro-CASE, 2010–. Non-exec. Dir, Ilika plc, 2009–18. Visiting Professor: Imperial Coll. London, 2002–; Univ. of Exeter, 2009–; Instituto Superior Técnico, Lisbon, 2009–. Chair, Wakeham Rev. of STEM Degree Provision and Graduate Employability, HEFCE and BIS, 2016. Sen. Vice-Pres., 2011–15, and Hon. Sec. Internat. Affairs, 2009–15, RAEng (Vice Pres., 2009); Pres., IChemE, 2011–12. FIC 2003. Trustee: Royal Anniversary Trust, 2010–; Rank Prizes Trust, 2010–. Hon. DSc: Lisbon, 1998; Exeter, 2007; Southampton Solent, 2007; Loughborough, 2010; Southampton 2011; Universidade Nova de Lisboa, 2012; Portsmouth, 2013. *Publications:* Intermolecular Forces: their origin and determination, 1981; Forces between Molecules, 1988; The Transport Properties of Fluids, 1987; International Thermodynamic Tables, vol. XI, 1989; Experimental Thermodynamics, vol. III, 1990; Commonly Asked Questions in Thermodynamics, 2011; numerous articles in learned jls. *Recreations:* power boats, cycling. *Address:* Beacon Down, Rewe, Exeter, Devon EX5 4DX.

**WAKEHURST, 3rd Baron** *cr* 1934, of Ardingly; **(John) Christopher Loder;** Chairman: Anglo & Overseas Trust PLC (formerly Anglo-American Securities Corporation), 1980–96; The Overseas Investment Trust PLC (formerly North Atlantic Securities Corporation), 1980–96; Morgan Grenfell Equity Income Trust PLC, 1991–95; *b* 23 Sept. 1925; *s* of 2nd Baron Wakehurst, KG, KCMG, and Dowager Lady Wakehurst, (Dame Margaret Wakehurst), DBE (*d* 1994); *S* father, 1970; *m* 1956, Ingeborg Krumbholz-Hess (*d* 1977); one *s* one *d*; *m* 1983, Brigid, *yr d* of William Noble, Cirencester. *Educ:* Eton; King's School, nr Sydney, NSW; Trinity College, Cambridge (BA 1948, LLB 1949, MA 1953). Served War as Sub Lieut RANVR and RNVR; South West Pacific, 1943–45. Barrister, Inner Temple, 1950. Chm., Morgan Grenfell Trust Managers Ltd, 1991–94; Chairman: Continental Illinois Ltd, 1973–84; Philadelphia National Ltd, 1985–90; Dep. Chm., London and Manchester Gp, 1981–95. Trustee, The Photographers' Gallery Ltd, 1979–90. *Heir: s* Hon. Timothy Walter Loder, *b* 28 March 1958. *Address:* Trillinghurst Oast, Ranters Lane, Goudhurst, Kent TN17 1HL. *T:* (01580) 211502. *Club:* Chelsea Arts.

**WAKELAM, Prof. Michael John Owen,** PhD; Director and Chief Executive, BBSRC Babraham Institute, since 2007; Fellow, Downing College, Cambridge, since 2007; *b* 15 July 1955; *s* of John Wakelam and Sheila Wakelam; *m* 1980, Jane Catherine Fensome; two *s*. *Educ:* Univ. of Birmingham (BSc Med. Biochem. 1977; PhD Biochem. 1980). Res. Fellow, Univ. of Konstanz, 1981–83; Beit Meml Res. Fellow, Imperial Coll., London, 1983–85; Lectr, 1985–90, Sen. Lectr, 1991–92, Reader, 1992–93, in Biochemistry, Univ. of Glasgow; Prof. of Molecular Pharmacology, Univ. of Birmingham, 1993–2006. Hon. Prof., Sch. of Medicine, Univ. of Birmingham, 2007–; Hon. Prof. of Lipid Signalling, Faculty of Clinical Medicine, Univ. of Cambridge, 2011–; Vis. Prof., KCL, 2012–. Morton Lectr, Biochemical Soc., 2018. Mem., MRC, 2004–08 (Chm., Molecular and Cellular Medicine Bd, 2004–08). *Publications:* contrib. to learned jls on signalling processes and lipid biochem. *Recreations:* reading, music, walking. *Address:* Babraham Institute, Babraham Research Campus, Cambridge CB22 3AT.

**WAKELEY, Amanda Jane,** OBE 2010; fashion designer; Founder and Creative Director, Amanda Wakeley, since 1990; *b* 15 Sept. 1962; *d* of Sir John Cecil Nicholson Wakeley, 2nd Bt. *Educ:* Cheltenham Ladies' Coll. Worked, in fashion industry, NY, 1983–85, for private commns, 1987–90; Founder, Amanda Wakeley lifestyle luxury brand, 1990; opened flagship store in Mayfair, 2014; fashion and jewellery collections sold globally. Co-Chm., Fashion Targets Breast Cancer Appeal Cttee, 1996– (raised over £14 million). Hon. DFA Chester, 2016. British Fashion Award for Glamour, 1992, 1993 and 1996. *Recreations:* skiing, ski touring, sailing, travel, creative world. *Address:* 18 Albemarle Street, W1S 4HR.

**WAKELEY, (Sir) Nicholas Jeremy,** (3rd Bt *cr* 1952, of Liss, Southampton); *b* 17 Oct. 1957; *er s* of Sir John Cecil Nicholson Wakeley, 2nd Bt, FRCS and of June (*née* Leney); *S* father, 2012, but his name does not appear on the Official Roll of the Baronetage; *m* 1991, Sarah Ann, *d* of Air Vice Marshal Brian Lewis Robinson, *qv*; four *s* one *d*. *Educ:* Uppingham. *Heir: s* Joshua Jeremy Wakeley, *b* 27 Sept. 1993.

**WAKELIN, Prof. Daniel Leslie,** PhD; Jeremy Griffiths Professor of Medieval English Palaeography, University of Oxford, since 2011; *b* Bury St Edmunds, 31 Jan. 1977; *s* of Roger and Jennifer Wakelin; civil partnership 2011, *m* 2016, Dr Joel Harvey. *Educ:* Ixworth Middle Sch.; Thurston Upper Sch.; Trinity Hall, Cambridge (BA 1st Cl. Hons English 1998; MPhil Medieval and Renaissance Lit. 1999; PhD English 2003). Jun. Res. Fellow, St Catharine's Coll., Cambridge, 2002–04; Lectr and Fellow in English, Christ's Coll., Cambridge, 2004–11; Lectr in English, Univ. of Cambridge, 2006–11. Charles Owen Vis. Prof. of Medieval Studies, Univ. of Connecticut, 2009. Gov., N Oxfordshire Acad., 2011–15. *Publications:* Humanism, Reading and English Literature 1430–1530, 2007; (with Alexandra Gillespie) The Production of Books in England 1350–1500, 2011; Scribal Correction and Literary Craft: English manuscripts 1375–1510, 2014; Designing English: early literature on the page, 2017; Revolting Remedies for Medieval England, 2017; (with Edward Wilson) A Middle English Translation from Petrarch's 'Secretum', 2018. *Recreations:* classic cinema, poetry, American history, travel, photography and the visual arts. *Address:* Faculty of English Language and Literature, University of Oxford, St Cross Buildings, Manor Road, Oxford OX1 3UL. *E:* daniel.wakelin@ell.ox.ac.uk.

**WAKELIN, Michael Paul;** Executive Producer, TBI Media, since 2010; Head of Programmes, Coexist House (formerly Abraham House, then Cambridge Coexist Programme), since 2010; Coexist House Project Lead (formerly Consultant, Inter-faith Programme, then Executive Associate in Public Education), Faculty of Divinity, University of Cambridge, since 2012; *b* 21 April 1961; *s* of Paul Oasland Wakelin and Rosemary Wakelin (*née* Sorrel); *m* 1997, Jacqueline Clare Jouannet; two *s* one *d*. *Educ:* Little Plumstead Primary Sch., Priors Court; Kingswood Sch., Bath; Birmingham Univ. (BA Hons Theol.). English teacher, Mokwon Univ., Taejon, S Korea, 1983–85; BBC Radio: researcher, 1986; producer, 1987; Exec. Producer, 1988–99; Series Producer, BBC TV, 1999–2006; Head of Religion and Ethics, BBC, 2006–09. Dir of Progs, Council of Christians and Jews, 2010–11; Founder Partner, Religious Literacy Partnership, 2012; Chair, Religion Media Centre, 2016–. Co-Dir, Insight Film Fest., 2010–13 (Patron, 2013–). Trustee: Premier Media, 2015–; Reckitt Trust, 2015–. *Publications:* J. Arthur Rank: the man behind the gong, 1996; contribs to acad. pubns. *Recreations:* bass guitarist for The Naked Covers, walking, cooking, supporting Norwich City, running (London Marathon, 2018). *E:* michael@michaelwakelin.co.uk. *W:* www.michaelwakelin.co.uk.

**WAKELING, Dawn;** Executive Director, Adults and Health (formerly Strategic Director, Adults, Communities and Health), London Borough of Barnet, since 2015; *b* London; *d* of Peter and Dorothy Wakeling; *m* 2006, Clare Chettle; one *s* one *d*. *Educ:* Univ. of Leeds (BA Hons English); Univ. of Cardiff (Postgrad. Dip. Drama); St Peter's Coll., Oxford (MSc). CQSW 1992. Social worker, 1992–96; Develt Manager, Mental Health Foundn, 1996–98; Dir, Mind, 1998–2002; Associate Dir, NHS Modernisation Agency, 2002–04; Dir, Strategy and Service Improvement, Newham Univ. Hosp., 2004–07; Asst Dir, 2007–09, Service Dir, Adult Social Care, 2009–11, Islington Council; Dep. Dir, 2011–12, Commng Dir, 2012–15, Adult Social Services and Health, Barnet Council. Chair, London Safeguarding Adults Bd, 2016–. Chair, Nat. Policy Network, 2014–, Safeguarding Policy Lead, London, 2015–, ADASS. *Recreations:* family, sailing, fitness, opera, books. *Address:* London Borough of Barnet, 2 Bristol Avenue, NW9 4EW. *T:* (020) 8359 4290. *E:* dawn.wakeling@barnet.gov.uk.

**WAKELING, Richard Keith Arthur;** Chairman, Polar Capital (formerly Henderson) Technology Trust PLC, 1996–2011; *b* 19 Nov. 1946; *s* of late Eric George Wakeling and Dorothy Ethel Wakeling; *m* 1971, Carmen; three *s*. *Educ:* Churchill Coll., Cambridge (MA). Called to the Bar, Inner Temple, 1971. Group Treasurer, BOC Group, 1977–83; Finance Dir, John Brown, 1983–86; Finance Dir, 1986–88, Acting Chief Exec., 1988–89, Charter Consolidated; Dep. Chief Exec., 1990, Chief Exec., 1991–94, Johnson Matthey. Dep. Chm., Celtic Group Holdings Ltd, 1994–97; Director: Costain, 1992–96; Laura Ashley Holdings, 1994–95; Logica, 1995–2002; Staveley Industries, 1995–99; Henderson Geared Income & Growth Trust (formerly HTR Income and Growth Split Trust), 1995–2003; Oxford Instruments plc, 1995–2001; MG plc, 1999–2000; Brunner Investment Trust plc, 2000–10. *Recreations:* mediaeval history and architecture, golf, music, gardening. *Address:* 46 The Bourne, Southgate, N14 6QS.

**WAKEM, Dame Beverley (Anne),** DNZM 2012; CBE 1990; Parliamentary Ombudsman, 2005–15, and Chief Ombudsman of New Zealand, 2008–15; *b* Wellington, NZ, 27 Jan. 1944; *d* of George Joseph Wakem and Sophie May Wakem; partner, Nicola Robyn Granville Chapman. *Educ:* St Mary's Coll., Wellington; Victoria Univ., Wellington (BA Hist. and Eng. 1968); Univ. of Kentucky (MA Communications 1973). FTCL 1967. Public Affairs Producer, Radio and TV, NZ Broadcasting Corp., 1963–72; Radio New Zealand: Exec. Producer, District Current Affairs, Wellington, 1974–75; Controller of Progs, 1975–84; Dir Gen., 1984–88; Chief Exec., 1988–91; Actg Chief Exec., NZ Broadcasting Corp., 1988; Wrightson Ltd: Commercial Dir, 1991; Gen. Manager, Human Resources and Corporate Affairs, 1992–96; Exec. Chm., Hill and Knowlton (NZ) Ltd, 1996–97; Dep. Chm., Remuneration Authy, 1997–2005. International Ombudsman Institute: Dir, 2008–14; Regl Vice-Pres., Aust. and Pacific, 2009–10; Pres., 2010–14. Dir, Pacific Ombudsman Alliance, 2008–14. Chm., Insce and Savings Ombudsman Commn, 2000–05; Member: Wkg Party on Teaching and Learning at a Distance, Educn Dept, 1975–76; Commn for the Future, 1975–82; Drug Adv. Cttee, 1980–82. Vice Pres., 1987, Pres., 1988–90, Asia Pacific Broadcasting Union. *Recreations:* theatre, opera. *Address:* 248 Flightys Road, RD1, Porirua 5381, New Zealand. *T:* 274495798. *E:* bevwakem@actrix.co.nz. *Clubs:* Wellington, Rotary (Pres., 2004–05) (Wellington).

**WAKSMAN, Hon. Sir David (Michael),** Kt 2018; **Hon. Mr Justice Waksman;** a Judge of the High Court, Queen's Bench Division, since 2018; *b* 28 Aug. 1957. *Educ:* Royal Grammar Sch., Newcastle Upon Tyne; Manchester Univ. (LLB Hons); St Catherine's Coll., Oxford (BCL). Called to the Bar, Middle Temple, 1982, Bencher, 2019; QC 2002;

**WAKSMAN, Prof. Gabriel**, PhD; FMedSci; FRS 2012; Courtauld Professor of Biochemistry, University College London, since 2007; Professor of Structural Molecular Biology and Director, Institute of Structural and Molecular Biology, University College London and Birkbeck, University of London, since 2003; *b* Corbeil Essonnes, France, 3 Sept. 1957; *s* of Roger Waksman and Rita Waksman (née Goldstein); *m* 1990, Susan Graham; two *s. Educ:* Univ. of Paris (BSc Genetics, BSc Physical Chem.; MSc Fundamental Biochem. 1980; PhD Fundamental Biochem. 1982). Washington University School of Medicine, Saint Louis: Asst Prof., 1993–98; Associate Prof., 1998–2000; Prof. of Biochem. and Molecular Biophysics, 2000; Alumni Endowed Prof. of Biochem. and Molecular Biophysics, 2000–02; P. Roy and Diana Vagelos Prof. of Biochem. and Molecular Biophysics, 2002–03; Hd, Dept of Biochem. and Molecular Biol., UCL and Hd, Dept of Biol Scis, Birkbeck, Univ. of London, 2006–. FMedSci 2008. Member: EMBO, 2007; German Acad. of Sci., 2013; MAE 2014. *Publications:* over 200 articles in scientific jls incl. Nature, Science and Cell. *Recreation:* long distance walking. *Address:* Anchor Cottage, Honor End Lane, Prestwood, Bucks HP16 9HG. *T:* (020) 7631 6833. *E:* g.waksman@ucl.ac.uk.

**WALBY, Christine Mary**, OBE 2005; Director of Social Services, Staffordshire County Council, 1991–96; independent consultant, 1997–2009; *b* 9 Feb. 1940; *d* of late Kathleen Walby (née Bradburn) and James Walby. *Educ:* University College of Wales, Aberystwyth (BA, DipEd); Manchester Univ. (Dip. Social Admin and Social Work); University College Cardiff (MSc Econ). Youth Leader Trainer, 1961–64; Social Worker, Children's Dept, Cheshire, 1964–70; Training Officer, Salford; Tutor, Manchester Univ.; Area Officer, Salford Social Services, 1970–74; Principal Officer, S Glam Social Services, 1974–81; Divl Dir, Berks Social Services, 1981–87; Dir, Social Services, Solihull MDC, 1987–91. Sen. Vis. Res. Fellow, Keele Univ., 1994–; Hon. Res. Fellow, Univ. of Wales Swansea, 1998–2006. Mem., Human Fertilization and Embryology Authy, 1991–93. Chm., Early Childhood Unit Adv. Gp, Nat. Children's Bureau, 1995–99; Trustee: Office for Children's Rights Comr, 1992–97; Children in Wales, 1998–2007 (Chm., 2002–); Bryn Melyn Gp Foundn, 2001–03; Triangle Trust 1949 Fund, 2004–06; Mem., Nat. Commn of Inquiry into Prevention of Child Abuse, 1994–96; Advr to Chair, Safeguarding Vulnerable Children Review, Welsh Assembly Govt, 2004–06; Chm., Bd of Dirs, Tros Gynnal, 2002–11 (Dir and Trustee, 2005–); Ind. Chm., Local Safeguarding Children Bd, Rhondda Cynon Taff, 2006–08. Mem. (Lab) Monmouthshire CC, 2008–12 (Chm., Children and Young People Select Cttee, 2010–12; Mem., Strong Communities Select Cttee, 2008–10). Hon. Life Mem. Council, NSPCC, 1993–. Chm., Homestart (Wales), 1999–2004. *Publications:* Who Am I?: identity, adoption and human fertilization (with Barbara Symons), 1990; contrib. professional jls. *Recreations:* walking, theatre, music, bird watching, holidays.

**WALCOTT, Prof. Richard Irving**, PhD; FRS 1991; FRSNZ; Professor of Geology, Victoria University, Wellington, New Zealand, 1985–99, now Emeritus; *b* 14 May 1933; *s* of James Farrar Walcott and Lilian Stewart (née Irving); *m* 1960, Genevieve Rae Lovatt; one *s* two *d. Educ:* Victoria Univ., Wellington (BSc Hons 1962; PhD 1965; DSc 1980). Meteorological Asst, Falkland Is Dependencies Survey, 1955–58; Post-doctoral Fellow, Geophysics Dept, Univ. of BC, 1966–67; Research Scientist: Earth Physics Br., Dept of Energy, Mines and Resources, Ottawa, 1967–74; Geophysics Div., Dept Sci. and Industrial Res., Wellington, NZ, 1975–84. FRSNZ 1982; Fellow, American Geophysical Union, 1993. Hector Medal, Royal Soc. NZ, 1994; Charles Whitten Medal, Amer. Geophysical Union, 1999. *Recreation:* gardening. *Address:* 24 Mahoe Street, Eastbourne, Wellington, New Zealand. *T:* (4) 5628040.

**WALD, Sir Nicholas (John)**, Kt 2008; DSc; FRCP, FFPH, FRCOG, FMedSci; FRS 2004; CBiol, FRSB; Professor of Environmental and Preventive Medicine, since 1983, and Chairman/Director, Wolfson Institute of Preventive Medicine, 1991–95 and 1997–2013, Bart's and The London School of Medicine and Dentistry, Queen Mary (formerly St Bartholomew's Hospital Medical College, then St Bartholomew's and The Royal London School of Medicine and Dentistry, Queen Mary and Westfield College), University of London; Hon. Consultant, St Bartholomew's Hospital, since 1983; *b* 31 May 1944; *s* of Adolf Max Wald and Frieda (née Shatsow); *m* 1966, Nancy Evelyn Miller; three *s* one *d. Educ:* Owen's Sch., EC1; University Coll. London; University Coll. Hosp. Med. Sch. (MB BS); DSc (Med) London 1987. FRCP 1986 (MRCP 1971); FFPH (FFCM 1982; MFCM 1980); FRCOG 1992 (addendum); CBiol, FRSB (FIBiol 2000). VSO, India, 1966. Ho. appts, UCH and Barnet Gen. Hosp., 1968–69; Med. Registrar, UCH, 1970; Member: MRC Sci. Staff, MRC Epidemiology and Med. Care Unit, 1971; Sci. Staff, ICRF (formerly DHSS) Cancer Epidem. and Clin. Trials Unit, 1972–82, Dep. Dir, 1982–83. Wellcome Vis. Prof. in Basic Med. Scis, at Foundn for Blood Res., USA, 1980, then Hon. Sen. Res. Scientist; Hon. Professor: UCL, 2012–; St George's, Univ. of London, 2014; Hon. Consultant and Adjunct Prof., Brown Univ., 2018. Hon. Dir, Cancer Screening Gp, CRC, 1989–2000. Chairman: MRC Smoking Res. Rev. Cttee, 1986–89; MRC Study Monitoring Cttee of Randomised Trial of Colo-rectal Cancer Screening, 1986–2009; MRC Volatile Substance Abuse Wkg Party, 1985–87; NE Thames Reg. Breast Cancer Res. Cttee, 1988–96; Nat. Inst. of Child Health and Human Develt Wkg Gp on Quality Control of Alpha-fetoprotein Measurement, 1978; Steering Cttee for MRC Multicentre Aneurysm Screening Study, 1997–; Adv. Gp on Ionising Radiation, HPA, 2004–11; Member: MRC Neurosciences Bd, 1962–86; MRC Steering Cttee of Randomised Trial of Multivitamins and Neural Tube Defects, 1983–92; DHSS Cttee on Med. Aspects of Contamination of Air, Soil and Water, 1985–89; DHSS Ctee on Carcinogenicity of Chemicals in Food, Consumer Products and the Environment, 1984–89; DHSS Ind. Sci. Cttee on Smoking and Health, 1983–91; DoH (formerly DHSS) Adv. Cttee on Breast Cancer Screening, 1986–99; Central R&D Cttee, 1991–95; CMO's Health of the Nation Wkg Gp, 1991–97; DoH Population Screening Panel, 1992–98; CMO's Scientific Cttee on Tobacco and Health, 1993–2002; Folic Acid Sub-gp, DoH Cttee on Med. Aspects of Food and Nutrition Policy, 1996–2000; Antenatal Sub-gp, DoH Nat. Screening Cttee, 1997–2005; Nat. Screening Cttee, HPV/LBC Pilots Steering Gp, 2000–03; Adv. Gp for Evaluation of UK Colorectal Cancer Screening Pilot, 2000–03; ACOST Med. Res. and Health Cttee, 1991–92; RCP Cttee on Ethical Issues in Medicine, 1988–2010; RCP Computer Cttee, 1988–92; Physiol. and Pharmacol. Panel, Wellcome Trust, 1995–2000; MRC Scientific Adv. Cttee on Gulf War Syndrome, 1996–97; Adv. Gp on Nuclear Test Veterans, 2000–02; Council of Trustees, Foundn for Study of Infant Deaths, 2000–04; Cttee on Environmental Tobacco Smoke, Nat. Acad. of Sci., USA, 1985–86. 140th Cutter Lectr on Preventive Medicine, Harvard Sch. of Public Health, 2004; Rayner Lect., RCP, 2009; Feldman Lect., 2010; Jephcott Lect., RSocMed, 2011; Croonian Lect., RCP, 2015. Inaugural Ed., Jl of Medical Screening, 1994–. Pres., Med. Screening Soc., 2002–. William Julius Mickle Fellow, Univ. of London, 1990. Founder FMedSci 1998; Member: Assoc. of Physicians of GB and Ire.; Natural Science Club, UCL (Pres., 2017). Hon. DSc (Med) UCL, 2005. Joseph P. Kennedy Jr Foundn Award for Scientific Res., 2000; Hamdan Award for Med. Res. Excellence, Hamdan Awards Scientific Cttee, UAE Univ., 2012. *Publications:* (ed) Antenatal and Neonatal Screening, 1984, 2nd edn (ed with Ian Leck) 2000; (ed with Sir Richard Doll) Interpretation of Negative Epidemiological Evidence for Carcinogenicity, 1985; The Epidemiological Approach: an approach to epidemiology in medicine, 1985, 4th edn 2004; (ed jtly) UK Smoking Statistics, 1988; (ed with Sir Peter Froggatt) Nicotine, Smoking and the Low Tar Programme, 1989; (ed with J. Baron) Smoking and Hormone Related Disorders, 1990; (jtly) International Smoking Statistics, 1993, 2nd edn (ed jtly) 2000; articles in sci. jls on screening for neural tube defects, Down's Syndrome and other disorders, on health effects of tobacco, on the aetiology and prevention of cancer, cardiovascular disease and congenital malformations. *Recreations:* family, discussion, boating, economics. *Address:* Wolfson Institute of Preventive Medicine, Bart's and The London School of Medicine and Dentistry, Charterhouse Square, EC1M 6BQ. *T:* (020) 7882 6269; 9 Park Crescent Mews East, W1W 5AF. *T:* (020) 7636 2721. *Club:* Athenæum.

**WALDECK, Pieter Willem, (Pim)**, Grand Cross of Honour, Order of House of Orange (Netherlands), 2006; Ambassador of the Netherlands to the Court of St James's, 2007–12; *b* 6 Nov. 1947; *s* of late Dr Karel Waldeck and Elisabeth Waldeck (née Koster); *m* 1976, Jonkvrouw Cordula Catharina Agatha Quarles van Ufford; one *s* two *d. Educ:* Vrijzinnig Christelijk Lyceum, The Hague; Univ. of Leiden (Master of Law; PhD 2017). Mem. Bd (Sales and Publicity), NBBS Student Travel, 1970–71; 2nd Lieutenant RNR, Naval Intelligence Service, 1973–75; entered Netherlands Foreign Service, 1975; Third Sec. (Political), Moscow, 1976–78; Second Sec., Develt Co-operation, ESCAP, Bangkok, 1978–81; First Sec., Hd of Econ. Section, Cairo, 1981–84; Private Sec. to HM Queen and HRH Prince Claus of Netherlands, 1984–88; Hd of Section, Dept of Eur. Integration, Min. of Foreign Affairs, 1988–92; Counsellor, Perm. Repn to EU, Brussels, 1992–97; Hd, Dept of Information, and Chief Spokesman, Min. of Foreign Affairs, 1997–2000; Principal Sec. to HM Queen of Netherlands, 2000–02; Grand Master of the House of HM Queen of Netherlands, 2002–06. Chair, Van den Berch van Heemstede Foundn, 2012–; Member: Adv. Bd, Netherlands Dance Th., The Hague, 2012–; Bd, Friends of Royal Picture Gall. Mauritshuis, The Hague, 2012–; Bd, Nat. Archives Soc., The Hague, 2014–. Grand Officer: Order of Isabella la Católica (Spain), 2001; Order of Three Stars (Latvia), 2006; Grand Cross: Order of Southern Cross (Brazil), 2003; Order of Merit (Chile), 2003; Order of White Elephant (Thailand), 2004; Order of Independence (Jordan), 2006; Order of the Crown (Belgium), 2006; Civil and Mil. Order of Merit, Adolf of Nassau (Luxembourg), 2006. *Publications:* Maarten van der Goes van Dirxland (1751–1826), Holland's First Minister of Foreign Affairs, 2017 (in Dutch); articles in Nederlands Juristenblad, Mars Et Historia, Tijdschrift voor Zeegeschiedenis, Jaarboek Die Haghe. *Recreations:* drawing, bird watching, (naval) history, golf, sailing. *Address:* Groenhovenstraat 8, 2596 HT The Hague, Netherlands. *Clubs:* Haagsche (Plaats Royaal), Nieuwe Littéraire Sociëteit de Witte (The Hague); Broekpolder Golf.

**WALDEGRAVE**, family name of **Earl Waldegrave** and **Baron Waldegrave of North Hill**.

**WALDEGRAVE**, 13th Earl *cr* 1729; **James Sherbrooke Waldegrave**; Bt 1643; Baron Waldegrave 1685; Viscount Chewton 1729; *b* 8 Dec. 1940; *e s* of 12th Earl Waldegrave, KG, GCVO and Mary Hermione (*d* 1995), *d* of Lt-Col A. M. Grenfell, DSO; *S* father, 1995; *m* 1986, Mary Alison Anthea (marr. diss. 1996), *d* of late Sir Robert Furness, KBE, CMG, and Lady Furness; two *s. Educ:* Eton Coll.; Trinity Coll., Cambridge. *Heir: s* Viscount Chewton, *qv. Address:* Chewton House, Chewton Mendip, Radstock BA3 4LL. *Club:* Leander.

**WALDEGRAVE OF NORTH HILL**, Baron *cr* 1999 (Life Peer), of Chewton Mendip in the county of Somerset; **William Arthur Waldegrave**; PC 1990; Provost of Eton College, since 2009 (Fellow, since 2007); *b* 15 Aug. 1946; *yr s* of 12th Earl Waldegrave, KG, GCVO and Mary Hermione (née Grenfell); *m* 1977, Caroline Burrows (*see* Caroline Waldegrave); one *s* three *d. Educ:* Eton Coll.; Corpus Christi Coll., Oxford (Hon. Fellow, 1991); Harvard Univ. (Kennedy Fellow). Fellow, All Souls Coll., Oxford, 1971–86 and 1999–. Central Policy Review Staff, Cabinet Office, 1971–73; Political Staff, 10 Downing Street, 1973–74; Head of Leader of Opposition's Office, 1974–75; GEC Ltd, 1975–81; a Man. Dir, Dresdner Kleinwort Wasserstein, 1998–2003; a Vice-Chm. and Man. Dir, 2003–08, Consultant, 2008–12, UBS. MP (C) Bristol West, 1979–97; contested (C) same seat, 1997. Parly Under-Sec. of State, DES, 1981–83, DoE, 1983–85. Minister of State for the Environment and Countryside, 1985–87, for Planning, 1986–88, and for Housing, 1987–88, DoE; Minister of State, FCO, 1988–90; Sec. of State for Health, 1990–92; Chancellor of the Duchy of Lancaster, 1992–94; Minister of Agric., Fisheries and Food, 1994–95; Chief Sec. to HM Treasury, 1995–97. Director: Waldegrave Farms Ltd, 1975–; Bristol and West plc (formerly Bristol and West Bldg Soc.), 1997–2006; Bank of Ireland Financial Services (UK) plc, 2002–06; Henry Sotheran Ltd, 1998–2015 (Chm., 2007–15); Biotech. Growth Trust plc (formerly Finsbury Life Scis Investment Trust, then Finsbury Emerging Biotech Growth Trust), 1998–2016 (Chm., 2012–16); Fleming Family and Partners Ltd, 2008–12; Coutts and Co., 2012– (Chm., 2014–); GW Pharmaceuticals plc, 2017–. Member: IBA Adv. Council, 1980–81; Internat. Adv. Bd, Teijin Ltd, 2006–08; Remuneration and Nomination Cttee, Bergesen Worldwide Gas ASA, 2006–08; Chm., Adv. Cttee, Royal Mint, 2011–. Chm., Nat. Mus. of Sci. and Industry, 2002–10; Mem., President's Adv. Cttee, Royal Soc., 2012–. Trustee: Rhodes Trust, 1992–2002 (Chm., 2002–11); Beit Meml Fellowships for Medical Res., 1998–2006; Mandela Rhodes Foundn, 2003–11; Dyson Sch. of Design Innovation, 2007–08; Strawberry Hill Trust, 2008–13; Cumberland Lodge, Windsor, 2009–17. Mem. Bd, Lewis Walpole Liby, Yale Univ., 2008–. Founder Trustee and Chm., Bristol Cathedral Trust, 1989–2002. Pres., Royal Bath and West Soc., 2006. Chancellor, Univ. of Reading, 2016–. JP Inner London Juvenile Court, 1975–79. *Publications:* The Binding of Leviathan, 1977; A Different Kind of Weather: a memoir, 2015. *Address:* 62 Hornton Street, W8 4NU; Provost's Lodge, Eton College, Windsor, Berks SL4 6DH. *Clubs:* White's, Beefsteak, Pratt's; Leander (Henley-on-Thames).

**WALDEGRAVE, Caroline Linda Margaret, (Lady Waldegrave of North Hill)**, OBE 2000; Founding Principal, since 1975, and Director, since 2008, Leith's School of Food and Wine Ltd (Managing Director, 1977–2008); Owner and Director, Dudwell Cookery School, since 2012; Co-owner and Director, Barley Mow Pub, Marylebone, since 2013; *b* 14 Aug. 1952; *y d* of late Major Philip Richard Miles Burrows and Molly Burrows (née Hollins); *m* 1977, Hon. William Waldegrave (*see* Baron Waldegrave of North Hill); one *s* three *d. Educ:* Convent of the Sacred Heart, Woldingham, Surrey; Postgrad. Dip. Psychodynamic Counselling. Mem., HEA, 1985–88. Chm., Guild of Food Writers, 1991–93; Pres., Hosp. Caterers Assoc., 2006–08. Advr, Nat. Life Story Collection, BL, 2014– (Trustee, 2005–14). Pres., Portobello Trust, 1987–2000. *Publications:* The Healthy Gourmet, 1986; Low Fat Gourmet, 1987; *jointly:* Leith's Cookery Course, 1980; Leith's Cookery School, 1985; Leith's Cookery Bible, 1991, 2nd edn 1996; Leith's Complete Christmas, 1992; Children's Cookery, 1993; Leith's Fish Bible, 1995; Leith's Easy Dinner Parties, 1995; Leith's Healthy Eating, 1996; Children's Fun to Cook Book, 1996; Sainsbury Book of Children's Cookery, 1997. *Recreations:* bridge, tennis. *Address:* Provost's Lodge, Eton College, Windsor, Berks SL4 6DH.

**WALDEN, David Peter**, CBE 2013; independent public policy consultant, since 2012; Director of Adult Services (formerly Adults and Regions), Social Care Institute for Excellence, 2009–12; *b* 23 Sept. 1954; *s* of Gerald Walden and Shirley Walden (*née* Rothfield); *m* 1981, Janet Day; one *s* one *d*. *Educ:* Newcastle upon Tyne Royal Grammar Sch.; St John's Coll., Oxford (BA Modern Hist. 1977). DHSS, subseq. DoH, 1977–2004: Principal, 1982; Management Side Secretary: Nurses' and Midwives' Whitley Council, 1982–85; NHS Consultants' Negotiating Body, 1985–86; Private Sec. to Dep. Chm., NHS Mgt Bd, 1986–87; Asst Sec., Doctors' Pay and Conditions, 1989–90; on secondment as Personnel Dir, Poole Hosp. NHS Trust, 1991–93; Head: Community Care Br., 1993–96; Health Promotion Div., 1996–99; Social Care Policy, 1999–2001; Dir, Health Services Develt, Anchor Trust, 2001–03 (on secondment); Dir, Office of Ind. Regulator for NHS Foundn Trusts, 2003–04; Dir of Strategy, Commn for Social Care Inspection, 2004–09. Dir, 2020health, 2012–15; Bd Mem., Affinity Trust, 2011–. Non-exec. Dir, Poole Hosp. NHS Foundn Trust, 2015–. Trustee: Barchester Healthcare Foundn, 2013–; Elderly Accommodation Counsel, 2014–15. *Address:* Glebe House, Trent, Sherborne, Dorset DT9 4SL. *T:* 07789 653522.

**WALDEN, George Gordon Harvey**, CMG 1981; writer; *b* 15 Sept. 1939; *s* of G. G. Walden; *m* 1970, Sarah Nicolette Hunt; two *s* one *d*. *Educ:* Latymer Upper Sch.; Jesus Coll., Cambridge; Moscow Univ. (post-graduate). Research Dept, Foreign Office, 1962–65; Chinese Language Student, Hong Kong Univ., 1965–67; Second Secretary, Office of HM Chargé d'Affaires, Peking, 1967–70; First Sec., FCO (Soviet Desk), 1970–73; Ecole Nationale d'Administration, Paris, 1973–74; First Sec., HM Embassy, Paris, 1974–78; Principal Private Sec. to Foreign and Commonwealth Sec., 1978–81; sabbatical year, Harvard, 1981; Head of Planning Staff, FCO, 1982–83; retired from HM Diplomatic Service, 1983. MP (C) Buckingham, 1983–97. PPS to Sec. of State for Educn and Science, 1984–85; Parly Under-Sec. of State, DES, 1985–87. Chm. of Judges, Booker Prize, 1995; Chm., Russian Booker Prize, 2003–10. Columnist: Evening Standard, 1991–2002; Times, 2009–10. *Publications:* Ethics and Foreign Policy, 1990; We Should Know Better: solving the education crisis, 1996; Lucky George (memoir), 1999; The New Elites: making a career in the masses, 2000; Who is a Dandy?, 2002; God won't save America, 2006; Time to Emigrate?, 2006; China: a wolf in the world?, 2008; as Joseph Clyde: A State of Fear, 2013; The Oligarch, 2015; The China Maze, 2017.
*See also* P. S. Morgan.

**WALDEN, William Michael**; Senior Counsel, Strategic Communications, Edelman UK and Ireland, since 2019; *b* Guernsey, 8 June 1971; *s* of Michael and Kathleen Walden; two *s* one *d*; *m* 2018, Camilla Groom. *Educ:* Elizabeth Coll., Guernsey; Univ. of Durham (BA Modern Hist. 1993). Reporter: Channel TV (ITV), 1993–95; BBC Spotlight, 1995–97; reporter and producer, ITN News at Ten, 1997–99; Sen. Producer, Home and Foreign news desks, BBC News, 1999–2012; Sports News reporter and producer, 1999–2001; Sen. Political Producer, 2001–03; Dep. Bureau Chief, Washington, 2003–06; Westminster News Ed., 2006–12; Sen. Advr, Dir of Communications and External Affairs and Official Spokesman for Mayor of London, 2012–16; Chief Advr, Policy and Communications to Boris Johnson, EU Referendum Campaign, 2016; Dir of Communications and Sen. Political Advr to Foreign Sec., 2016; Man. Dir, Public Affairs and Govt Relns, Edelman UK, 2016–19. Mem., Old Elizabethan Assoc. Trustee, London's Air Ambulance, 2016–. *Recreations:* family, golf, cricket, shooting, amateur artist, exploring Britain's coastline. *Address:* Edelman UK, 105 Victoria Street, SW1E 6QT. *Club:* MCC.

**WALDEN-SMITH, Karen Jane; Her Honour Judge Walden-Smith**; a Circuit Judge, since 2010; Specialist Senior Chancery Circuit Judge, since 2013; Deputy High Court Judge, since 2013; Designated Civil Judge, County Court in London, since 2016; *b* Crawley, W Sussex, 17 Dec. 1966; *d* of late Edward Walden-Smith and of Eileen Walden-Smith (*née* White); *m* 2000, Prof. James Russell Raven, *qv*; two *s*. *Educ:* Hazelwick Comprehensive Sch., Crawley; Clare Coll., Cambridge (BA 1989; MA 1993). Called to the Bar, Lincoln's Inn, 1990 (Hardwicke, Shelford and Wolfson Major Scholar; Inns of Court Studentship; Sir Louis Gluckstein advocacy prize), Bencher, 2013 (Mem. Bar Rep. Cttee, 2005–13); Recorder, 2004–10; a Judge, Upper Tribunal (Lands Chamber), 2011–; Diversity and Community Relations Judge, 2011–. Founder Mem., Property Bar Assoc. (Mem. Cttee, 2004–10; Sec., 2007–09); Barrister Mem., Bar Council/Bar Standards Bd Disciplinary Panels, 2004–10. Mem., Public Speaking Cttee, 2008–12, and Treas., local br., ESU, 2010–12. Parish Councillor, 2005–13; Gov., local primary sch., 2005–10. *Publications:* (contrib.) Butterworth's Forms and Precedents, vol. 33, 2008; contrib. articles to legal jls. *Recreations:* theatre, reading, art, having fun with sons. *Address:* Central London Civil Justice Centre, Thomas More Building, Royal Courts of Justice, WC2A 2LL. *E:* HHJ.karen.walden-smith@ejudiciary.net.

**WALDMAN, Jennifer Kate**, CBE 2017; Director, 14–18 NOW: WWI Arts Commission, Imperial War Museum, since 2013; *b* Hampstead, 28 June 1960; *d* of Stanley and Naomi Waldman; *m* Richard Bull; two *s* two *d*. *Educ:* Camden Sch. for Girls; St Anne's Coll., Oxford (BA Hons PPP; MA). Adminr, Foco Novo Th. Co., 1983–86; theatre officer, Arts Council, 1986–89; Consultant, JWAM, 1989–91, 1995–99; Dir, Arts Centre Progs, Southbank Centre, 1991–95; Consultant, Somerset Hse, 1999–2011; Creative Producer, London 2012 Fest., Cultural Olympiad, LOCOG, 2011–12. *Recreations:* theatre, art, dance, outdoor events, music, reading, walking, family. *Address:* 14–18 NOW, Imperial War Museum, Lambeth Road, SE1 6HZ. *T:* (020) 7091 3114. *E:* jenny.waldman@1418Now.org.uk. *Club:* Two Brydges.

**WALDMANN, Carl Samuel**, FRCA; FFICM; Consultant in Intensive Care Medicine and Anaesthesia, and Director, Intensive Care Unit, Royal Berkshire Hospital, since 1986; Dean, Faculty of Intensive Care Medicine, since 2016; *b* London, 25 March 1951; *s* of Leon and Rena Waldmann; *m* Tanya; three *d*. *Educ:* Forest Sch.; Sidney Sussex Coll., Cambridge (Open Schol.; BA 1972); London Hosp. Med. Coll. (MB BChir 1975). FRCA 1980; EDIC 1993; FFICM 2011. RAF Cadetship; house posts and SHO Anaesthetics, London Hosp., 1975–77; UMO, RAF Brize Norton, 1977–79; Specialist in Anaesthetics, RAF Ely, 1979–82; Sen. Lectr in Intensive Care Unit Anaesthetics, Whipps Cross Hosp. and London Hosp., 1982–85; Sen. Registrar, Gt Ormond St Hosp., 1985–86. Formerly Editor: Jl Intensive Care Soc., until 2004; Care of the Critically Ill. Sir Andrew Humphrey Meml Award, 1978. *Publications:* (ed) Oxford Desk Reference: Law and Ethics in Intensive Care, 2007. *Recreations:* fencing, ski-ing, water ski-ing, tennis, football (crowd doctor for Leyton Orient FC). *Address:* 2 Dewe Lane, Burghfield, Reading RG30 3SH. *T:* (0118) 322 7257. *E:* cswald@aol.com. *Clubs:* Royal Air Force; Leyton Orient Football.

**WALDMANN, Prof. Herman**, FRCPath, FRCP; FRS 1990; FMedSci; Professor and Head of Department of Pathology, 1994–2012, Oxford University, now Emeritus Professor; Fellow of Lincoln College, Oxford, since 1994; *b* 27 Feb. 1945; *s* of Leon and Rene Ryfka Waldmann; *m* 1971, Judith Ruth Young. *Educ:* Sir George Monoux Grammar Sch., Walthamstow; Sidney Sussex Coll., Cambridge (BA; Hon. Fellow, 2008); London Hosp. Med. Coll. (MB BChir); PhD Cantab. FRCPath 1992; FRCP 2010. Cambridge University: Dept of Pathology, 1971–94; Fellow, King's Coll., 1985–94; Kay Kendall Prof. of Therapeutic Immunology, 1989–93. Founder FMedSci 1998. Hon. Fellow: QMW, 1996; King's Coll., Cambridge, 2009. Dist. Prof. Lect., Univ. of Iowa, 2007. Hon. ScD Cambridge, 2008. Graham Bull Prize for Clinical Res., RCP, 1991; José Carreras Award, European Hematology Assoc., 2005; JDRF Excellence in Clinical Res. Award, 2005; Thomas E. Starzl Prize in Surgery and Immunol., 2007; Scrip Lifetime Achievement Award, 2007. *Publications:* Limiting Dilution Analysis (with Dr I. Lefkovits), 1977, 2nd edn 1998; The Immune System (with Dr I. McConnell and A. Munro), 1981; (ed) Monoclonal Antibodies, 1988; many scientific papers. *Recreations:* family, (less) food, friends, travel, music, walking without falling. *Address:* Sir William Dunn School of Pathology, South Parks Road, Oxford OX1 3RE. *E:* herman.waldmann@path.ox.ac.uk.
*See also* C. S. Waldmann.

**WALDNER, Benita Maria F.**; *see* Ferrero-Waldner.

**WALDRON, Prof. Jeremy James**, DPhil; FBA 2011; Chichele Professor of Social and Political Theory, University of Oxford, 2010–14; Quondam Fellow, All Souls College, Oxford, since 2014 (Fellow, 2010–14); University Professor and Professor of Law, New York University, since 2006; *b* Invercargill, NZ, 13 Oct. 1953; *s* of Rev. Francis Herbert Waldron and Joyce Annette Waldron; *m* 1974, Helen Faye McGimpsey (marr. diss. 1987); one *s*; partner, Prof. Carol Sanger. *Educ:* Univ. of Otago (BA Hons 1974; LLB Hons 1978); University Coll., Oxford (DPhil Law 1986). Darby Fellow in Pol Theory, Lincoln Coll., Oxford, 1980–82; Lectr in Pols, Univ. of Edinburgh, 1983–87; Prof. of Law, Univ. of Calif. Berkeley, 1987–96; Univ. Prof. and Prof. of Law, Columbia Univ., 1997–2006. *Publications:* The Dignity of Legislation, 1999; Law and Disagreement, 1999; God, Locke and Equality, 2002; Torture, Terror and Trade-offs, 2010; The Harm in Hate Speech, 2012; Dignity, Rank and Rights, 2012; One Another's Equals, 2017; articles on legal and political philos. in learned jls. *Recreations:* travel, theatre, music. *Address:* 448 Riverside Drive, New York, NY 10027, USA. *E:* jeremy.waldron@nyu.edu.

**WALDRON, William Francis**; QC 2006; a Recorder, since 2000; *b* 27 Oct. 1957; *s* of William Henry Waldron, QC and Rosemary Waldron; *m* 2007, Julie Case; one *s*. *Educ:* St Edward's Coll., Liverpool; Univ. of Wales Inst. of Sci. and Technol. (LLB 1979). Broadcaster, CBC Commercial Radio Station, Cardiff, 1980–85. Called to the Bar, Gray's Inn, 1986, Bencher, 2011; in practice specialising in catastrophic injury law. Judge, Mental Health Review Tribunal (Restricted Panel), 2012–. Chair of Advocacy Trng, Northern Circuit, 2010–; Dep. Chair (Circuits), Advocacy Trng Council, 2014–16. Dep. Gov. (Circuits), Inns' Coll., 2016–. *Recreations:* Everton FC (lifelong, fanatical and ever-hopeful fan), acoustic guitar, flying (private pilot's licence/IMC), sailing. *Address:* Exchange Chambers, Derby Square, Liverpool L2 9XX. *T:* (0151) 236 7747. *E:* waldronqc@exchangechambers.co.uk. *Club:* Porthmadog Sailing.

**WALE, Kevin Ernest**; President and Managing Director, General Motors China Group, 2005–12; Chief Country Operations Officer, China, India and ASEAN, General Motors, 2012; *b* 30 Oct. 1954; *m* 1976, Marilyn Joy Baensch; two *s*. *Educ:* Melbourne Univ. (BCom Hons); General Motors Inst., USA. General Motors: joined Finance Dept, Holden, Australia, 1975; Corp. Finance Dept, NY, 1983–85; various posts, Finance Div., subseq. Dir of Finance and Strategic Planning, Holden, Australia, 1985–93; Dir of Sales, Marketing and Aftersales, Holden, Australia, 1993–98; Exec. in Charge, General Motors Asia Pacific (Pte) Ltd, Singapore, 1998–2001; Chm. and Man. Dir, Vauxhall Motors Ltd, and Vice-Pres., General Motors Europe, 2001–05; Mem., European Strategy Bd, 2001. *Recreations:* golf, cricket, motor sports.

**WALES, Archbishop of**, since 2017; **Most Rev. John David Edward Davies**; Bishop of Swansea and Brecon, since 2008; *b* 6 Feb. 1953; *s* of William Howell Davies and Doiran Rallison Davies; *m* 1986, Joanna Lucy Davies (*née* Aulton); one *s* one *d*. *Educ:* Southampton Univ. (LLB 1974); Coll. of Law; St Michael's Coll., Llandaff (DipTh English 1984); Univ. of Wales (LLM Canon Law 1995). Admitted Solicitor, 1977; private practice, 1975–82. Ordained deacon, 1984, priest, 1985; Asst Curate, Chepstow, 1984–86; Curate-in-charge, Michaelston-y-Fedw and Rudry, 1986–89; Rector, Bedwas and Rudry, 1989–95; Vicar, St John Evangelist, Newport, 1995–2000; Dean of Brecon, 2000–08. KStJ 2017 (CStJ 2010). Sub-Prelate, Priory for Wales, 2010–). *Recreations:* cooking, golf, music (wide taste), playing the organ, theatre, opera, reading, current affairs, sport (especially Test Match Special and Peter Alliss), planning walks for the family (and accompanying them when feeling energetic), entertaining my family by trying to convince them of the inestimable benefits of knowing Latin and of appreciating other lost glories of the past. *Address:* Ely Tower, Castle Square, Brecon, Powys LD3 9DJ. *T:* (01874) 622008.

**WALES, Andrew Nigel Malcolm**; QC 2012; a Recorder, since 2010; *b* Edinburgh, 27 July 1970; *s* of David Wales and Wendy Wales; *m* 2002, Alice Irene Wrangham; one *s* one *d*. *Educ:* Dulwich Coll.; Trinity Coll., Cambridge (BA 1990); Univ. of Virginia Sch. of Law (LLM 1991). Called to the Bar, Gray's Inn, 1992; in practice as a barrister specialising in commercial law, 1993–. *Recreations:* family, reading. *Address:* 7 King's Bench Walk, Temple, EC4Y 7DS. *T:* (020) 7910 8300. *E:* clerks@7kbw.co.uk.

**WALES, Prof. David John**, PhD, ScD, FRS 2016; Professor of Chemical Physics, University of Cambridge, since 2009; Fellow, Downing College, Cambridge, since 1990; *b* Epping, Essex, 21 Sept. 1963; *s* of John and Patricia Wales; *m* 1990, Dr Caroline Anne Brown; one *s* one *d*. *Educ:* Newport Free Grammar Sch.; Gonville and Caius Coll., Cambridge (Open Schol.; BA 1985); Univ. of Cambridge (MA 1988; PhD 1988; ScD 2004). Res. Fellow, Downing Coll., Cambridge, 1987–93; ESU Lindemann Trust Fellow, Univ. of Chicago, 1989; Lloyd's of London Tercentenary Fellow, 1990; Royal Soc. Univ. Res. Fellow, 1991–98; Lectr, 1998–2004, Reader in Chem. Physics, 2004–08, Univ. of Cambridge. Visiting Professor: Univ. de Paris-Sud, Orsay, 1999; Harvard Univ., 1999; Boston Univ., 2006; Univ. Paul Sabatier, Toulouse, 2006; Univ. de Lyon, 2011; Universidad de la Laguna, Tenerife, 2017. Meldola Medal and Prize, 1992, Tilden Medal and Prize, 2015, RSC. *Publications:* (with D. M. P. Mingos) Introduction to Cluster Chemistry, 1990; Energy Landscapes, 2003; contribs to peer-reviewed jls. *Recreations:* hiking, running, guitar, bridge. *Address:* Downing College, Regent Street, Cambridge CB2 1DQ. *T:* (01223) 336354. *E:* dw34@cam.ac.uk.

**WALES, Jimmy**; Founder, Wikipedia.org, 2001; Co-Founder and President, Wikia Inc., since 2004; *b* Huntsville, Ala, 7 Aug. 1966; *s* of Jimmy and Doris Wales; one *d*; *m* 2012, Kate Garvey; one *d*. *Educ:* Auburn Univ. (BA Finance); Univ. of Alabama (MA Finance). Res. Dir, Chicago Options Assoc., 1994–2000; Founder, Nupedia, 2000. Founder and Chm. Emeritus, Wikimedia Foundn, 2003. Board Member: iCommons, 2005; Creative Commons, 2006–. Co-Chairman: World Econ. Forum on Middle E, 2008; People's Operator, 2014–. Fellow, Berkman Center for Internet and Soc., Harvard Law Sch., 2005. Hon. LLD Knox Coll., Ill, 2006. Young Global Leader, World Econ. Forum, 2007; President's Medal, British Acad., 2017. *Publications:* (contrib.) Advances in Futures and Options Research, 1994. *Recreations:* international travel, free speech supporter, free culture advocate, contributor and active editor on Wikipedia, commerce and technology. *Address:* Wikimedia Foundation, 149 New Montgomery Street, 3rd Floor, San Francisco, CA 94105, USA. *Fax:* (415) 8820495. *E:* jwales@wikia.com.

**WALES, Prof. Kathleen Margaret**; Special Professor in English, University of Nottingham, since 2008; *b* 8 Feb. 1946; *d* of Richard Derwent and Yvonne Derwent (*née* Atkins); *m* 1st, 1971, Brian Wales (marr. diss. 1988); one *s*; 2nd, 1993, David Bovey. *Educ:* Darlington High Sch. for Girls; Royal Holloway Coll., Univ. of London (BA 1st Cl. Hons English). Royal Holloway College, later Royal Holloway and Bedford New College, University of London: Lectr in English Lang., 1968–88; Sen. Lectr, 1988–94; Reader, 1994–95; Prof., 1995–96; Hd, English Dept, 1995–96; University of Leeds: Prof. of Modern English Lang., 1996–2005; Dean of Learning and Teaching, Faculty of Arts, 2000–03; Dir, Centre for Medieval Studies, 2002–03; Res. Prof. in English, Univ. of Sheffield, 2005–08. Sen. Res. Fellow, British Acad./Leverhulme Trust, 1992–93; Visiting Research Fellow: Lucy Cavendish Coll., Univ. of Cambridge, 1999–2000, 2004; Centre for Res. in Arts, Social Scis and Humanities, Univ. of Cambridge, 2004–05; Leverhulme Emeritus Res. Fellow, Inst. of English Studies, Univ. of London, 2005–06. Member: Exec. Cttee, Council for Coll. and Univ. English, 1998–2002; Adv. Bd, Inst. of English Studies, Univ. of London, 2000–05; Cttee of Mgt, British Inst. in Paris, 2002–04; Peer Review Coll., AHRC, 2005–08 (Mem., PG Panel 5, 2006–07); Leverhulme Trust Adv. Panel, 2006–13; Internat. Adv. Bd, Aix-Marseille Univ., 2014–. Gov., Trinity and All Saints Coll., Leeds, 2001–04. Mem., Inst. of Tourist Guiding, 2016–. FRSA 1996; FEA 2001. Ed., Jl Lang. and Lit., 1996–2005. *Publications:* Dictionary of Stylistics, 1989, 3rd edn 2011; The Language of James Joyce, 1992; (ed) Feminist Linguistics in Literary Criticism, 1994; Personal Pronouns in Present-Day English, 1996; (ed jtly) Shakespeare's Dramatic Language: a reader's guide, 2000; Northern English: a cultural and social history, 2006; (ed jtly) Literature and Language Learning in the EFL Classroom, 2015; Dictionary of Cambridge, 2019; numerous book chapters; contrib. articles to learned jls and children's joke books. *Recreations:* buying and selling at antique fairs and flea markets, keeping fit, tour guiding round Cambridge, Fairport Convention. *Address:* 2 The Orchards, Great Shelford, Cambs CB22 5AB. *T:* (01223) 840506.

**WALES, Sir Robert Andrew, (Sir Robin)**, Kt 2000; first elected Mayor of Newham, 2002–18; Senior Adviser, Policy Exchange, since 2018; two *c*. *Educ:* Glasgow Univ. (BSc). Formerly with BT, responsible for developing credit and fraud mgt systems. Newham Borough Council: Mem. (Lab), 1982–86 and 1992–2018; Leader of Council, 1996–2002. Chairman: Assoc. of London Govt, 2000–06. Vice Chm., then Chm., Culture, Tourism and Sport Bd, LGA, 2006–09; Mem. Bd, LOCOG, 2006–13 (Chm., Remuneration Cttee, 2006–13); Chm., Host Boroughs Partnership (formerly Host Boroughs), 2006–18; Member: Olympic Park Regeneration Steering Gp, 2007–12; Olympic Park Legacy Cttee, 2009–12; Bd, London Legacy Develt Corp., 2012–18; Bd, E20 Stadium LLP, 2012–16. Chm., Red Door Ventures Ltd, 2014–15.

**WAŁĘSA, Lech**, Hon. GCB 1991; Founder and Head of Lech Wałęsa Institute Foundation, since 1995; President of Poland, 1990–95; *b* Popowo, 29 Sept. 1943; *s* of late Bolesław Wałęsa and Feliksa Wałęsa; *m* 1969, Danuta; four *s* four *d*. *Educ:* Lipno primary and tech. schools; trained as electrician. Lenin Shipyard, Gdańsk, 1966–76, 1980–90 (Chm., Strike Cttees, 1970, 1980); founder Chm., Nat. Co-ordinating Commn of Ind. Autonomous Trade Union Solidarity (NSZZ Solidarność), 1981–82; in custody, 1981–82; returned to Gdańsk Shipyard, 1983; Leader, (outlawed) Solidarity, 1983–88, (re-instated) Solidarity, 1988–90. Founder and Pres., Christian Democratic Party of Third Republic, Poland, 1997–2001. Dr *hc*, including: Alliance Coll., Cambridge, Mass, 1981; Harvard, 1983; Gdańsk, 1990; Connecticut State, 1996. Nobel Peace Prize, 1983. Presidential Medal of Freedom (USA); Grand Cross, Legion of Honour (France); Order of Merit (Italian Republic); Order of Pius, 1st Cl. (Holy See); Grand Ribbon, Order of Leopold (Belgium). *Publications:* A Path of Hope: An Autobiography, 1987. *Address:* Lech Wałęsa Institute Foundation, ul. Krucza 24/26, 00526 Warsaw, Poland.

**WALEY-COHEN, Sir Stephen (Harry)**, 2nd Bt *cr* 1961, of Honeymead, Co. Somerset; Managing Director, Mousetrap Productions, 1994–2018 (non-executive Director, since 2018); *b* 22 June 1946; *s* of Sir Bernard Nathaniel Waley-Cohen, 1st Bt and Hon. Joyce Constance Ina Waley-Cohen (*d* 2013); *S* father, 1991; *m* 1st, 1972, Pamela Elizabeth (marr. diss.), *yr d* of J. E. Doniger; two *s* one *d*; 2nd, 1986, Josephine Burnett, *yr d* of late Duncan M. Spencer; two *d*. *Educ:* Wellesley House Sch.; Eton (Oppidan Scholar); Magdalene Coll., Cambridge (MA Hons). Financial journalist, Daily Mail, 1968–73; Publisher, Euromoney, 1969–83; Chief Exec., Maybox Theatres, 1984–89; Chairman: Thorndike Holdings, management training, 1989–98; Bridge Underwriting Agents (formerly Willis Faber & Dumas (Agencies)), 1992–99 (Dir, 1988–99); Policy Portfolio, 1993–97; Portsmouth & Sunderland Newspapers, 1998–99 (Dir, 1994–99); First Call Gp, 1996–98; Director: Badgworthy Land Co., 1982–; St Martin's Theatre, 1989–; Theatresoft, 1992–97; Theatre Investment Fund, 1992–2017; Exeter Selective Assets (formerly Preferred Capital) Investment Trust, 1992–2003; Usha Martin Education Systems (formerly Usha Martin Infotech), 2008–13; D & S Mgt Ltd, 2009–; Managing Director: Victoria Palace Th., 1989–2014; Vaudeville Th., 1996–2001; Savoy Th. Mgt, 1997–2005; Ambassadors Th., 2007–18. Chm., Mousetrap Foundn for the Arts, 1996–; Mem., SOLT (formerly SWET), 1984– (Mem., Finance Cttee, 1989–2010; Chm., 1996–2002; Pres., 2002–05); Chm., Olivier Awards Cttee, 1995–2002. Pres. Council, JCA Charitable Foundn (formerly Jewish Colonisation Assoc.), 1995– (Mem. Council, 1985–); Chairman: Exec. Cttee, British American Project for Successor Generation, 1986–92; Mowbray Trust for Reproductive Immunology, 1996–2017. Chm., Combined Theatrical Charities, 2009–; Trustee: Theatres Trust, 1998–2004; Garrick Charitable Trust, 2004– (Chm., 2009–); Royal Theatrical Fund, 2009–. Patron, Front Row (Old Etonian th. and film assoc.), 2014–. Member: Public Affairs Cttee, British Field Sports Soc., 1972–92; Cttee, Devon & Somerset Staghounds, 1974–2009. Vice Pres., Exmoor Soc., 2015–. Member: UCL Finance Cttee, 1984–89; Council, RADA, 2003– (Chm., 2007–). Governor, Wellesley House Sch., 1974–97. Member, Committee: Friends of Wormwood Scrubs, 2016– (Chm., 2018–); Wormwood Scrubs Charitable Trust, 2016–. Contested (C) Manchester, Gorton, Feb. and Oct. 1974. Hon. PhD Ben Gurion Univ. of the Negev, 2011. *Recreations:* family, theatre, hunting. *Heir: s* Lionel Robert Waley-Cohen [*b* 7 Aug. 1974; *m* 2007, Octavia Green; two *d*]. *Address:* 1 Wallingford Avenue, W10 6QA. *T:* (020) 8968 6268; Honeymead, Simonsbath, Somerset TA24 7JX. *T:* (01643) 831242. *Club:* Garrick.

**WALFORD, Dr Diana Marion**, CBE 2002; Principal, Mansfield College, Oxford, 2002–11; Pro-Chancellor and Chair, Board of Trustees, Regent's University London, since 2015; *b* 26 Feb. 1944; *d* of late Lt-Col Joseph Norton, LLM, and Thelma Norton (*née* Nurick); *m* 1970, Arthur David Walford, LLB; one *s* one *d*. *Educ:* Calder High Sch. for Girls, Liverpool; Liverpool Univ. (George Holt Medal, Physiol.; J. H. Abram Prize, Pharmacol.; BSc (1st Cl. Hons Physiol.) 1965; MB ChB 1968; MD 1976); London Univ. (MSc (Epidemiology) 1987); MA Oxon 2003. FRCP 1990 (MRCP 1972); FRCPath 1986 (MRCPath 1979, FFPath 1989, FFPH (FPHM 1994). Ho. Officer posts, Liverpool Royal Inf., 1968–69; Sen. Ho. Officer posts and Sen. Registrar, St Mary's Hosp., Paddington, and Northwick Park Hosp., Harrow, 1969–75; MRC Research (Training) Fellow, Clin. Res. Centre, 1975–76; Sen. MO 1976–79, PMO 1979–83, SPMO (under Sec.), 1983–89, Dep. CMO, 1989–92, DHSS, subseq. Dept of Health; Dir, PHLS, 1993–2002. Hon. Consultant Haematologist, Central Middlesex Hosp., 1977–87. Non-executive Director: NHS Blood and Transplant Authy, 2005–09; UCLH NHS Foundn Trust, 2011–17. Founder Member: British Blood Transfusion Soc., 1983–95; Faculty of Med. Leadership and Mgt, 2011–16. Mem. Council, LSHTM, 2009–18 (Dep. Chm., 2010–18); Gov., Ditchley Foundn, 2000–. Trustee, Sue Ryder (formerly Sue Ryder Care), 2008–17. Mem., State Honours Cttee, 2010–17. FRSocMed; FRSA. *Publications:* chapters on haematological side effects of drugs in: Meyler's Side Effects of Drugs, 9th edn 1980; Side Effects of Drugs Annual, 1980; Drug-Induced Emergencies, 1980; articles on alpha-thalassaemia. *Recreations:* theatre, painting, travel. *Address:* 290 West End Lane, West Hampstead, NW6 1LN.

**WALFORD, Prof. Geoffrey**, PhD; Professor of Education Policy, University of Oxford, 2000–09, now Emeritus; Fellow, Green Templeton College (formerly Green College), Oxford, 1995–2009, now Emeritus; *b* 30 April 1949. *Educ:* Univ. of Kent (BSc Physics 1971; PhD 1975); Open Univ. (BA Sociol. and Educn 1975; MSc 1985; MBA 1996); St John's Coll., Oxford (MPhil Sociol. 1978; MA 1995); Inst. of Educn, Univ. of London (MA Educnl Admin 1986); DLitt Oxon 2016. Aston University: Lectr in Sociol. of Educn, Dept of Educnl Enquiry, 1979–83; Lectr in Educn Policy and Mgt, 1983–90, Sen. Lectr in Sociol. and Educn Policy, 1990–94, Aston Business Sch.; University of Oxford: Lectr in Educnl Studies (Sociol.), 1995–97; Reader in Educn Policy, 1997–2000; Univ. Jun. Proctor, 2001–02. Jt Ed., Brit. Jl Educnl Studies, 1998–2002; Ed., Oxford Review of Educn, 2003–10; Dep. Ed., Ethnography and Educn, 2006–. *Publications:* books include: Life in Public Schools, 1986; Restructuring Universities: politics and power in the management of change, 1987; Privatization and Privilege in Education, 1990; (with H. Miller) City Technology College, 1991; (ed) Doing Educational Research, 1991; Choice and Equity in Education, 1994; (ed) Researching the Powerful in Education, 1994; Educational Politics: pressure groups and faith-based schools, 1995; (ed with R. Pring) Affirming the Comprehensive Ideal, 1997; (ed) Doing Research about Education, 1998; (ed) Studies in Educational Ethnography, annually, 1998–2007; Policy, Politics and Education: sponsored grant-maintained schools and religious diversity, 2000; Doing Qualitative Educational Research, 2001; Private Education: tradition and diversity, 2005; Markets and Equity in Education, 2006; (ed) How to do Educational Ethnography, 2008; (ed jtly) The Sage Handbook of Measurement, 2010; (ed jtly) Education, Privatisation and Social Justice, 2014; (ed jtly) Non-State Actors in Education in the Global South, 2018. *Recreations:* travel, walking. *Address:* Department of Education, University of Oxford, 15 Norham Gardens, Oxford OX2 6PY. *T:* (01865) 274141.

**WALFORD, His Honour John de Guise**; a Circuit Judge, 1993–2015; *b* 23 Feb. 1948; *s* of late Edward Wynn Walford and of Dorothy Ann Walford; *m* 1977, Pamela Elizabeth Russell; one *s* one *d*. *Educ:* Sedbergh Sch.; Queens' Coll., Cambridge (MA). Called to the Bar, Middle Temple, 1971; practice on NE Circuit, 1974; Asst Recorder, 1985–89; Recorder, 1989–93. Standing Counsel (Criminal) to DHSS, NE Circuit, 1991–93. Chancellor, Dio. of Bradford, 1999–2014. *Recreations:* cricket, tennis, opera, watching Middlesbrough FC. *Clubs:* Hawks (Cambridge); Free Foresters.

**WALFORD, Lionel Kingsley**, PhD; FInstP; Assessor for Civil Service Fast Stream, since 1999; *b* 19 May 1939; *s* of late Edward Walford and Muriel (*née* Davies); *m* 1963, Linda Jones; one *d* (and one *d* decd). *Educ:* Whitchurch Grammar Sch., Cardiff; Univ. Coll. of South Wales and Monmouthshire (BSc 1st Cl. Hons Physics, Univ. of Wales, 1960); St Catharine's Coll., Cambridge (PhD 1963). FInstP 1972. Southern Illinois University, USA: Asst Prof., 1963–67; Associate Prof., 1967–72; Prof. of Physics, 1972–78; Research Consultant, McDonnell Douglas Corp., 1964–72; joined Welsh Office, 1978: Principal, 1978–84; Sen. Principal seconded to WDA, 1984–85; Dir, Manpower Services in Wales, 1985–88; Asst Sec., 1988–94, Under Sec. (Hd, then Dir), 1994–99, Welsh Office Agriculture Dept. Chairman: Lantra Council for Wales, 2009–15; Agric. Adv. Panel for Wales, 2016–; Ind. Mem., Agricl Wages Bd for England and Wales, 2007–13; Chm., Welsh Levy Bd, 2008–12. *Publications:* numerous articles in jls on applied physics; one US patent. *E:* lionel.walford@cantab.net.

**WALKER**, family name of **Barons Walker of Aldringham** and **Walker of Gestingthorpe**.

**WALKER OF ALDRINGHAM**, Baron *cr* 2006 (Life Peer), of Aldringham in the County of Suffolk; **Field Marshal Michael John Dawson Walker**, GCB 2000 (KCB 1995); CMG 1997; CBE 1990 (OBE 1982); DL; Chief of the Defence Staff, 2003–06; *b* 7 July 1944; *s* of William Hampden Dawson Walker and Dorothy Helena Walker (*née* Shiach); *m* 1973, Victoria Margaret Holme; two *s* one *d*. *Educ:* Milton Sch., Bulawayo; Woodhouse Grove Sch., Yorks; RMA Sandhurst. Commissioned Royal Anglian Regt, 1966; Regtl and Staff duties, 1966–82; Staff Coll., 1976–77; MA to CGS, 1982–85; CO 1 Royal Anglian Regt, 1985–87; Comdr, 20th Armoured Brigade, 1987–89; COS, 1 (Br) Corps, 1989–91; GOC NE District and Comdr, 2nd Inf. Div., 1991–92; GOC Eastern District, 1992; ACGS, MoD, 1992–94; Comdr, ACE Rapid Reaction Corps, 1994–97; Comdr, Land Component Peace Implementation Force, Bosnia, 1995–96; C-in-C, Land Comd, 1997–2000; ADC Gen. to the Queen, 1997–2006; CGS, 2000–03. Gov., Royal Hosp. Chelsea, 2006–11. Colonel Commandant: Queen's Div., 1991–2000; AAC, 1994–2004; Col, Royal Anglian Regt, 1997–2002 (Dep. Col, 1991–97). DL Gtr London, 2007. Hon. LLD UEA, 2002; Hon. DSc Cranfield, 2003. *Recreations:* ski-ing, sailing, shooting, golf, family. *Address:* House of Lords, SW1A 0PW.

**WALKER OF GESTINGTHORPE**, Baron *cr* 2002 (Life Peer), of Gestingthorpe in the County of Essex; **Robert Walker**, Kt 1994; PC 1997; a non-permanent Judge, Court of Final Appeal of Hong Kong, since 2009; *b* 17 March 1938; *s* of late Ronald Robert Antony Walker and Mary Helen Walker (*née* Welsh); *m* 1962, Suzanne Diana Leggi; one *s* three *d*. *Educ:* Downside Sch.; Trinity Coll., Cambridge (BA; Hon. Fellow, 2006). Called to Bar, Lincoln's Inn, 1960, Bencher 1990, Treas., 2010; QC 1982; in practice at Chancery Bar, 1961–94; a Judge of the High Court of Justice, Chancery Div., 1994–97; a Lord Justice of Appeal, 1997–2002; a Lord of Appeal in Ordinary, 2002–09; a Justice of the Supreme Court of the UK, 2009–13. Chm., H of L Select Cttee on HS2 Bill, 2016; H of L Select Cttee on Scrutiny of Secondary Legislation, 2018–19. *Address:* House of Lords, SW1A 0PW.

**WALKER, Prof. Alan Christopher**, CBE 2014; DLitt; FBA 2011; Professor of Social Policy and Social Gerontology, since 1985, and Co-Director, Institute for Healthy Lifespan, since 2019, University of Sheffield (Director, New Dynamics of Ageing Programme, 2005–15); *b* London, 20 April 1949; *s* of Alfred Charles and Joyce Margaret Walker; *m* 1972, Carol Anne Davey; one *s* one *d*. *Educ:* Smallberry Green Secondary Sch.; Spring Grove Grammar Sch.; Univ. of Essex (BA Hons Govt and Sociol. 1972; DLitt Sociol. 1990). Res. Asst, 1972–74, Res. Officer, 1974–75, Univ. of Essex; Sen. Res. Officer, Nat. Children's Bureau, 1975–77; Lectr in Social Policy, 1977–84, Sen. Lectr, 1983–84, Reader, 1984–85, Univ. of Sheffield. Non-exec. Dir, 1993–99, Chair, 1999–2003, Community Health Sheffield NHS Trust; Chair: Sheffield Care Trust, 2003–08; Sheffield Health and Social Care NHS Trust, 2008–16. FAcSS 1999. FRSA 1994. Hon. Fellow, Gerontological Soc. of America, 2016. Hon. DSocSc Hong Kong Baptist 2006. *Publications:* (ed with P. Townsend) Disability in Britain, 1981; Unqualified and Underemployed: handicapped young people and the labour market, 1982; (ed) Public Expenditure and Social Policy: an examination of social spending and social priorities, 1982; (ed) Community Care: the family, the state and social policy, 1982; Social Planning, 1984 (Japanese edn 1995); (ed with C. Phillipson) Ageing and Social Policy: a critical assessment, 1986; (ed with C. Walker) The Growing Divide: a social audit 1979–1987, 1987 (Japanese edn 1994); (jtly) After Redundancy: the experience of economic insecurity, 1988; (with H. Qureshi) The Caring Relationship: family care of elderly people, 1989; (ed jtly) The Social Economy and the Democratic State, 1989; (jtly) Age and Employment: policies, attitudes and practices, 1993; (ed) The New Generational Contract: intergenerational relations, old age and welfare, 1996; (with L. Warren) Changing Services for Older People: the Neighbourhood Support Units innovation, 1996; (ed jtly) Sociology of Aging: international perspectives, 1996; (with T. Maltby) Ageing Europe, 1997; (ed with C. Walker) Britain Divided: the growth of social exclusion in the 1980s and 1990s, 1997; (ed jtly) The Social Quality of Europe, 1997; Ageing and Welfare Change in Europe: prospect and future, 1997; (ed) European Home and Community Care 1998/99, 1998; (ed jtly) Politische Beteiligung älter Menschen in Europa, 1997; (with P. Taylor) Combating Age Barriers in Employment: a European portfolio of good practice, 1998; (ed with G. Naegele) The Politics of Old Age in Europe, 1999; (ed jtly) Social Quality: a vision for Europe, 2001; (ed with C. Hagan Hennessy) Growing Older: quality of life in old age, 2004 (Japanese edn 2009); (ed) Growing Older in Europe, 2005; (ed with C. K. Wong) East Asian Welfare Regimes in Transition: from Confucianism to globalisation, 2005; (ed) Understanding Quality of Life in Old Age, 2005; (ed jtly) Aging, Globalisation and Inequality: the new critical gerontology, 2006; (ed with H. Mollenkopf) Quality of Life in Old Age: international and multidisciplinary perspectives, 2007; (ed with C. Aspalter) Securing the Future for Old Age in Europe, 2008; (ed with G. Naegele) Social Policy in Ageing Societies: Britain and Germany compared, 2009; (ed jtly) The Peter Townsend Reader, 2010; (ed jtly) Fighting Poverty, Inequality and Injustice, 2011 (ed with L. van der Maesen) Social Quality: from theory to indicators, 2012; The New Science of Ageing, 2014; (ed with L. Foster) The Political Economy of Ageing and Later Life: critical perspectives, 2014; (ed with C. Aspalter) Active Ageing in Asia, 2015; (ed with L. Wang) Comparative Social Quality Between Taiwan and Korea, 2015; (ed) The New Dynamics of Ageing, 2 vols, 2018; (ed) The Future of Ageing in Europe, 2019. *Recreations:* my grandchildren Mabel and Bruce, walking, reading fiction, cooking, gardening, ballet, theatre, cinema, sculpture, music, trying not to support Arsenal FC. *Address:* Department of Sociological Studies, University of Sheffield, Elmfield, Northumberland Road, Sheffield S10 2TU. *T:* (0114) 222 6466/67. *E:* a.c.walker@sheffield.ac.uk.

**WALKER, Alexandra Margaret Jane;** psychoanalytic psychotherapist; Director, Human Resources, Inland Revenue, 2000–03; *b* 31 Oct. 1945; *d* of late Frederic Douglas Walker and Hertha Julie (née Freiin Gemmingen von Massenbach); one *d*; *m* 2017, Roger William Carter. *Educ:* Nikolaus Cusanus Gymnasium, Bonn; Lady Margaret Hall, Oxford (Schol.; BA Lit. Hum.); Univ. of Roehampton (MA Psychoanalytic Studies 2011); Heythrop Coll., Univ. of London (MA Christian Theol. 2016). Joined MoD as admin. trainee, 1973; Principal, 1976; on secondment to Plessey Co., 1979–81; LSE as Nancy Seear Fellow in Industrial Relns, 1981–82; Asst Sec. and Hd of Civilian Mgt (Industrial Relns), 1983–86; rcds 1987; Counsellor, British Embassy, Bonn, 1988–92; Asst Under-Sec. of State (Service Personnel), 1993–97; Dir Gen. Future Hd Office, 1997–2000. Chm., Foundn for Psychotherapy and Counselling, 2009–12. *Recreations:* walking, geology, amateur string quartets (cello), singing.

**WALKER, Alisdair James;** HM Diplomatic Service: Ambassador to Eritrea, since 2019; *b* London, 14 Sept. 1965; *s* of James Alexander Walker and Alison Margaret Walker; *m* 1992, Susan Mary; two *s* one *d*. *Educ:* St Paul's Sch., Barnes; Birmingham Univ. Entered FCO, 1989; Asst Desk Officer, Econ. Relns Dept, FCO, 1989–90; Desk Officer, E Africa Dept, FCO, 1990–91; Third Sec. (Pol), Islamabad, 1991–94; Asst Mgt Officer, Moscow, 1995–99; Desk Officer, Internal Audit Dept, 1999–2000, Quality and Efficiency Unit, 2000–02, Human Rights Dept, 2002–04, FCO; Second Sec. (Pol), Abuja, 2004–07; Team Leader, Japan, Korean Peninsula and Mongolia Section, Far Eastern Dept, FCO, 2007–11; Counsellor (Pol), Seoul, 2011–15; Hd, China Internal Section, E Asia Dept, FCO, 2015–18. *Recreations:* walking, local church. *Address:* British Embassy, 66–68 Mariam Ghimbi Street, Zip Code 174, PO Box 5584, Asmara, Eritrea. *E:* alisdair.walker@fco.gov.uk.

**WALKER, Andrew Angus;** HM Senior Coroner, North London (Coroner, Greater London Northern District, 2007); *b* Guildford, 8 Oct. 1964; *s* of Dr Andrew Allan Walker and Dr Janet Walker; *m* 1999, Rebecca Anne Byrne; one *s* one *d*. *Educ:* Westminster Univ. (LLB, BSc). Called to the Bar, Middle Temple, 1994; in private practice, 1994–2006; Door Tenant, 10 Kings Bench Walk, Temple, 2006–. *Recreation:* regulator and turret clock maker. *Address:* North London Coroner's Court, 29 Wood Street, High Barnet EN5 4BE.

**WALKER, Prof. Andrew Charles,** PhD; FRSE; Secretary and Treasurer, Carnegie Trust for the Universities of Scotland, since 2013; *b* Wembley, 24 June 1948; *s* of Maurice Frederick Walker and Margaret Florence Walker (née Rust); *m* 1972, Margaret Elizabeth Mortimer; one *s* one *d* (twins). *Educ:* Kingsbury Co. Grammar Sch.; Univ. of Essex (BA, MSc; PhD 1972). FInstP 1987. NRCC Postdoctoral Fellow, Ottawa, 1972–74; SRC Fellow, Univ. of Essex, 1974–75; SSO, UKAEA Culham Lab., 1975–83; Heriot-Watt University: Lectr in Physics, 1983; Reader, then Prof. of Modern Optics, 1985–2013, now Prof. Emeritus; Dir, Postgrad. Studies, 1998–2001; Dep. Principal (Resources), 2001–06; Vice-Principal, 2006–10; Sen. Dep. Principal, 2010–13; Dir, Heriot-Watt Malaysia Sdn Bhd, 2011–13 (CEO, 2011–12). Mem., SERC/DTI Advance Devices and Materials Cttee, 1992–94; Dir, Technol. Ventures Scotland, 2002–05. Institute of Physics: Mem. Cttee and Hon. Sec., Quantum Electronics Gp, 1979–85; Chm., Scottish Br., 1991–97 (Mem. Cttee, 1985–88). Royal Society of Edinburgh: FRSE 1994; Mem. Council and Sec. for Meetings, 1998–2001; Vice-Pres., 2001–04; Fellowship Sec., 2005–08. Non-exec. Dir and Chm., Terahertz Photonics Ltd, 1998–2000; non-exec. Dir, SeeByte Ltd, 2008–13. Trustee: RSE Scotland Foundn, 2002–05 (Chm., 2004–05); Scottish Building Fedn Edinburgh and Dist Charitable Trust, 2005–19. Non-exec. Dir, Edinburgh Business Sch., 2001–15. *Publications:* over 200 articles and letters in field of lasers and optoelectronics. *Recreations:* sailing (Cdre, Cramond Boat Club), music (piano). *Address:* Carnegie Trust for the Universities of Scotland, Andrew Carnegie House, Pittencrieff Street, Dunfermline KY12 8AW. *E:* a.c.walker@carnegie-trust.org; (home) 57 Cramond Glebe Road, Edinburgh EH4 6NT.

**WALKER, Andrew Douglas;** Senior Partner, Lovells, 2000–04; *b* 6 May 1945; *s* of Malcolm Douglas Walker and Jean Catherine Walker (née Ross-Scott); *m* 1973, Hilary Georgina Smith. *Educ:* Giggleswick Sch.; Exeter Coll., Oxford (MA 1966). Admitted Solicitor, England and Wales, 1970, Hong Kong, 1982; articled, 1968–70; Solicitor, 1970–71, Wilkinson Kimbers & Staddon; Lovell, White & King: Solicitor, 1971–75; Partner, 1975; Hong Kong office, 1982–87; Managing Partner, 1987–88; Lovell White Durrant (formed from merger with Durrant Piesse): Managing Partner, 1988–93; Sen. Partner, 1996–2000; Lovells formed 2000, from merger with Boesebeck Droste. *Recreations:* opera, classical music, ornithology. *Club:* Hong Kong.

**WALKER, Andrew John;** company director; *b* 27 Sept. 1951; *s* of late John Kenneth Walker, MD and Mary Magdaline (née Browne); *m* 1981, Pippa Robinson; two *s* one *d*. *Educ:* Ampleforth Coll., York; Gonville and Caius Coll., Cambridge (MA Engrg). FIMechE 2003. Chief Executive: SWALEC, 1993–96; McKechnie plc, 1997–2001; Chairman: Bioganix plc, 2004–09; Brintons Ltd, 2008–11 (Dir, 2006–11); Metalrax plc, 2010–13; Mainstay Gp Ltd, 2013–15; Director: Ultra Electronics Hldgs plc, 1996–2009 (Sen. Ind. Dir; Chm., Audit and Remuneration Cttees); Halma plc, 2003–07 (Sen. Ind. Dir; Chm., Audit and Remuneration Cttees); API Gp plc, 2003–15 (Sen. Ind. Dir; Chm., Audit and Remuneration Cttees); Manganese Bronze Hldgs plc, 2003–12 (Chm., Audit Cttee); Delta plc, 2005–10 (Sen. Ind. Dir; Chm., Audit Cttee); Porvair plc, 2005–14 (Sen. Ind. Dir; Chm., Remuneration Cttee); fountains plc, 2005–08 (Chm., Audit Cttee); Synnovia (formerly Plastics Capital) plc, 2007– (Chm., Audit Cttee, 2008–); May Gurney plc, 2009–13 (Chm., Remuneration Cttee); Stemcor Hldgs Ltd, 2014–15. Liveryman, Engineers' Co. *Address:* Synnovia plc, Room 1.1, London Heliport, Bridges Court Road, SW11 3BE. *Clubs:* Farmers; 20-Ghost.

**WALKER, Andrew John;** Director General of Human Resources and Change, House of Commons, 2011–16; *b* 4 Jan. 1955; *s* of Edward Geoffrey Walker and Raymonde Dorothy Walker; *m* 1987, Alison Aitkenhead; two *s* one *d*. *Educ:* Newcastle-under-Lyme High Sch.; Univ. of Birmingham (BA Ancient Near Eastern Studies). Inland Revenue, 1976–89; Principal, Fiscal Policy Gp, HM Treasury, 1989–91; Asst Dir, Human Resources Strategy and Planning, Inland Revenue, 1992–96; House of Commons: Dir of Finance and Admin, 1997–2007; Dir Gen., Resources, 2008–11. Adv. work for overseas parlts, with Westminster Foundn for Democracy, 2016–. Chair, Cttee for Revalidation of Occupational Health Physicians, Faculty of Occupational Medicine, 2017–. Dir, Christadelphian Mag. and Publishing Assoc., 2014–. CPFA 2008; FCIPD 2012. *Publications:* (with Emma Crewe) An Extraordinary Scandal, 2019. *E:* walkeraj55@gmail.com.

**WALKER, Andrew Paul Dalton;** QC 2013; *b* Chester, 22 Sept. 1968; *s* of Richard and Linda Walker; *m* 2003, Emma Bensted. *Educ:* King's Sch., Chester; Haberdashers' Aske's Sch., Elstree; Trinity Coll., Cambridge (BA 1990; MA). Called to the Bar, Lincoln's Inn, 1991, Bencher, 2016. Chair, Bar Council, 2018 (Mem., 2005–18; Vice-Chair, 2017). Trustee, Industry and Parliament Trust, 2013–. *Recreations:* wine, walking, gun dogs, conservation, historic buildings. *Address:* Maitland Chambers, 7 Stone Buildings, Lincoln's Inn, WC2A 3SZ. *T:* (020) 7406 1200, *Fax:* (020) 7406 1300. *E:* awalker@maitlandchambers.com. *Club:* Oxford and Cambridge.

**WALKER, Angus Henry;** Senior Consultant, Europe Economics, 2006; *b* 30 Aug. 1935; *s* of late Frederick William Walker and of Esther Victoria (née Wrangle); *m* 1st, 1968, Beverly Phillpotts (see B. J. Anderson) (marr. diss. 1976); 2nd, 1979, Ann (née Griffiths), *widow* of Richard Snow; two *d* and two step *d*. *Educ:* Erith Grammar Sch., Kent; Balliol Coll., Oxford (Domus Scholar; 1st Cl. Hons BA Mod. Hist. 1959; Stanhope Prize, 1958; MA 1968). Nat. Service, 1954–56 (commnd RA). Senior Scholar, St Antony's Coll., Oxford, 1959–63; HM Diplomatic Service, 1963–68: FO, 1963–65; First Sec., Washington, 1965–68. Lectr, SSEES, London Univ., 1968–70; Univ Lectr in Russian Social and Political Thought, Oxford, and Lectr, Balliol Coll., 1971–76; Fellow, Wolfson Coll., Oxford, 1971–76; Dir, SSEES, London Univ., 1976–79; British Petroleum Co. Plc, 1979–84; Dir, Corporate Strategy, British Telecom PLC, 1985–88; Managing Director: Strategic Planning Associates, 1988–91; A. T. Kearney, 1991–94; Partner, Mitchell Madison Gp, 1996–98. Co-opted Mem., Arts Sub-Cttee, UGC, for enquiry into Russian in British Univs, 1978–79; Governor, Centre for Economic Policy Res., 1986–89. Chairman: HemiHelp, 2004–11; Hampstead Garden Suburb Trust, 2007–13. FIET (FIEE 2002; CompIEE 1988). *Publications:* trans. from Polish: Political Economy, by Oskar Lange, vol. 1, 1963; Marx: His Theory in its Context, 1978, 2nd edn 1989. *Address:* Barclays Bank plc, 126 Station Road, Edgware HA8 7RY. *Club:* Reform.

**WALKER, Hon. Anna Elizabeth Blackstock, (Hon. Mrs Walker),** CB 2003; Chairman, Office of Rail and Road (formerly Office of Rail Regulation), 2009–15; *b* 5 May 1951; *d* of Baron Butterworth, CBE; *m* 1983, Timothy Edward Hanson Walker, *qv*; three *d*. *Educ:* Benenden Sch., Kent; Bryn Mawr Coll., USA; Lady Margaret Hall, Oxford (MA History). British Council, 1972–73; CBI, 1973–74; joined Department of Trade, 1975: Commercial Relations and Exports Div. (ME), 1975; Post and Telecommunications Div., 1976; Private Sec. to Sec. of State for Industry, 1977–78; Shipping Policy Div. (Grade 7), 1979–82; Finance Div., 1983–84; Interdeptl Rev. of Budgetary Controls, 1985; Cabinet Office (on secondment), 1986; Personnel Div. (Grade 6), 1987–88; Competition Policy Div. (Grade 5), 1988–91; Dir, Competition, 1991–94, Dep. Dir Gen., 1994–98, Oftel; Dep. Dir Gen., 1998, Dir Gen., 1998–2001, Energy, DTI; Dir Gen., Land Use and Rural Affairs, DEFRA, 2001–03; Chief Exec., Healthcare Commn, 2004–09. Chm., Ind. Review of Charging for Household Water and Sewerage Services, 2008–09 (Report, 2009). Non-executive Director: Welsh Water, 2011–; S London and the Maudsley NHS Foundn Trust, 2016–. Mem., Competition Appeal Tribunal, 2017–. Member, Council: Consumer Focus (formerly NCC), 2008–12; Which?, 2013– (Dep. Chm., 2017–). Chm., Young Epilepsy (formerly Nat. Centre for Young People with Epilepsy), 2009–16; Chair, St George's Hosp. Charity, 2016–. Trustee: Operahouse Music Projects, 2004–16; Women in Rail, 2016–18. *Recreations:* family, travel, theatre, cycling. *E:* anna@aebwalker.com.

**WALKER, Annabel;** see Carr, E. A.

**WALKER, Anthony Stanley L.;** see Lau-Walker.

**WALKER, Gen. Sir Antony (Kenneth Frederick),** KCB 1987; Director-General, British Institute of Facilities Management, 1998–2001; *b* 16 May 1934; *o s* of late Kenneth Walker and Iris Walker; *m* 1961, Diana Merran Steward (marr. diss. 1983); one *s* one *d*; *m* 1991, Sqn Ldr Hannah Watts, WRAF. *Educ:* Merchant Taylors' School; RMA Sandhurst. Commissioned into Royal Tank Regt, 1954; served BAOR, Libya, Ghana, Northern Ireland, Hong Kong, Cyprus; Instructor, Staff Coll., 1971–73; CO 1st Royal Tank Regt, 1974–76 (despatches); Col GS HQ UK Land Forces, 1976–78; Comdr Task Force Golf (11 Armd Bde), 1978–80; Dep. Mil. Sec. (A), 1980–82; Comdr, 3rd Armoured Div., 1982–84; Chief of Staff, HQ UKLF, 1985–87; Dep. CDS (Commitments), MoD, 1987–89; Comdt, RCDS, 1990–92. Sec.-Gen., Opsis (Nat. Assoc. for Educn, Trng and Support of Blind and Partially Sighted People), 1992–96. Mil. Advr, Porton Internat. plc, 1992–94; Sen. Mil. Advr, Electronic Data Systems Ltd, 1994; Business Develt Dir, John Mowlem. Col Comdt, Royal Tank Regt, 1983–94 (Rep., 1985–91). Mem. Council, RUSI, 1982–85 and 1990–94. Governor, Centre for Internat. Briefing, Farnham Castle, 1987–91. Chairman: Army Bobsleigh Assoc., 1983–92; British Bobsleigh Assoc., 1992–98 (Mem. Council, 1989–); President: Services' Dry Fly Fishing Assoc., 1988–92; Combined Services' Winter Sports Assoc., 1990–92. Mem., Council of Management, Salisbury Festival, 1988–96 (Vice-Chm., 1990–93; Chm., 1994–96). Trustee, Tank Mus., 1994. *Recreations:* bird watching, fly-fishing, music, practical study of wine. *Club:* Royal Air Force (Associate).

**WALKER, Prof. Brian Robert,** MD; FRCPE; FRSE; FMedSci; Pro-Vice-Chancellor, Research Strategy and Resources, Newcastle University, since 2017; *b* Glasgow, 12 July 1963; *s* of J. Grant Walker and Marjorie S. Walker; *m* 1990, Jane Mew; two *s*. *Educ:* Glasgow Acad.; Univ. of Edinburgh (BSc 1984; MB ChB 1986; MD 1992). FRCPE 1999. Jun. doctor, Edinburgh and Glasgow, 1986–89; University of Edinburgh: MRC Trng Fellow, 1990–93; Lectr in Medicine, 1992–96; BHF Sen. Res. Fellow, 1996–2006; Prof. of Endocrinol., 2001–17; Hd, BHF Centre for Cardiovascular Sci., 2009–17; Dean of Res., Coll. of Medicine and Veterinary Medicine, 2015–17. Hon. Consultant Physician: Lothian

Health Univ. Hosps Div., 1996–2017; Newcastle-upon-Tyne Hosps Trust, 2017–. FRSE 2011; FMedSci 2017. *Publications:* (ed) Davidson's Principles and Practice of Medicine, 20th edn 2006 to 22nd edn 2014. *Recreations:* choral singing, cycle touring. *Address:* Executive Office, Newcastle University, King's Gate, Newcastle upon Tyne NE1 7RU. *T:* (0191) 208 7701. *E:* brian.walker@ncl.ac.uk.

**WALKER, (Brian) Stuart**, RDI 1989; freelance film production designer, since 1990; *b* 5 March 1932; *s* of William and Annie Walker; *m* 1st, 1961, Adrienne Elizabeth Atkinson (marr. diss. 1997); two *d*; 2nd, 2000, Francesca Boyd; one *s. Educ:* Blackpool Sch. of Art (Intermediate Exam. in Arts and Crafts; Nat. Diploma in Painting (1st cl. Hons)); RA Schs (RA Dip.). BBC Television, 1958–90: Design Assistant, 1958; Designer, 1961; Sen. Designer, 1970. BAFTA Award for TV Design, 1983, 1990; RTS Award for Production Design, 1988. *Address:* c/o Casarotto Marsh Ltd, Waverley House, 7–12 Noel Street, W1F 8GQ. *T:* (020) 7287 4450.

**WALKER, Brian Wilson**; consultant in ecology and development, since 1996; Executive Director, Earthwatch Europe, 1989–95; *b* 31 Oct. 1930; *s* of Arthur Walker and Eleanor (*née* Wilson); *m* 1954, Nancy Margaret Gawith; one *s* five *d. Educ:* Heversham Sch., Westmorland; Leicester Coll. of Technol.; Faculty of Technol., Manchester Univ. Management Trainee, Sommerville Bros, Kendal, 1952–55; Personnel Manager, Pye Radio, Larne, 1956–61; Bridgeport Brass Ltd, Lisburn: Personnel Manager, 1961–66; Gen. Manager (Develt), 1966–69; Gen. Manager (Manufg), 1969–74; Dir Gen., Oxfam, 1974–83; Dir, Independent Commn on Internat. Humanitarian Issues, 1983–85; Pres., Internat. Inst. for Envmt and Develt, 1985–89. Chairman: Band Aid—Live Aid Projects Cttee, 1985–90; SOS Sahel, 1988–95. Founder Chm., New Ulster Movt, 1969–74; Founder Pres., New Ulster Movt Ltd, 1974. Member: Standing Adv. Commn on Human Rights for NI, 1975–77; World Commn on Food and Peace, 1989–95; Preparing for Peace, Westmorland Quakers, 2000–07. Mem., Editl Cttee, World Resources Report, 1985–95. Trustee: Cambodia Trust, 1989–95; Internat. Inst. for Environment and Develt, 1989–95; Artizan Trust, 1992–99; Nginn Karet Foundn, 1996–2002; Chm., Arnside Parish Plan Trust, 2003–07. Chm., Kent Estuary Labour Party, 2005–08. Chm. Govs, Dallam Sch., Cumbria, 1996–2003; Chm., Dallam Trust, 2003–11. Eponymous annual lecture inaugurated Oxford Univ., 1996. Hon. MA Oxon, 1983. Kt, Sov. Order of St Thomas of Acre; Kentucky Colonel, 1996. *Publications:* Authentic Development—Africa, 1986; various political/religious papers on Northern Ireland problem and Third World subjects. *Recreations:* gardening, Irish politics, classical music, active Quaker. *Club:* Athenæum.

**WALKER, Carl**, GC 1972; Police Inspector, 1976–82; *b* 31 March 1934; English; *m* 1955, Kathleen Barker; one *s. Educ:* Kendal Grammar Sch., Westmorland. RAF Police, 1952–54 (Corporal). Lancashire Police, Oct. 1954–March 1956, resigned; Blackpool Police, 1959–82 (amalgamated with Lancashire Constabulary, April 1968); Sergeant, 1971. Retired 1982, as a result of the injuries sustained from gunshot wounds on 23 Aug. 1971 during an armed raid by thieves on a jeweller's shop in Blackpool (GC). *Address:* 9 Lawnswood Avenue, Poulton-le-Fylde, Blackpool FY6 7ED.

**WALKER, Caron Ann**; Director, Collection and Production, Office for National Statistics, 2012–14; *b* Newport, S Wales, 4 June 1959; *d* of Michael Maguire and Gloria Maguire; *m* 1985, Graeme Walker; one *s* one *d. Educ:* Univ. of Southampton (BSc Maths with Actuarial Studies 1980). Business Statistics Office, then Central Statistical Office, later Office for National Statistics: Asst Statistician, 1981–86; Statistician, 1987–96; Sen. Statistician, 1996–2000; Dep. Dir, 2000–04; Temp. Dir, 2005–08; Dep. Dir, 2008–09; Dep. Dir, Nat. Statistician's Office, 2009–11; Temp. Dir, Sources, 2011–12. *Recreations:* judo black belt 4th dan, watching Manchester United, family, walking, theatre, music.

**WALKER, Sir Charles (Ashley Rupert)**, KBE 2019 (OBE 2015); MP (C) Broxbourne, since 2005; *b* 11 Sept. 1967; *s* of late Timothy Walker and of Carola Walker (*née* Ashton) (she *m* 1976, Rt Hon. Sir Christopher John Chataway, PC); *m* 1995, Fiona Jane Newman; two *s* one *d. Educ:* American Sch. of London; Univ. of Oregon (BSc Pol Sci. 1990). Communications Dir, CSG plc, 1997–2001; Director: Blue Arrow Ltd, 1999–2001; LSM Processing Ltd, 2002–04. Mem., Wandsworth LBC, 2002–06. Contested (C) Ealing North, 2001. *Recreations:* fishing, cricket. *Address:* House of Commons, SW1A 0AA. *T:* (020) 7219 3000. *E:* charles.walker.mp@parliament.uk. *Clubs:* Waltham Cross Conservative; Hoddesdon Conservative.

**WALKER, Maj. Gen. (Charles) Roland (Vincent)**, DSO 2010; Operations Director, Ministry of Defence, since 2018; *b* Nairobi, Kenya, 14 May 1970; *s* of Patrick Walker and late Daphne Walker (*née* Armour; she later *m* 7th Marquess of Conyngham); *m* 1998, Kate Leonore White-Thomson; three *d. Educ:* Dragon Sch.; Harrow Sch.; Royal Agricl Coll. (BSc Hons); RMA, Sandhurst; Cranfield Univ. (MA). Irish Guards, 1993; operational tours, NI, 1994–2000; acsc 2001–03; operational tours, Iraq, 2003–07; CO, 1st Bn Grenadier Guards, 2008–10, incl. operational tour, Afghanistan, and Queen's Birthday Parade, 2010; Bde Comd, 12 Armd Infantry Bde, 2013–15; Hd, Strategy, Army HQ, 2015–18. Regtl Lt Col, Grenadier Guards, 2017–; Col Comdt, RAVC, 2017–. Freeman, Ironmongers' Co., 2018. Pres., Armed Forces Equitation Assoc., 2017–. *Recreations:* field sports, ski-ing, triathlon sports, walking, riding, family. *E:* charles.walker495@mod.gov.uk. *Club:* Cavalry and Guards.

**WALKER, Christopher Charles**, FRCS; Consultant Plastic and Reconstructive Surgeon, 1983–2008; Medical Director, Mid Essex Hospitals NHS Trust, 2001–07; President, British Association of Plastic, Reconstructive and Aesthetic Surgeons, 2007; *b* 26 April 1945; *s* of Cyril and Evelyn Vera Walker; *m* 1981, Marlene Dawn Menner; one *d. Educ:* Univ. of Newcastle upon Tyne (MB BS 1968). FRCS 1974. SHO, Surgery Rotating, United Norwich Hosp., 1971–74; Registrar, Gen. Surgery, Leicester Royal Infirmary, 1974–75; MRC Res. Registrar, Burns Project, Mt Vernon Hosp., 1975–76; Registrar in Plastic Surgery, Mt Vernon Hosp. and UCH, 1976–80; Sen. Registrar in Plastic Surgery, Manchester Hosps, 1980–83; Consultant Plastic Surgeon: St Andrews Centre, Billericay, 1983–2008 (transf. to Broomfield Hosp., Chelmsford, 1998); Queen Elizabeth Children's Hosp. and Royal London Hosp., 1983–2001; Whipps Cross Hosp., 1983–2008. Founder and Chm., Broomfield Hosp. Arts Project, 1997–; Trustee, Changing Faces, 2008–. *Recreations:* jazz and classical music, wine and food, travel, art.

**WALKER, Sir Christopher (Robert Baldwin)**, 5th Bt *cr* 1856, of Oakley House, Suffolk; *b* 25 Oct. 1969; *s* of Sir (Baldwin) Patrick Walker, 4th Bt and of Rosemary Ann Walker (*née* Hollingrake); *S* father, 2005; *m* 2013, Keryn Barnes; one *s* one *d. Educ:* Diocesan Coll., Cape Town. Leading Seaman, South African Marine Corps, 1994–96; Sales Manager, 1996–2006; Dir, CSS Security and Technol. Centre, Ni9htwatcher Distribution, 2007–08; Sales Dir, Betafence SA, 2008–17. *Heir:* *s* Connor John Baldwin Walker, *b* 26 April 2017. *Address:* 28A Lewis Drive, Constantia, Cape Town 7806, South Africa.

**WALKER, (Christopher) Roy**, CB 1992; Chief Officer, Joint Nature Conservation Committee, 1993–96; *b* 5 Dec. 1934; *s* of late Christopher Harry Walker and Dorothy Jessica Walker; *m* 1961, Hilary Mary Biddiscombe; two *s. Educ:* Sir George Monoux Grammar Sch., E17; Sidney Sussex Coll., Cambridge (BA); Université Libre de Bruxelles. National Service, Essex Regt, 1952–54. BoT, 1958; CSD, 1968; Private Sec. to Lord Privy Seal, 1968–71; DTI, 1973; Dept of Energy, 1974; Cabinet Office, 1974; Dept of Energy, 1975; Under Secretary: DES, 1977; Dept of Employment, 1986; seconded as Dir, Business in the Cities, 1989; Dep. Head of Sci. and Technol. Secretariat, Cabinet Office, 1989–92. Chm., Rockdale Housing Assoc., Sevenoaks, 2003–07. *Recreations:* hill walking, sailing. *Club:* Chipstead Sailing (Sevenoaks).

**WALKER, Prof. Clive Phillip**, PhD, LLD; Professor of Criminal Justice Studies, University of Leeds, 1993–2014, now Emeritus; *b* Hartlepool, 10 Feb. 1954. *Educ:* Univ. of Leeds (LLB 1975); Univ. of Manchester (PhD 1982; LLD 2015). Admitted as solicitor, 1976; in practice as solicitor, 1976–78; Lectr, Univ. of Manchester, 1978–83; University of Leeds: Lectr, 1983–89; Sen. Lectr, 1989–92; Reader, 1992; Dir, Centre for Criminal Justice Studies, 1987–2000; Hd, Sch. of Law, 2000–05 and 2010. Visiting Professor: Univ. of Louisville, 1993; George Washington Univ., 1995; Univ. of Miami, 2000; Univ. of Connecticut, 2003; Stanford Univ., 2006; Univ. of Washington, 2006; Univ. of Melbourne, 2007; Inst. of Advanced Legal Studies, Univ. of London, 2009; Univ. of NSW, 2012; Univ. of Toronto, 2016. Special Adviser: to Parly Jt Cttee on Civil Contingencies Bill, 2003–04; to Ind. Reviewer of Terrorism Legislation, 2011–19; to Biometrics Wkg Gp, 2019–. Hon. QC 2016. *Publications:* The Prevention of Terrorism in British Law, 1986, 2nd edn 1992; (with G. Hogan) Political Violence and the Law in Ireland, 1989; (ed with K. Starmer) Justice in Error, 1993; (ed) Crime, Criminal Justice and the Internet, 1998; (ed with K. Starmer) Miscarriages of Justice, 1999; (jtly) The Internet, Law and Society, 2000; The Anti-Terrorism Legislation, 2002, 3rd edn 2014; (jtly) The Right to Speak Ill: defamation, reputation and free speech, 2006; (with J. Broderick) The Civil Contingencies Act 2004: risk, resilience and the law in the United Kingdom, 2006; Terrorism and the Law, 2011; (with R. L. Weaver) Free Speech in an Internet Era, 2013; (ed with C. King) Dirty Assets: emerging issues in the regulation of criminal and terrorist assets, 2014; (ed) Contingencies, Resilience and Legal Constitutionalism, 2015; (ed with G. Lennon) Routledge Handbook of Law and Terrorism, 2015; (ed jtly) The Palgrave Handbook of Criminal and Terrorism Financing Law, 2018; contrib. chapters in books and papers to learned jls. *Address:* School of Law, University of Leeds, Leeds LS2 9JT. *T:* (0113) 343 5033. *E:* law6cw@leeds.ac.uk.

**WALKER, Sir David (Alan)**, Kt 1991; Chairman: Barclays Bank PLC, 2012–15; Winton Capital, 2015–19; SETL, since 2016; *b* 31 Dec. 1939; *m* 1963, Isobel Cooper (*d* 2018); one *s* two *d. Educ:* Chesterfield Sch.; Queens' Coll., Cambridge (MA; Hon. Fellow, 1989). Joined HM Treasury, 1961; Private Sec. to Joint Permanent Secretary, 1964–66; seconded to Staff of International Monetary Fund, Washington, 1970–73; Asst Secretary, HM Treasury, 1973–77; joined Bank of England as Chief Adviser, then Chief of Economic Intelligence Dept, 1977; a Dir, 1981–93 (non-exec., 1988–93); Chairman: Johnson Matthey Bankers, later Minories Finance, 1985–88; SIB, 1988–92; Agricl Mortgage Corp., 1993–94; Dep. Chm., Lloyds Bank plc, 1992–94; Dir, Morgan Stanley Inc., 1994–97; Exec. Chm., Morgan Stanley Gp (Europe) plc, subseq. Morgan Stanley Dean Witter (Europe) Ltd, 1994–2000; Chm., Morgan Stanley Internat. Inc., 1995–2000; Mem., Mgt Bd, Morgan Stanley Dean Witter, 1997–2000; Sen. Advr, 2001–04, 2006–12, Exec. Chm., 2004–05, Morgan Stanley Internat. Ltd, later plc. Chairman: Steering Gp, Financial Markets Gp, LSE, 1998–; Review of Disclosure and Transparency in Private Equity, 2007; Review of Corporate Governance in UK Banks and Other Financial Instns, 2009. Bd Mem., CEGB, 1987–89; Chm., RVC Greenhouse Fund, 1999–; non-executive Director: National Power, 1990, 1993–94; British Invisibles, 1993–97; Reuters Holdings, 1994–2000; Legal & General Assce Co., 2002–11 (Vice-Chm., 2004–11). Mem., 1993–, Treas., 1998–, and Trustee, 2007–, The Group of Thirty. Chairman: London Investment Bankers' Assoc., 2002–04; Moroccan British Business Council, 2000–07. Nominated Mem., Council of Lloyd's, 1988–92 (Chm., Inquiry into LMX Spiral, 1992). Co. Chm., Univ. of Cambridge 800th Anniversary Campaign, 2005–11. Governor, Henley Management Coll., 1993–99. Chm., Community Links, East End charity, 1995–2011. Hon. FKC 2008. FRSA 1987; CCMI (CBIM 1986). Hon. LLD Exeter, 2002. *Recreations:* music, long-distance walking. *Clubs:* Garrick, Walbrook.

**WALKER, Air Marshal Sir David (Allan)**, KCVO 2011 (MVO 1992); OBE 1995; DL; non-executive Director, Alexander Mann Solutions, since 2015; an Extra Equerry to the Queen, since 2005; *b* 14 July 1956; *s* of late Allan Walker and Audrey Walker (*née* Brothwell); *m* 1983, Jane Alison Fraser Calder. *Educ:* City of London Sch.; Univ. of Bradford (BSc). RAF univ. cadet, 1974; RAF Coll., 1977–78; Equerry to the Queen, 1989–92; Loan Service, S Africa, 1994; Comd, RAF Halton, 1997–98; Director: Corporate Communication (RAF), 1998–2002; Personnel and Trng Policy (RAF), 2002–03; AOC RAF Trng Gp and Chief Exec., Trng Gp Defence Agency, 2003–04; retd in rank of Air Marshal, 2011. Senior Adviser: HSBC Gp Hldgs, 2013–14; Barclays Bank plc, 2014–15; PwC, 2014–18; Dir, Strategic Difference Ltd, 2014–17; Mem., Adv. Bd, Auticon, 2017–. Master of HM Household, 2005–13. Vice-Patron, Royal Internat. Air Tattoo, 2014; Vice Pres., 2005–12). Hon. President: London Wing, ATC, 2012–17; Montrose Air Heritage Centre, 2015–. Hon. Air Cdre 603 (City of Edinburgh) Sqn, RAuxAF, 2015–. Trustee, Savoy Educnl Trust, 2013–18. DL Glos, 2015. Hon. DLitt W London, 2014. *Recreations:* walking dogs, keeping fit(ish), old cars, shooting, military history. *Address:* Alexander Mann Solutions, 7–11 Bishopsgate, EC2N 3AQ. *Clubs:* Brooks's, Royal Air Force (Vice Pres., 2011–17; Pres., 2017–).

**WALKER, David Critchlow**, CMG 1993; CVO 1988 (MVO 1976); HM Diplomatic Service, retired; Chairman, Impact UK, since 2003; *b* 9 Jan. 1940; *s* of John Walker and Mary Walker (*née* Cross); *m* 1965, Tineke van der Leek; three *s. Educ:* Manchester Grammar Sch.; St Catharine's Coll., Cambridge (BA, MA, DipEd). Assistant Lecturer, Dept of Geography, Manchester Univ., 1962; Commonwealth Relations Office, 1963; Third Secretary, British Embassy, Mexico City, 1965; Second Secretary, Brussels, 1968; First Secretary: FCO, 1970; Washington, 1973; First Sec., later Counsellor, FCO, 1978–83; Consul General, São Paulo, 1983–86; Minister, Madrid, 1986–89; Counsellor, FCO, 1989–92; High Comr, Ghana, and non-resident Ambassador, Togo, 1992–96; High Comr, Bangladesh, 1996–99. *Address:* 7 The Crescent, Thirsk YO7 1DE.

**WALKER, David Frederick**; Contributing Editor, Guardian Public, since 2010 (Founding Editor, 2004–08); Chair, Oxford Health NHS Foundation Trust, since 2019; *b* Aberdeen, 8 Nov. 1950; *s* of John and Irene Walker; *m* 1974, Karen Irving (marr. diss. 1995); one *s. Educ:* Corby Grammar Sch.; St Catharine's Coll., Cambridge (BA); Univ. of Sussex (MA); Ecole Pratique des Hautes Etudes. Trainee, 1974–76, Chief Reporter, 1976, THES; Harkness Fellow, US Congress, Univ. of Calif, Berkeley, 1977; writer, Economist, 1979–81; Local Govt corresp., Leader Writer, then Whitehall corresp., The Times, 1981–87; Chief Leader Writer, London Daily News, 1987–88; presenter, Analysis prog., BBC Radio 4, 1988–93; Urban Affairs corresp., BBC, 1993–96; Chief Leader Writer, Independent, 1996–98; Analysis Ed. and Leader Writer, Guardian, 1998–2004; Man. Dir, Communications and Public Reporting, Audit Commn, 2008–10; Hd of Policy, Acad. of Social Scis, 2014–16. Member: ESRC, 2007–13; Ethics and Governance Council, UK Biobank, 2014–18. Non-executive Director: Places for People, 1999–2004; Central and NW London NHS Foundn Trust, 2011–19 (Dep. Chm., 2016–19). Mem. Council, Royal Holloway, Univ. of London, 2019–. Trustee: Nat. Centre for Social Res., 2001–08; Nuffield Trust, 2005–08; Franco-British Council, 2008–16. *Publications:* (with J. Tunstall)

Media Made in California, 1981; Municipal Empire, 1983; (jtly) Sources Close to the Prime Minister, 1984; Public Relations in Local Government, 1998; (with Polly Toynbee): Did Things Get Better?, 2001; Better or Worse, 2005; Unjust Rewards, 2009; The Verdict, 2010; Cameron's Coup: how the Tories took Britain to the brink, 2015; Exaggerated Claims: the ESRC after 50 years, 2016; Dismembered: how the attack on the state harms us all, 2017. *Recreations:* tennis, woodwind. *Address:* 2 Eton College Road, NW3 2BS. *E:* davidwlkr0@gmail.com. *W:* www.twitter.com/Exauditor77. *Clubs:* Reform; Wood Vale Tennis.

**WALKER, David Ralph,** FFPH; Medical Director, University Hospitals of Morecambe Bay Foundation Trust, since 2015; *b* 28 Oct. 1962; *s* of David and Ada Walker; *m* 1995, Elisabeth Ann Martin; two *d*. *Educ:* Nottingham High Sch.; Univ. of Newcastle upon Tyne Med. Sch. (BMedSci 1986; MB BS 1987; MSc 1994). MRCP 1991; MFPHM 1995, FFPH 2006. Trng posts in medicine and public health, Newcastle upon Tyne, 1987–94; Vis. Scientist, Centers for Disease Control, Atlanta, Ga, 1994–95; Consultant in Communicable Disease Control and Dep. Dir of Public Health, Co. Durham and Darlington HA, 1996–2001; Actg Dir of Public Health, Newcastle and N Tyneside HA, 2001–02; Dir of Public Health and Med. Dir, Co. Durham and Tees Valley Strategic HA, 2002–06; Actg Regl Dir of Public Health for NE of England, 2005–06; Regional Director of Public Health: E Midlands, 2006–11; NHS Midlands and East, 2011–13; Dep. CMO for England, 2013–15. Vis. Prof. of Public Health, Univ. of Lincoln, 2010–17. Chair, UK Nat. Screening Cttee, 2013–16. *Publications:* articles in med. jls. *Recreations:* ski-ing, boogie-woogie piano playing. *Address:* University Hospitals of Morecambe Bay Foundation Trust, Westmorland General Hospital, Burton Road, Kendal, Cumbria LA9 7RG.

**WALKER, Rt Rev. David Stuart;** *see* Manchester, Bishop of.

**WALKER, Maj.-Gen. Derek William Rothwell;** Manager, CBI Overseas Scholarships, 1980–89, retired; *b* 12 Dec. 1924; *s* of Frederick and Eileen Walker; *m* 1950, Florence Margaret Panting; two *s* (and one *s* decd). *Educ:* Mitcham County Grammar Sch.; Battersea Polytechnic. FIMechE 1970–89; FIEE 1971–89. Commissioned REME, 1946; served: Middle East, 1947–50 (despatches 1949); BAOR, 1951–53; Far East, 1954–56 (despatches 1957); Near East, 1960–62; Far East, 1964–67; psc 1957. Lt-Col 1964, Col 1970, Brig. 1973. Appts include: Comdr, REME Support Group, 1976–77; Dir, Equipment Engineering, 1977–79. Mem. Council, IEE, 1975–79; Pres., SEE, 1979–81. *Recreations:* fishing, sailing, wine-making. *Address:* 20 Moor Lane, Strensall, York YO32 5UQ.

**WALKER, Rt Rev. Dominic Edward William Murray,** OGS; DL; Bishop of Monmouth, 2003–13; an Hon. Assistant Bishop, Diocese of Swansea and Brecon, since 2013, Diocese of Llandaff, since 2018, and Diocese of Monmouth, since 2019; *b* 28 June 1948; *s* of Horace John and Mary Louise Walker. *Educ:* Plymouth Coll.; King's Coll. London (AKC); Heythrop Coll., London (MA); Univ. of Wales (LLM). Ordained priest, 1972; Asst Curate, St Faith, Wandsworth, 1972–73; Domestic Chaplain to the Bishop of Southwark, 1973–76; Rector, Newington, 1976–85; Rural Dean, Southwark and Newington, 1980–85; Vicar, Team Rector, and Rural Dean of Brighton, 1985–97; Canon and Prebendary, Chichester Cathedral, 1985–97; Area Bishop of Reading, 1997–2003. Mem., CGA, 1967–83; Mem., OGS, 1983– (Superior, 1990–96). Vice-Pres., 2001–10, Hon. Vice-Pres., 2010–, RSPCA; Pres., Anglican Soc. for Welfare of Animals, 2008–. Governor: Univ. of Wales Newport, 2003–10; St Michael's Coll., Llandaff, 2003–13. DL Gwent, 2014. Hon. DLitt Brighton, 1998. *Publications:* The Ministry of Deliverance, 1997. *Address:* 2 St Vincent's Drive, Monmouth NP25 5DS.

**WALKER, Prof. Donald,** FRS 1985; Professor of Biogeography, Institute of Advanced Studies, Australian National University, Canberra, 1969–88; *b* 14 May 1928; *s* of Arthur Walker and Eva (*née* Risdon); *m* 1959, Patricia Mary Smith (*d* 2013); two *d*. *Educ:* Morecambe Grammar School; Sheffield Univ. (BSc); MA, PhD Cantab. Commission, RAF (Nat. Service), 1953–55. Research Scholar and Asst in Res., later Sen. Asst, Sub-Dept of Quaternary Res., Cambridge Univ., 1949–60; Fellow of Clare College, 1952–60 (Asst Tutor, 1955–60); Reader in Biogeography, ANU, 1960–68; Head of Dept of Biogeography and Geomorphology, ANU, 1969–88. Hon. Prof., Chinese Acad. of Science, 1986–. *Publications:* articles on plant ecology, palaeoecology and related topics in sci. jls. *Recreations:* pottery, architecture, prehistory.

**WALKER, Elizabeth Mary; Her Honour Judge Walker;** a Circuit Judge, since 2019; *b* Leamington Spa, 11 March 1972; *d* of Raymond and Judith Stanton; partner, Christopher Adams; two *c*. *Educ:* King's High Sch. for Girls, Warwick; Durham Univ. (BA Hons Law). Called to the Bar, Gray's Inn, 1994; in practice as a barrister, St Paul's Chambers, Birmingham, 1994–2019. *Recreations:* theatre, opera, travel, cookery, snooker. *Address:* Wolverhampton Combined Court, Pipers Row, Wolverhampton WV1 3LQ.

**WALKER, George Robert,** OBE 1992; Director-General, International Baccalaureate Organisation, 1999–2006; *b* 25 Jan. 1942; *s* of William Walker and Celia Walker (*née* Dean); *m* 1968, Jennifer Anne Hill; one *s* one *d*. *Educ:* Watford Boys' Grammar Sch.; Exeter Coll., Oxford (MA, MSc); Univ. of Cape Town (LRSM). Science teacher, Watford Grammar Sch., 1966–68; Salters' Inst. Schol., 1968–69; Lectr in Educn, Univ. of York, 1969–73; Dep. Headmaster, Carisbrooke High Sch., 1973–76; Headmaster: Heathcote Sch., Stevenage, 1977–81; Cavendish Sch., Hemel Hempstead, 1981–91; Dir-Gen., Internat. Sch. of Geneva, 1991–99. Chm., Centre for Study of Comprehensive Schs, 1980–85. Member: HMC, 1982–99; Nat. Curriculum Sci. Working Gp, 1987–88. Educn Advr to ICI plc, 1990–91. Hon. Sen. Vis. Fellow, Univ. of York, 1988–91; Vis. Prof., Univ. of Bath, 1997–2009. Mem. Council, Univ. of York, 2002–05. Hon. DEd Bath, 2003. *Publications:* (jtly) Modern Physical Chemistry, 1981, 3rd edn 1986; Comprehensive Themes, 1983; (ed jtly) International Education in Practice, 2002; To Educate the Nations, 2002; To Educate the Nations 2, 2004; International Education and the International Baccalaureate, 2004; Educating the Global Citizen, 2006; An A to Z of School Leadership, 2007; M. T. Maurette: pioneer of international education, 2009; Challenges from a New World, 2010; (ed) The Changing Face of International Education, 2011; Glimpses of Utopia, 2013; Oxford and the Wills of Cecil Rhodes, 2016; (ed jtly) The International Baccalaureate: 50 years, 2018. *Recreation:* classical music. *Address:* 5 Elwes Close, Stoke by Clare, Suffolk CO10 8FF.

**WALKER, Gordon;** *see* Walker, T. G.

**WALKER, Prof. Greg,** PhD; FRHistS, FEA; FRSE; Regius Professor of Rhetoric and English Literature, University of Edinburgh, since 2010; *b* Coventry, 8 Sept. 1959; *s* of Arthur Walker and Hilda Walker; *m* 1985, Sharon Joynt; two *c*. *Educ:* Horndean Sch.; Univ. of Southampton (BA English and Hist.; PhD 1986). British Acad. Postdoctoral Fellow, Univ. of Southampton, 1986–89; Lecturer: in English Lit., Univ. of Queensland, 1989–90; Univ. of Buckingham, 1991; University of Leicester: Lectr, 1991–95; Reader, 1995–98; Prof. of English, 1998–2007; Masson Prof. of English Lit., Univ. of Edinburgh, 2007–10. Mem., AHRC, 2011–. FRHistS 1988; FEA 2002; FSA 2011; FRSE 2017. *Publications:* John Skelton and the Politics of the 1520s, 1988; Plays of Persuasion, 1991; Persuasive Fictions, 1996; The Politics of Performance in Early Renaissance Drama, 1998; (ed) Medieval Drama: an anthology, 2000; Alexander Korda's Private Life of Henry VIII, 2003; Writing under Tyranny, 2007; (with E. M. Treharne) The Oxford Handbook of Medieval Literature in English, 2010; (with Thomas Betteridge) The Oxford Handbook of Tudor Drama, 2012; Reading Literature Historically, 2013; (ed) The Oxford Anthology of Tudor Drama, 2014; (with J. J. McGavin) Imagining Spectatorship, 2016. *Recreations:* supporting Nottingham Forest FC; progressive rock music, dog walking, light irony. *Address:* English Department, University of Edinburgh, 50 George Square, Edinburgh EH8 9LH. *T:* (0131) 650 3049. *E:* greg.walker@ed.ac.uk.

**WALKER, Sir Harold (Berners),** KCMG 1991 (CMG 1979); HM Diplomatic Service, retired; *b* 19 Oct. 1932; *s* of late Admiral Sir Harold Walker, KCB, RN, and Lady Walker (*née* Berners); *m* 1st, 1960, Jane Bittleston (marr. diss.); one *s* two *d*; 2nd, 2004, Anne Savage (*née* Gourlay). *Educ:* Winchester; Worcester Coll., Oxford (BA 1955; MA). 2nd Lieut RE, 1951–52. Foreign Office, 1955; MECAS, 1957; Asst Political Agent, Dubai, 1958; Foreign Office, 1960; Principal Instructor, MECAS, 1963; First Sec., Cairo, 1964; Head of Chancery and Consul, Damascus, 1966; Foreign Office (later FCO), 1967; First Sec. (Commercial), Washington, 1970; Counsellor, Jedda, 1973; Dep. Head, Personnel Operations Dept, FCO, 1975–76, Head of Dept, 1976–78; Corpus Christi Coll., Cambridge, 1978; Ambassador to Bahrein, 1979–81, to United Arab Emirates, 1981–86, to Ethiopia, 1986–90, to Iraq, 1990–91; retd 1992. Member: Commonwealth War Graves Commn, 1992–97; Bd, CARE International UK, 1992–2001 (Chm., 1994–97); Pres., CARE Internat., 1997–2001; Chm., RSAA, 2001–08. President: Friends of Imperial War Mus., 1992–97; British Soc. for Middle Eastern Studies, 2006–10. Chm., Bahrain Soc., 1993–99. Mem. of Corp., Woking Sixth Form Coll., 1996–99. Trustee, Next Century Foundn, 2012–14. Chm., Blythe Sappers, 2013. Associate Fellow, RUSI, 1992–97. *Address:* 45 St Leonards Road, SW14 7LY. *E:* walker.turaco@btinternet.com. *Club:* Oxford and Cambridge.

**WALKER, Helen Mary;** Chief Executive, Carers UK, since 2018; *b* Shrewsbury, 12 April 1969; *d* of Roy and Joan Walker. *Educ:* London Sch. of Econs and Pol Sci. (BA Hons Geog. 1990; MPhil 1996). Briefing Officer, SOAS, 1995–2000; Hd of Fundraising, Hospitality Action, 2000–02; Dir, Fundraising, SSAFA, 2002–08; Chief Exec., TimeBank, 2008–18. FRSA. *Recreations:* volunteer mentor and trustee, football, walking, dogs, theatre. *Address:* Carers UK, 20 Great Dover Street, SE1 4LX. *T:* (020) 7378 4933. *E:* helen.walker@carersuk.org.

**WALKER, Iain;** HM Diplomatic Service; High Commissioner to Ghana and non-resident Ambassador to Benin, Burkina Faso and Togo, since 2017; *b* Dundee, 6 Dec. 1976; *s* of Alfred Walker and Mabel Walker; *m* 2007, Claire; two *s* one *d*. *Educ:* Univ. of Dundee (LLB Hons). ACA 2003. Ernst & Young; GOAL, 2002–04; DEFRA, 2004–08; Cabinet Office, 2006–08; PricewaterhouseCoopers, 2008–10; Dep. Finance Dir, 2010–12, Dir, Finance, 2012–17, FCO. Trustee, GOAL, 2004–12. *Recreations:* triathlon, golf, family. *Address:* Foreign and Commonwealth Office, King Charles Street, SW1A 2AH. *E:* iain.walker@fco.gov.uk.

**WALKER, Rev. Dr James Bernard;** Chaplain, 1993–2011, and Associate Director, Student Services, 2005–11 (Assistant Director, 1998–2005), St Andrews University; *s* of Rev. Dr Robert B. W. Walker and Grace B. Walker; *m* 1972, Sheila; three *s*. *Educ:* Hamilton Academy, Lanarkshire; Edinburgh Univ. (MA 1st cl. Hons Mental Philosophy 1968; BD 1st cl. Hons Systematic Theol. 1971); Merton Coll., Oxford (DPhil 1981). Church of Scotland minister, ordained 1975, Dundee; Associate Minister, Mid Craigie Parish Church linked with Wallacetown Parish Church, Dundee, 1975–78; Minister, Old and St Paul's Parish Church, Galashiels, 1978–87; Principal, Queen's Coll., Birmingham, 1987–93. Chm., St Andrews Town Commn on Housing, 2012–13 (report, Housing Need and Housing Pressures in St Andrews, 2013). *Publications:* Israel—Covenant and Land, 1986; (contrib.) Politique et Théologie chez Athanase d'Alexandrie (ed C. Kannengiesser), 1974; (contrib.) God, Family and Sexuality (ed D. W. Torrance), 1997. *Recreations:* golf, tennis, swimming, hill walking. *Address:* St Andrews.

**WALKER, Prof. James Johnston,** MD; FRCPSGlas, FRCPEd, FRCOG; Professor of Obstetrics and Gynaecology, University of Leeds, since 1994; *b* 17 March 1952; *s* of James and Catherine Walker; *m* 1976, Ann Mary Young; two *d*. *Educ:* High Sch. of Dundee; Univ. of Glasgow (MB ChB 1976; MD 1992). MRCOG 1981, FRCOG 1994; MRCP 1981; FRCPSGlas 1991; FRCPEd 1994. Jun. doctor, Obstetrics and Gynaecol., Glasgow, 1976–83; University of Glasgow: Res. Fellow in Obstetrics and Gynaecol., 1983–84; Lectr in Obstetrics and Gynaecol., 1984–87; Sen. Lectr, 1987–93; Reader, 1993. Clin. Advr (Obstetrics) to Nat. Patient Agency, 2003–11; Nat. Professional Advr (Maternity), Care Quality Commn, 2016. Member: Morecambe Bay Enquiry, 2014; Nat. Maternity Rev., 2015. Chm., Centre for Maternal and Child Enquiries, 2009–11. Sen. Vice Pres., RCOG, 2010–13. *Publications:* (with N. F. Gant) Hypertension in Pregnancy, 1997; (jtly) Problem-based Obstetrics and Gynaecology, 2003; (jtly) Pre-eclampsia, 2003; over 250 peer-reviewed articles in Obstetrics and Gynaecol. *Recreations:* travelling, cooking, swimming. *Address:* 12 Shire Oak Road, Headingley, Leeds LS6 2DE. *T:* (0113) 278 9599, *Fax:* (0113) 234 3450. *E:* j.j.walker@leeds.ac.uk. *Club:* Royal Society of Medicine.

**WALKER, Jane Helen;** *see* Darbyshire, J. H.

**WALKER, Janet Sheila;** Bursar, Eton College, since 2011; *b* Felton, 21 April 1953; *d* of David Walker and Sheila Walker (*née* Rapps); *m* 2017, Peter Corbett. *Educ:* Somerville Coll., Oxford (BA 1st Cl. PPE 1975); Institut des Hautes Études Internationales, Nice (Dip.). ACA 1979. Price Waterhouse, 1976–79; Chief Accountant, Handmade Films, 1980–81; Cost Controller, Channel 4, 1981–82; Hd, Programme Finance, Thames TV, 1982–84; London Films and Limehouse, 1984–87; Financial Dir, British Screen Finance, 1987–88; UK Rep., EURIMAGES Film Funding Orgn, 1987–88; Dep. Dir, Finance, Channel 4, 1988–94; Financial Controller for Regl Broadcasting, BBC, 1994–96; Financial Dir, Granada Media Gp, 1996–98; Dir, Finance and Business Affairs, Channel 4 Television, 1998–2003; Commercial and Finance Dir, Ascot Racecourse, 2003–10. Non-executive Director: Pizza Express plc, 1999–2003; Henderson High Income Trust plc, 2007–19. Mem., Design Council, 2006–10. Mem. Bd, Young Vic Th., 1997–2005. Mem. Council, Royal Holloway, Univ. of London, 2009–10. Mem., Audit Cttee, RHS, 2017–. Trustee, BAFTA, 2013–15. *Recreations:* walking, gardening, travel, reading. *Address:* Eton College, Windsor SL4 6DJ.

**WALKER, Janey Patricia Winifred, (Mrs H. F. Mykura);** Member, Content Board, Ofcom, since 2011; *b* 10 April 1958; *d* of Brig. Harry Walker and Patricia Walker; *m* 1997, Hamish Finlayson Mykura, *qv*; twin *d*. *Educ:* Brechin High Sch.; Benenden Sch.; York Univ. (BA Hist./Politics); Univ. of Chicago (Benton Fellow); London Business Sch. (Sen. Exec. Prog.). BBC News and Current Affairs, 1983–89; The Late Show, BBC, 1990–94; Editor, Edge prog., WNET, and dir, BBC NY, 1994–95; Wall to Wall TV, London, 1995–96; Channel 4 Television: Commng Ed. Arts, 1996–99; Man. Ed. Commng, 1999–2010; Hd of Educn, 2006–10; Dir, Internat. Gateway for Gifted Youth (IGGY), Univ. of Warwick, 2011–13; Man. Dir, Indie Trng Fund, 2014–16. Dep. Chair, Bd of Govs, Univ. of Brighton, 2014– (Acting Chair, 2018); Trustee, Univ. of Brighton Academies Trust, 2015–. *Recreations:* walking, art, keeping chickens.

**WALKER, Jeremy Colin Maclaren**; Chair, Your Climate, 2012–16; Member, North York Moors National Park Authority, since 2013; b 12 July 1949; m 1968, Patricia June Lockhart; two s one d. Educ: Brentwood Sch., Essex; Univ. of Birmingham (BA 1971). Dept of Employment, 1971–73; Pvte Sec. to Chm., MSC, 1974–75; HSE, 1975–76; Econ. Secretariat, Cabinet Office, 1976–78; MSC, 1978–82; Exchange Officer, Australian Dept of Employment and Industrial Relations, 1982–84; Manpower Services Commission: Regl Employment Manager, 1984–86; Hd, Community Prog. and New Job Trng Scheme, 1986–88; Regl Dir, Yorks and Humberside, Trng Agency and Dept of Employment, 1988–94; Regl Dir, Govt Office for Yorks and the Humber, 1994–99; Chief Exec., N Yorks CC, 1999–2005. Chairman: Yorks Regl Flood Defence Cttee, 2005–09; Adv. Cttee for Yorks and the Humber, Forestry Commn, 2007–13; Slowing the Flow Partnership, 2008–18; Yorks Derwent Partnership, 2016–18; Mem., Yorks Flood and Coastal Cttee, 2016–. Mem. Bd, Envmt Agency, 2009–15. Member: Bd, Yorks and Humberside Arts, 1994–99; N Yorks TEC, 1999–2001; Court, Univ. of York, 2001–18; Court, Univ. of Leeds, 2002–11 (Mem. Council, 1992–2000); Nat. Employment Panel, 2002–05. Trustee: W Yorks Police Community Trust, 1996–99; York and N Yorks Community Trust, 2000–04. Recreations: walking, family, gardening.

**WALKER, John**; see Walker, N. J.

**WALKER, John Eric Austin**; see Austin, J. E.

**WALKER, Sir John (Ernest)**, Kt 1999; DPhil; FRS 1995; Founding Director, MRC Mitochondrial Biology (formerly MRC Dunn Human Nutrition) Unit, Cambridge, 1998–2012, now Director Emeritus; Fellow, Sidney Sussex College, since 1997, and Professor of Molecular Bioenergetics, since 2002, University of Cambridge; b Halifax, Yorks, 7 Jan. 1941; s of late Thomas Ernest Walker and Elsie (née Lawton); m 1963, Christina Jane Westcott; two d. Educ: Rastrick Grammar Sch., W Yorks; St Catherine's Coll., Oxford (BA Chem.; DPhil 1969; Hon. Fellow, 1998). Research Fellow, Univ. of Wisconsin, 1969–71; NATO Res. Fellow, CNRS, Gif-sur-Yvette, France, 1971–72; EMBO Res. Fellow, Pasteur Inst., Paris, 1972–74; Staff Scientist, MRC Lab. of Molecular Biol., Cambridge, 1974–98. Mem., EMBO, 1983. Smith-Kline Beecham Vis. Prof. to USA, Royal Soc. of Med. Foundn, 1995; Hon. Prof., Peking Union Med. Coll., Beijing, 2001–; Lee Kong Chian Dist. Prof., Nanyang Technol Univ., Singapore, 2010; Vis. Prof., Dept of Life Scis, Imperial Coll. London, 2013. Hon. Member: Biochem. Soc., 1998; British Biophysical Soc., 2000. Foreign Member: Royal Netherlands Acad. of Arts and Scis, 1999; l'Accademia Nazionale dei Lincei, Rome, 2003–; For. Associate, NAS, 2004–; Hon. Gentle Scientist, Mitochondrial Physiology Soc., Austria, 2012. Millennium Fellow, RSC 2000; Fellow, Science Mus., London, 2009. Hon. FRSB (FIBiol 2002); Hon. FMedSci 2013 (Founder FMedSci 1998); Hon. FRS NZ 2013. MAE 1998. Hon. DSc: Bradford, 1998; Buenos Aires, 1998; Huddersfield, 1998; UMIST, 1999; Oxon, 1999; Groningen, 1999; Leeds, 1999; London, 2002; Sussex, 2003; Liverpool, 2004; UEA, 2006; Moscow State, 2007; Toyo, Japan, 2007; Paul Sabatier, France, 2007; KIIT, Bhubaneswar, India, 2015. Johnson Foundn Prize, Univ. of Pennsylvania, 1994; Ciba Medal and Prize, Biochem. Soc., 1995; Peter Mitchell Medal, European Bioenergetics Conf., 1996; Gaetano Quagliariello Prize for Mitochondrial Res., Univ. of Bari, 1997; Nobel Prize for Chemistry, 1997; Messel Medal, SCI, 2000; RSC Award for Biomembrane Chemistry, 2003; Lifetime Achievement Award, GeneExpression Systems Inc., Massachusetts, 2008; Ahmed Zewail Medal, Wayne State Univ., Detroit, 2010; Skou Award, Aarhus Univ., 2011; Keilin Meml Medal (and Lect.), Biochem. Soc., 2011; Gold Seal, Univ. of Bari Aldo Moro, 2011; Copley Medal, Royal Soc., 2012. Publications: research papers and reviews in scientific jls. Recreations: cricket, opera music, walking. Address: MRC Mitochondrial Biology Unit, Wellcome-MRC Building, Cambridge Biomedical Campus, University of Cambridge, Hills Road, Cambridge CB2 0XY. T: (01223) 252701, Fax: (01223) 252705.

**WALKER, John Robert**, CBE 2009; company director; b E Rainton, 3 Nov. 1946; s of John and Alice Walker; m 1990, Patricia Anne Henderson; one d and one d from previous marriage. Educ: Houghton Grammar Sch. CPFA 1969. Jun. Accountancy Asst, Hetton UDC, 1964–69; Accountancy Asst, Houghton UDC, 1969–70; Sen. Auditor, Sunderland CBC, 1970–73; Tyne and Wear County Council, 1973–85: Gp Auditor; Principal Audit/Technical Asst; Sen. Gp Accountant; Chief Accountant; Asst County Treas.; Chief Finance Officer, Northumbria Police, 1985–87; Finance Dir, Teesside Develt Corp., 1987–90; Mgt Consultant, Stoy Hayward, 1990–94; English Partnerships: Chief Accountant, 1994–96; Dir, Finance and Commercial Services, 1996–98; Finance and Admin Dir, 1998–2007; Regl Dir for NE, Yorks and E Midlands, 2003–04; Chief Operating Officer, 2004–07; Chief Exec., 2007–08. Comr for English Heritage, 2010–14. Non-executive Director: Esh Hldgs, 2009–17; Wynyard Park Develts, 2009; Gentoo Gp, 2009–16. Recreations: walking, cycling. Address: Drift House, North Street, West Rainton, Houghton Le Spring, Tyne and Wear DH4 6NU. T: (0191) 584 5452. E: johnrwalker@yahoo.com.

**WALKER, Julian Guy Hudsmith**, CB 1991; independent engineering consultant, since 1994; Director General, Policy and Special Projects, Ministry of Defence, 1992–94, retired; b 2 Oct. 1936; s of Nathaniel and Frieda Walker; m 1960, Margaret Burns (née Jamieson). Educ: Winchester College; Southampton Univ. (BSc Mech Eng). CEng, FIMechE. Hawker Aircraft Co., 1958–61; Logistic Vehicles, FVRDE, WO, subseq. MoD, 1961–69; Ministry of Defence: Special Projects, MVEE, 1970–80; Head, Vehicle Engrg Dept, 1980–84; Scientific Adviser (Land), 1984–87; Dir, Estabts and Research (B), 1987–89; Head, RARDE, Chertsey, 1989–92. Recreations: vintage cars, photography, wood-turning, Wombling, solving practical problems.

**WALKER, Linda, (Mrs P. B. Walker)**; see Sutcliffe, Linda.

**WALKER, Lorna Margaret S.**; see Secker-Walker.

**WALKER, Lorna Stuart**, CChem, FCIWEM; Director, Lorna Walker Consulting Ltd, since 2004; b 2 Jan. 1952; d of Eric and Anne Walker; m 1992, Gareth James Young. Educ: Univ. of Cape Town (BSc Chem. and Maths; MSc Civil Engrg). MRSC; CChem 1978; FCIWEM 1978; MCIWM 1993; CWEM 2012. Dir, Ove Arup & Partners Ltd, 1977–2004. Vis. Prof. of Engrg Design for Sustainable Develt, Univ. of Sheffield, 2003–. Mem., CABE, 2006–11. Mem., UK Urban Taskforce, 1997–. Comr, Infrastructure Planning Commn, 2010–12; Examining Inspector, Nat. Infrastructure Directorate, Planning Inspectorate, 2012–. Academician, Acad. of Urbanism, 2011. FRSA. Hon. DEng Sheffield, 2007. Publications: (contrib.) London's Environment: prospects for a sustainable world city, 2001; (contrib.) Manufactured Sites, 2005. Recreations: gardening, reading, travelling. Address: Lorna Walker Consulting Ltd, 5 Heathfield Road, SW18 3HX. T: 07789 768033. E: lwalker@lornawalker.co.uk.

**WALKER, Sir Malcolm (Conrad)**, Kt 2017; CBE 1995; Founder, Executive Chairman, since 2012, and Chief Executive, 2005–17, Iceland Foods Ltd; Chairman, Individual Restaurant Company, since 2011; b 11 Feb. 1946; s of Willie Walker and Ethel Mary Walker; m 1969, Nest Rhianydd; one s two d. Educ: Mirfield Grammar Sch. Trainee Manager, F. W. Woolworth & Co., 1964–71; Jt Founder, Iceland Frozen Foods, 1970; Chief Exec., 1973–2000, Chm., 1973–2001, Iceland Frozen Foods plc, subseq. Iceland Gp plc; Founder and CEO, Cooltrader Ltd, 2001–06. Non-exec. Dir, DFS Furniture Co. plc, 1993–2004. Recreations: ski-ing, sailing, shooting, business, home and family.

**WALKER, Marina F.**; see Frolova-Walker, M.

**WALKER, Martin John**; a District Judge (Magistrates' Courts), 2002–17; b 18 Sept. 1952; s of Eric and Olive Walker; m 1997, Rosalind Ann Jones; one d; one s one d from former marriage. Educ: Sheffield Univ. (LLB). Admitted solicitor, 1977; County Prosecutor; in practice as solicitor, Bakewell, 1981–2001. Recreations: boating, herbs.

**WALKER, Dr Michael John**; Founder, Chief Executive Officer and Director, Pomegranate Education Ltd, since 2015; Headmaster, Felsted School, 2008–15; b 24 Nov. 1955; s of Stephen Thomas Walker and Sheila Walker (née Ereaut); m 1st, 1977, Rita Bridget Carpenter (marr. diss. 2004); one s two d; 2nd, 2007, Corinne Anne Francis (marr. diss. 2014); 3rd, 2016, Maria Elena Munoz. Educ: Corpus Christi Coll., Cambridge (BA Hons Hist. 1977; CertEd 1979; MA 1980; PhD 1985). Asst Prof. of History, Birmingham-Southern Coll., Birmingham, Alabama, 1977–78; Asst Master, Dulwich Coll., 1982–86; Hd of History, Gresham's Sch., Norfolk, 1986–89; King Edward VI Grammar School, Chelmsford: Sen. Teacher, 1989–90; Dep. Head (Middle Sch.), 1990–92; Dep. Head (Sixth Form), 1992–99; Headmaster, 1999–2008. Member: Leading Edge Prog. Nat. Steering Gp, 2003–05; Forum for Learning and Res. Enquiry in Essex, 2003–05; Evaluation and Knowledge Transfer Wkg Gps, 2003–04; working with DfES Innovations Unit: leading Nat. Heads' Gp, 2004–07; leading Next Practice project on Higher Order Teaching Skills, 2005–06; Mem., Steering Gp, ARIA Project (UK-wide Assessment Reform Gp on evaluation of assessment develt projects), 2006–08. Mem., HMC, 2008–15. Dir, London Academies and Enterprise Trust, 2012–14; Chm. and Dir, Renewable Educn Ltd, 2016–; Dir of Educn UK, Kaiwen Educn, 2018–. Vice-Pres., Helen Rollason Cancer Care Trust, 2001–. Mem., World Bd, and Dir, Eur. Reg., Round Square, 2013–15 (Mem., 2009–15; Dep. Dir, 2012–13); Trustee: Friends of Round Square, 2012–19; Sparkle Malawi Charity, 2015–16; Greensward Charitable Trust, Acads Enterprise Trust Sponsor, 2015–17. Governor: Jack Petchey Acad., 2012–14; Sutton Valence Sch., 2012–16 (Internat. Coordinator, 2016–18). FRSA 2006. Recreations: family life, painting, drawing, tennis, squash, walking, travel, reading, theatre, gardening, restoration of historic buildings, village PCC and festival cttees. Clubs: East India; Essex.

**WALKER, Michael John**, CBE 2007; District Judge, 1994–2016, seconded to Office of the Senior Presiding Judge, Royal Courts of Justice, 2007–16; b 8 July 1951; s of late Albert George Walker and of Joan Walker; m 1st, 1974, Jill Sandham (marr. diss. 1980); one s; 2nd, 1982, Elaine G. Robinson; two d. Educ: Sir John Deane's Grammar Sch., Northwich, Cheshire; Univ. of Kent (BA Hons Law 1972); Law Soc. Finals Hons 1973. Articled clerk, 1973–75, Solicitor, 1975–78, Norton Rose; Solicitor, then Partner, Carpenter & Co., (Solicitors), Wallington, 1979–94. Member: Judges' Council, 2002–16; Bd, HM Courts Service, 2008–11; Bd, HM Courts and Tribunals Service, 2011–16. Hon. Sec., Assoc. of HM District Judges (formerly Assoc. of Dist Judges), 2000–11. Mem. Bd, Internat. Inst. for Justice Excellence, 2018–. Hon. Bencher, Gray's Inn, 2014. Gov., Wallington High Sch. for Girls, 1988–2017. Publications: Jordan's Civil Court Service, 3rd edn 2000 to 36th edn 2016; Blackstone's Civil Practice, (contrib.) 5th edn 2004 to 10th edn 2010, (consultant ed.) 11th edn 2011 to 19th edn 2019. Recreations: pottering around in the garden, listening to classical music and, in between times, enjoying food and wine and dreaming of Italy.

**WALKER, Sir Michael Leolin F.**; see Forestier-Walker.

**WALKER, Hon. Sir Miles Rawstron**, Kt 1997; CBE 1991; Chief Minister, Isle of Man, 1986–96; b 13 Nov. 1940; s of George Denis Walker and Alice (née Whittaker); m 1966, Mary Lilian Cowell; one s one d. Educ: Arbory Primary Sch.; Castle Rushen High Sch.; Shropshire Coll. of Agric. Company Dir, farming and retail dairy trade, 1960–. Mem. and Chm., Arbory Parish Comrs, 1970–76; Mem., House of Keys for Rushen, 1976–2001. Hon. LLD Liverpool, 1994. Address: Magher Feailley, Main Road, Colby, Isle of Man IM9 4AD. T: (01624) 833728.

**WALKER, Prof. Neil Craig**, PhD; FBA 2012; FRSE; Regius Professor of Public Law and the Law of Nature and Nations, University of Edinburgh, since 2008; b 5 July 1960; s of William Walker and Catherine Walker; m 1993, Gillian Couse; one s one d, and one s from former marriage. Educ: Univ. of Strathclyde (LLB 1st cl. 1981; PhD 1991). Lectr in Const. Law, 1986–92, Sen. Lectr, 1992–95, Univ. of Edinburgh; Prof. of Legal and Const. Theory, Univ. of Aberdeen, 1996–2000; Prof. of Eur. Law, European University Inst., Florence, 2000–08. Global Prof. of Law, New York Univ., 2011; Vis. Prof. of Law, Yale Univ., 2014; Franqui Internat. Chair, Leuven, 2017. FRSE 2011. Hon. LLD Uppsala, 2011. Publications: Managing the Police: law, organisation and democracy, 1986; The Scottish Community Charge, 1989; Policing the European Union, 1996; Policing in a Changing Constitutional Order, 2000; Civilizing Security, 2007; Intimation of Global Law, 2015; articles and collections on questions of constit. law and theory. Recreations: literature, sport, anything convivial. Address: School of Law, University of Edinburgh, Old College, South Bridge, Edinburgh EH8 9YL.

**WALKER, (Noel) John**; strategic development consultant; Managing Director, John Walker Consultants Ltd, since 1999; b 18 Dec. 1948; s of Robert and Nora Walker; m 1979, Pamela Gordon; two s. Educ: Liverpool Univ. (BSc 1970); Trent Polytechnic (DipTP 1972). Planning Officer, Hartlepool BC, 1972–74; Sen. Planner, Cleveland CC, 1974; travelled abroad, 1974–75; Milton Keynes Development Corporation: Employment Planner, 1975–76; Head of Policy Evaluation, 1976–78; Dep. Planning Manager, 1978–79; Planning Manager, 1979–80; Dir of Planning, 1980–87; Dep. Gen. Manager, 1987–92; Chief Exec., Commn for the New Towns, 1992–99; Dir, Competition for future use of Millennium Dome, 1999–2000; Chief Exec., BURA, 2000–02. Chairman: Bucks Manpower Cttee, 1982–83; Milton Keynes IT Exchange, 1983–86; Central Milton Keynes Project Bd, 2003–07; Milton Keynes and S Midlands Funding Gp, 2004–10; Eco Towns Challenge Gp, 2008; Whitehill and Bordon Ecotown Delivery Board, 2010–13; Planning and Infrastructure Gp, SE Midlands LEP, 2010–13. Founder Mem., Nat. Energy Foundn, 1988– (Trustee, 1999–2005; Chm., 2012–17; Pres., 2017–). Dep. Chm., Milton Keynes Housing Assoc., 1986–89; Board Member: Milton Keynes Marketing, 1992–93; Telford Develt Agency, 1992; Peterborough Develt Agency, 1992–94; Ind. Bd Mem., Milton Keynes Develt Partnership, 2013–18; Associate Dir, Garden City Develts CIC, 2014–. Chm., Green Gauge Trust, 2009–17; Trustee: Bletchley Park Trust, 2000–04; Milton Keynes Parks Trust, 2000–10; Milton Keynes Theatre and Gallery Co., 2002–08. Advr, ODPM, 2002–06; Develt Advr, TCPA, 2003–09. FRSA 1997. Hon. DArts De Montfort, 1998. Recreations: gardening, travelling, pottery, ski-ing. Address: Fullers Barn, The Green, Loughton, Milton Keynes MK5 8AW.

**WALKER, Sir Patrick (Jeremy)**, KCB 1990; *b* 25 Feb. 1932; *s* of late Reginald Plumer Walker, sometime Chief Accountant, East African Railways, and Gladys Walker; *m* 1955, Susan Mary Hastings; two *s* one *d*. *Educ*: King's Sch., Canterbury; Trinity Coll., Oxford (MA). Uganda Admin, 1956–62; Security Service, 1963–92, Dir Gen., 1988–92. Chm., Bd, N Northants Together, 2005–06; Dep. Chm., Bd, N Northants Develt Co., 2007–17 (Co-Chm., 2006–07). Member: Iraq Commn, Foreign Policy Centre, 2007; Council, Overseas Service Pensioners' Assoc., 2010–17. Trustee: Leonard Cheshire Foundn, 1994–2003 (Internat. Chm., 1995–2000; Vice Pres., 2003–); Northants Victoria County Records Trust, 2000–05. Gov., UC Northampton (formerly Nene Coll. of Higher Educn), 1997–2005 (Chm. Govs, 2000–05). Hon. Fellow, Univ. of Northampton, 2006. *Recreations*: music, African history, art. *Club*: MCC.

**WALKER, Paul Ashton**; non-executive Chairman: Perform Group plc; Halma plc, since 2013; Ashtead Group, since 2018; *b* 17 May 1957. *Educ*: Univ. of York (BA). ACA. With Arthur Youngs, 1979–84; joined Sage, 1984; Chief Executive: Sage Gp plc, 1994–2010; Sage Software Ltd. Chm., WANdisco, 2014–16; non-executive Director: Diageo plc, 2002; Experian plc, 2010–.

**WALKER, Dr Paul Crawford**; Regional Medical Officer, North East Thames Regional Health Authority, 1977–85; *b* 9 Dec. 1940; *s* of Joseph Viccars Walker, KHS, and Mary Tilley (*née* Crawford); *m* 1963, Barbara Georgina Bliss; three *d*. *Educ*: Queen Elizabeth Grammar Sch., Darlington; Downing Coll., Cambridge (MA); University College Hospital Med. Sch. (MB, BChir); Edinburgh Univ. (DipSocMed); Harvard Bus. Sch. (Program for Health Systems Management, 1980). FFPH (FFCM 1980). Dep. Medical Officer of Health and Dep. Principal Sch. MO, Wolverhampton County Borough Council, 1972–74; District Community Physician, Staffordshire AHA, 1974–76; Area MO, Wakefield AHA, 1976–77; Dist Gen. Manager, Frenchay HA, 1985–88; Hon. Consultant in Community Medicine, Bristol and Weston HA, 1988–89; Dir of Public Health, Norwich HA, 1989–93; Sen. Lectr in Applied Epidemiology, Univ. of Wales Coll. of Medicine, 1993–94; Dir of Public Health, Powys and Ceredigion Health Bds, 2003–05. Hon. Sen. Lectr, Dept of Community Medicine, LSHTM, 1983–85; Co-Dir, Centre for Health Policy Res., UEA, 1990–93; Vis. Prof., QMC, London Univ., 1985; Visiting Fellow: UWE, 1999–2003; Univ. of Glamorgan, 2004–09. Governor, Moorfields Eye Hosp., 1981–82; Vice-Chm., Professional Adv. Gp, NHS Trng Authy, 1986–88; Member: Bd of Management, LSHTM, 1983–85; Adv. Council on Drug Misuse, 1983–87; Exec. Cttee, Greater London Alcohol Adv. Service, 1978–85; NHS Computer Policy Cttee, 1984–85; Editl Bd, Jl of Management in Medicine, 1985–88; Norwich HA, 1989–93; Frenchay Mental Handicap Trust, 1986–88; Frenchay Mental Health Trust, 1986–88; Norwich and Norfolk Care Trust, 1991–93; Frenchay Community Care Trust, 1994–97; Peckham Pioneer Health Centre Ltd, 1994–96; Powys Local Health Alliance, 1999–2002; Ceredigion Local Health Gp, 2001–03. Chm., Welsh Food Alliance, 1998–2002; Director: S Bristol Advice Services, 1998–2000; Bristol Health Co-op., 1999–2000; Dir/Trustee, Lles Cymru Wellbeing Wales, 2010–. Chairman: Socialist Health Assoc., 2003–08; Transform Drug Policy Foundn, 2007–11; Sec., Public Health Assoc. Cymru, 1998–2004 (Chm., 2004–). Trustee, UK Public Health Assoc., 2006–10. Mem. (Lab), Bristol CC, 1995–99; Member: Avon and Som Police Authy, 1998–99; Avon Probation Cttee, 1997–99. JP Epping and Ongar, 1980–85. Captain, RAMC (V). Jt Editor, Health Matters and healthmatters website, 2008–. *Publications*: Healthy Norfolk People, 1990; (ed) Helping People with Disabilities in East Anglia, 1991; From Public Health to Wellbeing: the new driver for policy and action, 2011; contribs to medical and health service jls. *Recreations*: music, natural history, railway history. *E*: paulcrawfordwalker@googlemail.com.

**WALKER, Hon. Sir Paul (James)**, Kt 2004; a Judge of the High Court of Justice, Queen's Bench Division, 2004–19; a President, Upper Tribunal (Administrative Appeals Chamber), 2009–12; *b* Wellington, NZ, 1954; *s* of James Edgar Walker and Dawne Walker (*née* McGowan); *m* 1988, Josephine Andrews; one *d*. *Educ*: St Peter's Coll., Adelaide; Magdalen Coll., Oxford (BA Law, BCL). Called to the Bar, Gray's Inn, 1979, Bencher, 2005; barrister in private practice, 1980–2004; QC 1999. Sen. Lectr in Law, Victoria Univ. of Wellington, 1994–96; Dir, NZ Inst. Public Law, 1996. Counsel to BSE Inquiry, 1998–2000. Mem. Adv. Bd, British Inst. of Internat. and Comparative Law, 2001–. Vis. Fellow, Victoria Univ. of Wellington, 2013. Fellow: Arbitrators and Mediators Inst., NZ, 1994. Mem. Adv. Bd, NZ Jl of Public and Internat. Law, 2003–. Mem., Sci. Cttee, Jl de Droit Comparé du Pacifique, 2012–. *Publications*: (ed with S. Rogers) Studies in Insurance Law, 1996; (ed jtly) Commercial Regulation and Judicial Review, 1998; (ed jtly) Judicial Review, 3rd edn 2005.

**WALKER, His Honour Richard**; a Circuit Judge, 1989–2006; *b* 9 March 1942; *s* of Edwin Roland Walker and Barbara Joan (*née* Swann); *m* 1969, Angela Joan Hodgkinson; two *d*. *Educ*: Epsom Coll.; Worcester Coll., Oxford (MA). Called to the Bar, Inner Temple, 1966; in practice at the Bar, 1966–89; Asst Boundary Comr, 1979–88; a Recorder, 1989. Judicial Mem., Mental Health Review Tribunal, 1991–2005. Commissary Gen., City and Dio. of Canterbury, 1995–2011. *Publications*: (ed jtly) Carter-Ruck on Libel and Slander, 3rd edn 1985, 4th edn 1992; The Treasure in a Field, 2012.

**WALKER, Richard John**, OBE 1998; Director, British Council, Hong Kong, 2017; *b* Reading, 1 Nov. 1952; *s* of George Lewis and Gwendolen Jayne Walker; *m* 1978, Lauren Michaela Barker, (writer, as Lauren O'Hara); one *s* one *d*. *Educ*: Woolverstone Hall; Guildford Coll.; St Peter's Coll., Oxford (BA Hons English Lang. and Lit.); Manchester Univ. (Dip. TEO, PGCE). English teacher, Internat. House, Spain and Kuwait, 1976–78; English Lectr, Manchester Univ. and Huddersfield Coll., 1979–83; Thai Govt English Advr, Bangkok, 1983–85; British Council: Dep. Dir, Literature Dept, London, 1985–87; Asst Dir, Lagos, 1987–89; on secondment to Internat. Educn Centre and Sen. Lectr, Coll. of St Mark and St John, Plymouth, 1989–92; Dir, Develt, 1992–94; First Sec. (Cultural), British High Commn, New Delhi, 1994–98; Dir, and Superintendent Gen., Cultura Inglesa, São Paulo, 1998–2000; Regl Dir, E Asia, London, 2000–05; Dir, Cyprus, 2005–07; Dir, Greece, 2007–11; Dir, EU Operations, Brussels, 2011–13; Dir, EU Operations and Business Transformation, London, 2013–16. Writer of drama, monologues and short stories, BBC Radio 3 and Radio 4, 1985–95. FRSA. *Publications*: Language for Literature, 1983; A Curious Child, 1989; (ed) Penguin History of English Literature, 1990; contrib. reviews and articles to THES, Literary Rev. *Recreations*: tennis, walking, travel, history, visual arts, literature. *Club*: Manchester United.

**WALKER, Robert M.**; Chairman: Ei Group (formerly Enterprise Inns) plc, since 2012; Eagle TopCo Ltd, since 2014; *b* 3 Feb. 1945; *s* of Arthur Norman Walker and Nancy (*née* Waugh); *m* 1970, Patricia Douglass; one *s* one *d*. *Educ*: Hampton Sch.; Magdalen Coll., Oxford (BA Hons Modern History 1966). Brand Manager, Procter & Gamble Ltd, 1966–70; Engagement Manager, McKinsey & Co. Inc., 1970–76; Div. Pres., PepsiCo Inc., 1976–99; Gp Chief Exec., Severn Trent plc, 2000–05 (non-exec. Dir, 1996–99). Chairman: Williams Lea Group Ltd, 2005–06; WH Smith plc, 2005–10; BCA Europe Ltd, 2007–09; Americana Internat. Hldgs, 2009–14; Travis Perkins plc, 2010–17; Dep. Chm., Camelot Ltd, 2018–. Non-executive Director: Thomson Travel Gp plc, 1998–2000; Wolseley plc, 1999–2007; Signet Gp plc, 2004–08; BAA plc, 2004–05; Williams Lea Hldgs Plc, 2006–09; Tate & Lyle, 2006–15 (Sen. Ind. Dir, 2010–15). Advr, Cinven, 2005–07. Gov., Hampton Sch., 2007–. *Clubs*: Oxford and Cambridge, Brooks's.

**WALKER, Robin Caspar;** MP (C) Worcester, since 2010; Parliamentary Under-Secretary of State: Northern Ireland Office, since 2019; Scotland Office, since 2019; *b* Worcs, 12 April 1978; *s* of Baron Walker of Worcester, PC, MBE and of Tessa (*née* Pout); *m* 2011, Charlotte Keenan. *Educ*: St Paul's Sch.; Balliol Coll., Oxford (Schol.; BA Ancient and Modern Hist. 2000). Chief Exec., Property Map Ltd, 2000–01; Res. Exec., i-Search Ltd, 2001–03; Finsbury Group: Exec., 2003–04; Sen. Exec., 2004–06; Associate Partner, 2006–09; Partner, 2009–10. Member: Welsh Affairs Select Cttee, 2011–12; BIS Select Cttee, 2012–15; Admin Select Cttee, 2015–16; PPS to Minister of State, NI, 2013–14, to Sec. of State, DEFRA, 2014–15, to Sec. of State for Educn, 2015–16; Parly Under-Sec. of State, DExEU, 2016–19. *Address*: House of Commons, SW1A 0AA.

**WALKER, Sir Rodney (Myerscough)**, Kt 1996; Chairman: Myerscough Holdings Ltd, since 1976; Lightsong Media Ltd (formerly Lightsong Ltd), since 2009; Romiro Group plc (formerly Sport Pathways, then Rom Pathways, Ltd), since 2011; *b* 10 April 1943; *s* of Norman and Lucy Walker; *m* 1974, Anne Margaret Aspinall; two *s*. *Educ*: Thornes House Grammar Sch. CEng. Founder Chm., Myerscough Holdings, 1976; activities incl. civil engrg, motor retail, and develt. Chairman: W Yorks Broadcasting, 1986–2002; Brands Hatch Leisure plc, 1996–99; Leicester City plc, 1997–2002 (now Hon. Life Pres.); Wembley Nat. Stadium Ltd, 2000–02; Spice Holdings plc, 2002–08; Goals Soccer Centres plc, 2002–13; World Snooker Ltd, 2003–09; Archial (formerly SMC) Gp, 2004–10; Brand Cellar Ltd, 2011–13; TdF HUB 2014 Ltd, 2013–14. Chair, Adv. Bd, FansBet Ltd, 2018–. Chairman: Rugby Football League, 1993–2002; Sports Council of GB, 1994–96; English Sports Council, 1996–98; UK Sports Council, 1998–2003; British Basketball League, 2016–. Mem., Wakefield HA, 1982–90; Chairman: Bradford Hosps NHS Trust, 1990–96; NHS Trust Fedn, 1993–95 (Pres., 1995–97). Chm., Wakefield Theatre Trust, 1981–99, now Hon. Life Pres.; Vice Chm., Yorks Sculpture Park, 1984– (Trustee, 1995–). Trustee: Nat. Coal Mining (formerly Nat. Mining) Mus. of England, 1993–2014; English Nat. Stadium Trust, 1998–; London Marathon Charitable Trust, 2005– (Chm., 2015–); Vice Chair, Wembley Nat. Stadium Trust, 2003–. Chair, Yorks Soc. Freeman, City of Wakefield, 2012. FInstD. DUniv Huddersfield, 2014. KLJ 1997. *Recreations*: golf, theatre, travel. *Address*: Tower House, Bond Street, Wakefield WF1 2QP. *T*: (01924) 374349; Pine Lodge, Home Farm, Woolley, Wakefield WF4 2JS. *T*: (01226) 384089.

**WALKER, Comdr Roger Antony Martineau–**, LVO 1994; RN; Clerk to Trustees, and Chief Executive, United Westminster Almshouses Foundation, 1997–2007; *b* 15 Oct. 1940; *s* of Antony Philip Martineau-Walker and Sheila Hazeal Mayoh Wilson; *m* Inger Lene Brag-Nielsen; two *s*. *Educ*: Haileybury and Imperial Service College, Hertford; BRNC Dartmouth. Commissioned RN, 1962; served Malta, Singapore and Sarawak, 1962–65; Torpedo and Antisubmarine Course, HMS Vernon, 1968; HMS Galatea, 1973–76; NDC Latimer, 1977–78; Naval and Defence Staff, MoD, 1978–83; Naval Manpower Planning, with special responsibility for introd. of longer career for ratings (2nd Open Engagement), 1983–85; operational staff (UK commitments), 1985–87; Head, Naval Sec's Policy Staff, 1987–90; Pvte Sec. to Duke and Duchess of Kent, 1990–93. Trustee, St Giles–in–the–Fields United Charity, 2008–11. Bursar, Royal Sch. for Daughters of the Army, 1995–96. Foundn Gov., Burdett Coutts and Townshend C of E Primary Sch., 1998–2002 (Trustee, 2004–12). Churchwarden, St Hubert's, Idsworth, 2008–16 (Building Manager, 2008–); Chm., Friends of Ch of St Hubert, Idsworth, 2016–18. *Recreations*: fly fishing, photographic conservation, music. *Address*: 13 The Peak, Rowlands Castle, Hants PO9 6AH. *Clubs*: Army and Navy; MR Car.

**WALKER, Ronald Jack;** QC 1983; a Recorder, since 1986; *b* 24 June 1940; *s* of Jack Harris Walker and Ann Frances Walker; *m* 1st, 1964, Caroline Fox (marr. diss. 1997); two *s*; 2nd, 1999, Clare Oonagh Jane Devitt; one *s* one *d*. *Educ*: Owen's School, London; University College London. LLB (Hons). Called to the Bar, Gray's Inn, 1962, Bencher, 1993. Mem. Gen. Council of the Bar, 1993–96 (Chm. Professional Conduct Cttee, 1993–94). Mem., Mental Health Review Tribunal, 2000–12. *Publications*: (with M. G. Walker) English Legal System, 1967, 11th edn as Walker & Walker's English Legal System, 2011; contributing ed., Bullen & Leake & Jacob's Precedents of Pleadings, 13th edn 1990; (ed) Butterworths Professional Negligence Service, 1999; Butterworth's Personal Injury Litigation Service: Asbestos Disease Claims, 2004. *Address*: 12 King's Bench Walk, Temple, EC4Y 7EL. *T*: (020) 7583 0811.

**WALKER, Roy;** *see* Walker, C. R.

**WALKER, Sir Roy Edward**, 6th Bt *cr* 1906, of Pembroke House, City of Dublin; *b* 10 Aug. 1977; *yr s* of Major Sir Hugh Ronald Walker, 4th Bt and Norna Walker (*née* Baird); *S* brother, 2006.

**WALKER, Sarah Elizabeth Royle, (Mrs R. G. Allum)**, CBE 1991; mezzo-soprano; *d* of Elizabeth Brownrigg and Alan Royle Walker; *m* 1972, Graham Allum. *Educ*: Pate's Grammar School for Girls, Cheltenham; Royal College of Music. FRCM 1987; LRAM. Prince Consort Prof. of Singing, RCM, 1993–; vocal performance consultant, GSMD, 1999–; joined vocal faculty, RAM, 2009–. Pres., Cheltenham Bach Choir, 1986–. Major appearances at concerts and in recital in Britain, America, Australia, New Zealand, Europe; operatic débuts include: Coronation of Poppea, Kent Opera, 1969, San Francisco Opera, 1981; La Calisto, Glyndebourne, 1970; Les Troyens, Scottish Opera, 1972, Wiener Staatsoper, 1980; Principal Mezzo Soprano, ENO, 1972–77; Die Meistersinger, Chicago Lyric Opera, 1977; Werther, Covent Garden, 1979; Giulio Cesare, Le Grand Théâtre, Genève, 1983; Capriccio, Brussels, 1983; Teseo, Sienna, 1985; Samson, NY Metropolitan Opera, 1986; numerous recordings and video recordings, incl. title rôle in Britten's Gloriana. FGS 2001 (FGSM 2000). Hon. RAM 2015. *Recreations*: interior design, encouraging her husband with the gardening. *Address*: Cheffings, Witheridge, Devon EX16 8QD. *T*: (01884) 860132. *E*: megamezzo@sarahwalker.com. *Club*: University Women's.

**WALKER, Simon Edward John**, CBE 2017; business advisor and consultant; Director General, Institute of Directors, 2011–17; *b* 28 May 1953; *s* of Louis Charles Vivian Walker and Joan Wallace Walker (*née* Keith); *m* 1980, Mary Virginia Strang; one *s* one *d*. *Educ*: South African Coll. Sch.; Balliol Coll., Oxford (BA PPE; Pres., Oxford Union, 1974; MA 1978). Personal Asst to Lord Sainsbury, 1974–75; reporter, TV NZ, Wellington, 1975–79; Knight Journalism Fellow, Stanford Univ., 1979–80; Communications Dir, NZ Labour Party, 1980–84; Director: Communicor Govt and PR, 1984–87; NZ Centre for Independent Studies, Auckland, 1987–89; Eur. Public Affairs, Hill & Knowlton PR, London, 1989–90; Man. Dir, Hill & Knowlton, Belgium, 1990–94; Partner, Brunswick PR, 1994–98 (on secondment to Policy Unit, 10 Downing St, 1996–97); Dir of Communications, British Airways, 1998–2000; Communications Sec. to the Queen, 2000–02; Dir of Corporate Mktg and Communications, Reuters, 2003–07; Chief Exec., British Private Equity and Venture Capital Assoc., 2007–11. Non-exec. Dir, Comair Ltd (SA), 2000–01; Lead non-exec. Dir, DIT, 2016–. Member: Better Regulation Commn, 2006–08; H of C Speaker's Cttee on Public Engagement, 2009–15. Dir, Eur. Confedn of

Dirs' Assocs, 2011–17; Chm., Global Network of Dirs' Insts, 2016–18. Mem., BUPA Assoc., 2015–. Gov., Westminster Foundn for Democracy, 2015–. Trustee: NZ-UK Link Foundn, 2003–08; Queen Elizabeth Diamond Jubilee Trust, 2017–. Gov., Hillary Summit (NZ), 2008–. FInstD 2016. Hon. DBA West of England, 2015; Hon. LLD Warwick, 2016. *Publications:* Rogernomics: reshaping New Zealand's economy, 1989; contrib. newspaper and mag. columns. *Recreations:* family, reading, music, travel. *Address:* 86 Brook Green, W6 7BD. *E:* simon.walker@communicor.co.uk. *Club:* Athenæum.

**WALKER, Stuart;** see Walker, B. S.

**WALKER, Susannah Mary;** a District Judge, Principal Registry, Family Division, 2006–14; Deputy District Judge, South Eastern and Western Circuits, 2015–16; *b* 6 Aug. 1948; *d* of late Ronald Jack Marsh and Mary Marsh; *m* 1973, Robert Adrian Walker; one *s* one *d*. *Educ:* Univ. of Birmingham (BSocSc 1969; DipSW 1971); City Univ., London (Dip Law 1984). Social worker, 1971–80; called to the Bar, Inner Temple, 1985; an Immigration Judge, 2003–06. Mem., Mental Health Rev. Tribunal, 1996–2010.

**WALKER, Terence William, (Terry Walker);** *b* 26 Oct. 1935; *s* of William Edwin and Lilian Grace Walker; *m* 1959, Priscilla Dart (marr. diss. 1983); two *s* one *d*; *m* 1983, Rosalie Fripp. *Educ:* Grammar Sch. and Coll. of Further Educn, Bristol. Employed by Courage (Western) Ltd at Bristol for 23 yrs, Mem. Chief Accountant's Dept. MP (Lab) Kingswood, Feb. 1974–1979; Second Church Estates Comr, 1974–79. Contested (Lab): Kingswood, 1983; Bristol NW, 1987. Member: Avon CC, 1981–96 (Vice-Chm., 1992–93; Chm., 1993–94), S Glos Unitary Council, 1996–2015 (Dep. Leader Labour Gp, 1996–2009); Chair, Avon Combined Fire Authy, 1996–2015. *Recreations:* cricket, football. *Address:* 43 The Furlong, Bristol BS6 7TF. *T:* (0117) 989 2694.

**WALKER, Thelma Doris;** MP (Lab) Colne Valley, since 2017; *b* 7 April 1957; *m* Rob Walker; two *c*. *Educ:* Marple Hall Grammar Sch.; Manchester Poly. (BEd 1978); Leeds Metropolitan Univ. (NPQH). Teacher: Stockport LEA, 1978–90; Kirklees Local Authy, 1990–2001 (Special Educnl Needs Co-ordinator); Headteacher: Flockton First Sch., 2001–06; Overthorpe C of E Sch., 2006–12; ind. educnl consultant, 2012–. Mem., Educn Cttee, H of C, 2017–. Chm., Kirklees Primary Heads, 2011. *Address:* House of Commons, SW1A 0AA.

**WALKER, Dr (Thomas) Gordon,** OBE 2000; FInstP; Chief Executive, Council for the Central Laboratory of Research Councils, 2000–01; retired; *b* 4 Nov. 1936; *s* of James Smart Walker and Mary Margaret McIntosh Walker; *m* 1960, Una May Graham Stevenson; one *s* one *d*. *Educ:* Uddingston Grammar Sch.; Univ. of Glasgow (BSc, PhD). Rutherford High Energy Laboratory, National Institute for Research in Nuclear Science, later Rutherford Appleton Laboratory, Science and Engineering Research Council: Res. Physicist, 1960–71; Gp Leader, 1971–80; Head: Instrumentation Div., 1980–83; Technology Div., 1983–87; Dep. Dir, 1987–94; Head, 1994–96; Dir, R&D, CCLRC, 1996–2000. Mem., Renewable Energy Adv. Cttee, DTI, 1980–2000. Chief Sci. Advr (Civil Defence), Oxfordshire CC, 1983–93. Chm., Mgt Cttee, Didcot CAB, 1991–97; Pres., Didcot Rotary Club, 1977–78. Chm., Harwell Parish Council, 1988–91. *Publications:* papers in sci. jls on experimental particle physics. *Recreations:* golf, gardening. *Club:* Frilford Heath Golf.

**WALKER, Timothy;** Lecturer in Plant Science, Somerville College, Oxford, since 1997; Stipendiary Lecturer: in Botany, Pembroke College, Oxford, since 2014; in Plant Sciences, Hertford College, Oxford, since 2015; *b* Chalfont St Giles, 10 July 1958; *s* of Gerald and Doreen Walker; *m* 1993, Jill Humphries; two *s* one *d*. *Educ:* Abingdon Sch.; University Coll., Oxford (BA Hons Botany 1980); Askham Bryan Coll., York (Nat. Cert. Horticulture 1983); Univ. of Oxford (Post Grad. Dip. Learning and Teaching in HE 2017). MHort (RHS) 1985. Gen. foreman, 1986–88, Horti Praefectus, 1988–2014, Univ. of Oxford Botanic Gdn. *Publications:* Euphorbias, 2002; Plants, 2012; Plant Conservation, 2014; How Plants Work, 2018. *Recreations:* walking, photography, gardening, natural history. *Address:* Somerville College, Oxford OX2 6HD.

**WALKER, Timothy Alexander,** AM 2000; Chief Executive and Artistic Director, London Philharmonic Orchestra, since 2003; *b* Hobart, Tasmania, 23 Nov. 1954; *s* of Keith James Walker and Elaine Walker (née Edwards). *Educ:* Riverside High Sch.; Launceston Matriculation Coll.; Univ. of Tasmania (BA Hons; DipEd; AMusA); Univ. of New England (DipFM). Concert Manager, Canberra Sch. of Music, 1981–87; Mktg Develt Manager, 1987–89, Gen. Manager, 1989–99, Australian Chamber Orch.; CEO and Artistic Dir, World Orchestras, 1999–2003. Member: Australian Internat. Cultural Council, 1999–2003; Adv. Council, Sydney Conservatorium of Music, 1995–2003. Dir, Internat. Soc. for Performing Arts, 1995–2001; Dep. Chm., Music Council of Australia, 1995–2001. Director: Assoc. of British Orchestras, 2004–07 (Chm., 2007–10); Trustee, ABO Trust, 2007–); London Music Masters, 2007–; Director: Henry Wood Hall Trust, 2003–; Rachmaninoff Foundn, 2012–. Hon. RCM, 2014. *Recreations:* travel, the arts. *Address:* London Philharmonic Orchestra, Level 4, 89 Albert Embankment, SE1 7TP. *T:* (020) 7840 4218, *Fax:* (020) 7840 4201. *E:* timothy.walker@lpo.org.uk. *Club:* Athenæum.

**WALKER, Hon. Sir Timothy (Edward),** Kt 1996; a Judge of the High Court of Justice, Queen's Bench Division, and a Judge of the Commercial Court, 1996–2002; *b* 13 May 1946; *s* of George Edward Walker, solicitor, and Muriel Edith Walker; *m* 1968, Mary (née Tyndall); two *d*. *Educ:* Harrow Sch. (Totland Entrance Schol.; Clayton Leaving Schol.); University Coll., Oxford (Plumptre Schol., 1965; 1st Cl. Hons Jurisprudence, 1967; MA). Asst Lectr in Law, King's Coll., London, 1967–68; Profumo Schol., Inner Temple, 1968; Eldon Law schol., 1969; called to the Bar, Inner Temple, 1968, Bencher, 1996; QC 1985; a Recorder of the Crown Court, 1986–96. *Address:* c/o Royal Courts of Justice, Strand, WC2A 2LL.

**WALKER, Timothy Edward Hanson,** CB 1998; Third Church Estates Commissioner, 2006–12; *b* 27 July 1945; *s* of late Harris and Elizabeth Walker; *m* 1st, 1969, Judith Mann (*d* 1976); one *d*; 2nd, 1983, Hon. Anna Butterworth (see Hon. A. E. B. Walker); two *d*. *Educ:* Tonbridge Sch.; Brasenose Coll., Oxford (BA Chemistry, 1967; MA, DPhil 1969). Weir Jun. Res. Fellow, University Coll., Oxford, and Exhibnr of Royal Commn of 1851, Oxford and Paris, 1969; Harkness Fellow, Commonwealth Fund of New York, 1971, Univ. of Virginia, 1971 and Northwestern Univ., 1972; Strategic Planner, GLC, 1974; Principal, Dept of Trade, 1977; Sloan Fellow, London Business Sch., 1983; Department of Trade and Industry: Asst Sec., 1983; Dir (Admin), Alvey Programme, 1983; Head, Policy Planning Unit, 1985; Principal Private Sec. to successive Secs of State for Trade and Industry, 1986; Under Sec., 1987; Dir, Inf. Engrg Directorate, 1987; Head, Atomic Energy Div., Dept of Energy, then DTI, 1989–95; Dep. Sec., 1995, and Dir Gen., Immigration and Nationality Directorate, 1995–98, Home Office; Comr and Dep. Chm., HM Customs and Excise, 1998–2000; Dir.-Gen., HSE, 2000–05. Non-exec. Dir, London Strategic Health Authy, 2006–09. UK Gov., IAEA, 1989–94; non-exec. Dir, Govt Div., UKAEA, 1994–95. Chm., Assembly of Donors, Nuclear Safety Account, EBRD, 1993–95; Mem., Sci. and Technol. Cttee, Internat. Risk Governance Council, 2004–12. Chm., Accountancy and Actuarial Discipline Bd, 2008–12; Exec. Dir, Financial Reporting Council, 2008–12. Non-exec. Dir, ICI Chemicals and Polymers Ltd, 1988–89. Mem., Audit Cttee, St John of Jerusalem Eye Hosp., 2013–. Governor, St Anne's Sch.,

Wandsworth, 1977–82; Council Member: Warwick Univ., 2000–06; Inst. of Employment Studies, 2001–05. Trustee: Prostate Cancer Charity, 2006–13; Lambeth Palace Library, 2007–12; De Morgan Foundation, 2007–12; Drinkaware, 2014–. CEng, FIET, FInstP 2003. FRSA 2000; CCMI 2002. Hon. Fellow, Warwick Manufacturing Gp, 2006–. Hon. DSc Cranfield, 2003. *Publications:* If You Can Read You Can Cook, 2009; Twixt the Commons, 2010; The First Clapham Saints, 2016; contribs to scientific jls. *Recreations:* cooking, African tribal art, seventeenth century history.

**WALKER, Sir Victor (Stewart Heron),** 6th Bt *cr* 1868, of Sand Hutton, York and Beachampton, Bucks; *b* 8 Oct. 1942; *s* of Sir James Heron Walker, 5th Bt and Angela Margaret (née Beaufort); *S* father, 2003; *m* 1st, 1969, Caroline Louisa (marr. diss. 1982), *d* of Lt-Col F. E. B. Wignall; two *s* one *d*; 2nd, 1982, Svea (*d* 2013), *o d* of Captain Ernst Hugo Gothard Knutson Borg; 3rd, 2014, Mrs Sarah Gaunt, *e d* of Geoffrey Gillott. *Educ:* Eton. 2nd Lt Grenadier Guards, 1962–65; Lt Royal Wilts Yeo., 1965–73. Mem., RYS, 1972–. *Heir: s* James Frederick Heron Walker, *b* 14 Feb. 1970.

**WALKER, Victoria Patricia Ann, (Mrs F. A. Woods Walker);** see Woods, V. P. A.

**WALKER, William George;** researcher and writer, since 2013; Member for Dunfermline, Scottish Parliament, 2011–Sept. 2013 (SNP, 2011–12; Ind, 2012–13); *b* Edinburgh, 31 March 1942; *s* of George Stenhouse Walker and Mary Heriot Watt Walker. *Educ:* Univ. of Edinburgh (BSc 1st Cl. Electrical Engrg 1963; MBA Corporate Strategy and Finance 1982); Illinois Inst. of Technol., Chicago (Post Grad. Cert. Computer Programming 1968). CEng, FIET, FCMI. Technical R&D, then sales and marketing, business develt and gen. mgt in hi-tech engrg and electronics sector serving healthcare, scientific, industrial and energy markets, shipbuilding, USA and Europe, 1963–2007. Mem. (SNP) Fife Council, 2007–12. *Publications:* Bill Walker: my story—a private and professional life, 2017. *Recreations:* gardening, walking, DIY, travel. *E:* williamgeorgewalker@gmail.com.

**WALKER, William MacLelland;** QC (Scot.) 1971; Social Security Commissioner, 1988–2003; a Child Support Commissioner, 1993–2003; *b* 19 May 1933; *s* of late Hon. Lord Walker; *m* 1957, Joan Margaret (*d* 2006), *d* of late Charles Hutchison Wood, headmaster, Dundee; one *d*. *Educ:* Edinburgh Academy; Edinburgh Univ. (MA, LLB). Advocate, 1957; Flying Officer, RAF, 1957–59; Standing Junior Counsel: Min. of Aviation, 1963–68; BoT (Aviation), 1968–71; Min. of Technology, 1968–70; Dept of Trade and Industry (Power), 1971; Min. of Aviation Supply, 1971. Hon. Sheriff, various Sheriffdoms, 1963–71. Chairman: Industrial Tribunals in Scotland, 1972–88; VAT Tribunals, 1985–88. *Recreations:* travel, photography. *Clubs:* Royal Air Force; New (Edinburgh).

**WALKER-ARNOTT, Deborah Clare;** see Ounsted, D. C.

**WALKER-ARNOTT, Edward Ian;** Consultant, Herbert Smith Freehills (formerly Herbert Smith), since 2000 (Senior Partner, 1992–2000); *b* 18 Sept. 1939; *s* of late Charles Douglas Walker-Arnott and Kathleen Margaret (née Brittain); *m* 1971, (Phyllis) Jane Ricketts; one *s* two *d*. *Educ:* Haileybury Coll.; London Univ. (LLB ext.); University Coll. London (LLM; Fellow, 1999; Vis. Prof., 2000–18). Admitted solicitor, 1963; Partner, Herbert Smith, 1968–2000. Dir, Sturge Hldgs, 1989–95. Mem., Cork Cttee on Review of Insolvency Law, 1977–82. Mem. Council of Lloyds, 1983–88 (Hon. Mem. 1988). Mem., Takeover Appeal Bd, 2014–. Mem. Bd, RNT, 2000–08. Governor: S Bank Bd, 1999–2009; The Wellcome Trust, 2000–10. Member, Governing Body: Haileybury Coll., 1969–98; Benenden Sch., 1987–93. Author, report for Arts Council of England on relationship with Royal Opera House, Covent Garden (Walker-Arnott Report), 1997; Chm., ind. inquiry panel reporting to Univ. of Greenwich Court on Woolwich Incident, 2014. Hon. QC 2013. *Recreations:* reading, gardening, watching sport. *Address:* Manuden Hall, Manuden, near Bishop's Stortford, Herts CM23 1DY. *Club:* City of London.

**WALKER-HAWORTH, John Leigh;** Chairman, Black Rock (formerly Merrill Lynch) Greater Europe Investment Trust plc, 2004–13 (non-executive Director, Merrill Lynch European Investment Trust plc, 2000–04); *b* 25 Oct. 1944; *s* of William and Julia Walker-Haworth; *m* 1976, Caroline Mary Blair Purves; two *s*. *Educ:* Charterhouse; Pembroke College, Oxford. Called to the Bar, Inner Temple, 1967. Dir, 1981–93, Vice Chm., 1993–95, S. G. Warburg & Co.; Man. Dir, 1995–97, Advr, 1997–2000, UBS Warburg; Man. Dir, Integrated Finance Ltd, 2005–07. Chm. and Dir, GB Gp plc, 2002–10. Dep. Chm., Takeover Panel, 1997–2006 (Dir-Gen., City Panel on Takeovers and Mergers, 1985–87). Gov., Sutton's Hosp., Charterhouse, 1997–2003; Mem., Governing Body, Charterhouse, 2000–11 (Chm., 2004–11). *Address:* 7 Chancellor House, Hyde Park Gate, SW7 5DQ.

**WALKER-OKEOVER, Sir Andrew Peter Monro,** 5th Bt *cr* 1886, of Gateacre Grange, co. Lancaster and Osmaston Manor, co. Derby; DL; *b* 22 May 1978; *s* of Sir Peter Ralph Leopold Walker-Okeover, 4th Bt and of Catherine Mary Maule (née Ramsay); *S* father, 2003; *m* 2007, Philippa Lucy Mettins, *yr d* of Lt-Col Charles Swabey; two *s*. DL Derbyshire, 2017. *Heir: s* Peter Charles Monro Walker-Okeover, *b* 6 Feb. 2010. *Address:* Okeover Hall, Ashbourne, Derbyshire DE6 2DE.

**WALKER-SMITH, Sir (John) Jonah,** 2nd Bt *cr* 1960, of Broxbourne, Co. Herts; a Recorder of the Crown Court, 1980–2005; *b* 6 Sept. 1939; *s* of Baron Broxbourne (Life Peer), QC, TD and Dorothy (*d* 1999), *d* of late L. J. W. Etherton; *S* to baronetcy of father, 1992; *m* 1974, Aileen Marie Smith; one *s* one *d*. *Educ:* Westminster School; Christ Church, Oxford. Called to Bar, Middle Temple, 1963. Mem., Westminster CC, 1968–86 (Chm. of Social Services, Housing and Finance Cttees). *Heir: s* Daniel Derek Walker-Smith, *b* 26 March 1980. *Club:* Garrick.

**WALL, Alfreda, (Mrs D. R. Wall);** see Thorogood, A.

**WALL, Brian Owen,** CEng, FRINA; RCNC; Chief Naval Architect, Ministry of Defence, 1985–90; *b* 17 June 1933; *s* of Maurice Stanley Wall and Ruby Wall; *m* 1960, Patricia Thora Hughes; one *s*. *Educ:* Newport High School, Mon; Imperial Coll. of Science and Technology; RN Coll., Greenwich. BSc Eng. ACGI. MoD Bath: Ship Vulnerability, 1958–61; Submarine Design, 1961–66; Head of Propeller Design, Admiralty Experiment Works, Haslar, 1966–71; Staff of C-in-C Fleet, Portsmouth, 1971–73; Submarine Support and Modernisation Group, MoD Bath, 1973–77; RCDS 1977; MoD Bath: Ship Production Div., 1978–79; Project Director, Vanguard Class, 1979–84; Dir, Cost Estimating and Analysis, 1985. Gov., Imperial Coll., London, 1991–99. *Recreations:* photography, chess, music, walking. *Address:* Wychwood, 39 High Bannerdown, Batheaston, Bath BA1 7JZ.

**WALL, Carmel Miriam; Her Honour Judge Carmel Wall;** a Circuit Judge, since 2015; *b* Auckland, NZ, 8 Dec. 1963; *d* of David and Rita Adler; *m* 1987, Mark Arthur Wall, *qv*; one *s* one *d*. *Educ:* Epsom Girls' Grammar Sch.; Girton Coll., Cambridge (BA 1985). Called to the Bar, Lincoln's Inn, 1986; First-tier Tribunal Judge: Social Entitlement Chamber, 2001–15; War Pensions and Armed Forces Compensation Chamber, 2014–15; a Dep. Dist Judge, 2006–09; a Recorder, 2009–15. *Recreations:* travel, theatre, cooking, eating. *Address:* Birmingham Civil and Family Justice Centre, Priory Courts, 33 Bull Street, Birmingham B4 6DS.

**WALL, Prof. Charles Terence Clegg,** FRS 1969; Professor of Pure Mathematics, 1965–99, and Senior Fellow, 1999–2002, Liverpool University; b 14 Dec. 1936; s of late Charles Wall, schoolteacher; m 1959, Alexandra Joy, d of late Prof. Leslie Spencer Hearnshaw; two s two d. Educ: Marlborough Coll.; Trinity Coll., Cambridge. PhD Cantab 1960. Fellow, Trinity Coll., 1959–64; Harkness Fellow, Princeton, 1960–61; Univ. Lectr, Cambridge, 1961–64; Reader in Mathematics, and Fellow of St Catherine's Coll., Oxford, 1964–65. SERC Sen. Fellowship, 1983–88. Royal Soc. Leverhulme Vis. Prof., CIEA, Mexico, 1967. Pres., London Mathematical Soc., 1978–80 (Mem. Council, 1973–80 and 1992–96); Hon. Mem., Irish Math. Soc. 2001. Fellow: Royal Danish Academy, 1990; Amer. Maths Soc., 2012. Sylvester Medal, Royal Soc., 1988. Publications: Surgery on Compact Manifolds, 1970; A Geometric Introduction to Topology, 1972; (with A. A. du Plessis) The Geometry of Topological Stability, 1995; Singular Points of Plane Curves, 2004; Differential Topology, 2016; papers on various problems in geometric topology, singularity theory, and related algebra. Recreations: reading, walking, gardening. Address: 5 Kirby Park, West Kirby, Wirral, Merseyside CH48 2HA. T: (0151) 625 5063.

**WALL, James Francis, (Frank),** CMG 1999; formerly Head of Shipping Policy 2 Division, Department for Transport; b 6 Jan. 1944; s of late James Wall, MA and Elizabeth Wall (née O'Sullivan); m 1970, Eileen Forrester McKerracher; two d. Educ: Belvedere Coll., SJ; University Coll., Dublin (BA 1966); Univ. of Liverpool (MCD 1968). MRTPI 1970. Asst to Prof. H. Myles Wright, Dublin Regl Planning Consultant, 1965–66; Planner then Sen. Planner, Antrim and Ballymena Develt Commn, 1968–71; Planning Officer, NI Min. of Develt, 1971–72; Asst, S Hants Plan Technical Unit, 1972–74; Sen. Planning Officer, Hants CC, 1974; Planning Officer, then Principal Planning Officer, DoE, 1974–82; Principal, 1982, Asst Sec., 1993, Dept of Transport; Hd of Shipping Policy 3, later 2, Div., Dept of Transport, then DETR, subseq. DTLR, later DfT, 1993–2004. Chairman: UK Search and Rescue Strategy Cttee, 2000; Shipping Task Force, 2001. Internat. Maritime Prize, IMO, 2002; Dist. Public Service Award, US Coast Guard, 2002. Publications: contrib. conf. proc. and articles in maritime law jls. Recreations: Flower Class Corvettes, the Boeing 707–348C. Address: Collingwood, Elvetham Road, Fleet, Hants GU51 4HH.

**WALL, Jasper V.,** PhD; Adjunct Professor, Department of Physics and Astronomy, University of British Columbia, since 2003; b 15 Jan. 1942; s of late Philip Errington Wall and Lilian Margaret (née Blackburn); m 1969, Jennifer Anne Lash; one s one d. Educ: Vankleek Hill Collegiate Inst.; Queen's Univ., Kingston (BSc 1963); Univ. of Toronto (MASc 1966); Australian Nat. Univ. (PhD 1970). Res. Scientist, Australian Nat. Radio Astronomy Observatory, Parkes, NSW, 1970–74; Leverhulme Fellow, RAS, 1974–75, Jaffé Donation Fellow, Royal Soc., 1975–79, Cavendish Lab.; Hd, Astrophysics and Astrometry Div., Royal Greenwich Observatory, 1979–87; Officer-in-Charge, Isaac Newton Gp of Telescopes, La Palma, Canary Is, 1987–90; Royal Greenwich Observatory: Hd, Technol. Div., 1990–91; Hd, Astronomy Div., 1991–95; Dep. Dir, 1991–93; Head, 1993–95; Dir, 1995–98. Vis. Reader, Univ. of Sussex, 1980–90; Vis. Prof., Univ. of Oxford, 1998–. FRAS 1975 (Mem. Council, 1992–96; Vice-Pres., 1996). Chm., Editl Bd, Astronomy & Geophysics, 1999–2002. Publications: (ed jtly) Modern Technology and its Influence on Astronomy, 1986; (ed jtly) Optics in Astronomy, 1993; (ed jtly) The Universe at High Redshifts, 1997; (with C. R. Jenkins) Practical Statistics for Astronomers, 2003, 2nd edn 2012; 180 papers in professional jls on radio sky surveys, observational cosmology and statistics for astronomers. Recreations: ski-ing, music. Address: Department of Physics and Astronomy, University of British Columbia, Vancouver, BC V6T 1Z1, Canada.

**WALL, Sir (John) Stephen,** GCMG 2004 (KCMG 1996; CMG 1990); LVO 1983; HM Diplomatic Service, retired; Official Government Historian, since 2007; campaigner for global LGBT rights; b 10 Jan. 1947; s of John Derwent Wall and Maria Laetitia Wall (née Whitmarsh); m 1975, Catharine Jane Reddaway (marr. diss. 2015), d of late G. F. N. Reddaway, CBE and of Jean Reddaway, OBE; one s. Educ: Douai Sch.; Selwyn Coll., Cambridge (BA; Hon. Fellow, 2000). FCO 1968; Addis Ababa, 1969–72; Private Sec. to HM Ambassador, Paris, 1972–74; First Sec., FCO, 1974–76; Press Officer, No 10 Downing Street, 1976–77; Asst Private Sec. to Sec. of State for Foreign and Commonwealth Affairs, 1977–79; First Sec., Washington, 1979–83; Asst Head, later Head, European Community Dept, FCO, 1983–88; Private Secretary: to Foreign and Commonwealth Secs., 1988–90; to the Prime Minister, 1991–93; Ambassador to Portugal, 1993–95; Ambassador and UK Perm. Rep. to EU, Brussels, 1995–2000; Head of European Secretariat, Cabinet Office, and EU Advr to the Prime Minister, 2000–04; Principal Advr to Cardinal Archbp of Westminster, 2004–05; Vice Chm., Business for New Europe, 2005–16. Official Govt historian, 2007–19. Mem. Council, UCL, 2005–14 (Chm., 2008–14). Chairman: Federal Trust, 2008–; Cumberland Lodge, 2009–19; Co-Chm., Belgo-British Conference, 2010–14. Trustee: Thomson Foundn, 2006–16; Franco-British Council, 2009–16; Kaleidoscope Trust, 2014– (Chair, 2017–). Officer's Cross, Order of Merit (Germany), 2009; Chevalier, Légion d'Honneur (France), 2009. Publications: A Stranger in Europe: Britain and the European Union from Thatcher to Blair, 2008; The Official History of Britain and the European Community, 1963–75, 2012 and 1975–1985, 2019. Recreations: walking, photography, reading.

**WALL, Jonathan;** Controller, BBC Radio 5 Live and 5 Live Sports Extra, since 2013; b Manchester, 24 July 1972; s of Malcolm Wall and Noreen Wall; two s. Educ: Univ. of Central England (BA Hons Media and Communication 1993); Falmouth Coll. of Arts (Postgrad. Dip. Broadcast Journalism 1994). Sports Prod., Radio Humberside, 1994–96; BBC: Sports Researcher, BBC TV Sport, 1996–98; Sports Prod., BBC Radio Sport, 1998–2002; Editor, 5 Live Sport, 2002–08; Dep. Controller, Radio 5 Live, 2008–13. Recreations: political studies, sport, media studies. Address: BBC, Quay House, MediaCityUK, Salford Quays, Salford M50 2QH. T: (0161) 335 6723. E: jonathan.wall.01@bbc.co.uk.

**WALL, Malcolm Robert;** Chairman: dock10, since 2014; Audioboom plc, 2014–19; Eagle Eye plc, since 2017 (Director, since 2014); Director, Malcolm Wall Media Ltd, since 2013; b 24 July 1956; s of Maj. Gen. Robert Percival Walter Wall, CB, and of Patricia Kathleen Wall; m 1985, Elizabeth Craxford; three d. Educ: Allhallows Sch., Lyme Regis; Univ. of Kent (BA Hons). Sales Dir, Anglia TV, 1987; Sales and Mktg Dir, Granada TV, 1988–92; Dep. CEO, Meridian Broadcasting, 1992–94; Man. Dir, Anglia TV, 1994–96; Dep. CEO, 1996–99, CEO, 1999–2000, United Broadcasting and Entertainment; Chief Operating Officer, United Business Media plc, 2000–05; Chief Executive Officer: ntl:Telewest, 2006; Content, Virgin Media, 2006–09; Abu Dhabi Media, 2011; Advr to Abu Dhabi Media Zone Authy, 2013–15; Man. Dir, Song Lin, 2013–14. Former Dir, Redshift Strategy Consulting. Chairman: Harlequin FC, 1997–2000 and 2009–11; Disciple Media Ltd, 2015–17; non-executive Director: Five, 2000–05; ITE plc, 2006–11; Creston plc, 2007–11; Image Nation LLC, 2013–. Member: RTS, 1995–; BAFTA, 2014–. Recreations: sport, reading, television. Address: The Close, 2 Longfield Drive, SW14 7AU. Clubs: Royal Automobile, MCC, Harlequin Football; Royal Fowey Yacht.

**WALL, Mark Arthur;** QC 2006; **His Honour Judge Wall;** a Circuit Judge, since 2014; b 4 March 1963; s of Arthur and Phyllis Wall; m 1987, Carmel Miriam Adler (see C. M. Wall); one s one d. Educ: King Charles I Sch., Kidderminster; St John's Coll., Cambridge (BA 1984). Called to the Bar, Lincoln's Inn, 1985, Bencher, 2013; in practice, specialising in criminal law; a Recorder, 2002–14; Leader, Midland Circuit, 2011–14; a Dep. High Ct Judge (Admin. Ct), 2013–. Mem., Bar Council, 2008–14. Recreations: theatre, travel, horse racing. Address: Birmingham Crown Court, 1 Newton Street, Birmingham B4 7NA. E: mwqc@btinternet.com.

**WALL, Gen. Sir Peter (Anthony),** GCB 2013 (KCB 2009); CBE 2002 (OBE 1994); DL; Chief of the General Staff, 2010–14; Aide-de-Camp General to the Queen, 2009–14; b 10 July 1955; s of late John Ramsay Wall and of Dorothy Margaret (née Waltho); m 1980, Fiona Anne Simpson; two s. Educ: Whitgift Sch.; Selwyn Coll., Cambridge (BA 1978; MA 1980); psc; hcsc. Commnd RE, 1974; sc 1987; COS 5 AB Bde, 1988–89; OC 9 Para Sqn, RE, 1990–92; CO 32 Engr Regt, 1994–96; Commander: 24 Airmob Bde, 1999; 16 Air Assault Bde, 1999–2001; Chief of Jt Force Ops, 2001–03; GOC 1st (UK) Armoured Div., 2003–05; Dep. Chief of Jt Ops (Ops), 2005–07, DCDS (Commitments), 2007–09, MoD; C-in-C, Land Forces, 2009–10; Chief Royal Engr, 2009–13. Colonel Commandant: REME, 2002–09; RE, 2003–13; Bde of Gurkhas, 2012–16. Director: Amicus Ltd, 2014–; General Dynamics Corp., 2016–. Pres., Combat Stress, 2014–. Patron, Team Army, 2014–. DL Som, 2015. Hon. FREng 2013; Hon. FICE 2013. Recreation: sport. Club: MCC.

**WALL, Sir Stephen;** see Wall, Sir J. S.

**WALLACE,** family name of **Barons Dudley, Wallace of Saltaire** and **Wallace of Tankerness.**

**WALLACE OF SALTAIRE,** Baron cr 1995 (Life Peer), of Shipley in the County of West Yorkshire; **William John Lawrence Wallace;** PC 2012; Professor of International Relations, London School of Economics, 1999–2005, now Emeritus; b 12 March 1941; s of William E. Wallace and Mary A. Tricks; m 1968, Helen Sarah Rushworth (see Dame H. S. Wallace); one s one d. Educ: Westminster Abbey Choir School (Sen. Chorister, 1954); St Edward's Sch., Oxford; King's Coll., Cambridge (Exhibnr, 1959; BA Hist. 1962); Nuffield Coll., Oxford; Cornell Univ. (PhD Govt 1968). Lectr in Govt, Univ. of Manchester, 1967–77; Dep. Dir, RIIA, 1978–90; Sen. Res. Fellow in European Studies, St Antony's Coll., Oxford, 1990–95; Prof. of Internat. Studies, Central European Univ., Budapest, 1994–97; Reader in Internat. Relns, LSE, 1995–99. House of Lords: Mem., Select Cttee on EU, 1997–2001 (Chair, Sub-Cttee on justice and home affairs, 1997–2000); Lib Dem spokesman: on defence, 1998–2001; on foreign affairs, 2001–10; govt spokesman: on educn, foreign affairs, and on work and pensions, 2010–11; on Cabinet Office, foreign affairs and defence, 2011–12; on Cabinet Office and FCO, 2012–15; a Lord in Waiting (Govt Whip), 2010–15; Dep. Leader, Lib Dem Gp, 2004–10. Contested (L): Huddersfield West, 1970; Manchester Moss Side, Feb. and Oct. 1974; Shipley, 1983 and 1987. Vice-Chm., Liberal Party Policy Cttee, 1977–87. Editor, Jl of Common Market Studies, 1974–78. Hon. Dr, Free Univ. of Brussels, 1992. Ordre pour la Mérite (France), 1995; Chevalier, Légion d'Honneur (France), 2005. Publications: Foreign Policy and the Political Process, 1972; The Foreign Policy Process in Britain, 1977; (ed with Helen Wallace, and contrib.) Policy-making in the European Union, 1977, 5th edn 2005; (with Christopher Tugendhat) Options for British Foreign Policy in the 1990s, 1988; The Transformation of Western Europe, 1990; Regional Integration: the West European experience, 1994; Why vote Liberal Democrat?, 1997. Address: House of Lords, SW1A 0PW.

**WALLACE OF SALTAIRE, Lady;** see Wallace, H. S.

**WALLACE OF TANKERNESS,** Baron cr 2007 (Life Peer), of Tankerness in Orkney; **James Robert Wallace,** FRSE; PC 2000; QC (Scot.) 1997; Leader of Liberal Democrats, House of Lords, 2013–16; b 25 Aug. 1954; s of late John F. T. Wallace and Grace Hannah Wallace (née Maxwell); m 1983, Rosemary Janet Fraser; two d. Educ: Annan Academy; Downing College, Cambridge (BA 1975, MA 1979); Edinburgh University (LLB 1977). Called to the Scots Bar, 1979; practised as Advocate, 1979–83. Contested Dumfriesshire (L), 1979; contested South of Scotland (L), European Parlt election, 1979. Vice-Chm. (Policy), Scottish Liberal Party, 1982–85; Leader, Scottish Liberal Democrats, 1992–2005. MP Orkney and Shetland, 1983–2001 (L 1983–88, Lib Dem 1988–2001). Liberal spokesman on defence, 1985–87; Deputy Whip, 1985–87, Chief Whip, 1987–88; first Lib Dem Chief Whip, 1988–92; Alliance spokesman on Transport, 1987; Lib Dem spokesman on employment and training, 1988–92, on fisheries, 1988–97, on Scottish affairs, 1992–99, on maritime affairs, 1994–97. Mem. (Lib Dem) Orkney, Scottish Parlt, 1999–2007. Scottish Executive: Dep. First Minister, 1999–2005; Minister of Justice, 1999–2003; Minister for Enterprise and Lifelong Learning, 2003–05. Director: Northwind Associates Ltd, 2007–10; Jim Wallace Consultancy Ltd, 2007–10. Advocate Gen. for Scotland, 2010–15; Dep. Leader, H of L, 2013–15. Chair, Regulatory Bd, ICAS, 2017– (Mem., 2017–). Mem. Bd, St Magnus Internat. Fest. (formerly Fest.) Ltd, 2007–14. Chair, Bd of Trustees, Reprieve, 2017–. Hon. Prof., Inst. of Petroleum Engrg, Heriot-Watt Univ., 2007–10. FRSE 2018. Hon. Bencher, Lincoln's Inn, 2016. Hon. DLitt Heriot-Watt, 2007; DUniv Open, 2009; Dr hc Edinburgh, 2009. Recreations: golf, music, travel. Address: Northwood House, Tankerness, Orkney KW17 2QS. T: (01856) 861383; House of Lords, SW1A 0PW. E: wallacej@parliament.uk. Clubs: Caledonian; Scottish Liberal (Edinburgh).

**WALLACE, Albert Frederick,** CBE 1963 (OBE 1955); DFC 1943; Controller of Manpower, Greater London Council, 1978–82; b 22 Aug. 1921; s of Major Frederick Wallace and Ada Wallace; m 1940, Evelyn M. White (d 2005); one s one d. Educ: Roan School, Blackheath, SE3. MIPM, MCMI, MILGA. Regular Officer, Royal Air Force, 1939–69: served war of 1939–45, with 40 Sqn, 93 Sqn, 214 Sqn, 620 Sqn; overseas service in Egypt (Canal Zone), S Rhodesia, India, Cyprus; sc 1944–45; NDC 1959–60; sowc 1963; retired in rank of Group Captain. Regional Advisory Officer, Local Authorities Management Services and Computer Cttee, 1969–71; Asst Clerk of the Council, Warwickshire CC, 1971–73; County Personnel Officer, W Midlands CC, and Dir, W Midlands PTA, 1973–78. Chevalier, Légion d'Honneur (France), 2015. Recreations: golf, bridge. Address: Flat 14, Kepplestone, Staveley Road, Eastbourne BN20 7JY. T: (01323) 730668.

**WALLACE, Angus;** see Wallace, W. A.

**WALLACE, Rt Hon. Ben;** see Wallace, Rt Hon. R. B. L.

**WALLACE, Sir David (James),** Kt 2004; CBE 1996; PhD; FRS 1986; FREng; FRSE; FInstP; Master, Churchill College, Cambridge, 2006–14; b 7 Oct. 1945; s of Robert Elder Wallace and Jane McConnell Wallace (née Elliot); m 1970, Elizabeth Anne Yeats; one d. Educ: Hawick High Sch.; Univ. of Edinburgh (BSc, PhD). FRSE 1982; FInstP 1991; FREng (FEng 1998). Harkness Fellow, Princeton Univ., 1970–72; Lecturer in Physics, 1972–78, Reader in Physics, 1978–79, Southampton Univ.; Tait Prof. of Mathematical Physics, 1979–93, Hd of Physics, 1984–87, Edinburgh Univ.; Vice-Chancellor, Loughborough Univ., 1994–2005; N. M. Rothschild & Sons Prof. of Mathematical Scis and Dir, Isaac Newton Inst. for Mathematical Scis, Univ. of Cambridge, 2006–11. Director: Edinburgh Concurrent Supercomputer, 1987–89; Edinburgh Parallel Computing Centre, 1990–93. Science and Engineering Research Council, subseq. Engineering and Physical Sciences Research Council: Chm., Physics Cttee, 1987–90; Chm., Science Bd, 1990–94; Mem. Council, 1990–98; Chm., Technical Opportunities Panel, 1994–98. European Commission: Physics Panel, Human Capital and Mobility Prog., 1991–94; Large Scale

Facilities Evaluation Panel, 1995–97; European Sci. and Technol. Assembly, 1997–98. Mem., Royal Commn for Exhibn of 1851, 2001–11. Chairman: CVCP/SCOP Task Force on sport in higher educn, 1995–97; Value for Money Steering Gp, HEFCE, 1997–2003; Member: Royal Soc. sci. and industl award Cttees, 1990–95; SHEFC, 1993–97; LINK Bd, OST, 1995–98; LINK/Teaching Co. Scheme Bd, 1999–2001; Chairman: e-Science Steering Cttee, OST, 2001–06; Teaching Co. Scheme Quinquennial Rev., 2001. Non-executive Director: Scottish Life Insurance Co., 1999–2001; Taylor & Francis Gp plc, 2000–04; UK eUnivs Worldwide Ltd, 2001–04. Chm., Council for Mathematical Scis, 2006–10; Chm. Adv. Bd, Internat. Centre for Math. Scis, 2017–. President: Physics Sect., BAAS, 1994; Inst. of Physics, 2002–04; Cambridge Soc. for Application of Res., 2014–17; Vice-Pres. and Mem. Council, RSE, 2013–17. Royal Society: Mem. Council, 2001–07; Treas. and Vice-Pres., 2002–07. Chm., RSE/IEEE James Clerk Maxwell Award, 2015. Mem. Court, St Andrews Univ., 2014–. Trustee: Royal Instn of GB, 2011–12; Bill McLaren Foundn, 2016–. Gov. and Trustee, John Lyon's Foundn (formerly Harrow Sch. Foundn), 2007–16. DL Leics, 2001–06. Hon. FIMA, 2009. Hon. DEng Heriot-Watt, 2002; Hon. DSc: Edinburgh, 2003; Leicester, 2005; Loughborough, 2006; Southampton, 2006; East Anglia, 2009. Maxwell Medal of Inst. of Physics, 1980. *Publications:* in research and review jls, in a number of areas of theoretical physics and computing. *Recreations:* exercise, eating well, mycophagy. *E:* djw75@hermes.cam.ac.uk.

**WALLACE, Fleming;** *see* Wallace, J. F.

**WALLACE, Graham Martyn,** FCMA; Mentor, since 2006, and Director, since 2018, Merryck & Co. (Chief Executive, 2006–08); *b* 26 May 1948; *s* of Ronald and May Wallace; *m* 1974, Denise Margaret Wallace (*née* Dyer); *one s one d. Educ:* Imperial College, London (BSc Eng; ACGI); Birkbeck Coll., London (MA London Studies 2005). Graduate trainee, Turner & Newall, 1969–72; Co. Accountant, Brandhurst Co. Ltd, 1972–74; various finance and mgt posts, Rank Xerox, 1974–83; Planning Manager, Imperial Gp, 1983–85; Finance Dir, Imperial Leisure and Retailing, 1985–86; Head of Finance and Planning, 1986–89, Finance Dir, 1989–92, Granada Gp plc; Chief Executive: Granada UK Rental, 1992–95; Granada Restaurants and Services, 1995–97; Cable & Wireless Communications plc, 1997–99; Cable and Wireless plc, 1999–2003. Non-executive Director: Barclays PLC, 2001–03; Barclays Bank PLC, 2001–03.

**WALLACE, Helen Richenda, (Mrs D. Papp);** Consultant Editor, BBC Music Magazine (Editor, 1999–2004); Programme Director, Kings Place Music Foundation; *b* 19 Nov. 1966; *d* of Dr Ian Wallace and Richenda Ponsonby; *m* 2000, David Papp; *one d. Educ:* St Peter's Coll., Oxford (MA English); Guildhall Sch. of Music and Drama (LGSM); London Coll. of Printing (Dip. Periodical Journalism). Features Ed., The Music Mag., 1991–92; Ed., The Strad, 1992–94; Dep. Ed., BBC Music Mag., 1994–99; Editor-in-Chief, South Bank mag., 2000. *Publications:* Fanfare (ed with D. Minshull), 1999; Spirit of the Orchestra, 2006; Boosey & Hawkes: the publishing story, 2007; The History and Future of Music, 2008.

**WALLACE, Dame Helen Sarah, (Lady Wallace of Saltaire),** DBE 2011; CMG 2000; FBA 2000; Centennial Professor, European Institute, London School of Economics and Political Science, 2007–10, Emeritus Professor, 2010–13; *b* 25 June 1946; *d* of Edward Rushworth and Joyce Rushworth; *m* 1968, William John Lawrence Wallace (*see* Baron Wallace of Saltaire); *one s one d. Educ:* St Anne's Coll., Oxford (MA Classics); Coll. of Europe, Bruges (Dip. Eur. Studies 1968); Univ. of Manchester (PhD 1975). Lectr, UMIST, 1974–78; Lectr, then Sen. Lectr, CS Coll., 1978–85 (on secondment to FCO, 1979–80); Dir, Eur. Programme, RIIA, 1985–92; Dir, 1992–98, Co-Dir, 1998–2001, Sussex European Inst.; Dir, Robert Schuman Centre, European University Inst., 2001–06. Dir, One Europe or Several? Programme, ESRC, 1998–2001. Member: Better Regulation Commn, 2006–08; Bd, British Library, 2015–19. Foreign Sec., British Acad., 2011–15. Serves on various editl and adv. bds. Hon. Dr: Aston; Loughborough; Sussex; Sciences-Po Paris; Athens. Chevalier, Ordre Nationale du Mérite (France), 1996. *Publications:* (ed jtly) Policy Making in the European Union, 1977, 7th edn 2015; (jtly) The Council of Ministers of the European Union, 1997, 2nd edn 2006; (ed) Interlocking Dimensions of European Integration, 2001; contrib. numerous articles on European integration. *Recreations:* gardening, travelling.

**WALLACE, Prof. Ian George,** PhD; FRSC, FREng, FIExpE; Professor and Head of School, 2009–15 and Pro Vice Chancellor, 2014–15, Cranfield Defence and Security, Professor Emeritus, 2016, Cranfield University, Defence Academy of the United Kingdom; *b* Gourock, Renfrewshire, 21 Feb. 1948; *s* of John Wallace and Annie Wallace; *m* 1997, Maureen Clapton; *two s two d. Educ:* Heriot-Watt Univ., Edinburgh (BSc Hons Chem 1973; PhD Chem. 1976). FRSC 2000. Ministry of Defence: Higher, then Sen. Scientific Officer, Explosives Res. and Develt Establishment, 1976–85; PSO, Procurement Exec., 1985–89; Dir Air Systems Controllerate Information Systems, 1989–92; Ordnance Scientific Advr to Chief Inspector of Naval Ordnance, 1992–97; Ministry of Defence: Dir Standardisation, Dir Safety Policy, Vice-Pres., Ordnance Bd, 1997–2000; Chief Inspector Explosives, Dir Ordnance Safety Gp, Defence Procurement Agency, 2000–01; Hd of Dept, Cranfield Univ., 2001–09. Member: Defence Nuclear Safety Cttee, 2005–15; Nuclear Res. Adv. Council, 2015–. FREng 2011; FIExpE 2012. *Publications:* 77 conf. papers and reports. *Recreations:* art, music, golf, tennis, sailing, football. *Address:* 28 Brookfield, Highworth, Swindon, Wilts SN6 7HY. *T:* 07973 290611. *E:* i.g.wallace@cranfield.ac.uk. *Clubs:* Defence Academy Golf; Highworth Tennis.

**WALLACE, Ivan Harold Nutt,** CB 1991; Senior Chief Inspector, Department of Education, Northern Ireland, 1979–95; *b* 20 Feb. 1935; *s* of late Harold Wallace and Annie McClure Wallace; *m* 1962, Winifred Ervine Armstrong; *two d. Educ:* Grosvenor High Sch., Belfast; QUB (BSc 1957). MRSC 1963. School Teacher: Leeds Central High Sch., 1957–60; Foyle Coll., Londonderry, 1960–69; Inspector of Schools, NI, 1969–75; Sen. Inspector, 1975–77; Staff Inspector, 1977–78; Chief Inspector, 1978–79. Hon. Prof., Sch. of Educn, QUB, 1996–2001. *Recreations:* music, walking.

**WALLACE, (James) Fleming;** QC (Scot) 1985; Counsel to Scottish Law Commission, 1979–93; *b* 19 March 1931; *s* of James F. B. Wallace, SSC and Margaret B. Gray, MA; *m* 1st, 1964, Valerie Mary (*d* 1986), *d* of Leslie Lawrence, solicitor, and Madge Lawrence, Ramsbury, Wilts; *two d;* 2nd, 1990, Linda Ann, solicitor, *d* of Robert Grant, civil engineer, and Alice Grant. *Educ:* Edinburgh Academy; Edinburgh University (MA 1951; LLB 1954). Served RA, 1954–56 (2nd Lieut); TA 1956–60. Admitted Faculty of Advocates, 1957; practised at Scottish Bar until 1960; Parly Draftsman and Legal Secretary, Lord Advocate's Dept, London, 1960–79. Part-time Chm., Industrial Tribunals, Scotland, 1993–2001. Volunteer, CAB, 2001–08. *Publications:* The Businessman's Lawyer (Scottish Section), 1965, 2nd edn 1973. *Recreations:* hill walking, choral singing, golf. *Address:* 6 Westholme, Hutton Rudby, Yarm, N Yorks TS15 0EA.

**WALLACE, Sir James (Hay),** KNZM 2011 (ONZM 2001); Chairman and Managing Director, Wallace Corporation Ltd Group, since 1975; Director, James Wallace Arts Trust, since 1992; *b* Cambridge, NZ, 23 Nov. 1937; *s* of James Dunning Wallace and Frances Lindsay Hay Wallace (*née* Hay). *Educ:* King's Coll., Auckland; The Browne and Nichols Sch., Cambridge, Mass; Univs of Otago and Auckland (LLB). Admitted solicitor, 1960; called to the Bar, 1961; with Buddle Weir, Auckland, 1959–61, Ellis Piers and Young Jackson, London, 1962–64; Co. Sec. and Co. Solicitor, Kerridge Odeon Corp. Gp, incl. Rank Xerox NZ Ltd, 1965–70; Co. Solicitor and Exec., Fisher and Paykel Ltd, 1971–74. Dir, various cos. Chm., Trustee and Settlor, James Wallace Arts Trust, 1992–. Member: Tongariro Nat. Park Bd; NZ Film Commn Bd; Council, Meat Industry Assoc. Fellow, Knox Coll., Univ. of Otago, 2008. NZ Pres., AFS. Patron, Trustee and Bd Mem., charitable arts orgns. Founding Pres., Graduates' Ski Club; Treas., Ski Council, NZ Ski Assoc. *Recreations:* ski-ing, travel, opera and other performing and visual arts (sometime Member, Royal Choral Society and Dorian Singers NZ). *Address:* Rannoch, 77 Almorah Road, Epsom, Auckland 1023, New Zealand. *Club:* Northern (Auckland).

**WALLACE, Dr James Stuart;** Senior Hydrologist, TropWATER (Centre for Tropical Water and Aquatic Ecosystem Research), James Cook University, 2013–18; *b* 20 June 1952; *s* of Joseph Wallace and Anne Wallace (*née* Keenan); *m* 1974, Josephine Marie Richardson; *one s three d. Educ:* Lisburn Tech. Coll.; Queen's Univ., Belfast (BSc 1973); Univ. of Nottingham (PhD 1978). NERC Institute of Hydrology: Envmtl Physicist, 1978–2004; Head: Vegetation Water Use Section, 1989–93; Hydrological Processes Div., 1993–96; Dir, 1996–2000; Dep. Dir, and Dir of Hydrology, NERC Centre for Ecol. & Hydrol., 2000–04; Team Leader, Floodplain Hydrology Gp, Land and Water Div., CSIRO, 2004–12. Vis. Prof. in Hydrology, Univ. of Reading, 1997–2005. Consultant to UNDP Global Envmt Facility, 1995; Hydrological Advr to UK Perm. Rep. to WMO, 1999–2003. Chairman: Jt UNESCO/WMO Task Force for Hydrology for Envmt, Life and Policy initiative, 1999–2005; UK Inter-Deptl Cttee on Hydrology, 2000–03; Member: Dirs Mgt Bd, EurAqua, 2001–03; Steering Cttee, NERC Centres for Atmospheric Sci., 2002–03; Bd, British Oxygen Co. Foundn, 2003–07. Vice-Pres., Internat. Cttee on Atmosphere-Soil-Vegetation Relns, 1996. FRMetS 2003. *Publications:* (ed jtly) Soil Water Balance in the Sudano-Sahelian Zone, 1991; (ed jtly) Hydrology and Water Law - Bridging the Gap, 2006; papers on hydrological processes in Qly Jl RMetS, Proc. Royal Soc., Jl Hydrology, Agric. and Forest Meteorology, Marine Pollution Bulletin, Marine and Freshwater Res. *Recreations:* grandchildren, gardening, golf. *Address:* Centre for Tropical Water and Aquatic Ecosystem Research, Building No 145, James Cook University, Townsville, Qld 4811, Australia. *E:* jim.wallace@mail.com.

**WALLACE, Joanna Jane;** Independent Case Examiner, Department for Work and Pensions, since 2013; *b* Chesterfield, 3 Sept. 1965; *d* of Joseph Barry and Margaret Wallace; *one d. Educ:* University Coll. London (BSc Hons 1987); Univ. of Calif, Berkeley (MBA 1991). Planner and Planning Manager, Kaiser Permanente, Calif, 1991–95; Dir, E Cheshire NHS Trust, 1995–97; Chief Executive: St Helens and Knowsley HA, 1997–2000; Christie NHS Trust, 2000–05; Aptium Cancer Care, 2006–08; Spire Manchester Hosp., 2009–12. Ind. Assessor, Ombudsman Services, 2015–. Mem., Nat. Sentencing Adv. Panel, MoJ, 2005–07. *Recreations:* yoga, cooking, life drawing and mixed media, Quaker Attender (Society of Friends).

**WALLACE, John Malcolm Agnew;** JP; Vice Lord-Lieutenant, Dumfries and Galloway (District of Wigtown), 1990–2003; *b* 30 Jan. 1928; *s* of John Alexander Agnew Wallace and Marjory Murray Wallace; *m* 1955, Louise Haworth-Booth; *one s two d. Educ:* Brooks Sch., USA; Harrow; West of Scotland Agricultural College. Farmer. JP Stranraer, 1970; DL Dumfries and Galloway, 1971. *Address:* Lochryan, Stranraer DG9 8QY. *T:* (01581) 200284.

**WALLACE, John Williamson,** CBE 2011 (OBE 1995); Principal, Royal Conservatoire of Scotland (formerly Royal Scottish Academy of Music and Drama), 2002–14; freelance soloist, composer, conductor; *b* 14 April 1949; *s* of Christopher Kidd Wallace and Ann Drummond Allan; *m* 1971, Elizabeth Jane Hartwell; *one s one d. Educ:* Buckhaven High Sch.; King's Coll., Cambridge (MA); York Univ.; Royal Acad. of Music (ARAM 1983; FRAM 1990). ARCM 1968, Hon. RCM 1985, FRCM 2008; FRSAMD 1993; FRNCM 2008. Asst Principal Trumpet, LSO, 1974–76; Prin. Trumpet, Philharmonia Orch., 1976–94; founded The Wallace Collection (brass-interest music gp), 1986; Principal Trumpet, London Sinfonietta, 1987–2001; Artistic Dir of Brass, RAM, 1993–2001. Trumpet solo recordings. Hon. DMus Aberdeen, 2007; Hon. DLitt Strathclyde, 2007; Hon. DMus St Andrews, 2014. Mercedes-Benz Prize, 1991; Assoc. of British Orchs Award, 2002. *Publications:* Five Easy Pieces, 1984; First Book of Trumpet Solos, 1985; Second Book of Trumpet Solos, 1985, 2nd edn 1987; Grieg's Seven Lyric Pieces, 1985; Kornukopia, 1986; Prime Number, 1990; Odd Number and Even Number, 1991; (jtly) Music Through Time, 1995; (ed jtly) Cambridge Companion to Brass Instruments, 1997; (jtly) The Trumpet, 2011. *Address:* 157B Camphill Avenue, Glasgow G41 3DR.

**WALLACE, Major Malcolm Charles Robarts;** Director of Regulation, British Horseracing Authority (formerly Jockey Club, then Horseracing Regulatory Authority), 1994–2008; Chairman: HPower Group, 2008–10; Martin Collins Group, since 2010; Director, M. C. R. Wallace (Racing, Equestrian and Sporting) Ltd, since 2008; *b* 12 June 1947; *s* of Lionel John Wallace, MBE, TD and Maureen Winefride (*née* Robarts); *m* 1st, 1974, Caroline Anne Doyne-Ditmas (marr. diss. 1990); *one s one d;* 2nd, 1991, Mrs Jane Thelwall; *two s. Educ:* Blackrock College, Co. Dublin. Student pupil with Lt-Col J. Hume-Dudgeon at Burton Hall, Co. Dublin, 1965–67; Mons Officer Cadet Sch.; commissioned RA, 1967; gun line officer, 18 Light Regt, Hong Kong; 3rd Regt RHA, 1969; King's Troop RHA, 1970 (long equitation course, RAVC Melton Mowbray); Troop Comdr, 19 Field Regt, 1974; Adjutant 101 Northumbrian Field Artillery, 1976; Staff Officer, HQ UKLF, 1978–82; Comd King's Troop RHA, 1982–85, retired. Dir Gen., BEF, 1985–94. Chef d'Equipe to British Internat. and Olympic Three Day Event Teams, 1979–84; Chef de Mission, Equestrian Team, Olympic Games, Seoul, 1988 and Barcelona, 1992. Chm., Burghley Horse Trials, 2002–10. Freeman, Saddlers' Co., 1985. *Publications:* The King's Troop Royal Horse Artillery, 1984. *Recreations:* field and equestrian sports, training gun dogs, Leicester Tigers supporter! *Address:* Fishponds Farm, Stoke Albany, Market Harborough, Leics LE16 8PZ. *T:* (01858) 535250, *T:* 07785 390325. *Club:* Cavalry and Guards.

**WALLACE, Margaret;** Member (Lab) Kilmarnock and Loudoun, Scottish Parliament, 1999–2007; *b* 6 April 1953; *d* of late George and Margaret Wallace; *m* 1974, Russell Jamieson (marr. diss. 2002); *one d. Educ:* Grange Acad.; Ayr Coll. Official for UNISON (formerly NUPE), 1979–99. Mem. Bd, E Ayrshire Employment Initiative, 1998–2003. Scottish Parliament: Member: Audit Cttee, 1999–2007; Health and Community Care Cttees, 1999–2003. Convener, Scottish Commn for Public Audit, 2001–07.

**WALLACE, Marjorie Shiona Douglas,** CBE 2008 (MBE 1994); Founder, and Chief Executive, SANE, mental health charity, since 1989; broadcaster, author, journalist; *d* of William Wallace and Doris Tulloch; *m* 1974, Count Andrzej Skarbek (*d* 2011); *three s;* partner, Thomas Alan Margerison (*d* 2014); *one d. Educ:* Roedean; Johannesburg; Parsons' Mead, Ashtead; University College London (BA Hons Psych and Phil; Fellow, 2004). Television: The Frost Programme, 1966–68; ITV religious programmes, 1966–68; LWT current affairs, 1968–69; Dir/reporter, current affairs, BBC TV, 1969–72; Insight team (Thalidomide campaign), feature writer, Sunday Times, 1972–89, incl. Forgotten Illness, mental illness campaign, The Times, 1985–89; Guardian Res. Fellow, Nuffield Coll., Oxford, 1989–91. Founded SANE, and Prince of Wales Internat. Centre for SANE Res., Oxford (opened 2003). Institute of Psychiatry: Member: Cttee of Management, 1989–2002; Ethics Cttee (Res.), 1991–2002; Adv. Bd, Design for Patient Dignity, 2009–10.

Trustee, UKCP, 2009–12. Chm., Friends of Open Air Theatre, 1991–2008. Patron, Hay Literary Festival, 2001–. Numerous internat. presentations and speeches, also broadcasts on TV and radio; TV documentaries: Whose Mind Is It Anyway?, 1988; Circles of Madness, 1994. Hon. Fellow, Dept of Psychiatry, Univ. of Oxford, 2018. Hon. FRCPsych 1997. Hon. Mem., World Psychiatric Assoc., 2017. Hon. DSc City, 2001. Campaigning Journalist of the Year, British Press Awards, 1982, 1986; John Pringle Meml Award, 1986; Book Trust Prize, 1987; Snowdon Special Award, 1988; Medical Journalist of the Year, 1988; Evian Health Award, 1991, and Best Use of Media award, 1995; Public Service award, British Neurosci. Assoc., 2002; Internat. Pioneer and Diversity Award, Muslim community, 2005; Healthcare Communications Advocate, Communiqué Awards, 2014; Outstanding Campaigner, Women of the Year Awards, 2016. *Publications:* On Giant's Shoulders, 1976 (also original BBC TV screenplay (Internat. Emmy award), 1979); (jtly) Suffer the Children: the story of Thalidomide, 1978; (jtly) The Superpoison, The Dioxin Disaster, 1980; The Silent Twins, 1986 (also BBC TV screenplay; Best Docudrama, USA, HBO, 1989); Campaign and Be Damned, 1991. *Recreations:* poetry, piano, Victorian ballads, opera, musicals, dining out. *Address:* SANE, St Mark's Studios, 14 Chillingworth Road, Islington, N7 8QJ. *T:* (020) 3805 1790. *Clubs:* Athenæum, Groucho.

**WALLACE, Rt Rev. Martin William;** Bishop Suffragan of Selby, 2003–13; an Honorary Assistant Bishop, Diocese of York, since 2013; *b* 16 Nov. 1948; *s* of Derek Philip William Wallace and Audrey Sybil Wallace (*née* Thomason); *m* 1971, Diana Christine Pratt; one *s* one *d*. *Educ:* Varndean Grammar Sch., Brighton; Taunton's Sch., Southampton; King's Coll., London (BD Hons; AKC; Winchester Schol.); St Augustine's Theol Coll., Canterbury. Ordained deacon, 1971, priest, 1972; Assistant Curate: Attercliffe, Sheffield, 1971–74; New Malden, Surrey, 1974–77; Vicar, St Mark's, Forest Gate, 1977–93 and Priest-in-charge, Emmanuel, 1985–89, All Saints, 1991–93, Forest Gate; Chaplain, Forest Gate Hosp., 1977–80; Rural Dean, Newham, 1982–91; Chelmsford Diocesan Urban Officer, 1991–93; Priest-in-charge, Bradwell and St Lawrence, 1993–97; Industrial Chaplain, Maldon and Dengie, 1993–97; Archdeacon of Colchester, 1997–2003. Hon. Canon, Chelmsford Cathedral, 1989–97. *Publications:* Healing Encounters in the City, 1987; City Prayers, 1994; Pocket Celtic Prayers, 1996; Celtic Reflections, 1996; Celtic Resource Book, 1998; (contrib.) Worship: window of the urban Church, 2007; In Good Company, 2009; The Alex, 2019. *Recreation:* local history. *Address:* 28 Alexandra Court, Bridlington YO15 2LB. *T:* (01262) 670265. *E:* mdw28@btinternet.com.

**WALLACE, Moira Paul,** OBE 1997; Provost, Oriel College, Oxford, 2013–18 (Hon. Fellow, 2018); *b* 15 Aug. 1961; *d* of Prof. and Mrs W. V. Wallace; *m* 2009, David Archer. *Educ:* Coleraine High Sch.; Emmanuel Coll., Cambridge (MA Mod. Langs 1983; Hon. Fellow 2014); Harvard Univ. (Kennedy Schol.; AM Comparative Lit. 1985). Joined HM Treasury, 1985; Private Sec. to Chancellor of Exchequer, 1987–90; Econ. Affairs Private Sec. to Prime Minister, 1995–97; Dir, Social Exclusion Unit, Cabinet Office, 1997–2002; Dir Gen., Criminal Justice Gp, Home Office, 2002–04; Chief Exec., Office for Criminal Justice Reform, 2004–05; Dir Gen., Crime, Policing and Counter Terrorism, then Crime Reduction and Community Safety Gp, Home Office, 2005–08; Permanent Sec., DECC, 2008–12. Vis. Fellow, Nuffield Coll., Oxford, 1999–2007; Vis. Prof. in Practice, Centre for Analysis of Social Exclusion, LSE, 2018–. Trustee: Nesta, 2017–; Kennedy Meml Trust, 2019–. Hon Fellow, TCD, 2014. *Address:* c/o Oriel College, Oxford OX1 4EW.

**WALLACE, Pauline;** financial regulator; Head, UK Public Policy and Regulatory Affairs, PricewaterhouseCoopers LLP, 2009–13; *b* London, 19 March 1954; *d* of Sidney Robert Wallace and Hilda Mary Wallace; *m* 1983, Ron Agy; one *s*. *Educ:* Harrow Co. Grammar Sch. for Girls; Univ. of Nottingham (BA French and German). ACA 1979. Trainee accountant, Spicer & Pegler, 1976–80; Under Sec., Accounting Standards Cttee, 1981–83; Technical Dir, Hong Kong Soc. of Accountants, 1983–86; Arthur Andersen: Sen. Manager, Hong Kong, 1986–89, 1991–95; Partner, 1995–2002; Partner, PricewaterhouseCoopers, 2002–13. Member: Accounting Standards Bd, 2010–16; Regulatory Decisions Cttee, Financial Conduct Authy, 2014–; ICAEW Ind. Regulatory Bd, 2016–; Determinations Panel, Pensions Regulator, 2017–. Dir and Chm., Audit Cttee, Paradigm Trust, 2013–. Gov., Middleton Sch., 2013–. *Publications:* Company Law in Hong Kong, 1986, 2nd edn 1990. *Recreations:* walking my dogs, cooking, reading novels, running, keeping fit.

**WALLACE, Richard Alexander;** Principal Finance Officer, Welsh Office, 1990–97; *b* 24 Nov. 1946; *s* of late Lawrence Mervyn and Norah Wallace; *m* 1970, Teresa Caroline Harington Smith (*d* 2006); three *c* (and one *c* decd). *Educ:* Bembridge and Sandown C of E Primary Schools; Clifton Coll. Prep. Sch.; Clifton Coll.; King's Coll., Cambridge (MA). Asst Master, Woking County GS for Boys, 1967; Min. of Social Security, 1968; Principal, DHSS, 1972, Asst Sec., 1981; transf. to Welsh Office, 1986; Under Sec., 1988.

**WALLACE, Richard David;** Executive Producer, since 2012 and Senior Vice President (TV and Production), since 2017, Syco Entertainment; *b* 11 June 1961; *s* of late Bill Wallace and of Maureen Wallace; *m* 2016, Tina Weaver; one *s*. *Educ:* Ratcliffe Coll., Leics. Leicester Mercury, 1979–83; EMI Records, 1983–84; Oxon Bucks News Agency, 1984–86; Daily Mail, 1986–88; The Sun, 1988–90; Daily Mirror: show business reporter, then show business ed., 1999–2000; Hd of News, 2000–02; US Ed., 2002–03; Dep. Ed., Sunday Mirror, 2003–04; Ed., Daily Mirror, 2004–12. Mem., Editors' Code of Practice Cttee, 2010–12. *Recreations:* travel, contemporary American literature. *Club:* Savile.

**WALLACE, Rt Hon. (Robert) Ben (Lobban),** PC 2017; MP (C) Wyre and Preston North, since 2010 (Lancaster and Wyre, 2005–10); Secretary of State for Defence, since 2019; *b* 15 May 1970; *m* 2001, Liza Cooke; two *s* one *d*. *Educ:* Millfield Sch., Somerset; RMA Sandhurst. Ski Instructor, Austrian Nat. Ski Sch., 1987–89; commissioned, Scots Guards, 1991; Platoon Comdr, 1991–93 (despatches, 1992); Ops Officer, 1993, Intelligence, 1994–97; Co. Comdr, 1997; served Windsor, London, N Ireland, Central America, BAOR, Egypt, Cyprus; retired 1998. EU Dir, QinetiQ, 2003–05. MSP (C) NE Scotland, 1999–2003; Mem., EU Cttee, health spokesman, Scottish Parlt. Shadow Minister of State for Scotland, 2006–10; PPS to Lord Chancellor and Sec. of State for Justice, 2010–12, to Minister without Portfolio, 2012–14; an Asst Govt Whip, 2014–15; Parly Under-Sec. of State, NI Office, 2015–16; Minister of State (Minister for Security, then Minister for Security and Econ. Crime), Home Office, 2016–19. Mem., Scottish Select Cttee, 2005–10, NI Grand Cttee, H of C, 2005–10; Chm., All Party Parly Gp on Iran, 2006–14. Mem., Queen's Body Guard for Scotland (Royal Co. of Archers), 2006–. *Recreations:* ski-ing, sailing, Rugby, horse racing. *Address:* House of Commons, SW1A 0AA; c/o Village Centre, Great Eccleston Village Centre, 59 High Street, Great Eccleston PR3 0YB. *Club:* Third Guards.

**WALLACE, Sharmila;** *see* Nebhrajani, S.

**WALLACE, Stephanie Vera;** *see* Hilborne, S. V.

**WALLACE, Victoria Louise;** DL; Director General and Secretary, Commonwealth War Graves Commission, since 2014; *b* Pembury, Kent, 12 March 1966; *d* of Michael John Stickland and Janet Catherine Stickland (*née* Allen); *m* 1997, Seán Michael Wallace; two *d*. *Educ:* Cranbrook Sch., Kent; Univ. of Exeter (LLB Hons). HM Diplomatic Service, 1987–99: Asst Desk Officer, Sci. Space and Telecoms, FCO, 1987; Thai lang. trng, SOAS, 1988; Vice Consul, Bangkok, 1989–92; Desk Officer, Security Policy Dept, FCO, 1992–94; Second Sec. (Pol), Dar es Salaam, 1994–97; Asst Dir, British Council, Dar es Salaam (on secondment), 1997–98; Hd, Wider Europe Resource Mgt Unit, FCO, 1998–99; Justices' Chief Exec., Sussex Magistrates' Courts, 1999–2004; Chief Exec., Leeds Castle Foundn, 2004–14. Non-exec. Dir, Kent Tourism Alliance, 2004–08. Mem. Council, Assoc. of Ind. Museums, 2012–. Ambassador, Kent Co. Agricl Soc., 2010–14. Trustee, Army Museums Ogilby Trust, 2014–18; Hon. Sec., Assoc. of Ind. Mus, 2016–. DL Kent, 2019. *Recreations:* travel, curating a cabinet of curiosities, historic buildings, shopping with my daughters. *Address:* Commonwealth War Graves Commission, 2 Marlow Road, Maidenhead, Berks SL6 7DX. *T:* (01628) 507152. *E:* victoria.wallace@cwgc.org. *See also* Maj. Gen. C. R. Stickland.

**WALLACE, (Wellesley) Theodore (Octavius);** a Judge of the Tax and Chancery Chamber of the Upper Tribunal, 2009–12; *b* 10 April 1938; *s* of late Dr Caleb Paul Wallace and Dr Lucy Elizabeth Rainsford (*née* Pigott); *m* 1988, Maria Amelia Abercromby, *d* of Sir Ian Abercromby, 10th Bt; one *s* one *d*. *Educ:* Charterhouse; Christ Church, Oxford. 2nd Lt, RA, 1958; Lt, Surrey Yeomanry, TA, 1959–62. Called to the Bar, Inner Temple, 1963 (Duke of Edinburgh Schol.). Mem., Lincoln's Inn (*ad eundem*), 1973. Chm., VAT and Duties (formerly VAT) Tribunal, 1989–2009 (pt-time, 1989–92); Special Comr of Income Tax, 1992–2009. Hon. Sec., Taxation of Sub-cttee, Soc. of Cons. Lawyers, 1974–92. Contested (C): Pontypool, Feb. 1974; S Battersea, Oct. 1974, 1979. *Publications:* (jtly with John Wakeham) The Case Against Wealth Tax, 1968. *Recreations:* bridge, lawn tennis, ski-ing. *Address:* 46 Belleville Road, SW11 6QT. *T:* (020) 7228 7740; Whitecroft, W Clandon, Surrey GU4 7TD. *T:* (01483) 222574.

**WALLACE, Prof. (William) Angus,** FRCS, FRCSE, FFSEM; Professor of Orthopaedic and Accident Surgery, School of Clinical (formerly Medical and Surgical) Sciences, University of Nottingham, 1985–2015, now Emeritus; *b* 31 Oct. 1948; *s* of late Dr William Bethune Wallace and Dr Frances Barret Wallace (*née* Early), Dundee; *m* 1971, Jacqueline Vera Studley; two *s* one *d*. *Educ:* Dundee High Sch.; Univ. of St Andrews (MB ChB 1972); FRCSE 1977; Cert. of Orthopaedic Higher Specialist Trng 1984; FRCSE (Orth) 1985; FRCS 1997; FFSEM 2006. Jun. House Officer, Dundee Royal Infirmary and Maryfield Hosp., 1972–73; Sen. House Officer, Derby, 1974–75; Registrar (Basic Surg. Trng), Newcastle and Gateshead Hosps, 1975–77; Orthopaedic Registrar, Nottingham Hosps, 1978–81; MRC Res. Fellow, 1979; Lectr (Hon. Sen. Registrar) in Orthopaedic Surgery, Univ. of Nottingham, 1981–84; Vis. Res. Fellow, Toronto Western Hosp., Canada, 1983; Med. Dir, North Western Orthotic Unit, and Med. Advr, Dept of Orthopaedic Mechanics, Univ. of Salford, 1984–85. Founder: Nottingham Univ. Hosp. Skills Centre, 2002 (Chm., 2002–15); Nat. Repository Centre, Nottingham City Hosp., 2011–15. Advr, Rail Accident Investigation Bd, 2007. Expert Medical Adviser: M1 Kegworth Air Crash, 1989; Grayrigg Train Derailment, 2007; Sandilands/Croydon Tram derailment, 2016. Founding Mem., Internat. Bd for Res. into Aircraft Crash Events, 2016–. Mem., ABC Club, 1988–. Member: RSocMed 1988; Council, RCSE, 1990–2000, 2004–07 (Vice-Pres., 1997–2000); Council, Faculty of Sport and Exercise Medicine, 2005–10, 2015–16; Internat. Bd for Shoulder Surgery, 1992–2019; Council, British Orthopaedic Assoc., 2008–10; Council, Inst. of Advanced Motorists, 2011– (Trustee, 2007–); Dean, Faculty of Medical Informatics, RSCE, 2000–05; E Midlands Regl Dir (formerly Dir for Professional Affairs, E Midlands), RCS, 2014–19. Chairman: Nat. Sports Medicine Inst. of UK, 1999–2003; Inter-Collegiate Bd in Trauma and Orthopaedic Surgery, 2002–05; Specialist Adv. Cttee for Trauma and Orthopaedic Surgery, 2008–10. President: British Elbow and Shoulder Soc., 2001–03 (Hon. Mem., 2016); Internat. Congress for Shoulder and Elbow Surgery, 2010. Inventor/co-inventor of surgical and medical devices; (jtly) developer, The Orthopaedic eLogbook, Faculty of Health Informatics, RCSE, 2002–. Dir, Mavric Ltd, 2018–; Consultant: LockDown Medical Ltd, 2008–14; JRI Orthopaedics Ltd, 2010–; Xiros Ltd, 2015–. Inventor or co-Inventor: Nottingham Surgilig, 1988 (renamed Lockdown, 2011); Interax knee replacement, 1989; Nottingham Shoulder Replacement, 1991; Infinity-Lock Button, 2015. Member, Editorial Board: Jl of Orthopaedic Surgery, 2006–; Orthopaedic Jl of Sports Medicine, 2013–; Mem., Internat. Scientific Adv. Bd, Obere Extremität, 2015–. Foundn Fellow, Faculty of Sports and Exercise Medicine (UK), 2005–14 (Hon. Fellow, 2017). Hon. Mem., British India Orthopaedic Soc., 2005. Hon. Fellow: Hong Kong Coll. of Orthopaedic Surgeons, 2011; Hungarian Orthopaedic Assoc., 2011; British Orthopaedic Assoc., 2017. Triennial Codman Meml Lectr, Internat. Bd of Shoulder and Elbow Surgery, 2016. Sir Walter Mercer Gold Medal, 1985, Sir Walter Mercer Meml Lectr and Medal, 2015, RCSE; Weigelt-Wallace Award for exceptional med. care, Univ. of Texas, 1995; Great Scot Sci. and Medicine Award, Sunday Mail, Scotland, 1995; People of the Year Award, RADAR, 1995. *Publications:* Shoulder Arthroscopy, 1992; (ed jtly) Medical Audit: rationale and practicalities, 1993; Management of Disasters and their Aftermath, 1994; Joint Replacement of the Shoulder and Elbow, 1998; A Handbook of Sports Medicine, 1999; over 350 articles in learned jls on osteoporosis, shoulder surgery, sports medicine and med. informatics. *Recreations:* narrow boating, information technology, DIY. *Address:* High Trees, Foxwood Lane, Woodborough, Nottingham NG14 6ED. *T:* (0115) 965 2372. *E:* Angus.Wallace@rcsed.ac.uk.

**WALLACE-HADRILL, Prof. Andrew Frederic,** OBE 2004; DPhil; FBA 2010; Principal Investigator, Impact of the Ancient City, European Research Council Advanced Project, University of Cambridge, since 2016; Scientific Director, Herculaneum Conservation Project, 2013–16 (Director, 2001–13); *b* 29 July 1951; *s* of John Michael Wallace-Hadrill and Anne (*née* Wakefield); *m* 1976, Josephine Claire Braddock; one *s* one *d*. *Educ:* Rugby Sch.; Corpus Christi Coll., Oxford (MA; Hon. Fellow 2009); St John's Coll., Oxford (DPhil; Hon. Fellow 2009). Fellow and Dir of Studies in Classics, Magdalene Coll., Cambridge, 1976–83; Lectr in Ancient History, Univ. of Leicester, 1983–87; Prof. of Classics, Reading Univ., 1987–2009; Dir, British Sch. at Rome, 1995–2009; Master, Sidney Sussex Coll., Cambridge, 2009–13; Dep. Vice-Chancellor, 2010–12, Dir of Res., Faculty of Classics, 2012–16, Univ. of Cambridge. Editor, Jl of Roman Studies, 1991–95. Hon. DLitt Reading, 2014. *Publications:* Suetonius: the scholar and his Caesars, 1983, 2nd edn 1995; (ed) Patronage in Ancient Society, 1989; (ed with J. W. Rich) City and Country in the Ancient World, 1991; Augustan Rome, 1993, 2nd edn 2018; Houses and Society in Pompeii and Herculaneum, 1994; (ed with R. Laurence) Domestic Space in the Roman World: Pompeii and beyond, 1997; The British School at Rome: one hundred years, 2001; Rome's Cultural Revolution, 2008; Herculaneum: past and future, 2011.

**WALLARD, Prof. Andrew John,** CBE 2011; PhD; Director, International Bureau of Weights and Measures, 2004–10, now Emeritus Director (Director Designate, 2002–03); *b* 11 Oct. 1945; *s* of late William John Wallard and Marjorie Meredith Wallard (*née* Briggs); *m* 1969, Barbara Jean Pritchard (*d* 2016); two *s*. *Educ:* Liverpool Inst. High Sch. for Boys; Univ. of St Andrews (BSc Hons 1968; PhD 1971). CPhys 2000; CEng 2000; FInstP 2000. Laser physicist, NPL, 1968–78; Chief Scientist's Unit, DTI, 1978–80; Mktg Unit, NPL, 1980–81; Department of Trade and Industry, 1981–90: Res. and Technol. Policy Div.; Sec. of State's Policy Unit; Electronics Applications Div.; Alvey/Information Engrg Directorate; ESPRIT prog.; Dep. Dir and Chief Metrologist, NPL, 1990–2002. Member: Central Policy Review Staff, 1980–82; Panel, CSSB, 1985–95; Steering Cttee, Ilkley R&D Conf., 1988–2002; Internat. Cttee for Weights and Measures, 1995–2002

(President Consultative Committee: for Photometry and Radiometry, 1995–2002; for Acoustics, Ultrasound and Vibration, 1999–2003); Bd Mem., Nat. Conf. of Standards Labs Internat., 2002–10. Council Mem., 1998–2001, Chm., 2001–03, Res. and Develt Soc.; Vice Pres., Inst. of Physics, 2001–04 (Council Mem., 1996–2001); Member, Science Council: Istituto di Metrologia "Gustavo Colonnetti", 2002–10; Istituto Elettrotecnico "Galileo Ferraris", 2002–10. Mem., Ext. Panel, Physics Dept, Univ. of Wales, Aberystwyth, subseq. Aberystwyth Univ., 1997–2010 (Hon. Vis. Prof., 2001–). Hon. Ed., Kaye and Laby (a table of physical and chem. constants), 2014–. Chm., Alice Ruston Housing Assoc., 1986–95; Mem., Send PCC, 1988–95; Gov., Send First Sch., 1995–99. FRSA. Fellow: Acad. of Scis of Turin, 2003; Russian Acad. of Metrology, 2007. Hon. DSc Huddersfield, 1999. Lifetime Achievement Award, Co. of Scientific Instrument Makers, 2000; Gold Medal, NPL, 2002; Wildhack Award, Nat. Conf. of Standards Laboratories Internat., 2009. *Publications:* contribs to various books and over 40 contribs to learned jls. *Recreations:* reading the newspapers, the garden, choosing wines, choral evensong. *Address:* Bureau International des Poids et Mesures, Pavillon de Breteuil, 92312, Sèvres Cedex, France. *T:* (4) 66335875, (1) 45077000. *E:* andrew.wallard@gmail.com; Mas Vacquier - La Bergerie, St André d'Olérargues, Gard 30330, France; 4 Chaucer House, Upper Edgeborough Road, Guildford GU1 2BD. *Club:* Athenæum.

**WALLENBERG, Jacob;** Chairman of the Board, Investor AB, since 2005; *b* 13 Jan. 1956; *s* of late Peter Wallenberg, Hon. KBE and Suzanne Fleming; one *s* two *d*. *Educ:* Wharton Sch., Univ. of Pennsylvania (BSc Econ 1980; MBA 1981). Officer, Swedish Naval Reserve. Joined J. P. Morgan, NY, 1981; Hambros Bank, London, 1983; Enskilda Securities, London, 1984, then with Skandinaviska Enskilda Banken, Sweden, 1985; Exec. Vice Pres., Investor AB, 1990–92; rejoined Skandinaviska Enskilda Bank Gp, 1993: Dep. Chief Operating Officer, 1994, Chief Operating Officer, 1995–97, Enskilda Div.; Pres. and CEO, 1997–98; Chm. of Bd, 1998–2005; Vice-Chm., 2005. Vice Chairman: Atlas Copco, 1998; SAS, 2001; Scandinavian Airlines, 2001; Board Member: ABB Ltd, 1999– (Vice Chm., 2015–); Coca-Cola Co., 2007–14; Ericsson, 2011– (Dep. Chm.). Mem. Bd, Knut and Alice Wallenberg Foundn, 1985–. *Recreations:* golf, sailing, ski-ing. *Address:* Investor AB, 10332 Stockholm, Sweden. *T:* (8) 6142000.

**WALLENBERG, Marcus;** Chairman: Skandinaviska Enskilda Banken, since 2005 (a Deputy Chairman, 2002–05); Saab AB, since 2006 (Vice Chairman, 1993–2006); *b* 2 Sept. 1956; *s* of Marc and Olga Wallenberg; *m* Fanny Sachs; four *c*. *Educ:* Georgetown Univ., Washington (BSc Foreign Service). Lieut, Royal Swedish Naval Acad., 1977. Citibank NA, New York, 1980–82; Deutsche Bank AG, Frankfurt and Hamburg, 1983; S. G. Warburg Co. Ltd, London, 1983; Citicorp, Hong Kong, 1984; Skandinaviska Enskilda Banken, Stockholm and London, 1985–90; Dir, Stora Feldmuhle AG, Düsseldorf, 1990–93; Investor AB: Exec. Vice Pres., 1993–99; Pres. and Chief Exec., 1999–2005; Vice Chm., 2015–. Chairman: Electrolux, 2007–14 (Dir, 2005–07); Luossavaara-Kiirunavaara AB, 2011–14. Holds numerous directorships. *Recreations:* sports, tennis, sailing, ski-ing, hunting. *Address:* Skandinaviska Enskilda Banken, Kungsträdgårdsgatan 8, 10640 Stockholm, Sweden.

**WALLER, Rt Hon. Sir (George) Mark,** Kt 1989; PC 1996; Lord Justice of Appeal, 1996–2010; Vice-President, Court of Appeal (Civil Division), 2006–10; Intelligence Services Commissioner, 2011–16; *b* 13 Oct. 1940; *s* of Rt Hon. Sir George Waller, OBE; *m* 1967, Rachel Elizabeth, *d* of His Honour Christopher Beaumont, MBE; two *s* (and one *s* decd). *Educ:* Oundle Sch.; Durham Univ. (LLB). Called to the Bar, Gray's Inn, 1964, Bencher, 1988 (Vice-Treas., 2008; Treas. 2009); QC 1979; a Recorder, 1986–89; a Judge of the High Court of Justice, QBD, 1989–96; Presiding Judge, NE Circuit, 1992–95; Judge i/c Commercial List, 1995–96. Chm., Judicial Studies Bd, 1999–2003. Pres., Council of Inns of Court, 2003–06. *Recreations:* tennis, golf. *Address:* Serle Court, 6 New Square, Lincoln's Inn, WC2A 3QS. *Clubs:* Garrick, MCC; Huntercombe Golf.

See also R. B. *Waller.*

**WALLER, Guy de Warrenne,** MA, MSc; Headmaster, Cranleigh School, 1997–2014; *b* 10 Feb. 1950; *s* of late Col Desmond de Warrenne Waller and of Angela Mary Waller (née Wright); *m* 1980, Hilary Ann Farmbrough; four *d*. *Educ:* Hurstpierpoint Coll.; Worcester Coll., Oxford (MA; Hon. Sec., OUCC; cricket blue, 1974; hockey blue, 1974, 1979); Wolfson Coll., Oxford (MSc). Head of Chemistry and Housemaster, Radley Coll., 1974–93; Headmaster, Lord Wandsworth Coll., 1993–97. Academic Director, EduReach Education, 2014–. *Publications:* Thinking Chemistry, 1980; Advancing Chemistry, 1982; Condensed Chemistry, 1985. *Recreations:* sports, keeping up with family and friends, chess, music. *Clubs:* MCC; Vincent's (Oxford); Oxford University Tennis.

**WALLER, Sir (John) Michael,** 10th Bt *cr* 1780, of Newport, Co. Tipperary; PhD; *b* 14 May 1962; *s* of Sir Robert William Waller, 9th Bt and Carol Anne Waller (née Hines); S father, 2000; *m* 1986, Maria Renee Gonzalez (marr. diss. 2012); four *s* three *d*. *Educ:* George Washington Univ. (BA 1985); Boston Univ. (MA 1989; PhD 1993). Vice Pres., Center for Security Policy, Washington, DC, 2000–; Walter and Leonore Annenberg Prof. of Internat. Communication, Inst. of World Politics, Washington, DC, 2001–13. *Publications:* The Third Current of Revolution, 1991; Secret Empire: the KGB in Russia today, 1994; Russia's Security Services: a checklist for reform, 1997; (ed) The Public Diplomacy Reader, 2007; (ed) Strategic Influence, 2007. *Heir: s* John Michael Waller, *b* 18 Feb. 1990.

**WALLER, Rt Hon. Sir Mark;** *see* Waller, Rt Hon. Sir G. M.

**WALLER, Martin Christopher;** Founder and Director, Andrew Martin International (formerly Andrew Martin), since 1978; *b* Mombasa, 4 Jan. 1956; *s* of Ernest Waller and Alethea Waller (née Ruggles-Brise); two *s* one *d*. *Educ:* Eton Coll. Founder, Andrew Martin, 1978. Member, Advisory Board: KLC Sch. of Design; Molton Brown. Mem., RGS. *Publications:* (jtly) Andrew Martin Design Review, vol. 1, 1998 to vol. 22, 2018; (jtly) Fusion Interiors, 2000; (jtly) Threads of Colour, 2002. *Recreation:* treasure hunting. *Address:* 38 Holland Park, W11 3RP. *T:* 07970 945848. *E:* martin@andrewmartin.co.uk.

**WALLER, Sir Michael;** *see* Waller, Sir J. M.

**WALLER, Peter Graham;** voluntary worker, since 2008; Director, Energy Group, Department for Business, Enterprise and Regulatory Reform (formerly Department of Trade and Industry), 2004–08; political researcher, University College London, 2008–17; *b* 3 Jan. 1954; *s* of Raymond and Phyllis Waller; *m* 1991, Erica Zimmer. *Educ:* King's Sch., Macclesfield; Mansfield Coll., Oxford (BA Jurisp. 1976). Dept of Prices and Consumer Protection, subseq. Departments of Industry and of Trade, then Department of Trade and Industry, 1976–2001: various posts incl. Private Sec. to Minister of Consumer Affairs, 1981–83; privatisation of Rolls Royce, British Steel and water industry, 1987–91; Dir, Mkt Intelligence Unit, 1990–91; policy on future of PO, 1991–95; Dir, Business Links Services, 1995–97, Business Links, 1997–99; Dep. Chief Exec., Small Business Service, 2000–01; Dep. Dir Gen., Oftel, 2002–03. Chair of Govs, secondary sch. *Recreations:* watching lower league football, gardening, Shakespeare, walking in London. *Address:* 22 Grove Park, Wanstead, E11 2DL. *E:* petergwaller@btinternet.com.

**WALLER, Philip Anthony,** CBE 2011; **His Honour Judge Philip Waller;** a Circuit Judge, since 2013; *b* 12 Oct. 1952; *s* of late Robert Waller and of Olive (née Deakin); *m* 1978, Linda Andrews; two *d*. *Educ:* Whitgift Sch.; Univ. of Exeter (LLB Hons 1974); Inns of Court Sch. of Law. Called to the Bar, Inner Temple, 1975, Bencher, 2011; with Reed, Smith, Shaw & McClay, Attorneys, Pittsburgh, USA, 1976; practised London, 1977–93; a District Judge, 1994–2004; Sen. District Judge of the Family Div., 2004–13; a Recorder, 2009–13. Chancellor, Dio. of Portsmouth, 2014–. Consulting Ed., Rayden and Jackson's Law and Practice in Divorce and Family Matters, 2006–; Adv. editor, Atkin's Court Forms, 2010–. *Recreations:* choral singing, early music, historic houses and gardens, wine, France. *Address:* Luton Family and County Court, 2nd Floor, Cresta House, Alma Street, Luton LU1 2PU.

**WALLER, Rev. Dr Ralph,** KBE 2018; Principal, 1988–2018, and Tutor in Theology, since 1988, Harris Manchester (formerly Manchester) College, now Emeritus Fellow, and Pro-Vice-Chancellor, 2010–18, University of Oxford; Director, Farmington Institute for Christian Studies, since 2001; *b* 11 Dec. 1945; *s* of Christopher Waller and Ivy (née Miller); *m* 1968, Carol Roberts; one *d*. *Educ:* John Leggott Grammar Sch., Scunthorpe; Richmond Coll. Divinity Sch., Univ. of London (BD); Univ. of Nottingham (MTh); King's Coll. London (PhD 1986); MA Oxon. VSO in India, teaching maths and PE, and House Master, Shri Shivajh Mil. Sch., Poona, 1967–68; Maths Master, Riddings Comprehensive Sch., Scunthorpe, 1968–69; Methodist Minister, Melton Mowbray, 1972–75; ordained, 1975; Minister, Elvet Methodist Ch, Durham City, and Methodist Chaplain, Univ. of Durham, 1975–81; Chaplain, St Mary's Coll. and St Aidan's Coll., Univ. of Durham, 1979–81; Chaplain, Tutor in Theol. and Resident Tutor, Westminster Coll., Oxford, 1981–88; University of Oxford: Chm., Faculty of Theol., 1995–97; Chm., Envmtl Cttee, 1997–2000; Mem., Hebdomadal Council, 1997–2000; Chm., Curators of the Univ. Parks, 2010–. Ecumenical Canon, Christ Church, Oxford, 2017–. Gov., Cumberland Lodge, 2007–. Hon. Fellow, Homerton Coll., Cambridge, 2011–; MacWilliam Fellow of Divinity, UWTSD, 2015–. Hon. DLitt Menlo Coll., Calif, 1994; Hon. DHum: Ball State Univ., Indiana, 1998; St Olaf, 2001; Indianapolis, 2006; Hon. DTheol Uppsala, 1999; Hon. DHL Christopher Newport, 2005; Hon. DD: Hartwick, 2003; UWTSD, 2015. UK Templeton Prize, 1993. *Publications:* (contrib.) Truth, Liberty and Religion, 1986; (ed with Benedicta Ward) Christian Spirituality, 1999; John Wesley: a personal portrait, 2003; (ed with Benedicta Ward) Joy of Heaven, 2003. *Recreations:* cycling and thinking about cycling. *Address:* Harris Manchester College, Mansfield Road, Oxford OX1 3TD. *T:* (01865) 271006. *Club:* Oxford and Cambridge.

**WALLER, Richard Beaumont;** QC 2012; *b* London, 5 Dec. 1969; *s* of Rt Hon. Sir (George) Mark Waller, *qv*; *m* 1997, Katharine; three *s* one *d*. *Educ:* Radley Coll.; Trinity Coll., Cambridge (BA 1992). Called to the Bar, Gray's Inn, 1994. *Recreations:* cricket, golf, pub walks. *Address:* 35 Chalcot Crescent, NW1 8YE. *T:* (020) 7722 1529, 07971 414469. *E:* rwaller@7kbw.co.uk. *Club:* Brooks's.

**WALLERSTEINER, Dr Anthony Kurt;** Headmaster, Stowe School, since 2003; *b* 7 Aug. 1963; *m* 1994, Valerie Anne Macdougall-Jones; one *s* two *d*. *Educ:* King's Sch., Canterbury (Sen. Schol.); Trinity Coll., Cambridge (Open Schol.; BA Hist. Tripos 1985; MA 1993); Univ. of Kent at Canterbury (PhD Hist. and Theory of Art 2001). Crawford Travelling Schol., 1984; Assistant Master: Bancroft's Sch., Woodford Green, 1986; Sherborne, 1986–89; St Paul's Sch., 1989–92; Hd of Hist., 1993–2000, Housemaster, 1999–2003, Tonbridge Sch. Council Mem., Tate St Ives, 2006–09. Governor: Ashfold Prep. Sch., 2004–; Winchester House Prep. Sch., 2004–; Summer Fields Prep. Sch., 2006–; Maidwell Sch., 2009–; Buckingham Sch., 2009–10. Chairman: Children in Crisis, 2015–18; Street Child, 2018–. *Publications:* (contrib.) The Head Speaks, 2008; (contrib.) Cradles of Success: Britain's traditional public schools, 2008; (contrib.) Stowe House: saving an architectural masterpiece, 2018; contrib. reviews to Burlington Mag. *Recreations:* Dorset craft beers and folk music, trials biking, Bob Dylan, modern art. *Address:* Kinloss, Stowe, Buckingham MK18 5EH.

**WALLEY, Joan Lorraine;** DL; Chairman, Aldersgate Group, 2015–17, now Hon. Chairman; *b* 23 Jan. 1949; *d* of late Arthur Walley and Mary Walley; *m* 1980, Jan Ostrowski; two *s*. *Educ:* Biddulph Grammar School; Hull Univ. (BA); University Coll. Swansea (Dip. Community Work). Alcoholics Recovery Project, 1970–73; Swansea City Council, 1974–78; Wandsworth Borough Council, 1978–79; NACRO, 1979–82. Mem., Lambeth Borough Council, 1982–86 (Chair: Health and Consumer Services Cttee, 1982–86; Assoc. of London Authorities Public Protection Cttee, 1982–86). MP (Lab) Stoke-on-Trent N, 1987–2015. Opposition front-bench spokesman on envmtl protection, 1988–90, on transport, 1990–95; Chm., Envmtl Audit Select Cttee, 2010–15 (Mem., 1997–2010); Mem., Liaison Select Cttee, 2010–15; Vice-Chairman: All Party Football Gp, 1997–2000 and 2005–15; All Party Eur. Gp, 2001–12; Chairman: All Party Lighting Gp, 2000–15; All Party Regeneration Gp, 2000–10; Associate Envmt Gp, 2002–05; Mem., Speaker's Panel, 2007–11. Mem., Electoral Commn, 2018–. Non-exec. Dir, NHS Combined Healthcare Trust, 2016–. Hon. Vice-Pres., Chartered Inst. (formerly Inst.) of Environmental Health Officers, 1987 (LH Mem., 2015). Former member: UNISON; Globe Internat. Hon. Pres., 235 (1st Stoke-on-Trent) Sqn, ATC, 1993–2015; Mem., Woodland Trust, 2016–. Freeman, Kidsgrove Town Council, 2014–. Patron, Haywood Acad. VI Form, 2015–; Hon. Patron: Staffs Ladsandads, 2017–; N Staffs Parkinsons Soc., 2017–. Mem., Council of Fellows, Keele Univ., 2015–. Fellow, Instn of Envmtl Scis, 2015–. DL Staffs, 2017. DUniv Staffs, 2007. *Club:* Port Vale Football.

**WALLEY, Prof. Thomas Joseph,** MD; CBE 2008; FRCP, FRCPI; FMedSci; Professor of Clinical Pharmacology, University of Liverpool, since 1994; *b* Dublin, 28 Aug. 1956; *s* of Thomas Walley and Margaret Walley. *Educ:* Belvedere Coll., Dublin; Nat. Univ. of Ireland (MB BCh BAO 1980; MD 1990). FRCPI 1993; FRCP 1995. Sen. Lectr in Clin. Pharmacol., Univ. of Liverpool, 1991–94. Consultant Physician, Royal Liverpool and Broadgreen Univ. Hosps Trust, 1991–. Director: NIHR Health Technol. Assessment Prog., 2004–15; NIHR Evaluation, Trials and Studies Prog., 2008–. FMedSci 2013. *Publications:* Medical Pharmacology, 1996, 3rd edn 2007; Regulation of Pharmaceuticals in Europe, 2004; Pharmacoeconomics, 2004; over 200 articles in learned jls. *Recreations:* sailing, Irish literature, military history. *Address:* University of Liverpool, 70 Pembroke Place, Liverpool L69 3GF. *T:* (0151) 794 8123, *Fax:* (0151) 794 8126. *E:* twalley@liv.ac.uk.

**WALLFISCH, Raphael;** 'cellist; *b* 15 June 1953; *s* of Peter Wallfisch, pianist and Anita Lasker-Wallfisch, 'cellist; *m* Elizabeth; two *s* one *d*. *Educ:* Univ. of Southern California; Royal Acad. of Music; studies with Amaryllis Fleming, Amadeo Baldovino, Derek Simpson and Gregor Piatigorsky. FRAM; FGS. London début, QEH, 1974. Professor: Zürcher Hochschule für Musik; RCM. 1st recordings of compositions by Bax, Strauss and others; numerous other recordings. Won Gaspar Cassadó Internat. Cello competition, 1977.

**WALLIAMS, David;** *see* Williams, D. E.

**WALLINGER, Mark**; artist; *b* Chigwell, 1959. *Educ*: Loughton Coll.; Chelsea Sch. of Art; Goldsmiths' Coll., London (MA 1985). Contemporary artist; work includes painting, sculpture, photography, video and installations. Henry Moore Fellow, British Sch. at Rome, 1998; Artist-in-residence for Year of the Artist, Oxford Univ., 2000–01; represented GB at Venice Biennale, 2001; Artist-in-residence, Edinburgh Coll. of Art, 2008. Work in *group exhibitions* includes: Manchester City Art Galls, 1996; ICA, 1996; Royal Acad., 1997; Century City, Tate Modern, 2001; Sanctuary, Gall. of Modern Art, Glasgow, 2003; The End, Whitney Mus. of Amer. Art, NY, 2007; On Time, Courtauld Inst., 2008; Blink!, Denver Art Mus., 2011; Metamorphosis, Nat. Gall., 2012; Thresholds, Tate Liverpool, 2012; Art under Attack, Tate Britain, 2013; RA Summer Exhibn, 2014, 2017; Out There, Somerset Hse, 2016; *solo exhibitions* include: Serpentine Gall., London, Ikon Gall., Birmingham, 1995; Anthony Reynolds Gall., London, 1997, 2003, 2004, 2010, 2013; Canary Wharf Window Gall., 1997; Palais des Beaux Arts, Brussels, Portikus, Frankfurt, 1999; Ecce Homo, The Fourth Plinth, Trafalgar Sq., 1999; British Sch. at Rome, Tate Liverpool, 2000; Milton Keynes Gall., Southampton City Art Gall., Univ. Mus. of Natural Hist., Oxford, Whitechapel Art Gall., 2001; Christmas Tree, Tate Britain, 2003; Carlier Gebauer, Berlin, 2003, 2004, 2007, 2010, 2014, 2016; Laing Gall., Newcastle, Neue Nat. Gall., Berlin, 2004; Galerie Krinzinger, Vienna, 2005, 2013, 2017; Donald Young Gall., Chicago, 2007; State Britain, Tate Britain, 2007; Kunstnernes Hus, Oslo, 2010; Mus. De Pont, Tilburg, 2011; SITE, Baltic, Gateshead, 2012; Freud Mus., London, 2016; Hauser and Wirth, London, 2016; Fruitmarket, Edinburgh, Dundee Contemp. Arts (travelling exhibn), 2017; The Human Figure in Space, Jerwood Gall., Hastings, 2018. *Film*: The Lark Ascending, 2004. Designed set, Undance, Sadler's Wells, 2011. Hon. Fellow, London Inst., 2002. Hon. Dr UCE, 2003. Turner Prize, 2007. *Publications*: (with M. Warnock) Art for All?: their policies and our culture; (ed jtly) On the Border: contemporary artists in Essex and Suffolk. *Address*: c/o Hauser & Wirth, 23 Savile Row, W1S 2ET.

**WALLINGTON, Esther**; Director General HR, HM Revenue and Customs, since 2016; *b* Wroughton, 20 Dec. 1975; *d* of Mark and Wendy Wallington; *m* 2008, Roger Hampson, *qv*; two *d*. *Educ*: BA Hons Generalist, UCL, 1998–99; HR Manager, Audit Commn, 1999–2003; Consultant, GatenbySanderson, 2004–06; Dep. Dir, Cabinet Office, 2007–11; Dep. Dir, 2011–14, HR Dir, 2014–16, MoD. FCIPD 2013. *Address*: 1 Grove Hall, 10–12 West Grove, Greenwich, SE10 8QT. *E*: estherwallington@icloud.com.

**WALLINGTON, Peter Thomas**; QC 2008; *b* Maidstone, Kent, 25 March 1947; *s* of Thomas Edwin and Doris Evelyn Wallington; *m* 1972, Barbara Alice Rowland. *Educ*: Hemel Hempstead Grammar Sch.; Trinity Hall, Cambridge (BA 1968; LLM 1969); Inns of Court Sch. of Law (Cert. of Hon. and CLE Scholar 1987). Lecturer in Law: Univ. of Edinburgh, 1969–72; Univ. of Liverpool, 1972–73; Asst Lectr, then Lectr in Law, Univ. of Cambridge, and Fellow, Trinity Hall, Cambridge, 1973–79; Prof. of Law, 1979–88, Hd, Dept of Law, 1979–86, Univ. of Lancaster; Prof. of Law and Hd, Dept of Law, Brunel Univ., 1988–91. Called to the Bar, Gray's Inn, 1987; in practice as barrister specialising in employment law, 1990–2018; pt-time Employment Judge, London E Reg., 2003–09, Scotland, 2009–18. Mem. editl team, Harvey on Industrial Relations and Employment Law, 2000–. *Publications*: Civil Liberties and a Bill of Rights (with Jeremy McBride), 1976; (ed) Butterworths Employment Law Handbook, 1979, 27th edn 2019; (jtly) Labour Law Cases and Materials, 1980; (ed and contrib.) Civil Liberties 1984, 1984; (jtly) The Police, Public Order and Civil Liberties: legacies of the miners strike, 1988; (with R. G. Lee) Blackstone's Public Law Statutes, 1988, 18th edn 2008; (contrib.) Supperstone and Goudie on Judicial Review, 1992, 3rd edn 2005; (contrib.) Tolley's Employment Law Handbook, 9th edn 1995 to 32nd edn 2018. *Recreations*: music, walking, reading. *Address*: c/o 11 KBW Chambers, 11 King's Bench Walk, Temple, EC4Y 7EQ. *T*: (01620) 892463. *E*: pwallington@btinternet.com.

**WALLIS, Andrew Jonathan**, OBE 2015; Founder and Chief Executive Officer, Unseen UK, since 2008; *b* Leeds, 13 April 1967; *s* of John Wallis and Kathleen Wallis; *m* 1990, Rosamund Askins; one *s* two *d*. *Educ*: Skinners' Sch.; St David's University Coll., Univ. of Wales (BA Hons Theol. 1989; Sen. Scholar Prize 1988). Asst Manager, Marks and Spencer, 1989–91; Business Analyst, London Electricity plc, 1991–93; Asst Leader, SW London Vineyard, 1993–95; Sen. Leader, Bristol Vineyard, 1995–2012; Commercial Manager, House of Fraser, 1995–2000; Proj. Manager, UWE, 2000–02. Associate, Deloitte UK, 2014–17. Treas. and Trustee, One25, 2009–12. Centre for Social Justice: Chm., Wkg Gp, 2011–13 (Report, It Happens Here, 2013); Fellow, 2014. FRSA 2014. *Recreations*: walking, fitness, music, dog, wine tasting, cooking, technology. *Address*: Unseen UK, Deben House, First Floor, 1–5 Lawrence Hill, Bristol BS5 0BY. *T*: 0303 040 2888. *E*: a.wallis@unseenuk.org.

**WALLIS, (Diana) Lynn**, OBE 2015; freelance ballet teacher, producer, coach and consultant; Artistic Director, Royal Academy of Dance (formerly of Dancing), 1994–2016; *b* 11 Dec. 1946; *d* of Dennis Blackwell Wallis and Joan Wallis. *Educ*: Tonbridge Grammar Sch. for Girls; Royal Ballet Upper Sch. FISTD. Royal Ballet Touring Co., 1965–68; Royal Ballet School: Ballet Mistress, 1969–81; Dep. Principal, 1981–84; National Ballet of Canada: Artistic Co-ordinator, 1984–86; Associate Artistic Dir, 1986–87; Co-Artistic Dir, 1987–89; Dep. Artistic Dir, English National Ballet, 1990–94. Hon. FRAD 2017. *Recreations*: music, theatre, cinema.

**WALLIS, Diana Paulette**; lawyer; President, European Law Institute, 2013–17; Member (Lib Dem) Yorkshire and the Humber, 1999–Jan. 2012, and Vice President, 2007–12, European Parliament; *b* 28 June 1954; *d* of John Frederick Wallis and Jean Elizabeth Wallis (*née* Jones); *m* 1989, Stewart David Arnold. *Educ*: N London Poly. (BA Hist.); Univ. of Kent at Canterbury (MA Local Govt); Coll. of Law, Chester. Admitted Solicitor, 1983. Mem. (Lib Dem) Humberside CC, subseq. E Riding of Yorks UA, 1994–99 (Dep. Leader, 1995–99). European Parliament: Member: Legal Affairs Cttee, 1999–2012; Petitions Cttee, 2004–12; Vice-Pres., delegn to Switzerland, Iceland and Norway, 1999–2004; Pres., delegn to Switzerland, Iceland, Norway and Eur. Econ. Area, 2004–07; Leader, Lib Dem European Parly Party, 2002–04, 2006–07. Accredited Mediator, 2012; MCIArb 2012. Sen. Fellow, Univ. of Hull Law Sch., 2013–. Mem. Bd, Internat. Mediation Inst., 2012–. Pres., Inst. of Translation and Interpreting, 2002–10. *Club*: National Liberal.

**WALLIS, Edmund Arthur**, CBE 2015; FREng; Chairman, Natural Environment Research Council, 2007–14; *b* 3 July 1939; *s* of late Reuben Wallis and of Iris Mary Cliff; *m* 1964, Gillian Joan Mitchell; two *s*. CEng 1978; MIET (MIEE 1971); MIMechE 1972; FREng (FEng 1995). Central Electricity Generating Board: Stn Manager, Oldbury Nuclear Power Stn, 1977–79; Dir of System Op., 1981–86; Divl Dir of Ops, 1986–88; PowerGen, subseq. Powergen: Chief Exec., 1988–2001 and 2002–03; Chm., 1996–2002; Dep. Chm., 2002–03. Chm., WS Atkins, 2005–10 (Dir, 2004–10); non-executive Director: BSI, 1992–97; LucasVarity plc, 1995–99 (Chm., 1998–99); London Transport, 1999–2003 (Chm., 2001–03); Ind. non-exec. Dir, Mercury European Privatisation Trust plc, 1994–2004; Mem. Adv. Bd, RWE, Germany, 1994–98. Lay Mem. Council, Aston Univ., 1992–98. Chm., Birmingham Royal Ballet Sch., 1996–2004; Mem. Bd, Birmingham Royal Ballet, 2005–10; Gov., Royal Ballet Sch., 2006–15. CCMI (CBIM 1991; AMBIM 1973).

**WALLIS, Eithne Victoria, (Lady Birt)**, CB 2004; Managing Director, Government Business (formerly Central Government Business Unit), Fujitsu Services UK, 2005–11; *b* 14 Dec. 1952; *d* of Ewing Walsh and late Marion Walsh; *m* 1st, 1977, Phillip Wallis (marr. diss. 2001); one *s* two *d*; 2nd, 2006, Baron Birt, *qv*. *Educ*: High Sch. for Girls, Dungannon, NI; Manchester Univ. (BA Econ 1973; MA Social Studies 1979). Probation Officer, 1979–87, mgt, 1987–94, Manchester; Asst Chief Probation Officer, Cambs, 1991–94; Dep. Chief Probation Officer, Inner London, 1994–97; Chief Probation Officer, Oxon and Bucks, 1997–2000; on secondment to Home Office, 2000; led team which created Nat. Probation Service for England and Wales, Dir Gen., 2001–04; Sen. Partner, Fujitsu Services UK, 2005. Chair, Bluelight Global Solutions Ltd. *Recreations*: reading, walking, gardening.

**WALLIS, (George James) Stewart**, OBE 2002; Executive Chair, Wellbeing Economy Alliance, since 2017; *b* 29 Aug. 1948; *s* of George and Jean Wallis; *m* 1987, Mary Jane Wallis; four *d* and one step *s*. *Educ*: Fitzwilliam Coll., Cambridge (MA Natural Sci. Tripos); London Business School (MSc Business and Econs 1976). Geologist and Financial Analyst, Rio Tinto Zinc Corp. Ltd, 1970–74; Industrial and Finance Economist, E Asia and Adminr Young Professional Prog., World Bank, Washington, DC, 1976–83; Dir and Gen. Manager, Special Products, 1983–86, Man. Dir, 1987–92, Robinson Packaging; Dep. Dir and Internat. Dir, Oxfam, 1992–2002; Livelihoods Dir, Oxfam GB and Livelihoods Lead, Oxfam Internat., 2002–03; Exec. Dir, new econs foundn, 2003–16. Hon. Prof., Inst. for Social Futures, Lancaster Univ., 2016–. Vice-Chair, WEF Global Agenda Council on Values, 2014–16; Trustee, WEF Global Challenge Initiative on Econ. Growth and Social Inclusion, 2015–17; Mem., WEF Global Future Council on Values, Technol. and Policy, 2016–18. Trustee: Overseas Develt Inst., 2003–15; New Econs Inst., 2007–17; Devon Community Foundn, 2016–; Dir, Devon Social Finance, 2017–18; Chair, Conservation Farming Trust, 2017–. Fellow, Club of Rome, 2015–. Hon. LLD Lancaster, 2016. *Publications*: (contrib.) Democracy and Capitalism, 2006; (contrib.) Surviving the Century, 2007; (with S. Spratt) From old economics to new economics: radical reform and a sustainable future, 2007; (contrib.) Why Love Matters, 2015; (contrib.) Peacefulness, 2017; (jtly) A Finer Future, 2018. *Recreations*: landscape photography, walking, reading, cinema. *Address*: Brakebrook, Parracombe, Barnstaple, Devon EX31 4RG. *T*: (01598) 763658. *E*: stewart@nexteconomy.org.uk.

**WALLIS, Prof. Kenneth Frank**, FBA 1994; Professor of Econometrics, University of Warwick, 1977–2001, now Emeritus; *b* 26 March 1938; *s* of late Leslie Wallis and Vera Daisy Wallis (*née* Stone); *m* 1963, Margaret Sheila Campbell; one *d* by previous partner. *Educ*: Wath-on-Dearne GS; Manchester Univ. (BSc, MScTech); Stanford Univ. (PhD). Mem. Exec., NUS, 1961–63. Lectr, then Reader, in Stats, LSE, 1966–77; Dir, ESRC Macroeconomic Modelling Bureau, 1983–99. Member: HM Treasury Academic Panel, 1980–2001 (Chm., 1987–91); Nat. Statistics Methodology Adv. Cttee, 2001–11. Member Council: Royal Stat. Soc., 1972–76; Royal Econ. Soc., 1989–94; Econometric Soc., 1995–97 (Fellow, 1975); British Acad., 2002–05. Fellow, Internat. Inst. of Forecasters, 2003. Hon. Dr Groningen, 1999. *Publications*: Introductory Econometrics, 1972; Topics in Applied Econometrics, 1973; (ed with D. F. Hendry) Econometrics and Quantitative Economics, 1984; Models of the UK Economy 1–4, 1984–87; (ed) Macroeconometric Modelling, 1994; Time Series Analysis and Macroeconometric Modelling, 1995; (ed with D. M. Kreps) Advances in Economics and Econometrics: theory and applications, 1997; articles in learned jls. *Recreations*: travel, music, gardening, swimming. *Address*: Department of Economics, University of Warwick, Coventry CV4 7AL. *T*: (024) 7652 3055. *E*: K.F.Wallis@warwick.ac.uk; 4 Walkers Orchard, Stoneleigh, Warwicks CV8 3JG. *T*: (024) 7641 4271.

**WALLIS, Lynn**; *see* Wallis, D. L.

**WALLIS, Maria Assumpta**, QPM 2002; Chief Constable, Devon and Cornwall Constabulary, 2002–06; *b* 13 Aug. 1955; *d* of late Philip and Margaret O'Donnell; *m* 1983, Michael Wallis. *Educ*: Bristol Univ. (BSc Jt Hons Sociol. and Social Admin). Metropolitan Police, 1976–94; Asst, then Dep. Chief Constable, Sussex Police, 1994–2002. *Recreations*: gardening, walking, reading. *Address*: c/o Devon and Cornwall Constabulary, Police HQ, Middlemoor, Exeter EX2 7HQ.

**WALLIS, Sir Peter (Gordon)**, KCVO 1992; CMG 1990; HM Diplomatic Service, retired; High Commissioner to Malta, 1991–94; *b* 2 Aug. 1935; *s* of late Arthur Gordon Wallis, DFC, BScEcon, and Winifred Florence Maud Wallis (*née* Dingle); *m* 1965, Delysia Elizabeth (*née* Leonard); three *s* one *d*. *Educ*: Taunton and Whitgift Schools; Pembroke Coll., Oxford (MA). Ministry of Labour and National Service, 1958; HM Customs and Excise, 1959 (Private Sec., 1961–64); HM Diplomatic Service, 1968; Tel Aviv, 1970; Nairobi, 1974; Counsellor (Econ. and Comm.), Ankara, 1977; RCDS, 1981; Cabinet Office, 1982; Hd, Perm. Under-Sec.'s Dept, FCO, 1983; Minister, Pretoria, 1987; Minister, British Liaison Office, 1989, and subseq. Acting High Comr, 1990, Windhoek, Namibia; Political Advr to Jt Comdr, British Forces in the Gulf, Jan.–April 1991, to Comdr, British Forces, SE Turkey and N Iraq, May–July 1991. Advr to Learmont Enquiry into Prison Security, 1995. Head, UK delegn to EC monitor mission, Balkans, 1996, 1997, 1998, 1999. Mem., Regl Adv. Council, subseq. Regl Audience Council, BBC West, 2005–09. Chm., 2004–07, Pres., 2009–18, Taunton and Dist Br., ESU. Mem., Taunton Area Cttee, Somerset CCC, 2005–11 (Vice-Chm., 2006–09; Actg Chm., 2009). Trustee: Friends of Somerset Churches, 2007–14; Somerset Cricket Mus., 2009– (Chm., 2014–). *Recreations*: reading, music, walking. *Address*: Parsonage Farm, Curry Rivel, Somerset TA10 0EP.

**WALLIS, Peter Ralph**; Deputy Controller, Aircraft Weapons and Electronics, Ministry of Defence, 1980–84; *b* 17 Aug. 1924; *s* of Leonard Francis Wallis and Molly McCulloch Wallis (*née* Jones); *m* 1949, Frances Jean Patricia Cowie; three *s* one *d*; *m* 2017, Elisabeth Irene Fischer. *Educ*: University College Sch., Hampstead; Imperial Coll. of Science and Technology, London (BScEng). CEng 1967; FIET (FIEE 1967); FIMA 1968. Henrici and Siemens Medals of the College, 1944. Joined Royal Naval Scientific Service 1944; work at Admty Signal and Radar Estab. till 1959, Admty Underwater Weapons Estab. till 1968; Asst Chief Scientific Advr (Research), MoD, 1968–71, Dir Gen. Research Weapons, 1971–75, Dir Gen. Guided Weapons and Electronics, 1975–78, Dir Gen. Research A (Electronics) and Dep. Chief Scientist (Navy), 1978–80. Vice Pres., Hampstead Scientific Soc., 1992– (Hon. Sec., 1974–90; Hon. Treas., 1988–2009). FCGI. Marconi Award, IERE, 1964. *Publications*: articles in Jl of IEE, IERE and Op. Res. Quarterly. *Recreations*: ski-ing, mountain walking, archæology, sailing, egyptology, geology, travel. *Address*: 22 Flask Walk, Hampstead, NW3 1HE. *Clubs*: Alpine Ski, Eagle Ski.

**WALLIS, Peter Spencer**; a District Judge (Magistrates' Courts) (formerly Metropolitan Stipendiary Magistrate), 1993–2010; a Recorder, 2000–15; a Deputy Judge Advocate, 2008–15; *b* 31 March 1945; *s* of Philip Wallis and Winifred Wallis; *m* 1970, Ann Margaret Bentham; one *s* one *d*. *Educ*: Maidstone Grammar Sch.; Lincoln Coll., Oxford (MA). Pilot, RAF, 1967–72. Admitted solicitor, 1976. Clerk to: Tonbridge and Malling Justices, 1977–88; Dover and Ashford Justices, 1988–93; Folkestone and Hythe Justices, 1990–93. An Asst Recorder, 1997–2000. Mem. Council, Justices' Clerks' Soc., 1983–93 (Pres.,

1993). *Publications:* The Transport Acts 1981 and 1982, 1982, 2nd edn 1985; Road Traffic: guide to Part I of the 1991 Act, 1991; General Editor, Wilkinson's Road Traffic Offences, 13th edn 1987 to 23rd edn 2007, Consultant Editor, 24th edn 2009 to 26th edn 2013. *Recreations:* flying, watching cricket, choral singing. *Club:* Royal Air Force.

**WALLIS, Robert;** Chief Executive, Transport Research Foundation and TRL Ltd, since 2013; *b* Bishop's Stortford, Herts, 11 July 1964; *s* of George and Catherine Ann Wallis; *m* 2009, Dr Julie Mullan. *Educ:* Leventhorpe Secondary Sch.; Cass Business Sch. (Strategic Thought Leadership and Innovation Prog. (Corporate) 2006). Shift Leader, ICT Data Centre and Ops, CAA, 1980–88; Internat. Sales and Prog. Delivery, EDS Inc., 1988–97; EDS Systems Engr Graduating Prog., 1989; Man. Dir, Transport Logistics and Commercial, CMG, 1997–2002; Dir, UK Business Develt, LogicaCMG, 2002–05; Man. Dir, Transport, EDS Inc., 2005–07; Hd of Transport, Hedra plc, 2007–08; Man. Dir, BSI, 2008–12. FInstD 2001; FCIHT 2013. *Address:* TRL Ltd, Crowthorne House, Nine Mile Ride, Wokingham, Berks RG40 3GA. *T:* (01344) 770001. *E:* rob.wallis@trl.co.uk.

**WALLIS, Dame Sheila (Ann),** DBE 2002; Director and Education Consultant, Wallis Partnership Ltd, 2002; *b* 13 Feb. 1940; *d* of John and Lilian Pearson; *m* 1964, Brian Wallis; two *s. Educ:* Chelsea Sch. of Human Movt; Univ. of London (BEd); Univ. of Brighton (MEd). Physical education teacher: Kings Manor Sch., Shoreham, 1962–64; Bognor Regis Grammar Sch., 1964–66; Davison High School for Girls: physical educn teacher, 1971–81; Dep. Headteacher, 1981–88; Headteacher, 1988–2002. Comr, NCC Commn into Public Services, 2003–. FRSA 1998. Hon. MEd Brighton, 2003. *Publications:* contribs to educn jls and govt papers. *Recreations:* jogging, swimming, travelling, cooking. *Address:* Drake House, River Road, Arundel, W Sussex BN18 9EY. *T:* and *Fax:* (01903) 882171.

**WALLIS, Simon Philip Zbigniew,** OBE 2015; Director, The Hepworth Wakefield, since 2008; *b* London, 7 Jan. 1967; *s* of Andrew Wallis and Malgosia Chelminska; *m* 2001, Deborah Marks; one *s* one *d. Educ:* Falmer Comp. Sch., Brighton; Varndean Sixth Form Coll., Brighton; Brighton Poly.; Chelsea Sch. of Art (BA Hons Fine Art); Univ. of Manchester (MA Art Gall. and Museum Studies). Curator: Kettle's Yard, Univ. of Cambridge, 1994–99; Tate Liverpool, 1999–2002; Sen. Exhibn Organiser, ICA, 2002–03; Dir, Chisenhale Gall., 2004–08. *Publications:* Hybrids, 2001; Remix, 2002; Folkert de Jong, 2004; Clare Woods, 2006; Philip Guston, 2006; Eva Rothschild, 2011. *Recreations:* photography, walking, jazz, chamber music, football, tennis, museums. *Address:* The Hepworth Wakefield, Gallery Walk, Wakefield, West Yorks WF1 5AW. *E:* simonwallis@hepworthwakefield.org.

**WALLIS, Stewart;** see Wallis, G. J. S.

**WALLIS, Stuart Michael;** Chairman: BCS Global Networks Ltd, since 2005; FGV Ltd, since 2016; *b* 8 Oct. 1945; *s* of Stanley Oswald Wallis and Margaret Ethel Wallis; *m* 1971, Eileen; one *s. Educ:* Hawesdown Sch., West Wickham, Kent. FCA, CTA. Roland Goodman & Co., 1962–68; Chrysler, 1968–71; Shipton Automation, 1971–73; Star Computer Services, 1973–74; Hestair Gp, 1974–85 (Main Board, 1977); Exec. Dir, Octopus, 1985–87; Main Board Dir, Bowater plc, 1988–94; Chief Exec., Fisons plc, 1994–95; Chairman: Sheffield Forgemasters Ltd, 1996–98; LLP Gp, 1996–98; Yorkshire Gp, 1996–2000; SSL Internat., 1996–2001; John Mansfield Gp, then Communisis plc, 1997–2003; Euramax Internat., 1997–2005; Hay Hall Gp Ltd, 1997–2004; Protherics plc, 1999–2008; Trident Components Gp, 1999–2005; Tetley Group Ltd, 1999–2000; ElektroTextiles, later Eleksen Ltd, 2000–03; Worldmark Internat., 2000–02; Simply Smart Gp Ltd, 2004–08; Plethora Solutions Hldgs plc, 2005–10; TSL Education Ltd, 2005–07; Ashridge Automobiles, 2006–18; LGC Hldgs Ltd, 2007–10; H. H. Associates, later H. H. Global, 2010–17; Egan Property Asset Mgt, 2011–13; Synseal Ltd, 2011–17; Edif Ltd, 2011–16. *Recreations:* golf, swimming, ski-ing, fishing. *Club:* Ashridge Golf.

**WALLIS, Sir Timothy (William),** Kt 1994; Managing Director, Alpine Deer Group; *b* 9 Sept. 1938; *s* of Arthur Wallis and Janice Blunden; *m* 1974, Prudence Ann Hazledine; two *s* (and two *s* decd). *Educ:* Christ's Coll., Christchurch. Founding Dir, Tourism Holdings Ltd. Mem. Council, NZ Deer Farmers' Assoc., 1977–84 (Hon. Life Mem.); founding Chm. and Hon. Life Mem., NZ Wapiti Soc. DCom (*hc*) Lincoln Univ., 2000. E. A. Gibson Award, 1980, for contribs to NZ aviation; Sir Arthur Ward Award, 1985, for contribs to agric.; Commem. Medal for services to deer industry, 1990; Sir Jack Newman Award, 1999, for outstanding contrib. to NZ tourism industry; Speights Southern Man Award, 2001; Laureate, NZ Business Hall of Fame, 2002; World Wide Gold Medal, RAeS, 2005. *Relevant publications:* Hurricane Tim: the story of Sir Tim Wallis, by Neville Peat, 2005; (for children) Winging It: the adventures of Tim Wallis, by Neville Peat, 2006. *Recreations:* scuba diving, hunting, fly fishing; represented West Coast-Buller 1958, S Canterbury 1959, at Rugby. *Address:* Benfiddich, Mount Barker, Wanaka 9192, New Zealand.

**WALLOP,** family name of **Earl of Portsmouth**.

**WALLS, Geoffrey Nowell;** Executive Director, Pearls of the Orient (Wholesale) (formerly International) Ltd, since 2006; *b* 17 Feb. 1945; *s* of Andrew Nowell Walls and Hilda Margaret Thompson; *m* 1975, Vanessa Bodger; one *s* three *d. Educ:* Trinity Grammar Sch., Melbourne; Univ. of Melbourne (BComm 1965). Australian Regular Army, 2nd Lieut RAAOC, 1966–69; Australian Trade Comr Service, 1970–79; served Jakarta, Singapore, Cairo, Beirut, Bahrain, Manila, Baghdad; Regional Dir, Adelaide, Commonwealth Dept of Trade, 1980–83; Gen. Manager, ATCO Industries (Aust) Pty Ltd, 1983–86; Agent Gen. for S Australia in London, 1986–98. CIH Ltd (formerly Clipsal Industries (Holdings) Ltd): Regl Manager, Sharjah, 1998–2000; Regl Dir, 2000–02; Exec. Dir, 2002–05; non-exec. Dir, 2005–07. Mem., S Australian Cricket Assoc. *Recreations:* golf, tennis, gardening. *Address:* Bollards, Ropes Lane, Fernhurst, Surrey GU27 3JD.

**WALLS, Stephen Roderick;** Partner, Next Wave Partners LLP, since 2007; *b* 8 Aug. 1947; *s* of late R. W. Walls and of D. M. Walls; *m;* two *s.* Accountant. Senior Auditor, Deloitte & Co., 1969; Group Chief Accountant, Lindustries, 1971; Financial Planning Exec., Vernons, 1974; Chesebrough Ponds: Finance Dir, UK and Geneva, 1975; Internat. Finance Dir, Geneva, 1981; Vice-Pres., Finance, 1981–87; Dir of Finance, 1987, Man. Dir, 1988–89, Plessey Co.; Chm., 1990–91, Chief Exec., 1990–92, Wiggins Teape Appleton, later Arjo Wiggins Appleton; Chm., The Albert Fisher Gp, 1992–97; Partner, Compass Partners Internat., 1998–2001. Chairman: VPS Hldgs Ltd, 2003–10; Pourshins plc, 2004–07; Petainer, 2009–14; Clearway Gp plc, 2016–. Chm., CHASE Children's Hospice, 2004–09. Mem., Financial Reporting Council, 1990–95. *Recreations:* running, music, shooting. *Address:* c/o Next Wave Partners LLP, 42 Wigmore Street, W1U 2RY. *Club:* Royal Automobile.

**WALLSTRÖM, Margot;** Minister for Foreign Affairs, Sweden, 2014–19; *b* 28 Sept. 1954; *m* 1984, Håkan Wallström; two *s. Educ:* Nordanå Upper Secondary Sch., Skellefteå. Adminr, Swedish Social Democratic Youth League, 1974–77; Accountant, 1977–79, Sen. Accountant, 1986–87, Alfa Savings Bank, Karlstad; MP (SDP), Sweden, 1979–85; Minister for: Civil Affairs, 1988–91; Culture, 1994–96; Health and Social Affairs, 1996–98; CEO, TV Värmland, 1993–94; Exec. Vice-Pres., Worldview Global Media, Sri Lanka, 1998–99. Mem., 1999–2010, a Vice-Pres., 2004–10, Eur. Commn; UN Special Rep. on Sexual Violence in Conflict, 2010–12. Mem. Exec. Cttee, Swedish SDP, 1993–99. Chm. Bd, Lund Univ., Sweden, 2012–14. Hon. Dr: Chalmers Univ., Sweden, 2001; Mälardalen Univ., Sweden, 2004. Comdr, Légion d'Honneur (France), 2014. *Publications:* (jtly) The People's Europe, or Why is it so Hard to Love the EU?, 2004.

**WALLWORK, John,** CBE 2012; DL; FRCSE; Consultant Cardiothoracic Surgeon, Papworth Hospital, 1981–2011 (Director of Transplantation, 1989–2006; Medical Director, 1997–2002); Chairman, Royal Papworth Hospital NHS Foundation Trust, since 2014; *b* 8 July 1946; *s* of Thomas and Vera Wallwork; *m* 1973, Elizabeth Ann Medley; one *s* two *d. Educ:* Accrington Grammar Sch.; Edinburgh Univ. (BSc Hons Pharm. 1966; MB ChB 1970); MA Cantab 1986. FRCSE 1974; FRCS 1992 *ad eundem,* FRCPE 1999, FRCP 2001. Surgical Registrar, Royal Infirmary, Edinburgh, 1975–76; Senior Registrar: Adelaide Hosp., SA, 1977–78; Royal Infirmary, Glasgow, 1978–79; St Bartholomew's Hosp., 1979–81; Chief Resident in Cardiovascular and Cardiac Transplant Surgery, Stanford Univ. Med. Sch., 1980–81. Hon. Prof. of Cardiothoracic Surgery, Cambridge Univ., 2002–11. Lister Prof., RCSE, 1985–86. FMedSci 2002. DL Cambs, 2007. *Publications:* (with R. Stepney) Heart Disease: what it is and how it is treated, 1987; (ed) Heart and Heart-Lung Transplantation, 1989; numerous papers on cardiothoracic and cardiopulmonary topics. *Recreations:* tennis, conversation, making phone calls from the bath. *Address:* 3 Latham Road, Cambridge CB2 7EG. *T:* (01223) 352827. *Club:* Garrick.

**WALMSLEY,** Baroness *cr* 2000 (Life Peer), of West Derby in the co. of Merseyside; **Joan Margaret Walmsley;** *b* 12 April 1943; *d* of Leo Watson and Monica Watson (*née* Nolan); *m* 1st, 1966, John Newan Caro Richardson (marr. diss. 1979); one *s* one *d*; 2nd, 1986, Christopher Roberts Walmsley (*d* 1995); one step *s* two step *d*; 3rd, 2005, Baron Thomas of Gresford, *qv. Educ:* Notre Dame High Sch., Liverpool; Univ. of Liverpool (BSc Hons Biology); Manchester Poly. (PGCE). Cytologist, Christie Hosp., Manchester, 1966–67; teacher, Buxton Coll., 1979–87; Mkting Officer, Ocean Youth Club, 1987–88; PR Consultant: Intercommunication, Manchester, 1988–89; Hill & Knowlton UK Ltd, 1989–97; Joan Walmsley Public Relations, 1997–99; Dir, Walmsley Jones Communications, 1999–2003. Co-Chair, Lib Dem Parly Cttee on Educn, Young People and Families (formerly Lib Dem spokesman on educn and children), H of L, 2004–12; Convenor of Lib Dem Peers, 2014–15; Lib Dem Health Spokesman, H of L, 2014–17; Dep. Leader, Lib Dem Peers, 2017–. *Recreations:* music, theatre, keeping fit, good company, gardening. *Address:* House of Lords, SW1A 0PW. *T:* (020) 7219 6047.

**WALMSLEY, Brian;** Under Secretary, Social Security Policy Group, Department of Social Security, 1990–94; *b* 22 April 1936; *s* of late Albert Edward Walmsley and Ivy Doreen Walmsley (*née* Black); *m* 1st, 1956, Sheila Maybury (marr. diss. 1993); two *d*; 2nd, 1994, Margaret Wilson. *Educ:* Prescot Grammar School. National Service, RAF, 1955–57. Joined Min. of Pensions and Nat. Insurance, 1957, later Min. of Social Security and DHSS; Sec. to Industrial Injuries Adv. Council, 1978–79; Asst Sec., 1979; Under Sec., 1985; Civil Service Comr, OMCS, Cabinet Office (on secondment), 1988–90. *Recreations:* following cricket, playing golf, reading, gardening. *Clubs:* MCC; Chester Golf.

**WALMSLEY, Prof. Ian Alexander,** PhD; FRS 2012; Provost, Imperial College London, since 2018; *b* 13 Jan. 1960; *s* of Richard M. and Hazel F. Walmsley; *m* 1986, Katherine Frances Pardee; two *s* one *d. Educ:* Imperial Coll., Univ. of London (BSc 1980); Univ. of Rochester, NY (PhD 1986). Res. Associate, Cornell Univ., NY, 1986–88; Institute of Optics, University of Rochester, New York: Asst Prof., 1988–94, Associate Prof., 1994–98, Prof., 1998–2000, of Optics; Dir, 2000; Oxford University: Prof. of Exptl Physics, 2001–05; Hooke Prof. of Physics, 2005–18; Head, Subdept of Atomic and Laser Physics, 2002–09; Pro-Vice-Chancellor (Res.), 2009–11, (Res., Academic Services and Univ. Collections), 2011–15, (Res. and Innovation), 2015–18; Dir, Networked Quantum Information Technologies Hub, 2014–19; Fellow, St Hugh's Coll., Oxford, 2001–18 (Hon. Fellow, 2018). Vis. Prof. of Physics, Ulm Univ., 1995; Sen. Vis. Fellow, Princeton Univ., 2002–05. Mem., UKRI-EPSRC, 2018–. Pres., Optical Soc. of America, 2018 (Fellow, 1997). FInstP 2004; Fellow, APS, 2000. Dr *hc*: Libre de Bruxelles, 2008; Paul Sabatier, Toulouse, 2010. Leibinger Innovationspreis, Berthold Leibinger Stiftung, 2006; Wolfson Res. Merit Award, Royal Soc., 2007; Joseph Keithley Award, APS, 2011; Thomas Young Medal, Inst. of Physics, 2011; Rumford Medal, Royal Soc., 2018. *Publications:* Light, 2015; contrib. to books and professional jls. *Recreations:* Tae Kwon Do (4th dan, World Assoc.), cycling, choral music. *Address:* Provost's Office, Faculty Building, Imperial College London, Exhibition Road, SW7 2AZ.

**WALMSLEY, Nigel Norman;** Chairman, Broadcasters' Audience Research Board Ltd, 2002–13; Deputy Chairman, Authority for Television on Demand (formerly Association for Video on Demand), 2010–16; Chairman, Ambassador Theatre Group Foundation, 2010–18; *b* 26 Jan. 1942; *s* of late Norman and Ida Walmsley; *m* 1969, Jane Walmsley, broadcaster, author and producer; one *d. Educ:* William Hulme's Sch.; Brasenose Coll., Oxford (BA English). Joined the Post Office, 1964; Asst Private Secretary to Postmaster General, 1967; Asst Director of Marketing, Post Office, 1973–75; Asst Sec., Industrial Planning Division of Dept of Industry, 1975–77; Director of Marketing, Post Office, 1977–81, Board Mem. for Marketing, 1981–82; Man. Dir, Capital Radio, 1982–91; Chief Exec., 1991–94, Chm., 1994–2001, Carlton TV; Exec. Dir, 1992–2001, Dep. Chief Exec., 2000–01, Carlton Communications plc; Chm., GMTV, 1994–96, 2000–01. Chm., Tourism SE, 2003–09. Board Member: Ind. Radio News, 1983–91; South Bank Centre, 1985–92 and 1997–2002; Director: The Builder Gp, 1986–92; General Cable plc, 1994–97; non-exec. Chm., Central Television, 1996–2001; non-executive Director: Energis plc, 1997–2002; ONdigital, subseq. ITV Digital, plc, 1997–2001; ITN, 2000–01; Ambassador Theatre Gp, 2001–04; de Vere plc, 2001–06; Eagle Rock, 2007–14 (Chm., 2002–07). Member Council: ASA, 2004–11; Postwatch, 2006–08; Mem., Rail Passengers' Council (Passenger Focus), 2005–13; Mem. Bd, London Ambulance Service PCT, 2010–11. Chm., GLAA, 1985–86; Vice Chm., Advertising Assoc., 1992–2003. *Recreation:* intensive inactivity. *Club:* City of London.

**WALMSLEY, Peter James,** MBE 1975; Director-General (formerly Director) of Petroleum Engineering Division, Department of Energy, 1981–89; *b* 29 April 1929; *s* of George Stanley and Elizabeth Martin Walmsley; *m* 1970, Edna Fisher; three *s* one *d. Educ:* Caterham Sch., Surrey; Imperial Coll., London (BSc; ARSM). Geologist: Iraq Petroleum Co., 1951–59; BP Trinidad, 1959–65; BP London, 1965–72; Exploration Manager, BP Aberdeen, 1972–78; Dep. Chief Geologist, BP London, 1978–79; Regional Exploration Manager, BP London, 1979–81. Chairman, Petroleum Exploration Soc. of Gt Britain, 1971–72; Pres., RSM Assoc., 1995–96. *Publications:* contribs to various learned jls on North Sea geology. *Recreation:* home and garden. *Address:* Elm Tree Cottage, 10 Great Austins, Farnham, Surrey GU9 8JG.

**WALMSLEY, Sir Robert,** KCB 1995; FREng, FIET; Chief of Defence Procurement, Ministry of Defence, 1996–2003; Chief Executive, Defence Procurement Agency, 1999–2003; *b* Aberdeen, 1 Feb. 1941; *s* of late Prof. Robert Walmsley, TD, FRCPE, FRCSE, and Dr Isabel Mary Walmsley; *m* 1st, 1967 (marr. diss. 2009); one *s* two *d*; 2nd, 2010, Alexandra Ashbourne. *Educ:* Fettes Coll.; RN Coll., Dartmouth; Queens' Coll., Cambridge (MA MechScis); RN Coll., Greenwich (MSc Nuclear Sci.). FIET (FIEE 1994); FREng (FEng 1998). HMS Ark Royal, 1962–63; HMS Otus, 1964–66; HMS Churchill,

1968–72; Ship Dept, MoD, 1973–74; HM Dockyard, Chatham, 1975–78; MoD, PE, 1979–80; Chm., Naval Nuclear Technical Safety Panel, 1981–83; Naval Staff, 1984; MoD, PE, 1985–86; Dir Operational Requirements (Sea), 1987–89; ACDS (Communications, Command, Control and Information Systems), 1990–93; Dir Gen. Submarines, Chief Naval Engr Officer and Sen. Naval Rep. in Bath, 1993–94; Controller of the Navy, in rank of Vice-Adm., 1994–96. Non-exec. Chm., Universal Credit, DWP, 2013–; non-executive Director: British Energy, 2003–09; Cohort plc, 2006–; Ultra Electronic Hldgs plc, 2009–; Independent Director: Gen. Dynamics, USA, 2004–15; EDO Corp., USA, 2004–08; Stratos Global, Canada, 2006–08; Chm., Major Projects Assoc., 2004–13; Sen. Advr, Morgan Stanley, 2004–12. Crown Rep., Crown Commercial Service, 2014–. Gov., St Mary's Primary Sch., Putney, 2019–. Hon. Col, 71st (Yeomanry) Signal Regt, 2001–07. Freeman, City of London, 1996; Liveryman, Co. of Engrs, 1999; Hon. Freeman, Co. of Shipwrights, 2001. FRSA 1997. Hon. FCIPS 2002. Hon. DSc Cranfield, 2002. *Recreations:* fly fishing, West Ham United FC, Scotland. *Address:* c/o Lloyds Bank, 110 Putney High Street, SW15 1RG. *Clubs:* Reform, Army and Navy; Hawks; Woking Golf.

**WALPOLE,** family name of **Baron Walpole**.

**WALPOLE,** 10th Baron *cr* 1723, of Walpole; **Robert Horatio Walpole;** Baron Walpole of Wolterton, 1756; *b* 8 Dec. 1938; *s* of 9th Baron Walpole, TD and Nancy Louisa, OBE, *y d* of late Frank Harding Jones; *S* father, 1989; *m* 1st, 1962, S. Judith Schofield (later S. J. Chaplin, OBE, MP; marr. diss. 1979; she *d* 1993); two *s* two *d*; 2nd, 1980, Laurel Celia, *o d* of S. T. Ball; two *s* one *d*. *Educ:* Eton; King's College, Cambridge (MA, Dip Agric). Member, Norfolk CC, 1970–81 (Chm. of various cttees). Elected Mem., H of L, 1999–2017. Chairman: Area Museums Service for South East England, 1976–79; Norwich School of Art, 1977–87; Textile Conservation Centre, 1981–88 (Pres. 1988); East Anglian Tourist Board, 1982–88. Hon. Fellow, St Mary's UC, Strawberry Hill, 1997. JP Norfolk, 1972. *Heir: s* Hon. Jonathan Robert Hugh Walpole [*b* 16 Nov. 1967; *m* 2006, Eileen Margaret Sean (separated), *d* of Edward James Quinn]. *Address:* Mannington Hall, Norwich NR11 7BB.
See also Hon. A. L. Walpole.

**WALPOLE, Hon. Alice Louise,** OBE 2017; HM Diplomatic Service; Assistant Secretary General and Deputy Special Representative of the Secretary General, United Nations Mission for Iraq, since 2017 (on loan); *b* Norwich, 1 Sept. 1963; *d* of Baron Walpole, *qv* and (Sybil) Judith Walpole (later Judith Chaplin, OBE, MP); *m* 1990, Dr Angel Carro Castrillo (marr. diss. 2010); three *s* three *d*. *Educ:* Norwich High Sch., GDST; New Hall, Cambridge (MA). Entered FCO, 1985; Desk Officer, Eastern Eur. Dept, FCO, 1985–86; Conf. Support Officer, UK Mission to UN, NY, 1986–87; Desk Officer, Information Dept, FCO, 1987; Third Sec., Develt, UK Rep. to EC, 1987–90; Swahili lang. trng, 1990; Second Sec. (Pol), Dar es Salaam, 1991–94; Desk Officer, Policy Planning Staff, FCO, 1994–96; Hd, Peacekeeping Unit, UN Dept, FCO, 1996–98; First Secretary: Eur. Defence, UK Delegn to NATO, 1998–2000; UK Rep. to EU, Brussels, 2000–01; Envmt, UK Mission to UN, NY, 2001–06; Deputy Head: Stabilisation Unit, 2006–08; Corporate Communication Gp, FCO, 2008–09; Consul Gen., Basra, 2009–11; Ambassador: to Luxembourg, 2011–16; to Republic of Mali and (non-resident) to Republic of Niger, 2016–17. *Recreations:* travelling, cinema, gardening, sewing. *E:* walpole@un.org.

**WALPORT, Sir Mark (Jeremy),** Kt 2009; PhD; FRCP, FRCPath, FMedSci; FRS 2011; Chief Executive, UK Research and Innovation, since 2018; *b* 25 Jan. 1953; *s* of Samuel Walport and Doreen Walport (*née* Music); *m* 1986, Julia Elizabeth Neild; one *s* three *d*. *Educ:* St Paul's Sch., London; Clare Coll., Cambridge (Hon. Fellow, 2012); Middlesex Hosp. Med. Sch., London (MA, MB BChir; PhD 1986). FRCP 1990; FRCPath 1997. House Officer, Middlesex Hosp. and Queen Elizabeth II Hosp., Welwyn, 1977–78; SHO, 1978–80; Hon. Registrar, Brompton Hosp., 1980; Registrar, Hammersmith Hosp., 1980–82; MRC Trng Fellow, MRC Mechanisms in Tumour Immunity Unit, Cambridge, 1982–85; Harrison-Watson Student, Clare Coll., Cambridge, 1982–85; Royal Postgraduate Medical School, subseq. Imperial College Faculty of Medicine: Sen. Lectr in Rheumatology, 1985–90; Reader in Rheumatological Medicine, 1990–91; Prof. of Medicine, 1991–2003; Vice Dean for Res., 1994–97; Hd, Div. of Medicine, 1997–2003; Hon. Cons. Physician, Hammersmith Hosp., 1985–2003; Dir, R&D, Hammersmith Hosps Trust, 1994–98; Dir, Wellcome Trust, 2003–13; Chief Scientific Advr to the Govt and Hd, Govt Office for Sci., BIS, 2013–17. Member: Scientific Adv. Bd, Cantab Pharmaceuticals, Cambridge, 1989–; R&D Adv. Bd, SmithKline Beecham, 1998–2003. Member: Council, British Soc. for Rheumatology, 1989–95 (Chm., Heberden Cttee, 1993–95); Wkg Cttee on Ethics of Xenotransplantation, Nuffield Bioethics Council, 1995–96; Council, British Soc. for Immunology, 1998–2000; Council for Sci. and Technol., 2004– (Co-Chm., 2013–17); Chairman: Ethics Cttee, Hammersmith and Queen Charlotte's SHA, 1990–94; Molecular and Cell Panel, Wellcome Trust, 1998–2000. Gov., Wellcome Trust, 2000–03; Trustee, Kennedy Meml Trust, 2015– (Chm., 2016–). Philip Ellman Lecture, RCP, 1995 (Graham Bull Prize in Clin. Sci., 1996); Harveian Oration, RCP, 2015. Founder FMedSci 1998 (Registrar, 1998–2003); Fellow, ICSTM, 2006; FIC 2006; Hon. FRSE 2015. Asst Ed., British Jl of Rheumatology, 1990–97; Series Ed., 1998–2001; Chm., Editl Bd, 2001–03, British Med. Bulletin; Ed., Clin. and Exptl Immunology, 1998–2000. Hon. DSc: Sheffield, 2006; KCL, 2007; Aberdeen, 2009; Leicester, 2012; Glasgow, 2013; Keele, 2013; Cranfield, 2013; DUniv York, 2011; Hon. DCL Newcastle upon Tyne, 2013. Roche Prize for Rheumatology, 1991. *Publications:* (ed jtly) Clinical Aspects of Immunology, 5th edn 1993; (jtly) Immunobiology, 3rd edn 1997 to 7th edn 2007; papers in sci. jls on immunology and genetics of rheumatic diseases. *Recreations:* natural history, food. *Address:* UK Research and Innovation, Department for Business, Energy and Industrial Strategy, 1 Victoria Street, SW1H 0ET.

**WALSALL, Archdeacon of;** *no new appointment at time of going to press.*

**WALSBY, Prof. Anthony Edward,** PhD; FRS 1993; Melville Wills Professor of Botany, University of Bristol, 1980–2006, now Professor Emeritus. *Educ:* Birmingham Univ. (BSc); PhD London. Asst Lectr, then Lectr in Botany, Westfield Coll., London Univ., 1965–71; Miller Fellow, Univ. of Calif at Berkeley, 1971–73; Lectr, then Reader, Department of Marine Science-Marine Biology, UCNW, Bangor, 1973–80. *Address:* University of Bristol, Tyndall Avenue, Bristol BS8 1TH. *E:* a.e.walsby@bristol.ac.uk.

**WALSH, Brendan;** see Walsh, P. B. F.

**WALSH, Colin Stephen;** Organist Laureate, Lincoln Cathedral, since 2002 (Organist and Master of the Choristers, 1988–2002); *b* 26 Jan. 1955. *Educ:* Portsmouth Grammar Sch.; St George's Chapel, Windsor Castle (Organ Scholar); Christ Church, Oxford (Organ Scholar; MA 1980; PGCE 1978). ARCM 1973; FRCO 1976. Asst Organist, Salisbury Cathedral, 1978–85; Master of the Music, St Alban's Cathedral, 1985–88. Recitals in UK (incl. Royal Festival Hall) and many other countries. Recordings incl. French organ music, esp. by Vierne. Hon. DMus Lincoln, 2013. *Recreations:* walking, dining out, theatre, travel. *Address:* 12 Minster Yard, Lincoln LN2 1PJ. *T:* (01522) 561646.

**WALSH, Dominic Gerard;** Chief Executive, Hospital Services Ltd, since 2015; *b* Belfast, 20 Oct. 1961; *s* of George Walsh and Philomena Walsh; *m* 1987, Carmel; one *s* one *d*. *Educ:* Belfast Royal Acad.; Queen's Univ. Belfast (BSc Hons, MBA). CEng; MIMechE. Chief. Exec., MSO Gp Ltd, 2002–14. Pres., BPIF, 2005–07. Chm., Sport NI, 2008–12; Mem. Bd, UK Sport, 2008–12. Trustee, Mary Peters Trust, 2009–. *Recreations:* Rugby, golf, soccer, being optimistic and cheerful as at worst it confuses people and at best is infectious. *Clubs:* Academy Rugby Football, Fortwilliam Golf.

**WALSH, Enda;** playwright; *b* Dublin, 1967; *m* Jo Ellison; one *d*. *Educ:* Greendale Community Sch.; Rathmines Coll. *Plays:* for Corcodera Theatre Co.: The Ginger Ale Boy, 1995; Disco Pigs, 1996; The Same, 2017; for Abbey Theatre Co.: Sucking Dublin, 1997; for Landmark Productions: Misterman, 1999; Ballyturk, 2014; Arlington, 2016; for Druid Theatre Co.: The Small Things, 2005; The Walworth Farce, 2006; How These Men Talk, 2008; Lyndie's Got a Gun, 2008; Gentrification, 2008; Penelope, 2010; Bedbound, Dublin Th. Fest., 2000; Chatroom, NT, 2005; The New Electric Ballroom, Edinburgh Fest. and world tour, 2005; The Twits (adaptation), Royal Court Th., 2015; *musicals:* Once: The Musical, 2011 (Tony Award for Best Book of a Musical, 2012); (with David Bowie) Lazarus, NY, 2015, King's Cross Th., 2016; Grief is the Thing with Feathers (adaptation), Barbican, 2019; writer of libretto and director of *operas:* The Last Hotel, 2015; The Second Violinist, 2017; writer and director of *installation pieces:* Room 303, 2014; A Girl's Bedroom, 2015; Kitchen, 2016; Bathroom, 2017; *films:* Disco Pigs, 2001; Hunger, 2008 (Best Feature Film Screenplay Award, Writers' Guild of GB, 2009); Chatroom, 2010. Hon. DLitt NUI, Galway, 2013. *Publications:* Disco Pigs and Sucking Dublin, 1997; Bedbound and Misterman, 2001; The Walworth Farce, 2007; The New Electric Ballroom and The Walworth Farce, 2009; The Small Things and Other Plays, 2011; Enda Walsh: Plays One, 2011; Misterman, 2012; Once, 2013; Enda Walsh: Plays Two, 2014; Ballyturk, 2014; The Small Things, 2014; Penelope, 2014; How These Desperate Men Talk, 2014; The New Electric Ballroom, 2014; Bedbound, 2014; Chatroom, 2014; Delirium, 2016; Arlington, 2016; (with David Bowie) Lazarus, 2016. *Address:* c/o Curtis Brown, Haymarket House, 28–29 Haymarket, SW17 4SP.

**WALSH, Fergus;** Medical Correspondent, BBC, since 2005; reporter, BBC Panorama, since 2012; *b* Leicester, 16 Sept. 1961; *s* of Michael Walsh and Ita Walsh (*née* Cogavin); *m* 2005, Véronique Maguin; one *s* two *d*. *Educ:* Royal Grammar Sch., High Wycombe; Univ. of Leeds (BA Hons Eng. Lit. 1983); Falmouth Coll. (Dip. Radio Journalism 1984). Freelance radio reporter, 1984–86; sub-editor, 1986–87, reporter, 1987–88, BBC Radio News; Home and Legal Affairs Corresp., BBC, 1988–90; reporter, BBC TV News, 1990–93; BBC News: Health Corresp., 1993–2000; Sci. Corresp., 2000–05. Hon. DCL Newcastle, 2009. *Recreations:* photography, road cycling, theatre, making espresso, gardening with my wife, playing croquet with my children. *Address:* BBC, Room 02D, New Broadcasting House, Portland Place, W1A 1AA. *E:* fergus.walsh@bbc.co.uk.

**WALSH, Rt Rev. (Geoffrey David) Jeremy;** Bishop Suffragan of Tewkesbury, 1986–95; an Honorary Assistant Bishop, Diocese of St Edmundsbury and Ipswich, since 2008; *b* 7 Dec. 1929; *s* of late Howard Wilton Walsh, OBE and Helen Maud Walsh (*née* Lovell); *m* 1961, Cynthia Helen, *d* of late F. P. Knight, FLS, VMH, and H. I. C. Knight, BEM; two *s* one *d*. *Educ:* Felsted Sch., Essex; Pembroke Coll., Cambridge (MA Econ.); Lincoln Theological Coll. Curate, Christ Church, Southgate, London, 1955–58; Staff Sec., SCM, and Curate, St Mary the Great, Cambridge, 1958–61; Vicar, St Matthew, Moorfields, Bristol, 1961–66; Rector of Marlborough, Wilts, 1966–76; Rector of Elmsett with Aldham, 1976–80; Archdeacon of Ipswich, 1976–86. Hon. Canon, Salisbury Cathedral, 1973–76. *Recreations:* gardening, bird-watching. *Address:* 6 Warren Lane, Martlesham Heath, Ipswich IP5 3SH. *T:* (01473) 620797.

**WALSH, Graham Robert,** FCA; Deputy Chairman, Moss Bros Group plc, 1999–2001 (Director, 1988–2001); *b* 30 July 1939; *s* of Robert Arthur Walsh and Ella Marian (*née* Jacks); *m* 1967, Margaret Ann Alexander; one *s* one *d*. *Educ:* Hurstpierpoint Coll., Sussex. Qualified as chartered accountant, 1962; joined Philip Hill Higginson Erlangers (now Hill Samuel & Co. Ltd), 1964; Director, Hill Samuel, 1970, resigned 1973; Dir, 1973–87, Head of Corporate Finance Div., and Mem. Management Cttee, 1981–87, Morgan Grenfell & Co. Ltd; Man. Dir, Bankers Trust Co., 1988–91; Director: Morgan Grenfell Group plc (formerly Morgan Grenfell Holdings), 1985–87; Armitage Shanks Group Ltd, 1973–80; Phoenix Opera Ltd, 1970–87; Ward White Group plc, 1981–89; Rush & Tompkins Gp plc, 1988–90; Haslemere Estates, 1989–92; Rodamco UK BV, 1992–98. Dir Gen., Panel on Takeovers and Mergers, 1979–81; Chm., Issuing Houses Assoc., 1985–87 (Dep. Chm., 1979 and 1983–85). Gov., Dulwich Coll. Prep. Sch., 1995–97. *Recreations:* opera, theatre, music, gardening.

**WALSH, Henry George;** Deputy Chairman, Building Societies Commission, 1991–95; *b* 28 Sept. 1939; *s* of James Isidore Walsh and Sybil Bertha Bazeley; *m* 1999, Elizabeth Long; one *d*; two *d* by previous *m*. *Educ:* West Hill High Sch., Montreal; McGill Univ.; Churchill Coll., Cambridge. HM Treasury, 1966–74; Private Secretary to Chancellor of the Duchy of Lancaster, 1974–76; HM Treasury, 1976–78; Cabinet Office Secretariat, 1978–80; Counsellor (Economic), Washington, 1980–85; HM Treasury: Hd of Monetary Policy Div., 1985–86; Hd of IMF and Debt Div., 1986–89; Hd of Financial Instns and Markets Gp, 1989–91. *Recreations:* golf, model railways, being taken for walks by Labrador retrievers. *Address:* 60 Roxburgh Road, SE27 0LD. *Clubs:* Model Railway; Dulwich and Sydenham Hill Golf.

**WALSH, Rt Rev. Jeremy;** see Walsh, Rt Rev. G. D. J.

**WALSH, Jill P.;** see Paton Walsh.

**WALSH, John;** Director, J. Paul Getty Museum, 1983–2000, now Director Emeritus; Vice-President, J. Paul Getty Trust, 1998–2000; *b* 9 Dec. 1937; *s* of John J. Walsh and Eleanor Walsh (*née* Wilson); *m* 1961, Virginia Alys Galston; two *s* one *d*. *Educ:* Yale Univ. (BA 1961); Univ. of Leyden, Netherlands; Columbia Univ. (MA 1965; PhD 1971). Lectr, Research Asst, Frick Collection, NY, 1966–68; Metropolitan Museum of Art, NY: Associate for Higher Educn, 1968–71; Associate Curator and Curator, 1970–75, Vice-Chm., 1974–75, Dept of European Paintings; Columbia University: Adjunct Associate Prof., 1972–75; Prof. of Art History, Barnard Coll., 1975–77; Mrs Russell W. Baker Curator of Paintings, Museum of Fine Arts, Boston, 1977–83. Visiting Professor of Fine Arts, Harvard, 1979; of History of Art, Yale Univ., 2003, 2011, 2015; Mem., Inst. for Advanced Study, Princeton Univ., 2001–02. Member: Governing Bd, Yale Univ. Art Gallery, 1975–; Bd of Fellows, Claremont Grad. Sch. and Univ. Center, 1988–2000; Bd of Dirs, Hammer Mus., 2008–. Member: Assoc. of Art Museum Dirs, 1983–2001 (Trustee, 1986–90; Pres., 1989); Amer. Antiquarian Soc., 1984–. Mem., Amer. Acad. of Arts and Scis, 1997. Trustee, Burlington Mag. Foundn, 1995–. Hon. LHD Wheaton Coll., 2000. *Publications:* Things in Place: landscapes and still lifes by Sheridan Lord, 1995; Jan Steen, The Drawing Lesson, 1996; (with D. Gribbon) The J. Paul Getty Museum and its Collections: a museum for the new century, 1997; numerous contribs to learned jls. *Address:* c/o J. Paul Getty Museum, 1200 Getty Center Drive, Ste 1000, Los Angeles, CA 90049-1679, USA. *Club:* Century Association (NY).

**WALSH, John Henry Martin**; Assistant Editor, Independent, 1998–2013; b 24 Oct. 1953; s of Martin Walsh and Anne Walsh (née Durkin); one s two d; m 2012, Angie O'Rourke. Educ: Wimbledon Coll.; Exeter Coll., Oxford (BA Hons); University Coll., Dublin (MA). Advertisement Dept, Tablet Magazine, 1977; Publicity Dept, Victor Gollancz, 1978–79; Associate Editor, The Director, 1979–83; freelance writer, 1983–87; Literary Editor, 1987, Features and Literary Editor, 1988, Evening Standard; Literary Editor, Sunday Times, 1988–92; Editor, Independent Magazine, 1993–95; Literary Editor, Independent, 1995–96. BBC Radio 4: Presenter, Books and Company, 1995–97; Team Captain, The Write Stuff, 1998–2014. Artistic Dir, Cheltenham Festival of Literature, 1997–98. Chm. Judges, Forward Poetry Prize, 2000. Pres., Authors' Club, 2008–. Publications: Growing Up Catholic, 1989; The Falling Angels, 1999; Are You Talking to Me?, 2003; Sunday at the Cross Bones, 2007. Recreations: road trips in USA, drinking Burgundy wine, talking to my children. Address: 4 Westbourne Park Villas, W2 5EA. T: 07881 625609; Telegraph House, North Marden, W Sussex PO18 9JX. Clubs: Groucho, National Liberal.

**WALSH, Rev. Mgr John Michael**; Principal Roman Catholic Chaplain to the Royal Air Force, 2007–10; Parish Priest: St Jerome's Roman Catholic Church, Formby, since 2012; St Anne's Roman Catholic Church, Freshfield, since 2016; b London, 22 June 1959; s of Vincent John and Elizabeth Philomena Walsh. Educ: St Raphael's RC Prim. Sch., Manchester; St George's RC Sec. Mod. Sch., Manchester; St Joseph's Coll., Upholland; St Cuthbert's Coll., Ushaw, Durham (CTh 1982); Pontifical Univ. of St Thomas Aquinas, Rome (STL 2012). Ordained priest, 1983; Assistant Priest: Metropolitan Cath. of Christ the King, 1983–89; St Mary's, Blackbrook, 1989–91; St Joseph's Penketh, 1991–92; Parish Priest, St Elizabeth's, Litherland, 1992–95; Community of St Laurence, Ampleforth, 1995–98; Parish Priest, St Michael's, Ditton, 1999–2003; Commnd as Chaplain, RAF, 2003; RAF Coll. Cranwell, 2003; RAF Brize Norton, 2003–04; RAF Halton, 2004–05; RAF Marham, 2005–07; RAF Coll. Cranwell, 2007; Vicar General, 2007. Adminr, Bishopric of the Forces, 2008–09. Papal Prelate of Honour, 2007. Recreations: aviation, reading, classical music.

**WALSH, Kate Louise R.**; see Richardson-Walsh.

**WALSH, (Mary) Noëlle**; Editor, The Good Deal Directory, since 1992; Director, The Value for Money Company Ltd, since 1992; b 26 Dec. 1954; d of late Thomas Walsh and of Mary Kate Ferguson; m 1988, David Heslam; one s one d. Educ: Univ. of East Anglia (BA Hons European Studies (History and German)). Editorial Asst, PR Dept, St Dunstan's Orgn for the War-Blinded, 1977–79; News Editor, Cosmopolitan, 1979–85; Editor, London Week newspaper, 1985–86; freelance writer, 1986; Dep. Editor, 1986–87, Editor, 1987–91, Good Housekeeping; Dep. Editor, You and Your Family, Daily Telegraph, 1992; Editor, The Good Deal Directory monthly newsletter, 1992–97; Founder: gooddealdirectory website, 2000; gooddealhouse website, 2004. Member: Network; 300 Group; Forum UK. FRSA. Publications: Hot Lips, the Ultimate Kiss and Tell Guide, 1985; (co-ed) Ragtime to Wartime: the best of Good Housekeeping 1922–39, 1986; (co-ed) The Home Front: the best of Good Housekeeping 1939–1945, 1987; (co-ed) The Christmas Book: the best of Good Housekeeping at Christmas 1922–1962, 1988; (ed jtly) Food Glorious Food: eating and drinking with Good Housekeeping 1922–1942, 1990; Things my Mother Should Have Told Me, 1991; Childhood Memories, 1991; (ed) The Good Deal Directory, annually, 1994–; (ed) The Good Deal Directory Food Guide, 1993; (ed) The Home Shopping Handbook, 1994; Baby on a Budget, 1995; Wonderful Weddings that won't cost a fortune, 1995; The Factory Shopping and Sightseeing Guide to the UK, 1996; The Good Mail Order Guide, 1996; contrib. to Sunday Times annual Good Deal Guide. Recreation: medieval Irish history. Address: Cottage by the Church, Filkins, Lechlade, Glos GL7 3JG.

**WALSH, Michael Jeffrey**; Senior Vice President, Business Development, Europe, Velti, 2011–13 (Vice President, 2009–11); b 1 Oct. 1949; s of Kenneth Francis Walsh and Edith Walsh; m 1983, Sally Elizabeth Hudson; one s one d. Educ: Hulme Grammar Sch., Oldham; Durham Univ. (BA Hons Geog.). Joined Young and Rubicam as grad. trainee, 1972; Dir, 1980–83; New Business Dir, 1981–83; Mem., Exec. Cttee, 1982–83; Ogilvy & Mather, 1983–2005: Man. Dir, 1986–89, Chm., 1989–90, UK; Chm., UK Gp, 1990–99 and 2002–05; CEO, Europe, Africa and Middle East, 1994–2005; non-exec. Dir, Ogilvy & Mather SA, 1985–2016. Exec. Dir, Brand Union, 2013. Non-exec. Dir, Archant, 2010–. Chm., UK Disasters Emergency Cttee, 2005–11. Bd Mem., MLA, 2006. Hon. Vice-Chm. and Trustee, BRCS, 1994–2004; Worldwide Trustee, WWF, 1996–99. Recreations: collecting children's books, antiques, golf, sailing. Clubs: Royal Automobile, Mark's; Royal West Norfolk Golf, Archerfield Golf.

**WALSH, Michael Thomas**; Head of Research, Community (formerly Iron and Steel Trades Confederation), 1999–2008; b 22 Oct. 1943; s of late Michael Walsh and Bridget (née O'Sullivan); m 1972, Margaret Patricia Blaxhall; two s two d. Educ: Gunnersbury Grammar Sch.; Exeter Coll., Oxford (Hon degree PPE). Internat. Dept, TUC, 1966; Deputy Overseas Labour Adviser, FCO, 1977–79; Head, Internat. Dept, TUC, 1980–99. Economic and Social Committee of the European Community: Mem., 1976–77 and 1979–80; Alternate Mem., Consultative Commn on Industrial Change, 2003; Mem., World of Work Cttee, Catholic Bishops' Conf. of England and Wales, 1992–2001; Dep. Mem., Exec. Cttee, Eur. Metalworkers' Fedn, 2003. Member: Wilton Park Academic Council, 1994–2003; Governing Body, Plater Coll., Oxford, 1995–2001; Grant-Making Body, Charles Plater Trust, 2007– (Trustee, 2017–). Publications: (ed) Report of International Confederation of Free Trade Unions, 1994–99; (ed) ISTC reports; contrib. professional and Catholic jls. Recreations: cricket, moral philosophy, historical research, music. Address: 77 Uvedale Road, Enfield EN2 6HD.

**WALSH, Noëlle**; see Walsh, M. N.

**WALSH, (Patrick) Brendan (Finbarr)**; Editor, The Tablet, since 2017; b Leeds, 22 Feb. 1954; s of Richard Walsh and Margaret Walsh, MBE; m 2016, Laura Margaret Keynes; three d. Educ: Austin Friars Sch., Carlisle; London Hosp. Med. Sch.; Lancaster Univ. (BA Religious Studies 1977); Bristol Univ. (MA Theol. 1978). Asst Ed., Catholic Truth Soc., 1979–87; Man. Ed., SPCK Publishing, 1987–94; Hd of Communications, CAFOD, 1994–99; Publishing Dir, Darton, Longman and Todd, 1999–2011; Literary Ed., The Tablet, 2011–17. Recreations: jigsaws, train sets, treating grazed knees, very occasional theatre-going. Address: The Tablet, 1 King Street Cloisters, Clifton Walk, W6 0GY. T: (020) 8748 8484. E: bwalsh@thetablet.co.uk.

**WALSH, Patrick Edward**; Founder, PEW Literary Agency, since 2016; b Zeist, Holland, 2 April 1965; s of Peter Walsh and Tina Walsh (née Posthuma-Jorna). Educ: Gonville and Caius Coll., Cambridge (Exhibnr; BA Law 1987). Jun. post, Watson Little, 1988–92; Christopher Little Agency, 1992–2000; Co-Founder and Chm., Conville & Walsh, literary agency, 2000–16. Mem. Bd, Jane Goodall Inst., 2017–. Recreations: fishing, scuba diving, reading, conservation, adventure. Address: 19 Little Russell Street, WC1A 2HL. E: patrick@pewliterary.com. Clubs: Ivy, Academy.

**WALSH, Most Rev. Patrick Joseph**; Bishop of Down and Connor, (RC), 1991–2008; b 9 April 1931; s of Michael and Nora Walsh. Educ: Queen's Univ. Belfast (MA); Christ's Coll., Cambridge (MA); Pontifical Lateran Univ., Rome (STL). Ordained 1956; Teacher, St MacNissi's Coll., Garron Tower, 1958–64; Chaplain, Queen's Univ., Belfast, 1964–70; Pres., St Malachy's Coll., Belfast, 1970–83; Auxiliary Bishop of Down and Connor, 1983–91. Recreations: walking, music, theatre. Address: 6 Waterloo Park North, Belfast BT15 5HW. T: (028) 9077 8182.

**WALSH, Paul S.**; Chairman: Compass Group, since 2014; Chime Communications Ltd, since 2016; b Manchester, 1 May 1955; s of Arthur and Anne Walsh; one s; m 2013, Julie Lewis. Educ: Manchester Poly. (accounting qualifications). GrandMet, subseq. Diageo plc: joined Brewing Div., 1982; Finance Dir, Intercontinental Hotels, 1986–90; Div. Chief Exec., Pillsbury, 1990–92; CEO, Pillsbury Co., 1992–2000; Mem. Bd, 1995–2013; Chief Operating Officer, 2000; CEO, 2000–13; Advr, 2013–14. Non-executive Director: Fedex Corp.; Centrica plc, 2005–09; Unilever, 2009–15; Avanti Communications plc, 2012– (Chm., 2013–); RM2 Internat., 2014–; HSBC Hldgs plc, 2016–17; McDonald's, 2019–; Mem. Bd, United Spirits Ltd, 2013–14. Mem., Prime Minister's Business Adv. Gp, 2010–12; Lead non-exec. Dir, DECC, 2011–16. Business Ambassador for food and drink industries, BIS, then BEIS, 2012–. Chm., Scotch Whisky Assoc., 2008–11. Gov., Henley Mgt Coll., 2003. Recreations: outdoor activities, sailing. Address: Compass Group, Compass House, Guildford Street, Chertsey KT16 9BQ.

**WALSH, Robin**; Controller, BBC Northern Ireland, 1991–94; b 6 Feb. 1940; s of Charles and Ellen Walsh; m 1964, Dorothy Beattie; two d. Educ: Foyle College, Londonderry; Royal Belfast Academical Instn. Reporter, Belfast Telegraph, 1958–65; Reporter/News Editor, Ulster TV, 1965–74; BBC: News Editor, NI, 1974–81; Dep. Editor, TV News, 1982–85; Managing Editor, News and Current Affairs—TV, 1985–88; Asst Controller, News and Current Affairs, Regions, 1988–90. Recreations: cricket, walking. Address: Holly Lodge, 3A Ballymullan Road, Crawfordsburn, Co. Down NI BT19 1JG. T: (028) 9185 2709.

**WALSH, Samuel Maurice Cossart**, AO 2010; Chief Executive Officer, Rio Tinto plc, 2013–16; b Brighton, Vic, 27 Dec. 1949; s of Maurice John Walsh and Winifred Margaret Lois Walsh; m 2002, Leanne Joy Roki; two s one d. Educ: Brighton Grammar Sch.; Taylor's Coll.; Univ. of Melbourne (BCom); Kettering Univ. FAIM 2005; FAICD 2005; FCIPSA 2011. Buyer, 1972–74, Purchasing Agent, 1974–76, Coordinator Purchasing Admin, 1976–78, Sen. Purchasing Agent, 1978–83, Purchasing Manager, 1983–86, Materials Manager, 1986–87, Holden; Dir, Product Develt and Supply, 1987–89, Exec. Dir Ops, 1989–91, Nissan; Rio Tinto: Managing Director: Comalco Foundry Products, 1991–93; Sales and Mktg, 1994–97; Ops, 1997–2000; Hamersley Iron, 2000–01; Chief Executive: Comalco Ltd, 2001–04; Rio Tinto Iron Ore, 2004–13. Dir, Seven West Media Ltd, 2008–12; Dir, Mitsui and Co., Japan, 2017–. Co-Chm., Australia-India CEO Forum, 2015–16. Chairman: Black Swan State Th. Co., 2009–13; Chamber of Arts and Culture, WA, 2010–13; Art Gall. of WA, 2016–18; Australia Council for the Arts, 2018–; Perth Diocesan Trust, 2016–; Royal Flying Doctor Service, WA, 2017–; Patron: Baden Powell Soc., 2009–; Univ. of WA Hackett Foundn, 2010–13; Black Swan State Th., WA, 2013–17; Australian Purchasing Managers' Index, 2013–16; Gold Corp. Aust. (The Perth Mint), 2019–. Trustee, Royal Opera Hse Covent Gdn Foundn, 2014–16. Vis. Fellow, Univ. of Oxford, 2016–18; Hon. Fellow, Univ. of Melbourne, 2015. FAusIMM 2005; FTSE 2012; FInstD 2015. Hon. DCom: Edith Cowan, 2010; WA, 2014. Citizen of the Yr Award, WA, 2007. Recreations: antiques, fine arts, opera, theatre, ballet, orchestra. Clubs: Weld (Perth); Melbourne Cricket; Royal Freshwater Bay Yacht.

**WALSH, Simon**; JP; barrister in private practice, since 1988; b 7 Jan. 1962; s of Thomas Walsh and Jean Walsh (née Morris). Educ: Manchester Grammar Sch.; Balliol Coll., Oxford (BA 1984, MA 1987); City Univ., London (Dip. Law 1986). MCIArb 1999. Called to the Bar, Middle Temple, 1987, Inner Temple, Lincoln's Inn, ad eundem. Chm., Valuation Tribunals, 1998–2008. City of London Corporation: Common Councilman, 1989–2000; Alderman, Ward of Farringdon Without, 2000–13; Chairman: Housing Cttee, 1995–98; Police Authy, 2002–05; Licensing Authy, 2007–10. Mem., London Fire and Emergency Planning Authy, 2008–11. Freeman, City of London, 1987–; Liveryman: Glovers' Co., 1989–; Fletchers' Co., 2001–; Court Assistant: Parish Clerks' Co., 2004–12 (Under Warden, 2008–09); Guild of Freemen, 2004–06. Parish Clerk, St Augustine Old Change, 1993–; Churchwarden, St Dunstan-in-the-West, 2002–. Chm., City Br., Royal Soc. of St George, 2004–05. Governor: City of London Sch., 1992–2000; City of London Sch. for Girls, 2005–06; (ex officio): Christ's Hosp., 2000–13; Bridewell Royal Hosp., 2000–13. Pres., Alumni Assoc., City Univ., 2001–05. JP City of London, 2000–10, Haringey, 2010. CLJ 1999. Recreations: the Commonwealth, civic responsibility, 19th century French novels, municipal tramways, promoting the survival of real ale. Address: 5 Essex Court, Temple, EC4Y 9AH. Clubs: City Livery, Farringdon Ward; Golden Lane Community Association Social.

**WALSH, His Honour Terence Michael**; a Circuit Judge, North East Circuit, 2001–12; b 10 March 1945; s of late Gerrard Walsh and Freda Alice Walsh (later Kay); m 1969, Pauline Totham; two s one d. Educ: Belle Vue Boys' Grammar Sch., Bradford. Admitted as solicitor, 1974; Sen. Partner, Chivers Walsh Smith, Solicitors, Bradford, 1991–2001. Dep. Registrar, later Dep. Dist Judge, 1984–94; Asst Recorder, 1989–94; Recorder, 1994–2001. Pres., Bradford Law Soc., 1990–91; Mem., Children's Panel, Law Soc., 1994–2001. Consulting Ed., Practitioner's Guides, 1991–2011. Publications: Child Care and the Courts, 1988; Child Protection Handbook, 1995. Recreations: history, cricket, music, walking.

**WALSH, Wilfred Thomas**; Chief Executive, Carpetright plc, since 2014; b Exeter, 22 June 1962; s of John and Eileen Walsh; m 1987, Joanne Carolyne Luck; two s. Educ: St Peter's RC Grammar Sch., Manchester; Univ. of Leeds (LLB Hons). Pepsi Cola Internat., 1990–94; Managing Director: HMV Germany, 1996–2000; Coral, 2000–08; Chm., Fortuna Entertainment Gp NV, 2009–14. Non-exec. Dir, Gala Coral Gp, 2010–. Recreations: season ticket holder at Exeter City FC, Manchester United FC, cycling, cinema, malt whisky, National Hunt and flat racehorse owner. E: wilfwalsh@itsjustit.co.uk.

**WALSH, Most Rev. William**; Bishop of Killaloe, (RC), 1994–2010; b 16 Jan. 1935; s of Bill Walsh and Ellen Maher. Educ: St Flannan's Coll., Ennis; St Patrick's Coll., Maynooth (BSc); Irish Coll., Rome; Lateran Univ., Rome (LTh, DCL); Univ. Coll., Galway (HDipEd). Ordained priest, 1959; postgrad. studies, 1959–63; Teacher of mathematics and physics, St Flannan's Coll., Ennis, 1963–88; Curate at Ennis Cathedral, 1988–94; Priest Dir, 1969–94, Pres., Nat. Exec., 1995–2010, ACCORD (formerly Catholic Marriage Adv. Council); Mem., Episcopal, R&D and Pastoral Commns, 2003–10. Publications: No Crusader, 2016; contribs to several books, religious jls and mags. Recreations: hurling (sometime coach/selector of club, college and county teams), golf, gardening, walking, choral singing. Clubs: Eire Og Hurling (Ennis); Ennis, Lahinch and Woodstock Golf.

**WALSH, Willie;** Chief Executive, International Airlines Group (formerly British Airways), since 2005; *b* 1961; *m* Caragh; one *d*. *Educ:* Ardscoil Rís Sch., Dublin; Trinity Coll., Dublin (MSc 1992). Joined Aer Lingus as cadet pilot, 1979, Captain, 1990; Chief Exec., Futura, 1998–2000; COO, 2000–01, CEO, 2001–05, Aer Lingus. Non-exec. Dir, Fyffes plc, 2004–07. Chm., Nat. Treasury Mgt Agency, Ireland, 2013– (Chm. Adv. Cttee, 2013–). Chm., A4E, 2018–. *Address:* International Airlines Group, Waterside (HAA2), PO Box 365, Harmondsworth, Middx UB7 0GB.

**WALSHAM, Prof. Alexandra Marie,** CBE 2017; PhD; FBA 2009; FRHistS, FAHA; Professor of Modern History, University of Cambridge, since 2010; Fellow, Trinity College, Cambridge, since 2010; *b* Hayle, Cornwall, 4 Jan. 1966; *d* of Bruce and Ann Walsham. *Educ:* Presbyterian Ladies' Coll., Melbourne; Univ. of Melbourne (BA 1987; MA 1990); Univ. of Cambridge (PhD 1995). Res. Fellow, Emmanuel Coll., Cambridge, 1993–96; University of Exeter: Lectr in Hist., 1996–2000; Sen. Lectr in Hist., 2000–05; Prof. of Reformation Hist. (Personal Chair), 2005–10. Leverhulme Trust Maj. Res. Fellow, 2015–18. Principal Investigator, Remembering the Reformation proj., Univs of Cambridge and York, 2016–. Ford Lectures in British Hist., Univ. of Oxford, 2018. FRHistS 1999; FAHA 2013. *Publications:* Church Papists: Catholicism, conformity and confessional polemic in early modern England, 1993; Providence in Early Modern England, 1999 (Longman History Today Prize; Morris D. Forkosch Prize, Amer. Histl Assoc., 2000); (ed with J. Crick) The Uses of Script and Print 1300–1700, 2004; (ed jtly) Richard Carew, The Survey of Cornwall (1602), facsimile edn, 2004; Charitable Hatred: tolerance and intolerance in England 1500–1700, 2006; (ed with P. Marshall) Angels in the Early Modern World, 2006; (ed with E. Jones) Syon Abbey and its Books 1400–1700, 2010; (ed) Relics and Remains, 2010; The Reformation of the Landscape: religion, identity and memory in Early Modern Britain, 2011 (Leo Gershoy Award, Amer. Histl Assoc., Wolfson Hist. Prize (jtly), Roland H. Bainton Prize, Sixteenth Century Studies Conf., 2011); Catholic Reformation in Protestant Britain, 2014; (ed jtly) Religion and the Household, 2014; (ed jtly) The Social History of the Archives: record keeping in early modern Europe, 2016; (ed jtly) Archives and Information in the Early Modern World, 2018; contrib. articles to learned jls, incl. Past and Present, English Histl Rev., Histl Jl, Jl Ecclesiastical Hist., Jl British Studies, Histl Res., Renaissance Qly, Church Hist., British Catholic Hist., Memory Studies. *Address:* Trinity College, Cambridge CB2 1TQ.

**WALSHAM, Prof. Geoffrey,** LittD; Professor of Management Studies, University of Cambridge, 2001–10, now Emeritus; *b* 10 June 1946; *s* of Harry Walsham and Charlotte Gladys Walsham; *m* 1970, Alison Jane Evans; three *s* one *d*. *Educ:* St Catherine's Coll., Oxford (BA Maths 1966; MA 1971); Warwick Univ. (MSc Maths 1968); Univ. of Cambridge (LittD 2010). Lectr in Maths, Mindanao State Univ., Philippines, 1966–67; OR Analyst, BP Chemicals, 1968–72; Lectr in OR, Univ. of Nairobi, Kenya, 1972–75; Cambridge University: Lectr in Mgt Studies, 1975–94; Fellow, Fitzwilliam Coll., 1979–94; Prof. of Information Mgt, Lancaster Univ., 1994–96; University of Cambridge: Dir, MBA course, 1997–98; Res. Prof. of Mgt Studies, 1998–2001. *Publications:* Interpreting Information Systems in Organizations, 1993; Making a World of Difference: information technology in a global context, 2001; jl articles in information systems, organisational studies, operational res. *Recreations:* mountain walking, travel. *Address:* Judge Business School, University of Cambridge, Cambridge CB2 1AG. *T:* (01223) 339606, *Fax:* (01223) 339701. *E:* g.walsham@jbs.cam.ac.uk.

**WALSHAM, Sir Gerald (Percy Robert),** 6th Bt *cr* 1831, of Knill Court, Herefordshire; *b* 7 Feb. 1939; *s* of Percy Robert Stewart Walsham, *g s* of 2nd Bt and Tamara (*née* Ellis); S cousin, 2011, but his name does not appear on the Official Roll of the Baronetage; *m* 1984, Evelyn Niebes. RAF (Flt Lt) retired. *Heir:* none.

**WALSINGHAM,** 9th Baron *cr* 1780; **John de Grey,** MC 1952; Lieut-Colonel, Royal Artillery, retired, 1968; *b* 21 Feb. 1925; *s* of 8th Baron Walsingham, DSO, OBE, and Hyacinth (*d* 1968), *o d* of late Lt-Col Lambart Henry Bouwens, RHA; S father, 1965; *m* 1963, Wendy, *er d* of E. Hoare, Southwick, Sussex; one *s* two *d*. *Educ:* Wellington Coll.; Aberdeen Univ.; Magdalen Coll., Oxford (BA Oxon, 1950; MA 1959); RMCS, Shrivenham (ptsc 1960). Army in India, 1945–47; Palestine, 1947; Oxford Univ., 1947–50; Foreign Office, 1950–51; Army in Korea, 1951–52; Hong Kong, 1952–54; Malaya, 1954–56; Cyprus, Suez, 1956; Aden, 1957–58; Royal Military Coll. of Science, 1958–60; Aden, 1961–63; Malaysia, 1963–65. Co. Dir, 1968–96; founded and ran three cos in farming, vegetable processing and water plants, 1970–98. FInstD 1978. *Publications:* On the Origins of Speaking, 2006; Lithic Language, 2013. *Heir: s* Hon. Robert de Grey [*b* 21 June 1969; *m* 1995, Josephine Elizabeth, *d* of Richard Haryott; one *s* two *d*]. *Address:* The Hassocks, Merton, Thetford, Norfolk IP25 6QP. *T:* (01953) 885385. *E:* hassocks@lineone.net.

**WALTER, Dame Harriet (Mary),** DBE 2011 (CBE 2000); actress; *b* 24 Sept. 1950; *d* of late Roderick Walter and Xandra Carandini de Trafford (*née* Lee). *Educ:* Cranborne Chase Sch.; LAMDA. Associate Artist, RSC, 1987–2015, now Hon. Associate Artist. Hon. DLitt Birmingham, 2001. Pragnell Shakespeare Award, 2007. *Theatre:* Ragged Trousered Philanthropists, Joint Stock Co., 1978; Hamlet, Cloud Nine, Royal Court, 1980; Nicholas Nickleby, RSC, 1980; Seagull, Royal Court, 1981; RSC seasons, 1981–83: Midsummer Night's Dream; All's Well That Ends Well (also on Broadway, 1983); The Castle, RSC, 1985; Merchant of Venice, Royal Exchange, Manchester, 1987; RSC seasons, 1987–89: Cymbeline; Twelfth Night; Three Sisters; Question of Geography (Best Actress, Olivier Awards, 1988); Duchess of Malfi, RSC, 1989–90; Three Birds Alighting on a Field, Royal Court, 1991–92, NY, 1994; Arcadia, 1993, The Children's Hour, 1994, National; Old Times, Wyndham's, 1995; Hedda Gabler, Chichester, 1996; Ivanov, Almeida, 1997; The Late Middle Classes, Watford and UK tour, 1999; Macbeth, RSC, 1999; Life x 3, RNT, 2000, transf. Old Vic, 2001; The Royal Family, Th. Royal, Haymarket, 2001; Much Ado About Nothing, RSC, 2002; Dinner, RNT, 2002, transf. Wyndham's, 2003; Us & Them, Hampstead, 2003; The Deep Blue Sea, Th. Royal, Bath and UK tour, 2003; Mary Stuart, Donmar Warehouse, transf. Apollo, 2005 (Best Actress, Evening Standard Th. Awards, 2005), NY 2009; Antony and Cleopatra, RSC, 2006; Women Beware Women, RNT, 2010; Julius Caesar, Donmar, 2012, NY, 2013; Henry IV, Donmar, 2014, NY, 2015; Boa, Trafalgar Studios, 2015; Death of a Salesman, RSC, 2015; Julius Caesar, Henry IV, The Tempest, Donmar, King's Cross, 2016, NY, 2017; *television:* The Imitation Game, 1980; Cherry Orchard, 1981; The Price, 1985; Lord Peter Wimsey, 1987; The Men's Room, 1991; Ashenden, 1991; A Dance to the Music of Time, 1997; Unfinished Business, 1998; Macbeth, 1999; George Eliot, 2002; Ballet Shoes, 2007; Little Dorrit, 2008; A Short Stay in Switzerland, 2009; Law and Order: UK, 2009–13; Downton Abbey, 2013–15; London Spy, 2015; The Crown, 2018; Black Earth Rising, 2018; Succession, The Spanish Princess, 2019; *films:* Turtle Diary, 1985; The Good Father, 1986; Milou en Mai, 1990; Sense and Sensibility, 1996; The Governess, 1998; Onegin, 1999; Villa des Roses, 2002; Bright Young Things, 2003; Chromophobia, 2004; Babel, 2005; Atonement, 2007; The Young Victoria, 2009; A Royal Affair, The Wedding Video, 2012; Suite Française, Man Up, 2015; Denial, Mindhorn, The Sense of an Ending, 2017; Sony Award for Best Actress, radio, 1988 and 1992. *Publications:* Other People's Shoes, 1999; Actors on Shakespeare: Macbeth, 2002; Facing It: reflections on images of older women, 2011; Brutus and Other Heroines, 2016; contribs to: Clamorous Voices, 1988; Players of Shakespeare, Vol. III, 1993; Mothers by Daughters, 1995; Renaissance Drama in Action, 1999; Living with Shakespeare, 2013. *Address:* c/o Hamilton Hodell, 20 Golden Square, W1F 9JL.

**WALTER, Natasha;** author and campaigner; Director, Women for Refugee Women, since 2007; *b* London, 20 Jan. 1967; *d* of Nicolas Walter and late Ruth Walter; partner, Mark Lattimer; one *s* one *d*. *Educ:* North London Collegiate Sch.; St John's Coll., Cambridge (BA 1st Cl. English Lit. 1988); Harvard Univ. (Frank Knox Fellow, 1988). Dep. Literary Ed., Independent, 1993–94; feature writer and columnist, Guardian, Independent and Observer, 1995–2007. Humanitas Vis. Prof. in Women's Rights, Univ. of Cambridge, 2015. *Publications:* The New Feminism, 1998; (ed) On the Move, 1999; Living Dolls: the return of sexism, 2010; A Quiet Life (novel), 2016. *Address:* c/o Anna Webber, United Agents, 12–26 Lexington Street, W1F 0LE. *E:* awebber@unitedagents.co.uk.

**WALTER, Neil Douglas,** CNZM 2002; *b* 11 Dec. 1942; *s* of Ernest Edward Walter and Anita Walter (*née* Frethey); *m* 1966, Berys Anne (*née* Robertson); one *s* two *d*. *Educ:* New Plymouth Boys' High School; Auckland University (MA). Second Sec., Bangkok, 1966–70; First Sec., NZ Mission to UN, NY, 1972–76; Official Sec., Tokelau Public Service, Apia, 1976–78; Minister, Paris and NZ Permt Deleg. to Unesco, 1981–85; Dep. High Comr for NZ in London, 1985–87; Asst Sec., Ministry of External Relations, NZ, 1987–90; NZ Ambassador to Indonesia, 1990–94; Dep. Sec., Ministry of Foreign Affairs and Trade, NZ, 1994–98; NZ Ambassador to Japan, 1998–99; NZ Sec. of Foreign Affairs and Trade, 1999–2002; Chair: Envmtl Risk Mgt Authy of NZ, 2003–08; NZ on Air, 2006–12; NZ Broadcasting Commn, 2007–12. *Recreations:* sport, reading.

**WALTER, Robert John;** *b* 30 May 1948; *s* of late Richard and of Irene Walter; *m* 1970, Sally Middleton (*d* 1995); two *s* one *d*; *m* 2011, Feride Alp. *Educ:* Lord Weymouth Sch., Warminster; Aston Univ. (BSc 1971). Formerly farmer, S Devon; Mem., Stock Exchange, 1983–86; internat. banker. Dir and Vice Pres., Aubrey G. Lanston & Co., Inc., 1986–97. Vice Pres., Cons. Gp for Europe, 1995–97 (Vice Chm., 1984–86; Dep. Chm., 1989–92; Chm., 1992–95). Contested (C) Bedwellty, 1979. MP (C) N Dorset, 1997–2015. Opposition spokesman on constitutional affairs and Wales, 1999–2001. Member: Health Select Cttee, 1997–99; Eur. Scrutiny Select Cttee, 1998–99; Internat. Develt Select Cttee, 2001–03; Treasury Select Cttee, 2003–05; Vice-Chm., Cons. Agric. Cttee, 1997–99; Sec., Cons. Eur. Affairs Cttee, 1997–99; Treasurer: All Party British-Japanese Parly Gp, 1997–2013; All Party Gp on Charities and Vol. Sector, 1997–2005; British-Caribbean Parly Gp, 1997–2014; Vice Chairman: All Party Gp on Lupus, 2000–05; All Party Human Rights Gp; Chairman: All Party Belgium Gp, 2008–15; All Party Egypt Gp, 2013–15. Mem., British-Irish Parly Assembly (formerly Body), 1997–2015 (Vice-Chair, 2010–15; Chm., Eur. Affairs Cttee, 2001–15); Member: Parly Assembly of Council of Europe, 2001–15 (Leader, UK Delegn, 2010–15; Vice-Pres., 2011–15; Chm., Eur. Democrat Gp, 2011–13); Assembly of WEU, 2001–11 (Chm., Defence Cttee, 2006–08; Leader, Federated Gp of Christian Democrats and European Democrats, 2006–15; Pres., Eur. Security and Defence Assembly, 2008–11); Pres., European Security and Defence Assoc., 2012–; Vice-Pres., IPU, 2013–15 (Chm., British Gp, 2010–13). Patron, Eurodefense UK, 2017–. Hon. Sec., 1999–2001, Rear Cdre, 2001–15, H of C Yacht Club. Chm. Bd of Governors, Tachbrook Sch., 1980–2000. Freeman, City of London, 1983; Liveryman, Needlemakers' Co., 1983. Hon. DLitt Aston, 2011. *E:* bobwalterx@gmail.com. *Clubs:* Carlton; Royal Western Yacht.

**WALTERS, Sir Dennis,** Kt 1988; MBE 1960; *b* 28 Nov. 1928; *s* of late Douglas L. Walters and Clara Walters (*née* Pomello); *m* 1st, 1955, Vanora McIndoe (marr. diss. 1969); one *s* one *d*; 2nd, 1970, Hon. Celia (*née* Sandys) (marr. diss. 1979); one *s*; 3rd, 1981, Bridgett (marr. diss. 2004), *d* of late J. Francis Shearer; one *s* one *d*. *Educ:* Downside; St Catharine's College (Exhibitioner), Cambridge (MA). War of 1939–45: interned in Italy; served with Italian Resistance Movement behind German lines after Armistice, 1943–44; repatriated and continued normal educn, 1944. Chm., Fedn of Univ. Conservative and Unionist Assocs, 1950; Personal Asst to Lord Hailsham throughout his Chairmanship of Conservative Party, 1957–59; Chm., Coningsby Club, 1959. Contested (C) Blyth, 1959 and Nov. 1960; MP (C) Westbury Div. of Wilts, 1964–92. Jt Hon. Sec., Conservative Party Foreign Affairs Cttee, 1965–71, Jt Vice-Chm., 1974–78; Jt Chm., Euro-Arab Parly Assoc., 1978–81; Mem., UK Parly Delegn to UN, 1966; UK Deleg. to Council of Europe and Assembly of WEU, 1970–73. Introduced Children and Young Persons (Amendment) Bill, 1985 (Royal Assent, 1986). Founder/Patron, Cons. ME Council, 2007– (Chm., 1980–92; Pres., 1992–2007). Director: The Spectator, 1983–84; Middle East Internat., 1971–90 (Chm., 1990–2006). Chm., Asthma Research Council, 1968–88; Vice Pres., Nat. Asthma Campaign, 1989–2001. Joint Chairman: Council for Advancement of Arab British Understanding, 1970–82 (Jt Vice-Chm., 1967–70); UK/Saudi Cultural Cttee, 1988–2007; Kuwait British Friendship Soc., 1996–2007 (Hon. Pres., 2007–); Mem., Kuwait Investment Adv. Cttee, 1969–; ME Consultant, JCB, 2005–. Governor, British Inst. of Florence, 1965–95. Comdr, Order of Cedar of Lebanon, 1969; Grande Ufficiale, Ordine al Merito Repubblica (Italy), 2012. *Publications:* Not Always with the Pack (autobiographical memoirs), 1989 (trans. Italian, rev. edn, as Benedetti Inglesi Benedetti Italiani, 1991). *Address:* Flat 43, 5 Sloane Court East, SW3 4TQ. *Clubs:* Boodle's, Hurlingham, Queen's.

**WALTERS, Geraint Wyn;** His Honour Judge Walters; a Circuit Judge, since 2015; *b* Glanamman, Carmarthenshire, 31 Dec. 1957; *s* of Thomas Eifion Walters and Dilys Walters; *m* 1986, Kathryn Ann Jenkins; three *d*. *Educ:* Ysgol Gyfun Ystalyfera; University Coll. of Wales, Aberystwyth (LLB Hons 1980); Inns of Court Sch. of Law. Called to the Bar, Gray's Inn, 1981; in practice as barrister, Angel Chambers, Swansea, 1981–2015 (Hd of Chambers, 2001–15); a Recorder, 2001–15. Asst Comr, Boundary Commn for Wales, 2001–15. Hon. Sec., then Chm., Guild for Promotion of Welsh Music, 1988–2002. Member: Gorsedd of Bards of Isle of Britain, 1975–; Arts Cttee, Inst. of Welsh Affairs, 1988–. Pres., Aberystwyth Law Students, 1979. *Recreations:* music, walking, gardening. *Address:* Cwmndwr House, Ynystawe, Swansea SA6 5BE.

**WALTERS, Ian,** CEng; FIMechE; Chief Executive, Action Mental Health, 2002–10; *b* 20 March 1943; *s* of John and Olive Walters; *m* 1968, Carol Ann Flanders; two *s* one *d*. *Educ:* Moseley Hall Grammar Sch., Cheadle; Univ. of Manchester (BSc; DipTechSc 1966). MIET (MIEE 1970); MIGEM (MIGasE 1972); FIMechE 1997. With Parkinson Cowan Measurement, rising to Factory Manager, Manchester, then Belfast, 1966–72; Dep. Principal, then Principal, Dept of Commerce, NI, 1972–80; Industrial Development Board for Northern Ireland: Dir, then Sen. Dir, IDB N America, NY, 1980–84; Executive Director: Food Div., 1985–89; Internat. Mktg Div., 1989–91; Internat. Repn Div., 1991–92; Corporate Services Group: Actg Dep. Chief Exec., 1992–93; Sen. Exec. Dir, Jan.–Oct. 1993; Dir, Business Support Div., 1993–95, Chief Exec., 1995–2001, Trng and Employment Agency, NI. Dir, Open Coll. Network, NI, 2014– (Chm., Finance and Gen. Purposes Cttee, 2015–). FCMI (MCMI; MBIM 1980); FRSA 2000. Mem., Governing Body, Belfast Metropolitan Coll., 2007–15 (Vice Chm., 2007–15). Hon. Treas., Arthritis Care, NI, 2011–17 (Trustee, 2015–17); Trustee, Arthritis Research UK, then Versus Arthritis, 2017–. Chm., Bd of Govs, Belvoir Park Primary Sch., 2011–14. Hon. Dr Rocky Mountain Coll., Montana, 1999. *Recreations:* photography, walking, gardening.

**WALTERS, John Latimer**; QC 1997; Judge of the First-Tier Tribunal and Deputy Judge of the Upper Tribunal, since 2009; b 15 Sept. 1948; o s of late John Paton Walters and Charlotte Alison Walters (née Cunningham); m 1st, 1970, Victoria Anne Chambers (marr. diss. 1987; she d 1996); 2nd, 1990, Caroline Elizabeth, d of late John Vipond Byles and of Doreen Violet Byles, Norwich; two d, and one step s. Educ: Rugby Sch.; Balliol Coll., Oxford (MA; Wylie Prize, 1970). Called to the Bar, Middle Temple, 1977 (Astbury Scholar); practice at Revenue Bar, 1978–. Special Comr and Chm. (part-time), VAT and Duties Tribunals, 2002–09. Local Preacher in the Methodist Church (Waveney Ecumenical Partnership). Recreations: gardening, painting, design and work embroidery, genealogy, singing, esp. hymns, formerly Lieder.

**WALTERS, Joyce Dora**; Headmistress, Clifton High School, Bristol, 1985–95; m 1st, 1979, Lt-Col Howard C. Walters (d 1983); one s; 2nd, 2004, Prof. Richard Lynn, qv. Educ: St Anne's College, Oxford (BA Lit.Hum.). Headmistress, St Mary's, Calne, 1972–85. Recreations: travelling, reading, cooking, bridge. Address: 4 Longwood House, Failand, Bristol BS8 3TL. T: (01275) 392092.

**WALTERS, Dame Julie**, DBE 2017 (CBE 2008; OBE 1999); actress; b 22 Feb. 1950; d of late Thomas and Mary Walters; m 1997, Grant Roffey; one d. Educ: Holly Lodge Grammar Sch., Smethwick; Manchester Polytechnic (Teaching Certificate). Theatre: Educating Rita, 1980 (Drama Critics' Most Promising Newcomer Award; Variety Club Best Newcomer); Having a Ball, Lyric, Hammersmith, 1981; Fool for Love, NT, 1984; Macbeth, Leicester Haymarket, 1985; When I was a Girl I used to Scream and Shout, Whitehall, 1986; Frankie and Johnny in the Clair de Lune, Comedy, 1989; The Rose Tattoo, Playhouse, 1991; All My Sons, RNT, 2000 (Best Actress, Laurence Olivier Awards, 2001); Acorn Antiques the Musical, Th. Royal, Haymarket, 2005; The Last of the Haussmans, NT, 2012. Films: Educating Rita, 1983 (Variety Club of GB's Award for best film actress; BAFTA Award for best actress; Hollywood Golden Globe Award); She'll be Wearing Pink Pyjamas, 1985; Car Trouble, 1986; Personal Services, 1987 (British Video Award, Best Actress); Prick Up Your Ears, 1987; Buster, 1988; Killing Dad, 1989; Stepping Out (Variety Club Best Film Actress), 1991; Just Like a Woman, 1992; Sister My Sister, 1995; Intimate Relations, 1996; Girls' Night, 1998; Titanic Town, 1999; Billy Elliot (Evening Standard Award, Best Actress; BAFTA Award, Best Supporting Actress), 2000; Harry Potter and the Philosopher's Stone, 2001; Before You Go, Harry Potter and the Chamber of Secrets, 2002; Calendar Girls, 2003; Harry Potter and the Prisoner of Azkaban, 2004; Wah-Wah, Driving Lessons, 2006; Becoming Jane, Harry Potter and the Order of the Phoenix, 2007; Mamma Mia!, 2008; Harry Potter and the Half-Blood Prince, 2009; Harry Potter and the Deathly Hallows, Pt 1, 2010, Pt 2, 2011; One Chance, 2013; Effie Gray, Paddington, 2014; Brooklyn, 2015; Paddington 2, Film Stars Don't Die in Liverpool, 2017; Mary Poppins Returns, Mamma Mia! Here We Go Again, 2018; Wild Rose, 2019; television: My Beautiful Son, 2001 (Best Actress, BAFTA, 2002); The Return, 2003; Canterbury Tales: The Wife of Bath, 2003 (Best Actress, BAFTA, 2004); Ahead of the Class, 2005; Ruby in the Smoke, 2006; series include: Wood and Walters, 1981–82; Victoria Wood as Seen on TV, 1985–87; The Secret Diary of Adrian Mole, 1985; Victoria Wood Series, 1989; GBH, 1991; Jake's Progress, 1995; Melissa, 1997; dinnerladies, 1998–99; films: Clothes in the Wardrobe, Wide Eyed and Legless, 1993; Bambino Mio, Pat and Margaret, 1994; Little Red Riding Hood, 1995; Brazen Hussies, 1996; Filth: The Mary Whitehouse Story, 2008; A Short Stay in Switzerland, 2009; Mo (Best Actress, BAFTA and Broadcasting Press Guild Awards), 2010; Henry IV, 2012; Henry V, 2012; serials: Oliver Twist, 1999; Murder, 2002 (BAFTA Award, Best Actress, RTS Best Actress, 2003); The Jury, 2011; Indian Summers, 2015, 2016; National Treasure, 2016; Coastal Railways with Julie Walters, 2017; also television plays, incl. monologues in series, Talking Heads, 1988, 1998. Show Business Personality of the Year, Variety Club of GB, 2001; Lifetime Achievement Award, South Bank Sky Arts Awards, 2013; Fellow, BAFTA, 2014. Publications: Baby Talk, 1990; Maggie's Tree (novel), 2006; That's Another Story (autobiog.), 2008. Recreations: reading, travel, walking. Address: c/o Independent Talent Agency Ltd, 40 Whitfield Street, W1T 2RH.

**WALTERS, Prof. Kenneth**, PhD, DSc; FRS 1991; Professor of Applied Mathematics, 1973–94, now Distinguished Research Professor, Institute of Mathematics, Physics and Computer Science (formerly of Mathematics and Physics), Aberystwyth University (formerly University of Wales, Aberystwyth); b 14 Sept. 1934; s of late Trevor Walters and Lilian (née Price); m 1963, Mary Ross Eccles; two s one d. Educ: University Coll. of Swansea (BSc 1956; MSc 1957; PhD 1959; DSc 1984; Hon. Fellow, 1992). Dept of Mathematics, University Coll. of Wales, Aberystwyth: Lectr, 1960–65; Sen. Lectr, 1965–70; Reader, 1970–73. Vis. Fellow, Peterhouse, Cambridge, 1996. Mem., Sci. Adv. Council for Wales, 2010–15. Pres., European Soc. of Rheology, 1996–2000; Chm., Internat. Cttee on Rheology, 2000–04. Church Warden, St Michael's, Aberystwyth, 1993–99, 2001–07. Founding FLSW 2010; Fellow, Soc. of Rheology, 2017. For. Mem., NAE, USA, 1995. Dr hc Joseph Fourier, Grenoble, 1998; Hon. DSc Strathclyde, 2011; Hon. Dr Aberystwyth, 2016. Gold Medal, British Soc. of Rheology, 1984; Weissenberg Award, European Soc. of Rheology, 2002. Publications: Rheometry, 1975; (ed) Rheometry: industrial applications, 1980; (with M. J. Crochet and A. R. Davies) Numerical Simulation of non-Newtonian Flow, 1984; (with H. A. Barnes and J. F. Hutton) An Introduction to Rheology, 1989; (with D. V. Boger) Rheological Phenomena in Focus, 1993; (with R. I. Tanner) Rheology: an historical perspective, 1998; The Way it Was, 2003; More Personal Stories from New Testament Times, 2012. Address: Institute of Mathematics, Physics and Computer Science, Aberystwyth University, Penglais, Aberystwyth, Ceredigion SY23 3BZ. T: (01970) 622750; 8 Pen y Graig, Aberystwyth, Ceredigion SY23 2JA. T: (01970) 615276.

**WALTERS, Lucy Mary Elizabeth**; see Crowe, L. M. E.

**WALTERS, Minette Caroline Mary**; DL; crime and historical writer, since 1992; b 26 Sept. 1949; d of Capt. Samuel Henry Desmond Jebb and Minette Colleen Helen Jebb (née Paul); m 1978, Alex Hamilton Walters; two s. Educ: Godolphin Sch.; Durham Univ. (BA). Magazine journalist, 1972–77; freelance journalist and writer, 1977–82. DL Dorset, 2019. Hon. DLitt: Bournemouth, 2005; Southampton Solent, 2006. John Creasey Award, 1992, Gold Dagger Award, 1994, 2002, CWA; Edgar Allen Poe Award, 1994. Publications: The Ice House, 1992; The Sculptress, 1993; The Scold's Bridle, 1994; The Dark Room, 1995; The Echo, 1997; The Breaker, 1998; The Shape of Snakes, 2000 (Palle Rosenkrantz Prize, Danish Acad. of Crime, 2001); Acid Row, 2001; Fox Evil, 2002; Disordered Minds, 2003; The Tinder Box, 2004; The Devil's Feather, 2005; Chickenfeed, 2006 (Quick Reads Award, 2006); The Chameleon's Shadow, 2007; A Dreadful Murder, 2013; The Cellar, 2015; The Last Hours, 2017; The Turn of Midnight, 2018. Recreations: crosswords, Scrabble, jigsaw puzzles, DIY, cinema, TV, walking, reading, cooking. Address: c/o Gregory & Co., Authors' Agents, David Higham Associates, Waverley House, 7–12 Noel Street, W1F 8GQ. T: (020) 7434 5900.

**WALTERS, Sir Peter (Ingram)**, Kt 1984; non-executive Director, Nomura International plc, 2004–10 (Senior Adviser, 2002–04); b 11 March 1931; s of late Stephen Walters and of Edna Walters (née Redgate); m 1st, 1960, Patricia Anne (née Tulloch) (marr. diss. 1991); two s one d; 2nd, 1992, Meryl Marshall. Educ: King Edward's Sch., Birmingham; Birmingham Univ. (BCom). NS Commn; RASC, 1952–54; British Petroleum Co., 1954–90: Man. Dir, 1973–90; Chm., 1981–90; Vice-Pres., BP North America, 1965–67; Chairman: BP Chemicals, 1976–81; BP Chemicals Internat., 1981; Blue Circle Industries PLC, 1990–96; SmithKline Beecham, subseq. Glaxo SmithKline: Dir, 1989–2000; Chm., 1994–2000; Jt Dep. Chm., 2000–02; Dep. Chm., Thorn EMI, later EMI, 1990–99 (Dir, 1989–99). Dir, 1981–89, Dep. Chm., 1988–89, Nat. Westminster Bank; Chm., Midland Bank, 1991–94; Dep. Chm., HSBC Hldgs, 1992–2001. Member: Indust. Soc. Council, 1975–90; Post Office Bd, 1978–79; Coal Industry Adv. Bd, 1981–85; Inst. of Manpower Studies, 1986–88 (Vice-Pres., 1977–80; Pres., 1980–86); Gen. Cttee, Lloyds Register of Shipping, 1976–90; President's Cttee, CBI, 1982–90; President: Soc. of Chem. Industry, 1978–80; Gen. Council of British Shipping, 1977–78; Inst. of Directors, 1986–92; Inst. Business Ethics, 2001–10. Chm. Governors, London Business Sch., 1987–91 (Governor, 1981–91); Governor Nat. Inst. of Economic and Social Affairs, 1981–90; Mem. Foundn Bd, 1982–83, Chm., 1984–86, Internat. Management Inst.; Trustee: Nat. Maritime Museum, 1983–90; E Malling Res. Station, 1983–2010; Inst. of Economic Affairs, 1986–2007. Pres., Police Foundn, 2001–10 (Chm., Trustees, 1985–2001). Hon. DSocSc Birmingham, 1986; DUniv Stirling, 1987. Comdr, Order of Leopold (Belgium), 1984. Recreations: golf, gardening, sailing. Address: 1 St James's Square, SW1Y 4PD. Clubs: Athenæum; West Sussex Golf.

**WALTERS, Rhodri Havard**, CB 2014; DPhil; Reading Clerk and Head of Corporate Services, House of Lords, 2007–14; b Merthyr Tydfil, 28 Feb. 1950; s of Havard Walters and Veigan Walters (née Hughes). Educ: Cyfarthfa Castle Grammar Sch., Merthyr Tydfil; Jesus Coll., Oxford (Meyricke Exhibnr; BA 1971; DPhil 1975). Clerk, Parliament Office, House of Lords, 1975–2014: on secondment to Cabinet Office as Private Sec. to Leader of the House and Govt Chief Whip, 1986–89; Civil Service Nuffield and Leverhulme Travelling Fellow, attached to US Congress, 1989–90; Clerk to Select Cttee on Sci. and Technol., H of L, 1990–93; Establishment Officer, 1993–2000; Clerk of Public Bills, 2000–02; Sec. to Ecclesiastical Cttee, 2000–03; Clerk: of Cttees, 2002–07; of the Overseas Office, 2002–14; of Jt Cttee on Draft H of L Reform Bill, 2011–12. Publications: How Parliament Works (with Robert Rogers), 1987, 7th edn 2015; (contrib.) The British Constitution in the Twentieth Century, 2003; Law in Politics, Politics in Law, 2013; articles in Econ. Hist. Rev., Welsh Hist. Rev., The Table. Recreations: rowing, gardening, ski-ing, church music. Address: 40 Cleveland Gardens, SW13 0AG. T: (020) 8878 7494. E: rhwalters@blueyonder.co.uk. Club: Garrick.

**WALTERS, Sam Robert**, MBE 1999; Artistic Director, Orange Tree Theatre, 1971–2014 (Founder, 1971); b 11 Oct. 1939; s of Denbigh Robert Walters and Elizabeth Walters (née Curry); m 1964, Auriol Smith; two d. Educ: Felsted Sch., Essex; Merton Coll., Oxford (MA PPE); LAMDA. Actor, 1963–67; Resident Dir, Worcester Repertory Co., Swan Theatre, 1967–69; Dir, Jamaica Theatre Co. and Jamaica Theatre Sch., 1970–71; freelance dir, West End, regl theatres, and in Israel and Holland, 1970–; at Orange Tree Theatre has dir. premières of plays by Alan Ayckbourn, Rodney Ackland, Harley Granville Barker, Vaclav Havel and James Saunders, amongst many others. Hon. Freeman, Richmond upon Thames, 2014. Hon. DLitt Kingston, 2009. Special Achievement Awards: Off West End Th. Awards, 2012; Peter Brook Empty Space Awards, 2013. Recreations: no time, alas, but now he may wish to acquire one or two.

**WALTHER, Robert Philippe**, FIA; Deputy Chairman, Nationwide Building Society, 2006–12 (Director, 2002–12); b 31 July 1943; s of Prof. D. P. Walther and Barbara (née Brook); m 1969, Anne Wigglesworth. Educ: Charterhouse; Christ Church, Oxford (MA). FIA 1970. Clerical Medical Investment Group: Investment Manager, 1974–85; Investment Dir, 1985–94; Dep. Man. Dir, 1994–95; Gp Chief Exec., 1995–2001; Chairman: JP Morgan Fleming (formerly Fleming Claverhouse Investment Trust), 1999–2005 (Dir, 1993–99); Fidelity European Values, 1999–2010 (Dir, 1993–2010). Dir, BUPA, 2004–09. Recreations: golf, sailing, bridge, fishing. Address: Ashwells Barn, Chesham Lane, Chalfont St Giles, Bucks HP8 4AS. T: (01494) 875575.

**WALTHO, Lynda Ellen**; Director, Midlands Confederation of Passenger Transport, since 2016; b 22 May 1960; d of Charles and Eunice Abbott; m Stephen J. Waltho (marr. diss. 2014); two s. Educ: Keele Univ.; Univ. of Central England (PGCE). School teacher, Birmingham, Sandwell and Dudley LEAs, 1981–94; Assistant to: Simon Murphy, MEP, 1995–97; Sylvia Heal, MP, 1997–2001; Agent, W Midlands Regional Labour Party, 2001–04; Principal Advr to Neena Gill, MEP, 2004–05. MP (Lab) Stourbridge, 2005–10; contested (Lab) same seat, 2010. PPS to Minister of State, NI Office, 2005–07, MoJ, 2007–10, to Prisons Minister, 2007–08; Dep. Minister for W Midlands, 2008–10.

**WALTON, His Honour Christopher Thomas**; a Circuit Judge, 1997–2014; b 20 March 1949; s of George Edward Chaytor Walton and Margaret Walton; m 1992, Brenda Margaret Laws. Educ: St Cuthbert's GS, Newcastle upon Tyne; Downing Coll., Cambridge (MA). Called to the Bar, Middle Temple, 1973; a recorder, 1992–97; North Eastern Circuit. Publications: (gen. ed.) Charlesworth & Percy on Negligence, 9th edn 1996, 14th edn 2018. Recreations: history (particularly local history), tennis, golf, music, Scottish art.
See also S. E. Wood.

**WALTON, Dawn**; Founder, Artistic Director and Chief Executive Officer, Eclipse Theatre Co., 2010–19; b London, 18 Feb. 1963; d of Selwyn and Monica Walton. Educ: St Ursula's Convent Grammar Sch., London; Goldsmiths' Coll., Univ. of London (BA Drama and Theatre Arts). Worked in sales and marketing industry specialising in IT and publishing, until 1998; Dir, Royal Court Th.; Actg Head, Studio-Nat. Th., 2006–07; freelance dir, theatre and film, 1998–; theatre includes: Oxford Street, Royal Court Th., 2006; The Hounding of David Oluwale, West Yorks Playhouse, 2009; Lyrical Feata: the letter with Jonzi D, Sadlers Wells, 2013; One Monkey Don't Stop No Show, Tricycle Th. and nat. tour, 2013; A Raisin in the Sun, Crucible Th. and nat. tour, 2016; Black Men Walking, Royal Exchange, Royal Court Th. and nat. tour, 2018; Salt, Edinburgh Fest., Royal Court Th., 2019 (The Stage Edinburgh Award, 2019); film includes: 10by10, 2012; Samuels Trousers, 2019; radio plays: The Last Flag, 2018; White Open Spaces, 2016. Founder: Revolution Mix, 2015–; Slate: Black.Arts.World, 2016–. Jerwood Young Director's Award, 2001; Tonic Award for Women in Theatre, 2017. Recreations: theatre, film, music, family. E: djbwalton@hotmail.com.

**WALTON, Ven. Geoffrey Elmer**; Archdeacon of Dorset, 1982–2000, now Archdeacon Emeritus; b 19 Feb. 1934; s of Harold and Edith Margaret Walton; m 1961, Edith Mollie O'Connor; one s. Educ: St John's Coll., Univ. of Durham (BA); Queen's Coll., Birmingham (DipTh). Asst Curate, Warsop with Sookholme, 1961–65; Vicar of Norwell, Notts, 1965–69; Recruitment and Selection Sec., ACCM, 1969–75; Vicar of Holy Trinity, Weymouth, 1975–82; RD of Weymouth, 1980–82; Non-Residentiary Canon of Salisbury, 1981–2000. Chairman: E Dorset Housing Assoc., 1991–2003; Dorset Scout Council, 1995–2013; Synergy Housing Gp, 2003–05. Recreations: conjuring, religious drama. Address: Priory Cottage, 6 Hibberds Field, Cranborne, Dorset BH21 5QL. T: (01725) 517167.

**WALTON, James Robert**; Director of Finance, Governance and Assurance (Section 151 Officer), Shropshire Council, since 2013; b Codsall, Staffs, 30 June 1971; s of James and Hilda Walton; m 1994, Eleanor Claire Doley; one s two d. Educ: Sandwell Coll.; Univ. of Wolverhampton (CIPFA 1996). Accountant roles, Wolverhampton MBC, 1989–99; Sen. Accountant roles, 2000–09, Asst Dir, 2009–13, Shropshire Council. Treasurer: Marches LEP, 2011–; W Mercia Energy, 2013–; Shropshire Fire and Rescue Service, 2013–;

**WALTON, John William Scott**; Director of Statistics, Board of Inland Revenue, 1977–85; b 25 Sept. 1925; s of late Sir John Charles Walton, KCIE, CB, MC, and late Nelly Margaret, Lady Walton, d of late Prof. W. R. Scott. *Educ*: Marlborough; Brasenose Coll., Oxford. Army (RA), 1943–47. Mutual Security Agency, Paris, 1952; Inland Revenue, 1954; Central Statistical Office, 1958, Chief Statistician, 1967, Asst Dir, 1972. *Publications*: (contrib. jtly) M. Perlman, The Organization and Retrieval of Economic Knowledge, 1977; (contrib.) ECB Workshop on Pensions, 2009; articles in The Review of Income and Wealth, Economic Trends, Business Economist, Statistical News. *Club*: Oxford and Cambridge.

**WALTON, Margaret Anita**; *see* Clark, M. A.

**WALTON, Peter David**; Director, Human Resources and Workplace Services, Department for Communities and Local Government (formerly Office of the Deputy Prime Minister), 2005–06; b 24 Feb. 1954; s of Kenneth Walton and Sheila Walton; m 1998, Margaret Anita Clark, qv. *Educ*: Robert Gordon's Coll., Aberdeen; Univ. of Durham (BA Hons (Geog.) 1975). Joined DoE, administrative trainee, 1975; various policy posts; Grade 7, 1980; various policy and finance posts, incl. secondment to RDA; sen. Civil Service posts in housing, finance, central policy planning and agency sponsorship, 1991–2001; Exec. Dir, Change Mgt, then Human Resources and Business Change, subseq. Orgnl Develt and Resources, ONS, 2001–05. Mem., 2013–, Vice Chm., 2015–, Puddletown Parish Council. Chm., Tolpuddle Village Hall, 2012–. *Recreations*: watching sport, music and opera, DIY, collecting and entertaining eccentric friends.

**WALTON, Richard Arthur**, CB 2003; PhD; FIMA; information assurance consultant, 2003–13; b 22 Sept. 1947; s of Lt Col Gordon Walton and Audrey Mary Walton (née Varah); m 1st, 1968, Jacqueline Elisabeth Roberts (d 1990); one d; 2nd, 1992, Mary Elizabeth Mackenzie. *Educ*: Shene Grammar Sch.; Univ. of Nottingham (BSc Hons Maths 1968; PhD 1971); Open Univ. (BA Hons 1987). FIMA 1999; CMath 1999; MBCS 2004; FIET 2005; CEng 2005. Lectr in Maths, N Staffordshire Poly., 1971–73; GCHQ: various posts, 1973–98; Dir, CESG (Nat. Technical Authy for Inf. Assurance), 1999–2002; Office of the e-Envoy, Cabinet Office, 2002–03. Vis. Prof., Royal Holloway, Univ. of London, 2002–. Mem., Elmley Castle Parish Council, 2004–15. Dir, Elmley Castle PubCo, 2016–. Honorary Treasurer: Elmley Castle Cricket Club, 1984–2004; Elmley Castle PCC, 2001–15. Mem., Inst. of Information Security Professionals, 2008–. Volunteer lock keeper, 2017–. *Recreations*: supporting cricket and Rugby, concerts, theatre. *E*: richard@walton-mackenzie.com. *Clubs*: Civil Service; New (Cheltenham).

**WALTON, Sarah Louise**; *see* Rowland-Jones, S. L.

**WALTON, Dr Suzy**, CDir, CSci, CPsychol; b Nottingham, 8 Dec. 1963; d of Michael Brett and Greta Brett (née Lowe); five s one d; partner, Andrew James Griffin. *Educ*: Nottingham Girls' High Sch.; Univ. of Herts (BSc 1st Cl. Hons 1994; MSc 1995); Cranfield Univ. (PhD Mil. Suicide 1999). CPsychol 1997; CSci 2007. Actress, Children of a Lesser God, 1983–85; producer, presenter and ed., Time Off (weekly travel prog.), LBC Radio, 1986–90; News Producer, Sky News, 1990–91; mil. psychologist, MoD, 1995–2000; Sen. Civil Servant, DTI, 2000; Cabinet Office: Prime Minister's Strategy Unit, 2000–04; Prime Minister's Delivery Unit, 2005–07. Member: Nat. Specialist Commng Gp, DoH, 2007–13; Ethics Gp, Nat. DNA Database, Home Office, 2007–14; Sci. Adv. Council, DEFRA, 2009–11; Bd, HEFCE, 2012–16; State Hons Cttee, Cabinet Office, 2012–. Member, Univ. of Westminster, 2005–14 (Dep. Chm., 2005–14); Internet Watch Foundn, 2008–14 (Dep. Chm., 2008–14); Combat Stress, 2008– (Chm., Clin. Governance (formerly Med. Services) Cttee, 2008–); Birmingham Children's Hosp., 2008–11; RSA, 2010–16 (Dep. Chm., 2010–16); IoD, 2013– (Chm., Accreditation and Standards Cttee, 2015–; Chm., Remuneration Cttee, 2018–); Regulatory Bd, ACCA, 2014– (Chm., Qualifications Bd, 2016–); Mem. Council, RSocMed, 2017– (Vice Pres., 2019–); Mem., Disciplinary Cttee, Judicial Conduct Investigations Office, 2015–. CDir 2008. FRSocMed. *Publications*: Suicide in the British Army, Parts 1–5, 1996–99. *E*: suzy.walton1@ntlworld.com.

**WALTON, William Stephen**; Chief Education Officer, Sheffield, 1985–90; b 28 March 1933; s of Thomas Leslie Walton and Ena Walton (née Naylor); adopted French nationality, 2008; m 1964, Lois Elicia Petts; three d (incl. twins). *Educ*: King's School, Pontefract; Univ. of Birmingham (BA). RAF, gen. duties (flying), 1951–55. Production Management, Dunlop Rubber Co., 1958–61; Derbyshire Local Educn Authy School Teacher, 1961–67; Educational Administration: Hull, 1967–70; Newcastle upon Tyne, 1970–79; Sheffield 1979–90. Visiting Professor: Univ. of Simon Fraser, BC, 1990–91; Univ. of Portland, Oregon, 1990–91. Pres., Soc. of Educn Officers, 1989–90; Chm., Sch. Curriculum Industry Partnership/Mini Enterprise Schs Project, 1990–95. Dir, Outward Bound, 1989–95. Registered Inspector of Schools, 1993–2003. Hon. Fellow, Sheffield City Polytechnic, 1990. *Recreation*: travel. *Club*: Royal Air Force.

**WAN, Joseph Sai Cheong**, FCA; FCIArb; Chief Executive Officer, Harvey Nichols Group Ltd, 1992–2014; b Hong Kong, 27 Feb. 1954; s of Yuk Lin Wan and Lai Bing Ho; m 1986, Flora Mei Yee; two d. *Educ*: St Louis Sch., Hong Kong. FCA 1984; FCIArb 2000. Qualified Asst, then Associate, Hong Kong Office, KPMG, 1978–87 (incl. one year in London office); Gp Finance Dir, Dickson Concepts Internat. Ltd, 1987–92. Chartered Arbitrator 2002. Fellow, Hong Kong Inst. Certified Public Accountants, 1986; FInstD 1989. FRSA. *Recreations*: reading (legal and finance), swimming, table tennis, travelling.

**WANAMAKER, Zoë**, CBE 2001; actor; b 13 May; d of late Sam Wanamaker, Hon. CBE, and Charlotte (née Holland); acquired British passport, 2001; m 1994, Gawn Grainger. *Stage includes*: A Midsummer Night's Dream, 69 Theatre Co., 1970; repertory at Royal Lyceum, 1971–72, Oxford Playhouse, 1974–75 and Nottingham, 1975–76; Royal Shakespeare Company: The Devil's Disciple, Ivanov, Wild Oats, 1976; Captain Swing, The Taming of the Shrew, Piaf, 1978 (NY, 1980); Once in a Lifetime, 1979 (Olivier Award/SWET Award); Comedy of Errors, Twelfth Night, The Time of your Life, 1983; Mother Courage (Drama magazine award), 1984; Othello, 1989; National Theatre: The Importance of Being Earnest, 1982; The Bay at Nice, Wrecked Eggs, 1986; Mrs Klein, 1988, transf. Apollo, 1989; The Crucible, 1990; Battle Royal, 1999; His Girl Friday, 2003; The Rose Tattoo, Much Ado About Nothing, 2007; The Cherry Orchard, 2011; West End: The Last Yankee, Young Vic, 1993; Dead Funny, Hampstead, transf. Vaudeville, 1994; The Glass Menagerie, Donmar, transf. Comedy, 1995; Sylvia, Apollo, 1996; The Old Neighbourhood, Duke of York's, 1998; Boston Marriage, Donmar, transf. New Ambassadors, 2001; All My Sons, Apollo, 2010 (whatsonstage.com Award); Passion Play, Duke of York's, 2013; Chichester: Electra, 1997 (Olivier Award, Variety Club Award, and Callaway Award, US Equity, 1998), transf. Princeton and NY, 1998–99; Stevie, Minerva, Chichester, 2014, transf. Hampstead, 2015; Loot, NY, 1986; Awake and Sing!, NY, 2006; Zorba, NY, 2015; Harlequinade, All On Her Own, Garrick Th., 2015; Elegy, Donmar Warehouse, 2016; The Birthday Party, Harold Pinter Th., 2018; Two Ladies, Bridge Th., 2019; *films include*: Inside the Third Reich, The Hunger, 1982; The Raggedy Rawney, 1987; Amy Foster, 1996; Wilde, 1996; Harry Potter and the Philosopher's Stone, 2001; Five Children and It, 2004; It's a Wonderful Afterlife, 2010; My Week with Marilyn, 2011; *television includes*: Strike, 1981; Richard III, 1982; Enemies of the State, 1982; The Edge of Darkness, 1984; Paradise Postponed, 1985; Once in a Lifetime, 1987; The Dog it was that Died, 1988; Prime Suspect, 1990; Love Hurts, 1991, 1992, 1993; The Blackheath Poisonings, 1991; Memento Mori, 1991; The Countess Alice, 1991; The Widowing of Mrs Holroyd, 1995; A Dance to the Music of Time, 1997; Leprechauns, 1999; David Copperfield, 1999; Gormenghast, 1999; My Family, 2000–11 (Best Sitcom Actress Rose d'Or, 2005); Adrian Mole: the Cappuccino Years, 2000; Miss Marple: A Murder is Announced, 2004; A Waste of Shame, 2005; Dr Who, 2005, 2006; Poirot: Cards on the Table, 2005, Mrs McGinty's Dead, 2008, The Third Girl, 2008, Halloween Party, 2010, Dead Man's Folly, Elephants Can Remember, 2013; Johnny and the Bomb, 2006; The Old Curiosity Shop, 2007; The Man, 2012; Wodehouse in Exile, 2013; Mr Selfridge, 2015; Babs, 2017; Girlfriends, 2018; Britannia, 2018, 2019; Inside No. 9, 2018; Killing Eve, 2019; has also appeared in radio plays. Patron, Prisoners of Conscience, 2003–; Vice Patron, The Actors' Centre, 2005–; Hon. Pres., Shakespeare's Globe, 2005–; Hon. Vice-Pres., Dignity in Dying (formerly Voluntary Euthanasia Soc.), 1994. Hon. DLitt: S Bank, 1993; Amer. Internat. Univ., London, 1999; UEA, 2012. BPG TV Award for Best Actress, 1992; Theatre Sch., DePaul Univ., Chicago, Award for Excellence in the Arts. 2004. *Address*: c/o Peggy Thompson, 1st & 2nd Floor Offices, 296 Sandycombe Road, Kew, Richmond, Surrey TW9 3NG.

**WANDSWORTH, Archdeacon of;** *see* Kiddle, Ven. J.

**WANG, Rachel Alexandra Louise**; Founder and Director, Chocolate Films, since 2003; b Sutton, 24 Nov. 1973; d of David and Yvonne Wang; m 2002, Mark Stuart Currie; one s one d. *Educ*: Wimbledon High Sch.; Wimbledon Sch. of Art (Foundn); Univ. of Bristol (BA Jt Hons Hist. of Art and Theol.); Univ. of Law (MA). Reg. Person, SFA 1999. Corporate Finance Exec., Beaumont Cornish Ltd, 1998–2002; Dir, Hybrid Prodns, 2002–03. Creative Dir, 1000londoners.com, 2014–. Non-exec. Dir, Movie Collective, 2018–. Board Member: Film Hub, Film London, 2014–; London Screen Archives, 2017–19. Mem., UK Council, Creative Industries Fedn, 2018–20. Trustee, NPG, 2017–. FRSA. Leadership Fellow, St George's, Windsor. Hon. DBA Middx, 2017; Hon. LLD Law, 2018. Freeman, City of London, 2017; Mem., Guild of Entrepreneurs, 2016–. *Recreations*: fine art, sandy beaches, hare-brained schemes. *Address*: Chocolate Films, Battersea Studios, 80–82 Silverthorne Road, Battersea, SW8 6HE. *T*: (020) 7793 4287. *E*: rachel@chocolatefilms.com.

**WANG Gungwu, Prof.**, CBE 1991; FAHA; University Professor, National University of Singapore, since 2007; Director, East Asian institute, Singapore, 1997–2007 (Chairman, 2007–18); Vice-Chancellor, University of Hong Kong, 1986–95; b 9 Oct. 1930; s of Wang Fo Wen and Ting Yien; m 1955, Margaret Lim Ping-Ting; one s two d. *Educ*: Anderson Sch., Ipoh, Malaya; Nat. Central Univ., Nanking, China; Univ. of Malaya, Singapore (BA Hons, MA); Univ. of London (PhD 1957). University of Malaya, Singapore: Asst Lectr, 1957–59; Lectr, 1959; University of Malaya, Kuala Lumpur: Lectr, 1959–61; Sen. Lectr, 1961–63; Dean of Arts, 1962–63; Prof. of History, 1963–68; Australian National University: Prof. of Far Eastern History, 1968–86, Emeritus Prof., 1988; Dir, Res. Sch. of Pacific Studies, 1975–80; Univ. Fellow, 1996–97. Rockefeller Fellow, 1961–62, Sen. Vis. Fellow, 1972, Univ. of London; Vis. Fellow, All Souls Coll., Oxford, 1974–75; John A. Burns Distinguished Vis. Prof. of History, Univ. of Hawaii, 1979; Rose Morgan Vis. Prof. of History, Univ. of Kansas, 1983; Dist. Professorial Fellow, Inst. of SE Asian Studies, 1999–2002; Dist. Fellow, Hong Kong Inst. for the Humanities and Social Scis, Univ. of Hong Kong, 2009; Rector, Cinnamon Coll., NUS, 2010–15. Dir, East Asian History of Science Foundation Ltd, 1987–95. MEC, Hong Kong, 1990–92. Co-Patron, Asia-Link, Melbourne, 1994–. Chairman: Australia-China Council, 1984–86; Envmt Pollution Cttee, HK, 1988–93; Adv. Council on the Envmt, 1993–95; Council for the Performing Arts, HK, 1989–94; Asia-Pacific Council, Griffith Univ., 1997–2001; Asia Scholarship Foundn, 2002–07; Internat. Adv. Council, Universiti Tunku Abdul Rahman, Malaysia, 2002–; Bd of Trustees, Inst. SE Asian Studies, 2002–; Singapore Higher Educn Accreditation Council, 2004–06; Bd, Lee Kuan Yew Sch. for Public Policy, 2005–17. Member: Commn of Inquiry on Singapore Riots, 1964–65; Internat. Adv. Panel, E-W Center, Honolulu, 1979–91; Cttee on Aust.-Japan Relations, 1980–81; Regional Council, Inst. of SE Asian Studies, Singapore, 1982–2002; Admin. Bd, Assoc. of SE Asian Instns of Higher Learning, 1986–92; Council, Chinese Univ. of Hong Kong, 1986–95; Exec. Council, WWF, HK, 1987–95; Council, Asia-Aust. Inst., Sydney, 1991–95, 1999–; Council, Asia Soc., HK, 1991–95; Council, IISS, 1992–2001; Nat. Arts Council, Singapore, 1996–2000; Nat. Heritage Bd, Singapore, 1997–2002; Nat. Library Bd, 1997–2003; Bd, Social Sci. Council, NY, 2000–06; Council, Nat. Univ. of Singapore, 2000–04; Bd, Inst. of Policy Studies, 2002–09; Vice-Chm., Chinese Heritage Centre, Singapore, 2000–12. Sen. Advr, Social Sci. Res. Council, Singapore, 2015–. President: Internat. Assoc. of Historians of Asia, 1964–68, 1988–91; Asian Studies Assoc. of Aust., 1979–80; Australian Acad. of the Humanities, 1980–83 (Fellow 1970); Hon. Corresp. Mem. for Hong Kong, RSA, 1987 (Fellow 1987; Chm., Hong Kong Chapter, 1992–95). Mem., Academia Sinica, 1992. For. Hon. Mem., Amer. Acad. of Arts and Scis, 1995; Hon. Mem., Chinese Acad. of Social Scis, 1996. Editor: (also Councillor) Jl of Nanyang Hsueh-hui, Singapore, 1958–68; (also Vice-Pres.), Jl of RAS, Malaysian Br., 1962–68; China, an internat. jl, 2002–07; Gen. Editor, East Asian Historical Monographs series for OUP, 1968–95. Hon. Fellow: SOAS, London Univ., 1996; Wolfson Coll., Cambridge, 2009. Hon. DLitt: Sydney, 1992; Hull, 1998; Hong Kong, 2002; Cambridge, 2009; Sunway, 2017; Hon. LLD: Monash, 1992; ANU, 1996; Melbourne, 1997; DUniv: Soka, 1993; Griffith, 1995. Darjah Dato' Paduka Makhota Perak, 2011; DHum Lingnan, 2017. *Publications*: The Nanhai Trade: a study of the early history of Chinese trade in the South China Sea, 1958, 2nd edn 1998; A Short History of the Nanyang Chinese, 1959; Latar Belakang Kebudayaan Pendudok di-Tanah Melayu: Bahagian Kebudayaan China (The Cultural Background of the Peoples of Malaysia: Chinese culture), 1962; The Structure of Power in North China during the Five Dynasties, 1963; (ed) Malaysia: a survey, 1964; (ed jtly) Essays on the Sources for Chinese History, 1974; (ed) Self and Biography: essays on the individual and society in Asia, 1975; China and the World since 1949: the impact of independence, modernity and revolution, 1977; (ed jtly) Hong Kong: dilemmas of growth, 1980; Community and Nation: essays on Southeast Asia and the Chinese, 1981; (ed jtly) Society and the Writer: essays on literature in modern Asia, 1981; Dongnanya yu Huaren (Southeast Asia and the Chinese), 1987; Nanhai Maoyi yu Nanyang Huaren (Chinese Trade and Southeast Asia), 1988; (ed with J. Cushman) Changing Identities of Southeast Asian Chinese since World War II, 1988; Lishi di Gongneng (The Functions of History), 1990; China and the Chinese Overseas, 1991 (Zhongguo yu Haiwai Huaren, 1994); The Chineseness of China: selected essays, 1991; Community and Nation: China, Australia and Southeast Asia, 1992; The Chinese Way: China's position in international relations, 1995; (ed with S. L. Wong) Hong Kong's Transition, 1995; (ed) Global History and Migrations, 1997; (ed) Xianggang shi Xinbian (Hong Kong History: new perspectives), 2 vols, 1997; (ed with S. L. Wong) Hong Kong in the Asia-Pacific Region, 1997; (ed with S. L. Wong) Dynamic Hong Kong: business and culture, 1997; (ed with L. C. Wang) The Chinese

Diaspora, 2 vols, 1998; China and Southeast Asia, 1999; (ed with J. Wong) Hong Kong in China, 1999; (ed with J. Wong) China: two decades of reform and change, 1999; The Chinese Overseas: from earthbound China to the quest for autonomy, 2000; Joining the Modern World: inside and outside China, 2000; (ed with Y. Zheng) Reform, Legitimacy and Dilemmas: China's politics and society, 2000; Don't Leave Home: migration and the Chinese, 2001; Sino-Malay Encounters, 2001; (ed) Wang Fo-wen Jinianji (Wang Fo-wen, 1903–1972: a memorial collection of poems, essays and calligraphy), 2002; To Act Is To Know: Chinese dilemmas, 2002; Wang Gengwu zixuanji: selected works, 2002; Bind Us In Time: nation and civilisation in Asia, 2002; Haiwai Huaren Yanjiu di Dashiye yu Xinfangxiang (Overseas Chinese Research: new directions), 2002; (ed with Y. Zheng) Damage Control: the Chinese Communist Party and the era of Jiang Zemin, 2003; (ed with I. Abrahms) The Iraq War and its Consequences, 2003; (ed jtly) Sino-Asiatica, 2003; Anglo-Chinese Encounters since 1800: war, trade, science and governance, 2003; Ideas Won't Keep: the struggle for China's future, 2003; Diasporic Chinese Ventures, 2004; (ed with C. K. Ng) Maritime China in Transition, 2004; (ed) Nation-building: five Southeast Asian histories, 2005; Yimin yu xingqi de Zhongguo, 2005; Divided China: preparing for reunification, 883–947, 2006; Lixiang bietu: jingwai kanzhonghua (China and its Cultures: from the periphery), 2007; Chuka Bunmei to Chugoku no yukue (Chinese Civilization and China's Position), 2007; (ed with Y. Zheng) China and the New International Order, 2008; (ed with Y. Zheng) Zhongguo de 'zhuyi' zhi zheng (China's Ideological Battles since the May Fourth Movement), 2009; (ed with W. Ong) Voice of Malayan Revolution: the CPM radio war against Singapore and Malaysia, 1960–81, 2009; Wang Gungwu: In Conversation with Asad-ul Iqbal Latif, 2010; Renewal: the Chinese State and the new global history, 2013; Huaren yu Zhongguo, 2013; Another China Cycle: committing to reform, 2014; Wudai Shiqi Beifang Zhongguo di Quanli Jiegou, 2014; The Eurasian Core and its Edges: dialogue with Wang Gungwu on the history of the world, 2015; Tianxia Huaren, 2016; Nanyang: essays on heritage, 2018; Home is not Here, 2018; China Re-Connects: joining a deep-rooted past to a New World Order, 2019; contribs to collected vols on Asian history; articles on Chinese and Southeast Asian history in internat. jls. *Recreations:* music, reading, walking. *Address:* East Asian Institute, Bukit Timah Campus, National University of Singapore, 469 Bukit Timah Road, Singapore 259756. *T:* 67752033, *Fax:* 67756607. *E:* eaiwgw@nus.edu.sg.

**WANGARATTA, Bishop of,** since 2008; **Rt Rev. (Anthony) John Parkes,** AM 2011; *b* Leamington Spa, Warwicks, 6 Aug. 1950; *s* of Dennis Arthur Parkes and Eleanor Margaret Parkes (*née* Burrill); *m* 1984, Margaret Anne O'Meara; one *s* one *d*. *Educ:* Warwick Sch.; Univ. of Sheffield (LLB Hons); St Mark's Nat. Theol Centre, Canberra (BTh Hons; Laurence Murchison Prize for Academic Excellence); Melbourne Coll. of Divinity (MTh 1995). Formerly in legal practice; ordained deacon, 1989; Asst Curate, All Saints, Ainslie, 1990; Asst Priest, Holy Trinity, Orange, NSW, 1991–93; Rector, Wellington, Dio. of Bathurst, 1993–96; Acting Archdeacon, 1996, Archdeacon, 1997, Young, NSW; Rector and Team Rector, Young District Anglican Ministry, 1996–98; Rector, All Saints, Ainslie, 1998–2003; Archdeacon: S Canberra, 1998–2001; Dio. of Canberra and Goulburn, 2001–03; Dean, St John's Cathedral, Brisbane, 2004–08; Asst Bishop, Dio. of Brisbane, 2007–08. Dir, Aust. Centre of Christianity and Culture, 2001–02. Mem., Gen. Synod of Anglican Church, 2001–. Mem., Appellate Tribunal, Anglican Ch of Australia, 2014–. Inaugural Chair, Careforce (Anglicare), Bathurst, 1992–. Mem. Bd, Trinity Coll., Univ. of Melbourne, 2012– (Chm., Theol Sch Cttee, 2012–). *Recreations:* reading, singing, fly fishing. *Address:* Bishop's Lodge, PO Box 457, Wangaratta, Vic 3676, Australia. *Clubs:* Melbourne (Melbourne); Albury (NSW).

**WANLESS, Peter Thomas,** CB 2007; Chief Executive, National Society for the Prevention of Cruelty to Children, since 2013; *b* 25 Sept. 1964; *s* of Thomas and Pam Wanless; *m* 1999, Beccy King; one *s*. *Educ:* Sheldon Sch., Chippenham; Univ. of Leeds (BA Hons Internat. History and Politics). HM Treasury, 1986–94; Private Sec. to Treasury Chief Sec., 1992–94; Head of Information, Dept of Employment, 1994–95; Head of Private Finance Policy, HM Treasury, 1996–98; Dir of Strategy and Communications, DfEE, subseq. DfES, 1998–2003; Dir of Secondary Educn, DfES, 2003–06; Dir of School Perf. and Reform, Sch. Standards Gp, DfES, subseq. DCSF, 2006–07; Dir, Families Gp, DCSF, 2007–08; Chief Exec., Big Lottery Fund, 2008–13. Chm., UK Lottery Forum, 2010–13. Non-exec. Mem. Cttee, Som CCC, 2014–. CCMI 2012. *Recreations:* Somerset County Cricket, Twitter. *Address:* National Society for the Prevention of Cruelty to Children, 42 Curtain Road, EC2A 3NH. *Club:* MCC.

**WANSBROUGH, Rev. Dom (Joseph) Henry,** OSB; Master, St Benet's Hall, Oxford, 1990–2004; Alexander Jones Professor of Biblical Studies, Liverpool Hope University, 2011–16; *b* 9 Oct. 1934; *s* of George Wansbrough and Elizabeth Wansbrough (*née* Lewis). *Educ:* Ampleforth Coll.; St Benet's Hall, Oxford (MA 1963); Univ. of Fribourg (STL 1964); Ecole Biblique Française, Jerusalem; Pontifical Biblical Commn, Rome (LSS 1965). Asst Master, 1965–90 and 2011–, Housemaster, 1969–90, Ampleforth Coll.; Chm., Oxford Fac. of Theology, 2001–03; Magister Scholarum of English Benedictines, 2002–09. Chairman: Catholic Biblical Assoc. of GB, 1985–91; Mgt Bd, Keston Inst., 1993–2001; Member: Pontifical Biblical Commn, 1996–2007; ARCIC III, 2011–18. Exec. Sec., Internat. Commn for Preparing an English Language Lectionary, 2006–17. Cathedral Prior: of Norwich, 2004–10; of Durham, 2010–. *Publications:* The Sunday Word, 1979; New Jerusalem Bible, 1985; The Lion and the Bull, 1996; The Passion and Death of Jesus, 2003; The Story of the Bible, 2006; The Use and Abuse of the Bible, 2010; The Sunday Word, 2012; The Psalms, 2014; Introducing the New Testament, 2015; Revised New Jerusalem Bible, 2019; numerous articles and reviews in The Times, The Tablet, Priests & People and TLS. *Recreations:* music, running. *Address:* Ampleforth Abbey YO62 4EN.

**WAPSHOTT, Nicholas Henry;** author and journalist; Senior Advisor, Europa Partners; *b* 13 Jan. 1952; *s* of Raymond Gibson Wapshott, DFC and Olivia Beryl Darch; *m* 1980, Louise Nicholson; two *s*. *Educ:* Dursley County Primary Sch.; Rendcomb Coll., Cirencester; Univ. of York (BA Hons). The Scotsman, 1973–76; The Times, 1976–84; The Observer, 1984–92, Political Editor, 1988–92; Editor: The Times Magazine, 1992–97; The Saturday Times, 1997–2001; North America Correspondent, The Times, 2001–04; Nat. and Foreign Ed., 2006–08, Contrib. Ed. and columnist, 2008–09, New York Sun; Sen. Ed., The Daily Beast, 2008–09; editl consultant, oprah.com, 2009–10; Internat. Ed., 2013–14, Opinion Ed., 2014–17, Newsweek. Columnist, Reuters, The New Statesman, 2011–14. *Publications:* Peter O'Toole, 1982; (with George Brock) Thatcher, 1983; The Man Between: a biography of Carol Reed, 1990; Rex Harrison, 1991; (with Tim Wapshott) Older: a biography of George Michael, 1998; Ronald Reagan and Margaret Thatcher: a political marriage, 2007; Keynes Hayek: the clash that defined modern economics, 2011; The Sphinx: Franklin Roosevelt, the isolationists and the road to World War II, 2014. *Recreations:* cinema, music, elephants. *Address:* c/o Raphael Sagalyn, The Sagalyn Agency, 4922 Fairmont Avenue, Suite 200, Bethesda, MD 20814, USA. *Club:* Garrick.

**WARBECK, Stephen;** freelance film and theatre composer, since 1977; *b* 21 Oct. 1953; *s* of Harold Robert Wood and Olive Patricia Wood; name changed to Warbeck, 1977. *Educ:* Lewes Priory Sch.; Bristol Univ. (BA Hons). Associate Artist, RSC, 1999. Scores composed include: *theatre:* An Inspector Calls, NT, 1992; RSC prodns incl. Alice in Wonderland, Pericles, Globe, 2005; Junkyard, Bristol Old Vic, 2017; Common, NT, 2017; *films:* Mrs Brown, 1997; Shakespeare in Love, 1999 (Oscar for Best Soundtrack); Billy Elliot, Quills, 2000; Captain Corelli's Mandolin, Charlotte Gray, 2001; Deséo, 2002; Blackball, Love's Brother, 2003; Two Brothers, Proof, Mickybo and Me, Oyster Farmer, 2004; On a Clear Day, 2005; Balcon Sur la Mer, 2010; Polisse, 2011; Doomsday, 2012; Papadopoulos & Sons, Jadoo, Day of the Flowers, 2013; Yellowbird, Keeping Rosy, Seve the Movie, The Tempest, 2014; The Children Act, King Lear, 2018; *television:* Indian Summers, Fungus the Bogeyman, The Dresser, Stephen Fry in Central America, 2015. *Recreation:* the hKippers (*sic*). *Address:* c/o Lynda Mamy, United Agents, 12–26 Lexington Street, W1F 0LE.

**WARBOYS, Prof. Brian Charles,** CEng, FBCS, CITP; Professor of Software Engineering, University of Manchester, 1985–2017, now Emeritus; *b* 30 April 1942; *s* of Charles Bernard and Vera Beatrice Warboys; *m* 1965, Gillian Whitaker; one *s* one *d*. *Educ:* Univ. of Southampton (BSc Maths). CEng 1990; FBCS 1996; CITP 1998. English Electric, subseq. ICL: Software Engr, 1963–71; Chief Designer, ICL mainframe computer VME operating system, 1971–79; Manager, Systems Strategy, Mainframes Div., 1979–84; Dir, Engrg, Office Systems Div., 1984–85; first ICL Fellow, 1984–89; Sen. ICL Fellow (pt-time), 1989–96. Visiting Professor: of Information Technol., Stirling Univ., 1984–87 (Hon. Prof., 1987–92); of Computer Sci., Univ. de Bretagne-Sud, 2005. *Publications:* Business Information Systems: a process approach, 1999. *Recreations:* playing golf badly, supporting Millwall Football Club and Sale Sharks Rugby Club, reading, spending time with my family and my four grandchildren. *Address:* School of Computer Science, University of Manchester, Manchester M13 9PL. *T:* (0161) 275 6182, *Fax:* (0161) 275 6204. *E:* brian@cs.manchester.ac.uk.

**WARBRICK, Prof. Colin John,** CMG 2016; Professor of Law, 2006–08, Barber Professor of Jurisprudence, 2007–08, Hon. Professor, 2008–12, now Emeritus Professor, University of Birmingham; *b* 7 Aug. 1943; *s* of George and Nancy Warbrick; *m* 1974, Rosemary Goodwin (*d* 2013); one *s* one *d*. *Educ:* Barrow-in-Furness Grammar Sch.; Corpus Christi Coll., Cambridge (LLB 1966; MA 1969); Michigan (LLM 1969; Fulbright Schol. and Ford Foundn Fellow). Law Department, University of Durham: Lectr, then Sen. Lectr, 1970–94; Prof. of Law, 1996–2006; Chm., 1998–2001. Vis. Prof., Coll. of Law, Univ. of Iowa, 1981–82, 1985; Sen. Associate, St Antony's Coll., Oxford, 2001. Consultant on Human Rights, Council of Europe, 1991–2002; Specialist Advr, Constitution Cttee, H of L, 2005–06. *Publications:* (ed with Vaughan Lowe) The United Nations and the Principles of International Law, 1993; (with David Harris and Michael O'Boyle) Law of the European Convention on Human Rights, 1995; (ed with S. Tierney) Towards an International Legal Community, 2006; (contrib.) Halsbury's Laws of England, vol. 61, 5th edn 2010; articles on internat. law and human rights. *Recreations:* Rugby, allotment. *Address:* 19 Nevilledale Terrace, Durham DH1 4QG. *T:* (0191) 384 7531. *E:* c.warbrick@bham.ac.uk.

**WARBURTON, David;** Senior National Officer: GMB (formerly General, Municipal, Boilermakers and Allied Trades Union), 1973–95; APEX (white collar section of GMB), 1990–95; *b* 10 Jan. 1942; *s* of Harold and Ada Warburton; *m* 1966, Carole Anne Susan Tomney; two *d*. *Educ:* Cottingley Manor Sch., Bingley, Yorks; Coleg Harlech, Merioneth, N Wales. Campaign Officer, Labour Party, 1964; Educn Officer, GMWU, 1965–66, Reg. Officer, 1966–73. Co-Chm., Crazy Horse Investment Trust, 2001–. Secretary: Chemical Unions Council; Rubber Industry Jt Unions, 1980–86; Chm., Paper and Packaging Industry Unions, 1988–92. Mem., Eur. Co-ord. Cttee, Chem., Rubber and Glass Unions, 1975–81. Chm., Chem. and Allied Industries Jt Indust. Council, 1973–86; Mem., Govt Industrial Workers Jt Consultative Cttee, 1988–92; Sec., Home Office Jt Indust. Council, 1989–; Treas., Electricity Supply Nat. Jt Council, 1990–; Member: Industrial Tribunal, 1995–99; Employment Tribunal, 1999–. Vice-Pres., Internat. Fedn of Chemical, Energy and Gen. Workers, 1986–94. Member: NEDC, 1973–86; Commonwealth Develt Corp., 1979–87; TUC Energy Cttee, 1978–92; Nat. Jt Council for Civil Air Transport, 1992–95; Chm., TUC Gen. Purposes Cttee, 1984–95; Dir, Union Liaison Services, 1995–2010. Nat. Sec., UK Friends of Palestine, 1983–2008. Campaign Dir, Friends of The Speaker, 1996–2000; Sponsor, Scottish Palestine Solidarity Campaign, 2015–; Dir/Trustee, Dunblane Develt Trust, 2018–. *Publications:* Pharmaceuticals for the People, 1973; Drug Industry: which way to control, 1975; UK Chemicals: The Way Forward, 1977; Economic Detente, 1980; The Case for Voters Tax Credits, 1983; Forward Labour, 1985; Facts, Figures and Damned Statistics, 1987. *Recreations:* music, American politics, flicking through reference books, films of the thirties and forties.

**WARBURTON, David John;** MP (C) Somerton and Frome, since 2015; *b* Burnham, Bucks, 28 Oct. 1965; *s* of John and Erica Warburton; *m* 2002, Harriet Katharine Baker-Bates; one *s* one *d*. *Educ:* Reading Sch.; Waingels Coll.; Royal Coll. of Music (Dip. RCM); King's Coll. London (MMus). Professional composer, 1992–95; Teacher of Music, Hurlingham and Chelsea Sch., and RCM Jun. Dept, 1995–99; Man. Dir, Music Solution Ltd, 1999–2002; Chief Exec., 2002–05, Chm., 2005–08, Pitch Entertainment Gp; Man. Partner, Oflang Partners LLP, 2008–15; Chm., MyHigh Ltd, 2012–15; non-exec. Chair, Vouch/Triple C Consulting, 2018–. PPS, DFE, 2017–18, DFID, 2018–. European Scrutiny Select Cttee, 2016–; Chair, All Party Parly Gp for Music, 2017; Co-Chair, All Party Parly Gp for Music Educn, 2017–. Chm., Wells Cathedral Sch. Parents' Assoc., 2010–14; Mem., Capital Exec. Cttee, Shakespeare's Globe Th., 2008–10. Trustee: Ups and Downs Southwest, 2013–16; Music for Youth, 2018–; British Music Youth Th. (formerly Youth Music Th.), 2018–; Nat. Youth Orch. of GB, 2018– (Chair, Develt Bd, 2018–). Patron, Royal Bath and West Soc., 2013–. Mem. Ct, Univ. of Bath, 2015–. Member: MENSA, 1994–; ESU, 2008–. FRSA. *Recreations:* playing the piano and thinking out loud, each of which to the constant annoyance of both friends and family. *Address:* House of Commons, SW1A 0AA.

**WARBURTON, Ivor William;** Vice President and General Manager Operations, Tangula Railtours, Shanghai, 2006–09; *b* 13 Aug. 1946; *s* of late Dennis and Edna Margaret Warburton; *m* 1969, Carole-Ann Ashton (marr. diss. 1982); three *d*. *Educ:* Dulwich Coll.; Queens' Coll., Cambridge (MA); Univ. of Warwick (MSc). FCILT (FCIT 1989); FCIM 1994. British Railways, 1968–97: graduate trainee, 1968–70; local ops posts, London Midland Region, 1970–73; Divl Passenger Manager, Bristol, 1974–78; Overseas Tourist Manager, 1978–82; Regional Passenger Manager, York, 1982–83; Dir, Passenger Marketing Services, 1984–85; Asst Gen. Manager, London Midland Region, 1985–87; Employee Relations Manager, 1987–88; Dir of Operations, 1988–90; Gen. Manager, London Midland Region, 1990–92; Dir, 1992–95, Man. Dir, 1995–97, InterCity West Coast; Dir, Business Develt and Industry Affairs, Virgin Rail Gp, 1997–99. Chm., Assoc. of Train Operating Cos, 1997–99. President: Railway Study Assoc., 1993–94; Retired Railway Officers' Soc., 2003–04; Alleyn Club, 2014–15. *Recreations:* Chinese language and culture, music, opera, handicapped scouting. *Address:* 34 St Clair's Road, Croydon CR0 5NE. *T:* (020) 8681 6421.

**WARBURTON, John Kenneth,** CBE 1983; Director General, Birmingham Chamber of Commerce and Industry, 1994 (Chief Executive, 1978–94); *b* 7 May 1932; *s* of Frederick and Eva Warburton; *m* 1960, Patricia Gordon (*d* 2009); one *d*. *Educ:* Newcastle-under-Lyme High Sch.; Keble Coll., Oxford (MA Jurisprudence). Called to Bar, Gray's Inn, 1977. London Chamber of Commerce, 1956–59; Birmingham Chamber of Commerce and

Industry, 1959–94. President, British Chambers of Commerce Executives, 1979–81; Member: Steering Cttee, Internat. Bureau of Chambers of Commerce, 1976–94; Nat. Council, Assoc. of British Chambers of Commerce, 1978–94; European Trade Cttee and Business Link Gp, BOTB, 1979–87; E European Trade Council, BOTB, 1984–93; Review Body on Doctors' and Dentists' Remuneration, 1982–92; MSC Task Gp on Employment Trng, 1987; Lord Chancellor's Birmingham Adv. Cttee, 1993–99; Ind. Remuneration Panel, Birmingham CC, 2001–07; Chm., Adv. Council, W Midlands Industrial Develt Assoc., 1983–86. Mediator, Centre for Dispute Resolution, 1994–. Director: National Garden Festival 1986 Ltd, 1983–87; National Exhibition Centre Ltd, 1989–95. Chm., Birmingham Macmillan Nurses Appeal, 1994–97; Dep. Chm., Birmingham Children's Hosp. Appeal, 1996–98. Vol. advr, BESO, Slovakia, 1994, and Mongolia, 1995. Companion, BITC, 1992–. Trustee, Holy Child Sch., Edgbaston, 1992–96; Gov., Newman Coll., 1993–2002 (Exec. Chm., 1999–2002; Hon. Life Fellow, 2003); Life Mem., Court, Birmingham Univ., 1981 (Gov., 1982–99). Hon. DUniv UCE, 1999. *Address*: Apartment 363, John Newman Drive, Hagley Road Village, 332–336 Hagley Road, Birmingham B17 8BP. *T*: (0121) 574 7893.

**WARBURTON, Jonathan**; Company Chairman, Warburtons Ltd, since 2001; *b* Bolton, Lancs, 1 June 1957; *s* of Derrick Warburton and Joyce Warburton; *m* 1990, Kim Latisevs; three *s* (incl. twins) one *d*. *Educ*: Millfield Sch. Sales Rep., Unilever, 1979–81; Warburtons Ltd: Sales Rep., 1981–84; Mktg and Sales Dir, 1984–92; Jt Man. Dir, 1992–2001. Non-exec. Dir, Samworth Bros Ltd, 1997–2017. Hon. DBA Manchester Metropolitan, 2002. *Recreations*: enthusiastic amateur sportsman, golfer, shooter, skier and traveller. *Address*: c/o Warburtons Ltd, Back O' Th' Bank House, Hereford Street, Bolton BL1 8HJ. *T*: (01204) 531004. *E*: jw@warburtons.co.uk, jw@burrowhall.com. *Clubs*: Royal and Ancient Golf (St Andrews), Trevose Golf, Royal Lytham and St Annes Golf.

**WARBY, Hon. Sir Mark (David John)**, Kt 2014; **Hon. Mr Justice Warby**; a Judge of the High Court of Justice, Queen's Bench Division, since 2014; *b* 10 Oct. 1958; *s* of David James Warby, FIMechE, and Clare Warby; *m* 1985, Ann Kenrick, OBE; one *s* two *d*. *Educ*: Bristol Grammar Sch.; St John's Coll., Oxford (Schol.; MA Jurisprudence). Called to the Bar, Gray's Inn, 1981, Bencher, 2007; QC 2002; a Recorder, 2009–14; a Dep. Judge, QBD (Admin. Court), 2013–14. Jt Hd of Chambers, 2011–14. Judge i/c Media and Communications List, 2017–; Dir, Sen. Judiciary Trng, 2018–; Mem., Judicial Data Protection Panel, 2018–; Chair: Judges' Council Communications Cttee, 2018–; High Court Judges' Assoc., 2019–. *Publications*: (jtly) The Law of Privacy and the Media, 2002, (ed jtly and contrib.) 3rd edn 2016; (contrib.) Blackstone's Guide to the Defamation Act 2013, 2013; (contrib.) Sport: law and practice, 3rd edn 2013. *Recreations*: surfing, guitar, tennis, cycling, architecture. *Address*: Royal Courts of Justice, Strand, WC2A 2LL. *Clubs*: Union; Butterfly Tennis; Crackington Haven Tennis.

**WARCHUS, Matthew**; theatre and film director; Artistic Director, Old Vic, since 2015; *b* 24 Oct. 1966; *s* of Michael Warchus and Rosemary Warchus. *Educ*: Bristol Univ. (BA 1st Cl. Hons Music and Drama). Associate Dir, W Yorkshire Playhouse, 1992–94. Plays directed include: Sejanus: his fall, Edinburgh, 1988; The Suicide, 1989, Coriolanus, 1990–91, NYT; Master Harold and the Boys, Bristol Old Vic, 1990; West Yorkshire Playhouse, 1992–94: Life is a Dream, 1992; Who's Afraid of Virginia Woolf, 1992; Fiddler on the Roof, 1992; The Plough and the Stars, 1993; Death of a Salesman, 1994; Betrayal, 1994; True West, 1994; Much Ado About Nothing, Queen's, 1993; The Life of Stuff, Donmar Warehouse, 1993; Henry V, 1994, The Devil is an Ass, 1995, RSC; Troilus and Cressida, Opera North, 1995; Volpone, RNT, 1995; Peter Pan, W Yorks Playhouse, 1995; The Rake's Progress, WNO, 1996; Art, Wyndham's, 1996, NY, 1998, Old Vic, 2017; Falstaff, Opera North and ENO, 1997; Hamlet, 1997, The Unexpected Man, Duchess, 1998, NY 2000, RSC; Life x 3, RNT, transf. Old Vic, 2000, NY, 2003; Follies, NY, 2001; The Winter's Tale, RSC, 2002; Così fan tutte, ENO, 2002; Our House (musical), Cambridge, 2002; Tell me on a Sunday, Gielgud, 2003; Buried Child, NT, 2004; Endgame, Albery, 2004; The Lord of the Rings, Th. Royal, 2007; Boeing Boeing, Comedy, 2007, NY, 2008; I Am Shakespeare, Chichester, 2007; Speed-the-Plow, Old Vic, 2008; The Norman Conquests, Old Vic, 2008, NY, 2009; God of Carnage, Gielgud, 2008, NY, 2009; La Bête, Comedy, transf. NY, 2010; Deathtrap, Noël Coward Th., 2010; Matilda, RSC, 2010, Cambridge Th., 2011, NY, 2013 (Olivier Award for Best Dir, 2012), UK and Ireland tour, 2018; Ghost The Musical, Piccadilly Th., 2011; Future Conditional, Old Vic, 2015; The Master Builder, The Caretaker, Groundhog Day, Old Vic, 2016; A Christmas Carol, Old Vic, 2017; Present Laughter, Lungs, Old Vic, 2019. Films: Simpatico (also screenplay), 1999; Pride, 2014. Hon. DLitt Bristol, 2010. *Address*: c/o Old Vic, The Cut, Waterloo, SE1 8NB.

**WARD**, family name of **Earl of Dudley** and of **Viscount Bangor**.

**WARD, Rt Hon. Sir Alan Hylton**, Kt 1988; PC 1995; a Lord Justice of Appeal, 1995–2013; *b* 15 Feb. 1938; *s* of late Stanley Victor Ward and of Mary Ward; *m* 1st, 1963 (marr. diss. 1982); one *s* two *d*; 2nd, 1983, Helen Madeleine Gilbert (*see* H. M. Ward); one *d* (and one twin *d* decd). *Educ*: Christian Brothers Coll., Pretoria; Univ. of Pretoria (BA, LLB); Pembroke Coll., Cambridge (MA, LLB; Hon. Fellow, 1998). Called to the Bar, Gray's Inn, 1964, Bencher, 1988, Treas., 2006 (Vice-Treas., 2005); QC 1984; a Recorder, 1985–88; a Judge of the High Court, Family Div., 1988–95; Family Div. Liaison Judge, Midland and Oxford Circuit, 1990–95. Formerly an Attorney of Supreme Court of South Africa. Mem., Matrimonial Causes Procedure Cttee, 1982–85. Consulting Editor, Children Law and Practice, 1991–2013. Hon. LLD: East Anglia, 2001; BPP University Coll., 2012. *Recreations*: as gamekeeper turned poacher, preaching the gospel, 'Mediate, don't Litigate', thinking of ways to keep myself amused. *E*: alanward@civilmediation.org. *Clubs*: Garrick, MCC.

**WARD, Anthony Richard Bangor**; Founder, Armajaro Holdings Ltd, since 1998; *b* Aldershot, 5 May 1960; *s* of Gen. Sir Richard Erskine Ward, GBE, KCB, DSO and Bar, MC and of (Stella) Elizabeth Ward; two *s* by Carolyn Ward; *m* 2013, Sophie Elizabeth Cowling. *Educ*: Marlborough Coll. Sime Derby Ltd, 1979–80; E. F. Hutton, 1980–82; V. Berg & Sons Ltd, 1982–89; J H Rayner (Cocoa) Ltd, 1989–94; Dir and Global Business Manager, Cocoa and Coffee, Phibro GmbH, 1994–98. Principal Portfolio Manager, CC+ Fund, 2007–17; Chm., Financial Express (Hldgs) Ltd, 1998–2018. Formerly Chairman: Eur. Cocoa Assoc.; Fedn of Cocoa Commerce Ltd. Formerly Director: LIFFE (Hldgs) ltd; LIFFE Admin and Mgt Ltd; London Commodity Exchange Ltd; Cocoa Assoc. of London. Chevalier, Ordre du Mérite Agricole (France), 2011. *Recreations*: sailing, ski-ing, shooting, tennis. *Clubs*: Queen's, Royal Automobile; Royal Thames Yacht, Sea View Yacht.

**WARD, Anthony Robert**; set and costume designer for theatre; *b* Birmingham, 6 Jan. 1957; *s* of Stanley and Jeanette Ward; civil partnership 2014, (Owen) Mark Thompson, *qv*. *Educ*: Wrekin Coll.; Wimbledon Coll. of Arts (BA Hons; Hon. Fellow, 2014). Productions include: Oklahoma!, Lyceum, 1999 (Olivier Award for Set Design), transf. NY; The Royal Family, Th. Royal Haymarket, 2001; Chitty Chitty Bang Bang, London Palladium, 2002, transf. NY; Gypsy, NY, 2003; The Night of the Iguanas, Lyric, 2005; Dying City, Lincoln Center, NY, 2007; Macbeth, Chichester, transf. Gielgud and Brooklyn Acad. of Music, 2007; Glengarry Glen Ross, Apollo, 2007; The Cherry Orchard, A Winter's Tale, Brooklyn Acad. of Music, 2009; Oliver!, Th. Royal Drury Lane, 2009; Mary Stuart, NY, 2009 (Tony Award for Costume Design); Sweeney Todd, Chichester, 2011, transf. Adelphi, 2012; Posh, Duke of York's, 2012; Josephine and I, Bush, 2013; Private Lives, Gielgud, 2013; Gypsy, Chichester, 2014, transf. Savoy, 2015; Women on the Verge of a Nervous Breakdown, Playhouse, 2015; Height of the Storm, Wyndham's, 2018, transf. NY, 2019; *for National Theatre*: Napoli Milionaria, 1991; Sweet Bird of Youth, 1994; The Way of the World and La Grande Magia, 1996 (Olivier Award for Costume Design); Othello, 1997; The Invention of Love, 1997; Oklahoma!, 1998; Remember This, 1999; My Fair Lady, 2001, transf. Th. Royal Drury Lane, 2002; Royal Hunt of the Sun, 2006; Exit the King, 2018; *for RSC*: Troilus and Cressida, 1990; The Alchemist, 1991; The Virtuoso, 1991; Artists and Admirers, 1992; The Winter's Tale, 1992; King Lear, 1993; The Tempest, 1993; A Midsummer Night's Dream, 1994 (Olivier Award for Costume Design, 1996); Cymbeline, 1997; Twelfth Night, 1997; The Lion, the Witch and the Wardrobe, 1998; The Secret Garden, 2001; Imperium, 2017, transf. Gielgud, 2018; *for Donmar Warehouse*: Assassins, 1992; Nine, 1996; To the Green Fields and Beyond, 2000; Uncle Vanya and Twelfth Night, 2002, transf. Brooklyn Acad. Music, 2003 (OBIE Award, Amer. Th. Wing); Mary Stuart, transf. Apollo, 2005; Small Change, 2008; A Doll's House, 2009; *for Royal Court*: The Arsonist, 2007; Rhinoceros, 2007; ENRON, Chichester, transf. Royal Court, 2009; Posh, 2010; *for Almeida Theatre*: The Rehearsal; A Hard Heart, 1992; Dona Rosita, 1997; The Novice, 2000; Marianne Dreams, 2007; *opera* includes: Manon Lescaut, Opera de Paris, Bastille and De Vlaamse Opera, 1991; Opera North: L'Étoile, 1991; Yollande, 1992; Gloriana, 1992; La Bohème, 1993; Peter Grimes, 2006; Tosca, De Vlaamse Opera, Antwerp, 1992; The Makropulos Case, Metropolitan Opera, NY, 1996; Il Ritorno d'Ulisse in Patria, Fest. de Aix-en-Provence, 2000; The Magic Flute, Glyndebourne, 2004; The Carmelites, ENO and WNO, 2005; Vienna State Opera: Alcina, 2010; Hansel & Gretel, 2015; Carousel, Opera North/Châtelet, Paris, 2017; Macbeth, ROH, 2018; *ballet and dance* includes: Matthew Bourne's Nutcracker!, Sadler's Wells and UK tour, 1992; Royal Ballet: Masquerade, 1999; Les Rendez-vous, 2000; Dance Variations, 2003; The Nutcracker, Royal Danish Ballet, 2011. *E*: anthonyward@mtspace.co.uk.

**WARD, Hon. Sir Austin**; *see* Ward, Hon. Sir L. A.

**WARD, Caroline Jane**; *see* Drummond, C. J.

**WARD, Cecil**, CBE 1989; JP; Town Clerk, Belfast City Council, 1979–89; *b* 26 Oct. 1929; *s* of William and Mary Caroline Ward. *Educ*: Technical High Sch., Belfast; College of Technology, Belfast. Employed by Belfast City Council (formerly Belfast County Borough Council), 1947–89; Asst Town Clerk (Administration), 1977–79. Mem., Local Govt Staff Commn, 1983–89. Member: Arts Council NI, 1980–85, 1987–89; Bd, Ulster Mus., 1989–95; Dir, Ulster Orchestra Soc., 1980–94 (Chm., 1990–94). Mem., Senate, QUB, 1990–2001. Mem., Bd, Mater Hosp., 1994–2002. JP Belfast, 1988. Hon. MA QUB, 1988. *Recreations*: music, reading, hill walking. *Address*: 24 Thornhill, Malone, Belfast, Northern Ireland BT9 6SS. *T*: (028) 9066 8950; Hatter's Field, Drumawier, Greencastle, Co. Donegal, Ireland.

**WARD, (Charles John) Nicholas**; *b* 1 Aug. 1941; *s* of late John Newman Ward and Vivienne Grainger Ward; *m* 1967, Deirdre Veronica Shaw; two *d*. *Educ*: Charterhouse; INSEAD (MBA 1968). FCA 1964. Early career spanned several cos engaged in textiles, venture capital, overseas trading, retailing, distribution, healthcare, leisure and property, subseq. Chairman or non-exec. dir of numerous cos in retail, textiles, healthcare, transport, stockbroking and fund mgt, coal mining, student accommodation, bio-fuels and agriculture and envmt sectors. Chairman: NHS Supplies Authy, 1995–98; Ryan Group Ltd, 1995–2004; ADAS Hldgs, 1998–2007; UPP Projects Ltd, 2006–07; Interactive Prospect Targeting Hldgs plc, 2008–10; Dep. Chm., Albert E. Sharp Hldgs, 1996–98; non-executive Director: Anglia and Oxford RHA, 1990–96; D1 Oils plc, 2010. Consultant to: Deutsche Bank, 1995–2014; Bank of Austria, 1995–2014; 3i, 1998–2007; Swiss Re, 2008–09. Ind. Mem., Steering Bd, Insolvency Service, DTI, 2004–06; Public Mem., Network Rail Ltd, 2011–13. Chairman: Make a Difference Team, 1994–96; The Volunteering Partnership, 1995–96; British Liver Trust, 1999–2004; CORGI Trust, 2005; Sulgrave Manor Trust, 2011–13; Co-Chm., The Volunteering Partnership Forum for England, 1996–97; Pres., Ind. Custody Visiting Assoc. (formerly Nat. Assoc. for Lay Visiting), 1996–2006 (Chm., 1992–96); Chm., Lay Visiting Charitable Trust, 1995–2019. Fellow, Inst. for Turnaround (formerly Soc. of Turnaround Professionals), 2001–11. Contested: (C) Liverpool Edge Hill, March and May 1979; (Ind) Westminster N, 2015; (Ind) Witney, Oct. 2016. Liveryman, Tylers' and Bricklayers' Co., 1963– (Master, 1991–92). Dist. Fellow, INSEAD, 2014. *Address*: Bacon House, Greatworth, Banbury, Oxon OX17 2DX. *T*: (07774 184762. *E*: nicholasward@variouscompanies.co.uk; Flat 12, 77 Warwick Square, SW1V 2AR.

**WARD, Christopher Gordon**; an Upper Tribunal Judge (Administrative Appeals Chamber) (formerly a Social Security and Child Support Commissioner), since 2008; *b* Bromley, 18 Sept. 1957; *s* of late Rev. Stanley Ward and of Mary Ward (*née* Lance); *m* 1990, Katharine Alyson Klopper; one *s* two *d*. *Educ*: Nottingham High Sch.; Jesus Coll., Cambridge (MA Hons); Coll. of Law. Admitted solicitor, 1982; Solicitor, Clifford-Turner, 1982–84; legal posts in local govt and voluntary sector, 1984–89; Solicitor, Nabarro Nathanson, 1989–98; Partner, Beachcroft Stanleys, later Beachcroft Wansbroughs, 1998–2005; London Bor. of Waltham Forest, 2006–08. Chm. (pt-time), Appeal Tribunals, 2002–08. *Publications*: contrib., principally on local govt, social security, EU and administrative law, to books and jls. *Recreations*: performing and listening to classical and traditional music, languages, racket sports. *Address*: c/o Upper Tribunal (Administrative Appeals Chamber), 5th Floor, Rolls Building, 7 Rolls Buildings, Fetter Lane, EC4A 1NL.

**WARD, Christopher John**; Joint Founder, 1983, and Chairman, 2006–17, Redwood London (formerly Redwood Publishing) (Editorial Director, 1983–2002; Vice-Chairman, 2002–06); *b* 25 Aug. 1942; *s* of John Stanley Ward and Jacqueline Law-Hume Costin; *m* 1st, 1971 (marr. diss.); one *s* two *d*; 2nd, 1990, Nonie Niesewand (*née* Fogarty). *Educ*: King's Coll. Sch., Wimbledon. Successively on staff of Driffield Times, 1959, and Newcastle Evening Chronicle, 1960–63; reporter, sub-editor, then feature writer and columnist, 1963–76, Daily Mirror; Assistant Editor: Sunday Mirror, 1976–79; Daily Mirror, 1979–81; Editor, Daily Express, 1981–83. Director: Acorn Computer plc, 1983–99; College Valley Estates, 2008–. Chm., Redwood Custom Communications, Toronto, 2007–08. Mem., Eur. Adv. Cttee to Chm., All Nippon Airways, 2003–10. Co-Chair, PPA, 2010–14. WWF: Trustee, 1994–2000; Chm., UK, 2002–08. Mem., Farne Is Cttee, 2004–. Mark Boxer award, British Soc. of Magazine Eds, 1995. *Publications*: How to Complain, 1974; Our Cheque is in the Post, 1980; And the Band Played On, 2011. *Recreations*: shooting, photography, weather-watching. *Address*: The Old Whaling House, Berwick-upon-Tweed TD15 1HP. *T*: (01289) 330646. *E*: cj.ward@btinternet.com. *Club*: Garrick.

**WARD, Christopher John Ferguson**; solicitor; *b* 26 Dec. 1942; *m* Janet Ward, JP, LLB; one *s* one *d* and two *s* one *d* by former marr. *Educ*: Magdalen College Sch.; Law Society Sch. of Law. MP (C) Swindon, Oct. 1969–June 1970; contested (C) Eton and Slough, 1979. Mem., Berks CC, 1965–81 (Leader of the Council and Chm., Policy Cttee, 1979–81). Gov., Chiltern Nursery Trng Coll., 1975–97 (Chm., 1988–91). Treas., United & Cecil Club, 1993 (Hon. Sec., 1982–87). *Address*: Ramblings, Maidenhead Thicket, Berks SL6 3QE.

**WARD, (Christopher) John (William);** Development Advisor, Welsh National Opera, since 2003; *b* 21 June 1942; *s* of late Thomas Maxfield and Peggy Ward; *m* 1st, 1970, Diane Lelliott (marr. diss. 1988); 2nd, 2008, Susan Corby. *Educ:* Oundle Sch.; Corpus Christi Coll., Oxford (BA LitHum); Univ. of East Anglia (Graduate DipEcon). Overseas and Economic Intelligence Depts, Bank of England, 1965; General Secretary, Bank of England Staff Organisation, 1973; Gen. Sec., Assoc. of First Div. Civil Servants, 1980; Head of Development, Opera North, 1988–94; Dir of Corporate Affairs, W Yorks Playhouse, 1994–97; Develt Dir, ENO, 1997–2002; Dir of Fundraising, Crafts Council, 2003–04. *Recreations:* opera, theatre, football. *Address:* c/o Welsh National Opera, Wales Millennium Centre, Bute Place, Cardiff CF10 5AL. *Club:* Swindon Town Supporters.

**WARD, Claire Margaret;** Director, Capewells Ltd Consultancy, since 2012; *b* 9 May 1972; *d* of Frank and Catherine Ward; *m* 2003, John Simpson; one *s* one *d*. *Educ:* Loreto Coll., St Albans; Univ. of Hertfordshire (LLB Hons); Brunel Univ. (MA). Trainee Solicitor, Pattinson & Brewer, 1995–97; qualif. Solicitor, 1998–. Mem. (Lab) Elstree and Borehamwood Town Council, 1994–98 (Mayor, 1996–97). MP (Lab) Watford, 1997–2010; contested (Lab) same seat, 2010. PPS to Minister of State for Health, 2001–05; an Asst Govt Whip, 2005–06; a Lord Comr of HM Treasury (Govt Whip), 2006–08; Vice-Chamberlain of HM Household, 2008–09; Parly Under-Sec. of State, MoJ, 2009–10. Mem., NEC, Lab. Party, 1991–95. Mem., Select Cttee on Culture, Media and Sports, 1997–2001. Jt Sec., All Party Film Industry Gp, 1997–2005. Chief Exec., Ind. Pharmacy Fedn, 2011–15. Non-exec. Dir, Sherwood Forest Hosps NHS Foundn Trust, 2013–. Chm., Pharmacy Voice, 2015–17. Patron, Young European Movement, 1999. FRSA. *Recreations:* family, films, food, travelling.

**WARD, Colin;** Associate, Capgemini, 2003–09; *b* 23 June 1947; *s* of Simon Myles Ward and Ella May McConnell; *m* 1969, Marjory Hall Milne. *Educ:* Daniel Stewart's Coll., Edinburgh; Heriot-Watt Univ. (BA 1970). CA 1974. Ernst & Young, Edinburgh, 1970–74; Price Waterhouse, Glasgow, 1974–75; BSC, 1975–77; SDA, latterly Chief Accountant, 1977–90; Student Loans Co., 1990–2003: Loans Dir, 1990–92; Asst Man. Dir, 1992–96; Main Board, 1994–2003; Chief Exec., 1996–2003. Loans Scheme consultant to Hungarian Govt, 1999–2000. CCMI 2003. *Recreations:* sailing, gardening, classical music.

**WARD, David;** Partner, 1964–98, Consultant, 1998–2009, Atkinson Ritson (formerly Atkinson & North), Solicitors, Carlisle; President, The Law Society, 1989–90; *b* 23 Feb. 1937; *s* of Rev. Frank Ward, Darfield, Yorks, and Elizabeth Ward (*née* Pattinson), Appleby, Westmorland; *m* 1978, Antoinette, *d* of Maj.-Gen. D. A. B. Clarke, CB, CBE; two *s* one *d*. *Educ:* Dame Allan's Sch., Newcastle upon Tyne; Queen Elizabeth Grammar Sch., Penrith; St Edmund Hall, Oxford (BA). Admitted solicitor, 1962. Articled Clerk, 1959, Assistant, 1962, Atkinson & North. Mem., Lord Chancellor's Adv. Cttee on Legal Educn and Conduct, 1991–97. Mem. Council, 1972–91, Vice-Pres., 1988–89, Law Soc.; Pres., Carlisle and District Law Soc., 1985–86. Pres., Carlisle Mountaineering Club, 1985–88. Methodist local preacher, 1955–. *Recreations:* mountaineering, choral and church music. *Address:* Mardale, Upton, Caldbeck, Wigton, Cumbria CA7 8EU. *T:* (01697) 478220.

**WARD, David;** *b* 24 June 1953; *m* 1974, Jacqueline Ann Dodd; two *s*. *Educ:* Boston Grammar Sch.; N Kesteven Grammar Sch.; Trent Poly. (CIPFA 1977); Univ. of Bradford (MBA 1981; MPhil 1984); Univ. of Leicester (MSc 1996). Accountant, Lincs CC, 1971–79; Leeds Polytechnic, later Leeds Metropolitan University: Prin. Lectr, 1985–2004; on secondment as Manager, Bradford Sports Partnership, 2004–10. Dir, Bantams Community Prog., 2005–. Mem. (Lib Dem) Bradford MDC, 1984–2010, 2016–. Contested (Lib Dem) Bradford N, Nov. 1990, 1992, 2001, 2005. MP (Lib Dem) Bradford E, 2010–15; contested (Lib Dem) same seat, 2015; contested (Ind) Bradford E, 2017. Member: Business, Innovation and Skills Select Cttee, 2010–12; Educn Select Cttee, 2012–15.

**WARD, David;** HM Diplomatic Service; High Commissioner to the Independent State of Samoa, since 2019; *b* 11 June 1968; *s* of Robert Norton Ward and Elizabeth Pestell Ward (*née* Byfield). *Educ:* Dame Allan's Boys' Sch., Newcastle upon Tyne; Magdalene Coll., Cambridge (BA 1989). Joined FCO, 1992; Tokyo, 1994–98, Second Sec. (Pol), 1995–98; FCO, 1998–2002; Dep. Hd of Mission, Kathmandu, 2002–05; Dep. Counsellor (Pol), Beijing, 2006–09; FCO, 2010–11; Dep. Hd of Mission, Tripoli, 2011–12; Dep. Hd, Provincial Reconstruction Team, Lashkar Gah, 2013–14; Ambassador to Eritrea, 2014–16; High Comr to Solomon Islands and non-res. High Comr to Republics of Vanuatu and Nauru, 2016–19. Mem., Japan Soc. *Recreations:* amateur piano, winter sports. *Address:* c/o Foreign and Commonwealth Office, King Charles Street, SW1A 2AH.

**WARD, David Gordon;** HM Diplomatic Service, retired; *b* 25 July 1942; *s* of late Major Gordon Alec Ward, MBE and Irene Ward; *m* 1st, 1966, Rosemary Anne Silvester (marr. diss. 1979); two *s* one *d*; 2nd, 1980, Margaret (*née* Martin); one *s* one *d*, and one step *s*. *Educ:* Rutlish Sch., Merton. With CRO, 1961–65; entered FCO, 1965; Montevideo, 1967–70; Dakar (also accredited to Nouakchott, Bamako and Conakry), 1970–74; FCO, 1974–76; Victoria, 1977–80; Libreville, 1980; Luxembourg, 1981–83; Consul, Oporto, 1983–87; FCO, 1988–90; Harare, 1990–95; FCO, 1995–98; Ambassador to Dominican Rep., 1998–2002 and (non-resident) to Haiti, 1999–2002; British Consul, Tenerife, 2002–07. Hon. Cavaleiro da Confraria do Vinho do Porto, 1986. Grand Silver Cross, Order of Merit of Duarte Sanchez and Mella (Dominican Republic), 2002. *Recreations:* theatre, visual arts, tennis, bridge. *E:* david_warduk@yahoo.co.uk.

**WARD, Dawn Patricia,** CBE 2015 (OBE 2007); Chief Executive and Principal, Burton and South Derbyshire College, since 2008; *b* Coventry, 28 March 1961; *d* of John Mernagh and Mary Mernagh; *m* 1996, Kenneth Ward; two *s*. *Educ:* Cardinal Wiseman Girls' Sch., Coventry; Oxford Brookes Univ. (MBA). Section Hd, Birmingham Coll. of Food, 1983–93; Vice Chm., 1993–95, Chm., 1995–97, British Assoc. of Beauty Therapy and Cosmetology; Vice Principal, Warwickshire Coll., 1998–2005; Principal and Chief Exec., Royal Forest of Dean Coll., 2005–08. Dep. Chm., Chartered Instn for FE (formerly Instn for FE), 2013–; Chm., Data Mgt Inf. Adv. Gp, Educn and Skills (formerly Skills) Funding Agency, 2014–18. Non-executive Director: EAL, 2011–; Staffline Gp PLC, 2018. Director: Burton and South Derbyshire Educn Trust, 2014–; UK Technical Vocational Qualifications, 2015–; Gtr Birmingham and Solihull LEP, 2015–; Highbury Burton Saudi Arabia, 2017–; Mem. Bd, D2N2 LEP, 2017–; Mem. Council, Gtr Birmingham Chambers of Commerce, 2014–. Mem. Council, C&G, 2010–. Trustee: League of Mercy, 2015–; YMCA (Birmingham), 2018. Gov., Repton Sch., 2016–. *Publications:* (jtly) Health and Beauty Therapy: a practical approach for NVQ level 3, 1995, 3rd edn 2004; (jtly) Good Practice in Salon Management, 1997. *Recreations:* ballet, reading, walking. *Address:* Burton and South Derbyshire College, Burton Town Centre Campus, Lichfield Street, Burton on Trent, Staffs DE14 3RL. *T:* (01283) 494401, *Fax:* (01283) 494801. *E:* dawn.ward@bsdc.ac.uk.

**WARD, (Elizabeth) Alison;** *see* Platt, E. A.

**WARD, Emma Marion, (Mrs R. H. Billey);** Director, European Union Exit Portfolio, Department for Business, Energy and Industrial Strategy, since 2017; *b* Harlow, 21 Aug. 1973; *d* of Malcolm G. Ward and Marion Ward; *m* 2004, Ray Hamilton Billey; one *s*. *Educ:* Chelmer Valley High Sch.; Middlesex Univ. (BA Hons); Fachhochschule für Technik un Wirtschaft, Reutlingen (Diplom Betriebswirt); Univ. of Manchester Inst. of Sci. and Technol. (MSc Internat. Business). Various posts, DTI, later BERR, then BIS, 2000–10; Exec. Dir, Shareholder Exec., 2010–11; Dir, Local Growth, BIS, 2012–14; Dir, Strategy and Growth, BIS, then BEIS, 2015–17. *Recreations:* music (pianist), pottery. *Address:* Department for Business, Energy and Industrial Strategy, 1 Victoria Street, SW1H 0ET. *T:* (020) 7215 4152. *E:* emma.m.ward@beis.gov.uk.

**WARD, Very Rev. Frances Elizabeth Fearn,** PhD; freelance writer and theologian, since 2018; Dean of St Edmundsbury, 2010–17; *b* Geelong, Vic, 16 Sept. 1959; *d* of Hubert Ward, *qv*; *m* 1986, Peter Powell; three *s* one *d*. *Educ:* King's Sch., Ely; Univ. of St Andrews (MTheol 1983); Univ. of Manchester (PhD 2000). Ordained deacon, 1989, priest, 1994; Tutor, Northern Coll. (URC and Congregational), 1993–98; Vicar, St Peter's, Bury, 1999–2005; Residentiary Canon, Bradford Cathedral, 2006–10. Vis. Theologian, Dio. of Carlisle and Carlisle Cathedral, 2018–. *Publications:* Lifelong Learning, 2005; (ed jtly) Studying Local Churches, 2005; (ed jtly) Theological Reflection Methods, 2005; (ed jtly) Theological Reflection Sources, 2007; Why Rousseau was Wrong: Christianity and the secular soul, 2013; Full of Character: a Christian approach to education for the digital age, 2018; (ed jtly) Holy Attention: preaching in today's church, 2019. *Recreations:* walking, sailing, reading, the Arts. *Address:* St Michael's Rectory, Dora Crescent, Workington, Cumbria CA14 2EZ. *E:* fefward@gmail.com.
*See also* V. J. Ward.

**WARD, Gareth Edward;** HM Diplomatic Service; Ambassador to Vietnam, since 2018; *b* Wrexham, 17 Jan. 1974; *s* of Ronald and Pauline Ward; *m* 2002, Elena Lukyanets; two *c*. *Educ:* Trinity Coll., Cambridge (BA Social Anthropol. 1995); London Sch. of Econs and Pol Sci. (MSc Social Policy 1996). Entered FCO, 1996; Desk Officer, Hungary and Bulgaria, FCO, 1996–97; Second Sec., Moscow, 1998–2002; Section Hd, Germany and Austria, 2003–04, Justice and Home Affairs, 2004–06, Europe Directorate, FCO; First Sec. and Hd, Foreign and Security Policy Team, Beijing, 2007–10; Consul Gen., St Petersburg, 2010–13; Hd, China Dept, FCO, 2013–18. *Address:* c/o Foreign and Commonwealth Office, King Charles Street, SW1A 2AH. *E:* gareth.ward@fconet.fco.gov.uk.

**WARD, Prof. Geoffrey Christopher,** PhD; Principal, Homerton College, Cambridge, since 2013; *b* Oldham, 18 Feb. 1954; *s* of Clifford Ward and Marjorie Ward; *m* 1992, Prof. Marion Wynne-Davies; two *s*. *Educ:* Manchester Grammar Sch. (Foundn Scholar); Clare Coll., Cambridge (BA 1st Cl. Hons Eng. 1975; PhD 2006). Lectr, 1978–93, Sen. Lectr, 1993–95, in Eng., Univ. of Liverpool; Prof. of Eng., 1995–2006, Dep. Principal, 2002–06, Univ. of Dundee; Royal Holloway, University of London: Prof. of Eng. and Creative Writing, 2006–13; Dean, Faculty of Arts, 2006–08; Vice Principal, 2008–13. Chm., Fitzwilliam Mus. Cambridge, 2014–. Occasional writer and presenter, broadcasts on Amer. writers, BBC Radio 3. Mem., Editl Bd, Cambridge Qly, 1992–. FRSA 2002 (Life Mem.). Hon. Fellow, Harris Manchester Coll., Oxford, 2013. *Publications:* Comeuppance (poetry), 1980; Statutes of Liberty: the New York School of Poets, 1993, 2nd edn 2001; Language Poetry and the American Avant-Garde, 1993; (ed) The Bloomsbury Guide to Romantic Literature, 1993; (ed jtly) Re: Joyce, 1998; The Writing of America: literature and cultural identity from the Puritans to the present, 2002; Worry Dream (poetry), 2013; You're Not Dead (novel), 2016. *Recreation:* beachcombing. *Address:* c/o Homerton College, Hills Road, Cambridge CB2 8PH. *T:* (01223) 747131. *E:* gw355@cam.ac.uk. *Clubs:* Athenæum, Oxford and Cambridge.

**WARD, Rev. Canon Prof. Graham John;** Regius Professor of Divinity, University of Oxford, since 2012; Fellow and Canon of Christ Church, Oxford, since 2012; *b* Salford, 25 Oct. 1955; *s* of John Herbert Ward and Mary Margaret Ward (*née* Hardman); *m* 1988, Mary Janet Jackson; one *s* one *d*. *Educ:* Salford Grammar Sch.; Fitzwilliam Coll., Cambridge (BA Hons 1979; MA; PGCE (Dist.) 1981; PhD 1994); Westcott Hse and Selwyn Coll., Cambridge. MA Oxon 1992. English master, John Lyon Sch., Harrow, 1981–84; Hd of Drama and Oral English, Latymer Sch., Edmonton, 1984–87; ordained deacon, 1990, priest, 1991; Chaplain Fellow and Tutor in Theol. and Philos., Exeter Coll., Oxford, 1992–95; Mem., Theol. Faculty Bd, Univ. of Oxford, 1993; Lectr (pt-time), Religious Studies Dept, Birmingham Univ., 1993–95; University of Cambridge: Dean and Dir of Studies for Theol. and Religious Studies, Peterhouse, 1995–97; Mem., Faculty of Divinity and Faculty of English, 1995–97; Manchester University: Sen. Fellow in Religion and Gender, 1997–98; Prof. of Contextual Theol. and Ethics, 1998–2010; Samuel Fergusson Prof. of Philosophical Theol. and Ethics, 2010–12; Director: Centre for Religion, Culture and Gender, 1998–2003; Centre for Religion and Political Culture, 2003–12; Hd, Sch. of Arts, Histories and Cultures, 2005–11; Res. Dir, Manchester Inst. for Res. in Religion and Civil Society, 2006–10. Ed., Lit. and Theol., 1990–2005. Vice-Pres., 2008–09, Pres., 2009–11, Soc. for Study of Theol.; Dir, Internat. Soc. of Religion and Lit., 2000–; Mem., Amer. Acad. of Religion, 1997–. Extraordinary Prof., Univ. of Stellenbosch, 2015–. Hon. Fellow, Exeter Coll., Oxford, 2012; Sen. Res. Fellow, Campion Hall, Oxford, 2016–. *Publications:* Karl Barth, Jacques Derrida and the Language of Theology, 1995; Theology and Contemporary Critical Theory, 1996 (trans. Greek, 2001); (contrib.) Oxford Companion to Christian Thought, 1999; Cities of God, 2000; True Religion, 2002; (jtly) God and Beauty, 2003; Christ and Culture, 2005; (trans. and ed with M. Hoelzl) Carl Schmitt's Political Theology II, 2008; The Politics of Discipleship, 2010 (trans. Chinese); Unbelievable: why we believe and why we don't, 2014; How the Light Gets In: ethical life, 2016; Unimaginable: what we can imagine and what we can't, 2018; Theology and Religion: why it matters, 2018; *edited:* The Postmodern God: a reader in contemporary philosophy of religion, 1997; (jtly) Radical Orthodoxy, 1998 (trans. Swedish); Michel de Certeau: The Reader, 1999 (trans. Chinese, 2001); The Blackwell Companion to Postmodern Theology, 2001 (trans. Portuguese, 2004); (with M. Hoelzl) Religion and Political Theory: a critical reader, 2006 (trans. Rumanian); (with M. Hoelzl) The New Visibility of Religion, 2008; (jtly) The Oxford Handbook of Theology and Modern European Thought, 2013; (trans. and ed with M. Hoelzl) Carl Schmitt's Dictatorship, 2014; contrib. chapters in books; contribs to jls incl. Lit. and Theol., Theol., Modern Theol., New Blackfriars, THES. *Recreations:* swimming, growing vegetables, cooking. *Address:* Christ Church, Oxford OX1 1DP.

**WARD, Graham Norman Charles,** CBE 2004; FCA; FEI; Chief Commissioner, Independent Commission for Aid Impact, 2010–15; non-executive Director, Civil Aviation Authority, since 2013; Vice-Chairman, World Energy Council, 2008–14 (Hon. Officer, 2014); *b* 9 May 1952; *s* of late Ronald Charles Edward Ward and Hazel Winifred Ward (*née* Ellis); *m* 1975, Ingrid Imogen Sylvia Baden-Powell (marr. diss. 1981); two *s*; *m* 1993, Ann Mistri; one *s*. *Educ:* Dulwich Coll.; Jesus Coll., Oxford (Boxing Blue; MA). ACA 1977, FCA 1983; CIGEM (CIGasE 1997); FEI (FInstE 1999). Price Waterhouse, subseq. PricewaterhouseCoopers: articled clerk, 1974–77; Personal Technical Asst to Chm., Accounting Standards Cttee, 1978–79; on secondment to HM Treasury, 1985; Partner, 1986; Dir, Electricity Services Europe, 1990–94; Direct Business Develt, 1993–94; Chm., World Utilities Gp, 1994–96; Dep. Chm., World Energy Gp, 1996–98; World Utilities

Leader, 1998–2000; Sen. Partner, World Energy and Utilities Gp, 2000–10. Member: Panel on Takeovers and Mergers, 2000–01; Financial Reporting Council, 2001–07 (Dep. Chm., 2000–01); Bd, UK India Business Council (formerly Indo British Partnership Network), 2005–13 (Vice-Chm., 2008–13); Financial Services Sector Adv. Bd, UK Trade & Investment, 2006–09. Chairman: Consultative Cttee of Accountancy Bodies, 2000–01; Power Sector Adv. Gp, UK Trade & Investment (formerly Trade Partners UK), 2001–04; Mem. Council, Soc. of Pension Consultants, 1988–90; Mem., Auditing Practices Bd, 2001–04 (Vice-Chm., 2003–04); Member: Cttee, British Energy Assoc., 1997–2004 (Vice-Chm., 1998–2001; Chm., 2001–04); Exec. Council, Parly Gp for Energy Studies, 1998–; Chairman: Young Chartered Accountants' Gp, 1980–81; London Soc. of Chartered Accountants, 1989–90 (Mem. Cttee, 1983–91); Chartered Accountants in the Community, 1996–2002; Member: Council, ICAEW, 1991–2003 (Vice-Pres., 1998–99; Dep. Pres., 1999–2000; Pres., 2000–01); Bd, Internat. Fedn of Accountants, 2000–06 (Pres., 2004–06). Vice Pres., Epilepsy Res. UK (formerly Epilepsy Res. Foundn), 1997–2015. Vice President: Univ. of Oxford Amateur Boxing Club, 1990–; Soc. of Conservative Accountants, 1992–2001; President: Jesus Coll. Assoc., 1990–91; Chartered Accountant Students' Soc. of London, 1992–96 (Vice-Pres., 1987–92). Governor: Goodenough Coll., 2004– (Vice Chm., 2016–); Dulwich Coll., 2008–19. Hon. Financial Advr, St Paul's Cathedral, 2008–18; Auditor, Duchy of Cornwall, 2001–10. FRSA 1996. Freeman: City of London, 1994; Co. of Chartered Accountants in England and Wales, 1994 (Mem., Ct of Assts, 1997–2015; Master, 2009–10). *Publications:* The Work of a Pension Scheme Actuary, 1987; Pensions: your way through the maze, 1988; (consultant ed) A Practitioner's Guide to Audit Regulation in the UK, 2004; (contrib.) The Handbook of International Corporate Governance, 2009. *Recreations:* boxing, Rugby, opera, ballet. *Address:* Civil Aviation Authority, 45–59 Kingsway, WC2B 6TE. *T:* (020) 7453 6757. *Clubs:* Carlton; Vincent's (Oxford).

**WARD, Prof. Harriet,** CBE 2012; PhD; Professor of Child and Family Research, Loughborough University, 2004–18, now Emeritus (Founding Director, Centre for Child and Family Research, 2002–14); Hon. Research Fellow, University of Oxford, since 2018; *b* Sheffield, 22 Sept. 1948; *d* of late Stephen Blaxland and Elizabeth Alice Blaxland (*née* Brierly); *m* 1974, Christopher David Ward; three *s. Educ:* Princess Helena Coll.; St Andrews Univ. (MA French Lang. and Lit.); Linacre Coll., Oxford (Dip. Social and Admin. Studies; CQSW 1973); Univ. of Bristol (PhD 1990). Social worker: London Bor. of Wandsworth, 1973–74; Exeter CC, 1974–75; Caithness CC, 1975–76; S Yorks CC, 1976–77; Res. Associate, 1989–91, Res. Fellow, 1991–96, Univ. of Bristol; Sen. Lectr, Dept of Social Work, Univ. of Leicester, 1996–99; Sen. Res. Fellow, Loughborough Univ., 1999–2004. Founder Mem., Internat. Res. Network on Transitions to Adulthood from Care, 2003–; Acad. Advr, MoD/DFE Res. Initiative on Safeguarding Children, 2005–12; Co-Dir, Childhood Wellbeing Res. Centre, 2010–14. Mem. Bd, Eur. Scientific Assoc. for Residential and Foster Care, 2007–. Trustee, Family Care, 2013–18. Vice Patron, Family Action, 2015–. *Publications:* (ed jtly) Looking After Children: assessing outcomes in child care, 1991; (ed) Looking After Children: research into practice, 1995; (ed with W. Rose) Approaches to Needs Assessment in Children's Services, 2002; Outcomes for Vulnerable Children, vol. 1 (ed with J. Scott), Promoting the Wellbeing of Children, Families and Communities, 2005, vol. 2 (jtly), Babies and Young Children in Care: life pathways, decision-making and practice, vol. 3 (jtly), Costs and Consequences of Placing Children in Care, 2008; (with C. Davies) Safeguarding Children Across Services: messages from research, 2012; (jtly) Safeguarding Babies and Very Young Children from Abuse and Neglect, 2012. *Recreations:* family and friends, English and French literature, theatre, films. *Address:* Rees Centre for Research in Fostering and Education, Department of Education, University of Oxford, 15 Norham Gardens, Oxford OX2 6PY. *T:* (01865) 274050. *E:* h.ward@lboro.ac.uk.

**WARD, Helen Madeleine, (Lady Ward);** Partner, Stewarts Law LLP, since 2012; *b* 28 May 1951; *d* of late Kenneth and of Ruth Gilbert; *m* 1983, Rt Hon. Sir Alan Hylton Ward, *qv*; one *d* (and one twin *d* decd). *Educ:* King Alfred Sch., Hampstead; Birmingham Univ. (LLB). Admitted Solicitor of the Supreme Court, 1978; Partner: Ward Bowie/Penningtons, 1978–94; Manches LLP, 1994–2012; a Dep. Dist Judge, 1992–2017. *Recreations:* family, friends, music, theatre, art. *Address:* Stewarts Law LLP, 5 New Street Square, EC4A 3BF. *T:* (020) 7936 8187. *E:* hward@stewartslaw.com.

**WARD, Hubert,** OBE 1996; MA; Headmaster (formerly Principal), English College, Prague, 1992–96; *b* 26 Sept. 1931; *s* of Allan Miles Ward and Joan Mary Ward; *m* 1st, 1958, Elizabeth Cynthia Fearn Bechervaise (*d* 2005); one *s* two *d*; 2nd, 2007, Judith Marion Hart (*née* Gay). *Educ:* Westminster Sch.; Trinity Coll., Cambridge. Asst Master (Maths), Geelong C of E Grammar Sch., Victoria, 1955–66; Asst Master (Maths), Westminster Sch., London, 1966–69; Headmaster, King's Sch., Ely, 1970–92. Mem. (L) Cambs CC, 1985–89. JP Cambs, 1976–92. *Publications:* (with K. Lewis) Starting Statistics, 1969. *Recreations:* rowing, sailing, bird-watching. *Address:* 1 The Green, Mistley, Manningtree, Essex CO11 1EU.
*See also Very Rev. F. E. F. Ward, V. J. Ward.*

**WARD, Janice Elizabeth, (Mrs J. C. Holmes),** CBE 2015; Founder and Chief Executive Officer, Corrotherm International Ltd, since 1992; *b* Southampton, 25 Sept. 1957; *d* of Owen George and Elizabeth Louise Ward; *m* 2005, Jonathan Charles Holmes; one *s* (and one *s* decd). *Educ:* BSc Mech. Engrg. Business Develt Manager, Amari Gp, 1982–86; UK Internat. Sales Dir, Cawsl Corp., USA, 1986–89; Man. Dir, Philip Cornes & Co. Ltd, 1989–92. Non-exec. Chair, AnTech Ltd, 2016–; non-executive Director: UKTI, 2012–15; Hardide plc, 2015–. Business Dir, Solent LEP, 2012–. Pres., Southampton Chamber of Commerce and Industry, 2010–13; non-exec. Dir, Hants Chamber of Commerce, 1993–. Member: Saudi British Jt Business Council, 2008–; UAE UK Business Council, 2015–. Judge: Queen's Awards for Enterprise, 2013–; Manufacturer of Year Awards, The Manufacturer, 2013–. Founding Trustee, Ben Voller G4 Fund, 2005–; Trustee, Southampton Cultural Develt Trust, 2009–. MIEx 1984. FInstD 2010. Hon. DEng Southampton Solent, 2015. *Recreations:* motor cycling, ski-ing, sailing, walking, collecting books, trying to make a change for the good if I can. *Address:* 1 Bramblebank Cottages, Calshot, Southampton SO45 1BR. *T:* (023) 8024 3424. *E:* jan.ward@corrotherm.co.uk.

**WARD, Jayne F.;** *see* Francis-Ward.

**WARD, John;** *see* Ward, C. J. W.

**WARD, Sir John (MacQueen),** Kt 2003; CBE 1995; FRSE; FIET; Chairman, Scottish Enterprise, 2004–09; *b* 1 Aug. 1940; *m* Barbara MacIntosh (decd); one *s* three *d. Educ:* Edinburgh Acad.; Fettes Coll. CA. FRSE 2005; FIET 2007. IBM UK Ltd: Plant Controller, 1966–75; Dir, Inf. Systems for Europe, 1975–79; Manufacturing Controller, 1979–81; Dir, Havant Plant, 1982–90 (numerous quality awards); Dir, UK Public Service Business, 1991–95; Res. Dir, Scotland and N England, 1991–96; Chairman: Scottish Homes, 1996–2002; Scottish Post Office Bd, 1997–2001; Macfarlane Gp (Clansman), subseq. Macfarlane Gp plc, 1998–2003. Chm., European Assets Trust, 1995–2015; non-exec. Chm., Dunfermline Building Soc., 1995–2007. Chairman: Scottish CBI, 1993–95; Scottish Qualifications Authy, 2000–04. Chm. or former Chm., advisory bodies and councils in Scotland. Trustee, Nat. Mus Scotland (formerly Nat. Mus of Scotland), 2005–12. FRSA 1999. *Recreations:* walking, DIY, reading, cycling. *Clubs:* New (Edinburgh); Bruntsfield Links Golf.

**WARD, Rev. Prof. (John Stephen) Keith,** FBA 2001; Regius Professor of Divinity, University of Oxford, 1991–2003; Canon of Christ Church, Oxford, 1991–2003; Professor of the Philosophy of Religion, Roehampton University, since 2017; *b* 22 Aug. 1938; *s* of John George Ward and Evelyn (*née* Simpson); *m* 1963, Marian Trotman; one *s* one *d. Educ:* UCW, Cardiff (BA 1962); Linacre Coll., Oxford (BLitt 1968); Trinity Hall, Cambridge (MA 1972); Westcott House, Cambridge. DD Oxon, 1998; DD Cantab, 1999. Ordained priest of Church of England, 1972. Lecturer in Logic, Univ. of Glasgow, 1964–69; Lectr in Philosophy, Univ. of St Andrews, 1969–71; Lectr in Philosophy of Religion, Univ. of London, 1971–75; Dean of Trinity Hall, Cambridge, 1975–82; F. D. Maurice Prof. of Moral and Social Theology, Univ. of London, 1982–85; Prof. of History and Phil. of Religion, King's Coll. London, 1985–91. Gresham Prof. of Divinity, 2004–08; Professorial Res. Fellow, Heythrop Coll., London, 2010–18. Jt Editor, Religious Studies, 1990–98. Jt Pres., World Congress of Faiths, 1992–2001. *Publications:* Ethics and Christianity, 1970; Kant's View of Ethics, 1972; The Divine Image, 1976; The Concept of God, 1977; The Promise, 1981; Rational Theology and the Creativity of God, 1982; Holding Fast to God, 1982; The Living God, 1984; Battle for the Soul, 1985; Images of Eternity, 1987; The Rule of Love, 1989; Divine Action, 1990; A Vision to Pursue, 1991; Religion and Revelation, 1994; Religion and Creation, 1996; God, Chance and Necessity, 1996; God, Faith and the New Millennium, 1998; Religion and Human Nature, 1998; Religion and Community, 2000; God: a guide for the perplexed, 2002; The Case for Religion, 2004; What the Bible Really Teaches, 2004; Pascal's Fire, 2006; Is Religion Dangerous?, 2006, new edn 2011; Christianity: a guide for the perplexed, 2007; Re-thinking Christianity, 2007; The Big Questions in Science and Religion, 2008; Religion and Human Fulfilment, 2008; Why There Almost Certainly Is a God: doubting Dawkins, 2008; The God Conclusion, 2009; The Word of God: the Bible after modern scholarship, 2010; More than Matter, 2010; Is Religion Irrational?, 2011; The Philosopher and the Gospels, 2011; Morality, Autonomy and God, 2013; The Evidence for God, 2014; Christ and the Cosmos: a reformation of trinitarian doctrine, 2015; Love is his Meaning: understanding the teaching of Jesus, 2017; The Christian Idea of God: a philosophical foundation for faith, 2017; The Mystery of Christ, 2018; Religion in the Modern World, 2019. *Recreations:* music, walking. *Address:* 39 Coopers Lane, Abingdon, Oxon OX14 5GU. *T:* (01235) 539799.

**WARD, Joseph Haggitt;** *b* 7 July 1926; *s* of Joseph G. and Gladys Ward; *m* 1961, Anthea Clemo (*d* 2010); one *s* one *d. Educ:* St Olave's Grammar School; Sidney Sussex College, Cambridge. Asst Principal, Min. of National Insurance, 1951; Private Sec. to Minister of Social Security, 1966–68; Asst Sec., 1968; Min. of Housing, later DoE, 1969–72; DHSS, 1972; Under-Sec. (pensions and nat. insce contributions), DHSS, 1976–86. *Recreations:* music, history of music, sequence dancing. *Address:* 34 Uffington Road, SE27 0ND. *T:* (020) 8670 1732.

**WARD, Sir Joseph James Laffey,** 4th Bt *cr* 1911; *b* 11 Nov. 1946; *s* of Sir Joseph George Davidson Ward, 3rd Bt, and Joan Mary Haden (*d* 1993), *d* of Major Thomas J. Laffey, NZSC; *S* father, 1970; *m* 1968, Robyn Allison, *d* of William Maitland Martin, Rotorua, NZ; one *s* one *d. Heir: s* Joseph James Martin Ward, *b* 20 Feb. 1971.

**WARD, Julian Anthony;** Headmaster, St Michael's Catholic Grammar School, Barnet, 2012–17; *b* Whalley, Lancs, 19 Jan. 1954; *m* 1979, Bernadette Crossin; one *s* two *d. Educ:* Pilgrim Grammar Sch., Bedford; Univ. of Manchester (BA Hons 1975); Bradford Univ. Business Sch. (DipBA 1976); Christ's Coll., Liverpool (PGCE 1977). Teacher of Economics: John Griffiths RC Boys' Sch., Wandsworth, 1977–81; Bishop Challoner RC Girls' Sch., Tower Hamlets, 1981–84; Sir John Cass Foundn and Redcoat Sch., Tower Hamlets, 1984–88; St Michael's Catholic GS, Barnet, 1988–2017. *Recreations:* walking, gardening, badminton. *Club:* Romford Golf.

**WARD, Julie Carolyn;** Member (Lab) North West Region, European Parliament, since 2014; *b* Ripon, 7 March 1957; *d* of Frederick and Sheila Ward; two *s. Educ:* RAF Seletar Secondary Sch.; Pilton Comprehensive Sch., Barnstaple; N Devon Coll.; Univ. of Newcastle upon Tyne (MEd 2012). Community Drama Worker, Mid-Pennine Arts, 1977–78; Community Drama Worker, Contact Theatre, Manchester, 1979–83; Asst Dir, Coventry Fest., 1984; Dir, Northern SHAPE, 1984–86; Founder and Dir, Jack Drum Arts, 1986–; Mem., Theatre for Young Audiences, 1999–2011; NE Regl Co-ordinator, ARROW and INDRA, 2009–11. Member, Board: Culture NE, 2004–08; Nat. Drama, 2011–; Regl Council Mem., Arts Council England, 2009–11; Mem., Co. Durham Cultural Partnership, 2011–13. Patron: Dance Syndrome; Performing Arts Network and Develt Agency. Churchill Fellow, 1995. FRSA 2015. *Publications:* Secret Lives, 1989; You're Not a Kid Anymore, 1989; I Can Fly, 1993; The Likes of Us, 1993; Stitches in Time, 1994; Parents Know It All, 1996; Wild Words for Wild Places, 2000; Stepping Up, 2000; Visions and Voices, 2002; Water Borne, Seed Blown, 2003; From Cuna Dun to Coundon Now, 2005; History of a Village: Sunniside, 2007. *Recreations:* theatre, music, arts and galleries, reading, writing poetry, swimming, Oxfam volunteer. *Address:* European Parliament, 60 Rue Wiertz, 1047 Brussels, Belgium; (office) Jactin House, 24 Hood Street, Manchester M4 6WX. *E:* contact@juliewardmep.eu.

**WARD, Keith;** *see* Ward, Rev. J. S. K.

**WARD, Keith David;** Chief Executive, British Medical Association, 2013–18; freelance consultant, since 2018; *b* London, 7 April 1960; *s* of Ronald and Rosalyn Ward; *m* 1990, Joanna Mary Martin; one *s* one *d. Educ:* St George's Sch., Harpenden; Hatfield Poly. (BA Hons Business). ACMA 1986; CGMA 2012. Project Accountant, British Aerospace, 1983–84; Financial Planning Manager, Dunn & Bradstreet, 1985–88; Finance Director: Datastream Internat., 1989–95; Primark Corp., 1996–2001; self-employed consultant, 2001–04; Finance Dir, 2004–06, Chief Operating Officer, 2007–10, C&G; Finance Dir, BMA, 2011–13. Trustee and Hon. Treas., London Youth, 2011–. Hon. MCGI 2011. *Recreations:* family, music, design, golf and other sport. *E:* keithward@gmail.com. *Club:* Berkhamsted Golf.

**WARD, Lawrence George;** Global Head of Security, PA Consulting Group, since 2015; *b* London, 20 June 1968; *s* of Theresa Ward; *m* 1996, Jayne Moreton; two *s. Educ:* Tring Sch.; Open Univ. (Dip. Mgt Studies 1996). Post Office: postal cadet, 1984–86; Operational Mgt, 1986–95; Area Ops Manager, Royal Mail, 1995–97; House of Commons: Postmaster, 1997–2002; Mail Security Consultant, 2002–06; Security Contract Manager, 2006–08; Asst Serjeant at Arms, 2008–12; Serjeant at Arms, 2012–15. *Recreations:* music, DIY, sailing, travel. *Address:* PA Consulting Group, 10 Bressenden Place, SW1E 5DN. *T:* (020) 7730 9000.

**WARD, Lee Anthony**; Director of Music, Liverpool Cathedral, since 2017; *b* Liverpool, 15 Aug. 1968; *s* of Terence Ward and Linda Dailey (later MacFarlane); *m* 2013, Daniel Cruz. *Educ*: Liverpool Bluecoat Sch.; Royal Coll. of Music (BMus London Univ.; ARCM 1989). ARCO 1989; LRAM 1989. Director of Music: London Oratory Sch., 1996–2012; Hampstead Parish Ch, 1998–2012; St Paul's Sch., São Paulo, Brazil, 2012–17. *Recreations*: dog walking, dining, concerts and theatre. *Address*: 8 Lady Chapel Close, Liverpool L1 7BZ. *E*: lee.ward@liverpoolcathedral.org.uk. *Club*: Savage.

**WARD, Hon. Sir (Lisle) Austin**, Kt 2006; Justice of Appeal, Bermuda, 2004–13; *b* 14 Nov. 1935; *s* of Sir Erskine Rueul La Tourette Ward, KA; *m* 1961, Francisca Sorhaindo; two *d*. *Educ*: Harrison Coll., Barbados. Called to the Bar, Middle Temple, 1962; Solicitor Gen., Bermuda, 1981–85; QC Bermuda 1983; Puisne Judge, Bermuda, 1985–93; Chief Justice, 1993–2004. *Publications*: Digest of Judgements of the Court of Appeal, 1985. *Address*: PO Box WK1, Warwick WKBX, Bermuda.

**WARD, His Honour Malcolm Beverley**; a Circuit Judge, Midland and Oxford Circuit, 1979–97; *b* 3 May 1931; *s* of Edgar and Dora Mary Ward; *m* 1958, Muriel Winifred (*d* 2018), *d* of Dr E. D. M. Wallace, Perth; two *s* two *d*. *Educ*: Wolverhampton Grammar Sch.; St John's Coll., Cambridge (Open Mathematical Schol.; MA, LLM). Called to the Bar, Inner Temple, 1956; practised Oxford (later Midland and Oxford) Circuit; a Recorder of the Crown Court, 1974–79. Gov., Wolverhampton Grammar Sch., 1972–2012 (Chm., 1981–2001). *Recreations*: music, (in theory) horticulture.

**WARD, Malcolm Stanley**; Founder and Managing Director, M60 Strategic Communications, since 2011; *b* 24 Sept. 1951; *s* of Hugh Ward and Rebecca Ward (*née* Rogerson). *Educ*: Gilberd School, Colchester. Dep. Editor, Gulf News, Dubai, 1978–79; Editor, Woodham and Wickford Chronicle, Essex, 1979–81; Dep. Editor, Gulf Times, Qatar, 1981–84; Dep. Editor, 1984–86, Dir and Editor, 1986–91, Daily News, Birmingham; Editor, Metro News, Birmingham, 1991–92; Ed., Evening News, Worcester, 1992–95; Man. Ed., The Peninsula, Qatar, 1995–98; News Ed., Gulf News, Dubai, 1998–2001; Account Dir, MCS Action, Dubai, 2001–06; Gp Account Dir, 2006–09, Dep. Man. Dir, 2009–11, JiWin, Dubai. *Recreations*: writing, travel, soccer, driving, tennis. *Address*: PO Box 440173, Dubai, UAE.

**WARD, Mary Angela**, MBE 1996; Co-Founder, and Artistic Director, 1974–2015, now Guardian and Ambassador, Chickenshed (formerly Chicken Shed Theatre Co.); *b* 2 Dec. 1944; *d* of Patrick O'Dwyer and Dot O'Dwyer (*née* Johnson); *m* 1971, Manus Ward; two *s*. *Educ*: Ilford Ursuline High Sch.; Digby Stuart Coll. Teacher, 1966–85; with Jo Collins, MBE, founded Chicken Shed Th. Co., 1974, with aim of producing pieces of theatrical and musical excellence to open the performing arts to all, incl. those denied access elsewhere. DUniv Middx, 1998. *Address*: c/o Chickenshed, 290 Chase Side, Southgate, N14 4PE. *T*: (020) 8351 6161, ext. 204.

**WARD, Michael**; writer and researcher; Chief Executive, British Urban Regeneration Association, 2008–09; *b* 15 Oct. 1949; *s* of late Donald Albert Ward and Mary Teresa Ward; *m* Hilary Knight; one *s* one *d*. *Educ*: Wimbledon Coll., London; University Coll., Oxford (BA PPE 1972); Birkbeck Coll., London (MA Social and Econ. Hist. 1980). Mem. (Lab), GLC, 1981–86 (Chm., Industry and Employment Cttee, 1981–86; Dep. Leader, 1985–86). Dir, Centre for Local Econ. Strategies, Manchester, 1987–2000 (Chm., 2009–17). Chm., Manchester City Labour Party, 1995–2000; Chief Executive: London Develt Agency, 2000–04; QMW Public Policy Seminars, Univ. of London, 2004–05; Kent Thameside Delivery Bd, 2005–08. Member: Poverty and Disadvantage Cttee, Joseph Rowntree Foundn, 2002–06; Bd, London Pensions Fund Authy, 2004–08 (Dep. Chm., 2005–08). Res. Fellow, Smith Inst., 2010–; Associate, Centre for London, 2013–. Chm., Twin and Twin Trading Ltd, 2011–17. *Publications*: reports for Smith Inst. *W*: www.michaelwardconsulting.co.uk.

**WARD, Michael Jackson**, CBE 1980; British Council Director, Germany, 1990–91, retired; *b* 16 Sept. 1931; *s* of late Harry Ward, CBE, and Dorothy Julia Ward (*née* Clutterbuck); *m* 1955, Eileen Patricia Foster; one *s* one *d*. *Educ*: Drayton Manor Grammar Sch.; University Coll. London (BA); Univ. of Freiburg; Corpus Christi Coll., Oxford. HM Forces, 1953–55; 2nd Lieut Royal Signals. Admin. Officer, HMOCS, serving as Dist Comr and Asst Sec. to Govt, Gilbert and Ellice Is; British Council, 1961–91: Schs Recruitment Dept, 1961–64; Regional Rep., Sarawak, 1964–68; Dep. Rep., Pakistan, 1968–70; Dir, Appointments Services Dept, 1970–72; Dir, Personnel Dept, 1972–75; Controller, Personnel and Appts Div., 1975–77; Representative, Italy, 1977–81; Controller, Home Div., 1981–85; Asst Dir-Gen., 1985–90. Hon. Mem., British Council, 1991. *Recreations*: music, world literature. *Address*: 1 Knapp Rise, Haslingfield, Cambridge CB23 1LQ. *E*: michaelward1@mac.com.

**WARD, Neil David**; independent business consultant, 2008–14; Director, Quality Transformation Ltd, 2008–11; *b* 14 March 1953; *s* of Tom Ward and Vera Ward (*née* Dowd); *m* 1979, Jane Gray; one *s* one *d*. *Educ*: St Francis Xavier's Coll., Liverpool; Wallasey Grammar Sch. HM Treasury, 1972–73; NI Office, 1973–87; DoH, 1987–89; Sen. Civil Service, 1989–91, 1994–; DSS, 1989–90; Chief Exec., Pegasus Retirement Homes (SE) Ltd, 1991–93; DWP (formerly DSS), 1994–99; Chief Exec., Appeals Service, 1999–2003; Department for Constitutional Affairs, subseq. Ministry of Justice: Dir, Judicial Appts, 2003–04; Dir, Criminal Justice, 2004–05; Dir, Crime, HM Courts Service, 2005–06; Chief Operating Officer, HM Courts Service, 2006–07; Interim Chief Exec., HM Courts Service, 2007–08; Prog. Dir, PAYE, HMRC, 2008–10. Asst Comr, Boundary Commn for England, 2011–12, 2016–17. *Recreations*: sport (golf and swimming and as a spectator of all sports), quizzes.

**WARD, Nicholas**; *see* Ward, C. J. N.

**WARD, Peter Simms**; a District Judge (Magistrates' Courts), Lancashire, 2006–13; *b* 20 June 1943; *s* of Norman and Marie Ward; *m* 1974, Monica Stalker; three *s*. *Educ*: Bolton Sch.; Bristol Univ. (LLB). Articled to J. J. Rothwell, Solicitor, Salford; admitted Solicitor, 1969; Partner, Rothwell & Evans, Solicitors, Salford, Gtr Manchester, 1969–94; Provincial Stipendiary Magistrate, subseq. Dist Judge (Magistrates' Courts), Merseyside, 1994–2001; Dist Judge (Magistrates' Courts), Manchester, 2001–06. *Recreations*: reading, walking, gardening. *E*: mstalkerward@fastmail.fm.

**WARD, Phillip David**; Chairman, Resource Futures Ltd, since 2011; *b* 1 Sept. 1950; *s* of Frederick William Ward and Phyllis Mavis Ward; *m* 1974, Barbara Patricia, (Pip), Taylor; two *d*. *Educ*: Sir John Talbot's GS, Whitchurch; Sheffield Univ. (BJur 1973). Department of the Environment, later Department of the Environment, Transport and the Regions: Admin. Trainee, 1973–78; Hackney/Islington Inner City Partnership, 1978–80; Principal, Local Govt Finance Directorate, 1980–85; Asst Sec., Local Govt Finance Review, 1985–90; Principal Private Sec. to Sec. of State for the Envmt, 1990–92; Dir (Under Sec.), Construction Sponsorship, 1992–97; Dir, Energy, Envmt and Waste, 1997–2001; Dir of Finance, then Prin. Finance Officer, DETR, subseq. DTLR, then ODPM, 2001–02; Dir, Local Govt Performance Unit, OPDM, 2002–04; Dir, Waste and Resources Action Prog. Ltd, 2004–11. Dir, OPRL Ltd, 2014–. *Recreations*: sailing, Rugby, cinema.

**WARD, Rear-Adm. Rees Graham John**, CB 2002; FIET; Managing Director, Eversfield Advisors Ltd, since 2013; *b* 1 Oct. 1949; *s* of John Walter Ward and Helen Burt Ward (*née* Foggo); *m* 1st, 1973, Christina Glen Robertson (marr. diss.); two *s*; 2nd, 1980, Phyllis Gentry Pennington; two *d*. *Educ*: Queens' Coll., Cambridge (MA); Cranfield Univ. (MSc 1981; MSc (Corp. Mgt) 2001). FIET (FIEE 1998). Joined RN, 1967; served: HMS Russel, 1972–73; HMS Brighton, 1977–79; MoD PE, 1981–83; jsdc 1984; HMS Ark Royal, 1984–87; Naval Asst to Controller of Navy, 1988–89; Asst DOR (Sea), 1990–92; MA to Chief of Defence Procurement, 1992–94; DOR (Sea), 1995–97; rcds 1998; hcsc 1999; ACDS, Operational Requirements (Sea Systems), 1999; Capability Manager (Strategic Deployment), MoD, 1999–2002; Chief Exec., Defence Communications Services Agency, 2002–07; Dir Gen. Inf. Systems and Services, Defence Equipment and Support, 2007. Dir Gen., Defence Manufrs Assoc., 2007–09; Chief Exec., ADS, 2009–11, ADS Gp, 2011–12; Proposals Dir, KBR, 2013–. Rep. GB and Scotland at athletics cross country running, 1972–77. CRAeS 2008. *Recreations*: reading, mountain biking. *Clubs*: Army and Navy; Hawks (Cambridge).

**WARD, Reginald George**; Director, Analysis and Research (formerly Statistics and Economic Office), Inland Revenue, 1994–2001; *b* 6 July 1942; *s* of Thomas George and Ada May Ward; *m* 1964, Chandan Mistry; two *s* one *d*. *Educ*: Leicester, Aberdeen and Oxford Universities; London Business Sch. Lectr in Economics, St Andrews Univ., 1965; Analyst, National Cash Register, 1969; Economist, ICL, 1970; DTI, 1971; Chief Statistician: HM Treasury, 1978; Cabinet Office, 1982; Dir, Business Statistics Office, DTI, 1986; Asst Dir, CSO, 1989–94. *Recreation*: sailing.

**WARD, Richard Churchill**, PhD; Chairman: Brit Insurance, 2014–18; Cunningham Lindsey Group, 2014–18; Senior Independent Director, Direct Line Group, since 2016; *b* 6 March 1957; *s* of Alan and Margaret Ward; *m* 1990, Carol Cole; two *s*. *Educ*: Wellington Coll.; Univ. of Exeter (BSc 1979; PhD 1982). Scientist, SERC, 1982–88; Sen. Manager, BP Research, 1988–91; Hd of Business Develt, BP Oil Trading Internat., 1991–94; Hd of Mktg, Tradition Financial Services, 1994–95; International Petroleum Exchange, subseq. ICE Futures: Dir, Product Develt and Res., 1995–96; Exec. Vice Pres., 1996–99; Chief Exec., 1999–2005; Vice Chm., 2005–06; Chief Exec., Lloyd's of London, 2006–13. Non-exec. Dir, Partnership Assce Gp, 2013–16. *Publications*: scientific res. papers in Chem. Soc. Rev., Jl of Applied Crystallography, Europhysics Letters, Molecular Physics, Nature, etc. *Recreations*: sailing, road cycling, ski-ing.

**WARD, Prof. Richard Samuel**, DPhil; FRS 2005; Professor of Mathematics, since 1991, Head, Department of Mathematical Sciences, 2004–07, University of Durham; *b* 6 Sept. 1951; *s* of late Walter Ward and Eileen Ward (*née* Phillips); *m* 1991, Rebecca Nora, *d* of Horace Basil Barlow, *qv*; one *s* one *d*. *Educ*: Rhodes Univ. (BSc Hons 1973, MSc 1974); St John's Coll., Oxford (DPhil 1977). Jun. Res. Fellow, Merton Coll., Oxford, 1977–79; Lectr and Fellow, TCD, 1979–82; Mem., Inst. for Theoretical Physics, Stony Brook, NY, 1982; Lectr, Sen. Lectr, then Reader, Univ. of Durham, 1983–91. Life Mem., Clare Hall, Cambridge. Jun. Whitehead Prize, LMS, 1989. *Publications*: (with R. O. Wells, Jr) Twistor Geometry and Field Theory, 1990; articles on mathematical physics in learned jls. *Recreations*: family, music, reading. *Address*: Department of Mathematical Sciences, University of Durham, Durham DH1 3LE. *T*: (0191) 334 3118. *E*: richard.ward@durham.ac.uk.

**WARD, Maj.-Gen. Robert William**, CB 1989; MBE 1972; DL; plantsman, landscape and garden design consultant, since 1992; *b* 17 Oct. 1935; *s* of late Lt-Col William Denby Ward and Monica Thérèse Ward (*née* Collett-White); *m* 1966, Lavinia Dorothy Cramsie; two *s* one *d*. *Educ*: Rugby School; RMA Sandhurst. Commissioned Queen's Bays (later 1st Queen's Dragoon Guards), 1955; served Jordan, Libya, BAOR, Borneo, NI, and Persian Gulf; MA to C-in-C BAOR, 1973–75; CO 1st Queen's Dragoon Guards, 1975–77; Col GS Staff Coll., 1977–79; Comdr 22 Armd Brigade, 1979–82; RCDS Canada, 1982–83; Asst Chief of Staff, Northern Army Group, 1983–86; GOC Western Dist, 1986–89, retd. Col, 1st Queen's Dragoon Guards, 1991–97; Hon. Col, Royal Mercian and Lancastrian Yeomanry, 1995–2001. Sec., Game Conservancy, Shropshire, 1993–2000; Chairman: Nat. Meml Arboretum, 1996–98; Shropshire Parks and Gardens Trust, 1996–2002. Pres., SSAFA, Shropshire, 1994–2016. DL Shropshire, 2000. *Recreations*: gardening, outdoor sports, country pursuits, travel, food, wine. *Clubs*: MCC, I Zingari.

**WARD, Rev. Robin**, PhD; Principal, St Stephen's House, Oxford, since 2006; *b* 24 Jan. 1966; *s* of late Peter Herbert Ward and of Maureen Ann Ward; *m* 1997, Ruth Suzanne (*née* Sheard); two *s*. *Educ*: Hassenbrook Sch.; City of London Sch.; Magdalen Coll., Oxford (BA 1987, MA 1991); St Stephen's House, Oxford; King's Coll. London (PhD 2003). Ordained deacon, 1991, priest, 1992; Assistant Curate: St Andrew Romford, 1991–94; St Andrew and St Francis, Willesden Green, 1994–96; Vicar, St John the Baptist, Sevenoaks, 1996–2006. Hon. Canon, and Hon. Canon Theologian, Rochester Cathedral, 2004–06, Canon Emeritus, 2006–. Proctor in Convocation, 2000–05. *Publications*: On Christian Priesthood, 2011; reviews in Jl of Theol Studies and Jl of Ecclesiastical Hist. *Recreation*: cultivation of rhododendrons. *Address*: St Stephen's House, 16 Marston Street, Oxford OX4 1JX. *T*: (01865) 247874. *Club*: Travellers.

**WARD, Rt Rev. Simon B.**; *see* Barrington-Ward.

**WARD, Simon Howe B.**; *see* Brooks-Ward.

**WARD, Simon John; His Honour Judge Ward**; a Circuit Judge, since 2016. *Address*: Wolverhampton Combined Court Centre, Pipers Row, Wolverhampton WV1 3LQ.

**WARD, Thomas**; Sheriff of North Strathclyde at Dunoon, since 2010; *b* Glasgow, 3 April 1953; *s* of Thomas and Mary Ward; *m* 1980, Ruth Zegleman; three *s*. *Educ*: St Mary's Coll., Blairs; St Aloysius Coll., Glasgow; Univ. of Dundee (LLB Hons). Partner, Blair & Bryden, Greenock, 1979–2000; Immigration Judge (pt-time), 2001–10; Mem. (pt-time), PMETB, 2005–10; Sheriff (pt-time), 2005–10. Legal Assessor: GMC, 2002–10; NMC, 2002–10. Mem., CICAP, 2001–10. *Recreations*: watching cricket, walking, visiting France. *Address*: 107 Finnart Street, Greenock PA16 8HN. *T*: (01475) 723055. *E*: sherifftward@scotcourts.gov.uk.

**WARD, Timothy Justin**; QC 2011; *b* Macclesfield, 16 Oct. 1966; *s* of Anthony and Sally Ward; *m* 1994, Catherine Temma Davidson; one *s* one *d*. *Educ*: Cheadle Hulme Sch.; University Coll. London (BA); Univ. of Southern Calif (MA); Trinity Coll., Cambridge. Called to the Bar, Gray's Inn, 1994, Bencher, 2016; in practice as barrister, specialising in EU, competition and public law. Jt Hd, Monckton Chambers, 2016–. Chm., Bar Eur. Gp, 2013–15. Ed. in Chief, Human Rights Law Reports: UK cases, 2000–. Barrister of Year, The Lawyer, 2013. *Publications*: (ed) Judicial Review and the Human Rights Act, 2000; (jtly) The Strasbourg Case Law: leading cases from the European Human Rights Law Reports, 2001; (jtly) Competition Litigation in the UK, 2005. *Recreations*: playing piano, elliptical cycling. *Address*: Monckton Chambers, 1–2 Raymond Buildings, Gray's Inn, WC1R 5NR. *T*: (020) 7405 7211.

**WARD, Tony,** OBE 1998; Group Services Director, BAA plc, 1999–2007 (Group Human Resources Director, 1997–99); *b* 20 Feb. 1950; *s* of Kenneth H. Ward and Elsie M. Ward; *m* 1972, Margaret Harrison; one *d*. *Educ:* Univ. of Leeds (BSc 1st Class Hons 1972). Personnel Manager, Stone Platt Industries, 1972–81; Personnel Director (Divisional), GrandMet, 1981–91; Dir of Human Resources, Kingfisher plc, 1992–97. Non-executive Director: SThree plc, 2006–16; OCS Gp Ltd, 2007–17. Mem., 1990–95, Dep. Chm., 1993–95, CRE. Chm., Equal Opportunities Panel, CBI; Mem. Council, Consumers' Assoc., 2011– (Dep. Chm., 2015–17); Mem. Bd, 2011–17, non-exec. Dir, 2017–, Which? Ltd. Ind. Advr, Ombudsman Services Ltd, 2017–. FCIPD 1991; FRSA 2000. *Recreations:* golf, yoga, art, cycling. *Club:* Lambourne.

**WARD, Vanessa Jane;** Managing Director and Education Consultant, Forward Education Ltd, since 2016; *b* Guildford, 20 Oct. 1964; *d* of Hubert Ward, *qv;* *m* 1989, Michael Petley; two *s*. *Educ:* King's Sch., Ely; Univ. of Edinburgh (MA Hons Eng. Lit. 1988); College of Law (CPE 1989; Law Soc. Finals 1991); Roehampton Inst., Univ. of Surrey (PGCE 1998); Nat. Coll. of Sch. Leadership (NPQH 2009). Admitted Solicitor, 1993. Trainee solicitor, 1991–93, Solicitor, 1993–96, Simkins Partnership; in-house Legal Advr, Judy Daish Associates, 1996; English Teacher, Nonsuch High Sch. for Girls, 1998–2001; Second i/c, English Dept, Wilson's Sch., 2001–02; Hd, English Dept, 2003–05, Asst Headteacher, 2005–08, Dep. Headteacher, 2008–10, St Philomena's Catholic High Sch. for Girls; Headteacher, Tiffin Girls' Sch., 2010–15; HM Inspector (Educn), Ofsted, 2015–16. Vice Chair, Royal Bor. of Kingston upon Thames Schs Forum, 2013–15. Gov., Tiffin Sch., 2007–10. Trustee: Thames Youth Orch., 2010–15; Beat (Beating Eating Disorders), 2014–15. *Recreations:* theatre, walking, reading, current affairs, DIY, camping.
*See also Very Rev. F. E. F. Ward.*

**WARD, William Alec;** HM Diplomatic Service, retired; *b* 27 Nov. 1928; *s* of William Leslie Ward and Gladys Ward; *m* 1955, Sheila Joan Hawking; two *s* two *d*. *Educ:* King's Coll. Sch., Wimbledon; Christ Church, Oxford. HM Forces, 1947–49. Colonial Office, 1952; Private Sec. to Permanent Under-Sec., 1955–57; Singapore, 1960–64; seconded to CRO, 1963; Karachi, 1964–66; Islamabad, 1966–68; joined HM Diplomatic Service, 1968; FCO, 1968–71; Salisbury, 1971–72; Dep. High Comr, Colombo, 1973–76; High Comr, Mauritius, 1977–81. *Recreations:* music, walking. *Address:* 19 Beech Court, South Walks Road, Dorchester DT1 1DX.

**WARDE, Prof. Alan,** PhD; FBA 2018; FAcSS; Professor of Sociology, University of Manchester, since 1999; *b* Newcastle upon Tyne, 18 Aug. 1949; *s* of Ernest Warde and Nancy Ward (*née* Smurthwaite). *Educ:* Dame Allan's Boys' Sch., Newcastle upon Tyne; Downing Coll., Cambridge (BA Hons); Univ. of Durham (MA); Univ. of Leeds (PhD 1976). Lectr, then Sen. Lectr, 1978–94, Reader, 1994–96, Prof., 1996–99, Lancaster Univ.; Co-Dir, ESRC Centre for Res. Innovation and Competition, Univ. of Manchester, 1999–2007. FAcSS 2011. *Publications:* Consensus and Beyond, 1982; Consumption, Food and Taste, 1997; Eating Out, 2000; Culture, Class, Distinction, 2009; The Practice of Eating, 2016; Consumption: a sociological analysis, 2017. *Recreations:* tennis, walking, music. *Address:* School of Social Sciences, University of Manchester, Oxford Road, Manchester M13 9PL. *E:* alan.warde@manchester.ac.uk.

**WARDELL, Gareth Lodwig;** environmental and planning consent consultant, since 2007; *b* 29 Nov. 1944; *s* of late John Thomas Wardell and Jenny Ceridwen Wardell; *m* 1967, Jennifer Dawn Evans; one *s*. *Educ:* London Sch. of Econs and Pol Science (BScEcon, MSc). Geography Master, Chislehurst and Sidcup Technical High Sch., 1967–68; Head of Econs Dept, St Clement Danes Grammar Sch., 1968–70; Sixth Form Econs Master, Haberdashers' Aske's Sch., Elstree, 1970–72; Educn Lectr, Bedford Coll. of Physical Educn, 1972–73; Sen. Lectr in Geography, Trinity Coll., Carmarthen, 1973–82. MP (Lab) Gower, Sept. 1982–1997. A Forestry Comr, 1999–2007. Mem. Bd, Envmt Agency, 1997–2004. Lay Mem., GMC, 1995–2008. *Publications:* articles on regional issues in British Econ. Survey. *Recreations:* cycling, cross-country running.

**WARDELL, Susan Toni,** CBE 2010; Vice President, Corporate Services, African Development Bank Group, 2012–15; *b* London, 12 Feb. 1954; *d* of Thomas Alfred Wardell and Joyce Ann Wardell (*née* Canter). *Educ:* Roehampton Inst. of Higher Educn, Univ. of London (BA 1st Cl. Hons Educn); Inst. of Educn, Univ. of London (MA Sociol. of Educn Double Dist.). Lectr in Sociol. and Psychol., Church Teacher's Coll., Jamaica, 1978–81; Principal Econ. and Employment Officer, London Bor. of Hackney, 1982–87; Field Dir, VSO Pacific Prog., 1987–91; Hd of Estimates and Resources Section, 1991–93, Prog. Manager, S Africa, 1993–99, ODA; Regl Dir, W and Southern Africa, Save the Children UK, 1996–99; Department for International Development: Head, Nepal, 1999–2001, Perf. and Effectiveness Dept, 2001–04, Southern Africa, 2004–06; Capability Rev. Manager, 2006–07; Dir, ME, Caribbean, Asia (N, Central, E) and Overseas Territories, 2007–10; Dir, Conflict, Humanitarian, Security, ME and N Africa, 2010–12; Chief Exec., Queen Elizabeth Diamond Jubilee Trust (on secondment), 2012. *Recreations:* listening to music, particularly African jazz, sailing, cricket, walking, cycling, theatre and arts.

**WARDLAW, Sir (Henry) Justin,** 22nd Bt *cr* 1631, of Pitreavie; *b* 10 Aug. 1963; *s* of Sir Henry John Wardlaw, 21st Bt, and of Julie-Ann, *d* of late Edward Patrick Kirwan; *S* father, 2005, but his name does not appear on the Official Roll of the Baronetage; *m* 1988, Rachel Jane, *y d* of James Kennedy Pitney; two *s* one *d*. Heir: *s* Henry James Wardlaw, *b* 8 Dec. 1999.

**WARDLAW, Prof. Joanna Marguerite,** CBE 2016; MD; FRCP, FRCR; FMedSci; FRSE; Professor of Applied Neuroimaging, since 2002, and Head, Division of Neuroimaging Sciences, since 2010, University of Edinburgh; Hon. Consultant Neuroradiologist, NHS Lothian, since 1994; *b* London, 4 Nov. 1958; two *c*. *Educ:* Park Sch., Glasgow; Univ. of Edinburgh (BSc Hons 1979; MB ChB Hons 1982; MD 1994). MRCP 1986, FRCP 1988; FRCR 1988. House Officer, Royal Infirmary of Edinburgh, 1982–83; SHO, Edinburgh, Eastern, Northern and Western Gen. Hosps, 1983–85; Registrar, Radiology, 1985–88, Sen. Registrar, Radiology, 1988–90, Edinburgh; MRC Res. Trng Fellow, Edinburgh, 1990–92; Consultant Neuroradiologist, Southern Gen. Hosp., Glasgow, 1992–94; Sen. Lectr, Univ. of Edinburgh, 1994–2002. Founder and Dir, Brain Res. Imaging Centre, Edinburgh, 1997–; Founder, Scottish Imaging Network, 2007. FMedSci 2005; Fellow: Eur. Soc. of Neuroradiol., 2008; Eur. Stroke Assoc., 2008; FRSE 2011; FAHA 2014. *Publications:* Stroke: a practical guide to management, 1998, 3rd edn, 2006; contribs to jls incl. Lancet, Stroke, Radiol., Neurol. *Recreations:* walking, cycling, theatre, art, film, travel, beachcombing, but most of all spending time with family. *Address:* Centre for Clinical Brain Sciences, Chancellor's Building, University of Edinburgh, 49 Little France Crescent, Edinburgh EH16 4SB. *Club:* Drumsheugh Baths.

**WARDLE, Charles Frederick;** immigration policy adviser and international consultant; *b* 23 Aug. 1939; *s* of late Frederick Maclean Wardle and Constance Wardle (*née* Roach); *m* 1964, Lesley Ann, *d* of Sidney Wells; one *d*. *Educ:* Tonbridge Sch.; Lincoln Coll., Oxford; Harvard Business Sch. MA Oxon 1968; MBA Harvard. Asst to Pres., American Express Co., NY, 1966–69; Merchant Banking, London, 1969–72; Chairman: Benjamin Priest Gp plc, 1977–84 (Dir, 1972–74, Man. Dir, 1974–77); Warne, Wright and Rowland, 1978–84. Mem. Council, CBI, 1980–84. MP (C) Bexhill and Battle, 1983–2001. PPS: to Sec. of State for Social Services, 1984–87; to Sec. of State for Scotland, 1990–92; Parly Under-Sec. of State, and Immigration Minister, Home Office, 1992–94, DTI, 1994–95. Member Select Committee: on Trade and Industry, 1983–84; on Treasury and Civil Service, 1990; on Public Accounts, 1995–2000. Public Affairs Dir, Harrods Ltd, 2000–02; claims settlement for Equitas Ltd with Libya, Iraq and UN Compensation Commn, 2003–06. Chm., Cons. One Nation Forum, 1989–90. Member: Commercial and Econ. Cttee, EEF, 1981–83; Midlands Cttee, IoD, 1981–83. FRGS 1977. *Recreations:* books, sport, travel. *Address:* Shepherds, Cranbrook, Kent TN17 3EN. *Clubs:* Farmers, Travellers.

**WARDLE, John;** *see* Wardle, R. J. S.

**WARDLE, (John) Irving;** Drama Critic, The Independent on Sunday, 1990–95; *b* 20 July 1929; *s* of John Wardle and Nellie Partington; *m* 1958, Joan Notkin (marr. diss.); *m* 1963, Fay Crowder (marr. diss.); two *s*; *m* 1975, Elizabeth Grist; one *s* one *d*. *Educ:* Bolton Sch.; Wadham Coll., Oxford (BA); Royal Coll. of Music (ARCM). Joined Times Educational Supplement as sub-editor, 1956; Dep. Theatre Critic, The Observer, 1960; Drama Critic, The Times, 1963–89. Editor, Gambit, 1973–75. Plays: The Houseboy, prod Open Space Theatre, 1974, ITV, 1982; devised A Kurt Tucholsky Cabaret, Arcola Th., 2010. *Publications:* The Theatres of George Devine (biog.), 1978; Theatre Criticism, 1992. *Recreation:* piano playing. *Address:* 51 Richmond Road, New Barnet, Herts EN5 1SF. *T:* (020) 8440 3671.

**WARDLE, Peter;** adviser on elections and democracy, since 2015; Chief Executive, Electoral Commission, 2004–15; *b* 3 July 1962; *s* of late Alec Peter Wardle and of Rev. Patricia Wardle (*née* Haker); *m* 2005, Jo Gray. *Educ:* Emanuel Sch.; Merton Coll., Oxford (BA Hons 1985). Inland Revenue, 1985–87; Private Sec. to Minister for Higher Educn and Sci., 1987–89; Inland Revenue: Principal, 1989–94; Asst Dir, 1994–98; Dir, Strategy and Planning, 1998–2000; Dir, Corporate Services, Cabinet Office, 2000–04. Non-exec. Dir, Basildon and Thurrock Univ. Hosp. NHS Foundn Trust (formerly Basildon and Thurrock Univ. Hosp. NHS Trust), 2004–12 (Vice Chm., 2007–10); Mem. Gp Audit and Risk Cttee, Circle (formerly Circle Anglia) Gp, 2008–16. Advr, Cambridge Conf. on Electoral Democracy, 2015–; Expert, Venice Commn, Council of Europe, 2015–. Member, Commonwealth Observer Mission: to Presidential and Parly Elections, Ghana, 2016; to Nat. Assembly Elections, Lesotho, 2017. Mem., High-Level Rev. Gp on Commonwealth Election Observation Guidelines, 2018. *Recreations:* fell-walking, cycling, music. *Club:* Royal Over-Seas League.

**WARDLE, Robert James;** Consultant, DLA Piper, 2008–13; *b* 23 Dec. 1951; *s* of late William James Wardle and Peggy Mary Wardle. *Educ:* Stamford Sch.; Univ. of Hull (LLB Hons). Admitted solicitor, 1976; articled clerk, 1974–76, asst solicitor, 1976–78, Greenwoods; Prosecuting Solicitor, Essex CC, 1978–80; Cambridgeshire County Council: Prosecuting Solicitor, 1980–86; Sen. Crown Prosecutor, 1986–88; Serious Fraud Office: Case Controller, 1988–92; Asst Dir, 1992–2003; Dir, 2003–08. *Recreations:* walking, shooting. *T:* (01733) 554929. *E:* wardle522@btinternet.com.

**WARDLE, Brig. (Robin) John (Stuart),** OBE 1987; DL; Chairman, NHS Staff College Council, since 2010; Vice Lord-Lieutenant, North Yorkshire, 2014–15; *b* Loxwood, Sussex, 7 Nov. 1944; *s* of Norman Henry Russell Wardle, TD and Joan Deardrie Wardle (*née* Hadden); *m* 1970, Sarah Jane Ingham; one *s* one *d*. *Educ:* Cheltenham Coll.; Queen's Univ., Kingston, Canada (Draper's Schol.); Mons Officer Cadet Sch. (Sen. Under Officer and Stick of Honour). Commnd Coldstream Guards, 1964; psc 1977; Acad. Adjt, RMA, 1980–83; CO, 1st Bn, Coldstream Guards, 1985–87; Comdr, 52 Lowland Bde, 1993–95. Chairman: Northallerton Health Services NHS Trust, 1996–2002; Craven and Harrogate PCT, 2002–06; NHS N Yorks and York, 2006–09. Chm. Trustees and Adv. Council, The Staff Coll. Charity: Leadership in Healthcare, 2016–. Freeman, Co. of Merchants to the Staple of England, 2008. DL N Yorks, 2004. Queen's Commendation for Brave Conduct, 1966. *Recreations:* yachting, gardening. *Address:* Bellwood Coach House, Littlethorpe, nr Ripon, N Yorks HG4 3AA. *T:* (01765) 602005. *E:* john_wardle@talk21.com. *Clubs:* Royal Yacht Squadron; Household Division Yacht (Cdre, 2010–17).

**WARE, Anna, (Mrs T. D. O. Ware);** *see* Pavord, A.

**WARE, Howard Elliott,** FRCS; Consultant Orthopaedic Surgeon, since 1994, and Director, Wellington Knee Surgery Unit, since 2010, Wellington Hospital; Consultant Orthopaedic Surgeon, and Head, Lower Limb Arthroplasty, Royal Free London NHS Foundation Trust, since 2014; *b* 2 Nov. 1955; *s* of David Frederick Ware and Ann Julia Ware; *m* 1979, Carol Frances Davis; one *s* two *d*. *Educ:* Lady Owen's Sch.; St Bartholomew's Med. Sch. (MB BS 1980). FRCS 1985; FRCS(Orth) 1992. Consultant Orthopaedic Surgeon: St Bartholomew's Hosp., 1992–94; Chase Farm Hosp., Enfield, 1994–2014. Med. Advr, Worldwide Healthcare Associates, 2014–. Hon. Sen. Lectr, Univ. of Dundee, 2001–. Inst. Chair, Orthopaedics and Rheumatology, Cleveland Clinic London, 2018–. Mem. Council, Conservative Health, 2017–. *Publications:* contribs to BMJ, Jl Bone and Joint Surgery. *Recreations:* travel, films, reading, gardening. *Address:* Wellington Knee Surgery Unit, Wellington Hospital South, Wellington Place, NW8 9LE. *T:* (020) 7586 5959. *Club:* Carlton.

**WARE, Joni;** *see* Lovenduski, J.

**WARE, Michael John,** CB 1985; QC 1988; barrister-at-law; Solicitor and Legal Adviser, Department of the Environment, 1982–92; *b* 7 May 1932; *s* of Kenneth George Ware and Phyllis Matilda (*née* Joynes); *m* 1966, Susan Ann Maitland; three *d*. *Educ:* Cheltenham Grammar Sch.; Trinity Hall, Cambridge (BA (Law), LLB). Called to Bar, Middle Temple. Nat. Service, 2/Lieut RASC, 1954–56. Board of Trade (later Dept of Trade and Industry): Legal Asst, 1957–64; Sen. Legal Asst, 1964–72; Asst Solicitor, 1972–73; Dir, Legal Dept, Office of Fair Trading, 1973–77; Under Secretary: Dept of Trade, 1977–81; DoE, 1982. Chm., Meat Hygiene Appeals Tribunals for England and Wales, 1993–2002.

**WAREHAM, Prof. Nicholas John,** PhD; FRCP, FFPH, FMedSci; Director, Medical Research Council Epidemiology Unit, since 2003; Professor, University of Cambridge, since 2013; *b* Gravesend, 1 March 1962; *s* of Michael Wareham and Christine Wareham; *m* 1985, Alison Butts; one *s* one *d*. *Educ:* Trinity Sch., Croydon; St Thomas's Hosp. Med. Sch., London (MB BS 1986); London Sch. of Hygiene and Tropical Medicine, Univ. of London (MSc 1991); Univ. of Cambridge (PhD 1997). FRCP 2003; FFPH (FFPHM 2003). MRC Clinician Scientist, 1997–2001; Wellcome Trust Sen. Clin. Fellow, Univ. of Cambridge, 2001–03. Hon. Consultant, Addenbrooke's Hosp., Cambridge, 1997–; Hon. Prof., Univ. of Cambridge, 2006–13. *Recreations:* cricket, hockey, watching Arsenal FC, musical theatre, opera. *Address:* MRC Epidemiology Unit, University of Cambridge, Box 285, Institute of Metabolic Science, Addenbrooke's Hospital, Cambridge CB2 0QQ. *T:* (01223) 330315, *Fax:* (01223) 330470. *E:* nick.wareham@mrc-epid.cam.ac.uk.

**WAREING, Michael Peter,** CMG 2010; FCA, FCCA; Chairman, Cobham plc, 2017–19 (Senior Independent Director, 2010–19); *b* Birmingham, 9 Feb. 1954; *s* of Anthony Peter and Margaret Florence Wareing; *m* 1998, Isabella Janusz; two *s* three *d* (and one *s* decd). *Educ:* Belmont Abbey Sch. FCA 1977; FCCA 1984; MCSI (MSI 1986). Partner, KPMG, 1985–2009; Chief Exec., Europe, ME and Asia, 2002–05; Internat. Chief Exec., 2005–09.

Dir, Wolseley plc, 2009–14; Sen. Ind. Dir, Intertek plc, 2011–17; Chm., Iraq Adv. Bd, G4S plc, 2011–12. Prime Minister's Envoy for Reconstruction of Southern Iraq, 2007–09; Chm., Basra Develt Commn, 2007–09; Internat. Investment Advr to Min. of Mines, Afghan Govt, 2011–15. Dir, BITC, 2008–12; Chm., BITC Internat., 2009–12. *Recreations:* horse riding (ex-amateur jockey), ski-ing, scuba diving, tennis.

**WARHURST, Pamela Janice**, CBE 2005; Chair: Pennine Prospects Rural Regeneration Co., since 2006; Incredible Edible Ltd, since 2009; Incredible Edible Todmorden Ltd, since 2013; *b* 12 Sept. 1950; *d* of Fred and Kathleen Short; marr. diss.; one *d*. *Educ:* Manchester Univ. (BA Hons Econ; MA Econs). Chm., Bear Healthfood Co-operative, 1985–. Mem. (Lab), Calderdale MBC, 1991–99 (Council Leader, 1995–99); Dep. Chair, Regl Assembly for Yorks and Humber, 1997–99; Yorks Rep., Cttee of the Regions in Europe, 1997–99; Dep. Chair, Countryside Agency, 1999–2006; Chair, Forestry Commn, 2010–12. Member, Board: Yorks Forward RDA, 1996–99; Natural England, 2006–10; Chm., Outta Place Ltd, 2012–14; Chm. and Mem. Bd, Handmade Parade Ltd, 2016–17. Chair: Calderdale NHS Trust, 1998–2000; Yorks Reg., RSA, 2011–. Hon. Fellow: Landscape Inst. 2012; Leeds Sustainability Inst. 2012. Ashoka Fellow, 2018. *Recreations:* cooking, travelling, dog walking. *Address:* 21 Mons Road, Todmorden, Lancs OL14 8EF. *T:* (01706) 819803. *E:* pamwarhurst@gmail.com.

**WARING, Sir (Alfred) Holburt**, 3rd Bt *cr* 1935; *b* 2 Aug. 1933; *s* of Sir Alfred Harold Waring, 2nd Bt, and Winifred (*d* 1992), *d* of late Albert Boston, Stockton-on-Tees; *S* father, 1981; *m* 1958, Ana, (Anita), *d* of late Valentin Medinilla, Madrid; one *s* two *d*. *Educ:* Rossall School; Leeds College of Commerce. Director: SRM Plastics Ltd; Waring Investments Ltd; Property Realisation Co. Ltd. *Recreations:* golf, squash, swimming. *Heir: s* Michael Holburt Waring, *b* 3 Jan. 1964. *Club:* Moor Park Golf (Rickmansworth).

**WARK, Prof. David Lee**, PhD; FRS 2007; FInstP; Professor in Experimental Particle Physics, University of Oxford; former Director, Particle Physics Department, STFC Rutherford Appleton Laboratory; Fellow, Balliol College, Oxford; *b* 8 June 1958; *s* of William L. Wark and Maxine V. Wark; *m* 1988, Sally Annette Martinez; one *s* one *d*. *Educ:* Indiana Univ. (BSc Physics 1980); California Inst. of Technol. (MS Physics 1982; PhD 1987). FInstP 2003. Postdoctoral Fellow, Los Alamos Nat. Lab., 1987–89; Res. Officer, 1990–92, Lectr in Phys, 1992–99, Oxford Univ.; Fellow, Balliol Coll., Oxford, 1992–99; Prof. of Phys, Univ. of Sussex and Rutherford Appleton Lab., 1999–2003; Prof. of Phys, Imperial Coll. London and Rutherford Appleton Lab., 2004. PPARC Lectr-Fellow, 1996–99. Chm., High Energy and Particle Phys Div., Eur. Phys. Soc., 2005–07. Rutherford Prize, Inst. of Phys, 2003. *Publications:* over 100 articles in learned jls. *Recreations:* reading, cooking, juggling, ski-ing, playing guitar (badly) and blues harp (worse). *Address:* Department of Physics, University of Oxford, Denys Wilkinson Building, Keble Road, Oxford OX1 3RH.

**WARK, Kirsty Anne**; journalist and television presenter, since 1976; *b* 3 Feb. 1955; *d* of James Allan Wark and Roberta Eason Forrest; *m* 1990, Alan Clements; one *s* one *d*. *Educ:* Wellington Sch., Ayr; Edinburgh Univ. (BA 1976). Joined BBC, 1976: radio then TV producer, politics and current affairs progs, 1977–90; formed independent prodn co., Wark Clements & Co. Ltd, with husband, 1990; Presenter: The Late Show, and Edinburgh Nights, 1990–93; Newsnight, Review Show (formerly Newsnight Rev.) and Newsnight Specials, 1993–; One Foot In The Past, 1993–2000; Words With Wark, 1995–99; Building a Nation, 1998; Gen. Elections, Scottish Gen. Elections and Referendum, and Rough Justice, 1998–; The Kirsty Wark Show, 1999–2001; Tales from Europe, 2004; Tales from Spain, 2005; The Book Quiz, 2008–09; A Question of Genius, 2009, 2010; The Review Show, 2010–; The Home Movie Road Show, 2010; A Question of Taste, 2012; The Man Who Collected the World: William Burrell, 2013; Kirsty Wark Meets Donna Tartt, 2013; Blurred Lines: the new battle of the sexes, 2014; The Summer Exhibition: BBC Arts at the Royal Academy, 2014–; Scotland's Art Revolution: The Maverick Generation, 2014; Our World: kidnapped for a decade, 2015; Edinburgh Nights, BBC2, 2015, 2016; BBC TV Proms, 2015; Walks with My Dog, 2017; The Menopause and Me, 2017; The Many Primes of Muriel Spark, 2018; series of interviews for BBC2 and BBC4, 2002–; finalist, Celebrity MasterChef, 2011; cameo role in films, Absolutely Fabulous: the movie, 2016, Carnage, 2016. Judge, Nat. Portrait of Year, 2017. Patron: Scottish Blind Golf Soc., 2000–; Maggie's Centre, 2001–; Cambodia Trust, 2001–; Crichton Foundn, 2001–; RIAS, 2001–; Ambassador: Nat. AIDS Trust, 2000–; The Prince's Trust, 2004– (Mem. Council, 2000–04). FRSE 2017. Hon. FRIAS 2000; Hon. FRIBA 2001. Hon. DLitt Abertay, 1995; Dr *hc* Edinburgh, 2000; Hon. LLD Aberdeen, 2001. Scotland Journalist of Year, 1993, Scotland Presenter of Year, 1997, Outstanding Contribn to Broadcasting, 2013, BAFTA Scotland; Scot of the Year, Scotland on Sunday, 1998; Richard Dimbleby Award for Best Presenter, Factual, Features and News, BAFTA, 2000. *Publications:* Restless Nation, 1997; The Legacy of Elizabeth Pringle (novel), 2014; The House by the Loch (novel), 2019. *Recreations:* reading, tennis, beachcombing, architecture, cooking, film, music. *Address:* c/o Black Pepper Media Ltd, PO Box 26323, Ayr KA7 9AY. *T:* (0141) 404 6355. *E:* info@blackpeppermedia.com.

**WARKE, Gary James**, MBE 2013; Education Specialist, Ministry of Education, United Arab Emirates, since 2018; *b* Coleraine, NI, 11 July 1967; *s* of William and Mary Warke; *m* 1997, Carol Ann Hawthorn; one *s* two *d*. *Educ:* Coleraine Academical Instn; Univ. of Ulster (BA Hons Eur. Business Studies; PGCE Econs and Business Studies); Univ. of Leeds (MEd). Lectr, Northampton Coll., 1993–97; Hd of Dept, Joseph Priestly Coll., Leeds, 1997–2000; Dir of Learning, Halton Coll., 2000–04; Dep. Chief Exec., Hull Coll., 2005–13; CEO, Hull Coll. Gp, 2013–17. Mem. Bd, Quality Assce Agency for Higher Educn, 2012–17. Dir, Humber LEP Ltd, 2013–17. *Recreations:* cycling, theatre, keyboard, travel, family.

**WARKE, Rt Rev. Robert Alexander**; Bishop of Cork, Cloyne and Ross, 1988–98; *b* 10 July 1930; *s* of Alexander and Annie Warke; *m* 1964, Eileen Charlotte Janet Minna Skillen; two *d*. *Educ:* Mountmellick National School; The King's Hospital; Trinity Coll., Dublin (BA 1952, BD 1960); Union Theol Seminary, New York (Dip. in Ecumenical Studies). Ordained, 1953; Curate: St Mark's, Newtownards, 1953–55; St Catherine's, Dublin, 1956–59; Rathfarnham, Dublin, 1959–64; Rector: Dunlavin, Hollywood and Ballymore-Eustace, 1964–67; Drumcondra, North Strand and St Barnabas, 1967–71; Zion, Dublin, 1971–88; Archdeacon of Dublin, 1980–88. *Publications:* St Nicholas Church and Parish, 1967; Light at Evening Time, 1986; The Passion according to St Matthew, 1990; Ripples in the Pool, 1993; In Search of the Living God, 2000; On Being a Bishop, 2004; In Focus, 2015. *Recreations:* following sport, theatre, reading. *Address:* 6 Kerdiff Park, Naas, Co. Kildare, Ireland.

**WARKENTIN, Juliet**; Chief Marketing Officer, Trouva, since 2019; *b* 10 May 1961; *d* of John and Germaine Warkentin; *m* 1991, Andrew Lamb (marr. diss.). *Educ:* Univ. of Toronto (BA History). Editor: Toronto Life Fashion Magazine, 1989–91; Drapers Record Magazine, 1993–96; Marie Claire, 1996–98; Man. Dir, Mktg and Internet Develt, Arcadia Gp plc, 1998–2000; Partner, The Fourth Room, 2000–02; Editl Dir, Redwood, 2002–07; Content Dir, WGSN, 2007–11; Co-founder and Chief Creative Officer, StylistPick.com, 2011–13; Dir, Brand and Creative, 2014–16, Marketing Dir, 2016–18, Amazon Fashion EU. FRSA 2004. National Magazine Award, Canada, 1990; PPA Business Editor of the Year, 1995. *Address:* 71A Regents Park Road, NW1 8UY.

**WARLOW, Prof. Charles Picton**, MD; FRCP, FRCPE, FRCPGlas, FMedSci; FRSE; Professor of Medical Neurology, 1987–2008, now Emeritus, and Hon. Consultant Neurologist, University of Edinburgh, since 1987; *b* 29 Sept. 1943; *s* of Charles Edward Picton Warlow and Nancy Mary McLennan (*née* Hine); *m* (marr. diss.); two *s* one *d*; partner, Cathie Sudlow; one *s* one *d*. *Educ:* Haileybury and Imperial Service Coll.; Sidney Sussex Coll., Cambridge (BA 1st Cl. Hons 1965; MB BChir with Dist. in Medicine 1968; MD 1975); St George's Hosp. Med. Sch. FRCP 1983; FRCPE 1987; FRCPGlas 1993; FRSE 2006. Clinical Reader in Neurology and Hon. Consultant Neurologist, Univ. of Oxford, 1977–86; Fellow, Green Coll., Oxford, 1979–86; Head, Dept of Clinical Neuroscis, Univ. of Edinburgh, 1990–93 and 1995–98. Pres., Assoc. of British Neurologists, 2001–03. Ed., Practical Neurology, 2001. Founder FMedSci 1998. *Publications:* Handbook of Clinical Neurology, 1991; (with G. J. Hankey) Transient Ischaemic Attacks of the Brain and Eye, 1994; (jtly) Stroke: a practical guide to management, 1996, 3rd edn 2008; (ed) Lancet Handbook of Treatment in Neurology, 2006. *Recreations:* sailing, photography, mountains, theatre.

**WARMAN, Matthew**; MP (C) Boston and Skegness, since 2015; Parliamentary Under-Secretary of State, Department for Digital, Culture, Media and Sport, since 2019; *b* Enfield, London, 1 Sept. 1981; *m* 2008, Dr Rachel Weaver. *Educ:* Haberdashers' Aske's Boys' Sch.; Univ. of Durham (BA Hons English Lit. 2004). The Telegraph: writer, 1999–2009; Consumer Technol. Ed., 2008–13; Technol. Ed. (Hd of Technol.), 2013–15. An Asst Govt Whip, 2019. *Recreations:* eating and consequential exercise. *Address:* House of Commons, SW1A 0AA. *T:* (020) 7219 8643. *E:* matt.warman.mp@parliament.uk.

**WARMINGTON, Sir Rupert (Marshall)**, 6th Bt *cr* 1908, of Pembridge Square, Royal Borough of Kensington; Chief Operating Officer, Neptune Networks Ltd, since 2019; *b* 17 June 1969; *s* of Sir David Marshall Warmington, 5th Bt and Susan Mary Warmington; *S* father, 2005; *m* 2002, Joanne Emma Mewse; two *s*. *Educ:* Charterhouse; Exeter Univ. (BA Hons). Dir, Fixed Income Dept, ABN AMRO, 1999–2004; Man. Dir, Tradeweb, 2004–17; Hd, Fixed Income Sales, Swiss Exchange, 2017–19. *Recreations:* golf, tennis, riding, cricket. *Heir: s* Oliver Charles Warmington, *b* 23 Oct. 2004.

**WARNE, (Ernest) John (David)**, CB 1982; Secretary, Institute of Chartered Accountants in England and Wales, 1982–90; *b* 4 Dec. 1926; *m* 1st, 1953, Rena Wolfe (*d* 1995); three *s*; 2nd, 1997, Irena Zajac. *Educ:* Univ. of London (BA (Hons)). Civil Service Commission, 1953; Asst Comr and Principal, Civil Service Commn, 1958; BoT, later DTI and Dept of Industry: Principal, 1962; Asst Sec., 1967; Under-Sec., 1972; Dir for Scotland, 1972–75; Under-Secretary: Personnel Div., 1975–77; Industrial and Commercial Policy Div., 1977–79; Dep. Sec., Dep Dir-Gen., OFT, 1979–82. *Recreations:* reading, collecting prints, languages. *Address:* 4 Priest Row, Wells, Somerset BA5 2PY. *T:* (01749) 674271.

**WARNE, (Frederick) John (Alford)**, CB 2000; Staff Counsellor, Serious Organised Crime Agency, 2007–13; *b* 7 March 1944; *m* 1st, 1967 (marr. diss. 1979); two *s*; 2nd, 2002, Elaine Carol Smith. *Educ:* Liskeard Grammar Sch., Cornwall. Home Office: Pvte Sec. to Minister of State, 1966–69; Principal, 1974–83; Asst Sec., 1984–93; Under-Sec., Police Dept, 1993–95; Dir, Organised Crime, 1996–98; Dir Gen., Organised Crime, Drugs and Internat. Gp, 1998–2002; Actg Perm. Sec., 2001–02, retd. Staff Counsellor, Security and Intelligence Agencies, 2004–09. Trustee, East Looe Town Trust, 2009– (Chm., 2011–17). *Recreations:* sport, gardening, walking, spending time with grandchildren, exploring Cornwall. *Address:* Glendower, Dawes Lane, Looe, Cornwall PL13 1JE.

**WARNER**, family name of **Baron Warner**.

**WARNER**, Baron *cr* 1998 (Life Peer), of Brockley in the London Borough of Lewisham; **Norman Reginald Warner**; PC 2006; *b* 8 Sept. 1940; *s* of Albert Henry Edwin Warner and Laura Warner; *m* 1961, Anne Lesley Lawrence (marr. diss. 1981); one *s* one *d*; *m* 1990, Suzanne Elizabeth Reeve (see S. E. Warner); one *s*. *Educ:* Dulwich College; University of California, Berkeley (MPH). Min. of Health, 1959; Asst Private Sec. to Minister of Health, 1967–68, to Sec. of State for Social Services, 1968–69; Executive Councils Div., DHSS, 1969–71; Harkness Fellowship, USA, 1971–73; NHS Reorganisation, DHSS, 1973–74; Principal Private Sec. to Sec. of State for Social Services, 1974–76; Supplementary Benefits Div., 1976–78; Management Services, DHSS, 1979–81; Regional Controller, Wales and S Western Region, DHSS, 1981–83; Gwilym Gibbon Fellow, Nuffield Coll., Oxford, 1983–84; Under Sec., Supplementary Benefits Div., DHSS, 1984–85; Dir of Social Services, Kent CC, 1985–91; Man. Dir, Warner Consultancy and Trng Services Ltd, 1991–97. Children's Social Care Comr, Birmingham CC, 2014–15. Advr to Govt on family policy and related matters, 1998–2001. Parly Under-Sec. of State, 2003–05, Minister of State, 2005–06, DoH. Mem., H of L Select Cttee on Sci. and Technol., 2007–12, on Adoption Legislation, 2012–13; Member, Joint Select Committee: on Draft Care and Support Bill, 2012–13; on Draft Modern Slavery Bill, 2013–14; on NHS Sustainability, 2016–17. Mem., Ind. Commn on Funding of Care and Support, 2010–11. Sen. Fellow in European Social Welfare and Chm., European Inst. of Social Services, Univ. of Kent, 1991–97. Chairman: City and E London FHSA, 1991–94; London Sports Bd, Sport England, 2003. Mem., Local Govt Commn, 1995–96. Chm., Expert Panel for UK Harkness Fellowships, 1994–97. Chairman: Nat. Inquiry into Selection, Develt and Management of Staff in Children's Homes, 1991–92 (report, Choosing with Care, 1992); Govt Task Force on Youth Justice, 1997–98; Youth Justice Bd for Eng. and Wales, 1998–2003; Provider Develt Agency, NHS London, 2007–09. Mem. Nat. Mgt Cttee, Carers Nat. Assoc., 1991–94. Trustee: Leonard Cheshire Foundn, 1994–96; MacIntyre Care, 1994–97; Royal Philanthropic Soc., 1992–99 (Chm., 1993–98); Chairman: Residential Forum, 1994–97; Include, 2000–01; NCVO, 2001–03. *Publications:* (ed) Commissioning Community Alternatives in European Social and Health Care, 1993; A Suitable Case for Treatment: the NHS and reform, 2011; Solving the NHS Care and Cash Crisis, 2014. *Recreations:* reading, cinema, theatre, exercise, travel. *Address:* House of Lords, SW1A 0PW.

**WARNER, Lady**; *see* Warner, S. E.

**WARNER, Prof. David Allan**, CBE 2009; FLSW; Senior Provost, University of Wales Trinity St David, 2012–14, now Emeritus Professor; Deputy Director; Oxford Centre for Higher Education Policy Studies, since 2001; Senior Research Fellow, Harris Manchester College, Oxford, 2013–14; *b* Coventry, 19 Sept. 1947; *s* of Raymond and Cecily Warner; partner, Prof. Ann Edworthy; one *d*. *Educ:* King Henry VIII Sch., Coventry; Warwick Univ. (BA 1970; MA 1971). Trainee quantity surveyor, 1965–67, sch. teacher, 1967, Coventry CC; Admin. Asst and Tutor, Univ. of Warwick, 1971–74; Sen. Admin. Asst, UEA, 1974–75; Asst Registrar, then Sen. Asst Registrar and Tutor, subseq. Sen. Lectr, Univ. of Warwick, 1975–85; Pro-Vice-Chancellor, UCE, 1985–98; Vice-Chancellor, Swansea Inst. Higher Educn, then Swansea Metropolitan Univ., 1998–2012. Commng Ed., Managing Univs and Colls book series, 1997–. FLSW 2013. *Publications:* An Educational Market Survey of Taiwan, 1988; (jtly) The Income Generation Handbook, 1992, 2nd edn 1997; How to Manage a Merger... or Avoid One, 1998; co-editor: Visual and Corporate Identity, 1989; Managing Educational Property, 1993; Human Resource Management in Higher and Further Education, 1995; Higher Education Management: the key elements, 1996; Higher Education and the Law: a guide for managers, 1998; The

State of UK Higher Education: managing change and diversity, 2001; Higher Education Law, 2002; Managing Crisis, 2003; (with Prof. A. Edworthy) Managing Stress for Carers and their Families, 2015. *Recreations:* reading, particularly ancient history, my family. *E:* davidwarner1909@gmail.com.

**WARNER, Deborah,** CBE 2006; free-lance theatre and opera director, since 1980; *b* 12 May 1959; *d* of Ruth and Roger Warner. *Educ:* Sidcot Sch., Avon; St Clare's Coll., Oxford; Central Sch. of Speech and Drama. Founder, 1980, and Artistic Dir, 1980–86, Kick Theatre Co.; Resident Dir, RSC, 1987–89; Associate Dir, Royal Nat. Theatre, 1989–98. *Productions:* Kick Theatre Co.: The Good Person of Szechwan, 1980; Woyzeck, 1981, 1982; The Tempest, 1983; Measure for Measure, 1984; King Lear, 1985; Coriolanus, 1986; Royal Shakespeare Co.: Titus Andronicus, 1987 (Laurence Olivier and Evening Standard Awards for Best Dir); King John, Electra, 1988; Electra (also in Paris), 1991; Royal National Theatre: The Good Person of Sichuan, 1989; King Lear, 1990; Richard II, 1995 (filmed, 1997); The Diary of One Who Vanished (also ENO), 1999; The PowerBook, 2002–03; Happy Days, European and USA tour, 2007–08; Mother Courage and Her Children, 2009; other productions: Wozzeck, Opera North, 1993 and 1996; Coriolan, Salzburg Fest., 1993 and 1994; Hedda Gabler, Abbey Theatre, Dublin, and Playhouse, 1991 (Laurence Olivier Award for Best Dir and Best Prodn); Don Giovanni, Glyndebourne Festival Opera, 1994 and 1995 (also Channel 4); Footfalls, Garrick, 1994; The Waste Land, Brussels, Dublin, Paris, Toronto, Montreal, NY, Cork, London, Adelaide, Brighton, Bergen, Perth, 1995–99 (televised, 1995); Une Maison de Poupée, Paris, 1996; The Turn of the Screw, Royal Opera, 1997; Bobigny (S Bank Arts Award; Evening Standard Award), 1998; Tower Project (London Internat. Fest. of Theatre), 1999; St John Passion, ENO, 2000; Medea, Abbey Th., Dublin, 2000, Queen's, 2001, USA tour and NY, 2002–03; The Angel Project, Perth Internat. Arts Festival, 2000 and NY, 2003; Fidelio, Glyndebourne, 2001, Châtelet, Paris, 2002, revived Glyndebourne, 2006; The Rape of Lucrece, Munich, 2004; Julius Caesar, Barbican, 2005; Dido and Aeneas, Vienna, 2006; La Voix Humaine, Opera North, 2006; Death in Venice, ENO, 2007, La Monnaie, Brussels, 2009, ENO, 2013; Messiah, ENO, 2009; The Waste Land, Wilton's Music Hall, 2009, Madrid Fest., 2010; Eugene Onegin, ENO, 2011; The Testament of Mary, NY 2013, Barbican, 2014; Between Worlds, ENO, Barbican, 2015; Der Sturm, Salzburg Fest., 2016; King Lear, Old Vic, 2016; Billy Budd, Teatro Real, Madrid, 2016, ROH, 2019; Le Testament de Marie, Comédie Française, Paris, 2016. *Film:* The Last September, 2000. Commandeur de l'Ordre des Arts et des Lettres (France), 2014 (Chevalier, 1992; Officier, 2000). *Recreation:* travelling. *Address:* c/o Askonas Holt, 15 Fetter Lane, EC4A 1BW. *T:* (020) 7400 1700; c/o The Agency, 24 Pottery Lane, Holland Park, W11 4LZ. *T:* (020) 7727 1346.

**WARNER, Edmond William,** OBE 2012; Chair, Palace for Life Foundation, since 2017; *b* Farnborough, Kent, 17 Aug. 1963; *s* of William John Warner and Kathleen Elizabeth Warner (*née* Rooke-Matthews); *m* 1988, Katharine Louise Wright; two *d*. *Educ:* St Olave's Grammar Sch., Orpington; Worcester Coll., Oxford (BA Hons PPE). Fund Manager, GT Management, 1985–87; Strategy Unit, UBS Phillips & Drew, 1987–89; Sen. Investment Dir, Thornton Management, 1989–91; Hd, Pan European Res., Baring Securities, 1991–93; Hd, Strategy and Econs, and Hd, Global Res., Dresdner Kleinwort Benson, 1993–97; Man. Dir, Natwest Markets, then BT Alex.Brown, 1997–99; Chief Executive: Old Mutual Securities, 1999–2001; Old Mutual Financial Services, 2001–03; IFX Gp, 2003–06; Chairman: Cantos Communications, 2007–10; LMAX, 2009–; Panmure Gordon, 2010–16 (non-exec. Dir, 2009–16); Standard Life Eur. Private Equity Trust, 2013–18 (non-exec. Dir, 2008–18); Air Partner, 2019–. Non-executive Director: Clarkson plc, 2008–19; Grant Thornton UK LLP, 2010– (Chm., 2016–); SafeCharge Internat. Gp, 2014–16. Chm., UK Athletics, 2007–17. *Publications:* Sport Inc.: why money is the winner in the business of sport, 2018. *Recreation:* running with the Fittleworth Flyers.

**WARNER, Francis (Robert Le Plastrier),** DLitt; poet and dramatist; Emeritus Fellow, St Peter's College, Oxford, since 1999; Hon. Fellow, St Catharine's College, Cambridge, since 1999; *b* Bishopthorpe, Yorks, 21 Oct. 1937; *s* of Rev. Hugh Compton Warner and Nancy Le Plastrier (*née* Owen); *m* 1st, 1958, Mary Hall (marr. diss. 1972); two *d*; 2nd, 1983, Penelope Anne Davis; one *s* one *d*. *Educ:* Christ's Hosp.; London Coll. of Music; St Catharine's Coll., Cambridge (Choral Exhibitioner; BA, MA); DLitt Oxon 2002. Supervisor in English, St Catharine's Coll., Cambridge, 1959–65; Staff Tutor in English, Cambridge Univ. Bd of Extra-Mural Studies, 1963–65; Oxford University: Fellow and Tutor, 1965–99, Fellow Librarian, 1966–76, Dean of Degrees, 1984–2006, and Vice-Master, 1987–89, St Peter's Coll.; University Lectr (CUF), 1966–99; Pro-Proctor, 1989–90, 1996–97, 1999–2000; Chm., Examiners, English Hon. Mods, 1993. Founder, Elgar Centenary Choir and Orch., 1957; cond. Honegger's King David, King's Coll. Chapel, 1958. Blitz Requiem perf. by Bach Choir and RPO (music by D. Goode), St Paul's Cath., 2013. Co-curator, Bacon/Moore: Flesh and Bone, Ashmolean Mus., 2013, Art Gall. of Ont, 2014. Foreign Academician, Acad. de Letras e Artes, Portugal, 1993. Hon. DMus William Jewell Coll., USA, 2012. Messing Internat. Award for distinguished contribs to Literature, 1972. Benemeriti Silver Medal, Kts of St George, Constantinian Order (Italy), 1990. *Publications:* poetry: Perennia, 1962; Early Poems, 1964; Experimental Sonnets, 1965; Madrigals, 1967; The Poetry of Francis Warner, USA 1970; Lucca Quartet, 1975; Morning Vespers, 1980; Spring Harvest, 1981; Epithalamium, 1983; Collected Poems 1960–84, 1985; Nightingales: poems 1985–96, 1997; Cambridge: a poem, 2001; Oxford: a poem, 2002; By the Cam and the Isis, 2005; with D. Goode: Blitz Requiem, 2013; Six Anthems and Other Compositions, 2014; Eight Sonnets—A Song Cycle, 2016; Christmas Cantata: a Legend's Carol, 2017; Four Songs of Time's Return, 2017; Anthem for Easter Day, 2019; prose: Beauty for Ashes: selected prose, 2012, 2nd edn 2013; plays: Maquettes, a trilogy of one-act plays, 1972; Requiem: Pt 1, Lying Figures, 1972, Pt 2, Killing Time, 1976, Pt 3, Meeting Ends, 1974; A Conception of Love, 1978; Light Shadows, 1980; Moving Reflections, 1983; Living Creation, 1985; Healing Nature: the Athens of Pericles, 1988; Byzantium, 1990; Virgil and Caesar, 1993; Agora: an epic, 1994; King Francis 1st, 1995; Goethe's Weimar, 1997; Rembrandt's Mirror, 2000; *edited:* Eleven Poems by Edmund Blunden, 1965; Garland, 1968; Studies in the Arts, 1968; *relevant publications:* by G. Pursglove: Francis Warner and Tradition, 1981; Francis Warner's Poetry: a critical assessment, 1988. *Recreations:* grandchildren, cathedral music, travel. *Address:* St Peter's College, Oxford OX1 2DL. *T:* (01865) 278900; St Catharine's College, Cambridge CB2 1RL. *T:* (01223) 338300. *Club:* Athenæum.

**WARNER, Sir Gerald (Chierici),** KCMG 1995 (CMG 1984); HM Diplomatic Service, retired; Intelligence Co-ordinator, Cabinet Office, 1991–96; *b* 27 Sept. 1931; *s* of Howard Warner and Elizabeth (*née* Chierici); *m* 1st, 1956, Mary Wynne Davies (*d* 1998), DMath, Prof., City Univ.; one *s* two *d*; 2nd, 2000, Catherine Mary Humphrey. *Educ:* St Peter's Coll., Oxford (BA; Hon. Fellow, 2017). 2 Lieut, Green Howards, 1949–50; Flight Lt, RAFVR, 1950–56. Joined HM Diplomatic Service, 1954; 3rd Sec., Peking, 1956–58; 2nd Sec., Rangoon, 1960–61; 1st Sec., Warsaw, 1964–66, Geneva, 1966–68; Counsellor, Kuala Lumpur, 1974–76; FCO, 1976–90, Asst Chief, SIS, 1987–90, retd. Mem., Police Complaints Authy, 1990–91. Mem., Adv. Bd, Tavistock Inst., 1998–; Chairman: Glos Council for Drugs and Alcohol, 1997–2009; Independence Trust, 2009–14; Trustee, Lifting the Blues Trust, 2015–. *Address:* c/o Coutts & Co., 440 Strand, WC2R 0QS.

**WARNER, Graeme Christopher;** Sheriff of Grampian, Highland and Islands, 1992–98; Part-time Sheriff, 2001–15 (Temporary Sheriff, 1985–91); *b* 20 Oct. 1948; *s* of Richard James Lewis Warner and Jean McDonald McIntyre or Warner; *m* 1st, 1976, Rachel Kidd Gear (marr. diss. 1994); one *s* one *d*; 2nd, 1996, Jean Raeburn. *Educ:* Belmont House, Glasgow; Strathallan, by Perth; Edinburgh Univ. (LLB). NP, WS. Law Apprentice, 1969–71; Law Assistant, 1971–72; Partner: Boyd, Janson & Young, WS, Leith, 1972–76; Ross Harper & Murphy, WS, Edinburgh, 1976–88; Macbeth, Currie & Co., WS, Edinburgh, 1989–91, Consultant, 1999–2000. Member: Parole Bd for Scotland, 2003–04; Mental Health Tribunal for Scotland, 2013–. Mem., Lothian Health Bd, 2012–15. *Recreation:* staying alive! *Address:* 6 Mortonhall Road, Edinburgh EH9 2HW. *T:* (0131) 668 2437.

**WARNER, Jeremy;** Columnist, since 2009, and Associate Editor, since 2013, The Daily Telegraph (Assistant Editor, 2009–13); *b* 23 Sept. 1955; *s* of Jonathan and Marigold Warner; *m* 1988, Henrietta Jane Franklin; one *s* two *d*. *Educ:* Magdalen Coll. Sch., Oxford; University Coll. London (BA 1st cl. Hons Hist. 1977). Reporter, The Scotsman, 1979–83; Business Correspondent: The Times, 1983–86; The Independent, 1986–91; City Editor, The Independent on Sunday, 1991–94; Business and City Editor, The Independent, 1994–2009. Specialist Writer of the Year, British Press Awards, 1990; Financial Journalist of the Year, Wincott Foundn, 1992; Special Award for outstanding contribn in defence of freedom of the press, Assoc. of British Editors, 1997. *Address:* The Daily Telegraph, 111 Buckingham Palace Road, SW1W 0DT. *T:* (020) 7931 2000.

**WARNER, Jocelyn;** textile designer, since 1986; *b* 16 April 1963; *d* of Brian and Jackie Warner; *m* 1993, Simon Bore; one *s*. *Educ:* Lewes Priory Sch.; Brighton Poly. (Foundn in Art); Camberwell Sch. of Arts and Crafts (BA Hons Textile Design); Central St Martin's Sch. of Art (MA Textile Design). Established: Jocelyn Warner Studio for printed textile design, 1986; Jocelyn Warner Ltd (contemporary wallpaper products and consultancy in surface design), 1999. Elle Decoration Award for Best in Wall Coverings, 2003. *Recreations:* looking at things, collecting bits and pieces from nature, taking photographs and scanning plants, walking, being with friends and family. *Address:* 4 The Old Dairy, Glynde, Lewes, E Sussex BN8 6SH. *W:* www.jocelynwarner.com.

**WARNER, His Honour John Charles;** a Circuit Judge, 1996–2015; Resident Judge, Wolverhampton Crown Court, 2007–15; *b* 30 Aug. 1945; *s* of late Frank Charles Warner and Kathleen Moyra Warner; *m* 1975, Kathleen Marion Robinson; one *s* one *d*. *Educ:* King Edward's Sch., Birmingham. Solicitor, 1969; Partner, Adie Evans & Warner, 1971–96; Asst Recorder, 1988–92; Recorder, 1992–96.

**WARNER, Prof. John Oliver,** OBE 2013; MD; FRCP, FRCPCH; FMedSci; Professor of Paediatrics, Imperial College London, since 2006; *b* 19 July 1945; *s* of Henry Paul Warner and Ursula Mina Warner; *m* 1st, 1968, Wendy Margaret Cole (marr. diss. 1989); one *s* two *d*; 2nd, 1990, Jill Amanda Price; two *d*. *Educ:* Sheffield Univ. Med. Sch. (MB ChB 1968; DCH 1970; MD 1979). FRCP 1986 (MRCP 1972); FRCPCH 1997. Gen. prof. trng, Children's Hosp. and Royal Hosp., Sheffield, 1968–72; Great Ormond Street Children's Hospital: Registrar, 1972–74; research, 1974–77; Sen. Registrar, 1977–79; Consultant, 1979–90, Sen. Lectr, 1979–88, Reader, 1988–90, London Cardiothoracic Inst., Brompton Hosp.; Prof. of Child Health, Univ. of Southampton, 1990–2006. NIHR Sen. Investigator, 2010–14; Early Years theme lead for NIHR Collaboration for Leadership in Applied Health Res. and Care NW London, 2013–. Hon. Prof., Univ. of Cape Town, 2014–. Pepys Lectr, 2011, Harry Morrow-Brown Lectr, 2014, British Soc. Allergy and Clin. Immunol. Pres., Academic Paediatric Assoc. of GB and Ireland, 2010–14. FMedSci 1999; Foundn FERS 2014. William Frankland Award for services to allergy, British Soc. Allergy Clin. Immunol., 2005; Lifetime Achievement Award, Eur. Respiratory Soc., 2009. *Publications:* A Colour Atlas of Paediatric Allergy, 1994; The Bronchoscope - Flexible and Rigid - in Children, 1995; (ed jtly) Textbook of Pediatric Asthma: an international perspective, 2001; over 400 papers in med. jls. *Recreations:* cricket, horse riding, polo. *Address:* The Jays, 17 Bingham Road, Winchester SO22 6GB. *Club:* MCC.

**WARNER, Keith Reginald;** freelance opera and theatre director, since 1989; *b* 6 Dec. 1956; *s* of Gordon Lawrence Warner and Sheila Ann Mary (*née* Collinson); *m* 1984, Emma Belinda Judith Besly. *Educ:* Bristol Univ. (BA Jt Hons English and Drama). Asst Dir, ENO, 1981–84; Associate Director: Scottish Opera, 1984–85; ENO, 1985–89; Associate Artistic Director, Opera Omaha, USA, 1991–94; Artistic Dir, Royal Opera, Copenhagen, 2011–12. Hon. DMus Bristol, 2017. *Recreations:* movie-going, reading, modern/contemporary art. *E:* KeithRWarner@aol.com.

**WARNER, Dame Marina (Sarah),** DBE 2015 (CBE 2008); FBA 2005; FRSL; writer and critic; Professor of English and Creative Writing, Birkbeck, University of London, 2014–17; Professor, School of Arts and Humanities, University of London, since 2014; Professorial Research Fellow, School of Oriental and African Studies, University of London, 2014–17; Associate Member, Faculty of English, University of Oxford; *b* 9 Nov. 1946; *d* of Esmond Pelham Warner and Emilia (*née* Terzulli); *m* 1st, 1971, Hon. William Shawcross, *qv*; one *s*; 2nd, 1981, John Dewe Mathews (marr. diss. 1999); 3rd, 2015, Graeme Bryce Segal, *qv*. *Educ:* Lady Margaret Hall, Oxford (MA Mod. Langs, French and Italian; Hon. Fellow, 2000). FRSL 1985. Getty Schol., Getty Centre for Hist. of Art and Humanities, Calif, 1987–88; Vis. Fellow, BFI, 1992; Whitney J. Oakes Fellow, Princeton Univ., 1996; Tinbergen Prof., Erasmus Univ., Rotterdam, 1991; Mellon Prof., Univ. of Pittsburgh, 1997; Visiting Professor: Univ. of Ulster, 1995; QMW, 1995–2008; Paris XIII, 2003; RCA, 2008–12; NYU Abu Dhabi, 2012; Distinguished Visiting Professor: Stanford Univ., 2000; NYU Abu Dhabi, 2014; Visiting Fellow: Trinity Coll., Cambridge, 1998; Humanities Res. Centre, Warwick Univ., 1999; All Souls Coll., Oxford, 2001; Hon. Res. Fellow, Birkbeck Coll., Univ. of London, 1999–2005; Prof., Dept of Lit., Drama and Visual Studies, subseq. Lit., Film and Theatre Studies, Univ. of Essex, 2004–14; Sen. Fellow, Erich Remarque Inst., NY Univ., 2006; Dist. Vis. Fellow, QMUL, 2009–12; Fellow, All Souls Coll., Oxford, 2013–15, then Quondam Fellow, Dist. Fellow, 2019–; Sen. Fellow, Italian Acad., Columbia Univ. 2013–; Vis. Schol., Center for Ballet and Arts, NY Univ., 2015; Fellow, Societas Europaea. Hon. Res. Fellow, Archive of Greek and Roman Performance, 2015; Weidenfeld Prof., Univ. of Oxford, 2016. Contributing Ed., London Rev. of Books, 2013–. Lectures: Reith, 1994; Tanner, Yale Univ., 1999; Clarendon, Oxford Univ., 2001; Robb, Auckland Univ., 2004; Beatrice Blackwood, Oxford, 2005; Sebald, UEA, 2007; Presidential, Stanford Univ., 2008; Jane Harrison, Cambridge Univ., 2008; Hussey, Oxford Univ., 2008; Graham Storey, Cambridge Univ., 2009; BIRTHA, Bristol Univ., 2009; Edward Saïd Meml, BM, 2010; Hughes, Birmingham, 2012; Freud Mus., 2012; Leconfield Italian Inst., 2012. Mem. Adv. Bd, Royal Mint, 1986–93. Member: Council, Charter 88, 1990–98; Cttee of Management, NCOPF, 1990–99 (Vice-Pres., 2000–); Adv. Council, British Liby, 1992–98; Cttee, London Liby, 1997–2000; Literature Panel, Arts Council, 1992–98; Council, Inst. of Historical Res., Univ. of London, 1999–2000; Cttee, PEN, 2001–04; Bd, NPG, 2008–; Council, British Sch. at Rome, 2008– (Vice-Pres., 2013–16). Chair, Man Booker Internat. Prize, 2015. Jt Curator, Metamorphing, Wellcome Trust exhibn at Sci. Mus., 2002–03; Curator, Only Make Believe: Ways of Playing, Compton Verney, 2004; Adv. Curator, Eyes, Lies and Illusions, Hayward Gall., 2006. Trustee: Artangel, 1997–2004; Orwell Foundn, 2004–09. President: Virgil Soc., 2004–05; British

Comparative Literature Assoc., 2010–16; RSL, 2017–. Patron: Med. Foundn for Victims of Torture, 2000–; Soc. for Story-telling, 2003–; Longford Trust, 2003–; Hosking Houses Trust, 2006–; Reprieve, 2008–; J-News, 2010–; Bloodaxe Poetry Books, 2014–. Hon. FRA 2018. Hon. DLitt: Exeter, 1995; York, 1997; St Andrews, 1998; Kent, 2005; Oxford, 2006; Leicester, 2006; KCL, 2009; Hon. Dr: Sheffield Hallam, 1995; North London, 1997; East London, 1999; RCA, 2004. British Acad. Medal, 2017. Chevalier de l'Ordre des Arts et des Lettres (France), 2000; Stella dell'Ordine della Solidarietà (Italy), 2005. Libretti: The Legs of the Queen of Sheba, 1991; In the House of Crossed Desires, 1996. Holberg Prize, 2015. *Publications:* The Dragon Empress, 1972; Alone of All Her Sex: the myth and the cult of the Virgin Mary, 1976, new edn 2013; Queen Victoria's Sketchbook, 1980; Joan of Arc: the image of female heroism, 1981, new edn 2013; Monuments and Maidens: the allegory of the female form, 1985; L'Atalante, 1993, repr. 2015; Managing Monsters: six myths of our time (Reith Lectures), 1994; From the Beast to the Blonde: on fairy tales and their tellers, 1994; The Inner Eye: art beyond the visible, 1996 (touring exhibn catalogue); No Go the Bogeyman: scaring, lulling and making mock, 1998; Fantastic Metamorphoses, Other Worlds (Clarendon Lectures), 2002; Signs and Wonders: essays on literature and culture, 2003; Phantasmagoria: spirit visions, metaphors, and media into the twenty-first century, 2006; Stranger Magic: charmed states after the Arabian Nights, 2012 (Nat. Book Critics' Circle Award, 2012; Truman Capote Award for Literary Criticism, Truman Capote Foundn, Sheykh Zayed Award, Cultural Foundn of Abu Dhabi, 2013); (ed with P. Kennedy) Scheherazade's Children: global encounters and The Arabian Nights, 2013; Once Upon a Time: a short history of fairy tale, 2014; Forms of Enchantment: writings on art and artists, 2018; Fairy Tale: a very short introduction, 2019; *fiction:* In a Dark Wood, 1977; The Skating Party, 1983; The Lost Father, 1988; Indigo, 1992; The Mermaids in the Basement, 1993; (ed) Wonder Tales, 1994; The Leto Bundle, 2001; Murderers I Have Known (short stories), 2002; Fly Away Home (short stories), 2015; *children's books:* The Impossible Day, 1981; The Impossible Night, 1981; The Impossible Bath, 1982; The Impossible Rocket, 1982; The Wobbly Tooth, 1984; *juvenile:* The Crack in the Teacup, 1979; pamphlet in Counterblasts series; short stories, arts criticism, radio and television broadcasting. *Recreations:* friends, travels, reading. *Address:* c/o David Godwin, 55 Monmouth Street, WC2H 9DG.

See also C. Shawcross.

**WARNER, Prof. Mark**, PhD; FRS 2012; Professor of Theoretical Physics, University of Cambridge, since 2001; Fellow, Corpus Christi College, Cambridge, since 1986; *b* New Zealand. *Educ:* Auckland Grammar Sch., NZ; Corpus Christi Coll., Cambridge (BA 1974); Univ. of London (PhD). Stanford Univ.; IBM Corp. EPSRC Sen. Res. Fellow, 2008–13. Hon. Fellow, Royal Soc. NZ, 2002. Maxwell Medal and Prize, Inst. of Physics, 1989; Alexander von Humboldt Res. Prize, 2000; EuroPhysics Prize, Eur. Physical Soc., 2003; Hopkins Prize, Cambridge Philosophical Soc., 2009; Colwyn Medal, IMMM, 2013; G. W. Gray Medal, British Liquid Crystal Soc., 2014. *Publications:* (ed jtly) Self Order and Form in Polymers, 1995; (ed with E. M. Terentjev) Liquid Crystal Elastomers, 2003, rev. edn 2007; (with A. Cheung) A Cavendish Quantum Mechanics Primer, 2012; articles in jls. *Address:* Department of Physics, University of Cambridge, Mott Building, Cavendish Laboratory, JJ Thomson Avenue, Cambridge CB3 0HE. *E:* mw141@cam.ac.uk.

**WARNER, Rt Rev. Martin Clive;** *see* Chichester, Bishop of.

**WARNER, Sir Philip (Courtenay Thomas)**, 4th Bt *cr* 1910, of Brettenham, Suffolk; *b* 3 April 1951; *e s* of Sir (Edward Courtenay) Henry Warner, 3rd Bt and of Jocelyn Mary, *d* of Sir Thomas Lubbock Beevor, 6th Bt; *S* father, 2011; *m* 1982, Penelope Anne Elmer; one *s* four *d*. *Educ:* Eton. Called to the Bar, Inner Temple, 1976. Dir, 1979–2013, Chm., 1993–2013, Warner Estate Hldgs PLC. *Heir:* *s* Charles Thomas Courtenay Warner, *b* 30 Sept. 1989.

**WARNER, Prof. Robert Ernest**, PhD; Vice-Chancellor, Plymouth Marjon University, since 2017; *b* Greenwich, 6 April 1956; *s* of Ernest and Joyce Warner; *m* 1978, Claire Liddell; two *s*. *Educ:* Reigate Grammar Sch.; Woking Grammar Sch.; Judd Sch., Tonbridge; Univ. of York (BA Hons English and Related Lit; MA English); Regent's Park Coll., Oxford (MA Theol.); King's Coll. London (PhD Theol. 2006). Ed., Hodder & Stoughton, 1979–83; Minister, BUGB, 1986–2003; Lectr, 2006–08, Hd of Dept, 2008–09, Univ. of Wales, Lampeter; University of Chester: Prof., 2009–17; Hd of Dept, 2009–10; Dean of Humanities, 2010–12; Exec. Dean of Humanities, 2012–17. *Publications:* Reinventing English Evangelicalism, 1996–2001, 2007; Secularization and its Discontents, 2010; (jtly) Christianity and the University Experience, 2013. *Recreations:* opera, classical music, theatre, photography, walking. *Address:* Plymouth Marjon University, Derriford, Plymouth PL6 8BH. *T:* (01752) 636700. *E:* rwarner@marjon.ac.uk.

**WARNER, Stephen Clifford; His Honour Judge Stephen Warner;** a Circuit Judge, since 2006; *b* 5 Aug. 1954; *s* of Jack and Marion; *m* 1979, Dr Amanda Craig; two *s*. *Educ:* Carmel Coll., Wallingford; St Catherine's Coll., Oxford (MA Hons). Called to the Bar, Lincoln's Inn, 1976, Bencher, 2017; in practice as barrister, 1976–2006; Asst Recorder, 1999–2000; Recorder, 2000–06. Legal Mem., First-tier Tribunal (Mental Health, Restricted Panel) (formerly Mental Health Review Tribunals (Restricted Panel)), 2009–. Trustee, Finchley Youth Music Centre, 2008– (Chair, 2018–). *Recreations:* cricket, music, walking, foreign travel. *Address:* c/o St Albans Crown Court, Bricket Road, St Albans, Herts AL1 3JW.

**WARNER, Suzanne Elizabeth, (Lady Warner)**, OBE 2006; Chairman, Botanic Gardens Conservation International, 1999–2005; *b* 12 Aug. 1942; *d* of Charles Clifford Reeder and Elizabeth Joan Armstrong Reeder; *m* 1st, 1967, Jonathan Reeve (marr. diss. 1980); one *s*; 2nd, 1990, Norman Reginald Warner (*see* Baron Warner); one *s*. *Educ:* Badminton Sch., Bristol; Univ. of Sussex (BA Hons History); Univ. of Cambridge (Dip. Criminology). Home Office Res. Unit, 1966–67; Personal Assistant to Sec. of State for Social Services, DHSS, 1968–70; Principal, DHSS, 1970–73; Central Policy Review Staff, 1973–74; Asst Sec., DHSS, 1979–85; Sec., 1985–88, Actg Chm., 1987–88, ESRC; Exec. Dir, Food from Britain, 1988–90; Chief Exec., Foundn for Educn Business Partnerships, 1990–91; Personal Advr to Dep. Chm., BT plc, 1991–93; Hd of Gp Govt Relations, 1993–96, Gp Dir of Govt Relations, 1996–97, Cable and Wireless plc; Dep. Chm., Broadcasting Standards Commn, 1998–2003. Member: Management Bd, Sci. Policy Support Unit, Royal Soc., 1991–93; Technology Foresight Steering Gp, OST, 1994–97; Council, Industry and Parlt Trust, 1994–97; Acad. Council, Wilton Park, 1995–2004 (Chm., 1999–2004); Bd, Envmt Agency, 2006–12 (Chm., Audit and Risk Cttee, 2009–12). University of Sussex: Mem. Adv. Bd, Sci. Policy Res. Unit, 1998–2007; Mem., Court, 2000–07; Vice-Chm. of Council, 2001–07. Non-executive Director: SE Thames RHA, 1993–94; S Thames RHA, 1994–96; Broadmoor Hosp. Authy, 1996–98. Trustee, April Trust, 2016–. *Recreations:* family life, cooking, gardening, reading, films.

**WARNOCK, (Alastair) Robert (Lyon); His Honour Judge Warnock;** a Circuit Judge, since 2003; *b* 23 July 1953; *s* of Alexander Nelson Lyon Warnock and Annabel Forest Lyon Warnock; *m* 1993, Sally May Tomkinson. *Educ:* Sedbergh Sch.; Univ. of East Anglia (BA History); Coll. of Law. Called to the Bar, Lincoln's Inn, 1977; Jun., Northern Circuit, 1980–81; Asst Recorder, 1996–2000, Recorder, 2000–03; Sen. Judge of the Sovereign Base Areas (Cyprus), 2012–17. Mem. Bd, Merseyside Probation Trust, 2013–15. Pres., SW Lancs Magistrates' Assoc., 2006–12. Pres., Royal Liverpool Village Play, 2000–14; Vice-Pres., Artisan Golfers' Assoc., 2002–. *Recreations:* golf, travel, food and wine, cricket. *Address:* c/o Queen Elizabeth II Combined Court Centre, Derby Square, Liverpool L2 1XA. *T:* (court) (0151) 473 7373. *E:* HHJ.Robert.Warnock@ejudiciary.net. *Clubs:* Artists' (Liverpool); Royal Liverpool Golf.

**WARNOCK, Andrew Ronald;** QC 2012; a Recorder, since 2019; *b* Magherafelt, Co. Londonderry, 31 Aug. 1970; *s* of Ronald John Warnock and Eleanor Heather Warnock (*née* Crooks); *m* 2003, Linda Clare Robb; two *s* one *d*. *Educ:* Cookstown High Sch.; Sidney Sussex Coll., Cambridge (BA 1992); Inns of Court Sch. of Law. Called to the Bar, Inner Temple, 1993, Bencher, 2017. Ind. Funding Adjudicator, 2006–16, Mem., Special Controls Rev. Panel, 2008–16, Legal Services Commn. Chm. Res., Soc. of Cons. Lawyers, 2013–16. *Publications:* (contributing ed.) Local Authority Liability, 1998, 6th edn 2015. *Recreations:* North Antrim coast, travel, scuba diving. *Address:* c/o 1 Chancery Lane, WC2A 1LF. *T:* (020) 7092 2900, *Fax:* (020) 7404 9876. *E:* awarnock@1chancerylane.com.

**WARNOCK, Robert;** *see* Warnock, A. R. L.

**WARNOCK-SMITH, Shân;** QC 2002; *b* 13 Sept. 1948; *d* of Thomas John Davies and Denise Dorothy Davies; one *s* one *d*; partner, Andrew De La Rosa. *Educ:* King's Coll., London (LLB Hons 1970, LLM 1972). Called to the Bar, Gray's Inn, 1971; admitted to Bar, Cayman Is, 2010; Lectr, Inns of Court Sch. of Law, 1970–72; Sen. Lectr, City of London Poly., 1972–80; in practice as barrister, specialising in trusts, estates and internat. wealth structuring, 1979–. Regular speaker and chm. at trust confs. *Publications:* contrib. articles to private client jls. *Recreations:* interior design, travel. *Address:* 5 Stone Buildings, Lincoln's Inn, WC2A 3XT. *T:* (020) 7242 6201, *Fax:* (020) 7831 8102. *E:* swarnocksmith@5sblaw.com; ICT Chambers, Grand Cayman. *T:* 9265211. *E:* sws@ictchambers.com.

**WARRELL, Prof. David Alan**, DM, DSc; FRCP, FRCPE, FMedSci; Professor of Tropical Medicine and Infectious Diseases, 1987–2006, now Emeritus, and Head, Nuffield Department of Clinical Medicine, 2002–04 (Deputy Head, 2004–06), University of Oxford; Fellow, St Cross College, Oxford, 1977–2006, Hon. Fellow, since 2007; International Director (Hans Sloane Fellow), Royal College of Physicians, 2012–16; *b* 6 Oct. 1939; *s* of late Alan and Mildred Warrell; *m* 1975, Dr Mary Jean Prentice; two *d*. *Educ:* Portsmouth Grammar Sch.; Christ Church, Oxford (MA, BCh 1964; DM 1970; DSc 1990). MRCS 1965; FRCP 1977; FRCPE 1999. Oxford Univ. Radcliffe Travelling Fellow, Univ. of Calif at San Diego, 1969–70; Sen. Lectr, Ahmadu Bello Univ., Zaria, Nigeria, 1970–74; Lectr, RPMS, London, 1974–75; Consultant Physician, Radcliffe Infirmary, Oxford, 1975–79; Founding Dir, Wellcome-Mahidol Univ. Oxford Tropical Medicine Research Programme in Bangkok, 1979–86; Founding Dir, Centre for Tropical Medicine, Univ. of Oxford, 1991–2001, now Emeritus. Hon. Clin. Dir, Alistair Reid Venom Res. Unit, Liverpool Sch. of Tropical Med., 1983–2009; Vis. Prof., Mahidol Univ., 1997–2006; Hon. Professor: Univ. Nacional Mayor de San Marcos, Lima, 2005–; of Tropical Medicine, Univ. of Medicine-1, Yangon, Myanmar, 2016–; Prof. Emeritus, Gorgas Inst., Univ. Peruana Cayetano Heredia, Lima, Peru, 2016; Adjunct Prof., Dept of Infectious Diseases, Xi'an Med. Coll., China, 2009–; Principal Fellow, Dept of Pharmacol., Univ. of Melbourne, 1997–. WHO Consultant on malaria, rabies and snake bite, 1979–; Dir, Global Snakebite Initiative, 2015–; Internat. Advr Myanmar Snakebite Mgt Project, Dept of Foreign Affairs and Trade, Australia, 2015–18. Chm., MRC's AIDS Therapeutic Trials Cttee, 1987–93; MRC's China-UK Res. Ethics Cttee, 2007–; Mem., MRC's Tropical Medicine Res. Bd, 1986–89; Advr to MRC on tropical medicine, 2001–06; Mem., FCO Pro Bono Medical Panel, 2002–. Hon. Consultant Malariologist to the Army, 1989–2018; Hon. Medical Adviser: RGS, 1993–2018; Earthwatch Internat., 2008–12; Health Advr, Hamish Ogston Foundn, 2018–. Pres., Internat. Fedn of Tropical Medicine, 1996–2000; Pres., RSTM&H, 1997–99. Delegate, OUP, 1999–2006. RCP Lectures: Marc Daniels, 1977; Bradshaw, 1989; Croonian, 1996; College, 1999; Harveian Oration, 2001; Lloyd-Roberts Lectr, RSocMed, 2004. FRGS 1989. Founder FMedSci 1998. Hon. Member: Assoc. Physicians of GB & Ireland, 2003; Amer. Soc. of Tropical Medicine and Hygiene, 2003; Instituto de Medicina Tropical Alexander von Humboldt, Universidad Peruana Cayetano Heredia, Lima, 2010. Hon. Fellow: Ceylon Coll. of Physicians, 1985; Royal Thai Coll. of Physicians, 2013; W African Coll. of Physicians, 2015; Coll. of Physicians and Surgeons, Mumbai, 2016; Hon. Fellow (Conservation), Zool Soc., 2009. Chalmers Medal, RSTM&H, 1981; Ambuj Nath Bose Prize, RCP, 1994; Busk Medal, RGS, 2003; Guthrie Medal, RAMC, 2004; Mary Kingsley Centenary Medal, Liverpool Sch. of Tropical Medicine, 2005; Osler Meml Medal, Univ. of Oxford, 2010; Redi Award, Internat. Soc. of Toxinology, 2012. Companion, Order of White Elephant (Thailand), 2004. *Publications:* Rabies—the Facts, 1977, 2nd edn 1986; (ed) Oxford Textbook of Medicine, 1983, 5th edn 2010; (ed) Essential Malariology, 3rd edn 1993 to 5th edn 2009; Expedition Medicine, 1998, 2nd edn 2002; Oxford Handbook of Expedition and Wilderness Medicine, 2008, 2nd edn 2015; (ed) Oxford Textbook of Medicine: infection, 2012; chapters in textbooks of medicine and herpetology; papers in learned jls (Lancet, New England Jl of Medicine, etc) on respiratory physiology, malaria, rabies, infectious diseases and snake bite. *Recreations:* book collecting, music, bird watching, hill walking. *Address:* University of Oxford, Nuffield Department of Clinical Medicine, John Radcliffe Hospital, Headington, Oxford OX3 9DU. *T:* (01865) 234664, *Fax:* (01865) 760683. *E:* david.warrell@ndm.ox.ac.uk.

**WARRELL, David Watson**, MD; FRCOG; urological gynaecologist, 1969–94; Chairman, Mid-Cheshire Hospitals NHS Trust, 1994–97; *b* 20 June 1929; *s* of late Charles Warrell and Sarah (*née* Gill); *m* 1955, Valerie Jean Fairclough; one *s* one *d*. *Educ:* Sheffield Univ. MB ChB 1953; MD 1964; FRCOG 1970. Sen. Lectr and Hon. Consultant Obstetrician and Gynaecologist, Jessop Hosp. for Women, 1965–69; St Mary's Hosp., Manchester, 1969–94: established Dept of Urological Gynaecology; Med. Dir, 1991–92, Chief Exec., 1992–94, Central Manchester Health Care Trust. Blair Bell Travelling Fellowship, 1967. *Publications:* chapters and papers on urinary control in women. *Address:* 36 Glenhills Court, Little Glen Road, Glen Parva, Leicester LE2 9DH.

**WARREN, Very Rev. Alan Christopher;** Provost of Leicester, 1978–92, now Provost Emeritus; *b* 27 June 1932; *s* of Arthur Henry and Gwendoline Catherine Warren; *m* 1957, Sylvia Mary (*née* Matthews); three *d*. *Educ:* Dulwich College; Corpus Christi Coll., Cambridge (Exhibnr, MA); Ridley Hall, Cambridge. Curate, St Paul's, Margate, 1957–59; Curate, St Andrew Plymouth, 1959–62; Chaplain of Kelly College, Tavistock, 1962–64; Vicar of Holy Apostles, Leicester, 1964–72; Coventry Diocesan Missioner, 1972–78; Hon. Canon, Coventry Cathedral, 1972–78; Proctor in Convocation, 1977–78, 1980–85. Mem., Cathedral Statutes Commn, 1981–85. Trustee, St Martin's, Birmingham, 1981–2011. Chm., Leicester Council of Christians and Jews, 1985–92; President: Leicester Council of Churches, 1985–92; Leicester Civic Soc., 1983–92. Tutor, Adult Educn, Norfolk, 1993–99; Dir of Music, W Norfolk Choral Soc., 1993–2000. Chm., Hunstanton Arts Fest. Cttee, 1994–99; Founder and Mem., Brancaster Music Fest., 2001–14. Mem., MCC, 1960–76. Pres., Alleyn Club, 1991–92 (Vice-Pres., 1990–91). *Publications:* Putting it Across, 1975; The Miserable Warren, 1991; Amazing Graces, 2012; Bits and Pieces, 2016; articles on church music, evangelism and sport in Church Times and other journals; *compositions:*

Incarnatus for Organ, 1960; Piano Sonata, 1996. *Recreations:* music, golf, steam trains. *Address:* 9 Queens Drive, Hunstanton, Norfolk PE36 6EY. *T:* (01485) 534533. *Clubs:* Free Foresters; Hunstanton Golf.
*See also R. H. C. Warren.*

**WARREN, Prof. Alan John,** PhD; FRCP, FRCPath; FMedSci; Professor of Haematology, University of Cambridge, since 2003; Honorary Consultant Haematologist, Cambridge University Hospitals NHS Foundation Trust (formerly Addenbrooke's NHS Trust), since 1997; *b* 22 Nov. 1961; *s* of John Rundle Warren and Marion Wallace Warren; *m* 1989, Nina Louise Johnman; one *s* one *d. Educ:* Univ. of Glasgow (BSc Hons (Biochem.) 1983; MB ChB 1986); Gonville and Caius Coll., Cambridge (PhD (Molecular Biol.) 1995). MRCP 1989, FRCP 2002; MRCPath (Haematol.) 1997, FRCPath (Haematol.) 2005. House officer posts, medicine and surgery, Royal Infirmary, Glasgow, 1986–87; Sen. House Officer, Western Infirmary Med. Rotation, Glasgow, 1987–89; Registrar in Haematol., Hammersmith and Ealing Hosps, London, 1989–91; MRC Laboratory of Molecular Biology, Cambridge: MRC Trng Fellow, 1991–94; MRC Clinician Scientist and Hon. Sen. Registrar, 1994–95; MRC Clinician Scientist, 1997–2000, and Hon. Consultant Haematologist, 1997–2003; MRC Sen. Clinical Fellow, 2000–03; Sen. Registrar in Haematol., Addenbrooke's Hosp., Cambridge, 1995–97. FMedSci 2005. *Publications:* articles of research in peer-reviewed primary scientific jls. *Recreations:* avid camellia collector, cycling. *Address:* Cambridge Institute for Medical Research, University of Cambridge, Cambridge Biomedical Campus, Wellcome-MRC Building, Hills Road, Cambridge CB2 0XY. *T:* (01223) 748488, *Fax:* (01223) 213556. *E:* ajw1000@cam.ac.uk.

**WARREN, Catherine;** *see* Graham-Harrison, C.

**WARREN, Rt Rev. Cecil Allan;** Rector, Old Brampton and Loundsley Green, 1983–88; Assistant Bishop, Diocese of Derby, 1983–88; *b* 25 Feb. 1924; *s* of Charles Henry and Eliza Warren; *m* 1947, Doreen Muriel Burrows. *Educ:* Sydney Univ. (BA 1950); Queen's Coll., Oxford (MA 1959). Deacon 1950, priest 1951, Dio. of Canberra and Goulburn; appointments in Diocese of Oxford, 1953–57; Canberra, 1957–63; Organising Sec. Church Society, and Director of Forward in Faith Movement, Dio. of Canberra and Goulburn, 1963–65; Asst Bishop of Canberra and Goulburn, 1965–72; Bishop of Canberra and Goulburn, 1972–83. *Publications:* A Little Foolishness: an autobiographical history, 1993. *Address:* Symesthorpe, 69 Stenner Street, Toowoomba, Qld 4350, Australia.

**WARREN, Sir David (Alexander),** KCMG 2012 (CMG 2007); HM Diplomatic Service, retired; Ambassador to Japan, 2008–12; Director, Aberdeen Japan Investment Trust, since 2015; *b* 11 Aug. 1952; *s* of late Alister Charles Warren and Celia Warren (*née* Golding); *m* 1992, Pamela, *d* of late Benjamin Ivan Pritchard and Violet Pritchard (*née* Sherman). *Educ:* Epsom Coll.; Exeter Coll., Oxford (MA English; Hon. Fellow, 2012; Pres., Oxford Union Soc., 1973). Entered HM Diplomatic Service, 1975; FCO, 1975–77; Third, later Second, then First Sec., Tokyo, 1977–81; FCO, 1981–87; First Sec. and Hd of Chancery, Nairobi, 1987–90; FCO, 1990–91; on secondment as Hd, Internat. Div., Sci. and Technol. Secretariat, later OST, then OPSS, Cabinet Office, 1991–93; Counsellor (Commercial), Tokyo, 1993–98; Hd, Hong Kong Dept, later China Hong Kong Dept, FCO, 1998–2000; Dir, Trade Partners UK, British Trade Internat., subseq. UK Trade and Investment, 2000–04; Dir, HR, FCO, 2004–07. Sen. Advr, Montrose Associates, 2014–. Vis. Prof., 2013–19, Hon. Prof., Sch. of E Asian Studies, 2019–, Sheffield Univ.; Vis. Prof., De Montfort Univ., 2013–14; Associate Fellow, RIIA, 2014–. Member: UK/Japan 21st Century Gp, 2013– (Dir, 2016–); Bd, Sainsbury Inst. for Study of Japanese Arts and Cultures, 2013–. Mem., 2013–, Chair, 2014–, Council, Univ. of Kent at Canterbury. Member, Advisory Council: LSO, 2013–; Migration Matters Trust, 2013–. Chair, Japan Soc., 2013–19. Trustee, Oxford Literary and Debating Union Trust, 2014–. Hon. DLitt: Sheffield, 2011; De Montfort, 2013. Grand Cordon, Order of the Rising Sun (Japan), 2018. *Publications:* contrib. articles to newspapers and jls. *Recreations:* books, jazz singing. *E:* David.Warren@japansociety.org.uk. *Club:* Oxford and Cambridge.

**WARREN, Frank John;** Chief Executive Officer, Sports Network Europe, since 1996; *b* London, 28 Feb. 1952; *s* of Frank and Iris Warren; *m* 1983, Susan Margaret Cox; four *s* two *d. Educ:* Highbury Co. Grammar Sch. Sport and boxing promoter and manager, 1978–; clients have included Nigel Benn, Frank Bruno, Chris Eubank, Mike Tyson, Ricky Hatton, Naseem Hamed, Joe Calzaghe and Amir Khan. Promoter, Frank Sinatra in London. Chm., Bedford RFC, 1996–99. Former Chm., London Arena. Founder and Dir, BoxNation TV, 2011–. *Recreations:* music, reading, art, sport. *Address:* Ground Floor, Turnford Place, Great Cambridge Road, Turnford, Herts EN10 6NH. *T:* (01992) 505550, *Fax:* (01992) 505552. *Club:* Royal Automobile.

**WARREN, Sir (Frederick) Miles,** ONZ 1995; KBE 1985 (CBE 1974); FNZIA; ARIBA; Senior Partner, Warren & Mahoney, Architects Ltd, 1958–94; *b* Christchurch, 10 May 1929. *Educ:* Christ's Coll., Christchurch; Auckland Univ. DipArch; ARIBA 1952; FNZIA 1965. Founded Warren & Mahoney, 1958. Award-winning designs include: Christchurch Town Hall and Civic Centre; NZ Chancery, Washington; Canterbury Public Library; Michael Fowler Centre, Wellington; St Patrick's Church, Napier; Ohinetahi, Governors Bay; Rotorua Dist Council Civic Offices; Mulholland Hse, Wanganui; Parkroyal Hotel, Christchurch. Pres., Canterbury Soc. of Arts, 1972–76. Gold Medal, NZIA, 1960, 1964, 1969, 1973; Nat. Awards, NZIA, 1980, 1981, 1983–86, 1988, 1989, 1990, 1991. *Publications:* Warren & Mahoney Architects, 1990; Miles Warren: an autobiography, 2008; Ohinetahi, 2014. *Recreation:* making a garden.

**WARREN, Prof. Graham Barry,** PhD; FRS 1999; Scientific Director, Max F. Perutz Laboratories, Vienna, 2007–17, now Professor Emeritus, University and Medical University of Vienna; Honorary Professor, MRC Laboratory for Molecular Cell Biology, University College London, since 2018; *b* 25 Feb. 1948; *s* of late Joyce Thelma and Charles Graham Thomas Warren; *m* 1966, Philippa Mary Adeline (*née* Temple-Cole); four *d. Educ:* Willesden County Grammar Sch.; Pembroke Coll., Cambridge (MA, PhD). MRC Fellow, Nat. Inst. for Med. Research, 1972–75; Royal Soc. Stothert Research Fellow, Dept of Biochemistry, Cambridge, 1975–77; Research Fellow, Gonville & Caius Coll., Cambridge, 1975–77; Group Leader then Senior Scientist, European Molecular Biology Lab., Heidelberg, 1977–85; Prof. and Hd of Dept of Biochemistry, Dundee Univ., 1985–88; Prin. Scientist, ICRF, 1989–99; Prof. of Cell Biology, Yale Univ. Med. Sch., 1999–2007. Mem., EMBO, 1986. Mem., Austrian Acad. Scis, 2011. *Publications:* papers in learned jls on cell biology. *Recreations:* city walking, photography. *Address:* MRC Laboratory for Molecular Cell Biology, University College London, Gower Street, WC1E 6BT. *E:* g.warren@ucl.ac.uk.

**WARREN, Joëlle Susan,** MBE 2016; Executive Chairman, Warren Partners Ltd, since 2010 (Managing Director, 1998–2010); Vice Lord-Lieutenant, Cheshire, since 2010; *b* Liverpool, 1 Nov. 1962; *d* of Rod and Tessa Howgate; *m* 1986, Andrew Mark Warren; two *s. Educ:* Withington Girls' Sch., Manchester; Univ. of Durham (BA Hons Econs 1984). ACIB 1987. Lloyds Bank plc: grad. trainee posts, 1984–86; Asst Manager, Corporate Banking Div., 1986–88; Manager: Stock Exchange Br., 1988–90; Portman Sq. Br., 1990–92; Trng, 1992–94; Partner, Howgate Sable, 1994–97. Bishops' Selection Advr, C of E, 2006–16. Gov. and Vice Chair, Manchester Metropolitan Univ., 2001–10. Chair: Cheshire Community Foundn, 2010–; York Crown Nominations Commn, 2019–. Non-exec. Dir, Chester Race Co., 2019–. Church Warden and Leadership Team, Christ Church Alsager, 2000–. DL Cheshire, 2010. *Recreations:* living life in all its fullness, Church, family, entertaining, ski-ing, walking, cycling. *Address:* Caledonian House, Tatton Street, Knutsford WA16 6AG. *T:* (01565) 656351, 07973 897536, *Fax:* (0845) 261 0606. *E:* jwarren@warrenpartners.co.uk.

**WARREN, John;** QC 1994; a Recorder, Midland and Oxford Circuit, 1993–2004; *b* 25 Aug. 1945; *s* of Frank Warren and Dora Warren (*née* Thomas); *m* 1968, Anne Marlor; one *s* one *d* (twins). *Educ:* Chadderton Grammar Sch., near Oldham; Univ. of Nottingham (LLB). Called to the Bar, Gray's Inn, 1968. *Recreations:* opera and classical music, supporting Nottingham Forest FC, doing The Times crossword with my wife, playing the classical guitar. *Address:* 39 Mear Drive, Borrowash, Derby DE72 3QW. *T:* (01332) 678996, 07710 214781.

**WARREN, John;** Regional Employment Judge (formerly Regional Chairman, Employment Tribunals), London South, 2003–08, fee-paid Judge, 2008–13; *b* 26 Sept. 1943; *s* of William John Warren and Phyllis Eliza Warren; one *s* one *d*. Solicitor. Pool Mem., Review Panel, Catholic Safeguarding Commn, 2009–. Mem., Surrey CC Sch. Appeals Panel. *Recreations:* walking, photography, gardening, touring by car, volunteer at RHS Wisley and Brooklands Mus.

**WARREN, (John) Robin,** AC 2007; MD; FAA; FRCPA; Pathologist, Royal Perth Hospital, 1968–99, now Emeritus Consultant Pathologist; Emeritus Professor, University of Western Australia, since 2005; *b* Adelaide, 11 June 1937; *s* of John Roger Hogarth Warren and Helen Josephine Warren (*née* Verco); *m* 1962, Winifred Teresa Williams (*d* 1998); four *s* two *d. Educ:* St Peter's Coll.; Univ. of Adelaide Sch. of Medicine (MB BS 1961; MD 2000). FRCPA 1967; FAA 2006. Jun. RMO, Queen Elizabeth Hosp., Woodville, 1961; Registrar in Haematology and Clinical Pathology, Inst. of Med. and Vet. Sci., Adelaide, 1962; Temp. Lectr in Pathology, Univ. of Adelaide, and Hon. Clinical Asst in Pathology, Royal Adelaide Hosp., 1963; Registrar in Clinical Pathology, 1964–66, in Pathology, 1966–68, Royal Melbourne Hosp. Member: AMA 1960; BMA 1960; Australian Soc. of Cytology, 1975; Internat. Acad. of Pathology, 1975. Honorary Member: Polish Soc. of Gastroenterology, 2000; German Soc. of Pathology, 2007. Hon. FRACP 2006. Hon. MD: Western Aust., 1997; Romana Studiorum, 2008; Sydney, 2012; DUniv Adelaide, 2006; Dr *hc*: Toyama, 2007; Otto-von-Guericke Universität, 2007. (Jtly) Warren Alpert Foundn Prize, Harvard Med. Sch., 1994; Western Aust. Br. Award, AMA, 1995; Dist. Fellows Award, RCPA, 1995; Medal, Univ. of Hiroshima, 1996; Paul Ehrlich and Ludwig Darmstaedter Award, Paul Ehrlich Foundn, 1997; Faulding Florey Medal, 1998; (jtly) Nobel Prize in Physiology or Medicine, 2005; Gold Medal, AMA, 2006; Western Australian of the Year, 2007; Medal of Hirosaki Univ. Sch. of Med., 2007; Distinguished Pathologist Medal, Internat. Acad. of Pathol. (Australia), 2008. *Publications:* contrib. numerous letters and articles in learned jls. *Recreations:* photography, philately, computer processing, music, sports (not active at present), rifle shooting and cycling. *Address:* 178 Lake Street, Perth, WA 6000, Australia. *T:* (8) 93289248, *Fax:* (8) 93289248. *E:* jrwarren@aapt.net.au.

**WARREN, Prof. Lynda May,** OBE 2017; PhD; FRSB; FLSW; Professor of Environmental Law, Aberystwyth University (formerly University of Wales, Aberystwyth), 1996–2003, now Emeritus; Member, Royal Commission on Environmental Pollution, 2005–11; *b* Croydon, 26 April 1950; *d* of Leonard Warren and Peggy Warren (*née* Tatnell); *m* 1986, Barry Archie Thomas; one *s. Educ:* Bedford Coll., Univ. of London (BSc 1971; PhD 1975); Univ. of London (LLB 1986 ext.); Univ. of Wales, Cardiff (MSc); Open Univ. (BA 2018). FRSB (FIBiol 1991). Senior Lecturer: in Marine Biol., Poly. of Central London, 1981–84; in Zool., Goldsmiths' Coll., London, 1984–89; Lectr, then Sen. Lectr in Law, Cardiff Law Sch., Univ. of Wales, Cardiff, 1989–95. Chairman: Salmon and Freshwater Fisheries Rev., 1998–2000; Wales Coastal and Maritime Partnership, 2007–12; Wildlife Trust of S and W Wales, 2009–15; Dep. Chm., JNCC, 2008–12; Member: Countryside Council for Wales, 1993–2003; Bd, EA, 2000–06; Cttee on Radioactive Waste Mgt, 2003–16 (Dep. Chm., 2016); Bd, British Geol Survey, 2004–11; Sci. Adv. Council, DEFRA, 2011–16; Natural Resources Wales, 2012–15; Ind. Envmtl Advr, Dŵr Cymru Welsh Water, 2012–13. Hon. Professor: Birmingham City Univ., 2010–13; Univ. of Birmingham, 2016–; Bangor Univ., 2016–. Hon. Sec., 2016–17, Chm., 2017–19, Welsh Assoc. of Churchill Fellows. FLSW 2018. Founding Editor: Law, Science and Policy (formerly Internat. Jl of Bioscience and the Law), 1996–2010; Envmtl Law Rev., 1999–2013. *Publications:* over 100 articles on law and science. *Recreations:* travel, reading, cinema, fashion. *Address:* Ynys Einion, Eglwys Fach, Machynlleth SY20 8SX. *T:* (01654) 781344, 07764 848230. *E:* lm.warren@btopenworld.com.

**WARREN, Marta Zofia;** *see* Kwiatkowska, M. Z.

**WARREN, Sir Miles;** *see* Warren, Sir F. M.

**WARREN, Nicholas John;** a Judge of the Upper Tribunal, 2010–15; *b* 24 June 1951; *s* of late Stanley and Barbara Warren; *m* 1976, Catherine Mackie; two *s* three *d. Educ:* Blessed John Rigby Grammar Sch., Wigan; St Catherine's Coll., Oxford (MA Juris.). Admitted solicitor, 1975; Solicitor: Arthur Smiths, Wigan, 1973–77; Child Poverty Action Gp, 1977–80; Family Rights Gp, 1980–81; Birkenhead Resource Unit, 1981–92; a Recorder, 1992–2010; full-time Chm., Social Security Tribunals, 1992–98, Regl Chm., 1998–2008. Pres., Gambling Appeals Tribunal, 2007–10; a Regl Tribunal Judge (Social Security), 2008–10; Pres., Gen. Regulatory Chamber of the First-tier Tribunal, 2011–15. Member: Lord Chancellor's Adv. Cttee on Legal Aid, 1992–95; Tribunal Procedure Cttee, 2008–11. Mem. Bd, Judicial Coll., 2011–15. Trustee, Cafod, 1993–2009. *Publications:* articles on social security and family law. *Recreations:* watching National Hunt racing and Tranmere Rovers FC, listening to Leonard Cohen. *Address:* 29 Grafton Street, Birkenhead CH43 4UJ. *T:* (0151) 652 2192.

**WARREN, Hon. Sir Nicholas Roger,** Kt 2005; a Judge of the High Court of Justice, Chancery Division, 2005–18; *b* 20 May 1949; *s* of Roger Warren and Muriel (*née* Reeves); *m* 1st, 1978 (marr. diss. 1989); two *s* one *d*; 2nd, 1994, Catherine Graham-Harrison, *qv. Educ:* Bryanston Sch.; University Coll., Oxford. Called to the Bar, Middle Temple, 1972, Bencher, 2001; QC 1993; a Recorder, 1999–2005; a Pres., Upper Tribunal (Tax and Chancery (formerly Finance and Tax) Chamber), 2009–15. *Recreations:* music, sailing. *E:* sir.nicholas.warren@ejudiciary.net.

**WARREN, Prof. Peter Michael,** PhD; FSA; FBA 1997; FLS; Professor of Ancient History and Classical Archaeology, 1977–2001, now Emeritus, and Senior Research Fellow, since 2001, University of Bristol; *b* 23 June 1938; *s* of Arthur George Warren and Alison Joan Warren (*née* White); *m* 1966, Elizabeth Margaret Halliday; one *s* one *d. Educ:* Sandbach Sch.; Llandovery Coll.; University College of N Wales, Bangor (Ellen Thomas Stanford Schol.; BA 1st Cl. Hons Greek and Latin); Corpus Christi Coll., Cambridge (Exhibnr; BA Classical Tripos Pt II 1962; MA 1966; PhD 1966; Fellow, 1965–68); student, British Sch. at Athens, 1963–65. FSA 1973. Research Fellow in Arts, Univ. of Durham, 1968–70; Asst Director, British Sch. at Athens, 1970–72; University of Birmingham: Lectr in Aegean

Archaeol., 1972–74; Sen. Lectr, 1974–76; Reader, 1976; Bristol University: Dean, Faculty of Arts, 1988–90; Pro-Vice-Chancellor, 1991–95; Fellow, 1995–96. Vis. Prof., Univ. of Minnesota, 1981; Geddes-Harrower Prof. of Greek Art and Archaeol., Univ. of Aberdeen, 1986–87; Neubergh Lectr, Univ. of Göteborg, 1986. Dir of excavations, Myrtos, Crete, 1967–68; Debla, Crete, 1971; Knossos, 1971–73, 1978–82, 1997. Mem., Rev. Panel, Italian Nat. Res. Council, 2009. Member: Managing Cttee, British Sch. at Athens, 1973–77, 1978–79, 1986–90, 1994–98, 1999–2004, 2006–10 (Chm., 1979–83, 2003–04; Vice-Pres., 2005–); Council, Soc. for Promotion of Hellenic Studies, 1978–81; President: Bristol Anglo-Hellenic Cultural Soc., 1987–97; Birmingham and Midlands Br., Classical Assoc., 1996–97. Bristol and Gloucestershire Archaeological Society: Vice-Chm. Council, 1980–81; Chm., 1981–84; Vice-Pres., 1989–93; Pres., 2000–01. Hon. Sec., Friends of British Sch. at Athens (UK), 2011–18. FLS 2018. Hon. Fellow: Historical, Folklore and Archaeol Soc. of Crete, 1980; Archaeol Soc. of Athens, 1987; Corresp. Fellow, Soc. for Cretan Historical Studies, 1992; Corresp. Mem., Österreichische Akad. der Wissenschaften, 1997; Internat. Hon. Mem., Amer. Acad. of Arts and Scis, 2017; For. Fellow, Onassis Public Benefit Foundn, 2007. Hon. Dr Univ. of Athens, 2000. Inst. for Aegean Prehistory Dist. Service Award, 2015. *Publications:* Minoan Stone Vases, 1969, repr. 2010; Myrtos, an Early Bronze Age Settlement in Crete, 1972; The Aegean Civilizations, 1975, 2nd edn 1989; Minoan Religion as Ritual Action, 1988; (with V. Hankey) Aegean Bronze Age Chronology, 1989; (with S. Alexiou) The Early Minoan Tombs of Lebena, Southern Crete, 2004; Ardtornish House: the architectural and decorative marbles and granite, 2012; (with G. Rethemiotakis) Knossos: a Middle Minoan III building in Bougadha Metochi, 2014; articles on Aegean Bronze Age, particularly Minoan archaeology, in archaeol, science and classical jls. *Recreations:* growing *Cistaceae* (Nat. Collection), Manchester United, history of Greek botany. *Address:* Claremont House, 5 Merlin Haven, Wotton-under-Edge, Glos GL12 7BA. *T:* (01453) 842290.

**WARREN, Peter Tolman,** CBE 1998; PhD; Executive Secretary, Royal Society, 1985–97; *b* 20 Dec. 1937; *s* of late Hugh Alan Warren and Florence Christine Warren (*née* Tolman); *m* 1961, Angela Mary (*née* Curtis); two *s* one *d*. *Educ:* Whitgift Sch., Croydon; Queens' Coll., Cambridge (MA, PhD); CGeol. Geological Survey of GB, 1962; Chief Scientific Adviser's Staff, Cabinet Office, 1972; Private Sec. to Lord Zuckerman, 1973–76; Science and Technology Secretariat, Cabinet Office, 1974–76; Safety Adviser, NERC, 1976–77; Dep. Exec. Sec., Royal Soc., 1977–85; Dir, World Humanity Action Trust, 1997–99, then Consultant, 1999–2001, Trustee, 2001–03 and Mem., Exec. Cttee, 2001–05, Stakeholder Forum for our Common Future; Adminr, Livery Schs Link, 2004–06. Founder and Chm., The Funding Exchange, 2013–15. Advr, Schs Funding Network, 2013–. Mem. Council, Parly and Scientific Cttee, 1992–2011 (Vice-Pres., 1995–97, 2001–04). Member: Council, GDST (formerly GPDST), 1989–2004; Ct of Governors and Council, Amgueddfa Cymru, Nat. Mus. of Wales (formerly Nat. Mus and Galls of Wales), 2000–06. Vice-President: Geol Soc., 1992–96; BAAS, 1997–2002; Chm., 2000–05, Vice-Pres., 2005–10, Pres., 2010–, Cambridge Soc. (Surrey Br.), later Cambridge Soc. of Surrey. Pres., Old Whitgiftian Assoc., 2008–09. Chm., Wingate Scholarships Cttee, 2005–12. Ct Asst, Co. (formerly Guild) of Educators, 2002– (Middle Warden, 2005–06; Upper Warden, 2006–07; Master, 2007–08). Editor, Monographs of Palaeontographical Soc., 1968–77. *Publications:* (ed) Geological Aspects of Development and Planning in Northern England, 1970; (co-author) Geology of the Country around Rhyl and Denbigh, 1984; papers on geology in learned jls. *Recreations:* geology, gardening. *Address:* 34 Plough Lane, Purley, Surrey CR8 3QA. *T:* (020) 8660 4087. *Club:* Athenæum.

**WARREN, Prof. Raymond Henry Charles,** MusD; Stanley Hugh Badock Professor of Music, University of Bristol, 1972–94; *b* 7 Nov. 1928; *s* of Arthur Henry Warren and Gwendoline Catherine Warren; *m* 1953, Roberta Lydia Alice Smith; three *s* one *d*. *Educ:* Bancroft's Sch.; Corpus Christi Coll., Cambridge (MA, MusD). Music Master, Woolverstone Hall Sch., 1952–55; Queen's University Belfast: Lectr in Music, 1955–66; Prof. of Composition, 1966–72; Resident Composer, Ulster Orchestra, 1967–72. Compositions incl. 3 symphonies, 3 string quartets, 6 operas and 4 song cycles. *Publications: compositions:* The Passion, 1963; String Quartet No 1, 1967; Violin Concerto, 1967; Songs of Old Age, 1971; Continuing Cities (oratorio), 1989; The Death of Orpheus (choral cantata), 2009; Cello Requiem, 2017; *book:* Opera Workshop, 1995. *Recreation:* walking. *Address:* 4 Contemporis, Merchants Road, Bristol BS8 4HB. *T:* (0117) 923 7687.
See also Very Rev. A. C. Warren.

**WARREN, Rebecca,** RA 2014; sculptor, since 1993; *b* Pinhoe, Exeter, 21 March 1965; *d* of William David Warren and Encarnación Brigida Warren (*née* Zarzalejo). *Educ:* Tunbridge Wells Girls' Grammar Sch.; West Kent Coll.; Paddington Tech. Coll.; Goldsmiths' Coll., Univ. of London (BA Hons Fine Art 1992); Chelsea Coll. of Art (MA Fine Art 1993). Artist in Residence, Ruskin Sch. of Art, Oxford Univ., 1993–94; Prof. of Painting and Sculpture, Kunstakademie, Dusseldorf, 2014–. Solo exhibitions include: Dark Passage, Kunsthalle Zurich, Zurich, 2004; Serpentine Gall., 2009; Renaissance Soc., Univ. of Chicago, 2010; Mus. Dhondt-Dhaenens, Ghent, 2012; The Living, Kunstverein München, Munich, 2013; The Main Feeling, Pas de Deux (Plaza Monument), Eagle Family Plaza, Dallas Mus. of Art, 2016; Fondation Vincent Van Gogh, Arles, 2017; Tate St Ives, 2017; Le Consortium, Dijon, 2018; Musée Delacroix, Paris, 2018; Belvedere 21, Vienna, 2020. *Publications:* Every Aspect of Bitch Magic, 2012; All That Heaven Allows, 2017. *Address:* c/o Maureen Paley, 21 Herald Street, E2 6JT.

**WARREN, Robin;** see Warren, J. R.

**WARREN, Rupert Miles;** QC 2012; *b* London, 13 Sept. 1969; *s* of George Warren and Diane Warren; *m* 2007, Emma Cawley; one *s* two *d*. *Educ:* Whitgift Sch.; Christ Church, Oxford (BA Lit.Hum. 1st). Called to the Bar, Gray's Inn, 1994; in practice as a barrister, specialising in planning law, Landmark Chambers, 1994– (Hd of Chambers, 2017–). *Publications:* (contrib. ed.) Encyclopedia of Planning Law and Practice, 2008–. *Recreations:* opera, theatre, writing, Chelsea FC. *Address:* Landmark Chambers, 180 Fleet Street, EC4A 2HG. *T:* (020) 7430 1221. *E:* rwarren@landmarkchambers.co.uk. *Club:* Travellers.

**WARREN EVANS, (John) Roger;** former lawyer and manager; Partner, Steele Evans Questors, 2014–16; *b* 11 Dec. 1935; *s* of Thomas and Mary Warren Evans; *m* 1966, Elizabeth M. James (*d* 2018); one *s* one *d*. *Educ:* Leighton Park Sch., Reading; Trinity Coll., Cambridge (BA History, 1st Cl.); London Sch. of Economics. Called to Bar, Gray's Inn, 1962. Television Interviewer, Anglia Television, 1960–61; Research Officer, Centre for Urban Studies, London, 1961; practice at Bar, 1962–69; Legal Correspondent, New Society, 1964–68; general management functions with Bovis Gp, in construction and develt, 1969–74, incl. Man. Dir, Bovis Homes Southern Ltd, 1971–74; Under-Secretary, DoE, 1975; Industrial Advr on Construction, DoE, 1975–76; Man. Dir, Barratt Develts (London), Ltd, 1977–79; Dir, Swansea Centre for Trade and Industry, 1979–85; Man. Dir, Demos Ltd, 1985–87; SavaCentre Property Develt Manager, 1987–88; Regl Property Dir, J. Sainsbury plc, 1988–94. Dir, Estates & Agency Hldgs plc, 1995–2004. Member: Welsh Consumer Council, 1992–95; Cttee, Community Selfbuild Agency, 1995–99. Mem. Bd, Assoc. of Self Employed, 1995–96. Immigration Advr, Office of Immigration Services Comr, 2005–14. Gov., Gillespie Primary Sch., Islington, 1993–96. Trustee: Inst. of Community Studies, 1975–2001; Mutual Aid Centre, 1975–2005 (Chm., 2003–05); Aquaterra Leisure, 1999–2005; Hygeia Trust, 1999–2005; Croeso Trust, 2000–05; Libri Trust, 2000–04; Mumbles Community Leisure Trust, 2003–05; Asylum Justice Trust, 2005–11, 2012–14 (Chm., 2005–11, 2012–14; Patron, 2014–); Dir and Sec., Neighbourhood Friends Mumbles Community Trust Ltd, 2016–17. Chair, Coll. of Questors, 2014–17. Member: Hackney BC, 1971–73; Mumbles Community Council, Swansea, 1999–2004; Mumbles Probus, 2015–. Sec., RBL, Mumbles, 2004–06. Convenor, Fabian Soc., Wales, 1999–2004. FCIOB 1976. Hon. Fellow, Coll. of Estate Mgt, 1982. *Recreations:* painting, writing, talking. *Address:* 23 St Peter's Road, Newton, Swansea SA3 4SB. *E:* roger@warrenevans.net.

**WARREN-GASH, Haydon Boyd;** HM Diplomatic Service, retired; Director, International Strategy, BTV, since 2015; *b* 8 Aug. 1949; *s* of late Alexis Patrick and Cynthia Warren-Gash; *m* 1973, Caroline Emma Bowring Leather; one *s* one *d*. *Educ:* Sidney Sussex Coll., Cambridge (MA Econs). Joined Foreign and Commonwealth Office, 1971; language training, SOAS, London Univ., 1972 (on secondment); Third Sec., Ankara, 1973–76; Second, subseq. First, Sec., Madrid, 1977–80; First Sec., FCO, 1980–82; Private Sec. to Minister of State, 1982–85; First Sec. (Commercial), Paris, 1985–89; Asst Head, Southern European Dept, FCO, 1989–91; Dep. High Comr, Nairobi, 1991–94; Hd, Southern European Dept, FCO, 1994–97; Ambassador to Côte d'Ivoire, to Niger, Burkina Faso and Liberia, 1997–2001; FCO, 2001–02; Ambassador to Morocco and Mauritania, 2002–05; to Columbia, 2005–08. Non-exec. Bd Mem., British and Colombian Chamber of Commerce, 2009– (Chm., 2013–17). *Recreations:* travel, opera and the arts, food and wine, nature and wildlife. *Club:* Muthaiga (Nairobi).

**WARRENDER,** family name of **Baron Bruntisfield.**

**WARRENDER, Rear Adm. William Jonathan,** CBE 2018; Flag Officer Sea Training, since 2018; *b* Firozpur, India, 28 Nov. 1968; *s* of William and Gillian Warrender; *m* 1992, Joanna Conway; two *s* one *d*. *Educ:* RN Engrg Coll. Manadon, Plymouth (BA Hons Maritime Defence Studies 1992); King's Coll. London (MA Defence Studies 2004). Joined RN, 1988; CO, HMS Cattistock, 1997–99; Principal Warfare Officer, HMS Cornwall, 2001–04; Commanding Officer: HMS Argyll, 2004–06; HMS Montrose, 2009; Comdr Sea Trng, 2009–11; CO, HMS Dauntless, 2011–12; UK Maritime Component Comdr (Bahrain), 2014–17; rcds 2018. Freeman, City of London, 2013. Officer, Legion of Merit (USA), 2017. *Recreation:* RN and Combined Services Hockey. *Address:* Flag Officer Sea Training, Grenville Block, HM Naval Base, Devonport, Plymouth PL2 2BG.

**WARRENS, Prof. Anthony Nigel,** PhD; DM; FRCP, FRCPath; PFHEA; Dean for Education, Professor of Renal and Transplantation Medicine, since 2010, and Director, Institute of Health Sciences Education, since 2012, Barts and The London School of Medicine and Dentistry, Queen Mary University of London; Hon. Consultant Physician, Barts Health NHS Trust, since 2010; *b* Glasgow, 24 Oct. 1959; *s* of Ian and Maisie Warrens; *m* 1990, Ruth Carole Burns; one *s* one *d*. *Educ:* Hutchesons' Grammar Sch., Glasgow; Univ. of Glasgow (BSc 1st Cl. Immunol. 1981); St John's Coll., Oxford (BM BCh 1984; DM 2006); Univ. of London (PhD 1996); Imperial Coll. London (Cert. Advanced Studies in Learning and Teaching 2004). MRCP 1987, FRCP 2000; FRCPath 2012. MRC Clinician Scientist Fellow, 1989–96; Post-doctoral Fellow, Massachusetts Gen. Hosp., Harvard Med. Sch., Boston, 1996–97; Imperial College London: Sen. Lectr, 1996–2006, Reader, 2006–08, Prof., 2008–10, Renal Section and Dept of Immunol., Div. of Medicine; Founding Hd, Grad. Entry MB BS prog., 2005–10; Hon. Consultant Physician, Renal Unit and Div. of Immunol., Imperial Coll. Healthcare NHS Trust (formerly Hammersmith Hosps NHS Trust), 2004–10; Dir, Clin. Immunol. Service, Hammersmith Hosp., 2011–14; Clin. Dir, Clin. Transplantation Lab., 2012–15, Clin. Dir, Educn Acad., 2013–16, Barts Health NHS Trust. Member: Human Tissue Authy, 2014–; Bd, Health Educn England N Central and E London team, 2014–16. Non-exec. Dir, Barking, Havering and Redbridge Univ. NHS Trust, 2011–13. Pres., British Transplantation Soc., 2013–15. Co-Chm. Govs, Immanuel Coll., Bushey, 2013–. PFHEA 2016 (FHEA 2007); Fellow, Eur. Bd of Surgery (Transplantation Medicine), Eur. Union of Med. Specialists, 2011. *Publications:* (jtly) Oxford Handbook of Clinical Medicine, 2nd edn 1989; (ed with R. I. Lechler) HLA in Health and Disease, 2nd edn 2000; (jtly) A Guide to the MRCP Part II Written Paper, 2nd edn 2004; contrib. peer-reviewed papers to jls incl. Blood, Jl Clin. Investigation, Amer. Jl Transplantation, Transplantation. *Recreations:* reading history, especially modern political biography, cinema, Jewish education. *Address:* Barts and The London School of Medicine and Dentistry, Garrod Building, Turner Street, E1 2AD. *T:* (020) 7882 2261. *E:* a.warrens@qmul.ac.uk. *Club:* Royal Society of Medicine.

**WARRILLOW, Timothy Daniel Gray;** Co-Founder and Chief Executive Officer, Fever-Tree plc, since 2005; *b* London, 13 Jan. 1975; *s* of Malcolm and Kate Warrillow; *m* 2002, Gemma; four *s*. *Educ:* Wellington Coll.; Newcastle Univ. Co-founder, Head Waiters, 1996–97; Account Dir, Summerfield, Wilmot Keene, advertising agency, 1997–2000; co-founder, business develt consultancy, 2000–14. *Recreations:* family, golf, squash, tennis, sailing, a very amateur foodie and cook, travels for fun and a lot for business. *Address:* Fever-Tree plc, 186–188 Shepherds Bush Road, W6 7NL. *T:* (020) 7349 4922. *Clubs:* Hurlingham, Queen's; Berkshire Golf; Beaulieu River Sailing.

**WARRINGTON, Bishop Suffragan of,** since 2018; **Rt Rev. Beverley Anne Mason;** *b* Germany; *d* of Cliff Mason and Thelma Mason. *Educ:* Trinity Coll., Bristol (BA Hons 2000). Ordained deacon, 2001, priest, 2003; Curate: St Paul's, Rusthall, 2001–02; St Margaret's, Rainham, 2002–05; Vicar, St John's, Norwood, 2005–12; Area Dean, Croydon N, 2010–12; Priest-in-charge, 2012–13, Vicar, 2013–16, All Saints, Bingley; Archdeacon of Richmond and Craven, 2016–18.

**WARRINGTON, Prof. Elizabeth Kerr,** FRS 1986; Professor of Clinical Neuropsychology, 1982–96, now Emeritus, and Hon. Consultant, since 1996, National Hospital for Neurology and Neurosurgery; *d* of late Prof. John Alfred Valentine Butler, FRS and Margaret Luis Butler; one *d*. *Educ:* University College London (BSc 1954; PhD 1960; DSc 1975; Fellow 1994). Research Fellow, Inst. of Neurology, 1956; National Hospital: Senior Clinical Psychologist, 1960; Principal Psychologist, 1962; Top Grade Clinical Psychologist, 1972–82. Dr *hc* Psicologia, Bologna, 1998; Univ. Louis Pasteur, Strasbourg, 2006; DUniv York, 1999. *Publications:* (with R. A. McCarthy) Cognitive Neuropsychology, 1990; numerous papers in neurological and psychological jls. *Recreation:* visiting granddaughters and great grandchildren. *Address:* Dementia Research Centre, Institute of Neurology, Queen Square, WC1N 3BG. *T:* (020) 3448 3291.

**WARRINGTON, Guy Murray;** HM Diplomatic Service; High Commissioner to Sierra Leone, 2016–19; *b* 23 Sept. 1963; *s* of Gordon and Vivien Warrington; *m* 2000, Karen Malia. *Educ:* London Sch. of Econs and Pol Sci. (BSc Econ). Joined FCO, 1986; Desk Officer, Central America and Mexico Dept, FCO, 1986–88; Second Secretary: Econs and Inf., Singapore, 1988–92; UKMIS to UN, NY, 1992–93; Head: Levant Section, Near East and N Africa Dept, FCO, 1993–95; Humanitarian and War Crimes Section, UN Dept, FCO, 1995–97; Specialised Agencies Section, UKMIS, Geneva, 1997–2001; Dep. Hd,

Drugs and Internat. Crime Dept, FCO, 2001–04; Minister Counsellor, Seoul, 2004–08; Consul Gen., Dubai, 2008–12; Dir, UKTI, 2012–16. *Recreations:* cricket, hillwalking, exploring. *Address:* c/o Foreign and Commonwealth Office, King Charles Street, SW1A 2AH. *Club:* Surrey County Cricket.

**WARRY, Peter Thomas,** PhD; CEng, FREng, FIET, FIMechE; FCMA; FSA; Chairman, Cobalt Health, since 2014; *b* 31 Aug. 1949; *s* of late William Vivian Warry and Pamela Warry; *m* 1981, Rosemary Furbank; one *d. Educ:* Clifton Coll.; Bristol; Merton Coll., Oxford (MA; Hon. Fellow, 2007); LLB London Univ.; Reading Univ. (PhD 2005). CEng 1979; FIET (FIEE 1995); FIMechE 1995; FCMA 1983; FREng 2006; CGMA 2012. Man. Dir, Self-Changing Gears Ltd, 1979–82; Gp Man. Dir, Aerospace Engineering plc, 1982–84; Director: Plessey Telecoms, 1986–87; Norcros plc, 1988–94; Nuclear Electric plc, 1995–96; British Energy plc, 1996–98; Chief Exec., Nuclear Electric Ltd, 1996–98. Non-executive Director: Heatherwood & Wexham Park Hosps NHS Trust, 1992–95; PTS Gp plc, 1995–98; Kier Gp plc, 1998–2004 (Chm., 2004–07); Office of the Rail Regulator, 1999–2004; Thames Water Utilities, 2001–05; River and Mercantile Gp plc, 2014–17. Chairman: Victrex plc, 1999–2008; BSS Gp plc, 2004–10 (non-exec. Dir, 1999–2003); Morrison Utility Services Gp Ltd, 2008–13; Mutual Energy (formerly Northern Ireland Energy Hldgs) Ltd, 2008–13; Keepmoat Gp (formerly Apollo Gp Hldgs Ltd), 2009–14. Chairman: PPARC, 2001–07; STFC, 2007–09. Special Advr, Prime Minister's Policy Unit, 1984–86; Mem., Deregulation Task Force, DTI, 1993–94; Chairman: Econ. Impact Gp (Warry Report), Office of Sci. and Innovation, 2006; AGR and PWR Liabilities Rev., DECC, 2014–15; Royal Mint, 2012–18. Indust. Prof., Warwick Univ., 1993–2017. Reading University: Mem. Council, 2006–11; Treas., 2009–11; Vis. Res. Fellow in Archaeology, 2011–. Mem. Council, Royal Acad. of Engrg, 2007–10. Trustee, Oxford Archaeology, 2009–. FRSA 2008; FSA 2013. Hon. DPhil Gloucestershire, 2017. *Publications:* A New Direction for the Post Office, 1991; Tegulae: manufacture, typology and use in Roman Britain, 2006; contribs to Archaeology, Economics and Engineering Jl. *Recreations:* tennis, walking, archeology, history. *E:* peter.warry@merton.oxon.org.

**WARSHAW, Justin Alexander Edward;** QC 2015; *b* Paddington, 7 Oct. 1970; *s* of Clive Warshaw and Michele Warshaw (*née* Steiner); *m* 2001, Stephanie Marshall; two *d. Educ:* Christ Church, Oxford (BA 1992). Called to the Bar, Gray's Inn, 1995; in practice as a barrister, specialising in divorce, 1995–. *Address:* 1 Hare Court, Temple, EC4Y 7BE. *T:* (020) 7797 7070. *Clubs:* MCC; North Hatley (Quebec).

**WARSHEL, Prof. Arieh,** PhD; FRSC; Distinguished Professor of Chemistry and Biochemistry, University of Southern California, Los Angeles, since 2011; *b* Kibbutz Sde-Nahum, British Mandate of Palestine, 20 Nov. 1940; *m* 1966, Tamar; two *d. Educ:* Technion, Israel Inst. of Technol., Haifa (BSc Chem. *summa cum laude* 1966); Weizmann Inst. of Sci., Rehovot, Israel (MSc Chem. Physics 1967; PhD Chem. Physics 1969). FRSC 2008. Mil. Service, Israel Defense Army, 1958–62; served Six-Day War, 1967, Yom Kippur War, 1973, in rank of Captain. Res. Fellow, Dept of Chem., Harvard Univ., 1970–72; Res. Associate, 1972–73, Sen. Scientist 1973–77, Weizmann Inst. of Sci.; EMBO Vis. Scientist, MRC Lab. of Molecular Biol., Cambridge (on leave of absence), 1974–76; Asst Prof. of Chem., USC, 1976–78; Associate Prof., Weizmann Inst. of Sci., 1977–78; University of Southern California, Los Angeles: Associate Prof. of Chem., 1979–84; Prof. of Chem., 1984; Prof. of Chem. and Biochem., 1991; Mem., Norris Cancer Center, 2004. Vis. Prof., Royal Inst. of Technol., Stockholm, 2006. Alfred P. Sloan Fellow, 1978–80; EMBO Sen. Fellow, Weizmann Inst. of Sci., 1981–82. Mem., NAS, 2009. Fellow, Biophysical Soc., 2000; FAAAS 2012. Tolman Medal, Southern Calif Section, Amer. Chem. Soc., 2003; Soft Matter and Biophysical Chem. Award, RSC, 2012; (jtly) Nobel Prize in Chem., 2013; Founders' Award, Biophysical Soc., 2014. *Publications:* Computer Modeling of Chemical Reactions in Enzymes and Solutions, 1991; contribs to learned jls. *Address:* Department of Chemistry and Biochemistry, University of Southern California, Los Angeles, CA 90089–1062, USA.

**WARSI, Baroness** *cr* 2007 (Life Peer), of Dewsbury in the County of West Yorkshire; **Sayeeda Hussain Warsi;** PC 2010; *b* 1971; *m* 1st (marr. diss.); one *d*; 2nd, 2009, Iftikhar Azam. *Educ:* Birkdale High Sch.; Dewsbury Coll.; Leeds Univ. (LLB). Admitted Solicitor, 1996. Chm., Savayra Foundn UK, 2002–. Comr, Joseph Rowntree Charitable Trust Destitution Inquiry, 2007. Vice Chm., 2005–07, Chm., 2010–12, Cons. Party. Contested (C) Dewsbury, 2005. Shadow Minister for Community Cohesion and Social Action, 2007–10; Shadow Minister for Sheffield, 2007–10; Minister of State (Minister without Portfolio), 2010–12; Sen. Minister of State, FCO and DCLG (Minister for Faith and Communities), 2012–14. *Publications:* The Enemy Within: a tale of Muslim Britain, 2017. *Address:* House of Lords, SW1A 0PW.

**WARSI, Perween,** CBE 2002 (MBE 1997); Managing Director, S&A Foods Ltd, 1987–2015; *b* 10 Aug. 1956; *m* 1972, Dr Talib Warsi; two *s*. Started S&A Foods from own kitchen, 1986; founded business, 1987; entered partnership with Hughes Foods Gp, 1988; with husband, completed mgt buy-out, 1991; S&A Foods began exporting, 1995; company created 1300 jobs in inner-city Derby, achieved annual growth rate of 40–50%, and recd 31 awards, 1995–2015 (incl. Gold and Silver Awards, Grocer Food and Drink Awards). Member: Govt Adv. Cttee on Competitiveness, 1997–; Nat. Cttee, CBI, 2004–. Everywoman Ambassador, 2008–. Member: Derby Renaissance Bd, 2010–; Derby Culture Bd, 2011–. Mem., Key Supporter Gp, Women's Aid. Patron, Leics Asian Business Assoc., 2011–. Hon. MBA Derby, 1997; Hon. DBA: Internat. Mgt Centres, 1999; Coventry, 2005; Hon. LLD Nottingham, 2006. Midlands Business Woman of Year Award, 1994; RADAR People of Year Award, 1995; Woman Entrepreneur of World Award, 1996; First Woman Lifetime Achievement Award, 2005.

**WARWICK, 9th Earl of,** *cr* 1759; **Guy David Greville;** Baron Brooke 1621; Earl Brooke 1746; *b* 30 Jan. 1957; *s* of 8th Earl of Warwick and of Sarah Anne Chester Greville (*née* Beatty; now Mrs Harry Thomson Jones); *S* father, 1996; *m* 1st, 1981, Susan McKinlay Cobbold (marr. diss. 1992); one *s*; 2nd, 1996, Louisa Heenan; one *s. Educ:* Summerfields; Eton; Ecole des Roches. *Recreation:* golf. *Heir: s* Lord Brooke, *qv. Club:* White's.

**WARWICK OF UNDERCLIFFE, Baroness** *cr* 1999 (Life Peer), of Undercliffe in the county of West Yorkshire; **Diana Warwick;** Chairman, National Housing Federation, since 2015; *b* 16 July 1945; *d* of Jack and Olive Warwick; *m* 1969. *Educ:* St Joseph's Coll., Bradford; Bedford Coll., Univ. of London (BA Hons). Technical Asst to the Gen. Sec., NUT, 1969–72; Asst Sec., CPSA, 1972–83; Gen. Sec., AUT, 1983–92; Chief Executive: Westminster Foundn for Democracy, 1992–95; Universities UK (formerly Cttee of Vice Chancellors and Principals), 1995–2009; Chm., Human Tissue Authy, 2010–14. Chm. Council, Property Ombudsman, 2017–. Member: Bd, Lattice plc, 2000–02; Mgt Bd, USS, 2001–09; Pension Protection Fund, 2011–. Mem., Cttee on Standards in Public Life, 1994–2000. Member: Bd, British Council, 1985–95; Employment Appeal Tribunal, 1987–99; Exec. and Council, Industrial Soc., 1987–2001; TUC Gen. Council, 1989–92; Council, Duke of Edinburgh's Seventh Commonwealth Study Conf., 1991; Chm., VSO, 1994–2003. Chm., Internat. Students' Hse, 2005–17. Gov., Commonwealth Inst., 1988–95. Trustee: Royal Anniversary Trust, 1991–93; St Catharine Foundn, Windsor, 1996–2008. Mem. and Vice Chm. Council, UCL, 2010–17; Mem. Council, Nottingham Trent Univ., 2014–. FRSA 1984. Hon. DLitt Bradford, 1993; DUniv Open, 1998; Hon. DSSc Royal Holloway, London, 2006; Hon. DPhil London Metropolitan, 2009; Hon. DEd Brunel, 2010. *Recreations:* theatre, opera, looking at pictures. *Address:* House of Lords, SW1A 0PW.

**WARWICK, Bishop Suffragan of,** since 2005; **Rt Rev. John Ronald Angus Stroyan;** *b* 5 May 1955; *s* of His Honour Ronald Angus Ropner Stroyan; *m* 1990, Mary (*née* Ferguson); two *d. Educ:* St Andrews Univ. (MTh 1976); Queen's Coll., Birmingham; Ecumenical Inst., Geneva; MA (Dist.) Univ. of Wales, 2007. Ordained deacon, 1983, priest, 1984; Curate, Coventry E Team, St Peter's, Hillfields, 1983–87; Vicar: St Matthew with St Chad, Smethwick, 1987–94; Bloxham with Milcombe and S Newington, 1994–2005; Area Dean, Deddington, 2002–05. Chm., Coventry Council of Churches, 1986–87. Mem., Rural Bishops' Panel, 2009. Pres., Community of Cross of Nails (UK), 2007–19. Mem., Internat. Commn for Anglican Orthodox Theol Dialogue, 2009–17. Co-Moderator, Coventry and Warwickshire Churches Together, 2009–12; Co-Chair, Reuilly Contact Gp, 2013–. Pres., Assoc. for Promoting Retreats, 2017–. *Publications:* Turned by Divine Love: starting again with God and with others, 2019; contribs to Credo in The Times; contribs to jls incl. The Way, Meditation Jl. *Recreations:* travel, walking, fishing, writing, the arts. *Address:* Warwick House, School Hill, Offchurch, Leamington Spa CV33 9AL. *T:* (01926) 427465. *E:* Bishop.Warwick@CovCofE.org.

**WARWICK, Archdeacon of;** no new appointment at time of going to press.

**WARWICK, Dawn Lesley;** Director, Children's Services, Wandsworth Borough Council, 2016–18; *b* Leeds; *d* of Geoffrey Warwick and June Warwick; *m* 1991, Colin Livingstone; one *s* one *d. Educ:* Univ. of Nottingham (BA Hons 1981; MA 1983; CQSW 1983); Kingston Business Sch. (DMS 1991). Social Worker, 1983–86, Sen. Social Worker, 1986–88, Leicestershire CC; Principal Officer (Mental Health), 1988–91, Sen. Manager, 1991–94, Hounslow LBC; Asst Dir, 1994–97, Dep. Dir, Social Services, Hillingdon LBC, 1997–2001; Dir, Social Services, 2001–07, Dep. Chief Exec., 2005–07, Slough BC; Dir, Adult Social Services, then Educn and Social Services, Wandsworth LBC, 2007–16. Asst Hon. Sec. and Trustee, ADSS, 2003–07; Asst Hon. Sec. and Trustee, 2007–, Co-Chm., Older People's Network, 2008–, ADASS. *Recreations:* gym, theatre, running, horse riding.

**WARWICK, Hannah Cambell Grant;** see Gordon, H. C. G.

**WARWICK, Kenneth Scott;** economics consultant; Director of Analysis, Department for Business, Innovation and Skills, 2009–11; *b* 23 April 1955; *s* of John Warwick and Mary Orr Warwick (*née* Osborne); *m* 1978, Susan Eileen Finch; one *s* one *d. Educ:* Christ's Coll., Cambridge (BA Hons 1976); Yale Univ. (MPhil 1982). Economist, MAFF, 1976–84; Econ. Advr, FCO, 1984–89; Economist, IMF, 1989–92; Senior Economic Adviser: FCO, 1992–96; DTI, 1996–2003; Dep. Chief Econ. Advr, DTI, then BERR, later BIS, 2003–09; Actg Dir Gen. Econs, BIS, 2010. Mem., Regulatory Policy Cttee, 2012–18. *Recreations:* golf, music, family history. *T:* 07823 535316. *E:* kenwarwick@btinternet.com. *Club:* West Byfleet Golf.

**WARWICK, Prof. Kevin,** PhD; FIET; Deputy Vice-Chancellor (Research), Coventry University, 2014–16, now Emeritus Professor; Professor of Cybernetics, University of Reading, 1988–2014, now Emeritus; *b* 9 Feb. 1954; *s* of Stanley and Jessie Allcock; *née* Kevin Warwick Allcock; adopted Warwick as surname by Deed Poll, 1974; *m* 1st, 1974, Sylvia Margaret Walsh (marr. diss. 1991); one *s* one *d*; 2nd, 1991, Irena Vorackova. *Educ:* Lawrence Sheriff Sch., Rugby; Aston Univ. (BSc); Imperial Coll., London (PhD 1982; DIC 1982); DSc (Eng) London 1993. FIET (FIEE 1987). British Telecom Apprentice, 1970–76; Res. Asst, Imperial Coll., London, 1982; Lectr, Newcastle upon Tyne Univ., 1982–85; Res. Lectr, Oxford Univ., 1985–87; Sen Lectr, Warwick Univ., 1987–88. FCGI 1992. Presenter, Royal Instn Christmas Lectures, 2000. Hon. Mem., Acad. of Scis, St Petersburg, 1999. DSc Czech Acad. of Scis, 1994; Hon. DSc: Aston, 2008; Coventry, 2008; Bradford, 2010; Bedfordshire, 2012; Portsmouth, 2012; Kingston, 2014; Skopje, 2015; Hon. DTech: Robert Gordon, 2011; Edinburgh Napier, 2015. Future of Health Technol. Award, MIT, 2000; Achievement Award, IEE, 2004; Mountbatten Medal, IET, 2008; Ellison-Cliffe Medal, RSocMed, 2011. *Publications:* (ed jtly) Neural Nets for Control and Systems, 1992; March of the Machines, 1997; In the Mind of the Machine, 1998; QI: The Quest for Intelligence, 2000; I, Cyborg, 2002; Artificial Intelligence: the basics, 2011; Turing's Imitation Game, 2016; contribs to books and jls on control, robotics, machine intelligence and cyborgs. *Recreations:* soccer (Viktoria Zizkov FC supporter), travel, theatre. *Address:* c/o Coventry University, Priory Street, Coventry CV1 5FB. *T:* (024) 7765 9893.

**WARWICK, Mark Granville;** QC 2013; *b* London, 11 Dec. 1951; *s* of Roy John Warwick and Marjorie Sylvia Warwick; *m* (marr. diss.); two *d. Educ:* Bexley Grammar Sch.; Univ. of Leeds (LLB Hons). Called to the Bar, Inner Temple, 1974; in private practice as a barrister, specialising in real property, 1975–; Hd, Selborne Chambers, 2015–. *Publications:* (jtly) Warwick and Trompeter on Break Clauses, 2011, 2nd edn 2016; contrib. to various legal jls. *Recreations:* foreign travel, running, walking. *Address:* Selborne Chambers, 10 Essex Street, WC2R 3AA. *T:* (020) 7420 9500, *Fax:* (020) 7420 9555. *E:* mark.warwick@selbornechambers.co.uk.

**WARWICK, Nicola Jane;** see Rushton, N. J.

**WASHINGTON, Denzel;** actor; *b* Mt Vernon, NY, 28 Dec. 1954; *s* of late Denzel Washington and of Lennis Washington; *m* 1983, Pauletta Pearson; two *s* two *d* (incl. twin *s* and *d). Educ:* Oakland Acad., New Windsor, NY; Fordham Univ. (BA 1977). American Conservatory Theater, San Francisco. *Theatre includes:* Coriolanus, 1979; Spell No 7; The Mighty Gents; One Tiger to a Hill; Ceremonies in Dark Old Men; When the Chickens Come Home to Roost, 1981; A Soldier's Play, 1981; Checkmates, 1988; Split Second; Richard III, 1990; Fences (Tony Award), 2010; A Raisin in the Sun, 2014; The Iceman Cometh, 2018; *films include:* Carbon Copy, 1981; A Soldier's Story, 1984; Power, 1986; Cry Freedom, 1987; For Queen and Country, The Mighty Quinn, Glory (Best Supporting Actor, Acad. Awards, 1990), 1989; Heart Condition, Love Supreme, Mo' Better Blues, 1990; Ricochet, 1991; Mississippi Masala, Malcolm X, 1992; Much Ado About Nothing, 1993; The Pelican Brief, Philadelphia, 1994; Crimson Tide, Virtuosity, Devil in a Blue Dress, 1995; Courage Under Fire, 1996; The Preacher's Wife, 1997; Fallen, He Got Game, 1998; The Siege, 1999; The Bone Collector, The Hurricane (Best Actor, Golden Globe Awards), 2000; Remember the Titans, 2001; Training Day (Best Actor, Acad. Awards), 2002; The Manchurian Candidate, Man on Fire, 2004; Inside Man, Déjà Vu, 2006; American Gangster, 2007; The Taking of Pelham 123, 2009; The Book of Eli, Unstoppable, 2010; Safe House, 2012; Flight, 2 Guns, 2013; The Equalizer, 2014; The Magnificent Seven, 2016; Fences (also dir), 2017; Roman J. Israel, Esq., The Equalizer 2, 2018; *director:* Antwone Fisher, 2002; *television includes:* Wilma, 1977; Flesh and Blood, 1979; St Elsewhere (series), 1982–88; License to Kill, 1984; The George McKenna Story, 1986.

**WASHINGTON, Neville James Cameron,** OBE 1992; Founder and Director, Washington Consulting, since 2010; *b* 8 May 1948; *s* of Peter Washington and Sybil Joan Washington (*née* Cameron); *m* 1980, Jennifer Anne Frideswide Kekewich; two *s* one *d. Educ:* Marlborough Coll.; Trinity Hall, Cambridge (MA). Research on chimpanzee behaviour, Gombe, Tanzania, 1969–70. Joined Queen's Own Highlanders (Seaforth & Camerons), 1971; Army Staff Coll., Camberley, 1982; jsdc 1987; comd 3rd Bn, UDR, 1987–89 (despatches); left Army in rank of Lieut-Col, 1992. Dir of Human Resources, Victoria Infirmary, Glasgow, 1992–94; Chief Exec., Coal Authy, 1994–97; Consultant, Norman Broadbent, 1998–2000; Partner, Odgers Ray & Berndtson, 2000–05; Dir, Harvey Nash Scotland, 2006–10. *Recreations:* sheep, sailing. *Address:* Rottenrow, Crosshands, by Mauchline, Ayrshire KA5 5TN.

**WASINONDH, Kitti;** Ambassador of Thailand to the Court of St James's, 2007–12; *b* 23 Nov. 1951; *m* Nutchanart; one *d*. *Educ:* Chulalongkorn Univ., Bangkok (Bachelor Pol Sci. 1974); Nat. Inst. Develt Admin, Bangkok (Master Develt Admin 1976); Univ. of Oxford (Cert. Diplomatic Studies 1981). Consul-Gen. of Thailand in Sydney, 2000–02; Director-General: Dept of ASEAN Affairs, 2003–06; Dept of Information, and Spokesman of Min. of Foreign Affairs, 2006–07. Dep. Chm., Foreign Affairs Cttee, Nat. Legislative Assembly, Thailand. Mem., Bd of Dirs, Thailand Sustainable Develt Foundn. *Recreation:* golf.

**WASS, Prof. John Andrew Hall,** MD; FRCP; Professor of Endocrinology, University of Oxford, since 1998; Fellow of Green Templeton College (formerly Green College), Oxford, 1995–2011, now Emeritus; Consultant Physician, Department of Endocrinology, Churchill Hospital, Oxford, since 1995; *b* 14 Aug. 1947; *s* of Samuel Hall Wass and June Mary Vaudine Wass (*née* Blaikie); *m* 1st, 1970, Valerie Vincent (marr. diss. 1997); one *s* one *d*; 2nd, 1998, Sally Smith. *Educ:* Rugby; Guy's Hosp. Med. Sch., Univ. of London (MB BS 1971; MD 1980). FRCP 1986. Sub-Dean, Med. Coll. and Prof. of Clin. Endocrinol., St Bartholomew's Hosp., London, 1989–95. Admissions Tutor, Green Coll., Oxford, 2001–03. Advr, Cancer Bacup, 1985–. Ed., Clin. Endocrinol. Jl, 1991–94. Linacre Fellow, 1994–98, Academic Vice-Pres., 2012–15, RCP. Chm., Soc. for Endocrinol., 2005–09; President: Eur. Fedn of Endocrine Socs, 2001–03; Pituitary Soc. (NY), 2006–07. Co-founder: Pituitary Foundn, 1994; Obesity Health Alliance (Mem., Strategy Gp, 2016). Gov., Purcell Sch., 2000–12. Chm., Bart's Choral Soc., 1992–95. Dist. Physician Award, Amer. Endocrine Soc., 2012. *Publications:* (jtly) Clinical Endocrine Oncology, 1997, 2nd edn 2008; Oxford Textbook of Endocrinology, 2002, 3rd edn 2020; Oxford Handbook of Endocrinology, 2002, 4th edn 2020; articles and chapters on acromegaly, pituitary tumours and osteoporosis. *Recreations:* music, theatre, wine, Scotland. *Address:* Department of Endocrinology, Churchill Hospital, Oxford OX3 7LJ. *T:* (01844) 358031. *E:* john.wass@nhs.net. *Club:* Garrick.

**WASS, Sasha, (Mrs N. R. A. Hall);** QC 2000; a Recorder, since 2000; *b* 19 Feb. 1958; *d* of Sir Douglas William Gretton Wass, GCB; *m* 1986, Nigel R. A. Hall; one *s* one *d*. *Educ:* Wimbledon High Sch.; Liverpool Univ. (LLB Hons). Called to the Bar: Gray's Inn, 1981, Bencher, 2003; Gibraltar, 2008; Cayman Is, 2012; Asst Recorder, 1997–2000. Criminal Bar Association: Mem. Cttee, 1992–; Treas., 1997–99; Dir of Educn, 2002. *Address:* 21 College Hill, EC4R 2RP. *T:* (020) 3301 0910.

**WASSALL, His Honour Philip Hugh;** a Circuit Judge, 2004–17; *b* 11 March 1950; *s* of late Derek William Wassall and Avril Mary Holden Wassall; *m* 1991, Julia Lesley; two *d*. *Educ:* Aldridge Grammar Sch.; Chelmsford Coll. (LLB Hons ext. London). Criminal Law Clerk, 1969–75; Articled Clerk, 1976–78; Solicitor, 1979–94; a District Judge (Magistrates' Courts) (formerly Provincial Stipendiary Magistrate, Devonshire), 1994–2004; a Recorder, 2000–04. *Recreations:* golf, music, fishing, food technology, managing teenagers, keeping fit.

**WASSERMAN,** family name of **Baron Wasserman.**

**WASSERMAN,** Baron *cr* 2011 (Life Peer), of Pimlico in the City of Westminster; **Gordon Joshua Wasserman;** *b* Montreal, 26 July 1938; *s* of late John J. Wasserman, QC, and Prof. Rachael Chait Wasserman, Montreal; *m* 1964, Cressida Frances (separated 2006), *yr d* of late Rt Hon. Hugh Gaitskell, PC, CBE, MP, and Baroness Gaitskell; two *d*. *Educ:* Westmount High Sch., Montreal; McGill Univ. (BA); New Coll., Oxford (MA). Rhodes Scholar (Quebec and New Coll.), 1959; Sen. Research Scholar, St Antony's Coll., Oxford, 1961–64; Lectr in Economics, Merton Coll., Oxford, 1963–64; Research Fellow, New Coll., Oxford, 1964–67; joined Home Office as Economic Adviser, 1967, Sen. Econ. Adviser, 1972, Asst Sec., 1977–81; Head, Urban Deprivation Unit, 1973–77; Civil Service Travelling Fellowship in USA, 1977–78; Under Sec., Central Policy Review Staff, Cabinet Office, 1981–83; Asst Under Sec. of State, Home Office (Head, Police Science and Technology Gp), 1983–95; Special Advr (Sci. and Technol.) to Police Comr, NY Police Dept, 1996–98; COS, 1998–2002, Special Advr to Police Comr, Philadelphia Police Dept, 1998–2003; Advr to HM Govt on Policing and Criminal Justice, 2010–12. Founder and Chm., Public Safety Forum, 2013–. Mem., US Justice Dept Adv. Panel on Sci. and Technol., 1996–2003; Chm., Rev., US Justice Dept Rev. of R&D post-11/11, 2005. Trustee (formerly Mem. Bd), Centre for Justice Innovation, 2013–; Trustee, YIVO UK, 2019–. Chm., Ion Track Inc., 2000–02; Chm. and CEO, Gordon Wasserman Gp LLC, 2003–; Jt Founder and Chm., Yes Please Foods GmbH, 2006–. Jt Chair, All Party Parly Gp on Basketball, 2017–. Member: Exec., ELITE Gp, 1993–96; Bd, SEARCH Gp Inc., USA, 1994–2000, 2004–07; Bd, Orchid Cellmark Inc., 2004–06; Bd, IntelliSense.io, 2017–; Chm., Hemera Data Science Ltd, 2018–. Trustee, McGill Univ. (Canada) Trust, 1995–96. Fellow, Koret Inst., USA, 1996–98. Vice-Pres., English Basket Ball Assoc., 1983–86; Chm., Basketball Foundn, 2015–. Pres., Inst. for Public Safety, Crime and Justice, Univ. of Northampton, 2014–16. *Recreations:* listening to music, reading, walking. *Address:* House of Lords, SW1A 0PW. *Clubs:* Reform, Beefsteak.

**WATANABE-O'KELLY, Prof. Helen,** FBA 2012; Professor of German, University of Oxford, since 1989; Fellow, Exeter College, Oxford, 1989–2013, now Emeritus; *b* Cork, Ireland, 2 June 1948; *d* of Michael J. O'Kelly and Claire O'Kelly (*née* O'Donovan); *m* 1st, 1975, Toshio Watanabe (marr. diss. 2003); two *d*; 2nd, 2008, Ekkehard Henschke. *Educ:* Ursuline Convent, Blackrock, Cork; University Coll., Cork (BA 1969, MA 1971, Nat. Univ. of Ireland); Univ. of Basel (Dr phil 1976). Lectr in German, Univ. of Reading, 1974–89. Founder and first Chair, Women in German Studies, 1988; Chair, RAE panel for German, Scandinavian and Dutch, 2005–08; Mem., Specialist Panel, German Excellence Initiative, 2007–13. Mem., Scientific Commn, Einstein Foundn, Berlin, 2009–. Hon. DLitt NUI, 2016. *Publications:* Melancholie und die melancholische Landschaft: Ein Beitrag zur Geistesgeschichte des 17. Jahrhunderts, 1978; Triumphal Shews: tournaments at German-speaking courts in their European context 1560–1730, 1992; The Cambridge History of German Literature, 1997; (ed with Pierre Béhar) Spectaculum Europaeum: theatre and spectacle in Europe, Histoire du Spectacle en Europe, 1580–1750, 1999; (with Anne Simon) Festivals and Ceremonies: a bibliography of works relating to court, civic and religious festivals in Europe 1500–1800, 2000; Court Culture in Dresden from Renaissance to Baroque, 2002; (jtly) Europa Triumphans: court and civic festivals in early modern Europe, 2004; (with Sarah Colvin) Women and Death: warlike women in the German literary and cultural imagination since 1500, 2009; Beauty or Beast?: the woman warrior in the German imagination from the Renaissance to the present, 2010; (ed with Adam Morton) Queens Consort, Cultural Transfer and European Politics, c. 1500–1800, 2016. *Recreations:* theatre, opera, cinema, music, walking around in Berlin. *Address:* Faculty of Modern Languages, 47 Wellington Square, Oxford OX1 2JF. *E:* helen.watanabe@mod-langs.ox.ac.uk.

**WATERFALL, Air Vice-Marshal Gary Martin,** CBE 2012 (OBE 2008); Chief of Staff (Operations), Permanent Joint Headquarters, 2016–19; *b* RAF Wegberg, Germany, 7 Jan. 1967; *s* of Eric Sydney Waterfall and Elizabeth Pamela Waterfall (*née* Rogers); *m* 1992, Yvonne Elisabeth Appleby; one *s* one *d*. *Educ:* King's Sch., Grantham. Harrier pilot, 3 (Fighter) Sqdn, 1990–94; Instructor and display pilot, Harrier OCU, 1994–96; pilot, RAF Aerobatic Team (Red Arrows), 1997–99; Harrier pilot, 1 (Fighter) Sqdn, 2000–01; OC 41 Operational Evaluation Sqdn, 2004–07; delegated release to Service Authy, 2007–09; Stn Comdr, RAF Cottesmore, 2009–11; Comdr, UK Air Component, Op. Ellamy, 2011; Air Officer, Combat, ISTAR Gp, 2012; Typhoon Force Comdr, 2013–14; AOC No 1 Gp, 2014–16. *Recreations:* cycling, private flying, travel. *Club:* Royal Air Force.

**WATERFALL, Simon,** RDI 2008; creative director; *b* Portsmouth, 1971; *s* of John and Jenny Waterfall. *Educ:* Brunel Univ. (BSc Hons); Royal Coll. of Art (MA). Co-Founder, Deepend Design, 1995–2001; Creative Director: Poke, London, 2001–09; Fray, 2010–12; Vice President and Creative Director: Intel Media, USA, 2012–14; Verizon, 2014–16. Pres., D&AD, 2007–08. Award for Interactive Design, BAFTA, 2006. *Clubs:* Shoreditch House Global; Claremont (USA).

**WATERFIELD, Prof. Michael Derek,** PhD; FRCPath, FMedSci; FRS 1991; Courtauld Professor of Biochemistry, 1991–2006, now Emeritus Professor of Biochemistry and Molecular Biology, Director of Research, 1986–2007, and Director, Proteomics Unit, 2004–07, Ludwig Institute for Cancer Research, University College London; *b* 14 May 1941; *s* of Leslie N. Waterfield and Kathleen A. (*née* Marshall); *m* 1982, Sally E. James, MB BS, PhD; two *d*. *Educ:* Brunel Univ. (BSc 1963); Univ. of London (PhD 1967). FRCPath 1994. Res. Fellow, Harvard Univ. Med. Sch., 1967–70; Sen. Res. Fellow, CIT, 1970–72; Hd, Protein Chem. Lab., ICRF Labs, 1972–86; Head, Dept of Biochem. and Molecular Biology, UCL, 1991–2001. Founder and Dir, Piramed, 2003–08. Founder FMedSci 1998. Hon. MD Ferrara, Italy 1991. *Publications:* numerous articles in scientific jls on biochem. and molecular biol. as applied to cancer research. *Recreations:* pottering about the garden and kitchen, and walking hills and dales. *Address:* Chantemerle, Speen Lane, Newbury, Berks RG14 1RJ.

**WATERFORD,** 9th Marquess of, *cr* 1789; **Henry Nicholas de la Poer Beresford;** Baron La Poer, 1375; Bt, 1668; Viscount Tyrone, Baron Beresford, 1720; Earl of Tyrone, 1746; Baron Tyrone (Great Britain), 1786; *b* 23 March 1958; *e s* of 8th Marquess of Waterford and Lady Caroline Wyndham-Quin, *yr d* of 6th Earl of Dunraven and Mount-Earl, CB, CBE, MC; *S* father, 2015; *m* 1986, Amanda, *d* of Norman Thompson; two *s* one *d*. *Educ:* Harrow School. *Heir:* s Earl of Tyrone, qv.

**WATERHOUSE, David Martin;** Regional Director for South Asia and Pacific, British Council, 1994–97; *b* 23 July 1937; *s* of Rev. John W. Waterhouse and Dr Esther Waterhouse; *m* 1966, Verena Johnson; one *s* two *d*. *Educ:* Kingswood Sch.; Bath; Merton Coll., Oxford (MA). Joined British Council, 1961; Enugu, Nigeria, 1962–65; Glasgow, 1965–68; Ndola, Zambia, 1968–71; Inst. of Educn, London Univ., 1971–72; Representative: Nepal, 1972–77; Thailand, 1977–80; Dir, Personnel Management Dept, 1980–85; Rep., Nigeria, 1985–89; Controller, Home Div., subseq. Dir, Exchanges and Training Div., British Council, 1989–91; Dir, Germany, 1991–93. Chairman: Hoffman de Visme Foundn, 1998–2002; Charles Wallace Pakistan Trust, 2007–12; Friends of Shrewsbury Mus. and Art Gall., 2007–. Vice-Pres., Royal Asiatic Soc., 2003–06. *Publications:* The Origins of Himalayan Studies: Brian Houghton Hodgson in Kathmandu and Darjeeling 1820–1858, 2004. *Recreations:* walking, music. *Address:* Courtyard Cottage, Council House Court, Shrewsbury SY1 2AU.

**WATERHOUSE, Dame Rachel (Elizabeth),** DBE 1990 (CBE 1980); PhD; Chairman, Consumers' Association, 1982–90 (Member Council, 1966–96, Deputy Chairman, 1979–82); *b* 2 Jan. 1923; *d* of Percival John Franklin and Ruby Susanna Franklin; *m* 1947, John A. H. Waterhouse; two *s* two *d*. *Educ:* King Edward's High Sch., Birmingham; St Hugh's Coll., Oxford (BA 1944, MA 1948); Univ. of Birmingham (PhD 1950). WEA and Extra-mural tutor, 1944–47. Birmingham Consumer Group: Sec., 1964–65, Chm., 1966–68, Mem. Cttee, 1968–2005; Member: Nat. Consumer Council, 1975–86; Consumers' Consultative Cttee of EEC Commn, 1977–84; Price Commn, 1977–79; Council, Advertising Standards Authority, 1980–85; NEDC, 1981–91; BBC Consultative Gp on Industrial and Business Affairs, 1984–89; Richmond Cttee on Microbiol Safety of Food, 1989–90; HSC, 1990–95; Adv. Cttee on Microbiological Safety of Food, 1991–95. Ministerial nominee to Potato Marketing Bd, 1969–81; Chm., Council for Licensed Conveyancers, 1986–89; Member: Home Office Working Party on Internal Shop Security, 1971–73; Adv. Cttee on Asbestos, 1976–79; Council for the Securities Industry, 1983–85; Securities and Investments Board, 1985–92; Organising Cttee, Marketing of Investments Bd, 1985–86; Council, Office of the Banking Ombudsman, 1985–95; Duke of Edinburgh's Inquiry into British Housing, 1984–85; Adv. Bd, Inst. of Food Res., 1988–93. Pres., Inst. of Consumer Ergonomics, Univ. of Loughborough, 1980–90 (Chm., 1970–80); Vice-President: Nat. Fedn of Consumer Gps, 1980–96; Birmingham Centre for Business Ethics, 1999–2005; Member: Council, Birmingham and Midland Inst., 1993 (Pres., 1992); Court of Govs, Univ. of Birmingham, 1992–2012; Provost, Selly Oak Colls, 1997–2000. Chm., Birmingham Gp, Victorian Soc., 1966–67, 1972–74; Vice-Chm., Lunar Soc., 1996–98 (Chm., 1990–96). Trustee: Joseph Rowntree Foundn, 1990–98; Affirming Catholicism, 1991–2001; Gov., Foundn of Lady Katherine Leveson, 2001–04. Hon. FGIA (Hon. CGIA 1988). Hon. DLitt Univ. of Technology, Loughborough, 1978; Hon. DSocSc Birmingham, 1990; Hon. DSc Aston, 1998. *Publications:* The Birmingham and Midland Institute 1854–1954, 1954; A Hundred Years of Engineering Craftsmanship, 1957; Children in Hospital: a hundred years of child care in Birmingham, 1962; (with John Whybrow) How Birmingham became a Great City, 1976; King Edward VI High School for Girls 1883–1983, 1983. *Address:* 8 Prestbury Court, Castle Rise, Prestbury, Macclesfield SK10 4UR.

**WATERHOUSE, Roger William;** Vice-Chancellor, University of Derby, 1992–2004; *b* 29 April 1940; *s* of Ronald Waterhouse and Dorthy May Waterhouse (*née* Holmes); *m* 1st, 1962, Mania Jevinsky (marr. diss.); one *s* two *d*; 2nd, 1979, Jacqueline Mary Dymond; one *s* one *d*. *Educ:* Corpus Christi Coll., Oxford (BA, MA Phil. & Psychol.). Lectr, Shoreditch Coll., 1961–62; Teacher, Kibbutz Ma'abarot, Israel, 1962–64; Hd of Econs, Myers Grove Comprehensive Sch., Sheffield, 1966–68; Asst Lectr, Lectr, Sen. Lectr and Principal Lectr, Hendon Coll. of Technol., 1968–73; Hd, Dept of Humanities and Dean of Humanities, Middx Poly., 1973–86; Dep. Dir (Acad. Planning), Wolverhampton Poly., 1986–89; Dir, Derbys Coll. of Higher Educn, 1989–92. Chairman: Derbyshire Careers Service Ltd, 1995–2001; High Peak Rural Action Zone, 2003–05. Mem., Peak Dist Artisans, 2014–. FRSA 1993. DUniv: Middlesex, 1998; Derby 2006. Name inscribed in Keren Hakayemet (Jewish Nat. Fund) Golden Book, 2004. *Publications:* A Heidegger Critique, 1981; jl articles on modern European philosophy, higher educn, credit accumulation and transfer. *Recreation:* wood-turning.

**WATERLOW, Sir Christopher Rupert,** 5th Bt *cr* 1873; Camera Supervisor, QVC, since 2014 (Senior Lighting Cameraman, 2000–14); Managing Director, Waterlow & Sons Ltd, since 2016; *b* 12 Aug. 1959; *s* of (Peter) Rupert Waterlow (*d* 1969) and Jill Elizabeth (*d* 1961), *e d* of E. T. Gourlay; *S* grandfather, 1973; *m* 2009, Shirley Patricia, *o d* of late Robert

Anderson and of Irene Anderson, Crawley. *Educ:* Stonyhurst Coll., Lancs; Ravensbourne Coll. (HND Broadcast Technical Ops, 1999). Fellow, Inst. of Videography, 2001; Mem., Guild of Television Cameramen, 2005. Mem., Standing Council of the Baronetage. *Publications:* VideoSkills: the core competencies of videography, 2008, 3rd edn 2011; The House of Waterlow: a printer's tale, 2013. *Recreations:* playing and listening to music, supporting Wasps RFC and San Francisco 49ers. *Address:* 59 Sissinghurst Close, Pound Hill, Crawley, W Sussex RH10 7FY. *Club:* Stonyhurst Association.

**WATERLOW, Sir (Thomas) James,** 5th Bt *cr* 1930, of Harrow Weald, Middlesex; *b* 20 March 1970; *o s* of Sir (James) Gerard Waterlow, 4th Bt and of Diana Suzanne Waterlow (*née* Skyrme); *S* father, 2013; *m* 1999, Theresa Walsh; two *d*. *Heir:* uncle John William Waterlow [*b* 14 Nov. 1945; *m* 1972, Camilla Dudley Farmer; two *s*].

**WATERMAN, Adrian Mark;** QC 2006; a Recorder, since 2003; *b* 24 March 1964; *s* of Brian and Pamela Waterman; *m* 1992, Dr Amanda Jones; one *s* one *d*. *Educ:* King Edward VI Sch., Stourbridge; QMC, Univ. of London (LLB Hons). Called to the Bar, Inner Temple, 1988. *Recreations:* music, movies, reading, cycling. *Address:* c/o KBW Chambers, The Engine House, 1 Foundry Square, Leeds LS11 5DL.

**WATERMAN, Dame Fanny,** DBE 2005 (CBE 2000; OBE 1971); FRCM; Chairman, Leeds International Pianoforte Competition, 1963–2015, now Life President and Founder Director Emeritus (Chairman of Jury, 1981–2015); *b* 22 March 1920; *d* of Myer Waterman and Mary Waterman (*née* Behrmann); *m* 1944, Dr Geoffrey Michael de Keyser (*d* 2001); two *s*. *Educ:* Allerton High Sch., Leeds; Tobias Matthay, Cyril Smith, Royal College of Music, London (FRCM 1972). Concert pianist, teacher of international reputation. Vice-President: European Piano-Teachers Assoc., 1975–; World Fedn of Internat. Music Competitions, 1992–2000; Trustee, Edward Boyle Meml Trust, 1981–96. Governor, Harrogate Fest., 1983–99; Vice-Pres., Harrogate Internat. Fest., 1999–. Founded (with Marion Harewood) Leeds International Pianoforte Competition, 1961. Member of International Juries: Beethoven, Vienna, 1977, 1993; Casagrande, Terni, 1978, 1994; Munich, 1979, 1986; Bach, Leipzig, 1980, 1984, 1988; Calgary, 1982; Gina Bachauer, Salt Lake City, 1982, 1984; Viña del Mar (Chm.), 1982, 1987, 1992; Maryland, 1983; Cologne, 1983, 1986, 1989, 1996; Pretoria, 1984, 1992; Santander, 1984; Rubinstein, Israel (Vice-Pres.), 1986, 1989; Tchaikowsky, Moscow, 1986; Vladigerov, Bulgaria, 1986; Lisbon, 1987, 1991; Canadian Broadcasting Corp., Toronto, 1989; first Internat. Pianoforte Competitions, China, 1994, and Korea, 1995; Casagrande, Italy, 2002; Hong Kong (Asia) Piano Open Comp., 2005 (Chm.); Clara Haskil Comp., 2005; International Piano Competitions: Horowitz, 2005; Chopin, 2005; Dublin, 2006; Hamamatsu, 2006. Piano Progress series on ITV Channel 4. Hon. MA 1966, Hon. DMus 1992, Leeds; DUniv York, 1995. Hon. Freeman, City of Leeds, 2004. Dist. Musician Award, ISM, 2000; World Fedn of Internat. Comps Lifetime Achievement Award, 2002; Yorks Soc. Lifetime Achievement Award, 2003; DFS Women of the Year Lifetime Achievement Award, 2016. *Publications:* (with Marion Harewood): series of Piano Tutors, 1967–: 1st Year Piano lessons: 1st Year Repertoire; 2nd Year Piano lessons: 2nd Year Repertoire; 3rd Year Piano lessons: 3rd Year Repertoire; Duets and Piano Playtime, 1978; Recital Book for pianists, Book 1, 1981; Sonatina and Sonata Book, 1982; Four Study Books for Piano (Playtime Studies and Progress Studies), 1986; (with Paul de Keyser) Young Violinists Repertoire books, 1–4; Fanny Waterman on Piano Playing and Performing, 1983; Music Lovers Diary, 1984–86; Merry Christmas Carols, 1986; Christmas Carol Time, 1986; Nursery Rhyme Time, 1987; Piano for Pleasure, Bks 1 and 2, 1988; Me and my Piano series, Book 1, 1988, Book 2, 1989, repertoire and duets, Books 1 and 2, 1992, superscales for the young pianist, 1995; Animal Magic, 1989; Monkey Puzzles, Books 1 and 2, 1990; (with Wendy Thompson) Piano Competition: the story of the Leeds, 1990; Young Pianist's Dictionary, 1992. *Recreations:* travel, reading, voluntary work, cooking. *Address:* Woodgarth, Oakwood Grove, Leeds LS8 2PA. *T:* (0113) 265 5771.

**WATERMAN, Peter Alan,** OBE 2005; DL; record producer; Chairman, Peter Waterman Entertainment Ltd (formerly PWL Empire), since 1983; *b* 15 Jan. 1947; *s* of John Waterman and Stella Waterman; *m* 1st, 1970, Elizabeth Reynolds (marr. diss. 1974; she *d* 2010); (one *s* decd); 2nd, 1980, Julie Reeves (marr. diss. 1984); one *s*; 3rd, 1991, Denise Gyngell (marr. diss. 2000); two *d*. *Educ:* Frederick Bird Secondary Sch. Disc jockey at local pubs and Mecca dance hall, 1961–83; arts and repertoire man for various record cos, 1973–; formed Loose Ends Prodns with Peter Collins, 1977–83; Founder Partner with M. Stock and M. Aitken, Stock Aitken Waterman, 1984–93. Judge, TV series, Pop Idol, 2000, 2003. Has produced numerous charity records. Waterman Railway Trust formed 1994. DL Cheshire, 2010. Hon. DBA Coventry, 2001; Hon. DMus Liverpool, 2004. Awards for songwriting and for records produced include: BPI Best British Producer Award, 1988; Music Week Top Producers Award, 1987, 1988 and 1989; Ivor Novello Award, 1987, 1988 and 1989. *Publications:* I Wish I Was Me: Pete Waterman (autobiog.), 2000; A Train is for Life, 2008; Just Like the Real Thing: modelling railways, 2009; Fame Factor, 2009. *Recreation:* railways: models and the real thing. *Address:* (office) Suite 5, 6 The Vineyard, SE1 1QL.

**WATEROUS, Johanna Elizabeth Martin,** CBE 2013; Senior Independent Director, RSA plc, 2014–17 (Independent Director, 2009–17); Chairman, Sandpiper CI, 2010–16; *b* Brantford, Ont, 12 Sept. 1957; *d* of Richard Norman Haan Waterous and Joan Martin Waterous; *m* 1990, Roger George Parry, *qv*; one *s*. *Educ:* Brantford Collegiate Inst.; Univ. of Western Ontario (BSc Hons Chem. and Maths 1979); Harvard Business Sch. (MBA 1985). Intelligence analyst, Royal Canadian Signal Corps, 1977–79; Res. Chemist, Dow Chemical Canada, 1979–83; Dir, Retail and Consumer Mktg Practice, McKinsey and Co., 1985–2008. Operating Partner, Duke Street LLP, 2009–16; non-exec. Dir, Wm Morrison Supermarkets plc, 2010–15; Sen. Ind. Dir, Rexam plc, 2012–16. Trustee, Royal Botanic Garden Kew, 2008–18; Mem., Commercial Bd, RHS, 2011–; Gov., Courtauld Inst. of Art, 2018–. *Recreations:* extreme gardening, reckless ski-ing, theatre, tennis. *E:* jwaterous@gmail.com. *Club:* Ocean (Bahamas).

**WATERPARK, 8th Baron** *cr* 1792 (Ire.); **Roderick, (Rory) Alexander Cavendish;** Bt 1755; airline pilot, British Airways, since 1991; *b* 10 Oct. 1959; *o s* of 7th Baron Waterpark and of Danièle Alice Cavendish (*née* Guirche); *S* father, 2013; *m* 1989, Anne, *d* of late Hon. Luke Asquith; two *s*. *Educ:* Harrow; Vassar. *Heir: s* Hon. Luke Frederick Cavendish, *b* 17 Sept. 1990. *Address:* London, SW6.

**WATERS, Alan Victor;** HM Diplomatic Service, retired; High Commissioner, Solomon Islands, 1998–2001; *b* 10 April 1942; *s* of late George and Ruth Waters; *m* 1977, Elizabeth Ann Newman; one *s* one *d*. *Educ:* Judd Sch., Tonbridge. Joined CO, 1958, CRO, 1961; Freetown, 1963–66; UKDEL to ECSC, Luxembourg, 1967–68; Prague, 1968–70; Anguilla, 1970–71; Peking, 1971–73; FCO, 1973–76; Second Secretary: Kinshasa, 1976–80; Bombay, 1980–83; FCO, 1984–86; First Secretary: FCO, 1986–87; Copenhagen, 1987–91; FCO, 1991–95; acting Adminr, Tristan da Cunha, 1995–96; First Sec., Islamabad, 1996–98. *Recreations:* walking, watching cricket.

**WATERS, Caroline Ann,** OBE 2010; Deputy Chair, Equality and Human Rights Commission, since 2013; Vice President, Carers UK, since 2013; *b* Birmingham, 21 July 1961; *d* of Thomas and Teresa Murphy; *m* 1989, Keith Waters. *Educ:* Swanshurst Sch., Birmingham; Birmingham Poly. (HNC Business Studies 1985). Joined BT, 1979, HR Dir, People & Policy, 1999–2013. Founding Dir, CW Consulting Box Ltd, 2012–; Associate, Marylebone Exec. Search, 2013–. Member, Board: UK Resource Centre for Women, 2007–12; Whole Educn, 2009–; Roffey Park Inst., 2010–; Incredibull Ltd, 2013–. Founder and Chair: Employers Forum on Belief, 2003–13; Employers for Fathers, 2005–11; Chm., Employers for Carers, 2003–13. Trustee, Employers Forum on Age, 2001–13. HR Dir of the Year, HR Excellence Awards, 2009. *Recreations:* walking, dog training, gardening, art. *Address:* CW Consulting Box Ltd, Meadow Bank, Church Road, Stevington, Bedford MK43 7QB.

**WATERS, Gen. Sir (Charles) John,** GCB 1995 (KCB 1988); CBE 1981 (OBE 1977); DL; Deputy Supreme Allied Commander, Europe, 1993–94; Aide-de-Camp General to the Queen, 1992–95; *b* 2 Sept. 1935; *s* of Patrick George Waters and Margaret Ronaldson Waters (*née* Clark); *m* 1962, Hilary Doyle Nettleton; three *s*. *Educ:* Oundle; Royal Military Academy, Sandhurst. Commissioned, The Gloucestershire Regt, 1955; GSO2, MO1 (MoD), 1970–72; Instructor, GSO1 (DS), Staff Coll., Camberley, 1973–74; Commanding Officer, 1st Bn, Gloucestershire Regt, 1975–77; Colonel General Staff, 1st Armoured Div., 1977–79; Comdr 3 Infantry Bde, 1979–81; RCDS 1982; Dep. Comdr, Land Forces, Falkland Islands, May–July 1982; Comdr 4th Armoured Div., 1983–85; Comdt, Staff Coll. Camberley, 1986–88; GOC and Dir of Ops, NI, 1988–90; C-in-C, UKLF, 1990–93. Col, The Gloucestershire Regt, 1985–91; Col Comdt, POW Div., 1988–91; Hon. Colonel: Royal Wessex Yeomanry, 1991–97; Royal Devonshire Yeomanry, 1991–97. President: (Army) Officers' Assoc., 1997–2006; Devon RBL, 1998–2002. Mem. Adv. Council, Victory Meml Mus., Arlon, Belgium, 1989–97; Mem. Council, Cheltenham Coll., 1991–2002; Chm. Council, Nat. Army Mus., 1997–2005; Gov., Colyton Primary Sch., 1997–2003. Pres., Honiton and Dist Agricl Assoc., 2004–05; Patron, Royal Albert Meml Mus., Exeter, 2006–. Admiral: Army Sailing Assoc., 1990–93; Infantry Sailing Assoc., 1990–93. Kermit Roosevelt Lectr, USA, 1992. FRSA 1993. JP: Axminster and Honiton, 1998; Central Devon, 1998–2006; DL Devon, 2001. *Recreations:* sailing, ski-ing, painting, gardening. *Address:* c/o Lloyds Bank, Colyton, Devon EX24 6JS. *Clubs:* Army and Navy; British Kiel Yacht.

**WATERS, David Ebsworth Benjamin;** QC 1999; *b* 24 April 1945; *s* of William Thomas Ebsworth Waters and Esther Jane Waters; *m* 1996, Sonia Jayne Bound. *Educ:* Greenhill Grammar Sch., Tenby. Admitted Solicitor, 1969; called to the Bar, Middle Temple, 1973, Bencher, 2002; Recorder, 1986–2009; Junior Treasury Counsel, 1989–94, Sen. Treasury Counsel, 1994–99, CCC. Chair, Mental Health Rev. Tribunal, 1999–2004. Legal Assessor to GMC, 2010–16. *Recreations:* golf, fishing, gardening. *Address:* 2 Hare Court, Temple, EC4Y 7BH. *T:* (020) 7353 3982. *Clubs:* MCC; Tenby Golf.

**WATERS, Donald Henry,** OBE 1994; CA; Chief Executive, 1987–97, and Deputy Chairman, 1993–97, Grampian Television PLC; *b* 17 Dec. 1937; *s* of late Henry Lethbridge Waters, WS, and Jean Manson Baxter; *m* 1962, June Leslie, *d* of late Andrew Hutchison; one *s* two *d*. *Educ:* George Watson's, Edinburgh; Inverness Royal Acad. Mem. ICA(Scot.) 1961; CA 1961. Dir, John M. Henderson and Co. Ltd, 1972–75; Grampian Television: Company Sec., 1975; Dir of Finance, 1979. Chairman: Glenburnie Properties, 1993–97 (Dir, 1976–93); Central Scotland Radio Ltd, 1994–96; Director: Scottish TV and Grampian Sales Ltd, 1980–98; Blenheim Travel, 1981–91; Moray Firth Radio, 1982–97; Independent Television Publications Ltd, 1987–90; Cablevision (Scotland) PLC, 1987–91; FirstBus (formerly GRT Bus Group), 1994–96; British Linen Bank, 1995–99; British Linen Bank Gp, 1995–99; Aberdeen Royal Hosp. NHS Trust, 1996–99; Scottish Post Office Bd, 1996–2003; Digital 3 and 4 Ltd, 1997–98; Scottish Media Group plc, 1997–2005; James Johnston of Elgin Ltd, 1999–2016; North Bd, Bank of Scotland, 1999–2001; Aberdeen Asset Mgt plc, 2000–11. Vis. Prof. of Film and Media Studies, Stirling Univ., 1991–. Mem., BAFTA, 1980– (Scottish Vice Chm., 1992–); Chm., Celtic Film and Television Assoc., 1994–96 (Trustee for Scotland, 1990–96); Dir, ITVA, 1994–97. Mem. Council, CBI Scotland, 1994–2001. Chairman: Police Dependent Trust, Aberdeen, 1991–96; Project Steering Gp, New Royal Aberdeen Children's Hosp., 1999–2002; Jt Chm., Grampian Cancer MacMillan Appeal, 1999–2003; Member: Council, Cinema and Television Benevolent Fund, 1986–99; Grampian & Islands Family Trust, 1986–2005. Gov., Univ. of Aberdeen, 1998–99. Burgess of Guild, Aberdeen, 1979– (Assessor, 1998–2001). FRTS 1998 (Mem., 1988); FRSA 1990. *Recreations:* gardening, travel, hill-walking. *Address:* Balquhidder, Milltimber, Aberdeen AB13 0JS. *T:* (01224) 867131. *E:* donaldwaters@btinternet.com. *Club:* Royal Northern and University (Aberdeen) (Chm., 1987–88).

**WATERS, Emily;** see Watson, Emily.

**WATERS, Gen. Sir John;** see Waters, Gen. Sir C. J.

**WATERS, Keith Stuart,** FCA; Clerk, Fishmongers' Company, 1994–2009 (Assistant Clerk, 1987–93); *b* 18 March 1951; *s* of late Thomas Charles Waters and of Elsie Lilian (*née* Addison); *m* 1976, Elizabeth Jane Weeks; one *s* two *d*. *Educ:* Leigh GS; Wigan Tech. Coll.; Univ. of Newcastle upon Tyne (BA 1973). FCA 1976. Deloitte Haskins & Sells, Manchester, 1973–77; audit senior, Peat Marwick Mitchell, Kingston, Jamaica, 1978; with Price Waterhouse: audit senior, Miami, Fla, 1979–80; Manager, Melbourne, Aust., 1980–82; Sen. Manager, London, 1982–85; Gp Financial Accountant, Guinness plc, 1985–87. Chm., Livery Cos Mutual Ltd, 1999–. Sec., Bd of Trustees, City and Guilds of London Art Sch., 1993–2008. Gresham's School, Holt: Clerk to Govs, 1993–2008; Dep. Chm., 2009–16; Chm., Gresham's Sch. Foundn, 2009–14. *Recreations:* theatre, concerts, ballet, tennis, watersports, running, food and wine. *Address:* The Cow Shed, Bard Hill, Salthouse, Norfolk NR25 7XB. *T:* (01263) 740227.

**WATERS, Lee;** Member (Lab) Llanelli, National Assembly for Wales, since 2016; Deputy Minister for Economy and Transport, since 2018; *b* Glanamman, Carmarthenshire, 12 Feb. 1976; *s* of Brian and Tegwen Waters; *m* 2001, Felicity Morgan; one *s* one *d*. *Educ:* Amman Valley Sch., Ammanford; Univ. of Wales, Aberystwyth (BSc (Econ) 1st Cl. Political Studies 1998). Political Sec. to Rt Hon. Ron Davies, MP, 1998–99; producer, BBC Wales News, 1999–2001; Chief Political Corresp., ITV Wales, 2001–07; Director: Sustrans Cymru, 2007–13; Inst. of Welsh Affairs, 2013–16. Mem., Welsh Political Archive Adv. Cttee, Nat. Liby for Wales, 2005–. Vice-Chm., Cross-Party Referendum Campaign, Yes for Wales, 2010–11. Hon. Fellow, Inst. of Welsh Affairs, 2016. *Recreations:* walking, cycling, reading. *Address:* National Assembly for Wales, Cardiff Bay, Cardiff CF99 1NA. *E:* lee.waters@assembly.wales. *Club:* Ammanford Social (Life Mem.).

**WATERS, Malcolm Ian;** QC 1997; *b* 11 Oct. 1953; *s* of late Ian Power Waters and Yvonne Waters (*née* Mosley); *m* 2002, Setsuko Sato. *Educ:* Whitgift Sch.; St Catherine's Coll., Oxford (MA, BCL). Called to the Bar, Lincoln's Inn, 1977; in practice, 1978–2019. *Publications:* (jtly) The Building Societies Act 1986, 1987; (ed jtly) Wurtzburg & Mills, Building Society Law, 15th edn, 1989 (with regular updates, 1990–2018); (ed jtly) The Law of Investor Protection, 2nd edn, 2003; (Cons. Ed.) Friendly Societies, 2007, Mutual Societies, 2008, Financial Institutions, 2015, Halsbury's Laws of England; (jtly) Retail Mortgages: law regulation and procedure, 2013. *Recreations:* music, opera.

**WATERS, Melanie Dawn,** OBE 2017; Chief Executive Officer, Help For Heroes, since 2016; *b* Aylesbury; *d* of David and Rose-Marie Reid; two step *d*. *Educ:* Univ. of Manchester (LLB Hons Law 1990); Open Univ. (MBA 2005). Automobile Association: Legal Advr, 1991–97; Patrol Team Manager, 1997–2000; Regl Sales Manager, 2000–02; Hd, Business Improvement, 2002–04; Ext. Affairs Dir, Enham Trust, 2004–07; Ops Dir, UNITE Gp plc, 2007–10; Chief Exec., Poppy Factory, 2010–16. *Recreations:* cycling, pilates, poetry, dancing. *Address:* Help For Heroes, 14 Parkers Close, Downton Business Centre, Downton, Salisbury, Wilts SP5 3RB. *E:* melanie.waters@helpforheroes.org.uk.

**WATERS, Sarah,** OBE 2019; PhD; author, since 1995; *b* 21 July 1966; *d* of Ron and Mary Waters. *Educ:* Univ. of Kent (BA Hons English and American Lit. 1987); Univ. of Lancaster (MA Contemp. Literary Studies 1988); Queen Mary and Westfield Coll., London (PhD 1995). Tutor, Open Univ., 1996–2000. *Publications:* Tipping the Velvet, 1998 (televised 2002); Affinity, 1999 (televised 2008); Fingersmith, 2002 (televised 2005; filmed as The Handmaiden, 2017); The Night Watch, 2006 (televised, 2011); The Little Stranger, 2009 (filmed 2018); The Paying Guests, 2014. *Recreations:* cinema, theatre. *Address:* c/o Greene & Heaton (Authors' Agents) Ltd, 37 Goldhawk Road, W12 8QQ. *T:* (020) 8749 0315.

**WATERSON, Prof. Michael John,** PhD; Professor of Economics, University of Warwick, since 1991; *b* 29 July 1950; *s* of Geoffrey and Christine Mary Waterson; *m* 1972, Sally Ann Davis; one *s* one *d*. *Educ:* Bude Grammar Sch.; Univ. of Warwick (BA 1971; PhD 1977); London Sch. of Econs (MSc Econ 1972). Lectr in Econs, 1974–86, Reader in Econs, 1986–88, Univ. of Newcastle upon Tyne; Prof. of Econs, Univ. of Reading, 1988–91. Gen. Ed., Jl Industrial Econs, 1994–99. Associate Fellow, ZEW Univ. of Mannheim, 2013–17. Member: Competition Commn, 2005–14; Econs Reference Gp, Cooperation and Competition Panel, 2010–16; Competition Appeal Tribunal, 2017–. Specialist Advr, H of L Subcttee B, 2005, 2006; Expert Advr, Eur. Res. Council, 2015–16; Ad hoc Advr on energy matters, Nat. Audit Office, 2013–15; Advr, Aventus Foundn, 2017–. Chairman: Utilities Appeals Panel, States of Guernsey, 2002–07; Rev. of Consumer Protection Measures in the Secondary Ticketing Market, 2015–16. Pres., Eur. Assoc. for Res. in Industrial Econs, 1999–2001. Mem., Scientific Adv. Bd, DIW Berlin, 2009–13. FRSA 1989. *Publications:* Economic Theory of the Industry, 1984; Regulation of the Firm and Natural Monopoly, 1988; (jtly) Buyer Power and Competition in European Food Retailing, 2002; (ed jtly) Empirical Industrial Organization, 2004; contrib. jls incl. Amer. Econ. Rev., Qly Jl Econs, Econ. Jl, Eur. Econ. Rev. *Recreations:* walking, playing musical instruments, travel, railway modelling. *Address:* Department of Economics, University of Warwick, Coventry CV4 7AL. *T:* (024) 7652 3427, *Fax:* (024) 7652 3032. *E:* michael.waterson@warwick.ac.uk.

**WATERSON, Nigel Christopher;** Chairman: Equity Release Council, 2012–17; Trustee Board, NOW: Pensions, 2011–19; *b* 12 Oct. 1950; *s* of James Waterson and Katherine (née Mahon); *m* 1999, Dr Barbara Judge; one *s* one *d*. *Educ:* Leeds Grammar Sch.; Queen's Coll., Oxford (MA Jurisprudence); College of Law. Called to the Bar, Gray's Inn, 1973; admitted solicitor, 1979. Pres., Oxford Univ. Cons. Assoc., 1970. Res. Asst to Sally Oppenheim, MP, 1972–73. Cllr, London Borough of Hammersmith, 1974–78. Chairman: Bow Gp, 1986–87 (Hon. Patron, 1993–95); Hammersmith Cons. Assoc., 1987–90; Hammersmith and Fulham Jt Management Cttee, 1988–90; Member: Cons. Gtr London Area Exec. Cttee, 1990–91; Soc. of Cons. Lawyers Exec. Cttee, 1993–97; Conservative Political Centre: Mem., Adv. Cttee, 1986–90; Mem., Gtr London Gen. Purposes Cttee, 1990–91. MP (C) Eastbourne, 1992–2010; contested (C) same seat, 2010. PPS to Minister of State, DoH, 1995, to Dep. Prime Minister, 1996–97; an Opposition Whip, 1997–99; Opposition spokesman on local govt and housing, 1999–2001, on trade and industry, 2001–02, on pensions, 2003–10. Mem., Select Cttee on Nat. Heritage, 1995–96; Vice Chairman: Cons. Backbench Tourism Cttee, 1992–97; Cons. Backbench Transport Cttee, 1992–97; Sec., Cons. Backbench Shipping and Shipbuilding Cttee, 1992–97; Vice Chairman: All-Party Daylight Extra Gp, 1993–97; All-Party British Greek Gp, 1993–2010; Sec., British Cyprus Gp, CPA, 1992–2010. Member: London West European Constituency Council, 1987–91; Management Cttee, Stonham Housing Assoc. Hostel for Ex-Offenders, 1988–90. Trustee: Internat. Longevity Council, 2010–; Age and Employment Network, 2011–14; Chm., Abbeyfield (E Sussex), 2011–15. Mem. Council, Soc. of Pension Professionals, 2011–19; Gov., Pension Policy Inst., 2012–. *Publications:* papers on an Alternative Manifesto, 1973, the future of Hong Kong, and on shipping. *Recreations:* walking, opera, reading, history, playing the piano, visiting France. *E:* nigel@nigelwaterson.com. *Clubs:* Coningsby, 1900.

**WATERSTON, Dr Charles Dewar,** FRSE; formerly Keeper of Geology, Royal Scottish Museum; *b* 15 Feb. 1925; *s* of Allan Waterston and Martha Dewar (née Robertson); *m* 1965, Marjory Home Douglas (*d* 2008). *Educ:* Highgate Sch., London; Univ. of Edinburgh (BSc 1st Cl. Hons 1947; Vans Dunlop Scholar, PhD 1949; DSc 1980). FRSE 1958. Asst Keeper, Royal Scottish Museum, 1950–63, Keeper, 1963–85. Member: Scottish Cttee, Nature Conservancy, 1969–73; Adv. Cttee for Scotland, Nature Conservancy Council, 1974–82; Chairman's Cttee, 1978–80, Exec. Cttee, 1980–82, Council for Museums and Galleries in Scotland; Adv. Cttee on Sites of Special Scientific Interest, 1992–95; Gen. Sec., RSE, 1986–91 (Mem. Council, 1967–70; Vice-Pres., 1980–83; Sec., 1985–86)); Hon. Sec., Edinburgh Geol Soc., 1953–58 (Pres., 1969–71). Chm., Judges Panel, Scottish Mus. of Year Award, 1999–2000. Keith Prize, 1969–71, Bicentenary Medal, 1992, RSE; Clough Medal, Edinburgh Geol Soc., 1984–85; (first) A. G. Brighton Medal, Geol Curators' Gp, 1992. *Publications:* (with G. Y. Craig and D. B. McIntyre) James Hutton's Theory of the Earth: the lost drawings, 1978; (with H. E. Stace and C. W. A. Pettitt) Natural Science Collections in Scotland, 1987; Collections in Context, 1997; (with D. Guthrie) The Royal Society Club of Edinburgh 1820–2000, 1999; (with A. Macmillan Shearer) Biographical Index of Former Fellows of the Royal Society of Edinburgh 1783–2002, 2 vols, 2006; Perth Entrepreneurs: the Sandemans of Springland, 2008; technical papers in jls, chiefly relating to extinct arthropods, the history of geology, genealogy and local history. *Address:* 51 Homescott House, 6 Goldenacre Terrace, Edinburgh EH3 5RE.

**WATERSTONE, Sir Timothy (John Stuart),** Kt 2018; Founder, Waterstone's Booksellers, 1982; *b* 30 May 1939; *s* of Malcolm Waterstone and Sylvia Sawday; *m* 1st, Patricia Harcourt-Poole (marr. diss.); two *s* one *d*; 2nd, Claire Perkins (marr. diss.); one *s* two *d*; 3rd, Mary Rose, (Rosie), *d* of Rt Hon. Michael Alison, PC and of Sylvia Mary (née Haigh); two *d*. *Educ:* Tonbridge; St Catharine's College, Cambridge (MA). Carritt Moran, Calcutta, 1962–64; Allied Breweries, 1964–73; W. H. Smith, 1973–81; Founder, Chm. and Chief Exec., Waterstone's Booksellers Ltd, 1982–93; Dep. Chm., Sinclair-Stevenson Ltd, 1989–92; Chairman: Priory Investments Ltd, 1990–95; Golden Rose Radio (London Jazz FM), 1992–93; Founder and Exec. Chm., Chelsea Stores Ltd (Daisy & Tom), 1996–2007 (acquired Early Learning Centre Hldgs, 2004); Founder Chm., HMV Media Gp plc (merged businesses of Waterstone's and HMV), 1998–2001; Member of Board: Yale Univ. Press, 1992–; Future Start, 1992–2009; Virago Press., 1995–96; Hill Samuel UK Emerging Cos Investment Trust PLC, 1996–2000; National Gallery Co. Ltd, 1996–2003; Downing Classic VCT, 1998–2003. Chm., DTI Working Gp on Smaller Quoted Cos and Private Investors, 1999. Chm., Shelter 25th Anniversary Appeal Cttee, 1991–92. Member: Bd of Trustees, English International (Internat. House), 1987–92; Bd, London Philharmonic Orch., 1990–97 (Trustee, 1995–98); Portman House Trust, 1994–96; Cttee, BL, 1995–97; Chairman: Acad. of Ancient Music, 1990–95; London Internat. Festival of Theatre, 1991–92; Elgar Foundn, 1992–98; Library Bd, KCL, 2000–02; Vis. Cttee, Cambridge Univ. Library, 2007–13. Co-Founder: BOOKAID, 1992–93; Moscow booksellers Bookberry, 2003. Adv. Mem., Booker Prize Management Cttee, 1986–93; Chm. of Judges, Prince's Youth Business Trust Awards, 1990. Chancellor, Edinburgh Napier (formerly Napier) Univ., 2007–15. *Publications: novels:* Lilley & Chase, 1994; An Imperfect Marriage, 1995; A Passage of Lives, 1996; In For a Penny, In For a Pound, 2010; *non-fiction:* Swimming Against the Stream, 2006; The Face Pressed Against a Window, 2019. *Recreation:* talking with Rosie Alison. *Club:* Garrick.

**WATERWORTH, Peter Andrew;** HM Diplomatic Service, retired; Governor of Montserrat, 2007–11; *b* 15 April 1957; *s* of Bobby and Betty Waterworth; *m* 1994, Catherine Margaret. *Educ:* Univ. of Durham (BA Hons); Downing Coll., Cambridge (LLB Hons 1982); Inns of Court Sch. of Law. Standing Adv. Commn on Human Rights, NI, 1979–81; called to the Bar; barrister, 1983–87; joined FCO, 1987; Asst Legal Advr, FCO, 1987–90; Legal Advr, Bonn, 1990–94; Middle Eastern Dept, FCO, 1994–96; First Sec., Rome, 1996–2000; NI Office, 2000–03; Pol Counsellor, Islamabad, 2003–05, Iraq, 2005; Dep. High Comr and Consul-Gen., Lagos, 2005–07. Chief Admin. Officer, Municipality of Jasper, Alta, Canada, 2012–14. Ski Professional, Whistler Blackcomb, 2016–17, Fernie, 2017–19, BC, Canada. *Recreations:* ski-ing, cooking, golf, hiking, reading.

**WATES, Andrew Trace Allan,** OBE 2013; Vice Lord-Lieutenant of Surrey, 2013–16; Chairman: Wates Group (formerly Wates Ltd), 2000–06; Wates Family Holdings, 2000–08; *b* 16 Nov. 1940; 4th *s* of Sir Ronald Wallace Wates and Phyllis Mary Wates (née Trace); *m* 1965, Sarah Mary de Burgh Macartney; four *s* (and one *s* decd). *Educ:* Oundle Sch.; Emmanuel Coll., Cambridge (BA Estate Mgt 1960). Joined Wates, 1964; Dir, Wates Construction, 1972–2000; Chairman: Wates Leisure Gp, later Pinnacle Leisure Gp, 1972–99; Wates Estate Agency Services, 1976–2000; Director: Wates Ltd, 1973–2000; Wates Hldgs, 1973–. Chairman: United Racecourses Ltd, 1996–2003; Leisure and Media plc, 2001–09; Gambado, 2004–; Director: Racecourse Hldgs Trust, 1996; Fontwell Park plc, 1991–2001. Vice Chm., Family Business Network Internat., 2004–13; Chairman: Inst. for Family Business, 2007–10; Inst. for Family Business Res. Foundn, 2010–15. Vice-Chm., Bd of Mgt, Royal Albert and Alexandra Sch., 2000–16. Pro-Chancellor, Univ. of Surrey, 2016–. Mem., Jockey Club, 1977–. High Sheriff, Surrey, 2003–04; DL Surrey, 2006. *Recreations:* horse-racing, shooting, fishing, golf. *Address:* Henfold House, Beare Green, Dorking, Surrey RH5 4RW. *T:* (01306) 631324. *Clubs:* White's, Turf.
*See also M. E. Wates, P. C. R. Wates, T. A. de B. Wates.*

**WATES, Sir Christopher (Stephen),** Kt 1989; BA; FCA; Chairman, Wates Holdings, 2000–05; Chief Executive, Wates Group (formerly Wates Building Group), 1984–2000; *b* 25 Dec. 1939; *s* of Norman Edward Wates and Margot Irene Sidwell; *m* 1965, Sandra Mouroutsos (marr. diss. 1975); three *d*; *m* 1992, Georgina Ferris McCallum. *Educ:* Stowe School; Brasenose College, Oxford (BA 1962; Rugby blue, 1961; Hon. Fellow, 1993). FCA 1975 (ACA 1965). Financial Director, Wates Ltd, 1970–76. Chm., Criterion Hldgs, 1981–96. Director: Electra Investment Trust, 1980–93; Equitable Life Assurance Society, 1983–94; Scottish Ontario Investment Co. Ltd, 1978–83; 3i Smaller Quoted Cos Trust (formerly North British Canadian Investment Co., then NB Smaller Cos Trust), 1983–98 (Chm., 1996–98); Wates City of London Properties plc, 1984–2000; Mem., 1980–89, Chm., 1983–89, English Industrial Estates Corp.; Chm., Keymer Brick & Tile Co. Ltd, 1985–89. A Church Comr, 1992–96. Gov. of Council, 1984–2006, Chm., 1997–2010, Goodenough Coll. (formerly London House for Overseas Graduates, then London Goodenough Trust) (Dep. Chm., 1989–96); Gov., Frewen Coll., 2004–06. Trustee: Chatham Historic Dockyard Trust, 1984–87; Science Museum, 1987–2002; Lambeth Palace Library, 1990–2005. Chm., Industrial Soc., 1998. FRSA 1988. Hon. Mem., RICS, 1990. *Address:* Tufton Place, Northiam, Rye, East Sussex TN31 6HL. *T:* (01797) 252125.

**WATES, Sir James (Garwood Michael),** Kt 2019; CBE 2012; Chairman, Wates Group, since 2013 (Director, since 1997; Deputy Chairman, 2006–13); *b* London, 9 April 1960; *s* of Michael Edward Wates, *qv*; *m* 1991, Laurie Lindsey; two *s*. *Educ:* Downside Sch.; Poly. of Central London; Harvard Business Sch. With Wates Gp, 1983–: Line Manager, Wates Construction Ltd, 1983–89; Man. Dir, Wates Integra Ltd, 1989–92; Gp Sales and Marketing Manager, Wates Construction Ltd, 1992–94; Chm., Nominations Cttee and Mem., Remuneration Cttee, Wates Gp, 1997–; Chm., Charles Barratt Interiors, 1999–2000; Exec. Chm., Wates Interiors Ltd, 2000–01. Non-exec. Dir, Argent Gp LLP, 2015–. Mem., UK Commn for Employment Skills, 2009–15. Chairman: Construction Confedn, 2006–09; UK Contractors Gp, 2009–15; Construction Skills, CITB, 2010–18; Build UK, 2015–17; Construction Council, CBI, 2018–; Co-Chm., Infrastructure Exports: UK, 2017–. Pres., British Council for Offices, 2012–13 (Vice Pres., 2010–12). Pres., Chartered Inst. of Building, 2010–11. Mem., Court of Govs, Univ. of Westminster, 2013–. Trustee: Queen Elizabeth's Foundn, 2004–17; BRE Trust, 2010–15 (Chm., 2015–); Chm., Tomorrow's Co., 2017–; Chm., Corporate Adv. Gp, Prince's Trust, 2017–. *Recreations:* golf, sailing, shooting, family. *Address:* Field Place, Hookhouse Lane, Dunsfold, Surrey GU8 4LR. *T:* (01483) 201125; Wates House, Station Approach, Leatherhead, Surrey KT22 7SW. *T:* (01372) 861262. *E:* james.wates@wates.co.uk. *Clubs:* Cavalry and Guards; Royal Ocean Racing; Walton Heath Golf.

**WATES, Michael Edward,** CBE 1998; Chairman, Wates Group (formerly Wates Ltd), 1974–2000; *b* 19 June 1935; 2nd *s* of Sir Ronald Wallace Wates and Phyllis Mary Wates (née Trace); *m* 1959, Caroline Josephine Connolly; four *s* one *d*. *Educ:* Oundle School; Emmanuel College, Cambridge (MA); Harvard Business Sch. (PMD 1963). Served RM, 1953–55. Joined Wates 1959; Director: Wates Construction, 1963; Wates Built Homes, 1966. Mem., Nat. Housebuilding Council, 1974–80. Chm., British Bloodstock Agency plc, 1986–92; Member: Council, Thoroughbred Breeders Assoc., 1978–82 (Chm., 1980–82); Horserace Betting Levy Bd, 1987–90. King's College Hospital: Deleg., Sch. of Medicine and Dentistry, 1983–2004; Chm., Equipment Cttee, 1983–91; Special Trustee, 1985 (Chm., Trustees, 1985). Hon. FRIBA. *Address:* Manor House, Langton Long, Blandford Forum, Dorset DT11 9HS. *T:* (01258) 455241.
*See also A. T. A. Wates, Sir J. G. M. Wates, P. C. R. Wates.*

**WATES, Paul Christopher Ronald,** FRICS; Managing Director, 1984–94, Chairman, 1994–2001, Wates City of London Properties plc; *b* 6 March 1938; 3rd *s* of Sir Ronald Wallace Wates and Phyllis Mary Wates (née Trace); *m* 1965, Annette Beatrice Therese Randag; three *s* three *d*. Chesterton & Sons, 1958–59; Nat. Service, 14th/20th King's Hussars, 1959–61; joined Wates Ltd, 1962; Director: Wates Gp, 1969–2006; Wates Holdings (formerly Wates Family Holdings), 1973–. Chm., C&G, 1991–99 (Vice Pres., 2006–; Hon. FCGI). Mem. Court, Clothworkers' Co. (Master, 2003). *Address:* Bellasis House, Mickleham, Dorking, Surrey RH5 6DH. *Clubs:* White's, Turf, Cavalry and Guards, MCC.
*See also A. T. A. Wates, M. E. Wates.*

**WATES, Timothy Andrew de Burgh;** DL; Director, Wates Group, since 2011; Chairman: Wates Developments, since 2011; Wates Family Council, since 2011; *b* Leamington Spa, 3 June 1966; *s* of Andrew Trace Allan Wates, *qv*; *m* 1995, Annabel Rogerson; one *s* three *d*. *Educ:* Radley Coll.; Univ. of Exeter (BA Hons); Emmanuel Coll., Cambridge (MBA 1994). Investment Analyst, Cazenove & Co., 1988–91; Wates Gp,

1991–: housing and construction roles, 1994–2000; Man. Dir, Wates Residential Develts, 2000–07; Chm., Wates Family Hldgs, 2007–11. Director: Tampopo Ltd, 2005–; Pedder Property Ltd, 2010–. Chm. Coast to Capital LEP, 2014–. Mem., Adv. Bd, Judge Business Sch., Cambridge Univ., 2016–; Prime Minister's UK Business Ambassador, 2012–18. Trustee: Wates Charitable Trusts, 2000–; Clink Charity, 2010–. Gov., local primary sch., 2005–12. DL Surrey, 2017. *Recreations:* family, food and wine, weekly game of indoor football, chauffeuring children, Crystal Palace Football Club. *Address:* Oldhouse, Ewhurst, Surrey GU6 7SE. *E:* tim.wates@wates.co.uk.

**WATHERSTON, John Anthony Charles,** CBE 2005; Registrar of the Privy Council, 1998–2005; *b* 29 April 1944; *yr s* of Sir David Watherston, KBE, CMG and Lady Watherston; *m* 1976, Jane (*née* Chaytor), widow of John Atkinson; one *s*, and one step *s* one step *d*. *Educ:* Winchester Coll.; Christ Church, Oxford (BA Jurisp. 1966; MA 1970); Heythrop Coll., Univ. of London (Postgrad. Cert. Christian Ethics 2010). Called to the Bar, Inner Temple, 1967; Lord Chancellor's Department: Legal Asst, 1970–74; Sec., Phillimore Cttee on Law of Contempt of Court, 1971–74; Sen. Legal Asst, 1974–80; Private Sec. to Lord Chancellor, 1975–77; Asst Solicitor (Grade 5), 1980–85, 1988–98; Sen. Crown Counsel, Attorney Gen.'s Chambers, Hong Kong, 1985–88. Consultant Registrar, Dubai Internat. Financial Centre Courts, 2005–06. Lay Reader, Chelsea Old Church, Dio. of London, 1995–; Mem., London Diocesan Synod, 2000–09. *Publications:* (contrib.) Halsbury's Laws of England, vol. 10, 4th edn, 2002; (ed and contrib.) Jowitt's Dictionary of English Law, 3rd edn, 2010. *Club:* Reform.
*See also* Baron Freyberg.

**WATHES, Prof. (Dorothy) Claire,** PhD; FRSB; FRASE; Professor of Veterinary Reproduction, Royal Veterinary College, since 1994; *b* Wallington, Surrey, 5 Aug. 1953; *d* of John Bulman and Maida Bulman (*née* Hunter); *m* 1978, Christopher Michael Wathes, OBE (*d* 2016); two *d*. *Educ:* Cheltenham Ladies Coll.; Univ. of Birmingham (BSc 1st Cl. Biol Sci 1974); Univ. of Nottingham (PhD 1978); Univ. of Bristol (DSc 1992). FRSB (FSB 2011). Postdoctoral Res. Asst, Babraham Inst., 1978–79; Lectr in Anatomy, 1979–90, Reader in Anatomy, 1990, Univ. of Bristol; Res. Gp Leader, Babraham Inst., 1990–93. Guest Prof., Huazhong Agricl Univ., Wuhan, China, 2009–12; Vis. Prof., Univ. of Reading, 2017–. Dir, Genesis Faraday Partnership, 2002–09. Chm., Investigating Gene Function Farm Animals Steering Cttee, Roslin Inst., 2000–08. Mem., Veterinary Adv. Cttee, Horserace Betting Levy Bd, 1997–2008. Mem. Council, RSB, 2016–. FRASE 2009. Res. Medal, RASE, 2009; Marshall Medal, Soc. for Study of Fertility, 2015. *Publications:* book chapters; contrib. over 200 refereed scientific pubns. *Recreations:* walking, dinghy sailing, riding, family. *Address:* Royal Veterinary College, Hawkshead Lane, North Mymms, Hatfield, Herts AL9 7TA. *T:* (01707) 666553. *E:* dcwathes@rvc.ac.uk.

**WATHEY, Prof. Andrew Brian,** CBE 2016; DPhil; FRHistS, FSA; Vice-Chancellor and Chief Executive, Northumbria University, since 2008; *b* Plymouth, 19 July 1958; *s* of Brian Edwin Wathey and Florence Jean Wathey (*née* Tompkins); *m* 1995, Charlotte Brown; one *s* one *d*. *Educ:* St Edmund Hall, Oxford (BA Hons 1st Cl. Music 1979; MA 1983; DPhil 1987). FRHistS 1986; FSA 1989. Jun. Res. Fellow, Merton Coll., Oxford, 1982–85; Res. Fellow, Downing Coll., Cambridge, 1985–88; Lectr in Music, Univ. of Lancaster, 1988–89; Royal Holloway, University of London: Lectr in Music, 1989–94; Sen. Lectr in Music, 1995; Reader in Music, 1995–99; Dean, Graduate Sch., 1996–98; Prof. of Music Hist., 1999–2008; Hd, Music Dept, 2000–02; Dean of Arts, 2002; Vice-Principal (Planning and Resources), 2003–06; Sen. Vice-Principal, 2006–08. Vis. Prof., Keio Univ., Tokyo, 1987; Vis. Res. Fellow, All Souls Coll., Oxford, 1998. Dep. Chm., Univ. Alliance, 2009–12. Mem. Council, All Party Parly Univ. Gp, 2014–. Chm., UK Standing Cttee on Quality Assessment, 2016–. Chm., Student Loans Co. Stakeholder Forum, 2010–17; non-exec. Dir, Student Loans Co., 2018–. FRSA 2005. *Publications:* Music in the Royal and Noble Households in Late Medieval England: studies of sources and patronage, 1989; Manuscripts of Polyphonic Music: the British Isles 1100–1400, 1993; (ed with M. Bent) Fauvel Studies: allegory, chronicle, music and image in Paris, Bibliothèque Nationale de France, MS Français 146, 1998. *Address:* Vice-Chancellor's Office, Northumbria University, Sutherland Building, College Street, Newcastle upon Tyne NE1 8ST. *T:* (0191) 227 4002. *E:* andrew.wathey@northumbria.ac.uk. *Club:* Reform.

**WATKIN, (Richard) Owen,** OBE 2006; DL; Chairman, Local Democracy and Boundary Commission for Wales (formerly Local Government Boundary Commission for Wales), 2012–19; *b* Aberystwyth, 12 Jan. 1947; *s* of T. Ll. Watkin and A. M. Watkin; *m* 1972, G. M. Watkin; two *c*. *Educ:* Cathays High Sch., Cardiff; University Coll. of Wales, Aberystwyth (LLB 1968); Univ. of London (DPA); Univ. of Wales Trinity St David (MA 2014). Solicitor, 1971–2005. Asst Solicitor, Cardiganshire CC, 1972–74; Sen. Solicitor, Dyfed CC, 1974; Ceredigion District Council, 1974–95: Asst Solicitor; Asst Dir, Admin; Dep. Dir, Admin; Dir, Admin; Chief Exec., Ceredigion CC, 1995–2006. DL Dyfed, 2009. *Recreations:* various.

**WATKINS OF TAVISTOCK,** Baroness *cr* 2015 (Life Peer), of Buckland Monachorum in the County of Devon; **Mary Jane Watkins,** PhD; Professor of Nursing, 2013–12, now Emeritus Professor of Healthcare Leadership, and Deputy Vice Chancellor, 2007–12, Plymouth University; *b* 5 March 1955; *d* of John and Joyce Strelley; *m* Roger Malcolm Watkins, FRCS; one *s* one *d*. *Educ:* Wolfson Sch. of Nursing, Westminster Hosp. (RGN 1976); S London and Maudsley Nursing Sch. (RMN 1979); Florence Nightingale Faculty of Nursing and Midwifery, King's Coll. London (PhD 1994). Nightingale Schol., 1985; work in community, in-patient mental health and acute settings providing non-emergency and emergency healthcare; Dean, Faculty of Health and Social Work, 2003–05, Pro Vice-Chancellor (Health), 2005–07, Plymouth Univ. Member: UK Central Council for Nursing and Midwifery and Health Visiting, 1996–2001; Council for Professions Supplementary to Medicine, 1997–2001; Mem., Appraisal Cttee, NICE, 2001–07. Chm., Collaboration for Leadership in Applied Health Res. and Care, SW Peninsula, NIHR, 2014–. Non-executive Director: SW Ambulance NHS Foundn Trust, 2008–16; Aster Gp Ltd, 2010–. Nurse Advr, Med. Adv. Panel, BUPA, 2006–. Pres., Florence Nightingale Foundn, 2016–. Chm., Acorn Acad. Schs, Cornwall, 2014–16. Ed., Jl Clin. Nursing, 1992–2000. *Address:* House of Lords, SW1A 0PW.

**WATKINS, Dr Alan Keith;** Chairman, Senior plc (formerly Senior Engineering Group), 1996–2001 (Director, 1994–2001; Deputy Chairman, 1995–96); *b* 9 Oct. 1938; *s* of late Wilfred Victor Watkins and Dorothy Hilda Watkins; *m* 1963, Diana Edith Wynne (*née* Hughes); two *s*. *Educ:* Moseley Grammar School, Birmingham; Univ. of Birmingham (BSc Hons, PhD). FIMMM (Mem. Council, 1990–95); CEng; FIMfgE (Vice-Pres., 1991). Lucas Research Centre, 1962; Lucas Batteries, 1969, subseq. Manufacturing Dir; Lucas Aerospace, 1975; Man. Dir, Aerospace Lucas Industries, 1987–89; Man. Dir and Chief Exec., Hawker Siddeley Gp, 1989–91; London Transport: Chief Exec., 1992–94; Vice-Chm., 1992–93; Dep. Chm., 1993–94. Director: Dobson Park Industries plc, 1992–95; Hepworth plc, 1995–98; Chm., High Duty Alloys Ltd, 1997–2000. Member: DTI Aviation Cttee, 1985–89; Review Bd for Govt Contracts, 1993–2002. Member Council: SBAC, 1982–89 (Vice-Pres., 1988–89); CBI, 1992–94. Vice-Pres., EEF, 1989–91, 1997–2001. *Recreations:* tennis, veteran and vintage cars, hot-air ballooning, photography.

**WATKINS, Barbara Janet;** *see* Fontaine, B. J.

**WATKINS, Brian,** CMG 1993; HM Diplomatic Service, retired; Immigration Judge, 1993–2007; *b* 26 July 1933; *s* of late James Edward Watkins and late Gladys Anne Watkins (*née* Fletcher); *m* 1st, 1957 (marr. diss. 1978); one *s*; 2nd, 1982, Elisabeth Arfon-Jones, *qv*; one *d*. *Educ:* London School of Economics (BSc Econ); Worcester College, Oxford. Solicitor. Flying Officer, RAF, 1955–58. HMOCS, Sierra Leone, 1959–63; Local Govt, 1963–66; Administrator, Tristan da Cunha, 1966–69; Lectr, Univ. of Manchester, 1969–71; HM Diplomatic Service, 1971; FCO, 1971–73; New York, 1973–75; seconded to N Ireland Office, 1976–78; FCO, 1978–81; Counsellor, 1981; Dep. Governor, Bermuda, 1981–83; Consul General and Counsellor (Economic, Commercial, Aid), Islamabad, 1983–86; Consul Gen., Vancouver, 1986–90; High Comr to Swaziland, 1990–93. First Pres., Council of Immigration Judges, 1997–2000, now Emeritus. Swazi Rep., 1993–2002, Royal Canadian Legion, Rep., 2002–, on Council, Royal Commonwealth Ex-Services League (Mem. Exec. Cttee, 1996–; Hon. Legal Advr, 2001–17); Patron, Friends of Swaziland Hospice (UK), 1997–; Chm., Swaziland Soc., 1998–2002; Trustee, S Asian Assoc. for Regl Co-operation Foundn (UK), 2001–07. Patron, Vancouver Welshmen's Choir, 1987–92; Trustee, Gwent Shrievalty Police Trust, 2003–09; Pres., Chepstow Rifle Club, 2006–15. Mem., Livery Co. of Wales (formerly Welsh Livery Guild), 2010–. High Sheriff Gwent, 2004–05. OStJ 1994 (Chm., Monmouthshire Council, 1996–2002; Mem., Welsh Chapter, 1996–2002). *Publications:* Feathers on the Brain!: a memoir, 2011. *Recreations:* reading history and spy stories, watching theatre, dancing. *Address:* c/o Royal Bank of Scotland, Drummonds Branch, Charing Cross, SW1A 2DX. *Clubs:* Athenæum, Royal Over-Seas League.

**WATKINS, David James,** CB 2002; Director, DJW Consulting (Northern Ireland) Ltd, 2004–13; *b* 3 Aug. 1948; *s* of John Walter Watkins and Elizabeth Watkins (*née* Buckley); *m* 1974, Valerie Elizabeth Graham; one *s* one *d*. *Educ:* Royal Belfast Academical Instn; Trinity Coll., Dublin (BA Hons Modern Langs). Public Expenditure Control Div., NI Dept of Finance and Personnel, 1972–77; State Aids Directorate, DGIV, Eur. Commn, 1978–79; NI Dept of Econ. Develt, 1979–86; Private Sec. to Sec. of State for NI, 1986–88; Dep. Chief Exec., IDB, 1989–92; Dir, Central Secretariat, 1992–98; Sen. Dir, and Dir of Policing and Security, NI Office, 1998–2004. *Recreations:* reading, gardening, holidays in France.

**WATKINS, Prof. David John;** Research Professor of Jewellery, Department of Goldsmithing, Silversmithing, Metalwork and Jewellery, Royal College of Art, 2006–09, now Emeritus (Professor of Metalwork and Jewellery, 1984–2006); sculptor and jewellery designer; *b* 14 Nov. 1940; *s* of Jack Watkins and Dorothy May Watkins (*née* Burgwin); *m* 1962, Wendy Anne Jopling Ramshaw, CBE, RDI (*d* 2018); one *s* one *d*. *Educ:* Wolverhampton Grammar Sch.; Reading Univ. (BA Fine Art 1963). Sculptor, musician, special effects model maker (incl. 2001: A Space Odyssey) and jewellery designer, 1963–71; own studios for jewellery and sculpture, 1971–; designer, Olympic medals, London 2012. Artist in Residence, Western Australian Inst. for Technol., 1978. Vis. Lectr, Berks Coll. of Art and Guildford Sch. of Art, 1964–66; Vis. Prof., Bezalel Acad., Jerusalem, 1984. *Solo exhibitions* include: American Inst. of Architects, Philadelphia, 1973; Goldsmiths' Hall, Electrum Gall., London, 1973; Arnolfini Gall., Bristol, 1977; Nat. Gall. of Victoria, Melbourne, 1978; Gall. Am Graben, Vienna, 1980; City Art Gall., Leeds, 1985; Stedelijk Mus., Amsterdam, 1986; Contemporary Applied Art, London, 1989; City Art Gall., Birmingham, 1990; Mikimoto Hall, Tokyo, 1993; Handwerksmesse, Munich, 1999; Galerie Louise Smit, Amsterdam, 2000; *group exhibitions* include: V&A Mus., 1976; Künstlerhaus, Vienna, 1980; Crafts Council, London, 1982 and 1996; NMOMA, Tokyo, 1983; Barcelona, 1987; Nat. Mus of Scotland, 1998; American Crafts Mus., NY, 2001; *work in major collections* including: American Craft Mus.; Australian Nat. Gall.; Birmingham City Mus. and Art Gall.; Crafts Council, London; Kunstgewerbe Mus., Berlin; Musée des Arts Décoratifs, Paris; Nat. Gall. of Victoria; Nat. Mus. of Modern Art, Tokyo; Nat. Mus of Scotland; Science Mus., London; V&A Mus. Crafts Council: Member: Membership Cttee, 1976–78; Collection Cttee, 1983–84. Mem., Bd of Trustees, Haystack Mt Sch. of Crafts, Maine, 1999–. FCSD 1984; FRSA 1991. Freeman, 1988, Liveryman, 1989, Co. of Goldsmiths. Diamonds Today Award, De Beers, 1974; Art for Architecture Award, RSA, 1995. *Publications:* The Best in Contemporary Jewellery, 1994; A Design Sourcebook: Jewellery, 1999; The Paper Jewelry Collection, 2000. *Recreations:* being in my studio, listening to jazz and classical music. *Address:* Royal College of Art, Kensington Gore, SW7 2EU. *T:* (020) 7590 4261.

**WATKINS, (Edward) Maurice,** CBE 2011; Senior Partner, Brabners LLP (formerly Brabners Chaffe Street LLP), solicitors, since 2006; *b* Manchester, 30 Nov. 1941. *Educ:* Manchester Grammar Sch.; University Coll. London (LLB, LLM; Hon. Fellow 2011). Admitted solicitor, 1966; Solicitor; Partner, 1968–2006, Sen. Partner, 1999–2006, James Chapman & Co., Solicitors. Director: Manchester United FC Ltd, 1984–2012; Manchester United plc, 1991–2004; Regl Chm., Coutts Bank, 2002–13. Chairman: Greyhound Bd of GB, 2008–14; Rugby League Eur. Fedn, 2012–; Barnsley FC, 2013–17; Dir, Rugby Football League, 2002–14 (report, Watkins Review of Rugby League Governance, 2012; Actg Chm., 2012). Dir, British Assoc. for Sport and Law, 1992– (Chm., 1992–2000; Pres., 2000–06, 2015–). Member, Legal Committee: Fédération Internationale de Natation, 2013–17; Ligue Européenne de Natation, 2015–. Chm. Govs, Manchester Grammar Sch., 2008–; Chairman: Manchester Foundn Trust Charity, 2009– (Chm., New Children's Hosp. Appeal, 2005–09); Breakthrough Breast Cancer NW Appeal, 2010–14; British Swimming, 2012–; New Islington Free Sch., 2013–; British Basketball Fedn, 2018–; Trustee, Professional Footballers Pension Scheme, 2014–; Mem., Nat. Olympic Cttee, British Olympic Assoc., 2015–. Hon. Mem. Council, Bradford Univ., 2015–. Hon. LLD Bolton, 2017. *Recreations:* most sports, raising money for charity (particularly in education and health). *Address:* Brabners LLP, 55 King Street, Manchester M2 4LQ. *T:* (0161) 836 8818, *Fax:* (0161) 836 8801. *E:* maurice.watkins@brabners.com. *Club:* Lancashire CC (Dir, 2012–).

**WATKINS, Elisabeth;** *see* Arfon-Jones, E.

**WATKINS, Dr George Edward,** CBE 2000; Chairman and Managing Director, Conoco (UK) Ltd, 1993–2002; Chairman, Petro Matad Ltd, 2012–15; *b* 19 Aug. 1943; *s* of George Robert Leonard Watkins and Laura Watkins; *m* 1966, Elizabeth Mary Bestwick; two *s*. *Educ:* Leeds Univ. (BSc Mining, MSc Geophysics; PhD Geophysics 1968); Stanford Univ., Calif (MS Mgt 1985). Geophysicist, Shell Internat. Petroleum Co., 1968–73; Conoco (UK) Ltd: Geophysicist, 1973–80; Dir, Exploration, 1980–84; Dir, Prodn, 1985–90; Vice Pres., Exploration Prodn, Conoco Inc., Houston, 1990–93. Non-executive Director: Abbot Gp plc, 2002–08; Paladin Resources plc, 2003–05; ITI Scotland Ltd, 2003–09; Defence Procurement Agency, 2005–07; Petroleum Services Network Ltd, 2006–11; Bridge Resources Corp., 2006–12; Panoro Energy ASA, 2012–14. Sloan Fellow, Stanford Univ., 1984–85. Chm., Scottish Enterprise Grampian, 2002–04. Chm., UK Oil & Gas Step Change in Safety, 1997–2000. Pres., UKOOA, 1996. Gov., Robert Gordon Univ., Aberdeen, 2005–12. Hon. DEng Heriot-Watt, 2001. Van Weelden Award, Eur. Assoc. Exploration Geophysicists, 1967. *Recreations:* cinema, gardening, walking, fishing, golf. *Address:* Springfield House, Sway Road, Brockenhurst, Hants SO42 7SG. *T:* (01590) 623308.

**WATKINS, Gerwyn Rhidian;** a District Judge (Magistrates' Courts) (formerly Stipendiary Magistrate), South Glamorgan, 1993–2009; *b* 22 Jan. 1943; *s* of late William Watkins and Margaret Watkins (*née* Evans); *m* 1966, Eleanor Margaret Hemingway; two *s*. *Educ*: Ardwyn Grammar Sch., Aberystwyth; University Coll. of Wales, Aberystwyth (LLB). Articled to Thomas Andrews, Bracknell, 1966–68; Court Clerk, Cardiff Magistrates' Court, 1968–71; Justices' Clerk: Bromsgrove and Redditch, 1971–74; Vale of Glamorgan, 1974–93. Pres., Barry Rotary Club, 1990–91.

**WATKINS, Maj.-Gen. Guy Hansard,** CB 1986; OBE 1974; Chief Executive, Royal Hong Kong Jockey Club, 1986–96; *b* 30 Nov. 1933; *s* of Col A. N. M. Watkins and Mrs S. C. Watkins; *m* 1958, Sylvia Margaret Grant; two *s* two *d*. *Educ*: The King's Sch., Canterbury; Royal Military Academy, Sandhurst. Commissioned into Royal Artillery, 1953; CO 39 Medium Regt RA, 1973; Comd Task Force 'B'/Dep. Comd 1 Armd Div., 1977; Director, Public Relations (Army), 1980; Maj. Gen. RA and GOC Artillery Div., 1982; Dir Gen., Army Manning and Recruiting, 1985; retd 1986. Col Comdt RA, 1986; Hon. Col, The Royal Hong Kong Regt (The Volunteers), 1993–95. Chm., Jubilee Sports Centre and Hong Kong Sports Inst., 1986–96. Director: British Bloodstock Agency, 1996–2001; Racecourse Holdings Trust, 1996–2003. *Recreations*: racing, golf, fishing. *Address*: Archway House, The High Street, Petworth, West Sussex GU28 0AU. *T*: (01798) 344559, *Fax*: (01798) 344693. *Clubs*: Hong Kong Jockey, Shek O (Hong Kong); W Sussex Golf.

**WATKINS, Prof. Hugh Christian,** MD, PhD; FRS 2017; FMedSci; Radcliffe Professor of Medicine, since 2016, and Head, Radcliffe Department of Medicine, since 2012, University of Oxford; Fellow, Merton College, Oxford, since 2016; *b* 7 June 1959; *s* of David Watkins, MB, BCh, and late Gillian Mary Watkins; *m* 1987, Elizabeth Bridget Hewett; one *s* one *d*. *Educ*: Gresham's Sch., Norfolk; St Bartholomew's Hosp. Med. Sch., London (BSc 1st Cl. Hons; MB, BS; Brackenbury & Bourne Prize in Gen. Medicine, 1984); PhD 1995, MD 1995, London. MRCP 1987, FRCP 1997. House Physician, Professorial Med. Unit, St Bartholomew's Hosp., 1984–85; Senior House Officer: in Medicine, John Radcliffe Hosp., Oxford, 1985–87; in Neurology, St Bartholomew's, 1987; Registrar, Medicine and Cardiology, St Thomas' Hosp., London, 1987–89; Lectr in Cardiological Scis, St George's, London, 1990–94, Hon. Sen. Lectr, 1995; Res. Fellow in Medicine, Harvard Med. Sch. and Brigham & Women's Hosp., Boston, 1990–94; Asst Prof. of Medicine, Harvard Med. Sch. and Associate Physician, Brigham & Women's Hosp., 1995; Field Marshal Alexander Prof. of Cardiovascular Medicine, Univ. of Oxford, 1996–2013; Fellow, Exeter Coll., Oxford, 1996–2015, now Emeritus. BHF Clinical Scientist Fellow, 1990; Sen. Investigator, NIHR, 2009. Goulstonian Lectr, RCP, 1998; Lectures: Thomas Lewis, British Cardiac Soc., 2004; Ransom, Nottingham, 2005; Lord Rayner Meml, RCP, 2010; Paul Dudley White, Amer. Heart Assoc., 2011. FMedSci 1999. Young Res. Worker Prize, British Cardiac Soc., 1992; Graham Bull Prize, RCP, 2003; Mackenzie Medal, British Cardiac Soc., 2018. *Publications*: papers in scientific jls incl. New England Jl Medicine, Jl Clinical Investigation, Cell, Nature Genetics. *Recreations*: photography, collecting Chinese and Japanese porcelain. *Address*: Radcliffe Department of Medicine, John Radcliffe Hospital, Oxford OX3 9DU. *T*: (01865) 234657, *Fax*: (01865) 234658.

**WATKINS, Jason Peter;** actor; *b* Albrighton, Shropshire, 28 Oct. 1962; *s* of Alan Watkins and Avis Watkins (*née* Saltsman, now Baldry); *m* 1st, 1995, Caroline Harding (marr. diss. 2002); two *s*; 2nd, 2014, Clara Francis; one *s* one *d* (and one *d* decd). *Educ*: Marlborough Primary Sch.; Hounslow Manor Comprehensive Sch.; Royal Acad. of Dramatic Art. *Theatre* includes: Royal Court: Rafts and Dreams, 1990; King Lear, 1993; Blue Heart, 1997; Boy Gets Girl, 2010; The Twits, 2015; National Theatre: A Laughing Matter, 2002; Landscape with Weapon, 2007; Our Class, 2009; Inadmissible Evidence, 2013; Royal Shakespeare Co.: The Plantagenets, 1990; A Servant to Two Masters, and US tour, 2001 (Helen Hayes Award, theatreWashington, 2002); Kafka's Dick, Filumena, Sir Peter Hall Season, Piccadilly, 1998; Habeas Corpus, Donmar Warehouse, 1996; The Late Henry Moss, Almeida, 2009; Frozen, Haymarket, 2018; *television* includes: Being Human, 2009–11; Trollied, 2011–18; The Lost Honour of Christopher Jefferies, 2014 (Best Performance by a Leading Actor, BAFTA, 2015); W1A, 2015–17; The Hollow Crown, 2016; Dr Who, 2016; Are You Being Served, 2016; Friday Night Dinner, 2017; Taboo, 2017–; Inside No 9, 2017; Line of Duty, 2017; A Very English Scandal, 2018; Watership Down, 2018; Hold the Sunset, 2018, 2019; The Crown, 2019; *films* include: High Hopes, 1987; Tomorrow Never Dies, 1997; Bridget Jones: The Edge of Reason, 2004; Confetti, 2007; Nativity!, 2009; Nativity 2: Danger in the Manger, 2012; Nativity 3: Dude, Where's My Donkey?, 2014; Hampstead, 2017; The Children Act, 2018; The Man Who Killed Don Quixote, 2018. Patron: SLOW, 2015–; Child Bereavement UK, 2017–; Ambassador, UK Sepsis Trust, 2013–. *Recreations*: dealing with my dyslexia, serial hand-walker, photography, secret cyclist, the justice system, compassion. *Address*: c/o United Agents, 12–26 Lexington Street, W1F 0LE. *E*: ruthyoungteam@unitedagents.co.uk.

**WATKINS, Prof. Jeffrey Clifton,** PhD; FMedSci; FRS 1988; FRSB; Hon. Professor of Pharmacology, 1989–99, and Leader of Excitatory Amino Acid Group, Department of Pharmacology, 1973–99, School of Medical Sciences (formerly The Medical School), Bristol (Hon. Senior Research Fellow, 1983–89), now Professor Emeritus; *b* 20 Dec. 1929; *s* of Colin Hereward and Amelia Miriam Watkins; *m* 1973, Beatrice Joan Thacher; one *s* one *d*. *Educ*: Univ. of Western Australia (MSc 1954); Univ. of Cambridge (PhD 1954). Research Fellow, Chemistry Department: Univ. of Cambridge, 1954–55; Univ. of Yale, 1955–57; Res. Fellow, 1958–61, Fellow, 1961–65, Physiology Dept, ANU; Scientific Officer, ARC Inst. of Animal Physiology, Babraham, Cambridge, 1965–67; Res. Scientist, MRC Neuropsychiatry Unit, Carshalton, Surrey, 1967–73; Senior Research Fellow, Depts of Pharmacology and Physiology, The Med. Sch., Bristol, 1973–83. MAE 1989; FRSB (FIBiol 1998); FMedSci 1999. Hon. FBPhS (Hon. FBPharmacolS 1996); Hon. Fellow, Univ. of Bristol, 2015. Wakeman Foundn Award for Dist. Res. in Neuroscis, 1992; Dana Foundn Award for Pioneering Achievement in Health, 1994; Bristol-Myers Squibb Award for Dist. Achievements in Neuroscience Res., 1995; Thudichum Medal, British Biochemical Soc., 2000; Wellcome Gold Medal, British Pharmacol Soc., 2001. *Publications*: The NMDA Receptor, 1989, 2nd edn 1994; approx. 250 pubns in learned jls, e.g. Jl of Physiol., Brit. Jl of Pharmacol., Nature, Brain Res., Exptl Brain Res., Eur. Jl of Pharmacol., Neuroscience, Neuroscience Letters, Jl of Neuroscience, Neuropharmacology. *Address*: 8 Lower Court Road, Lower Almondsbury, Bristol BS32 4DX. *T*: (01454) 613829.

**WATKINS, Maurice;** see Watkins, E. M.

**WATKINS, Paul Rhys;** 'cellist and conductor; Artistic Director, Great Lakes Chamber Music Festival, since 2015; Member, Emerson String Quartet, since 2013; *b* 4 Jan. 1970; *s* of John Watkins and Esther Elizabeth Picton Watkins; *m* 1993, Jennifer Laredo; two *d*. *Educ*: Yehudi Menuhin Sch.; St Catharine's Coll., Cambridge. Finalist, BBC Young Musician of Year, 1988; Principal 'Cellist, BBC SO, 1990–98; Mem. ('cellist), Nash Ensemble, 1998–2013. Music Dir and Principal Conductor, English Chamber Orch., 2009–13; Principal Guest Conductor, Ulster Orch., 2009–12. Prof., RAM, 1996–2002. Vis. Prof. of Cello, Yale Univ., 2018–. Featured soloist, Masterworks, BBC TV, 1999. Solo and conducting appearances with LSO, LPO, Philharmonia Orch., English Chamber Orch., Gewandhausorchester Leipzig, Hong Kong Philharmonic, Detroit Symphony, Melbourne Symphony, Netherlands Philharmonic, Swedish Chamber Orch.; soloist, First Night of the Proms, 2007; solo début, Carnegie Hall, 2010; conducting début, BBC Proms, 2010. Recordings: 14 solo recordings, 2001–12; début recording as conductor, BBC SO, 2004. Winner, Leeds Conducting Competition, 2002. *Recreations*: wine, sleep, Lego. *Address*: c/o Thomas Walton, IMG Artists, Capital Tower, 91 Waterloo Road, SE1 8RT. *T*: (020) 7957 5800. *E*: twalton@imgartists.com.

**WATKINS, Penelope Jill, (Mrs M. J. Bowman);** a District Judge (Magistrates' Courts) (formerly Stipendiary Magistrate), Mid-Glamorgan, 1995–2014, and South Wales, 1996–2014; a Recorder, 2000–14; *b* 19 April 1953; *d* of Laurence Gordon Watkins and Dorothy Ernestine Watkins; *m* 1977, Michael James Bowman. *Educ*: Howell's Sch., Llandaff; Henbury Sch., Bristol; Somerville Coll., Oxford (BA Jurisp. 1974; MA). Called to the Bar, Lincoln's Inn, 1975; Inner London Magistrates' Courts Service: Dep. Chief Clerk, serving at London Courts, 1976–90; Dep. Training Officer, 1983–86; Justices' Clerk: Wells Street, 1990–91; Camberwell Green, 1991–95. An Asst Recorder, 1998–2000. *Recreations*: reading, music, travel.

**WATKINS, Peter Derek,** CB 2019; CBE 2004; FRAeS; Director General Strategy and International, Ministry of Defence, 2017–18; *b* 8 Feb. 1959; *s* of Vivian Derek Watkins and Eunice Mary Watkins (*née* Wilkinson). *Educ*: Strode's Sch., Egham; Peterhouse, Cambridge (BA Hist. 1980). FRAeS 2008. Joined MoD, 1980; various posts, 1980–90; Private Sec. to Minister for Defence Procurement, 1990–93; Dir (Finance and Secretariat) Air, 1994–96; Counsellor (Defence Supply and Aerospace), Bonn/Berlin, 1996–2000; Team Leader, Smart Acquisition, 2000–01; Private Sec. to Defence Sec., 2001–03; Comd Sec., RAF Strike Comd, 2004–06; Fellow, Weatherhead Center for Internat. Affairs, Harvard Univ., 2006–07; Dir Gen. Typhoon, 2007–08, Dir Operational Policy, 2008–11, MoD; Dir Gen., Defence Acad., 2011–14; Dir Gen. Security Policy, MoD, 2014–17. Vis. Prof., KCL, 2019–. FInstD 2016. Liveryman, Coachmakers' Co., 2008–. *Recreations*: overseas travel, historic buildings. *E*: peterdwatkins@msn.com.

**WATKINS, Peter Rodney;** Office for Standards in Education Inspector, 1993–98; *b* 8 Oct. 1931; *s* of late Frank Arthur Watkins and Mary Gwyneth Watkins (*née* Price); *m* 1971, Jillian Ann Burge (marr. diss. 1998); two *d*. *Educ*: Solihull Sch.; Emmanuel Coll., Cambridge (Exhibnr; Hist. Tripos Pts I and II 1952, 1953; Cert. in Educn 1954; MA 1957). Flying Officer, RAF, 1954–56; History Master, East Ham Grammar Sch., 1956–59; Sixth Form Hist. Master, Brentwood Sch., 1959–64; Sen. Hist. Master, Bristol Grammar Sch., 1964–69; Headmaster, King Edward's Five Ways Sch., Birmingham, 1969–74; Headmaster, Chichester High Sch. for Boys, 1974–79; Principal, Price's Sixth Form Coll., Fareham, 1980–84; Dep. Chief Exec., Sch. Curriculum Develt Cttee, 1984–88, Nat. Curriculum Council, 1988–91. Exec., SHA, 1980–84. Chm., Christian Educn Movement, 1980–87. Reader, St Peter's, Bishop's Waltham, dio. of Portsmouth, 1989–2010. Gov., St Luke's C of E Aided Sch., Portsmouth, 1992–2003 (Chm. 1998–2003). *Publications*: The Sixth Form College in Practice, 1982; Modular Approaches to the Secondary Curriculum, 1986; St Barnabas' Church, Swanmore 1845–1995, 1995; Swanmore since 1840, 2001; Jerusalem or Athens?, 2005; Not Like Uncle Tom: an autobiography, 2006; Bishop's Waltham: parish, town and church, 2007; The Villages of the Meon Valley: aspects of their history, 2010. *Recreations*: travel, walking, writing, local history, theology. *Address*: 1 Greenways, Spring Lane, Swanmore, Southampton SO32 2RL. *T*: (01489) 894789. *E*: p.watkins31@btinternet.com.

**WATKINSON, Dame Angela (Eileen),** DBE 2013; *b* 18 Nov. 1941; *m* 1961, Roy Michael Watkinson (marr. diss.); one *s* two *d*. *Educ*: Wanstead County High Sch.; Anglia Poly. (HNC 1989). Bank of NSW, 1958–64; Special Sch. Sec., Essex CC, 1976–88; Cttee Clerk, Barking and Dagenham BC, 1988–89; Cttee Manager, Basildon DC, 1989–94. Member (C): Havering BC, 1994–98; Essex CC, 1997–2001. MP (C) Upminster, 2001–10, Hornchurch and Upminster, 2010–17. An Opposition Whip, 2002–04 and 2006–10; Shadow Minister: for Health and Educn in London, 2004–05; for Local Govt and Communities, 2005; a Lord Comr of HM Treasury (Govt Whip), 2010–12. Mem., Work and Pensions Select Cttee, 2013–15. Member: Parly Assembly, Council of Europe, 2012–15; Cttee on Standards in Public Life, 2013–17. Patron: Romford Autistic Gp Support, 2001–17; ADD+UP, 2001–17. Freeman, City of London, 2004.

**WATLING, Giles Francis;** MP (C) Clacton, since 2017; *b* Chingford, Essex, 18 Feb. 1953; *s* of late Jack Stanley Watling and Patricia Hicks; *m* 1979, Vanda June; twin *d*. *Educ*: Forest Sch., Snaresbrook. Director and producer; actor: television includes: Gideon CID, 1964–67; How's Your Father?, 1979–80; Bread, 1988–91; The Tutankhamun Conspiracy, 2001. Mem. (C), Tendring DC, 2015–. Mem., Digital, Culture, Media and Sport Cttee, H of C, 2017–. Contested (C) Clacton, Oct. 2014, 2015. Vice Chm., Royal Theatrical Fund. *Recreations*: sailing, guitarist, theatre, cinema, walking. *Address*: House of Commons, SW1A 0AA. *E*: giles.watling.mp@parliament.uk. *Clubs*: Garrick; Frinton Cricket; Walton and Frinton Yacht; Frinton War Memorial.

**WATMORE, Ian Charles;** First Civil Service Commissioner, since 2016; *b* 5 July 1958; *s* of late Dr Kenneth Watmore and Kathleen Watmore; *m* 1987, Rev. Georgina; four *s*. *Educ*: Trinity Sch. of John Whitgift, Croydon; Trinity Coll., Cambridge (BA 1980). UK Man. Dir, Accenture, 2000–04; Govt CIO and Hd, e-Govt Unit, Cabinet Office, 2004–05; Chief Advr to Prime Minister on Delivery and Hd, Prime Minister's Delivery Unit, 2005–07; Permanent Sec., DIUS, 2007–09; Chief Exec., FA, 2009–10; Chief Operating Officer, 2010–11, Permanent Sec., 2011–12, Cabinet Office. Board Member: e-skills uk, 2000–06; English Inst. for Sport, 2002–15; England Rugby 2015, 2011–16; Inf. Comr's Office, 2012–16; Gov., Church Comrs, 2014–18. Non-exec. Chair, Quantum Sports, 2014–; non-exec. Dir, Cambridge Univ. Information Services, 2014–. Mem., Adv. Bd, Westminster Business Sch., 2010–13. Pres., Mgt Consultants Assoc., 2003–04. Chm., Migraine Trust, 2010–19 (Trustee, 2008–19). Mem. Council, Chester Cathedral, 2017–. Hon. DLitt Westminster, 2009. *Recreations*: golf, new technology, rock music, football, dog walking.

**WATSON,** family name of **Barons Manton** and **Watson of Richmond**.

**WATSON OF INVERGOWRIE,** Baron *cr* 1997 (Life Peer), of Invergowrie in Perth and Kinross; **Michael Goodall Watson;** *b* 1 May 1949; *s* of late Clarke Watson and Senga (*née* Goodall); *m* 2004, Clare Thomas; one *s*. *Educ*: Invergowrie Primary Sch., Dundee; Dundee High Sch.; Heriot-Watt Univ., Edinburgh (BA 2nd Cl. Hons Econs and Industrial Relns). Development Officer, WEA, E Midlands Dist, 1974–77; full-time official, ASTMS, then MSF, 1977–89. Director: PS Communications Consultants Ltd, Edinburgh, 1997–99; Dundee United FC, 2003–05; Caledonia Consulting, Edinburgh, 2007–12. MP (Lab) Glasgow Central, 1989–97. Mem., Public Accounts Cttee, 1995–97. Opposition spokesman on educn, H of L, 2015–. Mem., Scottish Exec. Cttee, Labour Party, 1987–90; Chm., PLP Overseas Develt Aid Cttee, 1991–97. Mem. (Lab) Glasgow Cathcart, Scottish Parlt, 1999–2005; Minister for Tourism, Culture and Sport, 2001–03. *Publications*: Rags to Riches: the official history of Dundee United Football Club, 1985; Year Zero: an inside view of the Scottish Parliament, 2001. *Recreations*: Dundee United FC, cycling, running. *Address*: House of Lords, SW1A 0PW.

**WATSON OF RICHMOND**, Baron *cr* 1999 (Life Peer), of Richmond in the London Borough of Richmond-upon-Thames; **Alan John Watson**, CBE 1985; Chairman: Corporate Television Networks (CTN), since 1992; Burson-Marsteller UK, 1994–2004; Burson-Marsteller Europe, 1996–2007; Raisin Social, since 2005; Director, Burson-Marsteller Worldwide, 1992–2004; *b* 3 Feb. 1941; *s* of Rev. John William Watson and Edna Mary (*née* Peters); *m* 1965, Karen Lederer; two *s. Educ*: Diocesan Coll., Cape Town, SA; Kingswood Sch., Bath, Somerset; Jesus Coll., Cambridge (Open Schol. in History 1959, State Schol. 1959; MA Hons; Hon. Fellow 2004). Vice-Pres., Cambridge Union; Pres., Cambridge Univ. Liberal Club. Research Asst to Cambridge Prof. of Modern History on post-war history of Unilever, 1962–64. General trainee, BBC, 1965–66; Reporter, BBC TV, The Money Programme, 1966–68; Chief Public Affairs Commentator, London Weekend Television, 1969–70; Reporter, Panorama, BBC TV, 1971–74; Presenter, The Money Programme, 1974–75; Head of TV, Radio, Audio-Visual Div., EEC, 1975–79; Dir, Charles Barker City Ltd, 1980–85 (Chief Exec., 1980–83); Dep. Chm., Sterling PR, 1985–86; Chairman: City and Corporate Counsel Ltd, 1987–94; Threadneedle Publishing Gp, 1987–94; Corporate Vision Ltd, 1989–98. Mem. Bd, Y & R Partnership, 1999–2002; Chm., Coca-Cola European Adv. Bd, 2003–06; Exec. Chm., Havas Media Gp UK, 2013–16. Mem., Exec. Bd, Unicef, 1985–92; Mem. Bd, POW Business Leaders Forum, 1996–99; non-exec. Dir, Community and Charities Cttee, BT Bd, 1996–2004. Pres., Liberal Party, 1984–85. Vice Chm., European Movt, 1995–2001. Chm., Jt Commonwealth Socs Council, 2003–13. Chairman: UK Koenigswinter Steering Cttee, 2003–10; British Accreditation Council, 2007–12. Presenter: You and 1992, BBC 1 series, 1990; The Germans, Channel 4, 1992; Key Witness, Radio 4, 1996. Vis. Prof. in English Culture and European Studies, Louvain Univ., 1990–; Vis. Fellow, Oriel Coll., Oxford, 2003–; Hon. Professor: German Studies, Birmingham Univ., 1997–; Political Studies, St Petersburg State Univ., 2003–; Business Studies, Korea Univ., 2004–; Churchill Fellow, Westminster Coll., Fulton, Mo, 2017–. Chairman: RTS, 1992–94 (Mem. Council, 1989–95; FRTS 1992); CBI Media Industries Gp, 1995–98. President: British-German Assoc., 2000– (Chm., 1992–2000); Franco-British Soc., 2012–. Pres., Heathrow Assoc. for Control of Aircraft Noise, 1992–95. Co-Chair, British Jamestown Cttee, 2006–08. Chairman: Chemistry Adv. Bd, Cambridge Univ., 1999–2008; Cambridge Foundn, 2005–; High Steward (Dep. Chancellor), Cambridge Univ., 2010–. Mem. Adv. Council: John Smith Meml Trust, 1998–2002; Univ. of Virginia Center for Politics, 2011–. Chm. of Govs, Westminster Coll., Oxford, 1988–94; Governor: Kingswood Sch., 1984–90; ESU, 1993– (Internat. Dep. Chm., 1995–99; Chm., 2000–05, now Emeritus; Churchill Medal, 2005; Vice Pres., Worldwide, 2012–); Trustee, British Studies Centre, Humboldt Univ., Berlin, 1998–2005; Patron: Richmond Soc., 2001–; Mus. of Richmond, 2002–. Fellow, Internat. Visual Communications Assoc., 1997. Protector, Habsburg-Lothringen Order of St Georg for GB and NI, 2015. Hon. FCIPR (Hon. FIPR 1998). Hon. DHL: St Lawrence Univ., 1992; Richmond American Internat. Univ., 2007; Hon Dr: Moldova Univ., 2007; Richmond American Internat. Univ., 2008; Tirana Univ., 2010; Hon. LLD: Bucharest, 2011; Birmingham, 2012. Grand Prix Eurodiaporama of EC for European TV Coverage, 1974; Commonwealth of Virginia Cert. of Public Recognition, 2007. Order of Merit (Germany), 1995, Grand Cross, 2001, Knight's Grand Cross, 2007; Order of Merit, Grand Cross (Romania), 2004; George Kastrioti Skanderbeg Medal (Albania), 2012; Knight of Habsburg-Lothringen Order of St Georg, 2015; Kt Comdr, Royal Constantinian Order of St Francis I, 2017. *Publications*: Europe at Risk, 1972; The Germans: who are they now?, 1992 (German, US, Japanese, Polish and Chinese edns); Thatcher and Kohl: old rivalries renewed, 1996; Jamestown: the voyage of English, 2007; The Queen and the USA, 2012; Churchill's Legacy: two speeches to save the world, 2017. *Recreations*: historical biography, wine, the Thames. *Address*: Cholmondeley House, 3 Cholmondeley Walk, Richmond upon Thames, Surrey TW9 1NS; Somerset Lodge, Nunney, Somerset BA11 4NP. *Clubs*: Brooks's, Royal Automobile, Kennel, Beefsteak, Oxford and Cambridge.

*See also* Hon. S. H. W. Watson.

**WATSON, Alan**, CBE 2001; Deputy Parliamentary Commissioner for Administration, 2000–03; Deputy Scottish Parliamentary Commissioner for Administration, 2000–02; Deputy Welsh Administration Ombudsman, 2000–03; *b* 23 Nov. 1942; *s* of late Dennis Watson and of Dorothy Watson; *m* 1st, 1966, Marjorie Eleanor Maid (marr. diss.); one *s* one *d*; 2nd, 1991, Susan Elizabeth Beare (*née* Dwyer); one step *s. Educ*: King Edward VI Grammar Sch., Morpeth. Min. of Pensions and Nat. Insce, later Min. of Social Security, then DHSS, 1962–76; Staff Inspection, CSD, 1976–80; Mgt Trng, DSS, 1980–84; Investigations Manager with Parly Comr for Admin, 1984–89; Personnel, DSS, 1989–92; Dir, Field Ops, with Contributions Agency, 1992–94; Dir of Investigations, with Parly Comr for Admin, 1994–2000. Dep. Ind. Football Ombudsman, 2008– (Dir, 2002–08, Dep. Chm., 2004–08, Ind. Football Commn). *Recreations*: cricket, football, football referee, walking, books.

**WATSON, Prof. Alan Andrew**, FRS 2000; FRAS; Professor of Physics, 1984–2003, now Emeritus, Research Professor, 2003–10, Visiting Professor, since 2010, University of Leeds; *b* 26 Sept. 1938; *s* of William John Watson and Elsie Robinson; *m* 1973, Susan Lorraine Cartman; one *s* one *d. Educ*: Daniel Stewart's College, Edinburgh; Edinburgh Univ. (BSc 1st cl. hons Physics 1960; PhD 1964). FInstP 1998. Asst Lectr, Univ. of Edinburgh, 1962–64; University of Leeds: Lectr, 1964–76; Reader in Particle Cosmic Physics, 1976–84; Chm., Physics Dept, 1989–93; Pro Vice-Chancellor, 1994–97; Hd, Dept of Physics and Astronomy, 1997–2000. Mem., Cosmic Ray Commn, IUPAP, 1991–95. Spokesman, Pierre Auger Observatory, Argentina, 2001–07, now Emeritus. Leverhulme Emeritus Fellow, 2011–12. Dr *hc* Santiago de Compostela, 2009. O'Ceallaigh Medal, Cosmic Ray Commn, IUPAP, 2011; Faraday Medal, InstP, 2011. *Publications*: contribs to Physical Review Letters, Astrophysical Jl, Jl of Physics, Nuclear Instruments and Methods, Astroparticle Physics, Nature, Physical Review D. *Recreations*: malt whisky tasting, golf, watching Scotland win Calcutta Cup games, theatre. *Address*: School of Physics and Astronomy, University of Leeds, Leeds LS2 9JT. *T*: 07870 109602. *E*: a.a.watson@leeds.ac.uk. *Club*: Crail Golfing Society.

**WATSON, Alistair Gordon**; Sheriff of North Strathclyde at Kilmarnock, since 2005; *b* Dundee, 1 July 1959; *s* of Robert and Isobel Watson; *m* 1985, Susan Gibson; one *s* two *d. Educ*: High Sch. of Dundee; Univ. of Dundee (LLB 1980; DipLP 1981). NP 1982. Solicitor, 1981–2005; Dir, Public Defence Solicitors' Office, 1998–2005. *Recreations*: family, photography, walking, gardening. *Address*: Kilmarnock Sheriff Court, St Marnock Street, Kilmarnock, Ayrshire KA1 1ED.

**WATSON, Sir Andrew**; *see* Watson, Sir J. A.

**WATSON, Prof. Andrew James**, PhD; FRS 2003; Royal Society Research Professor, College of Life and Environmental Sciences, University of Exeter, since 2013; *b* 30 Nov. 1952; *s* of Leslie John Watson and Ena Florence Watson (*née* Bence); *m* 1978, Jacqueline Elizabeth Pughe; two *s. Educ*: Steyning Grammar Sch.; Imperial Coll., London (BSc Physics 1975); Univ. of Reading (PhD 1978). Research Scientist: Dept of Atmospheric and Oceanic Sci., Univ. of Michigan, Ann Arbor, 1978–81; Marine Biological Assoc., Plymouth, 1981–88; Res. Scientist and Project Leader, Plymouth Marine Lab., 1988–95; Prof. of Envmtl Sci., 1996–2009, Royal Soc. Res. Prof., Sch. of Envmtl Sci., 2009–13, UEA. Visiting Scientist: Lamont-Doherty Geol Observatory, Columbia Univ., 1985, 1987; Woods Hole Oceanographic Inst., 2000. *Publications*: numerous articles and papers in scientific jls. *Recreations*: acoustic and electric guitar, cycling, walking. *Address*: Laver Building, College of Life and Environmental Sciences, University of Exeter, North Park Road, Exeter EX4 4QE. *T*: (01392) 723792.

**WATSON, Rt Rev. Andrew John**; *see* Guildford, Bishop of.

**WATSON, Maj.-Gen. Andrew Linton**, CB 1981; Lieutenant Governor and Secretary, Royal Hospital, Chelsea, 1984–92; *b* 9 April 1927; *s* of Col W. L. Watson, OBE, and Mrs D. E. Watson (*née* Lea); *m* 1952, Mary Elizabeth, *d* of Mr and Mrs A. S. Rigby, Warrenpoint, Co. Down; two *s* one *d. Educ*: Wellington Coll., Berks. psc, jssc, rcds. Commnd The Black Watch, 1946; served, 1946–66: with 1st and 2nd Bns, Black Watch, in UK, Germany, Cyprus and British Guiana; with UN Force, Cyprus; as GSO 2 and 3 on Staff, UK and Germany; GSO 1 HQ 17 Div./Malaya Dist, 1966–68; CO 1st Bn The Black Watch, UK, Gibraltar and NI, 1969–71; Comdr 19 Airportable Bde, Colchester, 1972–73; RCDS, 1974; Comdr British Army Staff, and Military Attaché, Washington, DC, 1975–77; GOC Eastern District, 1977–80; COS, Allied Forces, Northern Europe, 1980–82. Col, The Black Watch, 1981–92. Chm., Inner London Br., Army Benevolent Fund, 1983–2000; Trustee, Royal Cambridge Home for Soldiers' Widows, 1992–2001. *Recreations*: golf, walking, classical music. *Address*: c/o Royal Bank of Scotland, 12 Dunkeld Road, Perth PH1 5RB. *T*: (01738) 21777. *Club*: Pitt.

*See also* T. D. H. Davies.

**WATSON, Sir Andrew Michael M.**; *see* Milne-Watson.

**WATSON, (Angus) Gavin**; freelance writer and editor; Secretary, Pevsner (formerly Buildings) Books Trust, 1997–2014; *b* 14 April 1944; *s* of late H. E. and M. Watson; *m* 1967, Susan Naomi Beal (marr. diss. 1991); two *s* (and one *d* decd). *Educ*: Carlisle Grammar School; Merton College, Oxford; Peterhouse, Cambridge. Joined Dept of the Environment, 1971; Private Office, Secretary of State, 1975–77; Asst Sec., 1980–86; Under Secretary, 1986–97; Head: Directorate of Public Housing Mgt and Resources, 1986–91; Water Directorate, June–July 1991; Directorate of Envmtl Policy and Analysis, 1991–94; Cities, Countryside and Private Finance Directorate, 1994–95; Govt Offices Central Unit, 1995–97; Chm., Fortunegate Community Housing, 1998–2004. Adjudicator, Nat. Rlwy Heritage Awards, 2003–. Mem. Council, Shropshire Archaeol and Histl Soc., 2017–. *Publications*: The Story of Bishop's Castle, 2016; contribs to Pevsner Architectural Guides. *Recreations*: looking at buildings, industrial archaeology, fell walking. *Address*: 19 Castle Street, Bishop's Castle, Shropshire SY9 5BU. *T*: (01588) 630444.

**WATSON, Anthony**, CBE 2006; Chairman, Marks & Spencer Pension Trust Ltd, 2006–11; *b* 2 April 1945; *s* of Lt Comdr Andrew Patrick Watson and Harriet Watson; *m* 1972, Heather Jane Dye; two *s* one *d. Educ*: Campbell Coll., Belfast; Queen's Univ., Belfast (BSc Hons Econ). ASIP (AIIMR 1972). Called to the Bar, Lincoln's Inn, 1976, Bencher, 2002. Dir, Touche, Remnant & Co., 1980–85; Chief Investment Officer, Citibank NA, 1985–91; Dir Internat. Investments, 1991–95, Man. Dir, 1995–98, AMP Asset Management plc; Chief Investment Officer, 1998–2001, Chief Exec., 2002–06, Hermes Pensions Mgt Ltd. Chm., Asian Infrastructure Fund Ltd, 1998–2010; Director: Virgin Direct Ltd, 1995–98; Innisfree plc, 1996–98; MEPC, 2000–06 (Chm., 2003–06); Securities Inst., 2000–06; Edinburgh Fund Managers plc, 2001–02; Investment Mgt Assoc. Ltd, 2002–05; Vodafone Gp PLC, 2006–14; Hammerson Gp PLC, 2006–16 (Sen. Ind. Dir, 2009–16); Witan Investment Trust PLC, 2006– (Sen. Ind. Dir, 2009–); Lloyds Banking Gp, 2009–17 (Sen. Ind. Dir, 2012–17); Member: Adv. Bd, Norges Bank Investment Mgt, 2006–; ACT Adv. Bd, 2006–18; Adv. Gp, 2008–09, Dir, 2009–14, Shareholder Exec., BERR, later BIS. Chm., Strategic Investment Bd (NI), 2002–09. Mem., Financial Reporting Council, 2004–07. Dir, Queen's Univ. Foundn Bd, 2003–15. Trustee: Women Caring Trust, 1996–2006; Lincoln's Inn Pension Fund, 2002–; Investment Property Educnl Trust, 2004–06. Hon. FCSI (Hon. FSI 2006); Hon. FCT 2019. Freeman, City of London, 2007; Liveryman, Leathersellers' Co., 2007 (Master, 2014–15). Hon. DSc Econs QUB, 2012. *Recreations*: golf, ski-ing, history, tennis, Rugby. *E*: tonywatson11@btinternet.com. *Clubs*: Royal Automobile, MCC; Royal St Davids Golf (Harlech).

**WATSON, Anthony David F.**; *see* Forbes Watson.

**WATSON, (Anthony) Dennis**; QC 2009; **His Honour Judge Dennis Watson**; a Circuit Judge, since 2012; *b* Crosby, June 1963; *s* of Keith Watson and Margaret Watson; *m* 1994, Nicola Jane Hunt; one *s* one *d. Educ*: Uppingham Sch.; Leeds Poly. (BA Hons Law 1984); Inns of Court Sch. of Law. Called to the Bar, Inner Temple, 1985; in practice on N Circuit, 1985–2012; Recorder, 2003–12. *Recreations*: golf, ski-ing, family. *Address*: Liverpool Crown Court, The Queen Elizabeth II Law Courts, Derby Square, Liverpool, Merseyside L2 1XA. *Clubs*: Royal Birkdale Golf (Capt., 2008), Royal & Ancient Golf, Royal Cinque Ports Golf.

**WATSON, Anthony Gerard**; Managing Director, PA Media (formerly Press Association), since 2008; *b* 28 May 1955; *s* of George Maurice Watson and Ann (*née* McDonnell); *m* 1st, 1982, Susan Ann Gutteridge (marr. diss. 1994); two *s* one *d*; 2nd, 1994, Sylvie Helen Pask; one *s* one *d. Educ*: St John Fisher Sch., Peterborough; N Staffs Polytechnic (BA Pol. and Internat. Relns). Journalist with E Midlands Allied Press, Peterborough, 1977–79; joined Westminster Press—Evening Despatch, Darlington, 1979, News Editor, 1983–84; Yorkshire Post, 1984–86; Researcher, World in Action, Granada TV, 1986–88; Dep. Editor, 1988–89, Editor, 1989–2002, Yorkshire Post; Head of Business Develt, 2003–04, Editl Dir, 2004–06, Ed.-in-Chief, 2007–08, Press Assoc. Trustee, Television for the Envmt, 2016–. Provincial Journalist of the Year, British Press Awards, 1987. *Address*: PA Media, The Point, 37 North Wharf Road, Paddington, W2 1AF.

**WATSON, Antony Edward Douglas**; QC 1986; *b* 6 March 1945; *s* of William Edward Watson and Margaret Watson (*née* Douglas); *m* 1972, Gillian Mary Bevan-Arthur; two *d. Educ*: Sedbergh School; Sidney Sussex College, Cambridge (MA). Called to the Bar, Inner Temple, 1968. Dep. Chm., Copyright Tribunal, 1994–97. *Publications*: (jtly) Terrell on Patents (1884), 13th edn 1982, 14th edn 1994. *Recreations*: wine, opera, country pursuits. *Address*: The Old Rectory, Milden, Suffolk IP7 7AF. *T*: (01449) 740227. *Club*: Boodle's.

**WATSON, Arthur James**, RSA 2005 (ARSA 1986); artist; Senior Lecturer in Contemporary Art Practice, Duncan of Jordanstone College of Art and Design, University of Dundee, since 1995 (Course Director of Fine Art, 1995–2018); President, Royal Scottish Academy, 2012–18 (Secretary, 2007–12); *b* Aberdeen, 24 June 1951; *s* of David Lyall Watson and Nance Harding Nicol; *m* 1st, 1972, Jennifer Moncrieff Sutherland Murray (marr. diss.); 2nd, 1981, Joyce Winifred Cairns, RSA (marr. diss.). *Educ*: Aberdeen Grammar Sch.; Gray's Sch. of Art, Aberdeen (Dip. Art 1973; Postgrad. Dip. 1974). Founder Artistic Dir, Peacock Printmakers (Aberdeen) Ltd, 1974–95. Mem., Awards to Artists Panel, 1982–84, Exhibns Panel, 1984–85, Combined Arts Cttee, 1985–89, Scottish Arts Council. Chair, Royal Scottish Acad. Foundn, 2013–18. Member, Board: Scottish Sculpture Workshop, 1980–99; 369 Gall., Edinburgh, 1985–87; Richard Demarco Gall., 1987–92 (Chm., 1990–92); Workshop and Studio Provision, Scotland, 1999–2013; Friends of Royal Scottish Acad., 2007–17; Trustee: Demarco Eur. Art Foundn, 1992–2006; Pier Arts Centre, Orkney, 2010–18. Patron: Grampian Hosps Art Trust, 2012–; Perthshire Art Assoc., 2013–.

Exhibited widely in UK, Poland, Hungary, Romania, Italy, USA and Japan; (jtly) represented Scotland at Venice Biennale, 1990; Singing for Dead Singers, five venues in Aberdeen, 2000; (with Doug Cocker) Leaving Jericho, 2003; 10 Dialogues: Richard Demarco, Scotland and the European Avant Garde, Royal Scottish Acad., 2010; Towards Double Diablerie exhibn and performance, Nagoya, 2010; (jt curator) The Water Hen: Kantor, Demarco and the Edinburgh Festival, Royal Scottish Acad., 2015; (jt curator) Ages of Wonder, Scotland's Art of 1540–Now, Royal Scottish Acad., 2018. Hon. Mem., Aberdeen Artists Soc., 2004; HRHA 2012; Hon. RWA 2016. *Recreations:* filing stuff, Scottish Traditional Song (particularly if sung by elderly ladies). *Address:* 5B Melville Street, Perth PH1 5PY. *T:* 07837 672337. *E:* a.j.watson@dundee.ac.uk; Royal Scottish Academy, The Mound, Edinburgh EH2 2EL. *T:* (0131) 624 6110.

**WATSON, Her Honour Barbara Joan;** a Circuit Judge, 2000–13; *b* 13 Oct. 1950; *d* of Gordon Smith Watson and Joan Watson; *m* 1975, James David Heyworth (marr. diss. 1982); one *s*. *Educ:* Nelson Grammar Sch., Lancs; Southampton Univ. (LLB Hons 1972). Called to the Bar, Gray's Inn, 1973; in practice as barrister, Northern Circuit, 1973–75 and 1981–2000; Lectr in Law, Manchester Poly., 1973–80; Asst Recorder, 1992–97; Recorder, 1997–2000; Hon. Recorder, Bor. of Burnley, 2004–13; Designated Family Judge for Lancs, 2007–11; Dep. High Court Judge, 2007–13. Mem., Council of Circuit Judges, 2008–11. *Recreations:* opera, travel, watching Rugby Union.

**WATSON, Charles;** Chairman, Teneo International, since 2015; *b* Dartmouth, 5 March 1962; *s* of Basil Watson and Heather Howard; *m* 1989, Fiona; one *s* one *d*. *Educ:* Sherborne Sch.; King's Coll. London (BA Hist.). Good Relations Ltd, 1984–87; Valin Pollen Ltd, 1987–89; Financial Dynamics, 1990–2011, Gp Chief Exec., 2001–11; Chm., Strategic Communications, Financial Dynamics, later FTI Consulting, 2011–12; Chairman: Karma Commns Gp Ltd, 2011–14; Atlas 90 Hldgs, 2012–14. Chairman: Bedales Schs Develt Trust; New Coll. of the Humanities, 2011–14. Trustee, Island Initiative, 2018–. *Recreations:* skiing, mountain climbing, fishing, sailing. *Clubs:* Conduit; Royal Cruising.

**WATSON, Prof. Christine Jannette,** PhD; FMedSci; Professor of Cell and Cancer Biology, University of Cambridge, since 2010; Fellow, Newnham College, Cambridge, since 2000; *b* Greenock, Scotland, 28 Feb. 1954; *d* of James Ferguson Gray and Jean Neil Gray (*née* Bell); *m* 1976, Gordon Russell Watson; one *s* one *d*. *Educ:* Greenock High Sch.; Univ. of Glasgow (BSc Hons); Imperial Coll. London (PhD 1986); Univ. of Cambridge (MA). Research Assistant: Beatson Inst. for Cancer Res., Glasgow, 1975–78; Laboratory of Cell Biol., Consiglio Nazionale delle Richerche, Rome, 1978–80; Dept of Biochemistry, Imperial Coll. London 1980–82; Postdoctoral Fellow: Chester Beatty Laboratories, Fulham Rd, London, 1985–86; Dept of Biochemistry, Univ. of St Andrews, 1986–89; Postdoctoral Fellow, 1989–92, Gp Leader, 1992–97, Roslin Inst.; Gp Leader, Univ. of Edinburgh, 1997–98; Lectr, 1998–2002, Sen. Lectr, 2002–05, Reader, 2005–10, Univ. of Cambridge; Vice-Principal, Newnham Coll., Cambridge, 2015–18. *Publications:* contrib. scientific papers. *Recreations:* horse riding, tennis, Italian language and culture, fine art, quilting, reading. *Address:* Department of Pathology, University of Cambridge, Tennis Court Road, Cambridge CB2 1QP. *T:* (01223) 333725. *E:* cjw53@cam.ac.uk.

**WATSON, Dr David,** CBE 2017; FREng; Director, IBM Research, UK, 2015–17; *b* Consett, Co. Durham, 5 May 1960; *s* of Gordon Watson and Mary Elizabeth Watson; *m* 1985, Julia Margaret Moriarty. *Educ:* Loughborough Univ. (BSc Hons Geog. 1981); Univ. of Southampton (PhD Geog. 1986). CEng 2012; FREng 2013. IBM UK Ltd: Res. Scientist and Programmer, 1984–97; Software Tech. Manager, 1997–2000; Software Develt Prog. Dir, 2000–01; Services and Technol. Prog. Dir, 2001–06; Dir, Emerging Technol. Services, 2007–15. Mem., EPSRC, 2009–17. *Publications:* (ed with R. A. Earnshaw) Animation and Scientific Visualization, 1993. *Recreations:* swimming, photography, cabinet making, walking, travel. *E:* drdave@btinternet.com.

**WATSON, David James P.;** *see* Pitt-Watson.

**WATSON, Dennis;** *see* Watson, A. D.

**WATSON, Very Rev. Derek Richard;** Dean of Salisbury, 1996–2002; *b* 18 Feb. 1938; *s* of Richard Goodman and Honor Joan Watson; *m* 1985, Sheila Anne Atkinson (*see* W. S. A. Watson). *Educ:* Uppingham Sch.; Selwyn Coll., Cambridge (MA 1965); Cuddesdon Coll., Oxford. Ordained deacon, 1964, priest, 1965; Asst Curate, All Saints, New Eltham, 1964–66; Chaplain, Christ's Coll., Cambridge, 1966–70; Domestic Chaplain to Bishop of Southwark, 1970–73; Vicar, St Andrews and St Mark's, Surbiton, 1973–78; Canon Treasurer, Southwark Cathedral and Southwark Dir of Ordinands and Post Ordination Training, 1978–82; Rector, St Luke and Christchurch, Chelsea, 1982–96. Preacher of Lincoln's Inn, 2007–17 (Hon. Bencher, 2017). Chm., Chelsea Festival, 1993–96. *Recreations:* gentle cycling, history and biography, London. *Address:* 83 Winchester Street, SW1V 4NU.

**WATSON, Edward,** MBE 2015; Principal Dancer, Royal Ballet, since 2005; *b* Bromley, 21 May 1976. *Educ:* Royal Ballet Sch., White Lodge; Royal Ballet Upper Sch. Joined Royal Ballet, 1994; First Artist, 1998–2001; Soloist, 2001–02; First Soloist, 2002–05. *Address:* Royal Ballet, Royal Opera House, Covent Garden, WC2E 9DD. *T:* (020) 7212 9165. *Club:* h.

**WATSON, Prof. Elaine Denise,** PhD, DSc; FRCVS; FRSB; Chief Executive Officer, Agri-Food and Biosciences Institute, 2016–17; *b* Ayrshire, 8 Sept. 1955; *d* of Alexander and Isabel Watson; *m* 1989, Dr Christopher Clarke (marr. diss. 2014); one *s*. *Educ:* Univ. of Glasgow (BVMS 1978; MVM 1979); Univ. of Bristol (PhD 1987); Univ. of Edinburgh (DSc 2002). FRCVS 1990; Dip. Eur. Coll. of Animal Reproduction. Res. Officer, MAFF Cattle Breeding Centre, Shinfield, 1979–82; Veterinary Res. Officer, AFRC Inst. for Res. on Animal Diseases, Compton, 1982–84; Res. Asst, Univ. of Bristol Sch. of Veterinary Sci., 1984–87; Asst Prof. of Equine Reproduction, Univ. of Pennsylvania, 1987–91; Royal (Dick) School of Veterinary Studies, University of Edinburgh: Sen. Lectr and Hd of Reproduction, 1991–95; Reader, 1995–99; Prof. of Veterinary Reproduction, 1999–2011; Hon. Prof., 2011–; Dean, 2003–11; Dean, Ross Univ. Sch. of Veterinary Medicine, St Kitts, WI, 2012–15. Vice Pres., DeVry Medical Internat., 2013–15. ARAgS 2013; FRSB (FSB 2014). *Publications:* (ed jtly) Equine Medicine, Surgery and Reproduction, 1997; contrib. scientific papers and abstracts. *Recreations:* cycling, walking, travel, cinema, books, good food and wine.

**WATSON, (Elizabeth) Joyce;** Member (Lab) Wales Mid and West, National Assembly for Wales, since 2007; *b* 2 May 1955; *d* of late William Roberts and Jean Roberts (*née* Rennie); *m* 1986; three *c*. *Educ:* Manorbier Sch.; Cosheston Sch.; Cardigan Comprehensive Sch.; Pembroke Coll.; Univ. of Wales, Swansea (BScEcon Politics). Self-employed, retail and hospitality trade, 1980–2002; Manager, Women's Voice, 2002–07. *Publications:* Not Bad for a Woman, 2002; Knowing No Boundaries—Local Solutions to an International Crime: trafficking of women and children in Wales, 2010. *Recreations:* coastal path walking with dog, reading, bird watching, family meals. *Address:* National Assembly for Wales, Cardiff CF99 1NA. *T:* 0300 200 7093. *Club:* Soroptimist.

**WATSON, Emily Margaret, (Mrs J. Waters),** OBE 2015; actress; *b* 14 Jan. 1967; *m* 1995, Jack Waters; one *s* one *d*. *Educ:* Bristol Univ. (BA Hons English). *Films:* Breaking the Waves, 1997 (Best Actress, Variety Club, Eur. Film Award, LA Film Critics Assoc. Award, Evening Standard Film Award; Most Promising Newcomer, London Film Critics' Circle Awards); Metroland, The Boxer, Hilary and Jackie (Best Actress, British Ind. Film Awards, London Film Critics' Circle Awards), 1998; Cradle Will Rock, 1999; Angela's Ashes (London Film Critics' Circle Award), The Luzhin Defense, Trixie, 2000; Equilibrium, 2001; Punch-Drunk Love, Gosford Park, Red Dragon (Best Supporting Actress, London Film Critics' Circle Awards, 2003), 2002; The Life and Death of Peter Sellers, 2004; Separate Lies, 2005; Wah Wah, The Proposition, Corpse Bride, Miss Potter, 2006; The Water Horse: Legend of the Deep, 2007; Synecdoche, New York, 2008; Within the Whirlwind, Cold Souls, Fireflies in the Garden, 2009; Cemetery Junction, 2010; Oranges and Sunshine, 2011; War Horse, Anna Karenina, 2012; The Book Thief, Belle, 2014; Testament of Youth, 2014; Theory of Everything, A Royal Night Out, Everest, 2015; Molly Moon and the Incredible Book of Hypnotism, 2016; Kingsman: The Golden Circle, 2017; On Chesil Beach, The Happy Prince, Monster Family, 2018; *television:* Mill on the Floss, 1997; The Memory Keeper's Daughter, 2008; Appropriate Adult, 2011 (Best Leading Actress, BAFTA, 2012); The Politician's Husband, 2013; A Song for Jenny, 2015; The Secret Life of Marilyn Monroe, 2015; The Dresser, 2015; Apple Tree Yard, 2017; Genius, 2017; Little Women, 2017; King Lear, 2018; Chernobyl, 2019; *theatre:* Uncle Vanya, Twelfth Night, Donmar Warehouse, 2002, Brooklyn Acad. of Music, NY, 2003. *Address:* c/o Independent Talent Group Ltd, 40 Whitfield Street, W1T 2RH.

**WATSON, (Francis) Paul;** QC 2002; **His Honour Judge Paul Watson;** a Circuit Judge, since 2012; *b* 10 Sept. 1953; *s* of Ray and Hilda Watson; *m* 1980, Sally; one *s*. *Educ:* Churcher's Coll., Petersfield; Leeds Poly. (BA Hons). Called to the Bar, Gray's Inn, 1978; Magistrate's Clerk, 1978–80; Army Officer, Army Legal Corps, 1980–85, retd in rank of Major; in practice as barrister, 1986–2012; a Recorder, 1998–2012. *Recreations:* sailing, avid supporter of Middlesbrough FC. *Address:* Sheffield Combined Court Centre, The Law Courts, 50 West Bar, Sheffield S3 8PH.

**WATSON, Gavin;** *see* Watson, A. G.

**WATSON, George William P.;** *see* Pascoe-Watson.

**WATSON, Gerald Walter;** Treasurer, Hempnall Group of Parishes, since 2005; *b* 13 Dec. 1934; *s* of Reginald Harold Watson and Gertrude Hilda Watson (*née* Ruffell); *m* 1961, Janet Rosemary (*née* Hovey); one *s* two *d*. *Educ:* King Edward VI Sch., Norwich; Corpus Christi Coll., Cambridge (MA). National Service, RAF Regt, 1953–55. War Office, 1958–64; MoD, 1964–69; Civil Service Dept, 1969–73; Northern Ireland Office, 1973–75; CSD, 1975–81; HM Treasury, 1981–86; Dir, Central Computer and Telecommunications Agency, 1987–89; Dep. Chm., Building Socs Commn, 1986–88; Partner, Banking Gp, Ernst & Young (formerly Arthur Young), 1989–98. Chm., Centaur Trust, 1999–2013. *Recreations:* opera and theatre going, equestrian sports.

**WATSON, Gillian Anne McGregor;** Senior Managing Director, Noble & Company Ltd (formerly ES Noble & Company Ltd), since 2013; *b* Ayr, 27 Nov. 1964; *d* of James Gray Watson and Patricia Anne McGregor Watson; *m* 1990, Peter Julian Boyle; two *s* one *d*. *Educ:* Wellington Sch., Ayr; Hutchesons' Grammar Sch., Glasgow; Univ. of Edinburgh (BScHons Maths); INSEAD (MBA). Sen. Analyst, Morgan Stanley Internat., 1986–90; Sen. Manager, Standard Chartered Asia Ltd, 1990–93; Hd, Gp Strategy, 1995–99, Vice Pres., Iberia, 1999–2000, Eastern Gp, subseq. TXU Europe; Dir, Corporate Strategy, Endesa SA, 2000–05; consultant, 2006–07; CEO, Giltech Ltd, 2008–13. Chairman: Gordon & MacPhail, 2016–; DC Alpha Investments SPC Ltd, 2018–; non-executive Director: Martin Currie Global Investment Fund, 2013–; Meallmore Ltd, 2014–; Scottish Friendly, 2018–. Mem. Bd, Scottish Enterprise, 2013–17; non-exec. Dir, Royal Edinburgh Mil. Tattoo Ltd, 2013–; Trustee: Royal Edinburgh Mil. Tattoo (Charities) Ltd, 2013–; Boswell Trust, 2013–. *Recreations:* family, keeping fit, reading, travel.

**WATSON, Sir Graham (Robert),** Kt 2011; Member (Lib Dem) South West Region, England, 1999–2014, also Gibraltar, 2004–14, European Parliament (Somerset and North Devon, 1994–99); *b* 23 March 1956; *s* of late Gordon Graham Watson and of Stephanie Revill-Johnson; *m* 1987, Rita Giannini; one *s* one *d*. *Educ:* City of Bath Boys' Sch.; Heriot-Watt Univ. (BA Hons Mod. Langs). Freelance interpreter and translator, 1979–80; Administrator, Paisley Coll. of Tech., 1980–83; Head, Private Office of Rt Hon. David Steel, MP, 1983–87; Sen. Press Officer, TSB Group, 1987–88; HSBC Holdings: Public Affairs Manager, 1988–91; Govt Affairs Manager, 1992–94. European Parliament: Chm., Justice and Home Affairs Cttee, 1999–2002; Member: Econ. and Monetary Affairs Cttee, 2004–09; Foreign Affairs Cttee, 2009–14; Member, delegations: to China, 2009–14; to India, 2009–14 (Chm.); Leader, Liberal Gp, 2002–09. Contested (Lib Dem) SW England, EP, 2014. Pres., Alliance of Liberals and Democrats for Europe (formerly Eur. Lib Dem and Reform Party), 2011–15. Chm., Climate Parliament (formerly e-Parliament), 2009–14. *Publications:* (ed) The Liberals in the North-South Dialogue, 1980; (ed) To the Power of Ten, 2000; (ed) Liberalism and Globalisation, 2001; Liberal Language, 2003; EU've Got Mail, 2004; Liberal Democracy and Globalisation, 2006; The Power of Speech, 2006; Building a Liberal Europe: the ALDE Project, 2010; Letters from Europe, 2012; Continental Drift, 2014; pamphlets; articles on politics in magazines and nat. newspapers. *Recreations:* sailing, walking. *Address:* 9/3 Merchiston Park, Edinburgh EH10 4PW.

**WATSON, Maj.-Gen. (Henry) Stuart (Ramsay),** CBE 1973 (MBE 1954); *b* 9 July 1922; *yr s* of Major H. A. Watson, CBE, MVO and Mrs Dorothy Bannerman Watson, OBE; *m* 1965, Susan (*d* 2012), *o d* of Col W. H. Jackson, CBE, DL; two *s* one *d*. *Educ:* Winchester College. Commnd 2nd Lieut 13th/18th Royal Hussars, 1942; Lieut 1943; Captain 1945; Adjt 13/18 H, 1945–46 and 1948–50; psc 1951; GSO2, HQ 1st Corps, 1952–53; Instr RMA Sandhurst, 1955–57; Instr Staff Coll. Camberley, 1960–62; CO 13/18 H, 1962–64; GSO1, MoD, 1964–65; Col GS, SHAPE, 1965–68; Col, Defence Policy Staff. MoD, 1968; idc 1969; BGS HQ BAOR, 1970–73; Dir Defence Policy, MoD, 1973–74; Sen. Army Directing Staff, RCDS, 1974–76. Col, 13th/18th Royal Hussars, 1979–90. Exec. Dir, 1977–85, Dep. Dir Gen., 1985–88, Inst. of Dirs; Dir, Treasurers' Dept, Cons. Central Office, 1992–94. *Recreation:* golf. *Address:* 18 Abbey Mews, Amesbury, Wilts SP4 7EX. *Clubs:* Cavalry and Guards; Huntercombe Golf.

**WATSON, Dr Iain Arthur;** Technical Director, Thales UK, 2007–10; *b* 21 Nov. 1947; *s* of Alastair Cameron Watson and Lilian Ellen Watson (*née* Smith); *m* 1st, 1968, Janet Marshall (marr. diss. 1995); one *s* one *d*; 2nd, 1998, Pamela Chambers (*née* Low). *Educ:* Stratford Grammar Sch.; Dundee Univ. (BSc Pure Maths 1970; MSc Maths 1972; PhD 1976). Ministry of Defence: Underwater Research, Portland, 1974–89; Director: IT Systems, 1989–91; IT Strategy, 1991–92; Fleet Support (Communications and Inf. Systems), 1992–97; Dir Gen., Command Inf. Systems, 1997–99; Integrated Project Team Leader, BOWMAN and Land Digitization, 1999–2002; Dep. Tech. Dir, Thales Underwater Systems, 2002–03; Exec. Dir, 2003–04, Dir, Information Superiority, 2004–06, Defence Procurement Agency. *Recreations:* dinghy sailing, basketball, car restoration, history.

**WATSON, Ven. Ian Leslie Stewart;** Archdeacon of Coventry, 2007–12, now Archdeacon Emeritus; b Carlton, Nottingham, 17 Sept. 1950; s of Leslie Arthur Watson and Joan Harrison Watson (née Bramley); m 1972, Denise Macpherson; one s one d. Educ: Nottingham High Sch.; Britannia Royal Naval Coll. (French Interpreter); Army Staff Coll.; Wycliffe Hall, Oxford. Officer, RM, 1969–79; ordained deacon, 1981, priest, 1982; Curate, St Andrew's Plymouth, with St Paul's, Stonehouse, 1981–85; Vicar (and Methodist Minister), Matchborough, 1985–89; Vicar, 1989–92, Team Rector, 1992–95, Woodley; Anglican Chaplain, Amsterdam and Noord Holland, 1995–2001; Chief Exec., Intercontinental Church Soc., 2001–07. Canon, Gibraltar Cathedral, 2002–07, now Canon Emeritus. Chm., All Netherlands Anglican Council, 1997–2001; Diocesan Dir of Ordinands, Benelux, 1998–2001; Mem., Archbishop's Bd of Mission and Partnership in World Mission, 2001–07. Officiating Chaplain, RN, 1981–85; Chaplain: Actors' Christian Union, 1981–85; Freedom Fields Gen. Hosp., Plymouth, 1981–85; City of Coventry Freeman's Guild, 2008–09; Warwickshire Fire and Rescue Service, 2009–12. Asst Mechanic, RNLI Plymouth Lifeboat, 1983–85; Retained Firefighter, Royal Berks Fire and Rescue Service, 1991–93. Chm., Soc. for Relief of Poor Clergy, 2010–. Pres., RBL, Welton Br., 2015–. Coach (Level 2), British Wheelchair Basketball Assoc., 2018–. Bishop Kirkby's Meml Lect., Australia, 2003. GSM (NI) 1973; Silver Jubilee Medal, 1977; Vellum Service Cert., RNLI, 1985. Recreations: sport (Rugby, cricket, golf, rock climbing and potholing, now sedentary due to disability), music (singing, cellist), fishing, boating (Mem., Derby Motor Boat Club), wheelchair sports (Chm., Steelers Wheelers Sports Club, Scunthorpe, 2014–). Address: The Cottages, 43 Station Road, Hibaldstow, Brigg DN20 9DY. T: (01652) 651040, 07714 214790. E: i.watson440@btinternet.com. Clubs: Nottinghamshire CC; Rotary International (Brigg).

**WATSON, Sir (James) Andrew,** 5th Bt cr 1866; b 30 Dec. 1937; s of Sir Thomas Aubrey Watson, 4th Bt and Ella Marguerite, y d of late Sir George Farrar, 1st Bt, DSO; S father, 1941; m 1965, Christabel Mary, e d of K. R. M. Carlisle and Hon. Mrs Carlisle; two s one d. Educ: Eton. Called to the Bar, Inner Temple, 1966; a Recorder, 1985–2003. Gov., RSC, 1990–2003. Chm., Warwicks Br., CPRE. Heir: s Roland Victor Watson, b 4 March 1966. Address: Talton Wing, Newbold-on-Stour, Stratford-upon-Avon, Warwickshire CV37 8UB.

**WATSON, Prof. James Dewey,** Hon. KBE 2002; Chancellor, Cold Spring Harbor Laboratory, 2003–07 (Director, 1968–94; President, 1994–2003); b 6 April 1928; s of James D. and Jean Mitchell Watson; m 1968, Elizabeth Lewis; two s. Educ: Univ. of Chicago (BS); Indiana Univ. (PhD); Clare Coll., Cambridge (Hon. Fellow, 1967). Senior Res. Fellow in Biology, California Inst. of Technology, 1953–55; Harvard University: Asst Prof. of Biology, 1956–58; Associate Prof., 1958–61; Prof. of Molecular Biology, 1961–76. Dir, Nat. Center for Human Genome Res., NIH, 1989–92. Newton-Abraham Vis. Prof., Oxford, 1994. Member: US National Acad. Sciences, 1962–; Amer. Acad. of Arts and Sciences, 1958; Royal Danish Acad. 1962; Amer. Philosophical Soc., 1977; Foreign Member: Royal Soc., 1981; Acad. of Scis, Russia (formerly USSR), 1989; NAS, Ukraine, 1995; Hon. Member: Nat. Acad. of Scis, India, 2001; Internat. Acad. of Humanism, 2004 (Humanist Laureate 2005); RIA, 2005. Hon. FIBiol 1995; Hon. Fellow, Tata Inst. of Fundamental Res., Bombay, 1996. Hon. degrees include: Hon. DSc: Chicago, 1961; Indiana, 1963; Long Island, 1970; Adelphi, 1972; Brandeis, 1973; Albert Einstein Coll. of Medicine, 1974; Hofstra, 1976; Harvard, 1978; Rockefeller, 1980; Clarkson Coll., 1981; SUNY, 1983; Rutgers, 1988; Bard Coll., 1991; Univ. of Stellenbosch, S Africa, 1993; Fairfield Univ., Conn, 1993; Cambridge, 1993; Oxford, 1995; Melbourne, 1996; Univ. of Judaism, LA, 1999; London, Illinois Wesleyan, 2000; Widener, Dartmouth, TCD, 2001; Barcelona, 2005; Hon. MD: Buenos Aires, 1986; Charles Univ., Prague, 1998; Hon. LLD Notre Dame, 1965; Dhc: Barcelona, 2005; Moscow State, 2009; Patras, Greece, 2011. Awards include: Nobel Prize for Physiology or Medicine (jointly), 1962; Carty Medal, US NAS, 1971; Kaul Foundn Award for Excellence, 1992; Copley Medal, Royal Soc., 1993; Nat. Biotechnol. Venture Award, 1993; Nat. Medal of Science, USA, 1997; Mendel Medal, Czechoslovakia, 1998; Univ. of Chicago Medal, 1998; Heald Award, Illinois Inst. of Technol., 1999; NY Acad. of Medicine Award, 1999; Univ. Medal, SUNY, 2000; UCL Prize, 2000; (jtly) Benjamin Franklin Medal, APS, 2001; Gairdner Award, 2002; Lotos Club Medal of Merit, 2004; Othmer Medal, Chemical Heritage Foundn, 2005. Liberty Medal, City of Philadelphia, 2000. US Presidential Medal of Freedom, 1977. Publications: (jtly) Molecular Biology of the Gene, 1965, 4th edn 1986; The Double Helix, 1968; (with John Tooze) The DNA Story, 1981; (with others) The Molecular Biology of the Cell, 1983, 3rd edn 1994; (with John Tooze and David T. Kurtz) Recombinant DNA: a short course, 1984, 2nd edn (with others) 1992; A Passion for DNA, 2000; Genes, Girls and Gamow (autobiog.), 2001; DNA: the secret of life, 2003; (ed and commentary) Darwin: the indelible stamp, 2005; Avoid Boring People: and other lessons from a life in science (autobiog.), 2007; scientific papers on the mechanism of heredity. Recreation: tennis. Clubs: Century, Piping Rock, Lotos, Brook (New York).

**WATSON, James Kay Graham,** PhD; FRS 1987; FRSC 1990; Principal Research Officer, National Research Council of Canada, 1987–2007, now Researcher Emeritus (Senior Research Officer, 1982–87); b Denny, Stirlingshire, 20 April 1936; s of late Thomas Watson and Mary Catherine (née Miller); m 1981, Carolyn Margaret Landon Kerr, e d of late Robert Reid Kerr and Mona (née Kerr). Educ: Denny High Sch.; High School of Stirling; Univ. of Glasgow (BScChem, PhD). Postdoctoral Fellow: UCL, 1961–63; Nat. Res. Council, Ottawa, 1963–65; Univ. of Reading, 1965–66; Lectr in Chem. Physics, Univ. of Reading, 1966–71; Vis. Associate Prof. of Physics, Ohio State Univ., Columbus, 1971–75; SRC Sen. Res. Fellow in Chemistry, Univ. of Southampton, 1975–82. Fellow, American Physical Soc., 1990. Award for Theoretical Chemistry and Spectroscopy, Chemical Soc., 1974; Plyler Prize, Amer. Phys. Soc., 1986; Joannes Marcus Marci Medal, Czech and Slovak Spectroscopic Soc., 1996; H. M. Tory Medal, Royal Soc. of Can., 1999; E. Bright Wilson Award in Spectroscopy, Amer. Chem. Soc., 2004. Publications: 165 articles on molecular physics and spectroscopy in learned jls. Recreations: music, golf, tree-watching. Address: 183 Stanley Avenue, Ottawa, ON K1M 1P2, Canada. T: (613) 7457928; (business) Steacie Laboratory, National Research Council of Canada, Ottawa, ON K1A 0R6, Canada. E: watamarack@aol.com.

**WATSON, Prof. Janet Constance Elizabeth,** PhD; FBA 2013; Leadership Chair for Language@Leeds, University of Leeds, since 2013; b Pudsey, Leeds, 31 May 1959; d of Peter Charles Ernest Watson and Constance Lucia Watson (née Coidan); m 1988, James Dickins; one s one d. Educ: Wyndham Sch., Egremont, Cumbria; Univ. of Exeter (BA Arabic and Islamic Studies 1984); Sch. of Oriental and African Studies, Univ. of London (Dip. Linguistics 1985; PhD Linguistics 1989). Temp. Lectr in Arabic, Univ. of Edinburgh, 1987–88; British Acad. Post-doctoral Fellow, Univ. of Durham, 1990–92; Temp. Lectr in Arabic, Univ. of Salford, 1992–94; Lectr, 1994–98, Sen. Lectr in Arabic, 1998–2005, Univ. of Durham; Prof. of Arabic Linguistics, Univ. of Salford, 2005–13. Vis. Prof. of Semitic Studies, Univ. of Heidelberg, 2003–04; Vis. Associate Prof. of Arabic, Univ. of Oslo, 2004–05. Publications: A Syntax of San'ani Arabic, 1993; Lexicon of Arabic Horse Terminology, 1996; Sbahtu! A Course in San'ani Arabic, 1996; (with J. Dickins) Standard Arabic: an advanced course, 1999; Wasf San'a: texts in San'ani Arabic, 2000; Phonology and Morphology of Arabic, 2002, 2nd edn 2007; (with Abd al-Rahman Mutahhar) Social Issues in Popular Yemeni Culture, 2002; (ed with L. Edzard) Grammar as a Window onto Arabic Humanism: a collection of articles in honour of Michael G. Carter, 2006; (ed jtly) Arabic in the City, 2007; (ed with J. Retsö) Relative Clauses and Genitive Constructions in Semitic, 2009; (ed) A. Sima, Mehri-Texte aus der jemenitischen Sharqīyah: Transkribiert unter Mitwirkung von Askari Hugayran Saad, 2009; (ed jtly) The Semitic Languages: an international handbook, 2011; The Structure of Mehri, 2012; (ed with O. Elmaz) Languages of Southern Arabia: suppl. to the Proceedings of Seminar for Arabian Studies 44, 2014; (jtly) A Comparative Cultural Glossary Across the Modern South Arabian Language Family, 2019; contrib. articles to Linguistic Inquiry, Phonology, Morphology, Zeitschrift für Arabische Linguistik, Jl Semitic Studies, Folia Orientalia, Lang. and Linguistics, Historiographia Linguistica. Recreations: cycling, horse riding, guinea pigs, walking, swimming, ski-ing, novels, learning new languages. Address: School of Languages, Cultures and Societies, University of Leeds, Leeds LS2 9JT. T: (0113) 343 7069. E: j.c.e.watson@leeds.ac.uk.

**WATSON, Ven. Jeffrey John Seagrief;** Archdeacon of Ely, 1993–2004, now Archdeacon Emeritus; b 29 April 1939; s of late John Cole Watson and Marguerite Freda Rose Watson; m 1969, Rosemary Grace Lea; one s one d. Educ: University College Sch., Hampstead; Emmanuel Coll., Cambridge (MA Hons Classics); Clifton Theol Coll., Bristol. Curate: Christ Church, Beckenham, 1965–69; St Jude, Southsea, 1969–71; Vicar: Christ Church, Winchester, 1971–81; Holy Saviour, Bitterne, 1981–93; Examining Chaplain to Bishop of Winchester, 1976–93; RD of Southampton, 1983–93; Hon. Canon: Winchester Cathedral, 1991–93; Ely Cathedral, 1993–2004. Mem., Gen. Synod, 1985–95; Chm., C of E Vocations Adv. Sub-Cttee, 1991–99; Chm., Ministry Div. Candidates' Panel, 1999–2009. Recreations: photography, barbershop singing, walking, travel. Address: 7 Ferry Road, Hythe, Southampton SO45 5GB. T: (023) 8084 1189.

**WATSON, Jennifer, (Jenny),** CBE 2017; Board Member: Financial Ombudsman Service, since 2017; Financial Reporting Council, since 2018; b 25 Jan. 1964; d of Ronald Watson and Phyllis Watson (née Avery). Educ: Coopers' Co. and Coborn Sch., Upminster; Sheffield Hallam Univ. (BA Communications Studies); Univ. of Westminster (MA 20th Century British Hist.). Promotions Manager, Liberty (NCCL), 1993–95; Campaign and Communications Manager, Charter 88, 1996–98; Media and PR Manager, Victim Support, 1999; Develt Dir, Human Rights Act Res. Unit, KCL, 2000–01; Dir and Co-Founder, 2004–05, Associate, 2007–08, Global Partners and Associates. Equal Opportunities Commission: Comr, 1999–2000; Dep. Chair, 2000–05; Chair, 2005–07; Chm., Electoral Commn, 2009–16. Member: Banking Code Standards Bd, 2001–06 (Dep. Chair, 2005–06); Cttee on Radioactive Waste Mgt, 2003–06; Audit Commn, 2007–10; Chair: Ind. Transparency Rev. Panel, Nirex UK, 2001–03; Ind. Complaints Panel, Portman Gp, 2013–; Nat. Online Self-Exclusion Scheme, 2018–. Non-exec. Dir, Reclaim Fund Ltd, 2019–. Dir, WRAP, 2007–14. Mem. Bd, Money Advice Trust, 2008–17; Trustee, Charities Aid Foundn, 2009–12. Chm., Fawcett Soc., 1997–2001. Chair, House of St Barnabas, 2018–. Mem., Mgt Cttee, Liby of Women, London Guildhall Univ., 2001–08. Gov., Mossbourne Parkside Acad., 2017–. Publications: (jtly) Human Rights Act Toolkit, 2003. Recreations: gardening, singing (Mem., London Philharmonic Choir), reading, walking.

**WATSON, Prof. Jeremy Daniel McKendrick,** CBE 2013; DPhil; CEng; FREng; Chief Scientist and Engineer, BRE, since 2014; Professor of Engineering Systems, and Vice Dean, Engineering Sciences, University College London, since 2013; b Worthing, 5 May 1952; s of Stanley Albert and Alice Rose Watson; m 1980, Penelope Noel Rannard; two s. Educ: Worthing Boys' High Sch.; Univ. of London (BSc, MSc); Univ. of Sussex (DPhil). Technol. Dir, BOC Edwards, 1996–2006; Dir, Global Res., Arup, 2006–14; Chief Scientific Advr, DCLG, 2009–12. Member: Governing Bd, Technol. Strategy Bd, 2006–10; Council, EPSRC, 2011–15. Hon. Prof., Faculty of the Built Envmt, UCL, 2011–. Dep. Pres., 2014–16, Pres., 2016–17, IET. FIET; FICE; FREng 2010. Publications: (with N. B. Jones) Digital Signal Processing Principles, Devices and Applications, 1990; Built for Living: understanding behaviour and the built environment through engineering and design, 2015. Recreations: hill walking, choral singing. Address: UCL Science, Technology, Engineering and Public Policy, Boston House, 36–38 Fitzroy Square, W1T 6EY.

**WATSON, John Grenville Bernard,** OBE 1998; Chairman, Bay Horse Marketing Services Ltd, since 1990; b 21 Feb. 1943; s of Norman V. Watson and Ruby E. Watson; m 1st, 1965, Deanna Wood (d 2009); one s two d; 2nd, 2016, Caroline Inglis-Taylor (née Bentley). Educ: Moorlands Sch., Leeds; Bootham Sch., York; College of Law, Guildford. Articled, 1962, qualified as solicitor, 1967; joined John Waddington Ltd as managerial trainee, 1968; Export Director, Plastona John Waddington Ltd, 1972; Marketing Dir, 1975, Man. Dir, 1977, Waddington Games Ltd, responsible for Security Printing Div., 1984–89, for Johnsen & Jorgensen, 1988–89; Director: John Waddington PLC, 1979–89; Goddard Kay Rogers (Northern) Ltd, 1989–92; Yorkshire Bldg Soc., 1995–2004; Chief Exec., Bradford City Challenge Ltd, 1992–97. Chairman: NYnet Ltd, 2010–18; PIF Ltd, 2010–; EAL Ltd, 2010–15. Chm., Bradford Community NHS Trust, 1996–2002. Mem., Leeds Develt Corp., 1988–92; Chairman: Heritage Lottery Fund, Yorks and Humber, 2005–11; Morley and Outwood Business Assoc., 2015–. Joined Young Conservatives, 1965; Chairman, Yorkshire YC, 1969; Personal Asst to Rt Hon. Edward Heath, 1970; Chm., Nat. YC, 1971; contested (C) York, general elections, Feb. and Oct. 1974. MP (C): Skipton, 1979–83; Skipton and Ripon, 1983–87. Chm., Conservative Candidates Assoc., 1975–79. Mem., Parly Select Cttee on Energy, 1980–82; PPS, NI Office, 1982–83; PPS, Dept of Energy, 1983–85. Chm., British Atlantic Gp of Young Political Leaders, 1982–84; Nat. Vice Pres., Young Conservative Orgn, 1984–86. Mem. (C), N Yorks CC, 2005–13. Pres., British Youth Council, 1980–83. Recreations: travel, property renovation. Address: Evergreen Cottage, Main Street, Kirk Deighton, Leeds LS22 4DZ. T: (01937) 588273.

**WATSON, Joyce;** see Watson, E. J.

**WATSON, Julian Howard R.;** see Richmond-Watson.

**WATSON, Lara Anne;** see Fielden, L. A.

**WATSON, (Leslie) Michael (Macdonald) S.;** see Saunders Watson.

**WATSON, Lynn Deborah;** see Roberts, L. D.

**WATSON, Marc;** Chairman, Aser Media, since 2015; Executive Chairman and Group Chief Executive Officer, Eleven Sports Network, since 2016; b Dunstable, 1 Nov. 1969; s of Christopher Watson and Susan Watson; m 2006, Rosina Ladd; three s. Educ: Deer Park Sch., Cirencester; Univ. of Hull (LLB); Inns of Court Sch. of Law. Called to the Bar, Inner Temple, 2003; lawyer, subseq. gen. counsel, Northern and Shell, 1996–99; Dir, Reel Enterprises, 1999–2007; Commercial Dir, BT Vision, 2007–09; Chief Exec., TV Gp, BT, 2009–14; Founding Exec., Premier Boxing Champions, 2014–17. Non-executive Director: Shed Media, 2009–11; Youview, 2011–13; Founder and Chm., Industrious Recruitment Ltd, 2012–18. Dir, Cotswold Barn Conversions Ltd, 2012–. E: mc100watson@gmail.com.

**WATSON, Prof. Oliver James,** PhD; Ieoh Ming Pei Professor of Islamic Art and Architecture, University of Oxford, 2011–16; Governing Body Fellow, Wolfson College, Oxford, 2011–16; *b* London, 4 Aug. 1949; *s of* William and Katherine Watson; *m* 1992, Susan McCormack; three *d*. *Educ:* University Coll. Sch., London; Univ. of Durham (BA Hons 1971); Sch. of Oriental and African Studies, Univ. of London (PhD 1977). V&A Museum: Asst Keeper, 1979–91, Chief Curator, 1991–2001, Dept of Ceramics; Chief Curator, Islamic Section, Asian Dept, 2001–05; Keeper, Eastern Art, Ashmolean Mus., Univ. of Oxford, 2005–08; Dir, Mus. of Islamic Art, Doha, Qatar, 2008–11. *Publications:* Persian Lustre Ware, 1985; British Studio Ceramics, 1990; Ceramics from Islamic Lands, 2004; contrib. articles to specialist jls. *Recreation:* music. *Address:* c/o Wolfson College, Linton Road, Oxford OX2 6UD.

**WATSON, Paul;** *see* Watson, F. P.

**WATSON, Prof. Paul,** PhD; FREng; FBCS; Professor of Computer Science, Newcastle University, since 2002; *b* Durham, 8 Oct. 1961; *s of* Robert and Jean Watson; *m* 1986, Andrea Kaye; one *s* one *d*. *Educ:* Pelton Roseberry Comprehensive Sch.; Manchester Univ. (BSc Hons Computer Engrg 1983; PhD Computer Sci. 1986). Lectr in Computer Sci., Manchester Univ., 1986–89; System Designer, ICL, 1990–95; Lectr in Computer Sci., 1995–99, Reader in Computer Sci., 1999–2002, Newcastle Univ. FBCS 2003; FREng 2017. *Recreations:* family and friends, reading, cricket. *Address:* School of Computing, Urban Sciences Building, Newcastle University, 1 Science Square, Newcastle upon Tyne NE4 5TG. *T:* (0191) 208 4148. *E:* Paul.Watson@ncl.ac.uk. *Club:* Chester-Le-Street Cricket.

**WATSON, Dr Paul Stephen;** Regional Director, Midlands and East, NHS England, 2012–19; *b* Liverpool, 7 April 1964; *s of* Ronald Watson and Sylvia Watson; *m* 1989, Mary Eileen Campbell Hogg; two *s*. *Educ:* Birkenhead Sch.; Gonville and Caius Coll., Cambridge (BA 1985; MB BChir 1988); Univ. of Leeds (MPH 1992). DCH 1990; FFPH 1996 (MFPHM 1992). Consultant in Public Health Medicine, Wakefield HA, 1993–96; Dir of Acute Services, Cambridge & Huntingdon HA, 1996–99; Dir, Public Health, N Essex HA, 1999–2002; Med. Dir and Dep. Chief Exec., Essex Strategic HA, 2002–06; Dir, Commissioning, and Dep. Chief Exec., East of England Strategic HA, 2006–10; Chief Exec., Suffolk PCT, 2010–12. *Publications:* articles and book chapters on public health and health service mgt. *Recreation:* medieval history. *E:* pauldoc7@aol.com.

**WATSON, Rt Rev. Peter Robert;** Archbishop of Melbourne and Metropolitan of the Province of Victoria, 2000–05; *b* 1 Jan. 1936; *s of* Noel Frederick and Helen Elizabeth Watson; *m* 1962, Margo Eleanor Deans; three *d*. *Educ:* Canterbury Boys' High Sch., Sydney; Sydney Univ. (BEc); Moore Theological Coll., Sydney (ThL). Asst Priest, St Paul's, Chatswood, 1961–63; Curate-in-Charge, Lalor Park and Seven Hills, 1963–73; Rector, Lalor Park and Seven Hills, 1973–74; RD of Prospect, 1968–74; Canon, Prov. Cathedral of St John, Parramatta, 1969–74; Rector: St Luke's, Miranda, 1974–84; St Thomas, North Sydney, 1984–89; Area Dean, North Sydney, 1986–89; Bishop of Parramatta, 1989–93, of South Sydney, 1993–2000; an Asst Bp of Sydney, 1989–2000. *Recreations:* caravanning, walking, travel, swimming. *Address:* 8/41 Rocklands Road, Wollstonecraft, NSW 2065, Australia. *T:* (2) 89040330.

**WATSON, Philip Stuart,** CBE 2006; RIBA; FCIH; public sector consultant; Chief Executive, Blackburn with Darwen Unitary Authority, 1996–2006; *b* Blackburn, 22 Feb. 1946; *s of* late Herbert and Aimée Watson; *m* 1973, Shirley Clark; one *s* two *d*. *Educ:* Wensley Fold Primary Sch., Blackburn; Queen Elizabeth's Grammar Sch., Blackburn; Sheffield Univ. (BArch Hons 1968). Chartered Architect 1970; RIBA 1970; FCIH 1976. Blackburn Borough Council: various posts from architect to Dep. Borough Architect, 1968–85; Asst Chief Exec., 1985–96; Dep. Chief Exec., 1994–96. Non-exec. Dir, NHS Blackburn with Darwen, 2008–10; Independent Chairman: Blackburn with Darwen and Bolton Building Schs for Future Local Educn Partnership, 2010–13; Gtr Manchester Healthier Together Shared Cttees in Common, 2013–; Lancs and S Cumbria Jt CCG, 2016–. Gov., Blackburn Coll., 2005– (Hon. Fellow 2011; Vice Chair, 2011–16; Chair, 2016–). Trustee, Blackburn Rovers Community Trust, 2017–. *Recreations:* Blackburn Rovers, running, crown green bowling, golf. *Address:* Westleigh, Lawley Road, Blackburn BB2 6SG. *Clubs:* Blackburn Golf; Alexandra Bowling; Railway Bowling.

**WATSON, Sir Robert (Tony),** Kt 2012; CMG 2003; PhD; FRS 2011; Professor of Environmental Sciences, and Director of Strategic Development, Tyndall Centre for Climate Change Research, University of East Anglia, since 2007; Sir Louis Matheson Distinguished Visiting Professor, Monash Sustainability Institute, Monash University, since 2012; Chief Scientific Adviser, Department for Environment, Food and Rural Affairs, 2007–12. *Educ:* Queen Mary Coll., Univ. of London (BSc 1st Cl. Chem. 1969; PhD 1973). Dir and Chief Scientist, Science Div., Office of Mission to Planet Earth, NASA; Associate Dir for Envmt, Office of Sci. and Technol. Policy, Exec. Office of the Pres. of USA; World Bank: Sen. Scientific Advr, then Dir, Envmt Dept; Hd, Envmt Sector Bd, 1997; Chief Scientist and Sen. Advr for Environmentally and Socially Sustainable Develt. Dir and Co-Chair, Internat. Assessment of Agricl Sci. and Technol. for Develt; Co-Chair: Internat. Scientific Assessment of Stratospheric Ozone, 1980–; Bd, Internat. Millennium Ecosystem Assessment, 2000–05; Chm., UNEP/WMO Intergovtl Panel on Climate Change, 1997–2002; Chm., Intergovtl Science-Policy Platform on Biodiversity and Ecosystem Services, 2016–. Member: BBSRC, 2007–09; NERC, 2007–12. *Publications:* (ed jtly) Land Use, Land Use Change and Forestry, 2001; (ed) Climate Change 2001, 2002; contribs to Jl Envmtl Monitoring, Environmentally Sustainable Develt Proc., Phil Trans. Royal Soc. B, Ambio. *Address:* Tyndall Centre, School of Environmental Sciences, University of East Anglia, Norwich NR4 7TJ.

**WATSON, Robin,** CEng, FIMechE; Chief Executive Officer, John Wood Group, since 2016; *b* Glasgow, 3 Feb. 1967; *s of* Laurence and Elizabeth Watson; *m* 1995, Lorraine Gunn; two *s* one *d*. *Educ:* Glasgow Coll. of Natural Studies (HND Marine Engrg); Heriot Watt Univ. (BEng Hons Offshore and Mech. Engrg); Strathclyde Univ. (MBA). CEng 1994; FIMechE 2015. Marine engr, Benline Steamers Ltd, 1984–90; petroleum engr, 1990–93, project engr and Asst Manager, 1993–2000, Mobil North Sea Ltd; Ops Manager, 2000–04, Ops Dir, 2004–09, Petrofac plc; Man. Dir, 2010–12, Div. CEO, 2012–15, Gp Chief Operating Officer, 2015–16, John Wood Gp. Fellow, Energy Inst. *Recreations:* family, sport, reading, cycling, vacations, travel, music. *Address:* John Wood Group, 15 Justice Mill Lane, Aberdeen AB11 6EQ. *T:* 07946 370914. *E:* robin.watson@woodgroup.com.

**WATSON, Sir Ronald (Mathew),** Kt 1997; CBE 1989; Member, Sefton Metropolitan Borough Council, 1974–91, 1992–2014 and since 2018 (C, 1974–91, 1992–2011 since 2018; Ind, 2011–14); Chairman, Southport and Ormskirk NHS Trust, 2007–14; *b* 24 May 1945; *s of* Ralph and Rheta Mary Watson; *m* 1966, Lesley Ann McLean; one *s* one *d*. *Educ:* South Shields GS; Waterloo GS. General Manager: Laycock Travel Services, 1972–79; Morrisons Travel Agents, 1979–92. Mem. (C), Southport CBC, 1969–74; Leader, Sefton MBC, 1983–87. Leader, Cons. Gp, AMA, 1992–97. Director: Southport Mktg and Enterprise Bureau, 1983–97; Liverpool Airport plc, 1993–97; non-exec. Dir, Southport & Formby, subseq. Sefton, HA, 1991–2001; Dep. Chairman: Cheshire and Merseyside Strategic HA, 2002–06; Cheshire W PCT, 2006–07. Mem. Bd, Merseyside Develt Corp., 1993–97; Trustee, NW Trng Council, 1996–. Local Government Association: Dep. Leader, Cons. Gp, 1996–2000; Vice-Chm., 1997–2000; Chm., Tourism Exec., 1998–2003; Chm., Envmt and Regeneration Exec., 2003–04; Dep. Chm., Regeneration Bd, 2005–06; Vice Chm., Urban Commn, 2006–10. Mem., EU Cttee of the Regions, 1998–2009. Consultant, Eur. Advice Unit, Barnetts, Solicitors, Southport, 1994–2007. Member: Audit Commn, 1995–2001; Mental Health Tribunal, 2002–16; Standards for England (formerly Standards Bd for England), 2006–12; Bd, Solicitors Regulation Authy, 2010–12; Cttee, Merseyside Br., Benenden Health Care, 2014–. Vice-Pres., British Resorts Assoc., 1998–. Trustee, Sefton Pensioners Advocacy Service, 2015–19. Founder Mem. and Fellow, Tourism Soc., 1978; Fellow, Inst. of Travel and Tourism, 1989. Mem., Sherlock Holmes Soc. of London, 2012–. *Recreation:* writer on jazz and blues. *Address:* 7 Carnoustie Close, Oxford Road, Birkdale, Southport PR8 2FB. *Club:* Athenæum (Liverpool).

**WATSON, Sharon;** Artistic Director, Phoenix Dance Theatre, since 2009; *b* Leeds, 30 Jan. 1967; *d of* Lascelles and Kathleen Donaldson; *m* 2001, Andrew Watson; one *s* one *d*. *Educ:* London Sch. of Contemp. Dance (Dance Dip.); Northern Sch. of Contemp. Dance, Leeds (BA Dance); Leeds Metropolitan Univ. (MA Performance Works). Spiral Dance Co., 1986; Extemporary Dance Th., 1986–89; Phoenix Dance Co., 1989–97; Northern Sch. of Contemp. Dance, 1997–2001; Phoenix Dance Th., 2001–06; Sage Gateshead, Newcastle upon Tyne, 2007; Northern Ballet Th., 2008–09. Northern Power Woman Award, 2015; Yorkshire Woman of Achievement in Business, 2016; Yorkshire Woman of the Year, 2016. *Recreations:* music, social dancing, City ventures. *Address:* Phoenix Dance Theatre, St Cecilia Street, Quarry Hill, Leeds LS2 7PA. *T:* (0113) 236 8130. *E:* sharon.watson@phoenixdancetheatre.co.uk; 107 Harehills Avenue, Leeds LS8 4HU.

**WATSON, Ven. Sheila Anne;** Archdeacon of Canterbury, 2007–16; Preacher of Lincoln's Inn, since 2017; *b* 20 May 1953; *d of* William Calderhead Atkinson and Margaret Atkinson (*née* Gray); *m* 1985, Derek Richard Watson, *qv*. *Educ:* Ayr Acad.; St Andrews Univ. (MA 1975, MPhil 1980); Corpus Christi Coll., Oxford; Edinburgh Theol Coll. Ordained deaconess, 1979, deacon, 1987, priest, 1994; Deaconess: St Saviour, Bridge of Allan and St John's, Alloa, 1979–80; St Mary, Monkseaton, 1980–84; Adult Educn Officer, Kensington Episcopal Area, 1984–87; Hon. Curate, St Luke and Christchurch, Chelsea, 1987–96; Selection Sec., 1992–93, Sen. Selection Sec., 1993–96, ABM; Advr, CME, 1997–2002, Dir of Ministry, 1998–2002, Dio. of Salisbury; Hon. Canon, Salisbury Cathedral, 2000–02; Archdeacon of Buckingham, 2002–07; non-residentiary Mem., Chapter of St Paul's Cathedral, 2017–. Hon. DD Kent, 2013. *Recreations:* ballet, walking, riding a Brompton. *Address:* 83 Winchester Street, SW1V 4NU. *E:* vensheilawatson@gmail.com.

**WATSON, Sonia Maxine, (Mrs David Bromfield),** OBE 2019; Chief Executive, Stephen Lawrence Charitable Trust, since 2014; *b* Aylesbury, Bucks, 1964; *d of* Hugh John and Joyce Edwina Watson; *m* 1998, David Bromfield; two *d*. *Educ:* Mereway Upper Sch.; Univ. of Hull (MBA (Dist.)). Barclays plc: leadership mgt trainee, 1986–92; Dir, 1992–98, Sen. Exec., 1998–2004, Strategy and Planning; Fellow, Office for Public Mgt, 2004–08; Dir, Watson & Watson, 2008–13. Governor: De Montfort Univ., 2017–; James Allen's Girls' Sch., 2018. Hon. FRIBA 2017. *Recreations:* travel, historical novels. *Address:* Stephen Lawrence Charitable Trust, 39 Brookmill Road, SE8 4HU. *T:* (020) 8100 2800. *E:* swatson@stephenlawrence.org.uk. *Club:* City Women's Network.

**WATSON, Hon. Stephen Hartwig Willoughby;** Chief Executive, CTN Communications, since 2000; *b* Dorking, Surrey, 21 Sept. 1966; *s of* Baron Watson of Richmond, *qv*; *m* 2004, Emma Grace Winsor-Cundell; one *s* one *d*. *Educ:* European Sch., Brussels; Kingswood Sch., Bath; Royal Holloway Coll., Univ. of London (BA Hons Hist. and Politics 1987). Asst producer, BBC, 1987; Gen. Manager, Corporate Vision Ltd, 1988–90; Managing Director: Burson-Marsteller, 1990–92; Corporate Television Networks Ltd, 1992–2000. Chm., Internat. Visual Communications Assoc., 1996–98. Chairman: British-German Assoc., 2007–18 (Pres., 2018–); Atlantic Future Forum, 2019–. Contested (C) Caerphilly, 2005. Hon. Comdr, 2013, Hon. Capt., 2015, Hon. Cdre, 2019, RNR; Hon. Capt., USS Sequoia Presidential Yacht, 2016. Trustee: Tusk Trust, 1995–2013 (Chm., 2013–); RN and RM Charity, 2015– (Vice Pres., 2018–). Order of Merit (Germany), 2015; Knight of Habsburg-Lothringen, Order of St George, 2016. *Recreations:* military history, wine, countryside. *Address:* Hidcote House, Hidcote Boyce, Chipping Campden, Glos GL55 6LT. *T:* (020) 7395 4460. *E:* stephen.watson@ctn.co.uk. *Clubs:* Brooks's, Navy, Royal Automobile.

**WATSON, Prof. Stephen Roger;** Principal, Henley Management College, 2001–05; Fellow of Emmanuel College, Cambridge, since 1968; *b* 29 Aug. 1943; *s of* John C. Watson and Marguerite F. R. Watson; *m* 1969, Rosemary Victoria Tucker; one *s* one *d*. *Educ:* University College Sch., Hampstead; Emmanuel Coll., Cambridge (BA 1964; MA 1968; PhD 1969; MMath 2011). Research Fellow, Emmanuel Coll., Cambridge, 1968–70; Shell International, 1970–71; Cambridge University: Univ. Lectr in Operational Research, Engineering Dept, 1971–86; Tutor, Emmanuel Coll., 1973–85; Peat, Marwick Prof. of Management Studies, 1986–94; Dir, Judge Inst. of Management Studies, 1990–94; Dean, Lancaster Univ. Mgt Sch., 1994–2001. Director: Cambridge Decision Analysts Ltd, 1984–95; Environmental Resources Management, 1989–95. Assoc. Dean, Reims Mgt Sch., Reims, 2005–09. Special Advr to Pres., Assoc. to Advance Collegiate Schs of Business, Tampa, Florida, 2005–12. Chm., Practical Action, 2006–13. *Publications:* Decision Synthesis (with D. M. Buede), 1987; papers in learned jls. *Recreations:* singing, development issues. *Address:* 33 De Freville Avenue, Cambridge CB4 1HW.

**WATSON, Maj.-Gen. Stuart;** *see* Watson, Maj.-Gen. H. S. R.

**WATSON, Thomas;** MP (Lab) West Bromwich East, since 2001; *b* 8 Jan. 1967; *s of* Tony and Linda Watson; *m* 2000, Siobhan Corby. *Educ:* Hull Univ. Fundraiser, Save the Children, 1988–89; Chair, Nat. Orgn of Labour Students, 1992–93; Dep. Gen. Election Co-ordinator, Labour Party, 1993–97; Nat. Political Organiser, AEEU, 1997–2001. An Asst Govt Whip, 2004–05 and 2007–08; a Lord Comr of HM Treasury (Govt Whip), 2005–06; Parly Under-Sec. of State, MoD, 2006; a Parly Sec., Cabinet Office, 2008–09; Shadow Minister for Cabinet Office, 2015–16; Shadow Sec. of State for Culture, Media and Sport, subseq. Digital, Culture, Media and Sport, 2016–. Dep. Chm., Labour Party and Campaign Co-ordinator, 2011–13; Dep. Leader, Labour Party, 2015– (Chm., 2015–17). *Publications:* Downsizing, 2020. *Recreation:* gardening. *Address:* House of Commons, SW1A 0AA. *Club:* Friar Park and West Bromwich Labour.

**WATSON, Thomas Sturges;** professional golfer, since 1971 (Champions tour, since 1999); *b* 4 Sept. 1949; *s of* Raymond Etheridge Watson and Sarah Elizabeth Watson (*née* Ridge); *m* 1973, Linda Tova Rubin (marr. diss. 1998); one *s* one *d*. *Educ:* Stanford Univ. (BS 1971). Championships include: Open, 1975, 1977, 1980, 1982, 1983; US Open, 1982; Masters, 1977, 1981; Mem., Ryder Cup team, 1977, 1981, 1983, 1989, Captain, 1993 and 2014. *Address:* 1901 W 47th Place, Suite 200, Shawnee Mission, KS 66205, USA.

**WATT, Alison Jane,** OBE 2008; RSA; FRSE; artist; *b* 11 Dec. 1966; *d of* James Watt and Annie Watt (*née* Sinclair); *m* 2000, Ruaridh Nicoll. *Educ:* Glasgow Sch. of Art (BA Fine Art 1987, MA Fine Art 1989). Associate Artist, Nat. Gall., 2006–08. *Solo exhibitions:* Contemporary Art Season, Glasgow Art Gall. and Mus., 1990; New Paintings, 1993,

Paintings, 1995, Monotypes, 1997, Flowers East, London; New Paintings, Charles Belloc Lowndes, Chicago, 1996; Fold, Fruitmarket Gall., Edinburgh, 1997, Aberdeen Art Gall. and Mus. and Leeds Metropolitan Gall., 1998; Shift, Scottish Nat. Gall. of Modern Art, 2000; New Paintings, Dulwich Picture Gall., 2002; Still (installation), Old St Paul's Ch, Edinburgh, 2004; Dark Light, Pier Arts Centre, Orkney, 2007; Phantom, Nat. Gall., London, 2008; Ingleby Gall., Edinburgh, 2011; Generation, Scottish Nat. Gall. of Modern Art, 2014; (retrospective) Perth Mus. and Art Gall., 2014; Parafin, London, 2016; A Shadow on the Blind, Abbott Hall Mus., 2018; Scottish Nat. Portrait Gall., 2020. FRSE 2017. First Prize for Painting, RA, 1986; BP Portrait Award, 1987; City of Glasgow Lord Provost Prize, 1993; Scottish Arts Council Award, 1996; Creative Scotland Award, 2004; ACE Award for Art in a Religious Space, 2005. *Publications:* catalogues for exhibitions and monographs. *Recreations:* visiting the Highlands, eating in great restaurants, cooking, walking. *Address:* c/o Ingleby Gallery, 6 Carlton Terrace, Edinburgh EH7 5DD. *T:* (0131) 556 4441, *Fax:* (0131) 556 4454. *E:* mail@inglebygallery.com.

**WATT, Prof. David Anthony,** PhD; Professor of Computing Science, University of Glasgow, 1995–2016, now Honorary Senior Research Fellow; *b* 5 Nov. 1946; *s* of Francis Watt and Mary Watt (*née* Stuart); *m* 1974, Helen Dorothy Day; one *s* one *d*; *m* 2000, Carol Ann Laing. *Educ:* Univ. of Glasgow (BSc (Eng) 1st Cl. Hons; Dip. Comp. Sci. (Dist.); PhD 1974). University of Glasgow: programmer, Computing Service, 1969–72 and 1974; Department of Computing Science: Lectr, 1974–85; Sen. Lectr, 1985–90; Reader, 1990–95; Head of Dept, 1993–96; Vice-Dean, Faculty of Sci., 1996–99. Vis. Associate Prof., Univ. of Calif, Santa Cruz, 1981–82; Vis. Res. Associate, Univ. of Calif, Berkeley, 1985; Vis. Prof., Univ. of Queensland. *Publications:* (with W. Findlay) Pascal: an introduction to methodical programming, 1978, 3rd edn 1985; (jtly) Ada: language and methodology, 1987; Programming Language Concepts and Paradigms, 1990; Programming Language Syntax and Semantics, 1991; Programming Language Processors: compilers and interpreters, 1993; (with D. Brown) Programming Language Processors in Java, 2000; (with D. Brown) Java Collections, 2001; Programming Language Design Concepts, 2004. *Recreations:* chess, cycling, science, history. *Address:* School of Computing Science, University of Glasgow, Glasgow G12 8QQ.

**WATT, Prof. Fiona Mary,** FRS 2003; Director, Centre for Stem Cells and Regenerative Medicine, King's College London, since 2012; Executive Chair, Medical Research Council, since 2018; *b* 28 March 1956; *d* of David Mackie Watt and Janet Elizabeth Watt (*née* MacDougall); *m* 1979, James Cuthbert Smith (*see* Sir J. C. Smith); two *s* one *d*. *Educ:* New Hall, Cambridge (BA Hons); Univ. of Oxford (DPhil 1979). Postdoctoral Associate, MIT, 1979–81; Head: Molecular Cell Biol. Lab., Kennedy Inst. of Rheumatology, 1981–86; Keratinocyte Lab., ICRF, then CRUK London Res. Inst., 1987–2006; Herchel Smith Prof. of Molecular Genetics, and Dep. Dir, Wellcome Trust Centre for Stem Cell Res., Univ. of Cambridge, 2006–12; Dep. Dir, Cancer Res. UK Cambridge Res. Inst., 2005–12. Mem. Bd, Francis Crick Inst., 2018–. *Publications:* numerous contribs to learned jls. *Recreations:* fishing, reading novels, gardening, modern art. *Address:* Centre for Stem Cells and Regenerative Medicine, Floor 28, Tower Wing, Guy's Hospital, Great Maze Pond, SE1 9RT. *E:* fiona.watt@kcl.ac.uk.

**WATT, Iain Alasdair;** non-executive Director, Edinburgh Dragon Trust plc, 1988–2012; *b* Edinburgh, 30 March 1945; *s* of Andrew Watt and Margaret Fawns Watt; *m* 1982, Lynne Neilson. *Educ:* Edinburgh Acad.; Univ. of Hull (BSc Econs). FCIBS. Bank of Scotland, 1969–86: bank clerk in branches, 1976–84; Manager, Investment Services; Pensions Funds Investment Manager; Dir, British Linen Bank, 1984; Edinburgh Fund Managers Group plc: Dir, 1986–2002; Chief Investment Officer, 1989–90, 2001–02; Man. Dir, 1989–90; Chief Exec., 1996–2002. Trustee, Nat. Mus of Scotland, 2007–14. *Recreations:* golf, tennis, bridge. *Address:* Sycamore Bank, North Queensferry, Fife KY11 1HE. *T:* (01383) 413645. *E:* iain.watt@sycamorebank.co.uk.

**WATT, Sir James H.;** *see* Harvie-Watt.

**WATT, James Wilfrid,** CVO 1997; HM Diplomatic Service, retired; Partner, Ambassador Partnership LLP, since 2015; *b* 5 Nov. 1951; *s* of late Anthony James MacDonald Watt and Sona Elvey (*née* White); *m* 1st, 1980, Elizabeth Ghislaine Villeneuve (*d* 1998), *d* of late Marcel Villeneuve and Lorna Oliver Tudsbery; one *s* one *d*; 2nd, 2004, Amal Saad, *d* of Ibrahim Saad and Alice Homsi. *Educ:* Ampleforth Coll., York; Queen's Coll., Oxford (BA Mod. Langs 1973). Kleinwort Benson, 1974–75; freelance broadcaster and interpreter, Madrid, 1975–77; entered HM Diplomatic Service, 1977; MECAS, 1978; FCO, 1979–80; Abu Dhabi, 1980–83; FCO, 1983–85; UK Permanent Mission to UN, NY, 1985–89; Dep. Hd, UN Dept and Hd, Human Rights Unit, FCO, 1989–92; Dep. Hd of Mission and Consul Gen., Amman, 1992–96; Dep. High Comr, Islamabad, 1996–98; Res. Studentship, SOAS, 1999–2000; Head, Consular Div., then Dir for Consular Services, FCO, 2000–03; Ambassador: to Lebanon, 2003–06; to Jordan, 2006–11; to Egypt, 2011–14. Chairman: Council for British Res. in the Levant, 2017–; Internat. Adv. Bd, Res. for Health in Conflict - Middle East and N Africa, 2018–. Non-exec. Dir, Cap-It Financial Ltd, 2014–; Chm., Scholarship Cttee, British Lebanese Assoc., 2015–; Trustee: Buddhist Soc., 2017–; London Middle East Inst., 2018–. *Club:* Athenæum.

**WATT, John Gillies McArthur;** QC (Scot.) 1992; *b* 14 Oct. 1949; *s* of Peter Julius Watt and Nancy (*née* McArthur); *m* 1st, 1972, Catherine (marr. diss. 1988), *d* of Robert Russell, Toronto, Canada; two *d*; 2nd, 1988, Susan, *d* of Dr Tom C. Sparks, Ardmore, Oklahoma, and Breckenridge, Colorado, USA. *Educ:* Clydebank High Sch.; Glasgow Univ.; Edinburgh Univ. (LLB 1971). Solicitor, 1974–78; Advocate at Scottish Bar, 1979; Advocate Depute *ad hoc*, 1990; Temporary Sheriff, 1991; called to the Bar, Middle Temple, 1992. *Recreations:* shooting, ski-ing, sailing, opera, golf. *Address:* 301 Country Club Road, Ardmore, OK 73401–1125, USA. *T:* (580) 798 4595, *Fax:* (580) 798 4595. *E:* jgmwatt1@cableone.net. *Clubs:* Lansdowne; Royal Western Yacht (Glasgow); Dornick Hills Country (Oklahoma).

**WATT, Maureen, (Mrs Bruce Donaldson);** Member (SNP) Aberdeen South and Kincardine North, Scottish Parliament, since 2011 (North East Scotland, April 2006–2011); *b* 23 June 1951; *d* of late Hamish Watt; *m* 1987, Bruce Donaldson; one *s* one *d*. *Educ:* Univ. of Strathclyde (BA Hons Politics 1972); Univ. of Birmingham (PGCE 1973). Teacher, Bulmershe Sch., Woodley, Reading, 1974–76; Personnel Asst, then Personnel Mgr, Deutag Drilling, Aberdeen, 1977–91; Assessor for Office of Comr for Public Appts in Scotland, 1999–2006. Scottish Parliament: Minister for Schs and Skills, 2007–09; for Public Health, 2014–16, for Mental Health, 2016–18; Convener: Rural Affairs and Envmtl Cttee, 2009–11; Infrastructure and Capital Investment Cttee, 2011–14. *Recreations:* gardening, yoga, swimming. *Address:* (office) 51 Victoria Road, Torry, Aberdeen AB11 9LS. *T:* (01224) 876743. *E:* Maureen.Watt.msp@parliament.scot.
*See also* S. B. Donaldson.

**WATT, Miranda Lucy Mary C.;** *see* Carruthers-Watt.

**WATT, Peter Martin;** Managing Director, Family Support Services, London Borough of Hammersmith and Fulham, since 2018; political commentator and blogger; *b* 20 July 1969; *s* of David Watt and Sandra Watt; *m* 2003, Vilma Bermudez; one *s* four *d*, and one step *d*. *Educ:* Inst. of Health, Bournemouth Univ. (RGN 1992); Open Univ. Business Sch. (Professional Cert. in Mgt 2004). Student nurse, Inst. of Health, Bournemouth Univ., 1989–92; Staff Nurse, then Sen. Staff Nurse, Poole Hosp. NHS Trust, 1992–96; Labour Party: Local Organiser, Battersea/Wandsworth, 1996–98; Nat. Elections Delivery and Local Recruitment Officer, 1998–2001; Membership Taskforce Leader, 2000–01; Regl Dir, Labour East, 2001–02; Taskforce Leader, Financial and Legal Compliance, 2003–05; Dir of Finance and Compliance, 2005; Gen. Sec., 2006–07; Chief Executive: The Campaign Co., 2008–10; Counsel and Care, 2011; Dir, Child Protection Advice and Support, 2011–14, Dir, Nat. Services, 2014–18, NSPCC. Chm., Kingston Foster Carers Assoc., 2008–. Foster carer (with wife), Kingston-upon-Thames BC. Jt author, Giving Victims a Voice, report into allegations of sexual abuse made against Jimmy Savile, 2013. *Publications:* Inside Out, 2010; (contrib.) What next for Labour?: ideas for a new generation, 2011. *Recreations:* watching sport (cricket and Liverpool Football Club in particular), reading crime novels.

**WATT, Thorhilda Mary Vivia A.;** *see* Abbott-Watt.

**WATT-PRINGLE, Jonathan Helier;** QC 2008; barrister; *b* 8 June 1958; *s* of Louis Roy Watt-Pringle and late Molly Alleyne Watt-Pringle (*née* Payn). *Educ:* Queen's Coll., Queenstown; Univ. of Stellenbosch (BA 1978; LLB 1980); Keble Coll., Oxford (Rhodes Scholar; BA 1983; BCL 1984; MA 1987). Advocate, Supreme Court of South Africa, 1984–86; called to the Bar, Middle Temple, 1987; in practice at London Bar, 1988–. Chm., Appeal Cttee, HFEA, 2009–15. *Recreations:* bridge, theatre, travel, cycling. *Address:* Temple Garden Chambers, 1 Harcourt Buildings, Temple, EC4Y 9DA. *E:* jwpringle@tgchambers.com. *Club:* Reform.

**WATTAM, Nicholas John;** a District Judge (Magistrates' Courts), since 2018; *b* Scunthorpe, 15 Oct. 1969; *s* of Paul and Jacqueline Wattam; *m* 1998, Gillian Hancock; one *s* one *d*. *Educ:* Univ. of Leicester (LLB Hons 1991); Coll. of Law. Admitted as solicitor, 1996; Dep. Dist Judge (Magistrates' Courts), 2009–18. *Publications:* (contrib.) Magistrates' Courts' Criminal Practice, 2000, 10th edn 2014; (contrib.) Stone's Justices' Manual, 2019. *Recreation:* hunting and gathering. *Address:* Guildford Magistrates' Court, Mary Road, Guildford GU1 4BS. *T:* (01483) 405300. *E:* djmc.nick.wattam@ejudiciary.net.

**WATTERS, David George;** Strategic Consultant, International Patient Organisation for Primary Immunodeficiencies, 2011–13 (Executive Director, 2005–11); *b* 14 Jan. 1945. *Educ:* Stromness Acad., Orkney Is. Church of Scotland lay worker, 1964–68; Social Worker, St Martin-in-the-Fields, 1968–73; Director: Threshold Centre, 1973–78; Alone In London Service, 1978–81; Gen. Sec., Haemophilia Soc., 1981–93; Gen. Sec., subseq. Chief Exec., Primary Immunodeficiency Assoc., 1994–2005. Chair: Downderry and Seaton Assoc., 2009–17; Quay Lane Surgery Patient Participation Gp, St Germans, 2012–16. Clerk, Sir Walter Moyle's Almshouses, St Germans, 2009–17. Trustee, St Germans Priory Trust, 2012–14. Churchwarden: All Saints, Tooting, 1978–84 and 1994–98; St Germans Gp Parish, 2015–17. Licensed Reader, Truro Dio., 2008–; Mem., Truro Diocesan Synod, 2016–; Lay Chair, E Wivelshire Deanery Synod, 2016–. JP Inner London, 1980–2000. *Recreations:* music, photography, birdwatching, travel, Cornwall, Orkney, theology, reading, cooking, community affairs, poetry. *Address:* Jasione, Front Road, Downderry, Cornwall PL11 3JY.

**WATTERSON, Hon. Juan Paul,** FCA; Speaker of the House of Keys, Isle of Man, since 2016; *b* Douglas, I of M, 4 July 1980; *s* of John Watterson and Alison Watterson; *m* 2010, Helena Perry; one *s* one *d*. *Educ:* Rushen Primary Sch.; Castle Rushen High Sch.; Univ. of Lincoln (BA Hons 1st Cl. Mgt 2001). ACA 2005, FCA 2015; CMgr, FCMI 2016. KPMG, 2001–06. Isle of Man Government: Mem., House of Keys, 2006–; Minister for Home Affairs, 2011–16; Chm., Communications Commn, 2011–16; Chm., Tynwald Public Accounts Cttee, 2006–11, 2016–. Chm., 2016–; Jt Pres., 2016–; I of M Br., CPA. Dir, Southern Befrienders, 2008–; Chairman: Southern Authorities Healthcare Cttee, 2011–; Rushen Heritage Trust, 2015–; Vice Chm., Port Erin Br., 2012–; Treas., I of M County, 2014–, RBL Tynwald Rep., North West RFCA, 2011–; I of M Armed Forces Champion, 2012–. Mem., Council, 2005–06, 2017–19, Members and Commercial Bd, 2015–, ICAEW. Hon. Col, I of M ACF, 2016–. *Publications:* Tynwaldballs, 2010; Tynwaldballs 2, 2015; articles in The Parliamentarian and Jl of Critical Postmodern Orgn Sci. *Recreations:* local history, collecting cufflinks, bad jokes. *Address:* Legislative Buildings, Douglas, Isle of Man IM1 3PW. *T:* (01624) 685500. *E:* juan.watterson@gov.im.

**WATTS,** family name of **Baron Watts**.

**WATTS, Baron** *cr* 2015 (Life Peer), of Ravenhead in the County of Merseyside; **David Leonard Watts;** *b* 26 Aug. 1951; *s* of Leonard and Sarah Watts; *m* 1972, Avril Davies; two *s*. *Educ:* Huyton Hey Secondary Sch. Labour Party Orgnr, until 1992; Researcher for John Evans, MP, 1992–97. MP (Lab) St Helens N, 1997–2015. PPS to Minister of State, MoD, 2000–01, to Minister of State (Minister of Transport), DfT (formerly DTLR), 2001–03, to Dep. Prime Minister, 2003–05; a Lord Comr of HM Treasury (Govt Whip), 2005–10; an Opposition Whip, 2010–15. Mem., Foreign Affairs Select Cttee, 2010–15. Chm., Parly Labour Party, 2012–15. *Recreations:* reading, football, travel.

**WATTS, Prof. Anthony,** PhD; DSc; FRSC; FInstP; FRSB; Professor of Biochemistry, 1996, and Associate Head, Department of Biochemistry, 2011, University of Oxford; C. W. Maplethorpe Fellow in Biological Sciences, 1983–2017, and Vice Principal, 2015, St Hugh's College, Oxford, now Emeritus Fellow; *b* 7 Jan. 1950; *s* of late Wilfred Thomas Watts and of Ingrid Hiltraud Watts; *m* 1972, Valerie Maud Lewis; one *s* two *d*. *Educ:* Ludlow Grammar Sch.; Leeds Univ. (BSc; PhD 1976). DSc Oxon 1995. FRSC 2011; FInstP 2011; FRSB (FSB 2011). Max Planck Res. Fellow, Göttingen, 1976–80; University of Oxford: Deptl Demonstrator, 1980–83; New Blood Lectr, 1983–88; BBSRC Sen. Res. Fellow, 1997–2002; Rutherford Appleton Laboratory, Didcot: Sen. Scientist, ISCis (formerly ISIS) Facility, 1996–; Dir, Nat. Biol Solid State NMR Facility, 1997–. Fulbright Fellow and Vis. Prof., Harvard Univ., 1987; Fellow, IACR, 1998; Willsmore Fellow, Melbourne Univ., 2000. Lectr, Aust. and NZ Magnetic Resonance Soc., 1998. Moses Gomberg Lectr, Univ. Michigan, 2001. Chm., ESF Network on Molecular Dynamics of Biomembranes, 1990–92; UK rep., Membrane Commn, IUPAB, 1994–; Mem. Cttee, then Chm., BBSRC Biol Neutron Adv. Panel and Mem., ISIS Scheduling Panels, 1995–99. Member: Cttee, Biochem. Soc. of GB, 1989–98; Cttee, Biophysical Soc., 1998– (Chm., 2002–07, 2010–); Fellow, 2011). Principal Ed., Biophysical Chem., 1994–2000; Managing Ed., European Biophysics Jl, 2000–. Fellow, Amer. Biophysical Soc., 2011. 350th Commemorative Medal, Helsinki Univ., 1990; SERC-CNRS Maxime Hanss Prize for Biophysics, 1992; Morton Medal, British Biochem. Soc., 1999; Award for Biomembrane Chem., 2001, Interdisciplinary Award, 2015, Royal Soc. Chem.; Anatrace Award, Biophysical Soc., 2015. *Publications:* (with J. J. H. H. M. de Pont) Progress in Protein-Lipid

Interactions, Vol. 1 1985, Vol. 2 1986; Protein-Lipid Interactions, 1993; over 320 peer reviewed scientific papers and numerous contribs to learned jls. *Address:* Biomembrane Structure Unit, Department of Biochemistry, South Parks Road, Oxford OX1 3QU. *T:* (01865) 613219. *E:* anthony.watts@bioch.ox.ac.uk.

**WATTS, Prof. Anthony Brian**, PhD, DSc; FRS 2014; Professor of Marine Geology and Geophysics, University of Oxford, since 1990; *b* 23 July 1945; *s* of late Dennis Granville Watts and Vera Mabel (*née* Fisher); *m* 1970, Mary Tarbit; two *d. Educ:* University Coll. London (BSc); Univ. of Durham (PhD); DSc Oxon 2003. Post-Doctoral Fellow, Nat. Res. Council of Canada, 1970–71; Res. Scientist, Lamont-Doherty Geol Observatory, Palisades, NY, 1971–81; Arthur D. Storke Meml Prof. of Geol Scis, Columbia Univ., NY, 1981–90. Fellow: Amer. Geophysical Union, 1986; Geol Soc. of Amer., 2006; Eur. Geoscis Union, 2008 (Arthur Holmes Medal, 2008); MAE 1999. A. I. Levorsen Meml Award, Amer. Assoc. Petroleum Geologists, 1981; Rosenstiel Award, Univ. of Miami, 1982; Murchison Medal, Geol Soc., 1993; George P. Woollard Award, Geol Soc. of America, 2005. *Publications:* Isostasy and flexure of the lithosphere, 2001; numerous articles in scientific jls. *Recreations:* cricket, carpentry. *Address:* Department of Earth Sciences, University of Oxford, South Parks Road, Oxford OX1 3AN. *T:* (01865) 272032.

**WATTS, Prof. Charlotte Helen**, CMG 2019; PhD; FMedSci; Professor of Social and Mathematical Epidemiology, London School of Hygiene and Tropical Medicine, University of London, since 2006; Chief Scientific Advisor, Department for International Development, since 2015; *b* Farnborough, Kent, 5 Oct. 1962; *d* of Mary and Peter Watts; *m* 1988, Dr Chris Carbone; two *s. Educ:* Falmouth Sch., Cornwall; Exeter Coll., Oxford (BSc Maths 1984); Marlboro Coll., Vermont, USA (MSc Maths 1986); Univ. of Warwick (PhD Maths 1990). Royal Soc. Postdoctoral Res. Fellow, Univ. of Oxford, 1991–93; London School of Hygiene and Tropical Medicine, Univ. of London: Lectr, 1994–2000; Lectr, Univ. of Zimbabwe (on secondment), 1994–97; Sen. Lectr, 2000–06; Sigrid Rausing Prof. of Gender, Violence and Health, 2006–11. Member: BBSRC, 2016–18; UKRI-MRC, 2018–. FMedSci 2015. *Publications:* contrib. over 250 reviewed papers to acad. jls. *Recreations:* long distance running, walking. *Address:* Department of Public Health and Policy, London School of Hygiene and Tropical Medicine, 15–17 Tavistock Place, WC1H 9SN. *E:* Charlotte.watts@lshtm.ac.uk.

**WATTS, Prof. Colin**, DPhil; FRS 2005; FRSE; FMedSci; Professor of Immunobiology, University of Dundee, 1998, now Emeritus; *b* 28 April 1953; *s* of George Watts and Kathleen Mary Watts (*née* Downing); *m* 1979, Susan Mary Light; one *s* two *d. Educ:* The Friends Sch., Saffron Walden; Univ. of Bristol (BSc Hons 1975); Univ. of Sussex (DPhil 1980). EMBO Fellow, UCLA, 1980–82; Beit Meml Fellow, MRC Lab. of Molecular Biol., Cambridge, 1982–85; Lectr, 1986–92, Reader, 1992–98, Univ. of Dundee. Mem., Basel Inst. for Immunology, 1991; E. de Rothschild & Y. Mayent Fellow, Institut Curie, 1999. Mem., EMBO, 1996. FRSE 1999; FMedSci 2009. Margaret Maclellan Prize, Tenovus Scotland, 2000; (jtly) Descartes Prize, EU, 2002. *Publications:* res. papers, reviews and commentaries in scientific jls. *Recreations:* music, cities, armchair sport. *Address:* School of Life Sciences, University of Dundee, Dundee DD1 5EH. *T:* (01382) 384233, *Fax:* (01382) 345783. *E:* c.watts@dundee.ac.uk.

**WATTS, Diana**; see Ellis, D.

**WATTS, Donald Walter**, AM 1998; PhD; FTSE; FRACI; FACE; Emeritus Professor, 1995, and Dean, Research and Postgraduate Studies, 1995–2003, University of Notre Dame Australia (Senior Policy Adviser to the Vice Chancellor, 2004–05); *b* 1 April 1934; *s* of late Horace Frederick Watts and Esme Anne Watts; *m* 1960, Michelle Rose Yeomans; two *s. Educ:* Hale Sch., Perth; University of Western Australia (BSc Hons, PhD); University College London. FRACI 1967. Post-Doctoral Fellow, UCL, 1959–61; University of Western Australia: Sen. Lectr, 1962; Reader, 1969; Associate Prof., 1971; Personal Chair in Physical and Inorganic Chemistry, 1977–79; Dir, W Australian Inst. of Tech., 1980–86, renamed Vice-Chancellor, Curtin Univ. of Tech., Jan.–June 1987; Pres. and Vice-Chancellor, Bond Univ., Australia, 1987–90, now Emeritus. Vis. Scientist, Univ. of S California, 1967; Visiting Professor: Australian National Univ., 1973; Univ. of Toronto, 1974; Japan Foundn Vis. Fellow, 1984. Chairman: Aust. Cttee of Dirs and Principals in Advanced Education Ltd, 1986–87; NT Employment and Trng Authy, 1991–93; CEO, 1990–95, Chm., 1993–95, NT Trade Develt Zone Authy. Member: Aust. Science and Technol. Council, 1984–90; Technology Develt Authority of WA, 1984–87; Chm., Australian Space Council, Canberra, 1993–95. Chairman: Advanced Energy Systems Ltd, 1997–2003 (Dir, 1995–2003); Technical Trng Inst. Pty Ltd, 2001–03; Woodside Valley Foundn, 2003–10. Hon. Fellow, Marketing Inst. of Singapore, 1987–95. Hon. DTech Curtin, 1987; Hon. DEd WA, 2001; DUniv Bond, 2009. *Publications:* Chemical Properties and Reactions (jtly) (Univ. of W Aust.), 1978 (trans. Japanese, 1987); (jtly) Chemistry for Australian Secondary School Students (Aust. Acad. of Sci.), 1979; (jtly) The School Chemistry Project—a secondary school chemistry syllabus for comment, 1984; Earth, Air, Fire and Water, and associated manuals (Aust. Acad. of Sci. Sch. Chem. Project), 1984; numerous papers on phys. and inorganic chemistry in internat. jls; several papers presented at nat. and internat. confs. *Recreations:* tennis (Mem. Interstate Tennis Team, 1952–53), squash (Mem. Interstate Squash Team, 1957–66), golf. *Address:* Unit 139, 3 Dean Street, Claremont, WA 6010, Australia. *Clubs:* Royal Kings Park Tennis (Perth); Nedlands Golf (Nedlands); Lake Karrinyup Golf (Karrinyup); Vines Resort (Swan Valley).

**WATTS, Edward, (Ted)**, FRICS; property advisor; Director, Cedar Rydal Ltd, since 2006; *b* 19 March 1940; *s* of Edward Samuel Window Watts and Louise Coffey; *m* 1960, Iris Josephine Frost; two *s* (one *d* decd). *Educ:* SW Essex Technical Coll. FRICS 1971 (ARICS 1962). Established own practice, Watts & Partners, 1967 (surveyors, architects and engineers), Chm., 1967–99. Founder Chm., Hyde Housing Assoc., 1967–70 (Mem., 1967–85; Hon. Life Pres., 2007). Director: People Need Homes, 1991–97; Avilla Develts Ltd, 1999–2013; non-executive Director: WSP Gp, 1993–2002; Thamesmead Town, 1994–2000; Mem. Adv. Bd, Property Hldgs, 1992–96. Chairman: Empty Homes Agency, 1997–2002; Tilfen Ltd, 1999–2001; Blackheath Preservation Trust Ltd, 2001–09. Member: ARCUK, 1991–97; Urban Villages Gp, 1992–96; Ministerial Adv. Bd, Property Advrs to the Civil Estate. Royal Institution of Chartered Surveyors: Pres., 1991–92; Mem., Gen. Council, 1982–95; Dir, RICS Journals Ltd, 1982–88 (Chm., 1986–88). Freeman, City of London, 1985. Hon. DSc London South Bank, 1992. *Recreations:* sailing, cruising. *Address:* Flexford Farm, South Sway Lane, Sway, Lymington, Hants SO41 6DP. *T:* (01590) 681053. *E:* ted.watts@flexfordfarm.co.uk. *Clubs:* Royal Cruising; Lymington Town Sailing; Royal Lymington Yacht.

**WATTS, Elizabeth Anne**; soprano; *b* Norwich, 16 Feb. 1979; *d* of Peter Frederick Watts and Rosemary Jane Watts; *m* 2012, Guy Charles Kemp Robinson. *Educ:* Norwich High Sch.; Univ. of Sheffield (BA 1st Cl. Hons Archaeol. and Prehistory); Royal Coll. of Music (Postgrad. Dip. Advanced Opera). FRCM 2017. Début at Royal Opera, Covent Garden, 2011; Artist in Residence, Southbank Centre, 2011; performed at Last Night of the Proms, 2014; recitals incl. Wigmore Hall, Concertgebouw, Amsterdam, Tonhalle, Zürich. Has made numerous recordings. Hon. DMus Sheffield, 2013. Kathleen Ferrier Award, 2006; BBC Cardiff Singer of World Rosenblatt Recital Song Prize, 2007; Borletti-Buitoni Trust Award, 2011. *Recreations:* green issues, gardening, Norwich City FC. *Address:* c/o Maxine Robertson Management, Shakespeare House, 168 Lavender Hill, SW11 5TG. *T:* (020) 7993 2917. *E:* jbb@maxinerobertson.com. *W:* www.elizabethwattssoprano.com.

**WATTS, Garry**, MBE 2009; FCA; Chairman: Spire Healthcare Group, since 2011; BTG plc, since 2012; Foxtons, since 2013; *b* London, 1956; *s* of late Jack Watts and of Patricia May Watts; one *s* two *d. Educ:* Hounslow Coll. FCA 1987. Trainee Accountant, 1975–81, Qualified Accountant, 1981–84, Thomson McLintock; Manager, Thomson McLintock, later KPMG, 1984–90; Partner, KPMG, 1990–95; Director: Medeva plc, 1996–2000; Celltech Gp plc, 1999–2000; Financial Dir, 2001–04, CEO, 2004–10, SSL Internat. plc. Non-executive Director: Protherics plc, 2004–08; Stagecoach plc, 2007–16; Coca-Cola Eur. Partners (formerly Coca-Cola Enterprises), 2010–17. Mem., Supervisory Bd, Medicines and Healthcare Products Regulatory (formerly Medicines Control) Agency, 1991–2008. *Recreations:* fishing, shooting, ski-ing, horseracing, gardening, opera. *Address:* Spire Healthcare Ltd, 3 Dorset Rise, EC4Y 8EN. *T:* (020) 7427 9007. *E:* garry.watts@spirehealthcare.com. *Club:* New (Edinburgh).

**WATTS, Graham Clive**, OBE 2008; Chief Executive, Construction Industry Council, since 1991 (Director, since 1989); dance writer and critic; *b* 5 Aug. 1956; *s* of Clifford Bertie Watts and late Monica Kathleen Watts; *m* 1981, Tamara Jemima Ingrid Esposito; two *d. Educ:* Bedford Modern Sch.; Westfield Coll., London (BA Hons Hist. 1979); University Coll., Chichester (MA module, dance, writing and criticism, 2005). Society of Architectural and Associated Technicians: Sec. for Educn and Membership, 1979–82; Chief Exec., 1983–86; Chief Exec., British Inst. of Architectural Technicians, 1986–91. Director: Nat. Centre for Construction, 1996–; Considerate Constructors Scheme, 2001–; Construction Umbrella Body (Hldgs) Ltd, 2003–; Construction Industry Council Approved Inspectors Register Ltd, 2014–; Constructionarium Ltd, 2017–. Chairman: Construction Skills Standards and Qualifications Strategic Cttee, 2007–13; Civil and Structural Engrs' Selection Panel, Centre for Music, 2017; Competence Wkg Gp, Ind. Rev. of Building Regulations and Fire Safety, 2018; Member: Strategic Forum for Construction, 2001– (Sec., 2002–10); Council and Strategic Partnership Panel, Sector Skills Council for Construction, 2006–15; Adv. Bd, Assoc. for Consultancy and Engrg, 2008–; Delivery Gp, 2013–15, Adv. Bd, 2019–, Construction Leadership Council; Mem., Grenfell Industry Response Gp, 2017–, Chm., Competence Steering Cttee, 2018–, MHCLG; Sec., All Party Parly Gp for Excellence in Built Envmt, 2010–. Mem., Governing Body, BRE Global, 2010–14; Mem., Awards Cttee, Chartered Assoc. of Building Engrs (formerly Assoc. of Building Engrs), 2010–. Trustee: Interbuild Fund, 1997–2003; Sir Ian Dixon Meml Trust, 2001–12; Happold Trust, 2002–15; Cervantes Th., 2019–. Vis. Prof., Univ. of Northumbria, 2000–12. Manager, British Fencing Team, 1995–2010; Performance Dir, British Fencing, 2000–10; Olympic Team Manager for Fencing, 2001–10, Team Manager, 2004 and 2008 Olympic Games; Commonwealth Bronze Medal, 1990; British Sabre Capt., 1992 Olympic Games and 7 World Championships; Chm., Sabre Club, 1988–2008; Internat. Fencing Referee, 1991–2010. Consultant Editor, PSA and Local Government Rev., 1993; columnist: Atrium, 1987–90; New Civil Engineer, 1996–99; dance writer and critic, writing for specialist dance magazines in the UK, Europe, North America, Japan and on internet; Associate Artistic Dir, Gala for Grenfell, Adelphi Th., 2017. Member: Soc. of Dance Research, 2005–; Chichester Gp of Dance Writers, 2005–; Critics' Circle, 2009– (Sec., 2010–11, Chm., 2011–, Dance Section; Mem. Council, 2011–); UNESCO Internat. Dance Council, 2011–. Sec., 2010, Chm., 2011–, Nat. Dance Awards; Judge: English Nat. Ballet Emerging Dancer Award, 2017; Construction News Community Engagement Award, 2018; Assoc. for Consultancy and Engrg Business Awards, 2018. MCMI 1983; FRSA 1983. Hon. Member: Chartered Inst. of Architectural Technologists, 1991; RICS 2001 (Chm., Nat. Procurement Framework Wkg Gp, 2015–; Mem., Construction Mkt Forum, 2015–). Liveryman, Paviors' Co., 2006–. Hon. Fellow: RIBA, 2000 (Mem., Fellowship Assessment Panel, 2015–); Assoc. of Building Engrs, 2000; Inst. of Building Control, 2000–01; Faculty of Building, 2003; CIBSE, 2006; Inst. of Clerks of Works and Construction Inspectors, 2010; British Inst. of Interior Design, 2012. Hon. Fellow, Chartered Inst. of Civil Engrg Surveyors, 2014. Peter Stone Award, Assoc. of Building Engrs, 1996; President's Medal, Chartered Inst. of Building, 2000; Silver Medal, British Fencing Assoc., 2005. *Publications:* (jtly) Architectural Technology: the constructive link, 1984; (with D. Klimentová) Agony and Ecstasy: my life in dance, 2013; Irina Kolesnikova, Prima Ballerina of St Petersburg Ballet Theatre, 2015; (contrib.) The Oxford Handbook of Contemporary Ballet, 2019; regular contrib. to Dancing Times, Dance Tabs, LondonDance, Dance Europe, Shinshokan Dance Mag., Bachtrack and others; contrib. articles to Building and many other jls and mags associated with built envmt. *Recreations:* ballet and all forms of dance, dance writing, reading (especially modern literature and biographies), my dogs, being in N Norfolk, voice and life of Maria Callas, British Spanish Society, Anglo Chilean Society, lifelong fan of Wolverhampton Wanderers FC, member of Penya Blaugrana London (supporter of FC Barcelona). *Address:* c/o Construction Industry Council, The Building Centre, 26 Store Street, WC1E 7BT. *T:* (020) 7399 7402, *Fax:* (020) 7399 7425. *E:* gwatts@cic.org.uk. *W:* www.twitter.com/CICCEO. www.twitter.com/GWDanceWriter.

**WATTS, Jane Angharad, (Mrs C. D. G. Ross)**, FRCO; concert organist, since 1980; *b* 7 Oct. 1959; *d* of J. Maldwyn Watts and J. Leonora Watts; *m* 1985, Callum David George Ross; one *s. Educ:* Royal Coll. of Music (ARCM 1978, LRAM 1979); postgrad. studies with Mme Marie-Claire Alain, Paris. FRCO 1980; GRSM 1981. Mem. Council, RCO, 1994–2000. Débuts: BBC Radio, 1980; BBC TV, 1981; RFH, with LPO, 1983, recital, 1986; BBC Prom. Concerts, 1988; US début, 1991; New York recital début, 2008; Organist and accompanist, Bach Choir, 1971–2010. Numerous engagements throughout UK, 1980–, with orchestras incl. BBC Nat. Orch. of Wales, LPO, Ulster Orch., London Mozart Players, etc; recital series incl. complete cycle of Widor Organ Symphonies, Brangwyn Hall, Swansea, 1999 and 2000 and St John's Smith Square, 2001; Duruflé series, Brangwyn Hall, 2002; has performed in USA, Europe, Hong Kong, Barbados, Australia and NZ, 1991–. Jury Mem., St Albans Internat. Organ Festival, 2005. Numerous recordings incl. recitals in Westminster Abbey, Salisbury Cathedral, Chartres Cathedral, Orleans Cathedral, Belfast, Glasgow, Sydney, Brisbane and Wellington; Handel and Popplewell organ concertos. First Performer of Year, RCO, 1986. *Recreations:* cookery, maintaining links with Wales and Welsh-speaking community. *Address:* c/o Callum Ross, Yr Ysgubor, 10 Bury Farm Close, Horton Road, Slapton, Bucks LU7 9DS. *T:* (01525) 222729. *Club:* London Welsh.

**WATTS, Mark Francis**; Director and co-owner: LP Brussels, since 2010; IDA Brussels, since 2016; *b* 11 June 1964; *s* of Albert Charles Watts and Carole Emmah Watts (*née* Fleischman); *m* 1st, 1988, Kim McEachan (marr. diss. 2003); two *s*; 2nd, 2003, Jessica D'Souza; one *d. Educ:* Maidstone Grammar Sch.; LSE (BSc Econ; MSc Econ). Planning Officer, Royal Borough of Kingston-upon-Thames, 1988–94. Associate Dir, Waterfront Partnership, 2004–09. MEP (Lab) Kent E, 1994–99, SE Region, 1999–2004; Spokesman on transport, EP, 1995–2004. Co-Chm., Eur. Transport Safety Council, 1996–2004; Sec., Labour Transport Gp, 2010–. Maidstone Borough Council: Councillor, 1986–96; Leader,

Lab. Gp, 1990–94. Co-founder, Labour Business, Brussels, 2015–. Pres., E Kent Eur. Movt, 1999–. Mem. Council, Univ. of Kent at Canterbury, 2006–12. Pres., Old Maidstonians Soc., 1996–97. FRSA 2009. *Recreations:* history, walking, cooking, spending time with friends and family. *Address:* LP Brussels, Rue d'Arlon 40, Brussels 1000, Belgium. *T:* and *Fax:* (2) 2350530. *E:* markwatts@lpbrussels.com.

**WATTS, Mela Lesley Jane,** CBE 2008; Director of Free Schools and University Technical Colleges (formerly Free Schools, University Technical Colleges and Studio Schools), Department for Education, since 2010; *b* Chalfont St Peter, 12 Sept. 1963; *d* of late Edward Watts and of Pamela Watts (*née* Burke). *Educ:* Dr Challoner's High Sch., Bucks; Portsmouth Poly. (BSc Hons Biol.). Joined DES (later DFE, then DFEE, subseq. DFES, then DCSF), 1986; estabd Funding Agency for Schs; Private Sec. to Minister of Sport; estabd Nursery Educn Voucher Scheme; Bill Manager, Special Educnl Needs and Disability Act 2002; Curriculum Div.; Principal Private Sec. to Sec. of State for Children, Schs and Families, 2004–08; Dir, Sch. Performance and Reform, 2008–10. *Recreations:* wine tasting, walking, travelling. *Address:* Department for Education, Sanctuary Buildings, Great Smith Street, SW1P 3BT. *T:* (020) 7783 8421. *E:* Mela.Watts@education..gov.uk.

**WATTS, Neil Robert;** Member, Advisory Board, Cifas, since 2016; Consultant, Alpha Plus Group, since 2017; *b* Middleton, near Manchester, 8 Dec. 1951; *s* of Kenneth Leach Watts and of Joan Watts (*née* Morgan); *m* 1983, Sadie Wood; one *s* one *d*. *Educ:* Chadderton Grammar Sch.; Magdalene Coll., Cambridge (BA 1973; MA 1976); Univ. of Leicester (PGCE Econs). Teacher of Econs, King Henry VIII Sch., Coventry, 1974–78; Hd of Econs and Business Studies, Hedingham Comp. Sch., Halstead, 1978–81; Hd of Sixth Form, Stowupland High Sch., Stowmarket, 1981–84; Dep. Headteacher, Northgate High Sch., Ipswich, 1985–88; Headteacher: Sudbury County Upper Sch., 1988–92; Northgate High Sch., Ipswich, 1992–2009; Consultant Headteacher, Suffolk CC, 2009–13. Mem. Council, 2004–11, Dep. Chm., 2009–11, Advertising Standards Authy; Public Mem., Press Complaints Commn, 2011–14; Mem., Complaints Cttee, IPSO, 2014–18; Member, Board: ARB, 2009–17; Ofqual, 2010–18. Chair, Suffolk Family Carers Partnership Bd, 2014–. Mem., Foundn Bd, Univ. of Suffolk, 2017–. DUniv Suffolk, 2016. Mem., Great Finborough Wine Club. *Publications:* Competition, Monopoly and Public Policy, 1982; Selected Topics in Applied Economics, 1987. *Recreations:* remaining optimistic whilst supporting Rochdale AFC, theatre, travel and sport. *T:* 07850 117831. *E:* wattsnrw@gmail.com. *Club:* Rochdale Exiles.

**WATTS, Rev. Sir Philip (Beverley),** KCMG 2003; FInstP, FEI, FRGS, FGS; Group Managing Director, 1997–2004, and Chairman, Committee of Managing Directors, 2001–04, Royal Dutch/Shell Group; Managing Director, 1997–2004, and Chairman, 2001–04, Shell Transport and Trading plc; *b* 25 June 1945; *s* of Samuel Watts and Phillippa (*née* Wale); *m* 1966, Janet Lockwood; one *s* one *d*. *Educ:* Wyggeston Grammar Sch., Leicester; Univ. of Leeds (BSc Hons Physics, MSc Geophysics); Open Univ. (DipRS); Oxford Brookes (BA Hons Religion and Theol. 2011); Oxford Univ. (Postgrad. Dip. Applied Theol. 2017). FInstP 1980; FEI (FInstPet 1990); FRGS 1998; FGS 1998. Sci. teacher, Methodist Boys High Sch., Freetown, Sierra Leone, 1966–68; joined Shell International, 1969: seismologist, Indonesia, 1970–74; geophysicist, UK/Europe, 1974–77; Exploration Manager, Norway, 1978–81; Div. Head, Malaysia, Brunei, Singapore, London, 1981–83; Exploration Dir, UK, 1983–85; Head, Exploration & Production Liaison–Europe, The Hague, 1986–88; Head, Exploration & Production Econs and Planning, The Hague, 1989–91; Man. Dir, Nigeria, 1991–94; Regl Co-ordinator—Europe, The Hague, 1994–95; Dir, Planning, Envmt and Ext. Affairs, London, 1996–97. Member: Exec. Cttee, World Business Council for Sustainable Develt, 1998–2003 (Chm., 2002–03); Governing Body, ICC UK, 1997–2004 (Chm., 1998–2004); ICC Exec. Bd (Worldwide), 1997–2000; CfBT Educn Trust, 2009–13. Dir, Boniface Multi-Acad. Trust, 2017–. Ordained deacon, 2011, priest, 2012; Curate, Binfield, Berks, 2011–13; Priest-in-charge, Waltham St Lawrence, Berks, 2013–17; Sen. Priest, Warfield, Berks, 2017–18. *Recreations:* travel, gardening, reading. *Club:* Travellers.

**WATTS, Rolande Jane Rita;** see Anderson, R. J. R.

**WATTS, Susan Janet;** science journalist and communicator; Head of Communications and Public Engagement, Rothamsted Research, 2017–18; *b* Crystal Palace, 13 July 1962; *d* of Derek Watts and Judith Ann Mary Watts (*née* Collett); *m*; two *s* two *d*. *Educ:* Haberdashers' Aske's Hatcham Girls' Sch.; Imperial Coll., London (BSc Physics); City Univ. (Dip. Journalism). Computer Weekly, 1985–89; New Scientist, 1989–91; Independent, 1991–95; BBC Newsnight, 1995–2013 (Sci. Ed., 2000–13); Hd of Communications and Public Engagement, MRC Clin. Scis Centre, then MRC London Inst. of Med. Scis, 2015–17. Trustee, Scottish Assoc. for Marine Sci., 2018–. *E:* susan.watts@susanwatts.org.

**WATTS, Vincent Challacombe,** OBE 1998; Founding Chairman, East of England Development Agency, 1998–2003; Vice-Chancellor, University of East Anglia, 1997–2002; *b* 11 Aug. 1940; *s* of Geoffrey Watts and Lilian Watts (*née* Pye); *m* 1st, 1967, Rachel Rosser (*d* 1998), Prof. of Psychiatry, UCL Med. Sch.; one *s* one *d*; 2nd, 2009, Hilary (*née* Miles). *Educ:* Sidcot Sch.; Peterhouse, Cambridge (MA 1966); Birmingham Univ. (MSc 1967). FCA 1976. Joined Andersen Consulting, 1963, Partner, 1976–97; seconded to: Dept of Health as Founder Mem., Operational Res. Unit, 1970–71; HM Treasury, 1974; Financial Management Unit, Cabinet Office/HM Treasury, 1982–85. Mem. Council, John Innes Centre, 1997–2010; Mem. Council and Chair, Audit Cttee, LSC, 2002–03. CMC 1986; FIC (FIMC 1986); CCMI 2001. FRSA 2001. Hon. LittD East Anglia, 2002. *Publications:* papers on performance evaluation in health services. *Recreations:* sailing, gardening, exploring. *Clubs:* Oxford and Cambridge; Jesters.

**WAUCHOPE, Sir Roger Hamilton D.;** see Don-Wauchope.

**WAUGH, Andrew Peter;** QC 1998; *b* 6 Nov. 1959; *m* 1980, Catrin Prys Davies; four *s*. *Educ:* City Univ. (BSc 1st Cl. Hons 1980; DipLaw 1981). Called to the Bar, Gray's Inn, 1982; in practice as barrister, 1982–; specialist in Intellectual Property Law. *Publications:* (ed jtly) Terrell on the Law of Patents, 18th edn, 2017. *Address:* 3 New Square, Lincoln's Inn, WC2A 3RS. *T:* (020) 7405 1111.

**WAUGH, Rev. Eric Alexander;** Consultant on Christian Education, Theology and Worldviews, Every Nation Leadership Institute, Cape Town, South Africa, 2015– (Dean, 1995–98, Vice-Chancellor, 1998–2003, His People Leadership Institute); *b* 9 May 1933; *s* of Hugh Waugh and Marion Waugh (*née* McLay); *m* 1955, Agnes-Jean (Sheena) Saunders; two *s*. *Educ:* Glasgow Univ.; Edinburgh Univ. (LTh). Local government officer, 1948–64. Assistant Minister, High Church, Bathgate, 1969–70; Missionary, Kenya Highlands, 1970–73; Minister, Mowbray Presbyterian Church, Cape Town, 1973–78; Missioner, Presbyterian Church of Southern Africa, 1978–85; Minister, City Temple, URC, 1986–91; Missioner, Kingdom Communications Trust, S Africa, 1992–95. *Recreations:* walking, fly fishing, acrylic painting. *Address:* 20 Queens Lane, Bridge of Allan, Stirling FK9 4NY. *T:* (01786) 834044. *E:* revericawaugh@gmail.com.

**WAUGH, Stephen Rodger,** AO 2003; cricketer; Captain, Australian Test Cricket Team, 1999–2004; Founder, Waugh Global Realty, 2015; *b* Sydney, NSW, 2 June 1965; *s* of Rodger and Beverley Waugh; *m* Lynette; one *s* two *d*. *Educ:* East Hills High Sch. Cricketer: with NSW, 1984–2004; with Somerset CCC, 1987–88; Mem., Australian Cricket Team, 1985–2004; Captain, One Day Internats team, 1997–2002; Mem. of winning team, World Cup, 1987; Captain of winning team, World Cup, 1999. Passed 10,000 Test runs, 2003. Life Member: BCCI, India; Bankstown Canterbury CC, NSW; Hon. Member: SCG; MCG. Allan Border Medal, 2001; Steve Waugh Medal, 2003. *Publications:* South African Tour Diary, 1995; Steve Waugh's West Indies Tour Diary, 1996; Steve Waugh's World Cup Diary, 1997; Steve Waugh's 1997 Ashes Diary, 1997; (with Nasser Hussain) Ashes Summer, 1997; Images of Waugh, 1998; Steve Waugh: no regrets—a captain's diary, 2000; Never Satisfied, 2000; Ashes Diary, 2001; Steve Waugh—Captain's Diary, 2002; Out Of My Comfort Zone (autobiog.), 2006; The Meaning of Luck, 2013. *Address:* c/o The Steve Waugh Foundation, PO Box 1119, Cronulla, NSW 2230, Australia. *W:* www.stevewaughfoundation.com.au.

**WAUMSLEY, Lance Vincent;** a Judge of the Upper Tribunal (Immigration and Asylum Chamber) (formerly a Vice President, Immigration Appeal Tribunal, later a Senior Immigration Judge, Asylum and Immigration Tribunal), 2003–12; *b* 30 July 1947; *s* of Leslie Vincent Waumsley and Cecilia Daisy Waumsley (*née* Burden); *m* 2006, Sherrie Lee (*née* McCargar); two step *s* one step *d*. *Educ:* Wycliffe Coll., Glos; Selwyn Coll., Cambridge (MA, LLM). Admitted solicitor, 1972; with Collyer-Bristow and Co., 1970–76; Partner: Halsey Lightly and Hemsley, 1976–84; Macdonald Stacey, subseq. incorporated in Kidd Rapinet, 1984–97; Adjudicator of Immigration Appeals, 1997–2003. Mem., Special Immigration Appeals Commn, 2005–12. Hon. Treas., Council of Immigration Judges, 2001–03. Sec., Yapp Welfare Trust and Yapp Educn and Res. Trust, 1997–; Trustee and Founder Mem., Arts and Entertainment (formerly Comic Heritage) Charitable Trust, 1993–2001; Mem., Soc. of Trust and Estate Practitioners, 1994–. *Recreations:* genealogy, music, reading, crosswords. *Address:* 656 Lamplighter Circle Se, Salem, OR 97302, USA.

**WAVERLEY,** 3rd Viscount *cr* 1952, of Westdean; **John Desmond Forbes Anderson;** *b* 31 Oct. 1949; *s* of 2nd Viscount Waverley and Myrtle Ledgerwood (*d* 2013); *S* father, 1990; *m* 1994; one *s*. *Educ:* Malvern. Elected Mem., H of L, 1999. Chm., Parly Gps on Kazakhstan, Kyrgyzstan, Tajikistan, Turkmenistan and Uzbekistan; Co-Chm., Mongolia Parly Gp. Chm., League of Gentlemen Consultants; Vice-Chm., British Azerbaijan Business Council; Hon. Co-Chm., Internat. Tax and Investment Centre, Washington, DC. Advr, CCC Gp of Cos. Mem., RIIA. Jubilee Medal, Kazakhstan, 2002. Grand Cross, Order of San Carlos (Colombia), 1998. *Recreations:* golf, walking. *Address:* c/o House of Lords, SW1A 0PW.

**WAVERLEY, Viscountess;** see Barrow, U. H.

**WAWRZYNSKI, Dame Dana R.;** see Ross-Wawrzynski.

**WAX, Kenneth Howard;** theatre producer; Chief Executive Officer, Kenneth H. Wax Ltd, since 1995; *b* Cheshire, 23 June 1967; *s* of Robert and Valerie Wax; *m* 2000, Daniella; three *c*. *Educ:* Carmel Coll.; Poly. of Central London (BA Hons). Prodn Asst, King's Head Th., 1991–93; Producer, Imagination, 1993–95. West End production credits include: Top Hat, Once on this Island, The Play that Goes Wrong, Peter Pan Goes Wrong, The Comedy about a Bank Robbery, La Strada, Six; shows for families include The Gruffalo, The Gruffalo's Child, Mr Popper's Penguins, What the Ladybird Heard, We're Going on a Bearhunt, Hetty Feather, The Tiger Who Came to Tea, Room on the Broom, The Worst Witch and Around the World in 80 Days. Mem. Bd, Soc. of London Th., 2016– (Pres., 2017–June 2020). *Recreations:* tennis, golf, supporter of Manchester City FC. *Address:* Kenny Wax Ltd, 3rd Floor, 62 Shaftesbury Avenue, W1D 6LT. *T:* (020) 7437 1736.

**WAX, Ruby,** Hon. OBE 2015; actor, comedian and writer; mental health speaker and campaigner; *b* 19 April 1953; *d* of Edward Wax and Berta Wax (*née* Goldmann); *m* 1988, Edward Richard Morison Bye; one *s* two *d*. *Educ:* Evanston High Sch.; Berkeley univ.; RSAMD. *Theatre:* Crucible, 1976; Royal Shakespeare Co., 1978–82; Stressed (one-woman show), UK, Australia and NZ tour, 2000; The Witches, Wyndhams Th., 2005; Ruby Wax: Losing It, Corn Exchange, Newbury, 2010, Menier Chocolate Factory, 2011, Duchess Th., 2011; Ruby Wax: Sane New World, UK tour, 2014; Ruby Wax: Frazzled, Leicester Square, 2017, and UK tour; Ruby Wax: How to be Human, Leicester Square, and UK tour, 2019; *television:* Not the Nine O'Clock News, 1982–83; Girls on Top, 1983–85; Don't Miss Wax, 1985–87; Hit and Run, 1988; Full Wax, 1987–92; Ruby Wax Meets…, 1996, 1997, 1998; Ruby, 1997, 1998, 1999, 2000; Ruby's American Pie, 1999, 2000; Hot Wax, 2001; The Waiting Game (quiz show), 2001, 2002; Life with Ruby (chat show), 2002; Commercial Breakdown, 2002; Ruby Wax With…, 2003; Ruby Does the Business, 2004; Ruby Wax's Mad Confessions, 2012; *films:* Miami Memoirs, 1987; East Meets Wax, 1988; Class of '69; Ruby Takes a Trip, 1992. Chancellor, Univ. of Southampton, 2019–. *Publications:* How Do You Want Me?, 2002; Sane New World, 2013; A Mindfulness Guide for the Frazzled, 2016; How To Be Human, 2018. *Address:* c/o Peters Fraser + Dunlop, 55 New Oxford Street, WC1A 1BS.

**WAXMAN, Prof. Jonathan Hugh,** MD; FRCP; Professor of Oncology, Imperial College, University of London, since 1999; *b* 31 Oct. 1951; *s* of David Waxman and Shirley Waxman (*née* Friedman); one *s* one *d*; *m* Naomi Heaton. *Educ:* Haberdashers' Aske's Sch., Elstree; University Coll. London (BSc); University Coll. Hosp. (MB BS 1975; MD 1986). MRCP 1978, FRCP 1988. House Officer, UCH and Addenbrooke's Hosp., Cambridge, 1975–76; SHO, UCH, London Chest Hosp. and St Mary's Hosp., London, 1976–78; Registrar, St Mary's Hosp., 1979–81; ICRF Res. Fellow, St Bartholomew's Hosp., 1981–86; Consultant Physician, Hammersmith Hosp., 1986–99. Founder Mem., All Party Gp on Cancer, 1998–. Founder and Life Pres., Prostate Cancer UK (formerly Prostate Cancer Charity), 1996–. *Publications:* The New Endocrinology of Cancer, 1987; The Molecular Biology of Cancer, 1989; Urological Oncology, 1992; Interleukin 2, 1992; Molecular Endocrinology of Cancer, 1996; The Fifth Gospel, 1997; Cancer Chemotherapy Treatment Protocols, 1998; Cancer and the Law, 1999; Treatment Options in Urological Oncology, 2002; The Prostate Cancer Book, 2002; Lecture Notes in Oncology, 2006, 3rd edn 2015; The Elephant in the Room, 2011; The Sweetest Pill, MacLeod's Introduction to Medicine, 2013; contrib. over 400 scientific papers and book chapters on cancer res. *Recreation:* family and friends. *Address:* Department of Oncology, Hammersmith Hospital, Du Cane Road, W12 0NN. *T:* (020) 8383 4651.

**WAY, Andrew Mark,** AM 2019; Chief Executive, Alfred Health, Melbourne, Vic, since 2009; *b* 27 Feb. 1959; *s* of Maxwell Andrew Way and Jane Kathleen Way (*née* Palliser). *Educ:* Bournemouth Sch.; Bristol Sch. of Nursing (RN); City Univ. (BSc Hons 1990); Keele Univ. (MBA 1994). Gen. Manager, St George's Hosp., London, 1993–95; Gen. Manager, 1995–2000, Chief Operating Officer, 2000–02, Hammersmith Hosps NHS Trust; Chief Executive: Heatherwood & Wexham Park Hosps NHS Trust, 2002–05; Royal Free Hampstead NHS Trust, 2005–09. FAICD. *Recreations:* swimming, ski-ing, bridge. *Address:* The Alfred, PO Box 315, Prahran, Vic 3181, Australia. *T:* (3) 90766000, *Fax:* (3) 90766434. *E:* andrew-way@bigpond.com.

**WAY, David Edward**, CBE 2011; adviser on skills and business development domestically and internationally; *b* Bridgwater, Somerset, 8 Jan. 1953; *s* of Edward Way and Dorothy Way; *m* 2003, Margaret Egan; one *s* one *d*. *Educ*: Doctor Morgan's Grammar Sch., Bridgwater; City Univ., London (BSc Econ 1974); London Sch. of Econs and Pol Sci. (MSc 1975). Mgt trainee, Dept of Employment, 1975–78; mgt posts, Jobcentre, 1978–85; Hd, Strategy, Employment Service, 1985–90; Ops Dir, Employment Service, Wales, 1990–92; Dir, Strategy and Corp. Develt, Govt Office for SW, 1992–97; Dir, Business and Learning, Govt Office for West Midlands, 1997–2001; Exec. Dir, Black Country Learning and Skills Council, 2001–04; Nat. Dir, Skills, Learning and Skills Council, 2004–08; Chief Operating Officer and Dep. Chief Exec., 2008–12, Chief Exec., 2012–14, Nat. Apprenticeship Service. Vis. Prof., Univ. of Winchester, 2013–19, now Emeritus Prof. Skills Advr, Energy and Utilities Skills Partnership, 2013–19; Adviser: to Inter-American Develt Bank, 2017–18; to Birmingham City Univ., 2017. Chair, Quality Panel, Nat. Skills Acad. for Rail, 2017–18. Apprenticeship Ambassador, PeoplePlus, 2018–19. Warden, St Mary Magdalene, Tanworth-in-Arden, 2011–18; Member: Deanery Synod, 2014–May 2020; Diocesan Synod, 2015–18. *Publications*: (ed) A Race to the Top: achieving three million more apprenticeships by 2020, 2016. *Recreations*: watching Somerset play cricket, walking, visiting National Trust houses and gardens, gardening, playing golf. *Address*: Tanworth-in-Arden, Warwickshire. *E*: way744@btinternet.com.

**WAY of Plean, George Alexander**; Baron of Plean in the County of Stirlingshire; Sheriff of Tayside Central and Fife, since 2009; *b* Edinburgh, 22 May 1956; *s* of Robert Blair Way and Annie Sanderson Way (*née* Gauld); *m* 1st, 1979, Rosemary Calder (marr. diss. 2009); one *s*; 2nd, 2012, Lynn Louisa Harrison, SSC. *Educ*: Boroughmuir Sch.; Univ. of Edinburgh (LLB Hons 1978); Pembroke Coll., Oxford (Masters Dip. Orgnl Leadership 2014; Oxford Saïd Prize 2016). Solicitor, then Sen. Partner, Beveridge & Kellas SSC, Leith, 1978–2008; Solicitor Advocate, 2003; Procurator Fiscal to Court of the Lord Lyon King of Arms, 2003–09. Member: Lord Coulsfield's Rev. of Civil Justice, 2005; Sheriff Court Rules Council, 2006–09; Scottish Govt Debt Action Forum, 2009. Pres., Soc. of Solicitors to Supreme Courts of Scotland, 2002–05; Mem. Council, Law Soc. of Scotland, 2009. Falkland Pursuivant Extraordinary, 2016–18; Carrick Pursuivant in Ordinary, 2018–. Scottish Law Agent, Shipwrecked Fishermen and Mariners' Royal Benevolent Soc., 1986–2009. Lt-Col, JAG, California State Mil. Reserve, 1986; Privy Counsellor to Royal House of Portugal, 2000. Sec., Standing Council of Scottish Clan Chiefs, 1985–2003. FSAScot 1985; FRSA 1986. Calif State Mil. Service Medal, 2000; Queen's Golden Jubilee Medal, 2002. OStJ 2017 (MStJ 1999). Comendador, Order of Our Lady of Vila Viçosa (Portugal), 1988; Knight, Order of Rose of Lippe (Germany), 1989; Cavaliere, Order of St Maurice and St Lazarus (Italy), 2002; Companion, SMO of Malta, 2004; Knight, Order of St Michael on the Wing (Portugal), 2018; Knight, Imperial Order of St Anna (Russia), 2018. *Publications*: Collins Clan and Family Encyclopaedia, 1994, 3rd edn 2018; Scottish Clans and Tartans, 1998; Homelands of the Clans, 1999; Collins Everyday Scots Law, 2000. *Recreations*: Scots heraldry and peerage, collecting, haunting auction rooms. *Address*: Sheriff Court House, 6 West Bell Street, Dundee DD1 9AD. *E*: sheriffgaway@scotcourts.gov.uk. *Clubs*: New (Edinburgh); Confederate Yacht (California).

**WAY, Nicholas John**, OBE 2016; consultant, since 2016; *b* 28 Aug. 1955; *s* of John Francis Way and Margaret Helen Laura Way (*née* Ewins); *m* 1987, Susan Clark; two *s* one *d*. *Educ*: Clare Coll., Cambridge (BA Econs 1978; MA 1982). MAFF, 1978–89; CLA, 1989–2005, Dir of Policy, 2001–05; Dir Gen., HHA, 2005–15. Mem. Bd, English Rural Housing Assoc., 1999–2005, 2010– (Vice-Chm., 2016–); Trustee: Heritage Alliance (formerly Heritage Link), 2005–15; Sulgrove Manor Trust, 2016–; CLA Pension Trust, 2017–; Mem. Council, Attingham Trust, 2005–15; Sec., Heritage Conservation Trust, 2005–15. Member: Adv. Council, Sch. of Rural Economy and Land Mgt, RAC, 2002–05; Res. Ethics Cttee, NHS Oxford, 2016–. *Recreations*: family, countryside, history and historic houses, football (spectator).
 See also P. E. Way.

**WAY, Patrick Edward**; QC 2013; *b* Solihull, 6 Feb. 1954; *s* of John Francis Way and Margaret Helen Laura Way (*née* Ewins); *m* 1978, Judith Anne, *d* of late Peter Orchard Williams, CBE; three *s*. *Educ*: Solihull Sch.; Univ. of Leeds (BA Hons). Admitted solicitor, 1979; Solicitor, Lawrence Graham, 1979–82; Asst Solicitor, 1982–85, Tax Partner, 1985–87, Nabarro Nathanson; Partner and Hd, Corporate Tax, Gouldens, 1987–94; called to the Bar, Lincoln's Inn, 1994; Member: 8 Gray's Inn Sq., 1994–2001; Gray's Inn Tax Chambers, 2001–14; Co-Founder, Field Ct Tax Chambers, 2014–. Mem., Attorney Gen.'s B Panel to the Crown, 2010–13. Dir, Richmond (Rugby) Football Club Ltd, 2010–. Founder Ed., Trusts and Estates, 1985–86; Tax Ed., BES Mag., 1986–94. *Publications*: Death and Taxes, 1985; (contrib.) Tolley's Tax Planning, 1985–2012; Maximising Opportunities under the BES, 1986; The BES and Assured Tenancies: the new rules, 1988; Tax Advice for Company Transactions, 1992; The Enterprise Investment Scheme, 1994; (ed and contrib.) Joint Ventures, 1994. *Recreations*: watching Richmond Rugby Club, contemporary art. *Address*: Field Court Tax Chambers, Gray's Inn, WC1R 5EP. *T*: (020) 3693 3700. *E*: pw@fieldtax.com. *Club*: Travellers.
 See also N. J. Way.

**WAYMAN, Caroline**; Chief Ombudsman and Chief Executive, Financial Ombudsman Service, since 2014; *b* Sunderland, 23 June 1975; *d* of Eric Wayman and Wendy Wayman; *m* 2017, Simon Horner. *Educ*: Weald of Kent Grammar Sch.; Nottingham Law Sch. (LLB Hons Law); Inns of Court Sch. of Law (BVC). Called to the Bar, Middle Temple, 1998; Adjudicator, Insurance Ombudsman Bureau, 1999; Financial Ombudsman Service: Service and Ops Manager, 2000–07; Lead Ombudsman, 2007–11; Principal Ombudsman and Legal Dir, 2011–14. Non-executive Member of Board: Claims Mgt Regulator, 2014–19; CPS, 2018–. *Recreations*: tennis, running, watching Rugby. *E*: caroline.wayman@financial-ombudsman.org.uk.

**WAYNE, Philip Brian**; Headmaster, Royal Grammar School, High Wycombe, since 2015; *b* Great Barr, Birmingham, 22 Dec. 1966; *s* of Brian and Lorna Wayne; *m* 1997, Elen Môn Jones; one *s* one *d*. *Educ*: Dartmouth High Sch.; Univ. of Manchester (MusB 1988); Univ. of Birmingham (PGCE); Nat. Coll. of Sch. Leadership (NPQH). ARCO 1985; LGSM 1992. Freelance musician, 1988–92; Dartmouth High School: Music Teacher, 1992–94; Dir of Music, 1994–99; Asst Head, 1999–2004; Dep. Headmaster, John Hampden GS, 2004–07; Headmaster, Chesham GS, 2007–15. Gov., Pipers Corner Sch. *Recreations*: family, food, cooking, organ and piano playing, sport. *Address*: Royal Grammar School, Amersham Road, High Wycombe, Bucks HP13 6QT. *T*: (01494) 524955. *E*: headmaster@rgshw.com. *Club*: Lansdowne.

**WEAIRE, Prof. Denis Lawrence**, PhD; FRS 1999; Erasmus Smith's Professor of Natural and Experimental Philosophy, 1984–2007, now Emeritus, and Fellow, 1987, now Emeritus, Trinity College, Dublin; *b* 17 Oct. 1942; *s* of Allen Maunder Weaire and Janet Eileen (*née* Rea); *m* 1969, Colette Rosa O'Regan; one *s*. *Educ*: Belfast Royal Acad.; Clare Coll., Cambridge (MA Maths; PhD 1968). Harkness Fellow, Calif and Chicago, 1964–66; researcher, Cavendish Lab., Univ. of Cambridge, 1966–69; Fellow, Clare Coll. Cambridge, 1967–69; Res. Fellow, Harvard Univ., 1969–70; Yale University: Instructor, 1970–72; Asst Prof., 1972–73; Heriot-Watt University: Associate Prof., 1973–74; Sen. Lectr, 1974–77; Reader, 1977–79; Prof. of Exptl Physics, UC Dublin, 1980–84 (Hd of Dept, 1983–84); Trinity College, Dublin: Hd of Dept, 1984–89, 2003–05; Dean of Science, 1989–92. Vis. Prof., Univ. of Auckland, 2012; Gledden Fellow, Univ. of Western Australia Perth, 2014. Ed., Jl Physics: Condensed Matter, 1994–97. Pres., Eur. Physical Soc., 1997–99 (Vice Pres., 1996–97 and 1999–2000). MRIA 1987; MAE 1998 (Vice Pres., 2005–08). Dr *hc* Tech. Univ., Lisbon, 2001. Cecil Powell Medal, Eur. Phys. Soc., 2001; Cunningham Medal, RIA, 2005; Holwech Medal, Inst. of Physics and French Phys. Soc., 2008. *Publications*: (ed jtly) Tetrahedrally Bonded Amorphous Semiconductors, 1974; (ed with D. Pettifor) The Recursion Method, 1985; (with P. G. Harper) Introduction to Physical Mathematics, 1985; (ed with C. Windsor) Solid State Science, 1987; (ed jtly) Tradition and Reform, 1988; (ed jtly) Epioptics, 1995; (ed) The Kelvin Problem, 1997; (ed with J. Banhart) Foams and Films, 1999; (ed jtly) Richard Helsham's Course of Lectures on Natural Philosophy, 1999; (with S. Hutzler) The Physics of Foams, 1999; (with T. Aste) The Pursuit of Perfect Packing, 2000, 2nd edn 2008; (ed jtly) George Francis Fitzgerald, 2009; (ed jtly) Hutchie, 2012; contrib. numerous scientific papers. *Recreations*: theatre, humorous writing. *Address*: 26 Greenmount Road, Terenure, Dublin, Republic of Ireland. *T*: (1) 4902063.

**WEALE, Prof. Albert Peter**, CBE 2013; PhD; FBA 1998; Professor of Political Theory and Public Policy, University College London, 2010–15, now Emeritus; *b* 30 May 1950; *s* of Albert Cecil and Margaret Elizabeth Weale; *m* 1st, 1976, Jane Leresche (marr. diss. 1987); 2nd, 1994, Janet Felicity Harris. *Educ*: St Luke's Primary Sch., Brighton; Varndean Grammar Sch., Brighton; Clare Coll., Cambridge (BA Theol.; PhD Social and Political Scis 1977). Sir James Knott Fellow, Dept of Politics, Univ. of Newcastle upon Tyne, 1974–76; University of York: Lectr, Dept of Politics, 1976–85; Asst Dir, Inst. for Res. in Social Scis, 1982–85; Prof. of Politics, UEA, 1985–92; Prof. of Govt, Univ. of Essex, 1992–2009. Chairman: Nuffield Council on Bioethics, 2008–12 (Mem., 1998–2004); Cttee on Ethical Issues in Medicine, RCP, 2014–19. Chm. Grants Cttee, 1997–2001, Mem. Mgt Cttee, 1997–2001, King's Fund. FRSA 1993. *Publications*: Equality and Social Policy, 1978; Political Theory and Social Policy, 1983; The New Politics of Pollution, 1992; Democracy, 1999, 2nd edn 2007; Democratic Citizenship and the European Union, 2005; Democratic Justice and the Social Contract, 2013; *jointly*: Lone Mothers, Paid Work and Social Security, 1984; Controlling Pollution in the Round, 1991; The Theory of Choice, 1992; Environmental Governance in Europe, 2000; *edited*: Cost and Choice in Health Care, 1988; (with L. Roberts) Innovation and Environmental Risk, 1991; (jtly) Environmental Standards in the European Community in an Interdisciplinary Framework, 1994; (with P. Lehning) Citizenship, Democracy and Justice in the New Europe, 1997; (with Michael Nentwich) Political Theory and the European Union, 1998; Risk, Democratic Citizenship and Public Policy, 2002; The Will of the People: a modern myth, 2018; articles in learned jls. *Recreations*: walking, music, the company of friends. *Address*: Department of Political Science, School of Public Policy, University College London, 29/30 Tavistock Square, WC1H 9QU.

**WEALE, Anthony Philip**; Secretary of Faculties, 1984–2005 and Academic Registrar, 1999–2005, University of Oxford; Fellow of Worcester College, Oxford, 1982–2005, now Emeritus; *b* 4 Dec. 1945; *s* of Geoffrey Arthur Weale and Jocelyn Mary Weale (*née* Weeks); *m* 1975, Katharine O'Connell; two *d*. *Educ*: Kimbolton Sch.; University Coll., Oxford (Scholar; BA 1st Cl. Jurisprudence (Martin Wronker Prize for Law), 1967; MA 1971). GKN Ltd, 1967–71; Admin. Service, Oxford Univ., 1971–2005 (Sec., Medical Sch., 1977–84). Treas., 1975–2018, Trustee, 2015–, Historic Towns Trust. Governor: Pusey House, Oxford, 1977–85; Kimbolton Sch., 2001–14; Bishop Wordsworth's Sch., 2008–16. Trustee: St Bartholomew's Sch. Foundn, Newbury, 2006–10; Sarum Coll., 2010–19 (Sec. to Trustees, 2007–10). *Recreations*: family, dabbling in military and political history, gardening, travel, talking to neighbours. *Address*: 40 Harnwood Road, Salisbury, Wilts SP2 8DB.

**WEALE, Rear Adm. John Stuart**, CB 2019; OBE 2009; Flag Officer Scotland and Northern Ireland and Assistant Chief Naval Staff Submarines, since 2015; *b* Glasgow, 14 July 1962; *s* of Victor and Maureen Weale; *m* 1986, Julie; one *s* three *d*. *Educ*: St Augustine's Coll.; Westminster Univ. (BSc Hons Life Scis); Cranfield Univ. (MDA). Joined RN 1985; qualified Submarine CO Course, 1995; i/c HMS Trafalgar, nuclear submarine, 1999; Lead Planning Officer, UK Maritime Battle Staff, 2006–07; COS Maritime Coalition Combined Task Force 158 Iraq, 2007–08; Dir Submarine Sea and Shore Trng, 2008–10; Team Leader, Submarine Trng and Educn Prog., 2010–12; Dep. Flag Officer Sea Trng, 2012–15. Mem., Assoc. of RN Officers. *Recreations*: family, fishing, small holding, reading, walking. *Address*: Catchfrench East Lodge, Saltash, Cornwall PL12 5BY. *E*: johnweale898@btinternet.com.

**WEALE, Martin Robert**, CBE 1999; Professor of Economics, King's College London, since 2016; *b* 4 Dec. 1955; *s* of late Prof. R. A. Weale and M. E. Weale. *Educ*: Clare Coll., Cambridge (BA 1977; ScD 2006). ODI Fellow, Nat. Statistical Office, Malawi, 1977–79; University of Cambridge: Research Officer, Dept of Applied Econs, 1979–87; Lectr, Faculty of Econs and Politics, 1987–95; Fellow, Clare Coll., 1981–95; Dir, NIESR, 1995–2010 (Sen. Res. Fellow, 2011–16); Mem., Monetary Policy Cttee, 2010–16. Prof. of Econs, QMUL, 2011–16. Houblon-Norman Fellow, Bank of England, 1986–87. Member: Stats Commn, 2000–08; Bd for Actuarial Standards, 2006–10; Econ. Experts Working Gp, ONS, 2016–. Hon. Treasurer, Alzheimer's Trust, 1992–2008. Trustee, Kennedy Meml Trust, 2010–. Hon. FIA 2001. Hon. DSc City, 2007. *Publications*: (with J. Grady) British Banking, 1986; (jtly) Macroeconomic Policy: inflation, wealth and the exchange rate, 1989; (with J. Sefton) Reconciliation of National Income and Expenditure, 1995; articles in learned jls. *Recreations*: bridge, music, travel. *Address*: 63 Noel Road, N1 8HE. *T*: (020) 7359 8210. *Club*: Athenæum.

**WEARE, Trevor John**, OBE 1990; PhD; Chairman, 1999–2007, Member of Board, 2007–09, HR Wallingford Group, Ltd; *b* 31 Dec. 1943; *s* of Trevor Leslie Weare and Edna Margaret (*née* Roberts); *m* 1964, Margaret Ann Wright; two *s*. *Educ*: Aston Technical Coll.; Imperial College of Science and Technology (BSc Physics, PhD). Post-doctoral Research Fellow: Dept of Mathematical Physics, McGill Univ., Montreal, 1968–70; Dept of Theoretical Physics, Univ. of Oxford, 1970–72; Sen. Scientific Officer, Hydraulics Res. Station, 1972; Principal Scientific Officer, 1975; Sen. Principal Scientific Officer, Head of Estuaries Div., 1978; Chief Scientific Officer, DoE, 1981; Chief Exec., Hydraulics Res. Ltd, then HR Wallingford Gp Ltd, 1984–99. *Publications*: numerous contribs to scientific jls on theoretical High Energy Nuclear Physics, and on computational modelling in Civil Engineering Hydraulics; archaeological paper in Oxoniensia. *Recreations*: music, walking, archaeology, golf, sailing. *Address*: 6 Smeathman Court, Hemel Hempstead, Herts HP1 1AH. *T*: (01442) 261827.

**WEARING, Gillian**, CBE 2019 (OBE 2011); RA 2007; artist; *b* 1963. *Educ*: Goldsmiths' Coll., Univ. of London (BA Hons Fine Art 1990). *Solo exhibitions*: Maureen Paley/Interim Art, London, 1994, 1996, 1999, 2003, 2014; Hayward Gall., 1995; Le Consortium, Dijon, 1996; Chisenhale Gall., London, Kunsthaus Zürich, 1997; Centre d'Art Contemporain, Geneva, 1998; De Vleeshal, Middleburg, The Netherlands, 1999; Serpentine Gall., Contemp. Art Center, Cincinnati, 2000; Regen Projects, LA, 2000, 2004, 2008, 2014; La Caixa, Madrid, Musée d'Art Moderne, Paris, 2001; Vancouver Art Gall., MCA Chicago,

2002; ICA Philadelphia, 2003; Franz Hals Mus., Haarlem, 2004; Bloomberg Space, London, 2005; Aust. Center for Contemp. Art, Melbourne, 2006; Galleria Civica di Arte Contemporanea, Trento, 2007; Musée Rodin, Paris, 2009; Tanya Bonakdar, NY, 2011; Whitechapel Gall. (retrospective), 2012; Museum Brandhorst, Munich, 2013; New Art Gall., Walsall, 2014; Instituto Valenciano de Arte Moderno, Valencia, 2015; NPG, London, Nat. Gall. of Denmark, Copenhagen, 2017; Cincinnati Art Mus., 2018; *group exhibitions* include: BT Young Contemporaries, UK tour, 1993; Brilliant! New Art from London, Walker Art Center, Minneapolis, 1995; Pandaemonium, London Fest. of Moving Images, ICA, 1996; Sensation, RA, 1997; Real/Life: New British Art, Japanese Mus. tour, 1998; Intelligence: New British Art, Tate Britain, London, 2000; Century City, Tate Modern, London, 2001; Remix: Contemporary Art and Pop, Tate Liverpool, 2002; Strange Days, Mus. of Contemporary Art, Chicago, 2003; Aftershock, Contemporary British Art 1990–2006, Guangdong Mus. of Art, Guangzhou, Capital Mus., Beijing, 2006; Global Feminisms, Brooklyn Mus., NY, 2007; The Reach of Realism, Mus. of Contemporary Art, N Miami; Role Models—Role Playing, Mus. der Moderne Salzburg, 2011; Salon der Angst, Kunsthalle Wien, Vienna, 2013; Perfect Likeness: Photography and Composition, Hammer Mus., LA, 2015; Thicker than Water, Kunstpalais, Erlangen, 2016; From Life, RA, 2017; Selves and others, SFMOMA, San Francisco, 2018; *public sculpture commissions*: A Real Birmingham Family, Birmingham, 2014; A Real Danish Family, Copenhagen, 2016; statue of Millicent Fawcett, Parliament Sq., London, 2018. Trustee, Tate Gall., 1999–2005. Turner Prize, 1997. *Address*: c/o Maureen Paley, 21 Herald Street, E2 6JT. *T*: (020) 7729 4112.

**WEATHERBY, Jonathan Roger;** Chairman, Weatherbys Bank Ltd, 1993–2017 (non-executive Director, since 2017), and Weatherbys Ltd (formerly Weatherbys Group Ltd), since 1993; *b* 30 Nov. 1959; *s* of late Christopher Nicholas Weatherby and Alison Beatrix (*née* Pease); *m* 1993, Sophie Frances Cliffe-Jones; two *s* two *d*. *Educ*: Eton Coll. Joined Weatherbys, 1979; Dir, 1988–. Mem., Jockey Club, 1997–. Trustee, Ascot Authority, 1998–; HM's Rep. at Ascot, 2011–. *Recreations*: horse-racing, soccer, hunting. *Address*: Weatherbys, Sanders Road, Wellingborough, Northants NN8 4BX. *T*: (01933) 304728. *Clubs*: White's, Turf.
See also Baron Daresbury, R. N. Weatherby.

**WEATHERBY, Roger Nicholas;** Chief Executive, Weatherbys Bank Ltd, since 2000; *b* Oxford, 6 Aug. 1962; *s* of late Christopher Nicholas Weatherby and Alison Beatrix Weatherby (*née* Pease); *m* 1998, Semantha Horne; two *s* two *d*. *Educ*: Eton Coll.; RMA Sandhurst; London Business Sch. (MSc Finance). Commnd 15/19 King's Royal Hussars, 1982. Internat. Sales, Cazenove and Co., 1985–96; Finance Dir, Weatherbys Gp Ltd, 1997–. Chairman: Racing Welfare, 2008–12 (Trustee, 2001–12); Racing Foundn, 2012–15. Mem., 2007–, Steward, 2013–14, Sen. Steward, 2014–19, Jockey Club. *Recreations*: country sports, family, exploration, horseracing, gardening. *Address*: Weatherbys Bank Ltd, Sanders Road, Wellingborough, Northants NN8 4BX. *T*: (01933) 304777. *E*: rweatherby@weatherbys.co.uk. *Clubs*: White's, Turf, Hertford Street.
See also Baron Daresbury, J. R. Weatherby.

**WEATHERHEAD, Alexander Stewart, (Sandy),** OBE 1985; TD 1964 (clasp 1973); Partner, 1960–97 and Senior Partner, 1992–97, Tindal Oatts & Rodger, then Tindal Oatts Buchanan and McIlwraith, subsequently Tindal Oatts, and Brechin Tindal Oatts, Solicitors, Glasgow (Consultant, 1997–98); *b* Edinburgh, 3 Aug. 1931; *er s* of Kenneth Kilpatrick Weatherhead and Katharine Weatherhead (*née* Stewart); *m* 1972, Harriett Foye, *d* of Rev. Dr Arthur Organ, Toronto, Canada; two *d*. *Educ*: George Watson's, Edinburgh; Larchfield Sch., Helensburgh; Glasgow Acad.; Glasgow Univ. MA 1955, LLB 1958. Served in RA, 1950–52, 2nd Lieut, 1950. Solicitor, 1958; Temp. Sheriff, 1985–92. Hon. Vice-Pres., Law Society of Scotland, 1983–84 (Mem. Council, 1971–84); Member: Royal Faculty of Procurators in Glasgow, 1960– (Mem. Council, 1992–2001; Dean, 1992–95; Hon. Mem., 1997); Council, Soc. for Computers and Law, 1973–86 (Vice-Chm., 1973–82; Chm., 1982–84; Hon. Mem., 1986); Mem., Royal Commn on Legal Services in Scotland, 1976–80. Trustee, Nat. Technol. and Law Trust (formerly Nat. Law Library Trust), 1979–86; Examr in Conveyancing, Univ. of Aberdeen, 1984–86. Dir, Glasgow Chamber of Commerce, 1992–95. Member: Local Res. Ethics Cttee, Royal Infirmary, Glasgow, 1999–2006; Multi Centre Res. Ethics Cttee for Scotland (B), 2005–06. Mem. Business Cttee, Gen. Council, Univ. of Glasgow, 2001–05 and 2007–11. Joined TA, 1952; Lt-Col Comdg 277 (A&SH) Field Regt, RA (TA), 1965–67; The Lowland Regt (RA(T)), 1967 and Glasgow & Strathclyde Univs OTC, 1971–73; Col 1974; TAVR Col Lowlands (West), 1974–76; ADC (TAVR) to the Queen, 1977–81; Member: TAVR Assoc. Lowlands, 1967–2000 (Vice-Chm., 1987–90; Chm., 1990–93); RFCA Lowlands, 2000–; RA Council for Scotland, 1972– (Vice Chm., 1997–2001; Patron, 2001–). Hon. Col, Glasgow and Strathclyde Univs OTC, 1982–98. Commodore, Royal Western Yacht Club, 1995–98 (Vice Cdre, 1991–95; Hon. Sec., 1981–84). *Recreations*: reading, music, tennis, sailing. *Address*: 52 Partickhill Road, Glasgow G11 5AB. *T*: (0141) 334 6277. *E*: sandywd@aol.com. *Clubs*: Royal Highland Yacht (Oban); Royal Western Yacht, Clyde Cruising (Glasgow).

**WEATHERILL, Barry Nicholas Aubrey,** CBE 2005; Consultant, Wedlake Bell, solicitors, since 2003; Chairman, IC Philanthropy Foundation, since 2016; *b* 17 July 1938; *s* of Percival Aubrey and Flora Evelyn Weatherill; *m* 1965, Wouterina Johanna Cornelia van den Bovenkamp; one *s* two *d*. *Educ*: Caldicott Sch.; Felsted Sch.; Clare Coll., Cambridge (BA 1962). Admitted solicitor, 1966; Wedlake Bell: Partner, 1966–2003; Finance Partner, 1975–81; Sen. Partner, 1984–94. Trustee, Guide Dogs for the Blind Assoc., 1975–2007 (Chm., 2000–07). All England Lawn Tennis Club: Mem., Cttee of Mgt, 1981–2002; Vice Pres., 2002–; Trustee, 2003–; Chm., Council of Internat. Lawn Tennis Clubs, 1991–2012 (Vice-Pres., 2014–); Dep. Pres., Internat. Lawn Tennis Club of GB, 2015– (Pres., 2008–16). *Recreations*: tennis, golf, gardening, music, investment. *Clubs*: Jesters; Hawks (Cambridge); All England Lawn Tennis and Croquet; International Lawn Tennis Club of GB, (and those of France, USA and the Netherlands); Berkshire Golf.

**WEATHERILL, Hon. Bernard Richard;** QC 1996; a Recorder, since 2000; *b* 20 May 1951; *er s* of Baron Weatherill, PC and of Lyn Weatherill; *m* 1st, 1977, Sally Maxwell Fisher (marr. diss. 2001); one *s* one *d*; 2nd, 2005, Diana Clare Forsyth. *Educ*: Malvern Coll.; Principia Coll., Illinois, USA; Kent Univ. (BA Hons). Called to the Bar, Middle Temple, 1974, Bencher, 2002; an Asst Recorder, 1998–2000. UK Legal Counsel and non-exec. Dir, Bluechain Payments Ltd, 2017–. Non-exec. Dir, A. Cohen & Co. plc, 1989–2000. Member: General Council of the Bar, 1990–95 (Mem., Professional Conduct Cttee, 1998–99); Council, Justice, 2010–16; Chm., Bar Services Co. Ltd, 2000–06; non-exec. Dir, Croydon Business Venture Ltd, 2009–. Mem. Council, Tennis and Rackets Assoc., 2010–17. FCIArb 1999. *Recreations*: lawn tennis, Real tennis, golf, wine, avoiding gardening, cultivating friendships. *Address*: Pallant Chambers, 12 North Pallant, Chichester, W Sussex PO19 1TQ. *Clubs*: Hurlingham (Trustee, 2000–19); All England Lawn Tennis, Bar Lawn Tennis Society, Jesters; Royal Wimbledon Golf, Lucifer Golfing Society; Radley College Real Tennis.

**WEATHERILL, Rt Rev. Garry John;** *see* Ballarat, Bishop of.

**WEATHERILL, Prof. Nigel Peter;** DL; PhD, DSc; CEng, FREng; FRAeS; FIMA; CSci; CMath; Vice-Chancellor, Liverpool John Moores University, 2011–18; *b* 1 Nov. 1954; *s* of Ernest and Barbara Weatherill; *m* 1976, Dr Barbara Ann Hopkins; one *s* one *d*. *Educ*: Whitcliffe Mount Grammar Sch., Cleckheaton, Yorks; Southampton Univ. (BSc 1st Cl. Hons Maths; PhD Maths 1979; DSc 1994). CEng 1996, FREng 2003; FIMA 1987; CMath 1991; FRAeS 1996; CSci 2005. Asst Team Leader, Regl Res. Team, Anglian Water Authy, Cambridge, 1979–81; Sen. Project Supervisor, Aircraft Res. Assoc., Bedford, 1981–87; Swansea University (formerly University of Wales, Swansea): Department of Civil Engineering: Lectr, 1987–90; Sen. Lectr, 1990–92; Reader, 1992–95; Prof. of Civil Engineering, 1995–2008; Hd of Dept, 1996–2001; Dir, Centre of Excellence in Computation and Simulation, 2000–08; Hd, Sch. of Engineering, 2001–07; Pro-Vice-Chancellor (Research), 2002–08; Hon. Fellow, 2009; Pro-Vice-Chancellor and Hd, Coll. of Engineering and Physical Scis, Univ. of Birmingham, 2008–11. Vis. Res. Fellow, Dept of Mechanical and Aerospace Engrg, Princeton Univ., 1985; Res. Consultant, Nat. Grid Generation Project, USA, NSF Engrg Res. Center, Mississippi State Univ., 1991–92, Adjunct Prof., 1992–98; Vis. Scientist-in-Residence, Inst. of High Performance Computing, A★Singapore, 2006–11. Chm., Royal Liverpool Philharmonic Soc., 2015–. Hon. Bencher, Middle Temple, 2018. Ed., Internat. Jl Numerical Methods in Fluids, 1999–2011. FRSA 2012. DL Merseyside 2016. *Publications*: (jtly) Multiblock Grid Generation, 1993; (jtly) Handbook of Grid Generation, 1999; (jtly) Probabilistic Methods in Fluids, 2003. *Recreations*: fly fishing, gardening, travelling.

**WEATHERILL, Prof. Stephen Robson;** Jacques Delors Professor of European Law, University of Oxford, since 1998; Fellow, Somerville College, Oxford, since 1998; *b* 21 March 1961. *Educ*: Queens' Coll., Cambridge (MA); Univ. of Edinburgh (MSc). Brunel Univ., 1985; Reading Univ., 1986–87; Manchester Univ., 1987–90; Nottingham Univ., 1990–97, Jean Monnet Prof. of European Law, 1995–97. *Publications*: Cases and Materials on EC Law, 1992, 10th edn as Cases and Materials on EU Law, 2012; (with P. Beaumont) EC Law, 1993, 3rd edn 1999; Law and Integration in the European Union, 1995; (with G. Howells) Consumer Protection Law, 1995, 2nd edn 2004; EC Consumer Law and Policy, 1997, 2nd edn 2005; (with H. Micklitz) European Economic Law, 1997. *Address*: Somerville College, Oxford OX2 6HD. *T*: (01865) 270600.

**WEATHERLEY, Christopher Roy,** MD; FRCS, FRCSE, FRCSE (Orth); Consultant Spinal Surgeon, Royal Devon & Exeter Hospital, since 1987; *b* 26 Sept. 1943; *s* of Dudley Graham Weatherley and Hilda Ada Weatherley (*née* Wilson). *Educ*: Queen Elizabeth's Sch., Crediton; Liverpool Univ. Med. Sch. (MB ChB; MD 1968). FRCSE 1973; FRCS 1974; FRCSE (Orth) 1984. Sen. Res. Associate, MRC Decompression Sickness Unit, Newcastle upon Tyne, 1973–76; Sen. Registrar in Orthopaedics, Robert Jones and Agnes Hunt Orthopaedic Hosp., 1979–87. Eur. Res. Fellow, Inst. Calôt, Berck-Plage, France, 1981–82; Consultant Spinal Surgeon, St Vincent's Hosp., Melbourne, 1985–86. Hon. Civilian Consultant, RN, 1991. Fellow, Brit. Orthopaedic Assoc., 1983; FRSocMed 1991. Member: Exec. Cttee, Brit. Scoliosis Soc., 1993– (Sec. and Treas., 1996–99; Pres., 2006–07); Council, Brit. Scoliosis Res. Foundn, 1998–; Eur. Cervical Spine Soc., 1984. Gold Medal Lectr, Old Oswestrians Annual Meeting, 2000. *Publications*: (reviewer) Gray's Anatomy, 40th edn 2008; contrib. chapters in books, editorials and papers on: decompression sickness and dysbaric osteonecrosis; spinal tumours; scoliosis; back pain; surgical approaches to the spine; spinal fusion; ankylosing spondylitis; stress fractures in fast bowlers. *Recreations*: the fine line, the creation of myths. *Address*: 1 The Quadrant, Wonford Road, Exeter, Devon EX2 4LE. *T*: (01392) 272951. *Club*: Royal Society of Medicine.

**WEATHERLEY, Mike;** Vice Chairman, Motion Picture Licensing Corporation, since 2015; *b* Clevedon, Som, 2 July 1957; *s* of Derrick and Kirsten Weatherley; two *s* one *d*. *Educ*: South Bank Univ. (BA Hons Business Studies). FCMA 1988. Finance Dir and Jt Owner, Cash Bases GB Ltd, 1994–2000; Financial Controller, Pete Waterman Ltd, 2000–05; Vice-Pres., Motion Picture Licensing Co. Ltd, 2007–10 (non-exec. Dir, 2010–13). Mem. (C) Crawley BC, 2006–07. Contested (C) Barking, 2001; Brighton Pavilion, 2005. MP (C) Hove, 2010–15. Intellectual Property Advr to the Prime Minister, 2013–14. *Recreations*: rock and heavy metal music, ski-ing (former instructor), football, motorbikes, intellectual property rights and politics.

**WEATHERSTON, (William) Alastair (Paterson),** CB 1993; Under Secretary, Scottish Office Education Department, 1989–95; *b* 20 Nov. 1935; *s* of William Robert Weatherston and Isabella (*née* Paterson); *m* 1961, Margaret Jardine (*d* 2004); two *s* one *d*. *Educ*: Peebles High Sch.; Edinburgh Univ. (MA Hons History). Asst Principal, Dept of Health for Scotland and Scottish Educn Dept, 1959–63; Private Sec. to Permanent Under Sec. of State, Scottish Office, 1963–64; Principal, Scottish Educn Dept, 1964–72, Cabinet Office, 1972–74; Assistant Secretary: SHHD, 1974–77; Scottish Educn Dept, 1977–79; Central Services, Scottish Office, 1979–82; Dir, Scottish Courts Admin, 1982–86; Fisheries Sec., Dept of Agric. and Fisheries for Scotland, 1986–89. Sec., Gen. Council, Univ. of Edinburgh, 1997–2001. Mem., Murrayfield Community Council, 2005–11. *Recreations*: reading, music. *Address*: 1 Coltbridge Terrace, Edinburgh EH12 6AB. *T*: (0131) 337 3339.

**WEATHERUP, Rt Hon. Sir Ronald Eccles,** Kt 2001; PC 2016; a Lord Justice of Appeal, Supreme Court of Judicature, Northern Ireland, 2015–17. *Educ*: Methodist Coll.; Queen's Univ., Belfast. Called to the Bar, NI, 1971; QC (NI) 1993; Judge of the High Court of Justice, NI, 2001–15. Jun. Crown Counsel, 1989–93, Sen. Crown Counsel, 1997–2001, for NI. Mem., NI Judicial Appts Commn, 2005. *Address*: c/o Royal Courts of Justice, Chichester Street, Belfast BT1 3JF.

**WEAVER, (Christopher) Giles (Herron),** FCA; Chairman: Charter European Trust, 2003–12; Helical Bar plc, 2005–12 (non-executive Director, 1993–2012); Tamar (formerly Kenmore) European Property Fund, 2006–14; *b* 4 April 1946; *s* of Lt Col John Weaver and Ursula (*née* Horlick); *m* 1975, Rosamund Betty Mayhew; two *s* two *d*. *Educ*: Eton Coll.; London Business Sch. (MSc 1973). FCA 1978. Dir, UK and Pensions Investment, Ivory & Sime, 1976–86; Man. Dir, Pension Mgt, Prudential Corp., 1986–90; Murray Johnstone Ltd, 1990: Chief Investment Officer, 1990–93; Man. Dir, 1993–99; Chm., 1999–2000. Chm., Murray Emerging Growth & Income Trust plc, 2001–05; non-executive Director: James Finlay, 1996–; Aberdeen Asset Management plc, 2000–13; IRP Property Investments Ltd (formerly ISIS Property Trust II Ltd), 2004–13; EP Global Opportunities Trust plc, 2011–. Trustee and Dep. Chm., Nat. Galls of Scotland, 1998–2005; Chm., HHA in Scotland, 1999–2004. Trustee: Lutyens Trust, 1986–; Flemings Wyfold Art Foundn, 2011–. *Recreations*: ski-ing, golf, tennis, bridge. *Address*: Hill Fort House, Drem, E Lothian EH39 5AZ. *T*: (01620) 880573. *Clubs*: Boodle's, Hurlingham, Queen's; New (Edinburgh); Hon. Company of Edinburgh Golfers (Muirfield).

**WEAVER, Susan Alexandra, (Sigourney);** actress; *b* New York, 8 Oct. 1949; *d* of late Sylvester Laflin, (Pat), Weaver and Elizabeth Weaver (*née* Inglis); *m* 1984, James Simpson; one *d*. *Educ*: Stanford Univ. (BA); Sch. of Drama, Yale Univ. (MFA). Founder, Goat Cay Productions. *Theatre includes*: Gemini, 1976, Crazy Mary, 2007, Playwrights Horizons, NY; Beyond Therapy, Marymount Manhattan Th., NY, 1981; Hurlyburly, Ethel Barrymore Th., NY, 1984; The Merchant of Venice, Classic Stage Co., NY, 1986; The Guys, 2002, Mrs Farnsworth, 2004, Flea Th., NY; The Mercy Seat, Acorn Th., NY, 2002. *Films include*: Annie Hall, 1977; Madman, 1978; Alien, 1979; Eyewitness, 1981; The Year of Living

Dangerously, 1982; Deal of the Century, 1983; Ghostbusters, 1984; Walls of Glass, Une Femme ou Deux, 1985; Half Moon Street, Aliens, 1986; Gorillas in the Mist (Best Actress, Golden Globe Awards, 1989), Working Girl (Best Supporting Actress, Golden Globe Awards, 1989), 1988; Ghostbusters II, 1989; Alien[3] (also co-prod.), 1492: Conquest of Paradise, 1992; Dave, 1993; Death and the Maiden, 1995; Jeffrey, Copycat, 1996; Snow White: a Tale of Terror, Alien: Resurrection (also co-prod.), 1997; Ice Storm, 1998; A Map of the World, Galaxy Quest, 1999; Company Man, 2000; Heartbreakers, 2001; The Guys, 2002; Tadpole, Holes, 2003; The Village, 2004; Imaginary Heroes, 2005; Snow Cake, The TV Set, Infamous, 2006; Vantage Point, The Girl in the Park, 2008; Avatar, 2009; You Again, 2010; Paul, Cedar Rapids, 2011; Red Lights, The Cabin in the Woods, The Cold Light of Day, 2012; Exodus: Gods and Kings, 2014; Chappie, 2015; A Monster Calls, 2017. *Address:* c/o United Talent Agency, 9336 Civic Center Drive, Beverly Hills, CA 90210–3604, USA; Goat Cay Productions, PO Box 38, New York, NY 10150, USA.

**WEBB, Sir Adrian (Leonard),** Kt 2000; DLitt; FLSW; Chair: National Lottery Community Fund (formerly Big Lottery Fund) Wales, since 2011 (non-executive Director, National Lottery Community Fund UK (formerly Big Lottery Fund UK), since 2011); Review of Higher Education in North East Wales, 2012–15; Vice-Chancellor, University of Glamorgan, 1993–2004; *b* 19 July 1943; *s* of Leonard and Rosina Webb; *m* 1st, 1966, Caroline Williams (marr. diss. 1995); two *s*; 2nd, 1996, Monjulee Dass. *Educ:* Birmingham Univ. (1st cl. Hons BSocSci 1965); LSE (MSc (Econ) 1966); DLitt Loughborough 1993. Lectr, LSE, 1966–74; Res. Dir, Personal Social Services Council, 1974–76; Loughborough University: Prof. of Social Policy, 1976–93; Dir, Centre for Res. in Social Policy, 1983–93; Dean, then Pro Vice-Chancellor, subseq. Sen. Pro Vice-Chancellor, 1986–93. Member: Nat. Cttee of Inquiry into Higher Educn (Dearing Cttee), 1996–97; BBC Broadcasting Council for Wales, 1998–2001; HM Treasury Public Sector Productivity Panel, 2000–06; Nat. Council, Educn and Learning in Wales, 2001–06; Beecham Review of Public Services in Wales, 2005–06; Administrative Justice and Tribunals Council, 2008–12 (Chair, Wales Cttee, 2013–15); Wales Comr, UK Commn for Employment and Skills, 2008–12; Chairman: Welsh Review Group (Nursing, Midwifery and Health Workers), 1999–2002; Higher Educn Wales, 2000–02; Rev. of Further and Post-16 Educn in Wales, 2006–07; Welsh Employment and Skills Bd, 2008–12. Non-executive Director: E Glamorgan NHS Trust, 1997–99; Mgt Bd, Nat. Assembly for Wales, 2003–08; Welsh Govt Bd, 2013–. Chm., Pontypridd & Rhondda NHS Trust, 2005–08. Chm., Wales Cttee, and Mem. Council, RSPB, 2017–. Founder Mem., Bevan Foundn, 2002–07. Gov., Thames Valley Univ., 2006–08. FCGI; FRSA; FLSW 2011. *Publications:* Change, Choice and Conflict in Social Policy, 1975; Planning Need and Scarcity: essays on the personal social services, 1986; The Economic Approach to Social Policy, 1986; Social Work, Social Care and Social Planning, 1987; Joint Approaches to Social Policy: rationality and practice, 1988; contribs on social policy and public admin to scholarly and professional periodicals. *Recreations:* walking, painting (water colour), ornithology.
See also G. T. Webb.

**WEBB, Catherine Sarah;** Director, Operations, HM Treasury, since 2019; *b* Wirral, 22 June 1979; *d* of David John Webb and Jane Catherine Webb. *Educ:* Hartford High Sch.; Sir John Deane's Sixth Form Coll.; Emmanuel Coll., Cambridge (BA Hons Econs 2000). HM Treasury, 2000–11, Hd, Work Incentives and Poverty Analysis team, 2008–11; Counsellor, Econ. and Trade Policy, British Embassy, Beijing, 2011–15; Dir, EU Internal Issues, Cabinet Office, 2015–16; Dir of Market Access and Budget, DExEU, 2016–17; Dir Policy, Europe Unit, Cabinet Office, 2017–18. *Recreations:* open water swimming, cinema, walking, cooking, family. *Address:* HM Treasury, 1 Horseguards Road, SW1A 2HQ.

**WEBB, Prof. Colin,** PhD; CEng, FIChemE; Professor of Chemical Engineering, University of Manchester, since 1994; *b* Hereford, 11 Oct. 1954; *s* of late Sidney Webb and Stella Webb; *m* 1984, Ann Elizabeth Kelly; one *s* one *d*. *Educ:* Leominster Grammar Sch.; Aston Univ. (BSc Chem. Engrg 1976; PhD 1980). CEng 1992; MIChemE 1992, FIChemE 1995; CSci 2003. University of Manchester Institute of Science and Technology, later University of Manchester: Res. Associate, 1979–83; Lectr, 1983–91, Sen. Lectr, 1991–94, in Chem. Engrg; Dir, Satake Centre for Grain Process Engrg, 1994–2004; Hd, Dept of Chem. Engrg, 2000–04; Associate Dean (Estates), 2004–05; Hd, Sch. of Chemical Engrg and Analytical Sci., 2005–07. Vis. Academic, Monash Univ., 1988. Process Technol. Examnr, Inst. of Brewing, 1998–2002; Vice-Pres. (Qualifications), 2012–15, Trustee and Mem. Council, 2012–18, IChemE. Fellow, Internat. Acad. of Food Sci. and Technol., 1999. Ed.-in-Chief, Biochemical Engineering Jl, 1998–. *Publications:* Process Engineering Aspects of Immobilised Cell Systems, 1986; Plant and Animal Cells: process possibilities, 1987; Studies in Viable Cell Immobilisation, 1996; Cereals: novel uses and processes, 1997; Comprehensive Biotechnology, vol. 2, Engineering Fundamentals, 2nd edn 2011; Food Industry Wastes: assessment and recuperation of commodities, 2013; over 270 articles in learned jls on biochem. engrg. *Recreations:* cycling, walking, watching football, checking e-mails, meeting friends I haven't seen for 25 years. *Address:* School of Chemical Engineering and Analytical Science, University of Manchester, C77, The Mill, Oxford Road, Manchester M13 9PL. *T:* (0161) 306 4379. *E:* colin.webb@manchester.ac.uk.

**WEBB, Prof. Colin Edward,** MBE 2000; DPhil; FRS 1991; FInstP; Professor, Department of Physics, University of Oxford, 1992–2002, now Emeritus; Senior Research Fellow, Jesus College, Oxford, 1988–2005, now Emeritus; Founder, since 1977, and non-executive Director, since 2015, Oxford Lasers Ltd (Chairman, 1977–2015); *b* 9 Dec. 1937; *s* of Alfred Edward Webb and Doris (née Collins); *m* 1st, 1964, Pamela Mabel Cooper White (*d* 1992); two *d*; 2nd, 1995, Margaret Helen (née Dewar); two step *d*. *Educ:* Univ. of Nottingham (BSc 1960); Oriel Coll., Oxford (DPhil 1964). FInstP 1985. Mem., Technical Staff, Bell Labs, Murray Hill, NJ, 1964–68; University of Oxford: AEI Res. Fellow in Physics, Clarendon Lab., 1968–71; Univ. Lectr, 1971–90; Tutorial Fellow, Jesus Coll., 1973–88; Reader, 1990–92, Prof., 1992, Dept of Physics; Hd of Atomic and Laser Physics, 1995–99. Visiting Professor: Dept of Pure and Applied Physics, Univ. of Salford, 1987–2002; Dept of Mechanical Engrg, Cranfield Univ., 1999–2002. Fellow, Optical Soc. of America, 1988. Gov., Launceston Coll., 2012–16; Trustee, Launceston Coll. and Bideford Coll. Multi-Academy Trust, 2016–. Hon. DSc Salford, 1996. Duddell Medal and Prize, 1985, Glazebrook Medal and Prize, 2001, Inst. of Physics; Clifford Paterson Lect. and Medal, Royal Soc., 1999. *Publications:* (Ed-in-Chief) Handbook of Laser Technology and Applications, 2003; (with S. M. Hooker) Laser Physics, 2010; contribs on lasers, laser mechanisms and applications to learned jls. *Recreations:* travel, photography, music, reading. *Address:* Clarendon Laboratory, Parks Road, Oxford OX1 3PU. *T:* (01865) 272254.

**WEBB, Prof. David Charles,** PhD; Professor of Finance, London School of Economics and Political Science, since 1991; *b* 13 July 1953; *s* of Charles Ronald Webb and Margaret Jane Webb (née Oldham). *Educ:* Hurworth Secondary Sch., Darlington; Grangefield Grammar Sch., Stockton-on-Tees; Univ. of Manchester (BA Econs 1974; MA Econs 1975); London School of Economics and Pol Sci. (PhD 1979). Lectr, Univ. of Bristol, 1978–84; London School of Economics and Political Science: Lectr, 1984–90; Reader in Econs, 1991; Director: Financial Mkts Gp Res. Centre, 1991–2008; UBS Pensions Res. Prog., 2001–06; Hd, Dept of Finance, 2009–14; Pro Dir Planning and Resources and Chief Financial Officer, 2014–. Vis. Associate Prof., Queen's Univ., Canada, 1982–84; Vis. Prof. of Economics, Univ. of Iowa, 1991. Consultant, Asian Develt Bank, 1998–; Mem., Adv. Bd, Centro de Estudios Monetarios y Financieros, Madrid, 1998–. Mem. Council, Royal Economic Soc., 2008–. Editor, Economica, 1989–97. *Publications:* articles in Econs and Finance, Qly Jl of Econs, Rand Jl of Econs, Internat. Econ. Review, Econ. Jl and Jl of Public Econs. *Recreation:* ski-ing. *Address:* Department of Finance, London School of Economics and Political Science, Houghton Street, WC2A 2AE. *T:* (020) 7955 6301.

**WEBB, Prof. David John,** MD, DSc; FRCPE, FRCP, FFPM, FMedSci, FBPhS; FRSE; FRSB; Christison Professor of Therapeutics and Clinical Pharmacology, since 1995, Director, Education Programme, Wellcome Trust Clinical Research Facility, since 1998, and Hypertension and Renal Theme Lead, University/British Heart Foundation Centre for Cardiovascular Science, since 2016, University of Edinburgh; Consultant Physician, Lothian University Hospitals NHS Trust, since 1990; *b* 1 Sept. 1953; *s* of Alfred William Owen Webb and Edna May Webb (née Parish); *m* 1st, 1984, Margaret Jane Cullen (marr. diss. 2007); three *s*; 2nd, 2009, Dr Louise Eleanor Bath. *Educ:* Dulwich Coll. (Kent Schol.); Royal London Hosp.; MB BS 1977, MD 1990, London; DSc Edinburgh 2000. MRCP 1980, FRCP 1994; FRCPE 1992; FFPM (FFPHM 1993); Hon. FFPM 2016); FBPhS (FBPharmacolS 2004), Hon. FBPhS 2018. House Officer posts, Royal London Hosp. scheme, 1977–78; Senior House Officer: Chelmsford Hosps, 1978–79; Stoke Mandeville Hosp., 1979–80; Registrar: Royal London Hosp., 1980–82; in Medicine, and MRC Clin. Scientist, MRC BP Unit, Western Infirmary, Glasgow, 1982–85; Lectr in Clin. Pharmacol., St George's Med. Sch., London, 1985–89; Sen. Registrar in Medicine, St George's Hosp., London, 1985–89; University of Edinburgh: Sen. Lectr in Medicine, 1990–95; Dir, Clin. Res. Centre, 1990–; Head: Dept of Medicine, 1997–98; Dept of Med. Scis, 1998–2001; Wellcome Trust Res. Leave Fellow, and Leader, Wellcome Trust Cardiovascular Res. Initiative, 1998–2001; Convenor, Cardiovascular Interdisciplinary Gp, 1999–2000; Hd, Centre for Cardiovascular Sci., 2000–04. Chm., Scottish Medicines Consortium, 2005–08 (Chm., New Drugs Cttee, 2001–05); Chair, Scientific Adv. Cttee, Nat. Inst. for Biol Standards and Control, 2014–; Jt Chair, Prescribing Safety Assessment Exec. Cttee, 2014–; Dir, Wellcome Trust Scottish Translational Medicine and Therapeutics Initiative, 2008–16; non-exec. Dir, Medicines and Healthcare products Regulatory Agency, 2013– (Dep. Chair, 2018–); Dep. Dir, Scottish Clinical Pharmacol. and Pathol. Prog., 2010–16. Vice-Pres., Clin. Div., Internat. Union for Pharmacol., 2004–. Res. Dir, High Blood Pressure Foundn, 1993– (Trustee, 1991–); Chair, Trustees, 2019–). President: Eur. Assoc. for Clin. Pharmacol. and Therapeutics, 2009; Scottish Soc. of Physicians, 2010; Vice-Pres., RCPE, 2007–09; Mem., Exec. Cttee, British Hypertension Soc., 1991–94; British Pharmacological Society: Mem., Exec. Cttee, 1994–98; Clin. Vice-Pres., 1995–98; Dir and Trustee, 1996–99 and 2004–; Chm., Cttee of Profs and Hds of Clin. Pharmacol. & Therapeutics, 2004–; Vice Pres., Meetings, 2012–13; Pres., 2016–17; Mem., Sectional Cttee 1, Acad. Med. Scis, 2000–02. Dir, Court, Edinburgh Acad., 2008–14. MAE 2017. Internat. Fellow, Amer. Heart Assoc., 1996; FMedSci 1999; FESC 2001; FRSE 2004; FBHS 2014; FRSB 2017. *Publications:* (with G. A. Gray) The Molecular Biology and Pharmacology of the Endothelins, 1995; (ed with P. J. T. Vallance) The Endothelium in Hypertension, 1996; (ed with P. J. T. Vallance) Vascular Endothelium in Human Physiology and Pathophysiology, 1999; (jtly) The Year in Therapeutics, Vol. 1, 2005. *Recreations:* summer and winter mountaineering, scuba diving, reading late at night. *Address:* Queen's Medical Research Institute, Centre for Cardiovascular Science, University of Edinburgh, E3.22, 47 Little France Crescent, Edinburgh EH16 4TJ. *T:* (0131) 242 9215. *E:* d.j.webb@ed.ac.uk; 75 Great King Street, Edinburgh EH3 6RN. *T:* (0131) 556 7145, 07770 966786. *Clubs:* Old Alleynian, Edinburgh Academical; Scottish Mountaineering.

**WEBB, Geraint Timothy;** QC 2013; *b* London, 17 July 1971; *s* of Sir Adrian Leonard Webb, *qv*; *m* 1999, Ilfa Charlotte, *d* of Sir David Paul Brandes Goldberg, *qv*; two *s* two *d*. *Educ:* Loughborough Grammar Sch.; Christ Church, Oxford (BA Mod. Hist. 1st Cl. 1992). Called to the Bar, Inner Temple, 1995; in practice as a barrister, specialising in commercial law, product liability, mass tort/group action claims and insurance law, Henderson Chambers, 2 Harcourt Bldgs, 1995–. *Recreations:* family, walking, photography, goldsmithing. *Address:* Henderson Chambers, 2 Harcourt Buildings, Temple, EC4Y 9DB. *T:* (020) 7583 9020. *E:* gwebb@hendersonchambers.co.uk.

**WEBB, Jonathan Mark,** MA; Headmaster, Ripon Grammar School, since 2017; *b* Thornhill, Dewsbury, W Yorks, 8 Dec. 1970; *s* of Rev. Nicholas Webb and Rev. Dr Norma Webb; *m* 2000, Helen Mary Park; two *s*. *Educ:* Batley Grammar Sch.; Christ's Coll., Cambridge (BA 1992; MA 1993); Leeds Univ. (PGCE). Teacher of History: Giggleswick Sch., 1994–99; Manchester GS, 1999–2003; Hd of History and Dir of Teaching and Learning, Pocklington Sch., 2003–12; Dep. Head, Durham Sch., 2012–17. *Recreations:* cricket, running, gardening, walking, music, travel, and all things historical and cultural. *Address:* Ripon Grammar School, Clotherholme Road, Ripon HG4 2DG. *T:* (01765) 602647. *E:* head@ripongrammar.com. *Club:* Lansdowne.

**WEBB, Justin Oliver;** Presenter, Today Programme, BBC Radio 4, since 2009; *b* 3 Jan. 1961; *s* of late Peter Woods and Gloria Webb (née Crocombe); *m* 1996, Sarah Gordon; one *s* two *d* (of whom one *s* one *d* are twins). *Educ:* London Sch. of Econs (BSc Econ 1983). BBC: Reporter: Radio Ulster, 1985–87; Today Prog., 1987–89; Foreign Affairs Corresp., TV News, 1989–94; Presenter: Breakfast TV News, 1994–98; One O'Clock TV News, 1998–99; Chief Europe Corresp., 1999–2002; Chief Washington Corresp., 2002–07; North America Ed., 2007–09. *Publications:* Have a Nice Day: a history of anti-Americanism, 2009; Notes on Them and US: reflections on relations between the UK and US, 2011; Cheers, America: how an Englishman learned to love America, 2013. *Recreations:* watching Bath Rugby, reading. *Address:* BBC Broadcasting House, Portland Place, W1A 1AA. *E:* justin.webb@bbc.co.uk.

**WEBB, Prof. (Leslie) Roy,** AO 2003; Vice-Chancellor, Griffith University, 1985–2001, Emeritus Professor, 2002; *b* 18 July 1935; *s* of Leslie Hugh Charles Webb and Alice Myra Webb; *m* 1966, Heather, *d* of late H. Brown; one *s* one *d*. *Educ:* Wesley College, Univ. of Melbourne (BCom 1957); Univ. of London (PhD 1962). FASSA 1986; FAIM 1989; FACE 1997. Sen. Lectr in Economics, Univ. of Melbourne, 1964–68; Reader in Economics, La Trobe Univ., 1968–72; University of Melbourne: Truby Williams Prof. of Economics, 1973–84; Prof. Emeritus, 1984; Pro-Vice-Chancellor, 1982–84; Chm., Academic Bd, 1983–84. Vis. Prof., Cornell, 1967–68. Chairman: Bd, Qld Tertiary Admissions Centre, 1986, 1991, 1992 (Mem., 1985–2001); Australian-Amer. Educnl Foundn (Fulbright Program), 1986–90 (Mem., 1985–89); Qld Non-State Schs Accreditation Bd, 2001–09; Library Bd of Qld, 2002–08; Member: Bd of Dirs, Australian Vice-Chancellors' Cttee, 1991–94; Cttee, Sir Robert Menzies Australian Studies Centre, Univ. of London, 1990–92; Bd of Govs, Foundn for Develt Co-operation, 1990–2007. Consultant, UN Conf. on Trade and Develt, 1974–75; Chm., Cttee of Inquiry into S Australian Dairy Industry, 1977; Mem., Council of Advice, Bureau of Industry Economics, 1982–84; Pres., Victoria Branch, Econ. Soc. of Aust. and NZ, 1976. DUniv: Qld Univ. of Technol., 2002; Griffith, 2002; Hon. DLitt Southern Qld, 2002. Award for outstanding achievement, US Inf. Agency, 1987. Joint Editor, The Economic Record, 1973–77. Cavaliere dell'Ordine al Merito (Italy), 1995. *Publications:* (ed jtly) Industrial Economics: Australian studies, 1982. *Recreations:* music, art. *Address:* 3 Davrod Street, Robertson, Qld 4109, Australia.

**WEBB, Lynn Margaret;** *see* Tayton, L. M.

**WEBB, Margaret Elizabeth Barbieri;** see Barbieri, M. E.

**WEBB, His Honour Nicholas John David;** a Circuit Judge, 2003–19; *b* 13 Oct. 1949; *s* of late David Frederick and of Joyce Mary Webb; *m* 1973, Jane Elizabeth; two *s*. *Educ:* Nottingham High Sch.; Downing Coll., Cambridge (BA 1971). Called to the Bar, Middle Temple, 1972; barrister, Midland and Oxford, later Midland Circuit, 1972–2003, specialising in crime and personal injury; Asst Recorder, 1996–2001, Recorder, 2001–03. Mem., Parole Bd, 2010–16. Chairman: Cambridge Univ. Conservative Assoc., 1971; Edgbaston Constituency Conservative Assoc., 1989–93; Dep. Chm., West Midlands Area Conservative Assoc., 1992–94. Contested (C) Birmingham Sparkbrook, 1979. *Recreations:* jazz (New Orleans to be-bop), cricket, medieval and modern history.

**WEBB, Nigel Mark;** Director, Member of Group Executive Committee, and Head of Developments, British Land Co. plc, since 2003; *b* Rotherham, 27 Nov. 1963; *s* of Geoffrey and Margaret Ellen Webb; *m* 1988, Philippa Ruth Sutton; two *s* one *d*. *Educ:* Rishworth Sch.; De Montfort Univ. (BSc Hons). Investment Surveyor, Edward Erdman, 1985–88; Develt Exec., Greycoat plc, 1988–92; Develt Dir, British Land Co. plc, 1992–2003. Mem., Leadership Gp, Prince's Trust for Built Envmt, 2014–. Trustee, V&A Mus., 2017–. *Recreations:* sport, family. *Address:* British Land, York House, 45 Seymour Street, W1H 7LX. *T:* (020) 7467 2860. *E:* nigel.webb@britishland.com.

**WEBB, Dame Patricia M.;** see Morgan-Webb.

**WEBB, Richard John;** Corporate Director, Health and Adult Services, North Yorkshire County Council, since 2014; *b* Portsmouth, 13 Feb. 1971; *s* of Harry and Joan Webb; *m* 2003, Stephanie, *d* of Eric and Bea Lare. *Educ:* Court Lane Sch., Portsmouth; Springfield Sch., Portsmouth; Portsmouth Sixth Form Coll.; Univ. of Durham (BA Hons Politics 1992). NHS nat. mgt trainee, Newcastle upon Tyne and N Tyneside, 1992–94; Operational Manager, Gateshead Healthcare NHS Trust, 1994–95; Service Manager, Learning Disabilities, 1995–97, Actg Divl Manager, Mental Health, 1997–98, N Tees Health NHS Trust; Gen. Manager, Learning Disabilities, Stockton on Tees BC and NHS, 1998–2000; Asst Dir (Adults), Social Services, Stockton on Tees BC, 2000–02; Dir, Service Develt, Stockton on Tees BC and N Tees PCT, 2002–05; Corporate Dir, Adult and Consumer Care, Telford and Wrekin Council, 2005–09; Exec. Dir, Communities, Sheffield City Council, 2009–14. Trustee and Hon. Sec., ADASS, 2011–. *Recreations:* walking, running, cycling, film, music, theatre, reading, travel. *Address:* c/o North Yorkshire County Council, County Hall, Northallerton, North Yorks DL7 8AD. *T:* (01609) 532217. *E:* richard.webb@northyorks.gov.uk. *Club:* Middlesbrough Football.

**WEBB, Richard Murton Lumley;** Chairman, Morgan Grenfell & Co. Ltd, 1989–96; *b* 7 March 1939; *s* of Richard Henry Lumley Webb and Elizabeth Martin (*née* Munro Kerr); *m* 1966, Juliet Wendy English Devenish; one *s* one *d*. *Educ:* Winchester Coll.; New Coll., Oxford (BA Modern Hist.). Mem., Inst. Chartered Accountants of Scotland, 1965. Brown Fleming & Murray, 1961–68; Director: Morgan Grenfell & Co. Ltd, 1973–96; Morgan Grenfell Gp PLC, 1988–96. Chairman: Medway Housing Society Ltd, 1996–2004; Wax Lyrical Ltd, 1997–99; Dir, Scottish Provident Instn, 1997–2001. *Address:* 12 Gwendolen Avenue, Putney, SW15 6EH. *Club:* Hurlingham.

**WEBB, Prof. Robert,** PhD, DSc; FRSE; Honorary Professor, School of Biosciences, University of Nottingham, 2012–17, now Emeritus Professor; *b* Nottingham, 18 June 1950; *s* of late Gordon David and of Audrey Irene Webb; *m* 1976, Jeanette Mary Caddick; two *s* one *d*. *Educ:* Arnold Co. High Sch., Nottingham; Notts Agricl Coll. (C&G Pig, Beef and Milk Prodn 1969); Univ. of Nottingham (BSc; PhD 1977); Univ. of Edinburgh (DSc 2012). Farmworker, 1968–70; Ford Foundn Fellow, Univ. of Michigan, 1977–79; Sen. Scientist, Dept of Obstetrics and Gynaecol., Univ. of Oxford, 1979–81; Principal Res. Scientist, Roslin Inst., Edinburgh, BBSRC, 1981–97; University of Nottingham: Prof. of Animal Scis, 1997–2012; Hd, Sch. of Biosciences, 2003–06; Dean, Faculty of Sci., 2007–08; Pro-Vice Chancellor (Res.), 2008–12; Principal and CEO, Scottish Agricultural Coll., subseq. Scotland's Rural Coll., 2012–13; Prof. of Agriculture, Univ. of Glasgow, 2012–13. Member: AgriTech Leadership Council, 2013–15; AgriFood Tech. Council, 2016–; Workforce and Skills Core Gp, Food and Drink Sector Council, 2018–. Chm., Ext. Adv. Bd, Future Food Beacon of Excellence, Univ. of Nottingham, 2018–. FRSE 2013. Hon. Fellow, Coll. of Medicine and Veterinary Medicine, Univ. of Edinburgh, 1996–2015. Marshall Medal, Soc. for Reproduction and Fertility, 2011. Editor-in-Chief: Jl of Reproduction and Fertility, 1999–2001; Reviews of Reproduction, 1999–2001; Inaugural Ed. in-Chief, Reproduction, 2001–04. *Publications:* contrib. papers to peer-reviewed scientific jls, books and conf. procs. *Recreations:* music, walking, trekking, sport.

**WEBB, Robert Stopford;** QC 1988; Chairman: Darktrace Ltd, since 2014; Luminance, since 2016; Senior Advisor, Brunswick Group LLP, since 2016; Door Tenant, Brick Court Chambers, 2009–12 and since 2016; *b* 4 Oct. 1948; *s* of late Robert Victor Bertram Webb, MC and Isabella Raine Webb (*née* Hinks); *m* 1975, Angela Mary Freshwater; two *s*. *Educ:* Wycliffe Coll.; Exeter Univ. (LLB 1970). Called to the Bar, Inner Temple, 1971 (Bencher, 1997), and Lincoln's Inn, 1996; Head of Chambers, 5 Bell Yard, 1988–98; a Recorder, 1993–98. General Counsel: British Airways, 1998–2009; Rolls-Royce plc, 2012–15. Chairman: Autonomy plc, 2009–12; BBC Worldwide, 2009–12; Sciemus Ltd, 2010–11; Sen. Ind. Dir, London Stock Exchange, 2001–15 (Chm., Remuneration Cttee, 2001–15); non-executive Director: Air Mauritius, 1998–2004; London First, 2002–09; Holdingham Gp (formerly Hakluyt and Co.) Ltd, 2005–19 (Chm., Remuneration Cttee, 2005–19; Sen. Ind. Dir, 2011–19); Emerging Health Threats Forum CIC (formerly Forum for Global Health Protection), 2006–12; BBC, 2007–12; Argent Gp plc, 2009–12. Chm., Air Law Gp, RAeS, 1988–93 (FRAeS 1992); English Bar Rep., Internat. Bar Assoc., 1994–99; Chm., Internat. Relations Cttee, Bar Council, 1997–98. Vis. Prof., Bournemouth Univ., 2009–11. Trustee: Migratory Salmon Fund, 1997–2015; Comic Relief, 2011–17. Fellow, Internat. Acad. of Trial Lawyers, 1990. Hon. Fellow, UNICEF, 2006–11. *Recreations:* golf, conservation. *Clubs:* Brooks's, Royal Automobile, Reform, Soho House, Flyfishers'; Royal Wimbledon Golf, Royal Lytham St Anne's Golf, Hampstead Golf, Prestbury Golf, Manor House Golf (Castle Combe).

**WEBB, Roy;** see Webb, L. R.

**WEBB, Simon,** CBE 1991; Executive Director, The Nichols Group, since 2010; *b* 21 Oct. 1951; *s* of Rev. Canon Bertie Webb and Jane Webb (*née* Braley); *m* 1975, Alexandra Jane Culme-Seymour (marr. diss. 2009); one *s* one *d*. *Educ:* King's Sch., Worcester (Schol.); Hertford Coll., Oxford (Meeke Schol.; MA; Edgell Sheppee Prize for Engrg and Econs). FICE 2014. Entered MoD, 1972: Asst Private Sec. to Minister of State, 1975; Principal, 1977; Public Enterprises, HM Treasury, 1982–85; Dir of Resources and Progs (Warships), MoD, 1985–88; Rand Corp., Santa Monica, Calif, 1988–89; Head, Agency Team, MoD, 1989; Private Sec. to Sec. of State for Defence, 1989–92; Minister (Defence Materiel), Washington, 1992–96; Dir Gen. Resources, PE, MoD, 1996–98; Team Leader, Smart Procurement, 1998–99; Asst Under Sec. of State (Home & Overseas), subseq. Dir Gen., Operational Policy, MoD, 1999–2001; Policy Dir, MoD, 2001–04; Dir Gen., Delivery and Security, 2004–07, Internat. Networks and Envmt, 2007–09, DfT. Dir, Major Projects Assoc., 2010–. Gov., Ditchley Foundn, 2008–19 (Hon. Gov., 2019–). *Publications:* Defense Acquisition and Free Markets, 1990. *Recreations:* cycling, gardens, church music. *Club:* Reform.

**WEBB, Rt Hon. Sir Steven (John),** Kt 2017; PC 2014; Director of Policy and External Communications, Royal London, since 2015; *b* 18 July 1965; *s* of Brian and Patricia Webb; *m* 1993, Rev. Helen Edwards; one *s* one *d*. *Educ:* Hertford Coll., Oxford (1st Cl. BA Hons PPE). Economist, Inst. for Fiscal Studies, 1986–95; Prof. of Social Policy, Bath Univ., 1995–97. MP (Lib Dem) Northavon, 1997–2010, Thornbury and Yate, 2010–15; contested (Lib Dem) same seat, 2015. Lib Dem spokesman on health, 2005–07, on envmt, energy, food and rural affairs, 2008, on energy and climate change, 2008–09, on work and pensions, 2009–10; Minister of State for Pensions, DWP, 2010–15. Lib Dem Manifesto Chair, 2007. *Publications:* (with Alissa Goodman and Paul Johnson) Inequality in the UK, 1997. *Recreations:* internet issues, church organ, oboe.

**WEBB, Prof. William Timothy,** PhD; FREng, FIET, FIEEE; Chief Executive Officer, Weightless SIG, since 2012; Consultant, Webb Search Ltd, since 2013; *b* Hersham, Surrey, 4 May 1967; *s* of Christopher and Genebeth Webb; *m* 1995, Alison Porter; two *d*. *Educ:* Southampton Univ. (BEng 1st Cl. Electronic Engrg 1989; PhD 1992); Southampton Univ. (MBA 1997). FIET 1995; FREng 2005; FIEEE 2008. Tech. Dir, Multiple Access Communications Ltd, 1989–93; Principal Consultant, Smith System Engrg Ltd, 1993–97; Hd, wireless local loop div., Netcom Consultants, 1997–98; Dir, Corporate Strategy, Motorola, 1998–2001; Managing Consultant, Wireless Practice, PA Consulting, 2001–03; Dir, Technol. Resources, Ofcom, 2003–11; Chief Tech. Officer, Neul, 2011–13. Visiting Professor: Centre for Communication Systems Res., Surrey Univ., 2003–16; De Montfort Univ., 2007–12; Southampton Univ., 2014–; TCD, 2014–18. Mem. Bd, Cambridge Wireless, 2009–17. Vice Pres., 2004–07 and 2009–12, Dep. Pres., 2013–14, Pres., 2014–15, IET; Royal Academy of Engineering: Mem., editl panel, Ingenia, 2007–; Mem., Ext. Engagement Cttee, 2010–13. Judge, Wall St Jl Innovation Awards, 2002–12. Hon. DSc: Southampton, 2015; Herts, 2019; Hon. DTech Anglia Ruskin, 2015. Mountbatten Medal, IET, 2018. *Publications:* (with L. Hanzo) Quadrature Amplitude Modulation, 1994, 2004; Introduction to Wireless Local Loop, 1998, 2000; Understanding Cellular Radio, 1998; The Complete Wireless Communications Professional, 1999; The Future of Wireless Communications, 2001; Wireless Communications: the future, 2007; (jtly) Essentials of Modern Spectrum Management, 2007; Being Mobile: future wireless technologies and applications, 2010; Understanding Weightless, 2012; Dynamic White Space Spectrum Access, 2013; Using Spectrum, 2015; The 5G Myth, 2017; Our Digital Future, 2018. *Recreations:* cycling, including some of the world's toughest sportives, such as the Cent Cols Challenge and the route of Tour de France. *E:* drwilliamwebb@gmail.com.

**WEBB-CARTER, Maj. Gen. Sir Evelyn (John),** KCVO 2000; OBE 1989; DL; Chief Executive, ABF The Soldiers' Charity (formerly Controller, Army Benevolent Fund), 2003–12; *b* 30 Jan. 1946; *s* of Brig. Brian Webb-Carter, DSO, OBE and Rosemary Webb-Carter (*née* Hood); *m* 1973, Hon. Anne Celia Wigram, *yr d* of 2nd Baron Wigram, MC; one *s* two *d*. *Educ:* Wellington Coll.; RMA Sandhurst. Commissioned Grenadier Guards, 1966; Commanded: 1st Bn Grenadier Guards, 1985–88; 19 Mechanised Bde, 1991–93; Multi National Div. (SW) in Bosnia, 1996–97; GOC London Dist and Maj. Gen. Comdg Household Div., 1997–2000. Special Advr to CRE, 2001–03. Regtl Lt-Col, Grenadier Guards, 1995–2000; Col, Duke of Wellington's Regt, 1999–2006; Hon. Regtl Col, King's Troop, RHA, 2001–11; Hon. Col, Glos ACF, 2011–17. Chairman: Mounted Infantry Club, 1993–; Waterloo Assoc. (formerly Assoc. of Friends of Waterloo Cttee), 2002–; Adv. Council, First Aid Nursing Yeomanry, 2003–12 (Vice Pres., 2012–); Commemoration Cttee, 200th Anniversary of Battle of Waterloo, 2007–15; Waterloo 200 Ltd, 2007–; Trustees, Brooke Hosp. for Animals, 2013–. Patron, Burnaby Blue Foundn, 2001–. Mem. Ct of Assts, Farriers' Co., 2004– (Liveryman, 2003–; Master, 2012–13). DL Glos, 2009. *Recreations:* hunting, military history, riding in foreign parts. *Address:* Horcott House, Fairford, Glos GL7 4BY. *Clubs:* Boodle's; Banja Luka Hunt (Bosnia).

**WEBBER;** see Lloyd Webber.

**WEBBER, Prof. Bryan Ronald,** PhD; FRS 2001; FInstP; Professor of Theoretical Physics, University of Cambridge, 1999–2010, now Emeritus; Fellow, Emmanuel College, Cambridge, since 1973; *b* 25 July 1943; *s* of Frederick Ronald Webber and Iris Evelyn Webber (*née* Hutchings); *m* 1968, Akemi Horie. *Educ:* Colston's Sch., Bristol; Queen's Coll., Oxford (MA); Univ. of Calif, Berkeley (PhD 1969). FInstP 1987. Physicist, Lawrence Berkeley Nat. Lab., Calif, 1969–71; Department of Physics, University of Cambridge: Res. Asst, 1971–73; Demonstrator, 1973–78; Lectr, 1978–94; Reader, 1994–99. Hon. PhD Lund, 2012. Dirac Medal for Theoretical Physics, Inst. of Physics, 2008; J. J. Sakurai Prize for Theoretical Physics, Amer. Physical Soc., 2012. *Publications:* (jtly) QCD and Collider Physics, 1996; contrib. articles on high energy physics. *Address:* Cavendish Laboratory, J. J. Thomson Avenue, Cambridge CB3 0HE. *T:* (01223) 337200.

**WEBBER, Howard Simon;** Chief Executive, Postwatch, 2006–08; *b* 25 Jan. 1955; *s* of Manny and Josie Webber; *m* 1978, Sandra Wagman; one *s*. *Educ:* Univ. of Birmingham (LLB 1976); Harvard Univ. (MPA 1987); King's Coll. London (MA 2011). Joined Home Office, 1976; seconded to Royal Commn on Criminal Procedure, 1979–80 and Cabinet Office, 1986; Harkness Fellow, USA, 1986–87; Prison Bldg Budget Manager, Home Office, 1987–88; Dir, Incentive Funding, 1988–91, Hd, Policy and Planning, 1991–94, Arts Council; Manager, Public Sector MBA, Cabinet Office, 1994; Hd, Voluntary Services Unit/Active Community Unit, Home Office, 1995–99; Chief Exec., Criminal Injuries Compensation Authy, 1999–2006. Advr, Business and Enterprise Cttee, H of C, 2009; Board Member: Metropolitan Housing Partnership, 2008–13; Kingston Liberal Synagogue, 2008–; PhonepayPlus, 2010–15; Royal Surrey Co. Hosp. NHS Foundn Trust, 2017–. Chair, Lambeth and Southwark Housing Assoc., 2015–. Mem., Standards Cttee, SRA, 2014–16. *Publications:* (jtly) A Creative Future: a national strategy for the arts and media, 1993. *Recreations:* travel, the arts. *E:* howardwebber@gmail.com.

**WEBBER, Rev. Lionel Frank;** Chaplain to the Queen, 1994–2001; Hon. Curate, St Mary, Burnham-on-Crouch, since 2005; *b* 12 July 1935; *s* of Nellie and Sydney Webber; *m* 1961, Jean Thomas; one *d*. *Educ:* Danetree Road Co. Secondary Sch., Ewell; Kelham Theol. Coll.; St Michael's Theol Coll., Llandaff. Ordained deacon, 1960, priest, 1961; Curate: The Saviour, Bolton, 1960–63; Holy Trinity, Aberavon, 1963–65; Rector, Stowell Meml Parish Ch, Salford, 1965–69; Vicar, Holy Trinity, Aberavon, 1969–74; Team Vicar, Stantonbury, Milton Keynes, 1974–76; Rector of Basildon, 1976–2001. Hon. Canon, Chelmsford Cathedral, 1984–2001. Chaplain, Vintage Sports Car Club. Life Vice Cdre, Royal Naval Sailing Assoc., 2008. *Recreations:* motor racing, sailing. *Address:* 12 Ramblers Way, Burnham-on-Crouch, Essex CM0 8LR.

**WEBBER, Timothy John;** visual effects supervisor and film director, and Chief Creative Officer, since 1998, Framestore Ltd; *b* 1965; *s* of Thomas John Webber and Margaret Denise Webber; *m* 2001, Fiona Jane Walkinshaw; two *s* one *d*. *Educ:* Summer Fields, Oxford; Marlborough Coll.; St Catherine's Coll., Oxford (BA). Joined Framestore Ltd, 1988, Partner, 1992–; visual effects supervisor of films: Harry Potter and the Goblet of

Fire, 2005; Children of Men, 2006; The Dark Knight, 2008; Where the Wild Things Are, 2009; Avatar, 2009; Gravity, 2013 (Oscar for Best Visual Effects (jtly), 2014; BAFTA for Best Special Visual Effects (jtly), 2014). Hon. FRPS 2014. Emmy Award, 1996, (jtly) 1998, 2000, (jtly) 2002; Progress Medal, RPS, 2014. *Recreations:* art, photography, cinema, croquet, family. *E:* timjwebber@gmail.com.

**WEBBON, Peter Michael,** PhD; Chief Executive, Animal Health Trust, 2007–13; *b* Leicester, 9 Jan. 1948; *s* of late Robert Ernest Webbon and Grace Webbon (*née* Salt); *m* 1st, 1970, Phyllis Mary Christine (marr. diss. 2008), *d* of late Major John Frederick Langdon, MC; one *s* three *d*; 2nd, 2012, Lynn Louise Hillyer, *d* of Roger Walkey; two *d*. *Educ:* Wyggeston Boys' Grammar Sch.; Royal Veterinary Coll., London (BVetMed Hons 1971; DVR 1975; PhD 1989). MRCVS. Res. Trng Scholar, Horserace Betting Levy Bd, 1971–74; Lectr, 1974–83, Sen. Lectr, 1983–96, RVC, London; Chief Vet. Advr, 1996–2001, Vet. Dir, 2002–06, Jockey Club; Chief Exec., HRA, 2006. Hon. Prof., RVC, 2007. Official veterinarian, FEI; Veterinary Advr, Internat. Stud Book Cttee. Chm., Equine Sector Council; Ind. Dir, Greyhound Bd of GB, 2015–. *Publications:* (ed and contrib.) A Guide to Diagnostic Radiography in Small Animal Practice, 1981; chapters in books on diagnostic imaging and equine medicine; articles in scientific and gen. jls; contrib. professional and lay societies. *Recreations:* keeping Ryeland sheep, gardening, ski-ing, golf. *E:* pwebbon@hotmail.co.uk.

**WEBBORN, Prof. Nick Anthony David John,** OBE 2016; Medical Director, Sportswise, Sussex Centre for Sport and Exercise Medicine, since 1997; Clinical Professor of Sport and Exercise Medicine, University of Brighton, since 2014; Chair and President, British Paralympic Association, since 2017; *b* Swansea, 8 Oct. 1956; *s* of Thomas John Haydn Webborn and Mary Frances Therese Webborn; *m* 1st, 1982, Susan Jane Mathers (marr. diss. 2007); two *s* two *d*; 2nd, 2012, Stephanie Elizabeth Anderson. *Educ:* Belmont Abbey Sch., Hereford; London Hosp. Med. Coll., Univ. of London (MB BS 1979); Queen Mary Coll., Univ. of London (MSc Sports Medicine 1996). MRCGP 1985; FFSEM 2003; FFSEM (UK) 2006. Served Med. Br., RAF, 1980–85. GP, Polegate, E Sussex, 1986–93; Lectr in Sports Medicine, Academic Dept of Sports Medicine, St Bartholomew's and Royal London Sch. of Medicine and Dentistry, QMW, Univ. of London, 1993–97; Medical Advisor: (pt-time) Nat. Sports Medicine Inst., UK, 1999–2003; British Paralympic Assoc., 2002–08; Sports Physician, English Inst. of Sport, SE Reg., 2003–05; Chief Medical Officer: ParalympicsGB, London 2012 Paralympic Games, 2010–12; UK Invictus Games Team, 2017. Hon. Clinical Prof., Sch. of Sport, Exercise and Health Scis, Loughborough Univ., 2018–. Member: Med. Adv. Gp, London 2012, 2003–08; Sports Medicine Wkg Gp, LOCOG, 2009–12. Member: Therapeutic Use Exemption Cttee, UK Anti-Doping, 2004–; Med. Cttee, Internat. Paralympic Cttee, 2014–; Prohibited List Expert Gp, World Anti-Doping Assoc., 2016–. *Publications:* book chapters; peer-reviewed contribs on sport and exercise medicine. *Recreations:* sport, music, opera, disabled rambler, family, wheelchair tennis (represented GB, 2005; Nat. Doubles Champion (Quad), 2005; highest world rankings: singles, 41, doubles, 28). *Address:* 1A Willingdon Park Drive, Eastbourne, E Sussex BN20 0BP. *T:* (01323) 520444. *E:* nickwebborn@sportswise.org.uk. *Club:* Royal Society of Medicine.

**WEBER, Prof. Axel Alfred;** Chairman: UBS AG, since 2012; UBS Group AG, since 2014; *b* Kusel, 8 March 1957; *m;* two *c*. *Educ:* Univ. of Constance (degree Econs and Mgt 1982); Univ. of Siegen (Doctorate 1987; Habilitation Econs 1994). Prof. of Econ. Theory, Rheinische Friedrich Wilhelms Univ., Bonn, 1994–98; Prof. of Applied Monetary Econs, Johann Wolfgang Goethe Univ., Frankfurt am Main, 1998–2001; Dir, Center for Financial Studies, Frankfurt am Main, 1998–2002; Prof. of Internat. Econs, Univ. of Cologne, 2001–04; Pres., Deutsche Bundesbank and Mem., Governing Council, European Central Bank, 2004–11. Mem., German Council of Economic Experts, 2002–04. *Address:* c/o UBS Group AG, Bahnhofstr. 45, PO Box, 8098 Zurich, Switzerland.

**WEBER, Catherine Elisabeth Dorcas;** *see* Bell, C. E. D.

**WEBER, Prof. Jonathan Norden,** PhD; FRCP, FRCPath, FMedSci; Dean, Faculty of Medicine, since 2018, and Director, Academic Health Science Centre, since 2016, Imperial College London; Jefferiss Professor of Genito-Urinary Medicine and Communicable Diseases, Imperial College and St Mary's Hospital, since 1991; *b* 29 Dec. 1954; *s* of Dr Geoffrey Norden Weber and Rosalie Weber; *m* 1996, Prof. Sophie Elisabeth Day; three *s*. *Educ:* Gonville and Caius Coll., Cambridge (BA 1976; PhD 2003); St Bartholomew's Med. Sch. (MB BChir 1979). FRCP 1993; FRCPath 1997. Wellcome Trust Res. Fellow, St Mary's Hosp. Med. Sch., 1982–85; Wellcome Trust Lectr in Cell and Molecular Biol., Inst. Cancer Res., 1985–88; Sen. Lectr, Dept of Medicine, RPMS, 1988–91; Imperial College London: Chm., Wright-Fleming Inst., 2000–04; Dean, St Mary's Campus, 2001–04; Hd, Div. of Medicine, 2004–09; Dir of Res., 2008, Vice Dean, 2009, Faculty of Medicine; Dir, Imperial NIHR Biomedical Res. Centre, 2009. Dir of Res., Imperial Coll. Healthcare NHS Trust, 2007. Chm. Governors, William Tyndale Primary Sch., 2007–12. FMedSci 2000. *Publications:* The Management of AIDS Patients, 1986; contribs to The Lancet, etc. *Recreations:* motor-bikes, boats. *E:* j.weber@imperial.ac.uk.

**WEBER, Jürgen;** Hon. Chairman, Supervisory Board, Deutsche Lufthansa AG, since 2013 (Chairman: Executive Board, 1991–2003; Supervisory Board, 2003–13); *b* 17 Oct. 1941; *m* 1965, Sabine Rossberg; one *s* one *d*. *Educ:* Stuttgart Tech. Univ. (Dipl. Ing. Aeronautical Engrg 1965); MIT (Sen. Mgt Trng 1980). Joined Lufthansa, 1967: Engrg Div., 1967–74; Director: Line Maintenance Dept, 1974–78; Aircraft Engrg Sub-div., 1978–87; Chief Operating Officer (Tech.), 1987–89; Dep. Mem., Exec. Bd, 1989–90; Chief Exec., Tech., 1990–91. Chm., Supervisory Bd, Bogner Sport GmbH; Member, Supervisory Board: Deutsche Post AG, 2003–08 (Chm., 2006–08); Bayer AG. *Recreations:* jogging, ski-ing. *Address:* c/o Deutsche Lufthansa AG, Von-Gablenz-Strasse 2–6, 50679 Cologne, Germany.

**WEBER, Prof. Richard Robert,** Jr, PhD; Churchill Professor of Mathematics for Operational Research, Cambridge University, 1994–2017; Fellow, Queens' College, Cambridge, since 1978; *b* 25 Feb. 1953; *s* of Richard Robert Weber and Elizabeth Bray. *Educ:* Walnut Hills High Sch., USA; Solihull Sch.; Downing Coll., Cambridge (BA 1974; MA 1978; PhD 1980). Cambridge University: Asst Lectr and Lectr in Engrg, 1978–92; Reader in Management Sci., Engrg, 1992–94; Dir, Statistical Lab., 1999–2009; Queens' College, Cambridge: Res. Fellow, 1977–78; Tutor, 1979–92; Dir of Studies (Maths) 1985–94; Vice Pres., 1996–2007 and 2018–. *Publications:* (with C. Courcoubetis) Pricing Communication Networks, 2003; (jtly) Multi-armed Bandit Allocation Indices, 2011; numerous articles on stochastic systems, scheduling and queueing theory. *Recreations:* hiking, travel. *Address:* Queens' College, Cambridge CB3 9ET. *T:* (01223) 335570.

**WEBSTER, Alistair Stevenson;** QC 1995; a Recorder, since 1996 (an Assistant Recorder, 1992–96); *b* 28 April 1953; *s* of His Honour Ian Stevenson Webster; *m* 1977, Barbara Anne Longbottom; two *d*. *Educ:* Hulme Grammar Sch., Oldham; Brasenose Coll., Oxford (BA Hons Jurisp.). Called to the Bar, Middle Temple, 1976, Bencher, 2004; practice on Northern Circuit, 1976–. Hon. Sec., Northern Circuit, 1988–93; Mem., Bar Council, 1995–96; Chm., Membership Cttee, Middle Temple, 2015–. Chm., Lib Dem Lawyers Assoc., 2011–14. Author of report into allegations relating to Lord Rennard, 2014. *Recreations:* cricket, tennis, ski-ing, football. *Address:* Lincoln House Chambers, Tower 12, The Avenue North, Spinningfields, 18–22 Bridge Street, Manchester M3 3BZ. *T:* (0161) 832 5701; 33 Chancery Lane, WC2A 1EN. *T:* (020) 7440 9950. *Clubs:* Garrick; Rochdale Racquets; Gentlemen Gardeners Cricket.

**WEBSTER, Andrew George;** QC (Scot.) 2018; Sheriff (part-time), since 2010; *b* Wick, Caithness, 20 July 1967; *s* of James Thomas Sutherland Webster and Margaret Wood Webster (*née* Steven); *m* 1992, Sheila Mairead Mann, WS; two *d*. *Educ:* Univ. of Aberdeen (LLB Hons; DipLP). Admitted as Advocate, 1992; Standing Jun. Counsel, MoD, 1997–2012; First Scottish Standing Counsel, 2012–. Chair, Pensions Appeal Tribunal, 2010–; Legally Qualified Chair: Med. Practitioners' Tribunal Service, 2017–; Scottish Social Services Council, 2017–; Mem., Police Appeals Tribunal, 2013–. Legal Assessor, Gen. Osteopathic Council, 2015–; Ind. Examr, ICAS, 2012–; Ind. Reviewer, Chartered Accountants Ireland, 2013–. FRSA. *Address:* Advocates Library, Parliament House, Edinburgh EH1 1RF. *T:* (0131) 226 5071. *E:* andrew.webster@advocates.org.uk.

**WEBSTER, Maj.-Gen. Bryan Courtney,** CB 1986; CBE 1981; Director of Army Quartering, 1982–86; *b* 2 Feb. 1931; *s* of Captain H. J. Webster, Royal Fusiliers (killed in action, 1940) and late M. J. Webster; *m* 1957, Elizabeth Rowland Waldron Smithers, *d* of Prof. Sir David Smithers; two *s* one *d*. *Educ:* Haileybury College; RMA Sandhurst. Commissioned Royal Fusiliers, 1951; ADC to GOC, 16 Airborne Div., 1953–55; served BAOR, Korea, Egypt, Malta, Gibraltar, Hong Kong; Directing Staff, Staff Coll., 1969–70; Comd 1st Bn Royal Regt of Fusiliers, 1971–73; Comd 8th Inf. Brigade, 1975–77 (despatches); Dep. Col, Royal Regt of Fusiliers (City of London), 1976–89; Nat. Defence Coll., India, 1979; Staff appts, Far East, MoD, incl. Dir of Admin. Planning (Army), 1980–82. Chm., Army Benevolent Fund, Surrey, 1986–2000. Mem. Council, Wine Guild of UK, 1995–2001. Pres., CPRE Hants, 2001–08. FCMI. Freeman, City of London, 1984. *Recreations:* ornithology, shooting, wine. *Address:* c/o HSBC, 69 High Street, Sevenoaks, Kent TN13 1LB.

**WEBSTER, Charles,** DSc; Senior Research Fellow, All Souls College, Oxford, 1988–2004, now Emeritus Fellow. Reader in the History of Medicine, University of Oxford, 1972–88; Director, Wellcome Unit for the History of Medicine, 1972–88; Fellow of Corpus Christi College, Oxford, 1972–88. FBA 1982–99. *Publications:* (ed) Samuel Hartlib and the Advancement of Learning, 1970; The Great Instauration, 1975; From Paracelsus to Newton, 1982; Problems of Health Care: the National Health Service before 1957, 1988; (ed) Aneurin Bevan on the National Health Service, 1991; (ed) Caring for Health, History and Diversity, 1993; Government and Health Care: the British National Health Service 1958–1979, 1996; The National Health Service: a political history, 1998. *Address:* All Souls College, Oxford OX1 4AL. *T:* (01865) 279379.

**WEBSTER, David Gordon Comyn;** Director, Temple Bar Investment Trust, 2009–18; Director, Amadeus IT Group SA (formerly Amadeus IT Holding SA), since 2010; *b* 11 Feb. 1945; *s* of Alfred Edward Comyn Webster and Meryl Mary Clutterbuck; *m* 1972, Pamela Gail Runnicles; three *s*. *Educ:* Glasgow Acad.; Glasgow Univ. (LLB). Lieut, RNR, retd 1970. Admitted Solicitor, 1968; Corporate Finance Manager, Samuel Montagu & Co., 1969–72; Finance Dir, Oriel Foods Ltd, 1973–76; Co-Founder and Finance Dir, 1977–89, Dep. Chm., 1989–97, Chm., 1997–2004, Argyll Gp, subseq. Safeway plc; Chairman: InterContinental Hotels Gp, 2004–12 (Dir, 2003–12); Makinson Cowell, 2004–14; Vuma Finance Ltd, 2010–; Telum Media Gp Pte Ltd, 2013–. Non-executive Director: Reed International plc, 1992–2002; Reed Elsevier, 1993–2002; Elsevier NV, 1999–2002. Member: Nat. Employers Liaison Cttee, 1992–2002; Appeals Cttee, Panel on Takeovers and Mergers, 2007–. Pres., Inst. of Grocery Distribn, 2001–02. Trustee, Nat. Life Story Collection, 2005–15. KStJ 2004. *Recreations:* military history, ski-ing, sailing, gardening, walking. *E:* dgcwebster@gmail.com.

**WEBSTER, His Honour David MacLaren;** QC 1980; a Circuit Judge, 1987–2003 (Resident Judge, Salisbury); Hon. Recorder of Salisbury, 2002–05; *b* 21 Dec. 1937; *s* of late John MacLaren Webster and Winning McGregor Webster (*née* Rough); *m* 1964, Frances Sally McLaren, RE, *o d* of late Lt-Col J. A. McLaren and of Mrs H. S. Scammell; three *s*. *Educ:* Hutchesons', Glasgow; Christ Church, Oxford (MA (Eng. Lang. and Lit.)); Conservatoire d'Art Dramatique and Sorbonne (French Govt Schol. 1960–61). Radio and television work in drama and current affairs, Scotland, incl. Dixon of Dock Green, A Nest of Singing Birds, and Muir of Huntershill, 1949–64; called to the Bar, Gray's Inn, 1964; Western Circuit; a Dep. Circuit Judge, 1976–79; a Recorder, 1979–87. Chairman: Salisbury & Dist Family Mediation Service, 1987–2001; Area Criminal Justice Liaison Cttee for Hants, Dorset and IoW, 1994–99; Area Criminal Justice Strategy Cttee, Hants and IoW, 2000–01. Member: Bar Council, 1972–74; Senate of Inns of Court and Bar, 1974–79, 1982–85 (Senate Representative, Commonwealth Law Conf., Edinburgh, 1977). Chm., Salisbury Safety Partnership, 1998–2004; Member: Salisbury Playhouse Develt Cttee, 2006–11; Standards Cttee for Wilts, 2009–12. Gold Medal, LAMDA, 1954; LRAM 1955. President, Oxford Univ. Experimental Theatre Club, 1958–59; Secretary, Mermaid's, 1958; Chm., Bar Theatrical Soc., 1976–86. Governor, Port Regis Sch., 1983–94. *Recreations:* theatre, sailing, cricket, reading, still training Pippin and Jazzmine. *Clubs:* Garrick, MCC; Bar Yacht.

**WEBSTER, Edward;** *see* Webster, K. E.

**WEBSTER, Evelyn Ann;** Chief Executive Officer, Guardian US and Guardian Australia, since 2017; *b* Wakefield, W Yorks, 12 May 1969. *Educ:* Univ. of Greenwich (BA Hons Business Studies with Mktg). IPC Media Ltd: Graduate Trainee, 1992; Client Services Exec., Marketforce, 1993; Mktg Manager, New Scientist, 1994; Asst Publisher, Sci. and Special Interest Gp, 1995–97; Publisher, Specialist Gp, 1997; Gp Publisher (Special Projects), 1998; Publishing Dir, Country and Equestrian titles, 1999–2003; Managing Director: IPC Country and Leisure Media, 2003–04; IPC Connect, 2004–08; Chief Exec., IPC Media Ltd, 2009–10 (Dir, 2003–10); Exec. Vice Pres., Time Inc., 2011–16. *Recreations:* running, yoga.

**WEBSTER, Rt Rev. Glyn Hamilton;** *see* Beverley, Bishop Suffragan of.

**WEBSTER, Janice Helen,** WS; Judge, First-tier Tribunal, Social Entitlement Tribunal (formerly part-time Chairman, Appeals Service), 1996–2015; legal expert to Council of Europe, 1993–97; *b* 2 April 1944; *d* of James Bell Reid and Janet (*née* Johnston); *m* 1968, R. M. Webster; two *d*. *Educ:* Edinburgh Univ. (LLB 1964). Solicitor and Notary Public. Legal Asst, then Sen. Solicitor, Falkirk Town Council, 1967–71; in private practice, Alston Nairn & Hogg, Edinburgh, 1971–74; Dep. Sec., Law Soc. of Scotland, 1974–80; Crown Counsel, then Magistrate, Govt of Seychelles, 1980–82; Law Society of Scotland, 1982–90 (Dep. Sec., Dir, European Affairs and Sec., Scottish Lawyers' European Gp); Dir Gen., CCBE, 1991–93; Consultant, Bell & Scott, WS, Edinburgh, 1994–96. Sec., Scottish Law Agents Soc., 1998–2004. Mem., Scottish Records Adv. Council, 1995–2000. Director: Scottish Archive Network, 1998–2002; Franco-British Lawyers' Soc. Ltd, 1998–2000; Chm., Scottish Soc. for Computers and Law, 2001–04. Member: Council, WS Soc., 1998–2000; Governing Council, Erskine Stewart's Melville, 1998–2002. Ed., Human

Rights and UK Practice, 1999–2009. Chm., Perth and Kinross, Order of St John Scotland, 2018–. MStJ 2017. *Publications:* (with R. M. Webster) Professional Ethics and Practice for Scottish Solicitors, 3rd edn 1996, 4th edn 2004. *Recreations:* singing, walking, gardening. *Club:* New (Edinburgh).

**WEBSTER, Vice-Adm. Sir John (Morrison)**, KCB 1986; RSMA; painter; President, Royal Naval Benevolent Trust, 1991–98; *b* 3 Nov. 1932; *s* of late Frank Martin Webster and Kathleen Mary (*née* Morrison); *m* 1962, Valerie Anne Villiers (*d* 2005); two *d* (one *s* decd). *Educ:* Pangbourne College. Joined RN, 1951; specialised navigation, 1959; RAN, 1959–61; HMS Lowestoft, 1961–63; BRNC Dartmouth, 1963–65; HMS Dido, 1965–67; RN Tactical Sch., 1967–69; in command HMS Argonaut, 1969–71; MoD Navy, 1971–73; RNLO Ottawa, 1974–76; in command HMS Cleopatra and 4th Frigate Sqdn, 1976–78; MoD, Director Naval Warfare, 1980–82; Flag Officer Sea Trng, 1982–84; C of S to C-in-C Fleet, 1984–86; Flag Officer Plymouth, Naval Base Comdr Devonport, Comdr Central Sub Area Eastern Atlantic and Comdr Plymouth Sub Area Channel, 1987–90; retired. Lt-Comdr 1963, Comdr 1967, Captain 1973, Rear-Adm. 1982, Vice-Adm. 1985. Younger Brother of Trinity House, 1970–. Life Mem., Armed Forces Art Soc., 2008 (Mem., 1967–2008; Chm., 1990–96). One-man exhibitions of paintings: Canada, 1976; Winchester, 1980; London, 1982, 1984, 1986, 1988, 1991, 1993, 1996, 1999, 2002, 2004, 2007, 2009, 2011; Jersey, 2006. Governor: Canford Sch., 1984–2003; Pangbourne College, 1990–2000 (Chm., 1992–2000); FBA, 2002–08. Associate, RSMA, 1998, RSMA 2001. *Recreations:* painting, travel. *Clubs:* Royal Cruising, Royal Naval Sailing Association.

**WEBSTER, Prof. (John) Paul (Garrett)**; Emeritus Professor of Agricultural Business Management, Imperial College London, since 2005; *b* 16 July 1942; *s* of Leonard Garrett Webster and Dorothy Agnes Webster (*née* White); *m* 1972, Dr Amanda Jane Hetigin; one *s* one *d*. *Educ:* Leys Sch., Cambridge; Reading Univ. (BSc); Wye Coll., London Univ. (PhD). FIAgrM 1995; FRAgS 2003. Wye College (merged with Imperial College of Science, Technology and Medicine, 2000): Department of Agricultural Economics, 1965–2005: Asst Lectr, 1965–67; Lectr in Agricl Econs, 1967–76; Sen. Lectr, 1976–81; Reader, 1981–91; Prof. of Agricl Business Mgt, 1991–2005. Visiting appointments: Makerere Univ., Uganda, 1970–71; Drapers Lectr, Univ. of New England, Australia, 1974–75; Economist, Internat. Rice Res. Inst., Philippines, 1980–81; Prof., Lincoln Univ., NZ, 1999–2000. Ind. Mem., Adv. Cttee on Pesticides, MAFF, 1992–99. Pres., Agricl Econs Soc., 1999–2000. President: City of Canterbury Swimming Club, 2004–06; E Invicta Amateur Swimming Assoc., 2007–08. FCMI (FBIM 1985); FRSA 1987. Hon. Freeman, Farmers' Co., 2000. *Publications:* articles in Jl Agricl Econs, Amer. Jl Agricl Econs, Farm Mgt, etc. *Recreations:* masters swimming (UK rankings; 100m French Open Champion 2012 (70+ age group), 2017 (75+ age group)). *Address:* 25 Chequers Park, Wye, Kent TN25 5BB. *Club:* Farmers.

**WEBSTER, Prof. (Keith) Edward**, PhD; Professor of Anatomy and Human Biology (formerly Professor of Anatomy), King's College, University of London, 1975–2000; *b* 18 June 1935; *e s* of Thomas Brotherwick Webster and Edna Pyzer; 1st marr. diss. 1983; two *s*; 2nd marr. diss. 1990. *Educ:* UCL (BSc 1957, PhD 1960); UCH Med. Sch. (MB, BS 1962). University Coll. London: Lectr in Anatomy, 1962–66; Sen. Lectr in Anat., 1966–74; Reader in Anat., 1974–75. Symington Prize, British Anatomical Soc., 1966. *Publications:* A Manual of Human Anatomy, Vol. 5: The Central Nervous System (with J. T. Aitken and J. Z. Young), 1967; papers on the nervous system in Brain Res., Jl of Comp. Neurol., Neuroscience and Neurocytology. *Recreations:* Mozart, Wagner and language: the deification of the unspeakable.

**WEBSTER, Leslie Elizabeth**, FSA; Keeper, Department of Prehistory and Europe, British Museum, 2003–07; *b* 8 Nov. 1943; *d* of James Lancelot Dobson and Elizabeth Marjorie Dobson (*née* Dickenson); *m* 1966, William Ian Webster; one *s* two *d*. *Educ:* Central Newcastle High Sch.; Westfield Coll., Univ. of London (Open Exhibnr; BA 1st Cl. Hons 1964). British Museum: Asst Keeper, Dept of British and Medieval Antiquities, 1964–69; Asst Keeper, 1969–85, Dep. Keeper, 1985–2002, Dept of Medieval and Later Antiquities, subseq. Dept of Medieval and Modern Europe; Actg Keeper, Dept of Medieval and Modern Europe, 2002–03. Hon. Vis. Prof. (formerly Vis. Prof.), Inst. of Archaeol., UCL, 2002–. Chair, Res. Adv. Panel, Staffs Hoard, 2011–14; Member: Adv. Panel, NHMF, 2012–; Reviewing Cttee for the Export of Works of Art, 2013–. Pres., Soc. for Medieval Archaeol., 2007–10; Vice-Pres., Royal Archaeol. Inst., 2007–12. UK rep., Koordinierend Ausschuss der Internationalen Arbeitsgemeinschaft für Sachsenforschung, 1986–99. FSA 1973. *Publications:* (ed) Aspects of Production and Style in Dark Age Metalwork, 1982; (jtly) The Golden Age of Anglo-Saxon Art 966–1066, 1984; (with J. Backhouse) The Making of England: Anglo-Saxon art and culture AD 700–900, 1991; (ed with M. Brown) The Transformation of the Roman World, 1997; (ed jtly) Form and Order in the Anglo-Saxon World AD 600–1100, 2009; (ed with J. Roberts) Anglo-Saxon Traces, 2011; Anglo-Saxon Art: a new history, 2012; The Franks Casket, 2012; (ed with A. Reynolds) Early Medieval Art and Archaeology in the Northern World, 2013; contrib. numerous articles to learned jls and chapters in monographs, on Anglo-Saxon material culture. *Recreations:* books, music, walking, cooking, France, whistling. *Address:* c/o Department of Prehistory and Europe, British Museum, Great Russell Street, WC1B 3DG.

**WEBSTER, Marion Frances;** *see* Sinclair, M. F.

**WEBSTER, Ven. Martin Duncan;** Archdeacon of Harlow, 2009–17; *b* Hornchurch, 1952; *m* Vicky; three *s*. *Educ:* Nottingham Univ. (BSc 1974); Lincoln Theol Coll. Ordained deacon, 1978, priest, 1979; Asst Curate, St Peter and St Michael's, Thundersley, 1978–81; Asst Curate, 1981–82, Team Vicar, 1982–86, Canvey Island Team Ministry; Vicar, All Saints, Nazeing, 1986–99; Rural Dean, Harlow, 1988–99; Team Rector, Holy Cross, Waltham Abbey, 1999–2009. Hon. Canon, Chelmsford Cathedral, 2000–09. *Recreations:* oil and acrylic landscape painting, coarse fishing, walking. *Address:* 22 Ashlands, Ford, Salisbury SP4 6DY. *T:* 07814 154572. *E:* m.webster609@btinternet.com.

**WEBSTER, Maj. Michael;** *see* Webster, R. M. O.

**WEBSTER, Patrick;** a Chairman, Industrial, then Employment, Tribunals, Cardiff Region, 1965–2000 (full-time Chairman, 1976–93); a Recorder, 1972–93; *b* 6 Jan. 1928; *s* of late Francis Glyn Webster and Ann Webster; *m* 1955, Elizabeth Knight; two *s* four *d*. *Educ:* Swansea Grammar Sch.; Rockwell Coll., Eire; St Edmund's Coll., Ware; Downing Coll., Cambridge (BA). Called to Bar, Gray's Inn, 1950. Practised at Bar, in Swansea, 1950–75; Chm., Medical Appeals Tribunal (part-time), 1971–75. *Recreations:* listening to music, watching rowing and sailing. *Address:* Langland, 24 Maillard's Haven, Penarth, South Glam CF64 5RF. *T:* (029) 2070 4758. *Clubs:* Penarth Yacht; Beechwood (Swansea).

**WEBSTER, Paul;** film producer; Director, Shoebox Films, since 2011; *b* 19 Sept. 1952. Co-Dir, Osiris Film, London, 1979–81; Founder, Palace Pictures, 1982–88; launched Working Title Films, LA, 1990–92; Head of Prodn, Miramax Films, 1995–97 (films incl. The English Patient, Welcome to Sarajevo, Wings of the Dove); Head of Film Div., Channel 4, subseq. Chief Exec., FilmFour Ltd, 1998–2002; Film Producer, Kudos Pictures, 2004–11. Producer: The Tall Guy, 1988; Drop Dead Fred, 1990; Bob Roberts, 1992; Romeo is Bleeding, 1993; Little Odessa, 1994; The Pallbearer, 1995; Gridlock'd, 1996; The Yards, 1998; Pride and Prejudice, 2005; Atonement, 2007; Eastern Promises, 2008; Crimson Wing, 2009; Brighton Rock, 2010; Salmon Fishing in the Yemen, Anna Karenina, 2012; Hummingbird, 2013; Locke, 2014; Pan, 2015; Executive Producer: The Motorcycle Diaries, 2004; Miss Pettigrew Lives for a Day, 2008; God's Own Country, 2017. Member: UK Film Council, 2000–03; BAFTA; Acad. of Motion Picture Arts and Scis; Producers Guild of America.

**WEBSTER, Paul;** *see* Webster, J. P. G.

**WEBSTER, Paul Frederick;** Editor, The Observer, since 2018 (Deputy Editor, 1996–2018); *b* London, 20 Aug. 1954; *s* of Peter and Barbara Webster; *m* Louise Phillips; two *d*. *Educ:* Poly. of North London (BSc Sociol. 1978); Birkbeck Coll., Univ. of London (MSc Politics and Sociol. 1979). Porter, Elizabeth Garret Anderson Hosp., 1972–75; Subed., Morning Star, 1979–84; Asst Ed., Marxism Today, 1979–84; Subed., Financial Weekly, 1984–85; Business Chief Subed., Sunday Times, 1985–86; The Guardian: Foreign Subed., 1986–89; Foreign Ed., 1989–94; Home Ed., 1994–96. *Address:* The Observer, Kings Place, 90 York Way, N1 9GU. *T:* (020) 3353 4744. *E:* Paul.Webster@observer.co.uk.

**WEBSTER, Philip George;** journalist, author and political consultant; Assistant Editor, and Editor, Red Box bulletin, The Times, 2015–16; *b* 2 June 1949; *s* of Bertie and Eva Webster. *Educ:* Rockland St Mary Primary Sch.; County GS; Wymondham Coll.; Harlow Coll. (NCTJ Cert.). Eastern Counties Newspapers, 1967–73; The Times: Parly Reporter, 1973–81; Pol Reporter, 1981–86; Chief Pol Correspondent, 1986–93; Pol Ed., 1993–2010; Ed., digital edns, 2010–14. *Publications:* Keelan: the story of a goalkeeper, 1979; Inside Story: politics, intrigue and treachery from Thatcher to Brexit, 2016. *Recreations:* golf, ski-ing, cricket, football, bridge. *Address:* 4 St Georges Square, Narrow Street, E14 8DL. *T:* 07774 617815. *Clubs:* Richmond Golf; Eaton Golf; Andrew Robson Bridge.

**WEBSTER, Maj. (Richard) Michael (Otley);** Secretary, The Royal Hampshire Regiment Trust, 2004–06; one of HM Body Guard, Honourable Corps of Gentlemen-at-Arms, 1993–2012 (Standard Bearer, 2010–12); *b* 11 Aug. 1942; *s* of late Brig. Frederick Richard Webster and Beryl Helena Sellars (*née* Otley); *m* 1971, Joanna Gay Enid Simpson, *d* of Lt-Col R. H. O. Simpson, DSO; two *s*. *Educ:* Charterhouse; RMA, Sandhurst. Commnd RA, 1962; 1 RHA, Germany and Aden, 1963–66; Army Staff Coll., 1975; CO, King's Troop, RHA, 1976–78. United Racecourses, 1979–96; Clerk of the Course: Kempton Park, 1980–96; Lingfield Park, 1986–87; Epsom, 1988–95; Chester, 2001–03; Clerk of the Course and Manager, Bangor-on-Dee, 1996–2003. Member: Horseracing Adv. Council, 1987–90; Nat. Jt Pitch Council, 2000–03. *Recreations:* cricket, racing, shooting, Soay sheep. *Address:* Coopers Farm, Hartley Wespall, Hook, Hants RG27 0BQ. *Club:* Army and Navy.

**WEBSTER, Robert;** Chief Executive, South West Yorkshire Partnership NHS Foundation Trust, since 2016; *b* Barrow-in-Furness, 26 Sept. 1968; *s* of Robert and Beryl Webster; *m* 2000, Jane Grace; one *s* one *d*. *Educ:* Newcastle Univ. (BSc Hons Stats 1987). Department of Health: Asst Statistician, NHS Dentistry, 1990–92; Asst Statistician and Section Hd, Medical Workforce Planning, 1992–93; Statistician and Section Hd, Corporate Analysis Team, 1994–96, Waiting, Patient's Charter and League Tables, 1996–97; Section Hd, Acute Services, 1998, Public Expenditure Team, 1998–2000; Nat. Dep. Dir, Gen. Medical Services, 2000–02; Nat. Dir, Primary Care Services, 2002–03; Prog. Dir, Primary Care Contracts, 2003–04; Nat. Dir, Workforce Capacity, 2004–06; Dir, Prime Minister's Delivery Unit, Cabinet Office, 2006–07; Chief Executive: NHS Calderdale, 2007–11; Leeds Community Healthcare NHS Trust, 2011–14; NHS Confedn, 2014–16. Vis. Prof., Leeds Beckett Univ., 2014–. Hon. Fellow, Queen's Nursing Inst. Trustee, Leeds Mencap, 2000–10. Hon. FRCGP 2016. *Recreations:* music, literature, gigs, food, travel, running, record shops, being a servant to my two children. *Address:* South West Yorkshire Partnership NHS Foundation Trust, Fieldhead, Ouchthorpe Lane, Wakefield WF1 3SP. *Club:* Royal Society of Medicine.

**WEBSTER, Prof. Robert Gordon**, FRS 1989; Professor of Virology and Molecular Biology, St Jude Children's Research Hospital, Memphis, USA, until 2015, now Emeritus; *b* 5 July 1932; *s* of Robert Duncan Webster and Mollie Sherriffs; *m* 1957, Marjorie Freegard; two *s* one *d*. *Educ:* Otago Univ., NZ (BSc, MSc); Australian Nat. Univ., Canberra (PhD). Virologist, NZ Dept of Agric., 1958–59; Postdoctoral Fellow, Sch. of Public Health, Univ. of Michigan, Ann Arbor (Fulbright Schol.), 1962–63; Res. Fellow, then Fellow, Dept of Microbiology, John Curtin Med. Sch., ANU, 1964–67; Associate Mem., then Mem., Dept of Virology and Molecular Biol., 1968–88, apptd Head of Dept and Rose Marie Thomas Prof., 1988, St Jude Children's Res. Hosp. Fogarty Internat. Sen. Fellow, Nat. Inst. for Med. Res., MRC, London, 1978–79. Mem., Nat. Acad. of Sci., USA, 1998. Hon. DSc St Andrews, 2015. *Publications:* contribs on influenza viruses etc to learned jls, incl. Virology, Nature, and Cell. *Recreations:* gardening, sea-fishing, walking. *Address:* Department of Infectious Diseases, St Jude Children's Research Hospital, 262 Danny Thomas Place, Memphis, TN 38105–3678, USA. *T:* (901) 5953400. *Club:* Royal Society of Medicine.

**WEBSTER, Prof. Robin Gordon MacLennan**, OBE 1999; RSA 2008 (ARSA 1995); RIBA; FRIAS; Partner, cameronwebster architects, since 2005; Professor of Architecture, Scott Sutherland School of Architecture, Robert Gordon University, Aberdeen, 1984–2004; *b* 24 Dec. 1939; *s* of Gordon Webster and Sheila Webster; *m* 1st, 1967, Katherine Crichton (*d* 2003); one *s* two *d*; 2nd, 2011, Pauline Lawrence. *Educ:* Glasgow Acad.; Rugby Sch.; St John's Coll., Cambridge (MA); University Coll., London (MA Arch). ARIBA 1967; FRIAS 1996. Partner, Spence & Webster, 1972–84; Principal, Robin Webster Associates, 1984–2004. Comr, Royal Fine Art Commn for Scotland, 1990–98. Chm., Alexander Thomson Soc., 2007–13; Trustee: Glasgow City Heritage Trust, 2006–13; Scottish Stained Glass Trust, 2015–. Pres., RIAS, 2018–. *Publications:* Stonecleaning, and the nature, soiling and decay mechanisms of stone, 1992. *Recreations:* looking at buildings, drawing. *Address:* 7 Walmer Crescent, Glasgow G51 1AT. *T:* 07970 165762. *E:* robin.webster@mac.com.

**WEBSTER, Stephen,** MBE 2013; designer of fine and silver jewellery; Founder and Creative Director, Stephen Webster Ltd, since 1989; Director, Garrard, since 2007; *b* Gravesend, 13 Aug. 1959; *m* 1998, Anastasia Vatnitsky; two *d*. *Educ:* Medway Coll. of Design. Established and ran jewellery studio and retail venture for Silverhorn Jeweller, Santa Barbara, Calif, 1986–89. Hon. MA Univ. of Creative Arts, 2007. Hon. Liveryman, City of London, 2009. British Luxury Jeweller of Year, 2000, 2001, 2003, 2005, Jewellery Designer of Year, 1997, 1999, 2006, Retail Jeweller. *Publications:* Goldstruck: a life shaped by jewellery, 2016. *Address:* 24 Albemarle Street, W1S 4HT. *T:* 0845 539 1800, 0845 539 1849. *E:* info@stephenwebster.com

**WEBSTER, Toby Crawford Gordon;** Founding Director, The Modern Institute, since 1997; *b* Glasgow, 4 Dec. 1968; *s* of Martyn and Shery Webster; *m* 2007, April; one *s* two *d*. *Educ:* Glasgow Sch. of Art (BA 1st Cl. Hons 1993). Mem. Cttee, Transmission Gall., 1995–97; Gall. Manager and Curator, Centre for Contemporary Arts, Glasgow, 1996–98. Board Member: Grizedale Arts, 2004–08; Common Guild, 2006–08. Hon. DLitt Glasgow Sch. of Art, 2015. *Publications:* My Head is on Fire but My Heart is Full of Love, 2002;

Strange I've Seen that Face Before, 2006. *Recreations:* walking, sailing, ski-ing, reading, raising children, talking to varied people, collecting art and looking at it. *Address:* The Modern Institute, 14–20 Osborne Street, Glasgow G1 5QN. *T:* (0141) 248 3711, *Fax:* (0141) 552 5988. *E:* mail@themoderninstitute.com.

**WECHSLER, David Keith;** Chief Executive, London Borough of Croydon, 1993–2007; *b* 17 June 1946; *s* of late Bernard James Victor Wechsler and Kathleen Nora Wechsler (*née* Ramm); *m* 1968, Muriel-Anne (Polly) Stuart; one *s* one *d*. *Educ:* Sloane Sch., Chelsea; Leicester Univ. (BA Social Sci.). London Borough of Croydon: grad. trainee, 1970–72; Corporate Planner, 1972–79; Hd, Exec. Office, 1979–87; Dep. Chief Exec., 1987–91; Dir, Econ. and Strategic Develt, 1991–93. Director: S London TEC, 1993–99; Croydon Business Venture, 1993–2007. Chm., Emergency Planning Sub-cttee, London Local Authorities, 2002–07. Dep. Regl Returning Officer, EP elections, 2004. Dir, London Mozart Players, 2007–16. *Publications:* articles on corporate planning and local govt mgt in specialist jls. *Recreations:* sailing, music, swimming, making ice cream.

**WEDDERBURN, Sir Andrew John Alexander O.;** *see* Ogilvy-Wedderburn.

**WEDELL, Prof. (Eberhard Arthur Otto) George;** Professor of Communications Policy, University of Manchester, 1983–92, Professor Emeritus since 1992; Vice President, European Institute for the Media, 1993–97 (Director, then Director-General, 1983–93); *b* 4 April 1927; *er s* of late Rev. Dr H. Wedell and Gertrude (*née* Bonhoeffer); *m* 1948, Rosemarie (*née* Winckler) (*d* 2010); three *s* one *d*. *Educ:* Cranbrook; London School of Economics (BSc Econ., 1947). Ministry of Education, 1950–58; Sec., Bd for Social Responsibility, Nat. Assembly of Church of England, 1958–60; Dep. Sec., ITA, 1960–61, Secretary, 1961–64; Prof. of Adult Educn and Dir of Extra-Mural Studies, Manchester Univ., 1964–75; Vis. Prof. of Employment Policy, Manchester Business Sch., 1975–83; Head, Employment Policy Div., European Commn, 1973–82. Emeritus Fellow, Leverhulme Trust, 1994–96. Contested (L) Greater Manchester West, 1979, (L-SDP Alliance) Greater Manchester Central, 1984, European Parly elections; Chm., British Liberals in EEC, 1980–82; Vice-President: Greater Manchester Liberal Party, 1984–88; EC-ACP Cultural Foundn, 1992–94. Chairman: Wyndham Place Trust, 1983–2001; Beatrice Hankey Foundn, 1984–2001; Christians and the Future of Europe, 1997–99. Director, Royal Exchange Theatre Company, 1968–89, Hon. Mem., 1989. Patron, Mosscare Housing Assoc., 1998–. FRSA; FRTS. Hon. MEd Manchester, 1968; Dr *hc* Internat. Journalistics Inst., Kazakhstan, 1994; Hon. DSocSc LSE, 2017. Lord of the Manor of Clotton Hoofield in the County Palatine of Chester. Letters Patent of Armorial Ensigns, 1997. Chevalier de l'Ordre des Arts et des Lettres (France), 1989; Verdienstkreuz (1 Klasse) des Verdienstordens (Germany), 1991; Comdr, Order of Merit (Portugal), 1993. *Publications:* The Use of Television in Education, 1963; Broadcasting and Public Policy, 1968; (with H. D. Perraton) Teaching at a Distance, 1968; (ed) Structures of Broadcasting, 1970; (with R. Glatter) Study by Correspondence, 1971; Correspondence Education in Europe, 1971; Teachers and Educational Development in Cyprus, 1971; (ed) Education and the Development of Malawi, 1973; (with E. Katz) Broadcasting in the Third World, 1977 (Nat. Assoc. of Educational Broadcasters of USA Book of the Year Award, 1978); (with G. M. Luyken and R. Leonard) Mass Communications in Western Europe, 1985; (ed) Making Broadcasting Useful, 1986; (with G. M. Luyken) Media in Competition, 1986; (ed and contrib.) Europe 2000: what kind of television?, 1988; (with P. Crookes) Radio 2000, 1991; (with R. Rocholl) Vom Segen des Glaubens, 1995 (trans. as A Memoir of Troubled Times, 2008); (ed and contrib.) No Discouragement, 1997; (with B. Luckham) Television at the Crossroads, 2001; A Post-War Half Century, 2012; The Samuel Meyer of Hanover Connection, 2015; contrib. Oxford DNB; general editor, Media Monographs, 1985–93. *Recreations:* gardening, theatre, reading. *Address:* 18 Cranmer Road, Manchester M20 6AW. *T:* (0161) 445 5106; Vigneau, Lachapelle, 47350 Seyches, France. *T:* (5) 53838871. *Club:* Athenæum.

**WEDGWOOD,** family name of **Baron Wedgwood**.

**WEDGWOOD,** 5th Baron *cr* 1942, of Barlaston; **Antony John Wedgwood;** *b* London, 31 Jan. 1944; *s* of late Dr John Wedgwood, CBE, FRCP and Margaret Webb Wedgwood (*née* Mason); *S* cousin, 2014; *m* 1970, Angela Margaret Mary, *d* of Dr Ernest Donald Page; one *s* two *d*. *Educ:* Marlborough Coll.; Trinity Coll., Cambridge (BA 1965; MA 1970). With Peat, Marwick, Mitchell & Co., later KPMG, 1966–2001 (Partner, 1981–2001). Member: Financial Reporting Review Panel, 2001–07; various professional cttees of Auditing Practices Bd, ICAEW. Trustee, Historic Churches Preservation Trust and Nat. Churches Trust, 2002–12. *Publications:* (jtly) A Guide to the Financial Services Act 1986, 1986; Tom Wedgwood of Waterloo, 2018. *Recreations:* reading, travel, old cars and wirelesses. *Heir:* s Major the Hon. Josiah Thomas Antony Wedgwood, RAMC, *b* 20 April 1978. *Address:* 10 Milner Place, N1 1TN. *Club:* Athenæum.

**WEDGWOOD, Sir Ralph (Nicholas),** 4th Bt *cr* 1942, of Etruria, Co. Stafford; PhD; Professor of Philosophy, University of Southern California, since 2012; *b* Vancouver, 10 Dec. 1964; *s* of Sir (Hugo) Martin Wedgwood, 3rd Bt and of Alexandra Mary, *er d* of Late Judge Alfred Gordon Clark; *S* father, 2010. *Educ:* Westminster Sch.; Magdalen Coll., Oxford (BA); King's Coll. London (MPhil); Cornell Univ. (PhD 1994). Asst Prof. of Philos., 1995–99, Associate Prof. of Philos., 1999–2002, MIT; Lectr in Philos., 2002–07, Prof. of Philos., 2007–11, Univ. of Oxford; Fellow, Merton Coll., Oxford, 2002–11. Visiting Research Fellow: Princeton Univ., 2005, 2018; Hebrew Univ. of Jerusalem, 2008; ANU, 2010; All Souls Coll., Oxford, 2018. Dist. Res. Prof., Univ. of Birmingham, 2013–17. *Publications:* The Nature of Normativity, 2007; The Value of Rationality, 2017; articles in learned philosophical jls. *Recreations:* hill-walking, music. *Heir:* uncle (John) Julian Wedgwood [*b* 17 June 1936; *m* 1961, Sheila Mary, *d* of late George Robert Meade; three *s*]. *Address:* School of Philosophy, University of Southern California, 3709 Trousdale Parkway, Los Angeles, CA 90089–0451, USA. *E:* wedgwood@usc.edu.

**WEDZICHA, Prof. Jadwiga Anna, (Wisia),** MD; FRCP, FMedSci, FERS; Professor of Respiratory Medicine, National Heart and Lung Institute, Imperial College London, since 2014; Honorary Consultant Physician, Royal Brompton Hospital, since 2014; *b* 17 Sept. 1953; *d* of Karol and Irena Wedzicha. *Educ:* Somerville Coll., Oxford (BA 1975); St Bartholomew's Hosp. Med. Coll., London Univ. (MB BS 1978; MD 1985). FRCP 1994. Consultant Physician, London Chest Hosp., 1988–96; Reader in Respiratory Medicine, 1996–2000, Prof. of Respiratory Medicine, 2000–05, Bart's and The London, Queen Mary's Sch. of Medicine and Dentistry; Prof. of Respiratory Medicine, UCL, 2005–14. Hon. Consultant Physician, Royal Free Hospital NHS Trust, 2005–14. Sen. Investigator, NIHR, 2011–. European Respiratory Society: Guidelines Dir, 2009–12; Chair, Pubns Cttee, 2010–14. Clinical Lead, Home Oxygen Services, England, 2009–13. Ed. in chief, Thorax, 2002–10; Ed., American Jl of Respiratory and Critical Care Medicine, 2015–. FMedSci 2013; FERS 2014; Fellow, American Thoracic Soc., 2018. *Publications:* (ed with M. Pearson) Chronic Obstructive Pulmonary Disease: critical debates, 2003; (ed with F. J. Martinez) Chronic Obstructive Pulmonary Disease Exacerbations, 2008; papers in New England Jl of Medicine, BMJ, American Jl of Respiratory and Critical Care Medicine, Thorax, Chest. *Recreations:* gardening, tennis, music. *Address:* National Heart and Lung Institute, Imperial College London, Guy Scadding Building, Dovehouse Street, SW3 6LY. *T:* (020) 7594 7947. *E:* j.wedzicha@imperial.ac.uk.

**WEEDEN, John,** CB 2003; a Recorder, 2012–14; *b* 21 June 1949; *s* of Denis Claude Weeden and Winifred Marion Weeden; *m* 1971, Marjanne Dita De Boer; three *s* two *d*. *Educ:* Brighton Coll.; Univ. of Bristol (LLB Hons). SSC 1973. Articled to Griffith Smith, Brighton, 1971–73, Asst Solicitor, 1973–74; joined RAF Legal Br. as Flight Lieut, 1974; worked in UK and Europe, undertaking court martial prosecutions and gen. legal work involving administrative, internat. and operational law; Deputy Director: Cyprus, 1984–87; Germany, 1991–92; Legal Services (RAF), MoD, 1992–97; Dir of Legal Services (RAF) and RAF Prosecuting Authy, MoD, 1997–2002; retd in rank of Air Vice Marshal. Comr, Criminal Cases Rev. Commn, 2002–12; Adjudicator, Solicitors Regulation Authy, 2008–13; Panel Chair, Conduct Cttees, Nursing and Midwifery Council, 2012–. Trustee, RAF Benevolent Fund, 2004–08. *Recreations:* golf, photography, cars.

**WEEDS, John Ian;** Head Teacher, Cranbrook School, since 2012; *b* Horsham, W Sussex, 21 Oct. 1962; *s* of Mike and Barbara Weeds; *m* 1990, Sarah Louise Turner; three *s*. *Educ:* Collyer's Sch., Horsham; Pembroke Coll., Cambridge (BA 1986); Durham Univ. (PGCE); Nottingham Univ. (MPhil); Roehampton Univ. (EdD 2014). Teacher of Classics: Hampton Sch., 1987–90; Bolton Sch., 1990–93; Hd of Classics and Housemaster, Bedford Sch., 1993–2000; Dep. Hd, Slough GS, 2000–06; Principal, Reading Sch., 2006–12. Mem., Guild of Mercers' Scholars. *Recreations:* travel writing, banjo or guitar according to mood, children's literature, philosophy. *Address:* School House, Cranbrook School, Waterloo Road, Cranbrook, Kent TN17 3JD. *T:* (01580) 715638. *E:* the_weeds@btinternet.com. *Club:* Lansdowne.

**WEEDY, Maj.-Gen. Michael Anthony C.;** *see* Charlton-Weedy.

**WEEKES, Anesta Glendora;** QC 1999; a Recorder, since 2000; *b* 10 June 1955; *d* of late Joseph Weekes and of Sarah Weekes. *Educ:* Keele Univ. (BA Hons). Called to the Bar, Gray's Inn, 1981, Bencher, 2003; in practice at the Bar, specialising in criminal law and public inquiries; Counsel to Stephen Lawrence Inquiry, 1999; Asst Recorder, 1999–2000. Arbitrator (part-time), Commonwealth Secretariat Arbitral Tribunal, 2000–. Dir, ENO, 2001–09. *Recreations:* music, opera, dance, travel books. *Address:* 33 Bedford Row, WC1R 4JH.

**WEEKES, Sir Everton (de Courcy),** KCMG 1995; GCM; OBE; international bridge player; former international cricketer; *b* Bridgetown, Barbados, 26 Feb. 1925. *Educ:* St Leonard's Sch., Bridgetown. First class début, 1944, for Barbados; played for Barbados, 1944–64 (Captain), for West Indies, 1947–58 (48 Test matches; 15 centuries, incl. 5 double centuries in England, 1950); on retirement from Test cricket, held world record for five consecutive centuries (*v* England and India), 1948–49, and for seven consecutive half-centuries. *Publications:* (with Hilary McD. Beckles) Mastering the Craft, 2007. *Address:* c/o West Indies Cricket Board of Control, Letchworth Complex, The Garrison, St Michael, Barbados, West Indies.

**WEEKES, Mark Vincent; His Honour Judge Weekes;** a Circuit Judge, since 2019; *b* York, 2 Nov. 1974; *s* of Tony Weekes and Bríd Coady Weekes; *m* 2010, Kelly Marie Edgson Wright; two *s*. *Educ:* Bootham Sch., York; Trinity Coll., Oxford (BA Hons 1997; MA); Univ. of Westminster (CPE 1998); Inns of Court Sch. of Law. Called to the Bar, Lincoln's Inn, 1999; in practice as barrister, specialising in criminal law, 1999–2019; a Recorder, 2016–19. *Recreations:* cricket, Rugby, cooking, family, procrastination via internet, time wasting. *Address:* Canterbury Combined Court, Law Courts, Chaucer Road, Canterbury CT1 1ZA.

**WEEKES, Thomas Charles;** QC 2016; *b* London, 18 May 1971; *s* of Brian Charles Mark Weekes and Ann Shaw Weekes. *Educ:* Broomfield Comprehensive Sch.; Woodhouse Sixth Form Coll.; New Coll., Oxford (BA 1st Cl. Hons PPE); City Univ. (DipLaw); Inns of Court Sch. of Law. Called to the Bar, Inner Temple, 1995; in practice as barrister, specialising in property law, 1997–. *Publications:* Property Notices, 2008, 2nd edn 2011; (jtly) Rights of Light, 3rd edn 2015. *Recreations:* playing football, food and wine, travel. *Address:* Landmark Chambers, 180 Fleet Street, EC4A 2HG. *T:* (020) 7430 1221, *Fax:* (020) 7421 6060. *E:* tweekes@landmarkchambers.co.uk. *Club:* Home House.

**WEEKS, Gillian Margaret, (Mrs Tony Dean),** OBE 2011; Owner and Director, Dean Weeks Consultants Ltd, since 2013; *b* Hull, 29 July 1955; *d* of Fred and Mavis Weeks; *m* 2002, Tony Dean; one step *s* one step *d*. *Educ:* St Hilda's Sch., Whitby; Hull Coll. of Technol. (OND Scis 1973); Hull Coll. of Higher Educn (HNC Biol. 1980); John Moores Univ., Liverpool (LLB Hons 1996). CEnv 2006. Waste Regulation Site Inspector, Tyne and Wear CC, 1980–83; Waste Regulation Licensing Officer, Humberside CC, 1983–85; Regulation and Envmt Dir, Cleanaway Ltd, 1985–2006; Regulatory Affairs Dir, Veolia Envmtl Services, 2006–13; Interim Policy Dir, Envmtl Services Assoc., 2010–11. Mem. Bd, Envmt Agency, 2014–. Mem., UK Envmtl Law Assoc., 1997–. Chair, Trustees, The Welcome (Knutsford) Ltd. Fellow, Industry and Parliament Trust, 2000. FCIWM 2007. *Recreations:* travel, ski-ing, walking. *Address:* 8 Trevone Close, Knutsford, Cheshire WA16 9EJ. *T:* 07740 958358. *E:* gill@deanweeks.co.uk.

**WEEKS, His Honour John Henry;** QC 1983; a Circuit Judge, 1991–2006; *b* 11 May 1938; *s* of Henry James and Ada Weeks; *m* 1970, Caroline Mary, *d* of Lt Col J. F. Ross; one *s* two *d*. *Educ:* Cheltenham Coll.; Worcester Coll., Oxford (MA). Called to Bar, Inner Temple, 1963, Bencher, 1996; in practice in Chancery, 1963–91. *Publications:* Limitation of Actions, 1989. *Recreation:* walking the dog. *Address:* Western Cottage, The Green, Calbourne, Isle of Wight PO30 4JG. *T:* (01983) 555101.

**WEEKS, Wilfred John Thomas,** OBE 2006; Chairman, European Public Affairs, Weber Shandwick, 2002–11; *b* 8 Feb. 1948; *s* of late William Weeks and Kathleen Weeks (*née* Penhale); *m* 1981, Anne Veronica Harrison; three *s*. *Educ:* Shebbear Coll.; KCL (BD Hons). Private Sec. to Rt Hon. Edward Heath, 1976–80; Jt Founder, GJW Govt Relns, 1980–2000; Chm., BSMG UK, 2000–02. Non-exec. Dir, Helical Bar, 2005–12. Chm., Friends of the Tate, 1990–99, Mem. Council, Tate Britain, 2000–03; Chairman: Dulwich Picture Gall., 2000–06 (Trustee, 1994–2006); Heritage Educn Trust, 2005–08; Spitalfields Fest., 2006–08; British Future, 2012–; Edward Heath Charitable Foundn, 2013–15; Trustee: LAMDA, 2000–10 (Chm. Develt Bd, 2002–06); Trust for London (formerly City Parochial Foundn and Trust for London), 2007–18; Buccleuch Living Heritage Trust, 2011–; Prison Advice and Care Trust, 2011–; Resource for London, 2011–; Gainsborough's House, 2014– (Chm., Develt Bd, 2015–); Gov., Charterhouse, 2016– (Chm., Develt Bd, 2013–18). Hon. Treas., Hansard Soc., 1996–2007. Goodman Award, Arts and Business, 2004. *Recreation:* gardening. *Address:* 50A Clapham Common North Side, SW4 0AB. *Club:* Garrick.

**WEEPLE, Edward John,** CB 2004; Chairman, Board of Management, Edinburgh's Telford College, 2007–10 (Member, 2003–07); Head of Lifelong Learning Group, Scottish Executive Enterprise, Transport and Lifelong Learning (formerly Enterprise and Lifelong Learning) Department, 1999–2003; *b* 15 May 1945; *s* of Edward Weeple and Mary Catherine (*née* McGrath); *m* 1970, Joan (*née* Shaw); three *s* one *d*. *Educ:* St Aloysius' Coll., Glasgow; Glasgow Univ. (MA). Asst Principal, Min. of Health, 1968–71; Private Sec. to Minister of Health, 1971–73; Principal: DHSS, 1973–78; Scottish Econ. Planning Dept, 1978–80; Assistant Secretary: SHHD, 1980–85; Dept of Agriculture and Fisheries for

Scotland, 1985–90; Under Sec., Scottish Office Industry Dept, 1990–95; Hd of Further and Higher Educn, Trng and Sci., then Lifelong Learning, Gp, Scottish Office Educn and Industry Dept, 1995–99. First Minister's Assessor, 2004–15, Trustee, 2015–, Carnegie Trust for Univs of Scotland; non-exec. Dir, Interactive Univ., 2005–09. Mem., Court, Heriot-Watt Univ., 2004–10 (Chm., Audit Cttee, 2009–10); Mem., Bd of Mgt, Garvald Edinburgh, 2009–10; Special Advr, Paisley Univ., 2005–07. Sec., Goodison Gp in Scotland, 2003–05. *Recreations:* saxophone, Edinburgh Concert Band (Sec., 2013–), hillwalking, film group. *Address:* 19 Lauder Road, Edinburgh EH9 2JG. *T:* (0131) 668 1150.

**WEERERATNE, (Rufina) Aswini;** QC 2015; *b* Colombo, Sri Lanka, 6 June 1963; *d* of Rienzie and Elaine Weereratne; *m* 1997, David Pallister; one *s. Educ:* Ursuline Convent Sch., Wimbledon; Sussex Univ. (BSc Exptl Psychol.); City Univ. (DipLaw); Inns of Court Sch. of Law; Sch. of Oriental and African Studies, Univ. of London (LLM Internat. Human Rights Law). Called to the Bar, Gray's Inn, 1986; in practice as a barrister, specialising in mental health law, human rights, and cases relating to vulnerable and mentally disabled people, including historic child abuse. Judge (pt-time) of First-Tier Tribunal (Health, Educn and Social Care Chamber), 2001–. Dep. Chm., Investigative Cttee, Gen. Pharmaceutical Council, 2014–. *Publications:* (jtly) Butterworth's New Law Guide to the Mental Capacity Act 2005, 2008; (Consultant Ed.) Halsbury's Laws of England, Mental Health Vol., 2004, 2012; contrib. articles to jls and the press. *Recreations:* baking bread, singing, playing tennis, a fluffy labradoodle. *Address:* 54 Doughty Street, WC1N 2LS. *T:* (020) 7404 1313, *Fax:* (020) 7404 2283. *E:* a.weereratne@doughtystreet.co.uk.

**WEETCH, Kenneth Thomas;** *b* 17 Sept. 1933; *s* of Kenneth George and Charlotte Irene Weetch; *m* 1961, Audrey Wilson (decd); two *d. Educ:* Newbridge Grammar Sch., Mon; London School of Economics (MSc(Econ)), London Inst. of Educn (DipEd). National Service: Sgt, RAEC, Hong Kong, 1955–57; Walthamstow and Ilford Educn Authorities and Research at LSE, 1957–64; Head of History Dept, Hockerill Coll. of Educn, Bishop's Stortford, 1964–74. Contested (Lab): Saffron Walden, 1970; Ipswich, 1987. MP (Lab) Ipswich, Oct. 1974–1987. PPS to Sec. of State for Transport, 1976–79. Member: Lab Select Cttee on Home Affairs, 1981–83; Select Cttee on Parly Comr for Administration, 1983–87. *Publications:* East Anglia: the great vote robbery, 1987. *Recreations:* walking, reading, watching Association football, playing the piano in pubs, eating junk food. *Club:* Silent Street Labour (Ipswich).

**WEETMAN, Prof. Anthony Peter,** MD, DSc; FRCP, FRCPE; FMedSci; Sir Arthur Hall Professor of Medicine, University of Sheffield, 1991–2016, now Emeritus (Pro-Vice-Chancellor for Medicine, 2008–15); *b* 29 April 1953; *s* of Kenneth Weetman and Evelyn Weetman (*née* Healer); *m* 1982, Sheila Thompson; one *s* one *d. Educ:* Univ. of Newcastle upon Tyne (BMedSci 1974; MB BS 1977; MD 1983; DSc 1991). FRCP 1990; FRCPE 2004. MRC Trng Fellow, Welsh Nat. Sch. of Medicine, 1980–84; MRC Travelling Fellow, NIH, Bethesda, USA, 1984–85; Wellcome Trust Sen. Res. Fellow in Clin. Sci., RPMS and Univ. of Cambridge, 1985–89; Lectr in Medicine, Univ. of Cambridge, 1989–91; Dean, Medical Sch., Univ. of Sheffield, 1999–2008. Hon. Consultant Physician: Hammersmith Hosp., 1986–87; Addenbrooke's Hosp., 1987–91; Northern Gen. Hosp., Sheffield, 1991–2001; Sheffield Teaching Hosps NHS Trust, 2001–15. Chm., UK Healthcare Educn Adv. Cttee, 2011–15. President: British Thyroid Assoc., 2005–08; Assoc. of Physicians, 2015–16; Chm., Medical Schs Council, 2009–13. FMedSci 1998. H. C. Jacobæus Prize, Nordisk Foundn, 2012; Paul Starr Award, American Thyroid Assoc., 2013. *Publications:* Autoimmune Endocrine Disease, 1991; papers on endocrine autoimmunity and disease, esp. concerning the thyroid. *Recreations:* fell walking (Munroist number 2342), squash, ski-ing. *Address:* Faculty of Medicine, Dentistry and Health, Barber House, 387 Glossop Road, Sheffield S10 2HQ. *T:* (0114) 222 8712, *Fax:* (0114) 222 8756. *E:* a.p.weetman@sheffield.ac.uk.

**WEGERIF, Prof. Rupert Boudewijn,** PhD; CPsychol; Professor of Education (2000), University of Cambridge, since 2017; *b* Dartford, 2 Sept. 1959; *s* of Boudewijn Wegerif and Gillian Mary Basil Cochrane; *m* 1998, Julieta Alejandra Pérez Linares; one *s. Educ:* Univ. of Kent (BA 1st Cl. Hons Philosophy with Social Anthropol. 1983); Bristol Univ. (PGCE RE and English 1991); Queen Mary and Westfield Coll., Univ. of London (MSc IT (Dist.) 1992); Open Univ. (PhD Psychol. and educnl Technol. 1996). Res. Fellow, Sch. of Educn, 1995–2001, Sen. Res. Fellow, Faculty of Educn and Lang. Studies, 2001–04, Open Univ.; Reader in Educn, Univ. of Southampton, 2004–06; Prof. of Educn, Univ. of Exeter, 2006–17. *Publications:* (ed jtly) Computers and Talk in the Primary Classroom, 1997; (jtly) Thinking Together: a programme of activities for developing speaking, listening and thinking skills for children aged 8–11, 2000, 2nd edn 2004; (with L. Dawes) Thinking and Learning with ICT: raising achievement in primary classrooms, 2004; (with S. Williams) Radical Encouragement: changing cultures of thinking, 2005; Dialogic, Dialogic and Technology: expanding the space of learning, 2007; Mind-Expanding: teaching for thinking and creativity, 2010; Dialogic: education for the internet age, 2013; (ed jtly) Science Education for Diversity, 2013; (ed jtly) The Routledge International Handbook of Research on Teaching Thinking, 2015; (with N. Phillipson) Dialogic Education: mastering core concepts through thinking together, 2017; (ed jtly) Theory of Teaching Thinking: international perspectives, 2018; contrib. papers to scientific jls incl. Thinking Skills and Creativity, Learning and Instruction, British Educnl Res. *Recreations:* travel, walking, films. *Address:* 5 Cavendish Court, Cavendish Road, Cambridge CB1 3FZ. *T:* (01223) 411696. *E:* rupertwegerif@gmail.com; Faculty of Education, University of Cambridge, 184 Hills Road, Cambridge CB2 8PQ.

**WEGG-PROSSER, Benjamin Charles;** Managing Partner, Global Counsel, since 2011; *b* Paddington, 11 June 1974; *s* of Stephen and Victoria Wegg-Prosser; *m* 2004, Yulia Khabibullina; two *s* one *d. Educ:* Southbank Sch.; Sheffield Univ. (BA Politics 1995). Res. asst, Office of Peter Mandelson, MP, 1995–97; political advr, Cabinet Office, 1997–98; Special Advr, DTI, 1998–99; Communications Manager, Pearson PLC, 1999–2000; Publisher: Slate UK, 2000; Guardian newspaper, 2000–05; Dir, Strategic Communications Unit, Office of the Prime Minister, 2005–07; Dir, Corporate Develt, SUP Media, 2007–10. *Recreations:* cooking, politics, football, travel, running. *Address:* Global Counsel, 5 Welbeck Street, W1G 9YQ. *T:* (020) 3667 6500. *Club:* Soho House.

**WEI,** Baron *cr* 2010 (Life Peer), of Shoreditch in the London Borough of Hackney; **Nathanael Ming-Yan Wei;** Founding Partner, The Shaftesbury Partnership, 2006–10, now Honorary Founding Partner; founding non-executive Director, Manchester China Forum, since 2013; *b* 19 Jan. 1977; *m* Cynthia; two *c. Educ:* Jesus Coll., Oxford. Consultant, McKinsey & Co.; Founder: Teach First, 2002; Future Leaders; Co-founder, Challenge Network; Hd, New Prog. Develt (Ventures), Absolute Return for Kids; Govt Advr on Big Society, Cabinet Office, 2010–11; Advr, Community Foundn Network, 2011–. House of Lords: Chm., All Party Parly Gp on E Asia Business, 2011–15; Vice Chm., All Party Parly Gp on China, 2011–; Mem., EU Internal Mkt Sub-cttee, 2015–. Non-exec. Dir and Chm., Greenacre Properties Ltd; Dir, LJ Real Estate Ltd; Member, Advisory Board: Future Planet Capital; Epic Hostels; Chm., Ninety Ltd. Founder, Diaspora Leadership Prog. Chm., Cons. Friends of the Chinese. Trustee, Asia House, 2011–. Young Global Leader, WEF, 2013. Fellow, Young Foundn. *Address:* House of Lords, SW1A 0PW. *W:* www.natwei.com.

**WEIDMANN, Dr Jens;** President, Deutsche Bundesbank, since 2011; Member, Governing Council, European Central Bank, since 2011; Chairman, Board of Directors, Bank for International Settlements, since 2015; *b* Solingen, Germany, 20 April 1968; *m* Dr Anja; one *s* one *d. Educ:* Univ. de Droit, d'Economie et des Sciences, Aix-Marseilles III and Rheinische Friedrich-Wilhelms Univ., Bonn (BA Econs 1993); Bonn Univ. (PhD 1997). Res. asst, Inst. for Internat. Econ. Policy, Univ. of Bonn, 1994–97; IMF, Washington, 1997–99; Sec. Gen., German Council of Econ. Experts, 1999–2003; Hd, Monetary Policy and Analysis Div. and Dep. Hd, Econs Dept, Deutsche Bundesbank, 2003–06; Hd, Dept for Econ. and Financial Policy, Federal Chancellor's Office, 2006–11; personal rep. of Federal Chancellor preparing for world econ. summits of G8 and G20 countries. Gov., IMF. Member: Steering Cttee, Financial Stability Bd; Bd of Dirs and Steering Cttee, European Systemic Risk Bd. *Address:* Deutsche Bundesbank, Wilhelm-Epstein-Strasse 14, 60431 Frankfurt am Main, Germany. *T:* (69) 95663511, *Fax:* (69) 95663077. *E:* info@bundesbank.de.

**WEIGHILL, Maj. Gen. Robert Peter Mark,** CBE 2012; independent defence and strategic risk consultant, since 2016; Head, Change Design and Delivery Portfolio Office, London Underground, Transport for London, since 2019; *b* London, 5 June 1961; *s* of late Peter Weighill and Rosemary Weighill; *m* 1989, Caroline Louise Payne; one *s* two *d. Educ:* St Neot's Prep. Sch.; Dauntsey's Sch.; RMA Sandhurst; King's Coll. London (MA Internat. Relns (Dist.) 2006); Manchester Business Sch. (Advanced Mgt Achievement Course 2015); Inst. of Dirs (Cert. Co. Direction 2016). Commnd RA, 1981; 2 Field Regt RA, 1983–86; 7th Regt RHA, 1987–89; Platoon Instructor, RMA Sandhurst, 1989–91; acsc 1992–93; SO2 J3 Jt Ops HQ British Forces HK, 1994–95; Batt. Comdr 22 Regt RA, 1996–97; SO1 Chief G3 Ops HQ ARRC, 1998–2000; CO 47th Regt RA, 2000–03; Asst Dir Concept Develt, MoD, 2003–05; RCDS 2006; Dep. Commanding Gen., Min. of Interior Transition Team, Iraq, 2007; Comdr RA 1 (UK) Armoured Div., 2008–09; Hd Jt Plans, Jt Force Comd Naples, NATO, 2010–12; Dir Ops, Operation Unified Protector, Libya, 2011; DCS (Plans), Jt Force Comd Naples, NATO, 2012–15. Hon. Regtl Col, 47th Regt RA, 2013–; Col Comdt, RA, 2017–. Dir, Alpha Integrate Ltd, 2015–. Chm., British Biathlon Union, 2017–. FCMI 2015. NATO Meritorious Service Medal, 2012. Legion of Merit (USA), 2007. *Publications:* (jtly) The Cauldron: NATO's campaign in Libya, 2018; contrib. articles in RUSI Defence. *Recreations:* ski-ing, running, military history.

**WEIGHTMAN, Michael William,** CB 2013; DPhil; FREng; HM Chief Inspector of Nuclear Installations, and Director, Health and Safety Executive, 2005–13; Chief Executive, Office for Nuclear Regulation, 2011–13; *b* 6 Feb. 1949; *s* of William Henry Weightman and Hilda Weightman; *m* 1974, Elizabeth Anne; two *s. Educ:* Lutterworth Grammar Sch.; Univ. of Sussex; Univ. of Bristol. BSc, MSc, DPhil. CEng; MInstP. HM Principal Inspector of Nuclear Installations, 1988; Hd, Nuclear Policy, HSE, 1995; HM Dep. Chief Inspector of Nuclear Installations, 2000–05. Non-exec. Dir, Nat. Nuclear Lab., 2014–. Chm., Potters Bar Rail Crash Investigation Bd, 2002; Hd, IAEA Internat. Fact Finding Mission to Japan on Fukushima Dai-ichi nuclear accident, 2011. MIOM. FREng 2010. *Recreations:* family, Rugby Union, village community, arts. *Club:* Chester Rugby Union Football.

**WEIGHTMAN, Prof. Peter,** PhD; Professor of Physics, University of Liverpool, since 1989; *b* Alfreton, Derbys, 21 Oct. 1944; *s* of Arthur and Gertrude Edith Weightman; *m* 1st, 1974, Anne Susan Kirby (marr. diss. 1993); two *s*; 2nd, 2001, Susan Clare Nobay. *Educ:* Univ. of Keele (BA 1st Cl. Hons Phys and Maths 1967; PhD 1970). Res. Fellow, Phys Dept, Univ. of Essex, 1970–71; University of Liverpool: Lectr, 1971–81, Sen. Lectr, 1981–85, Reader, 1985–89, Dept of Phys; Dep. Dir, 1988–98, Dir, 1998–2001, Interdisciplinary Res. Centre in Surface Sci.; Dir, Grad. Sch. in Engrg and Physical Sci., 1994–98. Fulbright Sen. Res. Scholar, Chem. Dept, Oregon State Univ., 1980–81. Mem. of numerous cttees of UK res. councils, SERC, EPSRC, CCLRC, STFC and MRC; UK Mem., High Technol. Panel, 1993–98, Physical and Engrg Sci. and Technol. Panel, 1999–2000, NATO; European Synchrotron Radiation Facility: Mem., Sci. Adv. Cttee, 1995–97, 1997–99; Mem. Council, 2000–03; Chm., Scientific Steering Cttee, UK Fourth Generation Light Source, 2000–08. Chm., Condensed Matter Physics Div., Inst. of Physics, 2008–. Mem. Council, European Physical Soc., 2007–10. Mott Medal and Prize, Inst. of Physics, 2006; Sen. Prize and John Yarwood Meml Medal, British Vacuum Council, 2011. *Publications:* 300 res. papers in learned jls. *Recreations:* reading history books, listening to music. *Address:* Physics Department, University of Liverpool, Oxford Street, Liverpool L69 3BX. *T:* (0151) 794 3871, *Fax:* (0151) 794 3441. *E:* peterw@liverpool.ac.uk.

**WEILL, Michel Alexandre D.;** *see* David-Weill.

**WEINBERG, Prof. Anton;** solo clarinettist; teacher of music; writer; broadcaster; consultant on personal performance issues; *b* 25 Nov. 1944; *s* of Louis and Gladys Weinberg; *m* 1987, Brenda Teresa Douglas; three *s* one *d. Educ:* Royal Acad. of Music (Associated Bd, Royal Schs of Music Schol.; 1st clarinettist to hold both Hawkes and Solomon prizes; LRAM); 5 yrs study with the late Hans Keller (Arts Council of GB Award). ARCM; ARAM 1987. Prof., GSMD, 1979–86; Prof. of Performance and Communication Skills course, 1983–85; Prof. of Music, Indiana Univ., 1984–90. Artistic Dir, Capitol Prodns Ltd, 1984–87; Music Dir, New Music Prodns, 1984–87; Founding Prof., Nat. Youth Orch. of Spain, 1984–86; Consultant: Jumping Sideways Ltd, 2002–; in woodwind and mouthpiece design, Dawkes Music Ltd, 2002–. Visiting Professor: Nat. Centre of Orchestral Studies, NY; Dartington Internat. Summer Sch. Various lecture progs, BBC Radio 3, 1970–94, incl. writer/presenter, Contrasting Styles of Playing, 1974; writer/presenter, In Short (series), BBC, 1978, 1979; Brahms, Muhlfeld and the Clarinet, BBC, 1983; Mozart and Another Salieri, 1984; The Keller Instinct, Channel 4, 1984–85; BBC broadcast on develt of stylistic personality in music students. Solo clarinettist, Wallfisch/Weinberg Trio, 1974–86. Distinguished Teacher, White House Commn on Presidential Scholars, USA, 1989. Represented UK in first Anglo-American cultural visits to China in 1970s. Cert. of Excellence, White House Commn of Educn, Washington, 1989. *Publications:* Unfinished Sentences, 1987; Clarinet and Saxophone Mouthpieces: what you need to know, 2008; Reshaping Thoughts, 2013; numerous articles in the Listener, Classical Music Mag. and Musical Times, 1970–84. *Recreations:* supporting my wife who is Founder and Chair of United Families and Friends Campaign (Deaths in Custody), art, furniture restoration techniques, travel, cooking, writing, my family. *Address:* Apt 17, 62 Ridgeway, Wimbledon Village, Wimbledon SW19 4RA. *T:* 07951 706687. *E:* anton.weinberg@btinternet.com.

**WEINBERG, Prof. Julius Rolf,** DM; FRCP, FFPH; Vice-Chancellor, Kingston University, 2011–16; *b* 27 Dec. 1954; *s* of Willy Wolfgang Weinberg and Jose Letitia Weinberg; two *s* one *d. Educ:* Queen's Coll., Oxford (BM BCh 1979; MA 1979; DM 1992); MSc London; Open Univ. (MEd 2011). FRCP 2001; FFPH (FFPHM 2002). Lectr and Sen. Registrar, Charing Cross Hosp. Sch. of Medicine, 1984–89; Lectr and Hon. Consultant, Univ. of Zimbabwe Sch. of Medicine, 1989–93; Consultant, WHO Mission to Bosnia, 1993–94; Consultant Epidemiologist, PHLS, 1994–99; City University: Pro Vice-Chancellor (Res.), 1999–2006; Dir, Inst. of Health Scis, 2002–06; Dep. Vice Chancellor, 2006–11; Actg Vice Chancellor, 2009–10. Vis. Prof., of Health Policy, City Univ., 1996–99. Chair, Ofsted, 2017–; Mem. Bd, Ofqual, 2012 (Dep. Chm., 2012–17); Trustee,

London Higher, 2012 (Chm., Access HE, 2012). Principal FHEA, 2014. *Publications:* (jtly) Communicable Disease Control Handbook, 2001, 2nd edn 2005; contrib. peer-reviewed jls on physiol. of shock, internat. outbreak control, modelling hosp. services and health informatics. *Recreations:* pottery, cycling, ski-ing.

**WEINBERG, Sir Mark (Aubrey),** Kt 1987; Chairman: St James's Place Group (formerly J Rothschild Assurance), 1991–2004 (Life President, 2004); *b* 9 Aug. 1931; *s* of Philip and Eva Weinberg; *m* 1st, 1961, Sandra Le Roith (*d* 1978); three *d*; 2nd, 1980, Anouska Hempel; one *s*. *Educ:* King Edward VII Sch., Johannesburg; Univ. of the Witwatersrand (BCom, LLB); London Sch. of Econs (LLM). Called to the Bar, South Africa, 1955. Barrister, S Africa, 1955–61; Man. Dir, Abbey Life Assurance Co., 1961–70; Hambro Life Assurance, subseq. Allied Dunbar Assurance: Man. Dir, 1971–83; Chm., 1984–90; Chm., Life Assce Hldg Corp., 1994–2003. Chairman: Pension Insce Corp. Hldgs, 2006–16; Atlas City Finance; Kernel Associates. Chm., Organizing Cttee, Marketing of Investments Bd, 1985–86; Dep. Chm., Securities and Investment Bd, 1986–90 (Mem., 1985–90). Sen. Advr, Stamford Associates Ltd, 2011–. Trustee, Tate Gall., 1985–92. Hon. Treas., NSPCC, 1983–91. *Publications:* Take-overs and Mergers, 1962, 5th edn 1989. *Recreation:* bridge. *Address:* Spencer House, 27 St James's Place, SW1A 1NR. *T:* (020) 7514 1960. *Clubs:* Army and Navy, Portland, Royal Automobile.

**WEINBERG, Prof. Steven,** PhD; Josey Regental Professor of Science, University of Texas, since 1982; *b* 3 May 1933; *s* of Fred and Eva Weinberg; *m* 1954, Louise Goldwasser; one *d*. *Educ:* Cornell Univ. (AB); Copenhagen Institute for Theoretical Physics; Princeton Univ. (PhD). Instructor, Columbia Univ., 1957–59; Research Associate, Lawrence Berkeley Laboratory, 1959–60; Faculty, Univ. of California at Berkeley, 1960–69; full prof., 1964; on leave: Imperial Coll., London, 1961–62; Loeb Lectr, Harvard, 1966–67; Vis. Prof., MIT, 1967–69; Prof., MIT, 1969–73; Higgins Prof. of Physics, Harvard Univ., and concurrently Senior Scientist, Smithsonian Astrophysical Observatory, 1973–83 (Sen. Consultant, 1983–). Morris Loeb Vis. Prof., Harvard Univ., 1983–; Dir, Jerusalem Winter Sch. of Theoretical Physics, 1983–94. Lectures: Richtmeyer, Amer. Assoc. of Physics Teachers, 1974; Scott, Cavendish Lab., 1975; Silliman, Yale Univ., 1977; Lauritsen, Calif Inst. of Technol., 1979; Bethe, Cornell, 1979; Schild, Texas, 1979; de Shalit, Weizmann Inst., 1979; Henry, Princeton, 1981; Harris, Northwestern, 1981; Cherwell-Simon, Oxford, 1983; Bampton, Columbia, 1983; Einstein, Israel Acad. of Arts and Sciences, 1984; Hilldale, Wisconsin, 1985; Dirac, Cambridge, 1986; Klein, Stockholm, 1989; Brittin, Colorado, 1992; Gibbs, Amer. Math. Soc., 1996; Bochner, Rice, 1997; Witherspoon, Washington, 2001; Messenger, Cornell, 2007; Phi Beta Kappa Oration, Harvard, 2008; Sackler, Niels Bohr Inst., Copenhagen, 2009; Clark, Univ. of Texas at Dallas, 2010. Mem., Science Policy Cttee, Superconducting Supercollider Lab., 1989–93. Mem., Bd of Dirs, Daedalus, 1990–. Fellow, Amer. Acad. of Arts and Scis; Member: US Nat. Acad. of Scis; Amer. Philosophical Soc.; Phil Soc. of Texas (Pres., 1994); IAU; Texas Inst. of Letters; For. Mem., Royal Soc.; Hon. MRIA. Hon. ScD: Knox Coll. 1978; Chicago, 1978; Rochester, 1979; Yale, 1979; City Univ. of New York, 1980; Clark, 1982; Dartmouth Coll., 1984; Columbia, 1990; Salamanca, 1992; Padua, 1992; Barcelona, 1996; Bates Coll., 2002; McGill, 2003; Rensselaer Poly. Inst., 2016; Rockefeller, 2017; Hon. PhD Weizmann Inst., 1985; Hon. DLitt, Washington Coll., 1985. J. R. Oppenheimer Prize, 1973; Heineman Prize in Mathematical Physics, 1977; Amer. Inst. of Physics—US Steel Foundn Science Writing Award, 1977; Elliott Cresson Medal of Franklin Inst., 1979; (jtly) Nobel Prize in Physics, 1979; Madison Medal, Princeton, 1991; US Nat. Medal of Sci., 1991; Gemant Prize, Amer. Inst. of Physics, 1997; Piazz Prize, govts of Sicily and Palermo, 1998; Lewis Thomas Prize, Rockefeller Univ., 1999; Humanist of the Year Award, Amer. Humanist Assoc., 2002; Benjamin Franklin Medal, Amer. Philosophical Soc., 2004; Trotter Prize, Texas A & M Univ., 2008; James Joyce Award, University Coll., Dublin, 2009. Hon. Citizen, Padua, 2007. *Publications:* Gravitation and Cosmology: principles and applications of the general theory of relativity, 1972; The First Three Minutes: a modern view of the origin of the universe, 1977; The Discovery of the Subatomic Particles, 1982; (jtly) Elementary Particles and the Laws of Physics, 1988; Dreams of a Final Theory, 1993; The Quantum Theory of Fields, vol. I, 1995, vol. II, 1996, vol. III, 2000; Facing Up, 2001; Glory & Terror, 2004; Cosmology, 2008; Lake Views, 2009; Lectures on Quantum Mechanics, 2012; To Explain the World: the discovery of modern science, 2015; Third Thoughts, 2018; Lectures on Astrophysics, 2019; numerous articles in learned jls. *Recreation:* reading history. *Address:* Physics Department, University of Texas, Austin, TX 78712, USA. *T:* (512) 4714394. *Clubs:* Saturday (Boston, Mass); Cambridge Scientific (Cambridge, Mass); Headliners, Tuesday (Austin, Texas).

**WEINER, Edmund Simon Christopher;** Deputy Chief Editor, Oxford English Dictionary, 1993–98 and since 2001 (Co-Editor, 1984–93; Principal Philologist, 1998–2001); Supernumerary Fellow, Kellogg College (formerly Rewley House), Oxford, since 1991; *b* 27 Aug. 1950; *s* of late Prof. Joseph Sidney Weiner and Marjorie Winifred (*née* Daw); *m* 1973, Christine Mary Wheeler (changed name by deed poll to Clare Mariella Howard, 2014); two *s* one *d*. *Educ:* Westminster; Christ Church, Oxford (BA Eng. Lang. and Lit.; MA). Lectr, Christ Church, Oxford, 1974–77; Mem. Staff, A Supplement to The Oxford English Dictionary, 1977–84. *Publications:* Oxford Guide to English Usage, 1983, 2nd edn (with A. Delahunty) 1993; (ed with John Simpson) The Oxford English Dictionary, 2nd edn, 1989; (with Sylvia Chalker) The Oxford Dictionary of English Grammar, 1994; (with Sidney Greenbaum) The Oxford Reference Grammar, 2000; (with Peter Gilliver and Jeremy Marshall) The Ring of Words: J. R. R. Tolkien and the Oxford English Dictionary, 2006; (contrib. jtly) From Elvish to Klingon, 2011; (contrib.) Corpora and Lexis: language and computers, 2018. *Recreations:* language, music, family life, the Church, history, cooking, gardening, elementary carpentry. *Address:* Oxford University Press, Great Clarendon Street, Oxford OX2 6DP. *T:* (01865) 556767.

**WEINIGER, Matthew Gideon;** QC 2014; Partner, since 2015, and Global Co-Head, International Arbitration, since 2015, Linklaters LLP; *b* Hull, E Yorks, 3 Oct. 1970; *s* of Noah Weiniger and Elaine Finestein (*née* March); *m* 1994, Suzanne Cohen; four *s* one *d*. *Educ:* Hymers Coll., Hull; Downing Coll., Cambridge (BA Law 1993). Admitted solicitor, 1996. Herbert Smith Freehills, 1994–2015; Mem., Internat. Arbitration Gp; Partner, Internat. Arbitration, 2003–15. *Publications:* (contrib.) Blackstone's Civil Practice, 1999–2014; (jtly) International Investment Arbitration: substantive principles, 2007, 2nd edn 2017. *Recreation:* sports. *Address:* Linklaters LLP, One Silk Street, EC2Y 8HQ. *T:* (020) 7456 5523, *Fax:* (020) 7456 2222.

**WEINSTEIN, Harvey,** Hon. CBE 2004; film producer; Co-Chairman, The Weinstein Company, 2005–17; *b* 19 March 1952; *s* of late Max Weinstein and Miriam Weinstein; *m* 1986, Eve (marr. diss. 2004); three *d*; *m* 2007, Georgina Chapman (marr. diss. 2018); one *d*. Co-Chm., Miramax Films Corp., 1979–2005. Films produced include: Playing for Keeps, 1986; Scandal, 1989; Strike it Rich, Hardware, 1990; A Rage in Harlem, 1991; The Crying Game, 1992; The Night We Never Met, Benefit of the Doubt, True Romance, 1993; Mother's Boys, Like Water for Chocolate, Pulp Fiction, Pret-a-Porter, 1994; Smoke, A Month by the Lake, The Crossing Guard, The Journey of August King, Things To Do In Denver When You're Dead, The Englishman Who Went Up A Hill But Came Down A Mountain, Blue in the Face, Restoration, 1995; Scream, The Pallbearer, The Last of the High Kings, Jane Eyre, Flirting with Disaster, The English Patient, Emma, The Crow: City of Angels, Beautiful Girls, 1996; Addicted to Love, Air Bud, Cop Land, Good Will Hunting, Scream 2, Jackie Brown, 1997; Velvet Goldmine, Shakespeare in Love, Rounders, The Prophecy II, A Price Above Rubies, Playing by Heart, The Mighty, Little Voice, Heaven, Halloween H20: Twenty Years Later, The Faculty, B. Monkey, Phantoms, Senseless, Ride, Wide Awake, Night Watch, 54, Talk of Angels, 1998; Guinevere, Allied Forces, Wasteland, She's All That, My Life So Far, The Yards, 1999; Scary Movie, Boys and Girls, The Crow: Salvation, Reindeer Games, Love's Labour's Lost, Scream 3, About Adam, Highlander: Endgame, Chocolat, Dracula, 2000; Bounce, Spy Kids, Texas, Scary Movie 2, The Others, The Fellowship of the Ring, 2001; Iris, Shipping News, Spy Kids 2, Equilibrium, Waking up in Reno, The Two Towers, Gangs of New York, Chicago, 2002; Human Stain, Kill Bill: Vol. 1, Confessions of a Dangerous Mind, Spy Kids 3-D, Scary Movie 3, The Return of the King, Cold Mountain, 2003; Kill Bill: Vol. 2, Fahrenheit 9/11, Shall We Dance, 2004; The Aviator, The Brothers Grimm, 2005; An Unfinished Life, Proof, Derailed, Scary Movie 4, 2006; Miss Potter, 2007; The Reader, 2008; The No 1 Ladies' Detective Agency (TV), Crossing Over, Inglourious Basterds, Halloween II, 2009; Piranha, 2010; The King's Speech, The Fighter, Scream 4, I Don't Know How She Does It, The Artist, 2011; Untouchable, Silver Linings Playbook, Django Unchained, 2012; Scary Movie 5, One Chance, 2013; Mandela: Long Walk to Freedom, August: Osage County, Paddington, 2014; Carol, Macbeth, Southpaw, The Hateful Eight, 2015; Lion, 2016. *Publications:* (with Robert Weinstein) The Art of Miramax: the inside story.

**WEINSTOCK, Anne Josephine,** CBE 1993; Executive Chair, Sheffield Futures, 2011–12; *b* 28 Dec. 1950; *d* of late Dr Kevin Maher and Brenda Maher; *m* 1976, Dr Harold Weinstock; one *s* two *d*. *Educ:* Manchester Victoria Univ. (BA Hons Econs). Manager: Stopover hostel for homeless girls, 1972–73; Lance Project for Single Homeless, 1973–75; Regl Manager, then Principal Organiser, NACRO, 1975–79; Mem., Home Office Parole Bd, 1979–84; Chief Exec., Rathbone Soc., later Community Industry, then Rathbone CI, 1985–99; Dir, Millennium Volunteers, 1999–2000 (on secondment); Chief Exec., Connexions Service, DfES, 2000–03; Dir, Supporting Children and Young People Gp, DfES, subseq. DCSF, 2003–08; Hd, Youth Task Force, DCSF, subseq. DFE, 2008–10. Director: Manchester TEC, 1989–98; Manchester Careers Partnership, 1995–98; Member: NW FEFC, 1995–98; Govt Skills Task Force, 1998–2000. Fellow, Univ. of Central Lancs, 2001. Trustee, Harmony Trust, 2018–. *Publications:* contrib. articles on raising standards in educn and trng, impact of league tables, alternative educn for disaffected youth, and encouraging young people to become volunteers. *Recreations:* running, walking, swimming, friends and family, reading.

**WEIR,** family name of **Baron Inverforth** and **Viscount Weir**.

**WEIR, 3rd Viscount** *cr* 1938; **William Kenneth James Weir;** Baron Weir 1918; Chairman: The Weir Group PLC, 1973–80 and 1983–99; Balfour Beatty (formerly BICC) plc, 1996–2003; CP Ships Ltd, 2001–03; Director: St James's Place Capital (formerly J. Rothschild Holdings) plc, 1985–2004 (Vice-Chairman, 1985–95); Canadian Pacific Railway Co., 1989–2004; *b* 9 Nov. 1933; *e s* of 2nd Viscount Weir, CBE, and Lucy (*d* 1972), *d* of late James F. Crowdy, MVO; *S* father, 1975; *m* 1st, 1964, Diana (marr. diss.), *o d* of Peter L. MacDougall; one *s* one *d*; 2nd, 1976, Mrs Jacqueline Mary Marr (marr. diss.), *er d* of late Baron Louis de Chollet; 3rd, 1989, Marina, *d* of late Marc Sevastopoulo; one *s*. *Educ:* Eton; Trinity Coll., Cambridge (BA). Sub-Lt, RNVR, 1955–56; Dir, BSC, 1972–76; Dir, British Bank of Middle East, 1973–80; Dir, 1977–91, Dep. Chm., 1991–96, BICC Ltd. Dir, 1970, Chm., 1975–82, Great Northern Investment Trust Ltd; Co-Chm., RIT and Northern plc, 1982–83; Chairman: Major British Exporters, 1992–2003; British Water, 1998–2000. Member: London Adv. Cttee, Hongkong & Shanghai Banking Corp., 1980–92; Court, Bank of England, 1972–84; Export Guarantees Adv. Council, 1992–98. Chm., Engrg Design Res. Centre, 1989–91; Pres., BEAMA, 1988–89, 1994–95; Vice Pres., China-Britain Business Council, 1994–2003. Chm., Patrons of Nat. Galls of Scotland, 1985–95. Mem., Queen's Body Guard for Scotland (Royal Co. of Archers). FRSA. Hon. FREng (Hon. FEng 1993). Hon. DEng Glasgow, 1993. *Recreations:* shooting, golf, fishing. *Heir: s* Hon. James William Hartland Weir [*b* 6 June 1965; *m* 2001, Benedicte Marie Françoise, *d* of Louis Virard]. *Address:* Rodinghead, Mauchline, Ayrshire KA5 5TR. *T:* (01563) 884233. *Club:* White's.

**WEIR, Hon. Lord; David Bruce Weir;** a Senator of the College of Justice in Scotland, 1985–97; *b* 19 Dec. 1931; *yr s* of late James Douglas Weir and Kathleen Maxwell Weir (*née* Auld); *m* 1964, Katharine Lindsay, *yr d* of Hon. Lord Cameron, KT, DSC; three *s*. *Educ:* Kelvinside Academy; Glasgow Academy; The Leys Sch., Cambridge; Glasgow Univ. (MA, LLB). Royal Naval Reserve, 1955–64, Lieut RNR. Admitted to Faculty of Advocates, 1959; Advocate Depute for Sheriff Court, 1964; Standing Junior Counsel: to MPBW, 1969; to DoE, 1970; QC (Scot.) 1971; Advocate Depute, 1979–82; Justice of Ct of Appeal, Botswana, 1999–2002; Hon. Sheriff, N Strathclyde at Campbeltown, 2004–. Chairman: Medical Appeal Tribunal, 1972–77; Pensions Appeal Tribunal for Scotland, 1978–84 (Pres., 1984–85); NHS Tribunal, Scotland, 1983–85; Member: Criminal Injuries Compensation Bd, 1974–79 and 1984–85; Transport Tribunal, 1979–85; Parole Bd, Scotland, 1989–92. Mem., Law Adv. Cttee, 1988–95, Chm., Scottish Law Cttee, 1994–95, British Council. Governor, Fettes Coll., 1986–99 (Chm., 1989–95). Mem. Bd, Scottish Internat. Piano Competition, 1997–2007. Vice-Chm., S Knapdale Community Council, 1998–2004. Mem. Council, RYA, 2005–08. *Publications:* (contrib.) The Laws of Scotland: Stair Memorial Encyclopaedia, 1990; (contrib.) The Baltic Sea Pilot, 3rd edn, 2010. *Recreations:* sailing, music. *Clubs:* New (Edinburgh); Royal Cruising; Royal Highland Yacht.
*See also* R. B. Weir.

**WEIR, Alison;** historian and novelist; *d* of Ronald James Matthews and Doreen Ethel (*née* Marston, now Cullen); *m* 1972, Rankin Alexander Lorimer Weir; one *s* one *d*. *Educ:* City of London Sch. for Girls; N Western Poly., London. Civil Service, 1974–83; Principal and Proprietor, Henry Tudor Sch. for Children with Special Needs, 1991–97. Chief Exec., Alison Weir Tours Ltd, 2010–. Hon. Life Patron, Historic Royal Palaces, 2011. FRSA 2003–16, 2018. *Publications:* Britain's Royal Families, 1989; The Six Wives of Henry VIII, 1991; The Princes in the Tower, 1992; Lancaster and York, 1995; Children of England: the heirs of Henry VIII, 1996; Elizabeth the Queen, 1998; Eleanor of Aquitaine, 1999; Henry VIII: King and Court, 2001; Mary, Queen of Scots and Murder of Lord Darnley, 2003; Isabella, She Wolf of France, Queen of England, 2005; Innocent Traitor, 2006; Katherine Swynford: the story of John of Gaunt and his scandalous Duchess, 2007; The Lady Elizabeth, 2008; The Lady in the Tower, 2009; The Captive Queen, 2010; Traitors of the Tower, 2010; (jtly) The Ring and the Crown: a history of royal weddings 1066–2011, 2011; Mary Boleyn: 'the great and infamous whore', 2011; A Dangerous Inheritance, 2012; Elizabeth of York, 2013; The Marriage Game, 2014; The Lost Tudor Princess, 2015; Katherine of Aragon: the true queen (novel), 2016; Anne Boleyn: a king's obsession (novel), 2017; Queens of the Conquest, 2017; Jane Seymour: the haunted queen, 2018; (jtly) A Tudor Christmas, 2018; Anna of Kleve: queen of secrets, 2019. *Recreations:* royal and aristocratic genealogy, reading, music, foreign travel, art, poetry, researching royal portraits, collecting nostalgia.

**WEIR, Maj. Gen. Colin Richard James**, DSO 2011; MBE 2009; General Officer Commanding 1st (UK) Division, since 2018; *b* Portadown, 2 March 1971; *s* of Herbie and Maud Weir; *m* 1998, Diane Campbell; three *s*. *Educ*: Portadown Coll.; Queen's Univ., Belfast (BA Hons); RMA, Sandhurst; Cranfield Univ. (MA). Joined Army, 1993; MA to GOC NI, 2006–07; COS 11, Light Bde, 2007–09; CO, 1st Bn, Royal Irish Regt, 2010–12; Comdr, 16 Air Assault Bde, 2015–17; Chief Ops Officer, Perm. Jt HQ, 2017–18. Col, Royal Irish Regt, 2019–. *Recreations*: history, music, fitness. *Address*: Danesmead House, 262 Fulford Road, York YO10 4PD. *T*: 07423 531288. *E*: colinrjweir@hotmail.com. *Club*: Naval and Military.

**WEIR, David Bruce;** *see* Weir, Hon. Lord.

**WEIR, Prof. David Thomas Henderson;** Chairman: Fourth Paradigm Consulting, since 2014; Editorial Advisory Board, Cambridge Scholars, since 2013; Professor of Intercultural Management, York St John University, since 2015; *b* 10 April 1939; *s* of late Johnstone Mather Weir and Irene Florence Brooks; *m* 1st, 1959, Janeen Elizabeth Whitson Fletcher; one *s* one *d*; 2nd, 1967, Mary Willows; one *s*. *Educ*: Ambrosden Sch.; Prebendal Sch., Aylesbury; St Philip's Sch.; Ilkley Grammar Sch.; Bradford Grammar Sch.; Queen's Coll., Oxford (Hastings Scholar, Sir William Akroyd's Scholar, MA, Dip PSA). Research and lecturing, MRC, Univs of Aberdeen, Leeds, Hull, Manchester, 1961–72; Sen. Lectr, Manchester Business Sch., 1972–74; University of Glasgow: Prof. of Organizational Behaviour, 1974–89; Head, Dept of Management Studies, 1981–89; Dean, Scottish Business Sch., 1977–79; Chm., Glasgow Business Sch., 1985–89; Dir and Prof. of Mgt, Univ. of Bradford Sch. of Mgt, 1989–97; Dean and Dir, Newcastle Business Sch., and Prof. of Mgt, Univ. of Northumbria at Newcastle, 1998–2000, now Prof. Emeritus; Prof. of Intercultural Mgt, Centre for Educn and Res. Applied to Mgt, France, 2001–07; Prof. of Intercultural Mgt, Liverpool Hope Univ., 2007–11; Prof. of Business and Enterprise, and Hd, Sch. of Business, Leadership and Enterprise, Univ. Campus Suffolk, 2011–14. Visiting Professor: Bolton Inst., 1993; Southampton Inst., 1994; (in Mgt Develt) Lancaster Sch. of Mgt, 2000–; Bristol Business Sch., 2002–; Lincoln Univ., 2011–; Edgehill Univ., 2014–; York St John, 2014–15; Hull Univ. Dist. Vis. Prof., eTQM Coll., Dubai, 2007; Affiliate Prof. of Mgt, Ecole Supérieure de Commerce, Rennes, 2007–13; Sen. Enterprise Fellow, Essex Univ., 2005–; Barrie Turner Meml Lectr, Middlesex Univ., 1998. Keynote address, Gulf Economic Summit, 2002. Dir, Gulliver Foods, 1980–81; Arbitrator, Dairy Industry, Scotland, 1985–89; Chm., Forever Broadcasting, Yorks, 2000–01. Consultant, World Bank, Unesco, SDA, Arthur Andersen and many companies; Strategic Advr, Emerald Gp, 2000–. Member: Sociology and Social Admin Cttee, SSRC, 1976–78; Cttee of Inquiry, Engrg Profession (Finniston Cttee), 1977–79; Teaching Co. Cttee, SERC, 1983–87 (Chm., 1986–87); CNAA, 1986–89; Incorp. of Gardeners of Glasgow, 1985; Conseil Scient. de l'Univ. des eaux de vie, Segonzac, 1989; Strategic Audit Panel for Review of Dutch Business Educn, Eur. Foundn for Mgt Educn, 1994–95. Chm., Assoc. of Business Schs, 1994–96; Mem. Council, Nat. Forum for Management Educn and Develt, 1994–96. Member Council: Prague Internat. Business Sch., 1992–99; Cyprus Internat. Business Sch., 1990–99. Pres., Emerald Acad. for Online Action and Learning, 2006–12. Fellow, Leadership Trust Foundn. CCMI (FBIM 1984); FRSA. Burgess, City of Glasgow, 1985; Ambassador for Bradford, 1996–. Halloran Prize, Acad. of Mgt, USA, 2012. *Publications*: with Eric Butterworth: Sociology of Modern Britain, 1970, 3rd edn 1980; Social Problems of Modern Britain, 1972; New Sociology of Modern Britain, 1984; Men and Work in Modern Britain, 1973; (with Camilla Lambert) Cities in Modern Britain, 1974; (jtly) Computer Programs for Social Scientists, 1972; (with E. Gittus) Key Variables in Sociological Research, 1976; (with Gerald Mars) Risk Management: theories and models, 2000; (with Gerald Mars) Risk Management: practice and prevention, 2000; (jtly) Critical Management into Critical Practice, 2009; (contrib.) Bards in the Bog (poetry), 2009; (with Nabil Sultan) From Critique to Action: the practical ethics of the organizational world, 2011; (ed jtly) The New Post-Oil Arab Gulf, 2011; (with Paresh Wankhade) Modern Policing, 2015; (jtly) Ethnographic Research and Analysis: anxiety, identity and self, 2017. *Recreations*: playing cricket, supporting Leeds United FC, listening to music, hill walking, wine appreciation, writing poetry, performing poetry. *Address*: Hadleigh House, Main Street, Skirpenbeck, York YO41 1HF. *E*: weir53@gmail.com. *Clubs*: Athenæum, Groucho; Riviera Cricket.

**WEIR, Fiona;** Chief Executive, Joseph Rowntree Reform Trust Ltd, since 2016; *b* Bellshill, N Lanarks, 20 Oct. 1959; *d* of John Morrison Weir and Wendy Elisabeth Christine Weir; partner, 1986, Toby Peter Shelley; two *s*. *Educ*: Lady Margaret Hall, Oxford (BA Hons PPE). Nat. organiser, Eur. Nuclear Disarmament, 1984–87; Sen. Climate Change and Air Pollution Campaigner, Friends of the Earth, 1988–95; Dir of Campaigns, Amnesty Internat. UK, 1995–2000; Hd, Public Affairs, Consumers' Assoc., 2000–02; Dir, Policy and Communications, Save the Children, 2002–07; freelance consultant to charities on strategy, communications and campaigning, 2007; Chief Exec., Gingerbread (formerly One Parent Families|Gingerbread), 2008–17. Mem., BBC Appeals Adv. Cttee, 2007–11. Mem. RSA. *Recreations*: family, food, films, travel, football (Arsenal). *Address*: Joseph Rowntree Reform Trust Ltd, The Garden House, Water End, York YO30 6WQ.

**WEIR, Dame Gillian (Constance)**, DBE 1996 (CBE 1989); concert organist; Prince Consort Professor, Royal College of Music, since 1999; *b* Martinborough, NZ, 17 Jan. 1941; *d* of Cecil Alexander Weir and Clarice M. Foy Weir (*née* Bignell); *m* 1st, 1967, Clive Rowland Webster (marr. diss. 1971); 2nd, 1972, Lawrence Irving Phelps (*d* 1999). *Educ*: Royal College of Music, London. LRSM, LRAM, LTCL; Hon. FRCO. Winner of St Albans Internat. Organ Competition, 1964; Début, 1965: Royal Festival Hall, solo recital; Royal Albert Hall, concerto soloist, opening night of Promenade Concerts; since then, internat. career as touring concert organist and harpsichordist; concerto appearances with all major British orchestras, also with Boston Symphony, Seattle Symphony, Württemberg Chamber Orch., and others; solo appearances at leading internat. Festivals, incl. Bath, Aldeburgh, Edinburgh, English Bach, Europalia, Europe and USA (AGO Nat. Conventions, RCCO Diamond Jubilee Nat. Convention, etc). Frequent radio and television appearances: BBC Third Prog., USA, Australasia, Europe, Far East; TV film, Toccata: two weeks in the life of Gillian Weir, 1981 (shown NZ TV 1982); presenter and performer, The King of Instruments, 6 part TV series BBC2 and Europe, Australia etc, 1989; many first performances, incl. major works by Fricker, Connolly, Camilleri, Messiaen. Dist. Vis. Artist, Peabody Conservatory of Music, Baltimore, 2004–12; retired from public performance, 2012; master-classes, adjudicator internat. competitions, UK, Europe, N America, Japan; exponent of and authority on Messiaen. President: Incorp. Assoc. of Organists, 1981–83; ISM, 1992–93; RCO, 1994–96 (Hon. Fellow and Mem. Council, 1977–); Hon. RAM 1989; Hon. FRCM 2000. Hon. Fellow: Royal Canadian Coll. of Organists, 1983; Hatfield Coll., Durham, 2014; Grey Coll., Durham, 2016; St Chad's Coll., Durham, 2017. Hon. Bencher, Middle Temple, 2012. Hon. Freeman, Musicians' Co., 2015. Hon. DMus: Victoria Univ. of Wellington, NZ, 1983; Hull, 1999; Exeter, 2001; Leicester, 2003; Aberdeen, 2004; London, 2009; Durham, 2013; Hon. DLitt Huddersfield, 1997; DUniv UCE, 2001. Internat. Performer of the Year Award, NY Amer. Guild of Organists, 1981; Internat. Music Guide's Musician of the Year Award, 1982; Turnovsky Prize for outstanding achievement in the arts, Turnovsky Foundn for the Arts, NZ, 1985; Silver Medal, Albert Schweitzer Assoc., Sweden, 1998; Evening Standard Award for outstanding performance, 1999; award-winning recordings include complete organ works of Messiaen, 1994, and of Franck, 1997. *Publications*: contributor to: Grove's Internat. Dictionary of Music and Musicians, 1980; The Messiaen Companion; musical jls and periodicals. *Recreation*: theatre. *W*: www.gillianweir.com.
*See also* Sir R. B. Weir.

**WEIR, Col James Mathieson Knight**, OBE (mil.) 1988; TD 1971 (clasp 1977); FRICS; DL; Vice Lord-Lieutenant of Rutland, 1997–2006; Chairman, Rutland County Council, 1997–99; *b* 3 March 1931; *s* of James Weir and Elspet Mathieson Weir (*née* Knight); *m* 1961, Mary, *d* of Thomas Maden; two *s*. *Educ*: George Heriot's Sch., Edinburgh; Heriot-Watt Coll. FRICS 1954. Nat. Service, 1954–57; RSME; commnd RE; served UK, Germany, Belgium and Holland. Territorial Army: RE in Scotland, 1958–74; attached 4 Armd Div., 1974–81; Territorial, Auxiliary & Volunteer Reserve Association: Mem., Council, 1996–2000; Mem. for E Midlands, 1983–2000; Chm., Leics and Rutland Cttee, 1996–2000; Chm., ACF Cttee, E Midlands, 1998–2000; Co. Comdt, Leics and Northants ACF, 1982–92 (Hon. Col, Leics, Northants and Rutland ACF, 1995–2002); Mem., ACFA Council, 1998–2002. Director: Mitchell Construction Kinnear Moodie Gp, 1966–73; Jeakins Weir Ltd, 1973–. Mem. Bd, Anglian Water Authy, 1981–87. Mem. (C), Leics CC, 1981–93 (Chm., Public Protection Cttee, 1989–93); Mem., Leics Police Authy, 1986–93; Chm., Rutland & Melton Police/Community Consultative Cttee, 1990–93; Mem. (C), Rutland DC, 1991–97 (Vice Chm., 1996–97). DL: Leics, 1984–97; Rutland, 1997. Chm., Leics and Rutland Campaign Army Benevolent Fund, 1989–99. Constituency Conservative Association: Chm., Rutland & Stamford, 1982–83; Rutland & Melton, 1983–85 and 1991–94. Trustee: Peterborough Cathedral Preservation Trust, 1988–2014; Oakham Sch., 1989–2011; Rutland Trust, 2006–. Governor: C of E Co. Primary Sch., Oakham, 1984–92; Rutland Sixth Form Coll., 1985–93; Vale of Catmose Coll., 1986–95. *Recreations*: golf, visual arts, Rugby Union. *Address*: Swooning House, Oakham, Rutland LE15 6JD. *T*: (01572) 724273. *Club*: Army and Navy.

**WEIR, Judith**, CBE 1995; composer; Master of the Queen's Music, since 2014; *b* 11 May 1954; *d* of Jack and Ishbel Weir. *Educ*: King's Coll., Cambridge (MA). Cramb Fellow, Glasgow Univ., 1979–82; Fellow-Commoner, Trinity Coll., Cambridge, 1983–85; Composer-in-Residence, RSAMD, Glasgow, 1988–91; Fairbairn Composer in assoc. with CBSO, 1995–98; Artistic Dir, Spitalfields Fest., 1998–2000 (Jt Artistic Dir, 1994–97). Associate Composer, BBC Singers, 2015–. Hambro Vis. Prof. of Opera Studies, Oxford Univ., 1999; Vis. Prof. of Composition, Princeton Univ., 2001; Fromm Foundn Vis. Prof., Harvard Univ., 2004; Vis. Res. Prof., Cardiff Univ., 2006–13. Hon. Fellow, Trinity Coll., Cambridge, 2019. Hon. FRSE 2018; Hon. FRSCM 2018. Hon. DMus Oxford, 2017. Critics' Circle Award, 1994; Lincoln Center Stoeger Award, 1996; South Bank Show Award, 2000; Queen's Medal for Music, 2007; Distinguished Musician Award, ISM, 2010; Ivor Novello Classical Music Award, 2015. *Publications*: compositions: King Harald's Saga, 1979; The Consolations of Scholarship, 1985; Missa Del Cid, 1988; Heaven Ablaze In His Breast, 1989; Music Untangled, 1991–92; Heroic Strokes of the Bow, 1992; Moon and Star, 1995; Forest, 1995; Piano Concerto, 1997; Storm, 1997; We are Shadows, 2000; The Welcome Arrival of Rain, 2002; Tiger under the Table, 2003; Piano Trio Two, 2004; Vertue, 2005; Winter Song, 2007; Concrete, 2008; Blue-Green Hill, 2012; I give you the end of a golden string, 2013; Day Break Shadows Flee, 2014; Good Morning, Midnight, 2014; In the Land of Uz, 2017 (British Composer Award, 2018); Oboe Concerto, 2018; *operas*: A Night at the Chinese Opera, 1987; The Vanishing Bridegroom, 1990; Blond Eckbert, 1994; Armida, 2005; Miss Fortune, 2011. *Address*: c/o Music Sales Ltd, 14–15 Berners Street, W1T 3LJ. *T*: (020) 7612 7400.

**WEIR, Michael;** *b* 24 March 1957; *s* of James and Elizabeth Weir; *m* 1985, Anne Jack; two *d*. *Educ*: Arbroath High Sch.; Aberdeen Univ. (LLB). Solicitor: Charles Wood and Son, Kirkcaldy, 1981–83; Myers and Wills, Montrose, 1983–84; J. & D. G. Shiell, Brechin, 1984–2001. Dean, Faculty of Procurators and Solicitors in Angus, 2001. Mem. (SNP), Angus DC, 1984–88. Contested (SNP) Aberdeen S, 1987. MP (SNP) Angus, 2011–17; contested (SNP) same seat, 2017. Pres., Aberdeen Univ. Student Nationalist Assoc., 1979; Mem., Nat. Exec., Young Scottish Nationalists, 1982.

**WEIR, Peter James;** barrister; Member (DemU) Strangford, Northern Ireland Assembly, since 2017 (Member for North Down, 1998–2017 (UU, 1998–2001, DemU, 2002–17)); *b* 21 Nov. 1968; *s* of late James Weir and of Margaret Lovell Weir. *Educ*: Ballyholme Primary Sch.; Bangor Grammar Sch.; Queen's Univ., Belfast (LLB Law and Accountancy; MSSc; Cert. Professional Legal Studies). Called to the Bar, NI, 1992; Lectr in Constitutional and Admin. Law, Univ. of Ulster, 1993. Mem., NI Forum, 1996–98. Minister of Education, NI, 2016–17. Northern Ireland Assembly: Member: Finance Cttee, 2007–15; Envmt Cttee, 2007–15; Assembly Commn, 2010–; Justice Cttee, 2011–13; Chm., Assembly Educn Cttee, 2015–16; Vice Chm., Employment and Learning Cttee, 2010–11. Chief Whip, DUP, 2010–16. Chm., Ulster Young Unionist Council, 1993–95. Mem., North Down BC, 2005–15. Pres., NI LGA, 2005–06; Member: S Eastern Educn and Liby Bd, 2005–11; NI Police Bd, 2006–10. Mem., Senate, QUB, 1997–2005. *Publications*: (jtly) The Anglo-Irish Agreement: three years after, 1988; (jtly) Unionism, National Parties and Ulster, 1991. *Recreations*: sport, history, reading. *Address*: 6 Vernon Park, Bangor, Co. Down BT20 4PH; (office) 6A North Street, Newtownards BT23 4DE. *T*: and *Fax*: (028) 9181 0858.

**WEIR, Peter Lindsay**, AM 1982; film director, since 1969; *b* 21 Aug. 1944; *s* of Lindsay Weir and Peggy Barnsley Weir; *m* 1966, Wendy Stites; one *s* one *d*. *Educ*: Scots Coll., Sydney; Vaucluse High Sch.; Sydney Univ. Short Film: Homesdale, 1971; Feature Films: The Cars That Ate Paris, 1973; Picnic at Hanging Rock, 1975; Last Wave, 1977; The Plumber (for TV), 1979; Gallipoli, 1980; The Year of Living Dangerously, 1982; Witness, 1985; The Mosquito Coast, 1986; Dead Poets Society, 1989; Green Card, 1991; Fearless, 1994; The Truman Show, 1998; Master and Commander, 2003; The Way Back, 2010. Chevalier, Ordre des Arts et des Lettres (France), 2010; Commander's Cross (Poland), 2011.

**WEIR, Robert Bruce;** QC (Scot.) 2010; a Temporary Judge, Court of Session, since 2017; Sheriff of Lothian and Borders at Edinburgh, since 2018; Specialist Sheriff, all-Scotland Sheriff Personal Injury Court, since 2018; *b* Edinburgh, 21 Feb. 1967; *s* of Hon. Lord Weir, *qv*; *m* 2002, Lesley-Anne Purdie; two *s*. *Educ*: Edinburgh Acad.; Univ. of Durham (BA Hons Hist. 1983); Univ. of Dundee (LLB Ord. 1991; DipLP 1992). Trainee solicitor, Maclay Murray & Spens, 1992; admitted Faculty of Advocates, 1995; Advocate Depute, 2005–08; Sheriff of S Strathclyde, Dumfries and Galloway at Hamilton, 2015–18. Served Tay Div., RNR, 1988–93. *Recreations*: sailing, hill-walking, violin, running. *Address*: 16 Dudley Crescent, Edinburgh EH6 4QN. *T*: (0131) 554 2453. *E*: robert.weir@advocates.org.uk. *Clubs*: Royal Forth Yacht; Scottish Bar Yacht.

**WEIR, Robert Thomas Macdonald;** QC 2010; a Recorder, since 2018; *b* London, 19 May 1969; *s* of Neil and Sue Weir; *m* 1995, Rachel Robert-Blunn; two *s* one *d*. *Educ*: Downside Sch.; Christ's Coll., Cambridge (BA 1st Cl. Law 1991); King's Coll. London (MA Med. Law and Ethics). Called to the Bar, Middle Temple, 1992, Bencher, 2019; in practice as barrister, specialising in personal injuries. *Recreation*: outdoor activities with family and friends. *Address*: Devereux Chambers, Ground Floor South, Queen Elizabeth Building, EC4Y 9BS. *T*: (020) 7353 7534. *E*: weir@devchambers.co.uk.

**WEIR, Sir Roderick (Bignell)**, Kt 1984; JP; Chairman, Rod Weir Co. Ltd; Director, New Zealand Enterprise Trust; *b* 14 July 1927; *s* of Cecil Alexander Weir and Clarice Mildred Foy; *m* 1952, Loys Agnes Wilson (*d* 1984); one *d*; *m* 1986, Anna Jane Mcfarlane. *Educ*: Wanganui Boys' Coll., NZ. Various positions to regional manager, Dalgety NZ Ltd, Wanganui, 1943–63; formed stock and station co., Rod Weir & Co. Ltd, 1963; formed Crown Consolidated Ltd, 1976; Dir, 1980–98, Chm., 1988–98, McKechnie Pacific Ltd; Chm., Danaflex Packaging Corp. Ltd, 1990–98; former Chm., Rangatira Ltd; former Dir, NZ SO. Former Patron, Massey Coll. Business & Property Trust. Past President: NZ Stock and Station Agents' Assoc.; ASEAN Business Council. Former Mem., NZ Inst. of Econ. Res. Inc.; former Board Member and Patron: Massey Univ. Foundn; Medic Alert; Wellington Sch. of Medicine; Wellington Med. Res. Foundn. Former Trustee: Link Foundn; Wanganui Old Boys' Assoc. Almoner, Wellington Cathedral of St Paul, 2000–. Hon. Consul-Gen., Austria, 1982–87. Dist. Fellow, Inst. of Dirs in NZ, 2003; FNZIM 1982. JP NZ 1972. Hon. DSc Massey, 1993. NZ Business Hall of Fame, 2010. *Recreations*: fishing, shooting, boxing. *Address*: The Grove, 189 Main Road, Waikanae, New Zealand. *T*: and *Fax*: (4) 2936373. *Clubs*: Wellington (Wellington); Levin (Levin).
*See also* Dame G. C. Weir.

**WEIR, Sarah St Clair**, OBE 2011; Chief Executive, Design Council, since 2017; *b* Edinburgh; *d* of Michael St Clair Weir and Marion Baldwin Weir (*née* Miller, later Cox); civil partnership 2005, Louise Hide. *Educ*: Birkbeck Coll., Univ. of London (BA Hist. of Art 1997; Hon. Fellow 2013). Aldgate Group Brokers: Jun. Asst, 1979–81; Broker, 1981–85; Asst Dir, 1985–88; Dir, 1988–91; Man. Dir, 1991–94; Fundraising Dir, RA, 1997–2001; Executive Director: Almeida Th., 2001–03; Arts Council England, 2003–07; Hd, Arts and Cultural Strategy, Olympic Delivery Authy, 2008–11; Dir, Arts and Culture, London Legacy Develt Corp., 2011–12; Chief Executive Officer: Legacy List (Olympic Park charity), 2012–13; Waddesdon Manor, 2013–16; Exec. Producer, Roundhouse, 2016. *Recreations*: reading, walking, travelling. *Address*: Design Council, Angel Building, 407 St John Street, EC1V 4AB. *T*: (020) 7420 6215. *E*: sarah.weir@designcouncil.org.uk.

**WEIR, Stuart Peter**; Senior Research Fellow, Human Rights Centre, Essex University, since 1991 (Director, 1991–2009, Associate Director, 2009–12, Democratic Audit); Visiting Professor, Essex University, since 1999; *b* 13 Oct. 1938; *e s* of Robert Hendry Weir, CB and Edna Frances (*née* Lewis); *m* 1st, 1963, Doffy Burnham; two *s*; 2nd, 1987, Elizabeth Ellen Bisset; one *s* two *d*. *Educ*: Peter Symonds Sch., Winchester; Brasenose Coll., Oxford (BA Hons Modern History). Feature writer, Oxford Mail, 1964–67; diarist, The Times, 1967–71; Dir, Citizens Rights Office, CPAG, 1971–75; Founding Editor, Roof magazine, 1975–77; Dep. Editor, New Society, 1977–84; Editor: New Socialist, 1984–87; New Statesman, 1987–88, New Statesman and Society, 1988–90. WEA and Adult Educn lectr, 1969–73. Founder Chair, Family Rights Gp, 1975; Founder, Charter 88, 1988, Exec. Mem., 1988–95 and 1997–; Chm., Charter 88 Trust, 1991–92. Associate Consultant, British Council, 1997–2001; Consultant, State of Democracy Project, Inst. for Democracy and Electoral Assistance, Stockholm, 1998–2002. Policy Vice Chair, Unlock Democracy, 2007–; Founder and Vice Chair, Cambridge Commons, 2014–. Member: Exec., CPAG and Finer Jt Action Cttee, 1970–84; (Founding), Labour Co-ordinating Cttee, 1979. Active in anti-racist and community groups, Oxford and Hackney, 1964–72; Mem. (Lab), London Bor. of Hackney Council, 1974–76. Mem., Human Rights Commn, Helsinki Citizens Assembly, 1990–92; Sen. Internat. Facilitator, EU Democracy and Governance Project, Namibia, 1994–95; Facilitator, Parly Reform Project, Zimbabwe, 1996–98; Head, UNDP Parly Assessment, Zimbabwe, 2002–03; consultant on Parly reform, Malawi, 2004–06. Special Advr, Public Admin Select Cttee, H of C, 2000–01, 2002–03. Trustee: Civil Liberties Trust, 1990–97; The Scarman Trust, 1997–99. Columnist: Community Care, 1973–75; London Daily News, 1987; script consultant: Spongers, BBC TV, 1977; United Kingdom, BBC TV, 1980–81; editorial consultant: The People's Parliament (series), C4, 1994–96; C4 Dispatches, Behind Closed Doors, 1995. *Publications*: (contrib.) Towards Better Social Services, 1973; Social Insecurity, 1974; Supplementary Benefits: a social worker's guide, 1975; (ed and contrib.) Manifesto, 1981; (contrib.) The Other Britain, 1982; (contrib.) Consuming Secrets, 1982; (with W. Hall) EGO-TRIP, 1994; (with W. Hall) Behind Closed Doors, 1995; Consolidating Parliamentary Democracy in Namibia, 1995; (with F. Klug and K. Starmer) The Three Pillars of Liberty: political rights and freedoms in the UK, 1996; (jtly) Making Votes Count, 1997; (with D. Beetham) Political Power and Democratic Control in Britain, 1998; (jtly) Voices of the People, 2001, 2nd edn 2005; (jtly) The IDEA Handbook on Democracy Assessment, 2001; (jtly) The State of Democracy, 2002; (jtly) Democracy Under Blair, 2003; (jtly) Not in Our Name, 2005; Unequal Britain: the human rights route to social justice, 2006; (jtly) The Rules of the Game: terrorism, community and human rights, 2007; (jtly) Power and Participation in Modern Britain, 2008; (jtly) Assessing the Quality of Democracy: a practical guide, 2008; The Unspoken Constitution, 2009; (jtly) Fairness Review of Cambridge, 2015; (jtly) The Cambridge Health Gap, 2016. *Recreations*: active in community politics, in Cambridge, and with Unlock Democracy; cooking, football, family.

**WEISMAN, Malcolm**, OBE 1997; Barrister-at-law; a Recorder of the Crown Court, since 1980; *s* of David and Jeanie Pearl Weisman; *m* 1958, Rosalie, *d* of Dr and Mrs A. Spiro; two *s*. *Educ*: Harrogate Grammar Sch.; Parmiter's Sch.; London School of Economics; St Catherine's Coll., Oxford (MA). Blackstone Pupillage Prize. Chaplain (Sqdn Ldr), Royal Air Force, 1956; called to Bar, Middle Temple, 1961; Head of Chambers, 1982–90. Asst Comr of Parly Boundaries, 1976–85; Special Adjudicator, Immigration Appeals, 1998–. Mem., Bar Disciplinary Cttee, Inner Temple, 1990–. Senior Jewish Chaplain, HM Forces, 1972; Religious advisor to small congregations, and Hon. Chaplain, Oxford, Cambridge and new universities, 1963–; Chm. and Sec.-Gen., 1981–92, Pres., 1993–, Allied Air Forces in Europe Chief of Chaplains Cttee; Sec., Former Chiefs of Chaplains Assoc., 1994; Mem. Exec., USA Jewish Chaplains Assoc., 1992–; Member: MoD Adv. Cttee on Chaplaincy, 1972–; Exec. Council, CCJ, 1998–; Exec. Council, Three Faiths Forum, 1998–. Mem., Cabinet of the Chief Rabbi, 1967–; Hon. Chaplain to: Lord Mayor of Westminster, 1992–93; Mayor of Barnet, 1994–95; Assoc. of Jewish Ex-Servicemen and Women, 1999–; Chaplain to Mayor: of Redbridge, 2005–06; of Montgomery, 2006–07; Officiating Chaplain to the Military, 2009; Chaplain to: HM Prisons, 1960s–; US Forces in UK, 2010–. Vice Pres., Council of Christians and Jews. Hon. Vice-Pres., Monash Br., RBL, 1992–. Mem., Senior Common Room, Essex, Kent and Lancaster Univs, 1964–; Fellow, Centre for Theol. and Soc. (formerly Inst. of Theology), Univ. of Essex, 1992– (Mem. Council, 2000–). Member of Court: Univ. of Lancaster, 1970–; Univ. of Kent, 1970–; Warwick Univ., 1983–; Univ. of East Anglia, 1985–; Essex Univ., 1990–; Sussex Univ., 1992–; Mem. Council, Selly Oak Coll., Birmingham, 1992–; Gov., 1980–, Trustee, 1994–, Parmiter's Sch.; Gov., Carmel Coll., 1995–98. Trustee: B'nai B'rith Music Fest., 1995–; Internat. Multi-faith Chaplaincy, Univ. of Derby, 2000; Jt Pres., Multi-Faith Centre, Univ. of Derby, 2017–. Patron: Jewish Nat. Fund (formerly Holy Land Trust), 1993–; Oxford Synagogue Choir, 2017–. Hon. Fellow, Univ. of Lancaster, 2006. B'nai B'rith Award for Outstanding Communal Service, 1980; Chief Rabbi's Award for Excellence, 1993; US Jewish Military Special Chaplains' Chaplain Award, 1998; Inter-faith Gold Medallion, Internat. CCJ, 2001; Outstanding Leadership Award, United Synagogue Rabbinic Conf., 2005; Special Award, Canadian Military Chaplains, 2008; Peterborough Inter-faith Award, 2009, 2011, 2013, 2015, 2016, 2017, 2018. Editor, Menorah Jl, 1972–. *Recreations*: travelling, reading, doing nothing. *Address*: 101 Brondesbury Park, NW2 5JL. *T*: (020) 8459 4372.

**WEISS, Althea McNish;** *see* McNish, A. M.

**WEISS, John Roger**, CB 2004; Deputy Chief Executive and Member of Management Board, Export Credits Guarantee Department, 2004–05; *b* 7 Dec. 1944; *s* of Ernest Weiss, Basel, and Betsy Weiss (*née* Hallam); *m* 1967, Hazel Kay Lang. *Educ*: St Helen's Coll., Thames Ditton. Tax Officer, Inland Revenue, 1961–64; ECGD, 1964–2005: Dir, Asset Management Gp, 1990–95; Gp Dir, Underwriting, 1995–2001; Dir, Business Gp, 2001–04. *Recreations*: music, walking. *Address*: Priory House, 47 Fortesque Street, Norton St Philip, Bath BA2 7PE.

**WEISS, Julian;** *see* Huck, S.

**WEISS, Prof. Nigel Oscar**, FRS 1992; Professor of Mathematical Astrophysics, Cambridge University, 1987–2004, now Emeritus; Fellow of Clare College, Cambridge, since 1965; *b* 16 Dec. 1936; *s* of Oscar and Molly Weiss; *m* 1968, Judith Elizabeth Martin; one *s* two *d*. *Educ*: Hilton College, Natal; Rugby School; Clare College, Cambridge (BA 1957; PhD 1962; ScD 1993). Research Associate, UKAEA Culham Lab., 1962–65; Cambridge University: Lectr, Dept of Applied Maths and Theoretical Physics, 1965–79; Reader in Astrophysics, 1979–87; Sen. Fellow, SERC, 1987–92; Chm., Sch. of Physical Scis, 1993–98. Visiting Professor: Sch. of Math. Scis, QMC, then QMW, London, 1986–96; Dept of Applied Maths, Univ. of Leeds, 2001–07; temporary appointments: MIT; Max Planck Inst. für Astrophysik, Munich; Nat. Solar Observatory, New Mexico; Harvard-Smithsonian Center for Astrophysics; Sci. Univ. of Tokyo; Ecole Normale Supérieure, Paris. Pres., Royal Astronomical Soc., 2000–02. Gold Medal, RAS, 2007. *Publications*: (with J. H. Thomas) Sunspots and Starspots, 2008; (with M. R. E. Proctor) Magnetoconvection, 2014; papers on solar and stellar magnetic fields, astrophysical and geophysical fluid dynamics and nonlinear systems. *Recreation*: travel. *Address*: Department of Applied Mathematics and Theoretical Physics, Centre for Mathematical Sciences, Wilberforce Road, Cambridge CB3 0WA. *T*: (01223) 337910; 13 Eltisley Avenue, Cambridge CB3 9JG. *T*: (01223) 355032.

**WEISS, Prof. Robert Anthony, (Robin)**, PhD; FRCPath; FRS 1997; Professor of Viral Oncology, University College London, 1999–2012, now Professor Emeritus; *b* 20 Feb. 1940; *s* of Hans Weiss and Stefanie Löwinsohn; *m* 1964, Margaret Rose D'Costa; two *d*. *Educ*: University College London (BSc, PhD; Fellow, 2006). Lecturer in Embryology, University Coll. London, 1963–70; Eleanor Roosevelt Internat. Cancer Research Fellow, Univ. of Washington, Seattle, 1970–71; Visiting Associate Prof., Microbiology, Univ. of Southern California, 1971–72; Staff Scientist, Imperial Cancer Research Fund Laboratories, 1972–80, Gustav Stern Award in Virology, 1973; Institute of Cancer Research: Dir, 1980–89; Prof. of Viral Oncology, 1984–98; Dir of Res., 1990–96; Hon. Fellow, 1999. Researching into viruses causing cancer and AIDS. Chm., Governing Body, Inst. of Animal Health, 2003–06. Pres., Soc. for Gen. Microbiol., 2006–09. For. Associate, US Nat. Acad. of Scis, 2013; Mem., Amer. Philos. Soc., 2018. Founder FMedSci 1998. Hon. Fellow, LSHTM, 2003. Hon. FRCP 1998. Hon. MD Uppsala, 2003. *Publications*: RNA Tumour Viruses, 1982, 2nd edn (2 vols) 1985; various articles on cell biology, virology and genetics. *Recreations*: music, natural history. *Address*: Division of Infection and Immunity, Cruciform Building 1.3, University College London, Gower Street, WC1E 6BT. *T*: (020) 8346 8014. *E*: r.weiss@ucl.ac.uk.

**WEISSBERG, Prof. Peter Leslie**, CBE 2017; MD, FRCP, FMedSci; Chairman, UK Biocentre, since 2017; Medical Director, British Heart Foundation, 2004–16; Fellow of Wolfson College, Cambridge University, since 1993; *b* 4 Oct. 1951; *s* of Edmund and Dorcas Alfreda Weissberg; *m* 1976, Alison (*née* Prowse), MB ChB; two *s*. *Educ*: Warwick Sch.; Univ. of Birmingham (MB ChB Hons 1976; MD 1985); MA Cantab 2009. MRCP 1978, FRCP 1992; FRCPE 1996. Lectr in Cardiovascular Medicine, Univ. of Birmingham, 1983–88; MRC Res. Fellow, Baker Inst., Melbourne, Australia, 1985–87; University of Cambridge: BHF Sen. Res. Fellow, 1988–92; Lectr in Medicine, 1993–94; BHF Prof. of Cardiovascular Medicine, 1994–2004. FESC 1994; FMedSci 1999. Hon. DSc Birmingham, 2013. *Publications*: numerous contribs to sci. jls. *Address*: Wolfson College, Barton Road, Cambridge CB3 9BB.

**WEISSELBERG, Tom;** QC 2014; *b* London, 3 Feb. 1971; *s* of Kiffer and Alison Weisselberg; *m* 1998, Kate Douglas; one *s* one *d*. *Educ*: Westminster Sch.; Merton Coll., Oxford (MA 1st Cl. 1993); City Univ. (CPE 1994). Called to the Bar, Inner Temple, 1995; in practice as barrister, 1996–, specialising in commercial and public law. Trustee, Early Opera Co., 2019–. *Recreations*: walking, theatre, opera, family. *Address*: Blackstone Chambers, Blackstone House, Temple, EC4Y 9BW. *T*: (020) 7583 1770. *E*: clerks@ blackstonechambers.com.

**WEITZENHOFFER, (Aaron) Max;** producer; President: Weitzenhoffer Productions, New York and London, since 1965; Weitzenhoffer Theatres Ltd, since 2001; Chairman, Nimax Theatres Ltd, since 2005; *b* 30 Oct. 1939; *s* of Aaron and Clara Weitzenhoffer; *m* 1st, Frances (*d* 1991); 2nd, 2000, Ayako Takanashi; one *s* one *d*. *Educ*: Univ. of Oklahoma (BFA Drama 1962). Productions include: Dracula, NY (Tony Award), 1978; Song and Dance, NY, 1985; The Will Rogers Follies (Tony Award), NY, 1991; Defending the Caveman, Apollo (Olivier Award), 2000; Feel Good, Garrick, 2001; One Flew over the Cuckoo's Nest, Gielgud, 2004; Who's Afraid of Virginia Woolf, Apollo, 2006; A Moon for the Misbegotten, NY, 2007; A Little Night Music, NY, 2010; Long Day's Journey into Night, Apollo (Olivier Award), 2012. Member: Amer. League of Theatres and Producers, 1977–; SOLT, 2001–. Regent, 2003–17, Prof. and Artistic Consultant, 2017–, Univ. of Oklahoma. Hon. DHL Oklahoma, 2000. *Recreation*: trying to keep up with my children. *Address*: Nimax Theatres Ltd, 11 Maiden Lane, WC2E 7NA. *T*: (020) 7395 0780, *Fax*: (020) 7240 4540. *E*: mweitzenhoffer@yahoo.com. *Clubs*: Friars, Century Association, Players (New York).

**WEITZMAN, Peter;** QC 1973; a Recorder of the Crown Court, 1974–98; *b* 20 June 1926; *s* of late David Weitzman, QC, and Fanny Weitzman (*née* Galinski); *m* 1954, Anne Mary Larkam; two *s* two *d*. *Educ*: Cheltenham Coll.; Christ Church, Oxford (Gibbs Schol. in Mod. Hist., Newdigate Prize, 1949; BA 1950). Lt RA, 1945–48. Called to Bar, Gray's Inn, 1952; Bencher, 1981; Leader, Midland and Oxford Circuit, 1988–92 (Dep. Leader, 1985–88). Mem., Senate of Inns of Court, 1980–81, 1984–92. Member: Mental Health Review Tribunal, 1986–98; Criminal Injuries Compensation Bd, 1986–2000; Criminal Injuries Compensation Appeals Panel, 2000–02. *Recreation*: hedging and ditching. *Address*: 21 St James's Gardens, W11 4RE; Little Leigh, Kingsbridge, Devon TQ7 4AG.
*See also* T. E. B. Weitzman.

**WEITZMAN, Thomas Edward Benjamin;** QC 2003; a Recorder, since 2009; *b* 11 Sept. 1959; *s* of Peter Weitzman, *qv*; *m* 1995, Maria Villegas; one *s* one *d*. *Educ*: St Paul's Sch.; New Coll., Oxford (BA Hons). Called to the Bar, Gray's Inn, 1984, Bencher, 2008; in practice, specialising in commercial, insurance and reinsurance and professional negligence law. *Recreations:* looking, reading, walking. *Address:* 3 Verulam Buildings, Gray's Inn, WC1R 5NT. *T:* (020) 7831 8441.

**WEIZMAN, Prof. Eyal**, PhD; FBA 2019; Professor of Spatial and Visual Cultures, since 2011, Founding Director, Centre for Research Architecture, since 2005, and Founder and Director, Forensic Architecture, since 2010, Goldsmiths (formerly Goldsmiths' College), University of London; *b* Israel, 26 July 1970; *s* of Meir and Rachel Weizman. *Educ:* Architectural Assoc.; London Consortium/Birkbeck Coll., London (PhD 2006). Unit Master, Bartlett Sch. of Architecture, London, 2000–02; Prof. of Architecture, Acad. of Fine Arts, Vienna, 2004–06. Global Schol., Princeton Univ., 2014–15. Founding Mem., architecture collective, DAAR, Beit Sahour/Palestine, 2007. Member: Technol. Adv. Bd, Internat. Criminal Court; Adv. Bd, ICA; Adv. Bd, B'Tselem, Jerusalem; Bd, Centre for Investigative Journalism. Member, Editorial Board: Third Text; Humanity Jl; Cabinet Mag.; Political Concepts. James Stirling Meml Lect. Prize, LSE and Canadian Centre for Arch., 2006–07; Prince Claus Architecture Prize, 2011; Beazley Design of the Year Award, 2017; Princess Margriet Award for Culture, European Cultural Foundn, 2017. *Publications:* Yellow Rhythms, 2000; (ed jtly) A Civilian Occupation, 2003; Adam Broomberg and Oliver Chanarin: Chicago, everything that happened, happened here first in rehearsal, 2006; Hollow Land, 2007; (jtly) The Objective Quality of the Problem: on the space of Palestine/Israel, 2008; The Least of All Possible Evils: a short history of humanitarian violence, 2011; (with T. Keenan) Mengele's Skull: the advent of forensic aesthetics, 2012; Forensic Architecture: notes from fields and forums, 2012; Architecture After Revolution, 2014; (with Ines Weizman) Before and After: documenting the architecture of disaster, 2014; FORENSIS, 2014; (with F. Sheikh) The Conflict Shoreline, 2015; (with T. Keenan) Images of Conviction: the construction of visual evidence, 2015; The Roundabout Revolution, 2015; (jtly) Negative Publicity: artefacts of extraordinary rendition, 2016; (contrib.) Kent Klich: Gaza works, 2017; Forensic Architecture: violence at the threshold of detectability, 2017. *Address:* Forensic Architecture, Department of Visual Cultures, Goldsmiths, University of London, New Cross, SE14 6NW.

**WELBANK, (John) Michael**, MBE 2014; RIBA; architect and planner, retired; *b* London, 2 Aug. 1930; *s* of William Stephenson Welbank and Alice Mary Welbank (*née* Robson); *m* 1952, Alison Mary Hopkins; two *s* one *d. Educ:* Highgate Sch.; University Coll., London (BA; DipTP). RIBA 1957; MRTPI 1959. Planning Officer, LCC, 1957–59; Architect, Min. of Educn, 1959–64; Associate, Shankland Cox Associates, 1965–71; Partner, Shankland Cox Partnership, 1972–89; Dir, EntecUK, 1990–97. Vis. Prof., Oxford Brookes Univ., 1992–97. Churchill Travelling Fellow, 1989. Mem., Envmtl Audit Bd, Northumbrian Water Gp, 1990–95. Chm. Council, British Consultants Bureau, 1985. Pres., RTPI, 1992. Governor: Mus. of London, 2008–; GSMD, 2008–10. Common Councilman, City of London Corp., 2005– (Chief Commoner, 2016–17; Chm., Planning and Transportation Cttee, 2014–17). Master, Chartered Architects' Co., 1994. FRSA. *Recreations:* hill walking, watercolour painting. *Address:* 1 The Porticos, 53–55 Belsize Avenue, NW3 4BN. *T:* (020) 7431 6789. *Club:* Reform.

**WELBY, Sir Bruno;** *see* Welby, Sir R. B. G.

**WELBY, Most Rev. and Rt Hon. Justin Portal;** *see* Canterbury, Archbishop of.

**WELBY, Sir (Richard) Bruno (Gregory)**, 7th Bt *cr* 1801; *b* 11 March 1928; *s* of Sir Oliver Charles Earle Welby, 6th Bt, TD, and Barbara Angela Mary Lind (*d* 1983), *d* of late John Duncan Gregory, CB, CMG; *S* father, 1977; *m* 1952, Jane Biddulph (*d* 2016), *y d* of late Ralph Wilfred Hodder-Williams, MC; three *s* one *d. Educ:* Eton; Christ Church, Oxford (BA 1950). *Heir: s* Charles William Hodder Welby [*b* 6 May 1953; *m* 1978, Suzanna, *o d* of Major Ian Stuart-Routledge, Harston Hall, Grantham; three *d*]. *Address:* Denton Manor, Grantham, Lincs NG32 1JX.

**WELCH, Andrew Richard;** theatre producer; Managing Director, Andrew Welch Ltd, 2005–16; *b* 5 Feb. 1949; *s* of Richard Joseph Welch and Ruth Jordan Welch; *m* 1980, Louisa Mary Emerson; two *s. Educ:* Bedford Sch., Bedford; UC of Swansea, Univ. of Wales (BA). Dir, Arts Centre, Univ. of Warwick, 1977–81; General Manager: Hong Kong Arts Centre, 1981–84; Theatre Royal, Plymouth, 1984–90; Man. Dir, Armada Prodns, 1987–2014; Producer, Carnival Films and Theatre Ltd, 1990–95; Chief Exec., Theatre of Comedy Ltd, 1996–98; Fest., subseq. Theatre, Dir, Chichester Fest. Th., 1998–2002; Gen. Dir, Dance Umbrella, 2002–04 (Mem. Bd, 1985–88). Chm., Michael Clark Dance Co., 2003–09. Trustee, Two Moors Fest. FRSA 2004. Hon. MA UC Chichester, 2002. *Recreations:* music, walking. *Address:* 6 Clifton Hill, Exeter EX1 2DL. *T:* (01392) 422975. *Club:* Garrick.

**WELCH, Prof. Graham Frederick**, PhD; Professor of Music Education, UCL Institute of Education, University College London (formerly Institute of Education, University of London), since 2001; *b* London, 25 Nov. 1947; *s* of George and Joyce Welch; *m* 1st Ann Whitwell (marr. diss.); two *s*; 2nd, 2001, Sally Thompson; one *s. Educ:* Froebel Inst., London (BEd, Cert Ed); Inst. of Educn, Univ. of London (MA; PhD 1983). Teacher: St Mary's Primary Sch., 1971–73; Smallwood Junior Sch., 1973–76; Dep. Headteacher, Beatrix Potter Primary Sch., 1976–84; Principal Lectr in Educn, Bristol Poly., 1985–89; Dean and Dir of Educnl Res., Roehampton Inst., later Univ. of Surrey, Roehampton, 1989–2001. Chair, Soc. for Educn, Music and Psychol. Res., 2000–. Mem., Rev. Coll. for Music, AHRC, 2007–15. Pres., ISME, 2010–12 (Hon. Life Mem.). Consultant to govt agencies in UK, Italy, UAE, Ukraine, Argentina and S Africa. Arts and Health Award (jtly), RSPH, 2011. *Publications:* The Misunderstanding of Music, 2001 (Greek edn 2008); (ed with L. Thurman) Bodymind and Voice: foundations of voice education, 2000; (ed with G. McPherson) The Oxford Handbook of Music Education, 2 vols, 2012, 2nd edn, 5 vols, 2018; (ed jtly) The Oxford Handbook of Singing, 2019; over 200 academic pubns. *Recreations:* walking, gardening. *Address:* 2 Backfields, Rectory Lane, Winchelsea, E Sussex TN36 4AB. *T:* (01797) 227750, 07785 535440. *E:* graham.welch@ucl.ac.uk.

**WELCH, Sir John K.;** *see* Kemp-Welch.

**WELCH, Sir John (Reader)**, 2nd Bt *cr* 1957; Partner, Wedlake Bell, 1972–96; Chairman, John Fairfax (UK) Ltd, 1977–90; *b* 26 July 1933; *s* of Sir (George James) Cullum Welch, 1st Bt, OBE, MC, and Gertrude Evelyn Sladin Welch (*d* 1966); *S* father, 1980; *m* 1962, Margaret Kerry, *o d* of late K. Douglass, Killara, NSW; one *s* twin *d. Educ:* Marlborough College; Hertford Coll., Oxford (MA). National service in Royal Signals, 1952–54 (2nd Lt; GSM with Canal Zone Clasp); TA, 1954–62 (Capt., Middlesex Yeomanry). Admitted a solicitor, 1960. Partner, Bell Brodrick & Gray, 1961–71. Ward Clerk of Walbrook Ward, City of London, 1961–74, Common Councilman, 1975–86 (Chm., Planning and Communications Cttee, 1981, 1982); Chm., Walbrook Ward Club, 1978–79; Hon. Solicitor, 1983–90, Pres., 1986–87, City Livery Club; Registrar of Archdeaconry of London, 1964–99. Governor: City of London Sch. for Girls, 1977–82; Haberdashers' Aske's Schs, Elstree, 1981–85 and 1990–91. FRSA. Liveryman, Haberdashers' Co., 1955 (Court of Assistants, 1973; Master, 1990–91, now Past Master Emeritus); Freeman, Parish Clerks' Co. (Master, 1967, now Past Master Emeritus); Clerk, Furniture Makers' Co., 1963–66. Chm., Cttee of Management, London Homes for the Elderly, 1980–90; Pres., Freemasons' Grand Charity, 1985–95; Sen. Grand Warden, United Grand Lodge of England, 1998–2000. CStJ 1981. *Recreations:* piano, walking. *Heir: s* James Douglass Cullum Welch, *b* 10 Nov. 1973. *Address:* 28 Rivermead Court, Ranelagh Gardens, SW6 3RU. *Club:* Hurlingham.

**WELCH, Ven. Stephan John;** Archdeacon of Middlesex, 2006–Jan. 2020; *b* 16 Oct. 1950; *s* of Ernest Ian Welch and Regina Welch; *m* 1990, Jennifer Clare (*née* Gallop); three *s. Educ:* Hull Univ. (BA French Lang. and Lit. 1974); Birmingham Univ. (Postgrad. Dip. in Theol. 1976); London Univ. (MTh 1998). Ordained deacon, 1977, priest, 1978; Curate, Christ Church, Waltham Cross, 1977–80; Priest-in-charge: Reculver, 1980–86; St Bartholomew, Herne Bay, 1982–86; Vicar: Reculver and St Bartholomew, Herne Bay, 1986–92; Hurley and Stubbings, 1992–2000; Priest-in-charge, St Peter, Hammersmith, 2000–06. Area Dean, Hammersmith and Fulham, 2001–06. *Recreations:* French language and literature, French wine, sailing, patristic theology.

**WELCHMAN, His Honour Charles Stuart;** a Circuit Judge, 1998–2013; *b* 7 April 1943; *s* of late Edward James Welchman and Marjorie (*née* Williams, later Parsons); *m* 1972, Rosemary Ann Fison, *d* of late Dr Thomas Notley Fison and Nancy Jean Laird Fison; one *s* one *d. Educ:* W Buckland Sch.; Exeter Tech. Coll.; University Coll. London (LLB Hons 1965). Called to the Bar, Gray's Inn, 1966 (Mould Scholar 1966), Bencher, 2011; an Asst Recorder, 1990–94; a Recorder, 1994–98. Mem., Restricted Patients Panel, Mental Health Review Tribunal, 2002–13. Mem., Exec. Cttee, Professional Negligence Bar Assoc., 1996–98. Contested (L): Esher, Oct. 1974, 1979; Putney, 1982. Best Individual Speaker, Observer Mace Nat. Debating Competition, 1965. *Recreations:* theatre, jazz, politics and political history, opera. *Address:* 21 Winsham Grove, SW11 6NB. *Clubs:* National Liberal (Mem., Gen. Cttee, 2016–; Vice Chm., Membership Cttee, 2017–); Surrey County Cricket.

**WELCHMAN, Zoe;** *see* Kourtzi, Z.

**WELD FORESTER,** family name of **Baron Forester**.

**WELDON, Sir Anthony (William)**, 9th Bt *cr* 1723; *b* 11 May 1947; *s* of Sir Thomas Brian Weldon, 8th Bt, and Marie Isobel (who *m* 1984, 6th Earl Cathcart, CB, DSO, MC), *d* of Hon. William Joseph French; *S* father, 1979; *m* 1980, Mrs Amanda Wigan (marr. diss. 2006), *d* of Major Geoffrey and Hon. Mrs North; two *d. Educ:* Sherborne. Formerly Lieutenant, Irish Guards. Dir, Bene Factum Publishing Ltd, 1983–; Asst Dir and Gen. Manager, ViRSA Educnl Trust, 2003–05. Vice Chm., Leinster Regt Assoc., 2015–. *Publications:* (ed) Breakthrough: handling career opportunities and changes, 1994; (jtly) Numeroids: any number of things you didn't know, 2008; Words of War: speeches that inspired heroic deeds, 2012; (jtly) The Drum Horse in the Fountain: and other tales of heroes and rogues in the Guards, 2018. *Recreations:* country sports, cricket, books, champagne. *Heir: cousin* Kevin Nicholas Weldon [*b* 19 April 1951; *m* 1973, Catherine Main; one *s*]. *Clubs:* White's, Pratt's, Stranded Whales.

**WELDON, Fay**, CBE 2001; writer; Professor of Creative Writing, Bath Spa University, since 2012; *b* 22 Sept. 1931; *d* of Frank Birkinshaw and Margaret Jepson; *m* 1962, Ron Weldon (*d* 1994); four *s*; *m* 1994, Nicolas Fox. *Educ:* Hampstead Girls' High Sch.; St Andrews Univ. (MA 1952). Has written or adapted numerous television and radio plays, dramatizations, and series, and ten stage plays. Prof. of Creative Writing, Brunel Univ., 2007–12. Chm. of Judges, Booker McConnell Prize, 1983. Hon. DLitt St Andrews, 1990; Hon. Dr: Birmingham; Worcester; Bath; Connecticut. *Libretto:* A Small Green Space, 1989. *Publications:* The Fat Woman's Joke, 1967; Down Among the Women, 1972; Female Friends, 1975; Remember Me, 1976; Little Sisters, 1977 (as Words of Advice, NY, 1977); Praxis, 1978 (Booker Prize Nomination); Puffball, 1980; Watching Me, Watching You (short stories), 1981; The President's Child, 1982; The Life and Loves of a She-Devil, 1984 (televised, 1986; filmed as She-Devil, 1990); Letters to Alice—on First Reading Jane Austen, 1984; Polaris and other Stories, 1985; Rebecca West, 1985; The Shrapnel Academy, 1986; Heart of the Country, 1987 (televised, 1987); The Hearts and Lives of Men, 1987; The Rules of Life, 1987; Leader of the Band, 1988; (for children) Wolf the Mechanical Dog, 1989; The Cloning of Joanna May, 1989 (televised, 1992); (for children) Party Puddle, 1989; Darcy's Utopia, 1990; (contrib.) Storia 4: Green, 1990; Moon over Minneapolis or Why She Couldn't Stay (short stories), 1991; Life Force, 1992; Growing Rich, 1992; Affliction, 1994; Splitting, 1995; (with David Bailey) The Lady is a Tramp: portraits of Catherine Bailey, 1995; Wicked Women (short stories), 1995; Worst Fears, 1996; (for children) Nobody Likes Me!, 1997; Big Women, 1998 (televised, 1998); A Hard Time to Be a Father (short stories), 1999; Godless in Eden: a book of essays, 1999; Rhode Island Blues, 2000; The Bulgari Connection, 2001; Auto Da Fay (autobiog.), 2002; Nothing to Wear & Nowhere to Hide (short stories), 2003; Mantrapped, 2004; She May Not Leave, 2005; What Makes Women Happy, 2006; The Spa Decameron, 2007; The Stepmother's Diary, 2008; Chalcot Crescent, 2009; Kehua!, 2010; Habits of the House, 2012; Long Live the King, 2013; The New Countess, 2013; Mischief (short stories), 2015; Before the War, 2016; Death of a She Devil, 2017; Why Will No-one Publish My Novel? A handbook for the rejected writer, 2018; After the Peace, 2018. *Address:* c/o Georgina Capel Associates Ltd, 29 Wardour Street, W1D 6PS.

**WELDON, Thomas Daryl;** Chief Executive, Penguin Random House UK, since 2013 (Chief Executive Officer, Penguin UK, 2011–13); *b* London, 9 Aug. 1963; *s* of Patrick Weldon and Pamela Weldon (*née* Grant); civil partnership 2006, Colquitto A. McDonnell. *Educ:* Westminster Sch.; St John's Coll., Oxford (BA Modern Hist.). Ed., Macmillan Publishers, 1985–88; Editl Dir, William Heinemann, 1989–96; Penguin UK: Publishing Dir, 1997–2001; Man. Dir, Gen. Div., 2001–09; Dep. Chief Exec., 2009–11. *Recreations:* horse racing, walking, travel, movies, exhibitions, restaurants. *Address:* 10 Chesterton Road, W10 5LX.

**WELEMINSKY, Judith Ruth;** Chair, Jewish Resource Centre, University of Roehampton, since 2012; Founder, 2014, and Chair, since 2015, Pro Israel, Pro Palestinian, Pro Peace; *b* 25 Oct. 1950; *d* of Dr Anton Weleminsky and Gerda Weleminsky (*née* Loewenstamm); *m* 2003, Robert James Armstrong Smith; two *d. Educ:* Birmingham Univ. (BSc Hons Psych); Lancaster Univ. (MA Organisational Psych). Personnel and Training Officer, Lowfield (Storage and Distribn), 1973–75; Community Relations Officer, Lambeth, 1975–78; Equal Opportunities Officer, Wandsworth, 1978–80; Employment Development Officer, NACRO, 1980–82; Dir, Nat. Fedn of Community Orgns, 1982–85; Dir, Nat. Schizophrenia Fellowship, 1985–90; Dir, NCVO, 1991–94; Associate, Centre for Voluntary Sector and Not for Profit Mgt, City Univ. Bus. Sch., 1994–97; Sen. Consultant, Compass Partnership, 1994–2005; Chief Executive: Mental Health Providers Forum, 2005–11; Three Wings Trust, 2012; Res. Microbiologist, UCL, 2017–. Partner, Mentoring Dirs, 1995–97. Member: Bd, Children and Family Court Adv. Support Service, 2001–04; Gen. Social Care Council, 2001–04. Trustee: Makaton Vocabulary Develt Project, 1998–2010; Makaton Charity, 2007–12; Renaissance Publishing, 2015–. Mem., S London Israel Forum, 2014– (Chm., 2015–). Council Mem., Wimbledon and Dist Synagogue, 2005–06, 2011–14 (Co. Sec., 2011–13); Chair, Israel Cttee, Wimbledon Synagogue, 2013–. FRSA. *Recreations:* family, friends, food. *E:* judywele@blueyonder.co.uk.

**WELFARE, Jonathan William**; Chief Executive, Elizabeth Finn Care (formerly Distressed Gentlefolk's Aid Association, then Elizabeth Finn Trust), 1998–2010; *b* 21 Oct. 1944; *s* of late Kenneth William Welfare and Dorothy Patience Athol Welfare (*née* Ross); *m* 1969, Deborah Louise Nesbitt; one *s* three *d*. *Educ*: Bradfield Coll., Berks; Emmanuel Coll., Cambridge (MA Econs and Land Economy 1969; boxing blue). Economist, Drivers Jonas & Co., 1966–68; Consultant, Sir Colin Buchanan and Partners, 1968–70; Economist and Corporate Planning Manager, Milton Keynes Develt Corp., 1970–74; Economist, then Dep. Chief Exec., S Yorks CC, 1974–84; Director: Landmark Trust, 1984–86; Oxford Ventures Gp, 1986–90; Man. Dir, Venture Link Investors, 1990–95; Chief Exec., Bristol 2000, 1995–96; mgt consultant, 1995–98. Director: Oxford Innovation, 1987–96; Granite TV, 1988–2003; Interconnect Ltd, 1990–94; Calidair Ltd, 1990–95; Meridian Software, 1990–95; English Community Care Assoc., 1999–2010; Elizabeth Finn Homes Ltd, 2005–10. Trustee: Oxford Trust, 1985–2001, 2011– (Chm., 1985–95); Northmoor Trust, 1986–99 (Chm., 1986–95); Turn2Us, 2007–10; Nominet Trust, 2009–12 (Chm., 2009–12); Gingerbread, 2014– (Chair, 2014–); Town and Manor of Hungerford, 2016–. FRSA 1992. Freeman: City of London, 1991; Co. of Information Technologists, 1991. *Recreations:* family, cricket, architecture, gardening. *Address:* The Garden House, R/O 34 Street, Hungerford, Berks RG17 0NF. *T:* (01488) 684228. *Club:* Hawks (Cambridge).

**WELLAND, Sir Mark (Edward)**, Kt 2011; PhD; FRS 2002; FREng, FIET, FInstP; Fellow and Master of St Catharine's College, Cambridge, since 2016; Professor of Nanotechnology, since 1999, and Head of Electrical Engineering, since 2015, University of Cambridge; *b* 18 Oct. 1955; *s* of John Michael Welland and Pamela June Welland (*née* Davey); *m* 1981, Dr Esme Lynora Otun; two *s* two *d*. *Educ:* Univ. of Leeds (BSc Physics 1979); Univ. of Bristol (PhD Physics 1984); MA Cambridge 1988. FInstP 2001; FREng 2002; FIET (FIEE 2002). Lectr in Electrical Engrg, 1986–95, Reader in Nanoscale Sci., 1995–99, Univ. of Cambridge; Fellow, St John's Coll., Cambridge, 1986–2016. Chief Scientific Advr, MoD, 2008–12. World Trade Vis. Scientist, IBM Res. Div., Yorktown Heights, USA, 1985–86. Turing Lect., IEE and BCS, 2002; Sterling Lectr, Russell Gp Univs, 2003; Materials Res. Soc. of India Lect., 2004; Max-Planck Soc. Lect., 2007. Foreign Mem., Danish Acad. of Scis, 2010. Foreign Fellow, Nat. Acad. of Scis, India, 2008. Hon. DSc Bristol, 2015. Gold Medal, Nat. Nuclear Security Admin, Dept of Energy, USA, 2011; Office of Sec. of Defense Medal for Exceptional Public Service, Dept of Defense, USA, 2011. *Publications:* numerous contribs to learned jls, Trans Royal Soc. and NATO pubns. *Recreations:* bee-keeping, squash, ski-ing. *Address:* Master's Lodge, St Catharine's College, Cambridge CB2 1RL. *E:* mew10@cam.ac.uk.

**WELLER, Sir Ian (Vincent Derrick)**, Kt 2015; MD; FRCP; Professor, Centre for Sexual Health and HIV Research, Department of Infection and Population Health, University College London (formerly at University College London Medical School, later Royal Free and University College Medical School of University College London), 1991–2011, now Emeritus Professor; *b* 27 March 1950; *s* of Derrick Charles William Weller and Eileen Weller; *m* 1972, Darryl McKenna; two *d*. *Educ:* Westlain Grammar Sch., Brighton; St Bartholomew's Hosp. Med. Sch. (BSc 1st Cl. Hons 1971; MB BS 1974; MD 1983). MRCP 1977, FRCP 1990. House physician, Med. Unit, St Bartholomew's Hosp. and house surgeon, Hackney Hosp., 1975; SHO rotation, Northwick Park Hosp., 1976–77; Med. Registrar rotation, St Mary's Hosp., London, 1977–79; Ingram Res. Fellow, then Hon. Lectr and MRC Trng Fellow, Acad. Dept of Medicine, Royal Free Hosp., 1979–82; Lectr and Hon. Sen. Registrar, Acad. Dept of Genito-Urinary Medicine, 1982–84, Wellcome Trust Sen. Lectr in Infectious Diseases, 1984–88, Middx Hosp. Med. Sch.; Reader in Genito-Urinary Medicine, UCL Med. Sch., 1988–91; Hd, Dept of Sexually Transmitted Diseases, UCL Med. Sch., subseq. Royal Free and University Coll. Med. Sch. of UCL, 1994–2003. Dir, Camden PCT, 2002–10 (Mem. and Dep. Chm., Ethics Cttee, 1995–2010). Member: UK Adv. Panel for Health Care Workers Infected with Blood Borne Viruses, DoH, 1993–2005 (Chair, tripartite wkg gp, 2007–); Genito-Urinary Specialist Cttee, RCP, 1994–2005; Adv. Gp to HEA, 1994–97; Jt Med. Adv. Cttee to HEFC, 2000–06; MRC Committees: AIDS Res. Co-ordinating Cttee, 1994–; AIDS Therapeutics Cttee, 1987–2000 (Dep. Chm.; Chm., Anti-viral Sub-gp); Data and Safety Monitoring Bd of two internat. breast cancer trials (IBISII and DCIS), and nat. trial in HIV infection; Vice Chair, Commn on Human Medicines (formerly Cttee on Safety of Medicines), 1999–2014; Chairman: Steering Gp, N Thames Regl AIDS/HIV Educn Prog., 1994–2001; internat. study steering cttees of many internat. trials in HIV/AIDS funded by MRC, DFID and Eur. and Developing Countries Clinical Trials Partnership in Uganda, Zimbabwe, Malawi, Zambia and Kenya, 2003–; HIV/Viral Diseases Scientific Adv. Gp, Cttee for Human Medicinal Products, EMEA, 2005–; Collaboration of Observational HIV Epidemiology Res. Europe, 2005–14; Specialist Adv. Gp on HIV and Viral Diseases, EMEA, 2006–14; Chm. of Scientific Cttee and organiser, Internat. Congress on Drug Therapy in HIV Infection, 1992–2012. Member: Eur./Australian Internat. Co-ordinating Cttee for trials in HIV infection and AIDS, 1989–2000; Internat. Sci. Adv. Gp, Agence Nationale de Recherches sur le SIDA, 2000–12; Bd, Internat. AIDS Soc., 2001–08 (Treas.); Ind. Expert Mem., Strategic Working Gp, Div. of AIDS, NIH, 2007–14. Mem. and Chm. of Bd, Terrence Higgins Trust, 1998–2001; Trustee, HIV Trust, 2011–14 (Chm., 2015–). Hon. FRCPGlas 2012. *Publications:* over 200 pubns in peer reviewed jls and numerous book chapters and review articles. *Recreations:* golf, walking, farming, soccer and horseball supporter. *Address:* Centre for Sexual Health and HIV Research, University College London, Mortimer Market Centre, Mortimer Market, off Capper Street, WC1E 6JP.

**WELLER, Prof. Marc**, Dr jur, Dr phil, PhD; Professor of International Law and International Constitutional Studies, University of Cambridge, since 2010; Fellow of Hughes Hall, Cambridge, since 1997; barrister; *b* Hamburg, 1960; *s* of Wulf P. G. and Antje Weller; *m* 2006, Leonora Visoka; one *s* one *d*. *Educ:* Univ. of Frankfurt (Dr jur); Univ. of Hamburg (Dr phil); Univ. of Cambridge (MA; PhD); Fletcher Sch. of Law and Diplomacy, Tufts Univ. (MALD). FCIArb; Accredited Mediator. Called to the Bar, Middle Temple; University of Cambridge: Mem., Faculty of Law, 1990–; Fellow, 1990–, Dir, 2010–16, Lauterpacht Centre (formerly Res. Centre) for Internat. Law; Dep. Dir, Centre for Internat. Studies, 1997–2000. Dir, Europ. Centre for Minority Issues, 2000–09; Sen. Mediation Expert, Dept of Pol Affairs, UN Secretariat, NY, 2011–12. Former Dir of Studies, Hague Acad. for Internat. Law; former Visiting Professor: Univ. of Paris; Keio Univ.; Vincent Wright Prof., Sciences Po, Paris, 2015–16. Halsbury Legal Award, 2014; Ius Gentium Prize for Res. and Pubn in Law, Amer. Soc. Internat. Law, 2017. *Publications:* (jtly) The Kuwait Crisis: basic documents, 1991; Democracy and Politics in Burma, 1993; Iraq and Kuwait: the hostilities and their aftermath, 1993; Regional Peace-keeping and International Enforcement: the Liberian crisis, 1994; (with Daniel Bethlehem) The Yugoslav Crisis in International Law: general issues, 1997; The Crisis in Kosovo 1989–99, 1999, 2nd edn 2001; The Kosovo Conflict: the conduct and termination of hostilities and the renewed search for a settlement, 2001; (ed with Jorn Kuehl) Minority Governance in Action, 2005; (ed with Stefan Wolff) Autonomy, Self-Governance and Conflict Resolution, 2005; (ed with Alexander H. E. Morawa) Mechanisms for the Implementation of Minority Rights, 2005; (ed) The Rights of Minorities: commentary on the European Framework Convention for the Protection of National Minorities, 2005; (ed with Stefan Wolff) Internationalized State-building after Violent Conflict: Dayton after ten years, 2007; (ed) Universal Minority Rights: a commentary on the jurisprudence of international court and treaty bodies, 2007; (ed with Barbara Metzger) Settling Self-determination Conflicts, 2008; Peace Lost: missed opportunities for conflict prevention in Kosovo, 2008; (ed with Stefan Wolff) Institutions for the Management of Ethnopolitical Conflict in Eastern and Central Europe, 2008; (ed jtly) The Protection of Minorities in the Wider Europe, 2008; Escaping the Self-determination Trap, 2008; Contested Statehood: Kosovo's struggle for independence (Shtetesia e kuntestuar), 2009; (ed with Katherine Nobbs) Asymmetrical State Design as a Tool of Ethnopolitical Conflict Settlement, 2010; Iraq and the Use of Force in International Law, 2010; (ed with Katherine Nobbs) Political Participation of Minorities, 2010; (ed) Handbook on the Use of Force in International Law, 2015; (jtly) The Protection of Civilians in International Law, 2016. *Recreations:* sailing, fencing, archery. *E:* mw148@cam.ac.uk.

**WELLER, Ven. Dr Susan Karen**; Archdeacon of Lichfield, and Archdeacon Missioner, Diocese of Lichfield, since 2019; *b* Beverley, 20 Aug. 1965; *d* of Brian and June Spence; *m* 1997, David Weller; one *d*. *Educ:* Wolfreton Sch.; Univ. of Leeds (BSc Botany and Zool. 1986); Univ. of Liverpool (PhD Marine Pollution 1989); Univ. of Oxford (BA Theol. 1995). Higher Scientific Officer, 1989–93; ordained deacon, 1996, priest, 1997; Curate, Caverswall, Weston Coyney and Dilhorne, 1996–99; Associate Minister: Wilnecote, 2000–05; Christ Church, Rio de Janeiro, 2005–11; Interim Minister: Wednesfield, 2012–14; Darlaston and Moxley, 2014; Archdeacon of Walsall, 2015–19. *Recreation:* travel. *Address:* Diocese of Lichfield, St Mary's House, The Close, Lichfield WS13 7LD. *T:* (01543) 306030.

**WELLESLEY**, family name of **Duke of Wellington** and of **Earl Cowley**.

**WELLESLEY, Viscount; Arthur Darcy Wellesley**; *b* 4 Jan. 2010; *s* and *heir* of Earl of Mornington, *qv*.

**WELLINGS, Prof. Paul William**, CBE 2012; PhD; Vice-Chancellor and Principal, University of Wollongong, New South Wales, since 2012; *b* 1 Nov. 1953; *s* of late William and Beryl Wellings; *m* 1990, Annette Frances Schmidt. *Educ:* Royal Grammar Sch., Lancaster; King's Coll. London (BSc Hons); Durham Univ. (MSc); Univ. of E Anglia (PhD 1980). NERC Res. Fellow, 1980–81; Res. Scientist, 1981–95, Chief of Div. of Entomol., 1995–97, CSIRO; First Asst Sec., Dept of Industry, Sci. and Resources, Australia, 1997–99; Dep. Chief Exec., CSIRO, Australia, 1999–2002; Vice Chancellor and Prof. of Population Ecology, Lancaster Univ., 2002–11. Chm., 1994 Gp, 2009–11. Board Member: Australian Nuclear Sci. and Technol. Orgn, 1996–99; Australian Centre for Internat. Agricl Res., 2000–02; HEFCE, 2006–11; UUK, 2006–11. Member, Board of Trustees: Guangdong Univ. of Foreign Studies, 2011–16; Univ. of Wollongong in Dubai, 2012. Univ. of Wollongong USA Foundn, 2013–. Member, Board: Cumbria Rural Regeneration Co., 2003–06; Bundanon Trust, 2015–; Member: New Colombo Plan Adv. Cttee, Canberra, 2013–; Res. Infra Rev. Wkg Gp, Canberra, 2014–15; Internat. Educn Adv. Bd, NSW, 2014–; Adv. Bd, Australian Res. Council, 2015–; Adv. Council, Global Foundn, 2015–; Innovation and Productivity Council, NSW, 2016–; Dep. Chair, Steering Cttee, Cttee for Sydney, 2017–18. Regl Develt Australia Illawarra, 2018–. FAICD 2001; FRSA 2004; FRSN 2018. Hon. DSc Lancaster, 2014; DUniv Surrey, 2019. DL Lancs, 2009. *Publications:* numerous contribs in fields of insect ecology and pest mgt. *Recreations:* cricket, fell-walking, visual arts. *Address:* University of Wollongong, Northfields Avenue, Wollongong, NSW 2522, Australia. *T:* (2) 42213909. *E:* wellings@uow.edu.au.

**WELLINGTON, 9th Duke of**, *cr* 1814; **Arthur Charles Valerian Wellesley**, OBE 1999; DL; Baron Mornington, 1746; Earl of Mornington, Viscount Wellesley, 1760; Viscount Wellington of Talavera and Wellington, Somersetshire, Baron Douro, 1809; Earl of Wellington, Feb. 1812; Marquess of Wellington, Oct. 1812; Marquess of Douro, 1814; Prince of Waterloo, 1815, Netherlands (now Belgium); Count of Vimeiro, Marquess of Torres Vedras and Duke of Victoria in Portugal; Duke of Cuidad Rodrigo in Spain, 1812 and a Grandee of Spain 1st class; Chairman, Richemont Holdings UK Ltd (formerly Vendôme Luxury Group Ltd), since 1993; Director: Compagnie Financière Richemont, 1999–2017 (International Consultant, since 2017); RIT Capital Partners plc, since 2010; *b* 19 Aug. 1945; *e s* of 8th Duke of Wellington, KG, LVO, OBE, MC and Diana Ruth Wellesley (*née* McConnel), MBE; *S* father, 2014; *m* 1977, Antonia von Preussen (*see* Duchess of Wellington); two *s* three *d*. *Educ:* Eton; Christ Church, Oxford. Deputy Chairman: Thames Valley Broadcasting, 1975–84; Deltec Panamerica SA, 1985–89; Guinness Mahon Hldgs, 1988–91; Director: Antofagasta and Bolivia Railway Co., 1977–80; Eucalyptus Pulp Mills, 1979–88; Transatlantic Hldgs, 1983–95; Global Asset Mgt Worldwide Inc., 1984–2013; Continental and Industrial Trust plc, 1987–90; Sanofi (formerly Sanofi-Synthélabo, then Sanofi-aventis) SA, 2002–14; Pernod Ricard SA, 2003–11; Chairman: Deltec Securities (UK) Ltd, 1985–89; Dunhill Holdings, 1991–93; Sun Life Corp., subseq. Sun Life and Provincial Hldgs plc, 1995–2000; Framlington Gp plc, 1994–2005. Comr, English Heritage, 2003–07. Chm. Council, King's Coll. London, 2007–16. Gov., Wellington Coll., 2015–. Trustee, RUSI, 2016–. MEP (C): Surrey, 1979–84; Surrey West, 1984–89; contested (C) Islington N, Oct. 1974; Mem., Basingstoke Borough Council, 1978–79. Elected Mem., H of L, 2015–. High Steward, Winchester Cathedral, 2013–. DL Hants, 1999. Grand Officer, Order of Merit (Portugal), 1987; Grand Cross, Order of Isabel the Catholic (Spain), 2000. *Heir: s* Earl of Mornington, *qv*. *Address:* Apsley House, Piccadilly, W1J 7NT; Stratfield Saye House, Hants RG7 2BZ.

**WELLINGTON, Duchess of; Antonia Elisabeth Brigid Luise Wellesley**, OBE 2008; President, Guinness Partnership (formerly Guinness Trust), since 2007 (Trustee, 1976–2007; Chairman, 1984–2007); Chairman, Royal Ballet School, since 2009; *b* 28 April 1955; *d* of late Prince Friedrich of Prussia and Lady Brigid (*née* Guinness; she *m* 2nd, Maj. A. P. Ness); *m* 1977, Marquess of Douro (*see* Duke of Wellington); two *s* three *d*. *Educ:* Cobham Hall, Kent; King's Coll., London (BA; FKC 2014). Director: Thames Valley Broadcasting, 1984–87; English Nat. Ballet, 1987–90; Scenarist, Frankenstein (ballet), Covent Garden, 1987. Mem. Cttee, London Library, 1981–86; Trustee: Getty Endowment Fund for Nat. Gall., 1985–92; Hermitage Develt Trust, Somerset House, 2000–05; NPG, 2004–12. Pres., Royal Hosp. for Neuro-disability, 1991–2001. Patron, Loddon Sch., 1996–. Fellow, Eton Coll., 2008–. *Address:* Stratfield Saye House, Hants RG7 2BZ; Apsley House, Piccadilly, W1J 7NT.

**WELLINGTON (NZ), Archbishop of**, (RC), since 2005; **His Eminence Cardinal John Atcherley Dew**; Metropolitan, and Military Ordinary, for New Zealand, since 2005; *b* 5 May 1948; *s* of Alfred George Dew and Joan Theresa Dew (*née* McCarthy). *Educ:* St Joseph's Coll., Masterton; Holy Name Seminary, Christchurch; Holy Cross Coll., Mosgiel (BTh 1975). Ordained deacon, 1975, priest, 1976; Asst Priest, St Joseph's Parish, Upper Hutt, 1976–79; Parish Priest, St Joseph's Cathedral Parish, Dio. Rarotonga, Cook Is, 1980–82; Leader, Archdiocesan Youth Ministry Team and Chaplain to Cook Is Maori Community, 1983–87; Dir, First Year Formation, Holy Cross Coll., Mosgiel, 1988–91; study leave, St Anselm, Kent, England, 1991–92; Parish Priest, St Anne's, Newtown, 1993–95; Auxiliary Bishop, Archdio. Wellington, 1995–2004; Co-adjutor Archbishop of Wellington, 2004. Cardinal, 2015. *Address:* Archdiocese of Wellington, PO Box 1937, Wellington 6140, New Zealand. *T:* (4) 4961766. *E:* j.dew@wn.catholic.org.nz.

**WELLINGTON (NZ), Bishop of,** since 2012; Rt Rev. Justin Charles Hopkins Duckworth; *b* Lower Hutt, NZ, 25 Nov. 1967; *s* of Leslie Duckworth and Alison Claire Duckworth; *m* 1991, Jennifer Boland; one *s* two *d*. *Educ*: Victoria Univ. (BSc 1989; BA Hons 1995); Massey Univ. (MPhil 1999); Melbourne Coll. of Divinity (BDiv 1999). Ordained deacon, 2005, priest, 2006; Asst Priest, Waikanae, 2006–12. *Publications*: (with Jenny Duckworth) Against the Tide, Towards the Kingdom, 2011. *Recreations*: running, tramping. *Address*: c/o Diocese of Wellington, PO Box 12046, Wellington 6144, New Zealand. *T*: (4) 4718597, *Fax*: (4) 4991360. *E*: justin@wn.ang.org.nz.

**WELLINK, Arnout Henricus Elisabeth Maria;** Executive Director, 1982–2011, and President, 1997–2011, De Nederlandsche Bank; *b* 27 Aug. 1943; *m* 1989, Monica Victoria Volmer; three *s* two *d*. *Educ*: Gymnasium B; Leyden Univ. (law degree 1968); Univ. of Rotterdam (PhD Econs 1975). Teaching asst in econs, and staff mem., Leyden Univ., 1965–70; Ministry of Finance: staff mem., 1970–75; Hd, Directorate Gen. for Financial and Econ. Policy, 1975–77; Treas. Gen., 1977–81. Mem. Bd of Dirs, 1997–2011, Pres., 2002–04, BIS, Basle (Mem., Banking and Risk Cttee, 2007–11); Chm., Basel Cttee on Banking Supervision, 2006–11; Member: Council, Eur. Monetary Inst., 1997–98; Gp of Ten Governors, Basel, 1997–2011; Governing Council and Gen. Council, 1999–2011, Audit Cttee, 2007–11, European Central Bank; Financial Stability Bd, 1999–2011; Trilateral Commn, 2000–11; Gov., IMF, 1997–2011. Ind. non-exec. Dir, Bank of China, 2012–18. Mem. Bd of Govs, Nat. Acad. for Finance and Economy, 2003. Chairman: Bd of Trustees, Mus. of Mauritius; King William I Foundn, 1997; Supervisory Bd (formerly Bd of Trustees), Nederlands Openlucht Mus., 2003; Supervisory Bd, Leiden Univ., 2008–16; Member: Bd, Foundn for Orthopaedic Patients' Interests, 1995; Foundn for Postgrad. Med. Trng in Indonesia, 1997; N. G. Pierson Fund Foundn, 1997–. Kt, Order of Lion (Netherlands), 1981; Comdr, Order of Orange-Nassau (Netherlands), 2011.

**WELLS, Dean of;** *see* Davies, Very Rev. J. H.

**WELLS, Archdeacon of;** *see* Gell, Ven. A. E.

**WELLS, Andrew Mark;** *b* 22 Feb. 1955; *s* of Richard Frederick Wells and Eunice Mary Wells (*née* Williams); partner, Pam Temple; one *d*. *Educ*: Bristol Grammar Sch.; St John's Coll., Cambridge (MA Maths 1976). Grad. trainee, 1976–83, Principal, Local Govt Finance, 1983–87, DoE; on loan as Principal, Econ. Secretariat, Cabinet Office, 1987–90; Department of the Environment: Divl Manager, Local Govt Rev. Team, 1990–92; Hd, London Policy Unit, 1992–93; Divisional Manager: Local Authy Housing, 1993–96; Water Supply and Regulation, 1996–99; on loan as Dir, Modernising Govt, Cabinet Office, 1999–2000; Dir, Regl Co-ordination Unit, Cabinet Office, then ODPM, 2000–03; Dir, New Homes and Sustainable Communities, ODPM, then DCLG, 2003–08; Dir, Planning, DCLG, 2009–11. Advr, London Legacy Develt Corp., 2011–12. Dir, Marine Mgt Orgn, 2013–19. Chm., Redbridge Homes, 2011–12; Director: Moat Homes Ltd, 2010–16; Catalyst Homes Ltd, 2017–. *Recreations*: walking, cycling.

**WELLS, Bowen;** international development specialist, since 2001; *b* 4 Aug. 1935; *s* of late Reginald Laird Wells and of Agnes Mary Wells (*née* Hunter); *m* 1975, Rennie Heyde; two *s*. *Educ*: St Paul's School; Univ. of Exeter (BA Hons); Regent St Polytechnic School of Management (Dip. Business Management). National Service, RN (promoted to Sub Lt), 1954–56. Schoolmaster, Colet Court, 1956–57; sales trainee, British Aluminium, 1957–58; Univ. of Exeter, 1958–61; Commonwealth Development Corporation, 1961–73; Owner Manager, Substation Group Services Ltd, 1973–79. Board Member: CARE UK, 2001–07; AMREF UK, 2001–07. MP (C) Hertford and Stevenage, 1979–83, Hertford and Stortford, 1983–2001. Parliamentary Private Secretary: to Minister of State for Employment, 1982–83; to Minister of State at Dept of Transport, 1992–94; an Asst Govt Whip, 1994–95; a Lord Comr of HM Treasury (Govt Whip), 1994–97. Member: For. Affairs Select Cttee, 1981–92; European Legislation Select Cttee, 1983–92; Chairman: Select Cttee on Internat. Develt, 1997–2001; UN Parly Gp, 1983–92; British-Caribbean Gp, 1983–95; Jt Hon. Sec., Parly Cons. Trade and Industry Gp, 1984–91 (Vice-Chm., 1983–84); Sec., All Party Overseas Develt Gp, 1984–94; Sec., Cons. Envmt Cttee, 1991–92; Mem., 1922 Exec.; Mem., British-American Gp, 1985. Mem. Exec. Bd, 2004–, Treas., 2010–15, Assoc. of Former MPs. Member: UK Br. Exec., CPA, 1984–2001 (Treas., 1997–2001); Exec. Cttee, Internat. CPA, 1994–98 (Treas., 1998–2001). Trustee, Industry and Parlt Trust, 1985–2001. Gov., Inst. of Development Studies, 1980–94; Mem. Bd, ODI, 1997–2008. Rep. of BVI, 2002–03. *Publications*: (jtly) Bridging the Gap, 2011. *Recreations*: music, walking, gardening, cooking, sailing. *Address*: Saltings, Harbour Road, Bosham, Chichester, W Sussex PO18 8JE. *Club*: Bosham Sailing.

**WELLS, Brigid;** *see* Wells, J. B. E.

**WELLS, Christopher;** *see* Wells, J. C. D.

**WELLS, Sir Christopher (Charles),** 3rd Bt *cr* 1944, of Felmersham, co. Bedford; *b* 12 Aug. 1936; *s* of Sir Charles Maltby Wells, 2nd Bt and of Katharine Boulton Wells; *S* father, 1996; *m* 1st, 1960, Elizabeth Florence Vaughan (marr. diss. 1983), *d* of I. F. Griffiths; two *s* two *d*; 2nd, 1985, Lynda Ann Cormack; one *s*. *Educ*: McGill Univ., Montreal (BSc); Univ. of Toronto (MD). MD in family practice, retired 1995. Assoc. Prof., Faculty of Medicine, Univ. of Toronto, 1975–95. *Heir*: *s* Michael Christopher Gruffydd Wells, *b* 24 Oct. 1966. *Address*: 1268 Seaforth Crescent, RR#3, Lakefield, ON K0L 2H0, Canada.

**WELLS, Hon. Clyde (Kirby);** Chief Justice of Newfoundland, 1999–2009; Counsel, Cox and Palmer, St John's, Newfoundland, since 2013 (Chairman of Board, 2014–18); *b* Buchans Junction, Newfoundland, 9 Nov. 1937; *s* of Ralph Pennell Wells and Maude Wells (*née* Kirby); *m* 1962, Eleanor, *d* of Arthur and Daisy Bishop; two *s* one *d*. *Educ*: All Saints Sch., Stephenville Crossing; Memorial Univ., Newfoundland (BA 1959); Dalhousie Univ. Law Sch. (LLB 1962). Served with Canadian Army, JAG's Office, 1962–64; called to the Bar, Nova Scotia, 1963, Newfoundland, 1964; Partner, Barry and Wells, and successor law firms, 1964–81; Senior Partner, Wells & Co., 1981–87; QC (Newfoundland) 1977; Counsel, O'Reilly, Noseworthy, 1996–98; Justice, Court of Appeal, Newfoundland, 1998–99. Dir, 1978–87, and Chm., 1985–87, Newfoundland Light & Power Co. Ltd. MHA (L): Humber East, 1966–71; Windsor-Buchans, Dec. 1987–1989; Bay of Islands, 1989–96; Minister of Labour, 1966–68; Leader of Liberal Party, 1987; Premier of Newfoundland and Labrador, 1989–96. Hon. LLD Memorial, Newfoundland, 1996. *Address*: Cox and Palmer, Suite 1100, Scotia Centre, 235 Water Street, St John's, NL A1C 1B6, Canada; 305–25 Bonaventure Avenue, St John's, NL A1C 6N8, Canada. *E*: ckwells@coxandpalmer.com.

**WELLS, Prof. David Arthur;** Professor of German, Birkbeck College, University of London, 1987–2006, now Emeritus; *b* 26 April 1941; *s* of Arthur William Wells and Rosina Elizabeth (*née* Jones). *Educ*: Christ's Hosp., Horsham; Gonville and Caius Coll., Cambridge; Univs of Strasbourg, Vienna and Münster. Mod. and Med. Langs Tripos, BA 1963, Tiarks Studentship 1963–64, MA, PhD Cantab 1967. Asst Lectr 1966–67, Lectr 1967–69, in German, Univ. of Southampton; Lectr in German, Bedford Coll., Univ. of London, 1969–74; Sec., London Univ. Bd of Staff Examiners in German, 1973–74; Lectr, Nat. Extension Coll., Cambridge, 1966–74; Prof. of German, QUB, 1974–87. Lecture tour of NZ univs, 1975. Mem., Managing Body, Oakington Manor Jun. Mixed and Infant Sch., London Bor. of Brent, 1972–74. Hon. Treasurer: Assoc. for Literary and Linguistic Computing, 1973–78; MHRA, 2001–09 (Hon. Sec., 1969–2001); Pres., Internat. Fedn for Modern Langs and Lits, 2005–08 (Sec.-Gen., 1981–2005). Jt Editor, The Year's Work in Modern Language Studies, 1976–2004 (Editor, 1982). FRSA 1983. *Publications*: The Vorau Moses and Balaam: a study of their relationship to exegetical tradition, 1970; The Wild Man from the Epic of Gilgamesh to Hartmann von Aue's Iwein, 1975; A Complete Concordance to the Vorauer Bücher Moses (Concordances to the Early Middle High German Biblical Epic), 1976; (contrib.) MHRA Style Guide: a handbook for authors, 2002; The Central Franconian Rhyming Bible, 2004; articles, monographs and reviews in learned jls. *Recreations*: travel, theatre, music. *Address*: School of Languages, Linguistics and Culture, Birkbeck College, 43 Gordon Square, WC1H 0PD. *T*: (020) 7631 6103.

**WELLS, David George;** Managing Director, Service, British Gas plc, 1993–96; *b* 6 Aug. 1941; *s* of George Henry Wells and Marian (*née* Trolley); *m* 1967, Patricia Ann Fenwick; two *s*. *Educ*: Market Harborough Grammar Sch.; Reading Univ. (BA). FCA 1966. Hancock, Gilbert & Morris, 1962–67; Esso Chemical Ltd, 1967–69; joined Gas Council, 1969; Investment Accountant (Investment Appraisal), 1970–73; British Gas Corporation: Chief Accountant, Admin, 1973–76; Chief Investment Accountant, 1976; Dir of Finance, SE Reg., 1976–83; Dep. Chm., W Midlands Reg., 1983–88; Regl Chm., S Eastern, 1988–93; Man. Dir, Regl Services, 1993. Director: Metrogas Bldg Soc., 1978–86 (Dep. Chm., 1979–83); Port Greenwich Ltd, 1989–. Chm., S London Trng and Enterprise Council, 1989–93. CIGEM (CIGasE 1988); CCMI (CBIM 1990); FRSA 1991. *Recreations*: world travel, walking, reading, photography, bridge, U3A activities, gardening. *Address*: 11 Parklands, Ewood, Surrey RH8 9DP.

**WELLS, Dominic Richard Alexander;** screenwriter and freelance journalist, since 2007; *b* 7 March 1963; *s* of late Prof. Colin M. Wells and of Catherine Wells; two *s*. *Educ*: Winchester Coll.; New Coll., Oxford (BA Hons Modern History). Gofer, Muller, Blond & White Publishing Ltd, 1985–86; Sub-Editor, London's Alternative Magazine, 1986–87; Time Out magazine: Sub-Editor, then Chief Sub-Editor, subseq. Dep. Editor, 1987–92; Editor, 1992–98; Editorial Dir, AOL Bertelsmann Online, 1999–2001; Editor in Chief, AOL UK, 2001–02; Ed., Play mag., 2002–03, The Eye, later The Knowledge mag., 2003–07, Saturday Times. Editor of the Year, BSME, 1992, 1994, 1995, 1998. *Recreation*: Texas Hold 'Em poker. *Address*: 3 Chantrey Road, SW9 9TD. *T*: (020) 3133 2060. *E*: DominicRAWells@aol.com.

**WELLS, Doreen Patricia, (Doreen, Marchioness of Londonderry);** dancer and actress; Ballerina of the Royal Ballet, 1955–74; Founder, Doreen Wells Summer Ballet School, East Bridgford Hill, since 2013; *m* 9th Marquess of Londonderry, (marr. diss. 1989; he *d* 2012); two *s*. *Educ*: Walthamstow; Bush Davies School; Royal Ballet School. Engaged in Pantomime, 1952 and 1953. Joined Royal Ballet, 1955; became Principal Dancer, 1960; has danced leading roles in Noctambules, Harlequin in April, Dance Concertante, Sleeping Beauty, Coppelia, Swan Lake, Sylvia, La Fille mal Gardée, Two Pigeons, Giselle, Invitation, Rendezvous, Blood Wedding, Raymonda, Concerto, Nutcracker, Romeo and Juliet, Concerto No 2 (Ballet Imperial); has created leading roles in Toccata, La Création du Monde, Sinfonietta, Prometheus, Grand Tour; also starred in West End musicals. Choreographer and Co-Dir, Canterbury Pilgrims for the Canterbury Fest., 2000; Reader, 600th anniv. of Geoffrey Chaucer, Southwark Cathedral and Westminster Abbey, 2000; Consultant, Images of Dance performing gp, London Studio Centre, 2005–. Founder Mem., Foundn of Purcell Sch., 2004–. Patron: British Ballet Orgn; ISTD Ballet; Chelmsford Ballet Co.; Liverpool Proscenium Youth Ballet Co.; Liverpool Th. Sch. and Coll. Ltd; Tiffany Sch. of Dancing; GB Fest. of Music and Dance; Casa dei Mezzo Music Fest., Crete. Pres., Radionic Assoc., 2004–. Hon. Prof. of Classical Ballet, Dublin Metropolitan Univ., 2011. Hon. MA, 2011, Hon. DLit, 2011, Dublin Metropolitan Univ. Adeline Genée Gold Medal, 1954. *Recreations*: music, theatre-going, charity fundraising.
*See also* Marquess of Londonderry.

**WELLS, Howard James Cowen,** OBE 2013; Vice-President, Sport and Recreation Alliance (formerly Central Council of Physical Education), since 2016 (Director, 2000–16; Chairman, 2001–05; Deputy Chairman, 2011–13); *b* 9 Jan. 1947; *s* of late Harold Arthur James Wells and Joan Wells (*née* Cowen, later Moore); *m* 1971, Linda Baines (marr. diss. 2017); one *s* one *d*. *Educ*: Leeds Univ. (BEd, Cert Ed); Carnegie Coll. (Dip. in Phys. Educn). Head of Boys' Phys. Educn, Brooklands Sch., Leighton Buzzard, 1970–72; Lectr-in-Charge of Phys. Recreation, Hitchin Coll., 1972–74; Dep. Dir, Bisham Abbey Nat. Sports Centre, 1975–81; Operations Manager, 1981–84, Chief Exec., 1984–89, Jubilee Sports Centre, Hong Kong; Chief Executive: Hong Kong Sports Develt Bd, 1989–96; UK Sports Council, 1996–98; Watford Assoc. FC, 1998–99; Ipswich Town FC, 1999–2000. CEO, Irish Football Assoc., 2005–08; Chief Exec., Sport Pathways Ltd, 2013–14. Non-executive Director: Premier Sport & Media Ltd, 2000–05; Sportsgate Ltd, 2002–05; Hello Communications Gp, 2018–19; Chairman: Rebben Ltd, 2007–19; Memorial Walls Ltd (County Cemetery Services Ltd), 2013–14; Adastra Sport Mgt, 2016–18; Dacorum Sports Network; Tring Athletic FC. Mem., Saudi Arabian-UK Memorandum of Understanding Gp in Sport, 1996–2010. Governor: Shatin Coll., Hong Kong, 1984–96; Ashlyns Sch., Berkhamsted, 1996–2003. *Publications*: Start Living Now, 1979. *Recreations*: Football Association (full qualifying coaching licence, 1973), theatre, travel. *Address*: Sport and Recreation Alliance, Burwood House, Caxton Street, SW1W 0QT. *Clubs*: Oriental, Scribes, Carbine.

**WELLS, Jack Dennis;** Vice President, Aircraft Owners and Pilots Association, since 2011 (Executive Director, 1991–2010; Vice-Chairman, 1996–98); Assistant Director, Central Statistical Office, 1979–88; *b* 8 April 1928; *s* of late C. W. Wells and H. M. Wells (*née* Clark); *m* 1st, 1953, Jean Allison; one *s* one *d*; 2nd, 1987, Cynthia Palmer. *Educ*: Hampton Grammar Sch.; Polytechnic of Central London. AIS 1955. Ministry of Fuel and Power, 1947; Royal Air Force, 1947–49; Min. of (Fuel and) Power, 1949–69; Private Secretary to Paymaster General, 1957–59; Chief Statistician, Dept of Economic Affairs, 1969; Min. of Technology, 1969; HM Treasury, 1970; Dept of (Trade and) Industry, 1971–79. Pres., CS Aviation Assoc., 1988–2009. Sec. and Dir, 1997–2002, Vice Pres., 2003–, Gen. Aviation Awareness Council. Vice Pres., Old Hamptonians Assoc., 2011– (Past Chm.). *Publications*: contribs to Long Range Planning, Economic Trends, Statistical News, Review of Income and Wealth, Jl of Banking and Finance, BIEC Yearbook. *Recreations*: watching cricket, jazz, travel. *Clubs*: Civil Service, MCC, Probus.

**WELLS, James Henry;** Member (DemU) South Down, Northern Ireland Assembly, since 1998; *b* 27 April 1957; *s* of Samuel Henry Wells and Doreen Wells; *m* 1983, Violet Grace Wallace; one *s* two *d*. *Educ*: Lurgan Coll.; Queen's Univ., Belfast (BA Hons Geog. 1979; DipTP 1981). Mem. (DemU) S Down, NI Assembly, 1982–86; research asst, RSPB, 1987–88; Asst Regl Public Affairs Manager, NI Reg., NT, 1989–98. Minister for Health, Social Services and Public Safety, NI, 2014–15. Contested (DUP) S Down, 2010, 2015. *Recreations*: birdwatching, hill-walking. *Address*: 12 Bridge Street, Kilkeel, Newry BT34 4AD.

**WELLS, James Nicholas M.;** *see* Murray Wells.

**WELLS, (Jennifer) Brigid (Ellen);** Chairman Assessor, Civil Service Selection Board, 1989–95; *b* 18 Feb. 1928; *d* of Dr Leonard John Haydon, TD, MA Cantab, MB BCh and Susan Eleanor Haydon (*née* Richmond), actress; *m* 1962, Ian Vane Wells (*d* 2017); three *d*. *Educ*: schools in UK, USA, Canada; Edinburgh Univ.; Lady Margaret Hall, Oxford (scholar; BA Mod. Hist.; MA); PG Dip. Couns., Univ. of Brighton, 1995. Commonwealth Relations Office, 1949; UK High Commn, NZ, 1952–54; Private Sec. to Parly Under-Sec. of State, CRO, 1954–56; MAFF, 1956–62; teaching: LCC, 1962–63; Haringey, 1967; Camden Sch. for Girls, 1969–75 (to Head of Dept); Head of Dept, St David's and St Katharine's, Hornsey, 1975–77; Headmistress, Brighton and Hove High Sch., GPDST, 1978–88. Qualified team inspector: OFSTED, 1994; ISI (formerly ARCS), 1995–2003. Chm. designate, W Sussex Ambulance NHS Trust, 1992–93. Member: Local Radio Council, 1980–82; Broadcasting Complaints Commn, 1986–93 (Chm., Jan.–June 1992); Chairman: Educn Cttee, GSA, 1987–88; SE Region, GSA, 1984–86. Project Manager (USA), GAP, 1989–91; Mem., British Atlantic Council, 1988–93; Governor, Woldingham Sch., 1989–97; Comr, Duke of York's Royal Mil. Sch., Dover, 1993–2004. Chm., Friends of GPDST (now GDST), 1991–2003. JP Inner London, 1972–77, Brighton and Hove, 1980–98. *Publications*: (ed jtly) The First Crossing, 2007; articles in learned jls. *Recreations*: gardening, travel. *Address*: 12 Greyfriars Court, Court Road, Lewes, E Sussex BN7 2RF. *T*: (01273) 281870.

**WELLS, Rt Rev. Joanne Caladine Bailey;** *see* Dorking, Bishop Suffragan of.

**WELLS, Sir John,** KNZM 2009 (DCNZM 2009); FCA; Founder, 1986, and non-executive Chairman, 2005–16, Bancorp Group (Executive Chairman, 1986–2005); *b* Wanganui, NZ, 21 July 1943; *s* of Charles and Mary Wells; *m* 1969, Sheryl Gavin; two *s*. *Educ*: Auckland Grammar Sch.; Auckland Univ. (ACA 1973). FCIS 1986. FCA 2016. NZI Financial Corporation: Ops Manager, 1973–76; Co. Sec. and Asst Gen. Manager, 1976–80; Chief Gen. Manager and Dir, 1973–86. Chairman: Greenpark Hldgs Ltd, 1993–; Sheffield Gp Ltd, 2006–10; Auckland City Property Enterprise, 2006–10; Fisher Funds Mgt Ltd, 2008–18; Sheffield N Island Ltd, 2010–18; Auckland Council Property Ltd, 2010–15; CBL Insurance Ltd, 2012–18; CBL Corp. Ltd, 2013–18; Develt Auckland Ltd, 2015–16; Assetinsure Pty Ltd and Assetinsure Hldgs Pty Ltd, 2016–18; Dir, Martin Jenkins & Associates Ltd, 2011–18 (Chm., 2016–); Member: Adv. Bd, Marsh Ltd, 2005–; Karapiro 2010 Ltd (World Rowing Championships), 2007–11. Chairman: NZ Finance Houses Assoc., 1980–84; Hillary Commn, 2001. Chairman: Sport and Recreation NZ, 2001–09; Auckland Stopover Local Organising Cttee, Volvo Ocean Race, 2010–12; Triathlon World Championships 2012 Ltd, 2010–13; World Masters Games 2017 Ltd, 2013–18; Member: Rugby World Cup 2011 Bid Cttee, 2005; RWC 2011 Estabt Bd, 2005–06; Rugby NZ 2011 Ltd, 2006–12. Chm., NZ Sports Foundn Charitable Trust, 2001–09; Trustee, Auckland Grammar Sch. Foundn Trust, 2011–; former Trustee, Life Educn Trust - Northern. Fellow, Chartered Accountants Australia and NZ, 2016. *Recreations*: all sports, cycling, walking. *Address*: PO Box 28540, Remuera, Auckland 1541, New Zealand. *T*: 93028522. *E*: john@jwells.co.nz.

**WELLS, Prof. John Christopher,** PhD; FBA 1996; FCIL; Professor of Phonetics, University College London, 1988–2006, now Emeritus; *b* 11 March 1939; *s* of Rev. Philip Cuthbert Wells and Winifred May (*née* Peaker); civil partnership 2006, Gabriel Parsons. *Educ*: St John's Sch., Leatherhead; Trinity Coll., Cambridge (BA 1960; MA 1964); University Coll., London (MA 1962; PhD 1971). FCIL (FIL 1982). University College London: Asst Lectr in Phonetics, 1962–65; Lectr, 1965–82; Reader, 1982–88; Head, Dept of Phonetics and Linguistics, 1990–2000. Sec., Internat. Phonetic Assoc., 1973–86 (Pres., 2003–); President: World Esperanto Assoc., 1989–95; Simplified Spelling Soc., 2003–. Mem., Esperanto Acad., 1971–. Editor, Jl Internat. Phonetic Assoc., 1971–87. Contribs to radio and TV programmes. *Publications*: Concise Esperanto and English Dictionary, 1969, 2nd edn 2008; (with G. Colson) Practical Phonetics, 1971; Jamaican Pronunciation in London, 1973; (jtly) Jen Nia Mondo 1, 1974 (trans. Italian, Icelandic, Swedish, Finnish); (jtly) Jen Nia Mondo 2, 1977; Lingvistikaj aspektoj de Esperanto, 1978, 2nd edn 1989 (trans. Danish, Korean, German); Accents of English (three vols and cassette), 1982; Geiriadur Esperanto/Kimra vortaro, 1985; (pronunciation editor) Universal Dictionary, 1987; (pronunciation editor) Hutchinson Encyclopedia, 8th edn 1988, and subsequent editions; Longman Pronunciation Dictionary, 1990, 3rd edn 2008; English Intonation: an introduction, 2006; Sounds Interesting: observations on English and general phonetics, 2014; Sounds Fascinating: further observations on English phonetics and phonology, 2016; articles in learned jls and collective works. *Recreations*: reading, walking, playing the melodeon. *Address*: 5 Poplar Road, SW19 3JR. *T*: (020) 8542 0302. *E*: j.wells@ucl.ac.uk.

**WELLS, (John) Christopher (Durant),** FRCA; Consultant in Pain Relief, 1982–2016; President, European Federation of IASP Chapters, 2014–17; *b* 5 Oct. 1947; *s* of late Colin Durant Wells and of Barbara Gwynneth Wells; *m* 1st, 1971, Sheila Frances Murphy (marr. diss. 2000); two *d*; 2nd, 2004, Susan Lynn Corness. *Educ*: Manchester Grammar Sch.; Liverpool Univ. (MB ChB 1970). LRCP 1970; MRCS 1970; LMCC 1974; FRCA (FFARCS 1978); Eur. Dip. Pain Medicine 2017. Consultant in Pain Relief: Spire (formerly BUPA N) Cheshire Hosp., Stretton, 2000–; Spire Liverpool Hosp.; BMI Beaumont Hosp., Bolton. Hon. Consultant, Pain Res. Inst., Liverpool, 1995–. Mem., guideline develt gp on low back pain, NG59, NICE. Dir, Pain Relief Res. Foundn, 1984–95. Director: Pain Matters Ltd, 2000–; Pain Management Co., 2006–. Trustee, World Inst. of Pain Foundn. Hon. Member: British Pain Soc., 2008–; Neuropathic Pain Special Interest Gp, 2010–; Internat. Assoc. for Study of Pain, 2016; Bulgarian Pain Assoc.; Ukrainian Assoc. for Study of Pain; Moldovan Pain Soc.; Lithuanian Pain Soc. Hon. Fellow of Interventional Pain Practice, 2001. *Publications*: (with C. Woolf) Pain Mechanisms and Management, 1991; (with G. Nown) In Pain?, 1993, 2nd edn as The Pain Relief Handbook, 1996; (with D. Jankowicz) Regional Blockade, 2001; contrib. to British Med. Bull. *Recreations*: curling (for Wales), ski-ing, boating. *Address*: (office) 12 Rodney Street, Liverpool L1 2TE. *T*: (0151) 708 9344, *Fax*: (0151) 306 3623. *E*: cxwells@aol.com.

**WELLS, Prof. Michael,** MD; FRCPath, FRCOG; Professor of Gynaecological Pathology, University of Sheffield, 1997–2014, now Emeritus; Consultant Histopathologist, Leeds Teaching Hospitals, since 2015; Locum Consultant Histopathologist, Bradford Teaching Hospitals, since 2018; *b* Wolverhampton, 7 Aug. 1952; *s* of John Thomas Wells and Lily Wells (*née* Ellis); *m* 1994, Lynne Margaret Walker; one *s* one *d*, and two step *s*. *Educ*: Univ. of Manchester (BSc Hons 1974; MB ChB 1976; MD 1986). FRCPath 1995; FRCOG (*ad eundem*) 2004. Hon. Consultant, United Leeds Teaching Hosps NHS Trust, 1983–93; Prof. of Gynaecol Pathol., Univ. of Leeds, St James's Univ. Hosp., 1994–96; Dir of Internat. Affairs, Faculty of Medicine, Dentistry and Health, Univ. of Sheffield, 2013–14; Hon. Consultant Histopathologist, Sheffield Teaching Hosps, 1997–2014. Associate Prof., Faculty of Medicine, Univ. of Nice, 2017. President: British Gynaecol Cancer Soc., 1994–97; Internat. Soc. of Gynecol Pathologists, 2003–05; Eur. Soc. of Pathol., 2009–11. Royal College of Pathologists: Mem. Council, 1998–2001, 2008–11; Mem., Exec. Cttee, 2008–11; Chm., Specialty Adv. Cttee on Histopathology, 2008–11; Vice Pres., 2011–14; Pres., British Div., Internat. Acad. of Pathol., 2012–14. Ed.-in-Chief, Histopathology, 2003–11. Mem., Upper Nidderdale Parish Council, 2019–. Cunningham Medal, 2014, President's Medal, 2017, British Div., Internat. Acad. of Pathol. *Publications*: Haines and Taylor Obstetrical and Gynaecological Pathology, (Asst Ed.) 4th edn 1995, (Co-Ed.) 5th edn 2003; over 230 original papers, review articles and book chapters. *Recreations*: singing (Mem., Ripon Choral Soc.), gardening, reading for pleasure, walking Oscar, Chocolate Labrador. *Address*: Thornhill, Ramsgill, Harrogate, N Yorks HG3 5RL. *T*: (01423) 755148. *E*: m.wells@sheffield.ac.uk. *Club*: Athenæum.

**WELLS, Michael Andrew;** Group Chief Executive, Prudential plc, since 2015 (Executive Director, 2011–15); *b* Ontario, Canada, 9 April 1960; *s* of Garnet and Constance Wells; *m* 1992, Lindsay; two *s*. *Educ*: San Diego State Univ. (BSc Econs). FINRA Principal. Pres., Jackson Nat. Life Distributors Inc., 1995–2001; Vice Chm., 2001–02, Chief Operating Officer, 2002–11, Pres. and CEO, 2011–15, Jackson Nat. Life Insce Co. Mem. Bd of Managers, Curian Capital LLC. *Recreations*: outdoors, music. *Address*: Prudential plc, 12 Arthur Street, EC4R 9AQ.

**WELLS, Nicholas Mark;** Chief Executive Officer, Whistl (formerly TNT Post UK), since 2003; *b* Wellingborough, 1959; *s* of Raymond Wells and Gwendoline Wells; *m* 1988, Ruth; one *s* two *d*. *Educ*: Univ. of Warwick (BA Hons 1980). Circular Distributors Ltd: Sales and Mktg Dir, 1987–94; Man. Dir, 1994–2003. Non-exec. Chm., Lifecycle Mktg, 2012–. *Recreations*: golf, ski-ing, family, travel, wine. *Address*: Whistl, Meridian House, Fieldhouse Lane, Marlow, Bucks SL7 1TB. *T*: (01628) 816757.

**WELLS, Petrie Bowen;** *see* Wells, Bowen.

**WELLS, Richard Burton,** QPM 1987; Chief Constable of South Yorkshire, 1990–98; Director, E-Quality Leadership, 1998–2007; *b* 10 Aug. 1940; *s* of Walter Percival Wells and Daphne Joan Wells (*née* Harris); *m* 1970, Patricia Ann Smith; one *s* one *d*. *Educ*: Sir Roger Manwood's Grammar Sch., Sandwich; Priory Sch. for Boys, Shrewsbury; St Peter's Coll., Oxford (Open Exhibnr 1959; BA 1962; MA 1965); principal educn, 36 yrs with the police service. Constable, Bow Street, 1962–66; Sergeant, Notting Hill, 1966–68; Special Course, Police Staff Coll., 1966–67; Inspector, Leman St, and Hendon Police Trng Sch., 1968–73; Chief Inspector, Notting Hill, 1973–76; Supt, Hampstead, 1976–79; Chief Supt, Hammersmith and New Scotland Yard, 1979–82; Sen. Command Course, Police Staff Coll., 1981; Comdt, Hendon Training Sch., 1982–83; Dep. Asst Comr, Dir of Public Affairs, New Scotland Yard, 1983–86; Dep. Asst Commissioner, OC NW London, 1986–90. Chairman: Media Adv. Gp, ACPO, 1992–98; Nat. Conf. of Police Press and PROs, 1994–98; Personnel and Trng Cttee, ACPO, 1996–98 (Sec., 1993–96). Sec., Provincial Police Award Selection Cttee, 1990–98. Member: Rathbone Corporate Partnership Gp, 1993–98; Selection Cttee, Fulbright Fellowship in Police Studies, 1991–98; Forensic Psychotherapy Course Adv. Gp, 1990–98; Barnsley City Challenge Bd, 1992–98; Sheffield Common Purpose Adv. Gp and Council, 1993–98. President: Young Enterprise Bd for S Yorks and S Humberside, 1993–98; Deepcar Brass Band, 1992–98; Patron: S Yorks Br., RLSS, 1990–98; Weston Park Hosp. Cancer Care Appeal, 1993–98. President: St Peter's Soc., Oxford Univ., 1989–96; Police Athletics Assoc. Men's Hockey, 1996–98 (Vice Pres., 1989–96). Mem., St John Council for S and W Yorks, 1990–98. Freeman, City of London, 1992. CCMI (CBIM 1991; Pres., Exeter & Torbay Br., 2004). Chm. Editl Bd, Policing Today, 1994–98. *Publications*: (contrib.) Leaders on Leadership, 1996; (contrib.) Learning Organisations in the Public Sector, 1997; (contrib.) On Work and Leadership, 1999. *Recreations*: T'ai Chi, cooking and jam-making, philately, genealogy, local history, scanning the medical horizon for new prostheses. *Address*: Bidwell Farm, Upottery, Devon EX14 9PP. *T*: (01404) 861122. *E*: rbwells@rbwells.uk.

**WELLS, Ven. Roderick John;** Archdeacon of Stow, 1989–2001, and of Lindsey, 1994–2001, now Archdeacon Emeritus; *b* 17 Nov. 1936; *s* of Leonard Arthur and Dorothy Alice Wells; *m* 1969, Alice Louise Scholl; one *s* two *d*. *Educ*: Durham Univ. (BA Hons Theol.); Hull Univ. (MA). Insurance clerk, 1953–55 and 1957–58. RAF, 1955–57 (Radar Mechanic). Asst Master, Chester Choir School, 1958–59; Asst Curate, St Mary at Lambeth, 1965–68, Priest-in-Charge 1968–71; Rector of Skegness, 1971–78; Team Rector, West Grimsby Team Ministry (Parish of Great and Little Coates with Bradley), 1978–89; Area Dean of Grimsby and Cleethorpes, 1983–89. *Recreations*: music (pianist and organist), walking, geology, golf. *Address*: 5 Wheatfield Way, Barleythorpe, Oakham, Rutland LE15 7UD.

**WELLS, Rosemary;** writer and illustrator of children's books, since 1968; *b* 29 Jan. 1943; *m* Thomas M. Wells; two *d*. Mem., Soc. of Illustrators, NY. Best Illustrated Book of the Year, New York Times (twice); Horn Book Book of the Year; Notable Book, American Library Assoc. (40 times); numerous other awards. *Publications* include: Noisy Nora, 1973; Benjamin and Tulip, 1973; Timothy Goes to School, 1981; Voyage to the Bunny Planet, 1992; Edward Unready for School, 1995; My Very First Mother Goose, 1996; Bunny Cakes, 1997; Bunny Money, 1997; The Bear Went Over the Mountain, 1998; The Itsy-Bitsy Spider, 1998; Max's Toys, 1998; Max's Bath, 1998; Yoko, 1998; Morris's Disappearing Bag, 1999; Max Cleans Up, 2000; Emily's First 100 Days of School, 2000; Timothy Goes to School, 2000; Mama, Don't Go!, 2001; The School Play, 2001; The Halloween Parade, 2001; Bunny Party, 2001; Ruby's Beauty Shop, 2003; Max Drives Away, 2003; Ruby's Tea for Two, 2003; My Kindergarten, 2004; Bunny Mail, 2004; The Gulps 2007; Red Moon at Sharpsburg, 2007; Otto Runs for President, 2008; Yoko Writes her Name, 2008; My Havana: memories of a Cuban boyhood, 2010; Max & Ruby's Bedtime Book, 2010; On the Blue Comet, 2010; Yoko's Show-and-Tell, 2011; Hands Off, Harry!, 2011; Max & Ruby's Treasure Hunt, 2012; Time Out for Sophie, 2013; Ivy Takes Care, 2013; Yoko Finds her Way, 2014.

**WELLS, Rev. Dr Samuel Martin Bailey;** Vicar, St Martin-in-the-Fields, London, since 2012; Visiting Professor of Christian Ethics, King's College London, since 2012; *b* Chatham, Ont, 24 April 1965; *s* of late Stephen Wells and Ruth Wells (*née* Moran); *m* 1994, Rt Rev. Dr Joanne Caladine Bailey (*see* Bishop Suffragan of Dorking); one *s* one *d*. *Educ*: Bristol Grammar Sch.; Merton Coll., Oxford (BA Modern Hist. 1987; MA 1995); Univ. of Edinburgh (BD Systematic Theol. 1991); Univ. of Durham (PhD Christian Ethics 1996). Ordained deacon, 1991, priest, 1992; Assistant Curate: St Luke's, Wallsend, 1991–95; St Andrew's, Cherry Hinton with All Saints, Teversham, 1995–97; Priest-in-charge, Earlham St Elizabeth, Norwich, 1997–2003; Rural Dean, Norwich South, 1999–2003; Priest-in-charge, Newnham St Mark, Cambridge, 2003–05; Dean of the Chapel, and Res. Prof. of Christian Ethics, Duke Univ., N Carolina, 2005–12. Theological Canon, Chichester Cathedral, 2004–09. Mem., Multi-Stakeholder Council, G20's Global Solutions Initiative, 2018–. Sen. Mem. and Hon. Chaplain, Wolfson Coll., Cambridge, 2003–05; Hon. Canon, Guildford Cathedral, 2018–. *Publications*: Transforming Fate into Destiny: the theological ethics of Stanley Hauerwas, 1998; (ed jtly) Faithfulness and Fortitude: in conversation with the theological ethics of Stanley Hauerwas, 2000; Community-Led Estate Regeneration and the Local Church, 2003; Improvisation: the drama of Christian ethics, 2004; (ed jtly) The Blackwell Companion to Christian Ethics, 2004, 2nd edn 2011; God's Companions: reimagining Christian ethics, 2006; Power and Passion: six characters in search of resurrection, 2007; Speaking the Truth: preaching in a pluralistic culture, 2008; (ed jtly) Praying for England: priestly presence in contemporary culture, 2008; (jtly) Living Out Loud, 2010; Liturgy Comes to Life, 2010; (jtly) Introducing Christian Ethics, 2010; Christian Ethics: an introductory reader, 2010; (jtly) Living Without Enemies: being present in the midst of violence, 2011; What Episcopalians Believe: an introduction, 2011; What Anglicans Believe: an introduction, 2011; Be Not Afraid, 2011; Crafting Prayers for Public

Worship: the art of intercession, 2013; Learning to Dream Again: rediscovering the heart of God, 2013; (with George Sumner) Esther and Daniel: Brazos commentary on the Bible, 2013; (with Abigail Kocher) Shaping the Prayers of the People: the art of intercession, 2014; A Nazareth Manifesto: being with God, 2015; How Then Shall We Live? Christian engagement with contemporary issues, 2016; (with A. Kocher) Eucharistic Prayers, 2016; (with A. Kocher) Joining the Angels' Song: Eucharistic prayers for Sundays and Holy Days, years A, B and C, 2016; Hanging by a Thread: the questions of the cross, 2016; Incarnational Ministry: being with the Church, 2017; (jtly) For Good: the Church and the future of welfare, 2017; (ed) Liturgy on the Edge: pastoral and attractional worship, 2018; (edd jtly) Who Is My Neighbour? The global and personal challenge, 2018; Incarnational Mission: being with the world, 2018; Speaking the Truth: preaching in a diverse culture, 2018; Face to Face: meeting Christ in friend and stranger, 2019; Walk Humbly: encouragements for living, working and being, 2019. *Recreations:* tennis, cricket, watching sports, reading, hill-walking. *Address:* 6 St Martin's Place, WC2N 4JJ. *T:* (020) 7766 1126. *E:* sam.wells@smitf.org.

**WELLS, Sir Stanley (William),** Kt 2016; CBE 2007; Professor of Shakespeare Studies, and Director of the Shakespeare Institute, University of Birmingham, 1988–97, now Emeritus Professor and Hon. Fellow; General Editor of the Oxford Shakespeare since 1978; Chairman, Shakespeare Birthplace Trust, 1991–2011, now Hon. President; *b* 21 May 1930; *s* of Stanley Cecil Wells, MBE, and Doris Wells; *m* 1975, Susan Elizabeth Hill, *qv*; two *d* (and one *d* decd). *Educ:* Kingston High Sch., Hull; University Coll., London (BA; Fellow, 1995); Shakespeare Inst., Univ. of Birmingham (PhD). FRSL 2014. Fellow, Shakespeare Inst., 1962–77; Lectr, 1962; Sen. Lectr, 1971; Reader, 1973–77; Hon. Fellow, 1979–88; Head of Shakespeare Dept, OUP, 1978–88. Sen. Res. Fellow, Balliol Coll., Oxford, 1980–88 (Hon. Fellow, 2014); Vis. Fellow, UCL, 2006–07. Consultant in English, Wroxton Coll., 1964–80. Chm., Membership Cttee, 1991–99, Collections Cttee, 1992–99, RSC; Mem., Exec. Council, 1976–, Exec. (formerly F and GP) Cttee 1991–, Educn Cttee, Royal Shakespeare Theatre (Gov., 1974–, Vice Chm. of Govs, 1991–2003, Hon. Gov. Emeritus, 2004–); Dir, Royal Shakespeare Theatre Summer Sch., 1971–98. Pres., Shakespeare Club of Stratford-upon-Avon, 1972–73, 2011–12; Chm., Internat. Shakespeare Assoc., 1996–2001, Mem. Exec., 2001– (Vice-Chm., 1991–96); Member: Council, Malone Soc., 1967–90; Exec. Cttee, Shakespeare Birthplace Trust, 1976–78, 1988– (Trustee, 1975–81, 1984–2004; Life Trustee, 2003–; Hon. Pres., 2011); Trustee, Rose Theatre, 1991–; Dir, Globe Theatre, 1992– (Trustee, 1998–2004); President: Wolverhampton Shakespeare Soc., 1992–93; Birmingham and Midland Inst., 2008–09. Governor, King Edward VI Grammar Sch. for Boys, Stratford-upon-Avon, 1973–77. Guest lectr, British and overseas univs; Lectures: British Acad. Annual Shakespeare, 1987; Hilda Hulme Meml, 1987; first annual Globe, 1990; Melchiori, Rome, 1991; Walter Clyde Curry Annual Shakespeare, Vanderbilt Univ., 1998. Hon. DLitt: Furman Univ., SC, 1978; Hull, 2005; Durham, 2005; Craiova, 2008; Warwick, 2008; Marburg, 2010; Hon. DPhil Munich, 1999. Walcott Award, LA, 1995. Associate Editor: New Penguin Shakespeare, 1967–; Oxford DNB, 1998–; Editor, Shakespeare Survey, 1980–99; Gen. Editor, Penguin Shakespeare, 2005–. Sam Wanamaker Award, Globe Th., 2010; Internat. Shakespeare Prize, Craiova Internat. Shakespeare Fest., 2014. President's Medal, British Acad., 2016. *Publications:* (ed) Thomas Nashe, Selected Writings, 1964; (ed, New Penguin Shakespeare): A Midsummer Night's Dream, 1967, Richard II, 1969, The Comedy of Errors, 1972; Shakespeare, A Reading Guide, 1969, 2nd edn 1970; Literature and Drama, 1970; (ed, Select Bibliographical Guides): Shakespeare, 1973 (new edn 1990), English Drama excluding Shakespeare, 1975; Royal Shakespeare, 1977, 2nd edn 1978; (compiled) Nineteenth-Century Shakespeare Burlesques (5 vols), 1977; Shakespeare: an illustrated dictionary, 1978, 2nd edn 1985, revised as Oxford Dictionary of Shakespeare, 1998; Shakespeare: the writer and his work, 1978; (ed with R. L. Smallwood) Thomas Dekker, The Shoemaker's Holiday, 1979; (with Gary Taylor) Modernizing Shakespeare's Spelling, with three studies in the text of Henry V, 1979; Re-Editing Shakespeare for the Modern Reader, 1984; (ed) Shakespeare's Sonnets, 1985; (ed with Gary Taylor *et al*) The Complete Oxford Shakespeare, 1986; (ed) The Cambridge Companion to Shakespeare Studies, 1986; (with Gary Taylor *et al*) William Shakespeare: a textual companion, 1987; An Oxford Anthology of Shakespeare, 1987; Shakespeare: a dramatic life, 1994, rev. edn as Shakespeare: the poet and his plays, 1997; (ed with E. A. Davies) Shakespeare and the Moving Image, 1994; (ed with R. Warren) Twelfth Night, 1994; (ed) Shakespeare in the Theatre: an anthology of criticism, 1997; (ed) Summerfolk, 1997; William Shakespeare: the quiz book, 1998; (ed) King Lear, 2000; (ed with C. M. S. Alexander) Shakespeare and Race, 2001; (ed with M. de Grazia) The Cambridge Companion to Shakespeare, 2001; (ed with Michael Dobson) The Oxford Companion to Shakespeare, 2001; (ed with C. M. S. Alexander) Shakespeare and Sexuality, 2001; Shakespeare For All Time, 2002; (ed with Lena Orlin) A Shakespeare Study Guide, 2002; Looking for Sex in Shakespeare, 2004; (with Paul Edmondson) Shakespeare's Sonnets, 2004; Shakespeare and Co., 2006; Is It True What They Say About Shakespeare?, 2007; (with P. Edmondson) Coffee with Shakespeare, 2008; Shakespeare Found!, 2009; (ed with Margreta de Grazia) New Cambridge Companion to Shakespeare, 2010; Shakespeare, Sex, and Love, 2010; (with P. Edmondson) Shakespeare Beyond Doubt, 2013; Great Shakespeare Actors, 2015; William Shakespeare: a very short introduction, 2015; (with P. Edmondson) The Shakespeare Circle, 2016; contrib. Shak. Survey, Shak. Qly, Shak. Jahrbuch, Theatre Notebook, Stratford-upon-Avon Studies, TLS, The Stage, NY Rev. of Books, etc. *Recreations:* music, theatre, the countryside. *Address:* 9 New Street, Stratford-upon-Avon, Warwicks CV37 6BX. *T:* 07769 336533. *E:* Stanley.Wells@shakespeare.org.uk.

**WELLS, Susan Elizabeth, (Lady Wells);** *see* Hill, S. E.

**WELLS, Timothy Nigel Carl,** PhD, ScD; Chief Scientific Officer, Medicines for Malaria Venture, Geneva, since 2007; *b* Derby, 30 March 1962; *s* of Carl Allan Walter Wells and Joan Hazel Wells (née Hughes); partner, Susan Jane Self; two *s* two *d*. *Educ:* Churchill Coll., Cambridge (BA Natural Scis 1984); Imperial Coll. London (PhD Chem. 1987); Univ. of Cambridge (ScD Biol. 2009). Dept Hd, Glaxo Inst. for Molecular Biol., Geneva, 1990–97; Hd, Res., Serono Internat., 1998–2007. FMedSci 2012. *Publications:* (with Michael J. Palmer) Neglected Diseases and Drug Discovery, 2012. *Address:* Medicines for Malaria Venture, 20 route de Pré-Bois, 1215 Geneva 15, Switzerland. *E:* timncwells@gmail.com.

**WELLS, Sir William (Henry Weston),** Kt 1997; FRICS; Chairman: ADL plc, since 2006; Marr Procurement Ltd, since 2016; *b* 3 May 1940; *s* of Sir Henry Wells, CBE, and Lady Wells; *m* 1966, Penelope Jean Broadbent; two *s* (and one *s* decd). *Educ:* Radley Coll.; Magdalene Coll., Cambridge (BA). Joined Chesterton, 1959, Partner, 1965–92; Chairman: Land and House Property Gp, 1977 (Dir, 1972–76); Frincon Holdings Ltd, 1977–87; Chesterton plc, 1992–97; Pres., Chesterton Internat. plc, London, 1998–2004. Chairman: Covenant Healthcare, 2005–10; CMG plc, 2007–16 (Dir, 2016–18); Ashley House plc, 2007–13; Pure Sports Medicine plc, 2007–16 (Dir, 2016–); St Wenceslas Property Adv. Bd, 2007–; SUSD (formerly CAM) plc, 2008–13; Mavinwood, subseq. Restore plc, 2009–18; Transform plc, 2010–14; Libra Holdco, 2011–14; The Practice plc, 2013–18; Facilities First, 2014–16; Director: London Life Assoc., 1984–89; AMP (UK) plc, 1994–2002; Pearl Gp Ltd (formerly Pearl Assurance), 1994–2005; Norwich and Peterborough Bldg Soc.,

1994–2003; NFC plc, 1996–2000; AMP (UK) Holdings, 1997–2005; NPI Ltd, 1999–2005; Nat. Provident Life Ltd, 1999–2005; Exel plc, 2000–05; Hillgate (220) Ltd, 2002–; HHG plc, 2003–05; ARC Fund Mgt, 2006–08; SQW Ltd, 2007–14; Dods plc, 2010–18; HCOne plc, 2011–; Skyfall Ltd, 2014–. Advisor: Healthcare at Home, 2008–; Dr Foster, 2008–10; ipp, 2009–16; Centene, 2018–; Mem. Council, NHS Trust Fedn, 1991–93 (Vice Chm., 1992–93). Chairman: Hampstead HA, 1982–90; Royal Free Hampstead NHS Trust, 1990–94; S Thames RHA, 1994–96; S Thames Region, NHS Exec., DoH, 1996–99; NHS Appointments Commn, 2001–07; Commercial Adv. Bd, DoH, 2003–07; Regl Chm., SE, NHS Exec., 1999–2001. Member: Board of Governors, Royal Free Hosp., 1968–74; Camden and Islington AHA, 1974–82; Chm., Special Trustees of Royal Free Hosp., 1979–2001; Member, Council: Royal Free Hosp. Sch. of Medicine, 1977–91; UMDS, Guy's and St Thomas' Hosps, 1994–98; St George's Hosp. Med. Sch., 1994–98; Univ. of Surrey, 1998–2015 (Vice Chm., 1999–2000, Chm., 2001–06; Pro-Chancellor, 2007–15); KCL, 1998–2001; City Univ., 1999–2001; Member: Delegacy, King's Coll. Sch. of Medicine and Dentistry, 1994–98; Council and Mgt Cttee, King's Fund, 1995–2010; Chm., Guy's and St Thomas' Charity, 2010–15. Trustee: Nat. Mus. of Science and Industry, 2003–11; Action Med. Res., 2005–07. Pres., Royal Free Hosp. Retirement Fellowship, 1994–; Vice President: RCN, 2006– (Hon. Treas., 1988–2005); Attend (formerly Nat. Assoc. of Leagues of Hosp. Friends), 2004– (Hon. Treas., 1992–2004). Mem. Council, Priory of England and the Is, 2000–02. Hon. FRCP 2002. *Recreations:* family, the ballet. *Club:* Boodle's.

**WELSBY, John Kay,** CBE 1990; Chief Executive, 1990–98, and Chairman, 1995–99, British Railways Board; *b* 26 May 1938; *s* of late Samuel and Sarah Ellen Welsby; *m* 1964, Jill Carole Richards; one *s* one *d*. *Educ:* Heywood Grammar Sch.; Univ. of Exeter (BA); Univ. of London (MSc). FCILT (FCIT 1990). Govt Economic Service, 1966–81; British Railways Board: Dir, Provincial Services, 1982–84; Managing Dir, Procurement, 1985–87; Mem. Bd, 1987–99; Director: London & Continental Rlys Ltd, 1999–2007; LCR Finance plc, 1999–2007. Chm., CIT, 1998–99. Pres., Inst. of Logistics and Transport, 1999–2002. Member: Business Adv. Council, Transport Dept, Northwestern Univ., Evanston, Ill., 1995–2000. CCMI (CIMgt 1991). Freeman, City of London, 1992; Liveryman, Carmen's Co., 1992. *Publications:* articles on economic and transport matters. *Recreations:* walking, music, swimming. *Address:* Stone Barn, Bow, Crediton, Devon EX17 6LB.

**WELSER-MÖST, Franz;** Music Director, Cleveland Orchestra, since 2002; General Music Director, Vienna State Opera, 2010–14; *b* 16 Aug. 1960. Music Dir, LPO, 1990–96; Chief Conductor, 1995–2002, Principal Conductor, 2002–05, Gen. Music Dir, 2005–08, Zürich Opera; conducts Bayerischer Rundfunk, Vienna Philharmonic, Salzburg Fest., Berlin Philharmonic and all major US orchestras; numerous recordings. Awards from USA and UK. *Address:* Enticott Music Management, 18 Hearne Road, W4 3NJ.

**WELSH, Andrew Paton;** Member (SNP) Angus, Scottish Parliament, 1999–2011; *b* 19 April 1944; *s* of William and Agnes Welsh; *m* 1971, Sheena Margaret Cannon; one *d*. *Educ:* Univ. of Glasgow (MA (Hons) History and Politics; DipEd, 1980); Open Univ. (Dip. French 2005). Teacher of History, 1972–74; Lectr in Public Admin and Economics, Dundee Coll. of Commerce, 1979–83; Sen. Lectr in Business and Admin. Studies, Angus Technical Coll., 1983–87. MP (SNP) South Angus, Oct. 1974–1979; contested (SNP) Angus E, 1983; MP (SNP) Angus E, 1987–97, Angus, 1997–2001. SNP Parly Chief Whip, 1978–79, 1987–97; SNP spokesman on: housing, 1974–78; self employed affairs and small businesses, 1975–79, 1987–2001; agriculture, 1976–79, 1987–2001; local govt, 1987–97; local govt, housing and educn, 1997–2001. Member: Scottish Affairs Select Cttee, 1992–2001; Speaker's Panel of Chairmen, 1997–2001. Scottish Parliament: Member: Corporate Body, 1999–2006; Commn of Accounts, 2000–07; Audit Cttee, 2007–09 (Convener, 1999–2003; Dep. Convener, 2004–07); Dep. Convener, Local Govt and Transport Cttee, 2003–04; Convener, Finance Cttee, 2007–11. SNP Exec. Vice Chm. for Admin, 1979–87; SNP Vice-Pres., 1987–2004. Mem., Angus District Council, 1984–87; Provost of Angus, 1984–87. Freeman of Angus, 2013. DL Angus, 2013. *Recreations:* music, horse riding, languages. *Address:* Montquhir Farm House, Carmyllie, Arbroath, Angus DD11 2QS. *Club:* Glasgow University Union.

**WELSH, Prof. Dominic;** *see* Welsh, J. A. D.

**WELSH, Frank Reeson,** FRHistS; writer; Director, Grindlays Bank, 1971–85; *b* 16 Aug. 1931; *s* of F. C. Welsh and D. M. Welsh; *m* 1954, Agnes Cowley; two *s* two *d*. *Educ:* Gateshead and Blaydon Grammar Schools; Magdalene Coll., Cambridge (schol.; MA). With John Lewis Partnership, 1954–58; CAS Group, 1958–64; Man. Dir, William Brandt's Sons & Co. Ltd, 1965–72; Chairman: Hadfields Ltd, 1967–79; Jensen Motors Ltd, 1968–72; Cox & Kings, 1972–76; Dir, Henry Ansbacher & Co., 1976–82. Member: British Waterways Board, 1975–81; Gen. Adv. Council, IBA, 1976–80; Royal Commn on Nat. Health Service, 1976–79; Health Educn Council, 1978–80. Dir, Trireme Trust, 1983–. Vis. Lectr and Alcoa Schol., Graduate Sch. of Business Studies, Univ. of Tennessee, Knoxville, 1979–85. CCMI. *Publications:* The Profit of the State, 1982; (contrib.) Judging People, 1982; The Afflicted State, 1983; First Blood, 1985; (with George Ridley) Bend'Or, Duke of Westminster, 1985; Uneasy City, 1986; Building the Trireme, 1988; Companion Guide to the Lake District, 1989, 2nd edn 1997; Hong Kong: a history (US edn as A Borrowed Place), 1993, 2nd edn 1997 (Chinese edn 2001, 2014); A History of South Africa, 1998; Dangerous Deceits, 1999; The Four Nations, 2002; Great Southern Land: a new history of Australia, 2004; (jtly) Victoria's Empire, 2007; The Battle for Christendom, 2008; A History of the World, 2011, 2nd edn 2013. *Recreations:* sailing, correcting Radio 4's pronunciation and grammar. *Address:* 33 rue St Bartélémy, 16500 Confolens, France. *Club:* Oxford and Cambridge.

**WELSH, Ian;** *see* Welsh, J. Mcw.

**WELSH, Prof. (James Anthony) Dominic,** DPhil; Professor of Mathematics, 1992–2005, and Chairman of Mathematics, 1996–2001, Oxford University; Fellow of Merton College, Oxford, 1966–2005, now Emeritus; *b* 29 Aug. 1938; *s* of late James Welsh and Teresa Welsh (née O'Callaghan); *m* 1966, Bridget Elizabeth Pratt; two *s* (and one *s* decd). *Educ:* Bishop Gore Grammar Sch., Swansea; Merton Coll., Oxford (MA DPhil); Carnegie Mellon Univ. (Fulbright Scholar). Bell Telephone Labs, Murray Hill, 1961; Oxford University: Jun. Lectr, Mathematical Inst., 1963–66; Tutor in Maths, Merton Coll., 1966–90; Reader in Maths, 1990–92. Vis. appts, Univs of Michigan, Waterloo, Calgary, Stockholm, North Carolina; John von Neumann Prof., Univ. of Bonn, 1990–91; Vis. Oxford Fellow, Univ. of Canterbury, NZ, 2005; Res. Visitor, Centre de Recerca Matemàtica, Barcelona, 2006–07. Chm., British Combinatorial Cttee, 1983–87. Hon. Dr Math. Waterloo, 2006. *Publications:* (ed) Combinatorial Mathematics and its Applications, 1971; (ed jtly) Combinatorics, 1973; Matroid Theory, 1976; (with G. R. Grimmett) Probability: an introduction, 1986, 2nd edn 2014; Codes and Cryptography, 1988, German edn 1991, Japanese edn 2004; (ed jtly) Disorder in Physical Systems, 1990; Complexity: knots, colourings and counting, 1993; (with J. Talbot) Complexity and Cryptography: an introduction, 2006; articles in math. jls. *Recreations:* most sports, walking. *Address:* Merton College, Oxford OX1 4JD. *T:* (01865) 276310.

**WELSH, John Mcwilliam, (Ian),** OBE 2015; Chief Executive, Health and Social Care (formerly Long Term Conditions) Alliance Scotland, since 2010; *b* 23 Nov. 1953; *m* 1977, Elizabeth McAndrew; two *s*. *Educ:* Prestwick Acad.; Ayr Acad.; Glasgow Univ. (MA Hons Eng. Lit. and Hist.); Jordanhill Coll. (Dip. in Educnl Mgt); Open Univ. (MA). Former professional football player, Kilmarnock FC; English teacher: James Hamilton Acad., Kilmarnock, 1977–80; Auchinleck Acad., 1980–97 (Dep. Head Teacher, 1992–97); Dir of Human Resources and Public Affairs, Prestwick Internat. Airport, 1997; Chief Executive: Kilmarnock FC, 1997–99 and 2000–01; Momentum Scotland, 2001–07; Dir, UK Services, Rehab Gp, 2007–10. Member (Lab): Kyle and Carrick Council, 1984–95 (Leader, 1990–92); S Ayrshire Council, 1995–99 (Leader); MSP (Lab) Ayr, 1999. Chairman: Scottish Adv. Cttee to Voluntary Sector NTO, 2002–05; Ayrshire Business in the Community, 2007–09; Ayr United Football Acad., 2007–18; E Ayrshire Jt Integration Bd, 2015–19; E Ayrshire Health and Social Care Partnership, 2015–19; Member of Board: Scottish Enterprise, Ayrshire, 2002–07; Irvine Bay Regeneration Co., 2007–10; Ayrshire and Arran NHS, 2011–19. Chm., Microtech Gp, 2016–18; Director: Borderline Theatre Co., 1990– (Chm., 2002–07); Prestwick Internat. Airport, 1992–97; Chm., Ayr Gaiety Partnership, 2010–. Mem. Ct, Univ. of W Scotland, 2007–17 (Chm., 2013–16; Hon. Prof., 2018). FRSA. DUniv West of Scotland, 2016. *Address:* Health and Social Care Alliance Scotland, Venlaw Building, 349 Bath Street, Glasgow G2 4AA; 35 Ayr Road, Prestwick, Ayrshire KA9 1SY.

**WELSH, Jolyon Rimmer;** HM Diplomatic Service; Senior Director, Consulum Strategic Communications Counsel, since 2014; *b* Manchester, 22 Dec. 1967; *s* of Frank Welsh and Imelda Welsh; *m* 1999, Susan Lynley Kelly; one *s* one *d*. *Educ:* Trinity Coll., Cambridge (BA Hons Hist. 1990; MA). Entered HM Diplomatic Service, 1990; G7 Unit, 1991; Far Eastern Dept, 1991–92; Second Sec., Colombo, 1992–95; W Eur. Dept, 1996; Human Rights Policy Dept, 1997–98; First Sec., UK Mission to the UN, NY, 1998–2002; Sanctions Unit, 2003; Middle E and N Africa Directorate, 2003–06; Hd, Public Diplomacy, 2006–08; Dep. High Comr, Canberra, 2008–12; Hd of Govt to Govt Contracting, FCO, 2012–14. Chevalier de la Légion d'honneur (France), 1996. *Publications:* (ed with D. Fearn) Engagement: public diplomacy in a globalised world, 2008. *Address:* 35 Prebend Mansions, Chiswick High Road, W4 2LU.

**WELSH, Michael John,** MBE 2014; non-executive Director, Lancashire Teaching Hospitals Trust, 2013–18; *b* 22 May 1942; *s* of Comdr David Welsh, RN, and Una Mary (*née* Willmore); *m* 1963, Jennifer Caroline Pollitt; one *s* one *d*. *Educ:* Dover Coll.; Lincoln Coll., Oxford (BA (Hons) Jurisprudence). Proprietors of Hays Wharf Ltd, 1963–69; Levi Strauss & Co. Europe Ltd, 1969–79 (Dir of Market Development, 1976). Chm., Chorley and S Ribble NHS Trust, 1994–98. MEP (C) Lancashire Central, 1979–94; contested (C) Lancashire Central, Eur. Parly elecns, 1994; Chm., Cttee for Social Affairs and Employment, Eur. Parlt, 1984–87. Mem. (C) Lancs CC, 1997–2013 (Leader, Cons. Gp, 2003–08). Chm., Positive Europe Gp, 1988–94; Chief Exec., Action Centre for Europe Ltd, 1995–2004. Chm., Lancs County Develts Ltd, 2009–13. Chm., Friends of St Laurence Ch, Chorley. *Recreations:* country walks, gardening, theatre, concerts. *Address:* Watercrook, 181 Town Lane, Whittle le Woods, Chorley, Lancs PR6 8AG. *T:* (01257) 276992. *Club:* Carlton.

**WELSH, Peter,** OBE 2001; CEng, FIET; Executive Director, United Kingdom Atomic Energy Authority (Dounreay Division), 1998–2003; *b* 25 March 1941; *s* of late Robert Welsh and Florence Welsh (*née* Gollege; later Armory); *m* 1964, Margaret Philips; two *s*. *Educ:* Sunderland Poly. (BSc 1st Cl. Hons Electrical Engrg 1966). CEng 1966; FIET (FIEE 2000). Manager: Dungeness A Power Station, CEGB, 1987–91; Hinkley Point A and B Power Station, Nuclear Electric Plc, 1991–95; Dir, Business Improvement, Magnox Electric Plc, 1995–98. Chm., Somerset TEC, 1994–96; Dir, Somerset Careers Bd, 1994–96; non-exec. Director: Trng Standards Council, 1998–2001; Sector Skills Develt Agency, 2002–06. Mem. Council, SW Reg., CBI, 1998–2001. Gov., Somerset Coll. of Art and Technol., 1995–98. *Recreations:* walking, ski-ing, golf, travel.

**WELTEKE, Ernst;** President, Deutsche Bundesbank, 1999–2004; *b* Korbach, 21 Aug. 1942. *Educ:* Univ. of Marburg; Univ. of Frankfurt am Main (grad. in econs). Apprentice agricl machine mechanic, 1959–62; Office of Prime Minister of Hesse, 1972–74; MP (SPD) Hesse, 1974–95; Minister of Econs, Transport and Technol., 1991–94; Minister of Finance, 1994–95; Pres., Land Central Bank, Hesse, and Mem., Central Bank Council, Deutsche Bundesbank, 1995–99. Chm., Parly Gp, SDP, 1984–Apr. 1987 and Feb. 1988–1991. Mem. Governing Council, European Central Bank, 1999–2004.

**WEMYSS, 13th Earl of,** *cr* 1633, **AND MARCH, 9th Earl of,** *cr* 1697; **James Donald Charteris;** DL; Lord Wemyss of Elcho, 1628; Lord Elcho and Methil, 1633; Viscount Peebles, Baron Douglas of Neidpath, Lyne and Munard, 1697; Baron Wemyss of Wemyss (UK), 1821; *b* 22 June 1948; *s* of 12th Earl of Wemyss and March, KT and Mavis Lynette Gordon (*née* Murray); *S* father, 2008; *m* 1st, 1983, Catherine Ingrid (marr. diss. 1988), *d* of Baron Moyne, *qv*, and Mrs Paul Channon; one *s* one *d*; 2nd, 1995, Amanda Claire, *y d* of late Basil Feilding. *Educ:* Eton; University College, Oxford (BA 1969, MA 1974); St Antony's Coll., Oxford (DPhil 1975); Royal Agricultural Coll., Cirencester (Diploma, 1978); MRICS (ARICS 1983). Page of Honour to HM Queen Elizabeth the Queen Mother, 1962–64. Mem., Royal Co. of Archers (Queen's Body Guard for Scotland), 1978–. Mem. Council, Nat. Trust for Scotland, 1987–92; Chm., Heart of England Reg., Hist. Houses Assoc., 1991–96. DL Glos, 2005. *Publications:* The Singapore Naval Base and the Defence of Britain's Eastern Empire 1919–42, 1981. *Heir: s* Lord Elcho, *qv*. *Address:* Stanway, Cheltenham, Glos GL54 5PQ. *T:* (01386) 584469. *Clubs:* Brooks's, Pratt's, Ognisko Polskie; Puffin's, New (Edinburgh).

**WEMYSS, Rear-Adm. Martin La Touche,** CB 1981; *b* 5 Dec. 1927; *s* of late Comdr David Edward Gillespie Wemyss, DSO, DSC, RN, and Edith Mary Digges La Touche; *m* 1st, 1951, Ann Hall (marr. diss. 1973); one *s* one *d*; 2nd, 1973, Elizabeth Lovedday Alexander; one *s* one *d*. *Educ:* Shrewsbury School. CO HMS Sentinel, 1956–57; Naval Intell. Div., 1957–59; CO HMS Alliance, 1959–60; CO Commanding Officers' Qualifying Course, 1961–63; Naval Staff, 1963–65; CO HMS Cleopatra, 1965–67; Naval Asst to First Sea Lord, 1967–70; CO 3rd Submarine Sqdn, 1970–73; CO HMS Norfolk, 1973–74; Dir of Naval Warfare, 1974–76; Rear-Adm., 1977; Flag Officer, Second Flotilla, 1977–78; Asst Chief of Naval Staff (Ops), 1979–81. Clerk to Brewers' Co., 1981–91. *Recreation:* gardening. *Address:* The Old Post House, Emberton, near Olney, Bucks MK46 5BX. *T:* (01234) 713838. *Club:* Army and Navy.

**WEN, Prof. Eric Lewis;** freelance writer and music producer; Professor of Music Theory, Curtis Institute of Music, Philadelphia, since 1999 (Chairman of Musical Studies, 2002–08); Professor of Music, Juilliard School of Music, New York, since 2014 (Lecturer, 2013–14); Lecturer, Graduate Center, City University of New York, since 2013; *b* 18 May 1953; *s* of Adam and Mimi Wen; *m* 1st, 1989, Louise Barder (marr. diss. 1998); two *d*; 2nd, 1999, Rachel Stadlen; one *s*. *Educ:* Columbia Univ. (BA); Yale Univ. (MPhil); Cambridge Univ. Lecturer: Guildhall Sch. of Music, 1978–84; Goldsmiths' Coll., Univ. of London, 1980–84; Mannes Coll. of Music, NY, 1984–86; Editor: The Strad, 1986–89; The Musical Times, 1988–90; Man. Dir, Biddulph Recordings, 1990–99; Edward Aldwell Prof. of Music, Mannes Coll. of Music, NY, 2008–13. *Publications:* (contrib.) Schenker Studies, 1989; (contrib.) Trends in Schenkerian Research, 1990; (ed) The Fritz Kreisler Collection, 1990; (contrib.) Cambridge Companion to the Violin, 1992; (ed) The Heifetz Collection, 1995; (contrib.) Schenker Studies 2, 1999; (ed) The Joseph Szigeti Collection, 2000; (ed) Hebrew Melodies, 2001; (ed) Masterpieces for Violin, 2005; (contrib.) Structure and Meaning in Tonal Music, 2006; (contrib.) Essays from the Third Schenker Symposium, 2006; (ed) Masterworks for Violin, 2006; (ed) Solos for Violin, 2006; (contrib.) Essays from the Fourth Schenker Symposium, 2008; (contrib.) Bach to Brahms, 2015; (contrib.) Schubert's Late Music: history, theory, style, 2016; Structurally Sound, 2017; Graphic Music Analysis, 2019; contrib. various music jls. *Recreations:* music, chess, cooking, legerdemain.

**WENBAN, Sarah Ann;** *see* Thane, S. A.

**WENBAN-SMITH, (William) Nigel,** CMG 1991; HM Diplomatic Service, retired; Secretary General, Commonwealth Magistrates' and Judges' Association, 1993–94; *b* 1 Sept. 1936; *s* of William Wenban-Smith, CMG, CBE; *m* 1st, 1961, Charlotte Chapman-Andrews (marr. diss 1975; she *m* 2nd, Sir Peter Evelyn Leslie); two *s* two *d*; 2nd, 1976, Charlotte Susanna Rycroft (*d* 1990); two *s*; 3rd, 1993, Frances Catharine Barlow; two step *d*. *Educ:* King's Sch., Canterbury; King's Coll., Cambridge (BA); MA Buckingham 2000. National Service, RN. Plebiscite Supervisory Officer, Southern Cameroons, 1960–61; Asst Principal, CRO, 1961–65 (Private Sec. to Parly Under Sec., 1963–64); Second Sec., Leopoldville, 1965–67; First Sec. and (1968) Head of Chancery, Kampala, 1967–70; FCO, 1970–74; Dublin, 1975; Commercial Sec., 1976–78, Commercial Counsellor, 1978–80, Brussels; on loan to Cabinet Office, 1980–82; Hd of E Africa Dept and Comr, British Indian Ocean Territory, FCO, 1982–85; National Defence Coll. of Canada, 1985–86; Deputy High Comr, Ottawa, 1986–89; High Comr, Malaŵi, 1990–93. Chm., Friends of the Chagos Assoc., 1996–2002. *Publications:* Chagos: a history, 2016. *Recreations:* walking, gardening, history of Chagos archipelago. *Address:* 29 Elaine Grove, NW5 4QH.

**WEND, Prof. Petra,** PhD; FRSE; Principal and Vice-Chancellor, Queen Margaret University, Edinburgh, 2009–19; *b* Gütersloh, Germany, 21 Jan. 1959; *d* of Peter and Thekla Wend; partner, Prof. Philip James; one *d*. *Educ:* Münster Univ. (Staatsexamen in Italian and French lang. and lit., and educn); Univ. of Leeds (PhD Italian Lang. and Lit. 1990). Middlesex Polytechnic, later Middlesex University: Lectr, Sen. Lectr, then Principal Lectr, 1989–97; Dep. Hd, Sch. of Langs, 1996–97 (Acting Hd, 1995); Dir of Curriculum, Learning and Quality, 1997–99; Dean, Faculty of Humanities and Educn, 1999–2002, Pro Vice-Chancellor (Learning and Teaching), 2000–02, Univ. of N London; Dir of Learning, Teaching and Student Affairs, London Metropolitan Univ., 2002–05; Dep. Vice-Chancellor and Dep. Chief Exec., Oxford Brookes Univ., 2005–09. Convener, Learning and Teaching Cttee, 2010–12, Vice-Convener, 2012–16, Universities Scotland; Chair, Nat. Implementation Bd, Teaching Scotland's Future, 2012–15. Member: QAA, 2010–16 (Mem., Scotland Cttee, 2011–16); Skills Cttee, Jt Govt and Scottish Funding Council, 2010–13; Scotland Cttee, British Council, 2011–18; Commn for Widening Access, 2015–16; Chm., Edinburgh Adv. Gp, Common Purpose, 2017–19. Member: Edinburgh Business Forum, 2010–17 (Chair, Productivity and Skills Sub-Gp, 2010–12); Goodison Gp Forum, 2012– (Dir, Gp Bd, 2017–); Edinburgh Partnership Bd, 2013–15; Trustee, 2016–, Mem., Ordinary Council, 2016–, and Mem., Educn Cttee, 2016–, RSE. Member: Council, Univ. of Hamburg, 2017–; Internat. Expert Gp, Transnational Univ. Leaders' Council, 2017–. Mem., Soc. of Renaissance Studies, 1991. FRSA 2009; FRSE 2015. *Publications:* The Female Voice: lyrical expression in the writings of the five Italian Renaissance poets, 1994; German Interlanguage, 1996, 2nd edn 1998; Geschäftsbriefe schnell und sicher formulieren, 2004; contrib. articles to learned jls on linguistics and on instnl strategies. *Recreations:* painting, sport, Arsenal FC (season ticket holder).

**WENDT, Henry,** Hon. CBE 1995; Chairman: SmithKline Beecham, 1989–94; Global Health Care Partners, DLJ Merchant Banking, 1997–2002; Arrail Dental (China) Ltd, 1999–2012; *b* 19 July 1933; *s* of Henry Wendt and Rachel L. (*née* Wood); *m* 1956, Holly Peterson; one *s* one *d*. *Educ:* Princeton Univ. (AB 1955). Joined SmithKline & French Labs, 1955: various positions in Internat. Div.; Pres., 1976–82; Chief Exec. Officer, 1982–87; Chm., 1987–89 (merger of SmithKline Beckman and Beecham, 1989). Director: Arjo Wiggins Appleton plc, 1990–92; Cambridge Labs plc, 1996–; West Marine Inc., 1997–2001; Wilson Greatbatch Ltd, 1997–2003; Computerised Med. Systems, 1997–; Charles River Labs, 2000–01; Prometheus Labs, 2000–03; Focus Technologies Inc., 2000–03. Chairman: Healdsburg Performing Arts Theatre, 2000–03; Sonoma County Community Foundn, 2001–04. Trustee: Philadelphia Museum of Art, 2004–99; Amer. Enterprises Inst., 1987–96. Order of the Rising Sun with Gold and Silver Star (Japan), 1994. *Publications:* Global Embrace, 1993. *Recreations:* sailing, flyfishing, tennis, viticulture. *Address:* 1400 Waverly Road, Unit #46, Gladwyn, PA 19035, USA. *Clubs:* Flyfishers'; New York Yacht (New York).

**WENDT, Robin Glover,** CBE 1996; DL; Vice-Chairman, Action for Children (formerly NCH), 2000–08; *b* 7 Jan. 1941; *er s* of late William Romilly Wendt and Doris May (*née* Glover), Preston, Lancs; *m* 1965, Prudence Ann Dalby; two *d*. *Educ:* Hutton GS, Preston; Wadham Coll., Oxford Univ. (BA 1962; MA 1992). Asst Principal 1962, Principal 1966, Min. of Pensions and Nat. Insurance; Principal Private Sec. to Sec. of State for Social Services, 1970; Asst Sec., DHSS, 1972; Dep. Sec., 1975, Chief Exec., 1979–89, Cheshire CC; Clerk of Cheshire Lieutenancy, 1979–90; Sec., ACC, 1989–97; Chief Exec., Nat. Assoc. of Local Councils, 1997–99. Sec., Manchester Airport Consultative Cttee, 1979–89. Member: Cheshire Area Manpower Bd, 1982–89; Social Security Adv. Cttee, 1982–2002; PCFC, 1989–93; Council, RIPA, 1989–92; Council for Charitable Support, 1991–97; DoH Wider Health Working Gp, 1991–97; Carnegie Third Age Enquiry, 1992–96; Adv. Bd, Fire Service Coll., 1992–96; Citizenship Foundn Adv. Council, 1993–97; Joseph Rowntree Foundn Income and Wealth Inquiry, 1993–95; Royal Commn on Long-Term Care of the Elderly, 1997–99; Bd, FAS, 1997–99; Council, Action for Children (formerly NCH Action for Children, then NCH), 1997–2008; Bd, YMCA Chester, 1997–2008; Benefits Agency Standards Cttee, 1999–2002; Joseph Rowntree Foundn Adv. Gp on Long-Term Care of the Elderly, 2003–06; NCH/Nat. Family and Parenting Inst./Joseph Rowntree Foundn Family Commn, 2005–06. Non-exec. Dir, NIMTECH, 2000–13. Mem., S Cheshire HA, 2001–02; Vice-Chm., Cheshire and Merseyside Strategic HA, 2002–04. Chairman: Cheshire Rural Forum, 2000–04; Chester in Partnership, 2001–06. Mem. Exec., Chester Music Soc., 1999–2008 and 2011–16; Chairman: Chester Summer Music Fest., 2001–08; Chester Fests, 2003–06; Dir, Chester Performing Arts Centre Ltd, 2006–08; Conductor, Cheshire CC Staff Choir, 2003–07. Pres., Cheshire Assoc. of Town and Parish Councils, 1997–2004. Sec., NW Says No Campaign, 2003–04. Trustee: Ind. Living Funds, 1993–2001; Vision Homes Assoc., 2011–16; Cheshire W Citizens Advice, 2012–16. Dir, Bowling Green Court Ltd, 2015– (Chm. 2016–). DL Cheshire, 1990. Hon. Citizen, Chester Co., Penn, 1984. Contributor (as Ted Browning), Tribune, 1999–2004. *Publications:* various letters, articles and reviews on public service issues; occasional music reviews. *Recreations:* music, reading, following sport, pursuing penal reform. *Address:* 25 Bowling Green Court, 2 Brook Street, Chester CH1 3DP. *T:* (01244) 340455. *E:* robin.wendt@icloud.com. *Club:* Chester FC.

**WENGE, Rt Rev. Giegere**, KBE 2017; Assistant Pastor, Lutheran Church of Papua New Guinea, since 2017; *b* Samanzing Village, PNG, 30 July 1946; *s of* Yowanu Wenge and Migere Kambelinga; *m* Lucy Saigeng; two *s* three *d. Educ*: BTh 1975; BA 1979; MTh 1991. Pastoral ministries; Lectr, later Principal, Seminary; Dept Sec.; Hd Bishop, Lutheran Church of PNG. *Address*: PO Box 2434, Lae Rural, Nawaeb District, Morobe Province, Papua New Guinea. *T*: 7331 9006.

**WENGER, Arsène**, Hon. OBE 2003; Chevalier, Légion d'Honneur, 2002; Manager, Arsenal Football Club, 1996–2018; *b* 22 Oct. 1949. *Educ*: Strasbourg Univ. (BEc 1974). Amateur football player, Mutzig, then Mulhouse, 1969–78; professional football player, Strasbourg, 1978–83 (Coach, Youth team, 1981–83); Player/Coach, Cannes, 1983; Manager: AS Nancy, 1984–87; AS Monaco, 1987–94; Nagoya Grampus Eight, Japan, 1995–96. Arsenal won Premier League and FA Cup, 1998, 2002, FA Cup, 2003, 2005, 2014, Premier League, 2004; Champions League finalists, 2006. Lifetime Achievement Award, Laureus World Sports Award, 2019.

**WENNER, Michael Alfred**; HM Diplomatic Service, retired; President, Wenner Communications (formerly Wenner Trading Co.), 1982–2002; *b* 17 March 1921; *s of* Alfred E. Wenner and of Simonne Roussel; *m* 1st, 1950, Gunilla Cecilia Ståhle (*d* 1986), *d* of Envoyé Nils K. Ståhle, CBE, and Birgit Olsson; four *s*; 2nd, 1990, Holly (Raven) Adrianne Johnson, *d* of Adrian W. Johnson and Ophelia A. Matley. *Educ*: Stonyhurst; Oriel College, Oxford (Scholar). Served E Yorks Regt, 1940; Lancs Fusiliers and 151 Parachute Bn, India, 1941–42; 156 Bn, N Africa, 1943; No 9 Commando, Italy and Greece, 1944–45. Entered HM Foreign Service, 1947; 3rd Sec., Stockholm, 1948–51; 2nd Sec., Washington, 1951–53; Foreign Office, 1953–55; 1st Sec., Tel Aviv, 1956–59; Head of Chancery, La Paz, 1959–61, and at Vienna, 1961–63; Inspector of Diplomatic Establishments, 1964–67; Ambassador to El Salvador, 1967–70. Commercial Advr, Consulate-Gen. of Switzerland in Houston, Texas, 1974–91. Founder, Academia Británica Cuzcatlea, El Salvador, 1970. Hon. Mem., Consular Corps of Houston, Texas, 1992–2008. *Publications*: Advances in Controlled Droplet Application, Agrichemical Age, 1979; So It Was (memoirs), 1993; (translated) Kidnapped by Brigands, by Isaac Friedli, 1995; Telephone Tales, 1996. *Recreations*: fly-fishing, old maps, choral singing, volunteer teaching, elocution. *Address*: The Old Coach House, Broadbottom, Hyde, Cheshire SK14 6AH; Laythams Farm, Slaidburn, Clitheroe, Lancs BB7 3AJ. *T*: (01200) 446677.

**WENSLEY, Prof. (John) Robin (Clifton)**, PhD; Professor of Policy and Marketing, University of Warwick, 1986–2012, now Professor Emeritus; Professor of Strategic Marketing, Open University, since 2013; *b* 26 Oct. 1944; *s of* George Leonard Wensley and Jeannette Marion Wensley; *m* 1970, Susan Patricia Horner; one *s* two *d. Educ*: Perse Sch., Cambridge; Queens' Coll., Cambridge (BA 1966); London Business Sch. (MSc; PhD). Lectr, then Sen. Lectr, London Business Sch., 1974–85; University of Warwick: Chm., Warwick Business Sch., 1989–94; Chair, Faculty of Soc. Studies, 1996–99; Dep. Dean, Warwick Business Sch., 2001–04; Dir, Advanced Inst. of Mgt Res., 2004–12. Chm. Council, Tavistock Inst. of Human Relns, 1998–2003; Council Mem., ESRC, 2001–04; Mem., Adv. Council, Warburg Inst., 2012–; Mem., Bd of Advrs, Faculty of Business and Law, Southampton Univ., 2013–. Member: Warwickshire Wildlife Trust, 1997–; Sustrans, 1997–. *Publications*: Strategic Marketing: planning, implementation and control, 1983; Interface of Marketing and Strategy, 1990; Rethinking Marketing, 1994; Handbook of Marketing, 2002; Effective Management in Practice: analytical insights and critical questions, 2013. *Recreations*: walking, DIY, reading, cycling. *Address*: 147 Leam Terrace, Leamington Spa CV31 1DF. *T*: (01926) 425022. *E*: robin.wensley@warwick.ac.uk.

**WENSLEY, Penelope Anne**, AC 2011 (AO 2001); Governor of Queensland, 2008–14; *b* Toowoomba, Qld, 18 Oct. 1946; *d of* Neil Wensley and Doris McCulloch; *m* 1974, Stuart McCosker; two *d. Educ*: Penrith High Sch.; Rosa Bassett Grammar Sch., London; Univ. of Queensland (BA 1st Cl. Hons 1967; Alumnus of Yr 1994). Joined Dept of Foreign Affairs, Australia, 1968; Third Sec., later Second Sec., then First Sec., Paris, 1969–73; Gen. Assembly, Aust. Mission to UN, NY, 1974–75; Dep. Hd of Mission, Mexico, 1975–77; Dep. High Comr, Wellington, 1982–85; Consul-Gen., Hong Kong and Macau, 1986–88; Department of Foreign Affairs and Trade: Asst Sec., E Asia Br., 1989–90; Principal Advr 1991–92; First Asst Sec., Internat. Orgns and Legal Div., 1992; Ambassador for the Environment, 1992–95; Ambassador and Perm. Rep. to UN, Geneva, 1993–95; Actg Dep. Sec., 1996; First Asst Sec., N Asia Div., 1996–97; Ambassador and Perm. Rep. to UN, NY, 1997–2001; High Comr to India, 2001–04, and Ambassador (non-resident) to Bhutan, 2003–04; Ambassador to France, 2005–08, and (non-resident) to Algeria, Mauritania and Morocco, 2005–08 and Monaco, 2007–08; First Asst Sec., Eur. Div., 2008. Chm., UN Fifth Cttee (Budget and Finance), 1999–2000; Co-Chm., UN Gen. Assembly Special Session on HIV/AIDS, 2001. Chairman: Council, Aust. Inst. of Marine Sci., 2015–; Adv. Cttee, Gt Barrier Reef 2050 Plan, 2015–; Dir, Lowry Inst. Nat. Patron, Soil Sci. Australia; Patron, Alumni Friends of Univ. of Qld. Fellow, Aust. Inst. of Internat. Affairs, 2015. Hon. Fellow, Envmt Inst. of Australia and NZ, 2014. Hon. DPhil: Queensland, 1994; Griffith, 2008; Queensland Univ. of Technol., 2011; James Cook Univ., 2013. Peace Medal, UN Assoc. of Australia, 1998. Grand Officer, Order of Merit (France), 2009. *Recreations*: reading, music, theatre, bush-walking, travel. *Clubs*: National Press (Canberra); Moreton (Brisbane).

**WENSLEY, Robin**; *see* Wensley, J. R. C.

**WENT, David**; Chairman, Irish Times Ltd, 2007–13; *b* 25 March 1947; *s of* Arthur Edward James Went and Phyllis (*née* Howell); *m* 1972, Mary Christine Milligan; one *s* one *d. Educ*: High Sch., Dublin; Trinity Coll., Dublin (BA Mod; LLB). Called to the Bar, King's Inns, Dublin, 1970. Graduate Trainee, Citibank, Dublin, 1970; Gen. Manager, Citibank, Jeddah, 1975–76; Dir 1976, Chief Exec. 1982, Ulster Investment Bank; Ulster Bank: Dep. Chief Exec., 1987; Chief Exec., 1988–94; Chief Exec., Coutts Gp, 1994–97; Man. Dir, Irish Life, 1998, Gp Chief Exec., 1999–2007, Irish Life & Permanent PLC. Non-executive Director: Vhi Healthcare, 2007–10; Goldman Sachs Bank (Europe) Ltd, 2007–13; Covestone Asset Mgt Ltd, 2017–; Element Financial Technology Ltd, 2017–; Johnson Hana Internat. Ltd, 2018–. Chm., NI Bankers' Assoc., 1988–89; President: Irish Bankers' Fedn, 1991–92; Inst. of Bankers in Ireland, 1993–94. Chm., Trinity Foundn, 2002–12. Hon. LLD Trinity Coll., Dublin, 2013. *Recreations*: tennis, reading. *Address*: Twyzel Lodge, Lordello Road, Rathmichael, Co. Dublin, Ireland. *Clubs*: Kildare Street and University (Dublin); Fitzwilliam Lawn Tennis; Killiney Golf.

**WENT, Rt Rev. John Stewart**; Bishop Suffragan of Tewkesbury, 1996–2013; House-for-duty Assistant Chaplain, Chenies with Little Chalfont, Latimer and Flaunden, 2013–18; an Honorary Assistant Bishop: Diocese of Oxford, since 2013; Diocese of London, since 2019; *b* 11 March 1944; *s of* Douglas and Barbara Went; *m* 1968, Rosemary Evelyn Amy (*née* Dunn); three *s. Educ*: Corpus Christi Coll., Cambridge (1st Cl Classics Pt I, starred 1st Theology Pt II; MA). Curate, Emmanuel, Northwood, Middx, 1969–75; Vicar, Holy Trinity, Margate, 1975–83; Vice-Principal, Wycliffe Hall, Oxford, 1983–89; Archdeacon of Surrey, 1989–95. Warden of Readers, Gloucester dio., 1996–2000. Chairman: Diocesan Council for Unity and Mission, Guildford, 1990–95; Vocation, Recruitment and Selection Cttee, C of E Ministry Div., 2002–08. Member Council: Bible Reading Fellowship, 1989–2015; World Vision, 1996–2006; Interserve, 2009–17 (Chm., 2015–16); Chm.,

British Tantur Trust, 2009–. *Publications*: (contrib.) Changing Rural Life: a Christian response to key rural issues (ed J. Martineau, L. J. Francis and P. Francis), 2004; contrib. to One in Christ and Rural Theology Jl. *Recreations*: music, photography, crosswords. *Address*: 31 Pandorea House, 35 Lismore Boulevard, NW9 4DL.

**WENTWORTH, Stephen**, CB 2003; Fisheries Director, Department for Environment, Food and Rural Affairs (formerly Fisheries Secretary, Ministry of Agriculture, Fisheries and Food), 1993–2003; *b* 23 Aug. 1943; *s of* Ronald Wentworth, OBE and Elizabeth Mary Wentworth (*née* Collins); *m* 1970, Katharine Laura Hopkinson; three *d. Educ*: King's College Sch., Wimbledon; Merton Coll., Oxford (MA 1970; MSc 1970); Open Univ. (Dip. Lit. 2005); Birkbeck, Univ. of London (MA Japanese Cultural Studies 2008; MA World History 2014). Joined Ministry of Agriculture, Fisheries and Food, 1967; seconded to CSSB, 1974, and to FCO, as First Sec., UK Perm. Repn to EEC, Brussels, 1976; Head of Beef Div., 1978; seconded to Cabinet Office, 1980; Head of: Milk Div., 1982; European Communities Div., 1985; Under-Sec. and Head of Meat Gp, 1986; Head of Livestock Products Gp, 1989; Head of EC and External Trade Policy Gp, 1991.

**WERNICK, Jane Melville**, CBE 2015; CEng, FREng, FIStructE, FICE; Consultant, engineersHRW incorporating Jane Wernick Associates, since 2017 (Director, 2015–17); *b* 21 April 1954; *d of* Doreen and Irving Wernick. *Educ*: Christchurch Primary Sch., Hampstead; Haberdashers' Aske's Sch., Acton; Southampton Univ. (BSc Civil Engrg). CEng 1985; MStructE 1985, FIStructE 1993; MICE 1989, FICE 2008; FREng 2009. Grad. engr, Ove Arup & Partners, 1976–80; project engr, Birdair Structures Inc., 1980–81; Ove Arup & Partners, 1981–98: Associate, 1984; Principal i/c LA Office, 1986–89; Associate Dir, London Office, 1989–98; Dir, Jane Wernick Associates Ltd, 1998–2015. Visiting Professor: Harvard Univ. Grad. Sch. of Design, 1995; Architecture Dept, Oxford Brookes Univ., 1999–2008; Bedford Vis. Prof., Rensselaer Poly. Inst., 1998; RAEng Vis. Prof. of Design, Civil Engrg Dept, Univ. of Southampton, 2001–14. Diploma Unit Master, AA, 1998–2003. Mem., Design Rev. Panel, 2001–06, Schools Design Rev. Panel, 2009–11, CABE; Mem., Nat. Design Rev. Panel, Design Council CABE, 2011–. Liveryman, Co. of Engrs, 2000. FRSA. Hon. FRIBA 2006. *Publications*: (contrib.) Lunar Bases and Space Activities of the 21st Century, Vol. 2, 1988; (contrib.) Arups on Engineering, 1996; (ed) Building Happiness: architecture to make you smile, 2008; contribs to Structural Engr, Architectural Research Qly. *Recreations*: making music, making art, making things, gardening, reading, socializing, travelling, snorkelling.

**WERNICK, Michael Bernard**; Clerk of the Privy Council and Secretary to the Cabinet, Canada, 2016–19; *b* Montreal, 3 Sept. 1957; *s of* Morris Wernick and Kathleen Wernick; *m* 1985, Wiebke Merck; two *c. Educ*: Univ. of Toronto (BA Econs 1979; MA Econs 1980). Joined Canadian public service, 1981; Dep. Sec. to Cabinet, 2003–06; Dep. Minister of Aboriginal and Northern Affairs, 2006–14; Dep. Clerk, Privy Council Office, 2014–15. Mem., Bd of Govs, Carleton Univ. Queen's Diamond Jubilee Medal, 2012. *Recreation*: diehard Arsenal supporter.

**WERRETT, Dr David John**; Chief Executive, Forensic Science Service, 2001–07; Managing Director, Cedere Ltd, since 2007; *b* 24 Oct. 1949; *s of* Kenneth John Werrett and Heather Victoria Werrett; *m* 2004, Rebecca Lesley; one *s* one *d*, and one step *s* one step *d. Educ*: Univ. of Birmingham (BSc; PhD 1974). With Forensic Sci. Service, 1974–2007 (Mem. Bd, 1986–2007). MInstD 2002. *Publications*: contrib. numerous scientific papers to jls, incl. Nature. *Recreations*: good food, good wine, good company, preferably on a sail boat. *Club*: Lyme Regis Sailing.

**WESCOTT, Mary Eileen Patricia, (Mo)**; *see* Flynn, M. E. P.

**WESSELY, Clare**; *see* Gerada, C.

**WESSELY, Sir Simon (Charles)**, Kt 2013; MD; FRCP, FRCPsych, FMedSci; Regius Professor of Psychiatry, since 2017, Head, Department of Psychological Medicine, 2005–14, and Vice Dean, Academic Psychiatry, Institute of Psychiatry, 2010–14; King's College London; President, Royal Society of Medicine, 2017–July 2020; *b* 23 Dec. 1956; *s of* Rudi and Wendy Wessely; *m* 1988, Dr Clare Gerada, *qv*; two *s. Educ*: King Edward VII Sch., Sheffield; Trinity Hall, Cambridge (BA 1978; Hon. Fellow, 2015); University Coll., Oxford (BM BCh 1981); London Sch. of Hygiene and Tropical Medicine (MSc 1989); MD London 1993. MRCP 1984, FRCP 1997; MRCPsych 1986, FRCPsych 2000. SHO in Gen. Medicine, Freeman Hosp., Newcastle upon Tyne, 1982–84; SHO, then Registrar, Maudsley Hosp., 1984–87; Sen. Registrar, Nat. Hosp. for Neurol., 1987–88; Wellcome Res. Trng Fellow in Epidemiol., 1988–91; Sen. Lectr, Dept of Psychol Medicine, GKT, 1991–96; Prof. of Epidemiol and Liaison Psychiatry, then Prof. of Psychol Medicine, Inst. of Psychiatry, KCL, 1996–2017; Director: Chronic Fatigue Syndrome Res. Unit, KCL, 1994–; Gulf War Illness Res. Unit, later King's Centre for Mil. Health Res., KCL, 1996–. Civilian Consultant Advr in Psychiatry, British Army, 2001–; Sen. Investigator, NIHR, 2008–; Member: Defence Scientific Adv. Council, 2008–; Judicial Appts Commn, 2017–. Chair, Ind. Rev. of Mental Health Act, 2017–18. Pres., RCPsych, 2014–17. FMedSci 1999. *Publications*: (jtly) Psychosis in the Inner City, 1998; Chronic Fatigue and its Syndromes, 1998; Clinical Trials in Psychiatry, 2003; From Shellshock to PTSD: a history of military psychiatry, 2005; Psychological Reactions to the New Terrorism: a NATO Russia dialogue, 2005; numerous contribs to learned jls on epidemiol., schizophrenia, chronic fatigue syndrome, unexplained symptoms and syndromes, somatisation, deliberate self-harm, Gulf War illness, military health, psychol aspects of terrorism, risk communication and med. history. *Recreations*: modern history, ski-ing, cycling to Paris, wasting time in Viennese cafes. *Address*: Department of Psychological Medicine, Weston Education Centre, Cutcombe Road, Camberwell, SE5 9RJ. *T*: (020) 7848 5411, *Fax*: (020) 7848 5408. *E*: simon.wessely@kcl.ac.uk.

**WESSON, Edward Michael**; Headmaster, Skinners' School, Tunbridge Wells, since 2013; *b* Nottingham, 15 July 1965; *s of* Tony and Angela Wesson; *m* 2009, Susie Kumpel; two *d. Educ*: Tonbridge Sch.; Trinity Hall, Cambridge (BA Law 1987). Freelance journalist, Paris, 1987–88; Teacher of Hist. and French, New Beacon Sch., 1988–89; journalist, Sevenoaks Chronicle, 1989–90; Teacher of Hist. and French, Wellington Sch., 1990–94; Hd of Sixth Form and Master i/c cricket, Hampton Sch., 1994–2006; Dep. Hd, Reigate GS, 2006–10; Headmaster, King's Sch., Tynemouth, 2010–13. Gov., Skinners' Kent Acad., 2013–. *Recreations*: cricket, gardening. *Address*: Skinners' School, St John's Road, Tunbridge Wells, Kent TN4 9PG. *T*: (01892) 520732. *E*: edward.wesson@skinners-school.org.uk. *Club*: MCC.

**WESSON, Jane Louise**; Independent Public Appointments Assessor, 2001–12; Chairman, Council for Healthcare Regulatory Excellence (formerly Council for the Regulation of Healthcare Professionals), 2003–07; *b* 26 Feb. 1953. *Educ*: Univ. of Kent (BA Hons Law). Solicitor of the Supreme Court; Solicitor, Hepworth & Chadwick, 1978–89; Consultant, Ashworth Tetlow & Co., 1995–2005. Chairman: Ind. Tribunal Service, 1992–99; Nat. Clinical Assessment Authy, 2000–02. Chm., Harrogate Healthcare NHS Trust, 1993–2000; Board Member: Northern Counties Housing Assoc., 1993–96; Anchor Housing, 2003–09; Nuffield Health (formerly Nuffield Hosps), 2005–14; Age UK (formerly Help the Aged and Age Concern), 2009–12. *Club*: Royal Automobile.

**WEST**; *see* Sackville-West, family name of Baron Sackville.

**WEST**, family name of **Baron West of Spithead**.

**WEST OF SPITHEAD**, Baron *cr* 2007 (Life Peer), of Seaview in the County of Isle of Wight; **Adm. Alan William John West**, GCB 2004 (KCB 2000); DSC 1982; PC 2010; *b* 21 April 1948; *m* 1973, Rosemary Anne Linington Childs; two *s* one *d*. *Educ*: Windsor Grammar Sch.; Clydebank High Sch. Joined RN 1965; BRNC Dartmouth; seagoing appts, 1966–73; CO HMS Yarnton, 1973; qualified Principal Warfare Officer, 1975; HMS Juno, 1976; HMS Ambuscade, 1977; RN Staff Course, 1978; qualified Advanced Warfare Officer, 1978; HMS Norfolk, 1979; CO HMS Ardent, 1980; Naval Staff, 1982; CO HMS Bristol, 1987; Defence Intell. Staff, 1989; RCDS 1992; Higher Comd and Staff Course, Camberley, 1993; Dir, Naval Staff Duties, 1993; Naval Sec., 1994–96; Comdr UK Task Gp, and Comdr Anti Submarine Warfare Striking Force, 1996–97; Chief of Defence Intelligence, 1997–2001; C-in-C Fleet, C-in-C E Atlantic and Comdr Allied Naval Forces N, 2001–02; Chief of Naval Staff and First Sea Lord, 2002–06; First and Principal Naval ADC to the Queen, 2002–06. Parly Under-Sec. of State for Security and Counter Terrorism, Home Office, 2007–10; Minister for Cyber Security, 2009–10. Chairman: Defence Adv. Bd, QinetiQ, 2006–07; Nat. Security Forum, 2008–10; Mem., Internat. Adv. Bd, HSBC, 2010–11. Trustee, Imperial War Mus., 2006–14. Chm., Cadet Vocational Qualification Orgn, 2006–12. Chancellor, Southampton Solent Univ., 2006–18. Yr Brother, Trinity House. President: Bollington Sea Cadet Corps; Ardent Assoc.; Ship Recognition Corps. Pres., Britannia Assoc., 2006–14; Knight Pres., Knights of the Round Table, 2009–. Member: RUSI, 1977–; St Barbara Assoc., 1978–; Royal Naval Sailing Assoc., 1984–; Anchorites, 1992–; Royal Naval Assoc., 2000–; Pepys Club, 2002–; Destroyer Club, 2002–; Pilgrims, 2003–. Patron: Care for St Anne's Limehouse, 2008–; Dockland Sinfonia, 2008–; Merchant Navy Medal Fund. Member: Master Mariners' Co., 2005. *Recreations*: sailing, military and local history. *Address*: House of Lords, SW1A 0PW. *Clubs*: Naval, Royal Navy of 1765 and 1785; Royal Yacht Squadron.

**WEST, Anthony**; *see* West, J. A. H.

**WEST, Brian John**; media consultant; Director and Chief Executive, Association of Independent Radio Companies, 1983–95; *b* 4 Aug. 1935; *s* of Herbert Frank West and Nellie (*née* Painter); *m* 1st, 1960, Patricia Ivy White (marr. diss. 1986); 2nd, 1987, Gillian Bond. *Educ*: Tiffin Sch., Kingston upon Thames. Sub-Lt (O), Fleet Air Arm, RN, 1956–58. Journalist, Richmond Herald, Surrey Comet and Western Morning News, 1952–60; Surrey Comet: Asst Editor, 1960–64; Editor, 1964–70; Editor, Leicester Mercury, 1970–74; Head of Advertising and PR, Littlewoods Orgn Plc, 1974–83. Founder Pres., Assoc. of European Radios, 1992–93; Council Mem., Advertising Assoc., 1987–95; Dir, Radio Jt Audience Res. Ltd, 1992–94. Churchill Fellow, 1995; Beaverbrook Foundn Fellow, 1995; Fellow, Radio Acad., 1995. *Publications*: Radio Training in the United States, 1996. *Recreations*: voluntary work, computers, music, horses and dogs, walking, gardening, photography, cherishing my wife. *Address*: Melrose, 33 Cwm Road, Dyserth, Denbighshire LL18 6BA. *T*: and *Fax*: (01745) 570568. *E*: brigil9@talktalk.net.

**WEST, Catherine Elizabeth**; MP (Lab) Hornsey and Wood Green, since 2015; *b* Mansfield, Vic, Australia; *m* 1996, Dr Colin Sutherland; one *s* one *d*. *Educ*: Univ. of Sydney (BA, BSW); Sch. of Oriental and African Studies, Univ. of London (MA Chinese Politics). Social worker, Australia; caseworker for David Lammy, MP, 2000. Mem., Islington LBC, 2000–14 (Leader of Opposition, 2004–10; Leader of Council, 2010–13). Chm., Transport and Envmt Cttee, London Councils, 2010–14. *Recreations*: swimming, cricket. *Address*: House of Commons, SW1A 0AA. *T*: (020) 7219 6141. *E*: catherine.west.mp@parliament.uk.

**WEST, Prof. Christopher David**; Chief Executive, Royal Zoological Society of Scotland, 2012–16; Partner, Pobblebonk Environmental, since 2016; *b* 16 Aug. 1959; *s* of Donald Frank Hartley West and Delia Handford West; *m* 1993, Diane Linda Keetch; two *s* three *d*. *Educ*: Poole Grammar Sch.; Purbeck Sch.; Royal Veterinary Coll., London (BVetMed 1983; Cert. Lab. Animal Sci. 1986). CBiol, MRSB (MIBiol 1985). Houseman, 1983, Registrar, 1985, Surgery Dept, RVC; Vet. Surgeon and Res. Scientist, Clinical Res. Centre, MRC, 1985–87; Gp Manager, ICI Pharmaceuticals, 1987–91; Named Vet. Surgeon, Zeneca-CTL, 1991–97; Chief Curator, Chester Zoo, 1997–2001; Zool Dir, Zool Soc. of London, 2001–05; Chief Exec., Royal Zool Soc. of Australia, 2006–12. Prof. of Zoology, Univ. of Adelaide, 2006–12; Prof. of Biodiversity Conservation, Flinders Univ., 2007–12. Vis. Prof. in Conservation Medicine, Vet. Faculty, Univ. of Liverpool, 2001; Vis. Lectr, Univ. of Gothenburg, 2002. Hon. Prof., Univ. of Edinburgh, 2014–16. Chm. Trustees, Wildlife Vets Internat., 2005–06. Chm., Jane Goodall Inst., Australia, 2007–11. *Publications*: papers in Animal Behaviour, Animal Welfare, etc. *Recreations*: organic gardening, visiting deserts, tree planting (to offset international travel), cooking curries, worrying about climate change, working for Chinese species conservation.

**WEST, Dominic Gerard Francis Eagleton**; actor; *b* Sheffield, 15 Oct. 1969; *s* of George West and Moya West; one *d* by Polly Astor; *m* 2010, Catherine FitzGerald; two *s* two *d*. *Educ*: Eton Coll.; Trinity Coll., Dublin (BA Hons); Guildhall Sch. of Music and Drama (BA Hons; Hon. Fellow 2012). *Films* include: 3 Joes, 1991; Richard III, 1995; 28 Days, 2000; Rock Star, 2001; Chicago, 2002; Mona Lisa Smile, 2003; The Forgotten, 2004; 300, 2007; Centurion, 2010; The Awakening, 2011; John Carter, 2012; Pride, 2014; Genius, Money Monster, 2016; Tomb Raider, The Square, 2018; Colette, 2019; *television* series include: The Wire, 2002–08; The Hour, 2011–12; Appropriate Adult, 2011 (Best Actor, BAFTA, 2012); The Affair, 2014–19; Les Misérables, 2018; TV film, Burton and Taylor, 2013. *Theatre* includes: The Seagull, Old Vic, 1996 (Ian Charleson Award); De La Guarda, Roundhouse, 1999; The Voysey Inheritance, NT, 2006; Rock 'n' Roll, Duke of York's, 2007; Life is a Dream, Donmar, 2009; Butley, Duchess, 2011; Othello, Sheffield Crucible, 2011; The River, Royal Ct, 2012; My Fair Lady, Sheffield Crucible, 2012; Les Liaisons Dangereuses, Donmar Warehouse, 2015. Hon. Dr: Sheffield Hallam, 2011; Sheffield, 2018. *Recreation*: boomerang. *Address*: c/o Tavistock Wood, 45 Conduit Street, W1S 2YN. *T*: (020) 7494 4767. *E*: wood@tavistockwood.com.

**WEST, Prof. Donald James**; Professor of Clinical Criminology 1979–84, now Emeritus, and Director 1981–84, University of Cambridge Institute of Criminology; Fellow of Darwin College, Cambridge, 1967–91, now Emeritus; Hon. Consultant Psychiatrist, National Health Service, 1961–86, retired; *b* 9 June 1924; *s* of John Charles and Jessie Mercedes West. *Educ*: Merchant Taylors' Sch., Crosby; Liverpool Univ. (MD). LittD Cambridge. FRCPsych. Research Officer, Soc. for Psychical Research, London, and pt-time graduate student in psychiatry, 1947–50; in hospital practice in psychiatry, 1951–57; Sen. Registrar, Forensic Psychiatry Unit, Maudsley Hosp., 1957–59; Inst. of Criminology, Cambridge, 1960–84. Founder, Cambridge Study in Delinquency Develt, 1961–. Leverhulme Emeritus Fellow, 1988–89. Mental Health Act Comr, 1989–97. Vice Pres., 1981–, and former Pres., British Soc. of Criminology; Pres., Soc. for Psychical Research, 1963–65, 1984–87, 1998–2000; Chm., Forensic Section, World Psychiatric Assoc., 1983–89; Chm., Streetwise Youth, 1986–92. *Publications*: Psychical Research Today, 1954, rev. edn 1962; Eleven Lourdes Miracles (med. inquiry under Parapsych. Foundn Grant), 1957; The Habitual Prisoner (for Inst. of Criminology), 1963; Murder followed by Suicide (for Inst. of Criminology), 1965; The Young Offender, 1967; Homosexuality, 1968; Present Conduct and Future Delinquency, 1969; (ed) The Future of Parole, 1972; (jtly) Who Becomes Delinquent?, 1973; (jtly) The Delinquent Way of Life, 1977; Homosexuality Re-examined, 1977; (ed, jtly) Daniel McNaughton: his trial and the aftermath, 1977; (jtly) Understanding Sexual Attacks, 1978; Delinquency: its roots, careers and prospects, 1982; Sexual Victimisation, 1985; Sexual Crimes and Confrontations, 1987; (jtly) Children's Sexual Encounters with Adults, 1990; Male Prostitution, 1992; (ed) Sex Crimes, 1994; (ed with R. Green) Sociolegal Controls on Homosexuality: a multi-nation comparison, 1997; Gay Life, Straight Work, 2012; various contribs to British Jl of Criminology, Criminal Behaviour and Mental Health, Jl Forensic Psychiatry and Jl Soc. for Psychical Res. *Recreations*: travel, parapsychology. *T*: (020) 7581 2875.

**WEST, Edward Mark**, CMG 1987; Deputy Director-General, Food and Agriculture Organization of the United Nations, 1986–89; *b* 11 March 1923; *m* 1948, Lydia Hollander; three *s*. *Educ*: Hendon County Sch.; University Coll., Oxford (MA). Served RA (W/Lieut), 1943; ICU BAOR (A/Captain), 1945. Asst Principal, Colonial Office, 1947; Private Sec., PUS, Colonial Office, 1950–51, Principal, 1951–58; Head of Chancery, UK Commn, Singapore, 1958–61; Private Secretary to Secretary of State, Colonial Affairs, 1961–62; Private Secretary to Secretary of State for Commonwealth and Colonial Affairs, 1963; Asst Sec., ODM, 1964–70; Food and Agriculture Organization: Director, Programme and Budget Formulation, 1970; Asst Dir-Gen., Administration and Finance Dept, 1974; Asst Dir-Gen., Programme and Budget Formulation, 1976; Special Rep., Internat. Conf. on Nutrition, 1992. *Address*: 10 Warwick Mansions, Cromwell Crescent, SW5 9QR.

**WEST, Emma Louise**; *see* Johnson, E. L.

**WEST, Lt-Col George Arthur Alston-Roberts-**, CVO 1988; Comptroller, Lord Chamberlain's Office, 1987–90 (Assistant Comptroller, 1981–87); an Extra Equerry to the Queen, since 1982; *b* 1937; *s* of Major W. R. J. Alston-Roberts-West, Grenadier Guards (killed in action 1940) and late Mrs W. R. J. Alston-Roberts-West; *m* 1970, Hazel, *d* of late Sir Thomas and Lady Cook. *Educ*: Eton Coll.; RMA, Sandhurst. Commissioned into Grenadier Guards, Dec. 1957; served in England, Northern Ireland, Germany and Cyprus; retired, 1980. Dir, Care Ltd, 1991–95. DL Warwicks, 1988. *Address*: Atherstone Hill Farm, Stratford-on-Avon, Warwicks CV37 8NF. *Club*: Boodle's.

**WEST, Rev. Canon Jeffrey James**, OBE 2006; FSA; Associate Minister, St Mary's, Banbury, since 2011 (Curate, 2007–11); *b* 15 Oct. 1950; *s* of late Walter Edward West and (Frances) Margaret West (*née* Tatam); *m* 1987, Juliet Elizabeth Allan. *Educ*: Bedford Modern Sch.; Worcester Coll., Oxford (BA PPE 1972; BPhil Politics 1974; MA 1976; DipTh 2006); Oxford Brookes Univ. (PGDipMin 2007); Ripon Coll., Cuddesdon. FSA 2011. Joined Ancient Monuments Inspectorate, Department of Environment, 1974: Asst Inspector, 1974–79; Inspector, 1979–81; seconded as Principal, Local Govt Finance, DoE, 1981–83; Principal Inspector of Historic Buildings, DoE, later English Heritage, 1983–86; English Heritage: Regl Dir of Historic Properties (Midlands and E Anglia), 1986–97; Actg Dir of Historic Properties, 1997–98; Dep. Dir of Conservation, and Dir, Conservation Mgt, 1998–2002; Policy Dir, 2002–05. Ordained deacon, 2007, priest, 2008; Area Dean of Deddington, 2012–17. Hon. Canon, Christ Ch Cathedral, Oxford, 2017–. Oxford Diocese: Member: Diocesan Synod, 2008–; Diocesan Adv. Cttee for the Care of Churches, 2009–; Bp's Council, 2016–18. Member: Council, Royal Archaeol Inst., 1980–83; Home Office Burials and Cemeteries Adv. Gp, 2001–05; Rural Affairs Forum for England, 2002–04; Exec. Cttee, ICOMOS (UK), 2006–12 (Mem., Res. and Recording Cttee, 1997–2004; Chm., Develt Cttee, 2009–12). Dir, BURA, 2004–07; Chm., Cotswolds Conservation Bd, 2009–14 (Vice-Chm., 2005–09). FRSA 2001. *Publications*: (with Nicholas Palmer) Haughmond Abbey, Shropshire: excavation of a 12th-century cloister in its historical and landscape context, 2014; contrib. articles, notes and reviews on individual historic bldgs and theory and practice of conservation in learned jls. *Recreation*: architectural and landscape history. *Address*: c/o St Mary's Centre, Horsefair, Banbury, Oxon OX16 0AA.

**WEST, (John) Anthony (Hawthorne)**; Vice Lord Lieutenant of Berkshire, 2015–16; *b* Reading, 1 Aug. 1941; *s* of John Lewis West and Camilla Hawthorne West (*née* Lydall); *m* 1966, Sarah Hamilton Mays-Smith; three *s*. *Educ*: Radley Coll.; Sch. of Law. Admitted as solicitor, 1964; in private practice as solicitor with Darley Cumberland, subseq. Cumberland Ellis Peirs, London, 1964–99; Solicitor to Carpenters' Co., 1978–99 (Liveryman, 1999). Member: Bd, Royal Alfred Seafarers' Soc., 1970–2000 (Vice Pres., 2000–); Council, Shipwrecked Mariners' Soc., 1995–2011 (Chm., 2002–08; Vice Pres., 2011–). Trustee: Radley Coll. War Meml Funds, 1968–2010 (Chm., 1989–2010); Freemasons' Fund for Surgical Res., 1984–2018 (Chm., 2010–18); Royal Merchant Navy Sch. Foundn/Bearwood Coll., 1985–97; Upper Thames Rowing Club, 1998–; Serth and Gates Charity, 2008–; former Trustee, Docklands Settlements; Founding Trustee, Charlie Waller Meml Trust, 1998–2005 (Treas., 1998–2004; Patron, 2005–). Governor: Clothworkers' Foundn, 1995–2012; Mary Hare Sch. for Deaf, 1995–2007 (Vice Chm., 2008; Vice Pres., 2009–). Mem., Court of Patrons, RCS, 2016–. Liveryman, Clothworkers' Co., 1980– (Mem. Ct, 1997–2017, now Asst Emeritus; Master, 2008–09). High Sheriff, 2004–05, DL, 2007, Berks. *Recreations*: sailing, golf (occasional), horseracing, Freemasonry, philately, bridge. *Address*: Remenham Manor, Henley-on-Thames, Oxon RG9 3DD. *T*: (01491) 574750; The Old Rectory, Gerrans, Truro, Cornwall TR2 5ES. *T*: (01872) 580102. *E*: jahwest@aol.com. *Clubs*: St Mawes Sailing, Huntercombe Golf.

**WEST, Kenneth**, CChem, FRSC; Deputy Chairman, ICI Fibres Division, 1980–84 (Technical Director, 1977–80); *b* 1 Sept. 1930; *s* of Albert West and Ethel Kirby (*née* Kendall); *m* 1980, Elizabeth Ann Borland (*née* Campbell); one step *s*, and three *d* by a previous marriage. *Educ*: Archbishop Holgate's Grammar Sch., York; University Coll., Oxford (BA). Customer Service Manager, ICI Fibres, 1960; Res. and Engrg Manager, FII, 1967; Director: South African Nylon Spinners, Cape Town, 1970; Fibre Industries Inc., N Carolina, 1974; Man. Dir, TWA, 1984–85; Dir, Water Res. Council, 1984–85. Dir, Seahorse Internat. Ltd, 1987–89. *Recreations*: sailing, flying, music, wine, amateur dramatics. *Address*: Ar Dhachaidh, Wood Side Farm, Coupar Angus, Blairgowrie, Perthshire PH13 9LP. *Club*: Oxford and Cambridge (Var Br.).

**WEST, Lawrence Joseph**; QC 2003; a Recorder, 2000–16; *b* 6 July 1946; *s* of Lionel Chaffey West and Catherine Agnes (*née* Daly); *m* 1972, Cathryn Hudson; two *s*. *Educ*: De La Salle Oaklands Sch., Toronto; Univ. of Toronto (BA 1967; LLB 1970); London Sch. of Econs (LLM 1971). MCIArb 2003. Called: to Law Soc. of Upper Canada, 1973; to the Bar, Gray's Inn, 1979. *Recreations*: chess, fencing and other arts of controlled violence. *Address*: Henderson Chambers, 2 Harcourt Buildings, Temple, EC4Y 9DB. *T*: (020) 7583 9020, *Fax*: (020) 7583 2686. *E*: lwest@hendersonchambers.co.uk.

**WEST, Mary Cecilia**; *see* Kenny, M. C.

**WEST, Prof. Michael Alun,** PhD; FBPsS; FCIPD; Professor of Organisational Psychology, University of Lancaster, since 2011 (Chair, Centre for Performance-Led HR, 2011–16); *b* Loughborough, 6 March 1951; *m* 2006, Gillian Hardy; one *s* two *d*; one *s* from previous marriage. *Educ:* Univ. of Wales Inst. of Sci. and Technol. (BSc Econ Hons 1973; PhD 1977). FBPsS 1992; FCIPD 2006. Aston Business School, Aston University: Res. Dir, 2001–06; Prof. of Organisational Psychol., 2001–11, now Emeritus; Exec. Dean, 2007–11. Adv. Consultant, Aston Organisational Development Ltd (Dir, 2004). FBAM 1999; FHEA 2007; FRSA. Fellow: Amer. Psychol Assoc., 1998; Internat. Assoc. of Applied Psychol., 2006. *Publications:* (jtly) The Transition from School to Work, 1983; (ed) The Psychology of Meditation, 1987; (jtly) Managerial Job Change: men and women in transition, 1988; (ed jtly) Innovation and Creativity at Work, 1990; (ed jtly) Women at Work: psychological and organizational perspectives, 1990; Effective Teamwork: practical lessons from organisational research, 1994, 2nd edn 2004; (ed) Handbook of Work Group Psychology, 1996; Developing Creativity in Organizations, 1997; (jtly) Effective Top Management Teams, 2001; (ed jtly) International Handbook of Organizational Teamwork and Cooperative Working, 2003; (with L. Markiewicz) Building Team-based Working: a practical guide to organizational transformation, 2004; The Secrets of Successful Team Management, 2004; (ed jtly) The Essentials of Teamworking: international perspectives, 2005; (jtly) Teamwork, teamdiagnose, teamentwicklung, 2005; (jtly) Aston Team Performance Inventory: management set, 2006. *Address:* Department for Organisation, Work and Technology, Charles Carter Building, University of Lancaster, Bailrigg, Lancaster LA1 4YX.

**WEST, Nigel;** *see* Allason, R. W. S.

**WEST, Paul,** QPM 2004; Managing Director, Policing First Ltd, since 2011; *b* 29 March 1958; *s* of Derrick and Constance West; *m* 1993, Rosemary Helen Goundry; three *s* three *d*. *Educ:* Durham Johnston Sch.; Pembroke Coll., Oxford (BA (Physics) 1979, MA 1983); Michigan State Univ. (MSc (Criminal Justice) 1987); Durham Univ. (MA (Human Resource Mgt and Develt) 1998). Joined Durham Constabulary, 1979: Constable, 1979–83; Sergeant, 1983–85; Insp., 1985–90; Harkness Fellow, 1986; Chief Insp. 1990–92; Supt, 1992–98; Thames Valley Police: Asst Chief Constable, 1998–2000; Dep. Chief Constable, 2000–03; Chief Constable, W Mercia Police, 2003–11. Ind. Mem., Judicial Appointments Commn, 2012–; Mem., Prison Service Pay Review Body, 2016–. Bishop's Advr on Criminal Justice Affairs, Dio. of Worcester, 2013–. *Recreations:* classical music (violin and viola), sports (partic. football), gardening, charity fundraising, poultry and small animal rearing, family.

**WEST, Peter Bernard,** CMG 2015; HM Diplomatic Service; High Commissioner to Uganda, since 2016; *b* 29 June 1958; *s* of late Bernard West and Alice West (*née* Bowen); *m* 1980, Julia Anne Chandler; two *s* (twins) one *d*. Joined FCO, 1977; Third Secretary: Buenos Aires, 1980–83; Auckland, 1984–85; Second, then First, Sec., FCO, 1986–91; First Sec. (Political/EU), Copenhagen, 1992–97; Dep. Hd, S Asian Dept, FCO, 1997–99; Counsellor and Dep. Hd of Mission, Bangkok, 2000–04; Consul-Gen., Melbourne, 2004–08; Dep. High Comr, Abuja, 2008–11; Dep. High Comr, Lagos, 2011–12; High Comr, Sierra Leone, 2013–16. *Recreations:* family, sport, travel. *Address:* c/o Foreign and Commonwealth Office, King Charles Street, SW1A 2AH. *Club:* Melbourne Football (Melbourne).

**WEST, Prof. Peter Christopher,** PhD; FRS 2006; FInstP; Professor, Department of Mathematics, King's College, London, since 1986; *b* 4 Dec. 1951; *s* of Ronald West and Martha West (now Williams); *m* 1980, Susan Amanda Back; one *s* one *d*. *Educ:* Imperial Coll., London (BSc 1973; PhD 1976). FInstP 2007. Postdoctoral Fellow: Ecole Normale Supérieure, Paris, 1976–77; Imperial Coll., London, 1977–78; Lectr, 1978–85, Reader, 1985–86, KCL. Visiting appointments: CIT, 1984; CERN, 1986–89, 2000; Chalmers 150th Anniv. Prof., Sweden, 1992. FKC 2007. *Publications:* Introduction to Supersymmetry and Supergravity, 1983, 2nd edn 1990; Introduction to Strings and Branes, 2012; more than 200 scientific pubns. *Recreations:* classical music, cycling, travelling in remote regions, gardening. *Address:* Department of Mathematics, King's College London, Strand, WC2R 2LS. *T:* (020) 7848 2224, *Fax:* (020) 7848 2017. *E:* peter.west@kcl.ac.uk.

**WEST, Prunella Margaret Rumney, (Mrs T. L. West);** *see* Scales, Prunella.

**WEST, Prof. Richard Gilbert,** FRS 1968; FSA; FGS; Fellow of Clare College, Cambridge, since 1954; Professor of Botany, University of Cambridge, 1977–91; *b* 31 May 1926; *m* 1958, one *s*; and, 1973, Hazel Gristwood (*d* 1997); two *d*. *Educ:* King's School, Canterbury; Univ. of Cambridge. Cambridge University: Demonstrator in Botany, 1957–60; Lecturer in Botany, 1960–67; Dir, Subdept of Quaternary Research, 1966–87; Reader in Quaternary Research, 1967–75; Prof. of Palaeoecology, 1975–77. Member: Council for Scientific Policy, 1971–73; NERC, 1973–76; Ancient Monuments Bd for England, 1980–84. Darwin Lecturer to the British Association, 1959; Lyell Fund, 1961, Bigsby Medal, 1969, Lyell Medal, 1988, Geological Society of London. Hon. MRIA. *Publications:* Pleistocene Geology and Biology, 1968, 2nd edn 1977; (jtly) The Ice Age in Britain, 1972, 2nd edn 1981; The Pre-glacial Pleistocene of the Norfolk and Suffolk coasts, 1980; Pleistocene Palaeoecology of Central Norfolk, 1991; Plant Life in the Quaternary Cold Stages, 2000; From Brandon to Bungay, 2009; Quaternary Research in Britain and Ireland, 2014; Evolution of a Breckland Landscape, 2015. *Address:* 3A Woollards Lane, Great Shelford, Cambs CB22 5LZ. *T:* (01223) 842578; Clare College, Cambridge CB2 1TL.

**WEST, Samuel Alexander Joseph;** actor and director; Artistic Director, Sheffield Theatres, 2005–07; Associate Artist, Royal Shakespeare Company, since 2013; *b* 19 June 1966; *s* of Timothy Lancaster West, *qv* and Prunella Margaret Rumney West (*see* Prunella Scales); partner, Laura Joanne Wade, *qv*; two *d*. *Educ:* Alleyn's Sch., Dulwich; Lady Margaret Hall, Oxford (BA Hons Eng. Lit.). First professional stage appearance, The Browning Version, Birmingham Rep., 1985; London début, Les Parents Terribles, Orange Tree, Richmond, 1988; West End début, A Life in the Theatre, Haymarket, 1989; *theatre* includes: Hidden Laughter, Vaudeville, 1990; Royal National Theatre: The Sea, 1991; Arcadia, 1993; Antony and Cleopatra, 1998; Cain (Byron), Chichester, 1992; The Importance of Being Earnest, Manchester, 1993; Henry IV parts I & II, English Touring Th., 1996; Richard II, 2000, Hamlet, 2001, RSC; Dr Faustus, The Master and Margarita, Chichester, 2004; Much Ado About Nothing, Crucible, Sheffield, 2005; Betrayal, Donmar Warehouse, 2007; Drunk Enough To Say I Love You?, NY, 2008; The Family Reunion, Donmar Warehouse, 2008; Enron, Chichester, transf. Royal Court, 2009, then Noël Coward, 2010; A Number, Menier, 2010; Uncle Vanya, Vaudeville, 2012; Ivanov, The Seagull, Chichester, 2014; Julius Caesar, Crucible, Sheffield, 2017; The Writer, Almeida, 2018; (opera) The Book of Disquiet, Coronet Th., 2016; Present Laughter, Th. Royal, Bath and tour, 2016; Kreutzer vs Kreutzer, RFH, 2016; narrator, Lélio, City Halls, Glasgow, 2019; director: The Lady's Not For Burning, Chichester, 2002; Les Liaisons Dangereuses, Bristol Old Vic, 2003; Cosi fan tutte, ENO, 2003; Three Women and a Piano Tuner, Chichester, 2004, Hampstead, 2005; Insignificance, Lyceum, Sheffield, 2005; The Romans in Britain, The Clean House, 2006, As You Like It, 2007, Crucible, Sheffield; Dealer's Choice, Menier, 2007; Waste, Almeida, 2008; Close the Coalhouse Door, Northern Stage, Newcastle, 2012; After Electra, Tricycle Th., 2015; The Watsons, Minerva Th., Chichester, 2018; *television* includes: serials: Stanley and the Women, 1990; Over Here, 1995; Out of the Past, 1998; Hornblower, 1998; Waking the Dead, 2002; Cambridge Spies, 2003; Foyle's War, 2004; E=mc$^2$, 2005; The Inspector Lynley Mysteries, 2006; The Long Walk to Finchley, 2008; Desperate Romantics, 2009; New Tricks, 2009; Garrow's Law, 2010; Any Human Heart, 2010; Poirot: Murder on the Orient Express, 2010; Law and Order, 2011; Eternal Law, 2012; Mr Selfridge, 2012, 2013, 2014, 2015; Fleming, 2014; W1A, 2015; Jonathan Strange and Mr Norrell, 2015; The Hollow Crown: The War of the Roses, 2016; Midsomer Murders, 2018; films: Frankie and Johnny, 1985; Voices in the Garden, 1991; A Breed of Heroes, 1995; Persuasion, 1995; Longitude, 2000; Random Quest, 2006; *films* include: Reunion, 1989; Howards End, 1991; Archipel (in French), 1992; Carrington, 1994; A Feast at Midnight, 1995; Jane Eyre, 1995; Stiff Upper Lips, 1996; The Ripper, 1997; Rupert's Land, 1997; Notting Hill, 1998; Pandæmonium, 1999; Iris, 2001; Van Helsing, 2003; Schweitzer, 2009; Hyde Park on Hudson, 2012; The Riot Club, 2014; Suffragette, 2015; Darkest Hour, 2018; On Chesil Beach, 2018; *radio* includes: more than 50 plays; regular reader for Words and Music. 100 audiobooks. Reciter and reader for concerts with orchs incl. LSO, BBC SO and CBSO. Member: Council, Equity, 1996–2000, 2008–14; Bd, Nat. Campaign for the Arts, 2006– (Chair, 2012–); Bd, Belarus Free Th., 2013–. *Recreations:* birding, travelling, poker, growing chillies, supporting AFC Wimbledon. *Address:* c/o United Agents, 12–26 Lexington Street, W1F 0LE. *T:* (020) 3214 0800. *Clubs:* Century, Groucho.

**WEST, Shani;** *see* Rhys-James, S.

**WEST, Prof. Shearer Carroll,** PhD; FRHistS; Vice-Chancellor, University of Nottingham, since 2017; *b* Rocky Mount, Va, 18 Jan. 1960; *d* of Edgar Allen West and Natalie Carroll West; *m* 1992, Nicholas Sinclair Davidson; one *d*. *Educ:* Coll. of William and Mary, Va (BA Art Hist. (major), English (minor) 1981); St Andrews Univ. (PhD Art Hist. 1986). FRHistS 1995. Sub-editor, Macmillan's Dictionary of Art, 1986–87; Lectr, 1987–96, Sen. Lectr, 1996, in Hist. of Art, Univ. of Leicester; University of Birmingham: Sen. Lectr and Hd, Dept of Fine Art, 1996–2000; Prof. of Art Hist., 2000–11; Hd, Sch. of Historical Studies, 2004–07; Actg Hd, Coll. of Arts and Law, 2008; Dir, Res., AHRC, 2008–11; Hd of Humanities Div., Univ. of Oxford, 2011–15; Fellow of Magdalen Coll., Oxford, 2011–15; Dep. Vice-Chancellor and Provost, Univ. of Sheffield, 2015–17. Trustee, NPG, 2018–. FHEA 2000; FRSA 2002. Hon. Fellow, Mansfield Coll., Oxford, 2010. *Publications:* Chagall, 1990 (trans. French 1991); The Image of the Actor: verbal and visual representation in the age of Garrick and Kemble, 1991; Fin de Siècle: art and society in the age of uncertainty, 1993; (ed with Marsha Meskimmon) Visions of the 'neue Frau': women and the visual arts in Weimar Germany, 1995; (ed) The Bloomsbury Guide to Art, 1996; (ed) The Victorians and Race, 1996; (ed) Italian Culture in Northern Europe in the Eighteenth Century, 1999; The Visual Arts in Germany, 1890–1937: utopia and despair, 2000; Portraiture, 2004; articles in learned jls incl. Art History, Eighteenth-Century Studies, Eighteenth-Century Life, Brit. Jl for Eighteenth-century Studies, Victorian Studies, Nineteenth-Century Theatre, Theatre Notebook, Jl of Victorian Culture. *Recreations:* running, swimming, classical music, theatre, opera, ballet. *Address:* University of Nottingham, University Park, Nottingham NG7 2RD. *Club:* Priory (Edgbaston, Birmingham).

**WEST, Dr Stephanie Roberta,** FBA 1990; Senior Research Fellow in Classics and Fellow Librarian, Hertford College, Oxford, 1990–2005, now Honorary Fellow; *b* 1 Dec. 1937; *d* of Robert Enoch Pickard and Ruth (*née* Batters); *m* 1960, Martin Litchfield West, OM, FBA (*d* 2015); one *s* one *d*. *Educ:* Nottingham High Sch. for Girls; Somerville Coll., Oxford (1st cl. Classics Mods 1958, 1st cl. Lit. Hum. 1960; Gaisford Prize for Greek Verse Composition 1959; Ireland Scholar 1959, Derby Scholar 1960); MA 1963, DPhil 1964, Oxon. Oxford University: Mary Ewart Res. Fellow, Somerville Coll., 1965–67; Lecturer: in Classics, Hertford Coll., 1966–90; in Greek, Keble Coll., 1981–2005. Foreign Mem., Polish Acad. of Arts and Scis, 2012. Mem. Council, GPDST, 1974–87. *Publications:* The Ptolemaic Papyri of Homer, 1967; Omero, Odissea 1 (libri I–IV), 1981; (with A. Heubeck and J. B. Hainsworth) A commentary on Homer's Odyssey v, 1988; Demythologisation in Herodotus, 2002; articles and reviews in learned jls. *Recreations:* opera, curious information. *Address:* 42 Portland Road, Oxford OX2 7EY. *T:* (01865) 556060.

**WEST, Dr Stephen Craig,** FMedSci; FRS 1995; Senior Group Leader, Francis Crick Institute, since 2015; *b* 11 April 1952; *s* of Joseph and Louise West; *m* 1985, Phyllis Fraenza. *Educ:* Univ. of Newcastle upon Tyne (BSc 1974; PhD 1977). Post-doctoral Research Associate: Univ. of Newcastle upon Tyne, 1977–78; Dept of Molecular Biophysics and Biochemistry, and Therapeutic Radiology, Yale Univ., 1978–83 (Res. Scientist, Dept of Therapeutic Radiology, 1983–85); Sen. Scientist, 1985–89, Principal Scientist, 1989–2015, ICRF, then Cancer Res. UK. Hon. Fellow, UCL, 1997–. Mem., EMBO, 1994; FMedSci 2000; Foreign Associate, NAS, 2016. Swiss Bridge Prize for Cancer Research, 2001, 2009; Louis-Jeantet Prize for Medicine, 2007; Novartis Lect. and Prize, Biochem. Soc., 2008; GlaxoSmithKline Prize, Royal Soc., 2010; Medal, Genetics Soc., 2012; Lifetime Achievement Award, Cancer Res. UK, 2018. *Publications:* over 250 res. articles in biochem. and molecular biol. *Recreations:* squash, ski-ing, music. *Address:* Francis Crick Institute, 1 Midland Road, NW1 1AT.

**WEST, Prof. Steven George,** CBE 2017; FChS, FCPodMed, FRSocMed; DL; Professor, since 1995, and Vice-Chancellor, President and Chief Executive Officer, since 2008, University of the West of England, Bristol; *b* Luton, 27 March 1961; *s* of Paul West and Jean West; *m* 1999, Samantha Watson; two *s* three *d*. *Educ:* Denbigh High Sch., Luton; Luton Sixth Form Coll.; Chelsea Sch. of Chiropody, Paddington Tech. Coll. (Grad. Dip. Chiropody 1982), Poly. of Central London (BSc 1st Cl. Hons Podiatry 1986); King's Coll. London. FChS 1990; MPodA 1992; FCPodMed 2009; MIPEM 1986. Sen. Chiropodist, Chiropody and Res. Unit, City and Hackney HA, 1982–84; Chelsea School of Chiropody, Paddington Technical College, later Paddington College: vis. clinical teacher, 1982–83; Lectr, 1984–87; Sen. Lectr, 1987–90; University of Huddersfield: Head of Podiatry and Associate Dean, 1990–95; Dean, Sch. of Human and Health Scis, 1992–95; University of the West of England, Bristol: Dean of Faculty, 1995–2005; Dean and Asst Vice-Chancellor, 1998–2001; Pro Vice-Chancellor (Resources and Planning), 2005–06; Dep. Vice-Chancellor, 2006–07. Non-exec. Dir, Office for Students, 2018–. Mem., Educn Honours and Diversity and Inclusion Honours Cttee, 2017–. Chairman: Univs South West, 2010–12; Univ. Alliance Mission Gp, 2012–16; West of England Academic Health Sci. Network, 2013–; SW Region CBI, 2014–16; Member, Board: Higher Educn Leadership Foundn, 2010–; UUK, 2011– (Chm., Health and Res. Cttee, 2011–; Chair, Mental Health in Higher Educn Working Gp, 2017–); Health Educn England SW, 2012–. Dir, Bristol UWE Healthcare Training Ltd, 2002–. Non-executive Director: Avon, Gloucester and Wilts Strategic HA, 2003–06; South West Strategic HA, 2006– (Vice-Chair, 2009–); South Strategic HA, 2011– (Chm., Patient and Care Standards Cttee, 2011–); Univ. Hosps Bristol NHS Foundn Trust, 2017–; Chm., NHS Regl Trng Bd, 2009–; Chair, W of England LEP, 2017–. Trustee, Bristol Urological Inst., 2007–; Regl Trustee, Prince's Trust, 2008–. Pres., Business West and Bristol Chamber of Commerce and Initiative, 2013–. Mem., Biol Engrg Soc., 1989. Fellow, Leadership Foundn, 2005. FRSocMed 2006. FRSA 2012. Mem., Soc. of Merchant Venturers,

Bristol, 2014–. DL Glos 2012. Hon. DLaws Bristol, 2014; Hon. DEd Taylor's, Malaysia, 2016. *Publications*: articles in podiatric and learned jls. *Recreations*: scuba diving, driving nice cars, swimming. *Address*: Vice-Chancellor's Office, University of the West of England, Bristol BS16 1QY. *T*: (0117) 328 2201. *E*: vicechancellor@uwe.ac.uk.

**WEST, Susan Fiona Dorinthea**; *see* Michie, S. F. D.

**WEST, Timothy Lancaster**, CBE 1984; actor and director; *b* 20 Oct. 1934; *s* of late Harry Lockwood West and Olive Carleton-Crowe; *m* 1st, 1956, Jacqueline Boyer (marr. diss.); one *d*; 2nd, 1963, Prunella Scales, *qv*; two *s*. *Educ*: John Lyon Sch., Harrow; Regent Street Polytechnic. Entered profession as asst stage manager, Wimbledon, 1956; first London appearance, Caught Napping, Piccadilly, 1959; Mem., RSC, 1964–66; Prospect Theatre Co., 1966–72: Dr Samuel Johnson, Prospero, Bolingbroke, young Mortimer in Edward II, King Lear, Emerson in A Room with a View, Alderman Smuggler in The Constant Couple, and Holofernes in Love's Labour's Lost; Otto in The Italian Girl, 1968; Gilles in Abelard and Heloise, 1970; Robert Hand in Exiles, 1970; Gilbert in The Critic as Artist, 1971; Sir William Gower in Trelawny (musical), Bristol, 1972; Falstaff in Henry IV Pts I and II, Bristol, 1973; Shpigelsky in A Month in the Country, Chichester, 1974 (London, 1975); Brack in Hedda Gabler, RSC, 1975; Iago in Othello, Nottingham, 1976; with Prospect Co.: Harry in Staircase, 1976, Claudius in Hamlet, storyteller in War Music, and Enobarbus in Antony and Cleopatra, 1977; Ivan and Gottlieb in Laughter, and Max in The Homecoming, 1978; with Old Vic Co.: Narrator in Lancelot and Guinevere, Shylock in The Merchant of Venice, 1980; Beecham, Apollo, 1980, NZ, 1983, Dublin, 1986; Uncle Vanya, Australia, 1982; Stalin in Master Class, Leicester, 1983, Old Vic, 1984; Charlie Mucklebrass in Big in Brazil, 1984; The War at Home, Hampstead, 1984; When We Are Married, Whitehall, 1986; The Sneeze, Aldwych, 1988; Bristol Old Vic: The Master Builder, 1989; The Clandestine Marriage, Uncle Vanya, 1990; James Tyrone in Long Day's Journey into Night, 1991, also at NT; Andrew in It's Ralph, Comedy, 1991; King Lear, Dublin, 1992; Willie Loman in Death of a Salesman, Theatr Clwyd, 1993; Christopher Cameron in Himself, Southampton, 1993; Sir Anthony Absolute in The Rivals, Chichester, 1994; Macbeth, Theatr Clwyd, 1994; Mail Order Bride, 1994, Getting On, 1995, W Yorks Playhouse; Twelve Angry Men, Comedy, 1996; Falstaff, in Henry IV Pts 1 and 2, Old Vic, 1997; Gloucester, in King Lear, RNT, 1997; The Birthday Party, Piccadilly, 1999; The Master Builder, tour, 1999; The External, tour, 2001; Luther, RNT, 2001; Lear in King Lear, tour, 2002, Old Vic, 2003; National Hero, Edinburgh and tour, 2005; The Life of Galileo, Birmingham Rep, 2005; The Old Country, Trafalgar Studio, 2006; Menenius in Coriolanus, RSC, 2007; The Collection, Comedy, 2008; The Winslow Boy, tour, 2009; Quartet, tour, 2010; A Number, Menier Chocolate Factory, 2010; Uncle Vanya, Chichester Festival Th., 2012; The Handyman, tour, 2012; The Vote, Donmar, 2015; King Lear, Bristol Old Vic, 2016; Narrator in The Fairy Queen, Barbican, 2016. *Directed*: plays for Prospect Co., Open Space, Gardner Centre, Brighton, and rep. at Salisbury, Bristol, Northampton and Cheltenham; HMS Pinafore, Carl Rosa Co., 2003; own season, The Forum, Billingham, 1973; Artistic Dir, Old Vic Co., 1980–81. *Television includes*: Edward VII, 1973; Hard Times, 1977; Crime and Punishment, 1979; Brass, 1982–84, 1990; The Last Bastion, 1984; The Nightingale Saga, Tender is the Night, 1985; The Monocled Mutineer, 1986; The Train, 1987; A Shadow on the Sun, 1988; The Gospels, Framed, 1992; Bramwell, 1998; Midsomer Murders, 1999; Murder in Mind, 2000; Bedtime, 2001, 2002, 2003; Going Postal, 2010; Coronation Street, 2013; Last Tango in Halifax, 2013; Great Canal Journeys, 2014–18; Eastenders, 2014–15; The Vote, 2015; Gentleman Jack, 2019; *plays*: Richard II, 1969; Edward II, The Boswell and Johnson Show, 1970; Horatio Bottomley, 1972; Churchill and the Generals, 1979 (RTS Award); The Good Doctor Bodkin Adams, 1986; What the Butler Saw, Harry's Kingdom, When We Are Married, Breakthrough at Reykjavik, 1987; Strife, The Contractor, 1988; Blore, MP, Beecham, 1989; Survival of the Fittest, 1990; Bye Bye Columbus, 1991; Reith to the Nation, Smokescreen, 1993; Hiroshima, Eleven Men Against Eleven, Cuts, 1995; The Place of the Dead, 1996; King Lear, 1997; Bleak House, 2005; A Room with a View, 2007; Exile, 2010. *Films*: The Looking-Glass War, 1968; Nicholas and Alexandra, 1970; The Day of the Jackal, 1972; Hedda, 1975; Joseph Andrews, and The Devil's Advocate, 1976; William Morris, 1977; Agatha, and The 39 Steps, 1978; The Antagonists, 1980; Murder is Easy, and Oliver Twist, 1981; Cry Freedom, 1986; Consuming Passions, 1987; Ever After, 1997; Joan of Arc, 1998; Iris, 2001; Beyond Borders, 2002; Villa des Roses, 2002; The Endgame, 2008. Compiles and dir. recital progs; sound broadcaster. Dir, All Change Arts Ltd, 1986–2006; Dir and Trustee, Nat. Student Drama Fest., 1990–2007; Pres., LAMDA, 2003–18 (Gov., 1992–). Pres., Soc. for Theatre Res., 1999–. FRSA 1992. DUniv Bradford, 1993; Hon. DLitt: West of England, 1994; East Anglia, 1996; Westminster, 1999; London, 2004; Hull, 2004; Hon. Dr Drama, RSAMD, 2004; Hon. DArts Kent, 2018. *Publications*: I'm Here, I Think, Where are You? (collected letters), 1994; A Moment Towards the End of the Play, 2001; (with Prunella Scales) So You Want to be an Actor?, 2005; Our Great Canal Journeys, 2018. *Recreations*: theatre history, travel, music, old railways, inland waterways. *Address*: c/o Gavin Barker Associates Ltd, 2D Wimpole Street, W1G 0EB. *Clubs*: Garrick, Groucho.
*See also* S. A. J. West.

**WEST CUMBERLAND, Archdeacon of**; *see* Pratt, Ven. Dr R. D.

**WEST HAM, Archdeacon of**; *see* Cockett, Ven. E. W.

**WEST-KNIGHTS, Laurence James**; QC 2000; *His Honour Judge West-Knights*; a Circuit Judge, since 2017; *b* 30 July 1954; *o s* of late Major Jan James West-Knights and Amy Winifred West-Knights (*née* Gott); *m* 1st, 1979 (marr. diss. 1983); 2nd, 1992 (marr. diss. 2013); one *s* two *d*. *Educ*: Perse Sch., Cambridge; Hampton Sch.; Emmanuel Coll., Cambridge (MA 1976). FCIArb 1993. RNR, 1979–94 (Lt Comdr 1993, retd). Called to the Bar, Gray's Inn, 1977, Bencher, 2004; W Circuit; in practice at the Bar, 1977–2017; Asst Recorder, 1995–99; Recorder, 1999–2017; IT Liaison and Chaplaincy Liaison Judge, Snaresbrook Crown Court, 2017–. Chm., Steering Cttee, IT Industry Enquiry into Govt IT Contracts, 2000; Member: Incorporated Council of Law Reporting, 1997–2005; IT and the Courts, 1998–2006 (Mem., Civil Litigation Wkg Party, 1997–2005); Founding Trustee and Exec. Dir, British and Irish Legal Information Inst., 2000–. Jt Chm., Soc. for Computers and Law, 2001–02 (Mem. Council, 1995–2001; Vice-Chm., 1996–2001); Vice Chm., of London Common Law and Commercial Bar Assoc., 2015–17. Lay Chm., PCC, Christ Church, Turnham Green, 1999–2001. Mem. Editl Bd, Jl of Judicial Studies Bd, 1997–2003. Writer, www.LawOnLine.cc, legal web site, 1997–2015. Winner, Kennett Shoot Trophy, 2003. *Publications*: (contrib.) Jordan's Civil Court Service, 1999–2017; numerous papers and articles on free access to the law via the Internet. *Recreations*: motorcycling, sailing, scuba diving, point-to-points, watching and listening to cricket, shooting, New Zealand, his children. *Address*: Snaresbrook Crown Court, 75 Hollybush Hill, Snaresbrook, E11 1QW. *T*: (020) 8530 0000. *Clubs*: Garrick, MCC; Pegasus (Pres., 2019–); Royal Naval Volunteer Reserve Yacht; Bar Yacht; Cambridge University Motorcycle.

**WESTABY, Prof. Stephen**, FRCS; Senior Cardiac Surgeon, John Radcliffe Hospital, 1986; Professor of Biomedical Sciences, Swansea University (formerly University of Wales, Swansea), since 2006; *b* 27 July 1948; *s* of Kenneth and Doreen Westaby; *m*; one *s* one *d*. *Educ*: Charing Cross Hosp. Med. Sch., Univ. of London (BSc Biochemistry 1969; MB BS 1972; MS 1986); PhD (Bioeng). FRCS 1986; FESC, FETCS, FICA. Surgical training: Addenbrooke's Hosp., Hammersmith Hosp., RPMS, Hosp. for Sick Children, Great Ormond Street, Harefield Hosp., Middlesex Hosp., Univ. of Alabama. Dist. Ralph Cicerone Prof., Univ. of California, 2006; adult and paediatric surgeon; specialist surgeon in congenital heart disease, thoracic aortic surgery, valvular and coronary heart disease; designated a pioneer in artificial heart technology by Jl of Amer. Heart Assoc.; developed first artificial heart res. prog., UK; established Oxford Heart Centre, John Radcliffe Hosp., internat. teaching centre for valve and aortic surgery; has performed over 11,000 open heart ops on adults and children. Member: Soc. for Thoracic Surgery, USA, 1995; Amer. Assoc. for Thoracic Surgery, 1998; European Assoc. for Cardiothoracic Surgery, 1998. Editor, Jl of Heart Failure Clinics of N Amer., surgical edn. *Publications*: editor/joint author: Wound Care, 1986; Stentless Bioprosthesis, 1995, 2nd edn 1999; Landmarks in Cardiac Surgery, 1997; Surgery of Acquired Aortic Valve Disease, 1997; Principles and Practice of Critical Care, 1997; Trauma Pathogenesis and Treatment, 1998; Ischemic Heart Disease: surgical management, 1998; Cardiothoracic Trauma, 1999; Fragile Lives, 2017; The Knife's Edge: the heart and mind of a cardiac surgeon, 2019; more than 50 chapters in books, and over 260 scientific papers. *Recreations*: writing, shooting.

**WESTAD, Prof. Odd Arne**, PhD; FBA 2011; Professor of History and Global Affairs, Yale University, since 2019; *b* Alesund, Norway, 5 Jan. 1960; *s* of Arne and Oddbjorg Westad; *m* 1985, Dr Ingunn Bjornson; one *s* one *d*. *Educ*: Univ. of Oslo (BA Hist., Phil. and Mod. Langs); Univ. of North Carolina (PhD Hist. 1990). Dir, Res., Nobel Inst., 1990–98; Prof. of Internat. History, 1998–2015, Hd, Internat. History Dept, 2004–07, Co-Dir, LSE IDEAS, 2008–15, LSE; S. T. Lee Prof. in US-Asia Relns, Kennedy Sch. of Govt, Harvard Univ., 2015–19. Visiting Professor: Hong Kong Univ., 1994; Univ. of Cambridge, 1998; New York Univ., 2002; Ca' Foscari Univ., Venice, 2012. *Publications*: Cold War and Revolution, 1993; (jtly) Beyond the Cold War: future dimensions in international relations, 1993; (jtly) The Soviet Union in Eastern Europe, 1994; The Fall of Détente, 1997; Brothers in Arms, 1998; Reviewing the Cold War: approaches, interpretations, theory, 2000; Decisive Encounters: the Chinese Civil War, 2003; (jtly) The Cold War: a history in documents and eyewitness accounts, 2003; The Global Cold War, 2005; (ed with M. Leffler) The Cambridge History of the Cold War, 3 vols, 2010; Restless Empire: China and the world since 1750, 2012; The Cold War: a world history, 2017. *Recreations*: hill walking, travel. *Address*: Jackson Institute for Global Affairs, Yale University, PO Box 208359, New Haven, CT 06520–8359, USA. *E*: oaw@oaw.cn.

**WESTBROOK, Rear Adm. Jonathan Simon**, CBE 2013 (MBE 1990); Director, Jon Westbrook Ltd, since 2013; Member, Armed Forces Pay Review Body, since 2014; *b* Chatham, Kent, 29 Aug. 1958; *s* of Derrick and Pam Westbrook; *m* 1980, Alison, (Jill), Finney; one *s* two *d*. *Educ*: Chester City Grammar Sch.; BRNC Dartmouth; NATO Defence Coll. Joined RN, as jun. seaman, 1975; HMS Bristol, 1978–79; HMS Soberton, 1981–82; HMS Sheffield, 1982; HMS Otter, 1983–85; HMS Superb, 1985–87; HMS Sovereign, 1987–88; HMS Torbay, 1988–90; Submarine Comd Course, 1990; XO, HMS Trenchant, 1991–93; Exchange USA, 1993–95; CO, HMS Talent, 1995–97; Comdr, UK Task Gp, 1997–98; MoD, 1998–2001; HMS Raleigh, 2001–02; Capt., FOST, 2002–04; MoD, 2004–07; Cdre, PJHQ, 2007–09; Comdr, Devonport Flotilla and Faslane Flotilla, 2009–11; Dep. Rear Adm., Submarines, 2010–11; COS Allied Maritime Comd, 2011–13. Sen. Bd Advr, Torchlight Solutions, 2013–; Bd Advr, Autonomous Surface Vehicles Ltd, 2013–. Dir, Parnall Foundn, 2018–. Member: British Assoc. for Shooting and Conservation, 1996–; Royal Naval Assoc., 2013–; President: Liskeard RBL, 2013–17; Naval Club, 2017–; Chm., Friends of Royal Navy Submarine Mus., 2014–. Associate FNI 2014. CCMI 2011. *Recreations*: shooting, fishing, the countryside, Blues music. *Address*: Caradon Town, Liskeard, Cornwall.

**WESTBROOK, Michael John David**, OBE 1988; composer, pianist and band-leader; *b* 21 March 1936; *s* of Philip Beckford Westbrook and Vera Agnes (*née* Butler); *m* 1976, Katherine Jane (*née* Duckham), singer, songwriter and painter; one *s* one *d* of previous marriage. *Educ*: Kelly Coll., Tavistock; Plymouth Coll. of Art (NDD); Hornsey Coll. of Art (ATD). Formed first band at Plymouth Art Sch., 1958; moved to London, 1962, and has since led a succession of groups incl. The Mike Westbrook Brass Band, formed with Phil Minton in 1973, The Mike Westbrook Orch., 1974–, Westbrook Trio (with Kate Westbrook and Chris Biscoe), formed in 1982, Kate Westbrook Mike Westbrook Duo, 1995–, Westbrook & Company, 1998–, The New Westbrook Orchestra, 2001–, The Village Band, 2004–, and The Uncommon Orchestra, 2015–. Has toured extensively in Britain and Europe, and performed in Australia, Canada, NY, Singapore and Hong Kong. Has written commissioned works for fests in Britain, France and other European countries, composed music for theatre, radio, TV and films, and made numerous LPs. Principal compositions/recordings include: Marching Song, 1967; Metropolis, 1969; Tyger: a celebration of William Blake (with Adrian Mitchell), 1971, also The Westbrook Blake, 1980 and Glad Day, 1999; Citadel/Room 315, 1974; On Duke's Birthday (dedicated to the memory of Duke Ellington), 1984; Off Abbey Road, 1988; Bean Rows and Blues Shots (saxophone concerto), 1991; Coming Through Slaughter (opera), 1994; Bar Utopia (lyrics by Helen Simpson), 1995; Blues for Terenzi, 1995; Cable Street Blues, 1997; The Orchestra of Smith's Academy, 1998; Classical Blues, 2001; Glad Day Live, 2014; Paris (solo piano), 2016; In Memory of Lou Gare, 2018; The Last Night at the Old Place (recorded 1968), 2018; Starcross Bridge (solo piano), 2018; Catania (recorded 1992), 2018; TV scores incl. Caught on a Train, 1983; film scores: Moulin Rouge, 1990; Camera Makes Whoopee, 1996; with Kate Westbrook: concert works incorporating European poetry and folk song, notably The Cortège, for voices and jazz orch., 1979, London Bridge is Broken Down, for voice, jazz orch. and chamber orch., 1987, and Chanson Irresponsable, 2001; Turner in Uri, 2003; also a succession of music-theatre pieces and recordings, with Kate Westbrook, including: Mama Chicago, 1978; Westbrook-Rossini, 1984; The Ass (based on poem by D. H. Lawrence), 1985; Pier Rides, 1986; Quichotte (opera), 1989; Goodbye Peter Lorre, 1991; Measure for Measure, 1992; Good Friday 1663 (TV opera; libretto by Helen Simpson), 1994; Stage Set, 1996; Love Or Infatuation, 1997; Platterback, 1998; Jago (opera), 2000; L'Ascenseur/The Lift, 2002; Art Wolf, 2003; The Nijinska Chamber, 2005; Waxeywork Show, 2006; Cape Gloss (opera), 2007; English Soup or the Battle of the Classic Trifle, 2008; Fine 'n Yellow, 2009; allsorts, 2009; The Serpent Hit, 2010; Three into Wonderfull, 2012; Five Voyages, 2012; Rossini Re-Loaded, 2013; A Bigger Show, 2013; Paintbox Jane: Raoul Dufy paints a portrait, 2016; Granite (soliloquy with text by Kate Westbrook), 2018. Hon. DMus Plymouth, 2004. *Recreations*: writing, drawing, walking on Dartmoor. *Address*: PO Box 92, Dawlish, Devon EX7 9WN. *E*: admin@westbrookjazz.co.uk. *Clubs*: Chelsea Arts, Vout-o-Reenees.

**WESTBROOK, Roger**, CMG 1990; HM Diplomatic Service, retired; Ambassador to Portugal, 1995–99; *b* 26 May 1941; *e s* of Edward George Westbrook and Beatrice Minnie Westbrook (*née* Marshall). *Educ*: Dulwich Coll.; Hertford Coll., Oxford (MA Modern History). Foreign Office, 1964; Asst Private Sec. to Chancellor of Duchy of Lancaster and Minister of State, FO, 1965; Yaoundé, 1967; Rio de Janeiro, 1971; Brasilia, 1972; Private Sec. to Minister of State, FCO, 1975; Head of Chancery, Lisbon, 1977; Dep. Head, News

Dept, FCO, 1980; Dep. Head, Falkland Is Dept, FCO, 1982; Overseas Inspectorate, FCO, 1984; High Comr, Negara Brunei Darussalam, 1986–91; Ambassador to Zaire, 1991–92; High Comr, Tanzania, 1992–95. UK Comr, EXPO 98, Lisbon. Chm., Spencer House, 2000–06. Chairman: Anglo-Portuguese Soc., 2000–04; FCO Assoc., 2003–09. Mem. Council, Book Aid Internat., 2002–. Pres., Hertford Soc., 2009–15. Chief Hon. Steward, Westminster Abbey, 2006–14. Archbp of Canterbury's Trustee, Bd of Dulwich Estate, 2015–. Freeman, City of London, 2002; Liveryman, Tylers' and Bricklayers' Co., 2002– (Master, 2014–15). *Recreations:* doodling, sightseeing, theatre, reading, dining. *Address:* 33 Marsham Court, Marsham Street, SW1P 4JY. *Club:* Travellers.

**WESTBURY**, 6th Baron *cr* 1861, of Westbury, co. Wilts; **Richard Nicholas Bethell**, MBE 1979; *b* 29 May 1950; *e s* of 5th Baron Westbury, CBE, MC and of Ursula Mary Rose (*née* James); *S* father, 2001; *m* 1st, 1975, Caroline Mary Palmer (marr. diss. 1991); one *s* two *d*; 2nd, 1993, Charlotte Sara Jane (marr. diss. 2004), *d* of John Temple Gore; 3rd, 2009, Hilary Luise Kindersley. *Educ:* Harrow; RMA Sandhurst. Major, Scots Guards, retd. *Heir: s* Hon. (Richard) Alexander (David) Bethell, *b* 21 Dec. 1986.

**WESTCOTT, David Guy;** QC 2003; *s* of Walter Dennis Westcott and Eileen Patricia Westcott; *m* Sara Paterson-Brown; one *s* one *d*. *Educ:* Cranleigh Sch.; Brasenose Coll., Oxford (BA Juris; BCL). Called to the Bar, Middle Temple, 1982, Bencher, 2014. Jt Hd, Outer Temple Chambers, 2012. Captain, GB Men's Hockey team (winners of Bronze Medal), LA Olympics, 1984. Mem., 1988–2009, Vice-Chm., 2006–09, Governing Body, Cranleigh Sch. *Recreations:* outdoor sports, theatre.

**WESTCOTT, Dr Nicholas James,** CMG 1999; HM Diplomatic Service, retired; Director, Royal African Society, since 2017; *b* 20 July 1956; *s* of Prof. John Hugh Westcott, FRS and Helen Fay Westcott (*née* Morgan); *m* 1989, Miriam Pearson; one *s* one *d*. *Educ:* Epsom Coll.; Sidney Sussex Coll., Cambridge (MA; PhD History 1982). Entered Foreign and Commonwealth Office, 1982; on secondment to EC, 1984–85; UK Perm. Rep. to EC, Brussels, 1985–89; FCO, 1989–93; Head of Common Foreign and Security Policy Unit, 1992–93; Dep. High Comr, Dar es Salaam, 1993–96; Head of Economic Relations Dept, FCO, 1996–98; Minister-Counsellor (Trade and Transport), Washington, 1999–2002; Head of IT Strategy, subseq. Chief Information Officer, FCO, 2002–07; High Comr to Ghana, and (non-resident) Ambassador to Côte d'Ivoire, Togo, Niger and Burkina Faso, 2008–11; Man. Dir for Africa, 2011–15, Man. Dir for Middle E and N Africa, 2015–17, Eur. Ext. Action Service (on loan). *Publications:* (contrib.) Africa and the Second World War, 1986; (with P. Kingston and R. G. Tiedemann) Managed Economies in World War II, 1991; articles in jls. *Recreations:* swimming, writing, music, travelling. *Address:* Royal African Society, 21 Russell Square, WC1B 5EA.

**WESTENRA,** family name of **Baron Rossmore**.

**WESTERMAN, Gillian Barbara, (Jill), (Mrs Martin Rapier),** CBE 2010; Principal and Chief Executive, Northern College for Residential Adult Education, 2007–18; *b* Wakefield, W Yorks, 30 Nov. 1955; *d* of Albert and Sheila Westerman; *m* 1999, Martin Rapier; two *d*. *Educ:* Wakefield Girls' High Sch.; Durham Univ. (BA English Lit. 1978); Birkbeck Coll., London Univ. (MA English Lit. 1984); Garnett Coll. (Cert Ed 1985). Tutor, W Midlands Travellers' Sch., 1975; TEFL tutor, Internat. Hse, Spain, 1978–79; refuge worker, Hackney Women's Aid, 1979–82; community worker, Springfield Project, 1982–84; Tutor: Bede Educn Centre, 1984–87; Camden Adult Educn Inst., 1987–91; Sen. Lectr, Kingsway Coll., 1992–93; Tutor, Rotherham Coll. of Art and Technol., 1993–94; Northern College for Residential Adult Education: Tutor, 1994–2000; Sen. Tutor, 2000–02; Prog. Dir, 2002–07. *Publications:* contrib. res. articles on leadership in adult and further educn. *Recreations:* finding the fun in things, reading, family, hill walking, cycling, dancing. *E:* jillwesterman1@gmail.com.

**WESTERN, Matthew Raymond;** MP (Lab) Warwick and Leamington, since 2017. *Educ:* Univ. of Bristol (BSc Geog. 1984). Peugeot Motor Co.: Fleet Sales Manager, 1992–95; Advertising and Media Manager, 1997–2002; Automobiles Peugeot: Manager, Internat. Communications Strategy, 2002–03; Regl Manager, 2003–04; Purchasing Manager, Peugeot Motor Co., 2004–08; owner, Oxygency, 2008–. Mem. (Lab), Warwickshire CC, 2013–. Mem., Internat. Trade Cttee, H of C, 2017–. *Address:* House of Commons, SW1A 0AA.

**WESTERN AUSTRALIA, Metropolitan of;** *see* Perth (Australia), Archbishop of.

**WESTGARTH, Peter Allen;** Chief Executive, Duke of Edinburgh's Award, 2005–19; *b* 17 May 1953; *s* of Allen and Elizabeth Westgarth; *m* 2007, Rachael Molsom; one *s* one *d* (twins); three *d* from previous marriage. *Educ:* City of Birmingham Sch. of Educn (Cert Ed). Secondary sch. teacher, Walbottle High Sch., 1974–75; advertising sales exec., Newcastle Chronicle, 1976; Exec. Manager, Help the Aged, 1976–80; Fundraising Manager, MIND, 1980–83; PR Officer, NE Co-op., 1983–86; UK Dir, Livewire, 1986–90; Chief Exec., Young Enterprise UK, 1990–2005. Hon. Pres., Young Enterprise Europe, 1991–98. Bata Lifetime Achievement Award for Young Enterprise Achievement, 2004; Queen's Award for Enterprise Promotion, 2006. *Recreations:* playing guitar, hill-walking, travel, BBQ, red wine, reading, and work.

**WESTHAVER, Rev. Dr George Derrick;** Principal, Pusey House, Oxford, since 2013; Fellow, St Cross College, Oxford, since 2013; *b* Halifax, NS, 5 May 1968; *s* of Reid Westhaver and Judy Gates; *m* 1994, Karen Conrod; two *d*. *Educ:* McGill Univ., Montreal; St Mary's Univ., Halifax, NS (BA 2002); Wycliffe Coll., Univ. of Toronto (MDiv 2008); Univ. of Durham (PhD 2013); MA Oxon 2013. Ordained deacon, 1997, priest, 1998; Asst Curate, St Andrew, Cherry Hinton and All Saints, Teversham, 1997–2000; Team Vicar, The Ramseys and Upwood Team Ministry, Dio. of Ely, 2000–03; Asst Minister, St Michael at the North Gate, Oxford, 2003–06; Chaplain, Lincoln Coll., Oxford, 2003–06; Rector, Parish of St George, Halifax, NS, 2007–13. *Recreations:* sport, travel, reading, walking, exploring the artistic expression of Christian doctrine in art and music, church crawling. *Address:* Pusey House, St Giles, Oxford OX1 3LZ. *E:* gwesthaver@gmail.com.

**WESTHEIMER, Prof. Gerald,** AM 2009; FRS 1985; Professor of Neurobiology, University of California, Berkeley, since 1989 (Professor of Physiology, 1967–89; Head of Division of Neurobiology, 1989–92); *b* Berlin, 13 May 1924; *s* of late Isaac Westheimer and Ilse Westheimer (*née* Cohn); Australian citizen, 1945. *Educ:* Sydney Tech. Coll. (Optometry dip. 1943, Fellowship dip. 1949); Univ. of Sydney (BSc 1947); Ohio State Univ. (PhD 1953); postdoctoral training at Marine Biol. Lab., Woods Hole, 1957 and at Physiolog. Lab., Cambridge, 1958–59. Practising optometrist, Sydney, 1945–51; faculties of Optometry Schools: Univ. of Houston, 1953–54; Ohio State Univ., 1954–60; Univ. of California, Berkeley, 1960–67. Associate: Bosch Vision Res. Center, Salk Inst., 1984–92; Neurosciences Res. Program, NY, 1985–95; Chairman: Visual Scis Study Sect., NIH, 1977–79; Bd of Scientific Counsellors, Nat. Eye Inst., 1981–83; Bd of Editors, Vision Research, 1986–91; service on numerous professional cttees. Guest Investigator, Lab. of Neurobiol. (formerly Adjunct Prof.), Rockefeller Univ., NY, 1994–. Fellow or Member, scientific socs, UK and overseas; Fellow, Amer. Acad. of Arts and Scis. Lectures: Sackler, in Med. Sci., Tel Aviv Univ., 1989; Perception, Eur. Conf. on Visual Perception, 1989; D. O. Hebb, McGill Univ., Canada, 1991; Ferrier, Royal Soc., 1992; Wertheimer, Frankfurt Univ., 1998. Hon. Prof., Univ. of Electronic Sci. and Technol., Chengdu, China, 2009–. Hon. DSc: New South Wales, 1988; SUNY, 1990; Hon. MD Tübingen, 2005. Tillyer Medal, Optical Soc. of America, 1978; Proctor Medal, Assoc. for Res. in Vision and Ophthalmology, 1979; von Sallmann Prize, Coll. of Physicians and Surgeons, Columbia Univ., 1986; Prentice Medal, Amer. Acad. of Optometry, 1986; Bicentennial Medal, Aust. Optometric Assoc., 1988; Collin Res. Medal, Optometrists Assoc. of Australia, 2009; Fry Medal in Physiol Optics, Ohio State Univ., 2014. *Publications:* research articles in sci. and professional optometric and ophth. jls; editl work for sci. jls. *Recreations:* chamber music (violin), foundation and history of sensory physiology. *Address:* 582 Santa Barbara Road, Berkeley, CA 94707, USA. *E:* gwestheimer@berkeley.edu. *Club:* Cosmos (Washington).

**WESTLEY, Stuart Alker,** MA; General Secretary, Association of Governing Bodies of Independent Schools, 2009–16; *b* 21 March 1947; *s* of Arthur Bancroft Westley and Gladys Westley; *m* 1979, Mary Louise Weston; one *d*. *Educ:* Lancaster Royal GS; Corpus Christi Coll., Oxford (BA 1969; MA 1972). Professional cricketer, 1969–71; Mathematics Teacher, King Edward VII Sch., Lytham, 1969–72; Housemaster and Dir of Studies, Framlingham Coll., 1973–84; Dep. Headmaster, Bristol Cathedral Sch., 1984–89; Principal, King William's Coll., IOM, 1989–96; Master of Haileybury, 1996–2009. *Recreations:* golf, fly fishing, gardening, architecture, choral and classical music. *Club:* East India, Devonshire, Sports and Public Schools.

**WESTMACOTT, Sir Peter John,** GCMG 2016 (KCMG 2003; CMG 2000); LVO 1993; HM Diplomatic Service, retired; Ambassador to United States of America, 2012–15; Vice Chairman and Partner, Tellus Matrix LLP, since 2016; *b* 23 Dec. 1950; *s* of late Rev. Prebendary Ian Field Westmacott and of Rosemary Patricia Spencer Westmacott; *m* 1st, 1972, Angela Margaret Lugg (marr. diss. 1999); two *s* one *d*; 2nd, 2001, Susan Nemazee. *Educ:* Taunton Sch.; New Coll., Oxford (MA; Hon. Fellow, 2012). Entered FCO 1972; served Tehran 1974, Brussels, 1978; First Sec., Paris, 1980; Private Sec. to Minister of State, FCO, 1984; Head of Chancery, Ankara, 1987; Dep. Private Sec. to Prince of Wales, 1990; Counsellor, Washington, 1993; Dir, Americas, FCO, 1997; Dep. Under-Sec. of State, FCO, 2000–01; Ambassador to: Turkey, 2002–06; France, 2007–12. Mem., Ind. non-exec. Oversight Cttee, Ernst & Young, 2017–. *Publications:* Turkey's European Journey, 2017. *Recreations:* tennis, ski-ing, travel.

**WESTMEATH,** 13th Earl of, *cr* 1621; **William Anthony Nugent;** Baron Delvin, by tenure temp. Henry II; by summons, 1486; Senior Master, St Andrew's School, Pangbourne, 1980–88; *b* 21 Nov. 1928; *s* of 12th Earl of Westmeath and Doris (*d* 1968), 2nd *d* of C. Imlach, Liverpool; *S* father, 1971; *m* 1963, Susanna Margaret, *o d* of His Honour James Leonard; two *s*. *Educ:* Marlborough Coll. Captain, RA, retired. Staff of St Andrew's Sch., Pangbourne, 1961–88. *Heir: s* Hon. Sean Charles Weston Nugent, *b* 16 Feb. 1965. *Address:* Farthings, Rotten Row Hill, Bradfield, Berks RG7 6LL. *T:* (0118) 974 4426.

**WESTMINSTER,** 7th Duke of *cr* 1874; **Hugh Richard Louis Grosvenor;** Bt 1622; Baron Grosvenor, 1761; Earl Grosvenor and Viscount Belgrave, 1784; Marquess of Westminster, 1831; *b* 29 Jan. 1991; *o s* of 6th Duke of Westminster, KG, CB, CVO, OBE, TD, CD and of Natalia Ayesha Grosvenor; *S* father, 2016. *Heir:* (to Dukedom) none; (to Marquessate in remainder) Earl of Wilton, *qv*.

**WESTMINSTER, Archbishop of, (RC),** since 2009; **His Eminence Cardinal Vincent Gerard Nichols;** *b* 8 Nov. 1945; *s* of Henry Joseph Nichols and Mary Nichols (*née* Russell). *Educ:* St Mary's College, Crosby; Gregorian Univ., Rome (STL PhL); Manchester Univ. (MA Theol); Loyola Univ., Chicago (MEd). Chaplain, St John Rigby VI Form College, Wigan, 1972–77; Priest, inner city of Liverpool, 1978–81; Director, Upholland Northern Inst., with responsibility for in service training of clergy and for adult Christian educn, 1981–84; Gen. Sec., RC Bishops' Conf. of England and Wales, 1984–91; Auxiliary Bishop of Westminster (Bishop in N London), 1992–2000; Titular Bishop of Othona, 1992–2000; Archbishop of Birmingham, (RC), 2000–09. Cardinal, 2014. Chm., Catholic Educn Service, 1998–; Chm., Dept of Catholic Educn and Formation, 1998–, Pres., 2009–, RC Bishops' Conf. of Eng. and Wales; Mem., Congregation for Bishops, 2013–. Advr to Cardinal Hume and Archbishop Worlock, Internat. Synods of Bishops, 1980, 1983, 1985, 1987. Deleg. of Bishops' Conf. to Synod of Bishops, 1994; Mem., Synod of Bishops for Oceania, 1998, for Europe, 1999. Chancellor, St Mary's Univ., Twickenham, 2014–. *Publications:* Promise of Future Glory, 1997; Missioners, 2007; St John Fisher: bishop and theologian in Reformation and controversy, 2011; Hope in Action, 2017; Faith Finding a Voice, 2018; Gospel in Art, 2018; articles in Priests and People, Business Economist. *Address:* Archbishop's House, Ambrosden Avenue, Westminster, SW1P 1QJ.

**WESTMINSTER, Auxiliary Bishops of, (RC);** *see* Hudson, Rt Rev. N. G. E.; McAleenan, Rt Rev. P.; Sherrington, Rt Rev. J. F.

**WESTMINSTER, Dean of;** *see* Hoyle, Very Rev. D. M.

**WESTMORLAND,** 16th Earl of, *cr* 1624; **Anthony David Francis Henry Fane;** Baron Burghersh, 1624; independent art adviser; Director: Phillips Auctioneers, 1994–2001; Bonhams Auctioneers, 2001–04; Watson Westmorland Ltd, since 2003; *b* 1 Aug. 1951; *s* of 15th Earl of Westmorland, GCVO and Jane, *d* of Lt-Col Sir Roland Lewis Findlay, 3rd Bt; *S* father, 1993; *m* 1985, Caroline Eldred, *d* of Keon Hughes; one *d*. *Educ:* Eton. Mem., Orbitex North Pole Expedn, 1990. FRGS. *Heir: b* Hon. Harry St Clair Fane [*b* 19 March 1953; *m* 1984, Tessa, *d* of Captain Michael Philip Forsyth-Forrest; one *s* one *d*]. *Address:* London, SW7. *Club:* Turf.

**WESTMORLAND AND FURNESS, Archdeacon of;** *see* Ross, Ven. V.

**WESTON, Alannah Elizabeth;** Chairman, Selfridges Group, since 2019 (Creative Director, Selfridges & Co., 2004–14; Deputy Chairman, Selfridges Group, 2014–19); *b* Dublin, 8 Jan. 1972; *d* of W(illard) Galen Weston, *qv* and Hon. Hilary Mary Weston, *qv*; *m* 2007, Alexander Desmond Sursock Cochrane, *s* and *heir* of Sir (Henry) Marc (Sursock) Cochrane, *qv*; two *d*. *Educ:* Havergal Coll., Toronto; Merton Coll., Oxford (MA English). Contrib. Ed., Telegraph mag., 1994–98; Press Officer, Burberry, 1998–2000; Creative Dir, Windsor, Florida, 2001–04. Dir, Zephyr Projects, 2003–04. Chm., Selfridges Gp Foundn, 2016–; Trustee: Reta Lila Howard Foundn and Reta Lila Weston Trust, 1998– (Chm. Trustees, 2011–14); Blue Marine Foundn, 2012–. *Publications:* The Beach, 2001; Christo and Jeanne-Claude: the Weston Collection, 2002; Ed Ruscha, 2003; Heel to Heal: the collection of paintings, drawings and photographs of Bruce Weber and Nan Bush, 2003; The Family, 2004; Peter Doig: works on paper, 2004; (jtly) A Book of Wonder, 2007. *Recreations:* travel, reading, riding, cycling, canoeing. *Address:* Selfridges & Co., 400 Oxford Street, W1A 1AB. *Clubs:* Soho House, Hertford Street; Windsor (Florida); Ojibway (Pointe au Baril, Ont).

**WESTON, Prof. Arthur Henry,** PhD, DSc; FMedSci; Leech Professor of Pharmacology, University of Manchester, 1990–2011, now Emeritus; *b* 31 May 1944; *s* of Arthur Edward Weston and Betty Nutt Weston (*née* Wetherell); *m* 1967, Kathleen Margaret Goodison; one *s* one *d*. *Educ:* Hymers Coll., Hull; Univ. of Manchester (BSc 1st Cl. Hons 1966, MSc 1968; PhD 1970; DSc 1994). Lectr in Pharmacol., 1970–75, Sen. Lectr, 1975–88, Reader, 1988–90, Univ. of Manchester. Alexander von Humboldt Fellow, Univ. of Marburg, 1974,

Univ. of Heidelberg, 1985; Vis. Prof., Univ. of Kyushu, 1987; Vis. Fellow, Magdalen Coll., Oxford, 2011–12. Trustee and Hon. Treas., British Pharmacol Soc., 2000–07; Pres., Fedn of Eur. Pharmacol Socs, 2006–08; Hon. Mem., Finnish Pharmacol Soc., 2008. FMedSci 2001; FBPharmacolS 2004–12, Hon. FBPhS (Hon. FBPharmacolS 2012). Mem., RHS. Gaddum Memorial Award, British Pharmacol Soc., 2008; Rodolfo Paoletti Medal, Fedn of Eur. Pharmacol Socs, 2014; Award of Merit, Crocosmia Forum, 2019. *Publications:* (jtly) Pharmacology of the Hypothalamus, 1978; (with T. C. Hamilton) Potassium Channel Modulators, 1992; contrib. original papers to British Jl Pharmacol., Jl Pharmacol. and Exptl Therapeutics, Nature, Naunyn Schmiedeberg's Archives of Pharmacol. *Recreations:* gardening, mechanical watches, visiting Germany. *Address:* Faculty of Life Sciences, University of Manchester, 3rd Floor, CTF Building, 46 Grafton Street, Manchester M13 9NT. *T:* (0161) 275 5490, *Fax:* (0161) 275 5600. *E:* arthur.weston@manchester.ac.uk.

**WESTON, Christopher John;** Life President, Phillips Son & Neale (Chairman and Chief Executive, 1972–98); Chairman and Chief Executive Officer, Plaxbury Group, since 1998; *b* 3 March 1937; *s* of Eric Tudor Weston and Evelyn Nellie Weston; *m* 1969, Josephine Annabel Moir; one *d*. *Educ:* Lancing Coll. FIA (Scot.). Director: Phillips, 1964–98; Foreign and Colonial Pacific Investment Trust, 1984–99; Hodder Headline Plc (formerly Headline Book Publishing PLC), 1986–99 (Chm., 1997–99); Foreign & Colonial Enterprise Trust plc, 1987–99. Vice-Pres., Quit - Soc. of Non Smokers, 1993–. FRSA (Mem. Council, 1985). *Recreations:* theatre, music. *Address:* 5 Hillside Close, Carlton Hill, NW8 0EF. *Club:* Oriental.

**WESTON, Rev. Canon David Wilfrid Valentine,** PhD; Residentiary Canon of Carlisle Cathedral, 1994–2005; Canon Librarian, 1995–2005, now Hon. Assistant Librarian; *b* 8 Dec. 1937; *s* of Rev. William Valentine Weston and Mrs Gertrude Hamilton Weston; *m* 1984, Helen Strachan Macdonald, *d* of James and Barbara Macdonald; two *s*. *Educ:* St Edmund's Sch., Canterbury; Lancaster Univ. (PhD 1993). Entered Nashdom Abbey, 1960; deacon, 1967, priest, 1968; Novice Master, 1969–74; Prior, 1971–74; Abbot, 1974–84; Curate, St Peter's, Chorley, 1984–85; Vicar, St John the Baptist, Pilling, 1985–89; Domestic Chaplain to Bishop of Carlisle, 1989–94; Actg Dean, Carlisle, 2003–04. Chm., Carlisle Tourism Forum, 1996–98. Freeman, City of London; Liveryman, Salters' Co. *Publications:* Carlisle Cathedral History, 2000; (ed jtly) Carlisle and Cumbria, 2004; Rose Castle and the Bishops of Carlisle 1133–2012, 2013. *Address:* The Pond House, Ratten Row, Dalston, Carlisle CA5 7AY.

**WESTON, Galen;** *see* Weston, W. G.

**WESTON, George Garfield;** Chief Executive, Associated British Foods plc, since 2005; *b* 4 March 1964; *s* of late Garfield Howard Weston and Mary Ruth Weston (*née* Kippenberger); *m* 1996, Katharine Mary Acland; three *s* one *d*. *Educ:* Westminster Sch.; New Coll., Oxford (MA PPE); Harvard Business Sch. (MBA). N. B. Love Mills, 1988–92; Managing Director: Westmill Foods, 1992–98; Allied Bakeries, 1999–2003; Chief Exec., George Weston Foods Ltd (Australia), 2003–05. Trustee, British Mus., 2019–. *Recreations:* tennis, gardening. *Address:* Associated British Foods plc, 10 Grosvenor Street, W1K 4QY. *T:* (020) 7399 6500.
*See also* A. C. Hobhouse, G. H. Weston.

**WESTON, Guy Howard;** Chairman, Garfield Weston Foundation, since 2000; *b* Sydney, NSW, 3 July 1960; *s* of late Garfield Howard Weston and Mary Ruth Weston; *m* 1986, Charlotte Emily Brunet; three *s* one *d*. *Educ:* Westminster Sch.; Merton Coll., Oxford (BA 1981; Hon. Fellow 2007); INSEAD (MBA 1988). Morgan Grenfell & Co. Ltd, 1984–87; Managing Director: Jacksons of Piccadilly Ltd, 1990–93; Ryvita Co. Ltd, 1993–2000. Chairman: Heals plc, 2001–12; Wittington Investments Ltd, 2002–. Trustee, Thrombosis Res. Inst., 2002–; Chairman: Garfield Weston Fund for Westminster Abbey, 2007–; Bodleian Liby Appeal Cttee, 2010–18. Hon. RCM 2019. Hon. LLD Buckingham, 2005; Hon. DSc Imperial Coll. London, 2008. *Recreations:* theatre, travel, history, sailing, ski-ing. *Address:* Garfield Weston Foundation, 10 Grosvenor Street, W1K 4QY. *Club:* Reial Club Nàutic Port de Pollença.
*See also* A. C. Hobhouse, G. G. Weston.

**WESTON, Hon. Hilary Mary,** CVO 2015; CM 2003; OOnt 2001; Lieutenant Governor of Ontario, 1997–2002; *b* 12 Jan. 1942; *d* of Michael Frayne and Noel Elizabeth Guerrini; *m* 1966, W(illard) Galen Weston, *qv*; one *s* one *d*. *Educ:* Loretto Abbey, Dalkey. Dep. Chm., Holt, Renfrew & Co., 1986–96; Design Dir, Windsor, Florida, 1988–96. Founder, Ireland Fund of Canada, 1979. Chm., Royal Ontario Mus. Renaissance Campaign, Toronto, 2002–09. Trustee, Foundn of Coll. of St George, Windsor Castle. Hon. Col, 437 Transport Sqdn, CFB Trenton & The Princess of Wales' Own Regt, Kingston, 1998–2002. Hon. DLittS Univ. of St Michael's Coll., Toronto, 1997; Hon. LLD: Western Ontario, 1997; UC of Cape Breton, 1999; Toronto, 2000; Niagara, York, 2002; Dublin, 2004; Queen's, Kingston, 2008; Concordia, Montreal, 2008; Hon. DLitt UCD, 2009. Woodrow Wilson Award for Public Service, 2005; Women of Distinction President's Award, YWCA, 2009. DStJ 1997. *Publications:* (jtly) In a Canadian Garden, 1989; (jtly) At Home in Canada, 1995; No Ordinary Time, 2006. *Recreations:* tennis, riding. *Address:* 22 St Clair Avenue East, Toronto, ON M4T 2S3, Canada. *T:* (416) 9354050; Fort Belvedere, Ascot, Berks SL5 7SD. *Club:* National (Toronto).
*See also* A. E. Weston.

**WESTON, Jeremy Paul;** QC 2011; a Recorder, since 2018; *b* Dorchester, 3 Sept. 1969; *s* of David and Ann Weston; *m* 2001, Kate Stilgoe; one *s* two *s*. *Educ:* Reading Blue Coat Sch.; Staffordshire Univ. (LLB Hons). Called to the Bar, Inner Temple, 1991; in practice as barrister, specialising in family law; 8 Fountain Court, 1992–96, St Ives Chambers, 1996–. *Recreations:* family, gardening, cooking, golf. *Address:* St Ives Chambers, Whittall Street, Birmingham B4 6DH. *T:* (0121) 236 0863, *Fax:* (0121) 236 6961. *E:* jeremy.weston@stiveschambers.co.uk.

**WESTON, Sir John;** *see* Weston, Sir P. J.

**WESTON, John Pix,** CBE 1994; FRAeS; FREng; Chairman: Brittpac, since 2010; Seven Technologies, since 2019; *b* 16 Aug. 1951; *s* of late John Pix Weston and Ivy (*née* Glover); *m* 1975, Susan West (*d* 2016); one *s* one *d*. *Educ:* King's Sch., Worcester; Trinity Hall, Cambridge (MA Eng.). CEng 1992; FRAeS 1992. British Aerospace, subseq. BAE SYSTEMS: undergrad. apprenticeship, 1970–74; sales appts on Jaguar and Tornado projects, 1974–82; on secondment to MoD Sales Orgn, 1982–85; Military Aircraft Division, Warton: ME Sales Manager, Project Manager, Al Yamamah Project and Exec. Dir, Saudi Ops, 1985–89; Dir, 1989–92; Man. Dir, 1990–92; Chm. and Man. Dir, British Aerospace Defence Ltd, 1992–96; Dir, 1994–2002; Gp Man. Dir, 1996–98; Chief Exec., 1998–2002. Chairman: Spirent plc, 2002–06; Acra Controls, 2003–11; INBIS plc, 2004–05; Ufi learn-direct Ltd, 2004–11; i-SOFT, 2005–07; MB Aerospace, 2007–15; AWS Ltd, 2008–12; Torotrak plc, 2011–15; Acesso Plc (formerly Lo-Q), 2011–18; Fibercore plc, 2012–17; Prodrive Composites Ltd, 2014–17; Windar Photonics, 2014–17. Vice-Pres., RUSI, 2000–17. FREng 2000; FRSA. Commander, Order of the Pole Star (Sweden), 2000. *Recreations:* ski-ing, photography, hill-walking. *E:* jpwweston2@gmail.com.

**WESTON, Dame Margaret (Kate),** DBE 1979; BScEng (London); CEng, FIET, FNucI; FMA; Director of the Science Museum, 1973–86; *b* 7 March 1926; *oc* of late Charles Edward and Margaret Weston. *Educ:* Stroud High School; College of Technology, Birmingham (now Univ. of Aston). Engineering apprenticeship, General Electric Co. Ltd, 1945–49; development work, very largely on high voltage insulation problems. Science Museum: Assistant Keeper, Dept of Electrical Engineering and Communications, 1955–61; Deputy Keeper, 1962; Keeper, Dept of Museum Services, 1967–72. Member: Ancient Monuments Bd for England, 1977–84; 1851 Commission, 1987–96; Museums and Galleries Commission, 1988–96; Steering Gp, Museum in Docklands, 1986–90. Member: SE Elec. Bd, 1981–90; BBC Sci. Consultative Gp, 1986–89. Chairman: Brunel Goods Shed Cttee, Stroud, 2004–07; Heritage Network (formerly Heritage Forum), Stroud, 2005–18; Mem. Hunterian Bd, RCS, 1981–2012; Trustee: Brooklands, 1987–2002; Fleet Air Arm Mus., 1992–2000; British Empire and Commonwealth Mus., Bristol, 1999–2002 (Chm., 1999–2002); Museum in the Park, Stroud, 2004–18 (Chm. Trustees, 2004–05). Horniman Public Museum and Public Park: Chm. Trust, 1990–96; Mem. Develt Cttee, 1996–2002; Pres., Friends, 1996–2003; Chm. Trustees, Horniman Mus. Trust, 1997–2002. Patron: Stroudwater Textile Trust, 2002–; Vale of Berkeley Railway, 2019–. Governor: Imperial Coll., 1974–90 (FIC 1975); Ditchley Foundn, 1984–2008 (Mem., Mgt Council, 1984–2003). Pres., 1985–2011, Patron, 2011–, Heritage Railways Assoc. (formerly Assoc. of Railway Preservation Socs, then Assoc. of Independent Railways and Preservation Socs); Mem., Adv. Panel, Railway Heritage Trust, 1987–2011. FMA 1976; Sen. Fellow, RCA, 1986; Fellow, Sci. Mus. Gp, 2018. FRSA (Mem. Council, 1985–90); CCMI. Hon. Fellow, Newnham Coll., Cambridge, 1986. Hon. DEng Bradford, 1984; Hon. DSc: Aston, 1974; Salford, 1984; Leeds, 1987; Loughborough, 1988; DUniv Open, 1987. *Address:* Ryland Lodge, Ashlane, Randwick, nr Stroud, Glos GL6 6EX. *T:* (01453) 766694.

**WESTON, Sir Michael (Charles Swift),** KCMG 1991; CVO 1979; JP; HM Diplomatic Service, retired; UK Permanent Representative to Conference on Disarmament, Geneva (with personal rank of Ambassador), 1992–97; *b* 4 Aug. 1937; *s* of late Edward Charles Swift Weston and Kathleen Mary Weston (*née* Mockett); *m* 1st, 1959, Veronica Anne Tickner (marr. diss. 1990); two *s* one *d*; 2nd, 1990, Christine Julia Ferguson; one *s* one *d*. *Educ:* Dover Coll.; St Catharine's Coll., Cambridge (Exhibitioner; BA, MA). Joined HM Diplomatic Service, 1961; 3rd Sec., Kuwait, 1962; 2nd Sec., FCO, 1965; 1st Secretary: Tehran, 1968; UK Mission, New York, 1970; FCO, 1974; Counsellor, Jedda, 1977; RCDS, 1980; Counsellor (Information), Paris, 1981; Counsellor, Cairo, 1984; Head of Southern European Dept, FCO, 1987; Ambassador to Kuwait, 1990–92. Member: UN Sec.-Gen.'s Gp of Experts on Small Arms, 1998–99; Special Immigration Appeals Commn, 1999–2007. Chm. Adv. Gp, Comprehensive Nuclear-Test-Ban Treaty Orgn, 2009–. JP West Kent, 2002. Decoration with Sash (First Cl.), Kuwait, 1991. *Recreations:* walking, gardening. *Address:* Beech Farm House, Beech Lane, Matfield, Kent TN12 7HG. *T:* (01892) 824666.

**WESTON, Sir (Philip) John,** KCMG 1992 (CMG 1985); HM Diplomatic Service, retired; British Permanent Representative to the United Nations, 1995–98; *b* 13 April 1938; *s* of Philip George Weston and Edith Alice Bray (*née* Ansell); *m* 1967, Margaret Sally Ehlers; two *s* one *d*. *Educ:* Sherborne; Worcester Coll., Oxford (1st Cl. Hons, Honour Mods Classics and Lit. Hum.; Hon. Fellow, 2003). Served with 42 Commando, Royal Marines, 1956–58. Entered Diplomatic Service, 1962; FO, 1962–63; Treasury Centre for Admin. Studies, 1964; Chinese Language student, Hong Kong, 1964–66; Peking, 1967–68; FO, 1969–71; Office of UK Permanent Representative to EEC, 1972–74; Asst Private Sec. to Sec. of State for Foreign and Commonwealth Affairs (Rt Hon. James Callaghan, Rt Hon. Anthony Crosland), 1974–76; Counsellor, Head of EEC Presidency Secretariat, FCO, 1976–77; Vis. Fellow, All Souls Coll., Oxford, 1977–78; Counsellor, Washington, 1978–81; Hd Defence Dept, FCO, 1981–84; Asst Under-Sec. of State, FCO, 1984–85; Minister, Paris, 1985–88; Dep. Sec. to Cabinet, Cabinet Office, 1988–89 (on secondment); Dep. Under-Sec. of State (Defence), FCO, 1989–90; Political Dir, FCO, 1990–91; Ambassador and UK Perm. Rep. to N Atlantic Council (NATO), 1992–95, to Perm. Council of WEU, 1992–95. Non-executive Director: BT Gp, 1998–2002; Rolls Royce Gp, 1998–2004; Hakluyt and Co. Ltd, 2001–07. Trustee: NPG, 1999–2008; Poetry Soc., 2005–08; Chm. Trustees, The Poetry Sch., 2005–08. Council Mem., IISS, 2001–05. Governor: Sherborne Sch., 1995–2007 (Chm., 2002–07); Ditchley Foundn, 1999–2011. Trustee, Amer. Associates of the Royal Acad. Trust, 1998–2004. Pres., Worcester Coll. Soc., 2003–12. Hon. Pres., Community Foundn Network (UK), 1999–2008. *Publications:* (contrib.) Take Five 04 (anthol. poems), 2004; Chasing The Hoopoe (poems), 2005; Echo Soundings (poems), 2012; poems in many magazines (various prizes). *Recreations:* poetry, bee-keeping, fly-fishing, running, birds. *Address:* 139 Queen's Road, Richmond, Surrey TW10 6HF. *Club:* Garrick.

**WESTON, Simon,** CBE 2016 (OBE 1992); motivational speaker, writer and performer, since 1985; *b* 8 Aug. 1961; *s* of Harold Hatfield and Pauline Hatfield; *m* 1990, Lucy Veronica (*née* Titherington); two *s* one *d*. *Educ:* Lewis Boys' Sch., Pengam, Mid Glam. Joined Welsh Guards, 1978; served Berlin, NI, Kenya and Falklands; Co-Founder and Vice Pres., Weston Spirit, 1988–2009. Documentaries: Simon's War, Simon's Peace, Simon's Triumph, Simon's Return, Simon's Journey, Simon's Heroes, BBC TV; Saving Simon, ITV. Vice Pres. and advocate, Royal Star and Garter Home, 1991. Pres., Fleming Fulton Special Needs Sch. Poultry Club, 1990. Freedom, City of Liverpool, 2002. Fellow, Univ. of Wales Sch. of Midwifery, 2001. Hon. Fellow: John Moores Univ., Liverpool, 2003; Open Univ., 2003; Cardiff Univ., 2005. Hon. degree in humanities, 1994, Hon. DHum, 2002, Glamorgan; Hon. Dr Heriot-Watt, 2008. *Publications:* autobiography: Walking Tall, 1989; Going Back, 1992; Moving On, 2003; novels: Cause of Death, 1995; Phoenix, 1996; *for children:* A Nod from Nelson, 2008; Nelson to the Rescue, 2010; Nelson at Sea, 2011; Get Fit With Nelson, 2013. *Recreations:* reading, keeping fit, music, watching sport, jogging. *Address:* Abingdon Management Company, Rosedale House, Rosedale Road, Richmond, Surrey TW9 2SZ. *T:* (020) 8939 9019, *Fax:* (020) 8939 9080.

**WESTON, Susan Elizabeth;** *see* Murray, S. E.

**WESTON, W(illard) Galen,** OC 1990; OOnt 2004; CVO 2018; Chairman, George Weston Ltd, Toronto, 1978–2016, now Chairman Emeritus (former President); former Executive Chairman, Loblaw Companies Ltd; *b* England, 29 Oct. 1940; *s* of W. Garfield Weston and Reta Lila (*née* Howard); *m* 1966, Hon. Hilary Mary Frayne (*see* Hon. H. M. Weston); one *s* one *d*. Chairman: Selfridges & Co., until 2019; Holt Renfrew & Co. Ltd; Brown Thomas; Wittington Investments Ltd; Vice-Chm., Fortnum & Mason plc (UK); Director: Associated British Foods (UK); Brown Thomas Group Ltd (Eire). Pres. and Trustee, W. Garfield Weston Foundation, Canada. Hon. LLD Univ. of Western Ont. *Recreations:* outdoor sports, contemporary arts. *Address:* George Weston Ltd, 22 St Clair Avenue East, Toronto, ON M4T 2S7, Canada. *T:* (416) 9222500, *Fax:* (416) 9224394. *Clubs:* Guards' Polo; Toronto, York (Toronto); Windsor (Florida); Deep Dale (NY).
*See also* A. E. Weston.

**WESTON, William John,** MVO 2002; independent management consultant to cultural, heritage and leisure sectors, retired; *b* 4 July 1949; *s* of Eric Gordon and Pauline Violet Weston; *m* 1978, Patricia April (decd); two *d*; *m* 1995, Jane Henriques; one step *s* one step *d*. *Educ*: Wymondham Coll., Norfolk; Royal Manchester Coll. of Music; Poly. of Central London. Concerts Manager, Bournemouth SO, 1971–73; City Arts Administrator, Southampton CC, 1973–77; Administrator, Irish Th. Co., Dublin, 1977–80; Exec. Dir and Creator, W Yorks Playhouse, Leeds, 1980–93; freelance TV producer, 1993–95; Gen. Manager, RSC, 1995–2000; Chief Exec., Royal Parks Agency, 2000–05. Non-exec. Dir, England Nat. Cttee, Forestry Commn, 2008–14. Chm., Heart of Teesdale Landscape Partnership, 2010–14; Member: Yorks Dales Nat. Park Authy, 2006–14; Barnard Castle Regeneration Partnership, 2011–14. Associate Dir, Georgian Th., Richmond, 2012–14. *Recreations:* the arts, walking, gardening, open spaces, jazz, sailing. *Address:* 93 Seacon Tower, 5 Hutchings Street, E14 8JX.

**WESTWELL, Alan Reynolds,** OBE 1996; PhD, MSc; CEng, MIMechE, MIET; FCILT; Managing Director and Chief Executive, Dublin Buses Ltd, 1997–2005; *b* 11 April 1940; *s* of Stanley Westwell and Margaret (*née* Reynolds); *m* 1967, Elizabeth Aileen Birrell; two *s* one *d*. *Educ*: Old Swan Coll.; Liverpool Polytechnic (ACT Hons); Salford Univ. (MSc 1983); Keele Univ. (PhD 1991). Liverpool City Transport Dept: progressively, student apprentice, Technical Asst, Asst Works Manager, 1956–67; Chief Engineer: Southport Corporation Transport Dept, 1967–69; Coventry Corp. Transport Dept, 1969–72; Glasgow Corp. Transport Dept, 1972–74; Director of Public Transport (responsible for bus/rail, airport, harbours), Tayside Regional Council, 1974–79; Dir Gen., Strathclyde PTE, 1979–86; Chm., Man. Dir and Chief Exec., Strathclyde Buses Ltd, 1987–90; Man. Dir and Chief Exec., Greater Manchester Buses Ltd, 1990–93, Greater Manchester Buses North Ltd, 1993–97. Professional Advr, COSLA, 1976–86. President: Scottish Council of Confedn of British Road Passenger Transport, 1982–83 (Vice-Pres., 1981–82); Bus and Coach Council, UK, 1989–90 (Vice Pres., 1985–88; Sen. Vice-Pres., 1988–89). Mem., Parly Road Transport Cttee, 1986–97. Chm., IMechE, Automobile Div., Scottish Centre, 1982–84; Mem. Council, CIT, UK, 1986–89 (Chm. Scottish Centre, 1983–84). International Union of Public Transport: Vice Pres., 1997; Member: Management Cttee, 1991–; Internat. Metropolitan Railway Cttee, 1979–86; Internat. Gen. Commn on Transport and Urban Life (formerly Internat. Commn, Traffic and Urban Planning), 1986–; UITP-EU (formerly European Action) Cttee, 1988–; Chm., UK Members, 1993–97. Hon. Vice Pres., UITP, 2003. Chm., Altrincham Probus Club, 2012–13. *Publications:* various papers. *Recreations:* swimming, music, reading. *Address:* 6 Amberley Drive, Hale Barns, Altrincham, Cheshire WA15 0DT. *T:* (0161) 980 3551.

**WESTWOOD,** family name of **Baron Westwood.**

**WESTWOOD, 4th Baron** *cr* 1944, of Gosforth; **William Fergus Westwood;** *b* 24 Nov. 1972; *s* of 3rd Baron Westwood and of Penelope, *e d* of Dr C. E. Shafto; *S* father, 2019.

**WESTWOOD, Dr Albert Ronald Clifton,** FREng; consultant in research and technology management, since 2000; Vice President, Research and Exploratory Technology, Sandia National Laboratories, 1993–96, now Emeritus; *b* 9 June 1932; *s* of Albert Sydney Westwood and Ena Emily (*née* Clifton); *m* 1956, Jean Mavis Bullock; two *d*. *Educ*: King Edward's Sch., Birmingham; Univ. of Birmingham (BSc Hons 1953; PhD 1956; DSc 1968). FInstP 1967; FIMMM (FIM 1998). Joined Research Institute for Advanced Studies, subseq. Martin Marietta Labs, Baltimore, 1958, Dir, 1974–84; Martin Marietta Corporation: Corporate Dir, R&D, 1984–87; Vice Pres., R&D, 1987–90; Corporate Vice Pres., Res. and Technol., 1990–93. Chm. and Chief Exec., CCLRC, UK, 1998–2000. Chairman: Commn on Engrg and Technical Systems, Nat. Res. Council, 1992–97; Cttee on Global Aspects of Intellectual Properties Rights in Sci. and Technol., Nat. Res. Council, 1992–93; and numerous govt, academic, civic, music and humanities councils and adv. bds. Mem. Bd, US Civilian R&D Foundn, 1995–2010. President: Industrial Res. Inst., US, 1989–90; Minerals, Metals and Materials Soc., 1990 (Fellow, 1990). Mem., Bd of Sci. and Technol., Univ. of New Mexico, 1995–2016 (Interim Pres., 2007). Fellow, Amer. Soc. for Materials Internat., 1974; FAAAS 1986; FREng (FEng 1996). Member: US NAE, 1980; Royal Swedish Acad. Engrg Scis, 1989; Russian Acad. Engrg, 1995; Georgia Acad. of Engrg, 2007. Pianist and arranger accompanying wife in concerts and recitals in US and around world. Has received numerous awards, prizes and lectureships in recognition of scientific and managerial contribs. *Publications:* (ed) Environment Sensitive Mechanical Behavior, 1966; (ed) Mechanisms of Environment Sensitive Cracking of Materials, 1977; about 125 scientific papers. *Recreations:* music, theatre, arts, travel. *Address:* 13539 Canada Del Oso, High Desert, Albuquerque, NM 87111, USA. *E:* arwestwood@aol.com.

**WESTWOOD, Dr David,** QPM 2001; Chief Constable, Humberside Police, 1999–2005; Owner, Just Things, Fairtrade shop, Ilminster, since 2012; *b* 1 April 1948; *s* of late Sqdn Ldr William Westwood and Judith Westwood (*née* Green); *m* 1969, Wendy Stevenson; three *s* one *d*. *Educ*: Collyer's Sch., Horsham; Lady Margaret Hall, Oxford (MA Juris.); Bristol Poly. (PhD 1991). Constable, Sussex Police, 1963–73; Constable to Supt, Avon and Somerset Police, 1973–92; Chief Supt, Humberside Police, 1992–95; Asst Chief Constable, Merseyside Police, 1995–97; Dep. Chief Constable, Humberside Police, 1997–99. Hd, Business Area for Race and Community Relns, ACPO, 2000–03. *Recreations:* theatre, organic gardening, Fairtrade. *Address:* Park View, Long Close, Ilminster, Somerset TA19 0EP. *E:* enquiries@just-things.co.uk.

**WESTWOOD, Nicola Ann;** *see* Sullivan, N. A.

**WESTWOOD, Dame Vivienne (Isabel),** DBE 2006 (OBE 1992); RDI 2001; fashion designer; *b* 8 April 1941; *née* Vivienne Isabel Swire; two *s*. In partnership with Malcolm McLaren, designed a series of influential avant-garde collections showcased at World's End (formerly named Let It Rock, Too Fast to Live Too Young to Die, Sex, Seditionaries), 430 King's Rd, Chelsea, 1971–82; opened Vivienne Westwood shop, 6 Davies St, W1, 1990, flagship shop, 44 Conduit St, W1, 1992, head office, Milan, 1998, shop, Los Angeles, 2011, and stores worldwide; collections include: Anglomania, 1993–; Vivienne Westwood Man (Milan), 1996–; Red Label, London, 1997–, Paris, 1998–, New York, 2000–; Gold Label, 1999–. Launched fragrances: Boudoir, 1998; Libertine, 2000; Boudoir Sin City, 2007; Let It Rock, 2007. Exhibitions at V & A Museum: (contrib.) Radical Fashion, 2001; (contrib.) Men in Skirts, 2002; (contrib.) Tiaras, 2002; Vivienne Westwood 36 Years in Fashion, 2004 and subseq. world tour; launched manifesto at Wallace Collection, 2007. Professor of Fashion: Acad. of Applied Arts, Vienna, 1989–91; Hochschule der Künste, Berlin, 1993–. Launched Climate Revolution, 2012. Trustee, Civil Liberties Trust, 2007–. Hon. Sen. FRCA 1992; Hon. FKC 2008; Dr *hc*: Heriot-Watt, 2008; RCA, 2008. British Designer of the Year, 1990, 1991, Outstanding Achievement in Fashion, 2007, British Fashion Council; Queen's Award for Export, 1998; Moët & Chandon Red Carpet Dresser, 2006; André Leon Talley Lifetime Achievement Award, SCAD Mus. of Art, 2015. *Publications:* (with Ian Kelly) Vivienne Westwood, 2014. *Address:* Vivienne Westwood Ltd, Westwood Studios, 9–15 Elcho Street, Battersea, SW11 4AU. *T:* (020) 7924 4747.

**WETHERED, Julian Frank Baldwin;** Director, International Division, United States Banknote Corporation, 1992–94; *b* 9 Nov. 1929; *s* of late Comdr Owen Francis McTier Wethered, RN retd and Betty (*née* Baldwin); *m* 1st, 1952, Britt Eva Hindmarsh (marr. diss. 1971); one *s* one *d*; 2nd, 1973, Antonia Mary Ettrick Roberts; two *s*. *Educ*: Eton Coll.; Jesus Coll., Cambridge (BA Hons Hist. 1952; MA); BA Hons Open Univ. 2002. National Service, RM, HMS Diadem, 1948–49. Trainee, Expandite Ltd, 1952–54; Sales Rep., Remington Rand, 1955–56; Thomas De La Rue and Co.: trainee, 1956; Mem., PA Study Team, 1957; Printing Preliminaries Manager, Currency Div., 1958–62; Special Rep., Africa, 1963–67; Manager, Banknote Printing Co., 1968–69; Regl Manager, FE, 1970–75; Associate Dir of Sales, Africa and FE, 1976–83; Regl Dir, FE, De La Rue Co. plc, 1984–88; Associate Dir of Sales, Thomas De La Rue & Co., 1989. Dir Gen., RoSPA, 1990–91. Dir, Whatman Far East Pte Ltd, 1987–88. Chm., Riding for the Disabled Assoc. of Singapore, 1987–88. Pres., British Business Assoc. of Singapore, 1988. FInstD; FRSA. *Recreations:* sailing, riding, the arts. *Address:* Brunton Barn, Collingbourne Kingston, Marlborough, Wilts SN8 3SE. *Club:* Travellers.

**WETHERELL, Gordon Geoffrey,** CMG 2011; HM Diplomatic Service, retired; Governor, Turks and Caicos Islands, 2008–11; *b* 11 Nov. 1948; *s* of late Geoffrey and Georgette Maria Wetherell; *m* 1981, Rosemary Anne Myles; four *d*. *Educ*: Bradfield Coll., Berks; New Coll., Oxford (BA 1969; MA 1975); Univ. of Chicago (MA 1971). Joined HM Diplomatic Service, 1973; FCO (concurrently British Embassy, Chad), 1973–74; E Berlin, 1974–77; First Sec., FCO, 1977; UK Delegn to Comprehensive Test Ban Negotiations, Geneva, 1977–80; New Delhi, 1980–83; FCO, 1983–85; on secondment to HM Treasury, 1986–87; Asst Head, European Communities Dept (External), FCO, 1987–88; Counsellor and Dep. Head of Mission, Warsaw, 1988–92; Counsellor (Politico-Military), Bonn, 1992–94; Hd, Personnel Services Dept, FCO, 1994–97; Ambassador: to Ethiopia and (non-resident) to Eritrea and Djibouti, 1997–2000; to Luxembourg, 2000–04; High Comr to Ghana, and (non-resident) Ambassador to Togo, Niger, Burkina Faso and Côte d'Ivoire, 2004–07. *Recreations:* tennis, reading, travel, Manchester United Football Club. *Club:* Oxford and Cambridge.

**WETTON, Hilary John D.;** *see* Davan Wetton.

**WETTON, Philip Henry Davan,** CMG 1993; HM Diplomatic Service, retired; Consul-General, Milan, 1990–96; *b* 21 Sept. 1937; *s* of late Eric Davan Wetton, CBE and Kathleen Valerie Davan Wetton; *m* 1983, Roswitha Kortner. *Educ*: Westminster; Christ Church, Oxford (MA). Unilever Ltd, 1958–65; FCO, 1965–68; served Tokyo, Osaka and FCO, 1968–73; Head of Division, later Director, Secretariat of Council of Ministers of European Communities, 1973–83; Counsellor, Seoul, 1983–87; FCO, 1987–90. Founded Philip Wetton Chair of Astrophysics, Oxford Univ., 2000; endowed Grad. Scholarship in Astrophysics, Christ Church, Oxford, 2005. *Recreations:* rowing, music, astronomy. *Address:* Aller's End, East Kennett, Marlborough, Wilts SN8 4EY.
*See also* H. J. Davan Wetton.

**WETZEL, Dave;** Chief Executive Officer and International Speaker on Transport, Taxation and Land Value Capture, Transforming Communities Consultancy, since 2008; *b* 9 Oct. 1942; *s* of Fred Wetzel and Ivy Donaldson; *m* 1973, Heather Allman; two *d*. *Educ*: Spring Grove Grammar Sch.; Southall Technical Coll., Ealing Coll., and the Henry George Sch. of Social Sciences (part-time courses). Student apprentice, Wilkinson Sword/Graviner, 1959–62; Bus Conductor/Driver, 1962–65, Bus Official, 1965–69, London Transport; Br. Manager, Initial Services, 1969–70; Pilot Roster Officer, British Airways, 1970–74 (ASTMS Trade Union Shop Steward); Political Organiser, London Co-op., 1974–81; Proprietor, Granny's Attic Antique Shop, Mevagissey, 1994–99; Partner, Yun Kim's family restaurant, 1997–2015. Member (Lab): for Hammersmith N, GLC, 1981–86 (Transport Cttee Chair, 1981–86); Hounslow Borough Council, 1964–68, 1986–94 (Dep. Leader and Chair, Environmental Planning, 1986–87; Leader, 1987–91). Vice-Chair, Transport for London, 2000–08 (Chair, Safety, Health and Envmt Cttee, 2004–08); Chair: London Buses, 2000–01; Transport Trading Ltd, 2000–01. Contested (Lab): Richmond upon Thames, Twickenham, 1979; Mevagissey, Restormel DC, 1995; St Austell West, Cornwall CC, 1997. Vice-Chm., Public Transport Cttee, AMA, 1993–94; Mem. Management Cttee, Hounslow Community Transport and Central London Dial-a-Ride, 1991–94; Mem. Bd, Capital Transport Campaign, London, 1991–94. Exec. Dir, DaRT (Dial-a-Ride and Taxicard Users), 1989–94. Pres., W London Peace Council, 1982–94; Pres., Labour Land Campaign, 1982–2016; Chair, Professional Land Reform Gp, 2004–; Hon. Gen. Sec., Internat. Union for Land Value Taxation and Free Trade, 2010–12 (Pres., 2013–15). Mem. Bd, Riverside Studios, Hammersmith, 1983–86. Founder and co-ordinator, Trade Union and Co-op Esperanto Gp, 1976–80. Pres., Thames Valley Esperanto Soc., 1982–94; Vice-Pres., Transport Studies Soc., London Univ., 1992–99 (Pres., 1991–92). Vice Chm., Mevagissey Chamber of Commerce, 1996–98. Member: Cttee, Mevagissey Folk Mus., 1995–99; Bd, London Transport Mus., 2007–08. Mem. Bd, Socialist Envmtl Resources Assoc., 2006–08. Mem. Editl Bd, Voice of the Unions, 1975–79; Editor, Civil Aviation News, 1978–81. FRSA 2001–08; FILT, then FCILT, 2002–12. *Recreations:* politics (Labour, 1960–69, 1971–2014; Green Party, 2014–), Esperanto, land reform. *Address:* 29 Riverdale Road, Hanworth, Feltham, Middx TW13 6NR. *T:* (020) 8568 9004, 07715 322926. *E:* Dave.C.Wetzel@gmail.com.

**WEYLAND, Joseph;** Ambassador of Luxembourg to United States of America, 2005–08; *b* 24 April 1943; *s* of Adolphe Weyland and Marie Kox; *m* 1st, 1969, France Munhowen; two *s*; 2nd, 1993, Bénédicte Boucqueau. *Educ*: Univ. of Paris (LLD; Dip. of Inst. d'Etudes Politiques). Foreign Ministry, Luxembourg, 1968; served Bonn and EEC, Brussels; Ambassador to UN, NY, 1982; Perm. Rep. to EEC, Brussels, 1985 (Mem., Intergovt Conf. leading to Single European Act, 1985, later Chm., Intergovt Conf. on Political Union leading to Treaty of Maastricht, 1991; Sec.-Gen., Foreign Ministry, Luxembourg, 1992; Ambassador to UK, 1993–2002; Ambassador to NATO and to Belgium, 2003–05. Mem., Reflection Gp, IGC, 1995. *Publications:* (jtly) Le Traité de Maastricht, 1993. *Recreations:* art, sports, music. *Club:* Rotary.

**WEYMAN, Anne Judith,** OBE 2000; FCA; mentor and adviser to chief executives and senior managers, since 2008; *b* 1 Feb. 1943; *d* of Stanley Weyman and Rose Weyman; *m* 1977, Christopher Leonard Bulford; one *d*. *Educ*: Tollington GS; Bristol Univ. (BSc Physics); London Sch. of Econs (BScSoc). FCA 1973. Articled Clerk and Audit Manager, Finnie, Ross, Welch & Co., Chartered Accts, 1964–68; Audit Manager, Foster Weyman & Co., Chartered Accts, 1968–69; Research Officer: LSE, 1972–74; Queen Mary's Hosp., Roehampton, 1974–77; Hd of Finance and Admin, Internat. Secretariat, Amnesty Internat., 1977–86; Dir of Inf. and Public Affairs and Co. Sec., Nat. Children's Bureau, 1986–96; Chief Exec., fpa (Family Planning Assoc.), 1996–2008. Chm., Pinter Publishers Ltd, 1989–95. Mem. (Lab), Westminster CC, 1978–82. Mem., NW Thames RHA, 1978–80; non-executive Director: Islington PCT, 2002–13 (Vice Chm., 2011–13); Haringey PCT, 2011–13; Vice Chair and Chair of Audit, Islington CCG, 2012–15. Vice-Chair: Sexual Health Strategy Reference Gp, 1999–2000; Ind. Adv. Gp on Sexual Health and HIV, 2003–10; Member: Ind. Adv. Gp on Teenage Pregnancy, 2000–07; Women's Nat. Commn, 1999–2003; Bd, Forum UK, 2008–10; GMC, 2009–12; Chm., Programme Develt Gp in Personal Social and Health Educn, 2007–10, and Programme Develt Gp on

Contraception, 2008–10, NICE. Vice Chair: Britain for Europe, 2017–; Eur. Movement, 2018–19. Trustee: Family & Parenting Inst., 2006–12 (Vice-Chair, 2011–12); Galapagos Conservation Trust, 2009–14 (Vice-Chair, 2013–14). Chair, Islington U3A, 2013–17. Hon. Pres., Sex Educn Forum (Founder, 1987). Hon. LLD Bristol, 2005. *Publications*: (with J. Westergaard and P. Wiles) Modern British Society: a bibliography, 1977; (with J. Unell) Finding and Running Premises, 1985; (with S. Capper and J. Unell) Starting and Running a Voluntary Group, 1989; (jtly) RCGP Handbook of Sexual Health in Primary Care, 1998, 2nd edn 2006; (with M. Duggan) Individual Choices, Collective Responsibility: sexual health, a public health issue, 1999; (jtly) Sexual and Reproductive Health and Rights in the UK: 5 years on from Cairo, 1999; articles on health, mental health and sex educn. *Recreations*: travel, theatre, cinema, walking.

**WEYMES, John Barnard**, OBE 1975; HM Diplomatic Service, retired; Managing Director, Cayman Islands News Bureau, Grand Cayman, 1981–83; *b* 18 Oct. 1927; *s* of William Stanley Weymes and Irene Innes Weymes; *m* 1978, Beverley Pauline Gliddon; three *c* by a previous marr. *Educ*: Dame Allan's Sch., Newcastle upon Tyne; King's Coll., Durham Univ., Newcastle upon Tyne. Served HM Forces, 1945–48. Foreign Office, 1949–52; 3rd Sec., Panama City, 1952–56; 2nd Sec., Bogotá, 1957–60; Vice-Consul, Berlin, 1960–63; Dep. Consul, Tamsui, Taiwan, 1963–65; 1st Sec., FCO, 1965–68; Prime Minister's Office, 1968–70; Consul, Guatemala City, 1970–74; 1st Sec., FCO, 1974–77; Consul-Gen., Vancouver, 1977–78; Ambassador to Honduras, 1978–81. *Recreations*: outdoor sport, partic. cricket; chess, reading. *Address*: Holmesdale, Lower Lane, Dalwood, Axminster, Devon EX13 7EG. *T*: (01404) 881114. *Club*: MCC.

**WEYMOUTH, Viscount; Ceawlin Henry Laszlo Thynn;** Director: Longleat Enterprises, since 2010; Cheddar Caves, since 2010; *b* 6 June 1974; *s* and *heir* of Marquess of Bath, *qv*, *m* 2013, Emma Clare McQuistan; two *s*. *Heir*: *s* Hon. John Alexander Ladi Thynn, *b* 26 Oct. 2014.

**WHALAN, Mark Andrew;** Taxing Master of the Senior Courts Costs Office (Costs Judge), since 2015; *b* Middlesbrough, 25 May 1965; *s* of Maurice and Marion Whalan; *m* 1994, Catherine Waugh; two *s* one *d*. *Educ*: Churchill Comprehensive Sch., Som; Univ. of Leeds (BA Hons Hist. 1986); City Univ., London (DipLaw 1987); Inns of Court Sch. of Law. Called to the Bar, Middle Temple, 1988; in practice as barrister, 1988–2015. *Publications*: Road Traffic Accident Claims, 1999; (contrib.) Curran's Personal Injury Pleadings, 3rd edn 2005; (ed jtly) Encyclopedia of Insurance Law (looseleaf), 2009–. *Recreations*: football, specifically following the England football team, home and away, worship in the C of E (Church Warden), art of the St Ives School. *Address*: 31 Beverley Crescent, Bedford MK40 4BX. *T*: (01234) 219357, 07715 803371. *E*: master.whalan@ejudiciary.net; whalanfamily@hotmail.com. *Clubs*: England Supporters, Bristol City Football; Somerset County Cricket.

**WHALEN, Sir Geoffrey (Henry),** Kt 1995; CBE 1989; FIMI, FIPD; Chairman, Camden Motors Ltd, 1996–2012; Director, Camden Ventures Ltd, 2012–17; *b* 8 Jan. 1936; *s* of Henry and Mabel Whalen; *m* 1961, Elizabeth Charlotte; two *s* three *d*. *Educ*: Magdalen College, Oxford (MA Hons Modern History). National Coal Board, Scotland (industrial relations), 1959–66; Divl Personnel Manager, A. C. Delco Div., General Motors, Dunstable, 1966–70; British Leyland, 1970–78; Personnel Dir, Leyland Cars, 1975–78; Personnel Dir, Rank Hovis McDougall Bakeries Div., 1978–80; Personnel and Indust. Rel. Dir, 1980–81; Asst Man. Dir, 1981–84; Talbot Motor Co.; Man. Dir, 1984–95, Dep. Chm., 1990–2003, Peugeot Motor Co. plc. Director: Coventry Bldg Soc., 1992–2006 (Chm., 1999–2005); Novar (formerly Caradon) plc, 1996–2005; Chm., Hills Precision Components Ltd, 1990–2001. Pres., SMMT, 1988–90 and 1993; Chm., Coventry and Warwicks TEC, 1990–94. FIMI 1986; FCGI 1989; CCMI (CBIM 1987). Hon. DBA Coventry Univ., 1995. Midlander of the Year Award, Bass Mitchells & Butlers Ltd, 1988; Midlands Businessman of the Year, 1992. Chevalier de la Légion d'Honneur (France), 1990. *Address*: Victoria Lodge, 8 Park Crescent, Abingdon, Oxon OX14 1DF. *Club*: Oxford and Cambridge.

**WHALEY, Prof. Joachim,** PhD, LittD; FBA 2015; FRHistS; Professor of German History and Thought, University of Cambridge, since 2013; Fellow, Gonville and Caius College, Cambridge, since 1987; *b* Dulwich, London, 25 Aug. 1954; *s* of John Whaley and Elselore Whaley; *m* 2000, Alice Castle. *Educ*: St Joseph's Acad., Blackheath, London; Christ's Coll., Cambridge (BA Hons Hist. 1975). PhD 1983, LittD 2013, Cantab. FRHistS 1984. University of Cambridge: Fellow and Lectr in Hist., Christ's Coll., 1976–78; Fellow and Lectr in Hist., Robinson Coll., 1978–86; Department of German: Asst Lectr, 1980–84; Lectr, 1984–2000; Sen. Lectr, 2000–13; Hd of Dept, 2001–05; Lectr in Mod. Langs, 1987–; Sen. Tutor, 1989–98, Gonville and Caius Coll. FHEA 2001. Pilkington Teaching Prize, Univ. of Cambridge, 2010. *Publications*: (ed) Mirrors of Mortality: studies in the social history of death, 1981, reissued 2011; Religious Toleration and Social Change in Hamburg 1529–1819, 1985 (trans. German, 1992); Germany and the Holy Roman Empire, 2 vols, 2012 (trans. German 2014); The Holy Roman Empire: a very short introduction, 2018 (trans. German 2018); articles in learned jls. *Recreation*: visiting historic houses and museums. *Address*: Gonville and Caius College, Cambridge CB2 1TA. *T*: (01223) 332454. *E*: jw10005@cam.ac.uk. *Clubs*: Athenæum, Lansdowne.

**WHALLEY, Dr Caroline Elizabeth,** CBE 2015; Founder, Elliot Foundation, since 2011, and Chair, Elliot Foundation Academies Trust; *b* Chesterfield, Derbys, 4 Jan. 1951; *d* of Jonathon Henry Weaver and Elizabeth Weaver (*née* Oag); *m* 1970, William Edgar Whalley (*d* 2015); two *s* (and one *s* decd). *Educ*: CNAA (Cert Ed 1974); Open Univ. (BA 1988); Adv. Dip. Applied Mgt 1989; MA 1990); University Coll. London (Dip. Clin. Hypnosis); Brunel Univ. (EdD 2000). Jl Publications, CUP, 1969–71; BBC Enterprises, 1974–77; Adult trng and access progs, UCLA, 1977–79; Industrial Arts design co., 1979–81; London Borough of Ealing: secondary sch. teacher, 1981–89; Advisory Teacher, TVEI, 1989–91; Project Co-ordinator, Recruitment, Induction and Retention, 1991–94; London Borough of Hillingdon: Mgt Develt Manager, 1994–98; Sen. Advr, Orgnl Develt, 1997–98; Chief Inspector, 1998–99; Chief Inspector and Dir, Schs, 1999–2002, Exec. Dir, 2002–04, London Bor. of Ealing; Dir, Educn and Trng, Babcock Internat., 2004–07; Academic Dir, Reed Learning, 2007–10; Sen. Consultant, Innovation Unit, DFE, 2007–10. Non-exec. Dir, Ealing PCT, 2006–09. Vis. Prof., Bedford Univ., 2013–16. Trustee, Shine, 2002–17; Mem., Floreat, 2015–. *Publications*: Mentoring: resources for school based development, 1993; Learning About Learning, 2000; contribs to TES, Mgt in Educn, Local Govt Chronicle. *Recreations*: silver smithing, painting, sculpture, writing. *E*: caroline.whalley@elliotfoundation.co.uk.

**WHALLEY, Jeffrey;** Chairman and Chief Executive, Gartland Whalley & Barker plc, 2005–08 (Director, 1995–2008); Chairman, Tangent (formerly Ofquest) Office Furniture Ltd, 2009–17; *b* 20 Nov. 1942; *s* of William Henry and Elsie Whalley; *m* 1st, 1965; three *s*; 2nd, 1996, Karn Jane Jamieson. *Educ*: Grammar School and Polytechnic. Managing Director: Dynamo Electrical Services, 1970–75; Whipp & Bourne Switchgear, 1975–80; FKI Electricals, 1980–87; Man. Dir and Dep. Chm., FKI Babcock, 1987–89; Jt Dep. Chm., Babcock International, 1989–95; Man. Dir, Gartland & Whalley Securities, later Gartland Whalley & Barker Ltd, 1989–95; Chairman: FKI, 1991–99; British Aluminium plc, 1996–2006; Whalley Jones Hldgs Ltd, 2009–16. Non-exec. Dir, Towcester Racecourse Ltd, 1998–2006. FRSA; FInstD. *Recreations*: tennis, fishing, football.

**WHALLEY, John Mayson,** FRTPI; FRIBA; PPLI; Principal, JMW International, since 1994; *b* 14 Sept. 1932; *s* of George Mayson Whalley and Ada Florence Cairns; *m* 1966, Elizabeth Gillian Hide; one *s* two *d*. *Educ*: Grammar Sch., Preston; Univ. of Liverpool (BArch, 1st Cl. Hons; Sir Charles Reilly Medal and Prize for thesis design, 1956; MCivic Des.); Univ. of Pennsylvania (MLandscape Arch). FLI 1970. Leverhulme and Italian Govt Fellowships for study in Scandinavia and Univ. of Rome, 1957; Fulbright Schol., 1958; Manchester Soc. of Architects Winstanley Fellowship, 1965. Asst architect to Sir Frederick Gibberd, Harlow, 1956; architect/landscape architect: Oskar Stonorov, Philadelphia, 1958–60; Grenfell Baines and Hargreaves Building Design Partnership, Preston, 1960–62; Associate, 1963–68, Sen. Partner, 1968–93, Derek Lovejoy & Partners. Design Co-ordinator, Kishiwada Port Develt Corp., Osaka, Japan, 1997–2001; Special Advr, Takemoto Foods Co. Ltd, 2013–. Chm., NW Region, RIBA, 1984–85; President: Manchester Soc. of Architects, 1980–81; Landscape Inst., 1985–87; Mem. Council, National Trust, 1989–94; Trustee and Dir, Rural Heritage (formerly Rural Bldgs Preservation) Trust, 1996–2002; Chm., Rivington Heritage Trust, 1997–2004; Pres., Preston Grammar Sch. Assoc., 2009–14. Civic Trust awards: W Burton Power Stn, 1968; Cheshire Constabulary HQ, 1969; Rochdale Canal, 1973; Royal Life Offices, Peterborough, 1992; design competitions 1st prizes: Cergy-Pontoise Urban Park, 1970; La Courneuve Regional Park, Paris, 1972; Liverpool Anglican Cathedral precinct, 1982; Urban Park, Vitoria-Gasteiz, 1991; Regional Park, Mito City, Japan, 1992; Garden Festivals: Liverpool, 1982; Stoke-on-Trent, 1983; Glasgow, 1985. Civic Trust awards assessor, 1970–94; UN Tech. Expert, Riyadh, 1975. Mem., Ordre des Architectes de France; FRSA. Contribs to radio and TV. *Publications*: Selected Architects Details, 1958; articles in professional jls. *Recreations*: using imagination – to play jazz piano, opening for Lancashire and England, playing twenty pounds salmon and owning French vineyard! *Address*: Dilworth House, Longridge, Preston, Lancs PR3 3ST. *T*: (01772) 783262. *E*: johnmwhalley@aol.com. *Clubs*: Ronnie Scott's; St James's (Manchester).

**WHALLEY, Robert Michael,** CB 2005; Independent Reviewer, Justice and Security (Northern Ireland) Act 2007, 2008–14; *b* 17 Feb. 1947; *s* of William Lambert Whalley and Edith Mary Whalley; *m* 1981, Teresa Jane, *yr d* of Dr D. W. Hall; three *d*. *Educ*: King Edward's Sch., Birmingham (Foundn Schol.); Pembroke Coll., Cambridge (MA; Searle Prize). Home Office, 1970–72; Private Sec. to Sec. of State for NI, 1972–73; Principal, 1975, Private Sec. to Perm. Sec., 1978–80, Home Office; Cabinet Office, 1980–82; Private Sec. to Lord President of the Council, 1983; Home Office: Asst Sec., Prison Dept, 1984–87; Emergency Planning Div., 1987–89; Sec., Hillsborough Stadium Disaster Inquiry, 1989–90; Personnel Dept, 1990–93; Dir, Immigration and Nationality Policy, 1993–2000; Hd of Unit, Organised and Internat. Crime Directorate, 2000–03; Dir, Crime Reduction and Community Safety Gp, 2003–05. Consulting Sen. Fellow, IISS, 2006–11; Vis. Fellow, Cranfield Univ., 2008–11; Visiting Lecturer: Swedish Nat. Defence Coll., 2007–; Geneva Centre for Security Policy, 2008–11; ETH Zürich, 2010–14; Loughborough Univ. in London, 2015–. Consultant, ICF Internat., 2010–17. *Recreations*: gardens, music. *Address*: c/o Home Office, 2 Marsham Street, SW1P 4DF.

**WHARFE, Dr James Richard;** independent environment consultant, since 2014; Senior Scientific Advisor, Environment Agency, 2010–14 (Head of Science Programmes, 2004–10); *b* Hertford, 7 Dec. 1947; *s* of late Harry Wharfe and Constance Wharfe (*née* Brown); partner, Caroline Budd; three *s* one *d*. *Educ*: Hertford Grammar Sch.; Sir John Cass Coll., Univ. of London (BSc 1st Cl. Hons Applied Biol.; PhD Envmtl Pollution 1976). Posts with DoE, MAFF and Welsh Water Authy; Regl Biologist, Southern Water Authy, 1981–87; Regl Scientist, NRA, 1988–96; Hd, Nat. Centre for Hazardous Substances, EA, 1997–2004. Chair, Sci. Adv. Gp, Resource Recovery from Waste prog., NERC, 2013–; Member: Ministerial Marine Sci. Coordinating Cttee, 2009–14; Sci. and Innovation Strategy Bd, 2010–13, Valuing Nature Prog. Adv. Gp, 2015–, Exec. Bd, Unconventional Hydrocarbons Prog., 2019, NERC; Res. and Innovation Steering Cttee, UK Water, 2013–15; Res. and Innovation Steering Gp, UK Water Partnership, 2015–; Science and Technology Facilities Council: Chair: Global 21st Century Networks Panel, 2019; Challenge Led Applied Systems Prog., 2019; Mem., Adv. Panel, Innovation Partnership Scheme, 2019. NERC Advr, UK Energy Res. Centre Funders Gp, 2014–. *Publications*: (ed jtly) Toxic Waste Impact on the Aquatic Environment, 1996; contrib. scientific papers to jls. *Recreation*: fitness fanatic. *Address*: 2 Cedar Chase, Cross Lane, Findon, W Sussex BN14 0US. *T*: (01903) 872696.

**WHARMBY, Debbie;** *see* Wiseman, D.

**WHARNCLIFFE, 5th Earl of,** *cr* 1876; **Richard Alan Montagu Stuart Wortley;** Baron Wharncliffe 1826; Viscount Carlton 1876; President, Royal Construction Services, Maine, USA; *b* 26 May 1953; *s* of Alan Ralph Montagu-Stuart-Wortley (*d* 1986) and Virginia Anne (*d* 1993), *d* of W. Martin Claybaugh; *S* cousin, 1987; *m* 1st, 1979, Mary Elizabeth Reed (*d* 2005); three *s*; 2nd, 2013, Jessica Caroline Rathbun. *Heir*: *s* Viscount Carlton, *qv*.

**WHARTON, 12th Baron** *cr* 1544–45; **Myles Christopher David Robertson;** *b* 1 Oct. 1964; *e s* of Baroness Wharton (11th in line) and Henry McLeod Robertson; *S* mother, 2000; *m* 2003, Barbara Kay, *d* of Colin Paul Marshall; one *d*. *Educ*: King's Coll., Wimbledon. *Heir*: *d* Hon. Meghan Ziki Mary Robertson, *b* 8 March 2006.

**WHARTON, James Stephen;** Chairman, UK Corporate and Public Affairs, Hume Brophy, since 2018; *b* Stockton-on-Tees, 16 Feb. 1984; *s* of Stephen Wharton and Karen Wharton. *Educ*: Yarm Sch., Yarm; St Peter's Sch., York; Durham Univ. (LLB Hons); Coll. of Law, York. Admitted solicitor, 2008; Solicitor, BHP Law, Darlington and Stockton. MP (C) Stockton S, 2010–17; contested (C) same seat, 2017. Parly Under-Sec. of State, DCLG, 2015–16, DFID, 2016–17. Advr, Aquind Ltd, 2017–. *Recreation*: walking, usually whilst delivering leaflets.

**WHARTON, Rt Rev. (John) Martin,** CBE 2011; Bishop of Newcastle, 1997–2014; an Honorary Assistant Bishop: Diocese of Europe, since 2016; Diocese of Southwark, since 2016; Diocese of London, since 2016; *b* 6 Aug. 1944; *s* of John and Marjorie Wharton; *m* 1970, Marlene Olive Duckett; two *s* one *d*. *Educ*: Van Mildert Coll., Durham (BA 1969); Linacre Coll., Oxford (BA 1971; MA 1976); Ripon Hall, Oxford, 1969. Ordained: deacon, 1972, priest, 1973; Assistant Curate: St Peter, Birmingham, 1972–75; St John the Baptist, Croydon, 1975–77; Dir of Pastoral Studies, Ripon Coll., Cuddesdon, 1977–83; Asst Curate, Cuddesdon, 1979–83; Exec. Sec., Bd of Ministry and Training, dio. of Bradford, 1983–91; Hon. Canon, Bradford Cathedral, 1984; Bishop's Officer for Ministry and Training, 1992; Residentiary Canon, Bradford Cathedral, 1992; Area Bishop of Kingston-upon-Thames, 1992–97. *Recreation*: sport. *Address*: 20 Thamespoint, Fairways, Teddington TW11 9PP.

**WHARTON, Malcolm,** CBE 2012; education business consultant, since 2012; Principal, Hartpury College, Gloucester, 1990–2012; *b* Penrith, 19 Nov. 1948; *s* of Robinson Wharton and Mary Wharton; *m* 1990, Sarah Newham; one *s* four *d*. *Educ:* Kirkby Stephen Grammar Sch.; Royal Agricultural Coll. (NDA Agric.); Univ. of Birmingham (PGCE); Coll. of St Mark and St John (BEd Hons). Lectr, Bicton Coll., 1973–84; Vice Principal, Duchy Coll., Cornwall, 1984–90. Rugby Football Union: Mem., Council, 2011–; Mem., 2013–, Chm., 2013–18, Community Game Bd; Chm. Council, BEF, 2018–. Chm., Rugby Football Foundn, 2015–. Trustee, British Eventing Charitable Trust, 2014–. *Recreations:* Rugby, fly fishing, sea fishing, eventing, dog walking. *Address:* Pendragon, Lodge Lane, Axminster, Devon EX13 5RT. *T:* (01297) 32020. *E:* malcolmwharton@hotmail.com.

**WHATELY, Helen Olivia Bicknell;** MP (C) Faversham and Mid Kent, since 2015; Parliamentary Under-Secretary of State, Department for Digital, Culture, Media and Sport, since 2019; *b* Surrey, 23 June 1976; *m* Marcus Whately; one *s* two *d*. *Educ:* Lady Margaret Hall, Oxford (BA PPE 1998). Consultant, PricewaterhouseCoopers, 1998–2001; Manager, Strategic Alliances Gp, AOL Europe, 2003–05; Sen. Manager, AOL UK, 2005–06; Advr to Shadow Sec. of State for Culture, Media and Sport, 2006–07; Engagement Manager, and Associate, McKinsey & Co., 2007–15. PPS to Minister of State for Trade and Investment, 2016–17, to Sec. of State for Educn and Minister for Women and Equalities, 2017–18, to Minister without Portfolio and Cons. Party Chm., 2018. Mem., Health Select Cttee, 2015–17; Co-Chair, All Pty Parly Gp on Health, 2015–; Vice-Chair, All Pty Parly Gp on Mental Health, 2015 (Chair, 2016–18). Dep. Chair, Cons. Party, 2019– (Vice-Chair for Women, 2018–19). Contested (C) Kingston and Surbiton, 2010. *Address:* House of Commons, SW1A 0AA.

**WHATELY, Kevin;** actor; *b* 6 Feb. 1951; *s* of late Richard Whately and Mary Whately (*née* Pickering); *m* 1984, Madelaine Newton; one *s* one *d*. *Educ:* Barnard Castle Sch.; Central Sch. of Speech and Drama. Theatre, incl. Old Vic Co., 1975–82; Gypsy, Chichester, 2014; *television:* rôles include: Neville in Auf Wiedersehen Pet, 1982–2002; Sgt Lewis in Inspector Morse, 1986–2001; Jack Kerruish in Peak Practice, 1992–95; Inspector Lewis in Lewis, 2005–15; Joe in Joe Maddison's War, 2010; *films:* rôles include: Hardy in The English Patient, 1996. Ambassador for: Prince's Trust, 1992–; Alzheimer's Soc., 2007–; Vice-Pres., Action for Children (formerly NCH), 2003–; Patron, Sparks, 1993–; Trustee: Winship Foundn, 2010–; Wavendon Foundn, 2017–. Ambassador for: Newcastle and Gateshead, 2002–; City of Sunderland, 2005–. Hon. Fellow, Royal Central Sch. of Speech and Drama, 2013. Hon. DCL Northumbria, 2000; Hon. DArts Bedfordshire, 2013. *Recreation:* charity golf (Captain, Variety Club of GB Golf Soc., 2013). *Address:* c/o Caroline Dawson Associates, 4th Floor, 167–169 Kensington High Street, W8 6SH. *T:* (020) 7937 2749, *Fax:* (020) 7937 5120. *Club:* Bamburgh Castle Golf.

**WHATLEY, Prof. Frederick Robert,** FRS 1975; Sherardian Professor of Botany, Oxford University, 1971–91; Fellow of Magdalen College, Oxford, since 1971; *b* 26 Jan. 1924; *s* of Frederick Norman Whatley and Maud Louisa (*née* Hare); *m* 1951, Jean Margaret Smith Bowie; two *d*. *Educ:* Bishop Wordsworth's Sch., Salisbury; (Scholar) Selwyn Coll., Cambridge University (BA, PhD). Benn W. Levy Student, Cambridge, 1947. Sen. Lectr in Biochemistry, Univ. of Sydney, 1950–53; Asst Biochemist, Univ. of California at Berkeley, 1954–58; Associate Biochemist, 1959–64; Guggenheim Fellowship (Oxford and Stockholm), 1960; Prof. of Botany, King's Coll., London, 1964–71. Vis. Fellow, ANU, 1979. *Publications:* articles and reviews in scientific jls. *Address:* 12 The Swallows, Patron's Way West, Denham Garden Village, Denham UB9 5PB.

**WHATMORE, Prof. Sarah Jane,** PhD, DSc; FBA 2014; Professor of Environment and Public Policy, since 2004, and Head, Social Sciences Division, since 2018, University of Oxford (Head, School of Geography and the Environment, 2012–15); Fellow, Keble College, Oxford, since 2012; *b* 25 Sept. 1959; *d* of late Col Denys Edwin Whatmore and of (Freda) Pauline Whatmore. *Educ:* University Coll. London (BA Hons 1st cl. (Geog.) 1981; MPhil Town Planning 1983; PhD (Geog.) 1988); Univ. of Bristol (DSc 2000); MA Oxon 2004. Policy Res. Officer, GLC, 1983–84; Res. Associate, Dept of Geog., UCL, 1984–87; Lectr, Dept of Geog., Univ. of Leeds, 1988–89; University of Bristol: Lectr, 1989–93, Reader, 1993–99, in Human Geog.; Prof. of Human Geog., 1999–2001; Prof. of Envmtl Geog., OU, 2001–04. Mem., Sci. Adv. Council, DEFRA, 2015–Dec. 2020 (Chm., Social Sci. Expert Gp, 2016–Dec. 2020). FRGS 1994 (Mem. Council, 2004–07; Vice Pres., 2014–16; Chm., RGS/IBG Annual Conf., 2015); FAcSS (AcSS 2002). Cuthbert Peek Award, RGS, 2003. *Publications:* Farming Women: gender, work and family enterprise, 1991; Hybrid Geographies: natures, cultures, spaces, 2002; (ed jtly) Using Social Theory: thinking through research, 2003; (with Thrift) Cultural Geography: critical concepts, 2004; (ed jtly) Dictionary of Human Geography, 5th edn 2009; (with Braun) Political Matter: technoscience, democracy and public life, 2010; numerous other ed vols, book chapters, papers in learned jls and policy reports. *Recreations:* gardening, antiquarian books, modern art. *Address:* Social Sciences Division, University of Oxford, Hayes House, 75 George Street, Oxford OX1 2BQ.

**WHATMOUGH, Rev. Michael Anthony, (Tony);** Vicar, St Michael and All Angels, Headingley, Leeds, since 2014 (Priest-in-charge, 2012–14); Team Rector, Headingley Team Ministry, since 2014; *b* 14 Oct. 1950; *s* of Derrick and Molly Whatmough; *m* 1st, 1975, Jean Macdonald Watt (marr. diss. 2004); two *s* two *d*; 2nd, 2006, Catherine, *d* of Richard and Margaret Ainley. *Educ:* Exeter Univ. (BA 1972); Edinburgh Univ. (BD 1981). ARCO 1972. Teacher of music, Forrester High Sch., Edinburgh, 1973–74; Sub-Organist, Old St Paul's Church, Edinburgh, 1973–78; Music Master, George Watson's Coll., Edinburgh, 1974–78; ordained deacon, 1981, priest, 1982; Curate, St Hilda and St Fillan, Edinburgh, 1981–84; Vis. Lectr in Music, Faculty of Divinity, Edinburgh Univ., 1981–84; Curate and Rector, Salisbury St Thomas, 1984–93; Rural Dean, Salisbury, 1990–93; Vicar, St Mary Redcliffe, Bristol, 1993–2005; Teacher of RE, Fair Oaks Business and Enterprise Coll., Rugeley, 2005–11; non-stipendiary priest, parishes of Coven and Bilbrook, Dio. Lichfield, 2008; Associate Minister, St Luke and St Barnabas, Cannock, with St Thomas, Huntingdon, 2010–12. *Recreations:* playing clavichord and organ, cooking, hill walking with our Springer Spaniel, singing. *Address:* Headingley Vicarage, 16 Shire Oak Road, Leeds LS6 2DE. *T:* (0113) 274 3238. *E:* tony@whatmough.org.uk.

**WHEADON, Richard Anthony;** Principal, Elizabeth College, Guernsey, 1972–88, retired; *b* 31 Aug. 1933; *s* of Ivor Cecil Newman Wheadon and Margarita Augusta (*née* Cash); *m* 1961, Ann Mary (*née* Richardson); three *s*. *Educ:* Cranleigh Sch.; Balliol Coll., Oxford (MA Physics). Commissioned RAF, 1955 (Sword of Honour); Air Radar Officer, 1955–57; Asst Master, Eton Coll., 1957–66; Dep. Head Master and Head of Science Dept, Dauntsey's Sch., 1966–71. Mem., Wilts Educn Cttee's Science Adv. Panel, 1967–71. Rowed bow for Oxford, 1954, for GB in European Championships and Olympic Games, 1956; Captain RAF VIII, 1956 and 1957; Olympic Selector and Nat. Coach, 1964–66. Contingent Comdr, Dauntsey's Sch. CCF, 1969–70; Sqdn Leader, RAFRO, 1970–. Reader, C of E, dio. of Winchester, 1995–2013, now Emeritus Reader; Member: Guernsey Standing Adv. Council for Religious Educn, 1997–2003; Diocesan Readers' Selection Bd, 1998–2013; Admin. Sec., 2001–03, Hon. Sec., 2003–05, Guernsey Readers' Centre. *Publications:* The Principles of Light and Optics, 1968. *Recreations:* French horn, photography, electronics, singing, sailing, words. *Address:* L'Enclos Gallienne, Rue du Court Laurent, Torteval, Guernsey, Channel Islands GY8 0LH. *T:* (01481) 264988.

**WHEARE, Thomas David,** MA; Headmaster of Bryanston School, 1983–2005; *b* 11 Oct. 1944; *s* of late Sir Kenneth Wheare, CMG, FBA, and Lady (Joan) Wheare; *m* 1977, Rosalind Clare Spice; two *d*. *Educ:* Dragon Sch.; Magdalen College Sch., Oxford; King's Coll., Cambridge (BA, MA); Christ Church, Oxford (DipEd). Assistant Master, Eton College, 1967–76; Housemaster of School House, Shrewsbury School, 1976–83. Chm., HMC, 2000 (Hon. Treas., 1993–98). Ed., Conference & Common Room, 2005–. FRSA 1989. *Recreations:* music, supporting Arsenal FC. *Address:* 63 Chapel Lane, Zeals, Warminster, Wilts BA12 6NP.

**WHEAT, Rev. Fr (Charles Donald) Edmund,** SSM; Assistant Curate (Non-Stipendiary Minister), St John, South Bank, diocese of York, 2003–07; *b* 17 May 1937; *s* of Charles and Alice Wheat. *Educ:* Kelham Theol Coll.; Nottingham Univ. (BA); Sheffield Univ. (MA). Curate, St Paul's, Arbourthorne, Sheffield, 1962–67; licensed, Dio. Southwell, 1967–70; Mem., SSM, 1969–; Chaplain, St Martin's Coll., Lancaster, 1970–73; Prior, SSM Priory, Sheffield, 1973–75; Curate, St John, Ranmoor and Asst Chaplain, Sheffield Univ., 1975–77, Chaplain 1977–80; Provincial, English Province, 1981–91, Dir, 1982–89, Provincial Bursar, 1992–98, Provincial of European Province, 1999–2001, SSM; Vicar, All Saints', Middlesbrough, 1988–95; Prior, St Antony's Priory, Durham, 1998–2001; Vicar, St Thomas', Middlesbrough, 2001–03; licensed, dio. of Oxford, 2011–16. Chaplain: Whitelands Coll., 1996–97; Order of the Holy Paraclete, Whitby, 1997–98, 2008–10. Mem., Gen. Synod, 1975–80. *Recreations:* reading, watching soap operas.

**WHEATCROFT,** Baroness *cr* 2010 (Life Peer), of Blackheath in the London Borough of Greenwich; **Patience Jane Wheatcroft;** Editor-in-Chief, The Wall Street Journal Europe, 2009–11; *b* 28 Sept. 1951; *d* of Anthony Wheatcroft and Ruth Wheatcroft (*née* Frith); *m* 1976, Anthony Salter; two *s* one *d*. *Educ:* Univ. of Birmingham (LLB). Dep. City Ed., The Times, 1984–86; Asst City Ed., Daily Mail, 1986–88; Ed., Retail Week, 1988–93; Dep. City Ed., Mail on Sunday, 1994–97; Business and City Ed., The Times, 1997–2006; Ed., The Sunday Telegraph, 2006–07. Columnist, Sunday Times, 2018–. Non-executive Director: Barclays plc, 2008–09; Shaftesbury plc, 2008–09; FCA Automobiles NV (formerly Fiat SpA), 2012–; St James's Place plc, 2012–; Mem., Adv. Bd, Huawei, 2011–14. Chm., Appointments and Oversight Cttee, FT, 2014–. Mem., Bd of Trustees, British Museum, 2010–18 (Dep. Chm., 2014–18). *Recreations:* ski-ing, opera, theatre.

**WHEATCROFT, Geoffrey Albert;** author; freelance journalist, since 1997; *b* 23 Dec. 1945; *s* of late Stephen Frederick Wheatcroft, OBE and Joy Wheatcroft (*née* Reed); *m* 1990, Sally, *d* of late Frank Muir, CBE and Polly Muir; one *s* one *d*. *Educ:* University Coll. Sch.; New Coll., Oxford (Schol.; MA Modern Hist.); London Coll. of Printing. In publishing, 1968–75: prodn asst, then publicity manager, Hamish Hamilton, 1968–70; editor: Michael Joseph, 1971–73; Cassell & Co., 1974–75; asst ed., 1975–77, Literary Ed., 1977–81, Spectator; reporting and researching in S Africa, 1981–84; Ed., Londoner's Diary, Evening Standard, 1985–86; columnist, Sunday Telegraph, 1987–91; feature writer, Daily Express, 1996–97. *Publications:* The Randlords, 1985; Absent Friends, 1989; The Controversy of Zion, 1996 (Amer. Nat. Jewish Book Award); Le Tour: a history of the Tour de France, 2003, 3rd edn 2013; The Strange Death of Tory England, 2005; Yo, Blair!, 2007. *Recreations:* bibliophily and hypochondria. *Address:* 11 Southstoke Road, Combe Down, Bath BA2 5SJ. *T:* (01225) 835540. *E:* wheaty@compuserve.com. *Clubs:* Garrick, Beefsteak, Colony Room, MCC.

**WHEATER, Prof. Howard Simon,** PhD; FRS(Can); FREng; FICE; CEng; Professor of Hydrology, 1993–2010, now Emeritus, Distinguished Research Fellow, 2010–18, and Senior Research Investigator, since 2018, Department of Civil and Environmental Engineering, Imperial College London; Canada Excellence Research Chair in Water Security, 2010–17, Research Chair Laureate, since 2018, and Founding Director, Global Institute for Water Security, 2011–18, University of Saskatchewan, Canada; *b* 24 June 1949; *s* of late Claude and Marjorie Wheater; *m* 1st, 1970, Elisabeth Anne (marr. diss. 2004); two *s*; 2nd, 2007, Prof. Valerie Susan Isham (marr. diss. 2010); 3rd, 2010, Prof. Patricia Ann Gober. *Educ:* Nottingham High Sch.; Queens' Coll., Cambridge (BA 1971, MA Engrg Scis); Univ. of Bristol (PhD 1977). CEng 1978; FICE 1999. Grad. apprentice, Aero Engine Div., Rolls-Royce Ltd, 1967–72; Res. Asst, Dept of Civil Engrg, Univ. of Bristol, 1972–78; Department of Civil and Environmental Engineering, Imperial College London: Lectr, 1978–87; Sen. Lectr, 1987–90; Reader, 1990–93; Hd, Envmtl and Water Resource Engrg, 1995–2010; Chm., Centre for Envmtl Control and Waste Mgt, 1995–2010; Dir, Envmt Forum, 2008–09. Consultant to Republic of Chile concerning Silala River dispute with Bolivia, at Internat. Court of Justice, 2016–. Mem. and Chair, nat. and internat. adv. panels and cttees, incl. MAFF, DEFRA, Envmt Agency, NERC, UNESCO. Consultant: Northern Oman Flood Study, 1981; to State of Nevada concerning proposed Yucca Mt nuclear waste repository, 2003–; Counsel and Advocate for Republic of Hungary at Internat. Court of Justice concerning GNBS Danube barrage system, 1993–97, for Republic of Argentina, Internat. Court of Justice concerning River Uruguay, 2006–10. Chairman: UNESCO Global Network for Water and Develt Inf. for Arid Lands prog., 2003–; Council of Canadian Academies Expert Panel on Sustainable Mgt of Water in Agricl Landscapes of Canada, 2011–13; Vice-Chm., Scientific Steering Gp, World Climate Prog., Global Energy and Water Experiment, 2010–13; Member: Internat. Ct of Arbitration, Indus Waters Treaty, 2010–13; Alberta Provincial Envmtl Monitoring Panel, 2011. Pres., British Hydrological Soc., 1999–2001. Fellow, Amer. Geophysical Union, 2010. Life Mem., Internat. Water Acad., Oslo. FREng 2003; FRS(Can) 2018. Prince Sultan bin Abdulaziz Internat. Water Prize, 2006; Dooge Medal, IAHS-UNESCO-WMO Internat. Hydrol. Prize, 2018. *Publications:* (ed jtly) Hydrology in a Changing Environment, 3 vols, 1998; (jtly) Rainfall-Runoff Modelling in Gauged and Ungauged Catchments, 2004; (jtly) Biosphere Implications of Deep Disposal of Nuclear Waste: the upwards migration of radionuclides in vegetated soils, 2007; (jtly) Hydrological Modelling in Arid and Semi-Arid Areas, 2008; (jtly) Groundwater Modelling in Arid and Semi-Arid Areas, 2010; 200 refereed papers. *Recreations:* sailing (dinghy racing and yacht cruising), music (orchestral trumpet player). *Address:* University of Saskatchewan, National Hydrology Research Centre, 11 Innovation Boulevard, Saskatoon, SK S7N 3H5, Canada. *E:* howard.wheater@usask.ca.

**WHEATER, Roger John,** OBE 1991; CBiol, FRSB; FRSE; Chairman, National Trust for Scotland, 2000–05; *b* 24 Nov. 1933; *m* 1963, Jean Ord Troup; one *s* one *d*. *Educ:* Brighton, Hove and Sussex Grammar Sch.; Brighton Tech. Coll. Commnd Royal Sussex Regt, 1953; served Gold Coast Regt, 1953–54; 4/5th Bn, Royal Sussex Regt (TA), 1954–56. Served Colonial Police, Uganda, 1956–61; Chief Warden, Murchison Falls Nat. Park, 1961–70; Director: Uganda Nat. Parks, 1970–72; RZSScot, 1972–98. Hon. Prof., Univ. of Edinburgh, 1993–. Mem. Editl Bd, Internat. Zoo Year Book, 1987–99. Consultant, World Tourist Orgn, UN, 1980–2000. Mem., Sec. of State for Scotland's Wkg Gp on Envmtl Educn, 1990–94. Mem., Co-ordinating Cttee, Nuffield Unit of Tropical Animal Ecol.; Chm., Beaver-Salmonid Wkg Gp, Nat. Species Reintroduction Forum, 2009–15; Member: Council, NT for Scotland, 1973–78 and 2000–05 (Mem., Exec. Cttee, 1982–87);

Bd, Scottish Natural Heritage, 1995–99 (Dep. Chm., 1997–99); Strategic Develt Fund Panel, Royal Soc. of Wildlife Trusts, 2008–12; Assessor, Council, Scottish Wildlife Trust, 1973–92 (Pres., 2007–09). Chm., Wkg Party on Zoo Licensing Act, 1981–84. Pres., Assoc. of British Wild Animal Keepers, 1984–99 (Chm., Membership and Licensing Cttee, 1984–91); Chairman, Advisory Committee: Whipsnade Wild Animal Park, 1999–2002; London Zoo, 2002–03. Chm., Fedn of Zool Gardens of GB and Ireland, 1993–96. Dep. Chm., Zoo Forum, 1999–2002; Chairman: Access Forum, 1996–2000; Tourism and Envmt Forum, 1999–2003. Chm., Eur. Assoc. of Zoos and Aquaria, 1994–97; Mem. Council, 1980, Pres., 1988–91, Internat. Union of Dirs of Zool Gdns. Vice-President: Eur. Network of Nat. Heritage Orgns, 2000–05; Scottish Heritage USA, 2001–05. Chm., Cammo Estate Adv. Cttee, 1980–95; Dir, Nat. Park Lodges Ltd; Mem., Uganda Nat. Res. Council; Vice-Chm., Uganda Tourist Assoc. Chm., Anthropoid Ape Adv. Panel, 1977–91. Mem. Council, 1991–92, 1995–99, 2000–03, Vice Pres., 1999, Zool Soc. of London; Mem. Bd, Royal Zool Soc. of Scotland, 2011–. Vice-Pres., World Pheasant Assoc., 1994–. Vice Chm., Edinburgh Br., ESU, 1977–81. Trustee: The Gorilla Orgn (formerly Dian Fossey Gorilla Fund), 1995–2010 (Chm., 2008–10); Thyne Scholarship, 1997– (ESU William Thyne Schol., 1975); and Founder Patron, Dynamic Earth, 1999–2012; Tweed Foundn, 2007–18; Chm., Heather Trust, 1999–2002. Pres., Tweedale Soc., 2007–18; Pres., Probus Club, Innerleithen, Walkerburn and Traquair, 2010–11 (Vice Pres., 2009–10). Gov., Mweka Coll. of Wildlife Mgt, Tanzania, 1970–72. FRSE 1985; FRSB (FIBiol 1987); FRSA 1995. Hon. FRSGS 1995; Hon. FRZSScot 1999. DUniv Open, 2004. *Publications:* numerous papers on wildlife mgt and conservation to professional jls. *Recreations:* country pursuits, painting, gardening. *Address:* 17 Kirklands, Innerleithen, Peeblesshire EH44 6NA. *T:* (01896) 830403. *E:* roger.wheater@btinternet.com. *Clubs:* Edinburgh Special Mobile Angling (Pres., 1982–86), Cockburn Trout Angling (Pres., 1997–2018).

**WHEATLE, Alex Alphonso,** MBE 2008; writer; *b* London, 3 Jan. 1963; *s* of Alfred Wheatle and Almira Gunter (née Panceta Da Costa); *m* 1999, Beverley Robinson; two *s* one *d*. *Educ:* John Ruskin Sch., Shirley, Croydon. *Publications:* Brixton Rock, 1999; East of Acre Lane, 2001; The Seven Sisters, 2002; Checkers, 2004; Island Songs, 2005; The Dirty South, 2008; Brenton Brown, 2011; *for young adults:* Liccle Bit, 2015; Crongton Knights, 2016 (Guardian Children's Fiction Prize); Straight Outta Crongton, 2017; The Kerb-Stain Boys, 2018. *Recreations:* cricket, football, chess, music, youth club work.

**WHEATLEY, Rt Hon. Lord; John Francis Wheatley;** PC 2007; a Senator of the College of Justice in Scotland, 2000–10; *b* 9 May 1941; *s* of John Thomas Wheatley (Baron Wheatley, PC) and late Agnes Nichol; *m* 1970, Bronwen Catherine Fraser; two *s*. *Educ:* Mount St Mary's Coll., Derbyshire; Edinburgh Univ. (BL). Called to the Scottish Bar, 1966; Standing Counsel to Scottish Develt Dept, 1971; Advocate Depute, 1975; Sheriff of Tayside Central and Fife, at Dunfermline, 1979–80, at Perth, 1980–2000; Temp. High Ct Judge, 1992; QC (Scot.) 1993. Chm., Judicial Studies Cttee, 2002–06. *Recreations:* gardening, music. *Address:* Braefoot Farmhouse, Crook of Devon, Fossoway, Kinross-shire KY13 7UL. *T:* (01577) 840212.

**WHEATLEY, Alan Edward,** FCA; Chairman, Burlington Chase Ltd, since 2008; *b* 23 May 1938; *s* of late Edward and of Margaret Wheatley (née Turner); *m* 1962, Marion Frances (née Wilson); two *s* one *d*. *Educ:* Ilford Grammar School. Chartered Accountant. Norton Slade, 1954–60, qualified 1960; joined Price Waterhouse, 1960; admitted to partnership, 1970; Mem., Policy Cttee, 1981–92; Sen. Partner (London Office), 1985–92; Chm., 3i Gp, 1992–93; Dep. Chm., Ashtead Gp, 1994–2003; Chm., Foreign and Colonial Special Utilities, subseq. Special Utilities, Investment Trust plc, 1993–2003. Non-executive Director: EBS Investments (Bank of England sub.), 1977–90; British Steel plc (formerly BSC), 1984–94; Babcock International Gp, 1993–2002; Legal & General Gp, 1993–2002; Forte, 1993–96; N M Rothschild & Sons, 1993–99; Chairman: New Court Financial Services Ltd, 1996–99; Utilico Investment Trust plc, 2003–07; Isis Solar Ltd, 2011–13; Sasial Technologies Ltd, 2007–14; Govt Dir, Cable & Wireless, 1981–84, non-exec. Dep. Chm., 1984–85. Mem., Ind. Develt Adv. Bd, 1985–92. Trustee, V&A Mus., 1996–99. Governor, Solefield School, 1985–95. *Recreations:* golf, bridge. *Club:* Wildernesse (Seal, Kent).

**WHEATLEY, Bruce David;** Programmes Director, Pensions Regulator, since 2019; *b* Brighton; *s* of Captain Walter Wheatley and Ana Wheatley; *m* 1978, Julia Fletcher; two *d*. *Educ:* Brighton, Hove and Sussex Grammar Sch. Practitioner in Prog., Project and Risk Mgt, Office of Govt Commerce; Financial Planning Cert., Chartered Insce Inst.; Cert. of Competence in Occupational Testing, BPsS. Waitrose Ltd: Mgt Trainee, 1976–77; Section Manager, 1977–83; Trng Manager, 1983–88; Proj. Manager, 1988–90; Prudential Assurance: HR Manager, 1990–92; Br. Manager, 1993–97; Sen. Proj. Manager, 1997–2000; HR Dir, Eurolink Consulting, 2000–01; Prog. Dir and IT Dir, Wynnwith Engrg, 2002–04; Prog. Manager, Enterprise Develt Prog., WS Atkins plc and BAA, 2004–05; Prog. Implementation Manager, Phoenix Prog., EDS plc and MoJ, 2006–07; Dir, Shared Services Prog., DIUS, later Dir, Finance Systems, BIS, 2008–09; Hd of Business Solutions, Res. Councils UK Shared Service Centre, 2010–11; Transition Dir, Sussex Health Informatics Service, NHS Sussex, 2012; Dep. Dir, Police ICT Directorate, Home Office, 2013–14; Chief Inf. Officer and Dir of Inf. Mgt and Technol., Central London Community Health NHS Trust, 2014–15; Dir of IT, Surrey and Borders Partnership NHS Foundn Trust, 2016; Chief Information Officer, Brighton and Sussex Univ. Hosp. NHS Trust, 2016–17; Dir of IT, Pensions Regulator, 2018. *Recreation:* nowadays mostly spent with our four gorgeous grandchildren. *Address:* 18 Woodland Avenue, Hove, E Sussex BN3 6BL. *T:* 07979 590864. *E:* brucewheatley@pavilion-it.co.uk.

**WHEATLEY, Catherine;** see Wood, C.

**WHEATLEY, Prof. David John,** MD; British Heart Foundation Professor of Cardiac Surgery, University of Glasgow, 1979–2006; Hon. Consultant Cardiac Surgeon, Glasgow Royal Infirmary, 1979–2006; *b* 2 Aug. 1941; *s* of John Henry Wheatley and Dorothy Wheatley (née Price); *m* 1964, Ann Marie Lamberth; two *d*. *Educ:* South African Coll., Cape Town; Univ. of Cape Town Med. Sch. (MB ChB 1964; ChM 1976; MD 1979). FRCSE 1969; FRCSGlas 1979; FRCPE 1997; FRCS 1998. Senior Registrar: Nat. Heart Hosp., London, 1972–73; Mearnskirk Hosp., Glasgow, 1974–76; Sen. Lectr, Royal Infirmary, Edinburgh, 1976–79. Special Prof., Dept of Cardiothoracic Surgery, Univ. of the Free State, SA, 2005–16; Hon. Prof., Sch. of Sci. and Engrg, Univ. of Dundee, 2018–. Dir, Wheatley Research Ltd, 2015–. Mem. Council, RCSE, 1986–90, 1992–97, 1997–2002; President: Soc. of Cardiothoracic Surgeons of GB and Ireland, 1996–98; European Assoc. for Cardiothoracic Surgery, 1998–99. Mem., Acad. of Med. Scis, 1998. FECTS 2002. *Publications:* Surgery of Coronary Artery Disease, 1986, 2nd edn 2003; author or jt author of 175 articles on cardiac surgery. *Recreations:* piano, classical music, opera. *Address:* 13 Lochend Drive, Bearsden, Glasgow G61 1ED. *T:* (0141) 942 1381.

**WHEATLEY, John Derek,** CBE 1993; Member, National Rivers Authority, 1989–96 (Chief Executive, 1991–92); *b* 24 July 1927; *s* of Leslie Sydney and Lydia Florence Wheatley; *m* 1956, Marie Gowers; one *s* one *d*. *Educ:* Sir Thomas Rich's Sch., Gloucester; Loughborough Coll., 1944–46 (Teacher's Cert.); Carnegie College of Physical Educn, 1952–53 (DipPE). Served RAF, 1946–52; Surrey Education Authority, 1953–54; Central Council of Physical Recreation: London and SE, 1954–58; Secretary, Northern Ireland, 1959–69; Principal Regional Officer, SW, 1970–72; Sports Council: Regional Director, SW, 1972–80; Director of Administrative Services, Headquarters, 1980–83; Dir Gen., 1983–88. Chm., Nat. Small-Bore Rifle Assoc., 1989–95. *Recreations:* gardening, music.

**WHEATLEY, Rt Hon. John Francis;** see Wheatley, Rt Hon. Lord.

**WHEATLEY, Oswald Stephen, (Ossie),** CBE 1997; Chairman, Sports Council for Wales, 1990–99; company director; *b* 28 May 1935; *s* of late Harold Wheatley and Laura Wheatley (née Owens); *m* 1st, 1964, Christine Mary Godwin (*d* 2000); one *s* (two *d* decd); 2nd, 2011, Janet Mary Parry-Jones. *Educ:* King Edward's Sch., Birmingham; Caius Coll., Cambridge (MA Econs and Law). 2nd Lieut, RA, 1954. Cambridge Cricket Blue, 1957–58; played for Warwicks CCC, 1957–60; Glamorgan CCC, 1961–69 (Captain, 1961–66); Chm., Glamorgan CCC, 1977–84. Test and County Cricket Board: Test Selector, 1972–74; Chairman: Discipline Cttee, 1978–83; Cricket Cttee, 1987–95; Mem., England Cttee, 1989–93; Chm., Cricket Foundn, 1996–2008. Member: Sports Council of GB, 1984–88 and 1990–96; UK Sports Council, 1997–99; Broadcasting Council for Wales, 1990–95; Sch. Exam and Assessment Council, 1992–93. Chm., Nat. Sports Medicine Inst., St Bartholomew's Hosp., 1991–96. Hon. Fellow, Cardiff Metropolitan Univ. (Hon. Fellow, Univ. of Wales Inst., 1995). Freeman, City of Newcastle-upon-Tyne, 1976. *Recreations:* sport, art. *Address:* 78 Adventurers Quay, Cardiff Bay, Cardiff CF10 4NQ. *Clubs:* MCC, Free Foresters; Cardiff and County; Glamorgan CC.

**WHEATLEY, Ven. Paul Charles;** Archdeacon of Sherborne and Priest in Charge of West Stafford with Frome Billet, 1991–2003, now Archdeacon Emeritus; *b* 27 May 1938; *s* of Charles Lewis and Doris Amy Wheatley; *m* 1963, Iris Mary Lacey; two *s* one *d*. *Educ:* Wycliffe Coll.; St John's Coll., Durham (BA 1961); Lincoln Theol Coll. Ordained deacon 1963, priest 1964; Curate, Bishopston, Bristol, 1963–68; Youth Chaplain, dio. of Bristol, 1968–73; Team Rector, Dorcan, Swindon, 1973–79; Rector, Ross, Hereford, 1979–81; Team Rector, Ross with Brampton Abbots, Bridstow, Peterstow, 1979–91; Prebendary, Hereford Cathedral, 1987–91; Ecumenical Officer, Hereford, 1987–91; Hon. Canon, Salisbury Cathedral, 1991–2003, now Hon. Canon Emeritus. *Recreations:* travel, gardening, opera. *Address:* The Farthings, Bridstow, Herefordshire HR9 6QF.

**WHEATLEY, Rt Rev. Peter William;** Area Bishop of Edmonton, 1999–2014; an Honorary Assistant Bishop: Diocese of Southwark, since 2013; Diocese of London, since 2015; Diocese of Chichester, since 2015; Priest-in-charge, Christ Church, St Leonards-on-Sea, since 2019; *b* 7 Sept. 1947; *er s* of late William Nobes Wheatley and Muriel (née Ounsted). *Educ:* Ipswich Sch. (Queen's and Foundn Schol.); Queen's Coll., Oxford (Styring Schol., MA); Pembroke Coll., Cambridge (MA); Coll. of the Resurrection, Mirfield; Ripon Hall, Oxford. Deacon 1973, priest 1974; Asst Curate, All Saints, Fulham, 1973–78; Vicar: Holy Cross with St Jude and St Peter, St Pancras, 1978–82; St James, W Hampstead, 1982–95; Priest-in-charge: St Mary, Kilburn, 1982–90; St Mary with All Souls, Kilburn, 1990–95; Curate-in-charge, All Souls, S Hampstead, 1982–90; Archdeacon of Hampstead, 1995–99. Proctor in Convocation and Mem. Gen. Synod, C of E, 1975–95. *Recreation:* music. *Address:* 47 Sedlescombe Road South, St Leonards-on-Sea, E Sussex TN38 0TB. *T:* (01424) 424814. *E:* peter.wheatley@outlook.com.

**WHEATLEY, Philip Martin,** CB 2004; consultant and expert witness on prison operations and their management, since 2016; Director, Wheatley & Roy Associates Ltd, management consultancy, 2012–17; *b* 4 July 1948; *s* of Alan Osborne Wheatley and Ida Mary Wheatley; *m* 1st, 1969, Merryll Angela Francis (marr. diss. 1989); one *s* one *d*; 2nd, 1990, Anne Eleanor Roy. *Educ:* Leeds Grammar Sch.; Sheffield Univ. (LLB Hons). HM Prison Service: Prison Officer, 1969–70; Asst Gov., 1970; Hull Prison, 1971–74; Prison Service Coll., 1974–78; Leeds Prison, 1978–82; Dep. Gov., Gartree Prison, 1982–86; Governor, Hull Prison, 1986–90; Prison Service Area Manager for E Midlands, 1990–92; Asst Dir, Custody Gp, Prison Service HQ, 1992–95; Dir of Dispersals, i/c 6 highest security prisons, 1995–99; Dep. Dir Gen., 1999–2003; Dir Gen., 2003–08; Chief Exec., then Dir Gen., Nat. Offender Mgt Service, MoJ, 2008–10. Non-exec. Dir, NI Prisons Bd, 2010 and 2011–; Member: NI Prison Review Team, 2010–11; Oversight Gp, Prison Officer Professionalisation Prog., 2018, Advr, 2019–, Scottish Prison Service. Associate consultant, G4S, 2011–18. Non-exec. Mem., Mgt Bd, Inst. of Criminology, Univ. of Cambridge, 2017–. Trustee: St Giles Trust, 2010–; Feltham Community Chaplaincy Trust, 2013–17. FRSA. *Recreations:* good wine, good food and holidays to enjoy them, history, current affairs, politics, criminology. *E:* pmwheatley@hotmail.co.uk. *Club:* Reform.

**WHEELDON, David John;** education consultant, since 2016; Headmaster, King Edward VI Five Ways School, Birmingham, 2003–12; Interim Executive Director, Schools of Foundation of King Edward VI in Birmingham, 2016; *b* Newcastle-under-Lyme, 28 Oct. 1949; *s* of John Wheeldon and Edna Wheeldon; *m* 1975, Janet Alexander (*d* 2014); two *s*. *Educ:* Alleyne's Grammar Sch., Uttoxeter, Staffs; Worcester Coll. of Educn (Cert Ed 1971); Univ. of Birmingham (BEd 1972); Birmingham Poly. (BA 1979); Open Univ. (AdvDip Educn Mgt 1987); Coventry Univ. (MSc 1996). Asst teacher, Oswestry High Sch. for Boys, 1972–74; King Edward VI Five Ways School: Hd of Dept of Social Scis and Gen. Studies, 1974–86; Hd of Sixth Form, 1986–89; Dep. Head, 1989–97; Head Master, Altrincham Grammar Sch. for Boys, 1997–2003. Associate Dir, CJHutt Associates, 2012–. Schools of Foundation of King Edward VI in Birmingham: Advr/Consultant, 2012–16; Mem. Bd, 2017–; Mem. Bd, King Edward VI Multi Academy Trust, 2017–. Mem. Exec., Grammar Schs Heads Assoc., 2008–12 (Associate Mem., 2012–). Governor: Bishop Vesey's Grammar Sch., 2012–15; King Edward VI Camp Hill Sch. for Boys, Birmingham, 2014–; King Edward VI Handsworth Sch., 2015– (Chm., 2017–). Mem., Birmingham Lunar Soc., 2011–. FRSA 1993–2014. *Recreations:* local history, antiques, travel, a lapsed bee keeper… and lapsed Rotarian. *Address:* 59 Hill Grove Crescent, Kidderminster, Worcs DY10 3AR. *T:* (01562) 741695. *E:* djwheeldon@btinternet.com. *Club:* Lansdowne.

**WHEELDON, Nusrat Munir;** see Ghani, N. M. Ul-.

**WHEELER, Baroness** *cr* 2010 (Life Peer), of Blackfriars in the City of London; **Margaret Eileen Joyce Wheeler,** MBE 2005; Director of Organisation and Staff Development, UNISON, 1993–2010; *b* 25 March 1949. With COHSE, later UNISON, 1973–2010. Former Mem., Commn on Social Justice. Former Mem., Enquiry Panel into productivity and high performance, DTI/Work Foundn; seconded to Nat. Care Strategy Team, DoH, 2009–11; Mem., Investors in People Adv. Bd, UK Commn for Employment and Skills, 2010–13. House of Lords: Opposition frontbench spokesperson on health and social care, 2010–; an Opposition Whip, 2010–14; an Opposition Sen. Whip, 2014–. Member, All-Party Parliamentary Group: on Stroke, 2010–; on Carers, 2010–. Mem., Specialised Health Care Alliance, 2013– (Chm., 2014–). Trustee: Blackfriars Settlement, 2003–. *Address:* House of Lords, SW1A 0PW.

**WHEELER, Rev. Canon Dr Andrew Charles;** Mission Pastor and Director of Mission Education, St Saviour's Church, Guildford, 2002–16; World Church Advisor (formerly World Mission Advisor), Guildford Diocese, 2006–19; *b* 14 April 1948; *s* of Charles Hildred Wheeler and Ruth Goss Wheeler (née Rhymes); *m* 1979, Susan Jane Snook; one *s* one *d*. *Educ:* Corpus Christi Coll., Cambridge (MA); Makerere Univ., Kampala (MA); Leeds

Univ. (PGCE); Trinity Coll., Bristol (BA Theol.). Asst Master in Hist., Harrogate Granby High Sch., 1972–75; theol teacher, for CMS, Bishop Gwynne Coll., Mundri, Sudan, 1977–86; ordained deacon, 1988, priest, 1988; Asst Curate, Aldbourne, Salisbury dio., 1988–89; Hon. Curate, with resp. for care of Sudanese refugees, 1989–92, Hon. Canon, 2005, All Saints Cathedral, Cairo; Theol Trng Co-ordinator, New Sudan Council of Churches, 1992–96; Sudan Church Res. Project Dir, 1996–2000; Archbishop's Sec. for the Anglican Communion, 2000–01. DD Lambeth, 2008. *Publications*: (Gen. Ed.) Faith in Sudan series, 13 vols, 1997–2000 (ed and contrib. to vols 1, 5 and 6); (jtly) Day of Devastation, Day of Contentment: the history of the Sudanese Church across 2000 years, 2000; (ed) Voices from Africa, 2002; Bombs, Ruins and Honey: journeys of the spirit with Sudanese Christians, 2006; Desire of Nations: the Magi, their journey and the child, 2015. *Recreations*: music, walking, squash.

**WHEELER, Andrew George**; QC 2017; *b* Amersham, Bucks, 17 Nov. 1964; *s* of Colin and Wendy Wheeler; *m* 1992, Kathryn Rowley; three *d*. *Educ*: John Hampden Grammar Sch., High Wycombe; N Staffs Poly. (LLB Hons 1986). Called to the Bar, Lincoln's Inn, 1988; in practice as barrister specialising in complex and commercial fraud, 1988–. *Recreations*: family, live music, cricket, football, ski-ing. *Address*: 7 Bedford Row Chambers, Bedford Row, WC1R 4BS. *T*: (020) 7400 7300. *E*: clerks@7br.co.uk.

**WHEELER, Anthony Ian**, AO 2014; Co-founder, 1973, and Joint Director, 1973–2007, Lonely Planet Publications; Co-Founder and Director, Planet Wheeler Foundation, since 2007; *b* 20 Dec. 1946; *s* of late Ian James Wheeler and Hilary Audrey Wheeler; *m* 1971, Maureen Dixon; one *s* one *d*. *Educ*: Warwick Univ. (BSc); London Business Sch. (MSc). *Publications*: Across Asia on the Cheap, 1973; South-East Asia on a Shoestring, 1975; Australia, 1977; New Zealand, 1977; West Asia on a Shoestring, 1978; Papua New Guinea, 1978; Burma, 1979; Sri Lanka, 1979; India, 1981; Malaysia, Singapore and Brunei, 1981; Bali and Lombok, 1984; Rarotonga and the Cook Islands, 1986; Islands of Australia's Great Barrier Reef, 1990; Nepal, 1990; Japan, 1991; Dublin, 1993; Britain, 1995; San Francisco, 1996; Tahiti and French Polynesia, 1996; Chasing Rickshaws, 1998; Tahiti and French Polynesia: diving and snorkeling, 2001; Time and Tide: the Islands of Tuvalu, 2001; Rice Trails, 2004; East Timor, 2004; Falkland Islands and South Georgia, 2004; Once While Travelling: the Lonely Planet story, 2005; Bad Lands: a tourist on the axis of evil, 2007; Dark Lands, 2013; On Travel, 2018; Islands of Australia, 2019. *Recreations*: walking, trekking, scuba diving, running, cycling, travel (as much as possible). *E*: tony@tonywheeler.com.au.

**WHEELER, Captain Arthur Walter**; RN retd; CEng; Keeper, HMS Belfast, 1983–88; *b* 18 Oct. 1927; *s* of Walter Sidney Wheeler and Annie Ethel Marsh; *m* 1st, 1957, Elizabeth Jane Glendinning Bowman (marr. diss. 1968); two *s*; 2nd, 1968, Mary Elvis Findon; one *s*. *Educ*: Woodhouse Sch., Finchley; HMS Fisgard, Torpoint; RN Engineering Coll., Manadon. FIMechE, MIMarE. Joined Royal Navy as artificer apprentice, 1943; served in cruiser Birmingham, 1947–50. Progressively, Sub Lieut 1950 to Captain 1974. Served in frigate Palliser and aircraft carriers Bulwark, Hermes and Ark Royal 1954–74; Sea Trng Staff at Portland, 1961–63; MoD, Ship Dept, 1966–70 and 1975–78; CSO(Engrg) to Flag Officer Third Flotilla, 1979–80; HMS Daedalus in comd, 1980–82, retired. Received into RC Church, 1987; returned to C of E, 2008. *Recreations*: music, reading, painting, walking.

**WHEELER, (Belinda) Christian**; *see* Rucker, B. C.

**WHEELER, David Arthur**; Founder and Editor, Hortus, since 1987; *b* Thrupp, Glos, 2 Oct. 1945; *s* of Arthur Wheeler and Lily Wheeler (*née* Eckford). *Educ*: none. Advertising Executive: Southern Evening Echo, Southampton, 1963–70; Observer, 1970–75; Advertising Manager, Spectator, 1975–79; Campaigns Dir, RSPCA, 1979–82; jobbing gardener, 1982–87. Founder, Convivium: the journal of good eating, 1993. Gold Veitch Meml Medal, RHS, 2009. *Publications*: (ed) By Pen and By Spade, 1990; (ed) The Generous Garden, 1991; Panorama of English Gardens, 1991; Over the Hills from Broadway: images of Cotswold gardens, 1991; (ed) The Penguin Book of Garden Writing, 1996. *Recreations*: gardening, travel, gastronomy, orchestral, chamber and instrumental music, opera, chasing moonbeams and the ghosts of Ottoman gardeners. *Address*: Hortus, Bryan's Ground, Presteigne, Herefordshire LD8 2LP. *E*: d.a.wheeler@hotmail.com.

**WHEELER, Frank Basil**, CMG 1990; HM Diplomatic Service, retired; *b* 24 April 1937; *s* of late Harold Gifford Wheeler and Winifred Lucy Wheeler (*née* Childs); *m* 1st, 1959, Catherine Saunders Campbell (*d* 1979); one *s*; 2nd, 1984, Alyson Ruth Lund (*née* Powell) (marr. diss. 1989); 3rd, 1991, Susana Plaza Larrea. *Educ*: Mill Hill Sch. HM Forces, 1956–58. HM Foreign Service, 1958–: Foreign Office, 1958–61; Third Sec., Moscow, 1961–63; Asst Private Sec. to Minister of State, FO, 1963–65; Second Sec., Berne, 1965–67; First Sec., FO (later FCO), 1967–72; Wellington, 1972–75; FCO, 1975–77; Counsellor and Head of Chancery, Prague, 1977–79; Inspector, 1979–82; Head of Personnel Policy Dept, FCO, 1982–84; Counsellor and Head of Chancery, UK Delegn to NATO, Brussels, 1984–86; Counsellor, on loan to DTI, 1986–89; Ambassador: to Ecuador, 1989–93; to Chile, 1993–97; Chm., British-Chilean Chamber of Commerce, 1997–2003. Dir, Vicor Inc., Florida, 2011–13. Internat. Advr, FA, 1997–2000. Grand Cross, Order of Merit (Chile), 1998. *Recreations*: music, tennis. *Address*: 28–30 Theobalds Road, WC1X 8NX; Ecuador.

**WHEELER, Fraser William**; HM Diplomatic Service, retired; consultant in international low carbon technology investment; Consultant, Forbury Investment Network; Sensitivity Reviewer, Foreign and Commonwealth Office; *b* 23 March 1957; *s* of Albert, (Bill), and Janet Wheeler; *m* 1988, Sarah Humphreys; one *s* one *d*. *Educ*: Univ. of Warwick (BA Hons Politics). Trainee, Deloitte, 1979–80; entered FCO, 1980; Defence Dept, FCO, 1980–82; Third Secretary: Accra, 1982–85; UK Mission to UN, Geneva, 1986–89; Desk Officer, Soviet Dept, 1990–91; Dep. Hd, Trade Section, Moscow, 1991–94; Dep. Consul Gen., Vancouver, 1995–2000; PR Consultant, Vancouver, 2000–01 (on special leave); Policy Planning Staff, 2001–03, Hd, Partnerships and Networks Gp, 2003–05, FCO; Hd, British Embassy Office, Basra, Iraq, 2005–06; High Comr to Guyana, and concurrently Ambassador to Suriname and CARICOM, 2006–10. Exec. Sec., Canada–UK Council, 2016–. Sen. Advr, Sure Chill. *Recreations*: the fruitless pursuit of the life of old Reilly, travel with a point to it, playing with a Harley Davidson, country walking in bad weather, smoky and cramped jazz bars, sport for fun, banter with the best of them over fine wine or good coffee.

**WHEELER, Heather**; MP (C) South Derbyshire, since 2010; Parliamentary Under-Secretary of State, Foreign and Commonwealth Office, since 2019; *b* Norwich, 14 May 1959; *d* of Charles Peter Clough Wilkinson and Freda Mary Wilkinson; *m* 1986, Robert James Wheeler; one *d*. *Educ*: Grey Coat Hosp., Westminster. ACII 1985. Placing Manager, RICS Insce Services Ltd, 1977–87. Member (C): Wandsworth BC, 1982–86; S Derbys DC, 1995–2011 (Leader, 2007–10). Contested (C) Coventry S, 2001, 2005. An Asst Govt Whip, 2016–17; a Lord Comr of HM Treasury (Govt Whip), 2017–18; Parly Under-Sec. of State, MHCLG, 2018–19. Member, Select Committee: on Standards and Privileges, 2010–13; on Communities and Local Govt, 2011–15. Chm., All Party Parly Local Govt Gp, 2010–. Mem. Exec., 1922 Cttee, 2011–14. *Recreations*: watching sport, DIY, listening to The Archers. *Address*: House of Commons, SW1A 0AA.

**WHEELER, Joanne Elizabeth**, MBE 2017; Director, Alden Legal (formerly Advisers) Ltd, since 2018; *b* Edinburgh, 4 Feb. 1971; *d* of Joseph Duff Wheeler and Elizabeth Anne Wheeler; *m* 2005, Alexander James Monk; three *d*. *Educ*: George Watson's Coll., Edinburgh; Univ. of Aberdeen (LLB Hons 1993; DipLP 1995); Rotterdam Univ. (LLM Law and Econs (with distinction) 1994); Univ. of Oxford (MSt Law and Econs 1996); BPP Law Sch. (Qualified Lawyers Transfer Test 1998); Queen Mary, Univ. of London (Dip. Telecommunications Law 2002). Admitted solicitor, Scotland, 1996, England and Wales, 1998; NP 1996. Trainee solicitor, McGrigor Donald, 1995–97; Assistant Solicitor: Slaughter and May, 1997–99; Baker & McKenzie, 1999–2001; Sen. Associate, Allen & Overy, 2001–03; Lawyer: ESA, Paris, 2003–06; OFCOM, 2006–07; Sen. Associate, Milbank Tweed Hadley & McCloy, 2007–09; Partner (communications, satellite and space law): CMS Cameron McKenna LLP, 2009–14; Bird & Bird LLP, 2014–18. Rep. of UK Govt to UN Cttee on the Peaceful Uses of Outer Space, 2011–15. Chm., Nat. Space Acad., 2018–; Trustee, Nat. Space Centre, 2018–. Co-Chm., Satellite Finance Network, 2009–; Chm., Space Cttee, Internat. Bar Assoc., 2014–17; Dep. Chm., Space Law (UK) Cttee, Internat. Law Assoc., 2007–; Sec. for UK Nat. Point of Contact, Eur. Centre of Space Law, 2001–. FRAS 2010; FRAeS 2017. Mem., Internat. Inst. of Space Law, 2001–. Columnist: Satellite Finance, 2011–; Via Satellite, 2013–. *Publications*: (contrib.) The International Space Station: commercial utilisation from a European perspective, 2006; (contrib.) Yearbook on Space Policy 2010/2011, 2013; contrib. articles in Scots Law Times, Jl of Aerospace Engrg, Harvard Internat. Rev., Satellite Finance, Via Satellite. *Recreations*: family, space law and policy, hiking, art, classic music, wildlife. *Address*: Alden Legal Ltd, 25 Southampton Buildings, WC2A 1AL. *T*: (020) 3488 3335. *E*: joanne.wheeler@wearealden.com.

**WHEELER, Rt Hon. Sir John (Daniel)**, Kt 1990; PC 1993; JP; DL; Chairman, Service Authorities for National Criminal Intelligence Service and National Crime Squad, 1997–2002; *b* 1 May 1940; *s* of late Frederick Harry Wheeler and of Constance Elsie (*née* Foreman); *m* 1967, Laura Margaret Langley; one *s* one *d*. *Educ*: county sch., Suffolk; Staff Coll., Wakefield. Home Office: Asst Prison Governor, 1967–74; Res. Officer (looking into causes of crime and delinquency and treatment of offenders), 1974–76; Dir-Gen., BSIA, 1976–88 (Hon. Mem., 1990). Dir, National Supervisory Council for Intruder Alarms, 1977–88. Chairman: Nat. Inspectorate of Security Guard Patrol and Transport Services, 1982–92; Security Systems Inspectorate, 1987–90; Inspectorate of the Security Industry, 1992–93; govt review of airport security, 2002; Airport Security and Policing Review, Fed. Govt of Aust., 2005; Dep. Chm., UK Border Security Adv. Cttee, 2007–08. Chm. and non-exec. dir, various cos, 1976–93. Chairman: Capital Link, 1997–2002; Adv. Bd, Avarae Global Coins plc, 2006–. MP (C) City of Westminster, Paddington Div., 1979–83, Westminster N, 1983–97. Minister of State, NI Office, 1993–97. Member: Home Office Crime Prevention Cttee, 1976–92; Cons. Party National Adv. CPC Cttee, 1978–80; Home Affairs Select Cttee, 1979–92 (Chm., 1987–92); Chairman: Home Affairs Sub-Cttee, Race Relations and Immigration, 1980–87; All Party Penal Affairs Gp, 1986–93 (Vice-Chm., 1979–86); Vice-Chairman: Cons. Home Affairs Cttee, 1987–92 (Jt Sec., 1980–87); British Pakistan Parly Gp, 1987–93; Chm., Cons. Greater London Area Members' Cttee, 1983–90 (Jt Sec., 1980–83). Mem., Lloyd's, 1986–97. Pres., Paddington Div., St John Ambulance, 1998–99 (Vice Pres., 1990–98). Trustee, Police Foundn, 2004– (Vice Chm., 2010–). Freeman, City of London, 1987. JP Inner London, 1978; DL Greater London, 1989; Rep. DL, LB of Merton, 1997–2015. James Smart Lecture, SHHD, 1991 (Silver Medal). KStJ 1997 (Mem. Council, Order of St John for London, 1990–2012; Mem., Chapter Gen., 1993–99; Registrar, 1997–99, Sub-Chancellor, 1999–2002, Order of St John; Trustee and Mem., 1999–2008, Chancellor, 2002–08, Priory Chapter of England and the Islands). Hilal-i-Quaid-i-Azam (Pakistan), 1991; Comdr, Order of Isabella the Catholic, 2017. *Publications*: Who Prevents Crime?, 1980; (jtly) The Standard Catalogue of the Coins of the British Commonwealth, 1642 to present day, 1986. *Recreation*: enjoying life. *Club*: Travellers (Chm., 2014–18).

**WHEELER, Sir John (Frederick), (Jim)**, 4th Bt *cr* 1920, of Woodhouse Eaves, co. Leicester; *b* 3 May 1933; *s* of Sir John Hieron Wheeler, 3rd Bt and Gwendolen Alice Wheeler (*née* Oram); *S* father, 2005; *m* 1963, Barbara Mary, *d* of Raymond Flint; two *s* one *d*. *Educ*: Bedales; London Sch. of Printing. *Heir*: *s* Lt-Col John Radford Wheeler [*b* 27 Dec. 1965; *m* 1991, Sarah, *d* of Comdr Tim Howard-Jones; two *s* two *d*]. *Address*: Round Hill, Aldeburgh, Suffolk IP15 5PG.

**WHEELER, (John) Stuart**; Founder, Chief Executive, 1974–2002, and Chairman, 1985–2003, IG Group (formerly IG Index); Treasurer, UK Independence Party, 2011–14; *b* 30 Jan. 1935; adopted by late Capt. Alexander Hamilton Wheeler and Betty Lydia Wheeler; *m* 1979, Teresa Anne Codrington (*d* 2016); three *d*. *Educ*: Eton Coll.; Christ Church, Oxford (LLB Hons). Nat Service, 2nd Lieut, Welsh Guards, 1953–55. Called to the Bar, Inner Temple, 1959, in practice as barrister, 1959–62; Asst Manager, Investment Dept, Hill Samuel, 1962–68; Manager, Investment Dept, J. H. Vavasseur, 1968–73; First Nat. Finance Corp., 1973. Contested (Trust) Bexhill and Battle, 2010. Coronation Medal, 1953. *Publications*: A Crisis of Trust, 2010; Winning Against the Odds: my life in gambling and politics (autobiog.), 2019. *Recreations*: tennis, bridge, poker. *Address*: Chilham Castle, Canterbury, Kent CT4 8DB. *T*: (01227) 733100. *Club*: Portland.

**WHEELER, Karen Stephanie**, CBE 2007; Director General, Borders, HM Revenue and Customs, since 2017; *b* Isleworth, London, 30 Nov. 1956; *d* of Reginald William Wheeler and June Heather Wheeler; *m* 2009, Stuart Lynas. *Educ*: Reigate Co. Sch. for Girls; Durham Univ. (BSc Physics). Change Mgt Manager, Andersen Consulting, 1988–95; Change Mgt Consultant, Practick Ltd, 1995–99; Sen. Manager, Penna Consulting, 1999–2003; Change Prog. Manager, DCA, 2003–06; Change Dir, 2006–08, Delivery Dir, 2008–09, MoJ; Digital Delivery Dir, Cabinet Office, 2009–10; Transition Dir, 2010–12, Dir Gen., Gp Ops and Assurance, 2012–14, DoH; Nat. Dir, Transformation and Corporate Ops, NHS England, 2014–17. *Recreations*: opera, jazz, choral singing, walking. *Address*: HM Revenue and Customs, 100 Parliament Street, SW1A 2BQ.

**WHEELER, Air Vice-Marshal Leslie William Frederick**; Independent Inspector for Public Inquiries and Chairman of Appointments Boards for Civil Service Commissioners and Ministry of Defence, 1984–94; *b* 4 July 1930; *s* of late George Douglas and Susan Wheeler; *m* 1961, Joan, *d* of late Harry and Evelyn Carpenter; two *d*. *Educ*: Creighton School, Carlisle. Commnd, 1952; Egypt and Cyprus, 1954–56; Specialist in Signals, 1958; Aden, 1958–60; V-force (Valiants), 1961–65; India (Staff Coll.), 1965–66; Headquarters Signals Command, 1966–69; OC 360 Sqdn, 1970–72; Dir, RAF Staff Coll., 1972–74; Electronic Warfare and Recce Operations, MoD, 1975–77; Stn Comdr, RAF Finningley, 1977–79; Air Cdre Policy & Plans, Headquarters RAF Support Comd, 1979–83; Dir-Gen., Personnel Services (RAF), MoD, 1983–84, retired. *Recreations*: walking, philately, genealogy. *Address*: c/o HSBC, English Street, Carlisle CA3 8JW.

**WHEELER, Dame Margaret Anne**; *see* Brain, Dame M. A.

**WHEELER, Michael Antony**; a District Judge (Magistrates' Courts), since 2009; a Recorder, since 2012; *b* Coventry, 23 May 1959; *s* of Alan James Wheeler and Doris Joan Wheeler; *m* 1986, Kim Lorna Osborne; one *s* one *d*. *Educ*: Bablake Sch., Coventry; Liverpool Poly. (BA Hons Law 1980). Admitted as solicitor, 1983; sole practitioner,

Michael Wheeler, Solicitor (criminal defence practice), 1995–2009; a Dep. Dist Judge (Magistrates' Courts), 2003–09. *Recreations:* clay pigeon shooting, running, golf, crosswords. *Address:* Wolverhampton Magistrates' Court, North Street, Wolverhampton WV1 1RA. *T:* (01902) 773151, *Fax:* 0870 739 4167. *E:* DJMC.Michael.Wheeler@ejudiciary.net.

**WHEELER, Nicholas Charles Tyrwhitt,** OBE 2018; Chairman, Charles Tyrwhitt, since 1986; *b* 20 Jan. 1965; *s* of John Vashon Tyrwhitt Wheeler and late Geraldine Noel Wheeler; *m* 1995, (Belinda) Christian Rucker, *qv*; one *s* three *d. Educ:* Eton Coll.; Univ. of Bristol (BSc 1987). Charles Tyrwhitt, 1986–; Bain & Co., 1987–89. *Recreations:* tennis, ski-ing, photography. *E:* nickw@ctshirts.co.uk. *Club:* Hurlingham.

**WHEELER, Prof. Nicholas John,** PhD; FAcSS, FLSW; Professor of International Relations, and Director, Institute for Conflict, Cooperation and Security, University of Birmingham, since 2012; *b* Hereford, 7 April 1962; *s* of John and Lola Wheeler; one *d. Educ:* Staffordshire Poly. (BA Hons Modern Studies (Internat. Relns and Econs) 1983); Southampton Univ. (MSc (Econ) Internat. Studies; PhD 1988). Tutor, Dept of Internat. Politics, University Coll. of Wales, Aberystwyth, 1985–86; Res. Fellow, Dept of War Studies, KCL, 1987–88; Res. Associate, Internat. Inst. for Strategic Studies, 1988–89; Lectr, Dept of Politics, Univ. of Hull, 1989–93; Department of International Politics, University of Wales, Aberystwyth, later Aberystwyth University: Lectr, 1993–97; Sen. Lectr, 1997–2002; Reader, 2002–04; Prof. of Internat. Politics, 2004–12; Dir, 2005–10, David Davies Meml Inst. of Internat. Studies. ESRC/AHRC Fellow, Global Uncertainties Prog., Res. Councils UK, 2009–13. FLSW 2011. *Publications:* (with I. Clark) The British Origins of Nuclear Strategy, 1945–55, 1989; (ed with T. Dunne) Human Rights in Global Politics, 1999; Saving Strangers: humanitarian intervention in international society, 2000; (ed with C. McInnes) Dimensions of Military Intervention, 2002; (ed with Jean-Marc Coicaud) National Interest Versus Solidarity: particular and universal ethics in international life, 2008; (with K. Booth) The Security Dilemma: fear, cooperation and trust in world politics, 2008; (jtly) Special Responsibilities: global problems and American power, 2012; Trusting Enemies: interpersonal relationships in international conflict, 2018. *Recreations:* swimming, walking, cycling. *Address:* College of Social Sciences, School of Government and Society, Muirhead Tower, University of Birmingham, Edgbaston, Birmingham B15 2TT.

**WHEELER, Prof. Quentin D.,** PhD; President, College of Environmental Science and Forestry, State University of New York, 2014–18; *b* 31 Jan. 1954; *s* of Quentin Wheeler and Hattie (*née* Philips); *m* 2004, Darlene Marie Platt; one *s* four *d. Educ:* Ohio State Univ., Columbus (BS 1976, MS 1977; PhD 1980). Cornell University: Prof., 1980–2004; Chm., Entomology, 1989–93; Dir, L. H. Bailey Hortorium, 1988–89. US National Science Foundation: Prog. Officer, 2001; Dir, Div. of Envmtl Biology, 2001–04; Keeper and Hd of Entomol., Natural History Mus., 2004–06; Arizona State University: Prof. of Natural History and the Envmt, Sch. of Life Scis, 2006–14; Vice Pres. and Dean, Coll. of Liberal Arts and Scis, 2006–11; Dir, Internat. Inst. for Species Exploration, 2007–14. Mem., Willi Hennig Soc. FAAAS 2003; FLS 2003; FRES 2004. *Publications:* Fungus/Insect Relationships: perspectives in ecology and evolution, 1984; Extinction and Phylogeny, 1992; Species Concepts and Phylogenetic Theory: a debate, 2000; What on Earth?: 100 of our planet's most amazing new species, 2013; The Future of Phylogenetic Systematics: the legacy of Willi Hennig, 2016; more than 100 articles in scientific jls. *Recreations:* furniture making, insect collecting, hiking, photography, wines and coffees.

**WHEELER, Raymond Leslie,** RDI 1995; FRAeS; FRINA; *b* 25 Oct. 1927; *s* of Edmund Francis Wheeler and Ivy Geraldine Wheeler; *m* 1950, Jean McInnes; one *s* two *d. Educ:* Southampton Univ. (BSc (Eng) 1948); Imperial Coll., London (MSc (Eng) 1953; DIC). FRAeS 1974; FRINA 1975. Apprentice, 1945–48, Aircraft stressman, 1953–62, Chief Stressman, 1962–65, Saunders Roe Ltd, then Saunders Roe Div. of Westland Aircraft Ltd; Chief Structural Designer and Project Engr, SRN4 (world's largest hovercraft), 1965; British Hovercraft Corp. Ltd, subseq. Westland Aerospace Ltd: Chief Designer, 1966–85; Technical Dir, 1972–85; Dir, 1985–91. President: IoW Hockey Club; IoW Br., RAeS; IoW Young Enterprise; E Cowes Br., RNLI. *Publications:* (with A. E. Tagg) From Sea to Air: the heritage of Sam Saunders, 1989; From River to Sea: the marine heritage of Sam Saunders, 1993; Saunders Roe, 1998; (with J. B. Chaplin) In the Beginning: the SRNI hovercraft, 2007; A 20th Century Engineer, 2011. *Recreations:* gardening, photography, pottery, painting, archaeology, sport. *Address:* Brovacum, 106 Old Road, East Cowes, Isle of Wight PO32 6AX.

**WHEELER, Gen. Sir Roger (Neil),** GCB 1997 (KCB 1993); CBE 1983; Constable, HM Tower of London, 2001–09; Chief of the General Staff, 1997–2000; Aide-de-camp General to the Queen, 1996–2000; *b* 16 Dec. 1941; *s* of Maj.-Gen. T. N. S. Wheeler, CB, CBE; *m* 1980, Felicity Hares; three *s* one *d* by former marriage. *Educ:* All Hallows Sch., Devon; Hertford Coll., Oxford (BA Hons 1964; MA 1974; Hon. Fellow 2002). Early Army service in Borneo and ME, 1964–70; Bde Major, Cyprus Emergency, 1974; Mem., Lord Carver's Staff, Rhodesia talks, 1977; Bn Comd, Belize, Gibraltar, Berlin and Canada, 1979–82; COS, Falkland Is, June–Dec. 1982; Bde Comd, BAOR, 1985–86; Dir, Army Plans, 1987–89; Comdr, 1st Armoured Div., BAOR, 1989–90; ACGS, MoD, 1990–92; GOC and Dir of Military Ops, NI, 1993–96; C-in-C, Land Comd, 1996–97. Col, Royal Irish Regt, 1996–2001; Col Comdt, Intell. Corps, 1996–2000. Hon. Colonel: QUB OTC, 2000–08; Oxford Univ. OTC, 2000–06. President: Army RFU, 1995–99; Army Rifle Assoc., 1995–2000; Mem. Council, NRA, 2000–02. Non-executive Director: Thales plc, 2001–11; Aegis Defence, 2003–11; Serious Organised Crime Agency, 2005–09. President: Ex Services Mental Welfare Soc., Combat Stress, 2001–09; Forces Pension Soc., 2006–13. Patron, Police Foundn, 2001–. Pres. and Patron, Lady Grover's Fund, 2003–19. Chm. Trustees, Tank Mus., Bovington, 2002–10. Trustee, Salmon and Trout Assoc., 2012–18. FRGS 2000. Liveryman, Painter-Stainers' Co. (Master, 2010–11). *Recreations:* fly-fishing, cricket, shooting, ornithology. *Clubs:* Army and Navy, Beefsteak.

**WHEELER, Sara Diane,** FRSL; writer; *b* 20 March 1961; *d* of John Wilfred Wheeler and Diane Pauline Wheeler (*née* Vernon, now Price); two *s. Educ:* Redland High Sch., Bristol; Brasenose Coll., Oxford (BA Hons). Hawthornden Fellow, 2010; Vis. Tutor, RHUL, 2014–15. Writer and presenter, BBC Radio 4 series, Captain Scott's Men, 2012. Chm., Judging Panel, Stanford Dolman Travel Book of Year Award, 2016–18. FRSL 1999 (Mem. Council, 2000–05). Trustee: London Liby, 2006–09 and 2014–; Sibs, 2010–. Contributing Ed., Literary Rev., 2009–. *Publications:* An Island Apart: travels in Evia, 1992; Travels in a Thin Country: a journey through Chile, 1994; Terra Incognita: travels in Antarctica, 1996; (ed jtly) Amazonian: the Penguin Book of women's new travel writing, 1998; Cherry: a biography of Apsley Cherry-Garrard, 2001; Too Close to the Sun: a biography of Denys Finch Hatton, 2006; The Magnetic North: notes from the Arctic Circle, 2009 (Best Adventure Travel Book, Banff Mountain Fest., 2011); Access All Areas: selected writings 1990–2010, 2011; O My America!: second acts in a new world, 2013; Mud and Stars: travels in Russia with Pushkin and other geniuses of the Golden Age, 2019. *Address:* c/o Aitken Alexander Associates, 291 Gray's Inn Road, WC1X 8EB. *E:* reception@aitkenalexander.co.uk. *Club:* Academy.

**WHEELER, Stuart;** *see* Wheeler, J. S.

**WHEELER, Canon Prof. Timothy Jerome;** DL; PhD; CPsychol; Principal and Vice-Chancellor, University of Chester, 2005–19, Professor and Vice-Chancellor Emeritus, 2020; *b* 22 Oct. 1950; *s* of George Edward Wheeler and Mary Wheeler (*née* Carter); *m* 1975, Marilyn Sutton Jones; three *d. Educ:* Colwyn Bay Grammar Sch.; University Coll. of N Wales, Bangor (BA 1972; PhD 1977); Llandrillo Coll. (FE Teacher's Cert.). CPsychol 1988. Lectr, then Sen. Lectr, Sheffield Poly., 1974–80; Hd of Sch. and Dean of Faculty, Dublin City Univ., 1980–85; Hd, Sch. of Social Scis, Robert Gordon's Inst. of Technol., Aberdeen, 1985; Hd, Communication and Media, Dorset Inst., subseq. Bournemouth Poly., 1986–91; Southampton Institute: Dir, Envmt Sch., 1991–96; Dep. Dir, 1996–97; Dir, 1997–98; Principal, Chester Coll., subseq. UC Chester, 1998–2005. Vis. Prof., Communication Studies, Calif State Univ., Sacramento, 1982; Sen. Schol., St John's Coll., Oxford, 1988; Visiting Professor: Xiamen Univ. of Sci. and Technol., 2014–; Beijing Foreign Studies Univ., 2015–; Shanghai Jiao Tong Univ., 2015–; Dalian Minzu Univ., 2015–; Zaozhuang Univ., 2019–; Jiangsu Univ., 2019–. Dep. Chm., UCAS, 1999–2005. Chair: NW Universities Assoc., 2007–10; Univ. of Chester Academies Trust, 2011–; Chair, Cathedrals Gp (formerly Church Univs and Colls Gp), 2009–11. Member: LLSC Cheshire and Warrington, 2001–08; Cheshire & Warrington Econ. Alliance, 2001–11; Warrington Collegiate, 2002–10; Diocesan Bd of Educn, 2002–; NW Regl Assembly and Exec., 2006–08; NW Leaders' Forum, 2008–11; NW Skills and Employment Bd, 2008–10; Jt Econ. Commn for the NW, 2008–10; Cheshire and Warrington LEP, 2011– (Dep. Chm., 2017–); Daresbury Econ. Action Zone, 2011–; C of E Bd of Educn, 2011–14; NW Business Leadership Team, 2012–; Cheshire Business Leaders, 2013–. Pres., Warrington Chamber of Commerce, 2007–10, 2011–12. Governor: S Cheshire Coll., 2002–14; Priestley Coll., 2011–14; Univ. C of E Acad., Ellesmere Port, 2009–12; Reaseheath Coll., 2016–; Coleg Cambria, 2016–. Lay Canon, 2003–, Mem. Chapter, 2004–14, Chester Cathedral. DL Cheshire, 2003. Freeman, City of London, 2017; Liveryman, Fruiterers' Co., 2017. Member Editorial Boards: Dyslexia: an Internat. Jl of Res. and Practice, 1996–; Internat. Jl of Corporate Communications, 1997–. *Publications:* Handbook of Safety Management, 1989; 120 contribs to scientific jls, chapters in books, reviews. *Recreations:* collector of antique oriental ceramics, keen interest in contemporary film, catholic tastes in music, active in a number of charities. *Clubs:* Chester Business; Cheshire Pitt.

**WHEELER, Prof. Timothy Robert,** PhD; Director, International, UK Research and Innovation, since 2018; *b* Overton, 8 Aug. 1963; *s* of Robert and Margaret Wheeler; *m* 2016, Ruth Smith; two *s* three *d. Educ:* Queen Mary's Coll., Basingstoke; Keele Univ. (BSc Biol. 1986); Reading Univ. (MSc Crop Physiol. 1987; PhD Agric. 1991). University of Reading: Res. Fellow, 1991–96; Lectr, 1996–2004; Reader, 2004–08; Prof. of Crop Science, 2008–16; Vis. Prof. of Agriculture, 2016–. Specialist Advr, H of L, 2009–10; Dep. Chief Scientific Advr, DFID, 2010–16; Dir, Res. and Innovation, NERC, 2016–18. Mem. Council, BBSRC, 2012–16. Hon. DSc Reading, 2017. *Publications:* over 180 contribs to scientific pubns on climate change, agriculture and food. *Recreations:* reading, running, surfing, vegetable growing, beekeeping. *Address:* UK Research and Innovation, Polaris House, North Star Avenue, Swindon SN2 1EU. *T:* (01793) 444000. *E:* tim.wheeler@ukri.org.

**WHEELHOUSE, Keith Oliver B.;** *see* Butler-Wheelhouse.

**WHEELHOUSE, Paul;** Member (SNP) Scotland South, Scottish Parliament, since 2011; Minister for Energy, Connectivity and the Islands, since 2018; *b* Dundonald, NI, 22 June 1970; one *s. Educ:* Stewart's Melville Coll., Edinburgh; Univ. of Aberdeen (MA Econ. Sci. 1992); Univ. of Edinburgh (MBA 1999). Asst Economist, then Econ. Consultant, Pieda plc, 1992–98; Econ. Consultant, then Sen. Econ. Consultant, DTZ Pieda Consulting/DTZ Consulting & Research, 1998–2009; Sen. Consultant, BiGGAR Economics Ltd, 2009–10; Dir, Paul Wheelhouse Consultancy Ltd. Scottish Parliament: Minister for Envmt and Climate Change, 2012–14, for Community Safety and Legal Affairs, 2014–16, for Business, Innovation and Energy, 2016–18; Member: Finance Cttee, 2011–12; Standards, Procedures and Public Appts Cttee, 2011–12. *Address:* Scottish Parliament, Edinburgh EH99 1SP.

**WHEEN, Francis James Baird;** author and journalist; *b* 22 Jan. 1957; *s* of late James Francis Thorneycroft Wheen and of Patricia Winifred Wheen (*née* Ward); *m* 1985, Joan Alison Smith, *qv* (marr. diss. 1993); partner, Julia Jones; two *s. Educ:* Copthorne Sch.; Harrow; Royal Holloway Coll., London (BA 1978; Hon. Fellow, 2008). Office boy, The Guardian, 1974–75; reporter: New Statesman, 1978–84; Private Eye, 1987–; columnist: Independent, 1986–87; Independent on Sunday, 1990–91; Observer, 1993–95; Esquire, 1993–98; Guardian, 1994–2001; Evening Standard, 2006–07. Panellist, News Quiz, BBC Radio, 1989–. Columnist of Year, Granada/What the Papers Say awards, 1997. *Publications:* The Sixties, 1982; World View, 1982; The Battle for London, 1985; Television: a history, 1985; Tom Driberg: his life and indiscretions, 1990; (ed) The Chatto Book of Cats, 1993; (ed) Lord Gnome's Literary Companion, 1994; Karl Marx, 1999 (Isaac Deutscher Prize); Hoo-Hahs and Passing Frenzies, 2002 (George Orwell Prize); Who Was Dr Charlotte Bach?, 2002; How Mumbo-Jumbo Conquered the World, 2004; Marx's Das Kapital: a biography, 2006; Strange Days Indeed: the golden age of paranoia, 2009. *Recreation:* cricket. *Address:* Sokens, Green Street, Pleshey, Chelmsford, Essex CM3 1HT. *T:* (01245) 231566. *Clubs:* MCC; Essex CC, High Roding Cricket.

**WHEEN, Natalie Kathleen;** broadcaster, writer and lecturer on olive oil; farmer, producer and retailer of organic olive oils, since 2009; Director, AVLAKI Ltd, since 2014 (Partner, AVLAKI Superb Organic Olive Oils, 2007–14); *b* Shanghai, China, 29 July 1947; *d* of late Edward Leslie Lee Wheen and Galina (*née* Yourieff). *Educ:* Downe House, Newbury; London Univ. (BMus 1967); Royal Coll. of Music (ARCM). BBC, 1968–80: radio studio manager; attachments as Asst Producer, BBC TV Music and Arts, 1970; Radio 3 Music Producer, Manchester and London, 1971–72; Asst Producer, Music Now, Radio 3, 1972–73; Producer, Music Now, Talking About Music and various documentaries, 1973–80 (Best Music Documentary, Imperial Tobacco Soc. Authors Awards for Radio, 1978); London Arts Corresp., Canadian Broadcasting; freelance broadcaster, 1980–; Presenter: Kaleidoscope, Radio 4, 1980–95; Mainly for Pleasure, subseq. In Tune, Radio 3, 1980–97; Music Review, World Service; Cardiff Singer of the World, BBC2, 1993, 1995 and 1997; presenter, Classic FM: Week-end Afternoons, 1999–2008; Access All Areas, 2000–01; Tonight at 11, 2001–03; Natalie Wheen's Full Works Concert, week-ends, 2008–10; special programme series, 2010–; contributor: The Food Programme, R4; The Influence of Effluent, R4, 1998; Compère, Gramophone Awards, 1995 and 1996; interviews, Third Ear, etc; interviewer and co-producer: Tippett's Time, C4, 1995; Visions of Paradise Intervals, R3, 1995; documentaries on arts subjects; performance, Talking Dirty (one woman show), 2007–; Plenary Guest Speaker on MacMillan's Music for DanSox conf. on Sir Kenneth MacMillan, 2019. Partner: Worsley Wheen prodns, 1983–88; ind. media prodn with Natalie Wheen & Associates. Contributing Editor, 3 mag., 1983–86. Jury Member: Sony Awards for Radio, 1994, 2003; Prudential Awards for the Arts, 1996; Masterprize, 2003; Kathleen Ferrier Scholarship, 2003; David Parkhouse Award, 2005. Director/Trustee: Hackney Music Develt Trust, 1995–2002; Creative Dance Artists Trust, 1995–96; Matthew Hawkins and the Fresh Dances Gp, 1995–97. Lectr and Workshop Leader in presentation and communication skills; Consultant, GSMD, 1991–92; Presenter, British Airways In-flight Light Classics Channel, 1991–95. Mem. Council, ENO Works, 1996–98. Governor, Downe House Sch., 1986–98. Contributor: www.theartsdesk.com,

2010–; Dancing Times. *Publications:* (jtly) A Life on the Fiddle: Max Jaffa's Autobiography, 1991; publications on trng and employment for Careers and Occupational Information Centre, and Dept of Employment; contribs to Spectator, Independent (Travel), Classic FM mag., Opera Now. *Recreations:* olives, fishing, laughter, anarchy. *Address:* AVLAKI Ltd, Unit 3372, PO Box 6945, London, W1A 6US. *E:* info@oliveoilavlaki.com.

**WHELAN, Michael George;** Director, Whelan Associates Ltd, 2006–11; *b* 13 Oct. 1947; *s* of George Henry Whelan and Vera Frances Whelan (*née* Davies); *m* 1st, 1968, Veronica Gemma Merron (marr. diss. 1986); one *s* one *d*; 2nd, 1987, Anne Vivien Williams, JP; one *s*. *Educ:* Univ. of London (BSc(Econ) Hons, MSc(Econ)). Operational Manager, Walton Hosp., Liverpool, then Good Hope Hosp., Sutton Coldfield, and Hope Hosp., Salford, 1964–72; Tutor in Management, and Principal Trng Officer, N Western RHA, 1972–74; Deputy Chief Officer: Tameside and Glossop HA, 1974–78; Surrey AHA, 1978–80; Chief Officer, SW Surrey HA, 1980–85; Gp Manager, Healthcare, KPMG Management Consultants, 1985–90; Partner, Pannell Kerr Forster, 1990–92; Chief Exec., Parkinson's Disease Soc., 1992–94; healthcare business consultant, 1994–97; Principal, Watson Wyatt Actuaries and Consultants, 1997–98; Chief Exec., Thomson, Snell & Passmore, Solicitors, 1998–2000; Practice Dir, T. V. Edwards (Solicitors), 2000–02; healthcare mgt consultant, 2002–03; Project Dir, Surrey and Sussex SHA, 2003–05; Registrar, Faculty of Dental Surgery, RCS, 2005; Chief Exec., Inst. of Optometry, 2007; Operational Manager (Medicine), Portsmouth NHS Trust, 2007–08. AIPM 1975; FHSM 1980. *Recreations:* music, entertaining, family, gardening, literature. *Address:* Chambord, 46 Pewley Way, Guildford, Surrey GU1 3QA.

**WHELAN, Prof. Michael John,** MA, PhD, DPhil; FRS 1976; FInstP; Professor of Microscopy of Materials, Department of Materials, University of Oxford, 1992–97, now Emeritus Professor; Fellow of Linacre College, Oxford, since 1967; *b* 2 Nov. 1931; *s* of William Whelan and Ellen Whelan (*née* Pound). *Educ:* Farnborough Grammar Sch.; Gonville and Caius Coll., Cambridge. FInstP 1976. Fellow of Gonville and Caius Coll., 1958–66; Demonstrator in Physics, Univ. of Cambridge, 1961–65; Asst Dir of Research in Physics, Univ. of Cambridge, 1965–66; Reader, Dept of Materials, Univ. of Oxford, 1966–92. Hon. Prof., Univ. of Sci. and Technol. Beijing, China, 1995. Hon. FRMS 2001; Hon. Fellow: Japanese Soc. of Microscopy, 2003; Microscopy Soc. of Amer., 2009. C. V. Boys Prize, Inst. of Physics, 1965; Hughes Medal, Royal Soc., 1988; Distinguished Scientist Award, Microscopy Soc. of Amer., 1998; Gjønnes Medal, Internat. Union of Crystallography, 2012. *Publications:* (jtly) Electron Microscopy of Thin Crystals, 1965; Worked Examples in Dislocations, 1990; (jtly) High-Energy Electron Diffraction and Microscopy, 2004; numerous papers in learned jls. *Recreation:* gardening. *Address:* 18 Salford Road, Old Marston, Oxford OX3 0RX. *T:* (01865) 244556.

**WHELAN, Prof. William Joseph,** PhD, DSc; FRS 1992; Professor of Biochemistry and Molecular Biology, University of Miami Miller School of Medicine (formerly University of Miami School of Medicine), 1967–2019, now Emeritus (Chairman of Department, 1967–91); *b* 14 Nov. 1924; *s* of William Joseph Whelan and Jane Antoinette Whelan (*née* Bertram); *m* 1st, 1951, Margaret Miller Birnie (*d* 1993); 2nd, 2009, Alina Akin. *Educ:* Univ. of Birmingham, England (BSc Hons 1944; PhD 1948; DSc 1955). Asst Lectr, Univ. of Birmingham, 1947–48; Asst Lectr and Sen. Lectr, UCNW, Bangor, 1948–55; Sen. Mem., Lister Inst. of Preventive Medicine, Univ. of London, 1956–64; Prof. and Head, Dept of Biochemistry, Royal Free Hosp. Sch. of Medicine, Univ. of London, 1964–67. Sec. Gen., FEBS, 1965–67. Co-Dir, Miami Winter Symposia, 1968–. Dir, Enterprise Florida Technol. Develt Bd (formerly Enterprise Florida Innovation Partnership), 1993–98. President: Portland Press Inc., 1994–98; Frontiers of Knowledge Inc., 1999–2003. Gen. Sec., 1978–83, Pres., 1997–2000, Internat. Union of Biochemistry and Molecular Biol. (formerly Internat. Union of Biochemistry). FAAAS 1989. Hon. MRCP 1985; Hon. Mem., Biochemical Soc., 1993. Hon. DSc La Trobe, 1997. Alsberg Medal, 1967; Ciba Medal, 1968; Saare Medal, 1979; FEBS Millennium Medal, 2000. Editor-in-Chief: Trends in Biochemical Sciences, 1975–78; BioEssays, 1984–89; Fedn Procs, 1986–87; FASEB Jl, 1987–96; IUBMB Life, 2000–. *Recreations:* publishing, travel. *Address:* 1420 Brickell Bay Drive, Apartment 1003, Miami, FL 33131, USA. *T:* (305) 3738039. *E:* wwhelan@miami.edu. *Club:* Athenæum.

**WHELER, Sir Trevor (Woodford),** 15th Bt *cr* 1660, of City of Westminster; *b* 11 April 1946; *s* of Sir Edward Woodford Wheler, 14th Bt, and Molly Ashworth, *e d* of Thomas Lever, Devon; *S* father, 2008; *m* 1974, Rosalie Margaret, *o d* of late Ronald Thomas Stunt; two *s*. *Educ:* St Edmund's Sch., Canterbury; St Mary's Sch., Nairobi. Air Traffic Control, RAF, 1966–71, CAA, 1971–2006. *Heir: s* Edward William Wheler [*b* 14 June 1976; *m* 2004, Monika Poleŝáková (marr. diss. 2014); one *s* one *d*. *Address:* 83 Middle Park, Inverurie, Aberdeenshire AB51 4QW. *T:* (01467) 622642. *E:* trevor.wheler@sky.com.

**WHELON, (Charles) Patrick (Clavell);** a Recorder of the Crown Court, 1978–97; *b* 18 Jan. 1930; *s* of Charles Eric Whelon and Margaret Whelon; *m* 1968, Prudence Mary (*née* Potter); one *s* one *d*. *Educ:* Wellington Coll.; Pembroke Coll., Cambridge (MA Hons). Called to Bar, Middle Temple, 1954. Liveryman of Vintners' Co., 1952–. *Recreations:* gardening, cartooning. *Address:* Russets, Pyott's Hill, Old Basing, Hants RG24 8AP. *T:* (01256) 469964.

**WHELTON, David William Courtenay,** OBE 2015; pianist, organist, music administrator; Managing Director, Philharmonia Orchestra, 1988–2016 (Hon. Member, since 2016); *b* 16 June 1954; *s* of William and Nora Whelton; *m* 1977, Caroline Rachel Gardner; one *s*. Mem. of Staff, GSMD, 1978–83; Dir of Music, Royal GS, Guildford, 1979–83; Music Officer, Yorks Arts Assoc., 1983–85; Principal Arts Officer, Leeds CC, 1985–86; Music Officer, Arts Council of GB, 1986–88. Director: Assoc. of British Orchestras, 1997–; Internat. Musicians Seminar, Prussia Cove, 1998–; Three Choirs Fest. Assoc., 2017–. Artistic Dir, Klosters Music Fest. 2017–. Chm., Leeds Conductors' Comp., 2005, 2009; Member Jury: Besançon Conductors Comp., 2001; Windsor Fest. Internat. String Comp., 2008, 2009, 2012, 2013, 2014, 2015; Sheepdrove Piano Comp., 2009, 2011, 2012, 2013, 2014, 2016, 2017, 2018, 2019; Svetlanov Internat. Conductors Comp., 2014; Khachaturian Internat. Conducting Comp., 2016. Member: Adv. Bd, Chateauville Foundn, 2012–; Council, RCM, 2018–; Adv. Bd, Idagio, 2019–. Pres., Amer. Friends of Philharmonia Orch., 2008–; Chm., Bedford Philharmonia Orch. Endowment trust, 2016–. Hon. Vice Pres., Ernst Bloch Soc., 2008–. Trustee: Mayfield Valley Arts Trust, 1986– (Chm., 2015–); Philharmonia Trust, 1988–; Hattori Foundn, 2011–; Anvil Arts, 2017–; Garrick Trust, 2019–; Radcliffe Trust, 2019–. Hon. RCM 2013; Hon. FRAM 2016; FRSA. Freeman, City of London, 2005; Mem., Musicians' Co. Assoc. of British Orchs Special Award, 2017. *Recreations:* gardening, architecture, history. *Address:* Freeland, 56 Crooksbury Road, Farnham, Surrey GU10 1QB. *Club:* Garrick.

**WHETNALL, Andrew Donard,** CB 1996; Director for Local Government, Office of the Deputy Prime Minister (formerly Department of the Environment, Transport and the Regions, then Department for Transport, Local Government and the Regions), 1996–2003; *b* 18 May 1948; *s* of late Donard and of Joan Whetnall (*née* Mummery); *m* 1972, Jane Lepel Glass; two *s* two *d*. *Educ:* King's Norton Grammar Sch.; Univ. of Sussex (MA). Joined DoE, 1975; Principal, Dept of Transport, 1980–83; Department of the Environment: Principal, 1983–87, Asst Sec., 1987–88, Inner Cities; Water Legislation, 1988–89; Head, Machinery of Govt Div., Cabinet Office, 1989–96 (Under Sec., 1993). Lay Mem., Information Rights Tribunal, 2005–. *Recreations:* reading, music.

**WHETSTONE, Rear-Adm. Anthony John,** CB 1982; Chairman, Bridgeworks Trust, 1999–2004; *b* 12 June 1927; *s* of Albert and Anne Whetstone; *m* 1951, Elizabeth Stewart Georgeson (*d* 2016); one *s* two *d*. *Educ:* King Henry VIII School, Coventry. Joined RN, 1945; specialised in submarines, 1949; Commanded: HMS Sea Scout, 1956–57; HMS Artful, 1959–61; HMS Repulse, 1968–70; HMS Juno, 1972–73; HMS Norfolk, 1977–78; Flag Officer Sea Training, 1978–80; Asst Chief of Naval Staff (Operations), 1981–83. Director-General: Cable TV Assoc., 1983–86; Nat. Television Rental Assoc., 1983–87. Dep. Sec., Defence Press and Broadcasting Cttee, 1987–92. Dir, DESC Ltd, 1991–96. Mem., Adv. Cttee on Historic Wreck Sites, 1996–2002. Nat. Pres., Submariners Assoc., 1988–2002. Chm. Trustees, Royal Navy Submarine Mus., 1990–98. FCMI (FBIM 1979). *Recreations:* gentle strolls, theatre (Chm., Civil Service Drama Fedn, 1985–92), music. *Address:* 17 Alverstoke Court, Alverstoke, Hants PO12 2LX. *Club:* Civil Service.

**WHETSTONE, Rachel Marjorie Joan;** Chief Communications Officer, Netflix, since 2018; *b* London, 22 Feb. 1968; *d* of Francis Whetstone and Linda Whetstone; *m* 2008, Steve Hilton; two *s*. *Educ:* Benenden Sch.; Univ. of Bristol (BA Hist.). Conservative Res. Dept, Conservative Central Office, 1990–94; One2one, Public Affairs, 1994–96; Special Advr to the Home Sec., 1994–97; Carlton Communications plc, 1996–2001; Political Sec. to Leader of the Opposition, 2003–05; Google Inc.: Dir, Communications, EMEA, 2005–08; Vice Pres., Global Communications, 2008–09; Vice Pres., 2009–11, Sen. Vice Pres., 2011–15, Global Communications and Policy; Sen. Vice Pres., Policy and Strategy, Uber, 2015–17; Vice Pres. of Communications for Instagram, Whatsapp and Messenger, Facebook, 2017–18. *Recreations:* gardening, riding, family, travel. *Address:* Tuscaloosa Avenue, Atherton, CA 94027, USA.

**WHEWAY, (Jonathan) Scott;** Chairman, AXA UK plc, since 2018; Independent non-executive Director, Centrica plc, since 2016; Senior Independent Director, Santander UK plc, since 2013; *b* Sheffield, 26 Aug. 1966; *s* of Barry and Cynthia Wheway; *m* 2000, Amanda Smith; one *s* one *d*. *Educ:* Rowlinson Sch., Sheffield. With Tesco plc, 1984–2003: Stores Dir, 1995–2000; Ops Dir, 2000–03; CEO, Japan, 2003; Man. Dir and Retail Dir, Boots the Chemist, 2003–07; CEO, Best Buy Europe, 2009–11. Non-exec. Dir, Aviva plc, 2007–17; Chm., Aviva Insce Ltd, 2015–17. Dir, British Retail Consortium, 2006–07. *Recreations:* mountains, cricket, technology, growing fruit, mending tractors. *Club:* Lansdowne.

**WHIPPLE, Hon. Dame Philippa Jane Edwards,** DBE 2015; **Hon. Mrs Justice Whipple;** a Judge of the High Court of Justice, Queen's Bench Division, since 2015; Presiding Judge, South Eastern Circuit, since 2018; *b* 7 May 1966; *d* of John Braham Scott Edwards and Veronica Mary Edwards; *m* 1992, Sam Whipple; three *s*. *Educ:* St Mary's Sch., Ascot; Merton Coll., Oxford (MA). Admitted solicitor, 1991; Solicitor, Freshfields, 1989–93; called to the Bar, Middle Temple, 1994, Bencher, 2012; in practice as barrister, specialising in tax, medical and admin. law, 1994–2015; a Recorder, 2007–15; QC 2010. Mem., Judicial Appts Commn, 2016–. *Address:* Royal Courts of Justice, Strand, WC2A 2LL.

**WHISH, Prof. Richard Peter;** Professor of Law, King's College London, 1991–2013, now Emeritus; *b* 23 March 1953; *s* of Thomas Stanton Whish and Avis Mary Whish (*née* Sullivan). *Educ:* Clifton Coll., Bristol; Worcester Coll., Oxford (BA 1st Cl. Hons 1974; BCL 1st Cl. Hons 1978). Qualified as solicitor, 1977; University of Bristol: Lectr in Law, 1978–88; Reader in Commercial Law, 1988–90; Partner, Watson, Farley and Williams (Solicitors), London, 1989–98. Mem., Exec. Council, Centre for European Law, KCL, 1991–. Chm., Adv. Body to Dir Gen. of Gas and Electricity Mgt, 2000–01. Member: Adv. Cttee, Centre for Study of Regulated Industries, 1991–2009; Adv. Panel, Dir Gen. of Fair Trading, 2001–03; non-executive Director: OFT, 2003–09; Energy Mkts Authy of Singapore, 2005–11. Member: Editl Bd, European Business Law Review, 1994–; Adv. Bd, Competition Law Jl, 2002–. FRSA 1995. Hon. QC 2014. *Publications:* (jtly) Conveyancing Solutions, 1987; (Gen. Ed.) Butterworth's Competition Law, 1991; Competition Law, 3rd edn 1993 to 8th edn 2015; (jtly) Merger Cases in the Real World: a study of merger control procedures, 1994; (ed) Halsbury's Laws of England, Vol. 47, 4th edn 1994; The Competition Act, 1998; numerous articles, case-notes and book reviews in legal periodicals and books. *Recreations:* opera and music, travelling (in particular in the sub-continent), gardening, conservation, Bristol Rovers FC. *Address:* 14 Glebe House, 15 Fitzroy Mews, W1T 6DP. *E:* richard.whish@kcl.ac.uk. *Club:* Groucho.

**WHISHAW, Anthony Popham Law,** RA 1989 (ARA 1980); RWA; *b* 22 May 1930; *s* of Robert Whishaw and Joyce (*née* Wheeler); *m* 1957, Jean Gibson; two *d*. *Educ:* Tonbridge Sch. (Higher Cert.); Chelsea Sch. of Art; Royal College of Art (ARCA 1955). Travelling Schol., RCA; Abbey Minor Schol.; Spanish Govt Schol.; Abbey Premier Schol., 1982; Lorne Schol., 1982–83. RWA 1992, Hon. RWA 2003. John Moores Minor Painting Prize, 1982; (jtly) 1st Prize, Hunting Group Art Awards, 1986. *One-man exhibitions:* Libreria Abril, Madrid, 1956; Roland Browse and Delbanco, London, 1960, 1961, 1963, 1965, 1968; ICA, 1971; New Art Centre, 1972; Folkestone Arts Centre, 1973; Hoya Gall., London, 1974; Oxford Gall., Oxford, 1974; ACME, London, 1978, 2010; Newcastle upon Tyne Polytech. Gall., 1979; (with Martin Froy) New Ashgate Gall., Farnham, 1979; Nicola Jacobs Gall., London 1981; From Landscape, Kettle's Yard, Cambridge, Ferens Gall., Hull, Bede Gall., Jarrow, 1982–84; Works on Paper, Nicola Jacobs Gall., 1983; Paintings, Nicola Jacobs Gall., 1984; Mappin Art Gall., Sheffield, 1985; Large Paintings, RA 1986; Reflections after Las Meninas (touring): Royal Acad., and Hatton Gall., Newcastle upon Tyne, 1987; Mead Gall., Warwick Univ., John Hansard Gall., Southampton Univ., and Spacex Gall., Exeter, 1988; Infaust Gall., Shanghai and Hamburg, 1989; Blason Gall., London, 1991; artspace, London, 1992, 1994 and 1995; RWA Bristol, 1993; Barbican, 1994 and tour, Mappin Gall., Sheffield, Royal Albert Meml Mus., Exeter, 1994; Newport Mus. and Art Gall., Bolton Metropolitan Mus. and Art Gall., 1995; Maclaurin Gall., Ayr, Huddersfield Gall., Royal Hibernian Acad. of Arts, Gallagher Gall., Dublin, Hatton Gall., Newcastle, 1994; Art First, London, 1997; Friends' Room, Royal Acad., 2000; Stephen Lacey Gall., London, 2000; Osborne Samuel Gall., London, 2007; Tate Britain, 2010; Kings Place Gall., London, 2010; Fine Art Soc., London, 2010; Browse and Darby, 2016; Art Space, 2016. *Group exhibitions:* Gimpel Fils, AIA Gall., Café Royal Centen., Towards Art (RCA), Camden Arts Centre, London, Ashmolean Mus., Oxford, 1957–72; Brit. Drawing Biennale, Teesside, 1973; British Landscape, Graves Art Gall., Sheffield, Chichester Nat. Art, 1975; Summer Exhibn, RA, 1974–2014; British Painting, 1952–77, RA, 1977; London Group, Whitechapel Open, 1978, A Free Hand, Arts Council (touring show), 1978; The British Art Show, Arts Council (touring), Recent Arts Council Purchases and Awards, Serpentine Gall., First Exhibition, Nicola Jacobs Gall., Tolly Cobbold (touring), 55 Wapping Artists, London, 1979; Four Artists, Nicola Jacobs Gall., Sculpture and Works on Paper, Nicola Jacobs Gall., Wapping Open Studios, Hayward Annual, Hayward Gall., Whitechapel Open, Whitechapel Gall., John Moore's Liverpool Exhibn 12, 1980, Exhibn 13, 1982, Walker Art Gall., Liverpool; London Gp, S London Art Gall., Wapping Artists, 1981; Images for

Today, Graves Art Gall., Sheffield, 1982; Nine Artists (touring), Helsinki, 1983; Tolly Cobbold/Eastern Arts Fourth (touring), 1983; Three Decades 1953–83, RA, 1983; Romantic Tradition in Contemporary British Painting (touring), Murcia and Madrid, Spain, and Ikon Gall., Birmingham, 1988; Cello Factory, London, 2010; RWA, Bristol, 2010; Richmond Hill Gall., London, 2010; St Paul's Crypt, London, 2010; Visual Centre for Contemporary Art, Carlow, Ireland, 2010. *Works in collections:* Arts Council of GB, Tate Gall., Coventry Art Gall., Leicester Art Gall., Nat. Gall. of Wales, Sheffield City Art Galls, Financial Times, Shell-BP, Museo de Bahia, Brazil, Nat. Gall. of Victoria, Melb., Seattle Mus. of Art, Bank of Boston, Chantrey Bequest, W Australia Art Gall., Bayer Pharmaceuticals, DoE, Nat. Westminster Bank, Power Art Gall., Aust. European Parlt, Ferens Art Gall., Museum, Murcia, Spain, Alliance & Leicester, Rosehaven PLC, Royal Academy, Linklater and Paines, Mus. of Contemp. Art, Helsinki, Christchurch, Kensington, Long Term Credit Bank of Japan, Andersen Consulting, Ashikaga Bank of Tokyo, Tetrapak, Zeneca, RWA, Deutsche Morgan-Grenfell, Mercury Asset Mgt, Ladbrokes, Crown Commodities, Stanhope, Baring Asset Mgt, St Anne's Coll., Oxford. *Recreations:* chess, badminton. *Address:* 7a Albert Place, Victoria Road, W8 5PD. *T:* (020) 7937 5197. *W:* www.anthonywhishaw.com.

**WHISHAW, Benjamin John;** actor; *b* Hitchin, Herts, 14 Oct. 1980. *Educ:* Royal Acad. of Dramatic Arts. Actor: *stage* includes: Hamlet, Old Vic, 2004; Bakkhai, Almeida, 2015; The Crucible, NY, 2016; Against, Almeida, 2017; Julius Caesar, Bridge Th., 2018; Norma Jeane Baker of Troy, The Shed, NY, 2019; *films* include: Perfume, 2006; Brideshead Revisited, 2008; Bright Star, 2009; The Tempest, 2010; Skyfall, 2012; Cloud Atlas, 2013; Lilting, Paddington, 2014; The Lobster, Suffragette, Spectre, In the Heart of the Sea, 2015; The Danish Girl, 2016; Paddington 2, 2017; Mary Poppins Returns, 2018; *television series* include: Criminal Justice, 2008; The Hollow Crown, 2012; The Hour, 2012; London Spy, 2015; A Very English Scandal, 2018 (Golden Globe for Best Actor in a Supporting Role, 2019; BAFTA Award for Best Supporting Actor, 2019; Best Supporting Actor in a Limited Series, Emmy Awards, 2019). *Address:* c/o Hamilton Hodell, 20 Golden Square, W1F 9JL. *T:* (020) 7636 1221, *Fax:* (020) 7636 1221. *E:* info@hamiltonhodell.co.uk.

**WHISTON, John Joseph;** Managing Director, Continuing Drama (formerly Creative Director, Soaps), ITV Studios, since 2011; *b* 10 Oct. 1958; *s* of Peter Rice Whiston and Kathleen Whiston (*née* Parker); partner, Nickie Lister; one *s* two *d. Educ:* Edinburgh Acad.; Balliol Coll., Oxford (BA Eng.). Follow spot operator, for Rowan Atkinson, 1982; joined BBC, 1982: gen. trainee, 1983–85; Producer, Music and Arts, 1985–94; Head: Youth and Entertainment Features, 1994–96; Entertainment and Features, 1996–98; Director of Programmes: Yorkshire Tyne Tees Prodns, 1998–2001; Granada Content (North), 2001–02; Dir, Drama, Children's, Arts and Features, Granada Content, subseq. Drama, Kids and Arts, Granada, 2002–05; Dir, ITV Prodns, 2005–09; Dir, ITV Studios, 2009–11. Motoring corresp., Vogue, 1991–93. *Recreations:* power tools, sailing dinghies, table tennis. *Address:* Ashcliffe, Tighnabruaich, Argyll PA21 2EJ. *T:* (01700) 811799.

**WHITAKER,** family name of **Baroness Whitaker**.

**WHITAKER,** Baroness *cr* 1999 (Life Peer), of Beeston in the county of Nottinghamshire; **Janet Alison Whitaker;** Deputy Chair, Independent Television Commission, 2001–03; *b* 20 Feb. 1936; *d* of late Alan Harrison Stewart and Ella Stewart (*née* Saunders); *m* 1964, Benjamin Charles George Whitaker, CBE (*d* 2014); two *s* one *d. Educ:* Nottingham High Sch. for Girls; Girton Coll., Cambridge (Major Scholar); Bryn Mawr Coll., USA (Farley Graduate Fellow); Harvard Univ. (Radcliffe Fellow). Teacher, Lycée Français de Londres, 1958–59; Editor, André Deutsch Ltd, 1961–66; Health and Safety Executive, 1974–88: Hd of Gas Safety, 1983–86; Hd of Nuclear Safety Admin, 1986–88; Department of Employment: Hd of Health and Safety Br., 1988–92; Hd of Sex Equality Div., 1992–96; Leader, UK delegn to Fourth UN Conf. on Women, 1995. Chair, Working Men's Coll. for Men and Women Corp., 1998–2001 (Fellow, 2010). Member: Sub Cttee on Social Affairs, Educn and Home Affairs, EU Select Cttee, H of L, 1999–2002; Jt Parly Cttee on Human Rights, 2000–03; Jt Parly Cttee on Corruption Bill, 2003; Jt Parly Cttee on Draft Bribery Bill, 2009; Vice-Chair, All-Party Groups: on Ethiopia, 2003–09; on Overseas Develt, 2005–; on Landmine Eradication, 2005–07; on Gypsy and Traveller Law Reform, 2006–; Vice-Chair: PLP Civil Rights Cttee, 2002–05; PLP Internat. Develt Cttee, 2003–10; Chair, Stakeholder Gp for Gypsy, Traveller and Roma Educn, DfE, 2013–. Co-Chair, Design in Public Procurement Inquiry, 2009; Vice Chair, Associate Parly Gp on Design and Innovation, 2011–17. Member: OECD Wkg Pty on Rôle of Women in the Economy, 1992–96; Employment Tribunals, 1996–2000; ACORD Gender Cttee, 1996–2002; SOS Sahel Mgt Cttee, 1997–2004 (Council, 2004–14); Immigration Audit Complaints Cttee, 1998–99; Bd and Trustee, Overseas Develt Inst., 2003–09; Chm., DFE Stakeholder Gp for Gypsy, Traveller and Roma Educn, 2013–15; Pres., Friends, Families and Travellers, 2013–. Chair, Camden Racial Equality Council, 1999. Assessor, Citizen's Charter Chartermark Unit, 1996. Dir, Tavistock & Portman NHS Trust, 1997–2001. Member: Friends Provident Cttee of Reference, 2000–08; Adv. Council, Transparency Internat. (UK), 2001–10; Adv. Council, British Inst. of Human Rights, 2005–; Council, African and W Eur. Parly Assoc., 2005–08; UNA-UK Adv. Panel, 2006–; Design Commn, 2011–17. Patron: Runnymede Trust, 1997–; British Stammering Assoc., 2003–; Student Partnerships Worldwide, 2005–; Hillcrest Community Centre, Newhaven, 2015–. Trustee: One World Trust, 2000–04 (Vice-Pres., 2004–); UNICEF UK, 2003–09. President: S Downs Soc., 2012–16; Adv. Council for Educn of Romany and other Travellers, 2014–; Newhaven Historical Soc., 2015–. Member: Fabian Soc., 1970; Humanists UK (formerly British Humanist Assoc.), 1970 (Vice-Pres., then Patron, 2004–). FRSA 1993–2014. Hon. FRIBA 2013. *Recreation:* travelling hopefully. *Address:* House of Lords, SW1A 0PW.

**WHITAKER, Claire Lois,** OBE 2015; Director: Serious, international music producers, since 1996; London International Jazz Festival, since 1996; Arts Programme Advisor, Paul Hamlyn Foundation, 2009–15 (Trustee, since 2016); *b* Heswall, Cheshire, 1 Dec. 1963; *d* of Raymond Spinks and Anne Flight; *m* 1989, Simon Whitaker; one *s* one *d. Educ:* City Univ. (MA Cultural Leadership 2009). Lending Officer, Natwest Corp. Banking Unit, 1982–89; Business Affairs Exec., Decca Records, 1989–90; Develt Dir, Southbank Centre, 1990–92; Dir, Africa 95, 1992–96. Advr, African Odyssey, Kennedy Center, 1997–2001; Representative: DCMS Live Music Forum, 2004–07; DCMS Music Export Gp, 2008–; Mem. Adv. Bd, Sing Up, 2007–. Chair, Steering Gp, ArtWorks, 2010–15. Member: London Music Bd, GLA, 2016–; Arts and Creative Economy Adv. Gp, British Council, 2016–; Music Educn Adv. Cttee, ABRSM, 2016–; Ind. Mem., Governing Body and Mem., Audit and Risk Cttee, Arts Univ. Bournemouth, 2018–; Ind. Mem., Customer and Community Network and Gp Audit Cttee, Aster Gp, 2019. Trustee, Cane Prize for African Writing, 1999–; Founder Judge, Young Marketeer of the Year, 1999, Fellow, 2010, Marketing Soc. Chm., Royal Commonwealth Soc., 2014–18 (Dep. Chm., 2007–13). Ambassador, Mayor of London's Cultural Leadership Bd, 2017–. *Recreations:* playing piano and flute, singing, ski-ing, reading. *Address:* Serious, 51 Kingsway Place, Sans Walk, Clerkenwell, EC1R 0LU. *T:* (020) 7324 1880. *E:* claire.whitaker@serious.org.uk.

**WHITAKER, David Haddon,** OBE 1991; Chairman, J. Whitaker & Sons, Ltd, 1982–97 (Director, 1966–97; Editorial Director, 1980–91); *b* 6 March 1931; *s* of late Edgar Haddon Whitaker, OBE and of Mollie Marian, *y d* of George and Louisa Seely; *m* 1st, 1959, Veronica Wallace (decd); two *s* two *d*; 2nd, 1976, Audrey Miller (marr. diss. 1979); 3rd, 1994, Marguerite van Reenen. *Educ:* Boscastle Infants' Sch.; Marlborough Coll.; St John's Coll., Cambridge. Joined family firm of publishers, J. Whitaker & Sons, Ltd, 1955; Dir, 1966; Editor, The Bookseller, 1977–79. Dir, Standard Book Numbering Agency Ltd, 1967–97 (introduced standard book numbering system in UK, 1967, internat. standard book numbering (ISBN), 1970); Member: Adv. Panel, Internat. Standard Book Numbering Agency (Berlin), 1979–97 (Chm., 1990–97); Adv. Panel, Registrar for Public Lending Right, 1983–93 (Chm., 1989–93); Standing Cttee on Technology, Booksellers' Assoc., 1984–89; Library and Information Services Council, 1985–89; Chairman: Information and Library Services Lead Body for Nat. Vocational Qualifications, 1992–95; British Nat. Bibliography Res. Fund, 1992–2001. Chairman: Soc. of Bookmen, 1984–86; Book Trade Electronic Data Interchange Standards Cttee, 1987–90. Trustee, 2002–07, Chm., 2007–17, Laser Foundn. Hon. Vice-Pres., LA, 1990. Hon. Fellow, Amer. Nat. Inst. of Standards Orgns, 1997. *Recreations:* reading, walking. *Address:* 4 Ufton Grove, N1 4HG. *T:* (020) 7241 3501. *Clubs:* Beefsteak, Garrick, Thames Rowing; Leander (Henley-on-Thames); Boscastle and Crackington Haven Gig.

**WHITAKER, (Edwin) John,** MBE 1991; show-jumper; *b* 5 Aug. 1955; *er s* of Donald Whitaker and Enid (*née* Lockwood); *m* 1979, Claire Barr; one *s* two *d*. British champion, 1992, 1993; other European championship wins: team and individual silver medals, 1983 (Ryan's Son); team gold and individual bronze, 1985 (Hopscotch); team gold and individual silver, 1987 (Milton); individual and team gold, 1989 (Milton); team bronze, 2007 (Peppermill), 2011 (Peppermill). World Cup gold medals, 1990, 1991 (Milton); Olympic individual and team silver medals, 1980, and team silver medal, 1984 (Ryan's Son); jumping Derby, 1983 (Ryan's Son), 1998 (Gammon), 2000 (Virtual Village Welham); King George V Gold Cup, 1986 (Ryan's Son), 1990 (Milton), 1997 (Virtual Village Welham); Aachen Grand Prix, 1997 (Virtual Village Welham); Rome Grand Prix, 2007 (Peppermill); Alltech Grand Prix, 2010 (Uniek). Leading Jumper of the Year, Horse of the Year Show, 1993, 1998; numerous other wins and awards. Dir, John Whitaker Internat. Ltd, 1998–. *Address:* c/o British Show Jumping Association, Stoneleigh, Warwicks CV8 2LR.
*See also M. Whitaker.*

**WHITAKER, Sir John James Ingham, (Sir Jack),** 4th Bt *cr* 1936, of Babworth, Nottinghamshire; farmer; *b* 23 Oct. 1952; *o s* of Sir James Herbert Ingham Whitaker, 3rd Bt, OBE and Mary Elisabeth Lander Whitaker (*née* Johnston); *S* father, 1999; *m* 1981, Elizabeth Jane Ravenscroft Starke; one *s* three *d. Educ:* Eton; Bristol Univ. (BSc). FCA; MIET. Pres., Royal Forestry Soc., 2013–15 (Treas., 1993–2008). High Sheriff, Notts, 2001. *Heir: s* Harry James Ingham Whitaker, *b* 16 March 1984. *Address:* Babworth Hall, Retford, Notts DN22 8EP.

**WHITAKER, Michael;** show-jumper; *b* 17 March 1960; *yr s* of Donald Whitaker and Enid (*née* Lockwood); *m* 1980, Veronique Dalems, *d* of Dino Vastapane (marr. diss.); *m* 2013, Melissa Braybrooke; one *s* two *d*. British champion, 1984, 1989; other European championship wins: Junior, 1978; team gold medal, 1985 (Warren Point); team gold, 1987 (Amanda); team gold and individual silver, 1989 (Monsanta); team silver and individual silver, 1995; team bronze, 1997; team gold (Viking), 2013; Olympic silver medal, 1984 (Amanda); Jumping Derby: 1980 (Owen Gregory); 1991 and 1992 (Monsanta); 1993 (My Messieur); King George V Gold Cup: 1982 (Disney Way); 1989 (Didi); 1992, 1994 (Midnight Madness); bareback high jump record, Dublin, 1980. *Address:* c/o British Show Jumping Association, Stoneleigh, Warwicks CV8 2LR.
*See also E. J. Whitaker.*

**WHITAKER, Steven Dixon;** Senior Master of the Senior Courts (formerly Supreme Court), Queen's Bench Division, and Queen's Remembrancer, 2007–14; *b* 28 Jan. 1950; *s* of George and Elsie Whitaker; *m* Tereska Anita Christiana Stawarz; one *s* one *d. Educ:* Burnley Grammar Sch.; Churchill Coll., Cambridge (MA). Called to the Bar, Middle Temple, 1973, Bencher, 2010–14; in practice as a barrister, specialising in property and professional negligence law, 1973–2002; Dep. Dist Judge, 1998–2002; Master of Supreme Court, QBD, 2002–07. Mem., Civil Procedure Rules Cttee, 2002–08. Liveryman, Glaziers' and Painters of Glass Co., 2008–14. Chief Consultant Editor, Atkin's Court Forms, 2008–14; Jt Gen. Editor, Civil Procedure (the White Book), 2011–14; Mem. Adv. Panel, Electronic Evidence and E-Disclosure Handbook, 2014. *Recreations:* music, poetry.

**WHITBREAD, Jasmine;** Chief Executive, London First, since 2016; *b* 1 Sept. 1963; *d* of Gerald and Ursula Whitbread; *m* 1994, Howard Exton-Smith; one *s* one *d. Educ:* Bristol Univ. (BA Hons English); Stanford Univ. (Exec. Prog.). Dir, Global Mktg, Cortex Corp., 1986–90; Mgt Trainer, Nat. Union of Disabled Persons of Uganda/VSO, 1990–92; Man. Dir, Thomson Financial, 1994–99; Regl Dir, W Africa, 1999–2002, Internat. Dir, 2002–05, Oxfam GB; Chief Exec., Save the Children UK, 2005–10; CEO, Save the Children Internat., 2010–15. Non-executive Director: BT plc, 2011–; Standard Chartered plc, 2015–. Hon. LLD Bristol, 2014. *Recreation:* competing with City of Oxford Rowing Club. *Address:* London First, Middlesex House, 34–42 Cleveland Street, W1T 4JE.

**WHITBREAD, Sir Samuel (Charles),** KCVO 2010; Director: Whitbread plc, 1972–2001 (Chairman, 1984–92); Whitbread Farms Ltd (formerly S. C. Whitbread Farms), since 1985; Lord-Lieutenant of Bedfordshire, 1991–2012; *b* 22 Feb. 1937; *s* of late Major Simon Whitbread and Helen Beatrice Margaret (*née* Trefusis); *m* 1961, Jane Mary Hayter; three *s* one *d. Educ:* Eton College. Beds and Herts Regt, 1955–57. Joined Board, Whitbread & Co., 1972, Dep. Chm., Jan. 1984. Director: Whitbread Investment Co., 1977–93; Sun Alliance Gp, 1989–92; Chm., Hertfordshire Timber Supplies, 2000–. Chm., Mid-Beds Conservative Assoc., 1969–72 (Pres., 1986–91). President: Shire Horse Soc., 1990–92; E of England Agricl Soc., 1991–92; St John Council for Beds, 1991–2012; Beds RFCA (formerly Beds TA&VRA), 1991–2012; Vice-Pres., E Anglia RFCA (formerly E Anglia TA&VRA), 1991–2000, 2005– (Pres., 2000–05). Bedfordshire: JP, 1969–83, 1991; High Sheriff, 1973–74; DL, 1974; County Councillor, 1974–82. FRSA 1986; FLS 1994; FSA 2007. Hon. LLD: De Montfort, 2002; Bedfordshire, 2007. Bledisloe Gold Medal, RASE, 1989. KStJ 1992. *Publications:* Straws in the Wind, 1997; Plain Mr Whitbread: seven centuries of a Bedfordshire family, 2007; February: birthday celebrations around the world, 2014. *Recreations:* shooting, painting, music. *Address:* Glebe House, Southill, Biggleswade, Beds SG18 9LL. *T:* (01462) 813272. *Club:* Brooks's.

**WHITBURN, Vanessa Victoria,** OBE 2014; Editor, The Archers, BBC Radio, 1991–2013; additional responsibility for Radio Drama in the Midlands, BBC, 1995–2013; freelance radio drama consultant, and drama producer and director, since 2013; *b* 12 Dec. 1951; *d* of late Victor D. Whitburn and Eileen Whitburn. *Educ:* Mount St Mary's Convent, Exeter; Univ. of Hull (BA Hons). Studio Manager, BBC, 1974–76; Asst Floor Manager, BBC TV, 1976–77; Producer and Sen. Producer, Radio Drama, Pebble Mill, 1977–88; Producer, Brookside, Channel 4, 1988–90; Producer and Director, BBC TV, Pebble Mill, 1990–91; additional responsibility: for Silver Street, 2004–09; for drama, Asian Network, 2010–13; Ed., Ambridge Extra, 2011–13. Consultant: Midwest Radio Theater Workshop, Missouri, 1985–; to ODA, on Ndiga Nacio (Kenyan radio soap opera), 1987–; to S African Broadcasting Corp. on radio soap drama, 2006–; Mem., Adv. Bd, Nat. Music Th. Festivals, USA, 2005–. Hon. DLitt Hull, 2012. *Publications:* The Archers: the official inside story, 1996. *Recreations:* opera, theatre, spending time with friends, travel.

**WHITBY,** Baron *cr* 2013 (Life Peer), of Harborne in the City of Birmingham; **Michael John Whitby;** Chairman and Managing Director, Skeldings Ltd, Smethwick (Director, 1992); *b* 6 Feb. 1948; *m* 1987, Gaynor Baldwin. Non exec. Dir, Marketing Birmingham Ltd, 2002–14. Mem. (C) Birmingham CC, 1997–2014 (Leader, 2004–12). Contested (C): Midlands W, European Parlt, 1989; Delyn, 1992.

**WHITBY, Bishop Suffragan of,** since 2014; **Rt Rev. Paul John Ferguson;** *b* 13 July 1955; *s* of Thomas and Joyce Ferguson; *m* 1982, Penelope Hewitt-Jones; two *s* one *d. Educ:* Birkenhead Sch.; New Coll., Oxford (BA 1976, MA 1980); Westminster Coll., Oxford (PGCE); King's Coll., Cambridge (BA 1984, MA 1988); Westcott Hse, Cambridge. FRCO 1975. Ordained deacon, 1985, priest 1986; Curate, St Mary's Chester, 1985–88; Chaplain and Sacrist, 1988–92, Precentor, 1992–95, Westminster Abbey; Precentor and Residentiary Canon, York Minster, 1995–2001; Archdeacon of Cleveland, 2001–14. *Publications:* (jtly) Sing His Glory, 1997; Great is the Mystery of Faith: exploring faith through the words of worship, 2011; reviews, articles on music and liturgy. *Address:* 21 Thornton Road, Stainton, Middlesbrough TS8 9DS. *T:* (01642) 593273.

**WHITBY, Mrs Joy;** Managing Director, Grasshopper Productions Ltd, since 1986; *b* 27 July 1930; *d* of James and Esther Field; *m* 1954, Anthony Charles Whitby (*d* 1975); three *s. Educ:* St Anne's Coll., Oxford. Schools Producer, BBC Radio, 1956–62; Children's Producer, BBC Television, 1962–67; Executive Producer, Children's Programmes, London Weekend Television, 1967–70; freelance producer and writer, 1970–76; Head of Children's Programmes, Yorkshire TV, 1976–85. Dir, Bd of Channel 4, 1980–84; Member: Adv. Panel for Youth, Nat. Trust, 1985–89; Bd, Unicorn Theatre, 1987–92. Trustee, Internat. Childcare Trust, 1995–97. Devised for television: Play School, 1964; Jackanory, 1965; The Book Tower, 1979; Under the Same Sky (EBU Drama Exchange), 1984. Key productions include: The Growing Summer, 1968; Catweazle, 1970. Independent film productions: Grasshopper Island, 1971; A Pattern of Roses, 1983; Emma and Grandpa, 1984; East of the Moon, 1988; The Angel and the Soldier Boy, 1989 (ACE Award, 1991); On Christmas Eve, 1992; The Mousehole Cat, 1993; The Story of Arion and the Dolphin, 1996; (with Alan Bennett and Richard Briers) Mouse and Mole (five-minute series), 1995–99; A Small Miracle, 2002; (stage prodn) Grasshopper Rhymes from Other Times, 2004; (with Alan Bennett, Richard Briers and Imelda Staunton) Mouse and Mole at Christmas Time, 2013. BAFTA Award and Prix Jeunesse: for Play School, 1965; for The Book Tower, 1980 (also BAFTA Award, 1983); Eleanor Farjeon Award for Services to Children's Books, 1979. *Publications:* Grasshopper Island, 1971, repr. 2017; Emma and Grandpa (4 vols), 1984, republd 2018; Hundreds of Bears for Ben, 2018. *E:* whitby165@btinternet.com.

**WHITBY, Mark,** FICE, FREng; Co-founder and Design Director, Whitby Wood Ltd, since 2017; *b* 29 Jan. 1950; *s* of George Whitby, MBE, FRIBA and Rhona Charmian Whitby (*née* Butler); one *s* by Alison Scott; *m* 1991, Janet Taylor; two *s* two *d. Educ:* Ealing Grammar Sch. for Boys; King's Coll., London (BSc). FICE 1992; FREng 1996. Founding Partner and Dir, Whitby Bird & Partners, then whitbybird, later Ramboll Whitbybird, subseq. Ramboll UK, 1984–2009; Dir, Davies Maguire + Whitby, 2010–15; Dir, Whitby & Mohajer Engrs, 2011–17. Major projects include: York and Lancaster Millennium Bridges, 2000; British Embassies in Dublin, 1995, Berlin, 2000, and Sana, 2006; Tate Modern Extension, 2016; City Island Bridge, Canning Town, 2017. Special Prof. of Sustainable Construction, Nottingham Univ., 2005–15; Vis. Prof. Bartlett Sch. of Architecture, UCL, 2014–19. Founder, Engineering Timelines, 1985–; Founder, The Engineering Club, 1990. Dir, Element Energy, 1999–2011; Chairman: Urban Design Alliance, 2001–02; EVO Energy, 2010–12. Pres., ICE, 2001–02. Mem., Nat. House Building Council, 2009–15. Trustee, Construction and Develt Partnership, 2007–. Gov., Building Centre Trust, 1997–2016. Hon. FRIBA 1999. *Recreations:* canoeing (Mem., Olympic Team, 1968), running (London Marathon 2001), 20th Century engineering history, the children.

**WHITCHURCH, Sir Graeme (Ian),** Kt 2006; OBE 1984; Senior Advisor, Leaders Benefits, National Parliament of Papua New Guinea, since 1970; Officer of the Parliamentary Service, Papua New Guinea, since 1970; *b* 8 Dec. 1945; *s* of late Roy Frederick Whitchurch and Alpha Aimee Whitchurch; *m* 1967, Kaia Edith Heni; three *s* three *d. Educ:* Punchbowl State Sch., Launceston, Tasmania; Launceston State High Sch. Civil Servant; PMG's Dept, Australia, 1961–64; Public Service of PNG, 1964–70. Mem., Rotary Club of Boroko, PNG, 1990–2007 (Pres., 1995–96). *Recreation:* Australian Rules Football (Life Mem., Koboni FC, Port Moresby). *Address:* PO Box 413, Konedobu, Papua New Guinea. *T:* (home) 6753211255, (office) 6753277789, *Fax:* 6753254346. *E:* gwhit@daltron.com.pg. *Clubs:* Papua (1912) (Mem. Cttee, 2002–07; Pres., 2009–), Aviat Social and Sporting (Life Mem., 1994, Pres., 1984–98), Royal Papua Yacht (Port Moresby).

**WHITE,** family name of **Baron Annaly**.

**WHITE, Sir Adrian (Edwin),** Kt 2015; CBE 1993; DL; CSci; Founder Chairman, Biwater Holdings Ltd (formerly Biwater plc), since 1968; Governor of the BBC, 1995–2000; *b* 25 July 1942; *s* of Raymond Gerard White and Lucy Mildred White (*née* Best); *m* 1971, Gillian Denise Evans; four *s* one *d. Educ:* Cray Valley Technical High; City of London Coll. Chartered Water Engineer; FCIWEM; CSci 2005. Biwater Holdings Ltd (formerly Biwater plc) (holding co. for Biwater International and other cos), 1968–. Gp Chm., British Water Industries Gp, 1992–93; Founder Chm., British Water, 1993–98; Chm., Cascal NV, 2009–10. Vice-Pres., Small Business Bureau, 1980–90; Governor, Engineering, World Economic Forum, 1989–2006; Mem., Overseas Projects Bd, DTI, 1993–95. Chm., Epsom Healthcare NHS Trust, 1990–94, 1997–99. President: Epsom Medical Equipment Fund, 1999–; Surrey Care Trust, 2007–. Founder: Denbies and St Kilda Charitable Trusts; Surrey Jobmatch, 2007; Chm., The Children's Trust, Tadworth, 2008–12. Founder, Denbies Wine Estate, 1985–. President: Dorking Swimming Club, 1988–; Dorking Scouts, 1988–; Surrey Performing Arts, 1996–; Friends of Dorking Hospital, 1999–; Dorking Soc. (formerly Dorking & District Preservation Soc.), 2006–. Mem., Surrey Scout Council, 2000–. Governor: Stanway Sch., 1984–94; Queen Elizabeth's Foundn (formerly Queen Elizabeth's Foundn for Disabled People), 1989–; Parkside Sch., 1994–96; Chm. Bd of Governors, Millfield Schs, 1997–2009. DL, 2002, High Sheriff, 2006–07, Surrey. Hon. Fellow, Regent's Park Coll., Oxford, 2005. DUniv Surrey, 2010. Winner, Free Enterprise Award, 1985. *Recreations:* family, golf, theatre. *Address:* Biwater Holdings Ltd, Biwater House, Station Approach, Dorking, Surrey RH4 1TZ. *T:* (01306) 740740; Denbies, Ranmore Common Road, Ranmore Common, Dorking, Surrey RH5 6SP. *T:* (01306) 886640.

**WHITE, Aidan Patrick;** Founder, and President, since 2018, Ethical Journalism Network (Director, 2011–18); General Secretary, International Federation of Journalists, 1987–2011; *b* Derry, N Ireland, 2 March 1951; *s* of Thomas White and Kathleen Ann McLaughlin. *Educ:* King's Sch., Peterborough. Journalist, reporter and sub-ed., Peterborough, Lincoln and Birmingham, 1968–74; sub-ed., London Evening News, 1974; chief sub-ed., Stratford Express Gp, 1975–77; Dep. Gp Ed., Stratford Express, 1977–79; journalist, The Guardian, 1980–87. Mem., Press Council, 1978–80. National Union of Journalists: Mem. Exec. Council, 1974, 1976, 1977; Treasurer, 1984–86; Chm., National Newspapers Council, 1981. Chm., EC Inf. Soc. Forum Wkg Gp, 1996–98. Chm., Appointments Panel, IMPRESS, 2015; Member: Steering Cttee, ETUC, 1997–2000; EU Expert Gp on Media Literacy, 2016–. Founder and Mem. Bd, Internat. News Safety Inst., 2003–12; Chm., Council of Global Unions, 2010–12. Trustee, Statewatch, 2011–18; Chm., Internews Europe, 2013–14. *Publications:* Making a World of Difference, 2006; Journalism, Civil Liberties and the War on Terror, 2006; To Tell You the Truth: ethical journalists initiative, 2008; Journalism as a Public Good, 2011; reports on ethics of journalism for UNESCO, UNICEF and Council of Europe. *Address:* 11 Vicarage Road, E15 4HD. *T:* 07946 291511. *E:* aidanpatrickwhite@gmail.com.

**WHITE, Aileen Elizabeth;** *see* Campbell, A. E.

**WHITE, Alan,** CMG 1985; OBE 1973; HM Diplomatic Service, retired; Ambassador to Chile, 1987–90; *b* 13 Aug. 1930; *s* of William White and Ida (*née* Hall); *m* 1st, 1954, Cynthia Maidwell (*d* 2004); two *s* one *d*; 2nd, 1980, Clare Corley Smith. SSC Army 1954 (Capt.); Hong Kong, 1959–63; MoD (Central), 1965; First Sec., FO (later FCO), 1966; Mexico City, 1969; First Sec., UK Disarmament Delegn, Geneva, 1974; Counsellor (Commercial), Madrid, 1976; Counsellor and Head of Chancery, Kuala Lumpur, 1980–83; Hd, Trade Relns and Exports Dept, FCO, 1983–85; Ambassador to Bolivia, 1985–87. *Recreations:* reading, travel. *Address:* c/o Foreign and Commonwealth Office, SW1A 2AH.

**WHITE, Alan,** FCA; Chairman: Hotter Ltd, since 2014; Ultra Finishings, since 2017; *b* 15 April 1955; *s* of Ronald and Margaret White; *m* 2009, Gillian Mills; one *s* one *d* by a previous marriage. *Educ:* Warwick Univ. (LLB). FCA 1979. Audit Senior, Arthur Andersen, 1976–79; Gen. Manager, Finance, Sharp Electronics, 1979–85; Finance Dir, N Brown Gp, 1985–99; Gp Finance Dir, Littlewoods plc, 1999–2002; Chief Exec., N Brown Gp plc, 2002–13. Chm., T. M. Lewin, 2015–16; non-executive Director: Topps Tiles plc, 2008–14; Direct Wines Ltd, 2013–16; fruugo.com Ltd, 2016–. *Recreations:* tennis, squash, ski-ing, waterski-ing, Manchester United.

**WHITE, Rt Rev. Alison Mary;** *see* Hull, Bishop Suffragan of.

**WHITE, Andrew;** QC 1997; *b* 25 Jan. 1958; *s* of Peter White and late Sandra Jeanette White (*née* Lovelace); *m* 1987, Elizabeth Denise Rooney; two *s. Educ:* University Coll. Cardiff (LLB Hons). Called to the Bar, Lincoln's Inn (Hardwick Schol., Megarry Schol.), 1980, Bencher, 2003; in practice at the Bar, 1981–; Hd of Chambers, 2011–17. Liveryman, Bakers' Co., 2015–. *Publications:* (contrib.) Encyclopaedia of Forms and Precedents, vol. 5: Building and Engineering Contracts, 5th edn (1986). *Recreations:* farming, sailing, music. *Address:* 1 Atkin Building, Gray's Inn, WC1R 5AT. *T:* (020) 7404 0102; Afflington Manor, Corfe Castle, Wareham, Dorset BH20 5HT. *Club:* Athenæum.

**WHITE, Air Vice-Marshal Andrew David,** CB 2003; DL; Chief Executive, National Security Inspectorate, 2006–10; *b* 2 Jan. 1952; *s* of Edward and Margaret White; *m* 1975, Christine Ann Spratt; two *s. Educ:* Loughborough Univ. (BTech Hons Aeronautical Engrg); RAF Cranwell. Joined RAF, 1970; served Nos 17, 151, 20 Sqdns, 1977–84; Flt Comdr, No 14 Sqdn, 1984–85; NATO staff, 1985–88; jsdc 1988; MoD staff, 1988–91; Sqdn Comdr, Nos 15 and 9 Sqdns, 1991–94; PSO to CAS, 1994–96; Station Comdr, RAF Cottesmore, 1996–99; Staff Officer, HQ Strike Comd, 1999–2003; AOC No 3 Gp, 2003–06. Non-exec. Dir, NATS, 2006–13. Chm. Govs, Cottesmore Co. Primary Sch., 1996–99. DL Northants, 2016. *Recreations:* golf, aviation, ski-ing, walking, Reserve and Cadet Forces. *Club:* Royal Air Force.

**WHITE, Rev. Canon Andrew Paul Bartholomew;** Anglican Chaplain to St George's, Baghdad, 2003–14, now Emeritus Vicar; Director, US Department of Defense and Iraqi Government Religious Sectarianism Programme, since 2007; *b* 29 June 1964; *s* of Maurice and Pauline White; *m* 1991, Caroline Spreckley; two *s. Educ:* Picardy Sch.; St Thomas' Hosp., London; Ridley Hall, Cambridge; Hebrew Univ., Jerusalem; Karliner Yeshiva, Mea Shearim, Jerusalem. Student Operating Dept Practitioner, St Thomas' Hosp., London, 1981–84; Operating Department Practitioner: Obstetrics, Derby City Hosp., 1984; St Thomas' Hosp., 1985–86 (Hon. Operating Dept Practitioner, 1990–97); ordained deacon, 1990, priest, 1991; Asst Curate, St Mark's Ch, Battersea Rise, London, 1990–93; Vicar, Ch of the Ascension, Balham Hill, London, 1993–98; Canon, Coventry Cathedral, and Dir, Internat. Centre for Reconciliation, 1998–2005. Archbishop of Canterbury's Special Representative: to Middle East, 2002–04; to Alexandria Process, 2004–09; Internat. Dir, Iraqi Inst. of Peace, 2003–. Pres. and CEO, Foundn for Relief and Reconciliation in the Middle East (formerly Foundn for Reconciliation in the Middle East), 2005–16; Vice Pres., Israel Trust of the Anglican Church, 2016–; Pres., Liverpool Christian Sch., 2017–. Advr to Mosaica Centre for Inter-Religious Cooperation, Jerusalem, 2004–; Sen. Inter-religious Advr to Iraqi Prime Minister, 2006. Vis. Lectr, Wheaton Coll., Illinois, 1999–; Vis. Fellow, Harvard Univ., 2008. Chm., Young Leadership Section, Internat. CCJ, 1990–95 (Prize for Intellectual Contribn to Jewish Christian Relns, 1993). Ambassador, Jerusalem MERIT, 2018–. Mem. for Balham, Wandsworth BC, 1998 (Dep. Chm., Social Services, 1998). Eric Lane Fellow, Clare Coll., Cambridge, 2003. Hon. PhD Gloucester, 2010. Anglo Israel Assoc. Prize, 1998; Sternberg Inter Faith Prize, Three Faith Forum, 2003; Tannenbaum Peace Prize, 2005; Cambridge Centre for Jewish Christian Relations Peacemaker Award, 2007; Prize for Peace, Woolf Inst., Cambridge, 2007; Iraq Peace Prize, Baghdad Shia Leaders; Civil Courage Prize, Train Foundn, 2010; Internat. First Freedom Award, First Freedom Center, 2011; Colson Center William Wilberforce Award, 2014. Grand Comdr and Companion of Honour, OSMTH, 2003; Cross of Valour, American OSMTH, 2005; GCStG, 2011. *Publications:* Iraq: people of hope, land of despair, 2003; Iraq: searching for hope, 2005 (Christian Book Award, 2006), rev. edn 2007; (with Hope Jones) By the Rivers of Babylon, 2008; The Vicar of Baghdad: fighting for peace in the Middle East, 2009 (Best Christian Book in Britain, Christian Resources Together, 2010); Suffer the Children, 2010; Faith Under Fire, 2010 (Ultimate Christian Liby Bk Award, 2012); Father Forgive, 2013; Jews and Christians, 2013; Suffering and Glory, 2014; The Older and Younger Brother: the tragic treatment of the Jews by the Christians, 2014; My Journey So Far, 2016; A Year with Andrew White, 2019; various newspaper articles and chapters in books on conflict resolution, Jewish Christian relns, interfaith issues, Israel/Palestine and the Middle East. *Recreations:* angora goats, cleaning, cooking, collecting crosses from around the world, collecting sebaha beads, fountain pens and books. *E:* apbw2@cam.ac.uk. *Clubs:* Carlton, Royal Over-Seas League; Alwyah (Baghdad).

**WHITE, Dr Anthony Alfred Leigh,** MBE 2004; Chairman, BW Energy Ltd, since 2009; a Commissioner, Crown Estate, 2011–17; *b* London, 15 March 1953; *s* of Joseph and Patricia White; *m* 1984, Anne Brewis; one *s* two *d. Educ:* Alleyn's Sch., Dulwich; Keble Coll., Oxford (BA 1st Cl. Physics; Johnson Meml Prize); Wolfson Coll., Oxford (DPhil 1977); City Univ. (MBA). Res. scientist, CEGB, 1979; Harkness Fellow, Los Alamos Lab., Electric Power Inst., Brown Univ., 1980–82; Strategy, Safety and Finance Depts, CEGB, 1982–88; Sen. Analyst, James Capel, Electricity Privatisation, 1989–92; National Grid: Hd, Transmission Develt, 1992–93; Mem., Exec., 1992–96; Hd, Corporate Strategy, 1994–96; Man. Dir, Kleinwort Benson and Citigroup, 1996–2002; Dir and Founder, Climate Change Capital, 2002–08. Member: Adv. Panel, UK Energy, 1993–2003; Sark Electricity Price

Control Commn, 2017–. Non-executive Director: Nat. Renewable Energy Centre, 2004–12; Low Carbon Contracts Co., 2011–. *Publications*: contribs to scientific jls, incl. Nature. *Recreations*: hiking, cooking, travelling. *Address*: The Old Vicarage, West Street, Long Buckby, Northants NN6 7QF. *T*: (01327) 843560. *E*: thewhitefamily@clara.co.uk.

**WHITE, Antony Dennis Lowndes**; QC 2001; *b* 22 Jan. 1959; *s* of Albert Dennis White and Marion Seymour White; partner, Kate Ursula Macfarlane; one *s* two *d*. *Educ*: Huish's Grammar Sch., Taunton; Clare Coll., Cambridge (MA). Called to the Bar: Middle Temple, 1983; Gibraltar, 1998; NI, 2016. *Publications*: (with S. Greer) Abolishing the Diplock Courts, 1986; *contributed to*: Justice Under Fire, 1988; The Jury Under Attack, 1988; Bullen & Leake & Jacob's Precedents of Pleadings, 14th edn, 2001 to 19th edn, 2019; Privacy and the Media: the developing law, 2002; Civil Appeals, 2002, 2nd edn 2013; Enforcing Contracts in Transition Economies, 2005; Freedom of Information Handbook, 2006, 2nd edn 2008; Information Rights, 4th edn 2014, 5th edn 2019. *Recreations*: classic cars and motorcycles, walking, swimming, cooking, wine, modern literature, contemporary art.

**WHITE, Bryan Oliver**; HM Diplomatic Service, retired; *b* 3 Oct. 1929; *s* of Thomas Frederick White and Olive May Turvey; *m* 1958, Helen McLeod Jenkins; one *s* two *d*. *Educ*: The Perse Sch.; Wadham Coll., Oxford (Lit.Hum.). HM Forces, 1948–49; FO, 1953; Kabul, Vienna, Conakry, Rio de Janeiro, the Cabinet Office, and Havana, 1953–79; Counsellor, Paris, 1980–82; Head of Mexico and Central America Dept, FCO, 1982–84; Ambassador to Honduras and (non-resident) to El Salvador, 1984–87; Consul-Gen., Lyon, 1987–89. *Recreation*: the Romance languages. *Address*: 14 Stonebridge Lane, Fulbourn, Cambridge CB21 5BW.

**WHITE, (Charles) John (Branford)**; HM Diplomatic Service, retired; Director for Development, Aquaculture Stewardship Council, since 2011; *b* 24 Sept. 1946; *s* of Frederick Bernard White and Violet Phyllis White (*née* Palmer); *m* 1975, Judith Margaret Lewis. *Educ*: Taunton Sch.; Brentwood Sch.; Pembroke Coll., Cambridge (Trevelyan Schol., MA); University Coll. London (MSc 1983). ODI Fellow, Govt of Botswana, 1968–71; ODA, 1971–77; Economic Advr, E Africa Develt Div., ODM, 1977–82; ODA, 1983–86; Asst Head, Economic Relations Dept, FCO, 1986–90; First Sec., Lagos, 1990–93; Dep. Hd of Mission, Consul Gen. and Counsellor, Tel Aviv, 1993–97; Hd, S Atlantic and Antarctic, subseq. UK Overseas Territories, Dept, FCO, and Comr (non-resident), British Antarctic Territory and British Indian Ocean Territory, 1997–2001; High Comr, Barbados and the Eastern Caribbean States, 2001–05. Dir for Develt, Marine Stewardship Council, 2006–10. Gov., Atlantic Coll., 2012–16. *Recreations*: walking, golfing, opera going. *Address*: 26 Turner House, Clevedon Road, Twickenham, Middx TW1 2TE. *Club*: Royal Mid-Surrey Golf.

**WHITE, Christopher**; Director, Institute for Industrial Strategy, King's College London, since 2018; *b* 28 April 1967. *Educ*: Univ. of Manchester (BE); Univ. of Bath (MBA). Work at Longbridge with MG Rover; freelance PR consultant. Mem. (C) Warwick DC, 2007–10. Contested (C): Birmingham Hall Green, 2001; Warwick and Leamington, 2005. MP (C) Warwick and Leamington, 2010–17; contested (C) same seat, 2017. PPS to Minister of State for Policing Crime and Criminal Justice, 2015–16, for Security, 2015–16. Chair, Cttee on Arms Export Controls, 2016–17; Member: Internat. Develt Select Cttee, 2010–15; Business, Energy and Industrial Strategy (formerly Business, Innovation and Skills) Select Cttee, 2015–17. Co-Chair, All Party Parly Gp on Manufg, 2010–17, on Charities and Volunteering, 2016–17; Chair, All Party Parly Gp on Video Games, 2014–17; Vice Chair, All Party Parly Gp on Poverty, 2010–15. Introd. Private Mem.'s Bill, resulting in Public Services (Social Value) Act, 2012. Pres., Warwicks Coll. Gp, 2017–. Mem. Bd and Vice Chm., Policy Connect, 2011–; Member: Bd, Social Enterprise UK, 2018–; Crown Rep. Voluntary, Community and Social Enterprise Adv. Panel, 2018–. Member: Cranfield Manufg Council, 2018–; Strategic Cttee, Council for Mathematical Scis. Dir, Art in the Park, 2018–. Trustee, Motionhouse Dance Charity, 2011–17.

**WHITE, Prof. Sir Christopher (John)**, Kt 2001; CVO 1995; PhD; FBA 1989; Director, Ashmolean Museum, Oxford, 1985–97; Fellow of Worcester College, 1985–97, and Professor of the Art of the Netherlands, 1992–97, now Professor Emeritus, Oxford University; *b* 19 Sept. 1930; *s* of late Gabriel Ernest Edward Francis White, CBE and Elizabeth Grace Ardizzone; *m* 1957, Rosemary Katharine Desages; one *s* two *d*. *Educ*: Downside Sch.; Courtauld Institute of Art, London Univ. BA (Hons) 1954, PhD 1970. Served Army, 1949–50; commnd, RA, 1949. Asst Keeper, Dept of Prints and Drawings, British Museum, 1954–65; Director, P. and D. Colnaghi, 1965–71; Curator of Graphic Arts, Nat. Gall. of Art, Washington, 1971–73; Dir of Studies, Paul Mellon Centre for Studies in British Art, 1973–85; Adjunct Prof. of History of Art, Yale Univ., 1976–85; Associate Dir, Yale Center for British Art, 1976–85. Dutch Govt Schol., 1956; Hermione Lectr, Alexandra Coll., Dublin, 1959; Adjunct Prof., Inst. of Fine Arts, New York Univ., 1973 and 1976; Conference Dir, European-Amer. Assembly on Art Museums, Ditchley Park, 1975; Visiting Prof., Dept of History of Art, Yale Univ., 1976; Vis. Curator, Courtauld Gall., 2011. Trustee: V & A Mus., 1997–2004; NACF, 1998–2005; Mauritshuis, The Hague, 1999–2008. Gov., British Inst. of Florence, 1994–2002. Dir, Burlington Magazine, 1981– (Chm., 1996–2002). Reviews Editor, Master Drawings, 1967–80. *Publications*: Rembrandt and his World, 1964; The Flower Drawings of Jan van Huysum, 1965; Rubens and his World, 1968; Rembrandt as an Etcher, 1969, 2nd edn 1999; (jtly) Rembrandt's Etchings: a catalogue raisonné, 1970; Dürer: the artist and his drawings, 1972; English Landscape 1630–1850, 1977; The Dutch Paintings in the Collection of HM The Queen, 1982, 2nd edn 2015; (ed) Rembrandt in Eighteenth Century England, 1983; Rembrandt, 1984; Peter Paul Rubens: man and artist, 1987 (Eugène Baie Prize, 1983–87); (jtly) Drawing in England from Hilliard to Hogarth, 1987; (jtly) Rubens in Oxford, 1988; (jtly) One Hundred Old Master Drawings from the Ashmolean Museum, 1991; (jtly) The Dutch and Flemish Drawings at Windsor Castle, 1994; Anthony van Dyck: Thomas Howard, the Earl of Arundel, 1995; Dutch, Flemish and German Paintings in the Ashmolean Museum, 1999; (ed jtly) Rembrandt by Himself, 1999; The Later Flemish Pictures in the Collection of HM The Queen, 2007; (jtly) The Dutch and Flemish Drawings in the Victoria and Albert Museum, 2014; film (script and commentary), Rembrandt's Three Crosses, 1969; various exhibn catalogues; contribs to Burlington Mag., Master Drawings, etc. *Address*: 34 Kelly Street, NW1 8PH. *T*: (020) 7485 9148; Shingle House, St Cross, Harleston, Norfolk IP20 0NT. *T*: (01986) 782264.

**WHITE, Prof. David Clifford Stephen**, CBE 2009; DPhil; documentary, portrait and natural environment photographer, since 2009; Director, Institute of Food Research, 2004–09; Vice Chairman of Trustees, Cavernoma Alliance UK, since 2019 (Chairman, 2013–19); *b* 8 March 1941; *s* of late Clifford George White and of Joyce Beatrice White (*née* Lawley); *m* 1st, 1965, Ailsa Pippin (marr. diss.); one *s* one *d*; one *s*; 2nd, 1987, Patricia Spallone. *Educ*: Berkhamsted Sch.; New Coll., Oxford (BA 1962; MA 1967; DPhil 1967). Deptl Demonstrator, Dept of Zool., Univ. of Oxford, 1967–71; Department of Biology, University of York: Lectr, 1971–86; Sen. Lectr, 1986–90; Reader, 1990–95; Prof., 1995–97; Head of Dept, 1990–97; Dir of Sci. and Technol., BBSRC, 1997–2004. Photographic exhibition: The Living Medieval Parish Churches of Norwich, Hostry of Norwich Cath., 2011; The Restoration and Renewal of St Stephen's Church, Norwich, St Stephen's Church, 2013; Life, Light and Insight, Blickling Hall, 2014. *Publications*: Biological Physics, 1973; The Kinetics of Muscle Contraction, 1973; The Living Mediaeval Parish Churches of Norwich, 2012; Priorities for Research into Cavernoma, 2016. *Recreations*: walking, photography. *Address*: 16 The Crescent, Chapelfield Road, Norwich NR2 1SA. *T*: (01603) 630489. *E*: whitedcs12@gmail.com. *W*: www.davidwhitephotography.co.uk.

*See also* A. F. Moore-Gwyn.

**WHITE, Sir David Harry**, Kt 1992; DL; Chairman, Mansfield Brewing, 1993–2000; Director, 1970–88, a Deputy Chairman, 1988–90, Chairman of Trustees, 1986–2000, National Freight Consortium; *b* 12 Oct. 1929; *s* of late Harry White, OBE, FCA, and Kathleen White; *m* 1971, Valerie Jeanne White; one *s* three *d* (and one *d* decd). *Educ*: Nottingham High Sch.; HMS Conway. Master Mariner's F. G. Certificate. Sea career, apprentice to Master Mariner, 1944–56; Terminal Manager, Texaco (UK) Ltd, 1956–64; Operations Manager, Gulf Oil (GB) Ltd, 1964–68; Asst Man. Dir, Samuel Williams Dagenham, 1968–70; Trainee to Gp Managing Director, British Road Services Ltd, 1970–76; Group Managing Director: British Road Services, 1976–82; Pickfords, 1982–84; NFC Property Gp, 1984–87; Chm., Nottingham HA, 1986–98; Director (non-executive): BR Property Bd, 1985–87; Y. J. Lovell Ltd, 1987–94; Hilda Hanson Ltd, 1996–2010; James Bell (Nottingham) Ltd, 1997–2010; Nottingham Forest FC, 1999–2004; Alkane Energy plc, 2000–04; non-exec. Chm., EPS Ltd, 1997–2000. Mem., British Coal Corp., 1993–94; Chm., Coal Authy, 1994–99. Mem. Editorial Bd, Nottingham Evening Post, 2003–10. Chairman: Nottingham Develt Enterprise, 1987–93; Bd of Governors, Nottingham Trent Univ. (formerly Nottingham Poly.), 1989–99. Trustee, Djanogly City Technology Coll., 1989–99. Hon. Pres., Notts County Branch, RSPCA, 1987–2010. Governor, Nottingham High Sch., 1987–99. DL Notts, 1989. Hon. DBA Nottingham Trent, 1999; Hon. DLaw Nottingham, 2011. *Recreations*: football supporter (Nottingham Forest), walking. *Address*: Whitehaven, 6 Croft Road, Edwalton, Nottingham NG12 4BW.

**WHITE, David Thomas, (Tom)**, CBE 1990; Principal and Chief Executive, NCH Action for Children (formerly National Children's Home), 1990–96; *b* 10 Oct. 1931; *s* of Walter Henry White and Annie White; *m* 1956, Eileen May Moore; two *d* (and one *s* decd). *Educ*: Council Primary and Maesydderwen Grammar Sch., Ystradgynlais, Swansea Valley; University Coll., Swansea (Social Sci.); London School of Economics (Social Work). Clerical Officer, CS, 1947–54; National Service, RAF, 1951–53. Social work and management posts, Devon CC, 1957–61; Dep. Children's Officer, Monmouthshire, 1961–65; Dep. County Children's Officer, Lancs, 1965–70; Dir of Social Services, Coventry, 1970–85; Dir of Social Work, Nat. Children's Home, 1985–90. Past President: Assoc. of Child Care Officers; Assoc. of Directors of Social Services; Gov., Nat. Inst. of Social Work, 1973–96 (Hon. Fellow, 1996); Chm., Nat. Foster Care Assoc., 1996–99. Mem. (Lab), Coventry CC, 1996–2004. Hon. DBA Coventry, 1998. Coventry Award of Merit, Coventry CC, 2002. *Publications*: (contrib.) Social Work, the Media and Public Relations, 1991. *Recreations*: gardening, golf, walking. *Address*: Heathcote House, Little Tew, Chipping Norton, Oxon OX7 4JE. *T*: (01608) 683873.

**WHITE, David Vines**; Somerset Herald of Arms, since 2004; Registrar, College of Arms, since 2014; *b* 27 Oct. 1961; *s* of late Peter Vines White and Sheila White (*née* Chatterton, *widow* of Lt Comdr (E.) John William Windley Baker, RN). *Educ*: Kelvinside Acad.; Marlborough Coll.; Pembroke Coll., Cambridge (MA); Courtauld Inst. (MA). Res. Asst, College of Arms, 1988–95; Rouge Croix Pursuivant, 1995–2004. Member, Council: British Record Soc., 1998–; Heraldry Soc., 2000–12 (Chm., 2006–09; Hon. Vice Pres., 2013–). Hon. Vice Pres., Cambridge Univ. Heraldic and Genealogical Soc., 2002–; Hon. Genealogist, Royal Victorian Order, 2010–. Trustee, Marc Fitch Fund, 2008–. Mem., Cook Soc., 2017–. *Address*: College of Arms, Queen Victoria Street, EC4V 4BT. *T*: and *Fax*: (020) 7248 1766. *E*: somerset@college-of-arms.gov.uk. *Club*: Travellers.

**WHITE, Rt Rev. Francis, (Frank)**; Assistant Bishop of Newcastle, 2010–16; an Honorary Assistant Bishop, Diocese of York, since 2017; *b* 26 May 1949; *s* of John Edward White and Mary Ellen White; *m* 1982, Alison Mary Dumbell (*see* Bishop Suffragan of Hull). *Educ*: St Cuthbert's GS, Newcastle upon Tyne; Consett Tech. Coll.; UWIST, Cardiff (BScEcon); UC Cardiff (DipSocSci); St John's Coll., Nottingham (Dip. Pastoral Studies); Nottingham Univ. (DipTh). Dir, Youth Action York, 1971–73; Detached Youth Worker, Manchester, 1973–77; Asst Curate, St Nicholas, Durham, 1980–84; Sen. Curate, St Mary and St Cuthbert, Chester-le-Street, 1984–87; Chaplain, Durham HA Hosps, 1987–89; Vicar, St John the Evangelist, Birtley, 1989–97; RD of Chester-le-Street, 1993–97; Archdeacon of Sunderland, 1997–2002; Bishop Suffragan of Brixworth, 2002–10. Proctor in Convocation, Gen. Synod of C of E, 1987–2000. Hon. Canon: Durham Cathedral, 1997–2002; Peterborough Cathedral, 2002–10; St Nicholas Cathedral, Newcastle, 2010–16. *Recreations*: birdwatching, walking, motor cars, theatre, soccer, cycling. *Address*: Hullen House, Woodfield Lane, Hessle, E Yorks HU13 0ES. *T*: (01482) 649019. *E*: white6.francis1949@gmail.com.

**WHITE, Frank Richard**; JP; former executive director and industrial relations adviser; Director, National Training College, GMB (formerly General, Municipal, Boilermakers and Allied Trades Union), 1988–2000; *b* 11 Nov. 1939; *m*; two *s* one *d*. *Educ*: Bolton Tech. Coll. Member: Bolton CC, 1963–74; Greater Manchester CC, 1973–75; Bolton MBC (formerly DC), 1986–2012 (Cabinet Mem. for HR, Perf. Mgt and Community Cohesion, 2001–12; Mayor, 2005–06). Member: GMB; IPM; Inst. of Management Services. Contested (Lab): Bury and Radcliffe, Feb. 1974; Bury North, 1983; Bolton NE, 1987. MP (Lab) Bury and Radcliffe, Oct. 1974–1983; PPS to Minister of State, Dept of Industry, 1975–76; Asst Govt Whip, 1976–78; Opposition Whip, 1980–82; opposition spokesman on church affairs, 1980–83. Chairman: All Party Paper Industry Gp, 1979–83; NW Lab Gp, 1979–83; Mem., NW Regional Exec., Labour Party, 1986–88. Director: Lancs Co-op. Develt Agency, 1984–; Bolton/Bury TEC, 1995–2004; Mem., Greater Manchester Police Authy, 1997–2004; Mem. Area Bd, United Norwest Co-op., 1994–2004. Chairman: Bolton FM Community Radio, 2005–12; Age Concern, Bolton, 2008–13. President: Bolton United Services Veterans' Assoc., 1988–2012; Bolton Male Voice Choir, 1992–2004; Vice-Pres., E Lancs Railway Preservation Soc., 1983–2005. Hon. Alderman, Bolton MBC, 2013. JP Bolton, 1968–2010 (Chm. Bench, 1993–95). Hon. Fellow, Bolton Inst., 1993. DUniv Bolton, 2010. *Address*: 23 Dovedale Road, Bolton, Lancs BL2 5HT.

**WHITE, Sir George (Stanley James)**, 4th Bt *cr* 1904, of Cotham House, Bristol; FSA; Keeper of the Collection of the Worshipful Company of Clockmakers, 1987–2018, now Keeper Emeritus; *b* 4 Nov. 1948; *s* of Sir George Stanley Midelton White, 3rd Bt, and Diane Eleanor, *d* of late Bernard Abdy Collins, CIE; *S* father, 1983; *m* 1st, 1974; one *d*; 2nd, 1979; one *s* one *d*; 3rd, 2006, Joanna, *d* of Kazimierz Migdal. *Educ*: Harrow School. Pres. Gloucestershire Soc., 1993; Member: Gloucester DAC for Care of Churches, 1985– (Clocks Advr, 1986–); Council, Bristol and Glos Archaeological Soc., 1987–2000 (Chm., 1992–95); Council, Nat. Trust, 1998–2004. Pres., British Horological Inst., 2001. Chm. Adv. Bd, Bristol Cars, 2011–14. Liveryman, Co. of Clockmakers, 1986– (Asst, 1994–; Master, 2001); Brother, Parish Clerks' Co., 2009–17. High Sheriff, Avon, 1989; JP Bristol, 1991–95. Parish Clerk, St Mary the Virgin, Aldermanbury, 2009–17. FSA 1988. Harrison

Medal, Clockmakers' Co., 2017. *Publications:* English Lantern Clocks, 1989; Tramlines to the Stars, 1995; The Clockmakers of London, 1998, enlarged edn 2018; contrib. Antiquaries' Jl, Antiquarian Horology, etc. *Heir: s* George Philip James White, *b* 19 Dec. 1987.

**WHITE, His Honour Graham Brian Newton;** a Circuit Judge, 2007–12; Judicial Member, Parole Board, since 2010; Chair, Medical Practitioners Tribunal Service and Health and Care Professions Tribunal Service, since 2017; *b* London, 6 Dec. 1942; *s* of Pat and Molly White; *m* 1971, Lesley Williams; five *s* two *d*. *Educ:* Uxendon Manor Co. Prim. Sch., Wembley; Haberdashers' Aske's Hampstead Sch.; College of Law; Univ. of London (LLB by private study 1966). Admitted solicitor, 1965; Dep. District Judge, 1979–2007; Asst Recorder, 1992–96; Recorder, 1996–2007. Mem. Council, Law Soc., 1989–2007; Pres., Herts Law Soc., 1995. *Recreation:* rock 'n' roll drummer. *E:* gwhitesol@btinternet.com.

**WHITE, Graham John;** Chairman, Marine Aviation and General (London) Ltd, since 2014 (Director, since 2011); *b* 4 June 1946; *s* of William Kenneth White and Evelyn White (née Marshall); four *d* (and one *d* decd). *Educ:* University Coll. Sch., Hampstead; Gonville and Caius Coll., Cambridge (BA 1968); Cranfield Sch. of Mgt (MBA 1973). Willis Faber Gp, 1968–83 (Gp Co. Sec., 1980); Man. Dir, Richard Beckett Underwriting Agencies Ltd, 1983–86; NY Rep., Merrett Syndicates Ltd, 1987–88; Dir, Jardine Thompson Graham Ltd, 1989–96; Chairman: Bankside Members' Agency Ltd, 1996–97; Murray Lawrence Members' Agency, 1997–98; Chief Exec., Amlin Pvte Capital Ltd, 1998–2000; Chairman: CBS Pvte Capital Ltd, 2000–06; Argenta Private Capital Ltd, 2011–15 (Dir, 2006–); Man. Dir, 2008–11); Director: CBS Insce Hldgs Ltd, 2000–07; Argenta Holdings plc, 2008–; Newton Follis Partnership Ltd, 2011–16. Mem., Enforcement Bd, Lloyd's of London, 2016– (Mem. Council, 2006–15; Dep. Chm., 2007–14); Vice Pres., Insurance Inst. of London, 2011– (Mem. Exec. Cttee, 2014–). Director: Music Platform Company Ltd, 2007–11 (Director: English Pocket Opera Ltd, 2002–07; Children's Music Workshop Ltd, 2006–07); City of London Fest., 2009–. Chm., Lloyd's Charities Trust, 2008–09; Trustee, Lloyd's Patriotic Fund, 2010–15. *Recreations:* snow-shoeing, golf, tennis, theatre, opera, watching Tottenham Hotspur. *Address:* Marine Aviation and General (London) Ltd, 1 Minster Court, EC3R 7AA. *T:* (020) 7398 4010, *Fax:* (020) 7398 4011. *E:* gwhite@ maglondon.com. *Clubs:* Travellers, City of London; Hampstead Golf, Saunton Golf, East Devon Golf, Lloyd's Golf.

**WHITE, Harvey,** DM; FRCS; Consulting Surgeon: Royal Marsden Hospital, since 1976; King Edward VII Hospital for Officers, since 1983; *b* 10 March 1936; *s* of Arthur White and Doris (née Dunstan); *m* 1965, Diana Mary Bannister; one *s* one *d*. *Educ:* Winchester Coll.; Magdalen Coll., Oxford (DM, MCh); St Bartholomew's Hosp. FRCS 1970. St Bartholomew's Hospital: Lectr in Physiol., 1966–71; Sen. Surgical Registrar, 1971–76; Chm., Div. of Surgery, Royal Marsden Hosp., 1987–89. Editor: Oxford Med. Gazette, 1956–57; St Bartholomew's Hosp. Jl, 1960–61; Clinical Oncology, 1983–84; European Jl of Surgical Oncology, 1985–87; Chm., Royal Society of Medicine Press Ltd, 1997–2005. Hunterian Prof., RCS, 1988; Hunterian Oration, 1993. Vice-President: Brit. Assoc. of Surgical Oncology, 1988; RSocMed, 2008–10; President: Med. Soc. of London, 1995–96; Hunterian Soc., 2004–05. Mem. Council, Cancer Relief Macmillan Fund, 1991–95. Lead Vice-Patron, Brendoncare Foundn of Elderly, 2014– (Chm., 1986–2003); Trustee, Duchess of Somerset's Almshouses, 1992. Ernest Miles Medal, Brit. Assoc. of Surgical Oncology, 1989; Royal Soc. of Medicine Medal, 2012. *Publications:* (jtly) The Greater Omentum, 1983, Russian edn 1989; (jtly) The Omentum and Malignant Diseases, 1984; An Atlas of Omental Transposition, 1987; contrib. to: History of Surgery, 1974; Royal Hospital St Bartholomew, 1974; Surgical Oncology for Nurses, 1978; The Laser in General Surgery, 1979; Oxford Companion to Medicine, 1986; European Handbook of Oncology, 1989; Aird's Companion to Surgery, 1992; A History of the London Clinic, 2007; ed. and contrib. various learned books, surgical and cancer jls. *Recreations:* working my Guide dog, writing, fishing. *Address:* 12 Belvedere House, 130 Grosvenor Road, SW1V 3JY. *T:* 07860 330444. *Clubs:* Garrick, Royal Society of Medicine.

**WHITE, Ian;** Member (Lab) Bristol, European Parliament, 1989–99; former Partner, McCarthy and White, solicitors. Contested (Lab) SW Reg., EP elecn, 1999.

**WHITE, Prof. Ian Hugh,** PhD; CEng, FREng, FIET; Vice-Chancellor and President, University of Bath, since 2019; *b* 6 Oct. 1959; *s* of Oliver Morrow White and Emily Greenaway White; *m* 1983, Margaret Rosemary Hunt; one *s* one *d*. *Educ:* Belfast Royal Acad.; Jesus Coll., Cambridge (BA 1980, MA 1984; PhD 1984). FREng 2006. Res. Fellow, 1983–84, Asst Lectr, 1984–90, Univ. of Cambridge; Prof. of Physics, Univ. of Bath, 1990–96; Prof. of Optical Communication Systems, 1996–2001, Hd, Dept of Electrical and Electronic Engrg, 1998–2001, Univ. of Bristol; Van Eck Prof. of Engrg, 2001–19, Pro-Vice-Chancellor, 2010–11, Univ. of Cambridge; Fellow, 2001–19, Master, 2011–19, Jesus Coll. Cambridge. Royal Soc. Leverhulme Res. Fellow, Univ. of Bath, then Bristol, 1995–96. *Publications:* numerous contribs on semiconductor optoelectronic components, optical communications and sensors to learned jls. *Recreations:* church, music. *Address:* University of Bath, Claverton Down, Bath BA2 7AY.

**WHITE, Rev. Ian Thomas;** President of the Methodist Conference, 2002–03; *b* 6 July 1939; *s* of Sydney White and Annie (née Heathcote); *m* 1967, Diana (née Casson); two *d*. *Educ:* Hartley Victoria Theol Coll., Manchester. Methodist Minister: Hull Trinity Circuit, 1965–69; Retford Circuit, 1969–72; Bristol South Circuit, 1972–78; Bristol Kingswood Circuit, 1978–87 (Supt Minister, 1981–87); Sec., Bristol Dist Synod, 1978–87; Chairman: Bristol Dist, 1987–98; Channel Is Dist, 1998–2004; Supt Minister, Jersey Circuit, 1998–2004. Moderator, Bristol Free Ch Council, 1989–93. Chm., Methodist Ministers' Housing Soc., 2009–12. *Recreations:* reading, jigsaws, current affairs, theatre, music. *Address:* 26 Aln Crescent, Newcastle upon Tyne NE3 2LU. *T:* (0191) 285 5975.

**WHITE, Jack Edwin P.;** *see* Palmer-White.

**WHITE, James Ashton V.;** *see* Vallance White.

**WHITE, Sir Jan Hew D.;** *see* Dalrymple-White.

**WHITE, Prof. Jean Christine,** CBE 2017; Chief Nursing Officer for Wales, and Nurse Director NHS Wales, Welsh Government, since 2010; *b* Bishopston, Gower, Wales, 19 Dec. 1960; *d* of late Brian Richard Clark and of Eleanor Patricia Clark; *m* 1985, Dr Andrew Mark White. *Educ:* W Glamorgan Sch. of Nursing, Swansea (SRN 1982); Univ. of Wales. Coll. of Cardiff Univ. (Cert Ed (FE)/RN Teacher 1989; PhD 2006); Swansea Inst. Higher Educn (BN 1992); Univ. of Glamorgan (MSc Health Care Mgt 1998). Student nurse, W Glamorgan Sch. of Nursing, Swansea, 1979–82; Theatre Staff Nurse: Singleton Hosp., Swansea, 1982–83; UCH, London, 1983–84; Theatre Staff Nurse, 1984–85, Theatre Sister, 1985–88, Morriston Hosp., Swansea; Tutor, W Glamorgan Sch. of Nursing and Midwifery, 1988–89; Lectr, Mid and W Wales Sch. of Nursing, 1989–91; Lectr, 1991–94, Sen. Lectr, 1994–2000, Univ. of Wales, Swansea; Actg Dir, Quality and Standards/Professional Advr, Welsh Nat. Bd for Nursing, Midwifery and Health Visiting, 2000–02; Professional Advr (Adult Nursing), 2002–04, Dir of Quality and Standards, 2004–06, Health Professions Wales; Nursing Officer, Welsh Assembly Govt, 2006–10. Expert Nurse Advr to WHO Eur. Reg., 2013–. Hon. Visiting Professor: Cardiff Univ., 2011–; Univ. of S Wales, 2016–;

Fellow: Swansea Univ., 2013; Bangor Univ., 2014. Hon. DSc Swansea, 2013. MStJ 2018. *Publications:* contrib. articles to professional nursing jls, incl. Eurohealth Observer, British Jl Nursing, Nursing Mgt, Nursing Times. *Recreations:* reading, hand embroidery, driving sports cars, Star Trek fan. *Address:* Nursing Directorate, Welsh Government Offices, Cathays Park, Cardiff CF10 3NQ. *T:* 0300 025 5517. *E:* jean.white@gov.wales.

**WHITE, Jeremy Nigel;** President, White Foundation, since 2001; Chairman, White Capital Partners, since 2009; Director: Integrity Capital plc, since 2015; Integrity Capital Advisors Ltd, since 2017; *b* 20 Jan. 1955; *s* of Colin Lawrence White and late Drusilla Marie Goodman; *m* 1989, Kim-Marie Klinger; one *s* three *d*. *Educ:* Leeds Grammar Sch.; Leeds Polytechnic (Dip. Management, Accounting and Finance, Marketing); City Univ. (MBA); Pepperdine Univ. (MA Educn and Psychology; Dist Alumni 1995). Man. Dir, RSS Gp, 1975–79; Chm., White Gp Electronics, 1979–85; Britannia Group: Jt Man. Dir, 1985–86; Pres., 1986–88; Chm., Data Safe Inc., 1988–94; Chief Exec. and Dep. Chm., Prince's Youth Business Trust, 1994–95; Dep. Chm., Youthnet UK, 1995–2000; Chm., Nettec plc, 1995–2001, 2003–06; Dir, Vizual Business Tools Ltd, subseq. OneclickHR plc, 1997–2003; Chm., Newfound International Resorts NV, 2006–08. Mem., Bd, British-Amer. Chamber of Commerce, S Calif, 1993–94, and other LA orgns, 1992–94. Member: Council, Industry and Parlt Trust, 1984–88 and 1995–2000; Young Enterprise Nat. Council, 1986–98; Adv. Council Educn and Trng, Inst. of Econ. Affairs, 1996–2000; DoI Business Links Accreditation Adv. Bd, 1996–98; Small and Medium Size Enterprises Task Gp and Basic Skills Gp, Univ. for Industry, 1999–2000; Economic Wkg Gp, Acad. for Develt of a Democratic Envmt, Malta, 2012–13; Business Start-up Council, Malta Enterprise, 2013–14; Mem., Strategy Bd, Cass Business Sch., 2012–. Trustee: Prince of Wales Award for Innovation, 1995–2014; Technology Coll. Trust, 1998–2000. Hon. Vis. Prof., Cass Business Sch., 2018–. Gov., Pepperdine Univ., 1993–; Member: Council, City Univ. Business Sch., 1995–99; Global Adv. Bd, Cass Business Sch., London, 2018–; Mem. Ct Govs, Univ. of Westminster, 1999–2002. Founder and Judge, World Sax Competition, Montreux, 2002–06. Produced film, Virtuosic Saxophones, 2002. Mem., BSES exp. to W Himalayas, 1989; flying records: Lisbon to LA, 1990; LA to Albuquerque, 1990; Buenos Aires to LA, 1991; La Paz to LA, 1991. FLS 2015. *Publications:* The Retail Financial Services Sector, 1985; 21st Century Schools—Educating for the Information Age, 1997. *Recreations:* private flying, collecting, jazz music, photography. *E:* info@whitefoundation.com. *Clubs:* Brooks's, Pilgrims; Royal Malta Yacht.

**WHITE, Prof. Jeremy Richard, (Jerry);** Professor in Modern London History, Birkbeck, University of London, since 2016 (Visiting Professor: in London History, 2004–09; in Modern London History, 2009–16); *b* 23 March 1949; *s* of John Robert White and Molly Loiseau; *m* 1st, 1981, Sandra Margaret Smith (marr. diss. 1995); two *s* one *d*; 2nd, 1995, Rosie Cooper; one *d*. *Educ:* Swanage Grammar Sch.; Cosham and Hackney Technical Colls. Sen. Public Health Inspector, Islington, 1970–81; Asst Borough Housing Officer, Haringey, 1981–84; London Borough of Hackney: Head, Environmental Health, 1984–87; Dir, Environmental Health and Consumer Protection, 1987–89; Chief Exec. and Town Clerk, 1989–95. Comr for Local Admin in England (Local Govt Ombudsman), 1995–2009. Vis. Prof., Sch. of Arts, Middlesex Univ., 1996–98. Associate Fellow, Centre for Social History, Univ. of Warwick, 1997–99. FRHistS 2008. Hon. DLitt London, 2005. *Publications:* Rothschild Buildings: life in an East End tenement block 1887–1920, 1980; The Worst Street in North London: Campbell Road, Islington, between the wars, 1986; Fear of Voting: local democracy and its enemies 1894–1994, 1994; (with Michael Young) Governing London, 1996; London in the Twentieth Century: a city and its people (Wolfson History Prize), 2001; London in the Nineteenth Century: a human awful wonder of God, 2007; London in the Eighteenth Century: a great and monstrous thing, 2012; (ed with Andrew Whitehead) London Fictions, 2013; Zeppelin Nights: London in the First World War, 2014 (Social History Book of the Year, Spear's Book Awards, 2014); Mansions of Misery: a biography of the Marshalsea Debtors' Prison, 2016. *Recreations:* reading, music, London. *Address:* Birkbeck, University of London, Malet Street, WC1E 7HX. *T:* (020) 7631 6000. *Club:* Reform.

**WHITE, John;** *see* White, C. J. B.

**WHITE, Rev. Canon John Austin,** CVO 2012 (LVO 2004); Canon, 1982–2012, now Canon Emeritus, and Vice-Dean, 2004–12, Windsor; *b* 27 June 1942; *s* of Charles White and Alice Emily (née Precious). *Educ:* The Grammar Sch., Batley, W Yorkshire; Univ. of Hull (BA Hons); College of the Resurrection, Mirfield. Assistant Curate, St Aidan's Church, Leeds, 1966–69; Asst Chaplain, Univ. of Leeds, 1969–73; Asst Dir, post ordination training, Dio. of Ripon, 1970–73; Chaplain, Northern Ordination Course, 1973–82. Dir of Clergy Courses, 1998–2012, Warden, 2000–03, St George's House, Windsor Castle; European Dep. for Dio. Mexico, Anglican Ch of Mexico, 2003–; Hon. Canon, Anglican Cathedral of N Mexico, 2012–. Chm., Windsor Fest., 1998–2015 (Pres., 2015–). Trustee, Manchester Acad. of Fine Arts, 2006–. Liveryman, Masons' Co., 2009–. *Publications:* (with Julia Neuberger) A Necessary End: attitudes to death, 1991; (with L. R. Muir) Nicolaus Ferrar: materials for a life, 1997; Phoenix in Flight, 1999; (with Mark Stenning) Spoken Light, 2007; (ed and contrib.) In the Spirit of the Age: sculptural restoration, 2016; (contrib.) Education and Extremism, 2018; poems and various articles. *Recreations:* medieval iconography, drama, Italy, cooking, poetry, Mexico. *Address:* 24 Camm Avenue, Windsor, Berks SL4 4NW.

**WHITE, Prof. John Edward Clement Twarowski,** CBE 1983; FSA; Durning-Lawrence Professor of the History of Art, University College London, 1971–90 (Vice-Provost, 1984–88; Pro Provost, 1990–95); *b* 4 Oct. 1924; *s* of Brigadier A. E. White and Suzanne Twarowska; *m* 1950, Xenia Joannides *d* 1991). *Educ:* Ampleforth College; Trinity College, Oxford; Courtauld Institute of Art, University of London. Served in RAF, 1943–47. BA London 1950; Junior Research Fellow, Warburg Inst., 1950–52; PhD Lond. 1952; MA Manchester 1963. Lectr in History of Art, Courtauld Inst., 1952–58; Alexander White Vis. Prof., Univ. of Chicago, 1958; Reader in History of Art, Courtauld Inst., 1958–59; Pilkington Prof. of the History of Art and Dir of The Whitworth Art Gallery, Univ. of Manchester, 1959–66; Vis. Ferens Prof. of Fine Art, Univ. of Hull, 1961–62; Prof. of the History of Art and Chm., Dept of History of Art, Johns Hopkins Univ., USA, 1966–71. Member: Adv. Council of V&A, 1973–76; Exec. Cttee, Assoc. of Art Historians, 1974–81 (Chm., 1976–80); Art Panel, Arts Council, 1974–78; Vis. Cttee of RCA, 1977–86; Armed Forces Pay Review Body, 1986–92; Chm., Reviewing Cttee on Export of Works of Art, 1976–82 (Mem., 1975–82). Trustee, Whitechapel Art Gall., 1976–93 (Vice-Chm., 1985–93); Trustee and Hon. Sec., London Shogyoji Trust, 1997–. Mem., Cttee, Burma Campaign Soc., 2003–09. Membre Titulaire, 1983–95, Membre du Bureau, 1986–92, Comité International d'Histoire de l'Art. *Publications:* Perspective in Ancient Drawing and Painting, 1956; The Birth and Rebirth of Pictorial Space, 1957, 3rd edn 1987 (trans. Italian 1971; trans. French 1992; trans. Spanish 1994); Art and Architecture in Italy, 1250–1400, 1966, 3rd edn 1993 (trans. Spanish 1989); Duccio: Tuscan Art and the Medieval Workshop, 1979; Studies in Renaissance Art, 1983; Studies in Late Medieval Italian Art, 1984; Poems Poèmes Poesie, 1992; Quartet Quartett Quartetto Quatuor, 1993; Trinity Trinita Trinité, 1994; You that I love, 1998; The Breath in the Flute, 2001 (English/Japanese bilingual text); On the Razor's Edge, 2004; New Moon, Old Moon, 2006; Enlightenment, 2010; Postscript, 2011; Pondskaters, 2014; Sunset, 2016; articles in Art History, Art Bulletin, Burlington Magazine, Jl of Warburg and Courtauld Institutes. *Address:* Flat 16, 27 Onslow Square, SW7 3NH. *Club:* Athenæum.

**WHITE, John William,** AO 2016; CMG 1981; DPhil; FRS 1993; FRSC; FAA; Professor of Physical and Theoretical Chemistry, Australian National University, Canberra, 1985–2014, now Emeritus (Pro Vice-Chancellor and Chairman, Board of Institute of Advanced Studies, 1992–94; Dean, Research School of Chemistry, 1995–98); *b* Newcastle, Australia, 25 April 1937; *s* of late George John White and of Jean Florence White; *m* 1966, Ailsa Barbara, *d* of A. A. and S. Vise, Southport, Qld; one *s* three *d. Educ:* Newcastle High Sch.; Sydney Univ. (MSc); Lincoln Coll., Oxford (1851 Schol., 1959; MA, DPhil). ICI Fellow, Oxford Univ.; Research Fellow, Lincoln Coll., 1962; University Lectr, Oxford, 1963–85, Assessor, 1981–82; Fellow, St John's Coll., Oxford, 1963–85 (Vice-Pres. 1973; Hon. Fellow, 1995). Neutron Beam Coordinator, AERE, Harwell, 1974; Asst Director, 1975, Director 1977–80, Institut Laue-Langevin, Grenoble. Argonne Fellow, Argonne Nat. Lab. and Univ. of Chicago, 1985; Christensen Fellow, St Catherine's Coll., Oxford, 1991; Distinguished Vis. Fellow, Victorian Inst. of Chemical Scis, 2007; Distinguished Vis. Prof., CSIRO, 2012. President: Soc. of Crystallographers, Aust., 1989–92; Royal Aust. Chemical Inst., 2000–02; Aust. Inst. of Nuclear Sci. and Engrg, 2004–07 (Vice Pres., 2002–04); Asia-Oceania Neutron Scattering Assoc., 2010–12 (Mem., Exec. Cttee, 2008–); Chairman: Nat. Cttee for Crystallography, Aust., 1992–2001; Neutron Scattering Commn, Internat. Union of Crystallography, 1994–99; Internat. Adv. Cttee on Japanese Atomic Energy Inst./High Energy Physics Lab. Jt Project, J-PARC (formerly Internat. Adv. Cttee, J-PARC project, Japan), 2001–10; Internat. Steering Cttee, Review of Australia's Antarctic Res., 2002; Ext. Review, 2004, 3rd Year Review, 2008, Australian Co-operative Res. Centre for Polymers; Review Cttee, NZ's Antarctic Sci. Report, 2005; Internat. Adv. Cttee, Bragg Inst., 2006–10; Member: Internat. Review Panel, 1998, Internat. Adv. Panel, 2001, Faculty of Science, Nat. Univ. of Singapore; Internat. Review Cttee, Jt Proposal of Japan Hadron Facility and Neutron Sci. Project, 1999; Internat. Cttee on Future of Neutron Sources, IUPAP, 2000; Internat. Adv. Panel, RAE, HEFC, 2001–02; Internat. Adv. Cttee, Central Lab. of the Res. Councils, 2002–; Chemicals and Plastics Sector Adv. Cttee, 2000–03, Emerging Sci. Oversight Cttee, 2004–06, CSIRO; Internat. Review Panel of Chemistry, Argonne Nat. Lab., 2004; Working Gp on Nuclear Physics, OECD, 2005–08; Foresight Cttee, KEK Tsukuba, Japan, 2008. Sec. for Sci. Policy, and Mem. Council, Aust. Acad. of Sci., 1997–2001. Chm., Dirs' Adv. Council, Intense Pulsed Neutron Source, Argonne Nat. Lab., and Univ. of Chicago, 1989–92. Pres., ISCAST Australia, 1991–2006. Chm., James Fairfax-Oxford Australia Scholarship Cttee, 1997–. Hon. Chm., Internat. Adv. Cttee, J-PARC, Tokai, Japan, 2013. Lectures: Tilden, Chemical Soc., 1975; Liversidge, Sydney Univ., 1985; Hinshelwood, Oxford Univ., 1991; Foundn, Assoc. of Asian Chemical Socs, 1991; H. G. Smith, RACI, 1997–98; T. G. H. Jones Meml, Univ. of Qld, 1998; Hudnall-Cars Distinguished, Univ. of Chicago, 1998; 50th Anniversary, Internat. Union of Crystallography, 1998; Founder's, St John's Coll., Oxford, 2007; Liversidge, Royal Soc. NSW, 2010; Kashiwa Public, Univ. of Tokyo, 2011. Member of Council: Epsom Coll., 1981–85; Wycliffe Hall, Oxford, 1983–85; St Mark's Nat. Theol Centre, Canberra, 1997–. Dist. Friend, Oxford Univ., 2008. FRSC 1982; FRACI 1985; FAIP 1986; FAA 1991. Marlow Medal, Faraday Soc., 1969; H. G. Smith Medal and Prize, 1997, Leighton Medal, 2005, RACI; Craig Medal, Aust. Acad. of Sci., 2005; AONSA Prize and Medal, 2016. *Publications:* over 300 pubns in scientific jls. *Recreations:* family, squash, skiing. *Address:* 2 Spencer Street, Turner, ACT 2612, Australia. *T:* (2) 62486836.

**WHITE, Sir John (Woolmer),** 4th Bt *cr* 1922; *b* 4 Feb. 1947; *s* of Sir Headley Dymoke White, 3rd Bt and Elizabeth Victoria Mary (*d* 1996), *er d* of late Wilfrid Ingram Wrightson; *S* father, 1971; *m* 1987, Joan Borland; one *s. Educ:* Hurst Court, Hastings; Cheltenham College; RAC, Cirencester. *Heir: s* Kyle Dymoke Wilfrid White, *b* 16 March 1988. *Address:* Salle Park, Reepham, Norwich, Norfolk NR10 4SG. *Clubs:* Athenæum, MCC; Starting Handle.

**WHITE, Keith George,** CBE 2009; consultant, since 2011; Senior Advisor, ES-KO Group, since 2015 (Chairman, ES-KO (UK) Ltd, 2009–15); Board Advisor, OTB Engineering Ltd, since 2016; Chief Executive, Crown Agents for Oversea Governments and Administrations Ltd, 2005–11; *b* 12 Oct. 1948; *s* of Arthur and Rose White; *m* 1971, Philomena Smith; one *s* one *d. Educ:* Bec Sch.; Kingston Poly. (BA London ext.); City of London Poly. (MA Business Law). Crown Agents: Corporate Sec., 1980–98; Dir, 1997–2011; Chief Operating Officer, 1997–2005. Vice Pres., HF Holidays Ltd, 2014– (Pres., 1987–2014); Chm., St Helena Line Ltd, 1992–2005; Dir, SITPRO Ltd, 2000–05. CO, Engr and Logistic Staff Corps, RE (V), 2007–16. VR 2000. FCILT 2005; FInstRE 2008. FRSA. *Recreations:* family, walking, browsing in walking kit shops, playing guitar. *T:* 07714 238454. *Clubs:* Victory Services, Royal Air Force.

**WHITE, Kenneth James,** MBE 2011; District Judge, Principal Registry of Family Division, 1991–2013; *b* 24 March 1948; *s* of Kenneth William John White and Pamela Blanche Emily White (*née* Seth); *m* 1971, Anne Christine Butcher; one *s* one *d. Educ:* Gosport County Grammar Sch., Hants; QMC, Univ. of London (LLB Hons 1969). Qualified as Solicitor, 1972; Partner, R. V. Stokes & Co., Solicitors, Portsmouth, 1974, Sen. Partner, 1991. Mem., Family Cttee, Judicial Studies Bd, 1999–2004. Mem., Portsmouth & Southsea Voluntary Lifeguards, 1968– (Pres. 1985–); Royal Life Saving Society UK: Vice-Pres., 1994–98; Pres., 1998–2004; Chm., Nat. Lifeguard Cttee, 1992–98; Mem., Commonwealth Council, 1998–2004; Pres., Wessex Br., 1981; Dir, Internat. Life Saving Fedn, 2000–09; Hon. Legal Advr, Internat. Life Saving of Europe, 2009–16. Knight, Order of Lifesaving, Internat. Lifesaving Fedn, 2011. *Publications:* (consulting editor) Family Court Reporter, 1992; (contrib.) Atkin's Court Forms, 1994–2013. *Recreations:* swimming, reading, travel, lifesaving, grandchildren.

**WHITE, Kevin Charles Gordon,** CB 2003; executive coach and mentor, since 2015; Director General, Human Resources, Home Office, 2007–15; *b* 20 July 1950; *s* of John Gordon White and Dorothy Marion White; *m* 1st, 1977, Louise Sarah Watt (marr. diss. 2011); three *s*; 2nd, 2018, Alison Allden, *qv. Educ:* Haberdashers' Aske's, Elstree; Univ. of E Anglia (BA Hons); Univ. of Warwick (MA). Senior CS posts in Dept for Employment, 1977–95; Human Resources Dir, Employment Service, 1995–2001; Gp Dir of Human Resources, DWP, 2001–07. FCIPD 1996. FRSA 2002. *Recreations:* music, cooking, theatre, golf, cigars. *Clubs:* Royal Over-Seas League, Soho Whisky.

**WHITE, Lindsey Anne;** *see* Clay, L. A.

**WHITE, Malcolm D.;** *see* Davis-White.

**WHITE, Marco Pierre;** chef and restaurateur; *b* 11 Dec. 1961; *s* of late Frank and Maria Rosa White; *m* 1st, 1988, Alexandra McCarthy (marr. diss.); one *d*; 2nd, 1992, Lisa Butcher (marr. diss.); 3rd, 2000, Matilda Conejero-Caldera; two *s* one *d. Educ:* Firtree Primary Sch.; Allerton High Sch., Leeds. Commis: Hotel St George, Harrogate, 1978; Box Tree, Ilkley, 1979; Chef de Partie: Le Gavroche, 1981; Tante Claire, 1983; Sous Chef, Manoir aux Quat' Saisons, 1984–85; Proprietor and Chef: Harveys, 1986–93; The Canteen Restaurant, Chelsea Harbour, 1992–96; Restaurant Marco Pierre White, 1993; Marco Pierre White's Criterion, 1995–2009; Quo Vadis, 1996–2001; Oak Room, Le Meridien, 1997–99; MPW Canary Wharf, 1997; Café Royal Grill Room, 1997; Mirabelle Restaurant, Curzon St, 1998; Belvedere, 1999; Wheeler's of St James's, 2002; Luciano, 2005; Proprietor, L'Escargot, 1995–2000; Jt Proprietor, Frankie's, 2004–; Jt Proprietor, Koffmann and Mr White's, Bath, 2018–. Michelin Stars 1988, 1990, 1995 (youngest and first GB winner of 3 Michelin stars). Television series: Hell's Kitchen, 2007, 2009; Marco's Great British Feast, 2008; The Chopping Block, USA, 2009; Marco's Kitchen Burnout, 2010. *Publications:* White Heat, 1990; Wild Food from Land and Sea, 1994; Canteen Cuisine, 1995; Glorious Puddings, 1998; The Mirabelle Cookbook, 1999; White Slave: the autobiography, 2006; Marco Pierre White's Great British Feast, 2008. *Recreations:* shooting, fishing, bird watching.

**WHITE, Martin Andrew C.;** *see* Campbell-White.

**WHITE, Maj.-Gen. Sir Martin (Spencer),** KCVO 2018; CB 1998; CBE 1991; Lord-Lieutenant of the Isle of Wight, 2006–19 (Vice Lord-Lieutenant, 1999–2006); *b* 25 March 1944; *s* of Harold Spencer White and Mary Elizabeth White; *m* 1966, Fiona Margaret MacFarlane; three *s* one *d. Educ:* Sandown GS, IoW; Welbeck Coll.; RMA Sandhurst. FCIT 1992; FILog 1993. Commnd, RASC/RCT, 1966; Staff Coll., Camberley, 1977–78; Comd 4 Div., Transport Regt, 1983–85; Directing Staff, Army Staff Coll., 1985–87; Command: Logistic Support Gp, 1987–89; Force Maintenance Area (Gulf), 1990–91; Transport 1(BR) Corps, 1991–92; RCDS, 1993; Dir of Support, HQ Allied Land Forces Central Europe, 1993–95; Dir-Gen., Logistic Support (Army), 1995–98. Senior Military Adviser: Ernst & Young, subseq. Cap Gemini Ernst & Young, 1999–2003; Deloittes, 2003–08. Col Comdt, RLC, 1998–2009. Hon. Colonel: Southampton Univ. OTC, 1999–2004; 165 Regt RLC, 2001–09. Governor, Ryde Sch., 1997–2006. Liveryman, Co. of Carmen, 1996–2007. DL Isle of Wight, 1998. CStJ 2010. *Publications:* Gulf Logistics: Black Adder's war, 1995. *Recreations:* cricket, sailing. *Address:* Oak Lodge, Seagrove Farm Road, Seaview, Isle of Wight PO34 5HU. *Clubs:* Victory Services; Royal Yacht Squadron; Sea View Yacht.

**WHITE, Mary Catherine;** *see* Restieaux, M. C.

**WHITE, Matthew Graham;** Partner, since 2005, and Head of Planning, London, since 2013, Herbert Smith Freehills LLP (formerly Herbert Smith LLP); *b* W Sussex, 30 March 1972; *s* of Graham White and Margaret White (*née* Leighs, later Broad); *m* 2001, Claire Cosgrave; one *s* two *d. Educ:* Imberhorne Comp. Sch., East Grinstead; Clare Coll., Cambridge (BA Hons Econs and Law 1994); Coll. of Law, York (DipLP 1995). Admitted as solicitor, 1997. Herbert Smith: trainee solicitor, 1995–97; Associate, 1997–2005. Trustee, Architecture Foundn, 2013–. LARTPI 2015. FRGS 2017. *Recreations:* cycling, triathlon, photography, The Archers. *Address:* Herbert Smith Freehills LLP, Exchange House, Primrose Street, EC2A 2EG. *T:* (020) 7466 2461. *E:* matthew.white@hsf.com.

**WHITE, Michael Charles;** Associate Editor, 1989–2016, and Assistant Editor (Politics), 2006–16, The Guardian; *b* 21 Oct. 1945; *y s* of Henry Wallis White, master mariner of St Just in Penwith, Cornwall and of Kay (*née* Wood); *m* 1973, Patricia Vivienne Gaudin; three *s. Educ:* Bodmin Grammar Sch.; University Coll. London (BA Hist. 1966; Fellow, 2002). Reporter: Reading Evening Post, 1966–70; London Evening Standard, 1970–71; The Guardian, 1971–2016: Parly Sketchwriter, 1977–84; Washington Corresp., 1984–88; Political Ed., 1990–2006. Columnist: Health Service Jl, 1977–84, 1992–2017; The New European, 2016–. Vis. Fellow, Woodrow Wilson Foundn, Princeton, NJ, 1990–2004. Hon. Fellow, UC Falmouth, 2006. What the Papers Say Sketchwriter of the Year Award, 1982; Political Writer Award, House Magazine, 2003. *E:* oapmikewhite@gmail.com. *Club:* Garrick.

**WHITE, Michael John;** critic, broadcaster and author; *b* 4 April 1955; *s* of Albert E. White and Doris M. White (*née* Harvey). *Educ:* Langdon Sch., London; Mansfield Coll., Oxford (MA Jurisp.). Called to the Bar, Middle Temple, 1978 (non-practising) (Harmsworth Scholar and Middle Temple Advocacy Prize). Contribs to Observer and Guardian; joined Independent, 1986; Music Critic, The Independent on Sunday, 1990–2000. Columnist: Catholic Herald, 2008–; (online) Daily Telegraph, 2009–; Opera Now, 2012–; Classical Music Mag., 2015–. Broadcasts for BBC Radio and TV, Channel 4, Classic FM (voted Britain's least boring music critic); presenter: Best of 3, R3, 1998–2000; Opera in Action, R3, 2000–02; Sound Barrier series, R4, 1999; opera libretti writer; awards judge. Lectr, Wigmore Hall and internat. fests. Member, Board of Directors: Spitalfields Fest., 1992–2000; London Internat. Piano Comp., 2002–. Created biographical website for soprano Jennifer Vyvyan, 2010. *Publications:* Wagner for Beginners, 1995; Opera and Operetta, 1997; Introducing Wagner: a graphic guide, 2013. *Recreations:* other people's dogs, the Church of England. *Address:* 16 Willow Road, Hampstead, NW3 1TJ.

**WHITE, Neville Helme;** Stipendiary Magistrate for Humberside, 1985–99; *b* 12 April 1931; *s* of Noel Walter White and Irene Helme White; *m* 1958, Margaret Jennifer Catlin (*d* 2013); two *s* one *d. Educ:* Newcastle-under-Lyme High School. RAF, 1949–51. Partner, Grindey & Co., Solicitors, Stoke-on-Trent, 1960–85. Pres., N Staffs Law Soc., 1980–81. Pres., Hull Boys' Club, 1985–99. *Recreations:* music, walking, gardening, reading, all sports, paintings. *Address:* 6 Whybrow Gardens, Castle Village, Berkhamsted HP4 2GU.

**WHITE, Sir Nicholas (John),** KCMG 2017; OBE 1999; MD, DSc; FRCP, FMedSci; FRS 2006; FBPhS; Chairman, Wellcome Trust Southeast Asian Tropical Medicine Research Programmes, since 2001; Professor of Tropical Medicine, Mahidol University, Bangkok, since 1995, and University of Oxford, since 1996; *b* 31 March 1951; *s* of John Carlisle White and Eileen Margaret White (*née* Millard); *m* 1997, Jitda; three *d. Educ:* Guy's Hosp. Med. Sch., London (BSc Pharmacol. 1971; MB BS 1st Cl. Hons 1974); MD 1984, DSc 1995, London Univ. FBPhS 2016. Dir, Wellcome Trust Mahidol Univ.-Oxford Tropical Medicine Res. Prog., 1986–2001. Hon. Consultant Physician, John Radcliffe Hosp., Oxford, 1986–. Co-Chm., WHO Antimalarial Treatment Guidelines Cttee, 2004–17; Chairman: Worldwide Antimalarial Resistance Network, 2009–16; Scientific Adv. Bd, Drugs for Neglected Diseases initiative, 2016–; Mem., Adv. Bd, Wellcome Innovations. Mem., US Nat. Acad. of Medicine, 2017. FMedSci 2001. Gairdner Global Health Award, Gairdner Foundn, Canada, 2010; Prince Mahidol Award, Prince Mahidol Award Foundn, 2010. *Publications:* over 1100 scientific articles in jls. *Recreations:* cricket, squash, guitar, gardening. *Address:* Faculty of Tropical Medicine, Mahidol University, 420/6 Rajvithi Road, Bangkok 10400, Thailand. *T:* (2) 2036301, *Fax:* (2) 3549169. *E:* nickw@tropmedres.ac. *Clubs:* British (Bangkok); Royal Bangkok Sports.

**WHITE, Sir Nicholas (Peter Archibald),** 6th Bt *cr* 1802, of Wallingwells, Nottinghamshire; *b* 2 March 1939; *s* of Captain Richard Taylor White, DSO (2 bars), RN (*d* 1995) and Gabrielle Ursula White (*née* Style) (*d* 1996); *S* uncle, 1996; *m* 1st, 1970, Susan Irene (*d* 2002), *d* of G. W. B. Pollock; two *s* one *d*, 2nd, 2007, Elaine Jeanne Hume, *d* of R. J. Dickson. *Educ:* Eton. Nat. Service, 2nd Lt 2/10th PMO Gurkha Rifles, 1957–59. Courage Ltd, 1959–84; wine trade, 1984–94; Gulf Eternit Industries, Dubai, UAE,

1994–2000; Future Pipe Industries Gp, 2001–06. Mem. (Ind), Tandridge DC, 2018–. *Recreations:* tennis, travelling, music. *Heir: s* Christopher David Nicholas White [*b* 20 July 1972; *m* 1st, 2004, Nathalie Hester (marr. diss. 2009); 2nd, 2010, Philippa Sarah Tayler]. *Address:* Little Westlands, Lingfield, Surrey RH7 6DE.

**WHITE, Prof. Nigel David,** PhD; Professor of Public International Law, since 2009, and Head, School of Law, since 2014, University of Nottingham; *b* Sheffield, 9 April 1961; *s* of David White and Barbara White; *m* 1987, Gillian Ann Hickey; two *s*. *Educ:* Carlton-le-Willows Comp. Sch., Nottingham; Pembroke Coll., Oxford (BA Hons Juris. 1982); Univ. of Nottingham (PhD 1988). University of Nottingham: Lectr in Law, 1987–95; Sen. Lectr in Law, 1995–99; Prof. of Internat. Orgns, 2000–05; Prof. of Internat. Law, Univ. of Sheffield, 2005–09. *Publications:* The United Nations and the Maintenance of International Peace and Security, 1990; The Law of International Organisations, 1996, 3rd edn 2016; Keeping the Peace, 1997; The United Nations System: toward international justice, 2002; Democracy Goes to War, 2009; Advanced Introduction to International Conflict and Security Law, 2014; The Cuban Embargo under International Law, 2014. *Recreations:* gardening, guitars, vinyl. *Address:* School of Law, University of Nottingham, University Park, Nottingham NG7 2RD. *T:* (0115) 846 8238, *Fax:* (0115) 951 5696. *E:* nigel.white@nottingham.ac.uk.

**WHITE, Patrick Rockliff;** Director, Metro Dynamics, since 2016; *b* Reading, 5 Oct. 1976; *s* of Ian White and Mary White; *m* 2008, Louise Dunkerley; one *s* one *d*. *Educ:* Thomas Adams Sch., Wem; Manchester Univ. (BA Hons Eng. Lit.); Vienna Univ. Cabinet Office, 1996–2003: various posts, incl. Defence and Overseas Secretariat and Civil Contingencies Secretariat; Exec. Dir, Policy, North West RDA, 2003–09; Cabinet Office: Principal Private Sec. to Minister for the Cabinet Office, 2009–10; Econ. and Domestic Secretariat, 2010–11; Dir, Local Govt Policy and Productivity, DCLG, 2011–16. *Recreations:* cycling, gardening, electronic music, English literature. *Address:* Metro Dynamics, 3 Waterhouse Square, 138 Holborn, EC1N 2SW. *T:* (020) 865 3082. *E:* patrick.white@metrodynamics.co.uk. *Club:* Reform.

**WHITE, Rt Rev. Paul Raymond;** an Assistant Bishop, Diocese of Melbourne (Bishop for Growth Areas), 2016–17 (Bishop of the Western Region, 2002–07; Bishop of the Southern Region, 2007–16; Chapter Bishop, St Paul's Cathedral, Melbourne, 2015–16); Permission to Officiate, since 2016; *b* Sydney, 31 March 1949; *s* of Ronald White and Betty White (*née* Shepherdson); *m* 1970, Robyn Jamieson, *d* of Robert Jamieson and Maxine Jamieson (*née* Lang); one *s* one *d*. *Educ:* Cronulla High Sch.; Bathurst Teachers' Coll.; St Mark's Coll., Canberra (BTh 1985, Dip. Min., 1986, ACT); Heythrop Coll., Univ. of London (MTh 1989). Teacher, NSW Dept of Educn, 1968–71; voluntary work in community-based progs made poss. by periods of paid work in business, industry and educn, 1971–82. Ordained deacon, 1985, priest, 1986; Asst Curate, N Goulburn, NSW, 1985–87; Lucas-Tooth Schol. and Acting Priest i/c, Reigate, UK, 1987–89; Rector, Queanbeyan, NSW, 1989–92; Vicar: Redhill, UK, 1992–96; E Ivanhoe, Vic, 1996–2000. Dir, Theol Educn, dio. Melbourne, 2000–07. *Recreation:* two grandsons. *Address:* 357 Barkly Street, Brunswick, Vic 3056, Australia.

**WHITE, Peter Richard;** non-executive Director, Reckitt Benckiser (formerly Reckitt & Colman), 1997–2008 (Chairman, Audit Committee, 1998–2006, and Member, Nomination Committee, 1999–2008); *b* 11 Feb. 1942; *m* 1968, Mary Angela Bowyer; one *s* one *d*. *Educ:* St Paul's School. FCA; FCIB, FCT. Price Waterhouse, 1965–69; Management Accountant, Chief Internal Auditor, Financial Controller, Treasurer, Abbey National Building Soc., 1970–82; Gen. Manager (Finance and Management Services), Alliance Building Soc., 1982–85; Alliance & Leicester Building Society: Gen. Manager (Admin. and Treasury), 1985–87; Dir and Gen. Manager (Develt and Treasury), 1987–89; Dep. Group Chief Exec. and Man. Dir, 1989–91; Gp Chief Exec., Alliance & Leicester Bldg Soc., subseq. Alliance & Leicester plc, 1991–99. Dir, 1990–99, Chm., 1996–99, Girobank plc; Dir, Alliance & Leicester Pensions Investments Ltd, 1989–99. Chairman: Metropolitan Assoc. of Buildings Socs, 1994–95; Council of Mortgage Lenders, 1995–98; Dep. Chm., BSA, 1995–96; Mem. Council, BBA, 1996–99. Trustee: Crimestoppers Trust, 1997–98; Develt Trust (for the Mentally Handicapped), 1997–99. Freeman, City of London, 1996. MInstD; CCMI. *Recreations:* golf, opera, arts. *Address:* 4 Osten Mews, SW7 4HW.

**WHITE, Peter Robert,** OBE 2006; FSA; Secretary, Royal Commission on the Ancient and Historical Monuments of Wales, 1991–2005; *b* 28 Nov. 1944; *y s* of late John Edward White and Lillie Agnes Lois White (*née* Powell); *m* 1973, Christine Margaret Joyce Robertson; two *d*. *Educ:* Eastbourne Grammar Sch.; Univ. of Leeds (BA History); Univ. of Southampton. FSA 1988; IHBC 1998. Asst Insp. of Ancient Monuments, MPBW, 1966–71; Insp., 1971–82, Prin. Insp., 1982–89, DoE; Head, Historic Buildings Listing, English Heritage, 1989–91. Member: Res. Cttee on Industrial Archaeol., Council of British Archaeol., 1969–91; Wkg Party on Industrial Archaeol., Council of Europe, 1984–89; Exec. Cttee, Soc. of Antiquaries of London, 1994–2002 (Mem. Council, 1992–94); Editl Bd, Cardiganshire County History, 1997–2005; Nat. Adv. Panel, Eur. Assoc. of Archaeologists, 1998–99; Chm., Industrial Archaeol. Panel, English Heritage, 2011–14 (Mem., 1991–2011). Hon. Res. Fellow, Univ. of Wales Lampeter, 2007–10. Vice-Pres., Royal Archaeol Inst., 1994–99 (Mem. Council, 1975–78, 1991–94). Chairman: Hafod Adv. Panel, Natural Resources (formerly Forestry Commn) Wales, 2006–16; Wales Cttee, Assoc. of Preservation Trusts, 2007–09; Ironbridge Heritage Foundn Ltd, 2013– (Trustee/ Dir, 2005–13). Chm., Ethical Standards Cttee, Dyfed-Powys Police Authy, 2009–12 (Vice-Chm., 2007–09). FRSA 1999–2019. Hon. Fellow, UC Northampton, 1999. *Publications:* (with Alan Cook) Sherborne Old Castle, Dorset: archaeological investigations 1930–1990, 2015; Stott Park Bobbin Mill, 2015; Sherborne Old Castle, 2016; contribs to books and learned jls, particularly on industrial archaeol. *Recreations:* walking, orchestral music. *E:* tyrafon@icloud.com.

**WHITE, Richard Michael,** MBE 1983; HM Diplomatic Service, retired; Head, Foreign and Commonwealth Office Outplacement Service (PROSPER), 2007–15; *b* 12 July 1950; *s* of late Geoffrey Richard White and of Frances Kathleen (*née* Kendrick); *m* 1979, Deborah Anne Lewis, *d* of late Kenneth H. Lewis, OBE and Jean Lewis (*née* Tearle); one *s* one *d*. *Educ:* King's Sch., Pontefract; Richmond Sch., Yorkshire. VSO, Senegal, 1968–69; entered HM Diplomatic Service, 1969: Attaché, UK Delegn to EEC, Brussels, 1971–74; Persian lang. studies, SOAS, and Yazd, Iran, 1974–75; Third Sec. (Commercial), Tehran, 1975–77; Second Sec. and Asst Private Sec. to Minister of State, Lord Privy Seal, FCO, 1978–79; FCO, 1979–80; Second Sec. (Commercial/Admin) and Consul, Dakar, 1980–84; First Secretary: (Technol.), Paris, 1984–88; FCO, 1988–92; Dep. High Comr, Valletta, 1992–95; FCO, 1996–2002, Hd, Migration and Visa Div., 1997–2000, Asst Dir, Personnel Services, 2000–02; Counsellor (Mgt), Paris, 2003–07. Mem. Bd, FCO Assoc., 2016–18. Volunteer, Citizens Advice, Tunbridge Wells, 2015–18. *Recreations:* family history, French cuisine, walking. *Address:* 8 Concord Close, Tunbridge Wells, Kent TN2 3PW. *E:* compostellan@hotmail.com.

**WHITE, Prof. Robert George,** PhD, DSc; FREng; Professor of Vibration Studies, University of Southampton, 1983–98, now Emeritus; *b* 11 Dec. 1939; *s* of N. A. J. White and G. M. White; *m* 1988, Patricia Margaret (*née* Sidley); one step *s* one step *d*. *Educ:* Farnborough Coll. of Technology; Southampton Univ. (PhD 1970; DSc 1992). FInstP 1981; FIOA 1985; FRAeS 1986; FREng (FEng 1995). RAE, Farnborough, 1957–67; Dir, Inst. of Sound and Vibration Res., 1982–89, Inst. of Transducer Technol., 1989–93, Hd of Dept of Aeronautics and Astronautics, 1995–98, Southampton Univ. Hon. FIOA 2003. (Jtly) Simms Prize, RAeS, 1982; Tyndall Medal, 1984, Engrg Medal, 2008, Inst. of Acoustics. *Publications:* (ed jtly) Noise and Vibration, 1982; 210 conf. papers and contribs to jls. *Recreations:* flying, walking. *Address:* 41 Lower Bere Wood, Waterlooville, Hants PO7 7NQ.

**WHITE, Prof. Robert Stephen,** FRS 1994; FGS; Professor of Geophysics, Cambridge University, since 1989; Fellow, St Edmund's College, Cambridge, since 1988; Founding Director, 2006, and Director, since 2012, Faraday Institute for Science and Religion at Westminster (formerly St Edmund's) College, Cambridge; *b* 12 Dec. 1952; 2nd *s* of James Henry White and Ethel Gladys (*née* Cornick); *m* 1976, Helen Elizabeth (*née* Pearce); one *s* one *d*. *Educ:* Market Harborough and West Bridgford Comprehensive Schs; Emmanuel Coll., Cambridge (Sen. Schol., 1972–74; Bachelor Schol., 1974–77; BA, MA, PhD). FRAS 1979; FGS 1989. Research Assistant: Berkeley Nuclear Labs, CEGB, 1970–71; Dept of Geodesy and Geophysics, Cambridge, 1978; postdoctoral schol., Woods Hole Oceanographic Instn, USA, 1978–79; Res. Fellow, Emmanuel Coll., Cambridge, 1979–82; Sen. Asst in Res., 1981–85, Asst Dir of Res., 1985–89, Dept of Earth Scis, Cambridge Univ. Cecil and Ida H. Green Schol., Scripps Instn of Oceanography, UCSD, USA, 1987; Guest Investigator, Woods Hole Oceanographic Instn, 1988. Adjunct Prof., Univ. of Iceland, 2009–; Harold Jeffreys Lectr, RAS, 2013. Fellow, American Geophysical Union, 2016. Bigsby Medal, Geol Soc., 1991; George P. Woollard Award, Geol Soc. Amer., 1997; Gold Medal, RAS, 2018. *Publications:* (with D. Alexander) Beyond Belief: science, faith and ethical challenges, 2004; (with N. Spencer) Christianity, Climate Change and Sustainable Living, 2007; Creation in Crisis: Christian perspectives on sustainability, 2009; (with J. A. Moo) Hope in an Age of Despair, 2013; Who is to Blame?: disasters, nature and acts of God, 2014; Creation Care and the Gospel: reconsidering the mission of the Church, 2016; papers in many internat. jls. *Recreations:* reading, walking, messing around in the garden and house. *Address:* Bullard Laboratories, Madingley Road, Cambridge CB3 0EZ. *T:* (01223) 337187, *Fax:* (01223) 360779.

**WHITE, Robin Bernard G.;** *see* Grove-White.

**WHITE, Roger,** FSA 1986; Executive Secretary, Garden History Society, 1992–96; *b* 1 Sept. 1950; *s* of Geoffrey and Zoë White. *Educ:* Ifield Grammar School; Christ's College, Cambridge (1st class Hons, Hist. of Art Tripos); Wadham College, Oxford. GLC Historic Buildings Div., 1979–83; Sec., Georgian Gp, 1984–91; Mem., Chiswick House Adv. Panel, 1991–2007. Trustee, Pell Wall Preservation Trust, 1994–98. Curator: John Piper: Georgian Arcadia, Marlborough Fine Art, 1987; Nicholas Hawksmoor and the Replanning of Oxford, RIBA, 1997, Ashmolean Mus., 1998; Europe and the English Baroque, V&A Mus., 2009. Chichele Lectr, All Souls Coll., Oxford, 1999; Hugh Shirreff Lect., Historic Houses Assoc., 2011. Contributing Ed., House and Garden, 1994–2015. *Publications:* John Vardy, 1985; Georgian Arcadia: architecture for the park and garden, 1987; The Architectural Evolution of Magdalen College, Oxford, 1993; Chiswick House and Gardens, 2001; The Architectural Drawings of Magdalen College, Oxford, 2001; Witley Court and Gardens, 2003, 2nd edn 2008; Belsay Hall, Castle and Gardens, 2005; (with Graham Byfield) Oxford Sketchbook, 2005; (ed) A Life of Frederick, Prince of Wales 1707–1751, 2007; Holkham Hall, 2010; (contrib.) William Kent: designing Georgian Britain, 2013; Cottages Ornés: the charms of the simple life, 2017; contribs to Architectural Hist., Jl of Garden Hist., Country Life, World of Interiors. *Recreation:* visiting and writing about historic buildings. *Address:* Tall Trees, The Avenue, Sherborne, Dorset DT9 3AH.

**WHITE, Dr Roger Henry,** FSA; archaeologist; Senior Lecturer, University of Birmingham, since 2002 (Academic Director, Ironbridge Institute, 2000–17); *b* London, 19 June 1959; *s* of Victor and Bessie White; *m* 1996, Francesca Bumpus; one *s* one *d*. *Educ:* Hampstead Comprehensive Sch.; Univ. of Liverpool (BA Ancient and Medieval Hist. and Archaeol. 1982; PhD Hist. 1987). FSA 2007. Lectr, Univ. of Liverpool, 1991–93; Leverhulme Res. Fellow, Univ. of Birmingham, 1994–97; Archaeol Project Manager, Birmingham Archaeology, 1997–2000. Mem., Adv. Cttee, Historic England (formerly English Heritage), 2011–17. Mem., Chartered Inst. of Archaeologists, 1987. *Publications:* (with P. Barker) Wroxeter: life and death of a Roman city, 1997, 3rd edn 2014; Britannia Prima, 2007. *Recreations:* gardening, walking, visiting museums and heritage sites. *Address:* Fry Building, University of Birmingham, Edgbaston, Birmingham B15 2TT. *T:* (0121) 414 5493. *E:* r.h.white@bham.ac.uk.

**WHITE, Sandra;** Member (SNP) Glasgow Kelvin, Scottish Parliament, since 2011 (Glasgow, 1999–2011); *b* 17 Aug. 1951; *d* of Henry Harley and Elizabeth Rodgers; *m* 1971, David White; two *s* one *d*. *Educ:* Garthamlock Sen. Sec. Sch.; Cardonald Coll. of Further Educn; Glasgow Coll. (Social Science degree). Clerkess, Gray Dunn, 1966–68; Timothy Whites, then Boots Chemist, 1968–73; Littlewoods Pools, 1973–88. Member (SNP): Renfrew DC, 1989; Renfrewshire CC, 1995–99. *Recreations:* walking, reading, gardening. *Address:* Scottish Parliament, Edinburgh EH99 1SP. *T:* (0131) 348 5000.

**WHITE, Sasha Nicolas;** QC 2013; *b* London, 8 Aug. 1967; *s* of late Michael Simon White and Sarah White; *m* 1997, Clare Heather Banks Skinner; two *s* one *d*. *Educ:* Bedales Sch.; Trinity Coll., Cambridge (BA Law 1990). Called to the Bar, Inner Temple, 1991; in practice as a barrister, specialising in planning law, Chambers of Lionel Read, QC, 1993–2002, Landmark Chambers, 2002–. Liveryman, Cordwainers' Co., 2000– (Renter Warden, 2012–13). *Publications:* Planning Appeals, 1997. *Recreations:* cricket, golf, tennis, football, Rugby, Northumberland, Scotland, running London Marathon. *Address:* Landmark Chambers, 180 Fleet Street, EC4A 2HG. *T:* (020) 7430 1221, *Fax:* (020) 7421 6060. *E:* sashawhite@landmarkchambers.co.uk. *Clubs:* Boodles, Royal Automobile, MCC; Kent County Cricket, Primrose Hill Cricket, Aston Rowant Cricket (Life Vice Pres., 2010–; Vice Chm., 2014–); Alnmouth Golf, Huntercombe Golf, Turnberry Golf; Arsenal Football, Rangers Football, London Scottish Football; Western Province Cricket (Cape Town).

**WHITE, Sharon Michele, (Mrs R. W. Chote);** Executive Chairman, John Lewis Partnership, since 2020; *b* 21 April 1967; *d* of Curtis Gustavus White and Bernice White; *m* 1997, Robert William Chote, *qv*; two *s*. *Educ:* Fitzwilliam Coll., Cambridge (BA Hons Econs 1988; Hon. Fellow, 2015); University Coll. London (MSc Econs 1993). HM Treasury, 1990–95; First Sec., Econ., Washington, 1995–97; Advr on Welfare Reform to the Prime Minister, 1997–99; Sen. Economist, World Bank, 1999–2002; Dir of Policy, DFID, 2003–06; Dir of Welfare to Work, DWP, 2006–09; Ministry of Justice: Chief Exec., Office for Criminal Justice Reform, 2009–10; Dir Gen., Strategy, 2010; Dir Gen., Law, Rights and Internat., 2010–11; Acting Dir Gen., Middle E and N Africa, DFID, 2011; Dir

Gen., Public Spending, 2012–13, Second Permanent Sec., 2013–15, HM Treasury; Chief Exec., Ofcom, 2015–20. Non-exec. Dir, Barratt Developments plc, 2018–. Dir, Sadler's Wells Trust Ltd, 2017–. *Recreation:* childcare. *Address:* John Lewis Partnership, Partnership House, Carlisle Place, SW1P 1BX.

**WHITE, Prof. Simon David Manton,** PhD; FRS 1997; Director, Max Planck Institute for Astrophysics, since 1994; *b* 30 Sept. 1951; *s* of David and Gwynneth White; *m* 1st, 1984, Judith Dianne Jennings (marr. diss. 1990); 2nd, 1994, Guinevere Alice Mei-Ing Kauffmann; one *s*. *Educ:* Christ's Hosp.; Jesus Coll., Cambridge (BA 1973; MA 1976; PhD 1977); Univ. of Toronto (MSc 1974). Lindemann Fellow, 1977–78, Sen. Res. Fellow, 1980–83, Univ. of Calif at Berkeley; Res. Fellow, Churchill Coll., Cambridge, 1978–80; Associate Prof., 1983–87, Prof., 1987–90, Univ. of Arizona; Sheepshanks Reader, Univ. of Cambridge, 1990–94. Scientific Mem., Max Planck Soc., 1994–. *Publications:* Morphology and Dynamics of Galaxies, 1983. *Recreations:* ski-ing, singing, violin, Morris Dancing. *Address:* Max Planck Institut für Astrophysik, Karl Schwarzschild Strasse 1, 85741 Garching bei München, Germany. *T:* (89) 300002211.

**WHITE, Stephen Fraser;** consulting engineer; *b* 13 May 1922; *s* of Robert and Iola White; *m* 1953, Judith Hamilton Cox; two *s* one *d*. *Educ:* Friars, Bangor; Nottingham Univ. BSc; FICE, MIWEM. War Service in Indian Electrical and Mechanical Engineers, discharged 1947. G. H. Hill and Sons, Consulting Civil Engineers, 1947–59; Cardiff Corporation, 1959–62; Engineering Inspector, Min. of Housing and Local Govt, 1962–70; Dir of Water Engineering, Dept of the Environment, 1970–77; Sen. Technical Advr to Nat. Water Council, 1977–83. *Recreations:* golf, bridge. *Address:* Rosehill, 4 Goodens Lane, Great Doddington, Northants NN29 7TY.

**WHITE, Prof. Stephen Leonard,** PhD, DPhil, LittD; FBA 2010; James Bryce Professor of Politics, University of Glasgow, 1991–2017, now Emeritus; *b* Dublin, 1 July 1945; *s* of William John White and Edna White (*née* McGuckin); *m* 1973, Ishbel MacPhie; one *s*. *Educ:* Trinity Coll., Dublin (BA 1st Cl. Hons Pols and Mod. Hist. 1967; Exhibnr, Foundn Scholar; LittD 2001); Univ. of Glasgow (PhD Soviet Studies 1973); Wolfson Coll., Oxford (MA, DPhil Pols 1987). University of Glasgow: Lectr in Politics, 1971–85; Reader in Politics, 1985–91; Sen. Associate Mem., Sch. of Central and E Eur. Studies, 1993–. Vis. Prof., Inst. of Applied Pols, Moscow, 1992–; Adjunct Prof. of Eur. Studies, Bologna Center, Johns Hopkins Univ., 2008–11. Pres., British Assoc. for Slavonic and E Eur. Studies, 1994–97. Founder AcSS 1999; FRSE 2002. Gen. Ed., Cambridge Russian, Soviet and Post-Soviet Monographs, 1990–2000; Ed., Jl of Communist Studies and Transition Politics, 1994–2011; Member, Editorial Board: Europe-Asia Studies, 1980–; Slavonica (formerly Scottish Slavonic Review), 1989–; Pol Sci. Qly, 1998–2004; Perspectives on Eur. Politics and Soc., 2000–04; Comparative Eur. Politics, 2003–; Internat. Politics, 2004–; Politics, 2006–; Post-Soviet Affairs, 2011–; Mem., Editl Cttee, BASEES/Routledge Series on Russian and E Eur. Studies, 2001–11. *Publications:* The USSR: portrait of a superpower, 1978; Political Culture and Soviet Politics, 1979; Britain and the Bolshevik Revolution: a study in the politics of diplomacy 1920–24, 1980; (ed with Dan Nelson) Communist Legislatures in Comparative Perspective, 1982; (jtly) Communist Political Systems: an introduction, 1982, 2nd edn 1987; (ed with W. B. Simons) The Party Statutes of the Communist World, 1984; The Origins of Detente: the Genoa conference and Soviet-Western relations, 1921–1922, 1986; (ed with Dan Nelson) Communist Politics: a reader, 1986; (ed with A. Pravda) Ideology and Soviet Politics, 1988; The Bolshevik Poster, 1988; Soviet Communism: programme and rules, 1989; (ed jtly) Gorbachev and Gorbachevism, 1989; (jtly) Communist and Postcommunist Political Systems, 3rd edn, 1990; (ed jtly) Developments in Soviet Politics, 1990, 3rd edn as Developments in Soviet and Post-Soviet Politics, 1994; Gorbachev in Power, 1990; (ed and contrib.) Handbook of Reconstruction in Eastern Europe and the USSR, 1991; Gorbachev and After, 1991, 4th edn 1993; (ed) New Directions in Soviet History, 1991; Developments in Central and East European Politics, 1993; (jtly) The Politics of Transition: shaping a post-Soviet future, 1993; (ed jtly) The Soviet Transition: from Gorbachev to Yeltsin, 1993; Russia Goes Dry: alcohol, state and society, 1996; (ed jtly) Developments in Russian Politics 4, 1997; (jtly) How Russia Votes, 1997; (jtly) Elections and Voters in Post-Communist Russia, 1998; Developments in Central and East European Politics 2, 1998; Russia's New Politics, 2000; (with Evan Mawdsley) The Soviet Elite from Lenin to Gorbachev: the CPSU Central Committee and its members 1917–1991, 2000; Communism and its Collapse, 2001; (ed with Dan Nelson) The Politics of the Postcommunist World, 2001; (ed with Rick Fawn) Russia After Communism, 2002; (ed jtly) Postcommunist Belarus, 2005; (jtly) Putin's Russia and the Enlarged Europe, 2006; (ed with Paul Webb) Party Politics in New Democracies, 2007; (jtly) Politics in Europe, 3rd edn 2003 to 6th edn 2015; (ed jtly) Developments in Central and East European Politics 4, 2007, 5, 2013; (ed) Media, Culture and Society in Putin's Russia, 2008; (ed) Politics and the Ruling Group in Putin's Russia, 2008; (ed jtly) Developments in Russian Politics 7, 2010; Understanding Russian Politics, 2011; (ed with Lena Jonson) Waiting for Reform under Putin and Medvedev, 2012; (ed jtly) Developments in Russian Politics 8, 2014; (with Valentina Feklyunina) Identities and Foreign Policies in Russia, Ukraine and Belarus, 2014. *Recreations:* film, theatre, travel. *Address:* (home) 11 Hamilton Drive, Glasgow G12 8DN; School of Social and Political Sciences, Adam Smith Building, Bute Gardens, University of Glasgow, Glasgow G12 8RT. *T:* (0141) 330 5352. *E:* stephen.white@glasgow.ac.uk.

**WHITE, Air Vice-Marshal Terence Philip,** CB 1987; DL; CEng, FIET; at leisure; *b* 1 May 1932; *s* of Horace Arthur White and Evelyn Annie White (*née* Simpson); *m* 1956, Sheila Mary (*née* Taylor) (*d* 2015); three *d*. *Educ:* Wellingborough Technical Inst.; Rugby Coll. of Technology and Arts; RAF Engineering College. Electrical engineering apprentice, BTH Co., 1948–53; Junior Design Engineer, BTH Co., 1953; commissioned RAF Signals Officer, 1954–56; RAF Permt commn, Elect. Engr, 1957; attached RAAF, 1958–60; RAF weapons, communications and radar appts, 1963–67; OC Wing, RAF, Fylingdales, 1967–70; RAF Staff Coll., 1971; commanded RAF N Luffenham, 1972–74; Mem., RCDS, 1975; Senior Elect. Engr, HQ RAF Strike Command, 1976–77; Dir, Engineering Policy MoD (Air), 1978–80; Air Officer, Engrg and Supply, HQ RAF Germany, 1981–82; AOC Maintenance Units and AO Maintenance, RAF Support Comd, 1983–87. Vice Chm. (Air), E Midlands TAVRA, 1988–98. Hon. Air Cdre, County of Lincoln RAuxAF Sqn, 1992–2005; Hon. County Rep., Lincs, RAF Benevolent Fund, 1995–2003. DL Lincoln, 1994. *Publications:* contribs to RAF and professional jls. *Recreations:* antiques, travel. *Address:* Eccleston, 45 Lansdown Road, Cheltenham, Glos GL51 6PT. *Club:* Royal Air Force.

**WHITE, Tom;** *see* White, D. T.

**WHITE, Rev. Canon Prof. Vernon Philip;** Canon Theologian, 2011–18, and Sub-Dean and Archdeacon, 2016–18, Westminster Abbey; Visiting Professor of Theology, King's College London, since 2011; *b* London, 16 March 1953; *s* of Raymond and Yvonne White; *m* 1977, Joy Valerie Hillyer; one *s*. *Educ:* Eltham Coll.; Clare Coll., Cambridge (BA 1975; MA 1979); Oriel Coll., Oxford (MLitt). Ordained deacon, 1977, priest, 1978; Tutor, Wycliffe Hall, Oxford, 1977–83; Lazenby Chaplain and Lectr, Exeter Univ., 1983–87; Dir of Ordinands, Dio. of Guildford, and Rector, Wotton and Holmbury St Mary, 1987–93; Chancellor of Lincoln Cathedral, 1993–2001; Special Lectr, Nottingham Univ., 1993–2001; Principal, Southern Theol Educn and Trng Scheme, 2001–11. Hon. Canon Theologian, Winchester Cath., 2006–11. *Publications:* The Fall of a Sparrow, 1985; Atonement and Incarnation, 1991; Paying Attention to People, 1996; Identity, 2002; Counterpoints, 2005; Life Beyond Death, 2006; Purpose and Providence: taking soundings in Western thought, literature and theology, 2015; articles in Theology. *Recreations:* mountain walking, 19th and 20th Century English literature, cricket.

**WHITE, Sir Willard Wentworth,** OM (Jamaica) 2000; Kt 2004; CBE 1995; singer, actor; President, Royal Northern College of Music, since 2008; *b* 10 Oct. 1946; *s* of Egbert and Gertrude White; *m* 1972; three *s* one *d*. *Educ:* Excelsior High Sch., Kingston, Jamaica; Juilliard Sch. of Music (BM). Guest singer, recitalist and recording artist, UK and overseas; singing rôles include Sarastro, Osmin, Sprecher, Leporello, Banquo, King Philip, Grand Inquisitor, Ferrando, Wotan, Klingsor, Hunding, Fafner, King Henry, Orestes, Porgy, Golaud, Pizarro, Prince Khovansky, Mephistopheles (Gounod's Faust and Berlioz's Damnation of Faust); Nekrotzar, Moses, four villains in Tales of Hoffman, Wanderer, Don Fernando, Schigolch; Alexander Gorjančikov, Maison des Morts; Arkel; Cadmus; Publio; Bottom; Doctor, Wozzeck; Tiresias, Messenger, Creonte; Timur; Seneca; *stage:* title rôle, Othello, RSC, 1989. Prime Minister of Jamaica's Medal of Appreciation, 1987.

**WHITE, Ven. William Robert S.;** *see* Stuart-White.

**WHITE-COOPER, (William) Robert (Patrick),** FCII; Director, Marsh & McLennan Companies, 1998–2000; *b* 17 March 1943; *s* of William Ronald White-Cooper and Alison Mary White-Cooper; *m* 1965, Jennifer Margaret Hayward; one *s* three *d*. *Educ:* Diocesan Coll., Cape Town. FCII 1970. Various exec. posts, Price Forbes Gp, S Africa, 1962–83; Chairman: Sedgwick UK Ltd, 1986–89; Sedgwick Europe Ltd, 1989–93; Sedgwick Noble Lowndes Gp, 1993–96; Chief Exec., Sedgwick Gp plc, 1997–98. Chm., Adv. Bd, Sapiens, 2004–07. Past President: Insce Inst. of London; Insce Inst. of Cape of Good Hope. Past Chm., Addaction, 2001–13. *Recreations:* tennis, golf, spectating cricket and Rugby, biographies, antiques. *Clubs:* MCC; Swinley Forest Golf, Wentworth; Kelvin Grove, Steenberg Golf, Western Province Cricket (Cape Town).

**WHITE-SPUNNER, Lt Gen. Sir Barnabas William Benjamin, (Sir Barney),** KCB 2011; CBE 2002; Director, Burstock Ltd, since 2015; *b* 31 Jan. 1957; *s* of late Benjamin Nicholson, (Tommy), White-Spunner and Elizabeth, (Biddy), White-Spunner; *m* 1989, Amanda Faulkner; one *s* two *d*. *Educ:* Eton; Univ. of St Andrews (MA 1978). Commnd Blues and Royals, 1979; Dep. Leader, British-Chinese Taklamakan Expedn, 1993; MA to CDS, 1994–96; CO Household Cavalry Regt, 1996–98; Dep. Dir Defence Policy, 1998–2000; Commander: 16 Air Assault Bde, 2000–02; NATO Op. Harvest Macedonia, 2001; Kabul Multi-Nat. Bde, 2002; Chief of Jt Force Ops UK, 2003–05; COS HQ Land Comd, 2005–07; GOC 3rd (UK) Div., 2007–09; GOC Multi Nat. Div., SE Iraq, 2008; Comdr Field Army, 2009–12. Co-ordinator, Ohrid Gp, 2018–. Exec. Chm., Countryside Alliance, 2012–15. Chairman: From Poverty to Opportunity, CAFOD, 2013–16; Sandpit Investments, 2013–; Adv. Bd, UK Fisheries, 2018–. Chm., Grand Mil. Race Cttee, 2011–. Pres., Soc. Army Histl Res., 2012–. Trustee, Nat. Army Mus., 2012–17. Corresp., The Field, 1992–2000; Ed., Baily's Hunting Directory, 1996–2009. Hon. Colonel: Kent and Sharpshooter Yeo., 2008–10; Tayforth Univs OTC, 2009–13; Colonel Commandant: HAC, 2010–13; Royal Yeo., 2010–17. Hon. Legionnaire 1st Cl., French Foreign Legion; Legion of Merit (USA), 2009; Knight's Cross (Hungary), 2018. *Publications:* Baily's Hunting Companion, 1994; Our Countryside, 1996; Great Days, 1997; Horse Guards, 2006; Of Living Valour: the story of the soldiers of Waterloo, 2015; Partition: the story of Indian independence and the creation of Pakistan in 1947, 2017. *Recreations:* history, hunting, racing, fishing. *Address:* c/o Headquarters, Household Cavalry, Horse Guards, Whitehall, SW1A 2AX. *Clubs:* Turf, Pratt's.

**WHITEFIELD, Gavin,** CBE 2011; Vice Lord-Lieutenant of Lanarkshire, since 2018; *b* 7 Feb. 1956; *s* of late Gavin Whitefield and Annie Whitefield; *m* 1981, Grace Tait; two *d*. *Educ:* DPA 1990; CPFA 1996. Audit Asst, Exchequer and Audit Dept, 1974–76; Clydesdale District Council: Asst Auditor, 1976–84; Computer Develt Officer, 1984–86; Principal Housing Officer (Finance and Admin), 1986–89; Asst Dir of Housing (Finance and Admin), Motherwell DC, 1989–95; Dir, Housing and Property Services, 1995–2000, Chief Exec., 2000–15, N Lanarks Council. Chm., Solace Scotland, 2007–08. DL Lanarkshire, 2016. *Recreations:* hill walking, football. *E:* gavinwhitef56@hotmail.com.

**WHITEFIELD, Karen;** Training Officer, Usdaw, since 2017; *b* 8 Jan. 1970; *d* of William and Helen Whitefield. *Educ:* Calderhead High Sch.; Glasgow Poly. (BA Hons Public Admin and Mgt). Civil Servant, Benefits Agency, 1992; Personal Asst to Rachel Squire, MP, 1992–99. Mem. (Lab) Airdrie and Shotts, Scottish Parlt, 1999–2011. Campaigns Officer, Usdaw, 2012–17. Contested (Lab) Falkirk, 2015. Mem., Girls' Bde, Scotland. *Recreations:* reading, travel, swimming.

**WHITEFORD, Eilidh,** PhD; *b* Aberdeen, 24 April 1969; *d* of Douglas Dodson Whiteford and Kathleen Whiteford (*née* MacLeod); *m* 2010, Stephen Smith. *Educ:* Banff Acad.; Univ. of Glasgow (MA Hons 1991; PhD 1998); Univ. of Guelph (MA 1994). Lectr in Scottish Literature and Academic Develt Officer, Univ. of Glasgow, 1999; Co-ordinator, Scottish Carers' Alliance, 2001–03; Campaigns Manager, Scotland, Oxfam, 2003–09. MP (SNP) Banff and Buchan, 2010–17; contested (SNP) same seat, 2017. *Recreation:* music.

**WHITEHEAD, Dr Alan Patrick Vincent;** MP (Lab) Southampton Test, since 1997; *b* 15 Sept. 1950; *m*; one *s* one *d*. *Educ:* Southampton Univ. (BA 1973; PhD 1976). Dep. Dir, 1976–79, Dir, 1979–83, Outset; Dir, British Inst. of Industrial Therapy, 1983–92; Prof. of Public Policy, Southampton Inst., 1992–97. Mem. (Lab), Southampton CC, 1980–92 (Leader, 1984–92). Parly Under-Sec. of State, DTLR, 2001–02; Shadow Minister for Energy and Climate Change, 2015–. Member: Select Cttee on Envmt, Transport and Regions, 1997–99, on constitutional affairs, 2003–10, on Energy and Climate Change, 2008–15; Envmtl Audit Select Cttee, 2010–15; Standards and Privileges Cttee, 2005–13; Chairman: All Party Ports Gp, 1998–2001; Parly Renewable and Sustainable Energy Gp, 2003–15; Parly Sustainable Resource (formerly Waste) Gp, 2003–15; British-Polish Parly Gp, 2008–15. Contested (Lab) New Forest, 1979; Southampton, Test, 1983, 1987, 1992. *Address:* House of Commons, SW1A 0AA. *T:* (020) 7219 3000.

**WHITEHEAD, Hon. Dame Annabel Alice Hoyer,** DCVO 2014 (CVO 2002; LVO 1987); Lady in Waiting to the Queen, since 2002; *b* Washington, DC, 1943; *d* of 1st Baron Inchyra, GCMG, CVO; *m* 1973, Christopher Whitehead (*d* 2018); one *s* one *d*. Lady in Waiting to Princess Margaret, 1971–2002. *Address:* Seend Lodge, Seend, Wilts SN12 6NU.

**WHITEHEAD, Edward Anthony, (Ted);** playwright; *b* 3 April 1933; *s* of Edward Whitehead and Catherine Curran; *m* 1st, 1958, Kathleen Horton (marr. diss. 1976); two *d*; 2nd, 1976, Gwenda Bagshaw. *Educ:* Christ's Coll., Cambridge (MA). Military Service, King's Regt (Infantry), 1955–57. *TV plays:* Under the Age; The Peddler; The Proofing Session; The Blonde Bombshell; *TV adaptations:* The Detective; Jumping the Queue; The Life and Loves of a She-Devil; Firstborn; The Free Frenchman; The Cloning of Joanna May; A Question of Guilt; Tess of the D'Urbervilles; The Mayor of Casterbridge; *stage adaptation:* The Dance of Death; *radio play:* Features Like Mine, 2005. Evening Standard Award, and George Devine Award, 1971; BAFTA Award, 1986. *Publications:* The

Foursome, 1972; Alpha Beta, 1972; The Sea Anchor, 1975; Old Flames, 1976; The Punishment, 1976; Mecca, 1977; World's End, 1981; The Man Who Fell in Love with his Wife, 1984; Collected Plays, 2005. *Recreations:* soccer, obituaries, cats. *Address:* c/o Mark Casarotto, Waverley House, 7–12 Noel Street, W1F 8GQ. *T:* (020) 7287 4450.

**WHITEHEAD, (Godfrey) Oliver,** CBE 1987; FICE; President, Smeatonian Society of Civil Engineers, 2012; *b* 9 Aug. 1941; *s* of late Clarence Whitehead and Mary Whitehead (*née* Gartside); *m* 1965, Stephanie McAllister; three *s* one *d*. *Educ:* Hulme Grammar Sch., Oldham; Univ. of Bradford (BSc Civil Engrg). FICE 1992. John Laing Plc, 1963–86: Man. Dir, John Laing Construction Ltd, 1982–86; Exec. Dir, John Laing Plc 1983–86; Chm., Jt Venture (Laing-Mowlem-ARC) which built Mt Pleasant Airport, Falkland Is, 1983–86; Chm., John Laing Internat., 1986; Exec. Dir, AMEC Plc, 1986–89; Gp Chief Exec., Babcock Internat. Gp PLC, 1989–93; Chief Exec., 1993–2003, Chm., 2002–07 (non-exec. Chm., 2003–07), Alfred McAlpine plc; Chairman: Minerva plc, 2007–11; Norland Managed Services Ltd, 2008–11. Non-exec. Dir, PSA, 1989–91. Manchester Ringway Developments PLC: Chm., 1987–89; Pres., 1989–2002. Col, 1996, CO, 2001, Engr and Logistics Staff Corps, TA (Major, 1984; Chm., Liaison Cttee, 1991–2000). Liveryman, Paviors' Co., 1986– (Master, 2007–08). *Recreations:* gardening, shooting, opera.

**WHITEHEAD, Joanne;** *see* Wicks, J.

**WHITEHEAD, Dame Margaret McRae,** DBE 2016; PhD; FFPH; FMedSci; WH Duncan Professor of Public Health, University of Liverpool, since 1999 (Head, Department of Public Health and Policy, 2010–17); *b* 28 Sept. 1948; *d* of William McRae Houston and Edna Houston; *m* 1970, John Whitehead; two *s*. *Educ:* Univ. of York (BA 1970); Karolinska Inst., Stockholm (PhD 1997). Hon. MFPHM 1993, FFPH 2001. Research Officer: Chester Beatty Cancer Res. Inst., London, 1971–72; MRC Clin. and Population Cytogenetics Unit, Edinburgh, 1973–75; Scottish Health Educn Unit, Edinburgh, 1976–78; independent researcher, 1978–99; University of Liverpool: Hd, Dept of Public Health, 1999–2005; Founding Hd, WHO Collaborating Centre for Policy Res. on the Determinants of Health Equity (formerly WHO Collaborating Centre for Policy Res. on Social Determinants of Health), 2005–. Vis. Fellow, King's Fund, London, 1993–99; Vis. Fellow, 1995–99, Vis. Prof., 2013–, Karolinska Inst., Stockholm. Consultant to ONS, London, 1995–97. Founder Mem., Global Health Equity Initiative, Rockefeller Foundn and Swedish Internat. Develt Agency, 1996–2000; Mem., Ind. Inq. into Inequalities in Health, 1997–98; Chm., Task Gp, Strategic Rev. of Health Inequalities in England post-2010, 2009–10; Sen. Advr, WHO Europ. Rev. of Social Determinants and the Health Divide, 2010–13; Chm., Ind. Inq. into Health Equity for N of England, 2014–15. FMedSci 2017. *Publications:* The Health Divide, 1988, 2nd edn 1992; (ed jtly) Tackling Inequalities in Health: an agenda for action, 1995; (ed jtly) Challenging Inequalities in Health: from ethics to action, 2001; articles in jls on inequalities in health; translations of seminal reports into over 20 langs. *Recreations:* family, theatre, art, gardening. *Address:* Department of Public Health and Policy, University of Liverpool, Whelan Building, The Quadrangle, Liverpool L69 3GB. *T:* (0151) 794 5280. *E:* mmw@liverpool.ac.uk.

**WHITEHEAD, Oliver;** *see* Whitehead, G. O.

**WHITEHEAD, Sir Philip Henry Rathbone,** 6th Bt *cr* 1889, of Highfield House, Catford Bridge, Kent; security specialist for Africa; *b* 13 Oct. 1957; *s* of Sir Rowland John Rathbone Whitehead, 5th Bt and of Marie-Louise (*née* Gausel); *S* father, 2007; *m* 1987, Emma Charlotte Milne Home (marr. diss. 2002); two *s*. *Educ:* Eton; Bristol Univ. (BSc Hons); RMA, Sandhurst. 1st Bn Welsh Guards, 1977; 22 SAS (R), 1982; Credit Suisse First, Boston, 1987; private security companies, 1994–. Mem., RGS. Gen. Service Medal, NI, 1980; Long Service and Good Conduct Medal, 1992. *Recreations:* travel, photography, flying (Mem., British Microlight Aircraft Assoc.), motorcycling. *Heir:* *s* Orlando James Rathbone Whitehead, *b* 8 Oct. 1994. *Address:* 15 Russell Close, W4 2NU. *Clubs:* Special Forces; Bridport Gentleman's Snooker.

**WHITEHEAD, Dr Roger George,** CBE 1992; nutrition consultant; Director, Dunn Nutrition Centre, Medical Research Council, Cambridge and Keneba, The Gambia, 1973–98; Fellow of Darwin College, Cambridge, 1973–2001, now Emeritus Fellow; *b* 7 Oct. 1933; *s* of late Arthur Charles Sanders Whitehead and Eleanor Jane Whitehead (*née* Farrer); *m* 1958, Jennifer Mary Lees; two *s* one *d*. *Educ:* Ulverston Grammar Sch.; Univ. of Leeds (BSc 1956; PhD 1959); MA Cantab 1973. FRSB (FIBiol 1973); Hon. MRCP 1986, Hon. FRCP 1993; Hon. FRCPCH 1997; Hon. FAfN 2012. Scientific Staff, MRC, 1959–98; Dir, Child Nutrition Unit, Kampala, 1968–73; Vice Master, Darwin Coll., Cambridge, 1989–99. Visiting Professor: KCL, 1992–; Oxford Brookes Univ., 2002–; Hon. Professor: Shenyang Univ., China, 1995–; Chinese Acad. of Preventive Medicine, 1995–; Fellow, Internat. Union of Nutritional Scis, 1997; Mem. Internat. Staff, Makerere Univ., Uganda, 2003–. Committee on Medical Aspects of Food Policy: Mem., 1975–91; Chm., Dietary Reference Panel, 1987–91; Mem., MAFF Food Adv. Cttee, 1988–95. Hon. Sen. Scientist, Human Nutrition Res., MRC, Cambridge, 1999–2015. FAO consultant, 2004–06. Pres., Nutrition Soc., 1989–92 (Hon. Mem., 2000; Hon. Fellow, 2016); Chm., British Nutrition Foundn, 1994–96 (Vice-Chm., 1993–94; Gov. Emeritus, 2005). Hon. DSc Ulster, 2000. Drummond Prize, Nutrition Soc., 1968; Unesco Science Prize, 1983; British Nutrition Foundn Prize, 1990; Nutricia Internat. Award for Nutritional Sci., 1994. *Publications:* (jtly) Protein-Energy Malnutrition, 1977; (ed) Maternal Nutrition during Pregnancy and Lactation, 1980; (ed) New Techniques in Nutritional Research, 1991; contribs to learned jls. *Recreations:* photography, licensed amateur radio operator, G3ZUK 5X5NA, C53U. *Address:* Church View, Church End, Weston Colville, Cambridge CB21 5PE. *T:* (01223) 290524. *E:* rogergwhitehead@aol.com.

**WHITEHEAD, Simon Christopher,** PhD; Consultant, Joseph Hage Aaronson LLP (formerly Hage Aaronson), since 2018 (Founding Partner, 2013–18); *b* Castle Donnington, 31 Jan. 1963; *s* of late John Whitehead and Patricia Helena Whitehead; *m* 1991, Frances Mary Somers; two *d*. *Educ:* Cranbrook Sch.; Univ. of Sydney (BA 1st cl. Hons 1985; LLB 1987; PhD 1993). St Paul's Coll. Council Scholar, 1985; Australian and Commonwealth Postgrad. Res. Award, 1987–91. Admitted solicitor, England and Wales, 1991, NSW, 1987, High Court of Australia, 1998; Partner and Hd of Civil Litigation, Saunders & Co., 1994–98; solicitor, NSW, 1998–2000; returned to practice in England, 2000; Partner and Hd of Litigation, PricewaterhouseCoopers Legal, 2002–03; Partner and Co-Hd of Trial (Europe), 2003–13, Partner in Charge, Internat., 2010–13, Dorsey & Whitney LLP. *Publications:* (contrib.) Roman Crossings: theory and practice in the Roman Republic, 2005; (ed) The Tax Disputes and Litigation Review, 2013, 7th edn 2019; articles in EC Tax Rev., Tax Jl, Solicitors' Jl, Taxation, Internat. Tax Rev., Tax Notes Internat., New Law Jl. *Recreations:* curing meat, homebrewing, engineering projects in honour of Merv Somers. *Address:* Joseph Hage Aaronson LLP, 280 High Holborn, WC1V 7EE. *T:* (020) 7851 8800. *E:* swhitehead@jha.com.

**WHITEHEAD, Stephen;** Corporate Relations Director, Crescent Capital Partners, since 2016; *b* Steeton, W Yorks, 12 Nov. 1963; *s* of Colin Whitehead and Shirley Whitehead. *Educ:* Ilkley Grammar Sch.; Univ. of Manchester (BA Hons American Hist. and Society). Hd, Communications, GlaxoWellcome, 1991–95; Gp Alcohol Policy Dir, Diageo plc, 1995–98; Corporate Affairs Dir, Eli Lilly & Co. Europe, 1998–2003; Group Corporate Affairs Director: Allied Domecq plc, 2003–05; Barclays plc, 2005–07; Gp Communications Dir, Prudential plc, 2007–11; CEO, ABPI, 2011–15. *Recreations:* theatre, cinema, walking, dogs, family. *Clubs:* Soho House, Home House.

**WHITEHEAD, Ted;** *see* Whitehead, E. A.

**WHITEHEAD, (Victoria) Jane;** *see* Bruton, V. J.

**WHITEHORN, Katharine Elizabeth, (Mrs Gavin Lyall),** CBE 2014; Columnist: The Observer, 1960–96 (Associate Editor, 1980–88); Observer Magazine, 2011–17; Agony Aunt, Saga Magazine, 1997–2016; *b* London; *d* of late A. D. and E. M. Whitehorn; *m* 1958, Gavin Tudor Lyall (*d* 2003); two *s*. *Educ:* Blunt House; Roedean; Glasgow High School for Girls, and others; Newnham Coll., Cambridge. Publisher's Reader, 1950–53; Teacher-Secretary in Finland, 1953–54; Grad. Asst, Cornell Univ., USA, 1954–55; Picture Post, 1956–57; Woman's Own, 1958; Spectator, 1959–61. Member: Latey Cttee on Age of Majority, 1965–67; BBC Adv. Gp on Social Effects of Television, 1971–72; Board, British Airports Authority, 1972–77; Council, Open Section, RSocMed, 1982–85. Director: Nationwide Building Soc., 1983–91; Nationwide Anglia Estate Agents, 1987–90. Vice-Pres., Patients Assoc., 1983–96. Rector, St Andrews Univ., 1982–85. Advr, Inst. for Global Ethics, 1993–2011. Mem., ESU. Hon. LLD St Andrews, 1985; Hon. DLitt London Guildhall, 2000. Woman That Makes A Difference Award, Internat. Women's Forum, 1992. *Publications:* Cooking in a Bedsitter, 1960; Roundabout, 1961; Only on Sundays, 1966; Whitehorn's Social Survival, 1968; Observations, 1970; How to Survive in Hospital, 1972; How to Survive Children, 1975; Sunday Best, 1976; How to Survive in the Kitchen, 1979; View from a Column, 1981; How to Survive your Money Problems, 1983; Selective Memory (autobiog.), 2007. *Address:* c/o 26 Holdenhurst Avenue, N12 0JB. *Clubs:* University Women's (Hon. Mem.), Royal Society of Medicine; Forum UK.

**WHITEHORN, William Elliott;** Deputy Chairman, Stagecoach Group plc, 2016–June 2020 (non-executive Director, 2011–June 2020); President, Chartered Institute of Logistics and Transport, 2016–17; *b* Edinburgh, 22 Feb. 1960; *s* of Donald Punyer Whitehorn and Marjorie Elliott Whitehorn; *m* 1st, 1987, Louise Mary Farquhar (marr. diss. 2014); one *s* one *d*; 2nd, 2015, Alison Ernst (*née* Horne). *Educ:* Edinburgh Acad.; Univ. of Aberdeen (MA Hons Hist. with Econs 1981). Pres., Aberdeen Univ. Student Union, 1981–82. Helicopter crewman, British Airways, 1982–84; grad. trainee, Thomas Cook, 1984–85; Mkt Intelligence Manager, TSB Bank plc, 1985; Account Dir, Lombard Communications, 1985–86; Investor Relns Manager, Virgin Gp, 1987–91; Special Projects Dir, Virgin Atlantic, 1990–2007; Brand Develt and Corporate Affairs Dir, Virgin Mgt, 1993–2007; Pres., Virgin Galactic, 2004–10; various non-exec. directorships, Virgin Gp, 1987–2007; Chairman: Loewy Gp, 2010–12; Speed Communications, 2011–17. Mem., Adv. Bd, Writtle Hldgs Ltd, 2012–; non-executive Director: SECC, Glasgow, 2010– (Chm., 2015–); Purplebricks Gp plc, 2012–; Sen. Ind. Dir, GVC Hldgs, 2017–. Mem., Sci. and Technol. Facilities Council, 2010–13; Chm. Bd, Transport Systems Catapult, 2013–. Chm., Scottish Gall., 2014–. FRAeS 2012; FCILT 2013; Fellow, Mktg Soc., 2015. Mem., Forresters' Assoc., Bisley. Space Medal (Geoffrey Pardoe Space Award), RAeS, 2010. *Recreations:* shooting, farming, hill-walking, scuba diving, sailing. *Address:* Stagecoach Group plc, 10 Dunkeld Road, Perth PH1 5TW. *T:* 07941 228844. *Club:* Caledonian.

**WHITEHOUSE, Prof. Colin Ralph,** PhD; CPhys, FInstP; FIMMM; FREng; independent consultant and adviser on science, technology and innovation, InnovationsST Ltd, since 2012; non-executive Chairman, Compound Semiconductor Centre (CSC) Ltd, Cardiff, since 2016; *b* 21 Aug. 1949; *s* of Clifford William Whitehouse and Edith Elizabeth Whitehouse (*née* Pearson); *m* 1973, Mary Elizabeth Wilks; two *d*. *Educ:* Queen Elizabeth Coll., London (BSc Physics 1970); Univ. of Birmingham (MSc Physics 1971); Univ. of Brighton/GEC Hirst Res. Centre (PhD Semiconductor Growth 1978). CPhys 1994; FInstP 1994; FREng 2002; FIMMM 2002. Res. scientist, GEC Hirst Res. Centre, Wembley, 1974–77; Sen. Res. Associate, Univ. of Newcastle upon Tyne, 1977–80; Higher SO, 1980–83, SSO, 1983–87, PSO, 1987–93, RSRE Malvern; University of Sheffield: Prof. of Electronic Materials, 1993–2003; Dir, EPSRC Nat. Centre for III–V Semiconductor Technologies, 1993–2003; Hd, Electronic and Electrical Engrg Dept, 1994–2000; Dir of Res., Engrg and Physical Scis Res. Div., 1996–99; Pro-Vice-Chancellor: for Res. and Internat. Affairs, 1999–2001; for Res. and Res. Exploitation, 2001–03; Council for the Central Laboratory of the Research Councils: Dir of Engrg, 2003–04; Dir, Daresbury Lab., 2004–06; Chief Technologist, 2005–06; Dep. Chief Exec., 2006–07; Science and Technology Facilities Council: Hd of Daresbury Lab., 2007–12; Mem., 2007–09; Dep. Chief Exec., 2007–12; Dir of Knowledge Exchange, 2007–08; Dir of Campus Strategy, 2008–12. Dep. Dir, UK IRC for Semiconductor Materials, 1993–98. Sci. Advr to Nu-Instruments Ltd, Wrexham, 2012–14. Visiting Professor: in Materials Sci., Univ. of Oxford, 2003–08; Sch. of Engrg, Univ. of Birmingham, 2005–. Member: UK North West Sci. Council, 2004–11; UK Yorks and Humberside Innovation Council, 2005–11; Knowledge Transfer and Economic Impact Gp, Res. Councils UK, 2006–08; Technology Strategy Bd, Res. Councils UK Strategy Gp, 2007–10; Northern Way Innovation Strategy Gp, 2008–11; FWO Hercules Foundn Sci. Bd, Brussels, 2009–. Member Board: Sheffield Univ. Enterprises Ltd, 1999–2003; White Rose Univs Res. Ltd, 1999–2003; Malvern Girls' Coll., 2000–06; CLIK, 2004–07; Microvisk, 2004–06; Halton Borough Chamber of Commerce and Enterprise, 2005–07; Daresbury Sci. and Innovation Campus, 2006–12; Didcot First, 2007–10; Quadrant, 2007–10; Oxford Economic Partnership, 2007–10; STFC Innovations, 2007–11; Spectrum, 2008–10; Res. and Develt Soc., 2008–16; STEMNET, 2008–14; Science Vale UK, 2009–12; Aalto Univ., Helsinki, 2012–; Member: Oxfordshire Local Enterprise Bd, 2010–12; Liverpool Knowledge Economy Gp, 2010–12; Adv. Council, Liverpool City Region LEP, 2012–; Welsh Govt Innovation Task and Finish Gp, 2012–13; Sci. and Innovation Cttee, Inst. of Physics, 2015–. *Publications:* numerous contribs to learned jl and prestigious conf. papers, relating to semiconductor materials, semiconductor processing, nanotechnology and nanoscience, next-generation devices and sensors, the knowledge economy, innovation and open innovation. *Recreations:* classical music, theatre, sports, gardening. *Address:* 3 Christchurch Road, Malvern, Worcs WR14 3BH. *T:* (01684) 572120. *E:* WhitehouseCR@aol.com.

**WHITEHOUSE, David Rae Beckwith;** QC 1990; *b* 5 Sept. 1945; *s* of late (David) Barry Beckwith Whitehouse, MA, MD, FRCS, FRCOG and Mary Beckwith Whitehouse, JP; *m* 1971, Linda Jane, *d* of Eric Vickers, CB and Barbara Mary Vickers; (one *s* decd). *Educ:* Ellesmere College; Choate Sch., Wallingford, Conn., USA; Trinity College, Cambridge (MA). English-Speaking Union Scholarship, 1964. Called to the Bar, Gray's Inn, 1969; in practice as a barrister specialising in criminal law and fraud cases, 1969–2011; Asst Recorder, 1983–87, Recorder, 1987–2010. Criminal cases include: Last Tango in Paris (obscene pubns); George Davis (five robbery trials and three appeals); Handless Corpse Murder; Cyprus Spy trial; murder trial of Lennie The Guv'nor McLean; Colombian Cartel and Mafia drug trials; Thomas ap Rhys Pryce murder trial; Christopher Langham case; defence of Adams, Arif, McAvoy, Richardson, Tibbs and Tobin families. Fraud cases include: Barlow Clowes (investment and co. takeover fraud); Norton plc (rights issue fraud); Abbey National plc (corruption); local authy frauds involving W Wilts and Brent Councils; John

(Goldfinger) Palmer (timeshare fraud); read The Sun for defamation and contempt, 1969–76. Member: Criminal Bar Assoc., 1969–2011; Central Criminal Court Bar Mess, 1970–2011. *Recreations:* the arts, esp. architecture, music and cinema; walking, wild gardening. *E:* dw@dwhitehouse.com. *Club:* Reform.

**WHITEHOUSE, Elly;** *see* Jansen, E.

**WHITEHOUSE, Prof. (Julian) Michael (Arthur),** MD; FRCP, FRCR, FRCPEd, FMedSci; Professor Emeritus, Imperial College School of Medicine, London, 2000; Vice Principal for Undergraduate Medicine, Imperial College School of Medicine and Professor of Medical Oncology, University of London, 1997–2000; *b* 2 June 1940; *s* of Arthur Arnold Keer Whitehouse and Kathleen Ida Elizabeth (*née* Elliston); *m* 1965, Diane France de Saussure; one *s* two *d*. *Educ:* Queens' Coll., Cambridge (BA 1963; MB, BChir 1966; MA 1967; MD 1975); St Bartholomew's Hosp. Med. Coll., London. FRCP 1979; FRCR 1992; FRCPEd 1994. Sen. Lectr and Actg Dir, ICRF Dept of Med. Oncology, and Hon. Consultant Physician, St Bartholomew's Hosp., London, 1975–76; Prof. of Med. Oncology and Dir, CRC Wessex Regl Med. Oncology Unit, Univ. of Southampton, and Hon. Consultant Physician, Southampton Gen. Hosp., 1976–97; Dean, Charing Cross and Westminster Med. Sch., 1997. Chm., Educn Trng Bd, Eur. Orgn for Res. and Treatment of Cancer, 1997–2001. Chm. Council, Paterson Inst., Christie Hosp., Manchester, 1997–2002; Member: Council, CRC, 1997–2002; GMC Fitness to Practise panel, 2000–15. Governor: Canford Sch., Dorset, 1986–2010; (and Mem. Council) St Swithun's Sch., Winchester, 1996–; City of London Sch., 2000–. FMedSci 2000. Hon. FACP 2019. *Publications:* CNS Complications of Malignant Disease, 1979; Recent Advances in Clinical Oncology, 1982, 2nd edn 1986; A Pocket Consultant in Clinical Oncology, 1983; Cancer Investigation and Management, 1984; Cancer: the facts, 1996; contrib. numerous papers in various jls on res. and treatment of cancer. *Recreations:* devising projects, ski-ing, sailing, travelling, genealogy. *E:* m.whitehouse@imperial.ac.uk. *Club:* Athenæum.

**WHITEHOUSE, Michael John,** OBE 2016; Chief Operating Officer, National Audit Office, 2009–17; *b* 14 Nov. 1957; *s* of late Bernard Joseph Whitehouse and Margaret Whitehouse (*née* Hutchings); civil partnership 2010, Michael Dust. *Educ:* King Edward VI Grammar Sch., Birmingham; Univ. of Exeter (BA Hons). CIPFA 1983. Joined Exchequer and Audit Dept, 1979; Dir, 1990–92; Min. of Finance, Zambia, 1992–94; Office of Auditor Gen., NZ, 1994–95; Dir, Value for Money Develt and Modernising Govt, 1996–2002; Asst Auditor Gen., Nat. Audit Office, 2002–09. Mem., Audit Cttee, Irish Audit Office, 2017–. Non-exec. Dir, and Chair, Audit Cttee, Medicines and Health Care Products Regulatory Agency, 2018–; non-exec. Dir, SE Coast Ambulance NHS Foundn Trust, 2018–. Trustee, Cruse Bereavement Care, 2015– (Hon. Treas., 2017–). *Recreations:* sport, travel, reading, theatre, history. *Address:* Wilton House, Old Woking Road, Pyrford, Surrey GU22 8PB. *E:* michael.jwhitehouse@btinternet.com.

**WHITEHOUSE, Paul;** writer, actor and producer; *m* Fiona (separated); two *d*. *Educ:* Univ. of E Anglia. Formerly plasterer. Dir, Tomboy Films Ltd. *Television includes:* writer (with Charlie Higson) and actor: Harry Enfield's Television Programme, 1990, 1992; Harry Enfield and Chums, 1994, 1997; The Fast Show, 1994–97 (also co-producer; Best Light Entertainment Perf., BAFTA Awards, 1998); Randall and Hopkirk, 1999; Happiness (also co-producer), 2001, 2003; writer (with Chris Langham) and actor, Help, 2005; writer and actor: Ruddy Hell! It's Harry and Paul, 2007; Harry and Paul, 2008, 2010, 2012 (Best Comedy Prog., BAFTA Awards, 2009); Bellamy's People (also co-dir), 2010; Nurse (also co-producer and co-dir), 2015; An Evening with Harry Enfield and Paul Whitehouse, 2015; Mortimer & Whitehouse: Gone Fishing, 2018–; actor, David Copperfield, 1999. *Films include:* Love's Labour's Lost, 2000; Kevin and Perry Go Large, 2000; Alice in Wonderland, 2010; Burke and Hare, 2010; Ghost Stories, 2018. *Theatre:* The Fast Show Live, Apollo, Hammersmith, 2002; The Fast Show Live: shamelessly plugging the DVD, Dominion, 2007; Legends!, tour, 2015; writer (with Jim Sullivan) and actor, Only Fools and Horses: The Musical, Th. Royal Haymarket, 2019. Writers' Guild of GB Award, British Comedy Awards, 2013. *Publications:* Mortimer & Whitehouse: gone fishing, 2019. *Address:* c/o Curtis Brown Group Ltd, Haymarket House, 28–29 Haymarket, SW1Y 4SP.

**WHITEHOUSE, Paul Chapple,** QPM 1993; Chairman, Gangmasters Licensing Authority, 2005–11; Chief Constable, Sussex Police, 1993–2001; *b* 26 Sept. 1944; *s* of Beatrice and Jack Whitehouse, Cambs; *m* 1970, Elizabeth Dinsmore; one *s* one *d*. *Educ:* Ipswich Sch.; Emmanuel Coll., Cambridge (BA 1967; MA 1969). VSO, Starehe Boys' Centre, Nairobi, 1963–64; Durham Constabulary, 1967–74; Northumbria Police, 1974–83; Asst Chief Constable, Greater Manchester Police, 1983–87; Dep. Chief Constable, W Yorkshire Police, 1987–93. Association of Chief Police Officers: Chairman: Communications Gp, 1995–2001; Personnel Mgt (formerly Personnel and Trng) Cttee, 1998–2001; Vice Chm., Media Adv. Group, 1994–2001; Member: Finance and Resources Cttee, 1994–2001; Inf. Mgt Cttee, 1995–2001. Chm., Brighton and Hove Common Purpose Adv. Gp, 1994–2001; Member Council: IAM, 1993–2002; NACRO, 1994–2007 (Vice-Chm., 2003–07); Centre for Crime and Justice Studies, 1997–2002. Chm., Nacro Pension Trustee, 2008–. Chairman: Starehe UK (formerly Starehe Endowment Fund (UK)), 1994–2013, now Trustee; Anti-Slavery Internat., 2011–14. Treasurer: Ludlow Assembly Rooms, 2002–07; Dutch Barge Assoc., 2002–12; Quakers and Business Gp, 2006–17; Bristol and Area Quaker Meeting, 2018–. Chair, Tim Field Foundn, 2015–; Trustee, Friends Trusts Ltd, 2013– (Chm., 2016–); Clerk: Friends Sch. Council, 2016–19; Audit Cttee, Britain Yearly Meeting Trustees, 2017–. Chm., W Somerset Railway Assoc., 2016–; Dir, Bristol Community Ferry Boats Ltd, 2016– (Chm., 2017–). Chm. of Govs, Sidcot Sch., 2007–16. *Recreations:* collecting people, IT, steam, disputation, keeping the peace. *Address:* 1 Slate Cottages, Manor Lane, Abbots Leigh, Bristol BS8 3RX. *T:* 07813 802783. *E:* paul@dunstanburgh.net. *Club:* Oxford and Cambridge.

**WHITEHOUSE, Sarah Alice;** QC 2014; a Recorder, since 2018; Deputy First Senior Treasury Counsel, Central Criminal Court, since 2018; *b* Kampala, Uganda, 13 Jan. 1961; *d* of Rev. Canon William Beadon Norman and Beryl Norman; *m* 1988, Andrew Timothy Brian Whitehouse (marr. diss. 2008); one *s* one *d*. *Educ:* Felixstowe Coll., Suffolk; St Andrews Univ. (MA Hons); Westminster Univ. (Postgrad. DipLaw). Asst Dir, Barclays de Zoete Wedd, 1989–91; called to the Bar, Lincoln's Inn, 1993; Sen. Treasury Counsel (Criminal), 2014–. *Publications:* (contrib.) Fraud (looseleaf), 2008; (contrib.) Millington & Sutherland Williams on The Proceeds of Crime, 2013; (contrib.) EU Law in Criminal Practice, 2013. *Recreation:* theatre. *Address:* 6KBW College Hill, 21 College Hill, EC4R 2RP. *T:* (020) 3301 0910. *E:* sarah.whitehouse@6kbw.com. *Club:* Carlton.

**WHITEHOUSE-JANSEN, Elly;** *see* Jansen, E.

**WHITELEY,** family name of **Baron Marchamley**.

**WHITELEY, Dame Jane (Elizabeth),** DBE 1990; *b* 14 July 1944; *d* of Major Charles Packe (killed in action, July 1944) and Hon. Margaret (*née* Lane Fox); *m* 1st, 1966, Ian Gow, TD, MP (*d* 1990); two *s*; 2nd, 1994, Lt-Col Michael Whiteley. *Educ:* St Mary's School, Wantage. Governor: three special schs in S London, 1968–72; Hankham CP Sch., 1976–85; St Bede's Sch., Eastbourne, 1980–87; Park Coll., Eastbourne, 1985–88; Grenville Coll., Bideford, 1997–2005; Mem. Council, Cheltenham Coll., 1996–98. Trustee: Ian Gow Meml Fund, 1990–2003; Exeter Cathedral Music Foundn Trust, 2005–14; Visitor: Henry Smith Charity, 2001–07; Trusthouse Charitable Foundn, 2005–07. Freeman, Bor. of Eastbourne, 1992. *Recreations:* playing organ and piano, reading. *Address:* Hornbeams, Tenterden Road, Biddenden, Kent TN27 8BJ.

**WHITELEY, Prof. Paul Frederick,** PhD; FBA 2012; FAcSS; Professor of Government, University of Essex, since 2001; *b* Batley, Yorks, 6 Feb. 1946; *s* of Frederick Whiteley and Constance Whiteley; *m* 1968, Susan Alice Everest; one *s* two *d*. *Educ:* Bournemouth Grammar Sch.; Univ. of Sheffield (BA Econ); Univ. of Essex (PhD 1984). Lecturer: Kingston Poly., 1971–78; Univ. of Bristol, 1978–88; Prof., Univ. of Arizona, 1988–90; Pamela Harriman Prof. of Govt, Coll. of William and Mary, Va, 1990–94; Prof. of Politics, Univ. of Sheffield, 1994–2001. FAcSS (AcSS 2011). *Publications:* Labour's Grassroots: the politics of party membership, 1992; True Blues: the politics of Conservative Party membership, 1994; Political Choice in Britain, 2004; Affluence, Austerity and Electoral Change in Britain, 2013; Brexit: why Britain voted to leave the European Union, 2017. *Recreations:* jogging, walking, film, popular science. *Address:* Department of Government, University of Essex, Wivenhoe Park, Colchester CO4 3SQ. *T:* (01206) 872641. *E:* whiteley@essex.ac.uk.

**WHITEMAN, Hon. Burchell Anthony,** OJ 2006; Senior Adviser, Office of the Governor-General of Jamaica (Senior Adviser, Office of the Prime Minister of Jamaica, 2012); High Commissioner of Jamaica in the United Kingdom, 2007–10; *b* May Pen, Jamaica, 21 Feb. 1938; *s* of Edgar James Whiteman and Merab Wilhelmina Whiteman (*née* Morgan); *m* 1970, Joline Ann Davis; two *d*. *Educ:* Munro Coll., Jamaica; University Coll. of the West Indies (BA Hons); Univ. of London; Univ. of Birmingham (MEd 1965; Dip. Educnl Admin 1974). Principal, York Castle High Sch., Jamaica, 1959–75; Principal, Brown's Town Community Coll., Jamaica, 1975–89; Minister of State, Jamaican Govt, 1989–91; Minister of Educn, 1992–2002; Minister of Information, 2002–06; Sen. Advr to the Gov. Gen. of Jamaica, 2006. Mem., Electoral Adv. Cttee, Jamaica, 2002–06. Chm., University Council of Jamaica, 2012–; Acting Pres., Univ. of Technol., Jamaica, 2014–15. Chm. Bd of Govs, Commonwealth of Learning, Vancouver, 2008– (Actg Chm., 2007–08; Mem., 2001–08). Hon. LLD: Univ. of Technol., Jamaica, 2013; Univ. of W Indies, 2015. Hon. Mem., Order of the Southern Cross (Brazil), 1998. *Recreation:* occasional writing. *E:* burchell.whiteman@gmail.com.

**WHITEMAN, Prof. John Robert,** PhD; CMath, FIMA; Professor of Numerical Analysis, since 1981, and Distinguished Professor, since 2004, Brunel University; Director, Brunel Institute of Computational Mathematics, 1976–2016; *b* 7 Dec. 1938; *s* of Robert Whiteman and Rita (*née* Neale); *m* 1964, Caroline Mary Leigh; two *s* (one *d* decd). *Educ:* Bromsgrove Sch.; Univ. of St Andrews (BSc); Worcester Coll., Oxford (DipEd); Univ. of London (PhD). FIMA 1970. Sen. Lectr, RMCS, Shrivenham, 1963–67; Assistant Professor: Univ. of Wisconsin, 1967–68; Univ. of Texas, Austin, 1968–70; Reader in Numerical Analysis, Brunel Univ., 1970–76; Richard Merton Gastprofessor, Univ. of Münster, 1975–76; Brunel University: Hd of Dept of Maths and Statistics, 1982–90; Vice Principal, 1991–96; Public Orator, 1999–2004. Visiting Professor: Univ. of Pisa, 1975; Univ. of Kuwait, 1986; Texas A & M Univ., 1986, 1988, 1989, 1990, 1992; Univ. of Stuttgart, 1989, 1992; Vis. Prof., 1996, Dist. Res. Fellow, 1997–2018, Univ. of Texas at Austin. Lectures: Geary, City Univ., 1986; Robert Todd Gregory, Univ. of Texas, Austin, 1990; Collatz Gedenkkolloquium, Hamburg Univ., 1991; Univ. of Stuttgart, 1995; Brunel, Brunel Univ., 2004; Ravenscroft, Co. of Glass Sellers, 2004; Maths Master Class, Royal Instn, 2008. Vice Pres., UK Inst. of Maths and Its Applications, 2004–05. Member: SERC Maths Cttee, 1981–86 and Science Bd, 1989–91; Bd of Dirs, Eur. Scientific Assoc. for Forming Processes, 1997–. Non-exec. Dir, Langdale Owners plc, 2004–17. Renter Warden, 2002, Prime Warden, 2003, Master, 2004, Co. of Glass Sellers (Chm., Charity Fund Trustees, 2008–). FRSA. Hon. DSc West Bohemia Univ., 1995. Editor, Numerical Methods for Partial Differential Equations, 1985–; Member, Editorial Board: Computer Methods in Applied Mechanics and Engrg; Communications in Applied Numerical Methods; Internat. Jl for Numerical Methods in Fluids; Jl of Mathematical Engrg in Industry; Jl of Engrg Analysis; Computational Mechanics Advances. *Publications:* (ed) The Mathematics of Finite Elements and Applications, vols 1–10, 1973, 1976, 1979, 1982, 1985, 1988, 1991, 1994, 1997, 2000, 2003; Finite Elements: an introduction to the method and error estimation, 2010; (jtly) Finite Element Methods: a posteriori error analysis and adaptivity, 2011; numerous works on numerical solution of partial differential equations, particularly finite element methods for singularities in elliptic problems and for problems of linear and non linear solid mechanics, incl. viscoelasticity and applications to problems of thermoforming. *Recreations:* walking, swimming, golf, orchestral and choral music. *Address:* Mathematics Department, Institute of Materials and Manufacturing, Brunel University, Uxbridge, Middx UB8 3PH. *T:* (01895) 265185. *E:* john.whiteman@brunel.ac.uk.

**WHITEMAN, Joslyn Raphael;** High Commissioner for Grenada in the United Kingdom, 2013–16; *b* Grenada, 19 Oct. 1939; *s* of late Francis Ignatius and Veronica Whiteman; *m* 1964, Lydia Theodora Purcell; two *s* two *d*. *Educ:* Presentation Brothers Coll., Grenada. Manager, insce office, London, 1969–87; self-employed, 1987–94; MP (New Nat. Party) St David, Grenada, 1999–2003. Minister of Agriculture, 1995–96, of Tourism, 1996–2000, of Information, 2000–01, of Implementation, 2001–03, Govt of Grenada; High Comr for Grenada in UK, 2004–05; Ambassador to China, 2005–08; proprietor, own business, 2008–13. Black Businessman of Year, Afro Caribbean Chamber of Industry and Commerce, 1988. *Recreations:* gardening, reading. *E:* millhavenhouse@hotmail.com.

**WHITEMAN, Peter George;** QC 1977; barrister-at-law; a Recorder, since 1989; a Deputy High Court Judge, since 1994; Attorney and Counselor at Law, State of New York; Professor of International Tax Law, University of Virginia, since 1980; *b* 8 Aug. 1942; *s* of David Whiteman and Betsy Bessie Coster; *m* 1st, 1971, Katherine Ruth (*née* Ellenbogen) (*d* 2009); two *d*; 2nd, 2017, Sally Patricia Mary Carter. *Educ:* Warwick Secondary Modern Sch.; Leyton County High Sch.; LSE (LLB, LLM with Distinction). Called to the Bar, Lincoln's Inn, 1967, Bencher, 1985; *ad eundem* Middle Temple, 1977. Lectr, London Univ., 1966–70. Mem., Faculty of Laws, Florida Univ., 1977; Visiting Professor: Virginia Univ., 1978; Univ. of California at Berkeley, 1980. Mem. Cttee, Unitary Tax Campaign (UK), 1982–. Pres., Dulwich Village Preservation Soc., 1987–97; Chm., Dulwich Jt Residents' Cttee, 1991–97. Member: Cttee, Dulwich Picture Gall., 1989–97 (Pres., Community Cttee, 2010); Adv. Cttee, Dulwich Estate Govs' Scheme of Management, 1988–97; Focus Gp, Patrons Cttee and Benjamin West Patrons Cttee, RA, 2010–. FRSA 1973. Mem. Bd, Univ. of Virginia Jl of Internat. Law, 1981–. *Publications:* Whiteman on Capital Gains Tax, 1967, 5th edn 2009; Whiteman on Income Tax, 1971, 4th edn 2009; No Bar to Success (autobiog.), 2016; contrib. British Tax Encyc. *Recreations:* opera, long distance travelling, tennis, mountain-walking, jogging, croquet. *Address:* QEB Hollis Whiteman Chambers, 1–2 Laurence Pountney Hill, EC4R 0EU. *T:* (020) 7933 8855, (020) 7283 7273.

**WHITEMAN, Robert Arthur;** Chief Executive, Chartered Institute of Public Finance and Accountancy, since 2013; *b* 4 Dec. 1961; *s* of late William Whiteman and of Joan Whiteman (*née* Elliott); *m* 1988, Hilary Barbara Cannon; two *s* one *d*. *Educ:* Univ. of Essex (BA Hons). IRRV 1988; CPFA 1995. W. H. Smith plc, 1983–86; London Borough of Newham, 1986–88; Corp. of London, 1988; Head of Revenues, London Borough of Camden,

1988–96; London Borough of Lewisham: Asst Dir of Finance, 1996–99; Exec. Dir for Resources, 1999–2005; Dep. Chief Exec., 2001–05; Chief Exec., London Bor. of Barking and Dagenham, 2005–10; Man. Dir, Improvement and Develt Agency, later Local Govt Improvement and Develt, 2010–11; Chief Exec., UK Border Agency, 2011–13; Dir Gen., Operational Systems Mgt, Home Office, 2013. Mem., non-exec. Bd, and Chm., Audit Cttee, DECC, 2009–13. Mem. Council, CIPFA, 2004–06. JP Newham, 1996–2005. *Publications*: regular contribs to local authy jls. *Recreations*: DIY, music, gardening. *Address*: Chartered Institute of Public Finance and Accountancy, 77 Mansell Street, E1 8AN.

**WHITEMAN, Ven. Rodney David Carter;** Archdeacon of Cornwall, 2000–05, now Archdeacon Emeritus; *b* Par, Cornwall, 6 Oct. 1940; *s* of Leonard Archibald Whiteman and Sybil Mary (*née* Morshead); *m* 1969, Christine Anne Chelton; one *s* one *d*. *Educ*: St Austell Grammar School; Pershore Coll. of Horticulture; Ely Theological Coll. Deacon 1964, priest 1965; Curate of Kings Heath, Birmingham, 1964–70; Vicar: St Stephen, Rednal, Birmingham, 1970–79; St Barnabas, Erdington, 1979–89; RD of Aston, 1981–89; Hon. Canon of Birmingham Cathedral, 1985–89; Priest-in-charge of Cardinham with Helland, 1989–94; Hon. Canon of Truro Cathedral, 1989–2005, now Canon Emeritus; Archdeacon of Bodmin, 1989–99. Trustee, Corp. of the Sons and Friends of the Clergy, 1996–2015. *Recreations*: gardening, music, historic buildings and monuments, walking. *Address*: 22 Treverbyn Gardens, Sandy Hill, St Austell, Cornwall PL25 3AW.

**WHITEN, Prof. (David) Andrew,** PhD; FBA 2000; FRSE; FBPsS; Professor of Evolutionary and Developmental Psychology, 1997, and Wardlaw Professor, 2000, University of St Andrews, now Emeritus Professor; *b* 20 April 1948; *s* of Bernard Wray Whiten and Maisie (*née* Gathercole); *m* 1973, Dr Sarah Challoner; two *d*. *Educ*: Sheffield Univ. (BSc 1st Cl. Hons Zool. 1969); Bristol Univ. (PhD 1973). FBPsS 1991. SSRC Conversion Fellow, Queen's Coll., Oxford, 1972–75; St Andrew's University: Lectr in Psychol., 1975–90; Reader, 1991–97; Leverhulme Res. Fellow, 1997, 2003–06; Royal Soc. Leverhulme Trust Sen. Res. Fellow, 2006–07. Vis. Prof., Zurich Univ., 1992; F. M. Bird Prof., Emory Univ., 1995–96; British Acad. Res. Reader, 1999–2001. FRSE 2001; Fellow, Cognitive Sci. Soc., 2013. Hon. DSc Heriot-Watt, 2015; DUniv Stirling, 2016; Hon. DSc Edinburgh, 2017. Jean-Marie Delwart Internat. Scientific Prize, Acad. Royale des Scis de Belgique, 2001; Rivers Meml Medal, RAI, 2007; Osman Hill Meml Medal, Primate Soc. of GB, 2010; Sir James Black Prize and Medal, 2013, Sen. Prize for Public Engagement, 2014, RSE. *Publications*: (ed) Natural Theories of Mind: evolution, development and simulation of everyday mindreading, 1991; (ed with E. Widdowson) Natural Diet and Foraging Strategy of Monkeys, Apes and Humans, 1992; (ed with R. Byrne) Machiavellian Intelligence: social expertise and the evolution of intellect, 1988; Machiavellian Intelligence II: extensions and evaluations, 1997 (trans. Japanese 2000); (ed jtly) Culture Evolves, 2012; contrib. many articles on evolution and develt of social intelligence and cultural transmission to learned jls. *Recreations*: friends, family, art, painting, film, music, garden. *Address*: School of Psychology & Neuroscience, University of St Andrews, St Andrews, Fife KY16 9JP.

**WHITEOAK, John Edward Harrison,** MA, CPFA; Managing Director (formerly Managing Partner), Whiteoak Associates Ltd (Public Sector Consultancy), 1998–2016; *b* 5 July 1947. *Educ*: Sheffield Univ. (MA). CPFA 1971. Cheshire County Council: Dep. County Treas., 1979–81; County Treas., 1981–94; Gp Dir, Resources, 1994–98; Treas., Cheshire Police Authy, 1995–98. Non-exec. Director: VALPAK Ltd, 1998–2004; Industrial Properties Ltd, 1997–2008. Lead negotiator on local govt finance for local authorities in England, 1994–97; lead finance advr to English County Councils, 1994–98. Member: Soc. of County Treasurers, 1981–89 (Pres., 1997–98); Accounting Standards Cttee, 1984–87. Chartered Institute of Public Finance and Accountancy: Mem., Technical Cttee, 1986–87 and 1991–2010; Mem., Accounting Panel, 1984–87 (Chm., 1987); Chm., Financial Reporting Panel, 1991–94; Chm., Corporate Governance Panel, 1994–2013; Pres., NW Region, 1994–95. *Publications*: (jtly) Public Sector Accounting and Financial Control, 1992; contrib. various professional and management journals. *Recreations*: bridge, tennis, social golf. *Clubs*: Royal Automobile; City (Chester); Chester Lawn Tennis.

**WHITEREAD, Dame Rachel,** DBE 2019 (CBE 2006); artist, sculptor; *b* 20 April 1963. *Educ*: Brighton Poly. (BA 1st Cl. Hons); Slade Sch. of Art (DipHE). Solo exhibitions include: Ghost, Chisenhale Gall., London, 1990; Stedelijk Van-Abbemuseum, Eindhoven, 1992; Mus. of Contemporary Art, Chicago, 1993; Kunsthalle, Basel, ICA, Philadelphia, ICA, Boston, 1994–95; retrospective, Tate Gall., Liverpool, 1996–97; Reina Sofia, Madrid, 1997; Venice Biennale (Award for Best Young Artist), 1997; Anthony d'Offay Gall., 1998; Serpentine Gall. and Scottish Nat. Gall. of Modern Art, 2001; Deutsche Guggenheim, Berlin, and Solomon Guggenheim Mus., NY, 2001–02; Room 101, V&A Mus., 2003–04; Mus. de Arte Moderna, Rio de Janeiro and São Paulo, 2004; Kunsthaus Bregenz, Austria, Gagosian Gall., London, Embankment for Turbine Hall, Tate Modern, 2005; Luhring Augustine Gall., NY, 2006; Donnaregina Mus. of Contemp. Art, Naples, 2007; Galleria Lorcan O'Neill, Rome, 2007; Centro Arte Contemporáneo, Málaga, 2007; Gagosian Gall., London, 2010; Drawings, Hammer Mus., LA, Nasher Sculpture Center, Dallas and Tate Britain, 2010; Galerie Nelson-Freeman, Paris, 2010; Long Eyes, Luhring Augustine Gall., NY, 2011; Looking On, Galleria Lorcan O'Neill, Rome, 2011; Detached, Gagosian Gall., London, 2013; Gagosian Gall., Geneva, 2014; Looking In, Luhring Augustine Gall., Chelsea, NY; Looking Out, Luhring Augustine Gall., Brooklyn, NY, 2015; Tate Britain, 2017. Public sculptures: Water Tower Project, NY, 1998; Holocaust Meml, Judenplatz, Vienna, 2000; Monument, Fourth Plinth, Trafalgar Sq., 2001; Tree of Life, Whitechapel Gall., 2012; Chicken Shed, Tate Britain, 2017. Deutscher Akademischer Austauschdienst, Berlin, 1992; Turner Prize, 1993; Eliette von Karajan Prize, Salzburg, 1996; McBean Distinguished Lectureship and Residency, San Francisco Art Inst., 2004; Nord LB Art Prize, 2004; August Seeling Sculpture Prize, Stiftung Wilhelm Lehmbruck Mus., Duisburg, 2007; Internat. Medal of Arts, US Dept of State, 2017. *Address*: c/o Lawrence Luhring, Luhring Augustine Gallery, 531 West 24th Street, New York, NY 10011, USA. *T*: (212) 206 9100, *Fax*: (212) 206 9055. *E*: info@luhringaugustine.com; c/o Gagosian Gallery, 20 Grosvenor Hill, W1K 3QD. *T*: (020) 7495 1500. *E*: london@gagosian.com.

**WHITEROD, Dr Lindsey Janet,** CBE 2018 (OBE 2014); Chief Executive Officer: Tyne Coast College, since 2017; Tyne Coast College Academy Trust, since 2017; *b* Gateshead, 2 Oct. 1970; *d* of James and Elsie Whiterod. *Educ*: Whickham Parochial Sch.; Whickham Sch. (Head Girl); Newcastle upon Tyne Poly. (LLB 1991; Law Soc. Finals 1995); Univ. of Sunderland (MBA 1998; MSc 2003); Newcastle Univ. (EdD 2014). Lectr, then Sen. Lectr in Law, S Tyneside Coll., 1994–2000; Dir, Sch. Business Mgt and Computing, Newcastle Coll., 2000–03; Dep. Principal and Dep. CEO, New Coll., Durham, 2003–09; Principal and CEO, S Tyneside Coll., 2009–17; CEO, S Tyneside Acad. Trust, 2012–17. Nat. Leader of Further Educn, 2018–. Vice Chair, S Tyneside Partnership Bd; Member: Bd, Opportunity NE, 2018–; S Tyneside Econ. Forum. MIET; MIMarEst. Nat. Leader of Year, Educate North, 2017. *Recreations*: ballroom and Latin dancing, tennis, golf, caravans, cats. *Address*: Tyne Coast College, St Georges Avenue, South Shields NE34 6ET. *T*: (0191) 427 3506. *E*: lindsey.whiterod@tynecoast.ac.uk.

**WHITESIDE, Bernard Gerrard,** MBE 1994; HM Diplomatic Service, retired; Ambassador to Ecuador, 2007–08; *b* 3 Oct. 1954; *s* of late Joseph Whiteside and Phoebe Anna (*née* Cummings). *Educ*: St Michael's Coll., Kirkby Lonsdale; Westfield Coll., Univ. of London (BA Hons French and Latin 1977); Univ. of London (Dip. Mediaeval Hist. 2006). Entered HM Diplomatic Service, 1979; Moscow, 1983–86; UK Disarmament Delegn, Geneva, 1986–89; News Dept, FCO, 1989–91; Bogotá, 1991–95; FCO, 1995–99; Russia Prog. Manager, DFID, 1999–2001; Ambassador to Moldova, 2002–06. Trustee, All We Can (formerly Methodist Relief and Develt Fund (MRDF)), 2010–14. *Recreations*: modern music, mediaeval history, the Lake District. *E*: bernardwhiteside@hotmail.com.

**WHITEWAY, Paul Robin;** HM Diplomatic Service, retired; independent consultant, since 2018; Senior Associate Director, GDP Global Development Ltd, since 2018; *b* 1 Dec. 1954; *s* of Frank Whiteway and Patricia (*née* Callaway); *m* 1st, 1980, Melanie Jane Blew (marr. diss.); one *d*; 2nd, 1996, Maha Georges Yannieh; one *s*. *Educ*: Henley Grammar Sch.; Merton Coll., Oxford (BA Hons Mod. History; MA). Joined FCO, 1977; Far Eastern Dept, 1977–79; Third, later Second Sec., Dublin, 1980–83; First Secretary: Nuclear Energy Dept, 1984–86; Port Stanley, 1986–87; Mexico and Central America Dept, 1987–88; seconded to MoD (Navy), 1988–90; Dep. High Comr, Uganda, 1990–93; Asst Head, Southern Africa Dept, 1993–96; Counsellor and Deputy Head of Mission: Syria, 1996–99; Chile, 2000–03; Dir Internat., Inward Investment Gp, 2003–06, Dir Internat. Sales, Business Gp, 2006–08, UK Trade and Investment; consultant in Foreign Direct Investment promotion, 2008–10; Dir, Ext. Relns, 2010–11, Dir, 2011–18, London Independent Diplomat. *Recreations*: history, travel, staying fit.

**WHITFIELD,** family name of **Baron Kenswood**.

**WHITFIELD, Adrian;** QC 1983; a Recorder of the Crown Court, 1981–2000; *b* 10 July 1937; *s* of Peter Henry Whitfield and Margaret Mary Burns; *m* 1st, 1962, Lucy Caroline Beckett (marr. diss.); two *d*; 2nd, 1971, Niamh O'Kelly; one *s* one *d*. *Educ*: Ampleforth Coll.; Magdalen Coll., Oxford (Demy; MA). 2nd Lieut, KOYLI (Nat. Service), 1956–58. Called to the Bar, Middle Temple, 1964, Bencher 1990, Treasurer 2005. *Publications*: contribs on legal matters in legal and medical pubns. *Recreations*: reading, visual arts, travel. *Address*: 47 Faroe Road, W14 0EL. *T*: (020) 7603 8982.

**WHITFIELD, Alan;** transport consultant, 1998–2014; *b* 19 April 1939; *s* of John J. Whitfield and Annie Fothergill-Rawe; *m* 1964, Sheila Carr; two *s*. *Educ*: Consett Grammar Sch., Durham; Sunderland and Newcastle Colls of Advanced Technology. MICE 1968; MIMunE 1969; FCIHT (FIHT 1984). Surveyor/Engr, NCB, 1956–62; Engrg Asst, Northumberland CC, 1962–70; Department of Transport: Main Grade Engr, 1970–73; Prin. Professional, 1973–76; Suptg Engr, 1976–80; Dep. Dir, Midlands Road Construction Unit, 1980–83; Dir (Transport), W Midlands Reg. Office, 1983–89; Regl Dir (Under Sec.), Eastern Region, DoE and Dept of Transport, 1989; Road Prog. Dir, Dept of Transport, 1989–94, Highways Agency, 1994–95 (acting Dep. Sec.). Director: Ove Arup & Partners, 1995–98; Ove Arup & Partners Internat., 1995–98; Chm., Arup Transport, 1996–98. Associate Consultant, Waterfront Partnership, 1998–2002. *Publications*: papers on cost benefit analysis, centrifugal testing soils, road design and construction, etc to IHT, ICE, Inst. Geo. Sci., etc. *Recreations*: restoration of old property, golf, choral singing, travel.

**WHITFIELD, Clovis;** Director, Whitfield Fine Art Ltd, since 1979; *b* 21 Oct. 1940; *s* of late Prof. John Humphreys Whitfield; *m* 1st, 1964, Sarah Oppenheim (marr. diss. 1986); two *d*; 2nd, 1986, Dr Irene Cioffi; one *s* one *d*. *Educ*: Corpus Christi Coll., Cambridge (MA 1962); Courtauld Inst. of Art, London. Vis. Prof., Indiana Univ., 1967–68; Associate Dir, Thomas Agnew & Sons Ltd, London, 1970–77; Director: Colnaghi, London, 1978–81, NY, 1983–84; Walpole Gall., London, 1987–91. Cavaliere al Merito (Italy), 1978. Exhibitions: (co-ordinator and joint editor) Painting in Naples: Caravaggio to Giordano, RA and Nat. Gall., Washington, 1982; Classicismo e Natura: la lezione di Domenichino, Capitoline Gall., (joint editor) Rome, 1996; Caravaggio's Friends and Foes, Whitfield Fine Art, 2010. *Publications*: Caravaggio's Eye, 2011 (trans. Italian, 2011); contrib. Burlington mag. *Recreation*: bee-keeping. *Address*: Whitfield Fine Art Ltd, 10 Pangbourne Avenue, W10 6BT. *T*: (020) 8964 8921. *E*: fineart@whitfieldfineart.com.

**WHITFIELD, Hugh Newbold,** FRCS; Consultant Urological Surgeon: London Clinic, 1979–2015; King Edward VII Hospital, since 1988; *b* 15 June 1944; *s* of George Joshua Newbold Whitfield and Audrey Priscilla Whitfield; *m* 1969, Penelope Joy Craig; two *s* (and one *s* decd). *Educ*: Gonville and Caius Coll., Cambridge (BA 1965, MA 1969; MB BChir 1968); St Bartholomew's Med. Coll., London (MA 1969, MChir 1978). FRCS 1972. Short service commn, RAMC, 1969–74; Res. Registrar, Inst. of Urology, London, 1974–76; Sen. Registrar, St Bartholomew's Hosp., 1976–79; Consultant Urological Surgeon: St Bartholomew's Hosp., 1979–93; Central Middlesex Hosp., 1993–2000; Reader in Urol., Inst. of Urol. and Nephrol., UCL, 1993–2001; Consultant Urol Surgeon, Royal Berks Hosp., 2001–06. Hon. Consultant Urologist, St Mark's Hosp. for Diseases of the Colon and Rectum, 1979–2006; Hon. Consultant: in Urol. to the Army, 1997–2012; in Paediatric Urol., Hosp. for Sick Children, Gt Ormond St, 1999–2006. Founder Dir, Ind. Med. Negligence Resolution, 2018–. Pres., Eur. Bd of Urology, 1998–2000. Ed., British Jl Urol. Internat., 1994–2002. *Publications*: Urology Pocket Consultant, 1985; Textbook of Genito-Urinary Surgery, 1985, 2nd edn 1998; Rob & Smith's Operative Surgery: Genito-Urinary Surgery, 1992; ABC in Urology, 1996, 2nd edn 2006; articles in urological jls. *Recreations*: music, golf, country pursuits, veteran rowing. *Address*: King Edward VII Consulting Rooms, Emmanuel Kaye House, 37a Devonshire Street, W1G 6QA. *T*: (020) 7935 3095, *Fax*: (020) 7467 4375. *E*: urology@whitfield.uk.net. *Clubs*: Garrick; Leander (Henley).

**WHITFIELD, John;** Consultant Solicitor, Ramsdens Whitfield Hallam, of Batley, Dewsbury and Mirfield, 2010–12 (Senior Partner, Whitfield Hallam Goodall, 1997–2010); *b* 31 Oct. 1941; *s* of Sydney Richard Whitfield and Mary Rishworth Whitfield; *m*; three *s*; *m* 1999, Janet Gissing (*née* Oldroyd). *Educ*: Sedbergh Sch.; Leeds Univ. (LLB). Solicitor: Bird & Bird, 1966–67; Whitfield Son and Hallam, then Whitfield Hallam Goodall, 1967–2010. MP (C) Dewsbury, 1983–87. Contested (C): Hemsworth, 1979; Dewsbury, 1987 and 1992. *Recreations*: fishing, shooting, walking with dogs, supporting Yorkshire Carnegie (Rugby Union). *Address*: Haugh Top Farm, Krumlin, Barkisland, Halifax HX4 0EL. *T*: (01422) 822994. *Clubs*: Tanfield Angling; Octave (Elland).

**WHITFIELD, Jonathan;** QC 2010; *b* 3 Sept. 1961; *s* of Ronald John Whitfield and Pamela Whitfield; *m* 1991, Joanna. *Educ*: St Mary's Coll., Southampton; London Metropolitan Univ. (BA Hons). Called to the Bar, Middle Temple, 1985; a Tribunal Judge, First-tier Tribunal (Mental Health), 2005–. Legal Assessor to GMC, 2007. *Recreations*: sailing, photography, music (banjo, flute, tabla), walking. *Address*: 54 Doughty Street, WC1N 2LS. *T*: (020) 7404 1313. *E*: j.whitfield@doughtystreet.co.uk.

**WHITFIELD, Martin;** MP (Lab) East Lothian, since 2017; *b* Newcastle, 1965; *m*; two *c*. Formerly lawyer specialising in personal injury law; primary sch. teacher, latterly in Prestonpans, until 2017. Mem., Sci. and Technol. Cttee, H of C, 2017–. *Address*: House of Commons, SW1A 0AA.

**WHITFIELD, Dr Michael,** CChem, FRSC; FGS; Vice President, Marine Biological Association, since 2000 (Director and Secretary, 1987–99); Director, Plymouth Marine Laboratory, 1994–96 (Deputy Director, 1988–94); b 15 June 1940; s of Arthur and Ethel Whitfield; m 1961, Jean Ann Rowe (d 1984); one s three d. Educ: Univ. of Leeds (BSc 1st cl. Hons Chem.; PhD Chem.). FRSC 1980; FRSB (FIBiol 1994); FGS 2001. Research Scientist, CSIRO Div. of Fisheries and Oceanography, Cronulla, NSW, 1964–69; Vis. Res. Fellow, KTH Stockholm, 1969, Univ. of Liverpool, 1970; Res. Scientist, Marine Biol. Assoc., 1970–87. Vice Pres., Sir Alister Hardy Foundn for Ocean Science, 1991–99; Pres., Challenger Soc. for Marine Science, 1996–98. FRSA 1992. Dr (hc): Göteborg, 1991; Plymouth, 2000. Publications: Ion-selective electrodes for the analysis of natural waters, 1970; Marine Electrochemistry, 1981; Tracers in the Ocean, 1988; Light and Life in the Sea, 1990; Aquatic Life Cycle Strategies, 1999; numerous papers in professional jls. Recreations: hill walking, bird watching, photography. Address: The Laboratory, Citadel Hill, Plymouth PL1 2PB. T: (01752) 633331.

**WHITFIELD, Prof. Roderick;** Percival David Professor of Chinese and East Asian Art, University of London, 1993–2002, now Professor Emeritus (Professor of Chinese and East Asian Art, and Head of Percival David Foundation of Chinese Art, 1984–93); b 20 July 1937; s of late Prof. John Humphreys Whitfield and Joan Herrin, ARCA; m 1st, 1963, Frances Elizabeth Oldfield, PhD (marr. diss 1983), e d of late Prof. R. C. Oldfield and Lady Kathleen Oldfield; one s two d; 2nd, 1983, Prof. Youngsook Pak, PhD, art historian, e d of late Pak Sang-Jon, Seoul. Educ: Woodbourne Acad.; King Edward's Sch., Birmingham; Sch. of Oriental and African Studies (Civil Service Interpreter, 2nd cl.); St John's Coll., Cambridge (BA Hons 1960, Oriental Studies Tripos; MA 1966); Princeton Univ. (MFA 1963, PhD 1965). Research Associate and Lectr, Princeton, 1965–66; Research Fellow, St John's Coll., Cambridge, 1966–68; Asst Keeper I, Dept of Oriental Antiquities, British Museum, 1968–84. Visiting Professor: Univ. of Heidelberg, 1996; Univ. of Helsinki, 1997; Univ. of Barcelona, 1998; Univ. of Oslo, 2002; City Univ. of Hong Kong, 2003; Univ. of Hong Kong, 2004; Yale Univ., 2007; ELTE Univ., Budapest, 2013; MaMa Charitable Foundn Vis. Prof. in Buddhist Studies, Hong Kong Univ., 2015. Teetzel Lectr, Univ. of Toronto, 1995; Keynote Lecturer: Freie Universitaet Berlin, 2013; Inaugural Conf. of Eur. Assoc. of Asian Art and Archaeology, 2014; Hungarian Acad. Scis, 2019. Pres., Circle of Inner Asian Art, 1996–; Mem. Internat. Adv. Bd, Buddhist Art and Conservation, Courtauld Inst. of Art, 2013–. Trustee, Inst. of Buddhist Studies, 1987–. Corresp. Fellow, Dunhuang Res. Acad., 1999–; Fellow, Palace Mus., Beijing, 2003–; Hon. Mem., Eur. Assoc. of Asian Art and Archaeol. Mem. Editl Bd, Artibus Asiae, 1992–; Sen. Ed., Internat. Jl of Korean Art, 2008–12. Publications: In Pursuit of Antiquity: Chinese paintings of Ming and Ch'ing dynasties in collection of Mr and Mrs Earl Morse, 1969; The Art of Central Asia: the Stein collection at the British Museum, 3 vols, 1983–85 (vol. I trans. Chinese, 2014); (ed) Treasures from Korea, 1984; (ed) Korean Art Treasures, 1986; (ed) Early Chinese Glass, 1988; Caves of the Thousand Buddhas, 1990; (ed) Problems in Meaning in Early Chinese Ritual Bronzes, 1993; Fascination of Nature: plants and insects in Chinese paintings and ceramics of the Yuan dynasty, 1993; Dunhuang, Caves of the Singing Sands: Buddhist Art from the Silk Road, 2 vols, 1995; (trans. jtly) The Arts of Central Asia: the Pelliot Collection in the Musée Guimet, 1996; (ed jtly) Exploring China's Past: new researches and discoveries in Chinese archaeology, 2000; (jtly) The Mogao Caves, 2000, 2nd edn as Cave Temples of Mogao at Dunhuang: art and history on the Silk Road, 2015; (jtly) Handbooks of Korean Art: pottery and celadon, 2002; (jtly) Buddhist Sculpture, 2002; (ed) Folk Painting, 2002; (contrib.) New Perspectives on China's Past: Chinese archaeology in the twentieth century, 2004; (trans. jtly) Korean Art from the Gompertz and other Collections in the Fitzwilliam Museum, 2004; (trans. and ed jtly) Korean True-View Landscape: paintings by Chŏng Sŏn (1676–1759), 2005; (contrib.) China at the Court of the Emperors, 2008; (contrib.) Il Celeste Impero, 2008; (contrib.) The Printed Image in China from the 8th to the 21st Centuries, 2010; (contrib.) What Makes a Masterpiece?: encounters with great works of art, 2010; (jtly) Catalogue of the Wou Lien-Pai Museum of Chinese Antiquities, 2011; (contrib.) Studies on Sino-Tibetan Buddhist Art, 2011; (contrib.) Bridges to Heaven: essays on East Asian art in honor of Professor Wen C. Fong, 2011; (contrib.) New Perspectives on Qingming shanghe tu, 2012; (ed and trans. jtly) Collected Works of Korean Buddhism, vol. IX: collection of Chinese poetry of the Great Monks of Korea, 2012; (contrib.) Glanz der Kaiser von China: Kunst und Leben in der Verbotenen Stadt, 2012; (ed jtly) A Lost Generation: Luo Zhenyu, Qing loyalists and the formation of modern Chinese culture, 2013; (contrib.) Qingming shanghe tu de gushi, 2013; (contrib.) Masterpieces of Chinese Painting, 8th to 12th centuries, 2013; (contrib.) Proceedings of the Dunhuang 2014 conference, 2016; (contrib.) Go Yuseop, A Study of Korean Pagodas, 2017; articles in Asiatische Studien, Artibus Asiae, Buddhica Britannica, Orientations, Burlington Magazine, British Liby Jl, Bukkyo Geijutsu (Ars Buddhica), Zijincheng, Dunhuang yanjiu, TLS, Arts of Asia and other jls. Address: 7 St Paul's Crescent, NW1 9XN. T: (020) 7267 2888.

**WHITFORD, Dr Philippa;** MP (SNP) Central Ayrshire, since 2015; b Belfast, 24 Dec. 1958; d of Philip Whitford and Elizabeth Whitford; m 1987, Hans Josef Pieper; one s. Educ: Douglas Acad., Milngavie; Univ. of Glasgow (MB ChB 1982; MD 1991). FRCSGlas 1986. Surgical training: Royal Victoria Hosp., Belfast, 1983–84; Belfast City Hosp., 1984; Glasgow Royal Infirmary, 1984–85; Registrar: Monklands Dist Gen. Hosp., Airdrie, 1985–86; Royal Hosp. for Sick Children, Glasgow, 1986–87; Canniesburn Hosp., Glasgow, 1987; Glasgow Royal Infirmary, 1987; Res. Fellow, Depts of Surgery and Biochem., Univ. of Glasgow, 1987–89; Registrar (Gen. Surgery), Inverclyde Royal Hosp., 1989–91; Volunteer Consultant Surgeon in Gen. Surgery and Urology, Ali Ahli Hosp., Gaza, 1991–92; Volunteer Health Care Planning and Gen. Surgery, Al Hamshary Hosp., Sidon, Lebanon Balsam Hosp., 1993; Sen. Registrar (Gen. Surgery and Breast Surgery), Aberdeen Royal Infirmary, 1994–96; Consultant Breast Cancer Surgeon, Crosshouse Hosp., Kilmarnock, 1996–2014. Lead clinician in breast cancer, Ayshire and Arran Health Bd, 1996–2010. SNP spokesperson for Health, 2017–; Mem., Health Select Cttee, 2015–17. Publications: articles on breast cancer and surgery in British Jl of Surgery, British Jl of Cancer, Eur. Jl of Cancer. Recreations: singing, playing cello, painting. Address: (office) 14 Eglinton Street, Irvine KA12 8AS. T: (01294) 311160. E: philippa.whitford.mp@parliament.uk.

**WHITING, Prof. Brian,** MD; FRCPGlas, FRCPE, FMedSci; Professor of Clinical Pharmacology, 1986–2001, Dean, Faculty of Medicine, and Head of Clinical Medicine Planning Unit, 1992–2000, University of Glasgow; b 6 Jan. 1939; s of late Leslie George Whiting and Evelyn Irene Edith Whiting (née Goss); m 1st, 1967, Jennifer Mary Tait (marr. diss. 1983); two d; 2nd, 1990, Marlene Shields (née Watson); two step s. Educ: Univ. of Glasgow (MB ChB 1964; MD 1970). FRCPGlas 1979; FRCPE 1996. House Officer, Western Infirmary and Stobhill Gen. Hosp., Glasgow, 1964; University of Glasgow: Department of Materia Medica: Hutchison Res. Schol., 1965; Registrar in Medicine, 1966–68; Lectr and Sen. Registrar in Clinical Pharmacol., 1969–77; Sen. Lectr and Consultant Physician, 1977–82; Reader in Clinical Pharmacol., 1982–86; Hd, Div. of Clinical Pharmacol., Dept of Medicine and Therapeutics, 1989–91. Dir, Clinical Pharmacokinetics Lab., Stobhill Gen. Hosp., Glasgow, 1980–90. Vis. Scientist, Div. of Clinical Pharmacol., Univ. of Calif, San Francisco, 1978–79; Internat. Union of Pharmacol. Vis. Consultant, India and Nepal, 1985; Visiting Professor of Clinical Pharmacology: Univ. of Auckland, 1987; (British Council) Japan, 1988; British Council and Internat. Union of Pharmacol., India and Nepal. 1990. Non-exec. Mem., Gtr Glasgow Health Bd, 1994–2000. Member: Assoc. of Physicians of GB and Ireland, 1985–; GMC, 1991–96. Founder FFPM (by Dist.) 1990; Founder FMedSci 1998. Publications: (ed jtly) Lecture Notes on Clinical Pharmacology, 1982, 6th edn 2001; contrib. numerous articles or book chapters, principally in field of clinical pharmacology. Recreations: painting, music (listening and composition); mountaineering. Address: 2 Milner Road, Glasgow G13 1QL. T: (0141) 959 2324.

**WHITING, (David) John,** CBE 2016 (OBE 2008); tax policy adviser, since 2017; Tax Director, Office of Tax Simplification, 2010–17; b Hull, Yorks, 20 March 1951; s of (Charles) Peter Whiting and Isabel Norah Whiting; m 1977, Susan Barbara Jones; three d. Educ: Hymers Coll., Hull; Univ. of Manchester (BSc Hons Maths 1972). FCA 1975; CTA 1978. Price Waterhouse, later PricewaterhouseCoopers, 1972–2009, Tax Partner, 1984–2009; Tax Policy Dir, Chartered Inst. of Taxation, 2009–13. Mem., First-tier Tribunal (Tax), 2009–13. Pres., Chartered Inst. of Taxation, 2001–02. Non-exec. Dir, HMRC, 2013–; Mem. Bd, Revenue Scotland, 2015–. Publications: (contrib.) Dimensions of Tax Design: the Mirrlees Review, 2011; contrib. articles in taxation jls incl. British Tax Review. Recreations: family life, bridge, history (particularly Richard III), watching cricket, music (especially Fairport Convention), DIY. Club: MCC.

**WHITING, Maj.-Gen. Graham Gerald M.;** see Messervy-Whiting.

**WHITING, John;** see Whiting, D. J.

**WHITLAM, Michael Richard,** CBE 2000; charity consultant, 2001–18; Director and Owner, Mike Whitlam - Solutions for Charity, consultancy, 2001–17; b 25 March 1947; s of late Richard William Whitlam and Mary Elizabeth Whitlam (née Land); m 1968, Anne Jane McCurley; two d. Educ: Morley Grammar Sch.; Tadcaster Grammar Sch.; Coventry Coll. of Educn, Univ. of Warwick (Cert. of Educn); Home Office Prison Dept Staff Coll. (Qual. Asst Governor Prison Dept); Cranfield Coll. of Technology (MPhil 1988). Biology teacher, Ripon, 1968–69; Asst Governor, HM Borstal, Hollesley Bay and HM Prison, Brixton, 1969–74; Dir, Hammersmith Teenage Project, NACRO, 1974–78; Dep. Dir/Dir, UK ops, Save the Children Fund, 1978–86; Chief Exec., RNID, 1986–90; Dir-Gen., BRCS, 1991–99; Chief Exec., Mentor Foundn (Internat.), 1999–2001; Chief Executive Officer: Internat. Agency for the Prevention of Blindness, 2002–05; Vision 2020 the Right to Sight, 2002–05. Special Charity Advr to Russam GMS, 2005–16. Board Member: Britcross Ltd, 1991–99; British Red Cross Events Ltd, 1991–99; British Red Cross Trading, 1991–99; REACH, 1997–; Chm., Sound Advantage plc, 1988–90. Chm., Ofcom Adv. Cttee for Older and Disabled People, 2004–10. Non-exec. Dir, Hillingdon PCT, 2004–11. Member: Exec. Council, Howard League, 1974–84; Community Alternative Young Offenders Cttee, NACRO, 1979–82; Exec. Council, Nat. Children's Bureau, 1980–86; Bd, City Literary Inst., 1989–90; Bd, Charity Appointments Ltd, 1990–99; Dir, Watford FC Community Educn Trust, 2007–17 (Vice Chm., 2010–17); Chairman: London Intermediate Treatment Assoc., 1980–83; and Founder, ACEVO (formerly ACENVO), 1988– (Mem. Policy and Res. Gp, 1994–99); Prisoners Abroad, 1999–2003; Chalker Foundn for Africa, 2007–15; Chm., CLICK Rukiga (link between Ickenham and Rukiga, Uganda), 2008–; Chair, Ickenham Police Ward Panel, 2011–15; Mem., Hillingdon Hosp. Major Incident Gp, 2016–. Trustee, CMS, 2012–15. FRSA 1995; CCMI (CIMgt 1997). Mem. PCC and Deanery Rep., St Giles Church, Ickenham; Bereavement Listener, Ickenham Churches Bereavement Gp. Publications: numerous papers on juvenile delinquency and charity management. Recreations: painting, walking, family activities, voluntary organisations, politics, visiting France, cooking. Address: 40 Pepys Close, Ickenham, Middx UB10 8NY. T: (01895) 678169. E: m.whitlam@btinternet.com.

**WHITLAM, Nicholas Richard;** company director; Chairman, Port Authority of New South Wales, 2014–18 (Chairman, 2005–16, and Chief Executive Officer, 2013–14, Port Kembla Port Corporation; Chairman: Sydney Ports Corporation, 2013–16; Newcastle Port Corporation, 2013–14); b 6 Dec. 1945; s of Hon. (Edward) Gough Whitlam, AC, QC and Margaret Elaine Whitlam, AO; m 1973, Sandra Judith Frye; two s one d. Educ: Sydney High Sch.; Harvard Coll. (AB cum laude); London Business Sch. (MSc). Morgan Guaranty Trust Co., 1969–75; American Express Co., 1975–78; Banque Paribas, 1978–80; Comr, Rural Bank of New South Wales, 1980–81, then Man. Dir, State Bank of New South Wales, 1981–87; Man. Dir, Whitlam Turnbull & Co. Ltd, 1987–90; Chm., Whitlam & Co., 1990–2002 and 2003–; Dep. Chm., Export Finance and Insurance Corp., 1991–94; Advr, Asian Capital Partners, 1993–96. Director: GreenCell Ltd, 2011–13; Crescent Wealth, 2015–. Proprietor, Mt Kembla Hotel, 2004–07. Board Member: Aust. Trade Commn, 1985–91; Integral Energy Aust., 1996–99. Pres., NRMA, 1996–2002 (Dep. Pres., 1995–96); Chm., NRMA Insce Ltd, 1996–2001. Chm., Lifetime Care and Support Authy, 2009–12 (Dir, 2006–12); Deputy Chairman: Workers' Compensation Insce Fund Investment Bd (formerly WorkCover Insce Investment Bd), 2005–12; WorkCover Authy, 2010–12. Board Member: Aust. Graduate Sch. of Management, 1982–97 (Chm., 1988–97); Aust. Sports Foundn, 1986–95; Mem., Adv. Council, SMART Infrastructure Facility, Univ. of Wollongong, 2017–. Chm., Sydney Symphony Orch., 1991–96; Mem. Symphony Council, 1996–2005; Trustee, Sydney Cricket and Sports Ground, 1984–88. DUniv NSW, 1996; Hon. DLitt Western Sydney, 2016. Publications: Nest of Traitors (with John Stubbs), 1974; Still Standing, 2004; Four Weeks One Summer, 2016. Recreations: swimming, cycling, reading. Address: PO Box 3072, Austinmer, NSW 2515, Australia. Clubs: Hong Kong; Tattersall's (Sydney) (Chm., 1993–96).

**WHITLEY, Edward John,** OBE 2013; Founder and Director, Whitley Asset Management, since 2001; Director: Ragleth Ltd, since 2005; Anglia Maltings Ltd, since 2005; b Shrewsbury, 6 June 1961; s of Edward and Penelope Whitley; m 1986, Araminta Ramsay; one s three d. Educ: Shrewsbury Sch.; St Anne's Coll., Oxford (Exhibnr; BA Hons English; Blue in Modern Pentathlon 1980). Manager, N M Rothschild & Sons Ltd, 1983–90; author, 1990–2000. Founder and Trustee, Whitley Fund for Nature, 1992– (Chm., 1992–); Trustee: Sheila Whitley Trust, 1988–; Whitley Animal Protection Trust, 1988–; Tavistock Trust for Aphasia, 2014–. Mem., George Eliot Fellowship, 2015–. Publications: The Graduates, 1986; Gerald Durrell's Army, 1992; Rogue Trader, 1996. Recreations: Shakespeare, fishing, tennis, exploration. Address: Whitley Asset Management, 116 Princedale Road, W11 4NH. T: (020) 7221 2145. Clubs: Vincent's; Plowden Fishing.

**WHITLEY, Edward Thomas;** Chairman, St Julian's Estate Ltd, 2009–18; b 6 May 1954; s of John Caswell Whitley and Shirley Frances Whitley (née Trollope); m 1984, Hon. Tara Olivia Chichester-Clark, d of Baron Moyola, PC (NI); one s. Educ: Harrow Sch.; Univ. of Bristol (BSc). Chartered accountant; Price Waterhouse, 1976–81; Cazenove & Co., 1981–2001, Partner, 1988–2001; CEO, Internat. Financial Services, London, 2001–07. Dir, Henderson Strata Investments plc, 1990–2005. Chm., Financial Services Sector Adv. Gp, 2005–06. Mem., Council of Mgt, Restoration of Appearance and Function Trust, 1999–2011; Trustee, World Trade Center Disaster Fund, 2001–06. Hon. Pres., S Derry Wildfowl and Game Preservation Soc., 2002–. FCSI 2010.

**WHITLEY, Susan Alison;** see Bradbury, S. A.

**WHITLEY, Dr Timothy John**; Managing Director, Applied Research, and Managing Director, Adastral Park, BT, since 2011; *b* Wrexham, 27 May 1965; *s* of Albert Edward and Peggy Maureen Whitley; *m* 1992, Teresa McManamon; four *d. Educ*: Chester Coll. of Further Educn (Tec III Telecommunications 1984); Univ. of Kent at Canterbury (BSc Physics 1987); Essex Univ. (PhD Optical Fibre Communications 1996). BT: trainee technician apprentice, 1981–84; Optical Res. Scientist, BT Labs, 1987–96; Tech. Architecture/Strategic Analyst, 1996–2007; Corporate Strategy Dir, 2007–11. Vis. Prof., Computer Sci. and Electronics Systems Engrg, Essex Univ., 2016–19; William Pitt Fellow, Pembroke Coll., Cambridge, 2018–. Mem., UKRI-EPSRC (formerly EPSRC), 2016–. Mem. Bd, New Anglia LEP, 2015–. *Publications*: contrib. peer-reviewed jl and conf. papers in field of optical fibre communications. *Recreations*: optical physics, walking, reading, family. *Address*: BT Laboratories, Adastral Park, Martlesham Heath, Ipswich, Suffolk IP5 3RE. *T*: (01473) 629963. *E*: Tim.whitley@bt.com.

**WHITLEY, Dr Zoé**; Senior Curator, Hayward Gallery, since 2019; *b* Washington, DC, USA, 30 Dec. 1979; *d* of Brian Whitley and Donna A. Richardson; *m* 2003, Shane Richmond; one *d. Educ*: Swarthmore Coll. (BA High Hons Art Hist. and French 2001); Royal Coll. of Art (MA Hist. of Design 2003); Univ. of Central Lancashire (PhD Contemp. Art 2018). Curator: Contemp. Progs, V&A, 2005–13; Contemp. British Art, Tate Britain, 2013–15; Internat. Art, Tate Modern, 2014–19; British Pavilion, La Biennale di Venezia, 2019. Founding Mem., Assoc. of Women in the Arts, 2017–. Trustee, Gasworks, 2019–. FRSA. *Publications*: The Graphic World of Paul Peter Piech, 2013; (with M. Godfrey) Soul of a Nation: art in the age of Black Power, 2017, 2nd edn 2019; Cathy Wilkes, 2019; (for children) Meet the Artist: Frank Bowling, 2019. *Recreations*: infrequent bouts of yoga, frequent baking for friends and family, too many hours lost in WhatsApp groups. *Address*: Hayward Gallery, Southbank Centre, Belvedere Road, SE1 8XX. *T*: (020) 7921 0717. *E*: zoe.whitley@southbankcentre.co.uk.

**WHITMARSH, Martin Richard**; Chief Executive, BAR Technologies, since 2017; *b* Lyndhurst, Hants, 29 April 1958; *s* of Kenneth Whitmarsh and Betty Whitmarsh; *m* 1996, Deborah Ann Kirby; one *s* one *d. Educ*: Portsmouth Poly. (BSc 1980). CEng, MRAeS 1995. Joined British Aerospace plc, 1980, Manuf. Dir, 1988–89; McLaren Racing Ltd: Hd of Ops, 1989–97; Man. Dir, 1997–2004; CEO, Formula 1 Team, 2004; Chief Operating Officer, 2005–10, Chief Exec., 2010–14, McLaren Gp; Dep. Chm., McLaren Automotive, 2010–14; Team Principal, Vodafone McLaren Mercedes Formula 1 Team, 2009–14; Chief Exec., Ben Ainslie Racing, then Land Rover BAR, 2015–17. Chm., Formula One Teams Assoc., 2010–14. Hon. LLD Portsmouth, 2009; Hon. DTech Southampton Solent, 2009. *Address*: BAR Technologies Ltd, East Street, Camber Quay, Portsmouth PO1 2JJ. *Club*: British Racing Drivers'.

**WHITMARSH, Prof. Timothy John Guy**, PhD; A. G. Leventis Professor of Greek Culture, University of Cambridge, since 2014; Fellow, St John's College, Cambridge, since 2014; *b* Chelmsford, 23 Jan. 1970; *s* of Guy Whitmarsh and Judy Whitmarsh; partner, Emily Kneebone; one *s* one *d. Educ*: Ashford Carbonell Primary Sch.; Moor Park Sch.; Malvern Coll.; King's Coll., Cambridge (BA Classics 1992; MPhil Classics 1994); St John's Coll., Cambridge (PhD Classics 1998). Jun. Res. Fellow, 1997–99, Fellow and Coll. Lectr, 1999–2001, St John's Coll., Cambridge; Newton Trust Lectr, Univ. of Cambridge, 1999–2001; University of Exeter: Lectr in Classics, 2001–03; Reader in Greek Lit., 2003–06; Prof. of Ancient Literatures, 2006–07; University of Oxford: Lectr in Greek Lang. and Lit., 2007–11; Prof. of Ancient Literatures, 2011–14; Fellow, Tutor and E. P. Warren Praelector, Corpus Christi Coll., 2007–14; Hon. Mem., Corpus Christi Centre for Study of Greek and Roman Antiquity, 2014–. Vis. Lectr, Univ. of Chicago, 2014–; Res. Associate, Univ. of Pretoria, 2015–. *Publications*: Greek Literature and the Roman Empire: the politics of imitation, 2001; (trans.) Achilles Tatius, Leucippe and Clitophon, 2001; Ancient Greek Literature, 2004; The Second Sophistic, 2005; (ed with Jason König) Ordering Knowledge in the Roman Empire, 2007; (ed) The Cambridge Companion to the Greek and Roman Novel, 2008; (ed jtly) Galen and the World of Knowledge, 2009; (ed) Local Knowledge and Microidentities in the Roman Greek World, 2010; Narrative and Identity in the Ancient Greek Novel: returning romance, 2011; Beyond the Second Sophistic: adventures in Greek postclassicism, 2013; (ed with Stuart Thomson) The Romance between Greece and the East, 2013; Battling the Gods: atheism in the ancient world, 2015; Dirty Love: the genealogy of the ancient Greek novel, 2018. *Recreations*: football, music, guitar. *Address*: Faculty of Classics, Sidgwick Avenue, Cambridge CB3 9DA. *T*: (01223) 335166.

**WHITMORE, Sir Clive (Anthony)**, GCB 1988 (KCB 1983); CVO 1983; Director, N. M. Rothschild & Sons Ltd, 1994–2010; *b* 18 Jan. 1935; *s* of Charles Arthur Whitmore and Louisa Lilian Whitmore; *m* 1961, Jennifer Mary Thorpe; one *s* two *d. Educ*: Sutton Grammar Sch., Surrey; Christ's Coll., Cambridge (BA). Asst Principal, WO, 1959; Private Sec. to Permanent Under-Sec. of State, WO, 1961; Asst Private Sec. to Sec. of State for War, 1962; Principal, 1964; Private Sec. to Permanent Under-Sec. of State, MoD, 1969; Asst Sec., 1971; Asst Under-Sec. of State (Defence Staff), MoD, 1975; Under Sec., Cabinet Office, 1977; Principal Private Sec. to the Prime Minister, 1979–82; Dep. Sec., 1981; Permanent Under-Secretary of State: MoD, 1983–88; Home Office, 1988–94. Director: Racal Electronics, 1994–2000; Boots Co., 1994–2001; Morgan Crucible Co. PLC, 1994–2004. Mem., Security Commn, 1998–2007. Chancellor, De Montfort Univ., 1995–97; Chm. Council, Inst. of Educn, Univ. of London, 1995–2000. *Recreations*: gardening, listening to music.

**WHITMORE, David John Ludlow**, FCA; Chief Executive Officer, Slater and Gordon Group, since 2018; *b* 20 July 1959; *s* of Dr John L. Whitmore and Joan C. Whitmore (*née* Hale); *m* 1984, Monica Mary Boyd; two *s* one *d. Educ*: Carisbrooke High Sch., IoW; Univ. of Warwick (BSc Hons Accounting and Financial Analysis). ACA 1984, FCA 1989; CPA(US) 1988. Joined Arthur Andersen, 1980; worked in: London, 1980–84; LA, 1984–86; World HQ, Chicago, 1986–87; LA, 1987–89; London, 1989–2002; Partner, 1991; Head, Commercial Assurance and Business Adv. Practice, 1995–97; Managing Partner: UK Assurance and Business Adv. Practice, 1997–2001; Global Assurance and Business Adv. Markets, 2001–02; Pres., Europe, Proudfoot Consulting, 2004; Chief Executive: 4 Future Gp, 2005–06; Compass Mgt Consulting Gp, 2007–11; Vice Chm., 2011–14, Pres., Americas, 2012–14, Information Services Gp, Inc.; Principal, 24 Haymarket Private Capital, 2015–18. Non-exec. Dir, Bevan Brittan LLP, 2009–17. Mem. Adv. Bd, Warwick Business Sch., 2001–12. *Recreations*: golf, tennis, ski-ing, bridge. *Clubs*: Royal Automobile; Liphook Golf.

**WHITMORE, Sir Jason**, 3rd Bt *cr* 1954; *b* 26 Jan. 1983; *s* of Sir John Henry Douglas Whitmore, 2nd Bt and Diana Elaine Whitmore (*née* Becchetti); *S* father, 2017.

**WHITMORE, Mark Graham**; museum consultant and historian, since 2015; Director of Collections and Research, Imperial War Museum, 2010–15 (Director of Collections, 2003–10); *b* 8 July 1952; *s* of late Prof. Raymond L. Whitmore, AM and of Ruth H. Whitmore; *m* 1975, Laura Diane Vincent; one *s* three *d. Educ*: Univ. of Queensland (BRTP Hons 1975); Univ. of Melbourne (MEnvS 1986). Urban and Envmtl Planner, Gutteridge, Haskins and Davey, 1983–87; Sen. Curator, Hist. and Technol., Qld Mus., 1987–90; Australian War Memorial: Sen. Curator, Military Technol., 1990–95; Asst Dir (Nat. Collection), 1995–2003. Museums Australia: Pres., ACT Br., 2000–03; Mem., Nat. Council, 2000–03. Trustee: Sir Winston Churchill Archive, 2006–15; Tank Mus., 2008–15. *Publications*: 'Mephisto' A7V Sturmpanzerwagen 506, 1989. *Recreations*: music, photography, art, travel, operating antique steam machinery, restoring classic cars.

**WHITNEY, David John**; Chairman, DHU Health Care (formerly Derbyshire Health United), since 2015; *b* 1 Sept. 1950; *s* of Leonard and Joyce Susannah Whitney; *m* 1979, Pauline Jane; one *s* two *d. Educ*: Exeter Univ. (BA Hons); London Univ. (MA). Dep. House Governor, Moorfields Eye Hosp., 1982–85; Regl Dir of Planning, Trent RHA, 1985–90; Chief Exec., Central Sheffield Univ. Hosps NHS Trust, 1991–2001; Dir, Clinical Mgt Unit, Keele Univ., 2001–06. Prof. Associate, Sheffield Sch. of Health and Related Res., Univ. of Sheffield, 1995–2012 (Hon. Prof., 2012–). Lay Trustee, RCS, 2014–. Chm., Weston Park Hosp. Cancer Care and Res. Fund, 2012–. *Recreations*: soccer, tennis, squash, art, music.

**WHITNEY, John Norton Braithwaite**, CBE 2008; Chairman: Friends Provident Charitable Foundation, 2002–06; Council, Royal Academy of Dramatic Art, 2003–07; *b* 20 Dec. 1930; *s* of Dr Willis Bevan Whitney and Dorothy Anne Whitney; *m* 1956, Roma Elizabeth Hodgson; one *s* one *d. Educ*: Leighton Park Friends' Sch. Radio producer, 1951–64; formed Ross Radio Productions, 1951, and Autocue, 1955; founded Radio Antilles, 1963; Founder Dir, Sagitta Prodns, 1968–82; Man. Dir, Capital Radio, 1973–82; Dir Gen., IBA, 1982–89; Dir, The Really Useful Group Ltd, 1990–97 (Man. Dir, 1989–90; Chm., 1990–95); Chm., Trans World Communications plc, 1992–94. Dir, Duke of York's Theatre, 1979–82. Chm., Friends' Provident Ethical Investment Trust plc, 1992–2000; Dir, Friends' Provident Life Office, 1982–2002 (Chm., Friends' Provident Stewardship Cttee of Reference, 1985–2000); Chairman: Radio Joint Audience Research Ltd, 1992–2002; Sony Music Pace Partnership (National Bowl), 1992–95; Enterprise Radio Hldgs Ltd, 1994–96; Radio Partnership, 1996–99; Caspian Publishing Ltd, 1996–2002; Director: VCI plc, 1995–98; Galaxy Media Corp. plc, 1997–2000; Far Pavilions Ltd, 1997–; Bird & Co. International, 1999–2001 (Chm.). Chm., Assoc. of Ind. Local Radio Contractors, 1973, 1974, 1975 and 1980. Wrote, edited and devised numerous television series, 1956–82. Chm., Sony Radio Awards Cttee, 1991–97; Vice Pres., Japan Festival 1991, 1991–92 (Chm., Festival Media Cttee, 1991); Trustee, Japan Educn Trust, 1993–; Member: Bd, NT, later RNT, 1982–94 (Trustee, Pension and Life Assce, RNT, 1994–2003); Films, TV and Video Adv. Cttee, British Council, 1983–89; RCM Centenary Develt Fund (formerly Appeals Cttee), 1982– (Chm., Media and Events Cttee, 1982–94); Bd, Open Coll., 1987–89; Council for Charitable Support, 1989–92; Bd, City of London Sinfonia, 1994–2001; Exec. Cttee, Musicians Benevolent Fund, 1995–2001; Council: Royal London Aid Society, 1966–90; TRIC, 1979–89 (Pres., 1985–86; Companion, 1989–); Fairbridge (formerly Drake Fellowship, then Fairbridge Drake Soc.), 1981–96 (Vice Pres., 1996–); RSA, 1994–99; Chm., British Amer. Arts Assoc., 1992–95. Pres., London Marriage Guidance Council, 1983–90; Vice President: Commonwealth Youth Exchange Council, 1982–83; RNID, 1988–; Chm., Trustees, Soundaround (National Sound Magazine for the Blind), 1981–2000 (Life Pres., 2000); Chm., Artsline, 1983–2000 (Life Pres., 2001); Trustee: Venture Trust, 1982–86; Hosp. Broadcasting Assoc. Patron, MusicSpace Trust, 1990–; Governor: English Nat. Ballet (formerly London Festival Ballet), 1989–91; Bd, Performing Arts and Technol. Sch., 1992–2001; Chm., Theatre Investment Fund, 1990–2001. Fellow and Vice Pres., RTS, 1986–89; Fellow, Radio Acad., 1996. FRSA; Hon. RCM. *Recreations*: chess, photography, sculpture. *Address*: 5 Church Close, Todber, Dorset DT10 1JH. *E*: johnnbwhitney@gmail.com. *Clubs*: Garrick, Whitefriars.

**WHITNEY, Sarah Jane**, FCA; *b* 1 July 1963; *d* of Michael Davies, CBE and Hester Davies (*née* Inglis); *m* 1989, David Whitney; three *s* one *d. Educ*: Sevenoaks Sch.; Univ. of Bristol (BSc Econs and Politics). ACA 1988. Price Waterhouse, 1985–89; Corporate Finance: Kleinwort Benson Ltd, 1989–91; Baring Brothers & Co. Ltd, 1991–93; Gp Finance Dir, Moat Housing Gp, 1993–96; Partner, Coopers & Lybrand, then PricewaterhouseCoopers, 1996–2003; Man. Dir, Consulting and Res., and Mem., Global Exec. Bd, DTZ Hldgs PLC, 2003–06; Exec. Dir and Mem., UK Bd, CBRE Gp Inc., 2006–12. Non-exec. Dir, St Modwen Properties plc, 2019–. Sen. Vis. Fellow, Dept of Land Economy, Univ. of Cambridge, 2012–. Mem., Supervisory Bd, Bilfinger Berger Global Infrastructure SICAV SA, 2019–. Mem. Council, UCL, 2017– (Treas., 2019–). Trustee: Land Restoration Trust, 2014–; Canal and River Trust, 2018–. *Recreations*: family and friends, fell walking, gardening, arts and heritage. *E*: sarahwhitneycontact@gmail.com.

**WHITSON, Sir Keith (Roderick)**, Kt 2002; Group Chief Executive, HSBC Holdings plc, 1998–2003 (Director, 1994–2003); *b* 25 March 1943; *s* of William Cleghorn Whitson and Ellen (*née* Wade); *m* 1968, Sabine Marita, *d* of Ulrich Wiechert; one *s* two *d. Educ*: Alleyn's Sch., Dulwich. FCIB. Joined Hong Kong and Shanghai Banking Corporation Ltd, 1961; Manager, Frankfurt, 1978–80; Manager, Indonesia, 1981–84; Asst Gen. Manager, Finance, Hong Kong, 1985–87; Chief Exec. Officer, UK, 1987–90, Exec. Dir, Marine Midland Bank, NY, 1990–92; Midland Bank: Dep. Chief Exec., 1992–94; Chief Exec., 1994–98; Dep. Chm., 1998–2003. Chairman: Merrill Lynch HSBC, 2000–02; HSBC Bank AS, 2001–03; Vice-Chm., HSBC Bank North America Inc., 2002–03; Director: HSBC Bank Argentina, 1997–2003; HSBC Bank USA, 1998–2003; HSBC Bank Canada, 1998–2003; Dep. Chm. Supervisory Bd, HSBC Trinkaus und Burkhardt Dusseldorf, 1993–2003. Non-executive Director: FSA, 1998–2003; Tetra Laval, 2005–14.

**WHITTAKER, Andrew Mark**; Group General Counsel, Lloyds Banking Group, 2013–15; *b* Rawtenstall, Lancs, 1956; *s* of Edmund and Margaret Whittaker; *m* 1993, Clare Margaret Porter; two *d. Educ*: Torquay Boys' Grammar Sch.; Balliol Coll., Oxford (BA 1977; MA 1980). Admitted as solicitor, 1980; in private practice as solicitor, 1977–82; Legal Asst, 1982–84, Sen. Legal Asst, 1984–85, DTI; Securities and Investments Board: Asst Dir, 1985–87; Dep. Dir, 1987–92; Hd, Internat. and Mkts Policy, 1993–95; Hd, Securities Mkt Supervision, 1995–97; Jt Actg Mkts Dir, 1997; Dep. Gen. Counsel, 1997–2000, Gen. Counsel, 2000–13, FSA. Short-term expert, IMF, 2016–17. Ind. non-exec. Dir, ICE Futures Europe, 2017– (Chm., Risk and Audit Cttee, 2017–). Member: Legal Services Bd, 2008–14; Ind. Regulatory Cttee, Abu Dhabi Global Markets, 2016–. Trustee, British Inst. of Internat. and Comparative Law, 2014– (Mem., Finance and Audit Cttee, 2016–19). Gen. Ed., Financial Services: Law and Practice, 1987–97; Cons. Ed., Butterworth's Financial Regulation Service, 1997–2006. *Publications*: (with G. Morse) The Financial Services Act 1986: a guide to the new law, 1987; contributor: Current Legal Problems, 1990; The Future for the Global Securities Market: legal and regulatory aspects, 1996; European Securities Markets: the Investment Services Directive and beyond, 1998; Commercial Law and Commercial Practice, 2003; Conflicts of Interest, 2005; Crisis and Recovery: ethics, economics and justice, 2010. *Recreations*: family, photography, travel. *Club*: Athenæum.
*See also* S. J. *Whittaker*.

**WHITTAKER, Craig**; MP (C) Calder Valley, since 2010; *b* Radcliffe, Lancs, 30 Aug. 1962; *s* of Frank Whittaker and Marjorie Whittaker; *m* 2011, Elaine Wilkinson; one *s* two *d* by a previous marriage. *Educ*: Belmont State High Sch., NSW. Restaurant Manager: Pizza Hut (Australia) Pty Ltd, 1980–84; Pizza Hut (UK) Ltd, 1984–85; Licensee: Liberty Taverns Ltd, 1985–86; J. W. Lees (Brewers) Ltd, 1986–88; Dir, Food Retail (Australia), Kezdem Pty Ltd, 1988–92; Retail Branch Manager, Wilkinson Home and Garden Stores, 1992–98; Retail

Gen. Manager, PC World, DSG Internat. plc, 1998–2009. Mem. (C) Calderdale MBC, 2003–04, 2007–11 (Lead Mem., Children and Young People, 2007–10). PPS to Minister for Immigration, Home Office, 2015–16, Sec. of State for Culture, Media and Sport, 2016–17; an Asst Govt Whip, 2017–18; a Lord Comr of HM Treasury (Govt Whip), 2018–19; Vice Chamberlain of HM Household (Govt Whip), 2019. Mem., Educn Select Cttee, 2010–15; Joint Chairman: All Party Parly Gp on Street Children, 2011–; All Party Parly Gp on Sexual Violence in Conflict, 2016–; Chm., All Party Parly Gp on Looked After Children and Care Leavers, 2012–15, on Adoption and Fostering, 2012–15. Chm., Together for Looked-after Children charity, 2011–. *Recreations:* scuba diving, travel. *Address:* House of Commons, SW1A 0AA. *T:* (020) 7219 7031, *Fax:* (020) 7219 1054. *E:* craig.whittaker.mp@parliament.uk.

**WHITTAKER, David John;** QC 2019; a Recorder, since 2004; *b* Knutsford, Cheshire, 11 Feb. 1962; *s* of John and Evelyn Whittaker; *m* 1995, Sarah Judd; one *s* two *d*. *Educ:* King's Sch., Macclesfield; University Coll. London (BA Hons); City Univ., London (DipLaw). Called to the Bar, Middle Temple, 1986; in practice as a barrister, specialising in crime and regulatory law. *Recreations:* tennis, ski-ing, cycling, reading. *Address:* 2 Hare Court, Temple, EC4Y 7BH. *T:* 07873 671972. *E:* davidwhittaker@2harecourt.com.

**WHITTAKER, John,** PhD; Senior Teaching Fellow, Department of Economics, University of Lancaster, since 2015; *b* 7 June 1945; *m*; four *s*. *Educ:* Queen Mary Coll., Univ. of London (BSc Physics 1966); Univ. of Cape Town (PhD Physics 1980; BA Econs 1982). Industrial Engr, Magnesium Elektron Ltd, Manchester, 1966–68; Sales Engr, 1968–72, Manager Controls Div., 1972–75, Bestobell Engrg Ltd, Cape Town; University of Cape Town: Lectr in Physics, 1978–85, in Econs, 1984–90; Associate Prof., Econs, 1990–93; Prin. Lectr, Econs, Staffs Univ., 1994–96; Sen. Lectr, Econs, 1996–2004, Vis. Fellow, 2004–15, Univ. of Lancaster. Mem. (UK Ind) NW Region, Eur. Parlt, 2004–09. Contested (UK Ind): Littleborough and Saddleworth, July 1995; Lancaster and Wyre, 1997, 2001; Wigan, Sept. 1999, 2005; NW Reg., EP, 1999. *Publications:* articles in jls.

**WHITTAKER, Prof. John Brian,** PhD, DSc; Professor of Ecology, University of Lancaster, 1987–2004, now Emeritus; *b* 26 July 1939; *s* of Roland Whittaker and Freda (née Lord); *m* 1st, 1964, Helen May Thorley (*d* 1998); two *s*; 2nd, 2007, Kathleen Wendy Cann. *Educ:* Bacup and Rawtenstall Grammar Sch.; Univ. of Durham (BSc, PhD, DSc). FRES 1979, Hon. FRES 2008. Res. Officer, Univ. of Oxford, 1963–66; University of Lancaster: Lectr, then Sen. Lectr, 1966–87; Hd, Dept of Biol Scis, 1983–86 and 1991–94. Mem., Adv. Cttee on Sci., NCC, 1978–81; Chm., Terrestrial Life Scis Cttee, NERC, 1991–95. Pres., British Ecol Soc., 2000–01 (Vice-Pres., 1987–89; Mem. Council, 1970–75, 1984–86); Member: Council, Freshwater Biol Assoc., 1988–91; Exec. and Council, UK Bioscis Fedn, 2002–06; Council, Royal Entomol Soc., 2005– (Vice-Pres., 2007–08). Hon. Fellow, Lancaster Univ., 2006. British Ecol Soc. Award, 2004. *Publications:* Practical Demonstration of Ecological Concepts, 1988; (ed jtly) Toward a More Exact Ecology, 1989; (with D. T. Salt) Insects on dock plants, 1998; (ed jtly) 100 Influential Papers: published in 100 years of the British Ecological Society journals, 2013; Hills and Mills: a story of a Lancashire family, 2016; contribs to books and jls in insect ecology. *Recreations:* Gillow furniture, fell-walking, family. *Address:* Department of Biological Sciences, Lancaster University, Lancaster LA1 4YQ. *T:* (01524) 65201.

**WHITTAKER, Penny Xenia;** see Gilbert, P. X.

**WHITTAKER, Sandra Melanie;** see Smith, Sandra M.

**WHITTAKER, Prof. Simon John,** DPhil, DCL; Professor of European Comparative Law, University of Oxford, since 2006; Fellow and Tutor in Law, St John's College, Oxford, since 1987; *b* Widnes, 5 Oct. 1958; *s* of Edmund Harry and Margaret Whittaker; *m* 1990, Judith Finch; two *s* one *d*. *Educ:* Torquay Boys' Grammar Sch.; St John's Coll., Oxford (BCL, MA; DPhil 1987; DCL 2008). Called to the Bar, Lincoln's Inn, 1987; in practice as barrister, Blackstone Chambers, Temple, 2009–14. Lectr in Laws, KCL, 1982–87; Lectr, 1987–2001, Reader in European Comparative Law, 2001–06, Univ. of Oxford. *Publications:* Liability for Products: English law, French law and European harmonization, 2005; (jtly) Principles of French Law, 1998, 2nd edn 2008; (contributing ed.) Chitty on Contracts, 26th edn 1989 to 33rd edn 2018; contrib. articles to acad. jls. *Recreations:* gardens, architecture. *Address:* St John's College, Oxford OX1 3JP. *T:* (01865) 277300.

See also A. M. Whittaker.

**WHITTAKER, Stanley Henry,** FCA, CGMA; Director of Finance and Planning, British Railways Board, 1988–91; *b* 14 Sept. 1935; *s* of Frederick Whittaker and Gladys Margaret (née Thatcher); *m* 1959, Freda Smith; two *s*. *Educ:* Bec School. ACA 1958, FCA 1969; ACMA 1971; CGMA 2012. Articled clerk, G. H. Attenborough & Co., Chartered Accountants, 1953–57; Sen. Assistant, Slater, Chapman & Cooke, 1960–62; Partner, Tiplady, Brailsford & Co., 1962–65; Finance Manager, NCB, 1965–68; British Railways: Finance Manager, 1968–74; Corporate Budgets Manager, 1974–78; Sen. Finance Manager, 1978–80; Chief Finance Officer, Western Reg., 1980–82; Director: Budgetary Control, 1982–86; Finance Develt, 1986–87; Group Finance, 1987–88. *Recreations:* flying, ski-ing, industrial archaeology, travel. *Address:* 12 Kennylands Road, Sonning Common, Reading, Berks RG4 9JT. *T:* (0118) 972 2951.

**WHITTAM, Richard;** see Whittam, W. R. L.

**WHITTAM, Prof. Ronald,** FRS 1973; Emeritus Professor, Leicester University, since 1983 (Professor of Physiology, 1966–83); *b* 21 March 1925; *e s* of Edward Whittam and May Whittam (née Butterworth), Oldham, Lancs; *m* 1957, Christine Patricia Margaret, 2nd *d* of Canon J. W. Lamb; one *s* one *d*. *Educ:* Council and Technical Schools, Oldham; Univ. of Manchester and Sheffield and King's College, Cambridge. BSc 1st Class Hons (Manchester); PhD (Sheffield and Cambridge); MA (Oxon). Served RAF, 1943–47. John Stokes Fellow, Dept of Biochem., Univ. of Sheffield, 1953–55; Beit Memorial Fellow, Physiological Lab., Cambridge, 1955–58; Mem. Scientific Staff, MRC Cell Metabolism Research Unit, Oxford, 1958–60; Univ. Lectr in Biochemistry, Oxford, 1960–66; Bruno Mendel Fellow of Royal Society, 1965–66; Dean of Fac. of Science, Leicester Univ., 1979–82. Mem. Editorial Bd of Biochem. Jl, 1963–67; Hon. Sec., 1969–74, Hon. Mem., 1986, Physiological Soc.; Mem. Biological Research Bd of MRC, 1971–74, Co-Chm., 1973–74; Member: Biological Sciences Cttee, UGC, 1974–82; Educn Cttee, Royal Soc., 1979–83; Chm., Biological Educn Cttee, Royal Soc. and Inst. Biol., 1974–77. *Publications:* Transport and Diffusion in Red Blood Cells, 1964; scientific papers dealing with cell membranes. *Recreation:* walking. *Address:* 9 Guilford Road, Leicester LE2 2RD.

**WHITTAM, (William) Richard (Lamont);** QC 2008; a Recorder, since 2009; a Deputy High Court Judge, since 2016; Justice of Appeal, Court of Appeal of Falkland Islands and South Georgia and South Sandwich Islands, since 2017; *b* 23 Nov. 1959; *s* of late William Wright Whittam and of Elizabeth Mary Whittam (née Lamont); *m* 1987, Carol Rosemary van Herwaarden; one *s* one *d*. *Educ:* Marple Hall Sch.; University Coll. London (LLB Hons); Inns of Court Sch. of Law. Called to the Bar, Gray's Inn, 1983, Bencher, 2013; Jun. Treasury Counsel, 1998–2002, First Jun. Treasury Counsel, 2002–06, Sen. Treasury Counsel, 2006–13, First Sen. Treasury Counsel, 2013–15, Central Criminal Court. Member: S Eastern Circuit Cttee, 1991–93; CPS Bar Standards Cttee, 2000–05. Ind. Examr, Inst. and Faculty of Actuaries, 2011–. Wanless Whittam Rev. for Home Office, looking at inf. held in connection with child abuse 1979–99, 2014. Mem., RFU Judiciary, 2014–. *Recreations:* pyrotechnics, waterski-ing, men's lacrosse, Rugby, golf. *Address:* 2 Bedford Row, WC1R 4BU. *Clubs:* Garrick; Denham Waterski.

**WHITTAM SMITH, Sir Andreas,** Kt 2015; CBE 2003; First Church Estates Commissioner, 2002–17; *b* 13 June 1937; *s* of Canon J. E. Smith and Mrs Smith (née Barlow); *m* 1964, Valerie Catherine, *d* of late Wing Comdr J. A. Sherry and of Mrs N. W. H. Wyllys; two *s*. *Educ:* Birkenhead Sch., Cheshire; Keble Coll., Oxford (MA; Hon. Fellow, 1990). With N. M. Rothschild, 1960–62; Stock Exchange Gazette, 1962–63; Financial Times, 1963–64; The Times, 1964–66; Dep. City Editor, Daily Telegraph, 1966–69; City Editor, The Guardian, 1969–70; Editor, Investors Chronicle and Stock Exchange Gazette, and Dir, Throgmorton Publications, 1970–77; City Editor, Daily Telegraph, 1977–85; Founder and Editor, The Independent, 1986–94; Editor-in-Chief, Independent on Sunday, 1991–94. Dir, 1986–98, Chief Exec., 1987–93, Chm., 1994–95, Newspaper Publishing plc; Director: Ind. News & Media (UK), 1998–2010; Independent Print Ltd, 2010–16 (Chm., 2014–16). Pres., BBFC, 1998–2002; Chairman: Financial Ombudsman Service Ltd, 1999–2003; With Profits Cttee, Prudential Assurance, 2005–14; Children's Mutual, 2006–10. Vice Pres., Nat. Council for One Parent Families, 1991– (Hon. Treas., 1982–86). Chm., Sir Winston Churchill Archive Trust, 1995–2000. Trustee, Architecture Foundn, 1994–2000. Hon. Fellow: UMIST, 1989; Liverpool John Moores, 2001. Hon. DLitt: St Andrews; Salford; City; Liverpool, 1992; Hon. LLD Bath. Wincott award, 1975; Marketing Man of the Year, Inst. of Marketing, 1987; Journalist of the Year, British Press Awards, 1987; Hemingway Europa Prize, 1988; Editor of the Year, Granada TV What the Papers Say award, 1989. *Recreations:* music, history, walking. *Address:* 154 Campden Hill Road, W8 7AS. *Club:* Garrick.

**WHITTELL, James Michael Scott,** CMG 1998; OBE 1984; Chief Executive, Interstate Programmes (2000) Ltd, 2004–19 (Founder and Chief Executive, Interstate Programmes Ltd, 1999–2004); Founder and Director, The Physics Factory, 2008–18; *b* 17 Feb. 1939; *s* of late Edward Arthur Whittell and Helen Elizabeth Whittell (née Scott); *m* 1962, Eleanor Jane Carling; three *s*. *Educ:* Gresham's School, Holt; Magdalen College, Oxford (MA, BSc); Manchester Univ. Teaching, Sherborne School, 1962–68, Nairobi School, 1968–72; British Council: Ibadan, Nigeria, 1973–76; Enugu, Nigeria, 1976–78; Director General's Dept, 1978–81; Rep., Algiers, 1981–85; Sec. to the British Council and Head, Director General's Dept, 1985–88; seconded to PM's Efficiency Unit, 1988; Rep., subseq. Dir, Nigeria, 1989–92; Dir, Africa and ME Div., 1992; Regl Dir, EC, later EU, 1993–96; Dir, British Council in Europe, 1996–99. *Recreations:* walking, mountaineering, books, music. *Address:* 15 Stratford Grove, SW15 1NU. *Club:* Alpine.

**WHITTEMORE, Prof. Colin Trengove;** Professor of Agriculture and Rural Economy, University of Edinburgh, 1990–2007, now Emeritus (Postgraduate Dean, College of Science and Engineering, 2002–07); *b* 16 July 1942; *s* of Hugh Ashcroft Whittemore and Dorothea Whittemore (née Nance); *m* 1966, Mary Christine Fenwick; one *s* three *d*. *Educ:* Rydal Sch.; Harper Adams Agricl Coll. (NDA); Univ. of Newcastle upon Tyne (BSc, PhD, DSc). FRSB (FIBiol 1989); FRSE 1994. Lectr, Univ. of Edinburgh, 1970–79; Head, Animal Production Adv. and Develt, E of Scotland Coll. of Agric., 1979–84; University of Edinburgh: Prof. of Animal Prodn, 1984–90; Head, Dept of Agric., 1989–90; Head, Inst. of Ecology and Resource Mgt, 1990–2000. Pres., British Soc. of Animal Sci., 1998–99 (Chm., Accreditation and Governance, 2013–). Sir John Hammond Award, British Soc. of Animal Prodn, 1983; Res. Gold Medal, RASE, 1984; Oscar della Suinicoltura, Assoc. Mignini, 1987; David Black Award, Meat and Livestock Commn, 1990. *Publications:* Practical Pig Nutrition (with F. W. H. Elsley), 1976; Lactation, 1980; Pig Production, 1980; Elements of Pig Science, 1987; The Science and Practice of Pig Production, 1993, 3rd edn 2006; Newlands, 2014; Curling, 2014; Farming Stories from the Scottish Borders, 2017; Animal Farming, 2018. *Recreations:* ski-ing, horses. *Address:* Rowancroft, 17 Fergusson View, West Linton, Peeblesshire EH46 7DJ. *Club:* Farmers.

**WHITTING, Ian Robert,** OBE 2011; HM Diplomatic Service; Deputy High Commissioner to Cyprus, since 2017; *b* 2 April 1953; *s* of Robert Stanley Whitting, ARIBA, and Mary Elizabeth (née Tindall); *m* 1986, Tracy Gallagher; two *d*. *Educ:* Chichester High Sch. for Boys. Joined FCO, 1972; Attaché, Moscow, 1975–76; Third Sec., Tunis, 1976–79; Press Attaché, Athens, 1980–83; FCO, 1983–85; Second Sec., Moscow, 1985–88; FCO, 1988–90; First Sec., Dublin, 1990–94; Dep. Hd of Mission, Abidjan, 1994–97; Dep. Hd, Africa Dept (Equatorial), and Sec. of State's Special Rep. for Great Lakes, 1998–2002; Hd, EU Dept (Bilateral), FCO, 2002–03; Dir, EU and Econ. Affairs, Athens, 2003–04; Counsellor, Dep. Hd of Mission and HM Consul-Gen., Athens, 2005–08; Ambassador: to Iceland, 2008–12; to Montenegro, 2013–17. *Recreations:* tennis, sailing, walking. *Address:* c/o Foreign and Commonwealth Office, King Charles Street, SW1A 2AH.

**WHITTING, John Justin;** QC 2011; *b* Claverdon, 15 Nov. 1966; *s* of Leonard and Barbara Whitting; *m* 1995, Emma Elizabeth Fallon; one *s* two *d*. *Educ:* King Edward VI Grammar Sch., Stratford on Avon; Oriel Coll., Oxford (BA Hons Juris.); King's Coll. London (LLM Commercial Law). Called to the Bar, Middle Temple, 1991; in practice as barrister, specialising in professional negligence, 1992–. *Recreations:* running, golf, my family. *Address:* The Old Rectory, Wimpstone, Warwicks CV37 8NS; 1 Crown Office Row, Temple, EC4Y 7HH. *E:* john.whitting@1cor.com. *Clubs:* Oxford and Cambridge; Leander (Henley-on-Thames).

**WHITTINGDALE, Rt Hon. John (Flasby Lawrance),** OBE 1990; PC 2015; MP (C) Maldon, since 2010 (Colchester South and Maldon, 1992–97; Maldon and East Chelmsford, 1997–2010); *b* 16 Oct. 1959; *s* of late John Whittingdale and of Margaret Esmé Scott Napier; *m* 1990, Ancilla Campbell Murfitt (marr. diss. 2008); one *s* one *d*. *Educ:* Sandroyd Sch.; Winchester Coll.; University Coll. London (BScEcon). Head of Political Section, Conservative Research Dept, 1982–84; Special Adviser to Sec. of State for Trade and Industry, 1984–87; Manager, N. M. Rothschild & Sons, 1987; Political Sec. to the Prime Minister, 1988–90; Private Sec. to Rt Hon. Margaret Thatcher, 1990–92. PPS to Minister of State for Educn, 1994–95, for Educn and Employment, 1995–96; an Opposition Whip, 1997–98; Opposition Treasury spokesman, 1998–99; PPS to Leader of the Opposition, 1999–2001; Shadow Sec. of State for Trade and Industry, 2001–02, for Culture, Media and Sport, 2002–03 and 2004–05, for Agriculture, Fisheries and Food, 2003–04; Sec. of State for Culture, Media and Sport, 2015–16. Member, Select Committee: on Health, 1993–97; on Trade and Industry, 2001; on Exiting the EU, 2016–; Chairman: Select Cttee on Culture, Media and Sport, 2005–15; Jt Cttee on Privacy and Injunctions, 2011–12. Mem., Parly Assembly, OSCE, 2017–; Chm., British Gp, IPU, 2018– (Vice Chm., 2017–18). Sec., Conservative Parly Home Affairs Cttee, 1992–94; Mem. Exec., Cons. 1922 Cttee, 2005–15 (Vice Chm., Cons. Party Bd, 2006–09. Parly Mem., Cons. Party Bd, 2006–09. Trustee, Royal Albert Hall Council, 2018–. FRSA 2008. *Recreations:* cinema, music. *Address:* c/o House of Commons, SW1A 0AA. *Club:* Essex.

**WHITTINGHAM, Nicholas Peter;** HM Diplomatic Service; Ambassador to Guatemala, and Ambassador (non-resident) to Honduras, since 2019; *b* Portsmouth, 6 April 1964; *s* of Peter John Whittingham and Linda Elizabeth Whittingham (*née* Bell); *m* 1999, Yuehping Yen. *Educ:* London Sch. of Econs and Pol Sci. (BSc Econ Internat. Relns 1994); Wolfson Coll., Cambridge (MPhil Latin American Studies 1995). Journalist, Portsmouth Evening News, 1988–90; entered FCO, 1995; Information Dept, FCO, 1995–2000; Consul, Guangzhou, 2001–03; First Sec., Beijing, 2004–07; Consul Gen., Chongqing, 2007–10; Pvte Sec. to Trade Minister, FCO, 2010–12; Counsellor, Beijing, 2013–14; Consul Gen., Wuhan, China, 2014–18. *Recreations:* mountain walking, diving, music, reading. *Address:* c/o Foreign and Commonwealth Office, King Charles Street, SW1A 2AH.

**WHITTINGSTALL, Hugh Christopher Edmund F.;** *see* Fearnley-Whittingstall.

**WHITTINGTON, Prof. Dorothy Allan,** CPsychol; Professor of Health Psychology, University of Ulster, 1999–2003, Professor Emeritus, 2005; *b* 14 Dec. 1941; *d* of Eric George Whittington and Margaret Cowan Whittington (*née* Allan). *Educ:* Hutchesons' Girls' Grammar Sch., Glasgow; Univ. of Glasgow (MA, MEd, Teaching Cert.). AFBPsS 1970; CPsychol 1988. Infant teacher, Glasgow primary schs, 1962–67; Lectr in Psychol., Callendar Park Coll. of Educn, Falkirk, 1967–72; Sen. Lectr in Educn, 1972–73, Principal Lectr in Psychol., 1973–84, Ulster Poly.; University of Ulster: Sen. Lectr in Psychol., 1984–94; Dir, Centre for Health and Social Res., 1990–95; Hd, Sch. of Health Scis, 1994–96; Dir, Health Care Distance Learning, 1997–2003. Mem., Nat. Council, Assoc. for Quality in Health Care, 1989–92; Dir, Trustee and Mem. Academic Council, Higher Educn Acad., 2008–10; Partner, Postgrad. Med. Educnl Trng Bd, 2008–10. Chairman, Advisory Group: Centre for Health Scis and Practice, Learning and Teaching Support Network, 2002–05; Centre for Medicine, Dentistry, Vet. Medicine and Health Scis, Higher Educn Acad., 2005–10. Dir of Educn, R&D, N Bristol NHS Trust, 2003–07; non-executive Director: Northern Health and Social Care Trust, NI, 2007–15; Health and Social Care Business Services Orgn, NI, 2016–. Co-founder, NI Parents' Advice Centre, 1978. Mem., Accreditation Panel, Pharmaceutical Soc. of NI, 2010–12; Mem., Accreditation Panel, and Associate, Gen. Pharmaceutical Council, 2012–. Associate, GMC, 2010–12. *Publications:* (jtly) Quality Assurance: a workbook for health professionals, 1992 (trans. Italian and Portuguese); with R. Ellis: A Guide to Social Skill Training, 1981; New Directions in Social Skill Training, 1983; Quality Assurance in Health Care, 1993; Quality Assurance in Social Care: an introductory workbook, 1998; contrib. papers and book chapters on social skill, communication in professional contexts, quality and governance in health and social care, needs assessment and prog. evaluation in primary and community care, patient and public involvement in health and social care planning, professional regulation and higher education. *Recreations:* sailing, music.

**WHITTINGTON, Prof. Geoffrey,** CBE 2001; Price Waterhouse Professor of Financial Accounting, Cambridge University, 1988–2001, now Emeritus; Fellow of Fitzwilliam College, Cambridge, 1966–72 and 1988–2001, now Life Fellow; Senior Research Fellow, Cambridge Centre for Finance (formerly Centre for Financial Analysis and Policy), Judge Business School, Cambridge, since 2006; Honorary Professor, University of Sussex, since 2014; *b* 21 Sept. 1938; *s* of late Bruce Whittington and Dorothy Gwendoline Whittington (*née* Gent); *m* 1963, Joyce Enid Smith; two *s*. *Educ:* Dudley Grammar Sch.; LSE (Leverhulme Schol.; BSc Econ); Fitzwilliam Coll., Cambridge (MA; PhD 1972; ScD 2009). FCA. Chartered Accountancy training, 1959–62; research posts, Dept of Applied Econ., Cambridge, 1962–72; Dir of Studies in Econs, Fitzwilliam Coll., Cambridge, 1967–72; Prof. of Accountancy and Finance, Edinburgh Univ., 1972–75; University of Bristol: Prof. of Accounting and Finance, 1975–88; Head of Dept of Econs, 1981–84; Dean, Faculty of Social Scis, 1985–87. Professorial Res. Fellow, Inst. of Chartered Accountants of Scotland, 1996–2001. Hon. Prof., Univ. of Sussex, 2014–. Part-time Econ. Adviser, OFT, 1977–83; part-time Mem., Monopolies and Mergers Commn, 1987–96; Accounting Standards Board: Acad. Advr, 1990–94; Mem., 1994–2001 and 2006–09; Member: Adv. Body on Fair Trading in Telecommunications, 1997–98; Internat. Accounting Standards Bd, 2001–06; Academic Adv. Panel, CMA (formerly Competition Commn), 2014–. Hon. DSc (SocSci) Edinburgh, 1998; DUniv Sussex, 2014. Dist. Academic of Year Award, British Accounting Assoc. and Chartered Assoc. of Certified Accountants, 1994; Chartered Accountants Founding Societies Centenary Award, 2003. *Publications:* Growth, Profitability and Valuation (with A. Singh), 1968; The Prediction of Profitability, 1971; Inflation Accounting, 1983; (with D. P. Tweedie) The Debate on Inflation Accounting, 1984; (ed jtly) Readings in the Concept and Measurement of Income, 1986; The Elements of Accounting, 1992; Profitability, Accounting Theory and Methodology, 2007; Value and Profit, 2017; contribs to jls and books in accounting, economics and finance. *Recreations:* music, walking, usual academic pursuits of reading my own books and laughing at my own jokes, visual arts. *Address:* Fitzwilliam College, Cambridge CB3 0DG. *Club:* Athenæum.

**WHITTINGTON, Joanna Sarah;** Director General, Energy and Security, Department for Business, Energy and Industrial Strategy, since 2018; *b* London, 17 Dec. 1966; *d* of Christopher and Sue Whittington. *Educ:* N London Collegiate Sch.; King's Sch., Canterbury; Somerville Coll., Oxford (BA Hons PPE); Univ. of Westminster (MSc Transport Planning and Mgt). Asst, Monopolies and Mergers Commn, 1989–90; Analyst, Intelligence Unit, The Economist, 1990–92; Sen. Analyst, MVA Consultancy, 1993–94; Economist, Office of the Rail Regulator, 1995–99; Partner, Ofgem, 1999–2014; Dir, Railway Mkts and Econs, 2014–16, Chief Exec., 2016–18, Office of Rail and Road. *Address:* Department for Business, Energy and Industrial Strategy, 1 Victoria Street, SW1H 0ET. *E:* joanna.whittington@beis.gov.uk.

**WHITTINGTON, Prof. Richard C.,** PhD; Professor of Strategic Management, University of Oxford, since 2002; Fellow of New College, Oxford, since 1996. *Educ:* Aston Univ. (MBA); Univ. of Manchester (PhD); MA Oxon. Lectr in Industrial Sociology, Imperial Coll., Univ. of London; Lectr, Sen. Lectr, then Reader in Marketing and Strategic Mgt, Warwick Business Sch., Univ. of Warwick; Reader in Mgt Studies, Univ. of Oxford, 1996–2002. Pierre de Fermat Distinguished Prof., Univ. of Toulouse, 2007–10. *Publications:* Corporate Strategies in Recession and Recovery, 1989; (jtly) Rethinking Marketing, 1999; What is Strategy - and Does it Matter?, 2nd edn 2000; (jtly) The European Corporation: strategy, structure, and social science, 2000; (jtly) The Handbook of Strategy and Management, 2001; (jtly) Innovative Forms of Organising, 2003; (jtly) Exploring Corporate Strategy, 8th edn 2007; (jtly) Strategy as Practice: research directions and resources, 2007; articles in learned jls. *Address:* Saïd Business School, University of Oxford, Park End Street, Oxford OX1 1HP.

**WHITTINGTON, Col the Rev. Richard Hugh,** MBE 1974; Senior Advisor, Winton Capital Management, 2013–17; *b* Brighton, 25 May 1947; *s* of Charles Henry Whittington and Violet May Whittington (*née* Hay); *m* 1970, Gisela Ingeborg; one *s* (one *d* decd). *Educ:* Dorothy Stringer Sch., Brighton; Army Apprentice Coll., Chepstow; Salisbury and Wells Theological Coll. (DipTh 1993). Commnd RE, 1970; Adjutant, 32 Engr Regt, 1974–75; psc 1980; OC 1 Field Sqdn, 1983–85; CO 26 Engr Regt, 1986–88; Sen. Instructor, Army Staff Coll., 1989–91. Ordained deacon, 1993, priest, 1994; Curate, St James, Enfield Highway, 1993–95; Rector, St Peter's, Ightham, 1995–2001; Chaplain, Royal Hosp. Chelsea, 2001–13. Mem., HM Bodyguard, Hon. Corps of Gentlemen at Arms, 1999– (Harbinger, 2015–17). *Recreations:* golf, ski-ing, tennis, shooting. *Address:* 60 Walker Drive, Faringdon SN7 7FZ. *T:* 07879 335536. *E:* rhw47@btinternet.com. *Clubs:* Cavalry and Guards; Frilford Heath Golf.

**WHITTINGTON-SMITH, Marianne Christine, (Mrs C. A. Whittington-Smith);** *see* Lutz, M. C.

**WHITTLE, Prof. Alasdair William Richardson,** DPhil; FBA 1998; Distinguished Research Professor of Archaeology, Cardiff University (formerly University of Wales College of Cardiff), 1997–2018, now Professor Emeritus; *b* 7 May 1949; *s* of late Charles and Grizel Whittle; three *d*. *Educ:* Christ Church, Oxford (BA, DPhil 1976). Lectr, UC Cardiff, then Univ. of Wales Coll. of Cardiff, 1978–97. Jt Ed., Proc. Prehistoric Soc., 1988–94. Leader: Avebury Area Excavation Project, 1987–93; The Times of Their Lives Project, 2012–17. Member: Panel for Archaeol., RAEs, 1996, 2001; Ancient Monuments Adv. Bd for Wales, 2000–10. *Publications:* Neolithic Europe, 1985; Scord of Brouster, 1986; Problems in Neolithic Archaeology, 1988; Europe in the Neolithic, 1996; Sacred Mound, Holy Rings, 1997; The Harmony of Symbols, 1999; The Archaeology of People, 2003; (jtly) Places of Special Virtue, 2004; (jtly) Histories of the Dead, 2007; (jtly) Building Memories, 2007; Neolithic on the Great Hungarian Plain, 2007; (jtly) Gathering Time, 2011; (ed jtly) The First Farmers of Central Europe, 2013; (ed jtly) Early Farmers, 2014; The Times of Their Lives, 2018. *Recreations:* golf, fishing, travel. *Address:* Department of Archaeology and Conservation, Cardiff University, John Percival Building, Colum Drive, Cardiff CF10 3EU.

**WHITTLE, Brian Ian;** Member (C) Scotland South, Scottish Parliament, since 2016; *b* Ayr, 26 April 1964; *s* of Ian and Carole Whittle; *m* 2008, Julia; three *d*. *Educ:* Marr Coll.; Glasgow Univ. (HNC Chem.); Kilmarnock Coll.; Open Univ. (MA Business). Director: PB Events Ltd, 2002–08; of Sport, 2006; Mii Hub Ltd, 2010–11; Insportive Ltd, 2011–13; Uniquedoc Ltd, 2013–16; CEO, My Sports Media Ltd, 2013–16. Mem. Bd, Scotland NSPCC. *Recreations:* coaching, golf, guitar. *Address:* Scottish Parliament, Edinburgh EH99 1SP. *E:* brian.whittle.msp@parliament.scot.

**WHITTLE, Eve;** *see* Salomon, E.

**WHITTLE, Lindsay Geoffrey;** Member (Plaid Cymru) South Wales East, National Assembly for Wales, 2011–16; *b* Caerffili, 24 March 1953; *s* of Thomas Ivor Whittle and Margaret May Whittle; one *d* by Adele Roberts. *Educ:* Cwm Ifor Primary Sch.; Caerffili Boys Grammar Tech. Sch.; Cardiff Univ. (Postgrad. Dip. Housing 1995). Archaeological excavator, 1970; aluminium foundry worker, 1971–82; Housing Manager, Hafod Housing Assoc., 1981–2006. Member (Plaid Cymru): Rhymney Valley DC, 1976–95; Caerffili CBC, 1976– (Leader of Opposition, 1995–99 and 2004–08; Leader, 1999–2004 and 2008–11). Contested (Plaid Cymru) Caerphilly, 2017. *Recreations:* regular attendee at Edinburgh Fringe Festival, gardening, antique collecting, and of course Rugby.

**WHITTLE, Prof. Martin John,** MD; FRCPGlas, FRCOG; Professor of Fetal Medicine, 1991–2006, and Associate Dean for Education, 2004–06, University of Birmingham (Head, Division of Reproductive and Child Health, 1998–2003), now Professor Emeritus; *b* 6 July 1944; *s* of Bruce and Eveline Whittle. *Educ:* William Grimshaw Secondary Modern Sch., London; Univ. of Manchester Med. Sch. (MB ChB 1972; MD 1980). FRCOG 1988; FRCPGlas 1988. House Physician and Surgeon, Manchester Royal Infirmary, 1972–73; Res. Fellow, LAC-USC Med. Center, Los Angeles, 1978–79; Lectr, Queen Mother's Hosp., Glasgow, 1979–82; Consultant Obstetrician and Gynaecologist, Queen Mother's Hosp. and Royal Samaritan Hosp., Glasgow, 1982–91; Consultant, Birmingham Women's Hosp., 1991–2006; Clinical Co-Dir, Nat. Collaborating Centre for Women and Children's Health, Nat. Inst. for Health and Clinical Excellence, 2006–09. Hon. MO, Jubilee Sailing Trust, 2010–19. *Publications:* (with J. M. Connor) Prenatal Diagnosis in Obstetric Practice, 1989, 2nd edn 1995; (with C. H. Rodeck) Fetal Medicine: Basic Science and Clinical Practice, 1999, 3rd edn 2019; novels: Just Another Trip, 2015; Tomorrow Must Wait, 2019; contrib. articles on fetal medicine and high-risk obstetric practice. *Recreations:* sailing, flying, diving, art, European history 1500–1800. *E:* mwhittle@doctors.net.uk.

**WHITTLE, Prof. Peter,** FRS 1978; Churchill Professor of Mathematics for Operational Research, University of Cambridge, 1967–94, now Emeritus; Fellow of Churchill College, Cambridge, 1967, now Emeritus; *b* 27 Feb. 1927; *s* of Percy and Elsie Whittle; *m* 1951, Käthe Hildegard Blomquist; three *s* three *d*. *Educ:* Wellington Coll., New Zealand. Docent, Uppsala Univ., 1951–53; employed New Zealand DSIR, 1953–59, rising to Senior Principal Scientific Officer; Lectr, Univ. of Cambridge, 1959–61; Prof. of Mathematical Statistics, Univ. of Manchester, 1961–67. Sen. Fellow, SERC, 1988–91. Mem., Royal Soc. of NZ, 1981–; For. Mem., NAE, 2016. Hon. DSc Victoria Univ. of Wellington, NZ, 1987. *Publications:* Hypothesis Testing in Time Series Analysis, 1951; Prediction and Regulation, 1963; Probability, 1970; Optimisation under Constraints, 1971; Optimisation over Time, 1982; Systems in Stochastic Equilibrium, 1986; Risk-sensitive Optimal Control, 1990; Probability via Expectation, 1992; Optimal Control: basics and beyond, 1996; Neural Nets and Chaotic Carriers, 1998; Networks: optimisation and evolution, 2007; contribs to Jl Roy. Statistical Soc., Proc. Roy. Soc., Jl Stat. Phys, Systems and Control Letters. *Recreations:* variable. *Address:* 268 Queen Edith's Way, Cambridge CB1 8NL.

**WHITTLE, Peter Robin;** author, journalist and broadcaster; Member, London Assembly, Greater London Authority, since 2016 (UK Ind, 2016–18; Brexit Alliance, since 2018); Founder and Director, New Culture Forum, since 2006; *b* London, 6 Jan. 1961; *s* of Peter Ernest Whittle and Joan Sylvia Whittle. *Educ:* Roan Boys' Sch.; Orpington Coll.; Univ. of Kent (BA Hons Hist. and Politics); Poly. of Central London. Broker, C. T. Bowring Ltd, 1987–89; Hd, Press and Mktg, Filmtrax Ltd, 1989–91; TV producer and dir of arts and factual progs for ITV, Channel 4, Channel Five, USA Networks, Fox Network, 1991–2003, incl. in LA, 1999–2003; critic, writer and cultural commentator for Sunday Times, LA Times, The Times and nat. and internat. pubns, 2000–06; TV and radio broadcaster on cultural and current affairs; host and producer, New Culture Forum's prog. on YouTube, So What You Are Saying Is…, 2019; columnist, Standpoint Mag., 2008–15. Leader UK Ind Gp, 2016–18, Brexit Alliance Gp, 2018–, London Assembly, GLA. Culture spokesman, 2013–18, Dep. Leader, 2016–17, UKIP. Contested (UK Ind): EP, 2014; Eltham, 2015; London Mayoral candidate, 2016. *Publications:* Look at Me: celebrating the self in modern Britain, 2008; Private Views: voices from the frontline of British culture, 2009; A Sorry State: self-denigration in British culture, 2010; Monarchy Matters, 2011; Being British: what's wrong with it?, 2012; Reel Life: Peter Whittle at the movies, 2014. *Recreations:* cinema, history, music, London life, swimming in hot climates. *Address:* Greater London Authority, City Hall, Queen's Walk, SE1 2AA. *E:* Peter.Whittle@london.gov.uk, prwhittle@btinternet.com.

**WHITTLE, Stephen Charles,** OBE 2006; Chairman, Broadcast Training and Skills Regulator, 2007–11; Controller of Editorial Policy, BBC, 2001–05; *b* 26 July 1945; *s* of Charles William Whittle and Vera Lillian Whittle (*née* Moss); *m* 1988, Claire Walmsley (marr. diss. 1999); *m* 2004, Eve Coulter Salomon, *qv*. *Educ:* St Ignatius College, Stamford Hill; University College London (LLB Hons). Asst Editor, New Christian, 1968–70;

Communications Officer, World Council of Churches, Geneva, 1970–73; Editor, One World, WCC, 1973–77; Asst Head, Communications Dept, WCC, 1975–77; BBC: Sen. Producer, Religious Programmes, Manchester, 1977–82; Producer, Newsnight, 1982; Editor, Songs of Praise and Worship, 1983–89; Hd of Religious Progs, 1989–93; Chief Advr, Editl Policy, Policy and Planning Directorate, 1993–96; Director: Broadcasting Standards Council, 1996–97; Broadcasting Standards Commn, 1997–2001. Member: Regulation Bd, Law Soc., subseq. SRA, 2005–11; GMC, 2009–13; Council, Public Concern at Work, 2010–. Gov., Eur. Inst. for the Media, 1997–2004. Chm., Adv. Gp, Healthwatch Southwark, 2016–. Trustee: Sandford St Martin Trust, 2002–11; Fifth Trust, 2010–; Time and Talents, 2016– (Chm., 2017–). Vis. Fellow, Reuters Inst. for Study of Journalism, Oxford Univ., 2007–. FRSA. Freeman, City of London, 1990. Sandford St Martin Award for contrib. to religious broadcasting, 1993. *Publications:* Tickling Mrs Smith, 1970; Privacy, Probity and Public Interest, 2009; contribs to Media Guardian and The Tablet. *Recreations:* cinema, theatre, music, reading, walking. *Address:* 4 Carmarthen Place, SE1 3TS.

**WHITTOW, Hugh John;** Editor, Daily Express, 2011–18; *b* Haverfordwest, 20 March 1951; *s* of Jack Whittow and Marion Whittow; *m* 1984, Lesley Grant; two *d*. *Educ:* Haverfordwest Grammar Sch. Reporter: Western Telegraph, Haverfordwest, 1968–71; Western Daily Press, Bristol, 1971; South Wales Echo, Cardiff, 1971–73; London Evening News, 1973–78; Daily Star, 1978–82; The Sun, 1982–87; Dep. Ed., Daily Star, 1987–2001; Launch Ed., Daily Star Sunday, 2002–03; Dep. Ed., Daily Express, 2003–11. Freeman of Haverfordwest, 1998. *Recreations:* family, ski-ing, Rugby, golf, walking our dog 'Darcey' on Newgale Beach. *E:* hugh.whittow@gmail.com.

**WHITTY,** family name of **Baron Whitty**.

**WHITTY, Baron** *cr* 1996 (Life Peer), of Camberwell in the London Borough of Southwark; **John Lawrence Whitty, (Larry);** PC 2005; *b* 15 June 1943; *s* of Frederick James and Kathleen May Whitty; *m* 1969, Tanya Margaret (marr. diss. 1986); two *s*; *m* 1993, Angela Forrester. *Educ:* Latymer Upper School; St John's College, Cambridge (BA Hons Economics). Hawker Siddeley Aviation, 1960–62; Min. of Aviation Technology, 1965–70; Trades Union Congress, 1970–73; General, Municipal, Boilermakers and Allied Trade Union (formerly GMWU), 1973–85; Gen. Sec., 1985–94, European Co-ordinator, 1994–97, Labour Party. A Lord in Waiting (Govt Whip), 1997–98; Parly Under-Sec. of State, DETR, subseq. DEFRA, 1998–2005. Chm., EU Internal Market Sub-cttee, H of L, 2015–. Chm., NCC, later Consumer Focus, 2006–10; Member: Nat. Water Services Regulation Authy, 2006; Bd, Envmt Agency, 2006–12; Adv. Cttee on Business Appts, 2019–; Chm., Commn on Vulnerable Energy Consumers, 2018. Chm., Eur. Assoc. for Study of Sci. and Technol., 2017–. Chairman: Chesshire Lehmann Fund, 2009–16; Road Safety Foundn, 2014–. Hon. Pres., Envmtl Protection UK, 2016–. *Recreations:* theatre, cinema, swimming, walking. *Address:* 61 Bimport, Shaftesbury, Dorset SP7 8AZ. *T:* (01747) 854619, 07704 675464.

**WHITTY, Prof. Christopher John MacRae,** CB 2015; FRCP; FMedSci; Chief Medical Officer, Department of Health and Social Care, since 2019; Consultant Physician, Hospital for Tropical Diseases and University College London Hospital, since 2001; *b* Gloucester, 21 April 1966; *s* of Kenneth Whitty and Susannah Whitty. *Educ:* Pembroke Coll., Oxford (BA 1988; DSc 2011); Wolfson Coll., Oxford (BM BCh 1991); London Sch. of Hygiene and Tropical Medicine, Univ. of London (DTM&H 1996; MSc 1996); Open Univ. (DipEcon); Northumbria Univ. (LLM 2005); Heriot-Watt Univ. (MBA 2010). FRCP 2004; FFPH 2009. Clinical and res. posts, UK, Africa and Asia, 1991–2001; Sen. Registrar, London, 1996–2001; Lectr, Univ. of Malawi, 1998–2000; Sen. Lectr, 2001–05, Prof. of Public and Internat. Health, 2005–19, Hon. Prof., 2019–, LSHTM; Chief Scientific Advr and Dir, Res. and Evidence, DFID, 2009–15; Interim Govt Chief Scientific Advr and Hd, Sci. and Engrg Profession, 2017–18; Chief Scientific Advr, DoH, then DHSC, and First Dep. Chief Med. Officer, 2016–19. Vis. Prof. of Public Health, 2014–18, Gresham Prof. of Physic, 2018–, Gresham Coll., London. FMedSci 2011.

**WHITTY, Niall Richard,** FRSE; Member, Scottish Law Commission, 1995–2000; *b* 28 Oct. 1937; *s* of Richard Hazleton Whitty and Muriel Helen Margaret Scott or Whitty; *m* 1977, Elke Mechthild Maria Gillis; three *s* one *d*. *Educ:* John Watson's Sch., Edinburgh; Morrison's Acad., Crieff; St Andrews Univ. (MA Hons 1960); Edinburgh Univ. (LLB 1963). Admitted solicitor, 1965. Legal Officer, 1967–70, Sen. Legal Officer, 1970–77, Asst Solicitor, 1977–94, Scottish Office; seconded to legal staff, Scottish Law Commn, 1971–94. Vis. Prof., Sch. of Law, Univ. of Edinburgh, 2000–. Gen. Editor, The Laws of Scotland, Stair Memorial Encyclopaedia, 2000–14. FRSE 2003. *Publications:* (ed with Reinhard Zimmermann) Rights of Personality in Scots Law: a comparative perspective, 2009; contrib. Stair Memorial Encyclopaedia, and legal jls. *Address:* St Martins, Victoria Road, Haddington, East Lothian EH41 4DJ. *T:* (01620) 822234.

**WHITWAM, Derek Firth,** CEng, FRINA; RCNC; General Manager, Portsmouth Naval Dockyard, 1981–85; *b* 7 Dec. 1932; *s* of Hilton and Marion Whitwam; *m* 1954, Pamela May (*née* Lander) (*d* 2018); one *s* one *d*. *Educ:* Royds Hall Sch., Huddersfield; Royal Naval Coll., Dartmouth; Royal Naval Engineering Coll., Manadon; Royal Naval Coll., Greenwich. Work on ship design, MoD (N) Bath, 1957–65; Rosyth Dockyard, 1965–68; Singapore Dockyard, 1968–70; DG Ships Bath, 1970–77; RCDS 1978; Production Manager, Rosyth Dockyard, 1979–80; Principal Dir of Planning and Policy, Chief Exec. Royal Dockyards, 1984–85; Dir, Quality Assce, MoD, 1985–88. *Publications:* papers for Trans Royal Inst. of Naval Architects. *Recreations:* golf, music, walking, reading. *Club:* Bath Golf.

**WHITWORTH, Francis John,** OBE 1994; Member, Economic and Social Committee of the European Communities, 1986–98; *b* 1 May 1925; *s* of late Captain Herbert Francis Whitworth, OBE, RNVR, and Helen Marguerite Whitworth (*née* Tait); *m* 1956, Auriol Myfanwy Medwyn Hughes; one *s* one *d*. *Educ:* Charterhouse (Jun. Schol.); Pembroke Coll., Oxford (Holford Schol.; MA Jurisprudence 1949). Served War, Royal Marines, 1943–46. Called to Bar, Middle Temple, 1950. Joined Cunard Steam-Ship Co., 1950; Personnel Director, 1965, Managing Dir Cunard Line, 1968, Group Admin. Dir, 1969; joined British Shipping Fedn as Dir, Industrial Relations, 1972; Dep. Dir-Gen., Gen. Council of British Shipping, 1980–87; Dir, Internat. Shipping Fedn, 1980–88; Mem., Nat. Maritime Bd, 1962–87. Chairman: Internat. Cttee of Passenger Lines, 1968–71; Atlantic Passenger Steamship Conf., 1970–71; Employers' Gp, Jt Maritime Commn of ILO, 1980–88; Employers' Gp, Internat. Maritime (Labour) Conf. of ILO, 1986–87; Social Affairs Cttee, Comité des Assocs d'Armateurs des Communautés Européennes, 1983–88; Nat. Sea Training Schs, 1980–87; Merchant Navy Officers' Pension Fund Trustees, 1987–93; Member: Industrial Tribunals for England and Wales, 1978–94; Council, Mission to Seafarers (formerly Missions to Seamen), 1985–2010; Vice-Pres., Marine Soc. and Sea Cadets, 2004–. FCMI (FBIM 1980; MBIM 1967). Freeman, City of London, 1999; Liveryman, Shipwrights' Co., 1999–. *Recreations:* racing, opera, music, cricket. *Address:* 5 Beaumont Green, Winchester SO23 8GF. *Club:* Oxford and Cambridge.

**WHITWORTH, Prof. Judith Ann,** AC 2001; DSc, MD, PhD; FRACP; FTSE; Director, John Curtin School of Medical Research, Australian National University, 1999–2008, Emeritus Professor and Visiting Fellow, since 2010; Director, Therapeutic Innovation Australia, since 2011; *b* 1 April 1944; *d* of Arthur Howard Whitworth and Margaret Edith Wilson Whitworth (*née* Dobbs); *m* 1981, John Ludbrook (marr. diss. 1992); one *d*; partner, Colin Nicholson Chesterman. *Educ:* St Michael's C of E Girls' Grammar Sch.; Univ. of Melbourne (MB BS 1967; MD 1974; PhD 1978; DSc 1992). FRACP 1975. RMO/Registrar, Royal Melbourne Hosp., 1968–71; Sen. Registrar, Queen Elizabeth Hosp., Adelaide, 1972; Winthrop Travelling Fellow, RACP, 1973; Vis. Registrar, Guy's Hosp., London, 1974–75; NHMRC Schol., Howard Florey Inst., 1975–77; Physician, 1978–81; Chm. Bd, Postgrad. Educn, 1983–91, Dep. Dir, Dept of Nephrology, 1990–91, Royal Melbourne Hosp.; Professorial Associate, Univ. of Melbourne, 1987–91; Prof. of Medicine, Univ. of NSW, 1991–99; CMO, Dept of Health and Family Services, 1997–99. Vis. Scientist, MRC Blood Pressure Unit, Glasgow, 1985; Naturalia et Biologia Fellow, Hosp. Tenon, Paris, 1985. Mem., NH&MRC Med. Res. Cttee, 1991–94 (Chm., 1994–97); Pres., High Blood Pressure Res. Council of Australia, 1998–2001; Co-Chair, NSW Health Care Adv. Council, 2006–11. Mem. Council, RACP, 1984–93; Pres., Australian Soc. for Med. Res., 1984; Kincaid Smith Oration, RACP, 2015. Member: WHO Global Adv. Cttee on Health Res., 2000–11 (Chm., 2004–11); Nominating Cttee, Internat. Soc. for Nephrology, 1990–93; Foundn Council, Global Forum for Health Res., 2004–11. Councillor, Internat. Soc. of Hypertension, 1992–2000. Member: Council, Charles Darwin Univ., 2003–06 and 2015–; Bd, Menzies Sch. of Health Res., 2004–06; Bd, Menzies Res. Inst., Tasmania, 2005–13. FTSE 2009; FAHMS; FAICD. Fellow, Janet Clarke Hall, Univ. of Melbourne, 2016. MD *hc*: Sydney, 2004; NSW, 2005; Hon. DSc Glasgow, 2008; Hon. DLitt Charles Darwin, 2011; Hon. LLD Melbourne, 2012. Smith Kline and French Award, Internat. Soc. for Hypertension, 1984; Howard Florey Inst. Medal, 1990; RACP Medal, 1994; ACT Australian of the Year, 2004; Kincaid-Smith Medal, Australian Kidney Foundn, 2010. Centenary Medal, Australia, 2003; John Curtin Medal, ANU, 2011. *Publications:* Dictionary of Medical Eponyms, 1987, 2nd edn 1996; The Kidney, 2nd edn 1987; Textbook of Renal Disease, 1987, 2nd edn 1994; Hypertension Management, 1990; Clinical Nephrology in Medical Practice, 1992; numerous contribs to med. and scientific pubns. *Recreations:* books, cricket, film, French. *Address:* PO Box 967, Edgecliff, NSW 2027, Australia. *T:* (2) 93261963. *Clubs:* Melbourne Cricket, Lord's Taverners.

**WHITWORTH-JONES, Anthony;** General Director, Garsington Opera, 2005–12; *b* 1 Sept. 1945; *s* of Henry Whitworth-Jones and Patience Martin; *m* 1974, Camilla (*née* Barlow); one *d*. *Educ:* Wellington College. Mem., Inst. of Chartered Accountants of Scotland. Thomson McLintock & Co., 1970–72; Administrative Dir, London Sinfonietta, 1972–81; Administrator, Glyndebourne Touring Opera and Opera Manager, Glyndebourne Fest. Opera, 1981–89; Gen. Adminr, then Gen. Dir, Glyndebourne Fest. Opera, 1989–98; Gen. Dir, The Dallas Opera, 2000–02; Artistic Dir, Casa da Musica, Porto, Portugal, 2004–05. Dir, SE Arts Bd, 1993–96. Chm., Michael Tippett Musical Foundn, 1998–. Member: Adv. Bd, Voices of Change, Dallas, 2001–02; Exec. Bd, Meadows Sch. of the Arts, Southern Methodist Univ., Dallas, 2001–02; Council, Spitalfields Fest., 2003–06; Bd, ENO, 2012–. Curator, Cubitt Sessions, King's Cross, 2015–. Trustee: Leonard Ingrams Foundn, 2006–16; Young Classical Artists Trust (formerly Young Concert Artists Trust), 2007–14. *Recreations:* enjoying the spirit and countryside of Wales, Portugal and Greece, arts in general, architecture, jazz, golf. *Address:* 60 Marquis Road, NW1 9UB. *T:* (020) 7267 3154. *E:* antwjones@gmail.com.

**WHOMERSLEY, Christopher Adrian,** CMG 2014; HM Diplomatic Service, retired; Deputy Legal Adviser, 2002–14, and Head, Maritime Policy Unit (formerly Law of Sea Section), 2008–14, Foreign and Commonwealth Office; consultant on international law, particularly law of the sea and deep sea mining; *b* 18 April 1953; *s* of Harry and Doreen Whomersley; *m* 1977, Jeanette Diana Szostak; one *s* two *d*. *Educ:* London Sch. of Economics (LLB); Christ's Coll., Cambridge (LLM). Called to the Bar, Middle Temple, 1981; entered FCO, 1977; Asst Legal Advr, 1977–91, Legal Counsellor, 1991–94, FCO; Legal Secretariat to Law Officers, 1994–97; Legal Counsellor, FCO, 1997–2002. Mem., UK Delegn to Channel Tunnel Intergovtl Commn, 1986–94, 1997–2014; Leader of UK Delegn to Bermuda II Negotiations, 1991–94, 1997–2004; Govt Agent before the European Court of Human Rights, 2000–04; Leader, UK Delegn to Assembly of States Parties, Internat. Criminal Court, 2003–10; Chm., UK Internat. Humanitarian Law Cttee, 2003–07. Member: Greenwich Forum, 2015–19; Adv. Bd, Centre for Marine Ecol Resilience and Geol Resources, Nottingham Trent Univ., 2017–. Vis. Prof., Xiamen Univ., China, 2015. *Recreations:* reading modern literature and history, philately, following Coventry City FC and Warwickshire CCC. *Address:* 26 The Avenue, Bedford Park, W4 1HT. *Club:* MCC.

**WHYBROW, Christopher John;** QC 1992; *b* 7 Aug. 1942; *s* of Herbert William Whybrow, OBE and Ruby Kathleen Whybrow (*née* Watson); *m* 1st, 1969, Marian Janet Macaulay (marr. diss. 1976); 2nd, 1979, Susan Younge (marr. diss. 1990). *Educ:* Colchester Royal Grammar Sch.; King's Coll., London (LLB). Called to the Bar, Inner Temple, 1965; in practice at the Bar, 1966–2009. A Dep. Upper Tribunal Judge (formerly a Dep. Social Security Comr), 1996–2011. *Publications:* (contrib.) Atkins Court Forms; contribs to Jl of Planning and Environment Law. *Recreations:* history, cricket, tennis, walking, gardening, country life, reading, conversation. *E:* C.whybrow180@btinternet.com. *Clubs:* Lansdowne, MCC; Leavenheath Cricket.

**WHYBROW, John William;** Chairman, Clayton Engineering, since 2019; *b* 11 March 1947; *s* of Charles Ernest James Whybrow and Doris Beatrice Whybrow (*née* Abbott); *m* 1968, Paula Miriam Hobart; one *s* one *d*. *Educ:* Hatfield Tech. GS; Imperial Coll., London (BSc Hons Mech. Engrg); Manchester Business Sch. (MBA); ACGI. English Electric, Rugby, 1968–70; Philips Electronics: Northern Operational Res. Gp, 1970–78; Ind. Engrg Head, Mullard Simonstone, 1979–82; Div. Manager, 1982–83, Plant Dir, 1983–87, Mullard Blackburn; Plant Dir, Hazel Grove, 1987–88; Man. Dir, TDS Circuits plc, 1988–90; Tech. Dir, Philips Components, 1990–91; Industrial Dir, 1991–93, Chm. and Man. Dir, 1993–95, Philips Electronics UK; Pres. and CEO, Philips Lighting Holding BV, 1995–2001; Exec. Vice-Pres., Main Bd, Royal Philips Electronics, 1998–2002. Chairman: Lumileds Lighting BV, 1997–2000; CSR plc, 2004–07 (Dir, 2003–07); Wolseley PLC, 2002–11 (Dir, 1997–2011); AZ Electronic Materials, 2010–14; non-executive Director: Teletext Hldgs, 1993–95; DSG Internat. (formerly Dixons) PLC, 2003–10. Chm., Petworth Cottage Nursing Home, 2002–13. Mem. Council, RNLI, 2012–. MInstD 1993. Order of Merit (Poland), 2002. *Recreations:* sailing, shooting. *Address:* Wild Harrys, Hayes Lane, Slinfold, Horsham RH13 0SL. *E:* john@thewhybrows.com. *Clubs:* East India, City Livery Yacht; Royal Solent Yacht.

**WHYTE, Anne Lynne;** QC 2010; *b* Wegberg, 19 June 1969; *d* of Peter Whyte and Carol Whyte (*née* Jones); *m* 2002, Simon Gorton. *Educ:* Luckley Oakfield Sch., Wokingham; Worcester Coll., Oxford (BA Hons Hist.; DipLaw). Called to the Bar, Lincoln's Inn, 1993, Bencher; in practice as a barrister, 1994–; a Dep. High Court Judge, 2016–. *Address:* Atlantic Chambers, 4–6 Cook Street, Liverpool L2 9QU. *T:* (0151) 236 4421. *E:* annewhyte@atlanticchambers.co.uk.

**WHYTE, Duncan**; consultant; Chairman, Ancala Midstream Acquisitions Ltd, since 2018; *b* 27 July 1946; *s* of Andrew Montgomery Whyte and Margaret Steedman Whyte; *m* 1971, Marion McDonald McCready; one *s*. *Educ*: Kilsyth Acad. CA 1968; ATII 1968. Trainee Chartered Accountant, Paterson and Benzies, 1963–69; Arthur Andersen & Co., 1969–83 (Man. Partner, Edinburgh office, 1980–83); Financial Dir, Kwikfit Hldgs plc, 1983–88; Scottish Power: Exec. Dir, 1988–99; Finance Dir, 1988–93; Chief Operating Officer, 1993–95; Exec. Dir, Multi Utility, 1995–99; Chief Exec., Weir Gp plc, 1999–2000. Non-executive Director: Motherwell Bridge Hldgs Ltd, 1997–2003; Internat. Energy Gp, 2016–; Islands Energy Gp, 2016–; Chairman: Wales and West Utilities Ltd, 2005–12; Green Highland Renewables Ltd, 2015–18. *Recreations*: golf, badminton, reading history.

**WHYTE, Hugh Francis D.**; see Durrant-Whyte.

**WHYTE, Prof. Iain Boyd**, PhD; FRSE; Professor of Architectural History, University of Edinburgh, 1996–2014 and since 2018; *b* 6 March 1947; *s* of Thomas Boyd Whyte and Mary Whyte (*née* Macpherson); *m* 1973, Deborah Smart; one *s* one *d*. *Educ*: Nottingham Univ. (BA 1969; MPhil 1971); Cornell Univ.; Jesus Coll., Cambridge (PhD 1979); Leeds Univ. (MA 1987). FRSE 1998. British Acad./Wolfson Fellow, 1976–77; Alexander von Humboldt-Stiftung Fellow, 1979–82; Leverhulme Trust Res. Fellow, 1985–87; University of Edinburgh: Lectr in Architectl Hist., 1988–93; Reader, 1993–95. Getty Schol., 1989–90; Getty Sen. Schol., 1998–2000; Sen. Prog. Officer, Getty Grant Prog., LA, 2002–04. Samuel H. Kress Prof., Center for Advanced Studies in Visual Arts, Nat. Gall. of Art, Washington, DC, 2015–16; Vis. Sen. Fellow, Alice Kaplan Inst. for Humanities, Northwestern Univ., 2011. Trustee, Nat. Galls of Scotland, 1998–2002. Co-Curator: Council of Europe Exhibn, Art and Power - Europe under the Dictators 1930–46, Hayward Gall., London, Centre de Cultura Contemporània, Barcelona, Deutsches Historisches Mus., Berlin, 1995–96; Darwin's Edinburgh exhibn, Talbot Rice Gall., Univ. of Edinburgh, 2009. Chm., Internat. Assoc. of Res. Centres in Hist. of Art, 2010–16. FRSA. Founder Editor, Art in Translation, 2009–. *Publications*: Bruno Taut and the Architecture of Activism, 1982 (German edn 1981); (ed) The Crystal Chain Letters, 1985 (trans. German 1986); Emil Hoppe, Marcel Kammerer, Otto Schönthal, 1989; (introd and co-trans.) Hendrik Petrus Berlage on Style 1886–1909, 1996; (jtly) John Fowler, Benjamin Baker: The Forth Bridge, 1997; Modernism and the Spirit of the City, 2003; Man-made Future: planning, education and design in mid-twentieth-century Britain, 2007; (jtly) Das Erhabene in Wissenschaft und Kunst: über Vernunft und Einbildungskraft, 2010; (jtly) Beyond the Finite: the sublime in art and science, 2011; (jtly) Metropolis Berlin: 1880–1940, 2013. *Recreations*: violin playing, sculling, amusing grandchildren. *Address*: 3 West Silvermills Lane, Edinburgh EH3 5BD. *T*: (0131) 556 4008. *Clubs*: Leander (Henley-on-Thames); New (Edinburgh); Akademischer Ruderclub zu Berlin (Berlin).

**WHYTE, Prof. Moira Katherine Brigid, (Mrs D. C. Crossman)**, OBE 2014; PhD; FRCP, FMedSci, FRSE; Sir John Crofton Professor of Respiratory Medicine, since 2014, Head of Edinburgh Medical School, since 2016, and Vice-Principal and Head of College of Medicine and Veterinary Medicine, since 2018, University of Edinburgh (Director, MRC Centre for Inflammation Research, 2015–18); *b* 25 Sept. 1959; *d* of Maurice and Anne Whyte; *m* 1988, David Christopher Crossman, *qv*; two *s*. *Educ*: Convent of Notre Dame, Plymouth; Plymouth Coll.; St Bartholomew's Hosp. Med. Coll., London (BSc 1st cl. Hons Anatomy 1981; MB BS 1984); Royal Postgraduate Med. Sch., London (PhD 1993). MRCP 1987, FRCP 1997. Jun. med. posts, London, 1984–87; Registrar in Respiratory Medicine, Dept of Medicine, Hammersmith Hosp., 1987–89; MRC Trng Fellow, RPMS, 1989–92; Sen. Registrar in Respiratory Medicine, Hammersmith Hosp., 1992–94; Wellcome Advanced Fellow and Hon. Consultant Physician, Univ. of Nottingham and ICRF, London, 1994–95; University of Sheffield: Prof. of Respiratory Medicine, 1996–2014; Sir George Franklin Prof. of Medicine, 2013–14; Hd, Section of Infection, Inflammation and Immunity, 2006–09; Hd, Dept of Infection and Immunity, 2009–14. Medical Research Council: Mem., Population and Systems Medicine Bd, 2010–14; Chm., Clinical Trng and Career Develt Panel, 2015–, Trng and Careers Gp, 2017–; Mem., Strategy Bd, 2017–. Member: Wellcome Trust Clinical Interest Gp, 1997–2002; Wellcome Trust Physiol Scis Panel, 2002–05. Chm., Scientific Cttee, British Lung Foundn, 2003–06. Mem., Dorothy Hodgkin Grants Panel, Royal Soc., 2006–12. Registrar, Acad. of Med. Scis, 2012–16. FMedSci 2005; FRSE 2018. *Publications*: papers on cell death in inflammation and inflammatory lung disease. *Recreations*: reading, my children's current hobbies. *Address*: MRC Centre for Inflammation Research, University of Edinburgh, Queen's Medical Research Institute, 47 Little France Crescent, Edinburgh EH16 4TJ. *T*: (0131) 242 9313, *Fax*: (0131) 242 6578. *E*: moira.whyte@ed.ac.uk.

**WIBBERLEY, Dr (Edward) John**, FRAgS; Principal, Rural Extension Agriculture Land Management, since 1989; *b* Quarndon, Derbys, 10 May 1947; *s* of Edward and Beatrice Enid Wibberley; *m* 1969, Jane. E. R. Weeks; two *s*. *Educ*: Ecclesbourne Grammar Sch., Duffield, Derbys; Univ. of Reading (BSc Hons Agric.; MSc Soil Microbiol.; MA Comparative Educn; PhD Agricl Extension 1992; Nuffield Scholar, 1988); London Sch. of Theol. (MTh Brunel Univ.); Univ. of Exeter (Cert. Theol.); Coll. of Preceptors, London (DipEd). FRAgS 1987; FRGS 2010. Lectr and Asst Warden, Askham Bryan Coll., York, 1969–70; Hd, Applied Sci., Berks Coll. of Agric., 1970–75; Hd of Agric., Gindiri, N Nigeria, 1975–76; Royal Agricultural College, Cirencester: Lectr, Sen. Lectr, Principal Lectr and Hd of Agric., 1976–89; Coordinator, Cirencester Cereal Study Gp, 1977–89. Visiting Professor: Comparative Agric. and Rural Extension, RAU (formerly RAC), Cirencester, 1999– (Vis. Fellow, 1989–99); Sch. of Agric., Policy and Develt, Univ. of Reading, 2016–; Adjunct Prof., Rural Extension Studies, Univ. of Guelph, Canada, 1995–98; Vis. Fellow, Agricl Extension and Rural Develt, Univ. of Reading, 1994–2004. British Council Diamond Jubilee Public Lect., Freetown, Sierra Leone, 2004; Ralph Melville Meml Lect., Tropical Agric. Assoc., 2010. Presenter, W Country Farming, HTV, 1989–92. Christian Stewardship Advr, Anglican Dio. Exeter and Dio. Portsmouth, 1993–2003. Mem., Area Gp, IoW, Envmt Agency, 1996–99. Coordinator, Steering Gp on Exploration of Professionalism in UK Agric., 2006–08. Sec. of State Appointee, Exmoor Nat. Park Authy, 2008–16; Chm., Exmoor Hill Farm Project, 2009–13; Deputy Chairman: Exmoor Parish and Consultative Forum, 2010–; Planning Cttee, Exmoor Nat. Park, 2013–15; Trustee, Exmoor Soc., 2015–. Member: Council, RASE, 2005–; Adv. Council, Sch. of Agric., Royal Agricl Univ. (formerly RAC), 2005–16; Faculty, Prince of Wales's Summer Sch. on Food and Farming, 2007–. UK Chm., Farm Crisis Network, 1998–2003; Chairman: Rural Issues Gp, IoW, 1999–2003; Devon Farming Community Network, 2014–; UK Agricl Christian Fellowship, 1977–79; Agriculturalist, UK Overseas Develt Cttee and Vice-Chm., Tearfund, 1977–89. Member, Board: African Enterprise, 1995–; Agri-Food Charities Partnership, 2015–17; Coordinator (CEO), Communications Unit for Africa, Rural Develt Counsellors through Christian Churches in Africa, 1996–2013 (Hon. Associate, 2013); UK Coordinator (CEO), Council for Awards of Royal Agricl Socs, 1999–2018. Chm., SW Br., Tropical Agric. Assoc., 2014–19. Chm., Carisbrooke Priory Trust, 1997–2000; Mem. Council, NT, 2014–; Trustee: Bicton Overseas Agricl Trust, 2004–11 (Hon. Associate, 2012); Sir Emrys Jones Meml Trust, 2019–. Mentor, Henry Plumb Foundn, 2012–. Governor: Long Ashton Res. Stn, Univ. of Bristol, 1986–89; Redcliffe Coll., Gloucester, 1997–2009. Trehane Award, Nuffield Farming Scholarships Trust, 1988. *Publications*: (with D. C. Joy) A Tropical Agriculture Handbook, 1979; Spring Wheat, 1984; Cereal Husbandry, 1989; (ed) Farming Fun and Wisdom: notes, quotes and anecdotes, 2001; Cereals, 2006; (contrib.) Just Food?: food and farming for a sustainable future, ed B. Butler, 2017; contrib. chapters in books; contrib. papers to jls incl. Internat. Jl Agricl Mgt. *Recreations*: family, walking, boating, gardening, the arts. *E*: ejwibberley@btinternet.com.

**WIBLIN, Derek John**, CB 1992; Under Secretary, Principal Establishment and Finance Officer, Crown Prosecution Service, 1988–93; *b* 18 March 1933; *s* of late Cyril G. H. Wiblin and of Winifred F. Wiblin; *m* 1960, Pamela Jeanne Hamshere; one *s* one *d*. *Educ*: Birmingham University (BSc Hons Chem. 1954). RAF, 1954–57. Courtaulds Ltd, 1957–58; joined DSIR Building Research Station, 1958; Civil Service Commission, 1967–71; Asst Sec., Local Govt Div., DoE, 1971–79; Ports Div., Dept of Transport, 1979–81; Estabs Div., DoE, 1981–83; Under Sec., Principal Estabt and Finance Officer, Lord Chancellor's Dept, 1984–88. Chm., First Division Pensioners' Gp, 1993–98. *Recreations*: making violins, collecting books. *Address*: 19 Woodwaye, Oxhey, Watford, Herts WD19 4NN. *T*: (01923) 228615. *Clubs*: Athenæum, Royal Air Force.

**WICKENS, Prof. Alan Herbert**, OBE 1980; FREng, FIMechE; Director of Engineering Research and Development, British Rail, 1984–89; *b* 29 March 1929; *s* of late Herbert Leslie Wickens and of Sylvia Wickens; *m* 1st, 1953, Eleanor Joyce Waggott (*d* 1984); one *d*; 2nd, 1987, Patricia Anne McNeil. *Educ*: Ashville Coll., Harrogate; Loughborough Univ. of Technol. (DLC Eng, BScEng London, 1951; DSc Loughborough, 1978). CEng, FIMechE 1971; MRAeS. Res. Engr, Sir W. G. Armstrong Whitworth Aircraft Ltd, Coventry, 1951–55; Gp Leader, Dynamics Analysis, Canadair Ltd, Montreal, 1955–59; Head of Aeroelastics Section, Weapons Res. Div., A. V. Roe & Co., Ltd, Woodford, 1959–62; British Rail: Supt, Res. Dept, 1962–67; Advanced Projs Engr, 1967–68; Dir of Advanced Projs, 1968–71; Dir of Labs, 1971–78; Dir of Research, 1978–84. Loughborough University of Technology: Industrial Prof. of Transport Technol., 1972–76; Prof. of Dynamics, Dept of Mechanical Engrg, 1989–92; Vis. Industrial Prof., Dept of Mech. Engrg, later Wolfson Sch. of Mech. and Manufg Engrg, 1993–2012. Vis. Prof., Dept of Mech. Engrg, Design and Manufacture, Manchester Metropolitan Univ., 1998–2001. Pres., Internat. Assoc. of Vehicle System Dynamics, 1981–86 (Hon. Mem., 2001); Chm., Office of Res. and Experiments, Union Internationale de Chemins de fer, 1988–90. Mem., Amer. Inst. Aeronautics and Astronautics, 1958. FBIS; FRSA. Hon. Fellow, Derbyshire Coll. of Higher Educn, 1984. Hon. DTech: CNAA, 1978; Loughborough, 2006; Hon. Dr Open Univ., 1980. George Stephenson Res. Prize, IMechE, 1966; (jtly) MacRobert Award, 1975. *Publications*: Fundamentals of Rail Vehicle Dynamics, 2003; papers on dynamics of railway vehicles, high speed trains and future railway technology, publ. by IMechE, Amer. Soc. of Mech. Engrs, Internat. Jl of Solids and Structures, and Jl of Vehicle System Dynamics. *Recreations*: gardening, travel, music. *Address*: Ecclesbourne Farmhouse, Ecclesbourne Lane, Idridgehay, Derbys DE56 2SB. *T*: (01773) 550368. *Club*: Royal Air Force.

**WICKER-MIURIN, Fields**, OBE 2007; Partner, Leaders' Quest Ltd, since 2002; *b* 30 July 1958; *d* of Warren Jake Wicker and Marie Peachee Wicker; *m* 1994, Dr Paolo Miurin. *Educ*: Univ. of Virginia (BA *cum laude* Foreign Affairs and French); Institut d'Etudes Politiques, Paris (Cert. d'Etudes Politiques); Johns Hopkins Sch. of Advanced Internat. Studies (MA Econs and Pol Affairs). Vice Pres., Philadelphia Nat. Bank, 1982–89; Partner and Hd Financial Services Practice, Europe, Strategic Planning Associates, 1989–94; Finance Dir and Dir of Strategy, London Stock Exchange, 1994–97; Partner and Vice Pres., Hd Global Financial Markets, AT Kearney, 1998–2000; Chief Operating Officer and Partner, Vesta Capital Advisors Ltd, 2000–02. Non-exec. Dir, 2002–08, Chm. Investment Cttee, 2002–06, BERR (formerly DTI); Member: Technol. Adv. Council, NASDAQ, 2000–04; Panel of Experts, Econ. and Monetary Affairs Cttee, EP, 2002–06; Internat. Adv. Council, Batten Sch. of Leadership, Univ. of Virginia, 2011–16. Non-executive Director: Utd Business Media plc, 1998–2004; Savills plc, 2002–10 (Chm., Audit Cttee, 2003–10); Royal London Gp, 2003–06 (Chm., Investment Cttee, 2003–06); Carnegie & Co. AB, 2003–07; CDC Gp plc, 2004–14 (Chm., Impact Cttee, 2010–14); BNP Paribas, 2011–; Ballarpur Internat. Graphic Paper Hldgs, 2011–16 (Sen. Ind. Dir, 2014–16; Chairman: Nominations Cttee, 2014–16; Remuneration Cttee, 2014–16; Corp. Social Responsibility Cttee, 2014–16); SCOR, 2013– (Chm., Corp. Social Responsibility Cttee, 2017–); SCOR UK, 2017–; Control Risks Gp, 2016–18; Prudential plc, 2018–; non-executive Director: MoJ, 2013–15; DCMS, 2016– (Chm., Audit and Risk Cttee, 2016–). Trustee: London Internat. Fest. of Theatre, 1997–2004; Arts & Business UK, 1998–2001; London Musici, 2000–03; Council, Tate Members, 2000–06; Brogdale Horticultural Trust, 2002–04. Governor, KCL, 2002–11 (Chm., Audit and Risk Cttee, 2002–11). Frequent speaker on leadership. FKC 2010. FRSA 1997. Global Leader for Tomorrow, World Econ. Forum, 1997. *Publications*: numerous articles about leadership and financial innovation. *Recreations*: the open countryside, dressage and training horses, opera, exploring new ideas and ways of seeing the world. *Address*: Leaders' Quest Ltd, 11–13 Worple Way, Richmond, Surrey TW10 6DG. *T*: (020) 8948 5200, *Fax*: (020) 8332 6423. *Clubs*: Athenæum (Mem., Investment Cttee, 2013–19), Lansdowne.

**WICKERSON, Sir John (Michael)**, Kt 1987; Partner, 1962–98, Consultant, 1998–2011, Ormerods (previously Ormerod, Morris & Dumont, later Ormerod Wilkinson Marshall, then Ormerod Heap & Marshall); President, Law Society, 1986–87; *b* 22 Sept. 1937; *s* of Walter and Ruth McKerson; *m* 1963, Shirley Maud Best; one *s*. *Educ*: Christ's Hospital; London University (LLB). Admitted solicitor, 1960; Mem. Council, Law Society, 1969 (Chm., Contentious Business Cttee; Vice-Pres., 1985–86). Member: Matrimonial Causes Rules Cttee, 1982–86; Royal Commn on Criminal Justice, 1991–93. Pres., London Criminal Courts Solicitors Assoc., 1980–81. Chairman: Mansell plc (formerly R. Mansell Ltd), 1994–2002; Investors' Compensation Scheme Ltd, 1996–2001; United Healthcare (Farnborough Hospital) Ltd, 2000–15; Hospital Co. (Darenth) Ltd, 2001–; Hospital Co. (Swindon and Marlborough) Ltd, 2002–11; Meridian Hospital Co. plc, 2013–. Chm., Croydon Community NHS Trust, 1991–98. Hon. Member: Amer. Bar Assoc., 1986; Canadian Bar Assoc., 1986; NZ Law Soc., 1987. *Publications*: Motorist and the Law, 1975, 2nd edn 1982. *Recreation*: golf. *Address*: 26 Eglise Road, Warlingham, Surrey CR6 9SE. *T*: (01883) 622126.

**WICKES, Charles G.**; see Goodson-Wickes.

**WICKHAM, Prof. Christopher John**, DPhil; FBA 1998; Chichele Professor of Medieval History, University of Oxford, 2005–16 (Chair, Faculty of History, 2009–12; Head, Humanities Division, 2015–16); Fellow of All Souls College, Oxford, 2005–16, now Emeritus; *b* 18 May 1950; *s* of Cyril George Wickham and Katharine Brenda Warington Wickham (*née* Moss); *m* 1990, Prof. Leslie Brubaker. *Educ*: Millfield Sch.; Keble Coll., Oxford (BA 1971; DPhil 1975). University of Birmingham: Lectr, 1977–87; Sen. Lectr, 1987–89; Reader, 1989–93; Prof. of Early Medieval History, 1993–2005. Mem., AHRC, 2018–. Jt Ed., Past & Present, 1994–2009. *Publications*: Early Medieval Italy, 1981; The mountains and the city, 1988; (with J. Fentress) Social memory, 1992; Land and power, 1994; Community and Clientele, 1998 (Italian edn 1995); Courts and Conflict, 2003

**WICKHAM, Daphne Elizabeth, (Mrs J. K. A. Alderson);** a District Judge (Magistrates' Courts) (formerly Metropolitan Stipendiary Magistrate), 1989–2012; a Recorder, 1997–2012; Deputy Chief Magistrate and Deputy Senior District Judge (Magistrates' Courts), 2003–12; b 31 Aug. 1946; d of late Major Harry Temple Wickham and Phyllis Wickham (née Roycroft); m 1983, John Keith Ameers Alderson. Educ: Sydenham High Sch.; Chislehurst and Sidcup Girls' Grammar School. Called to the Bar, Inner Temple, 1967. Recreation: laughter. Address: Chief Magistrate's Office, Westminster Magistrates' Court, 181 Marylebone Road, NW1 5BR. Club: Reform.

**WICKHAM, David Ian;** Director, Singlehurst Consulting Ltd, since 2003; Chairman, Mhub Ltd, 2011; b 23 Oct. 1957; s of Edwin and Betty Wickham; m 1982, Joanne Frances Carter; two s. Educ: St Olave's Grammar Sch., Orpington; S London Coll. (HND Business Studies). Various develt roles in UK, Europe and S Pacific to 1985; Mktg Dir, C&W Systems Ltd, Hong Kong, 1985–87; Mercury Communications Ltd: Gen. Manager, Residential and Operator Services, 1987–91; Mktg Dir, Business and Consumer Services, 1991–94; Man. Dir, Partner Services, 1994–96; Ops Dir, 1996–97; Man. Dir, Internat. and Partner Services, Cable & Wireless Communications Ltd, 1997–98; Chief Exec., Global Network, Cable and Wireless plc, 1998–99; Energis plc: Chief Operating Officer, 1999–2001; Chief Exec., 2001–02; Dep. Chief Exec., 2002; CEO, Vtesse Networks Ltd, 2012–14. Chairman: Telecom Direct Ltd, 2003–08; 3c plc, 2004–06; YAC Ltd, 2005–06 (non-exec. Dir, 2003–04, 2006–07); Synchronica plc, 2006–08. Recreations: golf, theatre, family, travel. Club: London Golf.

**WICKHAM, Janie;** see Dee, J.

**WICKHAM, Rt Rev. Robert James;** see Edmonton, Area Bishop of.

**WICKRAMASINGHE, Prof. (Nalin) Chandra,** PhD, ScD; Professor, 2000–10 and 2011–14, and Emeritus Professor of Applied Mathematics and Astronomy, since 2006, Cardiff University; Director, Buckingham Centre for Astrobiology, and Hon. Professor, University of Buckingham, since 2011 (Director, Cardiff Centre for Astrobiology, 2000–10); Hon. Professor, Sir John Kotelawala Defence University, since 2017; Hon. Professor and Director, Sri Lanka Centre for Astrobiology, University of Ruhuna, since 2017; b 20 Jan. 1939; s of Percival Herbert Wickramasinghe and Theresa Elizabeth Wickramasinghe; m 1966, Nelum Priyadarshini Pereira; one s two d. Educ: Royal Coll., Colombo, Sri Lanka; Univ. of Ceylon (BSc); Univ. of Cambridge (MA, PhD, ScD). Commonwealth Scholar, Trinity Coll., Cambridge, 1960; Powell Prize for English Verse, 1961; Jesus College, Cambridge: Research Fellow, 1963–66; Fellow, 1967–73; Tutor, 1970–73; Staff Mem., Inst. of Theoretical Astronomy, Univ. of Cambridge, 1968–73; Prof. and Hd of Dept of Applied Maths and Astronomy, UC, Cardiff, 1973–88; Prof., Sch. of Maths, UWCC, subseq. Cardiff Univ., 1988–2000. Visiting Professor: Vidyodaya Univ. of Ceylon, Univ. of Maryland, USA, Univ. of Arizona, USA, Univ. of Kyoto, Japan, 1966–70; Univ. of W Ontario, 1974, 1976; Inst. of Space and Astronautical Studies, Japan, 1993; Univ. of WI, Kingston, Jamaica, 1994; Peradeniya Univ., Sri Lanka, 2014; Vis. Fellow, Churchill Coll., Cambridge, 2015–16. UNDP Cons. and Scientific Advisor to President of Sri Lanka, 1970–81; Dir, Inst. of Fundamental Studies, Sri Lanka, 1982–83 (Vis. Prof., 1997–). Collaborator with Prof. Sir Fred Hoyle, and propounder with Hoyle of the theory of the space origin of life and of microorganisms. Hon. Prof., Glamorgan Univ., 2007. Hon. DSc: Soka Univ., Japan, 1996; Ruhuna Univ., Sri Lanka, 2004. Dag Hammarskjöld Gold Medal in science, Académie Diplomatique de la Paix, 1986; Scholarly Achievement Award, Inst. of Oriental Philosophy, Japan, 1989; Internat. Peace and Culture Award, Soka Gakkai, 1993; Sahabdeen Internat. Award for Science, A. M. M. Sahabdeen Trust Foundn, 1996; John Snow Lecture Medal, Assoc. of Anaesthetists of GB and Ire., 2004. Vidya Jyothi (Sri Lanka), 1992. Publications: Interstellar Grains, 1967; (with F. D. Kahn and P. G. Mezger) Interstellar Matter, 1972; Light Scattering Functions for Small Particles with Applications in Astronomy, 1973; The Cosmic Laboratory, 1975; (with D. J. Morgan) Solid State Astrophysics, 1976; Fundamental Studies and the Future of Science, 1984; (with F. Hoyle and J. Watkins) Viruses from Space, 1986; (with Daisaku Ikeda) Emergent Perspectives for 2000 AD, 1992; (with D. Ikeda) The Wonders of Life and the Universe, 1993; Glimpses of Life, Time and Space: an anthology of poetry, 1994; Cosmic Dragons: life and death of our planet, 2001; A Journey with Fred Hoyle, 2005, 2nd edn 2013; Quest for the Origins of Life, 2014; A Destiny of Cosmic Life: chapters in the life of an astrobiologist, 2014; (with F. Hoyle): Lifecloud: the origin of life in the universe, 1978; Diseases From Space, 1979; The Origin of Life, 1980; Evolution From Space, 1981; Space Travellers, the Bringers of Life, 1981; From Grains to Bacteria, 1984; Living Comets, 1985; Archaeopteryx, the Primordial Bird: a case of fossil forgery, 1986; Cosmic Life Force, 1987; Theory of Cosmic Grains, 1991; Our Place in the Cosmos: the unfinished revolution, 1993; Life on Mars?: the case for a cosmic heritage, 1997; (with F. Hoyle) Astronomical Origins of Life: steps towards panspermia, 2000; (with J. T. Wickramasinghe and W. M. Napier) Comets and the Origin of Life, 2010; The Search for Our Cosmic Ancestry, 2015; Where Did We Come From? Life of an astrobiologist, 2015; Vindication of Cosmic Biology, 2015; (with Theodore Walker, Jr) The Big Bang and God: an astrotheology, 2015; (with Robert Bauval) Cosmic Womb, 2017; (with K. Wickramasinghe and Gensuke Tokoro) Our Cosmic Ancestry in the Stars: the panspermia revolution and the origins of humanity, 2019; over 300 articles and papers in astronomical and scientific jls; contributor to anthologies of Commonwealth Poetry, incl. Young Commonwealth Poets '65, ed P. L. Brent, 1965. Recreations: photography, poetry—both writing and reading, history and philosophy of science. Address: 24 Llwyn Y Pia Road, Lisvane, Cardiff CF14 0SY. E: ncwick@gmail.com.

**WICKREMESINGHE, Sarath Kusum;** Chairman, 2008–09, Adviser to the Board, since 2012, Senkadagala Finance Company Ltd, Colombo; b 26 Jan. 1928; m 1953, Damayantha Hulugalle (d 2011). Educ: St Thomas' Coll., Mt Lavinia; Univ. of Ceylon (BSc Hons Physics). Exec. in ICI (Export) Ltd, Colombo, 1951–66; Chief Exec., 1966–80, Chm., 1966–94, ICI associate co. in Sri Lanka; Chm., subsid. and associate cos, Coates Internat., 1982–84, BAT, 1985–91, and Standard Chartered Bank, 1989–94; High Comr for Sri Lanka in London, 1995–99; Chairman: Sri Lankan Airlines Ltd, 1999–2002; National Development Bank Ltd, Colombo, 1999–2008. Address: 8 Claessen Place, Colombo 5, Sri Lanka. Club: Sri Lanka Turf.

**WICKS, Geoffrey Leonard;** a District Judge (Magistrates' Courts) (formerly Metropolitan Stipendiary Magistrate), 1987–2002 (a Deputy District Judge (Magistrates' Courts), 2002–09); Immigration Adjudicator (part-time), 1996–2003; b 23 July 1934; s of late Leonard James Wicks and Winifred Ellen Wicks; m 1st, 1959, Catherine Margaret Shanks (marr. diss. 1977); one s one d; 2nd, 1978, Maureen Evelyn Neville (d 2012); 3rd, 2018, Maureen Ann Ingram. Educ: Tollington Sch., N10; Law Society's Sch. of Law, London. Admitted Solicitor, 1957. National Service, 1957–59. Asst Solicitor, LCC, 1959–60; Asst Solicitor, 1960–61, Partner, 1961–79 (Abu Dhabi office, 1978), Oswald Hickson, Collier & Co., Solicitors, London, Chesham, Amersham, Slough; Principal, Geoffrey Wicks & Co., Solicitors, Chesham, Hemel Hempstead, 1979–82; Partner, Iliffes, Solicitors, London, Chesham, 1982–87. Chairman: Family Courts, 1991–97; Youth Courts, 1991–2002; Mem., Inner London Magistrates' Courts Cttee, 1995–99, 2000–01. Mem., Home Sec.'s Task Force for Youth Justice, 1997–98. Ind. Adjudicator (pt time), HM Prisons, 2002–09. Member: Chesham Round Table, 1962–75 (Chm. 1968–69, Area Chm. Area 42, 1972–73); Chesham Rotary Club, 1974–77. Recreations: opera, ballet. Address: c/o Chief Magistrate's Office, Westminster Magistrates' Court, 181 Marylebone Road, NW1 5BR.

**WICKS, Joanne;** QC 2010; b Thornbury, 25 April 1967; d of David James Wicks and Sheila Esther Wicks; m 1997, John Whitehead; two s. Educ: Cotham Grammar Sch., Bristol; W Bridgford Comprehensive Sch., Nottingham; Hertford Coll., Oxford (BA 1st Cl. Hons Juris.; BCL). Called to the Bar, Lincoln's Inn, 1990; in practice as barrister (self-employed), specialising in chancery commercial work, esp. property litigation and professional negligence, 17 Old Bldgs, Lincoln's Inn, 1990–97, Wilberforce Chambers, Lincoln's Inn, 1997–. Publications: (ed) Butterworth's Property Law Handbook, 7th edn 2007 to 9th edn 2011. Recreation: chatting. Address: Wilberforce Chambers, 8 New Square, Lincoln's Inn, WC2A 3QP. T: (020) 7306 0102, Fax: (020) 7306 0095. E: jwicks@wilberforce.co.uk.

**WICKS, Sir Nigel (Leonard),** GCB 1999 (KCB 1992); CVO 1989; CBE 1979; Chairman, BBA, 2012–15; non-executive Director, Edinburgh Investment Trust plc, 2005–19; b 16 June 1940; s of late Leonard Charles and Beatrice Irene Wicks; m 1969, Jennifer Mary (née Coveney) three s. Educ: Beckenham and Penge Grammar Sch.; Portsmouth Coll. of Technology; Univ. of Cambridge (MA); Univ. of London (MA). The British Petroleum Co. Ltd, 1958–68; HM Treasury, 1968–75; Private Sec. to the Prime Minister, 1975–78; HM Treasury, 1978–83; Economic Minister, British Embassy, Washington, and UK Exec. Dir, IMF and IBRD, 1983–85; Principal Private Sec. to the Prime Minister, 1985–88; Second Perm. Sec. (Finance), HM Treasury, 1989–2000. Chm., CRESTCo, 2001–02; Dep. Chm., 2002–06, Chm., 2006–12, Euroclear plc; Mem. Bd, BNOC, 1980–82; non-exec. Dir, Morgan Stanley Bank Internat. Ltd, 2004–06. Comr, Jersey Financial Services Commn, 2007–12. Chairman: Cttee on Standards in Public Life, 2001–04; Scrutiny Cttee, Actuarial Profession, 2004–06; Selection Panel for Appts, Judicial Appts Commn, 2005–06. Gov., King's Coll. Sch., Wimbledon, 1993–2005. Hon. LLD: Bath, 1999; Portsmouth, 2002.

**WICKSTEAD, Myles Antony,** CBE 2006; Visiting Professor of International Relations, King's College London, since 2015; Hon. Associate Professor, University of Exeter, since 2015; b 7 Feb. 1951; s of John Horace Wickstead and Eva Mary Wickstead (née Fouracre); m 1990, Shelagh Paterson; one s one d. Educ: Blundell's Sch.; St Andrews Univ. (MA 1st Cl. Hons Eng. Lang. and Lit. 1974); New Coll., Oxford (MLitt). Joined ODM, 1976; Asst Private Sec. to Lord Privy Seal, FCO, 1979–80; Asst to UK Exec. Dir, IMF/IBRD, 1980–84; Principal, ODA, 1984–88; Private Sec. to Minister for Overseas Develt, 1988–90; Head: EC and Food Aid Dept, ODA, 1990–93; British Develt Div. in Eastern Africa, 1993–97; UK Alternate Exec. Dir, World Bank, and Counsellor (Develt), Washington, 1997–2000; Ambassador to Ethiopia and (non-res.) to Djibouti, 2000–04; Hd of Secretariat, Commn for Africa, 2004–05. Vis. Prof., Internat. Relns, Open Univ., 2005–15. Specialist Advr, Internat. Develt Select Cttee, 2010–13. Chm. Bd, One World Media, 2009–14; Member: Adv. Council, Wilton Park, 2006–19; Council, Baring Foundn, 2007–18; Comic Relief Internat. Grants Cttee, 2008–13; Bd, Internat. Inspiration, 2009–17; Bd, Enterprise for Develt, 2014–17; Bd, Royal African Soc., 2019–; Gov., Westminster Foundn for Democracy, 2006–12. Chm., Joffe Charitable Trust, 2018–. Hon. DEd Leeds Metropolitan, 2009; DUniv Open, 2011; Hon. DLitt Ulster, 2011. Address: The Manor House, Great Street, Norton sub Hamdon, Som TA14 6SJ. T: (01935) 881385. Club: Muthaiga (Nairobi).

**WICKSTEED, Elisabeth Helen,** Clerk to City Livery Club, since 2014; b 24 June 1964; d of late Andrew and of Monica Hutchinson; m 2001, Michael Wicksteed. Educ: Univ. of York (BA Hons). Lord Chancellor's Dept, 1987–98; Private Sec. to Lord Chancellor, 1997–98; Dep. Sec., Sierra Leone Arms Investigation, June–July 1998; Econ. and Domestic Secretariat, 1998–2002, Legislative Prog. Manager, 2000–02, Cabinet Office; Home Office: Hd, Crime Reduction Progs and Partnership Unit, subseq. Asst Dir, Crime Reduction Delivery Team, 2002–04; Hd, Violent Crime Unit, 2004–06; Hd, HR Strategy and Policy, 2006–07; Institute of Cancer Research: Registry Officer, 2008–09; Quality, Governance and Events Manager, subseq. Quality and Governance Manager, 2009–11; Asst Dir, Academic Services (Quality and Governance), 2011–13; Asst Dir and Hd of Registry, 2013–14. Temp. Project Officer, Victoria Univ. of Wellington, NZ, 2018. Volunteer performer, Opening Ceremony, Olympic Games, London, 2012. Publications: (ed) Private Ire, 2007; (ed) The Brithdays Book, 2009. Address: City Livery Club, Bell Wharf lane, EC4R 3TB.

**WIDDECOMBE, Rt Hon. Ann (Noreen);** PC 1997; writer and broadcaster; Member (Brexit) South West Region, European Parliament, since 2019; b 4 Oct. 1947; d of late James Murray Widdecombe, CB, OBE and Rita Noreen (née Plummer). Educ: La Sainte Union Convent, Bath; Univ. of Birmingham; Lady Margaret Hall, Oxford (BA Hons, MA). Marketing, Unilever, 1973–75; Senior Administrator, Univ. of London, 1975–87. Contested (C): Burnley, 1979; Plymouth, Devonport, 1983. MP (C) Maidstone, 1987–97, Maidstone and The Weald, 1997–2010. PPS to Tristan Garel-Jones, MP, Nov. 1990; Parly Under-Sec. of State, DSS, 1990–93, Dept of Employment, 1993–94; Minister of State: Dept of Employment, 1994–95; Home Office, 1995–97; Shadow Sec. of State for Health, 1998–99; Shadow Home Sec., 1999–2001. Hon. Fellow, Canterbury Christ Church Univ., 2009. DUniv Birmingham, 2012. Dame, Order of St Gregory the Great (Holy See), 2013. Publications: Layman's Guide to Defence, 1984; Strictly Ann (memoir), 2013; Sackcloth and Ashes, 2013; novels: The Clematis Tree, 2000; An Act of Treachery, 2002; Father Figure, 2005; An Act of Peace, 2005; The Dancing Detective, 2014. Recreations: reading, researching Charles II's escape, walking. Address: Widdecombe's Rest, Haytor, Newton Abbot, Devon TQ13 9XT. T: (01364) 661154.

**WIDDICOMBE, David Graham;** QC 1965; a Recorder, 1985–96; a Deputy High Court Judge, 1983–96; b 7 Jan. 1924; s of Aubrey Guy Widdicombe and Margaret (née Puddy); m 1961, Anastasia Cecilia (née Leech) (marr. diss. 1983); two s one d. Educ: St Albans Sch.; Queens' Coll., Cambridge (BA 1st cl. Hons; LLB 1st cl. Hons; MA). Called to the Bar, Inner Temple, 1950, Bencher, 1973; Attorney at Law, State Bar of California, 1986; retired from legal practice, 2004. Mem., Cttee on Local Govt Rules of Conduct, 1973–74; Chairman: Oxfordshire Structure Plan Examination in Public, 1977; Cttee of Inquiry into Conduct of Local Authority Business, 1985–86. Publications: (ed) Ryde on Rating, 1968–83. Address: 5 Albert Terrace, NW1 7SU. T: (020) 7586 5209. Club: Athenæum.

**WIDDIS, Hugh;** Departmental Solicitor and Head of Government Legal Service for Northern Ireland, since 2015; b St Albans, Herts, 9 July 1970; s of Dr T. Widdis and M. K. F. Widdis; m 2002, Briony M. R. Crozier; one s two d. Educ: St Michael's Coll., Dublin; University Coll. Dublin (BCL 1991); Queen's Univ. Belfast (LLM 2009). Called to the Bar: King's Inns, Dublin, 1993; Inn of Court of NI, 1994; in practice as barrister, NI, 1994–98; Legal Advr, CGU Insce, 1999–2000; Northern Ireland Assembly: res. officer, 2000–02; Legal Advr, 2002–07; Dir, Legal Services, 2007–15; Permanent Sec., Dept of Finance, NI,

2017–18. Ind. Mem., Audit and Risk Cttee, Nat. Assembly for Wales, 2013–. Gov., Banbridge Acad., 2014–. *Recreations:* family, mountains, trees. *Address:* Departmental Solicitor's Office, Victoria Hall, 12 May Street, Belfast BT1 4NL. *T:* (028) 9025 1221. *E:* hugh.widdis@finance-ni.gov.uk.

**WIDDOWSON, Prof. Henry George;** Professor of English Linguistics, University of Vienna, 1998–2001, now Hon. Professor; *b* 28 May 1935; *s* of George Percival Widdowson and Edna Widdowson; *m* 1st, 1966, Dominique Dixmier (marr. diss.); two *s*; 2nd, 1997, Barbara Seidlhofer. *Educ:* Alderman Newton's Sch., Leicester; King's Coll., Cambridge (MA); Univ. of Edinburgh (PhD). Lectr, Univ. of Indonesia, 1958–61; British Council Educn Officer, Sri Lanka, 1962–63; British Council English Language Officer, Bangladesh, 1963–64, 1965–68; Lectr, Dept of Linguistics, Univ. of Edinburgh, 1968–77; Prof. of Educn, Univ. of London, at Inst. of Educn, 1977–2000, now Prof. Emeritus; Prof. of Applied Linguistics, Univ. of Essex, 1993–98. Chm., English Teaching Adv. Cttee, British Council, 1982–91; Mem., Kingman Cttee of Inquiry into Teaching of English Language, 1986–88. Advr for Applied Linguistics, OUP, 1978–2008. Editor, Jl of Applied Linguistics, 1980–85. Dr *hc* Oulu, 1994; Lorraine, 2012; Salento, 2016. Cross of Honour (1st Cl.) for Sci. and Art (Austria), 2015. *Publications:* Stylistics and the Teaching of Literature, 1975 (Japanese edn 1989); Teaching Language as Communication, 1978 (French edn 1981, Ital. edn 1982, Japanese edn 1991); Explorations in Applied Linguistics I, 1979; Learning Purpose and Language Use, 1983 (Italian edn 1986); Explorations in Applied Linguistics II, 1984; (with Randolph Quirk) English in the World, 1985; Aspects of Language Teaching, 1990; Practical Stylistics, 1992 (Japanese edn 2004); Linguistics, 1996 (Korean edn 2000); Defining Issues in English Language Teaching, 2003; Text, Context, Pretext, 2004; Discourse Analysis, 2007; Selected Works on Applied Linguistics, 2009; editor of series: English in Focus; Communicative Grammar; Language Teaching: a scheme for teacher education; Oxford Introductions to Language Study; numerous book chapters, encyclopedia entries, papers in various jls. *Recreations:* poetry, gardening, bird-watching. *Address:* Institut für Anglistik, Universität Wien, Universitätcampus AAKH/Hof 8, Spitalgasse 2–4, 1090 Vienna, Austria. *T:* (1) 3197268.

**WIDE, His Honour Charles Thomas;** QC 1995; a Circuit Judge, 2001–11; a Senior Circuit Judge, 2011–16; *b* 16 April 1951; *s* of late Nicholas Scott Wide, MC, and of Ruth Mildred Norton Wide; *m* 1979, Hon. Ursula Margaret Bridget Buchan, *qv*; one *s* one *d*. *Educ:* The Leys Sch., Cambridge; Exeter Univ. (LLB); Wolfson Coll., Cambridge (Adv. Dip. Theol.). Called to the Bar, Inner Temple, 1974, Bencher, 2010; Midland and Oxford Circuit Junior, 1983; Standing Counsel to: HM Customs and Excise (Crime), 1989–95; Inland Revenue (Crime), 1991–95; Asst Recorder, 1991–95; Recorder, 1995–2001; Resident Judge, Northampton, 2003–11. Mem., Criminal Procedure Rule Cttee, 2004–12. Reader, Dio. of Peterborough, 2007–. *Recreation:* fell walking.

**WIDE, Hon. Ursula Margaret Bridget;** *see* Buchan, Hon. U. M. B.

**WIEMAN, Prof. Carl Edwin,** PhD; Professor of Physics, Stanford University, since 2013; *b* Oregon, 26 March 1951; *s* of N. Orr Wieman and Alison Wieman; *m* 1984, Sarah Gilbert. *Educ:* MIT (BS 1973); Stanford Univ. (PhD 1977). Asst Res. Scientist, Dept of Physics, 1977–79, Asst Prof. of Physics, 1979–84, Univ. of Michigan; University of Colorado, Boulder: Associate Prof., 1984–87, Prof., 1987–97, Distinguished Prof., 1997–2013, of Physics; Dir, Sci. Educn Initiative, 2006–13; Fellow, Jt Inst. for Lab. Astrophysics, Boulder, 1985 (Chm., 1993–95); Prof. of Physics and Dir, Carl Wieman Sci. Educn Initiative, UBC, 2007–13. Associate Dir for Sci., Office of Sci. and Technol. Policy, Exec. Office of Pres. of USA, 2010–12. (Jtly) Nobel Prize for Physics, 2001. *Publications:* Improving How Universities Teach Science, 2017. *Address:* Department of Physics, 382 Via Pueblo Mall, Stanford University, Stanford, CA 94305-4060, USA.

**WIENER, Elizabeth Anne, (Libby);** Political Correspondent, ITN, since 2003; *b* Stockton-on-Tees, 2 March 1959; *d* of late Hans Wiener and of Irene Wiener; *m* 1995, Dr Bruce Kirkham; one *s* two *d*, and one step *s*. *Educ:* Hendon Sch.; Univ. of Leeds (BA Hons Hist. 1981); Centre for Journalism Studies, Cardiff (Postgrad. Dip. Journalism 1982). Reporter, Southern Evening Echo, Southampton, 1982–85; producer, BBC TV South, 1985–87; ITN: producer, 1987–88; Home Affairs Corresp., 1988–91; Europe Corresp., 1991–94; Australia Corresp., 1995–2000; Royal Corresp., 2000–02. *Recreations:* reading, art, theatre, swimming, ski-ing, travelling to the antipodes. *Address:* ITN, Press Gallery, House of Commons, SW1A 0AA. *T:* (020) 7430 4990. *E:* libby.wiener@itn.co.uk.

**WIESCHAUS, Prof. Eric Francis,** PhD; Professor of Molecular Biology, since 1987, and Squibb Professor, since 1993, Princeton University; *b* 8 June 1947; *s* of Leroy Wieschaus and Marcella Wieschaus (*née* Carner); *m* 1983, Trudi Schüpbach; three *d*. *Educ:* Univ. of Notre Dame, Indiana (BS 1969); Yale Univ. (PhD 1974); Univ. of Zürich. Postdoctoral Fellow, Zool. Inst., Univ. of Zürich, 1975–78; EMBO Fellowship, France, 1976; Vis. Researcher, Center of Pathology, Univ. of California, Irvine, 1977; Group Leader, EMBL, Heidelberg, 1978–81; Asst Prof., 1981–83, and Associate Prof., 1983–87, Princeton Univ. Fellow, Amer. Acad. of Arts and Scis; Mem., Nat. Acad. of Scis. Awards include: John Spangler Niclaus Prize, Yale, 1974; NIHHD Merit Award, 1989; Nobel Prize in Physiology or Medicine (jtly), 1995. *Publications:* From Molecular Patterns to Morphogenesis: the lessons from Drosophila, in the Nobel Prize 1995 (ed T. Fransmyr), 1996; numerous contribs to Jl of Cell Biology and other sci. jls. *Address:* Department of Molecular Biology, Princeton University, Washington Road, Princeton, NJ 08544, USA.

**WIESEL, Prof. Torsten Nils,** MD; Secretary-General, Human Frontier Science Program, 2000–09; Vincent & Brooke Astor Professor and Head of Laboratory of Neurobiology, 1983–98, and President, 1991–98, now Emeritus, Rockefeller University; *b* 3 June 1924; *s* of Fritz S. Wiesel and Anna-Lisa Wiesel (*née* Bentzer); *m* 1st, 1956, Teeri Stenhammar (marr. diss. 1981); 2nd, 1973, Ann Yee (marr. diss. 1981); one *d*; 3rd, 1995, Jean Stein; *m* 2008, Lizette Mususa Reyes. *Educ:* Karolinska Inst., Stockholm (MD 1954). Instructor, Dept of Physiol., Karolinska Inst., 1954–55; Asst, Dept of Child Psychiatry, Karolinska Hosp., Stockholm, 1954–55; Fellow in Ophthalmol., 1955–58, Asst Prof. of Ophthalmic Physiol., 1958–59, Johns Hopkins Univ. Med. Sch.; Harvard Medical School: Associate in Neurophysiol. and Neuropharmacol., 1959–60; Asst Prof., 1960–67; Prof. of Physiol., 1967–68; Prof. of Neurobiol., 1968–74; Chm., Dept of Neurobiol., 1973–82; Robert Winthrop Prof. of Neurobiol., 1974–83. Dir, Leon Levy and Shelby White Center for Mind, Brain & Behavior, Rockefeller Univ., 1999–. Scientific Advr, Bristol Myers-Squibb Corp. Lectures: Ferrier, Royal Soc., 1972; Grass, Soc. for Neurosci., 1976. Co-Chm., Bd of Govs, Okinawa Inst. of Sci. and Technol., 2002–. Member: Amer. Physiol Soc.; AAAS; Amer. Acad. of Arts and Scis; Amer. Philosophical Soc.; Soc. for Neurosci (Pres. 1978–79); Nat. Acad. of Scis; Swedish Physiol Soc.; Harvard Bd of Overseers; Foreign Mem., Royal Soc., 1982; Hon. Mem., Physiolog. Soc., 1982. Has received hon. degrees from univs in Sweden, Norway, Italy and USA. Awards and Prizes: Dr Jules C. Stein, Trustees for Research to Prevent Blindness, 1971; Lewis S. Rosenstiel, Brandeis Univ., 1972; Friedenwald, Assoc. for Res. in Vision and Ophthalmology, 1975; Karl Spencer Lashley, Amer. Phil. Soc., 1977; Louisa Gross Horwitz, Columbia Univ., 1978; Dickson, Pittsburgh Univ., 1979; Ledlie, Harvard Univ., 1980; Soc. for Scholars, Johns Hopkins Univ., 1980; Nobel Prize in Physiology or Medicine, 1981; US Nat. Medal of Science, 2005. *Publications:* (contrib.) Physiological and Biochemical Aspects of Nervous Integration, 1968; (contrib.) The Organization of the Cerebral Cortex, 1981; (with David Hubel) Brain and Visual Perception: the story of a 25 year collaboration, 2004; contribs to professional jls, symposia and trans of learned socs. *Address:* Rockefeller University, 1230 York Avenue, New York, NY 10065, USA. *T:* (212) 3277093. *Club:* Harvard (Boston).

**WIGAN, (Desmond Patrick) Neil,** OBE 2016; HM Diplomatic Service; Ambassador to Israel, since 2019; *m* Yael Banaji; one *s* one *d*. *Educ:* Univ. of Oxford (BA Hist.); Univ. of London (MSc Econs); Sch. of Advanced Internat. Studies, Johns Hopkins Univ. (Postgrad. Dip.). Entered FCO, 2000; Desk Officer, EU Econ. Policy, EU Dept (Internal), FCO, 2000–02; Head: Political Section, Tel Aviv, 2002–06; Arab Israel and N Africa Gp, FCO, 2006–08; Dep. Dir for Wider World, Foreign and Defence Policy Secretariat, Cabinet Office, 2008–09; Ambassador to Democratic Rep. of Congo and Rep. of Congo, 2010–13; Ambassador (non-resident) to Somalia, 2013–15; Dir, Africa, FCO, 2016–19. *Address:* c/o Foreign and Commonwealth Office, King Charles Street, SW1A 2AH.

**WIGAN, Sir Michael (Iain),** 6th Bt *cr* 1898, of Clare Lawn, Mortlake, Surrey and Purland Chase, Ross, Herefordshire; journalist and author; *b* 3 Oct. 1951; *s* of Sir Alan Lewis Wigan, 5th Bt, and of Robina, 2nd *d* of Sir Iain Colquhoun of Luss, 7th Bt, KT, DSO; *S* father, 1996; one *s* by Lady Alexandra Hay; *m* 1989, Julia Teresa, *d* of late John de Courcy Ling, CBE; three *s* one *d*. *Educ:* Eton; Exeter Coll., Oxford. *Publications:* The Scottish Highland Estate: preserving an environment, 1991; Stag at Bay, 1993; The Last of the Hunter Gatherers, 1998; Grimersta: the story of a great fishery, 2001; The Salmon: the extraordinary story of the king of fish, 2013. *Recreations:* deer stalking, fishing, literature. *Heir:* *s* Fergus Adam Wigan, *b* 30 April 1990. *Address:* Borrobol, Kinbrace, Sutherland KW11 6UB. *T:* (01431) 831264.

**WIGAN, Neil;** *see* Wigan, D. P. N.

**WIGAN AND WEST LANCASHIRE, Archdeacon of;** *see* McKenzie, Ven. J. G.

**WIGDORTZ, Brett Harris,** OBE 2013; Founder and Chief Executive Officer, Tiney, since 2018; *b* New Jersey, USA, 9 Oct. 1973; *s* of Larry Wigdortz and Judith Wigdortz; *m* 2005, Nicole Jacobs; one *s* two *d*. *Educ:* Univ. of Richmond (BA Econs); Univ. of Hawaii (MA Econs). Researcher, East-West Center, Honolulu, 1995–97; freelance journalist, 1998–99; Mgt Consultant, McKinsey & Co., Indonesia, Singapore and the Philippines, 2000–02; Founder and CEO, Teach First, 2002–17, now Hon.; Pres. Co-Founder and Dep. CEO, Teach for All, 2007–10. Chair, Nat. Citizen Service Trust, 2018–. Hon. LLD: Warwick, 2016; Birmingham City, 2017. *Publications:* Success Against the Odds, 2012. *Recreations:* family and friends, sailing, travelling, youth football team coaching. *Address:* 53 Fortis Green, N2 9JJ.

**WIGFIELD, Timothy B.;** *see* Byram-Wigfield.

**WIGGHAM, Hon. (Edward) Barrie,** CBE 1991; JP; Hong Kong Commissioner, USA, 1993–97; *b* 1 March 1937; *s* of Edward and Agnes Wiggham; *m* 1961, Mavis Mitson (*d* 2003); two *d* (one *s* decd). *Educ:* Woking Grammar Sch.; Queen's Coll., Oxford (MA Mod. Langs). Hong Kong Government: Admin. Officer, 1961–63; Dist Officer, New Territories, 1963–71; postings in finance, econ., security and information branches, 1971–79; Comr for Recreation and Culture, 1979–83; Regl Sec., 1983–86; seconded to British Embassy, Peking, 1986; Sec., General Duties, 1986–90; Mem. Gov's Exec. Council, 1989–92; Sec. for CS, 1990–93. JP Hong Kong, 1973. *Recreations:* music, people. *Address:* Cefn Mably Lodge, Old St Mellons, Cardiff CF3 6LP. *Clubs:* Hong Kong, Foreign Correspondents'; George Town, National Press (Washington).

**WIGGIN, Sir Richard Edward John,** 6th Bt *cr* 1892, of Metchley Grange, Harborne, Staffs; *b* Guildford, 1 July 1980; *o s* of Sir Charles Rupert John Wiggin, 5th Bt and Mary Burnett-Hitchcock (*née* Chambers); *S* father, 2012; *m* 2013, Phillipa Helen Bean; one *d*. *Educ:* Harrow Sch. *Heir:* *uncle* Benjamin Henry Edward Wiggin, *b* 23 Aug. 1951. *Address:* Honington Hall, Shipston-on-Stour, Warwickshire CV36 5AA.

**WIGGIN, William David;** MP (C) North Herefordshire, since 2010 (Leominster, 2001–10); *b* 4 June 1966; *s* of Sir Alfred William, (Jerry), Wiggin, TD and of Rosemary Janet (*née* Orr, now Dale Harris); *m* 1999, Camilla Chilvers; two *s* one *d*. *Educ:* Eton; UCNW, Bangor (BA Hons Pure Econs). Trader: Rayner Coffee Internat., 1988–90; Mitsubishi Corp., 1990–91; Union Bank of Switzerland, 1991–94; Associate Dir, Dresdner Kleinwort Benson, 1994–98; Manager, Commerzbank, 1998–2001. Opposition spokesman on envmt, 2003, on agric. and fisheries, 2005–09; Shadow Sec. of State for Wales, 2003–05; Opposition Whip, 2009–10; an Asst Govt Whip, 2010–12. Chm., Cttee of Selection, 2015–. Contested (C) Burnley, 1997. *Recreations:* motor bikes, Hereford cattle, country sports. *Address:* House of Commons, SW1A 0AA. *Clubs:* Pratt's, Hurlingham.

**WIGGINS, (Anthony) John,** CMG 2002; consultant on public financial management, control and audit, since 2002; *b* 8 July 1938; *s* of late Rev. Arthur Wiggins and of Mavis Wiggins (*née* Brown); *m* 1962, Jennifer Anne Walkden; one *s* (and one *d* decd). *Educ:* Highgate Sch.; The Hotchkiss Sch., Lakeville, Conn, USA; Oriel Coll., Oxford (MA). Assistant Principal, HM Treasury, 1961; Private Sec. to Permanent Under Sec., Dept of Economic Affairs, 1964–66; Principal: Dept of Economic Affairs, 1966–67; HM Treasury, 1967–69; Harkness Fellow, Harvard Univ., 1969–71 (MPA 1970); Asst Sec., HM Treasury 1972–79; Principal Private Sec. to Chancellor of the Exchequer, 1980–81; Under Sec., Dept of Energy, 1981–84 (Mem. of BNOC, 1982–84); Under Sec., Cabinet Office, 1985–87; Under Sec., 1987–88, Dep. Sec., 1988–92, DES, subseq. DFE, on secondment to HM Treasury, 1992; Mem., Ct of Auditors of European Communities, 1993–2001. Sec. to Royal Opera House Develt Bd, 1987–93 (Sec. to cttees, 1982–87). *Recreations:* mountaineering, ski-ing, opera. *Address:* Clayhanger Farm, Wadeford, Chard, Somerset TA20 3BD. *T:* (01460) 61610.

**WIGGINS, Bernard;** *see* Cornwell, B.

**WIGGINS, Sir Bradley (Mark),** Kt 2013; CBE 2009 (OBE 2005); professional cyclist, Team WIGGINS, 2015–16; *b* Ghent, Belgium, 28 April 1980; *s* of Garry and Linda Wiggins; *m* 2004, Catherine; one *s* one *d*. Professional cyclist: La Française des Jeux team, 2002–04; Credit Agricole team, 2004–05; Confidis team, 2006–07; Team High Road, 2008; Team Garmin-Slipstream, 2009; Team Sky, 2010–15. Bronze Medal, Team Pursuit, Sydney Olympics, 2000; Gold Medal, Individual Pursuit, Silver Medal, Team Pursuit, Bronze Medal, Madison, Athens Olympics, 2004; Gold Medal, Individual Pursuit, Gold Medal, Team Pursuit, Beijing Olympics, 2008; Gold Medal, Individual Time Trial, London Olympics, 2012; Gold Medal, Team Pursuit, Rio de Janeiro Olympics, 2016; Gold Medal, Individual Pursuit, 2003, 2007, 2008, Team Pursuit, 2007, 2008, 2011, Madison, 2008, 2016, Track World Championships; Silver Medal, Individual Time Trial, Road World Championships, 2011; 4th place, Tour de France, 2009; 3rd place, Vuelta a España, 2011; winner, Tour de France, 2012; winner, Tour of Britain, 2013; Silver Medal, Individual Time Trial, Road World Championships 2013; winner, Tour of Calif, 2014; Silver Medal, Team Pursuit, Commonwealth Games, Glasgow, 2014; 3rd place, Tour of Britain, 2014; Gold Medal, Individual Time Trial, Road World Championships, 2014; Gold Medal,

Team Pursuit, Eur. Track Championships, Switzerland, 2015; winner, Ghent Six Day Race, 2016. BBC Sports Personality of the Year Award, 2012. *Publications:* In Pursuit of Glory, 2008; My Time (autobiog.), 2012; My Hour (autobiog.), 2015. *Address:* c/o M&C Saatchi Merlin, 15 Golden Square, W1F 9JG.

**WIGGINS, Prof. David,** FBA 1978; Wykeham Professor of Logic, and Fellow of New College, Oxford University, 1994–2000, now Emeritus Fellow; *b* 8 March 1933; *s* of late Norman Wiggins and Diana Wiggins (*née* Priestley); *m* 1969, Hideko Ishiguro (marr. diss); *m* 1979, Jennifer Hornsby (marr. diss.); one *s*; *m* 2010, Phillida Gili. *Educ:* St Paul's Sch.; Brasenose Coll., Oxford (BA 1955; MA 1958; Hon. Fellow 2010). Asst Principal, Colonial Office, London 1957–58. Jane Eliza Procter Vis. Fellow, Princeton Univ., 1958–59; Lectr, 1959, then Fellow and Lecturer, 1960–67, New College, Oxford; Prof. of Philosophy, Bedford Coll., Univ. of London, 1967–80; Fellow and Praelector in Philosophy, University Coll., Oxford, 1981–89; Prof. of Philosophy, Birkbeck Coll., Univ. of London, 1989–94. Visiting appointments: Stanford, 1964 and 1965; Harvard, 1968 and 1972; All Souls College, 1973; Princeton, 1980; New York Univ., 1988; Boston Univ., 2001; Fellow, Center for Advanced Study in the Behavioral Sciences, Stanford, 1985–86. Mem., Ind. Commn on Transport, 1973–74; Chm., Transport Users' Consultative Cttee for the South East, 1977–79. Pres., Aristotelian Soc., 1999–2000. Mem., Institut International de Philosophie. For. Hon. Mem., Amer. Acad. of Arts and Scis, 1992. DUniv York, 2005. *Publications:* Identity and Spatio-Temporal Continuity, 1967; Truth, Invention and the Meaning of Life, 1978; Sameness and Substance, 1980; Needs, Values, Truth, 1987, 3rd edn 1998, rev. 2002; Sameness and Substance Renewed, 2001; Ethics: twelve lectures on the philosophy of morality, 2006; Solidarity and the Root of the Ethical, 2008; Continuants: their activity, their being, and their identity: twelve essays, 2016; philosophical articles in Philosophical Review, Analysis, Philosophy, Synthèse, Phil Qly, Ratio, Proc. Aristotelian Soc., Mind, Eur. Jl of Philosophy; articles on environmental and transport subjects in Spectator, Times, Tribune, and ed collections.

**WIGGINS, John;** *see* Wiggins, A. J.

**WIGGLESWORTH, Jack;** Chairman, London International Financial Futures Exchange, 1995–98; Deputy Chairman, Durlacher Corp. plc, 2002–05; *b* 9 Oct. 1941; *s* of Jack Wigglesworth and Gladys Maud Wigglesworth; *m* 1970, Carlota Josefina Paéz; one *s* one *d*. *Educ:* Jesus Coll., Oxford (MA). Gilt Desk Economist and Bond Salesman, Phillips & Drew, 1963–71; Gilt Desk Bond Salesman, 1971–86, Partner, 1973–86, W. Greenwell & Co.; London International Financial Futures and Options Exchange: Founder Mem., Wkg Party 1980–81; Mem., Steering Cttee, 1981–82; Dir, 1982–98; Designed Gilt Contract, 1982; Chm., Membership and Rules Cttee, 1988–92; Dep. Chm., 1992–95. Dir of Marketing, Citifutures Ltd, 1993–97; Chairman: ABN Amro Futures Ltd, 1997–99; CableNet Internat., 2001–03; LitComp plc, 2002–03; London Asia Capital plc, 2003–09; LOPPEX, 2010–. Director: Stace Barr Angerstein plc, 1997–2001; Clivia Ltd, 1998–2002; Capital Value Brokers Ltd, 1998–2005. Mem., London Stock Exchange, 1968–91; Director: Securities Inst., 1992–2003; Futures and Options Assoc., 1995–2000; Financial Services NTO, 2001–06. Member: Financial Services Adv. Gp, QCA, 1999–2001; Adv. Bd, OMFIF, 2012–. Chm., Hackney Educn Action Zone, 1999–2004; Member: Business Sch. Council, London Guildhall Univ., 1998–2002; Council, Gresham Coll., 1999–2011. Master, World Traders' Co., 2006–07. Hon. DSc City, 1998. *Recreations:* music, films, computers, gardening. *Address:* 3 Deacons Heights, Elstree, Herts WD6 3QY. *T:* (020) 8953 8524. *Clubs:* Athenæum, City of London.

**WIGGLESWORTH, Mark Harmon;** orchestral conductor; *b* 19 July 1964; *s* of Martin Wigglesworth and Angela (*née* Field). *Educ:* Bryanston Sch.; Manchester Univ. (BMus); Royal Acad. of Music. Winner, Kondrashin Comp., 1989. Founder and Music Dir, Première Ensemble, 1989–; Associate Conductor, BBC SO, 1991–93; Music Director: Opera Factory, 1991–94; BBC Nat. Orch. of Wales, 1996–2000; Prin. Guest Conductor, Swedish Radio SO, 1998–2001; Music Dir, ENO, 2015–16. Débuts: Glyndebourne Fest. Opera, 2000; ENO, 2001; Royal Opera House, Covent Gdn, 2002; Metropolitan Opera, NY, 2005; Bayerische Staatsoper, Munich, 2011; has conducted many orchestras incl. Berlin Philharmonic, Royal Concertgebouw, NY, LA Philharmonic, Boston, Cleveland, Philadelphia, Chicago, San Francisco, Montreal Symphony, Minnesota Orch., Sydney Symphony, Melbourne Symphony, Tokyo Symphony, Hong Kong Philharmonic, London Philharmonic, London Symphony, La Scala, Santa Cecilia; also at BBC Proms and Hollywood Bowl; recordings include complete Shostakovich Symphony cycle with Netherlands Radio Philharmonic. *Address:* c/o Intermusica Artists' Management, 9 Kingsway, WC2B 6XF.

**WIGGLESWORTH, Raymond;** QC 1999; a Recorder, 1990–2018; *b* 24 Dec. 1947; *s* of Kenneth Holt Wigglesworth and Marguerite (*née* Lonsdale); *m* 1982, Amanda Jane Littler; two *s* one *d*. *Educ:* Manchester Univ. (LLB). Called to the Bar, Gray's Inn, 1974; in practice on Northern Circuit, 1974–2016; Asst Recorder, 1987–90; Standing Counsel to HM Customs and Excise, 1995–99. *Recreations:* mountaineering, ski-ing, golf, sailing. *Club:* Wilmslow Golf.

**WIGGLESWORTH, Prof. Sarah Heath,** MBE 2003; RIBA; RDI 2012; architect; Founder and Director, Sarah Wigglesworth Architects, since 1994; Professor of Architecture, University of Sheffield, 1997–2016; *b* London, 16 May 1957; *d* of Gordon Hardy Wigglesworth and Cherry Diana Heath Wigglesworth; partner, Prof. Jeremy William Till, *qv. Educ:* Camden Sch. for Girls; Newnham Coll., Cambridge (BA 1979; MA; DipArch 1983). RIBA 1984; ARB 1985. Studio Tutor, Univ. of Cambridge, 1985–87; Lectr, 1989–92, Sen. Lectr, 1992–98, Kingston Univ. *Publications:* (ed jtly) Desiring Practices: architecture, gender and the interdisciplinary, 1996; (ed with J. Till) The Everyday and Architecture, 1998; (ed) Around and About Stock Orchard Street, 2011. *Recreations:* making things, food (growing, cooking, eating), cycling. *Address:* Sarah Wigglesworth Architects, 10 Stock Orchard Street, N7 9RW. *T:* (020) 7607 9200. *E:* sarah@swarch.co.uk.

**WIGGLESWORTH, William Robert Brian;** Director, Reedheath Ltd, 1994–2012; Joint Director, International Institute for Regulations in Telecommunications, Westminster University, 1998–2006 (City University, 1994–98); *b* 8 Aug. 1937; *s* of Sir Vincent Wigglesworth, CBE, FRS; *m* 1969, Susan Mary (MBE 2015), *d* of late Arthur Baker, JP, Lavenham; one *s* one *d*. *Educ:* Marlborough; Magdalen College, Oxford (BA). Nat. Service, 2nd Lieut, Royal Signals, 1956–58. Ranks, Hovis McDougall Ltd, 1961–70: trainee; Gen. Manager, Mother's Pride Bakery, Cheltenham; PA to Group Chief Exec.; Gen. Manager, Baughans of Colchester; Board of Trade, 1970; Fair Trading Div., Dept of Prices and Consumer Protection, 1975; Posts and Telecommunications Div., 1978, Inf. Tech. Div., 1982, Dept of Industry; Dep. Dir Gen. of Telecommunications, 1984–94, Actg Dir, 1992–93. Prin. Advr, Telecoms Forum, Internat. Inst. of Communications, 1994–97; Mem. Bd, UKERNA, 1994–98. *Recreations:* fishing, gardening, history. *Address:* Millfield House, Heath Road, Polstead, Colchester CO6 5AN. *T:* (01787) 210029.

**WIGGS, His Honour (John) Samuel;** a Circuit Judge, Western Circuit, 1995–2014; *b* 23 Nov. 1946; *s* of late Kenneth Ingram Wiggs and of Marjorie Ruth Wiggs (*née* Newton); *m* Elizabeth Jones (decd); *m* Kerry Martley; two *d*, and two step *d*. *Educ:* Chigwell Sch.; Southampton Univ. (LLB). Called to the Bar, Middle Temple, 1970; in practice, London, 1971–95; Recorder, 1991; Resident Judge, Bournemouth, 1999–2007, Bournemouth and Dorchester, 2007–13; pt-time Judge, Mental Health Tribunals, 2014–. Chancellor, Dio. of Salisbury, 1997–2016. *Recreations:* playing the bassoon and saxophone, church choir singing, gardening. *Address:* Courts of Justice, Deansleigh Road, Bournemouth, Dorset BH7 7DS. *T:* (01202) 502800, *Fax:* (01202) 502801.

**WIGGS, Roger Sydney William Hale;** Group Chief Executive, Securicor plc, 1996–2001, non-executive Director, 2001–03; *b* 10 June 1939; *s* of Sydney Thomas Wiggs and Elizabeth Alice Wiggs (*née* Coomber); *m* 1st, 1963, Rosalind Anne Francis (*d* 2004); four *s*; 2nd, 2008, Sally Elizabeth Mote (*née* Buzzard). *Educ:* Tiffin Sch., Kingston upon Thames. Admitted Solicitor, 1962; Partner, Hextall, Erskine & Co., 1963–74; Overseas Dir, Securicor Ltd, 1974–80; Man. Dir, Securicor Internat. Ltd, 1980–89; Dir, 1977, Dep. Gp Chief Exec., 1985–88, Gp Chief Exec., 1988–96, Securicor Gp plc, and Security Services plc. Non-exec. Dir, Crown Agents for Oversea Govts and Admins Ltd, 1997–2005. *Recreations:* sport, particularly soccer, Rugby, motor racing.

**WIGGS, Samuel;** *see* Wiggs, J. S.

**WIGHT, Ven. Dennis Marley;** Archdeacon of St Davids, 2013–18; Priest-in-charge, Wiston and Walton East, 2015–18; *b* 1953. *Educ:* Southampton Univ. (BTh 1987); Sarum and Wells Theol Coll. Ordained deacon, 1985, priest, 1986; Curate, Gillingham, 1985–87; Vicar, Christ Church, Coseley, 1990–94; Rector, Stoke Prior, Wychbold and Upton Warren, 1994–2002; Rural Dean, Droitwich, 1996–99; Vicar, Dale and St Brides with Marloes, 2002–10; Area Dean, Roose, 2005–10; Diocese of St Davids: Warden of Ordinands, 2009–11, 2012–13; Bishop's Chaplain, 2010–14; Dir of Ministry, 2010–18. Hon. Canon, St Davids Cath., 2009–18. *Address:* 6 Llys Holcwm, Ferryside SA17 5SY.

**WIGHT, Robin,** CVO 2000; President, WCRS and Engine Group, since 2008 (Chairman, WCRS, 1983–2008); Founder and Chairman, The Ideas Foundation, since 2002; *b* 6 July 1944; *s* of late Brig. I. L. Wight and of C. P. Wight; *m* (1st marr. diss.); two *s* one *d*; 2nd (marr. diss.); one *s* one *d*; 3rd (marr. diss.); two step *c*; 4th, 2013, Countess Paola von Csaky. *Educ:* Wellington Coll.; St Catharine's Coll., Cambridge. Copywriter: Robert Sharp and Partners, 1966; CDP and Partners, 1967; Creative Director: Richard Cope and Partners, 1968; Euro Advertising, 1968; Creative Partner, Wight, Collins, Rutherford, Scott, 1979. Marketing Adviser to Rt Hon. Peter Walker, 1982–84. Chm., Duke of Edinburgh Award Charter for Business, 1992–2000. Mem. Council, Arts & Business (formerly ABSA), 1994–97 (Chm., 1997–2005). Contested (C) Bishop Auckland, 1987. Hon. Col, 77th Brigade (inf. activities gp), 2018. *Publications:* The Day the Pigs Refused to be Driven to Market, 1972; The Peacock's Tail and the Reputation Reflex, 2008. *Address:* Engine, 60 Great Portland Street, W1W 7RT. *Club:* Chelsea Arts.

**WIGHTMAN, (Andrew Norman) Scott,** CMG 2009; Director for External Affairs, Scottish Government, since 2019; *b* 17 July 1961; *s* of Andrew James Scott Wightman and Joan MacDonald Wightman (*née* Campbell); *m* 1988, Anne Margaret Roberts; two *d*. *Educ:* George Heriot's Sch., Edinburgh; Edinburgh Univ. (MA Hons French and Contemp. European Instns). FCO, 1983; Second Sec., Peking, 1986; Cabinet Office, 1989; FCO, 1991; First Sec., Paris, 1994; Asst Dir, Personnel Policy, FCO, 1998; Minister and Dep. Hd of Mission, Rome, 2002–06; Dir for Global and Econ. Issues, FCO, 2006–08; Dir, Asia Pacific, FCO, 2008–10; Ambassador to Republic of Korea, 2011–15. *Address:* c/o Scottish Government, Victoria Quay, Edinburgh EH6 6QQ.

**WIGHTMAN, Very Rev. David;** *see* Wightman, Very Rev. W. D.

**WIGHTMAN, John Watt,** CVO 1998; CBE 1986; RD; WS; Chairman, Craig & Rose plc, 1994–2000; Solicitor to the Queen in Scotland, 1983–99; *b* 20 Nov. 1933; *s* of Robert Johnson Wightman and Edith Wilkinson (*née* Laing); *m* 1962, Isla Fraser MacLeod; one *s* two *d*. *Educ:* Daniel Stewart's Coll.; Univ. of St Andrews (MA); Univ. of Edinburgh (LLB). Partner, Morton Fraser, WS, 1961–99. Cdre, RNR, 1982–85; Chairman: Lowland TAVRA, 1992–95; Regl Adv. Cttee for S Scotland, Forestry Commn, 1998–2004. Dir, Douglas Haig Memorial Homes, then Trustee, Haig Housing Trust, 1998–2013; Dir, Earl Haig Fund Scotland, 2000–04. *Recreations:* sailing, fishing, ornithology. *Address:* 58 Trinity Road, Edinburgh EH5 3HT. *T:* (0131) 551 6128. *Clubs:* Naval; Royal Scots (Edinburgh).

**WIGHTMAN, Scott;** *see* Wightman, A. N. S.

**WIGHTMAN, Very Rev. (William) David;** Provost of St Andrew's Cathedral, Aberdeen, 1991–2002; Priest in charge of St Ninian, Aberdeen, 1991–2002; *b* 29 Jan. 1939; *s* of William Osborne Wightman and Madge Wightman; *m* 1963, Karen Elizabeth Harker; two *s* two *d*. *Educ:* Alderman Newton's GS, Leicester; George Dixon GS, Birmingham; Univ. of Birmingham (BA Hons Theol.); Wells Theol Coll. Ordained deacon, 1963; priest, 1964; Curate: St Mary and All Saints, Rotherham, 1963–67; St Mary, Castlechurch, Stafford, 1967–70; Vicar: St Aidan, Buttershaw, Bradford, 1970–76; St John the Evangelist, Cullingworth, Bradford, 1976–83; Rector: St Peter, Peterhead, 1983–91; St John Longside, St Drostan, Old Deer and All Saints, Strichen, 1990–91; Chaplain, HM Prison, Peterhead, 1989–91; Dir, Training for Ministry, Dio. of Aberdeen and Orkney, 1989–94. Hon. Canon, Christ Church Cathedral, Hartford, Conn, USA, 1991. *Recreations:* fishing, choral music, swimming, gardening. *Address:* 66 Wold Road, Pocklington, E Yorks YO42 2QG. *T:* (01759) 301369.

**WIGIN, Caroline Rosemary;** Her Honour Judge Wigin; a Circuit Judge, since 2019; *b* Leeds, July 1961; *d* of David and Elisabeth Wigin; partner, Adrian Havercroft; one *s* one *d*. *Educ:* Leeds Girls' High Sch.; Marlborough Coll.; Exeter Univ. (LLB). Called to the Bar, Inner Temple, 1984; Pt-time Tribunal Judge, 1999–2019; a Recorder, 2004–19. *Recreations:* collecting portraits of middle aged women, walking in cities. *Address:* St Albans Crown Court, Bricket Road, St Albans AL1 3JW.

**WIGLEY,** family name of **Baron Wigley**.

**WIGLEY, Baron** *cr* 2011 (Life Peer), of Caernarfon in the County of Gwynedd; **Dafydd Wigley;** PC 1997; industrial economist; President, National Library of Wales, 2007–11; Hon. President, Plaid Cymru, since 2006; *b* 1 April 1943; *s* of late Elfyn Edward Wigley, sometime County Treasurer, Caernarfonshire CC; *m* 1967, Elinor Bennett (*née* Owen), *d* of late Emrys Bennett Owen, Dolgellau; one *s* one *d* (and two *s* decd). *Educ:* Caernarfon Grammar Sch.; Rydal Sch., Colwyn Bay; Manchester Univ. Ford Motor Co., 1964–67; Chief Cost Accountant and Financial Planning Manager, Mars Ltd, 1967–71; Financial Controller, Hoover Ltd, Merthyr Tydfil, 1971–74. Chm., ADC Ltd, 1981–91. Mem., Merthyr Tydfil Borough Council, 1972–74. MP (Plaid Cymru) Caernarfon, Feb. 1974–2001. Mem., Select Cttee on Welsh Affairs, 1983–87. Vice-Chairman: Parly Social Services Gp, 1985–88; All-Party Disablement Gp, 1992–2001; British-Slovene Parly Gp, 1993–2001; Mem., Standing Cttee on Eur. Legislation, 1991–96. Sponsor, Disabled Persons Act, 1981. Pres., Plaid Cymru, 1981–84 and 1991–2000. National Assembly for Wales: Mem. (Plaid Cymru) Caernarfon, 1999–2003; Leader, Plaid Cymru, 1999–2000;

Chm., Audit Cttee, 2002–03. Contested (Plaid Cymru), N Wales, Eur. Parly elecns, 1994. Vice-Pres., Nat. Fedn of Industrial Develt Authorities, 1981–2001. Chairman: Ymddiriedolaeth Hybu Gwyddoniaeth Cyf, 2002–06; Una Cyf, 2004–08; non-exec. Dir, Gwernafalau Cyf, 2001–; Member: Adv. Bd for Wales, BT, 2003–07; S4C Authority, 2003–06. Pres., CAB, Gwynedd, 2003–09; Chm., N Wales Crimebeat, 2003–09. Pro-Chancellor, Univ. of Wales, 2003–06; Chm., Adv. Bd, Sch. of Business (formerly Sch. of Business and Regl Develt), Bangor Univ. (formerly Univ. of Wales, Bangor), 2003–. Pres., Spastic Soc. of Wales, 1985–90; Jt Pres., Mencap Wales, 1997–; Vice Pres., Royal Mencap Soc., 2014–; Trustee, Hope House, 2003–10. Pres. (unpaid), S Caernarfonshire Creamery, 1988–2003. Mem., Writers' Guild, 2000–. Fellow, UCNW, Bangor, 1994. Hon. LLD: Wales, 2002; Glamorgan, 2003. *Publications:* An Economic Plan for Wales, 1970; O Ddifri, 1992; Dal Ati, 1993; A Democratic Wales in a United Europe, 1995; A Real Choice for Wales, 1996; Maen i'r Wal, 2001. *Address:* Hen Efail, Bontnewydd, Caernarfon, Gwynedd LL54 7YH. *E:* dafydd_wigley@hotmail.com.

**WIGLEY, Prof. Dale Brian,** PhD; FRS 2004; Professor of Structural Biology, Imperial College London, since 2015; *b* 10 May 1961; *s* of Brian Wigley and Joan Wigley. *Educ:* Univ. of York (BSc Hons (Biochem.) 1985); Univ. of Bristol (PhD (Biochem.) 1988). Post-doctoral Fellow: Univ. of Leicester, 1988–90; Univ. of York, 1990–92; Lectr, 1993–97, Reader, 1997–2000, Univ. of Oxford; Principal Scientist, CRUK, Clare Hall Labs, 2000–10; Prof. of Protein Crystallography, Inst. of Cancer Res., 2010–14. Mem., EMBO, 2002. *Recreation:* fly-fishing. *Address:* Section of Structural Biology, Department of Medicine, Imperial College London, South Kensington Campus, SW7 2AZ. *E:* d.wigley@imperial.ac.uk.

**WIGLEY, Robert Charles Michael;** Chairman: UK Finance, since 2017; Vesta Global Holdings Ltd, since 2017; Secure Broadcast, since 2017; Accloud plc, since 2018; VST Enterprises, since 2019; *b* 4 Feb. 1961; *s* of Harold and Elizabeth Margaret Wigley; *m* 1996, Sarah Joan Molony; three *s. Educ:* Sch. of Mgt, Univ. of Bath (BSc Business Admin 1983). FCA 1986. Dir, Morgan Grenfell plc, until 1996; Man. Dir, Merrill Lynch Internat., 1996–2004; Chm., EMEA, Merrill Lynch, 2004–09; Chm., Merrill Lynch Internat. Bank Ltd, 2005–09; Operating Partner, Advent Internat., 2009–11. Non-executive Director: Royal Mail Gp plc, 2003–06 (Chm., Audit Cttee, 2003–06); Court, 2006–09, Risk Policy Cttee, 2006–09, Bank of England; LCH Clearnet Gp Ltd, 2005–09; Euroclear plc, 2007–09; Orca Exploration Inc., 2010–12; Altitude Med. Systems Inc., 2011–14; Qatar Financial Centre Authy, 2012– (Chm., Audit Cttee, 2012–); Bink (formerly Loyalty Angels) Ltd, 2015–17 (Chm., 2017–); Remora Ltd., 2016–; Symphony Environmental plc, 2018– (Mem., Adv. Bd, 2015–17); Member: Internat. Business Adv. Bd, British Airways plc, 2012–14; Adv. Bd, Tetronics Internat. Ltd, 2012–17; Chairman: Sovereign Reversions plc, 2009–10; hibu (formerly Yell Gp) plc, 2009–14; Stonehaven Search LLP, 2010–17; Expansys, 2010–14; Skrill Hldgs Inc., 2011; NetOTC Hldgs, SARL, 2012–16; Captive Minds Gp Communications Ltd, 2013–15; First Global Trust Bank (formerly Llamabrook) plc, 2013–16; Tantalum Corp. plc, 2014–16; Justinvesting Ltd, 2014–17; Victoria Beckham Ltd, 2016–17. Dep. Chm., BITC, 2005–10 (Chm., Educn Leadership Team, 2005–09); Co-Proprietor, Margot Restaurant, 2017–. Member: Sen. Practitioner Cttee, FSA, 2005–10; Panel on Takeovers and Mergers, 2007–09, 2019– (Mem., Remuneration Cttee); Adv. Bd, London Corp., 2005–10; Adv. Council, Business for New Europe, 2006–12; Chancellor's High Level Gp of Key London Financial Stakeholders, 2006–09; Nat. Council for Educnl Excellence, 2007–10; Mayor of London's Panel of Economic Advrs, 2008–14; Ministerial Wkg Gp on Sch. Governance for Sec. of State, DCSF, 2008–09; Challenge Panel, DCMS Tailored Review of Historic England, 2019–; Corporate Bd, CRUK, 2019–; Chairman: Nat. Educn Employer Taskforce, 2009–11; Green Investment Bank Commn, 2010; Adv. Bd, Green Investment Bank, 2011–12; Prime Minister's Ambassador for UK Business, 2011–12; Founder Comr, Blockchain Commn for Sustainable Develt, UN, 2019–. Author of commissioned reports: (for Mayor of London) London, Winning in a Changing World, 2008; (for Nat. Council of Educn Excellence) Governing Our Schools, 2008. Vis. Fellow, Saïd Business Sch., 2008–, Chm., Global Adv. Gp, Centre for Corporate Reputation, 2007–16, Univ. of Oxford; Mem., Adv. Bd, Doughty Centre for Corp. Responsibility, Cranfield Sch. of Mgt, 2008–15. Hon. Fellow, Judge Business Sch., Univ. of Cambridge, 2015–. Member: Court, Internat. Bankers' Co., 2006– (Master, 2009–10); Council, RCM, 2012–19. Trustee: Whizz Kidz Ltd, 2000–06; Peter Jones Foundn, 2011–18. CCMI 2019. Hon. DBA Bath, 2008. *Recreations:* squash, tennis, vintage cars, fine wine, opera. *Address:* (office) 5th Floor, 1 Angel Court, EC2N 2BR. *Clubs:* Royal Automobile, Queen's (Dir and Chm., Estates Cttee, 2014–), 5 Hertford Street; Aston Martin Owners.

**WIGNALL, Michael Thomas;** Chef Patron: The Angel at Hetton, since 2018; Cove, since 2019; *b* Preston, Lancs, 23 May 1967; *s* of Alan Wignall and Catherine Wignall (*née* Dunn); *m* 2015, Johanna Bethan Cole; one *s* one *d. Educ:* St Cuthbert Mayne High Sch., Preston; Preston Coll. Jun. sous chef, Heathcotes, Longridge, 1987–89; Head Chef: The Old Beams, Waterhouses, 1993–95 (Michelin Star); Waldo's, Cliveden, 1996–98 (Michelin Star); Michael's Nook, Grasmere, 1998–2002 (Michelin Star); Exec. Head Chef, The Devonshire Arms, N Yorks, 2002–07 (Michelin Star); Head Chef, Michael Wignall at The Latymer, Pennyhill Park Hotel, 2007–15; Creative Dir, Football Café, 2013–16; Exec. Chef, Gidleigh Park Hotel, Devon, 2016–18. Pop-up restaurants: Stockholm, 2013; Selfridges, London, 2014. Charity event, India, Creative Services Support Gp, 2013; Bobby Moore Fund, 2014, 2015. A judge, BBC MasterChef: The Professionals, 2013, 2014. Best dessert under 21s and best overall entrant, Salon Culinaire, 1986; winner, Northwest Chefs Circle, 1987; Best Restaurant Newcomer of the Yr, Good Food Guide, 2009; winner, SW, Britain's Best Dish, ITV, 2010; Michael Wignall at The Latymer awarded 2 Michelin Stars, 2012, 5 AA Rosettes, 2012; Gidleigh Park Hotel awarded 2 Michelin Stars, 2016, 5 AA Rosettes, 2017. *Recreations:* wakeboarding, snowboarding, heliboarding, downhill mountain biking, Lotus sport, photography, surfing. *Address:* 1 Mount View, Airton, Skipton, N Yorks BD23 4AU. *E:* Michael.Wignall@outlook.com.

**WIGODER, Hon. Charles;** Executive Chairman, Telecom Plus plc, since 2009; *b* London, 2 March 1960; *s* of Baron Wigoder, QC; *m* 1988, Elizabeth Duke-Cohan; one *s* three *d. Educ:* Westminster Sch.; Univ. of Kent (BA 1981). Chartered Accountant 1984. Chartered Accountant, KPMG, 1981–84; Investment Analyst, Grieveson Grant, 1984–85; Head, Corporate Finance and Development: Carlton Communications plc, 1985–87; Quadrant Gp plc, 1987–88; Founder and Chief Exec., Peoples Phone, 1988–95; Chief Exec., Telecom Plus plc, 1996–2009. Hon. Dr of Laws Kent, 2010. *Recreations:* bridge, theatre, ballet, opera, philanthropy. *Address:* Utility Warehouse, Network HQ, 508 Edgware Road, NW9 5AB. *T:* (020) 8955 5002. *E:* charles@wigoder.com. *Clubs:* TGRs; Cercle de l'Union Interalliée (Paris).

**WIGRAM,** family name of **Baron Wigram.**

**WIGRAM,** 3rd Baron *cr* 1935, of Clewer; **Andrew Francis Clive Wigram,** MVO 1986; *b* Wellington, NZ, 18 March 1949; *s* of 2nd Baron Wigram, MC and Margaret Helen Wigram; *S* father, 2017; *m* 1st, 1974, Gabrielle Diana Moore (marr. diss. 2010); three *s* one *d;* 2nd, 2011, Henrietta Mary Charrington. *Educ:* Winchester Coll.; Royal Mil. Acad. Sandhurst; Royal Agricl Coll., Cirencester. Served Army, Grenadier Guards, 1979–86; Equerry to the Duke of Edinburgh, 1982–86; farmer. Mem., HM Bodyguard, Hon. Corps of Gentlemen at Arms, 2000–12. Mem., Co. of Pikemen and Musketeers, HAC. Hon. Asst, Cordwainers' Co.; Co. of Watermen and Lightermen. Steward, Henley Royal Regatta. *Heir: s* Hon. Harry Richard Clive Wigram [*b* 20 May 1977; *m* 2012, Nicola Jane Harding; two *d*]. *Address:* Winchfield House, Hook, Hants RG27 8BS. *Clubs:* Pratts, Beefsteak, Honourable Artillery Company; Leander (Henley-on-Thames).

**WIGRAM, Sir John (Woolmore),** 9th Bt *cr* 1805, of Walthamstow, Essex; Director, JW Consultancy Ltd, since 2013; *b* 25 May 1957; *s* of late Peter Woolmore Wigram and of Sylvia Mary Wigram; *S* cousin, 2003; *m* 1996, Sally Jane Winnington; three *s. Educ:* Bedford Coll., London Univ. (BA Hons Hist.); Insead, Fontainebleau (MBA). Davidson Pearce, 1981–84; Leo Burnett, 1984–87; Davis Wilkins, 1987–91; CLK, 1993–96; Doner Cardwell Hawkins, 1996–98; ARC, 1998–2003; Dir, Rise Communications, 2003–06; Worldwide Planning Dir, Publicis, 2006–09; Dir, BPRI, 2010–13. *Heir: s* James Woolmore Wigram, *b* 10 Feb. 1997.

**WIGSTON, Air Chief Marshal Michael,** CBE 2013; Chief of the Air Staff, since 2019; Aide-de-Camp to the Queen, since 2019; *b* Portsmouth, 25 Feb. 1968; *s* of Michael Vernon Wigston and Pamela Florence Wigston (*née* Workman); *m* 1994, Kate Louise Nielson; one *s* one *d. Educ:* Friars Sch., Bangor; Oriel Coll., Oxford (MA Engrg Sci. 1992); King's Coll. London (MA Defence Studies 2004). Commnd RAF, 1986; Tornado GR1/4 pilot: II(AC) sqdn, 1992; 14 Sqdn, 1995; 31 Sqdn, 1998; II(AC) Sqdn, 1999; Officer Commanding: 12(B) Sqdn, 2005; 903 Expeditionary Air Wing, Basra, 2007; Ops Directorate, MoD, 2008; Targeting and Information Ops, MoD, 2010; Dir Air Ops, ISAF Jt Comd, Kabul, 2011; Tornado Force Comdr, 2013; PSO to CDS, 2013–15; Adminr, Sovereign Base Areas, and Comdr, British Forces Cyprus, 2015–17; Asst Chief of Air Staff, 2017–18; Dep. Comdr Capability and Air Mem. for Personnel and Capability, HQ Air Comd, 2018–19. *Recreation:* sailing. *Address:* HQ Air Command, RAF High Wycombe, Bucks HP14 4UE.

**WIKELEY, Nicholas John;** an Upper Tribunal Judge (Administrative Appeals Chamber) (formerly a Social Security and Child Support Commissioner), since 2008; *b* Farnborough, Kent, 27 Sept. 1957; *s* of Nigel Derek Telford Wikeley and Olga Mary Wilson Wikeley (*née* Naylor); *m* 1983, Clare Elaine Phillips; two *s* one *d. Educ:* Sevenoaks Sch.; Trinity Hall, Cambridge (Exhibnr; BA 1980). Called to the Bar, Gray's Inn, 1981; Lectr, 1984–92, Sen. Lectr, 1992–94, Faculty of Law, Univ. of Birmingham; Prof. of Law, 1994–2008, now Emeritus, Dean of Faculty, 1996–99, Univ. of Southampton. Pt-time Chm., Social Security Appeal Tribunals, 1992–2008; Dep. Social Security and Child Support Comr, 2000–18. Society of Legal Scholars: Hon. Sec., 2001–06; Vice-Pres., 2008–09; Pres., 2009–10. *Publications:* (jtly) Judging Social Security, 1992; Compensation for Industrial Disease, 1993; (jtly) Child Support in Action, 1998; (with A. Ogus) The Law of Social Security, 4th edn 1995, 5th edn 2002; Child Support Law and Policy, 2006; (jtly) Social Security Legislation: vol. 1, Non Means Tested Benefits and Employment and Support Allowance, annually, 2009–18; vol. 2, Income Support, Jobseeker's Allowance, State Pension Credit and the Social Fund, annually 2000–18; vol. 4, Tax Credits, Child Trust Funds and HMRC-Administered Social Security Benefits, annually 2003–18; vol. 5, Universal Credit, annually, 2013–18; contrib. articles to learned jls. *Recreations:* ferries, Danish islands, Swedish crime novels. *Address:* Upper Tribunal, Administrative Appeals Chamber, 5th Floor, Rolls Building, 7 Rolls Buildings, Fetter Lane, EC4A 1NL. *Club:* Tottenham Hotspur Football.

**WIKSTRÖM, Prof. Per-Olof Helge,** PhD; FBA 2011; Professor of Ecological and Developmental Criminology, University of Cambridge, since 2001; Fellow, Girton College, Cambridge, since 1997; *b* Uppsala, Sweden, 30 July 1955; *s* of late William Wikström and Signe Wikström (*née* Lindeberg); *m* 1991, Suzanna Maxe; four *d. Educ:* Stora Brynässkolan; Stenebergsskolan; Vasaskolans Gymnasium; Univ. of Stockholm (BA 1976; PhD 1985; Docent 1988). Various res. associate and lectr posts, Dept of Criminol., Univ. of Stockholm, 1979–90 (Dep. Hd of Dept, 1987–90); Sen. Res. Officer, 1985–90, Dir, Res. Dept, 1990–94, Nat. Council for Crime Prevention, Sweden; Principal Res. Fellow, Res. Unit, Nat. Police Coll., Sweden, 1995–96; Adjunct Prof. of Sociol. of Crime, Univ. of Stockholm, 1993–96; Univ. Lectr, 1997–99, Reader, 1999–2001, Inst. of Criminol., Univ. of Cambridge. Visiting Professor: Univ. of Malmö, 2007–12; Univ. of Münster, 2008. Member: Bd, Scandinavian Res. Council for Criminol., 1992–97; Scientific Commn of Internat. Soc. for Criminol., 1995–99; Bd, Eur. Soc. Criminol., 2000–01 and 2004–05. Fellow: Center for Advanced Study in Behavioral Scis, Stanford Univ., 2002; Amer. Soc. Criminol., 2010. Hon. Dr Universidad Nacional de Educación a Distancia, Madrid, 2017. Northern Schol. Award, Univ. of Edinburgh, 1991; Sellin-Glueck Award, Amer. Soc. Criminol., 1994; Stockholm Prize in Criminology, 2016. *Publications:* Everyday Violence in Contemporary Sweden: ecological and situational aspects, 1985; Crime and Measures against Crime in the City, 1990; Urban Crime, Criminals and Victims, 1991; Integrating Individual and Ecological Aspects of Crime, 1993; Integrating Crime Prevention Strategies: propensity and opportunity, 1995; Criminal Deterrence and Sentence Severity, 1998; The Explanation of Crime: context, mechanisms and development, 2006; Adolescent Crime: individual differences and life styles, 2006; Breaking Rules: the social and situational dynamics of young people's urban crime, 2012; contrib. chapters in books and papers to jls incl. Criminol., Eur. Jl of Criminol., Jl of Quantitative Criminol. *Recreations:* news, coffee, golf. *Address:* Institute of Criminology, University of Cambridge, Sidgwick Avenue, Cambridge CB3 9DA. *T:* (01223) 335378. *E:* pow20@cam.ac.uk. *Club:* Gog MaGog Golf.

**WILBOURNE, Rt Rev. David Jeffrey;** Assistant Bishop of Llandaff, 2009–17; an Honorary Assistant Bishop, Diocese of York, since 2017; *b* Chesterfield, 15 Sept. 1955; *s* of Rev. Geoffrey Wilbourne and Eileen Wilbourne; *m* 1983, Rachel Margaret Powell; three *d. Educ:* Jesus Coll., Cambridge (MA 1981); Westcott House, Cambridge. Ordained deacon, 1981, priest, 1982; Asst Curate, Stainton-in-Cleveland, 1981–85; Rector, Monk Fryston and S Milford, 1985–91; Domestic Chaplain to Archbishop of York, and Dir of Ordinands, Dio. of York, 1991–97; Vicar, Helmsley, York, 1997–2009; Canon of York Minster, 2008–09; Priest-in-charge, Upper Ryedale, 2009. *Publications:* Archbishop's Diary, 1995; A Vicar's Diary, 1998, 3rd edn 2002; A Virgin's Diary, 1999; A Summer's Diary, 2001, 2nd edn, 2002; You Were Made for Me, 2001; The Helmsley Chronicles, 2012; Expecting Christ, 2013; The Voice of Jesus, 2014; Shepherd of Another Flock, 2017; Jesus Christ Superstar, 2020; Just John: the authorised biography of Archbishop John Habgood, 2020. *Recreations:* cycling, hill-walking, writing, New Testament textual criticism. *Address:* 8 Bielby Close, Scarborough YO12 6UU.

**WILBRAHAM;** see Bootle-Wilbraham, family name of Baron Skelmersdale.

**WILBRAHAM, Sir Richard B.;** see Baker Wilbraham.

**WILBY, David Christopher;** QC 1998; a Recorder, since 2000; a Deputy High Court Judge, since 2008; *b* 14 June 1952; *s* of Alan Wilby and late June Wilby; *m* 1976, Susan Arding; one *s* three *d. Educ:* Roundhay Sch., Leeds; Downing Coll., Cambridge (MA). Called to the Bar, Inner Temple, 1974, Bencher, 2002; Mem., North Eastern Circuit. Member: Judicial Studies Bd, 2005–09; Criminal Injuries Compensation Tribunal (formerly Appeals Panel), 2007–. Arbitrator, PIcARBS, 2016–. Member: Exec. Cttee, Professional Negligence Bar Assoc., 1995–2009; Bar Council, 1996–99; Chm., Bar Conf., 2000. Member: Commonwealth Lawyers Assoc., 1995; Internat. Assoc. of Defense Counsel,

1998; Associate Mem., American Bar Assoc., 1996; Chm., Northern Administrative Law Assoc., 2008–. Editor: Professional Negligence and Liability Law Reports, 1995–; Professional Negligence Key Cases, 1999–; HSE sect., Atkin's Court Forms, 2002, 2006 and 2010. *Publications:* The Law of Damages, 2003, 2nd edn 2010; (contrib.) Munkman, Employers Liability, 14th edn 2006 to 16th edn 2013. *Recreations:* being in France, golf, Rugby, Association Football. *Address:* Old Square Chambers, 10–11 Bedford Row, WC1R 4BU. *T:* (020) 7269 0300; Park Lane Plowden Chambers, 19 Westgate, Leeds LS1 2RD. *T:* (0113) 228 5000. *Clubs:* Moortown Golf, Pannal Golf, Royal Cinque Ports Golf.

**WILBY, Peter John;** Editor, New Statesman, 1998–2005; *b* 7 Nov. 1944; *s* of Lawrence Edward Wilby and Emily Lavinia Wilby; *m* 1967, Sandra James; two *s. Educ:* Kibworth Beauchamp Grammar Sch., Leics; Univ. of Sussex (BA Hons). Reporter, Observer, 1968–72; Education Correspondent: Observer, 1972–75; New Statesman, 1975–77; Sunday Times, 1977–86; Educn Editor, Independent, 1986–89; Independent on Sunday: Home Editor, 1990–91; Dep. Editor, 1991–95; Editor, 1995–96; Books Editor, New Statesman, 1997–98. Columnist, New Statesman, 2005–. *Publications:* Parents' Rights, 1983; Sunday Times Good University Guide, 1984; Sunday Times Good Careers Guide, 1985; Eden, 2006; (ed with Henry Pluckrose): The Condition of English Schooling, 1981; Education 2000, 1982. *Recreations:* reading, cooking, lunching. *Address:* 51 Queens Road, Loughton, Essex IG10 1RR.

**WILCE, Penelope Jane;** *see* Reed, P. J.

**WILCOCK, Christopher Camplin,** CB 1997; Director, Financial Advisory Services, PricewaterhouseCoopers (formerly Price Waterhouse), 1997–99; *b* 13 Sept. 1939; *s* of late Arthur Camplin Wilcock and Dorothy (*née* Haigh); *m* 1965, Evelyn Clare Gollin; two *d. Educ:* Berkhamsted and Ipswich Schs; Trinity Hall, Cambridge (BA 1st Cl. Hons; MA). FO, 1962–63; MECAS, 1963–64; 3rd Sec., Khartoum, 1964–66; FO, 1966–68; 2nd Sec., UK Delegn to NATO, 1968–70; FO, 1970–72; Hosp. Bldg Div., DHSS, 1972–74; Petroleum Prodn, subseq. Continental Shelf Policy Div., Dept of Energy, 1974–78, Asst Sec. 1976; Electricity Div., 1978–81; on secondment to Shell UK Ltd, 1982–83; Department of Energy, subseq. of Trade and Industry: Hd of Finance Br., 1984–86; Dir of Resource Management (Grade 4), 1986–88; Grade 3, 1988; Hd of Electricity Div. A, 1988–91; Hd of Electricity Div., 1991–94; Hd of Electricity and Nuclear Fuels Div., 1994–95; Hd of Nuclear Power Privatization Team, 1995–96. Order of the Two Niles, Fifth Cl. (Sudan), 1965. *Recreation:* reading.

**WILCOCK, Prof. Gordon Keith,** DM; FRCP; Professor of Geratology (formerly Clinical Geratology), 2006–12, now Emeritus, Director, Clinical Dementia Research Programme, until 2012, and Director, Oxford Project to Investigate Memory and Ageing, 2008–16, University of Oxford; Emeritus Consultant in Clinical Geratology, Oxford University Hospitals NHS Trust, 2013; *b* 5 Sept. 1945; *m* 1969, Louise Molden; three *s* two *d. Educ:* St Catherine's Coll., Oxford; London Hosp. Med. Coll. (BSc 1st cl. Hons 1967); Oxford Univ. Med. Sch. (BM BCh 1970; DM 1977). FRCP 1984. MRC Clinical Res. Fellow, Dept of Regius Prof. of Medicine, Oxford, 1973–75; Sen. Registrar in Geriatric Medicine, Cambridge, 1976; Consultant Physician to Depts of Geriatric and Gen. Medicine, Oxfordshire HA (Teaching), 1976–84; Clinical Lectr in Geriatric and Gen. Medicine, Univ. of Oxford, 1978–84; Prof. of Care of the Elderly, Univ. of Bristol, and Hon. Consultant Physician, N Bristol NHS Trust, at Frenchay Hosp., 1984–2006. Invited Public Lectr, Royal Instn, 2001–04. Visiting Professor in Geriatric Medicine: Univ. of Hong Kong, 2000, 2009; UWE; Beijing Univ. of Chinese Medicine (Academic Master, 111 Project, 2008–12). Founder Chm., Alzheimer's Soc., 1979–86 (Vice Pres., 1987–2015; Trustee, 2015–); Vice Pres. for Academic Affairs, British Geriatrics Soc. 2012–15. Chm., Med. Adv. Cttee, Sir Halley Stuart Trust, 2003–. Gov., BUPA Foundn, 2004–09. Hon. DSc UWE, 2006. Dhole-Eddlestone Meml Prize, BGS, 2006; Silver Medal, European Region of Internat. Assoc. for Gerontology and Geriatrics, 2015; Clinical Trials in Alzheimer's Disease Lifetime Achievement Award, 2015. *Publications:* (with J. M. Gray) Our Elders, 1981; (with A. Middleton) Geriatric Medicine, 1980, 2nd edn 1989; (jtly) Geriatric Problems in General Practice, 1982, 2nd edn 1991; Living with Alzheimer's Disease, 1990, 2nd edn 1999 (Italian edn 1992); (ed jtly) Oxford Textbook of Geriatric Medicine, 2000; contrib. over 300 articles on Alzheimer's disease and dementia in med. and scientific jls. *Recreations:* ornithology, photography, beekeeping. *Address:* Nuffield Department of Clinical Neuroscience, Level 6, John Radcliffe Hospital, Oxford OX3 9DU. *E:* wilcock@doctors.org.uk.

**WILCOCKS, Rear-Adm. Philip Lawrence,** CB 2007; DSC 1991; DL; Owner and Director, CEMPA (Leadership) Ltd, since 2009; *b* 14 April 1953; *s* of Lt Comdr Arthur Wilcocks, RN and Marjorie Wilcocks; *m* 1976, Kym; two *s. Educ:* Oakham Sch.; Wallington County Grammar Sch.; Univ. of Wales (BSc). Navigation Officer, HMS Torquay, 1977–78; CO, HMS Stubbington, 1978–80; Warfare Officer, HMS Ambuscade (incl. Falklands Campaign), 1980–84; HMS Newcastle/York, 1984–89; CO, HMS Gloucester (incl. Gulf War), 1990–92; MoD, 1992–98; Capt., 3rd Destroyer Sqdn, HMS Liverpool, 1998–99; Dir Naval Ops, MoD, 1999–2001; Cdre, Maritime Warfare Sch. 2001–04; Dep. Chief of Jt Ops (Operational Support), PJHQ, 2004–06; FO Scotland, Northern England and NI, and FO Reserves, 2006; COS (Capability) to C–in–C Fleet and Rear Adm. Surface Ships, 2007–08. President: HMS Hood Assoc., 2009–; Type 42 Destroyer Assoc., 2013–. Churchwarden, Dore Abbey, 2010–. Mem., Bishop's Council, Dio. of Hereford, 2013–. Gov., Hereford Cathedral Sch., 2015– (Chm., 2017–). DL Herefordshire, 2013. *Recreations:* walking, cycling, hill climbing. *Clubs:* Royal Navy of 1765 and 1785, Destroyer.

**WILCOCKSON, Ven. Stephen Anthony;** Archdeacon of Doncaster, 2012–19; *b* Connahs Quay, N Wales, 15 May 1951; *s* of Stephen Donald Wilcockson and Edna Wilcockson; *m* 1986, Heather Mitchell; one *s* one *d. Educ:* Park High Sch., Birkenhead; Nottingham Univ. (BA Hons French); Oxford Univ. (MA Theol.); Sheffield Hallam Univ. (Post-Grad. Dip. Coaching and Mentoring). Ordained deacon, 1976, priest, 1977; Curate, Pudsey Parish Church, 1976–78. Sen. Curate, All Saints, Wandsworth, 1978–81; Vicar: St Peter, Rock Ferry, 1981–86; St Mark, Lache-cum-Saltney, Chester, 1986–95; St Paul, Howell Hill, Surrey, 1995–2009; Rural Dean, Epsom, 2000–07; Parish Develt Officer, Dio. of Chester, 2009–12. *Recreations:* sport, music, walking, reading. *Address:* 75 Orion Way, Doncaster DN4 8AE. *T:* (01302) 374563. *E:* stevewilcockson@yahoo.com.

**WILCOX, Baroness** *cr* 1995 (Life Peer), of Plymouth in the County of Devon; **Judith Ann Wilcox;** *d* of John and Elsie Freeman; *m* 1st, 1961, Keith Davenport; one *s*; 2nd, 1986, Sir Malcolm George Wilcox, CBE (*d* 1986). *Educ:* St Dunstan's Abbey, Devon; St Mary's Convent, Wantage; Plymouth Polytechnic. Management of family business, Devon, 1969–79; Financial Dir, Capstan Foods, Devon, 1979–84; Chm., Channel Foods, Cornwall, 1984–89; Pres. Dir Gen., Pêcheries de la Morinie, France, 1989–91; Chm., Morinie et Cie, France, 1991–94. Chm., Nat. Consumer Council, 1990–96; Comr, Local Govt Commn, 1992–95; Mem., Prime Minister's Adv. Panel to Citizen's Charter Unit, 1992–97; Chm., Citizen's Charter Complaints Task Force, 1993–95. Board Member: AA, 1991–2010; Inland Revenue, 1991–96; PLA, 1993– (Vice-Chm., 2000–); non-executive Director: Carpetright plc, 1997–2010; Cadbury Schweppes plc, 1997–2007; Johnson Services PLC, 2004–10. Shadow Spokesman on Energy and Climate Change, H of L,

2008–10; Parly Under-Sec. of State, BIS, 2010–12; Chm., H of L Sci. Select Cttee Enquiry into Aircraft Cabin Envmt, 2000–01; Member: Tax Law Review Cttee, 1989–2000; H of L Select Cttee on Europe, Envmt, Public Health and Consumer Affairs, 1996, on Sci. and Technol., 2000–02, on EU, 2015–; EU Energy and Envmt Sub-Cttee, 2015–; Lord Chancellor's Review of Court of Appeal, 1996; Vice-Chm., All Party Parly Gp on Fisheries, 2014–, on Consumer Affairs and Trading Standards, 2015–. Parly Deleg. to Council of Europe, 2012–15. President: NFCG; Inst. of Trading Standards Admin; Mem., Governing Body, Inst. of Food Res. Vice-Pres., Guide Assoc. Gov., Imperial Coll. London, 2006–10; Chm. of Govs, Falconwood Acad., 2008–10. Chairman: Trustees, Community of St Mary Virgin, 2012–17; Diocesan Adv. Cttee for London, 2012–17. FRSA. *Recreations:* sailing, walking, calligraphy, bird-watching, film, theatre. *Address:* House of Lords, SW1A 0PW. *Clubs:* Athenæum; St Mawes Sailing.
*See also* Hon. S. N. Davenport.

**WILCOX, Claire, (Mrs J. F. Stair);** Senior Curator, Furniture, Textiles and Fashion (formerly Fashion), Victoria and Albert Museum, since 2009; Professor in Fashion Curation, London College of Fashion, University of the Arts London, since 2014; *b* London, 7 Oct. 1954; *d* of Sydney William and Margaret Jean Wilcox; *m* 1992, Julian Francis Stair, *qv*; two *d* (one *s* decd). *Educ:* Godolphin and Latymer Sch.; Exeter Univ. (BA Hons English Lit. 1977); Gerrit Rietveld Acad. of Art, Amsterdam; Camberwell Sch. of Art (BA Hons 1987); Univ. of East Anglia (Mus. Leadership Prog. 2010). Curatorial Asst, V&A Mus., 1979–83; Curator, Brixton Artists' Collective, 1987; freelance writer and curator, 1987–99; Curator, 1999–2004, Sen. Curator, Modern Fashion, 2004–08, Acting Hd of Contemporary Progs, 2008–09, V&A Mus. Member: Mgt Council, British Fashion Council, 2006–10; Peer Review Coll., AHRC, 2010–14. Trustee, Council, Royal Sch. of Needlework, 2010–14. Hon. Dr Middlesex, 2017. *Publications:* (with V. Mendes) Modern Fashion in Detail, 1991, 5th edn 2009; A Century of Style: bags, 1997; Handbags, 1999, 2nd edn 2008; (ed jtly) The Ambassador: fashion and trade in post-war Britain, 2012; exhibition catalogues. *Recreations:* reading, planting, daydreaming. *Address:* c/o Victoria and Albert Museum, SW7 2RL. *T:* (020) 7942 2000. *E:* c.wilcox@vam.ac.uk.

**WILCOX, His Honour David John Reed;** a Judge of the Technology and Construction Court of the High Court, 1998–2012; a Judge of the Employment Appeal Tribunal, 1999–2012; *b* 8 March 1939; *s* of Leslie Leonard Kennedy Wilcox and Margaret Ada Reed Wilcox (*née* Rapson); *m* 1st, 1962, Wendy Feay Christine Whiteley (*d* 2003); one *s* one *d*; 2nd, 2005, Roberta Piera Prosio de Pardo. *Educ:* Wednesbury Boys' High Sch.; King's Coll., London (LLB Hons). Called to the Bar, Gray's Inn, 1962. Directorate, Army Legal Services (Captain): Legal Staff, 1962–63; Legal Aid, Far East Land Forces, Singapore, 1963–65. Crown Counsel, Hong Kong, 1965–68; Lectr in Law, Univ. of Hong Kong, 1966–68; Member, Hong Kong Bar, 1968; in practice, Midland and Midland and Oxford Circuits, 1968–85; Hd of Chambers, College St, Nottingham, 1973–85; a Recorder of the Crown Court, 1979–85; a Circuit Judge, 1985–98; an Official Referee, 1996–98. Resident Judge, Great Grimsby Combined Court Centre, 1989–94; County Court Judge: Lincs and S Humberside, 1989–94; Birmingham, 1994–96; Care Judge, Birmingham, 1994–96. Appeal Judge, Special Chamber Privatisation related matters EU Rule of Law Mission, Supreme Court, Kosovo, 2013–14. Lord Chancellor's Rep., Humberside Probation Cttee, 1989–94. Chm., Nottingham Friendship Housing Assoc., 1970–75. Trustee and Vice-Pres., Pug Dog Welfare and Rescue Assoc., 2013– (Treas., 2012–13); Dir, John Townsend Trust, 2015–16. *Recreations:* pugs, gardening, travel. *E:* wilcoxdjr@hotmail.com.

**WILCOX, Rt Rev. David Peter;** an Honorary Assistant Bishop, Diocese of Chichester, 1995–2017; *b* 29 June 1930; *s* of John Wilcox and Stella Wilcox (*née* Bower); *m* 1956, Pamela Ann Hedges; two *s* two *d. Educ:* Northampton Grammar School; St John's Coll., Oxford (MA); Lincoln Theological Coll. Deacon 1954, priest 1955; Asst Curate, St Peter's, St Helier, Morden, Surrey, 1954–56; Asst Curate, University Church, Oxford and SCM Staff Secretary in Oxford, 1956–59; on staff of Lincoln Theological Coll., 1959–64; USPG Missionary on staff of United Theological Coll., Bangalore, and Presbyter in Church of S India, 1964–70; Vicar of Great Gransden with Little Gransden, dio. Ely, 1970–72; Canon Residentiary, Derby Cathedral and Warden, E Midlands Joint Ordination Training Scheme, 1972–77; Principal of Ripon College, Cuddesdon and Vicar of All Saints', Cuddesdon, 1977–85; Bishop Suffragan of Dorking, dio. Guildford, 1986–95. Assisting in parish of St Mary's, Willingdon, Eastbourne, 1995–. *Recreations:* walking, music, art, painting. *Address:* 4 The Court, Hoo Gardens, Willingdon, Eastbourne BN20 9AX. *T:* (01323) 506108.

**WILCOX, Dame Esther Louise;** *see* Rantzen, Dame E. L.

**WILCOX, Rt Rev. Peter Jonathan;** *see* Sheffield, Bishop of.

**WILCZEK, Prof. Frank Anthony,** PhD; Herman Feshbach Professor of Physics, Massachusetts Institute of Technology, since 2000; *b* 15 May 1951; *s* of Frank John Wilczek and Mary Rose Wilczek (*née* Cona); *m* 1973, Elizabeth Jordan Devine; two *d. Educ:* Univ. of Chicago (BS 1970); Princeton Univ. (MA 1972; PhD 1974). Princeton University: Asst Prof., 1974–76; Vis. Fellow, Inst. for Advanced Study, 1976–77; Asst Prof., 1977–78; Associate Prof., 1978–80; Prof., 1980–81, 1989–2000; Prof., Univ. of Calif, Santa Barbara, 1980–88. (Jtly) Nobel Prize in Physics, 2004. *Publications:* A Beautiful Question, 2015; articles in learned jls. *Address:* Center for Theoretical Physics, Massachusetts Institute of Technology, 77 Massachusetts Avenue, Cambridge, MA 02139-4307, USA; (home) 4 Wyman Road, Cambridge, MA 02138–2218, USA.

**WILD, Dr David;** Director of Public Health, South West Thames Regional Health Authority, 1989–90, retired; *b* 27 Jan. 1930; *s* of Frederick and Lena Wild; *m* 1954, Dr Sheila Wightman; one *s* one *d. Educ:* Manchester Grammar Sch.; Univ. of Manchester (MB, ChB); Univ. of Liverpool (DPH; FFCM, DMA). Deputy County Medical Officer, 1962, Area Medical Officer, 1974, West Sussex; Regional MO, 1982–86, Dir of Prof. Services, 1986–89, SW Thames RHA. Non-exec. Dir, Worthing DHA, 1990–95. Dir, Inf. Unit for Conf. of Med. Royal Colls and their Faculties in UK, 1991–93. Editor (with Dr Brian Williams), Community Medicine, 1978–84. *Publications:* contribs Jl Central Council of Health Educn, Medical Officer, Archives of Disease in Childhood. *Recreation:* conversation. *Address:* 16 Brandy Hole Lane, Chichester, Sussex PO19 5RY. *T:* (01243) 527125. *E:* davidwild9238@yahoo.com.

**WILD, David Connell;** Founder and Chairman, Lodestone Communications, since 2012; *b* Littleborough, 20 June 1965; *s* of Brian and Mary Wild; *m* 1997, Susan Davis; one *s* one *d. Educ:* Todmorden High Sch.; Queens' Coll., Cambridge (BA Natural Scis 1986). Asst Ed., RSC, 1987–89; Principal Officer: W Yorks Waste Mgt, 1990–94; Envmt Agency, 1994–98; Account Exec., GPC, 1998–99; Dir of Communications, Nirex, 1999–2007; Partner, Jefferson Communications, 2007–12. Chairman: Unison, Wakefield MDC, 1992–94; Trade Unions, Envmt Agency, 1995–99. Mem., Adv. Bd, Demos, 2014–. Dir, RegistHERtoVote, 2016–. *Publications:* contrib. Demos Qly. *Recreations:* guitars, literature, politics, botanical prints (Curtis's Londinensis), painting. *Address:* Lodestone Communications, Second Home, 68–80 Hanbury Street, E1 5JL. *E:* david.wild@lodestonecommunications.com. *Clubs:* Reform, Ronnie Scott's.

**WILD, (John) Robin;** Chief Dental Officer, Department of Health, 1997–2000; Consultant in Dental Public Health, Dumfries and Galloway Health Board, 2005–07; *b* 12 Sept. 1941; *s* of John Edward Brooke Wild and Teresa (*née* Ballance); *m* 1965, Eleanor Daphne Kerr; two *d* (one *s* decd). *Educ:* Sedbergh Sch., Cumbria; Edinburgh Univ. (BDS); Dundee Univ. (DPD). DGDP RCS; FDS RCSE. Dental practice, 1965–71; Dental Officer, E Lothian CC, 1971–74; Chief Admin. Dental Officer, Borders Health Bd, 1974–87; Regl Dental Postgrad. Advr, SE Scotland, 1982–87; Dep. Chief Dental Officer, Scottish Office, 1987–93; Chief Dental Officer and Dir of Dental Services, NHS, Scottish Office, 1993–97. Pres., Council of European Chief Dental Officers, 1999–2000; Vice Pres., Commonwealth Dental Assoc., 1997–2003. JP Scottish Borders, 1982–2011; Chairman: Scottish Borders Justices Cttee, 2000–05; Dist Courts Assoc., 2002–04; Member: Disciplinary Panel, Inst. and Faculty of Actuaries, 2001–; Judicial Council for Scotland, 2007–09. Life FRSocMed; Fellow, BDA; Founding Fellow, Inst. of Contemp. Scotland. *Publications:* contribs to Scottish Office Health Bulletin. *Address:* Braehead Stables, St Boswells, Roxburghshire TD6 0DE. *T:* (01835) 823203. *Clubs:* Royal Society of Medicine, Frontline.

**WILD, Prof. Raymond,** DSc, PhD; consultant, since 2001; Principal, Henley Management College, 1990–2001; *b* 24 Dec. 1940; *s* of Alice Wild and Frank Wild; *m* 1965, Carol Ann Mellor; one *s* one *d*. *Educ:* Stockport College; Bradford University (PhD (Mgt), MSc (Eng), MSc (Mgt)); DSc Brunel, 1988; WhF. Engineering apprentice, Crossley Bros, 1957–62, design engineer, 1962–63, research engineer, 1963–65; postgrad. student, Bradford Univ., 1965–66; production engineer, English Electric, 1966–67; Res. Fellow then Senior Res. Fellow, Bradford Univ., 1967–73; Dir of Grad. Studies, Admin. Staff Coll., Henley, 1973–77, Mem., Senior Staff, Henley Management Coll., 1973–2001; Brunel University: Dir, Special Engineering Programme, 1977–84; Hd, Dept of Engrg and Management Systems, 1977–86; Hd, Dept of Prodn Technology, 1984–86; Hd, Dept of Manufacturing and Engrg Systems, 1986–89; Pro-Vice-Chancellor, 1988–89. DUniv Brunel, 2001. Editor-in-Chief, Internat. Jl of Computer Integrated Manufacturing Systems, 1988–91. *Publications:* The Techniques of Production Management, 1971; Management and Production, 1972, trans. Greek 1984; (with A. B. Hill and C. C. Ridgeway) Women in the Factory, 1972; Mass Production Management, 1972; (with B. Lowes) Principles of Modern Management, 1972; Work Organization, 1975; Concepts for Operations Management, 1977; Production and Operations Management, 1979, 5th edn 1994; Operations Management: a policy framework, 1980; Essentials of Production and Operations Management, 1980, 5th edn 2002; (ed) Management and Production Readings, 1981; Read and Explain (4 children's books on technology), 1982 and 1983, trans. French, Swedish, German, Danish; How to Manage, 1983, 2nd edn 1995; (ed) International Handbook of Production and Operations Management, 1989; (ed) Technology and Management, 1990; Operations Management, 2001; Essentials of Operations Management, 2001; papers in learned jls. *Recreations:* writing, restoring houses, travel, painting. *Address:* Broomfield, New Road, Shiplake, Henley-on-Thames, Oxon RG9 3LA. *T:* (0118) 940 4102.

**WILD, Robin;** see Wild, J. R.

**WILDASH, Richard James,** LVO 1997; HM Diplomatic Service; Head of Europe (North) Department, Foreign and Commonwealth Office, since 2018; *b* 24 Dec. 1955; *s* of Arthur Ernest Wildash and Sheila Howard Wildash; *m* 1981, Elizabeth Jane Walmsley; two *d*. *Educ:* Corpus Christi Coll., Cambridge (MA). Joined HM Diplomatic Service, 1977; FCO, 1977–79: Third Secretary: E Berlin, 1979–81; Abidjan, 1981–84; Second Sec., FCO, 1984–88; First Secretary: Harare, 1988–92; FCO, 1992–94; New Delhi, 1994–98; Dep. High Comr, Kuala Lumpur, 1998–2002; High Comr, Cameroon and Ambassador (non-res.), Equatorial Guinea, Gabon, Central African Republic and Chad, 2002–06; High Comr, Malawi, 2006–09; Ambassador to Angola and concurrently to São Tomé and Príncipe, 2010–14; Dep. Head of Mission, Riyadh, 2014–18. AIL 1977, MCIL (MIL 1990). FRGS 1991; FLS 2013; FZS 2016. *Recreations:* the arts, travel, the natural world. *Address:* Flat 5, 26 Medway Street, SW1P 2BD. *E:* wildash@tusker.co.uk.

**WILDBLOOD, Stephen Roger;** QC 1999; **His Honour Judge Wildblood;** a Circuit Judge, since 2007; Designated Family Judge, Avon, North Somerset and Gloucestershire, since 2013; *b* 18 Aug. 1958; *s* of F. R. J. Wildblood and late P. A. M. Wildblood; *m*; one *s* one *d*; *m* 2003, Emma Jane Bassett; two *s* two *d*. *Educ:* Sheffield Univ. (LLB). Called to the Bar, Inner Temple, 1980; Asst Recorder, 1997–2000; Recorder, 2000–07; Dep. High Court Judge, 2004–07. Legal Mem., Mental Health Review Tribunal, 2003–09. *Publications:* (ed jtly) Encyclopedia of Financial Provision in Family Matters, 1998. *Recreations:* sport, reading, languages. *Address:* Bristol Civil and Family Justice Centre, Redcliff Street, Bristol BS1 6GR.

**WILDE, Imogen;** Director, British and Foreign School Society, 2009–16; Consultant, Anderson Quigley, since 2017; *b* 22 Jan. 1949; *d* of late John William Luxton and Eva Luxton; *m* 1978, Patrick John Wilde (*d* 1999); two *d*. *Educ:* Colston's Girls' Sch., Bristol; Durham Univ. (BA Hons Hist. 1969). Postgrad. res., Inst. of Historical Research, 1969–71; joined Department of Education and Science, 1971; Sec. to Warnock Cttee on Educn of Children with Special Educnl Needs, 1975–78; Principal Private Sec. to Sec. of State for Educn and Sci., 1982–83; DES, subseq. DFE, 1983–91; Asst Sec., UGC (on secondment), 1986–88; British Petroleum plc (on secondment), 1988–91; various posts DFE, subseq. DfEE, 1991–99, incl. Divl Manager, HE Funding and Orgn, 1997–99; Dir, Curriculum and Communications, subseq. Assessment, Curriculum and e Learning in Schools, DfEE, subseq. DfES, 1999–2002; Dir, Norman Broadbent, 2003–07; Dir, 2007–11, Associate, 2011–17, Educn Practice, Harvey Nash plc. *Address:* Anderson Quigley, Tintagel House, 92 Albert Embankment, SE1 7TY. *T:* 07857 989768. *E:* imogen@andersonquigley.com.

**WILDE, John;** HM Diplomatic Service, retired; High Commissioner to Botswana, 1998–2001; *b* 6 Oct. 1941; *s* of John William and Clara Wilde; *m* 1965, Jeanette Grace Reed; one *s* one *d*. *Educ:* Malet Lambert Sch., Hull. Foreign Office, 1959; served Conakry, Pretoria, Kuwait, Tripoli, FCO and Zagreb, to 1976; Singapore, 1976–79; FCO, 1979–82; Asst to Dep. Governor, Gibraltar, 1982–85; jsdc, 1985; First Sec., FCO, 1985–87; Dep. High Comr, Lilongwe, 1987–91; FCO, 1991–95 (Mem., EC Monitor to former Yugoslavia, 1991; ECMM Service Medal, 1994); High Comr, The Gambia, 1995–98. *Recreations:* golf, music, reading. *Address:* 115 Main Street, Willerby, E Yorks HU10 6DA.

**WILDEN, Jonathan James;** Chief Executive Officer, Folio Education Trust, since 2018 (Executive Headteacher, WCGS Academy, then Opia Trust, later Folio Education Trust, 2015–18); *b* Ipswich, Suffolk, 8 Jan. 1976; *s* of John Edward and Margaret Patricia Wilden; *m* 2005, Joann Marie Croudace (separated, 2017); two *s* one *d*. *Educ:* St Joseph's Coll., Ipswich; Univ. of Wales, Lampeter (BA Hons Geog.); Univ. of Bath (PGCE); Univ. of Sussex (DipEd); Inst. of Educn (NPQH). Teacher of Geography: St Andrew's Sch., Leatherhead, 1998–99; Riddlesdown High Sch., Croydon, 1999–2003; Subject Leader for Geog., Wimbledon Coll., 2003–09; Dep Headteacher, Evelyn Grace Acad., Brixton, 2009–10; Dep. Headteacher, 2010–13, Headmaster, 2013–18, Wallington Co. Grammar Sch.; Founding Headteacher, Coombe Wood Sch., 2014–18. *Recreations:* children, triathlon and adventure racing, climbing Munros, open water swimming, looking out of windows. *Clubs:* Lansdowne; Tri Surrey Triathlon (Co-Founder and Chm., 2012–16) (Sanderstead, Surrey).

**WILDGOOSE, James Richmond,** DPhil; Head, Scotland Office, 2005–07; *b* 17 April 1949; *s* of Thomas Wildgoose and Annie Wildgoose; *m* 1982, (Charlotte) Dorothy Campbell; one *s* one *d*. *Educ:* Melville Coll., Edinburgh; Univ. of Edinburgh (BSc 1971); DPhil Oxon 1978. Economist and policy postings, MAFF, 1975–90; Chief Economist, Agric. and Fisheries Dept, Scottish Office, 1990–96, Hd of Profession, 1994–95; Rural Affairs Department, Scottish Office, then Scottish Executive: Hd, Food Safety Animal Health and Welfare Div., 1996–2000; Hd, CAP Mgt Div., 2000–02; Hd, Agricl Policy and Food Div., 2002–05. Member: Scottish Food Adv. Cttee, 2009– (Chm., 2012–); Bd, Food Standards Agency, 2011–15. *Recreations:* golf, mentoring at local primary school, chair of support group for lung condition (bronchiectasis), involvement in local Church of Scotland, travel.

**WILDING, Alison,** OBE 2019; RA 1999; sculptor; *b* Blackburn, Lancs, 7 July 1948; *m*. *Educ:* Nottingham Coll. of Art; Ravensbourne Coll. of Art and Design, Bromley, Kent; Royal Coll. of Art. Solo exhibitions include: Serpentine Gall., London, 1985; MOMA, NY, 1987; retrospective, Tate Gall., Liverpool, 1991; New Art Centre, Roche Court, Wilts, 1997, 2000; Northern Gall. for Contemp. Art, Sunderland, 1998; Henry Moore Foundn Studio, Dean Clough Galls, Halifax, 2000; Acanthus Asymmetrically, 2017; group exhibitions in UK, Ireland and Canada. Sculpture in public places incl. Ambit, Sunderland, 1999. *Address:* c/o Karsten Schubert, 46 Lexington Street, W1F 0LP.

**WILDING, Barbara,** CBE 2006; QPM 2000; Chief Constable, South Wales Police Authority, 2004–09; *m* Jeffrey E. Rees, QPM; two *d*. *Educ:* London Sch. of Econs (Dip. Criminology, 1980). WPC, States of Jersey Police; Detective, Metropolitan Police; Asst Chief Constable, Personnel, 1994–96, Crime, 1996–98, Kent Constabulary; Dep. Asst Comr, Corporate Strategic Resourcing, 1998–2000, Security and Protection Comd, 2000–03, Metropolitan Police. Member: RIIA, 2001–; RCDS, 2003–; Nat. Exec. Inst., FBI, 2005–; Adv. Bd, BITC Wales, 2006–09; Council, Prince's Trust Cymru, 2006–09; Bd, Big Lottery Cymru, 2006–14; Internat. Adv. Gp, Cardiff Business Sch., 2008–11; Adv. Bd, Out of Trouble Prison Reform Trust, 2009–12; Council, High Sheriff Assoc., 2012–18. Founder, Univ. Police Sci. Inst., Univ. of S Wales (formerly Glamorgan Univ.) and Cardiff Univ., 2007–. Gov., Cardiff Metropolitan Univ. (formerly UWIC), 2010–18 (Chm., 2011–18; Chancellor, 2015–). Trustee: S Wales Police Youth Trust, 2009–12; Nat. Crimebeat, 2010–18 (Chm., 2013–18); Butler Trust, 2014–. Life Member: ACPO, 2010; British Assoc. of Women Police, 2010. Vice President: Age Cymru, 2010; Cardiff Business Club, 2011. Liveryman, Livery Co. of Wales (formerly Mem., Welsh Livery Guild), 2006. CCMI 2005. FRSA 2006–18. High Sheriff, Mid Glamorgan, 2011–12. Hon. Fellow: Cardiff Univ., 2007; Swansea Univ., 2009. DUniv Glamorgan, 2008. *E:* rt.associates@live.co.uk. *Club:* Athenæum.

**WILDING, Christine Mary;** Director, British Institute of Florence, 1998–2003; *b* 7 Oct. 1941; *d* of Lionel Walter Haines and Marjorie Gibson Haines (*née* Hall); *m* 1964, Malcolm David Wilding (marr. diss. 1999); two *s* one *d*. *Educ:* Univ. of Leeds (BA Italian 1962). Language teaching posts, 1963–78; Res. Asst, Univ. of Aston, 1979–82; Sec., Jt Council of Lang. Assocs, 1982–89; Dir, Assoc. for Lang. Learning, 1989–97. Vis. Lectr, Univs of Warwick and Aston in Birmingham, 1977–79. Co-ordinator, Fest. of Langs and Young Linguists Awards, 1982–92. Sec., Bd of Trustees, Studio Arts Coll. Internat., Florence, 2015–. Chevalier, Ordre des Palmes Académiques (France), 1988. *Publications:* research papers and articles to promote use of foreign langs in business, and to motivate language learning. *Recreations:* family, cooking, walking, art history, SACI, Italy, meeting people, travel. *Address:* Les Cèdres, 1 rue des Tilleuls, 74500 Amphion-les-Bains, Haute Savoie, France. *T:* (04) 50810868. *E:* cwilding04@gmail.com.

See also Prof. R. D. Wilding.

**WILDING, His Honour Keith;** a Circuit Judge, 2013–19; *b* London, 9 Feb. 1953; *s* of Sidney and Lilian Wilding; *m* 1973, Jane Catherine Flanagan; two *d*. *Educ:* London Nautical Sch.; Coll. of Law, London. Admitted as solicitor, 1977; a Dep. Dist Judge, 1991–2002; a Dist Judge, 2002–13. *Recreations:* family, Rugby, golf, theatre, cinema. *Club:* Old Albanian Rugby Football.

**WILDING, Prof. Richard David,** OBE 2013; PhD; FIET; FCILT; FCIPS; PFHEA; Professor and Chair of Supply Chain Strategy (formerly Professor and Chair of Supply Chain Risk Management), Cranfield School of Management, Cranfield University, since 2010; *b* Sheffield, 8 May 1965; *s* of Dr Malcolm David Wilding and Christine Mary Wilding, *qv*; *m* 1990, Janice Caroline Lowe; one *s* one *d*. *Educ:* Princethorpe Coll., Princethorpe, Rugby; Univ. of Sheffield (BSc Tech. Hons); Univ. of Warwick (PhD Engrg 1998). Prodn Manager, Steetley Brick and Concrete Products Ltd, Newcastle-under-Lyme, 1987–89; systems engr, IMI Refiners Ltd, Walsall, 1989–91; Fellow, 1991–93, Sen. Fellow, 1993–97, and Principal Fellow in Logistics and Supply Chain Mgt, 1997–98, Warwick Mfg Gp, Univ. of Warwick; Cranfield School of Management, Centre for Logistics and Supply Chain Management, Cranfield University: Lectr, 1998–2000; Sen. Lectr, 2000–02; Director: In-company Progs, 2002–04; Customised Progs, 2004–06; Prof. and Chair of Supply Chain Risk Mgt, 2006–10. Visiting Professor: RMIT, 2008–10; Internat. Univ. of Logistics and Transport, Wroclaw, 2017–. Institute of Logistics and Transportation Research Network, CILT: Mem., Dirs' Forum, 1991–2010, Exec. Cttee, Leaders in Supply Chain, UK, 2010– (Co-Chm., 2012–16); Founding Mem., Steering Cttee, 1994; Tech. Advr, careers video, 1998–99; Bd Dir and Trustee, 2011–; Chm., CILT, 2015–. Advr on ops mgt and supply chain texts to Internat. Thompson Publishing and Wiley Publishing, 1999–. Vice Patron, Beds Garden Carers, 2012–. Freeman: City of London, 2013; Carmen's Co., 2012 (Liveryman, 2013). PFHEA 2016 (Fellow, Inst. for Learning and Teaching in HE 2001, later FHEA); FCILT 2006; FIET 2007; FCIPS 2014. Dist. Service Award, Eur. Supply Chain Distinction Awards, 2008; Individual Contribution Award, Eur. Supply Chain Excellence Awards, 2010; Viscount Nuffield Silver Medal for Achievement in Design and Production, IET, 2013; Logistics100 Award, SHD Logistics, 2017; Lifetime Contribn to Trng and Develt in Logistics, Talent in Logistics Awards, 2017. *Publications:* contributor: Idol-Lottery (poetry), 1997; The Gower Handbook of Purchasing Management, 3rd edn 2002; World Market Series Business Briefings: global purchasing and supply chain strategies 2004, 2004; (jtly) The Financial Times Handbook of Management, 3rd edn 2004; (jtly) Managing Business Risk: a practical guide to protecting your business, 3rd edn 2006; articles in British Jl Mgt, Internat. Jl Physical Distribn and Logistics Mgt, Eur. Jl Mktg, Jl Mktg Mgt, Supply Chain Mgt, FT. *Recreations:* gym, walking, pinball and jukebox, cleaning cars (car detailing), very amateur magician, BBQs, supporting local Church. *Address:* Cranfield School of Management, Cranfield, Bedford MK43 0AL. *T:* (01234) 751122. *W:* www.richardwilding.info.

**WILDMAN, Maj. Gen. Murray Leslie,** CBE 2001; business consultant, 2001–12; Director General, Whole Fleet Management, Ministry of Defence, 1999–2001; *b* 10 Feb. 1947; *s* of late Peter Wildman and Margery Wildman (*née* Littlechild) and step *s* of Elizabeth Susan Wildman (*née* White); *m* 1974, Lindsay Anne Johnson. *Educ:* Reading Sch.; Royal Military Coll. of Sci. (BSc (Eng) 1969). CEng 1987; Eur Ing 1991; FIET (FIEE 1991). Army service, 1968–2001, mainly in engrg and equipt support field; rcds 1993; Dir, Equipt Support, MoD, 1993–96; Defence Advr, Pretoria, S Africa, 1996–99. Dir, Defence Business

Solutions Ltd, 2001–12. Non-exec. Dir, G3 Systems Ltd, 2003–08. Chm., CCF Assoc., 2004–11. Chm., ABF Fundraising Cttee, Wilts, 2001–12. President: TA Rifle Assoc., 2006–14; Old Redingensians Assoc., 2010. *Recreations:* ski-ing, classic cars. *Clubs:* Victory Services; Alpbach Visitors Ski; MG Owners.

**WILDOR, Sarah;** ballet dancer; *b* 1972; *m* Adam Cooper, *qv*; one *s* one *d*. *Educ:* Royal Ballet Sch. Royal Ballet, 1991–2001: soloist, 1994; Principal, 1999; main rôles include: Juliet, in Romeo and Juliet; Giselle; Ondine; Manon; Anastasia; Cinderella; Titania, in The Dream; Lise, in La Fille Mal Gardée; with Adventures in Motion Pictures, Cinderella, 1998; The Two Pigeons, Scottish Ballet, 2002; (and acted) Contact, Queen's, 2002; On Your Toes, RFH, 2003; Les Liaisons Dangereuses, Japan, then Sadler's Wells, 2005; You Can't Take It With You, Southwark Playhouse, 2007; Shall We Dance, Sadler's Wells, 2009.

**WILDS, Ven. Anthony Ronald;** Archdeacon of Plymouth, 2001–10, now Archdeacon Emeritus; Associate Priest, Marnhull, Salisbury, 2015–18; *b* 4 Oct. 1943; *s* of Ernest and Eva Wilds; *m* 1967, Elizabeth Mary Prince; three *d*. *Educ:* Univ. of Durham (BA 1964); Bishops' Coll., Cheshunt. Ordained deacon, 1966, priest, 1967, Asst Curate, Newport Pagnell, 1966–72; Priest in charge, Chipili, Zambia, 1972–75; Vicar: Chandlers Ford, Hants, 1975–85; Andover, Hants, 1985–97; Rector, Solihull, W Midlands, 1997–2001. *Recreations:* travel, walking, gardening, Rugby Union. *Address:* 10 St Luke's Road, Midsomer Norton, Radstock, Som BA3 2EJ.

**WILDSMITH, Prof. John Anthony Winston, (Tony),** MD; FRCA, FRCPE, FRCSE, FDSRCS; Foundation Professor and Head of Department of Anaesthesia, University of Dundee, 1995–2007, now Emeritus; Hon. Consultant Anaesthetist, Tayside University (formerly Dundee Teaching) Hospitals NHS Trust, 1995–2007; *b* 22 Feb. 1946; *s* of Winston Wildsmith and Phyllis Wildsmith (*née* Jones); *m* 1969, Angela Fay Smith; three *d*. *Educ:* King's Sch., Gloucester; Edinburgh Univ. Med. Sch. (MB ChB 1969; MD 1982). FRCA (FFARCS 1973); FRCPE 1996; FRCSE 2005; FDSRCS 2008. Grad. Res. Fellow, Dept of Physiology and Anaesthetics, Univ. of Edinburgh, 1971–72; Rotating Registrar in Anaesthesia, Edinburgh Trng Scheme, 1972–75; Lectr in Anaesthesia, Univ. of Edinburgh, 1975–77; Royal Infirmary of Edinburgh: Consultant Anaesthetist, 1977–95; part-time Sen. Lectr, 1977–95; Clin. Dir of Anaesthesia, Theatres and Intensive Care, 1992–95. Vis. Lectr in Anaesthesia, Harvard Med. Sch., 1983–84. President: Scottish Soc. of Anaesthetists, 2003–04; History of Anaesthesia Soc., 2008–10; Dundee Med. Club, 2008–09. Mem. Council, RCAnaes, 1997–2007 (Hon. Archivist, 2012–15; Ed., Lives of Fellows Project, 2015–). *Publications:* edited jointly: Principles and Practice of Regional Anaesthesia, 1987 (trans. German 1991), 4th edn 2013; Induced Hypotension, 1991; Conduction Blockade for Postoperative Analgesia, 1991; Anaesthesia for Vascular Surgery, 2000; chapters and papers on aspects of regional anaesthesia, acute pain relief, induced hypotension and history of anaesthesia. *Recreations:* travel, wine, model railways. *Address:* 6 Castleroy Road, Broughty Ferry, Dundee DD5 2LQ. *T:* (01382) 732451. *Club:* Royal Automobile.

**WILES, Sir Andrew (John),** KBE 2000; PhD; FRS 1989; Regius Professor of Mathematics, University of Oxford, since 2018 (Royal Society 2010 Anniversary Research Professor, Mathematical Institute, 2011–18); Fellow, Merton College, Oxford, since 2011; *b* 11 April 1953; *s* of Rev. Prof. Maurice Frank Wiles, FBA; *m*; two *d*. *Educ:* Merton Coll., Oxford (BA 1974; MA 1988; Hon. Fellow); Clare Coll., Cambridge (MA 1977; PhD 1980). Jun. Res. Fellow, Clare Coll., Cambridge, 1977–80; IAS, Princeton Univ., 1981; Prof. of Maths, Princeton Univ., 1982–88; Guggenheim Fellow, Paris, 1985–86; Royal Society Res. Prof. in Maths and Professorial Fellow of Merton Coll., Oxford Univ., 1988–90; Prof. of Maths, 1990, Eugene Higgins Prof., 1994, James S. McDonnell Prof. of Maths, 2009, now Emeritus, Princeton Univ. Solved and proved Fermat's Last Theorem, 1994. For. Mem., US NAS, 1996; Hon. Mem., LMS, 2001. Hon. DSc: Oxon, 1999; Cambridge, 2010. (Jtly) Jun. Whitehead Prize, LMS, 1988; Royal Medal, 1996, Copley Medal, 2017, Royal Soc.; IMU Silver Plaque, 1998; Abel Prize, Norwegian Acad. of Sci. and Letters, 2016. *Publications:* Modular elliptic curves and Fermat's Last Theorem, in Annals of Mathematics, 1995; contrib. to learned jls. *Address:* Mathematical Institute, University of Oxford, Andrew Wiles Building, Radcliffe Observatory Quarter, Woodstock Road, Oxford OX2 6GG.

**WILES, Clive Spencer;** a District Judge (Magistrates' Courts) (formerly Stipendiary Magistrate), Middlesex, 1996–2013; *b* 1 Dec. 1942; *s* of late Ernest George Wiles and of Emily Louise Wiles (*née* Cummings); *m* 1966, Marie Susan Glasgow; two *s*. *Educ:* Leggatts Sch., Watford. Articled clerk to Clerk to Justices, Watford, 1962–67; admitted Solicitor, 1968; Solicitor, subseq. Partner, Ellis Hancock, Watford, later Hancock Quins, 1968–96. *Recreations:* golf, walking, gardening, reading, photography.

**WILES, Harry;** HM Diplomatic Service, retired; Ambassador to Nicaragua, 2000–02; *b* 17 June 1944; *s* of John Horace Wiles and Margaret, (Peggy), Wiles; *m* 1966, Margaret Bloom; two *d*. *Educ:* Hull Grammar Sch. Joined Foreign Office, 1964: Ankara, 1966–68; Paris, 1969–72; Algiers, 1972–75; FCO, 1975–78; Vice Consul, Bilbao, 1978–81; Third Sec. (Admin), Jedda, 1981–83; Second Secretary: (Admin), Riyadh, 1983–84; (Commercial), Abu Dhabi, 1984–88; Second, later First, Sec., on loan to ECGD, 1988–90; Consul (Commercial) and Dep. Consul Gen., Barcelona, 1990–94; First Sec. (Commercial), Buenos Aires, 1994–98; Dep. Hd of Security Comd, FCO, 1998–2000. *Recreations:* golf, Rugby League (spectating), music, reading, gardening.

**WILES, Air Vice-Marshal Matthew John Gethin,** CB 2013; CBE 2008; FCILT; FCIPS; FCIPD; Chief Executive, Leidos UK, since 2016; *b* 9 Feb. 1961; *s* of Wallace and Elizabeth Anne Wiles; *m* 1989, Rebecca White; one *d*. *Educ:* Fakenham Grammar Sch.; Open Univ. (MBA 2000). Jun. logistics roles, 1982–90; PSO to DG Support Mgt (RAF), 1990–92; OC Supply and Movts Sqn, RAF Odiham, 1992–94; RAF Advanced Staff Course, 1995; Wing Comdr Resources, HQ Strike Comd, 1995–96; Head of Tri Star/Royal Sqn Support Authy, 1996–98; Prog. Dir, Defence Logistics Orgn, 1998–2001; RCDS, 2002; Asst Dir Internat., MoD (Air Staff), 2002–04; Dir Supply Chain Support, Defence Logistics Orgn, 2004–06; HCSC 2005; ACOS Personnel and Logistics, UK Perm. Jt HQ, 2006–07; Hd, RAF Logistics (formerly Supply) Branch, 2007–11; Dir Gen. Jt Supply Chain, later Dir Jt Support Chain, Defence Equipment and Support, 2008–10; Comd Exec. Officer, HQ Air Comd, 2010–11; Air Sec. and COS Personnel, HQ Air Comd, 2011–13. Man. Dir, Serco Defence, 2014–16. FCILT 1998; FCIPS 2009; FCIPD 2013. Trustee, British Forces Foundn, 2014–. *Recreations:* collecting (and sampling) fine wine, horse riding, travel, keeping up with my family. *E:* matt.wiles@leidos.com. *Club:* Royal Air Force (Chm., Bd of Trustees, 2008–10, 2012–14; Vice-Pres., 2014–17).

**WILES, Paul Noel Porritt,** CB 2005; Biometrics Commissioner, since 2016; *b* 24 Dec. 1944; *m* 1989, Merlyn Alice Greenhalgh (*née* Morton); one *s* one *d*, and three step *s*. *Educ:* London Sch. of Economics (BSc Econ. 1967); Trinity Hall, Cambridge (Dip Criminol. 1968). Lectr in Sociology, LSE, 1969–70; Res. Fellow, Inst. of Criminology, Univ. of Cambridge, 1970–72; University of Sheffield: Lectr in Criminology, 1972–76, Sen. Lectr, 1976–88; Dir, Centre for Criminological and Socio-legal Studies, 1985–89; Prof. of Criminology, 1988–99; Dean, Faculty of Law, 1990–96. Vis. Prof. of Criminology, Univ. of Oxford, 2006–09; Fellow, Wolfson Coll., Oxford, 2006–09. Dir of Res., 1999–2002, Chief Scientific Advr and Dir of Res., Develt and Statistics, 2002–10, Home Office; Govt Chief Social Scientist, 2007–10; Advr, Sentencing Council, 2010–15. Member: Local Govt Boundary Commn for England, 2010–16; Bd, Nat. Centre for Social Res., 2010–16; Bd, Food Standards Agency, 2012–16. Gov., Sheffield Hallam Univ., 2016–. Mem., Mechanics Inst., Eyam, 1979–. *Publications:* monographs, contribs to books, and papers in learned jls on criminology and socio-legal studies. *Recreation:* fell walking. *Address:* Office of the Biometrics Commissioner, PO Box 72256, SW1P 9DU.

**WILEY, Francesca, (Mrs Carl Slater);** QC 2015; *b* London, 1971; *d* of Stewart and Catherine Wiley; *m* 1993, Carl Slater; one *s* one *d*. *Educ:* Trinity Coll., Oxford (BA). Called to the Bar, Gray's Inn, 1996; in practice as barrister, 1996–, specialising in family, children and criminal law. *Recreations:* ski-ing, sailing, cinema, music. *Address:* 1GC, 10 Lincoln's Inn Fields, WC2A 3BP. *T:* (020) 7797 7900. *E:* wiley@1gc.com.

**WILFORD, Daisy Georgia;** *see* Goodwin, D. G.

**WILFORD, (Jacqueline Lee) Penelope;** *see* Woods-Wilford, J. L. P.

**WILFORD, Michael James,** CBE 2001; RIBA; architect; Senior Partner, Michael Wilford Architects, since 2000; *b* 9 Sept. 1938; *s* of James Wilford and Kathleen Wilford; *m* 1960, Angela Spearman; two *s* three *d*. *Educ:* Kingston Tech. Sch.; Northern Poly. Sch. of Architecture; Regent St Poly. Planning Sch. (Hons DipArch with Dist.). Sen. Asst to James Stirling and James Gowan, 1960–63; Associate Partner, with James Stirling, 1964–71; Partner, James Stirling, Michael Wilford and Associates, 1971–92; Senior Partner: Michael Wilford and Partners, 1993–2000; Wilford Schupp Architekten, 2002–13. Major projects include: Staatsgalerie, Stuttgart, 1983; Clore Gall., Tate Gall., 1986; Tate Gall., Liverpool, 1988; No 1 Poultry, 1996; The Lowry, Salford, 2000; British Embassy, Berlin, 2000; Esplanade, Theatres on the Bay, Singapore, 2001; History Mus., Stuttgart, 2002; Carnegie Liby and Acad., Peace Palace, The Hague, 2007; British Embassy, Tbilisi, 2010; Carnegie Visitor Centre, Peace Palace, The Hague, 2012. Vis. Prof., Sch. of Architecture, Liverpool Univ., 2010–. Hon. Mem., Bund Deutscher Architekten, 1997. Hon. FAIA 2006. Hon. DLitt: Sheffield, 1987; Salford, 2002; Hon. DSc: Newcastle, Australia, 1993; Leicester, 2011. *Publications:* Recent Work of James Stirling, Michael Wilford and Associates, 1990; James Stirling, Michael Wilford and Associates Design Philosophy and Recent Projects, 1990; The Museums of James Stirling and Michael Wilford, 1990; James Stirling and Michael Wilford Architectural Monograph, 1993; James Stirling, Michael Wilford and Associates Buildings and Projects 1975–1992, 1994; Wilford-Stirling-Wilford, 1996; Michael Wilford and Partners, 1999; Michael Wilford - Selected Buildings and Projects 1992–2012, 2014; Stirling + Wilford: American buildings, 2014. *Recreation:* earth moving and landscaping. *E:* michaelwilford@michaelwilford.com.

**WILIAM, Eurwyn,** PhD; FSA; Chairman: Royal Commission on Ancient and Historical Monuments in Wales, 2009–19 (Vice-Chairman, 2003–06; Member, 1993–2006); Nantgarw China Works Trust (Trustee, 2007–19); *b* 26 Feb. 1949; *s* of Griffith Owen Williams and Morfudd (*née* Griffith); surname changed to Wiliam, 1970; *m* 1974, Mary Middleton; one *s* one *d*. *Educ:* Botwnnog Grammar Sch.; Univ. of Wales Cardiff (BA Hons Archaeol. 1970); Univ. of Manchester (MA 1972; PhD 1980). FSA 1993. Welsh Folk Museum, National Museum of Wales: Asst Keeper, 1971–76, Asst Keeper in charge, 1976–80, Keeper, 1980–84, Dept of Buildings; Keeper, Dept of Buildings and Domestic Life, 1984–91; Curator, 1991–94; Amgueddfa Cymru - Nat. Mus. Wales (formerly Nat. Mus and Galls of Wales): Assistant Director: Museums Develt, 1994–96; Collections and Res., 1996–99; Dir of Collections and Res. and Dep. Dir-Gen., 1999–2009, now Emeritus Keeper; Acting Dir-Gen., 2002–03. Mem., Historic Buildings Council for Wales, 1994–2004; non-exec. Dir, Council of Museums in Wales, 2003–04; Vice-Pres., ICOMOS UK, 2007–10. Pres., Welsh Mills Soc., 1990–. Chm., Ethnology and Folk Life Section, Guild of Grads, Univ. of Wales, 1993–2005 (Pres., 2005–). Hon. Prof., Sch. of Hist. and Archaeol., Univ. of Wales Cardiff, 1993–2005. Trustee, Strata Florida Trust, 2016–. *Publications:* Traditional Farm Buildings in North-East Wales 1550–1900, 1982; The Historical Farm Buildings of Wales, 1986; Home-made Homes, 1988; Hen Adeiladau Fferm, 1992; Welsh Long-houses, 1992; Welsh Cruck Barns, 1994; The Welsh Cottage, 2010; Y Bwthyn Cymreig, 2010; numerous articles in learned jls. *Recreations:* books, antiques, art, travel. *Address:* 42 St Fagans Drive, St Fagans, Cardiff CF5 6EF.

**WILK, Christopher David;** Keeper, Furniture, Textiles and Fashion Department, Victoria & Albert Museum, since 2001; *b* 28 Dec. 1954; *s* of Maurice Wilk and Norma Wilk (*née* Bloomberg); *m* 1st, 1980, Susan Harris (marr. diss. 1983); 2nd, 1984, Ann Curtis (marr. diss. 1997); two *d*; 3rd, 2002, Carolyn Sargentson; one *s*. *Educ:* Vassar Coll. (AB 1976); Columbia Univ. (MA 1979). Researcher, 1976–78, Curatorial Asst, 1978–79, NY Mus. of Modern Art; freelance curator and writer, 1979–82; Asst Curator, 1982–87, Associate Curator, 1987–88, Brooklyn Mus.; Victoria and Albert Museum: Asst Keeper, 1988–90; Curator and Head of Dept, 1990–96; Chief Curator, Furniture and Woodwork Dept, and British Galls Project, 1996–2001. Member: Adv. Council, The Art Fund (formerly NACF), 1992–; Adv. Bd, American Mus. in Bath, 2005–12; Member Council: Attingham Trust, 1989–2003; 20th Century Soc., 1990–97; Furniture History Soc., 1992–2002 (Chm., Ingram Fund, 1995–2002, Reviews Ed., 1995–2006); Trustee: Emery Walker Trust, 2007–; Isokon Trust, 2005–11. Editl Advr, Studies in the Decorative Arts, 1993–2009. *Publications:* Thonet: 150 years of furniture, 1980; Marcel Breuer: furniture and interiors, 1981; Frank Lloyd Wright: the Kaufmann Office, 1993; (ed) Western Furniture, 1996; (ed) Creating the British Galleries at the V&A: a study in museology, 2004; (ed) Modernism: designing a new world, 2006; Plywood: a material story, 2017; contribs to learned jls. *Recreations:* cycling, soccer (Brentford FC), music. *Address:* Furniture, Textiles and Fashion Department, Victoria and Albert Museum, SW7 2RL. *T:* (020) 7942 2286.

**WILKEN, Sean David Henry;** QC 2010; barrister; *b* Bromley, 20 Aug. 1967; *s* of J. H. F. Wilken and E. W. Wilken; *m* 1999, Theresa Anne Villiers (marr. diss.); partner, Julia Smith; one *s*. *Educ:* Hulme Grammar Sch., Oldham; Brasenose Coll., Oxford (BA Hons 1989); City Univ., London (DipLaw 1990). Called to the Bar, Middle Temple, 1991; in practice as a barrister, 1993–; Counsel, Attorney Gen.'s A Panel, 2003–10. UK Legal Rep., Fedn Internat. du Ski, 2010. *Publications:* Waiver, Variation and Estoppel (jtly), 1998, 3rd edn as The Law of Waiver, Variation and Estoppel, 2012. *Recreations:* ski-ing, climbing, hiking, fencing, diving, photography. *Address:* 39 Essex Chambers, 81 Chancery Lane, WC2A 1DD. *T:* (020) 7832 1111, *Fax:* (020) 7353 3978. *E:* sean.wilken@39essex.com. *Clubs:* Lansdowne, Ivy.

**WILKES, Rev. David Edward,** CB 2008; OBE 1995; Chaplain-General to the Land Forces, 2004–08; *b* 7 June 1947; *s* of Edward and Mary Wilkes; *m* 1967, Dianne Butters; two *s* one *d*. *Educ:* Sandbach Sch., Cheshire; Hartley Victoria Coll. (Methodist Ch Theol Coll.), Manchester. Ordained Methodist minister, 1976; Worsley, 1973–78, Kettering and Corby, 1978–80, Methodist Circuit; Chaplain, HM Forces, 1980–: Sen. Chaplain, NI, 1993–95; Dep. Chaplain-Gen., 2000–04. Ecumenical Canon, Ripon Cathedral, 2005–08, now Canon Emeritus. QHC, 2000–08. Regtl Chaplain, Yorks Regt Assoc., 2011–. *Recreations:* fly-fishing, walking, reading, travelling, Rugby Union supporter. *Address:* 3 Snowden Close, Beverley, E Yorks HU17 0WG.

**WILKES, Prof. John Joseph,** FSA; FBA 1986; Yates Professor of Greek and Roman Archaeology, University College London, 1992–2001, Professor Emeritus, since 2001; *b* 12 July 1936; *s* of Arthur Cyril Wilkes and Enid Cecilia Eustance; *m* 1980, Dr Susan Walker; (one *s* decd). *Educ:* King Henry VIII Grammar Sch., Coventry; Harrow County Grammar Sch.; University Coll. London (BA); Univ. of Durham (St Cuthbert's Society) (PhD). FSA 1969. Research Fellow, Univ. of Birmingham, 1961–63; Asst Lectr in History and Archaeology, Univ. of Manchester, 1963–64; Lectr in Roman History, 1964–71, Sen. Lectr 1971–74, Univ. of Birmingham; Prof. of Archaeology of the Roman Provinces, Univ. of London, 1974–92. Chm., Faculty of Archaeology, Hist. and Letters, British Sch. at Rome, 1979–83. Vis. Fellow, Inst. of Humanistic Studies, Pennsylvania State Univ., 1971. Mem., Ancient Monuments Bd for Scotland, 1981–91. Hon. Vice-Pres., Soc. for Promotion of Roman Studies, 1978; President: London and Middx Archaeological Soc., 1982–85; Assoc. for Roman Archaeology, 2010–18. Corresp. Mem., German Archaeol Inst., 1976. Governor, Mus. of London, 1981–95. Member: Council, British Sch. at Rome, 1988–96; Mgt Cttee, British Sch. at Athens, 1990–97. Editor, Britannia, 1980–84. *Publications:* Dalmatia (Provinces of Roman Empire series), 1969; (jtly) Diocletian's Palace: joint excavations in the southeast quarter, Pt 1, Split, 1972; (ed jtly) Victoria County History of Cambridgeshire, vol. VII, Roman Cambridgeshire, 1978; Rhind Lectures (Edinburgh), 1984; Diocletian's Palace, Split (2nd Ian Saunders Meml Lecture, expanded), 1986; (jtly) Stageath: excavations within the Roman Fort 1973–1986, 1989; The Illyrians, 1992; (jtly) Excavations at Sparta 1988–95, reports 1994–98; (ed jtly) Epigraphy and the Historical Sciences, 2012; papers, excavation reports and reviews in learned jls of Britain, Amer., and Europe. *Recreations:* listening to music, watching Association football.

**WILKES, Ven. Michael Jocelyn James P.;** *see* Paget-Wilkes.

**WILKES, Richard Geoffrey,** CBE 1990 (OBE (mil.) 1969); TD 1959; DL; FCA; company director; Director, Cassidy, Davis Insurance Group, 1989–99 (Chairman, 1998–99); Partner, Price Waterhouse, Chartered Accountants, 1969–90; *b* 12 June 1928; *s* of Geoffrey W. Wilkes and Kathleen (née Quinn); *m* 1953, Wendy Elaine, *d* of Rev. C. Ward; one *s* three *d*. *Educ:* Repton (Exhibnr). ACA 1952; FCA 1957. Partner, Bolton Bullivant, Chartered Accountants, Leicester, 1953–69. Pres., Leics and Northants Soc. of Chartered Accountants, 1967–68; Mem. Council, Inst. of Chartered Accountants in England and Wales, 1969–90 (Dep. Pres., 1979–80; Pres., 1980–81); Chairman: UK Auditing Practices Cttee, 1976–78; CA Compensation Scheme, 1990–98; International Federation of Accountants: UK Rep.; Mem. Council, 1983–87; Dep. Pres., 1985–87; Pres., 1987–90; Mem., Internat. Auditing Practices Cttee, 1978–79; Adviser on self-regulation, Lloyd's of London, 1983–85. Governor, CARE for the Mentally Handicapped, 1972–98 (Chm., 1995–98). Commnd RHA, 1947; served TA, RA and Royal Leics Regt, 1948–69; CO 4/5th Bn Royal Leics Regt (TA), 1966–69; Col TAVR E Midlands Dist, 1969–73; ADC (TAVR) to the Queen, 1972–77. Dep. Hon. Col, Royal Anglian Regt (Leics), 1981–88; Vice Chm., E Midlands TA&VRA, 1980–89 (Chm., Leics Co. Cttee, 1980–89); Chm., E Midlands TAVRA Employers Liaison Cttee, 1990–98. Comdt, Leics Special Constab., 1972–79. Chm., Leics SSAFA, 1991–98 (Treas., 1969–91). Mem., Court, Worshipful Co. of Chartered Accountants in England and Wales, 1977–98 (Master, 1991–92). DL Leics, 1967. Internat. Award, ICA, 1990. *Recreations:* shooting, sailing, gardening. *Club:* Army and Navy.

**WILKES, Very Rev. Robert Anthony;** Vicar, St Michael at the North Gate with St Martin and All Saints, Oxford, 2013–17 (Priest-in-charge, 2009–13); City Rector, Oxford, 2009–17; part-time Chaplain, Campsfield Immigration Removal Centre, 2016–19; *b* 2 Sept. 1948; *s* of Leslie Robert Wilkes and Diana Napier Wilkes; *m* 1974, Sheila Katherine Hare; one *s* three *d*. *Educ:* Pocklington Sch., York; Trinity Coll., Oxford (MA Lit.Hum.); Wycliffe Hall, Oxford. Ordained deacon, 1974, priest, 1975; Curate, 1974–77, Vicar, 1977–81, St Oswald, Netherton, Bootle; Chaplain and Press Officer to Rt Rev. David Sheppard, Bp of Liverpool, 1978–85; Mission Partner, then Regl Sec., CMS, ME and Pakistan, 1985–98; Priest-in-charge, then Team Rector, Mossley Hill, Liverpool, 1998–2006; Dean of Birmingham, 2006–09. Chm., Ch of Pakistan Partners Forum, 1987–97; Focal person, ME Forum, CTBI, 1993–97; Pres., Internat. Assistance Mission, Afghanistan, 1992–97. Chairman: Lifelong Learning, Liverpool Dio., 2000–03; Merseyside Council of Faiths, 2005–06. Trustee: St Michael's and All Saints' Charities, 2009–17; Restore, Oxford, 2013– (Chm., 2018–); Asylum Welcome, Oxford, 2014–17 (Chm., 2015–17); Faith to Share, 2014– (Chm., 2016–). *Recreations:* singing, fell walking, swimming.

**WILKIE, Hon. Sir Alan (Fraser),** Kt 2004; a Judge of the High Court, Queen's Bench Division, 2004–17; Presiding Judge North Eastern Circuit, 2007–10; *b* 26 Dec. 1947; *s* of late James and Helen Wilkie; *m* 1972, Susan Elizabeth Musgrave; one *s* one *d*. *Educ:* Hutchesons' Grammar Sch., Glasgow; Manchester Grammar Sch.; Balliol Coll., Oxford (BA, BCL). Lecturer in Law: Exeter Coll., Oxford, 1971–72; Southampton Univ., 1972–74; called to the Bar, Inner Temple, 1974, Bencher, 2001; QC 1992; an Asst Recorder, 1992–95; a Recorder, 1995–97; a Circuit Judge, 1997–2004; a Law Comr, 2000–04. Mem., Judicial Appts Commn, 2012–16; Judicial Comr of Investigative Powers Commn, 2017–. *Recreations:* music, films, watching football, playing 5-a-side, cycling.

**WILKIE, Prof. Alex James,** FRS 2001; PhD; Fielden Professor of Pure Mathematics, University of Manchester, 2007–15, now Emeritus; *b* 1 Aug. 1948; *s* of late Alan George Wilkie and Hilda Grace Wilkie (née Mitchell); *m* 1987, Catrin Roberts; one *s* one *d*. *Educ:* University Coll. London (BSc); Bedford Coll., London (MSc, PhD 1972). Lectr in Maths, Univ. of Leicester, 1972–73; Res. Fellow in Maths, Open Univ., 1973–78; Jun. Lectr in Maths, Oxford Univ., 1978–80 and 1981–82; Res. Fellow in Maths, Univ. Paris VII, 1982–83; SERC Advanced Res. Fellow, 1983–84, Lectr in Maths, 1984–86, Univ. of Manchester; Reader in Math. Logic, 1986–2007, and titular Prof., 1996–2007, Univ. of Oxford; Fellow, Wolfson Coll., Oxford, 1986–2007, now Emeritus. Leverhulme Emeritus Fellow, 2015–17. Vis. Asst Prof. in Maths, Yale Univ., 1980–81. Carol Karp Prize, Assoc. for Symbolic Logic, 1993, 2013. *Publications:* contrib. numerous papers in maths and mathematical logic jls. *Address:* Mathematical Institute, University of Oxford, Andrew Wiles Building, Radcliffe Observatory Quarter, Woodstock Road, Oxford OX2 6GG.

**WILKIE, Prof. Andrew Oliver Mungo,** FRCP; FMedSci; FRS 2013; FRSB; Nuffield Professor of Pathology, University of Oxford, since 2003; *b* 14 Sept. 1959; *s* of late Douglas Robert Wilkie, FRS and June Rosalind Wilkie (née Hill); *m* 1989, Jane Elizabeth Martin; two *s*. *Educ:* Arnold House Sch.; Westminster Sch.; Trinity Coll., Cambridge (BA 1980, MA 1984); Merton Coll., Oxford (BM BCh 1988; DM 1992). MRCP 1986, FRCP 1998; DCH 1987; FRSB (FSB 2013). MRC Trng Fellow, Univ. of Oxford, 1987–90; Clinical Res. Fellow, Inst. of Child Health, London, 1990–91; Sen. Registrar, Inst. of Medical Genetics, Cardiff, 1992–93; Wellcome Trust Advanced Trng Fellow, 1993–95, then Sen. Res. Fellow in Clinical Sci., 1995–2003, Univ. of Oxford. Hon. Consultant in Clinical Genetics, Oxford Univ. Hosps (formerly Oxford Radcliffe Hosps) NHS Trust, 1993–. Wellcome Sen. Investigator, 2014–19. Galton Lectr, Galton Inst., 2014. Mem., EMBO, 2006. FMedSci 2002. Oon Internat. Award, Downing Coll., Cambridge, 2002; Carter Medal, Clinical Genetics Soc., 2018. *Publications:* articles on genetic mechanisms of skull and limb malformations, and on mutations associated with paternal age effect in learned jls, inc. Nature, Cell, Nature Genetics, Science. *Recreations:* ornithology, Munros (mainly in winter), wild camping, visual arts, Test Match Special. *Address:* Weatherall Institute of Molecular Medicine, John Radcliffe Hospital, Headington, Oxford OX3 9DS. *T:* (01865) 222619, *Fax:* (01865) 222500. *E:* andrew.wilkie@imm.ox.ac.uk.

**WILKIE, Kim Edward Kelvin,** RDI 2009; landscape architect, since 1984; *b* 30 Oct. 1955. *Educ:* Winchester Coll.; New Coll., Oxford (MA); Univ. of California, Berkeley (MLA). MLI (ALI 1987). Marketing Manager, Unilever, 1978–81; Associate, Land Use Consultants, 1984–89; Principal, Kim Wilkie (formerly Kim Wilkie Associates), 1989–. Awards: Amer. Soc. of Landscape Architects, 1984; Francis Tibbalds, RTPI, 1994; Landscape Inst., 1995; RTPI, 1996; Centenary, Country Life, 1997; for Place Design, Envmtl Design Res. Assoc., US, 1999. Hon. FRIBA 2002. Dist. Alumnus, Univ. of Calif, Berkeley, 2016. *Publications:* Thames Landscape Strategy: Hampton to Kew, 1994; Indignation!, 2000; Led by the Land, 2012. *Address:* Franklin Farm, Dean Lane, Bishop's Waltham SO32 1FX.

**WILKIE, Nicholas Adam Barnes;** Chief Executive, National Childbirth Trust, 2015–19; *b* Manchester, 5 May 1975; *s* of David Wilkie and Ann Wilkie (née Clucas); *m* 2006, Rebecca Barnes; two *s* one *d*. *Educ:* Wrekin Coll.; Christchurch Grammar Sch., Perth, Australia; Trinity Hall, Cambridge (BA Hist. 1997); Cass Business Sch. (MSc Voluntary Sector Mgt 2008). Trainee, Charities Adv. Trust, 1997–99; youth worker, Dalston Youth Project, 1999–2000; res. asst, Rt Hon. Paul Goggins, MP, 2000; Hd, Sustainable Funding, NCVO, 2000–05; on secondment as Policy Advr, HM Treasury, 2002; Associate, Young Foundn, 2005–06; Chief Exec., London Youth, 2006–12; Parental Leave and Policy Advr, Cabinet Office, 2012–13; Dir, UK Progs, Save the Children, 2013–15. Non-executive Director/Trustee: Social Enterprise UK, 2002–05; Round Chapel Neighbourhood Project, 2002–10; FutureBuilders, 2003–05; London Youth Rowing, 2006–13; Jimmy Dixon Trust, 2012–; West London Zone, 2016–. Mem., Baring Foundn Panel on independence of voluntary sector, 2010–15. Liveryman, Tallow Chandlers' Co., 2015–. Mem., Asparagus Club. *Publications:* (jtly) The Magic Roundabout: how charities can make their money go further, 2003; (jtly) Hunch: a vision for youth in post-austerity Britain, 2011. *Recreations:* mountains, novels, coffee, cricket.

**WILKIN, Richard Cecil,** LVO 1979; MBE (mil.) 1976; DL; Secretary, Estates Business Group, since 2005; *b* 17 Sept. 1944; *s* of late Comdr Henry Egbert Peter Wilkin, RN, and Frances Anne Wilkin (née Chichester; she *m* 1984, Vice Adm. Sir (Robert) Alastair Ewing, KBE, CB, DSC); *m* 1st, 1983, Jane Susan Elliott (marr. diss. 1989), *d* of Sir Roger James Elliott, FRS; 2nd, 2002, Sally Ashley Brown, *d* of Col Ashley Brown, OBE, RM. *Educ:* Eton; RMA Sandhurst. Commnd HM Armed Forces 17th/21st Lancers, 1964; served Rhine Army, Berlin, Libya, British Forces Gulf, Cyprus; Captain 1968; GSO III HQ NI, 1973 (despatches 1974); retired 1975. Joined HM Diplomatic Service, 1975; UK Delegn to Rhodesia Constitutional Conf., Geneva, 1976; First Sec. (Political and Press), Lusaka, 1978; E Caribbean, 1988; attached MoD, 1990; Counsellor, FCO, 1992; retired 1996. Dir Gen., HHA, 1996–2005. Member: Country Land and Business Assoc. Tax Cttee, 1998–; Council, Attingham Trust, 1999–2005; British Tourism Develt Cttee, 2000–05; Exec. Cttee, Historic Envmt Review, 2001–05; NT Wessex Cttee, 2003–10 (Chm., 2006–10). Trustee: Heritage Link, 2002–05; Nat. Heritage Meml Fund, 2006–12 (Chm., Finance Cttee, 2009–12); Wolfeton Riding House, 2012–17; Etches Collection, 2013–17. DL Dorset, 2012. *Recreations:* fishing, painting, fine art and architecture, restoring historic buildings, motor cars, National Hunt racing. *Address:* c/o Messrs C. Hoare & Co., 37 Fleet Street, EC4P 4DQ. *Clubs:* Farmers; New (Edinburgh).

**WILKIN, Rt Rev. Rose Josephine H.;** *see* Hudson-Wilkin.

**WILKINS, Baroness** *cr* 1999 (Life Peer), of Chesham Bois in the county of Buckinghamshire; **Rosalie Catherine Wilkins;** *b* 6 May 1946; *d* of late Eric Frederick Wilkins and Marjorie Phyllis Elizabeth Wilkins. *Educ:* Univ. of Manchester (BA). PA to Dir, Central Council for the Disabled, 1971–74; Information Officer, MIND (Nat. Assoc. for Mental Health), 1974–78; presenter/researcher, Link magazine programme and documentaries, ATV Network and Central Television, 1975–88; freelance video and documentary producer/presenter on disability issues, 1988–96; Information Officer, Nat. Centre for Independent Living, 1997–99. Mem., H of L, 1999–2015. Vice-Chairman: All Party Parly Gp on Disability, 2004–15; All Party Parly Gp on Deafness, 2005–15. Pres., Coll. of Occupational Therapists, 2003–08. Snowdon Award (for outstanding work for the benefit of disabled people), Action Research, 1983. *Recreations:* friends, gardening, theatre, cinema.

**WILKINS, John Anthony Francis,** MBE 1998; Editor of The Tablet, 1982–2003; *b* 20 Dec. 1936; *s* of Edward Manwaring Wilkins and Ena Gwendolen Francis. *Educ:* Clifton Coll., Bristol (Scholar); Clare Coll., Cambridge (State Scholar, 1954; Major Scholar and Foundn Scholar; Classical Tripos 1959, Theol Tripos 1961; BA 1961; MA 2004). Served 1st Bn Glos Regt, 1955–57 (2nd Lieut). Planning Div., Marine Dept, Head Office of Esso Petroleum, London, 1962–63; Asst Editor: Frontier, 1964–67; The Tablet, 1967–72; features writer, BBC External Services, 1972–81; Producer, Radio 4, 1978. Vis. Fellow, Clare Coll., Cambridge, 1996. MA Lambeth, 2004; Hon. DD London, 2015. Ondas Radio Prize, 1973; John Harriott Meml Prize, ITC, 1996; Christian Culture Gold Medal, Assumption Univ., Windsor, Canada, 2001. *Publications:* (ed) How I Pray, 1993; (ed) Understanding Veritatis Splendor, 1994; (ed jtly) Spiritual Stars of the Millennium, 2001; (with Gerald O'Collins) Lost in Translation: the English language and the Catholic Mass, 2017. *Recreation:* ornithology.

**WILKINS, Prof. Malcolm Barrett,** FRSE 1972; Regius Professor of Botany, University of Glasgow, 1970–2000, now Emeritus; *b* 27 Feb. 1933; *s* of Barrett Charles Wilkins and Eleanor Mary Wilkins (née Jenkins); *m* 1959, Mary Patricia Maltby; one *s* (one *d* decd). *Educ:* Monkton House Sch., Cardiff; King's Coll., London. BSc 1954, 1955; PhD London 1958; AKC 1958; DSc 1972. Lectr in Botany, King's Coll., London, 1958–64; Rockefeller Foundn Fellow, Yale Univ., 1961–62; Research Fellow, Harvard Univ., 1962–63; Lectr in Biology, Univ. of East Anglia, 1964–65; Prof. of Biology, Univ. of East Anglia, 1965–67; Prof. of Plant Physiology, Univ. of Nottingham, 1967–70; Glasgow University: Dean, Faculty of Science, 1984–87; Chm., Sch. of Biol Scis, 1988–92. Darwin Lectr, British Assoc. for Advancement of Science, 1967. Member: Biol. Sci. Cttee of SRC, 1971–74; Governing Body: Hill Farming Res. Orgn, 1971–80; Scottish Crops Research Inst., 1974–89; Glasshouse Crops Res. Inst., 1979–88; W of Scotland Agricl Coll., 1983–92; Exec. Cttee, Scottish Field Studies Assoc.; British Nat. Cttee for Biology, 1977–82; Life Science Working Gp, ESA, 1983–89 (Chm., 1987–89); Microgravity Adv. Cttee, ESA, 1985–89; NASA Lifesat Science Cttee, 1986–91; Court, Glasgow Univ., 1993–97. Vice-Pres., RSE, 1994–97 (Mem. Council, 1989–92). Trustee, Royal Botanic Gdn, Edinburgh, 1990–99 (Chm., 1994–99; Hon. Fellow, 1999). Adv. Council, Scottish Agricl Coll. Corresp. Mem., Amer. Soc. of Plant Physiologists, 1985. Dir, West of Scotland Sch. Co.; Chm., Laurel Bank Sch. Co. Ltd. Cons. Editor in Plant Biology, McGraw-Hill Publishing Co., 1968–80; Managing Editor, Planta, 1977–2001. *Publications:* (ed) The Physiology of Plant Growth and Development, 1969; (ed) Advanced Plant Physiology, 1984;

Plantwatching, 1988; papers in Jl of Experimental Botany, Plant Physiology, Planta, Nature, Proc. Royal Soc. *Recreations:* fishing, model engineering. *Address:* 4 Keats House, Belwell Place, Four Oaks, Sutton Coldfield B74 4AZ. *T:* (0121) 323 3242. *E:* Profmwilkins@hotmail.com. *Club:* Caledonian.

WILKINS, Prof. Martin Russell, MD; FRCP; FMedSci; Professor of Clinical Pharmacology, since 1999, Head, Department of Medicine, since 2013; Vice Dean (Research), Faculty of Medicine, since 2017, Director, NIHR–Wellcome Trust (formerly McMichael) Clinical Research Facility, since 2000, and Director, British Heart Foundation Centre of Research Excellence, since 2019, Imperial College London; Consultant Physician, Hammersmith Hospital, since 1990; *b* Wellington, Som, 29 Dec. 1956; *s* of Alan Thomas and Brenda Maureen Wilkins; *m* 1979, Jenny Anne Palfrey; two *s*. *Educ:* Birmingham Univ. Med. Sch. (MB ChB 1979; MD 1988). FRCP 1995. House Surgeon, Manor Hosp., Walsall, 1979; House Physician, 1980, SHO, 1980–82, Selly Oak Hosp., Birmingham; Registrar, 1982–83, Sheldon Res. Fellow, 1983–84, Lectr, 1984–87, Birmingham Univ. Medical Sch.; Sen. Lectr in Clin. Pharmacol., Royal Postgraduate Med. Sch., London, 1990–97; Reader in Clin. Pharmacol., Imperial Coll. Sch. of Medicine, 1997–99; Director: Imperial Coll. Clinical Res. Office, 2004–10; Clinical and Investigative Scis, Imperial Coll. Healthcare NHS Trust, 2008–13. BHF/AHA Travelling Res. Fellow, St Louis, Missouri, 1987–89. Visiting Professor: Chao-Yang Hosp., Beijing, 2010; Liebig Univ. Giessen, 2014. FBPhS 2012; FMedSci 2015. *Publications:* contribs to med. jls, mostly on pulmonary hypertension. *Recreation:* watching football. *Address:* NIHR–Wellcome Trust Clinical Research Facility, Imperial College London, Hammersmith Hospital, Du Cane Road, W12 0NN. *E:* m.wilkins@imperial.ac.uk. *Club:* Bear.

WILKINS, Nancy; barrister-at-law; *b* 16 June 1932; two *s* one *d* (and one *s* decd). *Educ:* School of St Helen and St Katharine, Abingdon, Berkshire. Called to the Bar, Gray's Inn, Nov. 1962; in practice, Midland Circuit, 1962–85; Dep. Circuit Judge, 1974–78; a Recorder, 1978–85; practised in solicitors' office, 1986–90; retired. *Publications:* An Outline of the Law of Evidence (with late Prof. Sir Rupert Cross), 1964, 5th edn 1980; Thomas of Moulton, 2002; Ayscoughfee: a great place in Spalding, 2007; All About Ivo Taillbois, 2010; Five Houses in Spalding, 2014; About Moulton, 2017. *Recreation:* beginning to grow old gracefully.

WILKINS, Prof. Raphael Ashley; President, College of Teachers, 2011–16; *b* Eltham, London, 14 Aug. 1951; *s* of Anthony Wilkins and Nina Wilkins; *m* 1975, Mary Harvey; one *d*. *Educ:* Goldsmiths' Coll., London (BSc 1973; PGCE 1974); Inst. of Educn, Univ. of London (DipEd 1976; MA 1979); Open Univ. (MSc 1985); Durham Univ. (MBA 1992); Lincoln Univ. (EdD 2002). ACP 1977, FCOT 2003; ACIS 1982, FCIS 2010. Teacher, Langley Park Sch. for Boys, 1974–78; Professional Asst, London Bor. of Sutton, 1978–79; Proj. Develt Officer, London Bor. of Newham, 1980–83; Principal Educn Officer, Royal Bor. of Kingston upon Thames, 1983–85; Select Cttee Specialist Asst, H of C, 1985–87; Educn Officer, Assoc. of London Authorities, 1987–88; Asst Dir of Educn, London Bor. of Sutton, 1988–97; Dir of Educn, Thurrock Council, 1997–2000; Dir, Raphael Wilkins Educnl Ltd, 2001–06; Hd, Consultancy and Knowledge Transfer, London Centre for Leadership in Learning, 2006–08; Asst Dir, Inst. of Educn, Univ. of London, 2008–14. *Publications:* Research Engagement for School Development, 2011; Education in the Balance: mapping the global dynamics of school leadership, 2014; articles in learned jls. *Recreations:* watercolour painting, clay pigeon shooting. *Address:* 66 Newgate, Barnard Castle DL12 8NJ. *T:* (01833) 630938. *E:* raphaelwilkins66@gmail.com.

WILKINS, Prof. Terence Arthur, PhD; CEng, FREng; CChem, FRSC; FInstMC; Professor of Nanomanufacturing Innovation, University of Leeds, 2005–17, now Emeritus; Founder, and Director and Chief Executive Officer, Leeds Nanomanufacturing Institute, 2005–17; *b* Wantage, Berks, 24 Oct. 1944; *s* of Arthur Leonard Wilkins and Doris Wilkins (*née* Joyce); *m* 1974, Kay Elizabeth Johnson; two *s* one *d*. *Educ:* King Alfred's Grammar Sch., Wantage; Northern Poly. (BSc Chem. 1969; PhD Catalyst Chem. 1973). CChem 1983; FRSC 1999. Sen. mgt posts in R&D, manufg and business develt, Amersham Internat., 1973–85; Dir Scientifique, Nobel Laureate Christian De Duve Inst. of Cellular and Molecular Pathol., Catholic Univ. of Brussels, 1985–88; Chief Tech. Officer, Chief Operating Officer, then CEO, ICI Diagnostics, 1988–92; ICI plc: Dir, Control and Measurement Engrg, 1992–98; Strategic Res. Dir, 1998–2000; Dir and Founder, ICI Global High-Throughput Res. Centre, 2000–04. Co-Chair, UK Nat. Nanotechnol. Strategy Forum, DEFRA, 2011–14. Member: Adv. Gp, UK Nat. Metrology System Policy Unit, 1992–2002; EC Standards Metrology and Testing High Level Expert Adv. Gp, Brussels, 1994–2002; Chm., EC Industrial Technologies (Nano, Materials, Bio and Prodn) Res. and Innovation Expert Adv. Gp, Brussels, 2002–20. FREng 2017. Freeman, City of London, 2002; Mem., Scientific Instrument Makers' Co., 2002. Hon. DTech London Metropolitan, 2018. Prince of Wales Personal Prize for Industrial Innovation and Prodn, 1985; Industrial Innovation Prize, BBC Wales, 1986; Prince of Wales Co. Prize for Industrial Innovation and Prodn, 1987; ICI Supreme Award for Innovation and Creativity in Engrg, Sci. and Technol., 1996; Callendar Silver Medal, Inst. of Measurement and Control, 2009; Soc. of Chem. in Industry Award, 2013. *Publications:* contrib. chapters in: Liquid Scintillation Counting, 1974; Radioimmunoassay in Clinical Biochemistry, 1978; Physiological Peptides and New Trends in Radioimmunology, 1981; The Direct Estimation of Free Hormones by a Simple Equilibrium Radioimmunoassay, 1981; Radioimmunoassay and Related Procedures in Medicine, 1982; Future Directions in Polymer Colloids, 1987; Complementary Immunoassays II, 1988; Managing Emerging Technologies for Socio-Economic Impact, 2015; Nanomaterials Characterisation, 2016; contribs to scientific pubns on medicine, nanotechnol., chem. engrg, envmtl engrg and UK/EU res. and innovation policy. *Recreations:* family, music (guitarist), theatre, ballet, art (painter), DIY, walking, travel, judo (former student middleweight champion, 1972). *Address:* Chemical and Process Engineering, University of Leeds, R2.17 Engineering Building, Clarendon Road, Leeds LS2 9JT. *T:* (0113) 343 2570. *E:* t.a.wilkins@leeds.ac.uk. *Club:* Civil Service.

WILKINSON, Rev. Canon Alan Bassindale, PhD, DD; lecturer and writer; honorary priest, Portsmouth Cathedral, 1988–2014 (Cathedral Chaplain, 1994–2001; diocesan theologian, 1993–2001); *b* 26 Jan. 1931; *s* of late Rev. J. T. Wilkinson, DD; *m* 1975, Fenella Holland; two *s* one *d* of first marriage. *Educ:* William Hulme's Grammar Sch., Manchester; St Catharine's Coll., Cambridge; College of the Resurrection, Mirfield. MA 1958, PhD 1959, DD 1997 Cambridge. Deacon, 1959; priest, 1960; Asst Curate, St Augustine's, Kilburn, 1959–61; Chaplain, St Catharine's Coll., Cambridge, 1961–67; Vicar of Barrow Gurney and Lecturer in Theology, College of St Matthias, Bristol, 1967–70; Principal, Chichester Theol Coll., 1970–74; Canon and Prebendary of Thorney, 1970–74; Canon Emeritus, 1975; Warden of Verulam House, Dir of Training for Auxiliary Ministry, dio. of St Albans, 1974–75; Lectr in Theology and Ethics, Crewe and Alsager Coll. of Higher Educn, 1975–78; Dir of Training, Diocese of Ripon, 1978–84; Hon. Canon, Ripon Cathedral, 1984; Priest-in-Charge, Darley with Thruscross and Thornthwaite, 1984–88; Tutor, Open Univ., 1988–96. Vis. Fellow, Chichester Inst. of Higher Educn, 1995–97; Fellow, George Bell Inst., Chichester, 1996–; Vis. Lectr, Portsmouth Univ., 1998–2005. Hulsean Preacher, 1967–68; Select Preacher, Oxford Univ., 1982. Mem., Bd of Educn, Gen. Synod, 1981–85; Vice-Chm., Leeds Marriage and Personal Counselling Service, 1981–83. Governor: SPCK, 1982–91; Coll. of Ripon and York St John, 1985–88. Scott Holland Trustee, 1993–95, 1998–2015 (Scott Holland Lectr, 1998). *Publications:* The Church of England and the First World War, 1978, 3rd edn 2014; Would You Believe It?, 1983; More Ready to Hear, 1983; Christian Choices, 1983; Dissent or Conform?, 1986, 2nd edn 2010; The Community of the Resurrection: a centenary history, 1992; (jtly) An Anglican Companion: words from the heart of faith, 1996, 3rd edn 2014; Christian Socialism: Scott Holland to Tony Blair, 1998; One Foot in Eden, 2011; Reflections for the Unfolding Year, 2017; contributor to: Cambridge Sermons on Christian Unity, 1966; Catholic Anglicans Today, 1968; A Work Book in Popular Religion, 1986; Chesterton and the Modernist Crisis, 1990; Britain and the Threat to Stability in Europe, 1993; Forever Building, 1995; The Changing Face of Death, 1997; The Impact of New Labour, 1999; Piety and Learning: the Principals of Pusey House 1884–2002, 2002; Walter Frere, 2011; also to: Faith and Unity, Sobornost, Preacher's Quarterly, London Quarterly Holborn Review, Theology, Clergy Review, New Fire, Church Times, Chesterton Review, Internat. Christian Digest, Modern Hist. Rev., Oxford DNB, Expository Times, Humanitas. *Recreations:* gardening, walking, cinema, Victorian architecture. *Address:* 8 Byron Court, Stockbridge Road, Chichester, W Sussex PO19 1ES. *T:* (01243) 839578.

WILKINSON, Alexander Birrell; QC (Scot.) 1993; Sheriff of Lothian and Borders at Edinburgh, 1996–2001; *b* 2 Feb. 1932; *o s* of late Captain Alexander Wilkinson, MBE, The Black Watch and Isabella Bell Birrell; *m* 1965, Wendy Imogen, *d* of late Ernest Albert Barrett and R. V. H. Barrett; one *s* one *d*. *Educ:* Perth Academy; Univs of St Andrews and Edinburgh. Walker Trust Scholar 1950, Grieve Prizeman in Moral Philosophy 1952, MA (Hons Classics) 1954, Univ. of St Andrews. National Service, RAEC, 1954–56. Balfour Keith Prizeman in Constitutional Law 1957, LLB (with distinction) 1959, Univ. of Edinburgh. Admitted to Faculty of Advocates, 1959; in practice at Scottish bar, 1959–69; Lecturer in Scots Law, Univ. of Edinburgh, 1965–69; Sheriff of Stirling, Dunbarton and Clackmannan at Stirling and Alloa, 1969–72; Prof. of Private Law, 1972–86, and Dean of Faculty of Law, 1974–76 and 1986, Univ. of Dundee; Sheriff of: Tayside, Central and Fife at Falkirk, 1986–91; Glasgow and Strathkelvin, 1991–96; Temp. Judge of Court of Session and High Court of Justiciary, 1993–2003. Chancellor: Dio. of Brechin, 1982–98; Dio. of Argyll and the Isles, 1985–98. Chairman: Central Scotland Marriage Guidance Council, 1970–72; Scottish Marriage Guidance Council, 1974–77; Legal Services Gp, Scottish Assoc. of CAB, 1979–83. Pres., Sheriffs' Assoc., 1997–2000 (Vice-Pres., 1995–97). Trustee, Gen. Synod of Scottish Episcopal Ch, 2005–. *Publications:* (ed jtly) Gloag and Henderson's Introduction to the Law of Scotland, 8th edn 1980, 9th edn 1987; The Scottish Law of Evidence, 1986; (jtly) The Law of Parent and Child in Scotland, 1993; (contrib.) Macphail's Sheriff Court Practice, 2nd edn 1998; (contrib.) Legal Systems of Scottish Churches, 2009; articles in legal periodicals. *Recreations:* collecting books and pictures, reading, travel. *Address:* 1 Weston Gardens, Haddington, East Lothian EH41 3DD. *T:* (01620) 822891. *Club:* New (Edinburgh).

*See also* W. P. Saunders.

WILKINSON, Prof. Andrew Robert, FRCP, FRCPCH; Professor of Paediatrics and Perinatal Medicine, University of Oxford, 1997–2011, now Emeritus; Fellow, All Souls College, Oxford, 1992–2011, now Emeritus; Director of Neonatal Medicine, John Radcliffe Hospital, Oxford, 1981–2011, now Emeritus Consultant; *b* 30 Oct. 1943; *s* of late Rev. Thomas Richard Wilkinson and (Winifred) Frances Wilkinson (*née* Steel). *Educ:* Heath Grammar Sch., Halifax; Univ. of Birmingham Med. Sch. (MB ChB 1968); Univ. of Calif, San Francisco; DCH (Eng) 1972; MA Oxon 1992. MRCP 1972, FRCP 1986; FRCPCH 1997, Hon. FRCPCH 2010. House officer: in medicine and surgery, Dudley Rd Hosp., Birmingham, 1968–69; in paediatrics, Warwick Hosp., 1969–70; SHO in medicine, Dudley Rd Hosp., Birmingham, 1970–71; Registrar in medicine, Stratford-on-Avon, 1971–72; Hse Officer in paediatrics, Gt Ormond St Hosp., 1972–73; SHO in neonatal medicine, Oxford, 1973–74; Registrar, Southampton, 1974; Nuffield Med. Res. Fellow, Univ. of Oxford, 1974–75; Fulbright Fellow, Cardiovascular Res. Inst., Univ. of Calif, San Francisco, 1975–77; Clin. Lectr in Paediatrics, Univ. of Oxford, 1978–81; Consultant Paediatrician, Oxfordshire HA, 1981–92; Clin. Reader in Paediatrics, Univ. of Oxford, 1992–97. Vis. Prof. of Paediatrics, Univ. of Southampton, 2011–. Member: Nat. Adv. Bd for Confidential Enquiry into Stillbirths and Deaths in Infancy, 1995–2000 (Interim Chm., 2000–03); Board: Nat. Neonatal Audit Prog., 2006–; Neonatal Data Analysis Unit, 2007– (Co-Chm., 2011–); Medicines for Neonates, 2008–16. Chairman: Children and Young People's Specialised Services Project, Welsh Assembly Govt, 2004–06; Mem., All Wales Standards for Neonatal Services, 2004–06. President: British Assoc. of Perinatal Medicine, 1999–2002; Neonatal Soc., 2003–06; Treas., Academic Paediatrics Assoc., 2015–. Royal College of Paediatrics and Child Health: Sec., 1993–97, Chm., 1997–98, Acad. Bd; Chm., Acad. Regl Advrs, 2006–11; Sir James Spence Medal, 2011; Council Trustee for Sen. Members, 2012–17. Trustee: Helen and Douglas Hse Hospice, Oxford, 2004–; Oxford Radcliffe Hosps Charitable Trust, 2005–15. Dir, Friends of Warneford Meadow, Town Green, 2012–. Mem. Cttee, Oxford Univ. RFC, 2014–. Knight 1st Cl., Order of the White Rose (Finland), 2003. *Publications:* over 200 papers, articles and chapters in textbooks on care of sick children and specifically in neonatal medicine. *Recreations:* sailing, hill walking, lawn maintenance. *Address:* All Souls College, Oxford OX1 4AL.

*See also* C. R. Wilkinson.

WILKINSON, Brian; *see* Wilkinson, W. B.

WILKINSON, Christopher, (Christopher Haydon); freelance director, since 2017; *b* London, 1 Dec. 1979; *s* of James Hugh Wilkinson, *qv*; partner, Iona Firouzabadi. *Educ:* Hampton Sch.; Fitzwilliam Coll., Cambridge (BA Hons Theol. and Religious Studies); Central Sch. of Speech and Drama (BA Hons Acting). Heller Fellow, Chichester Fest. Th., 2007; Regl Th. Dir Bursary, Salisbury Playhouse, 2007–08; Associate Dir, Bush Th., 2009–11; Artistic Dir, Gate Th., 2012–17. Clore Fellow, 2017. *Publications:* (ed jtly) Conversations on Religion, 2007; (ed jtly) Conversations on Truth, 2008; (ed jtly) Identity and Identification, 2010; The Art of the Artistic Director, 2019; contribs to Guardian, FT, Scotsman, Prospect Mag., New Statesman, Independent, Stage. *E:* christopherhaydon@hotmail.co.uk.

WILKINSON, Christopher John, OBE 2000; RA 2006; Principal (formerly Chairman), Wilkinson Eyre (formerly Chris Wilkinson) Architects Ltd, since 1989; Partner, Wilkinson Design Studios LLP, since 2012; *b* 1 July 1945; *s* of Edward Anthony Wilkinson and Norma Doreen Wilkinson; *m* 1976, Diana Mary Edmunds; one *s* one *d*. *Educ:* St Albans Sch.; Regent Street Poly. (DipArch). RIBA; FCSD. Architect: Foster Associates, 1973–74; Michael Hopkins Architects, 1975–79; Richard Rogers Partnership, 1979–83; founded Chris Wilkinson Architects, 1983; partnership with James Eyre, 1986–; formed Wilkinson Eyre Architects, 1999. *Projects include:* Stratford Market Depot, 1997 (FT Architecture Award, British Construction Industry Building Award, RIBA Commercial Architecture Award, Structural Steel Design Awards, Industrial Buildings Award, 1997; Civic Trust Design Award, 1998) and Stratford Station, for Jubilee Line Extension, 1998 (RIBA Category Award, 1999; Civic Trust Award, 2000); South Quay Footbridge, 1997 (AIA Excellence in Design Award, 1997; Civic Trust Design Award, 1998); Hulme Arch, 1997; Challenge of Materials Gall., Science Mus., 1997; HQ for Dyson Appliances Ltd, 1999;

Explore at Bristol, 2000 (RIBA Award, 2001); Gateshead Millennium Bridge, 2002 (RA/Bovis Grand Award, 1997; RIBA Stirling Prize, 2002); Magna Millennium Project, Rotherham (RIBA Stirling Prize, 2001); Liverpool Arena and Conf. Centre, King's Dock (RIBA Award); Nat. Waterfront Mus., Swansea (RIBA Award); Anglia Poly. Univ. Campus and Business Sch., Chelmsford; City & Islington Coll.; Audi Regl HQ, Hammersmith; Empress State Bldg, Earls Court; John Madejski Acad., Reading, 2007; Bristol Brunel Acad., 2007; Bath Bus Station, 2009; Bridge Learning Campus, 2009; Earth Scis Dept, Oxford Univ., 2010; Hauser Forum, Cambridge Univ., 2010; Guangzhou Internat. Finance Centre, 2010 (Best Tall Bldg in Asia and Australasia, Council on Tall Bldgs and Urban Habitat, 2011; Lubetkin Award, 2012); Media City Bridge, 2011; Humanities Dept and Maths Dept, QMUL, 2012; Basketball Arena, London Olympic Games, 2012; From Landscape to Portrait, RA Courtyard, 2012; Brislington Enterprise Coll.; Mary Rose Final Voyage Mus., Portsmouth (RIBA Award, 2014; Civic Trust Award, 2014); Gardens by the bay, Singapore (World Building of Year Award, 2012; Lubetkin Award, 2013); Internat. Architect Award, 2013); Univ. of Exeter Forum Project; Worthing New Pools; Siemens Urban Sustainability Centre, London; The Polygon, West Town, Cairo; Swinburne Univ. Advanced Manufg Centre, Melbourne; Maggie's Centre, Oxford; Royal Docks Cable Car; Landscape to Portrait sculpture, RA Courtyard, 2012; Dyson Shop, Oxford Street, 2016; Dyson R&D Bldg, Malmesbury, 2017; King's Cross Gas Holders, 2018; *current projects:* Battersea Power Station; Crown Sydney; 45 Bay Street, Toronto; 150 Leadenhall Street. Mem. Council, Steel Construction Inst., 1998–2001; Comr, English Heritage, 2007–11 (Mem. Urban Panel, 2000–09); Founding Cttee, London Fest. of Architecture, 2004–; Mem., RA Architecture Cttee, 2006–; Chm., RA Client Cttee (formerly Works Cttee), 2012–. Patron, Nat. Trust Design Awards, 2011–. RIBA Lectr, 1996, 2001; Vis. Prof., 1997–98, Mies van der Rohe Lectr, 2003, Illinois Inst. of Technol., Chicago; Vis. Prof., Harvard Grad. Sch. of Design, 2004. Work exhibited: Union of Architects, St Petersburg, 2008; British Design Innovation in the Modern Age, V&A, 2012; IX Venice Biennale; Royal Acad.; Science Mus.; RIBA; Architecture Foundn; Design Council Millennium Products touring exhibn; Love Architecture Fest., Turner Contemporary Mus., Margate, 2013; Lookout. Architecture with a View, Swiss Architecture Mus., Basel, 2013–14; Practical Utopias, AIA Centre, NY, 2013–14; The Brits Who Built the Modern World, RIBA, 2014; solo exhibn, Thinking Through Drawing, Royal Acad., 2015. External Examiner: Univ. of Westminster, 1996–99; Mackintosh Sch. of Art, 2000–04; Bartlett Sch. of Architecture, 2012–. Hon FAIA 2007. Hon. DLit Westminster, 2002; Hon. Dr Oxford Brookes, 2007. Designer of the Year, CSD, 1996; FX Designer of the Year, 2001; over 150 design awards. *Publications:* Supersheds, 1991, 2nd edn 1995 (trans. Japanese 1995); (with James Eyre) Bridging Art and Science, 2001; Exploring Boundaries, 2007; Tectonics: a building for earth sciences, 2011; Wilkinson Eyre Architects: works, 2014; The Sketchbooks of Chris Wilkinson, 2015; contribs World Architecture, Architects Jl. *Recreations:* golf, painting, travel, olive farm in Tuscany. *Address:* 52 Park Hall Road, SE21 8BW. *T:* (020) 8761 7021. *Clubs:* Chelsea Arts; FABS; Dulwich and Sydenham Golf.

**WILKINSON, Christopher Richard;** Adviser, Internet Governance, Directorate General, Information Society and the Media (formerly Telecommunications Information Market and Exploitation of Research) (DG XIII), Commission of the European Communities, 1993–2005, now Hon. Director, European Commission; Head of Secretariat, Governmental Advisory Committee, Internet Corporation for Assigned Names and Numbers, 2002–05 (EU Representative, 1999–2002; Vice-Chairman, 2001–02); *b* 3 July 1941; *s* of late Rev. Thomas Richard Wilkinson and Winifred Frances Wilkinson (*née* Steel). *Educ:* Hymers Coll., Kingston upon Hull; Heath Grammar Sch., Halifax; Selwyn Coll., Cambridge (MA). Commonwealth Economic Cttee, 1963–65; OECD, Paris and Madrid, 1965–66; World Bank, Washington DC and Lagos, 1966–73; EEC: Head of Division: Directorate Gen. for Regional Policy, 1973–78; Directorate Gen. for Internal Market and Industrial Affairs, 1978–82; Directorate Gen. for Telecommunications, Information Industries and Innovation, 1983–93. Mem., Internet Policy Oversight Cttee, 1997–2000; Dir, Bd, EURid, 2010–14 (Mem., Strategic Cttee, 2010–14); Chm., Internet Soc. European Co-ordinating Council, 2007–12. Vis. Fellow, Center for Internat. Affairs, Harvard Univ., 1982–83. Vice-Pres., European School Parents Assoc., Brussels, 1974, 1976–77, Alicante, 2005–06; Pres., Interparents, Assoc. of the Parents' Assocs of European Schs, 2008–09. *Recreations:* walking, gardening, cooking.
See also A. R. Wilkinson.

**WILKINSON, Clive Victor;** Chairman, John Taylor Hospice, 2011–17; *b* 26 May 1938; *s* of Mrs Winifred Jobson; *m* 1961, Elizabeth Ann Pugh; two *d*. *Educ:* Four Dwellings Secondary Sch., Quinton; Birmingham Modern Sch. Birmingham City Council: Member, 1970–84; Leader, 1973–76 and 1980–82; Leader of Opposition, 1976–80, 1982–84. Dir, Nat. Exhibn Centre, 1973–84; Financial and Commercial Dir, Birmingham Rep. Theatre, 1983–87. Chm., CoSIRA, 1977–80; Dep. Chairman: AMA, 1974–76; Redditch Develt Corp., 1977–81. Chairman: Sandwell DHA, 1986–94; Wolverhampton Health Care NHS Trust, 1995–97; W Midlands Region, NHS Exec., DoH, 1997–2001; Birmingham Heartlands and Solihull NHS Trust, subseq. Heart of England NHS Foundn Trust, 2001–11. Member: Develt Commn, 1977–86; Electricity Consumers Council, 1977–80; Audit Commn, 1987–96; Black Country Develt Corp., 1989–92; Local Govt Commn, 1992–95; Midlands Industrial Assoc., 1978– (Chm., 1980–88). Non-exec. Dir, FSA, 2001–13. Chairman: Birmingham Civil Housing Assoc., 1979–2011; Customer Services Cttee, Severn Trent Region, Office of Water Services, 1990–2001. Mem. Council, Univ. of Birmingham, 1974–84. Trustee, Bournville Village Trust, 1982–2017. Hon. Alderman, City of Birmingham, 1984. *Recreation:* watching Birmingham City Football Club. *Address:* 53 Middle Park Road, Birmingham B29 4BH. *Club:* Barnt Green Cricket (Chm., 2019–).

**WILKINSON, Rev. Prof. David Adam,** PhD; Principal, St John's College, since 2006, Professor, since 2011, University of Durham; *b* 16 May 1963; *s* of late Adam and Margaret Wilkinson; *m* 1992, Alison Mary Russell; one *s* one *d*. *Educ:* Greencroft Comprehensive Sch., Co. Durham; Univ. of Durham (BSc 1984, PhD 1987 and 2004); Fitzwilliam Coll., Cambridge (MA 1989); Wesley House, Cambridge. FRAS 1989. Methodist Minister, Letchworth, 1990–91; Methodist Minister and Univ. Chaplain, Liverpool, 1991–99; University of Durham: Fellow in Christian Apologetics, St John's Coll., 1999–2004; Wesley Res. Lectr in Theol. and Science, Dept of Theol. and Religion, 2004–06. *Publications:* God, the Big Bang and Stephen Hawking, 1993, 2nd edn 1996; Thinking Clearly About God and Science, 1996, 2nd edn 1997; Alone in the Universe: the X-Files, aliens and God, 1997; A New Start: hopes and dreams for the millennium, 1999; The Power of the Force: the spirituality of the Star Wars films, 2000; Holiness of the Heart, 2000; God, Time and Stephen Hawking, 2001; Creation, 2002; The Case Against Christ, 2006; The Call and the Commission, 2009; Reading Genesis After Darwin, 2009; Christian Eschatology and the Physical Universe, 2010; Science, Religion and the Search for Extraterrestrial Intelligence, 2013; When I Pray, What Does God Do?, 2015. *Recreations:* Star Wars, the Simpsons, Newcastle United. *Address:* St John's College, 3 South Bailey, Durham DH1 3RJ. *T:* (0191) 334 3500, *Fax:* (0191) 334 3501. *E:* david.wilkinson@durham.ac.uk.

**WILKINSON, David Anthony,** CB 1994; Lay Member, Information Tribunal, since 2005; *b* 27 Nov. 1947; *s* of Ambrose Wilkinson and Doreen (*née* Durden); *m* 1973, Meryl, *d* of Edison and Margaret Pugh; three *d*. *Educ:* Boteler Grammar Sch., Warrington; Wigan and District Mining and Technical Coll.; Bedford Coll., Univ. of London (BA History); London School of Economics; Moscow State Univ. Department of Education and Science, 1974–92: Under Sec., and Hd of Sci. Br., 1989–92; Under Sec., OST, then OPSS, Cabinet Office, 1992–94; RCDS, 1995; Dir, Machinery of Govt and Standards Gp, OPS, 1996–98, Hd of Central Secretariat, 1998–2000, Cabinet Office; Dir of Regl Policy, DETR, 2000–01; Business Co-ordinator, Civil Contingencies Secretariat, Cabinet Office, 2001–02; Sec., Govt Communication Review Gp, Cabinet Office, 2002–03. *Address:* 74 Station Road, Shalford, Guildford GU4 8HD. *Club:* AFC Wimbledon.

**WILKINSON, Dr David George;** Group Leader, Francis Crick Institute, since 2015; *b* 8 March 1958; *s* of George Arthur Wilkinson and Barbara May Wilkinson (*née* Hayton); *m* 1991, Qiling Xu. *Educ:* Aylesbury Grammar Sch.; Hymers Coll., Hull; Univ. of Leeds (BSc Hons 1979, PhD 1983). Postdoctoral Fellow, Fox Chase Cancer Center, Philadelphia, 1983–86; MRC National Institute for Medical Research: Postdoctoral Fellow, 1986–88; scientific staff, 1988–2015; Hd, Div. of Develtl Neurobiol., and Genetics and Develt (formerly Genes and Cellular Controls) Gp, 2000–15. Mem., EMBO, 2000. Editor in Chief: Mechanisms of Develt, 2010–; Gene Expression Patterns, 2010–. FMedSci 2000. *Publications:* (ed) In Situ Hybridisation, 1992, 2nd edn 1998; (ed jtly) Extracellular Regulators of Differentiation and Development, 1996; contrib. numerous scientific articles to various jls. *Recreations:* natural history, music, poetry. *Address:* Francis Crick Institute, 1 Midland Road, NW1 1AT. *T:* (020) 3796 1638.

**WILKINSON, Sir David Graham Brook;** *see* Wilkinson, Sir Graham.

**WILKINSON, Prof. David Gregor, (Greg),** FRCP Ed; FRCPsych; consultant psychiatrist: in independent and medico-legal practice, since 2005; Royal Liverpool and Broadgreen University Hospitals NHS Trust, since 1994; Professor of Liaison Psychiatry, Liverpool University, 1994–2005; *b* 17 May 1951; *s* of David Pryde Wilkinson and Joan (*née* McCabe); *m* 1984, Christine Mary Lewis; three *s* one *d*. *Educ:* Lawside Acad., Dundee; Edinburgh Univ. (BSc, MB ChB); MPhil London. FRCPEd 1989; FRCPsych 1991. House Physician and Surgeon, Royal Infirmary, Edinburgh, 1975–76; Sen. House Physician, Leith Hosp., 1976–78; Registrar, Maudsley Hosp., 1978–81; Sen. Registrar, Maudsley Hosp. and KCH, 1981–83; Res. Worker and Lectr, then Sen. Lectr, Inst. of Psychiatry, Univ. of London, 1983–89; Sen. Lectr and Reader, Academic Sub-dept of Psychol Medicine in N Wales, 1989–91; Prof. of Psychiatry, London Hosp. Med. Coll., London Univ., 1992–94. Editor, Brit. Jl of Psychiatry, 1993–2003. *Publications:* Mental Health Practices in Primary Care Settings, 1985; (jtly) Mental Illness in Primary Care Settings, 1986; (jtly) The Provision of Mental Health Services in Britain, 1986; Coping with Stress, 1987, 2nd edn as Understanding Stress, 1993; Depression, 1989; Recognising and Treating Depression in General Practice, 1989; (jtly) The Scope of Epidemiological Psychiatry, 1989; Recognising and Treating Anxiety in General Practice, 1992; Talking About Psychiatry, 1993; (jtly) Psychiatry and General Practice Today, 1994; (jtly) A Carers Guide to Schizophrenia, 1996, 2nd edn 2000; (ed jtly) Textbook of General Psychiatry, 1998, 2nd edn 2007; (jtly) Critical Reviews in Psychiatry, 1998, 2nd edn 2000; (jtly) Seminars in Psychosexual Disorders, 1998; (jtly) Treating People with Depression, 1999; Treating People with Anxiety and Stress, 1999; articles in general and specialist med. jls. *Recreations:* family, rural pursuits. *Address:* Craig y Castell, Bryniau, Dyserth, Denbighshire LL18 6DE. *T:* (01745) 571858. *Club:* Athenæum.

**WILKINSON, Endymion Porter,** PhD; independent scholar, since 2018; *b* 15 May 1941; *s* of late George Curwen Wilkinson and Pamela Algernon Wilkinson (*née* Black). *Educ:* King's Coll., Cambridge (BA 1964; MA 1967); Princeton Univ. (PhD 1970). Teacher, Peking Inst. of Languages, 1964–66; Lectr in History of Far East, SOAS, London Univ., 1970–74; joined European Commn, 1974: Head of Economic and Commercial Section, EU Tokyo Delegn, 1974–79; China Desk, Brussels, 1979–82; Dep. Head, EU SE Asia Delegn, Bangkok, 1982–88; Head, Asia Div., Brussels, 1988–94; Ambassador and Hd of EU Delegn to China and Mongolia, EC, 1994–2001. Sen. Fellow, Asia Center, 2001–07, Res. Associate, Fairbank Center, 2007–18, Harvard Univ. Visiting Professor: Peking Univ., 2001–04 and 2007–14; Tsinghua Univ., 2005. Stanislas Julien Prize, Académie des Belles-Lettres et Inscriptions, Paris, 2014. *Publications:* The History of Imperial China: a research guide, 1973; Studies in Chinese Price History, 1980; Japan versus Europe: a history of misunderstanding, 1982 (trans. Japanese, Chinese, French, German and Italian); Japan versus the West, 1991; Chinese History: a manual, 1998, 2nd edn 2000; Chinese History: a new manual, 2013, 5th edn 2017; translations: The People's Comic Book, 1973; Landlord and Labour in Late Imperial China, by Jing Su and Luo Lun, 1978. *Recreations:* Chinese history, finalizing memoirs, learning Thai, swimming. *E:* epw2012@gmail.com.

**WILKINSON, Fiona Helen,** FCA; Director, Fiona Wilkinson Ltd, since 2012; President, Institute of Chartered Accountants in England and Wales, 2019–June 2020; *b* Rochester, Kent, 17 Feb. 1954; *d* of William Frank Potter and Lorna Winifred Potter; *m* 1980, Stephen James Robb Wilkinson; one *s* two *d*. *Educ:* Devonport High Sch. for Girls, Plymouth; Royal Holloway Coll., Univ. of London (BA Hons 1976). FCA 1980. Trainee, then Manager, Touche Ross, 1976–87; Principal, Fiona Wilkinson, 1989–2012. Vice Pres., 2017–18, Dep. Pres., 2018–19, ICAEW. Mem., Accountants' Co., 2019–. *Recreations:* theatre, especially musical theatre and ballet, family, looking after 17th century house.

**WILKINSON, Sir Graham,** 3rd Bt *cr* 1941; Managing Director, S.E.I.C. Services (UK) Ltd, 1985–89; *b* 18 May 1947; *s* of Sir David Wilkinson, 2nd Bt, DSC, and Sylvia Anne, *d* of late Professor Bosley Alan Rex Gater; *S* father, 1972; *m* 1977, Sandra Caroline Rossdale (marr. diss. 1996); two *d*; *m* 1998, Hilary Jane Griggs, *d* of late W. H. C. Bailey, CBE. *Educ:* Millfield; Christ Church, Oxford. Orion Royal Bank Ltd, 1971–85 (Dir, 1979–85); non-executive Director: Galveston-Houston Co., USA, 1986–89; Sovereign Management Corp., USA, 1987–94; Lamport Gilbert Ltd, 1992–97. Pres., Surrey County Agricultural Soc., 2006–08; Mem. Council, RASE, 2005–10. Gov., Queen's Gate Sch. Trust, 1989–2005. Master, Farmers' Co., 2006–07. KStJ 2003. *Clubs:* Vincent's (Oxford); Royal Ocean Racing; Royal Yacht Squadron.

**WILKINSON, Graham Paul;** a District Judge (Magistrates' Courts), since 2009; *b* Barking, Essex, 1 Nov. 1968; *s* of Trevor and Pamela Wilkinson; *m* 2008, Adelle; one step *d*. *Educ:* Judd Sch., Tonbridge; Trent Poly. (LLB Hons); Coll. of Law, York. Articled clerk, 1991–93, Solicitor, 1993–99, Russell-Cooke, Potter & Chapman, Putney; Solicitor, then Partner, EBR Attridge, 1999–2009. *Recreations:* walking, natural history, film, supporting West Ham United. *Address:* c/o Wolverhampton Magistrates' Court, The Law Courts, North Street, Wolverhampton WV1 1RA. *T:* (01902) 329003.

**WILKINSON, Greg;** *see* Wilkinson, David Gregor.

**WILKINSON, Rev. Canon Guy Alexander,** CBE 2012; Non-stipendiary Minister, St Mary Magdalene, Eardisley with Bollingham, Willersley, Brilley, Michaelchurch, Whitney, Winforton, Almeley and Kinnersley, Diocese of Hereford, since 2019; *b* 13 Jan. 1948; *m* 1971, Tessa Osbourn; four *s* one *d*. *Educ:* Magdalene Coll., Cambridge (BA 1969); Ripon

Coll., Cuddesdon. Commn of Eur. Communities, 1973–80; Dir, 1980–85, non-exec. Dir, 1985–87, Express Foods Gp; ordained deacon 1987, priest 1988; Curate, Caludon, Coventry, 1987–90; Priest i/c, 1990–91, Rector, 1991–94, Ockham with Hatchford; Domestic Chaplain to Bishop of Guildford, 1990–94; Vicar, Small Heath, Birmingham, 1994–99; Archdeacon of Bradford, 1999–2004; Archbishop of Canterbury's Sec. for Inter Religious Relns, 2005–10; C of E Nat. Advr, 2005–10; Area Dean, Hammersmith and Fulham, 2012–15; Vicar, St Andrew's, Fulham Fields, 2012–15; Bishop of Salisbury's Inter Faith Advr, 2016–18. Co. Sec., Near Neighbours, 2008–14; Chair: Faiths Forum for London, 2010–13; Adv. Bd, Catalyst, 2017–; Trustee: St Ethelburga Centre for Reconciliation and Peace, 2013–17; Near Neighbours.

**WILKINSON, Prof. Guy Roderick,** DPhil; FRS 2018; Professor of Physics, University of Oxford, since 2010; Tutorial Fellow, Christ Church, Oxford, since 2001; b Ashton-under-Lyne, 16 Oct. 1968; s of Edmund Wilkinson and Anne Wilkinson (née Smith); m 2008, Dr Paula Collins; three d. Educ: Bishops Stortford Coll., Herts; Imperial Coll. London (BSc Physics 1989); Magdalen Coll., Oxford (DPhil Particle Physics 1993). Postdoctoral Associate, Univ. of Oxford, 1993–96; Res. Fellow, CERN, 1996–99; PPARC Advanced Fellow, affiliated to Univ. of Oxford, 1999–2004; Lectr, Univ. of Oxford, 2004–. Spokesperson of LHCb Collaboration and CERN Guest Prof., 2014–17. James Chadwick Medal and Prize, Inst. of Physics, 2017. Recreations: mountains, literature, music. Address: Particle Physics, Department of Physics, University of Oxford, Denys Wilkinson Building, Keble Road, Oxford OX2 3RH. E: guy.wilkinson@physics.ox.ac.uk.

**WILKINSON, Rt Hon. Dame Heather;** see Hallett, Rt Hon. Dame H. C.

**WILKINSON, James Hugh;** freelance journalist and broadcaster; b 19 Sept. 1941; s of Hugh Davy Wilkinson and Marjorie Wilkinson (née Prout); m 1978, Rev. Elisabeth Ann Morse; two s. Educ: Westminster Abbey Choir Sch.; King's Coll., London (BSc Hons); Inst. of Educn, Univ. of Cambridge (CertEd). Health and Sci. Corresp., Daily Express, 1964–71; Sci. and Air Corresp., BBC Radio News, 1974–83; Sci. Corresp., BBC News and Current Affairs, 1983–99. Vis. Fellow, Inst. of Food Res., 1992–96. Mem., Educn Cttee, CRC, 1977–82; Mem., Adv. Bd, CIBA Foundn Media Resource Service, 1994–99 (Mem., Steering Cttee, 1985–94). Hon. Steward, Westminster Abbey, 1999– (Sec., Brotherhood of St Edward, 1984–99). Mem., Editl Cttee, Sci. and Public Affairs Jl, 1989–99. Founder Mem., Med. Journalists' Assoc. (Chm., 1972–74). FSA 2010. Glaxo Wellcome Sci. Writers' Award, 1996. Publications: The Conquest of Cancer, 1973; Tobacco: the truth behind the smokescreen, 1986; Green or Bust, 1990; Westminster Abbey: 1000 years of music and pageant, 2003; Westminster Abbey Souvenir Guide, 2006; The Royal Wedding: Westminster Abbey official souvenir, 2011; The Queen's Coronation: the inside story, 2011; To Drink, to Sing: a short history of the Noblemen and Gentlemen's Catch Club, 2014; booklets about aspects of Westminster Abbey incl. Poet's Corner and the Coronation Chair. Recreations: music, bookbinding, editing The Westminster Abbey Review. Club: Oxford and Cambridge.
See also C. Haydon.

**WILKINSON, Jeffrey Vernon;** management consultant; Consultant, Apax Partners & Co. (formerly Alan Patricof Associates), 2000–07 (Director, 1986–2000; Partner, 1988–2000); Chairman of several private companies, 1985–2007; b 21 Aug. 1930; s of late Arthur Wilkinson and Winifred May Allison; m 1955, Jean Vera Nurse; two d. Educ: Matthew Humberstone Foundation Sch.; King's Coll., Cambridge (BA Hons, MA; Fellow Commoner, 2001–). Sorbonne. FBCS. Joined Joseph Lucas as graduate apprentice, 1954; Director, CAV, 1963; Director and General Manager, Diesel Equipment, CAV, 1967; Director: Simon Engineering, 1968; Joseph Lucas, 1974; Dir and Gen. Manager, Lucas Electrical, 1974; Divisional Man. Dir, Joseph Lucas Ltd, 1978; Jt Gp Man. Dir, Lucas Industries plc, 1979–84; Chm. and CEO, Spear & Jackson plc, 1992–2000. Chairman: Automotive Components Manufacturers, 1979–84; Plastics Processing EDC, 1985–87; Mem. Council and Exec., SMMT, 1979–84. CCMI. Liveryman, Wheelwrights Company, 1971–2006. Mem., 2002–, Chm., 2004–07, Develt Cttee, King's Coll., Cambridge. Recreations: reading, theatre, art. Address: Hillcroft, 15 Mearse Lane, Barnt Green, Birmingham B45 8HG. T: (0121) 447 7750.

**WILKINSON, John Nicholas Ralph;** Partner, Cooley LLP, since 2015; b Nottingham, 7 Oct. 1964; s of Ronald James Wilkinson and June Christine Wilkinson; m 1998, Barbara Radha; one s two d. Educ: Bilborough Sixth Form Coll.; Imperial Coll. London (BSc Chem.); Coll. of Law (CPE 1993). Admitted Solicitor, 1995. Development Chemist: Laporte Industries, 1986–89; AstraZeneca, 1989–91; trainee solicitor, 1993–95, solicitor, 1995–98, Lovells; Legal Counsel, Cancer Res. Technol., 1998–2000; Partner: Bird & Bird LLP, 2000–05; Reed Smith LLP, 2005–15. Recreations: family, fishing, windsurfing, making things. Address: Cooley LLP, Dashwood House, 69 Old Broad Street, EC2M 1QS. T: (020) 7556 4387, Fax: (020) 7900 3819. E: jwilkinson@cooley.com.

**WILKINSON, Jonathan Peter,** CBE 2015 (OBE 2004; MBE 2003); Rugby Union football player; Managing Director, Fineside Ltd, since 2009; Rugby pundit, Sky Sports, since 2014; b 25 May 1979; s of Philip Wilkinson and Philippa Wilkinson; m 2013, Shelley Jenkins. Educ: Lord Wandsworth Coll., Hants. Player (fly half): Newcastle Falcons RFU Club, 1997–2009; Toulon Rugby Club, 2009–14 (Captain, 2011–12, 2013–14; Jt Captain, 2012–13; winners, Heineken Cup, 2013, 2014); Member, England Rugby Team, 1998–2011 (91 caps); member, winning team: Five Nations Championship, 1999; Six Nations Championship, 2000, 2001, 2003; World Cup, 2003; played World Cup, 2011; captain, winning team, Top 14 French Championship, 2014. Member, British Lions tour, Australia, 2001, NZ, 2005. World record internat. points scorer (1246 points). Freedom: City of Newcastle Upon Tyne, 2004; Town of Bandol, France, 2013; City of Toulon, France, 2014. Hon. DCL Northumbria, 2004; DUniv Surrey, 2009. Player of the Year, Internat. Rugby Players Assoc., 2002, 2003; Player of the Year, Internat. Rugby Bd, 2003; BBC Sports Personality of the Year, 2003; European Player of the Year, Eur. Rugby Cup, 2013. Publications: Lions and Falcons: my diary of a remarkable year, 2001; My World (autobiog.), 2004; How to Play Rugby My Way, 2005; (with Steve Black) Tackling Life, 2008; (with Owen Slot) Jonny: my autobiography, 2011. W: www.jonnywilkinson.com.

**WILKINSON, Rev. Canon Keith Howard;** Steward of the Livings, Eton College, since 2017 (Conduct, 2008–16); b 25 June 1948; s of Kenneth John Wilkinson and Grace Winifred (née Bowler); m 1972, Carolyn Gilbert; two d. Educ: Beaumont Leys Sch.; Gateway Sch., Leicester; Univ. of Hull (BA Hons); Emmanuel Coll., Cambridge (Lady Romney Exhibnr, MA status); Westcott House, Cambridge. Hd of Religious Studies, Bricknell High Sch., 1970–72; Hd of Faculty (Humanities), Kelvin Hall Comprehensive Sch., Kingston upon Hull, 1972–74; Deacon 1976; Priest 1977; Asst Priest, St Jude, Westwood, Peterborough, 1977; Asst Master and Chaplain, Eton Coll., Windsor, 1979–84; Sen. Chaplain and Hd of Religious Studies, Malvern Coll., 1984–89; Sen. Tutor, Malvern Coll., 1988–89; Headmaster: Berkhamsted Sch., 1989–96; King's Sch., Canterbury, 1996–2007. Hon. Canon, Canterbury Cathedral, 1996–2007, now Canon Emeritus. Publications: various articles and reviews. Recreations: films, theatre, music, walking, buildings and building, ecology. Address: Eton College, Windsor SL4 6DW. Clubs: East India, Lansdowne.

**WILKINSON, His Honour Kenneth Henry Pinder;** a Circuit Judge, 1996–2005; Designated Family Judge, Merseyside, 2002–05; b 5 Aug. 1939; s of late Henry Wilkinson and Alice Wilkinson; m 1966, Margaret Adams; two s one d. Educ: Wigan GS; Univ. of Manchester (LLB Hons). Admitted solicitor, 1965; in private practice, 1965–80; Dep. Dist Registrar, 1977–80; Dist Judge, 1980–96; Asst Recorder, 1990–93; Recorder, 1993–96. Chm. (part-time), Industrial Tribunal, 1977–80; Member: Matrimonial Causes Rule Cttee, 1978–80; County Court Rule Cttee, 1988–92. Mem., Family Law Cttee, Law Soc., 1976–80. Publications: (jtly) A Better Way Out, 1979; (contrib.) Personal Injury Litigation Service, 1984; (with I. S. Goldrein) Commercial Litigation: pre-emptive remedies, 1987, 3rd edn 1996; (with M. De Haas) Property Distribution on Divorce, 1989; (Consult. Ed.) County Court Litigation, 1993. Recreations: gardening, music, walking, watching sport, birdwatching. Address: School House, Chorley Road, Bispham, Ormskirk, Lancs L40 3SL.

**WILKINSON, Leon Guy,** FCIB; a General Commissioner of Income Tax, City of London, 1989–2003; part-time Member, VAT Tribunal, 1989–2004; b 6 Nov. 1928; s of Thomas Guy and Olive May Wilkinson; m 1953, Joan Margaret; one s one d. Educ: Bude Grammar Sch. CMS Oxon. Lloyds Bank: Regional Gen. Man., N and E Midlands, 1976–79; Asst Gen. Man., 1979–83; Gen. Man. (Finance), 1984–86; Chief Financial Officer, 1986–88. Recreation: sports. Clubs: MCC, Royal Over-Seas League; Nevill Golf (Tunbridge Wells).

**WILKINSON, Rear-Adm. Nicholas John,** CB 1994; Press Complaints Commissioner, 2005–08; Cabinet Office Historian, 2005–10; freelance lecturer on modern history, 2010–15; b 14 April 1941; s of late Lt-Col Michael Douglas Wilkinson, RE and Joan Mary Wilkinson (née Cosens); m 1st, 1969, Penelope Ann Stephenson (marr. diss. 1996; she d 2003); three s one d; 2nd, 1998, Juliet Rayner (née Hockin). Educ: English School, Cairo; Cheltenham College; BRNC Dartmouth. Served HM Ships Venus, Vidal and Hermes, 1960–64; RN Air Station, Arbroath, 1964–65; HMS Fife, 1965–67; Asst Sec. to Vice-Chief of Naval Staff, 1968–70; HMS Endurance, 1970–72; Army Staff Course, 1973 (Mitchell Prizewinner); Clyde Submarine Base, 1974–75; Sec. to ACNS (Policy), 1975–77; HMS London, 1977–78; Asst Dir, Naval Officer Appts (SW), 1978–80; Trng Comdr, HMS Pembroke, 1980–82; NATO Defence Coll., Rome, 1982–83; MA to Dir, NATO Internat. Mil. Staff, 1983–85; RCDS, 1986; Dir, Defence Logistics, 1986; Sec. to First Sea Lord, 1989–90; Sen. Mil. Mem., Defence Organisation Study and Project Team, 1991–92; Dir Gen. of Naval Manpower and Trng, 1992–94; Chief Naval Supply and Secretariat Officer, 1993–97; Comdt, JSDC, 1994–97; mgt consultant, 1998–99; Maj.-Gen., RCDS, 1999; Sec., Defence, Press and Broadcasting Adv. Cttee (DA Notice Sec.), 1999–2004. Chm., Assoc. RN Officers, 1998–2004; Member Council: Forces Pension Soc., 1994–2005; Victory Services Assoc., 1998–2008 (Chm., 2001–08). Trustee, Greenwich Foundn, 2003–10. Mem., Develt Council, Trinity Coll. of Music, 2001–05; Ambassador, Trinity Laban Conservatoire of Music and Dance, 2005–. Chm., Adv. Cttee, Maritime Inst., Univ. of Greenwich, 2003–14. Gov., Princess Helena Coll., 1994–2004. President: Royal Naval Assoc. (Swindon), 1999–; Swindon Sea Cadets, 1999–2019; Great Bedwyn Cricket Club, 2010–. Publications: Secrecy and the Media, 2009; (contrib.) Spinning Intelligence, 2009; articles in the Naval Review and media publications. Recreations: cricket, opera. Address: 37 Burns Road, SW11 5GX. Clubs: Savile (Chm., 2008–14), Victory Services (Chm., 2001–08; Vice Pres., 2008–), MCC (Mem., Memship Cttee, 2000–03, 2005–14).

**WILKINSON, Nigel Vivian Marshall;** QC 1990; a Recorder, since 1992; a Deputy High Court Judge, since 1997; b 18 Nov. 1949; s of late John Marshall Wilkinson and Vivien Wilkinson; m 1974, Heather Carol Hallett (see Rt Hon. Dame Heather Hallett); two s. Educ: Charterhouse; Christ Church, Oxford (Holford exhibnr; MA). Called to the Bar, Middle Temple, 1972, Bencher, 1997; Astbury Scholar, 1972; Midland and Oxford Circuit, 1972–; an Asst Recorder, 1988–92; Hd of Chambers, 2008–12. Dep. Chm., Appeals Cttee, Cricket Council, 1991–97. Gov., Brambletye Sch., 1992–98. Member: Almost Modern Order of Purchasers; Sen. Golfers' Soc. Recreations: cricket, golf, theatre. Address: Mint House, The Mint, Rye, E Sussex TN31 7EW. Clubs: Garrick, MCC; Vincent's (Oxford); I Zingari, Butterflies CC, Invalids CC, Armadillos CC, Rye Golf (Captain, 2012–13), Royal and Ancient Golf (St Andrews), Hon. Co. of Edinburgh Golfers.

**WILKINSON, Vice Adm. Peter John,** CB 2010; CVO 2007; Deputy Chief of Defence Staff (Personnel), 2007–10; b 28 May 1956; s of Sir Philip (William) Wilkinson and Eileen Patricia Wilkinson (née Malkin); m 1981, Tracey Kim Ward; two d. Educ: Royal Grammar Sch., High Wycombe; St David's Coll., Lampeter, Univ. of Wales (BA 1978). FCIPD 2003. Joined RN, 1975; trng, 1975–80; qualified submarines, 1980; Torpedo Officer, HMS Onslaught, 1981; Staff, C-in-C Fleet, 1982; trng courses, 1983; Tactics and Sonar Officer, HMS Resolution, 1984–86; Navigating Officer, HMS Churchill, 1986–87; submarine comd course, 1987; CO, HMS Otter, 1988–89; Staff of Captain (SM) Sea Trng, 1989–90; CO, HMS Superb, 1991–92; Comdr (SM), Maritime Tactical Sch., 1992–94; CO, HMS Vanguard, 1994–96; Asst Dir, Nuclear Policy, MOD, 1996–99; Capt., 2nd Submarine Sqn, 1999–2001; Director: RN Service Conditions, 2001–03; RN Life Mgt, 2003–04; Naval Sec., and Dir Gen., Human Resources (Navy), 2004–05; Defence Services Sec., 2005–07. Dir, Hook Park Consulting Ltd, 2011–13. Member: RNSA, 2011–; Council, Forces Pension Soc., 2011–17 (Chm., 2014–17). Pres., RN Football Assoc., 2004–10; Hon. Vice Pres., FA, 2004–10; Nat. Pres., RBL, 2012–16. Patron, Loch Class Frigates Assoc., 2012–. Chm., Seafarers UK, 2010–. Clerk, Cooks' Co., 2011–. Hon. Fellow, Univ. of Wales Trinity St David, 2013. Recreations: genealogy, gardening, watching all sports. Address: c/o Naval Secretary, Leach Building, Whale Island, Portsmouth, Hants PO2 8ER. Club: Army and Navy (Dir, 2016–18).

**WILKINSON, Rhiannon Jane;** Head, Whittle School and Studios, Shenzhen Campus, China, since 2019; b Ashton under Lyne, Lancs, 8 March 1962; d of David Fell and Letty Fell; m 2000, Donald Wilkinson; two s, and one step d. Educ: Fairfield High Sch. for Girls, Droylsden; St Hugh's Coll., Oxford (BA Hist.); Univ. of Bath (PGCE 1984); Manchester Univ. (MEd 2004). Teacher of History: King Edward VI Coll., Totnes, 1984–87; Bramhall High Sch., Stockport, 1987–91; Head of Hist., 1991–93, Head of Sixth Form, 1993–97, Shatin Coll., Hong Kong; Deputy Head: Cheadle Hulme, 1998–99; Jerudong Internat. Sch., Brunei, 2000–04; Dir of Studies, 2004–09, Housemistress, 2007–09, Haileybury; Principal, Harrogate Ladies' Coll., 2009–13; Headmistress, Wycombe Abbey School, 2013–19. Recreations: travel, theatre, reading, food. E: rwilkinson@whittleschool.org.

**WILKINSON, Richard Denys,** CVO 1992; HM Diplomatic Service, retired; Ambassador to Chile, 2003–05; b 11 May 1946; y s of late Denys and Gillian Wilkinson; m 1982, Maria Angela Morris; two s one d. Educ: Eton Coll. (King's Schol.); Trinity Coll., Cambridge (MA, MLitt, Wace Medallist); Ecole Nat. des Langues Orientales Vivantes, Univ. de Paris; Ecole des Langues Orientales Anciennes, Inst. Catholique de Paris. Hayter Postdoctoral Fellow in Soviet Studies, SSEES, London, 1971; joined Diplomatic Service, 1972: Madrid, 1973; FCO, 1977; Vis. Prof., Univ. of Michigan, Ann Arbor, 1980; FCO, 1980; Ankara, 1983; Mexico City, 1985; Counsellor (Information), Paris, 1988; Head of Policy Planning Staff, FCO, 1993–94; Head of Eastern Dept, FCO, 1994–96; Ambassador to Venezuela,

1997–2000; Dir, Americas and Overseas Territories, FCO, 2000–03. Hd of Spanish, Winchester Coll., 2007–11. Chm. Govs, Univ. of Winchester, 2011–16. *Publications*: articles and reviews in learned jls. *Recreations*: sightseeing, oriental studies. *Address*: 1 Westley Close, Winchester, Hants SO22 5LA. *Club*: Oxford and Cambridge.

**WILKINSON, Dr Robert Edward**; Principal, Hills Road Sixth Form College, Cambridge, 2002–08; *b* 23 Jan. 1950; *s* of Sydney Arthur Wilkinson and Winifred Wilkinson (*née* Hawker); *m* 1974, Diana Viader; one *s* two *d*. *Educ*: Bexley-Erith Tech. High Sch. for Boys, Bexley; University Coll., Swansea (BA 1971; PhD 1982); PGCE Oxford. Teacher of Hist., Scarborough Sixth Form Coll., 1975–82; Hd of Hist., John Leggott Coll., Scunthorpe, 1982–89; Vice Principal, Hills Rd Sixth Form Coll., Cambridge, 1989–94; Principal, Wyggeston & Queen Elizabeth I Coll., Leicester, 1994–2002. Registered Inspector, FEFC, 1995–2001; Addnl Inspector, Ofsted, 2001–04. Gov., Beaminster Sch., Dorset, 2010–16. *Recreations*: bird-watching, walking, music, opera, theatre, history.

**WILKINSON, Robert Purdy**, OBE 1990; *b* 23 Aug. 1933; *s* of Robert Purdy and Lily Ingham Wilkinson; *m* 1957, June (*née* Palmer); two *d*. *Educ*: Univ. of Durham (BA; DipEd 1957). Kleinwort Sons & Co., 1958–62; Estabrook & Co., 1962–64; Partner, W. I. Carr Sons & Co., 1966–81. Stock Exchange: Mem. Council, 1978–81; Cttee Chm., 1980–81; Stock Exchange Inspector, 1981–84; Dir of Surveillance, Stock Exchange, 1984–90; Dir of Enforcement and Dep. Chief Exec., Securities Assoc., 1987–90. Dir, Tradepoint, 1994–2001; Chm., Bovill Ltd, 2003–05. Consultant: Morgan Grenfell Internat., 1991; S Africa Financial Markets Bd, 1991; Johannesburg Stock Exchange, 1991; DTI Inspector, 1987, 1989, 1991; Invesco Gp, 1997–2003 (Dir, 1994–97). Mem., Financial Services Tribunal, 1991–94; Special Advisor: Assoc. of Swiss Stock Exchanges, 1991; Czech Ministry of Finance, 1995; Bulgarian Ministry of Finance, 1997–99; Romanian Securities Commn, 1997–99; Tallinn Stock Exchange, 1999; Jordan Securities Commn, 1999–2002. Testified US Congress Cttee, 1988. Chm. of Govs, Sevenoaks Sch., 1992–2002; Chairman: Sevenoaks Sch. Foundn, 2003–12; Chevening C of E Sch., 2009–10. *Publications*: various articles on securities regulation and insider dealing. *Recreations*: schools' sport, education, church affairs.

**WILKINSON, Sarah Fay**; Chief Executive, NHS Digital, since 2017; *b* Chester, 2 May 1970; *d* of Peter and Gloria Wilkinson; partner, 1991, Martin Clive Charlton; two *s*. *Educ*: Chichester Coll. of Technol.; Imperial Coll. London (BSc Maths 1991); London Business Sch. (MBA 2001). Exec. Dir, Lehman Brothers Ltd, 1995–2007; Managing Director: Deutsche Bank AG, 2007–10; UBS AG, 2010–12; Credit Suisse AG, 2012–15; Chief Digital, Data and Technol. Officer, Home Office, 2015–17. Non-executive Director: Holmesdale Bldg Soc., 2013–15; Police ICT Co., 2015–18; NatWest Markets, 2018–. *Publications*: contrib. articles to technol. jl. *Recreations*: family, cycling, books, cooking. *Address*: c/o NHS Digital, 80 London Road, SE1 6LH. *E*: nhsd.ceo@nhs.net.

**WILKINSON, Simon B.**; *see* Browne-Wilkinson.

**WILKINSON, Susan Jane**, MBE 2013; Chief Executive Officer, The Reading Agency, 2014–19; *b* Barnsley, S Yorks, 10 May 1959; *d* of Albert and Beryl Wilkinson; *m* 1997, Peter John McDonough; three step *s*. *Educ*: Hall Balk Sch., Barnsley; Clare Coll., Cambridge (Exhibnr; BA Hons Hist. 1980; PGCE Dist.); Univ. of Leicester (Postgrad. Cert. Mus. Studies). Teacher, Dr Challoner's High Sch., 1982–85; Educn Officer, HM Tower of London, 1985–91; CEO, S Eastern Mus Educn Unit, 1991–99; Dir of Policy, MLA, 1999–2012; Hd, Acad. and Govt Alliances, UK Elsevier, 2013–14. Trustee: Handel and Hendrix in London, 2012–17; Yorkshire Sculpture Park, 2013–; Historic Royal Palaces, 2017–. *Publications*: (with G. Durbin and S. Morris) A Teacher's Guide to Learning from Objects, 1990; (with S. Allen) A Teacher's Guide to Using Homes and Houses, 1999; (with S. Clive) Developing Cross Curricular Learning in Museums and Galleries, 2000; contribs to learned jls incl. Nat. Heritage, Mus Jl. *Recreations*: reading, travel, theatre, walking, cooking. *Address*: 8 Copthall Drive, Mill Hill, NW7 2NB. *T*: 07971 253550. *E*: susan-wilkinson1@hotmail.co.uk.

**WILKINSON, Prof. Toby Alexander Howard**, PhD; FSA, FRHistS; Egyptologist and author; Professor of Egyptology and Deputy Vice Chancellor, University of Lincoln, since 2017; Bye Fellow, Clare College, Cambridge, since 2018 (Fellow, 2003–17); *b* Fareham, 25 March 1969; *s* of William Frederick Howard Wilkinson and Ann Elizabeth Wilkinson (*née* Rathbone); civil partnership 2006, *m* 2016, Michael Timothy Eric Bailey. *Educ*: Portsmouth Grammar Sch.; Downing Coll., Cambridge (BA 1st cl. Hons 1990; Thomas Mulvey Prize 1990; MA 1994); Christ's Coll., Cambridge (PhD 1994). Lady Wallis Budge Jun. Res. Fellow, Christ's Coll., Cambridge, 1993–97; Leverhulme Trust Special Res. Fellow, Univ. of Durham, 1997–99; Develt Dir, and Fellow, Christ's Coll., Cambridge, 1999–2003; Develt Dir, Clare Coll., Cambridge, 2003–11; Chm., Cambridge Colls Develt Gp, 2007–11; Hd, Internat. Strategy Office, 2011–15, Dir, Internat. Strategy, 2015–17, Univ. of Cambridge. Trustee, Thomas Wall Trust, 2014–; Chm., Lincolnshire Educnl Trust, 2017–. Gov., Ipswich Sch., 2015–. FSA 2017. *Publications*: State Formation in Egypt, 1996; Early Dynastic Egypt, 1999; Royal Annals of Ancient Egypt, 2000; Genesis of the Pharaohs, 2003; The Thames and Hudson Dictionary of Ancient Egypt, 2005; Lives of the Ancient Egyptians, 2007; (ed) The Egyptian World, 2007; The Rise and Fall of Ancient Egypt, 2010 (Hessell-Tiltman Prize); The Nile: downriver through Egypt's past and present, 2014; Writings from Ancient Egypt, 2016; (with Julian Platt) Aristocrats and Archaeologists, 2017; numerous articles in learned jls. *Recreations*: writing, gardening, travel, history. *Address*: University of Lincoln, Brayford Pool, Lincoln LN6 7TS; c/o Rogers, Coleridge and White Ltd, 20 Powis Mews, W11 1JN.

**WILKINSON, Tom**, OBE 2005; actor; *b* 5 Feb. 1948; *m* 1998, Diana Hardcastle; two *d*. *Educ*: Univ. of Kent (BA); Royal Acad. of Dramatic Art. *Theatre includes*: The Cherry Orchard (tour); Peer Gynt; Brand; Three Sisters; Uncle Vanya; Henry IV; Henry V; Julius Caesar; The Merchant of Venice; As You Like It; Hamlet, RSC, 1981; King Lear, Tom and Viv, 1983, My Zinc Bed, 2000, Royal Court; Ghosts, 1986 (Critics' Circle Award, 1986), An Enemy of the People, 1988 (Critics' Circle Award, 1988), Young Vic; The Crucible, White Chameleon, 1991, RNT. *Films include*: Sylvia, Wetherby, 1985; Sharma and Beyond, 1986; Paper Mask, 1990; In the Name of the Father, 1993; Priest, A Business Affair, 1994; Sense and Sensibility, 1995; The Ghost and the Darkness, 1996; Jilting Joe, Oscar and Lucinda, Smilla's Sense of Snow, Wilde, The Full Monty, 1997; The Governess, Shakespeare in Love, Rush Hour, 1998; Molokai: The Story of Father Damien, Ride with the Devil, 1999; The Patriot, Essex Boys, Chain of Fools, 2000; In the Bedroom, Another Life, Black Knight, 2001; The Importance of Being Earnest, Before You Go, 2002; Girl with a Pearl Earring, 2003; If Only, Eternal Sunshine of the Spotless Mind, Stage Beauty, Piccadilly Jim, A Good Woman, 2004; Ripley Under Ground, Batman Begins, The Exorcism of Emily Rose, A Good Woman, Separate Lies, 2005; The Night of the White Pants, The Last Kiss, 2006; Dedication, Michael Clayton, 2007; Cassandra's Dream, RocknRolla, 2008; Valkyrie, Duplicity, 2009; The Best Exotic Marigold Hotel, The Samaritan, 2012; The Lone Ranger, 2013; The Grand Budapest Hotel, Belle, 2014; Selma, Unfinished Business, Good People, 2015; The Choice, Snowden, 2016; Denial, 2017; The Happy Prince, Dead in a Week (Or Your Money Back), 2018. *Television includes*: Prime Suspect, 1991; All Things Bright and Beautiful, 1994; Martin Chuzzlewit, 1994; The Gathering Storm, 2002. *Address*: c/o Lou Coulson Associates Ltd, 1st Floor, 37 Berwick Street, W1F 8RS.

**WILKINSON, Prof. (William) Brian**, DSc, PhD; FGS; FICE; FCIWEM; Senior Consultant, Solutions to Environmental Problems, since 1999; *b* 20 Jan. 1938; *s* of James Edmund Wilkinson and Gladys (*née* Forster); *m* 1962, Gillian Warren; two *s* one *d*. *Educ*: Univ. of Durham (BSc Hons Civil Engrg, BSc Hons Geol.; DSc 2016); Univ. of Manchester (PhD 1968). FGS 1974; FCIWEM (FIWEM 1984); FICE 1989. Asst engr, Babtie Shaw and Morton, Consulting Engrs, 1961–63; Lectr, Dept of Civil Engrg, Univ. of Manchester, 1963–69; Sen. Engr, Water Resources Bd, 1969–74; Sen. Principal Hydrologist, Severn Trent Water Authy, 1974–75; Hd, Water Resources Div., Water Res. Centre, 1975–83; Prof. of Civil Engrg, RMCS, Cranfield Univ., 1983–88; Dir, Inst. of Hydrology, 1988–94; Dir, Centre for Ecology and Hydrology, 1995–99, NERC. Visiting Professor: in Hydrol., Univ. of Reading, 1989–; in Dept of Civil Engrg, Univ. of Newcastle upon Tyne, 2000–. Dir, Oxford Vacs, 1997–99. Mem. and Project Co-ordinator, Ind. Rev. Gp for Decommissioning Brent N Sea Platforms, 2007–; Advr, Safety Health and Envmt Cttee, Transport for London, 2007–10. Fellow, Russian Acad. of Nat. Sci., 1997. *Publications*: (ed) Groundwater Quality, Measurement, Prediction and Protection, 1976; (ed jtly) Applied Groundwater Hydrology, 1991; (ed) Groundwater Problems in Urban Areas, 1994; numerous articles covering geotechnics and envmtl sci. *Recreations*: classical music, violin, viola, French wines, water colour painting, choral singing, archaeology, Shukokai karate (black belt, 1st Dan). *Address*: Millfield House, High Street, Leintwardine, Craven Arms, Shropshire SY7 0LB. *T*: (01547) 540356. *E*: gb.wilk@dsl.pipex.com.

**WILKINSON, Dr William Lionel**, CBE 1987; FRS 1990; FREng; a Director, British Nuclear Fuels plc, 1984–94; *b* 16 Feb. 1931; *s* of Lionel and Dorothy Wilkinson; *m* 1955, Josephine Anne Pilgrim (*d* 2018); five *s*. *Educ*: Christ's Coll., Cambridge (MA, PhD, ScD). Salters' Res. Schol., Christ's Coll., Cambridge, 1953–56; Lectr in Chem. Engrg, UC Swansea, 1956–59; UKAEA Production Gp, 1959–67; Prof. of Chem. Engrg, Univ. of Bradford, 1967–79; British Nuclear Fuels Ltd: Dep. Dir, 1982–84; Technical Dir, 1984–86; Dep. Chief Exec., 1986–92; non-exec. Dir, 1992–94; Dep. Chm., Allied Colloids plc, 1992–98 (non-exec. Dir, 1989–98). Vis. Prof. of Chemical Engrg, Imperial Coll., London, 1980–2004. Chm., British Nuclear Industry Forum, 1992–97; Pres., Eur. Atomic Forum, 1994–96. Member: SRC, 1981–85; ACOST, 1990–95. FIChemE (Pres., 1980); FREng (FEng 1980). Liveryman, Salters' Co., 1985. Hon. DEng Bradford, 1989. *Publications*: Non-Newtonian Flow, 1960; contribs to sci. and engrg jls on heat transfer, fluid mechanics, polymer processing, process dynamics and nuclear fuel processing. *Recreations*: bridge, gardening. *Address*: Tree Tops, Legh Road, Knutsford, Cheshire WA16 8LP. *T*: (01565) 653344. *Club*: Athenæum.

**WILKS, Ann**; *see* Wilks, M. A.

**WILKS, Maj. Gen. Carew Lovell**, CB 2014; CBE 2007; CEng, FIET; Vice President, General Dynamics Land Systems, since 2018; *b* Cuckfield, Sussex, 10 May 1960; *s* of Richard Lovell Wilks and Sheila Gillian Jean Wilks (*née* Bowack, now Olford); *m* 1983, Janey Prior-Willeard; two *s*. *Educ*: Malvern Coll.; Lincoln Coll., Oxford (MA Engrg Sci.); RMA Sandhurst; RSME. CEng 1992; FIET 2007. Commnd RE, 1978; Troop Comdr, 1983–86; on secondment to industry, 1987–88; Adjt, 28 Amphibious Engr Regt, 1989–90; Berlin Works Office, 1991–93; OC 5 Field Sqdn, 1994–96; Project Manager, MoD Procurement Exec., 1996–98; OC 529 Specialist Team RE (Air Support), 1998–99; Directing Staff, RMCS, 1999–2000; CO, 25 Engr Regt, NI, 2000–02; Team Leader, Combat Support Vehicles, 2002–04; Director: Army Infrastructure Orgn, 2004–07; Energy Ops, Iraq, 2007–08; Hd, Individual Capability, MoD, 2008–11; Dir Land Equipment, MoD, 2011–13; Chief Operating Officer, NIMR LLC, 2013–17. Pres., Instn of RE, 2012–17. *Recreations*: overland travel, dinghy sailing, shooting, deer management. *E*: carew.wilks@btinternet.com. *Club*: Naval and Military.

**WILKS, Jonathan Paul, (Jon)**, CMG 2012; HM Diplomatic Service; Ambassador to Iraq, 2017–19; *b* Callow End, Worcs, 30 Sept. 1967; *s* of Douglas Edwin Ian Wilks and Veronica Kay Wilks (*née* Mills); *m* 2015, Hon. Patricia Marie Haslach. *Educ*: Chase High Sch., Malvern; Durham Univ. (BSc Natural Scis 1989; MA Dist. Middle East Politics 2000); St Antony's Coll., Oxford (MPhil Internat. Relns 2002). FRGS 1996. Entered FCO, 1989; Asst Desk Officer, Iran Desk, 1990–91; Arabic lang. trng, London, 1991–92, Cairo, 1992–93; Second Sec., Khartoum, 1993–96; First Sec., Riyadh, 1996–99; on secondment to Cabinet Office Assessments Staff, 2002–03; Deputy Head: British Office, Baghdad, 2003; Iraq Policy Unit, FCO, 2004; Security Policy Gp, FCO, 2005–07; Regl Arabic Spokesman, Dubai, 2007–09; Dep. Hd of Mission, Baghdad, 2009–10; Ambassador to Yemen, 2010–11; HCSC 2012; UK Special Rep. to the Syrian Opposition, 2012–13; UK Special Rep. for Syria, 2014; Ambassador to Oman, 2014–17. Iraq Reconstruction Medal, 2004. *Recreations*: horse racing, music. *Address*: c/o Foreign and Commonwealth Office, King Charles Street, SW1A 2AH. *Clubs*: Travellers, National Liberal.

**WILKS, (Margaret) Ann**, CBE 2004; Secretary, Financial Reporting Council, and Financial Reporting Review Panel, 1998–2004; *b* 11 May 1943; *d* of Herbert Robson and Margaret Robson (*née* Culbert); *m* 1977, Victor Wilks; two *d*. *Educ*: Putney High Sch., GPDST; Lady Margaret Hall, Oxford (BA Modern Hist., BPhil American Hist.); Univ. of Pennsylvania (Thouron Schol.). Asst Principal, Min. of Power and DTI, 1968–71; Department of Trade and Industry: Private Sec. to Perm. Sec. (Trade) and Parly Sec., 1971–72; Principal, 1972–73; journalist, Economist, 1973–74; Principal: DTI, 1974–76; Cabinet Office, 1976–78; (pt-time) DTI, 1982–84; (pt-time) Asst Sec., DTI, 1984–96 (Hd, Industrial Develt Unit, and Sec., Industrial Develt Adv. Bd, 1991–96); Dir, Metals, Minerals and Shipbuilding, DTI, 1996–98. Mem., Tribunal Panel, Financial Reporting Council Disciplinary Scheme (formerly Accountancy Investigation and Discipline Bd, then Accountancy and Actuarial Discipline Bd), 2004–13. Chm., Hornsey Town Hall Community Partnership Bd and Creative Trust, 2018–11. Trustee, 2002–11, and Chm. of Govs, 2004–11, Nat. Centre for Young People with Epilepsy, Lingfield. Trustee, Victorian Soc., 2015–. Mem. Cttee, Thouron Scholarship, 1974–80. *Publications*: contribs to British Jl of Middle Eastern Studies, Jl of Royal Asiatic Soc. *Recreations*: tennis, cookery, theatre, walking, sightseeing. *Address*: 28 Berkeley Road, N8 8RU.

**WILKS, Prof. Stephen Robert Mark**, PhD; Professor of Politics, 1990–2013, now Emeritus, and Deputy Vice Chancellor, 1999–2002 and 2004–05, University of Exeter; *b* 2 Jan. 1949; *s* of late Ernest Gordon Fawcett Wilks and Florence Wilks (*née* Wilson); *m* 1976, Philippa Mary Hughes; three *d*. *Educ*: Buckhurst Hill Co. High Sch.; City of Westminster Coll.; Univ. of Lancaster (BA); Univ. of Manchester (PhD 1980). FCA 1978. Chartered Accountant, Fryer Whitehill and Co., London, 1968–72; University of Liverpool, Department of Political Theory and Institutions: Lectr, 1978–86; Sen. Lectr, 1986–89; Reader, 1989–90. Vis. Prof., Faculty of Law, Kyoto Univ., 1989. Member: ESRC, 2001–05 (Chm., Res. Priorities Bd, 2001–05); Competition Commn, 2001–09; Competition Appeal Tribunal, 2011–. *Publications*: Industrial Crisis (ed with K. Dyson), 1983; Industrial Policy and the Motor Industry, 1984, 2nd edn 1988; (ed with M. Wright) Comparative Government-Industry Relations, 1987; (ed with B. Doern) Comparative

Competition Policy, 1996; (ed with B. Doern) Regulatory Institutions in Britain and North America, 1998; In the Public Interest: competition policy and the Monopolies and Mergers Commission, 1999; (ed jtly) Reforming Public and Corporate Governance, 2002; The Political Power of the Business Corporation, 2013. *Recreations:* walking, wine, gardening, tea. *Address:* Newlands, Millhayes, Stockland, Devon EX14 9DG. *E:* srmwilks@gmail.com.

**WILL, Prof. Robert George**, CBE 2000; MD; FRCP; Professor of Clinical Neurology, University of Edinburgh, since 1998; Consultant Neurologist, Western General Hospital, Edinburgh, since 1987; Co-ordinator, European Creutzfeldt-Jakob Disease Surveillance, since 2002; *b* 30 July 1950; *s* of George and Margaret Will; *m* 1976, Jayne; one *s* one *d*. *Educ:* Glenalmond Coll.; St John's Coll., Cambridge (MB BChir 1974; MA, MD 1985); London Hosp. Med. Coll. FRCP 1994. London Hosp., Nat. Hosp., Queen Sq. and N Middx Hosp., 1974–79; res. at Univ. of Oxford, 1979–82; Registrar, St Thomas' Hosp., 1982–84; Sen. Registrar, Nat. Hosp., Queen Sq. and Guy's Hosp., 1994–97. Dir, Nat. CJD Surveillance Unit, 1990–2002. FMedSci 2001. FRSA 1998. *Publications:* contrib. articles on Creutzfeldt-Jakob Disease. *Address:* 4 St Catherine's Place, Edinburgh EH9 1NU. *T:* (0131) 667 3667.

**WILLACY, Michael James Ormerod**, CBE 1989; Managing Director (formerly Managing Partner), Michael Willacy Associates Ltd, 1990–2010; *b* 7 June 1933; *s* of James and Marjorie Willacy (*née* Sanders); *m* 1st, 1961, Merle Louise de Lange; two *s* one *d*; 2nd, 1985, Victoria Stuart John; three *s* one *d*. *Educ:* Taunton Sch., Somerset. FCIPS. Purchasing Agent, Shell Venezuela, 1964–73; Procurement Advr, Shell Internat., The Hague, 1974–77; Supt, Shell Stanlow, 1978–80; Manager, Shell Wilmslow, 1981–83; Gen. Man., Shell Materials Services, 1983–85; Dir, Central Unit on Purchasing, 1985–90, Procurement Advr, 1991–92, HM Treasury. Chairman: Macclesfield Chamber of Commerce, 1981–83; Macclesfield Business Ventures, 1982–83. Old Tauntonian Association: Gen. Sec., 1978–91; Pres., 1988–89; Vice-Pres., 1990–; Gov., Taunton Sch., 1993–2008; Chm., St Dunstan's Abbey Sch., Plymouth, 1997–2004; Hon. Vice-Pres., Plymouth Coll., 2005–. *Recreations:* golf, travel, gardening. *Address:* 2 Erme Park, Ermington, Ivybridge, Devon PL21 9LY. *Clubs:* Old Tauntonian Association (Taunton); Bigbury Golf (Chm., 2007–10).

**WILLANS, David William**; His Honour Judge Willans; a Circuit Judge, since 2018; *b* Brighton, 29 Oct. 1969; *m* 2005, Tara McAndrew; one *s* three *d*. *Educ:* Cardinal Newman Sch., Hove; University Coll. London (BSc Econs); City Univ., London (LLB Law). Called to the Bar, Lincoln's Inn, 1995; a District Judge, 2013–18. *Address:* West London Family Court, Gloucester House, 4 Dukes Green Avenue, Feltham, Middx TW14 0LR.

**WILLARD, Kathryn Charlotte Louise**; Director, Partnership Development, Stobart Group, since 2006; *b* Hertford, 29 April 1962; *d* of Derek William Frederick Willard and Pamela Joy Willard; one *s* one *d*. Apprentice, Th. Royal, Stratford East, 1982–85; Associate Dir, Liverpool Playhouse, 1986–91; Founder and Dir, Brouhaha, 1991–94; Expert, Eur. Commn, 1995–2002; CEO, Rural Regeneration Cumbria, 2002–06. Non-exec. Dir, Liverpool City Reg. LEP, 2012–17. Chair: Atlantic Gateway, 2014–19; Opportunity S Essex, 2014–. Mem., Arts Council, 2017– (Chm., North Area, 2017–). Trustee, Liverpool Everyman and Playhouse Theatres Trust, 2016–18. FRSA. *Recreations:* travel, wine, food and new adventures. *Address:* Stobart Group, The Terminal, Aviation Way, Carlisle Lake District Airport, Carlisle CA6 4NZ. *T:* 07775 898959. *E:* kate.willard@stobartgroup.com. *Club:* Farmers.

**WILLASEY-WILSEY, Timothy Andrew**, CMG 2007; HM Diplomatic Service, retired; International Advisor: Royal Bank of Scotland and Natwest, since 2008; Coutts, since 2011; *b* 12 Sept. 1953; *s* of Maj.-Gen. Anthony Patrick Willasey-Wisey, CB, MBE, MC, and of Dorothy Willasey-Wilsey (*née* Yates); *m* 1983, Alison Middleton Mackie; three *s*. *Educ:* Shrewsbury Sch.; Univ. of St Andrews (MA 1st Cl. Hons Mod. Hist. 1976). Teacher, English Sch., Addis Ababa, 1971–72; Metal Box Ltd, 1976–81: Export Sales Manager, 1977–79; Factory Mgt, 1979–81; joined HM Diplomatic Service, 1981; FCO, 1981–83; First Sec., Luanda, 1983–86; Hd of Chancery, later Dep. Hd of Mission, San Jose, Costa Rica, 1986–89; also Consul, San Jose and Managua, Nicaragua, 1986–89; FCO, 1989–93; Counsellor (Political), Islamabad, 1993–96; FCO, 1996–99; Counsellor, UK Mission to UN, Geneva, 1999–2002; Dir, FCO, 2002–08. Vis. Sen. Res. Fellow, Dept of War Studies, KCL, 2012–. Mem. Council, RIIA, Chatham House, 2016–. Ext. Expert, Indian Council on Global Relns, 2013–. Asst Ed., The Victorian Web, 2014–. *Recreations:* history, travel, reading, cricket. *Address:* c/o Royal Bank of Scotland, 250 Bishopsgate, EC2M 4RB. *Clubs:* Royal Over-Seas League, MCC.

**WILLBY, Christopher Roy**, CEng; Director, Hazardous Installations Directorate, Health and Safety Executive, 2003–05; *b* 11 March 1945; *s* of Brian George Willby and Jean Marjorie Willby; *m* 1967, Sheila Burton (marr. diss. 1991); two *d*. *Educ:* Temple Moor Grammar Sch., Leeds; Univ. of Manchester Inst. of Sci. and Technol. (BSc Hons); Leeds Poly. (DMS). CEng, MInstE 1983. Asst Engr, Southern Project Gp, CEGB, 1966–70; Section Hd, UKAEA Risley, later NNC, 1970–78; Engrg Manager for subsid. co., Hickson Gp, 1978–82; Health and Safety Executive: Principal Inspector, 1982–87, Superintendent Inspector, 1987–91, NII; Dep. Chief Inspector, Nuclear and Radioactive Waste Policy, 1991–98; Regl Dir, Yorks and NE, 1998–2002. Chm., Potters Bar Rail Inquiry Bd, 2007–09. Co. Sec., Welsh Highland Rly Ltd, 2006–. *Recreations:* gardening, walking, theatre, renovating old motorcycles. *E:* chris.willby@hotmail.co.uk.

**WILLCOCKS, Prof. Dianne Marie**, CBE 2008; DL; Leadership Consultant and Emeritus Professor, York St John University, since 2010; *b* 5 May 1945; *d* of late Jack and Georgina Kitson; *m* 1965, Peter Willcocks (marr. diss. 1984); two *d*. *Educ:* Ealing Coll. of Higher Educn (DipM 1966); Univ. of Surrey (BSc Hons Human Scis 1976). Dir of Res., then Dean, Envmtl and Social Scis, Poly., then Univ., of N London, 1980–93; Prof. of Social Gerontology, Univ. of N London, 1992–93; Asst Principal, Sheffield Hallam Univ., 1993–99; Principal, York St John Coll., later York St John Univ. Coll., then Vice-Chancellor, York St John Univ., 1999–2010; Dir, Governor Develt Progs, Leadership Foundn for HE, 2011–14. Mem. Bd, HEFCE, 2006–09. Vice-Chairman: York Teaching Hosp. Foundn Trust, 2010–19; Joseph Rowntree Foundn, 2011–; Chairman: Bd, York Th. Royal, 2003–13; York Mediale Fest., 2017–. Gov., London Metropolitan Univ., 2010–18; Vice-Chm., Rose Bruford Coll., 2010–17 (Hon. Fellow, 2017). Trustee, York Museums Trust, 2018–. Chm., Wilf Ward Family Trust, 2019–. DL N Yorks, 2010. Hon. Dr Sheffield Hallam, 2012; Hon. DEd York St John, 2018. *Publications:* (jtly) Private Lives in Public Places, 1987; (jtly) Residential Care Revisited, 1997; (contrib.) Access to Success and Social Mobility through Higher Education, 2018. *Recreations:* family, friends, fitness. *Address:* 61 Rowntree Wharf, York YO1 9XA. *T:* (01904) 670884. *E:* d.willcocks@sircles.net.

**WILLCOCKS, Jonathan Peter**; freelance conductor and composer, since 1975; *b* Worcester, 9 Jan. 1953; *s* of Sir David Valentine Willcocks, CBE, MC; *m* 1999, Dr Alice Emerson; three *s* two *d*. *Educ:* Clifton Coll.; Trinity Coll., Cambridge (BA 1974; MA 1976; PGCE). Director of Music: Portsmouth Grammar Sch., 1975–78; Bedales Sch., 1978–89; Dir, Jun. Acad., RAM, 1989–2008. Musical Director: Portsmouth Choral Union, 1975–2012; Chichester Singers, 1979–; Southern Pro Musica, 1990–; Guildford Choral Soc., 2012–; Conductor, Leith Hill Musical Fest., 2016–. Hon. RAM 1996. Compositions include major choral works, works for children's choir, shorter pieces and instrumental works. *Recreations:* golf, theatre, eating and drinking. *Address:* 3 The Square, Compton, Chichester, W Sussex PO18 9HA. *T:* (023) 9263 1369. *E:* jonathan@jonathanwillcocks.com. *Clubs:* Liphook Golf, St Enodoc Golf.

**WILLCOCKS, Lt.-Gen. Sir Michael (Alan)**, KCB 2000 (CB 1997); CVO 2009; Independent Reviewer (formerly Charter Commissioner), Press Complaints Commission, 2009–12; Gentleman Usher of the Black Rod and Serjeant-at-Arms, House of Lords, and Secretary to the Lord Great Chamberlain, 2001–09; *b* 27 July 1944; *s* of late Henry Willcocks and Georgina Willcocks (*née* Lawton); *m* 1st, 1966, Jean Paton Weir (separated 2004; marr. diss. 2018); one *s* two *d*; 2nd, 2018, Penelope Jane Beels (*née* Aedy). *Educ:* St John's Coll.; RMA Sandhurst; London Univ. (BSc Hons). Commnd RA, 1964; served Malaya, Borneo, NI, Germany, 1965–72; Instructor, RMA Sandhurst, 1972–74; MoD, 1977–79; Comd M Battery, RHA, 1979–80; Directing Staff, Staff Coll., 1981–83; CO, 1st Regt, RHA, 1983–85; Dep. ACOS, HQ UKLF, 1985–87; ACOS, Intelligence/Ops, HQ UKLF, 1988; CRA, 4th Armd Div., 1989–90; rcds 1991; ACOS, Land Ops, Joint War HQ, Gulf War, 1991; Dir Army Plans and Programme, 1991–93; Dir Gen. Land Warfare, 1993–94; COS Allied Command Europe Rapid Reaction Corps, 1994–96; COS Land Component Implementation Force, Bosnia-Herzegovina, 1995–96; ACGS, MoD, 1996–99; Dep. Comdr (Ops), Stabilisation Force, Bosnia-Herzegovina, 1999–2000; UK Mil. Rep. to NATO and the EU, 2000–01. Comr, Royal Hosp., Chelsea, 1996–99. Col Comdt, RA, 2000–05; Representative Col Comdt, RA, 2004–05. Hon. Col, 1 RHA, 1999–2006. Director: IKOS CIF, 2010–15; IKOS AM, 2016–. Mem., European-Atlantic Gp, 1994–. Mem., Pilgrims, 2002–. Trustee, Lifeline Energy (formerly Freeplay Foundn), 2006–13. MSM (USA), 1996, 2000. Hon. DLitt Hull, 2008. Kt Comdr, Sacred Military Order of St George, 2006; PJK 2006. *Publications:* Airmobility and the Armoured Experience, 1989. *Recreations:* books, music, fishing, sailing, shooting. *Clubs:* Beefsteak, National Liberal, Pitt, Saints and Sinners, Farmers.

**WILLEMS, Julia Ann**; *see* Cheetham, J. A.

**WILLEMS, Lodewijk**; Chief Executive Officer, Edwards & Willems, since 2013; *b* 6 April 1948; *s* of Frans and Leona Willems-Hendrickx; *m* 1976, Lindsay Edwards; three *s* one *d*. *Educ:* Univ. of Brussels (Licentiate Pol Science and Internat. Relns 1971); Yale Univ. (MA Pol Science 1975). Entered Belgian Diplomatic Service, 1976; Dep. Perm. Rep., IAEA, Vienna, 1977; Advr to Dep. Prime Minister and Minister for Econ. Affairs, 1977–81; Dep. Sec. Gen., Benelux Econ. Union, 1981–85; Political Counsellor, Kinshasa, 1985–88; Chef de Cabinet to Minister for Econ. Affairs, 1988–91; Dep. Perm. Rep. to EU, 1991–92; Chef de Cabinet to Minister of Foreign Affairs, 1992–94; Perm. Rep. (Ambassador rank), UN, Geneva, 1994–97; Ambassador: to UK, 1997–2002; to Germany, 2002–06. Fortis Bank, later BNP Paribas Fortis: Dir of External Affairs, then Dir of Ext. and Govtl Affairs, 2006–13; Advr to CEO and Chief Operating Officer, 2013–15. Chm., Internat. Relns Commn, Fédération des Entreprises de Belgique/Verbond van Belgische Ondernemingen, 2008–14; Board Member: BASF Antwerp, 2006–15; Flanders Festival, 2008–. Commn for Relief of Belgium Fellow, Belgian-American Educnl Foundn, 1973. Grand Officier, Order of Leopold II (Belgium), 2005. *Recreations:* theatre, classical music.

**WILLEMS, Marc Paul Bernard Albert**; QC 2015; a Recorder, since 2005; *b* Manchester, 6 May 1966; *s* of Bernard and Berthe Willems; *m* 1991, Julia Ann Cheetham, *qv*; two *s* one *d*. *Educ:* St Bede's Coll., Manchester; Nottingham Univ. (BA Law 1989); Inns of Court Sch. of Law. Called to the Bar, Lincoln's Inn, 1990; in practice as barrister specialising in personal injury and clinical negligence. *Recreations:* cycling, running, family, France, music concerts. *Address:* Cobden House Chambers, 19 Quay Street, Manchester M3 3HN. *T:* (0161) 833 6000, *Fax:* (0161) 833 6001. *E:* marc.willems@cobden.co.uk. *Clubs:* Bareges Cycling, Edge Cycling.

**WILLERS, Marc Lawrence George**; QC 2014; *b* Newton, Cambs, 28 Nov. 1964; *s* of Peter Willers and Diane Waters (*née* Dobrashian); *m* 1999, Zoe Uney; one *d*. *Educ:* Haydon Sch., Middx; Chelmer Coll. of Higher Educn (LLB). Called to the Bar, Lincoln's Inn, 1987; in practice as a barrister, specialising in human rights law, 1987–. *Publications:* (ed jtly) Gypsy and Traveller Law, 2004, 2nd edn 2007; Ensuring Access to Rights for Roma and Travellers, 2009, 3rd edn 2014. *Recreations:* sport, theatre, travelling, cooking, Gypsy music. *Address:* Garden Court Chambers, 57–60 Lincoln's Inn Fields, WC2A 3LJ. *T:* (020) 7993 7600, *Fax:* (020) 7993 7700. *E:* marcw@gclaw.co.uk.

**WILLESDEN, Area Bishop of**, since 2001; **Rt Rev. Peter Alan Broadbent**; *b* 31 July 1952; *s* of Philip and Patricia Broadbent; *m* 1974, Sarah Enderby; one *s*. *Educ:* Merchant Taylors' Sch., Northwood, Middx; Jesus Coll., Cambridge (MA 1978); St John's Coll., Nottingham (DipTh 1975). Ordained deacon, 1977, priest 1978; Assistant Curate: St Nicholas, Durham City, 1977–80; Emmanuel, Holloway, 1980–83; Chaplain, Poly. of N London, 1983–89; Vicar, Trinity St Michael, Harrow, 1989–94; Archdeacon of Northolt, 1995–2001; Acting Bishop: of Edmonton, 2015; of London, 2017–18. Proctor in Convocation, London, 1985–2001. Member: Archbishops' Council, C of E, 1999–2000; Central Governing Body, City Parochial Foundn, 1999–2003; Gen. Synod, 2004–. Chm. Council, St John's Coll., Nottingham, 2002–10. Trustee, Church Urban Fund, 2002–11. Mem. (Lab) Islington BC, 1982–89. *Publications:* contrib. to theol books and jls. *Recreations:* football, theatre and film, railways. *Address:* 173 Willesden Lane, NW6 7YN. *T:* (020) 8451 0189, *Fax:* (020) 8451 4606. *E:* bishop.willesden@btinternet.com.

**WILLETT, Prof. Keith Malcolm**, CBE 2016; FRCS; Professor of Orthopaedic Trauma Surgery, University of Oxford, since 2004; Fellow, Wolfson College, Oxford, since 2004; Medical Director for Acute Care and Emergency Preparedness, NHS England, since 2012; *b* 9 Sept. 1957; *s* of Aubrey and Ruth Willett; *m* 1980, Lesley Kiernan; three *s*. *Educ:* Charing Cross Hosp. Med. Sch., Univ. of London (MB BS 1981). LRCP, MRCS 1981, FRCS 1985. Fellow in Trauma, Sunnybrook Health Sci. Center, Toronto, 1991–92; Consultant, Nuffield Orthopaedic Centre, Oxford, 1992–95; Consultant Orthopaedic and Trauma Surgeon, John Radcliffe Hospital, 1992–2004, Hon. Consultant, 2004–; Nat. Clinical Dir for Trauma Care, NHS, 2009–12. Hon. FRCSE 2015. *Publications:* research papers on functional outcomes after injury and surgical interventions. *Recreations:* football, hiking. *Address:* Kadoorie Centre for Critical Care Research and Education, John Radcliffe Hospital, Oxford OX3 9DU. *T:* (01865) 223101.

**WILLETT, Michael John**, FRAeS; Board Member, Civil Aviation Authority and Group Director, Safety Regulation, 1992–97; *b* 2 Oct. 1944; *s* of Reginald John Willett and Nora Else Willett; *m* 1st, 1967, Gillian Margaret Pope (marr. diss. 1998); two *s* one *d*; 2nd, 1998, Paulene Ann Parkinson. *Educ:* Grammar Sch., Tottenham; Open Univ. (BA Hons); Open Business Sch. (MBA). RAF, 1963–71; Airline Captain, Laker Airways, 1973–82; Flight Ops Inspectorate, CAA, 1982–92. Member (C): W Sussex CC, 1999–2001; Horsham DC, 2015–19. Liveryman, Hon. Co. of Air Pilots (formerly GAPAN), 1991– (Master, 2003–04). *Recreations:* horse riding, guitar playing. *Club:* Royal Air Force.

**WILLETT, Prof. Peter,** PhD, DSc; Professor of Information Science, University of Sheffield, since 1991; *b* 20 April 1953; *s* of David and Patricia Willett; *m* 1978, Marie-Therese Gannon; one *d*. *Educ*: Exeter Coll., Oxford (MA); Univ. of Sheffield (MSc 1976; PhD 1979; DSc 1997). Lectr, 1979–86, Sen. Lectr, 1986–88, Reader, 1988–91, Univ. of Sheffield. Pres., Chemical Structure Assoc., 1998–2002. Chm., Bd of Govs, Cambridge Crystallographic Data Centre, 2001–03. *Publications*: Similarity and Clustering in Chemical Information Systems, 1987; (with J. Ashford) Text Retrieval and Document Databases, 1988; (with E. M. Rasmussen) Parallel Database Processing, 1990; Three-Dimensional Chemical Structure Handling, 1991; (jtly) Readings in Information Retrieval, 1997; (with Y. C. Martin) Designing Bioactive Molecules, 1998; over 550 articles, reports, and book chapters. *Recreations*: classical music, current affairs, military history. *Address*: Information School, University of Sheffield, 211 Portobello Street, Sheffield S1 4DP. *T*: (0114) 222 2633, *Fax*: (0114) 278 0300. *E*: p.willett@sheffield.ac.uk.

**WILLETTS,** family name of **Baron Willetts**.

**WILLETTS,** Baron *cr* 2015 (Life Peer), of Havant in the County of Hampshire; **David Lindsay Willetts;** PC 2010; President, Resolution Foundation, since 2019 (Executive Chair, 2015–19); *b* 9 March 1956; *s* of late John Roland Willetts and of Hilary Sheila Willetts; *m* 1986, Hon. Sarah Harriet Ann, *d* of Lord Butterfield; one *s* one *d*. *Educ*: King Edward's Sch., Birmingham; Christ Church, Oxford (BA 1st cl. Hons PPE). Res. Asst to Nigel Lawson, MP, 1978; HM Treasury, 1978–84: Pvte Sec. to Financial Sec., 1981–82; Principal Monetary Policy Div., 1982–84; Prime Minister's Downing Street Policy Unit, 1984–86; Dir of Studies, Centre for Policy Studies, 1987–92. MP (C) Havant, 1992–2015. PPS to Chm. of Cons. Party, 1993–94; an Asst Govt Whip, 1994–95; a Lord Comr of HM Treasury (Govt Whip), 1995; Parly Sec., Office of Public Service, Cabinet Office, 1995–96; HM Paymaster General, 1996; Opposition front bench spokesman on employment, 1997–98; Shadow Secretary of State: for educn and employment, 1998–99; for social security, 1999–2001; for work and pensions, 2001–05; DTI, 2005; for Educn and Skills, 2005–07; for Univs and Skills (formerly Innovation, Univs and Skills), 2007–10; Minister of State (Minister for Univs and Sci.), BIS, 2010–14. Consultant Dir, 1987–92, Chm., 1997, Cons. Res. Dept; Hd of Policy Co-ordination, Cons. Party, 2003–04. Director: Retirement Security Ltd, 1988–94; Electra Corporate Ventures Ltd, 1988–94; Economic Advr, Dresdner Kleinwort Benson, 1997–2007; Sen. Advr, Punter Southall, 2005–09. Non-exec. Director: Surrey Satellite Technology, 2015–; Biotech Growth Trust, 2015–; Sen. Advr, 2U, 2016–; Chair, Verditek Ltd, 2018–. Mem. Adv. Bd, British Council, 2001–05. Vis. Fellow, Nuffield Coll., Oxford, 1999–2007; Visiting Professor: Pensions Inst., Cass Business Sch., 2005–09; Policy Inst., KCL, 2014–. Non-exec. Dir, Nat. Centre for Univs and Business, 2015–17; Member, Board: Francis Crick Inst., 2015–18; UK Res. and Innovation, 2017–; Chair: Sanger Inst., 2017–; Council for Sci. and Technol., 2018–. Member: Social Security Adv. Cttee, 1989–92; Global Commn on Ageing, 2000–09. Chm., British Sci. Assoc., 2015–18. Trustee, Sci. Mus. Gp, 2015–18. Member: Parkside HA, 1988–90; Lambeth, Lewisham and Southwark FPC, 1987–90. Mem., Prog. Cttee, 1998–2010, Gov., 2004–19, Hon. Gov., 2019, Ditchley Foundn. Mem. Council, Inst. for Fiscal Studies, 2003–. Mem., Sen. Common Room, Christ Church, Oxford, 2007–. Chancellor, Univ. of Leicester, 2018–. Hon. Mem., Salters' Co., 2016. Hon. Fellow, Nuffield Coll., Oxford, 2015. FAcSS 2014. Hon. FMedSci 2016; Hon. FRSC 2018; Hon. FRS 2018. *Publications*: Modern Conservatism, 1992; Civic Conservatism, 1994; Blair's Gurus, 1996; Why Vote Conservative?, 1997; (jtly) Is Conservatism Dead?, 1997; Welfare to Work, 1998; After the Landslide, 1999; Tax Credits: do they add up?, 2002; Old Europe?: demographic change and pension reform, 2003; Conservatives in Birmingham, 2008; The Pinch: how baby-boomers took their children's future - and why they should give it back, 2010, 2nd edn 2019; A University Education, 2017; paper, The Role of the Prime Minister's Policy Unit, 1987 (Haldane Medal, RIPA); various pamphlets. *Recreations*: swimming, reading. *Address*: House of Lords, SW1A 0PW.

**WILLI, Prof. Andreas Jonathan,** DPhil; Diebold Professor of Comparative Philology, University of Oxford, since 2005; Fellow of Worcester College, Oxford, since 2005; *b* Altstätten, Switzerland, 17 Dec. 1972; *s* of Thomas Willi and Ina Willi-Plein; *m* 2005, Helen Kaufmann; one *s* two *d*. *Educ*: Primarschule Peters, Basel; Humanistisches Gymnasium, Basel; Universität Basel (lic.phil. Classics, Slavonic Langs/Lits 1997); Université de Lausanne; Univ. of Michigan; Univ. de Fribourg (lic.phil. Comparative Philology 1998); Corpus Christi Coll., Oxford (DPhil Classics 2001). Oberassistent, Classics, 2001–04, Privatdozent für Klassische Philologie, 2007–, Univ. of Basel. *Publications*: (ed) The Language of Greek Comedy, 2002; The Languages of Aristophanes, 2003; Sikelismos: Sprache, Literatur und Gesellschaft im griechischen Sizilien, 2008; (ed jtly) Laws and Rules in Indo-European, 2012; (ed) Sprachgeschichte und Epigraphik, 2017; Origins of the Greek Verb, 2018; (ed) Formes et fonctions des langues littéraires en Grèce ancienne, 2019. *Address*: Worcester College, Oxford OX1 2HB.

**WILLIAMS;** see Rees-Williams.

**WILLIAMS;** see Sims-Williams.

**WILLIAMS,** family name of **Barons Williams of Elvel** and **Williams of Oystermouth**, and **Baronesses Williams of Crosby** and **Williams of Trafford**.

**WILLIAMS OF CROSBY,** Baroness *cr* 1993 (Life Peer), of Stevenage in the County of Hertfordshire; **Shirley Vivian Teresa Brittain Williams,** CH 2017; PC 1974; Co-founder, Social Democratic Party, 1981, President, 1982–88; Leader, Liberal Democrats, House of Lords, 2001–04; Public Service Professor of Elective Politics, John F. Kennedy School of Government, Harvard University, 1988–2000, now Emeritus; *b* 27 July 1930; *d* of late Prof. Sir George Catlin, and late Mrs Catlin, (Vera Brittain); *m* 1st, 1955, Prof. Bernard Arthur Owen Williams, FBA (marr. diss. 1974; he *d* 2003); one *d*; 2nd, 1987, Prof. Richard Elliott Neustadt (*d* 2003). *Educ*: eight schools in UK and USA; Somerville Coll., Oxford (scholar; MA, Hon. Fellow, 1970); Columbia Univ., New York (Smith-Mundt Scholar, 1952). General Secretary, Fabian Soc., 1960–64 (Chm., 1980–81). Contested: (Lab) Harwich, Essex, 1954 and 1955, and Southampton Test, 1959; (SDP) Crosby, 1983; (SDP/Alliance) Cambridge, 1987. MP: (Lab) Hitchin, 1964–74; (Lab) Hertford and Stevenage, 1974–79; (first-elected SDP MP) Crosby, Nov. 1981–1983; PPS, Minister of Health, 1964–66; Parly Sec., Min. of Labour, 1966–67; Minister of State: Education and Science, 1967–69; Home Office, 1969–70; Opposition spokesman on: Social Services, 1970–71, on Home Affairs, 1971–73; Prices and Consumer Protection, 1973–74; Sec. of State for Prices and Consumer Protection, 1974–76; Sec. of State for Educn and Science, 1976–79; Paymaster General, 1976–79. Mem., H of L, 1993–2016; Dep. Leader, Liberal Democrat Party, H of L, 1999–2001. Bd Mem., Rand Corp., Europe, 1993–2001. Chm., OECD study on youth employment, 1979; Member: Council of Advrs to Praesidium, Ukraine, 1991–97; Adv. Council to UN Sec.-Gen. for Fourth World Women's Conf., Beijing, 1995; EC Comité des Sages, 1995–96; Council, Internat. Crisis Gp, 1998–2004; Internat. Adv. Cttee, Council on Foreign Relns, NY; Comr, Internat. Commn on Nuclear Non-proliferation and Disarmament, 2008–10. Advr on Nuclear Non-proliferation to Rt Hon. Gordon Brown, 2007–10. Mem., Labour Party Nat. Exec. Cttee, 1970–81. Visiting Fellow, Nuffield Coll., Oxford, 1967–75; Res. Fellow, PSI, 1979–81; Visiting Faculty, Internat. Management Inst., Geneva, 1979–88; Fellow, Inst. of Politics, Harvard, 1979–80 (Mem., Sen. Adv. Council, 1986–99; Acting Dir, 1989–90); Director: Turing Inst., Glasgow, 1985–90; Learning by Experience Trust, 1986–94; Educn Develt Centre, Newton, Mass, 1991–98; Internat. Mgt Inst., Kiev, 1990–2000; Project Liberty, 1990–98; Bd Mem., Moscow Sch. of Political Studies, 1993–2007. Co-Pres., RIIA, 2002–06. Chm. of Judges, Nat. Teaching Awards, 2007–10. Trustee: The Century Foundn (formerly Twentieth Century Fund), NY, 1978–; IPPR, 2001–10. Lectures: Godkin, Harvard, 1980; Rede, Cambridge, 1980; Janeway, Princeton, 1981; Regents', Univ. of Calif., Berkeley, 1991; Erasmus, Notre Dame, 2001–02. Hon. Fellow, Newnham Coll., Cambridge, 1977. Hon. DEd CNAA, 1969; Hon. Dr Pol Econ.: Univ. of Leuven, 1976; Radcliffe Coll., Harvard, 1978; Leeds, 1980; Bath, 1980; Hon. LLD: Sheffield, 1980; Southampton, 1981; Liverpool, 2008; Cambridge, 2009; Hon. DLitt Heriot-Watt, 1980; Hon. DSc Aston, 1981; Hon. Dr Monterey Inst., Calif, 2006. *Publications*: Politics is for People, 1981; Jobs for the 1980s; Youth Without Work, 1981; (jtly) Unemployment and Growth in the Western Economies, 1984; A Job to Live, 1985; Snakes and Ladders: a diary of a political life, 1996; (contrib.) Realizing Human Rights, ed Power and Alison, 2000; (contrib.) Making Globalization Good, 2003; God and Caesar, 2003; Climbing the Bookshelves, 2009. *Recreations*: music, poetry, hill walking.

**WILLIAMS OF ELVEL,** Baron *cr* 1985 (Life Peer), of Llansantffraed in Elvel in the County of Powys; **Charles Cuthbert Powell Williams,** CBE 1980; PC 2013; *b* 9 Feb. 1933; *s* of late Dr Norman Powell Williams, DD, and Mrs Muriel de Lérisson Williams (*née* Cazenove); *m* 1975, Jane Gillian (*née* Portal), DL; one step *s*. *Educ*: Westminster Sch.; Christ Church, Oxford (MA); LSE. Nat. Service, KRRC, 1955–57 (2nd Lieut, 1956–57). British Petroleum Co. Ltd, 1958–64; Bank of London and Montreal, 1964–66; Eurofinance SA, Paris, 1966–70; Baring Brothers and Co. Ltd, 1970–77 (Man. Dir, 1971–77); Chm., Price Commn, 1977–79; Man. Dir 1980–82, Chm. 1982–85, Henry Ansbacher & Co. Ltd; Chief Exec., Henry Ansbacher Holdings PLC, 1982–85. Parly Candidate (Lab), Colchester, 1964. House of Lords: Dep. Leader of Opposition, 1989–92; Opposition spokesman on trade and industry, 1986–92, on energy, 1988–90, on defence, 1990–97, on the envmt, 1992–97. Founder Mem., Labour Econ. Finance and Taxation Assoc. (Vice-Chm., 1975–77, 1979–83). Director: Pergamon Holdings Ltd, 1985–91; Mirror Group Newspapers Ltd, 1985–91, Mirror Group Newspapers PLC, 1991–92. Pres., Campaign for Protection of Rural Wales, 1989–95 (Vice-Pres., 1995–2009; Pres., Radnor Branch, 1995–2014). Chm., Mid Wales Chamber Orch., 2009–13; Trustee, Cambrian Music Trust, 2009–14. Patron, Llandrindod Wells Spa Town Trust, 1995–. *Publications*: The Last Great Frenchman: a life of General de Gaulle, 1993; Bradman: an Australian hero, 1996; Adenauer, the Father of the new Germany, 2000; Pétain, 2005 (Elizabeth Longford Prize for Histl Biog., 2006); Harold Macmillan, 2009; Gentlemen and Players: the death of amateurism in cricket, 2012; Max Beaverbrook: not quite a gentleman, 2019. *Recreations*: cricket (Oxford Univ. CC, 1953–55, Captain 1955; Essex CCC, 1953–59), music. *Address*: House of Lords, SW1A 0PW. *T*: (020) 7219 6054. *Clubs*: Beefsteak, Reform, MCC.

*See also Archbishop of Canterbury*.

**WILLIAMS OF OYSTERMOUTH,** Baron *cr* 2013 (Life Peer), of Oystermouth in the City and County of Swansea; **Rt Rev. and Rt Hon. Rowan Douglas Williams;** Royal Victorian Chain, 2012; PC 2002; DPhil, DD; FBA 1990; Master, Magdalene College, Cambridge, 2013–Sept. 2020; an Assistant Bishop, Diocese of Ely, since 2013; *b* 14 June 1950; *s* of Aneurin Williams and Nancy Delphine Williams; *m* 1981, Hilary Jane Paul; one *s* one *d*. *Educ*: Dynevor School, Swansea; Christ's College, Cambridge (BA 1971, MA 1975); Christ Church and Wadham College, Oxford (DPhil 1975; DD 1989). Lectr, College of the Resurrection, Mirfield, 1975–77; ordained deacon, 1977, priest, 1978; Chaplain, Tutor and Director of Studies, Westcott House, Cambridge, 1977–80; Cambridge University: Univ. Lectr in Divinity, 1980–86; Fellow and Dean of Clare Coll., 1984–86; Lady Margaret Prof. of Divinity, and Canon of Christ Church, Oxford, 1986–92; Bishop of Monmouth, 1992–2002; Archbishop of Wales, 2000–02; Archbishop of Canterbury, 2002–12. Hon. Asst Priest, St George's, Cambridge, 1980–83; Canon Theologian, Leicester Cathedral, 1981–92; Hon. Canon, Ely Cathedral, 2014–. Examining Chaplain to Bishop of Manchester, 1987–92. Chm., Bd of Trustees, Christian Aid, 2003–. Chancellor, Univ. of S Wales, 2013–. Lectures: Gifford, Edinburgh Univ., 2013; Tanner, Harvard Univ., 2014; Hulsean, Cambridge Univ., 2016; Du Bose, Univ. of the South, Sewanee, 2016; Payton, Fuller Theol Seminary, 2018. Overseas Mem., Acad. of Athens, 2018. FRSL 2004. Hon. Fellow: UC, Swansea, 1993; Clare Coll., Cambridge, 1994; Univ. of Wales Coll., Newport, 2000; UC, Cardiff, 2002; UC, Aberystwyth, 2005. Hon. DTheol: Erlangen, 1999; Uppsala 2017; Hon. DD: Nashotah Hse, USA, 2000; Exeter, 2001; Aberdeen, 2002; Kent, 2003; Wales, 2003; Bonn, 2006; Cambridge, 2006; DUniv. Open, 2004; York 2016; Hon. DCL Oxford, 2005; Hon. Dr: St Vladimir's Orthodox Seminary, NY, 2010; Athens, 2010; Catholic Univ. Leuven, 2011; Hon. Dr Pastoral Theology Anglia Ruskin, 2013; Hon. DTh Nijmegen, 2014; Hon. DHL Fordham, NY, 2014; Hon. LLD Warwick 2016; Hon. DD Yale, 2018; Hon. DArts Winchester, 2018. Presidential Decree, Order of Friendship (Russia), 2009; Star of Pakistan, 2012; Benedict Medal, St Mary's Univ., Twickenham, 2018. *Publications*: The Wound of Knowledge, 1979; Resurrection, 1982; The Truce of God, 1983; (with Mark Collier) Beginning Now; peacemaking theology, 1984; Arius: heresy and tradition, 1987; (ed) The Making of Orthodoxy, 1989; Teresa of Avila, 1991; Open to Judgement, 1994; After Silent Centuries (poems), 1994; Sergii Bulgakov: towards a Russian political theology, 1999; On Christian Theology, 1999; Lost Icons, 2000; Christ on Trial, 2000; (ed jtly) Love's Redeeming Work: the Anglican quest for holiness, 2001; Remembering Jerusalem (poems), 2001; (ed jtly) The New Dictionary of Pastoral Studies, 2002; Ponder These Things: praying with icons of the Virgin, 2002; The Poems of Rowan Williams, 2002; The Dwelling of the Light, 2003; Silence and Honey Cakes, 2003; Anglican Identities, 2004; Why Study the Past?, 2005; Grace and Necessity, 2005; Tokens of Trust: an introduction to Christian belief, 2007; Wrestling with Angels: conversations in modern theology, 2007; Dostoevsky: language, fiction and faith, 2008; Headwaters (poems), 2008; A Margin of Silence: the Holy Spirit in Russian Orthodox theology, 2008; (ed jtly) Crisis and Recovery, 2010; A Silent Action, 2011; Faith in the Public Square, 2012; The Lion's World, 2012; Choose Life, 2013; Being Christian, 2014; The Poems of Rowan Williams, 2014; The Edge of Words: God and the habits of language, 2014; Meeting God in Mark, 2014; The Other Mountain (poems), 2014; Meeting God in Paul, 2015; On Augustine, 2016; The Tragic Imagination, 2016; God with us: the meaning of the cross and resurrection—then and now, 2017; Holy Living: the Christian tradition for today, 2017; Being Human: bodies, minds, persons, 2018; Christ the Heart of Creation, 2018; Luminaries: twenty lives that illuminate the Christian Way, 2019; *translation*: (with Gwyneth Lewis) The Book of Taliesin, 2019; contribs to Theologische Realencyklopädie, Jl of Theological Studies, Downside Review, Eastern Churches Review, Sobornost, New Blackfriars, New Statesman, Prospect. *Recreations*: music, fiction, languages. *Address*: The Master's Lodge, Magdalene College, Cambridge CB3 0AG.

**WILLIAMS OF TRAFFORD,** Baroness *cr* 2013 (Life Peer), of Hale in the County of Greater Manchester; **Susan Frances Maria Williams;** Minister of State, Home Office, since 2016; Minister for Equalities, since 2018; *b* Cork, Ireland, 16 May 1967; *d* of John Henry McElroy and Mary McElroy; *m* 2005, Alexander Williams; one *s* two *d*. *Educ*: La Sagesse High Sch., Jesmond, Newcastle upon Tyne; Huddersfield Poly. (BSc Hons Applied Nutrition). Nutritionist, Multiple Sclerosis charity, 1992–2002. Mem. (C) Trafford MBC,

1998–2011 (Leader, 2004–09). NW Chm., Heritage Lottery Fund, 2011–12; CEO, Atlantic Gateway, 2012–14; Dir, NW Rail Campaign, 2011–14. A Baroness in Waiting (Govt Whip), 2014–15; Parly Under-Sec. of State, DCLG, 2015–16. Contested (C) Bolton West, 2010. *Recreations:* hill walking in Scotland, backgammon, pub quizzes. *Address:* House of Lords, SW1A 0PW.

**WILLIAMS, Adèle;** *see* Williams, J. A.

**WILLIAMS, Adrian Spencer Vaughan,** CBE 2003; Headteacher, Bury St Edmunds County Upper School, 1985–2005; *b* 23 May 1945; *s* of Bill and Eileen Williams; *m* 1972, Janet Daniels; one *s* two *d. Educ:* Colston's Sch., Bristol; St Catharine's Coll., Cambridge (BA 1967, MA 1971; DipEd). Asst teacher, King's Coll. Sch., Wimbledon, 1968–74; Hd, History Dept, Frome Coll., Som., 1974–79; Dep. Headteacher, Eggbuckland Sch., Plymouth, 1979–84. Lay Canon, St Edmundsbury Cathedral, 2005–10 (Lay Canon Emeritus, 2011–). Chairman: Connect Education Business (formerly Suffolk Educn Business Partnership), 2007–16; William and Ellen Vinten Trust, 2009–15; Trustee: Guildhall Feoffment Trust, 1988–2015; St Nicholas' Hospice, 1997–2015 (Chm., 2012–15); Lund Trust, 2005–. *Recreations:* (nearly) all things French, relentless pursuit of the misuse of the apostrophe, watching cricket and Ipswich Town Football Club. *Address:* Gatehouse, 1 Byfield Way, Bury St Edmunds, Suffolk IP33 2SN. *T:* (01284) 763339. *E:* asvjew@gmail.com.

**WILLIAMS, Rt Rev. Alan;** *see* Brentwood, Bishop of, (R.C).

**WILLIAMS, Alan Lee,** OBE 1973; Director, Atlantic Council, 1993–2007 (Director, 1972–74 and 1992–93, Chairman, 1980–83, British Atlantic Committee); *b* 29 Nov. 1930; *m* 1st, 1954, Molly Steer (marr. diss. 1958); 2nd, 1963, Karen Holloway (marr. diss. 1971); two *s*; 3rd, 1974, Jennifer Ford (*née* Bunnett); two step *d. Educ:* Roan Sch., Greenwich; Ruskin Coll., Oxford. National Service, RAF, 1951–53; National Youth Officer, Labour Party, 1956–62. Dir-Gen., E-SU, 1979–86; Warden and Chief Exec., Toynbee Hall, 1987–92. MP (Lab) Hornchurch, 1966–70, Havering, Hornchurch, Feb. 1974–1979; PPS to Sec. of State for Defence, 1969–70, 1976; PPS to Sec. of State for NI, 1976–78; Chm., Parly Lab. Party Defence Cttee, 1976–79. Member: Parly Assembly, Council of Europe and WEU, 1967–70; N Atlantic Parly Assembly, 1974–79; FO Adv. Cttee on Disarmament and Arms Control, 1975–79; Council, RUSI, 1975–78; Adv. Council on Public Records, 1977–84; Chm., Delegn to 4th Cttee of UN, NY, 1969; Chm., Transport on Water Assoc., 1974–2016; Deputy Director, European Movement, 1970–71; Vice Pres., European-Atlantic Gp, 1983–; Pres., Atlantic Treaty Assoc., 2000–03; Chm., European Working Gp of Internat. Centre for Strategic and Internat. Studies, Washington, 1987–99 (Mem., 1974–); Member: Council, RUSI, 1968–79; Trilateral Commn, 1976–2002. Chm., Beveridge Foundn, 2006–14. Vis. Prof., Queen Mary Univ. of London, 2003–16. Chairman: Cedar Centre, Isle of Dogs, 1991–2008; Toynbee Housing Assoc., 1993–99. Chm. of Govs, City Coll., 1990–. Freeman: City of London, 1969; Co. of Watermen and Lightermen, 1952–. Fellow, QMW, 1993. FRSA 1987. DLitt (*hc*) Schiller Internat. Univ., 1987. Golden Laurel Branch (Bulgaria), 2002. *Publications:* Radical Essays, 1966; Europe or the Open Sea?, 1971; Crisis in European Defence, 1973; The European Defence Initiative: Europe's bid for equality, 1985; The Decline of Labour and the Fall of the SDP, 1989; Islamic Resurgence, 1991; Prospects for a Common European Foreign and Security Policy, 1995; NATO's Future in the Balance: time for a rethink, 1995; NATO and European Defence: a new era of partnership, 1997; NATO's Strategy for Securing the Future, 1999; (with Geoffrey Lee Williams) A Couple of Duffers Go to War, 2011. *Recreations:* reading, history, walking. *Address:* 6 North Several, Blackheath, SE3 0QR. *Clubs:* Reform, Pilgrims, Mid-Atlantic (Chm., 2006–), English-Speaking Union.

**WILLIAMS, Dr Alan Wynne;** freelance solar energy research; *b* 21 Dec. 1945; *s* of late Tom and Mary Hannah Williams; *m* 1973, Marian Williams. *Educ:* Carmarthen Grammar School; Jesus College, Oxford (BA Chem. 1st cl. hons; DPhil). Senior Lecturer in Environmental Science, Trinity College, Carmarthen, 1971–87. MP (Lab) Carmarthen, 1987–97, Carmarthen E and Dinefwr, 1997–2001; contested Carmarthen E and Dinefwr, 2001. *Recreations:* reading, watching sport. *Address:* 79 Parklands Road, Ammanford, Carmarthenshire SA18 3TD.

**WILLIAMS, Sir Alastair Edgcumbe James D.;** *see* Dudley-Williams.

**WILLIAMS, Aled Tudno;** President, Eurojust, 2010–12; *b* Newton Abbot, Devon, 11 Aug. 1947; *s* of Llew and Sian Williams; *m* 1975, Mercedes Morillo; two *d. Educ:* King Edward VI Grammar Sch., Chelmsford; Gonville and Caius Coll., Cambridge (BA 1968; MA 1972). Admitted as solicitor, 1984; Crown Prosecutor, 1986–2012; UK Liaison Magistrate to Spain, 2002–06; Dep. Hd Nat. Mem., 2006–08, UK Nat. Mem., 2008–12, Eurojust. Lay Observer, 2013–. Order of San Raimundo de Peñafort (Spain), 2006. *Recreations:* theatre, reading, walking. *Club:* Oxford and Cambridge.

**WILLIAMS, Alexander,** CB 1991; FInstP; Government Chemist, 1987–91; *b* 30 March 1931; *s* of Henry and Dorothy Williams; *m* 1957, Beryl Wynne Williams (*née* Williams); one *s. Educ:* Grove Park Grammar Sch., Wrexham; University College of North Wales, Bangor (BSc). National Service, REME, 1953–55; Monsanto Chemicals, 1955–56; Southern Instruments, Camberley, 1956–59; National Physical Laboratory: Div. of Radiation Science, 1959–78; Head, Div. of Mechanical and Optical Metrology, 1978–81; Under Sec., Res. and Technology Policy Div., DTI, 1981–87. Dir, Assoc. of Official Analytical Chemists, 1989–93. Pres., British Measurement and Testing Assoc., 1995–2001. Freeman, City of London, 1997; Liveryman, Co. of Scientific Instrument Makers, 1997–. *Publications:* (with P. J. Campion and J. E. Burns) A Code of Practice for the Detailed Statement of Accuracy, 1973; (ed with H. Günzler) Handbook of Analytical Techniques, 2001; numerous papers on measurements of radio-activity etc and quality assce in analytical chem., to Internat. Jl of Applied Radiation and Isotopes, Nucl. Instruments and Methods, Accreditation and Quality Assurance, etc. *Recreations:* bell-ringing, music, opera, walking.

**WILLIAMS, (Alun) Craig;** *b* Welshpool, 7 June 1985; *s* of David Williams and Andrea Williams; *m* 2013, Cathe Bath; one *s* one *d*. Mem. (C), Cardiff CC, 2008–15 (Chm., Economy Cttee, 2012–15). MP (C) Cardiff N, 2015–17; contested (C) same seat, 2017. Dir, Cardiff Bus, 2011–15. *Recreations:* Rugby, real ale, walking, Welsh springer spaniels, school governor (primary). *Clubs:* Carlton; Cardiff and County.

**WILLIAMS, Prof. Alun Edward,** PhD; Professor of Veterinary Diagnostic Pathology, since 2009 and Director of Teaching, Department of Veterinary Medicine, since 2013, University of Cambridge; Fellow, Wolfson College, Cambridge, since 2009; *b* York, 6 Nov. 1960; *s* of Arthur and Margaret Williams; *m* 1995, Marianna Fletcher; one *s* one *d*. *Educ:* Univ. of Glasgow (BVMS 1985; MRCVS 1985); Wolfson Coll., Cambridge (PhD 1989). Diplomate, Eur. Coll. of Vet. Pathologists, 1998; Post Grad. Cert. in Med. Educn, Univ. of Cambridge, 2016. AFRC Vet. Schs Fellow, Univ. of Cambridge, 1985–89; MRC Univ. Res. Fellow, Univ. of Oxford, 1989–90; Principal Res. Scientist and Named Vet. Surgeon, Inst. for Animal Health, Edinburgh, 1990–97; Sen. Lectr, 1997–2001, Reader, 2001–03, Dept of Veterinary Pathol., Univ. of Glasgow; Prof. of Pathol. and Infectious Diseases, RVC, Univ. of London, 2003–09 (Hd of Dept, 2003–07). FHEA 2009. *Recreations:* music (performing in orchestras and choirs), growing vegetables. *Address:* Department of Veterinary Medicine, University of Cambridge, Madingley Road, Cambridge CB3 0ES. *T:* (01223) 337640. *E:* aw510@cam.ac.uk.

**WILLIAMS, Angela Joy,** CMG 2005; Director, United Nations Relief and Works Agency Affairs, Syrian Arab Republic, 1998–2004; *b* 24 Sept. 1944; *d* of Douglas Granville Needham and Annie Needham (*née* Balshaw); *m* 1984, Edward Hunter Williams; two step *s* one step *d. Educ:* Bolton Sch. Girls' Div.; Univ. of Birmingham (BSocSci Hons 1966); American Univ. of Beirut (post-grad. Middle Eastern Studies). VSO, Ghana, 1966–68; Asst Educn Officer, Community Relns Commn, 1969–71; UN Relief and Works Agency for Palestine Refugees in the Near East, 1971–2004: Chief of Secretariat, 1980–83; Chief of External Relns, 1984–85; Dep. Dir of Ops, Gaza, 1985–88; Dir, Relief and Social Services, 1988–98. Music in Me: Dir, Prog. Implementation, 2005–08; Consultant, 2008–09. Trustee, Damask Rose Trust, 2008–11. *Recreations:* exploring cultural diversity and cross-cultural communication through reading, writing, music, photography and travel. *Address:* 3–111 Echo Drive, Ottawa, ON K1S 5K8, Canada. *T:* (613) 2308610. *E:* ajwilliams_241@hotmail.com.

**WILLIAMS, Anna Maureen, (Mrs G. H. G. Williams);** *see* Worrall, A. M.

**WILLIAMS, Sir Anthony Geraint,** 3rd Bt *cr* 1953, of Cilgeraint, co. Caernarvon; *b* 22 Dec. 1958; *s* of Sir Robin Philip Williams, 2nd Bt, and of Wendy Adèle Marguerite, *o d* of late Felix Joseph Alexander; *S* father, 2013; *m* 1990, Rachel Jane, *e d* of Norman Jennings; three *s* one *d. Heir: s* Thomas Alexander Philip Williams, *b* 30 Aug. 1992.

**WILLIAMS, Anthony Neville;** Managing Partner (formerly Managing Director), Jomati Consultants LLP (formerly Jomati Ltd), since 2002; *b* 8 July 1956; *s* of late David Leslie Williams and Rose Williams (*née* Mingay); *m* 1979, Johannah McDonnell; one *s* one *d. Educ:* Southampton Univ. (LLB 1978). Admitted Solicitor, England, 1981, Hong Kong, 1985; Solicitor and Barrister, Victoria, Australia, 1986. Solicitor: Turner Garrett & Co., 1981; Coward Chance, 1981–87, Clifford Chance (following merger), 1987–2000: Hong Kong office, 1984–90; Partner, 1988–2000; Man. Partner, Moscow office, 1995–97; Firmwide Man. Partner, 1998–2000; Man. Partner Worldwide, Andersen Legal, 2000–02. Vis. Prof., Univ. of Law, 2015–. Mem. Bd, SRA, 2016–. *Publications:* (jtly) Intellectual Property in the People's Republic of China, 1986; (jtly) The Hong Kong Banking Ordinance, 1987; (contrib.) Butterworths Guide to the Legal Services Act 2007, 2009; numerous articles on law firm mgt strategy. *Recreations:* horse racing, cricket, wine. *Address:* Jomati Consultants LLP, 3 Amen Lodge, Warwick Lane, EC4M 7BY. *E:* tony.williams@jomati.com.

**WILLIAMS, Dr Anthony Peter;** HM Inspector of Constabulary (non-police), 1993–96; *b* 18 June 1936; *s* of late Dr Emlyn Williams, OBE, Principal, Hendon Coll. of Technology, and Gwyneth Mair Williams (*née* Williams); *m* 1964, Vera Georgiadou; one *s* one *d. Educ:* St Paul's Sch., London; Keble Coll., Oxford (BA 1961; MA 1965); Birkbeck Coll., London (PhD 1971). Research and teaching, 1961–67; Principal Psychologist, CSSB, 1967–71; Consultant, Hay-MSL Ltd, 1971–76; Head of Personnel, BOC Gases, 1976–78; Consultant and Manager, Hay Associates, NY, 1979–84; Dir of Personnel, World Bank, 1984–88; Worldwide Partner and Dir, Hay Management Consultants, 1989–93. Vis. Sen. Fellow, 1997–2003, Vis. Prof., 2003–, Sir John Cass Business Sch., City of London (formerly City Univ. Business Sch.). Mem., Corporate Governance Wkg Party, Assoc. of Investment Trust Cos, 1999–2000. *Publications:* Just Reward?: the truth about top executive pay, 1994; Who Will Guard the Guardians?: corporate governance in the Millennium, 1999; (with Bill Pitkeathley) Executive Express: a swift and practical route to tomorrow's top jobs, 2006; Bill's Saga: the story of the financial exploitation of a helpless sufferer in a nursing home by his 'carer', 2015; numerous articles in professional and management jls. *Recreations:* international affairs, use of language, travel, cultural diversity, opera, good food and wine, intelligent conversation, asking difficult questions. *Address:* 49 Talbot Road, W2 5JJ. *Clubs:* Athenæum, Oxford and Cambridge.

**WILLIAMS, (Arthur) Ronald,** OBE 1991; Chief Executive, Publishers Association, 1998–2007; *b* 29 Oct. 1942; *s* of late Alfred Arthur Williams, OBE and Marjory Williams (*née* Heenan); *m* 1st, 1968, Lynne Diana Merrin; two *d*; 2nd, 1993, Antoinette Catherine Naldrett. *Educ:* Rossall Sch., Lancs; Selwyn Coll., Cambridge (Exhibnr, Trevelyan Scholar; MA). HM Diplomatic Service, 1964–79, served Jakarta, Singapore, Budapest and Nairobi (First Sec.); Chief Exec., Timber Growers UK, 1981–87; Exec. Dir, Forestry Industry Council of GB, 1987–97. Mem., Exec. Cttee, Fedn of European Publishers, 1998–2007; Dir, Digital Content Forum (UK), 2003–07. Ambassador, Highlands and Islands Enterprise, 1994–98. FRSA. *Publications:* Montrose: cavalier in mourning, 1975; The Lords of the Isles, 1985; The Heather and the Gale, 1997; Sons of the Wolf, 1998; The Portrait of Montrose in Warwick Castle, 2014. *Recreations:* fly-fishing, walking, writing, portrait miniatures, Heritage sites. *Address:* Sea Villa, The Promenade, Laxey, Isle of Man IM4 7DF. *T:* (01624) 860059.

**WILLIAMS, Benjamin James;** QC 2015. *Educ:* Colston's Sch., Bristol (Foundn Schol.); Exeter Coll., Oxford (Stapeldon Schol.; BA 1st Cl. 1992; MA 1998); City Univ. (Postgrad. DipLaw 1993); Inns of Court Sch. of Law (Inns of Court Studentship Schol., 1994). Called to the Bar, Lincoln's Inn, 1994 (Hardwicke Entrance Schol., 1994; CPE Schol., 1994; Droop Schol., 1995); in private practice as barrister, 1995–. *Recreations:* walking, cooking, restaurants, opera, books. *Address:* 4 New Square, Lincoln's Inn, WC2A 3RJ.

**WILLIAMS, Betty;** *see* Williams, Elizabeth.

**WILLIAMS, Betty Helena;** *b* 31 July 1944. *Educ:* Talysarn Primary Sch.; Ysgol Dyffryn Nantlle; Coleg y Normal, Bangor (BA (Hons) Wales, 1995). Member (Lab): Llanllyfni Parish Council, 1967–83; Gwyrfai Rural DC, 1970–74; Arfon BC, 1973–91 (Mayor, 1990–91); Gwynedd CC, 1976–93. Contested (Lab) Caernarfon, 1983, Conwy, 1987 and 1992. MP (Lab) Conwy, 1997–2010. Mem., Welsh Affairs Select Cttee, 1997–2005. Vice Pres., Univ. of Wales, Bangor, 2001–06 (Hon. Fellow, 2000). Ordained deacon, 1996; Deacon, Seion Chapel, Talysarn, 1996–. Pres., Gwynedd Citizens Advice, 2010–; Member: Bd, Mantell Gwynedd, 2010–; Bd, N Wales Advice and Advocacy Assoc., 2015–. Pres., Lleisiau Traeth Lane, 2007–17. Member: Gorsedd y Beirdd (White Robe), 2006–; Llandudno and Dist Soroptimist Internat., 2010–15.

**WILLIAMS, Brian Owen,** CBE 2011; MD; FRCP, FRCPE, FRCPGlas; President, Royal College of Physicians and Surgeons of Glasgow, 2006–09; Interim Postgraduate Dean, West of Scotland, NHS Education for Scotland, 2012–13; *b* 27 Feb. 1947; *s* of William and Joan Williams; *m* 1970, Martha Carmichael; two *d*. *Educ:* Kings Park Sch., Glasgow; Univ. of Glasgow (MD 1984). FRCPGlas 1983; FRCP 1989; FRCPE 1991; FCPS 1996; FRCSLT 1996; FRCPI 1999; FRACP 2007. Consultant Geriatrician, 1977–2010; Consultant Geriatrician, Gartnavel Gen. Hosp., Glasgow, 1982–. President: British Geriatric Soc., 1998–2000; EU Geriatric Medicine Soc., 2000–02. Hon. Prof., Univ. of Glasgow, 2007–. Chairman: Bd of Govs, Hutchesons' Grammar Sch., Glasgow, 2013–17; Abbeyfield

Societies in Scotland, 2013–17; Member: Bd, Abbeyfield UK, 2017–; W Scotland Adv. Bd, Salvation Army, 2019–. Hon. DSc Glasgow Caledonian, 2007. *Recreations:* music, literature, gardening, Rotarian. *Address:* 15 Thorn Drive, High Burnside, Glasgow G73 4RH. *T:* (0141) 634 4480. *E:* brianwilliams@gmx.com.

**WILLIAMS, Rear Adm. Bruce Nicholas Bromley,** CBE 2008 (OBE 2002); Editor and Chief Executive Officer, The Naval Review, since 2017; *b* Liverpool, 3 Nov. 1957; *s* of Dr Cecil William Llewellyn Williams and Judith Elizabeth Williams; *m* 1985, Julia Anne Quick; one *s* two *d*. *Educ:* Kingswood Sch., Bath; Lancaster Univ. (BSc Hons Ecol.). Commnd RN, 1980; served HMSs Kingfisher, Argonaut, Galatea, Danae, Brilliant, 1981–92; RNSC, 1992; Asst Defence Advr, RN Liaison Officer and CO, Naval Party 1022 Singapore, 1993–96; COS Co-ordinator, UK PJHQ, Northwood, 1996–98; CO, HMS Norfolk, 1998–2000; Desk Officer, Directorate Policy Planning, 2000–01; Asst Dir, Directorate Naval Ops, 2001–03; CO, HMS Campbeltown, 2003–04; Dep. Flag Officer, Sea Trng, 2005; Commander: Coalition Task Force 58 (Iraq-N Gulf), 2005–06; UK Task Gp and Dep. Comdr, UK Maritime Force, 2006–07; Coalition Task Force 150 (Indian Ocean), 2006–07; Dep. Comdt, JSCSC, 2007–09; ADC to the Queen, 2008–09; COS and Sen. UK Rep., Allied Maritime HQ, Naples, 2009–11; Dep. Dir Gen. EU Mil. Staff, 2011–14. Vis. Sen. Res. Fellow, KCL, 2015–. Non-exec. Dir, The Military Mutual, 2014–. Vice-Pres., CCF Assoc., 2015–. Dir, Ubique Ltd, 2015–. Mem., South Hush Parish Council, 2016–. Younger Brother, Trinity House, 2006. CCMI 2008. QCVS 1999; General Service Medals: NI, 1982; NATO Article 5, 2003; Afghanistan Campaign, 2004; Iraq Campaign, 2006. *Recreations:* sailing, walking. *T:* 07585 771479. *E:* bruce.williams@live.co.uk, bruce.williams@themilitarymutual.com, editor@naval-review.com.

**WILLIAMS, Sir Charles (Othniel),** Kt 2000; Executive Chairman, C. O. Williams Construction and group of companies, since 1969; *b* 24 Nov. 1932; *s* of Elliot Williams and Lillian Williams; *m* 1st, 1956, Diane Walcott (marr. diss. 1999); two *s* one *d*; 2nd, 2000, Mary-Ann Gemmell (*née* Stewart-Richardson). *Educ:* Lodge Secondary Sch., Barbados. Overseer, Brighton Plantation, St George, 1951–54; Under Manager: Hothersall Plantation, St John, 1954–56; Guinea Sugar Factory, St John, 1956; Manager, Foster Hall Plantation, St Joseph, 1956–60; leased Foster Hall, 1960–75; founded: C. O. Williams, 1960; C. O. Williams Construction Co. Ltd, 1969; Co-Founder, Ready Mix/Ready Block Ltd, 1969; Director: Ready Mix Ltd, 1970–; Williams Industries Inc., 1973–; Fairway Developments, 1990–; Exec. Chm. and major shareholder, Dixie Farms Ltd, 1995; Co-Developer and Director: Port St Charles, residential marina, 1996; Apes Hill Golf and Polo Club, 2005. Champion breeder of thoroughbred horses in Barbados, 2005, 2009, 2010, 2011, 2012. Master Entrepreneur of the Year, Ernst & Young Awards, 1997. *Recreations:* polo, deep-sea fishing, horse-racing. *Address:* Bromefield Plantation House, St Lucy, Barbados. *Clubs:* Sloane; Port St Charles Yacht (Barbados); Barbados Polo (Capt., 1969–2004), Barbados Turf, Barbados Yacht, Carlton Cricket (Barbados), Wanderers Cricket (Barbados).

**WILLIAMS, Chris Morgan;** DL; Chief Executive, Buckinghamshire County Council and Clerk to the Lieutenancy, 2000–16; Chief Executive, South East England Councils, 2009–16; Management Consultant, Morgan Dell Management, since 2016; Chairman, Buckinghamshire and Milton Keynes Natural Environment Partnership, since 2017; *b* Rhayader, Powys, Wales, 26 Nov. 1948; *s* of Harold and May Williams; *m* 1st, 1973, Julie Gleave (marr. diss. 2008); two *d*; 2nd, 2013, Clare Hedger; two step *s*. *Educ:* Lanchester Poly., Coventry (BA Hons); Univ. of Sussex (MA). MRTPI 1976. Co. Planning Officer, E Sussex, 1989–96; Dir, Envmtl Services, Bucks CC, 1996–2000. Vis. Res. Fellow, Univ. of Sussex, 1992–. Pres., Co. Planning Officers' Soc., 1993–94. DL Bucks. MCMI. *Recreations:* travel, wine, Rugby. *Address:* 16 Chadbone Close, Aylesbury, Bucks HP20 2PS.

**WILLIAMS, Rt Rev. Christopher;** see Williams, Rt Rev. J. C. R.

**WILLIAMS, Christopher Beverley,** FRCP, FRCS; Consultant Physician in Gastrointestinal Endoscopy: Endoscopy Unit, London Clinic, 1975–2013; Wolfson Unit for Endoscopy, St Mark's Hospital for Colorectal and Intestinal Disorders, 1975–2003, then Hon. Consultant; *b* 8 June 1938; *s* of late Denis John Williams, CBE, MD, FRCP and Dr Joyce Beverley Williams (*née* Jewson); *m* 1970, Christina Janet Seymour, MB, FRCP, *d* of Reginald S. Lawrie, MD, MS, FRCS, FRCP, and Jean E. Lawrie, CBE, MB; one *s* one *d*. *Educ:* Dragon Sch.; Winchester Coll.; Trinity Coll., Oxford (BA Hons Physiol., BM BCh, MA); UCH. MRCS 1965, FRCS 1999; LRCP 1965, MRCP 1968, FRCP 1983. House appointments: UCH, 1965; Whittington and Brompton Hosps, 1966; SHO, Nat. Hosp. for Nervous Diseases, and Hammersmith Hosp., 1966–67; Registrar, UCH, 1968–70; Registrar, 1970–72, Res. Fellow and Hon. Sen. Registrar, 1972–74, St Mark's Hosp.; Consultant Physician, St Bartholomew's Hosp., 1975. Hon. Consultant Physician (Endoscopy): Royal Free Hosp.; Great Ormond Street Hosp. for Sick Children; King Edward VII Hosp. for Officers; St Luke's Hosp. for the Clergy. Vis. Prof., Sydney Univ., 1973; demonstrations, teaching courses and invited lectures world-wide on colonoscopy and colorectal cancer prevention; Foundn Lectr, British Soc. of Gastroenterology, 1976, 1995 (Vice-Pres., Endoscopy, 1987). Mem., Soc. of Apothecaries, 1956–. Mem., several internat. editl bds. *Publications:* (ed jtly) Colorectal Disease, 1981; (jtly) Practical Gastrointestinal Endoscopy, 1983, 7th edn as Cotton and Williams' Practical Gastrointestinal Endoscopy, 2014 (trans. Italian 1980, German 1985, French 1986, Spanish 1992, Portuguese, 1998, Korean, 2003, Turkish 2010); (jtly) Annual of Gastrointestinal Endoscopy, annually 1988–97; (ed jtly) Colonoscopy: principles and practice, 2003, 2nd edn 2009 (trans. Portuguese 2010); numerous articles and chapters on colonoscopy, colorectal disease and teaching methodology. *Recreations:* travel, fine wine, good food, the arts. *Address:* 17 Pavilion Court, Frognal Rise, Hampstead, NW3 6PZ. *T:* (020) 7435 4030. *E:* christopher@candcwilliams.co.uk.

**WILLIAMS, Christopher Guy;** Partner, Perella Weinberg Partners, since 2015; *b* Carshalton, 24 May 1965; *s* of John Monro Williams and Sheila Marion Williams; *m* 1993, Amanda Jane Waggott; three *s*. *Educ:* Christ's Hosp. Sch.; Birmingham Univ. (BSc Hons Chem. Engrg). Hill Samuel & Co. Ltd, 1987–89; Vice Pres., Bankers Trust Internat., 1989–92; Man. Dir and Co-Head, European Banks Advisory, Goldman Sachs, 1992–2005; Co-Head, Global Financial Instns, Citicorp, 2005–09; Vice Chm., Investment Banking EMEA, Credit Suisse, 2009–14; Exec. Vice Chm., Global Financial Instns, Credit Suisse, 2014–15. Mem. Council, ICSTM, 2016–. Donation Gov., Christ's Hosp., 2008–. Mem., Amicable Soc. of Blues, 2012–. *Recreations:* daydreaming, rock music, harvesting apples. *Address:* Perella Weinberg Partners, 20 Grafton Street, W1S 4DZ. *T:* (020) 7268 2800.

**WILLIAMS, Dr Christopher John Hacon,** FRCP; Consultant Medical Oncologist, Bristol Haematology and Oncology Centre, 2003–11 (Clinical Director, 2003–07); *b* 3 Aug. 1946; *s* of Owen Henry Williams and Joyce May Hacon Deavin; *m* 1970, Susan Tennant (marr. diss. 1995); two *d*; *m* 1999, Mary Quirk. *Educ:* Reed's Sch., Surrey; London Univ., St Mary's Hosp. (MBBS); DM Southampton 1980; Metanoia Inst. and Middlesex Univ. (MSc Creative Writing for Therapeutic Purposes, 2018). Jun. posts, London Hosps, 1971–74; Jun. Registrar, Med. Oncology, St Bartholomew's, 1974–75; Postdoctoral Res. Fellow, Stanford Univ., 1975–77; Res. Fellow, 1977–80, Sen. Lectr and Hon. Consultant Physician in Medical Oncology, 1980–96, Southampton Univ.; Dir, Cochrane Cancer Network, Inst. of Health Scis, Oxford, 1996–2003. Chairman: MRC Gynaecol Cancer Working Party, 1989–93; MRC Cancer Therapy Cttee, 1994–97; steering cttees and ind. data monitoring cttees for large-scale trials in breast, ovarian and prostate cancer; Member: Protocol Rev. Cttee, EORTC, 1993–2003; Oncology Trials Adv. Cttee, MRC, 1997–2003; Steering Gp, Cochrane Collaboration, 1998–2002; Co-ordinator, ICON trials for ovarian carcinoma, 1991–96. Mem., Council, Inst. of Health Scis, Oxford, 1997. Mem. Bd of Editors, Annals of Oncology, 1996; Co-ordinating Ed., Cochrane Gynaecol Cancer Collaborative Rev. Gp, 1997–2011. *Publications:* Recent Advances in Clinical Oncology, 1982; All About Cancer, 1983; Lung Cancer: the facts, 1984, 3rd edn (with S. Falk) 2009; Cancer Investigations and Management, 1985; Cancer: a guide for patients and family, 1986; (with R. B. Buchanan) Medical Management of Breast Cancer, 1987; Textbook of Uncommon Cancer, 1988; Cancer Biology and Management, 1989; (with J. S. Tobias) Cancer: a colour atlas, 1991; Introducing New Treatments for Cancer, 1992 (Medical Textbook of the Year, 1993); Supportive Care of the Cancer Patient, 1997; (jtly) Cancer: a comprehensive guide, 1998; Evidence-based Oncology, 2003; One Day in the Life of an Executioner, 2012; papers on new therapies for cancer, esp. clinical trials and systematic reviews. *Recreations:* wildlife and landscape photography, theatre, music, films, books, gathering art objects, creative writing. *Address:* Spring Vale, Mill Hill, Brockweir, Chepstow NP6 7NW. *E:* chrisjhwilliams@btinternet.com.

**WILLIAMS, Prof. Christopher Mark,** PhD; FRHistS, FLSW; Head, College of Arts, Celtic Studies and Social Sciences, University College Cork, since 2017; *b* Griffithstown, Monmouthshire, 9 March 1963; *s* of Peter Hale Williams and Josephine Anne Williams; *m* 1st, 1985, Siobhan Elizabeth McClelland (marr. diss. 1993); one *s*; 2nd, 2003, Sara Louise Spalding; two *s*. *Educ:* Churchfields Comp. Sch., Swindon; Balliol Coll., Oxford (BA Mod. Hist. 1985); University Coll., Cardiff (PhD 1991). Lectr in Hist., University Coll., Cardiff, then Cardiff Univ., 1988–2001; Prof. of Mod. and Contemp. Wales, Univ. of Glamorgan, 2001–04; Prof. of Welsh Hist., 2005–13, Dir, Res. Inst. for Arts and Humanities, 2010–13, Swansea Univ.; Prof. of History, and Head, Sch. of History, Archaeology and Religion, Cardiff Univ., 2013–17. Mem., Royal Commn on Ancient and Historical Monuments of Wales, 2008–18. FRHistS 2004; FLSW 2016. *Publications:* Democratic Rhondda: politics and society, 1885–1951, 1996; Capitalism, Community and Conflict: the South Wales Coalfield, 1898–1947, 1998; With Dust Still in His Throat: A. B. L. Coombes anthology, 1999, 2nd edn 2014; B. L. Coombes, 1999; The Labour Party in Wales, 1900–2000, 2000; These Poor Hands: the autobiography of a miner working in South Wales, 2002, 2nd edn 2011; A Companion to Nineteenth-Century Britain, 2004; Postcolonial Wales, 2005; Debating Nationhood and Government in Britain, 1885–1945, 2006; Wales and War: society, politics and religion in the nineteenth and twentieth centuries, 2007; Gwent County History: Vol. 4, Industrial Monmouthshire, 1780–1914, 2011, Vol. 5, The Twentieth Century, 2013; Robert Owen and his Legacy, 2011; The Richard Burton Diaries, 2012 (Richard Burton: Die Tagebucher, 2013); The Art of the Possible: politics and governance in modern British history: essays in memory of Duncan Tanner (1958–2010), 2015. *Recreations:* hillwalking, cycling. *Address:* College of Arts, Celtic Studies and Social Sciences, O'Rahilly Building, University College Cork, Cork, Ireland.

**WILLIAMS, Claire Victoria,** OBE 2016; Deputy Principal, Williams Grand Prix Engineering Ltd, since 2013; *b* Windsor, 21 July 1976; *d* of Sir Francis Owen Garbett, (Sir Frank), Williams, *qv*; *m* 2018, Marc Harris; one *s*. *Educ:* Univ. of Newcastle upon Tyne (BA Politics 1999). Press Officer, Silverstone Circuit, 2000–02; Williams Formula 1 Racing Team: Communications Officer, 2002–10; Hd of Communications, 2010–12; Dir, Mktg and Communications, 2012–13. Vice Pres., Spinal Injuries Assoc., 2016–. Patron, F1 in Schs, 2014–. Ambassador, Dare to be Different, 2016–. *Recreations:* family, travel, baking. *Address:* Williams F1, Grove, Wantage, Oxon OX12 0DQ. *T:* (01235) 777700. *E:* Personnel@williamsf1.com. *Club:* British Racing Drivers' (Associate).

**WILLIAMS, Prof. Clyde,** OBE 2009; PhD; Professor of Sports Science, Loughborough University, 1986–2008, now Emeritus; *b* Maesteg, Glamorgan, 11 Aug. 1940; *s* of Thomas John Williams and Elsie May Williams; *m* 1964, Joan Bryant; three *d*. *Educ:* Bridgend Tech. Coll.; Univ. Coll. of Wales, Aberystwyth (BSc Chem. 1964; DipEd 1965); Washington State Univ. (MSc Exercise Physiol. 1969); Univ. of Aberdeen (PhD Physiol. 1978). Chemistry Master, Devizes Grammar Sch., 1965–67; Lectr, Dept of Physiol., Univ. of Aberdeen, 1970–78; Loughborough University: Sen. Res. Fellow, 1978–83; Sen. Lectr, 1983–86; Pro-Vice-Chancellor, 1995–98. Founder Chm., 1984–87, Chm., 2002–04, non-exec. Dir, 2014–16, British Assoc. of Sport Scis, subseq. British Assoc. of Sport and Exercise Scis; Founder Chm., Bd for Registration of Professionals in Sport and Exercise Nutrition, British Dietetic Assoc., 2005; Dep. Chm., Bd of Dirs, Nat. Inst. of Sports Medicine, 1999; Chm., sub-panel for sport-related subjects, HEFCE RAE 2008. Internat. Vis. Prof., Vrije Univ., Brussels, 2011; E. W. Barker Vis. Prof., Inst. of Educn, Nanyang Tech. Univ., Singapore, 2013; Vice Chancellor's Fellow and Adjunct Prof., Victoria Univ., Melbourne, 2013–19; Vis. Prof., Univ. of Suffolk, 2016–. Chm., Scientific Adv. Bd, Manchester Inst. of Health and Performance, 2016–. FRSA 2016. Hon. Fellow, Fac. of Sport and Exercise Medicine, RCP and RCPE, 2011. Hon. Fellow, Aberystwyth Univ., 2009. Hon. DSc Loughborough, 2015; Hon. Dr Victoria, Melbourne, 2016. *Publications:* (ed jtly) Foods, Nutrition and Sports Performance, 1992; (ed jtly) Oxford Textbook of Sports Medicine, 1994, 2nd edn 1998; (ed jtly) ABC of Sport and Exercise Medicine, 1995, 3rd edn 2005; approx. 250 articles mainly on nutritional influences on exercise performance in jls incl. Medicine and Sci. in Sport and Exercise, Jl of Applied Physiol., Nature, Eur. Jl of Sports Medicine, Eur. Jl of Applied Physiol., Scandinavian Jl of Sport and Exercise Medicine, Amer. Jl of Clin. Nutrition, Brit. Jl of Nutrition, Jl of Sports Sci., Brit. Jl of Sport and Exercise Medicine. *Recreations:* tennis, cycling for charity, hillwalking, theatre, travel, family. *Address:* 2 Tynedale Road, Loughborough, Leics LE11 3TA. *T:* (01509) 214151. *E:* c.williams@lboro.ac.uk. *Club:* Charnwood Lawn Tennis (Chm, 2014–16).

**WILLIAMS, Ven. Colin Henry;** Archdeacon of Germany and Northern Europe and Archdeacon of the East, 2015–19; *b* 12 Aug. 1952; *s* of William Henry Williams and Blanche Williams. *Educ:* King George V Grammar Sch. for Boys, Southport; Pembroke Coll., Oxford (BA 1973; MA 1977); Coll. of Law, Chester; St Stephen's House, Oxford (BA Oxon 1981). Asst Solicitor, Gibson, Russell & Adler, solicitors, Wigan, 1974–78; ordained deacon 1981, priest 1982; Asst Curate, St Paul Stoneycroft, Liverpool, 1981–84; Team Vicar, St Aidan, Walton, 1984–89; Domestic Chaplain to Bishop of Blackburn, and Chaplain, Whalley Abbey Retreat and Conf. Centre, 1989–94; Vicar, St Chad, Poulton-le-Fylde, 1994–99; Archdeacon of Lancaster, 1999–2005, now Archdeacon Emeritus; Gen. Sec., Conf. of European Churches, 2005–10; Team Rector, Ludlow Team Ministry, 2010–15. Canon, Cathedral Chapter, Dio. of Europe, 2007–10, 2016–19. Mem., Gen. Synod of C of E, 1995–2005. Mem., Meissen Commn, 1996–2005. Mem., Council for Christian Unity, 2003–05. Hon. Canon, Blackburn Cathedral, 1999–2005, now Canon Emeritus; Hon. Canon and Preb., Hereford Cathedral, 2014–15. *Recreations:* walking, singing, developing knowledge of all things German. *Address:* Flat 1, 3 Ash Drive, Poulton-le-Fylde, Lancs FY6 8DZ. *E:* colinw834@gmail.com.

**WILLIAMS, Coram;** Chief Financial Officer, Pearson plc, since 2015; *b* Aberystwyth, 8 Jan. 1974; *s* of Karel and Gwenda Williams; *m* 2001, Juliane Fürst; two *d*. *Educ:* Penglais Sch., Aberystwyth; Christ Church, Oxford (BA PPE); London Business Sch. (MBA). Road tester, Autocar, 1997–98; Consultant, Arthur Andersen, 1998–2002; Finance Dir,

ELT, Pearson Educn, 2002–05; Hd, Financial Planning, Pearson plc, 2005–08; Chief Financial Officer: Penguin Gp, 2008–13; Penguin Random House, 2013–15. Mem. Bd, Guardian Media Gp, 2017– (Chm., Audit Cttee, 2017–). Trustee, NESTA, 2009–12. *Recreations:* opera, literature, cycling, fast cars. *Address:* Pearson plc, 80 Strand, WC2R 0RL. *E:* coram.williams@pearson.com.

**WILLIAMS, Craig;** *see* Williams, A. C.

**WILLIAMS, Craig H.;** *see* Howell Williams.

**WILLIAMS, Sir Daniel (Charles),** GCMG 1996; QC 1996; Governor-General of Grenada, 1996–2008; international legal consultant, since 2009; Founder and Head, Danny Williams and Co., since 1974; *b* 4 Nov. 1935; *s* of Adolphus D. Williams and Clare Stanislaus; *m* 1960, Cecilia Patricia Gloria Modeste; one *s* three *d*. *Educ:* Primary and comprehensive schs, Grenada; LLB London Univ.; Council of Legal Educn, London. Called to the Bar, Lincoln's Inn, 1968; Barrister, 1969–70, 1974–84, 1990–96; Magistrate, St Lucia, 1970–74; MP (New Nat. Party) St David's, Grenada, 1984–89; Minister of Health, Housing and Envmt, 1984–89; Minister of Legal Affairs, and Attorney Gen., 1988–89; Acting Prime Minister, July 1988. Sec., Grenada Bar Assoc., 1977–81. Held several lay positions in RC Ch, incl. Chm., Dio. Pastoral Council. Was active Scout, incl. Dist Comr and Dep. Chief Comr; Chief Scout, 1996–2009. Founder and Mem., Grenada Foundn for Needy Students, 1996–. Sole Sponsor, Danny Williams annual cricket tournament for six primary schs in St David's, Grenada, 1985–2010. *Publications:* Index of Laws of Grenada 1959–79; (contrib.) Modern Legal Systems Cyclopedia: Central America and the Caribbean, vol. 7, 1985; The Office and Duties of the Governor-General of Grenada, 1998; A Synoptic View of the Public Service of Grenada, 1999; Prescriptions for a Model Grenada, 2000; God Speaks, 2001; The Layman's Lawbook, 2002; The Love of God, 2004; Government of the Global Village, 2007. *Recreations:* lawn tennis, gardening. *Clubs:* St George's Lions (Pres.) (St George's); Vieux Fort Lions (Pres.) (St Lucia).

**WILLIAMS, Darius James;** *see* James, Darius.

**WILLIAMS, Prof. David,** FRS 1984; Emeritus Honorary Professor, Wales Institute of Mathematical and Computational Sciences, since 2009; Professor of Mathematical Sciences, Bath University, 1992–99, now Emeritus; *b* 9 April 1938; *s* of Gwyn Williams and Margaret Elizabeth Williams; *m* 1966, Sheila Margaret Harrison; two *d*. *Educ:* Jesus College, Oxford (DPhil; Hon. Fellow, 2008); Grey College, Durham. Instructor, Stanford Univ., 1962; Lectr, Durham Univ., 1963; Shell Research Lectr, Statistical Lab., and Res. Fellow, Clare Coll., Cambridge, 1966; Lectr, 1969, Prof. of Maths, 1972, University Coll., Swansea; Prof. of Mathematical Stats and Professorial Fellow, Clare Coll., Cambridge Univ., 1985–92; (part-time) Res. Prof. of Maths, Univ. of Wales Swansea, later Swansea Univ., 1999–2008. Vis. Fellow, Bath Univ., 1991–92. Hon. Fellow, UC, Swansea, 1991–. *Publications:* Diffusions, Markov processes, and martingales, vol. 1, Foundations, 1979, 2nd edn (with L. C. G. Rogers) 1994, vol. 2 (with L. C. G. Rogers), Itô calculus, 1987; Probability with martingales, 1991; Weighing the odds, 2001; papers in Séminaire de probabilités and other jls. *Recreations:* music, cycling, walking.

**WILLIAMS, David;** Chairman, Horbury Group, since 2009; *b* 22 Nov. 1950; *s* of Stanley and Ethel Williams; *m* 1972, Joan Elizabeth Martin; three *s*. *Educ:* Sheffield Coll. of Further Educn (HNC Business Studies 1972). Joined Sheffield Insulations Ltd, 1983, Sales and Mktg Dir, 1988; Dir, Main Bd, 1993, Dep. Chief Exec., 2001, Gp Chief Exec., 2002–08, Sheffield Insulations Gp plc, subseq. SIG plc. Sen. Industrial Advr, Permira, 2008–14. Mem. Adv. Bd, Sheffield Univ. Business Sch., 2006–. Dep. Chm., Sheffield Children's Hosp. Foundn Trust, 2010–15 (non-exec. Dir, 2007). Member: Northern, RSPB; I of M Marshalls Assoc. *Recreations:* motorcycling, bird watching, shooting, walking, travel, gardening, golf, music of Bob Dylan, control of grey squirrels and magpies. *Club:* Vincent Owners.

**WILLIAMS, Prof. David Arnold,** OBE 2000; PhD, DSc; CPhys, FInstP; FRAS; Perren Professor of Astronomy, University College London, 1994–2002; *b* 9 Sept. 1937; *s* of James Arnold Williams and Frances Barbara Williams (*née* Begg); *m* 1964, Doreen Jane Bell; two *s*. *Educ:* Larne Grammar Sch.; Queen's Univ., Belfast (BSc, PhD); Manchester (DSc). CPhys 1968; FInstP 1994; FRAS 1967. Maths Dept, Manchester Coll. of Sci. and Technol., 1963–65; NASA Goddard Space Flight Center, Md, USA, 1965–67; Lectr, Sen. Lectr, Reader, Maths Dept, 1967–84, Prof. of Theoretical Astrophysics, 1984–94, UMIST. Pres., RAS, 1998–2000. *Publications:* (with J. E. Dyson) The Physics of the Interstellar Medium, 1980, 2nd edn 1997; (with W. W. Duley) Interstellar Chemistry, 1984; (with T. W. Hartquist) The Chemically Controlled Cosmos, 1995; (with T. W. Hartquist) The Molecular Astrophysics of Stars and Galaxies, 1998; (with T. W. Hartquist) The Cosmic-Chemical Bond, 2013; (with S. Viti) Observational Molecular Astronomy, 2013; (with C. Cecchi-Pestellini) The Chemistry of Cosmic Dust, 2016; contrib. numerous articles in learned jls. *Recreations:* hill-walking, choral singing, beer and wine. *Address:* Department of Physics and Astronomy, University College London, Gower Street, WC1E 6BT.

**WILLIAMS, Hon. Sir David (Basil),** Kt 2017; **Hon. Mr Justice Williams;** a Judge of the High Court, Family Division, since 2017; *b* Bedford, 18 June 1964; *s* of John Williams and Barbara Williams; *m* 2000, Siobhan Hoy; two *s* one *d*. *Educ:* Cedars Upper Sch., Leighton Buzzard; Univ. of Leicester (LLB); Inns of Court Sch. of Law (BVC). Exec. Officer, Legal Aid Bd, 1986–89; called to the Bar, Inner Temple, 1990; in practice as a barrister: 3 Dr Johnson's Bldgs, 1990–2000; 4 Paper Bldgs, 2000–17 (mediator, 2007–17); QC 2013; a Recorder, 2016–17. Contested (Lab) Wycombe, 2015. Member: Labour Party, 1987–; Soc. of Labour Lawyers, 1990–. Contrib. Ed., Butterworths Family Law Service, 2012–; Mem., Editl Bd, Internat. Family Law Jl, 2013–; Ed., Rayden and Jackson, 2015–. *Publications:* articles in Family Law Jl and Internat. Family Law. *Recreations:* motorcycles, cycling, football (Arsenal), modern European history. *Address:* Royals Courts of Justice, Rolls Building, Fetter Lane, EC4A 1NL.

**WILLIAMS, David Edward, (David Walliams),** OBE 2017; actor and writer, since 1992; *b* London, 20 Aug. 1971; *s* of Peter and Kathleen Williams; *m* 2010, Lara Stone; one *s*. *Educ:* Reigate Grammar Sch.; Bristol Univ. (BA Hons Drama). *Television* appearances include: Rock Profile, 1999–2000; Little Britain, 3 series, 2003–06 (Best Comedy Perf., RTS, 2003; Best TV Comedy, British Comedy Awards, 2004; Best Comedy Prog., 2003, 2004, Best Comedy Perf., 2004, BAFTA); Little Britain Abroad, 2005–06; Little Britain USA, 2008; Capturing Mary, 2007; Frankie Howerd: Rather You Than Me, 2008; Come Fly with Me, 2010; Mr Stink, 2012; Big School, 2013, 2014; Gangsta Granny, 2013; The Boy in the Dress, 2014; Partners in Crime (series), 2015; Ratburger, 2017; Grandpa's Great Escape, 2018; Judge, TV series, Britain's Got Talent, 2012, 2013, 2014, 2015, 2016, 2017, 2018; Billionaire Boy, 2015; Walliams & Friend, 2016; Presenter, Perspectives on Roald Dahl, 2012; *film* includes: Stardust, 2007; Dinner for Schmucks, 2010; Great Expectations, 2012; The Look of Love, 2013; *theatre*: Little Britain Live, UK and Australian tour, 2005–07; No Man's Land, Duke of York's, 2008; A Midsummer Night's Dream, Noel Coward Th., 2013. *Publications:* The Boy in the Dress, 2008 (adapted for stage, 2019); Mr Stink, 2009; Billionaire Boy, 2010 (adapted for stage, 2018); Gangsta Granny, 2011 (adapted for stage, 2017); Ratburger, 2012; Camp David (autobiog.), 2012; Demon Dentist, 2013; The Slightly Annoying Elephant, 2013; Awful Auntie, 2014 (adapted for stage, 2017); The First Hippo on the Moon, 2014 (adapted for stage, 2016); The Queen's Orang-Utan (for Comic Relief), 2015; Grandpa's Great Escape, 2015; The Bear Who Went Boo, 2015; The Midnight Gang, 2016 (adapted for stage and television, 2018); Bad Dad, 2017; The Ice Monster, 2018; Fing, 2019; The World's Worst Teachers, 2019. *Recreation:* swimming (swam the Channel, 2006, in 10.5 hours, raising over £1million for Sport Relief; swam 140 mile stretch of River Thames, 2011, raising £2.5million for Sport Relief). *Address:* Troika Talent Agency, 180 Great Portland Street, W1W 5QZ.

**WILLIAMS, Prof. David Edward,** PhD; FRSC; FRSNZ; FNZIC; Professor of Chemistry, University of Auckland, since 2006; *b* 6 Feb. 1949; *s* of William and Gertrude Williams; *m* 1972, Lindsay Mary Sutherland; one *s* one *d*. *Educ:* Lynfield Coll., Auckland; Univ. of Auckland (BSc; MSc Hons; PhD 1974). CChem 1977, FRSC 1986; FRSNZ 2009; FNZIC 2007. Gp Leader, Solid State Chemistry, Harwell Lab., UKAEA, 1980–90; Chief Scientist in Applied Electrochemistry, AEA Technol., 1990–91; University College London: Thomas Graham Prof. of Chemistry, 1991–2002; Hd, Dept of Chemistry, 1999–2002; Vis. Prof. of Chemistry, 2002–; Chief Scientist, Unipath Ltd, 2002–06. Hon. Vis. Prof., Royal Instn of GB, 2002–. *Publications:* (ed jtly) Techniques and Mechanisms in Gas Sensing, 1991; approx. 260 papers in jls of chemistry and materials sci. *Recreation:* yachting. *Address:* Department of Chemical Sciences, University of Auckland, Private Bag 92019, Auckland, New Zealand. *E:* david.williams@auckland.ac.nz.

**WILLIAMS, Prof. David Franklyn,** PhD, DSc; FREng; Professor, and Director of International Affairs, Wake Forest Institute of Regenerative Medicine, North Carolina, since 2008; *b* 18 Dec. 1944; *s* of late Henry Sidney and Margaret Williams; *m* 2001, Margaret Mary O'Donnell; three *s*. *Educ:* Thornbury Grammar Sch.; Univ. of Birmingham (BSc 1965; PhD 1969; DSc 1982). CEng, FIPEM 1982; FIMMM (FIM 1982). University of Liverpool: Department of Clinical Engineering: Lectr, 1968–78; Sen. Lectr, 1978–84; Prof., 1984–2001; Hd of Clinical Engrg, 1984–2007; Prof. of Tissue Engrg, 2001–07, now Emeritus; Dir, UK Centre for Tissue Engrg, 2004–07; Pro-Vice-Chancellor, 1997–2001. Hon. Consultant Scientist, Royal Liverpool Univ. Hosp., 1990–2007. Visiting Professor: Shanghai Jiao Tong Med. Univ., 2008–; Christiaan Barnard Dept of Cardiothoracic Surgery, Cape Town, 2008–; Grad. Sch. of Biomedical Engrg, Univ. of NSW, 2008–; Guest Prof., Tsinghua Univ., Beijing, 2007–. Mem., CCLRC, 2001–04. Chm., Strait Access Technologies Pty Ltd, S Africa, 2012–. Pres., Tissue Engrg and Regenerative Medicine Internat. Soc., 2013–15. FREng 1999; MAE 1999; Fellow, American Inst. for Med. and Biol Engrg 2000; Foreign Fellow, Indian NAE, 2014. Ed.-in-Chief, Biomaterials, 1996–2014. *Publications:* include: Implants in Surgery, 1973; Biocompatibility of Implant Materials, 1976; Materials in Clinical Dentistry, 1979; Biocompatibility, 14 vols, 1981–86; Definitions in Biomaterials, 1987; Concise Encyclopaedia of Medical and Dental Materials, 1990; The Williams Dictionary of Biomaterials, 1999; Essential Biomaterials Science, 2014; A Decade of Transition, 2016; over 400 papers in learned jls. *Recreations:* painting, photography, travel, writing poetry. *Address:* One Sheffield Place, Winston-Salem, NC 27104, USA. *T:* (336) 6718895. *E:* dfwillia@wfubmc.edu. *Club:* Athenæum.

**WILLIAMS, David Frederick,** PhD; Executive Director, Digital, National Facilities and Collections, Commonwealth Scientific and Industrial Research Organisation, since 2014; Director: Pawsey Supercomputing Centre, since 2014; National Computational Infrastructure, since 2014; Australian Academic Research Network, since 2014; International Centre for Radio Astronomy Research, since 2015; Chairman, National Information and Communications Technology Australia, since 2018; *s* of Frederick Sefton Williams and Dorothy Williams (*née* Banks); *m* 1985, Jeannie Elizabeth Rickards; one *s* two *d*. *Educ:* Hutton Grammar Sch., Preston; Univ. of Reading (BSc 1974; PhD 1978). Lectr, Dept of Geography, Reading Univ., 1977–78; Clyde Surveys, 1978–82; NERC, 1982–89; BNSC, DTI, 1989–96; Hd, Strategy and Internat. Relns, Eur. Orgn for the Exploitation of Meteorol Satellites, Darmstadt, 1996–2006; United Kingdom Space Agency: Dir Gen., British Nat. Space Centre, 2006–10; Acting Chief Exec., 2010–11; Chief Exec., 2011–12; Gp Exec., Inf. Services Gp, CSIRO, 2012–14. Chm., European Space Agency, 2010–12; Dir, AARNet Pty Ltd, 2014–. Member: Steering Cttee, Global Climate Observing System, 2000–11; Internat. Acad. of Astronautics, 2012–. Trustee, Nat. Space Centre, Leicester, 2006–12. *Publications:* various articles in jls. *Recreations:* football, gardening, renovation. *Address:* CSIRO North Ryde, Riverside Corporate Park, 5 Julius Avenue, North Ryde, NSW 2113, Australia. *T:* (2) 9490 5620.

**WILLIAMS, Rt Rev. David Grant;** *see* Basingstoke, Bishop Suffragan of.

**WILLIAMS, David Huw Anthony;** QC 2008; *b* Neath, W Glamorgan, 26 Feb. 1964; *s* of late Thomas Brinley Williams and Mair E. Williams (*née* Anthony); *m* 1994, Denise Dolan; two *s*. *Educ:* Gnoll Prim. Sch., Neath; Cefn Saeson Sch., Neath; Univ. of Wales, Swansea (BSc Hons 1983). Called to the Bar, Inner Temple, 1988; in practice as barrister specialising in crime and fraud. *Publications:* (contrib.) Fraud: law, practice and procedure, 2004; Smith's Law of Theft (with David Ormerod), 9th edn 2019. *Recreations:* tennis, Welsh Rugby, film, reading, theatre (particularly the work of Stephen Sondheim). *Address:* Fulcrum Chambers Ltd, The Shard, 25th Floor, 32 London Bridge Street, SE1 9SG.

**WILLIAMS, David John,** QPM 1992; Chief Constable, British Transport Police, 1997–2001; Associate Director, Reliance Security Services Ltd, 2001–02; *b* 7 April 1941; *s* of late John Isaac Williams and Edith (*née* Stoneham); *m* 1962, Johanna Murphy; two *s*. *Educ:* Ystalyfera Grammar Sch.; University Coll. London (LLB Hons). Called to the Bar, Middle Temple, 1977. Metropolitan Police, 1960–84; FBI Nat. Acad., 1982; on secondment to Home Office Inspectorate, 1983; Herts Constabulary, 1984–89; Dep. Chief Constable, 1989–91, Chief Constable, 1991–97, Surrey Police; Nat. Exec. Inst., USA, 1994. Chm., Traffic Cttee, ACPO, 1995–97. Mem. Council, St John Ambulance, Herts, 2004–11; Dir and Trustee, Relate, N London, 2004–07; Chm., Child Accident Prevention Trust, 2007–09; Gov./Trustee, Corps of Commissionaires Trust, 2008–09; Patron, Isabel Hospice, 2006–. Chm. and Trustee, Three Valleys Male Voice Choir, 2011–13. Friend: Royal Opera Hse; Royal Acad. of Arts. OStJ 1995. Queen's Commendation for Bravery, 1976; Police Long Service and Good Conduct Medal, 1982. *Recreations:* music, Rugby football, walking, choir singing, opera, art.

**WILLIAMS, David John,** FRCP, FRCPE, FRCS, FRCSE, FRCA, FRCEM; JP; Clinical Director, Accident & Emergency Services, Guy's and St Thomas' Hospitals NHS Trust, 1993–2000; *b* 23 April 1938; *s* of Frank Williams, CBE and Kathleen Williams; *m* 1977, Ann Andrews (*née* Walker-Watson); one *s* one *d*, and one step *s* one step *d*. *Educ:* Highgate Sch.; Hotchkiss Sch., USA; Trinity Coll., Cambridge (MA, MB, BChir); St Thomas' Hosp. Med. Sch. MRCP 1970, FRCP 1982; MRCGP 1972; FRCEM (FFAEM 1993); FRCS 1997; FRCPE 1998; FRCSE 1999; FRCA 2000. Jun. med. posts, St Thomas' Hosp., Kingston Hosp., Guy's-Maudsley Neurosurgical Unit, 1964–65; RMO, Nat. Heart Hosp., 1966, Middlesex Hosp., 1967–70; Registrar, Maudsley Hosp., 1970–71; GP, 1971–72; Consultant, Accident and Emergency Medicine: Middlesex Hosp., 1973–84; St Thomas' Hosp., 1984–2000. Clin. Advr, Health Service Comr, 2000–05; Mem., Criminal Injuries Compensation Tribunal (formerly Appeals Panel), 2000–12; Sen. Medical Mem., Tribunal Service (formerly Appeals Tribunals), 2006–13. Sec., Casualty Surgeons Assoc., 1978–84; President: British Assoc. for A&E Medicine, 1987–90; Intercollegiate Faculty of A&E

Medicine, 1993–97; Eur. Soc. for Emergency Medicine, 2004–07 (Vice-Pres., 2000–04); Chairman: UEMS Cttee on Emergency Medicine, 2005–12; Eur. Bd of Emergency Medicine, 2010–16; Pres., UEMS Section on Emergency Medicine, 2012–16. Invited Member Council: RCP, 1994–2000; RCS, 1994–2000; Royal Coll. of Anaesthetists, 1994–2000. JP Sutton, 2004–08. Fellow, Internat. Fedn of Emergency Medicine, 2000; Hon. Member: Amer. Coll. Emergency Physicians, 1990; Amer. Acad. of Emergency Medicine, 2005; German Assoc. for Emergency Medicine, 2010; Czech Soc. for Emergency and Disaster Medicine, 2013; Hon. Life Mem., British Assoc. for A&E Medicine, 1998–2008; Hon. FRSocMed 2001. Silver Decoration of Honour, UEMS, 2018. *Recreations:* reading, collecting books, theatre, travel, playing bridge. *Address:* 154 Durham Road, West Wimbledon, SW20 0DG. *T:* (020) 8946 3785.

**WILLIAMS, (David John) Delwyn;** company director; *b* 1 Nov. 1938; *s* of David Lewis Williams and Irena Violet Gwendoline Williams; *m* 1963, Olive Elizabeth Jerman; one *s* one *d*. *Educ:* Welshpool High School; University College of Wales, Aberystwyth. LLB. Sometime Solicitor and company director. MP (C) Montgomery, 1979–83; former Member: Select Cttee on Wales; Statutory Instruments Cttee; Jt Sec., All-Party Leisure and Recreation Industry Cttee. Contested (C) Montgomery, 1983. Former Mem., British Field Sports Soc. *Recreations:* race horse owner; cricket, golf, small bore shooting.

**WILLIAMS, David Lincoln;** Chairman and Managing Director, Costa Rica Coffee Co. Ltd, 1988–2002; *b* 10 Feb. 1937; *s* of Lewis Bernard Williams and Eileen Elizabeth Cadogan; *m* 1959, Gillian Elisabeth, *d* of William Phillips; one *s* one *d*. *Educ:* Cheltenham College. Served RA Gibraltar, 1955–57. Chairman: Allied Windows (S Wales) Ltd, 1971–85; Cardiff Broadcasting PLC, 1979–84; Allied Profiles Ltd, 1981–96; Chm. and Man. Dir, John Williams of Cardiff PLC, 1983–88 (Dir, 1968–88). Chm., Cox (Penarth), 1987–94. President, Aluminium Window Assoc., 1971–72. Member: CBI Welsh Council, 1986–89; Welsh Arts Council, 1987–94 (Chm., Music Cttee, 1988–94). Chm., Vale of Glamorgan Festival, 1978–95 and 2004–18 (Pres., 1995–2004); Director: Cardiff Bay Opera House Trust, 1994–2001; WNO, 1994–2001 (Nat. Chm., 1980–2000, Vice-Pres., 2005–18, Friends of WNO). Freeman, City of London, 1986; Liveryman, Founders' Co., 1986. *Recreations:* opera, wheelchair gardening. *Address:* Rose Revived, Llantrithyd, Cowbridge, Vale of Glamorgan CF71 7UB. *T:* (01446) 781357. *Club:* Cardiff and County (Cardiff).

**WILLIAMS, Prof. David Michael,** PhD; FRCPath, FDSRCS; Professor of Global Oral Health, Bart's and the London School of Medicine and Dentistry, Queen Mary University of London, since 2011; Professor of Pathology, University of Southampton, 2004–11, now Emeritus (Dean, Faculty of Medicine, Health and Life Sciences, 2004–10; Vice Provost, 2010–11); *b* 4 Nov. 1946; *s* of late Reginald Albert Williams and Mary Williams (*née* Holland); *m* 1970, Gillian Elizabeth Regester; one *s* one *d*. *Educ:* Plymouth Coll.; London Hosp. Med. Coll., Univ. of London (BDS Hons 1969; MSc 1972; PhD 1976). FRCPath 1991; FDSRCS 1994. London Hospital Medical College: Sen. Lectr in Oral Pathology, 1982–89; Reader in Oral Pathology, 1989–93; Prof. of Oral Pathology, 1994–2004, Dean of Clinical Dentistry, 1994–98, Dep. Warden, 1998–2001, St Bartholomew's and Royal London Sch. of Medicine and Dentistry, QMW, Univ. of London, subseq. Bart's and The London, Queen Mary's Sch. of Medicine and Dentistry; Vice-Principal, Queen Mary, Univ. of London, 2001–04; Hon. Consultant: Bart's and the London NHS Trust (formerly Royal London Hosp., then Royal Hosps NHS Trust), 1982–2004; Southampton Univ. Hosps NHS Trust, 2004–11 (non-exec. Dir, 2005–11); non-exec. Dir, S Central Ambulance Service NHS Foundn Trust, 2012–18 (Chm., Quality and Safety Cttee, 2015–18). Chm., Dentistry Sub-panel 2008 RAE. Member: GDC, 1998–2003 (Chm., Registration Sub-Cttee, 1999–2003); Health and Sci. Cttee, BDA, 2015–; Sci. Cttee, FDI, 2015– (Vice-Pres., 2015–18); Adv. Bd, Bridge2Aid, 2016–. Pres., British Soc. for Dental Res., 2002–04; International Association for Dental Research: Pres., Pan-European Fedn, 2004–05; Vice-Pres., 2007–08; Pres.-elect, 2008–09; Pres., 2009–10. Mem., numerous editl bds. *Publications:* (jtly) Pathology of Periodontal Disease, 1992; (ed jtly) The Challenge of Oral Disease: a call for global action, 2nd edn, 2015; numerous articles in learned jls. *Recreations:* golf, scuba diving, hill walking, sailing, painting in watercolours, fine wines. *Address:* Bart's and the London School of Medicine and Dentistry, Queen Mary University of London, Turner Street, Whitechapel, E1 2AD. *E:* d.m.williams@qmul.ac.uk. *Club:* Athenæum.

**WILLIAMS, Rev. David Michael;** JP; Vicar, Benefice of St Giles, Great Coxwell, with St Mary the Virgin, Buscot, All Saints, Coleshill, and St Michael and All Angels, Eaton Hastings, 2014–19 (Priest-in-Charge, 2011–14); Tutor in Foundations for Denominational Ministry, Department of External Studies, St John's School of Mission (formerly St John's College), Nottingham, 2013–19; Permission to Officiate, Dioceses of Guildford, Oxford and Southwark, since 2019; *b* 6 April 1950; *s* of David Woodget Williams and Edith Olive Williams (*née* Hance); *m* (marr. diss.). *Educ:* Exeter Univ. (BA Hons 1971); UCL (Dip. Liby and Inf. Studies 1974); London Univ. (MA 1977); Univ. of Kent (Dip. Applied Christian Theology 2008). On staff, Council for the Care of Churches, 1972–73, 1974–87; Church of England: on staff, 1987–94, Sec., 1994–99, Central Bd of Finance; Clerk to the Gen. Synod, 1999–2011; Dir, Central Services, 1999–2002, Hd, Central Secretariat, 2002–11, Archbishops' Council. Ordained deacon 2008, priest 2009; Area Dean, Vale of White Horse, Dio. of Oxford, 2015–18. FSA 1981; FRSA 1982. JP: SE Surrey, 1986; Oxon, 2012. *Publications:* articles in jls on hist. of English parochial libraries; contrib. to study guide for St John's Sch. of Mission. *Recreations:* numismatics, ecclesiology, art and architecture, horticulture, cycling, walking. *Address:* Pine Cottage, Harrow Road West, Dorking, Surrey RH4 3BE.

**WILLIAMS, David Oliver;** General Secretary, Confederation of Health Service Employees, 1983–87; *b* 12 March 1926; *m* 1949, Kathleen Eleanor Jones, Dinorwic; two *s* five *d* (and one *s* decd). *Educ:* Brynrefail Grammar Sch.; North Wales Hospital, Denbigh (RMN 1951). COHSE: full-time officer, Regional Secretary, Yorkshire Region, 1955; National Officer, Head Office, 1962; Sen. National Officer, 1969; Asst General Secretary, 1974. Chairman: Nurses and Midwives Whitley Council Staff Side, 1977–87; General Whitley Council Staff Side, 1974–87. Member: NEC, Labour Party, 1981–83; TUC Gen. Council, 1983–87. Occasional Tech. Advr to WHO. Jubilee Medal, 1977. *Recreations:* walking, birdwatching, swimming, music. *Address:* 1 King's Court, Beddington Gardens, Wallington, Surrey SM6 0HR. *T:* (020) 8647 6412.

**WILLIAMS, Air Vice-Marshal David Owen C.;** *see* Crwys-Williams.

**WILLIAMS, Sir David (Reeve),** Kt 1999; CBE 1990; Member (Lib Dem), Richmond upon Thames Borough Council, 1974–2014 (Leader, 1983–2001; Cabinet Member, 2001–02, 2006–10); *b* 8 June 1939; *s* of Edmund George Williams and May Williams (*née* Partridge); *m* 1964, Christine Margaret Rayson. *Educ:* St Cuthbert's Soc.; Univ. of Durham (BA Hons Politics and Econs). Computer systems analyst, 1961–95: IBM UK Ltd, 1961–70; Insurance Systems and Services, 1970–78; David Williams and Associates, 1978–91; Teleglobe Insce Systems Ltd, 1991–95. Dep. Chm., and Leader, Lib Dem Gp, LGA, 1996–2001. *Recreations:* collecting books, particularly about Lloyd George, listening to jazz, particularly Charlie Parker. *Address:* 8 Arlington Road, Petersham, Richmond, Surrey TW10 7BY. *T:* (020) 8940 9421.

**WILLIAMS, David Whittow;** Chief Executive, Amari Plastics plc, since 2004; *b* 18 Aug. 1957; *s* of David Whittow Williams and Eileen Williams; *m* 1992, Helle Nordensgaard. *Educ:* Birkenhead Sch.; Mansfield Coll., Oxford (MA). Exec. Vice Pres., Melwire Inc., 1982–86; Mkting Dir, Vickers Healthcare, 1986–88; Eur. Business Develt Manager, Blue Circle Cement, 1988–90; Business Develt Dir, Blue Circle Home Products plc, 1991–94; Man. Dir, Potterton/Myson, 1994–96; Chief Executive: Magnet, 1996–99; Berisford, subseq. Enodis plc, 1999–2001. *Recreations:* hockey, tennis, cricket.

**WILLIAMS, Dr (David) Wynford,** CB 2007; Chairman, Public Weather Service Customer Group, since 2013; *b* 19 July 1946; *s* of late Thomas Elwyn Williams and of Nancy Williams; *m* 1969, Dilys Arthur; one *s* one *d*. *Educ:* Amman Valley Grammar Sch., Ammanford; University Coll., Swansea (BSc 1967, PhD 1971). CPhys 1987, CEng 1987; FInstP 1981; FRAeS 1981; FIMarEST 2006. Scientist: ASWE, MoD, 1971–81; British Naval Staff, Washington, 1981–84; Ministry of Defence: ACOS (Operational Analysis), C-in-C Fleet, 1984–87; Supt, RAE Ranges, 1987–91; Dir, A&AEE Boscombe Down, 1991–95; rcds 1996; Dir, Sea Systems Sector, DERA, 1997–2000; Chief Exec., UK Hydrographic Office, and UK Nat. Hydrographer, 2001–06. Chm., Pelydryn Ltd, 2008–13. Pres., Inst. of Marine Engrg, Sci. and Technol., 2007–08. Non-exec. Dir, S Wales Probation Trust, 2007–. Chm., Bath and Wells Diocesan Bd of Finance, 2006–10. *Recreations:* Rugby, golf, music (orchestral and choral). *E:* wyn.dil@sky.com.

**WILLIAMS, Delwyn;** *see* Williams, D. J. D.

**WILLIAMS, Sir Dillwyn;** *see* Williams, Sir E. D.

**WILLIAMS, Rev. Doiran George;** Non-Stipendiary Minister, Greater Whitbourne, since 1993; *b* 27 June 1926; *s* of Rev. Dr Robert Richard Williams and Dilys Rachel Williams; *m* 1st, 1949, Flora Samitz (decd); one *s* one *d*; 2nd, 1977, Maureen Dorothy Baker; one *d*. *Educ:* Hereford Cathedral Sch.; Colwyn Bay Grammar Sch.; Liverpool Coll.; John F. Hughes Sch., Utica, NY. Served Army (Infantry), 1944–47. Called to the Bar, Gray's Inn, 1952; practised in Liverpool, 1952–58; Dept of Dir of Public Prosecutions, 1959, Asst Dir, 1977–82, Principal Asst Dir of Public Prosecutions, 1982–86; Chm., Med. Appeal Tribunals, 1987–98. Sec., Liverpool Fabian Soc., 1956–58. Reader: Liverpool Dio., 1953–58; London Dio., 1959–63; Southwark Dio., 1963–88; Hereford Dio., 1988–93; Mem., Southwark Readers' Bd, 1977–88. Ordained deacon, 1993, priest, 1994. *Recreations:* arts, mountains, sport, wine. *Address:* Howberry, Whitbourne, Worcester WR6 5RZ.

**WILLIAMS, Sir Donald Mark,** 10th Bt *cr* 1866; *b* 7 Nov. 1954; *s* of Sir Robert Ernest Williams, 9th Bt, and Ruth Margaret, *d* of Charles Edwin Butcher, Hudson Bay, Saskatchewan, Canada; *S* father, 1976; *m* 1982, Denise, *o d* of Royston H. Cory; three *d* (one *s* decd). *Educ:* West Buckland School, Devon. *Heir: b* Barton Matthew Williams [*b* 21 Nov. 1956; *m* 1st, 1980, Karen Robinson (marr. diss.); one *s* one *d*; 2nd, 1985, Sarah (marr. diss.); one *d*]. *Address:* Upcott House, Barnstaple, N Devon EX31 4DR.

**WILLIAMS, Edmund Morys;** QC 2018; *b* Southport, 6 May 1975; *s* of Emrys and Susan Williams; *m* 2010, Carla Revere; two *d*. *Educ:* Bexhill 6th Form Coll.; Nottingham Univ. (BA Hons Hist. 1997); Nottingham Law Sch. (CPE, BVC 2000). Called to the Bar, Inner Temple, 2000; in practice as barrister, 2000– (sabbatical, Cairo to Cape Town, 2005–06). Founder and Dir, Assurety Trng, 2011–. Contested (Lab) Meriden, 2010. Founder and Trustee, Cricket Without Boundaries, 2005–. *Recreations:* history, cricket, travel, being a modern dad, coaching cricket in Africa and the Middle East. *Address:* Cloisters, 1 Pump Court, Temple, EC4Y 7AA. *T:* (020) 7827 4029, *Fax:* (020) 7827 4100. *E:* ew@cloisters.com.

**WILLIAMS, Prof. Sir (Edward) Dillwyn,** Kt 1990; FRCP, FRCPath, FMedSci, FLSW; Professor of Histopathology, 1992–96, now Emeritus, and Hon. Senior Visiting Fellow, Department of Public Health, since 2010, University of Cambridge; *b* 1 April 1929; *s* of Edward Williams and Ceinwen Williams (*née* James); *m* 1st, 1954, Ruth H. (marr. diss. 1973); one *s* two *d* (and one *s* decd); 2nd, 1976, Dilwen Williams (marr. diss. 2001); one *s* one *d*. *Educ:* Christ's Coll., Cambridge (MA, MD; Hon. Fellow, 1991); London Hospital Med. Coll. Jun. appts, London Hosp. and RPMS; successively Lectr, Sen. Lectr, Reader, in Morbid Anatomy, RPMS; Prof. of Pathology, 1969–92, Vice-Provost, 1982–84, Univ. of Wales Coll. of Medicine. Consultant Pathologist, Cardiff, 1969–92. Res. Fellowship, Harvard Univ., 1962–63. President: RCPath, 1987–90; BMA, 1998–99; Hd and Prin. Investigator of WHO's Internat. Reference Centre for Endocrine Tumours, 1972–; Chairman: Welsh Sci. Adv. Cttee, 1985–92; Conference of Medical Royal Colleges, 1988–90; Mem., GMC, 1987–93. Chairman: Scientific Project Panel of Chernobyl Tissue Bank, 1998–2004; Agenda for Res. on Chernobyl Health, 2010–. Mem., Sci. Scholarships Cttee, Royal Commn for Exhibn of 1851, 2000–12. Corresp. Mem., Amer. Thyroid Assoc.; President: Thyroid Club of GB, 1987–90; European Thyroid Assoc., 1993–96. Founder FMedSci 1998; Founder FLSW 2010. Lifetime Achievement Award and Totovic Medal, German Internat. Acad. of Pathology, 2016. *Publications:* International Histological Classification of Tumours: histological typing of endocrine tumours, 1980; Pathology and Management of Thyroid Disease, 1981; Current Endocrine Concepts, 1982; numerous contribs to learned jls in field of endocrine pathology and carcinogenesis, identifying cell of origin, humoral and genetic associations of medullary carcinoma of thyroid, clonality studies of thyroid and colon, radiation and thyroid cancer, in particular recently on thyroid carcinoma following Chernobyl nuclear accident. *Recreations:* natural history in general, birdwatching in particular, mountain walking. *Address:* 9 Cow Lane, Fulbourn, Cambs CB21 5HB. *T:* (01223) 880738.

**WILLIAMS, Eleanor Jane;** *see* Milner-Gulland, E. J.

**WILLIAMS, Elizabeth, (Betty);** working for peace, since 1976; Founder and President, World Centers of Compassion for Children International, since 1997; *b* 22 May 1943; *m* 1st, 1961, Ralph Williams (marr. diss.); one *s* one *d*; 2nd, 1982, James T. Perkins. *Educ:* St Dominic's Grammar School. Office Receptionist. Co-founder and Leader, NI Peace Movement, 1976–78; Chm., Inst. for Asian Democracy, Washington, DC; Patron, Internat. Peace Foundn, Vienna. Hon. LLD, Yale Univ., 1977; Hon. HLD, Coll. of Sienna Heights, Michigan, 1977. Nobel Peace Prize (jtly), 1976; Carl-von-Ossietzky Medal for Courage, 1976; Eleanor Roosevelt Award; Frank Foundn Child Assistance Internat. Oliver Award; Peace Building Award, Together for Peace Foundn, 1995. Paul Harris Fellow, Rotary Internat., 1995. *Publications:* Madness in My Country, 2009. *Recreation:* gardening.

**WILLIAMS, Felicity Ann;** Senior Regional Official, National Association of Schoolmasters/Union of Women Teachers, since 2008; General Secretary, Wales Trade Union Congress, 2004–08 (Assistant General Secretary, 2000–04); *b* 29 Oct. 1960; *d* of Ivan and Doris Parker; *m* 1981, David Williams. *Educ:* Univ. of Bristol. FIBMS 1988. Biomed. scientist, then Dep. Hd of Microbiology 1988–97, Welsh Blood Service. *Recreations:* travel, reading, good food and wine, theatre.

**WILLIAMS, Prof. Fiona;** *see* Williams, J. F.

**WILLIAMS, Sir Francis Owen Garbett, (Sir Frank),** Kt 1999; CBE 1987; Managing Director, 1992–2012, Team Principal, since 2012, Williams Grand Prix Engineering Ltd; *b* 16 April 1942; *s* of Owen Garbett Williams; *m* 1974, Virginia Jane, *d* of Raymond Berry; three *c*. *Educ*: St Joseph's Coll., Dumfries. Racing driver to 1966, competing first in Austin A40; grand prix team management, 1969–; Formula One with Brabham BT 26A; founded Frank Williams Racing Cars, 1975; first Grand Prix race, with FW07, Silverstone, 1979; won Constructors' Cup, 1980, 1981, 1986, 1987, 1992, 1993, 1994, 1996, 1997; introduced active ride system, 1988, semi-automatic 6-speed gear box, 1991. Helen Rollason Award, BBC Sports Personality of the Year, 2010. *Address*: Williams Grand Prix Engineering Ltd, Grove, Wantage, Oxon OX12 0DQ.
*See also* C. V. Williams.

**WILLIAMS, Frank John;** actor and playwright; *b* 2 July 1931; *s* of William Williams and Alice (*née* Myles). *Educ*: Ardingly Coll.; Hendon County Sch. *Theatre* includes: Stage Manager and actor, Gateway Theatre, London, 1951; *writer*: No Traveller, 1958; The TV Murders, 1960; The Substitute, 1961; Murder by Appointment, 1985; Alibi for Murder, 1989; Murder Weekend, 1993; Mask for Murder, 1993; The Playing Fields, 2003; *actor*: The Cresta Run, Royal Court, 1965; The Waiters, Watford, 1967; Dad's Army, Shaftesbury, and tour, 1975–76; The Editor Regrets, tour, 1978; Stage Struck, 1980, The Winslow Boy, 1982, Vienna; Lloyd George Knew My Father, tour, Middle East and Far East, 1993; A Midsummer Night's Dream, Almeida, and tour, 1996–97; *television* includes: The Call Up, 1952; The Queen came by, 1955; The Army Game, 1958–61; Anna Karenina, 1961; Diary of a Young Man, 1964; After Many a Summer, 1967; Dad's Army, 1969–77; How Many Miles to Babylon, 1981; Grey Granite, 1982; Love's Labour Lost, 1984; You Rang M'Lord, 1989–92; Stella, 2016; *films* include: Shield of Faith, 1954; The Extra Day, 1955; The Square Peg, 1958; The Bulldog Breed, 1960; Dad's Army, 1970; Jabberwocky, 1976; The Human Factor, 1979; Fall of an Empire, 2014; Dad's Army, 2016. Member: Gen. Synod, 1985–2000; Crown Appts Commn, 1992–97; Trustee, Annunciation Trust, 1995–2006. Mem., Equity Council, 1984–88, 1990–94, 1998–2010; Dir, Equity Charitable Trust (formerly Equity Trust Fund), 1992–2013. *Publications*: Vicar to Dad's Army, 2002. *Recreations*: theatre, cinema, collecting boys' school books. *Address*: 31 Manor Park Crescent, Edgware, Middx HA8 7NE. *T*: (020) 8952 4871.

**WILLIAMS, Prof. Gareth,** MD, ScD; FRCP, FRCPE; Professor of Medicine, University of Bristol, 2003–13, now Emeritus Professor and Honorary Senior Research Fellow in English (Dean, Faculty of Medicine and Dentistry, 2003–08); *b* 17 March 1952; *s* of Sir Alwyn Williams, FRS, and Joan Williams (*née* Bevan); *m* 1983, Caroline Anne Evans; one *s* one *d*. *Educ*: Royal Belfast Academical Instn (Sir Hans Sloane Medal 1970); Clare Coll., Cambridge (Open and Foundn Scholar); Middlesex Hosp. Med. Sch. (MB BChir Hons Medicine and Pharmacol. 1977); Univ. of Cambridge (MD 1986; ScD 2003). FRCP 1991; FRCPE 1999. Jun. hosp. posts, Middlesex, Hammersmith and Brompton Hosps, London, and Hôpital Cantonal, Geneva, 1977–79; Res. Registrar, Guy's Hosp., London, 1980–83; Med. Registrar, Ealing and Hammersmith Hosps, 1983–85; R. D. Lawrence Res. Fellow, British Diabetic Assoc., 1986–88; University of Liverpool: Sen. Lectr, 1988–92, Reader, 1992, in Medicine; Prof. of Medicine, 1995–2003; Hon. Consultant Physician, Royal Liverpool Univ. Hosp., 1988–92; Foundn Prof. of Medicine and Hon. Consultant Physician, Univ. Hosp. Aintree, Liverpool, 1995–2003. Lectures: Henry Cohen Hist. of Medicine, Liverpool Med. Inst., 2011; Gresham Coll., London, 2011, 2013; Milroy, RCP, 2012; Charter, Royal Soc. Biol., 2016; FitzPatrick, RCP, 2017; Haldane-Tait, Scottish Soc. of History of Medicine, 2017. Non-exec. Dir, United Bristol Healthcare Trust, 2005–07. Member: Obesity Leadership Gp, Coalition for Better Health, 2009–10; Expert Rev. Gp, History of Medicine and Med. Humanities, Wellcome Trust, 2011–14. Vis. Prof., Fac. of Medicine, Univ. of Alberta, 1988–89. UK Pres., Anglo-French Med. Soc., 1993–2000; Mem. Council, Eur. Soc. for Clinical Investment, 1996–2000 (Vice-Pres., 2000); Chm., MEDINE (Med. Educn in Europe), 2004–07. Trustee, Jenner Trust and Dr Jenner's House (formerly Jenner Mus.), 2009–11 (Chm., 2010–11). Editl Bd, Peptides, 1994–2003. Mem. Cttee, Med. Writers' Gp, Soc. of Authors, 2001– (Chm., 2007). Ambassador, British Polio Fellowship, 2013–. Dr *hc* Angers, 2007. Novartis UK Award for Achievement in Diabetes, 1999. *Publications*: (ed jtly) Textbook of Diabetes, 1990, 2nd edn 1995 (BMA Medicine Book of the Yr; Soc. of Authors prize), 3rd edn 2004; (ed jtly) Handbook of Diabetes, 1992, 3rd edn 2004; (contrib.) Oxford Textbook of Medicine, 4th edn 2004 to 5th edn 2010; (ed jtly) Obesity: science to practice, 2009; Angel of Death: the story of smallpox, 2010; Paralysed with Fear: the story of polio, 2013; A Monstrous Commotion: the mysteries of Loch Ness, 2015; Unravelling the Double Helix: the lost heroes of DNA, 2019; papers on diabetes, neuroendocrinology and obesity in sci. and med. jls, and articles of gen. medicine interest. *Recreations*: playing music (reputable and disreputable), exploring Gloucestershire by bike, bird-watching, French, microlite flying, writing fiction. *Address*: Yellow, Rockhampton, Berkeley, Glos GL13 9DY. *E*: Gareth.Williams@bris.ac.uk. *Clubs*: Twenty (Liverpool); Flying Shack (Staverton).

**WILLIAMS, Gareth Charlton;** Director of Strategy, since 2014, and Company Secretary, since 2011, Eurostar International Ltd (Regulatory Affairs Director, 2011–14); *b* Crawley, Sussex, 25 March 1968; *s* of late Vivian Graham Williams and of Margaret Aileen Williams; *m* 2014, Joanne Claire Corsar. *Educ*: Ipswich Sch.; Webb Sch. of Calif; Nottingham Univ. (BA Hons Hist. 1990). Various posts, Govt Office for London, Office of Passenger Rail Franchising and DfT, 1991–2000; Hd, Envmt Agency Sponsorship, DEFRA, 2000–02; Divl Manager, Disability and Work, DWP, 2002–04; Department for Transport: Divisional Manager: Rail Finance, 2004–05; Rail Strategy, 2005–07; London and Continental Railways Restructuring and Sale, 2007–11. *Recreations*: writing trashy screenplays, cooking pretentious dinners, eating the Michelin Guide, ski-ing, scuba diving. *Address*: Eurostar International Ltd, Times House, Bravingtons Walk, N1 9AW. *Club*: National Liberal.

**WILLIAMS, Prof. Gareth Lloyd;** Professor of Educational Administration, Institute of Education, University of London, 1984–2001, now Emeritus; *b* 19 Oct. 1935; *s* of Lloyd and Katherine Enid Williams; *m* 1960, Elizabeth Ann Peck; two *s* one *d*. *Educ*: Creeting St Mary; Framlingham; Cambridge Univ. (MA). Res. Officer, Agricl Econs Res. Inst., Oxford Univ., 1959–62; Res. Fellow, OECD, Athens, 1962–64; Principal Administrator, OECD, Paris, 1964–68; Associate Dir, Higher Educn Res. Unit, LSE, 1968–73; Prof. of Educnl Planning, Univ. of Lancaster, 1973–84. Visiting Professor: Melbourne Univ., 1981–82; Coll. of Europe, 1994–. Specialist Adviser to Arts and Educn Sub-Cttee to House of Commons Cttee on Expenditure, 1972–76; Consultant to OECD, ILO, UNESCO, and World Bank. Member: Council, Policy Studies Inst., 1979–85; Governing Council for Soc. for Res. into Higher Educn, 1970– (Chm., 1978–80, 1986–88). Mem. Bd, Red Rose Radio PLC, 1981–92. FRSA 1982. *Publications*: (with Greenaway) Patterns of Change in Graduate Employment, 1973; (with Blackstone and Metcalf) The Academic Labour Market in Britain, 1974; Towards Lifelong Learning, 1978; (with Zabalza and Turnbull) The Economics of Teacher Supply, 1979; (with Woodhall) Independent Further Education, 1979; (with Blackstone) Response to Adversity, 1983; Higher Education in Ireland, 1985; (with Woodhall and O'Brien) Overseas Students and their Place of Study, 1986; Changing Patterns of Finance in Higher Education, 1992; The Enterprising University, 2004. *Address*: 2 Kempton Road, Lancaster LA1 4LS. *T*: (01524) 66002.

**WILLIAMS, Sir Gareth R.;** *see* Rhys Williams, Sir A. G. L. E.

**WILLIAMS, Geoffrey;** QC 2003; barrister; *b* 29 April 1954; *s* of Trevor and Eunice Williams; partner, Kathy Wiley; two *s*. *Educ*: Jones' W Monmouth Grammar Sch., Pontypool; Trent Polytech., Nottingham (BA Hons Law); Coll. of Law, Chester (2nd cl. Hons Solicitors' Finals). Admitted solicitor, 1978; Partner, specialising in regulatory and disciplinary law, solicitors' firm, 1980–98; Sen. Partner, Geoffrey Williams & Christopher Green, Solicitor Advocates, 1998–2013; called to the Bar, Gray's Inn, 2013. Higher Rights of Audience (Civil), 1997. *Recreations*: sport (particularly racing, cricket and Rugby), current affairs. *Address*: Farrar's Building, Temple, EC4Y 7BD. *T*: (020) 7583 9241. *E*: law@gwcg.globalnet.co.uk. *Club*: Royal Automobile.

**WILLIAMS, Prof. Geraint Trefor,** OBE 2011; MD; FRCP, FRCPath, FMedSci; FLSW; Professor of Pathology, Cardiff University (formerly University of Wales College of Medicine), 1991–2016, now Emeritus; *b* 10 Sept. 1949; *s* of late Rev. William Trefor Williams and of Eleanor Doris Williams (*née* Evans), Cefngorwydd; *m* 1974, Vivienne Elizabeth Jones; two *d*. *Educ*: Builth Wells Grammar Sch.; Univ. of Wales, Cardiff, and Welsh National Sch. of Medicine (BSc 1st cl. Hons Physiol. 1970; MB BCh Hons 1973; MD 1981). MRCP 1975, FRCP 1991; FRCPath 1991. Jun. med. appts, Univ. Hosp. of Wales, Cardiff, and Hammersmith and Brompton Hosps, London, 1973–76; Lectr in Pathology, St Bartholomew's Hosp. and St Mark's Hosp., London, 1976–79; Sen. Lectr, 1980–88, Reader, 1988–91, Univ. of Wales Coll. of Medicine; Admissions Sub-Dean, Cardiff Univ. Medical Sch., 2004–10. Hon. Consultant Histopathologist, Cardiff and Vale Univ. Health Bd (formerly Cardiff and Vale NHS Trust), 1980–2011. Mem., Cttee on Carcinogenicity of Chemicals in Food, Consumer Products and the Envmt, DoH, 1993–2003; Chm., Welsh Scientific Adv. Cttee, Welsh Assembly Govt, 2000–04. Mem. Council, RCPath, 2004–07; Mem. Council, 1985–88, Vice Pres., 1999–2002, Assoc. of Clinical Pathologists; Chm., Pathology Sect., British Soc. of Gastroenterology, 1996–99; Member, Executive Committee: Pathological Soc. of GB and Ire., 1996–99; Eur. Soc. of Pathology, 1991–95; Councillor, 2004–06, Pres. elect, 2006–08, Pres., 2008–10, British Div., Internat. Acad. of Pathology. Trustee, Tenovus Cancer Care, 2015–. FMedSci 2002; FLSW 2011. Hon. Mem. RCR, 2003. *Publications*: (jtly) Morson and Dawson's Gastrointestinal Pathology, 3rd edn 1990 to 5th edn 2013; (ed) Current Topics in Pathology: Gastrointestinal Pathology, 1990; (jtly) Tumors of the Intestines, 2003; numerous contribs to learned jls on gut pathology and carcinogenesis. *Recreations*: ornithology, photography, music, cat watching. *Address*: 11 Cyncoed Crescent, Cardiff CF23 6SW. *E*: GTWilliams@doctors.org.uk.

**WILLIAMS, Glyn,** CB 2019; Director-General, Policy and International, Borders, Immigration and Citizenship System, Home Office, since 2017; *b* Stoke-on-Trent, 19 Dec. 1961. *Educ*: Holden Lane High Sch.; Stoke-on-Trent Sixth Form Coll.; Univ. of Manchester (BA 1st Cl. Hons French and German 1984). DTI, 1985–93; UK Mission to UN, 1993–98; Department of Trade and Industry: Dep. Dir, EU Employment Law, 1998–2001; Director: Employment Relns, 2001–03; Export Control, 2003–06; Dir, Visa Services, UK Border Agency, 2006–10; Home Office: Hd, Migration Policy, 2010–13; Director: Asylum Ops, 2013–14; Immigration and Border Policy, 2014–17.

**WILLIAMS, Prof. Glynn Anthony,** FRSS, FRCA; sculptor; Professor of Sculpture, Royal College of Art, 1990–2009, now Emeritus (Head, School of Fine Art, 1995–2009); *b* 30 March 1939; *s* of Idris Merion Williams and Muriel Elizabeth Purslow; *m* 1963 (marr. diss. 2001); two *d*. *Educ*: Wolverhampton Grammar Sch.; Wolverhampton Coll. of Art (NDD Sculpture Special Level); British Sch. in Rome (Rome Scholar). Head of Sculpture Departments: Leeds Coll. of Art, later Leeds Polytechnic, 1968–75; Wimbledon Sch. of Art, 1976–90. 24 one-man exhibns incl. retrospective, Margam Park, S Wales, 1992; numerous group exhibns incl. British Sculpture of 20th Century, Whitechapel Gall., 1981; rep. GB, Kotara Takamura Grand Prize Exhibn, Japan, 1984; work in collections: Arts Council of GB; Bottisham Village Coll., Cambridge; Bradford City Art Gall.; British Sch. in Rome; Grisedale Theatre in the Forest, Cumbria; Hakone Open Air Mus., Japan; Hampshire Sculpture Trust; Haroldwood Hosp., Essex; Hemel Hempstead Arts Trust; Henry Moore Centre for Sculpture, Leeds; Hove Mus. and Art Gall.; Hull City Art Gall.; Leeds City Council; Lincoln City Council; London Borough of Hounslow; Middlesbrough Council; Milton Keynes Develt Corp.; Nat. Portrait Gall.; Newport (Gwent) Educn Cttee; Northern Arts Assoc.; Peterborough Develt Corp.; Southern Arts Assoc.; Tate Gall.; V&A; Welsh Arts Council; Welsh Sculpture Trust; Wolverhampton Educn Cttee; Yorkshire Arts Assoc. Commissions: 14′ bronze meml to Henry Purcell, Flowering of the English Baroque, City of Westminster, 1995; Lloyd George Meml, Parliament Sq., 2007. Trustee, Forest of Dean Sculpture Trail, 2012. FRCA 1991; FRSS (FRBS 1992). FRSA 1996. Hon. Fellow, Wolverhampton Polytechnic, 1989. *Publications*: contribs to arts magazines, jls, TLS. *Recreations*: cooking, crosswords, music. *Address*: c/o Bernard Jacobson Gallery, 28 Duke Street, St James's, SW1Y 6AG. *Club*: Chelsea Arts.

**WILLIAMS, Gordon;** *see* Williams, James G.

**WILLIAMS, Prof. Gordon,** OBE 2011; FRCS; Consultant Urologist, Bethel Hospital and Medical School, Addis Ababa, Ethiopia, 2012–18; Advisor in Medical Education, Ministry of Health, Ethiopia, 2015–18; *b* 27 June 1945; *s* of Charles and Marjorie Williams; *m* 1st, 1968, Susan Gubbins (marr. diss. 1989); two *d*; 2nd, 1989, Clare Forbes (marr. diss. 2005); 3rd, 2014, Sintayehu Oumer Mohammed; two *d*. *Educ*: Bishop Vesey's Grammar Sch., Sutton Coldfield; University Coll. London (MB BS 1968). FRCS 1973; FRCSEd *ad eundem* 2001; Hon. FRCSGlas 2004. Consultant Urologist and the surgery of renal failure, Hammersmith Hosp., 1978–2007. Chairman: Specialist Adv. Cttee Urology, 2000–04; Jt Cttee of Higher Surgical Trng, 2003–07; Prof. of Surgery, and Dean, St Paul's Millennium Med. Sch., Addis Ababa, 2007–08; Med. Dir, Addis Ababa Fistula Hosp., 2008–12. Trustee, Wings of Healing. Mem. numerous editl bds. King James IV Professor of Surgery, RCSE, 2005. Albert Schweitzer Internat. Teaching Award, Internat. Soc. of Urology, 2006; St Peter's Medal, British Assoc. of Urological Surgeons, 2008; Sir James Young Simpson Medal, RCSE, 2011; Frederick Salmon Medal, RSM, 2013. *Publications*: Urological Oncology (with J. Waxman), 1991; contrib. 32 chapters in books and over 200 articles. *Recreations*: eating Indian food, helping the developing world provide surgical care to rural areas and with such poverty and deprivation trying to understand how there could possibly be a God. *Address*: PO Box 420, Code 1056, Addis Ababa, Ethiopia.

**WILLIAMS, Air Vice-Marshal Graham Charles,** AFC 1970 and Bar 1975; FRAeS; Director, Lockheed Martin UK (formerly Loral International Inc., then Lockheed Martin International), 1993–2004; Commandant General, RAF Regiment and Director General of Security (RAF), 1990–91; *b* 4 June 1937; *s* of Charles Francis Williams and Molly (*née* Chapman); *m* 1962, Judith Teresa Ann Walker; one *s* one *d*. *Educ*: Marlborough College; RAF College, Cranwell. FRAeS 1984. 54 Sqn, 229 OCU, 8 Sqn, Empire Test Pilots' School, A Sqn, A&AEE, 1958–70; RAF Staff Coll., 1971; OC 3 Sqn, Wildenrath, 1972–74; Junior Directing Staff (Air), RCDS, 1975–77; OC RAF Brüggen, 1978–79; Group Captain Ops, HQ RAF Germany, 1980–82; CO Experimental Flying Dept, RAE, 1983; Comdt, Aeroplane and Armament Exptl Estabt, 1983–85; Dir, Operational Requirements, MoD,

1986; ACDS, Operational Requirements (Air), 1986–89. Harmon Internat. Trophy for Aviators, USA, 1970. *Publications:* Rhapsody in Blue: an RAF fighter pilot's life in the Cold War (autobiog.), 2016. *Recreations:* old cars, golf. *Address:* 5 Martinsley Lodge, Uppingham Road, Preston, Oakham, Rutland LE15 9NZ. *Club:* Royal Air Force.

**WILLIAMS, Gwyneth**; Controller, BBC Radio 4 and BBC Radio 4 Extra (formerly BBC Radio 7), 2010–19; *b* 14 July 1953; *d* of Prof. Owen Williams and Beryl Williams (*née* Harrett); *m* 1982, David Nissan; one *s* one *d*. *Educ:* St John's High Sch., Pietermaritzburg, Natal; St Hugh's Coll., Oxford (BA Hons PPE 1975; Dip. Soc. Anth. 1976; Hon. Fellow, 2011). Current affairs talks writer, BBC Bush House, 1976; Res. Asst, ODI, 1977; BBC: Prod., The World Tonight, 1979; career break to be with children, 1984–89; Prod. and Ed., various progs on Radio 4 and Radio Five Live, 1989–94; Editor: Foreign Affairs Radio, 1994; Home Current Affairs, Bi-media, 1996; Reith Lectures, 1999–2007; various special series and progs on Radio 4 and World Service; Hd, World Current Affairs, BBC News, 2004; Dir, BBC World Service English, 2007–10. Mem. Editl Bd, Political Qly, 1996–2004. Trustee, Topsy Foundn, 2014–. *Publications:* Third World Political Organizations, 1981, 2nd edn 1987; (with Brian Hackland) The Contemporary Political Dictionary of Southern Africa, 1988, 2nd edn 2015. *Recreations:* reading, music, dog walking. *Address:* 13 King Henry's Road, NW3 3QP. *T:* (020) 7586 2748.

**WILLIAMS, Heather Jean**; QC 2006; barrister; a Recorder, since 2018; a Deputy High Court Judge, since 2018; *b* 1963; *d* of Leonard Archibald Williams and Dorothy Jean Williams; *m* 1997, Trevor William Bragg; one *s* one *d*. *Educ:* King's Coll. London (LLB 1st cl. Hons 1984). Called to the Bar, Gray's Inn, 1985 (Scarman Scholarship 1985), Bencher, 2012; in practice as a barrister, 1987–. Pt-time Judge (formerly Chm.), Employment Tribunals, 2005–. *Publications:* (jtly) Police Misconduct: legal remedies, 4th edn 2005. *Recreations:* listening to music, attending concerts and festivals, spending time with my children, yoga, reading. *Address:* Doughty Street Chambers, 53–54 Doughty Street, WC1N 2LS. *T:* (020) 7404 1313, *Fax:* (020) 7404 2283/4. *E:* h.williams@doughtystreet.co.uk.

**WILLIAMS, Helen Elizabeth Webber**, MA; Principal, RNIB New College, Worcester, 1995–2000; *b* 28 April 1938; *o d* of Alwyn and Eleanor Thomas; *m* 1962, Dr Peter Williams (marr. diss. 1974); one *s* one *d*. *Educ:* Redland High Sch., Bristol; Girton Coll., Cambridge (MA; DipEd). Assistant English Mistress: St Paul's Girls' Sch., 1962–63; St George's Sch., Edinburgh, 1963–64; Edinburgh University: Asst Lectr, Dept of English, 1964–67; Lectr in English and Dir of Studies, Faculty of Arts, 1967–78; Headmistress, Blackheath High Sch., 1978–89; High Mistress, St Paul's Girls' Sch., 1989–92; Trevelyan Fellow, Trevelyan Coll., Univ. of Durham, 1993; English teacher, The Brearley Sch., NY, 1993–94. Member: HMC, 1994–2000; Governing Body, SOAS, 1988–96; Council, City Univ., 1990–92; Governing Body, Stowe Sch., 1992. *Publications:* (ed) T. S. Eliot: The Wasteland, 1968. *Recreations:* music, drama, cookery, gardening. *Address:* 4/2 Advocates Close, The Royal Mile, Edinburgh EH1 1PS.

**WILLIAMS, Helen Mary, (Mrs D. M. Forrester)**, CB 2006; Director, School Curriculum and Pupil Well-Being, Department for Education (formerly Department for Education and Skills, then Department for Children, Schools and Families), 2006–11; *b* 30 June 1950; *d* of late Graham Myatt and of Mary (*née* Harrison); *m* 1st, 1975, Ian Vaughan Williams (marr. diss. 1982); 2nd, 1993, David Michael Forrester, *qv*; one *s* one *d*. *Educ:* Allerton High Sch., Leeds; St Hilda's Coll., Oxford (MA Hons Mod. Hist.). Joined DES, 1972; Private Sec. to Joan Lester and to Margaret Jackson, 1975–76; Asst Sec., DES, subseq. DFE, 1984–93; Under-Sec., then Dir, OST, Cabinet Office, subseq. DTI, 1993–98; Dir, Sch. Orgn and Funding, DFEE, subseq. DFES, 1999–2002; Department for Education and Skills: Dir, Primary Educn and e Learning, 2002–04; Co-Dir, Sch. Standards, 2004–06. Trustee, Girls Day Sch. Trust, 2013–19. Governor: Greig City Acad., Haringey, 2011–19 (Chair, 2016–19); Prior Weston Primary Sch., Islington, 2012–15; mentor of care system leavers, 2012–15; Mem., St Mary Magdalene Educnl Trust, 2013–15. *Recreations:* bell-ringing, playing the piano, hill-walking, family history. *E:* helen.mary.forrester@gmail.com.

**WILLIAMS, (Henry) Nigel**, FRSL; author and broadcaster; *b* 20 Jan. 1948; *s* of late David Ffrancon Williams and Sylvia Margaret Williams (*née* Hartley); *m* 1973, Suzan Elizabeth Harrison; three *s*. *Educ:* Highgate Sch.; Oriel Coll., Oxford (MA Hist.). BBC: gen. trainee, 1969–73; Producer/Dir, Arts Dept, 1973–85; Editor: Bookmark, 1985–92; Omnibus, 1992–96; writer/presenter, 1997–2000. *Plays:* Class Enemy, Royal Court, 1978 (Most Promising Playwright Award, Plays and Players mag.); Sugar and Spice, Royal Court, 1980; Line 'Em, NT, 1980; Trial Run, Oxford Playhouse, 1980; My Brother's Keeper, Greenwich, 1985; Country Dancing, RSC, 1987; Lord of the Flies (adapted), RSC, 1996; My Face, NT, 2008; *television plays* include: Charlie, 1980; Breaking Up, 1986; The Last Romantics, 1990; Skallagrig, 1994 (BAFTA Award); Dirty Tricks, 2000 (Internat. Emmy Award); Bertie and Elizabeth, 2002; Uncle Adolf, 2005; Elizabeth I, 2005 (Emmy Award for outstanding mini-series, 2006; Golden Globe Award for best mini-series, 2007); Footprints in the Snow, 2005; HR, 2006; Wodehouse in Exile, 2013; Catherine the Great, 2019; *radio:* HR (series), 2009; HR2 (series), 2010; HR3 (series), 2011; HR4 (series), 2013; HR5 (series), 2014; Looking for Billy, 2016; *films:* Seawolf, 2009; BP Centenary Film, 2009; Moby Dick (adapted screenplay), 2011. FRSL 1994. *Publications:* (novels) My Life Closed Twice, 1978 (Somerset Maugham Award); Jack Be Nimble, 1980; Star Turn, 1985; Witchcraft, 1987; Black Magic, 1988; The Wimbledon Poisoner, 1990; They Came from SW19, 1992; East of Wimbledon, 1993; 2½ Men in a Boat, 1993; Scenes from a Poisoner's Life, 1994 (televised); From Wimbledon to Waco, 1995; Stalking Fiona, 1997; Fortysomething, 1999 (adapted for television, 2003); Hatchett and Lycett, 2002; Unfaithfully Yours, 2013; R.I.P., 2015. *Recreations:* swimming, drinking, walking, talking, family, dogs, Harry. *Address:* 18 Holmbush Road, Putney, SW15 3LE.

**WILLIAMS, Hugh Richard Bonneville, (Hugh Bonneville)**; actor; *b* London, 10 Nov. 1963; *s* of John Pritchard Williams, FRCS and late Patricia Williams; *m* 1998, Lulu Evans (*née* Conner); one *s*. *Educ:* Sherborne Sch.; Corpus Christi Coll., Cambridge (BA Theol. 1985). Actor: *theatre:* Midsummer Night's Dream, Romeo and Juliet, Arms and The Man, Open Air Th., Regent's Park, 1986; French Without Tears, Leicester Haymarket, 1987; Taking Steps, The Circle, Taming of the Shrew, Look Back in Anger, Dick Whittington, Siege, Colchester Mercury, 1987–88; Yerma, School for Wives, Entertaining Strangers, Juno and the Paycock, School for Scandal, The Devil's Disciple, NT, 1987–94; Two Gentlemen of Verona, The Virtuoso, 'Tis Pity She's a Whore, The Alchemist, Amphibians, Hamlet, RSC, 1991–93; Habeas Corpus, Donmar Warehouse, 1995; My Night with Reg, Criterion/Playhouse, 1996; The Handyman, Chichester Fest. Th. and tour, 1998; Us and Them, Hampstead, 2003; Cloaca, Old Vic, 2004; An Enemy of the People, Chichester Festival Th., 2016; Shadowlands, Chichester Festival Th., 2019; numerous TV and film appearances, 1990–; *television* includes: Mosley, 1998; Take a Girl Like You, 2000; The Cazalets, 2001; The Gathering Storm, 2002; Tipping the Velvet, 2002; Daniel Deronda, 2002; Love Again, 2003; The Robinsons, 2005; Tsunami: The Aftermath, 2006; The Diary of a Nobody, 2007; DSI Iain Barclay in Five Days, 2007 and Hunter, 2009; Freezing, 2007–08; Filth: The Mary Whitehouse Story, 2008; Bonekickers, 2008; Lost in Austen, 2009; Miss Austen Regrets, 2009; Ben Hur, 2010; The Silence, 2010; Downton Abbey, 2010, 2011, 2012, 2013, 2014, 2015; Twenty Twelve, 2011, 2012; Rev, 2011, 2012, 2014; Mr Stink, 2012; W1A, 2014, 2015, 2017; Galavant, 2015; The Hollow Crown: the Wars of the Roses, 2016; *films* include: Frankenstein, 1994; Notting Hill, Mansfield Park, 1999; Iris, 2002; Stage Beauty, 2004; Asylum, 2005; Scenes of a Sexual Nature, 2006; French Film, 2008 (Best Actor, Monte Carlo Comedy Film Fest., 2008); Glorious 39, 2009; Burke & Hare, From Time to Time, 2010; Third Star, 2011; The Monuments Men, Paddington, 2014; Viceroy's House, Paddington 2, Breathe, 2017; The Corrupted, Downton Abbey, 2019. Co-producer, Beautiful Thing, Duke of York's Th., 1994; co-writer and producer (with Christopher Luscombe): Half Time, Donmar Warehouse and tour, 1994. Patron: Scene and Heard, 2008–; Nat. Youth Th. of GB, 2013–. *Recreation:* enjoys getting cross about health and safety. *Address:* c/o Gordon & French Ltd, 12–13 Poland Street, W1F 8QB. *E:* mail@gordonandfrench.co.uk. *W:* www.hughbonneville.uk. *Clubs:* Garrick, Soho House.

**WILLIAMS, Hugo Mordaunt**; writer; *b* 20 Feb. 1942; *s* of late Hugh Williams, actor and playwright, and Margaret Vyner; *m* 1965, Hermine Demoriane; one *d*. *Educ:* Eton College. Asst Editor, London Magazine, 1961–70; Arts Editor, New Review, 1973–74; television critic, 1983–88, and poetry editor, 1984–93, New Statesman; theatre critic, The Sunday Correspondent, 1989–91; columnist, TLS, 1988–2014; film critic, Harpers & Queen, 1993–98; poetry editor, The Spectator, 2008–. Henfield Writer's Fellowship, Univ. of East Anglia, 1981. Awards (for poetry): Eric Gregory, 1965; Cholmondeley, 1970; Geoffrey Faber Memorial Prize, 1979; Queen's Gold Medal for Poetry, 2004. *Publications: poems:* Symptoms of Loss, 1965; Sugar Daddy, 1970; Some Sweet Day, 1975; Love-Life, 1979; Writing Home, 1985; Selected Poems, 1989; Self-Portrait With A Slide, 1990; Dock Leaves, 1994; Billy's Rain (T. S. Eliot Prize), 1999; Collected Poems, 2002; Dear Room, 2006; West End Final, 2009; I Knew the Bride, 2014; Lines Off, 2019; *travel:* All the Time in the World, 1966; No Particular Place to Go, 1981; *journalism:* Freelancing, 1995; *edited:* Curtain Call, 101 Portraits in Verse, 2001; John Betjeman, Selected Poems, 2006. *Address:* 3 Raleigh Street, N1 8NW. *T:* (020) 7226 1655.

**WILLIAMS, Hywel**; MP (Plaid Cymru) Arfon, since 2010 (Caernarfon, 2001–10); *b* 14 May 1953; *s* of late Robert Williams and of Jennie Page Williams; *m* 1st, 1977, Sian Davies (marr. diss. 1998); three *d*; 2nd, 2010, Dr Myfanwy Davies; one *s* one *d*. *Educ:* Ysgol Glan y Mor, Pwllheli, Gwynedd; UC Cardiff (BSc Hons Psychol. 1974); UCNW, Bangor (CQSW 1980). Approved Social Worker (Mental Health), 1984. Social Worker: Child Care and Long Term Team, Social Services Dept, Mid Glam CC, 1974–76; Mental Health Team, Social Services Dept, Gwynedd CC, 1976–78 and 1980–84; Welsh Office funded project worker, 1985–91, Hd of Centre, 1991–93, N and W Wales Practice Centre, UCNW, Bangor; freelance lectr, consultant and author in social work and social policy, 1994–2001. CCETSW Cymru: Mem. Welsh Cttee and Chm., Welsh Lang. Sub-cttee, 1989–92; Mem., Welsh Lang. Pubns Adv. Panel, 1992–93. *Publications:* (contrib.) Social Work in Action in the 1980s, 1985; (compiled and ed) A Social Work Vocabulary, 1988; (gen. ed.) Child Care Terms, 1993; (contrib. and gen. ed.) Social Work and the Welsh Language, 1994; (compiled and ed) An Index of Trainers and Training, 1994; (contrib. and ed jtly) Gofal: a training and resource pack for community care in Wales, 1998; Speaking the Invisible, 2002. *Recreations:* walking, cinema, reading. *Address:* House of Commons, SW1A 0AA. *T:* (020) 7219 5021; 8 Stryd Y Castell, Caernarfon, Gwynedd LL15 1SE. *T:* (01286) 672076; 70 Stryd Fawr, Bangor, Gwynedd LL57 1NR. *T:* (01248) 372948.

**WILLIAMS, Prof. Hywel Charles**, PhD, DSc; FRCP, FMedSci; Professor of Dermato-Epidemiology, University of Nottingham, since 1998; Director, NIHR Health Technology Assessment Programme, since 2016 (Director-designate, 2015); *b* Swansea, 15 July 1958; *s* of Elwyn Williams and Mair Lloyd Williams; *m* 1984, Molly Chan; one *d*. *Educ:* Cymer Afan Comp. Sch.; Glan Afan Comp. Sch.; Charing Cross Hosp. Med. Sch., Univ. of London (BSc Anatomy 1979; MB BS (Dist.) 1982); London Sch. of Hygiene and Tropical Medicine (MSc 1990); St Thomas' Hosp., Univ. of London (PhD 1994); Univ. of Nottingham (DSc 2013). FRCP 1995. Jun. doctor trng at Charing Cross Hosp., Kingston Hosp., Hammersmith Hosp., King's Coll. Hosp. and St Thomas' Hosp., 1982–93; University of Nottingham: Sen. Lectr in Dermato-Epidemiol., 1994–98; Co-Dir, Centre of Evidence Based Dermatol., 2002–; Hon. Consultant Dermatologist, Nottingham Univ. Hosps NHS Trust, 1994–. NIHR Sen. Investigator, 2008; Chm., NIHR Health Technol. Assessment Commng Bd, 2010–15; Dep. Dir, NIHR Health Technol. Assessment Prog., 2010–15. FMedSci 2014. Gold Distinction Award, NHS, 2013; Sir Archibald Gray Medal, British Assoc. of Dermatologists, 2017. *Publications:* The Challenge of Dermato-Epidemiology, 1997; Atopic Dermatitis: the epidemiology, causes and prevention of atopic eczema, 2000; Evidence-Based Dermatology, 2004, 3rd edn 2014; over 500 articles in learned jls. *Recreations:* gardening (especially delphiniums, cacti, orchids), classic cars (Member, Midland Lotus Owners Club), jazz (trombone and keyboards), marine tropical fish. *Address:* Department of Dermatology, C Floor South Block, Queen's Medical Centre, Nottingham University Hospitals NHS Trust, Nottingham NG7 2UH. *T:* (0115) 823 1048, *Fax:* (0115) 823 1046. *E:* hywel.williams@nottingham.ac.uk.

**WILLIAMS, Prof. (James) Gordon**, FRS 1994; FREng; Professor of Mechanical Engineering, Imperial College, London, 1990–2003, now Emeritus (Head, Department of Mechanical Engineering, 1990–2000); *b* 13 June 1938; *s* of John William and Eira Williams; *m* 1960, Ann Marie Joscelyne; two *s* one *d*. *Educ:* Imperial Coll. (BScEng, PhD, DScEng); FCGI; FREng (FEng 1982). RAE, Farnborough, 1956–61; Imperial College: Asst Lectr, 1962–64; Lectr, 1964–70; Reader, 1970–75; Prof. of Polymer Engrg, 1975–90. Vis. Prof., Univ. of Sydney, 2001–. *Publications:* Stress Analysis of Polymers, 1973, 2nd edn 1981; Fracture Mechanics of Polymers, 1984. *Recreations:* gardening, mountains (walking and skiing), golf. *Address:* Mechanical Engineering Department, Imperial College London, Exhibition Road, South Kensington, SW7 2BX. *T:* (020) 7594 7200.

**WILLIAMS, Jane**; former independent adviser to further education; Executive Director for Further Education and 14 to 19 (formerly Skills and Regeneration, later Further Education, Regeneration and Delivery), Becta (formerly British Education Communications Technology Agency), 2007–11; *b* 13 April 1953; *d* of John and Gwenllian Williams; *m* 1993, Robert Walker; one *s* one *d*. *Educ:* Univ. of Bristol (BA Hons); Univ. of Birmingham (Cert Ed). Teacher, Swanshurst Sch., 1975–78; Lectr, Bournville Coll., 1979–81; Sen. Lectr, Telford Coll., 1981–84; Principal Lectr, Accredited Training Centre, Telford, 1984–89; Asst Principal, Solihull Coll., 1989–92; Vice Principal, North Warwickshire Coll., Nuneaton, 1992–96; Principal: Wulfrun Coll., Wolverhampton, 1996–99; City of Wolverhampton Coll., 1999–2002; Dir, Teaching and Learning, and Head, Standards Unit, subseq. Dir, Improvement Gp, DFES, 2003–07. Chairman: Focus Housing Assoc., 2000–02; Wolverhampton Strategic Partnership, 2002; Ind. Quality Bd, Energy and Utility Skills, 2013–15. Mem. Bd, NHS (formerly NHS W Midlands) Quality Review Service, 2019– (Lay Mem., 2015; Chm., Quality Assurance Gp, 2015–19). Mem. Bd, Ufi Ltd, 2008–12. Mem., Corporation, Birmingham Metropolitan Coll., 2010–14 (Vice Chair, 2010–14). Trustee, Royal Birmingham Conservatoire Assoc. (formerly Birmingham Conservatoire Assoc.), 2015–. FRSA 1999–2016. Hon. DEd Wolverhampton, 2003. *Recreations:* music, travel, painting. *E:* jw@jane-williams.co.uk.

**WILLIAMS, (Jean) Adèle**, (Mrs A. Patience); DL; **Her Honour Judge Williams**; a Circuit Judge, since 2000; *b* 28 July 1950; *d* of David James Williams and Dorothy Williams; *m* 1975, Andrew Patience, *qv*; one *s* one *d*. *Educ*: Llanelli Girls' Grammar Sch.; University Coll. London (LLB). Called to the Bar, Gray's Inn, 1972; in practice on S Eastern Circuit, 1972–2000; a Recorder, 1995–2000; Resident Judge, Canterbury Crown Court, 2008–16; Hon. Recorder of Canterbury, 2016. Sen., Kent Bar Mess, 1997–2000. DL Kent, 2015. *Recreations*: cinema, theatre, holidays, conversation. *Address*: Maidstone Crown Court, The Law Courts, Barker Road, Maidstone, Kent ME16 8EQ.

**WILLIAMS, Jennifer Mary, (Jenny)**; Commissioner and Chief Executive, Gambling Commission (formerly Gaming Board for Great Britain), 2004–15; *b* 26 Sept. 1948; *d* of Baron Donaldson of Lymington, PC, and Dame (Dorothy) Mary Donaldson, GBE; *m* 1970, Michael Lodwig Williams, *qv*; three *s*. *Educ*: New Hall, Cambridge (BA 1970). Joined Home Office, 1973; Dir, PSA Privatisation and Strategy, DoE, 1990–93; Dir, Railways Privatisation and Regulation Directorate, Dept of Transport, 1993–97; Dir, Local Govt Finance Policy, DoE, later DETR, 1997–98; Dir, Company, later Business, Tax Div., Bd of Inland Revenue, 1998–2000; Dir Gen., Judicial Gp, and Sec. of Commns, LCD, 2001–03. Non-exec. Dir, Northumbrian Water Gp PLC, 2006–10. Ind. Dir, Greyhound Regulatory Bd, 2015–; Member: Bd, Fundraising Regulator, 2016–; Adv. Bd, Univ. of Nevada Las Vegas Internat. Center for Gaming Regulation, 2016–. Board Member: The Connection at St Martin's, 2004–16 (Vice-Chm., 2012–16); Nat. Campaign for the Arts, 2004–07. Trustee: Internat. Assoc. of Gaming Regulators, 2011–14; Fight for Sight, 2016–]. Non-exec. Dir, Morley Coll., 1993–2000. *Address*: 46 Durand Gardens, SW9 0PP.

**WILLIAMS, John**, AO 1987; OBE 1980; guitarist; *b* Melbourne, 24 April 1941. Studied with father, Segovia and at the Accademia Musicale Chigiana, Siena and RCM, London; since when has given recitals, concerts, and made TV and radio appearances worldwide. Mem., Sky, 1979–84. Artistic Dir, South Bank Summer Music, 1984 and 1985; Artistic Dir, Melbourne Arts Fest., 1987. Wide range of recordings with other musicians including Julian Bream, John Dankworth and Cleo Laine, NYJO, Itzhak Perlman, Inti Illimani, etc, and many orchestras. Hon. FRCM; Hon. FRNCM. *Recreations*: people, living, chess, table-tennis, music. *Address*: c/o Askonas Holt Ltd, 15 Fetter Lane, EC4A 1BW.

**WILLIAMS, John**; Visiting Fellow, Department of War Studies and Centre for Strategic Communication, King's College London, since 2017; *b* 20 Feb. 1954; *s* of Roy and Barbara Williams; *m* 1976, Pamela Blackburn; two *s* one *d*. *Educ*: Sir Roger Manwood's Sch., Sandwich. Reporter: Chatham News, 1973–77; Birmingham Evening Mail, 1977–80; Industrial Corresp., 1980–85, Political Corresp., 1985–93, London Evening Standard; political columnist, Daily Mirror, 1993–98; Dep. Hd, News Dept, FCO, 1998–2000; Press Sec., FCO, 2000–04; Dir, Communications, FCO, 2004–06; freelance consultant to Palestinian Authy, Syrian Opposition and others, 2006–19. *Publications*: Victory, 1997; Robin Cook: principles and power, 2015; (jtly) Strategic Communication, 2018. *Recreations*: gardening, guitar, books, family, walking. *Address*: Cherry Trees, Fore Street, Weston, Hitchin, Herts SG4 7AS. *T*: (01462) 790536.

**WILLIAMS, John**, FRICS; Director, Aston Rose Chartered Surveyors, since 2000; *b* 18 March 1968; *s* of David and Chantal Williams. *Educ*: Epsom Coll.; Univ. of Reading (BSc Hons Est. Mgt 1990). ARICS 1992, FRICS 1998. Dir, Ernest Owers & Williams, 1986–2000. Royal Institution of Chartered Surveyors: Nat. Jun. Org. Cttee, 1988–2003, Chm., Nat. Jun. Org., 2000–01; Member: Gen. Council, 1999–2001; Internat. Governing Council, 2001–06; Sen. Vice Pres., 2004–05. Nat. Judge, RICS Awards, 2016. Lionheart: Steward, 1988–2000; Fundraising Cttee, 1989–2001; Trustee, 2000–07. Liveryman, Chartered Surveyors' Co., 2002– (Property, Advertising, Mktg and Design Awards Cttee (PAMADA), 2002–07). *Recreations*: ski-ing, reading, film, cooking. *Address*: Aston Rose, St Albans House, 57/59 Haymarket, SW1Y 4QX. *T*: (020) 7629 1533, *Fax*: (020) 7925 2492. *E*: johnwilliams@astonrose.co.uk.

**WILLIAMS, (John Bucknall) Kingsley**; solicitor, retired; *b* 28 July 1927; *s* of Charles Kingsley Williams and Margaret Elizabeth (*née* Bucknall); *m* 1st, 1961, Brenda (*née* Baldwin) (marr. diss. 2001); two *s*; 2nd, 2001, Eleanor Marion Yates. *Educ*: Kingswood Sch., Bath; Trinity Hall, Cambridge (MA, LLB). Partner, Dutton Gregory & Williams, Solicitors, Winchester, 1956–91. Chm., Wessex RHA, 1975–82. Member: Winchester City Council, 1966–73; Hampshire CC, 1973–75; Assoc. of County Councils, 1973–75. Chairman: Exec. Cttee, NHS Supply Council, 1980–82; Adv. Cttee, Wessex Inst. of Public Health Medicine, 1991–96. Chm. Council, Southampton Univ., 1987–98 (Mem., 1977–98); Chm. of Governors, Winchester Sch. of Art, 1986–96. DUniv Southampton, 1999. *Address*: Danesacre, Worthy Road, Winchester, Hants SO23 7AD. *T*: (01962) 852594.

**WILLIAMS, John Charles**, OBE 1997; PhD; FREng; Secretary and Chief Executive, Institution of Electrical Engineers, 1989–99; *b* 17 July 1938; *s* of Frank and Miriam Williams; *m* 1968, Susan Winifred Ellis; two *s* one *d*. *Educ*: High Wycombe Royal GS; Queen Mary Coll. (BScEng (1st Cl. Hons), 1960; PhD 1964; Fellow, 1995). Philips Research Labs, 1964–78; GEC Marconi Space and Defence Systems, Stanmore, 1978–80; GEC Central Res. Labs, Wembley, 1980–82; GEC Marconi Res. Centre, Gt Baddow, 1982–88. Freeman, City of London, 1996. FREng (FEng 1990). Hon. FIEE 2000. *Recreations*: traditional jazz, contract bridge, walking, gardening, tennis, listening to his family play music, enjoying company of his grandson Arturo, learning the art of church bell ringing. *Address*: Beightons, Bassetts Lane, Little Baddow, Chelmsford, Essex CM3 4DA. *T*: (01245) 225092. *E*: johnchaswilliams@btinternet.com.

**WILLIAMS, Rt Rev. (John) Christopher (Richard)**; Bishop of The Arctic, 1991–2002; *b* 22 May 1936; *s* of Frank Harold and Ceridwen Roberts Williams; *m* 1964, Rona Macrae (*née* Aitken); one *s* one *d*. *Educ*: Manchester Grammar Sch.; Univ. of Manchester (BA Comm); Univ. of Durham, Cranmer Hall (DipTh). Ordained: deacon, Stretford, England, 1960; priest, Sugluk, PQ, 1962; Missionary, Diocese of The Arctic: Sugluk, PQ, 1961–72; Cape Dorset, NWT, 1972–75; Baker Lake, NWT, 1975–78; Archdeacon of The Keewatin, 1975–87; Rector, Yellowknife, NWT, 1978–87; Bp Suffragan, 1987–90, Coadjutor Bp, 1990, Dio. of The Arctic. Hon. DD: Emmanuel and St Chad Coll., Saskatoon, 1997; Wycliffe Coll., Toronto Univ., 2000. Queen's Diamond Jubilee Medal, 2013. *Recreations*: stage and piano, Canada 55+ Games (swimming). *Address*: 4916–44th Street, Yellowknife, NT X1A 1J8, Canada.

**WILLIAMS, John Eirwyn F.**; *see* Ffowcs Williams.

**WILLIAMS, Hon. Sir John G.**; *see* Griffith Williams.

**WILLIAMS, John Leighton**; QC 1986; a Recorder of the Crown Court, 1985–2014; a Deputy High Court Judge, 1995–2014; *b* 15 Aug. 1941; *s* of Reginald John Williams and Beatrice Beynon; *m* 1969, Sally Elizabeth Williams; two *s*. *Educ*: Neath Boys' Grammar School; King's College London (LLB); Trinity Hall, Cambridge (MA). Called to the Bar, Gray's Inn, 1964, Bencher, 1994 (Vice-Treas., 2009; Treas. 2010). Mem., Criminal Injuries Compensation Bd, 1987–2002. Mem. Council, Med. Protection Soc., 1998–2007. *Address*: c/o Farrar's Building, Temple, EC4Y 7BD. *T*: (020) 7583 9241.

**WILLIAMS, John Llewellyn**, CBE 1999; FRCS, FRCSE, FDSRCS, FDSRCSE, FRCA; Consultant Oral and Maxillofacial Surgeon, St Richard's Hospital, Chichester, Worthing and Southlands Hospitals, Worthing and St Luke's Hospital, Guildford, 1973–2003, now Hon. Consultant Emeritus; Vice-President, Royal College of Surgeons of England, 1997–99; *b* 24 Jan. 1938; *s* of David John Williams and Anne Rosamund Williams (*née* White); *m* 1960, Gillian Joy Morgan; three *d*. *Educ*: Christ's Hosp.; Guy's Hosp. Med. Sch. (MB BS, BDS). FDSRCS 1966; FRCSE 1991; FRCS 1996; FRCA 2000; FDSRCSE *ad hominem* 2000. Registrar in Oral and Maxillofacial Surgery, Plymouth, 1970; Sen. Registrar, Westminster Hosp., UCH and Queen Mary's, Roehampton, 1970–73; Postgrad. Tutor, BMPF, 1973–95; Hon. Consultant: Queen Mary's, Roehampton, 1974–2003; King Edward VII Hosp., Midhurst, 1974–2006; Hon. Clinical Tutor, Guy's and St Thomas', subseq. Guy's, King's and St Thomas' Hosps' Med. and Dental Sch. of KCL, 1976–2003. Hon. Consultant to Army, Cambridge Hosp., 1992–. Chairman: Nat. Cttee of Enquiry into Peri-operative Deaths, 1998–2003; Cttee on Safety of Devices, Med. Devices Agency, DoH, 2001–09; non-exec. Dir, Medicines and Healthcare Products Regulatory Agency Bd, 2009–. Dean, Faculty of Dental Surgery, RCS, 1996–99; Vice Chm., Acad. of Med. Royal Colls, 1998–2000; President: Eur. Assoc. for Cranio-Maxillofacial Surgery, 1998–2000; BAOMS, 2000; Internat. Assoc. of Oral and Maxillofacial Surgeons, 2005–07 (Pres.-elect, 2003–05); Chm., Oral and Maxillofacial Surgery Foundn, 2007–. Mem. Ct of Patrons, RCS, 2004–. Hon. Fellow: Amer. Assoc. Oral and Maxillofacial Surgeons, 1998; Aust. and NZ Assoc. of Oral and Maxillofacial Surgeons, 1999; Hon. Life Mem., BDA, 2010. Evelyn Sprawson Prize, RCS, 1961; Down Surgical Prize, BAOMS, 1996; John Tomes Medallist, BDA, 1998; Colyer Gold Medallist, RCS, 2000. *Publications*: (with N. L. Rowe) Maxillofacial Injuries, Vols I and II, 1985, 2nd edn 1994; (with P. Stoelinga) 50 Years of the IAOMS: the development of the specialty, 2012; contribs to Brit. Dental Jl, RCS Annals. *Recreations*: gardening (garden open under Nat. Gardens Scheme), sailing (RYA Race Training Instructor). *Address*: Cookscroft, Bookers Lane, Earnley, Chichester, W Sussex PO20 7JG. *T*: (01243) 513671. *Clubs*: Oral Surgery of Great Britain; Hayling Island Sailing.

**WILLIAMS, Prof. (John) Mark (Gruffydd)**, DSc; FBPsS; FBA 2008; FMedSci; Professor of Clinical Psychology, University of Oxford, 2004–13, now Emeritus, and Honorary Research Fellow, since 2014; Fellow of Linacre College, Oxford, 2004–13, now Emeritus; Director, Oxford Mindfulness Centre, 2008–13; *b* 23 July 1952; *s* of John Howard Williams and Anna Barbara Mary Williams (*née* Wright); *m* 1973, Phyllis Patricia Simpson; one *s* two *d*. *Educ*: Stockton-on-Tees Grammar Sch.; St Peter's Coll., Oxford (BA 1973; MSc 1976; MA 1977; DPhil 1979; DSc 1998); E Anglian Ministerial Trng Course. FBPsS 1984. Lecturer in: Psychology, Magdalen Coll., Oxford, 1977–79; Applied Psychology, Univ. of Newcastle upon Tyne, 1979–82; Scientist, then Sen. Scientist, MRC Applied Psychol. Unit, Cambridge, 1983–91; University College of North Wales (Bangor) subseq. University of Wales, Bangor: Prof. of Clinical Psychology, 1991–97; Dir, Centre for Medical and Health Scis, subseq. Inst. for Med. and Social Care Res., 1997–2002; Pro Vice-Chancellor, 1997–2001; Wellcome Principal Res. Fellow, Dept of Psychiatry, Univ. of Oxford, 2003–12. Member: Grants Cttee, Neuroscis Bd, MRC, 1992–96; Neuroscis & Mental Health Panel, Wellcome Trust, 1997–2001; Panel Mem. for Psychology, RAE 2001. Ordained deacon, Ely, 1989, priest 1990; Asst Curate (NSM), Girton, 1989–91; permission to officiate, dio. of Bangor, 1991–2003; Asst Curate, 2003–08, Associate Priest (NSM), 2008–10, Wheatley. Hon. Canon, Christchurch Cathedral, Oxford, 2011. Gov., NE Wales Inst. of Higher Educn, 1999–2001. FMedSci 2004. *Publications*: Psychological Treatment of Depression, 1983, 2nd edn 1992; (jtly) Cognitive Psychology and Emotional Disorders, 1988, 2nd edn 1997; (with F. Watts) The Psychology of Religious Knowing, 1988; (jtly) Cognitive Therapy and Clinical Practice, 1989; Cry of Pain: understanding suicide and self-harm, 1997; (with Z. Segal and J. D. Teasdale) Mindfulness-based Cognitive Therapy for Depression: a new approach to preventing relapse, 2002; Suicide and Attempted Suicide, 2002; (jtly) The Mindful Way Through Depression: freeing yourself from chronic unhappiness, 2007; (with D. Penman) Mindfulness: a practical guide to finding peace in a frantic world, 2011; (with J. Kabat-Zinn) Mindfulness: diverse perspectives on its meanings, origins and applications, 2013; (jtly) The Mindful Way Workbook, 2013; Cry of Pain: understanding suicide and the suicidal mind, 2014; (jtly) Mindfulness and the Transformation of Despair: working with people at risk of suicide, 2015; (jtly) Mindfulness-Based Cognitive Therapy with People at Risk of Suicide, 2017; papers in scientific jls on psychological models and treatment of depression and suicidal behaviour. *Recreations*: piano, walking, playing with grandson. *Address*: Oxford Mindfulness Centre, Department of Psychiatry, University of Oxford, Warneford Hospital, Oxford OX3 7JX.

**WILLIAMS, John Peter Rhys**, MBE 1977; FRCSEd; Consultant in Trauma and Orthopaedic Surgery, Princess of Wales Hospital, Bridgend, 1986–2004; *b* 2 March 1949; *s* of Peter Williams, MB, BCh and Margaret Williams, MB, BCh; *m* 1973, Priscilla Parkin, MB, BS, DObst, RCOG, DA; one *s* three *d*. *Educ*: Bridgend Grammar School; Millfield; St Mary's Hosp. Med. School. MB, BS London 1973; LRCP, MRCS, 1973; Primary FRCS 1976; FRCSEd 1980. University Hosp., Cardiff, Battle Hosp., Reading, St Mary's Hosp., London, 1973–78; Surgical Registrar, 1978–80, Orthopaedic Registrar, 1980–82, Cardiff Gp of Hosps; Sen. Orthopaedic Registrar, St Mary's Hosp., London, 1982–86. Played Rugby for Bridgend, 1967–68, 1976–79 (Captain, 1978–79), 1980–81, for London Welsh, 1968–76; 1st cap for Wales, 1969 (Captain, 1978); British Lions tours 1971, 1974; a record 55 caps for Wales, to 1981; won Wimbledon Lawn Tennis Junior Championship, 1966. *Publications*: JPR (autobiog.), 1979; JPR: Given the Breaks - My Life in Rugby (autobiog.), 2006. *Recreations*: sport and music. *Address*: Llansannor Lodge, Llansannor, near Cowbridge, South Glamorgan CF71 7RX. *Club*: Lord's Taverners.

**WILLIAMS, John Towner**; composer of film scores; *b* 8 Feb. 1932. *Educ*: Juilliard Sch., NY. Conductor, Boston Pops Orchestra, 1980–93, then Laureate. Hon. DMus: Berklee Coll. of Music, Boston, 1980; St Anselm Coll., Manchester, NH, 1981; Boston Conservatory of Music, 1982; Hon. DHL S Carolina, 1981; Hon. Dr of Fine Arts Northeastern Univ. (Boston), 1981; Hon. DMus: William Woods Coll., USA, 1982; Juilliard Sch., 2004. 40 Acad. Award nominations and five Awards for: Fiddler on the Roof (filmscore arrangement), 1971; Jaws, 1976; Star Wars, 1978; E. T., 1983; Schindler's List, 1994; 18 Grammies, 2 Emmys, 14 Golden Globes and many other awards. Kennedy Center Honor, 2004. *Composer of film scores* including: The Secret Ways, 1961; Diamond Head, 1962; None but the Brave, 1965; How to Steal a Million, 1966; Valley of the Dolls, 1967; The Cowboys, 1972; The Poseidon Adventure, 1972; Tom Sawyer, 1973; Earthquake, 1974; The Towering Inferno, 1974; Jaws, 1975; Jaws 2, 1976; The Eiger Sanction, 1975; Family Plot, 1976; Midway, 1976; The Missouri Breaks, 1976; Black Sunday, 1977; Star Wars, 1977; Close Encounters of the 3rd Kind, 1977; The Fury, 1978; Superman, 1978; Dracula, 1979; The Empire Strikes Back, 1980; Raiders of the Lost Ark, 1981; E. T. (The Extra Terrestrial), 1982; Return of the Jedi, 1983; Indiana Jones and the Temple of Doom, 1984; Empire of the Sun, 1988; Indiana Jones and the Last Crusade, Born on the Fourth of July, 1989; Home Alone, 1990; Hook, JFK, 1991; Home Alone 2, Far and Away, 1992; Jurassic Park, 1993; Schindler's List, 1994; The Lost World, Seven Years in Tibet, 1997; Amistad, Saving Private Ryan, 1998; Star Wars, Episode I: The Phantom Menace, Angela's Ashes, 1999; The Patriot, 2000; AI, Harry Potter and the Philosopher's Stone, 2001; Star

Wars, Episode II: Attack of the Clones, Minority Report, Harry Potter and the Chamber of Secrets, 2002; Catch Me if You Can, 2003; The Terminal, Harry Potter and the Prisoner of Azkaban, 2004; Star Wars, Episode III: Revenge of the Sith, War of the Worlds, 2005; Munich, 2005; Memoirs of a Geisha, 2006; Indiana Jones and the Kingdom of the Crystal Skull, 2008; Harry Potter and the Half-Blood Prince, 2009; War Horse, 2012; Lincoln, 2013; The Book Thief, 2014; Star Wars: The Force Awakens, 2015; The BFG, 2016; The Post, 2018; many TV films. Lifetime Achievement Award, American Film Inst., 2016. *Address*: c/o Gorfaine/Schwartz Agency Inc., 4111 W Alameda Avenue, Suite 509, Burbank, CA 91505, USA.

**WILLIAMS, Rev. Prof. John Tudno,** PhD; FLSW; Professor of Biblical Studies, 1973–2003, Principal, 1998–2003, United Theological College, Aberystwyth; Moderator of the General Assembly, Presbyterian Church of Wales, 2006–07 (Moderator of the Association in the South, 2002–03); *b* 31 Dec. 1938; *s* of late Rev. Arthur Tudno Williams and Primrose (*née* Hughes Parry); *m* 1964, Ina Lloyd-Evans; one *s* one *d*. *Educ*: Liverpool Inst. High School; Colfe's GS, Lewisham; Jesus Coll., Oxford (MA); UCW, Aberystwyth (PhD); United Theol Coll., Aberystwyth. Ordained as Welsh Presbyterian Minister, 1963; Minister in Borth, Cards, 1963–73; Part-time Lecturer: United Theol Coll., 1966–73; UCW (Religious Studies), 1976–87; Tutor responsible for Religious Studies, external degree through medium of Welsh, UCW, 1984–2003; Dean, Aberystwyth and Lampeter Sch. of Theology, 1985–87, 1994–97. Vis. Prof., Acadia Divinity Coll., Nova Scotia, 1997. Margaret and Ann Eilian Owen Fellow, Nat. Liby of Wales, 2001–; Hon. Res. Fellow, Univ. of Wales Trinity St David (formerly Univ. of Wales Lampeter), 2003–. Moderator, Free Church Federal Council, 1990–91. Secretary: Theology Section, Univ. of Wales Guild of Graduates, 1967–2003; Educn Cttee, Gen. Assembly of Presbyterian Church of Wales, 1979–2000; Bd of Trustees, Davies Lecture, 1983– (Lectr, 1993). External examr, QUB, Sheffield Univ., Univ. of Glos and Univ. of Wales, Bangor; examiner in religious studies and member of various educn cttees. Mem., Aberystwyth Town Council, 1979–87. FLSW 2012. Hon. DD Wales, 2006. *Publications*: Cewri'r Ffydd (Heroes of the Faith), 1974, 2nd edn 1979; Problem Dioddefaint a Llyfr Job (The Problem of Suffering and the Book of Job), 1980; Yr Epistol Cyntaf at y Corinthiaid (Commentary on I Corinthians), 1991; Y Llythyrau at y Galatiaid a'r Philipiaid (Commentary on the Letters to the Galatians and to the Philippians), 2001; contrib. to: Studia Biblica, 1978, Vol. ii 1980; C. H. Dodd, The Centenary Lectures, 1985; You Shall Be My Witnesses: festschrift for A. A. Trites, 2003; Protestant Nonconformity in the Twentieth Century, 2003; Ecumenical and Eclectic: festschrift for Alan Sell, 2007; The Reception of the Hebrew Bible in the Septuagint and the New Testament, 2013; Dictionary of Welsh Biography; contrib. T. & T. Clark Companion to Nonconformity, 2013; articles in Welsh jls, Expository Times; contrib. Hanes Methodistiaeth Galfinaidd Cymru (The History of Welsh Calvinistic Methodism), Vol. IV, 2017; Diwinyddiaeth Paul (Paul's Theology), 2019; *festschrift*: The Bible in Church, Academy and Culture: essays in honour of the Reverend Dr John Tudno Williams (ed Alan P. Sell), 2011. *Recreations*: music (singing), Welsh language and culture. *Address*: Brynawel, Capel Seion, Aberystwyth SY23 4EF. *T*: (01970) 880489.

**WILLIAMS, Dr Jonathan Hugh Creer,** FSA, FRHistS, FLSW; Deputy Director, British Museum, since 2013; *b* 19 Aug. 1967; *s* of Hugh Williams and Ann Williams (*née* Creer); *m* 2001, Konstanze Scharring; one *s* one *d*. *Educ*: Birkenhead Sch.; University Coll., Oxford (MA Classics); St Hugh's Coll., Oxford (DPhil Ancient Hist. 1994). Lectr in Ancient Hist., St Anne's Coll., Oxford, 1992–93; British Museum: Curator, Iron Age and Roman Coins, 1993–2005; Internat. Policy Manager, 2006–07; Keeper, Dept of Prehistory and Europe, 2007–12; Dir of Collections, 2012–13. Member, Board: British Mus. Co., 2009–; Fulham Palace Trust, 2011–14; Mem., UNESCO UK Culture Cttee, 2009–11. Sec., Royal Numismatic Soc., 2001–05. FRHistS 2005; FSA 2007; FLSW 2015. Hon. DArts Kingston, 2016. *Publications*: (ed jtly) Money, A History, 1997, 2nd edn 2007; (with C. Cheesman) Rebels, Pretenders and Imposters, 2000; Beyond the Rubicon: Gauls and Romans in Republican Italy, 2001; articles on ancient hist. and coins in learned jls. *Address*: Directorate, British Museum, Great Russell Street, WC1B 3DG. *E*: jwilliams@britishmuseum.org.

**WILLIAMS, Jonathan R.;** *see* Rees-Williams.

**WILLIAMS, Prof. (Jonquil) Fiona,** OBE 2004; PhD; FBA 2016; FAcSS; Professor of Social Policy, University of Leeds, 1996–2012, now Professor Emeritus; *b* Rugby, 22 July 1947; *d* of Leonard and Celia Williams; one *s* one *d*. *Educ*: Ilkley Grammar Sch.; Bedford Coll., Univ. of London (BSc Hons Sociol. and Social Admin 1968); Open Univ. (PhD 1993). Commonwealth Schol., Univ. of Ibadan, 1968–70; pt-time Lectr, Kilburn Poly., 1970–72; Lectr, N London Poly., 1972–75; pt-time Lectr, 1981–85, Res. Officer, 1985–87, Plymouth Poly.; Res. Officer, Leeds Poly., 1987–88; Lectr, 1988–92, Sen. Lectr, 1992–95, Open Univ.; Prof. of Applied Social Studies, Bradford Univ., 1995–96; Prof., Social Policy Res. Centre, 2010–14, Hon. Prof., 2014–, Univ. of NSW; Res. Associate, Centre on Migration, Policy and Society, Univ. of Oxford, 2012–. Dir, ESRC Res. Gp, Care, Values and the Future of Welfare, 1999–2005. Social Scis Ed., Jl of British Acad., 2017–. FAcSS 2003; FRSA. *Publications*: Social Policy: a critical introduction: issues of race, gender and class, 1989; (ed jtly) 'Know me as I am': an anthology of prose, poetry and art from people with learning disabilities, 1990; (ed jtly) Community Care: a reader, 1993, 2nd edn 1997; (ed jtly) Welfare Research: a critical review, 1999; Rethinking Families, 2004; (jtly) Gendering Citizenship in Western Europe, 2007; contribs on gender, race, social policy, migration and the ethics of care. *Recreations*: writing poetry (founder member, The Wharfedale Poets, 2010–), walking, wild swimming, gardening, family and friends, listening to music, cinema.

**WILLIAMS, Dame Josephine,** DBE 2007 (CBE 2000); DL; Chair, Alder Hey Children's NHS Foundation Trust, since 2019; *b* 8 July 1948; *d* of Frank Heald and Catherine Heald; *m* 1980, Robert Williams; two step *s*. *Educ*: Univ. of Keele (BA Hons Sociol. and Soc. Studies 1970; Dip. Applied Soc. Work 1971). Social Services in North West, for 20 yrs; Director Social Services: Wigan MBC, 1992–97; Cheshire CC, 1997–2002; Chief Exec., Royal Mencap Soc., 2002–08. Comr, 2008–12, Chair, 2010–13, Care Quality Commn; Chair, Prison Reform Trust, 2009–11. Pres., Assoc. of Dirs of Social Services, 1999–2000. Trustee: EveryChild, 2004–16 (Vice Chair, 2011–13; Chair, 2013–16); Dartington Hall Trust, 2010–. FCGI 2009. DL Cheshire, 2009. *Recreations*: running, tennis, ballet, travel, cooking for family and friends.

**WILLIAMS, Dame Judi;** *see* Dench, Dame J. O.

**WILLIAMS, Prof. Julie,** CBE 2012; PhD; Professor of Neuropsychological Genetics, since 2001, and Director, Dementia Research Institute, since 2017, Cardiff University; *b* Merthyr Tydfil, 11 Sept. 1957; *d* of Eric Valentine Baker and Jean Terry Baker; *m* 1976, John Glenville Williams; two *d*. *Educ*: Cardiff Univ. (BSc Occupational Psychol.; PhD). Cardiff University: Hd, Neurodegeneration Section, MRC Centre for Neuropsychiatric Genetics and Genomics; Dean of Res., Med. Sch. Former Mem., MRC Neurosci. and Mental Health Bd. Chief Scientific Adviser: Alzheimer's Research UK, 2008; for Wales, 2013–17. *Publications*: over 140 articles in jls incl. Lancet, Nature Genetics, New England Jl of Medicine. *Address*: Haydn Ellis Building, Cardiff University, Maindy Road, Cathays, Cardiff CF24 4HQ. *E*: williamsj@cardiff.ac.uk.

**WILLIAMS, Juliet Susan Durrant,** CBE 2009; Founder Director, Strategic Management Resources Ltd, since 1991; *b* 17 April 1943; *d* of Robert Noel Williams and Frances Alice Williams (*née* Durrant). *Educ*: Cheltenham Ladies' Coll.; Bedford Coll., Univ. of London (BSc Hons Geog. with Econs); Hughes Hall, Cambridge (PGCE (Dist.)). Commng Ed., Macmillan, 1966–68; Ed., Geographical Mag., 1968–73; Marketing Dir and Gen. Manager, Readers' Union, 1973–78; CEO, Marshall Cavendish Mail Order, 1978–82; Man. Dir, Brann Direct Marketing, 1983–89; CEO, Marketing Communications Div., BIS Gp, 1985–91; Chairman: Alden Gp Ltd, 1993–2007; Waddie & Co., Edinburgh, 1996–99. Chairman: SW RDA, 2002–09; SW Regl Employment and Skills Partnership, 2005–09; Dir, VisitBritain, 2005–09. Non-exec. Dir, Oxfam, 1984–90. Mem., Industrial Develt Adv. Bd, DTI, 2003–09. Chm. of Govs, Univ. (formerly Univ. Coll.) of St Mark and St John, Plymouth, 2012–15. FRGS 1968. DUniv Oxford Brookes, 2005; Hon. PhD Gloucestershire, 2010. *Publications*: papers and articles in jls, magazines and newspapers. *Recreations*: writing, sport (esp. sailing, motorsport, Welsh Rugby), the sea, the countryside, walking, gundogs. *Address*: PO Box 54, Newton Abbot, Devon TQ12 5AP. *T*: (01626) 361655, 07831 097946. *E*: juliet@strategic-management-resources.co.uk.

**WILLIAMS, Katherine Frances Maria D.;** *see* Dienes-Williams.

**WILLIAMS, Katherine Lyndsay;** *see* Mavor, K. L.

**WILLIAMS, Prof. Katherine Ruth, (Kate),** DPhil; historian and writer. *Educ*: Edgbaston High Sch., Birmingham; Somerville Coll., Oxford (BA Hons; DPhil); Queen Mary, Univ. of London (MA); Royal Holloway, Univ. of London (MA). Lectr in Creative Writing, Royal Holloway, Univ. of London; Prof. of Public Engagement with History, Univ. of Reading, 2015–. *Publications*: England's Mistress: the infamous life of Emma Hamilton, 2006; Becoming Queen: Princess Charlotte and Queen Victoria, 2008; (jtly) The Ring and the Crown: a history of royal weddings 1066–2011, 2011; The Pleasures of Men (novel), 2012; Young Elizabeth: the making of our Queen, 2012; Josephine: desire, ambition, Napoleon, 2013; The Storms of War: 1914–1918, 2014; The Edge of the Fall, 2016; The House of Shadows, 2018; Rival Queens: the betrayal of Mary, Queen of Scots, 2018. *Recreations*: dry and dusty documents, family trees, parish registers, living in the past, drinking hot water. *Address*: Department of History, University of Reading, Whiteknights, PO Box 217, Reading RG6 6AH.

**WILLIAMS, Kathryn;** *see* Maitland, K.

**WILLIAMS, Kathryn Jean;** *see* Wade, K. J.

**WILLIAMS, Katrina Jane,** CB 2016; Deputy Permanent Representative, UK Permanent Representation to the European Union, since 2017; *b* 30 July 1962; *d* of Ian Clive Williams and June Elizabeth Williams (*née* Dedman); *m* 2005, Paul Allen Green. *Educ*: Cheadle Hulme Sch.; Lady Margaret Hall, Oxford (BA Hons English Lang. and Lit.). MAFF, London, 1983–93; First Sec. (Agriculture), UK Perm. Representation to EU, 1993–96; Hd of Br., EU Div., MAFF, 1996–98; Principal Private Sec. to Minister of Agriculture, Fisheries and Food, 1998–99; Counsellor (Agric., Fisheries and Food), UK Perm. Repn to EU, Brussels, 1999–2003; Dep. Hd, Eur. Secretariat, Cabinet Office, 2003–06; Department for Environment, Food and Rural Affairs: Dir, Transmissible Spongiform Encephalopathies, later Food and Farming, 2006–08; Dir Gen., Food and Farming, 2008–12; Dir Gen., Strategy, Evidence and Customers, 2012–13; Dir Gen., Internat., Sci. and Resilience, DECC, then BEIS, 2013–17. Hon. Nat. Chm., Civil Service Retirement Fellowship, 2004–09. *Address*: c/o Foreign and Commonwealth Office, King Charles Street, SW1A 2AH.

**WILLIAMS, Keith Ronald,** FRIBA; architect; Design Director and Founder, Keith Williams Architects, since 2001; *b* 21 April 1958; *s* of Ronald Albert Williams and Sheila Lillian Grace Williams (*née* Dobson); *m* 2002, Vanessa Lillian Shrimpton. *Educ*: Kingston Grammar Sch.; Kingston Sch. of Architecture (BA Hons 1979); Greenwich Sch. of Architecture (DipArch Hons 1982). RIBA 1984, FRIBA 2016; MRIAI 2004. Sheppard Robson, 1984–85; Terry Farrell & Partners, 1985–87; Partner, Pawson Williams Architects, 1987–2000. Major works include: Earth Galls Masterplan, Natural Hist. Mus., London, 1995–96; remodelling of Birmingham Repertory Th., 1996–99; Athlone Civic Centre, Co. Westmeath, Ire., 2001–04; Unicorn Th., London, 2001–05; The Long House, St John's Wood, London, 2001–06; Clones Liby and County HQ, Co. Westmeath, 2004–08; new Wexford Opera House, 2005–08; Luan Art Gall., Athlone, Ireland, 2005–12; new Marlowe Th., Canterbury, 2007–11; Novium Mus., Chichester, 2007–12; Clare County Library and Art Gallery, Ennis, 2016–. Mem., Design Council CABE (formerly Nat. Design Review Panel, CABE), 2008–. Ext. Examr, Dept of Architecture, Univ. of Strathclyde, 2010–13; Mem., Nat. Panel Jury, Civic Trust Awards, 2011– (Chm., 2015–); Chm., Lewisham Design Rev. Panel, 2013–; Co-Chm., Design South East, 2014–. Hon. Prof. of Arch., Zhengzhou Univ., China, 2010. FRSA 2005. Richmond Soc. Award, 2004; RIAI Awards, 2005, 2006, 2007, 2009; RIBA Awards, 2005, 2006, 2008, 2009; OPUS Arch. and Construction Award, Bank of Ireland, 2005, 2008; Irish Concrete Soc. Award, 2005; Public Bldg Architect of the Yr, BD, 2006, 2008; AIA Award, 2006, 2010; Chicago Athenaeum Prize, 2006, 2008; Merit Award, US Inst. for Th. Technol., 2007; Copper in Arch. Award, Copper Develt Assoc., 2008; Quadrennial Award for Practical Design Excellence, Soc. of Theatre Consultants, 2010; Civic Trust Award, 2010; LAMA Nat. Impact Award, 2010; RIBA Downland Award, 2012; two Civic Trust Awards and Civic Trust Michael Middleton Special Award, 2013; RIAI Best Cultural Bldg Award, 2013; Civic Trust Award, 2014; RIBA Regl Award, 2014; RIBA Nat. Award, 2014. *Publications*: Keith Williams: architecture of the specific, 2009; numerous internat. and nat. articles, etc. *Recreations*: cricket, ski-ing, sailing, opera, travel, art, food. *Address*: Keith Williams Architects, 74 Long Lane, SE1 4AU. *T*: (020) 7843 0070. *E*: studio@keithwilliamsarchitects.com. *Club*: Architecture (Mem. Cttee, 2017–).

**WILLIAMS, Kenneth Robert,** CVO 2003; CBE 2002; QPM 1992; HM Inspector of Constabulary, North of England and Northern Ireland, 2002–09; *b* 28 April 1944; *s* of Sydney Williams and Margaret Elizabeth Williams (*née* Howell); *m* 1969, Jean Margaret Ballantyne; two *d*. *Educ*: Wellacre Sch., Flixton; BA Soc. Scis Open Univ. Greater Manchester Police: Constable, Salford S Div., Salford City Police, 1963–68; Sergeant, N Manchester Div., 1968–72; Patrol Inspector, Salford Div., 1973–74; Inspector, then Chief Inspector, HQ, 1974–76; Sub-Divl Comd, Bolton Div., 1976–78; N Manchester Div., 1978–79; directing staff, Police Staff Coll., Bramshill, 1979–81; Greater Manchester Police: Sub-Divisional Command: Manchester Central Div., 1981; Manchester Internat. Airport, 1981–84; Departmental Command: Computer Project Branch HQ, 1984–85; Ops Support Branch HQ, 1985–86; Divl Comd, N Manchester, 1986–87; Sen. Comd course, Police Staff Coll., Bramshill, 1987; Asst Chief Constable, Greater Manchester Police, 1987–90; Dep. Chief Constable, Durham Constabulary, 1990–93; Chief Constable, Norfolk Constabulary, 1993–2002. *Recreations*: swimming, walking, reading, music. *Address*: 440 Unthank Road, Norwich NR4 7QH.

**WILLIAMS, Kingsley;** *see* Williams, J. B. K.

**WILLIAMS, Kirsty;** *see* Williams, V. K.

**WILLIAMS, Prof. Laurence Glynn,** OBE 2018; CEng, FREng, FIMechE, FNucI; Professor of Nuclear Safety and Regulation, University of Central Lancashire, 2010–14, now Emeritus; Senior Research Investigator, Imperial College London, since 2018 (Senior Research Fellow, 2014–18); *b* 14 March 1946; *s* of Hugh Williams and Ruby Williams (*née* Lawrence); *m* 1976, Lorna Susan Rance (marr. diss. 1997); one *s* one *d*. *Educ:* Liverpool Poly. (BSc Hons Mech. Engrg); Univ. of Aston in Birmingham (MSc Nuclear Reactor Technol. 1972). CEng 1976; FIMechE 1991; FNucI (FINucE) 1998; FREng 2004. Design engr, Nuclear Power Gp, 1970–71; nuclear engr, CEGB, 1973–76; Health and Safety Executive: Nuclear Installations Inspectorate: Inspector, 1976–78; Principal Inspector, 1978–86; Superintending Inspector, 1986–91; Dep. Chief Inspector, 1991–96; Div. Head, Safety Policy Directorate, 1996–98; HM Chief Inspector of Nuclear Installations and Dir, Nuclear Safety Directorate, 1998–2005; Mem. Bd, 1999–2005; Nuclear Decommissioning Authority: Dir, Nuclear Safety, Security and Envmt (formerly Nuclear Safety and Security), 2005–08; Chief Engr, 2007–08. Nuclear safety and security consultant, 2008–10. Chair: Cttee on Radioactive Waste Mgt, DECC, later BEIS, 2012–17; Defence Nuclear Safety Cttee, MoD, 2013–18 (Mem., 2006–13). Mem., Civil Nuclear Police Authy, 2007–08; UK Mem., Higher Scientific Council, European Nuclear Soc., 2011–. Chm., UN/IAEA Commn on Safety Standards, 2000–05; Pres., UN Jt Convention on Safety of Spent Fuel and Radioactive Waste Mgt, 2003–06; Chm., EC High Level Panel for: EURATOM FP7 and FP7+2 ex-post evaluation, 2015–16, interim evaluation, 2016–17, fusion and fission res. prog., 2014–18; Advr on Nuclear Safety, EBRD, 1996–2019; Member: Safety Review Gp, 1996–2019; Internat. Adv. Gp on Chernobyl, 1996–2019; Singapore Nuclear Safety Adv. Panel, 2017–; Chm., Expert Adv. Gp on NW Russia, 2005–12. Chm., Internat. Nuclear Regulators' Assoc., 2000–02. Chair: Regulatory and Safety Cttee, Tokomak Energy, 2018–; Design Review of Safety Work Package, Eurofusion, 2019. Vis. Prof., KCL, 2012–15; Vis. Sen. Fellow, Nat. Nuclear Lab., 2012–; Hon. Prof., Univ. of Bangor, 2019–. Chm., Editl Cttee, Nuclear Inst., 2012–. *Recreations:* cycling, keeping fit, walking, music, theatre, supporting Liverpool Football Club. *Address:* Centre for Nuclear Engineering, Department of Materials, Imperial College London, South Kensington Campus, SW7 2AZ. *E:* laurence.williams@imperial.ac.uk.

**WILLIAMS, Lia Jane;** actress and director; *b* Birkenhead, 26 Nov. 1964; *d* of Bernard and Brenda Williams; one *s*. *Educ:* Arts Educnl Sch., Tring Park, Herts. Actress: *television* includes: Mr Wroe's Virgins, 1993; Seaforth, 1994; The Uninvited, 1997; Imogen's Face, 1998; May 33rd, 2004; Doc Martin, 2009; Secret State, 2012; The Missing, 2016; Strike, 2017; The Crown, 2016–17; Kiri, 2018; The Capture, 2019; His Dark Materials, 2019; *films* include: Dirty Weekend, 1993; The King is Alive, 2001; The Truth Commissioner, 2016; The Foreigner, 2017; *theatre* includes: The Revengers' Comedies, Scarborough, 1989 (Critics Circle Award for Most Promising Newcomer, 1991); Skylight, NT, 1995; The Father, Ustinov, Bath, 2014; A Streetcar Named Desire, Gate, Dublin, 2014; Oresteia, Almeida, transf. Trafalgar, 2015; Mary Stuart, Almeida, transf. Duke of York's, 2018; The Prime of Miss Jean Brodie, Donmar, 2018; The Night of the Iguana, Noël Coward Th., 2019. Director: short films: Feathers, 2002; The Stronger, 2007 (SAE Digital Short Award, Raindance Film Fest., 2007); Dog Alone, 2009; documentary, Nanaboshung, 2016; theatre: The Matchbox, Liverpool Playhouse and The Tricycle, 2012; Ashes to Ashes, Harold Pinter Th., 2017. Patron, Clean Break, 2015–. *Recreations:* scuba diving, art, travel, film. *E:* tiltinglia21@hotmail.com. *Club:* h.

**WILLIAMS, Manon Bonner;** *see* Antoniazzi, M. B.

**WILLIAMS, Maria Lisa;** executive audio producer, since 1997; Head of Development, Loftus Media, 2015–19; *b* Southampton, 13 Dec. 1967; *d* of Peter and Jennifer Williams; *m* 1995, Warren Hatter; one *s* one *d*. *Educ:* Chipping Sodbury Comprehensive Sch.; Univ. of Birmingham (BA Hons English Lang. and Lit.). Exec. Producer, Speech and Campaigns, BBC Radio 1, 1997–2004; Dep. Ed., Woman's Hour, BBC Radio 4, 2004–06; Exec. Producer, Saturday Live, BBC Radio 4, 2006–08 (Gold Sony Award winner, 2008); Hd of Progs, Wise Buddah, 2008–11; Founder and Dir, Sound Women, 2011–16. Fellow, Radio Acad., 2014. *Recreations:* post-punk, box-sets, K-Pop, swimming in Tooting Bec Lido. *T:* 07814 378264. *E:* maria@maria-williams.com.

**WILLIAMS, Marjorie Eileen,** CB 2005; Tax Expert, International Monetary Fund, since 2006; *b* 18 Dec. 1946; *d* of Leslie Vernon Cuttle and Mary Fleming Cuttle (*née* Howie); *m* 1970, Graham Terence Williams. *Educ:* Reading Univ. (BSc Hons Geog. with Geol. 1968); Centre for W African Studies, Birmingham Univ. (postgrad. studies). Joined Inland Revenue, 1972; Regl Dir, SW Reg., 1994–96; Dir, Large Business Office, 1996–2000, Capital and Savings Tax Policy, 2000–03; Dir, Local Services, Bd of Inland Revenue, subseq. HM Revenue and Customs, 2003–06. *Publications:* Birdwatching in Lesbos, 1992. *Recreations:* birdwatching, gardening, Romanian needlework. *E:* maggiewcb@btinternet.com.

**WILLIAMS, Mark;** *see* Williams, J. M. G.

**WILLIAMS, Mark Fraser;** Teacher, since 2017, and Deputy Headteacher, Llangors Church in Wales School; *b* 24 March 1966; *s* of Ronald and Pauline Williams; *m* 1997, Helen Refna Wyatt; one *s* three *d* (of whom one *s* one *d* are twins). *Educ:* University Coll. of Wales, Aberystwyth (BSc Econ 1987); Rolle Faculty of Educn, Univ. of Plymouth (PGCE 1993). Res. Asst to Lib, then Lib Dem, Peers and Constituency Asst to Geraint Howells, MP, 1987–92; Primary School Teacher: Madron Daniel Sch., Penzance, 1993–96; Forches Cross Sch., Barnstaple, 1997–2000; Dep. Hd, Llangors Church in Wales Sch., nr Brecon, 2000–05. MP (Lib Dem) Ceredigion, 2015–17; contested (Lib Dem) same seat, 2017. Lib Dem spokesman on schools, 2005–06, on Wales, 2005–17; Dep. Leader, 2015–16, Leader, 2016–17, Welsh Lib Dems. Mem., Welsh Affairs Select Cttee, 2005–17. Co-Chm., Lib Dem Backbench Cttee for political and constitutional reform, 2010–12, for Welsh Affairs, 2012–17. Contested (Lib Dem): Monmouth, 1997; Ceredigion, Feb. 2000, 2001. Pres., Ceredigion Lib Dems, 1999–2000; Welsh Lib Dem spokesman on agriculture and rural affairs, 2015–. Chm., N Ceredigion Forum for Elderly Care. Trustee, Hospice at Home Aberystwyth Volunteers. Pres., SW Wales RBL. *Recreations:* gardening, reading, biographies, walking.

**WILLIAMS, Ven. Martin Clifford L.;** *see* Lloyd Williams.

**WILLIAMS, Martin John,** CVO 1983; OBE 1979; HM Diplomatic Service, retired; High Commissioner, New Zealand, Governor (non-resident) of Pitcairn, Henderson, Ducie and Oeno Islands, and High Commissioner (non-resident), Samoa, 1998–2001; *b* 3 Nov. 1941; *s* of John Henry Stroud Williams and Barbara (*née* Benington); *m* 1964, Susan Dent; two *s*. *Educ:* Manchester Grammar Sch.; Corpus Christi Coll., Oxford (BA). Joined Commonwealth Relations Office, 1963; Private Sec. to Permanent Under Secretary, 1964; Manila, 1966; Milan, 1970; Civil Service College, 1972; FCO, 1973; Tehran, 1977; FCO, 1980; New Delhi, 1982; Rome, 1986; Hd of S Asian Dept, FCO, 1990; on secondment to NI Office as Asst Under-Sec. of State (Political), Belfast, 1993; High Comr, Zimbabwe, 1995–98. UK Consultant to NZ Antarctic Heritage Trust, 2002–12; Chm., NZ-UK Link Foundn, 2004–08. *Recreations:* music, gardening, woodworking. *Address:* Russet House, Lughorse Lane, Yalding, Kent ME18 6EG. *Club:* Royal Over-Seas League.

**WILLIAMS, Prof. Martin Lloyd,** PhD; FIEnvSc; Professor, Environmental Research Group, King's College London, since 2010; *b* Mountain Ash, Wales, 22 Nov. 1947; *s* of Chester Lloyd Williams and Muriel Williams; *m* 1982, Rosemary Anne Hudlestone; two *s*. *Educ:* Mountain Ash Grammar Sch.; University Coll., Cardiff (BSc 1st Cl. Hons Chem. 1968); Univ. of Bristol (PhD Chem. 1971). FIEnvSc 2008. Res. Fellow, Univs of British Columbia and Bradford, 1971–75; Hd, Air Pollution Modelling, Warren Spring Lab., 1975–81; Tech. Asst to Chief Scientist, DTI, 1981–82; Hd, Air Pollution Div., Warren Spring Lab., 1982–93; Hd, Air Quality Sci. Unit, DoE, 1993–2002; Hd, Atmospheric Quality and Industrial Pollution, DEFRA, 2002–10. Vis. Prof., Univ. of Southampton, 2007–. Mem., Air Quality Expert Gp, 2012–, Chm., Air Quality Modelling Steering Gp, 2014–, DEFRA. Chm., Exec. Body, UNECE Convention on Long Range Transboundary Air Pollution, 2005–14; Co-Chair, WHO Air Quality Guidelines Develt Gp, 2017–; Advr to World Bank on air pollution, 2017–. Burntwood Lect. and John Rose Award for Envmtl Sci., Instn of Envmtl Sci., 2007. *Publications:* numerous scientific papers in specialist jls. *Recreations:* drawing, painting, cycling, walking, guitar, ukelele, banjo. *Address:* Environmental Research Group, King's College London, Franklin Wilkins Building, 150 Stamford Street, SE1 9NH. *T:* (020) 7848 3844. *E:* martin.williams@kcl.ac.uk. *Club:* Verulam Cycling.

**WILLIAMS, Martin Wykeham;** Director, Office of Manpower Economics, since 2014; *b* Manchester, 15 May 1959; *s* of David John Wykeham Williams and Marjorie Williams (*née* Turnbull); *m* 1990, Eve Samson; one *s* one *d*. *Educ:* Winchester Coll.; Trinity Hall, Cambridge (BA Hist. 1980); École Nat. d'Admin, Paris (Dip. Internat. Public Admin 1990). Department of Employment, later Employment Department Group, then Department for Education and Employment, subseq. Department for Education and Skills: MSC and HSC, 1982–97; Hd of Strategy, 1997–2000; Grade 5, Sch. Workforce, 2000–03; Higher Educn (HE Act), 2003–06; Parents Policy, 2006–07; Dir, Higher Educn Strategy, DIUS, then Dir, Higher Educn, BIS, 2007–12; Dir, Educn and Procurement Industrial Strategies, and Office of Life Scis, BIS, 2012–14. Chair: The Brix at St Matthews, 1994–2005 (Trustee, 2005–16); St Jude's Primary Sch., Lambeth, 2005–10. Trustee: Working With Men, 2009–16; Fulbright Commn, 2009–14. *Recreations:* trombone, English concertina, fell-walking. *Address:* Office of Manpower Economics, Fleetbank House, 2–6 Salisbury Square, EC4Y 8JX. *T:* (020) 7211 8109. *E:* martin.williams@beis.gov.uk.

**WILLIAMS, Sir Max;** *see* Williams, Sir W. M. H.

**WILLIAMS, Major Michael Ingouville,** MBE 2001; Lord Lieutenant, East Lothian, since 2014 (Vice Lord Lieutenant, 2010–14); *b* Winchester, 15 March 1946; *s* of Roger Williams and Norah Williams; *m* 1971, Barbara Mary Campbell Williams; two *s* one *d*. *Educ:* Bradfield Coll.; RMA, Sandhurst. Commnd RTR, 1966; retd as Major, 1985. Farmer, E Lothian, 1986–2014. DL E Lothian, 1997. *Recreations:* farm conservation, forestry, golf, shooting, walking, countryside management. *Address:* Duncastle, Eaglescairnie Mains, Gifford, Haddington E Lothian EH41 4HN. *T:* (01620) 810491. *E:* mw.eagles1@gmail.com.

**WILLIAMS, Michael John;** journalist, writer; Editor, New Musical Express, 2012–18; *b* Wrexham, 4 Feb. 1979; *s* of Peter Williams and Sandra Williams; *m* Eleanor Stevenson; two *s*. *Educ:* Univ. of Wales, Aberystwyth (Film and TV Studies 2000). Editor, Kruger Mag., 2003–10; New Musical Express: Features Editor, 2010–11; Dep. Editor, 2011–12. Editor of the Year, British Soc. of Mag. Editors, 2016. *Recreation:* curtain twitching.

**WILLIAMS, Rev. Canon Michael Joseph;** Vicar of Bolton, 1999–2007, and Priest-in-charge, St Philip, Bolton le Moors, 2004–07; *b* 26 Feb. 1942; *s* of James and Edith Williams; *m* 1971, Mary Miranda Bayley; one *s* one *d*. *Educ:* St John's College, Durham (BA in Philosophy 1968). Apprentice Mechanical Engineer, then Engineer, with W & T Avery, Birmingham, 1958–63 (HNC in Mech. Eng 1962). Deacon 1970, priest 1971; Curate, then Team Vicar, St Philemon, Toxteth, 1970–78; Director of Pastoral Studies, St John's Coll., Durham, 1978–88; Principal, Northern Ordination Course, 1989–99; Area Dean, Bolton, 2001–05; Permission to Officiate, Diocese of Manchester, 2008–. Hon. Tutor in Pastoral Theology, Univ. of Manchester, 1990–2000. Hon. Canon: Liverpool Cathedral, 1992–99; Manchester Cathedral, 2000–07, now Canon Emeritus. Reviewer, Clergy Rev. Panel, Dio. of Manchester, 2014–17. Mem., EU Energy Transparency Task Gp, 2013–15. Part-time Lectr, Liverpool Hope Univ., 2007–09; Tutor, Southern Theol Educn and Trng Scheme, 2013–15. Chaplain, Bolton Normandy Veterans Assoc., 2004–10; Advr, Bolton Chaplaincy Training Course, 2010–13. Hon. Mem., Bolton Royal Artillery Assoc., 2008–11. Pres., Northern Fedn for Trng in Ministry, 1991–93. Chm. Trustees, Hands Around The World, 2014–17 (volunteer, 2009–13); volunteer, Bolton Steam Mus., 2012–. *Publications:* The Power and the Kingdom, 1989. *Address:* 51 Cotswold Drive, Horwich, Bolton BL6 7DE.

**WILLIAMS, Michael Lodwig,** CB 2003; consultant on government debt and cash management, since 2003; Chief Executive, UK Debt Management Office, 1998–2003; *b* 22 Jan. 1948; *s* of John and Eileen Williams; *m* 1970, Jennifer Mary Donaldson (*see* J. M. Williams); three *s*. *Educ:* Wycliffe Coll., Stonehouse, Glos; Trinity Hall, Cambridge (BA 1969; MA); Nuffield Coll., Oxford. Min. of Finance, Lusaka, Zambia, 1969–71; HM Treasury, 1973–2003: on secondment to Price Waterhouse, 1980–81; Under Sec., then Dep. Dir, Industry, 1992–98. Non-exec. Dir, Euroclear UK and Ireland Ltd (formerly CRESTCo Ltd), 1998–2002, 2004–13. *T:* (020) 7735 8694. *E:* mike.williams@mj-w.net.

**WILLIAMS, Prof. Michael Maurice Rudolph;** consultant engineer; Professor of Nuclear Engineering, University of Michigan, 1987–89; Professor of Nuclear Engineering, 1970–86, now Emeritus, and Head of Department, 1980–86, Queen Mary College, London University; *b* 1 Dec. 1935; *s* of late M. F. Williams, RAFVR and G. M. A. Williams (*née* Redington); *m* 1958, Ann Doreen Betty; one *s* one *d*. *Educ:* Ewell Castle Sch.; Croydon Polytechnic; King's Coll., London (State Scholar, 1954); Queen Mary Coll., London. BSc, PhD, DSc; CEng; FNucI; CPhys, FInstP. Asst Experimental Officer, AWRE, Fort Halstead, 1954–55; Engr with Central Electricity Generating Board, 1962; Research Associate at Brookhaven Nat. Lab., USA, 1962–63; Lectr, Dept of Physics, Univ. of Birmingham, 1963–65; Reader in Nuclear Engrg, 1965–70, Dir, Nuclear Reactor, 1980–83, QMC, London Univ.; Prin. Scientist, Electrowatt Engrg Services (UK) Ltd, 1989–95. Vis. Professor, Imperial Coll., London, 2002, 2010–. Augustin-Frigon Lecture, École Polytechnique de Montréal, 2001. Mem., Adv. Cttee on Safety of Nuclear Installations, 1983–86. UN Advr on Engrg Educn in Argentina, 1979–89. Vice-Pres., Instn of Nuclear Engrs, 1971–73. Mem., Electrical Engrg Coll., EPSRC, 1995–97. Chm. of Governors, Ewell Castle Sch., 1976–79; Mem., Academic Bd, RNC, Greenwich, 1975–86. Foreign Mem., Royal Soc. of Arts and Scis, Goteborg, Sweden, 2008–. Exec. Editor, Annals of Nuclear Energy, 1973–2013. Fellow, American Nuclear Soc. (Arthur Holly Compton Award, 1994; Eugene P. Wigner Award, 2000; G. C. Pomraning Award, 2011; Seaborg Medal, 2018). *Publications:* The Slowing Down and Thermalization of Neutrons, 1966; Mathematical Methods in Particle Transport Theory, 1971; Random Processes in Nuclear Reactors, 1974; Aerosol Science, 1991; contribs to Proc. Camb. Phil. Soc., Nucl. Science and Engrg, Jl Nuclear Energy, Jl Physics, Annals of Nuclear Energy. *Address:* 6 Lincoln Close, Eastbourne, E Sussex BN20 7TZ.

**WILLIAMS, Michael Roger,** CB 2017; Director, Business and International Tax (formerly Business and Indirect Tax), HM Treasury, since 2010; *b* 2 July 1957; *s* of Roger Williams and Margaret Laura Williams (*née* Dawes). *Educ:* Bradford Grammar Sch.; Balliol Coll., Oxford (MA Physics 1978). Entered Inland Revenue, 1978: various tax inspector posts, 1978–93; Principal Inspector, Large Business Office, 1993–97; Asst Dir, Company Tax, then Personal Tax, 1997–99; Hd, Social Security Team, HM Treasury, 1999–2001; Dep. Dir, Internat., IR, 2001–04; Dir, Internat. Tax, 2004–07, Personal Tax and Welfare Reform, 2008–10, HM Treasury. *Recreations:* visiting France, reading, ice skating, going to the gym. *Address:* HM Treasury, 1 Horse Guards Road, SW1A 2HQ. *T:* (020) 7270 5000. *E:* mike.williams@hmtreasury.gsi.gov.uk.

**WILLIAMS, Nicholas Michael Heathcote;** QC 2006; **His Honour Judge Heathcote Williams;** a Circuit Judge, since 2014; *b* 5 Nov. 1954; *s* of Sir Edgar Trevor Williams, CB, CBE, DSO, and Gillian Williams (*née* Gambier-Parry); *m* 1987, Corinna Mary Mitchell; two *s* one *d. Educ:* St Catharine's Coll., Cambridge (Briggs Scholar; BA 1975); RMA Sandhurst. Commnd and served Royal Green Jackets, 1977–80. Called to the Bar, Inner Temple, 1976; in practice at the Bar, 1980–2014; a Recorder, 2000–14. *Recreations:* reading, art, film, sport (particularly cricket). *Address:* Woolwich Crown Court, 2 Belmarsh Road, SE28 0EY. *Clubs:* Rifles, MCC.

**WILLIAMS, Sir Nicholas Stephen, (Sir Nick),** Kt 2013; Principal, BRIT School for the Performing Arts and Technology, 2002–12; Chief Executive Officer, Future Schools Trust, 2014–16; education adviser, since 2012; *b* Solihull, 29 Dec. 1953; *s* of John Williams and Jane Williams; *m* 1990, Joanna Arkwright; one *s* three *d. Educ:* Univ. of Kent (BA Hons Amer. Lit.); King's Coll., London (PGCE). Teacher of English and Media, Battersea County Sch., Wandsworth, 1977–85; Hd of English, Dunraven Sch., Lambeth, 1985–89; Educn Advr, ILEA, 1989–90; Schs Inspector, London Bor. of Southwark and Ofsted, 1990–95; Dep. Headteacher, Pimlico Sch., Westminster, 1995–96; Headteacher, Thomas Tallis Sch., Greenwich, 1996–2001. DFE (formerly DCSF) Academies Educn Advr, 2008–15. Consultant Leader, London Leadership Centre, 2004–10. Trustee: Centre for Learning in Primary Educn, 1993–96; Imperial War Mus., 2008–16; E London Acad. of Music, 2014–16. Chm. Govs, Crescent Primary Sch., 2011–; Founder and Gov., Birmingham Ormiston Acad., 2011–. FRSA 1998. *Publications:* various educnl articles. *Recreations:* arts, education, family.

**WILLIAMS, Nicola;** Service Complaints Ombudsman for the UK Armed Forces, since 2016 (Service Complaints Commissioner for the Armed Forces, 2015–16); *b* London; *b* 24 Oct.; *d* of Andrew Matthew Sylvester Williams and Waveney Leonie Williams. *Educ:* Poly. of the South Bank (BA Hons Law 1984); Inns of Court Sch. of Law. Called to the Bar, Lincoln's Inn, 1985; barrister in private practice, 1985–2001; Complaints Comr, Cayman Is, 2009–15; a Recorder, 2009–. Member: Bd, Police Complaints Authy, 2001–04; Ind. Police Complaints Commn, 2004–09. *Publications:* Without Prejudice (novel), 1997. *Recreations:* dancing, film, music, travel. *Address:* Office of the Service Complaints Ombudsman for the UK Armed Forces, PO Box 72252, SW1P 9ZZ. *T:* (020) 7877 3444. *E:* EA@scoaf.org.uk.

**WILLIAMS, Nigel;** *see* Williams, H. N.

**WILLIAMS, Very Rev. Nigel Howard;** Dean of St Asaph, since 2011; *b* St Asaph; *m* Nia; two *d. Educ:* Llysfasi Agricultural Coll.; St Michael's Coll., Llandaff; Univ. of Wales, Cardiff. Depot Manager, Wynnstay Farmers, Llanrwst; ordained deacon, 1995, priest, 1996; Asst Curate, St Mary's, Denbigh, 1995–97; Rector, Llanrwst and Llanddoget, 1998–2004; Vicar, St Paul's, Colwyn Bay, 2004–08; Area Dean, Rhos, 2004–09; Vicar, Colwyn Bay with Bryn y Maen, 2008–11. Archbishop's Advr on Rural Ministry. *Address:* Cathedral Office, High Street, St Asaph LL17 0RD. *T:* (01745) 582245.

**WILLIAMS, Nigel L.;** *see* Leader-Williams.

**WILLIAMS, Nigel Lamplough,** CEng; FIMarEST; Secretary, Royal Commission for the Exhibition of 1851, since 2010; *b* Yeovil, 15 July 1953; *s* of late Rear Adm. David Apthorp Williams, CB, DSC and Susan Eastlake Williams (*née* Lamplough); *m* 1986, Sarah Joanna Christie; one *s* one *d. Educ:* Cheltenham Coll.; BRNC Dartmouth; RNEC Manadon (BSc). MIMarE 1980; CEng, 1980; FIMarEST 2005. Served Royal Navy: HM Ships Torquay, Apollo, Bristol, Intrepid, 1976–82; Asst Naval Attaché, Bonn, 1983–85; HMS Aurora, 1985–87; on staff: FO Scotland and NI, 1987–89; Second Sea Lord, 1989–92; Capt. in Charge, Hong Kong, 1992–94; Cdre (E), HM Yacht Britannia, 1994–96; Dir Trng, HMS Sultan, 1996–99; Captain 1999; staff of Second Sea Lord, 1999–2002; Superintendent Fleet Maintenance, Portsmouth, 2002–04; Dir, Naval Officer Appts (E), 2004–06; Job Evaluation Judge (Navy), 2006–08. Freeman, City of London, 2011; Liveryman, Shipwrights' Co., 2012 (Clerk, 2008–10; Freeman, 2011). Mem., RNSA, 1970–. *Recreations:* sailing, ski-ing, music. *Address:* c/o Royal Commission for the Exhibition of 1851, Sherfield Building, Imperial College London, SW7 2AZ. *Clubs:* Royal Yacht Squadron, Royal London Yacht.

**WILLIAMS, Prof. Sir Norman Stanley,** Kt 2015; FRCS, FRCP, FRCPE, FMedSci, FRCA; Professor of Surgery, 1986–2016 and Director of Surgical Innovation, 2011–16, Academic Surgical Unit, and Director, National Centre for Bowel Research and Surgical Innovation, 2011–16, Barts and The London School of Medicine and Dentistry, Queen Mary University of London (formerly London Hospital Medical College, London University), 1986–2016 (Head, Academic Surgical Unit, 1986–2011); President, Royal College of Surgeons of England, 2011–14; Senior Clinical Adviser, Secretary of State for Health, 2015–18; Chairman, National Clinical Improvement Programme, since 2018; *b* 15 March 1947; *s* of Jules Williams and Mabel Sundle; *m* 1977, Linda Feldman; one *s* one *d. Educ:* Roundhay Sch., Leeds; London Hosp. Med. Coll., Univ. of London (MB BS, MS). LRCP; MRCS, FRCS 1975; FRCP 2013; FRCPE 2014; FRCA 2014. House and Registrar appts, London Hosp., 1970–76; Registrar, Bristol Royal Infirmary, 1976–78; Res. Fellow and Lectr, Leeds Gen. Infirmary, 1978–80; Res. Fellow, UCLA, 1980–82; Sen. Lectr, Leeds Gen. Infirmary, 1982–86. Fulbright Scholar, UCLA, 1980; Ethicon Foundn Fellow, RCS, 1980; Moynihan Fellow, Assoc. of Surgeons of GB and Ireland, 1985. President: Ileostomy and Internal Pouch Support Group, 1992–2008; European Digestive Surgery, 1997–98; Chm., UK Co-ordinating Cttee of Cancer Res. Sub-Cttee on Colorectal Cancer, 1996–2001. Mem., Steering Gp, Nat. Cancer Res. Network, 2001–03. Non-executive Director: Private Healthcare Inf. Network, 2015–; St George's NHS Foundn Hosp., 2016–. Mem. Council, 2005–, Chm., Acad. and Res. Bd, 2006–11, RCS. Pres., Soc. of Academic and Res. Surgery, 2009–11. Vice-Chm., British Jl of Surgery, 1995–2001. FMedSci 2004. Hon. Fellow, Amer. Surgical Assoc., 2008; Hon. FACS 2013; Hon. FDS 2014; Hon. FRCSI 2014. Hon. DSc Leeds, 2019. Patey Prize, Surgical Res. Soc., 1978; Nessim Habif Prize, Univ. of Geneva, 1995; Galen Medal in Therapeutics, Soc. of Apothecaries, 2002; (jtly) Cutler's Surgical Prize, 2011; Lifetime Achievement Award, British Assoc. of Surgical Oncology, 2018. *Publications:* (jtly) Surgery of the Anus, Rectum and Colon, 1993 (BUPA and Soc. of Authors Med. Writer's Gp Prize), 4th edn 2018; (ed jtly) Bailey and Love's Short Practice of Surgery, 22nd edn 1995 to 27th edn 2018; (ed) Colorectal Cancer, 1996; scientific papers. *Recreations:* long distance swimming, Rugby football, cinema, reading about crime, fact and fiction.

**WILLIAMS, Paul;** MP (Lab) Stockton South, since 2017; *b* 23 Aug. 1972; *s* of William Williams and Susan Ann Williams (*née* Burtenshaw); partner, Vicky Holt; two *d. Educ:* Univ. of Newcastle upon Tyne (MB BS 1996; MSc Health Scis (Public Health) 2005); Univ. of Liverpool (Dip. Tropical Medicine and Hygiene 2001). Jt Founder and doctor, Arrival Practice, 2002–06; Med. Superintendent, Bwindi Community Hosp., Uganda, 2006–10; GP: Woodbridge Med. Practice, 2011–12; A&B Med. Practice, 2013–16; Tennant St Med. Practice, 2015–17; GP Clin. Lead in Public Health, Tees Valley Public Health Shared Services, 2013–15; CEO, Hartlepool and Stockton Health Ltd, 2015–17. Mem., Health and Social Care (formerly Health) Select Cttee, H of C, 2017–. *Recreations:* triathlon, live music; cycled length of the Tour de France (2014) unsupported. *Address:* House of Commons, SW1A 0AA.

**WILLIAMS, Dr Paul David;** Chief Executive, Seafish Industry Authority, 2010–15; *b* Urmston, Manchester, 29 Jan. 1958; *s* of Stanley and June Williams; *m* 1993, Christine Kendall. *Educ:* William Hulme Grammar Sch., Manchester; Hatfield Poly. (BSc); Univ. of Manchester (PhD 1983). Res. Fellow, Univ. of Manchester, 1984–88; Manager, Plant Biotech Ltd, 1988–92; Project Manager, Proteus, Macclesfield, 1992–95; Manager, Ewos Tech. Centre, Scotland, 1995–2000; Man. Dir, Ewos Innovation, Norway, 2000–03; Res. Dir, Seafish Industry Authy, 2003–10. Non-executive Member, Board: Gangmasters Licensing Authy, 2015–; Food Standards Agency, 2016–19. *Publications:* contrib. res. papers on aquaculture and fisheries issues. *Recreations:* fly fishing, reading, walking.

**WILLIAMS, Rt Rev. Paul Gavin;** *see* Southwell and Nottingham, Bishop of.

**WILLIAMS, Paul Maurice,** OBE 2014; RDI 2005; RIBA; Director, Stanton Williams Architects, since 1985; *b* 8 Oct. 1949; *s* of Maurice Williams and Joan Williams (*née* Neighbour); *m* 1984, Beth Stockley; one *s* one *d. Educ:* Birmingham Coll. of Art (BA Hons; HDipAD). RIBA 2002. V&A Museum, 1975–80, Hd of Design, 1978–80: exhibns incl. Fabergé, Biedermeier, Renaissance Jewels and Tudor Miniatures; Design Consultant, Royal Liby, Windsor, 1978–87 (worldwide touring exhibns, Leonardo da Vinci Anatomical and Nature Study Drawings); private practice, 1980–85: exhibns incl. Romanesque, Matisse, Renoir, Hayward Gall.; Japanese Gall., V&A; formed partnership Stanton Williams Architects with Alan Stanton, 1985. *Award-winning projects* include: Design Mus. Galls, London, 1989; Issey Miyake Retail Shops, London, 1990–99; Triforium Mus., Winchester Cath., 1992; Leo Burnett Office Bldg, 60 Sloane Ave, London, 1994; Four Brindley Place, Birmingham, 1999; Wellcome Trust Millennium Seed Bank, Sussex, 2000; Whitby Abbey Visitor Centre, Yorks, 2002; Compton Verney Art Gall., 2004; Tower Hill Environs Scheme, London, 2004; Casa Fontana, Switzerland, 2004; Belgrade Th. Extension, 2008; Cadbury Offices, Bournville, 2009; Sainsbury Lab., Cambridge, 2011; Central Saint Martins, Univ. of Arts, London, 2012; Eton Manor, London, 2012; Waddesden Bequest Gall., BM, 2015; Victoria Hall, King's Cross, 2016; Musée d'arts de Nantes, 2017; Islamic Galleries, BM, 2018; Royal Opera House, Covent Garden, 2018. Exhibitions include: Art of Ancient Mexico, Yves Klein, Jasper Johns, Leonardo da Vinci, Romanesque Art, Hayward Gall.; Gothic, Bronze, RA; Bridget Riley, Tate Britain and De La Warr Pavilion; Gerhard Richter, 2009, Giacometti, NPG; Masterpieces of Chinese Painting, V&A. Architectural Advr, Heritage Lottery Fund, 1998–2002; Advr/Enabler, CABE, 2002–11; Member: Architectural Adv. Panel, Kensington and Chelsea, 2008–; St Paul's Cathedral, 2009–. External Examiner, Schools of Architecture: Westminster Univ., 1993–96; Plymouth Univ., 2000–04; Dundee Univ., 2005–07; Birmingham Univ., 2009–13; lectured and taught in Europe and USA. Trustee: Whitechapel Art Gall., 1994–99; SPACE, 2011–. FRSA. Hon. Dr Univ. of Arts, London, 2012. *Publications:* work published and exhibited widely in architectural books and jls. *Recreations:* the arts, all sports. *Address:* Stanton Williams, 36 Graham Street, Islington, N1 8GJ. *T:* (020) 7880 6400, *Fax:* (020) 7880 6401. *E:* p.williams@stantonwilliams.com.

**WILLIAMS, Sir Paul Michael,** Kt 2011; OBE 2000; DL; Prior for Wales, Order of St John of Jerusalem, since 2017 (Chancellor, 2011–12, Registrar, 2012–14, Bailiff of St David's, 2014–17); *b* Cardiff, 25 June 1948; *s* of Leonard and Marion Williams; *m* 1982, Glenys Williams, JP. *Educ:* St Illtyd's Coll., Cardiff; Glamorgan Poly. (DMS). Joined NHS as clerk, Welsh Hosp. Bd, 1966; Asst Dist Gen. Manager, Mid Glamorgan HA; CEO, Bridgend and Dist NHS Health Trust, 1993–99; Chief Executive: Bro Morgannwg NHS Trust; Abertawe Bro Morgannwg Univ. NHS Trust; Dir Gen., Health and Social Services, and Chief Exec., NHS Wales, Welsh Govt, 2008–11. Non-exec. Dir, Natural Resources Wales, 2012–. Trustee: St John Cymru—Wales, 2008–; RVS, 2011–; Royal Masonic Benevolent Instn, 2011– (Chm., RMBI Care Co., 2015–); Masonic Charitable Foundn, 2016–. Fellow, UWIC, 2010. High Sheriff, 2007–08, DL 2010, S Glamorgan. CCMI; CIHM. KStJ 2015 (CStJ 2011). Hon. Dr S Wales, 2013. *Recreations:* fly fishing, walking, music. *Address:* 191 Cyncoed Road, Cyncoed, Cardiff CF23 6AJ. *Clubs:* Army and Navy; Cardiff County.

**WILLIAMS, Dr Paul Randall,** CBE 1996; DL; FInstP; Chairman and Chief Executive, Council for Central Laboratory of Research Councils, 1995–98; *b* 21 March 1934; *s* of Fred and Eileen Westbrook Williams; *m* 1957, Marion Frances Lewis; one *s* one *d. Educ:* Baines Grammar School; Loughborough College (BSc London external; DLC); Liverpool Univ. (PhD). ICI Research Fellow, Liverpool Univ., 1957; Research Physicist, British Nat. Bubble Chamber, 1958–62; Rutherford Lab., SRC, 1962–79 (Dep. Div. Head, Laser Div., 1976–79); Science and Engineering Research Council: Head, Astronomy, Space and Radio Div., 1979–81; Head, Engineering Div., 1981–83; Dep. Dir, 1983–87, Dir, 1987–94, Rutherford Appleton Lab.; Dir, Daresbury and Rutherford Appleton Lab., EPSRC, 1994–95. Chm., Abingdon Coll. Corp., 1993–95. Local Preacher, Methodist Church. DL Oxfordshire, 1998. Hon. DSc Keele, 1996. Glazebrook Medal, Inst. of Physics, 1994. *Recreations:* listening to music, choral singing, travel. *Address:* 5 Tatham Road, Abingdon, Oxon OX14 1QB. *T:* (01235) 524654.

**WILLIAMS, Pauline Margaret,** FFPM, FMedSci; Senior Vice President, and Head of Global Health Research and Development, GlaxoSmithKline, since 2017; *b* Hull, 11 March 1967; *d* of Michael and Dorothy Walker; partner, Gregor Anderson; two *s. Educ:* Univ. of Wales Coll. of Medicine (MB BCh 1990); Dip. Pharmaceutical Medicine, RCP, 1995. FFPM 2014. Clin. Pharmacol. Physician, Glaxo Wellcome, 1995–2001; GlaxoSmithKline: Head: Discovery Medicine, 2001–07; Academic Discovery Performance Unit, 2007–12; Maternal and Neonatal Health Unit, 2012–17. Mem., UKRI-MRC (formerly MRC), 2017–. FMedSci 2018. *Recreations:* cookery, reading. *Address:* GSK Medicines Research Centre, Gunnels Wood Road, Stevenage, Herts SG1 2NY. *T:* (01438) 762075. *E:* pauline.m.williams@gsk.com.

**WILLIAMS, Maj. Gen. Peter Gage,** CMG 2005; OBE 1994 (MBE 1984); Head of NATO Military Liaison Mission, Moscow, 2002–05; Editor, The Guards Magazine, 2009–13; *b* 25 June 1951; *s* of Col G. T. G. Williams; *m* 1982, Anne Rankine; one *s* two *d. Educ:* Eton; Magdalene Coll., Cambridge (BA 1972). Commnd Coldstream Guards, 1969; Sultan of Oman's Forces, 1976–78; served NI and Berlin; psc; MA to SACEUR, 1990–92; CO 1st Bn Coldstream Guards, 1992–94; served NI (despatches), Bosnia, with MoD Intelligence; ocds (Aust.), 1999 (Fellow, 1999); Dep. Mil. Rep., EU Mil. Cttee,

2001–02. Patron, British Ex-Servicemen's Assoc., Western Australia, 2009–; Chm., BRIXMIS Assoc., 2010. Mem., Chartered Inst. of Linguists, 1996 (Associate Mem., 1981). Gov., Rendcomb Coll., 2011. Legion of Merit (USA), 2005. *Recreations:* tourism, military history. *Address:* Northcot House, Highworth, Wiltshire SN6 7BW.

**WILLIAMS, Sir Peter (Michael),** Kt 1998; CBE 1992; PhD; FRS 1999; FREng; Chairman: Daiwa Anglo-Japanese Foundation, since 2012 (Trustee, since 2009); Kromek plc, since 2015; *b* 22 March 1945; *s* of Cyril Lewis and Gladys Williams; *m* 1970, Jennifer Margaret Cox; one *s. Educ:* Hymers College, Hull; Trinity College, Cambridge (MA, PhD). Mullard Research Fellow, Selwyn College, Cambridge, 1969–70; Lectr, Dept of Chemical Engineering and Chemical Technology, Imperial College, 1970–75; VG Instruments Group, 1975–82 (Dep. Man. Dir, 1979–82); Oxford Instruments Group plc, 1982–99: Man. Dir, 1983–85; Chief Exec., 1985–98; Chm., 1991–99; Master, St Catherine's Coll., Oxford, 2000–02. Chm., Isis Innovation Ltd, Oxford Univ., 1997–2001; non-executive Director: GKN plc, 2001–10; WS Atkins plc, 2004–11. Chairman: PPARC, 1994–99; Trustees, Science Mus., 1996–2002; Engrg and Technol. Bd, 2002–06; NPL, 2002–14. Mem., Council for Sci. and Technology, 1993–98; President: Inst. of Physics, 2000–02; BAAS, 2002–03. Supernumerary Fellow, St John's Coll., Oxford, 1988–2000. Chancellor, Univ. of Leicester, 2005–10. FREng (FEng 1996). FIC 1997; FCGI 2002. Hon. FIChemE 2003; Hon. FIET (Hon. FIEE 2004); Hon. FCMI 2007; Hon. FIMechE 2008. Hon. Fellow: Selwyn Coll., Cambridge, 1997; UCL, 1997; St Catherine's Coll., Oxford, 2002. Hon. DSc: Leicester, 1995; Nottingham Trent, 1995; Loughborough, 1996; Brunel, 1997; Wales, 1999; Sheffield, 1999; Salford, 2003; Staffordshire, 2004; City, 2007; Hull, 2010; Bedfordshire, 2010. Guardian Young Business Man of the Year, 1986. *Publications:* numerous contribs to jls relating to solid state physics. *Recreations:* ski-ing, walking.

**WILLIAMS, Peter Richard Michael;** Joint Founder and Chief Executive Officer, Jack Wills, clothing and homeware, 1999–2013 and 2015–18; *b* Bolton, 12 July 1974; *s* of Michael and Diana Williams; *m* 2003, Laura; two *s* one *d. Educ:* King Edward's Sch., Birmingham; University Coll. London (BSc). Launched Aubin & Wills, 2008. Mem., Young President's Orgn. *Recreations:* family and sport. *Address:* 94 Lansdowne Road, W11 2LS.

**WILLIAMS, Peter Robert,** CBE 2009; consultant on quality assurance in higher education; Chief Executive, Quality Assurance Agency for Higher Education, 2002–09 (Acting Chief Executive, 2001–02); *b* 20 April 1948; *s* of Gilbert David Williams and Phyllis Williams, Oxford; *m* 1st, 1979, Katherine Pickles (marr. diss.); 2nd, 1987, Fiona Pollock-Gore; two *s. Educ:* City of Oxford High Sch.; Univ. of Exeter (BA Hons English 1969). Mgt trainee, Hazell, Watson and Viney Ltd, 1969–70; Admin. Asst, Univ. of Surrey, 1970–74; University of Leicester: Sen. Admin. Asst, 1974–79; Asst Registrar, 1979–82, Sec., 1982–84, Medical Sch.; Dep. Sec., British Acad., 1984–90; Director: CVCP Academic Audit Unit, 1990–92; of Quality Audit, 1992–94; of Quality Assurance, 1994–97, HEQC; of Institutional Review, QAA, 1997–2001. British Accreditation Council for Independent Further and Higher Education: Member: Council, 1998–2018; Exec. Cttee, 2000–18; Chm., 2012–18; Pres., 2019–; European Association (formerly European Network) for Quality Assurance in Higher Education: Mem., Steering Cttee, 2000–04; Mem. Bd, 2004–08; Vice-Pres., 2004–05, Pres., 2005–08. Mem., Educn Honours Cttee, 2010–17. Chm., Accreditation Rev. Cttee, Nat. Commn for Academic Accreditation and Assessment, Saudi Arabia, 2011–16; Special Advr, Sir John Cass's Foundn, 2016–. Mem. Cttee, 1981–84, Chm., Leicester Gp, 1981–84, Victorian Soc. Gov., Cardiff Metropolitan Univ. (formerly UWIC), 2009–16 (Vice Chm., Bd of Govs, 2012–14, 2015–16; Chm., Audit Cttee, 2012–16; Hon. Fellow, 2017); Trustee: Richmond, American Internat. Univ. in London, 2012–19 (Mem. 2010–12, Chm., 2012–14, Bd of Academic Advrs (formerly Bd of Academic Govs); Chm., Academic Cttee, 2014–19); Norfolk Archives and Heritage Develt Foundn, 2017– (Chm., 2017–); The Educators' Trust, 2018–. Mem. Bd, Improving Dispute Resolution Adv. Service, 2010–15 (Dep. Chm., 2011–12). Lord Upjohn Lect., Assoc. of Law Teachers, 2009. Hon. Treas., Little Malvern Priory, 2010–16. Fellow, Univ. of Worcester, 2009. FRSA 2002–19. Hon. Fellow, Coll. of Teachers, 2011. Hon. LLD: Higher Educn Trng and Awards Council, Ireland, 2008; Leicester, 2010; Hon. PhD Gloucestershire, 2010. Freeman, City of London, 2012; Freeman, then Liveryman, Co. (formerly Guild) of Educators, 2002 (Ct Asst, 2002–; Master, 2014–15). *Publications:* articles in books and jls on quality assurance and higher educn. *Recreations:* classical music, books, pictures, English topography and history. *Address:* The Old Hall, Crostwight, North Walsham, Norfolk NR28 9PA. *E:* piersplowman2@gmail.com. *Club:* City Livery.

**WILLIAMS, Peter Wodehouse;** Chairman, Superdry, since 2019; *b* 18 Dec. 1953; *s* of John and Claire Williams; *m* 1981, Gwen Knight; two *s. Educ:* Univ. of Bristol (BSc Maths). ACA 1978. Audit Senior, Arthur Andersen, 1975–78; Consultant, Accenture, 1978–82; Financial Controller, Aiwa (UK) Ltd, 1982–84; Finance Dir, Bandive Ltd, 1984–87; Finance Divl Manager, Freemans plc, 1987–91; Finance Dir, 1991–2003, Chief Exec., 2003–04, Selfridges plc; Chief Exec., Alpha Gp (formerly Alpha Airports), 2006–08; Director: JJB Sports plc, 2009; Maltby Investments Ltd, 2010. Non-executive Director: Capital Radio plc, 2003–05; GCap Media plc, 2005–08; Asos plc, 2006–13; Cineworld Gp plc, 2006–15; Silverstone Hldgs Ltd, 2009–14; Sportech plc, 2011–16; London Transport Mus., 2012–17; non-executive Chairman: Blacks Leisure, 2011–12; Erno Lazlo, 2011–13; Without Prejudice, 2012–14; Brissi, 2013–; Mister Spex, 2013–; OfficeTeam, 2013–14; Jaeger, 2014–15; Rightmove plc, 2014–19; boohoo.com plc, 2014–19; U+I, 2015–; Sophia Webster Ltd, 2016–; DP Eurasia N. V., 2017–. Member: Bd of Mgt, British Retail Consortium, 2003–04; Design Council, 2006–17. Member: Business Adv. Bd, Comic Relief, 2002–14; Finance Cttee, British Red Cross, 2002–08. Trustee: GCap Charities (formerly Capital Charities), 2003–10. *Recreations:* film, tennis, ski-ing, Southampton Football Club, shopping. *Address:* 3 Rayners Road, SW15 2AY. *T:* (020) 8788 5346. *E:* peterwodehousewilliams@outlook.com. *Clubs:* Home House; Bank of England Sports.

**WILLIAMS, Sir Philip;** *see* Williams, Sir R. P. N.

**WILLIAMS, Rhodri John;** QC 2010; *b* Cardiff, 3 Jan. 1963; *s* of David Barry Williams, QC and Angela Joy Williams; *m* 1991, Rachel Margaret Williams; one *s* two *d. Educ:* Cardiff High Sch.; Exeter Coll., Oxford (BA Hons Mod. Langs 1985; MA 2002); Poly. of Central London (Dip. Law 1986). Called to the Bar, Gray's Inn, 1987, Bencher, 2015; in practice as barrister, specialising in EU law, and public and admin. law, 1987–. Fonctionnaire, Commn of EC, 1992–97. Mem., Editl Bd, Public Procurement Law Rev., 2000–. *Recreations:* Rugby, fencing, walking. *Address:* Henderson Chambers, 2 Harcourt Buildings, Temple, EC4Y 9DB. *T:* (020) 7583 9020, *Fax:* (020) 7583 2686. *E:* clerks@hendersonchambers.co.uk. *Clubs:* Oxford and Cambridge; Cardiff and County.

**WILLIAMS, Prof. Richard Andrew,** OBE 2009; PhD; FREng, FTSE; FRSE; FIChemE, FIMMM; Principal and Vice-Chancellor, Heriot-Watt University, since 2015. *Educ:* King's Sch., Worcester; Imperial Coll. London (BEng Hons Mineral Technol. 1982; PhD Diamond Processing 1988). FIChemE 1995; FIMMM 1995; CEng; FREng 2000; CSci. Res. Metallurgist, Anglo American plc, SA, 1980–81; researcher, De Beers Industrial Diamonds, 1982–86; Sen. Lectr in Chem. Engrg, UMIST, 1986–94; RAEng/Rio Tinto Prof. of Minerals Engrg, Camborne Sch. of Mines, Univ. of Exeter, 1995–99; University of Leeds: Anglo American Prof. of Mineral and Process Engrg, 1999–2011; Pro-Vice-Chancellor (Enterprise/Internat. Strategy), 2005–11; University of Birmingham: Pro-Vice-Chancellor and Hd, Coll. of Engrg and Physical Scis, 2011–15; Prof. of Energy and Mineral Resource Engrg, 2013–15. RISE Fellow, EPSRC, 2014. Vis. Prof., Univ. of NSW, 2006–15; Hon. Professor: Chinese Acad. Scis, Beijing, 2011–; Taylor's Educn Gp, Malaysia, 2014–17; Tianjin Univ. of Finance and Economy, 2017–. Director: Industrial Tomography Systems plc, 1997–; Structure Vision Ltd, 2003–; Leeds Innovation Centre Ltd, 2005–10; Medilink UK Ltd, 2007–10; Dispersia Ltd, 2007–11; Manufg Technol. Centre Ltd, 2011–15; Alta Innovations Ltd, 2011–15; Resilience Partners Ltd, 2011–; Alta Birmingham China Ltd, 2012–15. Dir, Leeds and N Yorks Chamber of Commerce Ltd, 2008–10. Dir, British Geological Survey, 2018–. Royal Academy of Engineering: Vice-Pres., 2005–08 and 2014–18; Trustee, 2014–18; President's Medal, 2019. Mem., Bd of Trustees, Carnegie Trust for Univs of Scotland, 2016–. FTSE 2008; FRSE 2017. *Address:* Heriot-Watt University, Edinburgh Campus, Edinburgh EH14 4AS. *Clubs:* Athenæum, Caledonian.

**WILLIAMS, Richard Charles John;** Founder Director, Williams Murray Hamm Ltd, 1997–2017; *b* 19 Oct. 1949; *s* of Herbert Charles Lionel Williams and Barbara Dorothy Williams; *m* 1973, Agnieszka Wanda Skrobanska; one *s* one *d. Educ:* Highgate Sch.; London College of Printing (DipAD 1973). Founder Dir, Design Bridge, 1986–95. Director: Design Business Assoc., 1989 and 2005; Writtle Hldgs; Mem., Design Council, 2005–10. Mem. (Esher Residents' Assoc.), Elmbridge BC, 2019–. *Publications:* (with Richard Murray and Garrick Hamm) The Little Book of Don'ts in Brand Design, 2002; (jtly) Seemed Like a Good Idea at the Time, 2009; (with Garrick Hamm) Blood, Sweat and Ideas, 2018. *Recreations:* motor sport, sailing.

**WILLIAMS, Richard Evan Huw; His Honour Judge Richard E. Williams;** a Circuit Judge, since 2018; *b* 17 Feb. 1959; *s* of Evan Howell Williams, FIChemE and Muriel Maynard Williams (*née* Cooke); *m* 1991, Lindsey Ann Duckworth; two *d. Educ:* Ysgol Gyfun Rhydfelen, Pontypridd; Univ. of Bristol (LLB Hons 1991). Metropolitan Police, 1978–88; called to the Bar, Lincoln's Inn, 1992; a barrister, 1992–2004; a Dep. Dist Judge (Magistrates' Courts), 2000–04; a Dist Judge (Magistrates' Courts), S Wales, later Gwent, 2004–18; a Recorder, 2012–18. Mem., Sentencing Council for England and Wales, 2014–17. *Recreations:* family, music, cycling. *Address:* Cardiff Crown Court, The Law Courts, Cathays Park, Cardiff CF10 3PG. *E:* hhj.richard.e.williams@ejudiciary.net.

**WILLIAMS, Prof. Richard James Willson,** OBE 2010; TD 1995; FRCPsych (Hon.), FRCPCH; Professor of Mental Health Strategy, Welsh Institute for Health and Social Care, University of South Wales (formerly University of Glamorgan), 1998–2014, now Emeritus; Honorary Consultant Disaster Psychiatrist and Public Mental Health Physician, Extreme Events and Health Protection Section, Public Health England (formerly Health Protection Agency), since 2012; *b* 5 Feb. 1949; *s* of Ernest James Williams and Eleanor May Willson Williams; *m* 1971, Janet May Simons; one *s* two *d. Educ:* Bristol Grammar Sch.; Univ. of Birmingham (MB ChB 1972); DPM 1976. MRCPsych 1976, FRCPsych 1990, Hon. FRCPsych 2014; MRCPCH 1996, FRCPCH 1997; DMCC 2009. House Physician, Selly Oak Hosp., Birmingham, 1972–73; House Surgeon, Worcester Royal Infirmary, 1973; Sen. House Officer in Psychiatry, Whitchurch Hospital Mgt Cttee, Cardiff, 1973–74; Registrar in Psychiatry, S Glamorgan AHA (T), 1974–77; Sen. Registrar in Child and Adolescent Psychiatry, S Glamorgan AHA (T) and Welsh Nat. Sch. of Medicine, 1977–80; Consultant Child and Adolescent Psychiatrist: Bristol Royal Hosp. for Sick Children, 1980–98; Aneurin Bevan Health Bd (formerly Gwent Healthcare NHS Trust), 1998–2014; Advanced Trauma Life Support Instructor, RCS, 1996–; Lead Officer for Disaster Mgt, RCPsych, 2008. Director: NHS Health Adv. Service, 1992–96; Drugs Adv. Service, 1992–96; Vice Chm., Mental Health Act Commn, 1997–2001. Special Advr on Child and Adolescent Mental Health to Welsh Assembly Govt, 1999–2010; Mem., Adv. Bd for Healthcare Standards in Wales, 2004–08 (Chm., Ethics Cttee, 2005–); Chm., Wales Collaboration in Mental Health, 2003–09; Vice Chm., Wales Cttee, Adv. Cttee on Clin. Excellence Awards, 2009–12; Member: Emergency Planning Clinical Leadership Adv. Gp, DoH, 2005; Cttee on the Ethical Aspects of Pandemic Influenza, UK Govt, 2006–; Pandemic Influenza Clin. and Operational Adv. Gp to UK's Chief Med. Officers, 2008–; Scientific Adviser on Psychosocial and Mental Healthcare: to Dir of Emergency Preparedness, DoH, 2006–13; to Jt Med. Cttee, NATO, 2007–09. Chm., Assoc. for Psychiatric Study of Adolescents, 1989–92. Gov. and Mem. Exec. Cttee, Inst. of Child Health, Univ. of Bristol, 1988–94 (Treas., 1989–91); Sen. Fellow, Health Services Mgt Centre, Univ. of Birmingham, 1996–99. Society of Apothecaries: Mem., Bd of Examrs, Dip. in Med. Care of Catastrophes, 1997–; Mem., Exec. Cttee, Faculty of Conflict and Catastrophe Medicine, 2006–. Hon. Professor: of Child and Adolescent Mental Health, Sch. of Public Health and Clinical Scis, Univ. of Central Lancs, 2006–11; of Disaster Healthcare, Robert Gordon Univ., 2009–13; Humanitarian and Conflict Response Inst., Univ. of Manchester, 2012–. Dir of Confs, 2001–07, Presidential Lead Officer for Disaster Mgt, 2008–14, RCPsych. Chm., 2004–06, Vice Chm., 2002–03, 2006–08, Acad. of Med. Royal Colls in Wales; Mem., Acad. of Med. Royal Colls, 2002–08. MIHM 1994; MInstD 1995. Ed., child and adolescent psychiatry, Current Opinion in Psychiatry, 1993–; Asst Ed., 1992–97, Mem. Editl Bd, 1997–, Jl of Adolescence. Served TA, 1967–2009 (Mem., Birmingham Univ. OTC, 1967–70; Commnd Officer, UK TA, 1970–2009; OC Basic Wing Bristol Univ. OTC, 1984–97; jsc 1997; CO Ambulance Train Gp RAMC (V), 1997–2001). Freeman, City of London, 2000; Liveryman, Soc. of Apothecaries, 2004– (Convener, DMCC, 2012–). Queen's Golden Jubilee Medal, 2002; VRSM, 2005. *Publications:* (ed jtly) A Concise Guide to the Children Act 1989, 1992; (ed and contrib.) Comprehensive Mental Health Services, 1994; (ed jtly) Suicide Prevention, 1994; (ed and contrib.) Comprehensive Health Services for Elderly People, 1994; (ed and contrib.) Drugs and Alcohol, 1994; (ed jtly and contrib.) Together We Stand, 1995; (ed jtly and contrib.) A Place in Mind, 1995; (ed jtly and contrib.) The Substance of Young Needs, 1996; (ed jtly) Safeguards for Young Minds, 1996, 2nd edn 2004; (ed jtly and contrib.) Heading for Better Care, 1996; (ed jtly and contrib.) Addressing the Balance, 1997; (ed jtly) Voices in Partnership, 1997; (ed jtly and contrib.) Forging New Channels, 1998; (jtly) Promoting Mental Health in a Civil Society, 2001; (jtly) Deaths of Detained Patients in England and Wales, 2001; (ed jtly) Child and Adolescent Mental Health Services, 2005; contrib. many chapters in books, major reports to govts and other authorities, and leading articles, editorials and papers in learned jls. *Recreations:* walking on Bodmin Moor, licensed radio amateur, preserved steam railways, military history, coastal powerboating. *Address:* Welsh Institute for Health and Social Care, Faculty of Life Sciences and Education, University of South Wales CF37 1DL. *T:* (01433) 483070. *E:* richard.williams@southwales.ac.uk. *Club:* Athenæum.

**WILLIAMS, Sir Robert Hughes, (Sir Robin),** Kt 2019; CBE 2004; FRS 1990; CPhys; FLSW; Vice-Chancellor, University of Wales, Swansea, 1994–2003, now Emeritus Professor; *b* 22 Dec. 1941; *s* of Emrys and Catherine Williams; *m* 1967, Gillian Mary Harrison; one *s* one *d. Educ:* Bala Boys' Grammar Sch.; University College of North Wales, Bangor (BSc, PhD, DSc). Res. Fellow, Univ. of Wales, 1966–68; Lectr, then Reader and Prof., New University of Ulster, 1968–83; Prof. and Hd of Dept of Physics, later Physics and Astronomy, 1984–94, Dep. Principal, 1993–94, Univ. of Wales Coll. of Cardiff. Visiting Professor: Max Planck Inst., Stuttgart, 1975; Xerox Res. Labs, Palo Alto, USA, 1979; IBM Res. Labs, Yorktown Heights, USA, 1982; Distinguished Res. Fellow, La Trobe Univ., Melbourne, 2003. Mott Lectr, Inst. of Physics, 1992. Member: Council, HEFCW, 2009–18 (Chm., Res. Cttee, 2010–18); Sci. Adv. Council for Wales, 2010– (Chm., 2015–18); Innovation Adv. Council for Wales, 2014–18; Chairman: Planning Bd to report on establishment of Y Coleg Cymraeg Cenedlaethol, 2009; Ser Cymru Delivery Bd, 2013–15. Mem. Council, Learned Soc. of Wales, 2010– (Founding Fellow, 2010). Mem. Council, Aberystwyth Univ., 2018–. Honorary Fellow: Univ. of Wales Cardiff, 1998; Bangor Univ. 1998; Aberystwyth Univ., 2015; Swansea Univ., 2004. Hon. FInstP 2014. Hon. DSc Ulster, 2003; Hon. DLaws Wales, 2005. Silver Medal, British Vacuum Council, 1988; Max Born Medal and Prize, German Physics Soc. and Inst. of Physics, 1989. *Publications*: Metal-Semiconductor Contacts (with E. H. Rhoderick), 1988; over 300 pubns in field of solid state physics and semiconductor devices. *Recreations*: walking, fishing, soccer. *Address*: Dolwerdd, Trerhyngyll, Cowbridge, Vale of Glamorgan CF71 7TN. *T*: (01446) 773402.

**WILLIAMS, Sir (Robert) Philip (Nathaniel),** 4th Bt *cr* 1915; DL; landowner; *b* 3 May 1950; *s* of Sir David Philip Williams, 3rd Bt and Elizabeth Mary Garneys, *d* of late William Ralph Garneys Bond; *S* father, 1970; *m* 1979, Catherine Margaret Godwin, *d* of Canon Cosmo Pouncey, Tewkesbury; one *s* three *d*. *Educ*: Marlborough; St Andrews Univ. MA Hons. Mem., Ind. Monitoring Bd, HM YOI, Portland, 2000–16 (Chm., 2007–09). Lay Canon, Salisbury Cathedral, 2010–15. Pres., Mill Street Housing Soc., Dorchester, 1985–; Vice Pres., Welshpool and Llanfair Light Railway, 2017–; Patron, Swanage Railway Trust, 2017–. JP W Dorset PSA (formerly Dorchester), 1992–2016; DL 1995, High Sheriff, 2016–17, Dorset. *Heir*: *s* David Robert Mark Williams, *b* 31 Oct. 1980. *Address*: Bridehead, Littlebredy, Dorchester, Dorset DT2 9JA. *T*: (01308) 482232. *Club*: MCC.

**WILLIAMS, Sir Robin;** *see* Williams, Sir Robert H.

**WILLIAMS, Maj.-Gen. Robin Guy,** CB 1983; MBE 1969; retired; Chief Executive Officer, Auckland Regional Trust Board, Order of St John, 1993–98; *b* 14 Aug. 1930; *s* of Dr John Upham and Dr Margaret Joan Williams; *m* 1953, Jill Rollo Tyrie; one *s* two *d*. *Educ*: Nelson Coll., New Zealand. psc(UK) 1963, jssc(AS) 1972, rcds(UK) 1976. Commissioned RMC, Duntroon, 1952; 1 Fiji Inf. Regt Malaya, 1953–54; Adjt/Coy Comd 2 NZ Regt Malaya, 1959–61 Chief Instructor Sch. of Inf. (NZ), 1964–65; BM 28 Comwel Inf. Bde, Malaysia, 1965–68; CO 1 Bn Depot (NZ), 1969; CO 1 RNZIR (Singapore), 1969–71; GSO1 Field Force Comd (NZ), 1972–73; C of S Field Force Comd (NZ), 1973–74; Col SD, Army GS, 1974–75; Comd Field Force, 1977–79; ACDS (Ops/Plans), 1979–81; DCGS 1981; CGS, 1981–84. Hon. Col 1 RNZIR, 1986–88; Col, RNZIR, 1988–90. Chm., Bell Helicopter (BH) Pacific, 1988–90. Vice-Chm., 1985–86, Chm., 1986–88, Operation Raleigh, NZ; Chief Executive: Order of St John (NZ), 1986–87; Auckland Div., Cancer Soc. of NZ, 1988–93. *Recreations*: golf, swimming, walking. *Address*: Apt 1A, 454, Edmund Hillary Retirement Village, 221 Abbotts Way, Remuera, Auckland 1050, New Zealand. *T*: (9) 5251167. *Club*: Northern (Auckland).

**WILLIAMS, Roderick Gregory Coleman,** OBE 2017; baritone, since 1992; *b* Barnet, Herts, 19 Nov. 1965; *s* of Adrian John and Norma-Rose Alesia Williams; *m* 1988, Miranda Jane Clasen; one *s* two *d*. *Educ*: Haberdashers' Aske's Sch., Elstree; Magdalen Coll., Oxford (BA); Inst. of Educn, Univ. of London (PGCE); Guildhall Sch. of Music and Drama. Hd, Choral Studies, Tiffin Boys' Sch., 1989–92. Has sung concert repertoire with BBC Orchestras and ensembles, incl. Royal Scottish Nat. Orch., Philharmonia, London Sinfonietta, Manchester Camerata, Royal Liverpool Philharmonic Orch., Hallé Orch., Britten Sinfonia, Bournemouth SO, Scottish Chamber Orch., Deutsches Symphonie-Orch. Berlin, Russian Nat. Orch., Orch. Philharmonique de Radio France, Ensemble Orchestral de Paris, Acad. Ancient Music, The Sixteen, Le Concert Spirituel, Rias Kammerchor, Bach Collegium Japan. Composer of works performed at Wigmore Hall, Barbican Hall, Purcell Room, including: O Adonai, 1998; Soundbites, 2000; Jazz Choral Evensong, 2006; O Brother Man - A New England Symphony, 2015. Artistic Dir, Leeds Lieder, 2016. *Recreations*: walking, composing. *Address*: c/o Groves Artists, 7 St George's Court, 131 Putney Bridge Road, SW15 2PA. *T*: (020) 8874 3222.

**WILLIAMS, Sir Rodney (Errey Lawrence),** GCMG 2014; KGN 2014; Governor-General of Antigua and Barbuda, since 2014; *b* Antigua and Barbuda, 2 Nov. 1947; *s* of Hon. Ernest Emanuel Williams and Irene B. Williams; *m* 2005, Sandra; three *s*. *Educ*: Antigua Grammar Sch.; Univ. of W Indies (Jamaica) (MB BS 1976); RAF Inst. of Aviation Medicine (Cert. Aviation Medicine 1978); Cert. Sports Medicine. Intern, Queen Elizabeth Hosp., Barbados, 1976–78; in private med. practice, Antigua and Barbuda, 1978–84. MP Antigua and Barbuda, 1984; Dep. Speaker, House of Reps, 1984–86; Minister: of Econ. Develt, Industry and Tourism, 1986–89; of Educn, Sports, Youth and Community Develt, 1989–94; of Tourism, Culture and Envmt, 1994–99; of Educn, Culture and Technol., 1999–2004. Member: Sports Medicine Assoc.; Airline Med. Dirs' Assoc.; Civil Aviation Med. Assoc. (Mem., Bd of Trustees, 2006–; Mem., Exec. Bd, 2010–); Amer. Aerospace Assoc. (Exec. Fellow, 2011). FRSocMed 1986; Fellow, US Civil Aviation Med. Assoc., 2007. KJStJ 2016 (KStJ 2014); Kt Grand Cross, Royal Order of Francis I, 2014. *Recreation*: tennis. *Address*: Government House, Independence Drive, St John's, Antigua, West Indies. *T*: 4620002/3/4. *E*: govgenab@gmail.com.

**WILLIAMS, Prof. Sir Roger,** Kt 2006; Vice-Chancellor of The University of Reading, 1993–2002; Chairman, Higher Education Funding Council for Wales, 2002–08 (Member, 1995–2008; Acting Chairman, 2000–02); *b* 21 March 1942; *s* of late M. O. Williams, MBE and W. Williams; *m* 1967, Rae Kirkbright; two *d*. *Educ*: Tredegar Grammar Sch.; Worcester Coll., Oxford (BA Nat. Scis (Physics), MA; Hon. Fellow, 1999); Univ. of Manchester (MA). Operational Res. Br., Nat. Coal Bd, 1963–64; Department of Government, University of Manchester: Res. Student, 1964–66; Asst Lectr, Lectr, Sen. Lectr, 1966–78; Prof. of Govt and Sci. Policy, 1979–93; Founding Dir, Policy Res. in Engrg, Sci. and Technol., 1979–93; Hd of Dept, 1984–88; Dean of Economic and Social Studies, 1989–92. NATO Envmtl Fellowship, 1977–79; Aust. Univs Fellowship, 1984; Vis. Prof., Univ. of Montreal, 1981. Sci. Advr, Sci. Council of Canada (on secondment), 1974–75; Advr, OECD, 1980–81; Specialist Advr, H of L Select Cttees on Sci. and Technology, 1986–92, on European Communities, 1990; Member: Adv. Bd, Sci. Policy Res. Unit, 1987–97; Cabinet Office Wkg Gp on internat. collaboration in sci. and technol., 1989–91. Chm., Jt SERC-ESRC Cttee, 1991–93; Member: ESRC, EPSRC and NERC Cttees; Quality Assurance Agency for Higher Educn, 1997–2002. Mem. Editl Bd, Government and Opposition, 1994–. Associate, Technical Change Centre, 1981–85. British Council Delegn to China, 1985. FLSW 2011. Hon. Fellow, Cardiff Univ., 2008. Hon. DCL Reading, 2002; Hon. DSc Glamorgan, 2008. *Publications*: Politics and Technology, 1972; European Technology, 1973; The Nuclear Power Decisions, 1980; Public Acceptability of New Technology, 1986; contrib. to approx. 22 books and more than 20 acad. articles. *Club*: Athenæum.

**WILLIAMS, Dr Roger,** FRS 2017; FMedSci; Programme Leader, MRC Laboratory of Molecular Biology, University of Cambridge, since 1992; *b* Fort Wayne, Indiana; *s* of William and Wanda Williams; *m* 1986, Olga Perišić. *Educ*: Purdue Univ. (BS); Eastern Washington Univ. (MS); Univ. of Calif, Riverside (PhD). Internat. Res. and Exchanges Bd Fellow, Dept of Theoretical Physics, Boris Kidrič Inst., 1986–87; NIH Postdoctoral Fellow, Dept of Chemistry, Cornell Univ., 1987–90; Res. Asst Prof., Center for Advanced Biotechnol. and Medicine, Rutgers Univ., 1990–92. FMedSci 2010. *Publications*: contribs to scientific jls. *Recreation*: long-distance running. *Address*: MRC Laboratory of Molecular Biology, Francis Crick Avenue, Cambridge CB2 0QH. *T*: (01223) 243548. *E*: rlw@mrc-lmb.cam.ac.uk.

**WILLIAMS, Roger Hugh,** CBE 2013; farmer, since 1969; *b* 22 Jan. 1948; *s* of Morgan Glyn Williams and Eirlys Williams; *m* 1973, Penelope James; one *s* one *d*. *Educ*: Llanfilo Co. Primary Sch.; Christ Coll., Brecon; Selwyn Coll., Cambridge (BA). Mem. (Lib Dem) Powys CC, 1981–2001, 2017–. MP (Lib Dem) Brecon Radnorshire, 2001–15; contested (Lib Dem) same seat, 2015. Dir, Develt Bd for Rural Wales, 1989–97. Chm., Brecon Beacons Nat. Park, 1991–96. *Recreations*: sport, walking. *Address*: Tredomen Court, Llanfilo, Brecon, Powys LD3 0RL.

**WILLIAMS, Prof. Roger Stanley,** CBE 1993; MD; FRCP, FRCS, FMedSci; Professor of Hepatology, King's College London, since 2015; Professor of Hepatology, University of London, 1994–2010; Director, Institute of Hepatology, Foundation for Liver Research, since 1996; *b* 28 Aug. 1931; *s* of Stanley George Williams and Doris Dagmar Clatworthy; *m* 1st, 1954, Lindsay Mary Elliott (marr. diss. 1977); two *s* three *d*; 2nd, 1978, Stephanie Gay de Laszlo; one *s* two *d*. *Educ*: St Mary's Coll., Southampton; London Hosp. Med. Coll., Univ. of London. MB, BS (Hons), MD; LRCP, MRCP, FRCP 1966; MRCS, FRCS 1988; FRCPE 1990; FRACP 1991. House appointments and Pathology Asst, London Hospital, 1953–56; Jun. Med. Specialist, Queen Alexandra Hospital, Millbank, 1956–58; Medical Registrar and Tutor, Royal Postgrad. Med. Sch., 1958–59; Lectr in Medicine, Royal Free Hospital, 1959–65; Consultant Physician, Royal South Hants and Southampton General Hospital, 1965–66; Consultant Physician, KCH, 1966–96; Dir, Liver Res. Unit, then Inst. of Liver Studies, KCH and Med. Sch., then King's Coll. Sch. of Medicine and Dentistry, 1966–96; Hon. Consultant Physician, UC Hosps NHS Trust, 1996–2011. Hon. Consultant: Foundn for Liver Res., 1974–; in medicine to the Army, 1988–. Member: Clinical Standards Adv. Gp, 1994–; Adv. Gp on Hepatitis, DHSS, 1980–; Transplant Adv. Panel, DHSS, 1974–83; WHO Scientific Gp on Viral Hepatitis, Geneva, 1972. Rockefeller Travelling Fellowship in Medicine, 1962; Legg Award, Royal Free Hosp. Med. Sch., 1964; Sir Ernest Finch Vis. Prof., Sheffield, 1974; Hans Sloane Fellow, RCP, 2004–; Hon. Prof., Birkbeck, Univ. of London, 2011–. Lectures: Melrose Meml, Glasgow, 1970; Goulstonian, RCP, 1970; Searle, Amer. Assoc. for the Study of Liver Diseases, 1972; Fleming, Glasgow Coll. of Physicians and Surgeons, 1975; Sir Arthur Hurst Meml, British Soc. of Gastroenterology, 1975; Skinner, Royal Coll. of Radiologists, 1978; Albert M. Snell Meml, Palo Alto Med. Foundn, 1981; Milford Rouse, Baylor Med. Center, Dallas, 1989; Norman Tanner Meml, St George's Hosp., 1992; Searle Special, St Bartholomew's Hosp., 1992; Datta Meml Oration, India, 1984; Quadrennial Review, World Congress of Gastroenterol., Sydney, 1990; Sir Jules Thorn, RCP, 1994. Vice-Pres., RCP, 1991–93; President: Internat. Med. Club, 1998–99; British Liver Trust, 2002–; Member: European Assoc. for the Study of the Liver, 1966– (Cttee Mem., 1966–70; Pres., 1983; Hon. Pres., 2008); Harveian Soc. of London (Sec., Councillor and Vice-Pres., 1963–70, Pres., 1974–75); British Assoc. for Study of Liver (formerly Liver Club) (Sec. and Treasurer, 1968–71; Pres., 1984–86); Royal Soc. of Medicine (Sec. of Section, 1969–71); British Soc. of Gastroenterology (Pres., 1989). Chm., Cons. Health, 2012–. FKC 1992; FMedSci 1999. Hon. FACP 1992; Hon. FRCPI 2001. Hon. Fellow, UCL, 2008. Gold Medal, Canadian Liver Foundn, 1992; Lifetime Achievement Award, British Assoc. for the Study of the Liver, 2003; Wyeth Senior Achievement Award for Clinical Transplantation, Amer. Soc. of Transplantation, 2004; Hans Popper Life Achievement Award, Internat. Liver Congress, Hong Kong, 2008; Distinguished Service Award, Internat. Liver Transplantation Soc., 2011; Distinguished Achievement Award, Amer. Assoc. for Study of Liver Disease, 2013. *Publications*: (ed) Fifth Symposium on Advanced Medicine, 1969; edited jointly: Immunology of the Liver, 1971; Artificial Liver Support, 1975; Immune Reactions in Liver Disease, 1978; Drug Reactions and the Liver, 1981; Variceal Bleeding, 1982; Antiviral Agents in Chronic Hepatitis B Virus Infection, 1985; The Practice of Liver Transplantation, 1995; International Developments in Health Care, 1995; Acute Liver Failure, 1996; Fulminant Hepatic Failure: seminars in liver disease, 2003; Clinical Dilemmas in Primary Liver Cancer, 2011; author of over 2000 scientific papers, review articles and book chapters. *Recreations*: tennis, sailing, opera. *Address*: Brickworth House, Whiteparish, Wilts SP5 2QE; 30 Devonshire Close, W1G 7BE; Institute of Hepatology, London, Foundation for Liver Research, 111 Coldharbour Lane, SE5 9NT. *Clubs*: Athenæum, Saints and Sinners, Royal Ocean Racing; Royal Yacht Squadron (Cowes).

**WILLIAMS, Ronald;** *see* Williams, A. R.

**WILLIAMS, Rt Rev. Ronald John Chantler;** Bishop of the Southern Region, and an Assistant Bishop, Diocese of Brisbane, 1993–2007; *b* 19 July 1938; *s* of Walter Chantler Williams and Constance Bertha Williams (*née* Pool); *m* 1963, Kathryn Rohrsheim; two *s* one *d*. *Educ*: Prince Alfred Coll., Adelaide; St John's Coll., Morpeth (ThL); St Mark's Coll., Adelaide Univ. (BA); Bristol Univ. (MSc 1974); Australian Management Coll., Mt Eliza (AMP). Ordained deacon, 1963, priest, 1964; Curate, Toorak Gardens, 1963–64; Australian Bd of Missions, Sydney, 1965; Domestic Chaplain, Bishop of Polynesia, 1966–67; Priest, Labasa, Fiji, 1967–71; Hon. Priest, Bedminster, Bristol, 1972–74; Dean of Suva, Fiji, 1974–79; Rector, Campbelltown, Adelaide, 1979–84; Priest to City of Adelaide and founding Dir, St Paul's Centre, 1984–93; Hon. Canon, St Peter's Cathedral, Adelaide, 1986–93. *Recreation*: jazz musician—double bass. *Address*: 42 Princess Street, Bulimba, Qld 4171, Australia. *T*: (7) 33999818. *E*: rk.will@bigpond.com.

**WILLIAMS, Ronald Millward,** CBE 1990; DL; Member, Essex County Council, 1970–93 and 1997–2005 (Chairman, 1983–86); *b* 9 Dec. 1922; *s* of George and Gladys Williams; *m* 1943, Joyce (*d* 2009); one *s* two *d*. *Educ*: Leeds College of Technology. Electrical Engineer, then Industrial Eng Superintendent, Mobil Oil Co. Ltd, 1954–82. Member: Benfleet Urban Dist Council, 1960–74 (Chm. 1963–66, 1972–74); Castle Point Dist Council, 1974–87 (Chm. 1980–81; Leader, 1981–87); Essex County Council: Leader Cons. Gp, 1977–83, 1986–87; Chairman: County Planning Cttee, 1981–83; County Highways Cttee, 1989–93; Envmtl Services Bd, 1998–2000; Exec. Mem., with strategic planning and transportation portfolio, 2000–01; Cabinet Mem., Highways and Transportation, 2001–03; Hon. Alderman, 2005. Chm., Southend Health Authority, 1982–90, Southend Health Care Services, NHS Trust, 1990–96. Chm., SE Essex Abbeyfield Soc., 1983–88. DL Essex, 1983. Hon. Freeman, Borough of Castle Point, 2006. *Recreations*: supporter, football, cricket, bowls, tennis; video filming of countryside.

**WILLIAMS, Roy,** CB 1989; Deputy Secretary, Department of Trade and Industry, 1984–94; *b* 31 Dec. 1934; *s* of Eric Williams and Ellen Williams; *m* 1959, Shirley, *d* of Captain and Mrs O. Warwick; one *s* one *d*. *Educ*: Liverpool Univ. (1st Cl. BA Econs). Asst Principal, Min. of Power, 1956; Principal, 1961; Harkness Commonwealth Fellow, Univs

**WILLIAMS, Rev. Samuel Lewis**; Minister, St Columba's United Reformed Church, Gosport, 1991–96; *b* 8 Jan. 1934; *s* of Thomas John Williams and Miriam Mary Williams (*née* West); *m* 1958, Mary Sansom (*née* Benjamin); one *s* one *d*. *Educ*: Pagefield College Public Day School, Newport, Gwent; Memorial Coll. (Congregational), Brecon. Local government officer, 1950–52; RAF, 1952–55; theol. training, 1955–58. Ordained Congregational (URC) Minister, 1958; Mill Street Congregational Church, Newport, Gwent, 1958–63; Bettws Congregational Church, 1963–66; Llanvaches Congregational Church, 1966–68; Free Churches Chaplain, St Woolas Hosp., Newport, 1964–68. Entered RN as Chaplain, 1968; served HMS: Seahawk, 1968–69; Hermes, 1969–70; Raleigh, 1970–71; Seahawk, 1971–73; Daedalus, 1973–74; served Malta, 1974–76; C-in-C Naval Home Comd staff, 1977–81; HMS Sultan, 1981–84; Flag Officer Scotland and NI staff, 1984–86; HMS Heron, 1986; Prin. Chaplain (Navy), Ch of Scotland and Free Churches, 1986–91; RN retired, 1991. QHC, 1986–91. *Recreations*: oil painting, golf, hill walking, music, gardening, Rugby. *Address*: 18 Brodrick Avenue, Gosport, Hants PO12 2EN. *T*: (023) 9258 1114.

**WILLIAMS, Sara Ann, (Sally)**; *see* Muggeridge, S. A.

**WILLIAMS, Sarah Rosalind**; *see* Palmer, S. R.

**WILLIAMS, Sean Mountford Graham**; Founder, shareholder and non-executive Director, Nosy Crow Ltd, since 2011; Senior Adviser, Boston Consulting Group, since 2018; Chairman: G.Network, since 2018; Grain Connect, since 2019; *b* London, 1 June 1963; *s* of Tony Williams and Sheelagh Williams; *m*; three *s* one *d*. *Educ*: Charterhouse; Worcester Coll., Oxford (BA 1986); Kennedy Sch. of Govt, Harvard Univ. (MPA 1990). Man. Dir, Williams Lea & Co., 1990–92; Gp Finance Dir, Williams Lea Gp, 1993–95; Special Advr, Prime Minister's Policy Unit, 1995–97; Partner, LEK Consulting LLP, 1997–2003; Exec. Dir, OFCOM, 2003–07; Exec. Dir, Markets and Projects, OFT, 2007–08; BT Group plc: Man. Dir, Strategy, Portfolio, Legal and Regulatory Services, 2008–11; Gp Dir, Strategy, Policy and Portfolio, then Chief Strategy Officer, 2011–17. Non-exec. Dir, Williams Lea Hldgs plc, 1995–2008. Trustee, Bodhi Coll., 2017–. Liveryman, Leathersellers' Co., 1989–. *Recreations*: cycling, meditation, singing, family. *Address*: 6 Coates Castle, Fittleworth, W Sussex RH20 1EU. *T*: (01798) 865164; 62 Warwick Square, SW1V 2AL. *T*: (020) 7630 9941. *E*: smgwilliams@btinternet.com.

**WILLIAMS, Serena Jameka**; tennis player; *b* Mich, USA, 26 Sept. 1981; *d* of Richard and Oracene Williams; *m* 2017, Alexis Ohanian; one *d*. *Educ*: Fort Lauderdale Art Inst. (degree in fashion design). Professional tennis player, 1995–: Grand Slam wins: (singles): US Open, 1999, 2002, 2008, 2012, 2013, 2014; French Open, 2002, 2013, 2015; Wimbledon, 2002, 2003, 2009, 2010, 2012, 2015; Australian Open, 2003, 2005, 2007, 2009, 2010, 2015, 2017; (doubles, with Venus Williams): French Open, 1999; US Open, 1999, 2012, 2013; Wimbledon, 2000, 2002, 2008, 2009, 2012; Australian Open, 2001, 2003, 2010; (mixed doubles, with Max Mirnyi) Wimbledon, US Open, 1998. Winner, Women's Tennis Assoc. Championships, 2001, 2009, 2012, 2013, 2014. Member: US Fedn Cup Team, 1999, 2003, 2007, 2012, 2013; US Olympic Team, Sydney, 2000 (Gold Medallist, doubles, with Venus Williams), Beijing, 2008 (Gold Medallist, doubles, with Venus Williams); London, 2012 (Gold Medallist singles and doubles, with Venus Williams); ranked world No 1, 2002, 2009, 2013, 2014. Player of the Year, Women's Tennis Assoc., 2002, 2008, 2009, 2012, 2013. Founder and designer, fashion label, Aneres, 2004–; launched Serena Williams Collection by Nike, apparel and footwear collection, 2005; numerous appearances as actress on TV progs. *Publications*: (with Venus Williams and Hilary Beard) Venus & Serena - Serving from the Hip: 10 rules for living, loving and winning, 2005; Queen of the Court (autobiog.), 2009. *Address*: c/o William Morris Endeavor Entertainment, 9601 Wilshire Boulevard, Beverly Hills, CA 90210, USA; c/o US Tennis Association, 70 West Red Oak Lane, White Plains, NY 10604, USA.

*See also* V. E. S. Williams.

**WILLIAMS, Sian Mary**; journalist and broadcaster; Channel 5 News Presenter, since 2016; *b* London, 28 Nov. 1964; *d* of John Price Williams and late Katherine Elizabeth Rees; *m* 2012, Paul Woolwich; one *s* one *d*; two *s* from previous marriage. *Educ*: Oxford Brookes Univ. (BA Hons English and History); Univ. of Westminster (MSc Psychol. (Dist.)); City, Univ. of London (DPsych). BBC Radio trng scheme, 1987–88; reporter, BBC Radio Merseyside, 1988–90; Sen. Producer, BBC Radio 4 World at One/PM, 1990–97; Editor, 1997, Sen. Presenter, 1997–99, BBC News 24; Special Corresp., BBC 6 O'Clock News, 1999–2001; Presenter, 2001–05, Main Presenter, 2005–12, BBC1 Breakfast; Co-host, Saturday Live, BBC Radio 4, 2012–13; BBC Events commentator, 2013–15; Presenter: BBC1 Sunday Morning Live, 2014–15; Save Money: Good Health, ITV; Secrets of Your Supermarket Food, C5; occasional presenter, BBC1 and BBC Radio 4 progs. Pres., Television and Radio Industries Club, 2007–08, 2009–10. Patron: Sparks; Hearing Link. Hon. Fellow, Cardiff Univ., 2012. Hon. DArt Oxford Brookes, 2017. *Publications*: Rise: surviving and thriving after trauma, 2016. *Recreations*: cinema, wine, walking. *Address*: c/o Sue Ayton, Knight Ayton Management, 29 Gloucester Place, W1U 8HX. *T*: (0203795 1806. *E*: info@knightayton.co.uk.

**WILLIAMS, Simon Huw Llewelyn**; Headmaster, Churcher's College, since 2004; *b* Hawarden, N Wales, 15 Oct. 1961; *s* of Dr Bill Williams and Judith Williams; *m* 1993, Alison Gemmell; two *s* one *d*. *Educ*: Kingswood Sch., Bath; Durham Univ. (BSc Biol Physiol.); Jesus Coll., Cambridge (PGCE); Keele Univ. (MA). Teacher of Biol. and Hd of Rugby, King's Coll. Sch., Wimbledon, 1984–93; Hd of Biol. and Hd of Sci., Newcastle-under-Lyme Sch., 1993–97; Dep. Hd, Warwick Sch., 1997–2004. *Recreations*: sport, DIY, outdoor pursuits, travel. *Address*: Churcher's College, Ramshill, Petersfield, Hants GU31 4AS. *T*: (01730) 263033. *E*: headmaster@churcherscollege.com.

**WILLIAMS, Rear Adm. Simon Paul**, CB 2017; CVO 2015; Naval Secretary, Assistant Chief of Naval Staff (Personnel) and Flag Officer Reserves, 2015–18; *b* Bristol, 13 July 1960; *s* of Philip Williams and June Williams; *m* 1986, Charlotte Jane Anderson; one *s* one *d*. *Educ*: Salisbury Cathedral Sch.; Kingsbridge Sch.; City Univ. (BSc (Hons) Systems and Mgt). PWO(CEW) 1990. Gunnery Officer, HMS Pollington, 1983–85; Navigating Officer, HMS Minerva, 1986–87; Exec. Officer, HMS Orkney, 1987–89; Principal Warfare Officer, HMS Sheffield, 1990–92; Amphibious Warfare Staff, 1992–94; Sea Trng Staff, 1995–96; CO HMS Brecon, 1997; Navy Plans, 1997–99; Equipment Plans, 1999–2000; CO HMS Sheffield, 2001–02; Asst Dir Strategy Naval Staff, 2002–04; CO HMS Cornwall, 2005–06; Dep. Dir Operational Capability, 2006–08; Dir Naval Personnel Strategy, 2008–11; Cdre Naval Core Trng and CO, BRNC, 2011–12; Defence Services Sec. and ACDS (Personnel and Trng), 2012–15. CCMI 2012. *Recreations*: amateur artisan dabbling in cars, decrepit houses and sundry equipments, driving cars and boats, experimenting in canal transits, cycling, camping. *E*: simonpw@hotmail.co.uk. *Club*: Royal Navy of 1765 and 1785.

**WILLIAMS, Rear Adm. Simon Thomas**, OBE 2004; Chairman, Clarion Defence and Security Ltd, since 2012; Director, RedDrig Ltd, since 2012; *b* Swansea, 22 March 1957; *s* of Derek and Catherine Williams; *m* 1984, Catherine White; two *s* one *d*. *Educ*: Reigate Grammar Sch.; City Univ., London (BSc Hons); King's Coll. London (MA). Joined RN, 1976; HM Submarines, 1981–88; Submarine Command Course, 1988; XO, HMS Turbulent, 1988–90; on exchange in USA, 1990–92; Commanding Officer: HMS Superb, 1992–94; Submarine Command Course, 1994–96; Staff, Flag Officer Submarines, 1996–98; Desk Officer, Navy Plans, MoD, 1998–2000; Asst Dir (ME), MoD, 2000–03; DACOS Fleet (Ops), 2003–05; UK Maritime Component Comdr, Bahrain, 2005–06; Dir, Strategic Plans, MoD, 2006–09; Sen. Directing Staff (Navy), RCDS, 2009–11. Non-executive Director: 3CN Ltd, 2012–17; Corp. Governance Gp, Welsh Govt, 2012–. *Recreations*: reading, walking.

**WILLIAMS, Stephen Geoffrey**; Chief Legal Officer and Group Secretary, Unilever plc and Unilever NV, 1986–2010; *b* Ilford, 31 Jan. 1948; *s* of Alfred Earnest Williams and Edith Betty Williams (*née* Harding); *m* 1972, Susan Jennifer Cottam; one *s*. *Educ*: Brentwood Sch., Essex; King's Coll., London (LLB Hons). Admitted as solicitor, 1972; solicitor, Slaughter and May, 1970–75; Attorney, ICI, 1975–86. Director: Bunzl plc, 1995–2004; Arriva plc, 2004–10; Whitbread plc, 2008–17; Croda International PLC, 2010–19; Eversheds, then Eversheds Sutherland LLP, 2011–17. Sen. Advr, Spencer Stuart LLP, 2011–. Mem., Companies Cttee, CBI, 1998–. Vice Chm., De La Warr Pavilion, 2015– (Chm., 2008–15). Member, Board: Leverhulme Trust, 2011–; Moorfields Hosp. Trust, 2012– (Dep. Chm., 2014–). FRSA. *Recreations*: contemporary fiction, vulgar automobiles, modern art and architecture. *Address*: 15 Queens Gate Gardens, SW7 5LY. *E*: stevewilliams247@gmail.com. *Clubs*: Royal Automobile, 2 Brydges Place.

**WILLIAMS, Stephen Michael**; Director (formerly Director of European Affairs), Channel Islands Brussels Office, since 2011; *b* 20 July 1959; *s* of Very Rev. H. C. N. Williams and of Pamela Williams; *m* 1983, Fiona Michele Hume; one *s* two *d*. *Educ*: Sidney Sussex Coll., Cambridge (BA 1980, MA). Entered Foreign and Commonwealth Office, 1981; Third, later Second, Sec., Sofia, 1984–87; EU Dept (Ext.), FCO, 1987–90; on secondment to Barclays Bank, 1990–91; Hd, Econ. and Commercial Sect., Oslo, 1991–95; First Sec. (Ext. Relns), UK Perm. Repn to EU, Brussels, 1995–98; Dep. Hd, EU Dept (Int.), FCO, 1998–2000; Minister and Dep. Hd of Mission, Buenos Aires, 2001–03; Hd, Latin America & Caribbean Dept, FCO, 2003–05; Dir, Americas, FCO, 2005–07; Ambassador to Bulgaria, 2007–11. *Recreations*: walking, sport, music. *Address*: Channel Islands Brussels Office, Rond Point Schuman 6/8, 1040 Brussels, Belgium. *T*: (2) 26391440. *E*: info@channelislands.eu.

**WILLIAMS, Stephen Roy**; *b* 11 Oct. 1966. *Educ*: Mountain Ash Comprehensive Sch., Glamorgan; Univ. of Bristol (BA 1988). Coopers and Lybrand, Bristol, 1988–95; Tax Manager: Kraft Jacobs Suchard Ltd, 1995; Grant Thornton, Cheltenham, 1996–98, Bristol, 1998–2001; Tax Accountant for Orange plc, Wincanton plc and RAC plc, 2001–05. Member (Lib Dem): Avon CC, 1993–96; Bristol CC, 1995–99. Contested (Lib Dem): Bristol S, 1997; Bristol W, 2001, 2017. MP (Lib Dem) Bristol W, 2005–15. Shadow Minister: for Public Health, 2005–06; for Further and Higher Education, 2006–07; for Schools, 2007; Shadow Sec. of State for Innovation, Univs and Skills, 2007–10; Parly Under-Sec. of State, DCLG, 2013–15. Member: Educn Select Cttee, 2005–07; Public Accounts Cttee, 2005–06; Children, Schs and Families Select Cttee, 2007–08; Political and Constitutional Reform Select Cttee, 2010–13; Chair: All Party Parly Gp on Smoking and Health, 2010–13; Lib Dem Backbench Treasury Cttee, 2010–13.

**WILLIAMS, Steven**; Co-Founder and Chief Executive Officer, Midas Public Relations, since 1990; *b* Plymouth, 27 Oct. 1953; *s* of Adm. Sir David Williams, GCB and of Philippa Beatrice Williams (*née* Stevens); *m* 1978, Ruth McCarthy; two *d*. *Educ*: St Edward's Sch., Oxford; Durham Univ. (BA). Publicity Manager, Leo Cooper Ltd, 1975–77; Publicity Dir, Heinemann, 1977–83; Steven Williams Consultancy, 1983–90. *Recreations*: cricket, tennis, gardening, reading, Italy. *Address*: 28 Waldemar Avenue, W13 9BY. *T*: 07899 920720. *E*: steven.williams@midaspr.co.uk. *Club*: Burntwood House Cricket.

**WILLIAMS, Stuart John**; Regional Employment Judge, Wales, 2009–15; a fee-paid Employment Judge, Wales Region, since 2015; *b* Caerleon, 8 April 1949; *s* of Arthur Williams and Ann Williams; *m* 1980, Lindsey Keatley; one *s* one *d*. *Educ*: Jones' West Monmouth Sch., Pontypool; Magdalen Coll., Oxford (BA Hons Mod. Langs); Sch. of Oriental and African Studies, Univ. of London (MA African Studies). VSO, 1970–72; Lector, British Council, Slovakia, 1972–73; Technical Translator, 1975–81; called to the Bar, Gray's Inn, 1981; pt-time Chm., Employment Tribunals, 1992–95; full-time Chm., Employment Tribunals, later Employment Judge, 1995–2009. *Recreations*: Rugby (passive only), cricket (still slightly active), singing (active and passive), gardening.

**WILLIAMS, Susan Elizabeth**, OBE 2000; Director of Nursing, Lanarkshire Primary Care NHS Trust, 2001–03; *b* 30 Oct. 1942; *d* of late Ernest George Fost and of Kathleen Beatrice Maud Fost; *m* 1st, 1964, Dennis Norman Carnevale (decd); one *s* one *d*; 2nd, 1977, Keith Edward Williams (marr. diss. 1996). *Educ*: Grammar School for Girls, Weston-super-Mare; Wolverhampton Polytechnic (Post-grad. DipPsych); Bristol Royal Hosps (RSCN, RGN, RNT); BEd (Hons), DipN London. Ward Sister, Royal Hosp. for Sick Children, Bristol, 1972–76; Nurse Tutor, Salop Area Sch. of Nursing, 1976–80; Sen. Tutor, Dudley AHA, 1980–83; Reg. Nurse (Educn and Res.), W Midlands RHA, 1983–87; Chief Nurse Advr/Dir of Nurse Educn, Bromsgrove and Redditch HA, 1987–88; Regl Dir of Nursing and Quality Assurance, W Midlands RHA, 1988–93; Dep. Dir of Nursing Management Exec., DoH, 1993–94; Dir of Nursing, Greater Glasgow Community and Mental Health NHS Trust, 1994–98; Nurse Advr to Greater Glasgow Health Bd, 1998–2001. Board Member: Erskine Hospital, 2001; Prince and Princess of Wales Hospice, 2003–05. *Recreations*: hill walking, photography, reading, listening to music, foreign travel.

**WILLIAMS, Susan Frances**; a District Judge, Magistrates' Courts, since 2002; *b* 27 Nov. 1955; *d* of Major John Trelawny Williams and Joyce Williams. *Educ*: Kent Coll.; Bristol Univ. (LLB Hons). Called to the Bar, Middle Temple, 1978; barrister in private practice specialising in criminal law, 1978–2002; a Recorder, 2006. Mem., Criminal Bar Assoc., 1987–2002. Member: Hall Cttee, Middle Temple, 1984–94; N London Bar Mess, 1994–2002 (Jun. for Wood Green Crown Court). *Recreations*: gardening (Mem., RHS), malt whisky tasting (Mem., Scotch Malt Whisky Soc.). *Address*: Highbury Corner Magistrates' Court, 51 Holloway Road, N7 8JA. *T*: (020) 7506 3150.

**WILLIAMS, Rt Rev. Thomas Anthony**; Auxiliary Bishop of Liverpool, (RC), Vicar General, and Titular Bishop of Mageo, since 2003; Apostolic Administrator, Archdiocese of Liverpool, 2013–14; *b* Liverpool, 10 Feb. 1948; *s* of late Richard and Margaret Williams. *Educ*: Christleton Hall, Chester; English Coll., Lisbon; St Joseph's Coll., Upholland. Ordained priest, 1972; Curate: St Francis of Assisi, Garston, 1972–75; Sacred Heart,

Liverpool, 1975–83 (Chaplain to Royal Liverpool Hosp.); Our Lady of Walsingham, Netherton, 1983–84; Parish Priest, Liverpool: Our Lady Immaculate, 1984–89 and 1999–2003; St Anthony's, 1989–2003. Mem., Catholic Bishops' Conf. of England and Wales, 2003– (Bishop responsible for Hosp. Chaplaincy, 2003–). Member: Archdiocesan Finance Adv. Cttee, 1977–2013; George Andrew Fund Cttee, 1994–; Liverpool City Centre Ecumenical Team, 1996–; Trustee: Archdiocese of Liverpool, 2003–; Nugent Care Soc., 2003–. Mem., Archdiocese of Liverpool Chapter of Canons, 2001. KC★HS 2008. *Recreations:* music, golf. *Address:* (office) 14 Hope Place, Liverpool L1 9BG.

**WILLIAMS, His Eminence Cardinal Thomas Stafford,** ONZ 2000; DD; Archbishop of Wellington, (RC), and Metropolitan of New Zealand, 1979–2005, now Emeritus Archbishop; *b* 20 March 1930; *s* of Thomas Stafford Williams and Lillian Maude Kelly. *Educ:* Holy Cross Primary School, Miramar; SS Peter and Paul Primary School, Lower Hutt; St Patrick's Coll., Wellington; Victoria University Coll., Wellington; St Kevin's Coll., Oamaru; Holy Cross Coll., Mosgiel; Collegio Urbano de Propaganda Fide, Rome (STL); University Coll., Dublin (BScSc); Hon. DD. Assistant Priest, St Patrick's Parish, Palmerston North, 1963–64; Director of Studies, Catholic Enquiry Centre, Wellington, 1965–70; Parish Priest: St Anne's Parish, Leulumoega, W Samoa, 1971–75; Holy Family Parish, Porirua, NZ, 1976–79. Cardinal, 1983. *Address:* 229/112 Parata Street, Waikanae 5036, New Zealand. *T:* (4) 2934684.

**WILLIAMS, Thomasina Jean;** *see* Miers, T. J.

**WILLIAMS, Prof. Timothy John,** PhD; FMedSci; FRS 2012; Asthma UK Professor of Applied Pharmacology and Head of Leukocyte Biology Section, National Heart and Lung Institute, Faculty of Medicine, Imperial College London, 1988–2010, now Professor Emeritus; *b* Gloucester, 31 March 1945; *s* of Francis Edward and Joyce Edith Williams; *m* 1st, 1968, Susan Jean Condie (marr. diss. 1983); one *s* one *d*; 2nd, 1988, Helen Mary Carey; two *d*. *Educ:* Sir Thomas Rich's Grammar Sch., Gloucester; University Coll. London (BSc Hons Physiol. 1968); Kennedy Inst. of Rheumatol. and University Coll. London (PhD Pharmacol. 1978). Lectr, Dept of Pharmacol., Inst. of Basic Med. Scis, RCS, 1979–84; MRC Sen. Career Scientist, Clin. Res. Centre, Northwick Park, Harrow, 1984–88; Jt Dir, KCL/Imperial Coll. London MRC and Asthma UK Centre in Allergic Mechanisms of Asthma, 2005–10; Campus Dean, Faculty of Medicine, S Kensington Campus, Imperial Coll. London, 2006–10. Exec. Dir and Hd of Asthma and Allergy, Novartis Insts for BioMed. Res., Horsham, 2010–11. For. Mem., Brazilian Acad. of Scis, 2007. FMedSci 2000. Hon. FBPhS 2015. Pfizer Academic Prize, 1984; Gaddum Meml Prize, British Pharmacol Soc., 2000; Jack Pepys Lectureship Award, British Soc. for Allergy and Clin. Immunol., 2003; Ulf von Euler Meml Lectureship Award, Karolinska Inst., Stockholm, 2010; Derek Willoughby Lectureship Award, William Harvey Inst., 2011; Paul Ehrlich Lectureship Award, Internat. Eosinophil Soc., Quebec City, 2011. *Publications:* contrib. chapters in books and 255 peer-reviewed papers, editorials and articles in scientific press; patents covering discovery of Eotaxin molecule. *Recreations:* photography, collecting optical instruments. *Address:* National Heart and Lung Institute, Faculty of Medicine, Sir Alexander Fleming Building, Imperial College London, S Kensington, SW7 2AZ. *T:* (020) 7594 3159, *Fax:* (020) 7594 3119. *E:* tim.williams@imperial.ac.uk.

**WILLIAMS, Rt Rev. Trevor Russell;** Bishop of Limerick and Killaloe, 2008–14; Chairman, Christian Aid Ireland, 2010–18; *b* Dublin, 29 June 1948; *s* of James Williams and Ada Clare Williams; *m* 1972, Joyce Milne; three *s*. *Educ:* Trinity Coll. Dublin (BA Natural Scis 1971); St John's Theol Coll., Nottingham (BA Theol. 1973; Dip. in Pastoral Theol. 1974). Ordained deacon, 1974, priest, 1975; Curate, St Mary's, Maidenhead, 1974–77; Asst Chaplain, QUB, 1977–80; Religious Broadcasting Producer, BBC Ulster, 1980–88; Rector, St John's Parish, Newcastle, Dio. of Down and Dromore, 1988–93; Leader, Corrymeela Community, 1993–2003; Rector, Holy Trinity and St Silas Joanmount with Immanuel Ardoyne, Dio. of Connor, 2003–08. Canon, St Patrick's Cathedral, Dublin, 2001–08. *Recreations:* sailing, computing, music. *Address:* 50 Murlough View, Dundrum, Co. Down BT33 0WE. *T:* (028) 4375 1838. *E:* bishoptrevor.williams@gmail.com.

**WILLIAMS, Venetia Mary;** racehorse trainer, since 1996; *b* 10 May 1960; *d* of late John Williams and Patricia Williams. *Educ:* Downe House Sch., Newbury. Trained winners of: King George VI Gold Cup, Kempton Park; Hennessy Gold Cup, Newbury; Welsh Grand Nat., Chepstow (twice); Scottish Champion Hurdle, Ayr; Grand Annual Chase, Cleeve Hurdle (3 times), Coral Cup, Racing Post Plate, Pertemps Final Hurdle and Festival Plate Chase (twice), Cheltenham; Ascot Chase; Grand National (Mon Mome, 2009). *Recreations:* ski-ing (snow and water), travel. *Address:* Aramstone, Kings Caple, Hereford HR1 4TU. *T:* (01432) 840646, 07770 627108. *E:* office@venetiawilliams.com.

**WILLIAMS, Venus Ebony Starr;** tennis player; *b* Calif, USA, 17 June 1980; *d* of Richard and Oracene Williams. Professional tennis player, 1994–: Grand Slam wins: (singles): Wimbledon, 2000, 2001, 2005, 2007, 2008; US Open, 2000, 2001; (doubles, with Serena Williams): French Open, 1999; US Open, 1999; Wimbledon, 2000, 2002, 2008, 2009, 2012; Australian Open, 2001, 2003, 2010; (mixed doubles, with Justin Gimelstob): Australian Open, French Open, 1998. Member: US Fedn Cup Team, 1995, 1999, 2003; US Olympic Team, Sydney, 2000 (Gold Medallist, singles and doubles), Athens, 2004, Beijing, 2008 (Gold Medallist, doubles, with Serena Williams); London, 2012 (Gold Medallist, doubles, with Serena Williams); ranked world No 1, 2002. Pres. and CEO, V Starr Interiors, 2002–; Founder and CEO, EleVen by Venus, 2007–. *Publications:* (with Serena Williams and Hilary Beard) Venus & Serena - Serving from the Hip: 10 rules for living, loving and winning, 2005; Come to Win, 2010. *Address:* EleVen by Venus, 7656 Byron Drive, Suite B5, Riviera Beach, FL 33404–3338, USA; c/o US Tennis Association, 70 West Red Oak Lane, White Plains, NY 10604, USA.
 *See also* S. J. *Williams*.

**WILLIAMS, Victoria Helen;** *see* McCloud, V. H.

**WILLIAMS, Victoria Kirstyn, (Kirsty),** CBE 2013; Member (Lib Dem) Brecon and Radnorshire, National Assembly for Wales, since 1999; Minister (formerly Cabinet Secretary) for Education, since 2016; *b* 19 March 1971; *d* of Edward G. Williams and Pamela M. Williams (*née* Hall); *m* 2000, Richard John Rees; three *d*. *Educ:* St Michael's Sch., Llanelli; Univ. of Manchester (BA Hons Amer. Studies 1993); Univ. of Missouri. Marketing and PR Exec., 1994–97. National Assembly for Wales: Chairman: Health and Social Services Cttee, 1999–2003 (Mem., 2003–05, 2011); Standards Cttee, 2003–08 (Mem., 2011); Sustainability Cttee, 2010–11; Member: Local Govt and Public Services Cttee, 2003–04; Economic Develt and Transport Cttee, 2005–08; Proposed Learner Travel Measure and Learning and Skills Measure Cttees, 2008; Finance Cttee, 2008. Lib Dem Business Manager, 2000–08; Leader, Welsh Liberal Democrats, 2008–16. Dep. Pres., Welsh Liberal Democrats, 1997–99. *Recreations:* horse riding, sport, farming. *Address:* National Assembly for Wales, Cardiff CF99 1NA. *T:* 0300 200 7277.

**WILLIAMS, Sir (William) Max (Harries),** Kt 1983; solicitor; Senior Partner, Clifford Chance, 1989–91 (Joint Senior Partner, 1987–89); *b* 18 Feb. 1926; *s* of Llwyd and Hilary Williams; *m* 1951, Jenifer (*d* 1999), *d* of late Rt Hon. E. L. Burgin, LLD, and Mrs Burgin, JP; two *d*. *Educ:* Nautical Coll., Pangbourne. Served 178 Assault Field Regt RA, Far East (Captain), 1943–47. Admitted Solicitor, 1950. Sen. Partner, Clifford Turner, 1984–87. Mem. Council, 1962–85, Pres., 1982–83, Law Society. Mem., Crown Agents for Oversea Govts and Administration, 1982–86; Lay Mem., Stock Exchange Council, 1984–93; Mem., Stock Exchange Appeals Cttee, 1989–2000. Director: Royal Insurance plc, 1985–95 (Dep. Chm., 1992–95); 3i Group plc, 1988–96 (Dep. Chm., 1993–96; Chm. Audit Cttee, 1991–96); Garden Pension Trustees Ltd, 1990–96; Royal Insurance Co. of Canada, 1991–95. Chairman: Review Bd for Govt Contracts, 1986–93; Police Appeals Tribunal, 1993–99. Member: Royal Commission on Legal Services, 1976–79; Cttee of Management of Inst. of Advanced Legal Studies, 1980–86; Council, Wildfowl Trust (Hon. Treasurer, 1974–80). Pres., City of London Law Soc., 1986–87. Mem., Amer. Law Inst., 1985–; Hon. Member: Amer. Bar Assoc.; Canadian Bar Assoc. Master, Solicitors' Co., 1986–87. Hon. LLD Birmingham, 1983. *Recreations:* golf, fishing, ornithology. *Address:* Orinda, Holly Lane, Harpenden, Herts AL5 5DY. *Club:* Garrick.

**WILLIAMS, Hon. Sir Wyn (Lewis),** Kt 2007; FLSW; a Judge of the High Court of Justice, Queen's Bench Division, 2007–17; President, Welsh Tribunals, since 2017; a Judge of the Courts of Appeal of Guernsey and Jersey, since 2018; *b* 31 March 1951; *s* of Ronald and Nellie Williams; *m* 1973, Carol Ann Bosley; one *s* one *d*. *Educ:* Rhondda County Grammar Sch.; Corpus Christi Coll., Oxford (MA). Called to the Bar, Inner Temple, 1974, Bencher, 2007; in practice at the Bar, Cardiff, 1974–88, and London, 1998–2004; QC 1992; a Recorder, 1992–2004; a Circuit Judge (specialist Chancery Circuit Judge for Wales and Chester Circuit), 2004–07; a Presiding Judge, Wales Circuit, 2012–15. Dep. Chm., Boundary Commn for Wales, 2012–16; Chairman: Lord Chancellor's Standing Cttee on Welsh Lang., 2012–15; Wales Trng Cttee, Judicial Coll., 2013–16. Justice in Wales Comr, 2017–. Mem., Disciplinary Panel, Internat. Rugby Bd, 1999–2011; Chm., Professional Rugby Game Bd for Wales, 2013–17. Pres., Pendyrus Male Choir, 2008–. FLSW 2013. Hon. LLD Glamorgan, 2012. *Recreations:* sport, particularly Rugby, music, reading. *Clubs:* Cardiff and County; Tylorstown Rugby Football.

**WILLIAMS, Wynford;** *see* Williams, D. W.

**WILLIAMS-BULKELEY, Sir Richard (Thomas),** 14th Bt *cr* 1661 of Penrhyn, Caernarvonshire; Vice Lord-Lieutenant of Gwynedd, 2006–14; *b* 25 May 1939; *s* of Sir Richard Harry David Williams-Bulkeley, 13th Bt, TD and Renée Arundell (*d* 1994), *yr d* of Sir Thomas Neave, 5th Bt; *S* father, 1992; *m* 1964, Sarah Susan, *er d* of Rt Hon. Sir Henry Josceline Phillimore, OBE; twin *s* one *d*. *Educ:* Eton. FRICS 1989. Captain, Welsh Guards, 1964. High Sheriff, 1993, DL 1998, Gwynedd. *Recreation:* astronomy. *Heir: s* Major Richard Hugh Williams-Bulkeley, Welsh Guards [*b* 8 July 1968; *m* 1995, Jacqueline, *er d* of David Edwards; two *s* one *d*].

**WILLIAMS-WYNN, Sir (David) Watkin,** 11th Bt *cr* 1688, of Gray's Inn; DL; *b* 18 Feb. 1940; *s* of Sir Owen Watkin Williams-Wynn, 10th Bt, CBE and Margaret Jean (*d* 1961), *d* of late Col William Alleyne Macbean, RA; *S* father, 1988; *m* 1st, 1967, Harriet Veryan Elspeth (marr. diss. 1981), *d* of Gen. Sir Norman Tailyour, KCB, DSO; two *s* twin *d*; 2nd, 1983, Victoria Jane Dillon (marr. diss. 1998), *d* of late Lt-Col Ian Dudley De-Ath, DSO, MBE; twin *s*. *Educ:* Eton. Lt Royal Dragoons, 1958–63; Major Queen's Own Yeomanry, 1970–77. DL 1970, High Sheriff, 1990, Clwyd. *Recreations:* foxhunting and other field sports. *Heir: s* Charles Edward Watkin Williams-Wynn, *b* 17 Sept. 1970. *Address:* Plas-yn-Cefn, St Asaph, N Wales LL17 0EY. *T:* (01745) 585515. *Clubs:* Pratt's, Cavalry and Guards.

**WILLIAMSON,** family name of **Baron Forres**.

**WILLIAMSON, Adrian John Gerard Hughes;** QC 2002; a Recorder, since 2004; a Deputy High Court Judge, since 2010; *b* 25 Nov. 1959; *s* of late Dennis Walter Williamson and Margaret Teresa Williamson; *m* 1983, Gillian Herrod; two *s* one *d*. *Educ:* Highgate Sch.; Trinity Hall, Cambridge (BA 1st Cl. Hons Law 1982, MA 1985, PhD 2014). Called to the Bar, Middle Temple, 1983, Bencher, 2018; in private practice as barrister, specialising in construction law, 1985–. Pt-time Supervisor in Law, Churchill Coll., Cambridge, 1982–84. Gov., St Thomas More Primary Sch., Saffron Walden, 1996–2003. FRHistS 2015. *Publications:* (contrib.) Keating on Building Contracts, 5th edn 1991 to 10th edn 2016; (ed jtly) Halsbury's Laws of England, vol. 4(3): Building Contracts, Building Societies, 2002; (gen. ed.) Keating on JCT Contracts, 2006; Conservative Economic Policymaking and the Birth of Thatcherism, 1964–1979, 2015. *Recreations:* family, Arsenal FC, squash, tennis, Labour politics, historical writing. *Address:* Keating Chambers, 15 Essex Street, WC2R 3AA. *T:* (020) 7544 2600, *Fax:* (020) 7240 7722. *E:* awilliamson@keatingchambers.com.

**WILLIAMSON, Aldon Thompson;** Head, Dame Alice Owen's School, 1994–2005; *b* 19 June 1944; *d* of Gordon Anderson Baxter and Margaret Sophia Baxter; *m* 1966, Prof. James Williamson; one *s* one *d*. *Educ:* Aberdeen Univ. (MA Hons); Inst. of Educn, Univ. of London (PGCE). Maths teacher, S Hampstead High Sch. (GPDST), 1967–69, Head of Maths, 1969–71; Dep. Head, Dame Alice Owen's Sch., 1983–89; Head, Leventhorpe Sch., Herts, 1989–94. FRSA 1997. *Recreations:* opera, art, reading.

**WILLIAMSON, Alisdair George James;** QC 2017; *b* Solihull, 14 Jan. 1970; *s* of Alexander Boyd Williamson and Margaret Williamson; *m* 2002, Lisa Godwin; one *s* one *d*. *Educ:* Exeter Sch.; Christ Church, Oxford (BA Hons 1991; MA 1995); City Univ. (DipLaw 1993). Called to the Bar, Middle Temple, 1994; in practice as barrister, specialising in crime. *Recreations:* running, tennis, cycling. *Address:* 3 Raymond Buildings, Gray's Inn, WC1R 5BH. *T:* (020) 7400 6400.

**WILLIAMSON, Andrew George,** CBE 1999; Chairman, Exeter Primary Care, since 2014; *b* 29 Feb. 1948; *s* of Albert and Jocelyn Williamson; *m* 1972, Mary Eleanor White; one *s* one *d*. *Educ:* Southern Grammar Sch., Portsmouth; Oxford Poly. (Dip. in Social Work; CQSW); Birmingham Univ. (Advanced Management Develt Prog., 1982). Residential Child Care, Portsmouth, 1967; Child Care Officer, Hants, 1969; social work management positions in Northumberland and Wandsworth; Asst Dir of Social Services, East Sussex, 1983; Dep. Dir, West Sussex, 1986; Dir of Social Services, Devon CC, 1990–99. Chairman: N and E Devon HA, 2000–02; Cornwall and Isles of Scilly PCT, 2006–13; Coastal W Sussex CCG, 2014–15; non-exec. Dir, SW Peninsular Strategic HA, 2002–06 (Vice-Chm., 2006). Member: Top Mgt Programme, 1992–; Criminal Justice Consultative Council, 1992–95; Sec. of State for the Home Dept's Youth Justice Task Force, 1997–; Co-Chm., MoJ/DCFS Inquiry into use of restraint in secure accommodation, 2008–10. Chm. of Devon and Cornwall Workforce Confedn, 2001–04. Adviser: Nat. Authy for Child Protection, Govt of Romania, 2000–; to Minister, HSS, States of Jersey, on services for children and young people, 2011–14. Hon. Sec., Assoc. of Dirs of Social Services, 1996–99. Trustee: Exeter Council Voluntary Service, 2016–; The Staff Coll.: leadership in healthcare. FRSA 1995. *Recreations:* reading, cricket, music, theatre. *Address:* Victoria House, Clyst St George, Exeter EX3 0RE. *T:* (01392) 879725.

**WILLIAMSON, Sir Brian;** *see* Williamson, Sir R. B.

**WILLIAMSON, Christopher;** MP for Derby North, 2010–15 and since 2017 (Lab, 2010–15 and 2017–19; Ind, since 2019); *b* Derby, 16 Sept. 1956; *s* of George Williamson and Eileen Williamson; *m* 1997, Lonny Wilsoncroft (*d* 2004); one *s* one *d*; partner, Maggie Amsbury. *Educ:* St John Fisher Primary Sch.; Castle Donington High Sch.; St Thomas More

Sch., Derby; Leicester Poly. (CQSW 1985). Mechanical engr apprentice, 1972–73; bricklayer, 1973–78; market trader, 1978–79; social work asst, 1979–83, social worker, 1983–86, Derby; Welfare Rights Officer, Derbys, 1986–2000. Mem. (Lab) Derby CC, 1991–2011 (Dep. Leader, 2000–02; Leader, 2002–03, 2005–08). Contested (Lab) Derby N, 2015. Shadow Minister for Communities and Local Govt, 2010–13, for Fire and Emergency Services, 2017–18. Mem., Select Cttee on Communities and Local Govt, 2013–15. Trustee, League Against Cruel Sports, 1979–. *Recreations:* watching Derby County, walking, rambling, cycling. *Address:* House of Commons, SW1A 0AA. *E:* derbyvegan@gmail.com.

**WILLIAMSON, Prof. Edwin Henry,** PhD; King Alfonso XIII Professor of Spanish Studies, University of Oxford, 2003–17, now Emeritus; Fellow, Exeter College, Oxford, 2003–17, now Emeritus; *b* 2 Oct. 1949; *s* of Henry Alfred Williamson and Renée Williamson (*née* Clarembaux); *m* 1976, Susan Jane Fitchie; two *d*. *Educ:* Edinburgh Univ. (MA; PhD 1980). Jun. Lectr in Spanish, TCD, 1974–77; Lectr in Spanish, Birkbeck Coll., Univ. of London, 1977–90; Forbes Prof. of Hispanic Studies, Univ. of Edinburgh, 1990–2003. Leverhulme Res. Fellow, 1995–96; British Acad. Res. Leave Award, 1996–97; Leverhulme Major Res. Fellow, 2015–17; Visiting Professor: Univ. of São Paulo, Brazil, 1997; Stanford Univ., Calif, 1999; Brettschneider Vis. Scholar, Cornell Univ., 2006; Univ. of Colorado, Denver, 2010; Dist. Vis. Scholar, UCLA, 2011. Corresponding Fellow, Real Academia Española, 2016. Comdr, Orden de Isabel la Católica (Spain). *Publications:* The Half-way House of Fiction: Don Quixote and Arthurian romance, 1984, 2nd edn 1986; El Quijote y los libros de caballerías, 1991; The Penguin History of Latin America, 1992, rev. edn 2009 (trans. Portuguese, 2012, Spanish 2014); Cervantes and the Modernists, 1994; Borges: a life, 2004 (trans. Spanish and Dutch, 2006, Romanian, 2007, Hungarian, 2010, Brazilian, 2011, Chinese, 2013); (ed jtly) Autoridad y poder en el Siglo de Oro, 2009; (ed) The Cambridge Companion to Jorge Luis Borges, 2013; (ed jtly) La autoridad política y el poder de las letras en el Siglo de Oro, 2013; articles in learned jls. *Recreations:* hill-walking, cinema, theatre, visual arts, exploring cities, going abroad. *Address:* Exeter College, Turl Street, Oxford OX1 3DP. *E:* edwin.williamson@exeter.ox.ac.uk.

**WILLIAMSON, Elizabeth Ann;** Executive Editor, Victoria History of the Counties of England, 2010–13 (Architectural Editor, 1997–2010); Reader in Architectural History, University of London, 2002–13; Senior Research Fellow, Institute of Historical Research, University of London, since 2013; *b* 10 May 1950; *d* of late Walter Felce Williamson and Elizabeth Joan (*née* Ford); *m* 1995, Malcolm Slade Higgs. *Educ:* High Sch., Stamford; Courtauld Inst. of Art, London (BA Hons (Hist. of European Art) 1973). Asst, then Dep. Ed., Buildings of England, Ireland, Scotland and Wales, Penguin Books, 1976–97. Historic England (formerly English Heritage): Comr, 2003–11; Mem., Adv. Cttee, 2003–11, London Adv. Cttee, 2003–07; Chm., Historic Parks and Gardens Panel, 2007–14; Mem., Designation Review Cttee, 2013–18. Editor and researcher, Pevsner Architectural Guides, Buildings of England: Sussex: West, 2014–19. FSA 1998. *Publications:* The Buildings of England: revisions of 6 vols in series, 1978, 1979, 1983, 1984, 1994, 2019, London Docklands, 1998; (with Anne Riches and Malcolm Higgs) The Buildings of Scotland: Glasgow, 1990; contribs to 25 vols in Victoria History of the Counties of England, 1998–2013, and to England's Past for Everyone, 2007–10. *Recreation:* places and buildings in fact and fiction. *Address:* c/o Institute of Historical Research, University of London, Senate House, WC1E 7HU.

**WILLIAMSON, Rt Hon. Gavin (Alexander),** CBE 2016; PC 2015; MP (C) South Staffordshire, since 2010; Secretary of State for Education, since 2019; *b* Scarborough, 25 June 1976; *s* of Ray and Beverley Williamson; *m* 2001, Joanne Elizabeth Eland; two *d*. *Educ:* Raincliffe Secondary Sch.; Scarborough Sixth Form Coll.; Univ. of Bradford (BSc Hons Social Scis). Glynwed Gp, 1998–2004; Gen. Manager, Aynsley China, 2004–08; Divl Man. Dir and Gp Dir, NPS Gp, 2008–10. Mem. (C) N Yorks CC, 2001–05. Contested (C) Blackpool N and Fleetwood, 2005. PPS to Minister of State for NI, 2011–12, to Sec. of State for Transport, 2012–13, to Prime Minister, 2013–16; Parly Sec. to the Treasury (Govt Chief Whip), 2016–17; Sec. of State for Defence, 2017–19. Mem., NI Affairs Select Cttee, 2010–11; Chm., All Party Parly Gp on Motor Neurone Disease, 2010–14; Co-Chm., Associate Parly Design and Innovation Gp, 2010–14. Mem., Exec. Cttee, UK Br., CPA, 2010–12. *Address:* House of Commons, SW1A 0AA.

**WILLIAMSON, Sir (George) Malcolm,** Kt 2007; FCIB; Chairman: Friends Life Group Ltd (formerly Friends Provident Holdings (UK) plc, then Friends Life Group plc), 2010–15 (Independent Director, 2009–15); Charter Court Financial Services Ltd, since 2017; Senior Independent Director, Aviva plc, 2015–17; *b* 27 Feb. 1939; *s* of George and Margery Williamson; *m* Hang Thi Ngo; one *s* one *d*, and one *s* one *d* by a previous marriage. *Educ:* Bolton School. FIB. Barclays Bank: various posts, 1957–80; Local Director, 1980–81; Asst Gen. Manager, 1981–83; Regional Gen. Manager, 1983–85; Bd Mem., Post Office, and Man. Dir, Girobank plc, 1985–89; Gp Exec. Dir, Standard Chartered Bank, 1989–91; Gp Man. Dir, 1991–93, Gp Chief Exec., 1993–98, Standard Chartered PLC; Pres. and CEO, Visa Internat., San Francisco, 1998–2004. Chairman: Nat. Australia Gp Europe Ltd, 2004–12; Clydesdale Bank PLC, 2004–12; Britannic Gp plc, 2004–05 (Dep. Chm., 2002); CDC Gp plc, 2004–09; SAV Credit Ltd, 2010–11; NewDay Ltd (formerly Progressive Credit Ltd), 2010–18 (non-exec. Dir, 2018–); NewDay Ltd (formerly Invicta Card Services Ltd), 2010–18; Resolution Ltd, 2013–14; non-executive Director: National Grid Group, 1995–99; British Invisibles, 1996–98; Gp 4 Securicor, subseq. G4S, plc, 2004–08; Nat. Australia Bank, 2004–12; JP Morgan Cazenove Hldgs, 2005–10; Resolution plc, 2005–08 (Dep. Chm., 2005–08); Signet Jewelers Ltd (formerly Signet Gp plc), 2006–12 (Chm., 2006–08); Internat. Business Leaders Forum, 2006–10. Chairman: Youth Business International (formerly Youth Business Internat. Adv. Bd, then The Prince's Youth Business Internat.), 2005–; Youth Business America, 2009–11 (non-exec. Dir, 2009–13). Mem. Council, Industrial Soc., 1996–98. Chairman: Strategy and Develt Bd, Cass Business Sch., 2008–; Governing Council, Centre for the Study of Financial Innovation, 2012–. Hon. DSc: City, 2010; ifs Sch. of Finance, 2013. *Recreations:* mountaineering, golf, chess. *Clubs:* Oriental; Rucksack, Pedestrian (Manchester).

**WILLIAMSON, Hazel Eleanor;** *see* Marshall, H. E.

**WILLIAMSON, Helen Sheppard, (Sarah);** *see* Kay, H. S.

**WILLIAMSON, Prof. Howard John,** CVO 2016; CBE 2002; PhD; Professor of European Youth Policy, University of South Wales, since 2005; *b* Hull, 25 Feb. 1954; *s* of John Frederick Williamson and Kathleen Thelma Williamson (*née* Bennett); *m* 2009, Charlotte Barrett Christiansen; one *s* two *d*. *Educ:* King Edward's Sch., Birmingham; University Coll., Cardiff (BSc (Econ) 1st Cl. Hons 1975; PhD 1982). Res. Officer, Univ. of Oxford, 1979–82; Researcher/Lectr, Cardiff Univ. (formerly UC, Cardiff, then Univ. of Wales Coll., Cardiff, later Univ. of Wales, Cardiff), 1983–2005; Jt Negotiating Cttee qualified youth and community worker, 1985; youth and community worker, 1985–2003. Vis. academic posts in Denmark, France, Croatia, Malta, China, Iran and Australia. Mem., Youth Justice Bd, 2001–08. Trustee: Duke of Edinburgh's Award, 2003–15; Duke of Edinburgh's Internat. Award Foundn, 2015–. Mem., Council of Europe High Level Task Force on Youth Work, 2018–. FRSA. *Publications:* Five Years, 1981; Toolmaking and Politics, 1987; Social Action for Young People, 1994; Children Speak, 1994; Youth and Policy: contexts and consequences, 1997; Supporting Young People in Europe, Vol. 1–Vol. 3, 2002–17; The Milltown Boys Revisited, 2004; The History of Youth Work in Europe, Vol. 1–Vol. 7, 2009–19; Thinking Seriously About Work, 2017. *Recreations:* motorcycling, football, music, horse riding, playing guitar. *Address:* Beech Trees, Forest Grove, Treforest, Pontypridd CF37 1UB. *T:* 07785 938879. *E:* howard.williamson@southwales.ac.uk.

**WILLIAMSON, Prof. Hugh Godfrey Maturin,** OBE 2015; FBA 1993; Regius Professor of Hebrew, and Student of Christ Church, Oxford University, 1992–2014; *b* 15 July 1947; *s* of Thomas Broadwood Williamson and Margaret Frances (*née* Davy); *m* 1971, Julia Eiluned Morris; one *s* two *d*. *Educ:* Rugby Sch.; Trinity Coll., Cambridge (BA 1st cl. Hons Theol., 1969; MA); St John's Coll., Cambridge; PhD 1975, DD 1986, Cantab. Cambridge University: Asst Lectr in Hebrew and Aramaic, 1975–79; Lectr, 1979–89; Reader, 1989–92; Fellow of Clare Hall, 1985–92. Chm., Anglo-Israel Archaeol Soc., 1990–2010. Pres., SOTS, 2004. Vice-Pres., British Acad., 2010–11. Corresp. Mem., Göttingen Akademie der Wissenschaften, 2008. *Publications:* Israel in the Books of Chronicles, 1977; 1 and 2 Chronicles, 1982; Ezra, Nehemiah, 1985; Ezra and Nehemiah, 1987; Annotated Key to Lambdin's Introduction to Biblical Hebrew, 1987; (ed jtly) The Future of Biblical Studies, 1987; (ed jtly) It is Written: essays in honour of Barnabas Lindars, 1988; Jesus is Lord, 1993; The Book Called Isaiah, 1994; (ed jtly) Wisdom in Ancient Israel: essays in honour of J. A. Emerton, 1995; Variations on a Theme: King, Messiah and Servant in the Book of Isaiah, 1998; (ed jtly) Reading from Right to Left: essays in honour of David J. A. Clines, 2003; (ed jtly) Prophetie in Israel, 2003; Studies in Persian Period History and Historiography, 2004; Confirmation or Contradiction?: archaeology and Biblical history, 2004; (ed jtly) Dictionary of the Old Testament Historical Books, 2005; Isaiah 1–5: a critical and exegetical commentary, 2006; (ed) Understanding the History of Ancient Israel, 2007; Holy, Holy, Holy: the story of a liturgical formula, 2008; (ed jtly) Interpreting Isaiah: issues and approaches, 2009; He Has Shown You What is Good: Old Testament justice then and now, 2012; Isaiah 6–12: a critical and exegetical commentary, 2018; (ed jtly) The Oxford Illustrated History of the Holy Land, 2018; contrib. to learned jls incl. Vetus Testamentum, Jl of Theol Studies, Jl of Biblical Lit., Jl of Semitic Studies, Jl for Study of OT, Palestine Exploration Qly, Zeitschrift für die alttestamentliche Wissenschaft, Oudtestamentische Studiën. *Recreations:* allotment tending, model yacht sailing. *Address:* 7 Chester Road, Southwold, Suffolk IP18 6LN. *T:* (01502) 722319.

**WILLIAMSON, James Hunter;** Sheriff, Tayside Central and Fife at Kirkcaldy, since 2009; *b* Edinburgh, 9 Feb. 1961; *s* of James Hunter Williamson and Elizabeth Williamson (*née* Brown); *m* 1992, Christine Margaret Gillan; two *d*. *Educ:* Broughton High Sch., Edinburgh; Univ. of Dundee (LLB). Partner, Lawson, Coull & Duncan Solicitors, Dundee, 1990–2009; pt-time Sheriff, 2003–09. Tutor in Criminal Advocacy, 1990–2003, Lectr in Criminal Procedure, 2000–03, Univ. of Dundee. *Recreations:* golf, architecture, football, backgammon, American pulp fiction circa 1930–1950. *Address:* 344 Blackness Road, Dundee DD2 1SD. *T:* (01382) 669603. *Clubs:* Downfield Golf; El Club De Golf Rosa de Sombrero (Champion, 2004, 2015).

**WILLIAMSON, Lucy Maria;** *see* Powell, L. M.

**WILLIAMSON, Sir Malcolm;** *see* Williamson, Sir G. M.

**WILLIAMSON, Martin Charles;** HM Diplomatic Service, retired; Head, Research Analysts, Foreign and Commonwealth Office, 2007–10; *b* 28 Jan. 1953; *s* of Charles Frederick Williamson and Marie Williamson; *m* 1978, Elizabeth Michelle Darvill; two *s*. *Educ:* Univ. of Keele (BA Hons 1975); London Sch. of Econs (MSc 1977); Univ. of Exeter (PhD 2018). Entered FCO, 1977; FCO, 1977–84; Res. Dept, IMF, 1984–87; Econ. Advr, FCO, 1987–89; Cabinet Office, 1989–91; OECD, 1991–94; Foreign and Commonwealth Office: Sen. Econ. Advr, 1994–99; Dep. Hd, Econ. Policy Dept, 1999; Hd, Resource Budgeting Dept, 1999–2003; Prism Team, 2003–04; Dep. High Comr, Wellington, 2004–06. Research student: Univ. of Kent, 2010–13; Univ. of Exeter, 2013–18. *Publications:* Acquisition of Foreign Assets by Developing Countries, 1986. *Recreations:* walking, gym, reading, music. *Address:* c/o Department of Politics, University of Exeter, Amory Building, Rennes Drive, Exeter, Devon EX4 4RJ. *E:* martin@martinwilliamson.plus.com.

**WILLIAMSON, Matthew;** designer; Founder and President, Matthew Williamson Ltd, since 1997; *b* Manchester, 23 Oct. 1971; *s* of Maureen and David Williamson. *Educ:* Central St Martins Coll. (BA Design and Printed Textiles 1994). First store opened, London, 2004, NY and Dubai, 2009; Creative Dir, Emilio Pucci, 2005–08. Retrospective exhibn, Matthew Williamson: 10 Years in Fashion, Design Mus., 2007. Elle Designer of Year, 2004; Red Carpet Designer of Year Award, British Fashion Awards, 2008. *Relevant publication:* Matthew Williamson, by Colin McDowell, 2010. *E:* estella@matthewwilliamson.co.uk.

**WILLIAMSON, Nigel;** writer; *b* 4 July 1954; *s* of Neville Albert and Anne Maureen Williamson; *m* 1976, Magali Patricia Wild; two *s*. *Educ:* Chislehurst and Sidcup Grammar School; University College London. Tribune: Journalist, 1982–84; Literary Editor, 1984; Editor, 1984–87; Editor: Labour Party News, 1987–89; New Socialist, 1987–89; The Times: political reporter, 1989–90; Diary Editor, 1990–92; Home News Editor, 1992–95; Whitehall correspondent, 1995–96; freelance interviewer and music writer, 1996–; contrib. ed., Uncut mag., 1997–; weekly columnist and contrib. ed., Billboard, 1999–; specialist music advr, British Council, 2002–. A Judge, Mercury Music Prize, 1999–2004. *Publications:* The SDP (ed), 1982; The New Right, 1984; (contrib.) The Rough Guide to World Music, 2000; Journey Through the Past: the stories behind the songs of Neil Young, 2002; The Rough Guide to Bob Dylan, 2004; (ed and contrib.) The Rough Guide Book of Playlists, 2005; The Rough Guide to the Blues, 2007; The Rough Guide to Led Zeppelin, 2007; The Rough Guide to the Best Music You've Never Heard, 2008; The Straight Ahead Guide to Bob Dylan, 2014; The Straight Ahead Guide to Led Zeppelin, 2014. *Recreations:* world music, cricket, gardening, opera. *Address:* Long Tilings, Hever Lane, Hever, Kent TN8 7ET. *T:* (01342) 851472.

**WILLIAMSON, Prof. Oliver E.,** PhD; Professor of Economics and Law, Graduate School, 1988–2004, now Emeritus, and Edgar F. Kaiser Professor of Business, Haas School of Business, 1998–2004, now Emeritus, University of California, Berkeley; *b* Superior, Wisconsin, 27 Sept. 1932; *s* of Scott and Lucille Williamson; *m* 1957, Dolores Celeni; three *s* two *d*. *Educ:* Massachusetts Inst. Technol. (SB 1955); Stanford Univ. (MBA 1960); Carnegie-Mellon Univ. (PhD 1963). Asst Prof. of Econs, Univ. of Calif, Berkeley, 1963–65; University of Pennsylvania: Associate Prof., 1965–68; Prof., 1968–83; Chair, Dept of Econs, 1971–72 and 1976–77; Dir, Centre for Study of Organizational Innovation, 1976–83; Charles and William L. Day Prof. of Econs and Social Sci., 1977–83; Gordon B. Tweedy Prof. of Econs of Law and Orgn, Yale Univ., 1983–88; Prof., Haas Sch. of Business, Univ. of Calif, Berkeley, 1988–98. Visiting Professor: Univ. of Warwick, 1973; Indiana Univ., 1987; of Econs and Transamerica Prof. of Business Admin, Univ. of Calif, Berkeley, 1988; Saarbrücken Univ., 1991; Paris 1 (Sorbonne), 1994; Dist. Vis. Prof., Univ. of Kyoto, 1989; Taussig Res. Prof. of Econs, Harvard Univ., 1987; Pritzker Dist. Vis. Prof., Northwestern Univ. Law Sch., 1993; Vis. Fellow, Res. Sch. of Social Scis, ANU, 1996. Distinguished Fellow: Industrial Orgn Soc., 2005; Amer. Econ. Assoc., 2007; Fellow: Econometrics Soc., 1977; Amer. Acad. Arts and Scis, 1983; Amer. Acad. Pol and Social Scis,

1997. Mem., NAS, 1994. (Jtly) Nobel Prize in Econs, 2009. *Publications:* The Economics of Discretionary Behaviour, 1964 (trans. Japanese); Corporate Control and Business Behaviour, 1970 (trans. Japanese); Markets and Hierarchies, 1975 (trans. Japanese); The Economic Institutions of Capitalism, 1985 (trans. Spanish, Italian, German, Russian, French, Polish); The Mechanisms of Governance, 1996 (trans. Italian); contribs to Amer. Econ. Rev., Jl Econ. Perspectives. *Address:* Walter A. Haas School of Business, University of California, Berkeley, CA 94720–1900, USA.

**WILLIAMSON, Dr Paul,** OBE 2016; FSA; FRHistS; Keeper of Sculpture, Metalwork, Ceramics and Glass, Victoria and Albert Museum, 2001–16, now Keeper Emeritus and Hon. Senior Research Fellow; *b* 4 Aug. 1954; *s* of late Peter Williamson and Mary Teresa Williamson (*née* Meagher); *m* 1984, Emmeline Mary Clare Mandley, MBE; one *s. Educ:* Wimbledon Coll.; Univ. of East Anglia (BA Hons; MPhil; LittD). Res., British Sch. at Rome, 1978; Major State Student, DES, 1978–79; Department of Sculpture, Victoria and Albert Museum: Asst Keeper, 1979–89; acting Keeper, 1989; Chief Curator, 1989–2001; Sen. Chief Curator, 1995–98; Dir of Collections, 2004–07; Acting Dep. Dir, 2013. Member: Wells Cathedral West Front Specialist Cttee, 1981–83; Wall Paintings Sub-Cttee, Council for the Care of Churches, 1987–90; Cttee, British Acad. Corpus of Romanesque Sculpture in Britain and Ireland, 1990–97; Lincoln Cathedral Fabric Adv. Council, 1990–2001; Internat. Adv. Bd, Courtauld Inst. of Art (Wall Paintings Conservation), 2005–; Expert Advr on Sculpture, Reviewing Cttee on Export of Works of Art, 1989–2016. Member, Consultative Committee: Sculpture Jl, 1997–; Burlington Mag., 2003– (Dir and Trustee, 2008–); Walpole Soc., 2004–. Lansdowne Vis. Prof., Univ. of Victoria, BC, 2001; Diskant Lectr, Philadelphia Mus. of Art, 2001. FSA 1983 (Mem. Council, 1997–2003; Vice-Pres., 1999–2003); FRHistS 2011. Trustee, Stained Glass Mus., Ely, 2005–09. Hon. Res. Fellow, Courtauld Inst. of Art, 2018–. *Publications:* An Introduction to Medieval Ivory Carvings, 1982 (trans. German); Catalogue of Romanesque Sculpture in the Victoria and Albert Museum, 1983; (ed) The Medieval Treasury: the art of the Middle Ages in the Victoria and Albert Museum, 1986, 3rd edn 1998; The Thyssen-Bornemisza Collection: medieval sculpture and works of art, 1987; Northern Gothic Sculpture 1200–1450, 1988; (ed jtly) Early Medieval Wall Painting and Painted Sculpture in England, 1990; Gothic Sculpture 1140–1300, 1995 (trans. Spanish 1997, trans. Portuguese, 1998); (ed) European Sculpture at the Victoria and Albert Museum, 1996; Netherlandish Sculpture 1450–1550, 2002; (ed jtly) Wonder: painted sculpture from medieval England, 2002; Medieval and Renaissance Stained Glass in the Victoria and Albert Museum, 2003; (ed jtly) Gothic: art for England 1400–1547, 2003; Medieval and Later Treasures from a Private Collection, 2005; (ed jtly) Medieval and Renaissance Treasures from the V&A, 2007; Medieval Ivory Carvings: early Christian to Romanesque, 2010; (ed) Object of Devotion: medieval English alabaster sculpture from the Victoria and Albert Museum, 2010; (with Glyn Davies) Medieval Ivory Carvings 1200–1550, 2014; The Wyvern Collection: medieval and renaissance sculpture and metalwork, 2018; The Wyvern Collection: medieval and later ivory carvings and small sculpture, 2019; contribs to numerous exhibn catalogues; articles and book reviews in learned jls. *Recreation:* travel. *E:* pwilliamson302@gmail.com.

**WILLIAMSON, Peter John;** Chairman of the Board, Solicitors Regulation Authority (formerly Regulation Board, Law Society of England and Wales), 2005–09; President, Law Society of England and Wales, 2003–04; Chairman, Independent Schools Inspectorate, 2012–17; *b* 20 Aug. 1947; *s* of late John Reginald Williamson and Margaret Audrey Williamson (*née* Morrison); *m* 1974, Patricia Anne Mitchell Miller; one *s* one *d. Educ:* Berkhamsted Sch. Admitted as solicitor, 1972; Partner: Kenneth Brown Baker Baker, subseq. Turner Kenneth Brown, 1974–91 (Man. Partner, 1986–90); Dawson & Co., subseq. Dawsons, 1991–98 (Consultant, 1998–2007). Dep. Dist Judge, 1995–2001; Asst Recorder, 1997–2000; Recorder, 2000–08. Law Society: Chm., Associate Mems Gp, 1970; Mem. Council, 1992–2005; Dep. Vice-Pres., 2001–02; Vice-Pres., 2002–03. Dir, Solicitors Indemnity Fund Ltd, 1995–2002 (Chm., 1997–2002). Pres., Holborn Law Soc., 1989–90. Mem., Disciplinary Cttee, 2011–18, a Tribunal Chm., 2014–18, ICAEW. Trustee, Slynn Foundn, 2010– (Chm., 2012–). Berkhamsted School (formerly Berkhamsted Collegiate School): Pres., Old Berkhamstedians Assoc., 1979–81; Gov., 1991–2012 (Chm. Govs, 1995–2012); Gov., Coll. of Law, 2002–05. *Recreations:* watching and reading about sport, particularly cricket, listening to classical music, travel. *E:* peter.williamson47@btinternet.com. *Clubs:* Lansdowne, MCC.

**WILLIAMSON, Peter Roger;** HM Diplomatic Service, retired; Chairman, Risk Resolution Group; *b* 20 April 1942; *s* of Frederick W. and Dulcie R. Williamson; *m* 1977, Greta Helen Clare Richards; one *s* one *d. Educ:* Bristol Grammar Sch.; St John's Coll., Oxford (MA). Journalist and teacher, Far East, 1965–66; joined FCO, 1966; Kuala Lumpur, 1970; 1st Sec., FCO, 1973; Hong Kong, 1975; FCO, 1979; Counsellor: Kuala Lumpur, 1985–88; FCO, 1988–92; on loan to Cabinet Office, 1992–94; Counsellor, Nairobi, 1994–97. *Recreations:* tennis, travel, theatre, cinema, forest and farmland management.

**WILLIAMSON, Philip Frederick,** CBE 2008; Chief Executive, Nationwide Building Society, 2002–07; Chairman, Investors in People UK, 2006–11; *b* 11 Dec. 1947; *s* of late Philip Gordon Williamson and of Elsie May Williamson; *m* 1993, Theresa Taylor; two *d. Educ:* Calday Grange Grammar Sch.; Newcastle Univ. (BA Hons Econ); Harvard Business Sch. FCIB 2002. Joined Lloyds Bank as grad. trainee, 1970; Dir, UK Land plc, 1988–91; Nationwide Building Society, 1991–2007: Divisional Director: Business Planning, 1994–95; Corporate Develt, 1996; Marketing and Commercial Dir, 1996–99; Retail Ops Dir, 1999–2001; Chm., Nationwide Life, 1999–2001. Chm., Acenden Ltd, 2011–18; non-executive Director: Visa Europe, 2006–07; In-Deed Online plc, 2011–13. Chairman: Council of Mortgage Lenders, 2000–01; Corporate Forum for Internat. Service, 2004–07; BSA, 2005–06; Founder Dir, Regulatory and Retail Faculty Bd, Inst. of Financial Services; UK Vice-Pres., Eur. Mortgage Fedn, 2004. *Recreations:* proficient golfer (12 handicap), stamp collecting, bird watching.

**WILLIAMSON, Richard Arthur;** Director, Midland Region, Crown Prosecution Service, 1987–89; *b* 9 Jan. 1932; *s* of George Arthur and Winifred Mary Williamson; *m* 1957, Christina Elizabeth, *d* of Harry Godley Saxton, Worksop, Notts, and Helena Saxton; two *s. Educ:* King Edward VI Grammar Sch., East Retford; Sheffield Univ. (statutory year). Solicitor, 1956. National Service, RN (Sub-Lieut), 1956–58. Asst Solicitor, Lancs CC, 1958–61; Sen. Asst Solicitor, Lincs (Lindsey) CC, 1961–65; private practice, Partner in Hetts, Solicitors, Scunthorpe, 1965–76; Prin. Prosecuting Solicitor, Greater Manchester, 1976–83; Chief Prosecuting Solicitor, Lincs, 1983–85; Asst Hd of Field Management, Crown Prosecution Service, 1985–87. Prosecuting Solicitors Soc. of England and Wales: Mem. Exec. Council, 1978–85; Treas., 1978–85; Chm., Hds of Office, 1984–85. Mem., York and the Humber War Pensions Cttee, 1997–2010. *Recreations:* family, theatre, gardening. *Address:* The Lookout, Back Street, Alkborough, near Scunthorpe, North Lincolnshire DN15 9JN. *T:* (01724) 720843.

**WILLIAMSON, Prof. Robert,** AO 2004; FRCP, FRCPath; FRS 1999; Director, Murdoch Children's Research Institute (formerly Murdoch Research Institute), Royal Children's Hospital, Melbourne, 1995–2006, now Honorary Senior Research Fellow; Research Professor of Medical Genetics, University of Melbourne School of Medicine, 1995–2005; *b* 14 May 1938; *s* of John and Mae Williamson; *m* 1st, 1962, Patricia Anne Sutherland (marr. diss. 1994); one *s* one *d;* 2nd, 1994, Robyn Elizabeth O'Hehir; one *s* one *d. Educ:* Bronx High School of Science, NY; Wandsworth Comprehensive School; University College London (BSc, MSc, PhD). FRCP 1990; FAA 2001. Lectr, Univ. of Glasgow, 1963–67; Sen. Scientist (Molecular Biol.), Beatson Inst. for Cancer Research, Glasgow, 1967–76; Prof. of Biochem., St Mary's Hosp. Med. Sch., London Univ., 1976–95. Sen. Fellow, Carnegie Instn of Washington, Baltimore, 1972–73. External Examr, Malaysia, Saudi Arabia. Member: UK Genetic Manipulation Adv. Cttee, 1976–91; Grants Cttees, MRC Cancer Research Campaign, 1976–95; Action Research for Crippled Child; Cystic Fibrosis Research Trust. Francqui Hon. Prof., Belgian Univs, 1995. Hon. MRCP 1986. Hon. MD Turku, 1987. Wellcome Award, Biochem. Soc., 1983; King Faisal Internat. Prize for Medicine, 1994. *Publications:* (ed) Genetic Engineering, vol. 1, 1981, vol. 2, 1982, vol. 3, 1982, vol. 4, 1983; articles in Nature, Cell, Procs Nat. Acad. of Scis, Biochemistry, Nucleic Acids Research. *Recreations:* reading, sport. *Address:* The Dean's Ganglion, Faculty of Medicine, University of Melbourne, 4/766 Elizabeth Street, Melbourne, Vic 3010, Australia. *T:* (3) 83444181. *E:* r.williamson@unimelb.edu.au.

**WILLIAMSON, Sir (Robert) Brian,** Kt 2001; CBE 1989; Chairman: London International Financial Futures and Options Exchange, 1985–88 and 1998–2003 (Director, 1982–89); Electra Private Equity PLC (formerly Electra Investment Trust plc), 2000–10 (Director, 1994–2010); Resolution PLC (formerly Resolution Life Group), 2004–05 (Director, 2004–08); *b* 16 Feb. 1945; *m* 1969, Diane Marie Christine de Jacquier de Rosée. *Educ:* Truro Sch.; Trinity College, Dublin (MA). Personal Asst to Rt Hon. Maurice Macmillan (later Viscount Macmillan), 1967–71; Editor, International Currency Review, 1971; Man. Dir, Gerrard & National Hldgs, 1978–89; Chairman: GNI Ltd, 1985–89; Gerrard & Nat. Hldgs, later Gerrard Gp PLC, 1989–98; Fleming Worldwide Investment Trust, 1998 (Dep. Chm., 1996–98); MT Fund Management Ltd, 2004–; R. J. Fleming & Co. Ltd, 2013–. Director: Fleming Internat. High Income Investment Trust plc, 1990–96; Court, Bank of Ireland, 1990–98; Barlows plc, 1997–98; HSBC Hldgs plc, 2002–12; Templeton Emerging Markets Investment Fund plc, 2002–03; Liv-Ex Ltd, 2005–; Open Europe, 2005–08; Waverton (formerly J. O. Hambro) Investment Mgt Ltd, 2010–15; Climate Exchange plc, 2007–10; Aggregated Micro Power Hldgs plc, 2012–; Incubex, 2017–; Vice Chm., Bergos Fleming, 2019–. Member: Bd, Bank of Ireland Britain Hldgs, 1986–90; Council, 1985–88, Council, Eur. Cttee, 1988–90, British Invisible Exports Council; FSA (formerly SIB), 1986–98; Supervisory Bd, NYSE Euronext (formerly Euronext NV), 2002–13. Sen. Advr, Fleming Family and Partners, 2003–09. Dir, Politeia, 1999–. Chm., Adv. Bd, Armed Forces (formerly Army) Common Investment Fund, 2002–09. Gov. at Large, Nat. Assoc. of Securities Dealers, USA, 1995–98; Mem., Internat. Markets Adv. Bd, NASDAQ Stock Market, 1993–98 (Chm., 1996–98). Mem. Governing Council, Centre for Study of Financial Innovation, 2000–. Mem., City of London Lord Mayor's Appraisal Panel, 2009–16. Mem. HAC, commissioned 1975. Dir, Rowing Mus., Henley Foundn, 1992–94. Mem., Royal Opera House Develt Cttee, 2004–09; Mem., Adv. Circle, Royal Opera House Foundn, 2009–12; Member, Council: St George's House, 1996–2002, St George's Chapel, 2002–; Dir, St George's House Trust (Windsor Castle), 1998–2002; Trustee: St Paul's Cathedral Foundn, 1999–2005; Winston Churchill Meml Trust, 2009–17; Edenbeg Trust Corporation Ltd (formerly Fallon Family Bd), 2012–. Freeman, 1994, HM Lieut, 2003, City of London. Contested (C) Sheffield Hillsborough, Feb. and Oct. 1974; prosp. parly cand., Truro, 1976–77. FRSA 1991. Hon. Bencher, Inner Temple, 2006. *Clubs:* Pratt's, White's; Leander; Durham Univ. Boat; Kildare Street and University (Dublin); Brook (New York); St Moritz Tobogganing (Pres., 2009–14).

**WILLIAMSON, Rt Rev. Robert Kerr, (Roy);** Bishop of Southwark, 1991–98; Honorary Assistant Bishop, Diocese of Southwell and Nottingham, since 1998; *b* 18 Dec. 1932; *s* of James and Elizabeth Williamson; *m* 1956, Anne Boyd Smith (*d* 2004); three *s* two *d. Educ:* Elmgrove School, Belfast; Oak Hill College, London. London City Missionary, 1955–61; Oak Hill Coll., 1961–63; Asst Curate, Crowborough Parish Church, 1963–66; Vicar: St Paul, Hyson Green, Nottingham, 1966–71; St Ann w. Emmanuel, Nottingham, 1971–76; St Michael and All Angels, Bramcote, 1976–79; Archdeacon of Nottingham, 1978–84; Bishop of Bradford, 1984–91. Chm., Central Religious Adv. Cttee to BBC and ITC, 1993–97; Co-Chm., Inter-Faith Network for the UK, 1994–99. *Publications:* Can You Spare a Minute?, 1991; Funny You Should Say That, 1992; For Such a Time as This, 1996; Joyful Uncertainty, 1999; Open Return, 2000; Not Least in the Kingdom, 2001; Wholly Alive, 2002; Loved By Love, 2004. *Recreations:* walking, bird watching, reading, music.

**WILLIAMSON, Prof. Robin Charles Noel,** FRCS; Professor of Surgery, Imperial College School of Medicine (formerly Professor and Head of Department of Surgery, Royal Postgraduate Medical School), University of London, 1987–2009, now Honorary; Demonstrator of Anatomy, Imperial College, London, since 2009; Chairman, London Clinic, 2012–16 (Member, Board of Trustees, since 2010); *b* 19 Dec. 1942; *s* of James Charles Frederick Lloyd Williamson and Helena Frances Williamson (*née* Madden); *m* 1967, Judith Marjorie (*née* Bull); three *s. Educ:* Rugby School; Emmanuel College, Cambridge; St Bartholomew's Hosp. Med. Coll. MA, MD, MChir (Cantab). Surgical Registrar, Reading, 1971–73; Sen. Surgical Registrar, Bristol, 1973–75; Clin. and Res. Fellow, Mass Gen. Hosp. Boston and Harvard Med. Sch., 1975–76; Consultant Sen. Lectr, Bristol, 1977–79; Prof. of Surgery, Univ. of Bristol, 1979–87. Consultant Surgeon, Hammersmith Hosp., 1987–2009; Deanery Tutor in Surgery, Imperial Coll. Med. Sch., 2008–12; Foundn Trng Prog. Dir, Imperial Coll. Healthcare NHS Trust, 2009–12. Mem., Cell Biology and Disorders Bd, MRC, 1987–91. Fulbright-Hays Sen. Res. Scholar, USA, 1975; Sen. Penman Vis. Fellow, South Africa, 1985; Paul Grange Vis. Fellow, Univ. of Monash, 1986; Hunterian Prof., RCS, 1981–82; Raine Vis. Prof., Univ. of Western Australia, 1983; Richardson Prof., Mass Gen. Hosp., 1985; Visiting Professor: Univ. of Lund, Sweden, 1985; Univ. of Hong Kong, 1987; Univ. of Hamburg, 1999; Johnson and Johnson Vis. Prof., Univ. of Calif, San Francisco, 1989; Edwin Tooth Guest Prof., Royal Brisbane Hosp., Qld, 1989; Totalisator Bd Vis. Prof., Nat. Univ. of Singapore, 1994. Lectures: Arris and Gale, RCS, 1977–78; Finlayson Meml, RCPSG, 1985; Sir Gordon Bell Meml, RACS, NZ, 1988; Stuart, RSocMed and RCSE, 2007; Farndon Meml, Soc. of Acad. and Res. Surgery, 2008; Stevens, RSocMed, 2011; Hunterian, 2011; Med. Soc. of London, 2013. Association of Surgeons of GB and Ireland: Moynihan Fellow, 1979; Mem. Council, 1993–99; Chm., Scientific Cttee, 1995–97; Vice Pres., 1997–98; Pres., 1998–99. Royal Society of Medicine: Associate Dean, 2001–02; Dean, 2002–06; Emeritus Dean, 2006–08; Pres., 2008–10. President: Pancreatic Soc. of GB and Ireland, 1984–85; Internat. Hepato-Pancreato-Biliary Assoc., 1996–98 (Sec. Gen., 1994–96); Assoc. of Upper Gastrointestinal Surgeons, 1996–98; European Soc. of Surgery, 1998; James IV Assoc. of Surgeons, 2002–06; Chm., Educn Cttee, British Soc. of Gastroenterology, 1981–87; Member: Med. Adv. Cttee, British Council, 1988–94; Clin. Res. and Trng and Career Panel, MRC, 1997–2003; Internat. Adv. Bd, Nat. Univ. of Singapore, 1998–2000; Res. Cttee, Mason Med. Res. Foundn, 1999–2010 (Chm., 2004–10); Sec. Gen., World Assoc. of Hepato-Pancreato-Biliary Surgery, 1990–94 (Treas., 1986–90); Jt Adv. Bd, Weill Cornell Medicine, Qatar, 2014–16. Examiner: Primary FRCS, 1981–87; Intercollegiate Bd in General Surgery, 1994–2002 (Mem., Intercollegiate Examng Bd in Gen. Surg., 1998–2002). Chm., Retired Fellows Soc., RSocMed, 2013–16. FRSocMed 2000. FRCSE (*ad hominem*) 2009;

Hon. FRCS Thailand, 1992. Hon. DSc Med. Mahidol Univ., Thailand, 1994. Hallett Prize, RCS, 1970; Research Medal, British Soc. of Gastroenterology, 1982; Bengt Ihre Medal, Swedish Soc. of Gastroenterology, 1998; Gold Medal, IHPBA, 2004. Sen. Ed., British Jl of Surgery, 1991–96 (Co. Sec., 1983–91); Ed., HPB, 1999–2003; Ed.-in-Chief, HPB Surgery, 2006–11. *Publications:* edited jointly: Colonic Carcinogenesis, 1982; General Surgical Operations, 2nd edn 1987; Emergency Abdominal Surgery, 1990; Surgical Management, 2nd edn 1991; Clinical Gastroenterology: gastrointestinal emergencies, 1991; Scott, An Aid to Clinical Surgery, 6th edn 1998; Hepatobiliary and Pancreatic Tumours, 1994; Upper Digestive Surgery: oesophagus, stomach and small intestine, 1999; Surgery, 2000; Surgery: core principles and practice, 2017; numerous papers in surgical and med. jls. *Recreations:* travel, military uniforms and history. *Address:* The Barn, 88 Lower Road, Gerrards Cross, Bucks SL9 8LB. *T:* (01753) 889816. *E:* r.williamson@imperial.ac.uk, robin.williamson@btinternet.com. *Club:* Oxford and Cambridge.

**WILLIAMSON, Rt Rev. Roy;** *see* Williamson, Rt Rev. Robert K.

**WILLIAMSON, Dr Sarah Joanne,** FREng; FICE; Technical Director, Laing O'Rourke, since 2012; *b* Workington, 14 March 1969; *d* of Philip and Heather Williamson; *m* David Ball. *Educ:* Liverpool John Moores Univ. (BSc 1st Cl. Hons Civil Engrg); Univ. of Birmingham (PhD 2000). MIStructE. Lectr, Univ. of Birmingham, 2003–06; Chief Engr, Atkins, 2006–12. FREng 2017. *Recreation:* outdoors. *Address:* Laing O'Rourke, Bridge Place 1, Dartford, Kent DA2 6SN. *T:* 07827 807099. *E:* swilliamson@laingorourke.com.

**WILLIAMSON, Prof. Stephen,** FREng; Deputy Vice-Chancellor (Research and Innovation), University of Surrey, 2009–13; *b* 15 Dec. 1948; *s* of Donald Williamson and Patricia K. M. Williamson (*née* Leyland); *m* 1970, Zita Mellor; one *s* two *d. Educ:* Burnage Grammar Sch., Manchester; Imperial Coll. of Science and Technology (scholarship, 1968; Sylvanus P. Thompson Prize, 1969; BScEng, ACGI, PhD, DIC; DScEng 1989). FIEEE 1995; FREng (FEng 1995). Lectr in Engrg, Univ. of Aberdeen, 1973–81; Sen. Lectr, 1981–85, Reader, 1985–89, Dept of Electrical Engrg, Imperial College; Prof. of Engrg, 1989–97, and Fellow, St John's Coll., 1990–97, Cambridge Univ.; Technical Dir, Brook Hansen, later Invensys Brook Crompton, 1997–2000; Prof. of Electrical Engrg, 2000–09, Hd, Sch. of Electrical Engrg and Electronics, 2003–09, UMIST, later Univ. of Manchester. Non-exec. Dir, Tesla Engrg, 2009–. Chm., Electrical, Controls, and System Electronics Adv. Bd, Rolls Royce, 2002–15; Member: Scientific Adv. Council, MoD, 2005–11; Bd of Trustees, IET, 2009–12; Res. and Knowledge Exchange Strategic Adv. Cttee (formerly Res. and Innovation Scientific Adv. Council), HEFCE, 2011–14. FCGI 1989. Institution of Electrical Engineers: John Hopkinson Premium, 1981; Crompton Premium, 1987, 1996, 1998; Swan Premium, 1989; Science, Educn and Technol. Div. Premium, 1991; Power Div. Premium, 1995; Achievement Medal, 2000; Nikola Tesla Award, IEEE, 2001. *Publications:* papers relating to induction machines. *Recreations:* reading, walking, gardening.

**WILLIAMSON, Prof. Timothy,** FRSE; FBA 1997; Wykeham Professor of Logic, Oxford University, since 2000; Fellow of New College, Oxford, since 2000 (Sub-Warden, 2018–19); *b* 6 Aug. 1955; *er s* of late Colin Fletcher Williamson and of Karina Williamson (*née* Side; she *m* 2nd, Prof. Angus McIntosh, FBA, FRSE); *m* 1st, 1984, Elisabetta Perosino (marr. diss. 2003); one *s* one *d*; 2nd, 2004, Ana Mladenović; one *s. Educ:* Henley Grammar Sch.; Balliol Coll., Oxford (Hon. Fellow 2014); Christ Church, Oxford (MA 1981; DPhil 1981); MA *aeg* Dublin 1986. FRSE 1997. Sen. Scholar, Christ Church, Oxford, 1976–80; Lectr in Philosophy, TCD, 1980–88; Fellow and Praelector in Philosophy, University Coll., and CUF Lectr in Philosophy, Univ. of Oxford, 1988–94; Prof. of Logic and Metaphysics, Edinburgh Univ., 1995–2000. Visiting Professor: MIT, 1994; Princeton, 1998–99; Visiting Fellow: ANU, 1990, 1995; Centre for Advanced Study, Oslo, 2004; Vis. Erskine Fellow, Univ. of Canterbury, NZ, 1995; Nelson Dist. Prof., 2003, Nelson Vis. Prof., 2013–15, Univ. of Michigan; Vis. Prof., Yale Univ., 2016–17; Townsend Visitor in Philos., Berkeley, 2006; Tang Chun-I Vis. Prof., Chinese Univ. of Hong Kong, 2007; Leverhulme Trust Major Res. Fellowship, 2009–12; A. Whitney Griswold Vis. Prof., Yale Univ., 2018–. Lectures: Henriette Herz, British Acad., 1996; Weatherhead, Tulane Univ., 1998; Jacobsen, UCL, 2001; Skolem, Oslo Univ., 2004; Jack Smart, ANU, 2005; Wedberg, Stockholm Univ., 2006; Gaos, Nat. Autonomous Univ. of Mexico, 2006; Hempel, Princeton, 2006; Amherst, Amherst Coll., 2009; Zeno, Utrecht Univ., 2009; Mesthene, Rutgers, 2010; Ortlieb, Claremont, 2012; Petrus Hispanus, Lisbon, 2012; Hägerström, Uppsala Univ., 2013; Kim Young-Jung, Seoul Nat. Univ., 2013; Nanqiang, Xiamen Univ., 2014; Ruth Manor, Tel-Aviv Univ., 2015; Bergmann, Univ. of Iowa, 2015; Beth, Amsterdam, 2015; Logic, Univ. of Conn, 2016; Saul Kripke, Columbia Univ. of NY, 2016; Royal Inst. Philosophy, London, 2016; Sainsbury, KCL, 2016; Wade, St Louis Univ., 2016; Whitehead, Harvard, 2017; Casalegno, Univ. of Milan, 2018; Gottlob Frege, Univ. of Tartu, 2018; Sanders, American Philosophical Assoc., Denver, 2019. President: Aristotelian Soc., 2004–05; Mind Assoc., 2006–07 (Vice-Pres., 2005–06); Vice-Pres., British Logic Colloquium, 2007–12. FRSA 2011. MAE 2014. For. Mem., Norwegian Acad. of Sci. and Letters, 2004; FHMAAAS 2007; Hon. Mem., RIA, 2014; Mem., Inst. Internat. de Philosophie, 2017. Dr *hc* Bucharest, 2015. *Publications:* Identity and Discrimination, 1990; Vagueness, 1994; Knowledge and its Limits, 2000; The Philosophy of Philosophy, 2007; Modal Logic as Metaphysics, 2013; Tetralogue: I'm right, you're wrong, 2015; Doing Philosophy: from common curiosity to logical reasoning, 2018; (with Paul Boghossian) Debating the A Priori, 2019; articles in Jl of Phil., Phil Rev., Mind, Jl of Symbolic Logic, Jl of Phil Logic, Studia Logica, etc; *relevant publications:* Williamson on Knowledge, ed P. Greenough and D. Pritchard, 2009; Williamson on Modality, ed M. McCullagh and J. Yli-Vakkuri, 2017. *Address:* New College, Oxford OX1 3BN. *T:* (01865) 279555.

**WILLIAMSON, Cdre Toby Justin,** MVO 1998; Clerk, Fishmongers' Company, since 2017; *b* Canterbury, Sept. 1964; *s* of John and Ailsa Williamson; *m* 1997, Polly Lyon; two *s. Educ:* King's Sch., Canterbury; Royal Naval Engrg Coll. (BEng); Jt Services Comd and Staff Coll. (MA). Served RN, 1983–2017: Equerry to the Queen, 1995–98; CO, Royal Naval Air Stn, Culdrose, 2010–11; Comdr Operational Trng, 2013–17. Mem., Fleet Air Arm Officers' Assoc., 1995. *Recreations:* maritime history, classical music, family, travel. *Address:* Fishmongers' Company, Fishmongers' Hall, London Bridge, EC4R 9EL. *T:* (020) 7626 3531. *E:* Toby.Williamson@fishhall.org.uk.

**WILLING, Dame Paula;** *see* Rego, Dame M. P. F.

**WILLINGHAM, Anne Julie;** *see* Desmet, A. J.

**WILLINK, Sir Edward (Daniel),** 3rd Bt *cr* 1957, of Dingle Bank, City of Liverpool; PhD; Director, Willink Transformations Ltd, since 2012; *b* Windsor, 18 Feb. 1957; *o s* of Sir Charles William Willink, 2nd Bt and of Elizabeth, *d* of Humfrey Andrewes; *S* father, 2009; *m* 2004, Sally Margaret Hooker. *Educ:* Eton; Magdalene Coll., Cambridge (BA 1978; MA); Surrey Univ. (PhD 2002). CEng, MIEE 1993. Chief Technical Consultant, Thales Res. and Technol., 2000–12. Chm., OCL/QVT Revision Task Force, Object Mgt Gp, 2011–. Committer, Eclipse Foundn, 2009–. *Publications:* various digital signal processing and software modelling workshop and conf. procs. *Recreation:* open source software. *Heir: cousin* Henry Augustine Willink [*b* 12 May 1971; *m* 2011, Aisha Mary Ellen Jung; three *s*].
*See also* S. J. L. Linnett.

**WILLIS,** family name of **Baron Willis of Knaresborough**.

**WILLIS OF KNARESBOROUGH,** Baron *cr* 2010 (Life Peer), of Harrogate in the County of North Yorkshire; **George Philip Willis;** *b* 30 Nov. 1941; *s* of George Willis and Hannah (*née* Gillespie); *m* 1974, Heather Elizabeth Sellars; one *s* one *d. Educ:* City of Leeds and Carnegie Coll.; Univ. of Leeds (Cert Ed 1963); Univ. of Birmingham (BPhil 1978). Asst teacher, Middleton Co. Secondary Boys' Sch., 1963–65; Head of History, Moor Grange Co. Secondary Boys' Sch., 1965–67; Sen. Master, Primrose Hill High Sch., Leeds, 1967–74; Dep. Hd, W Leeds Boys' GS, 1974–78; Head Teacher: Ormsby Sch., Cleveland, 1978–82; John Smeaton Community Sch., 1983–97. MP (Lib Dem) Harrogate and Knaresborough, 1997–2010. Front bench spokesman on further and higher educn, 1997–99, on educn and employment, 1999–2001, on educn and skills, 2001–05. Mem., Educn and Employment Select Cttee, 1999–2001; Chm., Innovation, Universities, Science and Skills (formerly Sci. and Technol.) Select Cttee, 2005–10. Treas., All-Party Gp on medical res., 2005–10. Chairman: Willis Commn on Nursing Educn (report, Quality with Compassion, publd 2012); Shape of Caring Rev. (publd 2015). Consultant: to Health Educn England on future of nursing, 2015–; to NMC on role of registered nurses, 2015–. Chairman: AMRC, 2010–15; Yorks and Humber Collab. for Leadership in Applied Health Res. and Care, NIHR, 2014–; NIHR Applied Res. Collaborations, 2019–; Mem., NERC, 2010–. Chm., eLearning Foundn, 2010–15. Hon. DSc: Salford, 2013; City, 2018. *Recreations:* Leeds United season ticket holder, dance (ballet), current affairs, fishing. *Address:* House of Lords, SW1A 0PW. *Club:* National Liberal.

**WILLIS, Prof. Anne Elizabeth,** OBE 2017; PhD; Director, Medical Research Council Toxicology Unit, since 2010; *b* London; *d* of Edward Willis and Winifred Willis; *m* 1996, Kenneth Siddle, *qv*; one *s. Educ:* Henrietta Barnett Sch., London; Univ. of Kent (BSc Biochem. 1984); Imperial Coll. London (PhD 1987). Res. Associate, Biochem., Univ. of Cambridge, 1988–92; Jun. Res. Fellow, 1988–92, Lectr, 1991–92, Churchill Coll., Cambridge; Lectr, 1992–2002, Reader, 2002–04, Prof., 2004, Univ. of Leicester; Prof. of Cancer Cell Biol., Univ. of Nottingham, 2004–10. *Recreation:* running. *Address:* MRC Toxicology Unit, Lancaster Road, Leicester LE1 9HN. *T:* (0116) 252 5611. *E:* aew5@le.ac.uk.

**WILLIS, Air Vice-Marshal Gerald Edward;** Director, Projects Defence Estates, 2003–04; *b* 25 Oct. 1949; *s* of John Morris Willis and Dorothy Maud Willis; *m* 1st, 1973, Janet Seaman (marr. diss. 1995); one *s* one *d*; 2nd, 1996, Angela Suter. *Educ:* Cardiff High Sch. for Boys; Univ. of Bristol (BSc Hons 1971). Asst Prodn Manager, GKN, 1971–73; commnd Engr Br., RAF, 1973; Dir, Corporate Develt, RAF Trng Gp Defence Agency, 1999–2000; Asst Comdt, Jt Services Comd and Staff Coll., 2000–01; Dir, Project Alexander Implementation Team, 2001–03. *Recreations:* choral singing, fishing, swimming, walking. *Address:* Fairford, Glos. *E:* gerrywillis@mail.com.

**WILLIS, Jane;** Director, Cross-cutting Interventions, Health and Safety Executive, 2009–15; *b* 26 Aug. 1955; *d* of Ernest and Lena England; *m* 1974, Howard Willis; one *s* one *d. Educ:* Watford Grammar Sch. for Girls; Open Univ. (BA Hons 1987). Joined Civil Service, 1973; Health and Safety Executive, 1988–2015: Head: Safety Policy Div., 1998–2002; Planning Efficiency and Finance Div., 2002–03; Strategic Policy, subseq. Strategic Prog., Dir, 2003–09. Gov., Watford Grammar Sch. for Girls, 2009– (Vice-Chm., 2017–18). Chm., Bushey Trefoil Guild, 2019–. *Recreations:* going to the ballet and theatre, gardening.

**WILLIS, John Edward;** Chief Executive, Mentorn, since 2017, and Creative Director, Tinopolis Group, since 2006 (Director, Tinopolis plc, since 2006); *b* 4 April 1946; *s* of Baron Willis and of Lady (Audrey Mary) Willis (*née* Hale); *m* 1972, Janet Ann Sperrin; one *s* one *d. Educ:* Eltham Coll.; Fitzwilliam Coll., Cambridge (MA); Bristol Univ. (PG Cert. in Film and TV). Yorkshire Television: journalist, 1970–75; Documentary Dir, 1975–82; Controller of Documentaries and Current Affairs, 1982–88; Channel Four Television: Controller of Factual Progs, 1988–89; Dep. Dir of Progs, 1990–92; Dir of Progs, 1993–97; Man. Dir, 1997–98, Chief Exec., 1998–2000, United (formerly United Film and Television) Productions; Man. Dir, LWT and United Prodns, 2000–01; Vice-Pres. for Nat. Programming, WGBH, 2002–03; Dir, Factual and Learning, BBC, 2003–06. Member, Board: Channel 5 Broadcasting, 1998–2000; ITN, 1999–2000. Chairman: Broadcasting Support Services, 1997–2002; Edinburgh Internat. Television Fest., 1998–2002; Internat. Television Enterprises Ltd Distributors, 1999–2000; Granada Wild (formerly United Wildlife), 1999–2001; Cosgrove Hall Ltd, 1999–2001; Dir, Sheffield Internat. Documentary Fest., 2007–. Vis. Industrial Prof. in Television, Univ. of Bristol, 1999–; Hon. Prof., Univ. of Stirling, 1997–. The Guardian: Ombudsman, 1998–2002; External Ombudsman, 2006–17; Chm., Complaints Rev. Panel, 2015–. Mem., Ind. Football Commn, 2002. Advr, Convergence Think Tank, DCMS and BERR, 2007–08. Trustee: Future Lab, 2006–12; BAFTA, 2007– (Dep. Chm., 2011–12, 2014–15; Chm., 2012–14); Disasters Emergency Cttee, 2008–14; One World Media, 2014– (Chm., 2014–). Chair of Govs, Royal Central Sch. for Speech and Drama, Univ. of London, 2017–. FRTS 1993; FRSA 1997. Numerous prizes and awards. *Publications:* Johnny Go Home, 1976; Churchill's Few: the Battle of Britain remembered, 1985. *Recreations:* cycling, soccer, cinema, theatre. *Address:* Mentorn Productions, Elsinore House, 77 Fulham Palace Road, W6 8JA.

**WILLIS, Prof. John Raymond,** PhD; FRS 1992; FIMA; Professor of Theoretical Solid Mechanics, University of Cambridge, 1994–2000 and 2001–07, now Emeritus; Fellow of Fitzwilliam College, Cambridge, 1966–72, 1994–2000 and 2001–07; *b* 27 March 1940; *s* of John V. G. and L. Gwendoline Willis; *m* 1964, Juliette Louise Ireland; three *d. Educ:* Imperial Coll., London (BSc, PhD); MA Cantab 1966. ARCS, DIC; FIMA 1966. Asst Lectr, Imperial Coll., 1962–64; Res. Associate, NY Univ., 1964–65; Cambridge University: Sen. Asst in Research, 1965–67; Asst Dir of Research, 1968–72; Dir of Studies in Maths, Fitzwilliam Coll., 1966–72; Bath University: Prof. of Applied Maths, 1972–94; Prof. of Maths, 2000–01. Editor-in-Chief, 1982–92, Jt Editor, 1992–, Jl Mechanics and Physics of Solids. Foreign Associate: NAE, 2004; French Acad. of Scis, 2009. Hon. DSc Bath, 2007. Timoshenko Medal, ASME, 1997; Prager Medal, Soc. of Engrg Sci., 1998; Solid Mechanics Prize, EUROMECH, 2012. *Publications:* papers on mechanics of solids in learned jls. *Recreations:* swimming, hiking, music. *Address:* Department of Applied Mathematics and Theoretical Physics, Centre for Mathematical Sciences, Wilberforce Road, Cambridge CB3 0WA. *T:* (01223) 339251.

**WILLIS, Prof. Katherine Jane,** CBE 2018; PhD; FGS; Professor of Biodiversity, University of Oxford, since 2013; Principal, St Edmund Hall, Oxford, since 2018; *b* London, 16 Jan. 1964; *d* of Edward George Willis and Winifred Ellen Willis (*née* Dymond); *m* 1992, Dr Andrew John Gant, *qv*; two *s* one *d. Educ:* Henrietta Barnett Sch., London; Univ. of Southampton (BSc Envmtl Sci. and Geog.); PhD Plant Scis Cantab 1989. FGS 2008. Plant Scis Ed., CUP, 1988–90; University of Cambridge: Trevelyan Res. Fellow, Selwyn Coll., 1990–94; NERC Postdoctoral Res. Fellow, Dept of Plant Scis, 1991–94; Royal Soc. Univ. Res. Fellow, Godwin Inst. for Quaternary Res. and Dir of Studies, Selwyn Coll., 1994–98; University of Oxford: Lectr, Sch. of Geog. and Envmt, 1998–2004; Reader, Centre for Envmt, 2004–06; Prof. of Long Term Ecology, 2006–08, Professorial Res. Fellow, 2009–10, Sch. of Geog. and Envmt; Fellow, Jesus Coll., 2009–10; Tasso

Leventis Prof. of Biodiversity and Dir, Biodiversity Inst., 2010–13; Fellow, Merton Coll., 2010–13; Dir of Sci., Royal Botanic Gdns, Kew (on secondment), 2013–18. Adjunct Prof., Biol Inst., Univ. of Bergen, Norway, 2007–15. Hon. Fellow: St Hugh's Coll., Oxford, 2015; Selwyn Coll., Cambridge, 2017. Fellow, Norwegian Acad. Scis and Letters, 2010 (Foreign Mem., 2010). Hon. Dr Bergen, 2017. Michael Faraday Prize, Royal Soc., 2015. *Publications:* The Evolution of Plants, 2002, 2nd edn 2014; Key Topics in Conservation Biology, 2013; Plants: from roots to riches, 2014; Biodiversity in the Green Economy, 2015. *Recreations:* singing, walking, gardening. *Address:* St Edmund Hall, Queen's Lane, Oxford OX1 4AR. *Club:* Oxford and Cambridge.

**WILLIS, Hon. Ralph,** AO 2011; Treasurer of Australia, Dec. 1990 and 1993–96; Chairman, Western Health, 2004–14; *b* 14 April 1938; *s* of S. Willis; *m* 1970, Carol Dawson; one *s* two *d. Educ:* Footscray Central Sch.; University High Sch.; Melbourne Univ. (BCom). Australian Council of Trade Unions: Research Officer, 1960–70; Industrial Advocate, 1970–72. MP (ALP) Gellibrand, Vic, 1972–98; instrumental in developing econ., finance and ind. relns policies for Opposition, 1976–83; Opposition spokesperson on: Ind. Relns, 1976–77; Econ. Affairs, 1977–83; Econ. Develt, Jan.–March 1983; Minister for Employment and Ind. Relns and Minister Assisting the Prime Minister for Public Service Matters, 1983–88; Minister for Transport and Communications, 1988–90; Minister of Finance, 1990–93. Chm., C+BUS Industry Superannuation Fund, 2000–09. *Recreations:* tennis, reading, football. *Address:* 24a Gellibrand Street, Williamstown, Vic 3016, Australia.

**WILLIS, Prof. Rebecca,** PhD; environmental consultant, since 2004; Professor in Practice, Lancaster University, since 2019; *b* 20 Feb. 1972; *d* of Dave and Jane Willis; *m* (marr. diss.); two *s. Educ:* King's Coll., Cambridge (BA Hons Social and Pol Scis 1994); Univ. of Sussex (MA Envmt, Develt and Policy 1996); Lancaster Univ. (PhD Sociol.). Policy Advr, EP, Brussels, 1997–98; Green Alliance: Hd of Policy, 1998–2001; Dir, 2001–04; Associate, 2004–. Vice Chm., Sustainable Develt Commn, 2004–11. Member: NERC, 2011–15; Scientific Adv. Cttee, RCUK Energy Prog., 2015–19. Freelance writer and policy consultant. *Publications:* See-through Science: why public engagement needs to move upstream (with James Wilsdon), 2004; Grid 2.0: the next generation, 2006; (with Nick Eyre) Demanding Less: why we need a new politics of energy, 2011; Paris 2015: getting a global agreement on climate change, 2014. *Recreations:* fell-walking, running, wild swimming. *Address:* 5 Bankfield, Kendal, Cumbria LA9 5DR. *W:* www.rebeccawillis.co.uk.

**WILLIS, Very Rev. Robert Andrew;** DL; Dean of Canterbury, since 2001; *b* 17 May 1947; *s* of Thomas Willis and Vera Rosina Willis (*née* Britton). *Educ:* Kingswood Grammar Sch.; Warwick Univ. (BA); Worcester Coll., Oxford (DipTheol); Cuddesdon Coll., Oxford. Ordained deacon, 1972, priest, 1973; Curate, St Chad's, Shrewsbury, 1972–75; Vicar Choral, Salisbury Cathedral and Chaplain to Cathedral Sch., 1975–78; Team Rector, Tisbury, Wilts, 1978–87; Chaplain, Cranborne Chase Sch. and RAF Chilmark, 1978–87; RD, Chalke, 1982–87; Vicar, Sherborne with Castleton and Lillington, 1987–92; Chaplain, Sherborne Sch. for Girls, 1987–92; RD, Sherborne, 1991–92; Dean of Hereford, 1992–2001; Priest-in-charge, St John the Baptist, Hereford, 1992–2001. Canon and Prebendary of Salisbury Cathedral, 1988–92; Proctor in Convocation, 1985–92, 1994–2015. Member: Council, Partnership for World Mission, 1990–2002; Cathedrals' Fabric Commn for England, 1994–2005; C of E Liturgical Commn, 1994–98; Chm., Deans' (formerly Deans' and Provosts') Conf., 1999–2015. Governor: Cranborne Chase Sch., 1985–87; Sherborne Sch., 1987–92; Chairman of Governors: Hereford Cathedral Sch., 1993–2001; King's Sch., Canterbury, 2001–. Mem. Council, Univ. of Kent, 2003–09. FRSA 1993. DL Kent 2011. Freeman, City of Canterbury, 2008. Hon. Fellow, Canterbury Christ Ch Univ., 2004; Hon. FGCM 2006. Hon. DD Yale, 2009; Hon. DCL Kent, 2011. KStJ 2009 (CStJ 2001; Sub ChStJ 1991; Sub Dean, 1999). Cross of St Augustine, 2012. *Publications:* (contrib.) Hymns Ancient and Modern, New Standard edn, 1983; (jtly) The Chorister's Companion, 1989; (contrib.) Common Praise, 2000; (contrib.) New English Praise, 2006; (contrib.) Sing Praise, 2011. *Recreations:* music, literature, travel. *Address:* The Deanery, 20 The Precincts, Canterbury, Kent CT1 2EP. *T:* (01227) 762862, *Fax:* (01227) 865222. *Club:* Oxford and Cambridge.

**WILLISCROFT, Elizabeth Susan, (Sue); Her Honour Judge Williscroft;** a Circuit Judge, since 2016; Designated Family Judge for Derby, since 2019; *b* Bridgwater, 24 March 1954; *d* of Richard Andrew and Mary Isobel Williscroft; partner, Dr Ann Tobin. *Educ:* Barrow-in-Furness Girls' Grammar Sch.; London Sch. of Econs nd Pol Sci. (LLB 1975). Admitted as solicitor, 1980; Solicitor: Alexander Johnson, Bethnal Green, 1980–83; AV Hammond & Co., Bradford, 1983–87; Partner, Williscroft & Co., Bradford, 1987–2008; a Dep. Dist Judge, 1995–2008; a Dist Judge, 2008–16. Mem., Assoc. of Women Judges, 2008–. *Recreations:* cycling, hiking, opera, jazz. *E:* family.derbycountycourt@justice.gov.uk. *Club:* Pinnacle.

**WILLISON, Ian Roy,** CBE 2005; Senior Research Fellow, Institute of English Studies, School of Advanced Study, University of London, since 1999; *b* 17 Aug. 1926; *s* of Charles Walter Willison and Daisy Willison (*née* Farmer). *Educ:* Colfe's Grammar Sch.; Peterhouse, Cambridge (BA 1948, MA 1953); Sch. of Librarianship and Archive Admin, UCL (Postgrad. Dip. 1953). Asst Keeper, Dept of Printed Books, BM, 1953–74; Dep. Keeper and Hd, Rare Books Br., then Hd, English Lang. Br., BL, 1974–87. Vis. Prof. of Histl Bibliography, Grad. Liby Sch., Univ. of Chicago, 1959; Cline Vis. Prof., Univ. of Texas at Austin, 1989. Sec., then Chm., Rare and Precious Books and Documents Section, Internat. Fedn of Liby Assocs, 1978–86; Chm., UK Book Trade Hist. Gp, 1985–98; Mem., Colloque d'Histoire Mondiale du Livre et de l'Edition, 2001–05. Benefactor and Trustee, Willison Foundn Charitable Trust, 2016–. Jt Gen. Ed., Cambridge History of the Book in Britain, 1999–. Hon. FCLIP (Hon. FLA 1988). *Publications:* (ed jtly) The New Cambridge Bibliography of English Literature, vol. 4 1900–1950, 1972; (ed jtly) Modernist Writers and the Marketplace, 1996; (ed jtly) Literary Cultures and the Material Book, 2007. *Recreation:* classical music. *Address:* Institute of English Studies, School of Advanced Study, University of London, Senate House, Malet Street, WC1E 7HU. *T:* (020) 7862 8707, *Fax:* (020) 7862 8720. *E:* ian.willison@sas.ac.uk.

**WILLISON, Prof. Keith Robert,** PhD; molecular biologist; Professor of Chemical Biology, Imperial College London, since 2012; *b* 12 Oct. 1953; *s* of late Dr Robin Gow Willison and of Gillian Margaret Willison (*née* Caven-Irving); *m* 1979, Jennifer Anne Bardsley; two *s. Educ:* New College Sch., Oxford; St Edward's Sch., Oxford (Schol.); Univ. of Sussex (BSc Hons 1975); St John's Coll., Cambridge (PhD 1979). MRC Schol., MRC Lab. of Molecular Biol., Cambridge, 1975–78; Postdoctoral Fellow, Cold Spring Harbor Labs, NY, 1979–81; Institute of Cancer Research: Res. Scientist, 1981–2011; Hd, Chester Beatty Labs, 1996–2005; Hd, Haddow Labs, 2002–05; Personal Chair in Molecular Cell Biol., at BPMF, subseq. Inst. of Cancer Res., Univ. of London, 1995–2011. Vis. Prof., Osaka Univ., 1990–91; Weston Vis. Prof., Weizmann Inst. of Sci., Rehovot, 2011–12; JSPS Vis. Prof., Hyogo Univ., 2013; Vis. Prof., Tokyo Inst. of Technol., 2017–; JSPS Bridge Fellow, Japan, 2020. Institute of Cancer Research: Member: Exec. Cttee, 1994–2000; Bd of Mgt, 1997–2000; Corp. Mgt Gp, 2000–05; Mem., Jt Res. Cttee, Royal Marsden NHS, subseq. NHS Foundn, Trust and Inst. Cancer Res., 2000–09. Mem. Council, Royal Marsden NHS, subseq. NHS Foundn, Trust, 2003–11. Mem., Governing Body, Charterhouse, 2004–17. FRSC 2013. *Publications:* contrib. papers to scientific jls on topics in genetics and protein biochem. *Recreations:* cricket (Mem., Presidents XI CC, Wimbledon, 1983–99), football. *Address:* Institute of Chemical Biology, Department of Chemistry, Imperial College London, Molecular Sciences Research Hub, White City Campus, Wood Lane, W12 0BZ. *T:* (020) 7594 5837. *Club:* Athenæum.

**WILLMAN, John;** editorial consultant, since 2009; *b* 27 May 1949; *s* of late John Willman and Kate Willman (*née* Thornton); *m* 1978, Margaret Shanahan; one *s* two *d. Educ:* Bolton Sch.; Jesus Coll., Cambridge (MA); Westminster Coll., Oxford (CertEd). Teacher, Brentford Sch. for Girls, Brentford, Middx, 1972–76; Financial Researcher, Money Which?, 1976–79; Editor, Taxes and Assessment (Inland Revenue Staff Fedn pubn), 1979–83; Pubns Manager, Peat, Marwick, Mitchell & Co., 1983–85; Gen. Sec., Fabian Soc., 1985–89; Jt Editor, New Socialist, 1989; Editor, Consumer Policy Review, 1990–91; Financial Times: Public Policy Editor, 1991–94; Features Editor, 1994–97; Consumer Industries Editor, 1997–2000; Banking Editor, 2000–01; Chief Leader Writer, 2002–06; Associate Editor, 2002–09; UK Business Editor, 2006–09. Visiting Research Fellow: IPPR, 1990–91; Social Market Foundn, 1997; Sen. Res. Fellow, Policy Exchange, 2009–10. Specialist Advisor: Treasury Cttee, H of C, 2011–15; Parly Commn on Banking Standards, 2012–13. Journalist of the Year, Financing Healthcare, Norwich Union, 1998; Financial Journalist of the Year, British Press Awards, 2001; Business Journalist of the Year, Best Banking Submission, 2002. *Publications:* Lloyds Bank Tax Guide, annually, 1987–2000; Make Your Will, 1989; Labour's Electoral Challenge, 1989; Sorting Out Someone's Will, 1990; The Which? Guide to Planning and Conservation, 1990; Work for Yourself, 1991; A Better State of Health, 1998. *T:* 07767 301225. *E:* johnwillman27@gmail.com.

**WILLMAN, Prof. Paul William,** DPhil; Professor of Management, London School of Economics, 2006–17, now Emeritus; *b* 24 Aug. 1953; *s* of late William Willman and Marjorie Willman; *m* 1997, Kathleen Pickett. *Educ:* St Catharine's Coll., Cambridge (BA, MA); Trinity Coll., Oxford (DPhil 1979). Lectr in Industrial Sociol., Imperial Coll., London, 1979–83; Lectr, Sch. of Mgt, Cranfield Inst. of Technol., 1983–84; London Business School: Asst, 1984–88; Associate Prof., 1988–91; Prof. of Organisational Behaviour, 1991–2000; Ernest Butten Prof. of Mgt Studies, Saïd Business Sch., Univ. of Oxford, 2000–06; Fellow, Balliol Coll., Oxford, 2000–06. Mem. Council, ACAS, 2014–17. *Publications:* Fairness, Collective Bargaining and Incomes Policy, 1982; (jtly) Power Efficiency and Institutions, 1983; (ed jtly and contrib.) The Organisational Failures Framework and Industrial Sociology, 1983; (jtly) Innovation and Management Control, 1985; (jtly) The Car Industry: labour relations and industrial adjustment, 1985; Technological Change, Collective Bargaining and Industrial Efficiency, 1986; (jtly) The Limits to Self-Regulation, 1988; Union Business, Trade Union Organisation and Financial Reform in the Thatcher Years, 1993; (jtly) Union Organisation and Activity, 2004; (jtly) Traders: managing risks and decisions in financial markets, 2004; Understanding Management, 2014; contrib. books and learned jls on industrial relations etc. *Recreations:* opera, parish churches, dogs, tennis. *Address:* 770 Wendt Terrace, Laguna Beach, CA 92651, USA.

**WILLMER, John Franklin;** QC 1967; Lloyd's Appeal Arbitrator in Salvage Cases, 1991–2000; *b* 30 May 1930; *s* of Rt Hon. Sir (Henry) Gordon Willmer, OBE, TD and Barbara, *d* of Sir Archibald Hurd; *m* 1st, 1958, Nicola Ann Dickinson (marr. diss. 1979); one *s* three *d*; 2nd, 1979, Margaret Lilian, *d* of Chester B. Berryman. *Educ:* Winchester; Corpus Christi Coll., Oxford. National Service, 2nd Lieut, Cheshire Regt, 1949–50; TA Cheshire Regt, 1950–51; Middlesex Regt, 1951–57 (Captain). Called to Bar, Inner Temple, 1955, Bencher, 1975. A Gen. Comr of Income Tax for Inner Temple, 1982–2005. Member: panel of Lloyd's Arbitrators in Salvage Cases, 1967–91; panel from which Wreck Commissioners appointed, 1967–79, reapptd 1987–2000; Admiralty Court Cttee, 1980–95. Leader, Admiralty Bar, 1992–95. Retired from practice at Bar, 1995, from practice as Arbitrator, 2003. Freeman, Arbitrators' Co., 1992. St Mellitus Medal, Dio. London, 2012. *Recreations:* walking, visiting ancient sites and buildings, amateur dramatics. *Address:* Flat 4, 23 Lymington Road, NW6 1HZ. *T:* (020) 7435 9245. *Club:* Oxford and Cambridge.

**WILLMORE, Prof. (Albert) Peter,** FRAS; Professor of Space Research, University of Birmingham, 1972–97, now Emeritus; *b* 28 April 1930; *s* of Albert Mervyn Willmore and Kathleen Helen Willmore; *m* 1st, 1963, Geraldine Anne Smith; two *s*; 2nd, 1972, Stephanie Ruth Alden; one *s* one *d. Educ:* Holloway Sch.; University Coll. London (BSc, PhD). Research interests: fusion res., AERE, 1954–57; upper atmosphere, using sounding rockets and satellites, esp. Ariel I (launched 1962), UCL, 1957–70; X-ray astronomy, using sounding rockets and satellites, UCL, 1970–72, Univ. of Birmingham, 1972–. Academician, Internat. Acad. of Astronautics, 1996. Tsiolkovsky Medal, USSR, 1987; Vikram Sarabhai Medal, COSPAR, 2004; Distinguished Service Medal, COSPAR, 2012. *Publications:* approx. 150 papers in learned jls, together with many other articles and reviews. *Recreations:* music, playing the violin (though this may not be music), literature, Bronze Age history, travel, sailing. *Address:* 38 Grove Avenue, Moseley, Birmingham B13 9RY. *T:* (0121) 449 2616.

**WILLMOT, Prof. Derrick Robert,** PhD; FDSRCPSGlas, FDSRCS; Specialist Orthodontist, Ferndale House Dental Practice, Chesterfield, since 2011; *b* Chesterfield, Derbys; *s* of Jack and Olive Willmot; *m* 1971, Patricia, *d* of Robert Creighton, San Luis, Minorca; two *s. Educ:* Chesterfield Boys Grammar Sch.; University Coll. London and UCH Dental Sch. (BDS 1970); PhD Sheffield 2000. LDS RCS 1969, FDS RCS 2007; FDSRCPSGlas 1978; DOrthRCS 1980, MOrthRCS 1988; DDO Glasgow 1980. Resident Dental Hse Surgeon, Royal Portsmouth Hosp., 1970; Partner, gen. dental practice, Ashbourne, Derbys, 1970–77; Registrar, then Sen. Registrar, UCH Dental Sch., 1977–84; Consultant Orthodontist: Chesterfield Royal Hosp., 1984–92; Sheffield Teaching Hosps NHS Trust, 1992–2010; Hon. Prof. of Orthodontics, Sheffield Univ., 2005–10, now Emeritus. Dean, Faculty of Dental Surgery, RCS, 2008–11. Pres., S Yorks Br., BDA, 1992–93. Vice Chm. Govs, Chesterfield Grammar Sch., 1988–92. Mem., Round Table, Ashbourne, St Albans, Chesterfield, 1972–87. Chm., Chesterfield 41 Club, 2013–14. Pres., Old Cestrefeldians, 2015–16. FHEA 2002. John Tomes Medal, BDA, 2001; Distinction Award, British Orthodontic Soc., 2011. *Publications:* contrib. peer reviewed scientific papers, abstracts, letters and book chapters. *Recreations:* fishing, shooting, gardening, Member of Chesterfield Scarsdale Rotary Club (Pres., 2000–01; Paul Harris Fellowship, 2017). *Address:* Ashcroft, Matlock Road, Walton, Chesterfield S42 7LD. *E:* d.willmot@sheffield.ac.uk. *Clubs:* Flyfishers'; Royal Society of Medicine.

**WILLMOTT, Prof. Andrew John,** PhD; Professor of Physical Oceanography, since 2014, and Head, School of Mathematics, Statistics and Physics, since 2017, Newcastle University (Head, School of Marine and Science Technology, 2014); *b* 1 Aug. 1954; *s* of David Edward Willmott and Margaret Ethel Willmott (*née* Punt); *m* 1979, Sasithorn Aranuvachapun; two *d. Educ:* Bristol Univ. (BSc 1st Cl. Hons Maths); Univ. of E Anglia (MSc; PhD Applied Maths 1978). Res. Fellow, Univ. of BC, 1978–81; Asst Prof., Naval Post-grad. Sch., Monterey, 1981–83; Lectr in Applied Maths, 1983–96, Reader in Geophysical Fluid Dynamics, 1991–96, Univ. of Exeter; Prof. of Applied Maths and Hd, Sch. of Computing and Maths, Keele Univ., 1996–2005; Dir, NERC Proudman Oceanographic Lab., 2005–10; Dir of Sci. and Technol., NERC Nat. Oceanography Centre, 2010–13; Prof. of

Physical Oceanography and Hd, Sch. of Marine and Sci. Technol., Newcastle Univ., 2014. Visiting Professor: Dept of Earth and Ocean Scis, Univ. of Liverpool, 2005–16; in Applied Maths, 2005, in Ocean and Climate Dynamics, 2013–16, Keele Univ. Mem., Panel for Earth System and Envmtl Scis, REF 2014. *Publications:* numerous contribs to refereed jls, and book chapters, on ocean dynamics and sea ice processes relating to polynya modelling. *Recreations:* racquet sports, hiking, gardening, wine tasting. *Address:* School of Mathematics, Statistics and Physics, Herschel Building, Newcastle University, Newcastle upon Tyne NE1 7RU. *E:* andrew.willmott@ncl.ac.uk. *Club:* Oceanography.

**WILLMOTT, Dennis James,** CBE 1988; QFSM 1981; Group Contingency Manager, 1988–93, and Fire Safety Consultant, 1993–98, Avon Rubber plc; *b* 10 July 1932; *s* of James Arthur Willmott and Esther Winifred Maude Willmott (*née* Styles); *m* 1958, Mary Patricia Currey; three *s. Educ:* St Albans County Grammar School. MIFireE. Regular Army Service, East Surrey Regt, 1950–51, Royal North Regt, 1951–57. London, Bucks, Hants and Isle of Wight Fire Brigades, 1957–74; Dep. Chief Officer, Wilts Fire Brigade, 1974–76; Chief Staff Officer, 1976–81, Dep. Chief Officer, 1981–83, London Fire Brigade; Chief Fire Officer, Merseyside Fire Brigade, 1983–88. Member: Kennet DC, 1991–2009 (Leader, 1999–2003; Chm., 2008–09); (C) Wilts CC, 1993–2009 (Chm., 2003–04). Chairman: Devizes Constituency Cons. Assoc., 1999–2002 (Vice Pres., 2002–); Wilts and Swindon Combined Fire Authy, 2000–09; SW Regl Mgt Bd, 2004–09; Chm. Bd of Dirs, SW Local Authy Controlled Co., 2007–09; Mem., Veteran's Adv. and Pensions Cttee for the SW, 2010–18. Pres., Wilts Retired Firefighters Assoc., 2014–. Member: Royal Norfolk Regtl Assoc.; Korean Veteran's Assoc. (SW). *Recreation:* walking. *Address:* 27 Highlands, Potterne, Devizes, Wilts SN10 5NS. *T:* (01380) 730115. *E:* djwillmott@btconnect.com. *Clubs:* Victory Services, Union Jack; Conservative (Devizes); Royal British Legion (Potterne).

**WILLMOTT, Maj.-Gen. Edward George,** CB 1990; OBE 1979; CEng, FICE, FInstRE; Panel Chairman, 2gether NHS Foundation Trust, since 2014; *b* 18 Feb. 1936; *s* of late T. E. Willmott and E. R. Willmott (*née* Murphy); *m* 1960, Sally Penelope (*née* Banyard); two *s* one *d. Educ:* Gonville and Caius Coll., Cambridge (MA). FICE 1989; CEng 1990; FInstRE 2015. Commissioned RE 1956; psc 1968; active service, N Borneo 1963, N Ireland 1969, 1970, 1971, 1972, 1977; comd 8 Field Sqdn, 1971–73; 23 Engr Regt, 1976; 2 Armd Div. Engr Regt, 1977–78; 30 Engr Bde, 1981–82; RCDS 1983; Dep. Comdt RMCS, 1984–85; Vice-Pres. (Army), Ordnance Bd, 1985–86; Pres., Ordnance Bd, 1986–88; Dir Gen., Weapons (Army), 1988–90. Chief Exec., CITB, 1991–98. Col Comdt, RE, 1987–97. Hon. Col 101 (London) Engr Regt (V), 1990–97. Chairman: Herefordshire Primary Care Trust, 2000–06; Hereford Futures Ltd, 2009–16; non-executive Director: Healthcare Purchasing Consortium, 2006–09; ESG Ltd, 2006–09. Pres., Instn of Royal Engrs, 1987–90. Master, Engineers' Co., 2004–05 (Warden, 2001–04). Mem. Council, Roedean Sch., 1994–2004. Gov., Hereford Cathedral Trust, 2015–. *Recreations:* gardening, fishing. *Club:* Oriental.

**WILLMOTT, Dame Glenis,** DBE 2015; Member (Lab) East Midlands Region, European Parliament, 2006–17; Leader, European Parliamentary Labour Party, 2009–17; *b* 4 March 1951; *d* of Cyril Montgomery Barden and Lily Barden; *m* 1999, Edward Charles Willmott; one *d*, and one step *s* one step *d. Educ:* Trent Poly. (HNC Med. Scis, Clin. Chem.; HNC Med. Scis, Haematol.). Med. scientist, King's Mill and Mansfield Hosps, 1968–87; Parly Asst, 1987–90; Pol Officer, 1990–2006, Organiser, 1992–95, Sen. Organiser, 1995–2006, GMB. Mem. (Lab), Notts CC, 1989–93. Sec., E Midlands Regl Trade Union and Labour Party Orgn, 1990–2006. Chair, Nat. Exec., Labour Party, 2016–17. *Recreations:* reading, pilates, cooking, crosswords and sudoku.

**WILLMOTT, Prof. Hugh Christopher,** PhD; FBA 2015; Research Professor of Organization Studies, Cardiff University, since 2005; Professor of Management, Cass Business School, City, University of London (formerly City University London), since 2014; *b* 17 Sept. 1950; *s* of David P. T. Willmott and Mary Elizabeth Willmott (*née* Kitchen); *m* 1977, Irena Niezgoda; three *d. Educ:* Univ. of Manchester (BSc 1st Cl. 1972; PhD 1977). Univ. of Aston, 1977–85; Prof. of Organizational Analysis, Manchester Sch. of Mgt, UMIST, 1995–2001; Diageo Prof. of Mgt Studies, Judge Inst. of Mgt, Cambridge Univ., 2001–05. Visiting Professor: Copenhagen Business Sch., 1989; Uppsala Business Sch., 1990; Univ. of Lund, Sweden, 1999–2004; Cranfield Univ., 2000–03. Hon. PhD Lund, 2011. *Publications:* (with M. Alvesson) Making Sense of Management, 1996; (with D. Knights) Management Lives, 1999; (ed jtly) Managing Knowledge, 2000; contrib. numerous articles to acad. jls. *Recreations:* cycling, walking, gardening, swimming. *Address:* Cass Business School, City, University of London, 106 Bunhill Row, EC1Y 8TZ.

**WILLMOTT, Rt Rev. Trevor;** Bishop Suffragan of Dover, 2010–19; Bishop for the Channel Islands, 2014–19; *b* 29 March 1950; *s* of Frederick and Phyllis Willmott; *m* 1973, Margaret Anne Hawkins; one *d. Educ:* St Peter's Coll., Oxford (MA); Fitzwilliam Coll., Cambridge (DipTh); Westcott House, Cambridge. Ordained deacon, 1974, priest, 1975; Asst Curate, St George's, Norton, 1974–78; Asst Chaplain, Oslo with Trondheim, 1978–79; Chaplain of Naples with Capri, Bari and Sorrento, 1979–83; Rector of Ecton, 1983–89; Diocesan Dir of Ordinands and Post Ordination Training, Peterborough, 1986–97; Canon Residentiary of Peterborough Cathedral, 1989–97; Archdeacon of Durham, 1997–2002; Bishop Suffragan of Basingstoke, 2002–09. *Recreations:* travel, cooking, the appreciation of good wine, sport, music.

**WILLOCHRA, Bishop of,** since 2012; **Rt Rev. John Stead;** *b* Bexleyheath, 11 March 1956; *s* of James Joseph Stead and Evelyn May Stead; *m* 1979, Janet Ellen, (Jan); two *s. Educ:* Deakin High Sch.; Univ. of Canberra (BEd); Sydney Coll. of Divinity (BTh). Archdeacon, Dio. of Canberra and Goulburn, 2004–09; Asst Bishop of Bathurst, 2009–12. Liaison Bishop, Mission to Seafarers, Australia, 2013–; Bishop Protector, First Order Soc. of St Francis, Province of the Divine Compassion, 2014–. Mem., Standing Cttee of General Synod, 2017–. Chair of Leaders, Christian Churches S Australia, 2018–. Nat. Clerical Chair, Anglican Men's Soc., 2012–. Mem., Alban Inst. Visitor, Soc. of the Sacred Mission (Australia), 2018–. *Recreations:* cooking, walking, watching movies. *Address:* PO Box 88, Gladstone, SA 5473, Australia.

**WILLOTT, Brian;** see Willott, W. B.

**WILLOTT, Rt Hon. Jennifer Nancy,** OBE 2018; PC 2014; Director of Enterprise and Innovation, St Mary's University, Twickenham, since 2017; *b* 29 May 1974; *d* of (William) Brian Willott, *qv;* *m* 2009, Andrew Poole; two *s. Educ:* Univ. of Durham (BA Hons Classics 1996); London Sch. of Econs (MSc Develt Studies 1997). Consultant, Adithi NGO, Bihar, 1995; Hd of Office, Lembit Öpik, MP, 1997–2000; Researcher, Nat. Assembly for Wales, 2000–01; Project Adminr, Derwen Fostering and Adoption Project, Barnardo's, 2001–03; Hd of Advocacy, UNICEF UK, 2001–03; Chief Exec., Victim Support S Wales, 2003–05. Mem., Merton BC, 1998–2000. Contested (Lib Dem) Cardiff Central, 2001. MP (Lib Dem) Cardiff Central, 2005–15; contested (Lib Dem) same seat, 2015. PPS to Sec. of State for Energy and Climate Change, 2010; an Asst Govt Whip, 2012–14; Parliamentary Under Secretary of State: Employment Relations and Consumer Affairs, 2013–14; Women and Equality, 2013–14. Member: Work and Pensions Select Cttee, 2005–10; Public Admin Select Cttee, 2005–10. Mem., Ind. Parly Standards Authy, 2016–; Chm., Consumer Panel, Civil Aviation Authy, 2018–. *Recreations:* travelling, music, singing, reading. *Address:* St Mary's University, Twickenham, Waldegrave Road, Strawberry Hill, Twickenham TW1 4SX.

**WILLOTT, (William) Brian,** CB 1996; PhD; Chair, Gwent Healthcare NHS Trust, 2003–08; *b* 14 May 1940; *s* of late Dr William Harford Willott and Dr Beryl P. M. Willott; *m* 1970, Alison Leyland Pyke-Lees; two *s* two *d. Educ:* Trinity Coll., Cambridge (MA, PhD). Research Associate, Univ. of Maryland, USA, 1965–67; Asst Principal, Board of Trade, 1967–69; Principal: BoT, 1969–73; HM Treasury, 1973–75; Asst Sec., Dept of Industry, 1975–78; Secretary: Industrial Development Unit, DoI, 1978–80; NEB, 1980–81; Chief Exec., British Technology Gp (NEB and NRDC), 1981–84; Head of IT Div., DTI, 1984–87; Hd of Financial Services Div., DTI, 1987–92; Chief Exec., ECGD, 1992–97; Chief Exec., WDA, 1997–2000. Vis. Prof., Univ. of S Wales (formerly Univ. of Glamorgan), 2000–08. Dir, Dragon Internat. Studios Ltd, 2002–. Dir, Wales Mgt Council, 2000–03. Mem. Council, Nat. Museums and Galls of Wales, subseq. Trustee, Nat. Museum Wales, 2001–10. Mem., Church of Wales Governing Body, 2012–15. Chm., Raglan Community Council, 2017–19. *Recreations:* music, reading, gardening. *Address:* Coed Cefn, Tregare, Monmouth NP25 4DT.

See also Rt Hon. J. N. Willott.

**WILLOUGHBY,** family name of **Baron Middleton.**

**WILLOUGHBY DE BROKE,** 21st Baron *cr* 1491; **Leopold David Verney;** *b* 14 Sept. 1938; *s* of 20th Baron Willoughby de Broke, MC, AFC, AE and Rachel (*d* 1991), *d* of Sir Bourchier Wrey, 11th Bt; *S* father, 1986; *m* 1st, 1965, Petra (marr. diss. 1989), 2nd *d* of Sir John Aird, 3rd Bt, MVO, MC; three *s;* 2nd, 2003, Alexandra, Comtesse du Luart. *Educ:* Le Rosey; New College, Oxford. Chairman: S. M. Theatre Co. Ltd, 1992–; Compton Verney Opera and Ballet Project, 1992–2002; St Martins Magazines plc, 1992–2008. President: Heart of England Tourist Bd, 1996–2005; CPRE Warwicks, 2005–; Patron, Warwicks Assoc. of Boys' Clubs, 1991–2004; Chm., Warwicks Hunt Ltd, 2005–12. Hon. Gov., RSC. Mem. Council, Anglo-Hong Kong Trust, 1989–2006. Mem., H of L Select Cttee on EC, 1996–2001; elected Mem., H of L, 1999. DL Warwickshire, 1999. *Heir: s* Hon. Rupert Greville Verney, *b* 4 March 1966. *Address:* Ditchford Farm, Moreton-in-Marsh, Glos GL56 9RD.

**WILLOUGHBY DE ERESBY,** Baroness (27th in line), *cr* 1313 (by some reckonings 28th in line); **Nancy Jane Marie Heathcote-Drummond-Willoughby;** *b* 1 Dec. 1934; *d* of 3rd Earl of Ancaster, KCVO, TD, and Hon. Nancy Phyllis Louise Astor (*d* 1975), *d* of 2nd Viscount Astor; *S* to Barony of father, 1983. Trustee, Nat. Portrait Gall., 1994–2004. Mem. (Ind.), South Kesteven DC, 1969–82. DL Lincs, 1993–2009. OStJ 2000. *Heir: co-heirs:* Lt-Col Sebastian St Maur Miller [*b* 7 Feb. 1965; *m* 1991, Emma Caroline Harries; one *s* one *d*]; Sir John Aird, Bt, *qv. Address:* Grimsthorpe, Bourne, Lincs PE10 0LZ.

**WILLS,** family name of **Barons Dulverton** and **Wills.**

**WILLS, Baron** *cr* 2010 (Life Peer), of North Swindon in the County of Wiltshire and of Woodside Park in the London Borough of Barnet; **Michael David Wills;** PC 2008; *b* 20 May 1952; *s* of Stephen Wills and Elizabeth Wills (*née* McKeowen); *m* 1984, Jill Freeman; three *s* two *d. Educ:* Haberdashers' Aske's Sch., Elstree; Clare Coll., Cambridge (BA 1st cl. Hons Hist.). HM Diplomatic Service, 1976–80; Researcher, 1980–82, Producer, 1982–84, LWT; Dir, Juniper Productions, 1985–97. MP (Lab) N Swindon, 1997–2010. Parliamentary Under-Secretary of State: DTI, 1999; DFEE, 1999–2001; Parly Sec., LCD, 2001–02; Parly Under-Sec. of State, Home Office, 2002–03; Minister of State, MoJ, 2007–10. *Publications:* as David McKeowen: Grip, 2005; Trapped, 2007. *Address:* House of Lords, SW1A 0PW.

**WILLS, Arthur William,** OBE 1990; DMus (Dunelm), FRCO (CHM), ADCM; composer; Organist and Director of Music, Ely Cathedral, 1958–90; Professor, Royal Academy of Music, 1964–92; *b* 19 Sept. 1926; *s* of Violet Elizabeth and Archibald Wills; *m* 1953, Mary Elizabeth Titterton; one *s* one *d. Educ:* St John's Sch., Coventry. Sub-Organist, Ely Cathedral, 1949; Director of Music, King's School, Ely, 1953–64. Mem. Council, RCO, 1966–95; Examr to Royal Schs of Music, 1966–2002. Recital tours in Canada, Europe, USA, Australia and New Zealand; recording artist. Composer, opera, Winston and Julia '1984' (unpublished). Hon. RAM, Hon. FLCM, FRSCM. *Publications:* (contrib.) English Church Music, 1978; Organ, 1984, 2nd edn 1993; Full with Wills (memoir), 2006; numerous musical compositions include: *organ:* Sonata, Trio Sonata, Christmas Meditations, Prelude and Fugue (Alkmaar), Tongues of Fire, Variations on Amazing Grace, Symphonia Eliensis, Concerto (organ, strings and timpani), The Fenlands (symphonic suite for brass band and organ; for orchestral brass and organ), Etheldreda Rag (organ or piano); Wondrous Machine! A Young Person's Guide to the Organ; *brass band:* Overture: A Muse of Fire; *guitar:* Sonata, Pavane and Galliard, Hommage à Ravel, Four Elizabethan Love Songs (alto and guitar), Moods and Diversions, The Year of the Tiger, Suite Africana, Concerto Lirico for Guitar Quartet; Concerto for guitar and organ; *chamber:* Sacrae Symphoniae: Veni Creator Spiritus; A Toccata of Galuppi's (counter-tenor and string quartet); *piano:* Sonata; *choral:* Missa Eliensis, The Child for Today (carol sequence), The Light Invisible (double choir, organ and percussion), Missa in Memoriam Benjamin Britten, An English Requiem, Jerusalem Luminosa (choir and organ), Ely (part-song for treble voices), Caedmon: a children's cantata; The Gods of Music (choral concerto), Missa Sancti Stephani; Missa Incarnationis; That Wondrous Birthday: three carols and a coda; Crossing the Bar; Remembrance: the world of light; Love bade me welcome (communion motet); *vocal:* When the Spirit Comes (four poems of Emily Brontë), The Dark Lady (eight Shakespeare Sonnets); Eternity's Sunrise (three poems of William Blake); *orchestra:* Symphony No 1 in A minor. *Recreations:* travel, antique collecting, Eastern philosophy. *Address:* Paradise House, 26 New Barns Road, Ely, Cambs CB7 4PN. *T:* (01353) 662084.

**WILLS, Sir David James Vernon,** 5th Bt *cr* 1923 of Blagdon, co. Somerset; *b* 2 Jan. 1955; *s* of Sir John Vernon Wills, 4th Bt, KCVO, TD and Diana Veronica Cecil, (Jane), (*née* Baker); *S* father, 1998; *m* 1999, Mrs Paula Burke. Master, Soc. of Merchant Venturers, 2005. *Heir: b* Anthony John Vernon Wills [*b* 10 Dec. 1956; *m* 1983, Katherine Wilks; three *s*]. *Address:* Langford Court, Langford, Bristol BS40 5DA.

**WILLS, Sir (David) Seton,** 5th Bt *cr* 1904, of Hazelwood and Clapton-in-Gordano; FRICS; *b* 29 Dec. 1939; *s* of Major George Seton Wills (*d* 1979) (*yr s* of 3rd Bt) and Lilah Mary, *y d* of Captain Percy Richard Hare; *S* uncle, 1983; *m* 1968, Gillian, twin *d* of A. P. Eastoe; one *s* three *d. Educ:* Eton. FRICS 1976. *Heir: s* James Seton Wills [*b* 24 Nov. 1970; *m* 2003, Katy Gascoigne-Pees; two *s* one *d* (of whom one *s* one *d* are twins)]. *Address:* Tower House, Hollington Lane, Woolton Hill, Newbury, Berks RG20 9XX.

**WILLS, Dean Robert,** AO 1994 (AM 1986); Chairman: Transfield Services Ltd, 2001–05; John Fairfax Holdings Ltd, 2002–05 (Director, 1994–2005); *b* 10 July 1933; *s* of Walter William Wills and Violet Wills (*née* Watts), 1955, Margaret Florence Williams, *d* of E. G. Williams; one *s* two *d. Educ:* Sacred Heart Coll., S Aust.; SA Inst. of Technology. AASA. Dir, 1974, Man. Dir, 1977–83, Chm., 1983–86, W. D. & H. O. Wills (Australia) Ltd; Amatil Ltd, later Coca-Cola Amatil Ltd: Dir, 1975–99; Dep. Chm., 1983–84; Man. Dir,

1984–94; Chm., 1984–99; Chm., Australian Eagle Insurance Co., 1986–89. Chairman: Nat. Mutual Life Assoc., 1997–2000 (Dir, 1991; Vice Chm., 1992–97); Nat. Mutual Hldgs Ltd, 1997–2000 (Dep. Chm., 1995–97); Coca-Cola Australia Foundn Ltd, 2002–05; Director: Australian Grand Prix Corp., 1994–2002 (Dep. Chm., 1994–2002); Westfield Hldgs/Westfield America Trust, 1994–2008. Member: Business Council of Aust., 1984–94 (Vice Pres., 1987–88, Pres., 1988–90); Bd of Aust. Graduate Sch. of Management, Univ. of NSW, 1985–92. Pres., 1991, Gov., 1992–94, Med. Foundn. Trustee, Mus. of Applied Arts and Sciences (Powerhouse Mus.), NSW, 1986–90. *Recreations*: tennis, performance cars. *Address*: 175 Forest Way, Belrose, NSW 2085, Australia.

**WILLS, Kathryn Ann**; see Matthews, K. A.

**WILLS, Nicholas Kenneth Spencer**; international consultant and company director; *b* 18 May 1941; *s* of Sir John Spencer Wills and Elizabeth Drusilla Alice Clare Garcke; *m* 1st, 1973, Hilary Ann Flood (marr. diss. 1983); two *s* two *d*; 2nd, 1985, Philippa Trench Casson, *d* of Rev. Donald and Marion Casson; one *d*. *Educ*: Rugby Sch.; Queens' Coll., Cambridge (MA; Hon. Fellow, 1990). ACA 1967, FCA 1977–2013. Binder Hamlyn & Co., 1963–67; Morgan Grenfell, 1967–70; BET plc, 1970–92 (Director, 1975–92; Man. Dir, 1982–91; Chief Exec., 1985–91; Chm., 1991–92). Managing Director: Birmingham & Dist Investment Trust, 1970–91; Electrical & Industrial Investment, 1970–91; National Electric Construction, 1971–91; Chairman: Argus Press Hldgs, 1974–83; Electrical Press, 1974–83; Boulton & Paul plc, 1979–84; Initial plc, 1979–87; BET Building Services Ltd, 1984–87; Dep. Chm., Nat. Mutual Home Loans, 1994–96; Director: Bradbury, Agnew & Co. Ltd, 1974–83; National Mutual Life Assce Soc., 1974–85, 1991–2002 (Dep. Chm., 1992–99; Chm., 1999–2002); Chm. Supervisory Bd, 2002–08); St George Assce Co. Ltd, 1974–81; Colonial Securities Trust Co. Ltd, 1976–82; Cable Trust Ltd, 1976–77; Globe Investment Trust plc, 1977–90; Drayton Consolidated, 1982–92; Tribune (formerly Barings Tribune) Investment Trust, 1992–2004; Hitchin Priory Ltd, 1992–2002 (Dep. Chm., 1994–99; Chm., 1999–2002); Onslow Trading and Commercial, 1994–99; Manchester Trading and Commercial, 1995–2000; Toye & Co., 1996–2013; SMC Gp plc, 1999–2009; American Chamber of Commerce (UK), 1985–2000 (Vice-Pres., 1988–2000); United World Colls (Internat.) Ltd, 1987–95; IQ-Ludorum plc, 2000–05; Solid Terrain Modeling Inc., 2000–11; Archial Gp plc, 2009–10; Member, Advisory Board: City and West End, National Westminster Bank, 1982–91; Charterhouse Buy-Out Funds, 1990–98. Member: Council, CBI, 1987–92 (Member: Overseas Cttee, 1987–90; Public Expenditure Task Force, 1988; Economic Affairs Cttee, 1991–96); Council, Business in the Community, 1987–92; Advisory Board: Fishman-Davidson Center for Study of Service Sector, Wharton Sch., Univ. of Pennsylvania, 1988–92; Centre of Internat. Studies, Cambridge Univ., 1999–2006 (Hon. Fellow, 2000). Mem. Adv. Council, Prince's Youth Business Trust, 1988–2004 (Hon. Treas., 1989–92); Mem., Investment Cttee, 1992–98); Chm., Internat. Trustees, Internat. Fedn of Keystone Youth Orgns, 1990–2002. Chm., Involvement & Participation Assoc., 1991–96. Chm., Mgt Cttee, Cambridge Rev. of Internat. Affairs, 1998–2003. Treasurer and Churchwarden, Church of St Bride, Fleet Street, 1978–2001; Asst, Co. of Haberdashers, 1981–(Master, 1997–98); Gov., Haberdashers' Aske's Schs, Elstree, 1989–98 (Chm., Girls' Sch. Cttee, 1994–97). Hon. Mem., Clan McEwan. CCMI; FCIM; FCT; FRSA. *Recreations*: snow shoeing downhill, trying to farm in the Highlands. *Clubs*: White's, Royal Automobile; Beaver Creek.

**WILLS, Sir Seton**; see Wills, Sir D. S.

**WILLS-GOLDINGHAM, Claire Louise Margaret**; QC 2012; *b* Gloucestershire, 12 Nov. 1965. *Educ*: Birmingham Univ. (LLB Hons). Called to the Bar, Inner Temple, 1988. Legal Mem., Mental Health Rev. Tribunal, 2006–; Panel Mem. Child and Adolescent Mental Health Services. Panel Judge, Side Saddle Assoc. Trustee, Kitty Barron Trust, Riding for Disabled, 2014. Dep. Ed., Family Law Weekly. Website Ed., Court of Protection Hub, 2015–. *Publications*: (jtly) Atkin's Court Forms (Family), 2002, 2006, 2011; (jtly) Encyclopaedia of Forms and Precedents, 2001–; (contrib.) Essential Family Practice, 2000, 2001, 2002; (contrib.) Jackson's Matrimonial Finance and Taxation, 2010; (jtly) Family Finance in Practice, 2006, 3rd edn 2011; Family Law Case Library (Finance), 2008, 2012; (jtly) Atkin's Court Forms (Infants), 2012; Court of Protection Made Clear, 2016; Atkin's Court Forms (Children), 2016; (contrib.) Financial Provision in Family Matter, 2017, (ed jtly) 2018. *Recreations*: horses, HGV licence. *Address*: Colleton Chambers, Colleton Crescent, Exeter EX2 4DG. *T*: (01392) 274898. *E*: CWGQC@colletonchambers.co.uk.

**WILMERS, Mary-Kay**; Editor, London Review of Books, since 1992; *b* 19 July 1938; *d* of Charles Wilmers and Cesia (*née* Eitingon); *m* 1968, Stephen Arthur Frears, *qv* (marr. diss. 1975); two *s*. *Educ*: Athénée Royal d'Uccle, Brussels; Badminton Sch., Bristol; St Hugh's Coll., Oxford (BA; Hon. Fellow 2002). Editor, Faber & Faber, 1961–68; Dep. Ed., The Listener, 1968–73; Fiction Ed., TLS, 1974–79; Dep. Ed., then Co-Ed., London Rev. of Books, 1979–92. Hon. FRSL 2017; Hon. FBA 2018. *Publications*: The Eitingons: a twentieth century story, 2009; Human Relations and Other Difficulties, 2018. *Address*: c/o London Review of Books, 28 Little Russell Street, WC1A 2HN. *T*: (020) 7209 1101.

**WILMOT, Sir Benjamin John E.**; see Eardley-Wilmot.

**WILMOT, Sir Henry Robert**, 9th Bt *cr* 1759; DL; *b* 10 April 1967; *s* of Sir Robert Arthur Wilmot, 8th Bt, and of Juliet Elvira, *e d* of Captain M. N. Tufnell, RN; *S* father, 1974; *m* 1995, Susan Clare, *er d* of late John Malvern, FRCSE, FRCOG; two *s* one *d* (of whom one *s* one *d* are twins). Trustee, Ocean Youth Trust (N), 2014–. DL N Yorks, 2015. *Recreation*: Trebuchet. *Heir*: *s* Oliver Charles Wilmot, *b* 12 July 1999. *Club*: Buck's.

**WILMOT-SMITH, Richard James Crosbie**; QC 1994; a Recorder, 2000–14; *b* 12 May 1952; *s* of late John Patrick Wilmot-Smith and Rosalys Wilmot-Smith (*née* Massy); *m* 1978, Jenny (marr. diss. 2005), *d* of late R. W. Castle and L. M. Castle; one *s* two *d*. *Educ*: Charterhouse; Univ. of N Carolina (Morehead Schol.; AB 1975). Called to the Bar, Middle Temple, 1978 (Benefactors Law Schol.), Bencher, 2003 (Treas., 2018); Asst Recorder, 1995–2000. Trustee, Free Representation Unit, 1997–2007. *Publications*: Encyclopedia of Forms and Precedents, 5th edn: (contrib. and ed) Vol. 5, Building and Engineering Contracts, 1986; (contrib.) Vol. 12, Contracts for Services, 1994; (ed jtly) Human Rights in the United Kingdom, 1996; Construction Contracts: law and practice, 2006, 3rd edn 2014. *Recreations*: music, theatre, cinema, horse racing and breeding, cricket. *Address*: 39 Essex Chambers, 81 Chancery Lane, WC2A 1DD. *T*: (020) 7832 1111. *Club*: Kent CC.

**WILMOTT, Anthony Raymond**, FSA; Senior Archaeologist, Historic England (formerly English Heritage), since 2002; *b* Derby, 24 Feb. 1956; *s* of Raymond Arthur Wilmott and Margaret Eileen Wilmott. *Educ*: High Storrs Grammar Sch., Sheffield; Univ. of Newcastle upon Tyne (BA Combined Studies (Hist. and Archaeol.)); Univ. of Birmingham (MA Medieval Archaeol.). MCIfA (MIFA 1982); FSA 2000. Archaeologist: Hereford and Worcester CC, 1977, 1978–79; Birmingham City Mus., 1977; Mus. of London, 1979–85; West Yorks CC, 1985–87; English Heritage, 1987–2002. Director of Excavations: Kenchester, Herefords, 1977–79; London Wall, 1983; Pontefract, W Yorks, 1985–86; Birdoswald Roman Fort, Cumbria, 1987–92, 1997–98, 2009; Whitby Abbey, N Yorks, 1993–95, 2002, 2007, 2014; Richborough, Kent, 2001, 2008; Maryport, Cumbria, 2011–15; small sites on Hadrian's Wall, 1996, 1999–2000. Seconded (seasonally) to Indiana Univ. excavations at Castle Copse, Wilts, 1983–86. Hon. Life Mem. and Vice-Pres., Pontefract and Dist Archaeol. Soc., 2016. Hon. Editor, Trans of London and Middx Archaeol Soc., 1982–87. Archaeologist of the Year, Current Archaeology awards, 2012. *Publications*: Excavations in the Middle Walbrook Valley, City of London 1929–60, 1991; Birdoswald: excavations of a Roman fort on Hadrian's Wall and its successor settlements 1987–92, 1997; (ed with P. Wilson) The Late Roman Transition in the North, 2000; Birdoswald Roman Fort: 800 years on Hadrian's Wall, 2001; The Roman Amphitheatre in Britain, 2008; (ed) Roman Amphitheatres and Spectacula: a 21st century perspective, 2009; (ed) Hadrian's Wall: archaeological research by English Heritage, 1976–2000, 2009; English Heritage guidebooks: Birdoswald Roman Fort, 1995, 2005; Richborough and Reculver, 2012; (with D. Garner) The Roman Amphitheatre of Chester vol. 1: the prehistoric and Roman archaeology, 2017; articles in archaeol jls and mags. *Recreations*: gardening, travel, Sir Thomas Tylesley's Regiment of Foote, sailing tall ships, archaeology. *Address*: Meadow View, Tindale Fell, Brampton, Carlisle CA8 2QG. *T*: 07808 461261. *E*: t.wilmott@mail.com.

**WILMOTT, Peter Graham**, CMG 1996; business consultant, 1996–2013; *b* 6 Jan. 1947; *s* of John Joseph Wilmott and Violet Ena Wilmott; *m* 1969, Jennifer Carolyn Plummer; two *d*. *Educ*: Hove Grammar Sch.; Trinity Coll., Cambridge (MA). Asst Principal, Customs and Excise, 1968; Second Sec., UK Delegn to EEC, Brussels, 1971; Principal, Customs and Excise, 1973; First Sec., UK Perm. Rep.'s Office to EEC, Brussels, 1977; Asst to UK Mem., European Ct of Auditors, Luxembourg, 1980; Asst Sec., Customs and Excise, 1983; a Comr of Customs and Excise, 1988; Dir-Gen. (Customs and Indirect Taxation), Commn of the EC, 1990–96; Partner, Prisma Consulting Gp SA, 1996–2000; First Vice-Prés., Office de Dévelt par l'Automatisation et la Simplification du Commerce Extérieur, Paris, 2004–08 (Prés., 2000–04). Director: Ad Valorem Internat. Ltd, 2000–08; SITPRO Ltd, 2001–07; GlobalLink Border Solutions Ltd, 2006–13. Chairman: Internat. VAT Assoc., 1998–2000; Europro, 2010–12. *Recreations*: travelling, building and mending things, languages. *Address*: La Boissière, 46170 Castelnau Montratier, France.

**WILMSHURST, Elizabeth Susan**, CMG 1999; Distinguished Fellow, International Law (formerly Head of International Law Programme, then Senior Fellow, International Law), Royal Institute of International Affairs (Chatham House), since 2015 (Associate Fellow, 2004–15); *b* 28 Aug. 1948; *d* of Owen David Wilmshurst and Constance Hope Wilmshurst (*née* Brand). *Educ*: Clarendon Sch., N Wales; King's Coll., London (LLB 1969, AKC 1969). Admitted Solicitor, 1972. Asst Lectr, Bristol Univ., 1973–74; HM Diplomatic Service, 1974–2003: Asst Legal Advr, FCO, 1974–86; Legal Counsellor: Attorney-Gen.'s Chambers, 1986–91; FCO, 1991–94, 1997–99; Legal Advr, UKMIS to UN, NY, 1994–97; Dep. Legal Advr, FCO, 1999–2003. Vis. Prof., UCL, 2004–12.

**WILMUT, Sir Ian**, Kt 2008; OBE 1999; PhD; FRS 2002; Chair, MRC (formerly Scottish) Centre for Regenerative Medicine, 2011–13 (Director, 2006–11), and Professor Emeritus, since 2012, and Senior Honorary Professorial Fellow, 2011, University of Edinburgh; *b* 7 July 1944; *s* of Leonard (Jack) and Eileen Mary Wilmut; *m* 1967, Vivienne Mary Craven (*d* 2015); two *d*, one adopted *s*; *m* 2017, Sara Murray Haddon. *Educ*: Nottingham Univ. (BSc 1967); Darwin Coll., Cambridge (PhD 1971). Post-doctoral Fellow, Unit of Reproductive Physiol. and Biochem., Cambridge, 1971–73; Animal Breeding Research Organisation, ARC, subseq. BBSRC Roslin Institute: res. posts, 1973–81; Principal Investigator, 1981–2000; Hd, Dept of Gene Expression and Develt, 2000–05; Prof. of Reproductive Sci., Univ. of Edinburgh, 2005. Hon. Prof., Edinburgh Univ., 1998. Hon. DSc Nottingham, 1998. FRSE 2000. *Publications*: (with Colin Tudge) The Second Creation, 2000; (with Roger Highfield) After Dolly: the uses and misuses of human cloning, 2006; contrib. papers to Nature and Science on cloning of Dolly the sheep, first animal produced from an adult cell, using procedure developed at Roslin Inst. and use of this procedure to introduce genetic changes in sheep. *Recreations*: walking in countryside, photography, music, gardening, reading. *Address*: MRC Centre for Regenerative Medicine, SCRM Building, University of Edinburgh, Edinburgh BioQuarter, 5 Little France Drive, Edinburgh EH16 4UU. *T*: (0131) 651 9500.

**WILSEY, Gen. Sir John (Finlay Willasey)**, GCB 1996 (KCB 1991); CBE 1985 (OBE 1982); DL; Chairman, Western Provident Association, 1996–2009; *b* 18 Feb. 1939; *s* of Maj.-Gen. John Harold Owen Wilsey, CB, CBE, DSO and Beatrice Sarah Finlay Wilsey; *m* 1975, Elizabeth Patricia Nottingham; one *s* one *d*. *Educ*: Sherborne Sch.; RMA Sandhurst. Commissioned, Devonshire and Dorset Regt, 1959; regtl service in Cyprus, Libya, British Guyana, Germany, Malta, UK; Instructor, RMA, 1967–68; Great Abbai (Blue Nile) Expedition, 1968; Staff Coll., 1973, Defence Policy Staff, MoD, 1974–75; Co. Comdr, 1976–77; BAOR and NI (despatches 1976); Directing Staff, Staff Coll., 1978–79; Comd 1st Bn Devonshire and Dorset Regt, 1979–82 (despatches 1981); COS, HQ NI, 1982–84; Comdr 1st Inf. Brigade, 1984–86; RCDS 1987; COS, HQ UKLF, 1988–90; GOC NI, 1990–93; C-in-C, UK Land Forces then Land Comd, 1993–96; Jt Comdr, British Forces in Former Republic of Yugoslavia, 1993–96; ADC Gen. to the Queen, 1994–96. Col, Devonshire and Dorset Regt, 1990–97; Col Comdt, POW Div., 1991–94. Hon. Col, Royal Jersey Militia Sqdn, RE, 1993–2006. Mem., Commonwealth War Graves Commn, 1998–2005 (Vice Chm., 2001–05). President: Army Winter Sports Assoc., 1993–97; Army Catering Corps Assoc., 1996–; Wilts ACF, 2006–09. Governor: Sherborne Sch., 1994–2001 (Vice-Chm., 1996–2001); Sherborne Sch. for Girls, 1996–2001; Sutton's Hosp., Charterhouse, 1996–2001; Comr, Royal Hosp. Chelsea, 1996–2002. Chm., Salisbury Cathedral Council, 2001–10. Patron, Hope and Home for Children, 1996–2006. Mem., Scientific Exploration Soc. DL Wilts, 1996. *Publications*: Service for the Nation: Seaford papers, 1987; H. Jones, VC, the Life and Death of an Unusual Hero, 2002; The Ulster Tales, 2011. *Address*: c/o Lloyds Bank, 9 Broad Street, St Helier, Jersey, CI. *Club*: Army and Navy.

**WILSEY, Timothy Andrew W.**; see Willasey-Wilsey.

**WILSHAW, Sir Michael (Norman)**, Kt 2000; Senior Adviser, Education Strategy, GEMS Education, since 2017; *b* 3 Aug. 1946; *s* of Norman and Verna Wilshaw; *m*; one *s* two *d*. *Educ*: Birkbeck Coll., London Univ. (BA Hons). Teacher, later Head of Department, Inner London comprehensive schools, 1968–81: St Michael's, Bermondsey; Edith Cavell, Hackney; St Thomas the Apostle, Peckham; Dep. Headteacher, Trinity High Sch., Redbridge, 1981–85; Headteacher, St Bonaventure's RC Comp. Sch., 1985–2004; Principal, Mossbourne Community Acad., 2004–11; Dir of Educn, ARK Schs, 2007–11; HM Chief Inspector of Schs, 2012–16. *Recreations*: sport of all kinds, reading, theatre and cinema.

**WILSHIRE, David**; *b* 16 Sept. 1943; *m* 1967, Margaret Weeks (separated 2000); one *s* (one *d* decd). *Educ*: Kingswood School, Bath; Fitzwilliam College, Cambridge. Partner, Western Political Research Services, 1979–2000; Co-Director, Political Management Programme, Brunel Univ., 1986–91; Partner, Moorlands Res. Services, 2000–07. Mem., Avon CC, 1977–81; Leader, Wansdyke DC, 1981–87. MP (C) Spelthorne, 1987–2010. Parliamentary

Private Secretary: to Minister for Defence Procurement, 1991–92; to Minister of State, Home Office, 1992–94; an Opposition Whip, 2001–05. Leader, Cons. Parly Delegn, 2005–10, Chm., Eur. Democrat Gp, 2009–10, Parly Assembly of Council of Europe. *Recreations:* gardening, cider making.

**WILSON**; *see* Marslen-Wilson.

**WILSON**, family name of **Barons Moran, Nunburnholme, Wilson of Dinton** and **Wilson of Tillyorn**.

**WILSON OF DINTON**, Baron *cr* 2002 (Life Peer), of Dinton in the County of Buckinghamshire; **Richard Thomas James Wilson**, GCB 2001 (KCB 1997; CB 1991); Master, Emmanuel College, Cambridge, 2002–12, now Life Fellow; *b* 11 Oct. 1942; *s* of late Richard Ridley Wilson and Frieda Bell Wilson (*née* Finlay); *m* 1972, Caroline Margaret, *y d* of Rt Hon. Sir Frank Lee, GCMG, KCB and Lady Lee; one *s* one *d. Educ:* Radley Coll.; Clare Coll., Cambridge (Exhibnr; BA 1964, LLB 1965; MA 2002). Called to the Bar, Middle Temple, 1965. Joined BoT as Asst Principal, 1966; Private Sec. to Minister of State, BoT, 1969–71; Principal: Cabinet Office, 1971–73; Dept of Energy, 1974; Asst Sec., 1977–82; Under Sec., 1982; Prin. Estabt and Finance Officer, Dept of Energy, 1982–86; on loan to Cabinet Office (MPO), 1986–87; Dep. Sec., Cabinet Office, 1987–90; Dep. Sec. (Industry), HM Treasury, 1990–92; Perm. Sec., DoE, 1992–94; Perm. Under-Sec. of State, Home Office, 1994–97; Sec. of the Cabinet and Head, Home Civil Service, 1998–2002. Chm., C. Hoare & Co., Bankers, 2006–16. Non-executive Director: BSkyB, 2003–13; Xansa plc, 2003–07. Mem. Council, Cambridge Univ., 2005–08. Syndic, Fitzwilliam Mus., 2005–11. Pres., Policy Leaders Fellowship, Centre for Sci. and Policy, 2010– . Trustee: Ewing Foundn, 1994–2015; Leeds Castle Foundn, 2002–06; Royal Anniversary Trust, 2003–06; Cicely Saunders Foundn, 2004–15; Dir, Cambridge Arts Th. Trust, 2008–12; Trustee, Cambridge Film Trust, 2014–16. Chm., Prince's Teaching Inst., 2006–09. Pres., CIPD, 2004–06. Mem. Council, Radley Coll., 1995–2010 (Chm., 2004–10). Chm., Bd of Patrons, Wilberforce Soc., 2010– ; Chm. of Friends, 2013– , Trustee, 2014– , Kettle's Yard. Chm., Cambridge Univ. Boat Club Foundn, 2014–18. Chm. Council, Ely Cathedral, 2016– . Hon. Fellow: Univ. of Cardiff, 1999; LSE, 2000; Univ. of Wales Coll., Newport, 2002. Hon. LLD: Birmingham, 2000; City, 2001; Exeter, 2003. *Recreations:* movies, small gardens, expanding my horizons. *Address:* Emmanuel College, Cambridge CB2 3AP.

**WILSON OF TILLYORN**, Baron *cr* 1992 (Life Peer), of Finzean in the District of Kincardine and Deeside and of Fanling in Hong Kong; **David Clive Wilson**, KT 2000; GCMG 1991 (KCMG 1987 CMG 1985); PhD; FRSE; Master of Peterhouse, Cambridge, 2002–08 (Hon. Fellow, 2008); Deputy Vice-Chancellor, University of Cambridge, 2005–08; President, Royal Society of Edinburgh, 2008–11; Registrar, Order of Saint Michael and Saint George, 2001–10; Lord High Commissioner, General Assembly, Church of Scotland, 2010–11; *b* 14 Feb. 1935; *s* of Rev. William Skinner Wilson and Enid Wilson; *m* 1967, Natasha Helen Mary Alexander; two *s. Educ:* Trinity Coll., Glenalmond; Keble Coll., Oxford (schol., MA; Hon. Fellow, 1987); PhD London 1973. FRSE 2000. National Service, The Black Watch, 1953–55; entered Foreign Service, 1958; Third Secretary, Vientiane, 1959–60; Language Student, Hong Kong, 1960–62; Second, later First Secretary, Peking, 1963–65; FCO, 1965–68; resigned, 1968; Editor, China Quarterly, 1968–74; Vis. Scholar, Columbia Univ., New York, 1972; rejoined Diplomatic Service, 1974; Cabinet Office, 1974–77; Political Adviser, Hong Kong, 1977–81; Hd, S European Dept, FCO, 1981–84; Asst Under-Sec. of State, FCO, 1984–87; Governor and C-in-C, Hong Kong, 1987–92. Chm., Scottish Hydro-Electric, then Scottish and Southern Energy, 1993–2000; Dir, Martin Currie Pacific Trust plc, 1993–2003. Mem. Board, British Council, 1993–2002 (Chm., Scottish Cttee, 1993–2002). Chm., Scottish Peers Assoc., 2000–02 (Vice Chm. 1998–2000). Chm. Trustees, Nat. Museums of Scotland, 2002–06 (Trustee, 1999–2006); Vice-Pres., Scotland's Churches Trust (formerly Scotland's Churches Scheme), 2015– (Trustee, 1999–2002, 2008–15); Trustee, Carnegie Trust for the Univs of Scotland, 2000–16. Member: Council, CBI Scotland, 1993–2000; Adv. Cttee on Business Appts, 2000–09 (Chm., 2008–09). Chancellor's Assessor, Court, Univ. of Aberdeen, 1993–97; Chancellor, Univ. of Aberdeen, 1997–2013; Member: Governing Body, SOAS, 1992–97; Council, Glenalmond Coll., 1994–2005 (Chm. Council, 2000–05). Oxford Univ. Somaliland Expedn, 1957; British Mt Kongur Expedn (NW China), 1981. President: Bhutan Soc. of UK, 1993–2008; Hong Kong Assoc., 1994–2013. Hon. Hong Kong Soc., 1994–2012; Vice Pres., RSGS, 1996– . Chm., Adv. Cttee, St Paul's Cathedral, 2009–15. Patron, Scottish Pilgrim Routes Forum, 2016– . Burgess, Guild of City of Aberdeen, 2004. Hon. LLD: Aberdeen, 1990; Chinese Univ. of Hong Kong, 1996. Hon. DLitt: Sydney, 1991; Abertay Dundee, 1994; Hong Kong, 2006; Dhc Edinburgh, 2011. KStJ 1987. *Recreations:* hill-walking, theatre, reading. *Address:* c/o House of Lords, SW1A 0PW. *Clubs:* Alpine; New (Edinburgh); Royal Northern and University (Aberdeen).

*See also* Hon. P. M. A. Wilson.

**WILSON OF CULWORTH**, Rt Hon. Lord; **Nicholas Allan Roy Wilson**, Kt 1993; PC 2005; a Justice of the Supreme Court of the United Kingdom, since 2011; *b* 9 May 1945; *s* of late Roderick Peter Garratt Wilson and Dorothy Anne Wilson (*née* Chenevix-Trench); *m* 1974, Margaret (*née* Higgins); one *s* one *d. Educ:* Bryanston School; Worcester College, Oxford (BA 1st cl. hons Jurisp. 1966; Hon. Fellow, 2008). Eldon Scholar, 1967. Called to the Bar, Inner Temple, 1967, Bencher, 1993; QC 1987; a Recorder, 1987–93; a Judge of the High Court, Family Div., 1993–2005; a Lord Justice of Appeal, 2005–11. Pres., Family Mediators Assoc., 1998–2013. Patron, Hardman Trust, 2018– . Hon. Dr Staffordshire, 2014. Editor-in-Chief, Family Court Practice, 2008– . *Address:* Supreme Court of the United Kingdom, Parliament Square, SW1P 3BD.

**WILSON, Sir Alan (Geoffrey),** Kt 2001; FRS 2006; FBA 1994; Director of Special Projects, Alan Turing Institute, since 2018 (Chief Executive, 2016–18); Executive Chairman, Ada Lovelace Institute, Nuffield Foundation, since 2018; *b* 8 Jan. 1939; *s* of Harry Wilson and Gladys (*née* Naylor); *m* 1987, Sarah Caroline Fildes. *Educ:* Corpus Christi Coll., Cambridge (MA; Hon. Fellow, 2004). Scientific Officer, Rutherford High Energy Lab., 1961–64; Res. Officer, Inst. of Econs and Statistics, Univ. of Oxford, 1964–66); Math. Adviser, MoT, 1966–68; Asst Dir, Centre for Environmental Studies, London, 1968–70; University of Leeds: Prof. of Urban and Regl Geog., 1970–2004; Pro-Vice-Chancellor, 1989–91; Vice-Chancellor, 1991–2004; Dir-Gen., Higher Educn, DfES, 2004–06; Master of Corpus Christi Coll., Cambridge, 2006–07; Prof. of Urban and Regl Systems, UCL, 2007–18. Hon. Prof., Urban and Regl Geog., Univ. of Cambridge, 2006–07. Mem., Kirklees AHA, 1979–82; Vice-Chm., Dewsbury HA, 1982–85; non-exec. Mem., Northern and Yorks RHA, 1994–96. Chm., AHRC, 2007–13; Mem., ESRC, 2000–04 (Vice-Chm. Environment and Planning Cttee, 1986–88). Chm., Sci. Adv. Council, Home Office, 2013–19; Chm., Lead Expert Gp, Govt Office for Sci. Foresight Project, Future of Cities, 2013–15. Non-exec. Dir, Banking Standards Bd, 2018– . Dir, GMAP Ltd, 1991–2001; non-exec. Dir, Prospective Labs Ltd, 2016– . MAE 1991; FAcSS (AcSS 2000). FCGI 1997; FIMA 2017. Honorary Fellow: UCL, 2003; Regional Sci. Assoc. Internat., 2007. Hon. DSc Pennsylvania State, 2002; DUniv Bradford, 2004; Hon. DEd Leeds Metropolitan, 2004; Hon. LLD: Leeds, 2004; Teesside, 2006; Hon. DSocSci, KCL, 2010); Hon. DLitt London, 2017. Gill Meml Award, RGS, 1978; Honours Award, Assoc. of Amer. Geographers, 1987; Founder's Medal, RGS, 1992; Lauréat d'Honneur, IGU, 2004; European Prize, Regl Sci. Assoc., 2004. *Publications:* Entropy in Urban and Regional Modelling, 1970; Papers in Urban and Regional Analysis, 1972; Urban and Regional Models in Geography and Planning, 1974; (with M. J. Kirkby) Mathematics for Geographers and Planners, 1975, 2nd edn 1980; (with P. H. Rees) Spatial Population Analysis, 1977; (ed with P. H. Rees and C. M. Leigh) Models of Cities and Regions, 1977; Catastrophe Theory and Bifurcation: applications to urban and regional systems, 1981; (jtly) Optimization in Locational and Transport Analysis, 1981; Geography and the Environment: Systems Analytical Methods, 1981; (with R. J. Bennett) Mathematical Methods in Geography and Planning, 1985; (ed jtly) Urban Systems, 1987; (ed jtly) Urban Dynamics, 1990; (ed jtly) Modelling the City, 1994; (jtly) Intelligent Geographical Information Systems, 1996; Complex Spatial Systems, 2000; Knowledge Power, 2010; The Science of Cities and Regions, 2012; (ed) Urban Modelling, 5 vols, 2013; (with J. Dearden) Explorations in Urban and Regional Dynamics, 2015; (ed) Global Dynamics, 2016; (ed) Geo-mathematical Modelling, 2016; (jtly) Collaborative Approach to Trade, 2017. *Recreation:* writing. *Address:* Alan Turing Institute, British Library, 96 Euston Road, NW1 2DB. *T:* (020) 3862 3327. *Club:* Athenæum.

**WILSON, (Alan) Martin;** QC 1982; a Recorder of the Crown Court, 1979–2005; *b* 12 Feb. 1940; *s* of late Joseph Norris Wilson and Kate Wilson; *m* 1st, 1966, Pauline Frances Kibart (marr. diss. 1975); two *d;* 2nd, 1976, Julia Mary Carter; one *d. Educ:* Kilburn Grammar Sch.; Nottingham Univ. (LLB Hons). Called to the Bar, Gray's Inn, 1963; in practice as a barrister, until 2010; door tenant, 7 Bedford Row, 2010– . Occasional Mem., Hong Kong Bar, 1988– ; admitted to Malaysian Bar, 1995; Temp. Advocate, IOM Bar, 2004. Trustee, Broadway Arts Fest., 2010–16 (Chm., 2015–16). *Publications:* The Little Book of Anger, 2012; Unbidden Guests, 2013. *Address:* 7 Bedford Row, WC1R 4BS.

**WILSON, Rt Rev. Alan Thomas Lawrence;** *see* Buckingham, Area Bishop of.

**WILSON, Alastair James Drysdale;** QC 1987; a Recorder, since 1996; *b* 26 May 1946; *s* of late A. Robin Wilson and of Mary Damaris Wilson; *m;* one *s* two *d. Educ:* Wellington College; Pembroke College, Cambridge. Called to the Bar, Middle Temple, 1968. *Recreations:* gardening, restoring old buildings, shopping at boot fairs, mending things. *Address:* Hogarth Chambers, 5 New Square, Lincoln's Inn, WC2A 3RJ. *T:* (020) 7404 0404, *Fax:* (020) 7404 0505. *E:* alastairwilson@hogarthchambers.com; Rainthorpe Hall, Tasburgh, Norfolk NR15 1RQ.

**WILSON, Alastair John;** Chief Executive, School for Social Entrepreneurs, since 2004; *b* Edinburgh, 22 Nov. 1968; *s* of Iain and Shirley Wilson. *Educ:* Milburn Acad., Inverness; Napier Univ. (BA Hons Business Studies); Sch. for Social Entrepreneurs (Fellow, 1998). Business Devel Manager, ICL, 1993–97; Founder and Manager, Homeless Direct, 1999–2003; Devel Dir, Sch. for Social Entrepreneurs, 2003–04. Dir, Tonic Housing CIC, 2015– . Trustee: Sheila McKechnie Foundn, 2007– ; Cabrach Trust, 2016– . *Recreations:* theatre, politics, travel, ski-ing. *Address:* School for Social Entrepreneurs, 2nd Floor, The Fire Station, 139 Tooley Street, SE1 2HZ. *E:* alastair.wilson@sse.org.uk.

**WILSON, Allan;** Member (Lab) Cunninghame North, Scottish Parliament, 1999–2007; *b* 5 Aug. 1954; *s* of Andrew Wilson and Elizabeth (*née* Lauchlan); *m* 1981, Alison Isabel Melville Liddell; two *s. Educ:* Spiers Sch., Beith. Trainee Officer, 1972–75, Area Officer, 1975–93, NUPE; Sen. Regl Officer, UNISON, 1993–94; Head of Higher Educn, UNISON (Scotland), 1994–99. Contested (Lab) Cunninghame N, Scottish Parlt, 2007 and 2011. Dep. Minister for Sport, the Arts and Culture, 2001, for Envmt and Rural Develt, 2001–04, for Enterprise and Lifelong Learning, 2004–07, Scottish Exec. *Recreations:* football, reading, golf. *Address:* 44 Stoneyholm Road, Kilbirnie, Ayrshire KA25 7JS. *Clubs:* Garnock Labour, Place Golf (Kilbirnie).

**WILSON, Air Chief Marshal Sir Andrew;** *see* Wilson, Air Chief Marshal Sir R. A. F.

**WILSON, Andrew;** *see* Wilson, R. A.

**WILSON, Prof. Andrew Ian,** DPhil; Professor of the Archaeology of the Roman Empire, University of Oxford, and Fellow of All Souls College, Oxford, since 2004; *b* 29 Feb. 1968; *s* of Anthony Keith Wilson, *qv; m* 1994, Heather Mary Claire Grabbe, *qv* (marr. diss. 2009); two *d. Educ:* Corpus Christi Coll., Oxford (BA (Lit.Hum.) 1991; MA 1996); Magdalen Coll., Oxford (DPhil 1998). Fellow by Exam., Magdalen Coll., Oxford, 1996–2000; Univ. Lectr in Roman Archaeol., Univ. of Oxford, and Fellow, Wolfson Coll., Oxford, 2000–04. Hon. Sec., 2001–08, Chm., 2008–11, Soc. for Libyan Studies; Foreign Corresp. Mem., Soc. Nat. des Antiquaires de France, 2004. Ed., Libyan Studies, 1998–2002. *Publications:* ed books, and numerous articles in archaeol jls. *Recreation:* moderate hedonism. *Address:* Institute of Archaeology, 36 Beaumont Street, Oxford OX1 2PG.

**WILSON, Andrew John;** Founding Partner, Charlotte Street Partners, since 2014; *b* Lanark, 27 Dec. 1970; *s* of Harry Arthur Wilson and late Dorothy Wilson (*née* Bunting); *m* 1st, 2004, Karen Isabella Doyle (marr. diss. 2014); two *s* one *d;* 2nd, 2017, Anna Croze (*née* Macdonald); two step *d. Educ:* Coltness High Sch., Wishaw; Univ. of St Andrews; Univ. of Strathclyde (BA Hons Econs and Politics). Economist, Government Economic Service: Forestry Commn, 1993–95; Scottish Office, 1995–96; Dir of Business for Scotland, 1996–97; Economist and Sen. Researcher, SNP, 1996–97; Economist, Royal Bank of Scotland, 1997–98; Royal Bank of Scotland Group: Hd of Gp Media Relns, 2003–05; Dep. Chief Economist, 2005–08; Hd of Gp Corporate Affairs, 2008–10; Hd of Gp Communications, 2010–12; Client Team Leader, WPP Gp, 2012–13. MSP (SNP) Central Scotland, 1999–2003; Scottish Parliament: Shadow Minister: Finance, 1999–2001; Economy and Transport, 2001; Economy, Enterprise and Lifelong Learning, 2001–03; contested (SNP) Cumbernauld and Kilsyth, 2003. Chair, Sustainable Growth Commn, 2016–18; Mem., Ind. Commn on Referendums, UCL, 2017–18. Columnist: Sunday Mail, 1999–2003; Scots Independent, 2001–03; Scotland on Sunday, 2012–16. Member: Inst. of Fiscal Studies, 2002– ; David Hume Inst., 2012– . Member: Develt Bd, Barnardo's (Scotland), 2008–10; Bd of Govs, Scottish Crop Res. Inst., 2009–11; Public Policy Adv. Bd, Univ. of Glasgow, 2013–17. Dir, Frame PR, 2015– . Trustee: John Smith Meml Trust, 2005–16; John Smith Centre for Public Service, 2016– ; Edinburgh Internat. Culture Summit, 2016– . Dir, Motherwell FC, 2010–15. FCIBS 2004; MInstD 2012. *Publications:* contribs to various jl and conf. papers. *Recreations:* golf, football, family, current affairs. *Address:* (office) Charlotte Building, Evelyn Yard, Fitzrovia, W1T 1QL; 16 Alva Street, Edinburgh EH2 4GG; (home) 2 Johnsburn Green, Balerno, Edinburgh EH14 7NB. *Clubs:* Ivy; New (Edinburgh).

**WILSON, Andrew Morley;** Chief Executive, North York Moors National Park Authority, since 2000; *b* Leamington Spa, 20 Feb. 1958; *s* of David and Elizabeth Wilson; *m* 1995, Helen Jayne Ashworth; two *d. Educ:* St Benedict's Sch.; Univ. of Southampton (BSc 1980). Mem. Exec., NUS, 1982; agric. officer, RSPB, 1982–85; researcher, Nat. Campaign for the Arts, 1986; Parly agric. advr, 1987; Sen. Policy Officer, CPRE, 1987–92; Hd, Park Mgt, Northumberland Nat. Park, 1992–2000. Mem. Bd, Natural England, 2009–14; Mem., National Forest Co., 2016– ; Chair, North York Moors Nat. Park Trust, 2017– . *Recreations:* birdwatching, growing hostas, reading history, skimming stones, my family. *Address:* North York Moors National Park Authority, The Old Vicarage, Bondgate, Helmsley, York YO62 5BP. *T:* (01439) 770657. *E:* a.wilson@northyorkmoors.org.uk.

**WILSON, Andrew Norman;** author; *b* 27 Oct. 1950; *s* of late Norman Wilson, Lt-Col RA, potter and industrialist, and Jean Dorothy Wilson (*née* Crowder); *m* Katherine Duncan-Jones, *qv*; two *d*; *m* 1991, Dr Ruth Alexandra Guilding; one *d*. *Educ*: Rugby; New College, Oxford (MA). Chancellor's Essay Prize, 1971, and Ellerton Theological Prize, 1975. Asst Master, Merchant Taylors' Sch., 1975–76; Lectr, St Hugh's Coll. and New Coll., Oxford, 1976–81; Literary Editor: Spectator, 1981–83; Evening Standard, 1990–97. Television work incl. (as presenter): Eminent Victorians, 1988; Jesus Before Christ, 1991; The Genius of Josiah Wedgwood, 2013; C. S. Lewis, 2014; Betjeman land, 2014; Return to Larkinland, 2015; Return to Eliotland, 2018; frequent contribs to radio. Mem., AAIL, 1988. FRSL 1981. *Publications: novels:* The Sweets of Pimlico, 1977 (John Llewellyn Rhys Memorial Prize, 1978); Unguarded Hours, 1978; Kindly Light, 1979; The Healing Art, 1980 (Somerset Maugham Award, 1981; Arts Council National Book Award, 1981; Southern Arts Prize, 1981); Who was Oswald Fish?, 1981; Wise Virgin, 1982 (W. H. Smith Literary Award, 1983); Scandal, 1983; Gentlemen in England, 1985; Love Unknown, 1986; Incline Our Hearts, 1988; A Bottle in the Smoke, 1990; Daughters of Albion, 1991; The Vicar of Sorrows, 1993; Hearing Voices, 1995; A Watch in the Night, 1996; Dream Children, 1998; My Name is Legion, 2004; A Jealous Ghost, 2005; Winnie and Wolf, 2007; The Potter's Hand, 2012; Resolution, 2016; Aftershocks, 2018; *for children:* Stray, 1987; Hazel the Guinea-pig, 1997; Furball and the Mokes, 2011; *non fiction:* The Laird of Abbotsford, 1980 (John Llewellyn Rhys Memorial Prize, 1981); A Life of John Milton, 1983; Hilaire Belloc, 1984; How Can We Know?, 1985; (jtly) The Church in Crisis, 1986; The Lion and the Honeycomb, 1987; Penfriends from Porlock, 1988; Tolstoy, 1988 (Whitbread Biography Award); Eminent Victorians, 1989; C. S. Lewis, a biography, 1990; Against Religion, 1991; Jesus, 1992; (ed) The Faber Book of Church and Clergy, 1992; The Rise and Fall of the House of Windsor, 1993; (ed) The Faber Book of London, 1993; Paul: the mind of the apostle, 1997; God's Funeral, 1999; The Victorians, 2002; Iris Murdoch as I Knew Her, 2003; London: a short history, 2004; After the Victorians, 2005; Betjeman, 2006; Our Times, 2008; Dante in Love, 2011; The Elizabethans, 2011; Hitler, 2012; Victoria, 2014; The Book of the People: how to read the Bible, 2015; The Queen, 2016; Charles Darwin, Victorian Mythmaker, 2017; Prince Albert: the man who saved the monarchy, 2019. *Address:* 5 Regent's Park Terrace, NW1 7EE. *Clubs:* Travellers, Beefsteak, Academy.
*See also* Viscount Runciman of Doxford.

**WILSON, Angela Christine;** *see* Smith, Angela C.

**WILSON, Anna Celia;** *see* Mallett, A. C.

**WILSON, Anthony Joseph, (Joe);** Member (Lab) North Wales, European Parliament, 1989–99; *b* 6 July 1937; *s* of Joseph Samuel Wilson and Eleanor Annie (*née* Jones); *m* 1st, 1959, June Mary Sockett (marr. diss. 1987); one *s* two *d*; 2nd, 1998, Sue Bentley (*d* 2012); 3rd, 2016, Marie-Josée Gianetti. *Educ:* Birkenhead Sch.; Loughborough Coll. (DLC); Univ. of Wales (BEd Hons). National Service, RAPC, 1955–57. Teacher: Vauvert Sec. Mod. Sch., Guernsey, 1960–64; Les Beaucamps Sec. Mod. Sch., Guernsey, 1964–66; Man., St Mary's Bay Sch. Journey Centre, Kent, 1966–69; Lectr in PE, Wrexham Tech. Coll., subseq. NE Wales Inst. of Higher Educn, 1969–89. Contested (Lab) Wales, EP elecn, 1999. *Recreations:* camping, boules, tennis. *Address:* 79 Ruabon Road, Wrexham, North Wales LL13 7PU. *T:* (01978) 352808. *E:* joewilson7779@gmail.com.

**WILSON, Anthony Keith;** Chief Executive of the Press, University Printer and Secretary, Press Syndicate, Cambridge University Press, 1992–99; Fellow of Wolfson College, Cambridge, 1994–2006, now Emeritus; *b* 28 Sept. 1939; *s* of late Sidney Walter Wilson and Doris Jessie Wilson (*née* Garlick), Streatham; *m* 1963, Christina Helen, *d* of late Ivor Gray Nixon and Margaret Joan Nixon (*née* Smith); two *s* one *d*. *Educ:* Lexden House Sch.; Dulwich Coll.; Corpus Christi Coll., Cambridge (Maj. Scholar; BA Hons Modern and Medieval Langs 1961; MA 1966). Longmans Green & Co. Ltd, 1961–64; Thomas Nelson & Sons Ltd, 1964–68; George Allen & Unwin Ltd, 1968–72; Cambridge University Press, 1972–99: Sen. Editor, R&D, 1972–73; Publishing Ops Dir, 1973–82; Dep. Sec., Press Syndicate, 1979–92; Actg Man. Dir, 1982–83, Man. Dir, 1983–92, Publishing Div.; Dep. Chief Exec., 1991–92. Royal Shakespeare Company: Gov., 1983–2008; Mem. Council, 1991–2000; Mem., Exec. Cttee, 1991–2000; Mem. Bd, 2001–06; Chm., Budget Cttee, 1991–96; Chm., Budget and Audit Cttee, 1996–2000; Chm., Audit Cttee, 2000–06. Gov., Perse Sch. for Girls, Cambridge, 1979–99 (Chm. Govs, 1988–99); Hon. Treas., Westcott House, Cambridge, 2000–09. FInstD 1978 (Life-Mem.). *Recreations:* very active Humanism, walking, talking, walking and talking. *Address:* Wolfson College, Cambridge CB3 9BB.
*See also* A. I. Wilson.

**WILSON, Anthony Thomas;** Director, Institute for Employment Studies, since 2018; *b* Kingston-upon-Thames, 21 Oct. 1978; *s* of Raymond Basil Wilson and Mary Teresa Wilson; *m* 2017, Elizabeth Marie Hickey; one *s* one *d*. *Educ:* Selwyn Coll., Cambridge (BA Hons 2000; MA). DWP, 2001–10; HM Treasury, 2010–11; Policy and Research Director: Centre for Econ. and Social Inclusion, 2011–15; Learning and Work Inst., 2016–18. Mem., Inst. for Employability Professionals, 2017. Member: Ramblers Assoc.; British Canoeing; Amnesty Internat. FRSA. *Recreations:* vinification, rambling, canoeing, Brighton and Hove Albion. *Address:* 40 Cleveland Road, Brighton BN1 6FG. *T:* 07504 054407. *E:* tony.wilson@employment-studies.co.uk.

**WILSON, Arthur Andrew;** Director of Planning and Finance, Bristol South & West Primary Care Trust, 2002–06; *b* 23 July 1946; *s* of late Arthur James Wilson and Hilda Mellor Wilson (*née* Kennedy); *m* 1968, Susan Ann Faulkner; one *s* one *d*. *Educ:* Moulton Sch., Northampton; Bath Spa Univ. (MA 2007). CIPFA; IHSM. W. H. Grigg & Co., 1963; Calne and Chippenham RDC, 1963–66; Berkshire CC, 1966–67; Bath City Council, 1967–73; Chief Accountant, Avon CC, 1973–76; Principal Asst Regl Treasurer, SW RHA, 1976–82; Dist Treasurer, Plymouth HA, 1982–84; South Western RHA: Regl Treasurer, 1984–91; Dep. Regl Gen. Manager, 1991–93; Chief Exec., Plymouth Hosps NHS Trust, 1993–2000; Prog. Dir, Avon, Glos and Wilts HA, 2000–02. Mem. Mgt Council, 1997–2000, Chm. Exec. Cttee, 1998–2000, UC of St Mark and St John, Plymouth. *Recreations:* golf, reading, listening to music, musical theatre, first editions of modern novels. *Address:* 38 Cambridge Road, Clevedon, N Som BS21 7DW. *T:* (01275) 342238.

**WILSON, Barbara Ann,** OBE 1998; PhD; FBPsS, FMedSci, FAcSS; Director of Research, Oliver Zangwill Centre, Princess of Wales Hospital, Ely, 1996–2007, now Visiting Scientist; Clinical Neuropsychologist, Raphael Medical Centre, since 2009; *b* 23 Oct. 1941; *d* of William David Forester and Miriam Clara Forester; *m* 1962, Michael John Wilson; one *s* one *d* (and one *d* decd). *Educ:* Univ. of Reading (BA 1st Cl. Hons 1975); MPhil 1977, PhD 1985, London. CPsychol 1977; FBPsS 1987; FMedSci 2001; FAcSS (AcSS 2002). Sen. Clinical Psychologist, Rivermead Rehab. Centre, Oxford, 1979–85; Principal Clinical Psychologist, Charing Cross Hosp., London, 1985–87; Reader in Rehabilitation Studies, 1987–90, Hon. Prof. of Rehabilitation Studies, 1995–, Univ. of Southampton; Sen. Scientist and Clinical Psychologist, MRC Cognition and Brain Sci. Unit, 1990–2007, now Vis. Scientist. Hon. ScD: UEA, 2005; Cordoba. May Davidson Award for Clin. Psychol., 1984; Dist. Scientist Award, British Psychol Soc., 2000; Professional of the Yr, Encephalitis Soc., 2002; Robert L. Moody Prize for Services to Rehabilitation, Univ. of Texas, 2006; Ramon Y Cahal Award for dist. contribs to neuropsychiatry, Internat. Neuropsychiatric Assoc., 2011; Lifetime Achievement Award: British Psychol Soc.; Internat. Neuropsychol Soc.; Nat. Acad. of Neuropsychol.; Encephalitis Soc. *Publications:* (jtly) Families in Other Places, 1974; Rehabilitation of Memory, 1987; (jtly) Selecting, Administering and Interpreting Cognitive Tests, 1996; (jtly) Coping with Memory Problems, 1997; Case Studies in Neuropsychological Rehabilitation, 1999 (Book of the Yr Award, British Psychol Soc., 2003); (jtly) The Handbook of Memory Disorders, 2002; (ed) Neuropsychological Rehabilitation: theory and practice, 2003; (jtly) Behavioural Approaches in Neuropsychological Rehabilitation, 2003; (jtly) The Essential Handbook of Memory Disorders for Clinicians, 2004; First Year: Worst Year: coping with the unexpected death of our grown up daughter, 2004; *edited jointly:* Clinical Management of Memory Problems, 1984, 2nd edn 1992; Self-Injurious Behaviour, 1985; Everyday Cognition in Adulthood and Late Life, 1989; Developments in the Assessment and Rehabilitation of Brain-damaged Patients, 1993; Handbook of Memory Disorders, 1995; Rehabilitation Studies Handbook, 1997; 8 neuropsychological tests; over 250 book chapters and articles in jls. *Recreation:* travel. *Address:* Oliver Zangwill Centre, Princess of Wales Hospital, Lynn Road, Ely, Cambs CB6 1DN. *E:* barbara.wilson00@gmail.com.

**WILSON, Barbara Jolanta Maria,** PhD; Director of Organisational Development and Personnel, Catholic Agency for Overseas Development, 2005–10; *b* 26 June 1947; *d* of late Edward Szczepanik and Anne Szczepanik (*née* Janikowska); *m* 1971, Peter Brian Wilson (*d* 1996); one *s* one *d*. *Educ:* King George V Sch., Hong Kong; Convent of the Sacred Heart, Tunbridge Wells; St Anne's Coll., Oxford (MA Maths); Keele Univ. (PhD 1975); Heythrop Coll., Univ. of London (MA Christian Spirituality 2011). Statistical Res. Unit in Sociol., Keele Univ., 1969–73; Welsh Office, 1974–99: Sen. Asst Statistician, 1974–76; Statistician, 1976–84; Principal, Local Govt Finance, 1984–86; Educn Dept, 1986–89; Head of: Resource and Quality Mgt Div., 1989–92; Community Care Div., 1992–96; Personnel, 1996–99; Principal Estabts Officer, April–Aug. 1999; Dep. Clerk, Nat. Assembly for Wales, 1999–2000; Dir of Res. and Develt, 2000–03, Dir for Public Service Develt, 2003–05, Welsh Assembly Govt. Founder Trustee and Treas., WAY (Widowed and Young) Foundn, 1997–2002. *Recreations:* walking, music, cooking.

**WILSON, Brian Alfred Samuel;** Member (Green) North Down, Northern Ireland Assembly, 2007–11; *b* 15 May 1943; *s* of Alfred and Sheila Wilson; *m* 1979, Anne Campbell; three *s* one *d*. *Educ:* Bangor Grammar Sch.; Open Univ. (BA Hons); Univ. of Strathclyde (MSc). Lectr, Belfast Inst. of Further and Higher Educn, 1976–2003. Mem., N Down BC, 1981–2015 (Alliance 1981–96, Ind. 1996–2004, 2011–15, Green 2004–11) (Alderman, 2001–11). *Recreations:* sports, walking. *Address:* 1 Innisfayle Drive, Bangor BT19 1DN. *T:* (028) 9145 5189. *E:* baswilson@hotmail.com.

**WILSON, Rt Hon. Brian David Henderson;** PC 2003; UK Business Ambassador, 2012–19; Chairman, Harris Tweed Hebrides, since 2007; Adviser, UK Board of Trade, since 2017; *b* 13 Dec. 1948; *s* of late John Forrest Wilson and Marion MacIntyre; *m* 1981, Joni Buchanan; two *s* one *d*. *Educ:* Dunoon Grammar School; Dundee Univ. (MA Hons); University College Cardiff (Dip. Journalism Studies). Publisher and founding editor, West Highland Free Press, 1972–97. MP (Lab) Cunninghame N, 1987–2005. Opposition front bench spokesman on Scottish affairs, 1988–92, on transport, 1992–94 and 1995–96, on trade and industry, 1994–95, on election planning, 1996–97; Minister of State: Scottish Office, 1997–98 and 1999–2001; (Minister for Trade), DTI, 1998–99; FCO, Jan.–June 2001; (Minister for Industry and Energy, then for Energy and Construction), DTI, 2001–03; Prime Minister's Special Rep. on Overseas Trade, 2003–06. Director: West Highland Publishing Co., 1972–97 and 2005–10; Amec Nuclear, 2005–14; Celtic plc, 2005–; Chairman: Airtricity UK, 2005–08; Mangersta Ltd, 2005–; Britain's Energy Coast, West Cumbria (formerly West Cumbria Vision), 2009–14; Havana Energy, 2010–. Visiting Professor: in Govt and Media, Glasgow Caledonian Univ., 2007–12; Internat. Public Policy Inst., Univ. of Strathclyde, 2016–. Mem. Bd, Community Land Scotland, 2010–. Hon. Pres., Industrial Power Assoc., 2005–. Led review of Support for Scottish Exporting, 2014. Hon. Fellow, Univ. of the Highlands and Islands, 2009. Hon. Keeper of the Quaich, Scotch Whisky Industry, 2014. First winner, Nicholas Tomalin Meml Award, 1975; UK Global Dir of the Year, IoD, 2011. *Publications:* Celtic: a century with honour, 1988; The Official History of Celtic Football Club, 2014, rev. edn 2017; (ed jtly) Remembering Sam: the life and times of Sam Galbraith, 2016; contribs to various newspapers and periodicals. *Address:* Cnoc na Meinn, 7A Mangersta, Isle of Lewis HS2 9EY. *E:* brianwilson@mangersta.net. *Clubs:* Soho House; Stoke Park; Archerfield.

**WILSON, Prof. Brian Graham,** AO 1995; Vice-Chancellor, University of Queensland, 1979–95; *b* 9 April 1930; *s* of Charles Wesley Wilson and Isobel (*née* Ferguson); *m* 1st, 1959, Barbara Elizabeth Wilkie; two *s* one *d*; 2nd, 1978, Margaret Jeanne Henry; 3rd, 1988, Joan Patricia Opdebeeck; three *s* (incl. twins). *Educ:* Queen's Univ., Belfast (BSc Hons); National Univ. of Ireland (PhD Cosmic Radiation). Post-doctoral Fellow, National Research Council, Canada, 1955–57; Officer in Charge, Sulphur Mt Lab., Banff, 1957–60, Associate Res. Officer, 1959–60; Associate Prof. of Physics, Univ. of Calgary, 1960–65, Prof., 1965–70, Dean of Arts and Science, 1967–70; Prof. of Astronomy and Academic Vice-Pres., Simon Fraser Univ., 1970–78. Pres., Internat. Develt Program of Australian Univs and Colls, 1991–93; Chairman: Australian Vice-Chancellors' Cttee, 1989–90 (Dep. Chm., 1987–88); Quality Assurance in Higher Educn, 1993–95. Founder and Chm., Uniquest Ltd, 1983–88. Member: Council, Northern Territory Univ., 1988–93; Council, Univ. of South Pacific, 1991–95. FTS 1990. Hon. LLD Calgary, 1984; DUniv Queensland Univ. Tech., 1995; Hon. DSc Queensland, 1995. Centenary Medal (Australia), 2001. *Publications:* numerous, on astrophysics and on higher educn issues, in learned jls. *Recreations:* golf, swimming. *Address:* Les Grezes, 11410 Montauriol, France. *E:* opdebeeck.wilson@orange.fr.

**WILSON, Brian William John Gregg,** MA; Headmaster, Campbell College, Belfast, 1977–87; *b* 16 June 1937; *s* of late Cecil S. and Margaret D. Wilson; *m* 1969, Sara Remington (*née* Hollins); two *d*. *Educ:* Sedbergh Sch., Yorks; Christ's Coll., Cambridge (MA; Otway Exhibnr and Scholar). Sec. and Capt., Cambridge Univ. Rugby Fives Club, 1959–60. NI short service commn, RIrF, 1955–57; Flt Lt, RAFVR (T), 1964–71. Asst Master, Radley Coll., 1960–65; Housemaster, King's Sch., Canterbury, 1965–73; Dir of Studies, Eastbourne Coll., 1973–76; Dep. Hd, St Mary's Sch., Wantage, 1989–97. Project Manager, Navan Fort Initiative Gp, 1987–88. Chief Examiner, Latin A Level, NI Schs Examinations Council, 1987–88. Mem. and Chm. Planning Cttee, Wantage Town Council, 1999–2000. Member, Management Committee: NISTRO, 1989–81; Adv. Council on Schs Industry Liaison, 1981–87; Central Religious Adv. Cttee, BBC/ITV, 1982–86; Researcher and Cttee Mem., Progressive Christianity Network, 2007–09. Hon. Sec., Ancient History Cttee, JACT, 1967–77; Treas., JACT Ancient History Bureau, 1998–2000. Guest Speaker, Swan Hellenic Cruises, 1998–2003. Secretary: Wantage PCC, 1999–2000; Cleeve PCC, 2001–04; Mem., Cleeve Parish Council, 2002–03; Chm., N Som Neighbourhood Watch Assoc., 2004–05. *Publications:* (with W. K. Lacey) Res Publica, 1970; (with D. J. Miller) Stories from Herodotus, 1973; (jtly) The Age of Augustus, 2003; A Faith Unfaithful, 2004; Experience is an Arch, 2007; (jtly) Tiberius to Nero, 2011; Hannibal's Invasion and Defeat, 2011; Lost Certainties, 2012; (jtly) Translation of The

Sarum Missal, 2014; (jtly) The Flavians, 2015; Rambles in Arcadia (3 vols), 2016; (jtly) Sparta, 2017. *Recreations:* fives, squash, golf, cricket, hockey, etc; translating, theology, stock market, drama, walking, birds, trees, letter-writing, rambling. *Address:* 9 Redwood Drive, Failand, Bristol BS8 3DU.

**WILSON, Rt Rev. Bruce Winston;** Bishop of Bathurst (NSW), 1989–2000; *b* 23 Aug. 1942; *s* of Alick Bruce Wilson and Maisie Catherine (*née* Pye); *m* 1966, Zandra Robyn Parkes; one *s* one *d*. *Educ:* Canterbury Boys' High School; Univ. of Sydney (MA); London Univ. (BD); Univ. of NSW (BA); Australian Coll. of Theology (ThL). Curacies, Darling Point and Beverly Hills, Sydney, 1966–69; Anglican Chaplain, Univ. of NSW, 1970–75; Rector of St George's, Paddington, Sydney, 1975–83; Director, St Mark's Theol Coll., Canberra, 1984–89; Asst Bishop, Diocese of Canberra and Goulburn, 1984–89. Exec., Nat. Council of Churches in Australia, 1994–2000. Co-editor, Market Place, 2005–08. *Publications:* The Human Journey: Christianity and modern consciousness, 1981; Can God Survive in Australia?, 1983; Reasons of the Heart, 1998. *Recreations:* jogging, motor car restoration, reading, cooking. *Address:* 84–88 Mount Street, Leura, NSW 2780, Australia.

**WILSON, Caroline Elizabeth,** CMG 2016; HM Diplomatic Service; Europe Director, Foreign and Commonwealth Office, since 2016; *b* Wimbledon, 12 Aug. 1970; *d* of Peter Wilson and Elizabeth Wilson. *Educ:* Sevenoaks Sch.; Downing Coll., Cambridge (BA 1992; Hon. Fellow, 2018); Inst. for Eur. Studies, Université Libre de Bruxelles (Licence Spéciale en droit européen 1994). Called to the Bar, Middle Temple, 1993, Bencher 2013. Entered FCO, 1995; First Secretary: Beijing, 1997–2000; UK Perm. Repn to EU, 2001–04; Private Sec. to Sec. of State for Foreign and Commonwealth Affairs, 2004–06; Dep. Dir, Eur. Secretariat, Cabinet Office, 2006–07; Minister Counsellor (Econ.), Moscow, 2008–12; Consul Gen., Hong Kong and (non-resident) Macao, 2012–16. *Recreations:* classical music, ice skating, foreign languages (Cantonese less 'recreational' than Italian). *Address:* c/o Foreign and Commonwealth Office, King Charles Street, SW1A 2AH. *E:* c.wilson@fco.gov.uk. *Club:* Athenæum.

**WILSON, Catherine, (Kate);** Founder and Managing Director, Nosy Crow, since 2010; *b* Edinburgh, 11 April 1964; *d* of Gerald and Margaret Wilson; *m* 2001, Adrian Soar; two *c*. *Educ:* British Sch. of Brussels; Worcester Coll., Oxford (BA English Lang. and Lit. 1985). Rights Asst, then Rights Manager, Faber & Faber, 1986–89; Rights Dir, Reed Children's Books, 1989–94; Man. Dir, Macmillan Children's Books, 1994–2004; Gp Man. Dir, Scholastic UK, 2004–09. Inspirational Business Mum of Year, MumpreneurUK Awards, 2011; Most Inspiring Digital Publishing Person, FutureBook Innovation Awards, 2014. *E:* kate@nosycrow.com.

**WILSON, Catherine Mary, (Mrs P. J. Wilson),** OBE 1996; FMA, FSA; Director, Norfolk Museums Service, 1991–98; *b* 10 April 1945; *d* of Arthur Thomas Bowyer and Kathleen May (*née* Hawes); *m* 1968, Peter John Wilson. *Educ:* Windsor County Grammar Sch. FMA 1984 (AMA 1972); FSA 1990. Museum Asst, Lincoln City Museums, 1964; Curator, Museum of Lincolnshire Life, 1972; Asst Dir (Museums), Lincs CC, 1983. Member: Museums and Galleries Commn, 1996–2000; Railway Heritage Cttee, 2000–10; E Midlands Regl Cttee, Heritage Lottery Fund, 2002–08. President: Soc. for Folklife Studies, 2000–02; Soc. for Lincs History and Archaeol., 2005–10. FRGS 1998. *Publications:* Lincolnshire's Farm Animals, 2012. *Recreations:* industrial archaeology, vernacular architecture, all local history.

**WILSON, Prof. Catherine Warren,** PhD; FRSC; Anniversary Professor of Philosophy, University of York, 2012–18; *b* New York, 28 March 1951; *d* of Robert F. Warren and Martha Helson; one *s* one *d*. *Educ:* Westtown Sch., Penn; Yale Univ. (BA Phil. 1972); Lady Margaret Hall, Oxford (BPhil Phil. 1974); Princeton Univ. (PhD Phil. 1977). FRSC 2003. University of Oregon: Asst Prof., 1978–84; Associate Prof., 1984–90; Prof., 1990–92; Professor: Univ. of Alberta, 1992–99; Univ. of BC, 1999–2005; Grad. Center, City Univ. of NY, 2005–09, 2014–18; Regius Prof. of Philosophy, Univ. of Aberdeen, 2009–12. Visiting Professor: Univ. of Notre Dame, 1990–91; Princeton Univ., 2008–09; Vis. Fellow Commoner, Trinity Coll., Cambridge, 2004–05; Visiting Fellow: All Souls Coll., Oxford, 2017; Wissenschaftskolleg zu Berlin, 2018. *Publications:* Leibniz's Metaphysics, 1989; The Invisible World, 1995, 2nd edn 2009; Descartes's Meditations, 2003; Moral Animals, 2004; Epicureanism at the Origins of Modernity, 2008; A Very Short Introduction to Epicureanism, 2015; Metaethics from a First Person Standpoint, 2016. *Address:* 28 Chelmsford Road, E18 2PL.

**WILSON, Cedric Gordon;** Member, Strangford, Northern Ireland Assembly, 1998–2003 (UKU 1998–99, NIU 1999–2003); Leader, Northern Ireland Unionist Party, 1999–2003; *b* 6 June 1948; *s* of Samuel Wilson and Elizabeth Wilson; *m* 1975, Eva Kverneland; one *s* two *d*. *Educ:* Hillcrest Prep. Sch.; Belmont Primary Sch.; Orangefield High Sch. Dir, Hollymount Develts Ltd, 1988. Mem., 1981–89, Dep. Mayor, 1982–83, Mayor, 1983–84, Castlereagh BC. *Recreations:* art, music, photography. *Address:* 12 Sandylands, Ballyhalbert, Newtownards, Co. Down BT22 1BT.

**WILSON, Prof. Charles Crichton, (Chick),** PhD, DSc; FInstP, FRSC; Professor of Physical Chemistry, since 2010, and Associate Dean, Research, Faculty of Science, since 2015, University of Bath (Director of Research, 2013–15); *b* 11 Oct. 1961; *s* of David Cherrie Wilson and Isabella Kennedy Wilson; *m* 2002, Victoria Marie Nield, DPhil. *Educ:* Craigbank Secondary Sch., Glasgow; Univ. of Glasgow (BSc Hons Chem. Physics 1982; DSc Chemistry 2004); PhD Physics Dundee 1985. FInstP 2002; FRSC 2002. Council for the Central Laboratory of the Research Councils: Sen. Scientist and Hd, ISIS Crystallography Gp, 1992–2004; Associate Scientist, 2003–06; Regius Prof. of Chemistry, 2003–10, Hd of Dept, 2009–10, Hon. Sen. Res. Associate, 2010–12, Univ. of Glasgow. Vis. Lectr, J. J. Thomson Physical Lab., Univ. of Reading, 1993–96; Vis. Prof. in Chemistry, Univ. of Durham, 2001–06; Adjunct Prof. of Chemistry, Univ. of Tennessee, Knoxville, 2006–. Dir, WestCHEM, 2008–10 (Dep. Dir, 2006–08). Pres., British Crystallographic Assoc., 2003–06. Thomas Graham Medal, Royal Philosophical Soc. of Glasgow, 2011. *Publications:* Single Crystal Neutron Diffraction from Molecular Materials, 2000; over 310 articles in learned scientific jls. *Recreations:* walking, running, reading, music (listening, not making), gardens, enthusing people about science. *Address:* Department of Chemistry, University of Bath, Bath BA2 7AY. *T:* (01225) 386143. *E:* C.C.Wilson@bath.ac.uk.

**WILSON, Charles Martin;** Managing Director, Mirror Group (formerly Mirror Group Newspapers) plc, 1992–98 (Editorial Director, 1991–92); Managing Director and Editor-in-chief, The Sporting Life, 1990–98; *b* 18 Aug. 1935; *s* of Adam and Ruth Wilson; *m* 1st, 1968, Anne Robinson, *qv* (marr. diss. 1973); one *d*; 2nd, 1980, Sally Angela O'Sullivan, *qv* (marr. diss. 2001); one *s* one *d*; 3rd, 2001, Rachel, *d* of Baroness Pitkeathley, *qv*. *Educ:* Eastbank Academy, Glasgow. News Chronicle, 1959–60; Daily Mail, 1960–71; Dep. Northern Editor, Daily Mail, 1971–74; Asst Editor, London Evening News, 1974–76; Editor, Glasgow Evening Times, Glasgow Herald, Scottish Sunday Standard, 1976–82; The Times: Exec. Editor, 1982; Dep. Editor, 1983; Editor, 1985–90; Internat. Develts Dir, News Internat. plc, 1990. Non-exec. Dir, Chelsea and Westminster NHS Trust, 2000–11. Mem., Newspaper Panel, Competition Commn, 1999–2006; Board Member: Youth Justice, 1998–2004; Countryside Alliance, 1998–2005, 2008–12; Countryside Alliance Foundn, 2012–; IPSO, 2014–. Mem., Jockey Club, 1993–. Trustee: WWF-UK, 1996–2002; Addaction, 1998–2016; Royal Naval Mus., 1999–2009; Nat. Mus. of Royal Navy, 2011–. *Recreations:* reading, riding, horse racing, countryside. *Address:* 23 Campden Hill Square, W8 7JY. *T:* 07831 623522.

**WILSON, Very Rev. Christine Louise;** Dean of Lincoln, since 2016; *b* Brighton, 26 March 1958; *d* of Ronald and late Dinah Bravery; *m* 1976, Alan Ronald Wilson; two *d* (and one *d* decd). *Educ:* Margaret Hardy Secondary Modern; Southern Dio. Ministerial Trng Scheme (DipTh 1994). Ordained deacon, 1997, priest, 1998; Curate, Henfield with Shermanbury and Woodmancote, 1997–2002; Team Vicar, Hove, 2002–08; Vicar, Goring-by-the-Sea, 2008–10; Archdeacon of Chesterfield, 2010–16. Mem., Gen. Synod. 2011–15; Regl Rep., House of Bishops, 2013–16. Chair: Cornerstone Community Centre, Hove, 2002–08; Brunswick Community Develt Project, Brighton and Hove, 2002–08; Peak Centre, 2010–16; Dir, Investors in Lincoln, 2016–. Non-executive Director: Ecclesiastical Insurance Group plc, 2012–; Ecclesiastical Insurance Office plc, 2012–. *Recreations:* gardening, travel, entertaining. *Address:* The Deanery, 11 Minster Yard, Lincoln LN2 1PJ. *E:* Dean@lincolncathedral.com.

**WILSON, Maj. Gen. Christopher Colin,** CB 2009; CBE 2004; Strategy Director, Thales Land and Air Systems, 2011–19; *b* 14 Sept. 1953; *s* of Brig. Colin David Hastings Wilson and Eileen Edna Wilson (*née* Fort); *m* 1988, Marguerite Rose Laurraine Stewart; two *d*. *Educ:* Sedbergh Sch.; RMA, Sandhurst. Commnd RA, 1973; Staff Coll., 1986; CO 47 Regt RA, 1993–95; CRA Land and Comdr 1st Artillery Bde, 1998–2000; Dir Capability Integration (Army), 2001–03; Dir RA, 2004; ADC, 2004; Sen. Directing Staff, RCDS, 2005–06; Dep. Comdr, Coalition Forces Comd (Afghanistan), 2006; Capability Manager (Battlespace Manoeuvre), 2006–10; Master Gen. of the Ordnance, 2006–10. Col Comdt, RA, 2005–12. Trustee, British Forces Broadcasting Service (formerly Services Sound and Vision Corp.), 2010– (Chm., 2018–). CGIA Mil. Technol. Officer, Legion of Merit (USA), 2009. *Recreations:* sailing, genealogy. *Address:* c/o Army and Navy Club, 36–39 Pall Mall, SW1Y 5JN. *Clubs:* Army and Navy; Royal Artillery Yacht (Rear Cdre, 1993–95).

**WILSON, Christopher G.;** *see* Grey-Wilson.

**WILSON, Clive Hebden;** Chairman, Shared Lives South West (formerly South West Adult Placement Scheme), 2004–13; *b* 1 Feb. 1940; *s* of Joseph and Irene Wilson; *m* 1976, Jill Garland Evans; two *d*. *Educ:* Leeds Grammar Sch.; Corpus Christi Coll., Oxford. Joined Civil Service, 1962; Ministry of Health: Asst Principal, 1962–67; Asst Private Sec. to Minister of Health, 1965–66; Principal, 1967–73; Assistant Secretary: DHSS, 1973–77; Cabinet Office, 1977–79; DHSS, 1979–82; Under Sec., DHSS, later DoH, 1982–98: Dir of Estabs (HQ), 1982–84; Child Care Div., 1984–86; Children, Maternity, Prevention Div., 1986–87; Medicines Div., 1987–90; Priority Health Services Div., subseq. Health Care (A) Div., 1990–92; on secondment from Department of Health: Hd of Health and Community Care Gp, NCVO, 1992–95; Dir, Office of Health Service Comr, 1995–96; Dep. Health Service Comr, 1996–98; Clerk Advr, H of C, 1998–2001; Independent Complaints Reviewer: Nat. Lottery Charities Bd, subseq. Community Fund, 1998–2004; New Opportunities Fund, 2000–04; Awards for All Scheme, 2000–05; Arts Council England, 2003–05; Big Lottery Fund, 2004–05; Lottery Forum, 2005–10. *Recreations:* walking, gardening.

**WILSON, Colin;** *see* Wilson, D. C. E.

**WILSON, Colin Alexander Megaw;** First Scottish Parliamentary Counsel, 2006–12; *b* 4 Jan. 1952; *s* of James Thompson Wilson and Sarah Elizabeth Howard Wilson (*née* Megaw); *m* 1987, Mandy Esca Clay (marr. diss. 2012); one *s* one *d*; *m* 2014, Catriona Sarah Weir Hardman. *Educ:* Glasgow High Sch.; Edinburgh Univ. (LLB Hons 1973). Admitted solicitor, Scotland, 1975; Asst Solicitor, then Partner, Archibald Campbell & Harley, WS, Edinburgh, 1975–79; Asst, later Depute, Parly Draftsman for Scotland, 1979–93; Asst Legal Sec. to Lord Advocate, 1979–99; Scottish Parly Counsel, 1993–2006. *Recreations:* choral singing, hill walking, nature conservation, reading.

**WILSON, Prof. Colin James Ness,** PhD; FRS 2015; FRSNZ; Professor of Volcanology, Victoria University of Wellington, since 2009; *b* Wantage, 19 July 1956; *s* of Donald Wilson and Joyce Wilson; *m* 1989, Katharine Horton; one *s* two *d*. *Educ:* Imperial Coll. London (BSc Hons 1977; PhD 1981). Post-doctoral Res. Fellow, Univ. of Auckland, 1981–87; Royal Soc. Univ. Res. Fellow, Univs of Cambridge and Bristol, 1987–93; Volcanologist, Inst. of Geol and Nuclear Sci., Taupo and Lower Hutt, 1993–2005; Prof. of Volcanol., Univ. of Auckland, 2005–09. FRSNZ 2001; Fellow, Amer. Geophysical Union, 2006. Rutherford Medal, Royal Soc. of NZ, 2017. *Publications:* articles in scientific jls. *Recreation:* sleeping. *Address:* School of Geography, Environment and Earth Sciences, Victoria University of Wellington, PO Box 600, Wellington 6140, New Zealand. *T:* (4) 4639510, *Fax:* (4) 4635168. *E:* colin.wilson@vuw.ac.nz.

**WILSON, Corraine;** *b* Ayr, 1963; *d* of John and Mary Wilson; one *s* one *d*. *Educ:* Ayr Acad.; West of Scotland Univ. New Deal Advr, DSS subseq. DWP, 1982–2003; project worker, Barnardo's, 2005–09; Police Custody Welfare Officer, Strathclyde Jt Police Bd, 2007–08; Dir, Caledonii Resources Ltd, 2012–15. Mem. (SNP) S Ayrshire Council, 2012–15. MP (SNP) Ayr, Carrick and Cumnock, 2015–17; contested (SNP) same seat, 2017.

**WILSON, Prof. David,** PhD; Professor of Criminology, Birmingham City University (formerly University of Central England, Birmingham), 1997–2017, now Emeritus; *b* 23 April 1957; *s* of late William and Margaret Wilson; *m* 1990, Anne Maguire; one *s* one *d*. *Educ:* Univ. of Glasgow (MA Hons 1979); Selwyn Coll., Cambridge (PhD 1984). Prison Governor, various prisons incl. HM Prisons Wormwood Scrubs, Grendon and Woodhill, 1983–97. Nat. Teaching Fellowship, England and Wales, Higher Educn Acad., 2012. Vice Chm., Howard League for Penal Reform, 1999–2014 (Chm., Commn on English Prisons, 2009–10). Presenter, BBC Television series: Crime Squad, 1999–2001; Leave No Trace, 2006; Who Killed Ivan the Terrible?, 2007; Identity, 2008; Jack the Ripper, 2018; David Wilson's Crime Files, 2019; presenter: Channel 5: Banged Up, 2009; Killers Behind Bars, 2012; First Kill, Last Kill, 2013; Bring Back Borstal, ITV1, 2015; Interview with a Murderer, Channel 4, 2016 (Broadcast Award, RTS, 2017). Editor, Howard Jl, 1999–2015. *Publications:* (jtly) The Prison Governor: theory and practice, 1998; The Longest Injustice: the strange story of Alex Alexandrowicz, 1999; Prison(er) Education: stories of change and transformation, 2000; (jtly) What Everyone in Britain Should Know about Crime and Punishment, 2001; (jtly) What Everyone in Britain Should Know about the Police, 2001; (jtly) Innocence Betrayed, 2002; (jtly) Images of Incarceration, 2004; (jtly) Student Handbook of Criminal Justice and Criminology, 2004; Death at the Hands of the State, 2005; Serial Killers: hunting Britons and their victims 1960–2006, 2007; (with P. Harrison) Hunting Evil, 2008; A History of British Serial Killing, 1888–2008, 2009; (with P. Harrison) The Last British Serial Killer, 2010; Looking for Laura: public criminology and hot news, 2011; Mary Ann Cotton: Britain's first female serial killer, 2013 (televised as Dark Angel, 2016); Pain and Retribution: a short history of British prisons, 1066 to the present, 2014; (with E. Yardley and A. Lynes) Serial Killers and the Phenomenon of Serial Murder, 2015; My Life with Murderers, 2019. *Recreations:* Rugby, tennis. *Address:* c/o Curtis Brown, 28–29 Haymarket, SW1Y 4SP. *T:* (020) 7393 4460. *E:* profw@globalnet.co.uk.

**WILSON, Dr David**; Principal and Director, David Wilson Fine Art Ltd, since 2012. *Educ*: Colchester Inst. of Higher Educn; Anglia Ruskin Univ. (BA Hons); Univ. of West of England; London Sch. of Econs and Pol Sci. (LLM); Univ. of Warwick (PhD 2011). Solicitor's clerk and articled clerk, Farrer & Co., 1983–86; admitted solicitor, Supreme Court, 1986; Solicitor: Holman, Fenwick & Willan, 1987–88; Gouldens, 1988–90; BAT Industries plc: Asst Solicitor, 1990–93; Gp Co. Sec., 1993–97; Dir, subsidiary cos; Co. Sec. and Gen. Counsel, Debenhams plc and Dir, Debenhams Retail plc, 1998–99; Co. Sec., PIA and IMRO, 2000–01; Registrar, Stock Exchange Quotations Cttee, 2000–01; self-employed contractor to Cazenove and Co., 2001; Gp Co. Sec. and Legal Dir, Safeway plc, and Dir and Sec., Safeway Stores plc, 2001–04; Trustee, 2005, Robert Woof Dir and Chief Exec., 2006–08, Wordsworth Trust; Dir of Policy and Strategy, 2008–09, Chief Exec., 2009–11, ICSA. Trustee, Henry Moore Foundn, 2010–. Antiquary, art historian and writer. FSA 2007. *Publications*: Guide to Best Practice for Annual General Meetings, 1996; A Portrait of Raja Rammohun Roy: a masterpiece in ivory, 2013; Johan Zoffany RA and The Sayer Family of Richmond: a masterpiece of conversation, 2014; articles on legal issues and corporate governance; articles on history and art of 18th and 19th centuries in acad. jls. *Recreations*: music, sport, art, history, literature. *Address*: David Wilson Fine Art Ltd, 328 Linen Hall, 162–168 Regent Street, W1B 5TD. *T*: (020) 7528 4786. *E*: info@davidwilsonfineart.com.

**WILSON, David Geoffrey**, OBE 1986; DL; Chairman, East Manchester Partnership, 1996–2006; Vice Lord-Lieutenant, Greater Manchester, 2003–08; *b* 30 April 1933; *s* of late Cyril Wilson and Winifred Wilson (*née* Sutton); *m* 1980, Dianne Elizabeth Morgan. *Educ*: Leeds Grammar Sch.; Oldham Hulme Grammar Sch. Williams Deacon's Bank, 1953–70 (Co. Sec., 1965–70); Co. Sec., 1970–72, Sen. Manager, 1973–81, Williams & Glyn's Bank; Regl Dir (NW), NEB, 1981–85; Dir of Banking (NW), British Linen Bank, 1986–91. Non-executive Director: Lancastrian Building Soc., 1991–92; Healthsure Gp Ltd, 1998–2003. Chm., Manchester Business Link Ltd, 1993–2000; Dir, 1998–2001, and Chm., 1999–2001, Business Link Network Co. Chairman: N Manchester HA, 1991–93; N Manchester Healthcare NHS Trust, 1993–97; Dir, Manchester Chamber of Commerce and Industry, 1974–2001 (Pres., 1978–80); non-exec. Dir, Manchester TEC, 1998–2001. Non-executive Director: Halle Concerts Soc., 1980–97 (Treas., 1986–92; Dep. Chm., 1992–97); NW Arts Bd, 1991–96. Pres., Manchester Literary and Philosophical Soc., 1981–83. Chairman: Manchester Settlement, 1999–2009; Manchester Outward Bound Assoc., 2002–; Pres., Gtr Manchester Victim Support and Witness Service, 2001–; Vice-Pres., St Ann's Hospice, 1991– (Sec., 1968–72; Treas., 1975–91). Mem. Court, Manchester Univ., 1980–99; Mem. Council, Salford Univ., 1996–2005; Governor: Salford Coll. of Technol., 1988–96; Manchester Coll. of Arts and Technol., 1999–2008. Hon. Consul for Iceland, 1981–. High Sheriff, 1991–92, DL 1985, Gtr Manchester. Hon. MA: Manchester, 1983; Salford, 1995. *Recreations*: gardening, music. *Address*: 28 Macclesfield Road, Wilmslow, Cheshire SK9 2AF. *T*: (01625) 524133, *Fax*: (01625) 520605. *E*: wilsondg@talk.com. *Clubs*: Army and Navy; Lancashire County Cricket.

**WILSON, Sir David (Mackenzie)**, Kt 1984; FBA 1981; Director of the British Museum, 1977–92; *b* 30 Oct. 1931; *e s* of Rev. Joseph Wilson; *m* 1955, Eva, *o d* of Dr Gunnar Sjögren, Stockholm; one *s* one *d*. *Educ*: Kingswood Sch.; St John's Coll., Cambridge (LittD); Hon. Fellow, 1985); Lund Univ., Sweden. Research Asst, Cambridge Univ., 1954; Asst Keeper, British Museum, 1954–64; Reader in Archaeology of Anglo-Saxon Period, London Univ., 1964–71; Prof. of Medieval Archaeology, Univ. of London, 1971–76; Jt Head of Dept of Scandinavian Studies, UCL, 1973–76 (Hon. Fellow, 1988). Slade Prof., Cambridge, 1985–86. Member: Ancient Monuments Bd for England, 1976–84; Historic Bldgs and Monuments Commn, 1990–97. Governor, Museum of London, 1976–81; Trustee: Nat. Museums of Scotland, 1985–87; Nat. Museums of Merseyside, 1986–2001. Crabtree Orator 1966. Member: Royal Swedish Acad. of Sci.; Royal Acad. of Letters, History and Antiquities, Sweden; Norwegian Acad. of Science and Letters; German Archaeological Inst.; Royal Gustav Adolf's Acad. of Sweden; Royal Soc. of Letters of Lund; Vetenskapssocieteten, Lund; Royal Soc. of Sci. and Letters, Gothenburg; Royal Soc. of Sci., Uppsala; Royal Norwegian Soc. of Sci. and Letters; FSA; MAE; Hon. MRIA; Hon. Mem., Polish Archaeological and Numismatic Soc.; Hon. FMA. Sec., Soc. for Medieval Archaeology, 1957–77; Pres., Viking Soc., 1968–70; Pres., Brit. Archaeological Assoc., 1962–68. Mem. Council, Nottingham Univ., 1988–94. Foundn Fellow, Birmingham Univ., 2008. Hon. FilDr Stockholm; Hon. Dr Phil: Aarhus; Oslo; Hon. DLitt: Liverpool; Birmingham; Nottingham; Leicester; Hon. LLD Pennsylvania. Félix Neubergh Prize, Gothenburg Univ., 1978; Gold Medal, Royal Gustav Adolf's Acad. of Sweden, 1994; Gold Medal, Soc. of Antiquaries, 1995. Order of Polar Star, 1st cl. (Sweden), 1977. *Publications*: The Anglo-Saxons, 1960, 3rd edn 1981; Anglo-Saxon Metalwork 700–1100 in British Museum, 1964; (with O. Klindt-Jensen) Viking Art, 1966; (with G. Bersu) Three Viking Graves in the Isle of Man, 1969; The Vikings and their Origins, 1970, 2nd edn 1980; (with P. G. Foote) The Viking Achievement, 1970; (with A. Small and C. Thomas) St Ninian's Isle and its Treasure, 1973; The Viking Age in the Isle of Man, 1974; (ed) Anglo-Saxon Archaeology, 1976; (ed) The Northern World, 1980; The Forgotten Collector, 1984; Anglo-Saxon Art, 1984; The Bayeux Tapestry, 1985, 2nd edn 2004; The British Museum: purpose and politics, 1989; Awful Ends, 1992; Showing the Flag, 1992; Vikingatidens Konst, 1995; Vikings and Gods in European Art, 1997; The British Museum: a history, 2002; (ed jtly) The Hoen Hoard, 2006; The Vikings in the Isle of Man, 2008; (ed jtly) Aggersborg: the viking-age settlement and fortress, 2014; Manx Crosses, 2018. *Address*: The Lifeboat House, Castletown, Isle of Man IM9 1LD. *T*: (01624) 822800. *Club*: Athenæum.

**WILSON, David William**, CBE 2011; DL; FCIOB; Chairman: Wilson Bowden PLC, 1987–2007; Beacon Hill Group (formerly Eastern Range Ltd) and subsidiary Davidsons Ltd, since 2004; Founder, David Wilson Foundation, since 1995; *b* 5 Dec. 1941; *s* of Albert Henry Wilson and Kathleen May Wilson; *m* 1st, 1964, Ann Taberner; one *s* one *d*; 2nd, 1985, Laura Isobel Knifton; two *s*. *Educ*: Ashby Boys' Grammar Sch.; Leicester Polytechnic. Created from scratch what is now Wilson Bowden PLC. Pres., Leics CCC, 2003–. DL Leics, 2008. Hon. Canon, Leicester Cathedral, 2009. FCIOB 2004. Hon. LLD: Leicester, 2004; De Montfort, 2010. *Recreation*: farming. *Address*: Lowesby Hall, Lowesby, Leics LE7 9DD. *T*: (0116) 259 5321.

**WILSON, Prof. Deirdre Susan Moir**, PhD; FBA 1990; Professor of Linguistics, University College London, 1991–2007, now Emeritus; Research Professor and Co-Director, Linguistic Agency project, Centre for the Study of Mind in Nature, University of Oslo, 2007–17; *b* 1941; *m* 1975, Dr Theodore Zeldin, *qv*. *Educ*: Somerville Coll., Oxford (BA 1964); Nuffield Coll., Oxford (BPhil 1967); Massachusetts Inst. of Technol. (PhD 1974). Lectr in Philosophy, Somerville Coll., Oxford, 1967–68; Harkness Fellow, MIT, 1968–70; University College London: Lectr in Linguistics, 1970–85; Reader, 1985–91; British Acad. Res. Reader, 1988. Hon. DLitt: Geneva, 2007; Oslo, 2014. *Publications*: Presuppositions and Non-truth Conditional Semantics, 1975; (with Neil Smith) Modern Linguistics: the results of Chomsky's Revolution, 1979; (novel) Slave of the Passions, 1991; (with Dan Sperber) Relevance: communication and cognition, 1995; (with Dan Sperber) Meaning and Relevance, 2012; contrib. to learned jls. *Address*: UCL Linguistics, Chandler House, 2 Wakefield Street, WC1N 1PF.

**WILSON, Derek Robert**; Chief Executive, Slough Estates, 1996–2002; *b* 10 Oct. 1944; *m* 1972, Maureen Thorpe; one *s* one *d*. *Educ*: Bristol Univ. (BA Econs and Accounting). FCA 1970. Deloitte Haskins & Sells, London and Geneva, 1966–72; Cavenham, 1973–78; Wilkinson Match, 1978–83; Dir of Finance, Cadbury Schweppes, 1983–86; Finance Dir, 1986, Gp Man. Dir, 1992–96, Slough Estates. Director: Candover Investments, 1994–2005; Westbury, 1996–2005. Trustee, Nat. Soc. for Epilepsy, 2003–14. Gov., St Mary's Sch., Gerrards Cross, 1996– (Chm. Govs, 2007–). *Recreation*: golf.

**WILSON, Des**; author; public affairs adviser; *b* 5 March 1941; *s* of Albert H. Wilson, Oamaru, New Zealand; *m* 1985, Jane Dunmore; one *s* one *d* by a previous marriage. *Educ*: Waitaki Boys' High Sch., New Zealand. Journalist-Broadcaster, 1957–67; Director, Shelter, Nat. Campaign for the Homeless, 1967–71; Head of Public Affairs, RSC, 1974–76; Editor, Social Work Today, 1976–79; Dep. Editor, Illustrated London News, 1979–81; Chm., 1981–85, Project Advr, 1985–89, CLEAR (Campaign for Lead-Free Air); Dir of Public Affairs, 1993–94, World Wide Vice Chm., Public Affairs, 1994, Burson-Marsteller; Dir of Corporate and Public Affairs, BAA plc, 1994–2000. Non-executive Director: Carphone Warehouse plc, 2000–03; Earls Court and Olympia Holdings, 2001–04. Chairman: Friends of the Earth (UK), 1982–86; Campaign for Freedom of Information, 1984–91; Citizen Action, 1983–91; Parents Against Tobacco, 1990. Member: Nat. Exec., Nat. Council for Civil Liberties, 1971–73; Cttee for City Poverty, 1972–73; Bd, Shelter, 1982–86 (Trustee, 1982–86); Council, Nat. Trust, 2001–02; Trustee, Internat. Year of Shelter for the Homeless (UK), 1985–87. Member: Bd, BTA, 1997–2004; UK Sports Council, 2000–02; Mgt Bd, ECB, 2003–04; Sen. Vice Chm., Sport England, 1999–2002 (Chm., Lottery Panel, 1999–2002). Columnist: The Guardian, 1968–70; The Observer, 1971–75; New Statesman, 1997–; regular contribution, Illustrated London News, 1972–85. Contested (L) Hove, 1973, 1974; Liberal Party: Mem. Council, 1973–74 and 1984–85; Mem., Nat. Exec., 1984–85; Pres., 1986–87; Pres., NLYL, 1984–85; Mem. Federal Exec., SLD, 1988; Gen. Election Campaign Dir, Lib Dems, 1990–92. ITN Environmentalist of the Decade, 1989; PR Week Outstanding Individual Award, 1992; Sheila McKechnie Foundn Lifetime Achievement Award, 2015. *Publications*: I Know It Was the Place's Fault, 1970; Des Wilson's Minority Report (a diary of protest), 1973; So you want to be Prime Minister: a personal view of British politics, 1979; The Lead Scandal, 1982; Pressure, the A to Z of Campaigning in Britain, 1984; (ed) The Environmental Crisis, 1984; (ed) The Secrets File, 1984; The Citizen Action Handbook, 1986; Battle for Power - Inside the Alliance General Election Campaign, 1987; Costa Del Sol (novel), 1990; Campaign (novel), 1992; Campaigning, 1993; (with Sir John Egan) Private Business, Public Battleground, 2002; Swimming with the Devilfish: under the surface of professional poker, 2006; Ghosts at the Table: a history of poker, 2007; Memoirs of a Minor Public Figure (autobiog.), 2011; Growing Old: the last campaign, 2014; Faces and Places (photographs), 2017. *Address*: 422 Harold Road, Hastings, E Sussex TN35 5HG.

**WILSON, Dominic**; *see* Wilson, J. D.

**WILSON, Donald**; Lord Lieutenant and Lord Provost of Edinburgh, 2012–17; Convener, Culture and Communities Committee, City of Edinburgh Council, since 2017; *b* Selkirk, 4 Dec. 1959; *s* of George Wilson and May Wilson; *m* 2016, Elaine Brand; one step *s* one step *d*. *Educ*: Galashiels Acad.; Univ. of Stirling (BA Hons); City Univ., London (MSc Information Sci.); Moray House Coll. of Educn (TQ Secondary). Teacher of Computing, 1984–2012; Adult Educn Tutor, 1984–2012; Actg Sen. Teacher, 1997–99, Curriculum Devel Officer, 1999–2001, ICT. Mem. (Lab) Edinburgh CC, 1999– (Bailie, 2007–12). Chm., 1999–2007, Pres., 2012–, Edinburgh Internat. Sci. Festl; Chairman: Edinburgh Sci. Foundn, 1999–2007; Edinburgh Convention Bureau, 2003–05; Edinburgh and Lothians Tourist Bd, 2003–05; Convener, Edinburgh SW Neighbourhood Partnership, 2007–12; Chairman and Director: Edinburgh Internat. Fest. Soc., 2012–; Edinburgh Royal Military Tattoo Ltd, 2012–. Comr, Northern Lighthouse Bd, 2012–. Chm., Transnational Demos Proj., 2001–. Dir and Trustee, Our Dynamic Earth Charitable Trust, 2012–. Gov., Edinburgh Trades Maiden Fund. Hon. Pres. or Patron of numerous charities and bodies in Edinburgh. Mem., Edinburgh Incorp. of Hammermen, 2017; Deacon Convener, Edinburgh Incorp. of Baxters, 2019. OStJ 2014. *Recreations*: film, opera, science fiction, computers, antiques. *Address*: City Chambers, High Street, Edinburgh EH1 1YJ. *T*: (0131) 529 4715. *E*: donald.wilson@edinburgh.gov.uk.

**WILSON, (Douglas) Colin (Edward)**; Deputy Government Actuary, since 2012 and Technical Director, Government Actuary's Department, since 2011; *b* Kingston-upon-Thames, 12 July 1962; *s* of Dr Eric Wilson and Joan Wilson; *m* 1986, Caroline Heslop; one *s* two *d*. *Educ*: King's College Sch., Wimbledon; Trinity Coll., Cambridge (BA Hons Maths 1983). FIA 1996; Chartered Enterprise Risk Actuary 2013. Technical Consultant, EDS-Scicon, 1983–93; trainee actuary, Prudential Ltd, 1993–96; Sen. Quantitative Analyst, 1996–98, Dir, Quantitative Res., 1998–2005, Prudential M&G Ltd; Sen. Consultant, Barrie & Hibbert Ltd, 2005–09; Chief Actuary (Investment and Risk), Govt Actuary's Dept, 2009–11. Member, Council: Inst. for Quantitative Investment Res., 2004–09; Inst. of Actuaries, 2002–08; Inst. and Faculty of Actuaries, 2013–18 (Pres., 2016–17). Actuarial advr, Local Govt Pension Scheme Adv. Bd, 2016–; Mem. Adv. Bd, Centre for Disaster Protection, 2018–. *Recreations*: violin playing, defending my flower beds from marauding puppies. *Address*: Government Actuary's Department, Finlaison House, 15–17 Furnival Street, EC4A 1AB. *T*: (020) 7211 2601. *E*: colin.wilson@gad.gov.uk.

**WILSON, Duncan Henry**, OBE 2007; FCA; FSA; Chief Executive, Historic England, since 2015; *b* London, 29 March 1957; *s* of Sir Anthony Wilson and late (Margaret) Josephine Wilson (*née* Hudson); *m* 1992, Kate Emms (marr. diss. 2017); three *s*. *Educ*: Sherborne Sch. for Boys, Dorset; Pembroke Coll., Oxford (MA PPE); Inst. of Archaeol., Univ. of Oxford (MPhil Eur. Archaeol.). FCA 1996; FSA 2009. Field archaeologist, 1983–84; trainee accountant, Coopers & Lybrand, 1984–87; Financial Controller, English Heritage, 1987–91; Defence, Industry and Resource Accounting Desks, HM Treasury, 1991–95; Hd, Libraries Div., DNH, 1995–97; Dir, Somerset Hse Trust, 1997–2002; Chief Executive: Greenwich Foundn for Old Royal Naval Coll., 2002–11; Alexandra Park and Palace Trust, 2011–15. Trustee: Royal Armouries, 2007–11; Churches Conservation Trust, 2008–17. Community Gov., Corelli Coll., Greenwich, 2004–07. FRSA. *Recreations*: classical singing and listening to music, restoring old buildings, gardening, dogs. *Address*: 3 Terrett's Place, N1 1QZ. *T*: (020) 7973 3247. *E*: duncan.wilson@HistoricEngland.org.uk.

**WILSON, Prof. Edward Osborne**, PhD; Pellegrino University Research Professor, 1997–2002, now Emeritus, and Hon. Curator in Entomology, since 1997, Harvard University (Curator in Entomology, 1972–97); *b* 10 June 1929; *s* of Edward O. Wilson, Sen. and Inez Freeman; *m* 1955, Irene Kelley; one *d*. *Educ*: Univ. of Alabama (BS 1949; MS 1950); Harvard Univ. (PhD 1955). Harvard University: Jun. Fellow, Soc. of Fellows, 1953–56; Asst Prof. of Biology, 1956–58; Assoc. Prof. of Zoology, 1958–64; Prof. of Zoology, 1964–76; Baird Prof. of Sci., 1976–94; Mellon Prof. of the Scis, 1990–93; Pellegrino University Prof., 1994–97. Hon. DSc Oxon, 1993; 32 other hon. doctorates. Nat. Medal of Sci., USA, 1978; Tyler Prize for Envmtl Achievement, 1984; Crafoord Prize, Swedish Royal Acad. of Sci., 1990; Internat. Prize for Biol., Japan, 1994; King Faisal Internat. Prize for Sci., 2000; Franklin Medal, Amer. Philosophical Soc., 2000, etc. *Publications*: (with R. H. MacArthur) The Theory of Island Biogeography, 1967; (jtly) A

Primer of Population Biology, 1971; The Insect Societies, 1971; Sociobiology: the new synthesis, 1975; On Human Nature, 1978 (Pulitzer Prize, 1979); (jtly) Caste and Ecology in the Social Insects, 1978; (jtly) Genes, Mind and Culture, 1981; (jtly) Promethean Fire, 1983; Biophilia, 1984; Success and Dominance in Ecosystems, 1990; The Diversity of Life, 1992; Naturalist (autobiog.), 1994; In Search of Nature, 1996; Consilience, 1998; Biological Diversity, 1999; The Future of Life, 2002; Pheidole in the New World: a hyperdiverse ant genus, 2003; Nature Revealed, 2006; The Creation, 2006 (Sci. and Literature Prize, Stevens Technol. Inst., 2007); with Bert Hölldobler: The Ants, 1990 (Pulitzer Prize, 1991); Journey to the Ants, 1994; The Superorganism, 2009 (Best Biology Book, Library Jl, 2009); The Leafcutter Ants, 2010; The Social Conquest of Earth, 2012; The Meaning of Human Existence, 2014; Half-Earth, 2016; The Origins of Creativity, 2017; contrib. learned jls. *Address*: Museum of Comparative Zoology, Harvard University, 26 Oxford Street, Cambridge, MA 02138–2902, USA. *T*: (617) 4952315.

**WILSON, Elizabeth Alice, (Mrs W. I. Wilson)**, OBE 1995; Chairman, Dumfries and Galloway Community NHS Trust, 1995–97; *b* 26 May 1937; *née* Edwards; *m* 1996, William Iain Wilson, MBE. *Educ*: Coleraine High Sch.; Univ. of Edinburgh (BSc Soc. Sci.); SRN, SCM. Staff Nurse, Midwife, Ward Sister and nurse management posts, 1958–72; Principal Nursing Officer, Edinburgh Northern Hosps Gp, 1972–74; Dist Nursing Officer, N Lothian, Lothian Health Bd, 1974–80; Chief Area Nursing Officer: Dumfries and Galloway Health Bd, 1980–88; Tayside Health Bd, 1988–94. Member: Nat. Bd for Nursing, Midwifery and Health Visiting, Scotland, 1983–93 (Dep. Chm., 1985–93); UK Central Council for Nursing, Midwifery and Health Visiting, 1983–88. Chm., Stranraer Cancer Drop In Centre Assoc., 1998–2008. Lady Capt., Stranraer Golf Club, 2015. Hon. Sen. Lectr, Univ. of Dundee, 1988–94. SSStJ 2003. *Publications*: papers on nursing.

**WILSON, Emily Helen;** Editor, New Scientist, since 2018; *b* Brighton, 4 June 1970; *d* of Richard Wilson and Jenny Jones; *m* 2013, Jonathan Absalom; two *s*. *Educ*: Sidcot Sch.; Hereford Sixth Form Coll.; Bristol Univ. (BSc 1st Cl. Chem.); Univ. of Wales Coll. of Cardiff (Postgrad. Dip. Journalism). Reporter: Daily Mirror, 1994–98; Daily Mail, 1998–2000; The Guardian: Health Ed., 2000–01; Asst Features Ed., 2002–04; Ed., Life (science supplement), 2004; Dep. Features Ed., 2005–07; Features Ed., 2008–10; G1 Ed., 2010–12; Network Ed., 2012–14; Ed.-in-Chief, Guardian Australia, 2014–18; Asst Ed., 2016–18. *Recreations*: walking, prehistoric stone tools. *Address*: New Scientist, 25 Bedford Street, WC2E 9ES. *T*: (020) 7611 1262. *E*: emily.wilson@newscientist.com.

**WILSON, Erik,** CBE 2019; Executive Director, Corporate and Support Services, and Board Member, Competition and Markets Authority, since 2013; *b* London, 29 Nov. 1963; *s* of Roy Wilson and Jean Wilson (now Norley). Prime Minister's Efficiency Unit, 1993; Sec. to Interception, Security and Intelligence Services Comrs, 1994–98; Home Office: Terrorism Bill Manager, Terrorism and Protection Unit, 1998–2000; Home Sec.'s Office, 2000–02; Office of Fair Trading: Principal Private Sec. to Sir John Vickers, 2002–04; Dep. Dir, Bd Secretariat, 2004–06; Director: Exec. Office and Human Resources, 2006–07; Exec. Office and Internat., 2007–12. *Recreations*: reading, family. *Address*: Competition and Markets Authority, The Cabot, 25 Cabot Square, E14 4QA. *E*: erik.wilson@cma.gsi.gov.uk.

**WILSON, Sir Franklyn (Roosevelt)**, KCMG 2016 (CMG 2003); chartered accountant; Chairman, Sunshine Holdings Ltd, since 2002; *b* Nassau, Bahamas, 27 March 1947; *s* of late Stanley A. Wilson and Della Jane Wilson; *m* 1972, Sharon Lockhart; two *s* two *d*. *Educ*: Dalhousie Univ. (BCom Hons 1968); Amer. Inst. of Banking (Basic Cert. 1971); Univ. of Miami (Grad. Studies in Mgt). MP (PLP) Grants Town, Bahamas, 1972–77; Opposition Leader, Senate of Bahamas, 1995–97. Chairman: Focol Hldgs Ltd; Arawak Homes Ltd; Sunshine Insce (Agents and Brokers) Ltd; Royal Star Assce Ltd; Sunshine Finance Ltd; Cotton Bay Developers Ltd. Member: Canadian Inst. Chartered Accts, 1970; Bahamas Inst. Chartered Accts (formerly Bahamian Accounting Assoc.), 1972. Chm. Council, Coll. of Bahamas, 2002–07; Mem. Council, Dalhousie Univ., 2010–. Founder: Young Presidents Orgn (Bahamas), 1977; Jun. Achievement (Bahamas), 1979; World Presidents Orgn (Bahamas), 1997. Trustee, Elmira Coll., NY, 2000–13. *Recreations*: tennis, reading. *Address*: 135 Eastern Road, Nassau, Bahamas; Sunshine Holdings Ltd, Sunshine House, East Shirley Street and Highland Terrace, Nassau, Bahamas. *T*: 5026500. *Clubs*: Lyford Cay, Old Fort Bay (New Providence).

**WILSON, Fraser Andrew,** MBE 1980; HM Diplomatic Service, retired; Executive Director, Prospect Burma, 2010–13; *b* 6 May 1949; *s* of William McStravick Wilson and Mary McFadyen Wilson (*née* Fraser); *m* 1981, Janet Phillips; two *s*. *Educ*: Bellahouston Acad.; Surrey Univ. (Dip. Russian Studies). Joined Diplomatic Service, 1967; served: FCO, 1967–70; Havana, 1970–71; SE Asia, 1971–73; Seoul, 1973–77; Salisbury, 1977–80; FCO, 1980–84; Moscow, 1984–85; First Sec. (Commercial), Rangoon, 1986–90; FCO, 1990–94; Dep. Consul Gen., São Paulo, 1994–98; Ambassador to Turkmenistan, 1998–2002; High Comr, Seychelles, 2002–04; Dep. Hd, Overseas Territories, FCO, 2004–06; Ambassador to Albania, 2006–09. *Recreations*: travelling, reading.

**WILSON, Geoffrey Alan,** OBE 2004; Chairman, Equity Land Ltd, 1994–2012; *b* 19 Feb. 1934; *s* of Lewis Wilson and Doris Wilson (*née* Shrier); *m* 1963, Marilyn Helen Freedman; one *s* two *d*. *Educ*: Haberdashers' Aske's School; College of Estate Management. FRICS. 2nd Lieut RA, 1955–56. Private practice, 1957–60; Director: Amalgamated Investment & Property Co., 1961–70; Sterling Land Co., 1971–73 (and co-founder); Greycoat, 1976–94 (Chm., 1985–94, and co-founder); Perspectives on Architecture (formerly Perfect Harmony) Ltd, 1993–98. Member: W Metropolitan Conciliation Cttee, Race Relations Bd, 1969–71; Council, Central British Fund for World Jewish Relief, 1993–97. Trustee: ORT Trust, 1980–85; Public Art Develt Trust, 1990–95; British Architectural Liby Trust, 1996–2000; AA Foundn, 1998–2002; Buildings at Risk Trust, 1998–2001. English Heritage: Comr, 1992–98; Chm., London Adv. Cttee, 1995–98; Chm., Urban Panel, 2000–03; Chm., Heritage Protection Review Steering Cttee, DCMS, 2004–08. Mem., Governing Council, UCS, 1991–95. Governor: Peabody Trust, 1998–2004; City Literary Inst., 1998–2002; Mus. of London, 2000–10. Hon. FRIBA 1995. *Recreations*: reading, architecture, art. *Address*: 5 Elm Walk, West Heath Road, NW3 7UP. *Club*: Reform.

**WILSON, Hon. Geoffrey Hazlitt,** CVO 1989; FCA, FCMA; Chairman, Southern Electric plc, 1993–96 (Director, 1989–96); *b* 28 Dec. 1929; *yr s* of 1st Baron Moran, MC, MD, FRCP, and Lady Moran, MBE; *m* 1955, Barbara Jane Hebblethwaite; two *s* two *d*. *Educ*: Eton; King's Coll., Cambridge (BA Hons). JDipMA. Articled to Barton Mayhew (now Ernst & Young), 1952; Chartered Accountant 1955; joined English Electric, 1956; Dep. Comptroller, 1965; Financial Controller (Overseas), GEC, 1968; joined Delta Group as Financial Dir, Cables Div., 1969; elected to Main Board as Gp Financial Dir, 1972; Jt Man. Dir, 1977; Dep. Chief Executive, 1980; Chief Exec., 1981–88; Chm., 1982–94. Director: Blue Circle Industries plc, 1980–97; Drayton English & International Trust, 1978–95; W Midlands and Wales Regl Bd, Nat. Westminster Bank PLC, 1985–92 (Chm., 1990–92); Johnson Matthey plc, 1990–97 (Dep. Chm., 1994–97); UK Adv. Bd, National Westminster Bank, 1990–92. Member: Council, Inst. of Cost and Management Accountants, 1972–78; Accounting Standards Cttee, 1978–79; Financial Reporting Council, 1990–93; London Metal Exchange, 1982–94; Chm., 100 Gp of Chartered Accountants, 1979–80 (Hon. Mem., 1985). Mem. Management Bd, Engineering Employers Fedn, 1979–83 (Vice-Pres., 1983–86 and 1990–94; Dep. Pres., 1986–90); Chm., EEF Cttee on Future of Wage Bargaining, 1980; Dep. Pres., 1986–87; Pres., 1987–88, Counsellor, 1989–94, BEAMA; Member: Administrative Council, Royal Jubilee Trusts, 1979–88, Hon. Treas., 1980–89; Council, Winchester Cathedral Trust, 1985–93; Council, St Mary's Hosp. Med. Sch., 1985–88. Vice-Chm., Campaign Appeal, 1994–97, Fellow Commoner, 1996–, King's Coll., Cambridge. CCMI. Mem. Ct of Assistants, Chartered Accountants' Co., 1982–95 (Master, 1988–89). OStJ 1996. *Recreations*: family, reading, walking, vintage cars. *Club*: Boodle's.

**WILSON, Prof. Geoffrey Victor Herbert,** AM 1998; PhD; Vice Chancellor and President, Deakin University, 1996–2002; *b* 23 Sept. 1938; *s* of Victor Hawthorne Wilson and Dorothy Eleanor Wilson (*née* Spooner); *m* 1961, Beverley Wigley; two *s* two *d*. *Educ*: Univ. of Melbourne (BSc 1958; MSc 1960; DSc 1977); PhD Monash Univ. 1964. FAIP, MACE, FTSE, FAIM. Postgrad. Schol., Univ. of Melbourne, 1958–60; Teaching Fellow, Monash Univ., 1960–63; Nuffield Foundn Travelling Fellow, Oxford Univ., 1963–65; Sen. Lectr in Physics, Monash Univ., 1965–71; University of New South Wales: Prof. of Physics, 1971–85, Dean, Faculty of Mil. Studies, 1978–86, Royal Mil. Coll.; Rector of University Coll., Aust. Defence Acad., 1984–91; Vice Chancellor, Central Queensland Univ., 1991–96. Director: Australian Maritime Coll., 2004–14; Forestry Cooperative Res. Centre, 2009–12. Chm. Bd, AMC Search, 2007–15. Vis. Prof., Free Univ. of Berlin, 1977–78. *Recreations*: gardening, theatre, physical recreation. *Address*: 35/12 Balcombe Road, Newton, Vic 3220, Australia.

**WILSON, Gerald Robertson,** CB 1991; FRSE; Treasurer, Royal Society of Edinburgh, 2012–17; Chairman, Scottish Biomedical Foundation, 1999–2004; Special Adviser, Royal Bank of Scotland, 2000–11; *b* 7 Sept. 1939; *s* of late Charles Robertson Wilson and Margaret Wilson (*née* Early); *m* 1963, Margaret Anne (*d* 2005), *d* of late John S. and Agnes Wight; one *s* one *d*. *Educ*: Holy Cross Academy, Edinburgh; University of Edinburgh. (MA). FRSE 1999. Asst Principal, Scottish Home and Health Dept, 1961–65; Private Sec. to Minister of State for Scotland, 1965–66; Principal, Scottish Home and Health Dept, 1966–72; Private Sec. to Lord Privy Seal, 1972–74, to Minister of State, Civil Service Dept, 1974; Asst Sec., Scottish Economic Planning Dept, 1974–77; Counsellor, Office of the UK Perm. Rep. to the European Communities, Brussels, 1977–82; Asst Sec., Scottish Office, 1982–84; Under Sec., Industry Dept for Scotland, 1984–88; Sec., Scottish Office Educn, later Educn and Industry, Dept, 1988–99. Non-exec. Dir, ICL (Scotland) Ltd, 2000–02; Advr, ScottishJobs.com, 2004–05. Chm., Scottish Biomed. Res. Trust, 1999–2003. Chm., E Scotland, RIPA, 1990–92. Vice Chm., Royal Scottish Nat. Orchestra, 2002–06 (Bd Mem., 1999–2002); Trustee, Royal Scottish Nat. Orchestra Foundn, 2006–17 (Chm., 2015–); Hon. Sec., Friends of the Royal Scottish Acad., 2009–17. Chm., Scottish Eur. Educnl Trust, 2006–12. Mem. Ct, Strathclyde Univ., 1999–2008 (Vice Chm., 2008–12; Hon. Fellow, 2011); Gov., George Watson's Coll., Edinburgh, 2000–08. Mem., Bd of Mgt, St Andrew's Children's Soc., 2002–11. Mem. Council, Fairbridge in Scotland, 2000–06 (Chm., 2006–11). DUniv Stirling, 1999. *Recreation*: music. *Address*: 17/5 Kinnear Road, Edinburgh EH3 5PG.

**WILSON, Gillian Brenda, (Mrs Kenneth Wilson);** *see* Babington-Browne, G. B.

**WILSON, Guy Murray,** MA; FSA; museum and historical consultant; *b* 18 Feb. 1950; *s* of late Rowland George Wilson and Mollie (*née* Munson; later Mrs Youngs); *m* 1972, Pamela Ruth McCredie; two *s* two *d*. *Educ*: New Coll., Oxford (MA); Manchester Univ. (Dip. Art, Gallery and Museum Studies). FSA 1984. Joined Royal Armouries, 1972; Keeper of Edged Weapons, 1978; Dep. Master of the Armouries, 1981–88; Master of the Armouries, 1988–2002. Member: British Commn for Military History, 1978–; Adv. Cttee on History Wreck Sites, 1981–99; Arms and Armour Soc. of GB, 1973– (Vice-Pres., 1995–); Arms and Armour Soc. of Denmark, 1978–; Meyrick Soc., 1980–; Internat. Napoleonic Soc., 2001–; Pres., Internat. Assoc. of Museums of Arms and Military Hist., 2002–03; Chairman: Internat. Cttee of Museums and Collections of Arms and Military Hist., 2003–10; Battle of Crécy Trust, 2007–; Leeds Peace Poetry, 2009–15. Dir, Genesis Trio Ltd, 2005–09. Writer, Arms in Action (TV series), 1998, 2000. FRSA 1992. *Publications*: Treasures of the Tower: Crossbows, 1975; (with A. V. B. Norman) Treasures from the Tower of London, 1982; (with D. Walker) The Royal Armouries in Leeds: the making of a museum, 1996; The Vauxhall Operatory: a century of inventions before the Scientific Revolution, 2009; (jtly) Arms and Armour in Shropshire Museums, 2017; contribs to museum and exhibn catalogues and to Jl of Arms and Armour Soc., Internat. Jl of Nautical Archaeol., Connoisseur, Burlington, Country Life, Museums Jl, Guns Rev., etc. *Recreations*: theatre, music, reading, walking. *Address*: Yeoman's Course House, Thornton Hill, Easingwold, York YO61 3PY.

**WILSON, (Iain) Richard,** OBE 1994; actor and director; *b* 9 July 1936; *s* of John Boyd Wilson and Euphemia (*née* Colquhoun). *Educ*: Greenock High Sch.; Royal Acad. of Dramatic Art. Associate Director: Royal Court, 2000–07; Sheffield Theatres, 2009–16. *Theatre* includes: Uncle Vanya, Edinburgh Traverse Th., 1968; Normal Service, Hampstead, 1979; Operation Bad Apple, 1982, An Honourable Trade, 1984, May Days, 1990, Royal Court; The Weekend, Strand, 1994; What the Butler Saw, NT, 1995; Waiting for Godot, Manchester Royal Exchange, 1999; The Play What I Wrote, West End, 2001–02; Whipping It Up, Bush Th., 2006, transf. New Ambassadors and tour, 2007; Twelfth Night, RSC Stratford and West End, 2009–10; A Little Hotel on the Side, Th. Royal, Bath, 2013; Krapp's Last Tape, Crucible Th., Sheffield, 2014; An Evening with Richard Wilson, Sheffield Crucible, 2015; Forty Years On, Chichester Fest. Th., 2017; *plays directed*: Heaven and Hell, 1981, Other Worlds, 1983, Royal Court; An Inspector Calls, Manchester Royal Exchange, 1986; A Wholly Healthy Glasgow, Manchester Royal Exchange, Royal Court and Edinburgh Fest., 1987, 1988; Prin, Lyric, Hammersmith, 1989; Imagine Drowning, Hampstead, 1991; Women Laughing, Manchester Royal Exchange, transf. Royal Court, 1992; Simply Disconnected, Chichester, 1996; Tom and Clem, Aldwych, 1997; Four Knights in Knaresborough, Tricycle Th., 1999; Primo, NT, Hampstead, NY and S Africa, 2004; East Coast Chicken Supper, Traverse Th., 2005; Astronaut Wives Club, NYT, 2006; Royal Court: Four, 1998; Toast, 1999; Mr Kolpert, I Just Stopped By to See the Man, 2000; Nightingale and Chase, 2001; Where Do We Live, Day in Dull Armour, Graffiti, 2002; Under the Whaleback, Playing the Victim, 2003; The Woman Before, 2005; Rainbow Kiss, 2006; That Face, The Pride, Sheffield Crucible, 2010; Lungs, Paines Plough co-prodn with Sheffield Crucible, 2011; Straight, Sheffield Crucible, transf. Bush Th., London, 2012; Smack Family Robinson, Rose Th., Kingston, 2013; May 08, GSMD, 2013; Love Your Soldiers, 2013, Blasted, 2015, The Nap, 2016, Sheffield Crucible; Fracked!, Chichester, 2016; Gig, RADA, 2019; *television series* include: My Good Woman, 1972; Crown Court, 1973–84; A Sharp Intake of Breath, 1979–81; Only When I Laugh, 1979–82; High and Dry, 1987; Tutti Frutti, 1987; One Foot in the Grave, six series, 1989–2000; High Stakes, 2001; Life - As We Know It, 2001; Jeffrey Archer: The Truth, 2002; King of Fridges, 2004; Born and Bred, two series, 2005; Doctor Who, 2005; A Harlot's Progress, 2006; The True Voice of Prostitution, 2006; Reichenbach Falls, 2007; Kingdom, two series, 2007–08; Merlin, 2008–12; New Tricks, 2009; Demons, 2009; Britain's Best Drives, 2009; Two Feet in the Grave, 2009; Dispatches, 2011; Playhouse Presents: Space Age, 2014; Richard Wilson on the Road, 2015; Trollied, 2015; TV film, Danny and the Human Zoo, 2015; A Midsummer Night's Dream, 2016;

*television directed* includes: Commitments, 1982; Remainder Man, 1982; Under The Hammer, 1984; A Wholly Healthy Glasgow, 1987; Changing Step, 1991; The Egg, 2002; Primo, 2008; *films* include: A Passage to India, 1984; Whoops Apocalypse, 1986; Prick Up Your Ears, 1987; How to Get Ahead in Advertising, 1989; Fellow Traveller, 1990; Carry on Columbus, 1992; Soft Top Hard Shoulder, 1993; The Man Who Knew Too Little, 1998; Women Talking Dirty, 2001; Love and Other Disasters, 2006. Rector, Glasgow Univ., 1996–99. Hon. DLitt Glasgow Caledonian, 1995; DUniv Sheffield Hallam, 2015. Top TV Comedy Actor, British Comedy Awards, 1991; Light Entertainment Award, BAFTA, 1991 and 1993; Award for Outstanding Contribn to TV and Film, BAFTA Scotland, 2013. *Recreations:* squash, collecting work of living Scottish painters. *Address:* c/o Conway van Gelder Grant Ltd, 8–12 Broadwick Street, W1F 8HW. *T:* (020) 7287 0077. *Clubs:* Royal Automobile, Groucho.

**WILSON, Prof. Ian Andrew,** DPhil, DSc; FRS 2000; FRSE; Hansen Professor of Structural Biology, Department of Molecular Biology and Skaggs Institute for Chemical Biology, Scripps Research Institute, since 1982; *b* 22 March 1949; *s* of George Alexander Wilson and Margaret Stewart Wilson (*née* McKillop). *Educ:* Perth Acad.; Univ. of Edinburgh (BSc 1st Cl. Hons 1971); Corpus Christi Coll., Oxford (DPhil 1976; DSc 2000). Jun. Res. Fellow, Corpus Christi Coll., Oxford, 1975–77; Res. Fellow in Biochem., 1977–80, Res. Associate, 1980–82, Harvard Univ.; Asst Mem., 1982–84, Associate Mem., 1984–90, Scripps Clinic and Res. Foundn. Adjunct Prof., UCSD, 1998–. FRSE 2008. *Recreations:* scuba diving, tennis, golf, opera. *Address:* Department of Molecular Biology, BCC206, Scripps Research Institute, 10550 North Torrey Pines Road, La Jolla, CA 92037, USA. *T:* (858) 7849706. *Club:* La Jolla Beach and Tennis.

**WILSON, Ian Matthew,** CB 1985; Under Secretary, Scottish Education Department, 1977–86; *b* 12 Dec. 1926; *s* of Matthew Thomson Wilson and Mary Lily Barnett; *m* 1st, 1953, Anne Chalmers (*d* 1991); three *s*; 2nd, 1996, Joyce Town (*d* 2012). *Educ:* George Watson's Coll.; Edinburgh Univ. (MA). Asst Principal, Scottish Home Dept, 1950; Private Sec. to Perm. Under-Sec. of State, Scottish Office, 1953–55; Principal, Scottish Home Dept, 1955; Asst Secretary: Scottish Educn Dept, 1963; SHHD, 1971; Asst Under-Sec. of State, Scottish Office, 1974–77. Sec. of Commns for Scotland, 1987–92. Dir, Scottish Internat. Piano Competition, 1997–2004. Mem., Bd of Govs, RSAMD, 1992–2000. Pres., Univ. of Edinburgh Graduates' Assoc., 1995–97. *Address:* 47 Braid Hills Road, Edinburgh EH10 6LD. *T:* (0131) 447 1802. *Club:* New (Edinburgh).

**WILSON, Ian Robert;** QC 2018; *b* Lancashire, 1970; *s* of Robert and Mary Wilson; *m* 2004, Claire Shelley; two *s*. *Educ:* Hawarden High Sch.; Corpus Christi Coll., Cambridge (BA 1991; LLM 1994). ARCM 1986. Called to the Bar, Middle Temple, 1995, *ad eund.* Gray's Inn, 2014; in practice as barrister, specialising in commercial law. Vice Chm., London Common Law and Commercial Bar Assoc., 2018–. *Publications:* (contrib.) Paget's Law of Banking, 14th edn 2014, 15th edn 2018; (contrib.) Bullen & Leake & Jacob's Precedents of Pleading, 14th edn 2001 to 19th edn 2019. *Recreation:* pianist and organist (professional/concert standard). *Address:* 3 Verulam Buildings, Gray's Inn, WC1R 5NT. *T:* (020) 7831 8441, *Fax:* (020) 7831 8479. *E:* iwilson@3vb.com.

**WILSON, Iona Elisabeth Lois;** *see* Jones, I. E. L.

**WILSON, Ivan Patrick;** Lay Member, First-tier Tribunal (Information Rights) (formerly Information Tribunal), 2003–12; *b* 24 Aug. 1941; *s* of William Wilson and Jessie (*née* Bateson); *m* 1966, Kathleen Mary Price; three *s*. *Educ:* Royal Sch., Dungannon; Academy, Omagh; Queen's Univ., Belfast. HM Treasury, 1965–95; Private Sec. to Perm. Sec., Overseas Finance, 1971–73; Press Office, 1973–76; Defence Policy and Budget Div., 1981–84; RCDS 1985; Information Systems, 1986–89; Under-Sec., Industry and Employment Gp, 1989–90; Dir, Govt Centre for Information Systems, 1990–93; Under Sec., Public Enterprises Gp, HM Treasury, 1993–95; Exec. Advr, ICL Enterprises, 1995–98; Partnership Sec., Freshfields, 1998–99; Interim Chief Exec., NI Policing Bd, 2001–02. *Recreations:* foreign travel, sport, walking, member of Manchester United Supporters Trust. *Address:* 88 Redhill Wood, New Ash Green, Longfield, Kent DA3 8QP. *T:* (01474) 874740.

**WILSON, Dame Jacqueline,** DBE 2008 (OBE 2002); author; Children's Laureate, 2005–07; *b* 17 Dec. 1945; *d* of late Harry Aitken and of Margaret Aitken (*née* Clibbons); *m* 1965, William Millar Wilson (marr. diss. 2004); one *d*. *Educ:* Coombe Girls' Sch. Journalist, D. C. Thomsons, 1963–65. Ambassador, Reading is Fundamental, UK, 1998–; Cttee Mem., Children's Writers and Illustrators Gp, Soc. of Authors, 1997–; Adv. Mem., Costa (formerly Whitbread) Book Awards Panel, 1997–; Judge: Rhône-Poulenc Prizes for Jun. Sci. Books, 1999; Orange Prize for Fiction, 2006; Prince Maurice Prize, 2006; Patron, Children's Film and TV Foundn, 2000–06; Pres., Book Trade Benevolent Soc., 2007–. Roehampton University: Vis. Prof. of Children's Literature, 2008–; Pro-Chancellor, 2011–13; Chancellor, 2014–. FRSL 2006. Hon. DEd: Kingston, 2001; Winchester, 2006; Roehampton, 2007; Hon. DLit Bath, 2006; Hon. DLaws Dundee, 2007. Special Award, British Academy Children's Awards, 2017. *Publications: fiction:* Hide and Seek, 1972; Truth or Dare, 1973; Snap, 1974; Let's Pretend, 1975; Making Hate, 1977; *for children:* Nobody's Perfect, 1982; Waiting for the Sky to Fall, 1985; Other Side, 1990; Take a Good Look, 1990; The Story of Tracy Beaker, 1991 (adapted for television, 2002); The Suitcase Kid, 1992 (Children's Book of the Year Award, 1993); Video Rose, 1992; The Mum-minder, 1993; The Werepuppy, 1993; The Bed and Breakfast Star, 1994; Mark Spark in the Dark, 1994; Twin Trouble, 1995; Glubbslyme, 1995; Jimmy Jelly, 1995; Dinosaur's Packed Lunch, 1995; Cliffhanger, 1995; Double Act, 1995 (Children's Book of the Year Award; Smarties Prize); My Brother Bernadette, 1995; Werepuppy on Holiday, 1995; Bad Girls, 1996; Mr Cool, 1996; Monster Story-teller, 1997; The Lottie Project, 1997; Girls in Love, 1997; Connie and the Water Babies, 1997; Buried Alive!, 1998; Girls Under Pressure, 1998; The Illustrated Mum (Guardian Children's Book of the Year Award), 1999 (adapted for television, 2003); Girls Out Late, 1999; The Dare Game, 2000; Vicky Angel, 2000; The Cat Mummy, 2001; Sleepovers, 2001; Dustbin Baby, 2001; Girls In Tears, 2002; Secrets, 2002; The Worry Website, 2002; Lola Rose, 2003; Midnight, 2003 (adapted for stage, 2005); The Diamond Girls, 2004; Best Friends, 2004 (adapted for television, 2006); Clean Break, 2005; Love Lessons, 2005; Candyfloss, 2006; Starring Tracy Beaker, 2006; Jacky Daydream (autobiog.), 2007; Kiss, 2007; My Sister Jodie, 2008; Cookie, 2008; My Secret Diary, 2009; Hetty Feather, 2009; Little Darlings, 2010; The Longest Whale Song, 2010; Lily Alone, 2011; Sapphire Battersea, 2011; The Worst Thing About My Sister, 2012; Four Children and It, 2012; Emerald Star, 2012; Queenie, 2013; Diamond, 2013; Opal Plumstead, 2014; Paws and Whiskers, 2014; The Butterfly Club, 2015; Katy, 2015; Little Stars, 2015; Clover Moon, 2016; Rent a Bridesmaid, 2016; Wave Me Goodbye, 2017 (adapted for stage, 2019); Hetty Feather's Christmas, 2017; My Mum Tracy Beaker, 2018; Dancing the Charleston, 2019; We Are The Beaker Girls, 2019. *Recreations:* talking to my daughter, reading, swimming, going to art galleries and films. *Address:* c/o David Higham Associates, 7th Floor, Waverley House, 7–12 Noel Street, W1F 8GQ. *T:* (020) 7434 5900.

**WILSON, James Millar;** Member (UU) Antrim South, Northern Ireland Assembly, 1998–2007; *b* 15 Dec. 1941; *s* of James Millar Wilson and Isobel Wilson; *m* 1965, Muriel Smyth; one *s* one *d*. *Educ:* Ballyclare High Sch.; Belfast Coll. of Technol. Engineer: Port Line Ltd, Merchant Navy, 1962–64; British Enkalon Ltd, 1964–73; partner, retail grocery business, 1972–88. Chief Exec., UU Party, 1987–98. Chief UUP Whip, 1998–2002, Dep. Speaker, 2002, NI Assembly. Dir, Bann System Ltd, 2002–. Mem., NI Water Council, 2000–08. Dir, Countryside Alliance, NI, 2003–08. Mem. Bd, Foyle and Carlingford Irish Lights, 2008–. Mem., UU Council, 1982–87 and 1998– (Mem. Exec. Cttee, 1985–87 and 1998–); Vice Pres., S Antrim UU Assoc., 1996–. *Recreations:* gardening, angling. *Address:* 1 Fairlands, Moorfields, Ballymena, Co. Antrim BT42 3HE. *E:* jim.wilson83@btopenworld.com.

**WILSON, Sir James (William Douglas),** 5th Bt *cr* 1906; farmer; *b* 8 Oct. 1960; *s* of Captain Sir Thomas Douglas Wilson, 4th Bt, MC, and Pamela Aileen, *d* of Sir Edward Hanmer, 7th Bt; *S* father, 1984; *m* 1985, Julia Margaret Louise, fourth *d* of J. C. F. Mutty, Mulberry Hall, Melbourn, Cambs; two *s* two *d*. *Educ:* London Univ. (BA Hons French). *Heir: s* Thomas Edward Douglas Wilson, *b* 15 April 1990.

**WILSON, Jennifer Chase E.;** *see* Edgar-Wilson.

**WILSON, Jeremy James O'Brien;** Managing Director, and Vice Chairman, Corporate Banking, Barclays Bank plc, 2009–19; Chairman, Barclays Bank Egypt, 2014–17; *b* Cape Town, SA, 9 Oct. 1949; *s* of Richard O'Brien Wilson and Anne Florence Wilson; *m* 1978, Joanna Jane Parker; two *s* two *d*. *Educ:* Pembroke Hse, Kenya; Nautical Coll., Pangbourne; Durham Univ. (BA Gen. (French, Geog., Anthropol.)). Dir, Barclays Bank plc; Dir, 2005–07, Chm., 2007–13, Bloomsbury Publishing plc. Chm., Govt Coordination Cttee, UK Payments Industry, 2013–. Dir, TheCityUK, 2011–16 (Chm., Audit & Risk Cttee, 2011–16); Chairman: Banking Envmt Initiative Wkg Gp, 2011–19; Whitechapel Think Tank, 2015–. Chm., Clearing House Automated Payments System, 2007–13. Bankers Association for Finance and Trade: Chm., Global Councils, 2006–09; Dir, 2009–15; Chm., Nominations Cttee, 2013–15. Dir, Barclays Bank Pension Fund Trustees Ltd, 2000–08. Mem., Vice Chancellor's 175 Appeal Cttee, Durham Univ., 2005–07. Chm., Majajani Primary Sch. Trust, 2005–. *Recreations:* cartoons, writing, rowing (support of), corporate sustainability, mowing, early waking, early bed. *Address:* The Globe, Farnham, Bishops Stortford, Herts CM23 1HR. *T:* 07970 123454, 07527 476642. *E:* jjob.wilson@btinternet.com. *Clubs:* Brooks's; Leander (Henley-on-Thames); Muthaiga Country (Nairobi).

**WILSON, Jill Christine;** *see* Rubery, J. C.

**WILSON, Joe;** *see* Wilson, Anthony J.

**WILSON, Most Rev. John;** *see* Southwark, Archbishop of, (RC).

**WILSON, John,** FRCM; conductor; *b* Gateshead, 25 May 1972; *s* of Brian Wilson and Margaret Wilson (*née* McKie). *Educ:* Royal Coll. of Music (GRSM; ARCM; FRCM 2011). Founder and Conductor, John Wilson Orch., 1994–; a Principal Conductor: Royal Northern Sinfonia (formerly Northern Sinfonia), 2009–; RTE Concert Orch., Dublin, 2014; Associate Guest Conductor, BBC Scottish SO, 2016–; regular conductor of most UK orchs. BBC Proms debut, Royal Albert Hall, 2007; operatic debut, Gilbert and Sullivan's Ruddigore, Opera North, 2010, UK tour, 2011; John Wilson Orch. BBC Proms debut, Royal Albert Hall, 2009. Orchestrations for film, radio and television incl. Beyond the Sea (film), 2004. Recordings with John Wilson Orch. *Recreations:* walking, cooking, reading, shouting at the television. *Address:* c/o Intermusica, 9 Kingsway, WC2B 6XF.

**WILSON, John Armstrong;** QC 2011; *b* Wigan, 8 Oct. 1958; *s* of Joe Wilson and late Ann Wilson (*née* Armstrong); *m* 1988, Susan Tilley. *Educ:* Ampleforth Coll.; St John Rigby Sixth Form Coll., Wigan; Pembroke Coll., Cambridge (BA Law 1980). Called to the Bar, Inner Temple, 1981; in practice as barrister, specialising in matrimonial, finance and cohabitation law. Mem., Family Procedure Rule Cttee, 2010–14. Member: Family Law Bar Assoc., 1995–; Chancery Bar Assoc., 2016–. Patron, Nat. Family Mediation, 2011–. MCIArb 2017. Mem., Soc. of Authors, 2016–. Fellow, Internat. Acad. of Family Lawyers, 2017–. FRSA 2014. Editor in Chief, Family Affairs, 2014–. *Publications:* Cohabitation Claims: Law, Practice and Procedure, 2009, 2nd edn 2014; (contrib.) Jackson's Matrimonial Finance and Taxation, 9th edn 2012, 10th edn 2019; (contrib.) Cases that Changed our Lives, vol. 2, 2015; (contrib.) Rayden and Jackson on Relationship Breakdown and Children, 2017; At the Dark Hour (novel), 2018. *Recreations:* spending time with my wife, the Alpes Maritimes, creative writing. *Address:* 1 Hare Court, Temple, EC4Y 7BE. *T:* (020) 7797 7070, *Fax:* (020) 7797 7435. *E:* jaw@1hc.com.

**WILSON, (John) Dominic;** Director General, Security Policy, Ministry of Defence, since 2018; *b* South Shields, 28 Oct. 1970; *s* of Stanley and Margaret Wilson; *m* 2002, Kate O'Connor; one *s* one *d*. *Educ:* Pocklington Sch.; Univ. of Liverpool (BA 1993); London Sch. of Econs and Pol Sci. (MSc 2012). Ministry of Defence: Operational Policy, Resources and Progs, 1993–2001; Private Sec. to Perm. Sec., 2001–04; Dep. Dir, Civilian Contingencies Secretariat, Cabinet Office, 2004–07; Dir, Policy Planning, 2007–09; Chief Officer, SBAA Cyprus, 2009–10; Director: Strategy and Resources, 2010–11; Security and Intelligence, Cabinet Office (on secondment), 2011–15; Operational Policy, 2015–17. *Recreations:* swimming, cycling, running, triathlon, travel. *Address:* Security Policy and Operations, Ministry of Defence, Main Building, Whitehall, SW1A 2HB. *T:* (020) 7218 2135.

**WILSON, John Gordon;** Member for Scotland Central, Scottish Parliament, 2007–16 (SNP, 2007–14, Ind, 2014–16); *b* 28 Nov. 1956; *s* of Thomas Wilson and Elizabeth Murray; *m* 1982, Frances M. McGlinchey; one *d*. *Educ:* Univ. of Glasgow (MA Social Scis 1987). Coachbuilder, W. Alexanders Co. Ltd, 1972–82; Project Co-ordinator, Castlemilk Housing Involvement Project, 1987–94; Dir, Glasgow Council of Tenant Assocs, 1994–97; Manager, Glasgow Tenants Resource Centre, 1997–98; Fieldwork Manager, Poverty Alliance, 1998–2001; Dir, Scottish Low Pay Unit, 2001–07. Contested (Green) Coatbridge and Chryston, Scottish Parlt, 2016. *E:* johnwilsonscot@hotmail.com.

**WILSON, His Honour John Warley;** a Circuit Judge, 1982–2001; *b* 13 April 1936; *s* of late John Pearson Wilson and Nancy Wade Wilson (*née* Harston); *m* 1962, Rosalind Mary Pulford. *Educ:* Warwick Sch.; St Catharine's Coll., Cambridge (MA). Served RA, 1954–56. Called to the Bar, Lincoln's Inn, 1960, in practice, 1960–82; a Recorder of the Crown Court, 1979–82. Dep. Chairman, West Midlands Agricultural Land Tribunal, 1978–82. *Recreations:* gardening, National Hunt racing. *Address:* Victoria House, Farm Street, Harbury, Leamington Spa CV33 9LR. *T:* (01926) 612572.

**WILSON, John Willoughby;** QC (NI) 1988; Master, Queen's Bench and Appeals, Supreme Court of Northern Ireland, 1993–2006; Clerk of the Crown for Northern Ireland, 1993–2006; *b* 4 Sept. 1933; *s* of late Willoughby Wilson and Martha (*née* Wood); *m* 1st, 1963, Rosemary Frances Turner (*d* 1999); one *s* two *d*; 2nd, 2006, Irenée Sarah, *widow* of Gordon Roger Cree; one step *s* one step *d*. *Educ:* Leys Sch.; Magdalene Coll., Cambridge (MA); Queen's Univ., Belfast (LLB). Called to the Bar, NI, 1960; in practice, 1960–66; Private Sec., 1966–79, Legal Sec., 1979–80, to Lord Chief Justice of NI; Asst Dir, NI Court Service, 1980–85; Master, High Court, Supreme Court of NI, 1985–93. Under Treas., NI Court of NI, 1997–2008; Hon. Bencher, 2008. Gov., Victoria Coll., Belfast, 1970–2012 (Chm., 1990–95). Chancellor, Dio. Connor, 1982–2007. *Recreations:* music, reading, cycling.

**WILSON, Kate**; see Wilson, Catherine.

**WILSON, Louise**; see Wilson, M. L.

**WILSON, Lynton Ronald**, OC 1997; Chairman, The Wilson Foundation, since 2001; President, 1990–96, Chief Executive Officer, 1992–98 and Chairman, 1993–2000, BCE Inc.; *b* Port Colborne, Canada, 3 April 1940; *s* of Ronald Alfred and Blanche Evelyn Wilson; *m* 1968, Brenda Jean Black; one *s* two *d*. *Educ*: Port Colborne High Sch.; McMaster Univ. (BA Hons 1962); Cornell Univ. (MA 1967). Dep. Minister, Min. of Industry and Tourism, Govt of Ontario, 1978–81; Pres. and CEO, 1981–88, Chm., 1988–89, Redpath Industries Ltd, Toronto; Man. Dir, North America, Tate & Lyle plc, 1986–89; Vice-Chm., Bank of Nova Scotia, Toronto, 1989–90; Chairman: CAE Inc., 1999–2013; Nortel Networks Corp., 2001–05 (now Chm. Emeritus). Dir, Supervisory Bd, Daimler AG (formerly DaimlerChrysler AG), 1998–2013; Chm., Mercedes-Benz (formerly Daimler Chrysler, then Daimler) Canadian Adv. Council, 2005–. Chancellor, Canadian Business Hall of Fame, 2013–16. Chancellor, McMaster Univ., 2007–13, now Chancellor Emeritus. Hon. D*hc* Montreal, 1995; Hon. LLD: McMaster, 1995; UC of Cape Breton, 1998; Mount Allison, 2000; Brock, 2003; Windsor, 2016; Hon. DCL Bishop's Univ., 1997. Vanier Medal, Inst. of Public Admin of Canada, 2014. *Recreation*: golf. *Address*: The Wilson Foundation, 1540 Cornwall Road, Suite 207, Oakville, ON L6J 7W5, Canada. *Clubs*: York, Toronto (Toronto); Rideau (Ottawa); Toronto Golf, Mount Royal; Sea Island, Ocean Forest Golf (Sea Island, Georgia).

**WILSON, (Marie) Louise**; Chairman, Signature Sponsorship Ltd (formerly Signature Sponsorship), since 1999; *b* Burnley, Lancs; *d* of Henry Anthony Wilson and Doreen Wilson (*née* Cass). *Educ*: Saints John Fisher and Thomas More RC High Sch.; St Theodore's RC VIth Form; Univ. of Nottingham (BA Hons Politics 1987). Andersen Consulting, 1987–89; Procter & Gamble, 1989–93; Pepsi-Co., 1993–94; Coca Cola Co., 1994–99. Client Services Dir, LOCOG, 2006– (Mem., 2006–09). University of Nottingham, 2007–: Mem. Council, 2008–; Chair: Strategy and Planning Cttee, 2012–14 (Mem., 2009–14); Laureate Awards, 2011, 2012; Member: Estates Planning Cttee, 2007–; Nominations Cttee, 2008–; Finance Cttee, 2009–; Campaign Bd, 2011–. Advanced Leadership Fellow, Harvard Univ., 2016–18. Mem. Bd, Mktg Gp of GB, 2012–. Trustee: David Ross Educn Acad. Trust, 2009–; Historic Royal Palaces, 2012– (Member: Remuneration Cttee, 2012–; Campaign Bd, 2013–; Chm. Search Cttee, 2014). FRSA 2002. *Recreations*: entertaining, heritage, historic houses, travelling, making music/singing, live concerts, theatre, art galleries, astrology, yoga. *Address*: The Coach House, Black Horse Yard, Windsor, Berks SL4 1LA. *E*: mlwilson@signaturesponsorship.com

**WILSON, Mark Andrew**; Group Chief Executive Officer, Aviva plc, 2013–18; *b* Rotorua, NZ, Aug. 1966; *s* of Herbert John Watters Wilson and Lynda Adele Wilson; *m* 1996, Antonia Basile (marr. diss. 2017); three *d*. *Educ*: Kelliher Econs Foundn (Econs Schol. 1983); Univ. of Waikato (BMS 1988). Mktg Manager, then Man. Dir, National Mutual Asset Mgt, later Man. Dir, NZ Permanent Trustees, National Mutual, NZ, 1988–99; AXA Asia Pacific Holdings: Chief Gen. Manager, 1999–2001; Chief Executive Officer: SE Asia, 2001–03; AXA China Reg. Ltd, 2003–06; Chief Operating Officer and Pres., 2007–09, CEO and Pres., 2009–10, AIA Gp. Non-exec. Dir, BlackRock, 2018–. UK New Zealander of Year, NZ Soc., 2016. *Recreations*: tennis, piano, art, Rugby.

**WILSON, Martin**; see Wilson, Alan M.

**WILSON, Martin Joseph**, FCA; Deputy Chairman, Ulster Bank, 2004–06 (Group Chief Executive, 1998–2004); *b* 13 March 1950; *s* of Michael and Elizabeth Wilson; *m* Paulette Palmer; one *s* two *d*. *Educ*: Oatlands Coll., Dublin. ACA 1975, FCA 1985; FIBI 1991. Articled Clerk, Fay McMahon & Co., Chartered Accountants, 1969–75; Sen. Audit Manager, KPMG, 1975–78; Chief Accountant, Bell Lines Ltd, 1978–80; Financial Controller, 1980–89, Head of Treasury, 1984–89, Ulster Investment Bank; Ulster Bank: Gp Treas., 1989–95; Dir, 1991; Dep. Gp Chief Exec., 1997–98; Chief Exec., Ulster Bank Mkts, 1995–97. Pres., ICAI, 2006–07. *Recreations*: golf, reading, music.

**WILSON, Sir Mathew John Anthony**, 6th Bt *cr* 1874, of Eshton Hall, Co. York; OBE 1979 (MBE 1971); MC 1972; *b* 2 Oct. 1935; *s* of Anthony Thomas Wilson (*d* 1979; 2nd *s* of Sir Mathew Richard Henry Wilson, 4th Bt) of Margaret (*d* 1980), *d* of late Alfred Holden; *S* uncle, 1991; *m* 1962, Janet Mary, *e d* of late E. W. Mowll, JP; one *s* one *d*. *Educ*: Trinity Coll. Sch., Ontario. Brig. KOYLI, retired 1983. Exec. Dir, Wilderness Foundn (UK), 1983–85. Former Vice-Pres., Internat. Wilderness Leadership Foundn. *Publications*: Taking Terrapin Home: a love affair with a small catamaran, 1994; The Bahamas Cruising Guide with the Turks and Caicos Islands, 1998; The Land of War Elephants: travels beyond the pale—Afghanistan, Pakistan, India, 2003; Seeking Havens, 2006. *Heir*: *s* Mathew Edward Amcotts Wilson [*b* 13 Oct. 1966; *m* 1995, Imogen Nancy, *yr d* of Richard Thomas Wilson; one *s* one *d*].

**WILSON, Michael**; see Wilson, T. M. A.

**WILSON, Michael Anthony**; Director: JVM Consultants Ltd, since 2007; Healthwatch Haringey, since 2013; Public Voice CIC, since 2015; *b* 19 Feb. 1948; *s* of Alan Wilson and Christina Wilson (*née* McFarlane); *m* 1st, 1972, Aileen Athey (marr. diss. 1991); one *s* one *d*; 2nd, 2008, Tanya Braznhikova. *Educ*: Aston Univ. (BSc Hons Behavioural Sci. 1972); DipTP 1979. MRTPI 1979; AIH 1984. Planning Asst, London Borough of Barnet, 1972–74; Res. and Inf. Officer, Harlow Develt Corp., 1974–80; Housing Manager, City of Glasgow, 1980–84; Dir of Housing and Envmtl Services, London Borough of Brent, 1984–92; Chief Exec., Waltham Forest Housing Action Trust, 1992–2002; Dir of Regeneration, NE London Strategic HA, 2002–06; Managing Dir, Mike Wilson Associates Ltd, 2002–09. Chairman: Sports Club Orient, 2003–10; Ocean Estate New Deal for Communities, 2004–07; Member Board: Waltham Forest Community-Based Housing Assoc., 2002–09; Leyton Orient Community Sports Prog., 2003–07. FRSA. JP Waltham Forest, 1999–2009. *Recreations*: watching football (Spurs), cinema, theatre, good food and wine, the children and grandchildren. *Address*: Hollyoaks Cottage, The Chilterns, Leighton Buzzard, Beds LU7 4QD.

**WILSON, Michael Anthony**, FRCGP; general practitioner; *b* 2 June 1936; *s* of late Charles Kenneth Wilson and Bertha Wilson; *m* 1st, 1959, Marlene (*née* Wilson) (marr. diss. 2011); two *s*; 2nd, 2012, Beryl May Hunt. *Educ*: Roundhay Grammar Sch., Leeds; Medical Sch., Univ. of Leeds (MB ChB 1958). DObst RCOG 1961; MRCGP 1965, FRCGP 1980. British Medical Association: Chm., Gen. Med. Services Cttee, 1984–90 (Dep. Chm., 1979–84); Pres., Yorkshire Regional Council, 1975–79; Mem. Council, 1977–90, 1992–2000; Vice-Pres., 2001–; Fellow, 1979. Member: GMC, 1989–2003; Standing Med. Adv. Cttee to DHSS, 1967–69, 1978–90 (Dep. Chm., 1986–90); NHS Clinical Standards Adv. Gp, 1990–93; Code of Practice Authy, Assoc. of British Pharmaceutical Industry, 1990–2013; Jt Consultants Cttee, 1991–97. Chm., BMA Pension Trustees Ltd, 1994–2000; Dir, Professional Affinity Group Services Ltd, 1987–2000. *Recreations*: golf, Rotary. *Address*: Court Ash, Woodacre Crescent, Bardsey, Leeds LS17 9DQ. *T*: (01937) 572381. *Clubs*: East India; Ampleforth Coll. Golf.

**WILSON, Michael Gregg**, OBE 2008; producer; Chairman, EON Productions, since 1983; *b* NY, 1942; *s* of Lewis Wilson and Dana Broccoli, and step *s* of Albert R., (Cubby), Broccoli; *m* 1965, Coila Jane Wilson; two *s*. *Educ*: Harvey Mudd Coll., Claremont, Calif (BS); Stanford Univ. (DJur). Legal Advr, Dept of Transportation, Washington, 1966–67; Partner, law firm, Surrey and Morse, Washington, 1967–74; joined legal dept, EON Productions, 1974; asst to Cubby Broccoli, The Spy Who Loved Me, 1977; Executive Producer: Moonraker, 1979; (and screenplay) For Your Eyes Only, 1981; (and screenplay) Octopussy, 1983; Producer: (and screenplay) A View to Kill, 1985; (and screenplay) The Living Daylights, 1987; (and writer) Licence to Kill, 1989; GoldenEye, 1995; Tomorrow Never Dies, 1997; The World is Not Enough, 1999; Die Another Day, 2002; Casino Royale, 2006; Quantum of Solace, 2008; Skyfall, 2012; Spectre, 2015. Chairman: Bd, Albert R. and Dana Broccoli Charitable Foundn, 2004–; Kraszna-Krausz Foundn, 2010–16; Science Mus. Foundn, 2012–16, now Trustee Emeritus. Trustee, NMSI, 2004–08 (Chm., Develt Cttee); Chm. Trustees, Nat. Media Mus. (formerly Nat. Mus. of Photography, Film and TV), 2004–12. Founder, Wilson Centre for Photography, London, 1998. Trustee: Carnegie Sci. Foundn; Harvey Mudd Coll., Claremont, CA; Cape Farewell, 2001–16, now Trustee Emeritus; The Art Fund, 2010– (Chm., Develt Cttee); Santa Barbara Museum of Art, 2016–. *Address*: c/o EON Productions Ltd, 138 Piccadilly, W1J 7NR.

**WILSON, Maj.-Gen. Michael Peter Bruce Grant**; Director, WISLON Field Sports Services, since 2008; Chief Executive, Security Industry Authority, 2007–08; *b* 19 Aug. 1943; *s* of Ian Henry Wilson and Catherine Collingwood Wilson; *m* 1967, Margaret Ritchie; two *s* one *d*. *Educ*: Duke of York Sch., Nairobi; Dip. Photogrammetry, UCL. FRICS 1995 (ARICS 1988); FRGS 1990. Commnd RE, 1966; served UK, Kenya, Uganda, Nigeria, BAOR, MoD; UK Exchange Officer, US Defense Mapping Agency, 1978; Sen. Instructor in Air Survey and Cartography, Sch. of Mil. Survey, 1981; Asst Dir, Mil. Survey Systems and Techniques Unit, 1983; CO 512 Special Team RE and Comdr, Geographic Staff, Washington, 1986; Comdr, 42 Survey Engr Gp, 1987; Dir, Geographic Ops, MoD, 1990; Dir-Gen., Mil. Survey and Chief Exec., Mil. Survey Defence Agency, 1993; Dir-Gen. Intelligence and Geographic Resources, MoD, 1995–96; Chief Executive: Defence Vetting Agency, 1996–2004; Gangmasters Licensing Authy, 2005–07. Col Comdt RE, 1997–2002. Chm., Yorkshire Retriever Field Trial Soc., 2017–. Mole catcher to the Vicar of Old Malton. FCMI. *Recreations*: mountaineering, rock climbing, shooting, stalking, fishing, golf, cricket. *Clubs*: Chartered Surveyor/Sapper; Ampleforth Golf (Captain, 2012–).

**WILSON, Prof. Nairn Hutchison Fulton**, CBE 2004; PhD; FDS; Professor of Restorative Dentistry and Dean and Head of King's College London Dental Institute (formerly Guy's, King's and St Thomas' Dental Institute, King's College London), 2001–12, Hon. Professor of Dentistry, 2012–16, now Emeritus; Deputy Vice Principal Health, King's College London, 2009–11; Lead, Dental Clinical Academic Group, King's Health Partners, 2010–11; *b* 26 April 1950; *s* of William Fulton Wilson and Ann Hutchison Wilson (*née* Stratton); *m* 1st, 1971, Madeleine Christina Munro (marr. diss. 1981); two *d*; 2nd, 1987, Margaret Alexandra Jones; one *s* one *d*. *Educ*: Strathallan Sch.; Univ. of Edinburgh (BDS 1973); Univ. of Manchester (MSc 1979; PhD 1985); Royal Coll. of Surgeons of Edinburgh (FDS 1977; DRD 1980). FACD 1990; FADM 1991; FDS RCS (*ad eundem*) 1994, Hon. FDS RCS 2010; FFGDP (UK) (*ad eundem*) 2002; FFDRCSI 2011; FDS RCPS 2016; FICD 2017. Lectr in Restorative Dentistry (Prosthetics), Univ. of Edinburgh, 1974–75; University of Manchester: Lectr in Conservative Dentistry, 1975–81; Sen. Lectr, 1981–86; Prof. of Restorative Dentistry, 1986–2001; Head, Dept of Conservative Dentistry, 1986–88, Dept of Restorative Dentistry, 1988–92; University Dental Hospital: Head, Unit of Operative Dentistry and Endodontology (formerly of Conservative Dentistry), 1982–2001; Dep. Dean, 1991–92; Dean and Clin. Dir, 1992–95; Pro-Vice-Chancellor, Univ. of Manchester, 1997–99. Hon. Vis. Prof. of Restorative Dentistry, Univ. of Manchester, 2001–04; Visiting Professor: Washington Univ., 1988–90; Airlangga Univ., 1991–94; Univ. of Florida, 1995–2000; Thammasat Univ., 2006–09; Osaka Dental Univ., 2011–. Hon. Consultant in Restorative Dentistry: Central Manchester Healthcare NHS Trust (formerly Central Manchester HA), 1982–2001; King's Coll. Hosp. NHS Trust, 2001–12; Consultant, Osteology Foundn, 2018–. Non-exec. Dir, N Manchester Healthcare NHS Trust, 1994–97. Dir, Univ. of Portsmouth Services Ltd, 2016–19. Dir, Med. and Dental Defence Union of Scotland, 2016–. Chairman: Jt Cttee for Specialist Trng in Dentistry, 1998–99, 2007–10; Oral and Dental Res. Trust, 2003–09; British Dental Editors Forum, 2004–08; Council of Hds and Deans of Dental Schs, 2006–08; Electoral Coll., BVA, 2016–19; Bd (formerly Transition Bd), Coll. of General Dentistry, 2017–; Adv. Bd, Univ. of Buckingham Dental Inst., 2019–; Mem., Strategic Planning Exec., Eur. Fedn of Periodontology, 2012–. Dean, Faculty of Dental Surgery, RCSE, 1995–98. President: British Assoc. of Teachers of Conservative Dentistry, 1992; Sect. of Odontology, Manchester Med. Soc., 1993–94; British Soc. for Restorative Dentistry, 1994–95; Eur. Sect., Acad. of Operative Dentistry, 1998–2000 (Life Mem., 2013); Educn Res. Gp, IADR, 1998–2000; GDC, 1999–2003; Eur. Fedn of Conservative Dentistry, 2003–05 (Hon. Mem., 2015); Sect. of Odontology, Royal Soc. of Med., 2008–09; Metropolitan Br., BDA, 2012–13; KCL Assoc., 2012–14; Royal Odonto-Chirurgical Soc. of Scotland, 2013–14 (Hon. Mem., 2017); BDA, 2015–16. Registrar, UK Public Health Register, 2012–15. Ext. Gov., Univ. of Portsmouth, 2012–19 (Dep. Chm., 2017–). Trustee: Oral Health Foundn (formerly British Dental Health Foundn), 2012–19; Nat. Exams Bd for Dental Nurses, 2014–; Oman Dental Coll., 2015– (Chm., 2016–). Patron: Dental Wellness Trust, 2011–; BDA Benevolent Fund, 2015–16 (Hon. Vice-Pres., 2017–); Sterling Dental Foundn, 2017–. Editor: Jl of Dentistry, 1986–2000 (Editor Emeritus, 2012–); Primary Dental Jl, 2015–17 (Chm., Editl Bd, 2012–15); ICDigest, 2017–; Ed. in Chief, Quintessentials in Dental Practice Series (44 vols), 2003–09; Chm., Editl Bd, Dental Practice, 2012–15. FKC 2006; FHEA 2007. Hon. Fellow: Coll. of Dental Surgeons of HK, 1999; Oman Dental Coll., 2012; Life Mem., American Acad. of Restorative Dentistry, 2012. Hon. DSc Portsmouth, 2010; Hon. Dr Dentistry Plymouth, 2018. Cultura Della Materia, Univ. of Brescia, 2011. *Publications*: (jtly) Advances in Operative Dentistry, vol. 1: contemporary clinical practice, 2001; vol. 2: challenges of the future, 2001; Minimally Invasive Dentistry, 2007; Clinical Dental Medicine 2020, 2009; Merger to Global Leader: King's College London Dental Institute 1998–2011, 2012; Principles and Practice of Esthetic Dentistry: vol. 1, essentials of esthetic dentistry, 2014; Manual of Clinical Procedures in Dentistry, 2018; contrib. chaps in contemporary texts and numerous papers in jls. *Recreations*: various. *Address*: 1 Oak Park, Alderley Edge, Cheshire SK9 7GS. *T*: 07815 997086.

**WILSON, Nicholas Allan Roy**; see Wilson of Culworth, Rt Hon. Lord.

**WILSON, Nigel Guy**, FBA 1980; Fellow and Tutor in Classics, Lincoln College, Oxford, 1962–2002; *b* 23 July 1935; *s* of Noel Wilson and Joan Lovibond; *m* 1996, Hanneke Marion. *Educ*: University Coll. Sch.; Corpus Christi Coll., Oxford (1st Cl. Classics (Mods) 1955; 1st Cl. Lit. Hum. 1957; Hertford Scholar 1955; Ireland and Craven Scholar 1955; Derby Scholar 1957; Hon. Fellow, 2013). Lectr, Merton Coll., Oxford, 1957–62. Jt Editor, Classical Rev., 1975–87. Ospite Linceo, Scuola normale superiore, Pisa, 1977; Visiting Professor: Univ. of Padua, 1985; Ecole Normale Supérieure, Paris, 1986. James P. R. Lyell Reader in Bibliog., Oxford Univ., 2002–03. Gaisford Lectr, 1983. Mem., Accademia

Ambrosiana, 2015. Hon. DLitt: Uppsala, 2001; Cyprus, 2013. Gordon Duff Prize, 1968; Premio Anassilaos, Reggio Calabria, 1999; Kenyon Medal, British Acad., 2015. *Publications*: (with L. D. Reynolds) Scribes and Scholars, 1968, 4th edn 2013; An Anthology of Byzantine Prose, 1971; Medieval Greek Bookhands, 1973; St Basil on the Value of Greek Literature, 1975; Scholia in Aristophanis Acharnenses, 1975; (with D. A. Russell) Menander Rhetor, 1981; Scholars of Byzantium, 1983, 2nd edn 1996; (with Sir Hugh Lloyd-Jones) Sophoclea, 1990; (ed with Sir Hugh Lloyd-Jones) Sophocles: Fabulae, 1990; From Byzantium to Italy, 1992, 2nd edn 2017; Photius: the Bibliotheca, 1994; Aelian: Historical Miscellany, 1997; Pietro Bembo: Oratio pro litteris graecis, 2003; Aristophanes: Comoediae, 2007; Aristophanea, 2007; A Descriptive Catalogue of the Greek Manuscripts of Corpus Christi College Oxford, 2011; (jtly) The Archimedes Palimpsest, 2011; Herodoti Historiae, 2015; Herodotea, 2015; Aldus Manutius: the Greek classics, 2016; (with M. L. Sosower) A Catalogue of the Greek Manuscripts of Magdalen College, Oxford, 2016; articles and reviews in various learned jls. *Recreations*: bridge, real tennis, wine. *Address*: Lincoln College, Oxford OX1 3DR. *T*: (01865) 279800, *Fax*: 279802.

**WILSON, Sir Patrick Michael Ernest David McN.**; *see* McNair-Wilson.

**WILSON, Pete**; Governor of California, 1991–98; Principal, Wilson Walsh George Ross LLC, since 2016; Of Counsel, Browne George Ross LLP, since 2016; *b* 23 Aug. 1933; *m* Betty Robertson (marr. diss.); *m* 1983, Gayle Edlund. *Educ*: Yale Univ. (BA); Univ. of California at Berkeley (JD). Admitted to California Bar, 1962. Mayor of San Diego, 1971–73; US Senator (Republican) from California, 1983–91. Former Man. Dir, Pacific Capital Gp Inc.; Of Counsel, Bingham McCutcheon, and Principal, Bingham Consulting Gp, 2004–14; Principal and Of Counsel, Morgan Lewis Consulting, 2014–16. Dist. Vis. Fellow, Hoover Inst., Stanford Univ., 1999–. *Address*: Wilson Walsh George Ross LLC, 2121 Avenue of the Stars, Suite 2800, Los Angeles, CA 90067, USA.

**WILSON, Prof. Peter Hamish**, PhD; Chichele Professor of the History of War, University of Oxford, since 2015; Fellow, All Souls College, Oxford, since 2015; *b* Croydon, 27 Nov. 1963; *s* of James Sturrock Wilson and Joan Elisabeth Wilson (née Hart); *m* 1997, Eliane Christine Meyer (marr. diss. 2017); two *s* one *d*. *Educ*: Univ. of Liverpool (BA Modern Hist. 1985); Jesus Coll., Cambridge (PhD Hist. 1990). Lecturer: in Modern Eur. Hist., Sunderland Poly., subseq. Univ. of Sunderland, 1990–93; in Early Modern Hist., Univ. of Newcastle upon Tyne, 1994–98; Reader, 1998–2001, Prof. of Early Modern Hist., 2001–06, Univ. of Sunderland; G. F. Grant Prof. of Hist., Univ. of Hull, 2007–15. *Publications*: War, State and Society in Württemberg, 1677–1793, 1995; German Armies: war and German politics 1648–1806, 1998; The Holy Roman Empire 1495–1806, 1999, 2nd edn, 2011; Absolutism in Central Europe, 2000; From Reich to Revolution: German history 1558–1806, 2004; (ed) 1848: the year of revolutions, 2006; (ed) Warfare in Europe 1815–1914, 2006; (ed) A Companion to Eighteenth-Century Europe, 2008; (ed jtly) The Bee and the Eagle: Napoleonic France and the end of the Holy Roman Empire, 1806, 2009; Europe's Tragedy: a history of the Thirty Years War, 2009; The Thirty Years War: a sourcebook, 2010; (ed jtly) The Holy Roman Empire, 1495–1806, 2011; (ed jtly) The Holy Roman Empire, 1495–1806: a European perspective, 2012; The Holy Roman Empire: a thousand years of Europe's history, 2016; Lützen, 2018. *Recreations*: 70s prog rock, travel, family, friends. *Address*: All Souls College, Oxford OX1 4AL.

**WILSON, Peter James**, OBE 2001; freelance cultural buildings consultant, since 2011; Capital Project Director, Hall for Cornwall, since 2017; *b* 19 Sept. 1947; *s* of James Arthur Wilson and Edith Mary Wilson (née Sillick); *m* 1971, Angela Mary Hawkes; one *s* two *d*. *Educ*: Eltham Coll.; Pembroke Coll., Cambridge (BA 1970). Tate Gallery: DES Studentship in Conservation, 1972–76 (Dip. Conservation, 1976); picture restorer, 1976–80; Head: Tech. Services, 1980–88; Gall. Services, 1988–94; Dir, Projects and Estates, 1994–2005 (incl. openings: Tate Gall. St Ives, 1993; Tate Gall. Liverpool Phase II, 1998; Tate Modern, 2000; Tate Britain Centenary Develt, 2001). Transformation Project Dir, RSC, 2005–11; Project Dir, Shakespeare Birthplace Trust, 2013–14. Associate Consultant: Lord Cultural Resources, Toronto, 2006–08; Tate Gall., 2014–; Associate Sen. Consultant, Lordculture Paris, 2008–13. Cultural Buildings Advr, West Kowloon Cultural District Authy, Hong Kong, 2011–16; Special Advr, Theatres Trust, 2011–; Client Advr, Made in London Team for Olympicopolis, 2015. Member: CABE Enabling Panel, 2001–04; Steering Cttee, Laban, 2001–04. Chm., Mus. Documentation Assoc., 1988–95. Mem. Bd, Lightbox, Woking, 2001–10. Gov., Compton Verney Art Gall. and Park, 2017–. Hon. FRIBA 2007. *Recreations*: visiting Cornish gardens, gardening, drawing, cycling, cooking, theatre-going, visiting museums and galleries.

**WILSON, Peter Michael**; Chairman, Gallaher Group Plc, 1997–2004 (Chief Executive, 1997–99); Chairman, Gallaher Ltd, 1994–2004 (Deputy Chairman, 1987–94; Chief Executive, 1994–99); *b* 9 June 1941; *s* of late Michael Wilson and Mary Wilson; *m* 1964, Lissa Trab; one *s* one *d*. *Educ*: Downside Sch.; Oriel Coll., Oxford (MA Hons Law). Marketing appts, Reckitt & Colman and Beecham Gp, 1963–69; joined Gallaher Ltd, 1969: Gen. Manager, Cigarette Marketing, 1974–79; Man. Dir, Gallaher (Dublin), 1979–81; Marketing Dir, Gallaher Tobacco Ltd, 1981–84; Jt Man. Dir, 1984–85, Dep. Chm., 1986, Gallaher Tobacco (UK) Ltd. Non-executive Director: Beam Inc. (formerly American Brands, then Fortune Brands Inc.), 1994–2014; Powergen plc, 2001–03; Somerfield plc, 2002–05; Kesa Electricals plc, 2003–11. *Address*: The Stable, Old Odiham Road, Alton, Hants GU34 4BW. *T*: (01420) 543892.

**WILSON, Hon. Peter Michael Alexander**, CMG 2013; HM Diplomatic Service; Ambassador to the Netherlands and Permanent Representative to the Organisation for the Prohibition of Chemical Weapons, since 2017; *b* London, 31 March 1968; *s* of Baron Wilson of Tillyorn, *qv*; *m* 2001, Mónica Quintas Ribeiro Roma Pereira; two *s* one *d*. *Educ*: Eton Coll.; Merton Coll., Oxford (BA Modern Hist.); Kennedy Sch. of Govt, Harvard Univ. (MPA); Westminster Univ. and Univ. of Internat. Business and Econs, Beijing (Operational Mandarin). Entered FCO, 1992; Second Sec. (Commercial), Beijing, 1995–98; Mem., Cabinet of Sir Leon Brittan, Vice Pres., EC, 1999; First Sec., UK Perm. Repn to EU, 1999–2002; Hd, Strategic Policy Team, FCO, 2003–04; Political Counsellor: Islamabad, 2005–06; Beijing, 2007–10; Dir, Asia Pacific, FCO, 2010–13; Dep. Perm. Rep., UK Mission to UN, New York, 2013–17. *Recreations*: walking, reading, photography. *Address*: c/o Foreign and Commonwealth Office, King Charles Street, SW1A 2AH. *E*: peter.wilson@fco.gov.uk.

**WILSON, Philip**; MP (Lab) Sedgefield, since July 2007; *b* 31 May 1959; *s* of Bernard Wilson and Ivy Wilson (née Woods); *m* (marr. diss. 1999); two *s*; *m* 2016, Kerrin Smith. *Educ*: Trimdon Secondary Modern Sch.; Sedgefield Comprehensive Sch. Civil Servant, Dept for Nat. Savings, 1978–87; res. asst to Rt Hon. Tony Blair, MP, 1987–94; Labour Party organiser, 1994–97; Political Asst to Gen. Sec., Labour Party, 1997–99; Consultant, Brunswick Gp, 1999–2002; Dir, Fellows' Associates, 2002–07. *Recreations*: jazz, reading, writing. *Address*: House of Commons, SW1A 0AA. *T*: (020) 7219 4966. *E*: phil.wilson.mp@parliament.uk.

**WILSON, Most Rev. Philip Edward**, DD; Archbishop of Adelaide, (RC), 2001–18; *b* 2 Oct. 1950; *s* of John and Joan Wilson. *Educ*: St Joseph's Coll., Hunters Hill, NSW; St Columba's Coll., Springwood; St Patrick's Coll., Manly; Catholic Inst. of Sydney (BTh 1974); JCL 1992, DD 1996, Catholic Univ. of America, Washington. Ordained priest, 1975; Asst Priest, E Maitland, 1975–77; studied RE, NY, 1977–78; Maitland Diocese: Dir of RE, 1978–80; Bishop's Sec. and Master of Ceremonies, 1980–83; Parish Priest, 1983–87; VG, Diocesan Management and Admin, 1987–90; Dir of Tribunal, 1993–94; Bp of Wollongong, 1996–2000; Coadjutor Archbp of Adelaide, 2000–01. Australian Catholic Bishops' Conference: Pres., 2006–12; Vice Pres., 2012; Chm., Justice, Ecol. and Develt Commn, 2012; Mem., Canon Law Commn, 2012. Co-Chm., Nat. Professional Standards Cttee, 2003. Chairman: Catholic Earthcare Australia, 2012; Caritas Australia, 2012. Hon. DLitt Newcastle, 2003. Prelate of Honour, 1995.

**WILSON, Primrose Eileen**, CBE 2007 (OBE 1997); engaged in voluntary projects; *b* 21 April 1947; *d* of Anthony and Sheelagh Clarke; *m* 1969, Edward Brice Wilson (CBE 2003); one *s* two *d*. *Educ*: Glengara Park Sch., Dun Laoghaire, Co. Dublin; Royal Victoria Hosp., Belfast (SRN); Open Univ. (BA Hons). MRIAI 2018. SRN, Royal Victoria Hosp., Belfast, 1969–75. Voluntary Co-ordinator, Eur. Heritage Open Days, 1997–2000. Chairman: Ulster Architectural Heritage Soc., 1987–94; Historic Bldgs Council (NI), 1994–2000. Trustee, Nat. Heritage Meml Fund, 2000–06; Chairman: Assoc. Preservation Trusts (NI), 2004–12; Follies Trust, 2006–. Hon. Mem., RSUA, 2000. *Publications*: (jtly) The Buildings of Armagh, 1992. *Recreations*: admiring, enjoying, conserving and restoring Ireland's and Britain's built heritage. *Address*: Marlacoo House, Portadown, Co. Armagh. *T*: (028) 3887 1238.

**WILSON, Richard**; *see* Wilson, I. R.

**WILSON, (Richard) Andrew**; author and writer, since 1989; Director and Partner, Wilson McWilliam Studio (formerly Associates) Garden and Landscape Design, 2008–18; Consultant, McWilliam Studio, Garden and Landscape Design, since 2018; Director, London College of Garden Design, since 2009; *b* St Helens, Lancs, 10 July 1959; *s* of Kevin and Edna Wilson; *m* 1985, Barbara Anne Martindale; two *d*. *Educ*: St Helens Cowley High Sch. for Boys; Manchester Poly. (BA Hons Landscape Design; Postgrad. DipLA). Landscape architect, BRB, 1984–91; Dir, Garden Design Studies and Vice Principal, Inchbald Sch. of Design, 1989–2003; Partner, Pockett Wilson Garden and Landscape Design, 1999–2006; Garden Designer, Andrew Wilson Associates, 2006–08; Prog. Dir, Garden Design, Guildford Coll., 2004–09. Visiting Lecturer: Garden Design, Univ. of Greenwich, 2003–06; Postgrad. Landscape Architecture, Birmingham City Univ. (formerly UCE), 2003–09. Founding Ed., Garden Design Jl, 1993–97. Columnist: Gardens Illustrated, 2006–10; ProLandscaper Mag., 2013–. Consultant, Bord Bia, Ireland for the Bloom Garden Show, 2006–. Ext. examr in garden design for Middx Univ., 1995–98, Univ. of Greenwich, 1998–2003, Writtle Coll., 1999–2002, Falmouth Coll., 2003–08; ext. examr, Univ. of Brighton, 2008–11. Assessor and judge for show gdns, 1994–13 (incl. Bloom Garden Show, Dublin, 2006–), Chair of Assessors, Chair of Gdns Panel and Judge, 2009–11, RHS; Mem. Selection Panel, Internat. Garden Fest., Chaumont sur Loire, 2012. Chm., Soc. of Gdn Designers, 1993–96. FSGD 1996. *Publications*: The Garden Style Source Book, 1989; The Creative Water Gardener, 1995; (contrib.) The Essential Garden Book, 1998; Influential Gardeners, 2002; The Book of Garden Plans, 2004; The Book of Plans for Small Gardens, 2007; (contrib.) The RHS Encyclopedia of Garden Design, 2009; The Gardens of Luciano Giubbilei, 2010; Contemporary Colour in the Garden, 2011; RHS Small Garden Handbook, 2013. *Recreations*: riding my motorbike, classical singing (tenor; Member of Weybridge Male Voice Choir, 2010–), swimming, good food, messing about on the beach/ in the surf in Cornwall, drawing and water-colour painting, travel, photography. *Address*: Laurel Cottage, 12 Bridge Road, Chertsey, Surrey KT16 8JL. *T*: (01932) 563293. *E*: r.a.wilson@btconnect.com, andrew@mcwilliamstudio.com, andrewwilson@lcgd.org.uk.

**WILSON, Richard Colin**; QC 2016; *b* Leicester, 20 Feb. 1975; *s* of Colin Graham Wilson and Jeanne Olivia Helyn Wilson; *m* 1999, Felicity Anne Mileham; two *s* two *d*. *Educ*: George Watson's Coll.; Univ. of Sheffield (LLB Hons); Queen Mary and Westfield Coll., Univ. of London (LLM); Inns of Court Sch. of Law. Called to the Bar, Middle Temple, 1996; Tax Consultant, Price Waterhouse, 1996–97; pupillage, 1997–99; in practice as a barrister, specialising in chancery law, 1999–. *Recreations*: country sports, ski-ing, following Heart of Midlothian FC, providing a taxi service for my children. *Address*: Serle Court, 6 New Square, Lincoln's Inn, WC2A 3QS. *T*: (020) 7242 6105. *E*: rwilson@serlecourt.co.uk. *Club*: National.

**WILSON, Prof. Richard Henry**, RA 2006; sculptor; Visiting Research Professor, University of East London, since 2004; Professor of Sculpture, Royal Academy of Arts, since 2011; *b* 24 May 1953; *s* of Arthur and Ivy Wilson; partner, Miyako Narita; one *s* one *d* with Silvia Ziranek, writer and performance artist. *Educ*: London Coll. of Printing (Foundn); Hornsey Coll. of Art (DipAD 1st 1974); Univ. of Reading (MFA 1976). Formed Bow Gamelan Ensemble with Anne Bean and Paul Burwell, 1983–91. Mem., Artistic Records Cttee, Imperial War Mus., London, 1999. DAAD Residency, Berlin, 1992; Henry Moore Fellowship in Sculpture, Univ. of East London, 2002–04; Maeda Vis. Artist, AA, London, 2003. *Solo exhibitions and commissions include*: 11 Pieces, 1976, 12 Pieces, 1978, Coracle Press Gall., London; Viaduct, Aspex Gall., Portsmouth, 1983; Sheer Fluke, 1985, 20:50, 1987, She Came in Through the Bathroom Window, 1990, Watertable, 1994, Matt's Gall., London; Hopperhead, Café Gall., London, 1985; Halo, The Aperto, Venice Biennale, 1986; Heatwave, Ikon Gall., Birmingham, 1986; One Piece at a Time, Tyne Bridge, Newcastle upon Tyne, 1987; Up a Blind Alley, Trigon Biennale, Graz, 1987; Leading Lights, Kunsthallen Brandts Klaedefabrik, Odense, 1989; Sea Level, Arnolfini Gall., Bristol, 1990; High-Tec, MOMA, Oxford, 1990; High Rise, São Paulo Biennial, Brazil, Great Britain/USSR, Kiev, Moscow, 1990; All Mod Cons, Edge Biennial, Newcastle, 1990; Take Away, Centre of Contemp. Art, Warsaw, 1990; Lodger, Valeria Belvedere, Milan, 1991; Swift Half and Return to Sender, Gal. de l'Ancienne Poste, Calais, 1992; Installation, Künstlerhaus Bethanien, Berlin, 1993; Deep End, LA/UK, Fest. MOCA, Los Angeles, 1994; Room 6 Channel View Hotel, Towner Art Gall., Eastbourne, 1996; Formative Processes, Gimpel Fils, London, 1996; Jamming Gears, Serpentine Gall., London, 1996; Going In/Off, Château de Sacy, Picardie, 1997; Hung, Drawn and Quartered, Städtisches Mus., Zwickau, 1997; Ha'Mumche Gall., Tel Aviv, 1999; Irons in the Fire, Globe Gall., South Shields, 1999; UK tour, 2002, Wapping Proj., London, 2003; Tate Christmas Tree, Tate Gall., London, 1997; Pipe Dreams, AA, London, 1999; Turbine Hall Swimming Pool, Clare Coll. Mission Ch, London, 2000; Butterfly, Wapping Proj., London, 2003; Queen & Gantry, Storey Gall., Lancaster, 2005; Curve Gall., London, 2006; 5 Piece Kit, Matthew Bown Gall., London, 2006; RIBA Drawing Show, Liverpool, 2007; Chris Westbrook Gall., London, 2007; Turning the Place Over (lead work for Liverpool, Eur. Capital of Culture 2008), Liverpool, 2007; RA Summer Show, 2007; Objects of Art, Matthew Brown Gall., London, 2007; Galleria Fumagalli, Bergamo, Italy, 2007; Meter's Running, Pula, Croatia, 2007; Richard Wilson, Edinburgh Fest., 2008; Force Quit, Workprojects, Bristol, 2009; 20:50, Sulaymanyah, Kurdistan, N Iraq, 2009. Saatchi Gall., 2010; Square the Block, LSE, 2009; Matthew Bown Gall., Berlin, 2010; Shack Stack, St James's Develt, Chelsea Dock, 2010; Vertu Global Art Commn, Shanghai, 2010; Hang On A Minute Lads, I've Got a Great Idea, De La Warr Pavilion, UK, 2012; Slipstream,

Heathrow Terminal 2, 2014; Stealing Space, Annely Juda Fine Art, London, 2017; *group exhibitions* include: Art of Our Time, Saatchi Collection, Royal Scottish Acad., Edinburgh, 1987; Saatchi Collection, London, 1991; Close Encounters of the Art Kind, V&A, 2001; Butterfly, Platform China, Beijing, 2006; Objects of Art, Matthew Bown Gall., London, 2007; Folkestone Triennial, 2008; Still-Film, Tate Britain, 2008; Royal Acad. Summer Show, 2008, 2009; *performance work*: Blast, Birmingham, 2007; Performance Fest., Staglinec, Croatia, 2008; Blast, Performance, Blackpool, 2009; *permanent works*: entrance to Utility Tunnel, Tachikawa Public Art Proj., Tokyo, 1994; Over Easy, The Arc, Stockton, 1999; Slice of Reality, North Meadow Sculpture Proj., Millennium Dome, London, 2000; Set North for Japan (74° 33' 2"), Echigo Tsumari Proj., Japan, 2000; Off Kilter, Millennium Sq., Leeds, 2001; Final Corner, World Cup Proj., Fukuroi City, 2002; Rock n' hole, Lincoln City and Archaeol. Mus., 2005; work in public collections inc. Weltkunst Collection at Irish Mus. of Mod. Art, Boise, BM, Govt Art, Arts Council England, British Council, Ulster Mus., Leeds Mus and Galls, Centre of Contemp. Art, Warsaw and Museet for Samstidskunst, Oslo. Hon. DFA Middx, 2008; Hon. Dr Arts UEL, 2010. *Recreations:* percussion, cinema, world musics, exhibitions. *Address:* 44 Banyard Road, SE16 2YA. *T:* (020) 7231 7312. *E:* richardwilson.sculptor@virgin.net.

**WILSON, Robert,** OBE 2008; professional footballer, 1964–74; Presenter: BBC Television Sport, 1974–94; ITV Sport, 1994–2003; *b* 30 Oct. 1941; *s* of William Smith Wilson and Catherine Wingate (*née* Primrose); *m* 1964, Margaret Vera Miles; two *s* (one *d* decd). *Educ:* Tapton House Grammar Sch.; Chesterfield Grammar Sch.; Loughborough Coll. (DipPE). PE teacher, 1963–64; represented England Schoolboys, 1957, Derbyshire Schs, 1957–60, and British Univs, 1960–63, at football; Mem., England Amateur Squad, 1960–63; professional footballer (goalkeeper), Arsenal FC, 1964–74 (winner: Euro Fairs Cup, 1970; League and Cup Double, 1971); internat. appearances for Scotland, 1971–72; Goalkeeping Coach, Arsenal FC, 1975–2003. Chm., London Football Coaches Assoc., 1990–2007. Co-founder, Willow Foundn Charity, 1999– (Life Pres., 2012). Gov., Univ. of Hertfordshire, 1997–2006. Hon. DLitt Loughborough, 1989; DUniv: Derby, 2001; Middlesex, 2004; Hon. DSc Hertfordshire, 2018. *Publications:* Goalkeeping, 1970; The Art of Goalkeeping, 1973; You've Got to be Crazy, 1989; Behind the Network (autobiog.), 2003; Googlies, Nutmegs and Bogies, 2006; Rucks, Pucks and Sliders, 2007; Life in the Beautiful Game, 2008. *Recreations:* reading, golf, boating, theatre.

**WILSON, Sir (Robert James) Timothy,** Kt 2011; DL; PhD; Vice-Chancellor and Chief Executive, University of Hertfordshire, 2003–10; *b* 2 April 1949; *s* of John and Joan Wilson; *m* 1972, Jackie Hinds; two *d*. *Educ:* Univ. of Reading (BSc Hons); Univ. of Lancaster (MA); Walden Univ., USA (PhD 1997). Lectr, then Sen. Lectr, Operational Res., Leeds Poly., 1974–84; Dir of Studies, Cranfield Inst. of Technol., 1984–87; Asst Dir, Leicester Poly., 1987–91; Hatfield Polytechnic, later University of Hertfordshire: Dep. Dir, 1991–92; Pro Vice Chancellor and Dep. Chief Exec., 1992–2002; Prof., 2002–10, now Emeritus. Chairman: Herts Prosperity Ltd, 2003–09; UH Holdings Ltd, 2008–10; Arden Univ., 2017–; Univ. Canada West, 2019–; Board Member: E of England Develt Agency, 2003–09; HEFCE, 2004–11. Head, Wilson Review of Univ.-Business Collaboration for UK govt, 2012. Dir, Raffles Univ., Singapore, 2008–10. Non-executive Director: Unite Gp plc, 2010–; University of Law Ltd, 2012–15. Chm., Herts LEP, 2011–12. Trustee: Garden House Hospice, 2012–; Unite Foundn, 2017–. DL Herts, 2011. FRSA 2008. Hon. DEd: Hertfordshire, 2013; Plymouth, 2014; Hon. DSc London S Bank, 2015. *Publications:* numerous articles in jls relating to mathematical modelling and higher educn mgt. *Recreations:* golf, Rugby Union. *E:* wilson.pendleton@gmail.com.

**WILSON, Robert Julian, (Robin),** MA; Headmaster, Trinity School of John Whitgift, Croydon, 1972–94; *b* 6 July 1933; *s* of late Prof. Frank Percy Wilson, FBA, and Joanna Wilson (*née* Perry-Keene); *m* 1957, Caroline Anne (*née* Maher); two *d* (and one *s* one *d* decd). *Educ:* St Edward's Sch., Oxford; Trinity Coll., Cambridge (MA). Lektor, Univ. of Münster, Westphalia, 1955–58; Assistant Master: St Peter's, York, 1958–62; Nottingham High Sch. (Hd of English), 1962–72. Mem. Cttee, HMC, 1987–94 (Chm., 1993); Vice-Chm., Academic Policy Cttee, 1990–92; Member: Council, GDST (formerly GPDST), 1994–2008; Cttee, GBA, 1999–2002. Governor: Brentwood Sch., 1995–2015; St Peter's Sch., York, 1996–2002. *Publications:* (jtly) Bertelsmann Sprachkursus English, 1959; (ed) The Merchant of Venice, 1971; articles on the teaching of English. *Recreations:* drama, travel, golf. *Address:* 22 Beech House Road, Croydon, Surrey CR0 1JP. *T:* (020) 8686 1915. *Clubs:* East India, Devonshire, Sports and Public Schools; Addington Golf.

**WILSON, Robert Nelson;** Chairman, A. Nelson & Co. Ltd, since 2001; *b* 23 July 1962; *s* of Robert Wiseman Wilson and Anne Wilson; *m* 1994, Nicola Jane Petrie; two *s* two *d*. *Educ:* St Columba's Coll., Dublin; Trinity Coll., Dublin (BA Hons Hist., MA); Harvard Business Sch. A. Nelson & Co.: Mktg Dir, 1990–93; Man. Dir, 1993–2001. Dir, Wigmore Pubns, 1991–. Trustee: Scottish Civic Trust, 2002–12; Prince's Foundn for Integrated Health, 2005–09; Prince's Initiative for Mature Enterprise, 2010–14; Little Sparta Trust, 2016–18; Royal Botanic Gardens Edinburgh, 2017–18; Chairman: Prostate Scotland, 2006–; Barcapel Foundn, 2006–; Creative Scotland, 2018–; Co-Founder, Jupiter Artland Foundn, 2006–; Trustee, The Art Room, 2013–17. Bd Dir, Edinburgh Arts Festival, 2010–18 (Chm., 2010–18). Gov., Kilgraston Sch., 2005–10. Mem., Royal Co. of Archers, 2013–. *Recreations:* art, golf, travel, shooting. *Address:* A. Nelson & Co., Nelson House, 83 Parkside, Wimbledon, SW19 5LP. *T:* (020) 8780 4200, *Fax:* (020) 8789 0141. *E:* RobertWilson@Nelsons.net. *Clubs:* Oriental, Sloane; New (Edinburgh); Bruntsfield Links Golfing Society; Golf House (Elie).

**WILSON, Robert Owen Biggs;** Chief Executive, Drugs Reform Research Group; *b* 4 Jan. 1965; *m* Jane; one *s* three *d*. *Educ:* Wallingford Sch.; Univ. of Reading (BA Hist.). Entrepreneur, health and communications. Mem. (C), Reading BC, 1992–96, 2004–06. MP (C) Reading E, 2005–17; contested (C) same seat, 2017. Shadow Minister for Higher Educn, 2007–09; an Opposition Whip, 2009–10; PPS to Sec. of State for Culture, Olympics, Media and Sport, 2010–12, for Health, 2012–13, to Chancellor of the Exchequer, 2013–14; Parly Sec., Cabinet Office, 2014–16; Parly Under-Sec. of State, DCMS, 2016–17. Contested (C): Bolton NE, 1997; Carmarthen W and S Pembs, 2001. Columnist, Daily Telegraph, 2017–. Non-executive Director: Consumer Council for Water, 2018–; Transport Focus, 2018–. Chm., Wheelpower, 2018–. Mem. Bd, Marine Mgt Orgn, 2018–. *Publications:* 5 Days to Power: the journey to coalition Britain, 2010; The Eye of the Storm, 2014.

**WILSON, Sir Robert (Peter),** KCMG 2000; Chairman, Riverstone Energy Ltd, 2013–16; *b* 2 Sept. 1943; *s* of late Alfred Wilson and Dorothy (*née* Mathews); *m* 1975, Shirley Elisabeth Robson; one *s* one *d*. *Educ:* Epsom Coll.; Sussex Univ. (BA). Harvard Business Sch. (AMP). With Dunlop Ltd, 1966–67; Mobil Oil Co. Ltd, 1967–70; RTZ Corporation plc, later Rio Tinto plc, 1970–2003: Dir, Main Bd, 1987–2003; Dir, Planning and Develt, 1987–89, Mining and Metals, 1989–91; Chief Exec., 1991–97; Chairman: Rio Tinto plc, 1997–2003; Rio Tinto Ltd, 1999–2003. Non-executive Director: The Boots Co. PLC, 1991–98; Diageo plc, 1998–2003; BP plc (formerly Britoil, then BP Amoco), 1998–2002; Economist Newspaper Ltd, later The Economist Gp, 2002–09 (Chm., 2003–09); BG Gp plc, 2002–12 (Chm., 2004–12); GlaxoSmithKline plc, 2003–13. Sen. Advr, Morgan Stanley, 2013–14. Chm., Internat. Council for Mining & Metals, 2002–03; Patron, Centre for Energy, Petroleum and Mineral Law and Policy, Dundee Univ., 2010–. FEI 2006; CCMI; FRSA. Hon. DSc: Exeter, 1993; Birmingham, 2002; Sussex, 2004; Hon. LLD Dundee, 2001. *Recreations:* theatre, opera, reading, wine.

**WILSON, Robert William Gordon,** OBE 2011; Principal Clerk of Select Committees, and Deputy Head, Committee Office, House of Commons, 2001–10; *b* 8 July 1946; *s* of late Gordon Chamberlain Wilson, CBE, and Winifred Wilson (*née* Low); civil partnership 2007, David Ira Wurtzel. *Educ:* Lancing Coll.; Christ Church, Oxford (Exhibnr; MA). A Clerk, H of C, 1967–: Clerk: of Eur. Legislation Cttee, 1981–86; of Envmt Cttee, 1986–87; of Foreign Affairs Cttee, 1987–91; Principal Clerk: of Financial Cttees and Treasury and Civil Service Cttee, 1991–92; of Domestic Cttees and Sec., H of C Commn, 1992–95; of Overseas Office, 1995–2001. Jt Sec., Assoc. of Secretaries-General of Parlts, 1977–84. Hon. Steward, Westminster Abbey, 1981–98, 2010–. Patron, Decorative Arts Soc., 2018– (Dep. Chm., 2004–11; Chm., 2011–17). Trustee, Erskine May Meml Fund, 2001–10. *Publications:* Guide to the Houses of Parliament, edns from 1988 to 2010. *Recreations:* theatre, opera, travel, swimming. *Address:* 35 Albany Mansions, Albert Bridge Road, SW11 4PG. *Club:* Athenæum.

**WILSON, Dr Robert Woodrow;** Senior Scientist, Harvard-Smithsonian Center for Astrophysics, since 1994; *b* 10 Jan. 1936; *s* of Ralph Woodrow Wilson and Fannie May Willis; *m* 1958, Elizabeth Rhoads Sawin; two *s* one *d*. *Educ:* Rice Univ. (BA Physics, 1957); Calif Inst. of Technol. (PhD 1962). Post-doctoral Fellowship, Calif Inst. of Technol., 1962–63; Mem. Technical Staff, Bell Labs, Holmdel, NJ, 1963–76; Head, Radio Physics Res. Dept, Bell Telephone Labs, Inc., later AT&T Bell Labs, 1976–94. Member: Phi Beta Kappa; Amer. Acad. of Arts and Sciences, 1978; US Nat. Acad. of Science, 1979. Hon. degrees: Monmouth Coll., 1979; Jersey City State Coll., 1979; Thiel Coll., 1980. Henry Draper Award, 1977; Herschel Award, RAS, 1977; (jtly) Nobel Prize for Physics, 1978. *Publications:* contrib. to Astrophys. Jl. *Address:* 9 Valley Point Drive, Holmdel, NJ 07733–1320, USA. *T:* (201) 6717807; Harvard-Smithsonian Center for Astrophysics, 60 Garden Street #42, Cambridge, MA 02138–1516, USA.

**WILSON, Robin;** *see* Wilson, R. J.

**WILSON, Robin Lee,** CBE 1992; FREng; consulting engineer; *b* 4 March 1933; *s* of late Henry Eric Wilson, OBE and Catherine Margaret Wilson; *m* 1956, Gillian Margaret, *d* of late L. J. N. Kirkby and Margaret Kirkby; one *s* two *d*. *Educ:* Glenalmond College; Univ. of Glasgow (BSc Eng. 1955). FICE 1966; FCIHT (FIHT 1966). Joined R. Travers Morgan & Partners, 1956, Partner, 1966, Sen. Partner, 1985; Dir and Gp Chm., Travers Morgan Ltd, Consulting Engineers, 1988–91; Chairman: New Builder Publications Ltd, 1989–94; Thomas Telford Ltd, publishers, 1990–94. Dir, Mid Kent Hldgs, 1994–97. Member Council: ICE, 1977–80, 1983–86, 1987–93 (Pres., 1991–92); ACE, 1985–88; Construction Industry Council, 1990–97 (Chm., 1994–96); Engrg Council, 1991–99 (Chm., Bd for Engineers' Regulation, 1994–99); Glenalmond Coll., 1985–2001 (Chm. Cttee, 1995–2001; Pres., Fellowship, 2011–17). Pres., Smeatonian Soc. of Civil Engineers, 2016. Minister's nominee, SE Council for Sport and Recreation, 1987–90. Chm., Coultershaw Trust, 2002–. Master, Paviors' Co., 2003–04. DSc *hc* City Univ., 1991. Coopers Hill Meml Prize, ICE, 1989; Instn of Highways and Transportation Award, 1990. *Publications:* papers in learned jls on highway engineering and related subjects. *Recreation:* sailing. *Address:* The Grove House, Little Bognor, Pulborough, Sussex RH20 1JT. *T:* (01798) 865774. *Club:* Itchenor Sailing.

**WILSON, Rodney Herbert William;** Executive Producer for BBC Classical Music, Television, 1998; *b* 21 June 1942; *s* of Herbert Herman Wilson and Vera Anne Faulkner. *Educ:* Windsor Grammar Sch. for Boys; Berkshire Coll. of Art (Intermediate Diploma); Camberwell Sch. of Art (NDD); Hornsey Coll. of Art (ATD). Asst Lectr, Loughborough Coll. of Art, 1965–69; Film Officer, 1970, Head of Film Section, 1980, Arts Council of GB; Dir, Dept of Film, Video and Broadcasting, Arts Council of England, 1986–98. Member: Film, Video and Television Adv. Cttee, British Council, 1983–98; Council, Edinburgh Film Festival, 1984–94; Festival Council, Art Film Fest., Slovakia, 1995–; RTS, 1994. Exec. Producer for Arts Council Films, 1970. *Recreations:* walking, doodling, photography.

**WILSON, Air Chief Marshal Sir (Ronald) Andrew (Fellowes), (Sir Sandy),** KCB 1991 (CB 1990); AFC 1978; Air Member for Personnel and Air Officer Commanding-in-Chief Personnel and Training Command, 1993–95; Air Aide-de-Camp to the Queen, 1993–95; *b* 27 Feb. 1941; *s* of late Ronald Denis Wilson and Gladys Vera Groombridge; *m* 1979, Mary Christine Anderson; one *d*, and one step *s* one step *d*. *Educ:* Tonbridge Sch.; RAF Coll., Cranwell. Flying Instr, 1963–65; No 2 Sqn, 1966–68; ADC to C-in-C, RAF Germany, 1967–68; Flt Comdr No 2 Sqn, 1968–72; RAF Staff Coll., 1973; HQ STC, 1974–75; CO No 2 Sqn, 1975–77; Air Plans, MoD, 1977–79; CO RAF Lossiemouth, 1980–82; Air Cdre Falkland Islands, 1982–83; Central Staff, MoD, 1983–85; Dir Ops Strike, MoD, 1985; Dir Air Offensive, MoD, 1986–87; SASO, HQ, RAF Strike Comd, 1987–89; AOC No 1 Group, 1989–91; Comdr, British Forces during Op. Granby, ME, Aug.–Dec. 1990; C-in-C, RAF Germany and Comdr Second ATAF, 1991–93; Mem., Air Force Bd, 1991–95. Pres., Aircrew Assoc., 1997–2003. Vice-Chm., Air League, 1997–2005. Mem. Council, Lord Kitchener Meml Fund, 1998–2018. Freeman, City of London, 1966; Liveryman, 1970, Mem. Court, 1984–87, 1994–, Master, 1999–2000, Worshipful Co. of Skinners. CCMI (CIMgt 1993); FRAeS 1994. *Recreations:* painting, antique restoration, genealogy, golf. *Club:* Royal Air Force.

**WILSON, Ruth Joanna;** actress; *b* Ashford, Middx, 13 Jan. 1982; *d* of Nigel and Mary Wilson. *Educ:* Notre Dame Sen. Sch., Cobham, Surrey; Esher Coll.; Nottingham Univ. (BA Hons). Actress: *television:* Jane Eyre, 2006; Capturing Mary, 2007; A Real Summer, 2007; The Doctor Who Hears Voices, 2008; The Prisoner, 2009; Small Island, 2009; Luther, 2010–13, 2019; The Affair, 2015 (Golden Globe Award, 2015), 2016, 2018; I am the Pretty Thing That Lives in the House, 2016; Mrs Wilson (also exec. prod.), 2019; His Dark Materials, 2019; *theatre:* Philistines, RNT, 2007; A Streetcar Named Desire, Donmar, 2009 (Best Supporting Actress, Olivier Awards, 2010); Through a Glass Darkly, Almeida, 2010; Anna Christie, Donmar, 2011 (Best Actress, Olivier Awards, 2012); The El Train (also dir), Hoxton Hall, 2013; Constellations, Samuel J Friedman Th., NY, 2015; Hedda Gabler, NT, 2016; King Lear, Cort Th., NY, 2019; *films:* Anna Karenina, 2012; The Lone Ranger, 2013; Saving Mr Banks, 2013; Locke, A Walk Among the Tombstones, 2014; Suite Française, 2015; How to Talk to Girls at Parties, Dark River, The Little Stranger, 2018. *Address:* c/o Troika Talent, 180 Great Portland Street, W1W 5QZ. *T:* (020) 7336 7868. *E:* info@troikatalent.com.

**WILSON, Rt Hon. Samuel, (Rt Hon. Sammy);** PC 2017; MP (DemU) East Antrim, since 2005; *b* 4 April 1953; *s* of Alexander and Mary Wilson. *Educ:* Methodist Coll., Belfast; The Queen's Univ., Belfast (BScEcon; PGCE). Teacher of Economics, 1975–83; Researcher in N Ireland Assembly, 1983–86. Councillor, Belfast CC, 1981–2010; Lord Mayor of Belfast, 1986–87 and 2000–01. Press Officer for Democratic Unionist Party, 1982–96. Contested (DemU): Strangford, 1992; Antrim E, 2001. Mem. (DemU) Belfast E, 1998–2003, E Antrim, 2003–Aug. 2015, NI Assembly; Minister of the Envmt, 2008–09, of Finance and Personnel, 2009–13, NI. Mem., Cttee on Exiting the EU, 2016–. *Publications:*

The Carson Trail, 1982; The Unionist Case—The Forum Report Answered, 1984; Data Response Questions in Economics, 1995. *Recreations:* reading, motor cycling, windsurfing, gardening. *Address:* East Antrim DUP, 116 Main Street, Larne BT40 1RG. *T:* (028) 2826 7722. *E:* barronj@parliament.uk.

**WILSON, Air Chief Marshal Sir Sandy;** *see* Wilson, Air Chief Marshal Sir R. A. F.

**WILSON, Simon Charles Hartley;** HM Diplomatic Service, retired; *b* 9 Aug. 1957; *s* of late Charles William Wilson and of Brenda Christine Wilson (*née* Hartley); *m* 1984, Heather Graine Richardson; two *s*. *Educ:* Newborough Sch., Liverpool; Liverpool Coll. Entered FCO, 1975; Attaché: Johannesburg, 1978–81; Helsinki, 1981–83; FCO, 1984–87; Vice Consul: Tehran, 1987; Riyadh, 1987–92; Second Sec. (Political), Lisbon, 1992–96; SE Asia Dept, FCO, 1997–2001; Dep. Hd of Mission, Bahrain, 2001–05; Dep. High Comr to Eastern India, at Kolkata, 2006–09. Mem. Bd, Dr Graham's Homes, Calcutta, 2007–09. Advr, Prosperitus Capital Partners, 2011–. Dir, RNVR Officers' Association Ltd, 2013–. Writer and presenter, documentary, Memories Bahrain, Bahrain TV, 2009; actor in film, Gumshuda - The Diamond Murders, 2010. Member: Cttee, Fulham and Hammersmith Asthma Soc., 1985–87; Chilbolton PCC, 1999–2001. *Publications:* articles on monarchy, ornithology, Bahrain history, HMS Hood, Roman Winchester, Portuguese history. *Recreations:* birding, taxidermy, philately, ambulist, nargileh, Edward VIII memorabilia, tennis, ski-ing, sports cars, Indian art, reading history. *Address:* Goodworth Clatford, Hants; Al Casale, 65010 Elice, Abruzzo, Italy. *E:* sheeshawilson@hotmail.com. *Clubs:* Naval (Chm., 2018–); Tollygunge, Bengal (Calcutta).

**WILSON, Sophie,** CBE 2019; FRS 2013; FREng; Senior Technical Director, Broadcom Corporation; *b* Leeds, 1957. *Educ:* Selwyn Coll., Cambridge (Computer Sci. and Maths; Hon. Fellow, 2016). Acorn Computers, 1979–99; co-founder, Element 14 Ltd, 1999, sold to Broadcom Corp., 2000; designed: Acorn Micro-Computer, 1978; BBC Microcomputer, BBC BASIC, 1980; instruction set for Acorn RISC Machine (ARM), 1983; Acorn Replay, video architecture for Acorn machines. Consultant, ARM Ltd, 1990. FREng 2008. Hon. DSc Cantab, 2017. *Address:* Broadcom Corporation, Unit 406 Science Park, Milton Road, Cambridge CB4 0WW.

**WILSON, Sir Thomas David,** 4th Bt *cr* 1920, of Carbeth, Killearn, co. Stirling; *b* 6 Jan. 1959; *s* of Sir David Wilson, 3rd Bt and of Eva Margareta Wilson (*née* Lindell); *S* father, 2014; *m* 1st, 1984, Valerie Stogdale (marr. diss. 2002); two *s*; 2nd, 2006, Briony Jane Roberts (*née* Clark). *Educ:* Harrow. *Heir: s* Fergus Wilson, *b* 24 April 1987.

**WILSON, Prof. Thomas Michael Aubrey,** PhD; CBiol, FRSB; FRSE; Honorary Professor, Warwick-HRI, University of Warwick, 2007–10 (Professor of Biological Sciences, 2004–07); *b* 10 Oct. 1951; *s* of Basil Francis Aubrey Wilson and Elisabeth Mathew Wilson (*née* Hogg); *m* 1975, Judith Lindsey Dring; two *s* one *d*. *Educ:* Univ. of Edinburgh (BSc 1st Cl. Hons Biol Sci. 1973); St John's Coll., Cambridge (PhD Biochem. 1976). CBiol 1995; FRSB (FIBiol 1998); FIHort 1999–2010; FRSE 1999. MRC Res. Fellow, Univ. of Nottingham, 1976–78; Lectr in Biochem., Univ. of Liverpool, 1979–83; SSO, 1983–86, PSO, 1986–89, John Innes Inst., Norwich; Prof., Rutgers Univ., NJ, 1989–92; Head of Virology, 1992–95, Dep. Dir, 1995–99, Scottish Crop Res. Inst., Dundee; Sci. Dir, 1999, CEO, 1999–2004, Horticulture Res. Internat. Hon. Lectr, UEA, 1985–92; Hon. Professor: Univ. of Dundee, 1993–99; Zhejiang Acad. Agricl Scis, China, 1993–; Univ. of Birmingham, 1999–2004; Univ. of Warwick, 1999–2004. Ed., Jl of Horticultural Sci. and Biotechnol., 2004–16. FRSA 2003–07. *Publications:* (with J. W. Davies) Genetic Engineering with Plant Viruses, 1992; Engineering Genesis, 1998; contrib. approx. 100 papers in specialist jls; also over 100 abstracts, proceedings and invited seminars.

**WILSON, Sir Timothy;** *see* Wilson, Sir R. J. T.

**WILSON, Prof. Timothy Hugh;** Barrie and Deedee Wigmore Research Keeper, Department of Western Art, Ashmolean Museum, Oxford, 2013–17, now Hon. Curator; Professorial Fellow, Balliol College, Oxford, 1990–2017, now Emeritus; Professor of the Arts of the Renaissance, University of Oxford, 2010–17, now Emeritus; *b* 8 April 1950; *s* of late Col Hugh Walker Wilson and Lilian Rosemary (*née* Kirke); *m* 1984, Jane Lott; two *s* one *d*. *Educ:* Winchester Coll.; Mercersburg Acad., USA; Corpus Christi Coll., Oxford (BA 1973; MA); Warburg Inst., London Univ. (MPhil 1976); Dept of Museum Studies, Leicester Univ. FSA 1989–2016. Res. Asst, Dept of Weapons and Antiquities, Nat. Maritime Mus., Greenwich, 1977–79; Asst Keeper (Renaissance collections), Dept of Medieval and Later Antiquities, BM, 1979–90; Keeper of Western Art, Ashmolean Mus., Oxford, 1990–2013. Trustee: Ruskin Foundn, 1994–2000; Oxford Preservation Trust, 2006–15; Cartoon Art Trust, 2010–15; Radcliffe Trust, 2011–; Oxford Civic Soc., 2017–19; Friends of Herefordshire Museums and Arts, 2017–. Fellow: Harvard Univ. Center for Renaissance Studies, Villa I Tatti, Florence, 1984; Accademia Raffaello, Urbino, 2003; Frick Center for the History of Collecting, NY, 2012. Hon. Fellow: Royal Soc. Painter-Printmakers, 1991; Accademia Pietro Vannucci, Perugia, 2008; Corresp. Fellow, Accademia Properziana del Subasio di Assisi, 2018. Liveryman, Fishmongers' Co., 2017. *Publications:* (jtly) The Art of the Jeweller, 1984; Flags at Sea, 1986, 2nd edn 1999; Ceramic Art of the Italian Renaissance, 1987; Maiolica, 1989, 2nd edn 2003; (ed) Italian Renaissance Pottery, 1991; (jtly) Systematic Catalogue of the National Gallery of Art: Western Decorative Arts, Part 1, 1993; (ed jtly) C. D. E. Fortnum and the Collecting and Study of Applied Arts and Sculpture in Victorian England, 1999; (jtly) Le maioliche rinascimentali nelle collezioni della Fondazione Cassa di Risparmio di Perugia, 2006–07; (jtly) Italian Renaissance Ceramics: a catalogue of the British Museum collection, 2009; Italian Maiolica in the Collection of the National Gallery of Victoria, 2015; (jtly) Treasures of the Goldsmith's Art, 2015; Maiolica: Italian Renaissance ceramics in the Metropolitan Museum of Art, 2016; Italian Maiolica and Europe, 2017; The Golden Age of Italian Maiolica-painting, 2018; articles in Apollo, Burlington Mag., Faenza, Jl Warburg and Courtauld Insts, Jl of Hist. of Collections, Ceramic Review, etc; contribs exhibition and museum catalogues. *Address:* Balliol College, Oxford OX1 3BJ; 4 Boults Close, Old Marston, Oxford OX3 0PP. *T:* (01865) 428677; Marlborough Cottage, Durlow Common, Herefordshire HR1 4JQ.

**WILSON, Dr William Laurence;** Member (SNP) Scotland West, Scottish Parliament, 2007–11; *b* 11 Dec. 1963; *s* of Samuel and Mary Wilson; *m* 2002, Julieta A. Pineda; one *s*. *Educ:* Glasgow Univ. (BSc Hons Zool.; MSc IT); Aberdeen Univ. (MSc Ecol.); Queen's Univ., Belfast (PhD). Biologist: Glasgow Univ., 1987; Berks, Bucks and Oxon Wildlife Trust and Oxford Univ., 1987–89; Res. Asst, QUB, 1989–91; Res. Officer, Ulster Univ., 1993–96; Res. Fellow, 1996–98, Project Manager, 1998–99, Glasgow Univ.; IT Asst, Glasgow Caledonian Univ., 2001; Systems Developer, Prudent/Standard Life, 2001–05; Statistician, Scottish Founding Council, 2005–07. Contested (SNP): Glasgow Anniesland, 1997, Paisley and Renfrewshire N, 2005; Glasgow Maryhill, Scottish Parlt, 1999, 2003. *Publications:* series of training booklets for researchers, 1999; (contrib.) Is There a Scottish Road to Socialism?, 2007; contrib. scientific jls. *Recreations:* reading, hill walking, travel.

**WILSON-BARNETT, Prof. Dame Jenifer, (Dame Jenifer Trimble),** DBE 2003; Professor of Nursing, 1986–2004, now Emeritus, and Founding Head of Florence Nightingale School of Nursing and Midwifery, 1999–2004, King's College, London (Head of Division of Nursing and Midwifery, 1994–99); *b* 10 Aug. 1944; adopted by Edith M. Barnett and Barbara M. Wilson; *m* 1975, Michael Robert Trimble. *Educ:* Chichester High School for Girls; St George's Hosp., London (student nurse), 1963–66; Univ. of Leicester, 1967–70 (BA Politics); Edinburgh Univ., 1970–72 (MSc); Guy's Hosp. Med. Sch., London (PhD 1977). FRCN 1984; FKC 1995. Staff Nurse, 1966, Nursing Sister, 1972–74, St George's Hosp.; Researcher, Guy's Hosp., 1974–77; Chelsea College: Lectr in Nursing, 1977; Sen. Lectr, 1983; Reader and Hd of Dept, 1984. Ed.-in-Chief, Internat. Jl of Nursing Studies, 2000–05. Chair, Chichester Cttee, Macmillan Cancer Support, 2013–. Patron, Selsey and Dist Carers Support Gp, 2007–17. Chair, St Mary, Our Lady, Sidlesham, Develt Gp, 2010–18. Hon. DSc: Hull, 2004; Kingston, 2006. Lifetime Achievement Award, British Jl Nursing, 2008. *Publications:* Stress in Hospital: patients' psychological reactions to illness and health care, 1979; (with Morva Fordham) Recovery from Illness, 1982; Patient Teaching, 1983; Nursing Research: ten studies in patient care, 1983; Nursing Issues and Research in Terminal Care, 1988; Patient Problems: a research base for nursing care, 1988; (with Sarah Robinson) Directions in Nursing Research, 1989; (with Jill Macleod Clark) Health Promotion and Nursing Research, 1993; (with Alison Richardson) Nursing Research in Cancer Care, 1996. *Recreations:* music, writing, 'singing'. *Address:* Jubilee Cottage, Mill Lane, Sidlesham, Chichester, W Sussex PO20 7NA. *Clubs:* Royal Automobile, Royal College of Nursing, Royal Society of Medicine.

**WILSON-JOHNSON, David Robert,** FRAM; baritone; Professor of Singing, Amsterdam Conservatorium, 2004–10; Director, Ferrandou Singing School; *b* 16 Nov. 1950; *s* of Sylvia Constance Wilson and Harry Kenneth Johnson. *Educ:* Wellingborough School; British Institute, Florence; St Catharine's College, Cambridge (BA Hons 1973); Royal Acad. of Music (Dove Prize), 1976). NFMS Award, 1977; Gulbenkian Fellowship, 1978–81. Royal Opera House, Covent Garden: We Come to the River (début), 1976; Billy Budd, 1982; L'Enfant et les Sortilèges, 1983; Le Rossignol, 1983; Les Noces, Boris Godunov, 1984; Die Zauberflöte, 1985; Werther, Turandot, 1987; Madam Butterfly, 1988; title rôle, St François d'Assise (Messiaen), 1988–89 (Evening Standard Award, 1989); Wigmore Hall recital début, 1978; Edinburgh Fest. début, 1980; BBC Proms début, 1981; Paris Opera début (Die Meistersinger), 1989; US début, Cleveland Orch., 1990; other roles include King Fisher (A Midsummer Marriage), King Priam (Tippett), Merlin (Albeniz), Oedipe (Enescu), The Nose (Shostakovitch); appearances at Netherlands Opera, Brussels, Geneva, Houston, New York, Turin, Salzburg, etc; many collaborations with Pierre Boulez, Frans Bruggen, Charles Dutoit, Robert King, Andre Previn, Simon Rattle, Gennadi Rozhdestvensky, David Owen Norris; numerous recordings, including works by Bach, Schönberg and Schubert. FRAM 1988 (ARAM 1982). *Recreations:* swimming, slimming, gardening and growing walnuts at Dordogne house. *Address:* Highfield Cottage, Overgate Road, Swayfield, Grantham, Lincs NG33 4LF. *T:* (01476) 550432; Prinsengracht 455, 1016 HN Amsterdam, Netherlands. *T:* (20) 7728104. *W:* www.davidwilsonjohnson.com.

**WILSON JONES, Prof. Edward,** FRCP, FRCPath; Professor of Dermatopathology, Institute of Dermatology, University of London, 1974–91, now Emeritus (Dean, 1980–89); *b* 26 July 1926; *s* of Percy George Jones and Margaret Louisa Wilson; *m* 1952, Hilda Mary Rees; one *s* one *d*. *Educ:* Oundle Sch.; Trinity Hall, Cambridge (MB, BChir 1951); St Thomas' Hosp., London. FRCP 1970; FRCPath 1975. National Service, Army, 1953–54. House Surgeon (Ophthalmic), St Thomas' Hosp., 1951; House Physician (Gen. Medicine), St Helier Hosp., Carshalton, 1951–52; House Physician (Neurology and Chest Diseases), St Thomas' Hosp., London, 1955; Registrar (Gen. Medicine), Watford Peace Meml Hosp., 1955–57; Registrar (Derm.), St Thomas' Hosp., 1957–60; Inst. of Dermatology, St John's Hosp. for Diseases of the Skin: Sen. Registrar (Derm.), 1960–62; Sen. Registrar (Dermatopath.), 1962–63; Sen. Lectr (Dermatopath.), 1963–74; Hon. Consultant, St John's Hosp. for Diseases of Skin, 1974–. Non-exec. Dir, Crockett & Jones Ltd. Founders Award, Amer. Soc. of Dermatopathology, 1997; Gray Medal, British Assoc. of Dermatology. *Publications:* (contrib.) Textbook of Dermatology, ed Rook, Wilkinson and Ebling, 3rd edn 1979; articles on dermatopath. subjects in British Jl of Derm., Arch. of Derm., Acta Dermatovenereologica, Dermatologica, Clin. and Exptl Derm., Histopath., and in Human Path. *Recreations:* art history, watercolour painting. *Address:* Featherstone House, 89 Wise Lane, NW7 2RH.

**WILTON,** 8th Earl of, *cr* 1801; **Francis Egerton Grosvenor;** Viscount Grey de Wilton 1801; Baron Ebury 1857; *b* 8 Feb. 1934; *s* of 5th Baron Ebury, DSO and Ann Acland-Troyte; *S* to Barony of father, 1957; *S* to Earldom of kinsman, 1999; is in remainder to Marquessate of Westminster; *m* 1st, 1957, Gillian Elfrida (Elfin) (marr. diss. 1962), *d* of Martin Soames, London; one *s*; 2nd, 1963, Kyra (marr. diss. 1973), *d* of late L. L. Aslin; 3rd, 1974, Suzanne Jean (*d* 2018), *d* of Graham Suckling, Christchurch, NZ; (one *d* decd). *Educ:* Eton; Univ. of Melbourne (PhD). *Recreation:* ornithology. *Heir: s* Viscount Grey de Wilton, *qv*. *Address:* PO Box 466, Mt Macedon, Vic 3441, Australia. *Clubs:* Oriental; Melbourne; Melbourne Savage (Melbourne); Hong Kong.

**WILTON, Andrew;** *see* Wilton, J. A. R.

**WILTON, Christopher Edward John,** CMG 2003; HM Diplomatic Service, retired; Director, DCW Consultants, since 2005; *b* 16 Dec. 1951; *s* of Sir (Arthur) John Wilton, KCMG, KCVO, MC and of Maureen Elizabeth Alison Wilton; *m* 1975, Dianne Hodgkinson; one *s* one *d*. *Educ:* Tonbridge Sch.; Manchester Univ. (Hons Near Eastern Studies); Chartered Insurance Inst. (Dip. Personal Finance 2012). Production Supervisor, Esso Petroleum, 1975–77; HM Diplomatic Service, 1977–98: FCO, 1977; Bahrain, 1978–81; FCO, 1981–84; Tokyo, 1984–88; on loan to Cabinet Office, 1988–90; Commercial Counsellor, Riyadh, 1990–94; Consul Gen., Dubai, 1994–97; Counsellor, FCO, and Comr (non-resident), British Indian Ocean Territories, 1998; Regl Man. Dir, GEC, later BAE Systems, 1999–2001 (on special leave); Counsellor, FCO, 2001–02; Ambassador to Kuwait, 2002–05. Middle East Advisor: to RBS, 2005–08; Selex Sensors and Airborne Systems Ltd, 2005–08; Sen. Advr, EMCIIS Ltd, 2008–10; Dir, Blue Sea UK Ltd, 2009–; Vice Chm., DTZ plc, 2009–10. Dir, Arab-British Chamber of Commerce, 2005–10; Chm. Adv. Council, London Middle East Inst., 2007–08. Chm., Raleigh Internat., 2007–12. Sen. Mentor, Advanced Comd and Staff Course, JSCSC, 2015–. Mem. (C), Petersfield Town Council, 2018–19. Trustee, Wallacea Trust, 2012–15; Chm. of Trustees, Rosemary Foundn Hospice at Home Care, 2014–; Chm. of Trustees, ShopMobility E Hants, 2017–. *Recreations:* walking, cooking, piano, choral singing, visiting islands. *Club:* Athenæum.

**WILTON, Helen B.;** *see* Bonser-Wilton.

**WILTON, (James) Andrew (Rutley),** FSA; Visiting Research Fellow, Tate Gallery, 2003–14 (Keeper and Senior Research Fellow, 1998–2002); *b* 7 Feb. 1942; *s* of Herbert Rutley Wilton and Mary Cecilia Morris (*née* Buckerfield); *m* 1976, Christina Frances Benn (marr. diss.); one *s*. *Educ:* Dulwich Coll.; Trinity Coll., Cambridge (MA). Assistant Keeper: Walker Art Gallery, Liverpool, 1965; Dept of Prints and Drawings, BM, 1967; Curator of Prints and Drawings, Yale Center for British Art, 1976; Asst Keeper, Turner Collection, BM, 1981; Curator, Turner Collection, 1985–89, Keeper of British Art, 1989–98, Tate Gallery. Hon. Curator of Prints and Drawings, Royal Acad., 2003. Trustee, Turner's House Trust (formerly Sandycombe Lodge Trust), 2005–17. Hon. Curator and Hon. Liveryman, Painter-Stainers' Co., 2003. FRSA 1973; FSA 2000. Hon. RWS 1985. *Publications:* Georges van Houten, 1967; Turner in Switzerland (with John Russell), 1976; British Watercolours 1750–1850, 1977; The Wood Engravings of William Blake, 1977; The Life and Work of J. M. W. Turner, 1979; The Art of Alexander and John Robert Cozens, 1979; William Pars: journey through the Alps, 1979; Constable's English Landscape Scenery, 1979; Turner and the Sublime, 1980; Turner Abroad, 1982; Turner in his Time, 1987; Painting and Poetry, 1990; The Swagger Portrait, 1992; The Great Age of British Watercolour, 1992; (ed jtly) Grand Tour, 1996; (ed jtly) Pictures in the Garrick Club: a catalogue, 1997; (ed jtly) The Age of Rossetti, Burne-Jones and Watts: symbolism in Britain, 1997; Five Centuries of British Painting, 2001; (ed jtly) American Sublime, 2002; Turner as Draughtsman, 2006; contribs to arts magazines. *Recreations:* music, architecture, travel. *Address:* 10 Farrington Place, Ashfield Lane, Chislehurst, Kent BR7 6BE. *Clubs:* Athenæum, Chelsea Arts.

**WILTON, Maxwell William M.;** *see* Moore-Wilton.

**WILTON, Dame Penelope (Alice),** DBE 2016 (OBE 2004); actress; *b* 3 June 1946; *m* 1st, Daniel Massey, actor (marr. diss.; he *d* 1998); one *d*, 2nd, 1991, Sir Ian Holm, *qv* (marr. diss. 2002). *Educ:* Drama Centre. *Theatre* includes: National Theatre, later Royal National Theatre: The Philanderer; Betrayal; Much Ado About Nothing; Man and Superman; Major Barbara, 1982; Sisterly Feelings; The Secret Rapture, 1988; Piano, 1990; Landscape, 1994; Sketches, 2002; The House of Bernarda Alba, 2005; Greenwich Theatre: Measure for Measure; All's Well That Ends Well; The Norman Conquests; King Lear, Nottingham Playhouse; The Deep Blue Sea, Almeida, 1992, transf. Apollo, 1993; Vita and Virginia, Chichester, 1992, transf. Ambassadors, 1993; The Cherry Orchard, RSC, 1995; Long Day's Journey into Night, Young Vic, 1996; A Kind of Alaska, Dublin, 1997, Donmar Warehouse, 1998; The Seagull, RSC, 2000; The Little Foxes, Donmar, 2001; Afterplay, Gielgud, 2002; Women Beware Women, RSC, 2006; Eh Joe, Duke of York's, 2006, Royal Lyceum Th., 2013; John Gabriel Borkman, Donmar, 2007; The Chalk Garden, The Family Reunion, Donmar, 2008; Hamlet, Wyndham's Th., 2009; Taken at Midnight, Chichester, 2014, transf. Th. Royal, Haymarket, 2015 (Best Actress, Olivier Awards, 2015); Fanny and Alexander, Old Vic, 2018; Pinter Three, Harold Pinter Th., 2018; The Bay at Nice, Menier Chocolate Factory, 2019; *television* includes: Othello; King Lear; Country; The Norman Conquests, 1977; The Tale of Beatrix Potter, 1983; Ever Decreasing Circles; Screaming; The Borrowers, 1992; The Deep Blue Sea, 1994; Landscapes, 1995; Talking Heads (Nights in the Gardens of Spain), 1998; Wives and Daughters, 1999; Victoria and Albert, 2001; Bob and Rose, 2001; Lucky Jim, 2003; Downton Abbey, 2010–15; South Riding, 2011; The Girl, 2012; Brief Encounters, 2016; After Life, 2019; *radio* includes: Jane and Prudence, 1994; North by Northamptonshire, 2011–12; *films* include: The French Lieutenant's Woman, 1981; Clockwise, 1986; Cry Freedom, 1987; The Secret Rapture, 1993; Carrington, 1995; Iris, 2002; Calendar Girls, 2003; Shaun of the Dead, 2003; Pride and Prejudice, 2005; Match Point, 2006; The History Boys, 2006; The Best Exotic Marigold Hotel, 2012; Belle, 2014; The Second Best Exotic Marigold Hotel, 2015; The BFG, 2016; The Guernsey Literary and Potato Peel Pie Society, 2018; Zoo, 2018; Downton Abbey, 2019. *Address:* c/o Independent Talent Group Ltd, 40 Whitfield Street, W1T 2RH.

**WILTS, Archdeacon of;** *see* Groom, Ven. S. A.

**WILTSHIRE, Earl of; Christopher John Hilton Paulet;** *b* 30 July 1969; *s* and heir of Marquess of Winchester, *qv*; *m* 1992, Christine, *d* of Peter Town; one *s* one *d*. Heir: *s* Lord St John, *qv*.

**WILTSHIRE, Deborah Ann;** *see* Charles, D. A.

**WIMBORNE, 4th Viscount** *cr* 1918; **Ivor Mervyn Vigors Guest;** Baron Wimborne 1880; Baron Ashby St Ledgers 1910; Bt 1838; *b* 19 Sept. 1968; *o s* of 3rd Viscount Wimborne and of his 1st wife, Victoria Ann, *o d* of Col Mervyn Vigors, DSO, MC; *S* father, 1993; *m* 2011, Ieva Imsa; one *d*. *Educ:* Eton. Heir: *uncle* Hon. Julian John Guest [*b* 12 Oct. 1945; *m* 1st, 1970, Emma Jane Arlette (marr. diss. 1978), *e d* of Cdre Archibald Gray, RN; 2nd, 1983, Jillian, *d* of late N. S. G. Bannatine].

**WINCHESTER, 18th Marquess of,** *cr* 1551; **Nigel George Paulet;** Baron St John of Basing, 1539; Earl of Wiltshire, 1550; Premier Marquess of England; *b* 23 Dec. 1941; *s* of George Cecil Paulet (*ggs* of 13th Marquess) (*d* 1961), and Hazel Margaret (*d* 1976), *o d* of late Major Danvers Wheeler, RA, Salisbury, Rhodesia; *S* kinsman, 1968; *m* 1967, Rosemary Anne, *d* of Major Aubrey John Hilton; two *s* one *d*. Heir: *s* Earl of Wiltshire, *qv*. *Address:* 6A Main Road, Irene, Centurion, 0062 Gauteng, South Africa.

**WINCHESTER, Bishop of,** since 2011; **Rt Rev. Timothy Dakin;** *b* Kongwa, Tanzania, 6 Feb. 1958; *s* of Rev. Canon Stanley Frederick Dakin and Judith Dakin (*née* Clark); *m* 1984, Sally Atkinson; one *s* one *d*. *Educ:* Schs in Tanzania and Kenya; University Coll. of St Mark and St John, Plymouth; King's Coll. London (BA Theol. and Phil.; MTh). Ordained deacon, 1993, priest, 1994; Principal, Carlile Coll., Kenya, 1993–2000; Curate, Nairobi Cath., 1993–2000; Gen. Sec., Church Mission Soc., 2000–11. *Recreations:* reading, walking, films, non-western Christianity. *Address:* Wolvesey, Winchester, Hants SO23 9ND. *T:* (01962) 854050. *E:* bishop.tim@winchester.anglican.org.

**WINCHESTER, Dean of;** *see* Ogle, Very Rev. C.

**WINCHESTER, Archdeacon of;** *see* Brand, Ven. R. H. G.

**WINCHESTER, Simon Bernard Adrian,** OBE 2006; writer and journalist, since 1967; *b* 28 Sept. 1944; *s* of Bernard Austin William Winchester and Andrée Freda Winchester (*née* de Wael); *m* 1st, 1966, Isobel Judith Brown (marr. diss. 1988); three *s*; 2nd, 1989, Catherine Evans (marr. diss. 1998); 3rd, 2007, Setsuko Sato; also one *d*. *Educ:* Hardye's Sch., Dorchester; St Catherine's Coll., Oxford (BA 1966, MA 1974; Hon. Fellow, 2009). Geologist: Falconbridge of Africa Ltd, Kilembe, 1966; Amoco Offshore Exploration, North Sea, 1967; reporter, then Science Corresp., The Journal, Newcastle upon Tyne, 1967–70; correspondent, variously NE England, NI, Washington, New Delhi, The Guardian, 1970–78; America Corresp., Daily Mail, 1978–80; Chief Foreign Feature Writer, then Asia Corresp., Sunday Times, 1980–84; Hong Kong Corresp., The Guardian, 1985–92; freelance journalist and writer, 1992–; Publisher, Art AsiaPacific, 2005–07; Ed., The Sandisfield Times, 2010–. Moderator, Town of Sandisfield, Massachusetts, 2017–. FRGS 1984; FGS 2000. Hon. LLD Dalhousie, 2010. Gold Medal, Royal Canadian Geographical Soc., 2016. *Publications:* In Holy Terror, 1974; American Heartbeat, 1976; Their Noble Lordships, 1981; Stones of Empire (photography), 1983; Prison Diary, Argentina, 1984; Outposts, 1985; Korea, 1988; The Pacific, 1991; Pacific Nightmare, 1992; Hong Kong: here be dragons, 1994; Small World, 1996; The River at the Centre of the World, 1997; The Surgeon of Crowthorne, 1998 (US edn as The Professor and the Madman); The Fracture Zone, 1999; America's Idea of a Good Time, 2001; The Map that Changed the World, 2001; The Meaning of Everything, 2003; Krakatoa, 2003; A Crack in the Edge of the World, 2005; Bomb, Book and Compass, 2008 (US edn as The Man Who Loved China); (ed) Best American Travel Writing, 2009; Atlantic, 2010; The Alice Behind Wonderland, 2011; Bering to Baja, 2012; Skulls, 2012; The Men who United the States, 2013; When the Earth Shakes, 2015; Pacific, 2015; When the Sky Breaks, 2016; East Coast: Arctic to Tropic, 2016; Oxford, 2017; Exactly, 2018 (US edn as The Perfectionists); The Mississippi, 2019. *Recreations:* bee-keeping, astronomy, stamp collecting, letterpress printing, hill-walking, being in Scotland west of the Caledonian Canal, being at sea anywhere, cider-making, cycle touring, carpentry. *Address:* c/o William Morris Endeavor Entertainment LLC, 11 Madison Avenue, New York, NY 10010, USA. *Clubs:* Travellers; Century, Coffee House (New York); China (Hong Kong).

**WINCHILSEA, 17th Earl of,** *cr* 1628, **AND NOTTINGHAM, 12th Earl of,** *cr* 1681; **Daniel James Hatfield Finch Hatton;** Bt 1611; Viscount Maidstone 1623; Bt 1660; Baron Finch, 1674; Custodian of the Royal Manor of Wye; *b* 7 Oct. 1967; *s* of 16th Earl of Winchilsea and 11th Earl of Nottingham, and of Shirley (*née* Hatfield); *S* father, 1999; *m* 1994, Shelley Amanda, *d* of Gordon Gillard; two *s* one *d*. *Educ:* Univ. of the West of England, Bristol. Heir: *s* Viscount Maidstone, *qv*.

**WINDEATT, Prof. Barry Alexander Corelli,** PhD, LittD; Professor of English, University of Cambridge, 2001–17; Fellow of Emmanuel College, Cambridge, since 1978; *b* 5 April 1950; *s* of Edwin Peter Windeatt and Queenie Gladys Windeatt (*née* Rusbridge). *Educ:* Sutton County GS, Surrey; St Catharine's Coll., Cambridge (BA 1971; MA 1975; PhD 1975; LittD 1996). Cambridge University: Res. Fellow, Gonville and Caius Coll., 1974–78; Asst Lectr in English, 1983–87; Lectr in English, 1987–95; Reader in Medieval Lit., 1995–2001; Tutor, 1982–95; Dir of Studies in English, 1979–98; Keeper of Rare Books, 1992–; Vice-Master, 2013–, Emmanuel Coll. *Publications:* (ed and trans.) Chaucer's Dream Poetry: sources and analogues, 1982; (ed) Geoffrey Chaucer, Troilus and Criseyde: A New Edition of The Book of Troilus, 1984, 2nd edn 1990; (trans.) The Book of Margery Kempe, 1985, new edn 2019; (ed with Ruth Morse) Chaucer Traditions, 1990; Oxford Guide to Chaucer: Troilus and Criseyde, 1992, 2nd edn 1995; (ed) English Mystics of the Middle Ages, 1994; Troilus and Criseyde: a new translation, 1998; (ed) The Book of Margery Kempe, 2000; (ed) Troilus and Criseyde, 2003; (ed with Charlotte Brewer) Traditions and Innovations in the Study of Medieval English Literature, 2013; Julian of Norwich: Revelations of Divine Love; a new translation, 2015; (ed) Revelations of Divine Love: parallel text edition, 2016; articles on medieval lit and culture. *Recreations:* opera, gardens, visual arts. *Address:* Emmanuel College, Cambridge CB2 3AP. *T:* (01223) 334200.

**WINDELER, John Robert;** Chairman, Quantum Alpha Ltd, since 2010; *b* 21 March 1943; *s* of Alfred Stewart Windeler and Ethela Windeler (*née* Bormuth); *m* 1965, Judith Lynn Taylor; two *s*. *Educ:* Ohio State Univ. (BA, MBA). Exec. Vice Pres., Irving Trust Co., 1969–89; Chief Financial Officer, Nat. Australia Bank, 1989–94; Dir, Alliance & Leicester Building Soc., subseq. Alliance & Leicester plc, 1995–2005, Dep. Chm., 1998–99, Chm., 1999–2005. Chm., Millen Gp, 2006; non-executive Director: BMS Associates Ltd, 1995–2005; RM plc, 2002–11. Gov., De Montfort Univ., 2005–10. *Recreations:* tennis, skiing, antiques. *Club:* Hurlingham.

**WINDER, Robert James;** writer; Section Editor, Independent on Sunday, 1998–2001; *b* 26 Sept. 1959; *s* of Herbert James Winder and Mary Ina (*née* Dalby); *m* 1989, Hermione Davies; two *s*. *Educ:* Bradfield Coll.; St Catherine's Coll., Oxford (BA English). Euromoney Publications, 1982–86; Dep. Lit. Ed., 1986–89, Lit. Ed., 1989–95, The Independent; Dep. Ed., Granta Publications, 1996–98. Trustee, Migration Mus. Project, 2011–. *Publications:* No Admission, 1988; The Marriage of Time and Convenience, 1994; Hell for Leather, 1996; Bloody Foreigners, 2004; The Final Act of Mr Shakespeare, 2010; Open Secrets, 2010; The Little Wonder: 150 years of Wisden, 2013; Half-Time: the glorious summer of 1934, 2015; The Last Wolf, 2017. *Recreations:* reading, writing, walking, talking, etc. *Address:* 125 Elgin Crescent, W11 2JH.

**WINDHAM, William Ashe Dymoke;** Chairman, Skelmersdale Development Corporation, 1979–85; (Deputy Chairman, 1977); *b* 2 April 1926; *s* of late Lt-Col Henry Steuart Windham and Marjory Russell Dymock; *m* 1956, Alison Audrey, *d* of late Maj. P. P. Curtis, MC and Ellinor Kidston; two *s* one *d*. *Educ:* Bedford Sch.; Christ's Coll., Cambridge (schol.; University prize; MA). Gen. Manager, Runcorn Div., Arthur Guinness Son & Co. (GB), 1972–84. Mem., Runcorn Develt Corp., 1975–77. Steward, Henley Royal Regatta, 1953– (Mem. Cttee of Mgt, 1972–94; Sen. Steward, 2002–); rowed for: winning Cambridge crews, 1947 and 1951; England, Empire Games, 1950; GB, European Championships, 1950 and 1951 (Gold Medal); Olympic Games, 1952; Leander, Grand Challenge Cup and Stewards' Challenge Cup, 1953. High Sheriff, Powys, 1996. *Recreations:* shooting, fishing, carpentry, gardening. *Clubs:* Hawks (Cambridge); Leander (Henley) (Pres., 1993–98).

**WINDLE, Prof. Alan Hardwick,** FRS 1997; FIMMM, FInstP; Professor of Materials Science, University of Cambridge, 1992–2009, now Emeritus; Fellow, Trinity College, Cambridge, since 1978; *b* 20 June 1942; *s* of Stuart George Windle and Myrtle Lillian (*née* Povey); *m* 1968, Janet Susan Carr; one *s* three *d*. *Educ:* Whitgift Sch.; Imperial Coll., London (BSc Eng. 1963; ARSM 1963); Trinity Coll., Cambridge (PhD 1966; ScD 2012). FIMMM (FIM 1992); FInstP 1997. Imperial College, University of London: ICI Res. Fellow, 1966–67; Lectr in Metallurgy, 1967–75; Cambridge University: Lectr in Metallurgy and Materials Sci., 1975–92; Hd of Dept of Materials Sci. and Metallurgy, 1996–2001; Trinity College, Cambridge: Lectr and Dir of Studies in Natural Scis, 1978–92; Tutor, 1983–91. Exec. Dir, Cambridge-MIT Inst., 2000–03; Dir, Pfizer Inst. for Pharmaceutical Materials Sci., 2005–13. Vis. Prof., N Carolina State Univ., 1980. Vice-Pres., Inst. of Materials, 2001. Comr, Royal Commn for Exhibition of 1851, 2001–10. Chm. Trustees, Mission Aviation Fellowship Europe, 2001–03. Gov., Whitgift Foundn, 1997–2001. Fellow, APS, 2001. Foreign Fellow, Nat. Acad. of Scis, India, 2007. Bessemer Medal, Imperial Coll., 1963; Silver Medal, RSA, 1963; Rosenhain Medal and Prize, Inst. Metals, 1987; Swinburne Medal and Prize, PRI, 1992; Founders' Prize, Polymer Physics Gp, Inst. of Physics, RSC and IMMM, 2007; Armourers' and Brasiers' Co. Prize, Royal Soc., 2007. *Publications:* A First Course in Crystallography, 1978; (with A. M. Donald) Liquid Crystalline Polymers, 1992, (with A. M. Donald and S. Hanna) 2nd edn 2006; contribs to learned jls mainly on polymer morphology, polymer glasses, polymer diffusion, liquid crystalline polymers, polymer modelling and the science and technology of carbon nanotubes. *Recreation:* model steam engines. *Address:* Trinity College, Cambridge CB2 1TQ.

**WINDLE, Terence Leslie William,** CBE 1991; Director, Directorate General for Agriculture, European Commission, 1980–91; *b* 15 Jan. 1926; *s* of Joseph William Windle and Dorothy Windle (*née* Haigh); *m* 1957, Joy Winifred Shield; one *s* two *d*. *Educ:* Gonville and Caius College, Cambridge (MA); London University (Colonial Course). Colonial/HMOCS: Nigeria, 1951–59; Zambia, 1959–69 (Under Sec., Min. of Natural Resources and Tourism); Home Civil Service, MAFF, 1969–73; Commn of EC, 1973–91. *Address:* rue du Fond Agny 20, 1380 Lasne, Belgium. *T:* (2) 6334410.

**WINDLESHAM, 4th Baron** *cr* 1937; **James Rupert Hennessy;** *b* London, 9 Nov. 1968; *o s* of 3rd Baron Windlesham, CVO, OBE and Prudence (*d* 1986), *d* of Lt-Col Rupert T. W. Glynn; *S* father, 2010; *m* 2004, Deborah Jane Wallace; one *s*. *Educ:* Eton Coll.; Bristol Univ. Hambros Bank Ltd, 1991–98; New Boston Partners Ltd, 1998–2007; MVP Asset Management, 2008–. *Recreations:* sport, reading. Heir: *s* Hon. George Rupert James Hennessy, *b* 19 Nov. 2006. *Address:* 65 Fulham Park Gardens, SW6 4LB. *E:* lord@windlesham.net. *Club:* White's.

**WINDSOR, Viscount; Robert Other Ivor Windsor-Clive;** company director and trustee; b London, 25 March 1981; s and heir of 4th Earl of Plymouth, qv; m 2015, Alice Rose Llewellyn; one s two d. Educ: Shrewsbury Sch.; Edinburgh Univ. (MA). Heir: s Hon. Edward Other Ivor Llewellyn Windsor-Clive, b 26 April 2019. Address: Oakly Park, Bromfield, Ludlow, Shropshire SY8 2JP. T: (01584) 856239. E: robert@oaklypark.co.uk.

**WINDSOR, Dean of;** see Conner, Rt Rev. D. J.

**WINDSOR, Dame Barbara (Anne),** DBE 2016 (MBE 2000); actress; b 6 Aug. 1937; d of John Deeks and Rose Deeks (née Ellis). Educ: Our Lady's Convent, London; Aida Foster Stage Sch. Theatre includes: Love from Judy, Palace; Fings Ain't Wot They Used T' Be, Garrick, 1959; Oh What a Lovely War, NY; Come Spy with Me, Whitehall; Sing a Rude Song, Garrick; The Threepenny Opera, Prince of Wales, 1972; The Owl and the Pussycat; Carry on London, Victoria Palace; A Merry Whiff of Windsor (one women show, UK and world tour); Twelfth Night, Chichester; Calamity Jane (UK tour); Entertaining Mr Sloane, Lyric, Hammersmith, 1981; The Mating Game; Guys and Dolls (tour). Television includes: The Rag Trade, 1961–63; Carry on Laughing, 1975; Worzel Gummidge, 1979; Peggy Mitchell in EastEnders, 1994–2003, 2005–10, 2016. Films include: Lost, 1956; Too Hot to Handle, 1959; Flame in the Street, 1961; On the Fiddle, 1961; Sparrers Can't Sing, 1963; Crooks in Cloisters, 1963; Carry on Spying, 1964; A Study in Terror, 1965; Carry on Doctor, 1968; Carry on Camping, Hair of the Dog, Chitty Chitty Bang Bang, 1969; Carry on Girls, 1971; The Boyfriend, 1971; Carry on Dick, 1974; Comrades, 1987; Double Vision; Alice in Wonderland, 2010. Radio series: Barbara Windsor's Ladies of Song, 2012. Numerous albums and radio performances. Freeman, City of London, 2010. Variety Club of GB Award, 1998; Best Actress, Manchester Evening News Awards, 1998; Best Actress, Nat. Soap Awards, 1999; RADAR People of the Year Award, 1999; BBC Hall of Fame Award, 2000; Gold Badge of Merit, BASCA, 2000; Outstanding Contrib. to Entertainment Award, Inside Soap, 2001. Publications: Laughter and Tears of a Cockney Sparrow; All of Me: my extraordinary life (autobiog.), 2000. Address: c/o Burnett Crowther Ltd, 10 Golden Square, W1F 9JA.

**WINDSOR, Dr Colin George,** FRS 1995; FInstP, FInstNDT; Consultant, Tokamak Energy Ltd, since 2013; b 28 June 1938; s of late George Thomas Macdonald Windsor and Mabel (née Rayment); m 1st, 1963, Margaret Lee (marr. diss. 2005); one s two d; 2nd, 2005, Mo Watkins. Educ: Beckenham Grammar Sch.; Magdalen Coll., Oxford (BA 1st Cl. Hons Physics; DPhil 1963). FInstP 1975; FInstNDT 1993. Magnetic resonance research, Clarendon Lab., Oxford, 1963; Res. Fellow, Yale Univ., 1964; Neutron scattering research, Harwell, 1964–96; Sen. Scientist, Nat. Non-Destructive Testing Centre, AEA Technology, 1988–96; Programme Area Manager, UKAEA, Fusion, 1996–98; Sen. Consultant, Penop, 1998–2001; Consultant, Culham Centre for Fusion Energy (formerly United Kingdom Atomic Energy Authority, Fusion) 1998–2014. Fellow: Japanese Soc. for Promotion of Sci., 1980; Neural Network Applications, 1987–. Hon. Prof. of Physics, Birmingham Univ., 1990. Publications: Pulsed Neutron Scattering, 1981; Four Computer Models, 1982; (ed jtly) Solid State Science, Past, Present and Predicted, 1987; contrib. to learned jls. Recreations: cycling to work, table tennis, sketching, singing, piano, organ, composing. Address: Tokamak Energy Ltd, 173 Brook Drive, Milton Park, Oxon OX14 4SD. T: (01235) 812083. E: colin.windsor@tokamakenergy.co.uk. W: https://colin-windsor.github.io/HomePage; (home) 116 New Road, East Hagbourne, Oxon OX11 9LD. Club: Oxford Naturist (Oxford).

**WINDSOR, Ven. (Julie) Fiona;** Archdeacon of Horsham, since 2014; b 2 Sept. 1959; d of Rev. Howell Jones and Margaret Jones; m 1979, Robin Windsor; one s one d. Educ: Ridley Hall, Cambridge; Chichester Univ. (MA Theol.). Ordained deacon, 2000, priest, 2001; Curate, Chertsey, 2000–04; Team Vicar, 2004–08, Team Rector, 2008–14, St Peter, Papworth; Bishop's Advr on Women's Ministry, Dio. of Ely, 2012–14. Hon. Canon, Ely Cathedral, 2012–14. Member: Gen. Synod of C of E, 2015–; Archdeacons' Nat. Forum, 2016–. Address: 20 Langley Lane, Ifield, Crawley, W Sussex RH14 0NA.

**WINDSOR, Michael John;** Headmaster, Abingdon School, since 2016; b Bristol, 25 May 1969; s of Geoffrey and Ursula Windsor; m 1997, Shanti Charles; two d. Educ: Bristol Cathedral Sch.; Durham Univ. (BA Hons German with French); Inst. of Educn, Univ. of London (PGCE); Birkbeck Coll., Univ. of London (MA Modern German Studies). TEFL teacher, British Sch., Bologna, 1992–96; teacher of modern langs, King's Coll. Sch., 1996–2003; Dep. Hd, Royal GS, Guildford, 2003–08; Headmaster, Reading Blue Coat Sch., 2008–16. Recreations: double bass (jazz, classical), running, swimming, cycling, 20th century German literature, travel. Address: Abingdon School, Park Road, Abingdon, Oxon OX14 1DE. T: (01235) 521563. E: heads.pa@abingdon.org.uk.

**WINDSOR-CLIVE,** family name of **Earl of Plymouth.**

**WINEGARTEN, Jonathan Isaac;** Chief Master of the Senior (formerly Supreme) Court, Chancery Division, 1998–2013 (a Master, 1991–2013); b 10 Dec. 1944; s of late Moshe Winegarten and Hannah Deborah Winegarten (née Cohen). Educ: Hasmonean Grammar Sch., Hendon (Head Boy); Gateshead Yeshiva; University Coll. London (LLB Hons 1967); Slabodka Yeshiva, Israel. Chm., Yavneh, 1966. Winston Churchill Award and called to the Bar, Middle Temple, 1969, ad eundem Lincoln's Inn, 1972 (Bencher, 1990); in practice, Chancery Bar, 1970–91. Accredited Civil and Commercial Mediator, ADR Gp, 2014. Member: Chancery Bar Assoc. Cttee, 1982, 1983; Supreme Court Procedure Cttee, 1992–2000; Judges' Council of England and Wales, 2008–12; Non-Contentious Probate Rules Cttee, 2009–; Adv. Panel, Chancery Modernisation Review, 2013. Member: Bd of Deputies, 1973–79; Council, Jews' Coll., 1989–2000; Elder, Fedn of Synagogues, 2015– (Vice Pres., 1989–2001). Pres., Shomrei Hadath Synagogue, 1982–2003 (Hon. Life Pres., 2004). Hon. Mem., The Institute, 2018. Freeman, City of London, 1992. Adv. Editor, Atkin's Court Forms, 1993–2015; Editor: Tristram and Coote's Probate Practice, 1995–2013; Civil Procedure (The White Book), 1999–2013. Publications: (ed) Collected works of Rabbi Z. H. Ferber (11 vols), 1983–92; (jtly) Modernising the Civil Courts: the judges' requirements, 2001. Recreations: violin playing, painting, esp. glass painting and etching, music, reading, publishing. Address: Radcliffe Chambers, 11 New Square, Lincoln's Inn, WC2A 3QB. E: clerks@radcliffechambers.com.

**WINELAND, Dr David J.;** Knight Research Professor, Department of Physics, University of Oregon, since 2018; b Milwaukee, Wisconsin, 24 Feb. 1944; m Sedna Quimby; two s. Educ: Encina High Sch., Sacramento; Univ. of California, Berkeley (BA 1965); Harvard Univ. (PhD Physics 1970). Res. Associate, Univ. of Washington, 1970–75; National Bureau of Standards, subseq. National Institute of Standards and Technology: physicist, Time and Frequency Div., 1975–2017; Project Leader, Ion Storage Gp, 1979–2017; Fellow, 1995–2017; Lectr, then Adjunct Prof., Dept of Physics, Univ. of Colorado, 2000–. Mem., NAS, 1992. Davisson-Germer Prize, 1990, Arthur L. Schawlow Prize in Laser Sci., 2001, Amer. Physical Soc.; Einstein Medal for Laser Sci., Soc. of Optical and Quantum Electronics, 1996; Frederick Ives Medal, Optical Soc. of America, 2004; Nat. Medal of Science (USA), 2007; (jtly) Benjamin Franklin Medal in Physics, Franklin Inst., 2010; (jtly) Nobel Prize in Physics, 2012. Publications: contribs to scientific jls, incl. Science, Nature, Physical Rev. Letters. Address: Department of Physics, 1274 University of Oregon, Eugene, OR 97403-1274, USA.

**WINEMAN, Vivian;** President, Board of Deputies of British Jews, 2009–15; Chairman, Mildmay Properties Ltd, since 2010; b London, 14 Feb. 1950; s of Joseph and Devorah Wineman; m 1994, Naomi Helen Greenberg; one s two d. Educ: City of London Sch.; Kerem B'Yavneh Rabbinical Acad.; Gonville and Caius Coll., Cambridge (BA 1971; MA 1975); University Coll. London (MA 2018). Admitted solicitor, 1975; Articled clerk, 1973–75, Asst Solicitor, 1975–77, Berwin Leighton; Solicitor, 1977–78, Partner, 1978–81, Clintons; Founder Partner, David Wineman, 1981–2008; DWFM Beckman Solicitors: Partner, 2008–10; Consultant, 2010–11. Sen. Vice Pres., Bd of Deputies of British Jews, 2006–09 (Chm., Defence and Gp Relations Div., 2006–09); Vice Pres., Eur. Jewish Congress, 2009–12 (Chair Council, 2012–16); Chair, Council of Members, Jewish Leadership Council, 2009–15. Vice Chair, 2007–13, Co-Chair, 2013–16, Inter Faith Network for UK; Mem., Adv. Bd, Three Faiths Forum, 2007–. Chairman: British Friends Peace Now, 1987–89; New Israel Fund UK, 1993–95. Dir, Conference for Jewish Material Claims against Germany, 2012–15 (Mem., Goodwill Guidelines Cttee, 2011–13; Mem., Governance Panel, 2014–15); Mem. Adv. Bd, Next Century Foundn, 2016–. Pres., Inst. Polish Jewish Studies, 2016–. Vice Pres., World Jewish Congress, 2013–15. Trustee: Holocaust Meml Day Trust, 2011–17; Council of Christians and Jews, 2015–; Next Century Foundn, 2018–; Patron: Norwood, 2018–; Kisharon, 2018–. Hon. Legal Counsel, High Premium Gp of Lloyds of London, 2004–. Kt (1st Cl.) Constantinian Order of King Francis 1, 2012. Publications: Contracts (Rights of Third Parties) Act 1999, 2001. Recreations: music, cycling, mountain walking. Address: 76 Meadway, NW11 6QH. Club: Royal Automobile.

**WINFIELD, Rev. Canon Flora Jane Louise;** DL; Archbishop of Canterbury's Special Representative to the Commonwealth, since 2017; m 1985, Ven. Jonathan Robin Blanning Gough, qv. Educ: Portsmouth High Sch. for Girls, GPDST; St David's Univ. Coll., Lampeter (BA Hons 1985); Ripon Coll., Cuddesdon, Oxford (Cert. Theol. 1989); Westminster Coll., Oxford (Dip. Applied Theol. 1996). Lay Worker, Christ Church Abbeydale, Glos, 1986–87; ordained deacon, 1989, priest, 1994; Parish Deacon, Stantonbury and Willen Ecumenical Parish, Milton Keynes, 1989–92; County Ecumenical Officer, Glos, 1992–94; Chaplain and Tutor, Mansfield Coll., Oxford, 1994–97; Sec. for Local Unity, and Advr to House of Bishops, C of E Archbishop's Council, 1997–2002; Canon Residentiary, Winchester Cathedral, 2002–05, now Canon Emerita; Asst Sec. Gen., 2005–06, Special Advr, 2006–, World Conference of Religions for Peace; Archbishop of Canterbury's Sec. for Anglican Relns, 2007–14; Priest-in-charge, St Mary-at-Hill, City of London, 2008–14; Anglican Communion Perm. Rep. to UN, Geneva, 2014–17. Hon. Chaplain, St Ethelburga's Centre for Reconciliation and Peace, 2008–13 (Special Advr, 2005–08); Sec. for Internat. Affairs, Churches Together in Britain and Ireland, 2006–09. Mem., Faith and Order Adv. Gp, C of E, 1991–2005. Chaplain: to HM Forces (V), 1997–; to Farriers' Co., 2004–; to Princess Royal's Volunteer Corps, 2007–. Trustee: St Andrew's Trust, 2003–; Community of St Mary the Virgin, Wantage, 2013–16. Gov., Sch. of St Helen and St Katharine, Abingdon, 1993–2009. FRSA 1998. DL Gtr London, 2011. Hon. DD Virginia Theol Seminary, 2010. Dame, Order of Francis (First Class). Publications: (with Elizabeth Welch) Travelling Together: a handbook on local ecumenical partnerships, 1995; Releasing Energy: how Methodists and Anglicans can grow together, 2000; Growing Together: working for unity locally, 2002; Working with Partner Churches in the Diocese: a handbook for new Bishops, 2002; It's the Thought that Counts in Unpacking the Gift: Anglican resources for theological reflection on the gift of authority, 2003; contributed to: European Women's Experience in the Church, 1991; Reconciliation in Religion and Society, 1994; Community, Unity, Communion: essays in honour of Mary Tanner, 1998; The Table of God's Generosity in Voices of this Calling: experiences of the first generation of woman priests, 2002; articles in Midstream, Ecumenical Review. Recreations: country pursuits, gardening, food, music. Club: Nikæan.

**WINFIELD, Susan Margaret,** OBE 2003; Lord-Lieutenant, Tyne and Wear, since 2015; b Sunderland, 18 May 1947; d of Richard Foster Heron and Margaret Marriott Heron; m 1974, Anthony Charles Winfield; one s one d. Educ: Central Newcastle High Sch.; Univ. of Newcastle upon Tyne (LLB 1968); Univ. of Nottingham (DipASS 1969). Durham Probation Service: Probation Officer, 1970–75; Sen. Probation Officer, 1975–82; Asst Chief Probation Officer, 1982–86; Northumbria Probation Service: Asst Chief Probation Officer, 1986–88; Dep. Chief Probation Officer and Dir of Service Delivery, 1988–2002; Chair, Sunderland Teaching PCT, 2002–13. Mem., Home Sec.'s Policy Adv. Cttee on Sexual Offences, 1976–86. Trustee and Manager, and Vice Chair, Bd of Managers, Aycliffe Young People's Centre, Darlington, 1988–2005. Trustee: Derwent Initiative, 1993–; Helix Arts, 2000–09; Community Foundn for Tyne and Wear and Northumberland, 2006–15 (Vice Pres., 2015–). High Sheriff Tyne and Wear, 2010–11. Publications: (contrib.) The Golden Age of Probation, 2014. Recreations: gardening, walking, singing, tennis, golf. Club: Northern Counties (Newcastle).

**WINFIELD, William Richard,** MA; Headmaster, Mill Hill School, 1995–2007; b 19 March 1947; s of William Arthur and Paula Constance Winfield; m 1986, Margaret Ruth Richards; one s one d. Educ: William Ellis Sch.; Royal Acad. of Music (Jun. Exhibnr); Clare Coll., Cambridge (BA Mod. and Med. Langs 1968; PGCE 1970; MA 1972). Lectr, Maison de l'Europe, Bordeaux, 1968–69; Mill Hill School: Asst Master, 1970–75; Head of Modern Langs, 1975–87; Dir of Studies, 1982–92; Dep. Headmaster, 1992–95. Chief Examr, French Studies, JMB, 1980–87. Publications: (jtly) Vocational French, 1985; contribs to jls on Section Bilingue and intensive language teaching. Recreations: chamber music, hill walking. Address: The Old School House, Church Road, Slapton, Leighton Buzzard LU7 9BX.

**WINGATE, Rev. Canon Andrew David Carlile,** OBE 2011; PhD; Director of Inter-Faith Relations (formerly Director of Ministry and Training and Bishop's Inter-Faith Adviser), Diocese of Leicester, 2000–10 (Co-ordinator of Lay Training, 2000–04); Director, St Philip's Centre for Study and Engagement in a Multifaith Society, Leicester, 2004–10; Canon Theologian of Leicester Cathedral, since 2000; Chaplain to the Queen, 2007–14; b 2 Aug. 1944; s of late Rev. Canon David Hugh Wingate and Olga Wingate; m 1967, Angela Beever; one s two d. Educ: Worcester Coll., Oxford (BA 1st class, MA, MPhil); Lincoln Theol Coll.; Univ. of Birmingham (PhD 1995). Asst Master, King Edward's Sch., Birmingham, 1968–70; ordained deacon, 1972, priest, 1973; Asst Curate, Halesowen Parish Church, 1972–75; Lectr, Tamil Nadu Theol Seminary, Madurai, S India, 1975–82; Principal: W Midlands Ministerial Training Course, Queen's Coll., Birmingham, 1982–90; United Coll. of the Ascension, Selly Oak, Birmingham, 1990–2000. Hon. Interfaith Advr, Dio. of Chichester, 2015–19, now Associate Interfaith Advr. Hon. Lectr in Theol., Univ. of Birmingham, 1998–2009; Hon. Lectr in Inter-Religious Relations, De Montfort Univ., 2009–. Hon. Fellow, Chichester Univ., 2016–. Hon. DArts De Montfort, 2007. Publications: Encounter in the Spirit: Muslim Christian dialogue in practice, 1988, 2nd edn 1991; The Church and Conversion, 1997; (ed) Anglicanism: a global communion, 1998; Does Theological Education Make a Difference?, 1999; Free to Be, 2002; Celebrating Difference: staying faithful – how to live in a multifaith world, 2005; (ed) Discipleship and

Dialogue: new frontiers in interfaith engagement, 2013; The Meeting of Opposites? Hindus and Christians in the West, 2014; (ed) Why Interfaith?: stories, challenges and reflections in Northern Europe, 2016; articles in theol jls. *Recreations:* tennis, swimming, golf, painting, mountain walking. *Address:* 25 Prince Charles Road, Lewes, E Sussex BN7 2HY.

**WINGFIELD**, family name of **Viscount Powerscourt**.

**WINGFIELD, Katrina Elizabeth;** Consultant, Bates Wells Braithwaite, since 2019; *b* Malvern, Worcs, 27 Jan. 1948; *d* of Frederick Wingfield and Elizabeth Wingfield; *m* 1983, Gareth Julian. *Educ:* Worcester Grammar Sch. for Girls; Univ. of Exeter (LLB). Admitted solicitor, 1974; Solicitor, 1974–77, Partner, 1977–2000, Walker Martineau Solicitors; Partner, 2000–13, Consultant, 2013–18, Penningtons Solicitors, then Penningtons Manches LLP. Tribunal Judge, Mental Health Tribunal, 1994–. Chair, Appeal Panel: Specialist Trng Authy of Royal Medical Colls, 1998–2005; PMETB, 2005–10; Dir, Appeals, GDC, 2004–; Chm., Registration and Certification Appeals, GMC, 2010–16. Chm., Regulatory Bd, Assoc. of Chartered Certified Accountants, 2008–14. *Recreations:* riding, swimming, sailing, walking the dog. *Address:* Bates Wells Braithwaite, 10 Queen Street Place, EC4R 1BE. *T:* (020) 7551 7777. *E:* k.wingfield@bwbllp.com.

**WINGHAM, Prof. Duncan John,** PhD; Executive Chair, Natural Environment Research Council, since 2018 (Chief Executive, 2012–18); *b* 12 Oct. 1957; *s* of Philip and Margaret Wingham; *m* 1987, Ivana Azanjac; one *d. Educ:* City of Bath Boys' Sch.; Univ. of Leeds (BSc Hons Phys 1979); Univ. of Bath (PhD 1985). Res. Seismologist, Seismograph Service Ltd, Kent, 1979–81; Res. Officer, Dept of Phys, Univ. of Bath, 1981–84; University College London: Res. Associate, Mullard Space Sci. Lab., 1985–86; Lectr, 1986–89, Sen. Lectr, 1989–93, Dept of Electronic and Electrical Engrg; Sen. Lectr, 1993–96, Prof. of Climate Phys, 1996–2005, Dept of Space and Climate Phys; Prof. and Hd, Dept of Earth Scis, 2005–12, now Hon. Prof.; Dir, NERC Centre for Polar Observation and Modelling, 2001–08. Lead Investigator, CryoSat, then CryoSat-2 Missions, ESA, 1999–2011. Chairman: Sci. and Innovation Bd, NERC, 2007–11; Steering Bd, UK Collaborative on Develt Scis, 2012–. *Publications:* articles in Nature, Science, Geophysical Res. Letters, Jl of Geophys Res., Jl of Glaciology, Earth & Planetary Sci. Letters, etc. *Address:* Natural Environment Research Council, Polaris House, North Star Avenue, Swindon SN2 1EU.

**WINKELMAN, Joseph William,** PPRE (RE 1982; ARE 1979); free-lance painter-printmaker, since 1971; President, Royal Society of Painter-Printmakers (formerly Royal Society of Painter-Etchers and Engravers), 1989–95; *b* 20 Sept. 1941; *s* of George William Winkelman and Cleo Lucretia (*née* Harness); *m* 1969, Harriet Lowell Belin; two *d. Educ:* Univ. of the South, Sewanee, Tenn (BA English 1964); Wharton School of Finance, Univ. of Pennsylvania; Ruskin Sch. of Drawing; Univ. of Oxford (Cert. of Fine Art 1971). Royal Society of Painter-Etchers and Engravers: Hon. Sec., 1982; Vice-Pres., 1986; Fellow, Printmakers' Council of GB, 1978 (Hon. Fellow, 1988). Former tutor for: Sch. of Architecture, Oxford Polytechnic; Ruskin Sch. of Drawing, Oxford Univ.; Dept for External Studies, Oxford Univ. Artist in Residence, St John's Coll., Oxford, 2004. Work in public collections including: BM; Tate Gall.; V&A; Mus. of London; Science Mus.; London Guildhall Liby; Royal Collection; Nat. Mus. of Wales; Ashmolean Mus., Oxford; Fitzwilliam Mus., Cambridge; Russian State Collection; Musée d'Art Contemporain, Chamalières; Lahti Museum, Finland; Iowa City Art Mus., USA; Bodleian Liby, Oxford; BL; L of C. Mem., Bd of Dirs, Bankside Gall., London, 2002–06. Chm., Oxford Art Soc., 1987–93 (Vice Pres., 1994–). Chm., Nat. Assoc. of Blood Donors, 1994–95. Gov., Windmill First Sch., Headington, Oxford, 1994–98. RBA, 1980–82; RWA, 1990–2006 (ARWA 1983). Hon. RWS 1997. *Publications:* (illustrated) Sewanee Poems, by Richard Tillinghast, 2010. *Recreations:* gardening, theatre, hill walking. *Address:* The Hermitage, 25 Old High Street, Headington, Oxford OX3 9HT. *T:* (01865) 762839. *E:* joe@winkelman.co.uk. *W:* www.winkelman.co.uk. *Club:* Oxford University Yacht.

**WINKETT, Rev. Lucy Clare;** Rector, St James's, Piccadilly, since 2010; *b* 8 Jan. 1968; *d* of Bryan and Cecilia Winkett. *Educ:* Dr Challoner's High Sch.; Selwyn Coll., Cambridge (BA (Hons) Hist. 1990); RCM (ARCM 1992); Queen's Coll., Birmingham (BD 1994). Ordained deacon, 1995, priest, 1996; Asst Curate, St Michael and All Angels, Manor Park, 1995–97; St Paul's Cathedral: Minor Canon, 1997–2003; Residentiary Canon and Precentor, 2003–10. Gov., Queen's Theological Foundn, Birmingham. Trustee, Nat. Churches Trust. Co-Founder, Leading Women. *Publications:* Our Sound is Our Wound, 2010. *Recreations:* reading, singing, cycling. *Address:* St James's Church, 197 Piccadilly, W1J 9LL. *T:* (020) 7734 4511.

**WINKLEMAN, Claudia;** television and radio presenter; Host, Sunday Night with Claudia Winkleman, BBC Radio 2, since 2016; *b* London, 15 Jan. 1972; *d* of Barry Winkleman and Eve Pollard, *qv*; *m* 2000, Kris Thykier; two *s* one *d. Educ:* City of London Sch. for Girls; New Hall, Cambridge (BA Hons Hist. of Art 1993). Television includes: host or presenter: Fanorama, 2001–02; Comic Relief Does Fame Academy, 2003–07; Strictly Come Dancing: It Takes Two, 2004–10; Hell's Kitchen, 2009; Let's Dance for Sport Relief, 2009–10; Strictly Come Dancing: The Results, 2010–; Film Show, 2010–16; The Great British Sewing Bee, 2013–; Strictly Come Dancing, 2014–; The Arts Show with Claudia Winkleman, BBC Radio 2, 2008–16; Britain's Best Home Cook, 2018. *Recreations:* sleeping, cuddling (and bothering) the children.

**WINKLEY, Sir David (Ross),** Kt 1999; DPhil; Founder and President, National Primary Trust, 1986–2006; *b* 30 Nov. 1941; *s* of late Donald Joseph Winkley and Winifred Mary Winkley; *m* 1967, Dr Linda Mary Holland; one *s* one *d. Educ:* King Edward's Sch., Birmingham; Selwyn Coll., Cambridge (MA); Wadham Coll., Oxford (DPhil 1975; Hon. Fellow 2006). Mem., Centre for Contemporary Cultural Studies, Univ. of Birmingham, 1965; Dep. Head, Perry Common Sch., 1968–71; Head, Grove Primary Sch., 1974–97. Fellow, Nuffield Coll., Oxford, 1981–82. Vis. Prof., Univ. of Huddersfield, 2003–; Hon. Professor: Univ. of Birmingham, 1999–; Univ. of Warwick, 2004–. Member: CATE, 1985–90; Stevenson Cttee on Information and Communication Technol., 1996. Founder and Chairman: Birmingham Children's Community Venture, 1967–; Health Exchange, 2008–; Founder, Children's Univ., 1992. DLitt Birmingham, 1999; DUniv UCE, 2000. *Publications:* Diplomats and Detectives, 1986; Handsworth Revolution, 2002; The Philosophy Group, 2010; Life Cycle, 2012; The Inspector, 2015; The Commission, 2018; numerous academic articles on educational and philosophical issues. *Recreations:* reading, music, piano playing, writing fiction.

**WINKWORTH-SMITH, (Michael) John;** mediator; Regional Managing Partner, Leeds Office, Dibb Lupton Alsop (formerly Dibb Lupton Broomhead), 1995–99; *b* 4 May 1944; *s* of late Frank Winkworth-Smith and Marjorie Beaumont Winkworth-Smith (*née* Smith); *m* 1974, Sarah Elisabeth Jackson; two *s* (one *d* decd). *Educ:* Ermysted's Grammar Sch., Skipton. Admitted solicitor, 1970; Partner, Broomhead Wightman & Reed, later Dibb Lupton Broomhead, then Dibb Lupton Alsop, 1972–99; Man. Partner, Birmingham Office, 1993–95. Treas., Royal Sheffield Instn for the Blind, 1972–78; Mem., Sheffield CVS, 1978–90; Dir, Broomgrove Trust, 1980–92; Chairman: Taptonholme Ltd, 1984–2000; Champion Hse, Derby Diocesan Youth Centre, 1988–93. Director: CEDR, 1991–99;

Japan Adv. Services Ltd, 1991–97; Consensus Mediation Ltd, 2004–11. Trustee, Sheffield Royal Soc. for the Blind, 2003–14. FRSA 1997. *Recreations:* family, farming, researching local history. *Address:* Churchdale Farm, Ashford-in-the-Water, Bakewell, Derbys DE45 1NX. *T:* (01629) 640912.

**WINN**, family name of **Baron St Oswald**.

**WINN, Allan Kendal,** FRAeS; Director, 2003–18, and Chief Executive Officer, 2015–18, Brooklands Museum; Vice-President, Brooklands Museum Trust, since 2018; *b* 19 March 1950; *s* of Atkinson Winn and Janet Winn; *m* 1994, Jacqueline Christina Worsley; one step *s* one step *d. Educ:* Nelson Coll., NZ; Univ. of Canterbury, Christchurch, NZ (BE(Mech), Diploma in Journalism). FRAeS 1996. Technical Editor, Consulting Engineer, 1975–77; Technical Editor, Editor, Man. Editor, Engineering Today, later New Technology, 1977–85; Editor: Commercial Motor, 1985–88; Flight International, 1989–98; Publisher, Flight International and Airline Business, 1998–2003. Chm., Assoc. of Friends of Brooklands Mus., 1995–2003. Mem. Heritage Wkg Gp, All Party Parly Gp on Aviation, 2019–. Mem. Exec. Cttee, Aviation Heritage UK, 2019–. Liveryman: Hon. Co. of Air Pilots (formerly GAPAN), 1999–; Coachmakers' and Coach Harness Makers' Co., 2008–. Sir Peter Masefield Gold Medal, British Assoc. Aviation Consultants, 2006; Jeffrey Quill Medal, The Air League, 2014. *Recreation:* vintage motor vehicles. *Address:* 39 Heathcote, Tadworth, Surrey KT20 5TH. *T:* (01737) 362760, 07979 516863. *Clubs:* Aviation of UK (Chm., 1991–97), Vintage Sports Car, Bentley Drivers.

**WINNICK, David Julian;** *b* Brighton, 26 June 1933; *s* of late Eugene and Rose Winnick; one *s*; *m* 1968, Bengi Rona (marr. diss.), *d* of Tarik and Zeynep Rona. *Educ:* secondary school; London Sch. of Economics (Dip. in Social Admin). Army National Service, 1951–53. Branch Secretary, Clerical and Administrative Workers' Union, 1956–62 (later APEX GMB; Mem. Exec. Council, 1978–88, Vice-Pres., 1983–88); Advertisement Manager, Tribune, 1963–66; employed by UKIAS, 1970–79 (Chm., 1984–90). Member: Willesden Borough Council, 1959–64; London Borough of Brent Council, 1964–66 (Chair, Children Cttee, 1965–66). Contested (Lab) Harwich, 1964; MP (Lab) Croydon S, 1966–70; contested (Lab): Croydon Central, Oct. 1974; Walsall N, Nov. 1976. MP (Lab) Walsall N, 1979–2017; contested (Lab) same seat, 2017. Member: Select Cttee on the Environment, 1979–83; Home Affairs Cttee, 1983–87, 1997–2017; Select Cttee on Procedure, 1989–97; Co-Chm., British-Irish Inter-Parly Body, 1997–2005 (Vice-Chm., 1993–97). *Recreations:* walking, cinema, theatre, reading. *Address:* 22 Mulgrave Road, NW10 1BT.

**WINNINGTON, Sir Anthony (Edward),** 7th Bt *cr* 1755, of Stanford Court, Worcestershire; *b* 13 May 1948; *s* of Col Thomas Foley Churchill Winnington, MBE and Lady Betty Marjorie Anson, *d* of 4th Earl of Lichfield; *S* uncle, 2003; *m* 1st, 1978, Karyn (marr. diss. 2007), *d* of F. H. Kettles; one *s* two *d*; 2nd, 2009, Alexandra Fawke, *d* of late Alexander B. MacColl. *Educ:* Eton. FCSI. High Sheriff, Worcs, 2015–16. *Heir: s* Edward Alan Winnington, *b* 15 Nov. 1987. *E:* winnington@aol.com. *Clubs:* Boodle's, Hurlingham.

**WINNINGTON-INGRAM, Edward John;** Managing Director, Mail Newspapers Plc (formerly Associated Newspapers Group), 1986–89, retired; *b* 20 April 1926; *s* of Rev. Preb. Edward Francis and Gladys Winnington-Ingram; *m* 1st, 1953, Shirley Lamotte (marr. diss. 1968); two *s*; 2nd, 1973, Elizabeth Linda Few Brown. *Educ:* Shrewsbury; Keble Coll., Oxford (BA). Served RN (Sub-Lieut), 1944–47. Joined Associated Newspapers, 1949; Circulation Manager, Daily Mail, 1960–65; Gen. Manager, Daily Mail Manchester, 1965–70; Dir, Associated Newspapers, 1971; Managing Director: Harmsworth Publishing, 1973; Mail on Sunday, 1982; Dir, Associated Newspapers Holdings, 1983; non-executive Director: NAAFI, 1987–93; Burlington Gp, 1988–92; Dir, Oxford Diocesan Pubns, 2000–08. Mem., Order of St Frideswide, 2009. *Recreations:* shooting, golf, Byzantine history, music, defending the 1662 Prayer Book. *Address:* Old Manor Farm, Cottisford, Brackley, Northants NN13 5SW. *T:* (01280) 848367. *Club:* Buck's (Chm., 1988–92).

**WINSER, Ellen;** *see* Winser, M. E.

**WINSER, Kim Lesley,** OBE 2006; Founder and Chief Executive Officer, Winser London Ltd, since 2012; *b* Helensburgh, 11 March 1959; *d* of Terence and Dorothy Haresign; one *s. Educ:* Purbrook Park Grammar Sch. Marks & Spencer plc: mgt trainee, 1978; Merchandiser, 1982–84; Merchandise Manager, 1984–89; Exec., Brooks Bros USA and Marks & Spencer Canada, 1989–93; Exec., UK Women's Casualwear, 1993–95; Dir, Womenswear, 1995–2000; President and Chief Executive Officer: Pringle of Scotland, 2000–06; Aquascutum, 2006–09; Chm., Agent Provocateur, 2009–11; Special Adviser: Net-A-Porter and French Sole, 2009–11; White Cloud Capital, 2010–; Advr, 3i, 2009–11. Ind. non-exec. Dir, Hongkong and Shanghai Hotels Ltd, 2016–. Contributor to Forbes, 2013–. Trustee, Natural Hist. Mus., 2013–. Hon. DLitt Heriot-Watt, 2002. *Recreations:* tennis, swimming, cars. *Address:* Winser London Ltd, 231 The Vale, Acton, W3 7QS. *T:* 0845 600 1521. *E:* emma@kimwinser.co.uk.

**WINSER, (Margaret) Ellen,** MBE 2012; Chair: Truro and Penwith College, since 2004; Truro & Penwith Academy Trust, since 2013; Vice Lord-Lieutenant for Cornwall, 2014–17; *b* London, 6 Sept. 1942; *d* of late Donald Blake Fraser, FRCS, FRCOG and Betsy Rose Fraser (*née* Henderson); *m* 1969, Thomas Ralph Winser (*d* 2014); two step *d* (one step *s* decd). *Educ:* Benenden Sch.; Girton Coll., Cambridge (BA 1964; MA 1972). James Capel & Co. (stockbrokers), 1967–90, Partner, 1973–90. Long distance sailing, 1990–95. Chairman: Liontrust Asset Mgt plc, 1996–2004; Sutton Harbour Hldgs plc, 1998–2007; Dir, Pendennis Shipyard Hldgs Ltd, 2004–09. Member: Objective One Cornwall Strategic Develt Gp, 2002–07; Bd, SW RDA, 2007–12. Mem. Council, Benenden Sch., 1972–2002. Gov., Univ. of Plymouth, 2005–10. Chm., Nat. Maritime Mus. Cornwall Trust, 2002–14; Dir/Trustee, Cornwall Care, 1997–2005; Trustee, Cornwall Air Ambulance Trust, 2015–. *Address:* Cuby House, Tregony, Cornwall TR2 5TN. *T:* (01872) 530117. *E:* ellen@cubyhouse.com.

**WINSHIP, Sir Peter (James Joseph),** Kt 2004; CBE 1998; QPM 1990; HM Inspector of Constabulary, 1995–2005; *b* 21 July 1943; *s* of late Francis Edward Winship and Iris May (*née* Adams); *m* 1st, 1963, Carol Ann McNaughton; two *s* one *d*; 2nd, 1989, Janet Mary Bird; one *d. Educ:* Bicester Grammar Sch.; St John's Coll., Oxford (BA Eng. Lang. and Lit.; MA). Oxfordshire Constabulary, 1962; Sergeant to Supt, Thames Valley Police, 1968–79; Graduate, FBI Acad., 1980; Chief Supt, Metropolitan Police, 1982; Asst Chief Constable, Thames Valley Police, 1984; Metropolitan Police: Dep. Asst Comr, Policy & Planning, 1987, No 1 Area HQ, 1988; Asst Comr, 1989–95; Management Support and Strategy Dept, 1989–91; Inspection and Review Dept, 1992–95. Dir, Police Extended Interviews, 1993–95. Chm., Technical and Res. Cttee, ACPO, 1992–95. Member: Exec. Council, London Fedn of Boys' Clubs, 1988–95; Exec. Cttee, Royal Humane Soc., 1989–95; Governing Bd, Revolving Doors Agency, 1993–95. Trustee, Police Rehabilitation Trust, 2002–. FCMI. *Publications:* articles in police jls and other periodicals on professionally related subjects, travel, and treatment of police in literature; essay on delinquency and social policy (Queen's Police Gold Medal, Essay Competition, 1969). *Recreations:* reading, gardening, music.

**WINSHIP, Sionaidh;** *see* Douglas-Scott, S.

**WINSKEL, Prof. Glynn**, ScD, PhD; Professor of Computer Science, University of Cambridge, since 2000; Fellow, Emmanuel College, Cambridge, since 2000; b 23 May 1953; s of Thomas Francis Winskel and Helen Juanita Winskel (née McCall); m 1982, Kirsten Krog Jensen; two d. Educ: Emmanuel Coll., Cambridge (BA, MA Maths, ScD Computer Sci. 1995); St Catherine's Coll., Oxford (MSc Maths); Univ. of Edinburgh (PhD Computer Sci. 1980). Res. Scientist, Carnegie-Mellon Univ., Pittsburgh, 1982–83; University of Cambridge: Lectr in Computer Sci., 1984–87; Reader, 1987–88; Fellow, King's Coll., 1985–88; Prof. of Computer Sci., 1988–2000, Dir, Basic Res. in Computer Sci., 1994–2000, Aarhus Univ., Denmark. Royal Soc. Leverhulme Sen. Res. Fellow, 2010–11. MAE 2011. Ed., Jl of Mathematical Structures in Computer Science. *Publications:* Formal Semantics of Programming Languages: an introduction, 1993; (contrib.) Handbook of Logic in Computer Science, 1994. *Recreations:* music, art, running, swimming. *Address:* University of Cambridge, Computer Laboratory, 15 JJ Thomson Avenue, Cambridge CB3 0FD.

**WINSLET, Kate Elizabeth**, CBE 2012; actress; b 5 Oct. 1975; d of Roger and late Sally Winslet; m 1st, 1998, Jim Threapleton (marr. diss. 2001); one d; 2nd, 2003, Samuel Alexander Mendes, qv (marr. diss. 2010); one s; 3rd, 2012, Ned Abel Smith (formerly Rocknroll); one s. Educ: Theatre Sch., Maidenhead. *Films include:* Heavenly Creatures, 1995; Sense and Sensibility (Best Supporting Actress, BAFTA), Jude, 1996; Hamlet, 1997; Titanic, 1998; Hideous Kinky, 1999; Holy Smoke, 2000; Quills, Enigma, 2001; Iris, 2002; The Life of David Gale, 2003; Eternal Sunshine of the Spotless Mind, Finding Neverland, 2004; Romance & Cigarettes, All the King's Men, Little Children, The Holiday, 2006; The Reader (Best Actress, Academy Awards and BAFTA; Best Supporting Actress, Golden Globe Awards), Revolutionary Road (Best Actress, Golden Globe Awards), 2009; Contagion, 2011; Carnage, 2012; Labor Day, 2013; Divergent, 2014; Insurgent, A Little Chaos, The Dressmaker, Steve Jobs (Best Supporting Actress, Golden Globe Awards and BAFTA), 2015; Triple 9, 2016; Collateral Beauty, 2017; The Mountain Between Us, 2017; Wonder Wheel, 2018; *television includes:* Mildred Pierce, 2011 (Best Actress, Emmy Awards, 2011; Best Actress, Golden Globe Awards, 2012). *Address:* c/o United Agents, 12–26 Lexington Street, W1F 0LE. *T:* (020) 3214 0800, *Fax:* (020) 3214 0801.

**WINSLOW, Peter Anthony**, CBE 2012; FCA; Executive Chairman, BGL Group, 2013–18 (Group Chief Executive, 1995–2013); Special Adviser to Board, BHL, since 2019; b London, 9 Feb. 1953; s of William Winslow and Babette Winslow; m 1977, Janet Young; one s one d. Educ: Uppingham Sch. FCA 1978. Chief Exec., HarperCollins UK, 1990–94. Non-exec. Dir, St Andrew's Healthcare, 1998– (Chm., 2014–19). *Recreations:* tennis, skiing, restaurants.

**WINSOR, Sir Thomas (Philip)**, Kt 2015; HM Chief Inspector: of Constabulary, since 2012; of Fire & Rescue Services, since 2017; b 7 Dec. 1957; twin s of late Thomas Valentine Marrs Winsor and Phyllis Margaret Winsor (née Bonsor); m 1989, Sonya Elizabeth Field (marr. diss. 2012); two d. Educ: Grove Acad., Broughty Ferry; Univ. of Edinburgh (LLB Scots Law 1979); Univ. of Dundee (Postgrad. Dip. Petroleum Law 1983). Admitted solicitor, 1981, NP 1981, WS 1984, Scotland; admitted solicitor, England and Wales, 1991; in general practice, Dundee, 1981–83; Assistant Solicitor: Dundas & Wilson, CS, 1983–84; Norton Rose, 1984–91; Partner, Denton Hall, 1991–99; Chief Legal Advr and Gen. Counsel, Office of Rail Regulator, 1993–95; Rail Regulator and Internat. Rail Regulator, 1999–2004; Partner, White & Case LLP, 2004–12. Hon. Lectr, Centre for Energy, Petroleum and Mineral Law and Policy, Univ. of Dundee, 1993–. Member: Law Soc. of Scotland, 1981–; Internat. Bar Assoc., 1983–; Univ. of Dundee Petroleum and Mineral Law Soc., 1987– (Pres., 1987–89); Soc. of Scottish Lawyers in London, 1987– (Pres., 1987–89); Law Soc. of England and Wales, 1991–. Ind. Review of Police Officer and Staff Remuneration and Conditions for Home Sec., 2010–12. Consulting Ed., Vol. 37 (Railways), Halsbury's Laws of England, 2007–. *Publications:* (with M. P. G. Taylor) Taylor and Winsor on Joint Operating Agreements, 1989; contrib. Legal Lines, The Right Side of the Tracks, articles in Modern Railways mag., 1996–99, 2005–09; contrib. articles in newspapers, books and learned jls on oil and gas, electricity, railways law and regulation, policing. *Recreations:* family, literature, theatre, opera, music, cycling, politics, Scottish constitutional history, law, works of Robert Burns. *Address:* HM Inspectorate of Constabulary and Fire & Rescue Services, 6th Floor, Globe House, 89 Eccleston Square, SW1V 1PN.

**WINSTANLEY, Rt Rev. Alan Leslie**; Team Rector, Shirwell, Exeter, 2012–14; an Honorary Assistant Bishop: Diocese of Exeter, 2012–14; Diocese of Chester, since 2015; b 7 May 1949; s of John Leslie Winstanley and Eva Winstanley; m 1st, 1972, Vivien Mary Parkinson (d 2013); one s one d (and one s decd); 2nd, 2014, Janet Elizabeth Bowyer. Educ: St John's College, Nottingham (BTh, ALCD). Ordained deacon 1972, priest 1973, Blackburn; Curate: St Andrew's, Livesey, Blackburn, 1972–75; St Mary's, Great Sankey, dio. Liverpool, with responsibility for St Paul's, Penketh, 1975–77; Vicar of Penketh, 1978–81; SAMS Missionary in Peru: Lima, 1981–85; Arequipa, 1986–87; Bishop of Peru and Bolivia, 1988–93; Vicar of Eastham, and Hon. Asst Bp, Dio. of Chester, 1994–2003; Vicar of Whittle-le-Woods, and Hon. Asst Bp, Dio. of Blackburn, 2003–12. *Recreations:* vintage aircraft, caravanning, steam locomotives. *Address:* 11 Thorneycroft Way, Crewe CW1 4FZ.

**WINSTANLEY, Charles Jeffery**, TD 1990; JP; DL; DBA; Chairman, NHS Lothian, 2007–13; b London, 6 March 1952; s of late Jeffery and Elisabeth Winstanley; m 1987, Columbine Hobart (marr. diss. 2009); one s one d; m 2018, Gillian Findlay, one step s one step d. Educ: Wellington Coll.; RMA Sandhurst; Henley Management Coll. (MBA 1992; DBA 1997). Lieutenant, 16th/5th Lancers, 1970–76; Major, Royal Yeomanry, 1977–95. Chm., Fitness to Practise Panel, GMC, 2000–07; Member: Nat. Consumer Council for Postal Services, 2002–08; Asylum and Immigration Tribunal, 2003–; Audit Cttee, UK Supreme Court, 2011–. Chm., Adv. Military Sub-Cttee, Honours and Decorations Cttee, Cabinet Office, 2018–. Non-executive Director: Norfolk and Norwich Univ. Hosp. NHS Trust, 1999–2006; MoD, 2010–14; Scottish Govt, 2010–13; Chairman: Norfolk Probation Bd, 2001–06; Edinburgh Leisure, 2010–15; Scottish Police Pension Bd, 2015–18; Contact Gp, 2018–. Chm. Bd, Acad. of Med. Royal Colls, 2016–. Mem., Scottish Adv. Cttee on Distinction Awards, 2008–11. Mem. Council, Erskine, 2012–. JP Thames and Central Norfolk, 1993–2006, supplementary list, 2006–; DL Gtr London, 1997. *Recreations:* motorcycling, sailing, fly fishing, oil painting. *E:* cjwinstanley@aol.com.

**WINSTANLEY, Prof. Peter Andrew**, MD; FRCP; Director of Strategic Projects, Liverpool School of Tropical Medicine, since 2016; b Liverpool, 26 May 1956; s of Reginald Joseph and Jessie Patricia Winstanley; m 1984, Maria Therese Roberts; two s one d. Educ: St Mary's Coll., Crosby; Liverpool Med. Sch., Univ. of Liverpool (MB ChB Hons 1979; MD 1989). DTM&H 1988; FRCP 1997. Tutor in Medicine, Univ. of Leeds, 1982–83; Lectr in Clin. Pharmacol., Univ. of Liverpool, 1983–89; MRC Res. Fellow, Nuffield Dept of Medicine, Univ. of Oxford, 1989–92; University of Liverpool: Prof. of Clin. Pharmacol., 1992–2007; Hd, Sch. of Clin. Scis, 2007–10; University of Warwick: Dean of Medicine, 2010–15; Chair, Faculty of Medicine, 2010–16. *Publications:* (with S. Constable) Medical Pharmacology, 1996, 8th edn 2007. *Recreation:* Roman history. *Address:* 105 Druids Cross Road, Liverpool L18 3HN.

**WINSTANLEY, Col Richard Dirdoe**, OBE 2007; Clerk to Worshipful Company of Drapers, since 2013; b London, 28 May 1964; s of John Winstanley, MC, TD and Jane Winstanley; m 1989, Caroline Jane Grey Edwards; one s one d. Educ: Wellington Coll.; RMA Sandhurst. Commnd Grenadier Guards, 1984; served 2nd Bn in Belize and NI, 1985–87; Anti-tank Platoon Comdr, 1st Bn, 1988–91; Adjt, 2nd Bn, 1991–93; Comdr, 1st Bn, 1993–95; Guards Co. Comdr, Army Trng Regt, Pirbright, 1995; Staff Coll., 1996; GSO, HQ UK Support Comd, Germany, 1997–99; Co. Comdr, 1st Bn, 1999–2001; Acad. Adjt, RMA Sandhurst, 2001–03; Mil. Asst to COS, HQ ISAF, 2003–04; GSO, HQ Theatre Troops, 2004–05; CO, Support Bn, Allied Rapid Reaction Force, 2005–07; i/c Army's Lesson Learned Cell, Warminster, 2007–08; i/c officer career mgt for Infantry, Armoured Corps and AAC, 2008–10; resp. for personnel mgt and regtl issues for infantry, 2010–12. *Recreations:* fishing, cycling, mahjong, gardening, shooting. *Address:* Drapers' Company, Drapers' Hall, Throgmorton Avenue, EC2N 2DQ. *E:* rwinstanley@thedrapers.co.uk. *Club:* Flyfishers'.

**WINSTANLEY, His Honour Robert James**; a Circuit Judge, 1996–2016; a Deputy Circuit Judge since 2016; b 4 Nov. 1948; s of late Morgan James Winstanley and Joan Martha Winstanley; m 1972, Josephine Langhorne; two s. Educ: St Catharine's Coll., Cambridge (MA 1970). Admitted Solicitor, 1973; Asst Solicitor, Dawson & Co., 1973–75; Partner, Winstanley-Burgess, Solicitors, 1975–96. Mem. Council, Law Soc., 1985–96. *Recreations:* golf, cricket, bridge. *Clubs:* MCC; Sudbury Golf.

**WINSTON**, family name of **Baron Winston**.

**WINSTON**, Baron cr 1995 (Life Peer), of Hammersmith in the London Borough of Hammersmith and Fulham; **Robert Maurice Lipson Winston**; Professor of Science and Society, Imperial College London, since 2008; Professor of Fertility Studies, University of London at Imperial College School of Medicine (formerly at the Institute of Obstetrics and Gynaecology, Royal Postgraduate Medical School), 1987–2005, now Professor Emeritus; formerly Consultant Obstetrician and Gynaecologist, Hammersmith Hospital; Director of NHS Research and Development, Hammersmith Hospitals NHS Trust, 1998–2005; b 15 July 1940; s of late Laurence Winston and Ruth Winston-Fox, MBE; m 1973, Lira Helen Feigenbaum; two s one d. Educ: St Paul's Sch., London; London Hosp. Med. Coll., London Univ. (MB, BS 1964). MRCS, LRCP 1964; FRCOG 1983 (MRCOG 1971); FRCP 2002. Jun. posts, London Hosp., 1964–66; Registrar and Sen. Registrar, Hammersmith Hosp., 1970–74; Wellcome Res. Sen. Lectr, Inst. of Obs and Gyn., 1974–78; Sen. Lectr, Hammersmith Hosp., 1978–81; Reader in Fertility Studies, RPMS, 1982–86. Vis. Prof., Univ. of Leuven, Belgium, 1976–77; Prof. of Gyn., Univ. of Texas at San Antonio, 1980–81; Clyman Vis. Prof., Mt Sinai Hosp., New York, 1985. Member, Steering Cttee, WHO: on Tubal Occlusion, 1975–77; on Ovum Transport, 1977–78; Mem., EPSRC, 2007–13 (Chm., Societal Issues Panel, 2007–13). Pres., Internat. Fallopius Soc., 1987–88. Mem. Council, Cancer Res. UK (formerly ICRF), 1998–2004. Vice Pres., Progress (all-party parly campaign for res. into human reprodn), 1992 (Chm., 1988–91). Mem. Bd, POST, 1998– (Vice-Chm., 2014–); Mem., Select Cttee on Sci. and Technol., H of L, 1997–2001 (Chm., 1998–2001), 2003–06 and 2010–; Mem., Scottish Science Adv. Council, 2010–. Founder Mem., British Fertility Soc., 1975–; Mem. Bd, Internat. Soc. for Stem Cell Res., 2004–; Pres., BAAS, 2004–05; Co-Chm., British-Israel Sci. Council 2017–. Dir, Atazoa Ltd, 2004–. Hon. Member: Georgian Obs Soc., 1983–; Pacific Fertility Soc., 1983–; Spanish Fertility Soc., 1985–; Israel Fertility Soc., 1990–. Mem. Council, RPMS, 1992–97; Vice-Pres., Royal Coll. of Music, 2017– (Chm. Council, 2008–17). Chancellor, Sheffield Hallam Univ., 2001–17; Mem. Council, Univ. of Surrey, 2008–12. Chm., Genesis Res. Trust, 2010–; Trustee: UK Stem Cell Foundn, 2010–; Royal Institution, 2012–18. Presenter, BBC TV: Your Life in their Hands, 1979–87; The Human Body, 1998; The Secret Life of Twins, 1999; A Child of Our Time, 2000–; Superhuman, 2000; Threads of Life, BBC TV, 2001; Human Instinct, BBC TV, 2002; Walking with Cavemen, 2003; The Human Mind, 2003; Frankenstein: birth of a monster, 2003; The Story of God, 2005; Child Against All Odds, 2006; Super Doctors, 2008; Frontiers of Medicine, 2008; presenter, Robert Winston's Musical Analysis, Science and Music, BBC Radio 4. Member, Editorial Board: Internat. Jl of Microsurgery, 1981–; Clinical Reproduction and Fertility, 1985–. Founder FMedSci 1998; FCGI 2011. Hon. Fellow: QMW, 1996; Inst. of Educn. Hon. FRCSE 2006; Hon. FIBiol 2006; Hon. FRCPSGlas, 2007; Hon. FREng, 2008; Hon. Fellow: Clinical Genetics Soc., 2013; Endocrine Soc., 2013. Hon. DSc: Cranfield, 2001; UMIST, 2001; Oxford Brookes, 2001; Strathclyde, 2002; St Andrews, 2002; Salford, 2003; Middlesex, 2003; Sunderland, 2003; Exeter, 2004; Southampton Inst., 2004; QUB, 2005; TCD, 2005; East Anglia, 2006; Auckland, 2008; De Montfort, 2008; Lincoln, 2009; Aberdeen, 2010; Loughborough, 2011; Surrey, 2011; Hon. Dr: Lancaster, 2005; Open, 2014; Birmingham City, 2015; Weizmann Inst., 2015. Chief Rabbinate Award for Contribn to Society, 1992–93; Victor Bonney Prize, RCS, 1991–93; Cedric Carter Medal, Clinical Genetics Soc., 1993; Michael Faraday Gold Medal, Royal Soc., 1999; Gold Medal, RSH, 1999; Gold Medal for Medicine in the Media, BMA, 1999; Wellcome Award for Sci. in the Media, 2001; Edwin Stevens Gold Medal, RSocMed, 2003; Viewers' and Listeners' Award for Best Individual Contrib. to Television, 2003; Maitland Medal, Inst. of Engineers, 2004; Gold Medal, N of England Zool Soc., 2004; Al-Hammadi Medal, RCSE, 2007; Peer of the Year, H of L, 2008. *Publications:* Reversibility of Sterilization, 1978; (jtly) Tubal Infertility, 1981; Infertility, a Sympathetic Approach, 1987; Getting Pregnant, 1990; The IVF Revolution, 2000; (jtly) Superhuman: the awesome power within, 2000; Human Instinct, 2002; The Human Mind, 2003; What Makes Me Me, 2004 (Aventis Prize, Royal Soc.); The Story of God, 2005; Child Against All Odds, 2006; It's Elementary, 2008; Evolution Revolution from Darwin to DNA, 2009; Bad Ideas?: an arresting history of our inventions, 2010; What Goes On in My Head, 2010; Science Experiments, 2011 (Young Peoples' Science Book Prize, Royal Soc.); Science Year by Year, 2013; That's Life, 2013; Utterly Amazing Science, 2014 (Young Peoples' Sci. Book Prize, Royal Soc.); Utterly Amazing Body, 2015; The Essential Fertility Guide, 2015; Home Lab: exciting experiments for budding scientists, 2016 (Young Peoples' Sci. Book Prize, Royal Soc.); Help Your Kids with Growing Up, 2017; My Amazing Body Machine, 2017; Science Squad, 2018; Ask a Scientist, 2019; scientific pubns on human and experimental reproduction. *Recreations:* theatre (directed award-winning Pirandello production, Each in his Own Way, Edinburgh Fest., 1969), festering, music, wine. *Address:* 11 Denman Drive, NW11 6RE. *T:* (020) 8455 7475. *Clubs:* Athenæum, Garrick, MCC.

**WINSTON, Prof. Brian Norman**, PhD; The Lincoln Professor, College of the Arts, University of Lincoln, since 2007 (Dean, Faculty of Media and Humanities, 2002–05; Pro-Vice-Chancellor, 2005–07); b 7 Nov. 1941; s of Reuben and Anita Winston; m 1978, Adèle Paul; one s one d. Educ: Kilburn Grammar Sch.; Merton Coll., Oxford (BA Laws; MA); Univ. of Lincoln (PhD 2007). Researcher, 1963–66, Prod. and Dir, 1963–66, 1969–71, Granada TV; Prod. and Dir, BBC TV, 1966–69; Lectr, Bradford Coll. of Art, 1972–73; Head of Gen. Studies, Nat. Film Sch., 1973–79; Res. Dir, Dept of Sociology, Glasgow Univ., 1974–76; Vis. Prof., 1976–77, Prof., 1979–86, Sch. of the Arts, NY Univ.; writer, WNET-TV, NY, 1984–85; Dean, Coll. of Communications, Pennsylvania State Univ., 1986–92; Dir, Centre for Journalism Studies, UWCC, then Univ. of Wales, Cardiff, 1992–97; Hd, Dept of Communication, Media and Design, then Sch. of Communication and Creative Industries, Westminster Univ., 1997–2002. Guest Prof., Beijing Normal

Univ., 2013–. Gov., BFI, 1995–2001. Emmy Award for documentary script writing, 1985. *Publications:* Dangling Conversations, vol. 1, the image of the media, 1973, vol. 2, hardware/software, 1974; (jtly) Bad News, 1976; (jtly) More Bad News, 1980; Misunderstanding Media, 1986; (jtly) Working with Video, 1986; Claiming the Real, 1995, rev. edn as Claiming the Real II, 2008; Technologies of Seeing, 1996; Media, Technology and Society: a history, 1998; Fires Were Started, 1999; Lies, Damn Lies and Documentaries, 2000; Messages, 2005; A Right to Offend, 2012 (Internat. Book Award on Human Rights, Vienna, 2013); (ed and contrib.) The BFI Documentary Film Book, 2013; The Rushdie Fatwa and After: a lesson to the circumspect, 2014; The Act of Documenting: documenting in the 21st century, 2017. *Recreations:* cooking, theatre. *Address:* 24a Minster Yard, Lincoln LN2 1PY; University of Lincoln, Brayford Pool, Lincoln LN6 7TS.

**WINSTONE, Norma Ann,** MBE 2007; jazz singer, since 1965; *b* Bow, E London, 23 Sept. 1941; *née* Norma Ann Short; *d* of Walter Short and Doris Short (*née* Ince, later Clark); *m* 1st, 1962, Ted Humphrey (marr. diss. 1972); 2nd, 1972, John Taylor (marr. diss. 1988; he *d* 2015); two *s*; 3rd, 2016, Hugh Mitchell. *Educ:* County High Sch., Dagenham. Recording artist, 1979–. Hon. Fellow, Trinity Laban Conservatoire of Music and Dance, 2010; Hon. Mem., RAM, 2013. *Recreations:* gardening, walking, family, cinema, music. *Address:* Tideway, 8 Wellington Parade, Walmer, Deal, Kent CT14 8AA. *T:* (01304) 367840. *E:* winstone.norma@gmail.com.

**WINTER, Rev. Canon David Brian;** Team Minister, Hermitage Team Ministry, 1995–2000; Hon. Canon, Christ Church Cathedral, Oxford, 1995–2000, now Canon Emeritus; *b* 19 Nov. 1929; *s* of Walter George Winter and Winifred Ella Winter; *m* 1st, 1961, Christine Ellen Martin (*d* 2001); two *s* one *d*; 2nd, 2004, Rosalind Anne Lee. *Educ:* Machynlleth County Sch.; Trinity County Grammar Sch., Wood Green; King's Coll., Univ. of London (BA, PGCE). Nat. Service, RAF, 1948–50. Teacher: Ware CE Secondary Sch., 1954–58; Tottenham County Grammar Sch., 1958–59; Editor, Crusade, 1959–70; freelance writer and broadcaster, 1970–71; BBC: Producer, Religious Broadcasting, 1971–75, Sen. Producer, 1975–82; Hd of Religious Progs, Radio, and Dep. Hd, Religious Broadcasting, 1982–87; Hd of Religious Broadcasting, 1987–89. Chm., Arts Centre Gp, 1976–82. Oak Hill Ministerial Trng Course, 1985–87. Ordained deacon, 1987, priest, 1988. Hon. Asst Curate, St Paul and St Luke, Finchley, 1987–89; Priest-in-Charge, Ducklington, 1989–95; Bishop's Officer for Evangelism, Dio. of Oxford, 1989–95. Editor, Bible Reading Fellowship, 1997–2001; Consulting Ed., People's Bible Commentary, 1998–2006. *Publications:* Ground of Truth, 1964; New Singer, New Song (biog. of Cliff Richard), 1967; (with S. Linden) Two a Penny, 1968; Closer than a Brother, 1971; Hereafter, 1972; (ed) Matthew Henry's Commentary on the New Testament, 1974; After the Gospels, 1977; But this I can believe, 1980; The Search for the Real Jesus, 1982; Truth in the Son, 1985; Living through Loss, 1985; Walking in the Light (confessions of St Augustine), 1986; Believing the Bible, 1987; Battered Bride, 1988; What happens after Death?, 1992; You Can Pray, 1993; What's in a Word, 1994; Mark for Starters, 1995; Where do we go from here?, 1996; Forty Days with the 'Messiah', 1996; Message for the Millennium, 1998; (ed) The Master Haunter (anthol.), 1998, re-issued as The Poets' Christ, 2000; Winter's Tale (autobiog.), 2001; With Jesus in the Upper Room, 2001; Hope in the Wilderness, 2003; Making Sense of the Bible, 2004; Old Words, New Life, 2005; The Nation's Favourite Prayers (anthol.), 2006; Journey to Jerusalem, 2007; Seasons of the Son: a journey through the Christian year, 2008; Pilgrim's Way: journeying through the year with the Bible, 2008; One-stop Guide to Christianity, 2009; The Road Well Travelled: exploring traditional Christian spirituality, 2009; Facing the Darkness and Finding the Light: reflections for troubled times from the Book of Revelation, 2011; The Highway Code for Retirement, 2012; At the End of the Day: enjoying life in the departure lounge, 2013; Heaven's Morning, 2016. *Recreations:* watching cricket, opera, theatre, talking. *Address:* 51 Nideggan Close, Thatcham, Berks RG19 4HS.

**WINTER, Prof. (David) Michael,** OBE 2005; PhD; Professor of Land Economy and Society (formerly of Rural Policy), University of Exeter, since 2002 (Director, Centre for Rural Policy Research (formerly Centre for Rural Research), 2002–16); *b* 10 Nov. 1955; *s* of David Winter and Nanette Winter (*née* Wellstead); *m* 1979, Hilary Susan Thomas; one *s* one *d*. *Educ:* Peter Symonds Coll., Winchester; Wye Coll., London (BSc Rural Envmt Studies 1977); Open Univ. (PhD 1986). Res. Asst, Univ. of Exeter, 1980–82; Res. Officer, Univ. of Bath, 1983–87; Dir, Centre for Rural Studies, RAC, Cirencester, 1987–93; Reader, then Prof., Countryside and Community Res. Unit, Cheltenham and Gloucester Coll. of Higher Educn, 1993–2001; Hd, Sch. of Geog., Archaeol. and Earth Resources, Univ. of Exeter, 2003–05. Member, Board: Countryside Agency, 2005–06; Commn for Rural Communities, 2006–13; Natural England, 2016–; Mem., Sci. Adv. Council, DEFRA, 2009–11; Vis. Prog. Dir, Wilton Park, 2010–15. Chm., 2001–04, Vice-Chm., 2004–08, Hatherleigh Area Proj.; Chairman: South West Rural Affairs Forum, 2002–07; N Devon Biosphere Partnership, 2012–; Uplands Alliance, 2015–17; Pres., Devon Rural Network, 2006–09 (Chm., 2002–06); Vice Pres., Community Council of Devon, 2008–13; Trustee/Dir, North Wyke Res., 2008–09. Res. Associate, Inst. of Grassland and Envmtl Res., 1998– (Mem., Bd of Govs, 2006–08); Member: Expert Panel for Nat. Ecosystem Assessment, 2009–14; Bd of Govs Rothamsted Res., 2014–; Bovine Tuberculosis Review Panel, DEFRA, 2018; UK Jt Nature Conservation Cttee, 2018–. Lay Canon, Exeter Cathedral, 2008–. *Publications:* (ed jtly) Agriculture: people and policies, 1986; (jtly) Countryside Conflicts, 1986; (ed with M. Bouquet) Who From Their Labours Rest, 1987; (jtly) The Voluntary Principle in Conservation, 1990; (jtly) Church and Religion in Rural England, 1991; Rural Politics, 1996; (with P. Gaskell) The Effects of the 1992 Reform of the Common Agricultural Policy on the Countryside of Great Britain, 1998; (ed with M. Lobley) What is Land For? The Food, Fuel and Climate Change Debate, 2009; (with M. Lobley and R. Wheeler) The Changing World of Farming in Brexit UK, 2018. *Recreations:* gardening, hedge-laying, walking, choral singing, music, Church, community, reading, Welsh Rugby. *Address:* Centre for Rural Policy Research, University of Exeter, Lazenby House, Prince of Wales Road, Exeter EX4 4PJ. *T:* (01392) 263837. *E:* d.m.winter@exeter.ac.uk. *Club:* Athenæum.

**WINTER, Sir Gregory (Paul),** Kt 2004; CBE 1997; PhD; FRS 1990; FMedSci; scientific researcher and consultant; Fellow, Trinity College, Cambridge, since 2019 (Master, 2012–19); *b* 14 April 1951; *m* 1974, Fiona Jane Winter (marr. diss. 2002); one *s* three *d*. *Educ:* Royal Grammar Sch., Newcastle-upon-Tyne; Trinity College, Cambridge (BA Natural Scis 1973; MA; PhD 1976). Early career in protein chemistry, later in recombinant DNA technology, and enzyme and antibody engrg; Fellow, Trinity College, Cambridge, 1976–80 and 1991–2012; MRC Laboratory of Molecular Biology: Staff Scientist, 1981–2014; Jt Hd, Div. of Protein and Nucleic Acid Chemistry, 1994–2008; Dep. Dir, 2006–11; Acting Dir, 2007–08; Dep. Dir, Centre for Protein Engrg, 1990–2010. Co-Founder and non-executive Director: Cambridge Antibody Technology, 1989–96; Domantis, 2001–06; Bicycle Therapeutics, 2009–; non-executive Director: Peptech (Australia), 2001–03; Biosceptre Internat. Ltd, 2016–. Trustee, Newton Trust. FMedSci 2006. Foreign Fellow, Aust. Acad. of Technol Scis, 2002; Foreign Mem., Royal Swedish Acad. of Engrg Scis, 2007. Hon. FRCP 2003; Hon. Mem., Biochem. Soc., 2007; Hon. FRSocMed, 2009. Dr *hc* Nantes, 2001; Hon. Dr rer. nat. ETH Zurich, 2002; Hon. DSc Aarhus, 2015. Novo Biotechnology Award, Denmark, 1986; Colworth Medal, Biochem. Soc., 1986; Behring Prize, FRG, 1989; Louis Jeantet Foundn Award for Medicine, Switzerland, 1989; Pfizer Award, 1989; Milano Award, Italy, 1990; Scheele Award, Swedish Acad. of Pharmaceutical Scis, 1994; Biochemical Analysis Prize, German Soc. for Clin. Chem., 1995; King Faisal Internat. Prize in Medicine, 1995; William B. Coley Award, Cancer Res. Inst., USA, 1999; Jacob Heskel Gabbay Award in Biotechnol. and Medicine, Brandeis Univ., 2002; Jean-Pierre Lecocq Award, Acad. of Scis, France, 2002; Nat. Biotechnology Ventures Award, USA, 2004; Baly Medal, RCP, 2005; Biochemical Soc. Award, 2006; Bioindustry Assoc. Award, 2008; Royal Medal, Royal Soc., 2011; Prince of Asturias Award, Spain, 2012; Canada Gairdner Internat. Award, 2013; Millennium Medal, MRC, 2013; Exner Medal, Österreichischer Gewerbeverein, 2015; Prince Mahidol Award for Medicine, Thailand, 2016; (jtly) Nobel Prize in Chemistry, 2018. *Publications:* articles in learned jls on protein and gene structure, enzymes, viral proteins, antibodies and peptides.

**WINTER, Henry Oliver;** Chief Football Writer, The Times, since 2015; *b* London, 18 Feb. 1963; *s* of John and Valerie Winter; *m* 1992, Catriona Elliott; one *s* one *d*. *Educ:* The Hall, Hampstead; Westminster Sch.; Edinburgh Univ. (MA Hist.); London Coll. of Printing (Cert. Journalism). Sports journalist, The Independent, 1987–94; Football Correspondent, Daily Telegraph, 1994–2015. Columnist, 4-4-2 Mag., 2000–; contrib. Sky Sports, BBC TV and Radio. *Publications:* (with D. Davies) FA Confidential, 2008; ghost writer: Kenny Dalglish: My Autobiography, 1997; John Barnes: The Autobiography, 1999; Steven Gerrard: The Autobiography, 2006; Kenny Dalglish: My Liverpool Home, 2010; Fifty Years of Hurt: the story of England football and why we never stop believing, 2016. *Recreations:* marathon-running, visiting WW II museums, cycling round Rutland Water, singing out of tune. *Address:* The Times, 1 London Bridge Street, SE1 9GF.

**WINTER, Michael;** *see* Winter, D. M.

**WINTER, Peter John,** MA; Head, Latymer Upper School, 2002–12; *b* 10 July 1950; *s* of Jack Winter and Ursula Winter (*née* Riddington); *m* 1979, Jennifer Adwoa; one *s* one *d*. *Educ:* Trinity Sch., Croydon; Wadham Coll., Oxford (MA French); Univ. of Reading (PGCE). Asst teacher, French and German, Latymer Upper Sch., 1973–79; Head of Modern Langs, Magdalen Coll. Sch., Oxford, 1979–86; Head of Modern Langs, 1986–90, Housemaster, Internat. Centre, 1987–93, Sevenoaks Sch.; Headmaster, King Edward's Sch., Bath, 1993–2002. Strategic Consultant, PORG Schs, Czech Republic, 2014–15. FRSA. *Recreations:* Chelsea FC, Test Match cricket, France, grandparenting. *Address:* 20 Oyster Wharf, 18 Lombard Road, SW11 3RJ; 60 rue de la Cité, 34480 Magalas, France.

**WINTER, Richard Thomas George,** CBE 2017; FCA; Partner, PwC LLP, since 1997; *b* 13 Feb. 1963; *s* of David and Margery Winter; *m* 1993, Esther Bello Garcia; two *s* two *d*. *Educ:* Harrow Sch.; University Coll. London (BA). ACA 1989, FCA 1999. PricewaterhouseCoopers, 1985–. Chair, Med. Emergency Relief Internat., 2013–16. Hon. Treas., Save the Children Fund, 2004–15. Mem. Council, Wycombe Abbey Sch., 2011–. Trustee: Internat. Rescue Cttee, 2017–; Humanitarian Leadership Acad., 2017–19. Gov., John Lyon Foundn, 2016–. *Recreations:* opera, music, theatre, motor racing (spectating). *Address:* PwC International Ltd, 1 Embankment Place, WC2N 6RH. *T:* 07802 756222. *E:* richard.t.winter@pwc.com. *Club:* Reform.
*See also* R. J. D. Winter.

**WINTER, Dr Robert James David,** OBE 2009; FRCP; Consultant Respiratory Physician, Cambridge University Hospitals (formerly Addenbrooke's Hospital and Papworth Hospital), Cambridge, 2000–15; Programme Director, Integrated Care, University College London Partners, 2015–16; *b* 11 March 1953; *s* of David Winter and Margery Joan Winter; *m* 1984, Elizabeth Jane Sowton (marr. diss. 2005); two *d*. *Educ:* Clifton Coll., Bristol; Royal Free Hosp. Sch. of Medicine, Univ. of London (BSc 1974; MB BS 1977; MD 1987). MRCP 1979, FRCP 1995. Registrar, UCL, 1981–84; MRC Trng Fellow, 1984–86; Sen. Registrar, Hammersmith Hosp., 1986–91; Consultant Physician, Barnet Hosp., 1991–2000; Medical Director: Addenbrooke's NHS Trust, subseq. Cambridge Univ. Hosps NHS Foundn Trust, 2002–08; NHS East of England, 2008–11; Dir, Cambridge Univ. Health Partners, 2011–13; Man. Dir, Eastern Academic Health Sci. Network, 2013–14. Associate Lectr, Univ. of Cambridge, 2001–15; Fellow, Hughes Hall, Cambridge, 2013–15. Jt Nat. Clinical Dir for Respiratory Disease, DoH, 2009–13. Mem. Exec. Cttee, and Trustee, British Lung Foundn, 1992–2002 (Vice Pres., 2010–); Trustee, Fund for Addenbrooke's, 2002–07. *Publications:* reports and articles on quality in health care delivery. *Recreations:* music, walking. *Address:* 29 High Street, Barrington, Cambridge CB22 7QX.

**WINTER, Robert Rickaby,** OBE 2012; Lord-Lieutenant and Lord Provost of Glasgow, 2007–12; *b* 31 March 1937; *s* of Thomas Rickaby Winter and Dona Smillie McKendrick Winter; *m* 1983, Sheena Morgan Duncan; one *d*; four *s* by a previous marriage. CSW; DPA. Dir of Social Work, Greenock and Port Glasgow, 1969–75; Dep. Dir of Social Work, 1975–95, Dir of Social Work, 1995–96, Strathclyde Regl Council; Sec., Assoc. of Dirs of Social Work, 1996–99. Mem., 1996–2005, Panel Chm., 2005–14, GMC. Mem., Gtr Glasgow Health Bd PCT, 1996–2005. Mem. (Lab), Glasgow City Council, 1999–2012. Hon. FRCPGlas 2009; Hon. FRIAS 2011. DUniv: Caledonian, 2011; Strathclyde, 2012. *Recreations:* walking, swimming, reading, football spectation.

**WINTER, Sophie;** *see* Raworth, S.

**WINTERBOTTOM, Prof. Michael,** MA, DPhil; FBA 1978; Corpus Christi Professor of Latin, University of Oxford, 1993–2001; Fellow, Corpus Christi College, Oxford, 1993–2001, now Emeritus; *b* 22 Sept. 1934; *s* of Allan Winterbottom and Kathleen Mary (*née* Wallis); *m* 1st, 1963, Helen Spencer (marr. diss. 1983); two *s*; 2nd, 1986, Nicolette Janet Streatfeild Bergel. *Educ:* Dulwich Coll.; Pembroke Coll., Oxford. 1st Cl. Hon. Mods and Craven Schol., 1954; 1st Cl. Lit. Hum. and Derby Schol., 1956; Domus Sen. Schol., Merton Coll., 1958–59; MA 1959, DPhil 1964 (Oxon). Research Lectr, Christ Church, 1959–62; Lectr in Latin and Greek, University Coll. London, 1962–67; Fellow and Tutor in Classics, Worcester Coll., Oxford, 1967–92; Reader in Classical Langs, Univ. of Oxford, 1990–92. Dhc Besançon, 1985. *Publications:* (ed) Quintilian, 1970; (with D. A. Russell) Ancient Literary Criticism, 1972; Three Lives of English Saints, 1972; (ed and trans.) The Elder Seneca, 1974; (ed with R. M. Ogilvie) Tacitus, *Opera Minora*, 1975; (ed and trans.) Gildas, 1978; Roman Declamation, 1980; (ed with commentary) The Minor Declamations ascribed to Quintilian, 1984; (with D. C. Innes) Sopatros the Rhetor, 1988; (with M. Brett and C. N. L. Brooke) rev. edn of Charles Johnson (ed), Hugh the Chanter, 1990; (ed) Cicero, *De Officiis*, 1994; (ed with R. A. B. Mynors and R. M. Thomson) William of Malmesbury, *Gesta Regum Anglorum*, 1998; (ed with R. M. Thomson) William of Malmesbury, Saints' Lives, 2002; (ed with T. Reinhardt) Quintilian Book 2, 2006; (ed) William of Malmesbury, *Gesta Pontificum Anglorum*, vol. 1, 2007; (ed with R. M. Thomson) William of Malmesbury, *Liber super explanationem Lamentationum Ieremiae prophetae*, 2011; (ed with M. Lapidge) The Early Lives of St Dunstan, 2012; (trans.) William of Malmesbury on Lamentations, 2013; (ed with R. M. Thomson) William of Malmesbury, the Miracles of the Blessed Virgin Mary, 2015; articles and reviews in jls. *Recreations:* walking, geology. *Address:* 53 Thorncliffe Road, Oxford OX2 7BA. *T:* (01865) 513066.

**WINTERFLOOD, Brian Martin**, MBE 2012; Founder, 1988, and President, 2009–17, Winterflood Securities Ltd (Managing Director, 1988–99; Chief Executive Officer, 1999–2002; Chairman, 2002–09); Chief Executive Officer, Winterflood Gilts, 1999–2002 (Managing Director, 1994–99); Chairman, Gilts and Securities, 2001–10; *b* 31 Jan. 1937; *s* of late Thomas G. Winterflood and of Doris M. Winterflood; *m* 1966, Doreen Stella McCartney; two *s* one *d*. *Educ*: Fray's Coll., Uxbridge. National Service, 1955–57. Messenger, Greener Dreyfus & Co., 1953–55; Bisgood Bishop & Co. Ltd, 1957–85: Partner, 1967–71; Dir, 1971–81; Man. Dir, 1981–85; Man. Dir, County Bisgood, 1985–86; County NatWest Securities Ltd: Dir, 1986–87; Exec. Dir, 1986–88, resigned, 1988. Director: Union Discount Co. of London, 1991–93; Close Brothers Group, 1995–2002; PROSHARE, 1998–2003; Monument Securities, 2002–06. Chm., Cttee of USM Initiative, Prince's Youth Bus. Trust, 1989–92; Jt Chm., UK Adv. Bd, EASD, 2000–01. Member: City Gp for Smaller Cos, now Quoted Cos Alliance, 1992–2000 (Mem. Exec. Cttee, 1992–96; Pres., 2010–16); City Disputes Practitioners Panel, 1994–2000; AIM Adv. Cttee, 1995–; AIM Appeals Cttee, 1995–98; Non FTSE 100 Wkg Party Cttee, 1996–98; Secondary Markets Cttee, 1996–98; Market Adv. Cttee, EASD, 2000–. Mem. Cttee, October Club, 1990–2002; Trustee, Stock Exchange Benevolent Fund, 1995–2016; Pres., Securities Industry Mgt Assoc., 2004, now Pres. Emeritus (Lifetime Achievement Award, 2008). Pres., Rehabilitation and Med. Res. Trust, 1998–2007 (Vice Pres., 1989, 2007–10; Patron, 2010–); Vice-Pres., Save the Children, 2004–09; Vice-Chm., Lord Mayor's Appeal, 2004; Ambassador, E London Bond Appeal, 2010. Gov., Reeds Sch., 2002–07 (Pres., Sch. Appeal, 1997–98; Hon. Vice Pres., 2007). Patron: Natural History Mus., 2015–; Mus. of London, 2015–; Variety, the Children's Charity. Member: Boost (City Life) Appeal, 2001–02; Guild of Internat. Bankers, 2002– (Court Emeritus, 2017); Order of St George, 2002–; Heart of the City Cttee, 2002–16. Winterflood Theatre, City of London Boys' Sch., 2008. Freeman, City of London, 2002. Liveryman, Internat. Bankers' Co., 2007–17 (Mem. Ct, now Emeritus). FCSI (FSI 1997); FRSA 2001. PLC Achievement Award, Price Waterhouse Coopers, 1994; Assoc. of Private Client Investment Managers and Stockbrokers Award, 2000; Lifetime Achievement Award: Variety Club, 2008; Grant Thornton Quoted Companies Awards, 2011; PLC Retirement Award, 2016. *Recreations*: family, work, travel. *Club*: City of London.

**WINTERS, Prof. (Leonard) Alan**, CB 2012; PhD; Professor of Economics, University of Sussex, since 1999; Director and Founder, UK Trade Policy Observatory, since 2016; *b* Walthamstow, 8 April 1950; *s* of Geoffrey Walter Horace Winters and Christine Agnes Winters (*née* Ive); *m* 1997, Zhen Kun Wang; one *s* two *d*. *Educ*: Chingford Co. High Sch.; Univ. of Bristol (BSc 1971); Fitzwilliam Coll., Cambridge (MA 1975; PhD 1979). Res. officer, Dept Applied Econs, Univ. of Cambridge, 1971–80; Lectr, Univ. of Bristol, 1980–86; Economist, World Bank, 1983–85; Professor of Economics: UC of N Wales, Bangor, 1986–90; Univ. of Birmingham, 1990–97; Res. Manager, 1994–99, Dir of Res., 2004–07, World Bank; Chief Economist, DFID, 2008–11. Chair, Global Devel Network, 2011–17. Mem., ESRC, 2015–18. Ed., World Trade Rev., 2008–. Chair, English Folk Dance and Song Soc., 1981–83. *Publications*: International Economics, 1982, 2nd edn 1991; Eastern Europe's International Trade, 1994; Handbook on International Trade and Poverty, 2001; Regionalisation and Development, 2002; contrib. chapters to acad. books and jl articles. *Recreations*: music, cricket, walking. *Address*: Jubilee Building, University of Sussex, Falmer, Brighton BN1 9SL. *T*: (01273) 678332. *E*: L.A.Winters@sussex.ac.uk.

**WINTERSON, Jeanette**, CBE 2018 (OBE 2006); FRSL; writer; Professor of New Writing, University of Manchester, since 2012; *b* 27 Aug. 1959; *m* 2015, Susie Orbach, *qv*. *Educ*: St Catherine's Coll., Oxford (BA Hons English). Hon. FRA 2012; FRSL 2016. Internat. Fiction Award, Fest. Letteratura, Italy, 1999; 25th Anniversary Medal for Prose, Hay Fest., 2012; Internat. Rapallo Carige Prize for Women, 2014; Lifetime Achievement Award, Univ. of St Louis, Mo, 2014. *Publications*: Oranges are not the only fruit, 1985 (Whitbread Prize, 1st Novel; numerous awards for screenplay, televised 1990); The Passion, 1987 (John Llewellyn Rhys Prize); Sexing the Cherry, 1989 (E. M. Forster Award, Amer. Acad. and Inst. of Arts and Letters); Written on the Body, 1992; Art and Lies, 1994; Great Moments in Aviation (screenplay), 1994; Art Objects: essays on ecstasy and effrontery, 1995; Gut Symmetries, 1997; The World and Other Places (short stories), 1998; The Powerbook, 2000 (adapted for stage, 2002); Lighthousekeeping, 2004; Weight, 2005; The Stone Gods, 2007; (ed) Midsummer Nights: new stories/old dreams (short stories), 2009; Why Be Happy When You Could Be Normal? (memoir), 2011 (Ind. Publishers' Award, Stonewall Award, 2012); The Daylight Gate (horror novella), 2012; The Gap of Time, 2015; Christmas Days (short stories), 2016; Frankissstein: a love story, 2019; *for children*: The King of Capri, 2002; Tanglewreck, 2006; The Lion, the Unicorn, and Me, 2009 (opera version perf. Washington Nat. Opera, 2013); The Battle of the Sun, 2009; Ingenious (screenplay), 2009. *Recreations*: opera, ballet, champagne. *Address*: c/o Caroline Michel, PFD, 55 New Oxford Street, WC1A 1BS. *E*: connect@jeanettewinterson.com.

**WINTERTON, 8th Earl** *cr* 1766 (Ire.); **(Donald) David Turnour**; Baron Winterton 1761 (Ire.); Viscount Turnour 1766 (Ire.); *b* 13 Oct. 1943; *s* of Cecil Noel Turnour, DFM, CD (*d* 1987), *yr b* of 7th Earl Winterton and Evelyn Isabel, *d* of Dr C. A. Oulton; *S* uncle, 1991; *m* 1st, 1968, Jill Pauline (marr. diss. 1997), *d* of late John Geddes Esplen; two *d*; 2nd, 2004, Vecide Brigitte Aktelligul. *Educ*: Waterloo Lutheran Univ., Ontario (BA). *Heir*: *b* Robert Charles Turnour [*b* 30 Jan. 1950; *m* 1st, 1974, Sheila (marr. diss. 1976), *d* of G. H. Stocking; 2nd, 1983, Patricia Ann, *d* of William Avery; two *d*].

**WINTERTON, (Jane) Ann, (Lady Winterton)**; *b* 6 March 1941; *d* of late Joseph Robert Hodgson and Ellen Jane Hodgson; *m* 1960, Nicholas Raymond Winterton (*see* Sir N. R. Winterton); two *s* one *d*. *Educ*: Erdington Grammar Sch. for Girls. MP (C) Congleton, 1983–2010. Opposition spokesman on nat. drug strategy, 1998–2001; Shadow Minister for Agriculture and Fisheries, 2001–02. Mem., Chairmen's Panel, 1992–98, 2005–10. Chm., 1992–2002, Vice-Chm., 2002–10, All Party Parly Pro-Life Gp. Fellow, Industry and Parlt Trust, 1987–2010. Pres., Congleton Div., St John Ambulance, 1984–; Vice Pres., Townswomen's Guilds, 1994–2004. *Recreations*: music, theatre, tennis, ski-ing. *Address*: Whitehall Farm, Mow Lane, Newbold Astbury, Congleton, Cheshire CW12 3NH.

**WINTERTON, Sir Nicholas (Raymond)**, Kt 2002; DL; *b* 31 March 1938; *o s* of late N. H. Winterton, Lysways House, Longdon Green, near Rugeley, Staffs; *m* 1960, Jane Ann Hodgson (*see* J. A. Winterton); two *s* one *d*. *Educ*: Bilton Grange Prep. Sch.; Rugby Sch. Commnd 14th/20th King's Hussars, 1957–59. Sales Exec. Trainee, Shell-Mex and BP Ltd, 1959–60; Sales and Gen. Manager, Stevens and Hodgson Ltd, Birmingham (Co. engaged in sale and hire of construction equipment), 1960–71. Chairman: CPC Cttee, Meriden Cons. Assoc., 1966–68; Midland Branch, Contractors Mech. Plant Engrs Assoc., 1968–69. Member: W Midlands Cons. Council, 1966–69, 1971–72; Central Council, Nat. Union of Cons. and Unionist Assocs, 1971–72. Contested (C) Newcastle-under-Lyme, Oct. 1969, 1970. MP (C) Macclesfield, Sept. 1971–2010. Chairman: Select Cttee on Health, 1991–92; Select Cttee on Procedure, 1997–2005; Member: Social Services Select Cttee, 1980–90; Select Cttee on Modernisation of H of C, 1997–2010; Liaison Select Cttee, 1997–2005; Chairmen's Panel, 1986–2010. Additional Dep. Speaker, for sittings in Westminster Hall, 1998–2005. Chairman, All Party Parliamentary: Gp for Cotton and Allied Textiles, 1979–97; Gp for Media, 1992–2000; British Danish Gp, 1992–2010; British Falklands Is Gp, 1997–2010; British Bahamas Gp, 1997–2010; British Austria Gp, 1999–2010; Joint Chairman: All Party Parly British Taiwan Gp, 1997–2010; W Coast Mainline Gp, 2001–10; Vice Chairman, All Party Parliamentary: British Swedish Gp, 1992–2010; British Indonesian Gp, 1992–2000; Anglo S Pacific Gp, 1997–2010; Road Transport Study Gp, 1997–2001; Clothing and Textiles Gp, 1997–2010; Manchester 2002 XVII Commonwealth Games Gp, 2000–02. Member Executive: 1922 Cttee, 1997–2010 (Vice-Chm., 2001–05; Treas., 2005–10); UK Br., CPA, 1997–2010 (Treas., 2004–07); Mem., Exec. Cttee, IPU, 2001–10 (Treas., 2007–10). Member: Exec. Cttee, Anglo-Austrian Soc., 1987–2000 (Chm., 1998–2000); Nat. Adv. Cttee, Duke of Edinburgh Award Scheme, 1973–99; Imperial Soc. of Knights Bachelor, 2002–. County Councillor, Atherstone Div. Warwickshire CC, 1967–72. President: Macclesfield Fermain Club, 1973–2010; Poynton Youth and Community Centre, 1971–2010; Upton Priory Youth Club, Macclesfield, 1992–2001; Macclesfield and Congleton District Scout Council, 2018–; Vice-President: Cheshire Scout Assoc.; E Cheshire Hospice; Nat. Assoc. of Local Councils, 1979–2001; Royal Coll. of Midwives; N Cheshire Cruising Club, 1997–2010. Hon. Mem., Macclesfield Lions Club, 1973–2010; Hon. Life Mem., Macclesfield Rugby Union Football Club; Patron: Macclesfield and District Sheep Dog Trials Assoc., 1972–2014; Internat. Centre for Child Care Studies, 1980–94; Civit Hills Open Air Theatre, 1996–2001; Elizabeth Trust, 1983–94; Poynton Male Voice Choir, 1997–2010; E Cheshire Br., Alzheimer's Soc., 1998–2010. President, Macclesfield Branch: Riding for the Disabled, 1987–2010; Multiple Sclerosis Soc., 1987–2010. Founder Pres., Bollington Light Opera Gp, 1978– (Hon. Life Vice. Pres., 2010). Life Member: Poynton Gilbert and Sullivan Soc.; Bollington Fest. Players. Liveryman, Weavers' Co., 1981 (Mem., Ct of Assts, 1992–2012; Upper Bailiff, 1997–98); Freeman of the City of London, 1981. Hon. Freeman, Borough of Macclesfield, 2002. DL Cheshire, 2006. SBStJ 2000. Order of Brilliant Star with Grand Cordon (Taiwan), 2008. *Recreations*: squash, tennis, swimming, horse riding, reading, walking, Rugby (spectator). *Clubs*: Cavalry and Guards, Lighthouse; Old Boys and Park Green (Macclesfield).

**WINTERTON, Rt Hon. Dame Rosalie, (Rt Hon. Dame Rosie)**, DBE 2016; PC 2006; MP (Lab) Doncaster Central, since 1997; *b* 10 Aug. 1958; *d* of Gordon and Valerie Winterton. *Educ*: Doncaster Grammar Sch.; Hull Univ. (BA Hons Hist.). Asst to John Prescott, MP, 1980–86; Parliamentary Officer: London Borough of Southwark, 1986–88; RCN, 1988–90; Man. Dir, Connect Public Affairs, 1990–94; Hd, private office of John Prescott, MP, 1994–97. Parly Sec., LCD, 2001–03; Minister of State: DoH, 2003–07; DfT, 2007–08; DWP, 2008–09; BIS and DCLG, 2009–10; Minister for Yorkshire and the Humber, 2008–10; Shadow Leader, H of C, 2010; Opposition Chief Whip, 2010–16; Second Dep. Chm. of Ways and Means, 2017–. *Recreations*: sailing, reading. *Address*: House of Commons, SW1A 0AA.

**WINTLE, Rev. Canon Ruth Elizabeth**; Hon. Assistant Priest, St John-in-Bedwardine, 1994–2006 (Parish Deacon, 1984–94); Canon Emeritus, Worcester Cathedral, since 1998 (Hon. Canon, 1987–97); *b* 30 Sept. 1931; *d* of John Wintle and Vera (*née* Lane). *Educ*: Clarendon Sch., Malvern, and Abergele, Wales; Westfield Coll., London (BA Hons French 1953); St Hugh's Coll., Oxford (MA Theol. 1972); St Michael's House, Oxford (IDC 1966). Teacher, St Hilda's Sch., Jamaica, 1953–60; Travelling Sec., Inter-Varsity Fellowship and Technical Colls Christian Fellowship, 1960–63; Accredited Lay Worker, St Andrew's Church, N Oxford, 1967–69; Tutor, St John's Coll., Durham, 1969–74; Deaconess (C of E), 1972; Selection Sec., ACCM, 1974–83; Organiser, Internat. Diakonia Conf., Coventry, 1983; Diocesan Dir of Ordinands, Worcester, 1984–92; ordained deacon, 1987, priest 1994; Bishop's Advr on Women's Ministry, Worcester, 1995–97. Mem., Third Order, SSF, 1990–. Mem., Bishop's Staff Meeting, Worcs, 1993–97. Member: Church Army Bd, 1985–2000; Crown Appointments Commn, 1990–95; Gen. Synod of C of E, 1990–95; Council, Retired Clergy Assoc., 1998–2004. Mem. Council, Malvern Coll., 1991–2000. Chm., Li Tim-Oi Foundn, 1993–2006. *Recreations*: reading, driving, ornithology. *Address*: 6 Coronation Avenue, Rushwick, Worcester WR2 5TF. *T*: (01905) 427109.

**WINTON, Rt Rev. Alan Peter**; *see* Thetford, Bishop Suffragan of.

**WINTON, Alexander**, CBE 1993; QFSM 1987; HM Chief Inspector of Fire Services for Scotland, 1990–93; *b* 13 July 1932; *s* of Alexander and Jean Winton; *m* 1957, Jean Dowie (*d* 2018); two *s*. MIFireE. Fireman, Perth, 1958–64; Station Officer: Perth, 1964–67; Lancashire, 1967–69; Assistant Divisional Officer: E Riding, 1969–72; Angus, 1972–73; Divisional Officer III: Angus, 1973–75; Tayside, 1975–76; Divl Comdr (DOI), Tayside, 1976–80; Temp. Sen. Divl Officer, 1980–81; Dep. Firemaster, 1981–85; Firemaster, Tayside Fire Bde, 1985–89. *Recreations*: golf, curling, reading. *Address*: 5 Ferndale Drive, Broughty Ferry, Dundee DD5 3DB. *T*: (01382) 778156.

**WINTON, Dr Douglas James**, FMedSci; Senior Group Leader, Cancer Research UK Cambridge Institute, University of Cambridge, since 2012; *b* Aberdeen, 13 April 1959; *s* of late James Winton and of Margaret Nelson Winton; *m* 2006, Jean Aline Miller. *Educ*: Eastwood High Sch.; Univ. of Glasgow (BSc Hons 1982); Univ. of Bristol (PhD 1986). Post-doctoral Res. Associate, Inst. of Cancer Res., Surrey, 1986–89; University of Cambridge: Sen. Post-doctoral Res. Associate, Dept of Pathol., 1989–96; Ind. Principal Investigator, Dept of Oncol., 1996–2007; Gp Leader, CRUK Cambridge Inst., 2007–12. Mem., EMBO, 2016–. FMedSci 2014. Mem., Stickmakers Guild. *Publications*: papers on stem cells, cancer and intestinal biol. *Recreations*: walking stick maker, travel, jam making, collecting books on islands, finding good coffee bars. *Address*: Cancer Research UK Cambridge Institute, University of Cambridge, Li Ka Shing Centre, Robinson Way, Cambridge CB2 0RE. *T*: (01223) 769783. *E*: doug.winton@cruk.cam.ac.uk.

**WINTOUR, Dame Anna**, DBE 2017 (OBE 2008); Editor, US Vogue, since 1988; Artistic Director, Condé Nast, since 2013; *b* 3 Nov. 1949; *d* of late Charles Vere Wintour, CBE; *m* 1984, Dr David Shaffer (marr. diss.); one *s* one *d*. *Educ*: Queen's College Sch., London; North London Collegiate Sch. Dep. Fashion Editor, Harpers and Queen Magazine, 1970–76; Fashion Editor, Harpers Bazaar, NY, 1976–77; Fashion and Beauty Editor, Viva Mag., 1977–78; Contributing Editor for Fashion and Style, Savvy Mag., 1980–81; Sen. Editor, New York Mag., NY, 1981–83; Creative Dir, US Vogue, 1983–86; Editor-in-Chief, Vogue, 1986–87; Editor, House and Garden, New York, 1987–88.

*See also* P. Wintour.

**WINTOUR, Patrick**; Diplomatic Editor, The Guardian, since 2016; *b* 1 Nov. 1954; *s* of late Charles Vere Wintour, CBE and Eleanor Trego Wintour (*née* Baker); *m* 2002, Rachel Mynfreda Sylvester, *qv*; two *s*, and one *s* one *d* by a previous marriage. *Educ*: Hall Sch., London; Westminster Sch.; Corpus Christi Coll., Oxford (BA). Journalist, New Statesman, 1976–82; The Guardian: Chief Labour Correspondent, 1983–88; Chief Political Correspondent, 1988–96 and 2000–06; Political Editor: The Observer, 1996–2000; The Guardian, 2006–16. *Publications*: Eddie Shah and the Newspaper Revolution, 1985; Labour Rebuilt, 1990. *Recreations*: piano, gardening. *Address*: The Guardian, Kings Place, 90 York Way, N1 9AG. *E*: Patrick.Wintour@theguardian.com. *Club*: Soho House.

*See also* Dame A. Wintour.

**WINTOUR, Rachel Mynfreda**; *see* Sylvester, R. M.

**WINYARD, Dr Graham Peter Arthur,** CBE 1999; FRCP; FFPH; Postgraduate Dean, Wessex Deanery, Department of Health, 1999–2007; *b* 19 Jan. 1947; *s* of Lyonel Arthur Winyard and Dorothy Elizabeth Payne; *m* 1st, 1979, Sandra Catherine Bent (*d* 2002); one *s* two *d*; 2nd, 2006, Jill Saltmarsh. *Educ:* Southend High Sch.; Hertford Coll., Oxford (MA); Middlesex Hosp. (BM, BCh); Sch. of Oriental and African Studies, Univ. of London (MA 2014). Sen. House Officer, United Oxford Hosps, 1973–75; Registrar in Community Medicine, 1975–77; Provincial Health Officer, Madang, PNG, 1977–79; Sen. Registrar in Community Medicine, Oxford RHA, and Lectr, LSHTM, 1979–82; Dist MO, Lewisham and N Southwark HA, 1982–87; SPMO, DHSS, later Dept of Health, 1987–90; Regl Med. Dir and Dir of Public Health, Wessex RHA, 1990–93; Dep. CMO and Dir Health Services, NHS Exec., DoH, 1993–98. Consultant Advr to Defence Medical Services, 2001–07. Hon. Prof. of Public Health Mgt, Univ. of Southampton, 1999–2007. Vice-Pres., FPH, 2004–07; Chm., Cttee of Postgrad. Deans UK, 2004–07. Member: Steering Gp, Healthcare Professionals for Assisted Dying, 2010–18; Bd, Dignity in Dying, 2013–16. Treas., Chithurst Buddhist monastery, 2010–19. Trustee, Winchester Homestart, 2019–. *Recreations:* Buddhist studies, meditation, music, campaigning on end of life issues.

**WISBECH, Archdeacon of;** *see* McCurdy, Ven. H. K.

**WISDEN, Prof. William,** PhD; FMedSci, FRSB; Professor of Molecular Neuroscience, since 2009, Co-Director, Centre for Neurotechnology, since 2014, and Founding Member, UK Dementia Research Institute, since 2017, Imperial College London; *b* Shoreham-by-Sea, W Sussex, 28 Jan. 1964; *s* of late William Wisden, MBE and Margaret P. Wisden; *m* 2004, Dr Bianca Kuehler; one step *d*. *Educ:* King's Manor Comprehensive Sch., Shoreham-by-Sea; Fitzwilliam Coll., Cambridge (BA 1st Cl. Zool. Natural Scis 1986); Clare Hall, Cambridge (PhD Neurobiol. 1989). EMBO Long-term Fellow, Univ. of Heidelberg, 1990–92; Res. Fellow, Clare Hall, Cambridge, 1993–96; Group Leader: MRC Lab. of Molecular Biol., Cambridge, 1993–2001; Univ. of Heidelberg, 2001–05; Prof. and Chair of Neurosci., Univ. of Aberdeen, 2005–09. Member: Neurosci. and Mental Health Cttee, Wellcome Trust, 2009–11; Neurosci. and Mental Health Bd, MRC, 2012–16. FRSB (FSB 2010); FMedSci 2014. *Recreations:* gardening, walking, theatre, art, cats, gnomes (garden), natural history. *Address:* Department of Life Sciences, Sir Ernst Chain Building, Imperial College London, Exhibition Road, SW7 2AZ. *T:* (020) 7594 9744. *E:* w.wisden@imperial.ac.uk.

**WISE,** family name of **Baron Wise**.

**WISE,** 3rd Baron *cr* 1951, of King's Lynn; **Christopher John Clayton Wise;** Director, Everysite, since 2010; *b* Banbury, Oxfordshire, 19 March 1949; *er s* of 2nd Baron Wise and of Margaret Anne (*née* Snead); *S* father, 2012; *m* 1988, Rosalind Myrtle Reed; two *s. Educ:* Aspro-Norwich Sch.; Southampton Univ. (BSc; PhD); Harper Adams Coll. (PGDip). Publisher, Procs of British Crop Protection Council, 1978–2003; Policy Dir, Nat. Fedn of Builders, 2003–06; Co. Sec., British Assoc. for Supported Employment, 2006–08; Ops Dir, Construction Industry Accredited Performance Scheme Ltd, 2008–10. Non-exec. Dir, BCPC, 1994–2003. Crop Sci. Advr, NFU, 1994–2003. *Publications:* (contrib.) Modern Crop Protection: developments and perspectives, 1993; contrib. Annals of Applied Biol. *Recreations:* caravanning, ski-ing, sailing. *Heir: s* Hon. Thomas Christopher Clayton Wise, *b* 6 June 1989. *Address:* Demeter House, Woodmancote, Cirencester, Glos GL7 7EF. *Club:* Farmers.

**WISE, Hon. Lady; Morag Barbara Wise;** a Senator of the College of Justice in Scotland, since 2013; Judge, Employment Appeal Tribunal, 2016–18; *b* 22 Jan. 1963; *d* of Leslie James Wise and late Barbara Gillies or Wise; *m* 1994, Alastair John Angus McEwan; one *s* two *d. Educ:* Univ. of Aberdeen (LLB 1st Cl. Hons 1985; DipLP 1986); McGill Univ., Montreal (LLM 1995). Solicitor in private practice, 1989–92; admitted Advocate, 1993; QC (Scot.) 2005; Temp. Judge, Ct of Session, 2008–13. Mem. Bd, Judicial Appts Bd for Scotland, 2016–. Chair: Advocates Family Law Assoc., 2007–13; Family Law Arbitration Gp (Scotland), 2011–13 (Hon. Pres., 2015–); Dir and Trustee, Family Mediation Lothian, 2008–12; Mem. Bd, Children in Scotland, 2017–. Hon. Pres., Employment Lawyers Assoc., 2016–. Gov., Fettes Coll., 2018–. Hon. LLD Aberdeen, 2015. *Publications:* (ed jtly) Gloag and Henderson, The Law of Scotland, 11th edn 2001 to 13th edn 2012; (contrib.) A Practical Guide to Human Rights Law in Scotland, ed Lord Reed, 2001; (contrib.) Gloag and Henderson, The Law of Scotland, 14th edn 2017. *Recreations:* singing, ski-ing (badly), socialising. *Address:* Court of Session, Parliament House, Parliament Square, Edinburgh EH1 1RQ. *T:* (0131) 225 2595. *E:* supreme.courts@scotcourts.gov.uk.

**WISE, Christopher Mark,** RDI 1998; FREng; FICE; Co-founder and Director, Expedition Engineering, since 1999; *b* 2 Nov. 1956; *s* of Jeffery and Jean Wise; one *s* by Elspeth Beard; two *s* one *d* by Catherine Ramsden. *Educ:* Reigate Grammar Sch.; Univ. of Southampton (BSc Hons 1979). MIStructE 1985; FREng 2003; FICE 2008. Joined Ove Arup and Partners, Consulting Engrs, 1979; Dir, Ove Arup Partnership, 1993–99; *projects include:* Torre de Collserola, Barcelona, 1992; Channel 4 HQ, 1995; Commerzbank HQ, Frankfurt, 1996; American Air Mus., Duxford, 1997; Millennium Bridge, London, 2000; Infinity Footbridge, Stockton (IStructE Supreme Award, 2009); Barcelona Bullring; 2012 Olympic Velodrome; Intesa Sanpaolo Bank HQ Tower, Turin; Greek Nat. Opera House; Library, Athens. Prof. of Civil Engrg Design, ICSTM, 1998–99; Davenport Prof., Sch. of Architecture, Yale Univ. 2006; Prof. of Civil Engrg Design, UCL, 2012–15. Mem., Design Council, 2005–11. Co-founder and Chm., Useful Simple Trust, 2008–. Reconstructions of Roman technology, for Secrets of Lost Empires series, BBC2 Colosseum, 1996; Caesar's Bridge, 1999. Columnist, Building Mag., 2009–. Master, Faculty of RDI, 2007–09. FRSA 1995. Hon. FRIBA 2001. Guthrie Brown Award, 1993, Oscar Faber Medal, 1996, Gold Medal, 2012, IStructE; Silver Medal, RAEng, 2007; Milne Medal, IABSE, 2010; Gold Medal, ICE, 2012. *Publications:* papers on engrg educn projects in IStructE jl. *Recreations:* abstract painting, guitar, cricket, soccer. *Address:* Expedition Engineering, The Clove Building, 4 Maguire Street, SE1 2NQ.

**WISE, Fiona;** independent health care business consultant; Executive Lead, Buckinghamshire, Oxfordshire and Berkshire West Sustainability and Transformation Partnership, since 2018; *b* 1 Aug. 1954; *d* of Duncan and Doreen Lamond; *m*; two *s. Educ:* Haberdashers' Aske's Girls' Sch., Acton; St Mary's Grammar Sch., Northwood. DipHSM. Dep. Unit Gen. Manager, Royal Free Hosp., 1984–88; Unit Gen. Manager, Enfield Priority and Community Care, 1988–93; Chief Exec., Enfield Community Care NHS Trust, 1993–2001; interim Chief Exec., Stoke Mandeville Hosp. NHS Trust, 2001–03; Actg Dir of Modernisation, Beds and Herts Strategic HA, 2003; Chief Exec., Ealing Hosp. NHS Trust, 2003–07; Chief Exec., NW London Hosps NHS Trust, 2007–12; Interim Chief Exec., Kettering Hosp. NHS Foundn Trust, 2017–18. *Recreations:* family, tennis, cooking. *E:* f.wise@btinternet.com.

**WISE, Gordon Scott Frank;** Joint Managing Director, Book Department and Senior Literary Agent, Curtis Brown Group Ltd, since 2005; President, Association of Authors' Agents, 2016–18; *b* Birmingham, 11 July 1968; *s* of Gordon Wise and Marjory Wise (*née* Wright); partner, 1994, civil partnership, 2006, *m* 2015, Michael McCoy. *Educ:* Christ's Hosp. Sch.; Edinburgh Univ. (MA Hons Hist. with English 1991); Univ. of Pennsylvania. Ed., Kodansha America, Inc., 1991–94; Sen. Ed., Boxtree Ltd, 1994–96; Editl Dir and Publisher, Pan Macmillan, 1996–2003; Publishing Dir, John Murray (Publishers) Ltd/ Hodder Headline, 2003–05. Jerusalem Book Fair Fellow, 2015. Member: Bd., Churchill Alliance, 2013–15; Bd, Alliance for Intellectual Property, 2014–18; Adv. Bd, London Book Fair, 2016–. Literary executor, estate of Mary Renault. Mem., Twentieth Century Soc. Literary Agent of Year, Booksellers Industry Awards, 2015. Gov., Christ's Hosp. Sch., 2013–. *Recreations:* architecture and design, theatre and the performing arts, appreciation of Frinton-on-Sea. *Address:* c/o Curtis Brown, 5th Floor, Haymarket House, 28 Haymarket, SW1Y 4SP. *Clubs:* Ivy, Soho House.

**WISE, Ian;** QC 2010; *b* Stoke-on-Trent, 8 July 1959; *s* of Derek Wise and Beryl Wise (*née* Haynes); *m* 1992, Denise; two *d. Educ:* Newcastle High Sch.; Open Univ. (BA); King's Coll. London (Dip. EC Law). Called to the Bar, Gray's Inn, 1992; Mem., Doughty Street Chambers, 1994–2014, Hd, public law team, 1998–2011; Mem., Monckton Chambers, 2014–. DUniv Open 2018. *Publications:* Enforcement of Local Taxation, 2000; (jtly) Children in Need: local authority support for children and families, 2011, 2nd edn, 2014. *Recreations:* various sports, family, walking my dog through woods and countryside. *Address:* Monckton Chambers, 1–2 Raymond Buildings, Gray's Inn, WC1R 5NR. *T:* (020) 7405 7211, *Fax:* (020) 7405 2084.

**WISE, Morag Barbara;** *see* Wise, Hon. Lady.

**WISE, Dr Richard,** FMedSci; Consultant Medical Microbiologist, City Hospital, Birmingham, 1974–2005; *b* 7 July 1942; *s* of late James Wise and Joan Wise; *m* 1979, Jane M. Symonds; one *d* (one *s* decd). *Educ:* Univ. of Manchester (MB ChB; MD 1980). Hon. Prof. of Clin. Microbiol., Univ. of Birmingham, 1995–; Civilian Consultant, Army, 1997–. Advr, Sci. and Technol. Cttee, H of L, 1997–99. Chm., Specialist Adv. Cttee on Antimicrobial Resistance, 2001–07; Mem., Nat. Expert Cttee on New and Emerging Diseases, 2005–07. Non-executive Director: Centre for Applied Microbiol Res., Porton Down, 1999–2003; Health Protection Agency, 2003–07. Pres., British Soc. Antimicrobial Chemotherapy, 1997–2000. Advr, European Centre for Disease Control, Stockholm, 2005–. Vice Chm., W Midlands, 2009–12, Herefordshire, 2011–, CPRE. Trustee, Hereford Nature Trust, 2002–10 (Dep. Chm., 2007–10). FMedSci 2003. Hon. FRCP 1997. *Publications:* numerous contribs on antibiotic therapy. *Recreations:* gardening, wine, food, France, walking, flying. *Address:* Springfield House, Breinton, Hereford HR4 7PB. *Clubs:* East India; Herefordshire Aero.

**WISE, Thomas Harold;** Member (UK Ind) Eastern Region, European Parliament, 2004–09; *b* 13 May 1948; *s* of Harold Stanley and Helen Wise; *m* 1974, Janet Featherstone; one *s* one *d. Educ:* Bournemouth Grammar Sch.; Bournemouth Coll. Police cadet, 1965, PC, 1967–70, Dorset Police; salesman, 1970–73, Nat. Accounts Exec., 1973–74, Aspro-Nicholas; Regl Manager, Cavenham Confectionery, 1974–78; salesman, 1978–82, Nat. Account Sales Manager, 1982–84, Melitta Benz; National Account Manager: Nestlé, 1984–85; Spillers, 1985–87; Pasta Foods, 1987–89; Sales and Mktg Manager, Chineham Internat., 1989–91; Man. Dir, Ostmann Spices, Brynmawr, 1991–94; Retail Sales Manager, Rio Pacific Foods, Watford, 1994–97; Sales Dir, Brand Mktg Internat., 1997–98; portfolio mgt, 1998–2000; Special Projects Manager, Itswine.com, 2000–01; Office Manager and Regl Organiser, E of England, UKIP, 2001–04. *Recreations:* travel, numismatics, wine appreciation.

**WISEMAN, Adam Philip Pasternak;** QC 2018; *b* Manchester, 6 March 1971; *s* of Richard Ansel Wiseman and late Sarah Anne Wiseman (*née* Levenson, later Anderson); *m* 2005, Jemma Rosanne Read; two *s* one *d. Educ:* Univ. of Exeter (BSc Hons Chem.; MSc Hons Psychol Res. Methods); Univ. of Westminster (Postgrad. DipLaw (Commendation)); Inns of Court Sch. of Law. Called to the Bar, Inner Temple, 1994; in practice as barrister, specialising in crime, inquests, inquiries and financial regulation, 1994–. *Recreations:* adventure, comedy. *Address:* Red Lion Chambers, 18 Red Lion Court, EC4A 3EB. *T:* (020) 7520 6000. *E:* adam.wiseman@18rlc.co.uk. *Club:* MCC.

**WISEMAN, Debbie,** OBE 2018 (MBE 2004); composer and conductor, film and television scores, since 1984; *b* 10 May 1963; *d* of Paul Wiseman and Barbara Wiseman; *m* 1987, Tony Wharmby. *Educ:* Henrietta Barnett Sch.; Trinity Coll. of Music, London (Saturday Exhibnr); Kingsway-Princeton Morley Coll., London; GSMD (GGSM 1984). *Film scores include:* Tom and Viv, 1994; Haunted, 1995; Wilde, 1997; Lighthouse, 1998; Tom's Midnight Garden, 1999; Before You Go, 2002; Freeze Frame, Arsène Lupin, 2004; The Truth About Love, 2005; Middletown, 2006; Flood, 2007; Lesbian Vampire Killers, The Hide, 2009; Edie, 2018; *television scores include:* The Good Guys, 1992–93; Warriors, 2000; Judge John Deed, 2001; My Uncle Silas, 2001; Othello, 2001; He Knew He Was Right, 2004; The Man-eating Leopard of Rudraprayag, 2005; Beaten, 2005; The Inspector Lynley Mysteries, 2005; Johnny and the Bomb, 2006; Jekyll, 2007; The Passion, 2008; Stephen Fry in America, 2009; Land Girls, 2009–11; Joanna Lumley's Nile, 2010; The Promise, 2011; Fry's Planet Word, 2011; Joanna Lumley's Greek Odyssey, 2011; Lost Christmas, 2012; Father Brown, 2013; WPC 56, 2013; A Poet In New York, 2014; Wolf Hall, 2015; The Coroner, 2015; Dickensian, 2016; The Queen's 90th Birthday Celebration, 2016; Shakespeare and Hathaway Private Investigators, 2017; *theatre:* Feather Boy: the musical, NT, 2006; Sweet Bird of Youth, Chichester Fest. Th., 2017; The Deep Blue Sea, Chichester Fest. Th., 2019. Vis. Prof., Composition for Screen course, RCM, 1998–. Composer in Residence, Classic FM, 2016–. President: Vaughan Williams Fest., 2018–; Making Music, 2019–. Hon. FTCL 2006; Hon. FGSM 2007; Hon. DMus Sussex, 2015. *Recreations:* swimming, table tennis, snooker. *Address:* c/o Music Matters International Ltd, Crest House, 102–104 Church Road, Teddington, Middlesex TW11 8PY. *T:* (020) 8979 4580, *Fax:* (020) 8979 4590. *E:* dwiseman10@aol.com.

**WISEMAN, Sir John William,** 11th Bt *cr* 1628; financial adviser, R. W. Pressprich & Co., Boston, since 1996; *b* 16 March 1957; *s* of Sir William George Eden Wiseman, 10th Bt, CB, and Joan Mary, *d* of late Arthur Phelps, Harrow; *S* father, 1962; *m* 1980, Nancy, *d* of Casimer Zyla, New Britain, Conn; two *d. Educ:* Millfield Sch.; Univ. of Hartford, Conn, USA. *Heir:* kinsman Thomas Alan Wiseman [*b* 8 July 1921; *m* 1946, Hildemarie Domnik (*d* 1991); (one *s* one *d* decd)].

**WISEMAN, Prof. Timothy Peter,** DPhil; FSA; FBA 1986; Professor of Classics, University of Exeter, 1977–2001, now Emeritus; *b* 3 Feb. 1940; *s* of Stephen Wiseman and Winifred Agnes Wiseman (*née* Rigby); *m* 1962, Doreen Anne Williams. *Educ:* Manchester Grammar Sch.; Balliol Coll., Oxford (MA 1964; DPhil 1967). FSA 1977. Rome Schol. in Classical Studies, British Sch. at Rome, 1962–63; University of Leicester: Asst Lectr in Classics, 1963–65; Lectr, 1965–73; Reader in Roman History, 1973–76. Vice-Pres., British Acad., 1992–94; President: Roman Soc., 1992–95; Jt Assoc. of Classical Teachers, 1998–99; Classical Assoc., 2000–01. Chm. Council, British Sch. at Rome, 2002–07. Vis. Associate Prof., Univ. of Toronto, 1970–71; Lansdowne Lectr, Univ. of Victoria (BC), 1987; Whitney J. Oates Fellow, Princeton, 1988 and 2008; Webster Lectr, Stanford, 1993. Hon. DLitt Durham, 1988. *Publications:* Catullan Questions, 1969; New Men in the Roman Senate, 1971; Cinna the Poet, 1974; Clio's Cosmetics, 1979; (with Anne Wiseman) Julius Caesar: the battle for Gaul, 1980; (ed) Roman Political Life, 1985; Catullus and his World, 1985; Roman Studies Literary and Historical, 1987; trans., Flavius Josephus, Death of an Emperor, 1991, 2nd edn (as The Death of Caligula), 2013; Talking to Virgil, 1992;

Historiography and Imagination, 1994; Remus: a Roman myth, 1995; Roman Drama and Roman History, 1998; (ed) Classics in Progress, 2002; The Myths of Rome, 2004; Unwritten Rome, 2008; Remembering the Roman People, 2009; (with Anne Wiseman) Ovid: times and reasons, 2011; The Roman Audience, 2015; How Old is Exeter?, 2016; Julius Caesar, 2016; The House of Augustus, 2019. *Address:* 22 Hillcrest Park, Exeter EX4 4SH. *T:* (01392) 273226.

**WISHART, Peter;** MP (SNP) Perth and North Perthshire, since 2005 (North Tayside, 2001–05); *b* 9 March 1962; *s* of Alex and Nan Wishart; *m* 1990, Carrie Lindsay (separated 2003); one *s*. *Educ:* Moray House Coll. of Educn. Community worker, 1984–85; musician with rock band, Runrig, 1985–2001. Chief Whip, SNP Gp, 2001–07, 2013–15; Mem., Scottish Affairs Select Cttee, 2008–10 and 2015– (Chm., 2015–). SNP spokesperson: for Culture, Media and Sport, 2001–15; Internat. Develt, 2001–10; for Constitution and Home Affairs, 2007–15; Shadow Leader of the House, 2015–. *Recreations:* music, hillwalking. *Address:* (office) 17–19 Leslie Street, Blairgowrie PH10 6AH; (office) 63 Glasgow Road, Perth PH2 0PE.

**WISHART, Ruth;** writer and broadcaster; *d* of Jack Wishart and Margaret Wishart; *m* 1971, Roderick McLeod (*d* 2004). *Educ:* Eastwood Sen. Secondary Sch.; Open Univ. (BA Hons Humanities 2008). Assistant Editor: Daily Record, 1975–78; Sunday Mail, 1978–82; Sunday Standard, 1982–83; Sen. Asst Ed., The Scotsman, 1986–88; Presenter, BBC Radio Scotland, 1986–2008; columnist, The Herald, 1998–2015. Chair: Centre for Contemporary Arts Glasgow, 1995–2003; Glasgow Common Purpose, 1998–2003; Dewar Arts Awards, 2002–. Trustee: Nat. Galls of Scotland, 2002–10; Columba 1400, 2006–12; Creative Scotland, 2010–18. Gov., Glasgow Sch. of Art, 1998–2003. FRSA. DUniv: Stirling, 1994; Open, 2017. *Recreations:* visual arts, theatre, sport, concerts, book festivals. *Address:* Clutha, Meikle Aiden Brae, Kilcreggan G84 0JD. *E:* ghillie168@gmail.com.

**WISTRICH, Enid Barbara,** PhD; Visiting Professor, School of Social Sciences (formerly of History and Politics), Middlesex University, 1997–2016; *b* 4 Sept. 1928; *d* of Zadik Heiber and Bertha Brown; *m* 1950, Ernest Wistrich, CBE (*d* 2015); one *s* one *d* (and one *s* decd). *Educ:* Froebel Institute Sch.; Brackley High Sch.; St Paul's Girls' Sch.; London School of Economics (BScEcon, PhD). Research Asst, LSE, 1950–52; Instructor, Mt Holyoke Coll., Mass, USA, 1952–53; Research Officer, Royal Inst. of Public Administration, 1954–56; Sen. Res. Officer, LSE, 1969–72; NEDO, 1977–79; Prin. Lectr, 1979–91, Reader in Politics and Public Admin, 1991–94, Middlesex Poly., subseq. Middlesex Univ. Vis. Lectr, Univ. of Waikato, NZ, 1989. Councillor (Lab): Hampstead Metropolitan Bor. Council, 1962–65; London Bor. of Camden, 1964–68 and 1971–74; GLC, ILEA, 1973–77. Mem., Hampstead Community Health Council, 1984–92 (Chm., 1986–88). Governor: British Film Inst., 1974–81 (also Actg Chm., 1977–78); National Film Sch., 1978–82. Chm. of Governors, Heathlands Sch. for Autistic Children, 1976–86. *Publications:* Local Government Reorganisation: the first years of Camden, 1972; I Don't Mind the Sex, It's the Violence: film censorship explored, 1978; The Politics of Transport, 1983; (jtly) The Migrants' Voice in Europe, 1999; (jtly) Regional Identity and Diversity in Europe, 2007; (jtly) Devolution and Localism in England, 2014; chapters and articles in various books and jls. *Recreations:* experiencing the arts, admiring nature. *Address:* 37B Gayton Road, NW3 1UB. *T:* (020) 7419 1742.
*See also* H. K. Wistrich.

**WISTRICH, Harriet Katherine;** Solicitor, Birnberg Peirce Ltd, since 2002; Director, Centre for Women's Justice, since 2016; *b* London, 18 June 1960; *d* of late Ernest Wistrich, CBE and Enid Barbara Wistrich, *qv*, civil partnership 2006, Julie Bindel. *Educ:* Hampstead Comprehensive Sch.; City of East London Coll.; New Coll., Oxford (BA Hons); Westminster Univ. (CPE). Work in film and video and trng, 1983–93; trainee solicitor, Winstanley Burgess, 1995–97; admitted as solicitor, 1997; with Thanki Novy Taube Solicitors, 1997–2002. *Publications:* (ed jtly) The Map of My Life: the story of Emma Humphreys, 2003; contribs to Guardian, Daily Mail, Huffington Post, Hampstead and Highgate Express, Metro and legal pubns. *Recreations:* travel, cinema, food and wine, discussing politics, Zumba, yoga. *Address:* 55 Rathcoole Gardens, N8 9NE; c/o Birnberg Peirce Ltd, 14 Inverness Street, NW1 7HJ. *T:* 07812 149293. *E:* harrietwistrich64@yahoo.co.uk, h.wistrich@centreforwomensjustice.org.uk.

**WITCHELL, Nicholas Newton Henshall;** Diplomatic Correspondent, since 1995, Royal Correspondent, since 1998, BBC News; *b* 23 Sept. 1953; *s* of late William Joseph Henshall Witchell and Barbara Sybil Mary Witchell (*née* Macdonald); two *d*; *m* 2014, Maria Frances Staples. *Educ:* Epsom Coll.; Leeds Univ. (LLB). Joined BBC, 1976: grad. news trainee, 1976–78; reporter: TV and radio, NI, 1978–82; TV Network News, 1982–83; Ireland Corresp., 1983–84; Presenter: Six O'Clock News, 1984–89; BBC Breakfast News, 1989–94; Associate Producer: News '39, 1989; News '44, 1994; News '45, 1995; Corresp., Panorama, 1994–95. Gov., Queen Elizabeth's Foundn (formerly Queen Elizabeth's Foundn for Disabled People), 1992– (Vice-Pres., 2010–). Hon. Patron, Queen Alexandra Hosp. Home, 2006–. Founding Trustee, Normandy Meml Trust, 2016–. FRGS 1990. Sony Radio Acad. Event Award, 2002. OStJ 1995. *Publications:* The Loch Ness Story, 1974. *Address:* BBC News, BBC Broadcasting House, Portland Place, W1A 1AA. *Club:* Reform.

**WITCHER, Sally Anne,** OBE 2006; PhD; Chief Executive Officer, Inclusion Scotland, since 2013; *b* 11 July 1960; *d* of late Michael James Witcher and of Janet Mary Witcher (*née* Ashford). *Educ:* Slade Sch. of Fine Art (BA Hons); University Coll. London; Edinburgh Univ. (MSc Policy Studies, PhD Social Policy 2006). Teacher, English as a Foreign Language, British Inst., Lisbon, 1984–85; freelance sculptor, 1985–87; Homeless Families Liaison Worker, Earls Court Homelessness Project, 1987–89; Campaign Worker, Disability Alliance, 1989–93; Dir, CPAG, 1993–98; freelance mgt and social policy consultant, 1998–2006. Chair, Disability Employment Adv. Cttee, DWP, 2002–06; Dep. Dir, Office for Disability Issues, DWP, 2006–10; freelance mgt and social policy consultant, 2010–13. Mem. Bd, Care Inspectorate (formerly Social Care and Social Work Improvement Scotland), 2011–15; Chair, Scottish Commn on Social Security, 2019–. *Publications:* (jtly) A Way out of Poverty and Disability, 1991; (jtly) Letters, Lobbies, Legislation: a guide to Parliamentary campaigning in Scotland, 1999; (jtly) Direct Payments: the impact on choice and control for disabled people, 2000; (jtly) Bodies Politic: a guide for voluntary organisations lobbying in Holyrood, Westminster and Brussels, 2002; Reviewing the terms of inclusion: transactional processes, currencies and context, 2003; Inclusive Equality: a vision for social justice, 2013.

**WITCOMB, Roger Mark,** OBE 2015; Panel Chairman, Competition and Markets Authority, 2014–16; *b* Devizes, 5 May 1947; *s* of Cyril and Jo Witcomb; *m* 1970, Marian Stone; two *s*. *Educ:* Eton Coll.; Merton Coll., Oxford (BA Maths 1968); Nuffield Coll., Oxford (MPhil Econs 1970). Economist, Bank of England, 1970–71; Fellow, Churchill Coll., Cambridge, 1972–74; Fellow, Gonville and Caius Coll., Cambridge, 1974–79; Res. Officer, Dept of Applied Econs, Univ. of Cambridge, 1976–79; Commercial Manager, BP, 1980–89; schoolmaster, Winchester Coll., 1989–90; Dir of Planning, 1990–96, Finance Dir, 1996–2000, Nat. Power; Headhunter, Saxton Bampfylde, 2001–02; Senior Adviser: CDC, 2002–04; Actis, 2004–07. Director: Anglian Water, 2002–10; Andrews & Partners, 2005–11; Infraco Ltd, 2005–11; Renewable Energy Hldgs, 2009–10. Mem., Competition Commn, 2009–14 (Chm., 2011–14). Chair, Ofgem RIIO–2 Challenge Gp, 2018–. Trustee, Opportunity Internat. UK, 2002–14, 2018– (Chm., 2004–06). Gov., Univ. of Winchester, 2004–11 (Chm., 2006–11). Hon. DBA Winchester, 2012. *Recreations:* music, golf, walking, cricket. *E:* roger@oldplough.com.

**WITCOMBE, Very Rev. John Julian;** Dean of Coventry, since 2013; *b* Wimbledon, 1 March 1959; *s* of Dr Dennis Witcombe, OBE, and Patricia Witcombe; *m* 1st, 1983, Rev. Maureen Edwards (*d* 1999); one *s* two *d*; 2nd, 2000, Rev. Ricarda Leask (*née* Anderson); two step *d*. *Educ:* Nottingham High Sch.; Emmanuel Coll., Cambridge (BA Hons Law 1980); St John's Coll., Nottingham (BA Hons Theol. 1983); Univ. of Nottingham (MPhil 1991). Ordained deacon, 1984, priest, 1985; Curate, St John's, Birtley, 1984–87; Team Vicar, St Barnabas, Inham Nook, 1987–91; Vicar, St Luke's, Lodge Moor, 1991–95; Team Rector, Uxbridge, 1995–98; Dean, St John's Coll., Nottingham, 1998–2005; Diocese of Gloucester: Dir of Ordinands, 2005–11; Dir of Discipleship and Ministry, 2011–13. Hon. Canon, 2009–10, Res. Canon, 2010–12, Glos Cath. *Publications:* Renewing the Traditional Church, 2002; The Curate's Guide, 2005; Hanging on to God, 2008. *Recreations:* hillwalking, family, theatre, galleries, film, music, travel. *Address:* Coventry Cathedral, 1 Hill Top, Coventry CV1 5AB. *T:* (024) 7652 1200. *E:* dean@coventrycathedral.org.uk.

**WITHALL, Maj.-Gen. William Nigel James,** CB 1982; Marketing Director, and Member, Board of Directors, Link-Miles Ltd, 1985–93 (Consultant, 1984); *b* 14 Oct. 1928; *s* of late Bernard Withall and Enid (*née* Hill); *m* 1952, Pamela Hickman; one *s* one *d*. *Educ:* St Benedict's. Army Engr Cadet, 1947–50; Mons OCS, 1950; Commnd RE, 1950; served in Hong Kong, Gulf States, Aden, Germany and India; Staff Coll., 1961; Sqdn Comd, 73 Fd Sqdn, 1964–66; Jt Services Staff Coll., Latimer, 1967; Mil. Asst to MGO, 1968–70; CO 26 Engr Regt, BAOR, 1970–72; Bde Comd, 11 Engr Bde, 1974–76; NDC, India, 1977; No 259 Army Pilots Course, 1978; Dir, Army Air Corps, 1979–83. Col Comdt RE, 1984–97. Chm., Army Football Assoc., 1980–81; Pres., Army Cricket Assoc., 1981–83; Hon. Life Vice Pres., Aircrew Assoc., 1986; Chm., RE Assoc., 1993–97. Chm., Chute Parish Council, 1995–2002. Freeman, City of London, 1981; Liveryman, Hon. Co. of Air Pilots (formerly GAPAN), 1981. *Recreations:* cricket (Army Cricket XI, 1957–67), squash, all games, reading, walking. *Address:* Linden House, Upper Chute, near Andover, Hants SP11 9EL. *Clubs:* MCC, I Zingari, Band of Brothers, Free Foresters, Stragglers of Asia.

**WITHERFORD, Stephen Michael;** Founder and Director, Witherford Watson Mann Architects, since 2001; *b* Stourbridge, W Midlands, 5 July 1967; *s* of Geoffrey and Gillian Witherford; partner, Jane Clift; two *d*. *Educ:* Summerhill Secondary Sch., Kingswinford; Dudley Coll. of Technol. (OND Building Construction 1T85); Plymouth Poly. (BA 1st Cl. Hons Arch. 1988); Univ. of Cambridge (DipArch 1991; Postgrad. Cert. Professional Practice in Arch. 1993). Conran Roche Architects, 1988–89; Eric Parry Architects, 1992–2002. Major projects include: Human Rights Action Centre, Amnesty Internat. UK, 2005; Bankside Urban Forest, 2007–; Whitechapel Gall., 2009; Olympic Legacy Masterplan Framework, 2012; Astley Castle, Nuneaton, 2012. Vis. Fellow, LSE, 2008–09. Member: CABE Olympic Design Rev. Panel, 2006–10; Design Adv. Gp, Mayor of London, 2013–16. Member: Adv. Council, Tate Modern, 2008–16; Faculty of Fine Arts, British Sch. in Rome, 2013–17. Artist Trustee, Tate Gall., 2015–. Stirling Prize, RIBA, for Astley Castle, 2013. *Recreations:* family, art, music, bird watching, walking. *Address:* Witherford Watson Mann Architects, Coate House, 1 Coate Street, E2 9AG. *T:* (020) 7613 3113. *E:* stephen.witherford@wwmarchitects.co.uk.

**WITHERIDGE, Rev. John Stephen,** MA; FRHistS; Headmaster of Charterhouse, 1996–2013; Hon. Chaplain and Associate Senior Member, Christ Church, Oxford, since 2016; Chaplain to the Queen, since 2017; *b* 14 Nov. 1953; *s* of late Francis Edward Witheridge and Joan Elizabeth Witheridge (*née* Exell); *m* 1975, Sarah Caroline, *d* of Rev. Peter Phillips; two *s* two *d*. *Educ:* St Albans Sch.; Univ. of Kent at Canterbury (BA 1st cl. Eng. and Theol.); Christ's Coll., Cambridge (BA 2nd cl. Theol Tripos; MA); Ridley Hall, Cambridge. Ordained deacon, 1979, priest, 1980; Curate, Luton Parish Church, 1979–82; Head of Religious Studies and Asst Chaplain, Marlborough Coll., 1982–84; Chaplain to Archbishop of Canterbury, 1984–87; Hon. Curate, St Martin-in-the-Fields, 1984–87; Conduct (Sen. Chaplain), Eton Coll., 1987–96. Associate Sen. Mem., Wadham Coll., Oxford, 2014–16. Chm., Lomans Trust, 2000–07; Vice-Pres., Eyeless Trust, 2001–07. Mem. Ct, Univ. of Surrey, 1997–2013. Governor: Brambletye Sch., 2008–12; Clifton Coll., 2009–13. FRHistS 2013. *Publications:* Frank Fletcher: a formidable headmaster, 2005; Excellent Dr Stanley: the life of Dean Stanley of Westminster, 2013; articles and reviews. *Recreations:* biography, gardening, grandchildren. *Address:* Minster Cottage, Church Street, Charlbury, Oxon OX7 3PR.

**WITHEROW, David Michael Lindley,** CBE 2004; Executive Chairman, Radio Authority, 2003 (Member, 1998–2003; Deputy Chair, 2000–03); *b* 19 July 1937; *s* of Dr James Witherow and Greta (*née* Roberts); *m* 1st, 1960, Ragnhild Kadow (marr. diss. 1994); two *d*; 2nd, 1994, Elizabeth Anne Wright, *qv*. *Educ:* King Edward's Sch., Birmingham (Foundn Schol.); Pembroke Coll., Cambridge (BA Hons 1960). Nat. service, RCS, 1955–57. Press Assoc., 1960–63; BBC, 1963–96: Ext. Services News, 1963–77, Editor, 1973–77; Editor, Weekly Progs, TV News, 1977–79; Chief Assistant, Regions, 1980; Head, then Gen. Manager, Monitoring Service, Caversham, 1980–85; Controller, Resources and Admin, Ext. Services, 1985–89; Dep. Man. Dir, 1989–94, Policy Consultant, 1994–96, World Service; Project Dir, Digital Audio Broadcasting Services, 1994–96. Pres., World (formerly Europ.) DAB Forum, 1995–97. *Recreations:* theatre, music. *E:* davidmlw2@hotmail.com.

**WITHEROW, John Moore;** Editor, The Times, since 2013; *b* Johannesburg, 20 Jan. 1952; *m* 1985 (marr. diss.); two *s* one *d*. *Educ:* Bedford Sch.; York Univ. (BA Hons Hist.). Reuters trainee, London and Madrid, 1977–80; home and foreign corresp., The Times, 1980–83; Sunday Times: Defence corresp., 1984–85; Diplomatic Corresp., 1985–87; Focus Ed., 1987–89; Foreign Ed., 1989–92; Man. Ed. (News), 1992–94; Actg Ed., 1994; Ed., 1995–2013. *Publications:* (with Patrick Bishop) The Winter War: the Falklands, 1982; The Gulf War, 1993. *Recreations:* tennis, sailing. *Address:* The Times, 1 London Bridge Street, SE1 9GF. *T:* (020) 7782 5640. *E:* john.witherow@thetimes.co.uk. *Clubs:* Soho House, Hurlingham, Ivy; Campden Hill Tennis.

**WITHERS, Prof. Charles William John,** PhD; FBA 2006; FRSE, FRGS, FRSGS, FRHistS; Professor of Historical Geography, University of Edinburgh, since 1994 (Head, Institute of Geography, 2006–09); Geographer Royal for Scotland, since 2015; *b* 6 Dec. 1954; *s* of John Alastair Withers and Mary Alicia Withers (*née* Green); *m* 1980, Anne Marshall Hamilton; two *s* one *d*. *Educ:* St Andrews Univ. (BSc Hons); Downing Coll., Cambridge (PhD 1982). FRGS 1978; FAcSS (AcSS 2001); FRHistS 2002; CGeog 2003; FRSGS 2011. University of Gloucestershire: Lectr, 1981–84; Principal Lectr, 1984–92; Prof., 1992–94; Hd of Dept, 1991–94; Associate Dean, 1992–94. MAE 2000. FRSE 2006. FRSA 2000. *Publications:* Gaelic in Scotland 1698–1981, 1984; The Highland Communities of Dundee and Perth 1797–1891, 1986; Gaelic Scotland, 1988; Discovering the Cotswolds, 1990; Urban Highlanders, 1998; Geography, Science and National Identity: Scotland since 1520, 2001; Placing the Enlightenment, 2007; Geography and Science in Britain 1831–1939, 2010; joint editor: Urbanising Britain, 1991; Geography and Enlightenment, 1999; Science and Medicine in the Scottish Enlightenment, 2002; Georgian Geographies,

2004; Geography and Revolution, 2005; Geographies of the Book, 2010; Geographies of Nineteenth-Century Science, 2011; (jtly) Scotland: mapping the nation, 2011; (jtly) Travels into Print: exploration, writing and publishing with John Murray, 1773–1859, 2015; Geography, Technology and Instruments of Exploration, 2015; (jtly) Scotland: mapping the islands, 2016; Zero Degrees: geographies of the Prime Meridian, 2017; numerous articles in learned jls. *Recreations:* hill-walking, theatre, reading, food and wine, watercolour painting. *Address:* Institute of Geography, University of Edinburgh, Drummond Street, Edinburgh EH8 9XP. *T:* (0131) 650 2559, *Fax:* (0131) 650 2524. *E:* c.w.j.withers@ed.ac.uk.

**WITHERS, Dr Paul Nigel;** Senior Independent Director: Devro plc, since 2011; Keller plc, since 2012; *b* Kingston-upon-Thames, 5 June 1956; *s* of Roy and Pauline Withers; *m* 1987, Gillian Halliday; one *s* one *d. Educ:* St Peter's Sch., York; Trinity Coll., Cambridge (BA 1st Cl. Maths 1978); Open Univ. (MSc); Linacre Coll., Oxford (DPhil Maths 2016). John Brown Engineers, 1978–84; BPB plc, 1985–90; Mktg Dir, 1990–96, Man. Dir, 1996–2000, British Gypsum Ltd; Director: BPB plc, 2000–06; Hyder Consulting plc, 2006–2014; Premier Farnell plc, 2007–16; Boat Race Co. Ltd, 2014–. Chm. Govs, Magdalen Coll. Sch., Oxford, 2018–. Sloan Fellow, London Business Sch., 1985. *Address:* Old Whitehill Barn, Tackley, Oxon OX5 3AB. *T:* 07778 673918. *E:* paul.n.withers@gmail.com. *Clubs:* Cambridge University Boat; Leander (Henley-on-Thames).

**WITHERS, Roger Dean;** Chairman, Safecharge Ltd, since 2014; *b* Bradfield, Berks, 15 Aug. 1942; *s* of Frederick Charles Withers and Norah Daisy Withers; *m* 1963, Patricia Margaret Fenn; one *s.* Associate, Booz, Allen and Hamilton, 1968–73; Divl Dir, Ladbroke plc, 1973–86; Bass plc: Divl Dir, 1986–98; Man. Dir, Coral, 1997–98; Chm., Bass Leisure, South Africa, 1996–99; Chairman: Littlewoods Leisure, 1999–2000; Arena Leisure plc, 2001–06; Playtech Ltd, 2006–13; Sportech plc, 2011–17 (Sen. non-exec. Dir, 2000–05). Non-exec. Dir, Inspired Entertainment Inc., 2016–. Advr, Scientific Games Inc., 2000–13. *Recreations:* game shooting, food and wine, classic cars. *Address:* PO Box 325, Aylesbury HP17 8BD. *T:* 07802 155255. *E:* rogerwithers@compuserve.com. *Club:* Oriental.

**WITHERS, Prof. Stephen George,** PhD; FRS 2012; FRS(Can) 2002; Professor of Chemistry and Biochemistry, University of British Columbia, since 1991 (Director, Center for High-Throughput Biology, 2006–13); *b* Horton, Somerset, 1 May 1953; *s* of William Eric George Withers and May Avril Withers; *m* 1986, Pamela Anne Miller; one *s. Educ:* Ilminster Grammar Sch.; Univ. of Bristol (BSc Chem. 1974; PhD Chem. 1977). Postdoctoral Fellow and Res. Associate, Univ. of Alberta, 1977–82; Asst Prof., 1982–87, Associate Prof., 1987–91, Univ. of BC. Scientific Dir, P.E.N.C.E., 2000–05. *Publications:* contribs to chem. and biochem. jls. *Recreations:* kayaking and canoeing, hiking, cabin life, reading, theatre. *Address:* Department of Chemistry, University of British Columbia, 2036 Main Mall, Vancouver, BC V6T 1Z1, Canada. *T:* 6048223402. *E:* withers@chem.ubc.ca.

**WITHEY, Anthony George Hurst,** CBE 1997; FCMA, CGMA; Chief Executive, Remploy Ltd, 1988–2000; *b* 4 Oct. 1942; *s* of Walter Ronald Withey and Laura Maria Withey (*née* Thomas); *m* 1967, Yvonne Jeanette Price Withey; one *s* one *d. Educ:* Bishop Gore Grammar Sch., Swansea; Wadham Coll., Oxford (BA Hons Modern Hist.); Henley Business Sch. (GMC). FCMA 1986; CGMA 2012. Gen. Manager, BXL Plastics Ltd, various divs, and Dir, various subsids, 1976–83; Gp Exec., Tarmac Bldg Products Ltd, 1983–85; Chief Exec., Polymers Div., Evered Holdings PLC, 1985–88. Director: Pan Graphics Industries Ltd, 1991–94; Linx Printing Technologies PLC, 1994–2005; Océ (UK) Ltd, 2000–10; Chm., Electron Technologies Ltd, 2003–08. Director: Morriston Hosp. NHS Trust, 1997–99; Swansea NHS Trust, 1999–2002. Dir, Internat. Orgn for Provision of Work to Disabled People, 1993–2000. Mem., S Wales Police Selection Panel, 1998–2002. Mem. Council, Industrial Soc., 1989–2000. Chm., Crawshay Court (Langland Bay) Mgt Co. Ltd, 2000–18. *Recreations:* squash, gardening, antiques, theatre. *Club:* Swansea Lawn Tennis and Squash Racquets.

**WITNEY, Nicholas Kenneth James;** Senior Policy Fellow, European Council on Foreign Relations, since 2008; *b* 14 Dec. 1950; *s* of Kenneth Witney and Joan Witney (*née* Tait); *m* 1st, 1977, Ann Margaret Ruskell (marr. diss. 2011); one *s* one *d;* 2nd, 2012, Lucy Jane Aspinall. *Educ:* Tonbridge Sch.; Corpus Christi Coll., Oxford (MA Lit.Hum). Joined Foreign and Commonwealth Office, 1973: E European and Soviet Dept, 1973; Arabic lang. trng, Lebanon and Jordan, 1974–76; Third, later Second, Sec., Baghdad, 1976–78; Second, later First, Sec. and Private Sec. to Ambassador, Washington, 1978–82; EC Dept, FCO, 1982–83; on secondment, later perm. transfer, to MoD, 1983–2007: Principal: defence policy Africa/Asia, 1983–85; Army budget and plans, 1985–87; Director: (Ops), Saudi Armed Forces Project, 1987–90; Nuclear Policy and Security, 1990–93; sabbatical at Rand Corp., Santa Monica, 1993–94; Hd, Housing Project Team, 1994–96; Dir-Gen., Mgt and Orgn, 1996–98; Asst Under-Sec. of State, Systems, 1998–99; Director-General: Equipment, 1999–2002; Internat. Security Policy, 2002–04; Chief Exec., European Defence Agency, 2004–07. Trustee, Asylos, 2014–18. *Publications:* The British Nuclear Deterrent after the Cold War, 1994; (jtly) Western European Nuclear Forces, 1995; (contrib.) The Oxford Handbook of War, 2012. *Recreations:* Rugby, sailing, acting, European history. *Address:* European Council on Foreign Relations, 159–165 Great Portland Street, W1W 5PA.

**WITNEY, Dr Simon Richard;** Special Counsel, Debevoise & Plimpton LLP, since 2017; *b* Epping, Essex, 28 Sept. 1967; *s* of Richard and Linda Witney; *m* 1995, Claire Turnbull; three *d. Educ:* Leverton Primary Sch., Waltham Abbey; Davenant Foundn Sch., Loughton; Hertford Coll., Oxford (BA Hons Juris 1989); Leicester Univ. (MPhil 1990); INSEAD, Fontainebleau (MBA 1995); London Sch. of Econs and Pol Sci. (PhD 2017). Admitted as solicitor, 1994; Associate, 1995–2001, Partner, 2001–13, SJ Berwin. Vis. Prof. in Practice, LSE, 2018–. Mem. Council, British Venture Capital Assoc., 2017–. *Address:* Great Chesterford, Essex.

**WITT, Karsten;** Joint Founder, and Managing Director, Karsten Witt Musik Management GmbH, since 2004; *b* Hamburg, 5 March 1952; *s* of Reimer Witt and Hilde Witt (*née* Vöge); *m* 1st, 1982, Anna Zeijl; three *s;* 2nd, 1996, Marie-Annick Le Blanc. *Educ:* Univ. of Hamburg (BA Philosophy of Sci.); Univ. of Constance (MA). Founder: Junge Deutsche Philharmonie (Nat. Student Orch.), 1974 (Manager, 1974–87); Deutsche Kammerphilharmonie, 1980 (Manager, 1980–89); Ensemble Modern, 1980 (Manager, 1980–91); Manager, ISCM (German Br.), 1986–90; Gen. Sec., Vienna Konzerthaus, 1991–96; Pres., Deutsche Grammophon, 1996–99; CEO, S Bank Centre, London, 1999–2002; Artistic Advr, Megaron Athens, 2005–08; projects with Shaksfin Asia, 2002–04. Governor: Deutsche Ensemble Akad., 1999–; GSMD, 2000–03; Wiener Konzerthausges., 2002–13. Curator, Allianz Cultural Foundn, 2001–08. Ehrenkreuz für Wissenschaft und Kunst (Austria), 1996; Silbernes Ehrenzeichen für Verdienste um das Land Wien, 1997; Cross of Merit (Hungary), 1999. *Address:* (office) Leuschnerdamm 13, 10999 Berlin, Germany.

**WITTENBERG, Nicola,** *see* Solomon, N.

**WITTY, Sir Andrew (Philip),** Kt 2012; Chief Executive, Optum, since 2018; *b* 1964; *m* Caroline; one *s* one *d. Educ:* Univ. of Nottingham (BA Econs 1985). Joined Glaxo, 1985; Dir, Pharmacy and Distribn; internat. product manager; Man. Dir, Glaxo S Africa; Area Dir, S and E Africa; Vice-Pres., Glaxo Wellcome; Sen. Vice Pres., Asia Pacific; Pres., GlaxoSmithKline Europe, 2003; Chief Exec., GlaxoSmithKline plc, 2008–17. Venture Partner, Hatteras Venture Partners, 2017–. Dir, United Health Gp, 2017–18; Mem., Bd of Dirs, G1 Therapeutics, 2017–; Mem. Bd, Synthego, 2017–. Non-exec. Dir, BIS, 2011–13. Pres., Eur. Fedn of Pharmaceutical Industries and Assocs, 2010–13. Chancellor, Univ. of Nottingham, 2013–18. Hon. FMedSci 2012. Public Service Medal, 2003, Public Service Star, 2012 (Singapore).

**WITTY, Mark F.;** *see* Featherstone-Witty.

**WLACHOVSKÝ, Miroslav;** Ambassador of Slovak Republic to the Kingdom of Denmark, since 2018; *b* Bratislava, 3 Feb. 1970; *s* of Karol Wlachovský and Miroslava Wlachovská; *m* 2009, Jaroslava Nováková; one *s. Educ:* Comenius Univ., Bratislava (Magister Philosophy and Sociology). Hd, Editl Dept and Editor-in-Chief of qly Internat. Issues, Slovak Inst. for Internat. Studies, 1994–95; Dir, Res. Centre, Slovak Foreign Policy Assoc., 1995–98; Dir, Analysis and Planning Dept, Min. of Foreign Affairs, Slovak Republic, 1998–2001; Foreign Policy Advr to Prime Minister of Slovak Republic, 2001–03; Hd, Political Section, 2003–05, Dep. Chief of Mission, 2005–07, Washington, DC; Dir, Strategic Planning Unit, Analysis and Planning Dept, Min. of Foreign Affairs, 2007–09; Sen. Human Rights Expert, Perm. Mission of Slovak Republic to Internat. Orgns, Vienna, 2009–11; Ambassador to the Court of St James's, 2011–15; Advr to Minister of Foreign and European Affairs, Slovak Republic, 2015–17; Hd of Strategic Communications Unit, Min. of Foreign and European Affairs, Slovak Republic, 2017–18. *Recreations:* cycling, swimming, hiking, travelling, music, film, cooking.

**WODEHOUSE,** family name of **Earl of Kimberley**.

**WODEHOUSE, Lord; David Simon John Wodehouse;** *b* 10 Oct. 1978; *s* and *heir* of Earl of Kimberley, *qv; m* 2016, Heidi Tonkin; one *s.*

**WOGAN, Patrick Francis Michael,** CMG 1991; HM Diplomatic Service, retired; Sensitivity Reviewer, Foreign and Commonwealth Office, 2008–19; *m* 1st, 1960, Rosmarie Diederich (marr. diss. 1988); one *s* one *d;* 2nd, 1988, Afsaneh Khalatbari. Joined FO, subseq. FCO, 1959; Second Sec., Bahrain, 1970; Second, then First, Sec., FCO, 1972; Brussels, 1976; FCO, 1981; Counsellor, FCO, 1983, Tehran, 1984; RCDS, 1987; Consul-Gen. and Dep. High Comr, Karachi, 1988; Ambassador to Iceland, 1991–93; Ambassador and Consul-Gen., Qatar, 1993–97. Officer of H of L, 1999–2004.

**WOJNAROWSKA, Prof. Fenella Theta,** DM; FRCP; Professor of Dermatology, University of Oxford, 1999–2009, now Emeritus; Consultant Dermatologist, Oxford Radcliffe NHS Trust, 1984–2009; *b* Oxford, 23 Oct. 1947; *d* of Kostek Wojnarowski and Muriel Wojnarowska; one *s; m* 2008, John Gardiner. *Educ:* Oxford High Sch. for Girls; Tonbridge Girls' Grammar Sch.; Somerville Coll., Univ. of Oxford (BA Animal Physiol.; MSc 1971; DM 1995); St Mary's Hosp. Med. Sch., London (BM BCh 1973). FRCP 1993. Dermatology trng, St John's Hosp. for Diseases of the Skin and St Mary's Hosp., London, 1977–84; Sen. Clin. Lectr, 1992–2002, Reader in Dermatol., 1996–99, Univ. of Oxford; Hon. Sen. Res. Fellow, Somerville Coll., Oxford, 2005–. Founder Mem., British Soc. for the Study of Vulval Disease, 1998– (Chm. and Pres., 2000–); Mem. Bd, Eur. Women's Dermatologic Soc., 1999–2009 (Pres., 2007–09). Chm., Tumour Site Specific Cancer Gp for skin, Thames Valley Cancer Gp, 2002–08. European Academy of Dermatology and Venereology: UK Bd Mem., 2004–09; Chm., Fostering Dermatology and Venereology Cttee, 2004–09; Member: Membership Cttee, 2004–06; CME Cttee, 2004–08; Exec. Cttee, 2008–10; Jt Ed., EADV News, 2004–07; Lead for Skin Diseases in Pregnancy Task Force, 2006–10. Mem., Guidelines Cttee, 2005–09, Lead on Eur. Guidelines for Safety of Topical Steroids in Pregnancy, 2006–11, Eur. Dermatology Forum. Maria M. Duran Lect., Internat. Soc. of Dermatology, 2006; Parkes Weber Lect., RCP, 2008; Gerald Levene Meml Lect., RSocMed, 2009. Chm., Bude and Dist U3A, 2013–16. Chm., Tresmeer Parish Council, 2013–16. Volunteer, Royal Med. Benevolent Fund, 2010–15; Bursary Sec., Oxford Univ. Cornwall Soc., 2014–; Mentor, Aspire Prog., Launceston Coll., 2016–; Cttee and Jt Prog. Co-ordinator, Café Scientifique, Launceston, 2016–. Gov., Launceston Coll., 2017–. Certificate of Appreciation, Internat. League of Dermatol Socs, 2009; Presidential Recognition Award, Internat. Soc. for Study of Vulvovaginal Disease, 2009. *Publications: contributions to:* Textbook of Dermatology, 3rd edn 1979 to 8th edn 2010; Textbook of Paediatric Dermatology, 2000, 2nd edn 2005; Kidney Transplantation, 5th edn 2001, 6th edn 2008; Dermatology, 2003, 2nd edn 2008; Oxford Textbook of Medicine, 4th edn 2005, 5th edn 2010; more than 300 articles in med. and scientific jls on autoimmune bullous disease, transplant dermatology and women's health (vulval disease, pregnancy dermatoses and their treatment). *Recreations:* gardening, walking, travel. *Address:* c/o Nuffield Department of Clinical Medicine, University of Oxford, Headington, Oxford OX3 9DU. *E:* fenella@northtregeare.com.

**WOLANSKI, Adam Michael Venantius,** QC 2019; *b* London, 1968; *s* of Adam and Anne Wolanski; *m* 2000, Alexandra Marzec; two *s. Educ:* Robinson Coll., Cambridge (BA Hons 1990); CPE 1992. Called to the Bar, Lincoln's Inn, 1995; in practice as a barrister, specialising in media law. *Publications:* (jtly) Law of Privacy and the Media, 2016. *Recreations:* ski-ing, cycling, windsurfing, gigs. *Address:* 5RB Chambers, Gray's Inn, WC1R 5AH.

**WOLF,** family name of **Baroness Wolf of Dulwich**.

**WOLF OF DULWICH,** Baroness *cr* 2014 (Life Peer), of Dulwich in the London Borough of Southwark; **Alison Margaret Wolf,** CBE 2012; Sir Roy Griffiths Professor of Public Sector Management, King's College London, since 2006 (Professor, since 2004); *d* of Herbert Kingsley Potter and Winnie Morrison (*née* Gove); *m* 1970, Martin Harry Wolf, *qv;* two *s* one *d. Educ:* Oxford High Sch.; Somerville Coll., Oxford (MA, MPhil). Res. Associate, Nat. Inst. of Educn, Washington, 1975–82; Res. Officer, 1983–85, Sen. Res. Officer, 1985–95, Prof., 1995–2004, Inst. of Educn, Univ. of London. Conducted Wolf Rev. of Vocational Educn, 2010–11, Advr, 2011–, DFE. Member, Council: UN Univ., 2003–11; KCL, 2011–19; Trustee: KCL Maths Sch., 2013– (Chm. of Govs, 2013–17); Friends of KCL Maths Sch., 2017–. Chm., Somerville Assoc., 2018–. Trustee: Abbeyfield Soc., Newbury, 2000–; Social Market Foundn, 2013–17. Hon. FKC 2013; Hon. FCGI 2017; Hon. Fellow, Birkbeck, Univ. of London. *Publications:* Does Education Matter?, 2002; An Adult Approach to Further Education, 2009; Education and Economic Performance, 2011; The XX Factor: how working women are creating a new society, 2013. *Recreations:* reading, walking, music. *Address:* Business School, King's College London, Bush House, 30 Aldwych, WC2B 4BG. *T:* (020) 7848 3724. *E:* alison.wolf@kcl.ac.uk.

*See also* R. Wolf.

**WOLF, Prof. (Charles) Roland,** OBE 2010; PhD; FMedSci; FRSE; FBTS; Strategic Director, School of Medicine, University of Dundee, since 2014; *b* 26 Feb. 1949; *s* of Werner Max Wolf and Elisabeth Wolf; *m* 1975, Helga Loth; one *s* one *d. Educ:* Univ. of Surrey (BSc Chem.; PhD Biochem. 1975). Vis. Fellow, Nat. Inst. of Envmtl Health Scis, N Carolina, 1977–80; Vis. Scientist, ICI Central Toxicology Labs, Macclesfield, 1980–81;

Hd of Biochemistry, Inst. of Toxicology, Univ. of Mainz, W Germany, 1981–82; Sen. Scientist, ICRF Med. Oncology Unit, Western Gen. Hosp., Edinburgh, 1982–86; Head, ICRF Molecular Pharmacology Gp, Univ. of Edinburgh, 1986–92; Dir, Univ. of Dundee Med. Res. Inst. (formerly Biomed. Res. Centre), 1992–2014; Hon. Dir, CRUK (formerly ICRF) Molecular Pharmacol. Unit, 1992–2011. FRSE 1995; FRSA 1999; FMedSci 2000. *Publications:* (ed jtly) Molecular Genetics of Drug Resistance, 1997; over 500 scientific papers on drug develt, toxicol., cancer res. *Recreations:* weaving, carpentry, piano playing, gardening, poetry, hiking. *Address:* School of Medicine, University of Dundee, Level 9, Jacqui Wood Cancer Centre, James Arnott Drive, Ninewells Hospital and Medical School, Dundee DD1 9SY. *T:* (01382) 383134.

**WOLF, Martin Harry,** CBE 2000; Associate Editor, since 1990, and Chief Economics Commentator, since 1996, Financial Times; *b* 16 Aug. 1946; *s* of Edmund Wolf and Rebecca Wolf (*née* Wijnschenk); *m* 1970, Alison Margaret Potter (*see* Baroness Wolf of Dulwich); two *s* one *d. Educ:* University College Sch.; Corpus Christi Coll., Oxford (MA 1st cl. Hons Mods 1967; 1st cl. Hons PPE 1969; Hon. Fellow, 2007); Nuffield Coll., Oxford (MPhil (BPhil Econs 1971); Hon. Fellow, 2010). World Bank: Young Professional, 1971; Sen. Economist, India Div., 1974–77, Internat. Trade Div., 1979–81; Dir of Studies, Trade Policy Res. Centre, 1981–87; Chief Economics Leader Writer, Financial Times, 1987–96. Hon. Prof., Economics Dept, Univ. of Nottingham, 2011– (Special Prof., 1993–2011); Vis. Fellow, Nuffield Coll., Oxford, 1999–2007. Member: NCC, 1987–93; Council, REconS, 1991–96; UK Govt Ind. Commn on Banking, 2010–11. Advr and Rapporteur, Eminent Persons Gp on World Trade, 1990. Hon. FKC 2012; Global Fellow, Columbia Univ., NY, 2013. Hon. DLitt: Nottingham, 2006; Kingston, 2010; Macquarie, 2012; Hon. DSc: (Econs) LSE, 2006; Warwick, 2009; Hon. Dr KU Leuven, 2018. (Jtly) Sen. Prize, Wincott Foundn, 1989 and 1997; RTZ David Watt Meml Prize, 1994; Decade of Excellence Award, 2003, Commentator of the Year, 2008, Business Journalist of the Year Awards; Newspaper Feature of the Year Award, 2003, AMEC Lifetime Achievement Award, 2007, Workworld Media Awards; Journalism Prize, Fundació Catalunya Oberta, 2006; Ludwig Erhard Prize, Ludwig Erhard Stiftung, 2009; Commentariat of the Year, Comment Awards, 2009; Jt Winner for columns in 'giant newspapers', Soc. of American Business Editors and Writers, 2009; Best Radio Prog., Wincott Awards, 2009, 2015; Internat. Award, Premio Ischia di Giornalismo, 2012; James Cameron Meml Trust Award for Journalism, 2012; Best Commentary Award, Overseas Press Club of America, 2014; Journalist of the Year, Green Ribbon Political Awards, 2014; Lifetime Achievement Award, Gerald Loeb Awards, 2019. Commemoration Medal (NZ), 1990. *Publications:* India's Exports, 1982; Why Globalization Works, 2004; Fixing Global Finance, 2008; The Shifts and the Shocks, 2014; numerous articles, mainly on internat. econ. policy. *Recreations:* opera, theatre. *Address:* 27 Court Lane, SE21 7DH. *T:* (020) 7873 3673/3421. *Club:* Reform.
*See also* R. Wolf.

**WOLF, Rachel;** Director, Public First, since 2016; *b* London, 1985; *d* of Martin Harry Wolf, *qv*, and Baroness Wolf of Dulwich, *qv*; *m* 2012, James Frayne; one *d. Educ:* Univ. of Cambridge (BA Natural Scis). DipEcon. Researcher, Boris Johnson, 2006–07; Political Advr, 2008, Educn Advr, 2008–09, Conservative Party; Dir, 2009–13, Chm. of Trustees, 2013–15, New Schs Network; Sen. Vice Pres., Amplify, 2013–15; Advr to the Prime Minister, 2015–16. Contested (C) Dulwich and W Norwood, 2017. *Recreations:* books, music. *Club:* Reform.

**WOLF, Roland;** *see* Wolf, C. R.

**WOLFE, Prof. Charles David Alexander,** OBE 2018; MD; FRCOG, FFPH, FRCP; Professor of Public Health Medicine, King's College London School of Medicine (formerly Guy's, King's and St Thomas' School of Medicine at King's College London), since 2002; Head, School of Population Health and Environmental Sciences, King's College London, since 2017 (Head, Division of Health and Social Care, 2004–17); *b* 30 July 1954; *s* of late Kenneth Wolfe and Doreen Hibbert Wolfe (*née* Anderson). *Educ:* Highgate Sch.; Royal Free Hosp. Sch. of Medicine, Univ. of London (MB BS 1978); MD London 1990. MRCOG 1985, FRCOG 1998; MFPHM 1991, FFPH (FFPHM 1996); FRCP 2017. Regtl MO, RAMC, 1980–85; United Medical and Dental Schools of Guy's and St Thomas' Hospitals: Res. Fellow in Obstetrics, 1985–87; Lectr in Public Health Medicine, 1988–92; Sen. Lectr, 1992–98; Reader, GKT, 1998–2002; Guy's and St Thomas' Hospital: Hon. Consultant in Public Health Medicine, 1992–; Clinical Dir, Women's Health, 1995–2000; Dir, R&D, 2000–. Lead for Public Health, King's Health Partners, 2011–. National Institute for Health Research: Chm., Res. for Patient Benefit Cttee, 2007–; Sen. Investigator, 2008–16, now Emeritus; Chm., NHS Confederation Health Services Res. Bd, 2010–. Mem. Bd, Stanley Thomas Johnson Foundn, Switzerland, 2003–13. *Publications:* Stroke Service and Research, 1996; Stroke Services: policy and practice across Europe, 2001; articles in med. jls on health service res. in stroke and women's health. *Recreations:* furniture restoration, classical music, opera. *Address:* Holly Lodge, Queen Street, New Buckenham, Norfolk NR16 2AL. *T:* (office) (020) 7848 6608. *E:* charles.wolfe@kcl.ac.uk.

**WOLFE, David Frederick Harris,** PhD; QC 2012; *b* Roodeport, South Africa, 9 June 1964; *s* of late (Frederick) John Harris and (Catherine) Ann Harris (*née* Pearson, later Wolfe), and step *s* of late Martin Stuart Wolfe; *m* 2009, Amanda Marguerite Illing; two *d. Educ:* Manchester Univ. (BSc MEng 1987); Univ. of Cambridge (PhD Engrg 1990); City Univ. (DipLaw 1991). Called to the Bar, Middle Temple, 1992; in practice as a barrister, Matrix, 1992–; pt-time Judge, Special Educnl Needs and Disability Tribunal, 2004–08. Chm. Bd, Press Recognition Panel, 2014–. Member, Board: Legal Services Commn, 2005–13; Legal Services Bd, 2008–13. Mem., Cambridgeshire CC, 1989–93. Gov., Leiston High Sch., later Alde Valley Sch., Suffolk, 2009–13. *Recreations:* friends and family, real ale, parties, ski-ing. *Address:* Flat 100, Vesage Court, Leather Lane, EC1N 7RF; Moya, The Street, Charsfield, Suffolk IP13 7PY. *T:* 07740 948536. *E:* davidwolfe@matrixlaw.co.uk.

**WOLFE, Gillian Anne,** CBE 2005 (MBE 1995); Director, Learning and Public Affairs, Dulwich Picture Gallery, 2009–15 (Head of Education, 1984–2008); freelance education consultant, since 1990; *b* 25 March 1946; *d* of late Noel Henry Humphrey and Anne (*née* Nicholls); *m* 1974, Dr Kenneth Maurice Wolfe; one *s* one *d. Educ:* Sydenham Girls' Sch.; Central Sch. of Art (Pre Diploma 1968); Stockwell Coll. (BEd Hons London 1972). Teacher: Rushey Gn Primary Sch., 1974; Greenwich Pk Secondary Sch., 1974–84. Advisory Teacher: for ILEA, 1984–89; for Southwark, 1989–2008; British Deleg., EC Council of Europe, Saltzburg, 1989; Advr, Kyoto and Tokyo Mus. Educn Project, 1996; Mem., Exec. Cttee, Nat. Heritage, 1997–2000; Judge, Mus. of Year Award, 1997–2000; Project Advr, American Fedn of Arts, 1998; Consultant, Royal Collection, 1999–2000; Specialist Advisor: Clore Foundn, 2001–; HLF, 2005–12; Comr, CABE, 2000–03, now Emeritus (Trustee, Educn Foundn, 2003–06); Mem., Steering Gp, Attingham Trust Survey on Learning in Historic Envmt, 2001–03; Chm., jt DCMS-DfES Adv. Cttee on developing envmt as an educn resource, 2003–04. Trustee: Historic Royal Palaces, 2002–05; Charleston Trust, 2009–15; Brighton Pavilion and Museums Foundn, 2010–16; Arts4Dementia, 2011–17; RIBA British Architects Trust, 2014– (Chm., Public Educn Cttee, 2015–); Mary Roxburghe Trust, 2016–19. Learning Advr, Historic Houses Assoc., 2012–. FRSA 2004. Hon. HLD St Norbert Coll., USA, 2006; Hon. Dr Canterbury Christ Church, 2014. NACF Award for Educn, 1987; Sustainable City Award, 2009; RSPH Award, 2012. *Publications:* (contrib.) Oxford Children's Encyclopaedia, 7 vols, 1991; Children's Art and Activity Books, 1997 (Gulbenkian Prize, 1992); (contrib.) Oxford Children's Pocket Encyclopaedia, 1999; Oxford First Book of Art, 1999 (Parent Choice Silver Hon. Award, USA, 2002); Look!: zoom in on art, 2002 (English Assoc. Award for Best Children's non-fiction book, 2007); Look!: body language in art, 2004; Look!: seeing the light in art, 2006; Look!: drawing the line in art, 2008; Look!: really smart art, 2010. *Recreations:* gardening, dance. *Address:* 31 Calton Avenue, SE21 7DE. *T:* (020) 8693 6995. *E:* gillian.wolfe@btinternet.com.

**WOLFE, John Henry Nicholas,** FRCS; Consultant Vascular Surgeon, St Mary's Hospital, London, 1984–2012, now Hon. Consultant; Hon. Consultant Vascular Surgeon, Royal Brompton Hospital, Great Ormond Street Hospital for Children and Edward VII Hospital for Officers, London, 1984–2016; *b* 4 June 1947; *s* of late Herbert Robert Inglewood Wolfe and Lesley Winifred (*née* Fox); *m* 1st, 1973, Jennifer Sutcliffe; three *s* two *d*; 2nd, 1994, Dorothy May Sturgeon. *Educ:* Eastbourne Coll.; St Thomas's Hosp. Med. Sch., London (MB BS 1971). MS 1981. FRCS 1975. Res. Fellow, Harvard Medical Sch., Brigham Hosp., 1981–82; Sen Registrar, St Thomas' Hosp., 1982–84; Consultant Surgeon, RPMS, Hammersmith, 1984. ICRC Surgical Instructor, 2016–. Hunterian Prof., RCS, 1983; Moynihan Fellow, Assoc. of Surgeons, 1985. Member: Speciality Adv. Bd, Assoc. of Surgeons, 1993–96; Specialities Board of Surgery: RCS, 1994–95; RCSE, 1994–96; Chm., Continuing Med. Educn Cttee, Eur. Div. Vascular Surgery, 1998–2001, Pres., Eur. Bd of Vascular Surgery, 2001–04, European Union of Med. Specialists, Brussels; Council Member: Vascular Soc. of GB and Ire., 1992–96 (Chm., Vascular Adv. Cttee, 1992–96; Pres., 2005–06); Assoc. of Surgeons of GB and Ire., 1998–2002; President: European Soc. of Vascular Surgery, 2007–08; World Fedn of Vascular Surgery, 2012–13. Honorary Member: Surgical Soc. of S Africa, 1991; Vascular Soc. of India, 2004; Swiss Vascular Soc., 2004; Soc. of Vascular Technologists, 2004; Vascular Soc. of Germany, 2005; Eur. Assoc. Vascular Surgical Trainees, 2006; Assoc. of Surgeons of India, 2007; Australasian Vascular Soc., 2012; Soc. of Vascular Surgery, USA, 2013. FRGS 1996. Freedom, City of London, 2007. *Publications:* (associate ed) Rutherford's Vascular Surgery, 1984; ABC of Vascular Diseases, 1992, Czech edn 1994, Italian edn 1995; articles on arterial, venous and lymphatic disease, and surgical training. *Recreations:* sailing, sculpture, rudimentary pond management, walking with children. *Address:* 6 Cleveland Avenue, W4 1SN. *T:* (020) 3441 8411. *E:* johnwolfevasc@gmail.com. *Clubs:* Chelsea Arts, Royal Ocean Racing.

**WOLFENDALE, Sir Arnold (Whittaker),** Kt 1995; PhD, DSc; FRS 1977; FInstP, FRAS; Professor of Physics, University of Durham, 1965–92, now Emeritus; Astronomer Royal, 1991–95; *b* 25 June 1927; *s* of Arnold Wolfendale and Doris Wolfendale; *m* 1st, 1951, Audrey Darby (*d* 2007); twin *s*; 2nd, 2015, Dr Dorothy Middleton. *Educ:* Univ. of Manchester (BSc Physics 1st Cl. Hons 1948, PhD 1953, DSc 1970). FInstP 1958; FRAS 1973. Asst Lectr, Univ. of Manchester, 1951, Lectr, 1954; University of Durham: Lectr, 1956; Sen. Lectr, 1959; Reader in Physics, 1963; Head of Dept, 1973–77, 1980–83, 1986–89. Vis. Lectr, Univ. of Ceylon, 1952; Vis. Prof., Univ. of Hong Kong, 1977–78; Kan Tong Po Vis. Prof. of Physics, City Univ. of Hong Kong, 1995; Prof. of Experimental Physics, Royal Instn of GB, 1996–2002. Lectures: H. C. Bhuyan Meml, Gauhati Univ., 1978 and 1993; B. B. Roy Meml, Calcutta Univ., 1978; Norman Lockyer, Exeter Univ., 1978; E. A. Milne, Oxford Univ., 1982; Rochester, Durham Univ., 1990 and 2006; A. W. Mailvaganam Meml, Colombo Univ., 1990; Perren, QMW, 1991; O'Neill, Glasgow, 1991; Durham Observatory Anniversary, 1992; Cormack, RSE, 1992; Robinson, Armagh, 1992; David Martin, Royal Soc./British Acad., 1992; Preston Guild, Univ. of Central Lancs, 1992; J. H. Holmes Meml, Newcastle Univ., 1993; Irvine Meml, Stirling, 1993; Tompion, Clockmakers' Co., 1993; Courtauld, Manchester Lit. and Phil., 1993; Minerva, Scientific Instrument Makers' Co., 1993; Hess, IUPAP Cosmic Ray Commn, 1993; Poynting, Univ. of Birmingham, 1994; Mme Curie, Inst. of Physics, 1995; Dee, Glasgow Univ., 1995; Harland, Univ. of Exeter, 1996; Temple Chevallier, Univ. of Durham, 1996; Carter Meml, Nat. Observatory of NZ, 1997; Charter, Inst. of Biology, 1997; Manley Meml, Univ. of Durham, 1997; Cockroft & Walton, Inst. of Physics, India, 1998; Wdowczyk Meml, Univ. of Lodz, Poland, 1998; Bakerian, Royal Soc., 2002; Appapillai Meml, Univ. of Peradeniya, 2003; Pniewski, Tech. Univ. of Warsaw, Plock, 2003. Home Office, Civil Defence, later Regl Scientific Advr, 1956–84. Chm., Northern Reg. Action Cttee, Manpower Services Commn's Job Creation Prog., 1975–78; Mem., SERC, 1988–94 (Chm., Astronomy and Planetary Sci. Bd, 1988–93; Chm., Particles, Space and Astronomy Bd, 1993–94). Chm., Cosmic Ray Commn, IUPAP, 1982–84. President: RAS, 1981–83; Antiquarian Horological Soc., 1993–2014; Inst. of Physics, 1994–96; European Physical Soc., 1999–2001. Pres., Durham Univ. Soc. of Fellows, 1988–94. Freeman: Clockmakers' Co., 1991 (Liveryman, 2006; Harrison Medal, 2006); Sci. Instrument Makers' Co., 1993. MAE 1998. Foreign Fellow: INSA, 1990; Indian Nat. Acad. Scis; For. Associate, RSSAf, 1995; Foreign Mem., Polish Acad. of Arts and Scis, 2010; Hon. Fellow: Lancashire Poly., 1991; Sri Lankan Acad. of Sci., 2010; Hon. Professor: Univ. of Yunnan, China, 1995; Univ. of Sci. and Technology, Hefei, China, 1995; Tata Inst. of Fundamental Res., 1996. Hon. DSc: Univ. of Potchefstroom for Christian Higher Educn, 1989; Lodz, 1989; Teesside, 1993; Newcastle upon Tyne, 1994; Paisley, 1996; Lancaster, 1996; Bucharest, 2000; DUniv: Open, 1995; Durham, 2001; SW Bulgaria, 2001; Turku, Finland, 2009; Bolton, 2009; Dip. *hc* Romanian Acad., 2000. Univ. of Turku Medal, 1987; Armagh Observatory Medal, 1992; Marian Smoluchowski Medal, Polish Phys. Soc., 1993; Powell Meml Medal, EPS, 1996. Silver Jubilee Medal, 1977; Fiorino d'Oro, Comune di Firenze, 2004; Chancellor's Medal, Univ. of Durham, 2011; Homi Bhabha Medal, IUPAP/Tata Inst. of Fundamental Res., 2011; INSA-Vainu Bappu Meml Award, Indian Nat. Acad. of Sci., 2013. *Publications:* Cosmic Rays, 1963; (ed) Cosmic Rays at Ground Level, 1973; (ed) Origin of Cosmic Rays, 1974; (ed jtly and contrib.) Origin of Cosmic Rays, 1981; (ed) Gamma Ray Astronomy, 1981; (ed) Progress in Cosmology, 1982; (with P. V. Ramana Murthy) Gamma Ray Astronomy, 1986, 2nd edn 1993; (with F. R. Stephenson) Secular Solar and Geomagnetic Variations in the last 1,000 years, 1988; (ed jtly) Observational Tests of Cosmological Inflation, 1991; original papers on studies of cosmic radiation, aspects of astrophysics and analysis of climate change. *Recreations:* walking, gardening, foreign travel. *Address:* Ansford, Potters Bank, Durham DH1 3RR. *T:* (0191) 384 5642.

**WOLFENSOHN, James David,** Hon. KBE 1995; Hon. AO 1987; Chairman and Chief Executive Officer, Wolfensohn Fund Management LLC (formerly Wolfensohn & Co. LLC), 2007–14; President, International Bank for Reconstruction and Development, 1995–2005; *b* Sydney, 1 Dec. 1933; *s* of Hyman Wolfensohn and Dora Weinbaum; *m* 1961, Elaine Botwinick; one *s* two *d. Educ:* Univ. of Sydney (BA, LLB); Harvard Business Sch. (MBA). Lawyer, Allen Allen & Hemsley; Officer, RAAF; former Exec. Dep. Chm. and Man. Dir, Schroders Ltd, London; former Man. Dir, Darling & Co., Australia; Pres., J. Henry Schroder Banking Corp., 1970–76; Pres., Salomon Brothers Internat., 1977–81; Pres., James D. Wolfensohn Inc., 1981–95; Chm. Internat. Adv. Bd, Citigroup Inc., 2005–. Special Envoy for Gaza Disengagement, 2005–06. Mem. Bd, Carnegie Hall, NY, 1970 (Chm. Bd, 1980–91, now Chm. Emeritus); Chm., Kennedy Center for the Performing

Arts, 1990–95, now Chm. Emeritus. Trustee: Inst. for Advanced Study, Princeton Univ., 1979 (Chm., 1986–2007, now Chm. Emeritus); Rockefeller Univ., 1985–94; Fellow: American Acad. of Arts and Scis; American Philosophical Soc. David Rockefeller Prize, Mus. of Modern Art, NY.

**WOLFF, Prof. Eric William,** PhD; FRS 2010; FRSC; Royal Society Research Professor of Earth Sciences, University of Cambridge, since 2013; *b* Bushey, Herts, 5 June 1957; *s* of Henry Wolff and Joan Agnes Wolff (*née* Whitehead); *m* 1983, Theresa Mary Ormiston. *Educ:* Quainton Hall Sch., Harrow; Merchant Taylors' Sch., Northwood; Churchill Coll., Cambridge (BA Nat. Sci. 1978); Univ. of Cambridge (PhD 1992). Contract glaciologist, British Antarctic Survey, 1978–84; Scientist, Water Research Centre, 1984–85; British Antarctic Survey: Res. Scientist, 1985–2000; Principal Investigator, 2000–09; Science Leader (Chemistry and Past Climate), 2009–13; Individual Merit Band 3, 2005–11, Band 2, 2011–13. Hon. Visiting Professor: Univ. of Southampton, 2011–13; UEA, 2012–. Chairman: Sci. Sub-gp, Eur. Project for Ice Coring in Antarctica, 2003–; Global Envmt Res. Cttee, Royal Soc., 2016–19; Co-Chm., Internat. Partnerships in Ice Core Scis, 2005–17; Member: Steering Cttee, Past Global Changes, 2007–13; UK Cttee, Future Earth, 2016–. Mem., Internat. Glaciol Soc., 1978– (Vice Pres., 2005–08). MRSC 1978, FRSC 2011; Member: Amer. Geophysical Union, 1992; Eur. Geoscis Union, 2004. Hon. Fellow, British Antarctic Survey, 2013–. Medal, Envmtl Chem. Gp, RSC, 2007; Louis Agassiz Medal, Eur. Geoscis Union, 2009; Lyell Medal, Geol Soc., 2012. *Publications:* over 200 papers in scientific jls. *Recreations:* alpine and coastal walking, ski-ing, good food, watching cricket, interglacials. *Address:* Department of Earth Sciences, University of Cambridge, Downing Street, Cambridge CB2 3EQ. *E:* ew428@cam.ac.uk.

**WOLFF, Prof. Jonathan;** Blavatnik Professor of Public Policy, Blavatnik School of Government, University of Oxford, since 2016; Fellow of Wolfson College, Oxford, since 2016; *b* 25 June 1959; *s* of Herbert Wolff and Doris Wolff (*née* Polakoff); *m* 2004, Elaine Collins; one *s*. *Educ:* University Coll. London (BA; MPhil). University College London: Lectr, 1986–92; Sen. Lectr, 1992–96; Reader, 1996–2000; Prof. of Philosophy, 2000–16; Dir, Centre for Philosophy, Justice and Health, 2008–13; Dean, Faculty of Arts and Humanities, 2012–16; Founding Dir, Philosophy Programme, Sch. of Advanced Study, Univ. of London, 1995–98. Member: Nuffield Council on Bioethics, 2008–14; Bd of Sci., BMA, 2014–16. Mem., Gambling Review Body, 2000–01; Trustee: Gambling Industry Charitable Trust, subseq. Responsibility in Gambling Trust, 2003–09; Responsible Gambling Trust, 2012–17. Pres., Aristotelian Soc., 2018–19 (Hon. Sec., 2001–07); Sec., British Philosophical Assoc., 2004–07. Editor, Procs of Aristotelian Soc., 1994–2000; columnist, Guardian, 2005–. *Publications:* Robert Nozick: property, justice and the minimal state, 1991; An Introduction to Political Philosophy, 1996, 3rd edn 2016; Why Read Marx Today?, 2002; (with Avner de-Shalit) Disadvantage, 2007; (ed with Mark Hannam) Southern Africa: 2020 vision, 2010; Ethics and Public Policy: a philosophical inquiry, 2011, 2nd edn 2019; The Human Right to Health, 2012; (ed) G. A. Cohen Lectures in the History of Philosophy, 2013; An Introduction to Moral Philosophy, 2018, 2nd edn 2020; (ed) Readings in Moral Philosophy, 2018. *Recreations:* reading, music, spectator sport, film, television. *Address:* Blavatnik School of Government, University of Oxford, Radcliffe Observatory Quarter, Woodstock Road, Oxford OX2 6GG. *T:* (01865) 614343. *E:* jonathan.wolff@bsg.ox.ac.uk.

**WOLFF, Michael,** RDI 2012; PPCSD; President, Michael Wolff and Company (formerly Newhouse Associates), since 1993; *b* 12 Nov. 1933; *s* of Serge Wolff and Mary (*née* Gordon); *m* 1st, 1976, Susan Kent (marr. diss.); one *d*; 2nd, 1989, Martha Newhouse (*d* 2011). *Educ:* Gresham's Sch., Holt, Norfolk; Architectural Association Sch. of Architecture. Designer: Sir William Crawford & Partners, 1957–61; BBC Television, 1961–62; Main Wolff & Partners, 1964–65; with Wolff Olins Ltd as a founder and Creative Director, 1965–83; Chm., Addison Design Consultants, 1987–92. Design Consultant to: W. H. Smith Gp, 1990–98; MFI Gp, 2000; Mothercare, 2000–; Consultant to: Citigroup, 1998–; Insead, 2003–; Pyjom, 2012–. Non-exec. Dir, Newell & Sorrell, 1995–98. Advr to UK Govt on Inclusive Design, 2011–. President: D&AD, 1991; SIAD, then CSD, 1985–87. Mem., Bd of Trustees, Hunger Project, 1979–2000; Trustee, Youth at Risk, 2012–. FRSA. *Recreations:* enjoying designing and enjoying an extended family of seven children and seven grandchildren. *Address:* 9 Cumberland Gardens, WC1X 9AG. *T:* (020) 7833 0007.

**WOLFFE, Hon. Lady;** Sarah Poyntell LaBudde Wolffe; a Senator of the College of Justice in Scotland, since 2014; *m* 1987, (Walter) James Wolffe, *qv*; two *s*. Admitted as solicitor, 1992; Legal Dept, Bank of Scotland, 1992–93; called to the Bar, 1994; in practice as barrister, specialising in commercial and public law; Standing Jun. Counsel, DTI, subseq. BERR, then DIUS, 1996–2008; Advocate Depute, 2007; QC (Scot.) 2008. Mem., Police Appeals Tribunal, 2013. Mem., Disciplinary Tribunal, Faculty of Advocates, 2005–08. *Address:* Parliament House, Edinburgh EH1 1RQ.

**WOLFFE, Sarah Poyntell LaBudde;** *see* Wolffe, Hon. Lady.

**WOLFFE, Rt Hon. (Walter) James;** PC 2016; QC (Scot.) 2007; Lord Advocate for Scotland, since 2016; *b* Dumfries, 20 Dec. 1962; *s* of late Antony C. Wolffe, MBE and of Alexandra L. Wolffe (*née* Graham); *m* 1987, Sarah Poyntell LaBudde (*see* Hon. Lady Wolffe); two *s*. *Educ:* Gatehouse of Fleet Primary Sch.; Kirkcudbright Acad.; Univ. of Edinburgh (LLB Hons; DipLP); Univ. of Oxford (BCL). Legal Asst to the Lord Pres. of the Court of Session, 1990–91; Advocate, 1992; First Standing Jun. Counsel to the Scottish Ministers, 2002–07; Advocate Depute, 2007–10; Sen. Advocate Depute, 2007–10; Vice-Dean, 2013–14, Dean, 2014–16, Faculty of Advocates; called to the Bar, Middle Temple, 2013, Bencher, 2015; Hon. Bencher, King's Inn, Dublin. Mem., Police Appeal Tribunal, 2013–16. Hd of UK Delegn to CCBE, 2013–15. Member: Scottish Council of Law Reporting, 2008–14 (Chm., 2011–14); Scottish Civil Justice Council, 2013–14. Co-Chair, Internat. Council of Advocates and Barristers, 2014–16. Trustee, Nat. Liby of Scotland, 2008–13. FRSE 2019; FSAScot. Hon. LLD Glasgow. *Publications:* contributions to: Finnie et al's Edinburgh Essays in Public Law, 1991; Stair Memorial Encyclopaedia of the Laws of Scotland; Gloag and Henderson's The Law of Scotland, 11th edn; Johnston and Zimmermann's Unjustified Enrichment Key Issues in Comparative Perspective, 2002; Macfadyen's Court of Session Practice; The Proposed Common European Sales Law - the Lawyers' View, 2013; UK Supreme Court Yearbook, vol. 8, 2018; articles in Public Law, Scots Law Times and Edinburgh Law Review. *Address:* Lord Advocate's Chambers, Crown Office and Procurator Fiscal Service, 29 Chambers Street, Edinburgh EH1 1LA. *E:* lordadvocate@gov.scot.

**WOLFSON,** family name of **Baron Wolfson of Sunningdale**.

**WOLFSON OF ASPLEY GUISE,** Baron *cr* 2010 (Life Peer), of Aspley Guise in the County of Bedfordshire; **Simon Adam Wolfson;** Chief Executive, Next plc, since 2001; *b* 27 Oct. 1967; *e s* of Lord Wolfson of Sunningdale, *qv*; *m* 2012, Eleanor, *d* of Hon. William Hartley Hume Shawcross, *qv*; two *s*. *Educ:* Radley Coll.; Trinity Coll., Cambridge. Dir, 1997–, Man. Dir, 1999–2001, Next plc. Trustee, Charles Wolfson Charitable Trust. *Address:* Next plc, Desford Road, Enderby, Leicester LE19 4AT. *T:* (0116) 284 2308.

**WOLFSON OF SUNNINGDALE,** Baron *cr* 1991 (Life Peer), of Trevose in the County of Cornwall; **David Wolfson,** Kt 1984; Chairman: Next plc, 1990–98; Great Universal Stores, 1996–2000; *b* 9 Nov. 1935; *s* of Charles Wolfson and Hylda Wolfson; *m* 1st, 1962, Patricia E. Rawlings (*see* Baroness Rawlings) (marr. diss. 1967); 2nd, 1967, Susan E. Davis (marr. diss. 2018); two *s* one *d*; 3rd, 2018, Alicia Anne Trevor; one *s*. *Educ:* Clifton Coll.; Trinity Coll., Cambridge (MA); Stanford Univ., California (MBA). Great Universal Stores, 1960–78, 1993–2000, Director, 1973–78 and 1993–2000; Secretary to Shadow Cabinet, 1978–79; Chief of Staff, Political Office, 10 Downing Street, 1979–85. Chm., Alexon Group PLC (formerly Steinberg Group PLC), 1982–86; non-executive Director: Stewart Wrightson Holdings PLC, 1985–87; Next, 1989–90; Compco Hldgs plc, 1995–2004; Fibernet Gp plc, 2001–06 (Chm., 2002–06). Chm., Charles Wolfson Charitable Trust, 1971–. Hon. Fellow, Hughes Hall, Cambridge, 1989. Hon. FRCR 1978; Hon. FRCOG 1989. *Recreations:* golf, bridge. *Clubs:* Portland; Sunningdale; Woburn Golf; Trevose Golf (N Cornwall).
*See also* Baron Wolfson of Aspley Guise.

**WOLFSON, David;** QC 2009; *b* Liverpool, 19 July 1968; *s* of Bernard and Rosalind Wolfson; *m* 1995, Louise, *d* of Jeffrey, (Jeff), and Rina Durkin; one *s* two *d*. *Educ:* King David High Sch., Liverpool; Yeshivat Hakotel, Jerusalem; Selwyn Coll., Cambridge (BA Hons 1991; MA 1994). Called to the Bar, Inner Temple, 1992 (Squire Schol.; Stuart of Rannoch Award; Inns of Court Sch. of Law Schol.; Inner Temple Major Schol.), Bencher, 2016; in practice as barrister, specialising in commercial law, 1993–. Director: Bar Mutual Indemnity Fund, 2005–16; Jewish Chronicle Trust Ltd, 2011– (Chm., 2019–); Benesco Charity Ltd, 2016–. Chm. Govs, Kerem Sch., London, 2012–19. Mem., Exec. Cttee, Soc. of Cons. Lawyers, 2014–. Trustee: Cambridge Univ. Jewish Soc., 2014–; Jewish Orthodox Feminist Alliance UK, 2017–. *Publications:* (ed and contrib.) Bank Liability and Risk, 1995; (contrib.) Arbitration in England, 2013. *Recreations:* travel, wine, learning *lishma*. *Address:* One Essex Court, Temple, EC4Y 9AR. *T:* (020) 7583 2000, *Fax:* (020) 7583 0118. *E:* david.wolfson@oeclaw.co.uk. *Club:* 67 Pall Mall.

**WOLL, Prof. Bencie,** PhD; FBA 2012; Professor of Sign Language and Deaf Studies, University College London, since 2005 (Director, Deafness Cognition and Language Research Centre, 2006–17); *b* 22 Feb. 1950; *d* of Lazar Benzion Woll and Fannie Zifkin Woll. *Educ:* Univ. of Pennsylvania (BA 1970); Univ. of Essex (MA 1971); Univ. of Bristol (PhD 1992). Sen. Lectr/Res. Fellow, Univ. of Bristol, 1973–95; Prof. of Sign Language and Deaf Studies, City Univ., London, 1995–2005. Vice Chm., Royal Assoc. for Deaf People, 2002–08. Trustee, UK Council on Deafness, 2011–. FAAAS 2016. *Publications:* (with J. Kyle) Sign Language: the study of deaf people and their language, 1985; (with R. Sutton-Spence) The Linguistics of BSL, 1999; (jtly) The Signs of a Savant, 2010; (with R. Pfau and M. Steinbach) Sign Language: an international handbook, 2012; (jtly) Research Methods in Sign Linguistics, 2015. *Recreations:* cats, Yiddish language and culture. *Address:* Deafness, Cognition and Language Research Centre, 49 Gordon Square, WC1H 0PD. *T:* (020) 7679 8670, *Fax:* (020) 7679 8691. *E:* b.woll@ucl.ac.uk. *Club:* Penn (New York).

**WOLLASTON, Helen Ruth;** Chief Executive, WISE, since 2012; *b* London, 4 May 1962; *d* of Eric and Oenone Wollaston; *m* 2011, Elisabeth, (Lisa), Smith. *Educ:* Manchester High Sch. for Girls; Univ. of Oxford (BA Hons French 1984); Univ. of Central England (Postgrad. Dip. Information Studies 1989); Open Univ. (Cert. Managing Not-for-Profit Orgns 1991); Leeds Metropolitan Univ. (Advanced Dip. PR 2014). Information Officer, Nat. Assoc. of Councils for Voluntary Service, 1990–96; Regl Develt Officer, 1996–97, Regl Manager, Yorks and Humber, 1997–2000, Nat. Lottery Charities Bd; Dir of Campaigns, EOC, 2000–07; Chm., YWCA England and Wales, 2008–12. Dep. Chm. and Sen. Ind. Dir, SW Yorks NHS Foundn Trust, 2009–15. Mem., Adv. Bd, Mgt Div., Leeds Univ. Business Sch., 2014–. Non-exec. Dir, Zero Waste Scotland, 2017–. Founder and Dir, Equal to the Occasion, 2007–. Member: Cruising Assoc.; Camping and Caravanning Club. *Recreations:* sailing, walking, organic gardening, cooking, reading. *Address:* WISE, Leeds College of Building, Hunslet Campus, Cudbear Street, Leeds LS10 1ET. *T:* (0113) 222 6072. *E:* h.wollaston@wisecampaign.org.uk.

**WOLLASTON, Sarah;** MP for Totnes, since 2010 (C, 2010–19; Ind, 2019; Lib Dem, since 2019); *b* 1962; *m* Adrian; one *s* two *d*. *Educ:* Tal Handaq Service Children's Sch., Malta; Watford Grammar Sch. for Girls; Guy's Hosp. Med. Sch. (BSc Pathol. 1983; MB BS 1986). DRCOG 1991; MRCGP 1992. Forensic med. examr, Devon and Cornwall Police, 1996–2001; GP, Chagford Health Centre, Devon, 1999–2010; Trainer, Peninsula Med. Sch., Plymouth, 2001–10; teacher, Exeter Postgrad. Centre until 2010. Mem., Health and Social Care (formerly Health) Select Cttee, 2010– (Chm., 2014–). *Address:* House of Commons, SW1A 0AA.

**WOLLEN, Siân;** *see* Davies, Siân.

**WOLMAR, Christian Tage Forter;** author and broadcaster, since 1997; *b* London, 3 Aug. 1949; *s* of Boris Semenovich Kougoulsky and Dagmar Birgit Wolmar (*née* Lindblom); one *d* by Sally Brooks; one *d* by Scarlett MccGwire; *m* 2017, Alice Deborah Maby. *Educ:* Lycée Français de Londres; Univ. of Warwick (BA Hons Econs 1971). Asst Editor, Marketing mag., 1972–73; Sports Writer, Hampstead and Highgate Express, 1973–74; Publications Officer, Release, 1976–79; Asst Editor, Roof mag., Shelter, 1979–82; PR Officer, London Bor. of Camden, 1982–84; News Editor, New Statesman, 1984; Local Govt Corresp., London Daily News, 1986–87; The Independent: reporter, 1989–91; Asst News Editor, 1991–92; Transport Corresp., 1992–97. Contested (Lab) Richmond Park, Dec. 2016. *Publications:* Points of View: censorship, 1990; Points of View: drugs, 1990; Drugs and Sport, 1992; Unlocking the Gridlock, 1997; The Great British Railway Disaster, 1997; Stagecoach, 1998; Forgotten Children, 2000; Broken Rails, 2001; Down the Tube, 2002; The Subterranean Railway, 2004; On the Wrong Line, 2005; Fire and Steam, 2007; Blood, Iron and Gold, 2009; Engines of War, 2010; The Great Railway Revolution, 2012; To the Edge of the World, 2013; The Iron Road, 2014; (ed jtly) Urban Access for the 21st Century, 2014; Are Trams Socialist?: why Britain has never had a transport policy, 2016; Railways and the Raj, 2017; Driverless Cars: on a road to nowhere, 2018; The Story of Crossrail, 2018. *Recreations:* cycling, cricket, tennis, running, ski-ing. *Address:* 48 Crayford Road, N7 0ND. *T:* 07931 504555. *E:* christian.wolmar@gmail.com. *W:* www.twitter.com/christianwolmar, www.christianwolmar.co.uk, www.wolmarforlondon.co.uk. *Clubs:* Beamers Cricket, Wood Vale Lawn Tennis.

**WOLMER, Viscount; William Lewis Palmer;** Managing Director, Blackmoor Estate; *b* 1 Sept. 1971; *s* and *heir* of 4th Earl of Selborne, *qv*; *m* 2001, Victoria Baum; two *s* one *d*. *Educ:* Eton Coll.; Christ Church, Oxford (BA 1993); Sch. of Oriental and African Studies, London Univ. (MA 1996); Univ. of Sussex (PhD 2001). Res. Officer, then Fellow, Inst. of Develt Studies, Univ. of Sussex, 1997–2007. *Publications:* From Wilderness Vision to Farm Invasions, 2007. *Heir: s* Hon. Alexander David R. Palmer, *b* 2002.

**WOLPERT, Prof. Daniel Mark,** DPhil; FRS 2012; FMedSci; Professor of Neuroscience, Mortimer B. Zuckerman Mind Brain Behavior Institute, Columbia University, New York, since 2018; *b* 8 Sept. 1963; *s* of Prof. Lewis Wolpert, *qv* and Elizabeth Wolpert (*née* Brownstein); *m* 1990, Mary Anne Shorrock; two *d*. *Educ:* Hall Sch.; Westminster Sch.; Trinity Hall, Cambridge (BA Hons Med. Scis 1985); Magdalen Coll., Univ. of Oxford (BM

BCh Clinical Medicine 1988); Lincoln Coll., Univ. of Oxford (DPhil Physiol. 1992). Med. House Officer, Oxford, 1988–89; MRC Trng Fellow, Univ. Lab. of Physiol., Univ. of Oxford, 1989–92; Fulbright Scholarship, 1992–95, Postdoctoral Associate, 1992–94, McDonnell-Pew Fellow in Cognitive Neurosci., 1994–95, Dept of Brain and Cognitive Sci., MIT; Institute of Neurology, University College London: Lectr, 1995–99, Reader in Motor Neurosci., 1999–2002; Prof. of Motor Neurosci. and Vice Chm., Sobell Dept of Motor Neurosci., 2002–05; Co-Dir, Inst. of Movt Neurosci., 1999–2005; Hon. Sen. Res. Fellow, UCL, 2005–08; 1875 Prof. of Engrg, Univ. of Cambridge, 2005–18; Fellow, Trinity Coll., Cambridge, 2005–18; Royal Soc. Noreen Murray Res. Prof. in Neurobiol., 2013–18. Francis Crick Prize Lect., Royal Soc., 2005; Fred Kavli Dist. Internat. Scientist Lect., Soc. for Neurosci., 2009. Golden Brain Award, Minerva Foundn, USA, 2010. FMedSci 2004. *Publications*: articles on neuroscience in learned jls. *Recreations*: travel, gadgets and games. *Address*: Columbia University, 3227 Broadway, Jerome L. Greene Science Center, MC9844, 4th Floor, Room L4–069, New York, NY 10027, USA. *E*: wolpert@columbia.edu. *W*: www.wolpertlab.com

**WOLPERT, Prof. Lewis**, CBE 1990; DIC, PhD; FRS 1980; FMedSci; FRSL; Professor of Biology as Applied to Medicine, London University, at University College London Medical School (formerly at Middlesex Hospital Medical School), 1966–2004, now Emeritus; *b* 19 Oct. 1929; *s* of William and Sarah Wolpert; *m* 1st, 1961, Elizabeth Brownstein; two *s* two *d*; 2nd, 1993, Jill Neville (*d* 1997); 3rd, 2016, Alison Hawkes. *Educ*: King Edward's Sch., Johannesburg; Univ. of Witwatersrand (BScEng); Imperial Coll., London (DIC; FIC 1996); King's Coll., London (PhD; FKC 2001). Personal Asst to Director of Building Research Inst., S African Council for Scientific and Industrial Research, 1951–52; Engineer, Israel Water Planning Dept, 1953–54; King's College, London: Asst Lectr in Zoology, 1958–60; Lectr in Zoology, 1960–64; Reader in Zoology, 1964–66; Hd of Dept of Biology as Applied to Medicine, later Dept of Anatomy and Biology as Applied to Medicine, Middlesex Hosp. Med. Sch., 1966–87. MRC: Mem. Council, 1984–88; Mem., 1982–88, Chm., 1984–88, Cell Bd; Chairman: Scientific Inf. Cttee, Royal Soc., 1983–88; COPUS, 1994–98; Biology Concerted Action Cttee, EEC, 1988–91. President: British Soc. for Cell Biology, 1985–91; Inst. of Information Scientists, 1986–87. Lectures: Steinhaus, Univ. of California at Irvine, 1980; van der Horst, Univ. of Witwatersrand, Johannesburg, 1981; Bidder, Soc. for Experimental Biology, Leicester, 1982; Swirling, Dana-Farber, Boston, 1985; Lloyd-Roberts, RCP, 1986; Royal Instn Christmas Lectures, 1986; R. G. Williams, Univ. of Pennsylvania, 1988; Bernal, Birkbeck Coll., 1989; Radcliffe, Warwick Univ., 1990; Redfearn, Leicester, 1991; Wade, Southampton, 1991; Robb, Univ. of Auckland, 1994; Samuel Gee, RCP, 1995; Hunterian Oration, 1996; Gerald Walters Meml, Bath Univ., 1997; Medawar, 1998, Faraday (also Award), 2000, Royal Soc.; Rose, Marine Biol. Lab., Woods Hole, Mass., 2001. Presenter: Antenna, BBC2, 1987–88; A Living Hell, BBC2, 1999; interviews with scientists, Radio 3, 1981–; radio documentaries: The Dark Lady of DNA, 1989; The Virgin Fathers of the Calculus, 1991. FMedSci 1998; FRSL 1999. Mem., Amer. Philos. Soc., 2002. For. Mem., Polish Acad. of Arts and Scis, 1998. Hon. MRCP, 1986. Hon. Fellow, UCL, 1995. Hon. DSc: CNAA, 1992; Leicester, 1996; Westminster, 1996; Bath, 1997; DUniv Open, 1998. Scientific Medal, Zoological Soc., 1968; Hamburger Award, Amer. Soc. of Develtl Biol., 2003; Waddington Medal, British Soc. of Develtl Biol., 2015; Royal Medal, Royal Soc., 2018. *Publications*: A Passion for Science (with A. Richards), 1988; Triumph of the Embryo, 1991; The Unnatural Nature of Science, 1992; (with A. Richards) Passionate Minds, 1997; Principles of Development, 1998; Malignant Sadness: the anatomy of depression, 1999; Six Impossible Things Before Breakfast, 2006; How We Live and Why We Die: the secret lives of cells, 2009; You're Looking Very Well: the surprising nature of getting old, 2011; Why Can't a Woman Be More Like a Man, 2014; approx. 200 articles on cell and developmental biology in scientific jls. *Address*: 63A Belsize Park Gardens, NW3 4JN.
*See also* D. M. Wolpert.

**WOLSELEY, Sir James Douglas**, 13th Bt *cr* 1745 (Ire.), of Mount Wolseley, Co. Carlow; *b* 17 Sept. 1937; *s* of James Douglas Wolseley (*d* 1960), and Olive, *d* of Carroll Walter Wofford; *S* kinsman, Sir Garnet Wolseley, 12th Bt, 1991, but his name does not appear on the Official Roll of the Baronetage; *m* 1st, 1965, Patricia Lynn (marr. diss. 1971), *d* of William R. Hunter; 2nd, 1984, Mary Anne, *d* of Thomas G. Brown. *Heir*: kinsman John Walter Wolseley [*b* 21 April 1938; *m* 1964, Patricia Ann Newland (marr. diss. 1978); two *s*].

**WOLSELEY, Sir Stephen Garnet Hugo Charles**, 12th Bt *cr* 1628; Business Development Manager, WorleyParsons, since 2017; *b* 2 May 1980; *s* of Sir Charles Garnet Richard Mark Wolseley, 11th Bt and Anita Maria Wolseley (*née* Fried); *S* father, 2018, but his name does not appear on the Official Roll of the Baronetage; *m* 2008, Mary-Kate, *d* of Anthony Quinlan, OBE; two *s*. *Educ*: Worth Abbey; Univ. of Southampton (BA Archaeol.); Royal Military Acad. Sandhurst. Commnd Captain, Irish Guards, 2003–12. *Heir*: *s* Nicholas William Garnet, *b* 11 Oct. 2010.

**WOLSTENCROFT, Ven. Alan**; Archdeacon of Manchester, Canon Residentiary of Manchester Cathedral, and Fellow of the College, 1998–2004, now Archdeacon and Canon Emeritus; *b* 16 July 1937; *s* of John Wolstencroft and Jean (*née* Miller); *m* 1968, Christine Mary Hall; one *s* one *d*. *Educ*: Wellington Tech. Sch., Altrincham; St John's Coll. of Further Educn, Manchester; Cuddesdon Coll., Oxford. Nat. Service, RAF, Nat. Mountain Rescue Team, 1955–57. Trainee Manager, W. H. Smith & Co., 1957–59; Regl Wine and Spirit Manager, Bass/Charrington Co., 1959–67; ordained deacon, 1969, priest, 1970; Assistant Curate: St Thomas, Halliwell, 1969–71; All Saints, Stand, 1971–73; Vicar, St Martin, Wythenshawe, 1973–80; Asst Chaplain, Wythenshawe Hosp., 1973–91; Rural, then Area, Dean of Withington, 1978–91; Vicar: St John the Divine, Brooklands, 1980–91; St Peter, Bolton, 1991–98. Manchester Retired Clergy and Widows/er Officer, 2004–. Synodal Sec., York Convocation, 2007–17. Theatre Chaplain, Actors' Church Union, 1975–2010; Religious Advr, Granada TV, 2000–10. Mem., Horwich Probus. *Recreations*: watching football, sport, theatre, reading, wines, beers, walking. *Address*: The Bakehouse, 1 Latham Row, Horwich, Bolton, Lancs BL6 6QZ. *T*: (01204) 469985. *Clubs*: Royal Air Force; Bolton Wanderers FC.

**WOLSTENHOLME, Andrew William Lewis**, OBE 2009; FREng, FICE, FRICS; Group Managing Director, Maritime and Land (UK), BAE Systems, 2018–19; *b* London, 5 March 1959; *s* of late Michael Ashmore Wolstenholme and Vivien Wolstenholme; *m* 1987, Caroline Barnes-Yallowley; five *s*. *Educ*: Univ. of Southampton (BSc Eng 1st Cl. Civil Engrg 1981); RMA Sandhurst; INSEAD (Advanced Mgt and Finance Progs 2009). Army: SSLC, RE, 1978; SSC, QRIH, 1981–83. Ove Arup and Partners, London, 1984–96, Dir, Proj. Mgt Gp, Hong Kong, 1993–96; BAA plc, 1996–2009: Dir, Capital Projects, 1998–2002; Prog. Dir, Terminal 5, Heathrow, 2002–08; Gp Construction Dir, 2008–09; Man. Dir, Balfour Beatty Mgt, 2009–10, Dir, Innovation and Strategic Capability, 2010–11, Balfour Beatty Gp plc. Dir, Inst. of Cancer Res., 2005–11; Chief Exec., Crossrail Ltd, 2011–18. Non-exec. Dir, Defence Equipment and Support, MoD, 2014–. Chm., Construction Leadership Council, 2015–. Mem. Council, Eastbourne Coll., 2009–15. FICE 2010; FREng 2013; FRICS 2013. Hon. DSc Southampton 2014. *Recreations*: watercolour painting, cooking, opera, tennis, walking, ukulele.

**WOLSTENHOLME, His Honour (John) Scott**; a Circuit Judge, 1995–2013; *b* 28 Nov. 1947; *s* of Donald Arthur Wolstenholme and Kaye (*née* Humphrys); *m* 1972, Lynne Harrison; three *s* one *d*. *Educ*: Roundhay Sch., Leeds; University Coll., Oxford (MA). Called to the Bar, Middle Temple, 1971; practised North Eastern Circuit, 1971–92; Chm., Industrial Tribunals, Leeds Region, 1992–95; a Recorder, 1991–95. Judicial Mem., Parole Bd, 2010–. *Recreations*: playing the drums, walking, ten grandchildren, Rotary.

**WOLSTENHOLME, Karen Suzanne**; HM Diplomatic Service, retired; Ambassador to the Democratic People's Republic of Korea, 2011–12; Investigating Officer, FCO Services, 2013–16; *b* Hammersmith, 16 Oct. 1962; *d* of late Peter and Teresa Vivian; *m* 1986, Jonathan David Wolstenholme (*d* 2011); one *s* two *d*. *Educ*: Penrhos Coll., Colwyn Bay; Open Univ. (MPA 2010). Entered FCO, 1980; Vice-Consul, Moscow, 1984–85; Asst Admin Officer, Harare, 1986–89; FCO, 1990–94; Second Sec., UK Repn to EU, Brussels, 1994–98; First Sec., Wellington, NZ and Dep. Gov., Pitcairn Is, 1998–2002; Dep. Hd, Conflict Prevention Unit, FCO, 2003; Team Leader: S Pacific, FCO, 2003–04; Nigeria, Ghana and Central Africa, FCO, 2004–06; Dep. UK Perm. Rep. to OPCW, The Hague, 2007–11. Governor: British Sch. in Netherlands, 2008–10; Lace Hill Acad., Buckingham, 2014–16. Sec., Salcombe WI, 2017–; Membership Sec., Nat. Trust South Hams Centre, 2018–. *Recreations*: genealogy, travel, cookery, family, volunteering (RNLI, Nat. Trust, Nat. Coastwatch Inst.), walking. *Club*: Civil Service.

**WOLSTENHOLME, Scott**; *see* Wolstenholme, His Honour J. S.

**WOLTON, Harry**; QC 1982; company director (planning and development consultancy), since 2012; *b* 1 Jan. 1938; *s* of late Harry William Wolton and Dorothy Beatrice Wolton; *m* 1971, Julie Rosina Josephine Lovell (*née* Mason); three *s*. *Educ*: King Edward's Sch., Birmingham (Foundn Scholar); Univ. of Birmingham. Called to the Bar, Gray's Inn, 1969; in practice as a barrister, 1969–2012; Hd of Chambers, No 5 Fountain Ct, 1984–95; a Recorder, 1985–2003; authorised to sit as a Dep. High Court Judge, 1990–2003. Dir, Bar Mutual Insurance Fund, 1997–2004. Trustee, Hon. Doctors Assoc., 2015–18. *Recreations*: dendrology, bibliophilia. *Address*: Waverley House, Edgeworth, Stroud GL6 7JE. *Club*: Garrick.

**WOLVERHAMPTON, Area Bishop of**, since 2007; **Rt Rev. Clive Malcolm Gregory**; *b* 25 Nov. 1961; *s* of late John Gregory and of Aurea Gregory; *m* 1997, Jenny Hyde; one *s* one *d*. *Educ*: Lancaster Univ. (BA Hons English 1984); Queens' Coll., Cambridge (BA Theology 1987, MA 1989); Westcott House Theol Coll. Ordained deacon, 1988, priest, 1989; Asst Curate, St John the Baptist, Margate, 1988–92; Sen. Chaplain, Univ. of Warwick, 1992–98; Team Rector, Coventry E, 1998–2007. Hon. MA Warwick, 1999. *Recreations*: walking, playing cricket, contemporary music. *Address*: 61 Richmond Road, Wolverhampton WV3 9JH. *T*: (01902) 824503. *E*: bishop.wolverhampton@lichfield.anglican.org.

**WOLVERTON, 8th Baron** *cr* 1869; **Miles John Glyn**; artist, art director, film-maker and animator; *b* London, 6 June 1966; *s* of Hon. Andrew John Glyn (*d* 2007) and of Celia (*née* Laws); *S* uncle, 2011; *m* 2007, Louise Riley (marr. diss. 2011); one *d*. *Educ*: Leicester Poly. (BA 1st cl. Hons Fine Art 1988); Bournemouth Univ. (MA 3D Computer Animation 2003). *Recreations*: table tennis, electronic music, camping, bicycling. *Heir*: half-*b* Jonathan Carlin Glyn, *b* 29 Jan. 1990. *Club*: London Fields Table Tennis.

**WOMACK, Joanna Mary**; Acting Bursar, Clare Hall, Cambridge, 2014; *b* 12 Sept. 1947; *d* of Laurence Paul Hodges and Mary Elizabeth Hodges (*née* Lyon); *m* 1971, Michael Thomas Womack; three *s*. *Educ*: James Allen's Girls' Sch., Dulwich; New Hall, Cambridge (MA 1st Cl. Hons Law). Admitted solicitor, 1972; solicitor, Herbert Smith & Co., 1972–75; New Hall, Cambridge: Coll. Lectr in Law, 1975–83; Fellow, 1975–90; Bursar, 1983–90; Emeritus Fellow, 1995; Trinity Hall, Cambridge: Bursar and Steward, 1990–93; Fellow, 1990–2003; Treasurer, Cambridge Univ., 1993–2003; Clare Hall, Cambridge: Bursar and Develt Dir, 2003–10; Emeritus Fellow, 2011. Gen. Comr of Tax, 1987–2008. Dir, Cambridge Building Soc., 1994–2006. Fellow and Acting Bursar, Murray Edwards Coll., Cambridge, 2013. Trustee: Cambridge Colleges Federated Pension Scheme, 2003–15 (Chm., 2006–15); Sir Halley Stewart Trust, 2003–; The Varrier-Jones Foundn, 2005–14; The Papworth Trust, 2006–15; Edward Storey Foundn, 2006–; Cambridge Building Soc. Retirement Plan, 2008– (Chm., 2009–18); King's Junior Voices, 2010–; Michaelhouse Centre Cambridge Ltd, 2017–. Member, Audit Committee: CUP, 2011–17; Comberton Acad. Trust, 2015–. Gov., Long Road VI Form Coll., Cambridge, 1992–2001. *Recreations*: family life, photography, hill-walking, choral singing, gardening. *Address*: Clare Hall, Herschel Road, Cambridge CB3 9AL. *T*: (01223) 332362.

**WOMBELL, Paul David**; independent photographic curator and writer; *b* 8 Oct. 1948; *s* of Clifford and Katherine Wombell; *m* 1995, Tricia Coral Buckley. *Educ*: St Martin's Sch. of Art, London (BA Fine Art). Midland Gp Art Centre, 1983–86; Director: Impressions Gall., York, 1986–94; The Photographers' Gall., London, 1994–2005; Festival Dir, Hereford Photography Festival, 2006–07. Guest Curator, Le Mois de la Photo à Montréal, 2013. Vis. Prof., 2003–07, Res. Prof., 2007–09, Univ. of Sunderland. Chm., Citigroup Photography Prize, 2003–05. *Publications*: Battle, Passchendale 1917, 1981; Photovideo: photography in the age of the computer, 1991; Sportscape, the evolution of sport photography, 2000; Blink, 2002; Local: the end of globalisation, 2007; 70s Photography and Everyday Life, 2009; Calves and Thighs: Juergen Teller, 2010; End Times: Jill Greenberg, 2012; Drone: the automated image, 2013. *Recreation*: life.

**WOMBWELL, Sir George (Philip Frederick)**, 7th Bt *cr* 1778; *b* 21 May 1949; *s* of Sir (Frederick) Philip (Alfred William) Wombwell, 6th Bt, MBE, and late Ida Elizabeth, *er d* of Frederick J. Leitch; *S* father, 1977, but his name does not appear on the Official Roll of the Baronetage; *m* 1974, (Hermione) Jane, *e d* of T. S. Wrightson; one *s* one *d*. *Educ*: Repton. *Heir*: *s* Stephen Philip Henry Wombwell [*b* 12 May 1977; *m* 2006, Helen-Sarah, *o d* of Terence William Pattinson; one *d*]. *Address*: Newburgh Priory, Coxwold, York YO61 4AS.

**WOMERSLEY, Prof. David John**, DLitt; FBA 2009; FRHistS; Thomas Warton Professor of English Literature, University of Oxford, since 2002; Fellow, St Catherine's College, Oxford, since 2002; *b* 29 Jan. 1957; *s* of late John Crossley Womersley and Joyce Womersley; *m* 1982, Carolyn Jane Godlee; one *s* two *d*. *Educ*: Strode's Sch., Egham; Trinity Coll., Cambridge (BA 1979; PhD 1983); DLitt Oxon 2015. FRHistS 1997; FEA 2003. Drapers' Co. Res. Fellow, Pembroke Coll., Cambridge, 1981–83; Lectr, Sch. of English, Univ. of Leeds, 1983–84; Fellow and Tutor in English Lit., Jesus Coll., Oxford, 1984–2002; Sen. Proctor, Univ. of Oxford, 2001–02. Governor: Dragon Sch., Oxford, 1998–2010; Harrow Sch., 2001–16. *Publications*: The Transformation of the Decline and Fall of the Roman Empire, 1988; Gibbon and the 'Watchmen of the Holy City': the historian and his reputation 1776–1814, 2002; Divinity and State, 2010; James II, 2015; *edited*: Edward Gibbon, The Decline and Fall of the Roman Empire, 3 vols, 1994, 7th edn 2004, facsimile edn, 6 vols, 1997, abridged edn 2000, 10th edn 2004; Edward Gibbon, Reflections on the Fall of Rome, 1995; Religious Scepticism: contemporary responses to Gibbon, 1997; Augustan Critical Writing, 1997; Edmund Burke, Pre-Revolutionary Writings, 1998; Restoration Drama: an anthology, 2000; Samuel Johnson, Selected Essays, 2003; James Boswell, Life of Johnson, 2008; Jonathan Swift, Gulliver's Travels, 2012; E. W. Montagu,

Reflections on the Rise and Fall of the Ancient Republicks, 2015; Samuel Johnson, 2018; John Brown: Estimate of the Manners and Principles of the Times and other writings, 2019; *edited collections of essays*: Gibbon: bicentenary essays, 1997; A Companion to English Literature from Milton to Blake, 2000; Cultures of Whiggism, 2005; Literary Milieux, 2008. *Recreations*: wine, yachting, cooking, dogs. *Address*: St Catherine's College, Manor Road, Oxford OX1 3UJ. *T*: (01865) 271714, *Fax*: (01865) 271768. *E*: david.womersley@ell.ox.ac.uk. *Clubs*: Athenæum, Saintsbury.

**WOMERSLEY, John**; *see* Womersley, W. J.

**WOMERSLEY, Sir Peter (John Walter),** 2nd Bt *cr* 1945; JP; human resources consultant, 1997–2001; *b* 10 Nov. 1941; *s* of Capt. John Womersley (*o s* of 1st Bt; killed in action in Italy, 1944), and of Betty, *d* of Cyril Williams, Elstead, Surrey; *S* grandfather, 1961; *m* 1968, Janet Margaret Grant (*d* 2016); two *s* two *d*. *Educ*: Aldro; Charterhouse; RMA, Sandhurst. Entered Royal Military Academy (Regular Army), 1960; Lt, King's Own Royal Border Regt, 1964; Captain, 1967; retd 1968; Personnel, then Human Resources, Manager, later Evaluation Project Manager, Human Resources, SmithKline Beecham, 1968–97. JP Steyning, 1991, Worthing and Dist, 1996. *Publications*: (with Neil Grant) Collecting Stamps, 1980. *Heir*: *s* John Gavin Grant Womersley, *b* 7 Dec. 1971.

**WOMERSLEY, (William) John,** DPhil; Director General, European Spallation Source, since 2016; *b* Torquay, Devon, 22 Sept. 1962; *s* of Leslie Womersley and Patricia Womersley; *Educ*: Torquay Boys' Grammar Sch.; Corpus Christi Coll., Cambridge (BA Hons 1st Cl. Nat. Scis 1983; MA Nat. Scis 1987); Corpus Christi Coll., Oxford (DPhil Experimental Particle Phys 1987). Asst Prof. of Physics, Florida State Univ., 1989–92; Scientist: SSC Lab., Texas, 1992–94; Fermi National Accelerator Lab., 1994–2004; Dir, Particle Physics, CCLRC Rutherford Appleton Lab., 2005–07; Dir, Sci. Strategy and Sci. Progs, 2007–11, Chief Exec., 2011–16, STFC. Vis. Prof., Univ. of Oxford, 2005–. FInstP 2006; Fellow, APS, 2002. *Recreations*: railways, travel, music. *Address*: European Spallation Source, Box 176, 22100 Lund, Sweden.

**WONG Kin Chow, Michael,** GBS 2001; JP; Chairman, Equal Opportunities Commission of Hong Kong, 2003; a Justice of Appeal of the High Court of Hong Kong, 1999–2001; *b* 16 Aug. 1936; *s* of late Wong Chong and Au Ting; *m* 1963, Mae (*née* Fong); two *s* two *d*. *Educ*: Univ. of Liverpool (LLB Hons 1961). Called to the Bar, Middle Temple, 1962; private practice, Hong Kong, 1962–65; Hong Kong Government: Crown Counsel, Legal Dept, 1966–69; Senior Crown Counsel, 1969–72; Asst Principal Crown Counsel, 1973; Presiding Officer, Labour Tribunal, 1973–75; Asst Registrar, Supreme Court, 1975–77; District Judge, 1977; a Judge of the High Court, then of the Court of First Instance of the High Court, Hong Kong, 1985–99. Chm., Release Under Supervision Bd, 1988–94. JP Hong Kong, 2002. *Address*: Flat B, 60th Floor, The Masterpiece, 18 Hanoi Road, Tsimshatsui, Kowloon, Hong Kong. *Clubs*: Chinese, Hong Kong, Hong Kong Jockey, Kowloon Cricket (Hong Kong).

**WONG Yin Song, Most Rev. James Richard;** *see* Indian Ocean, Archbishop of.

**WONG, Andrea;** President, International Production, Sony Pictures Television, and President, International, Sony Pictures Entertainment, 2011–17; *b* Los Gatos, Calif; *d* of Manford and Wanda Wong. *Educ*: Massachusetts Inst. of Technol. (BS Electrical Engrg 1988); Stanford Grad. Sch. of Business (MBA 1993). Analyst, First Boston Corp., 1988–90; strategic planning analyst, PepsiCo, 1990–91; researcher, ABC News, 1993–94; Exec. Asst to Pres., ABC TV, 1994–96; Vice Pres. and Exec. Asst to Pres., ABC Inc., 1996–98; Vice Pres., 1998–2000, Sen. Vice Pres., 2000–04, Exec. Vice Pres., 2004–07, Alternative Programming, Specials and Late Night, ABC Entertainment; Pres. and CEO, Lifetime Networks, 2007–10. Gov., BFI, 2014–. *Recreations*: food, drink, leisure, travel. *Clubs*: 5 Hertford Street, George, 67 Pall Mall, Soho House.

**WONG, Natasha Pui-Wai;** QC 2017; *b* London, 30 Dec. 1964; *d* of Wong Peng-Fun and Anneliese Osterspey; *m* 2015, Gregory James Campbell; one *s*. *Educ*: Lycée Français Charles de Gaulle, London; Kingston Poly. (BSc Hons Sociol.); Middlesex Univ. (CPE); Inns of Court Sch. of Law. Called to the Bar, Middle Temple, 1993; in practice as barrister, 1993–; a Recorder, 2014–16. *Recreations*: music, travel. *Address*: 5 King's Bench Walk, Temple, EC4Y 7DN. *T*: (020) 7353 5638.

**WONNACOTT, John Henry,** CBE 2000; artist; *b* 15 April 1940; *s* of John Alfred Wonnacott and Ethel Gwendoline Wonnacott (*née* Copeland); *m* 1974, Anne Rozalia Wesolowska; one *s* two *d*. *Educ*: Slade Sch. of Fine Art, London. *Solo exhibitions* include: Minories, Colchester, 1977; Rochdale Art Gall. and tour, 1978; Marlborough Fine Art, London, 1980, 1985, 1988; Scottish NPG, Edinburgh, 1986; Agnew's, London, 1992, 1996, 2005, 2011; Wolsey Art Gall., Christchurch Mansion, Ipswich, 1998; Hirschl & Adler, NY and Agnew's, London, 1999–2000; NPG (Royal Family etc), 2000; Clare Hall, Cambridge, 2013; St John's Coll., Oxford, 2013; Chambers Fine Art, NY, 2014; Norwich Castle Mus., 2014; Norwich Univ. of Arts, 2014; Focal Point Gall., Southend-on-Sea, 2019; *group exhibitions* include: Painting and Perception, MacRoberts Arts Centre Gall., Univ. of Sterling, 1971; British Painting '74, Haywood Gall.; British Painting 1952–77, RA, 1977; Britain Salutes New York, Marlborough Fine Art, 1983; The Hard-Won Image, Tate Gall., 1984; Foundn Veranneman invites Marlborough, Foundn Veranneman, Kruishoutem, 1986–87; Monet to Freud, Sotheby's, London, 1989; Salute to Turner, Agnew's, London, 1989; The Pursuit of the Real, British Figurative Painting from Sickert to Bacon, Manchester City Art Galls, Barbican Art Gall. and Glasgow City Art Gall., 1990; The New Patrons, Twentieth Century Art from Corporate Collections, Christie's, London, 1992; Contemp. Portraits from Suffolk to Essex, Gainsborough's House, Sudbury, 1995; Contemp. British Artists Celebrate One Hundred Years of the Nat. Trust, Christie's, London, 1995; Painting the Century, NPG, 2001; A Sea of Faces, Nat. Maritime Mus., London, 2001; Visions of London, Art Space Gall., 2004; Annual Exhibn, RP (Ondaatje Prize for Portraiture), 2006–19; work in public collections including: Arts Council, British Council, Imperial War Mus., H of C, NPG, Nat. Maritime Mus., Nat. Trust, Tate Gall., DTI, London; Metropolitan Mus., NY; Christchurch Mus., Ipswich; Scottish NPG; Norwich Castle Mus.; Rochdale Art Gall., Manton Collection, The Clark, Williamstown. Hon. RP 2001. Conversations Prize, RP, 2015. *Address*: 5 Cliff Gardens, Leigh on Sea, Essex SS9 1EY. *W*: www.johnwonnacott.co.uk.

**WONNACOTT, Mark Andrew;** QC 2013; *b* London, 1967; *s* of Richard Wonnacott and Sheila Wonnacott. *Educ*: Perth Acad.; University Coll. London (LLB 1988); Birkbeck, Univ. of London (BA 2016). Called to the Bar, Lincoln's Inn, 1989; in practice as a barrister, 1989–. *Publications*: Drafting Property Pleadings, 1997; Possession of Land, 2006; History of the Law of Landlord and Tenant, 2012; What is a Reversion on a Lease?, 2014. *Recreation*: teasing academics and annoying judges. *Address*: Wilberforce Chambers, 8 New Square, Lincoln's Inn, WC2A 3QP. *T*: (020) 7306 0102.

**WONNACOTT, Prof. Simone Maria;** Vice-Chancellor, Leeds Arts University, since 2017; *b* Herts, 1966; *d* of John and Gillian Wonnacott; *m* Prof. David Russell; one *s* one *d*. *Educ*: Leeds Beckett Univ. (Postgrad. Dip. Personnel Mgt 1988); Univ. of Leeds (MBA 2007). Leeds College of Art: Dir, Corporate Services, 2002–04; Dep. Principal, 2004–09; Principal, 2009–17. FCIPD; FRSA. *Recreations*: travel, food, family, the arts, music, theatre, pilates, running. *Address*: Leeds Arts University, Blenheim Walk, Leeds LS2 9AQ. *T*: (0113) 202 8000.

**WOO, Kwok-Hing,** GBS 2002; CBE 1996; Commissioner on Interception of Communications and Surveillance, Hong Kong, 2006–12; *b* 13 Jan. 1946; *s* of late Woo Leung and Leung Yuk-Ling; *m* Rowena Tang; two *s* two *d*. *Educ*: Univ. of Birmingham (LLB); University College, London (LLM). Called to the Bar, Gray's Inn, 1969; QC (Hong Kong), 1987; in private practice, Hong Kong, 1970–92; a High Court Judge, then Judge of the Ct of First Instance, High Ct, 1992–2000; a Justice of Appeal, 2000–03; Vice-Pres., Ct of Appeal, 2004–11. Chairman: Boundary and Election Commn, Hong Kong, 1993–97; Electoral Affairs Commn, 1997–2006; Commissioner: of Inquiry into Garley Bldg Fire, 1997; of Inquiry on New Airport, 1998–99. *Address*: c/o 66a Deep Water Bay Road, Hong Kong. *Clubs*: Hong Kong Jockey, Hong Kong, Hong Kong Country.

**WOO, Sir Leo (Joseph),** Kt 1993; MBE 1984; Chairman and Chief Executive, Dragon Resources Ltd, since 2006; *b* 17 Oct. 1952; *s* of Gabriel Bernard Woo and Molly Woo; *m* 1973, Emilyn Cha; one *s* two *d*. *Educ*: De La Salle Oakhill Coll., Sydney. Former Chm. and Chief Exec., Woo Hldgs Gp. *Address*: PO Box R399, Royal Exchange, NSW 1225, Australia.

**WOO, Prof. Patricia Mang Ming,** CBE 2005; PhD; FRCP, FRCPCH, FMedSci; Professor of Paediatric Rheumatology, University College London, 1994–2010, now Emeritus; Consultant Physician, Great Ormond Street and University College London Hospitals, 1994–2010, now Hon. Consultant Physician, Great Ormond Street Hospital Foundation NHS Trust and University College Hospital Foundation NHS Trust; *b* 12 Feb. 1948; *d* of Woo Hing Tak and Woo Lam Chiu Wah. *Educ*: Charing Cross Hosp. Med. Sch., Univ. of London (BSc 1969; MB BS 1972); Darwin Coll., Cambridge (PhD 1979). FRCP 1991; FRCPCH 1997. House physician and house surgeon, Charing Cross Hosp., 1973–74; Senior House Officer: Brompton Hosp., 1974; Northwick Park Hosp., 1974–75; MRC Clin. Trng Fellow and Hon. SHO, Cambridge Univ., 1975–78; Registrar, Northwick Park Hosp., 1979–81; Sen. Registrar, Guy's Hosp., 1981–83; Res. Fellow, Harvard Med. Sch., 1983–85; MRC Clin. Scientist and Consultant Physician, Northwick Park Hosp., 1985–94. FMedSci 2001. *Publications*: (jtly) Paediatric Rheumatology Update, 1989; (ed jtly) Oxford Textbook of Rheumatology, 1993, 3rd edn 2004; Paediatric Rheumatology in Clinical Practice, 2007; 230 original contribs to rheumatology, medical and scientific jls; 74 reviews, editorials and book chapters. *Recreations*: music, ski-ing, golf, sailing. *Address*: Rayne Building, University College London, 5 University Street, WC1E 6JF. *T*: (020) 7679 6364, *Fax*: (020) 7679 6212.

**WOO, Sir Po-Shing,** Kt 1999; FCIArb; Founder, Woo Kwan Lee & Lo, Solicitors & Notaries, Hong Kong, 1973; *b* 19 April 1929; *s* of late Seaward Woo, JP, and of Ng Chiu Man; *m* 1956, Helen Woo Fong Shuet Fun; four *s* one *d*. *Educ*: La Salle Coll., Hong Kong; King's Coll., London (LLB 1956; FKC 1995). Admitted Solicitor, England and Hong Kong, 1960; NP 1966; admitted as Barrister and Solicitor, Supreme Court of Victoria, Australia, 1983. Hon. Prof., Nankai Univ. of Tianjin, China, 1995. Dir of numerous companies in Hong Kong. Member: Inst. Admin. Mgt, 1975; Inst. Trade Mark Agents, 1978. Founder, Po-Shing Woo Charitable Foundn, 1994. Patron: Woo Po-Shing Gall. of Chinese Bronze, Shanghai Mus., 1996–; Sir Po-Shing Woo Auckland Observatory Bldg, 1998–. Fellow, Hong Kong Mgt Assoc., 2000. FCIArb 1966; FCMI (FIMgt 1975); FInstD 1975; World Fellow, Duke of Edinburgh's Award, 1994. Hon. LLD City Univ. of Hong Kong, 1995. Chevalier, Ordre des Arts et des lettres (France), 2004. *Recreations*: travelling, antiques (incl. Chinese paintings, bronze and ceramic), race-horse owner (incl. Derby winners, Helene Star, 1993, and Helene Mascot, 2008). *Clubs*: Royal Automobile; Hong Kong Jockey, Hong Kong (Hong Kong).

**WOOBEY, Paul,** CEng; Director, Information and Communications Technology, Wellcome (formerly Wellcome Trust) Sanger Institute, since 2014; *b* Leeds, 9 May 1956; *s* of Eric and Irene Woobey; *m* 1976, Alison Edwardson; one *s*. *Educ*: High Sch., Glasgow; Univ. of Glasgow (BSc Atomic Physics and Maths). CEng 1979; MInstP. Scientific Officer (Reactor Physics), AEA, 1978–83; Res. Scientist, Rutherford Labs, 1983–86; Vice Pres., Global Infrastructure, GE Healthcare, 1986–2000; Chief Information Officer, EMEA Corporate IT, Pfizer, 2000–08; Chief Inf. Officer, 2008–13, Dir, Strategy and Standards, 2011–13, ONS. MBCS 1979. *Address*: Wellcome Sanger Institute, Wellcome Genome Campus, Hinxton, Cambridge CB10 1SA. *T*: (01223) 499902. *E*: paul.woobey@sanger.ac.uk.

**WOOD,** family name of **Earl of Halifax** and **Baron Wood of Anfield**.

**WOOD OF ANFIELD,** Baron *cr* 2011 (Life Peer), of Tonbridge in the County of Kent; **Stewart Martin Wood,** PhD; Fellow in Practice, Blavatnik School of Government, University of Oxford, since 2015; Chairman, United Nations Association-UK, since 2016; *b* Tunbridge Wells, 25 March 1968; *s* of Brian James Wood and Gisela Wood; two *s*. *Educ*: Judd Sch., Tonbridge; University Coll., Oxford (BA 1989; MA); Harvard Univ. (PhD 1997). Fulbright Schol., 1989–90; Jun. Res. Fellow, St John's Coll., Oxford, 1995–96; Fellow and Tutor in Politics, Magdalen Coll., Oxford, 1996–2011. Special Advr to Chancellor of the Exchequer on Treasury's Council of Economic Advrs, 2001–07; Special Advr to Prime Minister on Foreign Policy, NI, Culture, Media and Sport, 2007–10; Hd of Communications, Rt Hon. Edward Miliband's Leadership Campaign, 2010; Advr to Rt Hon. Edward Miliband, Office of the Leader of the Opposition, 2010–15; Shadow Minister without Portfolio, Cabinet Office, 2011–15. Mem., Internat. Relns Cttee, H of L, 2016–. Mem., Marshall Aid Commemoration Commn, 2016–. Director: Janus Henderson Diversified Income Trust, 2017–; The Good Law Project, 2019–. *Publications*: (ed jtly) Options for Britain: a strategic policy review, 1996; contrib. articles to pol sci. jls and ed vols on pol economy and public policy in Western Europe. *Recreations*: film, theatre, football, cricket, alt-country music. *Address*: c/o House of Lords, SW1A 0PW. *T*: (020) 7219 5854. *E*: stewart.wood@parliament.uk.

**WOOD, Adam Kenneth Compton;** HM Diplomatic Service, retired; Lieutenant-Governor, Isle of Man, 2011–16; *b* 13 March 1955; *s* of Kenneth Wood and Cynthia Wood; *m* 1993, Katie Richardson; one *d*. *Educ*: Oriel Coll., Oxford (BA Hons). Kenya Programme Manager, ODA, Nairobi, 1988–93; Advr to Dir Gen., EC, 1993–96; Hd, DFID SE Asia, Bangkok, 1996–2000; Counsellor (Develt), UKREP, Brussels, 2000–02; High Commissioner: Uganda, 2002–05; Kenya, 2005–08; Dir (Africa), FCO, 2008–10. *Recreations*: birding, golf, tennis.

**WOOD, Prof. Adrian John Bickersteth,** CBE 2005; Professor of International Development, University of Oxford, 2005–11, now Emeritus; *b* 25 Jan. 1946; *s* of John Henry Francis Wood and Mary Eva Bickersteth Wood (*née* Ottley); *m* 1971, Joyce Miriam Teitz; two *d*. *Educ*: King's Coll., Cambridge (BA, PhD 1973); Harvard Univ. (MPA).

Fellow, King's College, Cambridge, 1969–77; Asst Lectr, then Lectr, Cambridge Univ., 1973–77; Economist, then Sen. Economist, World Bank, 1977–85; Professorial Fellow, Inst. Develt Studies, Univ. of Sussex, 1985–2000; Chief Economist, DFID, 2000–05. *Publications:* A Theory of Profits, 1975; A Theory of Pay, 1978; (jtly) China: long-term development issues and options, 1985; North-South Trade, Employment and Inequality, 1994; contrib. articles to learned jls. *Recreations:* music, tennis. *Address:* Court House, The Green, Rottingdean, Brighton BN2 7HA.

**WOOD, Alan John,** CBE 2005; FREng; Chairman, Siemens Holdings plc, 2007–12; *b* 20 March 1947; *s* of Joseph Wood and Ivy Wood (*née* Larcombe); *m* 1973, Jennifer Margaret Lynn; two *d. Educ:* King Edward VII Sch., Sheffield; Manchester Univ. (BSc 1st Cl. Hons 1968; Hon. LLD 2003); Harvard Univ. (MBA 1975). MIMechE 1973, FIMechE 2002. Unilever plc, 1968–73; Head of Production, Crittall Construction, 1975–78; Man. Dir, Small Electric Motors, 1978–81; joined Siemens, 1981: Siemens AG, 1981–82; Production Dir, 1982–84, Man. Dir, 1984–87, Siemens Measurements Ltd; Managing Director: Electronic Components & Telecom Networks, 1987–91; Energy & Industry, 1991–98; Chief Exec., Siemens plc, 1998–2007. Chairman: North West Reg., CBI, 1996–98; Nat. Mfg Council, CBI, 2000–02; German-British Chamber of Industry and Commerce, 2001–12; Econ. Policy Cttee, EEF, 2003–05; South East Reg., CBI, 2005–07. Pres., EEF, 2005–08. FREng 2005. Hon. DTech Loughborough, 2009. Bundesverdienstkreuz Erste Klasse, 2008. *Recreations:* family, travel, gardening.

**WOOD, Sir Alan Thorpe Richard,** Kt 2018; CBE 2011; Director, Children Services, London Borough of Hackney, 2006–15; Chair, What Works Centre for Children's Social Care, since 2018; *b* Romford, 4 April 1954; *s* of Henry Thorpe Peter Wood and Isabel Patricia Smith; one *s* one *d. Educ:* Stepney Green Comprehensive Sch.; York Univ. (BA Hons Social Scis); Birmingham Univ. (PGCE); Inst. of Educn, Univ. of London (Dip. SEN). History teacher, 1977–90; Hd, Pupil Support and Special Educnl Needs, Southwark LBC, 1990–97; Dep. Dir of Educn, 1997–2000, Dir of Educn, 2000–01, Lambeth LBC; Dir of Educn, Hackney LBC, 2001–02; Chief Exec., Learning Trust, 2002–06. Pres., Assoc. of Dirs of Children's Services, 2014–15. Mem., Youth Justice Bd, 2018–. *Recreations:* cycling, cinema, reading.

**WOOD, Alexandra Frances Sara;** Leader, since 2013, and Creative Director, since 2016, City of London Sinfonia; *b* Maidenhead, 15 Jan. 1977; *d* of Anthony and Sara Wood; *m* 2002, David Cuin; one *s* one *d. Educ:* Abbey Sch., Reading; Selwyn Coll., Cambridge (BA Music); Royal Coll. of Music (Adv. Postgrad. Dip.). Mills Williams Jun. Fellow, Royal Coll. of Music, 2000–01. Visiting Professor: RHUL, 2002–07; Leeds Coll. Music, 2006–08; Birmingham Conservatoire, 2006–12. Leader, Aurora Orch., 2008–; regular leader, Birmingham Music Gp and London Sinfonietta, 2006–. *Recreations:* ballroom dancing, ice skating fan.

**WOOD, Aloun;** *see* Ndombet-Assamba, A.

**WOOD, Dr Andrew Charles,** OBE 2013; DL; Chief Executive, Adnams plc, since 2010; *b* London, 1960; *s* of Charles Wood and Doris Wood (*née* Lewin); *m* 1985, Sonya Clabburn; one *d. Educ:* Brockley Co. Grammar Sch.; Anglia Poly. Univ. (MBA 1994); Cranfield Univ. (DBA 2007). Norwich Union Inscc Gp, 1976–94; Adnams plc: Customer Services, 1994–2000; Sales and Mktg Dir, 2000–06; Man. Dir, 2006–10. Non-exec. Chm., SG Wealth Mgt, 2014–. Chairman: Norcas, 2005–12; New Anglia LEP, 2010–14; Visit E Anglia, 2018–; non-exec. Dir, Thorpeness and Aldeburgh Hotels Ltd, 2018–. DL Norfolk, 2018. Hon. DBA Anglia Ruskin, 2010; Hon. DSc Cranfield, 2013; Hon. DCL E Anglia, 2014. *Address:* 59 Drewray Drive, Taverham, Norwich NR8 6XS. *E:* wood.andy1@gmail.com.

**WOOD, Sir Andrew (Marley),** GCMG 2000 (KCMG 1995; CMG 1986); HM Diplomatic Service, retired; Senior Adviser: ITE, since 2002; Associate Fellow, Chatham House, since 2008; *b* 2 Jan. 1940; *s* of Robert George Wood; *m* 1st, 1972, Melanie LeRoy Masset (*d* 1977); one *s*; 2nd, 1978, Stephanie Lee Masset; one *s* one *d. Educ:* Ardingly Coll.; King's Coll., Cambridge (MA 1965). Foreign Office, 1961; Moscow, 1964; Washington, 1967; FCO, 1970; seconded to Cabinet Office, 1971; First Sec., FCO, 1973; First Sec. and Hd of Chancery, Belgrade, 1976; Counsellor, 1978; Hd of Chancery, Moscow, 1979; Hd of W European Dept, 1982, Hd of Personnel Operations Dept, 1983, FCO; Ambassador to Yugoslavia, 1985–89; Minister, Washington, 1989–92; Chief Clerk, FCO, 1992–95; Ambassador to Russian Fedn and to Moldova, 1995–2000. Director: The PBN Co., 2002–11 (Chm., 2007–10); Mechel, 2004–06. Director: Foreign and Colonial Trust, 2000–07; Russo-British Chamber of Commerce, 2000–07 (Chm., 2005–06); Member, Advisory Council: British Expertise (formerly British Consultants Bureau), 2000–08; Renaissance Capital, 2003–08; Adviser: European Round Table, 2004–09; Toyota Europe, 2007–09; Special Representative: BP, 2002–14; Petrofac, 2012–13. Pres., King's Coll. (Cambridge) Assoc., 2006–14. Trustee, Victor Zorza Hospice Trust, 2000–12. *Publications:* (with Lilia Shevstova) Change or Decay: Russia's dilemma and the West's response, 2011; pubns with Chatham Hse, American Interest.

**WOOD, Anne,** CBE 2000; Founder, Ragdoll Productions Ltd, since 1984; *b* 18 Dec. 1937; *d* of Jack Savage and Eleanor Savage (*née* Thomson); *m* 1959, Barrie Wood; one *s* one *d. Educ:* Tudhoe Colliery Primary Sch.; Alderman Wraith Grammar Sch.; Bingley Teachers' Trng Coll. Teacher, Spennymoor Secondary Modern Sch., 1959–65; Founder: Books for Your Children mag., 1965, Ed. and publisher, 1965–95; Fedn of Children's Book Gps, 1969; Consultant, Tyne Tees TV, 1977–79; Children's Producer, Yorkshire TV (The Book Tower, Ragdolly Anna), 1979–82; Hd, Children's Progs, TV-am (originator of Rub a dub tub, Roland Rat), 1982–84. FRTS 1998. Eleanor Farjeon Award, 1969; Ronald Politzer Award, 1974; BAFTA Awards, 1979 and 1982, Prix Jeunesse, 1980, for The Book Tower; BAFTA Awards, 1996 and 1997, for Tots TV; Japan Prize, 1997, BAFTA Award, 1998, Most Edgy Children's Prog. in Last Fifty Years, Prix Jeunesse, 2014, for Teletubbies, and BAFTA Award, 2002, for Teletubbies Everywhere; Veuve Clicquot Business Woman of Year Award, 1999; Olswang Business Award, Women in Film & Television, 2003; Japan Foundn President's Prize, 2004, for Open a Door; BAFTA Awards, 2007 and 2008, and Best Children's TV Prog., Voice of the Listener and Viewer Excellence in Broadcasting Awards, 2010, for In the Night Garden; BAFTA Award for Best Ind. Production Co., 2008; Lifetime Achievement Award, Mother and Baby mag., 2010; BAFTA Award for Dipdap, 2011; North-West Awards for Twirlywoos, RTS, 2015, 2016, 2017; Best Production for Young Children Ages 2–5 Years for Twirlywoos, 33rd Chicago Internat. Children's Film Fest., 2016. Hon. DLitt: Birmingham, 2013; Sheffield, 2015; Warwick, 2017. *Recreations:* reading, gardening. *Address:* Ragdoll Productions Ltd, Timothy's Bridge Road, Stratford upon Avon, Warwickshire CV37 9NQ. *T:* (01789) 404100.

**WOOD, Anthony,** PhD; FMedSci; FRSC; Senior Vice President, Medicinal Science and Technology (formerly Platform Technology and Science), GlaxoSmithKline, since 2017; *b* Gateshead, 12 Sept. 1965; *s* of Alan Wood and Linda Winifred Wood; *m* 2008, Dr (Jane) Sarah Houlton; one *s* by a previous marriage. *Educ:* Newcastle Univ. (BSc Hons 1987; PhD 1990). Pfizer: Scientist, Dept of Discovery Chemistry, 1992–99; Manager, 1999–2001; Dir, 2001–04; Hd, Chemistry, 2004–07; Hd, Chemistry and Exploratory Medicinal Scis, 2007–08; Senior Vice-President and Head: Worldwide Medicinal Chemistry, 2008–15; Worldwide Medicinal Scis, 2015–17. Mem., EPSRC, 2010–13. Discovered maraviroc (Selzentry), a new HIV medicine. Malcolm Campbell Prize, RSC, 2005; Heroes of Chemistry Award, ACS, 2008; PhRMA Discoverers Award, 2010; UCB-Ehrlich Award, Eur. Fedn of Medicinal Chemistry, 2010. *Publications:* (ed) Annual Reports in Medicinal Chemistry, vol. 41, 2006. *Recreations:* mountain biking, cooking. *Address:* GlaxoSmithKline, Medicines Research Centre, Gunnels Wood Road, Stevenage, Herts SG1 2NY.

**WOOD, Sir Anthony John P.;** *see* Page Wood.

**WOOD, Anthony Richard;** HM Diplomatic Service, retired; *b* 13 Feb. 1932; *s* of late Rev. T. J. Wood and of Phyllis Margaret (*née* Bold); *m* 1st, 1966, Sarah Drew (marr. diss. 1973); one *s* one *d*; 2nd, 2006, Charlotte Olivia Ryder (*née* Strutt). *Educ:* St Edward's Sch.; Worcester Coll., Oxford (BA). HM Forces, 1950–52. British Sch. of Archaeology in Iraq, Nimrud, 1956; joined HM Foreign Service, 1957; served: Beirut, 1957; Bahrain, 1958; Paris, 1959; Benghazi, 1962; Aden, 1963; Basra, 1966; Tehran, 1970; Muscat, 1980; Counsellor, FCO, 1984–87. *Publications:* Time in the Levant: a life in the Middle East, 2019. *Recreations:* walking, singing, The Bach Choir. *Clubs:* Army and Navy, Rifle Officers'.

**WOOD, Ven. Antony Charles M.;** *see* MacRow-Wood.

**WOOD, Prof. Bernard Anthony,** PhD, DSc; Director, Center for the Advanced Study of Human Paleobiology, and University Professor of Human Origins, since 2006, and Professor of Human Evolutionary Anatomy, since 1997, George Washington University (Henry R. Luce Professor of Human Origins, 1997–2006); Hon. Senior Scientist, Smithsonian Institution, since 1997; *b* 17 April 1945; *s* of Anthony Wood and Joan Wood (*née* Slocombe); *m* 1st, 1965, Hazel Francis (marr. diss. 1980); one *s* one *d*; 2nd, 1982, Alison Richards (marr. diss. 2003); one *d*; 3rd, 2008, Sally Furze (marr. diss. 2015). *Educ:* King's Sch., Gloucester; Middlesex Hosp. Med. Sch., Univ. of London (BSc 1966; MB BS 1969; PhD 1975; DSc 1996). Lectr, Charing Cross Hosp. Med. Sch., 1973–74; Middlesex Hospital Medical School: Asst Lectr, 1971–73; Lectr, subseq. Sen. Lectr, 1974–78; Reader in Anatomy, 1978–82; S. A. Courtauld Prof. of Anatomy, 1982–85; Derby Prof. of Anatomy, 1985–97, and Dean, Faculty of Medicine, 1996–97, Univ. of Liverpool. Non-executive Director: Royal Liverpool and Broad Green NHS Trust, 1994–96; Liverpool HA, 1996–97. West Meml Lecture, Univ. of Wales, Cardiff, 1996. Chairman: Science-based Archaeol. Cttee, SERC, 1992–95; Science-based Archaeol. Strategy Gp, NERC, 1995–96; President: Primate Soc., 1986–89; Anatomical Soc. of GB and Ireland, 1996–97; Vice-Pres., Royal Anthropological Inst., 1989–92. *Publications:* (ed) Food Acquisition and Processing in Primates, 1984; (ed) Major Topics in Primate and Human Evolution, 1986; Koobi Fora Research Project: hominid cranial remains, 1991; (ed) Wiley-Blackwell Encyclopedia of Human Evolution, 2011; articles on palaeoanthropology, hominid palaeobiology, and human morphology in scientific jls. *Recreations:* English salt glaze stoneware, Verdi, Bach. *Address:* Center for the Advanced Study of Human Paleobiology, George Washington University, Science and Engineering Hall, 800 22nd Street NW, Suite 6000, Washington, DC 20052, USA.

**WOOD, Prof. Bernard John,** PhD; FRS 1998; Research Professor, University of Oxford, 2007–17, now Emeritus; *b* 10 May 1946; *s* of Sidney James Wood and Marjorie Ethel Wood; *m* 1st, 1968, Susan Brightmore (marr. diss.); two *d*; 2nd, 1982, Kristin Vala Ragnarsdottir (marr. diss.); one *s* one *d*; 3rd, 2004, Susan Prosser. *Educ:* Northern Poly. (BSc London); Univ. of Leeds (MSc); Univ. of Newcastle upon Tyne (PhD 1971). Lectr in Geol., 1973–78, Reader, 1978–79, Univ. of Manchester; Principal Scientist, Rockwell Hanford Ops, Richland, Washington, 1980–81; Prof., Northwestern Univ., 1982–89; Prof. of Earth Sciences, Univ. of Bristol, 1989–2005; Fedn Fellow, Nat. Key Centre for Geochem. Evolution and Metallogeny of Continents, Macquarie Univ., 2005–07. Vis. Prof., Univ. of Chicago, 1979–80. Award, Mineralogical Soc. of America, 1984; Schlumberger Medal, Mineralogical Soc. of GB, 1991; Holmes Medal, Eur. Union of Geoscis, 1997; Murchison Medal, Geol. Soc., 1997; Goldschmidt Medal, Geochem. Soc., 2003; Hess Medal, American Geophys. Union, 2013; Roebling Medal, Mineralogical Soc. of America, 2014. *Publications:* (with D. G. Fraser) Elementary Thermodynamics for Geologists, 1976; (with J. R. Holloway) Simulating the Earth, 1988. *Address:* Department of Earth Sciences, University of Oxford, South Parks Road, Oxford OX1 3AN.

**WOOD, Catherine;** QC 2011; a Recorder, since 2007; *b* Walsall, 27 Aug. 1963; *d* of late Bernard Michael Wood and of Margaret R. Wood; *m* 1991, Simon Derek John Wheatley, *s* of late Derek Peter Francis Wheatley, QC; three *s* one *d. Educ:* Queen Mary's High Sch. for Girls, Walsall; Queen Mary Coll., Univ. of London (LLB). Called to the Bar, Middle Temple, 1985; in practice as a barrister, 1985–; 4 Paper Buildings, 1993–. *Recreations:* family, friends, cricket, Mallorca, parkrun. *Address:* 4 Paper Buildings, Temple, EC4Y 7EX. *T:* (020) 7427 5200, *Fax:* (020) 7353 4979. *E:* cw@4pb.com. *Clubs:* London Irish; St George's Hill Lawn Tennis.

**WOOD, Charles;** Chief Executive, London Borough of Brent, 1986–95; *b* 16 May 1950; *s* of Sir Frank Wood, KBE, CB and Lady (Olive May) Wood (*née* Wilson); *m* Carolyn Hall; three *s* two *d. Educ:* King's College London (BSc Hons); Polytechnic of Central London (DipTP). Engineer, GLC, 1971–76; Planner, and Dep. Dir of Housing, London Borough of Hammersmith and Fulham, 1976–82; Dir of Develt, London Borough of Brent, 1982–86. *Recreations:* walking, tennis.
See also W. J. Wood.

**WOOD, Charles Gerald,** FRSL 1984; writer for films, television and the theatre, since 1962; *b* 6 Aug. 1932; *s* of John Edward Wood, actor and Catherine Mae (*née* Harris), actress; *m* 1954, Valerie Elizabeth Newman, actress; one *s* one *d. Educ:* King Charles I Sch., Kidderminster; Birmingham Coll. of Art. Corp., 17/21st Lancers, 1950–55; Factory worker, 1955–57; Stage Manager, advertising artist, cartoonist, scenic artist, 1957–59; Bristol Evening Post, 1959–62. Member: Drama Adv. Panel, South Western Arts, 1972–73; Council, BAFTA, 1991–93. Consultant to Nat. Film Develt Fund, 1980–82. *Wrote plays:* Prisoner and Escort, John Thomas, Spare, (Cockade), Arts Theatre, 1963; Meals on Wheels, Royal Court, 1965; Don't Make Me Laugh, Aldwych, 1966; Fill the Stage with Happy Hours, Nottingham Playhouse, Vaudeville Theatre, 1967; Dingo, Bristol Arts Centre, Royal Court, 1967; H, National Theatre, 1969; Welfare, Liverpool Everyman, 1971; Veterans, Lyceum, Edinburgh, Royal Court, 1972; Jingo, RSC, 1975; Has 'Washington' Legs?, Nat. Theatre, 1978; Red Star, RSC, 1984; Across from the Garden of Allah, Comedy, 1986; adapted Pirandello's Man, Beast and Virtue, Nat. Theatre, 1989 and The Mountain Giants, Nat. Theatre, 1993; Dumas's The Tower, Almeida, 1995. *Screenplays include:* The Knack, 1965 (Grand Prix, Cannes; Writers Guild Award for Best Comedy); Help!, 1965; How I Won the War, 1967; The Charge of the Light Brigade, 1968; The Long Day's Dying, 1969; Cuba, 1980; Wagner, 1983; Red Monarch, 1983; Puccini, 1984; Tumbledown, 1988 (Prix Italia, RAI Prize, 1988; BAFTA, Broadcasting Press Guild and RTS awards, 1989); Shooting the Hero, 1991; An Awfully Big Adventure, 1995; (with Richard Eyre) Iris, 2001; (with Richard Eyre) The Other Man, 2008; Will, 2009; *adapted:* Bed Sitting Room, 1973. Numerous *television* plays incl. Prisoner and Escort, Drums Along the Avon, Drill Pig, A Bit of a Holiday, A Bit of an Adventure, Do As I Say, Love Lies Bleeding, Dust to Dust; creator of Gordon Maple in series, Don't Forget to Write; Company of Adventurers (series for CBC), 1986; My Family and Other Animals (series for

BBC), 1987; The Settling of the Sun, 1987; Sharpe's Company, 1994; A Breed of Heroes, 1994; (with John Osborne) England My England, 1996; Sharpe's Regiment, 1996; Sharpe's Waterloo, 1997; Mute of Malice, 1997; Briefs Trooping Gaily, 1998; Monsignor Renard, 2000. Evening Standard Awards, 1963, 1973. *Publications*: plays: Cockade, 1965; Fill the Stage with Happy Hours, 1967; Dingo, 1967; H, 1970; Veterans, 1972; Has 'Washington' Legs?, 1978; Tumbledown, 1987; Man, Beast and Virtue, 1990; The Mountain Giants, 1993; (trans.) Dumas, The Tower, or Marguerite of Bourgogne, 1995; Plays One, 1997; Plays Two, 1997; Plays Three, 2005. *Recreations*: military and theatrical studies; gardening. *Address*: c/o Sue Rodgers, Independent Talent Group Ltd, 40 Whitfield Street, W1T 2RH. *T*: (020) 7636 6565. *Clubs*: Royal Over-Seas League, British Playwrights' Mafia.

**WOOD, Charlie Browne Martin**; entertainment producer; Founder and Director, Underbelly, since 2001; *b* London, 28 Feb. 1973; *s* of Simon Wood and Clare Wood (*née* Fitzalan Howard); *m* 2011, Henrietta, (Hatta), Byng, *d* of Viscount Torrington, *qv*; two *s* one *d*. *Educ*: Eton Coll.; Edinburgh Univ. (MA Hons); Coll. of Law (LLB). Admitted solicitor, 2002; Andersen Legal, 2000–02; Solicitor, DLA Piper, 2002–06. Director: Underbelly Fest., London, 2009–; Edinburgh's Hogmanay, 2017–. *Recreations*: fatherhood, entertainment. *Address*: c/o Underbelly Ltd, 36 Hatton Garden, EC1N 8EB. *T*: (020) 7307 8480. *Clubs*: White's, Soho House.

**WOOD, Rear Adm. Christopher Lainson**, CB 1991; *b* 9 Feb. 1936; *s* of Gordon and Eileen Wood; *m* 1962, Margot Price; two *s* (one *d* decd). *Educ*: Pangbourne College. Seaman Officer, RN, 1954; joined submarine service, 1958; CO's qualifying course, 1966; in comd, HMS Ambush, 1966–68; JSSC, 1970; nuclear submarine training, 1971; in comd, HMS Warspite, 1971–73; Staff of FO Submarines, 1973–75; Staff of Dir, Naval Op. Requirements, 1975–77; Underwater Weapons Acceptance, 1978–81; Dep. Dir, Naval Op. Requirements, 1981–83; Dir Gen., Underwater Weapons, 1983–85; Dir Gen., Fleet Support, 1986–88; ACDS, Operational Requirements (Sea Systems), 1988–91. Dir, ALVA, 1992–96. *Recreations*: reading, fishing, sporting interests, voluntary service.

**WOOD, Christopher Terence**; HM Diplomatic Service; Consul-General, Shanghai, since 2019; *b* Wolverhampton, 19 Jan. 1959; *s* of Terry and late Joyce Wood. *Educ*: Cotwall End Prim. Sch., Sedgley; High Arcal Grammar Sch., Sedgley; Fitzwilliam Coll., Cambridge (BA Hons Mod. and Medieval Langs 1981). Desk Officer, W Eur. Dept, FCO, 1981–82; lang. trng, London and Hong Kong, 1982–84; Asst Pol Advr, Hong Kong Govt, 1984–87; Hong Kong Dept, FCO, 1987–89; Security Co-ordination Dept, FCO, 1989–91; DoE, subseq. DETR, 1992–98, Private Sec. to Minister of State, 1995–98; Econ. and Domestic Secretariat, Cabinet Office, 1998–2001; ODPM, 2001–02; Consul-Gen., Guangzhou, 2003–06; Dir, Americas, FCO, 2007–08; Dep. Hd of Mission, Beijing, 2008–12; Dir, British Office (formerly British Trade and Cultural Office), Taipei, 2013–16; Dep. Hd, EU Delegn to China and Mongolia, European Ext. Action Service, 2016–19. *Recreations*: cinema, theatre, swimming. *Address*: c/o Foreign and Commonwealth Office, King Charles Street, SW1A 2AH.

**WOOD, Ven. Claire**; Archdeacon of Loughborough, since 2017; *b* 1963. *Educ*: St Albans and Oxford Ministry Course. Ordained deacon, 2006, priest, 2007; Curate, St Peter and St Paul, Buckingham, 2006–09; Rector, St Peter and St Paul, Olney, 2009–17; Area Dean, Newport, 2015–17. *Address*: c/o Diocesan Office, St Martins House, 7 Peacock Lane, Leicester LE1 5PZ.

**WOOD, Rt Rev. Clyde Maurice**, BA, ThL; Bishop of North Queensland, 1996–2002; *b* 7 Jan. 1936; *s* of Maurice O. Wood and Helen M. Wood; *m* 1957, Margaret Joan Burls; two *s* one *d*. *Educ*: Perry Hall, Melbourne (ThL 1964); Monash Univ. (BA 1974). Deacon 1965, priest 1965; Curate: St John's, Bentleigh, 1965–66; St Paul's, Ringwood, 1966–67; in Dept of Evangelism and Extension, 1967–70; Curate-in-Charge: St Philip's, Mount Waverley, 1967–70; Armadale/Hawksburn, 1971–73; Rector and Canon Res., Christ Church Cathedral, Darwin, 1974, Dean 1978–83; on leave, Rector St Timothy's Episcopal Church, Indianapolis, USA, 1981; Bishop of the Northern Territory, 1983–92; Bishop of the Western Region, and Asst Bishop, dio. of Brisbane, 1992–96. OStJ 1980; ChStJ 1985. *Recreations*: golf, sailing. *Address*: 23 Degan Court, Middle Ridge, Qld 4350, Australia.

**WOOD, David**, OBE 2004; actor, playwright, writer, composer, theatrical producer and director; *b* 21 Feb. 1944; *s* of Richard Edwin Wood and Audrey Adele Wood (*née* Fincham); *m* 1975, Jacqueline Stanbury; two *d*. *Educ*: Chichester High Sch. for Boys; Worcester Coll., Oxford. BA (Hons). Acted with OUDS and ETC at Oxford; first London appearance in ETC prodn, Hang Down Your Head and Die (also co-writer), Comedy, 1964; later performances include: A Spring Song, Mermaid, 1964; Dr Faustus (OUDS), 1966; Four Degrees Over, Edinburgh Festival and Fortune, 1966 (also contrib. lyrics and sketches); repertory, 1966–69; RSC's After Haggerty, Aldwych 1970, and Criterion 1971; A Voyage Round My Father, Greenwich, 1970, Toronto, 1972; Me Times Me, tour, 1971; Mrs Warren's Profession, 1972, and revue Just the Ticket, 1973, Thorndike, Leatherhead; The Provok'd Wife, Greenwich, 1973; Jeeves, Her Majesty's, 1975; Terra Nova, Chichester, 1980. *Films include*: If…, 1968; Aces High, 1975; Sweet William, 1978; North Sea Hijack, 1979. *TV plays and series include*: Mad Jack, Fathers and Sons, Cheri, The Vamp, Sporting Scenes, Disraeli, The Avengers, Van der Valk, Danger UXB, Huntingtower, Enemy at the Door, Jackanory, Jim'll Fix It, When the Boat Comes In, The Brack Report, Tricky Business, Watch, Longitude. Wrote various theatre revues in collaboration with John Gould; music and lyrics, The Stiffkey Scandals of 1932, Queen's, 1967 (revived as The Prostitutes' Padre, Norwich Playhouse, 1997); with John Gould formed Whirligig Theatre, touring children's theatre company, 1969; for Whirligig directed many of own plays on tour and at Sadler's Wells Theatre, annually 1979–2004; has directed nat. tours and West End productions for Clarion Productions, including The BFG, 1991–92, 1993–94, 2001–03 and 2009, The Witches, 1992–93 and 1996–97, Noddy, 1993–94, and More Adventures of Noddy, 1995–96, Guess How Much I Love You, 2010; has performed David Wood Magic and Music Show in theatres all over UK, incl. Polka Theatre, Arts Theatre and Purcell Room, 1983–; David Wood's Storytime, Rose Th., Kingston and Arts, 2010; wrote The Queen's Handbag, for children's Party at the Palace for the Queen's 80th birthday, 2006 (also televised); wrote (with Richard Taylor) The Go-Between (musical, based on book by L. P. Hartley), W Yorks Playhouse, 2011 (Best Musical Prodn, UK Th. Awards, 2012), Apollo, 2016; Goodnight Mister Tom (adaptation of book by Michelle Magorian), Chichester Fest. Th., then tour, 2013 (Olivier Award for Best Entertainment and Family, 2013). Trustee: Action for Children's Arts, 1998– (Chm., 1998–2017; Pres., 2017–); Story Mus., Oxford, 2003–. Formed, jointly: Verronmead Ltd, ind. TV producing co., 1983; Westwood Theatrical Productions Ltd, 1986; W2 Productions Ltd, 1995. *TV series scripts*: Chips' Comic; Chish 'n' Fips; Seeing and Doing; The Gingerbread Man; Watch; *screenplays*: Swallows and Amazons, 1974; Back Home, 1989; Tide Race, 1989; *radio play*: Swallows and Amazons, 1999. Hon. MA Chichester, 2008; J. M. Barrie Award, Action for Children's Arts, 2017. *Publications*: *musical plays for children*: (with Sheila Ruskin) The Owl and the Pussycat went to see…, 1968; (with Sheila Ruskin) Larry the Lamb in Toytown, 1969; The Plotters of Cabbage Patch Corner, 1970; Flibberty and the Penguin, 1971; The Papertown Paperchase, 1972; Hijack over Hygenia, 1973; Old Mother Hubbard, 1975; The Gingerbread Man, 1976; Old Father Time, 1976; (with Tony Hatch and Jackie Trent) Rock Nativity, 1976; Nutcracker Sweet, 1977; Mother Goose's Golden Christmas, 1977; Tickle, 1978; Babes in the Magic Wood, 1978; There Was an Old Woman…, 1979; Cinderella, 1979; Aladdin, 1981; (with Dave and Toni Arthur) Robin Hood, 1981; Dick Whittington and Wondercat, 1981; Meg and Mog Show, 1981; The Ideal Gnome Expedition, 1982; Jack and the Giant, 1982; The Selfish Shellfish, 1983; (with ABBA and Don Black) Abbacadabra, 1984; (with Dave and Toni Arthur) Jack the Lad, 1984; (with Peter Pontzen) Dinosaurs and all that Rubbish, 1985; The Seesaw Tree, 1986; The Old Man of Lochnagar (based on book by HRH the Prince of Wales), 1986; (with Dave and Toni Arthur) The Pied Piper, 1988; Save the Human, 1990; The BFG (based on book by Roald Dahl), 1991; The Witches (based on book by Roald Dahl), 1992; Rupert and the Green Dragon, 1993; Noddy (based on books by Enid Blyton), 1994; More Adventures of Noddy, 1995; Babe, the Sheep-Pig (based on book by Dick King-Smith), 1998; The Forest Child (children's opera based on book by Richard Edwards), 1998; The Twits (based on book by Roald Dahl), 1999; David Wood Plays 1, 1999; David Wood Plays 2, 1999; Spot's Birthday Party (based on books by Eric Hill), 2000; Tom's Midnight Garden (based on book by Philippa Pearce), 2000; Fantastic Mr Fox (based on book by Roald Dahl), 2001; James and the Giant Peach (based on book by Roald Dahl), 2001; Clockwork (opera, based on book by Philip Pullman), 2004; The Lighthouse Keeper's Lunch (based on book by Ronda and David Armitage), 2005; Danny the Champion of the World (based on book by Roald Dahl), 2005; Lady Lollipop (based on book by Dick King-Smith), 2005; Fimbles Live! (based on TV series), 2006; The Tiger Who Came to Tea (based on book by Judith Kerr), 2008; George's Marvellous Medicine (based on book by Roald Dahl), 2009; Guess How Much I Love You (based on book by Sam McBratney), 2010; Goodnight Mister Tom (based on book by Michelle Magorian), 2011; Shaun's Big Show (Shaun the Sheep) (based on Aardman Animations TV series), 2011; The Forest Child (based on book by Richard Edwards), 2012; The Magic Finger (based on book by Roald Dahl), 2013; *books for children*: The Gingerbread Man, 1985; (with Geoffrey Beitz) The Operats of Rodent Garden, 1984; (with Geoffrey Beitz) The Discorats, 1985; Chish 'n' Fips, 1987; Sidney the Monster, 1988; Save the Human, 1991; The BFG: plays for children, 1993; Meg and Mog: plays for children, 1994; The Christmas Story, 1996; (with Peters Day) The Phantom Cat of the Opera, 2000; The Witches: plays for children, 2001; The Twits: plays for children, 2003; Jack and the Baked Beanstalk, 2007; (with Dana Kubick) A Present for Father Christmas, 2008; Danny the Champion of the World: plays for children, 2009; Cinderella, 2012; The Porridge Pincher, 2012; with Richard Fowler: Play-Theatres, 1987; Happy Birthday, Mouse, 1991 (USA 1990); Baby Bear's Buggy Ride, 1993; Pop-up Theatre (Cinderella), 1994; Bedtime Story, 1995; The Magic Show, 1995; Mole's Summer Story, 1997; Silly Spider, 1998; Mole's Winter Story, 1998; Funny Bunny's Magic Show, 2000; The Toy Cupboard, 2000; Under the Bed, 2006; Scary Mary, 2012; *book for adults*: (with Janet Grant) Theatre for Children: guide to writing, adapting, directing and acting, 1997; Chi High, Chichester Festival Theatre and Me (memoir), 2017; Filming If… (memoir), 2018; articles in Drama, London Drama, Stage, ArtsBusiness, Encore. *Recreations*: crosswords, conjuring (Mem. of the Inner Magic Circle with Gold Star), collecting old books. *Address*: c/o Casarotto Ramsay Ltd, Waverley House, 7–12 Noel Street, W1F 8GQ. *T*: (020) 7287 4450, *Fax*: (020) 7287 9128.

**WOOD, Rear-Adm. David John**, CB 1998; CEng, FRAeS; defence aviation consultant; *b* 12 June 1942; *s* of John Herbert Wood and Nesta (*née* Jones); *m* 1966, Hilary Jolly; two *s* one *d*. *Educ*: St Paul's Sch.; BRNC Dartmouth; RNEC Manadon (BScEng 1965). Joined BRNC 1960; service in 892, 846, 707 Sqdns and HMS Ark Royal, 1967–73; Aircraft Dept (Navy), 1973–76; Air Engineer Officer, Lynx IFTU, 1976–77; Army Staff Course, 1978; Helicopter Procurement, MoD (PE), 1979–81; Naval Sec's Dept, MoD, 1981–84; Staff of FONAC, 1984–86; NATO Defence Coll., 1986–87; Asst Dir, EH101, MoD (PE), 1987–89; Dir, Aircraft Support Policy (Navy), 1989–91; Dir, Maritime Projects, MoD (PE), 1991–95; DG Aircraft (Navy), MoD, 1995–98. Mem. Council, RAeS, 1996. Trustee, Bishop's Palace, Wells, Som, 2010– (Chm., 2013–). *Recreations*: cross-country and long distance running, choral singing.

**WOOD, David M.**; see Muir Wood.

**WOOD, His Honour David Russell**; a Circuit Judge, 1995–2013; *b* 13 Dec. 1948; *s* of Christopher Russell Wood and Muriel Wynn Wood (*née* Richardson); *m* 1979, Georgina Susan Buckle; two *s* one *d*. *Educ*: Sedbergh Sch.; Univ. of East Anglia (BA). Called to the Bar, Gray's Inn, 1973; Recorder, 1989–95. Pres., Council of Circuit Judges, 2008. *Recreations*: country pursuits, tennis, walking, music. *Club*: Northern Counties (Newcastle upon Tyne).

**WOOD, Maj.-Gen. Denys Broomfield**, CB 1978; Independent Inquiry Inspector, 1984–93; General Commissioner for Taxes, 1986–98; *b* 2 Nov. 1923; *s* of late Percy Neville Wood and Meryl Broomfield; *m* 1948, Jennifer Nora Page (*d* 1999), *d* of late Air Cdre William Morton Page, CBE; one *s* two *d*. *Educ*: Radley; Pembroke Coll., Cambridge (MA). CEng, FIMechE. Commissioned into REME, 1944; war service in UK and Far East, 1944–47; Staff Captain, WO, 1948–49; Instructor, RMA, Sandhurst, 1949–52; Staff Coll., 1953; DAA&QMG, 11 Infantry Bde, 1955–57; OC, 10 Infantry Workshop, Malaya, 1958–60; jssc 1960; Directing Staff, Staff Coll., 1961–63; Comdr, REME, 3rd Div., 1963–65; Operational Observer, Viet Nam, 1966–67; Col GS, Staff Coll., 1967–69; idc 1970; Dir, Administrative Planning, 1971–73; Dep. Military Sec. (2), 1973–75; Dir of Army Quartering, 1975–78. Exec. Sec., 1978–82, Sec., 1982–84, CEI. Col Comdt, REME, 1978–84. Lay Mem., Law Soc. Adjudication Cttee, 1986–92. Volunteer Speaker for Nat. Trust, 1999–2011. FRSA. *Recreations*: walking, gardening, reading. *Address*: 20 Franklin Court, Brook Road, Wormley, Godalming, Surrey GU8 5US. *T*: (01428) 681829.

**WOOD, Derek Alexander**, CBE 1995; QC 1978; a Recorder, 1985–2007; Principal, St Hugh's College, Oxford, 1991–2002, now Hon. Fellow; *b* 14 Oct. 1937; *s* of Alexander Cecil Wood and Rosetta (*née* Lelyveld); *m* 1st 1961, Sally Teresa Clarke (marr. diss. 2001); two *d*; 2nd, 2001, Barbara Kaplan (*née* Spector). *Educ*: Tiffin Boys' Sch., Kingston-upon-Thames; University Coll., Oxford (MA, BCL; Hon. Fellow, 2002). Called to the Bar, Middle Temple, 1964 (Bencher, 1986; Treas., 2006; Dir of Advocacy, 2011–16). Department of the Environment: Mem., Adv. Gp on Commercial Property Develt, 1975–78; Mem., Property Adv. Gp, 1978–94; Mem., Working Party on New Forms of Social Ownership and Tenure in Housing, 1976; Chairman: Review of Rating of Plant and Machinery, 1991, 1997–98; Property Industry's Working Gp on Code of Practice for Commercial Leases, 1995; Standing Adv. Cttee on Trunk Road Assessment, Dept of Transport, 1987–94. Drafter of new Code of Statutes, 2002, and Regulations, 2002–04, Univ. of Oxford; Chm., review of bar vocational course, 2008, pupillage, 2009, continuing professional develt, 2010, Bar Standards Bd. Dep. Chm., Soc. of Labour Lawyers, 1978–90. Chm., Chislehurst Constituency Labour Party, 1972–76, 1979–84. Chm., Oxfordshire Community Foundn, 1995–2001; Trustee, Attlee Foundn, 2003–10 (Chm., 2004–10). Mem. Council, London Bor. of Bromley, 1975–78. Gov., Quintin Kynaston Sch., 2003–12; Chm. Govs, Inns of Court Coll. of Advocacy, 2016–. Fellow, CAAV, 1988; FCIArb 1993. FRSA 1992. Hon. RICS (Hon. ARICS 1991; Mem., Governing Council, 2003–06). *Publications*: (jtly) Handbook of Arbitration Practice, 2nd edn 1993 to 4th edn 2003; (contrib.) Landlord and Tenant Law: past, present and future, 2006; (contrib.) The Judicial House of Lords, 2009. *Recreation*: music. *Address*: Falcon Chambers, Falcon Court, EC4Y 1AA. *Clubs*: Athenæum, Royal Automobile.

**WOOD, Donald Edward,** CBE 2005; Chairman, Orders of St John Care Trust, since 2013 (Trustee, 2007–12); *b* 10 May 1945; *s* of Thomas Wood and Mary (*née* Burton); *m* 1970, Barbara Schumacher; three *s* three *d*. *Educ:* King's Coll. Sch., Wimbledon; Bristol Univ. (BSc Hons (Civil Engrg) 1966); Manchester Business Sch. (DipBA 1970). W S Atkins & Partners, 1966–69; Rio Tinto Zinc Corp., 1970–73; Circle 33 Housing Trust, 1973–74; GEP Project Management, 1974–76; Dir, New Islington & Hackney Housing Assoc., 1976–87; Chief Exec., later Gp Chief Exec., London & Quadrant Housing Trust, 1987–2008. Mem. Nat. Council, Nat. Housing Fedn, 1985–91; Chm., London Connection, 1991–99; Exec. Chm., London Housing Foundn, 2008–13 (Bd Mem., 1999–2008); Board Member: Focus Housing Gp, 1995–98; English Churches Housing Gp, 1999–2002; Homes and Communities Agency, 2008–12; Quintin Hogg Trust, 2013–. Member Management Committee: St Luke's House Community Centre, 1980–85; Carr-Gomm Soc., 1988–91. Cttee Mem., Catholic Inst. for Internat. Relns, 1976–81. Chm., Barn Educn Assoc., 1977–82; Gov., Queen's Sch., Kew, 1979–83; Mem. Bd of Govs, St Mary's Coll., Twickenham, 2000–03. KM 2012. *Recreations:* music, family. *Address:* 6 The Avenue, Kew Gardens, Richmond, Surrey TW9 2AJ. *T:* (020) 8940 7043. *E:* wood.don6@gmail.com.

**WOOD, Dudley Ernest,** CBE 1995; Secretary, Rugby Football Union, 1986–95; *b* 18 May 1930; *s* of Ernest Edward and Ethel Louise Wood; *m* 1955, Mary Christina Blake (*d* 2010); two *s*. *Educ:* Luton Grammar School; St Edmund Hall, Oxford (MA Modern Languages). Sen. Manager, ICI, 1954–86. Rugby Football: Oxford Blue, 1952, 1953; played Rugby for Bedford, Rosslyn Park, Waterloo, and Streatham-Croydon, 1949–65; Pres., Surrey County RFU, 1983–85. Pres., St Edmund Hall Assoc., 1996–99. Pres., Bedfordshire CCC, 1998–2006; Hon. Life Mem., Squash Rackets Assoc., 1984. Hon. DArts De Montfort, 1999. *Recreations:* walking in the park, watching cricket, attending reunions and socializing. *Address:* Mead Hall, Little Walden, Saffron Walden, Essex CB10 1UX. *Clubs:* East India, Lord's Taverners.

**WOOD, Eric;** Finance Director (formerly Finance Officer), University of Bristol, 1979–91; *b* 22 Sept. 1931; *s* of late Herbert Francis and Eva Wood; *m* 1955, Erica Twist (*d* 2018); three *d*. *Educ:* West Hartlepool Grammar Sch.; Blandford Grammar Sch.; St Peter's Coll., Oxford (MA). CPFA. National Service, Army, 1950–51. Finance Depts, Cheshire, Durham and Notts County Councils, 1954–65; Finance Dept, London Transport, 1965–67; Asst Treasurer, GLC, 1967–73; Dir, CIPFA, 1973–79. *Publications:* articles in prof. accountancy press. *Recreations:* ski-ing, squash, hill-walking, bridge. *Address:* 6 Royal York Mews, Royal York Crescent, Clifton, Bristol BS8 4LF. *T:* (0117) 946 6311.

**WOOD, Graham Nash;** QC 2002; **His Honour Judge Graham Wood;** a Circuit Judge, since 2011; a Deputy High Court Judge (Administrative Court), since 2010; a Senior Circuit Judge and Designated Civil Judge, since 2014; *b* 21 May 1957; *s* of late Benjamin Leslie Wood and Mary Valerie Wood; *m* 1984, Janet Helen Winstanley; three *s*. *Educ:* Liverpool Coll.; Leeds Univ. (LLB Hons). Called to the Bar, Middle Temple, 1979, Bencher, 2010; in practice as barrister, specialising in medical, public law, human rights and criminal fraud, 1980–2011. Asst Recorder, 1997–2000; Recorder, 2000–11. Legal Assessor: GDC, 2006–11; GMC, 2009–11. Tribunal Judge, Mental Health Rev. Tribunal (Restricted Patients Panel), 2007–. Dep. Chancellor, Dio. of Chester, 2008–; Chancellor, Dio. of Liverpool, 2018– (Dep. Chancellor, 2002–18). Chm. Govs, Liverpool Coll., 2009–12. Lay Reader, Church of England. *Publications:* (jtly) Bingham's Negligence Cases, rev. edn 1994, 4th 2002. *Recreations:* sailing, supporting Liverpool FC, writing novels and short stories in the hope that one day something may be published. *Address:* Liverpool Civil and Family Court, 35 Vernon Street, Liverpool L2 2BX. *E:* woodqc@btinternet.com.

**WOOD, (Gregory) Mark,** CBE 2017; FCA; non-executive Chairman, Digitalismedia, since 2010; *b* 26 July 1953; *s* of William Albert and Anne Wood; *m* 2009, Lisa Claire Walden; one *s* two *d* by a previous marriage. *Educ:* Cambridgeshire Coll. of Arts and Technol. (BA Hons Econ). FCA 1979. Work with Price Waterhouse, Commercial Union, Barclays, BZW, British & Commonwealth; Chairman: Wagon Finance Ltd, 1991–94; Safeguard Insce Services, 1991–94; Divl Chief Exec., UK Retail Financial Services, MAI plc, 1991–94; Man. Dir, AA Insce, Financial Services and Retail, 1994–96; Chief Exec., AXA Equity & Law, 1997; Gp Chief Exec., AXA in the UK (formerly Sun Life & Provincial Hldgs), 1997–2001; Chief Exec., Prudential Assurance Co. Ltd, 2001–05; Exec. Dir, Prudential PLC, 2001–05; Founder and Chief Exec., 2006–09, Dep. Chm., 2009–11, Paternoster Assurance; non-exec. Chm., 2010–13, CEO, 2013, JLT Benefit Solutions; CEO, JLT Employee Benefits, 2013–15. Non-executive Chairman: Digitalis Reputation, 2010–; Chaucer Syndicates, 2011–14; PensionBee, 2016–; Carbon8, 2016–17; Walbrook Hldgs, 2016–; The Innovation Gp, 2017–19; Utility Bidder, 2018–; non-exec. Dir, RAC Ltd, 2011–. Dep. Chm., ABI, 1999–2001 (Chm., Gen. Insce Cttee, 1999–2001); Chm., Govt's Property Crime Reduction Action Team, 1999–2001. Chm. Trustees, NSPCC, 2010–19 (Trustee, 1999–2007; Dep. Chm., 2003–07). Chm. Govs, Amesbury Sch., 2002–07. MCSI (MSI 1998). Hon. DBA Anglia Ruskin, 2010. *Recreations:* tennis, ski-ing. *Address:* Burtons Farm, Burtons Lane, Chalfont St Giles HP8 4BB. *E:* wood@walbrookadvisors.co.uk. *Club:* Royal Automobile.

**WOOD, Hugh Bradshaw;** composer; University Lecturer in Music, Cambridge University, and Fellow of Churchill College, Cambridge, 1977–99; *b* 27 June 1932; *s* of James Bonar Wood and Winifred Bradshaw Wood; *m* 1960, Susan McGaw; one *s* one *d* (and one *d* decd). *Educ:* Oundle Sch.; New Coll., Oxford (Major Scholar; 2nd Cl. Hons Modern History, 1954). ARCM (private study with Dr W. S. Lloyd Webber), 1955. Studied: composition with Iain Hamilton, and harmony and counterpoint with Anthony Milner, 1956–58; composition with Mátyás Seiber, 1958–60; taught at: Morley Coll., 1958–67; Royal Acad. of Music, 1962–65; Univ. of Glasgow (Cramb Res. Fellow), 1966–70; Univ. of Liverpool, 1971–75; Univ. of Leeds, 1975–76; teacher, Dartington Summer Sch. of Music, 1959–74. *Main compositions: for orchestra:* Scenes from Comus (with soprano and tenor), 1965; Concerto for Cello, 1969; Chamber Concerto, 1971; Concerto for Violin, No 1, 1972, No 2, 2005; Symphony, 1982; Concerto for Piano, 1991; Variations for Orchestra, 1997; Serenade and Elegy (for string quartet and string orch.), 1999; Epithalamion, 2015; *chamber music:* Variations for Viola and Piano, 1958; String Quartet No 1, 1962, No 2, 1970, No 3, 1976, No 4, 1993, No 5, 2001; Piano Trio, 1984; Horn Trio, 1989; Clarinet Trio, 1997; Overture for Trio, 2005; *for voice(s) and ensembles:* Logue Songs, 1961; Song Cycle to Poems of Pablo Neruda, 1974; Cantata, 1989; Tenebrae, 2003; From the Pisan Cantos, 2012; *songs:* Robert Graves Songs, 4 sets, 1976–93; Robert Graves cycle, 2006. Hon. DMus Liverpool, 2006. *Recreation:* thinking about going to Greece. *Address:* 32 Woodsome Road, NW5 1RZ. *T:* (020) 7267 0318.

**WOOD, Humphrey;** *see* Wood, J. H. A.

**WOOD, Sir Ian (Clark),** KT 2018; GBE 2016 (CBE 1982); Kt 1994; FRSE; Chairman, 1981–2012, and Chief Executive (formerly Managing Director) 1967–2006, John Wood Group plc (formerly John Wood & Son); Chairman, J. W. Holdings Ltd, since 1981; Chairman, Opportunity North East, since 2015; Founder Chairman, Oil & Gas Technology Centre, since 2016; *b* 21 July 1942; *s* of John Wood and Margaret (*née* Clark); *m* 1970, Helen Macrae; three *s*. *Educ:* Aberdeen Univ. (BSc Psychology, First Cl. Hons 1964). Joined John Wood & Son, 1964. Dir, Royal Bank of Scotland, 1988–97. Chairman: Aberdeen Beyond 2000, 1986–90; Grampian Enterprise, 1990–94. Member: Aberdeen Harbour Bd, 1972–89; Sea Fish Industry Authority, 1981–87; Offshore Industry Adv. Bd, 1989–93; Offshore Industry Export Adv. Gp, 1989–93; British Trade Internat. Oil and Gas Export Bd (formerly Oil & Gas Projects & Supplies Office), 1994–2000 (Chm., 1997–2000); Bd, Scottish Develt Agency, 1984–90; Scottish Econ. Council, 1988–98; Scottish Enterprise Bd, 1995–2000 (Chm., 1997–2000); Bd, Scottish Business Forum, 1998–99; Scottish Sub-Cttee, UGC, subseq. UFC, 1988–91; SHEFC, 1991–97; Nat. Trng Task Force, 1988–91; PILOT, 2000–06; Scottish Sea Fisheries Council, 2007–. Chancellor, Robert Gordon Univ., 2004–. Chm., Commn on Developing Scotland's Young Workforce, 2013–; Chm., UK Continental Shelf Maximising Recovery Rev., 2013–14. Chm. and Sen. Trustee, The Wood Foundation (formerly Sir Ian Wood Family Charitable Trust, then Wood Family Trust), 2007–. CCMI (CBIM 1983); FCIB 1998; FRSE 2000; FSQA; FRSA; Fellow, Scottish Vocational Educn Council. Hon. LLD Aberdeen, 1984; Hon. DBA Robert Gordon, 1998; Hon. DTech Glasgow Caledonian, 2002; Hon. DEng Heriot-Watt, 2012; Hon. DSc Strathclyde, 2013. Scottish Free Enterprise Award, 1985; (jtly) Scottish Business Achievement Award Trust Award, 1992; Corporate Elite Leadership Award, 1992; Corporate Elite World Player Award, 1996; Business Ambassador for Scotland, Scottish Business Insider, 2002; Chief Exec. of the Year, Business Insider/PricewaterhouseCoopers, 2003; Glenfiddich Spirit of Scotland Award for Business, 2003; Entrepreneurial Exchange Philanthropist of the Year Award, 2008; Offshore Energy Centre Hall of Fame, Houston, 2009; Wallace Award, American Scottish Foundn, 2012; Lifetime Achievement Award, Oil and Gas UK, 2012; Chm. of the Year, Broadwalk Asset Mgt LLP, 2012. Silver Jubilee Medal, 1977; Cadman Medal, Energy Inst., 2010; President's Award, SCDI, 2011; Royal Medal, Royal Soc. of Edinburgh, 2013; Lifetime Achievement Award: Northern Star Business Awards, 2014; Oil Council, 2014; Beacon Award for Philanthropy, Beacon Fellowship, 2015; Great London Scot Award for Lifetime Achievement, London Scottish, 2016. *Recreations:* family, art, tennis. *Address:* Marchmont, 42 Rubislaw Den South, Aberdeen AB15 4BB. *T:* (01224) 313625.

**WOOD, James Alexander Douglas;** QC 1999; a Recorder, since 2000; *b* 25 June 1952; *s* of Alexander Blyth Wood and Cynthia Mary Wood (*née* Boot); two *s* by Ros Carne; *m* 1999, Janet Allbeson. *Educ:* Haileybury Coll.; Warwick Univ. (LLB 1974). Called to the Bar, Middle Temple, 1975; criminal defence barrister specialising in civil liberties and human rights; has appeared in many leading terrorist cases and miscarriages of justice, incl. both appeals of Birmingham 6, and Carl Bridgwater case; Asst Recorder, 1998–2000. *Publications:* The Right to Silence, 1989; Justice in Error, 1993; reports. *Recreations:* travel, painting. *Address:* Doughty Street Chambers, 54 Doughty Street, WC1N 2LS. *T:* (020) 7404 1313. *Club:* Blacks.

**WOOD, James Douglas Graham,** FRSL; Staff Writer, The New Yorker, since 2007; *b* 1 Nov. 1965; *s* of Dennis William Wood and Sheila Graham Wood (*née* Lillia); *m* 1992, Claire Denise Messud; one *s* one *d*. *Educ:* Eton Coll.; Jesus Coll., Cambridge (BA 1st cl. Hons (Eng. Lit.) 1988). Chief Literary Critic, The Guardian, 1991–95; Sen. Editor, The New Republic, 1995–2007. Weidenfeld Vis. Prof. of Eur. and Comparative Lit., Oxford Univ., 2011. Vis. Lectr, subseq. Prof. of the Practice, Harvard Univ., 2003–. Mem. Editl Bd, London Review of Books, 1995–. Fellow, Amer. Acad. of Arts and Scis, 2007. FRSL 2011. Young Journalist of the Year, British Press Awards, 1990; Award in Literature, AAAL, 2001; Nat. Mag. Award for Criticism, American Soc. of Mag. Eds, 2009. *Publications:* The Broken Estate: essays on literature and belief, 1999; The Book Against God (novel), 2003; The Irresponsible Self: on laughter and the novel (essays), 2004; How Fiction Works, 2008; The Fun Stuff (essays), 2013; The Nearest Thing to Life (essays), 2015; Upstate, 2018; Serious Noticing: selected essays, 2019. *Recreations:* playing the piano, reading. *Address:* c/o Jonathan Cape Ltd, 20 Vauxhall Bridge Road, SW1V 2SA.

**WOOD, Prof. James Lionel Norman,** PhD; FRCVS; Alborada Professor of Equine and Farm Animal Science, since 2008, and Head, Department of Veterinary Medicine, since 2013, University of Cambridge; Fellow, Wolfson College, Cambridge, since 2009; *b* Wegberg, Germany, 19 May 1963; *s* of Lt-Col Lionel David Wood and Belinda Mary Wood; *m* 2004, Rosamund Anne Rivett; two *d*. *Educ:* University Coll. London (BSc Physiol. and Basic Medicine Scis 1985); Royal Veterinary College (BVetMed 1988); London Sch. of Hygiene and Tropical Medicine (MSc Epidemiol. 1991); Open Univ. (PhD 1998); MA Cantab 2009. MRCVS 1988, FRCVS 2017. Veterinary Res. Officer, Central Veterinary Lab., 1990; Animal Health Trust, Newmarket: Equine Epidemiologist, 1990–93; Hd of Epidemiology, 1993–2004; Dir, Cambridge Infectious Diseases Consortium, Univ. of Cambridge, 2005–10. Mem., Adv. Council, DEFRA, 2017–. Mem., Standing Tech. Cttee, European Commn for Control of Foot-and-Mouth Disease, 2019–. Pres., Soc. for Vet. Epidemiol. and Preventive Medicine, 2003; Hon. Pubns Officer, British Equine Vet. Assoc., 2005–. Trustee: Survival Internat., 1990– (Chm., 2009–); Animal Health Trust, 2005–10; Charity Trustee, Univ. of Cambridge Vet. Sch. Trust, 2014–16. Diplomat, Eur. Coll. of Vet. Public Health, 2002. Hon. Res. Fellow, Zoological Soc. of London, 2014–. Mem. Council, RCVS, 2014–. FRSocMed 1998–2008; FSS 2005; FRSB (FSB 2012). *Publications:* author or co-author of more than 250 papers in scientific and learned jls. *Recreations:* walking, cooking, boating, cycling. *Address:* Department of Veterinary Medicine, University of Cambridge, Madingley Road, Cambridge CB3 0ES. *T:* (01223) 337600. *E:* jlnw2@cam.ac.uk.

**WOOD, James Peter,** FRCO, FRAM; conductor, composer, musicologist and former percussionist; *b* 27 May 1953; *s* of Peter Ley Wood and Elizabeth Gillian Wood; *m* 1977, Penelope Anne Irish (marr. diss. 2010); one *s* one *d*. *Educ:* Radley Coll.; Sidney Sussex Coll., Cambridge (BA 1975); Royal Acad. of Music. ARCO 1968, FRCO 1971; ARAM 1990, FRAM 2000. Dir, New London Chamber Choir, 1982–2007; Prof. of Percussion, Internat. Ferienkürse für Neue Musik, Darmstadt, 1982–94; Dir, Critical Band, 1990–. Worked with: BBCSO; Netherlands Radio Symphony Orch.; London Sinfonietta; Ensemble InterContemporain (Paris); L'Itinéraire (Paris); Ensemble 2e2m (Paris); Champ d'Action (Antwerp); Ictus (Brussels); MusikFabrik (Cologne); Percussion Gp The Hague; Amadinda (Budapest); Ju Percussion Gp (Taipei); Netherlands Radio Choir; Netherlands Chamber Choir; Berlin Radio Choir; WDR Choir; RIAS Kammerchor; Rundfunk Chor, Berlin; Tokyo Philharmonic Choir. *Compositions* include: Rogosanti, 1986; Stoicheia, 1988; Oreion, 1989; Two Men Meet, each presuming the other to be from a distant planet, 1995; The Parliament of Angels, 1996; Mountain Language, 1998; Jodo, 1999; Autumn Voices, 2001; Hildegard, 2002–04; De telarum mechanicae, 2007; Cloud-Polyphonies, 2011; Sea Dances, 2012; Gulliver, 2014; Stylistic reconstruction of Gesualdo, Sacrae Cantiones, Liber Secundus, 2011; Lamentations, 2015; Sei Canti, 2016; Khamush, 2016. *Recreations:* mountain hiking, wine, instrument building, carpentry, gardening, cooking. *Address:* Dorfstrasse 32, 14913 Schlenzer, Germany. *T:* (33) 74680508. *E:* james.wood@gmx.net. *W:* www.choroi.net.

**WOOD, Sir (James) Sebastian (Lamin),** KCMG 2014 (CMG 2002); HM Diplomatic Service; Ambassador to Federal Republic of Germany, since 2015; *b* 6 April 1961; *s* of John Lamin Wood and Gillian Margaret Wood (*née* Neason, now Bohan); *m* 1990, Sirinat Pengnuam; one *s* three *d*. *Educ:* Emanuel Sch.; Magdalen Coll., Oxford (BA Hons Maths and Philos. 1982). FCO, 1983–85; Second Sec., Bangkok, 1985–89; Second, then First Sec., FCO, 1989–92; First Sec., Sino-British Jt Liaison Gp, Hong Kong, 1992–96; Security

Policy Dept, FCO, 1996–97; Dep. Hd, UN Dept, FCO, 1998; Principal Private Sec. to Cabinet Sec., Cabinet Office, 1998–2000; Fellow, Weatherhead Centre for Internat. Affairs, Harvard Univ., 2000–01; Counsellor, Washington, 2001–05; Dir, Asia-Pacific, FCO, 2005–08; Advr on Global Corporate Develt, Rolls Royce, 2008–09 (on secondment); Ambassador to the People's Republic of China, 2010–15. *Recreations:* Bach, blues and jazz guitar, long walks with the dog. *Address:* c/o Foreign and Commonwealth Office, King Charles Street, SW1A 2AH.

**WOOD, John,** CB 1989; Solicitor, Morgan Lewis & Bockius, 1997–99; *b* 11 Jan. 1931; *s* of Thomas John Wood and Rebecca Grand; *m* 1958, Jean Iris Wood; two *s*. *Educ:* King's College Sch., Wimbledon. Admitted Solicitor, 1955. Director of Public Prosecutions: Legal Assistant, 1958; Sen. Legal Asst, 1963; Asst Solicitor, 1971; Asst Director, 1977; Principal Asst Dir, 1981; Dep. Dir, 1985–87; Head of Legal Services, Crown Prosecution Service, 1986–87; Dir of Serious Fraud Office, 1987–90; DPP, Hong Kong, 1990–94; Consultant Solicitor, Denton Hall, 1995–97. Pres., Video Appeals Cttee, 1996–2011. *Recreations:* cricket, Rugby football, music, theatre.

**WOOD, John David;** Chief Executive, 2012–19, and Director of Environment, 2002–19, Hertfordshire County Council; *b* London, 9 June 1962; *s* of Cliff Wood and Barbara Wood; *m* 1989, Annmarie Leeming; three *s*. *Educ:* Highams Park Sen. High Sch.; City Univ. (BSc Hons Civil Engrg). MICE 1985. Trainee, then Asst Engr, Lambeth LBC, 1980–88; Sen. Engr, Newham LBC, 1988–91; Hertfordshire County Council: Principal Transport Engr, 1991–96; Hd of Forward Planning, 1996–2000; Asst Dir, Strategy, 2000–02; Dep. Chief Exec., 2009–12. *Recreations:* socialising with family and friends, playing sport (especially tennis), walking the dog.

**WOOD, (John) Humphrey (Askey);** a Managing Director, Consolidated Gold Fields plc, 1979–89; Chairman, Vitec (formerly Vinten) Group plc, 1991–99; *b* 26 Nov. 1932; *s* of late Lt-Col Edward Askey Wood and Irene Jeanne Askey Wood; *m* 1st, 1965, Jane Holland; one *s*; 2nd, 1981, Katherine Ruth Stewart Reardon (*née* Peverley); one step *s* one step *d*. *Educ:* Abberley Hall; Winchester College; Corpus Christi College, Cambridge. MA (Mech. Scis). De Havilland Aircraft Co. Ltd, 1956; Hawker Siddeley Aviation Ltd, 1964, Dir and Gen. Manager, Manchester, 1969–76; Man. Dir, Industrial and Marine Div., Rolls-Royce Ltd, 1976–79; Chm., Amey Roadstone Corp., 1979–86. Director: Gold Fields of South Africa Ltd, 1986–89; Blue Tee Corp., USA, 1986–89; non-executive Director: Birse Gp plc, 1989–95; Albrighton plc, 1990–96 (Chm., 1993–96); Ennstone plc, 1996–98. Butten Trustee, PA Consulting Gp, 1991–97. Vice-Pres., Nat. Council of Building Material Producers, 1985–89. Mem. Council, CBI, 1983–89. Chm., SW Rivers Assoc., 2002–11 (Vice Pres., 2011–); Trustee, Westcountry Rivers Trust, 2002–14; Mem., SW Reg. Fisheries, Ecology and Recreation Adv. Cttee, Envmt Agency, 2002–08. *Recreations:* salmon conservation, fly fishing, sailing, painting, gardening. *Address:* North Lodge, Hildon, Broughton, Stockbridge SO20 8DG. *T:* (01794) 301 831.

**WOOD, Prof. John Nicholas,** PhD, DSc; FMedSci; FRS 2009; Professor of Molecular Neurobiology, University College London, since 2000; *b* Plymouth, 23 Nov. 1950; *s* of late Charles Wood and Dorothy Wood; *m* 2005, Min Liu, PhD; one *d*. *Educ:* Univ. of Leeds (BSc 1971); Univ. of Warwick (MSc 1972; PhD 1976; DSc 1997). Post Doctoral Scientist, Institut Pasteur, Paris, 1976–79; Sen. Scientist, Wellcome Foundn, 1981–84; Hd of Neuroimmunol., Sandoz Inst. for Med. Res., 1984–95; Reader in Neurosci., UCL, 1995–2000. Visiting Professor: Neurobiol., Harvard Univ., 1984; Seoul Nat. Univ., 2012–; Univ. Cote D'Azur, 2018–. FMedSci 2009. Grand Prix Scientifique de l'Institut de France, 2009. *Publications:* Capsaicin in the Study of Pain, 1996; Molecular Basis of Pain Induction, 2000; The Neurobiology of Pain, 2018. *Recreations:* jazz, travel, sailing. *Address:* Wolfson Institute for Biomedical Research, University College London, Gower Street, WC1E 6BT. *T:* (020) 7679 6954, *Fax:* (020) 7679 6609. *E:* j.wood@ucl.ac.uk. *Clubs:* House of St Barnabus; Hurlingham Yacht.

**WOOD, Prof. John Vivian,** CBE 2007; PhD, DMet; FIMMM, FInstP, FREng; Secretary General, Association of Commonwealth Universities, 2010–17; *b* 10 Sept. 1949; *s* of Vivian Wood and Lois Wood (*née* Hall); *m* 1976, Alison Lee; one *s* one *d*. *Educ:* St Lawrence Coll., Ramsgate; Sheffield Univ. (BMet 1971, DMet 1994); Darwin Coll., Cambridge (PhD 1975). CEng 1984; FIMMM (FIM 1989); CPhys, FInstP 1998; FREng 1999. Goldsmiths' Jun. Res. Fellow, Churchill Coll., Cambridge, 1974–78; Lectr, then Sen. Lectr in Materials, Open Univ., 1978–89; University of Nottingham: Cripps Prof. and Hd, Dept of Materials Engrg, 1989–2001; Dean of Engrg, 1998–2001; Chief Exec., CCLRC (on secondment), 2001–07; Principal, Faculty of Engrg, 2007, Internat. Relns Advr, 2008–10, Imperial Coll. London. Chairman: Internat. Network for Availability of Scientific Pubns, 2009–15; Oxeta, 2011–; Director: M4 Technologies, 1994–2013; Maney Publg, 2003–12; Bio Nano Consulting, 2008–. Chairman: UK Foresight Panel on Materials, 1997–2001; Eur. Strategy Forum for Res. Infrastructure, 2002–08; Eur. Res. Area Bd, 2008–12; Res. Information Network, 2012–16; Adv. Bd, ATTRACT, 2015–; Co-Chm., Res. Data Alliance, 2012–; Member: Eur. Res. and Innovation Bd, 2012–14; EC Res. Innovation and Sci. Bd, 2014–. Consultant, CERN, 2016–. Mem. Council, RAEng, 2008–11. Trustee: Industrial Trust, 2000–13; Tomorrow Project, 2006–13; Daphne Jackson Trust, 2008–16; CRAC, 2013–. Hon. Professor: of Materials, Imperial Coll. London, 2010–; of Nanotechnol., UCL, 2014–17; of Materials, Brunel Univ.; Liverpool Hope Univ., 2017–; World Univ. of Bangladesh, 2017–. Hon. DSc: Tech. Univ. of Cluj-Napora, Romania, 1994; A. H. Rahman Univ., Chennai, 2014; Kwame Nkrumah Univ. of Sci. and Technol., Ghana, 2015. Grunfeld Medal, 1986, Ivor Jenkins Award, 2000, Inst. Materials; William Johnson Internat. Gold Medal, Internat. Conf. of Advanced Materials and Processes, 2001. *Publications:* (contrib.) Ultra Rapid Quenching of Metals, 1978; contrib. numerous res. pubns and patent applications. *Recreations:* woodlands, chamber music and serious contemporary music, affordable wine, reading. *E:* attract747@gmail.com. *Club:* Foundation Universitaire (Brussels).

**WOOD, Jonathan Paul Richard;** Headteacher, The Judd School, since 2017 (Deputy Headteacher, 2013–17); *b* Norwich, 13 March 1976; *s* of Paul and Kate Wood; one *s* one *d*. *Educ:* Norwich Sch.; Univ. of Nottingham (BSc Maths 1997; PGCE Secondary Maths 1998). NPQH 2008. Teacher of Maths, Bridgford Sch., Nottingham, 1998–2001; supply teacher, 2002–03; Hd of Year, Latymer Sch., Edmonton, 2003–06; Asst Headteacher, 2006–11, Dep. Headteacher, 2011–13, Wirral GS for Girls. *Recreations:* enjoy tennis, theatre, travel, dining and cooking, countryside walks, spending time with family and friends. *Address:* The Judd School, Brook Street, Tonbridge, Kent TN9 2PN. *Clubs:* Lansdowne; Leigh Tennis (Kent).

**WOOD, Dr (Kathryn) Louise,** CBE 2019; Director, Science, Research and Evidence, Department of Health and Social Care (formerly Department of Health), since 2016; *b* Stockport, 1963; *d* of Prof. Graham Charles Wood, FRS, FREng and of Freda Nancy Wood. *Educ:* Smithills Grammar Sch., Bolton; Univ. of Edinburgh (BSc Hons); Univ. of London (PhD Biomed. Sci.). Hd, Pharmacovigilance Co. Liaison Unit, 1990–92, Co-ordinator, Med. Dictionary for Regulatory Activities Project, 1993–96, Medicines Control Agency; Strategic Develt Co-ordinator, Post-Licensing Div., 1996–99, Dir, Gen. Practice Res. Database Div., 1999–2004, Medicines and Healthcare Products Regulatory Agency; Dep. Dir and Hd, Innovation and Industry R&D Relns, 2005–09, Dep. Dir and Hd, Infrastructure of Growth, 2009–15, R&D Directorate, DoH; Dir, Policy and Public Affairs, Assoc. of Med. Res. Charities (on secondment), 2015–16. Hon. FFPM 2010. *Publications:* contribs on central control of gastric motility, med. terminology and GP Res. Database. *Recreations:* travel, dining out. *Address:* Department of Health and Social Care, Science, Research and Evidence Directorate, 39 Victoria Street, SW1H 0EU. *T:* (020) 7210 6248. *E:* louise.wood@dhsc.gov.uk.

**WOOD, Lana Claire; Her Honour Judge Lana Wood;** a Circuit Judge, since 2018; *b* Meriden, 12 Oct. 1969; *d* of Adam and Christine Wood; *m* 1997, Edward Longstaff; two *c*. *Educ:* King Edward VI High Sch. for Girls, Birmingham (Foundn Scholar); Selwyn Coll., Cambridge (BA Law 1992); St Hilda's Coll., Oxford (BCL 1995). Called to the Bar, Gray's Inn, 1993 (Scholar); in practice as barrister, 9 Stone Bldgs, Lincoln's Inn, 1995–2012; Dep. Dist Judge, 2004–12; Dist Judge, 2012–18. Trustee, Relate London NW and Herts, 2017– (Vice-Chair, 2017–). Gov., Watford GS for Boys, 2012–18.

**WOOD, Prof. Laurie,** PhD; Professor, 2000–10, and Executive Director, Enterprise and Development, 2007–10, University of Salford; Chairman, Museum of Science and Industry, Manchester, 2001–11; Director, Laurie Wood Associates, 2010–15; *b* Manchester, 25 Dec. 1952; *d* of Walter and Muriel Brown; *m* 1972; one *d*. *Educ:* Fairfield High Sch. for Girls; Manchester Poly. (BA 1st Cl. Hons Business Studies 1982); Victoria Univ. of Manchester (PGCE 1986); Univ. of Salford (PhD 1993). Dip. Mktg CIM 1982; Chartered Marketer 1998. Asst to Gp Mktg Manager, CWS Packaging Technol. Gp, 1971–73; accounting and mktg consultant, 1973–75; Mktg Services Manager, Nat. Westminster Bank, Manchester, 1975–80; Nat. Develt Manager, CWS Milk Gp, Manchester, 1982–84; Sen. Lectr, Mktg and Planning and Industrial Liaison Tutor, Manchester Poly., 1984–87; University of Salford: Sen. Lectr in Strategic Mgt and Mktg Information Systems, 1987–2000; Dir, Centre for Audience Develt Res., 1997–2001; Associate Dean, Enterprise, Faculty of Business and Informatics, 1999–2001; Dir, Acad. Enterprise and Chief Exec., Univ. of Salford Enterprises, 2001–07. Chm., UK Mktg Council, 2000–02; Bd Mem., UK Sci. Enterprise Centres, 2006–09. Non-exec. Dir, Tameside and Glossop Acute Services NHS Trust, 1997–2000. Chm., Arts About Manchester, 1993–97. Mem. Bd, Acad. Mktg Res., 2001–. Chartered Institute of Marketing: Internat. Vice Chm., 1996–99, Internat. Chm., 1999–2001; Dir, Commercial Bd, 1997–2002; Professorial Senate Mem., 2001–06; Internat. Trustee, 2004–; Benevolent Fund Trustee, 2009–; Hon. Fellow, 2001. Trustee and Dep. Chm., Communications, Advertising and Mktg Foundn, 2000–02. MMRS 1987; MInstD 2006. FRSA 1997; FCMI 2003; FHEA 2007. Freeman, City of London, 2001; Liveryman, Marketors' Co., 2001. *Publications:* contribs to learned jls in field of mktg and communications. *Recreations:* reading, film and music, family. *Address:* The Rivals, 39 Springmeadow Lane, Uppermill, Oldham OL3 6HL. *T:* (01457) 878582, 07767 270473. *E:* lauriewood@btinternet.com.

**WOOD, Leanne;** Member (Plaid Cymru) Rhondda, National Assembly for Wales, since 2016 (South Wales Central, 2003–16); *b* 13 Dec. 1971; *d* of Jeff Wood and Avril Wood; one *d* by Ian Brown. *Educ:* Univ. of Glamorgan (BA Hons Public Admin); Univ. of Wales, Cardiff (Dip. in Social Work). Probation Officer, Mid Glamorgan Probation Service, 1997–2000; pt-time Pol Researcher to Jill Evans, MEP, 2000–01; Univ. Lectr, Social Work and Social Policy, Cardiff Univ., 2000–03 (pt-time, 2000–02); pt-time Community Support Worker, Cwm Cynon Women's Aid, 2001–02. Shadow Minister for Social Justice, 2003, for Housing and Regeneration, Nat. Assembly for Wales. Leader, Plaid Cymru, 2012–18. Mem. (Plaid Cymru) Rhondda Cynon Taf CBC, 1995–99. *Address:* National Assembly for Wales, Cardiff Bay, Cardiff CF99 1NA. *T:* 0300 200 7200. *E:* leanne.wood@assembly.wales.

**WOOD, Louise;** see Wood, K. L.

**WOOD, Maj. Gen. Malcolm David,** CBE 2002 (MBE 1988); Director General Joint Supply Chain, Defence Equipment and Support (formerly Director General Logistics (Supply Chain), Defence Logistics Organisation), 2003–08; *b* 14 May 1953; *s* of late Stanley Andrew Wood and of Elsie Blackley Wood (*née* Stamper); *m* 1977, Nora Ann (*née* Smith) (*d* 2008); three *d*; *m* 2010, Catalina; one *s*. *Educ:* Hampton Sch.; RMA, Sandhurst; St John's Coll., Cambridge (MA). Staff Officer, Grade 2, UKCICC, 1986–87; Comdr, 32 Ordnance Co., 1988–89; Staff Officer, Grade 2, Personnel Br., 1990; CO, 5 Ordnance Bn, 1991–93 (mentioned in despatches, 1993); Directing Staff, Army Staff Coll., 1993–94; Dep. COS, 3 UK Div., 1995–96; Director: Logistic Support Services, 1997; Materiel Support (Army), 1998–99; Comdr, 101 Logistic Bde, 2000–01; rcds 2002. Col Comdt, RLC, 2006–19. President: Council, RAOC; Conductors' Br., RLC Assoc.; Friends of RLC Mus. Trustee, ABF The Soldiers' Charity. QCVS 1996. *Recreations:* Army Football (former Chm.), supporter of Burnley FC and Lancs CCC.

**WOOD, Mark;** see Wood, G. M.

**WOOD, Mark William;** Chairman: Knowledge Motion, since 2016; Nominet, since 2017; *b* 28 March 1952; *s* of Joseph Hatton Drew Wood and Joyce Wood; *m* 1st, 1986, Helen Lanzer (*d* 2007); one *s* one *d*; 2nd, 2010, Jane Louise Jones (*d* 2012). *Educ:* Univs of Leeds (BA Hons), Warwick (MA) and Oxford. Joined Reuters, 1976; corresp. in Vienna, 1977–78, East Berlin, 1978–81, Moscow, 1981–85; Chief Corresp., West Germany, 1985–87; Editor, Europe, 1987–89; Editor-in-Chief, 1989–2000; Hd, strategic media investments and alliances, 2000–02. Dir, Reuters Hldgs, 1990–96; Chm., Reuters Television, 1992–2002; Independent Television News: Dir, 1993–2009; Chm., 1998–2009; Chief Exec., 2003–09; Chief Exec., Future Publishing UK, 2010–11; Chief Exec., 2011–14, non-exec. Dir, 2014–, Future plc; Chief Exec., Ten Alps plc, 2014–16. Non exec. Dir, Citywire, 2002–; Mem., Adv. Bd, PWC, 2015–. Chairman: Library and Inf. Commn, 1999–2000 (Mem., 1995–2000); Vice Chm., 1998–99); MLA (formerly Resource: Council for Museums, Archives and Libraries), 2003–08 (Bd Mem., 2000–08); Member: Commonwealth Press Union, 1996–2000; Rathenau Gesellschaft, Germany, 1999–. *Recreations:* opera, ski-ing, supporting Spurs, tennis, theatre. *Address:* Nominet, Minerva House, Edmund Halley Road, Oxford Science Park, Oxford OX4 4DQ. *Clubs:* Garrick, h.

**WOOD, Sir Martin (Francis),** Kt 1986; OBE 1982; FRS 1987; DL; Hon. President, Oxford Instruments Group plc, since 2000 (Deputy Chairman, 1983); Fellow, Wolfson College, Oxford, 1967–94. Hon. Fellow, 1994; *b* 19 April 1927; *s* of late Arthur Henry Wood and Katharine Mary (*née* Cumberlege); *m* 1955, (Kathleen) Audrey (OBE 2006), *d* of Rev. John Howard Stanfield; one *s* (one *d* decd) and one step *s* one step *d*. *Educ:* Gresham's; Trinity Coll., Cambridge (BA Engrg, MA); Imperial Coll. (RSM) (BSc); Christ Church, Oxford (MA; Hon. Student, 2003). Nat. Service, Bevin Boy, S Wales and Derbyshire coalfields, 1945–48. Mgt Trainee, NCB, 1954–55; Sen. Res. Officer, Clarendon Lab., Oxford Univ., 1955–69; Founder, Oxford Instruments Ltd, 1959 (co. floated, 1983). Chm., Nat. Cttee for Superconductivity, SERC/DTI, 1987–92; Member: ABRC, 1983–89; ACOST, 1990–93; NRPB, 1991–96; Council, Central Lab. of the Res. Councils, 1995–98. Co-Founder, CONECTUS, 1994. Pres., FARM/Africa Ltd, 2000 (Vice-Chm. Council, 1985); Mem. Council, Royal Soc., 1995–97. Founder Trustee, Northmoor Trust (for nature conservation); Sylva Foundn (to promote sustainable forest mgt); Founder, Oxford Trust (for encouragement of study and application of science and technol.); Director: Oxford Econ. Partnership; Oxford Technol. Venture Trust. Lectr, UK and abroad. DL Oxon, 1985. Hon. FREng (Hon. FEng 1994). Hon. Fellow: UMIST, 1989; Cardiff Univ., 1998. Hon. DSc: Cranfield Inst. of Technol., 1983; Nottingham, 1996; Oxford Brookes, 2000; Hon. DTech Loughborough Univ. of Technol., 1985; Hon. DEng Birmingham, 1997; DUniv Open, 1999; Hon. DCL Oxon, 2004; Hon. Dr York, 2004. Mullard Medal (jtly), Royal Soc., 1982. *Publications:* articles in prof. jls. *Address:* c/o Oxford Instruments Group plc, Tubney Woods, Abingdon, Oxon OX13 5QX.

**WOOD, Sir Michael (Charles),** KCMG 2004 (CMG 1995); barrister; HM Diplomatic Service, retired; *b* 5 Feb. 1947; *s* of Walter Wood and Hilda Wood (*née* Forrester). *Educ:* Solihull Sch.; Trinity Hall, Cambridge (MA, LLM); Free Univ., Brussels. Called to the Bar, Gray's Inn, 1968, Bencher, 2000. HM Diplomatic Service, 1970–2006: Asst Legal Advr, FCO, 1970–81; Legal Advr, Bonn, 1981–84; Legal Counsellor, FCO, 1986–91 and 1994–96; Counsellor (Legal Advr), UK Mission to UN, NY, 1991–94; Dep. Legal Advr, FCO, 1996–99; Legal Advr, FCO, 1999–2006. Sen. Fellow, Lauterpacht Centre for Internat. Law, Univ. of Cambridge, 2006–. Mem., UN Internat. Law Commn, 2008–. Mem. Editl Cttee, British Yearbook of Internat. Law, 2001–. *Publications:* (with I. D. Hendry) The Legal Status of Berlin, 1987; (with A. Pronto) The International Law Commission 1999–2009, Vol. IV 2010; articles on internat. law. *Recreations:* walking, music, travel. *Address:* 20 Essex Street, WC2R 3AL.

**WOOD, Prof. Michael David;** film maker, broadcaster and historian; Director, Maya Vision International Ltd, since 1989; Professor of Public History, University of Manchester, since 2013; *b* Manchester, 23 July 1948; *s* of George Wood and Elsie Bell; *m* 1988, Rebecca Ysabel Dobbs; two *d. Educ:* Manchester GS (Foundn Scholar); Oriel Coll., Oxford (Open Scholar; BA Hons; Postgrad. Scholar). Journalist: ITV, 1973–76; BBC, 1976–79; documentary film maker: BBC, 1979–86; Central TV, 1987–91. Has made over 100 documentaries for British and US TV. FRHistS 2001; FSA 2008. Gov., RSC, 2004–16. Trustee, Historic Royal Palaces, 2019–. DUniv Open, 2003; Hon. DLitt: Birmingham, 2005; Lancaster, 2007; Stafford, 2008; Sunderland, 2009; Leicester, 2011; Hon. Dr Manchester, 2015. Numerous awards; Medlicott Medal, Histl Assoc., 2011; President's Medal, British Acad., 2015. *Publications:* In Search of the Dark Ages, 1981, 6th edn 2005; (contrib.) Ideal and Reality in Carolingian and Anglo-Saxon England, 1983; In Search of the Trojan War, 1985, 6th edn 2005; Domesday, 1986, 5th edn 2005; Legacy, 1992, 3rd edn 2005; The Smile of Murugan, 1995, 3rd edn as A South Indian Journey, 2007; In the Footsteps of Alexander the Great, 1997, 3rd edn 2005; In Search of England, 1999; Conquistadors, 2000, new edn 2010; In Search of Shakespeare, 2003, expanded edn 2005; (contrib.) Chidambaram, 2004; In Search of Myths and Heroes, 2005; The Story of India, 2007, expanded edn 2008; (contrib.) Lay Intellectuals in the Carolingian World, 2008; The Story of England, 2010; (contrib.) England and the Continent in the Tenth Century, 2011; (contrib.) 100 Years of Royal Books and Manuscripts, 2013; (contrib.) The Impact of History, 2015; Queen Sembiyan Mahadevi, 2016. *Recreations:* theatre, music, reading history, walking in Greece. *Address:* Maya Vision International Ltd, 9 Newbury Street, EC1A 7HU. *T:* (020) 7796 4842.

**WOOD, Rear Adm. Michael George,** CBE 1995; JP; DL; logistic support consultant, since 2003; *b* 8 June 1948; *s* of late George William Wood and Margaret Jean Wood (*née* Cottier); *m* 1972, Judith Vivienne Tickle; one *s* two *d. Educ:* Plymouth Coll.; BRNC Dartmouth; RNEC Manadon. BSc, CNAA; CEng, FIMechE. Joined RN, 1968; served HM Ships Tenby, Torquay, Hermes, HM Yacht Britannia, Minerva, Cleopatra, Argonaut, and ashore at RNC Greenwich, Raleigh, RNEC and staff of Flag Officer Sea Training, 1968–85; exchange with US Navy, 1986–88; SMEO to Captain Seventh Frigate Sqn, 1988–90; jsdc 1990; Naval Asst to First Sea Lord, 1991–92; rcds 1993; staff of FO Portsmouth, 1994; Captain Fleet Maintenance, Devonport, 1994–96; Sec. to Chiefs of Staff Cttee, 1996–98; Dir Naval Logistic Policy, MoD, 1998–99; Dir Gen. Fleet Support (Ops and Plans), MoD, 1999–2000; Dir Gen. Defence Logistics (Ops and Business Develt), subseq. Dir Gen. Ops (Defence Logistics Orgn), MoD, 2000–03; Chief Naval Engr Officer, 2001–03. Senior Military Adviser: Mowlem plc, 2003–06; Carillion plc, 2006–10. Hon. Life Mem., Plymouth Area Business Council, 2005–. Chm., Devonport Naval Base Visitors Centre and Museum Trust, 2005–14. Gov., Drake Foundn, 2009–. Pres., RN Engrs Quart Club, 2004–13; Vice Pres., Combined Services Hockey Assoc., 2004–11. Chm. Trustees, China Fleet Club, 2013–. JP Plymouth, 2009 (Dep. Chm., S and W Devon Magistrates' Bench, 2013–); DL Cornwall, 2014. *Recreations:* family, sailing, travelling, ski-ing, tennis. *Address:* c/o Naval Secretary, Fleet Headquarters, Whale Island, Portsmouth PO2 8BY. *Club:* Royal Naval Sailing Assoc.

**WOOD, Michael John Andrew;** a District Judge (Magistrates' Courts), Durham, 2004–12; *b* 26 March 1950; *s* of Leslie Harold Thomas Wood and Irene Mary Wood; *m* 1973, Margaret (*née* Bellamy); three *d. Educ:* Headlands Sch., Bridlington; Univ. of Newcastle upon Tyne (LLB Hons 1972; J. H. Renoldson Meml Prize). Admitted solicitor, 1975; Assistant Solicitor: Messrs Linsley & Mortimer, 1975–77; Messrs Hay & Kilner, 1977–79; sole practitioner, Messrs Michael J. Wood & Co., 1979–2004. Dep. Dist Judge (Civil), 1993–99; Actg Stipendiary Magistrate, 1998–2000; Dep. Dist Judge (Magistrates' Courts), 2000–04. *Recreations:* golf, painting (watercolours), classic cars. *Club:* Whickham & District 41.

**WOOD, Michael Jon;** MP (C) Dudley South, since 2015; *b* 17 March 1976; *s* of Brian Wood and Jacqueline Susan Wood (*née* Priest); *m* 2008, Laura Chadderton; one *s* one *d. Educ:* Old Swinford Hosp. Sch.; Univ. of Wales, Aberystwyth (BScEcon Hons Econs and Law 1997); Cardiff Univ. (Postgrad. DipLaw 1999). Asst to Earl of Stockton, MEP, 1999–2002; Policy Advr, Eur. Parlt, 2002–06; Sen. Researcher, JDS Associates, 2006–08; Constituency Organiser, Cons. Party, 2009–10; Caseworker to Andrew Griffiths, MP, 2010–11; Parly Asst, H of C, 2011–14. Mem. (C) Dudley MBC, 2014–16. *Address:* House of Commons, SW1A 0AA.

**WOOD, Michael Mure;** QC 1999; a Recorder, since 1999; Advocate, Public Defender Service, since 2014; *b* 22 Oct. 1953; *o s* of John Craig Mure Wood and Jean Margaret Wood; *m* 1st, 1978, Marianne Smith (marr. diss. 2012); one *d*; 2nd, 2012, Suzanne Eleanor Jane Dixey; one *s. Educ:* Rugby Sch.; Southampton Univ. (LLB Hons). Called to the Bar, Middle Temple, 1976, Bencher, 2012; an Asst Recorder, 1994–99; admitted: Grand Court, Cayman Is., 2004–06, 2014–16; Dubai Internat. Financial Centre Court, 2007. Mem. Panel, Acting Grand Court Judges, Cayman Is, 2015–. Member: Criminal Bar Assoc. Cttee, 1992–94; Bar Human Rights Cttee, 1995–2000. *Publications:* articles for Criminal Bar Assoc. and Law Commn. *Recreations:* food, wine, travel, golf. *Address:* Public Defender Service, Ministry of Justice, Petty France, Westminster, SW1H 9AJ. *T:* 07841 816611. *E:* mwoodqc@hotmail.com. *Club:* Bar Golfing Soc.

**WOOD, Michael Roy;** *b* 3 March 1946; *s* of late Rowland L. Wood and Laura M. Wood; *m* 1999, Christine O'Leary; two step *d*; one *s* one *d* by a previous marriage. *Educ:* Nantwich and Acton Grammar Sch.; Salisbury and Wells Theol Coll. (CTh 1974); Leeds Univ. (CQSW 1981); Leeds Metropolitan Univ. (BA 1989). Probation officer, Liverpool, Bradford, Leeds, and social worker, Calderdale, Leeds, 1965–97. Mem. (Lab), Kirklees DC, 1980–88. Contested (Lab) Hexham, 1987. MP (Lab) Batley and Spen, 1997–2015.

**WOOD, Nicholas Leslie;** Executive Chairman, Leach and Burton Ltd, 1988–2012; *b* 25 Sept. 1948; *s* of Harold Edward Wood and Joyce Winifred Wood (*née* Clark); *m* 1974, Elizabeth Ann Ketteridge; two *s. Educ:* Forest Sch.; Sch. of Pharmacy, Univ. of London (BPharm). FRPharmS; FIPharmM. Community pharmacy br. manager, 1974–82, Man. Dir, 1982–2000, N. L. Wade Ltd. Gen. Sec., 1999–2003, Pres., 2007–15, Inst. of Pharmacy Mgt. Member Council: Royal Pharmaceutical Soc., 1985–97, 2003–05 (Vice-Pres., 1992–93; Pres., 1993–94, 2004–05); Pet Health Council, 1990–97; Fedn Internat. Pharmaceutique, 1992–97; Commonwealth Pharmaceutical Assoc., 1995–97. Member: Standing Pharmaceutical Adv. Cttee, DoH, 1987–96; Jt Formulary Cttee, British Nat. Formulary, 1987–2007 (Dep. Chm., 1995–2007); Nurse Prescribers Formulary Cttee, 1998–2007; Health Policy Cttee, N Essex HA, 1999–2002; Council for Healthcare Regulatory Excellence, 2004–05. Mem. Council, Sch. of Pharmacy, Univ. of London, 1993–99, 2000–09 (Vice-Chm., 2006–09). Membership Sec., Lib Dem Health Assoc., 1988–92. Fellow, Sch. of Pharmacy, 2010. Freeman, City of London, 1970; Liveryman, Soc. of Apothecaries, 1990– (Mem., Court of Assts, 1995–; Chm., Charity Cttee, 2000–07; Master, 2008–09; Gideon de Laune Lectr, 2009; Curator, 2013–). *Recreations:* motor boating, medical and family history, gardening, playing rock guitar badly. *Address:* Tintern House, Melton Road, Woodbridge, Suffolk IP12 1NH. *Clubs:* East India; Woodbridge Cruising.

**WOOD, Nicholas Marshall; His Honour Judge Nicholas Wood;** a Circuit Judge, since 2007; *b* Sydney, 8 Oct. 1955; *s* of Geoffrey Ingham Wood and Hazel Esther Wood; *m* 1989, Sophie McCallum Kneebone; one *s* one *d. Educ:* Leeds Grammar Sch.; Queen's Coll., Oxford (BA Hons 1976; MA 1978); Indiana Univ. Sch. of Law (LLM 1978). Called to the Bar, Middle Temple, 1980; in practice as barrister specialising in criminal law: Francis Taylor Bldg, 1982–95; QEB Hollis Whiteman Chambers, 1995–2007; Asst Recorder, 1997–2000; Recorder, 2000–07. Sec., Criminal Bar Assoc., 1996–98; Vice Chm., Remuneration Cttee, Bar Council, 2003–05. *Recreations:* hill-walking, cricket, football, cinema, theatre. *Address:* Isleworth Crown Court, 36 Ridgeway Road, Isleworth TW7 5LP. *T:* (020) 8380 4500.

**WOOD, Peter Anthony;** Finance Director, Standard Chartered Bank, 1993–2000; *b* 4 Feb. 1943; *s* of Roger Sydney Wood and Winifred May (*née* Hine); *m* 1965, Janet Catherine Brown; one *s* one *d. Educ:* Oldershaw Grammar Sch.; Manchester Univ. (BSc Hons maths); Birkbeck Coll., London Univ. (MSc Stats). ACIB; FCT; FSS. NCB, 1964–66; Barclays Bank, 1966–93: Treas., 1985–91; Finance Dir, 1991–93. *Recreations:* golf, birdwatching. *Club:* Wildernesse (Sevenoaks).

**WOOD, Prof. Peter Anthony,** PhD; CGeog; Professor of Geography, University College London, 1996–2005, now Emeritus; *b* 24 Aug. 1940; *s* of Peter Barron Wood and Mary Theresa Wood. *Educ:* Univ. of Birmingham (BSc 1961; PhD 1966). CGeog 2002. University College London: Asst Lectr, 1965–68; Lectr, 1968–82; Sen. Lectr, 1982–92; Reader, 1992–96; Hd, Dept of Geog., 1997–2002. Sec., Council of British Geog., 2010–16. Co-Chair, Chartered Geog. Assessors Panel, RGS, 2003–14; Chair, Frederick Soddy Trust, 2015– (Chair, RGS Adv. Bd, 2018–). Hon. FRGS 2015. *Publications:* (with G. M. Lomas) Employment Location in Regional Economic Planning, 1970; (with K. E. Rosing) Character of a Conurbation: a computer atlas of the West Midlands Conurbation, 1971; (jtly) Housing and Labour Migration in England and Wales, 1974; Industrial Britain: the West Midlands, 1974; (ed with H. D. Clout) London: problems of change, 1986; (ed with P. Damesick) Regional Problems, Problem Regions and Public Policy in the United Kingdom, 1987; (with J. N. Marshall) Services and Space: aspects of urban and regional development, 1995; (ed) Consultancy and Innovation: the business service revolution in Europe, 2002; (jtly) The Competitive Performance of English Cities, 2006; (contrib.) Handbook of Innovation and Services, 2010; (contrib.) Global Migration, Ethnicity and Britishness, 2011; (contrib.) University Evolution, Entrepreneurial Activity and Regional Competitiveness, 2016; numerous contribs to Trans of IBG, Progress in Human Geog., Geog., Regl Studies, Envmt and Planning A, Internat. Small Business Jl, Entrepreneurship and Regl Develt, Geoforum, Global Networks, L'Espace Géographique, Tijdschrift voor Econ. En Sociaale Geografie, Papers in Regl Sci., Service Industries Jl, Growth and Change, Jl Studies in Internat. Educn, Higher Educn Policy. *Recreations:* music, opera, golf, travel. *Address:* Department of Geography, University College London, 26 Bedford Way, WC1H 0DS. *T:* (020) 7679 8843.

**WOOD, Sir Peter (John),** Kt 2016; CBE 1996; Chairman: Esure, since 2000 (Chief Executive, 2000–12); GoCompare.com, since 2016; *m* (marr. diss.); six *d.* Founder, 1985, Chief Exec., 1985–96, Chm., 1996–97, Direct Line Insurance. Non-executive Director: Plymouth Rock Corp., USA, 1995–; The Economist Newspaper Ltd, 1998–2003; Chm., W-One Internat., 2016–. *Address:* Esure, The Observatory, Reigate, Surrey RH2 0SG.

**WOOD, Philip,** CB 1997; OBE 1979; Director General, Office of the Deputy Prime Minister (formerly Department of the Environment, Transport and the Regions, then Department for Transport, Local Government and the Regions), 1997–2003; *b* 30 June 1946; *s* of late Frank and Eleanor Wood; *m* 1971, Dilys Traylen Smith; one *s. Educ:* Queen Elizabeth Grammar Sch., Wakefield; Queen's Coll., Oxford. Entered Civil Service, 1967; Min. of Transport, 1967–70; DoE, 1970–75; a Private Sec. to the Prime Minister, 1975–79; Dept of Transport, 1979–97: Sec. to Armitage Inquiry into Lorries and the Envmt, 1980; Under Sec., 1986–95; seconded to BRB, 1986–88; Dep. Sec., 1995–97.

**WOOD, Philip Richard,** CBE 2015; Special Global Counsel, 2002–18, and Head, Global Law Intelligence Unit, 2009–18, Allen & Overy LLP; *b* Livingstone, N Rhodesia, 20 Aug. 1942; *s* of Frank Leslie Wood and Mary Florence Wood (*née* Dews); *m* Marie-Elisabeth Marciniak; three *s* one *d. Educ:* St John's Coll., Johannesburg; Univ. of Cape Town (BA 1963); Univ. of Oxford (MA English Lit.). Joined Allen & Overy, 1967: admitted Solicitor, 1970; Partner, 1973–2002; Hd, Banking Dept, 1992–98. Yorke Dist. Fellow, Cambridge Univ., 2001–. Visiting Professor: QMW, subseq. QMUL; of Internat. Financial Law, Univ. of Oxford, 2002–; LSE, 2003–08; Vis. Fellow, Bingham Centre for Rule of Law, 2013–. Founder, World Univs Comparative Law Project, 2010. Hon. QC 2010. Hon. LLD Lund. *Publications:* The Fall of the Priests and the Rise of the Lawyers, 2016; 18 books on internat. financial law; contrib. articles to jls. *Recreations:* marathon-running, book-writing, travelling, speaking, digging paths, non-fiction, popular piano. *Address:* Knowle Grange, Hound House Road, Shere, Surrey GU5 9JH. *T:* (01483) 202108, 07785 500831. *Club:* Reform.

**WOOD, (René) Victor;** Director: Sun Life Corp. plc, 1986–96; Wemyss Development Co. Ltd, 1982–2006; *b* 4 Oct. 1925; *e s* of late Frederick Wood and Jeanne Wood (*née* Raskin); *m* 1950, Helen Morag (*d* 2013), *o d* of the Dr David S. Stewart. *Educ:* Jesus Coll., Oxford (BA 1948; Queen Elizabeth I Fellow, 2014). FFA. Chief Exec., 1969–79, Chm. 1974–79, Hill Samuel Insurance and Shipping Holdings Ltd; Chm., Lifeguard Assurance, 1976–84. Director: Haslemere Estates, 1976–86; Coalite Gp, 1977–89; Chandros Insce Co., 1979–89; Colbourne Insce Co., 1980–90; Criterion Insce Co., 1984–90; Scottinvest SA, 1985–95; Wemyss Hotels France SA, 1985–95; Les Résidences du Colombier SA, 1985–93; Domaine de Rimauresq SARL, 1985–2006; Worldwide and General Investment Co., 1992–2008. Vice-Pres., British Insurance Brokers' Assoc., 1981–84. *Publications:* (with

Michael Pilch): Pension Schemes, 1960; New Trends in Pensions, 1964; Pension Scheme Practice, 1967; Company Pension Schemes, 1971; Managing Pension Schemes, 1974; Pension Schemes, 1979. *Address:* Helen Morag House, c/o Roca Corba 37, Can Diumenge – Escaldes, Andorra AD700. *T:* 869149.

**WOOD, Prof. Richard Dean,** PhD; FRS 1997; Grady F. Saunders Distinguished Professor in Molecular Biology, M. D. Anderson Cancer Center, University of Texas, since 2008; *b* 3 June 1955; *s* of Robert Dean Wood and Maxine Louise (*née* Hargis); *m* 1975, Enid Alison Vaag. *Educ:* Farmington High Sch., New Mexico; Westminster Coll., Salt Lake City (BS 1977); Univ. of Calif, Berkeley (PhD 1981). Grad. Fellow, NSF, 1977–80; Postdoctoral Fellow, Yale Univ., 1982–85; Imperial Cancer Research Fund: Postdoctoral Fellow, 1985–88; Res. Scientist, 1988–92; Sen. Scientist, 1992–95; Principal Scientist, 1995–2001; Richard Cyert Prof. of Molecular Oncology and Leader, Molecular and Cellular Biology (formerly Oncology) Prog., Univ. of Pittsburgh Cancer Inst., 2001–08. Hon. Prof., UCL, 1998. Mem., EMBO, 1998. Trustee, Marie Curie Cancer Care, 2000–01 (Chm., Scientific Cttee, 2000–01). Mem., Acad. of Medicine, Engrg and Scis, Texas, 2017. FAAAS 2018. Meyenburg Award for Cancer Res., 1998; Westminster Coll. Alumni Award, 1999. *Publications:* DNA Repair and Mutagenesis, 2nd edn 2006; papers in scientific res. jls. *Recreations:* playing bass, jazz, acoustic music, cycling, hiking. *Address:* Department of Epigenetics and Molecular Carcinogenesis, University of Texas, M. D. Anderson Cancer Center, PO Box 389, 1808 Park Road 1C, Smithville, TX 78957, USA.

**WOOD, Richard John;** HM Diplomatic Service; Ambassador to Norway, since 2018; *b* Great Yarmouth, 27 Aug. 1967; *s* of John Michael Wood and Christine Barbara Wood; *m* 2008, Xavier Piot. *Educ:* Lynn Grove High Sch., Gt Yarmouth; E Norfolk Sixth Form Coll., Gt Yarmouth; Leeds Poly. (BA Hons Eur. Langs and Instns 1990). Entered FCO, 1991; Second Sec. (Pol), Cape Town and Pretoria, 1993–98; Press Officer for Africa, News Dept, FCO, 1998–2001; Europe Directorate, FCO, 2001–02; First Sec. (Human Rights), UK Mission, NY, 2002–07; Consul General: Cape Town, 2007–11; Basra, 2011–12; Dep. Hd, Internat. Orgns Dept, FCO, 2012–14; Hd, Sanctions and Econ. Diplomacy, Prosperity Directorate, FCO, 2014; Counsellor (Foreign and Security Policy), Washington, 2014–15; Hd, Northern and Central Europe Dept, FCO, 2015–18. *Recreations:* languages, walking, baking. *Address:* British Embassy, Thomas Heftyes Gate 8, 0244 Oslo, Norway. *T:* 23132700. *E:* ukinnorway@fco.gov.uk.

**WOOD, Prof. Robert Anderson,** FRCSE, FRCPE, FRCPGlas, FRCPsych; Postgraduate Dean, and Professor in Clinical Medicine, University of Aberdeen Medical School, 1992–99; *b* 26 May 1939; *s* of late Dr John Fraser Anderson Wood and Janet Meikle Wood (*née* Hall); *m* 1966, Dr Sheila Margaret Pirie; one *s* three *d*. *Educ:* Edinburgh Academy; Univ. of Edinburgh (BSc Hons, MB ChB). FRCPE 1976; FRCSE 1994; FRCPGlas 1997; FRCPsych 1999. House Officer, Royal Infirmary, Edinburgh, 1963–64; Asst Lectr, Univ. of Edinburgh, 1964–65; Registrar and Sen. Registrar in Medicine, Dundee Teaching Hosps, 1965–69; Lectr in Therapeutics, Univ. of Aberdeen, 1969–72; Sen. Lectr in Therapeutics, 1972–92, Dep. Dir, Postgrad. Med. Educn, 1986–92, Univ. of Dundee; Consultant Physician, Perth Royal Infirmary, 1972–92. Member: Criminal Injuries Compensation Tribunal (formerly Appeals Panel), 2000–11; Advocates Disciplinary Tribunal, 2000–. HM Inspector of Anatomy for Scotland, 2007–14. Trustee, RCPE, 2005– (Mem. Council, 1990–92; Dean, 1992–95; Treas., 1999–2003). Mem. Bd, Med. and Dental Defence Union of Scotland, 2003–09 (Mem. Council, 1992–2003; Mem. Mgt Cttee, 1997–2003). *Publications:* papers on clinical pharmacology and medical education. *Recreations:* golf, sheep-husbandry. *Address:* Ballomill House, Abernethy, Perthshire PH2 9LD. *T:* (01738) 850201. *E:* robertwood127@btinternet.com. *Clubs:* Royal & Ancient Golf (St Andrews); Craigie Hill Golf (Captain, 1999–2001) (Perth); Elie Golf House (Fife); Blairgowrie Golf.

**WOOD, Air Vice-Marshal Robert Henry,** OBE 1977; *b* 24 Jan. 1936; *s* of Jack Cyril Wood and May Doris Wood; *m* 1957, Amy Cameron Wright; one *s* one *d*. *Educ:* Maldon Grammar School; cfs, psc, ndc, rcds. Commnd RAF, 1956; served Nos 617 and 88 Sqns, 1957–63; CFS, 1965–67; No 44 Sqn, 1967–69; attended Indian Staff Coll., 1970; MA to COS Far East Command, Singapore, 1970–71; PSO to Air Sec., 1972; NDC, Latimer, 1973; OC 51 Sqn, 1974; MoD Policy and Plans Dept, 1977; OC RAF Cranwell, 1978; OC RAF Linton-on-Ouse, 1979; Gp Capt. Flying Trng, HQ RAFSC, 1981–83; Dir Personal Services 1 (RAF), 1983–85; RCDS, 1985; Dep. Comdt, RAF Staff Coll., Bracknell, 1986; AOC and Comdt, RAF Coll., Cranwell, 1987–89; retd 1990. Director: Airways Flight Trng, 1992; British Red Cross, Leicestershire, 1993–96. *Recreations:* golf, music. *Clubs:* Royal Air Force; Luffenham Heath Golf (Captain, 2004).

**WOOD, Prof. Robert James Knoyle,** PhD; CEng, FREng; FIMechE, FIMMM, FICorr; Professor of Surface Engineering and Tribology, since 2004, and Associate Dean (Research), Faculty of Engineering and Physical Sciences (formerly Engineering and Environment), since 2015, University of Southampton; *b* Barnstaple, Devon, 23 Sept. 1960; *s* of David Wood and Sheila Wood (*née* Eales-White). *Educ:* Blundell's Sch., Tiverton; City Univ., London (BSc Hons Mech. Engrg); Univ. of Southampton (PhD Mech. Engrg 1987). CEng 1992; FIMechE 2002; FIMMM 2003; FREng 2016; FICorr 2017. Res. Fellow, Dept of Chemistry, Univ. of Southampton, 1987–89; Tribologist, BP Res., 1989–93; University of Southampton: Res. Fellow, 1993–96, Sen. Fellow, 1996–98, Lectr, 1998–2000, Dept of Mech. Engrg; Sen. Lectr, Sch. of Engrg Scis, 2000–04; Dir, Res. Inst. for Industry, 2000–08; Founder and Dir, Nat. Centre for Advanced Tribology, Southampton, 2008–15. Vis. Prof., Lanzhou Inst. of Chem. Physics, Chinese Acad. of Sci., 2008–. Ed.-in-Chief, Surface Topography: Metrology and Properties, Inst. of Physics Jl, 2016–. FHEA 2002. *Publications:* Multifunctional Materials for Tribological Applications, 2014; contrib. papers to learned jls incl. Wear, Tribol. Internat., Surface Coatings Technol., Jl Materials Sci., Diamond and Related Materials, Tribol. Letters, Corrosion Sci., Jl Power Sources, Proc. IMechE, Engrg Tribol., Tribol. Lubrication Technol., Philosophical Mag., Philosophical Trans Royal Soc., Jl Physics D Applied Physics, Langmuir, Nanotechnol. *Recreations:* jogging, walking, golf, tennis. *Address:* National Centre for Advanced Tribology at Southampton, Engineering Sciences, Faculty of Engineering and Physical Sciences, University of Southampton, Highfield, Southampton SO17 1BJ. *T:* (023) 8059 4881. *E:* r.wood@soton.ac.uk.

**WOOD, Hon. Sir Roderic (Lionel James),** Kt 2004; a Judge of the High Court of Justice, Family Division, 2004–16; *b* 8 March 1951; *s* of Lionel James Wood and Marjorie Wood (*née* Thompson). *Educ:* Nottingham High Sch.; Lincoln Coll., Oxford. Called to the Bar, Middle Temple, 1974; Bencher, 2001. QC 1993; a Recorder, 1997–2002; a Circuit Judge, 2002–03; Family Div. Liaison Judge for Wales, 2007–12. Member: Cttee, Family Law Bar Assoc., 1988–2002; Bar Council, 1993–95; Professional Conduct Cttee of the Bar, 1993–2000 (Vice-Chm., 1997–98; Chm., 1999–2000); Legal Aid and Fees Cttee, Gen. Council of the Bar, 1995–98 (Vice-Chm., Family, 1998); Court of Appeal (Civil Div.) User Cttee, 1995–2000. Jt Chm., Barristers/Clerks Liaison Cttee, 1994–95. Mem., Editl Bd, Longman Practitioner's Child Law Bull., 1993–94. *Recreations:* music, theatre, travel.

**WOOD, Roger Nicholas Brownlow;** Chairman, Reliance HiTech, 2009–11; *b* 21 July 1942; *s* of Reginald Laurence Charles Wood and Jean Olive Wood; *m* 1st, 1966, Julia Ellen Mallows (*d* 2013); two *d*; 2nd, 2016, Malainak Thongma. *Educ:* Sherborne Sch.; Grad. Sch. of Management, Northwestern Univ., USA. With ICL, 1962–89 (Dir, ICL (UK) Ltd, 1987–89); Man. Dir, STC Telecoms Ltd, 1989–91; Gp Vice Pres., NT Europe SA, 1991–93; Dir Gen. Adjoint, Matra Marconi Space NV, 1993–96; Man. Dir, British Gas Services Ltd, 1996–2001; Dir, Centrica plc, 1996–2004; Man. Dir, Automobile Assoc., 2001–04. Director: Paypoint plc, 2000–; Reliance plc, 2006–09. Mem., Parly Space Cttee, 1993–96. FBCS 1991; FCMI (FIMgt 1984); FInstD 1990. *Recreations:* music, Provence, Thai culture. *Address:* 16 Albany Reach, Queens Road, Thames Ditton, Surrey KT7 0QH. *Club:* Molesey Boat.

**WOOD, Maj.-Gen. Roy;** Trustee, Map Action, since 2008 (International Director, 2006–11; Chairman, 2011–15); *b* 14 May 1940; *s* of Alec and Lucy Maud Wood; *m* 1963, Susan Margaret Croxford; two *s*. *Educ:* Farnham Grammar Sch.; Welbeck College; RMA; Cambridge Univ. (MA); University College London (MSc 1971). FRICS; FRGS. Commissioned RE 1960; Mapping Surveys, Sarawak, Sierra Leone and Sabah, 1964–70; Instructor, Sch. of Military Survey, 1972–75; MoD, 1975–77; OC 14 Topo. Sqn, BAOR, 1977–79; CO Mapping and Charting Establt, 1979–81; Defense Mapping Agency, USA, 1981–83; MoD, 1984; Comdr, 42 Survey Engr Gp, 1985–87; Dir, Military Survey, 1987–90; Dir Gen., Military Survey, MoD, 1990–94. Col Comdt, RE, 1994–2003; Hon. Col, 135 Ind. Topographic Sqn RE (V), 1994–99. Chm., Geo-UK Ltd, 1994–2005. Pres., Photogrammetric Soc., 1993–95; Chairman: Assoc. for Geographic Information, 1996–97; RE Assoc., 2000–03; BSES, 2003–08; Pres., Defence Surveyors' Assoc., 2012–. Member: Cttee of Mgt, Mt Everest Foundn, 2002–08; Council, RGS, 2008–11. Gov., Winchcombe Sch., 2017–. *Publications:* articles on surveying and mapping in professional and technical jls. *Recreations:* rowing, hill walking, travel. *Clubs:* Geographical; Upper Thames Rowing.

**WOOD, Sir Samuel Thomas H.;** *see* Hill-Wood.

**WOOD, Scott F.;** *see* Furssedonn-Wood.

**WOOD, Sir Sebastian;** *see* Wood, Sir J. S. L.

**WOOD, Simon Edward; His Honour Judge Simon Wood;** a Circuit Judge, since 2008; *b* North Shields, 23 Oct. 1958; *s* of late Walter Scott Wood and of Shirley Wood (*née* Bittermann); *m* 1984, Catherine Mary, *d* of late George Edward Taylor Walton and Margaret Walton; four *s*. *Educ:* Chorister Sch., Durham; Royal Grammar Sch., Newcastle upon Tyne; Univ. of Newcastle upon Tyne (LLB Hons 1980). Called to the Bar, Middle Temple, 1981 (Harmsworth Schol.); in practice on NE Circuit, 1982–2008; Asst Recorder, 1998–2000; Recorder, 2000–08. NE Circuit Rep., Council of HM Circuit Judges, 2015–19 (Jun. Vice-Pres., 2019). Pres., N of England Medico Legal Soc., 2017–19 (Vice-Pres., 2015–17). Dep. Chancellor, Dio. of Newcastle, 2013–. Gov., Royal GS, Newcastle upon Tyne, 1999–2009. Trustee, Northern Sinfonia Trust, 2008–13 (Chm. Trustees, 2011–13). Lay Chapter Mem. and Lay Canon, Durham Cathedral, 2018–. *Publications:* (ed with Christopher Walton) Charlesworth & Percy on Negligence, 12th edn 2010; A German Heritage: the story of two immigrant families on Tyneside, 2018. *Recreations:* music (mem., Chorus of the Royal Northern Sinfonia (formerly Northern Sinfonia Chorus), 1983–), playing the piano, family history, walking. *Address:* The Law Courts, The Quayside, Newcastle upon Tyne NE1 3LA. *T:* (0191) 201 2000, *Fax:* (0191) 201 2001.
*See also* C. T. Walton.

**WOOD, Sotiroula Maria, (Roula);** *see* Konzotis, S. M.

**WOOD, Timothy John Rogerson;** Chairman, Autotronics plc, 1998–2000; *b* 13 Aug. 1940; *s* of Thomas Geoffrey Wood and Norah Margaret Annie (*née* Rogerson); *m* 1969, Elizabeth Mary Spencer; one *s* one *d*. *Educ:* King James's Grammar Sch., Knaresborough, Yorks; Manchester Univ. (BSc Maths). Joined Ferranti Ltd as Lectr in Computer Programming, 1962; joined ICT Ltd (later ICL), 1963; subseq. involved in develt of ICL systems software; Sen. Proj. Management Consultant advising on introdn of large computer systems, 1977; Sen. Proj. Manager on application systems, 1981; resigned from ICL, 1983. MP (C) Stevenage, 1983–97; contested (C) same seat, 1997. PPS to: Minister for Armed Forces, 1986–87; Minister of State, 1987–89, Sec. of State, 1989–90, Northern Ireland; Asst Govt Whip, 1990–92; Lord Comr of HM Treasury (Govt Whip), 1992–95; Comptroller of HM Household, 1995–97. Chm., Wokingham Cons. Assoc., 1980–83; President: Bracknell Cons. Assoc., 1998–2003; E Devon Cons. Assoc., 2016–; Vice Chairman: National Assoc. of Cons. Graduates, 1975–76; Thames Valley Euro Constituency Council, 1979–83; Mem., Bow Gp, 1962– (Mem. Council, 1968–71). Member: (C) Bracknell DC, 1975–83 (Leader, 1976–78); (C) E Devon DC, 2007–15 (Hon. Alderman, 2015–). Mem. Bd, Bracknell Develt Corp., 1977–82. Governor: Princess Helena Coll., 2000–09 (Vice Chm., 2005–09); Littleham Sch., 2004–18 (Chm., 2005–11). *Publications:* Bow Group pamphlets on educn, computers in Britain, and the Post Office. *Recreations:* gardening, chess, reading. *Club:* Carlton.

**WOOD, Victor;** *see* Wood, R. V.

**WOOD, Rt Rev. Wilfred Denniston,** KA 2000; Area Bishop (formerly Bishop Suffragan) of Croydon, 1985–2002; *b* Barbados, WI, 15 June 1936; *s* of Wilfred Coward and Elsie Elmira Wood; *m* 1966, Ina Eileen, *d* of L. E. Smith, CBE, Barbadian MP; three *s* two *d*. *Educ:* Combermere Sch. and Codrington Coll., Barbados. Lambeth Dip. in Theol., 1962. Ordained deacon, St Michael's Cath., Barbados, 1961; ordained priest, St Paul's Cath., London, 1962. Curate of St Stephen with St Thomas, Shepherd's Bush, 1962–66, Hon. Curate, 1966–74; Bishop of London's Officer in Race Relations, 1966–74; Vicar of St Laurence, Catford, 1974–82; RD of East Lewisham, 1977–82; Archdeacon of Southwark, 1982–85; Hon. Canon of Southwark Cathedral, 1977–85. Mem., General Synod, 1987–91. Chairman: Martin Luther King Meml Trust; Cttee on Black Anglican Concerns, 1986–91. Member: Royal Commn on Criminal Procedure, 1978–80; Archbishop of Canterbury's Commn on Urban Priority Areas, 1983–85; Housing Corp. Bd, 1986–95. Non-exec. Dir, Mayday Healthcare NHS Trust, 1993–2002 (Vice-Chm., 2000). JP Inner London, 1971–85. Hon. Freeman, London Bor. of Croydon, 2002. Hon. DD Gen. Theol Seminary, NY, 1986; DUniv Open, 2000; Hon. LLD West Indies, 2002. *Publications:* (contrib.) The Committed Church, 1966; (with John Downing) Vicious Circle, 1968; Keep the Faith, Baby!, 1994; Faith for a Glad Fool, 2010. *Recreations:* listening to audio-books, poetry and music, cricket; armchair follower of most sports. *Address:* 69 Pegwell Gardens, Christ Church, Barbados, West Indies. *T:* 4201822. *E:* wilfredwoodbarbados@gmail.com.

**WOOD, William James;** QC 1998; *b* 10 July 1955; *s* of Sir Frank Wood, KBE, CB, and Lady (Olive May) Wood (*née* Wilson); *m* 1986, Tonya Mary Pinsent; one *s* one *d*. *Educ:* Dulwich Coll.; Worcester Coll., Oxford (BA, BCL, both 1st cl.); Harvard Law Sch. (LLM). Called to the Bar, Middle Temple, 1980, Bencher, 2006. Member: Internat. Acad. of Mediators, 2012–; Civil Justice Council, 2014–. Adjunct Prof. of Dispute Resolution, Hong Kong Shue Yan Univ., 2014–. *Recreations:* fishing, bird-watching. *Address:* The Old Rectory, Church Lane, Charlbury, Oxon OX7 3PX; Brick Court Chambers, 7–8 Essex Street, WC2R 3LD.
*See also* C. Wood.

**WOOD, William Murray,** TD 2003; Sheriff of Tayside, Central and Fife at Perth, since 2014; *b* Fraserburgh, 1963; *s* of William Murray Diack Wood and Madelina Jack Wood (*née* Anderson); *m* 1990, Monica McLaughlin; two *s* one *d*. *Educ:* High Sch. of Dundee; Univ. of Aberdeen (LLB 1984; DipLP 1985); RMA, Sandhurst. Commnd Regular Army, 1986; served with 1st Bn, Gordon Highlanders, 1986–90. Trainee and solicitor, Inverness, 1990–93; admitted as solicitor, 1991; Solicitor, Alloa, Hamilton and Uddingston, 1993–2012. Fee Paid Immigration Judge, 2001–13; Convener, Mental Health Tribunal for Scotland, 2005–13; Chair, Pensions Appeal Tribunal for Scotland (War Pensions), 2008–13; Fee Paid Dep. Upper Tribunal Judge (Immigration and Asylum Chamber), 2010–13; Fee Paid Social Security Judge, 2012–13; pt-time Sheriff, 2012–13; Floating Sheriff of Tayside, Central and Fife at Stirling, 2013. Served TA, 1990–2013; Lt Col, 2006; i/c Glasgow and Strathclyde Univs OTC, 2006–08. Mem., Guildry of Stirling, 2013–. *Recreations:* obligatory gardening, moderate running and cycling, light squash, reading, films. *Address:* Sheriff's Chambers, Sheriff Court House, Tay Street, Perth PH2 8NL.

**WOOD, His Honour William Rowley;** QC 1997; a Circuit Judge, 2002–19; *b* 22 March 1948; *s* of Dr B. S. B. Wood and Elizabeth Wood; *m* 1973, Angela Beatson-Hird; one *s* two *d*. *Educ:* Bradfield Coll., Berks; Magdalen Coll., Oxford (MA). Called to the Bar, Gray's Inn, 1970. A Recorder, 1990–2002. Chm., Birmingham DAC, 1999–2006. *Recreations:* sailing, tennis, theatre. *Clubs:* Buckland (Birmingham); Bentley Drivers; Edgbaston Priory Lawn Tennis.

**WOODALL, Abigail R.;** *see* Rokison-Woodall, A.

**WOODARD, Rear-Adm. Sir Robert (Nathaniel),** KCVO 1995; DL; Flag Officer Royal Yachts, 1990–95; an Extra Equerry to the Queen, since 1992; *b* 13 Jan. 1939; *s* of Francis Alwyne Woodard and Catherine Mary Woodard (*née* Hayes); *m* 1963, Rosamund Lucia, *d* of Lt-Col D. L. A. Gibbs, DSO and Lady Hilaria Gibbs (*née* Edgcumbe); two *s* one *d*. *Educ:* Lancing College; Coll. of Air Warfare. Joined Royal Navy as Cadet, 1958; specialised in flying; served HM Ships Undaunted, Ark Royal, Eagle, Victorious, Bulwark in 800, 801, 845, 846 and 848 Sqns (active service Malaya, Borneo); DS, BRNC Dartmouth, 1971–73; Commands: 771 Sqn, 1973–74; 848 Sqn, 1974–75; HMS Amazon, 1978–80; Dir, JMOTS, 1981–83; HMS Glasgow, 1983–84; HMS Osprey, 1984–86; MoD Op. Requirements, 1986–88; Cdre, Clyde, 1989–90. Dir, Woodard (Western Div.) plc, 1985–2005; Fellow, Western Div., 1985–2005, Trustee, 2001–11, Vice Pres., 2011–, Woodard Corp.; Patron, Sir Robert Woodard Acad., 2009–. Vice-Pres., Falmouth Br., Royal Naval Assoc. Pres., SSAFA, Cornwall, 1995–. Chm., Regl Cttee, Devon and Cornwall, NT, 1997–2002. Chairman of Governors: King's Coll., Taunton, 2000–05; King's Hall, Pyrland, 2000–05; Vice-Chm., Govs, Bolitho Sch., Penzance, 1994–2010. Pres., Helford River Children's Sailing Trust, 1997–2014; Pres., Type 21 Club, 2014–; Member: Fleet Air Arm Officers' Assoc.; Buccaneer Aircrew Assoc. Younger Brother, Trinity House, 1994–. DL Cornwall, 1999. FCMI (FBIM 1979); MInstD 1995. Comdr, Ordre Nat. du Mérite (France), 1992. *Recreations:* grandchildren, shooting, fishing, painting, sailing, mowing, home life, laughter. *Club:* Port Navas Yacht.

**WOODBRIDGE, Anthony Rivers;** Senior Partner, The Woodbridge Partnership, 1997–2009; Consultant Solicitor, Thomas A Deegan, 2011–18; *b* 10 Aug. 1942; *s* of late John Nicholas Woodbridge and Patricia Madeleine (*née* Rebbeck); *m* 1976, Lynda Anne Nolan; one *s*. *Educ:* Stowe; Trinity Hall, Cambridge (MA). Admitted solicitor, 1967; Partner, Woodbridge & Sons, Uxbridge, 1969–83; Sen. Partner, Turberville Woodbridge, 1983–97. Company Secretary: Abbeyfield Uxbridge Soc. Ltd, 1974–2000 (Vice-Chm., 1996–98); Burr Brown Internat. Ltd, 1992–96. Adminr, Uxbridge Duty Solicitor Scheme, 1983–91. Clerk to Gen. Comrs of Income Tax, 1985–2009. Mem., Hillingdon HA, 1990–92; Chairman: Hillingdon Community Health NHS Trust, 1992–94; Harrow and Hillingdon Healthcare NHS Trust, 1994–2001; Stoke Mandeville Hosp. NHS Trust, 2001–02; Hillingdon Hosp. NHS Trust, 2002–05. Trustee, The Hillingdon Partnership Trust, 1994–2003 and 2011– (Chm., 2014–). Hon. Solicitor: Samaritans, Hillingdon, 1973–2009; Age Concern, Hillingdon, 1989–2009. Mem., Law Soc., 1967–. Mem. Ct, Brunel Univ., 1995–2000, now Life Mem. Ct. FInstD 1999. Gov., Fulmer Sch., Bucks, 1984–2003 (Chm. Govs, 1988–94). DUniv Brunel, 2000. *Recreations:* walking, cycling, touring. *Address:* 16 Fairfield Park Road, Fairfield Park, Bath, Avon BA1 6JN. *T:* (01225) 329650, 07802 414590. *E:* tonywoodbridge@hotmail.com.

**WOODBURN, Christopher Hugh,** FCA; Chief Executive, General Insurance Standards Council, 1999–2005; *b* 6 Nov. 1947; *s* of Leonard Arthur and Phyllis Lydia Woodburn; *m* 1972, Lesley Avril Mohan; two *d*. *Educ:* St John's Sch., Leatherhead. FCA 1972. Articled Clerk and Audit Senior, Deloitte & Co., 1966–72; London Stock Exchange, 1972–88 (Hd, Financial Regulation, 1987–88); Securities Assoc., 1988–91 (Dep. Chief Exec., 1990–91); SFA, 1991–99 (Chief Exec., 1997–99). Hon. FCII 2006. *Recreations:* sailing, history. *Address:* Oak House, Heathfield Road, Burwash, E Sussex TN19 7HN. *T:* (01435) 883196.

**WOODCOCK, Prof. Ashley Arthur,** OBE 2006; MD; FRCP; FMedSci; Professor of Respiratory Medicine, since 1998, and Associate Dean, Clinical Affairs, since 2016, University of Manchester; Consultant Respiratory Physician, University Hospital of South Manchester, since 1988; Clinical Director, North West Lung Centre, since 2013; *b* Stoke-on-Trent, 13 April 1951; *s* of Arthur and Vera Woodcock; *m* 1974, Fiona; two *s* one *d*. *Educ:* Hanley High Sch., Stoke-on-Trent; Univ. of Manchester (BSc 1972; MB ChB 1975; MD 1982). FRCP 1992. Consultant Physician: Bandar Seri Begawan Brunei, SE Asia; Manchester Royal Infirmary, 1985; University of Manchester: Head, Sch. of Translational Medicine, 2008–12; Head, Inst. of Inflammation and Repair, 2012–15. Co-chair: Med. Tech. Options Cttee to Montreal Protocol for Protection of Ozone Layer, 1996–2013; Technol. and Econ. Assessment Panel, UN Envmt Prog./Montreal Protocol for Protection of Ozone Layer, 2015–. FMedSci 2008. *Publications:* contribs on treatment of asthma, allergy and respiratory symptoms. *Recreations:* golf, walking in Wales. *Address:* University Hospital South Manchester, Southmoor Road, Manchester M23 9LT. *E:* ashley.woodcock@manchester.ac.uk. *Clubs:* Hale Golf, Aberdovey Golf.

**WOODCOCK, John Charles,** OBE 1996; cricket writer; *b* 7 Aug. 1926; *s* of late Rev. Parry John Woodcock and Norah Mabel Woodcock (*née* Hutchinson). *Educ:* Dragon Sch., St Edward's Sch., Oxford; Trinity Coll., Oxford (MA; DipEd; OUHC *v* Cambridge, 1946, 1947). Manchester Guardian, 1952–54; cricket writer, The Times, 1954–; Cricket Corresp. to Country Life, 1962–91; Editor, Wisden Cricketers' Almanack, 1980–86; has covered over 40 Test tours, 1950–98, to Australia, 18 times, S Africa, W Indies, New Zealand, India, Pakistan and Sri Lanka. Mem., MCC Cttee, 1988–91 and 1992–95 (Trustee, 1996–99; Life Vice-Pres., 2001). Pres., Cricket Writers' Club, 1986–2005. Patron of the living of Longparish. Hon. Fellow, Winchester Univ., 2012. Sports Journalist of the Year, British Press Awards, 1987. *Publications:* The Ashes, 1956; (with E. W. Swanton) Barclays World of Cricket, 1980 (Associate Editor, 2nd edn 1986, Consultant Editor, 3rd edn 1986); The Times One Hundred Greatest Cricketers, 1998. *Recreations:* the countryside, golf. *Address:* The Old Curacy, Longparish, Andover, Hants SP11 6PB. *T:* (01264) 720259. *Clubs:* MCC; Vincent's (Oxford); St Enodoc Golf.

**WOODCOCK, John Zak;** MP for Barrow and Furness, since 2010 (Lab Co-op, 2010–18; Ind, since 2018); *b* Sheffield, 14 Oct. 1978; *m* 2004, Amanda Telford; two *d*. *Educ:* Edinburgh Univ. (MA 2002). Journalist, Scotsman; Special Adviser: to Rt Hon. John Hutton, MP, 2005; to Cabinet Sec., 2005; to Sec. of State for Work and Pensions, 2005–07; to Sec. of State for Business, Enterprise and Regulatory Reform, 2007–08; to the Prime Minister, 2009. Shadow Transport Minister, 2010–13; Shadow Defence Minister, 2015. Member: Defence Select Cttee, 2010, 2013–15; Home Affairs Cttee, 2018–19. *Address:* House of Commons, SW1A 0AA.

**WOODCOCK, Vice Adm. Sir Jonathan;** *see* Woodcock, Vice Adm. Sir S. J.

**WOODCOCK, Michael, (Mike);** JP; company director, consultant, researcher and writer; *b* 10 April 1943; *s* of Herbert Eric Woodcock and Violet Irene Woodcock; *m* 1st, 1969, Carole Ann (*née* Berry) (*d* 2011); one *s* one *d*; 2nd, 2017, Candida Ann (*née* Croson). *Educ:* Queen Elizabeth's Grammar Sch., Mansfield, Notts; DLitt IMCB, 1988. Successively: Accountant, Personnel Officer, Management Development Adviser, Head of Small Business Development Unit, Consultant, Vice-Pres. of US Corp., Founder of six UK companies. Underwriting Mem. of Lloyd's, 1984–. Proprietor of Estates in Scotland: Glenrinnes; Rigg; Carron Bridge; Corbiewells. MP (C) Ellesmere Port and Neston, 1983–92. Member: Trade and Industry Select Cttee, 1984–87; Home Affairs Select Cttee, 1987–92; Secretary: Cons. Smaller Business Cttee, 1990–92; All Party Transpennine Gp of MPs, 1990–92. Parly Advr, Chamber of Coal Traders, 1985–93. Nat. Vice Pres., Ramblers' Assoc., 1993–. Vis. Prof., Univ. of Lancaster Mgt Sch., 1992–96; Vis. Fellow, Leeds Business Sch., 1994–97. Pres. and Chm. of Council, Royal Masonic Trust for Girls and Boys, 2008–16; Gov., Royal Masonic Sch. for Girls, 2013–; Trustee: Royal Masonic Instn for Girls Endowment Trust, 2013–18; Masonic Charitable Foundn, 2016–18; Chm. of Trustees, Lifelites, 2010–. Companion, IMCB, 1990. JP Mansfield, Notts, 1971. *Publications:* People at Work, 1975; Unblocking Your Organisation, 1978 (UK, USA and Holland); Team Development Manual, 1979 (UK, USA and Indonesia); Organisation Development Through Teambuilding, 1981 (UK and USA); The Unblocked Manager, 1982 (UK, USA and four foreign edns); 50 Activities for Self Development, 1982 (UK, USA and eight foreign edns); Manual of Management Development, 1985; 50 Activities for Teambuilding, 1989 (UK, USA and 11 foreign edns); (jtly) Clarifying Organisational Values, 1989 (UK and Sweden); 50 Activities for Unblocking Your Organisation, vol. 1, 1990, vol. 2, 1991; The Self Made Leader, 1990; Unblocking Organisational Values, 1990; Change: a collection of activities and exercises, 1992; The Woodcock Francis series of Management Audits, 1994; Teambuilding Strategy, 1994 (UK and India); The Teambuilders Toolkit, 1996; The Problem Solvers Toolkit, 1996; The New Unblocked Manager, 1996; 25 Interventions for Improving Team Performance, 1997; Developing Your People, 1998; Interventions for Developing Managerial Competencies, 1998; Management Skills Assessment, 1999; The Agile Organisation, 1999; Audits for Organisational Effectiveness, 2004; Team Metrics: resources for measuring and improving team performance, 2005. *Recreation:* walking. *Address:* Stubben Edge Hall, Ashover, Derbys S45 0EU.

**WOODCOCK, Vice Adm. Sir (Simon) Jonathan,** KCB 2018; OBE 2008; Second Sea Lord and Deputy Chief of the Naval Staff, 2015–18; *b* Sandown, IoW, 5 July 1962; *s* of Roger Fairhurst Woodcock and Phyllis Margaret Woodcock; *m* 1985, Joanna Leigh Clarke; one *s* one *d*. *Educ:* Ryde Sch.; Britannia Royal Naval Coll.; RNEC Manadon (BSc Hons Eng). CEng 1996; MIMechE 1996. Joined RN, 1980; Hd, Machinery Trials Unit, 1999–2001; Comdr (Marine Engrg), HMS Ark Royal, 2001–03; COS to Capability Manager (Precision Attack), 2003–05; Captain: RN Sch. of Marine Engrg, 2005–08; HMS Raleigh, 2008–09; rcds 2010; Hd, Pay and Manning, MoD, 2010–12; Cdre, Naval Personnel, 2012; Naval Sec. and ACNS (Personnel), 2012–15. Trustee: RN Benevolent Trust, 2009–15; MSSC, 2018–; Chm., Greenwich Hosp. Trust, 2015–18. Younger Brother, Trinity House, 2016. FCIPD 2014–18. *Recreations:* country sports, ski-ing, gardening, bee keeping. *Address:* c/o Office of the Naval Secretary, Leach Building, Whale Island, Portsmouth PO2 8BY.

**WOODCOCK, Thomas,** CVO 2011 (LVO 1996); DL; FSA; Garter Principal King of Arms, since 2010; Genealogist, Order of the Bath, since 2010; *b* 20 May 1951; *s* of late Thomas Woodcock, Hurst Green, Lancs, and Mary, *d* of William Woodcock, Holcombe, Lancs; *m* 1998, Lucinda Mary Harmsworth, *d* of late Lucas Michael Harmsworth King. *Educ:* Eton; University Coll., Durham (BA); Darwin Coll., Cambridge (LLB). FSA 1990. Called to Bar, Inner Temple, 1975, Bencher, 2010. Research Assistant to Sir Anthony Wagner, Garter King of Arms, 1975–78; Rouge Croix Pursuivant, 1978–82; Somerset Herald, 1982–97; Norroy and Ulster King of Arms, 1997–2010. Advr on Naval Heraldry, 1996–; Inspector of Regtl Colours and of RAF Badges, 2010–. Chm., Harleian Soc., 2004–; Pres., Lancs Parish Register Soc., 2004–. DL Lancs, 2005. *Publications:* (with John Martin Robinson) The Oxford Guide to Heraldry, 1988; (ed with D. H. B. Chesshyre) Dictionary of British Arms: Medieval Ordinary, vol. 1, 1992, vol. 2 (ed with Hon. J. Grant and I. Graham), 1996, vol. 3 (ed with Sarah Flower), 2009, vol. 4 (ed with Sarah Flower), 2014; (with John Martin Robinson) Heraldry in National Trust Houses, 2000. *Address:* College of Arms, 130 Queen Victoria Street, EC4V 4BT. *T:* (020) 7236 3634, (020) 7248 1188. *Clubs:* Travellers, Beefsteak, Pratt's.

**WOODDISSE, Maj. Gen. Ralph William,** CBE 2013 (MBE 2007); MC 1999; Assistant Chief of the General Staff, since 2018; *b* Dhekelia, Cyprus, 8 Jan. 1970; *s* of John and Ann Wooddisse; *m* 2000, Louise Auld; three *d*. *Educ:* Denstone Coll.; University Coll. London (BA Hons); Cranfield Univ. (MA). Joined Army, 1991; CO, 2nd Bn Royal Anglian Regt, 2009–11; Comdr, 38 (Irish) Bde, 2013–15; ACOS J3, PJHQ, 2015–17; GOC 1st (UK) Div., 2017–18. *Recreations:* cross country running, orienteering, ski-ing. *T:* 07547 272069. *E:* ralphw@hotmail.co.uk.

**WOODFORD, Air Vice-Marshal Anthony Arthur George,** CB 1989; Home Bursar and Fellow, Magdalen College, Oxford, 1992–2001; *b* 6 Jan. 1939; *s* of Arthur and May Woodford; *m* 1965, Christine Barbara Tripp; one *s* two *d*. *Educ:* Haberdashers' Aske's Hampstead School; RAF College, Cranwell. BA Hons Open Univ. 1978. Commissioned pilot, 1959; served Nos 12, 44, 53, 101 Sqns and 4017th CCTS USAF; Asst Air Attaché, British Embassy, Washington, 1978–81; Comdr RAF St Mawgan, 1982–83; Comdr British Forces Ascension Island, 1982; ADC to the Queen, 1982–83; RCDS 1984; HQ Strike Command: Air Cdre Plans, 1985–87; AOA, 1987–89; ACOS Policy, SHAPE, 1989–92, retd. *Address:* Filkins Moor, Filkins, Lechlade, Glos GL7 3JJ. *Club:* Royal Air Force.

**WOODFORD, F(rederick) Peter,** PhD; FRCPath; FRSC; FIPEM; FSA; Chief Scientific Officer, Department of Health (formerly of Health and Social Security), 1984–93; *b* 8 Nov. 1930; *s* of Wilfrid Charles Woodford and Mabel Rose (*née* Scarff); *m* 1964, Susan Silberman, NY; one *d*. *Educ:* Lewis Sch., Pengam, Glam; Balliol Coll., Oxford (Domus Exhibnr; BA (Hons Chem.) 1952; MA 1955). PhD Leeds 1955. FRCPath 1984; CChem, FRSC 1990; FIPEM (FBES 1993; MBES 1991). Res. Fellow and Sen. Lectr, Leiden Univ., 1958–62; Vis. Scientist/Lectr, Univ. of Tennessee Med. Sch. and NIH, USA, 1962–63; Guest Investigator, Rockefeller Univ., NY, 1963–71; Scientific Historian, Ciba Foundn, and Scientific Associate, Wellcome Trust, 1971–74; Exec. Dir, Inst. for Res. into Mental and Multiple Handicap, 1974–77; PSO (Clin. Chem.), DHSS, 1977–84. Distinguished Visitor,

Royal Free Hosp. Sch. of Med., 1994–2016; Gov., Royal Free London NHS Foundn Trust (formerly Royal Free Hosp. NHS Trust), 2012–14 (Shadow Gov., 2008–11). Mem., Quality of Life Panel, Camden Council, 2009–12. Editorial Consultant: Clin. Res. Inst., Montreal, 1970–90; Inst. of Pharmacology, Milan Univ., 1995–. Chm., Council of Biology Editors (USA), 1969–70; Managing/Executive Editor: Jl of Atherosclerosis Res., 1960–62; Jl of Lipid Res., 1963–69; Procs of Nat. Acad. of Scis, USA, 1970–71; Editl Consultant, King's Fund Centre for Health Service Develt, 1990–93; Pubns Editor, Camden History Soc., 1993–2016 (meetings co-ordinator, 2008–12, 2013–16; website manager, 2010–16; publisher, Hampstead Manorial 17C and 18C Court Records, 2010–). Student Gov., City Lit. Inst., 1999–2001. Chm., Hampstead Music Club, 1996–99; Patron, Cavatina Chamber Music Trust, 2003–; Patron Friend, Hampstead Town Hall. FSA 2010. First non-med. ARCP, 2000; Hon. Fellow, Assoc. of Clin. Biochemistry, 2005. Hon. DSc Salford, 1993. Waverley Gold Medal for scientific writing, RSA, 1955; Meritorious Award, Council of Biology Editors, USA, 1984. *Publications*: Scientific Writing for Graduate Students, 1969, 4th edn 1986; Medical Research Systems in Europe, 1973; The Ciba Foundation: an analytic history 1949–1974, 1974; Writing Scientific Papers in English, 1975; In-Service Training series: of Physiological Measurement Technicians, 1988; of Medical Physics Technicians, 1989; of Medical Laboratory Assistants, 1991; of Rehabilitation Engineering Technicians, 1992; (ed) From Primrose Hill to Euston Road, 1995; Atherosclerosis X, 1995; A Constant Vigil: 100 years of the Heath and Old Hampstead Society, 1997; (ed) Streets of Bloomsbury and Fitzrovia (a historical survey), 1997; (ed) East of Bloomsbury, 1998; How to Teach Scientific Communication, 1999; (ed) Streets of Old Holborn, 1999, 2nd edn 2010; (ed) The Streets of Hampstead, 3rd edn, 2000; (ed) The Good Grave Guide to Hampstead Cemetery, Fortune Green, 2000; (ed) Streets of St Giles, 2000, 2nd edn 2012; (ed) Victorian Seven Dials, 2001; (ed) 200 Years of Local Justice in Hampstead and Clerkenwell, 2001; (ed) The Railways of Camden, 2002; (ed jtly) Streets of St Pancras, 2002; (ed jtly) 20th-Century Camden Recalled, 2002; (ed jtly) Streets of Camden Town, 2003; (ed jtly) Streets of Kentish Town, 2005; (ed) Wartime St Pancras, 2006; (ed jtly) Streets of Gospel Oak and West Kentish Town, 2006; (ed) The Greville Estate: the history of a Kilburn neighbourhood, 2007; (ed) Buried in Hampstead, dec. edn, 2007; (ed jtly) Streets of Highgate, 2007; (ed jtly) George Morland: a London artist in eighteenth-century Camden, 2008; (ed) Streets of Belsize, 2009; (ed) A Better Life: oral histories of Italian immigrants to Clerkenwell, London from 1850, 2011; The King's Cross Fraudster Leopold Redpath: his life and times, 2013; (ed jtly) Streets of Bloomsbury, 2016; Belsize Remembered, 2017; articles on scientific writing, lipids of the arterial wall, editing of biomed. jls, prevention and treatment of handicapping disorders, screening for spina bifida, quality in pathology labs, costing and ethics in clin. chem., history of Heath and Old Hampstead Soc., 18th-century doctors in Bloomsbury, clinical significance of antioxidants, institutional invasion of Queen Square, London between 1846 and 2011, life in Hampstead in the 17th century, inspiration for Debussy's Golliwogg's Cakewalk, misrepresentation of Sir William Langhorn's 1715 will. *Recreations*: piano recitals, editing scientific and historical articles and books, tutoring grandchildren. *Address*: 1 Akenside Road, NW3 5BS.

**WOODFORD, Neil Russell,** CBE 2013; Head of Investment, Woodford Investment Management, since 2014; *b* Cookham, 2 March 1960. *Educ*: Univ. of Exeter (BA Econs and Agricl Econs 1981); London Business Sch. (postgrad. studies in finance). Fund Manager, Eagle Star, 1987–88; Hd, UK Equities, and Fund Manager, Invesco Perpetual, 1988–2014. *Address*: Woodford Investment Management, 9400 Garsington Road, Oxford OX4 2HN. *T*: (01865) 809000. *E*: info@woodfordfunds.com.

**WOODFORD, Stephen William John;** Chief Executive, Advertising Association, since 2016; *b* 11 Feb. 1959; *s* of John and Barbara Woodford; *m* 1988, Amelia Wylton Dickson; two *s* two *d*. *Educ*: Tomlinscote Sch., Frimley; City Univ. (BSc Hons). Grad. trainee, Nestlé Co. Ltd, 1980–82; Account Manager, Lintas Advertising, 1982–85; Account Dir, Waldron Allen Henry & Thompson, 1985–89; Account Dir, subseq. Gp Account Dir, WCRS, 1989–91; Dep. Man. Dir, Leo Burnett, 1991–94; Client Services Dir, 1994–95, Man. Dir, 1995–99, CEO, 1999–2005, WCRS; CEO, Engine, 2005–07; Chm. and CEO, DDB London, 2007–12; Chairman: adam&eveDDB, 2012–13; Lexis Agency, 2013–16; Livity, 2016–. Co-founder and non-exec. Dir, Ffrees Family Finance, 2011–. Non-exec. Dir, Brighton and Sussex Univ. Hosps NHS Trust, 2013–15. Mem. Bd, Creative Skillset, Learning and Skills Council for creative industries, 2011–15. Pres., Inst. Practitioners in Advertising, 2003–05; Pres. and Trustee, Nat. Advertising Benevolent Soc., 2009–12. Trustee: Changing Faces Charity, 2003–15 (Chm., 2003–07); History of Advertising Trust, 2015–. *Recreations*: family, riding, running, the countryside. *Address*: Advertising Association, 7th Floor North, Artillery House, 11–19 Artillery Row, SW1P 1RT.

**WOODFORD-HOLLICK, Susan Mary;** *see* Hollick, Lady.

**WOODGATE, Terence Allan,** RDI 2003; furniture and lighting designer; *b* 5 Feb. 1953; *s* of Charles and Ethel Woodgate; *m* 1979, Paula Casey; two *s*. *Educ*: Westminster Coll.. London Coll. of Furniture. Work exhibited in perm. collections of Museu d'Art Decoratives, Barcelona and V&A Mus. British Design Award, Design Council, 1992; Red Dot Best of the Best Award, Design Zentrum Nordrhein Westfalen, Germany, 1992; Industrie Form Ecology Award, Germany, 1995. *T*: 07798 813095. *E*: terence@terencewoodgate.com. *W*: www.studiowoodgate.com.

**WOODHALL, David Massey,** CBE 1992; Partner, The Woodhall Consultancy, 1992–2010; *b* 25 Aug. 1934; *s* of Douglas J. D. and Esme Dorothy Woodhall; *m* 1954, Margaret A. Howarth; two *s*. *Educ*: Bishop Holgate's Sch., Barnsley; Royds Hall, Huddersfield; Henley Administrative Staff Coll. Dip. Leeds Sch. of Architecture and Town Planning. West Riding CC, 1951–60; Cumberland CC, 1960–63; Northamptonshire CC, 1963–82: County Planning Officer, 1971–80; Asst Chief Executive, 1980–82; Chief Exec., Commn for New Towns, 1982–92. Dir, Adnams Co. plc, 1986–2006. Consultant, Caws and Morris, Chartered Surveyors, 1992–2004. A Countryside Comr, 1996–99; Mem., Countryside Agency, 1999–2001. *Recreations*: National Hunt racing, landscape, food and wine. *Address*: 2 Hardingstone Lane, Hardingstone, Northampton NN4 6DE. *T*: (01604) 764654.

**WOODHALL, Gary; His Honour Judge Woodhall;** a Circuit Judge, since 2018; *b* Hartlepool, 11 Jan. 1975; *s* of Dennis and Margaret Woodhall; *m* 2002, Rachael Elizabeth; one *s*. *Educ*: Billingham Campus Sch.; Trinity Hall, Cambridge (BA 1996). Called to the Bar, Gray's Inn, 1997; a Recorder, 2016–18. *Recreations*: theatre, acting, reading, music. *Address*: Queen Elizabeth II Law Courts, Derby Square, Liverpool L2 1XA.

**WOODHAM, Prof. Jonathan Michael;** Professor of History of Design, 1993–2015, now Emeritus, Director, Centre for Research Development (Arts and Architecture), 1998–2015, Director of Research and Development (Arts and Humanities), 2012–15, and Associate Head, School of Architecture and Design, 2016–17, University of Brighton; international consultant and research advisor for design history and design studies agendas, since 2017; *b* 8 June 1950; *s* of Ronald Ernest Woodham and Kathleen Isabel Woodham (*née* Malone); *m* 1981, Amanda Grace Callan Smith; two *s*. *Educ*: Downside Sch.; Edinburgh Coll. of Art, Univ. of Edinburgh (MA 1st cl. Hons (Fine Art) 1973); Courtauld Inst. of Art, London (MA (British Romantic Art) 1974). Lectr, 1974–75, Sen. Lectr, 1975–82, in Hist. of Art and Design, Staffordshire Polytech.; Brighton Polytechnic, later University of Brighton: Course Dir, Hist. of Design, 1982–93; Dir, Design Hist. Res. Centre, 1993–2001. Member: Hist. of Art and Design Bd, 1984–87, Register of Special Advrs, 1987–92, CNAA; Quality Assessment Panel, 1996–98, RAE Panel, 2001, HEFCE; Postgrad. Qualifications Res. Panel, Visual Arts & Media, AHRB, 1998–2004; Bd, Internat. Conference for Design Hist. and Design Studies, 1999–; AHRC Peer Review Coll., 2004–15; ESRC Peer Review Coll., 2010–; Social Scis and Humanities Res. Council Canada, 2008, 2011; Icelandic Res. Fund, 2011, 2012; Panel Mem., AHRC Block Grant Partnerships, 2011; AHRC Strategic Reviewer, 2011–15. Mem., Hong Kong Accreditation Council, 1987–2008; Expert Scientific Adviser: Culture and Soc. Panel, Acad. of Finland, 2003–09 and 2016; Political Sci. Panel, Acad. of Finland, 2017. Chm., Design Hist. Soc., 1995–97. Member, Editorial Board: Jl of Design History, 1987–2004 (Mem., Editl Adv. Bd, 2004–); Design Issues, 1994–; Art Design and Communication in Higher Educn, 2002–10; Design History (Japan), 2003–; Animation: an Interdisciplinary Jl, 2006–15; Jl of Media and Communications, 2012–. *Publications*: The Industrial Designer and the Public, 1983; Twentieth-Century Ornament, 1991; Twentieth-Century Design, 1997; Design and Popular Politics in the Postwar Period: the Britain Can Make It Exhibition 1946, 1999; Oxford Dictionary of Modern Design, 2004; (ed jtly) Image, Power and Space: studies in consumption and identity, 2007; (ed jtly) Art and Design at Brighton 1859–2009: from arts and manufactures to the creative and cultural industries, 2009; Jiří Pelcl - Czech Design, 2012; contribs to jls, incl. Jl of Design Hist., Design Issues, Design Hist. Japan, Temes de Disseny, L'Arca, Design, Crafts, and Architecture, Design and Culture, and to Procs British Acad. 2010. *Recreations*: cookery, gardening, travel, drinking wine, voluntary work for the Real Junk Food Project, Brighton. *Address*: 116 Hollingbury Park Avenue, Brighton BN1 7JP. *T*: (01273) 506319. *E*: j.m.woodham@brighton.ac.uk.

**WOODHAMS, Stephen Robert;** designer (gardens and exteriors); design director, since 1990; Founder, Stephen Woodhams Design Ltd, London and Ibiza, since 2008; *b* 17 July 1964; *s* of late Robert and Joy Woodhams. *Educ*: RHS Certificate. Paul Temple Ltd, 1982; buyer, Moyses Stevens, 1984; Dir, Horticultural Innovations, 1986; Founder, Woodhams Ltd, 1990–2007, Woodhams Landscapes Ltd, 1994–2007. Accredited RHS Judge, 2009. *Publications*: Flower Power, 1999; Portfolio of Contemporary Gardens, 2000; Garden Design Solutions, 2015. *Recreations*: photography, running. *T*: (020) 7735 3798. *E*: stephen@stephenwoodhams.com. *Club*: Blacks.

**WOODHEAD, Vice-Adm. Sir (Anthony) Peter,** KCB 1992; DL; Prisons' Ombudsman, 1994–99; *b* 30 July 1939; *s* of Leslie and Nancy Woodhead; *m* 1st, 1964, Carol (*d* 2016); one *s* one *d*; 2nd, 2018, Margaret. *Educ*: Leeds Grammar Sch.; Conway; BRNC Dartmouth. Seaman Officer; Pilot, 1962; Aircraft Carriers, Borneo Campaign; CO, HM Ships Jupiter, 1974, Rhyl, 1975; NDC 1976; Naval Plans Div., MoD, 1977; CSO to Flag Officer, Third Flotilla, 1980; COS to FO Comdg Falklands Task Force, 1982; Captain, Fourth Frigate Sqdn, 1983; RCDS 1984; Dir, Naval Ops, 1985; CO HMS Illustrious, 1986; Flag Officer: Flotilla Two, 1988; Flotilla One, 1989. Dep. SACLANT, 1991–93. Lay Reader: Guildford, 1991; Chichester, 1997. Pres., Marriage Resource, 1995–2004. Dep. Chm., BMT, 1996–2011. Chm., Crime Reduction Initiatives, 2001–10; Member: Security Vetting Appeals Panel, 1997–2009; Armed Forces Pay Review Body, 2001–04. Dir, Beaconlight Trust, 2004–13. Gov., Aldro Sch., 1996–2013; Trustee, Kainos prison therapeutic community, 1999–2013. DL E Sussex, 2012. *Recreation*: ball games. *Club*: Royal Navy of 1765 and 1785.

**WOODHEAD, David James;** education consultant, 2004–15; National Director, Independent Schools Council Information Service (formerly Independent Schools Information Service), 1985–2004; Deputy General Secretary, Independent Schools Council, 1998–2004; *b* 9 Nov. 1943; *s* of late Frank and Polly Woodhead; *m* 1974, Carole Underwood; two *s*. *Educ*: Queen Elizabeth Grammar Sch., Wakefield; Univ. of Leicester (BA Hons). Journalist: Cambridge Evening News (educn corresp.), 1965–68; Sunday Telegraph, 1968–75; ILEA Press Office: Press Officer, 1975–78; Chief Press Officer, 1978–85; Hon. Press Officer, London Schs Symphony Orch., 1975–84. Led UK Repn at first internat. conf. on private schs in China, Beijing, 1999. Trustee: Jt Educnl Trust, 1988–2004; Oratory Gp, 1995–98; EAC Educnl Trust, 2005–13; Founder-Trustee, Nat. Youth String Orch. (formerly Nat. ISIS Strings Acad., then Nat. Youth Strings Acad.), 1995–. Mem., Dresden Trust, 1994– (Trustee, 2005–18; Jt Vice Chm., 2011–13; Founder, Dresden Scholars' Scheme, 2001). Member: NW Herts Community Health Council, 1976–79; Adv. Develt Bd, Rudolf Kempe Soc. for Young Musicians, 2000– (Trustee, 2004–); Adv. Bd, Global Educn Mgt Systems Ltd, 2005–07 (Special Advr, 2007–09); British-German Assoc. Youthbridge Cttee, 2008–17; European Movement Surrey Cttee, 2015–. University of Leicester: Schs and Colls Liaison Consultant, 2005–15; Mem. Council, 2000–09; Mem. Court, 2000–09; Life Mem. Court, 2009. Consultant, Cherwell Schs Gp, 2010–12. Governor: Battle Abbey Sch., 1988–91; St John's Sch., Leatherhead, 1994–2011 (Vice-Chm., 2006–11; Chm., Educn Cttee, 2001–10); Feltonfleet Prep. Sch., Cobham, 1998–2001; City of London Sch. for Girls, 2002–06; Purcell Sch., 2004–13; Hon. Gov., Wakefield Grammar Sch. Foundn, 2004–09. FRSA 1990. Medal of Honour, Soc. for Reconstruction of the Frauenkirche, Dresden, 2007. *Publications*: Choosing Your Independent School, annually, 1985–99; (ed) Good Communications Guide, 1986, 2nd edn 1989; The ISC Guide to Accredited Independent Schools, annually, 2000–04; (contrib.) Education in the UK, 2002; (ed jtly and contrib.) A Trust for Our Times: the story of the Dresden Trust, 2015; numerous newspaper and magazine articles and letters. *Recreations*: family, classical music, opera (a Wagner fanatic), books, German and Austrian history, travel.

**WOODHEAD, Prof. Linda Jane Pauline,** MBE 2013; Professor of Sociology of Religion, since 2006, and Director, Institute for Social Futures, since 2015, Lancaster University; *b* Taunton, 15 Feb. 1964; *d* of Ronald Woodhead and Penelope Woodhead; *m* 2007, Alexander Mercer. *Educ*: Richard Huish Coll., Taunton; Emmanuel Coll., Cambridge (BA Theol. and Religious Studies 1985). Lectr, Ripon Coll., Cuddesdon, 1988–92; Lancaster University: Lectr, 1992–2000; Sen. Lectr, 2000–06. Dir, AHRC/ESRC Religion and Society Prog., 2007–13; Mem., ESRC, 2013–16. Co-Founder and Organiser, Westminster Faith Debates, 2012–. Pres., Modern Church, 2014–20. FAcSS, 2016; Fellow, Internat. Soc. for Sci. and Religion, 2017–. Hon. DD Uppsala 2009; Hon. PhD: Zurich 2014; MF Norwegian Sch. of Theol., 2017; Agder 2017. *Publications*: (ed jtly) Diana: the making of a media icon, 1999; (ed jtly) Religion in Modern Times, 2000; (ed) Reinventing Christianity: nineteenth century contexts, 2001; (ed jtly) Religions in the Modern World: traditions and transformations, 2002, 2nd edn 2009; (ed) Peter Berger and the Study of Religion, 2002; (ed jtly) Predicting Religion, 2003; (ed jtly) Congregational Studies in the UK, 2004; Christianity: a very short introduction, 2004; An Introduction to Christianity, 2004; (with Paul Heelas) The Spiritual Revolution, 2005; (with Ole Riis) A Sociology of Religious Emotions, 2010; (ed with Rebecca Catto) Religion and Change in Modern Britain, 2012; (ed jtly) Everyday Lived Islam in Europe, 2013; (ed) The Westminster Faith Debates, 2013; (ed jtly) A Sociology of Prayer, 2015; (with Andrew Brown) That Was the Church that Was, 2016. *Recreations*: friends and social media, American muscle cars, fashion, gardening, sleeping. *Address*: Department of Politics, Philosophy and Religion, Lancaster University LA1 4YD. *T*: (01524) 510819. *E*: l.woodhead@lancaster.ac.uk.

**WOODHEAD, Prof. Martin,** PhD; Professor of Childhood Studies, Open University, 2003–14, now Emeritus; *b* Birmingham, 4 Dec. 1949; *s of* Maurice Woodhead and Eunice Woodhead; *m* 1974, Judith M. Park; three *s* one *d. Educ:* Moseley Grammar Sch., Birmingham; Univ. of Manchester (BA 1st Cl. Hons Psychol. 1971); Univ. of Leicester (MA 1972); Open Univ. (PhD 1984). NFER, 1973–77; Faculty of Educn, Open Univ., 1977–2014. Sen. Associate, Univ. of Oxford/Young Lives Study, 2005–. Advr, All Our Children, BBC TV series, 1984–90; Consultant, UN Cttee on the Rights of the Child, 2005; Chm., Adv. Bd, Early Childhood Prog., Open Soc. Foundn, 2008–15; Trustee, UNICEF UK, 2012– (Vice Chm., 2014–18). Co-Editor, Children and Society Jl, 2003–11. *Publications:* Intervening in Disadvantage, 1976; Pre-school Education in Western Europe, 1979; In Search of the Rainbow, 1996; (ed jtly) Cultural Worlds of Early Childhood, 1998; (ed jtly) Changing Childhoods: local and global, 2003. *E:* martinwoodhead@me.com.

**WOODHEAD, Vice-Adm. Sir Peter;** *see* Woodhead, Vice-Adm. Sir A. P.

**WOODHEAD, Robin George;** Chairman, Sotheby's International, since 2008 (Chief Executive, 2000–08); *b* 28 April 1951; *s of* Walter Henry Woodhead and Gladys Catherine (*née* Ferguson); *m* 1980, Mary Fitzgerald Allen, *qv* (marr. diss. 1991). *Educ:* Mt Pleasant Sch., Salisbury, Rhodesia; UC of Rhodesia and Nyasaland (LLB Hons London ext.). Admitted Solicitor, 1978; Man. Dir, Premier Man Ltd, 1980–86; Chief Executive: Nat. Investment Gp, 1986–90; London Commodity Exchange, 1991–97; Man. Dir, 1998–99, Chief Exec., 1999–2000, Sotheby's Europe; Chief Exec., Sotheby's Europe and Asia, 2000–06. Chairman: Internat. Petroleum Exchange, 1980–86; Hofesh Shechter Co., 2008–. Chairman: Rambert Dance Co., 1995–2000; Music Research Inst., 1997–2000. Dep. Chm. and Gov., S Bank Centre, 2004–. Trustee and Chm., David Rattray Meml Trust, 2007–; Trustee, African Arts Trust, 2011–. *Recreations:* game reserve development in Zululand, riding, music, visual arts, performing arts. *Address:* Sotheby's, 34–35 New Bond Street, W1A 2AA. *T:* (020) 7293 6066.

**WOODHOUSE,** family name of **Baron Terrington.**

**WOODHOUSE, Rev. Canon Alison Ruth;** Vicar, St Luke's, Formby, 1995–2007; Chaplain to the Queen, 2005–13; *b* 14 Aug. 1943; *d of* Harold and May Woodhouse. *Educ:* Bedford Coll. of Educn (Cert Ed 1964); DipTh London Univ. 1971 (ext.). Primary sch. teacher, Huncoat CP Sch., Accrington, 1964–68; licensed as Parish Worker, Lichfield dio., 1971; ordained deaconess, 1978, deacon, 1987, priest, 1994; Parish Deacon, then Curate, Burscough Bridge, 1987–95; Area Dean, Sefton, 2000–05. Hon. Canon, Liverpool Cathedral, 2002–07, now Canon Emeritus. *Recreations:* family history research, reading, music, walking. *Address:* 16 Fountains Way, Liverpool L37 4HF.

**WOODHOUSE, Ven. Andrew Henry,** DSC 1945; MA; Archdeacon of Hereford and Canon Residentiary, Hereford Cathedral, 1982–91, now Archdeacon Emeritus; *b* 30 Jan. 1923; *s of* H. A. Woodhouse, Dental Surgeon, Hanover Square, W1, and Woking, Surrey, and Mrs P. Woodhouse; unmarried. *Educ:* Lancing Coll.; The Queen's Coll., Oxford. MA 1949. Served War, RNVR, 1942–46 (Lieut). Oxford, 1941–42 and 1946–47; Lincoln Theological Coll., 1948–50. Deacon, 1950; Priest, 1951; Curate of All Saints, Poplar, 1950–56; Vicar of St Martin, West Drayton, 1956–70; Rural Dean of Hillingdon, 1967–70; Archdeacon of Ludlow and Rector of Wistanstow, 1970–82. *Recreations:* photography, walking. *Address:* Orchard Cottage, Bracken Close, Woking, Surrey GU22 7HD. *T:* (01483) 760671. *Club:* Naval.
*See also* R. M. Woodhouse.

**WOODHOUSE, Ven. (Charles) David (Stewart);** Archdeacon of Warrington, 1981–2001, now Emeritus; Vicar of St Peter's, Hindley, 1981–92; *b* 23 Dec. 1934; *s of* Rev. Hector and Elsie Woodhouse. *Educ:* Silcoates School, Wakefield; Kelham Theological College; Lancaster Univ. (MA 1995). Curate of St Wilfrid's, Halton, Leeds, 1959–63; Youth Chaplain, Kirkby Team Ministry, Diocese of Liverpool, 1963–66; Curate of St John's, Pembroke, Bermuda, 1966–69; Asst Gen. Secretary, CEMS, 1969–70; Gen. Sec., 1970–76; Rector of Ideford, Ashcombe and Luton and Domestic Chaplain to Bishop of Exeter, 1976–81. Hon. Canon, Liverpool Cathedral, 1983. *Address:* 8 Upton Close, Lowton WA3 2JS.

**WOODHOUSE, Charles Frederick,** CVO 1998; DL; Partner, Farrer and Co., Solicitors, 1969–99 (Consultant, 1999–2001); Solicitor to the Duke of Edinburgh, 1983–2001; *b* 6 June 1941; *s of* late Wilfrid Meynell Woodhouse and Peggy Woodhouse (*née* Kahl); *m* 1969, Margaret Joan Cooper (*d* 2017); one *s* two *d. Educ:* Marlborough; McGill Univ.; Peterhouse, Cambridge (BA Hons 1963; MA Hons). Hon. Legal Advr, Commonwealth Games Council for England, 1983–2007; Legal Advr, CCPR, 1971–99 (Mem., Inquiry on Amateur Status, 1986–88). Pres., British Assoc. for Sport and Law, 1997–2000; Founder and Chm., Sports Dispute Resolution Panel, 1997–2007. Dir, Santos USA Corp., 1992–2002. Chm., Rural Regeneration Cumbria, 2003–06; Dir, Cumbria Vision Ltd (formerly Cumbria Vision Renaissance Ltd), 2006–08. Mem., Royal Parks Rev. Gp, 1992–96. Chairman: Cheviot Trust, 1991–97; Rank Pension Plan Trustee Ltd, 1992–2001; Trustee: Mulberry Trust, 1988–; Aim Foundn, 1988–2007; LSA Charitable Trust, 1991–2016; Brian Johnston Meml Trust, 1996–99; Yehudi Menuhin Meml Trust, 1999–2001; Cumbria Community Foundn, 2002–08; Hospice at Home, Carlisle and N Lakeland, 2002–11; Athletics Foundn, 2004–15; Lowther Castle and Gardens Trust, 2007–11. Governor: Nelson Thomlinson Sch., Wigton, 2003–11; St Bees Sch., 2004–08. DL Cumbria, 2007. *Publications:* articles on sports law, incl. The Law and Sport, 1972; The Role of the Lawyer in Sport, 1993; contrib. to Jl British Assoc. for Sport and Law. *Recreations:* cricket, golf, gardens and trees, Owen's Southsea, Cumbria's historic environment, writing (Mem., Mungrisdale Writers). *Address:* Quarry Hill House, Boltongate, Mealsgate, Cumbria CA7 1AE. *T:* (01697) 371225. *E:* cfwoodhouse@btinternet.com. *Clubs:* Oxford and Cambridge, MCC; Hawks (Cambridge); Worplesdon Golf; Silloth on Solway Golf (Capt., 2010); Aldeburgh Golf; Free Foresters, Guildford Cricket (Pres., 1991–2002); Surrey County Cricket, Lord's Taverners.

**WOODHOUSE, Ven. David;** *see* Woodhouse, Ven. C. D. S.

**WOODHOUSE, James Stephen;** Director, ISIS East, 1994–2000; *b* 21 May 1933; *s of* late Rt Rev. J. W. Woodhouse, sometime Bishop of Thetford, and late Mrs K. M. Woodhouse; *m* 1957, Sarah, *d of* late Col Hubert Blount, Cley, Norfolk; three *s* one *d. Educ:* St Edward's Sch.; St Catharine's Coll., Cambridge. BA (English) Cantab, 1957; MA 1961. Nat. Service, 14th Field Regt RA, 1953. Asst Master, Westminster Sch., 1957; Under Master and Master of the Queen's Scholars, 1963; Headmaster, Rugby Sch., 1967–81; Headmaster, Lancing Coll., 1981–93. Chairman: NABC Religious Adv. Cttee, 1971–93; Bloxham Project, 1972–77; Head Masters' Conf., 1979; Joint Standing Cttee of HMC, IAPS and GSA, 1981–86; Vice-Chm., E-SU Schoolboy Scholarship Cttee, 1973–77. Director: The Norfolk Boat, 1993–2012; Holkham Pageant, 1994. Mem. Council (formerly Cttee of Mgt), RNLI, 1994–2006. Trustee and Dir, Assoc. for Educn and Guardianship of Internat. Students, 2001–13. Gov., Norwich Cathedral Inst., 2000–11. *Recreations:* sailing, music, hill walking. *Address:* Welcome Cottage, Wiveton, Holt, Norfolk NR25 7TH.

**WOODHOUSE, Prof. John Henry,** PhD; FRS 2000; Professor of Geophysics, 1990–2014, now Emeritus, and Head of Department of Earth Sciences, 2000–03, 2011–12, University of Oxford; Fellow of Worcester College, Oxford, 1990–2014; *b* 15 April 1949; *s of* G. B. Woodhouse. *Educ:* Southall Grammar Sch.; Bristol Univ. (BSc 1970); King's Coll., Cambridge (MA, PhD 1975). Fellow, King's Coll., Cambridge, 1974–78; Vis. Asst Res. Geophysicist, Inst. of Geophysics and Planetary Physics, Univ. of Calif., San Diego, 1976–77; Asst Prof., 1978–80, Associate Prof., 1980–83, Prof. of Geophysics, 1983–90, Harvard Univ. Chm., Commn on Seismological Theory, Internat. Assoc. of Seismol. and Physics of Earth's Interior, 1983–87. Fellow, Amer. Geophys. Union (Macelwane Award, 1984; Inge Lehmann Medal, 2001). Beno Gutenberg Medal, Eur. Geoscis Union, 2008; Gold Medal for Geophysics, RAS, 2010. *Publications:* many contribs to learned jls. *Address:* Department of Earth Sciences, Parks Road, Oxford OX1 3AN; Worcester College, Oxford OX1 2HB.

**WOODHOUSE, Prof. John Robert,** FBA 1995; Fiat Serena Professor of Italian Studies, Oxford, 1989–2001; Fellow, Magdalen College, Oxford, 1990–2001, now Emeritus; *b* 17 June 1937; *s of* Horace Woodhouse and Iris Evelyn Pewton; *m* 1967, Gaynor Mathias. *Educ:* King Edward VI Grammar School, Stourbridge; Hertford College, Oxford (MA, DLitt); Univ. of Pisa; PhD Wales. Nat. Service, RAF, 1955–57. Asst Lectr in Italian, Univ. of Aberdeen, 1961–62; British Council Scholar, Scuola Normale Superiore, Pisa, 1962–63; Asst Lectr and Lectr, UCNW, Bangor, 1963–66; Lectr and Sen. Lectr, Univ. of Hull, 1966–73; Oxford University: Univ. Lectr in Italian and Fellow of St Cross Coll., 1973–84; Lectr at Jesus Coll., 1973, St Edmund Hall, 1975, Brasenose Coll., 1976; Fellow, 1984–89, Supernumerary Fellow, 1991, Pembroke Coll.; Founding Chm., Oxford Italian Assoc., 1990–2010. Harvard Old Dominion Foundn Fellow, Villa I Tatti, 1969; Founding Fellow, Centro Studi Dannunziani, Pescara, 1979; Corresponding Fellow: Accad. lett. ital. dell'Arcadia, 1980; Accad. della Crusca, 1991; Commissione per i Testi di Lingua, Bologna, 1992; Sen. Res. Fellow, Center for Medieval and Renaissance Studies, UCLA, 1985; Fellow: Huntington Liby, Calif., 1986; Newberry Liby, Chicago, 1988. Mem., Exec. Cttee, Soc. for Italian Studies, 1979–85 and 1989–95; Pres., MHRA, 2008 (Mem., Exec. Cttee, 1984–94; Hon. Life Mem., 1994). Editor (Italian), Modern Language Review, 1984–94; Mem., Editl Bd, Italian Studies, 1987–91. Gov., British Inst. of Florence, 1991–2001. Serena Medal, British Academy, 2002. Cavaliere Ufficiale, Order of Merit (Italy), 1991. *Publications:* Italo Calvino: a reappraisal and an appreciation of the trilogy, 1968; (ed) Italo Calvino, Il barone rampante, 1970; (ed) V. Borghini, Scritti inediti o rari sulla lingua, 1971; (ed) V. Borghini, Storia della nobiltà fiorentina, 1974; Baldesar Castiglione, a reassessment of the Cortegiano, 1978; (ed) G. D'Annunzio, Alcyone, 1978; (ed with P. R. Horne) G. Rossetti, Lettere familiari, 1983; (ed jtly) G. Rossetti, Carteggi, I, 1984, II, 1988, III, 1992, IV, 1996, V, 2002, VI, 2006; (ed jtly) The Languages of Literature in Renaissance Italy, 1988; From Castiglione to Chesterfield: the decline in the courtier's manual, 1991; (ed) Dante and Governance, 1997; Gabriele D'Annunzio: defiant archangel, 1998 (trans. Italian, 1999; Premio D'Annunzio, 2000); Gabriele D'Annunzio tra Italia e Inghilterra, 2003; Il Generale e il Comandante: Checcherini e D'Annunzio a Fiume, 2004; L'Ottavo Giurato: Giuseppe Sovera con D'Annunzio a Fiume, 2008; articles in learned jls. *Recreation:* gardening. *Address:* Magdalen College, Oxford OX1 4AU.

**WOODHOUSE, Rev. Jonathan,** CB 2014; Chaplain-General, HM Land Forces, 2011–14; Chaplain, and MA Tutor in Ethics and Chaplaincy, Moorlands College, since 2015; *b* Cardiff, 29 March 1955; *s of* Herbert and Joan Woodhouse; *m* 1978, Jackie Evetts; one *s* one *d. Educ:* Whitchurch Grammar Sch.; London Bible Coll.; Spurgeon's Coll.; BA Hons CNAA; Open Univ. (BSc); MTh Wales. Ordained to Baptist Ministry, 1980; Asst Minister, Eastbourne, 1980–85; Minister, Selsdon, 1985–90; Regtl Chaplain in Germany, Cyprus, UK and Hong Kong, 1990–2000; Chaplain, HQ Land Comd, 2000–01; Staff Chaplain to Chaplain Gen., Upavon, 2001–02; Senior Chaplain: 16 Air Assault Bde, Colchester, 2002–05; RMA Sandhurst, 2005–06; Asst Chaplain-Gen., Germany, 2006–08; Dep. Chaplain-Gen., 2008–11. Convenor, United Navy, Army and Air Force Bd, 2015–. QHC 2008–14. *Recreations:* enjoyable interest in Cardiff City FC, Welsh Rugby, England cricket, downhill ski-ing at a Padre's pace. *Address:* Henbury, New Inn Road, Bartley, Hampshire SO40 2LR. *T:* (023) 8081 3776. *E:* jonandjackie@hotmail.com.

**WOODHOUSE, Prof. Kenneth Walter,** MD; FRCP; Professor of Geriatric Medicine, 1990–2012, now Emeritus, and Professor of Medicine, 2010–12, now Emeritus, School of Medicine, Cardiff University (formerly University of Wales College of Medicine); *b* 18 July 1954; *s of* Walter and Marion Woodhouse; *m* 1994, Judith Paul; three *s. Educ:* Southampton University Med. Sch. (BM Hons 1977); Univ. of Newcastle upon Tyne (MD 1985). FRCP 1990. MRC Trng Fellow, 1980–83; MRC Travelling Fellow, Karolinska Inst., 1984–85; Sen. Lectr in Medicine (Geriatrics) and Clinical Pharmacol., and Consultant Physician, Univ. of Newcastle upon Tyne, 1985–90; University of Wales College of Medicine (later School of Medicine, Cardiff University): Vice Dean of Medicine, 1997–2000; Dean of Medicine, 2000–04; Pro Vice-Chancellor, 2004–10. Member: Cttee on Safety of Medicines, 1998–2005; Pharmacovigilance Cttee, MHRA, 2006–12; Chm., Nat. Commng Bd, Health Commn Wales, 2002–08. *Publications:* (ed jtly) Topics in Ageing Research in Europe, vol. 13, The Liver, Metabolism and Ageing, 1989; (with J. Pascual) Hypertension in Elderly People, 1996; (with M. Hasan) Managing Hypertension in Practice, Book 2, The Elderly Hypertensive Patient, 1997; (ed jtly) Drug Therapy in Old Age, 1998; (ed jtly) Brocklehurst's Textbook of Geriatric Medicine and Gerontology, 2010. *Recreations:* hill walking, scout leader, science fiction.

**WOODHOUSE, Michael;** *see* Woodhouse, R. M.

**WOODHOUSE, Prof. the Hon. Nicholas Michael John,** PhD; FInstP, FIMA; Professor of Mathematics, University of Oxford, 2006–10, now Emeritus (Chairman of Mathematics, 2001–10; Deputy Head, Mathematical, Physical and Life Sciences Division, 2011–12); Fellow of Wadham College, Oxford, 1977–2016, now Emeritus (Sub-Warden, 2014–16); President, Clay Mathematics Institute, since 2012; *b* Knebworth, Herts, 27 Feb. 1949; *s of* 5th Baron Terrington, DSO, OBE and Lady Davina Woodhouse (*née* Lytton), *widow of* 5th Earl of Erne; *m* 1973, Mary Jane Stormont Mowat, *qv*; one *s. Educ:* Christ Church, Oxford (BA 1970); King's Coll. London (MSc 1971; PhD 1973). FInstP 2002; FIMA 2004. University of Oxford: Lectr, 1977–97; Reader, 1997–2006; Sen. Tutor, Wadham Coll., 1982–86; Mem., North Commn of Inquiry, 1994. Fellow, Eton Coll., 1995–2007. Mem. Council, 2008–2009, Treas., 2002–09, London Mathematical Soc.; Pres., Clay Math. Inst., 2012–18. *Publications:* Geometric Quantization, 1979, 2nd edn 1991; Introduction to Analytical Dynamics, 1987; (with L. J. Mason) Integrability, Self-duality, and Twistor Theory, 1995; Special Relativity, 2003; General Relativity, 2007. *Recreations:* walking, gardening. *Address:* Wadham College, Oxford OX1 3PN. *T:* (01865) 277900. *E:* Nick.Woodhouse@maths.ox.ac.uk.
*See also* Baron Terrington.

**WOODHOUSE, (Ronald) Michael,** CVO 2000; Chairman, Rexam PLC (formerly Bowater), 1993–96 (Director, 1988–96); Chairman, Prince's Trust Volunteers, 1991–2000; *b* 19 Aug. 1927; *s of* Henry Alfred Woodhouse and Phyllis Woodhouse (*née* Gemmell); *m* 1955, Quenilda Mary (*d* 1997), *d of* Rt Rev. Neville Vincent Gorton; one *s* three *d. Educ:* Lancing Coll.; Queen's Coll., Oxford (BA Mod. History). Courtaulds plc, 1951–91: Dir,

1976–91; Dep. Chm., 1986–91; Man. Dir, 1972–79, Chm., 1979–84, Internat. Paint Co.; Chm., British Cellophane Ltd, 1979–86. A Director: RSA Exam. Board, 1991–95; RSA Exams and Assessment Foundn, 1995–97; Mem., Prince's Trust Council, 1995–2000. Dir, London Mozart Players, 1990–97; Mem. Council of Mgt, Friends of Royal Acad., 1996–2003; Trustee, Royal Acad. Pension Fund, 1997–2003. CCMI (CBIM 1978); FRSA 1979. *Recreations:* walking in Lake District, watching Rugby and cricket, opera, music, gardening, art, reading. *Address:* Tankards, Wonersh, Guildford, Surrey GU5 0PF. *T:* (01483) 892078; Dalehead, Hartsop, Patterdale, Cumbria CA11 0NZ. *Clubs:* Carlton; Vincent's (Oxford).

*See also Ven. A. H. Woodhouse.*

**WOODING JONES, Ven. Andrew David;** Archdeacon of Rochester, since 2018; *b* Manchester, 17 Aug. 1961; *s* of Gerald and Joan Wooding Jones; *m* 1986, Margaret Olley; one *s* one *d*. *Educ:* Skinners' Sch., Tunbridge Wells; Huddersfield Poly. (HND Hotel and Catering Admin); Oak Hill Theol Coll. (BA Theol and Pastoral Studies 1991); Univ. of Hull (MBA Church and Charity Mgt 2001). Ordained deacon, 1991, priest, 1992; Curate, St John's, Welling, 1991–95; Team Vicar, St Thomas', Crookes, Sheffield, 1995–2000; Resident Dir, Ashburnham Christian Trust, 2000–12; Curate, Ashburnham and Penshurst, 2001–12; Chief Exec., World Prayer Centre, Birmingham, 2012–14; Dir, Incognito Sussex, 2014–18; permission to officiate, Dio. of Rochester, 2014–18. Advocate, Small Missional Communities, Lee Abbey, 2017–. *Publications:* Running the Race Marked Out for Us, 2009. *Recreations:* running, reading, being outdoors. *Address:* Diocese of Rochester, St Nicholas Church, Boley Hill, Rochester, Kent ME1 1SL. *T:* (01634) 560000. *E:* andrew.wooding.jones@rochester.anglican.org; Lytlewood, Riding Lane, Hildenborough, Kent TN11 9LR.

**WOODLEY, Anthony;** Adviser, Unite the Union, since 2013 (Executive Officer, 2011–13; Joint General Secretary, 2007–11; General Secretary, Transport and General Workers' Union, 2003–07, on merger with Amicus); *b* 2 Jan. 1948; *s* of George Woodley. Ellesmere Port factory, Vauxhall Motors, 1967–89; Dist Official, 1989–91, Nat. Official, 1991–2002, Dep. Gen. Sec., 2002–03, TGWU. *Address:* Unite the Union, Unite House, 128 Theobalds Road, WC1X 8TN.

**WOODLEY, Karin Lee;** Chief Executive, Cambridge House, since 2013; *b* London, 11 Aug. 1961; *d* of late Wilfred Trevor Woodley and Hon. Juliet Priscilla Mary Duncombe; one *s*; *m* 2008, Michael Kenneth Herbert (marr. diss. 2015). *Educ:* Goldsmiths Coll., Univ. of London (BMus Hons 1982). Chief Exec., Minorities' Arts Adv. Service, 1985–89; Partner, Keya Associates, 1987–90; Dep. Dir, Camden Arts Centre, 1990–2000; Dir, Tabernacle Centre for Arts and Learning, 2000–05; Chief Executive: Stephen Lawrence Charitable Trust, 2005–09; ContinYou, 2010–13. Mem., ESRC, 2015–18. Director: Inst. of Race Relns, 1984–87; Cultural Partnerships Ltd, 1985–88; Nat. Campaign for the Arts Ltd, 1985–89; Chair: (and Founder) Haringey Black Arts Forum, 1983–87; Haringey Arts Council, 1984–89; (and Founder) Arts Media Gp, 1985–90; Black Art Gall., 1989–93; Funding Panel, Royal Bor. of Kensington and Chelsea Neighbourhood Renewal Fund, 2003; (and Founder) Race Equality Partnership, Kensington and Chelsea, 2004–08; Vice Chair: W Midlands Ethnic Minority Arts Service, 1984–89; London South Bank Univ. Student Union, 2014–18; Community Southwark, 2015–; non-executive Director: Legal Services Bd Consumer Panel, 2009–13; Office of the Public Guardian, 2018–; Advisory Member: Educn Cttee, Royal Opera House, 1988–91; Credit Framework Steering Gp, Learning Skills Council, 2002–05; Member: Exec. Cttee, GLAA, 1988–92; Exec. Cttee, British-Amer. Proj., 1999–2001; Community Advr, Scotland Yard Gold Task Gp for Notting Hill Carnival Policing Strategy, 2001–05. Trustee: Metronomes Steel Orch. Ltd, 2004–09; Harrow Club, 2004–07; Locality, 2013–; Magdalene Coll. Youth Trust, 2013–. Visiting Lecturer: Poly. of Central London, 1988; Wolverhampton Poly., 1989; Kingsway Coll., 1991; Univ. of Amsterdam, 1993; Dillard Univ., 2003; Birkbeck, Univ. of London, 2002–05; Siberian Federal Univ., 2010. Associate Trainer, Nat. Police Improvement Assoc., 2010–11. Governor: Coleridge Prim. Sch., 1996–2001 (Treas., 1996–2001); Alexandra Park Comp. Sch., 2003–05. Judge: London Educn Partnership Awards, 2007–08; Business in Community Opportunity Now Awards, 2008–09; Creating the Future Awards, Home and Communities Acad., 2009; Parly Premiership Rugby Community Awards, 2011. Fellow, British-Amer. Proj., 1996; FRSA 2015. Mem., Inst. of Fundraising, 2013. *Publications:* articles in jls incl. Regeneration Mag., British Amer. Arts Assoc. Jl, Black Arts in London mag., Disability Arts in London mag., City Limits mag. *E:* kwoodley@ch1889.org.

**WOODLEY, Keith Spencer,** OBE 2014; FCA; chartered accountant; *b* 23 Oct. 1939; *s* of Charles Spencer Woodley and Hilda Mary Woodley (*née* Brown); *m* 1962, Joyce Madeleine Toon; one *s* two *d*. *Educ:* Stationers' Co. Sch. Articled Clerk, Senior Deloitte Plender Griffiths & Co., 1959–69; Partner, Deloitte Haskins & Sells, 1969–90: Nat. Personnel Partner, 1978–82; Mem., Partnership Bd, 1985–90. Complaints Commissioner: SIB, 1990–95; SFA, 1990–2001; FIMBRA, 1990–2001; LSE, 1994–2009; PIA, 1995–2001; Ind. Investigator, Investors' Compensation Scheme, 1991–2002. Director: Royscot Trust, 1990–96; National & Provincial Building Soc., 1991–96; Abbey National Plc, 1996–2010 (Dep. Chm., 1999–2004); Abbey National Treasury Service Plc, 1998–2002; Alliance & Leicester plc, 2008–10; Santander UK plc, 2010–11. Member Council: ICAEW, 1988–98 (Pres., 1995–96); NACAB, 1991–94 and 1997–99 (Hon. Treas., 1991–94); Univ. of Bath, 1996–2013 (Treas., 2002–07; Pro-Chancellor, 2008–13). Trustee, Methodist Ministers' Pension Scheme, 1998–2016. Gov., Kingswood Sch., Bath, 2004–10. *Recreations:* theatre, music, hill walking. *Address:* 9 Hollytrees, Church Crookham, Fleet, Hants GU51 5NL.

**WOODLEY, Leonard Gaston;** QC 1988. *Educ:* Univ. of London (Dip. Internat. Affairs). Called to the Bar, Inner Temple, 1963, now Bencher; a Recorder, 1989–2000. Called to Trinidad and Tobago Bar. Mem., Royal Commn on Care of the Elderly, 1997–99. Chm., Laudat Enquiry under Mental Health Act; Mem., internat. enquiry into illegal hanging in Trinidad. First black person to be appointed QC and Recorder. Patron, Plan Internat. UK. *Recreations:* sports, music.

**WOODLEY, Sonia;** QC 1996; a Recorder, 1985–2016; *b* 8 Oct. 1946; *d* of Stanley and Mabel Woodley; *m* 1973, Stuart McDonald (marr. diss. 1986; he *d* 2007); two *s* one *d*. *Educ:* Convent High Sch., Southampton. Called to the Bar, Gray's Inn, 1968, Bencher, 2004. *Recreations:* travel, gardening.

**WOODMAN, Ellis James;** Director, Architecture Foundation, since 2015; *b* Lutterworth, 22 July 1972; *s* of Richard Woodman and Veronica Woodman (*née* McNab, now Morriss); civil partnership 2009, Rupert Christiansen. *Educ:* Ardvreck Sch.; Gordonstoun; Robinson Coll., Cambridge (BA Arch. 1993); N London Univ. (DipArch 1997). Architect, Panter Hudspith, 1997–2003; Building Design: Buildings Ed., 2003–09; Dep. Ed., 2009–10; Ed., 2011–14; Architecture Critic, Daily Telegraph, 2017–. Curator, British Pavilion, Venice Architecture Biennale, 2008. Mem., Art Workers' Guild, 2014. Mem., Adv. Cttee, Architects' Lives, British Liby, 2016–. Trustee: Studio Voltaire, 2017–; Docomomo UK, 2017–. *Publications:* Modernity and Reinvention: the architecture of James Gowan, 2008; contrib. architectural criticism to Architectural Rev., Building Design, Architects' Jl. *Recreations:* looking at buildings and art, swimming, opera, cinema, ardent flemophile. *Address:* 6 Offley Road, SW9 0LS. *T:* 07881 858414. *E:* ellis@architecturefoundation.org.uk.

**WOODMAN, Janet;** *see* Beer, J.

**WOODMAN, Rev. Dr Simon Patrick;** Minister, Bloomsbury Central Baptist Church, since 2018 (Joint Minister, 2012–18); *b* Sevenoaks, 5 Aug. 1972; *s* of Colin and Davida Woodman; *m* 1994, Elizabeth Mary Gleed. *Educ:* Judd Sch.; Sheffield Univ. (BA Biblical Studies 1994); Bristol Baptist Coll.; Univ. of Bristol (MLitt 2001); Cardiff Univ. (PhD 2012). Minister, Countersip Baptist Church, Bristol, 1999–2004; Tutor in Biblical Studies, S Wales Baptist Coll., Cardiff, 2004–12; Sen. Hon. Tutor in Biblical Studies, Cardiff Univ., 2004–12. Associate Baptist Chaplain, KCL, 2013–. Jt Editor, Baptist Qly, 2012–. FHEA 2008. *Publications:* The Book of Revelation, 2008; (ed jtly) The 'plainly revealed' Word of God: Baptist hermeneutics in theory and practice, 2011; (ed jtly) Prayers of the People, 2011; (ed jtly) The Book of Revelation: currents in British research on the apocalypse, 2015; (jtly) The Courage to be Baptist: a statement on Baptist ecclesiology and human sexuality, 2017. *Recreations:* reading, photography, drinking coffee, playing the guitar, watching Formula 1, subverting empire. *Address:* Bloomsbury Central Baptist Church, 235 Shaftesbury Avenue, WC2H 8EP. *T:* (020) 7240 0544. *E:* simon@bloomsbury.org.uk.

**WOODROFFE, Simon,** OBE 2006; Founder: YO! Sushi, 1997; YO! Company, 2002; Yotel, 2007; YO! Home, 2012; *b* 14 Feb. 1952; *s* of John and Pippa Woodroffe; one *d*. *Educ:* Marlborough (two 'O' levels). Roadie, 1970–75; stage designer, 1975–85; TV Exec., SuperChannel, 1985–92; skier, Chamonix, 1992–95. Appeared on Dragons' Den, BBC TV, 2005. *Publications:* The Book of YO!, 2004. *Recreations:* polo, climbing, sailing. *Address:* Houseboat Victory, Cheyne Walk, SW10 0DG.

**WOODROOFE, Susan;** Principal, The Grammar School at Leeds, since 2016; *b* North Shields, 5 March 1966; *d* of Alan Lang and Jean Lang (*née* Greenwell, later Wallace); *m* 1987, Martin Woodroofe; one *s* one *d*. *Educ:* York Coll. for Girls; Univ. of Liverpool (BA Hons 1987); Univ. of Durham (PGCE 1988); Inst. of Educn, Univ. of London (NPQH 2008); Univ. of Buckingham (MEd 2016). Teacher of English, Westfield Sch., Newcastle upon Tyne, 1988–90; Hd of Year, Emmanuel Coll., Gateshead, 1990–93; Hd of Lower Sch. and SEN Coordinator, Sutton GS for Boys, Sutton, 1993–98; Dep. Hd, Holy Trinity Sch., Crawley, 1998–2000; British School of Brussels: Asst Hd, 2004–06; Vice Principal and Hd of Secondary Sch., 2006–11; Principal, 2011–16. Governor: Froebelian Sch., 2017–; Royal GS, Newcastle upon Tyne, 2018–. *Recreations:* theatre, cinema, politics and current affairs, church. *Address:* The Grammar School at Leeds, Alwoodley Gates, Harrogate Road, Leeds LS17 8GS. *T:* (0113) 229 1552. *E:* sw@gsal.org.uk. *Club:* Lansdowne.

**WOODROW, William Robert, (Bill),** RA 2002; sculptor; *b* 1 Nov. 1948; *s* of late Geoffrey W. Woodrow and Doreen M. (*née* Fasken); *m* 1970, Pauline Rowley; one *s* one *d*. *Educ:* Barton Peveril GS, Eastleigh; Winchester Sch. of Art; St Martin's Sch. of Art (DipAD); Chelsea Sch. of Art. Trustee: Tate Gall., 1996–2001; Imperial War Mus., 2003–11. Chm., Roche Court Educnl Trust, New Art Centre, Salisbury, 2011–17. Gov., Univ. of the Arts, London, 2003–08. Solo exhibns in UK, Europe, Australia, USA and Canada, 1972–, including: Fools' Gold, Tate Gall., London, 1996; Regardless of History, for Fourth Plinth, Trafalgar Square, 2000; The Beekeeper, S London Gall. and Mappin Art Gall., Sheffield, 2001, and Glynn Vivian Art Gall., Swansea, 2002; Bill Woodrow: Sculpture, Waddington Galleries, London, 2006; Brood—Sculpture from The Beekeeper series 1996–2007, Great Hall, Winchester, 2007; Skulpturen und Zeichnungen, 2008, Revelator, 2012, Lullin & Ferrari, Zürich; Bill Woodrow: Sculptures 1981–1988, Waddington Custot Galls, London, 2011; Bill Woodrow - Sculpture, RA, 2013; work in group exhibitions worldwide, including: British Sculpture in the 20th Century, Whitechapel Art Gall., 1981; An International Survey of Recent Painting and Sculpture, Mus. of Modern Art, NY, 1984; Skulptur Im 20. Jahrhundert, Basle, Switzerland, 1984; Carnegie Internat. Mus. of Art, Pittsburgh, 1985; British Sculpture since 1965, USA tour, 1987; Great Britain–USSR, Kiev and Moscow, 1990; Metropolis, Berlin, 1991; Arte Amazonas, Rio de Janeiro, Brasilia, Berlin, Dresden and Aachen, 1992–94; Ripple across the Water, Tokyo, 1995; Un Siècle de Sculpture Anglaise, Jeu de Paume, Paris, 1996; Forjar el Espacio, La Palmas, Valencia and Calais, 1998–99; Bronze, Holland Park, 2000–01; Field Day, Taipei Fine Arts Mus., Taiwan, 2001; Turning Points: 20th Century British Sculpture, Tehran Mus. of Contemp. Art, Iran, 2004; Drawing and Works on Paper from the Collection, Irish Mus. of Modern Art, Dublin, 2005; Eldorado, Mus. of Modern Art, Luxembourg, 2006; In Focus: Living History, Tate Modern, London, 2006; Sculpture in the Close, Jesus Coll., Cambridge, 2007; Punk. No One is Innocent, Kunsthalle Wien, Vienna, 2008; Modern British Sculpture, RA, 2011; A One Day Walk, Kröller-Müller Mus., Netherlands, 2014; Seeing Round Corners, Turner Contemp., Margate, 2016; Object Love, Mus. Hedendaagse Kunst De Domijnen, Netherlands, 2018. Represented GB at Biennales of Sydney, 1982, Paris, 1982 and 1985, São Paulo, 1983 and 1991, Havana, 1997. Anne Gerber Award, Seattle Mus. of Art, USA, 1988. *Publications:* The Sculpture of Bill Woodrow, 2013. *E:* bill@billwoodrow.com.

**WOODRUFF, Prof. (David) Philip,** PhD, DSc; FRS 2006; Professor of Physics, University of Warwick, since 1987; *b* 12 May 1944; *s* of Cyril and Dora Woodruff; *m* 1969, Angela Grundy; two *s*. *Educ:* Univ. of Bristol (BSc 1st Cl. Hons Physics 1965); Univ. of Warwick (PhD Physics 1968; DSc 1983). Lectr, 1969–83, Sen. Lectr, 1983–87, in Physics, Univ. of Warwick. Consulting Scientist, Bell Labs, NJ, 1979, 1981, 1985; Vis. Scientist, 1982 and 2002–11, Scientific Consultant, 1998–2011, Fritz-Haber-Inst., Berlin; EPSRC Sen. Res. Fellow, 1998–2003. *Publications:* The Solid/Liquid Interface, 1973; Modern Techniques in Surface Science, 1986, 3rd edn 2016; over 500 articles in scientific jls. *Recreations:* gardening, walking, cookery, travel. *Address:* Physics Department, University of Warwick, Coventry CV4 7AL. *T:* (024) 7652 3378, *Fax:* (024) 7615 0897. *E:* d.p.woodruff@warwick.ac.uk.

**WOODS, Very Rev. Alan Geoffrey,** TD 1993; Clergy Retirement Officer, Sherborne Area, Salisbury Diocese, 2010–16; Dean of Gibraltar, 2003–08, now Emeritus; Archdeacon of Gibraltar, 2005–08; *b* 18 July 1942; *s* of Samuel and Grace Woods; *m* 1968, Barbara (*née* Macdonald); three *d*. *Educ:* Bristol Cathedral Sch.; Salisbury Theol Coll. ACCA 1965, FCCA 1980. Auditor, Goodyear Tyre & Rubber Co., 1965–67. Ordained deacon, 1970, priest, 1971; Curate, St Francis, Ashton Gate, Bristol, 1970–73; Swindon Archdeaconry Youth Chaplain and Warden, Legge House Residential Youth Centre, 1973–76; Priest i/c, Neston, 1976–79; Team Vicar, Greater Corsham, 1979–81; Priest i/c, Charminster, 1981–83; Vicar: Charminster and Stinsford, 1983–90; Calne and Blackland, 1990–96; Sen. Chaplain, Malta and Gozo, and Chancellor, St Paul's Cathedral, Valletta, 1996–2003; Vicar Gen. to Bishop in Europe, 2003–05; Priest i/c, Malaga, 2006–07. Rural Dean: Dorchester, 1985–90; Calne, 1990–96. CF (TA), 1980–94; Chaplain: Dorchester Hosps, 1986–87; St Mary's Sch., Calne, 1990–96; Canon and Preb., Salisbury Cathedral, 1992–96. *Recreations:* travel, music. *Address:* 6 Maumbury Square, Weymouth Avenue, Dorchester DT1 1TY. *T:* (01305) 264877.

**WOODS, Albert John**, OBE 2012; Vice Chairman, British Olympic Association, 1999–2013, now Hon. Life Vice President; *b* Nottingham, 6 June 1949; *s of* Thomas Woods and Ourania Woods; *m* 1987, Helen Armitage. *Educ*: Nottingham High Sch.; Peoples Coll. of Further Educn (ONC Mechanical and Electrical Engrg 1968). Man. Dir, Maltby Heating Engineers, 1970–2017. Vice Chm., Nova Educnl Trust, 2015–. President: British Canoeing (formerly British Canoe Union), 1992–2017; Eur. Canoe Assoc., 1993–; Mem. Bd of Dirs, Internat. Canoe Fedn, 1988– (Mem., Exec. Bd, 2016–). Hon. MSc Nottingham Trent, 2005. *Recreations*: canoeing, shooting, koi carp. *Address*: 35 Killerton Park Drive, West Bridgford, Nottingham NG2 7SB. *T*: (0115) 984 5068. *E*: albert.woods@britishcanoeing.org.uk. *Clubs*: Midland Canoe; Old Nottinghamians Rifle.

**WOODS, Prof. Andrew William**, PhD; FRS 2017; BP Professor of Petroleum Science, BP Institute, University of Cambridge, since 2000; Fellow, St John's College, Cambridge, since 2000; *b* 2 Dec. 1964; *s of* Prof. William Alfred Woods and Dorothy Elizabeth Woods; *m* 1996, Dr Sharon Jane Casey; three *s* one *d*. *Educ*: St John's Coll., Cambridge (BA 1st Cl. Maths 1985, Part III Maths 1986, MA 1988; PhD Applied Maths 1989). Green Scholar, Scripps Instn of Oceanography, UCSD, 1989–90; University of Cambridge: Res. Fellow, 1988–90, Teaching Fellow, 1991–96, St John's College; Lectr, Inst. of Theoretical Geophysics, 1991–96; Prof. of Applied Maths, Univ. of Bristol, 1996–99. Italgas Prize, Turin, 1997; Marcello Carapezza Prize, Gp. Nat. per la Volcanologia, Rome, 1997; Wager Medal, IAVCEI, 2002. *Publications*: (jtly) Volcanic Plumes, 1997. *Address*: BP Institute, Bullard Laboratories, Madingley Rise, Madingley Road, University of Cambridge, Cambridge CB3 0EZ. *T*: (01223) 765702.

**WOODS, Dr David Randle**, DPhil; FRSSAf; Chairman, SANTRUST, since 2006; *b* Pietermaritzburg, 18 July 1940; *s of* Arthur Phillips Woods and Katherine Isabella Woods (*née* Straffen); *m* 1965, Anne Charlotte Abbott; one *s* one *d*. *Educ*: Michaelhouse Sch.; Rhodes Univ. (BSc Dist. Botany; BSc Hons Dist. Botany); University Coll., Oxford (DPhil 1966). Rhodes Schol., Natal, 1963–66; Asst Lectr in Microbiol., Dept of Botany and Microbiol., QMC, 1966–67; Rhodes University: Sen. Lectr in Microbiol., 1967–71; Prof. and Head of Microbiol., 1972–79; University of Cape Town: Dir, Microbial Genetics and Industrial Microbiol. Res. Unit, 1975–96; Prof. and Head of Dept of Microbiol., 1980–87; Fellow, 1985; Dep. Vice-Chancellor, 1988–96; Dir, Foundn for Res. Develt/Univ. of Cape Town Microbial Genetics Res. Unit, 1980–96; Vice-Chancellor, Rhodes Univ., 1996–2006. Research Fellow: Institut Pasteur, Paris, 1973–74; Dept of Biochem. Trondheim Univ., Norway, 1974–75; R. F. Cherry Prof. for Dist. Teaching, Baylor Univ., USA, 1992–93. Member, Editorial Board: Jl Bacteriol., 1987–89; Anaerobe Microbiol., 1994–98. Chm., Bacteriol. and Applied Microbiol. Div., and Mem., Exec. Bd, Internat. Union of Microbiol Socs, 1995–99. Member: S African Soc. for Microbiol., 1970 (Pres., 1982–84); S African Soc. for Biochem., 1970–96; Amer. Soc. for Microbiol., 1980; Acad. of Sci. of SA, 1995–. FRSSAf 1987; Fellow: Acad. of Sci. of SA, 1994; Amer. Acad. Microbiol., 1995. Hon. DCL Oxford, 2003; Hon. DLaws Rhodes, 2007. *Publications*: (ed) The Clostridia and Biotechnology (series), 1993; jt author numerous res. papers. *Recreations*: squash, reading, music, hiking.

*See also T. P. Woods.*

**WOODS, Eldrick, (Tiger)**; golfer; *b* 30 Dec. 1975; *s of* late Lt-Col Earl Woods and of Kultida Woods; *m* 2004, Elin Nordegren (marr. diss. 2010); one *s* one *d*. *Educ*: Western High Sch., Anaheim, Calif; Stanford Univ. Professional golfer, 1996–; wins include: US Masters, 1997 (youngest winner), 2001 (first player ever to hold all four major professional titles concurrently), 2002, 2005, 2019; US PGA Championship, 1999, 2000, 2006, 2007, 2018; US Open, 2000, 2002, 2008; The Open, St Andrews, 2000, 2005, Hoylake, 2006; numerous other tournaments; Mem., US Ryder Cup Team, 1997, 1999, 2002, 2004, 2006, 2010, 2012, 2018, a Vice-Captain (non-playing), 2016; Presidential Medal of Freedom (USA), 2019. *Publications*: (jtly) How I Play Golf, 2001. *Address*: PGA Tour, 112 PGA Tour Boulevard, Ponte Vedra Beach, FL 32082, USA.

**WOODS, Elisabeth Ann**; a Commissioner, HM Customs and Excise, 1991–97; *b* 27 Oct. 1940; *d of* late Norman Singleton, CB and Cicely Margaret Singleton (*née* Lucas); *m* 1976, James Maurice Woods. *Educ*: South Hampstead High Sch.; Girton Coll., Cambridge (BA Hons Cl. 1 Modern Languages, 1963). Asst Principal, Min. of Pensions and Nat. Insurance, 1963–69 (Asst Private Sec. to the Minister, and Private Sec. to Permanent Sec.); Principal, DHSS, 1969–76 (Sec. to Cttees on Nursing and on Allocation of Resources to Health Authorities); Asst Sec., DHSS, 1976–88 (responsible for mental handicap policy, later for liaison with health authorities, finally for aspects of supplementary benefit); seconded to HM Treasury, 1980–82; Grade 3, DHSS Central Resource Management, 1988; Hd of Finance, DSS, 1988–91; HM Customs and Excise: Dir, VAT Control, 1991–94; Dir, Ops (Compliance), 1994–97; pt-time consultant on mgt and policy issues for UK and overseas govt depts and other orgns, 1998–2005. Non-executive Director: S Wilts PCT, 2003–06; NHS Wilts (formerly Wilts PCT), 2007–13. Chair, George Herbert in Bemerton Gp, 2013–14; Mem., HFEA, 1999–2002 (Chm., Audit Cttee, 2000–02). Mem., Wilts Children and Young People's Trust Bd, 2007–13; Gov., Salisbury Foundn Trust, 2007–13; Volunteer advr, Salisbury CAB, 1999–; Mem., Salisbury Civic Soc. Gen. Purposes Cttee, 2012–. *Recreations*: walking, travel, reading, cooking, being with friends. *Address*: West Wing, 43 Church Lane, Lower Bemerton, Salisbury SP2 9NR. *E*: lisandjames@gmail.com.

**WOODS, Gordon Campbell**, MA; Warden, Glenalmond College, Perth, 2003–15; *b* 5 Nov. 1955; *s of* late Ian and Margot Woods; *m* 1984, Emma, *d of* late Michael Godwin and Elizabeth Godwin; one *s* one *d*. *Educ*: Durham Sch.; Mansfield Coll., Oxford (BA Geog., MA 1978; PGCE 1979). Shrewsbury School, 1979–2003: Hd of Geog., 1984–89; Master i/c Rowing, 1988; Housemaster, 1989–99; Second Master (Dep. Hd), 1999–2003. Member: Bd of Mgt, SCIS, 2004–14; Exec. Cttee, Boarding Schs Assoc., 2010–14. Chm., Field Studies Working Gp, Geographical Assoc., 1989. Co. Sec., Shrewsbury Drapers, 2017–. Governor: Cargilfield Prep. Sch., 2003–15; Malsis Prep. Sch., 2003–14; Belhaven Hill Prep. Sch., 2015–18; Prestfelde Sch. 2016–; Shrewsbury Sch., 2018–. *Recreations*: golf, railways (steam), industrial archaeology, watching live sport, rowing, coaching, photography. *Club*: Leander (Henley-on-Thames).

**WOODS, Maj.-Gen. Henry Gabriel**, CB 1979; MVO 2014; MBE 1965; MC 1945; Vice Lord-Lieutenant, North Yorkshire, 1985–99; Vice-President, St William's Foundation, since 1998 (Secretary, then Director, 1984–98); *b* 7 May 1924; *s of* late G. S. Woods and F. C. F. Woods (*née* McNevin); *m* 1953, Imogen Elizabeth Birchenough Dodd; two *d*. *Educ*: Highgate Sch. (Scholar); Trinity Coll., Oxford (Exhibnr; MA 1st Cl. Hons Mod. History). psc, jssc, rcds. Commnd 5th Royal Inniskilling Dragoon Guards, 1944; served NW Europe, 1944–45; Korea, 1951–52; Adjt, 1952–53; Sqdn Leader, 1954–55 and 1962–64; Army Staff Coll., 1956; Jt Services Staff Coll., 1960; Mil. Asst to Vice CDS, MoD, 1962–64; comd 5th Royal Inniskilling Dragoon Gds, 1965–67; Asst Mil. Sec. to C-in-C BAOR, 1968–69; Comdt, RAC Centre, 1969–71; RCDS, 1972; Mil. Attaché, Brit. Embassy, Washington, 1973–75; GOC NE Dist, 1976–80, retd. Head, Centre for Industrial and Educnl Liaison (W and N Yorks), 1980–87. Chairman: SATRO Panel, 1982–83; W and N Yorks Regl Microelectronics Educn Programme, 1982–86; Yorks and Humberside Industry/Educn Council, 1982–87; Bradford and W Yorks Br., BIM, 1982–84; N Yorks Scouts, 1982–2000; Yorks Region, Royal Soc. of Arts, 1982–92 (Mem. Council, 1984–92); Vice Chm., W Yorks Br. Exec. Cttee, Inst. of Dirs, 1985–91; Mem., Yorks Br. Exec. Cttee, BAAS, 1982–87. Vice Pres., Duke of York's Community Initiative, 2012– (Trustee, 2011–12). Trustee, Second World War Experience Centre, 1998–. Mem. Council, RUSI, 1981–84. Mem. Court, Univ. of Leeds, 1980–2001 (Mem. Council, 1980–91). Chm., 5th Royal Inniskilling Dragoon Guards Regtl Assoc., 1979–92; Pres., Royal Dragoon Guards Regtl Assoc., 1992–. Pres., York and Humberside Br., Royal Soc. of St George, 1986–88; Member: Trinity Soc., 1947–; Oxford Soc., 1987– (Pres., York Br., 1997–2001). FRSA 1982–2018; MInstD; FCMI. Hon. Mem., Yorks Reg., RIBA, 1994. Mayor, Co. of Merchants of Staple of England, 1991–92; Mem., Merchant Adventurers of the City of York. DL N Yorks, 1984–2006. Hon. DLitt Bradford, 1988. Officier, Ordre de Léopold, Belgium, 1965; Chevalier, Légion d'Honneur (France), 2015. *Publications*: Change and Challenge: the story of 5th Royal Inniskilling Dragoon Guards, 1978; contrib. Everyone's War: tanks - a brief history. *Recreation*: military history. *Address*: Grafton House, Tockwith, York YO26 7PY. *T*: (01423) 358735. *Club*: Ends of the Earth (UK section).

**WOODS, Prof. John David**, CBE 1991; PhD; Professor of Oceanography, Department of Earth Science and Engineering (formerly Department of Earth Resources Engineering, then T. H. Huxley School of the Environment, Earth Sciences and Engineering), Imperial College, University of London, 1994–2006, now Emeritus Professor of Oceanography and Complex Systems; Adjunct Fellow, Linacre College, Oxford, since 1991; *b* 26 Oct. 1939; *s of* late Ronald Ernest Goff Woods and Ethel Marjorie Woods; *m* 1971, Irina (marr. diss. 1996), *y d of* Bernd von Arnim and Elizabeth Gräfin Platen-Hallermund; one *s* one *d*. *Educ*: Imperial College, Univ. of London. BSc Physics 1961, PhD 1965. Research Asst, Imperial Coll., 1964–66; Sen., later Principal, Research Fellow, Meteorol Office, 1966–72; Prof. of Physical Oceanography, Southampton Univ., 1972–77; Ordinarius für Ozeanographie, Christian Albrechts Universität und Direktor Regionale Ozeanographie, Kiel Institut für Meereskunde, Schleswig-Holstein, 1977–86; Dir, Marine and Atmospheric Sci., NERC, 1986–94; Imperial College, London: Hd, Dept of Earth Resources Engrg, 1994–97; Dean, Graduate Sch. of the Envmt, 1994–97. Vis. Prof. Atmospheric Scis, Miami Univ., 1969; Hon. Prof. of Oceanography, Southampton Univ., 1994–. Jt Founding Dir, Foto Zerüi, 2005–. Member: NERC, 1978–92; Meteorol Res. Cttee, Meteorol Office, 1976–77, 1987–96; OST Foresight Marine Panel, 1996–2006. Council Member: Underwater Assoc., 1967–72 (Hon. life mem., 1987); RMetS, 1972–75; RGS, 1975–77, 1987–92 (Vice-Pres., 1989–91; Patron's Medal, 1996); Member, international scientific committees for: Global Atmospheric Research Prog., 1976–79; Climate Change and the Ocean, 1979–84; World Climate Research Prog., 1980–86; World Ocean Circulation Experiment, 1983–89 (Chm., 1984–86); Internat. Geosphere Biosphere Prog., 1987–91; Global Ocean Observing System, 1994– (Chm., Eur. Consortium, 1994–); Global Envmt Facility, 1994–98; Lead Author, Intergovtl Panel for Climate Change, 1989. Associate, Italian Nat. Res. Council, 2008. MAE 1988. Lectures: Iselin, Harvard, 1989; Linacre, Oxford, 1991; Adye, Fellowship of Engrg, 1991; European Geophys. Soc., Edinburgh, 1992; Bruun, Unesco, 1993, 1999. Inventor and developer of Virtual Ecology Workbench, 1992–2007. Hon. DSc: Liège, 1980; Plymouth, 1991; Southampton, 2004. L. G. Groves Prize, MoD, 1968; Medal of Helsinki Univ., 1982. *Publications*: (with J. Lythgoe) Underwater Science, 1971; (with E. Drew and J. Lythgoe) Underwater Research, 1976; (with N. Pinardi) Ocean Forecasting, 2002; The Joy of Swimming, 2010; Ix-Xlendi and its Ancient Shipwrecks, 2011; Winter water colours, 2012; Spring water colours, 2013; papers on atmospheric physics and oceanography in learned jls. *Recreations*: history, photography (www.fotozerui.com), filmmaking (vimeopro.com/goff/alps). *Address*: Department of Earth Science and Engineering, Imperial College, SW7 2AZ. *T*: (020) 7594 7414. *Clubs*: Athenæum, Geographical, Royal Over-Seas League.

**WOODS, Kenneth Allen**; 'cellist; Principal Conductor and Artistic Director, English Symphony Orchestra, since 2013; *b* Madison, Wisconsin, 6 June 1968; *s of* Prof. R. Claude Woods and Charlotte O. Woods; *m* 2004, Suzanne Casey; one *s* one *d*. *Educ*: James Madison Meml High Sch.; Indiana Univ. Sch. of Music (BM Cello Performance 1991); Univ. of Wisconsin-Madison Sch. of Music (MM Cello Performance 1993); Univ. of Cincinnati Coll.-Conservatory of Music (DMA-ABD Conducting and Cello). Conducting Asst, Cincinnati SO, 1998–99; Asst Prof. of Cello and Conducting, and Hd of Strings and Chamber Music, Eastern Oregon Univ., 1999–2002; Music Director: Grande Ronde Symphony, 1999–2002; Oregon E Symphony, 2000–09; Principal Guest Conductor, Orch. of the Swan, 2009–14. Artistic Dir, Colorado MahlerFest, 2016–. Cellist: Taliesin Piano Trio, 1993–98; Quatuor Masala, 1996–99; Ensemble Epomeo, 2008–. Mem., Bd of Dirs, Conductors' Guild, 2001–02. Hon. Patron, Hans Gál Soc., 2014–. *Recreations*: writing (fiction, poetry, political analysis and blogging on music), composition and song-writing, cycling, camping, time with family, film, cooking, wine, beer and good coffee. *Address*: c/o English Symphony Orchestra, 16–20 Deansway, Worcester WR1 2ES. *T*: 07973 906206. *E*: ken@kennethwoods.net. *W*: www.kennethwoods.net.

**WOODS, Sir Kent (Linton)**, Kt 2011; MD; FRCP; Professor of Therapeutics, University of Leicester, 1996–2013, now Emeritus; *b* 5 June 1948; *s of* Stephen and Mary Woods; *m* 1970, Rose Whitmarsh; three *s* (one *d* decd). *Educ*: Lawrence Sheriff Sch., Rugby; Clare Coll., Cambridge (MA, MB BChir 1972; MD 1980 (Horton Smith Prize)); Birmingham Univ.; Harvard Sch. of Public Health (SM Epidemiology 1983). MRCP 1974, FRCP 1988. Clinical trng posts, Birmingham, 1972–75; Sheldon Res. Fellow and MRC Trng Fellow, 1975–78; Lectr in Clinical Pharmacology, Birmingham Univ., 1978–84; MRC Travelling Fellow, Harvard, 1982–83; Sen. Lectr in Clinical Pharmacology, 1984–94, Reader, 1994–96, Univ. of Leicester. Regl Dir of R&D, Trent, NHS Exec., DoH, 1995–99; Dep. Dir, 1998, Dir, 1999–2003, NHS Health Technol. Assessment Programme. Chief Exec., Medicines and Healthcare products Regulatory Agency, 2004–13; Chm., Eur. Medicines Agency, 2011–15. Sen. Med. Trustee and Chm., Adv. Council, BHF, 2015–. Hon. Consultant Physician, Leicester Royal Infirmary, 1984–2013. FMedSci 2008. Hon. FFPM 2009; Hon. FBPhS 2015. *Publications*: contrib. numerous papers to med. and scientific jls, mainly on cardiovascular topics. *Recreations*: family, travel, books. *Club*: Athenæum.

**WOODS, Prof. Mary D.**; *see* Dixon-Woods.

**WOODS, Maurice Eric**; Regional Chairman, Employment (formerly Industrial) Tribunals (Bristol), 1990–98; *b* 28 June 1933; *s of* late Leslie Eric Woods and of Winifred Rose Woods (*née* Boniface); *m* 1956, Freda Pauline Schlosser; two *s* two *d*. *Educ*: Moulsham Secondary Modern Sch., Chelmsford. LLB London. National Service (Army), 1951–53. Clerk with Essex CC, 1948–51; Police Constable, Essex Police Force, 1954–59; Claims Assistant, Cornhill Insce, 1959–61; Solicitors' Clerk and Articled Clerk, Barlow Lyde and Gilbert, 1961–65; admitted Solicitor, 1965; private practice, 1965–84; Dep. County Court Registrar, 1977–84; Chairman: Suppl. Benefit Appeal Tribunals and Social Security Appeal Tribunals, 1981–84; Industrial Tribunals, Bristol, 1984–90. *Recreation*: painting.

**WOODS, Prof. Ngaire Tui**, CBE 2018; DPhil; Founding Dean, Blavatnik School of Government, since 2011, and Professor of Global Economic Governance, since 2011, University of Oxford; Fellow, University College, Oxford, since 1993; *b* Wellington, NZ, 13 Feb. 1963; *d of* N. Rowland Woods and Tui Clark; *m* 1995, Prof. Eugene Lawrence Rogan, *qv*; one *s* one *d*. *Educ*: Univ. of Auckland (BA, LLB Hons); Balliol Coll., Oxford

(MPhil; DPhil 1992). Jun. Res. Fellow, New Coll., Oxford, 1990–92; University of Oxford: Lectr in Internat. Relns, Dept of Politics and Internat. Relns, 1993–2008; Prof. of Internat. Political Econ., 2008–11; Academic Dir, Blavatnik Sch. of Govt, 2011; Founder, Global Economic Governance Prog., 2003. Vis. Lectr, Govt Dept, Harvard Univ., 1992. *Publications:* (ed and contrib.) Explaining International Relations since 1945, 1996; (ed jtly and contrib.) Inequality and World Politics, 1999; (ed) The Political Economy of Globalization, 2000; The Globalizers: the IMF, the World Bank and their borrowers, 2006; (ed with J. Welsh) Exporting Good Governance, 2007; (ed with D. Brown) Making Self-Regulation Effective in Developing Countries, 2007; (ed with W. Mattli) The Politics of Global Regulation, 2009; (ed with L. Martinez) Networks of Influence, 2009. *Recreations:* sailing, ski-ing, hiking. *Address:* University College, High Street, Oxford OX1 4BH. *T:* (01865) 616699. *E:* dean@bsg.ox.ac.uk.

**WOODS, Nigel Dermot,** FRICS; Chief Executive and Commissioner of Valuation for Northern Ireland, Valuation and Lands Agency, 1998–2007; *b* 21 Feb. 1947; *s* of Victor and Sheila Woods; *m* 1974, Alison Grant; one *s* two *d*. *Educ:* Bangor Grammar Sch. FRICS 1983 (ARICS 1970). Worked in estate agency, Belfast, 1964–67; with Valuation Office, subseq. Valuation and Lands Agency, 1967–2007. Vis. Prof., Sch. of Built Envmt, Univ. of Ulster, 2003–. *Recreations:* golf, bridge. *Club:* Bangor Golf.

**WOODS, Robert Barclay,** CBE 2003; Chief Executive, Peninsular and Oriental Steam Navigation Co., 2004–06 (Executive Director, 1996–2006); *b* 23 Sept. 1946; *s* of Robert Wilmer Woods and Henrietta Wilson; *m* 1975, Georgiana Garton; three *s* one *d*. *Educ:* Winchester Coll.; Trinity Coll., Cambridge (MA); Harvard Business Sch. (SMP). Joined P&O Gen. Cargo Div., 1971; seconded to J. Swire & Sons, Japan, 1972–73; Overseas, subseq. P&O, Containers: Dubai, 1980–84; Gen. Manager, FE Trade, 1984–86; Trade Dir, Aust. and NZ, 1986–89; Dir, 1987; Managing Director: P&O Containers, 1990–96; P&O Nedlloyd, 1997–2003; Chairman: P&O Ports, 2002–06; P&O Ferries, 2003–. Chm., Southampton Container Terminal, 1989–; non-executive Director: J. Swire & Sons, 2002–15; Cathay Pacific Airways, 2006–10; Caledonia Investments plc, 2011–16; Advr, Dubai Ports World, 2006– (Dir, 2014–). Chm., Maritime London, 2007–10. Chm., Far Eastern Freight Conf., 1996–2003; President: Chamber of Shipping, 2002–04; Inst. of Chartered Shipbrokers, 2014–16. Chairman: Council of Trustees, Oxford House Community Centre, 1993–2005; Sea Cadet Council, 2005–17; Council, Mission to Seafarers, 2007–17. Younger Brother, Trinity House, 2005–. Hon. Capt. RNR, 2002–. Fellow, Winchester Coll., 2007–17. Hon. DUniv Anglia Ruskin, 2007. *Recreations:* field sports, music, vintage cars and aircraft, sailing. *Address:* Old Rectory, Frilsham, Newbury, Berks RG18 9XH. *T:* (01635) 201249. *E:* robert.woods@dpworld.com. *Clubs:* White's; Vintage Sports-Car; Keyhaven Yacht.

**WOODS, Sir Robert (Kynnersley),** Kt 2000; CBE 1986; Judge, District Court of New South Wales, 2000–11; *b* 12 Nov. 1939; *s* of Frederick Kynnersley Smythies Woods, OBE and Ruth Cecilia Woods (née Shaw). *Educ:* Univ. of Sydney (LLB). Solicitor, NSW, 1966–69; Legal Officer, PNG Govt, 1969–81; Justice, Nat. and Supreme Courts of PNG, 1982–99. PNG Scout Association: Scout Leader, 1969–74; Scout Comr, 1974–2000 (Leader Trainer, 1992–96); Chief Comr, 1996–99. Chancellor, Anglican Dio. of Bathurst, NSW, 2003–. KStJ 2004. *Address:* 26 Gobolion Street, Wellington, NSW 2820, Australia. *T:* (2) 68453707.

**WOODS, Robert Stockley;** Director, HM Treasury, since 2014; *b* Southport, 20 Oct. 1966; *s* of John and Mary Woods; *m* 1999, Maria del Carmen Frieyro de Lara; two *d*. *Educ:* Rainford High Sch.; Girton Coll., Cambridge (BA Hons Econs 1988); Warwick Univ. (MSc Econs). HM Treasury: Head: Forecast Report and Modelling Br., 1992–95; Monetary Policy Br., 1996–98; EU Econs and EMU Br., 1999–2001; Fiscal and Macroeconomic Policy, 2002–06; Global Econs, 2006–08; Dir, Macroeconomics, and Chief Macroeconomist, 2008–10; Head, Macro Financial Analysis Div., 2010–12; Head, Conjunctural Assessment and Projections Div., 2012–14; Project Leader, Monetary Analysis Directorate, Bank of England, 2014. *Publications:* contribs to learned jls. *Recreations:* swimming, tennis, football, piano, reading, gardening, socialising with friends and family. *Address:* HM Treasury, Horse Guards Road, SW1A 2HQ. *E:* robert.woods@hmtreasury.gov.uk.

**WOODS, Prof. Robert Thomas,** FBPsS, FAcSS; Professor of Clinical Psychology of the Elderly, 1996–2017, now Emeritus, and Co-Director, Dementia Services Development Centre, 1999–2017, Bangor University (formerly University of Wales, Bangor); *b* 9 April 1952; *s* of Walter T. W. Woods and Kathleen Ellen Woods (née Brooks); *m* 1972, Joan Doreen Foster; one *s* one *d*. *Educ:* Gravesend Sch. for Boys; Churchill Coll., Cambridge (BA 1973; MA 1977); Univ. of Newcastle-upon-Tyne (MSc 1975). CPsychol 1988; FBPsS 1992. Clinical psychologist, Newcastle Gen. Hosp., 1975–80; Lectr, then Sen. Lectr, Inst. of Psychiatry, Univ. of London and Hon. Clinical Psychologist, Maudsley and Bethlem Royal Hosps, 1980–92; Head, Psychol. Services for Older People, Camden and Islington Community Health Services NHS Trust, 1992–96; Hon. Sen. Lectr in Psychol., UCL, 1992–96; Hon. Clinical Psychologist, Betsi Cadwaladr University Health Bd (formerly Gwynedd Community Health, then NW Wales, NHS Trust), 1996–2017. Mem., Med. and Scientific Adv. Panel, Alzheimer's Soc. (formerly Alzheimer's Disease Soc.), 1987–2007, and Alzheimer's Disease Internat., 1997–; Ambassador, Alzheimer's Soc., 2007–. Associate Specialist Advr, Health Adv. Service 2000, 1998–2003. Associate Editor, Aging and Mental Health, 1997–. FAcSS (AcSS 2014). 25th Anniversary Award, Alzheimer's Soc., 2004; M. B. Shapiro Award, BPsS, 2006; Barry Reisberg Award, Hearthstone Alzheimer Care, USA, 2011. *Publications:* (with U. Holden) Reality Orientation, 1982, 3rd edn as Positive Approaches to Dementia Care, 1995; (with C. Lay) Caring for the Person with Dementia: a guide for families and other carers, 1982, 3rd edn 1994; (with P. Britton) Clinical Psychology with the Elderly, 1985; Alzheimer's Disease: coping with a living death, 1989; (ed) Handbook of the Clinical Psychology of Ageing, 1996, (ed with L. Clare) 2nd edn, 2008; (ed) Psychological Problems of Ageing, 1999; (with J. Keady and D. Seddon) Involving Families in Care Homes, 2007; (ed jtly) Cognitive Stimulation Therapy for Dementia: history, evolution and internationalism, 2018. *Recreations:* football, cooking. *Address:* Dementia Services Development Centre, Bangor University, Ardudwy, Holyhead Road, Bangor, Gwynedd LL57 2PZ. *T:* (01248) 383719.

**WOODS, Roberta C.;** *see* Blackman-Woods.

**WOODS, Tiger;** *see* Woods, E.

**WOODS, Timothy Phillips,** MA, DPhil; Head of History, Trent College, 1985–2004; *b* 24 Dec. 1943; *s* of late Arthur Phillips Woods and Katherine Isabella Woods; *m* 1969, Erica Lobb. *Educ:* Cordwalles Prep. Sch., Natal; Michaelhouse Sch., Natal; Rhodes Univ. (BA Hons, MA; UED); Oxford Univ. (DPhil). Cape Province Rhodes Scholar, 1968; Felsted School: Asst Master, 1971; Head of History, 1975; Headmaster, Gresham's Sch. 1982–85. *Recreations:* golf, gardening, music, history and architecture of cathedrals. *Address:* 63 Curzon Street, Long Eaton, Nottingham NG10 4FG. *T:* (0115) 972 0927. *Club:* Vincent's (Oxford).

*See also* D. R. Woods.

**WOODS, Victoria Patricia Ann, (Vicki), (Mrs F. A. Woods Walker);** Contributing Editor, Vogue (USA), since 1994; *b* 25 Sept. 1947; *d* of Frederick Woods and Barbara Joan (née Hinchliffe); *m* 1980, Frank A. Walker; one *s* one *d*. *Educ:* Lancaster Girls' Grammar Sch.; Univ. of Lancaster (BA). Sub-editor, Harpers & Queen, 1970–73; Chief sub-editor, Radio Times, 1973–75; Exec. Editor, Harpers & Queen, 1975–79; Associate Editor, then Dep. Editor, Tatler, 1982–87; Femail Editor, Daily Mail, 1987–89; Contributing Editor, Vogue (USA) and Associate Editor, Spectator, 1989–91; Editor, Harpers & Queen, 1991–94.

**WOODS-WILFORD, Dr (Jacqueline Lee) Penelope;** Chief Executive, British Lung Foundation, since 2012; *b* London, 3 May 1963; *d* of Peter Woods and Lucia Woods; *m* 2011, Julian Wilford; one *d*. *Educ:* Sidney Sussex Coll., Cambridge (BA 1984; MA 1987); Guy's Hosp. Med. Sch. (MB BS 1987); INSEAD Business Sch. (MBA 1992). Jun. doctor, NHS, 1987–89; mgt consultant, Arthur Andersen, Booz Allen and ISO Healthcare, 1989–2000; Sen. Vice Pres., BTG plc, 2000–07; Chief Exec., Picker Inst. Europe, 2009–12. Angel investor and non-exec. dir, private and public sectors, 1998–. FRSocMed; FRSA. *Recreations:* travel, family, designing and building beautiful homes, exploring France. *Address:* British Lung Foundation, 73–75 Goswell Road, EC1V 7ER. *T:* (020) 7688 5566. *E:* penny.woods@blf.org.uk.

**WOODSTOCK, Viscount; William Jack Henry Bentinck;** Count of the Holy Roman Empire; Head of Pathway Delivery (formerly Career Specialist, then Head of Careers), Makers Academy, since 2014; *b* 19 May 1984; *s* and *heir* of Earl of Portland, *qv*. *Educ:* Harrow Sch.; Heythrop Coll., Univ. of London (BA Hons Philosophy 1st cl.). Co-founder: Ragged Project (London), 2010–11; Levantine Links, 2010–14; Develt Manager, IDEA UK, 2011–12. Key Account Manager, Enternships Ltd, 2012–14. Dir, ISOWORG, 2014–. Mem. Cttee, BCS Entrepreneurs, 2012–; Catalyst, Global Wkg Gp on Decent Work for Youth, ILO, 2012–13; Head of Marketing, Business Governance Solutions, 2014; Member: Steering Gp, SEE Change, UnLtd, 2013–; Adv. Bd, EdTech UK, 2015–; Steering Gp, Learning Futures Prog., Educn and Trng Foundn, 2015–. Advisor: E-Skills UK, then The Tech Partnership, 2012–; Advocate, Tech London Advocates, 2013– (Chm., Supporting Educn Gp, 2013–); Course Leader, Accelerator Acad., 2013–; Becon, Beconomy, 2013–; Mentor: Wayra UK, 2014–; Wayra UnLtd, 2014–. World of Difference winner, Vodafone Foundn, 2011. Croupier, London Clubs Internat., 2005–08. *Heir:* *b* Hon. Jasper James Mellowes Bentinck, *b* 1988.

**WOODTHORPE BROWNE, Robert,** MBE 2014; Managing Director, Robert Browne and Partners, since 1984; *b* Little Gaddesden, Herts, 26 May 1943; *m* 1966, Barbara Zwiauer; one *s*. *Educ:* Birkbeck Coll., Univ. of London (BA Hons Spanish); Univ. de Barcelona (Estudios Hispánicos); Univ. de Poitiers. Chief Underwriter, Reinsurance Co. of Mauritius, 1969–73; Man. Dir, Africa and Middle East, Sedgwick Gp, 1973–84; Exec. Dir, Citicorp Insce Brokers, subseq. Nelson Hurst, 1988–96; Exec. Dir, Bain Hogg, subseq. Aon Gp, 1996–2002. Chm., IGSpaces, 2016–. Contested (Lib Dem): Harlow, 1979; Kensington and Chelsea, 1997, Nov. 1999; Mid Worcs, 2001; Sedgefield, 2005; Staffordshire S, 2015; European Parliament: Central London, 1997; East of England, 1999; Chairman: Lib Dem Parly Candidates Assoc., 1998–2001; Federal Internat. Relns Cttee, Lib Dems, 2006–. Pres., Supervisory Bd, City Insurance, Romania, 2019–. Member: Cttee, British German Assoc., 2000–; Cttee, Gresham Soc., 2002–; Council, RIIA, 2011–17. Court Asst, World Traders' Co., 2006– (Master, 2016–17). Chm., Past Masters' Assoc., 2017–. Vice Pres. Liberal Internat., 2008–. Trustee, Tuberous Sclerosis Assoc., 2018–. FRGS 1980. *Recreations:* forestry, 17th century English ceramics, theatre, international travel. *Address:* 136 Colaherne Court, Redcliffe Gardens, SW5 0DY. *T:* 07770 605978. *E:* robertbrowne@cix.co.uk. *Club:* National Liberal.

**WOODWARD, Alison Jane; Her Honour Judge Alison Woodward;** a Circuit Judge, since 2018; *b* Sheffield, 23 Feb. 1970. *Educ:* Cheadle Hulme Sch.; Sheffield Univ. (LLB Hons 1991). Called to the Bar, Gray's Inn, 1992; in practice as barrister, Cobden Hse (formerly Hollins) Chambers, Manchester, 1992–2001, Deans Court Chambers, Manchester, 2001–18; a Recorder, 2012–18.

**WOODWARD, Dame Barbara (Janet),** DCMG 2016 (CMG 2011); OBE 1999; HM Diplomatic Service; Ambassador to the People's Republic of China, since 2015; *b* 29 May 1961; *d* of late Arthur Claude Woodward, MC, FRICS, and of Rosemary Monica Gabrielle Woodward (née Fenton). *Educ:* Univ. of St Andrews (MA Hons (Hist.) 1983); Yale Univ. (MA (Internat. Relns) 1990). Joined HM Diplomatic Service, 1991; Asst European Corresp., FCO, 1991–93; Second, then First, Sec., Moscow, 1994–98; Hd, EU Enlargement Section, FCO, 1999–2001; Dep. Hd, Human Rights Policy Dept, FCO, 2001–03; Political Counsellor, Beijing, 2003–06; Minister and Dep. Hd of Mission, Beijing, 2006–09; Internat. Dir, UK Border Agency, 2009–11; Dir Gen., Econ. and Consular, FCO, 2011–14. Chm., Adv. Bd, Hua Dan, 2009– (Mem., 2006–). Patron: Inspiring Women (China), 2015–; Generation UK, 2015–. *Recreations:* sport (competitive swimming, mountain biking, tennis), bridge. *Address:* c/o Foreign and Commonwealth Office, King Charles Street, SW1A 2AH. *Club:* Otter Swimming (Hon. Sec., 1998–2002).

**WOODWARD, Christopher John Paul;** Director, Garden Museum (formerly Museum of Garden History), since 2006; *b* Welwyn Garden City, 13 Sept. 1969; *s* of David Woodward and Janet Woodward (née Musther); *m* 2000, Anna Bacigalupi (marr. diss. 2011); one *s*. *Educ:* Hitchin Boys' Sch.; Peterhouse, Cambridge (BA Hist. of Art 1990). Asst Curator, Sir John Soane's Mus., 1995–2000; Dir, Holburne Mus. of Art, Bath, 2000–05. Trustee: Heritage Lottery Fund, 2006–13; Nat. Heritage Meml Fund, 2006–13. *Publications:* In Ruins, 2001. *Recreations:* open water swimming (crossing of Hellespont and the Strait of Gibraltar, and River Thames from Oxford to London), ruins, gardening. *Address:* c/o Garden Museum, Lambeth Palace Road, SE1 7LB. *T:* (020) 7401 8865.

**WOODWARD, Sir Clive (Ronald),** Kt 2004; OBE 2002; Director of Sport, British Olympic Association and Director of Olympic Performance, Team GB in Beijing 2008, Vancouver 2010 and London 2012, 2006–12; Founder and Chairman, Hive Learning; *b* 6 Jan. 1956; *m* Jayne; two *s* one *d*. *Educ:* HMS Conway; Loughborough Univ. Rugby Football Union player: début for England U-23, 1976; 21 England caps, 1980–84; British Lions tours, 1980, 1983; Leicester RFC, 1979; Manly, Australia, 1985; Coach: Henley RFC, 1993–95; London Irish RFC, 1995; Bath RFC, 1996–97; Head Coach: England Rugby Football Union team, 1997–2004; winning England team, World Cup, 2003; British Lions tour, NZ, 2005; Technical Dir, Southampton FC, 2005–06; a Dep. Chef de Mission, GB Team, London Olympics, 2012. Dir, Leicester RFC, 2008–. Hon. Pres., British Assoc. of Ski (later Snowsport) Instructors, 2007–12; Mem., Perf. Mgt Gp, Amateur Boxing Assoc. of England, 2008–. *Publications:* Winning!: the story of England's rise to Rugby World Cup glory, 2004.

**WOODWARD, David John,** CMG 2000; Director, Cross Government Studies, National Audit Office, 2006–09; *b* 12 Dec. 1949; *s* of Lionel John Innes Woodward and Ethel Woodward; *m* 1st, 1973, Agnes Kane (marr. diss. 1985); 2nd, 1985, Yvonne Yee Fun Wong; one *s*. *Educ:* Reigate Grammar Sch.; Woolwich Poly.; City of London Poly. (Dip. Auditing and Accounting). With BR, 1969–75; Nat. Audit Office, 1975–2009: Associate Dir, 1987–93; Director: Internat., London, 1993–94; Audit Ops, UN HQ, NY, and Chm.

Tech. Gp, UN Panel of External Auditors, 1995–2001; Conseiller Maître en Service Extraordinaire, Cour des Comptes, France (on exchange), 2001–02; UK Mem., Internat. Bd of Auditors for NATO, Brussels, 2002–06 (Chm., 2003–05). Treas., Hounslow Bor. Neighbourhood Watch Assoc., 2015–18. Gov., Grove Park Primary Sch., 2014– (Chm., Resources Cttee, 2014–18). *Recreations:* English history, exploring the River Thames. *E:* woodwardaccount@yahoo.co.uk.

**WOODWARD, Edward Gareth;** Executive Vice Chairman, Manchester United Football Club, since 2012; *b* Chelmsford, Essex, 9 Nov. 1971; *s* of David Garry Woodward and Susan Carol Woodward (*née* Mayo); *m* 2001, Isabelle Nicole Caprano; one *s* one *d* (twins). *Educ:* Brentwood Sch.; Bristol Univ. (BSc Physics 1993). ACA 1996. Corporate Tax, PricewaterhouseCoopers, 1993–99; Mergers and Acquisitions, Robert Fleming & Co., 1999–2000, J. P. Morgan, 2000–05; with Manchester United FC, 2005–. *Recreation:* food and wine. *Address:* Manchester United Football Club, Old Trafford, Sir Matt Busby Way, Manchester M16 0RA. *T:* (020) 7484 1202. *E:* emma.challoner@manutd.co.uk.

**WOODWARD, Prof. (Frank) Ian,** PhD; Professor of Plant Ecology, Department of Animal and Plant Sciences, University of Sheffield, since 1991; *b* 15 Dec. 1948; *s* of Frank Clement Woodward and Gwenda Agnes Woodward (*née* Allen); *m* 1972, Pearl May Chambers; one *s* one *d*. *Educ:* Mansfield Coll., Oxford (BA Hons Botany 1970); Univ. of Lancaster (PhD 1973); MA Cantab 1979. NERC Res. Fellow, Univ. of Lancaster, 1973–75; Higher Scientific Officer, Grassland Res. Inst., 1975–76; Lectr, Dept of Plant Scis, UWCC, 1976–79; Lectr, Dept of Botany, 1979–91, Fellow, Trinity Hall, 1981–91, Univ. of Cambridge. Henry J. Oosting Lectr, Duke Univ., USA, 1996. FLS 1990; FAAAS 2003. W. S. Cooper Award, Ecological Soc. of America, 1991; Marsh Award for Climate Change Res., British Ecol Soc., 2010. *Publications:* Principles and Measurements in Environmental Biology, 1983; Climate and Plant Distribution, 1987 (trans. Japanese 1993); Vegetation and the Terrestrial Carbon Cycle: modelling the first 400 million years, 2001; Global Change and the Terrestrial Biosphere, 2011; numerous articles in jls on influences of climate and carbon dioxide on plants and vegetation. *Recreations:* wood turning, music. *Address:* 16 Ecclesall Road South, Ecclesall, Sheffield S11 9PE. *T:* (0114) 266 0399.

**WOODWARD, Guy Andrew;** Deputy Editor, Harrods Publishing, since 2014; *b* Birmingham, 30 May 1973; *s* of Ray Woodward and Susan Woodward; *m* 2012, Vanessa Miller. *Educ:* King Edward's Sch., Edgbaston; Univ. of Manchester (BMus). Editor, AB Europe, 1997–2001; Sub-Editor, Sport, The Guardian, 2001–03; Dep. Editor, 2003–06, Editor, 2006–12, Decanter; Editor, Food and Travel, 2012–14; Associate Editor, Le Pan Mag., 2015–17; Consultant Editor, Club Oenologique, 2018–. Mem. Cttee, BSME, 2012– (Vice Chm., 2013; Chm., 2014). Advr, All-Party Parly Wine and Spirit Gp Enquiry into impact of tax changes on UK wine industry, 2009. Broadcaster on wine, TV progs, BBC News, Market Kitchen, 2010–12, This Morning, 2010–12. *Publications:* freelance writing on sport, travel and wine for The Guardian, Independent, Daily Mail, Observer, FT, Independent on Sunday, Esquire, ShortList, TIME Mag., Christie's, Condé Nast Traveller; columnist, Harpers Wine & Spirit. *Recreations:* wine, sport (football, tennis), music (classical), gambling. *Address:* Harrods Publishing, 68 Hammersmith Road. *T:* W14 8YW.

**WOODWARD, Ian;** *see* Woodward, F. I.

**WOODWARD, Rev. Canon Dr James Welford;** Principal, Sarum College, Salisbury, since 2015; *b* Durham, 23 Feb. 1961; *s* of Colin Woodward and Patricia Woodward (*née* Welford). *Educ:* Spennymoor Grammar Sch.; King's Coll. London (BD 1982; AKC 1982); Westcott House, Cambridge; STh Lambeth 1985; Univ. of Birmingham (MPhil 1991); Open Univ. (PhD 1999). Ordained deacon, 1985, priest, 1986; Curate, Consett, 1985–87; Bishop of Oxford's Domestic Chaplain, 1987–90; Hd of Chaplaincy, Queen Elizabeth Hosp., Birmingham, 1990–96; Priest-in-charge, Middleton and Wishaw, 1996–98; Bishop of Birmingham's Advr for Health and Social Care, 1996–2001; Master, Foundn of Lady Katherine Leveson and Vicar, St Mary the Virgin, Temple Balsall, 1998–2009; Dir, Leveson Centre for Study of Aging, Spirituality and Social Policy, Temple Balsall, 2000–09; Canon Steward, St George's Chapel, Windsor, 2009–15; Hon. Canon and Preb., Salisbury Cathedral, 2015–. Associate Lectr, Dept of Health and Social Welfare, Open Univ., 1992–2001; Associate Res. Fellow, Warwick Business Sch., Univ. of Warwick, 2002–05; Vis. Prof. of Theology, Winchester Univ., 2017–; Hon. Lectr, Dept of Theology, Univ. of Birmingham, 1993–2005; Hon. Res. Fellow, Practical Theology, Univ. of Cardiff, 1999–2003. Non-exec. Dir, Solihull PCT, 2003–06. Trustee, St Martins Trust, Birmingham, 2013–. Lay Mem., Patient Liaison Cttee, RCAnaes, 2000–03. Gov., SCM Press Trust Ltd, 1994–99; Chm. Govs, Salisbury Cathedral Sch., 2017–. *Publications:* Embracing the Chaos: theological reflections on AIDS, 1990; Encountering Illness: voices in pastoral and theological perspective, 1995; Finding God in Illness, 1997; (with S. Pattison) The Blackwell Reader in Pastoral and Practical Theology, 1999; Befriending Death, 2005; Services for Weekdays: readings, reflections and prayers, 2006; Praying the Lectionary: prayers and reflections for every week's readings, 2006; Valuing Age: mission and ministry among older people, 2008; Between Remembering and Forgetting: the spiritual dimensions of dementia, 2010; (with P. Gooder and M. Pryce): Journeying with Mark, 2011; Journeying with Luke, 2012; Journeying with Matthew, 2013; Journeying with John, 2014; (jtly) Developing a Relational Model of Care for Older People: creating environments for shared living, 2018. *Recreations:* modern political biography, cooking, photography, Wales, walking, art, cinema. *Address:* Sarum College, 19 The Close, Salisbury, Wilts SP1 2EE.

**WOODWARD, John Collin;** Chairman, Park Circus, since 2016; MetFilm, since 2016; *b* 18 Feb. 1961; *s* of Anthony and Anne Woodward; *m* 2000, Emma Jeffery; one *s* one *d*. *Educ:* Shiplake Coll.; Poly. of Central London (BA Hons Media Studies). Co-ordinator, 25% Campaign, 1986–87; Dir, Independent Access Steering Cttee, 1987–88; Dep. Dir, Independent Producers Programme Assoc., 1988–90; Chief Executive: Producers Assocs, 1990–92; Producers Alliance for Cinema and Television, 1992–98; Dir, BFI, 1998–99; CEO, UK Film Council (formerly Film Council), 1999–2010; Man. Dir, Arts Alliance, 2010–17. Member: Govt Film Policy Rev. Gp, 1997; Film Policy Rev. Action Cttee, 1998; former Mem., Video Consultative Council, BBFC. *Recreations:* fatherhood, cinema, reading. *Club:* Ivy.

**WOODWARD, Prof. Mark,** PhD; FMedSci; Professor of Statistics and Epidemiology, University of Oxford, since 2013; Professor of Medical Statistics, University of New South Wales, since 2017; *b* Birmingham, 8 June 1955; *s* of John and Dorothy Margaret Woodward; *m* 1981, Lesley Megan Audrey Francis; two *s*. *Educ:* King Edward's Grammar Sch., Aston, Birmingham; Univ. of Birmingham (BSc); Univ. of Reading (MSc; PhD 1980). Statistics and Operational Res. Officer, Berks AHA, 1979–81; Tech. Cooperation Officer, ODA, Zimbabwe, 1981–83; Lecturer: Univ. of Reading, 1984–88; Univ. of Dundee, 1988–89; Dir, Trng and Develt Centre, Inst. of Statisticians, 1989–90; Sen. Lectr, Univ. of Reading, 1990–2000; Professor: of Biostatistics, Univ. of Sydney, 2000–06; of Medicine, Mt Sinai Sch. of Medicine, New York Univ., 2006–10; of Biostatistics, Univ. of Sydney, 2010–17. FMedSci 2018. *Publications:* Statistics for Health Management and Research, 1988; Epidemiology: study design and data analysis, 1999, 3rd edn 2014; contribs to jls. *Recreations:* Aston Villa, Warwickshire County Cricket Club. *Address:* 57 Town Furze, Headington, Oxford OX3 7EW. *T:* 07408 841174. *E:* markw@georgeinstitute.org.au.

**WOODWARD, Nicholas Frederick; His Honour Judge Nicholas Woodward;** a Circuit Judge, since 2001; *b* 12 March 1952; *s* of Frederick Cyril Woodward and Joan Woodward; *m* (marr. diss.); one *s*. *Educ:* Trent Poly., Nottingham (BA). Called to the Bar, Lincoln's Inn, 1975; in practice as barrister, Chester, 1977–2001. *Address:* Chester Crown Court, The Castle, Chester CH1 2AN. *Club:* City (Chester).

**WOODWARD, Patricia Mary Alice;** *see* Bey, P. M. A.

**WOODWARD, Paul Scott;** Chairman, Buckinghamshire Care Ltd, 2013–16; *b* Cardiff, 16 July 1950; *s* of William and Jean Woodward; two *s* three *d*. *Educ:* St John's Coll. Sch., Cambridge; Worksop Coll. CA 1973. Articled clerk, 1967–72, tax accountant, 1972–73, Everetts; Investment Analyst, ICI Pension Fund, 1973–74; Eur. Project Accountant, SGB Gp Ltd, 1974–76; Beecham Pharmaceuticals: Finance Manager, Internat. Div., 1976–79; Area Manager, Saudi Arabia, 1979–81, Francophone Africa, 1981–83; Manager, Gulf States, Yemen and Egypt, 1983–85; Gen. Manager, ME, 1985–90; Business Develt Dir, Europe, SmithKline Beecham, 1990–95; Schering Healthcare Ltd: Mktg Dir, 1995–2000; CEO, 2000–06; CEO, Sue Ryder Care, then Sue Ryder, 2007–14. Mem., Eur. Bd, Schering AG, 2000–06. Vice Chm., FPA, 2007–12 (former Chm., Finance and Audit Sub-Cttee, 2007–12). Chm., St John's Coll. Choir Assoc., Cambridge, 2009–14. Trustee: Voluntary Orgns Disability Gp, 2010–14; St Peter and St James Charitable Trust, 2012–14; St Elizabeth Hospice, Ipswich, 2015–; Compassion in Dying, 2017–. Chm., Fressingfield Neighbourhood Plan, 2018–. Hon. Fellow, Coll. of Pharmacy Practice, 2006. *Recreations:* ski-ing, sailing, music, reading. *Address:* The Vicarage, Tansy Meadow, Fressingfield, Suffolk IP21 5RQ. *E:* paulscottwoodward@yahoo.co.uk.

**WOODWARD, Robert Stanley Lawrence;** Chairman, Met Office, since 2018; *b* 30 Nov. 1959; *s* of Frederick Stanley Woodward and Freda Mary Williams; *m* 2009, Patricia Mary Alice Bey, *qv*. *Educ:* Marr Coll., Troon; Univ. of Durham (BSc 1980); Univ. of Edinburgh (MBA 1981). Deloitte & Touche, 1986–97: Partner, Deloitte & Touche Consulting, 1992–97; Man. Dir, Braxton Associates, 1995–97; Man. Dir, UBS Warburg, 1997–2001; Commercial Dir, Channel 4 Television, 2001–05; Sen. Advr, Longacre Partners, 2005–07; Chief Exec., SMG plc, then STV Gp plc, 2007–17. Chm., Ebiquity plc, 2018–; non-exec. Dir, Blancco Technol. Gp plc (formerly Regenersis plc), 2013– (Chm., 2017–). Trustee, NESTA, 2009–16. Pro Chancellor and Chm. Council, City, Univ. London (formerly City Univ., London), 2012–18 (Mem. Council, 2006–18; Dep. Pro Chancellor, 2009–12; Hon. Rector, 2018); Chm., Glasgow Caledonian Univ., 2018–. Chm., Developing Young Workforce Nat. Gp, 2015–. Comr, Northern Lighthouse Bd, 2017–. Member: Council, NYT, 2006–12; BAFTA, 2010–; Trustee, RTS, 2016–. FRSA 2010. *Recreations:* photography, ski-ing, travel, cheese-making. *Address:* Crawfordston Farm, Maybole, Ayrshire KA19 7JS. *T:* (01655) 750215. *Clubs:* MCC; Glasgow Art.

**WOODWARD, Roger Robert,** AC 1992; OBE 1980; concert pianist, conductor, writer and composer; Professor of Keyboard Literature and Performance Practice, San Francisco State University, since 2004 (Founding Director, School of Music, 2002–04); *b* Sydney, 20 Dec. 1942; *s* of Francis William Wilson Woodward and Gladys Alma Bracken; *m* 1989, Patricia May Ludgate (marr. diss. 2009), *d* of Edward and Hazel Ludgate; two *s* one *d*. *Educ:* Chopin Nat. Acad., Warsaw; Univ. of Sydney (DMus 1999). Débuts: Polish Nat. Philharmonic Orch., Warsaw, 1967; RPO, RFH, London, 1970; since then has appeared with major orchestras and conductors incl. Claudio Abbado, Zubin Mehta, Lorin Maazel, Kurt Masur, Witold Rowicki, Charles Mackerras, Erich Leinsdorf, Charles Dutoit, Walter Susskind, and at principal concert centres and festivals in Europe, USA, Japan, China, Australia, NZ; performed complete works of Beethoven, Chopin and Debussy; premières of works by Xenakis, Donatoni, Dillon, Stockhausen, Takemitsu, Feldman, Radulescu, Boyd, Meale, Sitsky. Founder and Artistic Director: London Music Digest, 1972; Alpha Centauri Chamber Ensemble, 1989; Sydney Spring Internat. Fest. of New Music, 1989; Koetschach Mauthen Musiktage (Austria), 1992; Joie et Lumière (Burgundy), 1997; Co-founder and Artistic Dir, Sydney Internat. Piano Comp., 1963; Co-founder, Music Teachers Assoc., NSW, 1975. Chair of Music, Univ. of New England, 2000. Has made numerous recordings; awarded Goethe Prize, Diapason d'Or and German Critics' Award. Order of Merit (Poland), 1993; Chevalier des Arts et des Lettres (France), 2005; Order of Solidarity (Poland), 2007; Gloria Artis Medal Gold Class (Poland), 2011. *Publications:* Beyond Black and White, 2013; numerous contribs to scholastic pubns. *W:* www.rogerwoodward.com.

**WOODWARD, Rt Hon. Shaun (Anthony);** PC 2007; *b* 26 Oct. 1958; *s* of Dennis George Woodward and late Joan Lillian (*née* Nunn); *m* 1987, Camilla Davan (marr. diss. 2018), *e d* of Rt Hon. Sir Timothy Sainsbury, *qv*; one *s* three *d*. *Educ:* Bristol Grammar Sch.; Jesus Coll., Cambridge (first class double MA). Parly Lobbyist, Nat. Consumer Council, 1981–82; BBC TV: Researcher, That's Life!, 1982–85; Producer: Newsnight, 1985–87; Panorama, 1988–89; Editor, That's Life!, 1989–91; Researcher, Lost Babies, 1983; Producer: Drugwatch, 1985; The Gift of Life!, 1987; Dir of Communications, Cons. Party, 1991–92; Vis. Professorial Fellow, QMW, 1992–96; Fellow, Inst. of Politics at Kennedy Sch., Harvard Univ., 1994–95. MP Witney, 1997–2001 (C, 1997–99, Lab, 1999–2001). MP (Lab) St Helens S, 2001–10, St Helens S and Whiston, 2010–15. Opposition front bench spokesman for London, 1999; Parly Under-Sec. of State (Minister for Security and Health Service), NI Office, 2005–06; Parly Under-Sec. of State (Minister for Creative Industries and Tourism), DCMS, 2006–07; Sec. of State for NI, 2007–10; Shadow Sec. of State for NI, 2010–11. Member, Select Committees: EU, 1997–99; Foreign Affairs, 1999–2001; Human Rights, 2001–05. Director: Jerusalem Productions, 1989–96; ENO, 1994–2002 (Chm., Redevelt Campaign, 1994–2002). Chairman: Understanding Industry, 1995–97; Oxford Student Radio, 1995–97; Chairman: LAMDA, 2017– (Dep. Chm., 2013–17; Chm., Capital Campaign, 2013–17); American Friends of LAMDA, 2017–; Hon. Chair, Hamptons Internat. Film Fest., 2013–15. Chm., Ben Hardwick Meml Fund, 1984–93; Trustee, 1993–2005, Dep. Chm., 1993–97, Childline; Mem., Bd of Dirs, Human Dignity Trust, 2012– (Dep. Chm., 2014–16; Chm., 2016–). Mem., Foundn Bd, RSC, 1998–2002; Mem., Fundraising Council, Southwark Cathedral, 2011–16; Dir, Marine Stewardship Council, 1998–2002. *Publications:* (with Ron Lacey) Tranquillisers, 1983; (with Esther Rantzen) Ben: the story of Ben Hardwick, 1985; (with Sarah Caplin) Drugwatch, 1986. *Recreations:* opera, architecture, gardening, reading, travel.

**WOODWARD, Sir Thomas (Jones), (Sir Tom Jones),** Kt 2006; OBE 1999; entertainer; *b* 7 June 1940; *s* of Thomas Woodward and late Freda (*née* Jones); *m* 1956, Melinda Trenchard (*d* 2016); one *s*. Singing début at age of 3; sang in clubs and dance halls; first hit record, It's Not Unusual, 1964; toured US, 1965; many internat. hit records, incl. Reload, 2000 (most successful album in career); radio and TV appearances, incl. series, This is Tom Jones, 1969–71; The Voice, 2012–15, 2016–; King of the Teds (TV play), 2012; Under Milk Wood, 2014; has toured worldwide. Score for musical play, Matador, 1987. *Films:* Mars Attacks, 1997; Agnes Brown, 1999. Appeared as character in Disney animated feature, Emperor's New Groove, 2000. Silver Clef Award, Nordoff Robbins Music

Therapy, 2001. Hon. FRWCMD (Hon. FWCMD 1994). MTV Video Award, 1988; Brit Award, 2003. *Publications:* Over the Top and Back: the autobiography, 2015. *Recreations:* music, history. *Address:* Tom Jones Enterprises, 1801 Avenue of the Stars, Suite 200, Los Angeles, CA 90067, USA. *T:* (310) 5520044. *E:* office@tomjones.com. *Clubs:* Home House; Friars (Los Angeles and New York).

**WOODWARD-CARLTON, Damian;** QC 2019; *b* London, 28 Sept. 1964; *s* of Dr Eric James Carlton and Dr Barbara Woodward-Carlton, MBE; *m* 1998, Julia Sharp; one *s* two *d*. *Educ:* Richmond Comprehensive Sch.; Univ. of Durham (BSc Psychol. 1986; MA 1988); RMA, Sandhurst; City Univ., London (DipLaw 1994). Change Mgt, Andersen Consulting, London and Chicago, 1989–93; called to the Bar, Inner Temple, 1995; in practice as barrister, specialising in public law and children, 1995–. Gov., Tufnell Park Primary Sch. *Recreations:* gardening, baking, pond swimming, amphibians, active supporter of local state schools. *Address:* 42 Bedford Row, WC1R 4LL. *T:* (020) 7831 0222. *E:* dwc@42br.com.

**WOODWARD GENTLE, Sally Claire;** Founder and Chief Executive Officer, Sid Gentle Films Ltd, since 2013; *b* Chatham, 6 Feb. 1964; *d* of Stan and Lorna Woodward; *m* 1995, Henry Gentle; two *s* one *d*. *Educ:* Goldsmiths' Coll., Univ. of London (BA Hons English and Drama 1986). Adminr, Chelsea Arts Club, 1986–87; Hd of TV, Limelight Films, 1988–95; Man. Dir, Kudos Prodns, 1995–2000; BBC, 2000–07: Hd of Develt, TV Drama; Exec. Producer, In-house Drama, then Creative Dir, In-house Drama; Creative Dir, Carnival Films, 2007–13; *productions include:* Whitechapel, 2009–13; Any Human Heart, 2010; Neil Gaiman's Likely Stories, 2016; The Durrells, 2016–18; SS-GB, 2017; Killing Eve, 2018–. Mem., BAFTA. FRTS 2019. *Recreations:* barefoot running, dogs, David Bowie. *Address:* Sid Gentle Films Ltd, 40 Whitfield Street, W1T 2RH. *T:* (020) 7034 2660. *E:* sally@sidgentle.com.

**WOODWARK, Susan Margaret;** *see* Sharland, S. M.

**WOOLARD, Christopher;** Executive Director of Strategy and Competition, since 2013, and Member, Board, since 2015, Financial Conduct Authority; *b* London, 17 March 1972; *s* of John Alan Woolard and Patricia Vera Woolard (*née* Brenchley); *m* 1997, Louise Drane; one *s* two *d*. *Educ:* King's Coll. London (BA; AKC); London Business Sch. (Sloan Fellow) MSc). Sen. Civil Servant, DTI, 1995–2005; Dep. Dir, BBC Trust, 2005–09; Gp Dir, Ofcom, 2009–13. Non-exec. Dir, Payment Systems Regulator, 2014–. *Publications:* (with D. Coyle) Public Value in Practice, 2009. *Address:* Financial Conduct Authority, 12 Endeavour Square, E20 1JN. *T:* (020) 7066 1000. *E:* Christopher.Woolard@fca.org.uk.

**WOOLARD, Edgar Smith;** Chairman, 1989–97, and Chief Executive Officer, 1989–96, Du Pont; *b* 15 April 1934; *s* of Edgar S. Woolard and Mamie (Boone) Woolard; *m* 1956, Peggy Harrell; two *d*. *Educ:* North Carolina State Univ. (BSc Indust. Eng. 1956). Joined Du Pont 1957; industrial engineer, Kinston, NC, 1957–59; group supervisor, industrial engrg, 1959–62; supervisor, manufg sect., 1962–64; planning supervisor, 1964–65; staff asst to Prodn Manager, Wilmington, 1965–66; product supt, Old Hickory, Tenn, 1966–69; engrg supt, 1969–70; Asst Plant Manager, Camden, SC, 1970–71; Plant Manager, 1971–73; Dir of products marketing div., Wilmington, 1973–75; Man. Dir, textile marketing div., 1975–76; Manager, corp. plans dept, 1976–77; Gen. Dir, products and planning div., 1977–78; Gen. Manager, textile fibers, 1978–81; Vice-Pres., textile fibers, 1981–83; Exec. Vice President, 1983–85; Vice Chm., 1985–87; Pres. and Chief Operating Officer, 1987–89. Former Director: Citicorp; N Carolina Textile Foundn; Dir, Acorn Energy, 2014– (Advr, 2010–14); Mem., Bd of Trustees, N Carolina State Univ., 1987–95; former member: Bd of Trustees, Winterthur Mus.; Med. Center of Delaware; Protestant Episcopal Theol Seminary, Virginia; Exec. Cttee, Delaware Roundtable; Bretton Woods Cttee; World Affairs Council; Business Roundtable. *Address:* c/o Du Pont, 1007 Market Street, Wilmington, DE 19898, USA.

**WOOLAS, Philip James;** Founder and Director, Wellington Street Partners Ltd, since 2011; *b* 11 Dec. 1959; *s* of late Dennis Woolas and of Maureen Woolas (*née* White); *m* 1988, Tracey Jane Allen; two *s*. *Educ:* Univ. of Manchester (BA Hons Philosophy 1981). Treas., 1983–84, Pres., 1984–86, NUS; journalist, Television South, 1987; Asst Prod., BBC Newsnight, 1988–90; Prod., Channel Four News, 1990–91; Head of Communications, GMB, 1991–97. MP (Lab) Oldham East and Saddleworth, 1997–Nov. 2010. PPS to Minister for Transport, 1999–2001; an Asst Govt Whip, 2001–02; a Lord Comr of HM Treasury (Govt Whip), 2002–03; Parly Sec., Privy Council Office, and Dep. Leader, H of C, 2003–05; Minister of State: (Minister for Local Govt and Community Cohesion), ODPM, subseq. DCLG, 2005–07; DEFRA, 2007–08; Minister of State (Minister for Immigration), HM Treasury and Home Office, 2008–10; Minister for the NW, 2009–10; Shadow Minister for Immigration, 2010. Chm., All Party Parly Clothing and Textile Gp, 1998–2001; Mem., PLP Leadership Campaign Team, 1997–99 (Dep. Chm., 1998–99). Chm., Tribune Publications Ltd, 1997–2001. Chm., ACE Centre, 2014–. FRSA 2007. *Recreations:* photography, reading, Roxy Music, French wine, cricket, Manchester United supporter. *Address:* 16 Church Walk, Brentford, Middlesex TW8 8DB. *Clubs:* Groucho; Lancashire County Cricket.

**WOOLER, Stephen John,** CB 2005; HM Chief Inspector, Crown Prosecution Service, 1999–2010 (became statutory independent inspectorate, 2000); *b* 16 March 1948; *s* of Herbert George Wooler and Mabel Wooler; *m* 1974, Jonquil Elizabeth Wilmshurst-Smith; one *s* one *d*. *Educ:* Bedford Modern Sch.; University Coll. London (LLB Hons 1969). Called to the Bar, Gray's Inn, 1969, Bencher, 2008; in practice at Common Law Bar, 1970–73; joined Office of Director of Public Prosecutions, 1973: Legal Asst, 1973–76; Sen. Legal Asst, 1976–82; Asst DPP, 1982–83; on secondment to Law Officers' Dept, 1983–87; Chief Crown Prosecutor (London North), 1987–89; on secondment to Law Officers' Dept, 1989–99: Dep. Legal Sec. to Law Officers, 1992–99. Asst Boundary Comr for England, 2011–14. Member: Lord Chancellor's Adv. Sub-Cttee for Bucks, 2012–14; for Thames Valley, 2014–19; Case Mgt Cttee, Financial Reporting Council, 2013–17; Ind. Bd, Legal Services Agency for NI (formerly NI Legal Services Commn), 2014–19. Review of Attorney Gen.'s Chambers for I of M Govt, 2012; Ind. Reviewer, RSPCA prosecution functions, 2013–14; Adv. Gp to the Victims' Comr, 2014–19. Mem., Adv. Bd, UCL Inst. for Criminal Law, 2009–. Trustee, Fremantle Trust, 2018–. *Recreations:* campanology, Rugby, walking, gardening. *Address:* 29 Vicarage Road, Marsworth, Tring, Herts HP23 4LT.

**WOOLEY, Prof. Trevor Dion,** PhD; FRS 2007; Professor of Pure Mathematics, University of Bristol, since 2007. *Educ:* Gonville and Caius Coll., Cambridge (BA Hons Maths 1987; Cert. of Adv. Study in Maths 1988; Imperial Coll. of Sci. and Technol., Univ. of London (PhD 1990). Department of Mathematics, University of Michigan: Asst Prof., 1991–95; Associate Prof., 1995–98; Prof., 1998–2007; Chm. of Dept, 2002–05. *Publications:* articles in jls. *Address:* Department of Mathematics, University of Bristol, University Walk, Clifton, Bristol BS8 1TW.

**WOOLF,** family name of **Baron Woolf.**

**WOOLF, Baron** *cr* 1992 (Life Peer), of Barnes in the London Borough of Richmond; **Harry Kenneth Woolf,** CH 2015; Kt 1979; PC 1986; Lord Chief Justice of England and Wales, 2000–05; Chartered Arbitrator/Mediator, since 2006; *b* 2 May 1933; *s* of late Alexander Woolf and Leah Woolf (*née* Cussins); *m* 1961, Marguerite Sassoon, *d* of late George Sassoon; three *s*. *Educ:* Fettes Coll.; University Coll., London (LLB; Fellow, 1981). Called to Bar, Inner Temple, 1954; Bencher, 1976. Commnd (Nat. Service), 15/19th Royal Hussars, 1954; seconded Army Legal Services, 1955; Captain 1955. Started practice at Bar, 1956. A Recorder of the Crown Court, 1972–79; Jun. Counsel, Inland Revenue, 1973–74; First Treasury Junior Counsel (Common Law), 1974–79; a Judge of the High Court of Justice, Queen's Bench Div., 1979–86; Presiding Judge, SE Circuit, 1981–84; a Lord Justice of Appeal, 1986–92; a Lord of Appeal in Ordinary, 1992–96; Master of the Rolls, 1996–2000; Judge, Hong Kong Court of Final Appeal, 2003–; Pres., Qatar Financial Services Court, 2006–. Held inquiry into prison disturbances, 1990, Part II with Judge Tumin, report 1991; conducted inquiry, Access to Justice, 1994–96; held inquiry into BAE Systems, 2008 (report: Business Ethics, Global Companies and the Defence Industry, 2008); Chm., LSE Inquiry into LSE's relationship with Libya, 2011. Member: Senate, Inns of Court and Bar, 1981–85; Bd of Management, Inst. of Advanced Legal Studies, 1985–94 (Chm., 1986–94); World Bank Internat. Adv. Council on Law and Justice, 2001–; Chairman: Lord Chancellor's Adv. Cttee on Legal Educn, 1986–91; Middx Adv. Cttee on Justices of the Peace, 1986–90; Lord Chancellor's Adv. Cttee on Public Records, 1996–2000; Council of Civil Justice, 1998–2000; Rules Cttee, 1998–2000; Bank of England's Financial Markets Law Cttee, 2005–; President: Assoc. of Law Teachers, 1985–89; Central Council of Jewish Social Services, 1987–2000; SW London Magistrates Assoc., 1987–93; Assoc. of Mems of Bds of Visitors, 1994–; Public Records Soc., 1996–2000. Vice-Pres., Royal Over-Seas League, 2001–. Pro-Chancellor, London Univ., 1994–2002. Chairman: Trustees, Butler Trust, 1992–96 (Trustee, 1991–96; Pres., 1996–); Special Trustees, St Mary's Hosp., Paddington, 1993–97; Magna Carta Trust, 1996–2000; Prison Reform Trust, 2011–. Patron: Jewish Mus., 1998–; Woolf Institute: Muslim, Jewish and Christian Inter-faith Relns, 2000–. Visitor: Nuffield Coll., Oxford, 1996–2000; UCL, 1996–2000 (Chm., Council, 2005–). Chancellor, Open Univ. of Israel, 2005–. Gov., Oxford Centre for Postgrad. Hebrew Studies, 1989–93. Hon. Mem., SPTL, 1988. Hon. Bencher, King's Inns, Dublin. Hon. FBA 2000; Hon. FMedSci 2002. Hon. Fellow, Leeds Poly., 1990. Hon. LLD: Buckingham, 1992; Bristol, 1992; London, 1993; Anglia Poly. Univ., 1994; Manchester Metropolitan, 1994; Hull, 2001; Richmond, 2001; Cambridge, 2002; Birmingham, 2002; Exeter, 2002; Wolverhampton, 2002; Hon. DSc Cranfield, 2001; Hon. DLit London. Hon. Freeman and Mem., Drapers' Co., 1999. *Publications:* Protecting the Public: the new challenge (Hamlyn Lecture), 1990; (ed with J. Woolf) Declaratory Judgement, 2nd edn, 1993, 3rd edn 2002; (ed jtly) de Smith, Judicial Review of Administrative Action, 5th edn, 1995, 7th edn (jtly) as de Smith's Judicial Review, 2008; (ed jtly) Principles of Judicial Review, 1999. *Address:* House of Lords, SW1A 0PW. *Clubs:* Athenæum, Garrick, Royal Automobile.
*See also* E. C. A. Woolf.

**WOOLF, Dame (Catherine) Fiona,** DBE 2015 (CBE 2002); DL; Partner, CMS Cameron McKenna Nabarro Olswang (formerly CMS Cameron McKenna), 1981–2019; President, Law Society, 2006–07 (Vice President, 2005–06); Lord Mayor of London, 2013–14; *b* 11 May 1948; *d* of Richard and Margaret Swain; *m* 1990, Nicholas Woolf; one step *s* one step *d*. *Educ:* Keele Univ. (BA Law 1970). Solicitor of Supreme Court, 1973. Coward Chance, 1973–78; CMS Cameron McKenna, 1981–, energy and projects practice, work on power sector restructurings, privatisations and power and transmission projects. Mem., Competition Commn, 2005–13. Non-exec. Dir, Affinity Water Ltd (formerly Three Valleys Water plc, then Veolia Water Central plc), 2006–13; Chair, Adv. Bd, Base London, 2014–15. Sen. Fellow, Harvard Univ., 2001–02. Pres., Chelsea Opera Gp, 2013 (Chm., 2008); Trustee: Raleigh Internat., 2007–16; Sci. Mus. Gp, 2015–. Gov., Guildhall Sch. of Music and Drama, 2011–14; Chancellor, Univ. of Law, 2014–18. Alderman, Candlewick Ward, City of London, 2007–18; Sheriff, City of London, 2010–11; DL Gtr London, 2016; Mem. Council, London Regt, 2011–19. Master, Plumbers' Co., 2018–19. Hon. Pres., Aldersgate Gp, 2014–. Hon. LLD: Coll. of Law, 2007; Keele, 2008; Hon. DSc City, 2014. DStJ 2013. *Publications:* Global Transmission Expansion: recipes for success, 2003; co-author of three World Bank pubns; many articles and papers in energy jls. *Recreations:* singing, music, furniture history, theatre, art, turned wood. *Club:* East India.

**WOOLF, Prof. Clifford John;** Professor of Neurology and Neurobiology, Harvard Medical School, since 2010 (Richard Kitz Professor of Anesthesia Research, 1997–2010); Director, F. M. Kirby Neurobiology Center, Children's Hospital Boston, since 2010; *b* 30 Jan. 1952; *s* of Jeffry and Lorna Woolf; *m* 1976, Fredia Maltz; two *s*. *Educ:* Univ. of the Witwatersrand, Johannesburg (MB, BCh, PhD). MRCP. Lectr, Middlesex Hosp. Med. Sch., London, 1979–81; Lectr, 1981–88, Reader, 1988–92, Prof. of Neurobiology, 1992–97, UCL. Director: Neural Plasticity Res. Gp, Massachusetts Gen. Hosp., 1997–2010; Neurobiology Prog., Harvard Stem Cell Inst., 2013–18. Schmidt Lectr, MIT, 2010. Hon. Fellow, Faculty of Pain Medicine, Coll. of Anaesthetists, Ireland, 2015. Distinguished Res. Award, Amer. Soc. for Anesthesia, 2004; Wall Medal, RCAnaes, 2009; Javits Award, NIH, 2011; F. E. Bennett Meml Lectureship Award, American Neurol Assoc., 2012; Magnes Medal (Israel), 2013; Frederick W. L. Kerr Basic Sci. Res. Award, American Pain Soc., 2015; Reeve-Irvine Res. Medal, 2017; Gill Award, 2017. *Publications:* numerous articles in scientific jls on the pathophysiology of pain and the regeneration of the nervous system. *Recreation:* mind surfing. *Address:* F. M. Kirby Neurobiology Center, Children's Hospital Boston, 300 Longwood Avenue, CLS 12258, Boston, MA 02115, USA.

**WOOLF, Eliot Charles Anthony;** QC 2018; *b* London, 29 July 1967; *s* of Baron Woolf, *qv*; *m* 2001, Jacqueline Auer; one *s* one *d*. *Educ:* Eton Coll.; Robinson Coll., Cambridge (MA Hist. of Art); City Univ., London (DipLaw). Called to the Bar, Inner Temple, 1993; in practice as a barrister specialising in clinical negligence and personal injury law. *Recreations:* music, art, cinema, travel, walking. *Address:* Outer Temple Chambers, 222 Strand, WC2R 1BA. *E:* eliot.woolf@outertemple.com. *Club:* Royal Automobile.

**WOOLF, Dame Fiona;** *see* Woolf, Dame C. F.

**WOOLF, Geoffrey David;** photographer; *b* 15 April 1944. *Educ:* Polytechnic of Central London (BSc Econ). Lecturer in History, Southgate Technical College, 1974–89; Gen. Sec., NATFHE, 1989–94; Trade Union Manager, LV Gp, 1996–97; Organiser, Prospect (formerly Inst. of Professionals, Managers and Specialists), 1997–2005. *Recreation:* politics. *Address:* 11 Queens Mews, Queen Street, Deal CT14 6HA. *E:* geoffwoolf@outlook.com.

**WOOLF, Prof. Gregory Duncan,** PhD; FBA 2017; Professor of Classics, and Director, Institute of Classical Studies, School of Advanced Study, University of London, since 2015; *b* Hemel Hempstead, 3 Dec. 1961; *s* of John Louis Woolf and Margaret Elizabeth Woolf (*née* Lewarne); *m* 1989, Johanna Weeks; one *s* one *d*. *Educ:* Bexhill Grammar Sch.; Christ Church, Oxford (BA); Trinity Coll., Cambridge (PhD 1991). Fellow: Christ's Coll., Cambridge, 1989–90; Magdalen Coll., Oxford, 1990–93; Brasenose Coll., Oxford,

1993–98; Prof. of Ancient Hist., Univ. of St Andrews, 1998–2014. FSA; FSAScot; MAE. *Recreation:* finding ways to be usefully difficult. *Address:* Institute of Classical Studies, School of Advanced Study, University of London, Senate House, Malet Street, WC1E 7HU. *E:* greg.woolf@sas.ac.uk.

**WOOLFE, Richard;** Creative Director, GooWoo Media, since 2017; *b* Brighton, 14 Aug. 1962; *s* of Julian Woolfe and Laurel Woolfe; *m* 1988, Hilary Berg (marr. diss.); one *s* one *d*. *Educ:* Brighton Coll.; Manchester Poly. (BEd Hons). Freelance reporter/producer, BBC Radio Sussex, 1985–86; Researcher, then Producer, later Exec. Producer, That's Life!, Hearts of Gold, Nat. Lottery Live, Noel's Christmas Presents, The Family Show, Good Fortune, BBC TV, 1986–96; Man. Dir, Real TV, 1996–97; Ed., Entertainment, Granada TV, 1998–99; Hd of Entertainment, Planet 24 Productions, 1999–2001; Dir of Television, Living TV, 2001–06; Dir of Progs, Sky 1, 2, 3, 2006–08; Channel Controller, Five, 2009–10; Creative Director: Prime Focus Productions, 2011–12; Prizeo.com, 2012–15; Dir, Woolfe TV, 2012–16. Member: RTS 2002; BAFTA 2007. *Recreations:* reading, wine. *Clubs:* Ivy, Soho House.

**WOOLFE, Steven Marcus;** Member for North West Region, European Parliament, 2014–19 (UK Ind, 2014–16; Ind, 2016–19); *b* Moss Side, Manchester, 9 Oct. 1967; *m*. *Educ:* St Bernard's RC Sch.; St Bede's RC Ind. Coll.; Univ. of Wales, Aberystwyth (LLB 1990); Inns of Court Sch. of Law. Called to the Bar, Inner Temple, 1992; in practice as barrister, specialising in commercial, criminal and common law, 1992–96; Legal and Compliance Analyst, UBS, 1996–97; Counsel: Taylor Wessing, 1997–99; DLA Piper, 1999–2000; Sen. Compliance Consultant and Partner, Aurelius Compliance Consultants, 2000–07; Dep. Hd, Compliance Dept, Standard Bank, 2003–04; Gen. Counsel, Boyer Allen Investment Mgt LLP, 2006–12; Gen. Counsel Consultant, MercuryJove Advrs, 2012–14. Sen. Legal Consultant, Barclays Capital, 2013. Sen. Compliance Advr, Aviva, 2014. UKIP spokesman on financial affairs and City of London, 2010–14, on econs, 2014, on migration and financial affairs, 2014–16. Contested (UK Ind) Stockport, 2015.

**WOOLFSON, Prof. Michael Mark,** FRS 1984; FRAS; FInstP; Professor of Theoretical Physics, University of York, 1965–94, now Emeritus; *b* 9 Jan. 1927; *s* of Morris and Rose Woolfson; *m* 1951, Margaret (*née* Frohlich); two *s* one *d*. *Educ:* Jesus College, Oxford (MA; Hon. Fellow, 1999); UMIST (PhD, DSc). Royal Engineers, 1947–49. Research Assistant: UMIST, 1950–52; Cavendish Lab., Cambridge, 1952–54; ICI Fellow, Univ. of Cambridge, 1954–55; Lectr, 1955–61, Reader, 1961–65, UMIST; Head of Dept of Physics, Univ. of York, 1982–87. Hughes Medal, Royal Soc., 1986; Patterson Award, Amer. Crystallographic Assoc., 1990; Aminoff Medal, Royal Swedish Acad. of Scis, 1992; Dorothy Hodgkin Prize, British Crystallographic Assoc., 1997; Ewald Prize, Internat. Union of Crystallography, 2002. *Publications:* Direct Methods in Crystallography, 1961; An Introduction to X-Ray Crystallography, 1970, 2nd edn 1997; The Origin of the Solar System, 1989; Physical and Non-Physical Methods of Solving Crystal Structures, 1995; An Introduction to Computer Simulation, 1999; The Origin and Evolution of the Solar System, 2000; Planetary Science, 2001, 2nd edn 2013; Mathematics for Physics, 2007; Formation of the Solar System, 2007, 2nd edn 2013; Everyday Probability and Statistics, 2008, 2nd edn 2012; Time, Space, Stars and Man, 2009; Materials, Matter and Particles, 2009; On the Origin of Planets, 2010; The Fundamentals of Imaging, 2011; Resonance, 2014; Time and Age, 2015; Colour, 2016; A Dialogue Concerning the Two Chief Models of Planet Formation, 2017; About Stars, 2019; papers in learned jls. *Recreation:* writing. *Address:* 61 Thackrah Court, Leeds LS17 8FQ. *T:* (0113) 469 2343.

**WOOLGAR, Prof. Stephen William,** PhD; FAcSS; Professor of Sociology and Marketing, and Head of Science and Technology Studies, University of Oxford, 2000, now Emeritus Professor; Fellow, Green Templeton College (formerly Green College), Oxford, 2000, now Emeritus Fellow; Professor of Science and Technology Studies, Linköping University, Sweden, since 2014; *b* 14 Feb. 1950; *s* of late William Thomas Woolgar, III, and Constance Lillian Stuart Woolgar (*née* Hinkes); *m* 1983, Jacqueline Stokes; three *d*. *Educ:* Brentwood Sch.; Emmanuel Coll., Cambridge (BA 1st Cl. Hons 1972; MA 1976; PhD 1978). Brunel University: Lectr in Sociol., 1975–88; Reader 1988–92; Prof. of Sociol., 1992–2000; Dir, Centre for Res. into Innovation, Culture and Technol., 1991–98; Hd, Dept of Human Scis, 1996–98; Dir, ESRC prog. Virtual Society? the social sci. of electronic technologies, Univ. of Oxford (formerly at Brunel Univ.), 1997–2002. Vis. Prof., McGill Univ., Canada, 1979–81; Exxon Fellow, MIT, 1983–84; Maître de Recherche Associé, Ecole Nationale Supérieure des Mines, Paris, 1988–89; ESRC Sen. Res. Fellow, 1994–95; Fulbright Sen. Schol., Dept of Sociol., UC San Diego, 1995–96. Member: OST Technology Foresight Panel: Leisure and Learning, 1994–96; IT, Electronics and Communications, 1996–99; Sociol. Panel, HEFCE RAE 1996 and 2001; Council, Consumers' Assoc., 2000–. FAcSS 2010. *Publications:* (with B. Latour) Laboratory Life: the construction of scientific facts, 1979, 2nd edn 1986; (ed) Knowledge and Reflexivity, 1988; Science: the very idea, 1988; (ed jtly) The Cognitive Turn: sociological and psychological perspectives on science, 1989; (ed with M. Lynch) Representation in Scientific Practice, 1990; (with K. Grint) The Machine at Work: technology, work and organisation, 1997; Virtual Society?: technology, cyberbole, reality, 2002; numerous articles. *Address:* Saïd Business School, University of Oxford, Park End Street, Oxford OX1 1HP. *T:* (01865) 288934. *E:* steve.woolgar@sbs.ox.ac.uk.

**WOOLHOUSE, Prof. Mark Edward John,** OBE 2002; FRSE; FMedSci; Professor of Infectious Disease Epidemiology, University of Edinburgh, since 2005; *b* Shrewsbury, 25 April 1959; *s* of late Prof. John George Woolhouse, CBE and of (Ruth) Carolyn Woolhouse; *m* 2004, Dr Francisca Mutapi; one *d*. *Educ:* New Coll., Oxford (BA Zool. 1980); Univ. of York (MSc Biol Computation 1981); Queen's Univ., Kingston, Ont (PhD Biol. 1985). Res. Fellow, Dept of Biol Scis, Univ. of Zimbabwe, 1985–86; MRC Trng Fellow, Dept of Biol., Imperial Coll. London, 1986–89; Department of Zoology, University of Oxford: Beit Meml Fellow for Med. Res., 1989–92; Royal Soc. Univ. Res. Fellow, 1992–97; Prof. of Veterinary Public Health and Quantitative Epidemiol., Centre for Tropical Veterinary Medicine, Univ. of Edinburgh, 1997–2005. FRSE 2004; FMedSci 2010. *Publications:* contrib. book chapters and articles to scientific jls. *Recreations:* walking, fishing, Everton FC. *Address:* Usher Institute of Population Health Sciences and Informatics, Ashworth Laboratories, Kings Buildings, University of Edinburgh, Charlotte Auerbach Road, Edinburgh EH9 3FL. *T:* (0131) 650 5456, *Fax:* (0131) 650 6564. *E:* mark.woolhouse@ed.ac.uk.

**WOOLHOUSE, Richard;** Head of Business Economics and Strategy Europe, Abbott Laboratories, since 2016; *b* Cambridge, 6 Aug. 1967; *s* of Geoffrey and June Woolhouse; *m* Susanna; one *s* two *d*. *Educ:* Fitzwilliam Coll., Cambridge (BA 1990; MA). PA, Financial Econ. Consultants, 1990–94; Economist/Strategist, Citibank: London, 1994–97; Hong Kong, 1997–98; London, 1998–2000; McKinsey & Co., London, 2000–02; Economist, HMRC/HM Treasury, 2002–04; Strategist, Credit Suisse First Boston, 2004–05; Public and Corporate Econ. Consultants, 2005–08; Economist: Centre for Cities, 2008–09; CBI, 2009–13; Chief Economist, BBA, 2013–16. *Recreation:* cricket. *Address:* Abbott Laboratories, Abbott House, Vanwall Road, Maidenhead SL6 4XE. *E:* richard.woolhouse@gmail.com.

**WOOLLAM, Her Honour Suzanna Elizabeth;** a Circuit Judge, 2001–06; *b* 6 Dec. 1946; *d* of late John Martin Woollam and Elizabeth Mary Woollam (*née* Brennan). *Educ:* various convents; Trinity Coll., Dublin (MA Philosophy 1969). Called to the Bar, Gray's Inn, 1975; law reporting for the Weekly Law Reports and Times Law Reports, 1975–77; Army Legal Service, 1977–79; Solicitor to Scotland Yard, 1980–88; Sen. Legal Asst, office of JAG, 1988–90; Asst JAG, 1990–2001. *Recreations:* walking, gardening, reading, films, theatre.

**WOOLLARD, John Ian;** a District Judge (Magistrates' Courts), Essex, since 2011; *b* 13 July 1954; *s* of Charles and Joy Woollard; *m* 1981, Angela Margaret Lee; one *s* one *d*. *Educ:* Brentwood Sch. Admitted Solicitor, 1977; Asst Solicitor, T. V. Edwards & Co., 1977–78; County Prosecuting Solicitors' Office, Essex, 1978–82; Partner, Mitchell Maudsley & Wright, Basildon, 1982–87; freelance solicitor advocate, 1987–98; a Stipendiary Magistrate, then Dist Judge (Magistrates' Courts), Hants, 1998–2006; a Dist Judge (Magistrates' Courts), NE London, 2006–11. *Recreations:* music, reading, tennis. *Address:* c/o Essex Magistrates' Courts, Osprey House, Hedgerows Business Park, Springfield, Chelmsford CM2 5PF. *T:* (01245) 313500.

**WOOLLEY, David Rorie,** QC 1980; barrister-at-law, 1962–2015; a Recorder of the Crown Court, 1982–94; *b* 9 June 1939; *s* of Albert and Ethel Woolley; *m* 1988, Mandy, *d* of Donald and Barbara Hutchison, Upper Dicker, Sussex. *Educ:* Winchester Coll.; Trinity Hall, Cambridge (BA Hons Law). Called to the Bar, Middle Temple, 1962, Bencher, 1988. Vis. Scholar, Wolfson Coll., Cambridge, 1982–87. Inspector, DoE inquiry into Nat. Gall. extension, 1984. *Publications:* Town Hall and the Property Owner, 1965; (jtly) Environmental Law, 2000, 2nd edn, 2009; (jtly) History of the Middle Temple, 2011; (contrib.) Pantaudi: nawab of cricket, 2013; contribs to various legal jls. *Recreations:* opera, mountaineering, Real tennis. *Address:* White Lodge, Lockeridge, Wilts SN8 4EQ. *Clubs:* MCC; Swiss Alpine.

**WOOLLEY, Janice Joanne;** *see* Graham, J. J.

**WOOLLEY, (John) Moger;** DL; Chairman, Bristol Water Holdings, 1998–2012; *b* 1 May 1935; *s* of Cyril Herbert Steele Woolley and Eveline Mary May Woolley; *m* 1960, Gillian Edith Millar; one *s* one *d*. *Educ:* Taunton Sch.; Bristol Univ., 1956–59 (BSc). National Service, 1954–56. Various management positions, DRG plc, 1959–89, Chief Exec., 1985–89; Chairman: Dolphin Packaging, 1990–95; API plc, 1992–2001; Brunel (Hldgs) plc (formerly BM Gp), 1992–2002. Non-executive Director: Staveley Industries, 1990–99; United Bristol Hosp. Trust, 1991–93; Avon Rubber, 1992–96. Chm. Council, 1997–2006, Pro-Chancellor, 2006–14, Univ. of Bristol. DL 2000, High Sheriff, 2002–03, Glos. Hon. Fellow, Univ. of Bristol, 2014. Hon. LLD Bristol, 2005. *Recreations:* cricket, hockey, golf, gardening. *Address:* Matford House, Northwoods, Winterbourne, Bristol BS36 1RS. *T:* (01454) 772180. *Clubs:* MCC; Merchant Venturers' (Bristol) (Master, 1998–99).

**WOOLLEY, Mary Elizabeth;** *see* Lewis, M. E.

**WOOLLEY, Moger;** *see* Woolley, (John) Moger.

**WOOLLEY, Sir Simon,** Kt 2019; Co-Founder and Director, Operation Black Vote, since 1996; *b* Leicester, 24 Dec. 1961; *s* of Daniel and Phyliss Fox; partner, Begona Juarros; one *s*. *Educ:* BA Hons Lit. and Spanish; MA Hons Spanish Lit. Mem., Equality and Human Rights Commn, 2009–12. Chair, At Home in Europe, Open Soc. Foundn, 2012–. Vis. Lectr, Nottingham Univ., 2006–. Hon. Dr Westminster, 2012. *Publications:* How to Achieve Better Black and Minority Ethnic Representation. *Recreations:* football, swimming. *Address:* 18A Victoria Park Square, E2 9PB. *E:* simon@obv.org.uk.
*[Created a Baron (Life Peer), 2019 but title not gazetted at time of going to press.]*

**WOOLLEY, Trevor Adrian,** CB 2007; non-executive Director, Oil and Pipelines Agency, since 2012; Deputy Chairman, Advisory Council, National Records and Archives, since 2017 (Member, since 2014); *b* 9 Aug. 1954; *s* of late Harry George Woolley and Doreen Vera Woolley (*née* O'Hale). *Educ:* Latymer Upper Sch., Hammersmith; Peterhouse, Cambridge (MA Hist.). Ministry of Defence, 1975–2012: Private Sec. to Sec. of Cabinet, 1986–90 (on secondment); Dir, Procurement Policy, 1990–93; Head, Resources and Progs (Army), 1993–97; Asst Under Sec. of State (Systems), 1997–98; Dir Gen., Resources and Plans, 1998–2002; Comd Sec., Land, 2002–03; Finance Dir, 2003–08; Dir Gen., Police Study Team, 2009–10; Chief of Corporate Services, then Dir Gen., Resources, Defence Equipment and Support Orgn, 2010–12. Lay Mem., Hounslow CCG, 2013–. *Publications:* Unnatural Selection: 50 years of England Test teams, 2015. *Recreations:* cricket, golf, travel, trekking. *E:* trvrwool@aol.com. *Club:* MCC.

**WOOLMAN, Hon. Lord;** Stephen Errol Woolman; a Senator of the College of Justice in Scotland, since 2008; *b* 16 May 1953; *s* of late Errol Woolman, architect, and Frances Woolman (*née* Porter); *m* 1977, Dr Helen Mackinnon; two *d*. *Educ:* George Heriot's Sch., Edinburgh; Aberdeen Univ. (LLB). Lectr, 1978–87, Associate Dean, Faculty of Law, 1981–84, Edinburgh Univ.; admitted to Faculty of Advocates, 1987; Standing Junior Counsel in Scotland: Office of Fair Trading, 1991–95; MoD (Procurement Exec.), 1995–96; Inland Revenue, 1996–98; QC (Scot.) 1998; Advocate Depute, 1999–2002. Chm., Scottish Council of Law Reporting, 2007–08; Dep. Chm., Boundary Commn for Scotland, 2009–15. Keeper, Advocates' Liby, 2004–08. Trustee, Nat. Liby of Scotland, 2004–08. Chm. Council, St George's Sch., Edinburgh, 2011–15. Hon. LLD Aberdeen, 2012. Liveryman, Woolmen's Co., 2014. *Publications:* An Introduction to the Scots Law of Contract, 1987, 6th edn 2018. *Recreations:* cinema, swimming. *Address:* Court of Session, Parliament House, Edinburgh EH1 1RQ. *Club:* New (Edinburgh).

**WOOLMAN, Andrew Paul Lander; His Honour Judge Woolman;** a Circuit Judge, since 2006; *b* 10 Feb. 1950; *s* of Sydney and Anita Woolman; *m* 1977, Telsa Phillipson; two *s* one *d*. *Educ:* Leeds Grammar Sch.; Pembroke Coll., Cambridge (BA 1971). Called to the Bar, Inner Temple, 1973; Asst Recorder, 1992–97; a Recorder, 1997–2006. *Recreations:* tennis, classics, football, music, theatre, fell-walking, talking. *Address:* c/o Preston Combined Courts, The Law Courts, Openshaw Place, Ringway, Preston, Lancs PR1 2LL. *T:* (01772) 844700.

**WOOLMAN, Stephen Errol;** *see* Woolman, Hon. Lord.

**WOOLMER,** family name of **Baron Woolmer of Leeds**.

**WOOLMER OF LEEDS,** Baron *cr* 1999 (Life Peer), of Leeds in the county of West Yorkshire; **Kenneth John Woolmer;** Partner: Halton Gill Associates, consultants on central and local government relations, 1999–2009 (Principal, 1979–97); Anderson McGraw, 2001–07; *b* 25 April 1940; *s* of Joseph William and Gertrude May Woolmer; *m* 1961, Janice Chambers; three *s*. *Educ:* Gladstone Street County Primary, Rothwell, Northants; Kettering Grammar Sch.; Leeds Univ. (BA Econs). Research Fellow, Univ. of West Indies, 1961–62; Teacher, Friern Rd Sec. Mod. Sch., London, 1963; Lecturer: Univ. of Leeds (Economics), 1963–66; Univ. of Ahmadu Bello, Nigeria, 1966–68; Univ. of Leeds, 1968–79; Dir, MBA Progs, 1991–97, Dean of Ext. Relns, 1997, Chm., subseq. Dean, 1997–2000, Sch. of Business and Econ. Studies, Leeds Univ., later Leeds Univ. Business Sch. Councillor: Leeds CC, 1970–78; West Yorkshire MCC, 1973–80 (Leader, 1975–77; Leader of Opposition, 1977–79). Chairman, Planning and Transportation Cttee, Assoc. of

Metropolitan Authorities, 1974–77. Contested (Lab) Batley and Spen, 1983, 1987. MP (Lab) Batley and Morley, 1979–83; Opposition spokesman on trade, shipping and aviation, 1981–83; Mem., Select Cttee on Treasury and Civil Service, 1980–81; Chm., 1981, Vice-Chm., 1982, PLP Economics and Finance Gp; House of Lords: Mem., 1999–2002, Chm., 2002–06, EU Sub Cttee B (Industry, Energy, Telecoms and Transport); Mem., EU Select Cttee, 2002–06; Mem., EU Sub Cttee A (Economic and Financial Affairs and Internat. Trade), 2007–12; Mem., Secondary Legislation Scrutiny Cttee, 2013–16. Dir, UK Japan 21st Century Gp, 2005–10; Mem., Internat. Adv. Bd, White Rose E Asia Centre, 2007–15. Dir, Leeds United AFC, 1991–96. Non-executive Director: Thornfield Develts Ltd, 1999–2002; Thornfield Ventures Ltd, 2002–04; Saiinfo plc, 2000–02; Courtcom Ltd, 2001–03. Chm. Govs, Leeds Metropolitan Univ., 2010–13; Mem. Adv. Bd, Warwick Business Sch., 2012–16.

**WOOLRICH, John;** composer; *b* 3 Jan. 1954; *s* of Derek Holland Woolrich and Una Woolrich (*née* MacDougall). *Educ:* Manchester Univ. (BA); Lancaster Univ. (MLitt). Northern Arts Fellow, Durham Univ., 1982–85; Composer in Residence, Nat. Centre for Orchestral Studies, 1985–86; Artistic Dir, Composers' Ensemble, 1989–; Composer in Association, Orch. of St John's, Smith Square, 1994–95; Dir of Concerts, Almeida Opera, 1999–; Artistic Associate, Birmingham Contemporary Music Gp, 2002–; Associate Artistic Dir, Aldeburgh Fest., 2005–10 (Guest Artistic Dir, 2004); Artistic Director: Dartington Internat. Summer Sch., 2010–13; Mirepoix Musique, 2013–. Lectr in Music, RHBNC, 1994–98; Prof. of Music, Brunel Univ., 2010–13. Vis. Fellow, Clare Hall, Cambridge, 1999–2001. Hon. FTCL 1996. *Compositions* include: orchestral: The Barber's Timepiece, 1986; The Ghost in the Machine, 1990; The Theatre Represents a Garden: Night, 1991; Concerto for Viola, 1993; Concerto for Oboe, 1996; Cello Concerto, 1998; Concerto for Orchestra, 1999; Violin Concerto, 2008; Falling Down, 2009; chamber music: Ulysses Awakes, 1989; Lending Wings, 1989; The Death of King Renaud, 1991; It is Midnight, Dr Schweitzer, 1992; A Farewell, 1992; Capriccio, 2009; Pluck from the Air, 2013; Call to the Mirrors, 2014; To the Silver Bow, 2014; A Book of Inventions, 2019. *Address:* c/o Faber Music, Bloomsbury House, 74–77 Great Russell Street, WC1B 3DA. *T:* (020) 7908 5310.

**WOOLTON, 3rd Earl of,** *cr* 1956; **Simon Frederick Marquis;** Baron Woolton, 1939; Viscount Walberton, 1953; Viscount Walberton, 1956; Head of Corporate Development, Europe, Middle East and Africa, Houlihan Lokey, since 2018; *b* 24 May 1958; *s* of 2nd Earl of Woolton and Cecily Josephine (later Countess Lloyd George of Dwyfor), *e d* of Sir Alexander Gordon Cumming, 5th Bt; *S* father, 1969; *m* 1st, 1987, Hon. Sophie Frederika (marr. diss. 1997), *o c* of Baron Birdwood; three *d*; 2nd, 1999, Mrs Carol Chapman (*née* Davidson). *Educ:* Eton College; St Andrews Univ. (MA Hons). Company director. Merchant banker, S. G. Warburg & Co. Ltd, 1982–88; Founder Director: Woolton Elwes Ltd, 1994–2000; New Boathouse Capital Ltd, 2000–08; Quayle Munro Ltd, 2008–18; Dir, Quayle Munro Hldgs Ltd, 2012–. Trustee: Woolton Charitable Trust; Titsey Foundn; Balcarres Heritage Trust; Keats-Shelley Meml Assoc., 2015–. Gov., Tonbridge Sch. Liveryman, Skinners' Co. *Recreation:* golf. *Address:* Broom Villa, 27 Broomhouse Road, SW6 3QU. *Clubs:* White's, Brooks's, MCC; Royal and Ancient; Swinley Forest Golf.

**WOOLWICH, Area Bishop of,** since 2017; **Rt Rev. Dr (Woyin) Karowei Dorgu;** *b* Nigeria, 1958. *Educ:* Coll. of Medicine, Univ. of Lagos (MB BS 1985); London Bible Coll. (BA 1993); Oak Hill Theol Coll. Ordained deacon, 1995, priest, 1996; Curate, St Mark, Tollington, 1995–98; Curate, 1998–2000, Team Vicar, 2000–12, Vicar, 2012–17, St John the Evangelist, Upper Holloway; Preb., St Paul's Cathedral, 2016–17. *Address:* Trinity House, 4 Chapel Court, Borough High Street, SE1 1HW. *T:* (020) 7939 9400.

**WOOLWICH, Sian Mary;** *see* Williams, S. M.

**WOOSNAM, Ian Harold,** OBE 2007 (MBE 1992); professional golfer, since 1976; golf course designer; *b* 2 March 1958; *s* of late Harold Woosnam and of Joan Woosnam; *m* 1983, Glendryth Mervyn Pugh; one *s* two *d*. *Educ:* St Martin's Modern Sch. 53 professional tournament wins, 1987–, including: World Cup (individual), 1987 and 1991; World Match Play, 1987, 1990 and 2001; PGA, 1988 and 1997; PGA Grand Slam of Golf, 1991; US Masters, 1991; British Masters, 1994. Hon. Mem., PGA European tour. Captain, Ryder Cup team, (winners) 2006. Pres., World Snooker, 1999–. *Publications:* Ian Woosnam's Golf Masterpieces, 1988; Power Golf, 1989, new edn 1991; Golf Made Simple: the Woosie Way, 1997; (with Edward Griffiths) Woosie: the autobiography, 2002. *Recreations:* snooker, water ski-ing, shooting. *Address:* 10 Henley Close, Oswestry, Shropshire SY11 2SW. *Clubs:* Llanymynech Golf, La Moye Golf.

**WOOTTON, Adrian,** OBE 2017; Chief Executive Officer: Film London, since 2003; British Film Commission, since 2011; *b* 18 May 1962; *s* of late Ronald Oliver Wootton and of Unity Wootton; *m* 1986, Karen Sarah Goodman; one *d*. *Educ:* Univ. of East Anglia (BA Hons English and Amer. Studies, MA Film Studies). Director: Bradford Playhouse and Film Theatre, 1986–89; Nottingham Media Centre Ltd, 1989–93; Hd, BFI Exhibn (incl. Exec. Hd, NFT and Dir, London Film Fest., 1993–2002); Dep. Dir, BFI, 2002–03. Founder, Dir and Chair, Shots in the Dark, Internat. Crime, Mystery and Thriller Fest., Nottingham, 1991–2001, 2018–; Dir, Crime Scene, fest. of crime and mystery genre, NFT, 2000–; Co-Curator, Soundtracking, Fest. of Popular Music and Cinema, Sheffield, 1999–2000; Chair of Bd, Sensoria Music and Film Fest., Sheffield, 2009–16; Curator, Cinema: Made in Italy, 2018–. Board Member: Skillset Craft and Tech. Skills Acad., 2011–; British Screen Adv. Council, 2011–; Mayor of London's Strategy Bd, 2012–16; Mem., Trade and Investment Bd, DIT, 2018–. Foreign Consultant, Noir in Fest., Italy, 1999–; Advr to Venice Film Fest., 2004–. Vis. Prof., Film and Media, Norwich University Coll. of the Arts, 2012–. Co-producer and writer, documentaries: Dickens on Film, 2012; All the World's A Screen, 2016. Member: BAFTA, 1996–; Eur. Film Acad., 2006–. Hon. DArts Norwich Univ. Coll. of the Arts, 2012; Hon. DLitt UEA, 2014. *Publications:* (contrib.) 100 Great Detectives, 1992; (ed jtly) Celluloid Jukebox, 1995; (ed) David Goodis, Black Friday and Selected Stories, 2006; contribs to arts magazines and Guardian newspaper. *Recreations:* film, literature, music, theatre. *Address:* Film London, The Arts Building, Morris Place, N4 3JG. *T:* (020) 7613 7676. *Clubs:* Groucho, Soho House.

**WOOTTON, Sir David (Hugh),** Kt 2013; Partner, Allen & Overy LLP, 1979–2015; Lord Mayor of London, 2011–12; *b* Bradford, W Yorks, 21 July 1950; *s* of James Wootton and Muriel Wootton (*née* Comfort); *m* 1977, Elizabeth Rosemary Knox; two *s* two *d*. *Educ:* Bradford Grammar Sch.; Jesus Coll., Cambridge (BA 1972; MA; Hon. Fellow, 2014). Admitted Solicitor, 1975; Hon. Bencher, Gray's Inn, 2011–; Asst Solicitor, Allen & Overy LLP, 1975–79. Dir, Local Partnerships LLP, 2009–11. Mem. Council, Nat. Trust, 2004–07. Pres., City of London Br., IoD, 2013–. Chairman: Misys Charitable Foundn, 2004–11; Local Partnership LLP, 2012–; Northern Ballet, 2013–; Morden Coll., 2013–; Cross-Sector Safety and Security Communications, 2013–; Vice-Chair, Saudi-British Jt Business Council, 2014–; Member: Inst. of Cancer Res., 2004–; Bd, Internat. Dispute Resolution Centre, 2012–; Bd, TheCityUK, 2016–; Brexit Law Cttee, 2017–; Bd, Co-operation Ireland, 2018–; Trustee: Jesus Coll., Cambridge Soc., 2008–18; King's Fund, 2008–14; St Paul's Cathedral Chorister Trust, 2009–16; Nat. Opera Studio, 2013–19; Chm. Trustees, Charles Dickens Mus., 2009–14 (Vice Chm., 2014–18). Governor: City of London Acad., Southwark, 2003–16; GSMD, 2004–13; King Edward's Sch., Witley, 2006–; Bradford Grammar Sch., 2012–; The Hon. The Irish Soc., 2015–18; Goodenough Coll., 2018–; Almoner, Christ's Hosp., 2008–09. Mem., Court of Common Council, 2002–05, Alderman, 2005–, Sheriff, 2009–10, City of London; Master: Fletchers' Co., 2005–06; City of London Solicitors' Co., 2010–11; Information Technologists' Co., 2015–16; Guild of Freemen, 2016–17; Glaziers' Co., 2016–17. Asst Grand Master, Utd Grand Lodge of England, 2014–. Pres., Soc. of Young Freemen, 2008–15. Renter Warden, Woolmen's Co., 2019–; Junior Warden, Watermen's Co., 2019–; Ct Asst, Bowyers' Co., 2018–. Pres., City Livery Club, 2014–15. Steward, Henley Royal Regatta, 2012–. KStJ 2011. Hon. DLaws City, 2012; Hon Dr Staffordshire, 2013. Hon. FGS, 2012. *Recreations:* opera, ballet, theatre, cinema, rowing, railway architecture. *Address:* City of London Corporation, Members' Room, Guildhall, EC2P 2EJ. *E:* dhwootton@gmail.com. *Clubs:* Athenæum, Oxford and Cambridge, Pilgrims, East India; Hawks (Cambridge); Leander; London Rowing.

**WOOTTON, Prof. (Harold) John,** CBE 1997; FREng; FICE; FCIHT; Rees Jeffreys Professor of Transport Planning, 1997–2001, Visiting Professor, 2001–15, University of Southampton; *b* 17 Nov. 1936; *s* of Harold Wootton and Hilda Mary (*née* Somerfield); *m* 1960, Patricia Ann Riley; two *s*. *Educ:* Queen Mary's Grammar Sch., Walsall; QMC, Univ. of London; Univ. of Calif, Berkeley. FCIHT (FIHT 1980); FCILT until 2014 (FCIT 1987; FILT 1999); CEng 1990, FREng 2000; FICE 1996. Lectr, Dept of Civil Engrg, Univ. of Leeds, 1959–62; Technical Dir, Freeman Fox Wilbur Smith, 1963–67; Jt Man. Dir, SIA Ltd, 1967–71; Chm., Wootton Jeffreys Consultants Ltd, 1971–91; Chief Exec., Transport and Road, subseq. Transport, Res. Lab., 1991–97. Visiting Professor in: Computing, KCL, 1987–89; Transport Studies, UCL, 1989–92. Pres., Instn of Highways and Transportation, 1997–98. Chm., Motorway Archive Trust, 2006–15; Mem., Public Policy Cttee, RAC Foundn, 2001–10. Trustee, Rees Jeffreys Road Fund, 2001–10. *Publications:* numerous papers on transport, planning and computer topics. *Recreations:* cricket, golf, Probus, photography, travel, investment strategies. *Address:* Transportation Research Group, Department of Civil Engineering and the Environment, University of Southampton, Highfield, Southampton SO17 1BJ. *T:* (023) 8059 2192.

**WOOTTON, John;** *see* Wootton, H. J.

**WOOTTON, Ronald William,** CBE 1991; Head of West and North Africa and Mediterranean Department, Overseas Development Administration, 1986–91; *b* 7 April 1931; *s* of late William George and Lilian Wootton; *m* 1954, Elvira Mary Gillian Lakeman; one *s* one *d*. *Educ:* Christ's College, Finchley. Served Royal Signals, 1950–52. Colonial Office, 1952–63; Commonwealth Relations Office, 1963–65; ODM/ODA, 1965–91: Head of Overseas Manpower and Consultancies Dept, 1976–79; Head of UN Dept, 1979–82; Head of British Develt Div. in the Pacific, 1982–85. Mem., Internat. Cttee, Leonard Cheshire Foundn, 1992–98. Chm., Caterham Probus, 2001–02; Pres., Ashburton Men's Probus, 2009–10 (Life Mem., 2015). *Address:* 4 Birchside Lane, Ashburton 7700, New Zealand.

**WOOTTON, Sarah Donaldson;** Chief Executive: Dignity in Dying, since 2008; Compassion in Dying, since 2008; *b* Shrewsbury, 30 Sept. 1966; *d* of Anthony James Wootton and Seonaid Moira Beaton Wootton; *m* 2012, Michael Faulkner; one *d*. *Educ:* Queen Anne Grammar Sch., York; Univ. of Sussex (BSc Neurobiol. 1988). Grad. trainee, SmithKline Beecham, 1990–92; Officer, Tequila Sales Promotion Agency, 1992–93; Volunteer Prog. Officer, CSV, 1994–97; Dir of Communications, FPA, 1997–2000; Hd of Communications and Change, EOC, 2001–07. Mem., Internat. Women's Forum, 2015–17. Mem., Fawcett Soc., 2016–. Trustee: Women's Resource Centre, 1995–99; Abortion Rights, 2000–05; Sheila McKechnie Foundn, 2017–. *Recreation:* over-thinking while over-drinking. *Address:* Dignity in Dying/Compassion in Dying, 181 Oxford Street, W1D 2JT. *T:* (020) 7479 7735. *E:* Sarah.Wootton@dignityindying.org.uk; c/o Sheila McKechnie Foundation, The Foundry, 17 Oval Way, SE11 5RR.

**WORCESTER, Marquess of; Henry Robert Fitzroy Somerset;** *b* 20 Jan. 1989; *s* and heir of 12th Duke of Beaufort, *qv*. *Educ:* Marlborough; Univ. of Bristol (BEng Civil Engineering, 2011; MSc Finance and Investment, 2012).

**WORCESTER, Bishop of,** since 2007; **Rt Rev. John Geoffrey Inge,** PhD; Lord High Almoner to the Queen, since 2013; *b* 26 Feb. 1955; *s* of Geoffrey Alfred and Elsie Inge; *m* 1st, 1989, Denise Louise Longenecker (*d* 2014); two *d*; 2nd, 2018, H-J Colston. *Educ:* Kent Coll., Canterbury; Univ. of Durham (BSc 1977; MA 1994; PhD 2002); Keble Coll., Oxford (PGCE 1979); Coll. of the Resurrection, Mirfield. Ordained deacon, 1984, priest, 1985; Asst Chaplain, Lancing Coll., 1984–86; Jun. Chaplain, 1986–89, Sen. Chaplain, 1989–90, Harrow Sch.; Vicar, St Luke, Wallsend, 1990–96; Canon Res., 1996–2003, and Vice-Dean, 1999–2003, Ely Cathedral; Bishop Suffragan of Huntingdon, 2003–07. Mem., Faith and Order Commn, 2010–16. Lead Bishop on Cathedrals and Church Buildings, 2014–19. Visitor: Community of the Holy Name, 2007–; Mucknell Abbey, 2009–. Trust Protector, Common Purpose, 2011– (Trustee, 2005–11). Pres., Three Counties Show, 2012. Hon. DLitt Worcester, 2011. *Publications:* A Christian Theology of Place, 2003; Living Love, 2007. *Address:* The Old Palace, Deansway, Worcester WR1 2JE. *Clubs:* Athenæum, Farmers; Worcestershire Cricket.

**WORCESTER, Dean of;** *see* Atkinson, Very Rev. P. G.

**WORCESTER, Archdeacon of;** *see* Jones, Ven. R. G.

**WORCESTER, Sir Robert (Milton),** KBE 2005; DL; Founder, Market & Opinion Research International (MORI) Ltd, 1969 (Managing Director, 1969–94; Chairman, 1973–2005); International Director, Ipsos, 2005–08; Senior Advisor, Ipsos MORI, since 2008; *b* 21 Dec. 1933; *s* of late C. M. and Violet Ruth Worcester, of Kansas City, Mo, USA; *m* 1st, 1958, Joann (*née* Ransdell) (decd); two *s*; 2nd, 1982, Margaret Noel (*née* Smallbone). *Educ:* Univ. of Kansas (BSc). Consultant, McKinsey & Co., 1962–65; Chief Financial Officer, Opinion Research Corp., 1965–69. Non-exec. Dir, Kent Messenger Gp, 2004–08; Chm., Maidstone Radio Ltd, 2004–06. Member, Advisory Board: Media Standards Trust, 2006–; GovNet, 2008–; Camelot Corp. Responsibility Adv. Bd, 2006–11. Pres., World Assoc. for Public Opinion Research, 1983–84. Vice President: Internat., Social Science Council, UNESCO, 1989–94; UNA, 1999–. Visiting Professor: City Univ., 1990–2002; LSE, 1992– (Gov., 1995–; Hon. Fellow, 2005; Chm., Emeritus Govs, 2015–); Strathclyde Univ., 1996–2001; Inst. of Contemp. British Hist., KCL; Hon. Prof., Warwick Univ., 2005–; Chancellor's Lectr, Univ. of Kansas, 2012–14 (Adjunct Prof., 2012–; Dist. Graduate, 2006). Mem., American Civil Liberties Union Nat. Bd, 1967–69; Chm., Pilgrims' Soc. of GB, 1993–2010 (Vice Pres., 2010–); Co-Chairman: Jamestown 2007 British Cttee, 2004–07; Magna Carta 2015 800th Anniversary Cttee, 2009–15; British Patron, Mayflower 400th Anniv., 2015–20; Vice Pres., European-Atlantic Gp. Governor: Ditchley Foundn; ESU. Comr, US-UK Fulbright Commn, 1995–2005. Vice-President: Royal Soc. of Wildlife Trusts, 1995–; Royal Soc. for Nature Conservation, 1995–; CPRE Kent; Pres., Envmtl Campaigns Ltd, 2002–06. Trustee: Magna Carta Trust, 1993– (Dep. Chm., 2009–); Wildfowl and Wetlands Trust, 2002–08 (Vice Pres., 2009–); WWF (UK), 1995–2001. Patron: Mkt Res. Soc., 2012–; Battlefields Trust, 2015–; Archive of Market and Social Res., 2017–; Kent Archaeol Soc.; Medway Archives; Pocahontas Trust; Chaucer in Canterbury Sculpture Project. Non-exec. Dir, Medway Maritime Hospital NHS Trust, 2002–04. Non-exec. Dir, What on Earth Publishing?, 2016– (Chm., 2017–); Chm., What on Earth Publishing? N America, 2016–; non-exec. Chm., Fly Through Films Ltd, 2015–. Mem., Adv. Council, Inst. of Business Ethics (Pres., 2010–13; Vice Pres., 2014–). Pres., Maidstone Museums' Foundn, 2016–. Member: Ct, Middlesex Univ., 2001–; Ct and Council, Univ. of Kent, 2002–13 (Chancellor, 2006–13; Hon. Prof. of Politics, 2002–). Kent Ambassador, Kent CC, 2008–. Freeman: City of London, 2001–; Stationers' Co., 2018–. DL Kent, 2004. Fellow: Market Res. Soc., 1997; Royal Statistical Soc., 2004. Founding Co-Editor, Internat. Jl of Public Opinion Research. Hon. FKC 2007. Hon. DSc Buckingham, 1998; Hon. DLitt Bradford, 2001; DUniv Middlesex, 2001; Hon. LLD Greenwich, 2002; Hon. DCL: Kent, 2006; Warwick, 2012. Hon. DLaws Richmond, Amer. Internat. Univ. in London, 2009. *Publications:* (ed) Consumer Market Research Handbook, 1972, 3rd edn 1986; (with M Harrop) Political Communications, 1982; (ed) Political Opinion Polling: an international review, 1983; (with Lesley Watkins) Private Opinions, Public Polls, 1986; (with Eric Jacobs) We British, 1990; British Public Opinion: history and methodology of political opinion polling, 1991; (with Eric Jacobs) Typically British, 1991; (with Samuel Barnes) Dynamics of Societal Learning about Global Environmental Change, 1991; (with Roger Mortimore): Explaining Labour's Landslide, 1999; Explaining Labour's Second Landslide, 2001; (with R. Mortimore and P. Baines) Explaining Labour's Landslip, 2005; (jtly) Explaining Cameron's Coalition: how it came about: an analysis of the 2010 General Election, 2011; (jtly) Explaining Cameron's Comeback, 2015; (jtly) Explaining Cameron's Catastrophe, 2017; contrib. Financial Times, Observer; papers in tech. and prof. jls. *Recreations:* castles, choral music, gardening. *Address:* Ipsos MORI, 3 Thomas More Square, E1W 1YW. *T:* (020) 3059 5000. *E:* rmworcester@yahoo.com. *Clubs:* Beefsteak, Reform, Walbrook, Ten Trinity Square; Brook (New York).

**WORDEN, Prof. (Alastair) Blair**, FBA 1997; Fellow, and Tutor in Modern History, St Edmund Hall, Oxford, 1974–95, now Emeritus Fellow; *b* 12 Jan. 1945; *s* of late Prof. Alastair Norman Worden and of Agnes Marshall Scutt; *m* 2014, Victoria Jane Drummond. *Educ:* St Edward's Sch., Oxford; Pembroke Coll., Oxford (BA 1966; MA 1971). Res. Fellow, Pembroke Coll., Cambridge, 1969–72; Fellow, and Dir of Studies in History, Selwyn Coll., Cambridge, 1972–74; Prof. of Early Modern History, Univ. of Sussex, 1996–2003. Vis. Prof. of Modern History, Univ. of Oxford, 2003–11; Res. Prof. of History, Royal Holloway Coll., Univ. of London, 2005–10. Trustee, London Liby, 2002–04. *Publications:* The Rump Parliament, 1974; (ed) Edmund Ludlow, A Voyce from the Watch Tower, 1978; (ed) Stuart England, 1986; (ed) David Wootton, Republicanism, Liberty and Commercial Society, part I, 1994; The Sound of Virtue: Philip Sidney's 'Arcadia' and Elizabethan politics, 1996; Roundhead Reputations: the English Civil Wars and the passions of posterity, 2001; Literature and Politics in Cromwellian England, 2007; The English Civil Wars, 2009; God's Instruments: political conduct in the England of Oliver Cromwell, 2012; (ed) Marchamont Nedham, The Excellencie of a Free-State, 2012; (ed) Hugh Trevor-Roper: the historian, 2016; articles on early modern English history and lit. *Address:* Dene Croft, 186 Heath Road, Leighton Buzzard LU7 3AT. *T:* (01525) 795491. *E:* blair.worden@history.ox.ac.uk.

**WORDSWORTH, Barry**; conductor; Music Director: Birmingham Royal Ballet, 1990–2008 (Music Director Laureate, since 2011); Royal Ballet, 1990–94 and 2007–15 (Principal Guest Conductor, since 2015); *b* 20 Feb. 1948; *s* of Ronald and Kathleen Wordsworth; *m* 1970, Ann Barber; one *s. Educ:* Royal College of Music. Conductor, Royal Ballet, 1974–84; Music Dir, New Sadler's Wells Opera, 1982–84; Musical Dir and Prin. Conductor, 1989–2015, Conductor Laureate, 2015–, Brighton Philharmonic Orch.; Prin. Conductor, 1989–2006, Conductor Laureate, 2006–, BBC Concert Orch. Joint winner, Sargent Conductor's Prize, 1970; Tagore Gold Medal, RCM, 1970. *Recreations:* swimming, photography, cooking. *Address:* c/o IMG Artists, Capital Tower, 91 Waterloo Road, SE1 8RT.

**WORDSWORTH, Prof. (Bryan) Paul**, FRCP; Clinical Reader in Rheumatology, since 1992, and Titular Professor of Rheumatology, since 1998, University of Oxford; Governing Body Fellow, Green Templeton College (formerly Green College), Oxford, 1992, now Emeritus; *b* 4 April 1952; *s* of Victor Pargiter Wordsworth and Dora Mary Wordsworth; *m* 1981, Christine Brow; two *s* one *d. Educ:* Whitgift Sch.; Westminster Med. Sch., London Univ. (MB BS 1975); MA Oxon 1992. MRCP 1978, FRCP 1996. Registrar in Rheumatology, Middx Hosp., 1978–80; Sen. Registrar in Rheumatology, Oxford Hosps, 1980–87; University of Oxford: Res. Fellow, Nuffield Depts of Pathology and Medicine, 1983–85 and 1987–92; Sen. Tutor, Green Coll., 1997–2000; Dean, Green Templeton Coll., Oxford, 2013–15. Gov., Whitgift Sch., 2014–. Michael Mason Prize, 1992, Heberden Orator, 2012, Distinguished Mem., 2016, British Soc. for Rheumatology. *Publications:* (with R. Smith) Clinical and Biochemical Disorders of the Skeleton, 2005, 2nd edn 2016; contribs to over 500 books and learned jls on musculoskeletal diseases and arthritis. *Recreation:* cricket. *Address:* Nuffield Orthopaedic Centre, Windmill Road, Headington, Oxford OX3 7LD. *T:* (01865) 737545.

**WORDSWORTH, Samuel Sherratt**; QC 2013; *b* Warborough, 27 June 1964; *s* of Jonathan Fletcher Wordsworth and Dorothy Ann Sherratt Wordsworth; *m* 2009, Claudia Josephs; one *s* two *d. Educ:* Magdalen College Sch., Oxford; University Coll. London (BA Hons 1st Cl.); London Sch. of Econs and Pol Sci. (LLM Internat. Law). Admitted as solicitor, 1991; Solicitor, Paris, 1991–97; Avocat à la Cour, barreau de Paris, 1994; called to the Bar, Lincoln's Inn, 1997; in practice as a barrister, 1997–; Mem., Attorney Gen.'s Panel of Counsel, 2002–13. Vis. Prof. KCL 2009–; Professeur Invité, Univ. de Paris, Paris X, 2011–12. *Publications:* (jtly) International Relations Law, in Halsbury's Laws of England, Vol. 61, 5th edn 2010. *Address:* Essex Court Chambers, 24 Lincoln's Inn Fields, WC2A 3ED. *T:* (020) 7813 8000, *Fax:* (020) 7813 8080. *E:* swordsworth@essexcourt.net.

**WORDSWORTH, Stephen John**, CMG 2011; LVO 1992; HM Diplomatic Service, retired; Executive Director, Council for At-Risk Academics, since 2012; *b* 17 May 1955; *s* of Christopher Wordsworth and Ruth Wordsworth (née Parrington); *m* 1981, Nichole Mingins; one *s. Educ:* St John's Sch., Porthcawl; Epsom Coll.; Downing Coll., Cambridge (MA). Joined HM Diplomatic Service, 1977; FCO, 1977–79; Third, later Second Sec., Moscow, 1979–81; FCO, 1981–83; First Sec. (Econ. and Commercial), Lagos, 1983–86; on loan to Cabinet Office, 1986–88; First Secretary: FCO, 1988–90; (Political), Bonn, 1990–94; Counsellor (Dep. Internat. Affairs Advr), SHAPE, Mons, 1994–98; FCO, 1998–2002, Hd, Eastern Adriatic Dept, 1999–2002; Minister and Dep. Hd of Mission, Moscow, 2003–06; Ambassador to Serbia, 2006–10. Hon. Dr Liberal Arts Arbertay, Dundee, 2014. Bundesverdienstkreuz (FRG), 1992. *Recreations:* travel, walking the dog, family history research, good food and drink.

**WORKMAN, Prof. Paul**, PhD; FRS 2016; FMedSci; Chief Executive and President, Institute of Cancer Research, since 2014; Harrap Professor of Pharmacology and Therapeutics, University of London, since 1997; *b* Cumbria, 30 March 1952; *s* of late Lancelot John Workman and Thomasina Workman; *m* 1975, Elizabeth Williams; one *s* one *d. Educ:* Workington Co. Grammar Sch.; Univ. of Leicester (BSc Hons 1973); Univ. of Leeds (PhD 1977). FRSB (FIBiol 2001); FRSC 2010. MRC Clinical Oncology Unit, Cambridge: Postdoctoral Scientist, 1976–79; Staff Scientist, 1979–87; MRC Special Appt, 1987–90; CRC Prof. of Experimental Cancer Therapy, Univ. of Glasgow, 1991–93; Hd, Biosci. Section, Zeneca Gp plc, 1993–97; Institute of Cancer Research: Chm., Section of Cancer Therapeutics, 1997–2011; Team Leader, Signal Transduction and Molecular Pharmacol. Team, 1997–; Dir, CRUK Cancer Therapeutics Unit, 1997–; Hd, Div. of Cancer Therapeutics, 2011–16; Dep. Chief Exec., 2011–14. Non-exec. Dir, Royal Marsden NHS Foundn Trust, 2014–. Founder: Chroma Therapeutics, 2001 (Consultant, Chm., Mem. Bd, and Mem. Sci. Adv. Bd, 2001–12); Piramed Pharma, 2003 (Consultant and Mem. Adv. Bd, 2003–08). European Organisation for Research and Treatment of Cancer: Mem. Council, 1987–93; Mem. Bd, 1991–93; Chm., Pharmacol. and Molecular Mechanisms Gp, 1987–91. Mem., Progs Cttee, CRUK (formerly Scientific Cttee, CRC), 1999–. UICC Vis. Fellow, Stanford Univ., 1990. Lectures: Bruce Cain Meml, NZ Cancer Soc., 2003; New Drug Develt Office Award, 2006; Tom Connors, British Assoc. for Cancer Res., 2009. Life Fellow, CRC, 1991. FMedSci 2002; FRSocMed 2007; Fellow, Eur. Acad. of Cancer Scis, 2014. Hon. DSc Leicester, 2009. Award for Excellence in Oncol. Res., Eur. Sch. of Oncol., 1985; George and Christine Sosnovsky Award, 2010, World Entrepreneur of the Year Award, 2012, RSC; Raymond Bourgine Award, Internat. Congress on Anticancer Treatment, 2014. Writer of blog, The Drug Discoverer, www.icr.ac.uk/blogs/the-drug-discoverer. *Publications:* papers on cancer res. and drug discovery in scientific jls. *Recreations:* family, music, sport, travel. *Address:* Institute of Cancer Research, 237 Fulham Road, SW3 6JB. *T:* (020) 7153 5209. *E:* paul.workman@icr.ac.uk. *Club:* Sloane.

**WORKMAN, Timothy (Henry)**, CBE 2007; a District Judge (Magistrates' Courts) (formerly Metropolitan Stipendiary Magistrate), 1986; Chief Magistrate and Senior District Judge (Magistrates' Courts), 2003–10 (Deputy Chief Magistrate and Deputy Senior District Judge, 2000–03); a Chairman, Inner London Youth Court (formerly Juvenile Panel), 1989–2010, and Family Proceeding Court, 1992–2010; a Recorder, 1994–2012; *b* 18 Oct. 1943; *s* of late Gordon and Eileen Workman; *m* 1971, Felicity Ann Caroline Western; one *s* one *d. Educ:* Ruskin Grammar Sch., Croydon. Probation Officer, Inner London, 1967–69; admitted Solicitor, 1969; Solicitor, subseq. Partner, C. R. Thomas & Son, later Lloyd Howorth & Partners, Maidenhead, 1969–85. Mem., Sentencing Guidelines Council, 2004–10. Exec. Vice-Pres., Commonwealth Magistrates' and Judges' Assoc., 2011–. Hon. Bencher, Gray's Inn, 2007. *Recreations:* woodturning, shepherding, pottery. *Address:* c/o Westminster Magistrates' Court, 181 Marylebone Road, NW1 5BR. *T:* (020) 3126 3100. *E:* timworkman@mail.com.

**WORMALD, Sir Christopher**, KCB 2017; Permanent Secretary, Department of Health and Social Care (formerly Department of Health), since 2016; *b* London, 30 Oct. 1968; *s* of Peter John Wormald, *qv*; *m* 1997, Claire McCoy; one *s* two *d. Educ:* Rutlish Sch.; St John's Coll., Oxford (BA 1990); Imperial Coll. London (MBA 1999). Department for Education, later Department for Education and Employment, then Department for Education and Skills: fast stream trainee, 1991–95; Team Leader, Finance Directorate, 1995–98; Standards and Effectiveness Unit, 1998–2001; Principal Private Sec. to Sec. of State, 2001–04; Policy Advr to Sec. of State, 2004–05; Dir of Academies and Capital, 2005–06; Dir Gen., Local Govt and Regeneration, DCLG, 2006–09; Dir Gen., Domestic Policy Gp and Hd of Econ. and Domestic Affairs Secretariat, 2009–11, Hd, Dep. Prime Minister's Office, 2010–12, Cabinet Office; Permanent Sec., DFE, 2012–16. Mem., ESRC, 2018–. *Address:* Department of Health and Social Care, 39 Victoria Street, SW1H 0EU.

**WORMALD, Peter John**, CB 1990; Director, Office of Population Censuses and Surveys, and Registrar General for England and Wales, 1990–96; *b* 10 March 1936; *s* of late H. R. and G. A. Wormald; *m* 1962, Elizabeth North; three *s. Educ:* Doncaster Grammar Sch.; The Queen's Coll., Oxford (MA). Assistant Principal, Min. of Health, 1958, Principal, 1963; HM Treasury, 1965–67, Asst Sec., 1970; Under Sec., DHSS, 1978; Dep. Sec., Dept of Health (formerly DHSS), 1987. *Recreations:* music, golf, contract bridge. *Club:* Oxford and Cambridge.

See also Sir C. Wormald.

**WORMALD, Richard Raphael**; QC 2019; *b* Bristol, 17 March 1967; *s* of Dr Christopher Wormald and Jean Wormald; one *s* three *d*; *m* 2014, Hannah Raphael; one *s* one *d. Educ:* Bristol Grammar Sch.; Univ. of York (BA English and Philosophy); City Univ. (MA Law). Called to the Bar, Gray's Inn, 1993 (Karmel Schol.); in practice as a barrister, specialising in criminal law and financial crime. Vis. Lectr, City Univ., 2008–. *Recreations:* sailing, paragliding, walking, music, reading, crosswords, my children. *Address:* 3 Raymond Buildings, Gray's Inn, WC1R 5BH. *T:* (020) 7400 6400. *E:* richard.wormald@3rblaw.com. *Clubs:* Savile; Royal Southern Yacht.

**WORMINGTON, Veronique Eira**; see Buehrlen, V. E.

**WORMWELL, Denis**; Chairman, CMAC Group, since 2018; *b* Colne, Lancs, 27 Aug. 1961; *s* of Peter and Kathleen Wormwell; *m* 2002, Amanda Whalley; two *s* two *d. Educ:* Colne Park High Sch.; Blackburn Coll. Univ. Centre (HNC Business Studies). Hd of Dept, Buoyant Upholstery, 1980–86; Overseas Area Manager, Club 18–30 Holidays, 1986–91; Sales Director: Elvington Ltd, 1991–95; Flying Colours Leisure Gp, 1995–98; Sales and UK Service Delivery Dir, Thomas Cook, 1998–2001; Chief Executive: Nat. Express Coaches, 2002–06; Nat. Express Bus, 2006–07; Shearings Holidays Gp, 2007–16. Non-exec. Dir, BTA, 2017–. Chm., VisitEngland, 2017–. *Recreations:* music, football, cinema, art. *Address:* CMAC Group, Suite 1, The Globe Centre, St James Square, Accrington, Lancashire BB5 0RE.

**WORNE, John Philip**; Chief Operating Officer for Arts and Sciences, King's College London, since 2015; *b* Sheffield, 15 Sept. 1968; *s* of Brian Patrick George Worne and Rita Worne; partner, Eleanor Street; one *s* one *d. Educ:* Jesus Coll., Oxford (BA Hons PPE 1990; MA). Graduate trainee, then Market Planner, Cable & Wireless plc, 1990–93; Hd, Mktg, then Hd, Advertising, Bouygues Telecom, France, 1993–98; Hd, Business Mobile and Data Products, Cable & Wireless UK, 1998–2000; Dir, Brand and Global Campaigns, Cable & Wireless Global, 2000–01; Public Service Reform Policy Advr, Cabinet Office, 2001–02; Dep. Dir, NHS and DoH Communications, 2002–05; Dir, Communications, Cabinet Office, 2005–07; Dir, Strategy, 2007–10, Dir, Corp. HQ, 2010–15, British Council. *Recreations:* family, dog, writing, arts, sciences philosophy and ethics, sports (especially cricket), current affairs. *Address:* King's College London, Strand, WC2R 2LS. *E:* john.worne@kcl.ac.uk. *W:* www.johnworne.com, www.twitter.com/johnworne. *Club:* MCC.

**WORRALL, Anna Maureen, (Mrs G. H. G. Williams)**; QC 1989; a Recorder, 1987–2003; *b* 16 Sept. 1938; *er d* of T. B. Worrall and S. F. Worrall (*née* Cushman); *m* 1964, (George Haigh) Graeme Williams, QC (*d* 2013); two *d. Educ:* Hillcrest Sch., Bramhall; Loreto Coll., Llandudno; Manchester Univ. Called to the Bar, Middle Temple (Harmsworth Scholar), 1959, Bencher, 1996; in practice, 1959–63 and 1971–2012; Lectr in Law, Holborn Coll. of Law, Language and Commerce, 1964–69; Dir, ILEA Educnl Television Service, 1969–71. Pres., Mental Health Review Tribunals, later a Judge, First-tier Tribunal, 1995–2011. Mem., Home Office Cttee on Review of Sexual Offences, 2002–03. *Recreations:* theatre, music, cooking, walking, travel. *Address:* Lamb Building, Ground Floor, Temple, EC4Y 7AS. *T:* (020) 7797 7788, *Fax:* (020) 7353 0535. *Club:* Reform.

**WORRALL, Denis John**, PhD; Chairman: Omega Investment Research Ltd (Chief Executive, 1990); African Business Advisors (Pty) Ltd; *b* 29 May 1935; *s* of Cecil John Worrall and Hazel Worrall; *m* 1965, Anita Ianco; three *s*. *Educ*: Univ. of Cape Town (BA Hons, MA); Univ. of South Africa (LLB); Cornell Univ. (PhD). Teaching and research positions, Univs of Natal, S Africa, Ibadan, Witwatersrand, California, Cornell; Rearch Prof. and Dir, Inst. of Social and Economic Research, Rhodes Univ., 1973. Senator, 1974; elected to Parlt, 1977; Chm., Constitutional Cttee, President's Council, 1981; Ambassador: to Australia, 1983–84; to the UK, 1984–87; Co-Leader, Democratic Party, 1988–90; MP (Democratic Party) Berea (Durban), South Africa, 1989–94. Advocate of Supreme Court of S Africa. *Publications*: South Africa: government and politics, 1970; The Independent Factor, 2018. *Recreations*: tennis, reading, music. *Address*: PO Box 23599, Claremont, 7700, South Africa.

**WORRALL, Peter Richard**, CB 2015; OBE 2000; CEng, FREng, FIMechE; Chief of Materiel (Joint Enablers), Defence Equipment and Support Organisation, Ministry of Defence, since 2011; *b* W Midlands, 1961; *s* of Frederick and Janet Worrall; *m* 1989, Claire Levenberg. *Educ*: King's Coll., London (BSc 1st Cl. Hons Mech. Engrg 1986; AKC 1986). CEng 1992; FIMechE 2000; FREng 2011; RCNC 1992. Ministry of Defence, 1980–: Team Leader, Challenger 2 Main Battle Tank, 1996–99; rcds 2000; Sen. Civil Service, 2000; Team Leader: Future Artillery Weapons Systems, 2000–02; Bowman and Land Digitisation, 2002–04; NATO Gen. Manager, NATO Eurofighter Typhoon and Tornado Mgt Agency, 2005–08; Dir, Defence Equipment and Support Orgn, 2008–11. Non-exec. Dir, HRW Ltd, 2009–. FAPM 2000; FCMI 2003. *Recreations*: horology, contemporary ceramics, Jack of many trades. *Address*: Chief of Materiel (Joint Enablers), Maple 2c #2219, Defence Equipment and Support Organisation, Abbey Wood, Bristol BS34 8JH. *Club*: Army and Navy.

**WORRALL THOMPSON, (Henry) Antony (Cardew)**; TV chef; restaurateur; *b* 1 May 1951; *s* of late Michael Worrall Thompson and Joanna Duncan; *m* 1st, 1974, Jill Thompson (marr. diss.); 2nd, 1983, Militza Millar (marr. diss.); two *s*; 3rd, 1996, Jacinta Shiel; one *s* one *d*. *Educ*: King's Sch., Canterbury; Westminster Hotel Sch. (HND). Head chef, Brinkley's Restaurant, Fulham Rd, 1978–80; head chef, Dan's Restaurant, Chelsea, 1980–81; opened Ménage à Trois, Knightsbridge, 1981; first chef/patron, restaurant at One Ninety, Queen's Gate, 1989 Best New Restaurant, Time Out, 1990; restaurants opened: Managing Director: Bistrot 190, 1990; dell 'Ugo, Frith St, 1992; Palio, Notting Hill Gate, 1992; Zoe, St Christopher's Place, 1993; Cafe dell 'Ugo, City of London, 1993; The Atrium, Westminster, 1994; Drones, Belgravia, 1995; De Cecco, Parsons Gn, 1995; The Greyhound Free House & Grill, 2005–; Kew Grill, 2005–; The Lamb Free House and Kitchen, 2006–09; Barnes Grill, 2006–09; Windsor Grill, 2007–14; chef/proprietor: Woz, N Kensington, 1997–99; Wiz, Holland Park, 1998–2002; Bistrorganic, N Kensington, 1999; Notting Grill, Holland Park, 2002–09. Restaurant consultant, Bombay, Melbourne, Stockholm and NY, 1981–88. Man. Dir, Simpson's of Cornhill Gp, 1995–97. Numerous TV appearances, incl. Ready, Steady, Cook, 1994–; Food and Drink prog., 1997–2003; Saturday Kitchen, 2003–06; Saturday Cooks, 2006–07; Daily Cooks Challenge, 2008–. FIH (FHCIMA 1989). Meilleur Ouvrier de GB, 1987. *Publications*: The Small and Beautiful Cookbook, 1984; (with M. Gluck) Supernosh, 1993; Modern Bistrot Cookery, 1994; 30 Minute Menus, 1995; Simply Antony, 1998; The ABC of AWT, 1998; Food and Drink Cookbook, 2002; Raw (autobiog.), 2003; How to Cook and Buy Real Meat, 2003; Healthy Eating for Diabetes, 2003; Antony Worrall Thompson's GI Diet, 2005; Antony's Weekend Cookbook, 2006; Barbecues and Grilling, 2006; The GL Diet Made Simple, 2006; AWT's The Diabetes Weight Loss Diet, 2007; The People's Cookbook, 2007; Saturday Cooks Cookbook, 2008; The Sweet Life, 2008; Fast Family Food, 2008; Antony Makes It Easy, 2010; The Essential Diabetes Cookbook, 2010 (Best Health and Nutrition Book, Cordon Bleu Media Awards, 2010); Slow Cooking, 2011; The Essential Low Fat Cookbook, 2011. *Recreations*: gardening, antiques, interior design, eating, cooking. *Address*: c/o Limelight Management, 10 Filmer Mews, 75 Filmer Road, SW6 7JF. *T*: (020) 7384 9950. *E*: antony@awtrestaurants.com. *W*: www.twitter.com/AntonyWT. *Club*: Groucho.

**WORSDALE, Godfrey James**, OBE 2016; Director, The Henry Moore Foundation, since 2015; *b* Doncaster, S Yorks, 19 Oct. 1967; *s* of John Raymond Worsdale and Alice Avril Worsdale; *m* 2001, Dr Alia Al-Khalidi; one *s* one *d*. *Educ*: Camberwell Coll. of Art (BA Hons Art Hist. 1989); HND Conservation Studies 1991). Curator, BM, 1991–95; Curator, 1995–99, Dir, 1999–2002, Southampton City Art Gall.; Director: Middlesbrough Inst. of Modern Art, 2002–08; BALTIC Centre for Contemporary Art, 2008–15. Trustee: Northern Canon, 2007–; ARC Stockton Arts Centre, 2015–; Chairman: Visual Art and Galls Assoc., 2010–15; Contemporary Visual Arts Network, 2010–15. Mem. Jury, Turner Prize, 2011. Patron, Crisis Commn, 2011–14. Vis. Fellow, Cleveland Coll. of Art and Design, 2015–. Gov., Univ. of Teesside, 2016–. FRSA 2011. Hon. DCL Northumbria, 2012. *Publications*: Douglas Allsop: Lacunae, 1995; Co-Operators, 1996; Chris Ofili, 1998, 2nd edn 1999; Martin Creed Works, 2000; (with E. Chaney) The Stuart Portrait: status and legacy, 2001; Graham Dolphin, 2005; Draw, 2007. *Recreation*: antiques - particularly glass. *Address*: The Henry Moore Foundation, Dane Tree House, Perry Green, Much Hadham, Herts SG10 6EE. *T*: (01279) 843333. *E*: godfrey.worsdale@henry-moore.org.

**WORSFOLD, Ven. Richard Vernon**; Archdeacon of Leicester, since 2018; *b* 17 July 1964; *s* of Peter and Joan Worsfold; *m* 1990, Jenny; two *s* one *d*. *Educ*: Exeter Univ. (LLB 1986); Cranmer Hall, Durham (BA 1994). Curate, St Andrew's, Countesthorpe, Blaby, 1995–99; Team Vicar, 1999–2001, Team Rector, 2001–09, Bradgate Team; Vicar, Martyrs, Leicester, 2009–18; Area Dean, City of Leicester, 2014–18. *Address*: St Martin's House, 7 Peacock Lane, Leicester LE1 5PZ. *E*: rworsfold@virginmedia.com.

**WORSLEY, Lord**; George John Sackville Pelham; *b* 9 Aug. 1990; *s* and heir of 8th Earl of Yarborough, *qv*. *Educ*: Eton Coll.

**WORSLEY, His Honour Daniel**; a Circuit Judge, 1999–2017; *b* 27 March 1948; *s* of Francis Arthur Worsley and Mary Worsley; *m* 1971, Virginia Caroline Wilkinson; one *s* one *d*. *Educ*: Ampleforth Coll.; Emmanuel Coll., Cambridge (BA). Called to the Bar, Gray's Inn, 1971; Barrister, 1971–99. *Publications*: Contrib. Ed., Halsbury's Laws of England, 4th edn, 1998; (jtly) I am Horatio Nelson, 2005; contrib. to legal textbooks. *Recreations*: East Anglia, sailing, fruit trees, wine, the Pyrenees.

**WORSLEY, Francis Edward, (Jock)**, OBE, 2002; non-executive Director, Brewin Dolphin Holdings plc, 2003–14; *b* 15 Feb. 1941; *s* of late Francis Arthur Worsley and Mary Worsley; *m* 1962, Caroline Violet (*née* Hatherell); two *s* two *d*. *Educ*: Stonyhurst College. FCA. Articled, Barton, Mayhew & Co., 1959–64; with Anderson Thomas Frankel, Chartered Accountants, 1964–69; Financial Training Co., 1969–93 (Chm., 1972–92). Dir, 1990–94, Dep. Chm., 1992–94, Lautro; Complaints Comr, SIB, then FSA, 1994–2001. Non-executive Director: Cleveland Trust PLC, 1993–99; Reece Plc, 1994–98; Accident Exchange Gp plc, 2004–05. Chm., Lloyds Members Agency Services Ltd, 1994–2012. Pres., Inst. of Chartered Accountants in England and Wales, 1988–89. Mem., Building Socs Commn, 1991–2002. Trustee, 1994–2002, Chm., 1998–2002, Cancer Res. Campaign; Trustee, Cancer Res. UK, 2002–03. *Recreations*: golf, wine, travel, cooking.

**WORSLEY, Lucy**, OBE 2018; DPhil; Chief Curator, Historic Royal Palaces, since 2003; *b* 18 Dec. 1973; *d* of Peter and Enid Worsley; *m* Mark Hines. *Educ*: New Coll., Oxford (BA Hons (Ancient and Mod. Hist.) 1995); Univ. of Sussex (DPhil (Art Hist.) 2001). FRHistS 2001. Administrator, Wind and Watermill Section, SPAB, 1995–97; Inspector of Ancient Monuments and Historic Bldgs, English Heritage, 1997–2002. Presenter, TV series: Elegance and Decadence: the age of Regency, 2011; If Walls Could Talk: the history of the home, 2011; Fit to Rule: how Royal illness changed history, 2013; A Very British Murder, 2013; The First Georgians: the German Kings who made Britain, 2014; Dancing Cheek to Cheek: an intimate history of dance, 2014; A Very British Romance, 2015; Empire of the Tsars: Romanov Russia, 2016; Six Wives with Lucy Worsley, 2016; American History's Biggest Fibs with Lucy Worsley, 2019; presenter: Tales from the Royal Bedchamber, 2013; Tales from the Royal Wardrobe, 2014; Lucy Worsley's 100 Years of the WI, 2015; Lucy Worsley's Reins of Power, 2015; Jane Austen: behind closed doors, 2017; Lucy Worsley's Nights at the Opera, 2017; Lucy Worsley's Fireworks for a Tudor Queen, 2018; Suffragettes with Lucy Worsley, 2018 (BAFTA Award for Best Specialist Factual, 2019); Victoria & Albert: the royal wedding, 2018; Queen Victoria: my musical Britain, 2019. *Publications*: Hardwick Old Hall, 1998; Bolsover Castle, 2000; Kirby Hall, 2000; The Official Illustrated History of Hampton Court Palace, 2005; Cavalier: a tale of passion, chivalry and great houses, 2007; Courtiers: the secret history of Kensington Palace, 2010; If Walls Could Talk: an intimate history of the home, 2011; A Very British Murder: the story of a national obsession, 2013; Eliza Rose (novel), 2016; My Name is Victoria (novel), 2017; Jane Austen at Home: a biography, 2017; Queen Victoria: daughter, wife, mother, widow, 2018; various articles in jls. *Recreation*: treasure hunts. *Address*: Hampton Court Palace, Surrey KT8 9AU. *T*: (020) 3166 6400. *E*: lucy.worsley@hrp.org.uk.

**WORSLEY, His Honour Paul Frederick**; QC 1990; a Circuit Judge, 2006–17; Senior Circuit Judge, 2007–17; *b* 17 Dec. 1947; *s* of late Eric Worsley, MBE, GM and of Sheila Mary Worsley (*née* Hoskin); *m* 1974, Jennifer Ann, JP, *d* of late Ernest Avery; one *s* one *d*. *Educ*: Hymers College, Hull; Mansfield College, Oxford (MA). Called to the Bar, Middle Temple, 1970 (Astbury Scholar), Bencher, 1999 (Reader, 2015); practised NE Circuit, 1970–2006; Asst Recorder, 1983–87; Recorder, 1987–2006; Additional Judge, Grand Court Cayman, 2015–. Mem., Parole Bd, 2007–14; Course Dir, Judicial Studies Bd, 2007–14. Governor: Scarborough Coll., 1996–2011; Leeds Girls' High Sch., 2001–05; Leeds Grammar Sch., 2005–08. Trustee, Stephen Joseph Theatre, 2011–15. Freeman: City of London, 2009; Coopers' Co., 2007 (Liveryman, 2011); Co. of Merchants of Staple of England, 2013. *Recreations*: Vanity Fair prints, opera, croquet, dogs, Georgian Silver, writing children's stories, crime novels. *Club*: Athenæum.

**WORSLEY, Rt Rev. Ruth Elizabeth**; see Taunton, Bishop Suffragan of.

**WORSLEY, Sir William (Ralph)**, 6th Bt *cr* 1838, of Hovingham, Yorkshire; DL; *b* York, 12 Sept. 1956; *s* of Sir William Marcus Worsley, 5th Bt and Hon. Bridget Assheton, *d* of 1st Baron Clitheroe, KCVO, PC; *S* father, 2012; *m* 1987, Marie-Noelle Dreesmann; one *s* two *d*. *Educ*: Harrow; RAC Cirencester. FRICS 1992; ARAgS 2012, FRAgS 2018. Consultant, Humberts, 1986–92; Director: Scarborough Building Soc., 1996–2009 (Chm., 2002–09); Brunner Investment Trust plc, 2000–14; Skipton Building Soc., 2009–11. Member: N York Moors Nat. Park Authy, 1994–98; Adv. Panel, Forestry Commn, 1998–2006; Indep. Panel on Forestry, 2011–12; Chairman: Howardian Hills Area of Outstanding Beauty Cttee, 2004–07, 2019–; Nat. Forest Co., 2016–. UK Nat. Tree Champion, 2018–. Lay Canon and Mem. Chapter, York Minster, 2018–. Pres., CLA, 2009–11 (Vice Pres., 2005–07; Dep. Pres., 2007–09). DL N Yorks, 2007. Lieut, QOY, 1975–80; Hon. Col, Yorks Sqdn, QOY, 2008–15. *Recreations*: walking, reading, ski-ing. *Heir*: *s* Marcus William Worsley, *b* 2 Nov. 1995. *Address*: Hovingham Hall, York YO62 4LU. *T*: (01653) 628771. *E*: office@hovingham.co.uk. *Club*: White's.

**WORSTHORNE, Sir Peregrine (Gerard)**, Kt 1991; writer; Editor, Comment Section, Sunday Telegraph, 1989–91; *b* 22 Dec. 1923; *s* of Col Koch de Gooreynd, OBE (who assumed surname of Worsthorne by deed poll, 1921), and Baroness Norman, CBE; *m* 1st, 1950, Claude Bertrand de Colasse (*d* 1990); one *d*; 2nd, 1991, Lady Lucinda Lambton (*see* L. Lambton), *d* of Viscount Lambton. *Educ*: Stowe; Peterhouse, Cambridge (BA); Magdalen Coll., Oxford. Commnd Oxf. and Bucks LI, 1942; attached Phantom, GHQ Liaison Regt, 1944–45. Sub-editor, Glasgow Herald, 1946; Editorial staff: Times, 1948–53; Daily Telegraph, 1953–61; Deputy Editor, Sunday Telegraph, 1961–76, Associate Editor, 1976–86, Editor, 1986–89. *Publications*: The Socialist Myth, 1972; Peregrinations: selected pieces, 1980; By the Right, 1987; Tricks of Memory (autobiog.), 1993; In Defence of Aristocracy, 2004. *Recreation*: reading. *Address*: The Old Rectory, Hedgerley, Bucks SL2 3UY. *T*: (01753) 646167. *Clubs*: Beefsteak, Garrick, Pratt's, City University.

*See also* Sir S. P. E. C. W. Towneley.

**WORSWICK, Dr Richard David**, CChem, FRSC; Chairman, Cobalt Light Systems Ltd, 2009–17; *b* 22 July 1946; *s* of (George) David (Norman) Worswick, CBE, FBA and of Sylvia Ellen Worswick; *m* 1970, Jacqueline Brigit Isobel Adcock; two *d* (and one *d* decd). *Educ*: New College, Oxford (BA Hons Nat. Sci. 1969; MA 1972; DPhil 1972). CChem, FRSC 1991. SRC post-doctorate res. asst, Inorganic Chem. Lab., Oxford, 1972–73; Res. Admin, Boots Co., Nottingham, 1973–76; Harwell Lab., UKAEA, 1976–91: marketing and planning, 1976–85; Head, Res. Planning and Inf. Services, 1985–87; Head, Safety Branch, 1988; Head, Envmtl and Med. Scis Div., 1988–90; Dir, Process Technology and Instrumentation, AEA Industrial Technology, 1990–91; Chief Exec., Lab. of Govt Chemist, DTI, 1991–96; Govt Chemist, 1991–2002. Chief Exec., 1996–2005, Dep. Chm., 2005–07, LGC Gp Hldgs plc (formerly LGC (Hldgs) Ltd); Chm., Pipeline Develts Ltd, 1998–2002. Mem., STFC, 2013–18. UK Entrepreneur of the Year (business products and services), Ernst & Young, 2003. *Publications*: LGC: the making of a company, 2011; research papers in sci. jls. *Recreations*: listening to music, playing the violin, walking.

**WORTHINGTON**, Baroness *cr* 2011 (Life Peer), of Cambridge in the County of Cambridgeshire; **Bryony Katherine Worthington**; Founder and Director, Sandbag Climate Campaign, since 2008; Executive Director, Europe, Environmental Defense Fund, since 2016; consultant on climate change and energy policy; *b* Wales; *m* 2010, Dr Srivas Chennu; one *s*. *Educ*: Queens' Coll., Cambridge (BA 1993). Fundraiser, Operation Raleigh; Leader, Friends of the Earth Climate Change Campaign, 2000; public awareness campaigns and drafting Climate Change Bill, DEFRA; Policy Advr to Scottish and Southern Energy. Shadow spokesperson on energy and climate change, 2011–15; an Opposition Whip, 2012–15. Non-exec. Dir, 10:10 Climate Campaign Gp. Mem., Guardian Sustainable Business Adv. Panel. Trustee, UNICEF UK, 2015–17. *Address*: House of Lords, SW1A 0PW.

**WORTHINGTON, Anthony, (Tony)**; *b* 11 Oct. 1941; *s* of late Malcolm and Monica Worthington; *m* 1966, Angela Oliver; one *s* one *d*. *Educ*: LSE (BA Hons); Univ. of Glasgow (MEd). Lecturer, Social Policy and Sociology: HM Borstal, Dover, 1962–66; Monkwearmouth Coll. of Further Educn, Sunderland, 1967–71; Jordanhill Coll. of Educn, Glasgow, 1971–87. Councillor, Strathclyde Region, 1974–87 (Chm., Finance Cttee, 1986–87). MP (Lab) Clydebank and Milngavie, 1987–2005. Opposition front bench spokesman: on educn and employment in Scotland, 1989–92; on overseas develt, 1992–93; on foreign affairs, 1993–94; on Northern Ireland, 1995–97; Parly Under-Sec. of State, NI

Office, 1997–98. Member: Home Affairs Select Cttee, 1987–89; Internat. Develt Select Cttee, 1999–2005; Treas., All Party Population and Develt Gp, 1989–97; Chm., All Party Gp on Overseas Develt, 2000–05. British Pres., Parliamentarians for Global Action, 2001–05; a Dir, Parliamentarians Network on the World Bank, 2002–05. Chm., Labour Campaign for Criminal Justice, 1987–89. *Recreation:* gardening. *Address:* 24 Cleddans Crescent, Hardgate, Clydebank G81 5NW. *T:* (01389) 873195. *Club:* Radnor Park Bowling.

**WORTHINGTON, Ian Alan,** OBE 1999; HM Diplomatic Service, retired; Ambassador to the Dominican Republic and (non-resident) to Haiti, 2006–09; *b* 9 Aug. 1958; *s* of Alan Worthington and Bette Worthington (*née* Wright). *Educ:* Parish Church Primary Sch., Spring Gardens, Stockport; Stockport Sch., Mile End. Joined FCO, 1977; Moscow, 1980–82; Lusaka, 1982–85; Second Sec., FCO, 1985–88; Second Sec., Seoul, 1988–91; Dep. Head of Mission, Vilnius, 1991–92; Second Sec., Kingston, 1992–95; Consul Gen., Ekaterinburg, 1995–98; FCO, 1998–2001; First Sec., Berlin, 2001–06. *Recreations:* family history, walking, languages, meeting new and interesting people. *Address:* 44 Forbes Road, Stockport SK1 4HN.

**WORTHINGTON, Sir Mark,** Kt 2014; OBE 2005; consultant; Construction Commissioner, High Speed Two, since 2018; *b* Leek, Staffs, 23 Jan. 1961; *s* of Percy and Marjorie Worthington. *Educ:* Westwood High Sch., Leek; King's Coll. London (BA MA Hist. 1982). Parly Advr, 1986–92; Private Sec. to Rt Hon. Baroness Thatcher, 1992–2013. Dir, Margaret Thatcher Foundn, 1992–2011. Chm., Freedom Assoc., 2014–18. *Recreations:* reading, history, politics, gardening, opera. *Address:* 96 Telford Avenue, SW2 4XG. *T:* (020) 3674 3969.

**WORTHINGTON, Prof. Michael Hugh,** PhD; Professor of Geophysics, 2001–11, and Senior Research Scientist, 2001–11, Oxford University; Supernumerary Fellow, Wolfson College, Oxford, 2002–11; *b* 16 June 1946; *s* of Air Vice-Marshal Sir Geoffrey Worthington, KBE, CB, and late Margaret Joan (*née* Stevenson); *m* 1975, Mary Archange Mackintosh; one *s* one *d. Educ:* Wellington Coll.; Durham Univ. (BSc 1968; MSc 1969); ANU (PhD 1973). Univ. Lectr in Geophysics, and Fellow of Exeter Coll., Oxford, 1973–85; Prof. of Geophysics, 1985–2001, Hd, Dept of Geol., 1993–97, ICSTM. Vis. Prof., Dept of Applied and Engrg Physics, Cornell Univ., 1978. Member: Soc. of Exploration Geophysicists; European Assoc. of Geoscientists and Engineers; FGS. William Smith Medal, Geol Soc., 2007. *Publications:* (jtly) Seismic Data Processing, 1986; contribs to professional jls. *Recreations:* sailing, painting.

**WORTHINGTON, Prof. Sarah Elizabeth,** FBA 2009; Downing Professor of the Laws of England, University of Cambridge, since 2011; Fellow, Trinity College, Cambridge, since 2011; *b* Barnsley, 18 Feb. 1955; *d* of Bernard and Frances Monks; *m* 1978, Peter Worthington; two *s* two *d. Educ:* Australian Nat. Univ. (BSc 1974); Univ. of Qld (DipEd 1977; LLB 1986); Univ. of Melbourne (LLM 1990); Wolfson Coll., Cambridge (PhD 1995). Departmental Tutor, Biochem. Dept, Univ. of Qld, 1975–77; Sen. Sci. Teacher, San Sisto Girls' Sch., 1978–79; Lectr in Law, Dept of Business Law, then Faculty of Law, 1988–92, Univ. of Melbourne; Lectr in Law, 1994–96, Sen. Lectr in Law, 1996–97, Dept of Law, Birkbeck Coll., London; Sen. Lectr in Law, 1997–2001, Reader, 2001–03, Prof. of Law, 2003–11, Dept of Law, and Pro-Dir, 2005–10, LSE. Professorial Fellow, Univ. of Melbourne, 2005–; Francqui Chair, Univ. of Leuven, 2009–10; Cheng Yu Tong Dist. Vis. Prof., Univ. of Hong Kong, 2010–. Called to the Bar, Middle Temple, 2005, Bencher, 2010; Academic Mem., South Sq. (formerly 3–4 South Sq.), Gray's Inn, 2005–; a Dep. High Court Judge, 2017–; Pres., Soc. of Legal Scholars, 2007–08. Member, Council: AHRC, 2010–13; British Acad., 2011–14, 2015– (Treas., 2015–); Mem., Panel of Recognised Internat. Market Experts in Finance, 2011–. Gov., London Business Sch., 2018–. Hon. QC 2010. FRSA 1995. Fellow, Australian Acad. of Law, 2015. Ed., Palmer's Company Law, 2003–; Syndic: CUP, 2012–; Cambridge Assessment, 2018–. *Publications:* Proprietary Interests in Commercial Transactions, 1996; Personal Property: text and materials, 2000; (ed) Commercial Law and Commercial Practice, 2003; Equity, 2004, 2nd edn 2006; (ed with L. Sealy) Sealy's Cases and Materials in Company Law, 8th edn 2007, 11th edn as Sealy and Worthington's Cases and Materials in Company Law, 2016; Equity and Property: fact, fantasy and morals, 2009; (ed with P. L. Davies) Gower and Davies, Principles of Modern Company Law, 9th edn 2012, 10th edn as Gower's Principles of Modern Company Law, 2016; (jtly) Law of Personal Property, 2013. *Recreations:* theatre, art, walking. *Address:* Faculty of Law, University of Cambridge, 10 West Road, Cambridge CB3 9DZ. *E:* sew1003@cam.ac.uk.

**WORTHINGTON, Stephen Anthony;** QC 2006; a Recorder, since 2001; *b* 14 April 1953; *s* of Dennis and Moya Worthington; *m* 1981, Julie Evans; two *s* one *d. Educ:* Trinity Coll., Cambridge (BA 1975). Called to the Bar, Gray's Inn, 1976, Bencher, 2009; barrister. *Recreations:* sport, wine, walking. *Address:* 12 King's Bench Walk, Temple, EC4Y 7EL. *T:* (020) 7583 0811, *Fax:* (020) 7583 7228. *E:* worthington@12kbw.co.uk.

**WOSNER, John Leslie;** Chairman and Senior Partner, PKF, accountants, 1999–2005; *b* 8 June 1947; *s* of Eugen and Lucy Wosner; *m* 1974, Linda Freedman; two *s* one *d. Educ:* Univ. of Sheffield (BA Econ 1969). FCA 1972; ATII 1973. Trained with Arthur Andersen & Co., 1969–74; PKF: joined, 1974; Partner, 1976–2005; Managing Partner, 1994–99. *Publications:* articles in British Tax Review, Taxation, Accountancy. *Recreations:* opera, country walking, history. *Club:* Travellers.

**WÖSSNER, Dr Mark Matthias;** Chairman, Supervisory Board: Heidelberger Druckmaschinen AG, 2004–11; Citigroup Global Markets Deutschland, 2002–08; *b* 14 Oct. 1938. *Educ:* Karlsruhe Technical University (DrIng). Management Asst, Bertelsmann AG, Gütersloh, 1968; Mohndruck (Bertelsmann largest printing operation): Production Manager, 1970; Technical Dir, 1972; Gen. Manager, 1974; Mem. Exec. Bd, Bertelsmann, 1976; Dep. Chm. of Bd, 1981, Chm. and CEO, 1983–98; Chm., Supervisory Bd, Bertelsmann AG, 1998–2000; Chm. and CEO, Bertelsmann Foundn, 1998–2000. Chm., Supervisory Bd, eCircle AG, 2000–10; Member, Supervisory Board: DaimlerChrysler AG, 1998–2009; Douglas Hldg AG, 2003–13; Aurelius Equity Opportunities, 2016–18 (Chm., 2016–18). Hon. Prof., Technical Univ. Munich, 2005–.

**WOTHERS, Peter David,** MBE 2014; PhD; FRSC; Teaching Fellow, Department of Chemistry, University of Cambridge, since 1996; Fellow, and Director of Studies, St Catharine's College, Cambridge, since 1997; *b* Swindon, 21 Jan. 1969; *s* of Geoffrey Wothers and June Wothers. *Educ:* Bedford Modern Sch.; St Catharine's Coll., Cambridge (BA Hons 1991; PhD 1996). FRSC 2005. Mem., UK Chemistry Olympiad, 1997–; Chm., Cambridge Chemistry Challenge, 2011–; Chm., Steering Cttee, Internat. Chemistry Olympiad, 2011–14. Sandars Readership in Bibliography, Univ. of Cambridge, 2017–18. Presenter: The Big Experiment, Discovery Channel, 2008; Royal Instn Christmas Lectures, 2012. Pres.'s Prize, 2011, Nyholm Prize for Educn, 2013, RSC. *Publications:* (jtly) Organic Chemistry, 2000; (with J. H. Keeler) Why Chemical Reactions Happen, 2003; (with J. H. Keeler) Chemical Structure and Reactivity, 2008, 2nd edn 2013. *Recreations:* collecting rare chemistry books 1500–1800, devising interesting chemistry questions, rowing, cycling. *Address:* St Catharine's College, Cambridge CB2 1RL. *T:* (01223) 336320. *E:* peter@wothers.com. *Club:* Hawks (Cambridge).

**WOTTON, John Prier;** Consultant, Allen & Overy LLP, 2007–12 (Partner, 1984–2007); *b* Hounslow, Middx, 7 May 1954; *s* of Arthur John Wotton and Persis Rubena (*née* Spearing); *m* 1976, Linde Diana Lester; one *s* two *d. Educ:* Latymer Upper Sch.; Jesus Coll., Cambridge (BA 1975). Admitted solicitor, 1978; Allen & Overy LLP, 1976–2012. Mem. Council, Law Soc. of England and Wales, 2007–13 (Pres., 2011–12; Chair, Educn and Trng Cttee, 2012–15). Mem., Co-operation and Competition Panel for NHS-funded Services, 2009–14; Mem., Reporting Panel, Competition Commn, 2013–14; Inquiry Chair (formerly Panel Dep. Chm.), CMA, 2014–19; External Expert, Monitor, then NHS Improvement, 2014–16. Gov., Latymer Foundn at Hammersmith, 2000–15. Mem. Council, Fauna & Flora Internat., 2006–19. Chair, CPRE Kent, 2019– (Trustee, 2016–); Chair, Kent Historic Buildings Cttee, 2016–; Vice-Chair, 2017–18). Trustee: Cranbrook Sch., 2017–; Great Dixter Trust, 2019–. Master, 2019–June 2020, City of London Solicitors' Co. Garden owner, Nat. Garden Scheme. *Publications:* articles on EU and competition law, media and utilities regulation. *Recreations:* cricket, gardening, conservation, music. *Address:* Goddards Green, Angley Road, Cranbrook, Kent TN17 3LR. *E:* jpwotton@gmail.com. *Clubs:* Travellers, MCC.

**WOUDHUYSEN, Deborah Jane;** see Loudon, D. J.

**WOUDHUYSEN, Prof. Henry Ruxton,** DPhil; FBA 2010; FSA; Rector, Lincoln College, Oxford, since 2012; *b* London, 24 Oct. 1954; *s* of Lewis Woudhuysen and Alice Woudhuysen (*née* Roberts); *m* 1987, Deborah Jane Loudon, *qv*; two *s. Educ:* St Paul's Sch., London; Pembroke Coll., Oxford (MA 1981; DPhil 1981; Hon. Fellow, 2014). Jun. Res. Fellow, Lincoln Coll., Oxford, 1979–82; Department of English, University College London: Lectr, 1982–95; Sen. Lectr, 1995–97; Prof. of English, 1997–2012; Hd of Dept, 2002–07; Dean, Faculty of Arts and Humanities, 2008–12; Lyell Reader in Bibliography, Univ. of Oxford, 2013–14. Member: Council, Malone Soc., 1984–; Council, Bibliographical Soc., 1985–88, 2001–06, 2008– (Vice-Pres., 2010–14; Pres., 2014–16); Curators of Bodleian Libraries, 2007–12, 2014–. Gov., City Lit, 2010–12. *Publications:* (ed with D. Norbrook) The Penguin Book of Renaissance Verse, 1509–1659, 1992; Sir Philip Sidney and the Circulation of Manuscripts, 1558–1640, 1996; (ed) Love's Labour's Lost, 1998; (ed) AEH AWP: a classical friendship, 2006; (ed with K. Duncan-Jones) Shakespeare's Poems, 2007; (ed with M. F. Suarez, SJ) The Oxford Companion to the Book, 2010; contribs to learned jls and to TLS on sales of books and manuscripts. *Address:* Lincoln College, Oxford OX1 3DR. *T:* (01885) 279804. *E:* rector@lincoln.ox.ac.uk.

**WRACK, Matt;** General Secretary, Fire Brigades Union, since 2005; *b* 23 May 1962. *Educ:* Open Univ. (BSc); London Sch. of Econs (MSc). Joined London Fire Brigade, 1983; served Silvertown, Ilford, Kingsland Fire Stations. Trades Union Congress: Mem., Gen. Council; Mem., Exec. Cttee. *Address:* Fire Brigades Union, Bradley House, 68 Coombe Road, Kingston-upon-Thames, Surrey KT2 7AE. *T:* (020) 8541 1765. *E:* matt.wrack@fbu.org.uk.

**WRAGG, John,** RA 1991 (ARA 1983); sculptor; *b* 20 Oct. 1937; *s* of Arthur and Ethel Wragg. *Educ:* York Sch. of Art; Royal Coll. of Art. *Work in public collections:* Israel Mus., Jerusalem; Tate Gall.; Arts Council of GB; Arts Council of NI; Contemp. Art Soc.; Wellington Art Gall., NZ; work in private collections in GB, America, Canada, France and Holland. *One-man exhibitions:* Hanover Gall., 1963, 1966 and 1970; Galerie Alexandre Iolas, Paris, 1968; York Fest., 1969; Bridge Street Gall., Bath, 1982; Katherine House Gall., Marlborough, 1984; Quinton Green Fine Art, London, 1985; Devizes Mus. Gall., 1994; England & Co., London, 1994; L'Art Abstrait, London, 1995; Handel House Gall., Devizes, 2000; Bruton Gall., Leeds, 2000; Sadlers Yard Gall., West Bay, 2009; *exhibitions:* Lord's Gall., 1959; L'Art Vivant, 1965–68; Arts Council Gall., Belfast, 1966; Pittsburgh Internat., 1967; Britische Kunst heute, Hamburg, Fondn Maeght, and Contemp. Art Fair, Florence, 1968; Bath Fest. Gall., 1977 and 1984; Artists Market, 1978; Biennale di Scultura di Arese, Milan, and King Street Gall., Bristol, 1980; Galerie Bollhagen Worpswede, N Germany, 1981 and 1983; Quinton Green Fine Art, London, 1984, 1985, 1986 and 1987; Best of British, Simpsons, 1993; Connaught Brown, London, 1993; Monumental '96, Belgium, 1996; Courcoux & Courcoux, 1997; Bruton Gall., Leeds, 1999; Bruton St Gall., London, 1999; Discerning Eye, Mall Galls, London, 2000; Cobham Fest., 2001; Bohun Gall., Henley-on-Thames, 2001; RWA Gall., 2001; Hotbath Gall., Bath, 2002. Sainsbury Award, 1960; Winner of Sainsbury Sculpture Comp., King's Road, Chelsea, 1966; Arts Council Major Award, 1977; Chantry Bequest, 1981. *Relevant publications:* chapters and articles about his work in: Neue Dimensionen der Plastik, 1964; Contemporary British Artists, 1979; British Sculpture in the Twentieth Century, 1981; Studio Internat., Art & Artiste, Sculpture Internat., Arts Rev., and The Artist. *Recreation:* walking. *Address:* 6 Castle Lane, Devizes, Wilts SN10 1HJ. *T:* (01380) 727087.

**WRAGG, William Peter;** MP (C) Hazel Grove, since 2015; *b* Stockport, 11 Dec. 1987; *s* of Peter Wragg and Julie Wragg. *Educ:* Poynton High Sch. and Sixth Form; Univ. of Manchester (BA Hist.); Liverpool John Moores Univ. (PGCE). Former primary sch. teacher. Mem. (C) Stockport Council, 2011–15. Member: Educn Select Cttee, 2016–; Backbench Business Cttee, 2016–; Procedure Cttee, 2017–. Mem., Exec. Cttee, 1922 Cttee, 2016–. *Address:* House of Commons, SW1A 0AA.

**WRAIGHT, Margaret Joan;** see Hustler, M. J.

**WRATTEN, Donald Peter;** Director, National Counties Building Society, 1985–96; *b* 8 July 1925; *er s* of late Frederick George and Marjorie Wratten; *m* 1947, Margaret Kathleen (*née* Marsh); one *s* one *d. Educ:* Morehall Elem. Sch. and Harvey Grammar Sch., Folkestone; London Sch. of Economics. Storehand, temp. clerk, meteorological asst (Air Min.), 1940–43; service with RAF Meteorological Wing, 1943–47. LSE, 1947–50. Joined Post Office, 1950; Private Sec. to Asst Postmaster Gen., 1955–56; seconded to Unilever Ltd, 1959; Private Sec. to Postmaster Gen., 1965–66; Head of Telecommunications Marketing Div., 1966–67; Director: Eastern Telecommunications Region, 1967–69; Exec. Dir, Giro and Remittance Services, 1969–74 (Sen. Dir, 1970–74); Sen. Dir, Data Processing Service, 1974–75; Sen. Dir, Telecom Personnel, 1975–81. Member: Industrial Adv. Panel, City Univ. Business Sch., 1974–81 (Chm., 1977–81); Court, Cranfield Inst. of Technology, 1976–81; Business Educn Council, 1977–83; Council: Intermediate Technology Develt Gp, 1982–85; Internat. Stereoscopic Union, 1987– (Vice-Pres., 2001–03); Pres., Stereoscopic Soc., 1996–98 (Vice-Chm., 1990–92; Chm., 1993–95). Pres., Radlett Soc. & Green Belt Assoc., 1996–2004 (Chm., 1989–96). *Publications:* The Book of Radlett and Aldenham, 1990. *Recreations:* 3-D photography, social history. *Address:* 11 Brampton Apartments, Brampton Valley Lane, Chapel Brampton, Northampton NN6 8GB. *T:* (01604) 850731.

**WRATTEN, Air Chief Marshal Sir William (John),** GBE 1998 (KBE 1991; CBE 1982); CB 1991; AFC 1973; Chief Military Adviser, Rolls-Royce Defence (Europe), 1998–2000; *b* 15 Aug. 1939; *s* of William Wellesley Wratten and Gwenneth Joan (*née* Bourne); *m* 1963, Susan Jane Underwood; two *s* two *d. Educ:* Chatham House Grammar Sch., Ramsgate; RAF Coll., Cranwell. OC, RAF Coningsby, 1980–82; Sen. RAF Officer, Falkland Is, 1982; RCDS, 1983; Dir, Operational Requirements (RAF), MoD, 1984–86; SASO, HQ 1 Gp, 1986–89; AOC No 11 Gp, 1989–91; Air Comdr British Forces ME, and Dep. to Comdr (on attachment), Nov. 1990–March 1991; Dir Gen., Saudi Armed Forces Project,

1992–94. AOC-in-C Strike Comd, and Comdr Allied Air Forces Northwestern Europe, 1994–97; Air ADC to the Queen, 1995–97. CCMI (CIMgt 1996). QCVSA 1968. Legionnaire, Legion of Merit (USA), 1993. *Recreation:* photography. *Address:* 14 College Road, Cheltenham GL53 7HX. *Club:* Royal Air Force.

**WRAXALL**, 4th Baron *cr* 1928, of Clyst St George, co. Devon; **Antony Hubert Gibbs;** *b* 19 Aug. 1958; *s* of 3rd Baron Wraxall, KCVO, CMG and Evelyn Veronica Gibbs (*née* Scott); *S* father, 2017; *m* 1st, 1988, Caroline Jane Gould (marr. diss. 1994); two *d*; 2nd, 1995, Virginia Gilchrist; two *s*. *Educ:* Eton Coll.; New Coll., Oxford. *Heir: s* Hon. Orlando Hubert Gibbs, *b* 19 May 1995.

**WRAXALL, Sir Charles (Frederick Lascelles)**, 9th Bt *cr* 1813; Assistant Accountant, Morgan Stanley International, since 1987; *b* 17 Sept. 1961; *s* of Sir Morville William Lascelles Wraxall, 8th Bt, and of Lady (Irmgard Wilhelmina) Wraxall; *S* father, 1978; *m* 1983, Lesley Linda, *d* of late William Albert and Molly Jean Allan; one *s* one *d*. *Educ:* Archbishop Tenison's Grammar School, Croydon. *Recreations:* choral singing (Mem., Choir Cttee), Mem., Mission Cttee, St Mary the Virgin, Ashford, watching football and cricket. *Heir: s* William Nathaniel Lascelles Wraxall, *b* 3 April 1987.

**WRAY, Prof. David;** Dean, Hamdan Bin Mohammed College of Dental Medicine (formerly Dubai School of Dental Medicine), 2012–15; Professor of Oral Medicine, Glasgow University, 1993–2011, now Emeritus; *b* 3 Jan. 1951; *s* of Arthur Wray and Margaret Wray (*née* Craig); *m* 1st, 1974, Alison Young (marr. diss. 1997); two *s*; 2nd, 1997, Alyson Urquhart (marr. diss. 2009); two *s* one *d*; 3rd, 2012, Jennifer Balfour. *Educ:* Uddingston Grammar Sch.; Glasgow Univ. (BDS 1972; MBChB 1976; MD 1982). FDSRCPSGlas 1979; FDSRCSE 1987. Fogarty Vis. Associate, NIH, Bethesda, 1979–81; Wellcome Res. Fellow, Royal Dental Sch., Univ. of London, 1982; Sen. Lectr, Dept of Oral Medicine and Pathology, Univ. of Edinburgh, 1983–93; Glasgow University: Associate Dean for Res., Dental Sch., 1995–2000; Dean of Dental Sch., 2000–05; Clinical Dir, Glasgow Dental Hosp., 2004–09. Hon. Consultant in Oral Medicine, Greater Glasgow and Clyde NHS (formerly North Glasgow NHS Trust), 1993–2011. Founder FMedSci, 1998. *Publications:* Oral Medicine, 1997; Oral Candidosis, 1997; Textbook of General and Oral Medicine, 1999; Textbook of General and Oral Surgery, 2003; (ed) Essential Dental Therapeutics, 2017. *Recreations:* golf, wine, cooking.

**WRAY, Edward James;** Co-Founder, 1999, and Chairman, 2006–12, Betfair Group plc; *b* Coulsdon, 27 March 1968; *s* of Philip and Brenda Wray; *m* 2003, Catherine Pickering; one *s* one *d*. *Educ:* Worcester Coll., Oxford (MA Hons Engr, Econs and Mgt). Joined JP Morgan, 1991; Vice Pres., 1994–99. *Recreations:* golf, sailing, horseracing, wine. *Address:* Matrix Complex, 91 Peterborough Road, SW6 3BU. *T:* (020) 7736 4699. *E:* edward.j.wray@gmail.com.

**WRAY, Nigel William;** non-executive Director: Prestbury Investment Holdings, since 2003; Chapel Down Group plc (formerly English Wines Group plc), since 2004; *b* 9 April 1948. *Educ:* Mill Hill Sch.; Univ. of Bristol (BSc). Chairman: Fleet Street Letter plc, 1976–90; Burford Hldgs plc, 1988–2001; Nottingham Forest plc, 1997–99; British Seafood Gp, 2006–10; Dir, Saracens Ltd, 1995– (Chm., 1996–); non-executive Director: Carlton Communications plc, 1976–97; Singer and Friedlander Gp plc, 1986–2001; Peoples Phone, 1989–96; Columbus Gp, 1991–2000; Urbium (formerly Trocadero, then Chorion) plc, 1995–2005; SkyePharma plc, 1995–2000; Domino's Pizza UK & IRL plc (formerly Domino's Pizza Group plc), 1997–2014; Carlisle Hldgs, 1998–2001; Hartford Gp, 1998–2000; Safestore plc, 1999–2003; Seymour Pierce Gp (formerly Talisman House) plc, 2000–04; Electric Word plc, 2000–06 (Chm., 2002–04); Invox plc, 2000–06; Extreme Gp, 2002–05; Play Hldgs Ltd, 2004– ; WILink.com (formerly Knutsford) plc, 2005–06 (non-exec. Chm., 1999–2005); Greenhouse Fund Ltd, 2006–07; Networkers International plc, 2006–15; Premier Team Hldgs, 2006– ; Franchise Brands Worldwide, 2008–18; non-exec. Chm., Environ Gp (Investments) plc (formerly Southern Bear plc), 2010–12. Hon. LLD Bristol, 2005. *Address:* Cavendish House, 18 Cavendish Square, W1G 0PJ. *T:* (020) 7647 7647.

**WREN, Simon William**, CBE 2003 (MBE 1997); Director of Communications, West Midlands Combined Authority, since 2018; *b* Stevenage, Herts, 10 May 1965; *s* of late Terence Roy Wren and Mary Christine Wren; *m* 2002, Sheila Elizabeth Houghton. *Educ:* King Harold Comprehensive Sch., Waltham Abbey. Ministry of Defence: various posts, 1985–2000; Chief Press Officer, 2000–02; Head of News: Dept for Transport, 2002–05; MoD, 2005–06; Home Office, 2006–11; Dir, Media and Communications, MoD, 2011–12; Dir, Communications, Home Office, 2012–17; interim Dir of Communication, FCO, 2018. *Recreation:* attending heavy metal concerts (Member of Motorheadbangers). *Club:* Tottenham Hotspur.

**WREN-LEWIS, Prof. Simon Jeremy Quentin;** Professor of Economic Policy, Blavatnik School of Government, University of Oxford, 2014–18, now Emeritus (Professor of Economics, 2007–14); Fellow and Tutor in Economics, Merton College, Oxford, 2007–14, now Emeritus; *b* London, 11 July 1953; *s* of John Wren-Lewis and Shirley Wren-Lewis; *m* 1979, Joanna Lynne Gura; two *s*. *Educ:* Cavendish Sch., Chiswick; Latymer Upper Sch., Hammersmith; Clare Coll., Cambridge (BA 1974); Birkbeck Coll., Univ. of London (MSc 1979). Economic Asst and Advr, HM Treasury, 1974–81; Sen. Res. Officer and Sen. Res. Fellow, NIESR, 1981–90; Lectr, Queen Mary Coll., Univ. of London, 1985; Prof. of Macroecon. Modelling, Univ. of Strathclyde, 1990–95; Prof. of Econs, Univ. of Exeter, 1995–2006. Res. Fellow, Centre for Econ. Policy Res., 1986–97; Member, Academic Panel: HM Treasury, 1986–95; ONS, 1997–2002; Member: Res. Grants Bd, ESRC, 1992–96; Adv. Panel, Office for Budget Responsibility, 2011– . Mem. Council, Royal Econ. Soc., 1998–2003. Consultant, Bank of England, 1999–2004; Vis. Prof., Reserve Bank of NZ, 2003–04. Mem., Econ. Adv. Cttee, Labour Party, 2015–16. Gov., NIESR, 1995– . *Publications:* papers on nat. and internat. macroecons in professional jls; The Lies We Were Told, 2018. *Recreations:* gardening, watching swallows, writing a blog. *Address:* Merton College, Oxford OX1 4JD. *T:* (01865) 271080, *Fax:* (01865) 271094.

**WRENBURY**, 4th Baron *cr* 1915, of Old Castle, Sussex; **William Edward Buckley;** *b* 19 June 1966; *s* of 3rd Baron Wrenbury and of Penelope Sara Frances Buckley (*née* Fort); *S* father, 2014; *m* 1996, Emma Clementson; two *s*. Teacher, Sherborne Sch.; Proctor, Oundle Sch. *Heir:* cousin Arthur Burton Buckley [*b* 2 May 1967; *m* 1992, Amanda Jane Ridley; one *s* two *d*].

**WRENCH, Peter Nicholas;** consultant and writer; *b* 5 April 1957; *s* of late Cyril Wrench and Edna Mary Wrench; *m* 1978, Pauline Jordan; two *d*. *Educ:* Clitheroe Royal Grammar Sch.; Royal Holloway Coll., London (BA). Home Office, 1980–2010: Private Sec. to Perm. Sec., 1987–88; Immigration and Nationality Dept, 1988–93; Organised and Internat. Crime Directorate, 1993–2000; Dep. Dir Gen., Immigration and Nationality Directorate, 2000–03; Dir of Resettlement, HM Prison Service, 2003–05; Dir of Strategy and Assurance, Nat. Offender Mgt Service, 2005–07; Sen. Dir, Simplification Project, Border and Immigration Agency, later UK Border Agency, 2007–10; Hd, Core Learning Prog., Nat. Sch. of Govt (on loan), 2010. Ind. Assessor of student finance appeals and complaints, DFE, 2015– . Member: Fitness to Practise Cttee, Gen. Pharmaceutical Council, 2010– (Dep. Chair, 2015–); Ind. Review Panel, Equitable Life Payments Scheme, HM Treasury, 2011–16; Planning, Resources and Performance Cttee, Bar Standards Bd, 2011–15; Audit Cttee, Office of Immigration Services Comr, 2012–18; Panel, Judicial Appts Commn, 2012–17; Disciplinary Panels, Judicial Conduct Investigations Office, 2012– ; Code Adjudication Panel (formerly Ind. Appeals Body), Phone-paid Services Authy (formerly PhonepayPlus), 2012– ; Disciplinary Tribunal, CILEx Regulation, 2015– ; Fitness to Practise Cttee (formerly Conduct and Competence Cttee), NMC, 2017– ; Chm., Professional Conduct Cttee, UK Council for Psychotherapy, 2012. Mem., Bd of Trustees, RoadPeace, 2014–18. *Publications:* (contrib.) Zusammenarbeit der Polizei- und Justizverwaltungen in Europa, 1996; (contrib.) Crime Sans Frontières: international and European legal approaches, 1998; Saint Dominic's Flashback, 2012. *Recreations:* obscure music, family, friends. *Address:* 38 Millers Road, Brighton BN1 5NQ. *W:* www.edenontheline.co.uk.

**WREXHAM, Bishop of, (RC)**, since 2012; **Rt Rev. Peter Malcolm Brignall;** *b* Whetstone, 5 July 1953; *s* of Charles V. Brignall and Marie E. Brignall (*née* Stilz). *Educ:* Finchley Catholic High Sch.; Barnet Coll. of Further Educn; Allen Hall Seminary; Univ. of Wales, Swansea (Dip. Med. Ethics 1993). Ordained deacon, 1977, priest, 1978; Deacon, St David's, Mold, 1977–78; Assistant Priest: Blessed Sacrament, Connah's Quay, 1978–79; Our Lady Star of the Sea, Llandudno, 1979–80; Chaplain, Univ. Coll. of N Wales, Bangor, 1979–84; Asst Priest, St David and St Patrick, Haverfordwest, 1984–85; Parish Priest: Knighton and Presteigne, 1985–89; Our Lady and St James, Bangor, 1989–99; Dean, Cathedral of Our Lady of Sorrows, Wrexham, 1999–2012. Member: Council, Coll. of Health Care Chaplains, 1998–2008; Historic Churches Cttee for Wales and Herefordshire, 2000–12; Liturgy Cttee, Bishops' Conf., 2010–12. Gov. and Trustee, Churches Tourism Network Wales, 2008–17. Chaplain: Bangor NHS Hosps, 1980–84, 1998–99; Carmelite Monastery, Presteigne, 1985–89; Wrexham NHS Hosps, 1999–2012. *Recreations:* food and cooking from source to plate, strolling with a purpose (natural history, historic routes, visiting antiquities), listening to classical music, learning to sign British Sign Language. *Address:* Bishop's House, Sontley Road, Wrexham LL13 7EW. *T:* (01978) 262726, *Fax:* (01978) 354257. *E:* curia@wrexhamdiocese.org.uk.

**WREXHAM, Archdeacon of;** *see* Lomas, Ven. J. D. P.

**WREY, Benjamin Harold Bourchier;** Chairman, Henderson Global Investors Ltd (formerly Henderson Administration Group and Henderson Investors), 1992–2004; Director, Henderson Global Investors (Holdings) plc, 1998–2005; *b* 6 May 1940; *s* of Christopher B. Wrey and Ruth Wrey (*née* Bowden); *m* 1970, (Anne) Christine (Aubrey) Cherry; one *d*. *Educ:* Blundell's Sch.; Clare Coll., Cambridge (Hons in Econs; MA). Legal and General Assurance Soc., 1963–66; Investment Dept, Hambros Bank, 1966–69; joined Henderson Administration, 1969; Director, 1971; Jt Man. Dir/Dep. Chm., 1982; Director: Henderson Electric and General Investment Trust plc (formerly Electric and General Investment Co.), 1977–2000; Henderson American Capital and Income Trust plc, 1996–99; CCLA Investment Management, 1999–2005. Chm., Institutional Fund Managers' Assoc., 1996–98 (Dep. Chm., 1994–96); Member: Institutional Investors Adv. Cttee, London Stock Exchange, 1994–2000; Exec. Cttee, Assoc. of Investment Trust Cos, 1997–2002 (Dep. Chm., 1999–2002); Investment Cttee, 1999–2010 (Chm., 2003–10), Council, 2003–10, BHF; Investment Cttee, Cambridge Univ. Assistants Pension Scheme, 2004– . Dir, 1998–2005, Chm., 2005–09, COIF Charities Funds. Mem., Adv. Council, Nat. Opera Studio, 1996–2005. *Publications:* articles on investment. *Recreations:* shooting (rep. Cambridge Univ., England and GB in full bore target rifle shooting; winner, Bisley Grand Aggregate, 1966, 1969; runner-up, HM The Queen's Prize, 1963, 1977), fishing, mountain-walking, ballet, photography. *Address:* 8 Somerset Square, Addison Road, W14 8EE. *Clubs:* Boodle's, City of London; Hurlingham.

**WREY, Sir (George Richard) Bourchier**, 15th Bt *cr* 1628, of Trebitch, Cornwall; *b* 2 Oct. 1948; *s* of Sir Bourchier Wrey, 14th Bt and Sybil Mabel Alice Wrey, *d* of Dr George Lubke, S Africa; *S* father, 1991; *m* 1981, Lady Caroline Lindesay-Bethune, *d* of 15th Earl of Lindsay; two *s* one *d*. *Educ:* Eton. *Recreation:* shooting. *Heir: s* Harry David Bourchier Wrey, *b* 3 Oct. 1984. *Address:* Hollamoor Farm, Tawstock, Barnstaple, Devon EX31 3NY. *T:* (01271) 373466.

**WRIGGLESWORTH**, family name of **Baron Wrigglesworth**.

**WRIGGLESWORTH**, Baron *cr* 2013 (Life Peer), of Norton on Tees in the County of Durham; **Ian William Wrigglesworth**, Kt 1991; Chairman, Durham Group (formerly Bluehall Properties), since 2014 (Chief Executive, 2008–14); Chairman, Port of Tyne, 2005–12 (Director, 2003–05); *b* Dec. 1939; *s* of Edward and Elsie Wrigglesworth; *m* 1967, Patricia Truscott; two *s* one *d*. *Educ:* Stockton Grammar Sch.; Stockton-Billingham Technical Coll.; Coll. of St Mark and St John, Chelsea. Formerly: Personal Assistant to Gen. Sec., NUT; Head of Research and Information Dept of Co-operative Party; Press and Public Affairs Manager of National Giro. Chm., Govt Policy Consultants Ltd, 1998–2000; Dep. Chm., John Livingston & Sons Ltd, 1987–95; Chm., UK Land Estates, 1995–2008; Dir, CIT Hldgs Ltd, 1987–2003; Divl Dir, Smiths Industries PLC, 1976–2000; Dir, Tyne Tees TV, 2002–06. Contested (SDP/Alliance) Stockton South, 1987. MP (Lab and Co-op, 1974–81, SDP, 1981–87) Teesside, Thornaby, Feb. 1974–1983, Stockton South, 1983–87. PPS to Mr Alec Lyon, Minister of State, Home Office, 1974; PPS to Rt Hon. Roy Jenkins, Home Secretary, 1974–76; Opposition spokesman on Civil Service, 1979–80; SDP spokesman on industry, 1981, on industry and economic affairs, 1983–87. First Pres., Liberal Democrats, 1988–90 (Treas., 2012–15). Chairman: Northern Reg., CBI, 1992–94; Newcastle-Gateshead Initiative, 1999–2004; Baltic Centre for Contemporary Art, Gateshead, 2004–09. Gov., Univ. of Teesside, 1993–2002. DL Tyne and Wear, 2005–13. Hon. DMus Northumbria, 2011; Hon. DBus Teesside, 2012. Freeman, City of London, 1995; Liverymen, Co. of Founders, 1994. *Address:* House of Lords, SW1A 0PW. *E:* wrigglesworthi@parliament.uk. *Clubs:* Reform, Groucho.

**WRIGHT**, family name of **Baron Wright of Richmond**.

**WRIGHT OF RICHMOND**, Baron *cr* 1994 (Life Peer), of Richmond-upon-Thames in the London Borough of Richmond-upon-Thames; **Patrick Richard Henry Wright**, GCMG 1989 (KCMG 1984; CMG 1978); HM Diplomatic Service, retired; *b* 28 June 1931; *s* of late Herbert H. S. Wright and Rachel Wright (*née* Green); *m* 1958, Virginia Anne Gaffney; two *s* one *d*. *Educ:* Marlborough; Merton Coll. (Postmaster), Oxford (MA; Hon. Fellow, 1987). Served Royal Artillery, 1950–51; joined Diplomatic Service, 1955; Middle East Centre for Arab Studies, 1956–57; Third Secretary, British Embassy, Beirut, 1958–60; Private Sec. to Ambassador and later First Sec., British Embassy, Washington, 1960–65; Private Sec. to Permanent Under-Sec., FO, 1965–67; First Sec. and Head of Chancery, Cairo, 1967–70; Dep. Political Resident, Bahrain, 1971–72; Head of Middle East Dept, FCO, 1972–74; Private Sec. (Overseas Affairs) to Prime Minister, 1974–77; Ambassador to: Luxembourg, 1977–79; Syria, 1979–81; Dep. Under-Sec. of State, FCO and Chm., Jt Intelligence Cttee, 1982–84; Ambassador to Saudi Arabia, 1984–86; Permanent Under-Sec. of State and Head of Diplomatic Service, 1986–91. Mem., Security Commn, 1993–2002. Member: H of L Sub-Cttee on Home Affairs, 2001–07 (Chm., 2004–07); EU Select Cttee, 2005–07; H of L Sub-Cttee on Law and Instns, 2007–12; Jt Cttee on Conventions, 2006; UK Delegn to Parly Assembly, Council of Europe, 2016– . Director: Barclays Bank plc,

1991–96; BP Amoco (formerly British Petroleum Co.), 1991–2001; De La Rue, 1991–2000; Unilever, 1991–99; BAA, 1992–98. Trustee, Home Start Internat., 1999–2007 (Chm., 2004–07). Chm., RIIA, 1995–99 (Mem. Council, 1992–99); Member: Council, RCM, 1991–2001 (FRCM 1994); Atlantic Coll., 1993–2000; ICRC Consultative Gp of Internat. Experts, 1992–95. Governor: Ditchley Foundn, 1986–2012; Wellington Coll., 1991–2001; Edward VII Hosp., 2005–07. KStJ 1990; Registrar, 1991–95, Dir of Overseas Relations, 1995–97, Order of St John of Jerusalem. House Mag. Award for Best Parly Speech of the Year, 2004. *Publications*: (contrib.) The Arabists of Shemlan, 2006; (contrib.) Envoys to the Arab World, 2009; Behind Diplomatic Lines, 2018. *Recreation*: cooking. *Address*: c/o House of Lords, Westminster, SW1A 0PW. *Club*: Oxford and Cambridge.
*See also Sir S. G. McDonald*.

**WRIGHT, Alan;** *see* Wright, R. A.

**WRIGHT, Alan John;** a Master of the Supreme Court, Supreme Court Taxing Office, 1972–91; *b* 21 April 1925; *s* of late Rev. Henry George Wright, MA and Winifred Annie Wright; *m* 1952, Alma Beatrice Ridding (*d* 2014); one *s* one *d* (and one *s* decd). *Educ*: St Olave's and St Saviour's Grammar Sch., Southwark; Keble Coll., Oxford. BA 1949, MA 1964. Served with RAF, India, Burma and China, 1943–46. Solicitor 1952; in private practice with Shaen Roscoe & Co., 1952–71; Legal Adviser to Trades Union Congress, 1955–71. Lay Reader, 1989. *Recreations*: Germanic studies, walking, travel, foreign languages. *Address*: 49 Grange Road, Billericay, Essex CM11 2RG.

**WRIGHT, Prof. Alexander William;** Head of Architecture, since 2008, and Professor of Architecture, since 2012, University of Bath; Principal, Alexander Wright Architects, since 1991; *b* Camberley, 3 Feb. 1964; *s* of Ronald Edward Wright and Margaret Pamela Beatrice Wright (*née* Moss, now Murphy); *m* 2004, Emma Jane Cooper; two *s*. *Educ*: France Hill Secondary Sch., Camberley; Univ. of Bath (BSc Hons Arch.); Univ. of Cambridge (DipArch); Harvard Univ. (Master of Design Studies). Harkness Fellow, 1988–89; Department of Architecture, University of Bath: Design Tutor, 2001–05; Dir of Studies for BSc, 2005–08. Chm., Standing Conf. of Heads of Schs of Architecture, 2012–16. Chair: Creating Excellence Design Rev. Panel, 2018–; QAA Adv. Gp on Architecture, 2019–. Expert Advr to Ministerial Adv. Gp, NI, 2012–. Member: Architects' Registration Bd, 2012–18; Bd, Built Envmt Professional Educn Project, 2014–17. Lay Mem., Bar Standards Bd, 2014–17. Adjudicator, Solicitors' Regulation Authy, 2015–. FHEA 2010. *Publications*: contrib. papers on architectural educn. *Recreations*: family, Texas hold 'em. *Address*: Department of Architecture and Civil Engineering, 6 East, University of Bath, Bath BA2 6NB. *T*: (01225) 386604. *E*: a.w.wright@bath.ac.uk. *Club*: Soho House.

**WRIGHT, Sir Allan Frederick,** KBE 1982; farmer, retired; *b* Darfield, 25 March 1929; *s* of Quentin A. Wright; *m* 1953, Dorothy June Netting; three *s* two *d*. *Educ*: Christ's Coll., Christchurch. Nat. Pres., Young Farmers' Clubs, 1957–58; President: N Canterbury Federated Farmers, 1971–74; Federated Farmers of NZ, 1977–81 (formerly Sen. Nat. Vice-Pres.). Mem., NZ Cricket Bd of Control, 1967–90; Manager, NZ Cricket Team to England, 1983; Pres., NZ Cricket, 1993–94 (Life Mem., 1993). Chairman: NZ Rail, 1991–94; Lincoln Hldgs Ltd, 1995–2003; The Crossings (Marlborough) Ltd, 1998–2006; Dir, Richina Pacific Ltd, 1996–2004 (Chm., 1998–2001); former Dir, Orion Ltd. Chancellor, Lincoln Univ., 1990–94 (Chm. Council, Lincoln Coll., 1985–89, Mem., 1974–89). Hon. DCom Lincoln, 1997. *Recreations*: cricket (played for N Canterbury), Rugby, golf.

**WRIGHT, Rev. Canon Andrew David Gibson;** Secretary General, Mission to Seafarers, since 2013; *b* Redditch, 18 May 1958; *s* of David and Anita Wright; *m* 1984, Julia Savage; one *s* three *d*. *Educ*: Dragon Sch., Oxford; St Edward's Sch., Oxford; Univ. of St Andrews (MTh 1981); Ridley Hall, Cambridge. Ordained deacon, 1983, priest, 1984; Assistant Curate: Church of the Good Shepherd, W Derby, 1983–86; Holy Trinity and St Barnabas, Carlisle, 1986–88; Vicar, St James with St Thomas, Wigan, 1988–91; Chaplain, Hd of Religious Studies, and Housemaster, St Edward's Sch., Oxford, 1991–2007; Mission Chaplain and Dir of Ops, Royal Nat. Mission to Deep Sea Fishermen, 2007–13. Canon, Cathedral Chapter, Dio. of Europe, 2016–. *Recreations*: walking, sailing, ski-ing, theatre, history. *Address*: The Mission to Seafarers, St Michael Paternoster Royal, College Hill, EC4R 2RL. *T*: (020) 7248 5202, *Fax*: (020) 7248 4761. *E*: andrew.wright@missiontoseafarers.org.

**WRIGHT, Andrew Paul Kilding,** OBE 2001; PPRIAS, RIBA; conservation architect and architectural historian in private practice, Andrew P. K. Wright, since 2001; Commissioner, Royal Fine Art Commission for Scotland, 1997–2005; *b* 11 Feb. 1947; *s* of Harold Maurice Wright, ARIBA and Eileen May Wright; *m* 1970, Jean Patricia Cross; one *s* two *d*. *Educ*: Queen Mary's Grammar Sch., Walsall; Univ. of Liverpool (BArch Hons). RIBA 1973; ARIAS 1976, FRIAS 1987; FSAScot 1998. Weightman & Bullen, Liverpool, 1970–72; Rowand Anderson Kininmonth & Paul, Edinburgh, 1972–73; Sir Basil Spence, Glover & Ferguson, Edinburgh, 1973–78; Law & Dunbar-Nasmith, 1978–2001: Partner, 1981–2001; Chm., 1999–2001. Dir, Exec. Bd, UK City of Architecture and Design, Glasgow 1999 Festival Co. Ltd, 1995–2004. Archt, dio. of Moray, Ross and Caithness, 1988–98; Cons. Archt, Mar Lodge Estate, NT for Scotland, 1996–99; Hon. Archtl Advr, Scottish Redundant Churches Trust, 1996–; Architectural Adviser: Holyrood Progress Gp, Scottish Parlt, 2000–04; Scottish Churches Trust (formerly Scottish Churches Architectural Heritage Trust), 2011–; Conservation Advr, Highland Historic Bldgs Trust (formerly Highland Bldgs Preservation Trust), 2001–. Member: Ancient Monuments Bd for Scotland, 1996–2003; Historic Envmt Adv. Council for Scotland, 2003–09 (Vice-Chm., 2003–06); Panel, Fundamental Review of Historic Scotland, 2003; Post Completion Adv. Gp, Scottish Parlt, 2004–06; non-exec. Mem., Adv. Cttee, Historic Scotland, 2012–15; Mem., Transition Adv. Bd, Historic Scotland and Royal Commn on Ancient and Histl Monuments of Scotland, 2013–15. Member Council: Inverness Archtl Assoc., 1981–90 (Pres., 1986–88); RIAS, 1986–94, 1995–99 (Vice-Pres., 1986–88; Convener, Memship Cttee, 1992–94; Pres., 1995–97); RIBA, 1988–94, 1995–97. Member: Ecclesiastical Archts and Surveyors Assoc., 1989; Conservation Adv. Panel, Hopetoun Hse Preservation Trust, 1997–2007 (Co-Chair, 2005–07); C of S Adv. Cttee on Artistic Matters, 2000–05; Arts and Crafts in Architecture Award Panel, Saltire Soc., 2001–06; Conservation Cttee, NT for Scotland, 2007–11. Trustee: Clan Mackenzie Charitable Trust, 1998–2018; Cawdor Maintenance Trust, 2010–; Cawdor Heritage Charity, 2010–; Scottish Lime Centre Trust, 2011–; Knockando Woolmill Trust, 2016–18; Historic Scotland Foundn, 2019–. Founding Fellow, Inst. of Contemp. Scotland, 2001; FRSA; FSA Scot. *Recreations*: cycling, fishing, industrial heritage, classical music. *Address*: Andrew P. K. Wright, Chartered Architect, 16 Moy House Court, Forres, Moray IV36 2NZ. *T*: (01309) 676655.

**WRIGHT, Dr Anne Margaret,** CBE 1997; Chair: National Lottery Commission, 2005–13; School Teachers' Review Body, 2008–11; *b* 26 July 1946; *d* of Herbert and Florence Holden; *m* 1970, Martin Wright; one *d*. *Educ*: Holy Trinity Ind. Grammar Sch., Bromley; King's Coll., London (BA Hons English I, 1967; Inglis Teaching Studentship, 1967–68; PhD 1970). Lectr in English, Lancaster Univ., 1969–71; Lectr, then Sen. Lectr, Principal Lectr and Reader in Modern English Studies, Hatfield Poly., 1971–84; British Acad. Res. Award, Univ. of Texas at Austin, 1979; Registrar for Arts and Humanities, CNAA, 1984–86; Dep. Rector (Academic), Liverpool Poly., 1986–90; Rector and Chief Exec., Sunderland Poly., 1990–92, Vice Chancellor and Chief Exec., Univ. of Sunderland, 1992–98; Chief Exec., UFI Ltd, 1998–2001; educational consultant, 2001–08. Member: English Studies Bd, 1978–84, Arts and Humanities Res. Sub-Cttee, 1979–84, CNAA; Cttee I of Cttee for Internat. Co-op. in Higher Educn, British Council, 1990–97; Council for Industry and Higher Educn, 1994–97; Armed Forces Pay Review Body, 2002–08; Bar Standards Bd, 2012–17; NMC, 2013–; Director: FEFC, 1992–97; Hong Kong UPGC, 1992–2003; HEQC, 1993–97. Member: EOC, 1997–98; Bd, English Partnerships, 2004–08. Chairman: City of Sunderland (formerly Wearside) Common Purpose, 1990–97; Nat. Glass Centre, 1997–98. Director: Everyman Theatre, Liverpool, 1988–90; The Wearside Opportunity, 1990–93; Northern Sinfonia, 1990–96; Northern Arts, 1991–95; Wearside TEC, 1992–98; Chair, Shaw Soc., 2017–; Chair of Trustees, Youth Music Theatre, 2009–11. CCMI (CIMgt 1994; Mem. Bd of Companions, 1999–2006); FRSA 1992. DL Tyne and Wear, 1997–2001. *Publications*: (ed jtly) Heartbreak House: a facsimile of the revised typescript, 1981; Literature of Crisis 1910–1922, 1984; Bernard Shaw's Saint Joan, 1984; articles in jls and entries in dictionaries of lit. biog. *Recreations*: singing, theatre, opera, the arts.

**WRIGHT, Prof. Anthony,** DM; FRCS; Professor of Otorhinolaryngology, University College London, 1991–2006, now Emeritus Professor of Otolaryngology (Director, Ear Institute (formerly Institute of Laryngology and Otology), 1991–2006); Consultant Ear, Nose and Throat Surgeon, Royal National Throat, Nose and Ear Hospital, 1993–2010; *b* 21 Nov. 1949; *s* of Arthur Donald and Hilda Wright; *m* 1989, Linda Steele; two *d*. *Educ*: Mill Hill Sch.; Emmanuel Coll., Cambridge (Sen. Schol.; Captain, Univ. Boxing Team, 1970; Full Blues, 1969, 1970); Lincoln Coll., Oxford (Full Blue, Boxing, 1972). DM Oxon 1986; LLM UWC Cardiff, 1995; FRCSE 1979; FRCS *ad eundem* 1995. Sen. Lectr in ENT Surgery, Inst. of Laryngology and Otology, 1984–89; Consultant ENT Surgeon, Royal Free Hosp., 1989–91. Queen's Award for Technol., 1998. *Publications*: Dizziness: a guide to disorders of balance, 1988; (ed with Harold Ludman) Diseases of the Ear, 6th edn 1997; scientific articles on the structure and function of the inner ear and on medico-legal aspects of ENT surgery. *Recreation*: still attempting to make coffee that tastes as good as it smells. *Address*: 4 Grange Road, Highgate, N6 4AP. *T*: (020) 8340 5593. *Clubs*: Athenæum; Hawks (Cambridge).

**WRIGHT, Anthony David;** *b* 12 Aug. 1954; *s* of late Arthur Wright and of Jean Wright; *m* 1988, Barbara Fleming; one *s* one *d*, and one step *d*. *Educ*: secondary modern sch. Engineer. Mem. (Lab) Great Yarmouth BC, 1980–82, 1986–98. Dir, Great Yarmouth Tourist Authority, 1994–97; Mem., Great Yarmouth Marketing Initiative, 1992–97 (Chm., 1996–97). MP (Lab) Great Yarmouth, 1997–2010; contested (Lab) same seat, 2010. Member: Public Admin Select Cttee, 2000–02; Trade and Industry Select Cttee, 2005–08; Business Enterprise and Regulatory Reform Cttee, 2008–10.

**WRIGHT, Rev. Canon (Anthony) Robert,** LVO 2010; Canon, 1998–2010, Sub-Dean, 2005–10 and Archdeacon, 2009–10, of Westminster; Rector of St Margaret's, Westminster, and Chaplain to the Speaker of the House of Commons, 1998–2010; *b* 24 April 1949; *s* of Kenneth William Wright and Christabel Annie Wright (*née* Flett); *m* 1970, Leah Helen Flower; one *s* one *d*. *Educ*: Lanchester Poly. (BA Hons Modern Studies); St Stephen's House, Oxford (CTh Oxon). Ordained deacon, 1973, priest, 1974; Curate: St Michael, Amersham, 1973–76; St Giles-in-Reading, 1976–78; Vicar: Prestwood, 1978–84; Wantage, 1984–92; RD of Wantage, 1984–92; Vicar of Portsea, 1992–98. *Recreations*: abstract painting, walking, reading.

**WRIGHT, Dr Anthony Wayland;** *b* 11 March 1948; *s* of Frank and Maud Wright; *m* 1973, Moira Elynwy Phillips; three *s* (and one *s* decd). *Educ*: Desborough County Primary Sch.; Kettering Grammar Sch.; LSE (BSc Econ 1st Cl. Hons); Harvard Univ. (Kennedy Schol.); Balliol Coll., Oxford (DPhil). Lectr in Politics, UCNW, Bangor, 1973–75; Lectr 1975, Sen. Lectr 1987, Reader 1989, in Politics, Sch. of Continuing Studies, Univ. of Birmingham. Educnl Fellowship, IBA, 1979–80; Chm., S Birmingham CHC, 1983–85. MP (Lab) Cannock and Burntwood, 1992–97, Cannock Chase, 1997–2010. PPS to the Lord Chancellor, 1997–98. Chm., Public Admin Select Cttee, 1999–2010. Hon. Prof., Univ. of Birmingham, 1999–; Vis. Prof. in Governance and Public Policy, UCL; Professorial Fellow, Birkbeck, Univ. of London. Jt Editor, Political Qly, 1994–. *Publications*: G. D. H. Cole and Socialist Democracy, 1979; Local Radio and Local Democracy, 1982; British Socialism, 1983; Socialisms: theories and practices, 1986; R. H. Tawney, 1987; (ed jtly) Party Ideology in Britain, 1989; (ed jtly) The Alternative, 1990; (ed jtly) Consuming Public Services, 1990; (ed jtly) Political Thought since 1945, 1992; Citizens and Subjects, 1993; (ed with G. Brown) Values, Visions and Voices, 1995; Socialisms: old and new, 1996; Who Do I Complain to?, 1997; Why Vote Labour?, 1997; (jtly) The People's Party, 1997; The British Political Process, 2000; British Politics: a very short introduction, 2003; contribs to learned jls. *Recreations*: tennis, walking, gardening.

**WRIGHT, Brian;** *see* Wright, G. B.

**WRIGHT, Caroline Jane; Her Honour Judge Caroline Wright;** a Circuit Judge, since 2009; *b* Oxford, 10 Aug. 1959; *d* of late Frederick and of Lilian Wright; *m* 1st, 1997, Dan Gardiner (marr. diss. 2002); one *s* one *d*; 2nd, 2007, Matthew John Hale. *Educ*: Oxford High Sch.; Univ. of York (BSc Psychol.); Univ. of Westminster (Dip. Law). Called to the Bar, Gray's Inn, 1983, Bencher, 2019; in practice as barrister, specialising in family and public law, Albion Chambers, Bristol, 1992–2003, 29 Bedford Row, London, 2003–09; Fee-paid Immigration Judge, 1998–2009; a Recorder, 2004–09. Mem., Bar Standards Bd, 2008–09. Tutor in family law, Judicial Coll., 2010–. *Recreations*: my diverse and entertaining family, painting, music, cycling, travel, swimming on Hampstead Heath and in the sea at Collioure, France. *Address*: Central Family Court, First Avenue House, 42–49 High Holborn, WC1V 6NP; Inner London Crown Court, Newington Causeway, SE1 6AZ. *E*: HHJ.Caroline.Wright@ejudiciary.net. *Club*: House of St Barnabas.

**WRIGHT, Caroline Janet Pamela;** Director General, British Educational Suppliers Association, since 2012; *b* 29 Dec. 1973; *d* of Peter Richard Wright and Janet Anne Wright; *m* 2007, Jonathan Rubidge; one *s* one *d*. *Educ*: Royal Holloway and Bedford New Coll., London (BSc Hons Geog.). Journalist, 1995–98; Communications Manager, Post Office, 1998–2000; Department of Trade and Industry: Dep. Dir of News, 2000–03; Hd, Strategic Communications, 2003; Hd, News and Mktg, Ofsted, 2003–05; Dir of Communications, Partnerships for Schs, 2005–06; Dir of Communications, DES, later DCSF, then DFE, 2006–11. Non-executive Director: Barking, Redbridge and Havering NHS Trust, 2011–13; EdTech Exchange, 2018–. *Address*: British Educational Suppliers Association, 20 Beaufort Court, Admirals Way, E14 9XL. *E*: caroline@besa.org.uk.

**WRIGHT, Christopher John;** Deputy Team Leader, Iraq Study, Ministry of Defence, 2009–10; *b* 22 March 1953; *s* of James Wright and Ruby Wright (*née* Galbraith); *m* 1995, Barbara Ann Spells. *Educ*: Royal Grammar Sch., Newcastle upon Tyne; Univ. of York (BA). Joined MoD, 1974; Private Sec. to Air Mem. for Supply and Orgn, 1981; Office of Manpower Econs, 1982–85; Private Sec. to Perm. Under-Sec. of State, 1987–90; Asst Sec., 1990; Head: Central Services, 1990–93; NATO and European Policy Secretariat, 1993–94;

Cost Review Secretariat, 1994–95; Dir of Orgn and Mgt Develt, 1995–98; Comd Sec., RAF Strike Comd, 1998–2001; Fellow, Center for Internat. Affairs, Harvard Univ., 2001–02; Hd, New Security Issues Prog., RIIA, 2002–04; Dir, Security and Intelligence, Cabinet Office, 2004–09. *Recreations:* reading, cinema, modern art, house refurbishment.

**WRIGHT, Christopher Norman,** CBE 2005; Director, Lasgo Chrysalis Ltd, 2011–13; Chairman: Chrysalis plc (formerly Chrysalis, later Chrysalis Group plc), 1969–2011; Digital Rights Group, 2007–13; non-executive Chairman, Chrysalis Records, since 2016; *b* 7 Sept. 1944; *s* of Walter Reginald Wright and Edna May (*née* Corden); *m* 1st, 1972, Carolyn Rochelle Nelson (marr. diss. 1999); two *s* one *d*; 2nd, 2003, Janice Ann Stinnes (*née* Toseland); one *d*. *Educ:* King Edward VI Grammar Sch., Louth; Manchester Univ. (BA Hons 1966); Manchester Business Sch. Co-Founder, Ellis Wright Agency, 1967; name changed to: Chrysalis, 1968; Chrysalis Gp plc, 1985. Chm., Loftus Road plc (incorp. Queen's Park Rangers Football and Athletic Club), 1996–2001; Founder, Shareholder and Dir, London Wasps RFC, 1996–2008 (Chm., 1996–2007); Chm., Portman Film and Television, 2004–07. Chm., British Phonographic Industry, 1980–83; Director: Phonographic Performance Ltd, 1980–94; Internat. Fedn of Phonographic Industry, 1981–95 (Vice-Pres., 1981–91); Blue Raincoat Songs, 2015–16. *Recreations:* playing tennis, breeding race horses, music, collecting art and fine wines, watching sport of all kinds. *Club:* Turf.

**WRIGHT, Prof. Crispin James Garth,** PhD, DLitt; FBA 1992; FRSE, FAAAS; Professor of Philosophy: New York University, since 2008; Stirling University, since 2015; *b* 21 Dec. 1942; *s* of Geoffrey Joseph Wright and Jean Valerie Holford; *m* 1985, Catherine Steedman (*née* Pain); two *s*, and one step *s* one step *d*. *Educ:* Birkenhead Sch.; Trinity Coll., Cambridge (BA Hons 1964; MA, PhD 1968); BPhil 1969, DLitt 1988, Oxon. Oxford University: Jun. Res. Fellow, Trinity Coll., 1967–69; Prize Fellow, All Souls Coll., 1969–71; Lectr, Balliol Coll., 1969–70; Lectr, UCL, 1970–71; Res. Fellow, All Souls Coll., Oxford, 1971–78; University of St Andrews: Prof. of Logic and Metaphysics, 1978–2008; Wardlaw Prof. 1997–2008; Dir, Arché Res. Centre, 1998–2009; Prof. of Phil., 1987–92, Nelson Prof. of Phil., 1992–94, Univ. of Michigan, Ann Arbor. Leverhulme Res. Prof., 1998–2003; Dir, Northern Inst. of Philosophy, 2009–15, Regius Prof. of Logic, 2013–15, Univ. of Aberdeen. FRSE 1996; FAAAS 2012. *Publications:* Wittgenstein on the Foundations of Mathematics, 1980; Frege's Conception of Numbers as Objects, 1983; Realism, Meaning and Truth, 1986; Truth and Objectivity, 1993; (with Bob Hale) The Reason's Proper Study, 2001; Rails to Infinity, 2001; Saving the Differences, 2003. *Recreations:* gardening, mountain-walking, running, P. G. Wodehouse, Liverpool FC. *Address:* Department of Philosophy, New York University, 5 Washington Place, New York, NY 10003, USA.

**WRIGHT, David;** *b* 22 Dec. 1966; *s* of Kenneth William Wright and Heather Wright; *m* 1996, Lesley Insole. *Educ:* Wolverhampton Poly. (BA Hons Humanities). MCIH 1994. With Sandwell MBC, 1988–2001 (Housing Strategy Manager, 1995–2001). MP (Lab) Telford, 2001–15; contested (Lab) same seat, 2015. An Asst Govt Whip, 2009–10; Opposition Whip, 2010–12. *Recreations:* watching football (AFC Telford Utd) and cricket (Surrey), visiting old towns and cities. *Clubs:* Wrockwardine Wood and Trench Labour, Dawley Social.

**WRIGHT, David Alan,** OBE 1983; HM Diplomatic Service, retired; Joint Head (formerly Assistant Director), PROSPER, Human Resources Command, Foreign and Commonwealth Office, 2002–15; *b* 27 May 1942; *s* of Herbert Ernest Wright and Ivy Florence (*née* Welch); *m* 1966, Gail Karol Mesling; four *s* one *d*. *Educ:* Surbiton Grammar Sch.; Univ. of Birmingham (BSocSc 1963). VSO, Chad, 1963; Inf. Officer, BoT, 1964; entered Foreign Office, 1965: Asst Private Sec. to Minister of State, FO, 1966–68; MECAS, 1968–70; Baghdad, 1970–73; Doha, 1973–76; on secondment to DHSS, 1976–78; FCO, 1978–80; Durban, 1980–83; Baghdad, 1983–87; FCO, 1987–92 (Head: Communications Dept, 1988–90; Inf. Systems Div. (Resources), 1990–92); Consul Gen., Atlanta, 1992–97; Ambassador and Consul Gen., Qatar, 1997–2002. Member: (C) Guildford BC, 2003–19 (Chm., Licensing, 2003–07; Lead Mem. for Community Safety, 2007–11; Dep. Leader, 2011–12). Mem., Surrey Probation Bd, 2006–09; Mem. Bd, 2003–, Vice Chm., 2007–14, Chm., 2014–, Surrey Hills Area of Outstanding Natural Beauty. Chairman: SurreySave Credit Union, 2012–16; W Sussex and Surrey Credit Union, 2017–. *Recreations:* jogging, pottery, travel, music. *Address:* Newlands House, Newlands Corner, Guildford GU4 8SE. *Club:* Royal Over-Seas League.

**WRIGHT, David Arthur,** FRCS; Consultant Otolaryngologist: Mount Alvernia Hospital, Guildford, 1970–2004; Royal Surrey County Hospital, 1970–99, now Consultant Emeritus; President, British Association of Otorhinolaryngologists and Head and Neck Surgeons, 1997–99; *b* 13 April 1935; *s* of Arthur Albert Wright and Ena May (*née* Caxton); *m* 1969, Hillery Drina Seex; one *s* one *d*. *Educ:* Repton; Jesus Coll., Cambridge (MB BChir, MA 1960); Guy's Hosp. LRCP 1959; MRCS 1959, FRCS 1966. Hon. Consultant Otolaryngologist: Cambridge Mil. Hosp., 1981–96; King Edward VII Hosp., Midhurst, 1995–2003. Ear, Nose and Throat Adviser: British Airways, 1987–97; CAA, 1994–; Army, 1999–. Asst Ed., Jl Laryngology and Otology, 1981–88. Pres., TWJ Otological Foundn, 2008– (Chm., 1974–2008). Sec. Gen., Eur. Bd Otolaryngology, 1998–2000. Member: BMA, 1960–98; Council, RCS, 1995–2000; Pres., Section of Otology, RSocMed, 1992; Hon. Mem., ENT UK, 2019. Examr, Intercollegiate Bd Otolaryngology, 1990–94. Mem. Senate, Royal Surgical Colls, 1997–2000 (Chm., Specialist Adv. Cttee, 1988–94). Patron, British Soc. of Hearing Therapists, 1999–; Master, British Academic Conf. in Otolaryngology, 2003–06. George Davey Howells Meml Prize, RSocMed, 1989; Walter Jobson Horne Prize, BMA, 1997; Gold Medal, British Assoc. of Otorhinolaryngologists, 1999. *Publications:* (ed) Scott-Brown's Otolaryngology, vol. 1, Basic Sciences, 5th edn 1988; chapters in text books; contrib. articles in med. jls on noise induced hearing loss, multi-channel hearing aids and functional endoscopic sinus surgery. *Recreations:* sailing, ski-ing, fly-fishing, golf; research project, Captain William Bligh's First Lieutenant (1765–1839). *Address:* No 1 Thames Bank, Thames Road, Goring-on-Thames, Oxon RG8 9AH. *T:* (01491) 871815, 07785 975650. *Clubs:* Royal Society of Medicine; Probus (Goring); Huntercombe Golf (Oxon).

**WRIGHT, Sir David (John),** GCMG 2002 (KCMG 1996; CMG 1992); LVO 1990; HM Diplomatic Service, retired; Adviser, Sumitomo Mitsui Banking Corporation Europe Ltd, since 2018; *b* 16 June 1944; *s* of J. F. Wright; *m* 1968, Sally Ann Dodkin; one *s* one *d*. *Educ:* Wolverhampton Grammar Sch.; Peterhouse, Cambridge (MA; Hon. Fellow, 2001). Third Secretary, FO, 1966; Third Sec., later Second Sec., Tokyo, 1966–72; FCO, 1972–75; Ecole Nationale d'Administration, Paris, 1975–76; First Sec., Paris, 1976–80; Private Sec. to Secretary of the Cabinet, 1980–82; Counsellor (Economic), Tokyo, 1982–85; Head of Personnel Services Dept, FCO, 1985–88; Dep. Private Sec. to HRH the Prince of Wales, 1988–90 (on secondment); Ambassador to Republic of Korea, 1990–94; Dep. Under-Sec. of State, FCO, 1994–96; Ambassador to Japan, 1996–99; Gp Chief Exec. (Perm. Sec.), British Trade Internat., 1999–2002. Vice-Chm., Barclays (formerly Barclays Capital), 2003–17; Sen. Advr, Barclays Internat., 2017–18; non-exec. Dir, Balfour Beatty, 2003–05; Chairman: Skarbek Associates, 2017–; Japan Market Adv. Gp, TheCityUK, 2017–; Member: Internat. Adv. Bd, All Nippon Airways, 2003–07; Internat. Adv. Council, China Develt Bank, 2010–. Chm., Govt Wine Cttee, 2004–. Vice-Pres., China Britain Business Council, 2003–09; Member: Bd, UK-Japan 21st Century Gp, 2003–18; Adv. Council, British Consultants and Construction Bureau, 2003–05. Chm. and Trustee, Daiwa Anglo-Japanese Foundn, 2001–04; Chm., UK-Korea Forum, 2008–14. Gov., RSC, 2004–08. Chm., Develt Cttee, Peterhouse, Cambridge, 2004–10; Chm., Governing Bd, Perse Sch., Cambridge, 2012–; Mem. Bd, 2020 Vision Campaign, Cambridge Biomed. Campus, 2011–13. Chm., Peterhouse Soc., 2010–13. Hon. LLD: Wolverhampton, 1997; Birmingham, 2000. Grand Cordon, Order of the Rising Sun (Japan), 1998. *Recreations:* golf, cooking, military history. *Address:* Meldreth, Cambs. *Clubs:* Garrick, Saintsbury.

**WRIGHT, Prof. (Douglas) Michael,** PhD; FBA 2016; FAcSS; Professor of Entrepreneurship, since 2011, and Director, Centre for Management Buyout Research, since 1986, Imperial College London; *b* Stockport, 11 April 1952; *s* of Douglas Leopold Wright and Nora Irene Wright (*née* Potts); *m* 1984, Maryse Ernestine Sallandrnze; one *s* one *d*. *Educ:* New Mills Grammar Sch.; Ealing Tech. Coll. (BA (Econ) 1973); Durham Univ. (MA 1978); Nottingham Univ. (PhD 1986). Prof. of Financial Studies, Univ. of Nottingham, 1989–2011; Hd, Dept of Innovation and Entrepreneurship, Imperial Coll. London, 2013–16. Vis. Prof., Univ. of Ghent, 2006–18. Editor: Jl Mgt Studies, 2003–09; Strategic Entrepreneurship Jl, 2011–16. Chm., Soc. for Advancement of Mgt Studies, 2015–. FRSA 1991; FBAM 1999; FAcSS 2011; FSMS 2017. Hon. Dr: Ghent, 2006; Derby, 2011. *Publications:* (with J. Coyne) Management Buyouts, 1985; (jtly) Academic Entrepreneurship in Europe, 2007; (with J. Gilligan) Private Equity Demystified, 2008, 3rd edn 2014; (jtly) Oxford Handbook of Corporate Governance, 2013; (jtly) Chicago Handbook of Tech Transfer and Academic Entrepreneurship, 2015; (with P. Westhead) The Habitual Entrepreneur Phenomenon, 2016; (jtly) Routledge Companion to Management Buyouts, 2018; (with I. Drori) Accelerators, 2018; (jtly) Student Entrepreneurship, 2019. *Recreations:* cycling Le Tourmalet and La Creuse, walking, ornithology, music of Bob Dylan, French films. *Address:* 100 Draycott Road, Breaston, Derby DE72 3DB. *T:* (01332) 874045. *E:* mike.wright@imperial.ac.uk.

**WRIGHT, Elizabeth Anne,** CMG 2015; Chair, Advisory Board, China Policy Institute, University of Nottingham, 2005–16 (Executive Chair, China Policy Institute, 2003–05); *b* Coventry, 6 Feb. 1946; *d* of John Wright and Anne Wright; *m* 1994, David Michael Lindley Witherow, *qv*. *Educ:* Nuneaton High Sch. for Girls; School of Oriental and African Studies, Univ. of London (BA Hons Chinese 1968; MA Area Studies 1971). Res. Officer, FCO, 1969–72; Second Sec., British Embassy, Beijing, 1972–75; Dep. Dir, 1976–78, Dir, 1978–84, Great Britain-China Centre; BBC World Service, 1984–2003: Hd, Chinese Service, 1989–93; Hd, Asia and Pacific Reg., 1993–2003. Trustee: Needham Res. Inst., 2009–; Governing Bd, SOAS, 2003–14 (Vice-Chm., 2011–14); Mem., Sen. Adv. Council, China Inst., 2016–); Chinadialogue, 2012–; Chm., Univs China Cttee, 2013–16. *Publications:* The Chinese People Stand Up, 1989. *Recreations:* classical music, opera, theatre, painting, fiction. *E:* ew25@soas.ac.uk.

**WRIGHT, Eric;** Chairman, Yorkshire and Humberside Development Agency (formerly Association), 1993–99; *b* 17 Nov. 1933; *s* of Alec Wright and Elsie (*née* Worthington); *m* 1st, 1955, Pauline Sutton (marr. diss. 1993); three *s* (and one *s* decd); 2nd, 1993, Hazel Elizabeth Story. *Educ:* Wolstanton Grammar Sch.; Keble Coll., Oxford (BA 1st Cl. Hons Mod. Hist.). 2nd Lieut RASC, 1955–57. Ministry of Fuel and Power, 1957–65; Civil Service Commission, 1965–67; Min. of Technology, 1968–70; Sloan Fellow, London Business Sch., 1970–71; Principal Private Sec. to Secretary of State, DTI, 1971–72; Dept of Trade, 1972–77; Dept of Industry, 1977–83; Under-Sec., 1979–; DTI, 1983–93 (Regl Dir, Yorks and Humberside, 1985–93). *Recreations:* music, tennis, chess. *Address:* 17 Foxhill Crescent, Leeds LS16 5PD. *T:* (0113) 275 4309.

**WRIGHT, Prof. Ernest Marshall,** PhD, DSc; FRS 2005; Professor of Physiology, since 1974, Sherman M. Mellinkoff Distinguished Professor of Medicine, since 1999, Distinguished Professor of Physiology, since 2004, School of Medicine, University of California, Los Angeles; *b* Belfast, N Ireland, 8 June 1940; *m* 1961, Brenda W. Keys; two *s*. *Educ:* Chelsea Coll. of Sci. and Technol., Univ. of London (BSc Physiol. and Chem. 1961); Univ. of Sheffield (PhD Physiol. 1964); Univ. of London (DSc Physiol. 1978). Res. Fellow, Biophysics, Harvard Univ., 1965–66; University of California, Los Angeles: Asst Prof. of Physiol., 1967–70; Associate Prof. of Physiol., 1970–74; Chair, Dept of Physiol., 1987–2000. Visiting Professor: Center for Advanced Studies, Nat. Poly. Inst., Mexico City, 1973; Max Planck Inst. for Biophysics, Frankfurt, 1974–75; Queen Elizabeth Coll., London, 1977. Senator Jacob K. Javits Neurosci. Investigator, 1985–92. Horace W. Davenport Dist. Lectr, Exptl Biol. 2000, San Diego, 2000. Mem., Adv. Bd, Broad Med. Res. Prog., 2001–. Chm., Physiol. Study Section, NIH, 1983–86; Councilor: Soc. of Gen. Physiologists, 1986–89; Gastrointestinal Sect. Steering Cttee, Amer. Physiol Soc., 1999–2002. Mem. Review Panel, Structural Biol., Nat. Center of Competence in Res., Swiss Nat. Sci. Foundn, 2002–. Fellow: Biophysical Soc., 2005; NAS, 2013. Mem., German Nat. Acad. Scis Leopoldina, 2006. Award for Sustained Achievement in Digestive Scis, Janssen/Amer. Gastroenterol. Soc., 2004. *Publications:* (with M. Martin) Congenital Intestinal Transport Defects, in Pediatric Gastrointestinal Disease, 4th edn 2004; (contrib.) Sugar Absorption, in Physiology of the Gastrointestinal Tract, 4th edn 2005; numerous articles in learned jls, incl. Nature, Science, Jl Biol Chem., Jl Membrane Biol., Jl Physiol., Biochemistry, Physiol Reviews. *Address:* Department of Physiology, David Geffen School of Medicine at UCLA, 10833 Le Conte Avenue, Los Angeles, CA 90095-1751, USA. *T:* (310) 8256905, *Fax:* (310) 2065661. *E:* ewright@mednet.ucla.edu.

**WRIGHT, Freya Patricia;** see Newbery, F. P.

**WRIGHT, (George) Brian;** JP; Head of Educational Broadcasting Services, BBC, 1989–93; *b* 9 April 1939; *s* of George Wright and Martha Blair Wright (*née* Dundee); *m* 1963, Joyce Avril Frances Camier; two *s*. *Educ:* Trinity Coll., Dublin (MA, HDipEd). Schoolmaster, 1961–67; Local Govt Administrator, 1967–69; BBC Educn Officer, Belfast, Nottingham, Birmingham, 1969–81; Chief Educn Officer, BBC, 1981–89. Occasional Lectr, Henley Management Coll., 1994–95. Mem., Lord Chancellor's Nottingham Div. Adv. Cttee, 1997–2001. Mem., City and Co. of Notts Adv. Bd, Salvation Army, 1999–2001. Burgess, Ancient Corp. of St Pancras, Chichester, 2015. JP Ealing, 1992–93, Nottingham, 1993. *Publications:* How Britain Earns Its Living, 1980; (with John Cain) in a class of its own, 1994; In the Name of Decent Citizens: the trials of Frank De Groot, 2006. *Recreations:* reading, crosswords, watching Rugby. *Address:* 56 Lyndhurst Road, Chichester, W Sussex PO19 7PE. *T:* (01243) 773432.

**WRIGHT, George Henry,** MBE 1977; Vice-Chairman, Wales Co-operative Development Centre, since 1985 (Chairman, 1983–85); Regional Secretary, Wales, Transport and General Workers Union, 1972–99; *b* 11 July 1935; *s* of William Henry and Annie Louisa Wright; *m* 1956, Margaret Wright; two *d*. *Educ:* Tinkers Farm Sch., Birmingham. Car worker, 1954–65. T&GWU: District Officer, West Bromwich, 1965–68; District Secretary, Birmingham, 1968–72. Gen. Sec., Wales TUC, 1974–84 (Chm., 1989–90). Member: MSC Wales, 1976–88; Employment Appeal Tribunal, 1985–; Welsh Trng Adv. Gp, 1989–; Bd, Welsh Develt Agency, 1994–; Central Arbitration Cttee, Dept of Employment, 1994–; Econ. and Social Cttee, EC, 1994–; S Wales Police Authority, 1994–. *Recreations:* fishing, gardening. *Address:* 5 Kidwelly Court, Caerphilly CF83 2TY. *T:* (029) 2088 5434.

**WRIGHT, Graeme Alexander**; Editor, Wisden Cricketers' Almanack, 1986–92 and 2000–02; *b* 23 April 1943; *s* of Alexander John Wright and Eileen Margaret Wright. *Educ*: St Patrick's Coll., Wellington, NZ; St Patrick's High Sch., Timaru, NZ; Univ. of Canterbury, Christchurch, NZ. Copywriter, NZ Broadcasting Corp., 1965–67; Sub-editor, BSI, 1968–69; Editor and writer, Publicare Ltd, 1969–72; Managing Editor, Queen Anne Press, 1973–74; freelance editor and writer, 1974–; cricket writer, Independent on Sunday, 1990–94; Dir, John Wisden & Co. Ltd, 1983–86. *Publications*: (with Phil Read) Phil Read, 1977; The Illustrated Handbook of Sporting Terms, 1978; Olympic Greats, 1980; (with George Best) Where do I go from here?, 1981; (with Patrick Eagar): Test Decade 1972–1982, 1982; Botham, 1985; (with Joe Brown) Brown Sauce, 1986; Merrydown: forty vintage years, 1988; Betrayal: the struggle for cricket's soul, 1993; Chelton: the first 50 years, 1997; (ed) Wisden on Bradman, 90th Birthday Edition, 1998; (ed) A Wisden Collection, 2004; (ed) Wisden at Lord's, 2005; (ed) Bradman in Wisden, 2008; Behind the Boundary: cricket at a crossroads, 2011; Mackie's Law, 2012; My House Book, 2017. *Recreations*: reading, thinking, coffee houses. *Address*: 14 Field End Road, Eastcote, Pinner, Middx HA5 2QL.

**WRIGHT, Helen Mary**, EdD; Headmistress, Ascham School, Sydney, 2013–14; Director, Global Thought Leadership, since 2014; international education adviser, recruitment consultant and executive coach; *b* Perth, 22 Aug. 1970; *d* of Gordon Kendal and Patricia Kendal (*née* Foggo); *m* 1993, Brian Wright; one *s* two *d*. *Educ*: James Gillespie's High Sch., Edinburgh; Lincoln Coll., Oxford (BA 1992; PGCE 1993); Univ. of Leicester (MA 1998); Univ. of Exeter (EdD 2004). French and German teacher, Reed's Sch., Cobham, 1993–95; Hd of Dept, Bishop's Stortford Coll., 1995–97; Hd of Dept and Dep. Housemistress, St Edward's Sch., Oxford, 1997–2000; Dep. Headmistress, 2000, Headmistress, 2001–03, Heathfield Sch., Ascot; Headmistress, St Mary's School, Calne, 2003–12. Teacher-educator and PGCE mentor, 1997–2000; Examr and Sen. Examr (Higher Level), Internat. Baccalaureate, 1999–2009; Inspector, ISI, 2000–12. Consultant, Scholastic Books, 1998–2001; Internat. Educn Advr, Australian Educn City, 2014–15; Associate Consultant, LSC Education, 2014–. Dir, Dalton Foundn Ltd (HK), 2014–; non-exec. Dir, Global Trails, 2015–; Director and Trustee: ESU (Scotland), 2014– (Chair, 2017–); Changing the Chemistry, 2015–18; Member, Advisory Board: Obrussa, 2014–16; 2-Way Learning, Australia, 2016–. Chair: World Leading Schs Assoc. Res. Gp, 2012–18; Assoc. for Educn and Guardianship of Internat. Students, 2018–. Member: Assoc. for Language Learning, 1993–2012; Ind. Schs' Modern Langs Assoc., 1993– (Mem. Cttee, 1997–2000; Ed. of Newsletter, 1997–2000; Patron, 2005–); ASCL (formerly SHA), 2000–12 (Mem. Council, 2009–12); GSA, 2001–12 (Mem. Council, 2009–12; Pres., 2011; Hon. Mem., 2012); Vice Chm., ISC, 2011–12. Mem. Council, Malvern Coll., 2015–. Mem. Bd, Oxford Univ. Soc., 2008– (Dep. Chm., 2016–) Mem. Editl Adv. Bd, Oxford Today, 2011–16. MInstD 2009. FRSA 2003. Freeman, Co. of Educators, 2015–; Mem., Merchants Co., Edinburgh, 2019–. Ed., Francophonie, 1999–2002. *Publications*: trans., Elizabeth Behr-Sigel, A Monk of the Eastern Church, 1999; French Fries My Brain!, 2001; Learning Through Listening, 2004; Decoding Your 21st Century Daughter, 2013; Powerful Schools: how schools can be drivers of social and global mobility, 2016; (contrib.) Early Childhood Education Redefined, 2018; (contrib.) The State of Independence, 2019; numerous articles and reviews. *Recreations*: reading, studying, travelling, making jam, indoor gardening, writing. *W*: www.drhelenwright.com, www.twitter.com/drhelenwright. *Club*: Caledonian.

**WRIGHT, Hugh Raymond**, MA; Chief Master, King Edward's School, Birmingham, 1991–98; *b* 24 Aug. 1938; *s* of Rev. Raymond Blayney Wright and Alice Mary Wright (*née* Hawksworth); *m* 1962, Jillian Mary McIldowie Meiklejohn; three *s*. *Educ*: Kingswood Sch., Bath; The Queen's Coll., Oxford (Bible Clerk; MA Lit.Hum.). Asst Master, Brentwood Sch., 1961–64; Cheltenham Coll., 1964–79: Hd of Classics, 1967–72; Housemaster, Boyne House, 1971–79; Headmaster, Stockport Grammar Sch., 1979–85; Gresham's School, Holt, 1985–91. Headmasters' Conference: Chm., 1995; Chm., NW Dist, 1983; Chm., Community Service Sub-Cttee, 1985–90 (Mem., 1980–90); Rep. on ISC (formerly ISJC) Europe Cttee, 1997–2001; Mem., Assisted Places Wkg Pty, 1992–97. Mem., Chaplaincy Team, Shepton Mallet Prison, 2001–13. Member: Bloxham Project Cttee, 1993–98 (Trustee, 1998–2006); Admty Interview Bd Panel, 1982–95; ABM (formerly ACCM), C of E, 1982–2012; GBA Cttee, 2000–03. Chm., Nat. Steering Cttee, Children's Univ., 1995–2001. Gov., Kingswood Sch., Bath, 1995–2006 (Chm., 1998–2006). Member: Cttee, Friends of Bath Internat. Fest., 1995–2013 (Chm., 2008–13); Cttee, Wilts Br., Butterfly Conservation, 2016–. Trustee, Wilts Victoria Co. Hist., 2019– (Sec., 2019–). Volunteer, Downside Abbey Liby. Co-writer, Into Your Satisfaction, diaries and music of Benjamin Britten, perf. Gresham's Sch., Holt, 2013. *Publications*: film strips and notes on The Origins of Christianity and the Medieval Church, 1980; Thomas Tropenell: builder of Great Chalfield, 2011; The Story of Great Chalfield: the lives and times of the owners and occupiers of the Manor 1553–1913, 2011; Widows, Wives and Daughters: the women who shaped the story of Great Chalfield, 2013; The Story of Great Chalfield 1487–2010: the first 550 years, 2017; The Webbs of Odstock 1466–1876, 2019; contribs The Greshamian, Conf. and Common Room. *Recreations*: music, playing the bassoon, theatre, walking, wildfowl, biographical research, butterflies, reading biographies and histories, travel by sea. *Address*: 5 The Paddock, Kingston Road, Bradford on Avon BA15 1FN. *Club*: East India.

**WRIGHT, Iain David**; Director of Corporate and Regional Engagement, Institute of Chartered Accountants of England and Wales, since 2018; *b* 9 May 1972; *m* Tiffiny; three *s* one *d*. *Educ*: Manor Comprehensive Sch., Hartlepool; University Coll. London (BA, MA). ACA 2003. Deloitte & Touche, 1997–2003; chartered accountant, One NorthEast, 2003–04. Mem. (Lab), Hartlepool BC, 2002–05. MP (Lab) Hartlepool, Sept. 2004–2017. Parly Under-Sec. of State, DCLG, 2007–09, DCSF, 2009–10. Chm., Select Cttee on Business, Innovations and Skills, 2015–17. Chief Exec., NE of England Process Industry Cluster, 2017–18. *Address*: Institute of Chartered Accountants of England and Wales, Chartered Accountants' Hall, Moorgate Place, EC2R 6EA.

**WRIGHT, Ian**, CBE 2015; Chief Executive (formerly Director General), Food and Drink Federation, since 2015; *b* Taplow, Berks, 4 April 1958; *s* of Peter Wright and Gladys Wright (*née* Green); *m* 1987, Judith Gilboy; one *s* one *d*. *Educ*: Desborough Sch., Maidenhead; St Catharine's Coll., Cambridge (BA Hons 1980; MA Hons 1984). Pres., Cambridge Students' Union, 1980–81. Political Officer, SDP, 1981–85; PR Consultant, 1985–94; Hd of PR, Boots Healthcare Internat., 1994–97; Dir of Communications, Boots the Chemist, 1997–2000; Dir of Communications, 2000–04, Corporate Relns Dir, 2004–14, Diageo plc. Advr to Leaders of Lib Dem Party, Paddy Ashdown, Menzies Campbell and Nick Clegg, 1994–2015. Mem., Food and Drink Sector Council, 2018–; Pres., CIPR, 2001. *Recreations*: walking, gardening, Rugby, third party politics, Crystal Palace FC. *E*: ian.wright@fdf.org.uk.

**WRIGHT, Prof. Ian Craig**, PhD; Deputy Vice-Chancellor, University of Canterbury, New Zealand, since 2016; *b* Wellington, NZ, 14 Dec. 1958; *s* of Peter Wright and Margaret Wright; *m* 1981, Barbara Stewart; one *s* one *d*. *Educ*: Wellington Coll., Wellington, NZ; Victoria Univ. of Wellington (BSc Hons 1981; PhD 1986). Jun. Lectr, Victoria Univ. of Wellington, 1982–86; Res. Scientist, NZ Oceanographic Inst., 1987–92; sabbatical, UK, 1993; National Institute of Water and Atmospheric Research, NZ: Res. Scientist, 1993–98; Principal Scientist, 1998–2004; Coasts and Oceans Centre Leader, 2004–08; National Oceanography Centre, UK: Gp Leader, 2008–10; Dep. Dir, Sci. and Technol., 2010–12; Dir, Sci. and Technol., 2013–16. *Publications*: over 75 articles in learned jls. *Recreations*: golf, gardening. *Address*: University of Canterbury, Ilam Campus, Christchurch 8140, New Zealand. *E*: ian.wright@canterbury.ac.nz.

**WRIGHT, Prof. Ian Peter**, PhD; Professor of Planetary Sciences, Open University, since 2005; *b* Birmingham, 28 Nov. 1956; *s* of Ronald Wright and Vera Wright; *m* 1986, Prof. Monica Mary Grady, *qv*; one *s*. *Educ*: King Edward VI Five Ways Grammar Sch.; Univ. of Birmingham (BSc Geol Scis 1978); Darwin Coll., Cambridge (PhD 1982). Post-doctoral Res., Univ. of Cambridge, 1982–83; Open University: Post-doctoral Res., 1983–88; Res. Fellow, 1988–96; Sen. Res. Fellow, 1996–2005. Fellow, Inst. of Advanced Study, Durham Univ., 2010. FRAS 1989. *Publications*: articles in scientific jls. *Recreations*: denizen of virtual worlds, theatre, music, gardening, cooking, art, outreach, education. *Address*: School of Physical Sciences, Open University, Walton Hall, Milton Keynes MK7 6AA. *T*: (01908) 653898. *E*: ian.wright@open.ac.uk.

**WRIGHT, Prof. Jack Clifford**, MA, BA; Professor of Sanskrit, 1964–96, Research Fellow, 1996–99, Research Associate, since 1999, Professor Emeritus, since 2000, and Hon. President, Centre of Jaina Studies, since 2004, School of Oriental and African Studies, University of London; *b* 5 Dec. 1933; *s* of late Jack and Dorothy Wright, Aberdeen; *m* 1958, Hazel Chisholm (*née* Strachan), Crathes, Banchory; one *s*. *Educ*: Robert Gordon's Coll., Aberdeen; Univ. of Aberdeen (MA Hons in French and German, 1955); University of Zürich; Univ. of London (BA Hons in Sanskrit, 1959). Lectr in Sanskrit, 1959–64, Head, Dept of Indology and Mod. Langs and Lits of S Asia, 1970–83, SOAS, Univ. of London. *Address*: Faculty of Languages and Cultures, School of Oriental and African Studies, University of London, Thornhaugh Street, Russell Square, WC1H 0XG.

**WRIGHT, James Robertson Graeme**, CBE 2001; DL; Vice-Chancellor, University of Newcastle upon Tyne, 1992–2000; *b* 14 June 1939; *s* of John Wright and Elizabeth Calder (*née* Coghill); *m* 1966, Jennifer Susan Greenberg; two *d*. *Educ*: Inverness Royal Acad.; Dundee High Sch.; Univ. of Edinburgh (MA 1st cl. Hons Classics 1961, Guthrie Fellowship in Classical Lit., C. B. Black Scholarship in New Testament Greek); St John's Coll., Cambridge (Major Scholar, BA 1st cl. Classical Tripos Pt II 1963, MA 1968, Henry Arthur Thomas Studentship, Denney Studentship, Ferguson Scholarship in Classics, 1962). University of Edinburgh: Asst Lectr in Humanity (Latin), 1965; Lectr, 1966–78; Sen. Warden, Pollock Halls of Residence, 1973–78; Mem., Univ. Court, 1975–78; St Catharine's College, Cambridge: Fellow, 1978–87; Professorial Fellow, 1987–91; Hon. Fellow, 1992–; Dir, Studies in Classics, 1978–87; Bursar, 1979–87; Cambridge Bursars' Committee: Sec., 1983–86; Chm., 1986–87; Sec.-Gen. of Faculties, Univ. of Cambridge, 1987–91. Non-executive Member: Cambridge Dist HA, 1990–91; Northern and Yorks RHA, 1994–96. Mem. Council, CVCP, 1996–2000. Chm., Higher Educn Management Statistics Gp, 1995–2000; Mem., SHEFC, 1992–99; Associate Comr, Hamlyn Nat. Commn on Educn, 1992–93; Dir, UCAS, 1997–2000; Chm. Exec. Cttee, UKCOSA: Council for Internat. Educn, 1998–2002. British Council: Mem., CICHE, 1993–2000; Mem., CICHE Cttee 2 (Asia and Oceans Reg.), 1992–94. Dir, Newcastle Initiative, 1993–2000; Chm., Connexions Tyne & Wear, 2002–08. Mem., Governing Body, Shrewsbury Sch., 1986–2000. Trustee: Nat. Heritage Meml Fund, 2000–06 (Chm., Audit Cttee, 2003–06); Homerton Coll., Cambridge, 2002–10; Chm., Homerton Sch. of Health Studies, 2003–05. Age Concern England, later Age UK: Trustee, 2001–05, 2007–13; Chm., 2002–05; Dir, Age Concern Hldgs, 2005–14 (Chm., 2007–14); Trustee, Age Concern Scotland, 2002–09; Chm., Age Scotland, 2009–13 (Trustee, 2009–13). DL 1995, High Sheriff, 2003–04, Tyne and Wear. Hon. LLD Abertay Dundee, 1999; Hon. DEd Naresuan, Thailand, 2000; Hon. DCL Newcastle upon Tyne, 2001. *Publications*: articles and reviews in classical jls. *Recreations*: walking, travel in France, food, wine. *Address*: 10 Montagu Avenue, Gosforth, Newcastle upon Tyne NE3 4JH. *Clubs*: Athenæum; Northern Counties (Newcastle upon Tyne).

**WRIGHT, James Roland**; High Commissioner for Canada in the United Kingdom, 2006–11; *b* Montreal, 19 July 1950; *s* of David Stuart Wright and Jean Gertrude Percy; *m* 1977, Donna Thomson, *d* of James Thomas and Marjorie McKeown; one *s* one *d*. *Educ*: McGill Univ., Montreal (BA 1972; MA 1973). Joined Dept of Foreign Affairs, Ottawa, 1976; Third Sec., Moscow, 1978–80; Soviet Desk Officer, E Eur. Div., Ottawa, 1980–83; First Sec., Washington, 1983–87; Office of the Prime Minister, Ottawa, 1987–89; Dir, Pol/Econ. Personnel Div., Ottawa, 1989–92; Minister, Pol and Public Affairs, London, 1992–96; Dir Gen., Central, E and S Europe Bureau, Ottawa, 1996–2000; Pol Dir and Asst Dep. Minister, Global and Security Br., Ottawa, 2000–04; Pol Dir and Asst Dep. Minister, Internat. Security Br., 2005–06. Sen. Advr, The World Remembers, 2012–; Mem. Bd, Citizen Advocacy, 2013–; Advr, Plan Inst., 2014–. Fellow, Norman Patterson Sch. for Internat. Affairs, Carleton Univ., 2012–. Hon. Dr Ulster, 2008. Queen's Diamond Jubilee Medal, 2013. *Recreations*: golf, tennis, ski-ing, hiking. *Address*: 89 Forward Avenue, Apt 601, Ottawa, ON K1Y 4M2, Canada. *E*: jameswrightca@gmail.com.

**WRIGHT, Rt Hon. Jeremy (Paul)**; PC 2014; QC 2014; MP (C) Kenilworth and Southam, since 2010 (Rugby and Kenilworth, 2005–10); *b* 24 Oct. 1972; *s* of John and Audrey Wright; *m* 1998, Yvonne Salter; one *s* one *d*. *Educ*: Taunton Sch.; Trinity Sch., NYC; Univ. of Exeter (LLB Hons). Called to the Bar, Inner Temple, 1996; in practice on Midlands and Oxford Circuit, specialising in criminal law, 1996–2005. An Opposition Whip, 2007–10; a Lord Comr of HM Treasury (Govt Whip), 2010–12; Parly Under-Sec. of State, MoJ, 2012–14; Attorney Gen., 2014–18; Sec. of State for Digital, Culture, Media and Sport, 2018–19. Mem., Select Cttee on Constitutional Affairs, 2005–07. Trustee, Community Develt Fund, 2007–09. *Recreations*: golf, music, cinema. *Address*: House of Commons, SW1A 0AA. *T*: (020) 7219 2008. *E*: jeremy.wright.mp@parliament.uk.

**WRIGHT, Sir (John) Michael**, Kt 1990; a Judge of the High Court of Justice, Queen's Bench Division, 1990–2003; Presiding Judge, South Eastern Circuit, 1995–98; *b* 26 Oct. 1932; *s* of Prof. John George Wright, DSc, MVSc, FRCVS, and Elsie Lloyd Razey; *m* 1959, Kathleen, *er d* of F. A. Meanwell; one *s* two *d*. *Educ*: King's Sch., Chester; Oriel Coll., Oxford (BA Jurisprudence 1956; MA 1978; Hon. Fellow, 2000). Served Royal Artillery, 1951–53; TA, 1953–57. Called to Bar, Lincoln's Inn (Tancred Student), 1957, Bencher 1983, Treasurer, 2003–04; QC 1974; a Recorder, 1974–90; Leader, SE Circuit, 1981–83; Chm. of the Bar, 1983–84 (Vice-Chm., 1982–83). Member: Bar Council, 1972–73; Senate of the Four Inns of Court, 1973–74; Senate of the Inns of Court and the Bar, 1975–84. Mem. Supreme Court Rules Cttee, 1973–74. Legal Assessor to the Disciplinary Cttee, RCVS, 1983–90; Vice-Chm., Appeal Cttee, ICA, 1989–90. Hon. Member: American Bar Assoc.; Canadian Bar Assoc. Trustee, Thalidomide Trust, 1997–2011 (Chm., 2008–11). Gov., Reigate Grammar Sch., 2004–08 (Chm. of Govs, 2004–08). *Recreations*: books, music. *Address*: Angel Shades, Angel Street, Petworth, W Sussex GU28 0BG.

**WRIGHT, John Robertson**; Chairman: XM International Associates Ltd, since 2004; Boomer Industries, since 2007; Qube GB Ltd, since 2012; Lagan Asphalt Ltd, since 2012; *b* 10 Sept. 1941; *s* of George Alexander Wright and Jean Robertson Wright (*née* Buchanan); *m* 1971, Christine Greenshields; one *s* one *d*. *Educ*: Daniel Stewart's Coll., Edinburgh. ACIBS; FIBI. Posts with Bank of Montreal, Canada and Hong Kong, Bank of North Lagos, Nigeria, Grindlays Bank Ltd, London, Calcutta and Colombo, Clydesdale Bank Ltd,

1958–74; Vice Pres., First Interstate Bank of California, 1974–79; Asst Gen. Manager, Internat. Div., Bank of Scotland, 1979–86; Dir and CEO, Oman International Bank, 1986–93; Chief Executive and Director: Northern Bank Ltd, 1993–96; Northern & National Irish Banks, 1996–97; Chief Exec. and Chief Gen. Manager, Gulf Bank KSC, Kuwait, 1997–98; Chief Exec., Clydesdale Bank plc and Yorkshire Bank, 1998–2001. Chairman: Edinburgh Fund Managers plc, 2001–02; Toughglass Ltd, 2002–06; BIC Systems Ltd, 2002–05; Claridge Ltd, Bermuda, 2006–07; EZD Ltd, 2006–07; Alphaplus Gp, 2008–11; non-executive Director: ECGD, 2001–06; Bank of N. T. Butterfield UK Ltd, 2001–; Bank of N. T. Butterfield, Bermuda, 2002–; Glasgow Univ. Retail Heritage Ltd, 2004–; Scottish Enterprise Borders, 2004–08; Alliance Housing Bank Ltd, Muscat, Oman, 2005–08; Kainos Ltd, 2006–13; Derby House Ltd, 2006–10; Sutherlands Ltd, 2006–09; Mazoon Electric Co., Oman, 2011–14; Majan Electric Co., Oman, 2011–14; Muscat Electric Distribn Co., Oman, 2011–; European Islamic Investment Bank, 2012–; Damac plc, 2013–; Dhofar Insce Co. Oman, 2017–. Director: Arab-British Chamber of Commerce, 1998–2010; Glasgow Chamber of Commerce, 1999–2005; Mem., Arab Financial Forum, 2005. External Mem., Audit Cttee, Scottish Borders Council, 2003–13. Vis. Prof. and Mem. Adv. Bd, Glasgow Univ. Business Sch., 2005–. Chm., Borders Coll., 2011–15. Trustee, Abbotsford House, Melrose, 2008–. *Recreation:* watching Rugby. *Clubs:* New (Edinburgh); Hong Kong; Edinburgh Academicals Sports, Hong Kong Football.

**WRIGHT, (John) Stephen;** Chairman, since 2008, and Managing Director, since 2018, Wright Music Management (formerly Van Walsum, then International Classical Artists); *b* 12 Feb. 1946; *s* of late Eustace McDonald Wright and Hilde Wright; *m* 1977, Jadwiga Maria Rapf (*d* 2007); two *s* one *d*. *Educ:* Dragon Sch., Oxford; Westminster; Magdalene Coll., Cambridge (Hons Mod. Langs and Law). Co-founder and Dir, Oxford and Cambridge Shakespeare Co., 1969–71; Dir, Shawconcerts Ltd, 1971–75; Dir, later Jt Man. Dir, Harold Holt, 1975–90; Man. Dir and Sen. Internat. Vice-Pres., IMG Artists Europe, later IMG Artists, 1991–2005. *Recreations:* cricket, wine, classic cars. *Address:* 32 Iffley Road, W6 0PA. *Clubs:* Garrick, Soho House, Savile.

**WRIGHT, Rt Rev. Kelvin;** Bishop of Dunedin, 2010–17; *b* Timaru, NZ, 14 April 1952; *s* of Norman Trevor Wright and Patricia Wright; *m* 1976, Clemency Underhill; one *s* two *d*. *Educ:* Aranui High Sch.; Univ. of Canterbury (BA 1973); Univ. of Otago (BD 1978); San Francisco Theol Seminary (DMin 1988). *Vicar:* Waihao Downs, 1982–85; Hillcrest, Hamilton, 1985–91; Sumner, Christchurch, 1991–93; Bishop's Chaplain for Ministry, Dio. of Waikato, 1994–98; Vicar, St John's, Roslyn, 1999–2010; Vicar Gen., Dio. of Dunedin, 2003–09. *Recreations:* photography, sailing. *Address:* 1 Glenfinnan Place, Anderson's Bay, Dunedin 9013, New Zealand. *T:* (3) 4544073. *Club:* Dunedin.

**WRIGHT, Leslie;** *see* Vinjamuri, L.

**WRIGHT, Lester Paul;** Under Secretary, Department for Culture, Media and Sport (formerly of National Heritage), 1992–99; *b* 2 July 1946; *s* of late Christopher Percy Wright and Mary Wright (*née* Sutton); *m* 1969, Jill Wildman (*d* 2008); one *s* (and one *s* decd). *Educ:* Bedford Sch.; Gonville and Caius Coll., Cambridge (BA 1967; PhD 1971); Harvard Univ.; Open Univ. (BSc 2007). Lectr in History, Univ. of Reading, 1970–71; Home Office, 1971; Asst Private Sec. to Home Sec., 1972; Harkness Fellow, Harvard Univ. and Univ. of California at Berkeley, 1976–77; Private Sec. to Perm. Under Sec., 1980–82; Asst Sec., 1983–92. *Recreations:* music, walking, looking at pictures. *Address:* 9 Broom Hall, High Street, Broom, Biggleswade, Beds SG18 9ND. *T:* (01767) 314633.

**WRIGHT, Margaret;** Development Executive, The Law Society, 1988–91; *b* 18 Oct. 1931; *d* of Harry Platt and Edith Baxter; *m* 1991, Bill Wright (*d* 1999). *Educ:* Bedford College, Univ. of London (BA Hons 1st Cl., History). Called to the Bar, Gray's Inn, 1956. Estate Duty Officer, Inland Revenue, 1952–63; Inst. of Professional Civil Servants, 1963–87 (Dep. Gen. Sec., 1980–87); Gen. Sec., Clearing Bank Union, 1987–88. Mem., Industrial Disputes Panel, Jersey, 1989–. *Recreations:* renovating old houses, travel, reading.

**WRIGHT, Martin;** Senior Research Fellow, Faculty of Health and Life Sciences, De Montfort University, Leicester, since 2007; Visiting Research Fellow, Sussex Law School (formerly Centre for, then School of, Legal Studies), University of Sussex, 1995–2007; *b* 24 April 1930; *s* of late Clifford Kent Wright and Rosalie Wright, Stoke Newington; *m* 1957, Louisa Mary Nicholls; three *s* one *d* (and one *d* decd). *Educ:* Repton (Scholar); Jesus Coll., Oxford (Exhibnr); PhD LSE, 1992. Librarian, Inst. of Criminology, Cambridge, 1964–71; Dir, Howard League for Penal Reform, 1971–81; NAVSS, later Victim Support, 1985–94: Information Officer, 1985–88; Policy Officer, 1988–94. Chm., Lambeth Mediation Service, 1989–92; Mem. Exec. Cttee, Mediation UK (formerly Forum for Initiatives in Reparation and Mediation), 1984–99; Board Member: Inst. for Food, Brain and Behaviour (formerly Natural Justice), 1999–2015; European Forum for Victim/Offender Mediation and Restorative Justice, 2000–06; Vice-Chm., Restorative Justice Consortium, 2001–07. Hon. Fellow, Inst. of Conflict Resolution, Sofia, Bulgaria, 2005. Eur. Restorative Justice Award, Eur. Forum, 2012. *Publications:* (ed) The Use of Criminological Literature, 1974; Making Good: Prisons, Punishment and Beyond, 1982, repr. 2008; (ed jtly) Mediation and Criminal Justice, 1989; Justice for Victims and Offenders: a restorative response to crime, 1991, 2nd edn 1996; Restoring Respect for Justice, 1999, 2nd edn 2008 (trans. Polish 2005, Russian 2007); Towards a Restorative Society, 2010; (ed jtly) Civilising Criminal Justice: an international restorative agenda for penal reform, 2013. *Recreation:* suggesting improvements. *Address:* 19 Hillside Road, SW2 3HL. *T:* (020) 8671 8037. *W:* www.martinwright.eu.

**WRIGHT, Sir Michael;** *see* Wright, Sir J. M.

**WRIGHT, Prof. Michael,** CBE 2010; DL; Vice-Chancellor, Canterbury Christ Church University, 2005–10, now Emeritus Professor; *b* 24 May 1949; *s* of Gordon Huddart Wright and Nancy (*née* Murgatroyd); *m* 1971, Pamela Stothart; one *s* one *d* (and one *s* decd). *Educ:* Durham Johnston Grammar Sch.; Bearsden Acad.; Univ. of Birmingham (LLB 1969, LLM 1970). Lectr in Law, Bristol Poly., 1970–79; Hd of Dept, Glasgow Coll. of Technology, 1980–83; Asst Principal, Napier Coll., subseq. Napier Poly., 1983–92; Dep. Vice Chancellor, Napier Univ., 1992–97; Principal, Canterbury Christ Ch Coll., subseq. Canterbury Christ Ch Univ. Coll., 1997–2005. Vice Pres., Inst. of Personnel and Develt, 1991–94. Member: Kent & Medway LSC, 2001–07; Kent (formerly Kent & Medway) Economic Bd, 2005–10; Dir, Kent & Medway Strategic HA, 2003–06. Comr, Duke of York's Royal Mil. Sch., 2000–12. Lay Canon, Canterbury Cathedral, 2004–14 (Mem. of Chapter, 2010–14); Mem. Council, Rochester Cathedral, 2007–10. Chm. Bd, Canterbury Arts Fest., 2011–14 (Vice Chm., 2009–11); Chm., Berwick Literary Fest., 2017–. Chm. Govs, Northbourne Park Sch., 2010–14; Chm., E Kent Coll. Governing Body (formerly Thanet Coll. Corporation), 2010–14. Chm., Lambeth Conference Co., 2012–. DL Kent, 2006. *Publications:* Labour Law, 1974, 4th edn (with C. J. Carr) 1984; articles in legal jls. *Recreations:* choral singing, golf. *E:* michael.wright@canterbury.ac.uk. *Clubs:* Nobody's Friends; Goswick Golf.

**WRIGHT, Michael;** *see* Wright, D. M.

**WRIGHT, Monica Mary;** *see* Grady, M. M.

**WRIGHT, Nathalie Marie Daniella;** *see* Lieven, N. M. D.

**WRIGHT, Nicholas;** playwright; *b* Cape Town, 5 July 1940; *s* of Harry and Winifred Wright. *Educ:* Rondebosch Boys' Sch.; London Acad. of Music and Dramatic Art. Casting Dir, 1967, Asst Dir, 1968, Royal Court Th.; Dir, Royal Court Th. Upstairs, 1969–70 and 1972–74; Jt Artistic Dir, Royal Court Th., 1975–77; Associate Dir, NT, 1984–89 and 1991–98. Member Board: Royal Court Th., 1992–2003; NT, 2003–09; Nat. Council for Drama Trng, 2005–07; NT Foundn, 2016–. *Plays:* Treetops, Riverside Studios, 1978 (George Devine Award); The Gorky Brigade, Royal Court Th., 1979; One Fine Day, Riverside Studios, 1980; The Crimes of Vautrin (after Balzac), Joint Stock, 1982; The Custom of the Country, RSC, 1983; The Desert Air, RSC, 1984; Mrs Klein, NT, 1988; Cressida, Almeida Th. at the Albery, 2000; Vincent in Brixton, NT, 2002 (Best New Play, Olivier Award); His Dark Materials (based on trilogy by Philip Pullman), NT, 2003, revived 2004; The Reporter, NT, 2007; He's Talking, NT Connections, 2008; Rattigan's Nijinsky, Chichester Fest., 2011; The Last of the Duchess, Hampstead Th., 2011; Travelling Light, NT, 2012; A Human Being Died That Night, Hampstead Th., 2013; The Slaves of Solitude (after Patrick Hamilton), Hampstead Th., 2017; 8 Hotels, Chichester Fest., 2019; *play adaptations:* Slave Island, RADA, 1985; Six Characters in Search of an Author, NT, 1987; Thérèse Raquin, Chichester Fest., 1990, NT, 2006; John Gabriel Borkman, NT, 1996; Naked, Almeida Th., 1998; Lulu, Almeida Th., 2001; Three Sisters, NT, 2003; Alice's Adventures in Wonderland, Royal Ballet, Covent Garden, 2011; Regeneration, Royal Northampton, 2014; television adaptations: Armistead Maupin's More Tales of the City, 1998; No 1 Ladies' Detective Agency (episodes), 2009; *opera libretti:* The Little Prince (after St Exupéry), premièred by Houston Grand Opera, 2003; Buzz on the Moon, C4, 2006; Marnie (after Winston Graham), 2017. The Art of the Play column, Independent on Sunday, 1993–94. *Publications:* 99 Plays, 1992; (with Richard Eyre) Changing Stages, 2000; *plays:* Five Plays (Treetops, One Fine Day, The Custom of the Country, The Desert Air, Mrs Klein), 2000; Cressida, 2000; Vincent in Brixton, 2002; His Dark Materials, 2003, rewritten version 2004; The Reporter, 2007; Rattigan's Nijinsky, 2011; The Last of the Duchess, 2011; Travelling Light, 2012. *Address:* c/o Judy Daish Associates, 2 St Charles Place, W10 6EG.

**WRIGHT, Sir Nicholas (Alcwyn),** Kt 2006; MD, PhD, DSc; FRCS, FRCP, FRCPath; Professor of Histopathology, 2011–18, now Emeritus, and Centre Lead, Centre for Tumour Biology, Barts Cancer Institute, 2013–18, Queen Mary University of London (Warden, Barts and The London (formerly Bart's and The London, Queen Mary's) School of Medicine and Dentistry, 2001–11); *b* 24 Feb. 1943; *s* of late Glyndwr Alcwyn Wright and Hilda Lilian (*née* Jones); *m* 1966, Vera, (Ned), Matthewson; one *s* one *d*. *Educ:* Bristol Grammar Sch.; Durham Univ. (MB BS 1965); Newcastle Univ. (MD 1974; PhD 1975; DSc 1984); MA (Oxon) 1979. FRCPath 1986; MRCP 1998, FRCP 2001; FRCS 1999. University of Newcastle upon Tyne: Demonstrator in Pathology, 1966–71; Res. Fellow, 1971–74; Lectr in Pathology, 1974–76; Sen. Lectr, 1976–77; Clinical Reader in Pathology, Univ. of Oxford, 1977, Nuffield Reader, 1978; Fellow, Green Coll., Oxford, 1979–80; Prof. of Histopathology, RPMS, 1980–96; Dir of Histopathology, Hammersmith Hosp., 1980–96; Dean, RPMS, 1996–97; Clin. Dir of Path., Hammersmith Hosps NHS Trust, 1994–96; Vice Principal for Res., 1996–2001, Dep. Principal, 1997–2001, ICSM, Univ. of London; Imperial Cancer Research Fund, later Cancer Research (UK): Asst Dir, 1988; Associate Dir, 1989; Dep. Dir, 1990; Dir of Clinical Res., 1991–96; Dir, Histopathology Unit, London Res. Inst., 1988–2011. Chm., Research for Health Charities Gp, 1994–96. Editor, Cell and Tissue Kinetics, 1980–87. President: Pathol Soc. of GB and Ireland, 2001–06; British Soc. for Gastroenterology, 2003–04 (Mem. Council, 1986, 1990); Mem. Council, RCPath, 1982, 1986, 1990. Lectures: Avery Jones, Central Middx Hosp., 1989; Kettle, RCPath, 1990; Showering, Southmead Hosp., 1991; Morson, 1991, Sir Arthur Hurst, 1997, British Soc. of Gastroenterology; Burroughs Wellcome, Yale Univ., 1993; Watson Smith, RCP, 1998; Sidney Truelove, Internat. Soc. for Inflammatory Bowel Disease, 1999; Dow, Dundee Univ., 2006. Fellow, Faculty of Medicine, Imperial Coll. London, 2011; Founder FMedSci 1998; Hon. Fellow, Canadian Coll. of Physicians and Surgeons, 2016. Hon. DSc: Hertfordshire, 2007; Durham, 2008; Bristol, 2011; Aston, 2015; Imperial Coll. London, 2017; Hon. MD St Andrews, 2008; Hon. LLD Dundee, 2012. *Publications:* Introduction to Cell Population Kinetics, 1977; (ed) Psoriasis: cell proliferation, 1982; The Biology of Epithelial Cell Populations, 1984; (ed) Colorectal Cancer, 1989; (ed) Oxford Textbook of Pathology, 1991; (ed) Clinical Aspects of Cell Proliferation, 1991; (ed) Molecular Pathology of Cancer, 1993; (ed) Growth Factors and Cytokines of the Gut, 1996; (ed) The Gut as a Model for Cell Molecular Biology, 1997; papers on cell proliferation and differentiation in the gut and the evolution of cancer. *Recreations:* Rugby football, cricket, military history, cooking. *Address:* Barts Cancer Institute, Barts and The London School of Medicine and Dentistry, Queen Mary University of London, Charterhouse Square, EC1M 6BQ. *T:* (020) 7882 3575. *Club:* Athenæum.

**WRIGHT, Capt. Sir Nicholas (Peter),** KCVO 2018 (CVO 2010; LVO 1994); RN; Private Secretary to the Princess Royal, 2002–18; an Extra Equerry to the Princess Royal, since 2019; *b* 11 Nov. 1949; *s* of late Lt Comdr Edward J. Wright and Peggy Wright; *m* 1976, Venetia, *d* of Vice-Adm. Sir Stephen Ferrier Berthon, KCB; one *s* three *d*. *Educ:* Ampleforth Coll. Joined BRNC Dartmouth, 1968; served HMS Whitby and HMS Diomede, 1969–73; Flag Lt to FO Medway, 1973–75; HMS Norfolk, 1976–77; Allied Forces, Northern Europe, Oslo, 1978–80; HMS Lowestoft, 1980–82; Asst Sec. to Second Sea Lord, 1982–84; Staff of BRNC Dartmouth, 1985–87; HMS Illustrious, 1987–89; Sec. to FO Portsmouth, 1989–91; JSDC RNC Greenwich, 1991; HM Yacht Britannia, 1992–94; Sec. to ACNS, 1995–97; CSO Personnel to FONA, 1998–2000; Exec. Asst to Dep. SACLANT, Virginia, 2000–02; retd RN, 2002. Trustee, Wardour Chapel Trust, 2014–. Younger Brother, Trinity House, 2013. *Recreations:* squash, ski-ing, tennis, cricket. *Address:* c/o Buckingham Palace, SW1A 1AA. *T:* (020) 7024 4199, *Fax:* (020) 7930 4180. *Club:* Jesters.

**WRIGHT, Rt Rev. Prof. (Nicholas) Thomas,** DPhil, DD; FRSE; Bishop of Durham, 2003–10; Research Professor of New Testament and Early Christianity, University of St Andrews, since 2010; *b* 1 Dec. 1948; *s* of Thomas Irwin Wright and Rosemary (*née* Forman); *m* 1971, Margaret Elizabeth Anne Fiske; two *s* two *d*. *Educ:* Sedbergh Sch.; Exeter Coll., Oxford (BA 1st cl. Hons LitHum 1971; MA 1975; DPhil 1981; DD 2000); Wycliffe Hall, Oxford (BA 1st cl. Hons Theology 1973). Ordained deacon, 1975, priest 1976; Jun. Res. Fellow, 1975–78, Jun. Chaplain, 1976–78, Merton Coll., Oxford (Hon. Fellow, 2004); Fellow and Chaplain, Downing Coll., Cambridge, 1978–81 (Hon. Fellow, 2003); Asst Prof. of New Testament Studies, McGill Univ., Montreal, and Hon. Prof., Montreal Dio. Theol Coll., 1981–86; Lectr in Theology, Oxford Univ., and Fellow, Tutor and Chaplain, Worcester Coll., Oxford, 1986–93; Dean of Lichfield, 1994–99; Canon of Westminster, 2000–03. Fellow, Inst. for Christian Studies, Toronto, 1992–; Canon Theologian, Coventry Cathedral, 1992–99. Visiting Professor: Hebrew Univ., Jerusalem, 1989; Harvard Div. Sch., 1999; Gregorian Univ., Rome, 2002; Fuller Theol Seminary, Pasadena, 2009; Vis. Res. Fellow, Merton Coll., Oxford, 1999. Gifford Lectures, Aberdeen Univ., 2018. Member: Doctrine Commn of C of E, 1979–81, 1989–95; Internat. Anglican Doctrinal and Theological Commn, 1991, 2001–08; Lambeth Commn, 2004. Presenter, various radio and television series, 1996–: Jesus Then and Now, BBC1, 1996; presenter and writer: Resurrection, Channel 4, 2004; Spring Journey, Radio 3, 2004; Evil, Channel 4, 2005; participant, The Brains Trust, Radio 3, 1999–2002. FRSE 2015. Hon. DD: Aberdeen, 2001; Wycliffe Coll., Toronto, 2006; Nashotah House, Wisconsin, 2007; Durham, 2007; St Andrews, 2009; Northumbria, 2010; London, 2010; St Mary's Univ., Baltimore, 2012; Fribourg, 2014; Univ. of the South, Sewanee, 2015; Huron Coll., Ont, 2015; Hon. DLitt Gordon Coll., Mass, 2003. Burkitt Medal for Biblical Studies, British Acad., 2014. *Publications:* Small Faith, Great God, 1978; The Work of John Frith, 1983; The Epistles of Paul to the Colossians and to Philemon, 1987; (ed jtly) The Glory of Christ in the New Testament, 1987; (with S. Neill) The Interpretation of the New Testament 1861–1986, 1988; The Climax of the Covenant, 1991; New Tasks for a Renewed Church, 1992; The Crown and the Fire, 1992; The New Testament and the People of God, 1992; Who Was Jesus?, 1992; Following Jesus, 1994; Jesus and the Victory of God, 1996; The Lord and His Prayer, 1996; What Saint Paul Really Said, 1997; For All God's Worth, 1997; Reflecting the Glory, 1998; (with M. Borg) The Meaning of Jesus, 1999; The Myth of the Millennium, 1999; (ed jtly) Romans and the People of God, 1999; Holy Communion for Amateurs, 1999, reissued as The Meal Jesus Gave Us, 2002; The Challenge of Jesus, 2000; Twelve Months of Sundays, Year C, 2000; (with Paul Spicer) Easter Oratorio, 2000; Twelve Months of Sundays, Year A, 2001; Luke for Everyone, 2001; Mark for Everyone, 2001; Paul for Everyone: Galatians and Thessalonians, 2002; Matthew for Everyone, 2002; Paul for Everyone: the prison letters, 2002; John for Everyone, 2002; Twelve Months of Sundays, Year B, 2002; (contrib.) New Interpreters Bible, vol. X, 2002; The Contemporary Quest for Jesus, 2002; The Resurrection of the Son of God, 2003; Paul for Everyone: 1 Corinthians, 2003; Paul for Everyone: 2 Corinthians, 2003; Quiet Moments, 2003; Hebrews for Everyone, 2003; For All the Saints?, 2003; Paul for Everyone: the pastoral letters, 2003; Paul for Everyone: Romans, 2004; (ed jtly) Dictionary for Theological Interpretation of Scripture, 2005; Scripture and the Authority of God, 2005, 2nd edn 2011; Paul: fresh perspectives, 2005; The Scriptures, the Cross and the Power of God, 2005; Simply Christian, 2006; Evil and the Justice of God, 2006; (jtly) The Resurrection of Jesus: John Dominic Crossan and N. T. Wright in dialogue, 2006; Judas and the Gospel of Jesus, 2006; The Cross and the Colliery, 2007; Surprised by Hope, 2007; Acts for Everyone, 2008; (with C. Evans) Jesus: the final days, 2008; (ed jtly) Theological Interpretation of the New Testament: a book-by-book survey, 2008; (with J. I. Packer) Anglican Evangelical Identity: yesterday and today, 2008; Justification: God's plan and Paul's vision, 2009; Lent for Everyone—Luke, 2009; Virtue Reborn, 2010; Lent for Everyone—Matthew, 2011; The New Testament for Everyone (new translation), 2011; Early Christian Letters for Everyone, 2011; Revelation for Everyone, 2011; Simply Jesus, 2011; Lent for Everyone—Mark, 2012; How God Became King, 2012; New Testament Prayers for Everyone, 2012; New Testament Wisdom for Everyone, 2013; The Case for the Psalms, 2013; Perspectives on Paul (Collected Essays, 1978–2013), 2013; Paul and the Faithfulness of God, 2013; Finding God in the Psalms: sing, pray, live, 2014; Surprised by Scripture, 2014; Simply Good News, 2015; The Paul Debate, 2015; Paul and his Recent Interpreters, 2015; God in Public, 2016; The Day the Revolution Began, 2016; Advent for Everyone: a journey through Matthew, 2016; Spiritual and Religious, 2017; Advent for Everyone: a journey with the Apostles, 2017; Advent for Everyone: a journey through Luke, 2018; Paul: a biography, 2018; History and Eschatology: Jesus and the promise of natural theology, 2019; (with Michael Bird) The New Testament in its World: an introduction to the history, literature and theology of the first Christians, 2019. *Recreations:* music, hill walking, poetry, golf, grandchildren. *Address:* St Mary's College, South Street, St Andrews, Fife KY16 9JU. *T:* (01334) 462850. *E:* ntw2@st-andrews.ac.uk.

**WRIGHT, Rev. Dr Nigel Goring;** Principal, Spurgeon's College, 2000–13, now Principal Emeritus and Senior Research Fellow; *b* Manchester, 13 May 1949; *s* of Charles Somerville Wright, MBE and Muriel Cooper Wright; *m* 1971, Judith Mary Biggin; one *s* one *d*. *Educ:* Manchester Central Grammar Sch.; Univ. of Leeds (BA 1970); Univ. of London (BD 1973); Univ. of Glasgow (MTh 1987); King's Coll., London (PhD 1994); Spurgeon's Coll. Ordained Minister, 1973; Minister, Ansdell Baptist Church, Lytham St Annes, 1973–86; Res. Fellow, Univ. of Glasgow, 1986–87; Lectr, Spurgeon's Coll., 1987–95; Sen. Minister, Altrincham Baptist Church, 1995–2000. Pres., Baptist Union of GB, 2002–03. FHEA; FRHistS 2012. *Publications:* You Are My God, 1982; The Church, 1983; The Radical Kingdom, 1986; The Fair Face of Evil, 1988; Challenge to Change, 1991; Charismatic Renewal, 1993; The Radical Evangelical, 1996; Power and Discipleship, 1996; Disavowing Constantine, 2000; New Baptists, New Agenda, 2002; A Theology of the Dark Side, 2003; Free Church, Free State, 2005; God on the Inside, 2006; Baptist Basics, 2008; The Real Godsend, 2009; Jesus Christ: the alpha and omega, 2010; Truth that Never Dies, 2014; Vital Truth: convictions of the Christian community, 2015; How to Be a Church Minister, 2018; *festschrift:* (ed Pieter J. Lalleman) Challenging to Change: dialogues with a radical baptist theologian: essays presented to Dr Nigel G. Wright on his sixtieth birthday, 2009. *Recreations:* walking, reading, travel. *Address:* 4 Chesterfield Close, Winsford, Cheshire CW7 2NS. *T:* (01606) 227828. *E:* nigelgoringwright@gmail.com.

**WRIGHT, His Honour Norman Alfred;** a Circuit Judge, 2006–18; a Deputy Circuit Judge, 2018–19; *b* 20 Jan. 1951; *s* of late Alfred Wright and Thea Wright (later Mason); *m* 1976, Susan Whittaker; one *s* one *d*. *Educ:* Bradford Grammar Sch.; Univ. of Liverpool (LLB 1973); College of Law. Called to the Bar, Gray's Inn, 1974 (Gerald Moody Entrance Schol. 1972; Albion Richardson Schol. 1974); in practice at the Bar, 1974–2006; Asst Recorder, 1994–99; a Recorder, 1999–2006; Liaison Judge, Burnley, Pendle and Rossendale Magistrates, 2007–12. Pt-time Tutor, Univ. of Liverpool, 1974–78. Member: Adv. Bd, Liverpool Univ. Law Sch., 2013–18; Bd, Liverpool Law Sch. Alumni Assoc., 2015–18. *Recreations:* oenology, golf, travel. *Club:* Heswall Golf.

**WRIGHT, Oliver;** Policy Editor, The Times, since 2016; *b* Manchester, 30 June 1973; *s* of Ian and Lydia Wright. *Educ:* Univ. of Edinburgh (MA Hons Pols and Mod. Hist.). Reporter, Sheffield Star, 1997–2000; The Times: Midlands Corresp., 2000–02; Health Corresp., 2002–04; Asst News Ed., 2004–05; Home News Ed., 2005–08; News Ed., 2008–10; Whitehall Ed., 2010–15, Political Ed., 2015–16, The Independent. *Recreations:* walking, failing newspaper shorthand examinations. *Address:* The Times, News Building, 1 London Bridge Street, SE1 9GF. *Club:* Shoreditch House.

**WRIGHT, Ven. Dr Paul;** Archdeacon of Bromley and Bexley, since 2003; Priest-in-Charge, St Augustine, Slade Green, since 2016; *b* 12 Feb. 1954; *s* of Cecil Edwin John Wright and Bessie Wright; *m* 1981, Jill Rosemary Yvonne Rayner; two *s* one *d*. *Educ:* King's Coll., London (BD, AKC 1978); Ripon Coll., Cuddesdon; Heythrop Coll., Univ. of London (MTh 1990); Univ. of Wales, Lampeter (DMin 2009). Ordained deacon, 1979, priest, 1980; Curate: St George, Beckenham, 1979–83; St Mary and St Matthias, Richmond, 1983–85; Chaplain, Christ's Ch., Richmond, 1983–85; Vicar, St Augustine, Gillingham, 1985–90; Rector, St Paulinus, Crayford, 1990–99; RD, Erith, 1994–97; Vicar, St John the Evangelist, Sidcup, 1999–2003. Hon. Canon, Rochester Cathedral, 1998–2003. FRSA 2016. *Recreations:* riding my Harley-Davidson, going to the cinema, France, walking Dolly the dog. *Address:* The Archdeaconry, The Glebe, Chislehurst, Kent BR7 5PX. *T:* (020) 8467 8743. *E:* archdeacon.bromley@rochester.anglican.org.

**WRIGHT, Prof. Paul Stanley,** PhD; FDSRCS, FFGDP(UK); Professor of Prosthetic Dentistry, Barts and The London (formerly Barts and The London, Queen Mary's) School of Medicine and Dentistry, Queen Mary, University of London, 2000–11, now Emeritus (Dean for Dentistry, 1999–2007); Consultant Adviser to the Chief Dental Officer, Department of Health, 2007–12; *b* 1 May 1946; *s* of late William and Eileen Wright; *m* 1970, Mary Lawrence; three *s*. *Educ:* London Hosp. Med. Coll. Dental Sch. (BDS; PhD 1980). FDSRCS 1973; FFGDP(UK) 2005. London Hospital Medical College Dental School, later Barts and The London, Queen Mary's School of Medicine and Dentistry, subseq. Barts and The London School of Medicine and Dentistry, Queen Mary, University of London: Lectr in Prosthetic Dentistry, 1972–80; Sen. Lectr in Prosthetic Dentistry, 1981–99; Hon. Consultant in Restorative Dentistry, 1982–2011; Specialist in Prosthodontics, 2000–11. Gen. dental practitioner (pt-time), 1970–2001. Founding Ed., Eur. Jl Prosthodontics and Restorative Dentistry, 1992–2003. Chairman: Council, Heads and Deans of Dental Schs, 2004–06; Central Commn, Academic Dental Staff, BDA, 2009–11. President: Eur. Prosthodontic Assoc., 2005–06; British Soc. of Gerodontology, 2007–08; Barts and The London Alumni Assoc., 2012–19. FHEA (ILTM 2002). Gold Medal, British Soc. for Study of Prosthetic Dentistry, 2011. *Publications:* (jtly) The Clinical Handling of Dental Materials, 1986, 2nd edn 1994; numerous contribs to jls. *Recreations:* swimming, ski-ing, gardening, family, touring in classic Jaguar replica. *T:* (01732) 456623, 07711 636952.

**WRIGHT, Rev. Canon Paul Stephen;** Sub-Dean, HM Chapels Royal, Deputy Clerk of the Closet, Sub-Almoner and Domestic Chaplain to the Queen, since 2015; *b* Winstanley, Wigan, Lancs 26 Dec. 1966; *s* of William and Dorothy Wright; *m* 2006, Georgina Elisabeth Peek; two *s* two *d*. *Educ:* Lancs Poly. (BA 1988); Liverpool Univ. (MA 1996); Westcott House, Cambridge; Cardiff Univ. (MTh 2011). Ordained deacon, 1993, priest, 1994; Curate, Up Holland, Lancs, 1993–96; Chaplain to the Forces, 1996–2015: Dover Castle, 2004–08; Guards Chapel, 2008–10; HQ ARRC, 2010–12; RMA Sandhurst, 2012–14; HM Chapels Royal, 2015; RAuxAF, 2015. Guest Curator, Soldiers of Solace, Talbot House, Belgium, 2015. Mem., Anglo-Belgian Soc. Vis. G. S. Beckwith Gilbert '63 Lectr, Princeton Univ., 2015–; Vice Chm., Royal Anglo-Belgian Benevolent Soc., 2016–. Chm., Old Talbot House Foundn, 2017–. *Recreations:* Battlefield history, Rugby League football and the Book of Common Prayer. *Address:* Chapel Royal, St James's Palace, SW1A 1BL. *Clubs:* Royal Air Force; Talbot House (Belgium).

**WRIGHT, Penelope Ann, (Mrs D. C. H. Wright);** see Boys, P. A.

**WRIGHT, Peter;** Editor Emeritus, Associated Newspapers, since 2012; *b* 13 Aug. 1953; *s* of late Nigel and of June Wright; *m* 1974, Dorothy Manders; three *s* one *d*. *Educ:* Marlborough Coll.; Clare Coll., Cambridge (MA History). Reporter, Evening Echo, Hemel Hempstead, 1976–79; Daily Mail: Reporter, 1979; Asst News Editor, 1980–85; Associate News Editor (Foreign), 1985; Asst Features Editor, 1986–88; Femail Editor, 1988–91; Asst Editor (Features), 1991; Associate Editor, 1992–95; Dep. Editor, 1995–98; Editor, Mail on Sunday, 1998–2012. Member: Editor's Code Cttee, 2004–08; Complaints Cttee, IPSO, 2014–; Defence Press and Broadcasting Adv. Cttee Review, 2014; Thomson Reuters Founders Share Co. Nomination Cttee, 2016–; Panel, Cairncross Review into Press Sustainability, 2018–; Comr, Press Complaints Commn, 2008–14. *Address:* Associated Newspapers, Northcliffe House, 2 Derry Street, W8 5TT.

**WRIGHT, Peter Duncan;** QC 1999; a Recorder, since 2001; *b* 2 Nov. 1957; *s* of Harvey Wright and Margaret Wright; *m* 1982, Stephanie Maria Mandziuk; one *s* two *d*. *Educ:* Hull Univ. (LLB Hons). Called to the Bar, Inner Temple, 1981. Sen. Treasury Counsel, 2006–10. *Recreations:* Rugby, travel. *Address:* 2 Hare Court, Temple, EC4Y 7BH. *T:* (020) 7353 5324.

**WRIGHT, His Honour Peter Malcolm;** a Circuit Judge, 2006–18; *b* 5 June 1948; *s* of late Malcolm Wright, QC, County Court Judge and Peggy Wright (*née* Prince), BEM; *m* 1975, Eleanor Charlotte Madge; one *s* one *d*. *Educ:* Kingswood Sch., Bath; Trinity Hall, Cambridge (BA 1971). Called to the Bar, Middle Temple, 1974 (Bencher, 2005); Tenant, Queen Elizabeth Bldg, Temple, 1975–2006; specialised in family law, clinical negligence and personal injury law; Asst Recorder, Western Circuit, 1998–2000; Recorder, 2000–06; Designated Family Judge, Watford and Herts, 2006–15. Legal Assessor, NMC, 1994–2006. Vice-Chm., Appeal Cttee, CIMA, 2001–05. Trustee, Lambeth Palace Liby, 2002–. Gov., Kingswood Sch., Bath, 1998–2016. *Recreations:* walking, sailing, music, gardening, country sports, Retriever training.

**WRIGHT, Peter Michael,** FRCO(CHM); Organist and Director of Music, Southwark Cathedral, 1989–2019; *b* 6 March 1954; *s* of late Dudley Cyril Brazier Wright and of Pamela Deirdre (*née* Peacock). *Educ:* Highgate Sch. (Music Schol.); Royal Coll. of Music (Exhibnr; ARCM); Emmanuel Coll., Cambridge (Organ Schol.; MA). LRAM. Sub-Organist, Guildford Cathedral, and Music Master, Royal Grammar Sch., Guildford, 1977–89. Conductor: Guildford Chamber Choir, 1984–94; Surrey Festival Choir, 1987–2001. Freelance conductor, recitalist (organ), adjudicator and broadcaster. Royal College of Organists: Mem. Council, 1990–2002; Hon. Sec., 1997–2002; Vice-Pres., 2003–05, 2008–; Pres., 2005–08; Mem. Council, Friends of Cathedral Music, 2001–04. Hon. Lay Canon, Southwark Cathedral, 2014–. FRSCM 2011. Hon. FGCM 2000. *Recreations:* travel, theatre, reading, good food. *Address:* 52 Bankside, SE1 9JE. *T:* (020) 7261 1291.

**WRIGHT, Sir Peter (Robert),** Kt 1993; CBE 1985; Director Laureate, The Birmingham (formerly Sadler's Wells) Royal Ballet, since 1995 (Director, 1987–95); *b* 25 Nov. 1926; *s* of Bernard and Hilda Mary Wright; *m* 1954, Sonya Hana (*d* 2007); one *s* one *d*. *Educ:* Bedales School; Leighton Park Sch. Dancer: Ballets Jooss, 1945–47, 1951–52; Metropolitan Ballet, 1947–49; Sadler's Wells Theatre Ballet, 1949–51, 1952–56; Ballet Master, Sadler's Wells Opera, and Teacher, Royal Ballet Sch., 1956–58; freelance choreographer and teacher, 1958–61; Ballet Master and Asst Dir, Stuttgart Ballet, 1961–63; BBC Television Producer, 1963–65; freelance choreographer, 1965–69; Associate Dir, Royal Ballet, 1969–77. Special Prof., Sch. of Performance Studies, Birmingham Univ., 1990–. Governor: Royal Ballet Sch., 1976–2002; Sadler's Wells Theatre, 1987–2001. Pres., Benesh Inst., 1993–; Vice Pres., Royal Acad. of Dancing, 1995–. *Creative Works:* Ballets: A Blue Rose, 1957; The Great Peacock, 1958; Musical Chairs, 1959; The Mirror Walkers, 1962; Quintet, 1962; Namouna, 1963; Designs for Dancers, 1963; Summer's Night, 1964; Danse Macabre, 1964; Variations, 1964; Concerto, 1965; Arpege, 1974; El Amor Brujo, 1975; Summertide, 1976; own productions of classics: Giselle: Stuttgart, 1966; Staatsoper Ballett, Cologne, 1967; Royal Ballet, 1968, 1985, 2014, 2018; Canadian National Ballet, 1970; Bavarian State Ballet, Munich, 1976; Dutch National Ballet, 1977; Houston Ballet, Texas, 1979; Staatsoper Ballett, Frankfurt, 1980; Ballet Municipale de Rio de Janeiro, Brazil, 1982; Royal Winnipeg Ballet, 1982; Star Dancers Ballet, Tokyo, 1989; Karlsruhe Ballet, 2004; The Sleeping Beauty: Staatsoper Ballett, Cologne, 1968; Royal Ballet, 1968; Bavarian State Ballet, Munich, 1974; Dutch National Ballet, 1981; Sadler's Wells Royal Ballet, 1984; Vienna State Opera Ballet, 1995; Ballet de Santiago, Chile, 2003; Coppelia: Royal Ballet Touring Co., 1976; Sadler's Wells Royal Ballet, 1979; Scottish Ballet, 1992; Star Dancers Ballet, Tokyo, 1997; Karlsruhe Ballet, 2005; Birmingham Royal Ballet, 2012; Swan Lake: Sadler's Wells Royal Ballet, 1981; Bavarian State Ballet, Munich, 1984; Birmingham Royal Ballet, 1991; Royal Swedish Ballet, 2001; Colon Teatro, Buenos Aires, 2013; Nutcracker: Royal

Ballet, 1984 (revised 1999, 2017); Birmingham Royal Ballet, 1990 (revised 2017); Star Dancers Ballet, Tokyo, 1998; Australian Ballet, Melbourne, 2007. FBSM (Conservatoire Fellow), 1991; Fellow, Birmingham Soc., 1995. Hon. DMus London, 1990; Hon. DLitt Birmingham, 1994. Evening Standard Award for Ballet, 1982; Queen Elizabeth II Coronation Award, Royal Acad. of Dancing, 1990; Digital Premier Award, 1991; Critics Circle Award, 1995; Nat. Dance Award for Outstanding Achievement, 2004; Critics' Circle Centenary Award for Lifetime Achievement in Dance, 2013. *Recreation:* all forms of theatre. *Address:* Flat 5, Wedderburn House, 95 Lower Sloane Street, SW1W 8BZ.

**WRIGHT, Phillip, (Phillip Rowntree);** Chief Financial Officer, Selladoor Worldwide Ltd, since 2018; *b* Ashington, 1987; *s* of Henry Miller Wright and Carol Elizabeth Wright; *m* 2016, Eloise Francesca Turner; one *d*. *Educ:* Liverpool Inst. for Performing Arts (BA Hons). Co-Founder and Commercial Dir, Sell A Door Th. Co., 2009–15; Co-Founder and Exec. Commercial Producer, Selladoor Worldwide, 2015–18. Chm. and Trustee, Future Stages, 2019–. *Recreations:* wood turning, DIY, wine tasting, family, cooking. *Address:* Selladoor Worldwide, Deptford Mission, 1 Creek Road, SE8 3BT. *T:* (020) 3355 8567. *E:* phillip@selladoor.com.

**WRIGHT, Richard Irwin V.;** *see* Vane-Wright.

**WRIGHT, Richard James;** QC 2013; a Deputy District Judge (Magistrates' Courts), since 2006; a Recorder, since 2012; *b* Ipswich, 1 July 1976; *s* of Gordon Wright and Andrea Wright (*née* Price, now Ridgeon); *m* 2011, Emma Haley; one *d*. *Educ:* Orwell High Sch., Felixstowe; Univ. of Leeds (LLB Hons 1997); Inns of Court Sch. of Law. Called to the Bar, Middle Temple, 1998, Bencher, 2015; Jun., NE Circuit, 2004. *Recreations:* countryside, beer, vintage tractors. *Address:* 6 Park Square, Leeds LS1 2LW. *T:* (0113) 245 9763, *Fax:* (0113) 242 4395. *E:* wrightqc@psqb.co.uk.

**WRIGHT, Sir Richard (Michael) C.;** *see* Cory-Wright.

**WRIGHT, Rev. Canon Robert;** *see* Wright, Rev. Canon A. R.

**WRIGHT, (Robert) Alan,** PhD; Public Sector Policy Adviser, Iron Mountain (UK), 2007–11; Director, Office of Manpower Economics, 2003–07; freelance pay and governance consultant, 2008–15; *b* 8 Oct. 1949; *s* of late John Haig Wright and Elsie Eileen Wright (*née* Hill); *m* 1975, (Veronica) Anne Dennis. *Educ:* Moseley Grammar Sch., Birmingham; Univ. of Birmingham (BA (Medieval and Mod. Hist.) 1971; PGCE 1975; PhD 1977). Joined Civil Service, 1975; Private Sec. to Chm. of MSC, 1982; Head: Secretariat, HSE, 1987–88; Admin, NII, 1988–91; Dir, Finance Policy, Employment Dept, 1991–94; Department of Trade and Industry: Director: Pay and Working Time, 1995–98; Coal Health Claims Unit, 1998–99; Finance, 2000–03. Member: Perf. and Best Value Cttee, Bar Standards Bd, 2007–11; Planning, Resources and Perf. Cttee, 2012. Volunteer: Elmbridge and Runnymede Talking News, 2009–; Surrey History Centre, 2010–; Planning Cttee, Weybridge Soc., 2017–. Trustee, ElmWey Learning Trust, 2015–. *Publications:* Their Day Has Passed: gypsies in Victorian and Edwardian Surrey, 2017. *Recreations:* history, modern literature, watching cricket and Rugby. *T:* 07956 919838.

**WRIGHT, Air Marshal Sir Robert (Alfred),** KBE 2004; AFC 1982; Controller, Royal Air Force Benevolent Fund, 2007–12; *b* 10 June 1947; *s* of Leslie Dominic Wright and Marjorie Wright; *m* 1970, Maggie Courtliff; one *s* one *d*. *Educ:* Maidstone Grammar Sch. No 8 (Day Fighter Ground Attack) Sqn (Hunters), 1969–71; No 17(F) Sqn (Phantoms), 1971–74; No 1 Tactical Weapons Unit (Hunters), 1974–76; Exchange Duty, USN (Phantoms), 1976–79; No 208 Sqn (Buccaneers), 1979–82; RAF Staff Coll., 1982; Operational Requirements Div., MoD, 1982–84; Directing Staff, RAF Staff Coll., 1984–87; OC, No 9 Sqn (Tornados), Bruggen, 1987–89; PSO to CAS, 1989–91; OC, RAF Bruggen, 1992–94; Asst COS, Policy and Plans, HQ AirNorthWest, 1994–95; Air Cdre Ops, and Dep. Dir Franco British Air Gp, HQ STC, 1995–97; MA to High Rep., Sarajevo, 1997–98; COS to Air Mem. for Personnel, and Dep. C-in-C, HQ PTC, 1998–2000; Asst COS (Policy and Requirements), Supreme HQ Allied Powers in Europe, 2000–02; UK Mil. Rep. to NATO and EU, 2002–06. President: RAF Athletics Assoc., 1998–2005; RAF Winter Sports Assoc., 2003–06; Combined Services Winter Sports Assoc., 2003–06; Naval 8/208 Sqn Assoc., 2003–. Liveryman, Hon. Co. of Air Pilots (formerly GAPAN), 2011. FRAeS 1997; FCMI 2006. *Publications:* contrib. articles to RUSI Jl. *Recreations:* golf, tennis, ski-ing, walking. *Clubs:* Royal Air Force; New (Cheltenham).

**WRIGHT, Robert Douglas John;** management consultant, retired; *b* 2 March 1951; *s* of Douglas Norman Wright and Nora Hermione Wright (*née* Hatton-Jones); *m* 1983, Jane Clare Augier; one *s* two *d*. *Educ:* Canford Sch.; Southampton Univ. (BSc Psychol. 1973). CSD, 1975–81; attachment to Canadian Govt, Ottawa, 1981–82; Cabinet Office (Mgt and Personnel Office), 1982–85; on secondment to Hong Kong Govt, Hong Kong, 1985–88; Cabinet Office (OPSS), 1988–94; Dir, Internat. Affairs, OST, 1994–98; Department of Trade and Industry: Director: Personnel Ops, 1999–2001; Coal Policy, 2001–02; Energy Strategy, 2002–04; Export Control and Non-Proliferation, 2004–07. Mem., Cabinet Office Security Vetting Appeals Panel, 2009–17; Ind. Mem., Civil Nuclear Police Authy, 2010–19. Sen. Consultant, Transparency Internat. UK, Defence and Security Prog. (formerly Transparency, Internat. Defence and Security Prog.), 2010–13. Dir, Wrighthand Ltd; 2007–13; Dir, Meadowcott Ltd, 2014–15. Associate: Nat. Sch. of Govt, 2007–12; Civil Service Coll. Ltd, 2012–13. Gov., Bohunt Community Sch., Liphook, 2002–08; Associate Gov., St Gregory's C of E Primary Sch., Marnhull, 2018–. Pt-time Editor, Shaftesbury Area Talking Newspaper for the Blind, 2017–. *Recreations:* family, vegetable growing, losing golf balls, staying alive. *Address:* Marnhull, Dorset DT10 1JX.

**WRIGHT, Roger William,** CBE 2015; Chief Executive, Snape Maltings (formerly Aldeburgh Music), since 2014; *b* 1956; *m*; two *c*. *Educ:* Chetham's Sch., Manchester; Royal Holloway College, London Univ. (BMus 1977; Pres., Students' Union, 1977–78; Hon. Fellow, 2002). Manager, then Dir, British Music Inf. Centre, 1978–87; Sen. Producer, BBC SO, 1987–89; Artistic Administrator, Cleveland Orch., 1989–92; Exec. Producer, then Vice-Pres., Deutsche Grammophon, 1992–97; Head of Classical Music, BBC, 1997–98; Controller, BBC Radio 3, 1998–2014; Dir, BBC Proms, 2007–14. FRCM 2007; Fellow, Radio Acad. *Publications* include: (with M. Finnissy) New Music 1989, 1989. *Address:* Snape Maltings, Snape Maltings Concert Hall, Snape, Saxmundham, Suffolk IP17 1SP.

**WRIGHT, Rosalind,** CB 2001; Independent Member, Regulatory Board, Association of Chartered Certified Accountants, 2012–18; *b* 2 Nov. 1942; *d* of late Alfred Kerstein and Felicie Kerstein; *m* 1966, Dr David Julian Maurice Wright; three *d*. *Educ:* University College London (LLB Hons). Called to the Bar, Middle Temple, 1964, Bencher, 2001; in practice at the Bar, 1965–69; Department of the Director of Public Prosecutions, then Crown Prosecution Service: Legal Asst, 1969–72; Sen. Legal Asst, 1972–81; Asst Dir, 1981–87 and Head of Fraud Investigation Gp (London), 1984–87; Head of Prosecutions, Securities Assoc., later SFA, 1987–94; Exec. Dir (Legal and Investor Protection Policy) and Gen. Counsel, SFA, 1994–97; Dir, Serious Fraud Office, 1997–2003. Chm., Fraud Adv. Panel, 2003–14; non-exec. Dir, OFT, 2003–07; Member: Supervisory Cttee, European Anti-Fraud Office, 2005–12 (Chm., 2005–07); Exclusion Cttee, European Investment Bank, 2012–. Independent Director: BIS (formerly DTI, then BERR) Legal Services Gp, 2002–08; Insolvency Service Steering Bd, 2006–11. Complaints Comr, London Metal Exchange, 2010–. Lay Member, Disciplinary Panel: Nat. Register of Public Sector Interpreters, 2012–; AAT, 2012–. Mem. of the Bar, NI, 1999–. Mem., Gen. Council of the Bar, 1998–2003. Chairman: Conduct Panel, CIMA, 2017–; Disciplinary Panel, ICAEW, 2018–. Trustee, 1999–2015, Vice Chm., 2003–15, Jewish Assoc. for Business Ethics. Hon. QC 2006. *Recreations:* music, theatre, Jewish jokes.

**WRIGHT, Hon. Ruth Margaret;** *see* Richardson, Hon. R. M.

**WRIGHT, Simon;** Chief Executive Officer, Nelson's Journey, since 2015; *b* 15 Sept. 1979; *Educ:* Dereham Neatherd High Sch.; Imperial Coll. London (BSc Maths); King's Coll. London (PGCE). Teacher of Maths, Alderman Peel High Sch., Wells Next the Sea, Norfolk, 2002–03; Campaigns Officer for Norman Lamb, MP, 2003–07. Mem. (Lib Dem) N Norfolk DC, 2003. MP (Lib Dem) Norwich S, 2010–15; contested (Lib Dem) same seat, 2015. Mem., Envmtl Audit Select Cttee, 2010–15.

**WRIGHT, Stephen;** *see* Wright, J. S.

**WRIGHT, Stephen James;** *see* Lowe, Stephen.

**WRIGHT, Sir Stephen (John Leadbetter),** KCMG 2006 (CMG 1997); HM Diplomatic Service, retired; Senior Adviser, Mitsui & Co. Europe plc, since 2011; *b* 7 Dec. 1946; *s* of late J. H. Wright, CBE and Joan Wright; *m* 1st, 1970 (marr. diss. 2000); one *s* one *d*; 2nd, 2002, Elizabeth Abbott Rosemont. *Educ:* Shrewsbury Sch.; The Queen's Coll., Oxford (BA Mod. History, 1968). HM Diplomatic Service, 1968; Havana, 1969–71; CS Coll., 1971–72; FCO, 1972–75; British Information Services, NY, 1975–80; UK Permanent Repn to EC, Brussels, 1980–84; FCO, 1984–85; seconded to Cabinet Office, 1985–87; Counsellor and Hd of Chancery, New Delhi, 1988–91; Counsellor (Ext. Relations), UK Perm. Repn to EC, Brussels, 1991–94; Asst Under Sec. of State, later Dir, EU affairs, FCO, 1994–97; Minister, Washington, 1997–99; Dir, Wider Europe, FCO, 1999–2000; Dep. Under-Sec. of State, FCO, 2000–02; Ambassador to Spain, 2003–07; Chief Exec., Internat. Financial Services London, 2008–10; Senior Adviser: TheCityUK, 2010–11; Good Governance Group (G3), 2008–14. *Recreations:* photography, rowing, books. *E:* stephenjlwright@gmail.com.

**WRIGHT, Stephen Neill;** Headmaster, Merchant Taylors' School, Northwood, 2004–13; *b* 4 Sept. 1956; *s* of Neill and Kathleen Wright; *m* 1985, Penelope Susan Gill; one *s* two *d*. *Educ:* King's Sch., Macclesfield; Queens' Coll., Cambridge (BA Hons (Hist.) 1979; PGCE 1980). Teacher, Woolverstone Hall Sch., Suffolk, 1980–83; Housemaster, Framlingham Coll., 1983–94; Dep. Headmaster, Judd Sch., Tonbridge, 1994–98; Headmaster, Borden Grammar Sch., Sittingbourne, 1998–2004. *Recreations:* gardening, National Trust volunteering.

**WRIGHT, Rt Rev. Thomas;** *see* Wright, Rt Rev. N. T.

**WRIGHT, Thomas Kendal,** CBE 2007; Chief Executive, Guide Dogs, since 2017; *b* 22 Feb. 1962; *s* of David Andrew Wright and Penelope Jane Wright; *m* 1986, Charlotte Annabel Mudford; one *d*. *Educ:* Marlborough Coll.; Ealing Coll. (BA Hons Business Studies 1985). Dip. Market Res.; DipM. Graduate trainee, various marketing roles, United Biscuits, 1981–87; Gp Product Manager, British Tissues, 1987–89; Gp Marketing Manager, Anchor Foods, 1989–95; R&D Dir, Carlsberg-Tetley, 1995–96; Sales and Marketing Dir, Center Parcs (UK), 1996–98; Marketing, Sales and Develt Dir, Center Parcs (NV), 1998–99; Man. Dir, Saga Holidays, 1999–2002; Dir, Saga Gp, 1999–2002; CEO, British Tourist Authy, later VisitBritain, 2002–09; Chief Exec., Age UK (formerly Age Concern England and Help the Aged), 2009–17. Non-exec. Dir, NICE, 2016–. Chm., Fuel Poverty Adv. Gp, 2015–16. Trustee: Imperial War Mus., 2004–12; Imperial War Mus. Develt Trust, 2012–; DEC, 2009–15; Royal Green Jackets Mus., 2011–; Doteveryone, 2012–; Leeds Castle Foundn, 2015–. *Recreations:* running, history, the countryside.

**WRIGHTSON, Sir (Charles) Mark (Garmondsway),** 4th Bt *cr* 1900; Chairman, Close Brothers Corporate Finance Ltd, 1999–2006 (Managing Director, 1996–99); *b* 18 Feb. 1951; *s* of Sir John Garmondsway Wrightson, 3rd Bt, TD, and Hon. Rosemary (*d* 1998), *y d* of 1st Viscount Dawson of Penn, GCVO, KCB, KCMG, PC; *S* father, 1983; *m* 1975, Stella Virginia, *d* of late George Dean; three *s*. *Educ:* Eton; Queens' Coll., Cambridge (BA 1972). Called to the Bar, Middle Temple, 1974. Hill Samuel & Co. Ltd, 1977–96 (Dir, 1984–96); Chm. of Trustees, Bowes Mus. 1989–. *Heir: s* Barnaby Thomas Garmondsway Wrightson [*b* 5 Aug. 1979; *m* 2008, Clare Nancy Louise, *d* of Hon. David Dugdale; two *s* (twins) one *d*]. *Address:* 39 Westbourne Park Road, W2 5QD.

**WRIGHTSON, Hilary Janet;** *see* Cross, H. J.

**WRIGHTSON, Prof. Keith Edwin,** PhD; FRHistS; FBA 1996; Randolph W. Townsend Professor of History, Yale University, since 2004 (Professor of History, 1999–2004); *b* 22 March 1948; *s* of Robert Wrightson and Evelyn Wrightson (*née* Atkinson); *m* 1972, Eva Mikušová; one *s* one *d*. *Educ:* Dame Allan's Boys' Sch., Newcastle upon Tyne; Fitzwilliam Coll., Cambridge (BA 1970; MA 1974; PhD 1974). FRHistS 1986. Research Fellow in Hist., Fitzwilliam Coll., Cambridge, 1972–75; Lectr in Modern Hist., Univ. of St Andrews, 1975–84; University of Cambridge: Univ. Lectr in Hist., 1984–93; Reader in English Social Hist., 1993–98; Prof. of Social Hist., 1998–99; Fellow, Jesus Coll., 1984–99 (Hon. Fellow, 2008). Visiting Professor: Univ. of Toronto, 1984, 1992; Univ. of Alberta, 1988; Centre for Northern Studies, Northumbria Univ., 2003–08; Univ. of Newcastle upon Tyne, 2008–14. Pres., N American Conference on British Studies, 2013–15 (Vice Pres., 2011–13). Hon. Prof., Univ. of Durham, 2008. Hon. DLitt: Durham, 2011; Newcastle, 2013. *Publications:* (with D. Levine) Poverty and Piety in an English Village, 1979, 2nd edn 1995; English Society 1580–1680, 1982; (ed jtly) The World We Have Gained, 1986; (with D. Levine) The Making of an Industrial Society, 1992; Earthly Necessities: economic lives in early modern Britain, 2000; Ralph Tailor's Summer: a scrivener, his city and the plague, 2011; (ed) A Social History of England, 1500–1750, 2017; numerous essays and articles on English social history. *Recreation:* modern jazz. *Address:* Department of History, Yale University, PO Box 208324, New Haven, CT 06520–8324, USA.

**WRIGHTSON, Sir Mark;** *see* Wrightson, Sir C. M. G.

**WRIGLEY, Andrea;** *see* Young, Andrea.

**WRIGLEY, Prof. Christopher John,** PhD; Professor of Modern British History, 1991–2012, now Emeritus, and Head of the School of History and Art History, 2000–03, Nottingham University; *b* 18 Aug. 1947; *s* of late Arthur Wrigley and Eileen Sylvia Wrigley; *m* 1987, Margaret Walsh. *Educ:* Goldsworth Primary Sch., Woking; Kingston Grammar Sch.; Univ. of E Anglia (BA 1968); Birkbeck Coll., London (PhD 1973). Lecturer in Econ. and Social Hist., QUB, 1971–72; Loughborough University: Lectr in Econ. Hist., 1972–78; Sen. Lectr, 1978–84; Reader, 1984–88; Reader in Econ. Hist., Nottingham Univ., 1988–91. Team Assessor (Hist.), Teaching Quality Assessment, HEFCE, 1993–94; Mem., Hist. Panel, HEFCE RAE, 1997, 2001; Coll. Mem. (Hist.), ESRC, 2002–05. Ed., The Historian, 1993–98. Member of Council: Historical Assoc., 1980–2008 (Pres., 1996–99); Econ. Hist. Soc., 1983–92, 1994–2000 and 2002–08; a Vice-President: RHistS, 1997–2001; Soc. for Study of Labour History, 2012– (Exec. Mem., 1983–2005; Vice Chm., 1993–97; Chm., 1997–2001); Trustee, Arkwright Soc., 2012–17 (Mem., Consultative

Council, 2011–12). Mem. (Lab) Leics CC, 1981–89 (Labour Chief Whip, 1985–86; Leader, Labour Gp, 1986–89); Mem. (Lab) Charnwood BC, 1983–87 (Dep. Leader, Labour Gp). Contested: (Lab) Blaby, 1983; (Lab and Co-op) Loughborough, 1987. CMILT (MILT 2000); AcSS 2001. Hon. LittD E Anglia, 1998. *Publications*: (ed jtly) The Working Class in Victorian Britain, 4 vols, 1973; David Lloyd George and the British Labour Movement, 1976, 2nd edn 1992; A. J. P. Taylor: a complete bibliography, 1980; (ed) A History of British Industrial Relations: Vol. 1: 1875–1914, 1982; Vol. 2: 1914–1939, 1986, 3rd edn 2018; Vol. 3: 1939–1979, 1996; (ed) William Barnes: the Dorset poet, 1984; (ed) Warfare, Diplomacy and Politics, 1986; Arthur Henderson, 1990; Lloyd George and the Challenge of Labour, 1990, 2nd edn 2018; (ed jtly) On the Move, 1991; Lloyd George, 1992; (ed) Challenges of Labour, 1993; (ed) A. J. P. Taylor: From Napoleon to the Second International, 1993; (ed) A. J. P. Taylor: From the Boer War to the Cold War, 1995; (jtly) An Atlas of Industrial Protest in Britain 1750–1990, 1996; (ed) British Trade Unionism 1945–95, 1997; (ed) A. J. P. Taylor: British Prime Ministers and other essays, 1999; (ed) A. J. P. Taylor: Struggles for Diplomacy: diplomatic essays, 2000; (ed) The First World War and the International Economy, 2000; Churchill: a biographical dictionary, 2002; British Trade Unions since 1933, 2002; (ed) A Companion to Early Twentieth-Century Britain, 2003; (ed jtly) The Emergence of European Trade Unionism, 2004; A. J. P. Taylor: radical historian of Europe, 2006; Churchill, 2006; (ed jtly) The Second Labour Government 1929–1931, 2011; (ed) The Industrial Revolution: Cromford, the Derwent Valley and the wider world, 2015; (ed) Industrialisation and Society in Britain: Cromford and beyond in the era of the Industrial Revolution, 2016; (ed) The Industrial Revolution and Industrialisation Revisited: Cromford, the Derwent Valley and beyond, 2017; (ed) The Changing Lives of Working People During the Industrial Revolution: the Derwent Valley and beyond, 2018; Industrialisation and Working People: Cromford, the Derwent Valley and beyond, 2019. *Recreations*: swimming, walking, music, visiting art galleries, reading even more history. *Address*: School of History, Nottingham University, Nottingham NG7 2RD. *E*: chris.wrigley@nottingham.ac.uk; (home) 8 Tavistock Road, West Bridgford, Nottingham NG2 6FH.

**WRIGLEY, Sir Edward Anthony, (Sir Tony),** Kt 1996; PhD; FBA 1980; Master of Corpus Christi College, Cambridge, 1994–2000; President, British Academy, 1997–2001; *b* 17 Aug. 1931; *s* of Edward Ernest Wrigley and Jessie Elizabeth Wrigley; *m* 1960, Maria Laura Spelberg; one *s* three *d*. *Educ*: King's Sch., Macclesfield; Peterhouse, Cambridge (MA, PhD). William Volker Res. Fellow, Univ. of Chicago, 1953–54; Lectr in Geography, Cambridge, 1958–74; Peterhouse, Cambridge: Fellow, 1958–74, Hon. Fellow, 1997; Tutor, 1962–64; Sen. Bursar, 1964–74; Co-Dir, Cambridge Gp for History of Population and Social Structure, 1974–94; Prof. of Population Studies, LSE, 1979–88; Sen. Res. Fellow, 1988–94, Dist. Fellow, 2002–05, All Souls Coll., Oxford; Prof. of Econ. History, Univ. of Cambridge, 1994–97. Leverhulme Emeritus Res. Fellow, 2008–09. Pres., Manchester Coll., Oxford, 1987–96. Mem., Inst. for Advanced Study, Princeton, 1970–71; Hinkley Vis. Prof., Johns Hopkins Univ., 1975; Tinbergen Vis. Prof., Erasmus Univ., Rotterdam, 1979. President: British Soc. for Population Studies, 1977–79; Econ. History Soc., 1995–98; Chm., Population Investigation Cttee, 1984–90; Treas., British Acad., 1989–95. Chm., Newton Trust, 2000–07. Editor, Economic History Review, 1986–92. Mem., Amer. Philosophical Soc., 2001; Hon. Foreign Mem., Amer. Acad. of Arts and Scis, 2001. Hon. LittD: Manchester, 1997; Sheffield, 1997; Bristol, 1998; London, 2004; Hon. DLitt: Oxford, 1999; Leicester, 1999; Hon. DSc Edinburgh, 1998. IUSSP Laureate, 1993; Founder's Medal, RGS, 1997; Leverhulme Medal, British Acad., 2005. *Publications*: Industrial Growth and Population Change, 1961; (ed) English Historical Demography, 1966; Population and History, 1969; (ed) Nineteenth Century Society, 1972; (ed) Identifying People in the Past, 1973; (ed with P. Abrams) Towns in Societies, 1978; (with R. S. Schofield) Population History of England, 1981; (ed jtly) The Works of Thomas Robert Malthus, 1986; People, Cities and Wealth, 1987; Continuity, Chance and Change, 1988; (ed with R. A. Church) The Industrial Revolutions, 1994; (jtly) English Population History from Family Reconstitution, 1997; Poverty, Progress and Population, 2004; Energy and the English Industrial Revolution, 2010; The Early English Censuses, 2011; The Path to Sustained Growth, 2016. *Recreation*: gardening. *Address*: 13 Sedley Taylor Road, Cambridge CB2 8PW. *T*: (01223) 247614.

**WRIGLEY, Prof. Neil,** PhD, DSc; FBA 2012; Professor of Geography, University of Southampton, 1991–2019, now Emeritus; *b* Denton, Lancs, 27 March 1948; *s* of Fred and Eva Wrigley; *m* 1st, 1972, Susan Broom (marr. diss. 1995); two *d*; 2nd, 1996, Michelle Lowe; two *s* one *d*. *Educ*: Audenshaw Grammar Sch., Lancs; University Coll. of Wales, Aberystwyth (BA 1st Cl. Hons 1970); St Catharine's Coll., Cambridge (PhD 1976); Univ. of Bristol (DSc 1990). Lectr in Geog., Univ. of Southampton, 1973–76; Lectr, then Reader in Geog., Univ. of Bristol, 1976–86; Prof. of City and Regl Planning, Univ. of Wales Coll. of Cardiff, 1986–91 (Hd of Dept, 1989–91); Hd of Dept of Geog., Univ. of Southampton, 1992–95, 1999–2001. Ed., Trans IBG, 1988–93; Founding Ed., Jl Econ. Geog., 2001–. Visiting Professor: UCSB, 1981; Boston Univ., 1981; Macquarie Univ., 1984; Karlsruhe Univ., 1985; UCLA, 1986, 1989; Univ. of Toronto, 1987, 2000; George Mason Univ., 1993; Univ. of Canterbury, NZ, 1995. Erskine Fellow, NZ, 1995; Vis. Schol., St Catharine's Coll., Cambridge, 1995–96; Sen. Res. Fellow, St Peter's Coll., Oxford, 1996–97; Leverhulme Trust Res. Fellow/Individual Award, 1997–99. Member: Res. Resources and Methods Cttee, 1983–91, Dir, Retail Ind. Business Engagement Network, 2008–13, ESRC; Future High Streets Forum, DCLG, then MHCLG, 2013–. Mem., Acad. Develt Bd, Worldwide Univs Network, 2001–03. Mem. Council, IBG, 1988–89; Chair, Royal Geographical Annual Conf. 2010, 2009–11. FAcSS (AcSS 2003). Ashby Prize, Pion Ltd, 2004; Murchison Award, RGS, 2008; Outstanding Impact in Business Prize, ESRC, 2014. *Publications*: (ed) Statistical Applications in the Spatial Sciences, 1979; (ed with R. J. Bennett) Quantitative Geography: a British view, 1981; Measuring the Unmeasurable: the analysis of quantitative spatial data, 1985; Categorical Data Analysis for Geographers and Environmental Scientists, 1985, 2nd US edn 2002; Store Choice, Store Location and Market Analysis, 1988, repubd 2014; (ed jtly) Urban Dynamics and Spatial Choice Behaviour, 1989; (ed with M. Lowe) Retailing, Consumption and Capital: towards the new retail geography, 1996, repr. 1998; (with M. Lowe) Reading Retail: a geographical perspective on retailing and consumption spaces, 2002; (ed with N. Coe) The Globalization of Retailing, 2 vols, 2009; (ed with E. Brookes) Evolving High Streets: resilience and reinvention, 2014; (with D. Lambiri) British High Streets: from crisis to recovery? a comprehensive review of the evidence, 2015; contrib. papers to internat. jls incl. Envmt & Planning A, Econ. Geog., Trans IBG, Jl Econ. Geog., Progress in Human Geog., Urban Studies, Regl Studies, Global Networks. *Recreations*: travel, wine, Manchester City FC, over-turning established academic pecking orders. *Address*: 18 St Thomas Street, Winchester, Hants SO23 9HJ. *T*: (01962) 865796; School of Geography and Environment, University of Southampton, Southampton, Hants SO17 1BJ. *T*: (023) 8059 3762. *E*: n.wrigley@soton.ac.uk.

**WRIGLEY, Sir Tony;** *see* Wrigley, Sir E. A.

**WRIXON-BECHER, Sir John William Michael;** *see* Becher.

**WROE, Dr Ann;** Obituaries Editor, The Economist, since 2003; *b* Maidstone, Kent, 8 Feb. 1951; *d* of Frank Bristow and Lorna Bristow (*née* Body); *m* 1981, Malcolm Wroe (*d* 2014); three *s*. *Educ*: Ursuline Convent, Wimbledon; Bedford Coll., London (BA 1st Cl. Hons Hist.); St Hilda's Coll., Oxford (DPhil 1975). BBC World Service, 1975–76; The Economist: US corresp., 1976–88; Books and Arts Ed., 1988–91; US Ed., 1991–2000; Briefings Ed., 2000–03. *Publications*: Lives, Lies and the Iran-Contra Affair, 1991; A Fool and His Money, 1995; Pilate: the biography of an invented man, 1999; Perkin: a story of deception, 2003; Being Shelley, 2007; Orpheus: the song of life, 2011; Six Facets of Light, 2016; Francis: a life in songs, 2018. *Recreations*: walking the Downs and watching the sea. *Address*: Flat 3a, 14 Lewes Crescent, Brighton BN2 1FH. *E*: annwroe@economist.com.

**WROTTESLEY,** family name of **Baron Wrottesley**.

**WROTTESLEY, 6th Baron** *cr* 1838; **Clifton Hugh Lancelot de Verdon Wrottesley;** Bt 1642; yacht broking, since 1997, property, since 2003, fine wine investment management, since 2005, and natural burial operator and landlord, since 2015; *b* Aug. 1968; *s* of Hon. Richard Francis Gerard Wrottesley (*d* 1970) (2nd *s* of 5th Baron) and of Georgina Anne (who *m* 1982, Lt-Col Jonathan L. Seddon-Brown), *er d* of Lt-Col Peter Thomas Clifton, CVO, DSO; *S* grandfather, 1977; *m* 2001, Sascha, *d* of Urs Schwarzenbach; three *s* one *d*. *Educ*: Eton; Edinburgh Univ. Commnd 1st Bn Grenadier Guards, 1990; Lieut, 1993, Capt. 1994; retd, 1995. Mem., Skinners' Co. *Heir*: *s* Hon. Victor Ernst Francis de Verdon Wrottesley, *b* Jan. 2004. *Address*: New Quadrant Partners Ltd, 22 Chancery Lane, WC2A 1LS. *Clubs*: White's, Turf; St Moritz Tobogganing; Corviglia Ski; Dracula (St Moritz).

**WROUGHTON, Sir Philip (Lavallin),** KCVO 2008; Lord-Lieutenant of Berkshire, 1995–2008; Chairman and Chief Executive, C. T. Bowring & Co. Ltd, 1988–96; *b* 19 April 1933; *s* of Michael Lavallin Wroughton and Elizabeth Angela Wroughton (*née* Rate); *m* 1957, Catriona Henrietta Ishbel MacLeod; two *d*. *Educ*: Eton Coll. Nat. Service, 1951–53, 2nd Lieut KRRC. Price Forbes & Co. Ltd, 1954–61; C. T. Bowring & Co. Ltd, 1961–96; Dir, Marsh & McLennan Cos, Inc., 1988–96 (Vice Chm., 1994–96); Chm., Venton Underwriting Agencies Ltd, 1996–99. Mem., Council of Lloyds, 1992–95. President: Newbury & Dist Agricl Soc., 1985–86; Berks Community Foundn, 1995–2008; SE RFCA, 2000–04; South of England Agricl Soc., 2008–09. Trustee, 1991–2000, Vice-Pres., 2000–12, Princess Royal Trust for Carers; Trustee, Prince Philip Trust, 1995–2008. Gov., St Mary's Sch., Wantage, 1986–2006. High Sheriff, Berks, 1977; DL Berks, 1994. Hon. LLD Reading, 2004. KStJ (Pres., Council of St John, Berks, 1995–2008). *Recreations*: shooting, racing. *Address*: North Lodge, Woolley Park, Wantage OX12 8NJ. *T*: (01488) 638214. *E*: plw@northlodge.biz. *Club*: White's.

**WU, Prof. Duncan,** DPhil; Professor of English, since 2008, and Raymond W. Wagner Professor of English Literature, since 2016, Georgetown University, Washington; *b* 3 Nov. 1961; *s* of Spencer Yin-Cheung Wu and Mary (*née* Sadler); *m* 1st, 1997, Caroline Beatrice Carey (marr. diss. 2008); 2nd, 2011, Catherine Mary Payling (MBE 2003). *Educ*: St Catherine's Coll., Oxford (MA; DPhil 1990). British Acad. Postdoctoral Res. Fellow, 1991–94; Reader in English Lit., 1995–98, Prof. of English Lit., 1998–2000, Univ. of Glasgow; Lectr in English Lit., 2000–03, Prof. of English Lang. and Lit., 2003–07, Univ. of Oxford; Fellow, St Catherine's Coll., Oxford, 2000–07. Trustee: Charles Lamb Soc., 1991–; Keats-Shelley Meml Assoc., 1998–. FRSA. *Publications*: Wordsworth's Reading 1770–1799, 1993; (ed with S. Gill) Wordsworth: a selection of his finest poems, 1994; Romanticism: an anthology, 1994, 4th edn 2012; Six Contemporary Dramatists: Bennett, Potter, Gray, Brenton, Hare, Ayckbourn, 1995; Romanticism: a critical reader, 1995; Wordsworth's Reading 1800–1815, 1996; William Wordsworth: the Five-Book Prelude, 1997; Women Romantic Poets: an anthology, 1997; A Companion to Romanticism, 1998; William Hazlitt, The Plain Speaker: key essays, 1998; The Selected Writings of William Hazlitt, 1998; Making Plays: interviews with contemporary British dramatists and directors, 2000; Wordsworth: an inner life, 2002; (ed with M. Demata) British Romanticism and the Edinburgh Review, 2002; The Blackwell Essential Literature Series, 7 vols, 2002; William Wordsworth: the earliest poems 1785–1790, 2002; Wordsworth's Poets, 2003; (ed jtly) Metaphysical Hazlitt: bicentenary essays, 2005; New Writings of William Hazlitt, 2007; Hazlitt: the first modern man, 2008; The Happy Fireside: Romantic poems about dogs and cats, 2011; Immortal Bird: the nightingale in Romantic poetry, 2011; Poetry of Witness: the tradition in English, 1500–2000, 2014; All that is worth remembering: selected essays of William Hazlitt, 2014; 30 Great Myths about the Romantics, 2015; John Keats and Percy Bysshe Shelley: the essential poems, 2016; Love Is My Religion: Keats on love, 2018; She Walks in Beauty: the best of Byron, 2019. *Recreations*: jazz, walking, cinema, visiting art museums and American Civil War battlefields, book collecting. *Address*: Department of English, 306 New North, Georgetown University, Washington, DC 20057–1131, USA. *E*: dw252@georgetown.edu.

**WU, Sir Gordon (Ying Sheung),** GBS 2004; KCMG 1997; Chairman, Hopewell Holdings Group, since 1972 (Managing Director, 1972–2001); *b* Hong Kong, 3 Dec. 1935; *s* of Chung Wu and Sum Wu (*née* Chang); *m* 1970, Kwok, (Ivy), San-Ping; two *s* two *d*. *Educ*: Princeton Univ. (BS Civil Engrg 1958). Architect; civil engr. Founder: Central Enterprises Co. Ltd, 1962; Gordon Wu and Associates, 1962; Hopewell Construction Co. Ltd, 1963; Hopewell Hldgs Ltd, 1972; Consolidated Electric Power Asia Ltd, 1993. *Projects* include: Hopewell Centre, Hong Kong (66 storey building); China Hotel, Guangdong, China; Shajiao B and C (coal-fired power stations), Guangdong, China; G-S-Z Superhighway (motorway linking Hong Kong and China). Vice Pres., Real Estate Developers Assoc. of Hong Kong, 1970–; Mem., Chinese People's Political Consultative Conf., 1983–2013 (Vice Chm., Cttee for Liaison with HK, Macao, Taiwan and Overseas Chinese, 2003–13). *Address*: Hopewell Holdings Ltd, 64th Floor, Hopewell Centre, 183 Queen's Road East, Hong Kong.

**WULF-MATHIES, Dr Monika;** Executive Vice President (formerly Managing Director), Corporate Public Policy and Sustainability (formerly Managing Director, Policy and Environment), Deutsche Post World Net, 2001–08 (Policy Adviser, Board of Management, since 2009); *b* 17 March 1942; *d* of Carl-Hermann Baier and Margott Meisser; *m* 1968, Dr Carsten Wulf-Mathies. *Educ*: Univ. of Hamburg (DrPhil 1968). Br. Asst, Federal Ministry of Econs, Germany, 1968–71; Hd, Dept for Social Policy, Federal Chancellery, 1971–76; joined Gewerkschaft Öffentliche Dienste, Transport und Verkehr (Public Services and Transport Workers' Union), 1971; Mem., Man. Exec. Cttee, 1976–95; Chm., 1982–95; Mem., European Commn, 1995–99. Policy Mem., Inst. for Study of Labour, Bonn, 2005–; Dep. Chm., Supervisory Bd, Univ. of Bonn, 2008–13; Mem. Senate, Leibniz Gemeinschaft, 2010–18. Pres., Beethoven-Stiftung für Kunst und Kultur, 2005–. *Recreations*: garden, painting in watercolours.

**WULFF, Christian;** President, Federal Republic of Germany, 2010–12; *b* Osnabrück, 19 June 1959; *s* of Rudolf Wulff and Dagmar Wulff; *m* 1st, 1988, Christiane Vogt (marr. diss.); one *d*; 2nd, 2008, Bettina Körner; one *s* and one step *s*. *Educ*: Univ. of Osnabrück (Law degree specialising in Econs 1986); Hanover (state exams in law). Legal trng, Oldenburg Higher Regl Court, 1987–90, then joined a law firm. Mem. (CDU), Osnabrück Council, 1986–2001 (Leader, CDU Gp, 1989–94). Landtag of Lower Saxony: Mem. (CDU),

1994–2010; Leader, CDU Parly Gp, 1994; Minister-Pres., 2003–10. Chm., Lower Saxony, CDU, 1994–2010; Dep. Federal Chm., CDU, 1998–2010. Patron, Nat. Orgn, German Multiple Sclerosis Soc., 2001–. Hon. Senator, Eur. Acad. of Scis and Arts, Salzburg. Hon. Dr Tongji Univ., Shanghai.

**WULWIK, Peter David; His Honour Judge Wulwik;** a Circuit Judge, since 2004; Principal Judge for estate agents' appeals to the First-Tier Tribunal (General Regulatory Chamber) and a Judge of the Upper Tribunal (Administrative Appeals Chamber), since 2009; a Judge of the Upper Tribunal (Tax and Chancery Chamber), since 2014; *b* 15 Sept. 1950; *s* of Eddie and Mona Wulwik; *m* 1975, Joanna Rosenberg; two *s* one *d*. *Educ:* St Marylebone Grammar Sch.; Univ. of London (LLB Hons ext.). Called to the Bar, Gray's Inn, 1972; Asst Recorder, 1995–2000; a Recorder, 2000–04. Part-time Chairman: London Rent Assessment Panel and Leasehold Valuation Tribunal, 1999–2004; Consumer Credit and Estate Agents Appeals Panel, 2003–. Pres., Consumer Credit Appeals Tribunal, 2008–09. *Publications:* (contrib.) Bennion's Consumer Credit Law Reports, 1990–2000; (contrib.) Goode's Consumer Credit Reports, 2000–04. *Recreations:* reading, opera, theatre, classical music, antique fairs, playing bridge, tennis, watching Tottenham Hotspur. *Club:* Farm Walk Tennis.

**WURTH, Hubert;** Permanent Representative of Luxembourg to the United Nations in Vienna and to the Organization for Security and Co-operation in Europe, since 2011; *b* Luxembourg, 15 April 1952; *s* of Ernest Wurth and Denise Wurth (*née* Conrath); *m* 1998, Francisca Passchier; two *d*. *Educ:* Univ. of Paris II (law degree 1975); Inst. of Political Studies, Paris (Dip. Internat. Relns 1976). Min. of Foreign Affairs, Luxembourg, 1978–89; Ambassador: to USSR, Poland, Finland and Mongolia, 1988–91; to Netherlands, 1992–98; Ambassador and Perm. Rep. to UN, NY, 1998–2003; Ambassador to France, OECD and UNESCO, 2003–07; Ambassador to the Court of St James's, and concurrently to Ireland and Iceland, 2007–11. Ambassador, Special Mission for Former Yugoslavia, 1996–98. *Recreations:* painter (self-taught), various exhibitions (incl. 'Dark', EU Commn Gall., London, 2008) and publications. *W:* www.wurthhubert.com.

**WÜTHRICH, Prof. Kurt,** PhD; Professor: of Biophysics, Eidgenössische Technische Hochschule, Zürich, since 1980; of Structural Biology, Scripps Research Institute, California, since 2001; Distinguished Senior Professor, ShanghaiTech University, since 2013; Adjunct Senior Professor, Daegu Gyeongbuk Institute of Science and Technology, since 2014; *b* 4 Oct. 1938; *s* of Herrmann Wüthrich and Gertrud Wüthrich-Kuchen; *m* 1963, Marianne Briner; one *s* one *d*. *Educ:* Univ. of Bern (MS Chemistry, Physics and Maths 1962); Univ. of Basel (PhD Chemistry 1964; Eidgenössisches Turn- und Sportlehrerdiplom 1964). Postdoctoral training: Univ. of Basel, 1964–65; Univ. of California, Berkeley, 1965–67; Mem., Tech. Staff, Bell Telephone Labs, Murray Hill, 1967–69; Eidgenössische Technische Hochschule, Zürich, 1969–: Asst Prof., 1972–76; Associate Prof., 1976–80; Chm., Dept of Biology, 1995–2000. Mem. Council, 1975–78, 1987–90, Sec. Gen., 1978–84, Vice Pres., 1984–87, IUPAB; Mem. Gen. Cttee, 1980–86, Standing Cttee on Free Circulation of Scientists, 1982–90, ICSU. Member: EMBO, 1984; Deutsche Akad. der Naturforscher Leopoldina, 1987; Academia Europea, 1989; Schweizerische Akad. der Technischen Wissenschaften, 2001; Schweizerische Akad. der Medizinischen Wissenschaften, 2002. Editor: Qly Rev. Biophysics, 1984–91, 1996–2001; Macromolecular Structures, 1990–2000; Jl Biomolecular NMR, 1991–2011. Hon. Member: Japanese Biochem. Soc., 1993; American Acad. of Arts and Scis, 1993; Nat. Magnetic Resonance Soc., India, 1998; Swiss Chemical Soc., 2003; World Innovation Foundn, 2003; Internat. Soc. Magnetic Resonance in Medicine, 2004; Hungarian Acad. of Sci., 2004; World Acad. of Young Scientists, 2004; Eur. Acad. Arts, Scis and Humanities, 2004; Latvian Acad. Scis, 2004; Groupement Ampère, 2004; NMR Soc. of Japan, 2004; Indian Biophysical Soc., 2005; Korean Magnetic Resonance Soc., 2005. Foreign Associate: US Nat. Acad. of Scis, 1992; Acad. of Scis, Inst. of France, 2000; RSChem, 2003; RSE, 2003. FAAAS 1998; Foreign Mem., Royal Soc., 2010. Foreign Fellow: Indian Nat. Sci. Acad., 1989; Korean Acad. of Sci. and Technol., 2005; Nordrhein-Westfälische Acad. der Wissenschaften, 2005; Hon. Fellow: NAS, India, 1992; Latvian Inst. of Organic Synthesis, Riga, 2008. Hon. Dr Chem.: Siena, 1997; Univ. del Norte, Asunción, Paraguay, 2007; Hon. PhD Zürich, 1997; Doctor *hc* Ecole Poly. Fédérale Lausanne, 2001; Valencia, 2004; Sheffield, 2004; King George's Med. Univ., Lucknow, 2005; Pécs, 2007; Lomonosov Moscow State Univ., 2007; Verona, 2007; Univ. René Descartes, Paris, 2007; Naples, 2012; Patras, 2015; Buenos Aires, 2015; Córdoba, Argentina, 2016. Friedrich Miescher Prize, Schweizerische Biochemische Ges., 1974; Shield, Fac. of Medicine, Tokyo Univ., 1983; P. Bruylants Medal, Catholic Univ. of Louvain, 1986; Stein and Moore Award, Protein Soc., USA, 1990; Louisa Gross Horwitz Prize, Columbia Univ., 1991; Gilbert N. Lewis Medal, Univ. of California, Berkeley, 1991; Marcel Benoist Prize, Switzerland, 1992; Dist. Service Award, Miami Winter Symposia, 1993; Prix Louis Jeantet de Médecine, Geneva, 1993; Kaj Linderstrøm-Lang Prize, Carlsberg Foundn, Copenhagen, 1996; Eminent Scientist of RIKEN, Tokyo, 1997; Kyoto Prize in Advanced Technol., 1998; Günther Laukien Prize, Exptl NMR Conf., 1999; Otto Warburg Medal, Soc. for Biochem. and Molecular Biol., Germany, 1999; World Future Award, M. Gorbatschow Foundn, 2002; (jtly) Nobel Prize for Chemistry, 2002; Swiss Soc. award, Swiss Awards, 2002; Ehrenpreis, Wallisellen, Switzerland, 2002; Johannes M. Bijvoet Medal, Utrecht Univ., 2008; Paul Walden Medal, Riga Tech. Univ., 2008; Jabir ibn Hyyan (Geber) Medal, Saudi Chemical Soc., 2009; Ralph and Helen Oesper Award, Univ. of Cincinnati, 2010; President's Gold Medal (India), 2012; Theodor Bücher Medal, FEBS, 2013; IUBMB Medal, 2015; Shanghai 1000 Talents Awards, 2016; Genome Valley Excellence Award, BioAsia, Hyderabad, 2017; Shanghai Internat. Sci. and Technol. Cooperation Award, 2018. *Publications:* NMR in Biological Research: Peptides and Proteins, 1976; NMR of Proteins and Nucleic Acids, 1986; NMR in Structural Biology: a collection of papers, 1995; over 800 contribs to learned jls. *Address:* Scripps Research Institute, Hazen Theory Building, 10640 John Jay Hopkins Drive, San Diego, CA 92121, USA; Institute of Molecular Biology and Biophysics, ETH Zürich, Otto Stern-Weg 5, 8093 Zürich, Switzerland.

**WYAND, Roger Nicholas Lewes;** QC 1997; a Recorder, since 2000; a Deputy High Court Judge, since 2004; *b* 31 Oct. 1947; *s* of John Blake Wyand and Diana Wyand (*née* Williams); *m* 1973, Mary Elizabeth Varley; three *s*. *Educ:* Lakefield Coll. Sch., Canada; Rugby Sch.; Downing Coll., Cambridge (MA Nat. Sci.). Called to the Bar, Middle Temple, 1973, Bencher, 2005; Asst Recorder (Patents County Court), 1994–2000. Vice-Chm., Intellectual Property Bar Assoc. *Recreations:* theatre, golf, Arsenal FC. *Address:* Hogarth Chambers, 5 New Square, Lincoln's Inn, WC2A 3RJ. *T:* (020) 7404 0404.

**WYATT, Prof. Adrian Frederick George,** DPhil; FRS 2000; Professor of Physics, 1976, now Emeritus, and former Director, Centre for Energy and the Environment (formerly Energy Studies Unit), University of Exeter; *b* 1 Oct. 1938. *Educ:* Univ. of Bristol (BSc 1960); DPhil Oxford 1963. Lectr, then Sen. Lectr, in Physics, Univ. of Nottingham, 1964–76. *Publications:* (ed with H. J. Lauter) Excitations in Two-dimensional and Three-dimensional Quantum Fluids, 1991; contrib. to learned jls. *Address:* School of Physics, University of Exeter, Stocker Road, Exeter EX4 4QL.

**WYATT, (Alan) Will,** CBE 2000; author; Chairman, ToniandRosi Films Ltd, 2010–14; *b* 7 Jan. 1942; *s* of Basil Wyatt and Hettie Evelyn (*née* Hooper); *m* 1966, Jane Bridgit Bagenal; two *d*. *Educ:* Magdalen College Sch., Oxford; Emmanuel Coll., Cambridge. Trainee reporter, Sheffield Telegraph, 1964; Sub-Editor, BBC Radio News, 1965; moved to BBC television, 1968; Producer: Late Night Line Up, In Vision, The Book Programme, B. Traven—a mystery solved, *et al*, 1970–77; Asst Hd of Presentation (Programmes), 1977; Hd of Documentary Features, 1981; Hd of Features and Documentaries Gp, 1987; Asst Man. Dir, 1988–91, Man. Dir, 1991–96, BBC Network Television; Chief Exec., BBC Broadcast, 1996–99. Chm., BBC Guidelines on Violence, 1983, 1987; Director: BARB, 1989–91; BBC Subscription TV, 1990–93; BBC Enterprises, 1991–94; BBC Worldwide Television, 1994–96; UKTV, 1997–99; Coral Eurobet, 2000–02; Vitec Gp plc, 2002–11; Racing UK, 2004–11; Amalgamated Racing, 2008–11 (Chm., 2010–11); Chairman: Human Capital Ltd, 2001–08; Goodwill Associates (Media) Ltd, 2003–13; Racecourse Media Gp, 2008–11. Vice-Chm., Shadow Racing Trust, 2003–07. Chairman: Adv. Bd, POLIS, 2006–09; Teaching Awards Trust, 2008–13. Governor: Univ. of the Arts London (formerly London Inst.), 1990–2007 (Chm., 1999–2007); Nat. Film and TV Sch., 1991–97; Magdalen Coll. Sch., Oxford, 2000–06. Vice-Pres., EBU, 1998–99. Trustee, Services Sound and Vision Corp., 2007–13; Trustee, Welsh Nat. Opera, 2013–. Prod. and dir, Toni and Rosi, BBC documentary film, 2012. FRTS 1992 (Vice-Pres., 1997; Pres., 2000–04). *Publications:* The Man Who Was B. Traven, 1980; (contrib.) Masters of the Wired World, 1999; The Fun Factory: a life in the BBC, 2003; Oxford Boy: a post-war townie childhood, 2018; numerous articles on broadcasting etc. *Recreations:* fell walking, horse racing, opera, theatre. *Address:* 46 Flanders Mansions, Flanders Road, W4 1NF. *E:* will.wyatt@btinternet.com. *Clubs:* Garrick, Century.

**WYATT, Caroline Jane;** presenter: Saturday PM, BBC Radio 4, since 2017; The World This Week, World Service Radio, since 2017; *b* Darlinghurst, 21 April 1967; *d* of David Joseph Wyatt, *qv* and Annemarie Wyatt (*née* Angst). *Educ:* Convent of the Sacred Heart, Woldingham; Southampton Univ. (BA Hons English and German); Rutgers Univ. (exchange prog.); City Univ. (Dip. Journalism). BBC: news trainee, 1991–92; asst producer, BBC World TV, 1993; Berlin stringer, 1994–97; Bonn Corresp., 1997–99; Berlin Corresp., 1999–2000; Moscow Corresp., 2000–03; Paris Corresp., 2003–07; Defence Corresp., 2007–14; Religious Affairs Corresp., 2014–16. Mem. Council, Chatham Hse, 2010–16; Mem., Adv. Bd, RUSI, 2017–. Trustee, Nat. Army Mus., 2014–17. Hon. DLitt Southampton, 2010; DUniv City, 2017. Op. Telic Medal, 2003. *Publications:* (contrib.) From Our Own Correspondent, 2005; (contrib.) More From Our Own Correspondent, 2008; (contrib.) Oxford Handbook of War, 2012; (contrib.) Contemporary Writing on Conflict: reportage, 2014. *Address:* c/o BBC Broadcasting House, Portland Place, W1A 1AA. *Club:* Naval and Military.

**WYATT, (Christopher) Terrel,** FREng, FICE, FIStructE; Chairman, W. S. Atkins plc, 1987–98; *b* 17 July 1927; *s* of Lionel Harry Wyatt and Audrey Vere Wyatt; *m*; four *s*; *m* 1990, Patricia Perkins. *Educ:* Kingston Grammar Sch.; Battersea Polytechnic (BScEng); Imperial Coll. (DIC). FICE 1963; FIStructE 1963; FREng (FEng 1980). Served RE, 1946–48. Charles Brand & Son Ltd, 1948–54; Richard Costain Ltd, 1955–87: Dir, 1970–87; Gp Chief Exec., 1975–80; Dep. Chm., 1979–80; Chm., Costain Group PLC, 1980–87. *Recreation:* sailing. *Address:* Ryderswells Farm, Uckfield Road, Lewes, E Sussex BN8 5RN.

**WYATT, David;** HM Diplomatic Service, retired; owner, The Lime Leaf restaurant, Basingstoke, 2007–18; *b* 18 April 1946; *s* of Ernest Wyatt and Eva Mabel Wyatt (*née* Hayles); *m* 1st, 1969, Rosemary Elizabeth Clarke (*d* 2000); one *s* one *d*; 2nd, 2002, Sunthian Phujarn. *Educ:* Sandown Grammar Sch. Entered Diplomatic Service, 1965; Lusaka, 1968–71; SOAS, 1971–72; Third Sec. (Commercial), Bangkok, 1972–76; Second Secretary: Yaoundé, 1976–77; FCO, 1977–79; NDC, 1980; First Secretary (Commercial), Athens, 1981–84; and Hd of Chancery, Bangkok, 1984–88; FCO, 1988–94; Dep. High Comr, Accra, 1994–98; Commercial Counsellor, Bangkok, 1999–2001; Dep. High Comr, Lagos, 2001–07. *Recreations:* running, gardening.

**WYATT, David Joseph,** CBE 1977; Chairman, Crown Bio Systems, 2004–05 (consultant, 2003); HM Diplomatic Service, 1949–85; *b* 12 Aug. 1931; *s* of late Frederick Wyatt and Lena (*née* Parr); *m* 1957, Annemarie Angst (*d* 1978); two *s* one *d*; 2nd, 1990, Dr Wendy Baron, *qv*. *Educ:* Leigh Grammar Sch. National Service, RAF, 1950–52. Entered Foreign Service, 1949; Berne, 1954; FO, 1957–61; Second Sec., Vienna, 1961; First Sec., Canberra, 1965; FCO, 1969–71; First Sec., Ottawa, 1971; Counsellor, 1974; seconded Northern Ireland Office, Belfast, 1974–76; Counsellor and Head of Chancery, Stockholm, 1976–79; Under Sec. on loan to Home Civil Service, 1979–82; UK Mission to UN during 1982 General Assembly (personal rank of Ambassador); Minister and Dep. Comdt, British Mil. Govt, Berlin, 1983–85. Acting Dir Gen., Jan.–July 1990, Dir, Internat. Div., 1985–92, Advr on Internat. Relations, 1992–99, BRCS; Chm., Internat. Red Cross/Red Crescent Adv. Commn, 1996–97. FRSA 1991.
*See also C. J. Wyatt.*

**WYATT, Derek Murray;** *b* 4 Dec. 1949; *s* of late Reginald Swithin Wyatt and of Margaret Eira (*née* Holmden); *m* (marr. diss.); one *d* one *s*; *m* 2015. *Educ:* St Luke's Coll., Exeter; Open Univ. (BA Hons); St Catherine's Coll., Oxford; Exeter Univ. (Cert. Ed 1971); King's College London (MA Internat. Relations 2018). History teacher, 1972–81; journalist and writer, 1982–84; editor, George Allen & Unwin Ltd, 1984–85; Dir and Publisher, William Heinemann Ltd, 1986–88; Dir, TSL Ltd, 1988–91; consultant, writer and journalist, 1992–94; Head of Programmes, Wire TV, 1994–95; Founder and Dir, Computer Channel, BSkyB, 1995–97. MP (Lab) Sittingbourne and Sheppey, 1997–2010. Mem., Select Cttee on Culture, Media and Sport, 1997–2005; Public Accounts Cttee, 2007. Chairman: All Party Parly Internet Gp (founder), 1997–2010; All Party Parly Rugby Union Cttee, 1997–2010; All Party Parly British Council Gp, 1998–2010; (also Founder) All Party Zimbabwe Gp, 2003–05; All Party London Olympic and Paralympic Gp 2012, 2004–10; Co-Chairman: All Party Adventure and Recreation in Society Gp, 2004–06; All Party Parly Communications Gp, 2007–10. Parliamentary Private Secretary: DCMS, 2007–09; FCO, 2009. Member: Exec. Bd, CAABU, 2008–12; Egypt British Business Council, 2010–12. Dir, Code Investing (formerly Crowdbnk), 2012–17; Chairman: Great Retail Revival Foundn, 2013–16; NICE NHS SE Innovation Hub, 2014–16; Chair, Foundn for Information Soc., 2016–18. Member: Bd, CITI, Columbia Univ., 2012–; Sounding Bd, Design Council, 2014–16; SE RFU Legacy Gp, Rugby World Cup 2015, 2013–15; Adv. Bd, Global Thinkers Forum, 2017–. Founder: Women's Sport (formerly Women's Sports Foundn, then Women in Sport), 1985; Oxford Internet Inst., 2000; Digital Day for the Nation, 2007–; Founder and Chair, Brain Campaign, 2017–. Ed.-at-Large, Atlantic Books, 2017–. Trustee: Major Stanley's (Trustee Gp for OURFC), 1986–2017 (Chm., 2013–17); Citizen's Online, 2005–09; Book Trust, 2015–18 (Chm., Develt Cttee, 2014–18); Mem., Liby Cttee, RIBA, 2013–16; Patron, Time Bank, 2008– (Trustee, 2004–08). Chm., Royal Trinity Hospice (formerly Trinity Hospice), 2011–17 (Patron, 2017–). UK Ambassador for Eur. Year of the Brain, 2014–15. Freeman, City of London, 2001; Liveryman, Co. of Information Technologists, 2012–16 (Mem., 2001–16). Commendation for work on sport and apartheid, UNO, 1987. Elected Representative New Media Award, New Statesman,

2006; Internet Hero Award, Internet Services Providers' Assoc., 2006; Winner, MPs Awards, British Computer Society, 2007 and 2008. *Publications:* Wisecracks from the Movies, 1987; The International Rugby Almanack 1994, 1993; The International Rugby Almanack 1995, 1994; Rugby Disunion, 1995; (with Colin Herridge) Rugby Revolution, 2003; (with Colin Herridge) Rugby 2011: the teams, the stats, the history of the World Cup, 2011. *Recreations:* Rugby (played for Oxford University, Barbarians, England), film, jazz, reading, software, travelling, writing. *E:* derekwyatt@aol.com. *W:* www.derekwyatt.co.uk. *Clubs:* Chelsea Arts; Vincent's (Oxford).

**WYATT, Prof. Derrick Arthur;** QC 1993; Professor of Law, 1996–2009, now Emeritus, and Visiting Professor of Law, 2009–14, University of Oxford; Fellow, St Edmund Hall, Oxford, since 1978; *b* 25 Feb. 1948; *s* of Iris Ross (formerly Wyatt, *née* Thompson) and step-*s* of Alexander Ross; *m* 1970, (Margaret) Joan Cunnington; one *s* one *d*. *Educ:* Alsop High Sch.; Emmanuel Coll., Cambridge (MA, LLB); Univ. of Chicago Law Sch. (JD). Lectr in law, Univ. of Liverpool, 1971–75; called to the Bar, Lincoln's Inn, 1972; Fellow, Emmanuel Coll., Cambridge, 1975–78; CUF Lectr in Law, Oxford Univ., 1978–96; in practice as barrister (door tenant), Brick Court Chambers, 1986–2018. Vis. Prof., Florida State Univ., 1987. Member: Vale of White Horse DC, 1983–87; Abingdon Town Council, 1983–87. Mem. Editl Cttee, British Yearbook of Internat. Law, 1992–2012; Mem. Editl Bd, Croatian Yearbook of European Law and Policy, 2005–; Mem. Strategic Bd, Navigating Brexit, 2018–. Mem. Panel, Kuala Lumpur Regl Centre for Arbitration, 2014–18. Has appeared in approx. 100 court cases before EU Courts; has given evidence on EU law issues to UK parlt, FCO, Bank of England and Financial Markets Law Cttee; has given evidence on Brexit issues to UK parlt cttees; rep. and advr, businesses in UK, Ireland, USA, Germany, Iran, and govts of UK, NI, Ireland, Cyprus. *Publications:* Wyatt and Dashwood's Substantive Law of the EEC, 1980, 6th edn as European Union Law, 2011; (ed with A. Barav) Yearbook of European Law, 1988–97; articles and reviews in learned jls. *Recreations:* walking, reading. *Address:* St Edmund Hall, Oxford OX1 4AR.

**WYATT, Hugh Rowland,** CVO 2009; Lord-Lieutenant of West Sussex, 1999–2008; *b* 18 Nov. 1933; *s* of late Brig. Richard John Penfold Wyatt, MC, TD and Hon. Margaret Agnes, *d* of 1st Baron Ebbisham, GBE; *m* 1959, Jane Ann Elizabeth Eden; one *s* two *d*. *Educ:* Winchester. 2nd Lieut, The Royal Sussex Regt, 1952–54; Captain, TA, 1954–61. Dir, McCorquodale plc, 1964–85; farmer. Chairman: Chichester Cathedral Trust, 1991–98; Chichester Dio. Bd of Finance, 1997–2001; Chichester Cathedral Council, 2001–09. High Sheriff of West Sussex, 1995–96. Pres., Royal Sussex Regtl Assoc., 1997–2008. KStJ 2001. *Recreations:* travel, opera. *Address:* The White Cottage, Nepcote, Findon, West Sussex BN14 0SD. *T:* (01903) 873328. *Club:* Sussex.

**WYATT, Matthew Stephen Spence;** Deputy Director, Middle East and North Africa, Department for International Development, since 2015; *b* 2 June 1961; *s* of Ralph William Peter Wyatt and Susan Jennifer Wyatt; *m* 1994, Simonetta Fucecchi; one *s* one *d*. *Educ:* Lady Margaret Hall, Oxford (BA PPE 1983); College of Europe, Bruges (Dip. Higher European Studies 1984). Head: E Europe and Central Asia Dept, DFID, 1999–2001; DFID, Kenya, 2001–04; Permanent Rep. to UN Food and Agric. Agencies, Rome, 2004–06; Asst Pres., Ext. Affairs Dept, IFAD, 2006–09; Hd, Climate and Envmt Dept, 2009–13, Hd, Syria Crisis Unit, 2013–14, DFID. *Recreations:* football, theatre, hiking. *Address:* Department for International Development, 22 Whitehall, SW1A 2EG. *Club:* Railway Wanderers (Nairobi).

**WYATT, Prof. Terence Richard, (Terry),** DPhil; FRS 2013; Professor of Physics, University of Manchester, since 2004; *b* Watford, 29 June 1957; *s* of Ernest Lawrence Wyatt and Pearl Evelyn Wyatt (*née* Sparkes); *m* 2001, Anne Marie Ryan; two *s*. *Educ:* Queen Elizabeth's Grammar Sch., Tamworth; Imperial Coll. London (BSc 1st Cl. Hons 1979; Govs' Prize for Phys 1979; ARCS); St Edmund Hall, Oxford (DPhil 1983). Computer programmer, Cosmic Ray and Space Phys Gp, Imperial Coll. London, 1975–76; research, Deutsches Elektron-Synchrotron, Hamburg, 1980–83; Res. Fellow, CERN, Geneva, 1984–86; Res. Associate, QMC, 1986–89; PPARC Advanced Res. Fellow, CERN/Univ. of Manchester, 1989–96; University of Manchester: Lectr in Phys, 1996–99; Reader in Phys, 1999–2004; PPARC Sen. Res. Fellow, 2003–06. Vis. Scientist, Fermi Nat. Accelerator Lab., 2002–03. Mem., Adv. Panel, Nurse Review, UK Res. Councils, 2015–. Mem., UK Cttee on CERN, BEIS (formerly BERR, then BIS), 2007–; Mem., Scientific Policy Cttee, 2007–, Chm., LHC Experiments Cttee, 2007–10, CERN. Member, Editorial Board: Eur. Phys. Jl C, 2010–; Progress of Theoretical and Experimental Physics, 2012–. Chadwick Medal and Prize, Inst. of Phys, 2011. *Publications:* approx. 800 articles in learned jls. *Recreations:* music (including playing the guitar), hill walking. *Address:* Particle Physics Group, School of Physics and Astronomy, University of Manchester, Oxford Road, Manchester M13 9PL. *T:* (0161) 275 4173, *Fax:* (0161) 275 0480. *E:* Terry.Wyatt@manchester.ac.uk. *W:* www.hep.man.ac.uk/u/wyatt.

**WYATT, Terrel;** see Wyatt, C. T.

**WYATT, Wendy, (Mrs D. J. Wyatt);** see Baron, O. W.

**WYATT, Will;** see Wyatt, A. W.

**WYBAR, Linda;** Headteacher, Tunbridge Wells Girls' Grammar School, since 1999; *b* 21 June 1959; *d* of late Thomas Smith Clough and of Mary Clough; *m* 1995, Geoffrey Wybar; two *s*. *Educ:* Blyth Grammar Sch.; Univ. of Hull (BA Hons Eng. Lang. and Lit. 1980; PGCE Dist. 1981); Open Univ. (MA Educn Mgt 1996). English Teacher: Rede Sch., Strood, 1981–82; Highworth Grammar Sch., Ashford, 1982–86; Hd of English, Norton Knatchbull Boys' Grammar Sch., Ashford, 1986–92; Dep. Headteacher, Highworth Grammar Sch., Sittingbourne, 1992–99. Chm., Kent and Medway Grammar Schs Assoc., 2004–. *Recreations:* reading modern fiction, theatre-going, wine-tasting, relaxing in Cornwall. *Address:* Tunbridge Wells Girls' Grammar School, Southfield Road, Tunbridge Wells, Kent TN4 9UJ. *T:* (01892) 520902, *Fax:* (01892) 536497. *E:* admin@twggs.kent.sch.uk.

**WYETH, Mark Charles;** QC 2009; *b* Kingsbury, London, 27 Sept. 1960; *s* of Derek Wyeth and Rosemary Jean Wyeth; *m* 1987, Mary Patricia Austin; one *s* two *d*. *Educ:* Abbotsfield Sch., Middx; Leicester Poly. (BA Hons Law); London Sch. of Econs (LLM Commercial Law). Called to the Bar, Inner Temple, 1983; Founder and Hd of Chambers, 2 Paper Buildings, Temple, 1988–99; 5 Paper Buildings, 1999–. Panel List QC, Serious Fraud Office, 2010–. Mem. Cttee, Bar Standards Bd, 2005–10. Organiser with Amer. Bar Assoc. Accreditation, London Law Consortium, 1991–. Chm., Disciplinary Appeals Cttee, CIPFA, 2010–13. Vis. Prof., Coll. of Law, Univ. of Iowa, 1995–. *Recreations:* founder of Club Ska records and films, bass player with Symarip, sleeve notes for various music CD and DVD releases, articles for music and sport periodicals, Chelsea Football Club. *Address:* 5 Paper Buildings, Temple, EC4Y 7HB. *T:* (020) 7583 6117, *Fax:* (020) 7353 0075. *E:* clerks@5pb.co.uk. *Clubs:* MCC, Bar Yacht.

**WYKE, Prof. John Anthony,** PhD; Professor, Faculty of Medicine, University of Glasgow, 1991–92, now Professor Emeritus; Director, Scottish Cancer Foundation, 2002–16 (Chairman, 2002–10); *b* 5 April 1942; *s* of late Eric John Edward Wyke and Daisy Anne Wyke (*née* Dormer); *m* 1968, Anne Wynne Mitchell; one *s*. *Educ:* Dulwich Coll.; St John's Coll., Cambridge (Schol.; VetMB, MA); Univ. of Glasgow; UCL (PhD). MRCVS. FRSE 1989. Postdoctoral res., Univ. of Washington and Univ. of Southern California, 1970–72; Imperial Cancer Research Fund: scientific staff, London, 1972–83; Head, ICRF Labs at St Bartholomew's Hosp., 1983–87; Asst Dir, 1985–87; Dir, Beatson Inst. for Cancer Res., 1987–2002. Dir, Worldwide Cancer Res. (formerly Assoc. for Internat. Cancer Res.), 2003–16. Mem. Council, RVC, 2008–12; Trustee, RSE Scotland Foundn, 2012–19. Founder FMedSci 1998. Hon. FRCVS 1999. Hon. Fellow, Univ. of Glasgow, 2004. *Publications:* more than 100 scientific articles. *Recreations:* hill walking, ski-ing, gardening. *Address:* 6 Ledcameroch Road, Bearsden, Glasgow G61 4AA. *E:* johnwyke@hotmail.co.uk.

**WYKES, Dr David Lewis;** Director, Dr Williams's Trust and Library, since 1998; Co-Director, Dr Williams's Centre for Dissenting Studies, 2004–15; *b* 29 June 1954; *s* of Christopher Lewis Wykes, FCA and Joan Margaret Wykes; *m* 1997, Dr Elizabeth Jane Clapp. *Educ:* Univ. of Durham (BSc); Univ. of Leicester (PhD 1987). Mem. of Ct, Leicester Univ., 1985–2015. Hon. Reader, QMUL, 2007–15. FRHistS 2002. *Publications:* (ed with Dr S. J. C. Taylor) Parliament and Dissent, 2005; (with Prof. I. Rivers) Joseph Priestley, Scientist, Philosopher, and Theologian, 2008; (with Prof. I. Rivers) Dissenting Praise: religious dissent and the hymn in England and Wales, 2011; (ed jtly) Protestant Dissent and Philanthropy in Britain, 1660–1914, 2020; numerous articles in academic and learned jls. *Recreations:* chamber music, walking, history. *Address:* Dr Williams's Library, 14 Gordon Square, WC1H 0AR. *T:* (020) 7387 3727.

**WYKES, Dame Hilary Margaret, (Dame Til),** DBE 2016; Professor of Clinical Psychology and Rehabilitation, since 1999, and Vice Dean, Psychology and Systems Science, since 2015, Institute of Psychiatry, Psychology and Neuroscience (formerly Institute of Psychiatry), King's College London; *b* Nantwich; *d* of William and Margaret Wykes; *m* 2006, Brinley Davies; two *s*. *Educ:* Univ. of Nottingham (BSc Hons Psychol. 1974); Univ. of Sussex (DPhil Psychol. 1978); Univ. of London (MPhil Clin. Psychol. 1985). SO, MRC Social Psychiatry Unit, Inst. of Psychiatry, 1978–83; clin. psychol. trainee, SE Thames HA and Inst. of Psychiatry, 1983–85; British Council Schol., Australia and NZ, 1985–86; Australia Res. Consultant, Dept of Health, NSW, 1985–86; Institute of Psychiatry: Lectr, Psychol. Dept, 1986–91; Sen. Lectr, 1991–96; Reader in Clin. Psychol., 1997–99. Dir, Mental Health Res. Network, Nat. Theme Lead for Mental Health and Jt Div. Dir, Clin. Res. Network, 2003–15. Sen. Spokesperson on Mental Health, NIHR Clin. Res. Network, 2016–17. FMedSci 2016. *Publications:* Psychosocial and Pharmacological Rehabilitation for Schizophrenia, 2003, 3rd edn 2012; Cognitive Remediation Therapy for Schizophrenia: theory and practice, 2005 (Japanese 2nd edn 2011); Schizophrenia: evolution and synthesis: Strungmann Forum Reports, 2014. *Address:* Department of Psychology, Institute of Psychiatry, Psychology and Neuroscience, King's College London, De Crespigny Park, SE5 8AF. *T:* (020) 7848 0596. *E:* til.wykes@kcl.ac.uk.

**WYLD, Baroness** *cr* 2016 (Life Peer), of Gosforth in the City of Newcastle upon Tyne; **Laura Lee Wyld;** Senior Adviser, Strategic Communications Alliance; *m*; three *d*. *Educ:* Univ. of Cambridge (BA Hist. 1999). Consultant, Lexington Communications, 2003–07; Consultant, 2007–09, Associate Dir, 2009–13, Fishburn Hedges; Hd, Prime Minister's Appts Unit, No 10 Downing Street, 2013–16. Mem. Bd, Ofsted, 2019–. Trustee, Urology Foundn, 2017–. *Address:* House of Lords, SW1A 0PW.

**WYLD, David John Charles;** Secretary General, International Law Association, 1993–2014; *b* Inverness, 11 March 1943; *s* of John Wyld and Helen Leslie Wyld; *m* 1st, 1970, Sally Morgan (marr. diss.); two *s*; 2nd, 1987, Caroline Alexander; three *d*. *Educ:* Harrow Sch.; Christ Church, Oxford (BA Eng. Lit. 1961); Coll. of Law; Queen Mary, Univ. of London (LLM Internat. Law 2007). Admitted as solicitor, 1974; Solicitor, Linklaters, 1974–79; Partner: Macfarlanes, 1980–2001; David Wyld & Co., 2001–13. Clerk to Governing Body, St Paul's Sch., 2013–. Chm., City of London Law Soc., 2000–04. *Recreations:* reading, walking, golf, theatre. *Address:* Ground Floor Flat, 20 Cresswell Road, Twickenham, Middx TW1 2DZ. *T:* 07771 531951. *E:* davidwyld1943@gmail.com. *Clubs:* Garrick; Berkshire Golf, Honourable Company of Edinburgh Golfers (Muirfield).
*See also* M. H. Wyld.

**WYLD, Martin Hugh,** CBE 1997; painting conservator; Chief Restorer, National Gallery, 1979–2009; *b* 14 Sept. 1944; *s* of John Wyld and Helen Leslie Melville; one *s* one *d*. *Educ:* Harrow School. Assistant Restorer, National Gallery, 1966. *Recreation:* travel. *Address:* Flat 5, 23 Clapham Common West Side, SW4 9AN. *T:* (020) 7978 5036. *Club:* MCC.
*See also* D. J. C. Wyld.

**WYLDBORE-SMITH, William Francis;** Vice Lord-Lieutenant of Wiltshire, since 2019; *b* Edenbridge, Kent, 15 Jan. 1948; *s* of John Henry Wyldbore-Smith and Robina Wyldbore-Smith (*née* Ward); *m* 1974, Prisca Faith Nourse; one *d*. *Educ:* Marlborough Coll. Admitted as solicitor, 1972; Solicitor: Theodore Goddard & Co., 1972–75; Osborne Clark, 1975–85, Partner, 1977–85; Partner, Things LLP (formerly Wood & Awdry, then Things Townsend Lee & Pembertons), 1986–2013. Chm., Wilts Out of Court Disposal Scrutiny Panel, 2014–19. Mem. Bd, Wilts and Bath HA, 1994–96. Chm., N Wilts Enterprise Agency, 1987; Mem. Bd, Great Western Enterprise, 1994. Pres., Glos and Wilts Law Soc., 2004–05. Under Sheriff, 1987–2005, DL, 2003, High Sheriff, 2013–14, Wilts. Vice Pres., Community First, 2012–; Trustee: Youth Action Wilts, 1994–2008; Plum Layton Charitable Trust, 2011–; Westcountry Rivers Trust, 2012–; Wilts Community Foundn, 2014–19 (Vice Chair, 2015–19); Marlborough Coll. Foundn, 2014– (Clerk, Council of Marlborough Coll., 2004–13); Chm., Brunel SEN Multi-Acad. Trust, 2018–. Patron, Uplands Enterprise Trust, 2014–; Vice Patron, Wilts Victoria Hist. Trust, 2014–. Literacy volunteer, Alton Close Primary Sch., Swindon, 2015–. Churchwarden. *Recreations:* gardening, family, life in the country. *Address:* Bremhill Manor, Calne, Wilts SN11 9LA. *T:* (01249) 814969. *E:* william@wyldbore.co.uk. *Club:* Brooks's.

**WYLDE, Dr Richard John,** FREng; Owner and Managing Director, Thomas Keating Ltd, scientific instrument manufacturers, since 1983; *b* London, 16 Feb. 1958; *s* of John Wylde and Nancy Wylde (*née* Stewart); *m* 1986, Lucy Wilcock; two *s*. *Educ:* Eton Coll.; Sidney Sussex Coll., Cambridge (BA Nat. Sci. 1979); Queen Mary Coll., Univ. of London (PhD Physics 1985). FIET 1999; FInstP 2013. Sen. Vis. Fellow, Dept of Phys, QMC, subseq. QMW, 1986–2002; Hon. Reader, Dept of Phys and Astronomy, Univ. of St Andrews, 2002–. Associate Scientist, ESA Planck Mission, 2009–. FREng 2013. Mem., Cave Diving Section, Nat. Speleological Soc. Liveryman, Innholders' Co., 1990–2018 (Ct Asst, 2018–). *Publications:* contrib. papers to microwave and antenna jls. *Recreations:* mapping underwater caves, ski touring, horse riding, quantum field theory. *Address:* Churchwood, Fittleworth, W Sussex RH20 1HP. *T:* (01798) 865324, *Fax:* (01403) 785464. *E:* r.wylde@terahertz.co.uk. *Clubs:* Athenaeum; Downhill Only (Wengen).

**WYLIE, Alexander Featherstonhaugh;** see Kinclaven, Hon. Lord.

**WYLIE, Andrew;** President, The Wylie Agency, since 1980; *b* 4 Nov. 1947; *s* of Craig and Angela Fowler Wylie; *m* 1969, Christina Meyer; one *s*; *m* 1980, Camilla Carlini; one *s* one *d*. *Educ*: St Paul's Sch.; Harvard Coll. (BA *magna cum laude* 1970). Established: Wylie Agency, NY, 1980; London office, 1996; Madrid office, 1999. Mem., Council on Foreign Relns, 2006–. *Recreations*: running, bicycling, tennis. *Address*: The Wylie Agency LLC, 250 West 57th Street, Suite 2114, New York, NY 10107, USA. *T*: (212) 2460069; The Wylie Agency (UK) Ltd, 17 Bedford Square, WC1B 3JA. *T*: (020) 7908 5900. *Clubs*: Knickerbocker, Harvard, River (New York); Southampton, Bathing Corporation, Meadow Club (Southampton, NY).

**WYLIE, Prof. Christopher Craig;** William Schubert Professor of Developmental Biology, and Director, Developmental Biology Division, Children's Hospital Medical Center, Cincinnati, 2000–13, now Emeritus Professor of Pediatrics; *b* 15 Sept. 1945; *s* of Joseph and Edna Wylie; *m* 1st, 1969, Christine Margaret Hall; 2nd, 1976, Janet Heasman; three *s* one *d*. *Educ*: Mombasa Primary Sch.; Duke of York Sch., Nairobi; Chislehurst and Sidcup County Grammar School for Boys; University College London (BSc, 1st cl. Hons Anatomy 1966; PhD Develtl Biol. 1971); MA Cantab 1991. Lectr in Anatomy, University College London, 1969; St George's Hospital Medical School: Sen. Lectr in Anatomy, 1975; Reader, 1983; Prof., 1985; F. J. Quick Prof. of Biol., Cambridge Univ., 1988–94, now Prof. Emeritus; Fellow, Darwin Coll., Cambridge, 1989–94; University of Minnesota: Martin Lenz Harrison Prof. of Develtl Biol. and Genetics, 1994–2000; Dir, Develtl Biol. Centre, 1994–2000; Dir, Develtl Genetics Prog., Sch. of Med., 1994–2000. Vis. Asst Prof. in Biology, Dartmouth Coll., 1975; Vis. Associate Prof. of Anatomy, Harvard Med. Sch., 1981. Editor in Chief, Development (internat. jl of develtl biol.), 1987–2003; Series Ed., Develtl and Cell Biol. Monographs, 1986–. President: Soc. for Develtl Biol., 1999–2000; Internat. Soc. for Differentiation, 2014–16. Waddington Medal, 2011, Lifetime Achievement Award, 2014, Soc. for Develtl Biol. *Publications*: (ed jtly) Development and Evolution, 1983; (ed jtly) Current Problems in Germ Cell Differentiation, 1983; (ed jtly) A History of Embryology, 1984; (ed jtly) Determinative Mechanisms in Early Development, 1986; 176 papers and review articles in sci. jls of biology. *Recreations*: relaxing with the family, racket sports, golf, history of biomedical science. *Address*: 66 Center Harvey Farm Road, Waterbury Center, VT 05677, USA.

**WYLIE, Dr Ian Martin;** Chief Executive, Royal College of Obstetricians and Gynaecologists, 2010–19; *b* 22 Oct. 1955; *s* of Charles Ronald Wylie and Margaret (*née* Catanach); *m* 1987, Siân Meryl Griffiths, *qv*; one *s*, and two step *d*. *Educ*: Bedford Modern Sch.; St Peter's Coll., Oxford (MA Hons) DPhil Oxon 1985. Manager, Homeless Services, Bloomsbury HA, 1982–84; Primary Care Officer, 1984–86, PR Consultant, 1986–88, City and Hackney HA; Press and Information Manager, Oxford CC, 1988–92; Dir, Public Relns, Oxford RHA, 1992–94; King's Fund: Hd, Communications, 1994–97; Dir, Corporate Affairs, 1997–2000; Chief Exec., BDA, 2001–05; Associate Prof., Faculty of Social Sci., Chinese Univ. of Hong Kong, 2006; Chief Exec., TreeHouse (nat. charity for autism educn), 2006–09; Sen. Officer, Service Planning and Develt, Hong Kong Hosp. Authy, 2009–10. Ind. Dir, College of Policing, 2018–. Chairman: Thames Vale Youth Orch., 2003–05; Autism Educn Trust, 2007–08. Trustee: Crouch End Festival Chorus, 2009–10; Faculty of Med. Leadership and Mgt, 2013–17. Parish Cllr, 2017–. *Publications*: Young Coleridge and the Philosophers of Nature, 1989; (with Sarah Harvey) Patient Power, 1999. *Recreations*: writing, opera, family, singing in Oxford Bach Choir. *Address*: 3 Canal Yard, Thrupp, Kidlington, Oxon OX5 1JZ. *Club*: Garrick.

**WYLIE, Rose,** OBE 2018; RA 2015; artist and painter, since 1951; *b* Hythe, Kent, 14 Oct. 1934; *d* of Alexander Forrest Wylie, OBE and Barbara Wylie (*née* Hewat Gillmon); *m* 1957, Roy Oxlade, artist, painter (*d* 2013); one *s* two *d*. *Educ*: Folkestone and Dover Sch. of Art (NDD 1956); Royal Coll. of Art (MA 1981). Foundn Lectr, Art Sch., Denbighshire Tech. Coll., 1965–68; Sen. Lectr Art Dept, Sittingbourne Coll. of Educn, 1972–79; Sen. Lectr (pt-time), Tunbridge Wells Adult Educn Centre, 1986–2000. Exhibitions include: retrospective, Jerwood Gall., Hastings, 2012; BP Spotlight, Tate Britain, 2013; Serpentine Gall., 2017; Lolita's House, David Zwirner Gall., 2018. Dupree Award, 1999, Charles Wollaston Award, 2015, RA; Paul Hamlyn Prize for Visual Arts, 2011; John Moores Painting Prize, 2014. *Recreations*: film, music, literature, art. *Address*: c/o UNION Gallery, 94 Teesdale Street, E2 6PU. *T*: (020) 3176 7303, *Fax*: (020) 7729 9461. *E*: info@union-gallery.com.

**WYLIE, Siân Meryl, (Mrs Ian Wylie);** *see* Griffiths, S. M.

**WYLLIE, Andrew,** CBE 2015; FREng; Chief Executive, Costain Group, 2005–19; *b* 24 Dec. 1962; *s* of Kenneth David Wyllie and Margaret Emily Wyllie; *m* 1990, Jane Morag Hudson; one *d*. *Educ*: Dunfermline High Sch.; Univ. of Strathclyde (BSc Hons 1984); London Business Sch. (MBA 1993). CEng 1991; FICE; FREng 2009; CCMI 2009. With Taylor Woodrow, 1984–2005, Man. Dir, Taylor Woodrow Construction Ltd, 2001–05. Non-executive Director: Scottish Water, 2009–17; Yorkshire Water, 2017–. Pres., ICE, 2018–19 (Vice Pres., 2015–16; Sen. Vice Pres., 2017–18). Fellow, British American Project, 2003–. FInstD.

**WYLLIE, Prof. Andrew David Hamilton,** FRS 1995; FRSE; FMedSci; Professor of Pathology, now Emeritus, and Fellow of St John's College, Cambridge University, 1998–2011. *Educ*: Aberdeen Univ. (BSc 1964; MB ChB 1967; PhD 1975). MRCP 1971; MRCPath 1975, FRCPath 1987; FRCPE 1993. Res. Fellow, Hammersmith Hosp., 1969; Res. Fellow, then Lectr in Pathol., Aberdeen Univ., 1970–72; Edinburgh University: Lectr, 1972–77; Sen. Lectr, 1977–85; Reader, 1985–92; Prof. of Experimental Pathology, 1992–98. FRSE 1991; FMedSci 1998. Hon. DSc Aberdeen, 1998. *Publications*: scientific papers on colorectal cancer and apoptosis.

**WYLLIE, Cameron Dickson;** Principal, George Heriot's School, 2014–17; *b* Edinburgh, 14 April 1957; *s* of George Wyllie and Janet Wyllie; partner, Kevin Stevens. *Educ*: George Heriot's Sch.; Univ. of Edinburgh (MA Hons English Lang. and Lit. 1979; DipEd 1980); Moray House Coll. (PGCE (Dist.) 1980). Teacher of English, 1980–91, Housemaster, 1988–91, Daniel Stewart's and Melville Coll.; George Heriot's School: Hd of English, 1991–95; Asst Hd Teacher, 1995–2002; Hd, Sen. Sch., 2002–14. Trustee: Circle, Scotland, 2018–; ESU, Scotland, 2018–; Scottish Schs Debating, 2018–; David Hume Inst., 2018–. Scottish schs' debating coach, 1991–97. Columnist: The Scotsman, 2018–; Holyrood Mag., 2018–. *Publications*: (ed) La Crème de la Crème, 2001. *Recreations*: cinema, Scottish art, American fiction, politics, food and drink, friends, gardening, blogging. *Address*: 3 Morton Street, Joppa, Edinburgh EH15 2EW. *T*: 07790 377428. *E*: cameron.d.wyllie@gmail.com. *W*: www.ahouseinjoppa.wordpress.com.

**WYLLIE, Very Rev. Hugh Rutherford;** Moderator of the General Assembly of the Church of Scotland, 1992–93; Minister at the Old Parish Church of Hamilton, 1981–2000; *b* 11 Oct. 1934; *s* of late Hugh McPhee Wyllie and Elizabeth Buchanan; *m* 1962, Eileen Elizabeth Cameron, MA Hons; two *d*. *Educ*: Shawlands Acad., Glasgow; Hutchesons' Grammar Sch., Glasgow; Univ. of Glasgow (MA; Pitcairn Miller Frame Awards, 1961, 1962; Frame Divinity Awards, 1991, 1992). The Union Bank of Scotland, 1951–53 (MCIBS). RAF Nat. Service, 1953–55. Licensed and ordained by Presbytery of Glasgow, 1962; Asst Minister, Glasgow Cathedral, 1962–65; Minister: Dunbeth Church, Coatbridge, 1965–72; Cathcart South Church, Glasgow, 1972–81. General Assembly: Convener: Stewardship and Budget Cttee, 1978–83; Stewardship and Finance Bd, 1983–86; Assembly Council, 1987–91; Member: Bd of Nomination to Church Chairs, 1985–91, 1993–99; Bd of Practice and Procedure, 1991–95; Bd of Communication, 1999–2003. Presbytery of Hamilton: Moderator, 1989–90; Convener, Business Cttee, 1991–95; Chaplain: Royal British Legion (Hamilton Br.), 1981–2001; Lanarks Burma Star Assoc., 1983–2001; Strathclyde Police 'Q' Div., 1983–2001. Master, Hamilton Hosp., 1982–2001; Vice-Chm., Lanarkshire Healthcare NHS Trust, 1996–99 (non-exec. Dir, 1995–99); Trustee, Lanarkshire Primary Care NHS Trust, 1999–2001. Established Centre for Information for the Unemployed, Hamilton, 1983; introduced Dial-a-Fact on drugs and alcohol, 1986; established Hamilton Church History Project, 1984–87; Pres., Glasgow Univ. SCM, 1958; Chm., SCM Scottish Council, 1958. Mem. Council, Scout Assoc., 1993–2004. Pres., Hamilton Burns Club, 1990. Hon. Freeman, District of Hamilton, 1992; Freeman, City of Winnipeg, Canada, 1992. Dr William Barclay Meml Fund Lectr, 1994. Hon. FCIBS 1997. Hon. DD Aberdeen, 1993. George and Thomas Hutcheson Award, Hutchesons' Grammar Sch., Glasgow, 2002. *Recreations*: gardening, the internet. *Address*: 18 Chantinghall Road, Hamilton ML3 8NP.

**WYLLIE, Prof. Peter John,** PhD; FRS 1984; Professor of Geology, California Institute of Technology, 1983–99, now Emeritus (Chairman, Division of Geological and Planetary Sciences, 1983–87; Academic Officer, 1994–99); *b* 8 Feb. 1930; *s* of George William and Beatrice Gladys Wyllie (*née* Weaver); *m* 1956, Frances Rosemary Blair; one *s* one *d* (and one *s* one *d* decd). *Educ*: Univ. of St Andrews. BSc 1952 (Geology and Physics); BSc 1955 (1st cl. hons Geology); PhD 1958 (Geology). Nat. Service, 1948–49: Aircraftsman First Cl. (Best Recruit, Basic Trng, Padgate, 1948). Heavyweight boxing champion, RAF, Scotland, 1949. Glaciologist, British W Greenland Expedn, 1950; Geologist, British N Greenland Expedn, 1952–54; Asst Lectr in Geology, Univ. of St Andrews, 1955–56; Research Asst, 1956–58, Asst Prof. of Geochemistry, 1958–59, Pennsylvania State Univ.; Research Fellow in Chemistry, 1959–60, Lectr in Exptl Petrology, 1960–61, Leeds Univ.; Associate Prof. of Petrology, Pennsylvania State Univ., 1961–65 (Acting Head, Dept Geochem. and Mineralogy, 1962–63); University of Chicago: Prof. of Petrology and Geochem., 1965–77; Master Phys. Scis, Collegiate Div., Associate Dean of Coll. and of Phys. Scis Div., 1972–73; Homer J. Livingston Prof., 1978–83; Chm., Dept of Geophysical Scis, 1979–82. Louis Murray Vis. Fellow, Univ. of Cape Town, 1987; Hon. Prof., Chinese Univ. of Geosciences, Beijing, 1996–. Man. Ed., Jl Petrology, 1965–67; Ed., Jl Geol., 1967–83; Ed.-in-Chief, Minerals and Rocks monograph series (25 vols), 1967–88. President: Mineralogical Soc. of America, 1977–78 (Vice Pres., 1976–77); Internat. Mineralogical Assoc., 1986–90 (Vice Pres., 1978–86); Internat. Union of Geodesy and Geophysics, 1995–99 (Vice Pres., 1991–95). Foreign Associate, US Nat. Acad. of Scis, 1981 (Chm. Cttee on Solid-Earth Sciences and Society, report published 1993); Fellow: Amer. Acad. of Arts and Scis, 1982; Amer. Geophys. Union; Geol Soc. Amer.; Mineral Soc. Amer., 1965; Corresp. Fellow, Edin. Geol. Soc., 1985–; Hon. Fellow, IUGG, 2015; Foreign Fellow: Indian Geophys. Union, 1987; Indian Nat. Sci. Acad., 1991; Nat. Acad. of Scis, India, 1992; Foreign Member: Russian (formerly USSR) Acad. of Scis, 1988; Chinese Acad. of Scis, 1996; Academia Europaea, 1996. Hon. Member: Mineralogical Soc. of GB and Ireland, 1986–; Mineralogical Soc. of Russia, 1986–; German Geological Soc., 2001–. Hon. DSc St Andrews, 1974. Polar Medal, 1954; Mineralogical Soc. of America Award, 1965; Quantrell Award for excellence in undergrad. teaching, Univ. of Chicago, 1979; Wollaston Medal, Geol Soc. of London, 1982; Abraham-Gottlob-Werner Medal, German Mineral. Soc., 1987; Roebling Medal, Mineralogical Soc. of America, 2001; Leopold von Buch Medal, Deutschen Geologischen Ges., 2001. *Publications*: Ultramafic and Related Rocks, 1967; The Dynamic Earth, 1971; The Way the Earth Works, 1976; (ed) Solid-Earth Sciences and Society, 1993; numerous papers in sci. jls. *Address*: Division of Geological and Planetary Sciences, B170 California Institute of Technology, Pasadena, CA 91125, USA.

**WYMAN, Peter Lewis,** CBE 2006; DL; FCA; Chairman: Sir Richard Sutton Ltd (formerly Sir Richard Sutton's Settled Estates), since 2011 (Director, since 2010); Care Quality Commission, since 2016; *b* 26 Feb. 1950; *s* of late John Bernard Wyman and Joan Dorethea Wyman (*née* Beighton); *m* 1978, Joy Alison Foster; one *s* one *d*. *Educ*: Epsom Coll. ACA 1973, FCA 1978. Chartered Accountant; articled clerk, Ogden Parsons & Co. and Harmood Banner, 1968–73; Deloitte Haskins & Sells, then Coopers & Lybrand, subseq. PricewaterhouseCoopers LLP: Manager, 1973–78; Partner, 1978–2010; Hd of Tax, 1993–98; Hd of External Relations, 1998–2000; Hd of Regulatory Policy, 2003–04; Hd of Professional Affairs and Regulatory Policy, 2004–09; Global Leader, Public Policy and Regulatory Matters, 2008–10; Chm., Yeovil District Hospital NHS Foundn Trust, 2011–15. Sen. Advr, Albright Stonebridge Gp LLC, 2010–15; Principal, Peter Wyman Private Clients, 2010–15. Mem. Cttee, London Soc. of Chartered Accountants, 1981–90 (Chm., 1987–88); Institute of Chartered Accountants in England and Wales: Mem. Council, 1991–2009; Chm., Faculty of Taxation, 1991–95; Chm., Educn and Trng Directorate, 1995–99; Chm., Professional Standards Office, 1999–2000; Mem., Exec. Cttee, 1996–2003; Vice Pres., 2000–01; Dep. Pres., 2001–02; Pres., 2002–03; Chm., Outstanding Achievement Award Selection Panel, 2011–14; International Federation of Accountants: Member: Transnat. Auditors' Cttee, 2006–08; Planning and Finance Cttee, 2006–08; Internat. Regulatory Liaison Cttee, 2008–10. Chairman: Common Content for Accountancy Qualifications Steering Gp, 2002–06; Consultative Cttee of Accountancy Bodies, 2002–03; Rev. Gp, Financial Reporting Adv. Bd, 2010–11; Dep. Chm., Financial Reporting Council, 2002–03. Special Advr on Deregulation and Taxation to Parly Under-Sec. of State for Corporate Affairs, 1993–94; Member: Deregulation Task Force, 1994–97; Panel on Takeovers and Mergers, 2002–03. External Overseer, Contributions Agency/IR Jt Working Prog., 1995–97; Member: Regulation of Accounting Profession Implementation Working Party, 1999–2001; Steering Gp, Rev. of Regulatory Régime of Accountancy Profession, 2003–04; Audit, Risk and Governance Cttee, RSA, 2005–11; EU Adv. Gp, City of London, 2004–09; Bd, Companies Hse, 2011–16 (Chm., Audit Cttee, 2011–16); Supervisory Bd, Focal & Co., 2012–14; Ind. non-exec. Dir, Pay.UK (formerly New Payment Systems Operator Ltd), 2017–; Chm., Public Responsibility Oversight Bd, Salad Gp, 2018–. Chm., Ind. Review of Funding of Debt Advice in England, Wales, Scotland and NI, 2017–18; Vice Chm., Ind. Review of Breast Cancer Screening, 2018–. Chairman: Somerset Community Foundn, 2009–15 (Dir, 2003–04; Vice-Pres., 2015–); Adv. Bd, Pasco Risk Mgt Ltd, 2011–13 (Mem., 2010–13). Dir, City of London Sinfonia, 2011–15. FRSA. Freeman, City of London, 1988; Freeman, 1988, Master, 2006–07, Almoner, 2011–14, Chartered Accountants' Co. Member: Council, Univ. of Bath, 2003–06 and 2009–17 (Mem., Finance Cttee, 2003–17; Treas., 2011–17; Vice-Chm., 2015–17); Adv. Bd, BPP Business Sch., 2010–11; Develt Adv. Council, Inst. Econ. Affairs, 2011–13. Gov., Aylwin Girls' Sch., Southwark, 2001–06 (Vice-Chm., 2001–03; Chm., 2003–06); Chm., F & GP Cttee, Harris Acad., Bermondsey, 2006–07; Trustee, Five Bridges Sch., Vauxhall, 2002–05. Trustee, Hestercombe Gdns Trust, 2010–11; Vice-Patron, Almhouse Assoc., 2017–. DL Somerset, 2015. Award for Outstanding Achievement, ICAEW, 2006; Award for Outstanding Industry Contribution, Accountancy Age, 2008;

Chancellor's Medal, Univ. of Bath, 2018. *Publications:* various professional jls on taxation and accountancy matters. *Recreations:* music, history, family history, equestrian sports, gardening. *Address:* Plainsfield Court, Plainsfield, Over Stowey, Somerset TA5 1HH. *T:* 07711 776128; Flat 1, Priory House, 3 Burgon Street, EC4V 5DR.

**WYN GRIFFITH, Martin Peter;** Commercial Director, Department for Business, Innovation and Skills, 2009–10; *b* 2 Feb. 1957; *s* of Hugh and Simone Wyn Griffith; *m* 2006, Jo; one step *s* one step *d*. *Educ:* Manchester Grammar Sch.; Univ. of Bristol (BA Jt Hons); Henley Mgt Coll. (MBA). EMI Records Ltd, 1978–84; Owner and Man. Dir, AWGO Ltd, 1984–92; Mktg Dir, EMI Music, 1994–96; Business Advr, 1996–97, Manager, 1997–99, and Chief Exec., 1999–2001, Business Link Wilts; Chief Exec., Business Link Berks and Wilts, 2001–02; Chief Exec., Small Business Service, DTI, later Enterprise Directorate, BERR, 2002–08; Dir, Service Transformation, BIS, 2008–09. Non-exec. Dir, Inst. of Family Business Res. Foundn, 2011–; Chm. Trustees, UnLtd, 2013–18 (Trustee, 2008–18). *Publications:* contribs on entrepreneurship in entertainment and the future for multimedia to Jl Strategic Mgt. *Recreations:* motor racing, ski-ing, golf, Manchester United.

**WYN-ROGERS, Catherine;** mezzo-soprano; *b* 24 July 1954; *d* of Geoffrey Wyn Rogers and Helena Rogers (*née* Webster). *Educ:* St Helena High Sch. for Girls, Chesterfield; Royal Coll. of Music. Studied with Meriel St Clair, Ellis Keeler and Diane Forlano. Performances: with various European orchs and choirs, incl. BBC SO, LPO, CBSO, RSNO, BBC Scottish Orch., RLPO, Accademia di Santa Cecilia, Rome, and Concertgebouw; with various opera cos incl. Royal Opera, Scottish Opera, WNO, Opera North, ENO, Bavarian State Opera and Teatro Real, Madrid; frequent appearances at BBC Proms, Aldeburgh, Salzburg and Edinburgh Fests; Glyndebourne début, 2013. Numerous recordings. *Address:* c/o Askonas Holt, 15 Fetter Lane, EC4A 1BW.

**WYNDHAM,** family name of **Baron Egremont and Leconfield**.

**WYNDHAM, Henry Mark;** Co-founder, Clore Wyndham Fine Art Ltd, since 2016; *b* London, 19 Aug. 1953; *s* of Hon. Mark Hugh Wyndham, OBE, MC and late Anne Wyndham; *m* 1978, Rachel Sarah Pritchard; three *s*. *Educ:* Eton; Univ. Paris Sorbonne. Dir, Christies, 1982; Proprietor, Henry Wyndham Fine Art, 1987–93; Chairman: Sotheby's UK, 1994–2004; Sotheby's Europe, 1997–2016. Trustee: Glyndebourne, 2004–14; Chatsworth House Trust, 2004–; Towner Art Gall., Eastbourne, 2014–; Imperial War Mus., 2016–; Samuel Courtauld Trust, 2016–. Mem., Curatorial Adv. Gp, Harley Foundn, 2016–. Member, International Council: Metropolitan Mus. of Art, 2017–; V&A Mus., 2017–. Mem. Court, Goldsmiths' Co., 2008–12. *Recreations:* many sports, tennis, golf, supporting Brighton and Hove Albion, travelling, music, going to the bottle bank, bonfires, growing vegetables, picking up rubbish off beaches on Colonsay, spending time with my family. *Address:* 18 St Leonards Terrace, SW3 4QG. *E:* henry@henrywyndham.com. *Clubs:* MCC (Mem. Cttee. 1988–91; Chm., Arts and Liby Cttee, 1993–98), White's, Pratt's, Saints & Sinners, Aberdino, Grillions, Oswald's.

**WYNESS, James Alexander Davidson;** Senior Independent Director, Spirent (formerly Bowthorpe) plc, 1999–2006 (Director, 1979–2006; Chairman, 2002); *b* 27 Aug. 1937; *s* of late Dr James Alexander Davidson Wyness and Millicent Margaret (*née* Beaton); *m* 1966, Josephine Margaret Worsdell; three *d*. *Educ:* Stockport Grammar Sch.; Emmanuel Coll., Cambridge (MA, LLB). National Service, 2 Lieut, RA. Articled Clerk, A. F. & R. W. Tweedie, 1964–66 (qualified 1965); Linklaters & Paines, 1966–97: Partner, 1970–97; Managing Partner, 1987–91; Jt Sen. Partner, 1991–93; Sen. Partner, 1994–96. Dir, Saracens Ltd, 1996–2008 (Chm., 1996–2002). Mem., Law Soc. Life Member: Saracens FC (RFU) (Captain, 1962–65); Middx RFU (County Champions, 1996); London Div. RFU. *Recreations:* visiting France, growing vegetables, Rugby football, reading. *Address:* c/o Linklaters, One Silk Street, EC2Y 8HQ.

**WYNFORD,** 9th Baron *cr* 1829, of Wynford Eagle, co. Dorset; **John Philip Robert Best;** chartered surveyor; Executive Partner, Wynford Eagle Partners, running family estate in Dorset, since 1981; *b* 23 Nov. 1950; *o s* of 8th Baron Wynford, MBE and Anne Daphne Mametz (*née* Minshull Ford); *S* father, 2002; *m* 1981, Fenella Christian Mary Danks; one *s* one *d*. *Educ:* Radley Coll.; Keele Univ. (BA Hons 1974); RAC Cirencester (MRAC 1977). MRICS (Land Agency Div.) 1979. *Recreations:* reading, music, fine claret, 17th century oak furniture. *Heir: s* Hon. Harry Robert Francis Best, *b* 9 May 1987. *Address:* The Manor, Wynford Eagle, Dorchester, Dorset DT2 0ER. *T:* (01300) 320763.

**WYNFORD-THOMAS, Prof. David,** PhD, DSc; FRCPath; Pro-Vice Chancellor, Dean of Medicine and Head of College of Medicine, Biological Sciences and Psychology, University of Leicester, 2008–15; *b* 28 Feb. 1955; *s* of Richard and Eunice Wynford-Thomas; *m* 2004, Theresa; one *s* two *d*. *Educ:* Welsh Nat. Sch. of Medicine (MB BCh Hons 1978; PhD 1981); DSc Wales 1995. FRCPath 1996. MRC/NIH Postdoctoral Res. Fellow, Univ. of Colorado, 1982–83; University of Wales College of Medicine: Lectr, 1983–86, Sen. Lectr, 1986–92, in Pathology; Prof. and Hd, Dept of Pathology, 1992–2005; Dean and Hd of Sch. of Medicine, Cardiff Univ., 2005–08. Hon. Consultant in Molecular Pathology, 1986–. FMedSci 2003. Subject Editor, British Jl of Cancer, 1995–. *Publications:* (ed with E. D. Williams) Thyroid Tumours, 1989; co-author of over 150 peer-reviewed papers in scientific and med. jls. *Recreations:* chess, walking, reading.

**WYNN,** family name of **Baron Newborough**.

**WYNN, Sir (David) Watkin W.;** *see* Williams-Wynn.

**WYNN, Terence;** Member (Lab) North West Region, England, European Parliament, 1999–2006 (Merseyside East, 1989–94, Merseyside East and Wigan, 1994–99); *b* 27 June 1946; *s* of Ernest Wynn and Lily (*née* Hitchen); *m* 1967, Doris Ogden; one *s* one *d*. *Educ:* Leigh Technical Coll.; Riversdale Technical Coll., Liverpool (OND); Liverpool Polytechnic (Combined Chief Engrs Cert); Salford Univ. (MSc Manpower Studies and Industrial Relns 1984). Seagoing Marine Engr Officer, MN, 1962–74; Engr Surveyor, ICI, Runcorn, 1975–76; Ship Repair Man., Manchester Dry Docks, 1976–78; Trng Advr, Shipbuilding ITB, 1978–82; Sen. Trng Exec., Marine Trng Assoc., 1982–89. Mem., Ethics Cttee, EC, 2010–. Trustee, Action for Children (formerly NCH), 2007–13. Adjunct Sen. Fellow, Nat. Centre for Res. on Europe, Univ. of Canterbury, NZ, 2007–. Methodist local preacher, 1978–. Mem. Bd, Trustees for Methodist Church Purposes, 2007–15; Mem., Central Finance Bd, Methodist Church, 2014–. Sec., Billy Boston Statue Trust, 2014–17. Performed playwright: Gerrumonside, Turnpike Theatre Co., Leigh, 1995; For The Love of the Game, Acad. of Live and Recording Arts, Mill at the Pier, Wigan, 2014, Chorley Little Th., 2018. *Publications:* Onward Christian Socialist, 1996; Where are the Prophets, 2007. *Recreation:* Rugby League supporter.

**WYNN-EVANS, Charles Andrew;** Partner, Dechert LLP, since 1997; a Fee-paid Employment Judge, Midlands West Region, since 2009; *b* Royal Leamington Spa, 12 Dec. 1967; *s* of Anthony Wynn-Evans and late Margaret Wynn-Evans; *m* 1997, Karen Wendy Alexandra, (Alex), McColl; one *s* one *d*. *Educ:* King Henry VIII Sch., Coventry; Univ. of Bristol (LLB 1988); Coll. of Law, Chester; Merton Coll., Oxford (BCL 1990). Titmuss, Sainer & Webb, later Dechert LLP: Trainee Solicitor, 1990–92; admitted solicitor, 1992; Solicitor, 1992–97. Member, Employment Law Committee: Law Soc. of England and Wales, 2007–; City of London Law Soc., 2008–. Ind. Person, London Bor. of Southwark, 2015–. *Publications:* Blackstone's Guide to the New Transfer of Undertakings Legislation, 2006; The Law of TUPE Transfers, 2013; articles in various jls. *Recreations:* tennis, cricket, watching Rugby, tending an allotment. *Address:* Dechert LLP, 160 Queen Victoria Street, EC4V 4QQ. *T:* (020) 7184 7545, *Fax:* (020) 7184 7001. *E:* charles.wynn-evans@dechert.com.

**WYNN OWEN, Philip,** CB 2008; Member, European Court of Auditors, Luxembourg, since 2014; *b* 10 June 1960; *s* of late Emrys and Ruth Wynn Owen; *m* 1989, Elizabeth Mary Fahey; three *s*. *Educ:* Maidstone Grammar Sch.; University Coll., Oxford (MA Mod. Hist.); London Business Sch. (MBA Dist.); Harvard Business Sch. (AMP 2008). HM Treasury, 1981–99: Asst Private Sec. to Chancellor of Exchequer, 1984–86; Private Sec. to Perm. Sec., 1991–93; Team Leader: Transport Team, 1993–96; Tax and Budget Team, 1996; Tax Policy Team, 1997–99; Director: Regulatory Impact Unit, Cabinet Office, 1999–2003; Financial Sector, HM Treasury, 2003–04; Director General: Strategy and Pensions, and Chair, Shared Services Business, DWP, 2004–09; Nat. Climate Change and Consumer Support, DECC, 2009–11; Dir Gen., Internat. Climate Change and Energy Efficiency, DECC, 2011–13; Acting Perm. Sec., DECC, 2012–13. Alternate Dir, EIB, 1994–96. Dean, Sustainable Use of Natural Resources Chamber, Eur. Ct of Auditors, 2016–18. Non-exec. Dir, Maidstone and Tunbridge Wells NHS Trust, 2008–13 (Dep. Chm., 2009–13). *Recreations:* cricket, tennis, running. *Clubs:* MCC; Leigh Cricket (Kent).

**WYNNE, Sir Graham (Robert),** Kt 2010; CBE 2003; Chief Executive, Royal Society for the Protection of Birds, 1998–2010; *b* 29 May 1950; *s* of late Arthur Robert Wynne and of Joan Brenda Wynne (*née* Chapman); *m* 1994, Janet Anne Stewart. *Educ:* Brentwood Sch., Essex; Pembroke Coll., Cambridge (BA Hons 1971; MA). DipTP 1975; MRTPI (RTPI 1975). Various planning posts, Lewisham, 1972–78; Shoreditch Area Team Leader, 1978–86, Hd, Planning Policy, 1986–87, Hackney; Reserves Dir, 1987–90, Conservation Dir, 1990–98, RSPB. Sen. Advr to Prince of Wales' Internat. Sustainability Unit, 2010–. Member: UK Biodiversity Steering Gp, 1994–2000; UK Round Table on Sustainable Develt, 1998–2000; Sustainable Develt Commn, 2000–03; Policy Commn on Future of Farming and Food, 2001–02; Cttee on Climate Change (Adaptation), 2009–18. Mem. Council, Birdlife Internat., 1998–2010. Trustee, Green Alliance, 2011–. *Publications:* Biodiversity Challenge: an agenda for conservation action in the UK, 1995; (contrib.) Conservation Science and Action, 1997; contrib. various RSPB and local authy pubns. *Recreations:* natural history, football, restoring a C16th house, gardening.

**WYRKO, David John,** QPM 1995; DL; Chief Constable of Leicestershire, 1997–2002; *b* 15 July 1948; *s* of late Wasyl John Wyrko and of Stella Doreen Wyrko (*née* Witts); *m* 1973, Beryl Case; one *s* one *d*. *Educ:* City of Bath Technical Sch.; Univ. of Surrey (BSc Electrical, Electronic and Control Engineering 1969). Police Constable to Chief Superintendent, Northants, 1972–91; Asst Chief Constable, Northants, 1991–93; Dep. Chief Constable, Leics, 1993–97. Co-Dir, Police Extended Interviews, 1999–2002. FBI Nat. Acad., Quantico, 1984; Cabinet Office Top Mgt Prog., 1995. Hon. Treas., 1994–98, Chm., Inf. Mgt Cttee, 1997–2000, ACPO; Mem., PITO Bd, 1997–2002. Sen. Vis. Fellow, Scarman Centre, Univ. of Leicester, 2003–. Council Mem., Shrievalty Assoc., 2005–07. Mem. Council, Leics and Rutland Wildlife Trust, 2007–11. Pres., Hope Against Cancer, 2012– (Chm. Trustees, 2007–11). High Sheriff, 2008–09, DL 2010, Leics. BUniv Surrey, 2011. *Recreations:* cabinet making, golf, cycling, gardening. *Address:* c/o Leicestershire Constabulary HQ, St John's, Narborough, Leics LE9 5BX. *T:* (0116) 222 2222.

**WYVER, Clare;** *see* Paterson, C.

# XYZ

**XI JINPING**; General Secretary, Central Committee, Communist Party of China, since 2012; President, People's Republic of China, since 2013 (Vice-President, 2008–13); Chairman, Central Military Commission, since 2013 (Vice-Chairman, 2010–13); *b* Fuping Co., Shaanxi Province, June 1953; *s* of Xi Zhongxun; *m* 1987, Peng Liyuan; one *d*. *Educ*: Tsinghua Univ., Beijing (BSc Chem. Engrg 1979; LLD 2002). Work as an educated youth, Liangjiahe Bde, Shaanxi Province, 1969–75; joined Communist Party, 1974; Sec., Gen. Office of State Council and Gen. Office of Central Mil. Commn (as officer in active service), 1979–82; Communist Party of China: Dep. Sec., 1982–83, Sec., 1983–85, Zhengding Co. Cttee, Hebei Province; Mem., Standing Cttee of Municipal Party Cttee and Vice Mayor, Xiamen, Fujian Province, 1985–88; Secretary: Ningde Prefectural Cttee, Fujian Province, 1988–90; Fuzhou Municipal Cttee, 1990–96; Fujian Provincial Committee: Mem., Standing Cttee, 1993–95; Dep. Sec., 1995–2002; Chm., Standing Cttee, Fuzhou Municipal People's Congress, Fujian Province, 1990–96; Actg Gov., 1999–2000, Gov., 2000–02, Fujian Province; Dep. Sec., 2002, Sec., 2002–07, Zhejiang Provincial Cttee, and Actg Gov., Zhejiang Province, 2002–03; Chm., Standing Cttee, Zhejiang Provincial People's Congress, 2003–07; Sec., Shanghai Municipal Cttee, 2007; Central Committee, Communist Party of China: Member: Standing Cttee of Central Cttee, 2007–10 and 2012–, Central Cttee, 2012–, Political Bureau; Secretariat, 2007–10; Pres., Party Sch., 2007–10; Sec. Gen., Nat. Congress, 2012–. *Publications*: The Governance of China, 2014. *Address*: Office of the President, Zhong Nan Hai, Beijing, People's Republic of China.

**YACOUB, Sir Magdi (Habib)**, OM 2014; Kt 1992; FRCS; FRS 1999; British Heart Foundation Professor of Cardiothoracic Surgery, National Heart and Lung Institute (formerly Cardiothoracic Institute), Imperial College London (formerly British Postgraduate Medical Federation, University of London), since 1986; Director of Research, Magdi Yacoub Institute (formerly Harefield Research Foundation), Heart Science Centre, since 2001; *b* Cairo, 16 Nov. 1935; *m*; one *s* two *d*. *Educ*: Cairo University. FRCS, FRCSE, FRCSGlas, 1962; LRCP 1966, MRCP 1986, Hon. FRCP 1990. Rotating House Officer, Cairo Univ. Hosp., 1958–59; Surgical Registrar, Postgrad. Surgical Unit, Cairo Univ., 1959–61; Resident Surgical Officer, 1962–63, Surgical Registrar, 1963–64, London Chest Hosp.; Rotating Sen. Surgical Registrar, Nat. Heart and Chest Hosps, 1964–68; Asst Prof. of Cardiothoracic Surgery, Chicago Univ., 1968–69; Consultant Cardiothoracic Surgeon, Harefield Hosp., Middx, 1969–92, Royal Brompton and Harefield NHS Trust, 1986–2001 (now Hon.); Consultant Cardiac Surgeon, Nat. Heart Hosp., 1973–89. Hon. Consultant: Royal Free Hosp. Med. Sch.; King Edward's Coll. of Medicine, Lahore, Pakistan; Hon. Prof. of Surgery, Univ. of Sienna; Hon. Prof. of Cardiac Surgery, Charing Cross and Westminster Hosp. Med. Schs. Has developed innovations in heart and heart-lung transplants. Founder and Pres., Chain of Hope, 1995–. Mem., Soc. Thoracic Surgeons; FRSocMed; Founder FMedSci 1998. Hon. DSc: Brunel, 1985; Amer. Univ. at Cairo, 1989; Loughborough, 1990; Hon. MCh Cardiff, 1986; Hon. PhD Lund, 1988. Editor: Annual of Cardiac Surgery; Current Opinion in Cardiology: coronary artery surgery. *Publications*: papers on pulmonary osteoarthropath, aortic valve homografts, surgical treatment of ischaemic heart disease, valve repairs, and related subjects. *Address*: Imperial College London, Heart Science Centre, Harefield, Middx UB9 6JH.

**YAKOVLEV, Prof. Alexandre**, PhD, DSc; FREng, FIET, FIEEE; Professor of Computer System Design, Newcastle University, since 2000; *b* St Petersburg, 9 April 1956; *s* of Vladimir Yakovlev and Irina Yakovlev; *m* 1980, Maria Rybak; one *s*. *Educ*: St Petersburg Electrical Engrg Inst. (MSc 1979; PhD 1982); Newcastle Univ. (DSc 2006). CEng 2015; FIET 2015; FIEEE 2016. Lectr (Asst Prof.), 1982–87, Dozent (Associate Prof.), 1987–90, St Petersburg Electrical Engrg Inst.; Lectr, 1991–97, Reader, 1997–2000, Newcastle Univ. FREng 2017. *Publications*: Self-Timed Control of Concurrent Processes, 1990; Concurrent Hardware: the theory and practice of self-timed design, 1993; Hardware Design and Petrinets, 2000; Logic Synthesis of Asynchronous Controllers and Interfaces, 2002. *Recreations*: family, genealogy, theatre, cinema, languages. *Address*: School of Engineering, Newcastle University, Newcastle upon Tyne NE1 7RU. *T*: (0191) 208 8184. *E*: alex.yakovlev@ncl.ac.uk.

**YALE, David Eryl Corbet**, FBA 1980; Reader in English Legal History, Cambridge University, 1969–93, now Emeritus; Fellow, Christ's College, Cambridge, since 1950; *b* 31 March 1928; *s* of Lt-Col J. C. R. Yale and Mrs Beatrice Yale (*née* Breese); *m* 1959, Elizabeth Ann, *d* of C. A. B. Brett, Belfast; two *s*. *Educ*: Malvern Coll., Worcs; Queens' Coll., Cambridge (BA 1949, LLB 1950, MA 1953). Called to the Bar, Inner Temple, 1951, Bencher, 2009; Asst Lectr and Lectr in Law, Cambridge Univ., 1952–69. Pres., Selden Soc., 1994–97. Hon. QC 2000. *Publications*: various, mainly in field of legal history. *Recreation*: fishing. *Address*: Christ's College, Cambridge CB2 3BU. *T*: (01223) 334900; Saethon, Porthmadog, Gwynedd LL49 9UR. *T*: (01766) 512129.

**YALLOP, (John) Mark**; Chair, Fixed Income, Currencies and Commodities Market Standards Board, since 2016; *b* Farnborough, Kent, 16 March 1960; *s* of Howard John and Mary Kathleen Yallop; *m* 1988, Rosemary Jane Moore; one *s* one *d*. *Educ*: Allhallows Coll., Devon; University Coll., Oxford (MA Hons Natural Scis 1982). Banking exec., Baring Brothers & Co. Ltd, 1982–85; Asst Dir, 1985–89, Dir, 1989–94, Morgan Grenfell & Co. Ltd; Deutsche Bank: Chief Operating Officer, Global Mkts, 1995–2000; Global Head, Money Markets/Repo, 1997–2000; Chief Operating Officer, Corporate and Investment Bank, 2001–02, Deutsche Bank Gp, 2002–04; Chief Operating Officer, ICAP plc, 2005–11; UK Chief Exec., UBS AG, 2013–14. Bank of England: Mem. Bd, Prudential Regulation Authy, 2014–17; Ext. Mem., Prudential Regulation Cttee, 2017–Nov. 2020; Mem. Bd, Financial Mkt Infrastructure Bd, 2017–. Ind. Dir, OpenFin Inc., 2017–. Non-exec. Dir, Centre for Social Justice, 2012–16. Chm., Develt Bd, University Coll., Oxford, 2016–18; Mem., Create the Change Bd, Francis Crick Inst., 2012–16. *Recreations*: ski-ing, sailing, cycling, painting, opera. *Address*: FICC Market Standards Board, 125 Old Broad Street, EC2N 1AR. *T*: (020) 3961 6156. *E*: mark.yallop@fmsb.com. *Clubs*: Royal Ocean Racing, Royal Dart Yacht.

**YAM Yee-Kwan, David**; a Judge of the Court of First Instance of the High Court (formerly Judge of the High Court), Hong Kong, 1994–2012; *b* 4 Oct. 1948; *s* of Yam Fat-Shing Frank and Ng Yuet-Hing Nora; *m* 1977, Dr Stella T. P. Wong; two *s*. *Educ*: Hong Kong Univ. (BSc 1971; LLB 1975); Inns of Court Sch. of Law. Called to the Bar, Middle Temple, and to Hong Kong Bar, 1976; in practice, 1977–87; District Court Judge, 1987–94. Chm., Insider Dealing Tribunal, 1995–97. *Recreations*: golf, music, travelling. *T*: 92727314. *Clubs*: Hong Kong Jockey, Shek O Country (Hong Kong).

**YAMANAKA, Prof. Shinya**, MD, PhD; Senior Investigator and L. K. Whittier Foundation Investigator, Gladstone Institute of Cardiovascular Disease, San Francisco, since 2007; Professor of Anatomy, University of California, San Francisco; Director, since 2008, and Professor, since 2012, Center for iPS Cell Research and Application, Kyoto University; *b* Osaka, Japan, 4 Sept. 1962; *s* of Shozaburo and Minako Yamanaka; *m* Chika; two *d*. *Educ*: Tennoji High Sch.; Kobe Univ. Sch. of Medicine (MD 1987); Osaka City Univ. Grad. Sch. of Medicine (PhD 1993). Resident, Osaka Nat. Hosp., 1987–89; Postdoctoral Fellow, 1993–95, Staff Res. Investigator, 1995–96, Gladstone Inst. of Cardiovascular Disease, San Francisco; Asst Prof., Dept of Pharmacol., Osaka City Univ., 1996–99; Associate Prof., 1999–2003, Prof., 2003–04, Nara Inst. of Sci. and Technol., Nara; Prof., Inst. for Frontier Med. Scis, Kyoto Univ., 2004–10; Prof. and Principal Investigator, Inst. for Integrated Cell-Material Scis, Kyoto Univ., 2007–12. Pres., Internat. Soc. for Stem Cell Res., 2012–13. Japan Soc. for Promotion of Sci. Prize, 2007; (jtly) Shaw Prize in Life Sci. and Medicine, 2008; (jtly) Robert Koch Prize, Koch Foundn, 2008; Canada Gairdner Internat. Award, 2009; (jtly) Albert Lasker Basic Med. Res. Award, Lasker Foundn, 2009; Kyoto Prize for Biotechnol. and Med. Technol., Inamori Foundn, 2010; March of Dimes Prize in Develt Biol., 2010; Imperial Prize, Japan Acad., 2010; (jtly) Wolf Prize in Medicine, Wolf Foundn, 2011; (jtly) Nobel Prize in Physiol. or Medicine, 2012; Millennium Technol. Award, Technol. Acad. Finland, 2012. *Publications*: contribs to scientific jls incl. Cell, Stem Cells, Nature, Cell Stem Cell. *Address*: Gladstone Institute, 1650 Owens Street, San Francisco, CA 94158-2261, USA; Institute for Integrated Cell-Material Sciences, Kyoto University, Yoshida Ushinomiya-cho, Sakyo-ku, Kyoto 606-8501, Japan.

**YAMEY, Prof. Basil Selig**, CBE 1972; FBA 1977; Professor of Economics, University of London, 1960–84, now Emeritus; Member (part-time), Monopolies and Mergers Commission, 1966–78; *b* 4 May 1919; *s* of Solomon and Leah Yamey; *m* 1st, 1948, Helen Bloch (*d* 1980); one *s* one *d*; 2nd, 1991, Demetra Georgakopoulou. *Educ*: Tulbagh High Sch.; Univ. of Cape Town; LSE. Served as Lieut, SAAF, 1941–45. Lectr in Commerce, Rhodes Univ., 1945; Senior Lectr in Commerce, Univ. of Cape Town, 1946; Lectr in Commerce, LSE, 1948; Associate Prof. of Commerce, McGill Univ., 1949; Reader in Economics, Univ. of London, 1950. Managing Trustee, IEA, 1986–91. Trustee: National Gall., 1974–87; Tate Gall., 1979–81; Member: Museums and Galls Commn, 1983–84; Cinematograph Films Council, 1969–73. Mem. Committee of Management: Courtauld Inst., 1981–84; Warburg Inst., 1981–84; Mem., Governing Body, London Business Sch., 1965–84. *Publications*: Economics of Resale Price Maintenance, 1954; (jt editor) Studies in History of Accounting, 1956; (with P. T. Bauer) Economics of Under-developed Countries, 1957; (jt editor) Capital, Saving and Credit in Peasant Societies, 1963; (with H. C. Edey and H. Thomson) Accounting in England and Scotland, 1543–1800, 1963; (with R. B. Stevens) The Restrictive Practices Court, 1965; (ed) Resale Price Maintenance, 1966; (with P. T. Bauer) Markets, Market Control and Marketing Reform: Selected Papers, 1968; (ed) Economics of Industrial Structure, 1973; (jt editor) Economics of Retailing, 1973; (jt editor) Debits, Credits, Finance and Profits, 1974; (with B. A. Goss) Economics of Futures Trading, 1976; Essays on the History of Accounting, 1978; (jt editor) Stato e Industria in Europa: Il Regno Unito, 1979; Further Essays on the History of Accounting, 1983; Arte e Contabilità, 1986; Análisis Económico de los Mercados, 1987; Art and Accounting, 1989; (ed) Luca Pacioli, Exposition of Double Entry Book-keeping, Venice 1494, 1994; (jt editor) Accounting History: some British contributions, 1994; articles on economics, economic history and law in learned journals. *Address*: 27B Elsworthy Road, NW3 3BT. *T*: (020) 7586 9344.

**YANDELL, Claire Louise**; see Armitstead, C. L.

**YANG, Chen Ning**, FInstP; physicist, educator; Einstein Professor and Director, Institute for Theoretical Physics, State University of New York at Stony Brook, New York, 1966–99, now Emeritus Professor and Director; Distinguished Professor-at-Large, Chinese University of Hong Kong, since 1986; Professor, Tsinghua University, Beijing, since 1998; *b* Hefei, China, 22 Sept. 1922; *s* of Ke Chuen Yang and Meng Hwa Lo; *m* 1950, Chih Li Tu (*d* 2003); two *s* one *d*; *m* 2004, Fan Weng. *Educ*: National Southwest Associated Univ., Kunming, China (BSc), 1942; University of Chicago (PhD), 1948. FInstP 1998. Institute for Advanced Study, Princeton, NJ: Member, 1949–55; Prof. of Physics, 1955–66; several DScs from universities. Member of Board: Rockefeller Univ., 1970–76; AAAS, 1976–80; Salk Inst., 1978–; Ben Gurion Univ.; Member: Amer. Phys. Soc.; Nat. Acad. Sci.; Amer. Philos. Soc., Sigma Xi; Brazilian, Venezuelan, Royal Spanish and Chinese Acads of Sci; Academia Sinica; Foreign Member: Royal Soc., 1992; Russian Acad. of Sciences, 1994. Nobel Prize in Physics, 1957; Rumford Prize, 1980; Nat. Medal of Science, 1986; Benjamin Franklin Medal, Amer. Phil Soc., 1993; Bower Prize, Franklin Inst., 1994; King Faisal Internat. Prize, 2001. *Publications*: contrib. to Physical Review, Reviews of Modern Physics. *Address*: Department of Physics, Chinese University of Hong Kong, Shatin, New Territories, Hong Kong; Tsinghua University, Beijing 100084, China.

**YANG, Prof. Fujia**; President, University of Nottingham, Ningbo, China, since 2004; Professor of Physics, Fudan University, since 1980; *b* Shanghai, 11 June 1936; *s* of Yang Shanqing and Zhu Qin; *m* Peng Xiuling; one *d*. *Educ*: Fudan Univ. (Physics degree 1958). Postdoctoral Researcher, Niels Bohr Inst., Copenhagen, 1963–65; Fudan University: Lectr; Pres., 1993–99; Niels Bohr Prof., Fudan Univ., 1999–2009. Dir, Shanghai Inst. of Nuclear Res., Chinese Acad. of Scis, 1987–2001; Chancellor, Univ. of Nottingham, UK, 2001–12. Chm., Shanghai Assoc. for Sci. and Technol., 1992–96; Vice Chm., Chinese Assoc. for Sci. and Technol., 2001–12. Academician, Chinese Acad. of Scis, 1991–. Fellow, 48 Group Club. Hon. degrees, Soka, New York State, Hong Kong, Nottingham,

Connecticut, Chinese Univ. Hong Kong and Misr Univ. of Sci. and Technol. *Publications:* Atom Physics, 1984, 2008; Atomic and Nuclear Physics, 1993; Applied Nuclear Physics, 1994; Quest for Excellence, 1995; (with J. H. Hamilton) Modern Atomic and Nuclear Physics, 1996; Boxue Duzhi, 2001; Chinese contemporary educator's work: Yang Fujia vol., 2006; Approaching to the top universities: comparison of Chinese and Western education, 2009; From Fudan to Nottingham, 2013; Liberal Arts Education, 2014, 4th edn 2017; Rich in Knowledge and Tenacious of Purpose, Inquiring with Earnestness and Reflecting with Self-Practice: Yang Fujia's thoughts on science and humanities, 2016. *Recreations:* reading, walking, swimming. *Address:* Fudan University, 220 Handan Road, Shanghai 200433, China. *E:* fjyang@fudan.edu.cn.

**YANG, Sir Ti Liang,** Kt 1988; Member Executive Council, Hong Kong Special Administrative Region, 1997–2002; Chairman, Exchange Fund Investment Ltd, 1998–2003; Chief Justice of Hong Kong, 1988–96; *b* 30 June 1929; *s* of late Shao-nan Yang and Elsie (*née* Chun); *m* 1954, Eileen Barbara (*née* Tam) (*d* 2006); two *s*. *Educ:* The Comparative Law Sch. of China; Soochow Univ., Shanghai; UCL (LLB Hons 1953; Fellow 1989). FCIArb 1990. Called to the Bar (with honours), Gray's Inn, 1954, Hon. Bencher, 1988. Magistrate, Hong Kong, 1956; Sen. Magistrate, 1963; Rockefeller Fellow, London Univ., 1963–64; District Judge, Dist Court, 1968; Judge of the High Court, Hong Kong, 1975; Justice of Appeal, Hong Kong, 1980; Pres., Court of Appeal of Negara Brunei Darussalam, 1988–92. Candidate for selection of Chief Exec., HKSAR, 1996. Chairman: Kowloon Disturbances Claims Assessment Bd, 1966, Compensation Bd, 1967; Commn of Inquiry into the Rainstorm Disasters, 1972; Commn of Inquiry into the Leung Wing-sang Case, 1976; Commn of Inquiry into the MacLennan Case, 1980; Mem., Law Reform Commn, 1980–96 (Chm., Sub-cttee on law relating to homosexuality, 1980). Mem., Chinese Lang. Cttee (Chm. Legal Sub-cttee), 1970. Chairman: University and Polytechnic Grants Cttee, 1981–84; Hong Kong Univ. Council, 1987–2001; Pro-Chancellor, Hong Kong Univ., 1994–2001. Chm., Hong Kong Red Cross, 1998–2012 (Pres., 2012–). Pres., Bentham Club. Hon. LLD: Chinese Univ. of Hong Kong, 1984; Hong Kong Poly., 1992; Hon. DLitt Hong Kong Univ., 1991. Order of Chivalry, First Class, SPMB, Negara Brunei Darussalam, 1990; Grand Bauhinia Medal (Hong Kong), 1999. *Publications:* (trans.) General Yue Fei, by Qian Cai (Qing Dynasty novel), 1995; (trans.) Peach Blossom Fan, (novel by Gu Shifan, 1948), 1998; (trans.) Officialdom Unmasked, (novel by Li Boyuan, 1903), 2001. *Recreations:* philately, reading, walking, oriental ceramics, travelling, music. *Address:* A10 Carolina Gardens, 20 Coombe Road, The Peak, Hong Kong. *Clubs:* Hong Kong, Hong Kong Country.

**YANG, Prof. Ziheng,** PhD; FRS 2006; R. A. Fisher Professor of Statistical Genetics, University College London, since 2010; *b* 1 Nov. 1964; *s* of Yi Yang and Weiying Wang; *m* 1991, Fan Yang; two *d*. *Educ:* Gansu Agricl Univ. (BSc 1984); Beijing Agricl Univ. (MSc 1987; PhD 1992). Lectr, Beijing Agricl Univ., 1992–97; postdoctoral res., Pennsylvania State Univ. and Univ. of Calif. at Berkeley; University College London: Lectr, 1997–2000; Reader, 2000–01; Prof. of Statistical Genetics, 2001–10. *Publications:* Computational Molecular Evolution, 2006; Molecular Evolution: a statistical approach, 2014. *Address:* Department of Genetics, University College London, Darwin Building, Gower Street, WC1E 6BT.

**YANNAKOUDAKIS, Marina;** Member (C) London Region, European Parliament, 2009–14; *b* London, 16 April 1956; *d* of Lefteris and Toulla Yallouros; *m* 1983, Zacharias Yannakoudakis; two *s* one *d*. *Educ:* Brunel Univ. (BSc Hons); Open Univ. (MA). Financial Dir, Viamare Travel Ltd, 1984–2008. Mem. (C), Barnet LBC, 2006–10. Contested (C) London Reg., EP, 2014. UK Mem., European Econ. and Social Cttee, 2014–. *Recreation:* family and friends.

**YANUKOVYCH, Viktor Fedorovych;** President of Ukraine, 2010–14; *b* Yenakiyeve, Donetsk Region, Ukraine, 9 July 1950; *m* Lyudmyla; one *s* (one *s* decd). *Educ:* Donetsk Poly. Inst. (Mech. Engrg 1980); Ukrainian Acad. of Foreign Trade (MA Internat. Law 2001). Regl transport exec. Gov., Donetsk Reg., 1997; Mem., Donetsk Regl Council, 1999; Prime Minister of Ukraine, 2002–04 and 2006–07; MP (Party of Regions), Ukraine, 2006. Leader, Party of Regions, 2003–10, now Hon. Leader. Fellow, Acad. of Econ. Scis of Ukraine. Order for Merit, 1st, 2nd and 3rd degrees, Honored Transport Worker of Ukraine.

**YAPP, John William;** HM Diplomatic Service, retired; High Commissioner, Belize, 2007–08; *b* 14 Jan. 1951; *s* of late William Yapp and Pamela Yapp (*née* Clarke); *m* 2010, Elizabeth Anne, *d* of late John March and of Loris March; one *s* four *d* by previous marriages. *Educ:* St Augustine's Coll., Ramsgate. Joined HM Diplomatic Service, 1971: Islamabad, 1973–75; Third Sec. (Consular), Kuala Lumpur, 1976–77; Asst Private Sec. to Ministers of State, FCO, 1978–80; Second Sec. (Commercial), Dubai, 1980–84; Second Sec. (Economic), The Hague, 1984–88; Jt Export Promotion Directorate, FCO/DTI, 1988–91; First Sec. (Political/PR), Wellington, NZ, 1992–95 (concurrently Dep. Governor, Pitcairn Is); Dep. Head, N American Dept, FCO, 1995–97; High Comr, Seychelles, 1998–2002; First Sec. (Political-Military), Washington, 2003; Dep. Hd, S Asia Gp, FCO, 2004–07. *Recreations:* photography, reading, cooking, Rugby Union (now as a spectator). *E:* jwyapp@hotmail.co.uk.

**YARBOROUGH, 8th Earl of,** *cr* 1837; **Charles John Pelham;** Baron Yarborough, 1794; Baron Worsley, 1837; *b* 5 Nov. 1963; *o s* of 7th Earl of Yarborough and Ann, *d* of late John Herbert Upton; *S* father, 1991; *m* 1990, Anna-Karin Zecevic, *d* of George Zecevic; four *s* one *d*. High Sheriff, Lincs, 2014–15. *Heir: s* Lord Worsley, *qv*. *Address:* Brocklesby Park, Lincs DN41 8FB.

**YARBOROUGH, Sir Anthony Edmund C.;** see Cooke-Yarborough.

**YARD, John Ernest,** CBE 2000; freelance consultant specialising in change management and outsourcing, since 2004; *b* 29 July 1944; *s* of Ernest Alfred and Kathleen Lilian Yard; *m* Jean Pamela Murray; one *s* one *d*; two *s* one *d* from a previous marriage. *Educ:* St Marylebone Grammar Sch. FBCS 2003; MCIPS 2004. Inland Revenue: Exec. Officer and PAYE Auditor, 1963–71; Inspector of Taxes, 1971–84; Dep. Dir (Systems and Policy), 1984–91; Dir of Change Mgt, 1992; Dir, Business Services (IT) Office, then Business and Mgt Services Div., subseq. Business Services Div., 1993–2004. *Recreations:* travel, eating, golf. *E:* john@johnyard.com.

**YARDE-BULLER,** family name of **Baron Churston**.

**YARMOUTH, Earl of; William Francis Seymour;** *b* 2 Nov. 1993; *s* and *heir* of Marquess of Hertford, *qv*. *m* 2018, Kelsey, *d* of Dr Andrew Wells. *Educ:* British Sch., Rio de Janeiro; Winterfold House Sch.; Shrewsbury Sch.; Haileybury Sch.; Royal Agricl Univ., Cirencester.

**YARNOLD, Elizabeth Anne,** OBE 2018 (MBE 2014); professional athlete, skeleton, 2009–18; *d* of Clive Yarnold and Judith Yarnold; *m* 2016, James Roche. *Educ:* Maidstone Grammar Sch. for Girls; Univ. of Gloucestershire (BSc Geog. and Sports Sci.). Skeleton: Bronze Medal, World Championships, 2012; World Cup Champion, 2013–14; Gold Medal, Women's Skeleton, Winter Olympics, Sochi, 2014; European Champion, 2015; World Champion, 2015; Bronze Medal, World Championships, 2017; Gold Medal, Women's Skeleton, Winter Olympics, Seoul, 2018. *Recreations:* cooking, music. *Address:* Sports Sphere, Unit 13, Baltimore House, Juniper Drive, Battersea Reach, SW18 1TS. *E:* info@sports-sphere.com.

**YARNOLD, Patrick;** HM Diplomatic Service, retired; professional genealogical and historical researcher; *b* 21 March 1937; *s* of late Leonard Francis Yarnold and Gladys Blanche Yarnold (*née* Merry); *m* 1961, Caroline, *er d* of late Andrew J. Martin; two *d*. *Educ:* Bancroft's School. HM Forces, 1955–57. Joined HM Foreign (now Diplomatic) Service, 1957; served: FO, 1957–60; Addis Ababa, 1961–64; Belgrade, 1964–66; FO (later FCO), 1966–70; 1st Sec., Head of Chancery, Bucharest, 1970–73; 1st Sec. (Commercial), Bonn, 1973–76; FCO, 1976–79; Counsellor (Economic and Commercial), Brussels, 1980–83; Consul-Gen., Zagreb, 1983–85; Counsellor and Head of Chancery, Belgrade, 1985–87; Hd of Defence Dept, FCO, 1987–90; Consul-Gen., Hamburg, 1990–94; Consul-Gen., Marseilles, 1995–97. *Publications:* Wanborough Manor: school for secret agents, 2009. *Recreations:* travel, photography, walking, local history, Chinese cooking, etc. *Address:* Cherry Cottage, The Street, Puttenham, Guildford, Surrey GU3 1AT.

**YARNTON, David Nigel;** Managing Director, Equinox Talent (formerly Global Talent Group), since 2012; *b* London, 25 Feb. 1959; *s* of Albert Edward Yarnton and Minnie Florence Evelyn Yarnton; *m* 1985, Sally Elizabeth Withers; one *s* one *d*. *Educ:* Defence Force Acad. (Duntroon Scholar); South Australian Inst. of Technol.; Australian Inst. of Mgt (Cert. Applied Mgt 1982); Univ. of New England (Co. Dirs Dip. 1990). Industrial Sales Rep., Stanley Tools, 1979–82; State Manager, Vic, Sidchrome Pty Ltd, 1982–84; State Sales Manager, Vic, British Paints Pty Ltd, 1984–86; Nat. Sales and Mktg Manager, Action Hi-Tech Pty Ltd, 1986; Gen. Manager and Dir, IAD Pty Ltd, 1987–95; Dir, Sales and Mktg, Nintendo Australia Ltd, 1995–2003; Gen. Manager, Nintendo UK, 2003–12. Non-executive Director: GfK Charttrack, 2007–12; Eyes on Athletes, 2012–; Gfinity, 2014–. Dir, Aust. Toy Assoc., 2000; Dir and Co-Founder, Interactive Entertainment Assoc. of Australia, 2002; Mem. Bd and Vice Chm., 2004–11, Chm., eSports Gp, 2014–, UK Interactive Entertainment Assoc.; Chm., Edge eSports, 2018–; Bd Advr, British Esports Assoc. Mem. Bd, Edinburgh Interactive Fest., 2004– (Chm., 2011–). Founder and Chm., British Inspiration Awards, 2009–. Associate, Aust. Inst. of Mgt, 1984; FAICD 1990; Hon. Mem., Acad. of Interactive Arts and Scis, LA, 1997. Athletics Coach, Level 1, Aust. Athletics Coaches Assoc., 1998. *T:* 07717 600800. *E:* dyarnton@aol.com.

**YARROW, Sir Alan (Colin Drake),** Kt 2016; JP; Chairman, Chartered Institute for Securities and Investment, 2009–18; Lord Mayor of London, 2014–15; *b* Johor Bahru, 1951; *s* of Colin Yarrow and Paula Yarrow; *m* 1975, Gilly; two *s*. *Educ:* Harrow; Manchester Business Sch. Work in graphic design studio, Paris, 1968; Grieveson Grant, later Kleinwort Benson: joined Grieveson Grant, stockbrokers, 1972; Mem., Stock Exchange, 1978; Partner, 1981; Hd, UK Institutional Sales, 1989–92; Hd, Global Distribution, 1992–94; Man. Dir, Kleinwort Benson Securities, 1994; Mem. Bd, Kleinwort Benson Gp, 1995; Global Hd, Equities, 1995; Mem. Mgt Bd, Dresdner Kleinwort Benson, 1995; Vice Chm., 2000; CEO, UK Reg., 2007–09; Chm., Kleinwort Benson Gp, 2010–14, Sen. Advr, 2014–17. Member: Takeover Panel, 2002–10 (Mem., Appeal Bd, 2016–); Chancellor of the Exchequer's High Level Stakeholder Gp, 2006–09; Dep. Chm., FSA Practitioners Panel, 2004–10. Chm., LIBA, 2004–09; Vice Pres. and Mem. Council, BBA, 2004–09. Non-executive Director: Complinet, 2002–10 (Chm., 2002–08); Baikal Global Ltd, 2009–10; Turquoise Global Hldgs Ltd, 2010–; Fixnetix, 2010–15; Institutional Protection Services Ltd, 2016–; Garden Bridge Trading Ltd, 2016–; Arbuthnot Banking Gp, 2016–. Mem., Adv. Bd, Commonwealth Enterprise and Investment Council, 2015–; Ind. Partnership Advr, James Hambro & Partners, 2017–. Trustee, Police Foundn, 2013–16. Vice-Pres., Royal Mencap Soc., 2014–. Hon. Chartered FCSI 2010; Hon. Fellow, ICSA 2015. Hon. DSc City, 2014. Gov., City of London Freemen's Sch., 2011–13; Almoner, Christ's Hosp., 2007–. City of London: Alderman, Ward of Bridge and Bridge Without, 2007–; Sheriff, 2011–12; HM Lieut, 2013–; JP 2007; Member, Committees: Libraries, 2007–09; Markets, 2007–09; Finance, 2009–10; Port Health and Envmtl Services, 2009–10; Planning and Transportation, 2010–12; Policy and Resources, 2013–14; Establishment, 2013–14; Standards, 2016–; Sir William Coxton Trust, 2016–. Liveryman: Fishmongers' Co., 2007; International Bankers' Co., 2008; Glaziers' Co., 2012; Hon. Liveryman, Launderers' Co., 2011. KStJ 2014. Order of the Aztec Eagle (Mexico), 2015. *Recreations:* tennis, golf. *Clubs:* Hurlingham, Boodle's, City of London, East India; Royal Wimbledon Golf.

**YARROW, Dr Alfred,** FFPH; Honorary Member, Epidemiology Unit, Ministry of Health, Jerusalem, 1987–96; *b* 25 May 1924; *s* of Leah and step *s* of Philip Yarrow; *m* 1953, Sheila Kaufman; two *d*. *Educ:* Hackney Downs Grammar Sch.; Edinburgh Univ. (MB, ChB); London Sch. of Hygiene and Trop. Medicine (Hons DPH). FFPH (Foundn FFCM 1972). Dep. Area MO, Tottenham and Hornsey, 1955–60; Area MO, SE Essex, 1960–65; MOH, Gateshead, 1965–68; Dir, Scottish Health Educn Unit, 1968–73; SMO, 1973–77, SPMO, 1977–84, DHSS. Temp. Consultant, WHO, 1975–76. Brit. Council Lectr, 1975; Council of Europe Fellow, 1978. *Publications:* So Now You Know About Smoking, 1975; Politics, Society and Preventive Medicine, 1986; scientific papers on demography, epidemiology, preventive medicine and health educn. *Recreations:* lawn bowls, travelling, reading. *Address:* 9/4 Nof Harim, Jerusalem 96190, Israel. *T:* 6438792.

**YARROW, Sir Ross (William Grant),** 4th Bt *cr* 1916; Managing Director (US Equities), Robert W. Baird Ltd, since 2009; *b* Inverness, 14 Jan. 1985; *s* of Richard Grant Yarrow and Sheila Elizabeth Yarrow; *S* grandfather, 2018; *m* 2012, Sally Marie Thompson; one *s* two *d* (incl. twin *s* and *d*). *Educ:* Edinburgh Acad.; Edinburgh Univ. (MA Econs 2007). Analyst, Credit Suisse, 2007–09. *Recreations:* Church, family, drumming, ski-ing, photography. *Heir: s* Henry Nathaniel Grant Yarrow, *b* 10 Aug. 2016.

**YARWOOD, Michael Edward,** OBE 1976; entertainer, since 1962; *b* 14 June 1941; *s* of Wilfred and Bridget Yarwood; *m* 1969, Sandra Burville (marr. diss. 1987); two *d*. *Educ:* Bredbury Secondary Modern Sch., Cheshire. First television appearance, 1963; *BBC TV:* Three of a Kind, 1967; Look—Mike Yarwood, and Mike Yarwood in Persons (series), 1971–82; *ATV:* Will the Real Mike Yarwood Stand Up? (series), 1968; *Thames:* Mike Yarwood in Persons, 1983–84; Yarwood's Royal Variety Show, the Yarwood Chat Show, and Mike Yarwood in Persons, 1986; *stage:* Royal Variety performances, 1968, 1972, 1976, 1981, 1987, 1993; One for the Pot, UK tour, 1988. Variety Club of Gt Britain award for BBC TV Personality of 1973; Royal Television Society award for outstanding creative achievement in front of camera, 1978. Mem., Grand Order of Water Rats, 1968. *Publications:* And This Is Me, 1974; Impressions of my life (autobiog.), 1986. *Recreations:* golf, tennis. *Club:* Lord's Taverners.

**YASAMEE, Heather Jacqueline, (Mrs S. J. Gagen),** CMG 2006; Assistant Director (Information Management), Directorate for Strategy and Information, Foreign and Commonwealth Office, 2004–06; *b* 12 Aug. 1951; *d* of Dennis Gordon Fenby and Betty Mitchell Fenby (*née* Linford); *m* 1st, 1979, Feroze Abdullah Khan Yasamee (marr. diss. 1999); 2nd, 2005, Stephen John Gagen, JP. *Educ:* Lawnswood High Sch. for Girls, Leeds; St Anne's Coll., Oxford (MA Mod. Hist.). Foreign and Commonwealth Office: joined, 1973; Historians, 1973–95, Hd of Historians, 1990–95; Editor, Documents on British

Policy Overseas, 1988–95; Departmental Record Officer, 1995–2006: Hd, Records and Histl Services, 1995–99; Hd, Records and Histl Dept, 1999–2003. *Publications*: (Asst Ed.) Documents on British Policy Overseas: Potsdam, 1984; Schuman Plan, 1986; London Conferences, 1987; (ed) German Rearmament, 1989; Korea, 1991; various articles. *Recreations*: family life, gardening. *Address*: 32 Station Road, SW19 2LP. *E*: heather@yasamee.com.

**YASIN, Mohammad;** MP (Lab) Bedford, since 2017; *b* 15 Oct. 1971. Mem. (Lab), Bedford BC, 2006– (Portfolio holder for Adult Services, 2015–17). *Address*: House of Commons, SW1A 0AA.

**YASS, Irving,** CB 1993; freelance transport policy consultant, since 2010; Policy Adviser, London First, 2008–09 (Director: Transport, 1995–2001; Policy, 2001–08); *b* 20 Dec. 1935; *s* of late Abraham and Fanny Yass; *m* 1962, Marion Leighton; two *s* one *d*. *Educ*: Harrow County Grammar School for Boys; Balliol Coll., Oxford (Brackenbury Schol.; BA). Assistant Principal, Min. of Transport and Civil Aviation, 1958; Private Sec. to Joint Parliamentary Secretary, 1960; HM Treasury, 1967–70; Asst Secretary, Dept of the Environment, 1971; Secretary, Cttee of Inquiry into Local Govt Finance, 1974–76; Dept of Transport, 1976–94 (Under Sec., 1982); Dir, Planning and Transport, Govt Office for London, 1994–95. *Address*: 61 West Heath Road, NW3 7TH. *T*: 0207 794 2221.

**YASSAIE, Sir Hossein,** Kt 2013; PhD; FREng; Chief Executive Officer, Imagination Technologies Ltd, 1998–2016; *b* Iran, 1956; adopted British nationality, 1984; *m* Maha; two *d*. *Educ*: Birmingham Univ. (BSc 1st Cl. Hons Electronics and Communications 1979; PhD 1982). FREng 2016. Res. Fellow, Birmingham Univ., 1982–84; with Inmos, subseq. STMicroelectronics, 1984–92; Chief Technol. Officer, 1992–98, Dir, 1995–2016, Imagination Technologies Ltd. Non-executive Director: Toumaz Gp (formerly Toumaz Ltd), 2009–; Ultrahaptics, 2016–; Chm., Pure Internat. Ltd, 2017–.

**YASSUKOVICH, Stanislas Michael,** CBE 1991; Chairman, S. M Yassukovich & Co. Ltd, 1997–2010; *b* 5 Feb. 1935; adopted British nationality, 1993; *s* of Dimitri and Denise Yassukovich; *m* 1961, Diana (*née* Townsend); two *s* one *d*. *Educ*: Deerfield Academy; Harvard University. US Marine Corps, 1957–61. Joined White, Weld & Co., 1961: posted to London, 1962; Branch Manager, 1967; General Partner, 1969; Managing Director, 1969; European Banking Co. Ltd: Managing Director, 1973; Group Dep. Chm., 1983. Sen. Advr, Merrill Lynch & Co., 1989–90; Dir, Merrill Lynch Europe Ltd, 1985–90 (Chm., 1985–90); Chairman: Flextech, 1989–97 (Dep. Chm., 1997–99; Dir, Telewest plc, 1999–2003); Park Place Capital, 1991–; Henderson Euro Trust PLC, 1992–2008; Hemingway Properties, 1993–98; Gallo & Co., 1995–98; Easdaq, 1997–2000; Manek Investment Management, 1998–2018; Cayzer Continuation PCC Ltd, 2004–15; Prometheus Energy, 2007–08; BMCE Internat. Hldgs plc (formerly Medicapital Hldgs Ltd), 2007–11; Vice-Chm., Bristol & West plc, 1991–99; Dep. Chm., ABC Internat. Bank, 1993–2007; Director: Mosimann's Ltd, 1989–98; Henderson plc, 1991–98; SW Water, 1992–99 (Dep. Chm., 1997–99); Tradepoint Financial Network, 1997–99; Atlas Capital Ltd, 2002–07; Fortis Investments SA, 2007–09. Jt Dep. Chm., Internat. Stock Exchange, 1986–89; Chm., Securities Assoc., 1988–91. Chairman: City Res. Project, 1991–95; City Disputes Panel, 1994–98. *Publications*: Two Lives: a social and financial memoir, 2016; Lives of the Luberon, 2019; articles in financial press. *Recreations*: writing, bridge. *Address*: 42 Berkeley Square, W1J 5AW. *T*: (020) 7318 0825. *Clubs*: Buck's, White's, Travellers (Paris).

**YATES, Prof. (Anthony) David;** Warden, Robinson College, Cambridge, since 2001; *b* 5 May 1946; *s* of Cyril Yates and Violet Ethel Yates (*née* Mann); *m* 1st, 1974, Carolyn Paula Hamilton (marr. diss. 1988); 2nd, 1992, Susanna Margaret McGarry. *Educ*: Bromley Grammar Sch. for Boys; St Catherine's Coll., Oxford (Exhibnr; BA 1967, MA 1971; Hon. Fellow, 2003). Admitted solicitor, 1972; Lecturer in Law, Univ. of Hull, 1969–72; Univ. of Bristol, 1972–74; University of Manchester: Lectr in Law, 1974–76; Sen. Lectr, 1976–78; Principal, Dalton Hall, 1975–80; Foundn Prof. of Law, 1979–87, Dean, Sch. of Law, 1979–84, and Pro-Vice-Chancellor, 1985–87, Univ. of Essex; Dir, Professional Develt, 1987–93, Dir of Strategy, 1993–97, Partner, 1993–2001, and Chief Operating Officer, 1997–2001, Baker & McKenzie. Visiting Professor: Univ. of Manchester, 1979; Univ. of NSW, 1985; Univ. of Essex, 1987–91; Parsons Vis. Fellow, 1985, Adjunct Prof. of Law, 2007–15, Univ. of Sydney. Mem., Educn and Trng Cttee, SRA, 2013–15. Mem., Law Soc., 1970– (Mem. Council, 1992–97). Chm. of Govs, Coll. of Law, England and Wales, 2009–12 (Gov., 2002–05; Dep. Chm., 2005–09). Hon. LLD Univ. of Law, 2013. FRSA 2006. *Publications*: Exclusion Clauses in Contracts, 1978, 2nd edn 1982; Leases of Business Premises, 1979; (with A. J. Hawkins) Landlord and Tenant Law, 1981, 2nd edn 1986; (with A. J. Hawkins) Standard Business Contracts, 1986; (Ed. in Chief) The Carriage of Goods by Land, Sea and Air, annually, 1993–2005; (with Malcolm Clarke) The Carriage of Goods by Land and Air, 2005, 2nd edn 2008. *Recreations*: opera, food, wine, Rugby football. *Address*: Warden's Lodge, Robinson College, Cambridge CB3 9AN. *Club*: Oxford and Cambridge.

**YATES, Brian Douglas;** Chairman, Probate Committee, Institute of Chartered Accountants in England and Wales, since 2013; *b* 1 May 1944; *s* of Bertram Yates and Barbara (*née* Wenham); *m* 1971, Patricia, *d* of Arthur Hutchinson, DFC; one *s*. *Educ*: Uppingham Sch.; Clare Coll., Cambridge (MA); London Business Sch. (MBA). CEng; Eur Ing. RHP Bearings, 1973–81; Thorn EMI, 1981–85; Dexion, 1985–88; Morris Material (formerly Morris Mechanical) Handling, 1988–2004. Member: Northampton BC, 1979–83; Hampshire CC, 1985–89. Mem. Council, 1986–, Chm., 1994–2007, Consumers' Assoc.; Consumer Dir, TrustMark, 2008–12; Member: Council, Ombudsman for Estate Agents, 1998–2005; Fitness to Practise (formerly Professional Conduct) Cttee, GMC, 2001–13; Genetics Insce Cttee, DoH, 2002–06; Hardship Panel, Assoc. of Investment Trust Cos, 2003–06; Immigration Appeal Tribunal, 2003–14; Insolvency Licensing Cttee, ICAEW, 2006–13; Fitness to Practise Cttee, NMC, 2009–17; Appeals Cttee, Law Soc. of Scotland, 2014–; Dir, Cavity Insulation Guarantee Agency, 2016–. Public Mem., Network Rail, 2008–11. Finance Cttee, Bar Council, 2018–. Mem., Lunar Soc., Birmingham. FRSA. *Recreations*: tennis, cross country ski-ing, orienteering. *Address*: 19 Park Avenue, Harpenden AL5 2DZ. *T*: (01582) 768484. *Clubs*: Athenæum, Royal Over-Seas League; Hatfield House Tennis, Harpenden Lawn Tennis.

**YATES, David;** *see* Yates, A. D.

**YATES, David James Francis;** QC 2019; *b* Wandsworth, 18 May 1979; *s* of late James and Margaret Yates; *m* 2007, Kathryn Grey; one *s* one *d*. *Educ*: Worth Sch., Sussex; Gonville and Caius Coll., Cambridge (BA 1st Cl. Classics; MA); City Univ. (Postgrad. DipLaw); Inns of Court Sch. of Law. Called to the Bar, Lincoln's Inn, 2004. *Recreations*: rowing, history, choral music. *Clubs*: Thames Rowing; Remenham (Henley-on-Thames).

**YATES, Prof. David William,** FRCS; Professor of Emergency Medicine, University of Manchester, 1990–2004, now Emeritus; *b* 19 Nov. 1941; *o s* of Bill and Lena Yates; *m* 1977, Veronica Mary Henderson; two *s*. *Educ*: Bradford Grammar Sch.; Emmanuel Coll., Cambridge (MB BChir 1967; MD 1990); St Thomas' Hosp., London; Univ. of Liverpool (MChOrth 1975). FRCS 1972. Med. posts in orthopaedic surgery; first Prof. of Emergency Medicine in UK, 1990. First Dean, Faculty of A&E Medicine, RCS, 1993–98. Founding Dir, Trauma Audit and Res. Network, 1990. *Address*: c/o Trauma Audit and Research Network, Salford Royal Hospital, Salford M6 8HD. *T*: (0161) 206 4397.

**YATES, Edgar;** *see* Yates, W. E.

**YATES, Ian Humphrey Nelson,** CBE 1991; Director, 1989–90, Chief Executive, 1975–90, The Press Association Ltd; *b* 24 Jan. 1931; *s* of James Nelson Yates and Martha (*née* Nutter); *m* 1956, Daphne J. Hudson, MCSP; three *s*. *Educ*: Lancaster Royal Grammar Sch.; Canford Sch., Wimborne. Royal Scots Greys, Germany and ME (National Service Commn), 1951–53. Management Trainee, Westminster Press Ltd, 1953–58 (Westmorland Gazette, and Telegraph & Argus, Bradford); Asst to Man. Dir, King & Hutchings Ltd, Uxbridge, 1958–60; Bradford and District Newspapers: Asst Gen. Man., 1960; Gen. Manager, 1964; Man. Dir, 1969–75; Dir, Westminster Press Planning Div., 1969–75. Chairman: Universal News Services Ltd, 1988–90; Tellex Monitors Ltd, 1988–90; CRG Communications Gp Ltd, 1990–91. President: Young Newspapermen's Assoc., 1966; Yorks Newspaper Soc., 1968. Member: Council, Newspaper Soc., 1970–75; Council, Commonwealth Press Union, 1977–90; Pres., Alliance of European News Agencies, 1987–88. FRSA 1989. *Recreations*: walking, reading, theatre.

**YATES, John Michael,** QPM 2006; Director of Global Security, The Westfield Group, since 2013; *b* Liverpool, 17 Feb. 1959; *s* of Dr Godfrey and Dr Muriel Yates; *m* 2012, Felicity Ross; one *d*; one *s* one *d* by previous marriage. *Educ*: Marlborough Coll.; King's Coll., London (BA Hons Medieval and Modern Hist.); Fitzwilliam Coll., Cambridge (Dip. Applied Criminol. 2003). Metropolitan Police Service, 1981–2011: Comdr, Crime, 2003–04; Dep. Asst Comr, and Dir of Intelligence, 2004–06; Asst Comr, Professional Standards, 2006–07; Hd of Serious and Organised Crime, 2008–09; Asst Comr, Specialist Ops, 2009–11; Sen. Consultant, G3 Security, 2013. ACPO lead for Rape and Serious Sexual Offences, 2003–09; Mem., Internat. Gp of Experts on Corruption, 2006–; Chair, Terrorism and Allied Matters, and nat. lead for Counter Terrorism, ACPO, 2009. *Recreations*: long-distance cycling, Liverpool Football Club, cooking.

**YATES, Nicholas Gilmore;** QC 2018; *b* London, 10 April 1972; *s* of Douglas Martin Yates and Gillian Yates; *m* 1998, Rebecca Ann Daldorph; three *d*. *Educ*: Aldenham Sch.; Trinity Coll., Cambridge (BA Theol. 1994; MA); City Univ., London (DipLaw 1995); Inns of Court Sch. of Law (BVC 1996). Called to the Bar, Inner Temple, 1996; in practice as barrister, specialising in high worth relationship generated disputes (mainly matrimonial finances cases). Mem., Family Law Bar Assoc., 1996–. *Recreations*: classical music (especially choral), singing (tenor), opera, cycling, wine, war poetry. *Address*: 1 Hare Court, Temple, EC4Y 7BE. *T*: (020) 7797 7070.

**YATES, Roger Philip;** Chief Executive Officer, Pioneer Investments, 2010–12 (non-executive Director, since 2012); *b* 4 April 1957; *s* of Eric Yates and Joyce Yates; *m* 2003, Catriona Louise Maclean; three *s* one *d*. *Educ*: Worcester Coll., Oxford (BA Hons Mod. Hist.); Univ. of Reading (postgrad. res.). GT Management plc, 1981–88, Dir, 1985; Chief Investment Officer: Morgan Grenfell Asset Mgt, 1988–94 (Dir, 1990–94); LGT Asset Mgt, 1994–98; Invesco Asset Mgt, 1998–99; Chief Exec. and Dir, Henderson Global Investors, 1999–2009; Chief Exec., Henderson Gp (formerly HHG), 2003–09 (Dir, 2003–09). Non-executive Director: IG Gp plc, 2006–; St James's Place plc, 2014– (Sen. Ind. Dir, 2018–); Director: JPMorgan Elect, 2008–; Electra Private Equity, 2012–15 (Chm., 2014–15). *Recreations*: ski-ing, golf, tennis, climbing.

**YATES, Prof. (William) Edgar,** MA, PhD; FBA 2002; Professor of German, University of Exeter, 1972–2001, now Emeritus; *b* 30 April 1938; *s* of Douglas Yates and Doris Yates (*née* Goode); *m* 1963, Barbara Anne Fellowes; two *s*. *Educ*: Fettes Coll. (Foundn Schol.); Emmanuel Coll., Cambridge (Minor Open Schol.; MA, PhD). 2nd Lieut, RASC, 1957–58. Lectr in German, Univ. of Durham, 1963–72; University of Exeter: Hd of Dept of German, 1972–86; Dep. Vice-Chancellor, 1986–89. Chairman: Univ. of Exeter Conf. of Univ. Teachers of German, 1991–93; Lewis Fry Meml Lectr, Univ. of Bristol, 1994. Vice-Pres., Wiener Shakespeare-Ges., 1992–2002; Member: Cttee, MHRA, 1980–2015; Council, English Goethe Soc., 1984–2009; Council, Internat. Nestroy-Ges., 1986– (Vice-Pres., 1997–). Germanic Editor, MLR, 1981–88; Editor, 1992–2001, Jt Editor, 2002–09, Nestroyana; Co-ordinating Gen. Editor, historisch-kritische Nestroy-Ausgabe, 1992–2012. Corresp. Fellow, Austrian Acad. of Scis, 1995. Gov., Exeter Sch., 1981–2011 (Chm., 1994–2008). J. G. Robertson Prize, Univ. of London, 1975. Ehrenkreuz für Wissenschaft und Kunst, 1. Klasse (Austria), 2001; Silver Medal, Schwechat, 2005. *Publications*: Grillparzer: a critical introduction, 1972; Nestroy: satire and parody in Viennese popular comedy, 1972; Humanity in Weimar and Vienna: the continuity of an ideal, 1973; Tradition in the German Sonnet, 1981; Schnitzler, Hofmannsthal, and the Austrian Theatre, 1992; Nestroy and the Critics, 1994; Theatre in Vienna 1776–1995: a critical history, 1996; (with B. Pargner) Nestroy in München, 2001; Bin Dichter nur der Posse: Johann Nepomuk Nestroy. Versuch einer Biographie, 2012; edited: Hofmannsthal: Der Schwierige, 1966; Grillparzer: Der Traum ein Leben, 1968; Nestroy: Stücke 12–14 (Hist.-krit. Ausgabe), 1981–82, Stücke 34, 1989, Stücke 18/I, 1991, Stücke 22, 1996, Stücke 17/II, 1998, (jtly) Stücke 2, 2000, (jtly) Nachträge (2 vols), 2007; (jtly) Viennese Popular Theatre, 1985; (jtly) Grillparzer und die europäische Tradition, 1987; Vom schaffenden zum edierten Nestroy, 1994; Nestroys Reserve und andere Notizen, 2000, 2nd edn 2003; (jtly) From Perinet to Jelinek, 2001; Der unbekannte Nestroy, 2001; Nestroys Alltag und dessen Dokumentation, 2001; (jtly) Hinter den Kulissen von Biedermeier und Nachmärz, 2001; (jtly) Briefe des Theaterdirektors Carl Carl und seiner Frau Margaretha Carl an Charlotte Birch-Pfeiffer, 2004; (jtly) Theater und Gesellschaft im Wien des 19. Jahrhunderts, 2006; numerous articles on Austrian literary and cultural history, on German literature of the Biedermeier period, and on German lyric poetry; *festschrift*: The Austrian Comic Tradition, 1998. *Recreations*: music, theatre, opera, French wine. *Address*: 7 Clifton Hill, Exeter EX1 2DL. *T*: (01392) 254713.

**YATES, William Hugh,** MBE 2007; Senior Partner, Knight Frank (formerly Knight Frank & Rutley), 1992–96; *b* 18 Dec. 1935; *s* of late Brig. Morris Yates, DSO, OBE and Kathleen Rosanna Yates (*née* Sherbrooke, later Mrs Hugh Cowan); *m* 1st, 1963, Celia Geraldine Pitman (marr. diss. 1972); one *s*; 2nd, 1979, Elisabeth Susan Mansel-Pleydell (*née* Luard); four step *s*. *Educ*: Lancing Coll.; RMA Sandhurst. FRICS. Commissioned, Royal Dragoons, 1955; ADC to Governor of Aden, 1959. Articled surveyor, Rylands & Co., 1961; Knight Frank & Rutley, 1964–96: Man. Dir, Geneva, 1968–72; Partner, 1972; Man. Partner, 1978–82; Head of Residential Div., 1982–92. Director: INCAS SA, 1970–78; European Property Investment Co. NV, 1973–81; Ecclesiastical Insurance Group, 1985–2006 (Dep. Chm., 1995–2006); Woolwich plc (formerly Woolwich Building Soc.), 1990–2000 (Dep. Chm., 1996–2000); Roxton Sporting Ltd, 2001–03. Save the Children Fund: Chm., Fund Raising Cttee, 1980–86; Hon. Treasurer, 1986–92; Dep. Chm., Suzy Lamplugh Trust, 2002–05. *Recreations*: riding, gardening, golf, music. *Address*: Upper Farm, Milton Lilbourne, Pewsey, Wilts SN9 5LQ. *T*: (01672) 563438. *Club*: Turf.

**YAXLEY, John Francis**, CBE 1990; HM Overseas Civil Service, 1961–94, retired; *b* 13 Nov. 1936; *s* of late Rev. Canon R. W. and Dorothy Yaxley; *m* 1960, Patricia Anne Scott; one *s*. *Educ*: Hatfield Coll., Durham Univ. National Service, 1958–60. Joined HMOCS, 1961; posts in New Hebrides and Solomon Islands, 1961–75; seconded FCO, 1975–77; Hong Kong, 1977–89: posts included Dir of Industry, Sec. for Econ. Services, and Dep. Financial Sec.; Comr, Hong Kong Govt, London, 1989–93. Mem., Salvation Army Nat. Adv. Bd, 1990–98; Chm., Oxford Diocesan Bd of Finance, 1996–2001. Mem. Council, Durham Univ., 1995–2001; Mem. Governing Body, Hatfield Coll., Durham, 1997–2001. Treasurer: W Mercia NADFAS, 1995–2000; Northleach DFAS, 2001–04. Trustee: Triumph over Phobia UK, 1995–2000; Oxford Historic Churches Trust, 2002–16 (Vice Chm., 2013–16); Trustee and Jt Financial Dir, Prayer Book Soc., 2005–06. *Publications*: The Population of the New Hebrides (with Dr Norma McArthur), 1968; (ed) Public Sector Reform in the Hong Kong Government, 1989. *Recreations*: walking, church crawling, history, gardening. *Address*: Old Housing, Fifield, Oxon OX7 6HF.

**YEA, Philip Edward**; Chairman, Equiniti Group plc, since 2017; *b* 11 Dec. 1954; *s* of John Yea and Beryl Yea (*née* Putman); *m* 1981, Daryl Walker; two *s* one *d*. *Educ*: Wallington High Sch.; Brasenose Coll., Oxford (MA Mod. Langs). FCMA. Perkins Engines, 1977–82; Klix (Mars), 1983; Guinness PLC, 1984–88; Cope Allmann plc, 1988–91; Dir, Financial Control, 1991–93, Finance Dir, 1993–97, Guinness PLC; Finance Dir, Diageo plc, 1997–99; Man. Dir, Investcorp, 1999–2004; Chief Exec., 3i Gp plc, 2004–09. Chm., Rose Partnership LLP, 2011–12. Non-executive Director: Halifax plc, subseq. HBOS plc, 1999–2004; Manchester United plc, 2000–04; Vodafone Gp, 2005–17 (Sen. non-exec. Dir, 2015–17); Aberdeen Asian Smaller Cos Investment Trust, 2014–; Rocket Internet SE, 2014–15; Marshall of Cambridge (Hldgs) Ltd, 2016–; Sen. non-exec. Dir, Computacenter, 2015–18; non-executive Chairman: bwin.party digital entertainment plc, 2014–16; Greene King, 2016–19. Mem., Adv. Gp, PricewaterhouseCoopers Services (UK), 2009–14. Sen. Business Advr to the Duke of York, 2009–14. Chm., British Heart Foundation, 2009–15 (Trustee, 2008–15). Ind. Dir and Trustee, Francis Crick Inst., 2011–18. *Recreation*: travel. *Address*: Farm Street Advisors Ltd, 73 West One House, 36A Riding House Street, W1W 7ER.

**YEANG, Dr Kenneth King Mun**; architect and planner; Principal, T. R. Hamzah & Yeang (Malaysia) Sdn Bhd, since 1976; *b* 6 Oct. 1948; *s* of Yeang Cheng Hin and Louise Yeang; *m* 1986, Priscilla Khoo; two *s* two *d*. *Educ*: Cheltenham Coll.; AA Sch., London (Grad. in Architecture 1971); Wolfson Coll., Cambridge (PhD 1981; Hon. Fellow, 2015). Principal, 2005–10, Chm., 2010–12, Llewelyn Davies Yeang. Major projects include: Menara Mesiniaga, Subang, Malaysia, 1992; Nat. Liby Building, Singapore, 2005; Mewah Oils HQ, Port Kelang, Malaysia, 2005; Gt Ormond St Hosp. Extension, 2010; Solaris, Singapore, 2010; Putrajaya 2C5 Mixed-use Complex, Malaysia, 2010. Graham Willis Vis. Prof., Sheffield Univ., 1994–98, 1999–2003; Distinguished Plym Prof., Univ. of Illinois, 2005–; Adjunct Prof., Tongji Univ., Shanghai, 2005–08. Hon. DLitt Sheffield, 2003. Aga Khan Award for Architecture, 1996; Malaysian Inst. of Architects Gold Medal, 2011; Merdeka Award, Govt of Malaysia, 2011. *Address*: T. R. Hamzah & Yeang Sdn Bhd, 8 Jalan Satu, Taman Sri Ukay, off Jalan Ulu Kelang, 68000 Ampang, Selangor, Malaysia. *T*: (603) 42571966, *Fax*: (603) 42561005. *E*: kynnet@kyeang.com.

**YEATMAN, Prof. Eric Morgan**, PhD; FREng, FIET, FIMMM, FIEEE; Professor of Micro-Engineering, since 2005, and Head, Department of Electrical and Electronic Engineering, since 2015, Imperial College London; *b* Oslo, 1 Feb. 1963; *s* of Richard Harry Martin Yeatman and Rannveig Havig Yeatman (*née* Omang); *m* 2002, Antonia Szigeti. *Educ*: Dalhousie Univ., Halifax (BSc 1983; MSc Phys 1986); Technical Univ. of Nova Scotia, Halifax (BEng 1985); Imperial Coll. of Sci., Technol. and Medicine, London (PhD 1989). FIET 2005; FIMMM 2005; FREng 2012; FIEEE 2013. Imperial College London: Lectr, 1989–96; Sen. Lectr, 1996–2001; Reader, 2001–05; Chm., Acad. Trng Cttee, Grad. Sch. of Engrg and Physical Scis, 2002–11; Dep. Hd, Dept of Electrical and Electronic Engrg, 2008–15; Mem., Adv. Bd, Inst. for Security Sci. and Technol., 2010–; Co-Dir, Digital Economy Lab., 2011–. Dir, 2001–, Chm., 2004–11, 2012–13, Microsaic Systems plc (formerly Microsaic Systems Ltd) (Actg Chief Exec., 2011–12). Member: Tech. Adv. Bd, Lambda Crossing, Caesarea, 2001–05; Adv. Bd, West Steag Partners, Essen, 2002–04; Tech. Adv. Bd, Young Associates, London, 2002–05. Advr, Wingate Scholarships, 2005–12; Chm., Internat. Adv. Cttee, Body Sensor Networks conf. series, 2009–; Acad. Dir, Vodafone Tech. Excellence Prog., 2011–; Chief Internat. Acad. Advr, Harbin Inst. of Technol., 2011–. Hon. Sec., Electronic Applications Divl Bd, Inst. of Materials, 1990–2002. Editor-in-Chief, Internat. Jl of Electronics, 1998–2001. Silver Medal, RAEng, 2011. *Publications*: over 200 articles in scientific jls and procs; book chapters; patents. *Recreations*: travel, walking, music, history. *Address*: Department of Electrical and Electronic Engineering, Imperial College London, Exhibition Road, SW7 2AZ. *T*: (020) 7594 6204, *Fax*: (020) 7594 6308. *E*: e.yeatman@imperial.ac.uk.

**YELLAND, David Ian**; Founder, Kitchen Table Partners Ltd, since 2015; *b* Harrogate, 14 May 1963; *s* of John Michael Yelland and Patricia Ann (*née* McIntosh); *m* 1st, 1996, Tania Farrell (*d* 2006); one *s*; 2nd, 2010, Charlotte, *d* of Prof. Jeremy Elston and Gill Elston; one *d*. *Educ*: Brigg Grammar Sch., Lincs; Coventry Univ. (BA Hons Econs 1984); Harvard Business Sch. (AMP 2003). Grad. trainee, Westminster Press, 1985; trainee reporter, Buckinghamshire Advertiser, 1985–87; industrial reporter, Northern Echo, 1987–88; gen. news and business reporter, North West Times and Sunday Times, 1988–89; city reporter, Thomson Regl Newspapers, 1989–90; joined News Corporation, 1990: city reporter, city editor and NY corresp., The Sun, 1990–93; Dep. Business Ed., Business Ed., Dep. Ed., New York Post, 1993–98; Editor, The Sun, 1998–2003; Sen. Vice Pres., News Corp., NY, 2003; Sen. Vice-Chm., Weber Shandwick UK and Ireland, 2004–06; Partner, Brunswick Gp LLP, 2006–15. Life Patron, NSPCC, 2007; Trustee and Mem. Bd, Action on Addiction, 2012–. FRSA 2003. *Publications*: The Truth About Leo, 2010. *Recreations*: swimming, sleeping, recovering, Manchester City FC. *T*: (020) 7652 4348. *E*: david@kitchentablepartners.com. *Clubs*: Savile, Royal Automobile, Soho House (New York).

**YELTON, Michael Paul**; His Honour Judge Yelton; a Circuit Judge, since 1998; a Justice of the Court of Appeal, St Helena, since 2015; *b* 21 April 1950; *s* of Joseph William Yelton and Enid Hazel Yelton; *m* 1973, Judith Sara Chaplin (*d* 2018); two *s* one *d*. *Educ*: Queen Elizabeth's Hospital Sch., Bristol; Colchester Royal Grammar Sch.; Corpus Christi Coll., Cambridge (BA 1971; MA 1973). Called to the Bar, Middle Temple, 1972; in practice at the Bar, 1973–98; Fellow and Dir of Studies in Law, Corpus Christi Coll., Cambridge, 1977–81. *Publications*: Fatal Accidents: a practical guide to compensation, 1998; (jtly) Martin Travers, 1886–1948: an appreciation, 2003; Trams, Trolleybuses, Buses and the Law, 2004; Peter Anson, 2005; Anglican Papalism 1900–1960, 2005; Alfred Hope Patten and the Shrine of Our Lady of Walsingham, 2006; Empty Tabernacles, 2006; (jtly) Anglican Church-Building in London 1915–1945, 2007; Alfred Hope Patten: his life and times in pictures, 2007; (jtly) West Mon, 2008; The Twenty One: an Anglo-Catholic rebellion in London, 2009; Outposts of the Faith: Anglo-Catholicism in some rural parishes, 2009; Blackwells of Earls Colne, 2009; An Anglo-Catholic Scrapbook, 2010; The South India Controversy and the Converts of 1955–6, 2010; Bedwas & Machen UDC, 2010; Gelligaer UDC, 2011; (jtly) Guide to the Family Procedure Rules, 2011; Caerphilly UDC, 2013; (jtly) Anglican Church Building in London 1946–2012, 2013; More Empty Tabernacles, 2014; Pontypridd UDC, 2016; All Manner of Workmanship, 2016; Martin Travers: his life and work, 2016; Aberdare UDC, 2017; St Silas, Pentonville: the first 150 years, 2017; contribs to transport jls. *Recreations*: ecclesiology, history of road passenger transport, Association football. *Address*: Cambridge County Court, 197 East Road, Cambridge CB1 1BA. *T*: (01223) 224500.

**YENTOB, Alan**; Creative Director, BBC, 2004–15; *b* 11 March 1947; *s* of Isaac Yentob and Flora Yentob (*née* Khazam); one *s* one *d* by Philippa Walker. *Educ*: King's School, Ely; Univ. of Grenoble; Univ. of Leeds (LLB). BBC general trainee, 1968; producer/director, 1970–; arts features, incl. Omnibus, and Arena (Best Arts Series, British Acad. Awards, 1982, 1983, 1984, BPG Awards, 1985); Editor, Arena, 1978–85; Co-Editor, Omnibus, 1985; Hd of Music and Arts, BBC TV, 1985–88; Controller: BBC2, 1988–93, responsible for progs incl. The Late Show, Have I Got News For You, Absolutely Fabulous, Rab C. Nesbitt; BBC1, 1993–96; Dir of Progs, BBC TV, 1996–97; Dir of Television, BBC, 1997–2000; Dir, Drama, Entertainment and Children's Progs, BBC, 2000–04. Member: Bd of Directors, Riverside Studios, 1984–91; BFI Production Board, 1985–93; Council, English Stage Co., 1990; Chm., ICA, 2002–10. Governor: Nat. Film and TV School, 1988; S Bank Bd, 1999; Trustee, Architecture Foundn, 1992; Patron, Timebank (Trustee, 2001). FRTS; Fellow, BFI, 1997. Hon. Fellow: RCA, 1987; RIBA, 1991. Programming Supremo of Year, Broadcast Prodn Awards, 1997. *Recreations*: swimming, books.

**YEO, Rev. (Christopher) Richard**, JCD; OSB; Novice Master, Monasterio Santa Maria de la Santísima Trinidad, Lurin, since 2018; *b* 7 July 1948; *s* of Peter and Patricia Yeo. *Educ*: Downside Sch.; Lincoln Coll., Oxford (MA; Hon. Fellow, 2010); St Benet's Hall, Oxford; Pontifical Gregorian Univ., Rome (JCD). Entered monastery, 1970; ordained priest, 1976; Sec. of Abbot Primate of the Benedictines, 1980–86; Parish Priest, Bungay, 1986–93; Official, Congregation for Consecrated Life, 1993–98; Abbot of Downside, 1998–2006; Abbot Pres., English Benedictine Congregation, 2001–17; Superior of Buckfast Abbey, 2007–09. *Publications*: The Structure and Content of Monastic Profession, 1982. *Address*: Monasterio Santa Maria de la Santísima Trinidad, Apto. 16–061, Lurin-Lima 16, Peru.

**YEO, Diane Helen**; charity consultant; Chairman, Encouragement Through the Arts and Talking, since 2014; *d* of Brian Harold Pickard, FRCS and late Joan Daisy Pickard; *m* 1970, Timothy Stephen Kenneth Yeo, *qv*; one *s* one *d*. *Educ*: Blackheath High Sch.; London Univ.; Institut Français de Presse. BBC Radio, 1968–74; Africa Educnl Trust, 1974–79; Girl Guides' Assoc., 1979–82; YWCA, 1982–85; Dir, Inst. of Charity Fundraising Managers, 1985–88; Charity Comr, 1989–95; Chief Exec., Malcolm Sargent Cancer Fund for Children, subseq. Sargent Cancer Care for Children, 1995–2001; Chief Exec., UK for UNHCR, 2001–03; Diane Yeo Associates not for profit consultancy, 2003–; Chief Executive: Muscular Dystrophy Campaign, 2003–05; Chelsea and Westminster Health Charity, 2005–08. Chm., Charity Standards Cttee, 1991–95 (Rowntree Report 1991); Member: Nathan Cttee on Effectiveness and the Voluntary Sector, 1989–90 (Report 1990); Adv. Council, NCVO, 1994–; Council and Audit Cttee, Advertising Standards Authy, 1997–2003; Fundraising Regulation Adv. Gp, Home Office (Charities Act 2003), 2001–. Chm., NCVO/Charity Commn Cttee on Trng of Trustees, 1989–92 (report, On Trust, 1990). Chm. Mgt Bd, 151 Proprietors Ltd, 2008–. Chm., SOS Westminster, 2010–; Ambassador, Save the Children, 1986; Patron, CANCERactive, 2004–. Chm., The Arts Educational Schools, 2004–13. Mem. Ct of Govs, Univ. of Westminster, 2008– (Dep. Chair, 2017–; Mem., Mgt Bd, Regent Street Cinema, 2015–). Judge, Third Sector Excellence Awards, 2006–. Contested (Change UK) SE, EP, 2019. FInstF; FRSA 1989. Paul Harris Fellow, Rotary Internat., 2000. Charity Accounts Award, ICAEW and Charities Aid Foundn, 2002; Local Campaign of the Year Award, Leonard Cheshire Disability, 2011. *Publications*: contribs to professional jls. *Recreations*: tennis, photography, piano, gardening.
*See also J. Yeo*.

**YEO, Jonathan**; artist; *b* London, 18 Dec. 1970; *s* of Timothy Stephen Kenneth Yeo, *qv* and Diane Helen Yeo, *qv*; *m* 2006, Shebah Ronay; two *d*. *Educ*: Westminster Sch.; Univ. of Kent. *Solo exhibitions*: Jonathan Yeo's Sketchbook, Eleven, London, 2006; Blue Period, 2008, You're Only Young Twice, 2012, Lazarides, London; Porn in the USA, Lazarides LA, 2010; (I've Got You) Under My Skin, Circle Culture Gall., Berlin, 2013; Jonathan Yeo Portraits, NPG, 2013–14; Lowry Gall., 2014, Laing Art Gall., 2014–15; Exposure, Circle Culture Gall., Berlin, 2014; Jonathan Yeo Portraits, Mus. of Nat. Hist. at Frederiksborg Castle, Denmark, 2016; Skin Deep, Bowes Mus., Co. Durham, 2018. Painting commissions include portraits of: Archbishop Trevor Huddleston, private collection, 1993; Tony Blair, William Hague and Charles Kennedy (triptych), H of C, 2001; Rupert Murdoch, NPG, 2006; Claire's Room (Grayson Perry), NPG, 2006–13; Prince Philip, Duke of Edinburgh, Muscular Dystrophy Campaign, 2008; Tony Blair, Lincoln's Inn, 2008; Sir Michael Parkinson, NPG, 2010; David Attenborough, Royal Collection, 2011; Girl Reading (Malala Yousafzai), Malala Fund, 2013; HRH Duchess of Cornwall, Clarence House, 2014; Helle Thorning Schmidt, Mus. of Nat. Hist. at Frederiksborg Castle, Denmark, 2016. Art consultant for Soho House, 2009–. Trustee, NPG, 2018–. Judge: Art Fund Prize for Mus, 2010; BP Portrait Award, 2014. *Relevant publications*: The Many Faces of Jonathan Yeo, 2013; In the Flesh, 2016. *E*: info@jonathanyeo.com. *Clubs*: Groucho, Soho House, Chelsea Arts.

**YEO, Rt Rev. Richard**; *see* Yeo, Rt Rev. C. R.

**YEO, Timothy Stephen Kenneth**; *b* 20 March 1945; *s* of late Dr Kenneth John Yeo and Norah Margaret Yeo; *m* 1970, Diane Helen Pickard (*see* D. H. Yeo); one *s* one *d*; one *d*. *Educ*: Charterhouse; Emmanuel Coll., Cambridge (Open Exhibnr 1962; MA 1971). Asst Treas., Bankers Trust Co., 1970–73; Director, Worcester Engineering Co. Ltd, 1975–86. Chief Exec., Spastics Soc., 1980–83, Mem., Exec. Council, 1984–86. MP (C) S Suffolk, 1983–2015. PPS to Sec. of State for Home Dept, 1988–89, to Sec. of State for Foreign Affairs, 1989–90; Parly Under Sec. of State, DoE, 1990–92, DoH, 1992–93; Minister of State, DoE, 1993–94. Opposition spokesman on local govt and envmt, 1997–98; Shadow Minister of Agric., 1998–2001; Shadow Culture, Media and Sport Sec., 2001–02; Shadow Trade and Industry Sec., 2002–03; Shadow Health and Educn Sec., 2003–04; Shadow Transport and Envmt Sec., 2004–05. Member: Social Services Select Cttee, 1985–88; Employment Select Cttee, 1994–96; Treasury Select Cttee, 1996–97; Chairman: Envmtl Audit Select Cttee, 2005–10; Energy and Climate Change Select Cttee, 2010–15; Jt Sec., Cons. Pty Finance Cttee, 1984–87. Captain, Parly Golfing Soc., 1991–95. Director: Genus plc, 2002–04; ITI Energy Ltd, 2006–12; Groupe Eurotunnel SA, 2007–; Chairman: AFC Energy plc, 2007–17; Eco City Vehicles plc, 2007–12; TMO Renewables Ltd, 2010–13; University of Sheffield Energy 2050 Industrial Adv. Bd, 2015–19; New Nuclear Watch Institute (formerly New Nuclear Watch Europe), 2014–. Hon. Treasurer, International Voluntary Service, 1975–78. Pres., Renewable Energy Assoc., 2012–15. Trustee: African Palms, 1970–85; Tanzania Development Trust, 1980–97; Victoria Univ., Kampala, 2010–14; Chm., Tadworth Court Trust, 1983–90. Golf Correspondent: Country Life, 1994–; Financial Times, 2004–08. Hon. Trade Ambassador for S Korea, 2016–. *Publications*:

Public Accountability and Regulation of Charities, 1983; Green Gold, 2010. *Recreation:* skiing. *Clubs:* Garrick, MCC; Royal and Ancient Golf (St Andrews); Royal St George's (Sandwich); Sunningdale Golf.
*See also* J. Yeo.

**YEOMAN, Maj.-Gen. Alan,** CB 1987; *b* 17 Nov. 1933; *s* of George Smith Patterson Yeoman and Wilhelmina Tromans Elwell; *m* 1960, Barbara Joan Davies; two *s* (one *d* decd). *Educ:* Dame Allan's School, Newcastle upon Tyne. Officer Cadet, RMA Sandhurst, 1952; commnd Royal Signals, 1954; served Korea, Malaysia, Singapore, Cyprus, UK, BAOR and Canada, 1954–70 (Staff Coll., 1963); CO 2 Div. Sig. Regt, BAOR, 1970–73; HQ 1 (BR) Corps, BAOR, 1973–74; MoD, 1974–77; Col AQ, HQLF Cyprus, 1978–79; Comd Trng Gp, Royal Signals and Catterick Garrison, 1979–82; Brig. AQ, HQ 1 (BR) Corps, BAOR, 1982–84; Comd Communications, BAOR, 1984–87; retd 1988. Dir, Army Sport Control Bd, 1988–95 (Army Rugby League Challenge Cup named Yeoman Cup, 1994). Col Comdt, Royal Corps of Signals, 1987–93. Hon. Col, 37th (Wessex and Welsh) Signal Regt, T&AVR, 1987–95. Chm., Royal Signals Assoc., 1995–2000. *Recreation:* bridge. *Address:* c/o Lloyds Bank, 3 South Street, Wareham, Dorset BH20 4LX.

**YEOMAN, Rt Rev. David,** PhD; Assistant Bishop of Llandaff, 2004–09, now Honorary; *b* 5 March 1944; *s* of Thomas Walter and Doreen Yeoman; *m* 1969, Janice Flower; one *s* one *d*. *Educ:* UC Cardiff (BTh; PhD 2004); St Michael's Coll., Llandaff. Local govt officer, 1963–66. Ordained deacon, 1970, priest, 1971; Curate: St John Baptist, Cardiff, 1970–72; Caerphilly, 1972–76; Vicar: Ystrad Rhondda, 1976–81; Mountain Ash, 1981–96; Rector, Coity with Nolton, 1996–2004; Archdeacon of Morgannwg, 2004–06. Chaplain: Princess of Wales Hosp., 1996–2004; Welsh Guards Assoc., Bridgend, 1996–2001; RBL, Bridgend, 2003–04. Priory Chaplain, St John Priory for Wales, 2010–. *Publications:* (jtly) Christ in AIDS, 1997; (contrib.) Sexuality and Spirituality, 2000. *Recreations:* reading, poetry, music, photography, theatre, sport. *Address:* 4 Llety Gwyn, Bridgend CF31 1RG. *T:* (01656) 649919. *Club:* Rotary International (Bridgend).

**YEOMAN, Prof. Michael Magson,** PhD; FRSE; Regius Professor of Botany, 1978–93, now Emeritus, and Curator of Patronage, 1988–93, University of Edinburgh; *b* 16 May 1931; *s* of Gordon Yeoman and Mabel Ellen (*née* Magson), Newcastle upon Tyne; *m* 1962, Erica Mary Lines; two *d*. *Educ:* Gosforth Grammar Sch.; King's Coll., Univ. of Durham (BSc 1952, MSc 1954, PhD 1960); FRSE 1980. National Service, Royal Corps of Signals, 1954–56. Demonstrator in Botany, King's Coll., Newcastle upon Tyne, 1957–59; Edinburgh University: Lectr in Botany, 1960; Sen. Lectr, 1968; Reader, 1973; Dean, Fac. of Science, 1981–84; Vice-Principal, 1988–91. Vis. Prof., NENU, Changchun, China, 1986–. Chm., Univs Council for Adult and Continuing Educn (Scotland), 1989–91. Member: Governing Bodies, Nat. Vegetable Res. Stn and Scottish Plant Breeding Stn, 1978–82; SERC Biological Scis Cttee, 1982–85; SERC Biotechnology Management Cttee, 1983–85; British Nat. Cttee for Biology, 1981–89. Chm., Edinburgh Centre for Rural Res., 1989–93; Governor: East of Scotland Coll. of Agriculture, 1984–93; Scottish Crops Res. Inst., 1986–89. Chm. Trustees, Edinburgh Botanic Gdn (Sibbald) Trust, 1996–2003 (Trustee, 1986–2003); Trustee, Royal Botanic Gdn, Edinburgh, 1992–98 (Chm., Scientific Adv. Bd, 1995–98). Convener, N Northumberland Gp, Scottish Rock Garden Club, 1999–2002. Mem. Council, RSE, 1985–91 (Fellowship Sec., 1986–91). Gov. and Chm., Ellingham C of E First Sch., 1993–99; Churchwarden, St Maurice, Ellingham, 1996–2000. Member Editorial Board: Jl of Experimental Botany, 1981–85; Plant Science Letters, 1974–83; New Phytologist, 1977–93 (Trustee); Botanical Jl of Scotland, 1992–99. *Publications:* (ed) Cell Division in Higher Plants, 1976; (jtly) Laboratory Manual of Plant Cell and Tissue Culture, 1982; (ed) Plant Cell Technology, 1986; contrib. scientific jls; chapters, articles and revs in books. *Recreations:* military history, photography, gardening, walking. *Address:* 116 Allerburn Lea, Alnwick, Northumberland NE66 2QP. *T:* (01665) 605822.

**YEOMANS, Prof. Julia Mary,** DPhil; FRS 2013; Professor of Physics, University of Oxford, since 2002; Pauline Chan Fellow and Tutor in Physics, St Hilda's College, Oxford, since 1983; *b* Derby, 15 Oct. 1954; *d* of Anthony Harold Hickling Yeomans and Edna Maud Yeomans; *m* 1989, Prof. Peter John Hore; four *d*. *Educ:* Manchester High Sch. for Girls; Somerville Coll., Oxford (BA Phys 1976); Wolfson Coll., Oxford (DPhil Theoretical Phys 1979). Postdoctoral Res. Associate, Cornell Univ., 1979–81; Lectr, Univ. of Southampton, 1981–83; University of Oxford: Lectr, 1995–98; Reader in Phys, 1998–2002. Member: Council, Eur. Phys. Soc., 2010–14; Commn C3, IUPAP, 2011–; Council, Royal Soc., 2017–. FInstP 2000. Gov., Francis Holland Schs, 2009–17. Eur. Phys. Jl E—Pierre-Gilles de Gennes Lect. Prize, 2013. *Publications:* Statistical Mechanics of Phase Transitions, 1992; articles on soft matter physics in learned jls. *Recreations:* family, hiking, orienteering. *Address:* Rudolf Peierls Centre for Theoretical Physics, University of Oxford, Clarendon Laboratory, Parks Road, Oxford OX1 3PU. *T:* (01865) 273992. *E:* julia.yeomans@physics.ox.ac.uk.

**YEOMANS, Lucy;** Editor-in-Chief, Net-A-Porter.com, 2012–19; Editor, Porter, 2014–19; *b* 1 Nov. 1970; *d* of Harry Hammond Light Yeomans and Margaret (*née* Boyle). *Educ:* Univ. of St Andrews (MA Hons Hist. of Art 1992). Ed., Boulevard mag., Paris, 1993–95; Lit. Ed. and Features Ed., The European, 1995–98; Features Ed., Dep. Ed. and Actg Ed., Tatler, 1998–2000; Ed., Harpers & Queen, later Harper's Bazaar, 2000–12. FRSA. *Recreations:* theatre, horse-riding, music, poetry. *Club:* Soho House.

**YERBURGH,** family name of **Baron Alvingham.**

**YIANNI, Steven John,** FREng; Chief Executive, Transport Systems Catapult, 2013–17; *b* Barnet, 9 April 1962; *s* of Antony Yianni and Marianne Yianni; *m* 1984, Pamela Lesley Paton; two *s* one *d*. *Educ:* Highgate Sch.; Haberdashers' Aske's Boys' Sch., Elstree; King's Coll., Cambridge (BA Engrg 1983; MA 1985); London Business Sch. (MBA 1990). CEng 1988; FIMechE 2002. Ford Motor Co.: graduate trainee, 1983–85; Develt Engr, 1985–87; Powertrain Product Planner, 1988–89; Sen. Strategy Analyst, 1990–91; J.C. Bamford Excavators Ltd: Gen. Manager, JCB Res., 1991–93; Engrg Manager, JCB Wheeled Loader Div., 1993–95, JCB Loadall Div., 1995–97; Gen. Manager, Hydraulic Ram Div., 1998–99; Dir, 1999–2007; Dir and Gen. Manager, JCB Transmissions, 1999–2004; Dir, JCB Engrg Ops, 2005–07; Dir, Engrg, Network Rail, 2008–13. Non-exec. Dir, AIRTO Ltd, 2017–. Chm., 2010–13, non-exec. Dir, 2013–, Welding Inst. FREng 2014; FWeldI 2018. *Recreations:* theatre, walking, family, running, swimming.

**YIP, Hon. Dame Amanda Louise,** DBE 2017; **Hon. Mrs Justice Yip;** a Judge of the High Court, Queen's Bench Division, since 2017; Presiding Judge, Northern Circuit, from Jan. 2020; *b* Liverpool, 23 April 1969; *d* of Rt Hon. Sir John William Kay, PC (Rt Hon. Lord Justice Kay) and Jeffa Kay; *m* 1991, David Yip; one *s* two *d*. *Educ:* Merchant Taylors' Sch. for Girls, Crosby, Liverpool; Emmanuel Coll., Cambridge (BA Law 1990). Called to the Bar, Gray's Inn, 1991; in practice as a barrister, Exchange Chambers, 1991–2017; a Recorder, 2009–17; QC 2011; a Dep. High Court Judge, 2013–17. *Recreations:* spending time with family and friends, recreational cycling, ski-ing. *Address:* Royal Courts of Justice, Strand, WC2A 2LL.

**YIP, Prof. George Stephen;** Professor of Marketing and Strategy, Imperial College Business School, Imperial College London, 2015, now Emeritus; *b* 24 Sept. 1947; *s* of Teddy Yip and Susie (*née* Ho); *m* 1970, Moira Winsland; one *s* one *d*. *Educ:* Peak Sch., Hong Kong; East Grinstead County Grammar Sch.; Dover Coll.; Magdalene Coll., Cambridge (BA Hons 1970; MA 1973); Cranfield Univ. (MBA 1976); Harvard Business Sch. (MBA 1976; DBA 1980). Account Executive, 1970–72, Account Supervisor, 1973–74, Lintas London; Product Manager, Birds Eye Foods, 1972–73; Business Manager, Data Resources Inc., 1976–78; Asst Prof., Harvard Business Sch., 1980–83; Sen. Associate, MAC Gp, 1983–86; Sen. Manager, Price Waterhouse, 1986–87; Vis. Associate Prof., Georgetown Univ., 1987–91; Adjunct Prof., UCLA, 1991–99; Beckwith Prof. of Mgt Studies, Judge Inst. and Fellow, Magdalene Coll., Univ. of Cambridge, 1998–2000; Prof. of Strategic and Internat. Mgt, 2001–06, Associate Dean, 2001–03, London Business Sch.; Vice-Pres., and Dir of Res. and Innovation, Capgemini Consulting, 2006–08; Dean, Rotterdam Sch. of Mgt, Erasmus Univ., 2008–11; Prof. of Strategy (formerly of Mgt) and Co-Dir, Centre on China Innovation, China Europe Internat. Business Sch., 2011–16. Visiting Professor: Stanford Business Sch., 1997; Imperial Coll. London Business Sch., 2011–15; Vis. Fellow, Templeton Coll., Oxford, 1998; Sen. Fellow, Advanced Inst. Mgt Res., 2003. Fellow: World Economic Forum, 1998; Acad. of Internat. Business, 1999. *Publications:* Barriers to Entry, 1982; Total Global Strategy, 1992; Asian Advantage, 1998; Strategies for Central and Eastern Europe, 2000; Managing Global Customers, 2007; Strategic Transformation, 2013; China's Next Strategic Advantage: from imitation to innovation, 2016; Pioneers, Hidden Champions, Changemakers and Underdogs: lessons from China's innovators, 2019; articles in internat. mgt and mkting jls. *Recreations:* theatre, opera, classical music, bridge, tennis, sailing.

**YONATH, Prof. Ada E.,** PhD; Martin S. and Helen Kimmel Professor of Structural Biology, Director, Mazer Center for Structural Biology, and Director, Kimmelman Center for Biomolecular Structure and Assembly, Weizmann Institute of Science; *b* Jerusalem, 22 June 1939; *d* of Hillel and Esther Lifshitz; one *d*. *Educ:* Hebrew Univ. of Jerusalem (BSc 1962; MSc 1964); Weizmann Inst. of Sci. (PhD 1968). Postdoctoral studies, Carnegie-Mellon Univ. and MIT, 1968–70; Weizmann Inst. of Sci., 1970–; Gp Leader, Max Planck Inst. for Molecular Genetics, 1979–84; Hd, Res. Unit for Ribosome Structure, Max Planck Unit of Structural Molecular Biol., DESY, Hamburg, 1986–2004. Vis. Prof., Univ. of Chicago, 1977–78. Mem., EMBO. Member: NAS; Amer. Acad. Arts and Scis; Israel Acad. Scis and Humanities; Eur. Acad. Scis and Art. (Jtly) Nobel Prize in Chem., 2009. *Address:* Department of Structural Biology, Weizmann Institute of Science, PO Box 26, Rehovot 76100, Israel.

**YONG, Rt Rev. Datuk Ping Chung;** Bishop of Sabah, 1990–2006; Archbishop of South East Asia, 2000–06; *b* 20 Feb. 1941; parents decd; *m* 1969, Julia Yong; two *d*. *Educ:* Meml Univ., Newfoundland (BA 1968); Queen's Coll., Newfoundland (LTh 1969). Ordained, Sabah, 1970; Canon, 1974–90, Archdeacon, 1976–90, Sabah. Chairman: ACC, 1984–90; Council of Churches of E Asia, 1996–99; President: Christian Fedn of Malaysia, 1997–2001; Council of Churches of Malaysia, 1997–2001; Sabah Council of Churches, 1997–2003. *Address:* c/o PO Box 10811, 88809 Kota Kinabalu, Sabah, Malaysia.

**YORK, Archbishop of,** 2005–June 2020; **Most Rev. and Rt Hon. John Tucker Mugabi Sentamu;** PC 2005; PhD; *b* 10 June 1949; *s* of John Walakira and Ruth; *m* 1973, Rev. Margaret (*née* Wanambwa); one *s* one *d*. *Educ:* Masooli, Kyambogo and Kitante Hill and Old Kampala Sch., Uganda; Makerere Univ. (LLB 1971); Selwyn Coll., Cambridge (Pattison Student; BA 1976; MA, PhD 1984; Hon. Fellow, 2005); Ridley Hall, Cambridge; Dip. in Legal Practice, Uganda, 1972. Advocate, Uganda High Ct, 1972–74. Ordained deacon and priest, 1979; Asst Chaplain, Selwyn Coll., Cambridge, 1979; Asst Curate, St Andrew, Ham, and Chaplain, HM Remand Centre, Latchmere House, 1979–82; Asst Curate, St Paul, Herne Hill, 1982–83; Priest-in-charge, Holy Trinity, and Vicar, St Matthias, Tulse Hill, 1983–84, Vicar of jt parish, 1985–96; Priest-in-charge, St Saviour, Brixton Hill, 1987–89; Area Bp of Stepney, 1996–2002; Bp of Birmingham, 2002–05. Hon. Canon, Southwark Cathedral, 1993–96. Mem., Gen. Synod of C of E, 1985–96 (Mem., Standing Cttee, 1988–96, Policy Cttee, 1990–96); Chm., Cttee for Minority Ethnic Anglican Concerns, 1990–99. Member: Young Offenders Cttee, NACRO, 1986–95; Council, Family Action (formerly Family Welfare Assoc.), 1989–96; Stephen Lawrence Judicial Inquiry, 1997–99; Chairman: Islington Partnership, 2002–04; EC1 New Deal for Communities, 2000–02; London Marriage Guidance Council, 2000–03 (also Pres.); Damilola Taylor Investigation and Prosecution Review, 2002; NHS Haemoglobinopathy Screening Prog., 2001–13; Living Wage Commn, 2013–14; Bayelsa State Oil and Envmtl Commn, 2019–; Sponsor, York Fairness Commn, 2011–12. President: Youth for Christ, 2004–20; YMCA, 2005–20. Trustee, John Smith Inst., 2002–11. Gov., Univ. of N London, 1997–2002; Chancellor: York St John Univ., 2006–; Univ. of Cumbria, 2007–. FRSA. Freeman: City of London, 2000; City of Montego Bay, 2007. Hon. Bencher, Gray's Inn, 2007. Hon. Fellow: Canterbury Christ Church UC, 2001; QMW, 2001; St Margaret's Coll., Dunedin, 2014. Harold Turner Vis. Fellow, Univ. of Otago, 2014. DUniv Open, 2001; Hon. DPhil Glos, 2002; Hon. DLitt West Indies, 2007; Hon. DCL Northumbria at Newcastle, 2008; Hon. DD: Birmingham, 2003; Hull, 2007; Cambridge, 2008; Nottingham, 2008; Wycliffe Coll., Toronto, 2009; Sewanee, Tennessee, 2010; London, 2010; Aberdeen, 2013; Huron Univ. Coll., London, Ont, 2013; Hon. LLD: Leicester, 2005; Teesside, 2009; Leeds, 2010; Hon. DLitt Sheffield, 2007; Hon. Dr: Birmingham City, 2008; DUniv York, 2010; Hon. DTheol Chester, 2009. Midlander of the Year, 2003; Yorkshire Man of the Year, 2007; Lifetime Achievement Award, Yorkshire Awards, 2019. *Recreations:* music, cooking, reading, Rugby, football, athletics. *Address:* Bishopthorpe Palace, Bishopthorpe, York YO23 2GE.

**YORK, Dean of;** *see* Frost, Rt Rev. J. H.

**YORK, Archdeacon of;** *no new appointment at time of going to press.*

**YORK, David;** independent consultant, since 2004; *b* 20 April 1950; *s* of George William York and Ann (*née* Morgan); *m* 1982, Lindsey Anne Murgatroyd (marr. diss. 2006). *Educ:* Manor Park Sch., Newcastle upon Tyne; Salford Univ. (BSc 1973). MICE 1976. Joined Dept of Transport, 1970; Project Engr, 1977–83; Principal Engr, 1983–87; Superintending Engr, 1987–90; Director: NW Network Mgt, 1990; Yorks and Humberside Construction Prog., 1990–93; Motorway Widening Unit, 1993–95; Dep. Road Prog. Dir, 1995–96, Road Prog. Dir, 1996; Highways Agency: Project Services Dir, 1996–2001; Operations Dir, 2001–03; Nat. Traffic Dir, 2003–04. *Recreations:* flying, scuba diving, golf. *E:* davidyork@davidyork.plus.com.

**YORK, Col Edward Christopher,** OBE 2015; TD 1978; Vice Lord-Lieutenant of North Yorkshire, 1999–2014; Chairman and Managing Director, Hutton Wandesley Farms Co., and others, 1984–2014; *b* 22 Feb. 1939; *o s* of late Christopher York and Pauline Rosemary York (*née* Fletcher); *m* 1965, Sarah Ann, *d* of late Major James Kennedy Maxwell, MC; one *s* one *d*. *Educ:* Eton Coll. 1st Royal Dragoons, 1957–64. Chm., Thirsk Racecourse Co., 1993–2008. Vice Pres., Northern Assoc. of Building Socs, 1987–91; Pres., Yorks Agricl Soc., 1989 (Mem. Council, 1970–99); Hon. Show Dir, 1992–96, Pres., 1997, Chm. of Council, 1998–2002, Vice Patron, 2003–, RASE; Mem., N Yorks Br., 1978–2005, RASE Rep. on Council, 1999–2002, CLA. Chm., Royal Armouries Develt Trust (Leeds),

1995–99. CO, Queen's Own Yeomanry, 1979–81 (Hon. Col, 1998–2003); Dep. Comdr, 15 (NE) Bde, 1981–85; ADC to the Queen, 1982–86; Col Comdt, Yeomanry, 1994–99. Chm., Yorks and Humberside RFCA (formerly TAVRA), 1998–2003; Vice-Chm. (Army), Council of RFCAs, 2001–04; Co. Chm., N Yorks Scouts, 1999–2008; President: Army Benevolent Fund, N Yorks, 1999–2015; SSAFA, N Yorks, 2003–14. Mem. Bd, Yorks Mus. of Farming, 1979–2001. Chm., Christopher Topham's Apprenticing Charity, 1974–2011; Trustee, Arthur Rank Centre, NAC, 2002–14; Gov., William Akroyd's Charity, 1996–2008; Patron, MIND, York, 2009–15. FRAgS 1998. DL 1988, High Sheriff, 1988, N Yorks. *Recreations:* racing, field sports. *Address:* Hutton Wandesley Hall, York YO26 7NA. *T:* (home) (01904) 738240, (office) (01904) 738755, *Fax:* (01904) 738468. *E:* ecy@huttonwandesley.co.uk. *Club:* Boodle's.

**YORK, Giles Tristan,** QPM 2015; Chief Constable, Sussex Police, since 2014; *b* Tonbridge, Kent, 10 Feb. 1967; *s of* Carl Peter Francis Andrew York and Deidre Gabrielle York (*née* MacDonald); *m* 1995, Sally Gail Hargreaves; one *s* two *d. Educ:* Judd Sch., Tonbridge; Univ. of Durham (BSc); Roffey Park, Sussex (MBA). With Kent Police, 1990–2004, Divl Comdr, Medway, 1999–2002, Hd, Special Br., 2002–04; Asst Chief Constable, S Wales Police, 2005–08; Dep. Chief Constable, Sussex Police, 2008–14. FRSA. *Recreations:* photography, Land Rover owner (Series 3). *Address:* Sussex Police Headquarters, Malling House, Church Lane, Lewes, E Sussex BN7 2DZ.

**YORK, Michael, (Michael York-Johnson),** OBE 1996; actor; *b* 27 March 1942; *s of* Joseph Johnson and Florence Chown; *m* 1968, Patricia Frances McCallum. *Educ:* Hurstpierpoint College; Bromley Grammar School; University College, Oxford (MA). *Stage:* Dundee Repertory Theatre, 1964; National Theatre Co., 1965; Outcry, NY, 1973; Bent, NY, 1980; Cyrano de Bergerac, Santa Fe, 1981; Whisper in the Mind, 1991; The Crucible, NY, 1992; Someone Who'll Watch Over Me, NY, 1993; Camelot, US tour, 2007; Strauss Meets Frankenstein, Long Beach, 2008; Lisztian Loves, 2011; My Fair Lady, 2012; King Lear, 2013; *films:* The Taming of the Shrew, Accident, 1966; Romeo and Juliet, 1967; Cabaret, England Made Me, 1971; The Three Musketeers, 1973; Murder on the Orient Express, 1974; Logan's Run, 1975; The Riddle of the Sands, 1978; Success is the Best Revenge, 1984; Dawn, 1985; Vengeance, 1986; The Secret of the Sahara, Imbalances, 1987; The Joker, Midnight Blue, The Return of the Musketeers, 1988; The Long Shadow, 1992; Rochade, 1992; Eline Vere, 1992; Wide Sargasso Sea, 1993; Discretion Assured, 1993; The Shadow of a Kiss, 1994; Gospa, 1995; Austin Powers, 1997; Wrongfully Accused, 1998; Lovers and Liars, The Omega Code, 1999; Borstal Boy, 2000; Megiddo, 2001; Austin Powers in Goldmember, 2002; Moscow Heat, 2004; Testimony, 2009; The Justice of Wolves, 2010; The Mill and the Cross, 2011; *television* includes: Jesus of Nazareth, 1976; A Man Called Intrepid, 1978; For Those I Loved, 1981; The Weather in the Streets, The Master of Ballantrae, 1983; Space, 1984; The Far Country, 1985; The Four Minute Mile, The Heat of the Day, 1988; Till We Meet Again, 1989; The Night of the Fox, 1990; Fall from Grace, 1994; September, 1995; Not of This Earth, 1996; The Ring, 1996; True Women, Dark Planet, The Ripper, 1997; The Search for Nazi Gold, A Knight in Camelot, 1998; Perfect Little Angels, 1999; The Haunting of Hell House, 2000; The Lot, 2001; Curb Your Enthusiasm, 2002; La Femme Musketeer, 2004; Icon, 2005; Law and Order: Criminal Intent, 2006; The Four Seasons, 2008; Coming Home, 2009; British Legends of Stage and Screen, 2012; The Simpsons 2016. Chm., Calif Youth Theatre, 1987–. Hon. DFA S Carolina, 1988. *Publications:* (contrib.) The Courage of Conviction, 1986; (contrib.) Voices of Survival, 1987; Travelling Player (autobiog.), 1991; A Shakespearean Actor Prepares, 2000; Dispatches from Armageddon, 2002; Are My Blinkers Showing?, 2005; The Readiness is All, 2018. *Recreations:* travel, music, collecting theatrical memorabilia. *W:* www.michaelyork.net.

**YORK-JOHNSON, Michael;** *see* York, M.

**YORKE,** family name of **Earl of Hardwicke.**

**YORKE, David Harry Robert,** CBE 1993; FRICS; Senior Partner, Weatherall Green & Smith, Chartered Surveyors, 1984–92 (Consultant, 1992–97); *b* 5 Dec. 1931; *s of* late Harry Yorke and Marie Yorke, Minera, N Wales; *m* 1955, Patricia Gwynneth Fowler-Tutt; one *d. Educ:* Dean Close Sch., Cheltenham; College of Estate Management; Open Univ. (BA (Hons) 2005). FRICS 1966 (ARICS 1956); FCIArb 1994. Articled to Tregear & Sons, 1948–54. 2nd Lieut RA, 1955–56. Weatherall Green & Smith, 1960–97, Partner, 1961. Dir, London Auction Mart, 1981–92; Chm., Belgravia Property Co. Ltd, 1993–95. Mem., Bristol Develt Corp., 1988–96; Dir, British Waterways Bd, 1988–2000 (Vice-Chm., 1998–2000). Royal Institution of Chartered Surveyors: Mem., Gen. Council, 1978–92; Pres., Gen. Practice Div., 1981–82; Pres., 1988–89; Chm., RICS Insurance Services, 1991–96. Mem. Council, British Property Fedn, 1990–94. Pres., British Chapter, Internat. Real Estate Fedn, 1974. Freeman, City of London, 1979; Liveryman, Co. of Chartered Surveyors, 1979. *Recreations:* reading, crosswords, occasional cookery, narrow boating. *Address:* Beech House, The Croft, Kintbury, Berks RG17 9TS. *T:* (01488) 608788. *E:* dhryorke@gmail.com. *Clubs:* Buck's, Sloane, East India.

**YORKE, John;** Managing Director, Angel Station TV, since 2015; *b* 9 July 1962; *s of* Sydney Yorke and Valerie Yorke. *Educ:* Univ. of Newcastle upon Tyne (BA 1st Cl. Hons English Lit. 1984). BBC Radio Five, Drama: Producer, 1990–92; Sen. Producer, 1992–93; Chief Producer, 1993–94; BBC 1: Script Editor, 1994, Series Script Editor, 1994, Story Editor, 1995–98, Eastenders; Producer, City Central, 1998–2000; Exec. Producer, Eastenders, 2000–03; Dep. Hd of Drama Series, BBC, 2003–04; Hd of Drama, Channel 4 Television, 2004–05; Controller, Continuing Drama Series and Head of Independent Drama, BBC, 2005–06; Controller, Drama Production, subseq. Drama Production and New Talent, BBC, 2006–12; Man. Dir, Company Pictures, 2013–15. Founder, BBC Writers' Acad., 2004. Vis. Prof., Univ. of Newcastle upon Tyne, 2007–. *Publications:* Into The Woods: a five act journey, 2013.

**YORKE, Robert Anthony,** FSA; finance director and management consultant, since 1981; *b* 27 June 1944; *s of* late Patrick Langdon Yorke and Pamela Mary (*née* Rudgard; later Mrs Robert Michael Clive); *m* 1975, Morag, *d of* late J. S. M. Dow; one *s* one *d. Educ:* Marlborough Coll.; Clare Coll., Cambridge (MA); London Business Sch. (MSc Econ). Financial Controller, Bowater Corp., 1975–77; Chief Exec., Ridham Freight Services, 1977–81; Finance Dir, London and Devonshire Trust Ltd, 1987–2009. Comr, RCHME, 1991–99; Member: Ancient Monuments Adv. Cttee, English Heritage, 1998–2003; English Heritage Adv. Cttee, 2003–04; Sussex Inshore Fisheries Conservation Authy, 2011. Chairman: Nautical Archaeol. Soc., 1987–91; Jt Nautical Archaeol. Policy Cttee, 1995– (Vice-Chm., 1988–95). FSA 2001. Gov., Coll. of Richard Collyer, Horsham, 2012–. *Publications:* contribs to learned jls. *Recreations:* nautical archaeology, tennis. *Address:* Silver Birches, Bashurst Hill, Itchingfield, Horsham, W Sussex RH13 0NY. *T:* (01403) 790311.

**YORKE, Thomas Edward;** singer and guitarist; *b* Wellingborough, Northants, 7 Oct. 1968; *m* 2003, Rachel Owen (*d* 2016); one *s* one *d. Educ:* Abingdon Sch., Oxon; Univ. of Exeter. Lead singer, Radiohead, 1991–. *Albums:* with Radiohead: Pablo Honey, 1993; The Bends, 1995; OK Computer, 1997 (Grammy Award, 1997); Kid A, 2000 (Grammy Award, 2000); Amnesia, 2001; Hail to the Thief, 2003; In Rainbows, 2007 (Ivor Novello Award, 2008; Grammy Award, 2008); The King of Limbs, 2011; A Moon Shaped Pool, 2016; solo: The Eraser, 2006; Tomorrow's Modern Boxes, 2014; Anima, 2019; with Atoms for Peace: Amok, 2013. *Address:* c/o XL Recordings, One Codrington Mews, W11 2EH.

**YOSHIDA, Miyako,** Hon. OBE 2007; Artistic Consultant, National Ballet of Japan, since 2018; *b* 28 Oct. 1965; *d of* Eiji Yoshida and Etsuko (*née* Fukuda). *Educ:* Royal Ballet Sch. Joined Sadler's Wells Royal Ballet, later Birmingham Royal Ballet, 1984; soloist, 1987; Principal, 1988; Principal Dancer, Royal Ballet, 1995–2010. *Performances* include leading rôles in: Swan Lake, Sleeping Beauty, The Nutcracker, Giselle, Elite Syncopations, La Fille Mal Gardée, Hobson's Choice, The Dream, Don Quixote, Paquita, Allegri Diversi, Theme and Variations, Concerto Barroco, Les Sylphides, Divertimento No 15, Danses Concertantes, Les Patineurs, Romeo and Juliet, The Firebird, Coppélia. Prix de Lausanne, 1983; Global Award, 1989; Nakagawa Einosuke Award, 1995; Akiko Tachibana Award, 1996, 2002; Arts Encouragement Prize for New Artists, Min. of Educn, Sci., Sports and Culture, 1997; Hattori Chieko Award, 1998; Artist for Peace, Unesco, 2004; Japan Soc. Award, 2007; Best Female Dancer, Dance Critics, 2007. *Recreations:* reading, watching films. *Address:* National Ballet of Japan, New National Theatre, 1–1–1 Hon-machi, Shibuya-ku, Tokyo 151–0071, Japan.

**YOUINGS, Ven. Dr Adrian;** Archdeacon of Bath, since 2017; *b* Romford, 30 July 1965; *s of* Michael Youings and Eileen Youings; *m* 1992, Francesca Hobbs; one *s* one *d. Educ:* Exeter Univ. (BSc Hons Biol Scis 1986); Bath Univ. (PhD Microbial Physiology 1990); Wycliffe Hall Theol Coll., Oxford (BTh). Lay Asst, St Ebbes Church, Oxford, 1990; Postdoctoral Res. Asst, Glycobiology Inst., Oxford, 1990–93; ordained deacon, 1996, priest, 1997; Asst Curate, St Paul's Church, Dorking, 1996–99; Sen. Curate, Emmanuel Church, S Croydon, 1999–2003; Rector, Trull with Angersleigh, 2003–17; Rural Dean, Taunton, 2015–17. *Publications:* contrib. Biochemical Jl. *Recreations:* West Ham United FC, amateur dramatics, school governor (primary), family, walking. *Address:* 56 Grange Road, Saltford, Bristol BS31 3AG. *T:* (01225) 873609. *E:* adbath@bathwells.anglican.org.

**YOUNG;** *see* Hughes-Young, family name of Baron St Helens.

**YOUNG,** family name of **Barons Kennet, Young of Cookham, Young of Graffham** and **Young of Norwood Green.**

**YOUNG OF COOKHAM,** Baron *cr* 2015 (Life Peer), of Cookham in the Royal County of Berkshire; **George Samuel Knatchbull Young,** CH 2012; PC 1993; Bt 1813; *b* 16 July 1941; *s of* Sir George Young, 5th Bt, CMG, and Elisabeth (*née* Knatchbull-Hugessen); *S* father as 6th Bt, 1960; *m* 1964, Aurelia Nemon-Stuart, er *d of* late Oscar Nemon, and of Mrs Nemon-Stuart, Boar's Hill, Oxford; two *s* two *d. Educ:* Eton; Christ Church, Oxford (Open Exhibitioner); MA Oxon, MPhil Surrey. Economist, NEDO, 1966–67; Kobler Research Fellow, University of Surrey, 1967–69; Economic Adviser, PO Corp., 1969–74. Councillor, London Borough of Lambeth, 1968–71; Mem., GLC, for London Borough of Ealing, 1970–73. MP (C) Ealing, Acton, Feb. 1974–1997, NW Hampshire, 1997–2015. An Opposition Whip, 1976–79; Parly Under Sec. of State, DHSS, 1979–81, DoE, 1981–86; Comptroller of HM Household, 1990; Minister of State, DoE, 1990–94; Financial Sec. to HM Treasury, 1994–95; Sec. of State for Transport, 1995–97; Shadow Leader, H of C, 1998–2000 and 2009–10; Lord Privy Seal and Leader, H of C, 2010–12; Parly Sec. to HM Treasury (Govt Chief Whip), 2012–14; a Lord in Waiting (Govt Whip), 2016–19. Chm., Acton Housing Assoc., 1972–79. Dir, Lovell Partnerships Ltd, 1987–90. Trustee, Guinness Trust, 1986–90. *Publications:* Accommodation Services in the UK 1970–1980, 1970; Tourism, Blessing or Blight?, 1973; I'm Keeping Young: the everyday life of an MP, 2015. *Recreation:* bicycling. *Heir:* (to Baronetcy) *s* George Horatio Young [*b* 11 Oct. 1966; *m* 1999, Marianne, *e d of* Dr Peter Toghill]. *Address:* House of Lords, SW1A 0PW.

**YOUNG OF GRAFFHAM,** Baron *cr* 1984 (Life Peer), of Graffham in the County of W Sussex; **David Ivor Young,** CH 2015; PC 1984; DL; Chairman, Young Associates Ltd, since 1996; *b* 27 Feb. 1932; *s of* late Joseph and of Rebecca Young; *m* 1956, Lita Marianne Shaw; two *d. Educ:* Christ's Coll., Finchley; University Coll., London (LLB Hons; Fellow, 1988). Admitted solicitor, 1956. Exec., Great Universal Stores Ltd, 1956–61; Chairman: Eldonwall Ltd, 1961–74; Manufacturers Hanover Property Services Ltd, 1974–84; Cable and Wireless, 1990–95; Neoscorp Ltd (formerly Inter Digital Networks), 1997–2002; CDT Holdings plc, 1997–99; Pixology Ltd, 1997; Autohit, then Accident Exchange Gp, plc, 2000–06; Spectrum Interactive plc, 2004; Euortel Ltd, 2006; Director: Town & City Properties Ltd, 1971–74; Salomon Inc., 1990–94; Business for Sterling. Chm., British ORT, 1975–80 (Pres., 1980–82); Pres., World ORT Union, 1990–93 (Chm., Admin. Cttee, 1980–84). Dir, Centre for Policy Studies, 1979–82 (Mem., Management Bd, 1977); Mem., English Industrial Estates Corp., 1980–82; Chm., Manpower Services Commn, 1982–84; Mem., NEDC, 1982–89. Industrial Adviser, 1979–80, Special Adviser, 1980–82, DoI; Minister without Portfolio, 1984–85; Sec. of State for Employment, 1985–87; Sec. of State for Trade and Industry, 1987–89; Dep. Chm., Cons. Party, 1989–90. Pres., Inst. of Directors, 1993–2002; Chairman: EU-Japan Business Forum (formerly EU-Japan Assoc.), 1991–97; W Sussex Econ. Forum, 1996–; formerly Dir, Prince of Wales Business Leaders Forum. Pres., Jewish Care, 1990–97 (formerly Mem., Community Foundn); Chairman: Internat. Council of Jewish Social and Welfare Services, 1981–84; Central Council for Jewish Community Services, 1993; Bd of Govs, Oxford Centre for Postgrad. Hebrew Studies, 1989–93. Chm., Chichester Festival Theatre Ltd, 1997–2012; Director: Royal Opera House Trust, 1990–95; South Bank Foundn Ltd; formerly Dir, Centre for Performing Arts; Chairman: London Philharmonic Trust, 1995–98; Council, UCL, 1995–2005. Hon. FRPS 1981. DL West Sussex, 1999. *Publications:* The Enterprise Years: a businessman in the Cabinet, 1990; Degrees of Isolation, 2005. *Recreations:* music, book-collecting, photography. *Address:* Young Associates Ltd, 100 Marylebone Road, NW1 5DX. *Club:* Savile.
*See also* Rt Hon. Sir B. A. Rix.

**YOUNG OF HORNSEY,** Baroness *cr* 2004 (Life Peer), of Hornsey in the London Borough of Haringey; **Lola Young,** OBE 2001; PhD; freelance arts and heritage consultant, since 2004; *b* 1 June 1951; *d of* Maxwell Fela Young and Yele Santos; *m* 1984, Barrie Birch; one *s. Educ:* Middlesex Univ. (BA Hons; PhD 1995). Social worker, London Bor. of Islington, 1971–73; actor, 1976–84; Co-Dir and Trng and Develt Manager, Haringey Arts Council, 1985–89; freelance arts consultant and lectr, 1989–91; Lecturer in Media Studies, Thames Valley Univ., 1990–92; Lectr, then Sen. Lectr, 1992–97, Prof. of Cultural Studies, 1997–2001, Emeritus Prof., 2002, Middx Univ.; Hd of Culture, GLA, 2002–04. Vis. Prof., Birkbeck, Univ. of London, 2004–07. Chm., Nitro, theatre co. (formerly Black Theatre Cooperative), 2004–09. Advr to Arts Council England, 1988–2002; Project Dir, Nat. Museum and Archives of Black History and Culture, 1997–2001. Mem., RCHME, 2000; Member, Board: Inst. of Internat. Visual Arts, 1994–2001; RNT, 2000–03; Resource: Council for Museums, Archives & Libraries, 2000–02; South Bank Centre, 2002–10; Somerset House, 2013–; Aid by Trade, 2013–; Member: English Heritage Blue Plaques sub-cttee, 2001–03; UK Cttee, Nat. Commn for UNESCO, 2009–11; Chairman: Arts Adv. Cttee, British Council, 2004–08; Commonwealth Gp on Culture and Develt, 2009–12; Cultural Diversity Panel, Arts Council; non-exec. Dir, Nat. Archives, 2007–10; Commissioner: Royal Commn on

Historic Manuscripts, 2000–01; Historic England (formerly English Heritage), 2011–17. Co-Chair, All Party Parly Gp on Ethics and Sustainability in Fashion, 2010–, on Sports, Modern Slavery and Human Rights, 2017; Member: EU Select Cttee, 2010–13; Jt Select Cttee on Reform of H of L, 2011–12; Select Cttee on Sexual Violence in Conflict, 2015–16; Constables Adv. Panel, Police Fedn, 2014–16; Bank of England Banknote Adv. Cttee, 2015–; Laming Review on Children in Care in Youth Justice System, 2016; Adv. Panel, Lammy Review into treatment of and outcomes for Black, Asian and Minority Ethnic individuals in Criminal Justice System, 2016; Expert Advr, Ind. Parly Review of Modern Slavery Act. Chair: Think Positive Age Well, 2010–13; Adv. Gp, The Young Review: improving outcomes for young black, mixed heritage and Muslim male offenders, 2013–; Agenda: the Alliance for Girls and Women at Risk, 2014–; Co-Chair, Foundn for Future London, 2018–; Ambassador: Cotton Made in Africa, 2010–; Ethical Fashion Forum, 2010–; Made-by, 2010–; Patron: Autograph (Assoc. of Black Photographers), 1997–; Post-Adoption Centre, 2004– (Mem. Mgt Cttee, 2000–03); Action Space, 2007–; Josephine Wolf Trust, 2007–; Anti-Slavery Internat., 2011–; Mem., Adv. Gp, Howard League for Penal Reform. Member, Judging Panel: Man Booker Prize, 2017 (Chair); Orange Prize for Literature (Chair); Caine Prize for African Literature; Art Fund Prize; Observer Ethical Awards. Mem., Ct of Govs, LSE, 2008–10. Hon. Dr: Middlesex, 2015; UAL, 2016; Sussex, 2016. Freeman, Tallow Chandlers' Co., 2012. FRSA 2000. *Publications:* Fear of the Dark: race, gender and sexuality in cinema, 1996; contrib. articles and chapters in edited books; contrib. articles to academic jls, incl. Women: A Cultural Rev., Cultural Studies from Birmingham, Oxford Art Jl, Parallax. *Recreations:* hiking, cinema, theatre, reading. *Address:* House of Lords, SW1A 0PW. *Clubs:* h, House of St Barnabas.

**YOUNG OF NORWOOD GREEN**, Baron *cr* 2004 (Life Peer), of Norwood Green, in the London Borough of Ealing; **Anthony Ian Young**, Kt 2002; *b* 16 April 1942; *m* 1st, 1962, Doreen Goodman (marr. diss. 1984); one *s* two *d*; 2nd, 1985, Margaret Newnham; one *s* one *d*. *Educ:* Kenmore Park Primary Sch.; Harrow County GS. Joined GPO as telecommunications apprentice, 1958; Union Br. Officer, 1967, Mem. NEC, 1978–89, PO Engrg Union; Gen. Sec., Nat. Communications Union, 1989–95; Jt Gen. Sec., 1995–98, Sen. Dep. Gen. Sec., 1998–2002, Communication Workers' Union. A Lord in Waiting (Govt Whip) and Parly Under-Sec. of State, DIUS, later BIS, 2008–10. Mem., Gen. Council, TUC, 1989–2002 (Pres., 2001–02); Eur. Co-Pres., Union Network Internat., 1999–2003 (Eur. Pres., Communications Internat., 1997–99). Trade Union Liaison Officer, Ethical Trading Initiative, 2002 (Vice Chm., 2002–14). Member: Employment Tribunal Steering Bd, 1997–2003; Wilton Park Academic Council, 1997–2006. A Governor, BBC, 1998–2002. Apprenticeship Ambassador, Nat. Apprenticeship Service, 2018–. Chm., One World Broadcasting Trust, 2002–09. Gov., Three Bridges Primary Sch., 2002 (Chm., 2017). *Recreations:* reading, music, cycling, tennis, skating, walking, spasmodic gardening and cooking. *Address:* House of Lords, SW1A 0PW.

**YOUNG OF OLD SCONE**, Baroness *cr* 1997 (Life Peer), of Old Scone, in Perth and Kinross; **Barbara Scott Young**; Chairman, Woodland Trust, since 2016; *b* 8 April 1948; *d* of George Young and Mary (*née* Scott). *Educ:* Perth Acad.; Edinburgh Univ. (MA Classics); Strathclyde Univ. (Diploma Sec. Sci.); DipHSM, 1971. Various posts, finally Sector Administrator, Greater Glasgow Health Bd, 1975–78; Dir of Planning and Develt, St Thomas' Health Dist, 1978–79; Dist Gen. Administrator, NW Dist, Kensington and Chelsea and Westminster AHA, 1979–82; Dist Administrator, Haringey HA, 1982–85; District General Manager: Paddington and N Kensington HA, 1985–88; Parkside HA, 1988–91; Chief Exec., RSPB, 1991–98; Chm., English Nature, 1998–2000; Vice-Chm., Bd of Govs, BBC, 1998–2000; Chief Exec., Envmt Agency, 2000–08; Shadow Chair, 2008–09, Chair, 2009–10, Care Quality Commission, DoH; Chief Exec., Diabetes UK, 2010–15. Member: BBC Gen. Adv. Council, 1985–88; Cttee, King's Fund Inst., 1986–90; Delegacy, St Mary's Hosp. Med. Sch., 1991–94; Cttee, Sec. of State for the Envmt's Going for Green initiative, 1994–96, UK Round Table on Sustainability, 1995–2000; Commn on Future of Voluntary Sector, 1995–96; Exec. Cttee, NCVO, 1997 (Mem., Trustee Bd, 1993–97); COPUS, 1996–97; Minister for Agriculture's Adv. Gp, 1997–98; EU Envmtl Adv. Forum, 1999–2001. Pres., Inst. of Health Services Management, 1987–88. Internat. Fellow, King's Fund Coll., 1985–87 and 1990. Non-exec. Dir, AWG plc, 1998–2001. Member: World Council, Birdlife Internat., 1994–98; Green Globe Task Force, 1997–98 Adaptation Sub-Cttee, Cttee on Climate Change, 2009–10. Patron, Inst. of Ecol and Envmt Management, 1993–; Vice President: Flora & Fauna Internat., 1998–; Birdlife Internat., 1999–; RSPB, 2000–; President: Cambs, Beds and Northants Wildlife Trust, 2002–; British Trust for Ornithology, 2005–13 (Vice Pres., 2004–05); S Georgia Heritage Trust, 2010–; Beds SO, 2013–. Trustee, IPPR, 1999–2009. Chancellor, Cranfield Univ., 2010–. Patron, Lantra, 2013–. Hon. RICS 2000; Hon. Fellow: Geologists Assoc., 2000; Sidney Sussex Coll., Cambridge, 2002; Hon. FCIWEM 2001; Hon. FRSE, 2017. DUniv: Stirling, 1995; York, St Andrews, Aberdeen, 2000; Open, 2001; Hon. DSc: Hertfordshire, 1997; Cranfield, 1998; Anglia Ruskin, 2009; Gloucestershire, 2009. *Recreations:* bad dressage rider, obsessive cinema goer and gardener. *Address:* House of Lords, SW1A 0PW.

**YOUNG, Andrea**, PhD; Director, Broadcasting, Media and Creative Industries, Department for Digital, Culture, Media and Sport (formerly Department for Culture, Media and Sport), since 2017; *b* Oadby, Leics, 30 July 1964; *d* of Alec Young and Janette Young; *m* 1994, Ave Wrigley; two *d*. *Educ:* Bristol Univ. (BSc Botany and Zoology 1982; PhD 1991). Hd, Sustainable Develt Unit, 2002–03, Hd, Farm Regulation, 2004–06, DEFRA; Hd, Econ. and Envmt, 2006–08, Actg Regl Dir, 2008, Govt Office for the East of England; Department for Environment, Food and Rural Affairs: Dir, Climate Change, Exotic Disease and Agency Relationship Portfolio, Food and Farming Gp, 2008–11; Dir, Strategy, 2011–12; Dir, Triennial Rev. Team, Envmt Agency and Natural England, 2012–13; Dir, Enterprise, 2013–14; Dir, Digital Economy Unit, DCMS and BIS, 2014–17. *Address:* Department for Digital, Culture, Media and Sport, 100 Parliament Street, SW1A 2BQ.

**YOUNG, Andrew**; Chairman, Andrew J. Young Foundation, since 2003; *b* New Orleans, La, 12 March 1932; *s* of Andrew J. Young and Daisy Fuller; *m* 1954, Jean Childs (*d* 1994); one *s* three *d*; *m* 1996, Carolyn Watson. *Educ:* Howard Univ., USA; Hartford Theological Seminary. Ordained, United Church of Christ, 1955; Pastor, Thomasville, Ga, 1955–57; Associate Dir for Youth Work, Nat. Council of Churches, 1957–61; Admin. Christian Educn Programme, United Church of Christ, 1961–64; Mem. Staff, Southern Christian Leadership Conf., 1961–70, Exec. Dir, 1964–70, Exec. Vice-Pres., 1967–70; elected to US House of Representatives from 5th District of Georgia, 1972 (first Black Congressman from Georgia in 101 years); re-elected 1974 and 1976; US Ambassador to UN, 1977–79; Mayor of Atlanta, 1982–89. Co-Chm., Atlanta Cttee for Olympic Games 1996. Chm., Law Cos Internat. Gp, Inc., 1990–93; Vice-Chm., Law Cos Gp, Inc., 1993–97; Co-Chm. and Co-founding Partner, GoodWorks Internat., 1997–2012. Pres., Nat. Council of the Churches of Christ, 2000–01. Chairman: Atlanta Community Relations Commn, 1970–72; National Democratic voter registration drive, 1976; during 1960s organized voter registration and community develt programmes. Mem. Bd of Dirs, Martin Luther King, Jr Center. Hon. Prof. of Policy Studies, Andrew Young Sch. of Policy Studies, Georgia State Univ. Holds numerous hon. degrees and awards, including: Presidential Medal of Freedom, 1980; Légion d'Honneur (France). *Publications:* A Way Out of No Way, 1994; An Easy Burden, 1996; Walk in My Shoes, 2010. *Address:* Andrew J. Young Foundation, 260 14th Street NW, Atlanta, GA 30318, USA.

**YOUNG, Dr Andrew Buchanan**, FRCPE; Deputy Chief Medical Officer, Scottish Office Department of Health (formerly Scottish Office Home and Health Department), 1989–97; *b* 11 Aug. 1937; *s* of Alexander and Elizabeth Young; *m* 1965, Lois Lilian Howarth; one *s* one *d*. *Educ:* Falkirk High School; Edinburgh Univ. (MB ChB). DTM&H. Supt, Presbyterian Church of E Africa Hosps, Kenya, 1965–72; Fellow in Community Medicine, Scottish Health Service, 1972–75; Scottish Home and Health Department: MO 1975; SMO 1978; PMO 1985. Pres., Edinburgh Medical Missionary Soc., 1992–97. QHP, 1993–96. *Recreations:* trying to learn computing, reading. *Address:* R12 The Oaks, 88 Main South Road, Christchurch 8042, New Zealand. *E:* abylly@xtra.co.nz.

**YOUNG, Andrew George**, OBE 2017; Strategy Actuary, Pensions Regulator, since 2009; *b* 15 June 1949; *s* of James Cameron Young and Agnes Young; *m* 1st, 1975, Victoria Leslie (marr. diss. 2009); one *s* three *d*; 2nd, 2010, Sara Victoria, two *d*. *Educ:* Univ. of Glasgow (BSc 1st Cl. Hons Maths, Natural Philosophy). Government Actuary's Dept, 1972–2009; Directing Actuary, 1995–2005; Sen. Consulting Actuary, 2005–09. *Recreations:* music, theatre, travel. *Address:* 95 Stanford Road, Brighton BN1 5PR. *T:* (01273) 563443.

**YOUNG, Prof. Andrew William**, PhD, DSc; FBA 2001; Professor of Neuropsychology, University of York, since 1997; *b* 14 March 1950; *s* of Alexander Young and Winnifred Doris Young; *m* 1976, Mavis Langham; one *s* two *d*. *Educ:* Bedford Coll., London (BSc 1971); PhD Warwick 1974; DSc London 1990. Lectr in Psychol., Univ. of Aberdeen, 1974–76; Lectr, then Reader in Psychol., Univ. of Lancaster, 1976–89; Prof. of Psychol., Univ. of Durham, 1989–93; Special Appt, MRC Scientific Staff, Applied Psychol. Unit, Cambridge, 1993–97. Bartlett Lect., Experimental Psychol. Soc., 2017 (Hon. Mem., 2018). Dr *hc* Liège, 2000. Cognitive Psychol. Award, 1994, 2007, 2014, President's Award, 1995, Book Award, 2001, Hon. Fellow, 2005, Lifetime Achievement Award, 2013, BPsS. *Publications:* (with A. W. Ellis) Human Cognitive Neuropsychology, 1988, 2nd edn 1996; (with V. Bruce) In the Eye of the Beholder: the science of face perception, 1998; (with V. Bruce) Face Perception, 2012. *Recreations:* jukebox collector and partially reformed trainspotter. *Address:* Department of Psychology, University of York, Heslington, York YO10 5DD. *T:* (01904) 323159.

**YOUNG, Prof. Archibald**, MD; FRCP, FRCPGlas, FRCPE; Professor of Geriatric Medicine, Edinburgh University, 1998–2007; *b* 19 Sept. 1946; *s* of Dr Archibald Young and Mary Downie Young (*née* Fleming); *m* 1st, 1973, Alexandra Mary Clark (marr. diss. 1995); one *s* one *d*; 2nd, 2006, Susann Mary Dinan. *Educ:* Glasgow Univ. (BSc 1st Cl. Hons 1969; MB ChB 1971; MD 1983). MRCP 1973, FRCP 1989; FRCPGlas 1985; FRCPE 1999. Hon. Consultant Physician in Rehabilitation Medicine, Nuffield Dept of Orthopaedic Surgery, Oxford Univ., 1981–85; Consultant Physician in Geriatric Medicine, Royal Free Hosp., 1985–87; Royal Free Hospital School of Medicine: Hon. Sen. Lectr, 1985–87, Sen. Lectr, 1987–88, in Geriatric Medicine; Prof. and Head, Univ. Dept of Geriatric Medicine and Hon. Consultant Physician, 1988–98. *Publications:* contribs to learned jls on effects of ageing, use and disuse on muscle and exercise physiology. *Recreation:* physical. *Address:* 45 Polton Road, Lasswade, Midlothian EH18 1LT. *Club:* Junior Mountaineering of Scotland.

**YOUNG, Charles Gerard M.**; *see* Mackworth-Young.

**YOUNG, Charmaine Carolyn**, CBE 2003; Chief Executive, Berkeley Foundation, 2013–16; *b* 24 July 1952; *d* of Leonard and Dolly Danks; *m* 1992, Robert Michael Young. *Educ:* Birmingham Polytech. (pt-time; ONC, HNC Bldg Construction). Architectural Technician, 1974–81, Project Team Leader, 1981–83, Birmingham CC; Asst Dir of Housing, Sheffield CC, 1983–89; Urban Renewal Manager, Wimpey Homes, 1989–96; Business Develt Dir, Lovell Partnerships, 1996–99; Regeneration Dir, St George Regeneration Ltd, 1999–2012; Dir, St George plc, 2010–12. Ind. Expert, Bd, Homes for London, 2012–. FInstD 2008; FCIOB 2017. *Publications:* (ed) Working Together: delivering growth through localism, 2011. *Recreations:* trying to recapture my youth, getting the construction industry to value women.

**YOUNG, His Honour Christopher Godfrey**; a Circuit Judge, 1980–97; a Deputy High Court Judge, 1992–97; *b* 9 Sept. 1932; *s* of late Harold Godfrey Young, MB, ChB, and Gladys Mary Young; *m* 1969, Jeanetta Margaret (*d* 1984), *d* of Halford and Dorothy Vaughan; one *s*. *Educ:* Bedford Sch.; King's Coll., Univ. of London (LLB Hons 1954; MA 1999). Called to the Bar, Gray's Inn, 1957; Midland and Oxford Circuit, 1959; a Recorder of the Crown Court, 1975–79; Resident Judge: Peterborough Crown Court, 1980–87; Leicester Crown Court, 1987–97. Mem., Parole Bd, 1990–93, 1997–2003 (Appraiser, 2003–05); Pt time Chm., Immigration Appeal Tribunal, 1997–98. Hon. Pres., De Montfort Univ. Sch. of Law, 1996–98. Postgraduate research: in Byzantine Studies, RHC, 1999–2005; in Faculty of Oriental Studies, Oxford Univ., 2005– (Mem., Pembroke Coll., Oxford). Mem., Cttee, Soc. for the Promotion of Byzantine Studies, 2004–07. Chm., Maidwell with Draughton Parish Council, 1973–76. *Recreations:* music, travel, Eastern Mediterranean. *Address:* Stockshill House, Duddington, Stamford, Lincs PE9 3QQ. *T:* (01780) 444658. *Club:* Athenæum.

**YOUNG, Colin**, CBE 1994 (OBE 1976); Senior Consultant, Ateliers du Cinéma Européen, since 1996 (Director, 1993–96); Director, National Film and Television School of Great Britain (formerly National Film School), 1970–92; *b* 5 April 1927; *s* of Colin Young and Agnes Holmes Kerr Young; *m* 1st, 1960, Kristin Ohman; two *s*; 2nd, 1987, Constance Yvonne Templeman; one *s* one *d*. *Educ:* Bellahouston Academy, Glasgow; Univs of Glasgow, St Andrews and California (Los Angeles). Theatre and film critic, Bon Accord, Aberdeen, 1951; cameraman, editor, writer, director, 1953–; producer, 1967–; UCLA (Motion Pictures): Instructor, 1956–59; Asst Prof., 1959–64; Assoc. Prof., 1964–68; Prof., 1968–70, Head, Motion Picture Div., Theater Arts Dept, UCLA, 1964–65; Chm., Dept of Theater Arts, 1965–70 (prod. film, The Village, 1968, for first academic prog. in ethnographic film). Res. Associate, Centre Nat. de Recherche Scientifique, Paris, 1984 and 1987; Andrew W. Mellon Vis. Prof. in Humanities, Rice Univ., Houston, Texas, 1985–86. Tutor, Arista Story Editing Workshops, 1996–2006. Vice-Chm., 1976–91, Chm., 1976–91, Edinburgh Film Festival; Chm., Edinburgh Internat. Film and Television Council, 1990–91; Governor, BFI, 1974–80. Member: Arts Council Film Cttee, 1972–76; Public Media Panel, Nat. Endowment for Arts, Washington, 1972–77; Gen. Adv. Council, BBC, 1973–78; Council of Management, BAFTA, 1974–81; Exec. Cttee, Centre International de Liaison des Ecoles de Cinéma et de Télévision, 1974–94 (Pres., 1980–94); Nat. Film Finance Corp., 1979–85; British Screen Adv. Council, 1990–; Bd, Moonstone Film Labs Internat., 1997–2007; Lottery Film Prodn Cttee, Scottish Arts Council, 1998–2000; Lottery Film Prodn Cttee, Scottish Screen, 2000–05. Consultant, Goldcrest Films & Television Ltd, 1985–86. FBKS 1975. Chm., Cttee on Educational Policy, UCLA, 1968–69. London Editor, Film Quarterly, 1970–91 (Los Angeles Editor, 1958–68). Hon. Gov., Nat. Film and Television Sch., 2007– (Mentor, documentary dept, 2006–). Michael Balcon Award, 1983, Fellow, 1993, BAFTA; Lifetime Achievement Award, British Ind.

Film Awards, 2000. Chevalier de l'Ordre des Arts et des Lettres (France), 1987. *Publications:* various articles in collections of film essays including Principles of Visual Anthropology, 1975; experimental film essay for Unesco, 1963; ethnographic film essays for Unesco, 1966, 1979; contribs to Film Quarterly, Sight and Sound, Jl of Aesthetic Education, Jl of the Producers Guild of America, Kosmorama (Copenhagen), etc. *Address:* Turret House, Ivy Hatch Court, Ivy Hatch, Sevenoaks, Kent TN15 0PQ.

**YOUNG, Sir Colville (Norbert),** GCMG 1994; MBE 1986; JP; DPhil; Governor-General of Belize, since 1993; *b* 20 Nov. 1932; *s* of Henry Oswald Young and Adney Wilhelmina (*née* Waite); *m* 1956, Norma Eleanor Trapp; three *s* one *d*. *Educ:* Univ. of West Indies (BA 1961); Univ. of York (DPhil 1971). Principal, St Michael's Coll., Belize, 1974–76; Lectr in English and Gen. Studies, Belize Tech. Coll., 1976–86; University College of Belize: Pres., 1986–90; Lectr, 1990–93. JP Belize, 1985, now supplementary list. *Publications:* Creole Proverbs of Belize, 1980, rev. edn 1988; From One Caribbean Corner (poetry), 1983; Caribbean Corner Calling, 1988; Language and Education in Belize, 1989; Pataki Full, 1990; contrib. poetry and drama in various anthologies; articles in Belizean Affairs, Jl Belizean Affairs, Belcast Jl, Caribbean Dialogue, Handbook on World Educn. *Recreations:* creative writing, playing and arranging steelband music. *Address:* Belize House, PO Box 173, Belmopan, Belize, Central America. *T:* (8) 222521, 223081, *Fax:* (8) 222050.

**YOUNG, David Edward Michael;** QC 1980; a Recorder, 1987–2006; *b* 30 Sept. 1940; *s* of George Henry Edward Young and Audrey Young; *m* 1968, Ann de Bromhead (*d* 2010); two *d*. *Educ:* Monkton Combe Sch.; Hertford Coll., Oxford (MA). Called to the Bar, Lincoln's Inn, 1966, Bencher, 1989; practised at Chancery Bar, specialising in intellectual property work. Dep. Judge, Patent County Court, 1990–2006; a Dep. High Court Judge, 1993–2006. Chm., Plant Varieties and Seeds Tribunal, 1987–2008. *Publications:* (co-ed) Terrell on the Law of Patents, 12th edn 1971 to 14th edn 1994; Passing Off, 1985, 3rd edn 1994. *Recreations:* gentleman farmer, francophile.

**YOUNG, David Ernest,** CBE 2007; Chairman, Higher Education Funding Council for England, 2001–07; *b* 8 March 1942; *s* of late Harold Young and Jessie Young (*née* Turnbull); *m* 1st, 1964, Norma Robinson (marr. diss. 1996); two *d*; 2nd, 1998, Margaret Pilleau. *Educ:* King Edward VII Sch., Sheffield; Corpus Christi Coll., Oxford (BA Hons). Ministry of Defence, 1963–82: Private Secretary to 2nd Perm. Sec., 1966–68; to CAS, 1968–70; to Minister of State for Defence, 1973–75; seconded to Central Policy Rev. Staff, Cabinet Office, 1975–77; Head of Defence Secretariat, 1979–82; John Lewis Partnership, 1982–2002: Finance Dir, 1987–2001; Dep. Chm., 1993–2002. Chm., John Lewis Partnership Trust for Pensions, 1989–2004. Director: Ocado plc, 2001–12; Orbit Gp, 2013–. Treas., Open Univ., 1998–2001; Hon. Treas., Soil Assoc., 2004–10. Mem. Adv. Panel, Greenwich Hosp., 2002–07. Trustee: RAF Mus., 1999–2005; Textile Ind. Children's Trust, 2000–08. Mem. Council, 2008–18, Treas., 2010–18, Sheffield Univ. Hon. DLitt Sheffield, 2005; Hon. DBA Beds, 2008. *Recreations:* theatre, food and wine, bridge, walking, croquet. *Address:* Gable Cottage, Fairmile, Henley on Thames RG9 2JX. *Club:* Phyllis Court (Henley on Thames).

**YOUNG, David John;** Chairman, Canongate Books Ltd, since 2017; *b* Ealing, Middx, 22 Jan. 1951; *s* of John and Marjorie Young; *m* 1996, Elizabeth Noble; one *s* two *d*. *Educ:* Merchant Taylors' Sch., Sandy Lodge; Watford Coll. of Technol. Man. Dir, Thorsons Publishing Gp, 1980–89; Divl Man. Dir, Harper Collins, 1989–92; Managing Director: Harper Collins Trade Div., 1992–96; Little Brown & Co., 1996–2000; CEO, Time Warner Book Gp UK, 2000–05; Chm. and CEO, Hachette Book Gp, USA, 2005–13; Dep. CEO, Hachette UK Ltd, 2013–15. Director: Tate Enterprises, 2016–; Scholastic Corp., NY, 2016–. Pres., Book Trade Benevolent Soc., 2013–16. *Recreations:* gardening, reading, collecting wine, attempting to learn Italian. *Address:* Mulberry, Pitch Place, Thursley, Godalming, Surrey GU8 6QW. *T:* (01428) 607716. *E:* djyoung51@gmail.com. *Clubs:* Garrick, Ivy.

**YOUNG, David Tyrrell;** Chairman, City and Guilds of London Institute, 1999–2006; *b* 6 Jan. 1938; *s* of late Tyrrell F. Young and Patricia M. Young (*née* Spicer); *m* 1965, Madeline Helen Celia Philips; three *d*. *Educ:* Charterhouse. Trained as Chartered Accountant; joined Spicer & Pegler, later Spicer & Oppenheim, 1965 (merged with Touche Ross, 1990): Partner 1968; Managing Partner, 1982; Sen. Partner, 1988–90; Dep. Chm., 1990–93. Chm., N Herts NHS Trust, 1995–2000. Director: Lombard Insce Gp, 1993–2000; Asprey, then Asprey & Garrard, 1993–2000; Wates City of London Properties, 1994–2000; Nomura Bank Internat., 1996–2010; Berkshire Hathaway Internat. Insce Ltd, 1998–2014; Marlborough Underwriting Agency, 2000–11; Capita Syndicate Mgt, 2001–08. Mem. Council, ICAEW, 1979–82. Mem. Court, Fishmongers' Co., 1981–. FRSA 1992. Hon. FCGI 1995. *Recreations:* golf, limited gardening. *Address:* East Barn, Blewbury Road, East Hagbourne, Oxon OX11 9EA. *T:* (01235) 810139. *Clubs:* Honourable Artillery Company, Royal Worlington Golf, Huntercombe Golf.

**YOUNG, Rt Rev. Donald Arthur;** Bishop of Central Newfoundland, 2000–04; *b* 11 Nov. 1944; *s* of Harold and Frances Young; *m* 1966, Sylvia Joan Spurrell; one *s* three *d*. *Educ:* Memorial Univ. of Newfoundland; Atlantic Sch. of Theology; Queen's Coll., St John's, Nfld (LTh). Ordained deacon, 1977, priest, 1977; Deacon in charge, Buchans, 1977; Rector: Buchans, 1977–81; Port Rexton, 1981–89; (pro tem.) Hermitage, 2011–12; (pro tem.) Deer Lake, 2013–14; Diocesan Progs and Exec. Officer, Central Newfoundland, 1989–2000; Tri-Diocesan Jt Cttee Officer, 2005–. *Address:* Box 48 - 410 Main Road, Norris Arm North, NL A0G 3N0, Canada. *T:* and *Fax:* (709) 6532864.

**YOUNG, Hon. Douglas;** *see* Young, Hon. M. D.

**YOUNG, Douglas;** *see* Young, R. M. D.

**YOUNG, Rt Hon. Edward,** CVO 2015 (LVO 2010); PC 2017; Private Secretary to the Queen and Keeper of the Queen's Archives, since 2017; *b* 24 Oct. 1966; *s* of Dr Edward Young and late Sally Rougier Young; *m* 2003, Nichola O'Brien Malone; one *d*. *Educ:* Reading Sch. (Boarder). Trade finance specialist, Internat. Services Br., Barclays, 1985–97; Project Manager, Barclays Corporate Euro Prog., 1997; Dep. Hd, Corporate Bank Public Relns, Barclays Bank plc, 1997–99; Adviser: to Shadow Chancellor, 1999–2000; to Leader of the Opposition, 2001; Hd, Corporate Communications, Granada plc, 2001–04; Asst Private Sec. to The Queen, 2004–07, Dep. Private Sec., 2007–17. *Address:* Buckingham Palace, SW1A 1AA.

**YOUNG, Edward;** Editor, Metro, since 2014; *b* Dar es Salaam, 7 Aug. 1961; *s* of Eric Young and Sheila Young (*née* Hutchinson); *m* 1989, Marie-Bénédicte Chantal Fournier; one *s* one *d*. *Educ:* Eastbourne Coll.; Fitzwilliam Coll., Cambridge (BA Hons Hist. 1983; MA). Reporter: Harrow Observer, 1983–86; Northern Echo, 1986–89; Dep. Night Ed., Today, 1989–95; Sub-ed., Daily Mail, 1995–98; Asst Ed./Night Ed., Sun, 1998–2002; Exec. Ed., Daily Express, 2002–04; Editor: London Lite, 2005–09; Mail Online, 2009–12; New York Daily News Online, 2012–14. *Recreations:* family, watching Rugby and Newcastle United. *Address:* Metro, Northcliffe House, 2 Derry Street, W8 5TT. *T:* (020) 7938 6000. *Club:* Reform.

**YOUNG, Eve J.;** *see* Jardine-Young, E.

**YOUNG, Rev. Prof. Frances Margaret,** OBE 1998; PhD; FBA 2004; Edward Cadbury Professor of Theology, University of Birmingham, 1986–2005; Methodist minister, since 1984; *b* 25 Nov. 1939; *d* of A. Stanley Worrall and Mary F. Worrall (*née* Marshall); *m* 1964, Robert Charles Young; three *s*. *Educ:* Bedford Coll., Univ. of London (BA); Girton Coll., Univ. of Cambridge (MA, PhD). Research Fellow, Clare Hall, Cambridge, 1967–68; University of Birmingham: Temp. Lectr, 1971–73; Lectr, 1973–82; Sen. Lectr, 1982–86; Hd, Dept of Theol., 1986–95; Dean, Faculty of Arts, 1995–97; Pro-Vice-Chancellor, 1997–2002. Hon. DD Aberdeen, 1994; Hon. DTh MF Norwegian Sch. of Theol., Oslo, 2008; DUniv Oxford Brookes, 2010; Hon. DD Liverpool Hope Univ., 2013. *Publications:* Sacrifice and the Death of Christ, 1975; (contrib.) The Myth of God Incarnate, 1977; From Nicaea to Chalcedon, 1983, 2nd edn 2010; Face to Face, 1985, 2nd edn 1990; (with David Ford) Meaning and Truth in 2 Corinthians, 1987; The Art of Performance, 1990; The Theology of the Pastoral Epistles, 1994; Biblical Exegesis and the Formation of Christian Culture, 1997; (ed) Encounter with Mystery, 1997; (ed jtly) The Cambridge History of Early Christian Literature, 2004; (ed jtly) The Cambridge History of Christianity: origins to Constantine, 2006; Brokenness and Blessing, 2007; (with Morna Hooker) Holiness and Mission, 2010; God's Presence: a contemporary recapitulation of Early Christianity, 2013; Arthur's Call: a journey of faith in the face of learning disability, 2014; Construing the Cross: type, sign, symbol, word, action, 2015; numerous articles, etc. *Recreations:* outdoor pursuits, music. *Address:* 142 Selly Park Road, Birmingham B29 7LH. *T:* (0121) 472 4841.

**YOUNG, Gavin Neil B.;** *see* Barr Young.

**YOUNG, Helen, (Mrs K. Rees),** FRMetS; broadcast meteorologist, 1993–2005, Broadcast Manager, 2000–05, BBC Weather Centre; *b* 10 June 1969; *d* of Derek and Lyn Young; *m* 1997, Keirth Rees; one *s* one *d*. *Educ:* Univ. of Bristol (BSc Geog.); Meteorological Office (qualified as forecaster). Dep. Manager, BBC Weather Centre, 1998–2000. *Recreations:* ski-ing, swimming, gardening.

**YOUNG, Prof. (Hobart) Peyton,** PhD; FBA 2007; Centennial Professor, London School of Economics and Political Science, since 2015; Fellow of Nuffield College, Oxford, since 2007; Research Principal, Office of Financial Research, US Treasury Department, since 2012; *b* 9 March 1945; *s* of Hobart Paul Young and Louise B. Young; *m* 1982, Fernanda F. Toueg; two *s*. *Educ:* Harvard Univ. (AB cum laude Gen. Studies 1966); Univ. of Michigan (PhD 1970). Prof. of Econs and Public Policy, Univ. of Maryland, 1981–94; Scott and Barbara Black Prof. of Econs, Johns Hopkins Univ., 1994–2007; James Meade Prof. of Econs, Univ. of Oxford, 2007–15. Sen. Fellow in Econ. Studies, Brookings Instn, 1998–2015; Ext. Prof., Santa Fe Inst., 2001–05, 2007–10; Fulbright Dist. Chair in Econs, Univ. of Siena, 2003–04. Pres., Game Theory Soc., 2006–08. Fellow, Econometric Soc., 1995; Mem., American Acad. of Arts and Scis, 2018. *Publications:* (with M. L. Balinski) Fair Representation: meeting the ideal of one man one vote, 1984, 2nd edn 2002; Equity in Theory and Practice, 1994; Individual Strategy and Social Structure: an evolutionary theory of institutions, 1998; Strategic Learning and Its Limits, 2004; articles in learned jls. *Address:* Nuffield College, Oxford OX1 1NF. *T:* (01865) 271086, *Fax:* (01865) 271094. *Clubs:* Oxford and Cambridge; Cosmos (Washington, DC); Chevy Chase.

**YOUNG, Ian Robert,** OBE 1985; PhD; FRS 1989; FREng; consultant; *b* 11 Jan. 1932; *s* of John Stirling Young and Ruth Muir Young (*née* Whipple); *m* 1956, Sylvia Marianne Whewell Ralph; two *s* one *d*. *Educ:* Sedbergh Sch., Yorkshire; Aberdeen Univ. (BSc, PhD). FIET; FREng (FEng 1988). Hilger & Watts Ltd, 1955–59; Evershed & Vignoles Ltd (and affiliates), 1959–76; EMI Ltd, 1976–81; GEC plc, 1981–97. Visiting Professor: of Radiology, RPMS, 1986; Dept of Electrical and Electronic Engrg, Imperial Coll. London, 2005–. Hon. FRCR 1990; Hon. Mem., Amer. Soc. of Neuroradiology, 1995; Hon. FRCP 2018. Hon. DSc Aberdeen, 1992. *Publications:* over 200 papers in Proc. IEE, Magnetic Resonance in Medicine, Magnetic Resonance Imaging, Jl Magnetic Resonance, Computer Assisted Tomography, etc; 50 separate patents; ed. 5 books. *Recreations:* bird watching, golf, gardening. *Address:* High Kingsbury, Kingsbury Street, Marlborough, Wilts SN8 1HZ. *T:* (01672) 516126.

**YOUNG, Prof. Ian Robert,** AO 2012; PhD; Kernot Professor of Ocean Engineering, University of Melbourne, since 2016; Hon. Professorial Fellow, L. H. Martin Institute, since 2016; Chief Executive, Conviro Pty Ltd, since 2016; *b* Cunnamulla, Qld, 17 Jan. 1957; *s* of Richard and Mary Stella Young; *m* 1985, Heather Beckwith; one *d*. *Educ:* James Cook Univ. (BE Hons; MEngSc; PhD 1984). FIEAust 1990, Hon. FIEAust 2011; FTSE 2000. Sen. Lectr, 1986–94, Prof. of Civil Engrg, 1994–98, Univ. of NSW; Exec. Dean, Faculty of Engrg, Computer and Mathematical Scis, 1999–2003, Pro Vice-Chancellor (Internat.), 2001–03, Univ. of Adelaide; Vice-Chancellor, Swinburne Univ. of Technol., 2003–11; Vice-Chancellor and Pres., ANU, 2011–16. Chm., Gp of Eight, 2014. Chair, Bd, VERNet Ltd, 2015–. Pres., CloudCampus Pty Ltd, 2016–. Fellow, Acad. of Technol Scis and Engrg, 2000. C. N. Barton Medal, Engineers Australia, 1979; Lorenz G. Staub Medal, Univ. of Minnesota, 1986; Centenary Medal (Australia), 2003. *Publications:* (with G. J. Holland) Atlas of the Oceans: wind and wave climate, 1996; Wind Generated Ocean Waves, 1999; contrib. papers to jls. *Address:* Melbourne School of Engineering, University of Melbourne, Parkville, Vic 3010, Australia. *E:* ian.young@conviro.com.au.

**YOUNG, James Edward D.;** *see* Drummond Young.

**YOUNG, John Adrian Emile;** Partner, Markby, Stewart & Wadesons, subseq. Cameron Markby Hewitt, 1965–95; *b* 28 July 1934; *s* of John Archibald Campbell Young and Irene Eugenie Young (*née* Bouvier); *m* 1959, Yvonne Lalage Elizabeth Bankes (*d* 2008); three *s* one *d*. *Educ:* Cranbrook Sch., Kent; London Univ. (LLB). Admitted solicitor, 1958; Asst Sec., Law Soc., 1958–64. Adjudicator (formerly Legal Officer), Office of the Banking Ombudsman, 1996–98. Nat Chm., Young Solicitors Gp, 1965–66; Pres., Assoc. Internat. des Jeunes Avocats, 1968–69; Law Society: Mem. Council, 1971–95; Dep. Vice-Pres., 1993–94; Vice-Pres., 1994–95; Mem. Council, Internat. Bar Assoc., 1983–94. FRSA 1989. Master, City of London Solicitors' Co., 1989–90. *Publications:* sundry legal articles. *Recreations:* music (runs local church choir), gardening, family! *Address:* Stonewold House, The Street, Plaxtol, Sevenoaks, Kent TN15 0QH. *T:* (01732) 810289.

**YOUNG, Sir John (Kenyon Roe),** 6th Bt *cr* 1821; *b* 23 April 1947; *s* of Sir John William Roe Young, 5th Bt, and Joan Minnie Agnes (*d* 1958), *d* of M. M. Aldous; *S* father, 1981; *m* 1977, Frances Elise, *o d* of W. R. Thompson; one *s* one *d*. *Educ:* Hurn Court; Napier College. Joined RN, 1963; transferred to Hydrographic Branch, 1970; qualified Hydrographic Surveyor, 1977; retired from RN, 1979; attended Napier Coll., 1979–80. Member: Hydrographic Soc.; Inst. of Purchasing Mgt. *Recreation:* fly fishing. *Heir: s* Richard Christopher Roe Young, *b* 14 June 1983.

**YOUNG, John Robert Chester,** CBE 1992; Nominated Member, 1996–2002, and Deputy Chairman, 1997–2002, Council of Lloyd's; Chairman, Lloyd's Regulatory Board, 1997–2002; *b* 6 Sept. 1937; *s* of Robert Nisbet Young and Edith Mary (*née* Roberts); *m* 1963, Pauline Joyce (*d* 1997); one *d* (and two *s* decd). *Educ:* Bishop Vesey's Grammar Sch.; St Edmund Hall, Oxford Univ. (MA); Gray's Inn, London. Joined Simon & Coates, members of the Stock Exchange, 1961; Partner, 1965; Dep. Sen. Partner, 1976; London Stock Exchange (formerly Stock Exchange, subseq. Internat. Stock Exchange): Mem.

Council, 1978–82; Dir of Policy and Planning, 1982–87; Vice-Chm. (non-exec.), Managing Bd, 1987–90. Chief Exec. and Dir, SFA (formerly Securities Assoc.), 1987–93; Dir, 1993–97, Chief Exec., 1993–95, SIB. Non-executive Director: Darby Gp plc, 1996–97; Elderstreet Millennium (formerly Gartmore) Venture Capital Trust, 1996–2006; E Surrey Healthcare (formerly E Surrey Hosp. and Community Healthcare) NHS Trust, 1992–96. Public Interest Dir, Financial Services Compensation Scheme Ltd, 2000–04. Mem. Ethics Cttee, Securities Inst., 1995–2009 (Hon. Fellow, 2003). Lay Mem., Legal Services Consultative Panel, DCA, subseq. MoJ, 2004–09. Advr, Royal Sch. for the Blind, 1997–2001. Formerly internat. athlete, Rugby player (England and British Lions) and England Rugby selector. *Recreations:* cooking, grandchildren, Rugby football. *Clubs:* Vincent's (Oxford); Harlequins, Achilles.

*See also* L. Botting.

**YOUNG, Sir John Robertson, (Sir Rob),** GCMG 2003 (KCMG 1999; CMG 1991); HM Diplomatic Service, retired; High Commissioner, New Delhi, 1999–2003; *b* 21 Feb. 1945; *s* of late Francis John Young and Marjorie Elizabeth Young; *m* 1967, Catherine Suzanne Françoise Houssait; one *s* two *d*. *Educ:* King Edward VI Sch., Norwich; Leicester Univ. (BA 1st Cl. Hons, French). Entered FCO, 1967; MECAS, Lebanon, 1968; Third Sec., Cairo, 1970; Second Sec., FCO, 1972; Private Sec. to Minister of State, 1975; First Sec., Paris, 1977; Asst Head, Western European Dept, FCO, 1982; Counsellor, Damascus, 1984; Head of Middle East Dept, FCO, 1987; Minister, Paris, 1991; Dep. Under-Sec. of State, 1994–98, and Chief Clerk, 1995–98, FCO. Comr, Commonwealth War Graves Commn, 2003–11. Non-executive Director: Hirco plc, 2006–10; Aguas de Barcelona, 2008–10; GDF SUEZ Energy Internat. (formerly Internat. Power), 2011–15. Chairman: Calcutta Tercentenary Trust, 2003–; Adv. Bd, World Appreciation of Music, 2008–. Mem., Conseil d'Admin, Fêtes Musicales en Touraine, 2012–15; Sec., Assoc. des Amis du Patrimoine Artannais, 2016–. Patron, Loomba Trust, 2005–; Trustee, Scots Asia Heritage Trust, 2016–. Hon. DLaws Leicester, 2001. *Recreations:* music, sailing, theatre, carpentry. *Address:* Les Choiseaux, La Planche des Chaqueneaux, 37260 Artannes-sur-Indre, France. *Clubs:* Beefsteak, Royal Over-Seas League.

**YOUNG, John Todd;** Co-Chair, Hogan Lovells, 2010–12 (Senior Partner, Lovells, 2004–10); *b* 14 Jan. 1957; *s* of Ian Taylor Young and Flora Leggett Young (*née* Todd); *m* 1981, Elizabeth Jane Grattidge (*d* 2016). *Educ:* Manchester Grammar Sch.; Sidney Sussex Coll., Cambridge (BA 1978; MA 1982). Admitted solicitor, 1981; Hogan Lovells (formerly Lovell, White & King, then Lovell White Durrant, later Lovells): articled clerk, 1979–81; Solicitor, 1981–87; Partner, 1987–2004; Hd, Corporate Insce Practice, 1997–2011; Hd, Financial Instns Gp, 2004–09. Non-executive Director: JLT Reinsurance Brokers Ltd, 2012–; Mitsui Sumitomo Insurance (London Mgt) Ltd, 2012–17; Forester Life Ltd, 2013– (Chm., 2017–); Solicitors Indemnity Fund Ltd, 2017– (Chm., 2018–). Trustee, Farm Africa, 2013–. Gov., Manchester Grammar Sch., 2014–. Liveryman, Solicitors' Co., 2009; Liveryman, Insurers' Co., 2014. *Publications:* (consultant ed.) A Practitioner's Guide to the FSA Regulation of Insurance, 2002, 4th edn 2011; numerous articles on insce related topics. *Recreations:* Scottish and Alpine mountaineering, trekking, ski-ing, wildlife and the environment. *E:* john@jty.scot. *Club:* Caledonian.

**YOUNG, John William Garne;** Group Chief Executive, Wolseley plc, 1996–2000; *b* 6 Jan. 1945; *s* of David Richard Young and Pamela Mary Young (*née* Garne); *m* 1971, Eleanor Louise Walsh; three *s*. *Educ:* Shaftesbury Grammar Sch. Apprentice, Tube Investment Gp, 1962–67; Man. Dir, P. J. Parmiter & Sons Ltd, 1967–85; Wolseley plc: Chief Exec., Agricl Div., 1982–90, Agricl, Photographic & Technical Services Div., 1990–95; Dep. Chief Exec., 1994–96. Pres., Agricl Engrs Assoc., 1987–88. Pres., Comité Européen de Constructeurs de Mechanisme Agricole, 1995–96. *Recreations:* fishing, golf. *Address:* Garne House, 23 Bimport, Shaftesbury, Dorset SP7 8AX.

**YOUNG, Jonathan Piers;** Editor, The Field, since 1991; *b* 23 Sept. 1959; *s* of Peter and Mavis Young; *m* 1993, Caroline Bankes; one *s* one *d*. *Educ:* Blundell's; Univ. of Leicester (BA). Ed., Shooting Times and Country Magazine, 1986–90. Liveryman, Gunmakers' Co., 1992 (Mem., Ct of Assts, 2012–; Master, 2017–18). *Publications:* A Pattern of Wings, 1989. *Recreations:* shooting, fishing, horsing around. *Address:* The Field, Pinehurst 2, Pinehurst Road, Farnborough Business Park, Farnborough, Hants GU14 7BF. *T:* (01252) 555222. *Clubs:* Tyburn Angling Society; Silkie.

**YOUNG, Air Marshal Julian Alexander,** CB 2013; OBE 2000; Chief of Materiel (Air), Defence Equipment and Support, since 2016; *b* Cambridge, 18 Dec. 1961; *s* of late Ronald Emsley Young and of Mrs Rosemary Eunice Young (now Perrin); *m* 1986, Helen Hewetson; two *s* one *d*. *Educ:* Royal Latin Sch., Buckingham; City Univ. (BSc Hons Air Transport Engrg); Cranfield Univ. (Master Defence Admin; MSc Leadership Studies); King's Coll. London (MA Internat. Studies). FREng 2016. RAF Univ. Cadet, 1980–85; Jun. Engr Officer, No 7 Sqdn, RAF Odiham, 1985–87; Engr Officer, No 78 Sqdn, RAF Mt Pleasant, 1987; OC No 1 Aircraft Repair Flt, Repair and Salvage Sqdn, RAF Abingdon, 1987–90; Sen. Engr Officer, No 18 Sqdn, RAF Gütersloh and RAF Laarbruch, 1990–93; PSO to AO Engrg and Supply, HQ Strike Comd, 1993–96; RAF Staff Coll., 1996; Harrier Support Authy, RAF Wyton, 1996–99; OC Engrg and Supply Wing, RAF Cottesmore, 1999–2000; Gp Captain, Logistics Policy and Strategy, 2000–02; CO, RAF Cosford, 2002–03; Dir, End-to-End Rev. Air Implementation and Defence Logistics Transformation Prog., 2003–06; rcds 2006; ACOS A4 Logistics, HQ Air Comd, 2007–09; Dir, Defence Support Review, 2009–10; Defence Career Partnering (placement in industry), 2010; COS Support, HQ Air Comd, 2010–11; Exec. Officer, HQ Air Comd and Chief Engr (Air Comd), 2011–12; Dir Technical, 2012–15, Chief Inf. Officer, 2013–15, Dir Helicopters, 2015–16, Defence Equipment and Support. *Recreations:* family, Impressionist art, military and British history, Radio 4, supporter of Peterborough United FC. *Address:* c/o RAF Personnel Management, HQ Air Command, RAF High Wycombe, Bucks HP14 4UE. *T:* 07704 186651. *E:* julian.young523@mod.uk. *Club:* Royal Air Force.

**YOUNG, Dr Kenneth William,** FREng; Technology Director, Manufacturing Technology Centre, since 2011; *b* York, 5 Dec. 1961; *s* of William Edward Young and Winifred Young; *m* 1987, Caroline Rosemary Edge; one *s* one *d*. *Educ:* Huntington Comprehensive Sch.; Nottingham Univ. (BSc Hons Mech. Engrg 1983; PhD 1986). Engineer: BYG Systems, 1986–90; Delcam, 1990–91; University of Warwick: Sen. Teaching Fellow, 1991–96; Principal Res. Fellow, 1996–2003; Reader, 2003–06; Prof., 2006–11. Visiting Professor: Loughborough Univ., 2011–; Coventry Univ., 2019–. FREng 2018. *Recreations:* shire horse breeder, carriage driving (Chm., W Midlands Driving Gp, 2017–), Mem., British Marathon Canoe Team, 1987–88. *Address:* Manufacturing Technology Centre, Pilot Way, Ansty Park, Coventry CV7 9JU. *T:* (024) 7670 1651. *E:* ken.young@the-mtc.org.

**YOUNG, Kirsty Jackson, (Mrs N. K. A. Jones);** Presenter, Desert Island Discs, BBC Radio Four, 2006–18; *b* 23 Nov. 1968; *d* of John and Catherine Young; *m* 1999, Nicholas Keith Arthur Jones, *qv*; two *d*. *Educ:* High Sch. of Stirling. Newsreader and news presenter, BBC Radio Scotland, 1990–93; news anchor and presenter, Scottish Television, 1993–95; reporter, Holiday and Film 96, BBC TV, 1995–96; News Anchor: Channel Five News, 1996–2000; ITV, 2000–01; Five News, Channel Five, 2001–07; presenter, Crimewatch UK, 2008–15. Pres., UNICEF (UK), 2016–. *Recreations:* family, food, laughter. *Address:* c/o KBJ, 22 Rathbone Street, W1T 1LG. *Club:* Soho House.

**YOUNG, Prof. Lawrence Sterling,** PhD, DSc; FRCPath, FRCP; FMedSci; FRSB; Director, Warwick Cancer Research Centre, and Pro-Dean, External Affairs, Warwick Medical School, University of Warwick, since 2017; *b* 28 Oct. 1958; *s* of Bernard Young and late Joan Young (*née* Black); *m* 1979, Alison Hilton; one *s*. *Educ:* Univ. of Birmingham (BSc 1981; PhD 1984; DSc 1998). MRCPath 1993, FRCPath 2000; FRSB (FSB 2009); FRCP 2012. University of Birmingham: Res. Fellow, 1984–89, Lectr and Sen. Lectr, 1989–94, Dept of Cancer Studies; Professor of Cancer Biology, 1994–2013; Head: Div. of Cancer Studies and Dir, Cancer Res. UK Inst. for Cancer Studies, 2001–07; Coll. of Medical and Dental Scis, 2008–12; Pro Vice-Chancellor, 2009–12; University of Warwick: Pro Vice-Chancellor for Res. and Capital Develt, 2013, for Academic Planning and Resources, 2013–16; Academic Vice-Pres., 2016–18. Adjunct Prof., Monash Univ., 2014; Vis. Prof., Cancer Center, Sun Yat-sen Univ., Guangzhou, 2014; Hon. Prof., Coll. of Med. and Dental Scis, Univ. of Birmingham, 2013–. Member: Med. and Scientific Adv. Panel, Leukaemia Res. Fund, 1996–99; Grants Cttee, CRC, 1996–2001; Molecular Cell Medicine Bd, MRC, 2003–07; Cancer Sub-panel, 2001 and 2008 RAEs; Yorks Cancer Res. Scientific Adv. Cttee, 2008–; Biol and Med. Scis Rev. Panel, British Council, 2015. Non-executive Director: Birmingham Children's Hosp., 2008–10; Alta Innovations, 2009–12; Biosciences Ventures, 2010–12; Alta Bioscience, 2010–12. Pres., Internat. Assoc. for Res. on Epstein-Barr Virus and Associated Diseases, 2008–10. Chm., CORE Res. Awards Cttee, 2010–. Mem., Lunar Soc., 2010–. FMedSci 2007 (Mem., Sectional Cttee 2, 2012–14). Hon. MRCP 1998. *Publications:* contrib. articles to learned jls on cancer, viruses and novel cancer therapies. *Recreations:* Gilbert and Sullivan operas, travel, poetry, learning to play the ukulele. *Address:* Warwick Medical School, University of Warwick, Coventry CV4 7AJ. *T:* (024) 7657 5238. *E:* L.S.Young@warwick.ac.uk.

**YOUNG, Hon. M. Douglas;** PC (Canada) 1993; QC (Canada) 2009; Chairman, Summa Strategies Canada, Inc., 1997; *b* 20 Sept. 1940; *s* of Douglas Young and Annie Young (*née* Wishart); *m* 1979, Jacqueline David; one *s* two *d*. *Educ:* St Thomas Univ. (BA 1972); Univ. of New Brunswick (LLB 1975); New Brunswick Teachers' Coll. Cert., 1957. Lawyer and businessman. MLA for Tracadie, New Brunswick, 1978–88; Leader, New Brunswick Liberal Party, 1981–83; Provincial Minister of Fisheries and Aquaculture, 1987–88; MP (L) Gloucester, renamed Acadie-Bathurst, 1988–97; Canadian Minister: of Transport, 1993–96; of Human Resources, 1996; of Nat. Defence and of Veteran Affairs, 1996–97. Hon. LLD St Thomas, 2013. *Recreations:* tennis, reading, travelling. *Address:* 1199 Jacques Cartier Drive, Beresford, NB E8K 1A6, Canada.

**YOUNG, Madeleine Mary, (Lady Young);** *see* Arnot, M. M.

**YOUNG, Malcolm, (Mal);** independent television producer, since 2011; *b* 26 Jan. 1957; *s* of late Charles Young, Liverpool, and of Maria (*née* Williams); *m* 2014, Mari Wilson. *Educ:* Liverpool Sch. of Art (DipAD). Design Manager, Littlewoods Orgn, 1975–81; actor/singer, 1981–84; Mersey Television, 1984–96: Design Asst on Brookside, then Asst Floor Manager and Floor Manager, 1986–91; Producer, Brookside and Dir, Brookside Prodns, 1991–95; Series Producer, Brookside, 1995–96 (also devised and produced And The Beat Goes On, Channel 4); Hd of Drama, Pearson TV, 1996–97; Hd of Drama Series, 1997–2001, Controller of Continuing Drama Series, 2001–04, BBC, responsible for: EastEnders, Casualty, Holby City, Waking the Dead, Doctors, Murder in Mind, In Deep, Judge John Deed, Down to Earth, Dalziel and Pascoe, and Dr Who; Dir of Drama, 19 TV, 2005–10; writer and creator: Born in the USA, for Fox TV (US), 2005; Austin Golden Hour, TV drama pilot for CW/Paramount (US), 2008; writer and executive producer: If I Can Dream, for Hulu, 2010; Desperate Scousewives, for Channel 4, 2012; The Young & The Restless, for CBS and Sony Pictures TV, 2017–; writer and creative consultant, Sony Pictures Internat. TV, 2012–; co-writer and creator: Young Americans, for ABC, 2013–14; Blocked, for NBC TV, 2014–15; storyline writer and consultant producer, River City, BBC Scotland, 2015; Founder and Co-Owner, Dynamo Prodns, 2012–15; Founder and Owner, Pool of Life Prodns, 2014–; Supervising Producer, 2016–17, Exec. Producer and Hd Writer, 2017–19, CBS/Sony Pictures Television, Hollywood, Calif. Prof., TV Scriptwriting, Glasgow Caledonian Univ., 2014–. Member: BAFTA, 1997–; RTS, 1999–; Writers Guild of Great Britain, 2013–; Writers Guild of America West, 2013–. Huw Wheldon Meml Lecture, RTS, 1999. Special Award for Creative Contribution to TV, British Soap Awards, 2004. *Publications:* Sinbad's Scrapbook, 1996. *Recreations:* music, tennis, snooker.

**YOUNG, Prof. Malcolm Philip,** PhD; Chief Executive, e-Therapeutics plc, 2007–16; *b* 11 Sept. 1960; *s* of James Guthrie Philips Young and Shirley Joyce Young (*née* Smith); *m* 1987, Deborah Anne Howse (marr. diss. 2015); one *s* two *d*. *Educ:* Bristol Univ. (BSc 1st cl. Hons (Psychol.) 1987); Univ. of St Andrews (PhD (Neurosci.) 1990). Royal Soc. Japan Sci. and Technol. Sci. Exchange Fellow, Riken Inst., Japan, 1990–91; Oxford University: MRC Res. Associate, 1991–92, Royal Soc. Univ. Res. Fellow, 1992–94, Univ. Lab. of Physiol.; British Telecommunications Jun. Res. Fellow, Brasenose Coll., 1993–94; Newcastle upon Tyne University: Dir, Inst. for Neurosci., 1999–2001; Prof. and Chair in Psychol., 1994–2009; Hd, Dept of Psychol., 1994–2001; Provost, Faculty of Sci., Agriculture and Engrg, 2001–05; Pro-Vice-Chancellor for Strategic Develt, 2005–07; Vis. Prof., Inst. of Neurosci., 2009–. Visiting Professor: Agency of Industrial Sci. and Technol., Tsukuba, Japan, 1995; Sch. of Computing and Maths, Keele Univ., 2017–. Chairman and Chief Technology Officer: In Rotis Technologies Ltd, 2001–07; e-Therapeutics plc, 2003–07; non-executive Chairman: Novotech Investment Ltd, 2007–; Searchbolt (formerly OGS Search) Ltd, 2007–13; Chairman: Lisles Research Ltd, 2012–; Nuchido Ltd, 2017–. Mem., Soc. for Neurosci., USA, 1990–. Ernst and Young Innovation Entrepreneur of the Year, N and Midlands, 2010. *Publications:* The Analysis of Cortical Connectivity, 1996; many articles in learned jls inc. Nature, Science, Procs of Royal Soc., Philosophical Transactions of Royal Soc., Jl of Neuroscience, etc. *Recreations:* sailing, ski-ing, hiking, music. *Address:* Nuchido, Dissington Hall, Dalton NE18 0AD.

**YOUNG, Marianne;** HM Diplomatic Service; Deputy Director, European Union Exit Strategy Department, Europe Directorate, Foreign and Commonwealth Office, since 2019; *b* UK, 8 Aug. 1971; *d* of James and Andrea Darch; *m* 2002, Barry Young; one *s* two *d*. *Educ:* St Teresa's Sch., Effingham; Wellington Coll.; Univ. of Warwick (BA); City Univ., London (Postgrad. Dip.). Grad. trainee, The Times, 1994–95; staff ed., then Asia Ed., Fairplay Gp Singapore, 1995–2000; Sen. Corresp., Fairplay Gp UK, 2000–01; entered FCO, 2001; deptl report writer, then Press Officer, Press Office, 2001–03; Hd, Great Lakes Section, then Hd, E Africa and Horn Section, Africa Directorate, 2003–05; Head: communications engaging with Islamic World Gp, 2005–06; Ext. Political Section, Pretoria and Dep. High Comr, Kingdoms of Lesotho and Swaziland, 2006–11; High Comr, Namibia, 2011–15; Dep. Hd (Climate), Sci., Innovation and Climate Dept, FCO,

2015–16; Dep. Head, Global Econ. Issues Dept, FCO, 2016–17; Hd, Future UKRep Brussels Change Prog., Europe Directorate, FCO, 2018. *Recreations:* literature, photography, scuba diving, travel, story writing. *Address:* c/o Foreign and Commonwealth Office, King Charles Street, SW1A 2AH.

**YOUNG, Melissa Zoë;** *see* Harrison, M. Z.

**YOUNG, Michael James;** QC 2017; Partner, Quinn Emanuel Urquhart & Sullivan LLP, since 2017; *b* Cleethorpes, 5 Jan. 1972; *s* of Derek and Jean Young; *m* 2017, Huw Morow-Griffin. *Educ:* Sidney Sussex Coll., Cambridge (BA Law 1993); Merton Coll., Oxford (BCL 1996); Inns of Court Sch. of Law. Admitted solicitor, 1996; Partner, Herbert Smith LLP, 2003–12; Partner and Co-Hd, Global Arbitration Practice, Allen & Overy LLP, Paris, 2012–17. Vice-Pres., ICC Court of Arbitration, 2015–. *Recreations:* sailing, reading, primatology, walking, food, travel. *Address:* Quinn Emanuel Urquhart & Sullivan LLP, 6 rue Lamennais, 75008 Paris, France. *T:* (01) 73446000, *Fax:* (01) 73446100. *E:* michaelyoung@quinnemanuel.com.

**YOUNG, Prof. Michael Warren,** PhD; Professor and Head, Laboratory of Genetics, since 1988, and Richard and Jeanne Fisher Professor and Vice President for Academic Affairs, since 2004, Rockefeller University; *b* Miami, Florida, 28 March 1949; *s* of Lloyd G. Young and Mildred T. Young; *m* 1978, Laurel Eckhardt; two *d*. *Educ:* Univ. of Texas, Austin (BA Biol. 1971; PhD Genetics 1975). Postdoctoral Fellow, Dept of Biochem., Stanford Univ. Sch. of Medicine, 1975–77; Rockefeller University: Asst Prof., Meyer Foundn Fellow, 1978–84; Associate Prof., 1984–88; Investigator, Howard Hughes Med. Inst., 1987–96; Hd, Rockefeller Unit, NSF Sci. and Technol. Center for Biol Timing, 1991–2001. Fellow, Amer. Acad. Microbiol., 2007. Member: NAS, 2007; Amer. Philosophical Soc., 2018; Genetics Soc. of America; Soc. for Res. on Biol Rhythms; NY Acad. Scis; Amer. Soc. for Microbiol.; Harvey Soc. Hayaishi Prize, Univ. of Tokyo, 2001; Ashoff/Pittendrigh Award for Pioneering Contribs to Field of Circadian Biol., Soc. for Res. on Biol Rhythms, 2006; Neurosci. Prize, Peter and Patricia Gruber Foundn, 2009; Louisa Gross Horwitz Prize, Columbia Univ., 2011; Canada Gairdner Internat. Award, 2012; Massry Prize, USC Keck Sch. of Medicine, 2012; Wiley Prize in Biomed. Scis, 2013; Shaw Prize in Life Sci. and Medicine, 2013; (jtly) Nobel Prize in Physiol. or Medicine, 2017. *Publications:* contrib. articles to professional scientific jls. *Recreations:* tennis, hiking/mountaineering. *Address:* Rockefeller University, Laboratory of Genetics, 1230 York Avenue, New York, NY 10065, USA. *T:* (212) 3278645, *Fax:* (212) 3277055.

**YOUNG, Sir Nicholas (Charles),** Kt 2009; charity adviser and mentor, since 2014; Chief Executive, British Red Cross, 2001–14; *b* 16 April 1952; *s* of late Leslie Charles Young and Mary Margaret Young (*née* Rudman); *m* 1978, Helen Mary Ferrier Hamilton; three *s*. *Educ:* Wimbledon Coll.; Birmingham Univ. (Hons LLB 2.1). Qualified Solicitor, 1977; Articled Clerk and Solicitor, Freshfields, 1975–78; Solicitor, later Partner, Turner, Martin & Symes, 1979–85; Sec. for Develt, Sue Ryder Foundn, 1985–90; Dir, UK Ops, BRCS, 1990–95; Chief Exec., 1995–2001 and Vice-Pres., 2001–, Macmillan Cancer Support (formerly Cancer Relief Macmillan Fund, later Macmillan Cancer Relief). Vice Chm., Nat. Council for Hospice and Specialist Palliative Care Services, 1996–99; Member: Exec. Cttee, Healthwork UK, 1998–2002; NCVO Charity Law Reform Gp, 1998–2001; NHS Modernisation Bd, 2000–01; Foreign Secretary's Human Rights Adv. Gp, 2010–14; Cabinet Office Nat. Honours Cttee, 2011–17; Trustee, 2000–, and Chm., 2005–, Monte San Martino Trust; Mem., Steering Cttee, The Giving Campaign, 2000–03; Member, Advisory Board: Nat. Council of Voluntary Orgns, 2010–; Freshfields Responsible Business, 2012–; Trustee: Disasters Emergency Cttee, 2001–14; Guidestar UK, 2003–06; Wimbledon Foundn, 2015–; Trustee and Dep. Chm., Humanitarian Forum, 2006–; Mem. and Vice Chm., Humanitarian Worker Meml Cttee, 2015–. Chm., Bredfield Neighbourhood Plan Wkg Gp, 2015–. Chm., Judging Panel, Asian Women of Achievement Awards, 2006–. Mem., Stumblers Assoc., 1978–. Gov., Wimbledon Coll., 1998–2000. Patron, Escape Lines Meml Soc., 2009–. MCMI 2009. Freeman, City of London, 2007. Queen's Badge of Honour, 2013, Hon. Vice Pres., 2014, British Red Cross. Cavaliere Ufficiale (Italy), 2016. *Publications:* Escaping with his Life, 2019. *Recreations:* theatre, walking, amateur dramatics, travel, reading, writing, music, guitar. *E:* youngs2city@yahoo.com. *Club:* MCC.

**YOUNG, Peter Lance;** Group Chief Executive, RMC Group, 1996–2000; *b* 26 June 1938; *s* of Harry Andrew Young and Ethel Freda Young; *m* 1962, Susan Mary Wilkes; three *s* one *d*. *Educ:* Chippenham Grammar Sch. Joined RMC Group, 1961; Dir, 1977; Dep. Man. Dir, 1992; Man. Dir, 1993. *Recreations:* tennis, gardening.

**YOUNG, Peter Michael Heppell,** OBE 1995; HM Diplomatic Service, retired; *b* 23 April 1939; *s* of late Denis and Constance Young; *m* 1st, 1969, Maria Laura Aragon; 2nd, Verona Buchan; two *s*. *Educ:* Haileybury Coll.; Williston Acad., USA (ESU Scholarship); Emmanuel Coll., Cambridge (MA). Chartered FCIPD. Royal Marines and Royal West Africa Frontier Force, later Queen's Own Nigeria Regt (2nd Lieut), 1958–60; FCO, 1964; served: Sofia, 1967–70; Geneva, 1970–72; Pretoria/Cape Town, 1972–74; FCO 1974–77; First Sec., Lagos, 1977–79; Dep. High Comr, Ibadan, 1979–80; Consul (Commercial), Lyon, 1981–84; FCO, 1985–89; Counsellor, Lagos, 1989–93; seconded to Dept of National Heritage (Events Director, D-Day and VE-Day 50th Annivs), 1993–95; High Comr, Bahamas, 1996–99. Pres., Bahamas Hon. Consular Corps, 2010–13. Dir, Nassau Inst.; former Mem., Exec. Cttee, Bahamas Nat. Trust. Mem. Bd, Tribune Media Gp, 2013–; Columnist, Tribune Newspaper, Nassau. *Recreations:* tennis, golf, African history. *Address:* PO Box EE 16944, Nassau, Bahamas. *Clubs:* Oxford and Cambridge, MCC; Lyford Cay, Royal Nassau Sailing (former Hon. Sec.); Nassau Lawn Tennis (Pres., 2012–13).

**YOUNG, Peyton;** *see* Young, H. P.

**YOUNG, Raymond Kennedy,** CBE 2007 (OBE 1989); Chairman, Architecture and Design Scotland, 2004–10; *b* 23 Jan. 1946; *s* of Sharp and Christina Neil (Neilina), Young; *m* 1972, Jean; three *s*. *Educ:* Univ. of Strathclyde (BArch Hons). FRIAS. Project Architect, ASSIST/Univ. of Strathclyde, 1971–74; Housing Corp., 1974–89 (Dir, Scotland); Dir North, and Dir Res. and Innovation, Scottish Homes, 1989–97; self-employed, 1997–2016. Hon. Sen. Res. Fellow, Dept of Urban Studies, Univ. of Glasgow, 1997–2009; Hon. Prof., Dept of Architecture, Univ. of Strathclyde, 2007–11. Mem., UK Sustainable Develt Commn, 2000–04. Non-exec. Dir, Historic Scotland, 2007–15. Gen. Trustee, Church of Scotland, 2012– (Chair, 2017–). *Publications:* Annie's Loo: the Govan origins of Scotland's community based housing associations, 2013; Affordable Homes in Rural Scotland: the role of housing associations, 2015; gen. professional pubns. *Recreations:* theatre, music, no sports. *Address:* Glenannia, Upper Granco Street, Dunning PH2 0RX.

**YOUNG, Richard;** photographer; Co-Founder and Co-Director, Richard Young Gallery, London, since 2008; *b* Welwyn Garden City, 17 Sept. 1947; *s* of David Young and Hilda Young; *m* 1985, Susan Walker; two *s* one *d*. Social photographer, 1974–. *Solo exhibitions* include: Richard Young: An Early Retrospective, Olympus Gall., London, 1979; By Invitation Only, 1981, PAPARAZZO!, 1989, Hamilton's Gall., London; Richard Young Two Thousand, Blains Fine Art, London, 1999; 15 Minutes: 30 Years Retrospective, The Hospital, London, 2004; Richard Young Gallery: Icons, 2009; GQ Man of the Year Awards 11 Year Retrospective, 2010; Pret-a-Photo II, 2011; Elizabeth Taylor, 2012, also Stephen Webster, LA and Colombaia Mus., Ischia, 2012; Rebels, Leica, LA, 2012, 2018, Leica, Boston, 2017; David Bowie, 2013; RY40, 2014; *group exhibitions* include: Olympus Gall., London, 1986; Four Stages of Innocence, RCA, 1993; Warholesque?, 2009, Pret-a-Photo, 2010, Richard Young Gall.; George Harrison, GRAMMY Mus., LA, 2011; photograph of Freddie Mercury inducted into NPG, 2013. Hon. Dr Univ. of Arts, London, 2013. Ischia Art Award, Ischia Global Film and Music Fest., 2012; Le Prix Champagne de la Joie de Vivre, 2013; Ordre des Coteaux de Champagne, 2014; Chairman's Award, UK Picture Editors' Guild, 2015; British Photographic Associateship, British Photography Awards, 2019. *Publications:* By Invitation Only, 1981; Paparazzo!, 1989; Shooting Stars, 2004; Nightclubbing, 2014. *Recreations:* walking, good food, music. *Address:* Richard Young Gallery, 4 Holland Street, W8 4LT. *T:* (020) 7937 8911. *E:* office@richardyoungonline.com. *Clubs:* Chelsea Arts, Groucho, Ivy.

**YOUNG, Sir Rob;** *see* Young, Sir J. R.

**YOUNG, Robert;** Principal, European Economic Research Ltd, 2004–13; *b* 27 March 1944; *s* of Walter Horace Young and Evelyn Joan Young; *m* 1965, Patricia Anne Cowin; one *s* one *d* (and one *s* decd). *Educ:* Magdalen College, Oxford (BA Hons 1965; MA 1996). Graduate apprentice, Rolls-Royce, 1965; IBM UK, 1969–71; Rolls-Royce Motors, 1971–81: Man. Dir, Military Engine Div., 1977–79; Dir and Gen. Manager, Diesel Div., 1979–81; Vickers, 1981–85 (Group Commercial Dir, 1981–83); Man. Dir, Crane Ltd, 1985–88; Chief Exec., Plastics Div., McKechnie plc, 1989–90; Dir, Beauford plc, 1990–92; Principal, Coopers & Lybrand, then PricewaterhouseCoopers, 1993–2001; Dir, LECG Ltd, 2001–04. Member: Central Policy Review Staff, 1983; No 10 Policy Unit, 1983–84; CBI W Midlands Regional Council, 1980–81 (Chm., CBI Shropshire, 1981); Monopolies and Mergers Commn, 1986–92; Fulbright Commn, 1994–2004. *Recreations:* Mozart, railways, cats, photography. *Address:* Cragdale House, Victoria Street, Settle, North Yorks BD24 9HD. *Club:* Oxford and Cambridge.

**YOUNG, Prof. Robert Joseph,** PhD; FRS 2013; FREng, FIMMM; FInstP; Professor of Polymer Science and Technology, University of Manchester (formerly University of Manchester Institute of Science and Technology), since 1986 (Head, School of Materials, 2004–09); *b* 29 May 1948; *s* of Joseph and Florence Young; *m* 1971, Sheila Winifred Wilson; two *d*. *Educ:* St John's Coll., Cambridge (MA, PhD). Res. Fellow, St John's Coll., Cambridge, 1973–75; Lectr in Materials, QMC, 1975–86. Wolfson Res. Prof. in Materials Science, Royal Soc., 1992–97. Visiting Professor: Hong Kong Poly. Univ., 2008–11, 2015–17; King Fahd Univ. of Petroleum and Minerals, Saudi Arabia, 2011–12. Zeneca Lect., 1996, BAAS Public Lect., 1997, Royal Soc. Panel Chm., HEFCE RAE, 1996, 2001. MAE 2015. FREng 2006. Silver Medal, Plastics and Rubber Inst., 1991; Griffith Medal, Inst. of Materials, 2002; Plueddemann Internat. Award, 2010; Leslie Holliday Prize, 2011, Swinburne Medal and Prize, 2012, Platinum Medal, 2019, IMMM. *Publications:* Introduction to Polymers, 1981, 3rd edn (jtly), 2011; (jtly) Fracture Behaviour of Polymers, 1983; more than 400 papers in learned jls. *Recreations:* tennis, piano, gardening; former athlete (four blues, 1967–70; British Univs' Sports Fedn 110m Hurdles Champion, 1970). *Address:* National Graphene Institute and School of Materials, University of Manchester, Oxford Road, Manchester M13 9PL. *T:* (0161) 306 3550, (0161) 306 1465.

**YOUNG, (Robert Macfie) Douglas,** TD 1980; WS; Vice Lord-Lieutenant of Inverness, since 2015; *b* Inverness, 23 Oct. 1948; *s* of late Robert Macfie Young and Margaret MacCaig Young; *m* 1979, Alexandra Mackenzie; one *s*. *Educ:* Inverness Royal Acad.; Drumtochty Castle Sch.; Fettes Coll.; Univ. of Aberdeen (LLB 1970). Admitted as solicitor, Scotland, 1973; WS 2000. Law Apprentice, Guild & Guild WS, Edinburgh, 1970–73; Partner, Innes & Mackay, Solicitors, Inverness, 1973–80; Solicitor: Chief Exec.'s Dept, Moray DC, 1980–88; Dept of Law and Admin, Highland Regl Council, 1988–96; Short Service Vol. Commn, HQ 1 (UK) Armd Div., ME, 1990–91; HQ ARRC, Bosnia-Herzegovina, 1996; Liaison Officer to HQ SFOR, HQ Multinat. Div. (SW), Bosnia-Herzegovina, 1996–97; UK Kosovo Diplomatic Observer Mission, OSCE Kosovo Verification Mission, 1998–99; Solicitor, Macleods WS, Solicitors, Inverness, 1999–2001; Liaison Officer to Kosovo Protection Corps, HQ Multinat. Bde Centre Kosovo, 2001–02. Served Territorial Army: commnd Scottish Div., 1970; Major, 1980; Lt Col, Highlanders (V), 1996–2002. Chm., British Armed Forces Fedn, 2006–16; Exec. Mem. and Chm., Northern Area Cttee, Highland RFCA, 2012–18. Sec., SSAFA Moray and Banffshire, 1984–88; Pres., SSAFA Inverness-shire and Western Isles, 2015–. Mem. Bd, Highlanders Mus., 2013–. Trustee: Queen's Own Highlanders Regtl Trusts, 2013–; Queen's Own Cameron Highlanders War Meml Youth Centre, 2014–. DL Inverness, 2000. MCMI 1989. FRSA 2007. *Recreations:* Scottish Highlands, British naval military and air force history, castles and churches. *E:* rmdouglasyoung@gmail.com.

**YOUNG, Sir Robin (Urquhart),** KCB 2002; Permanent Secretary, Department of Trade and Industry, 2001–05; Chairman: London 2017 Ltd, since 2016; London Championships Ltd, since 2016; *b* 7 Sept. 1948; *s* of late Col Ian U. Young and Mary Young; *m* 1998, Madeleine Mary Arnot, *qv*. *Educ:* Fettes Coll., Edinburgh; University Coll., Oxford (BA 1971). Joined DoE, 1973; Private Sec. to Parly Sec., Planning and Local Govt, 1976; Private Sec. to Minister of Housing, 1980–81; Local Govt Finance, 1981–85; Private Sec. to successive Secs of State, 1985–88; Under Secretary: Housing, 1988–89; Envmt Policy, 1989–91; Local Govt Review, 1991–92; Local Govt, DoE, 1992–94; Dep. Sec., 1994–98; Regl Dir, Govt Office for London, 1994–97; Hd of Econ. and Domestic Affairs Secretariat, Cabinet Office, 1997–98; Permanent Sec., DCMS, 1998–2001. Chairman: Dr Foster Intelligence Ltd, 2006–11; Euro RSCG Apex Commns, 2006–11; First Columbus Investments, 2007–09; A4e Ltd, 2012–15; Circle Housing Gp, 2009–16; Clarion Housing, 2016–18. Non-executive Director: Bovis Construction Ltd, 1989–94; Dr Foster Ltd, 2005–15; A4e Ltd, 2007–12; Cambridge Cleantech Ltd, 2012–. Chairman: E of England Sci. and Industry Council, 2006–09; E of England Internat. Ltd, 2006–10; Board Member: IoD, 2007–14; Film London, 2012–19; Adv. Bd, Solar Cloth Co. Ltd, 2014–16. *Recreations:* cinema, house in France. *Address:* 47 Moreton Terrace, SW1V 2NS.

**YOUNG, Roger;** President, FPL Group Inc., 1999, retired; *b* 14 Jan. 1944; *s* of Arnold and Margaret Young; *m* 1970, Sue Neilson; one *s* two *d*. *Educ:* Gordonstoun Sch.; Edinburgh Univ. (BSc Engrg); Cranfield Business Sch. (MBA). Rolls-Royce Ltd, 1961–72; Alidair Ltd, 1972–73; Wavin Plastics Ltd, 1973–76; Aurora Holdings Ltd, 1976–80; Low & Bonar plc, 1980–88; Chief Exec., Scottish Hydro-Electric plc, 1988–98. Non-executive Director: Friends Ivory & Sime (formerly Ivory & Sime) plc, 1993–99; Bank of Scotland, 1994–99. *Recreations:* family, flying, hill walking.

**YOUNG, Roger Dudley;** Chairman, Clex Developments, 1976–2017; *b* 7 Jan. 1940; *s* of Henry G. Young and Winifred G. Young; *m* 1st, 1965, Jennifer J. Drayton (marr. diss. 2010); one *s* two *d*; 2nd, 2011, Hilary C. Vaughan (*née* Rushworth). *Educ:* Dulwich Coll. Drayton Group, 1958–69; Imperial Group, 1969–73; Robert Fleming, 1971–73; Director: Henry Ansbacher Group, 1973–82; Touche Remnant Group, 1982–85; Chief Executive: Bank Julius Baer (London), 1985–89; March Group, 1989–91; Dir Gen., Inst. of Mgt, 1992–98. Dir Gen., Inst. of Enterprise, 1998–2001. Chairman: Andrews and Partners Ltd,

2000–05; Andrews Estate Agents Ltd, 2000–05; Bicon Hldgs Ltd, 2000–13; Lunar (formerly Apollo) Diagnostics Ltd, 2005–07; Chic Sheds Ltd, 2014–17; non-exec. Dir, PMP Plus, subseq. Apollo Medical Partners, Ltd, 2000–05. Dir, Ipswich Hosp. NHS Trust, 1992–99. Trustee, 1998–2005, Chm., 2000–03, World in Need, subseq. Andrews Charitable Trust Ltd. CCMI; FRSA. *Recreations:* investing in and supporting new ventures, sculpture, travel. *Address:* Hardy House, 32 Benton Street, Hadleigh, Ipswich IP7 5AT. *T:* (01473) 828878. *Club:* Honourable Artillery Company.

YOUNG, Hon. Sir Ronald (Leslie), KNZM 2016; a Judge of the High Court, New Zealand, 2001–15; a Judge of the Court of Appeal: Vanuatu, since 2006; Solomon Islands, since 2016; *b* Dunedin, NZ, 18 July 1951; *s* of Leslie Thomas and Mary Elizabeth Young; *m* 2002, Katherine Anne Lillian Bicknell; two *s* (and one *s* decd); one step *d*. *Educ:* Otago Boys High Sch.; Univ. of Otago (LLB 1974). Called to the Bar and admitted as solicitor, NZ, 1975; McCaw, Lewis, Chapman Lawyers, 1975–88, Partner, 1978–88; Dist Court Judge, 1988–2001 (Chief Dist Court Judge, 1993–2001). Pres., Electoral Commn, 2000–01. Mem., Criminal and Civil Appeal Div., Court of Appeal, 2005–15; Chm., Criminal Practice Cttee, 2007–15; Chair, NZ Parole Bd, 2018–. Commemorative Medal (New Zealand), 1990. *Recreations:* walking, reading, music, gardening, golf, travel. *Address:* 121 Humphries Street, RD1 Greytown 5794, New Zealand. *T:* 63048553, 21464396. *E:* youngbicknell@xtra.co.nz. *Clubs:* Wellington; Royal Wellington Golf, Martinborough Golf.

YOUNG, Sally; *see* MacDonald, S.

YOUNG, Prof. Stephen John, PhD; FREng; Professor of Information Engineering, Cambridge University, 1995–2017, now Emeritus; Fellow of Emmanuel College, Cambridge, since 1985; Senior Member, Technical Staff, Apple Computer Inc., since 2015; *b* 23 Jan. 1951; *s* of John Leonard Young and Joan Young (*née* Shaw); *m* 1976 (marr. diss. 1996); two *d*; *m* 1999, Sybille Wiesmann. *Educ:* Maghull GS; Jesus Coll., Cambridge (MA, PhD). FIET, CEng; FREng 2002; FIEEE 2009. Res. Engr, GEC Hirst Res. Centre, 1973–74; Univ. Lectr in Computation, UMIST, 1977–84; Lectr in Engrg, 1984–95, Reader, 1995, Cambridge Univ.; Tech. Dir, Entropic Cambridge Res. Lab., 1996–99; Architect, Microsoft Corp., 1999–2001; Cambridge University: Chm., Sch. of Technol., 2002–04; Hd of Inf. Engrg, 2002–09; Sen. Pro-Vice Chancellor, 2009–15. Chairman: Phonetic Arts Ltd, 2008–10; VocalIQ Ltd, 2011–15. Member of Council: Univ. of Cambridge, 2006–09; RAEng, 2006–. Chm., Speech and Lang. Tech. Cttee, IEEE, 2009–10. Fellow, Internat. Speech Communication Assoc., 2008 (Medal for Scientific Achievement, 2010). Tech. Achievement Award, Eur. Assoc. for Signal Processing, 2013; James L. Flanagan Award, IEEE, 2015. FRSA. Editor, Computer Speech and Language, 1993–2005. *Publications:* Real Time Languages, 1982; An Introduction to Ada, 1985; (ed) Corpus-based Methods, 1997; articles in jls. *Recreations:* ballet, film, music. *Address:* Apple Computer Inc., 90 Hills Road, Cambridge CB2 1PG. *T:* 07734 129069.

YOUNG, Sir Stephen Stewart Templeton, 3rd Bt *cr* 1945; QC (Scot.) 2002; Sheriff Principal of Grampian, Highland and Islands, 2001–12; *b* 24 May 1947; *s* of Sir Alastair Young, 2nd Bt, and Dorothy Constance Marcelle (*d* 1964), *d* of late Lt-Col Charles Ernest Chambers, and *widow* of Lt J. H. Grayburn, VC, Parachute Regt; *S* father, 1963; *m* 1974, Viola Margaret Nowell-Smith, *d* of Prof. P. H. Nowell-Smith and Perilla Thyme (she *m* 2nd, Lord Roberthall, KCMG, CB); two *s*. *Educ:* Rugby; Trinity Coll., Oxford; Edinburgh Univ. Voluntary Service Overseas, Sudan, 1968–69. Sheriff: of Glasgow and Strathkelvin, March–June 1984; of N Strathclyde at Greenock, 1984–2001. *Heir:* *s* Charles Alastair Stephen Young, *b* 21 July 1979. *Address:* Beechfield, Newton of Kinkell, Conon Bridge, Ross-shire IV7 8AS.

YOUNG, Timothy Mark Stewart; Director of Education, Rank Foundation, since 2007; *b* 6 Oct. 1951; *s* of Sir Brian Walter Mark Young and Fiona Marjorie Young (*née* Stewart); *m* 1990, Dr Alison Mary Keightley, MRCP, FRCR; two *s*. *Educ:* Eton (King's Schol.); Magdalene Coll., Cambridge (BA 1974; MA 1978); Bristol Univ. (PGCE 1975). Asst Master, Eton, 1975–83 and 1985–87; Asst Master, Wanganui Collegiate Sch., NZ, 1984; Teacher, Harvard Sch., Los Angeles, 1987–88; Housemaster, Eton, 1988–92; Headmaster, Royal Grammar Sch., Guildford, 1992–2006. Hon. Treas., HMC, 1999–2002. Mem. Court, Univ. of Surrey, 1992–2006. Governor: Abbots Hosp., 1992–2006; Westminster Sch., 2005–15. Consultant, Internat. Inst. of Educn, 2010–12. Trustee, Young Carers Develt Trust, 2011–. *Recreations:* music, cinema, travel, Watford FC. *Address:* Cobbetts, Mavins Road, Farnham, Surrey GU9 8JS. *Club:* East India, Devonshire and Public Schools.

YOUNG, Timothy Nicholas; QC 1996; barrister; *b* 1 Dec. 1953; *s* of William Ritchie Young and Patricia Eileen Young; *m* 1981, Susan Jane Kenny; two *s* one *d*. *Educ:* Malvern Coll.; Magdalen Coll., Oxford (BA, BCL). Called to the Bar, Gray's Inn, 1977, Bencher, 2004; in practice at the Commercial Bar, 1977–. Vis. Lectr, St Edmund Hall, Oxford, 1977–80. *Publications:* Voyage Charters, 1993, 4th edn 2014. *Recreations:* watercolours, drawing, cricket, golf, guitar, theatre, television. *Clubs:* Thebertons Cricket, Worcs CC; Dulwich and Sydenham Golf.

YOUNG, Toby Daniel Moorsom; journalist and author; *b* 17 Oct. 1963; *s* of Baron Young of Dartington and Sasha Young; *m* 2001, Caroline Bondy; three *s* one *d*. *Educ:* Creighton Comp. Sch.; King Edward VI Comp. Sch.; William Ellis Comp. Sch.; Brasenose Coll., Oxford (BA 1986); Harvard Univ.: Trinity Coll., Cambridge. Teaching Fellow, Graduate Sch. of Arts and Scis, Harvard, 1987–88; Teaching Asst, Soc. and Pol Scis Fac., Univ. of Cambridge, 1988–90; Editor, The Modern Review, 1991–95; Contrib. Editor, Vanity Fair, 1995–98; Drama Critic, 2001–06, Associate Editor, 2007–, Editorial Dir, Supplements, 2015–16, Editor, Spectator Life, 2015–17, The Spectator; Restaurant Critic, ES magazine, 2002–07; blogger, Daily Telegraph, 2010–15. Trustee, 2004–10, Ambassador, 2010–, Orbis UK; CEO, 2014–16, Dir, 2014–18, W London Free Sch. Academy Trust (Co-Founder, Chm. Govs and Trustee, 2011–14); Trustee, Knowledge Schs Foundn Trust; Dir, New Schs Network, 2017–18. Vis. Fellow, Univ. of Buckingham, 2011–14. Mem., Fulbright Commn, 2013–18. *Plays* (co-author): How to Lose Friends and Alienate People, 2003 (co-prod. of film, 2008); Who's the Daddy?, 2005 (Best New Comedy, Theatregoers' Choice Awards, 2006); A Right Royal Farce, 2006; *TV drama* (co-author and co-prod.), When Boris Met Dave, 2009. *Publications:* How to Lose Friends and Alienate People, 2001; The Sound of No Hands Clapping, 2006; How to Set Up a Free School, 2011; What Every Parent Needs to Know, 2014. *Recreation:* food and drink. *E:* tobyyoung@mac.com. *Club:* Soho House.

YOUNG, Sir William Neil, 10th Bt *cr* 1769; Chairman, Napo Pharmaceuticals Inc., 2007–14; *b* 22 Jan. 1941; *s* of Captain William Elliot Young, RAMC (killed in action 27 May 1942), and Mary (*d* 1997), *d* of late Rev. John Macdonald; *S* grandfather, 1944; *m* 1965, Christine Veronica Morley, *o d* of late R. B. Morley, Buenos Aires; one *s* one *d*. *Educ:* Wellington Coll.; Sandhurst. Captain, 16th/5th The Queen's Royal Lancers, retired 1970. Dir, Kleinwort Benson International Investment Ltd, 1982–87; Head: Investment Management, Saudi Internat. Bank, 1987–91; ME Dept, Coutts & Co., 1991–94; Dir, Barclays Private Bank Ltd, 1994–99. Chm., High Ham Br., RBL, 2004–15; Pres., Langport Br., RBL, 2015–. Gov., High Ham Sch., 2010–16. *Recreations:* tennis, gardening. *Heir:* *s* William Lawrence Elliot Young [*b* 26 May 1970; *m* 2001, Astrid Bartsch, Vienna; one *s* one *d*].

YOUNGE, Patrick Anthony; Co-founder and Managing Director, Sugar Films Ltd, since 2015; *b* Greenwich, 14 Feb. 1964; *s* of Patrick Colonso Younge and Reba Anelda Younge (*née* Stoute); *m* 1st, 1994, Jill Carter (marr. diss. 2007); one *s* one *d*; 2nd, 2010, Amy Girdwood; one *s*. *Educ:* Nobel Comprehensive Sch., Stevenage; University Coll. Cardiff (BSc Hons Mineral Exploitation). VP Education, NUS, 1987–89; London Weekend Television, 1991–94; BBC News and Current Affairs, 1994–99; Commng Ed., Channel 4 TV, 1999–2001; Hd, Progs and Planning, BBC Sport, 2001–05; Pres. and Gen. Manager, Travel Channel Media, USA, 2005–10; Chief Creative Officer, BBC Production, 2010–13; Founder and Dir, WeCreate Associates, 2014–16. Gov., Univ. of W London, 2014–. FRTS; FRSA. *Recreations:* cinema, sport, reading. *E:* patrickyounge@gmail.com.

YOUNGER, family name of Viscount Younger of Leckie.

YOUNGER OF LECKIE, 5th Viscount *cr* 1923, of Alloa, Clackmannanshire; James Edward George Younger; Bt 1911; Parliamentary Under-Secretary of State, Ministry of Housing, Communities and Local Government, since 2019; *b* 11 Nov. 1955; *e s* of 4th Viscount Younger of Leckie, KT, KCVO, TD, PC, DL and Diana Rhona (*née* Tuck); *S* father, 2003; *m* 1988, Jennie Veronica (*née* Wootton); one *s* two *d*. *Educ:* Cargilfield Sch., Edinburgh; Winchester Coll.; St Andrews Univ. (MA Hons Medieval Hist. 1979); Henley Mgt Coll. (MBA 1993). MCIM 1994. Personnel Mgr, Coats Patons, 1979–84; Recruitment Consultant, Angela Mortimer Ltd, 1984–86; Exec. Search Consultant, Stephens Consultancies, 1986–92; Director: MacInnes Younger, 1992–94; HR, UBS Wealth Mgt, 1994–2004; Culliford Edmunds Associates, 2004–07; Consultant, Eban Internat., 2007–10. Chm., Bucks Cons. Constituency Assoc., 2006–10. Member: Assoc. of Cons. Peers, 2006–; Area Bd, Oxon and Bucks Conservatives, 2008–13; Scottish Peers Assoc., 2014–; Chm., Milton Keynes Conservatives, 2011–13. Elected Mem., H of L, 2010. Cons. Party Whip, 2011–12; a Lord in Waiting (Govt Whip), 2012–13; Parly Under-Sec. of State, BIS, 2013–14; a Lord in Waiting (Govt Whip), 2015–19; spokesman on educn, Scotland, Wales and NI, DEFRA and DCMS, H of L, 2014–. Vice Pres., War Widows' Assoc., 2012–. Mem., Royal Co. of Archers (Queen's Body Guard for Scotland). Pres., 2012–16, Vice-Pres., 2016–, Highland Soc. of London; Pres., Buckingham Cons. Patrons Club; Hon. Pres., Kate Kennedy Club Life Members Assoc., St Andrews Univ. *Recreations:* sailing, tennis, shooting, Highland dancing, ski-ing, country pursuits, cricket. *Heir:* *s* Hon. Alexander William George Younger, *b* 13 Nov. 1993. *Address:* The Old Vicarage, Dorton, Aylesbury, Bucks HP18 9NH. *T:* (01844) 238396. *E:* jeg.younger@virgin.net. *Club:* White Hunters Cricket (Hampshire).

YOUNGER, Sir Alexander (William), KCMG 2019 (CMG 2011); Chief, Secret Intelligence Service, since 2014; *b* 4 July 1963; *m* 1993, Sarah Hopkins; one *s* one *d* (and one *s* decd). Served Army. Second Sec., FCO, 1991; First Secretary: UK Mission to IAEA, Vienna, 1995–98; FCO, 1998–2002; (Pol), Dubai, 2002–05; Counsellor, FCO, 2005–14. *Address:* PO Box 1300, London, SE1 1BD.

YOUNGER, Sir David; *see* Younger, Sir J. D. B.

YOUNGER, (James) Samuel, CBE 2009; Chair, CILEx Regulation, since 2015; *b* 5 Oct. 1951; *s* of Rt Hon. Sir Kenneth Gilmour Younger, KBE, PC and Elisabeth Kirsteen (*née* Stewart); *m* 1984, Katherine Anne Spencer; one *s*. *Educ:* Westminster Sch.; New Coll., Oxford (BA Hons). Asst Editor, Middle East International, 1972–78; BBC World Service: Sen. Asst, Central Current Affairs Talks, 1979–84; Sen. Producer and Exec. Producer, Current Affairs, 1984–86; Asst Head, Arabic Service, 1986–87; Head, Current Affairs, 1987–89; Head, Arabic Service, 1989–92; Controller, Overseas Services, 1992–94; Director of Broadcasting, 1994; Man. Dir, 1994–99; Dir-Gen., BRCS, 1999–2001; Chm., Electoral Commn, 2001–08. Chair, QAA, 2004–09; Interim Chief Executive: Shelter, 2009; Electoral Reform Soc., 2010; Bell Educnl Trust, 2010; Chief Exec., Charity Commn, 2010–14. Chair, VSO, 2018– (Vice Chair, 2014). Ind. Mem., Standards Cttee, GLA, 2008–12. Mem. Council, ASA, 2014–. Mem. Adv. Gp, Marston Hldgs Ltd, 2016–. Mem. Council, Univ. of Sussex, 1998–2007 (Chm. Council, 2001–07). Public Interest Observer, Chartered Inst. of Taxation, 2015–18. Dir, English Touring Opera, 1999–2010. Gov., Commonwealth Inst., 1998–2005. Patron, Windsor Leadership Trust, 1998–. *Recreations:* sport, choral singing.

YOUNGER, Captain Sir (John) David (Bingham), KCVO 2013 (LVO 2007); Lord-Lieutenant of Tweeddale, 1994–2014 (Vice Lord-Lieutenant, 1992–94); Co-founder and Managing Director, Broughton Brewery Ltd, 1979–95; *b* 20 May 1939; *s* of Major Oswald Bingham Younger, MC, A and SH, and Dorothea Elizabeth Younger (*née* Hobbs); *m* 1962, Anne Rosaleen Logan (*d* 2012); one *s* two *d*. *Educ:* Eton Coll.; RMA Sandhurst. Regular Army, Argyll and Sutherland Highlanders, 1957–69; Scottish and Newcastle Breweries, 1969–79. Dir, Broughton Ales, 1995–96. Chairman: Belhaven Hill Trust, 1986–94; Scottish Borders Tourist Board, 1989–91; Peeblesshire Charitable Trust, 1994–2014; Bowmen Ltd, 2008–15. Director: Queen's Hall (Edinburgh) Ltd, 1992–2001; Eastgate Theatre and Arts Centre (Peebles) Ltd, 2014–19 (Chm., 2015–19). Vice Pres., RHASS, 1994. Mem., Queen's Body Guard for Scotland, Royal Company of Archers, 1969– (Sec., 1993–2007; Brig., Ensign, 2010). River Tweed Comr, 2002–16. President: Lowland RFCA, 2006–14; Peebles Br., RBL Scotland, 2014–19; SSAFA (formerly SSAFA Forces Help) (Borders), 2016–. Trustee, Chambers Instn, 2012–15. DL Tweeddale, 1987. *Recreation:* the countryside. *Address:* Mansemanet, Broughton, Peeblesshire ML12 6HF. *T:* (01899) 830570.

YOUNGER, Samuel; *see* Younger, J. S.

YOUNGER-ROSS, Richard; Member (Lib Dem), Devon County Council, 2013–17; *b* 29 Jan. 1953; *m* 1982, Susan Younger. *Educ:* Walton-on-Thames Secondary Modern Sch.; Ewell Tech. Coll. (HNC); Oxford Poly. Architectural consultant, 1970–90; design consultant, 1990–2001. Joined Liberal Party, 1970 (Mem. Council, 1972–82). Contested (Lib Dem): Chislehurst, 1987; Teignbridge, 1992, 1997. MP (Lib Dem) Teignbridge, 2001–10; contested (Lib Dem) Newton Abbot, 2010, 2015.

YOUNGER THIERIOT, Sir Andrew William, 5th Bt *cr* 1911, of Auchen Castle, co. Dumfries; *b* 14 Jan. 1986; *s* of Sir Julian William Richard Younger, 4th Bt and Deborah Anne Younger (*née* Wood); *S* father, 2019.

YOUNGHUSBAND, Jan; Commissioning Editor, BBC Music and Events, since 2009; *b* Portsmouth, 8 May 1954; *d* of John Younghusband and Joyce Younghusband (*née* Browning); one *s*. *Educ:* Portsmouth High Sch.; Millfield Sch.; Royal Holloway Coll., London. Asst Prodn Manager, Glyndebourne, 1974–79; Prodn Manager, Nuffield Th., Southampton, 1979–80; Asst Producer to Peter Hall, NT, 1980–88; freelance television producer and writer, 1988–2000; Commissioning Ed., Channel 4, 2000–09, Arts and Performance, 2001–09. Mem., BAFTA, 2002–. *Publications:* Orchestra, 1990; Concerto, 1991; A Genius in the Family, 1997. *Recreations:* playing the piano, reading, ski-ing, golf.

**YOUNGSON, Prof. George Gray,** CBE 2009; PhD; FRCSEd; Professor of Paediatric Surgery, University of Aberdeen, 1999–2010, now Emeritus; *b* Glasgow, 13 May 1949; *s* of Alexander Keay Youngson, MBE and Jean O'Neil Youngson; *m* 1973, Sandra Jean Lister; one *s* two *d*. *Educ*: Buckhaven High Sch.; Aberdeen Univ. (MB ChB 1973; PhD 1979). FRCSEd 1977. Lectr in Surgery, 1975–83, Resident in Cardiothoracic Surgery, 1977–79, Univ. of Western Ontario; Fellow in Paediatric Surgery, Hosp. for Sick Children, Toronto, 1981–82; Consultant Gen. Surgeon, Aberdeen Royal Infirmary, 1984–88; Consultant Paediatric Surgeon, Royal Aberdeen Children's Hosp., 1984–2010. Mem. Council, RCSE, 2005–10 (Vice Pres., 2009–12). Hon. FRCPE 2011. *Publications*: Emergency Abdominal Surgery, 1996; Enhancing Surgical Performance: a primer in non-technical skills, 2015. *Recreations*: squash, golf, hill walking, bagpipes, guitar. *Address*: Birken Lodge, Bieldside, Aberdeen AB15 9BQ; Royal College of Surgeons of Edinburgh, Nicolson Street, Edinburgh EH8 9DG. *T*: (0131) 527 1642. *E*: ggyrach@abdn.ac.uk. *Clubs*: Deeside Golf (Aberdeen); Kippie Lodge Sports and Country.

**YOUSAF, Humza;** Member (SNP) Glasgow Pollok, Scottish Parliament, since 2016 (Glasgow, 2011–16); Cabinet Secretary for Justice, since 2018; *b* Glasgow, 7 April 1985; *s* of Muzaffar Yousaf and Shaaista Yousaf; *m* 2010, Gail Lythgoe. *Educ*: Glasgow Univ. (BA Hons Politics). Parliamentary researcher: to Bashir Ahmad, MSP, 2007–09; to Anne McLaughlin, MSP, 2009; Parly aide to Rt Hon. Alex Salmond, MSP, 2009–10; Communications and Policy Officer, SNP, 2010–11. Minister for Ext. Affairs and Internat. Develt, 2012–14, for Europe and Internat. Develt, 2014–16, for Transport and the Islands, 2016–18, Scottish Parlt. *Recreations*: football, running, badminton, riding my motorbike. *Address*: Scottish Parliament, Holyrood, Edinburgh EH99 1SP. *E*: Humza.Yousaf.msp@parliament.scot.

**YOUSAFZAI, Malala;** campaigner for education; *b* Swat Valley, Pakistan, 12 July 1997; *d* of Ziauddin Yousafzai and Toor Pekai Yousafzai. Co-Founder, Malala Fund. Nat. Youth Peace Prize, Pakistan, 2011; Tipperary Internat. Peace Award, Tipperary Peace Convention, 2012; Premi Internacional Catalunya, Spain, 2013; Simone de Beauvoir Prize, Éditions Gallimard and Culturesfrance, 2013; Ambassador of Conscience Award, Amnesty Internat., 2013; Sakharov Prize for Freedom of Thought, EP, 2013; Internat. Children's Peace Prize, KidsRights Foundn, 2013; Anna Politkovskaya Award, Reach All Women in War, 2013; (jtly) Nobel Peace Prize, 2014. *Publications*: (with C. Lamb) I Am Malala: the girl who stood up for education and was shot by the Taliban, 2013 (trans. 40 langs); (with P. McCormick) I Am Malala (young readers' edn), 2014; Malala's Magic Pencil, 2017; We Are Displaced, 2019.

**YOXALL, Basil Joshua;** Master of the Senior (formerly Supreme) Court, Queen's Bench Division, since 2002; *b* 24 April 1952; *s* of Cecil Ezra Yoxall-Harary and Grace Yoxall-Harary; *m* 1981, Sally Anne Eagle; two *s* one *d*. *Educ*: Wallington Grammar Sch.; St Catharine's Coll., Cambridge (MA). Called to the Bar, Inner Temple, 1975; known professionally as Basil Yoxall; in practice as barrister, specialising in common law, 1975–2002. *Publications*: (ed jtly) The White Book Service: Civil Procedure, annually 2004–; (contrib.) Atkin's Court Forms (on Judgments and Orders), 2004, 2014. *Recreations*: cinema, classical music, history. *Address*: Royal Courts of Justice, Strand, WC2A 2LL. *Club*: Travellers.

**YOXALL-HARARY, Basil Joshua;** *see* Yoxall, B. J.

**YU, David;** Chief Product Officer, Funding Circle, since 2015; *b* Seattle, 6 Nov. 1967; *s* of Donald and Jean Yu; *m* 1995, Philana Dee Chow. *Educ*: Univ. of Calif, Berkeley (BS Electrical Engrg and Computer Sci.); Stanford Univ. (MS Computer Sci.). Engrg Dir, Zip2 Corp., 1997–99; Vice-Pres., Engrg, Alta Vista Co., 1999–2001; Betfair Group Ltd: Chief Technol. Officer, 2002–05; Chief Operating Officer, 2005–06; CEO, 2006–11. *Recreations*: travel, photography, food and wine.

**YU, Prof. Hai-Sui,** DPhil, DSc; Pro-Vice Chancellor (International), University of Leeds, since 2016; *b* 12 Aug. 1961; *s* of Dahei Yu and Xinghua Xiao; *m* 1988, Xiu-Li Guan; one *s* one *d*. *Educ*: Shijiazhuang Railway Univ., China (BE Civil Engrg 1985); Imperial Coll. London (MSc Rock Mechanics 1987; DIC 1987); St Anne's Coll., Oxford (DPhil Soil Mechanics 1990); Univ. of Newcastle, NSW (DSc Geomechanics 2000). FREng 2011. University of Newcastle, New South Wales: Lectr in Civil Engrg, 1991–94; Sen. Lectr in Civil Engrg, 1994–98; Associate Prof. of Civil Engrg, 1998–2000; University of Nottingham: Prof. of Geotech. Engrg, 2001–16; Founding Dir, Nottingham Centre for Geomechanics, 2002–16; Dep. Hd, 2003–07, Hd, 2007–08, Sch. of Civil Engrg; Dean, Faculty of Engrg, 2008–11; Pro-Vice Chancellor, 2011–16. *Publications*: Cavity Expansion Methods in Geomechanics, 2000; Plasticity and Geotechnics, 2006; (ed with W. Wu) Modern Trends in Geomechanics, 2006; (ed jtly) Advances in Transportation Geotechnics, 2008; Memories of My Heart: Hai-Sui's Poems (in Chinese), 2012. *Recreations*: poetry (writing and reading), walking, literature. *Address*: Level 13, Marjorie and Arnold Ziff Building, University of Leeds, Woodhouse Lane, Leeds LS2 9JT. *T*: (0113) 343 6702. *E*: pvc.int@leeds.ac.uk.

**YU, Rt Rev. Patrick Tin-Sik;** Lecturer in Practical Theology, Minghua Theological College, and Bishop in Residence, Hong Kong Sheng Kung Hui, since 2017; *b* 8 July 1951; *s* of Cheung Tok Yu and Sin Yuk Law; *m* 1978, Kathy Cheung; one *s* two *d*. *Educ*: McMaster Univ. (BA Hons 1974); Wycliffe Coll., Univ. of Toronto (MDiv 1981); Toronto Sch. of Theology (DMin 1997). Ordained priest, 1982; Asst Curate, Church of Epiphany, 1981–83; Incumbent: Parish of Coldwater-Medonte, 1985–90; St Theodore of Canterbury, 1990–97; St Timothy Agincourt, 1997–2006; a Suffragan Bishop of Toronto (Area Bishop of York-Scarborough), 2006–17. Sec., Adv. Cttee for Postulants for Ordination, N and W Ontario, 1983–87; Co-ord. of Internship and Instructor, Supervised Ministry, Wycliffe Coll., Univ. of Toronto, 1995–2006. Convenor, Evangelism and Church Growth Initiative, Anglican Communion, 2010–15. Hon. DD Wycliffe Coll., 2006. *Publications*: Being Christian in Multi-Faith Context, 1997, new edn 2013; The Wycliffe Internship Manual, 2000; (contrib.) Canadian Anglicanism at the Dawn of a New Century, 2001; (contrib.) The Homosexuality Debate: faith seeking understanding, 2003; (in Chinese) Preaching the True and Living Word, 2009. *Recreations*: cooking, travel, music.

**YUEH, Linda,** DPhil; economist. *Educ*: Yale Univ. (BA); Harvard Univ. (MPP); New York Univ. (JD Law); Univ. of Oxford (MA; DPhil Econs). Attorney, Paul, Weiss, Rifkind, Wharton & Garrison, 1997–99; Economics Ed., Bloomberg TV, 2010–12; Chief Business Correspondent, BBC, 2013–15. Adjunct Prof. of Econs, London Business Sch., 2009–; Fellow in Econs, St Edmund Hall, Oxford, 2007–; Vis. Prof. of Econs, Peking Univ., 2013–15; Vis. Prof., LSE IDEAS, 2019–20. Chair, Royal Commonwealth Soc., 2018–. FRSA. *Publications*: (with Graeme Chamberlin) Macroeconomics, 2006; (jtly) Globalisation and Economic Growth in China, 2006; (ed) The Law and Economics of Globalisation, 2009; (ed) The Future of Asian Trade and Growth, 2009; The Economy of China, 2010; Enterprising China: business, economic and legal development since 1979, 2011; (ed) China and Globalisation, 4 vols, 2012; China's Growth: the making of an economic superpower, 2013; China's Macroeconomic Policy, 4 vols, 2015; The Great Economists: how their ideas can help us today, 2018.

**YUKON, Bishop of,** since 2010; **Rt Rev. Larry Robertson;** *b* Toronto, 11 July 1954; *m* 1976, Sheila; three *s*. *Educ*: St John's Coll., Winnipeg (BMin, DD); Church Army, Canada (Evangelist Dip.). Ordained priest, 1986; Lay Evangelist, later Priest, Dio. of the Arctic; Suffragan Bishop of the Arctic, 1999–2010. *Address*: Diocese of Yukon, Box 31136, Whitehorse, Yukon, Y1A 5P7, Canada. *E*: synodoffice@klondiker.com.

**YULE, Prof. William,** PhD; Professor of Applied Child Psychology, King's College London, 1987–2005, now Emeritus; *b* Aberdeen, 20 June 1940; *s* of Peter Cocker Yule and Mary Ann Yule (*née* Moir); *m* 1st, 1967, Vivien Walters (marr. diss. 1971); 2nd, 1972, Bridget Ann Osborn; one *s* one *d*. *Educ*: Aberdeen Grammar Sch.; Aberdeen Univ. (MA Psychol. 1962); Univ. of London Inst. of Psychiatry (Dip. Abnormal Psychol. 1963); Univ. of London (PhD Psychol. 1979). MRC Social Psychiatry Res. Unit, 1963–64; Res. Officer, 1965–68, Lectr, 1969, Univ. of London Inst. of Educn; Institute of Psychiatry: Lectr, 1969–73; Sen. Lectr, 1973–80; Reader, 1980–87; Hon. Clin. Psychologist, Bethlem Royal and Maudsley Hosp., 1969–2005 (Hd, Clin. Psychol. Services, 1979–94); Hon. Consultant in Clin. Psychol. to British Army, 2000–10; Vis. Lectr in Clin. Psychol., Univ. of Colombo, Sri Lanka, 2008–10. Fellow, Leverhulme Trust, 2005–06, now Emeritus. Hon. FBPsS 2006. Hon. LLD Roehampton, 2011. Lifetime Achievement Award, Internat. Soc. for Traumatic Stress Studies, 2005; Aristotle Prize, Eur. Fedn of Psychol Assocs, 2007. *Publications*: (jtly) A Neuropsychiatric Study in Childhood, 1970; (ed with J. Carr) Behaviour Modification for the Mentally Handicapped, 1980; (ed jtly) The Lead Debate: the environment, toxicology and child health, 1986; (ed with M. Rutter) Language Development and Disorders, 1987; (jtly) Treatment of Autistic Children, 1987; (with O. Udwin) Infantile Hypercalcaemia and Williams Syndrome: guidelines for parents, 1988; (with A. Gold) Wise Before the Event: coping with crises in school, 1993; (ed jtly) International Handbook of Phobic and Anxiety Disorders in Children and Adolescents, 1994; (ed with G. O'Brien) Behavioural Phenotypes, 1995; (ed jtly) Perspectives on the Classification of Specific Developmental Disorders, 1998; (ed) Post Traumatic Stress Disorder, 1999; (ed with J. Green) Research and Innovation on the Road to Modern Child Psychiatry: vol. 1: Festschrift for Professor Sir Michael Rutter, 2001; (jtly) Fostering Changes: how to improve relationships and manage difficult behaviour: training pack, 2005; (jtly) Managing Difficult behaviour: a handbook for foster carers of the under 12s, 2008; (jtly) Post Traumatic Stress Disorder: cognitive therapy with children and young people, 2010. *Recreations*: watercolour painting, theatre, family, reading detective stories, gardening, people watching. *Address*: Institute of Psychiatry, Psychology and Neuroscience, (PO78), De Crespigny Park, SE5 8AF. *E*: william.yule@kcl.ac.uk.

**YUNUS, Muhammad,** PhD; Founder, 1983, and Managing Director, 2000–11, Grameen Bank, Bangladesh; Chairman, Yunus Centre, since 2008; *b* Chittagong, 28 June 1940; *s* of Haji Muhammad Dula Meah and Sufia Khatun; *m* 1980, Afrozi; one *d*; one *d* by former marriage. *Educ*: Chittagong Collegiate Sch.; Chittagong Coll.; Dhaka Univ. (BA 1960; MA 1961); Vanderbilt Univ. (Fulbright Scholar; PhD 1969). Res. Asst, Bureau of Econs 1961; Lectr in Econs, Chittagong Coll., 1962–65; Asst Prof. of Econs, Middle Tennessee State Univ., 1969–72; Dep. Chief, Gen. Econs Div., Planning Commn, Govt of Bangladesh, 1972; Associate Prof. of Econs and Hd, Dept of Econs, Chittagong Univ., 1972–75; Prof. of Econs, Chittagong Univ. and Dir, Rural Econs Prog., 1975–89. Project Dir, Grameen Bank, Bangladesh, 1976–83. Chancellor, Glasgow Caledonian Univ., 2012–17. Hon. DLitt Glasgow Caledonian, 2008. (Jtly) Nobel Peace Prize, 2006. Presidential Medal of Freedom (USA), 2009. *Publications*: Banker to the Poor, 1999; (jtly) Creating a World Without Poverty, 2008; A World of Three Zeros, 2017. *Address*: c/o Grameen Bank, Mirpur–2, Dhaka 1216, Bangladesh.

**YURKO, Allen Michael;** Chairman, Aquam Corporation, since 2017; *b* 25 Sept. 1951; *s* of Mike Yurko and Catherine (*née* Ewanishan); *m* 1991, Gayle Marie Skelley; two *s* one *d*. *Educ*: Lehigh Univ. (BA Bus. and Econs); Baldwin-Wallace Coll.–USA (MBA). Divl Controller, Joy Mfg, 1978–81; Gp Controller, Eaton Corp., 1981–83; Chief Financial Officer and Gp Vice-Pres., Mueller Hldgs, 1983–89; Robertshaw Controls: Vice-Pres. of Finance, 1989–90; Pres., 1990–91; Pres. and Chief Operating Officer, Siebe T. & A. Controls, 1991–92; Siebe plc: Chief Operating Officer, 1992–93; CEO, 1994–9; Chief Exec., Invensys plc, 1999–2001; Partner: Compass Partners, 2002–07; DLJ Merchant Banking Partners, 2007–10; Industry Exec., Avista Capital Partners, 2010–17. Non-exec. Dir, Tate & Lyle plc, 1996–2005. *Recreations*: boating, golf, sports cars, theatre. *Address*: Aquam Corporation, 7710 Kenamar Court, Suite B, San Diego, CA 92121, USA. *Clubs*: Annabel's; Sunningdale Golf.

**YUVAL-DAVIS, Prof. Nira,** PhD; FAcSS; Professor, 2003–17, now Emeritus, and Director, 2009–17, now Honorary Director, Centre of Research on Migration, Refugees and Belonging, University of East London; *b* Tel-Aviv, 22 Aug. 1943; *d* of Itzhak and Rivka Yuval; *m* Alain Hertzmann; one *s* by a previous marriage. *Educ*: Hebrew Univ., Jerusalem (BA Sociol. and Psychol. 1966; MA 1st Cl. Sociol. 1972); Sussex Univ. (PhD Sociol. 1979). Res. Fellow, Richardson Inst. for Conflict and Peace Res., London, 1973–74; Sociol. Div., Thames Poly., later Univ. of Greenwich, 1974–2003, Prof. of Gender and Ethnic Studies, 1995–2003; Prof. and Dir, Post-Grad. Studies Prog. in Gender, Sexualities and Ethnic Studies, Sch. of Humanities and Social Scis, Univ. of E London, 2003–09. Arts Faculty Vis. Prof., ANU, 1998; Visiting Professor: Dept of Behavioural Scis, Ben-Gurion Univ., Israel, 2000; Dept of Sociol., Tel-Aviv Univ., 2002; Univs of Aalborg and Roskilde, Denmark, 2007; Maria Jahoda Vis. Prof., Dept of Women's Studies, Ruhr Univ., 2003; Benjamin Meacker Vis. Prof., Dept of Sociol., Bristol Univ., 2004; Guest Prof. (pt-time). Res. Centre for Gender Studies, Univ. of Umeå, Sweden, 2009–; Hon. Prof., Faculty of Social Scis, Aalborg Univ., Denmark, 2012–; Professorial Res. Associate, Centre for Gender Studies, SOAS, Univ. of London; Vis. Fellow, Dept of Sociol., Hebrew Univ., Jerusalem, 1980–81; Elizabeth Poppleton Vis. Fellow, Peace Res. Centre, ANU, 1989; Morris Ginsburg Fellow, Dept of Sociol., LSE, 1990–91; Visiting Research Fellow: Inst. of Social Studies, The Hague, 1992; Dept of Sociol., Univ. of Umeå, Sweden, 2000; Schol. in Residence, Havens Centre, Dept of Sociol., Univ. of Wisconsin, Madison, 2003; Rockefeller Fellow, prog. on Gender, Globalization and Human Security, Grad. Sch., CUNY and USA Nat. Council for Res. on Women, 2004. Mem., Sociol. Sub-panel, RAE, 2008, REF, 2014. Pres., Res. Cttee on Racism, Nationalism and Ethnic Relns RC05, Internat. Sociol Assoc., 2002–06. Founder Member: Women Against Fundamentalism, 1989; Internat. Res. Network of Women in Militarized Conflict Zones, 1993. FAcSS (acSS 2003). Dist. Award for Excellence in Res. and Practice, Internat. Sociol. Assoc., 2018. Ed., book series, Politics of Intersectionality, 2009–; Mem. internat. editl bds of 8 learned jls, incl. Signs; Jl of Women in Culture and Soc., and Sociol. of Race and Ethnicity. *Publications*: (ed jtly) Israel and the Palestinians, 1975; (ed jtly) Power and the State, 1978; Israeli Women and Men: divisions behind the unity, 1982; Worlds Apart: women under immigration and nationality laws in Britain, 1985; (ed with F. Anthias) Women - Nation - State, 1989; (ed with H. Bresheeth) The Gulf War and the New World Order, 1991; (with F. Anthias) Racialised Boundaries: race, nation, gender, colour and class and the anti-racist struggle, 1992; (ed with G. Sahgal) Refusing Holy Orders: women and fundamentalism in Britain, 1992; (ed jtly) Women and Citizenship in Europe: borders, rights and duties, 1992; (ed with D. Stasiulis) Unsettling Settler Societies: articulations of gender, ethnicity, race and class, 1995; (ed jtly) Crossfires: nationalism, racism and gender in Europe, 1995; Gender and Nation, 1997; (ed with P.

Werbner) Women, Citizenship and Difference, 1999; (ed with A. Imam) Warning Signs of Fundamentalisms, 2004; (ed jtly) Situating the Politics of Belonging, 2006; The Politics of Belonging: intersectional contestations, 2011; (ed with P. Marfleet) Racism, Migration and the Politics of Belonging, 2012; (ed with S. Dhaliwal) Women Against Fundamentalism: stories of dissent and solidarity, 2014; (ed with G. Wymess and K. Cassidy) Racialized Bordering Discourses on European Roma, 2017; (with G. Wemyss and K. Cassidy) Bordering, 2019; books and articles trans. more than 10 langs. *Recreations:* reading, dancing, visual and audio art and entertainment, sea, sun and sand. *Address:* Centre of Research on Migration, Refugees and Belonging, School of Social Sciences, University of East London, Docklands Campus, E16 2RD. *T:* (020) 7249 9718. *E:* n.yuval-davis@uel.ac.uk.

YVON, Christopher; HM Diplomatic Service; UK Permanent Representative to Council of Europe, Strasbourg (with personal rank of Ambassador), since 2016; *b* 11 Nov. 1969; *m* 2011, Aneta Michalska; one *s* two *d*. *Educ:* Marling Grammar Sch., Stroud. Entered FCO, 1989; Migration and Visa Dept, FCO, 1989–91; Attaché, Prague, 1991–93; Hong Kong Dept, FCO, 1994; Visa Officer, Bangkok, 1995; Vice Consul, Riyadh, 1995–99; Second Sec., Port Louis, 1999–2002; Desk Officer, Human Rights Policy Dept, FCO, 2003–04; Hd, Sanctions Team, 2005–06, Dep. Hd, 2007–10, Internat. Orgns Dept, FCO; Ambassador to Macedonia, 2010–14; Charge d'Affaires, Ljubljana, 2014–15. *Recreations:* snooker, cinema, cycling. *Address:* c/o Foreign and Commonwealth Office, King Charles Street, SW1A 2AH. *E:* christopher.yvon@fco.gov.uk. *Clubs:* Rileys Snooker (Vic); Lions (Macedonia).

ZACHARIAH, Joyce Margaret; Secretary of the Post Office, 1975–77; *b* 11 Aug. 1932; *d* of Robert Paton Emery and Nellie Nicol (*née* Wilson); *m* 1978, George Zachariah (marr. diss. 2006). *Educ:* Earl Grey Sch., Calgary, Canada; Hillhead High Sch., Glasgow; Glasgow Univ. (MA 1st cl. Hons French and German, 1956). Post Office: Asst Principal, 1956; Private Sec. to Dir Gen., 1960; Principal, 1961; Asst Sec., 1967; Dir, Chairman's Office, 1970. *Address:* Kelvinbrae, Wisborough Lane, Storrington, W Sussex RH20 4ND.

ZACKLIN, Ralph, CMG 2006; international law consultant; *b* 13 Oct. 1937; *s* of Joseph and Anna Zacklin; *m* 1961, Lyda Aponte; two *s*. *Educ:* University Coll. London (LLB Hons; Hon. Fellow, 2012); Columbia Univ. (LLM); Institut des Hautes Etudes Internationales, Geneva (PhD). Dir, Internat. Law Prog., Carnegie Endowment for Internat. Peace, NY, 1967–73; United Nations: Office of Legal Affairs, UN Secretariat, NY, 1973–2005; Officer-in-Charge, Office of High Comr for Human Rights, Geneva, 1997; Asst Sec. Gen. for Legal Affairs, 1998–2005. Sen. Advr, Macro Adv. Partners LLP, 2013. Legal Consultant, ICRC, 2010–11, 2013. Chm., UN Ind. Panel on Accountability, 2008–15; Member: Kyrgyzstan Inquiry Commn, 2010–11; UN Ind. Special Inquiry Commn for Timor Leste, 2006–07; UN Ind. Inquiry into violent demonstration against UN peacekeepers, Gao, Mali, 2015. Sen. Fellow, Faculty of Law, Univ. of Melbourne, 2006–08 (Sir Ninian Stephen Vis. Scholar, 2013). *Publications:* Amendment of the Constitution Instruments of the United Nations and Specialized Agencies, 1968, 2nd edn 2005; The Challenge of Rhodesia, 1969; The United Nations and Rhodesia, 1974; The Problem of Namibia in International Law, 1981; The United Nations Secretariat and the Use of Force in a Unipolar World: power v principle, 2010; articles in various jls. *Recreations:* travel, sports, reading, music. *Address:* 400 Central Park West, New York, NY 10025, USA. *T:* (212) 2220680. *E:* ralph@zacklin.com. *Club:* Yale (New York).

ZAFFAR, Dame Naila, DBE 2010; Executive Principal, Ambassador Schools, 2014–16; *b* Nairobi, 27 April 1955; *d* of Abdul Karim and Mumtaz Begum; *m* 1975, Shaukat Zaffar; two *d*. *Educ:* Fairfax Grammar Sch.; Wentworth Castle Coll., Barnsley (CertEd); Bradford and Ilkley Coll. (BEd 1st Cl. Hons). Teacher: West Bowling Lang. Centre, Bradford, 1983–84; Newby Primary Sch., Bradford, 1984–85; Atlas Primary Sch., Bradford, 1985–88; Teacher Fellowship, Bradford and Ilkley Coll., 1988–89; Dep. Headteacher, Feversham Primary Sch., Bradford, 1989–92; Headteacher, Copthorne Primary Sch., 1992–2012; Exec. Headteacher, Lapage Primary Sch., Bradford, 2009–10; Vice Principal, Sch. of Research Sci., Dubai, 2012–13. Mem., Gen. Teaching Council for England, 2000–05; Primary Strategy Consultancy Leader, 2004–07; Inspector, OFSTED, 2006–. *Recreation:* spending time with grandchildren. *E:* nzaffar@ymail.com.

ZAFIROPOULOS, Vassilis; Ambassador of Greece to the Court of St James's, 1996–99, retired; *b* Corfu, 24 Jan. 1934; *s* of Sarantis and Helen Zafiropoulos; *m* 1963; one *s*. *Educ:* Univ. of Athens. Joined Greek Civil Service, 1962; Min. of Finance, 1962–67; Head of Press Affairs, UN Information Centre for Greece, Israel, Turkey and Cyprus, 1967–71; joined Greek Diplomatic Service, 1971; Third Sec., Min. of Foreign Affairs, 1971–73; Second Sec., Liège, 1973–76; First Sec., Nicosia, and Dir, Greek Press Office in Cyprus, 1976–78; Counsellor, Nicosia, 1978–80; Counsellor (Political), London, 1980–84; Head of Cyprus Affairs, Min. of Foreign Affairs, 1984–86; Minister and Dep. Permt Rep. to NATO, Brussels, 1986–90; Ambassador to Australia and New Zealand, 1991–93; Permt Rep. to NATO, 1993–96. Special Rep., Greek Presidency of EU, S Caucasus, 2003. DUniv N London, 1998. Higher Comdr, Order of Phoenix (Greece). *Recreation:* tennis. *Address:* 20B Sirinon Street, Athens 175 61, Greece.

ZAHAWI, Nadhim; MP (C) Stratford-on-Avon, since 2010; Parliamentary Under-Secretary of State, Department for Business, Energy and Industrial Strategy, since 2019; *b* Baghdad, 2 June 1967; *s* of Harith and Najda Zahawi; *m* 2004, Lana Saib; two *s* one *d*. *Educ:* University Coll. London (BSc Chem. Eng.). Marketing Director: Global Inc. Ltd, 1990–95; Allen (Hinckley) Ltd, 1995–98; Eur. Mktg Dir, Smith & Brooks Ltd, 1998–2000; CEO and Co-founder, YouGov plc, 2000–10. Non-exec. Dir, SThree plc, 2008–; Chief Strategy Officer, Gulf Keystone, 2015–. Parly Under-Sec. of State for Children and Families, DfE, 2018–19. Mem., Foreign Affairs Select Cttee, 2014–18. Mem. (C), Wandsworth BC, 1994–2006. Patron, Peace One Day, 2008–. *Publications:* (with M. Hancock) Masters of Nothing: the crash and how it will happen again unless we understand human nature, 2011. *Recreations:* show jumping, cinema, spending time with family and friends. *Address:* House of Commons, SW1A 0AA. *Club:* Soho House.

ZAHEDI, Sir Saeed, Kt 2017; OBE 2000; RDI 2013; PhD; CEng, FREng; FIMechE; Chief Technical Officer, and Technical Director, Chas A. Blatchford & Sons Ltd, since 2013 (Technical Director, 2005–13); *b* Tehran, 23 May 1957; *s* of Ahmad Zahedi and Mehri Zahedi (*née* Mahloudji); *m* 1988, Shirin Sadeghian; one *s* two *d*. *Educ:* Poly. of Central London (BSc Hons Mech. Engrg); Univ. of Strathclyde (PhD Biomed. Engrg 1978). CEng 1985, FREng 2010; FIMechE 1998; CDir. Chas A. Blatchford & Sons Ltd: Res. Asst, 1979–85; Sen. Med. Physicist, 1985–88; Project Coordinator, 1988–92; Design Gp Leader, 1992–98; Res. Manager, 1998–2000; Hd of Technol., 2000–04; R&D Manager and Dir Designate, 2004–05. Visiting Professor: Univ. of Surrey, 2006–; Bournemouth Univ. Vice-Chm., Internat. Soc. for Prosthetics and Orthotics, 2013–. Chm., Manufg Cttee, American Orthotic and Prosthetic Assoc., 2007–10. Mem., ISO CEN, BSI, 1999–. Fellow, LSE. *Publications:* Advances in Prosthetics, 1996; Conference of European Society of Biomechanics, 1996; Review of Current Advances in Prosthetics, 1997; Atlas of Amputation and Limb Deficiencies, 2004; Principle of Design, 2004; Design Masters, 2008; contrib. articles to jls. *Recreations:* practical philosophy, economics with justice, mountaineering. *Address:* 10 Washington Road, Barnes, SW13 9BH. *T:* (020) 8748 2418, 07715 071086. *E:* Saeed.Zahedi@ic24.net.

ZAMBELLAS, Adm. Sir George (Michael), GCB 2016 (KCB 2012); DSC 2001; DL; FRAeS; First Sea Lord and Chief of the Naval Staff, 2013–16; First and Principal Naval Aide-de-Camp to the Queen, 2013–16; *b* 4 April 1958; *s* of late Michael George Zambellas and of Rosemary Frederique Zambellas (*née* Lindsay); *m* 1982, Amanda Jane LeCudennec; three *s*. *Educ:* Shabani Primary Sch., Zimbabwe; New College Sch.; Peterhouse Sch., Zimbabwe; Stowe; Univ. of Southampton (BSc Hons Aeronautical and Astronautical Engrg 1980). FRAeS 2009. Served 814, 829 and 815 Naval Air Sqdns, 1982–89; RN staff course, 1990; Command: HMS Cattistock, 1991; HMS Argyll, 1995; Corporate Planner, MoD, 1997; Comd HMS Chatham, 1999; HCSC, 2001; Dep. Flag Officer Sea Trng, 2002; PSO to CDS, 2002–05; Comdr Amphibious Task Gp, 2005–06; C of S (Fleet Transformation), 2006–07; Comdr, UK Maritime Force, 2007–08; COS (Ops), 2008–10; Dep. C-in-C Fleet, COS Navy Comd HQ and Chief Naval Warfare Officer, 2011; Fleet Comdr and Dep. Chief of Naval Staff, 2012; NATO Maritime Comdr (Northwood), 2012–13. Vice-Adm. of the UK, 2012. Gentleman Usher to the Sword of State, 2018–. Chairman: praXec Ltd, 2016–; CobWeb Cyber Ltd, 2017–; Galaxkey Ltd, 2018–; Sen. Advr, Liquid Robotics, 2017–; Dir, Agorai LLC, 2018–. Mem., Council of Mgt, White Ensign Assoc., 2016–; Pres., Shipwrecked Mariners' Soc., 2016–. Gov., Harrow Sch., 2009–19. Elder Brother, Trinity House, 2016; Upper Freeman, Hon. Co. of Air Pilots (formerly GAPAN), 2012; Freeman, Shipwrights' Co., 2014. DL Dorset, 2013. Hon. DSc Southampton, 2014.

ZAMBELLO, Francesca; theatre and opera director; Artistic Director, Washington National Opera, since 2013 (Artistic Advisor, 2011–12); *b* New York, 24 Aug. 1956. *Educ:* American Sch. of Paris; Colgate Univ. (BA). Assistant Director: Lyric Opera of Chicago, 1981–82; San Francisco Opera, 1983–84; Co-Artistic Dir, The Skylight, opera and music th. co., Milwaukee, 1984–91; Artistic Advr, San Francisco Opera; Gen. and Artistic Dir, Glimmerglass Opera, NY, 2010–. Dir of prodns at major theatre and opera cos in Europe and USA incl. Royal Opera House, Bastille Opera, Houston Grand Opera, Bolshoi Opera and NY Metropolitan Opera. Prodns incl. Fidelio, Tosca, War and Peace, Turandot, Arianna, Madama Butterfly, Iphigénie en Tauride, La Traviata, Emmeline, Tristan und Isolde, Boris Godunov, Dialogues of the Carmelites, Luisa Miller, Napoleon, Prince Igor, Peter Grimes, Queen of Spades, Of Mice and Men, The Bartered Bride, Thérèse Raquin, Don Giovanni, Les Troyens, Lady in the Dark, Street Scene, La Bohème, Carmen, Cyrano, Die Walküre, William Tell and The Tsarina's Slippers. Olivier awards for: Khovanshchina, ENO, 1994; Billy Budd, 1995, Paul Bunyan, 1998, Royal Opera House. Chevalier, Ordre des Arts et des Lettres (France), 2008. *Address:* c/o Opus 3 Artists, 470 Park Avenue South, 9th Floor North, New York, NY 10016, USA.

ZANDER, Prof. Michael, FBA 2005; Professor of Law, London School of Economics, 1977–98, now Emeritus; *b* 16 Nov. 1932; *s* of late Dr Walter Zander and Margarete Magnus; *m* 1965, Betsy Treeger; one *d* one *s*. *Educ:* Royal Grammar Sch., High Wycombe; Jesus Coll., Cambridge (BA Law, double 1st Cl. Hons; LLB 1st Cl. Hons; Whewell Scholar in Internat. Law); Harvard Law Sch. (LLM). Solicitor of the Supreme Court. National Service, RA, 1950–52, 2nd Lieut. Cassel Scholar, Lincoln's Inn, 1957, resigned 1959; New York law firm, 1958–59; articled with City solicitors, 1959–62; Asst Solicitor with City firm, 1962–63; London Sch. of Economics: Asst Lectr, 1963; Lectr, 1965; Sen. Lectr, 1970; Reader, 1970; Convener, Law Dept, 1984–88, 1997–98. Legal Correspondent, The Guardian, 1963–87. Mem., Royal Commn on Criminal Justice, 1991–93. Hon. QC 1997. Hon. LLD KCL, 2010. Halsbury Legal Award for Lifetime Contribn, 2015. *Publications:* Lawyers and the Public Interest, 1968; (ed) What's Wrong with the Law?, 1970; (ed) Family Guide to the Law, 1971, 2nd edn 1972; Cases and Materials on the English Legal System, 1973, 10th edn 2007; (with B. Abel-Smith and R. Brooke) Legal Problems and the Citizen, 1973; Social Workers, their Clients and the Law, 1974, 3rd edn 1981; A Bill of Rights?, 1975, 4th edn 1996; Legal Services for the Community, 1978; (ed) Pears Guide to the Law, 1979; The Law-Making Process, 1980, 7th edn 2015; The State of Knowledge about the English Legal Profession, 1980; The Police and Criminal Evidence Act 1984, 1985, 8th edn 2018; A Matter of Justice: the legal system in ferment, 1988, rev. edn 1989; The State of Justice, 2000; over 300 articles in jls incl. Criminal Law Rev., Mod. Law Rev., Law Soc.'s Gazette, New Law Jl, Criminal Law & Justice Weekly, Solicitors' Jl, Amer. Bar Assoc. Jl. *Address:* 12 Woodside Avenue, N6 4SS. *T:* (020) 8883 6257. *E:* mandbzander@gmail.com.

ZANI, John Andrew; a District Judge (Magistrates' Courts), Inner London, since 2001; *b* 1953. *Educ:* Highgate Sch.; Coll. of Law. Admitted solicitor, 1977; Partner, 1979, Sen. Partner, 1986–2000, Whitelock & Storr. Chm., Professional Matters Sub-Cttee, Holborn Law Soc., 1994–96. Mem. Founder Cttee, British Italian Law Assoc., 1982. Chm., Old Cholmeleian CC, 1990–. *Recreations:* cricket, football, the arts. *Address:* c/o Westminster Magistrates' Court, 181 Marylebone Road, NW1 5BR.

ŽANTOVSKÝ, Michael; Executive Director, Václav Havel Library, Prague since 2015; *b* Prague, 3 Jan. 1949; *s* of Jiri Žantovský and Hana Žantovska; *m* 2001, Jana Nosekova; two *s* two *d*. *Educ:* Charles Univ., Prague (MA 1973); McGill Univ., Montreal. Freelance translator and author, 1980–88 (trans. into Czech works of contemporary English and American fiction, poetry, drama and non-fiction); Prague corresp., Reuters, 1988–90; Press Sec. and spokesman for Pres., Czech and Slovak Fed. Republic, 1990–92; Ambassador, of Czech and Slovak Fed. Republic, 1992, then Czech Republic, 1993–96, to USA; Chm., Cttee on Foreign Affairs, Defence and Security, Senate of Parlt, 1996–2002; Ambassador to Israel, 2003–09; Ambassador to the Court of St James's, 2009–15. Founding Mem., Civic Forum (umbrella orgn that coordinated overthrow of communist regime), 1989; Pres., Civic Democratic Alliance, 1997 and 2001. Co-founder, Prog. of Atlantic Security Studies, 2003. Pres., Aspen Inst., Prague, 2012–15. Founding Mem., Czech chapter, PEN, 1989. *Publications:* Havel: a life, 2014. *Address:* Václav Havel Library, Ostrovní 13, 110 00 Prague 1, Czech Republic.

ZAOUI, Michael Alexandre; Co-Founder and Partner, Zaoui & Co., since 2013; *b* Fez, Morocco, 30 Dec. 1956; *s* of Charles Zaoui and Violette Zaoui (*née* Cohen); *m* 1995, Anna Benhamou; one *s* one *d*. *Educ:* Institut d'Etudes Politiques, Paris (Diploma); Univ. de Paris (Masters Law); Univ. Panthéon-Sorbonne, Paris (DESS Dr Law); London Sch. of Econs and Political Sci. (post-grad. res. prog.); Harvard Business Sch. (MBA). Banque Rothschild, Paris, 1978–81; Mgt Consultant, MAC Gp, London, 1983–85; Morgan Stanley: Vice Pres., NY, 1986–90; Exec. Dir, 1991–93; Man. Dir, London, 1993–97; Co-Hd, 1997–99, Chm., 1999–2008, Eur. M&A; Vice Chm., Institutional Securities Gp, London, 2006–08; advr to major corporations and investors, 2009–12. Dir of several privately owned cos. Counsellor, Commerce Extérieur de la France, London, 2011–. Gov., Southbank Centre, London, 2012–. Mem., Bd of Dean's Advrs, Harvard Business Sch., 2007–; Mem., Belfer Internat. Council, 2012–. Mem., Littauer Soc., 2014–, Kennedy Sch. of Govt, Harvard Univ. *Recreations:* symphony music, opera, classical and contemporary art, history, sport, cycling. *Address:* Zaoui & Co., 11 Hill Street, W1J 5LF. *T:* (020) 7290 5580. *Clubs:* Annabel's, Harry's Bar and Mosimann's.
*See also* Y. Zaoui.

ZAOUI, Yoël; Co-Founder and Partner, Zaoui & Co., since 2013; *b* Casablanca, 11 Jan. 1961; *s* of Charles Zaoui and Violette Zaoui (*née* Cohen); one *s* one *d*. *Educ:* HEC, Paris; Univ. Paris-Dauphine (DEA Dr Finance 1983); Stanford Univ. (MBA 1988). Sen. Auditor,

Arthur Andersen, Paris; Goldman Sachs, 1988–2012: Partner, 1998–2012; Co-Hd, then Hd, Eur. M&A; Co-Hd, then Hd, Eur. Investment Banking; Mem., Mgt Cttee, 2008–12; Global M&A. *Recreations:* sports, reading, travel. *Address:* Zaoui & Co., 11 Hill Street, W1J 5LF. *T:* (020) 7290 5585.
See also M. A. Zaoui.

ZAPATERO, José Luis Rodríguez; *see* Rodríguez Zapatero.

ZARA, Robert Joseph; a District Judge (Magistrates' Courts), Birmingham, 2004–17, and Family Court, Coventry, 2014–17; a Deputy District Judge (Family Court), Coventry and Northampton, 2017–19; *b* 20 July 1947; *s* of Alfred and Naomi Zara; *m* 1st, 1986, Alicia Edkins (*d* 2000); one *s*; 2nd, 2004, Catherine Edwards. *Educ:* Tonbridge Sch.; Bristol Univ. (LLB 1969). Community Lawyer, Coventry Community Develt Project, 1973–75; Solicitor: Coventry Legal and Income Rights Service, 1975–81; in private practice in Coventry, 1981–2002; a District Judge (Magistrates' Cts), Nottingham, 2002–04. Freelance lectr and author on magistrates' courts law and practice. *Publications:* (contrib.) Handbook for Widows, 1978; (contrib.) Survival Guide for Widows, 1986; (with Howard Riddle) Essential Magistrates' Courts Law, 2019; contrib. occasional articles and book reviews to New Law Jl. *Recreations:* bridge, crosswords (blogs regularly at www.fifteensquared.net), digging my allotment, walking my dog.

ZARNECKI, Prof. Jan Charles, (John), PhD; Professor of Space Science, Open University, 2004–13, now Emeritus; Director, International Space Science Institute, Berne, 2013–17; *b* London, 6 Nov. 1949; *s* of Jerzy, (George), Zarnecki and Anne Leslie Zarnecki (*née* Frith); *m* 1st, 1976, Gillian Elizabeth Fairbanks (marr. diss. 1993); one *s* one *d*; 2nd, 2009, Catherine Philomena O'Donoghue. *Educ:* Highgate Sch., London; Queens' Coll., Cambridge (Open Exhibnr; BA 1971); Mullard Space Science Lab., University Coll. London (PhD 1977). FRAS 1972; MInstP 1978, FInstP 2012; CPhys 2001. Res. Asst, Mullard Space Sci. Lab., UCL, 1974–79; Sen. Systems Engr, Dynamics Gp, British Aerospace, 1979–81; Unit for Space Sciences, University of Kent: Sen. Experimental Officer, 1981–85; Lectr, 1985–87; Sen. Lectr, 1987–96; Reader, 1996–2000; Reader, Planetary and Space Scis Res. Inst., Open Univ., 2000–04. Space projects include: Faint Object Camera for Hubble Space Telescope, 1979–81; Co-investigator for Dust Impact Detection System on Giotto Comet Halley Probe, 1982–92; Principal Investigator, Surface Sci. Package on Huygens Probe Titan, 1992–2006. Royal Astronomical Society: Mem. Council, 1995–98; Vice-Pres., 2009–11; Pres., 2016–18. Member: Solar System Wkg Gp, ESA, 1995–98 (Chm., 2014–16); Eur. Space Sci. Cttee, ESF, 1997–2000; PPARC, 2005–07; Council, Inst. of Physics, 2013–17; Chair, Space Sci. Adv. Cttee, ESA, 2017–19. Mem., Shareholder's Cttee, Eurotunnel plc, 2003–06. Mem. Bd, Milton Keynes Gall., 2002–06. Mem. IAU, 1982–. Gold Medal, RAS, 2014; Massey Award, COSPAR, 2018. *Publications:* over 200 scientific and technical articles. *Address:* Planetary and Space Sciences Research Institute, Open University, Walton Hall, Milton Keynes MK7 6AA. *T:* (01908) 659599, *Fax:* (01908) 655667. *E:* j.c.zarnecki@open.ac.uk.

ZEALLEY, Dr Helen Elizabeth, OBE 1998; MD; FRCPEd, FFPH; Director of Public Health and Chief Administrative Medical Officer, 1988–2000, Executive Director, 1991–2000, Lothian Health Board; *b* 10 June 1940; *d* of late Sir John Howie Flint Brotherston and Lady Brotherston; *m* 1965, Dr Andrew King Zealley; one *s* one *d*. *Educ:* St Albans High Sch. for Girls; Edinburgh Univ. (MB, ChB 1964; MD 1968). FRCPEd 1987; FFPH (FFPHM 1980). Virologist, City Hosp., Edinburgh, 1965–70; Consultant in Public Health Medicine, Lothian Health Bd, 1974–88, with a special interest in the health of children. Non-exec. Dir, NHS Health Scotland, 2003–09; Board Member: Scottish Envmtl Protection Agency, 2006–13; Central Scotland Green Network, 2011–14; Hon. Fellow, Scottish Envmt LINK, 2011– (Pres., 2008–11). Vice-President: Med Act, 1980–2014; Early Education, 1998–2006. Chm., Friends of the Earth, Scotland, 2003–08. Mem. Court, Edinburgh Univ., 1992–98. QHP 1996–2000. Kentucky Colonel, 1961. Hon. DCCH 1993. *Recreations:* family, gardening, sailing, ski-ing. *Address:* Viewfield House, 12 Tipperlinn Road, Edinburgh EH10 5ET. *T:* (0131) 447 5545.

ZEBEDEE, Graham; HM Diplomatic Service; Director, Department for International Trade (on secondment), since 2017; *b* Southampton, 27 Nov. 1973; *s* of Roger Zebedee and Brenda Zebedee; *m* 2009, Lucy Katherine Ryan; one *s* one *d*. *Educ:* Wadham Coll., Oxford (BA Phys and Philos.). Joined FCO, 1999; UK Perm. Rep. to EU, 1999–2000; EC (on secondment), 2001–02; Counter-Proliferation Dept, FCO, 2003–05; Kabul, 2005–07; Dep. Hd, Africa Directorate, FCO, 2007–10; Hd, Nat. Security Unit, 2010–13, Hd, Border and Visa Policy, 2013–15, Home Office (on secondment); Ambassador to the Democratic Republic of Congo and (non-resident) to the Republic of Congo and Central African Republic, 2015–17. *Recreations:* mountains, marathons, managing messy mealtimes. *Address:* c/o Department for International Trade, 3 Whitehall Place, SW1A 2AW. *E:* graham.zebedee@trade.gov.uk.

ZEDNER, Prof. Lucia Helen, DPhil; FBA 2012; Professor of Criminal Justice, University of Oxford, since 2005; Senior Research Fellow, All Souls College, Oxford, since 2016; *b* Kingston, Surrey, 20 Feb. 1961; *d* of Thomas and Ruby Zedner; *m* 1998, Prof. Joshua Getzler; two *d*. *Educ:* Univ. of York (BA); Nuffield Coll., Oxford (DPhil). Prize Res. Fellow, Nuffield Coll., Oxford, 1984–89; Lectr in Law, LSE, 1989–94; Lectr, 1994–99, Reader, 1999–2005, Law Faculty, Univ. of Oxford; Fellow, Corpus Christi Coll., Oxford, 1994–2016. Adjunct Prof., Faculty of Law, Univ. of NSW, 2007–17. Member: Res. Coll., ESRC, 2005–08; Adv. Panel, Leverhulme Trust, 2013–16; Projects Cttee, 2013–15; Law Selection Cttee, 2014–17, British Acad. Mem., Editl Bd, Clarendon Series in Criminol., Oxford Univ. Press., 1994– (Gen. Ed., 2010–12). Overseas Fellow, Australian Acad. of Law, 2015. *Publications:* Women, Crime and Custody in Victorian England, 1991; (with J. Morgan) Child Victims, Crime, Impact and Criminal Justice, 1992; (ed with Andrew Ashworth) The Criminological Foundations of Penal Policy, 2003; Criminal Justice, 2004; (ed with Benjamin Goold) Crime and Security, 2006; Security, 2009; (ed with Julian Roberts) Principles and Values in Criminal Law and Criminal Justice, 2012; (ed jtly) Prevention and the Limits of the Criminal Law, 2013; (with Andrew Ashworth) Preventive Justice, 2014; (ed jtly) Changing Contours of Criminal Justice, 2016; chapters in books. *Address:* All Souls College, Oxford OX1 4AL.

ZEEMAN, Prof. Nicolette, PhD; Professor of Medieval and Renaissance English, University of Cambridge, since 2016; Fellow, King's College, Cambridge, since 1995; *b* Cambridge, 3 Dec. 1956; *d* of Sir (Erik) Christopher Zeeman, FRS and Elizabeth Zeeman (*née* Jones, later Salter); *m* 1988, Jonathan Burt; one *s* one *d*. *Educ:* Mill Mount Grammar Sch., York; Clare Coll., Cambridge (BA 1979); Univ. of Pennsylvania; King's Coll., Cambridge (PhD 2000). Jun. Res. Fellow, Newnham Coll., Cambridge, 1984–87; Lectr, King's Coll., Cambridge, 1995–2012; Newton Trust Lectr, 2000–05, Lectr, 2012–14, Sen. Lectr, 2014–15, Faculty of English, Univ. of Cambridge. Fellow, Radcliffe Inst. for Advanced Studies, Harvard, 2014–15. *Publications:* (ed with D. Pearsall) Elizabeth Salter, Fourteenth-Century English Poetry, 1983; (ed with D. Pearsall) Elizabeth Salter, English and International Studies in the Literature, Art and Patronage of Medieval England, 1988; (ed jtly) Images, Idolatry and Iconoclasm in the Late Middle Ages, 2001; Piers Plowman and the Medieval Discourse of Desire, 2006; (ed jtly) Uncertain Knowledge: scepticism, relativism and doubt in the Middle Ages, 2014; (ed with J. M. Massing) King's College Chapel 1515–2015: art, music and religion in Cambridge, 2014; contrib. essays to books and jls. *Recreations:* art, films, music, gardening. *Address:* King's College, Cambridge CB2 1ST. *T:* (01223) 331458. *E:* nz202@cam.ac.uk.

ZEFF, Jonathan Charles; independent policy and strategy consultant; Director, Zeff Associates Ltd, since 2017; *b* London, 23 May 1966; *s* of Brian and Paula Zeff; *m* 1996, Alison Beat; one *s* one *d*. *Educ:* University Coll. Sch., London; Univ. of Warwick (BA Hons Maths). Admin Trainee, 1991–94, Employment Service Review Leader, 1995, Dept for Employment; Asst Dir, Employment Relns, DTI, 1995–98; Department for Culture, Media and Sport: Head: Film Policy, 1998–99; Nat. Lottery Div., 1999–2001; Policy Innovation and Delivery Unit, 2001–03; Broadcasting Policy, 2003–08; Director: Media, 2008–11; Broadband, Spectrum and Communications, 2011–14; BBC Trust, 2014–15. *Recreations:* contemporary literature, theatre, music, playing piano and video games, country walks, Queens Park Rangers FC.

ZEICHNER, Daniel Stephen; MP (Lab) Cambridge, since 2015; *b* Beckenham, 9 Nov. 1956; *s* of Eric Zeichner and Mary Zeichner (*née* Mead); partner, Barbara, (Budge), Ziolkowska. *Educ:* King's Coll., Cambridge (BA 1979). Milk roundsman, Co-op, 1976; trainee computer programmer, Cambs CC, 1979–81; computer programmer, Perkins Engines, Peterborough, 1981; Database Adminr, Pye Electronics, Cambridge, 1982; computer programmer, Whitbread, Reading and London, 1983; estabd and ran Red and Green Nurseries, Norfolk, retail and wholesale herbaceous plant specialists, 1983–91; computer programmer and systems designer, Norwich Union, 1984–91; Political Assistant: to John Garrett, MP, 1992–97; to Clive Needle, MEP, 1995–99; Labour Link Policy and Campaigns Officer, UNISON, 2002–15. Mem. (Lab), S Norfolk DC, 1995–2003. Shadow Transport Minister, 2015–17. Mem., Transport Select Cttee, 2017–. *Recreations:* enjoying music, especially at Cambridge's Kettles Yard, Cambridge United season ticket holder. *Address:* House of Commons, SW1A 0AA. *T:* (01223) 423252. *E:* daniel.zeichner.mp@parliament.uk.

ZEIDMAN, Martyn Keith; QC 1998; His Honour Judge Zeidman; a Circuit Judge, since 2001; a Senior Circuit Judge, since 2017; Resident Judge, Snaresbrook Crown Court, since 2017; *b* Cardiff, 30 May 1952; *s* of Abe and Jennie Zeidman; *m* 1977, Verity, *d* of His Honour Aron Owen; one *s* one *d*. *Educ:* Univ. of London (LLB Hons ext.). Called to the Bar, Middle Temple, 1974; Asst Recorder, 1995–99; a Recorder, 1999–2001. Hon. Recorder of Redbridge, 2017–. Pres., Mental Health Review Tribunal (Restricted Cases), 1998–2010. Chm., Jewish Marriage Council, 2004–15. Judicial Mem., London Courts Bd, 2007–10. *Publications:* A Short Guide to The Landlord & Tenant Act 1987, 1987; A Short Guide to The Housing Act 1988, 1988; Steps to Possession, 1989; A Short Guide to The Courts and Legal Services Act 1990, 1990; A Short Guide to The Road Traffic Act 1991, 1991; Making Sense of The Leasehold Reform Housing & Urban Development Act 1993, 1994; Archbold Practical Research Papers on: Law of Mistake, 1997; Law of Self Defence, 1997. *Recreations:* family, studying Jewish religious texts, cycling. *Address:* Snaresbrook Crown Court, The Court House, Hollybush Hill, E11 1QW.

ZEILER, Gerhard; Chief Revenue Officer, WarnerMedia and President, WarnerMedia International Networks, since 2019; *b* Vienna, 20 July 1955. *Educ:* Univ. of Vienna (Psychol., Sociol. and Educnl Sci.). Freelance journalist, 1979; Press Spokesman for Minister for Educn and the Arts, subseq. for Chancellor of Austria, 1979–86; Sec.-Gen., ORF (Public Broadcasting Corp. of Austria), 1986–91; Chief Executive Officer: Tele 5, Germany, 1991–92; RTL II, Germany, 1992–94; ORF, 1994–98; RTL Television, Cologne, 1998–2005; RTL Gp, 2003–12; Mem. Exec. Bd, Bertelsmann AG, 2005–12; Pres., Turner Broadcasting System Internat., 2012. Personality of Year Award, MIPCOM, 2004; Brandon Tartikoff Legacy Award, Nat. Assoc. TV Prog. Execs, USA, 2011. *Address:* WarnerMedia, 30 Hudson Yards, New York, NY 10001, USA.

ZEKI, Prof. Semir, FRS 1990; Professor of Neuroesthetics, University College London, since 2008 (Fellow, 2000); *b* 8 Nov. 1940; *m* 1967, Anne-Marie Claire Blestel; one *d* one *s*. *Educ:* University College London (BSc Anat. 1964; PhD 1967). Asst Lectr, UCL, 1966–67; Res. Associate, St Elizabeth's Hosp., Washington DC, 1967–68; Asst Prof., Univ. of Wisconsin, 1968–69; Lectr in Anatomy, UCL, 1969–75; Henry Head Res. Fellow, Royal Soc., 1975–80; University College London: Reader in Neurobiol., 1980–81; Prof. of Neurobiol., 1981–2008; Co-hd, Wellcome Dept of Cognitive Neurol., 1996–2001. Vis. Professorial Fellow, RPMS, Hammersmith Hosp., 1991–96. Visiting Professor: Duke Univ., 1977; Ludwig Maximilians Univ., Munich, 1982–87; Univ. of California, Berkeley, 1984, 2003 and 2006; St Andrews, 1985; Vis. Upjohn Prof., Erasmus Univ., Brussels, 1997–98; Visiting Scholar: J. Paul Getty Mus., 1996; Center for Advanced Study, Stanford, 2001. Lectures include: David Marr, Cambridge Univ., 1989; Philip Bard, Johns Hopkins Univ., 1992; Ferrier, Royal Soc., 1995; Woodhull, Royal Instn, 1995; Royal Soc. Humphry Davy, Acad. des Scis, Paris, 1996; Carl Gustave Bernhard, Royal Swedish Acad., 1998. Member: Neuroscience Res. Program and Neurosci. Inst., NY, 1985–; Wellcome Trust Vision Panel, 1985–93 (Chm., 1987–93); Bd of Scientific Govs, Scripps Res. Inst., Calif., 1992–2012; Nat. Sci. Council of France, 1998–2002. Trustee: Fight for Sight, 1992–97; Minerva Foundn, Berkeley, 1995–2012; Guarantor, Brain, 1994–2006. Mem., Cttee of Honour, Paris DFAS, 1996–. Ed., Philosophical Trans of Royal Soc., series B, 1997–2003. Exhibn, Bianco su bianco: oltre Malevich, Museo Pecci d'arte contemporanea, Milan, 2011. Founder FMedSci 1998; MRI, 1985; Member: Academia Europaea, 1990; Eur. Acad. of Scis and Arts, 1992; Amer. Phil Soc., 1998; Hon. Mem., Italian Primatological Assoc., 1988. Hon. DSc: Aston, 1994; Aberdeen, 2008; Athens, 2012. Minerva Foundn Prize, USA, 1985; Prix Science pour l'Art, LVMH, Paris, 1991; Rank Prize, 1992; Zotterman Prize, Swedish Physiol Soc., 1993; Electronic Imaging Award, Internat. Soc. for Optical Engrg, 2002; King Faisal Internat. Prize in Sci. (Biology), King Faisal Foundn, 2004; Erasmus Medal, Academia Europea, 2008; Segerfalk Award, Segerfalk Foundn, 2009; Aristotle Medal, World Psychiatric Fedn, 2011; Rome Prize, Atena Onlus Foundn, 2012. *Publications:* A Vision of the Brain, 1993; (with Balthus) La Quête de l'Essential, Paris, 1995; Inner Vision: an exploration of art and the brain, 1999; Splendors and Miseries of the Brain, 2008; (with Ludovica Lumer) La bella e la bestia: arte e neuroscienza, 2011; articles on vision and the brain in professional jls. *Recreations:* reading (esp. about the darker side of man), music, deep sleep. *Address:* Wellcome Department of Imaging Neuroscience, University College London, WC1E 6BT. *T:* (020) 7679 7316. *Clubs:* Athenæum, Garrick.

ZELDIN, Dr Theodore, CBE 2001; FBA 1995; FRSL, FRHistS; President, Oxford Muse, since 2001; Fellow, St Antony's College, Oxford, 1957–2001; *b* 22 Aug. 1933; *s* of Jacob Zeldin, civil engr, and Emma Zeldin, dentist; *m* 1975, Deirdre Wilson, *qv*. *Educ:* Aylesbury Grammar Sch.; Birkbeck Coll., London (BA 1951); Christ Church, Oxford (schol.; BA 1954; MA); St Antony's Coll., Oxford (DPhil 1957). Oxford University: Lectr, Christ Church, and Univ. Lectr in Modern Hist., 1959–76; Dean, Sen. Tutor, and Tutor for Admissions, St Antony's Coll., 1963–76; Dir, Future of Work Project, 1997–2000. Res. Fellow, CNRS, Paris, 1952–53; Visiting Professor: Harvard Univ., 1969–70; Univ. of Southern Calif, 1980–83. Mem., EC Cttee for Eur. Voluntary Service, 1997–99; Vice-Pres., Culture Europe, 2000–. Pres., Planning Commn, Nord-Pas-de-Calais, 1993–95; Advr, French Millennium Commn, 1999; Hon. President: Centre du Paysage, France,

2000; Maison du Temps et de la Mobilité, Belfort, 2001. Pres., Internat. Fest. of Geography, 1999; Chm., Oxford Food Symposium; Member: Council, Vivendi-Universal Inst de Prospective; Adv. Council, Demos; Mgt Cttee, Soc. of Authors; Attali Commission pour la Libération de la Croissance Française, 2007–11. Trustee: Wytham Hall Med. Charity for the Homeless; Amar Internat. Appeal for Refugees. MAE 1993. Wolfson Prize for History. Comdr, Ordre des Arts et des Lettres (France); Comdr, Légion d'Honneur (France), 2012. *Publications:* The Political System of Napoleon III, 1958; (ed) Journal d'Emile Ollivier, 1961; Emile Ollivier and the Liberal Empire of Napoleon III, 1963; Conflicts in French Society, 1971; France 1848–1945: vol. 1, Ambition, Love and Politics, 1973, vol. 2, Intellect, Taste and Anxiety, 1977, both vols re-issued 1993 as History of French Passions; The French, 1983; Happiness (novel), 1987; An Intimate History of Humanity, 1994; Flirtations (filmscript), 1994; Conversation, 1998; The Hidden Pleasures of Life, 2015; contrib. nat. press and learned jls. *Recreations:* painting, gardening, mending things. *Address:* Tumbledown House, Cumnor, Oxford OX2 9QE.

**ZELENSKY, Igor Anatolyevich;** ballet dancer; Artistic Director, Bayerische Staatsballett, since 2016; *b* Georgia, 13 July 1969; *m* Yana Serebryakova; three *c*. *Educ:* Tbilisi Sch. of Choreography; Vaganova Sch. of Choreography, St Petersburg. With Kirov (now Mariinsky) Ballet, 1989–2013 (Principal, 1991–2013); with New York City Ballet, 1992–97; guest dancer: Deutsche Oper, Berlin, 1990–; Royal Ballet, 1996– (Principal, 1997–2001); also with companies in Europe, Asia and America; rôles include Basil in Don Quixote, Siegfried in Swan Lake, Solor in La Bayadère, Albrecht in Giselle; leading rôles in Romeo and Juliet, Apollo, Le Corsaire, Manon, Sleeping Beauty; Asst Dir, Athens Opera House, 2001–06; Artistic Director: Novosibirsk State Academic Opera and Ballet Theatre, Siberia, 2006–15; Moscow Stanislavsky Ballet, 2011–16.

**ZELLICK, Adam David Russell;** QC 2017; *b* London, 4 June 1977; *s* of Prof. Graham John Zellick, *qv*, and Jennifer Zellick (*see* Prof. J. Temkin); *m* 2011, Deborah Crosbie; two *d*. *Educ:* City of London Sch. (Corporation Schol.); Gonville and Caius Coll., Cambridge (Sir William McNair Law Prize; Frere Smith Prize for Law; Sen. Schol., Squire Schol., BA; Tapp Postgrad. Schol. in Law; MA); Inns of Court Sch. of Law, City Univ. (DipLaw). Called to the Bar: Middle Temple, 2000 (Queen Mother Schol.; Sachs Prize); BVI, 2014. Res. Asst, Law Commn, 2000–01; Supervisor in Law, Gonville and Caius Coll., Cambridge, 2001–02; in practice at commercial bar, 2002–. Contributor and law reporter, Civil Procedure Reports, 2003–08. Mem., Editl Bd, Counsel, 2012–16. Freeman, City of London, 1999; Liveryman, Drapers' Co., 2008 (Freeman, 1998). *Publications:* (contrib.) Civil Aviation, in Atkin's Court Forms, 2006, 2010; (contrib.) Bullen and Leake and Jacob's Precedents of Pleadings, 14th edn 2000. *Address:* Fountain Court Chambers, Fountain Court, Temple, EC4Y 9DH. *T:* (020) 7583 3335. *E:* az@fountaincourt.co.uk. *Club:* Totteridge Millmillians Cricket.

**ZELLICK, Prof. Graham John,** CBE 2009; PhD; FAcSS; President, Valuation Tribunal for England, 2009–15; Member, Investigatory Powers Tribunal, since 2013; *b* 12 Aug. 1948; *s* of R. H. and B. Zellick; *m* 1975, Jennifer Temkin, *qv*; one *s* one *d*. *Educ:* Christ's Coll., Finchley; Gonville and Caius Coll., Cambridge (MA, PhD; Hon. Fellow, 2001); Stanford Univ. Called to the Bar, Middle Temple, 1992, Bencher, 2001 (Reader, 2013); Assoc. Mem., 3 Verulam Bldgs, Gray's Inn, 1993–2010. Ford Foundn Fellow, Stanford Law Sch., 1970–71; Queen Mary College, later Queen Mary and Westfield College, London: Lectr, 1971–78; Reader in Law, 1978–82; Prof. of Public Law, 1982–88; Dean of Faculty of Laws, 1984–88; Head, Dept of Law, 1984–90; Drapers' Prof. of Law, 1988–91; Prof. of Law, 1991–98, now Emeritus; Sen. Vice-Principal and Acting Principal, 1990–91; Principal, 1991–98; Vis. Prof. of Law, 2007–12; University of London: Dean, Faculty of Laws, 1986–88; Dep. Chm., Academic Council, 1987–89; Dep. Vice-Chancellor, 1994–97; Vice-Chancellor and Pres., 1997–2003. Vis. Fellow, Centre of Criminology, 1978–79, and Vis. Prof. of Law, 1975, 1978–79, Toronto Univ.; Vis. Scholar, St John's Coll., Oxford, 1989; Hon. Prof., Sch. of Law, Univ. of Birmingham, 2004–11; Dist. Vis. Fellow, NZ Law Foundn, 2010. Lectures: Noel Buxton, NACRO, 1983; Webber, Jews' Coll., London, 1986; Sir Gwilym Morris, UWIST, Cardiff, 1986; Wythe, Coll. of William and Mary, Va, 1989; Atkin, Reform Club, 2000; White, Indiana Univ., 2002; Van Der Zyl, Leo Baeck Coll., London, 2003; Lund, British Acad. Forensic Scis, 2006. Editor: European Human Rights Reports, 1978–82; Public Law, 1981–86; Member of Editorial Board: British Jl of Criminology, 1980–90; Public Law, 1981–91; Howard Jl of Criminal Justice, 1984–87; Civil Law Library, 1987–91. Member: Council and Exec. Cttee, Howard League for Penal Reform, 1973–82; Jellicoe Cttee on Bds of Visitors of Prisons, 1973–75; Sub Cttee on Crime and Criminal Justice, 1984–88, and Sub Cttee on Police Powers and the Prosecution Process, 1985–88, ESRC; Lord Chancellor's Legal Aid Adv. Cttee, 1985–88; Newham Dist Ethics Cttee, 1985–86; Data Protection Tribunal, 1985–96; Lord Chancellor's Adv. Cttee on Legal Educn, 1988–90; S Thames RHA, 1994–95; E London and the City HA, 1995–97; Criminal Injuries Compensation Appeals Panel, 2000–03; Competition Appeal Tribunal (formerly Competition Commn Appeal Tribunals), 2000–03; Criminal Justice Council, 2003–06; Valuation Tribunal Service Bd, 2009–15; Chm., Criminal Cases Review Commn, 2003–08; Electoral Comr, 2001–04. Chairman: Prisoners' Advice and Law Service, 1984–89; Legal Cttee, All-Party Parly War Crimes Gp, 1988–91; Dep. Chm., Justice Cttee on Prisoners' Rights, 1981–83. Dir, UCAS, 1994–97. Chairman: Cttee of Heads of Univ. Law Schs, 1988–90; E London Strategic Forum for Nat. Educn and Trng Targets, 1993–95; Vice-Chm., Acad. Study Gp for Israel and ME, 1995–2003; Mem. Council, CVCP, 1993–97. Pres., West London Synagogue, 2000–06 (Chm., Senate, 2006–14); Member: Council: UCS, 1983–92; City and East London Confedn for Medicine and Dentistry, 1991–95; St Bartholomew's Hosp. Med. Coll., 1991–95; Council of Govs, London Hosp. Med. Coll., 1991–95; Court of Governors: Polytechnic of Central London, 1973–77; Polytechnic of N London, 1986–89; Univ. of Greenwich, 1994–97; Chairman: Bd of Govs, Leo Baeck Coll., 2005–06; Bd of Trustees, Richmond, Amer. Internat. Univ. in London, 2005–06 (Trustee, 2002–06; Acad. Gov., 1999–2003); Governor: Pimlico Sch., 1973–77; Tel Aviv Univ., 2000–09 (Chm., Lawyers' Gp, 1984–89, and Trustee, 1985–87, Tel Aviv Univ. Trust); Visitor, Bancroft's Sch., 2009–10. Mem. Council, Spitalfields Heritage Centre, 1992–98; Patron, Redress Trust, 1993–2014; Trustee: William Harvey Res. Inst., 1995–2000; Samuel Courtauld Trust, 1997–2003; Gov., William Goodenough Trust, 1997–2003; Chm., Reform Club Conservation Charitable Trust, 2003–13. JP Inner London (N Westminster), 1981–85. Freeman, City of London, 1992; Mem., Ct of Assts, Drapers' Co., 2000– (Freeman, 1992; Liveryman, 1995; Master, 2009–10; Renter Warden, 2013–14). CCMI (FBIM 1991; CIMgt 1997); FRSA 1991; FRSocMed 1996; Founding FICPD, 1998; FAcSS (AcSS 2000). Fellow, Heythrop Coll., Univ. of London, 2005. Hon. QC 2010. Hon. Fellow: Soc. of Advanced Legal Studies, 1997; Burgon Soc., 2001 (Patron, 2009–16; Pres., 2016–); Leo Baeck Coll., 2007; Hon. FRAM 2003. Hon. LHD New York, 2001; Hon. LLD Richmond, Amer. Internat. Univ. in London, 2003; Birmingham, 2006; Hon. DLit London, 2010. *Publications:* Justice in Prison (with Sir Brian MacKenna), 1983; (ed) The Law Commission and Law Reform, 1988; (contrib.) Halsbury's Laws of England, 4th edn 1982; contribs to collections of essays, pamphlets, the national press, and professional and learned periodicals incl. British Jl of Criminology, Civil Justice Quarterly, Criminal Law Rev., Modern Law Rev., Public Law, Univ. of Toronto Law Jl, William and Mary Law Rev., Medicine, Sci. and the Law, Manitoba Law Jl. *Address:* 63 Hampstead Way, NW11 7DN; Wykeham House, Wothorpe, Stamford PE9 3LA. *E:* graham.zellick@gmail.com.
*See also* A. D. R. Zellick.

**ZELLICK, Jennifer, (Mrs G. J. Zellick);** *see* Temkin, J.

**ZEMAN, Miloš;** President of the Czech Republic, since 2013; *b* 28 Sept. 1944; *m* 1st, 1971 (marr. diss. 1978); one *s*; 2nd, 1993; one *d*. *Educ:* Sch. of Economics, Kolín; Univ. of Economics, Prague (graduated *summa cum laude* 1969). Worked at engrg plant Tatra Kolín, 1963–67; teacher of econ. forecasting, Univ. of Econs, Prague, 1969; Sportpropag Co., 1971–84; Agrodat, 1984–89; Economic Forecasting Inst., 1990. Mem., Federal Assembly, 1990–92 (Civic Forum, 1990–92, Czech Social-Democratic Party, 1992) (Chm., Budget Cttee). Leader, Czech Social-Democratic Party, 1993–2001; Chm., Chamber of Deputies, Parliament of Czech Republic, 1996; Prime Minister, 1998–2002. Founder, Party of Citizen Rights, 2009 (Leader, 2010; Hon. Chm., 2010). *Publications:* All My Mistakes in Politics (memoir), 2005. *Address:* Office of the President, Pražskýhrad, 11908 Prague 1, Czech Republic.

**ZEPHANIAH, Benjamin Obadiah Iqbal;** writer and poet; Professor of Poetry and Creative Writing, Brunel University, since 2011; *b* 15 April 1958; *s* of Oswald Springer and Leneve Faleta Wright. *Educ:* Broadway Comprehensive Sch., Birmingham; Glen-Parva Borstal, Leicester. Poet, 1977–. DUniv: N London, 1998; Staffordshire, 2001; Open, 2004; Hon. DLitt: W England, 1999; South Bank, 2002; E London, 2003; Leicester, 2004; Hon. DArts Oxford Brookes, 2002; Hon. MA Northampton, 2003. *Publications: poetry:* Pen Rhythm, 1980; The Dread Affair, 1985; Inna Liverpool, 1988; City Psalms, 1992; Propa Propaganda, 1996; School's Out, 1997; (ed) Bloomsbury Book of Love Poems, 1999; Too Black Too Strong, 2001; To Do Wid Me, 2013; *prose:* Rasta Time in Palestine, 1990; Kung Fu Trip, 2011; *for children:* Talking Turkeys, 1994; Funky Chickens, 1996; Wicked World, 2000; A Little Book of Vegan Poems, 2000; (with Prodeepta Das) We are Britain, 2002; When I Grow Up, 2011; *novels:* Face, 1999; Refugee Boy, 2001; Gangsta Rap, 2004; Teacher's Dead, 2007; Liam, 2012; Terror Kid, 2014; The Life and Rhymes of Benjamin Zephaniah (autobiog.), 2018. *Recreation:* collecting money. *Address:* PO Box 1153, Spalding, Lincs PE11 9BN.

**ZERHOUNI, Elias A., MD;** Professor of Radiology and Biomedical Engineering, and Senior Adviser, Johns Hopkins University School of Medicine, 2009, now Professor Emeritus; President, Global Research and Development, Sanofi, 2011–18 (Member, Executive Committee and Management Committee, 2011–18); *b* 12 April 1951. *Educ:* Univ. of Algiers Sch. of Medicine (MD 1975). Johns Hopkins University School of Medicine: Residency in Diagnostic Radiol., 1975–78 (Chief Resident, 1977–78); Instructor, 1978–79, Asst Prof., 1979–81, Dept of Radiol.; Asst Prof., 1981–83, Associate Prof., 1983–85, Dept of Radiol., Eastern Virginia Med. Sch.; Johns Hopkins University School of Medicine: Associate Prof., 1985–92; Prof. of Radiol., 1992–2002; Prof. of Biomedical Engrg, 1995–2002; Chm., Dept of Radiol., 1996–2002; Exec. Vice Dean, Vice Dean for Clin. Affairs and Pres., Clin. Practice Assoc., 1996–99; Vice Dean for Res., 1999–2002; Exec. Vice Dean, 2000–02. Vice Chm. and Dir, Body Imaging Section, De Paul Hosp., Eastern Virginia Med. Sch., 1982–85; Johns Hopkins Medical Institutions: Co-Dir, MRI and Body CT, and Co-ordinator of Clin. Res., 1985–88; Dir, Divs of Thoracic Imaging and MRI, 1988–96; Radiologist-in-Chief, Johns Hopkins Hosp., 1996–2002; Dir, Nat. Insts of Health, USA, 2002–08. Sen. Fellow for Global Health, Bill & Melinda Gates Foundn, 2009–; Dir, Foundn for Nat. Insts of Health, 2019–. Mem., Bd of Trustees, King Abdullah Univ. of Sci. and Technol., 2009–. Dr Emeritus, Univ. of Algiers, 2005. Fellow, Internat. Soc. for Magnetic Resonance in Medicine, 1998–. *Publications:* contrib. chapters to books; numerous contribs to peer-reviewed jls incl. Radiol., Jl Thoracic Imaging, JCAT, Circulation, Jl MRI.

**ZERNICKA-GOETZ, Prof. Magdalena,** PhD; FMedSci; Wellcome Trust Senior Research Fellow, Gurdon Institute, since 2002, and Professor of Mammalian Development and Stem Cell Biology, since 2010, University of Cambridge; *b* Warsaw, 30 Aug. 1963; *d* of Boguslaw and Danuta Zernicki; *m* 2000, Prof. David Moore Glover, *qv*; one *s* one *d*. *Educ:* Univ. of Warsaw (PhD). Adjunkt, Dept of Embryol., Univ. of Warsaw, 1993–97; University of Cambridge: EMBO Fellow, 1995–97; Lister Sen. Res. Fellow, Gurdon Inst., 1997–2002; Sen. Res. Fellow, Sidney Sussex Coll., 1997–2003; Reader in Develtl Biol., 2007–10. FMedSci 2013. *Publications:* contribs to scientific jls. *Address:* Department of Physiology, Development and Neuroscience, University of Cambridge, Downing Street, Cambridge CB2 3DY. *T:* (01223) 763291. *E:* mz205@cam.ac.uk.

**ZETLAND, 4th Marquess of,** *cr* 1892; **Lawrence Mark Dundas;** Bt 1762; Baron Dundas, 1794; Earl of Zetland, 1838; Earl of Ronaldshay (UK), 1892; DL; *b* 28 Dec. 1937; *e s* of 3rd Marquess of Zetland, DL and Penelope, *d* of late Col Ebenezer Pike, CBE, MC; *S* father, 1989; *m* 1964, Susan, 2nd *d* of late Guy Chamberlin, Oatlands, Wrington Hill, Wrington, Bristol, and late Mrs Chamberlin; two *s* two *d*. *Educ:* Harrow School; Christ's College, Cambridge. Late 2nd Lieut, Grenadier Guards. Founding Dir, British Horseracing Bd, 1993–97. DL N Yorks, 1994. *Heir: s* Earl of Ronaldshay, *qv*. *Address:* The Orangery, Aske, Richmond, N Yorks DL10 5HE. *T:* (01748) 823222. *Clubs:* All England Lawn Tennis and Croquet, Jockey (Steward, 1992–94).

**ZETTER, Paul Isaac,** CBE 1981; Chairman, Zetters Group Ltd, 1972–2000; *b* 9 July 1923; *s* of late Simon and Esther Zetter; *m* 1954, Helen Lore Morgenstern; one *s* one *d*. *Educ:* City of London Sch. Army, 1941–46. Family business, 1946–2000; became public co., 1965. Chm., Southern Council for Sport and Recreation, 1985–87; Member: Sports Council, 1985–87; National Centres Bd, Sports Council, 1987–88; Governor, 1975–, and Hon. Vice-Pres., 1985–, Sports Aid Foundation (Chm., 1976–85); Vice-Chm., World Ice Skating Championships, 1994–95. Trustee: Thames Salmon Trust, 1988–92; Foundn for Sports and Arts, 1991–96 (Chm., Sports Working Party, 1991–94). President: John Carpenter Club, 1987–88; Restricted Growth Assoc., 1993–96. Liveryman, Glovers' Co., 1981–2009; Freeman, City of London, 1981. Olympic torch bearer, W Sussex, 2012. *Publications:* It Could Be Verse, 1976; Bow Jest, 1992; Zero Risk, 2000; Global Warming, 2001; London Roundabout, 2007. *Recreations:* National Hunt horse racing (owner), walking, writing. *Address:* 27 Loxford Court, Elmbridge, Cranleigh, Surrey GU6 8TR.

**ZEUS, Tamara Catherine;** *see* Harvey, T. C.

**ZHELUDEV, Prof. Nikolay I.,** PhD; DSc; FRS 2018; FInstP; Professor of Physics and Astronomy, since 2000, and Deputy Director, Optoelectronics Research Centre, since 2006, University of Southampton; Professor, and Founding Co-Director, Photonics Institute, Nanyang Technological University, Singapore, since 2014; *b* Moscow, 23 April 1955. *Educ:* Lomonosov Moscow State Univ. (MSc 1978; PhD 1981; DSc 1992). FInstP 1994. Gp Leader, Nonlinear Optics Lab., Moscow State Univ., 1981–91; Lectr in Physics, 1991–94, Reader, 1994–2000, Univ. of Southampton; Principal Investigator and Coordinator, EPSRC NanoPhotonics Portfolio Centre, 2004; Dir, EPSRC UK prog. on

Nanostructured Photonic Metamaterials, 2009. Foreign Mem., NAE USA, 2019. Ed.-in-Chief, Jl Optics, 2008–. FOSA 2004. *Publications*: research pubns and books. *Address*: Optoelectronics Research Centre, University of Southampton, Highfield Campus, Southampton SO17 1BJ.

ZHU, Prof. Zi-Qiang, PhD; FREng, FIET, FIEEE; Professor of Electrical Machines and Control Systems, since 2000, Head, Electrical Machines and Drives Research Group, since 2008, Founding Academic Director, Sheffield Siemens Wind Power Research Centre, since 2009, and Royal Academy of Engineering/Siemens Research Chair, since 2014, University of Sheffield; *b* Zhejiang, China, 23 Sept. 1962; *s* of Xiaoniao Zhu and Xinhua Chen; *m* 1987, Summer Zhenping Xia; one *d*. *Educ*: Zhejiang Univ., China (BEng 1st Cl. 1981; MSc 1984); Univ. of Sheffield (PhD 1991). FIET 2012. Asst Lectr, 1984–86, Lectr, 1986–89, Dept of Electrical Engrg, Zhejiang Univ., China; Department of Electronic and Electrical Engineering, University of Sheffield: Vis. Res. Fellow, 1988–89; Res. Associate, 1989–92; Sen. Res. Scientist/Sen. Res. Officer, 1992–2000. Founding Director: Sheffield China Railway Rolling Stock Corp. Electric Drive Technol. Res. Centre (Fast Train propulsion), 2014–; Sheffield Midea Jt Res. Lab. of Electric Motors and Drives Technol., 2017–. Consultant Prof., Shanghai Univ., 1999–; Vis. Prof., Hong Kong Univ., 1999, 2000; Guest Prof., 2001–, Guangbiao Prof., 2005–11, Qian-Ren Prof. (B), 2011–14, 2014–18, Zhejiang Univ.; Guest Professor: Northeastern Univ., China, 2001–06; Southeast Univ., China, 2002–; Tianjin Univ., China, 2003–; Nanjing Univ. of Aeronautics and Astronautics, China, 2003–; Huazhong Univ. of Sci. and Technol., China, 2005–07; Naval Univ. of Engrg, China, 2008–10; Harbin Inst. of Technol., China, 2008–; Tsinghua Univ., China, 2009–12; Chinese Acad. of Sci., Inst. of Electrical Engrg, China, 2011–; Shenyang Univ. of Technol., China, 2011–14; Vis. Prof., Univ. of Wisconsin-Madison, 2007. FIEEE 2009; FREng 2016. *Publications*: Analysis and Control of Noises from Electrical Machines, 1987; (Ed.-in-Chief) Modern Electric Vehicles, Electric Drives and Power Electronics, 2005; (contrib.) Encyclopaedia of Automotive Engineering, 2014; contrib. papers to jls incl. IEEE Trans, IET Proc.; referred conf. papers. *Recreations*: painting, hiking. *Address*: 26 Moorbank Road, Sheffield S10 5TR. *T*: (0114) 222 5195, (office) (0114) 222 5360. *E*: Z.Q.Zhu@sheffield.ac.uk, Z.Q.Zhu@ieee.org.

ZIA, Hon. Khaleda; Prime Minister of Bangladesh, 1991–96 and 2001–06; *b* 15 Aug. 1945; *m* 1960, Gen. Ziaur Rahman (*d* 1981), President of Bangladesh; two *s*. *Educ*: Surendranath Coll., Dinajpur. Vice-Chm., 1982–84, Chm., 1984–, Bangladesh Nat. Party.

ZIEGLER, Philip Sandeman, CVO 1991; author; *b* 24 Dec. 1929; *s* of Major Colin Louis Ziegler, DSO, DL, and Mrs Dora Ziegler (*née* Barnwell); *m* 1st, 1960, Sarah Collins; one *s* one *d*; 2nd, 1971, (Mary) Clare Charrington; one *s*. *Educ*: Eton; New Coll., Oxford (1st Cl. Hons Jurisprudence; Chancellor's Essay Prize). Entered Foreign Service, 1952; served in Vientiane, Paris, Pretoria and Bogotà; resigned 1967; joined William Collins and Sons Ltd, 1967, Editorial Dir 1972, Editor-in-Chief, 1979–80. Chairman: The London Library, 1979–85; Soc. of Authors, 1988–90; Public Lending Right Adv. Cttee, 1994–97. FRSL 1975; FRHS 1979. Hon. DLitt: Westminster Coll., Fulton, 1988; Buckingham, 2000. *Publications*: Duchess of Dino, 1962; Addington, 1965; The Black Death, 1968; William IV, 1971; Omdurman, 1973; Melbourne, 1976 (W. H. Heinemann Award); Crown and People, 1978; Diana Cooper, 1981; Mountbatten, 1985; Elizabeth's Britain 1926 to 1986, 1986; The Sixth Great Power: Barings 1762–1929, 1988; King Edward VIII, 1990; Harold Wilson: the authorised life, 1993; London at War 1939–45, 1995; Osbert Sitwell, 1998; Britain Then and Now, 1999; Soldiers: fighting men's lives, 1901–2001, 2001; Rupert Hart-Davis: man of letters, 2004; Legacy: the Rhodes Trust and the Rhodes Scholarships, 2008; Edward Heath: the authorised biography, 2010 (Elizabeth Longford Prize, Soc. of Authors, 2011); Queen Elizabeth II: a photographic portrait, 2010; Olivier, 2013; George VI: the dutiful king, 2014; Between the Wars: 1919–1939, 2016; *edited*: the Diaries of Lord Louis Mountbatten 1920–1922, 1987; Personal Diary of Admiral the Lord Louis Mountbatten 1943–1946, 1988; From Shore to Shore: the diaries of Earl Mountbatten of Burma 1953–1979, 1989; (with Desmond Seward) Brooks's: a social history, 1991. *Address*: 22 Cottesmore Gardens, W8 5PR. *T*: (020) 7937 1903. *E*: philipziegler@me.com. *Club*: Brooks's.

ZILKHA, Selim Khedoury; Principal: Zilkha Renewable Energy, 2001–05; Zilkha Biomass, 2005–16; *b* 7 April 1927; *s* of Khedoury Aboodi Zilkha and Louise (*née* Bashi); *m* (marr. diss.); one *s* one *d*. *Educ*: English Sch., Heliopolis, Egypt; Horace Mann Sch. for Boys, USA; Williams Coll., USA (BA Major Philos.). Dir, Zilkha & Sons Inc., USA, 1947–87; Chm. and Man. Dir, Mothercare Ltd and associated cos, 1961–82; Dir, Habitat Mothercare Gp, 1982; Chairman: Amerfin Co. Ltd, GB, 1955–68; Spirella Co. of Great Britain Ltd, 1957–62; Chm./Jt Man. Dir, Lewis & Burrows Ltd, 1961–64; Chairman and Chief Executive Officer: Towner Petroleum Co., Houston, 1983–85; SKZ Inc., Houston, 1986; Zilkha Energy Co., Houston, 1987–98; non-executive Director: Sonat Inc., 1998–2000; El Paso Energy and Gas, 2000–02. Owner, Laetitia Winery and Vineyard, 2002–19. Founder, Zilkha Neurogenetic Inst., 2002. Hon. DHL USC, 2016. *Recreations*: bridge, tennis. *Address*: 750 Lausanne Road, Los Angeles, CA 90077–3316, USA. *Club*: Portland.

ZILLMAN, Dr John William, AO 1996; Director of Meteorology, Australia, 1978–2003; President, World Meteorological Organization, 1995–2003; Vice-Chancellor's Fellow, School of Earth Sciences, University of Melbourne, 2009–12 (Professor of Earth Sciences, 1999–2009); *b* 28 July 1939; *s* of late Charles H. S. Zillman and of Thelma Flora Fraser. *Educ*: Nudgee Coll.; Univ. of Queensland (BSc Hons 1960); BA 1970); Melbourne Univ. (MSc 1971); Univ. of Wisconsin (PhD 1972). Australian Bureau of Meteorology: forecaster and research scientist, 1957–74; Asst Dir (Res.), 1974–78. Perm. Rep. of Australia with WMO, 1978–2004 (Mem., Exec. Council, 1979–2004); Chm., Steering Cttee for Global Climate Observing System, 2006–09. President: Royal Soc. of Victoria, 1993–94; Aust. Acad. of Technol Scis and Engineering, 2003–06 (Vice-Pres., 1995–98); Internat. Council of Acads of Engrg and Technol Scis, 2005; Aust. Nat. Academics Forum, 2005–06. *Publications*: (ed jtly) Climate Change and Variability: a southern perspective, 1978; (ed jtly) Climate of the South Pacific, 1984; numerous contribs to learned jls. *Recreations*: reading, music. *Address*: GPO Box 1289, Melbourne, Vic 3001, Australia. *T*: (3) 96694250. *Club*: Melbourne (Melbourne).

ZIMMER, Hans Florian; film score composer; Co-founder and Partner, Remote Control Productions (formerly Media Ventures Entertainment Group); *b* Frankfurt-am-Main, 12 Sept. 1957; *m* Vicki Carolyn (marr. diss.); one *d*; *m* Suzanne; one *s*. Keyboard player with Buggles (album, The Age of Plastic, 1980), with Ultravox, with Krisma (album, Cathode Mama, 1981); formerly Asst to Stanley Myers, London; Hd of Music Dept, DreamWorks SKG, 1994–. *Film scores include*: with Stanley Myers: Moonlighting, 1982; Eureka, Success is the Best Revenge, 1984; Insignificance, 1985; My Beautiful Laundrette, 1986; score producer, The Last Emperor, 1986; sole composer: A World Apart, 1988; Rain Man, Black Rain, Driving Miss Daisy, 1989; Bird on a Wire, Days of Thunder, Pacific Heights, Green Card, 1990; Regarding Henry, Thelma & Louise, Backdraft, 1991; The Power of One, A League of their Own, Toys, 1992; True Romance, Cool Runnings, 1993; I'll Do Anything, The Lion King (Acad. Award; Golden Globe Award), Drop Zone, Renaissance Man, 1994; Nine Months, Something to Talk About, Beyond Rangoon, Crimson Tide (Grammy Award, 1996), 1995; Broken Arrow, The Rock, The Fan, Muppet Treasure Island, 1996; Preacher's Wife, 1996; The Peacemaker, As Good as it Gets, 1997; Prince of Egypt, 1998; The Thin Red Line, Chill Factor, The Last Days, 1999; The Road to El Dorado, Gladiator (Golden Globe Award), Mission Impossible 2, An Everlasting Piece, 2000; Pearl Harbor, Hannibal, 2001; Black Hawk Down, 2002; Pirates of the Caribbean: The Curse of the Black Pearl, The Last Samurai, Something's Gotta Give, 2003; King Arthur, Thunderbirds, Shark Tale, 2004; The Da Vinci Code, Pirates of the Caribbean: Dead Man's Chest, 2006; The Simpsons Movie, Pirates of the Caribbean: At World's End, 2007; Kung Fu Panda, The Dark Knight, Frost/Nixon, 2008; Sherlock Holmes, 2009; Inception, 2010; The Dark Knight Rises, 2012; Man of Steel, 2013; 12 Years a Slave, 2014; Interstellar, 2014; Batman v Superman: Dawn of Justice, 2016; Dunkirk, Blade Runner 2049, The Boss Baby, Hidden Figures, Kung Fu Panda 3, Inferno, 2017; Widows, 2018; The Lion King, 2019. *TV series scores include*: Through the Wormhole, 2011–16; Planet Earth II, 2016; The Crown, 2016–; Blue Planet II, 2017. Composer of the Year and Outstanding Contribution to Music, Classic BRIT Awards, 2013. *Address*: Remote Control Productions, 1547 14th Street, Santa Monica, CA 90404, USA.

ZIMMER, Prof. Robert J., PhD; President, and Professor, Department of Mathematics, University of Chicago, since 2006. *Educ*: Brandeis Univ. (AB 1968); Harvard Univ. (AM 1971; PhD 1975). University of Chicago: L. E. Dickson Instructor of Maths, 1977–79; Associate Prof., 1979–80; Prof., Dept of Maths, 1980–2002; Vice-Pres. for Res. and for Argonne Nat. Lab., 2000–02; Provost, Brown Univ., 2002–06. *Publications*: Ergodic Theory and Semisimple Groups, 1984; Essential Results of Functional Analysis, 1990. *Address*: Office of the President, University of Chicago, 5801 S Ellis Avenue, Suite 501, Chicago, IL 60637, USA. *E*: president@uchicago.edu.

ZIMMERMAN, Robert Allen, (Bob Dylan); singer, musician and composer, since 1960; *b* 24 May 1941; *s* of Abe Zimmerman and Beatrice Rutman; *m* 1965, Sarah Lowndes (marr. diss. 1978); three *s* one *d*, and one step *d*; *m* 1986, Carolyn Y. Dennis (marr. diss. 1992); one *d*. *Educ*: Hibbing High Sch., Minn; Univ. of Minnesota. Albums include: Bob Dylan, 1962; The Free Wheelin' Bob Dylan, 1963; The Times They Are A-Changin', 1964; Another Side of Bob Dylan, 1964; Bringing It All Back Home, 1965; Highway 61 Revisited, 1965; Blonde on Blonde, 1966; John Wesley Harding, 1967; Nashville Skyline, 1969; Self Portrait, 1970; New Morning, 1970; Dylan, 1973; Planet Waves, 1974; Before the Flood, 1974; The Basement Tapes, 1975; Blood on Tracks, 1975; Desire, 1976; Street Legal, 1978; Slow Train Coming, 1979; Saved, 1980; Shot of Love, 1981; Infidels, 1983; Empire Burlesque, 1985; Biograph, 1985; Knocked Out Loaded, 1986; Down in the Groove, 1988; Oh Mercy, 1989; Under the Red Sky, 1990; Bootleg Series, vols 1–3, 1991; Good as I Been to You, 1992; World Gone Wrong, 1993; Time Out of Mind, 1997; Bootleg Series, vol. 4, 1998; Love and Theft, 2001; Bootleg Series, vol. 5, 2002, vol. 6, 2004, vol. 7, 2006; Modern Times, 2006; Together Through Life, 2009; Christmas in the Heart, 2009; Tempest, 2012; The Basement Tapes Complete, 2014; Shadows in the Night, 2015; Fallen Angels, 2016; Triplicate, 2017. Actor in films: Pat Garrett and Billy the Kid, 1973; Hearts of Fire, 1987; Masked and Anonymous, 2003. Exhibitions of paintings and drawings: Drawn Blank Series, Halcyon Gall., 2008 and 2010; Bob Dylan: Face Value, NPG, 2013; Mood Swings, Halcyon Gall., 2013; Bob Dylan, Halcyon Gall., 2018. Nobel Prize for Literature, 2016. Presidential Medal of Freedom (USA), 2012; Officier, Légion d'Honneur (France), 2013. *Publications*: Tarantula, 1966; Writings and Drawings, 1973; Lyrics: 1962–85, 1985; Drawn Blank, 1994; Lyrics: 1962–1997, 1999; Lyrics: 1962–2001, 2004; Chronicles, vol. 1 (autobiog.), 2004. *Address*: c/o Jeff Rosen, PO Box 870, New York, NY 10276, USA.

ZINKERNAGEL, Prof. Rolf Martin, MD, PhD; Professor of Experimental Immunology, and Director, Institute of Experimental Immunology, University of Zürich, 1992–2008, now Emeritus; *b* 6 Jan. 1944; *s* of Robert Zinkernagel and Susanne Zinkernagel-Staehlin; *m* 1968, Kathrin Lüdin; one *s* two *d*. *Educ*: Mathematisch-Naturwissenschaftliches Gymnasium; Univ. of Basel (MD 1970); Univ. of Zürich; ANU (PhD 1975). Extern, Glen Cove Community Hosp., Long Island, NY, 1966; Intern, Surgical Dept, Clara-Spital, Univ. of Basel, 1969; Fellow: Lab. for Electron Microscopy, Inst. of Anatomy, Univ. of Basel, 1969–70; Inst. of Biochemistry, Univ. of Lausanne, 1971–73; Vis. Fellow, Dept of Microbiology, John Curtin Sch. of Med. Res., ANU, 1973–75; Asst Prof., subseq. Associate Prof., 1976–79, Prof., 1979, Dept of Immunopathology, Res. Inst. of Scripps Clinic, Calif; Adjunct Associate Prof., Dept of Pathology, UCSD, 1977–79; Associate Prof., 1979–88, Prof., 1988–92, Dept of Pathology, Univ. Hosp., Univ. of Zürich. Member: Swiss Soc. of Allergy and Immunology, 1971–; Amer. Assoc. of Immunologists, 1977–; Swiss Soc. of Pathology, 1981–; Sci. Adv. Council, Cancer Res. Inst., 1988–; Academia Europea, 1989–; Founding Cttee, Max-Planck-Inst. of Infectiology, 1990–92; US Acad. of Scis, 1996–; Foreign Mem., Royal Soc., 1998. Member: editl bd, numerous jls; numerous scientific adv. bds. Hon. DSc Liège, 1996. Awards include: Cloëtta Stiftung, Zürich, 1981; Paul Ehrlich Preis, Frankfurt, 1983; Lasker Award, 1995; (with Peter Doherty) Nobel Prize in Physiology or Medicine, 1996. *Address*: Institute of Experimental Immunology, University of Zürich, University Hospital, Schmelzbergstrasse 12, 8091 Zürich, Switzerland.

ZIOLKOWSKI, Prof. Antoni Marjan, PhD; FRSE; FREng; Professor of Petroleum Geoscience, University of Edinburgh, since 1992; *b* London, 14 July 1946; *s* of Stanislaw Ignacy Ziolkowski and Theodora Ziolkowska (*née* Crakanthorp); *m* 1978, Kathleen Crowley; two *s* one *d*. *Educ*: William Ellis Sch.; Chislehurst and Sidcup Co. Grammar Sch.; Trinity Hall, Cambridge (BA 1968, MA 1972; PhD 1971); London Sch. of Econs and Pol Sci. (MSc 1975). Staff Mem., Seismic Discrimination Gp, Lincoln Lab., MIT, 1971–73; HQ Geophysicist, NCB, 1976–80; Consultant, BNOC, 1980–82; Prof. of Applied Geophysics, Delft Univ. of Technol., Netherlands, 1982–92; Tech. Dir, MTEM Ltd, Edinburgh, 2004–07; Chief Scientist, Electromagnetics, 2007–09, Geosci. and Engrg, 2009–10, Petroleum Geo-Services, Edinburgh. EAGE FRSE 1995; FREng 2017. *Publications*: Deconvolution, 1982; (with Guido Baeten) The Vibroseis Source, 1990; (with Evert Slob) Introduction to Controlled Source Electromagnetic Methods, 2019. *Address*: (home) 17 Gordon Terrace, Edinburgh EH16 5QR; Grant Institute, School of Geosciences, University of Edinburgh, King's Buildings, James Hutton Road, Edinburgh EH9 3FE. *T*: (0131) 650 8511, *Fax*: (0131) 668 3184. *E*: Anton.Ziolkowski@ed.ac.uk. *Club*: Oxford and Cambridge.

ZISSERMAN, Prof. Andrew Peter, PhD; FRS 2007; Microsoft/Royal Academy of Engineering Professor of Computer Vision Engineering, University of Oxford, since 2006; Fellow of Brasenose College, Oxford. *Educ*: Fitzwilliam Coll., Cambridge (BA 1978; PhD); MA Oxon. Univ. of Edinburgh, 1984–87; Univ. of Oxford, 1987–, Prof. of Engrg Sci., 1999–2006. *Publications*: (with Andrew Blake) Visual Reconstruction, 1987; (with Richard Hartley) Multiple View Geometry in Computer Vision, 2nd edn 2004. *Address*: Department of Engineering Science, University of Oxford, Parks Road, Oxford OX1 3PJ.

ZISSMAN, Sir Bernard (Philip), Kt 1996; Chairman: Cerebrum Private Equity Ltd, since 2011; AQC Consulting Ltd (formerly AbbeyQC Ltd), since 2013; JWZ LLP, since 2013; Lambton Clothing Company LLP, since 2017; *b* 11 Dec. 1934; *s* of Hannah and David Zissman; *m* 1958, Cynthia Glass; one *s* two *d*. *Educ*: King Edward's Grammar Sch., Five Ways. Sales Dir, 1960–70, Man. Dir, 1970–85, Zissman Bros (Birmingham); Dir, Hyatt

Regency (Birmingham), 1992–95; Chm., Communication Hub Ltd, 1995–97; Dir of Communications, Bucknall Austin, 1996–99; Chief Exec., Confident Communications, 1997–. Chairman: CDI Gp Ltd, 1999–2016; Private Equity Builders (formerly Business Angels Bureau Ltd), 2005– (Dep. Chm., 2004–05); Early Equity plc, 2008–10; Rewired PR Ltd, 2011–14. Non-executive Director: Severn Trent Water Authy, 1983–89; Birmingham Broadcasting, 1994–2000; Capolito Roma, 1996–99. Chm., Good Hope NHS Hosp. Trust, 1998–2004. Birmingham City Council: Mem. (C), 1965–95; Lord Mayor, 1990–91; Leader, Conservative Gp, 1992–95; Hon. Alderman, 1995–. Pres., Edgbaston Cons. Assoc., 2013–16 (Chm., 1996–99). Member: Council, Birmingham Chamber of Commerce and Industry, 1991–2009; W Midlands Police Authy, 1994–95. Chairman: Adv. Bd, Japan Centre, Birmingham Univ., 1992–2001; Midlands Cttee, Princess Royal Trust for Carers, 1999–2006; Millennium Point Trust, 2007–12. Mem., Regl Council, Nat. Meml Arboretum, 2008–18. Trustee, CBSO, 1992–. Life Mem., Fedn of Clothing Designers and Execs, 1991–. Patron, Marie Curie Hospice, Solihull, 2012–. Freeman, City of London. President: Birmingham Hebrew Congregation, 1999–2004; Repr. Council, Birmingham and Midland Jewry, 2006–18 (Mem., 1992–2000). Hon. LLD Birmingham, 1997; DUniv Central England, 2000. *Publications:* A Knight Out with Chamberlain in Birmingham, 2002; Herzl's Journey, 2008. *Recreations:* family, photography, travel. *Address:* 14 Walled Garden Court, Hampton Road, Stanmore HA7 3GE. *T:* (020) 3759 1795.

**ZITCER, Diane;** *see* Kenwood, D.

**ZITTER, Guy;** Group Managing Director, Mail Newspapers, 2008–14; *b* London, 26 Feb. 1954; *s* of late Gerald Zitter and of Ina Zitter; *m* 1987, Julie Polk; one *s* one *d*. *Educ:* Edinburgh Univ. (BSc Commerce; Cert. Advertising and Mktg). Sen. Finance Officer, Seychelles Govt, 1976–77; night club proprietor, 1977–79; sales exec., Sunday Express, 1980–81; restaurant proprietor, 1981–84; Mail on Sunday: Sen. Sales Exec., 1981–83; Sales Manager, 1983–84; Advertising Manager, 1984–89; Daily Mail: Advertisement Dir, 1989–94; Man. Dir, 1994–2008. Chm., People Bank Ltd, 1996–99; Director: Free Publishing Services, 1995–98; Metro, 2003–14; Evening Standard, 2003–08; Boiling Oil Ltd, 2014–; Core London, 2018–. Non-exec. Dir, Easy Property, 2014–17. Gilt Cross, Scout Assoc., 1966. *Recreations:* ski-ing, shooting, fishing, fine wine, Cuban cigars. *E:* guy.zitter@hotmail.com. *Club:* St Moritz Yacht.

**ZOLLINGER-READ, Paul John,** CBE 2012; Chief Medical Officer, BUPA, 2012–19; *b* Birmingham, 18 Feb. 1962; *s* of Eric Ernest Read and Mary Irene Read; *m* 1988, Heidi Carris Zollinger; one *s* one *d*. *Educ:* Gonville and Caius Coll., Cambridge (BA 1983); Guy's Hosp. (MB BS 1986). Dip. Geriatric Medicine 1989; DRCOG 1990; Dip. Child Medicine 1991; MRCGP. Gp Partner, Braintree, Essex, 1991–2012. Dir, Modernisation Agency, NHS, 2000–02; Chief Executive Officer: Braintree Care Trust, 2002–06; Chelmsford PCT, 2004–06; NE Essex PCT, 2006–10; Gt Yarmouth and Waveney PCT, 2009; Cambs NHS, 2010–11; NHS Peterborough, 2010–11; Director: E of England SHA, 2010–12; Midlands and E SHA, 2012. Med. Advr and Primary Care Lead, King's Fund, 2011–12. Hon. PhD Anglian Ruskin, 2013. *Publications:* contrib. Lancet. *Recreations:* long distance running, playing piano, photography, family. *Address:* Flaglands, 25 Queen Street, Castle Hedingham, Essex CO9 3HA. *T:* 07515 507855. *E:* paul.zollingerread@btinternet.com.

**ZOUCHE,** 18th Baron *cr* 1308, of Haryngworth; **James Assheton Frankland;** Bt 1660; company director; President, Multiple Sclerosis Society of Victoria, 1981–84; *b* 23 Feb. 1943; *s* of Major Hon. Sir Thomas William Assheton Frankland, 11th Bt, and Mrs Robert Pardoe (*d* 1972), *d* of late Captain Hon. Edward Kay-Shuttleworth; *S* to father's Btcy, 1944; *S* grandmother, 17th Baroness Zouche, 1965; *m* 1978, Sally Olivia, *y d* of R. M. Barton, Bungay, Suffolk; one *s* one *d*. *Educ:* Lycée Jaccard, Lausanne. Served 15/19th the King's Royal Hussars, 1963–68. Mem. (C), Somerset CC, 2009–13. *Heir: s* Hon. William Thomas Assheton Frankland, *b* 23 July 1984. *Address:* The Abbey, Charlton Adam, Somerton, Somerset TA11 7BE.

**ZUCKER, His Honour Kenneth Harry;** QC 1981; a Circuit Judge, 1989–2005; *b* 4 March 1935; *s* of Nathaniel and Norma Zucker; *m* 1961, Ruth Erica, *y d* of Dr H. Brudno; one *s* one *d*. *Educ:* Westcliff High Sch.; Exeter Coll., Oxford, 1955–58 (MA). Served in Royal Air Force, 1953–55. Bacon Scholar, Gray's Inn, 1958; called to Bar, Gray's Inn, 1959; Atkin Scholar, Gray's Inn, 1959. A Recorder, 1982–89. *Recreations:* reading, walking, photography, bookbinding, table tennis.

**ZUCKERMAN, Adrian;** *see* Zuckerman, A. A. S.

**ZUCKERMAN, Prof. Arie Jeremy,** MD, DSc; FRCP, FRCPath, FMedSci; Professor of Medical Microbiology in the University of London, 1975–2014, now Emeritus, and Principal and Dean, Royal Free Hospital School of Medicine, then Royal Free and University College Medical School, 1989–99; *m* 1951, Alice Adamson (*d* 2011); one *s* one *d*. *Educ:* Birmingham Univ. (BSc 1953; MSc 1962; DSc 1973); London Univ. (MB BS 1957; MD 1963; DipBact 1965). MRCS, LRCP, 1957; DObst, RCOG, 1958; MRCPath 1965, FRCPath 1977; MRCP 1977, FRCP 1982. Ho. Surg., Royal Free Hosp., 1957–58; Ho. Phys., 1958, Casualty Surg. and Admissions Officer, 1958–59, Whittington Hosp.; Flt Lieut, then Sqn Leader, Medical Branch, RAF, 1959–62: Unit MO and Tutor in Aviation Medicine, Advanced Flying Sch., 1959–60; Epidemiol Res. Lab., PHLS, 1960–62; seconded to Dept of Pathol., Guy's Hosp. Med. Sch., 1962–63; Sen. Registrar, PHLS, 1963–65; London School of Hygiene and Tropical Medicine: Sen. Lectr, Dept of Bacteriol. and Immunol., 1965–68; Reader in Virology, 1968–72; Prof. of Virology, 1972–75; Dir, Dept of Med. Microbiol., 1975–88; Member Council: Univ. of London, 1995–99 (Mem. Court, 1992–95); UCL, 1995–2003. Chm., Conf. of Metropolitan Deans, 1992–95. Hon. Consultant Microbiologist: UCH, 1982–89; Royal Free Hosp., 1989–2003; Hon. Consultant Virologist: Charing Cross Hosp., 1982–95; NE Thames Regl Blood Transfusion Centre, Brentwood, 1970–94; Nat. Blood Authy, 1994–99. Department of Health: Mem., expert adv. gps, 1970–2007; Mem., Adv. Gps on hepatitis, HIV/AIDS, transfusion-transmitted viruses and liver disease strategy, 1970–2011; World Health Organisation: Consultant on hepatitis, 1970–2005; Expert Adv. Panel on Virus Diseases, 1974–2005; Dir, Collaborating Centre for Ref. and Res. on Viral Diseases, 1990–2006; Dir, Collaborating Centre for Ref. and Res. on Viral Hepatitis, London, 1974–89. Non-exec. Dir, Royal Free Hampstead NHS Trust, 1990–99; Dir, Anthony Nolan Bone Marrow Trust, 1999–2003. Mem. Council, Zool Soc. of London, 1989–92. Chm., Hepatitis B Foundn UK, 2006–12. Founder FMedSci 1998. Stewart Prize, BMA, 1981; James Blundell Medal and Award, British Blood Transfusion Soc., 1992. Editor: Jl of Med. Virology, 1976–2015; Jl of Virological Methods, 1979–2015. *Publications:* Virus Diseases of the Liver, 1970; Hepatitis-associated Antigen and Viruses, 1972, 2nd edn as Human Viral Hepatitis, 1975 (trans. Japanese 1980); (with C. R. Howard) Hepatitis Viruses of Man, 1979 (trans. Japanese 1981); A Decade of Viral Hepatitis: abstracts 1969–1979, 1980; (ed) Viral Hepatitis: clinics in tropical medicine and communicable diseases, 1986 (trans. Chinese 2013); (ed jtly) Principles and Practice of Clinical Virology, 1987 (trans. Italian 1992), 6th edn 2009; (ed) Viral Hepatitis and Liver Disease, 1988; (ed) Recent Developments in Prophylactic Immunization, 1989; (ed) Viral Hepatitis, 1990 (trans. Spanish 1991); (ed with H. Thomas) Viral Hepatitis: scientific basis and clinical management, 1993, 4th edn 2013 (trans. Turkish 2006, Chinese 2007); (ed) Prevention of Hepatitis B in the Newborn, Children and Adolescents, 1996; (ed) Hepatitis B in the Asian-Pacific Region, vol. 1, 1997, vol. 2, 1998, vol. 3, 1999; (ed jtly) Diabetes and Viruses, 2012; contribs to many learned jls. *E:* arie.zuckerman@ucl.ac.uk.

**ZUCKERMAN, Prof. (Azriel) Adrian (Sorin);** Professor of Civil Procedure, University of Oxford, 2006–14, now Emeritus; Fellow and Praelector in Jurisprudence, University College, Oxford, 1973–2011, now Emeritus Fellow; *b* Bucharest, Romania, 18 Jan. 1943; *s* of Bercu-Avram and Anna Zuckerman; *m* 1st, 1969, Orna Rabinowitz (marr. diss. 1972); one *d*; 2nd, 1995, Lady Joanna Edwina Doreen Knatchbull, *d* of 7th Baron Brabourne, CBE and Countess Mountbatten of Burma, CBE, CD; one *s*. *Educ:* Natanya Municipal Sch.; Hebrew Univ., Jerusalem (LLB, LLM); Univ. of Oxford (MA). Jun. Res. Fellow, Balliol Coll., Oxford, 1971–73. *Publications:* The Principles of Criminal Evidence, 1989; (ed) Reform of Civil Procedure: essays on access to justice, 1995; (ed) Justice in Crisis (essays), 1999; Civil Procedure, 2003, 3rd edn as Zuckerman on Civil Procedure, 2013; (with P. Roberts) Criminal Evidence, 2004, 2nd edn 2010. *Recreations:* sailing, opera, gardening, perfecting espresso coffee. *Address:* Law Faculty, St Cross Building, Manor Road, Oxford OX1 3UL. *T:* (01865) 271490. *E:* adrian.zuckerman@univ.ox.ac.uk. *Club:* Brooks's.
*See also* Earl Mountbatten of Burma, Hon. P. W. A. Knatchbull.

**zu GUTTENBERG, Karl-Theodor Freiherr;** Founder and Chairman, Spitzberg Partners LLC, New York, since 2013; *b* 5 Dec. 1971; *m* 2000, Stephanie Gräfin von Bismarck-Schönhausen; two *d*. *Educ:* Univ. of Bayreuth (Law); Univ. of Munich (Pol Sci.). Mil. service, Light Mt Infantry, Mittenwald (non-commnd officer of reserve). Hd, family business, Munich until 2002 (worked in Frankfurt, NY and Berlin); Mem., Bd of Dirs, Rhön-Klinikum AG, 1996–2002. Mem., Bundestag, 2002–11; Speaker, CDU/CSU Parly Gp, 2005–08; Mem., Foreign Affairs Cttee, 2005–08; spokesman of CDU/CSU Parly Gp on disarmament, non-proliferation and arms control, 2005–08; Chm., CSU Foreign Policy Expert Cttee, 2005–08; Federal Minister of Econs and Technol., 2009, of Defence, 2009–11. Chm., CSU Upper Franconian Dist Exec., 2007–11; Sec. Gen., CSU, 2008–09. Distinguished Statesman, Center for Strategic and Internat. Studies, 2011–.

**ZUKERMAN, Pinchas;** conductor, concert violinist and violist; Music Director, National Arts Centre Orchestra, Canada, 1999–2015, now Conductor Emeritus; *b* Tel Aviv, Israel, 16 July 1948; *s* of Yehuda and Miriam Zukerman; *m* 2004, Amanda Forsyth; two *d* from former marriage. *Educ:* Juilliard School of Music. Début, USA, 1963, Europe, 1970. Violin soloist with every major orchestra in USA and Europe; tours of USA, Europe, Israel, Scandinavia, Australia; extensive recordings. Music Director: South Bank Festival, 1978–80; St Paul Chamber Orch., 1980–87; Principal Guest Conductor: Dallas SO, 1993–95 (Principal Conductor, Internat. Summer Music Fest., 1990–95); RPO, 2009–. First prize, Leventritt Internat. Violin Competition, 1967. *Address:* c/o Kirshbaum Demler & Associates, 711 West End Avenue, New York, NY 10025, USA. *T:* (212) 2224843.

**ZUMA, Jacob Gedleyihlekisa,** Hon. GCB 2010; President: of South Africa, 2009–18; African National Congress, 2007–17; *b* Inkandla, KwaZulu-Natal, 12 April 1942; *s* of Gcinamazwi Zuma and Nokubhekisisa Zuma; *m* 1973, Sizakele Khumalo; *m* Kate Mantsho (*d* 2000); *m* Nkosazana Dlamini (marr. diss. 1998); *m* 2008, Nompumelelo Ntuli; *m* 2010, Thobeka Madiba; *m* 2012, Gloria Bongekile Ngema; twenty *c*. Mem., ANC, 1958–; arrested and convicted for conspiring to overthrow govt, 1963 and sentenced to 10 years imprisonment on Robben Island; after release in 1973, mobilised internal resistance and re-establt of ANC underground structures, 1974–75; based in Swaziland, then Mozambique, 1975–87; returned to SA, 1990; African National Congress: Mem., Nat. Exec. Cttee, 1977–; Dep. Sec. Gen., 1991–94; Nat. Chm., Council, 1995–97; Dep. Pres., 1997–2007. Mem., Exec. Council, Econ. Affairs and Tourism, KwaZulu-Natal Provincial Govt, 1994–99; Leader, Govt Business, Nat. Assembly, 1997–2005; MP (ANC), 1999–2005; Dep. Pres., SA, 1999–2005.

**ZUMLA, Prof. Sir Alimuddin,** Kt 2017; Grand Comdr, Order of Dist. Service, First Div. (Zambia), 2012; PhD; FRCP, FRCPE, FRCPath; FRSB; Professor of Infectious Diseases and International Health, UCL Medical School (formerly Royal Free and University College Medical School), University College London, since 1998; Consultant Infectious Diseases Physician, University College London Hospitals NHS Foundation Trust, since 1994; Honorary Consultant, Royal Free Hospital NHS Foundation Trust, since 2000; *b* Fort Jameson, Zambia, 1955; *s* of Ismail Bagas and Aminaben Zumla; *m* 1986, Farzana Gulam Bhuta; two *s* one *d*. *Educ:* Univ. of Zambia (BSc Human Biol. (Dist.) 1976; MB ChB 1979); London Sch. of Hygiene and Tropical Medicine, Univ. of London (MSc Tropical Medicine 1981 (Frederick Murgatroyd Medal and Prize); PhD 1987 (Alan Woodruff Medal)). MRCP 1984, FRCP 1994; FRCPE 1999; FRCPath 2009; FRSB (FSB 2012). Clin. Fellow and SHO in Gen. Medicine, RPMS, Hammersmith Hosp., 1981–83; Registrar in Gen. Medicine, Royal Northern Hosp., London, 1983–84; Beit Meml Res. Fellow and Hon. Registrar, LSHTM, 1984–87; Registrar, Rush Green and Oldchurch Hosps, Romford, 1987–88; Sen. Registrar and Hon. Lectr, Depts of Medicine and Immunol., RPMS, Hammersmith Hosp., 1988–92; Associate Prof., Center for Infectious Diseases, Univ. of Texas Health Sci. Center at Houston, Med. Sch. and Sch. of Public Health, Houston, Texas, 1992–94; University College London: Sen. Lectr, 1994–95, Reader in Infectious Diseases, 1995–98, Dept of Medicine, Royal Free and University Coll. Med. Sch.; Dir, Centre for Infectious Diseases and Internat. Health, 1994–2011. Visiting Professor: Univ. of Zambia Sch. of Medicine, 1992–; Univ. of Cape Town, 2007–; Univ. of Amsterdam, 2011; Hon. Professor: Liverpool Sch. of Tropical Medicine and Hygiene, 2003–08; Centre for Internat. Child Health, Inst. of Child Health, 2004–. Fellow, African Acad. of Scis, 2017. Hon. MD Karolinska Inst., Sweden, 2016. Bayer UK Award, British Soc. for Study of Infection, 1991; Weber-Parkes Trust Medal and Prize, RCP, 1999; Albert Chalmers Medal and Prize, Royal Soc. of Tropical Medicine and Hygiene, 2000; Windrush Award for Professional Achievement, Windrush Anserhouse, 2003; Gold Award, 2004, Platinum Award, 2008, NHS Adv. Cttee on Clin. Excellence Awards; Ibn Sina (Avicenna) Award for Excellence in Medicine and Sci., Muslim News Health Professional Awards, 2005; Zambia Med. Assoc. Medal, 2006; Bharuch Spinoza Award, Univ. of Amsterdam, 2011; India Internat. Foundn Award, 2011; Kochon Prize, Stop TB Partnership, 2011; Clinical Sci. Prize, Karolinska Inst., Sweden, 2012; Lifetime Achievement Award, Zambia Min. of Health, 2012; Best Internat. Collaboration Award, Times Higher Educn, 2013; Donald MacKay Medal, RSTM&H, 2014; Clinical Excellence Award for World Class Res., UCL Hosps NHS Foundn Trust, 2015; Sen. Investigator Award, NIHR, 2017; Union Medal, Internat. Union against TB and lung diseases, 2018. Ed., Current Opinions in Pulmonary Diseases Infectious Diseases (annually), 1998–. *Publications:* (jtly) A Guide to the MRCP Part 2 Written Examination, 1993, 2nd updated edn, as A Guide to the MRCP Part 2 Written Paper, 2006; (jtly) Multiple Choice Questions for the MRCP Part 1 Exam, 1993; (jtly) 100 Short Cases for the MRCP Clinical Exam, 1994; (ed jtly) AIDS and Respiratory Medicine, 1997; (ed with D. J. James) Granulomatous Disorders, 1999; (ed with O. P. Sharma) Tropical Lung Disease: clinics in chest medicine, 2002; (ed with M. Gandy) The Return of the White Plague: global poverty and the new tuberculosis, 2003; (ed with G. C. Cook) Manson's Tropical Diseases, 21st edn, 2003, 22nd edn 2009; (ed jtly) Tuberculosis: a comprehensive clinical treatise, 2009; (ed jtly) Perspectives in Medicine: tuberculosis, 2015; contribs to WHO reports and internat. guidelines; over 560 peer-reviewed pubns cited on PubMed. *Recreations:* cricket, philately, gardening, wildlife conservation. *Address:* UCL Medical School, University College London, Royal Free Campus, Division of Infection and Immunity, Centre for Clinical Microbiology, 2nd Floor, Royal Free Hospital, Rowland Hill Street, NW3 2PF. *T:* 07901 638375. *E:* a.zumla@ucl.ac.uk. *Club:* MCC.

**zur HAUSEN, Prof. Harald,** MD; Scientific Director, German Cancer Research Centre, Heidelberg, 1983–2003, now Professor Emeritus; *b* Gelsenkirchen, Germany, 11 March 1936; *m* 1st, 1964; three *s*; 2nd, Dr Ethel-Michele de Villiers. *Educ:* Univ. of Bonn; Univ. of Hamburg; Univ. of Düsseldorf (MD 1960). Internships in Wimbern, Isny, Gelsenkirchen and Düsseldorf, 1960–62; Research Fellow: Inst. of Microbiol., Univ. of Düsseldorf, 1962–65; Div. of Virology, Children's Hosp. of Philadelphia, 1966–69; Asst Prof., Univ. of Pennsylvania, 1968; Sen. Scientist, Inst. of Virology, Univ. of Würzburg, 1969–72; Chm. and Prof. of Virology, Univ. of Erlangen-Nürnberg, 1972–77; Chm. and Prof. of Virology, Univ. of Freiburg, 1977–83. Ed.-in-Chief, Internat. Jl of Cancer, 2000–09. Mem. Bd of Dirs, UICC, 2006–10. Vice-President: German Nat. Acad. for Natural Scis and Medicine, 2003–10; Eur. Acad. of Cancer, 2010–. (Jtly) Nobel Prize in Physiology or Medicine, 2008. Special Order of Merit with Star (Germany). *Address:* German Cancer Research Centre, im Neuenheimer Feld 280, 69120 Heidelberg, Germany.

**ZUYDAM, (David) Mel;** Chief Financial Officer, P3 Logistic Parks, since 2018; *b* Colombo, Sri Lanka, 29 Sept. 1961; *s* of late Willem Zuydam and of Sheila Zuydam (*née* Toff); *m* 2003, Melissa Christina Sophie Jones; one *s* one *d*. *Educ:* Kingsmead Sch., Wirral; Clifton Coll., Bristol; Univ. of Edinburgh (BSc Hons 1984). ACA 1991, FCA 2001. Subsidiary Finance Dir, Stylo plc, 1991–97; Balfour Beatty plc, 1997–2002: Financial Controller; Subsidiary Finance Dir; E Commerce Dir; Subsidiary Finance Dir, Serco plc, 2002–03; Consultant, EEF, 2003–04; Finance Dir, Highways Agency, DfT, 2004–08; Chief Financial Officer, Grontmij NV, 2009–12; Principal, ProSynergy, 2012–15; Chief Financial Officer, CH2m Inc., 2015–17. Non-exec. Mem., Audit Cttee, DFID, 2007–. Associate Dir, Technical Apprentice Consortium, Assoc. of Consulting Engrs, 2018–. Trustee: Y Care Internat., 2015–; Mercy Ships, 2018–. Volunteer, Disabled Sailing, RYA, 1995–2008; Shore Crew RYA 2.4m class Paralympic sailing team, 1995–2008; youth sailing instructor, Koninklijke Watersport Vereeniging, Loosdrecht, Netherlands, 2012–15. Examiner, St Anne's Church, Wandsworth, 2005–. MInstD 2010. *Recreations:* having fun with my wife, daughter and son, singing (Mem., Oxford Bach Choir, 2015–), sailing, flying (private pilot licence, 1997); Three Peaks Challenge (1997 and 2008); fundraising for UNICEF; Windsor Half Marathon 2017 for Save the Children Yemen appeal. *E:* mel@zuydam.com.